THE WORLD ALMANAC

AND BOOK OF FACTS

2019

WORLD ALMANAC BOOKS

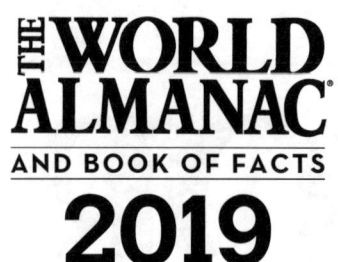

THE WORLD ALMANAC
AND BOOK OF FACTS
2019

Senior Editor: Sarah Janssen
Editor: M. L. Liu
Index Editor: Nan Badgett
Contributors: Francis X. Clooney, Emily J. Dolbear, Robert Famighetti, Marshall Gerometta, Jacqueline Laks Gorman, Richard Hantula, Marc Kissel, Donhae Koo, Laurence A. Marschall, John Mastroberardino, William A. McGeveran Jr., Janet M. Olson, John Rosenthal, S. Ross, Helene Salmon, Peter J. Schmidtke, George W. Smith IV, Edward A. Thomas, Valerie J. Weber, Lori P. Wiesenfeld, Dale Williams

Production: Newgen North America
Design and Production, Year in Pictures: QBS Learning
Design, Cover: Takeshi Takahashi
Photo Research: Edward A. Thomas

For Infobase:
Editorial Director: Laurie E. Likoff
Project Editor: Edward A. Thomas

Front cover: Shutterstock (unless otherwise noted); Foles: AP Images, Gregory Payan; Tesla: SpaceX; Black Panther: Newscom, Marvel Studios/Walt Disney Pictures; Prince Harry/Meghan Markle: AP Images, KGC-03/STAR MAX/Ipx. **Back cover:** Shutterstock (unless otherwise noted); March for Our Lives: AP Images, Joe Skipper; Trump/Kim: AP Images, Evan Vucci; McCain funeral: AP Images, Ross D. Franklin; Wildfires: AP Images, Marcio Jose Sanchez.
Interior pages: Photos are AP Images unless otherwise noted. **Courtesy of the Boston Public Library:** The Great Molasses Flood: Leslie Jones Collection, 333. **Jimmy Carter Library and Museum:** Carter, 503. **William J. Clinton Presidential Library:** 669. **Everett Collection:** Domino: Mirrorpix/Courtesy, 814; Franklin: LF Photoshot, 814; Graham: John G. Zimmerman Archive, 814; Hunter: Mary Evans/Ronald Grant, 814; Kidder: TM and Copyright © 20th Century-Fox Film Corp., 184; Rae: © NBC/Courtesy, 815; Reynolds: © Universal/Courtesy, 815; Roth: Bettmann, 815; Simon: © Paramount/Courtesy, 815. **FEMA:** Northridge earthquake, 455. **Gerald R. Ford Presidential Library and Museum:** Ford, 503. **Getty Images:** Family separation: John Moore, 193, 199; Afghan ambulance attack: Wakil Kohsar/AFP, 194; Russian spies: Matt Cardy, 195; Indonesia disasters: Jewel Samad/AFP, 197; Democratic congressional candidates: Scott Eisen, 200; Korean presidents: Inter-Korean Summit Press Corps/Pool/Anadolu Agency, 674; Bruno Mars: Lester Cohen/NARAS, 812; James Shaw: Jason Davis, 813; Annan: Joel Saget/AFP, 814; Bannister: Mrs. Dulce R. Stuart, 814; Le Guin: Dan Tuffs, 815; Mandela: Jeff Overs/BBC News & Current Affairs, 815; Naipaul, Wolfe: Ulf Andersen, 815; Roth: Bettmann, 815; Spade: David Howells/Corbis, 815. **Lyndon Baines Johnson Library and Museum:** Vietnam War protest, 450; Johnson, 502. **Library of Congress:** 444; 446; 448; March on Washington, 450; U.S. presidents, unless otherwise noted, 496-504; 648; 659; 661; 662; 665. **NASA:** 451. **National Archives and Records Administration:** 447; D-Day: Army Signal Corps Collection, 449; 463; 465; Grant, 499; 664. **NOAA:** Hurricane Camille, 328. **National Park Service:** Constitutional Congress, 442. **Newscom:** Syrian chemical attack: Syrian Civil Defense White Helmets/Zuma Press, 194; Trail of Tears: Picture History, 443; Aleppo boy: Mahmoud Raslan/Zuma Press, 673; Black Panther: Marvel Studios/Walt Disney Pictures/Album, 812; BTS: PG/BauerGriffin.com/MEGA, 812. **Ronald Reagan Presidential Foundation and Library:** 453. **Reuters:** Cloned monkeys: Chinese Academy of Sciences and released by China Daily, 816. **City of St. Petersburg/Flickr:** 459. **Shutterstock:** Roseanne, 193; 650-652; 656; 671; Bourdain, 814; Hawking, 814. **SpaceX:** Tesla, 816. **U.S. Army:** Spc. Mary L. Gonzalez, CJTF-101 Public Affairs, 670. **U.S. Coast Guard:** 456. **USGS:** Hawaii volcano: Hawaiian Volcano Observatory, 199; Water on Mars: Astrogeology Science Center, Arizona State University, ESA, INAF. Graphic rendering by Davide Coero Borga, 816. **U.S. Senate:** McCain, 815. **Victoria and Albert Museum:** 657. **White House:** Pete Souza, 457, 458; 461; George W. Bush, Eric Draper, 504; Obama, Pete Souza, 505; Trump, 505; Bush, 814. **White House Historical Society:** Madison, 496. **Yale University:** Transcontinental railroad: Yale Collection of Western Americana, Beinecke Rare Book and Manuscript Library, 445.

The World Almanac®
An imprint of Infobase
132 West 31st Street
New York, NY 10001
www.worldalmanac.com
almanac@infobase.com
Follow us on Facebook, Twitter, and Instagram

Hardcover	International Standard Serial Number	Paperback
ISBN-13: 978-1-60057-220-3	0084-1382	ISBN-13: 978-1-60057-222-7
ISBN-10: 1-60057-220-0		ISBN-10: 1-60057-222-7

The World Almanac® and Book of Facts is distributed to the trade by Simon & Schuster and to schools and libraries at special discounts by Infobase. For further information, contact (800) 322-8755 or www.Infobase.com.

The World Almanac® and Book of Facts 2019
Book printed and bound by LSC Communications, Kendallville, IN
Date printed: November 2018
Printed in the United States of America
LSC 10 9 8 7 6 5 4 3 2 1

CONTENTS

2018 SPECIAL FEATURES AND YEAR IN REVIEW

2018: YEAR IN PICTURES 193, 809

THE WORLD ALMANAC AND BOOK OF FACTS 2019

Top 10 News Topics of 2018

1. Democrats Make Gains in Midterm Elections. In an election, Nov. 6, marked by high turnout, a historically high number of women candidates, and a strategic emphasis on health care, Democrats picked up about 30 seats to gain control of the House of Representatives; in 2019, for the first time, the House will have at least 100 female members. Democrats also gained governorships, including in Midwestern battleground states Michigan and Wisconsin. Republicans tightened control on the U.S. Senate, defeating Democratic incumbents in several states that Pres. Donald J. Trump won in 2016, including Indiana, Missouri, and North Dakota. In Texas, incumbent Sen. Ted Cruz (R) held off a strong challenge from Beto O'Rourke (D). In a series of pre-election rallies, Pres. Trump emphasized an anti-immigration message, alleging (without evidence) that Democrats supported "caravans" of largely Central American asylum seekers traveling toward the U.S. On Oct. 26, a Florida man was arrested for allegedly sending more than a dozen bombs to prominent Democrats as well as to CNN.

2. U.S. Policies Seek to Limit Both Undocumented and Authorized Immigration. Under a Jan. 25, 2017, executive order expanding U.S. Immigration and Customs Enforcement's (ICE) apprehension priorities, ICE arrested more than 143,000 undocumented immigrants in fiscal year 2017 (up from 114,000 in FY2016) and almost 120,000 in 9 months in FY2018. Atty. Gen. Jeff Sessions announced, Apr. 6, 2018, a "zero tolerance" policy, essentially calling for prosecution of all unauthorized border crossers. The policy led to separation at the border of more than 2,600 children from detained family members. Although a federal judge, June 26, ordered the government to reunite all families within 30 days, about 245 of the children remained separated as of Oct. 15. Sec. of State Mike Pompeo announced, Sept. 17, that the U.S. would admit a maximum of 30,000 refugees in FY2019, down from 45,000 for FY2018, and 110,000 for FY2017. In a series of actions, Sept. 2017-May 2018, the Trump administration ended temporary protected status (TPS)—effectively, work authorization and relief from deportation—for more than 400,000 people in the U.S. from El Salvador, Haiti, Nicaragua, Sudan, Nepal, and Honduras. A federal court ruling, Oct. 3, 2018, temporarily blocked ending TPS for the first four countries pending legal challenges.

3. Mueller Investigation Gains Legal Victories, Witness Cooperation. Special counsel Robert S. Mueller III's investigation into Russian interference in the 2016 U.S. election, possible Trump campaign coordination with that effort, and related matters produced new indictments, convictions, and guilty pleas. On Aug. 21, Trump's personal attorney Michael Cohen pleaded guilty to 8 counts, including campaign finance violations, in connection with actions (allegedly made at Trump's direction) to cover up, before the 2016 election, Trump's alleged extramarital affairs with two women. Also Aug. 21, former Trump campaign chairman Paul Manafort was convicted of tax evasion and bank fraud in connection with his earlier political consulting in Ukraine. Manafort pleaded guilty to additional charges Sept. 14 and agreed to cooperate with Mueller's investigation. On Dec. 1, 2017, former Trump national security adviser Michael Flynn pleaded guilty to lying to the FBI communicating with a Russian official prior to Trump's inauguration; Flynn also agreed to cooperate with the Mueller probe. On July 13, 2018, 12 Russian intelligence officers were indicted for hacking Democratic campaign email accounts. Atty. Gen. Sessions, who had recused himself from overseeing Mueller, resigned at Trump's request, Nov. 7; Trump named Matthew G. Whitaker, a critic of the Mueller probe, acting atty. gen.

4. Korean Nuclear Negotiations Begin. After a year of heightened U.S.-North Korean tensions and threats, largely related to North Korea's missile and nuclear weapons programs, Pres. Trump and North Korean leader Kim Jong Un met in a summit in Singapore June 12. The meeting produced a general statement to "work toward complete denuclearization of the Korean Peninsula," with the details to be fleshed out in further negotiations. As those talks proceeded, U.S. intelligence officials and the International Atomic Energy Agency concluded North Korea was continuing its nuclear program.

5. Kavanaugh Replaces Kennedy on U.S. Supreme Court. After a divisive confirmation process, the Senate voted, 50-48, to confirm federal appeals court Judge Brett Kavanaugh Oct. 6 as the 114th U.S. Supreme Court justice. Kavanaugh was expected to give the Court a consistent conservative majority. He replaced Justice Anthony Kennedy, often a swing vote in key 5-4 rulings; Kennedy had announced his retirement June 27. Opposition to the nomination (announced by Pres. Trump July 9) strengthened in Sept., when an allegation became public that Kavanaugh had sexually assaulted Christine Blasey Ford in 1982, when both were high school students; a second woman, Deborah Ramirez, accused Kavanaugh of aggressive sexual behavior when they were in college. Kavanaugh denied both allegations, and the Senate concluded that a reopened but apparently limited FBI background check (completed Oct. 4) failed to corroborate the charges.

6. Parkland, FL, School Shooting Renews Calls for Gun Control. On Feb. 14, a 19-year-old former student using a legal semiautomatic rifle killed 17 (14 of them students) at Marjory Stoneman Douglas High School in Parkland, FL. The incident prompted renewed gun-control campaigns—including March for Our Lives demonstrations held Mar. 24—often led by surviving students, though they produced limited results. Florida's legislature in Mar. raised the gun-purchase age to 21 but voted down a ban on assault rifles. Florida and other states implemented waiting periods for gun purchases and banned bump stocks, devices that allow semiautomatic weapons to fire faster. Both the Natl. Rifle Assn. and Pres. Trump advocated the controversial step of arming school personnel. On Oct. 27, a gunman, apparently motivated by anti-Semitism and opposition to immigration, killed 11 people at a synagogue in Pittsburgh; Trump again called for armed guards.

7. #MeToo Movement Leads to Legal Action. Public allegations of sexual assault and other sexual misconduct—frequently referred to in shorthand using the social-media hashtag #MeToo—led to criminal charges and other disciplinary actions. Movie producer Harvey Weinstein was indicted, May and July, on charges of rape and other sex crimes. Since Oct. 2017, scores of women had accused Weinstein of sexual harassment or abuse. Following guilty pleas in Nov. 2017, former USA Gymnastics and Michigan State Univ. physician Larry Nassar was sentenced, Jan. 24 and Feb. 5, to 40-175 and 40-125 years in prison, respectively; hundreds of women had accused Nassar of sexual abuse. Comedian Bill Cosby, accused of sexual assault by dozens of women, was convicted, Apr. 26, of assaulting one victim; he was sentenced, Sept. 25, to 3-10 years in prison.

8. U.S. Withdraws From Iran Nuclear Deal; Regional Conflicts Continue. Citing Iran's role in regional conflicts and continued missile development, Pres. Trump announced, May 8, a U.S. withdrawal from the multiparty 2015 agreement to limit Iran's ability to develop nuclear weapons. The withdrawal triggered renewed U.S. sanctions against Iran, which international inspectors said was complying with the agreement. In Syria, where Iran backed Pres. Bashar al-Assad, government forces (also aided by Russia) had succeeded in regaining control of large areas of the country by Oct. 2018. Since 2011, Syria's civil war had claimed more than 500,000 lives and displaced over 13 million people. In Yemen, Iran-backed Shiite Houthi rebels continued to battle government forces supported by a coalition of mostly Sunni nations led by Saudi Arabia; the war produced a humanitarian crisis affecting over 22 million Yemenis. Saudi policies in Yemen and elsewhere came under increased international scrutiny following the Oct. 2 killing, in the Saudi consulate in Istanbul, Turkey, of Saudi dissident and journalist Jamal Khashoggi.

9. Trump Implements Aggressive Trade Policy. Attempting to reduce trade deficits and stimulate U.S. manufacturing, the Trump administration imposed a series of tariffs. Levies on steel and aluminum imports took effect against China and other nations Mar. 23, and against Canada, Mexico, and the EU June 1; the latter three imposed, June-July, tariffs on U.S. goods. Tariffs on about $250 bil worth of goods from China, accused by Trump of unfair trade practices, took effect July-Sept.; China implemented retaliatory tariffs. The tariffs raised concerns about higher prices for U.S. consumer goods and reduced U.S. exports. Negotiations to change NAFTA, begun in 2017 at U.S. insistence, produced, Sept. 30, 2018, a draft accord to be named the U.S.-Mexico-Canada Agreement (USMCA). The new draft left much of NAFTA intact but revised auto industry regulations, among other changes.

10. Norway Triumphs at the Olympics, and France at the World Cup. Pyeongchang, South Korea, hosted the Winter Olympics, Feb. 9-25. Norway won the most medals, a record-high 39, and tied with Germany for the most gold medals (14). The men's soccer World Cup tournament, hosted by Russia June 14-July 15, was won by France, with a 4-2 victory over underdog Croatia; midfielder Luka Modrić of Croatia was named the tournament's best overall player. Holding off 4th-quarter drives by the defending champion New England Patriots, the Philadelphia Eagles won Super Bowl LII, 41-33, on Feb. 4—their first Super Bowl win.

Number Ones

World's most populous country . . . . China, 1.38 billion population in 2018 *(p. 730)*
World's most populous urban area. . . . . Tokyo, Japan, 37.5 million population in 2018 *(p. 729)*
World's wealthiest person. . . . . American Jeff Bezos, $112.0 billion net worth as of Mar. 2018 *(p. 55)*
Most-visited U.S. social networking website. . . . . Facebook/Messenger, 207.3 million unique visitors in June 2018 *(p. 303)*
Most-used U.S. search engine . . . . Google, 11.5 billion searches (63.4% of all searches) in June 2018 *(p. 303)*
Most popular U.S. mobile app . . . . YouTube, 79.2% of U.S. smartphone users reached in June 2018 *(p. 303)*
U.S. airline that carried the most passengers. . . . . Southwest Airlines, 157.7 million passengers in 2017 *(p. 95)*
World's busiest airport by passenger traffic . . . . . . Hartsfield-Jackson Atlanta Intl. Airport, 103.9 million passengers in 2017 *(p. 95)*
World's most-visited amusement park . . . . Magic Kingdom at Walt Disney World, Florida, 20.5 million visitors in 2017 *(p. 97)*
Nations with the most days off of work per year. . . . . Austria and Malta, 38 days off *(p. 734)*
Most popular recording artist by digital singles . . . . Drake, 142.0 million units sold as of Aug. 2018 *(p. 260)*
Most pirated artist. . . . . Drake, 21.6 million peer-to-peer transactions in 2017 *(p. 260)*
Highest-rated prime-time TV show. . . . . . . *The Big Bang Theory*, watched in 11.3% of TV-owning households in 2017-18 *(p. 263)*
Highest-rated syndicated TV show. . . . . *Judge Judy*, watched in 7.2% of TV-owning households in 2017-18 *(p. 263)*
Highest-rated cable TV show. . . . . *The Walking Dead*, watched in 6.7% of TV-owning households in 2017-18 *(p. 264)*

Surprising Facts

U.S. student loan debt topped $1,386.4 billion in 2017, and 19% of that debt was owed by persons aged 50 and older. *(p. 390)*

Of high school students who drove a car at least once in the 30 days before they were surveyed, 39.2% said they had texted or emailed while driving. Only 5.5% drove when they had been drinking alcohol. *(p. 176)*

Americans paid an average of 26.0% of their gross wage earnings in income tax and Social Security contributions in 2017; Belgians, who had some of the highest personal income tax rates, paid 40.5%. *(p. 733)*

The U.S. divorce rate has declined fairly steadily since it peaked at 5.3 per 1,000 pop. in 1981; in 2016, it was 3.2. The U.S. marriage rate has been hovering around an all-time low of 6.8-6.9 per 1,000 pop since 2009. *(p. 170)*

U.S. workers with professional degrees had a lower unemployment rate (1.5%) and higher median weekly earnings ($1,836) than workers with any other level of education in 2017 (more than double the median earnings of all workers at $907). *(p. 113)*

The number of refugees in the world increased from 11.4 million in 2007 to 19.9 million in 2017. The number of internally displaced persons (IDPs) increased even more steeply, from 13.7 million in 2007 to a record-high 39.1 million in 2017. *(p. 735)*

The U.S. hosted more international migrants than any other country in 2017 with 49.8 million, up from 34.8 million in 2000. Second to the U.S., Saudi Arabia hosted 12.2 million international migrants in 2017, more than double its 2000 number of 5.3 million. *(p. 734)*

In 1950, the U.S. produced 75.7% of the world's motor vehicles manufactured that year; by 2017, that number had dropped to 11.5% (up from a low of 9.5% in 2009). *(p. 86)*

19.7% of female high school students reported being bullied electronically (e.g., bullied via texting, Instagram, Facebook, or other social media) in 2017; the rate for high school boys was 9.9%. *(p. 388)*

Employed U.S. women's earnings were equal to 73.9% of men's earnings in 2017. Women's earnings came closest to matching men's in the construction industry, where their earnings were 90.6% of men's, but women made up only 9.7% of construction industry employees. *(p. 113)*

Milestone Birthdays, 2019

90
Frank Gehry, Feb. 28
Dick Button, July 18
Bob Newhart, Sept. 5
Barbara Walters, Sept. 25
Ed Asner, Nov. 15

80
Francis Ford Coppola, Apr. 7
Harvey Keitel, May 13
Ian McKellen, May 25
Dick Vitale, June 9
Lou Brock, June 18
Carl Yastrzemski, Aug. 22
Lily Tomlin, Sept. 1
Ralph Lauren, Oct. 14
F. Murray Abraham, Oct. 24
John Cleese, Oct. 27
Margaret Atwood, Nov. 18
Tina Turner, Nov. 26
John Amos, Dec. 27

70
George Foreman, Jan. 10
Haruki Murakami, Jan. 12

Jessica Lange, Apr. 20
Billy Joel, May 9
Lionel Richie, June 20
Meryl Streep, June 22
Elizabeth Warren, June 22
Bill O'Reilly, Sept. 10
Bruce Springsteen, Sept. 23
Sigourney Weaver, Oct. 8
Bonnie Raitt, Nov. 8
John Boehner, Nov. 17
Jeff Bridges, Dec. 4
Tom Waits, Dec. 7

60
Roger Goodell, Feb. 19
Flavor Flav, Mar. 16
David Hyde Pierce, Apr. 3
Emma Thompson, Apr. 15
Morrissey, May 22
Mike Pence, June 7
Hugh Laurie, June 11
Vincent D'Onofrio, June 30
Magic Johnson, Aug. 14
Jason Alexander, Sept. 23
Emeril Lagasse, Oct. 15

Allison Janney, Nov. 19
Val Kilmer, Dec. 31

50
Jason Bateman, Jan. 14
Dave Grohl, Jan. 14
Jennifer Aniston, Feb. 11
Javier Bardem, Mar. 1
Jake Tapper, Mar. 12
Paul Rudd, Apr. 6
Renée Zellweger, Apr. 25
Cate Blanchett, May 14
Emmitt Smith, May 15
Peter Dinklage, June 11
Ice Cube, June 15
Jennifer Lopez, July 24
Edward Norton, Aug. 18
Matthew Perry, Aug. 19
Jack Black, Aug. 28
Tyler Perry, Sept. 13
Zach Galifianakis, Oct. 1
Gwen Stefani, Oct. 3
Brett Favre, Oct. 10
Sean Combs, Nov. 4
Matthew McConaughey, Nov. 4

Ken Griffey Jr., Nov. 21
Jay-Z, Dec. 4

40
Drew Brees, Jan. 15
Jordan Peele, Feb. 21
Adam Levine, Mar. 18
Claire Danes, Apr. 12
Kourtney Kardashian, Apr. 18
Kate Hudson, Apr. 19
Rosario Dawson, May 9
Chris Pratt, June 21
Mindy Kaling, June 24
Aaron Paul, Aug. 27
John Krasinski, Oct. 20
Tiffany Haddish, Dec. 3

30
Alia Shawkat, Apr. 18
Chris Brown, May 5
Daniel Radcliffe, July 23
James Harden, Aug. 26
Brie Larson, Oct. 1
Taylor Swift, Dec. 13

STATISTICAL SPOTLIGHT

U.S. Weather Disasters and Costs, 1980-2018

Source: National Centers for Environmental Information, National Oceanic and Atmospheric Administration, U.S. Dept. of Commerce

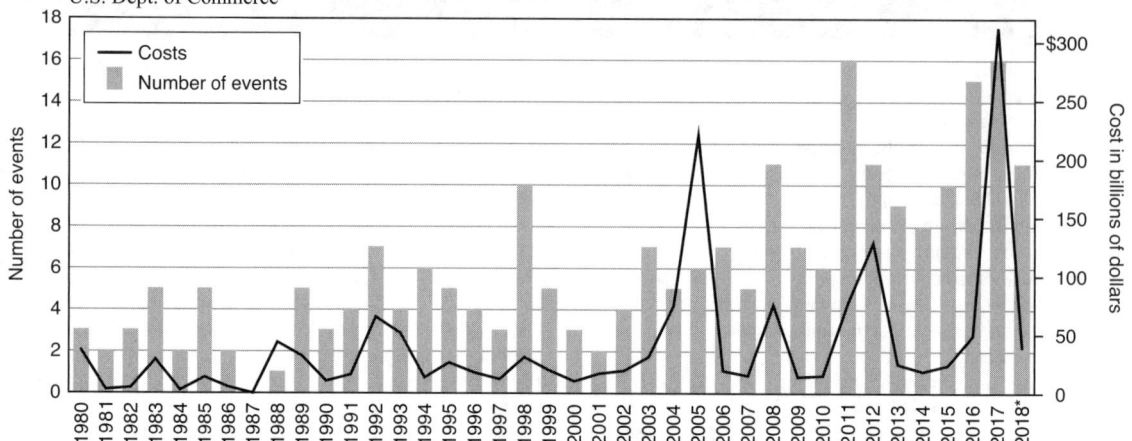

* = Compiled using preliminary data as of Oct. 9, 2018. **Note:** Disasters include drought, flooding, freeze, severe storm, tropical cyclone, wildfire, and winter storm events with losses exceeding $1 billion (previous years adjusted for inflation).

Refugees and Individuals Granted Asylum in the U.S., 1975-2018

Source: U.S. Dept. of Homeland Security, U.S. Dept. of Justice, U.S. Dept. of State

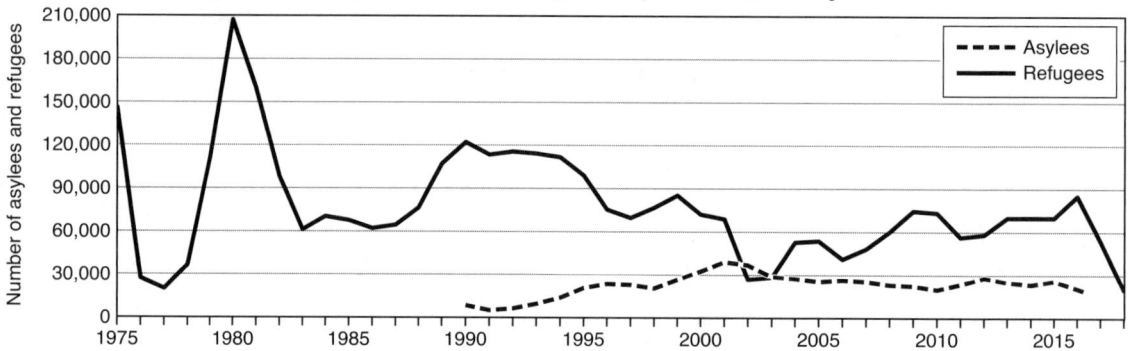

Note: Excludes Amerasians (children born in Cambodia, Korea, Laos, Thailand, or Vietnam after Dec. 31, 1950, and before Oct. 22, 1982, and fathered by a U.S. citizen) except in fiscal years 1989-91.

Immigrants Apprehended, Removed, or Returned by the U.S., 1940-2016

Source: Office of Immigration Statistics, U.S. Dept. of Homeland Security

Apprehensions include U.S. Border Patrol apprehensions for all years; U.S. Immigration and Customs Enforcement (ICE) administrative arrests are included for 1952 and on. Counting methods vary. **Removals** are the compulsory and confirmed movement of an inadmissible or deportable foreign national out of the U.S. based on a removal order. When a foreign national leaves without a removal order having been issued, that is counted as a **return**.

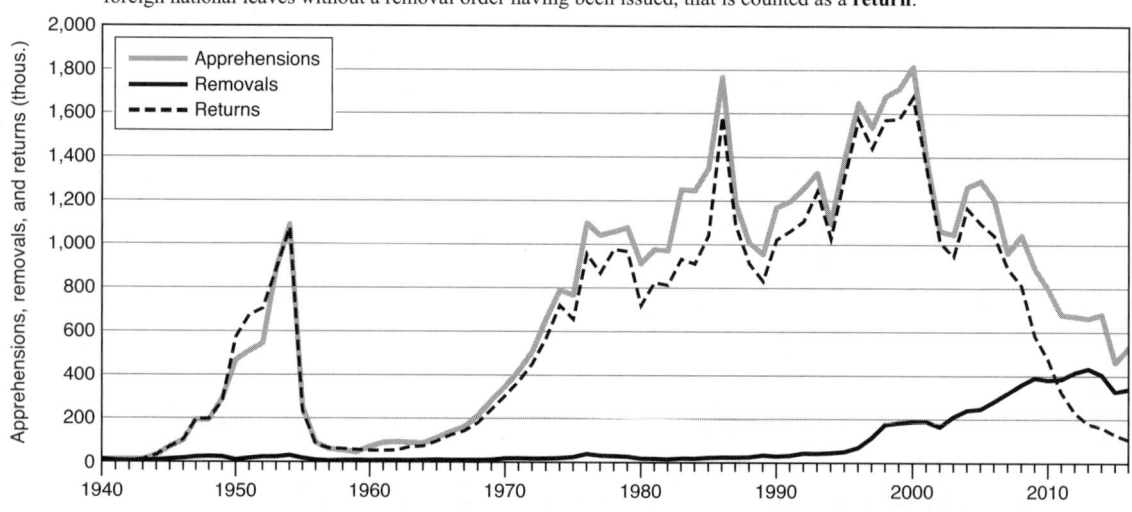

Revenue Effects of Major Tax Bills, 1978-2017

Source: Office of Tax Analysis, U.S. Dept. of the Treasury; Congressional Budget Office

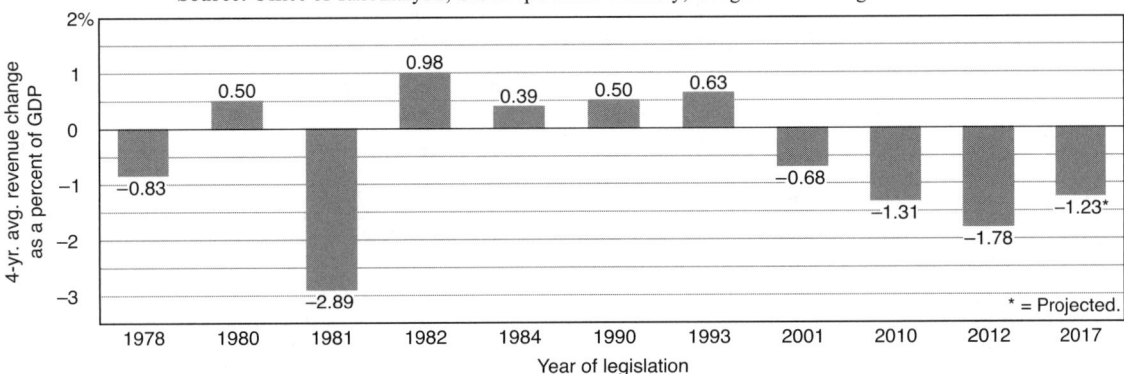

Presidential Approval Rating Over First Years in Office, 1989-2018

Source: Gallup poll on the question,
"Do you approve or disapprove of the way [president's name] is handling his job as president?"

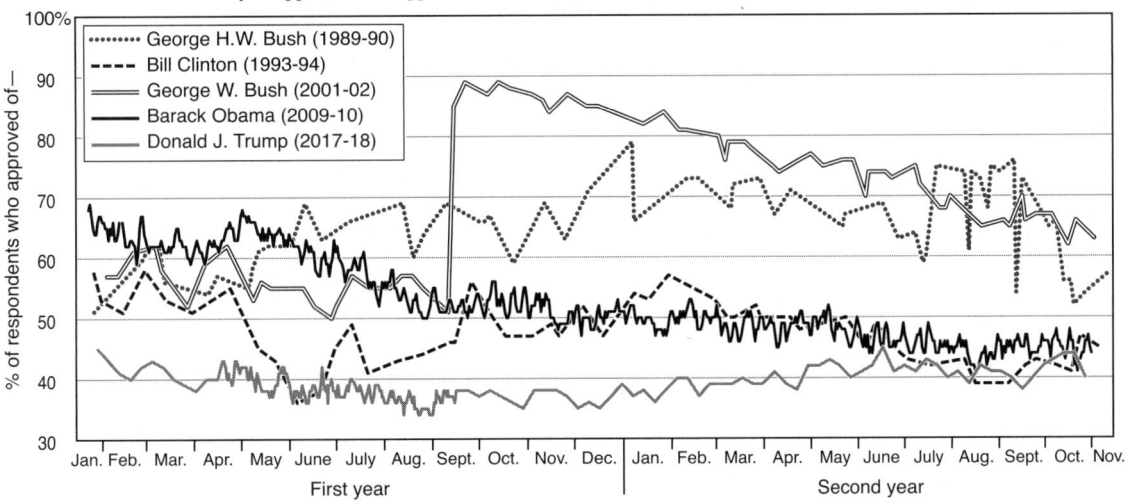

Note: Frequency of polling tended to increase over time, but Gallup ceased daily polling on this question in Jan. 2018.

Rate of Drug Overdose Deaths by State, 2016

Source: *Annual Surveillance Report of Drug-Related Risks and Outcomes—United States, 2018*, Centers for Disease Control and Prevention (CDC), U.S. Dept. of Health and Human Services

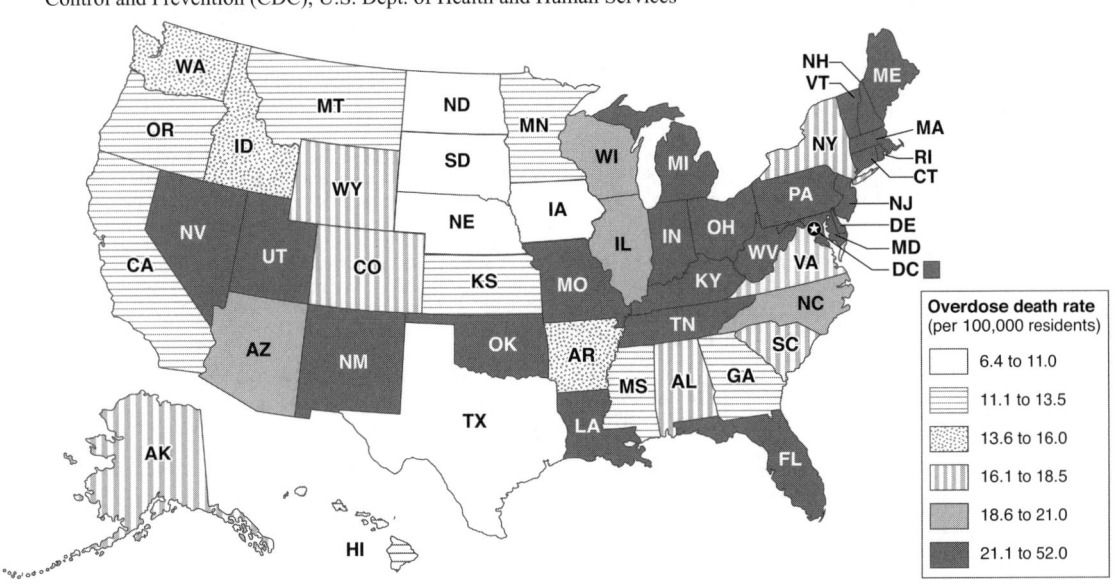

Democrats Take House; Republicans Increase Hold on Senate

Democrats scored a major victory Nov. 6, 2018, gaining control of the U.S. House of Representatives and adding a check on the unified Republican government that had held both the legislative and executive branches since the inauguration of Pres. Donald Trump in 2017. But Republicans increased their majority in the Senate in a split midterm election that offered a portrait of a divided electorate.

The Split Victory

Voter turnout, estimated at the highest for a midterm in 50 years even before all votes were counted, was considered a key factor for both parties. The Democrats had an edge as the opposition party in a midterm election—an historic advantage—but needed to defend nearly three times as many Senate seats as those held by Republicans. In the end, the GOP picked up at least three seats that had been previously held by Democratic incumbents in Indiana, Missouri, and North Dakota. Losing only one seat—held by a Nevada incumbent—Republicans thus increased their majority. The GOP also had a chance at retaining a seat in Arizona, where some ballots were still uncounted, as well as another pickup in Florida, where the incumbent Democratic senator called for a recount. A special election to fill a Republican-held seat in Mississippi was to be decided by a Nov. 27 runoff, required when no candidate won an outright majority.

In the House, where a takeover by Democrats had been widely anticipated, candidates from that party won at least five more seats than was required for a majority, adding a net total of at least 30 seats as of Nov. 9, with results from about 10 races outstanding. Marking a historic first, more than 100 female legislators would serve in the House in 2019, up from 84. Women also set other records in the 2018 election cycle, including number who filed to run and number who became party nominees for House, Senate, and governor races.

Democrats gained at least 7 governors' seats, including Kansas, Nevada, Michigan, and hard-fought Wisconsin, for 23 total. Based on preliminary results, Democrats also made modest gains in state legislature control, securing complete control of state government in 14 states; Republicans would control all of government in at least 20.

The results were widely considered to amount to a setback for the administration of Pres. Trump. Though he held a post-election press conference Nov. 7 during which he offered to cross party lines, he also threatened to investigate House Democrats if they used their newfound majority in the chamber to investigate allegations of collusion between his 2016 presidential campaign team and Russia or to look into his business dealings.

Electorate Issues and Concerns

The thematic undercurrent of the midterms was, as always, a referendum on the president and current leadership. An AP-NORC Center for Public Affairs Research poll in mid-Oct. found that 29% of Americans were "somewhat dissatisfied" and another 30% "very dissatisfied" over the direction of the country. Pres. Trump's approval rating, according to the RealClearPolitics (RCP) polling average, stood at 44% as voters headed to the polls. Gallup poll results released in early Nov. found that 34% of respondents wanted their vote to be a message in opposition to the president, with only 26% intending it as a message of support. In a *Washington Post*-ABC News poll of registered voters published Nov. 4, respondents by a 50%-34% margin believed Democrats would do a better job ensuring adequate health care, the biggest issue for voters, according to most polls. Democrats were also given a 5-point advantage on immigration (a top issue), but respondents favored Republicans for border security (by a 49%-39% margin) and on handling the economy (48%-39%). Respondents overwhelmingly, by a 32-point edge, said they trusted Democrats over Republicans to address climate change.

While tactics varied by state, Democrats focused roughly half of congressional campaign ads on health care (most notably, protecting or expanding Obamacare provisions, including coverage of pre-existing health conditions, and lowering prescription drug prices). To a lesser extent, Democrats targeted voters with ads concerning taxes, Trump's trade policy (including the effect of tariffs on agricultural exports), and traditional party priorities such as public education, gun control, and environmental protection, among others.

In contrast, Republican incumbents and challengers focused election advertising on touting Trump's tax cuts, passed by Congress in late 2017, and highlighting the country's relatively strong economy and favorable unemployment numbers and job growth. Most GOP candidates by the close of campaigning also pledged to protect Americans with pre-existing conditions, despite recent past efforts in the GOP-controlled Congress to eliminate or significantly weaken such coverage. Though TV ads accusing Democrats of favoring an "open border" with Mexico abounded—especially late in the campaign season—most GOP candidates' focus on immigration paled in comparison to Pres. Trump's.

Trump during campaign rallies frequently warned voters against a "migrant caravan" of Central Americans, claiming without proof that it included gang members and "unknown Middle Easterners." (In early Nov., CNN, NBC, Facebook, and Fox News all either outright rejected or aired and then dropped a Trump campaign ad, criticized as racist, associating the caravan with convicted police killer Luis Bracamontes, an undocumented immigrant.) Late Oct. actions by the president—derided by critics as political fearmongering—included proposals that would end birthright citizenship for children of noncitizens and deny entry to asylum seekers; on Oct. 29, Trump ordered 5,200 active troops to the southern U.S. border in advance of the caravan, at that point 1,000 mi away. Moderates feared Trump's hardline actions and rhetoric would harm candidates in states with large Hispanic populations—including Nevada and Arizona—and, without much success, implored him to highlight the strengthening economy to capture suburban swing votes.

According to a CNN exit poll taken of random midterm voters, Democrats captured the largest share of women's votes, with 59% supporting Democrats and 40% Republicans (the largest split since 1982). The same poll reported an extremely wide disparity of voter approval for Trump along party lines, with 90% of Democratic voters disapproving, and 88% of Republicans approving of his presidency.

Election Spending

The nonpartisan Center for Responsive Politics (CRP) projected that reportable total spending on the 2018 congressional elections would exceed $5.2 bil, far surpassing the $3.85 bil spent on the 2014 midterms. According to their estimates, "Team Blue" (Democratic candidates, parties, committees, and outside groups supporting them) would outspend "Team Red" (their GOP counterparts), 53.54%-46.46%. The CRP estimated that outside groups (funded mostly by a handful of megadonors) would account for about $1.1 bil in spending ($571 mil on House races), or around 21% of the election money spent, compared to less than 15% in 2014. These outside contributions were split nearly evenly between conservative and liberal groups. The biggest outside contributors supporting Republicans were the Congressional Leadership Fund, Senate Leadership Fund, and America First; the biggest Democrat-supporting outside contributors were the Senate Majority PAC, House Majority PAC, and Majority Forward.

Progressives Emerge From Primaries

An early theme in 2018 was the number of progressive candidates with varying degrees of political experience who upset more centrist or incumbent Democrats in primary races. Garnering the most widespread attention, Democratic Socialist Alexandria Ocasio-Cortez won a June primary race against longtime Rep. Joe Crowley—who outspent her 18 to 1—before she went on to become the youngest woman to win a House seat, at 29. Other longshot progressives who won primaries and then House seats included 32-year-old African-American nurse Lauren

Balance of Power, 2018

(as of Nov. 10, 2018)

Party	Senate Before	Senate After	House Before	House After	Governors Before	Governors After
Dem....	47	44	193	226	16	23
Rep. ...	51	51	235	198	33	25
Ind....	2[1]	2[1]	0	0	1	0

Note: Three Senate seats (AZ, FL, MS), 11 House seats, and two state governorships (FL, GA) were undecided. (1) Both independent senators were expected to continue caucusing with the Democrats.

Underwood (D, IL); Native American attorney and former professional mixed-martial arts fighter Sharice Davids (D, KS); and Boston City Council member Ayanna Pressley, the first black woman elected to represent Massachusetts in Congress. Other progressive Democratic primary winners were less successful: Bernie Sanders-backed Tallahassee Mayor Andrew Gillum appeared to have narrowly lost the Florida governorship (pending a recount), and pro-gun Native American Paulette Jordan, a two-term state lawmaker in GOP-stronghold Idaho, was roundly defeated in her bid for governor.

Key Senate Results

Republicans defended all but one of nine GOP-held seats up for reelection, while capturing at least three others from so-called "red state" Democrats, whose party defended 26 seats.

Voters in Republican-dominated North Dakota ousted first-term Sen. Heidi Heitkamp (D), already considered highly vulnerable ahead of her vote in Oct. against Pres. Trump's U.S. Supreme Court nominee, Brett Kavanaugh. U.S. Rep. Kevin Cramer, a supporter of Trump's ongoing trade conflict with China despite its negative impact on his state's farm exports, soundly defeated Heitkamp, 55.4%-44.6%. Sen. Joe Donnelly (D), who also opposed Kavanaugh's confirmation, lost in Indiana by roughly 8 points to state legislator Mike Braun. According to preliminary exit polls, more than half of those surveyed said Donnelly's Kavanaugh vote was an important factor in their decision.

The GOP also celebrated a win against Democratic Missouri Sen. Claire McCaskill, criticized by GOP challenger and Missouri Atty. Gen. Josh Hawley over her opposition to Kavanaugh. But McCaskill noted that she had voted with Trump, who won her state by nearly 19 points, roughly half the time, and said the president should use available means to secure the border. Hawley won, 51.5%-45.5%, supported by more than $30 mil in outside money opposing McCaskill.

Sen. Ted Cruz (R, TX) fended off a strong challenge by underdog U.S. Rep. Beto O'Rourke (D), 50.9%-48.3%, in a race projected earlier in 2018 to be noncompetitive. Visiting all 254 state counties by early summer, O'Rourke raised over $69 mil, the most ever by a Senate candidate and more than twice as much as Cruz.

In two closely watched "toss-up" races in pro-Trump states, second-term Sen. Jon Tester (D, MT) was reelected by a little over 3 points, while Sen. Joe Manchin (D, WV), who was the only Democrat to vote to confirm Kavanaugh, was reelected by a 49.5%-46.3% margin over Patrick Morrisey (R).

Tarnished and unpopular two-term Sen. Bob Menendez (D, NJ)—whose corruption trial on charges for which he was "severely admonished" by the Senate Ethics Committee ended in a mistrial—was easily reelected by New Jersey's majority anti-Trump voters.

Sen. Dean Heller (NV), the sole Republican senator fighting for reelection in a state not won by Trump, faced off against first-term Rep. Jacky Rosen. Rosen criticized Heller as an opportunist for embracing Trump, whom he earlier said he was "99 percent against." The president's hardline immigration stance worried GOP strategists given Nevada's growing Hispanic population, which makes up more than 28% of the state. Outside-group spending totaled over $65 mil, about $40 mil of it in favor of Heller, who lost 50.4%-45.4%.

Eight-term Rep. Marsha Blackburn (R, TN) easily won the seat of retiring Sen. Bob Corker (R, TN), establishing her as the state's first woman senator. GOP 2012 presidential nominee Mitt Romney cruised to victory for the Utah seat of retiring longtime Sen. Orrin Hatch (R).

Fellow Arizona Reps. Martha McSally (R) and Kyrsten Sinema (D) faced off in a hotly contested race for retiring GOP Sen. Jeff Flake's seat that would give the state its first female U.S. senator. McSally ads highlighted Sinema's anti-war activist past in contrast with McSally's service as a fighter pilot; in her defense, Sinema cited her record on defense spending. As of Nov. 9, Sinema led McSally 49.3%-48.3%, with ballots yet to be counted.

In the most expensive Senate contest (over $181 mil spent, more than $89 mil from outside groups), three-term Sen. Bill Nelson (D, FL) faced the state's outgoing term-limited governor, Rick Scott (R). The acrimonious race included misleading ads on both sides, covering issues from gun control to the effect of environmental deregulation on tourism. Scott as of Nov. 9 narrowly led 50.1%-49.9%, and the race appeared headed for a recount.

Notable House Races

A large number of House members (36 Republicans, 18 Democrats) did not seek reelection, including House Speaker Paul Ryan (R, WI) and Trey Gowdy (R, SC). But as in the three previous midterm elections, about 99% of House incumbents (all but four) seeking renomination were successful. Those who lost their seats in the primaries included, most notably, 10-term Rep. Crowley (D, NY), who lost to Ocasio-Cortez, and former South Carolina governor and two-term Rep. Mark Sanford (R), defeated in his primary by pro-Trump challenger Katie Arrington, who in turn narrowly lost Nov. 6 to political novice Joe Cunningham (D).

Backlash against the Trump administration in suburban districts, particularly by women voters, and sometimes in traditionally Republican strongholds, was believed to have played a crucial role in the Democrats' takeover of the House. Women elected in these districts included Lizzie Fletcher, a political newcomer who defeated nine-term incumbent Rep. John Culberson (R) by more than 5 points in a competitive Houston, TX, district. Similarly, first-time candidate Kendra Horn (D) unseated Rep. Steve Russell (R, OK) in a district won by the president by close to 14 points in 2016. Nonprofit director Debbie Mucarsel-Powell (D), who came to the U.S. as a teen from Ecuador, won a southern Florida seat from two-term Rep. Carlos Curbelo (R).

Ilhan Omar (D, MN), a former refugee from Somalia, and Palestinian-American Rashida Tlaib (D, MI) became the first two Muslim women to win seats in Congress. Marking another milestone, Debra Haaland (D, NM) and Sharice Davids (D, KS) were the first two Native American women elected to Congress.

Adding star power to its upset-win, former NFL football player Colin Allred (D) defeated 11-term Rep. Pete Sessions (R) in suburban Dallas, TX. And in a race that set congressional fundraising records in Washington state (over $28 mil raised, collectively), pediatrician Kim Schrier (D) narrowly defeated former state Sen. Dino Rossi (R) for the open 8th district seat previously held by retiring Rep. Dave Reichert (R).

Governors' Races

Of the 36 governors' seats at stake in 2018, Republicans were defending 26 to the Democrats' 9. (Alaskan Gov. Bill Walker, an independent, ended his campaign Oct. 19.) Though the overwhelming majority of incumbents, such as Democrats Andrew Cuomo (NY) and David Ige (HI) and Republicans Kay

---

Campaign Spending, 2017-18

Source: Federal Election Commission, for Jan. 1, 2017-Nov. 1, 2018 unless otherwise noted

Between Jan. 1, 2017, and Oct. 31, 2018, a combined $4.67 billion in campaign spending was reported by candidates ($1.99 bil), political action committees (PACs) ($1.66 bil), and political party committees ($1.02 bil).

Rank	Senate candidate	Spending (mil)
1.	Rick Scott (R, FL)	$66.50
2.	Beto O'Rourke (D, TX)	60.31
3.	Claire McCaskill (D, MO)	32.38
4.	Bob Hugin (R, NJ)	27.71
5.	Ted Cruz (R, TX)	27.48
6.	Bill Nelson (D, FL)	24.53
7.	Tammy Baldwin (D, WI)	24.46
8.	Doug Jones (D, AL)	22.92
9.	Jacky Rosen (D, NV)	20.82
10.	Kyrsten Sinema (D, AZ)	20.25

Rank	House candidate	Spending (mil)
1.	Jon Ossoff (D, GA)	$31.19
2.	David Trone (D, MD)	15.87
3.	Paul Ryan (R, WI)	15.16
4.	Scott Wallace (D, PA)	11.77
5.	Gil Cisneros (D, CA)	10.52
6.	Devin G. Nunes (R, CA)	9.94
7.	Greg Gianforte (R, MT)	8.78
8.	Conor Lamb (D, PA)	8.16
9.	Karen Handel (R, GA)	8.07
10.	Steve Scalise (R, LA)	8.05

Note: Not all candidates shown were up for election in Nov. 2018. Campaign spending by candidates does not reflect spending on candidates' behalf by other groups.

Ivey (AL), Asa Hutchinson (AR), and Charlie Baker (MA) easily won, a few faced strong challenges. Due mainly to term limits, 18 races (13 previously held by Republicans) were open and saw a number of tightly fought contests.

Two-term Wisconsin Gov. Scott Walker (R), known for his controversial fight with teachers' unions and for surviving a 2012 recall election, narrowly lost to the state superintendent of public instruction Tony Evers (D). Evers heavily criticized Walker over education funding and his rejection of federal Medicaid expansion funds. Between mid-Aug. and early Oct., GOP spending (including from outside groups) on TV ads swelled to $9.2 mil, compared to $4.8 mil by Evers and Democratic groups. In the only other general election race that unseated a governor, billionaire J.B. Pritzker (D) trounced GOP Illinois Gov. Bruce Rauner (R), 54.2%-39.2%, amid a lagging economy outside metro Chicago and an increasingly underfunded public employee pension system. The race set a record as the costliest gubernatorial contest ever, at $284 mil ($175 mil by Pritzker).

Staunch Trump ally and national voting fraud crusader Kris Kobach (R) defeated sitting Gov. Jeff Colyer in the Kansas primary but lost to four-term state Sen. Laura Kelly (D), who ran as a moderate in a state Trump won by over 20 points. Democrats celebrated victories in four other Republican-held states: Maine, won by state Atty. Gen. Janet Mills; Michigan, by former state rep. and sen. Gretchen Whitmer; Nevada, by local county commission chair and NRA-critic Steve Sisolak; and New Mexico, won by three-term U.S. Rep. Michelle Lujan Grisham.

Despite campaign appearances by former Pres. Barack Obama, Democrats fell short in Ohio (50.7%-46.4%) and narrowly lost Florida (49.6%-49.2%, pending a recount). In the latter race, one of the most closely watched nationally, Pres. Trump, who won the state by only 1.2 points in 2016, branded Andrew Gillum (D) a "thief" over corruption allegations, and Gillum's GOP opponent, Rep. Ron DeSantis, made an on-air "monkey this up" reference to Gillum, who is black, that critics said was racially charged. Democrats came within striking distance (3.0 points) in Iowa, won by Gov. Kim Reynolds (R), and 3.4 points in South Dakota, clinched by Rep. Kristi Noem (R).

Stacey Abrams (D), the first black female gubernatorial nominee by a major party, refused to concede to Georgia Sec. of State Brian Kemp (R) until all votes were counted. (The margin stood at 50.3%-48.7%, as of Nov. 9.) Kemp, whose office had been sued over a strict "exact-match" voter registration law, was ordered by a federal judge Nov. 2 to allow about 3,100 primarily minority residents, who had been barred, to cast votes. Without citing evidence, Kemp two days before Election Day alleged Democrats hacked into the state's voter files.

In other news-making races, Rep. Jared Polis (D) became the nation's first openly gay governor in Colorado, and in Vermont, Christine Hallquist (D), the first openly transgender major-party nominee for governor, lost to incumbent Gov. Phil Scott (R).

Ballot Issues

There were more than 150 statewide measures on Nov. 6 ballots. Perennial swing-state Florida restored voting rights to about 1.5 mil felons not convicted of murder or sexual offenses. (The move likely will disadvantage the GOP, since those affected were three times as likely to be Democratic voters, according to a *Tampa Bay Times/Miami Herald* analysis.) Voters in Colorado, Michigan, Missouri, and Utah all passed citizen-led redistricting measures aimed at limiting gerrymandering.

Following a contentious campaign to fund homeless-reduction efforts in San Francisco, CA, that pitted rival tech firm CEOs against one another, San Francisco voters easily approved a citywide tax on companies with over $50 mil in sales to fight the homeless crisis. Arkansas and Missouri voted to increase the state minimum wage.

Voters in the Republican strongholds of Idaho, Nebraska, and Utah approved expanding Medicaid. Alabama and West Virginia chose to prohibit publicly funding abortions, and Alabama extended "personhood" to fetuses, while voters in Oregon rejected an anti-abortion provision. Michigan legalized recreational marijuana use, the first Midwestern state to do so; Missouri and Utah approved marijuana for medical use, but North Dakota voters declined to pass a similar measure.

Two years after rejecting a carbon tax, Washington state voters by a 56%-44% margin again voted down what would have been the nation's first statewide fee on emitters. U.S. oil companies contributed most of the over $31 mil spent to thwart the measure, about twice what its supporters raised.

Campaign Trail Quotes, 2018

"Sadly, the left seems consumed with anger and hatred. They're angry at me. They're angry at the president. They are angry at all of you. They are angry with just about anyone who dares to agree with Republicans."
—**Gov. Scott Walker** (R, WI), speaking at state GOP convention, May 12, in Milwaukee.

"Donald Trump and the billionaire class should consider this victory a warning shot. The blue wave is coming."
—Democratic House nominee **Debra Haaland** after her June 5 primary win in New Mexico; she was one of the first two Native American women elected to the U.S. House.

"[I've] always said, 'I didn't run for Congress. I didn't run for the Senate. I'm not in Washington. My focus—what they hired me to do—was run the state of Maryland.'"
—**Gov. Larry Hogan** (R), who was reelected governor in blue-state Maryland, in interview with *NY Times* published Aug. 4.

"If you don't like what's going on right now, and you shouldn't—do not complain. Don't hashtag. Don't get anxious. … Don't put your head in the sand. Don't boo. Vote!"
—Former Pres. **Barack Obama**, Sept. 7, speaking at the Univ. of Illinois at Urbana-Champaign.

"We are seeing tens of millions of dollars flooding in … from liberals all over the country who desperately want to turn the state of Texas blue. They want us to be just like California, right down to tofu and silicon and dyed hair."
—**Sen. Ted Cruz** (R, TX), Sept. 8, campaigning in Katy, TX.

"You can't pick your family."
—**U.S. Rep. Paul Gosar** (R, AZ) in a tweet, Sept. 22, reacting to a televised ad in which six of his nine siblings denounced him and endorsed his Democratic challenger. (Gosar won.)

"There is nothing that unifies all stripes of Republicans more than a court fight. [Democrats] stupidly handed us the best issue they possibly could going into the fall election."
—**Senate Majority Leader Mitch McConnell** (R, KY), speaking to the *NY Times* after the Senate voted, Oct. 6, to confirm appointment of Judge Brett Kavanaugh to the U.S. Supreme Court.

"This will be an election of Kavanaugh, the caravan, law and order, and common sense."
—**Pres. Donald Trump** at a campaign rally in Montana, Oct. 18.

"My grandmother used to say, a hit dog will holler."
—Florida gubernatorial candidate **Andrew Gillum** (D), in Oct. 24 debate, in widely cited response to defense mounted by former U.S. Rep. Ron DeSantis (R) against charges of racism.

"I'm here today because of the men and … women who were lynched, who were humiliated … who were repressed and oppressed, for the right, for the equality, at the polls. … Their blood has seeped into my DNA, and I refuse to let their sacrifices be in vain."
—Media magnate **Oprah Winfrey**, campaigning Nov. 1 in Georgia for gubernatorial candidate Stacey Abrams (D).

"Yesterday's election was not only a vote to protect America's health care; it was a vote to restore the health of our democracy."
—**House Minority Leader Nancy Pelosi** (D, CA), at a news conference on Capitol Hill, Nov. 7.

"I want to probe senior administration officials across the government who have abused their positions of power and wasted taxpayer money, as well as President Trump's decisions to act in his own financial self-interest rather than the best interests of the American people."
—U.S. Rep. **Elijah Cummings** (D, MD), speaking Nov. 7 as prospective chair of the House Oversight Committee.

"Those that worked with me in this incredible Midterm Election, embracing certain policies and principles, did very well. Those that did not, say goodbye! Yesterday was such a very Big Win, and all under the pressure of a Nasty and Hostile Media!"
—**Pres. Trump** on Twitter, Nov. 7.

Members of the 116th Congress: U.S. Senate

Source: © Associated Press; all rights reserved. 2018 results are preliminary as of Nov. 7-9, 2018.

51 Republicans, 44 Democrats, 2 independents (who caucus with Democrats). Results in three races were still pending and are listed in italics. Terms are for six years and end Jan. of the year preceding the senator's name in the following table. Annual salary: $174,000; President Pro Tempore, Majority Leader, and Minority Leader: $193,400. To be eligible to serve in the Senate, a person must be at least 30 years old, a U.S. citizen for at least nine years, and a resident of the state from which elected. Boldface denotes the 2018 election winner. Third-party or independent candidates receiving fewer than 50,000 votes are not necessarily listed.

* = Incumbent. D = Democrat; R = Republican; DFL = Dem.-Farmer-Labor; Ind. = Independent; LB = Libertarian; NPL = Nonpartisan League.

Term ends	Senator/candidate (party); service from	2018 election results
Alabama		
2021	Doug Jones (D); 1/3/2018	
2023	Richard Shelby (R); 1/6/1987	
Alaska		
2021	Dan Sullivan (R); 1/6/2015	
2023	Lisa Murkowski (R); 12/20/2002	
Arizona		
2023[1]	Jon Kyl (R); 9/5/2018	
2025	*Kyrsten Sinema (D)*	*932,870*
	Martha McSally (R)	*923,260*
Arkansas		
2021	Tom Cotton (R); 1/6/2015	
2023	John Boozman (R); 1/5/2011	
California		
2023	Kamala Harris (D); 1/3/2017	
2025	**Dianne Feinstein* (D); 11/10/1992**	3,358,152
	Kevin de León (D)	2,820,615
Colorado		
2021	Cory Gardner (R); 1/6/2015	
2023	Michael Bennet (D); 1/22/2009	
Connecticut		
2023	Richard Blumenthal (D); 1/5/2011	
2025	**Christopher S. Murphy* (D); 1/3/2013**	771,927
	Matthew Corey (R)	527,263
Delaware		
2021	Christopher Coons (D); 11/15/2010	
2025	**Thomas R. Carper* (D); 1/3/2001**	217,358
	Robert B. Arlett (R)	137,123
Florida		
2023	Marco Rubio (R); 1/5/2011	
2025	*Rick Scott (R)*	*4,094,763*
	Bill Nelson* (D); 1/3/2001	*4,079,692*
Georgia		
2021	David Perdue (R); 1/6/2015	
2023	Johnny Isakson (R); 1/4/2005	
Hawaii		
2023	Brian Schatz (D); 12/26/2012	
2025	**Mazie K. Hirono* (D); 1/3/2013**	276,133
	Ron Curtis (R)	111,977
Idaho		
2021	Jim Risch (R); 1/6/2009	
2023	Mike Crapo (R); 1/6/1999	
Illinois		
2021	Richard J. Durbin (D); 1/7/1997	
2023	Tammy Duckworth (D); 1/3/2017	
Indiana		
2023	Todd C. Young (R); 1/3/2017	
2025	**Mike Braun (R)**	1,079,984
	Joe Donnelly* (D); 1/3/2013	907,081
	Lucy Brenton (LB)	82,205
Iowa		
2021	Joni Ernst (R); 1/6/2015	
2023	Chuck Grassley (R); 1/5/1981	
Kansas		
2021	Pat Roberts (R); 1/7/1997	
2023	Jerry Moran (R); 1/5/2011	
Kentucky		
2021	Mitch McConnell (R); 1/3/1985	
2023	Rand Paul (R); 1/5/2011	
Louisiana		
2021	Bill Cassidy (R); 1/6/2015	
2023	John Kennedy (R); 1/3/2017	
Maine		
2021	Susan M. Collins (R); 1/7/1997	
2025	**Angus King* (Ind.); 1/3/2013**	316,121
	Eric L. Brakey (R)	202,620
	Zak Ringelstein (D)	60,626

Term ends	Senator/candidate (party); service from	2018 election results
Maryland		
2023	Chris Van Hollen (D); 1/3/2017	
2025	**Ben Cardin* (D); 1/4/2007**	1,361,967
	Tony Campbell (R)	659,120
	Neal Simon (Ind.)	79,548
Massachusetts		
2021	Ed Markey (D); 7/16/2013	
2025	**Elizabeth A. Warren* (D); 1/3/2013**	1,540,825
	Geoff Diehl (R)	914,071
	Shiva Ayyadurai (Ind.)	85,803
Michigan		
2021	Gary Peters (D); 1/6/2015	
2025	**Debbie Stabenow* (D); 1/3/2001**	2,118,600
	John James (R)	1,889,577
Minnesota		
2021[2]	**Tina Smith* (DFL); 1/3/2018**	1,370,375
	Karin Housley (R)	1,095,777
	Sarah Wellington (Ind.)	95,634
2025	**Amy Klobuchar* (DFL); 1/4/2007**	1,566,015
	Jim Newberger (R)	940,454
	Dennis Schuller (Ind.)	66,264
Mississippi		
2021[3]	*Cindy Hyde-Smith* (R); 4/9/2018*	*368,536*
	Mike Espy (D)	*360,112*
	Chris McDaniel (R)	*146,013*
	Tobey Bartee (D)	*12,707*
2025	**Roger F. Wicker* (R); 12/31/2007**	515,131
	David Baria (D)	342,905
Missouri		
2023	Roy Blunt (R); 1/5/2011	
2025	**Josh Hawley (R)**	1,245,732
	Claire McCaskill* (D); 1/4/2007	1,101,377
Montana		
2021	Steve Daines (R); 1/6/2015	
2025	**Jon Tester* (D); 1/4/2007**	218,145
	Matt Rosendale (R)	213,935
Nebraska		
2021	Ben Sasse (R); 1/6/2015	
2025	**Deb Fischer* (R); 1/3/2013**	393,720
	Jane Raybould (D)	259,751
Nevada		
2023	Catherine Cortez Masto (D); 1/3/2017	
2025	**Jacky Rosen (D)**	486,794
	Dean Heller* (R); 5/9/2011	438,516
New Hampshire		
2021	Jeanne Shaheen (D); 1/6/2009	
2023	Maggie Hassan (D); 1/3/2017	
New Jersey		
2021	Cory Booker (D); 10/31/2013	
2025	**Robert Menendez* (D); 1/18/2006**	1,470,799
	Bob Hugin (R)	1,211,408
New Mexico		
2021	Tom Udall (D); 1/6/2009	
2025	**Martin Heinrich* (D); 1/3/2013**	364,749
	Mick Rich (R)	208,657
	Gary Johnson (LB)	104,887
New York		
2023	Charles Schumer (D); 1/6/1999	
2025	**Kirsten E. Gillibrand* (D); 1/27/2009**	3,699,442
	Chele Chiavacci Farley (R)	1,855,011
North Carolina		
2021	Thom Tillis (R); 1/6/2015	
2023	Richard Burr (R); 1/4/2005	
North Dakota		
2023	John Hoeven (R); 1/5/2011	
2025	**Kevin Cramer (R)**	178,876
	Heidi Heitkamp* (D-NPL); 1/3/2013	143,737

Term ends	Senator/candidate (party); service from	2018 election results
Ohio		
2023	Rob Portman (R); 1/5/2011	
2025	**Sherrod Brown* (D); 1/4/2007**	**2,286,730**
	Jim Renacci (R)	2,011,832
Oklahoma		
2021	James M. Inhofe (R); 11/21/1994	
2023	James Lankford (R); 1/6/2015	
Oregon		
2021	Jeff Merkley (D); 1/6/2009	
2023	Ron Wyden (D); 2/6/1996	
Pennsylvania		
2023	Pat Toomey (R); 1/5/2011	
2025	**Bob Casey Jr.* (D); 1/4/2007**	**2,724,451**
	Lou Barletta (R)	2,098,713
	Dale Kerns (LB)	50,110
Rhode Island		
2021	Jack Reed (D); 1/7/1997	
2025	**Sheldon Whitehouse* (D); 1/4/2007**	**228,679**
	Robert G. Flanders Jr. (R)	143,293
South Carolina		
2021	Lindsey Graham (R); 1/7/2003	
2023	Tim Scott (R); 1/3/2013	
South Dakota		
2021	Mike Rounds (R); 1/6/2015	
2023	John Thune (R); 1/4/2005	
Tennessee		
2021	Lamar Alexander (R); 1/7/2003	
2025	**Marsha Blackburn (R).**	**1,224,042**
	Phil Bredesen (D)	981,667
Texas		
2021	John Cornyn (R); 12/2/2002	

Term ends	Senator/candidate (party); service from	2018 election results
2025	**Ted Cruz* (R); 1/3/2013**	**4,240,942**
	Beto O'Rourke (D)	4,017,851
	Neal M. Dikeman (LB)	65,161
Utah		
2023	Mike Lee (R); 1/5/2011	
2025	**Mitt Romney (R)**	**475,034**
	Jenny Wilson (D)	239,341
Vermont		
2023	Patrick Leahy (D); 1/3/1975	
2025	**Bernie Sanders* (Ind.); 1/4/2007**	**183,108**
	Lawrence Zupan (R)	74,405
Virginia		
2021	Mark Warner (D); 1/6/2009	
2025	**Timothy M. Kaine* (D); 1/3/2013**	**1,883,375**
	Corey A. Stewart (R)	1,361,984
	Matt J. Waters (LB)	61,494
Washington		
2023	Patty Murray (D); 1/3/1993	
2025	**Maria Cantwell* (D); 1/3/2001**	**1,144,970**
	Susan Hutchison (R)	808,873
West Virginia		
2021	Shelley Moore Capito (R); 1/6/2015	
2025	**Joe Manchin III* (D); 11/15/2010**	**288,808**
	Patrick Morrisey (R)	269,872
Wisconsin		
2023	Ron Johnson (R); 1/5/2011	
2025	**Tammy Baldwin* (D); 1/3/2013**	**1,471,904**
	Leah Vukmir (R)	1,183,061
Wyoming		
2021	Michael B. Enzi (R); 1/7/1997	
2025	**John Barrasso* (R); 6/22/2007**	**136,329**
	Gary Trauner (D)	61,254

(1) Kyl was appointed to fill the seat vacated by Sen. John McCain (R), who died in office Aug. 25, 2018. A special election was expected to be held in 2020 to fill the seat for the duration of the term. (2) Smith was appointed to fill the seat vacated by Sen. Al Franken (DFL), who resigned effective Jan. 2, 2018. Result of special election held Nov. 6, 2018, to fill the seat for the duration of the term. (3) Hyde-Smith was appointed to fill the seat vacated by Sen. Thad Cochran (R), who resigned his seat effective Apr. 1, 2018. Result of special election held Nov. 6, 2018, to fill the seat for the duration of the term; a runoff between Espy and Hyde-Smith was scheduled for Nov. 27, 2018.

Members of the 116th Congress: U.S. House of Representatives

Source: © Associated Press; all rights reserved. 2018 results are preliminary as of Nov. 7-9, 2018.

226 Democrats, 198 Republicans. Results in 11 races were still pending and are listed in italics. Terms are for two years ending on Jan. 3, 2021. Annual salary, $174,000; Majority Leader and Minority Leader, $193,400; Speaker of the House, $223,500. To be eligible to serve in the House, a person must be at least 25 years of age, a U.S. citizen for at least seven years, and a resident of the state from which elected. Boldface denotes the 2018 election winner. Third-party or independent candidates receiving fewer than 10,000 votes are not necessarily listed.

* = Incumbent; ** = Incumbent in another district. D = Democrat; R = Republican; DFL = Dem.-Farmer-Labor; Ind. = Independent; LB = Libertarian; NPA = No party affiliation; NPL = Nonpartisan League; NPP = No party preference; RF = Reform.

Dist.	Representative/candidate (party)	2018 election results
Alabama		
1	**Bradley Byrne* (R)**	**151,150**
	Robert Kennedy Jr. (D)	87,540
2	**Martha Roby* (R)**	**138,581**
	Tabitha Isner (D)	86,580
3	**Mike Rogers* (R).**	**147,480**
	Mallory Hagan (D)	83,145
4	**Robert Aderholt* (R).**	**183,958**
	Lee Auman (D)	46,370
5	**Mo Brooks* (R).**	**156,532**
	Peter Joffrion (D).	99,694
6	**Gary Palmer* (R).**	**190,501**
	Danner Kline (D).	83,935
7	**Terri A. Sewell* (D)**	**Unopposed**
Alaska		
	Don Young* (R)	**126,655**
	Alyse S. Galvin (Ind.)	107,165
Arizona		
1	**Tom O'Halleran* (D)**	**111,886**
	Wendy Rogers (R)	97,958
2	**Ann Kirkpatrick (D)**	**125,349**
	Lea Marquez Peterson (R)	109,759
3	**Raúl M. Grijalva* (D)**	**78,308**
	Nicolas Pierson (R).	49,331
4	**Paul A. Gosar* (R).**	**156,086**
	David Brill (D)	67,346

Dist.	Representative/candidate (party)	2018 election results
5	**Andy Biggs* (R)**	**125,782**
	Joan Greene (D).	83,894
6	**David Schweikert* (R).**	**122,974**
	Anita Malik (D)	95,105
7	**Ruben Gallego* (D).**	**67,796**
	Gary Swing (Green)	12,647
8	**Debbie Lesko* (R).**	**123,681**
	Hiral Tipirneni (D)	94,583
9	**Greg Stanton (D).**	**100,618**
	Stephen L. Ferrara (R)	68,604
Arkansas		
1	**Rick Crawford* (R)**	**138,436**
	Chintan Desai (D).	57,459
2	**French Hill* (R)**	**131,712**
	Clarke Tucker (D)	115,564
3	**Steve Womack* (R)**	**148,088**
	Joshua Mahony (D)	74,278
4	**Bruce Westerman* (R)**	**135,300**
	Hayden Shamel (D)	63,271
California		
1	**Doug LaMalfa* (R)**	**110,236**
	Audrey Denney (D).	86,137
2	**Jared Huffman* (D)**	**135,375**
	Dale K. Mensing (R)	46,731
3	**John Garamendi* (D)**	**87,643**
	Charlie Schaupp (R).	65,628

Dist.	Representative/candidate (party)	2018 election results
4	**Tom McClintock* (R)**	**120,601**
	Jessica Morse (D)	97,345
5	**Mike Thompson* (D)**	**121,689**
	Anthony Mills (NPP)	34,279
6	**Doris O. Matsui* (D)**	**58,007**
	Jrmar Jefferson (D)	14,781
7	**Ami Bera* (D)**	**54,097**
	Andrew Grant (R)	48,597
8	**Paul Cook* (R)**	**66,136**
	Tim Donnelly (R)	43,589
9	**Jerry McNerney* (D)**	**56,188**
	Marla Livengood (R)	47,316
10	*Jeff Denham* (R)*	*56,701*
	Josh Harder (D)	*55,414*
11	**Mark DeSaulnier* (D)**	**110,188**
	John Fitzgerald (R)	43,053
12	**Nancy Pelosi* (D)**	**161,212**
	Lisa Remmer (R)	27,231
13	**Barbara Lee* (D)**	**106,951**
	Laura Wells (Green)	14,983
14	**Jackie Speier* (D)**	**75,585**
	Cristina Osmeña (R)	23,325
15	**Eric Swalwell* (D)**	**81,428**
	Rudy L. Peters Jr. (R)	34,953
16	**Jim Costa* (D)**	**44,769**
	Elizabeth Heng (R)	37,480
17	**Ro Khanna* (D)**	**72,765**
	Ron Cohen (R)	27,590
18	**Anna G. Eshoo* (D)**	**100,440**
	Christine Russell (R)	40,135
19	**Zoe Lofgren* (D)**	**75,959**
	Justin James Aguilera (R)	32,149
20	**Jimmy Panetta* (D)**	**95,124**
	Ronald Paul Kabat (NPP)	25,236
21	**David G. Valadao* (R)**	**35,416**
	TJ Cox (D)	30,577
22	**Devin G. Nunes* (R)**	**75,111**
	Andrew Janz (D)	59,528
23	**Kevin McCarthy* (R)**	**89,568**
	Tatiana Matta (D)	45,152
24	**Salud Carbajal* (D)**	**96,088**
	Justin Fareed (R)	75,578
25	**Katie Hill (D)**	**90,298**
	Steve Knight* (R)	84,272
26	**Julia Brownley* (D)**	**96,489**
	Antonio Sabato Jr. (R)	65,894
27	**Judy Chu* (D)**	**104,414**
	Bryan Witt (D)	28,740
28	**Adam B. Schiff* (D)**	**127,153**
	Johnny J. Nalbandian (R)	39,188
29	**Tony Cárdenas* (D)**	**78,470**
	Benito "Benny" Bernal (R)	20,592
30	**Brad Sherman* (D)**	**124,383**
	Mark S. Reed (R)	49,887
31	**Pete Aguilar* (D)**	**61,747**
	Sean Flynn (R)	48,234
32	**Grace Flores Napolitano* (D)**	**79,335**
	Joshua M. Scott (R)	39,600
33	**Ted W. Lieu* (D)**	**144,380**
	Kenneth Weston Wright (R)	67,939
34	**Jimmy Gomez* (D)**	**70,695**
	Kenneth Mejia (Green)	24,593
35	**Norma J. Torres* (D)**	**58,982**
	Christian Leonel Valiente (R)	28,282
36	**Raul Ruiz* (D)**	**57,675**
	Kimberlin Brown Pelzer (R)	44,616
37	**Karen Bass* (D)**	**134,719**
	Ron J. Bassilian (R)	17,972
38	**Linda T. Sánchez* (D)**	**91,031**
	Ryan Downing (R)	45,115
39	*Young Kim (R)*	*78,667*
	Gil Cisneros (D)	*74,793*
40	**Lucille Roybal-Allard* (D)**	**61,357**
	Rodolfo Cortes Barragan (Green)	17,454
41	**Mark Takano* (D)**	**43,929**
	Aja Smith (R)	28,749
42	**Ken Calvert* (R)**	**61,833**
	Julia C. Peacock (D)	42,245

Dist.	Representative/candidate (party)	2018 election results
43	**Maxine Waters* (D)**	**97,911**
	Omar Navarro (R)	31,188
44	**Nanette Diaz Barragán* (D)**	**65,748**
	Aja L. Brown (D)	28,961
45	*Mimi Walters* (R)*	*99,639*
	Katie Porter (D)	*95,602*
46	**Lou Correa* (D)**	**47,763**
	Russell Rene Lambert (R)	27,600
47	**Alan Lowenthal* (D)**	**86,427**
	John Briscoe (R)	52,131
48	*Harley Rouda (D)*	*98,259*
	Dana Rohrabacher* (R)	*93,503*
49	**Mike Levin (D)**	**76,135**
	Diane L. Harkey (R)	69,031
50	**Duncan D. Hunter* (R)**	**66,934**
	Ammar Campa-Najjar (D)	56,481
51	**Juan Vargas* (D)**	**43,387**
	Juan M. Hidalgo Jr. (R)	21,323
52	**Scott Peters* (D)**	**91,206**
	Omar Qudrat (R)	58,821
53	**Susan A. Davis* (D)**	**79,839**
	Morgan Murtaugh (R)	42,445

Colorado

Dist.	Representative/candidate (party)	2018 election results
1	**Diana DeGette* (D)**	**147,329**
	Charles "Casper" Stockham (R)	53,382
2	**Joe Neguse (D)**	**212,332**
	Peter Yu (R)	121,200
	Nick Thomas (Ind.)	12,270
3	**Scott R. Tipton* (R)**	**159,878**
	Diane Mitsch Bush (D)	133,345
4	**Ken Buck* (R)**	**181,513**
	Karen McCormick (D)	111,312
5	**Doug Lamborn* (R)**	**138,434**
	Stephany Rose Spaulding (D)	90,143
6	**Jason Crow (D)**	**151,239**
	Mike Coffman* (R)	125,963
7	**Ed Perlmutter* (D)**	**150,385**
	Mark Barrington (R)	92,630

Connecticut

Dist.	Representative/candidate (party)	2018 election results
1	**John B. Larson* (D)**	**163,934**
	Jennifer T. Nye (R)	93,257
2	**Joe Courtney* (D)**	**178,873**
	Danny Postemski Jr. (R)	102,326
3	**Rosa L. DeLauro* (D)**	**151,792**
	Angel Cadena (R)	92,856
4	**Jim Himes* (D)**	**165,278**
	Harry Arora (R)	106,156
5	**Jahana Hayes (D)**	**140,908**
	Manny Santos (R)	110,954

Delaware

Dist.	Representative/candidate (party)	2018 election results
	Lisa Blunt Rochester* (D)	**227,333**
	Scott Walker (R)	125,381

Florida

Dist.	Representative/candidate (party)	2018 election results
1	**Matt Gaetz* (R)**	**215,980**
	Jennifer M. Zimmerman (D)	105,998
2	**Neal Dunn* (R)**	**199,112**
	Bob Rackleff (D)	96,068
3	**Ted Yoho* (R)**	**176,286**
	Yvonne Hayes Hinson (D)	129,153
4	**John Rutherford* (R)**	**247,197**
	George "Ges" Selmont (D)	122,512
5	**Al Lawson* (D)**	**180,105**
	Virginia Fuller (R)	89,664
6	**Michael Waltz (R)**	**187,705**
	Nancy Soderberg (D)	145,546
7	**Stephanie Murphy* (D)**	**182,949**
	Mike Miller (R)	134,253
8	**Bill Posey* (R)**	**217,931**
	Sanjay Patel (D)	142,209
9	**Darren Soto* (D)**	**171,941**
	Wayne Liebnitzky (R)	124,460
10	**Val Demings* (D)**	**Unopposed**
11	**Daniel Webster* (R)**	**239,242**
	Dana Cottrell (D)	127,933
12	**Gus M. Bilirakis* (R)**	**194,436**
	Chris Hunter (D)	132,695
13	**Charlie Crist* (D)**	**182,563**
	George Buck (R)	134,183

Dist.	Representative/candidate (party)	2018 election results
14	**Kathy Castor* (D)**	Unopposed
15	**Ross Spano (R)**	151,063
	Kristen Carlson (D)	133,686
16	**Vern Buchanan* (R)**	196,965
	David Shapiro (D)	163,996
17	**Greg Steube (R)**	193,185
	Allen L. Ellison (April Freeman)[1] (D)	117,074
18	**Brian Mast* (R)**	183,376
	Lauren Baer (D)	153,543
19	**Francis Rooney* (R)**	211,321
	David Holden (D)	127,952
20	**Alcee L. Hastings* (D)**	Unopposed
21	**Lois Frankel* (D)**	Unopposed
22	**Ted Deutch* (D)**	172,220
	Nicolas Kimaz (R)	106,303
23	**Debbie Wasserman Schultz* (D)**	154,052
	Joe Kaufman (R)	95,220
	Tim Canova (NPA)	12,900
24	**Frederica S. Wilson* (D)**	Unopposed
25	**Mario Diaz-Balart* (R)**	128,611
	Mary Barzee Flores (D)	84,034
26	**Debbie Mucarsel-Powell (D)**	119,723
	Carlos Curbelo* (R)	115,644
27	**Donna Shalala (D)**	130,636
	Maria Elvira Salazar (R)	115,546

Georgia

Dist.	Representative/candidate (party)	2018 election results
1	**Earl L. "Buddy" Carter* (R)**	143,931
	Lisa M. Ring (D)	104,406
2	**Sanford D. Bishop Jr.* (D)**	135,707
	Herman West Jr. (R)	92,132
3	**Drew Ferguson* (R)**	191,700
	Chuck Enderlin (D)	100,733
4	**Henry C. "Hank" Johnson Jr.* (D)**	225,359
	Joe Profit (R)	60,646
5	**John Lewis* (D)**	Unopposed
6	**Lucy McBath (D)**	159,268
	Karen Handel* (R)	156,396
7	*Rob Woodall* (R)*	*139,804*
	Carolyn Bourdeaux (D)	*138,934*
8	**Austin Scott* (R)**	Unopposed
9	**Doug Collins* (R)**	224,412
	Josh McCall (D)	57,823
10	**Jody Hice* (R)**	190,080
	Tabitha A. Johnson-Green (D)	111,938
11	**Barry Loudermilk* (R)**	191,529
	Flynn D. Broady Jr. (D)	118,053
12	**Rick W. Allen* (R)**	148,092
	Francys Johnson (D)	100,986
13	**David Scott* (D)**	220,662
	David Callahan (R)	69,347
14	**Tom Graves* (R)**	175,482
	Steven Lamar Foster (D)	53,841

Hawaii

Dist.	Representative/candidate (party)	2018 election results
1	**Ed Case (D)**	134,603
	Cam Cavasso (R)	42,480
2	**Tulsi Gabbard* (D)**	153,132
	Brian Evans (R)	44,816

Idaho

Dist.	Representative/candidate (party)	2018 election results
1	**Russ Fulcher (R)**	193,980
	Cristina McNeil (D)	92,824
2	**Mike Simpson* (R)**	170,280
	Aaron Swisher (D)	110,386

Illinois

Dist.	Representative/candidate (party)	2018 election results
1	**Bobby L. Rush* (D)**	176,560
	Jimmy Lee Tillman II (R)	49,976
	Thomas Rudbeck (Ind.)	16,506
2	**Robin Kelly* (D)**	183,816
	David Merkle (R)	43,875
3	**Daniel Lipinski* (D)**	155,940
	Arthur J. Jones (R)	56,350
4	**Jesus "Chuy" Garcia (D)**	134,522
	Mark Wayne Lorch (R)	21,083
5	**Mike Quigley* (D)**	197,162
	Tom Hanson (R)	62,039
6	**Sean Casten (D)**	156,346
	Peter J. Roskam* (R)	139,667
7	**Danny K. Davis* (D)**	199,625
	Craig Cameron (R)	27,776

Dist.	Representative/candidate (party)	2018 election results
8	**Raja Krishnamoorthi* (D)**	124,908
	Jitendra "JD" Diganvker (R)	65,576
9	**Jan Schakowsky* (D)**	202,372
	John D. Elleson (R)	74,910
10	**Brad Schneider* (D)**	151,860
	Douglas R. Bennett (R)	80,361
11	**Bill Foster* (D)**	140,907
	Nick Stella (R)	80,775
12	**Mike Bost* (R)**	134,009
	Brendan Kelly (D)	116,985
13	**Rodney Davis* (R)**	135,680
	Betsy Dirksen Londrigan (D)	131,958
14	**Lauren Underwood (D)**	142,261
	Randall M. "Randy" Hultgren* (R)	131,819
15	**John M. Shimkus* (R)**	177,682
	Kevin Gaither (D)	69,234
16	**Adam Kinzinger* (R)**	149,205
	Sara Dady (D)	100,789
17	**Cheri Bustos* (D)**	139,461
	William W. "Bill" Fawell (R)	86,218
18	**Darin LaHood* (R)**	193,543
	Junius Rodriguez (D)	93,330

Indiana

Dist.	Representative/candidate (party)	2018 election results
1	**Peter J. Visclosky* (D)**	121,800
	Mark Leyva (R)	58,903
2	**Jackie Walorski* (R)**	117,901
	Mel Hall (D)	88,588
3	**Jim Banks* (R)**	158,355
	Courtney Tritch (D)	86,420
4	**Jim Baird (R)**	148,603
	Tobi Beck (D)	83,200
5	**Susan W. Brooks* (R)**	175,768
	Dee Thornton (D)	126,586
6	**Greg Pence (R)**	138,557
	Jeannine Lee Lake (D)	73,004
7	**André Carson* (D)**	116,673
	Wayne "Gunny" Harmon (R)	69,047
8	**Larry Bucshon* (R)**	157,209
	William Tanoos (D)	86,409
9	**Trey Hollingsworth* (R)**	144,541
	Liz Watson (D)	98,292

Iowa

Dist.	Representative/candidate (party)	2018 election results
1	**Abby Finkenauer (D)**	169,348
	Rod Blum* (R)	152,940
	Troy Hageman (LB)	10,228
2	**Dave Loebsack* (D)**	171,054
	Christopher Peters (R)	133,010
3	**Cindy Axne (D)**	169,886
	David Young* (R)	164,656
4	**Steve King* (R)**	157,221
	J.D. Scholten (D)	146,698

Kansas

Dist.	Representative/candidate (party)	2018 election results
1	**Roger Marshall* (R)**	149,708
	Alan LaPolice (D)	69,076
2	**Steve Watkins (R)**	124,895
	Paul Davis (D)	120,421
	Kelly Standley (LB)	14,402
3	**Sharice Davids (D)**	164,253
	Kevin Yoder* (R)	136,104
4	**Ron Estes* (R)**	138,856
	James A. Thompson (D)	93,384

Kentucky

Dist.	Representative/candidate (party)	2018 election results
1	**James Comer* (R)**	172,166
	Paul Walker (D)	78,849
2	**S. Brett Guthrie* (R)**	171,700
	Hank Linderman (D)	79,994
3	**John A. Yarmuth* (D)**	172,999
	Vickie Yates Brown Glisson (R)	101,929
4	**Thomas Massie* (R)**	162,943
	Seth Hall (D)	90,533
5	**Harold "Hal" Rogers* (R)**	172,359
	Kenneth S. Stepp (D)	45,965
6	**Andy Barr* (R)**	154,468
	Amy McGrath (D)	144,730

Dist.	Representative/candidate (party)	2018 election results
Louisiana		
1	**Steve Scalise* (R)**	**192,526**
	Tammy M. Savoie (D)	44,262
	Lee Ann Dugas (D)	18,552
2	**Cedric Richmond* (D)**	**190,066**
	Jesse Schmidt (NPA)	20,463
	Belden "Noonie Man" Batiste (Ind.)	17,255
3	**Clay Higgins* (R)**	**136,871**
	Mildred "Mimi" Methvin (D)	43,727
	Josh Guillory (R)	31,387
	Rob Anderson (D)	13,477
4	**Mike Johnson* (R)**	**139,307**
	Ryan Trundle (D)	72,923
5	**Ralph Abraham* (R)**	**149,010**
	Jessee Carlton Fleenor (D)	67,113
6	**Garret Graves* (R)**	**186,502**
	Justin DeWitt (D)	55,078
	Andie Saizan (D)	21,619
Maine		
1	**Chellie Pingree* (D)**	**187,054**
	Mark I. Holbrook (R)	101,600
	Martin J. Grohman (Ind.)	27,914
2	*Bruce Poliquin* (R)*	*131,466*
	Jared F. Golden (D)	*129,556*
	Tiffany Bond (Ind.)	*16,500*
Maryland		
1	**Andy Harris* (R)**	**176,595**
	Jesse Colvin (D)	109,617
2	**C.A. Dutch Ruppersberger* (D)**	**157,764**
	Liz Matory (R)	74,493
3	**John P. Sarbanes* (D)**	**186,207**
	Charles Anthony (R)	78,167
4	**Anthony G. Brown* (D)**	**194,129**
	George McDermott (R)	50,292
5	**Steny H. Hoyer* (D)**	**200,425**
	William A. Devine III (R)	78,117
6	**David Trone (D)**	**142,656**
	Amie Hoeber (R)	97,330
7	**Elijah Cummings* (D)**	**187,462**
	Richmond Davis (R)	53,615
8	**Jamie Raskin* (D)**	**190,973**
	John Walsh (R)	90,193
Massachusetts		
1	**Richard E. Neal* (D)**	**Unopposed**
2	**Jim McGovern* (D)**	**172,196**
	Tracy Lyn Lovvorn (R)	82,439
3	**Lori Loureiro Trahan (D)**	**171,303**
	Rick Green (R)	92,744
	Michael Mullen (Ind.)	12,473
4	**Joseph P. Kennedy III* (D)**	**Unopposed**
5	**Katherine M. Clark* (D)**	**216,363**
	John Hugo (R)	67,550
6	**Seth Moulton* (D)**	**196,253**
	Joseph S. Schneider (R)	92,672
	Mary Jean Charbonneau (Ind.)	10,048
7	**Ayanna Pressley (D)**	**Unopposed**
8	**Stephen F. Lynch* (D)**	**Unopposed**
9	**Bill Keating* (D)**	**175,967**
	Peter D. Tedeschi (R)	120,663
Michigan		
1	**Jack Bergman* (R)**	**185,752**
	Matthew W. Morgan (D)	144,203
2	**Bill Huizenga* (R)**	**168,843**
	Rob Davidson (D)	131,195
3	**Justin Amash* (R)**	**162,038**
	Cathy Albro (D)	124,981
4	**John Moolenaar* (R)**	**178,511**
	Jerry Hilliard (D)	106,539
5	**Daniel T. Kildee* (D)**	**164,521**
	Travis Wines (R)	99,269
	Kathy Goodwin (Working Class)	12,645
6	**Fred Upton* (R)**	**147,437**
	Matt Longjohn (D)	134,069
	Stephen J. Young (U.S. Taxpayers)	11,923
7	**Tim Walberg* (R)**	**158,885**
	Gretchen Driskell (D)	136,410
8	**Elissa Slotkin (D)**	**172,878**
	Mike Bishop* (R)	159,804

Dist.	Representative/candidate (party)	2018 election results
9	**Andy Levin (D)**	**181,844**
	Candius Stearns (R)	112,309
10	**Paul Mitchell* (R)**	**182,870**
	Kimberly Bizon (D)	106,098
	Jeremy Peruski (NPA)	11,373
11	**Haley Stevens (D)**	**179,976**
	Lena Epstein (R)	155,331
12	**Debbie Dingell* (D)**	**172,988**
	Jeff Jones (R)	69,743
13[2]	**Rashida Tlaib (D)**	**127,238**
	Sam Johnson (Working Class)	15,837
14	**Brenda Lawrence* (D)**	**197,105**
	Marc S. Herschfus (R)	36,592
Minnesota		
1	**Jim Hagedorn (R)**	**146,202**
	Dan Feehan (DFL)	144,891
2	**Angie Craig (DFL)**	**177,971**
	Jason Lewis* (R)	159,373
3	**Dean Phillips (DFL)**	**202,402**
	Erik Paulsen* (R)	160,838
4	**Betty McCollum* (DFL)**	**216,701**
	Greg Ryan (R)	97,696
	Susan Pendergast Sindt (Ind.)	13,764
5	**Ilhan Omar (DFL)**	**267,690**
	Jennifer Zielinski (R)	74,437
6	**Tom Emmer* (R)**	**192,946**
	Ian Todd (DFL)	122,333
7	**Collin C. Peterson* (DFL)**	**146,649**
	Dave Hughes (R)	134,651
8	**Pete Stauber (R)**	**159,388**
	Joe Radinovich (DFL)	141,972
	Skip Sandman (Ind.)	12,768
Mississippi		
1	**Trent Kelly* (R)**	**154,447**
	Randy Wadkins (D)	74,241
2	**Bennie G. Thompson* (D)**	**148,977**
	Troy Ray (Ind.)	44,921
	Irving Harris (RF)	13,398
3	**Michael Guest (R)**	**155,840**
	Michael Ted Evans (D)	90,193
4	**Steven Palazzo* (R)**	**133,805**
	Jeramey Anderson (D)	56,371
Missouri		
1	**Wm. Lacy Clay* (D)**	**216,479**
	Robert Vroman (R)	45,255
2	**Ann Wagner* (R)**	**190,008**
	Cort VanOstran (D)	174,486
3	**Blaine Luetkemeyer* (R)**	**211,000**
	Katy Geppert (D)	106,478
4	**Vicky Hartzler* (R)**	**185,245**
	Renee Hoagenson (D)	93,861
5	**Emanuel Cleaver II* (D)**	**173,592**
	Jacob Turk (R)	100,695
6	**Sam Graves* (R)**	**199,580**
	Henry Robert Martin (D)	97,515
7	**Billy Long* (R)**	**195,872**
	Jamie Daniel Schoolcraft (D)	88,642
	Benjamin T. Brixey (LB)	10,833
8	**Jason Smith* (R)**	**190,826**
	Kathy Ellis (D)	65,043
Montana		
	Greg Gianforte* (R)	**232,588**
	Kathleen Williams (D)	200,084
	Elinor Swanson (LB)	12,440
Nebraska		
1	**Jeff Fortenberry* (R)**	**137,632**
	Jessica McClure (D)	90,551
2	**Don Bacon* (R)**	**121,466**
	Kara Eastman (D)	114,154
3	**Adrian Smith* (R)**	**162,968**
	Paul Theobald (D)	49,473
Nevada		
1	**Dina Titus* (D)**	**99,892**
	Joyce Bentley (R)	46,465
2	**Mark E. Amodei* (R)**	**167,427**
	Clint Koble (D)	120,091

Dist.	Representative/candidate (party)	2018 election results
3	**Susie Lee (D)**	**147,048**
	Danny Tarkanian (R)	121,505
4	**Steven A. Horsford (D)**	**120,888**
	Cresent Hardy (R)	101,748

New Hampshire

Dist.	Representative/candidate (party)	2018 election results
1	**Chris Pappas (D)**	**154,510**
	Eddie Edwards (R)	129,291
2	**Ann McLane Kuster* (D)**	**150,915**
	Steven Negron (R)	113,404

New Jersey

Dist.	Representative/candidate (party)	2018 election results
1	**Donald Norcross* (D)**	**136,540**
	Paul E. Dilks (R)	73,702
2	**Jeff Van Drew (D)**	**122,562**
	Seth Grossman (R)	108,822
3	*Andy Kim (D)*	*150,311*
	Tom MacArthur (R)*	*146,887*
4	**Chris Smith* (R)**	**156,271**
	Joshua Welle (D)	119,394
5	**Josh Gottheimer* (D)**	**148,021**
	John J. McCann Jr. (R)	116,505
6	**Frank Pallone Jr.* (D)**	**121,502**
	Richard J. Pezzullo (R)	72,337
7	**Tom Malinowski (D)**	**137,446**
	Leonard Lance* (R)	131,549
8	**Albio Sires* (D)**	**104,418**
	John R. Muniz (R)	25,359
9	**Bill Pascrell Jr.* (D)**	**121,236**
	Eric P. Fisher (R)	50,499
10	**Donald M. Payne Jr.* (D)**	**149,566**
	Agha Khan (R)	17,911
11	**Mikie Sherrill (D)**	**148,618**
	Jay Webber (R)	115,816
12	**Bonnie Watson Coleman* (D)**	**145,274**
	Daryl Kipnis (R)	67,389

New Mexico

Dist.	Representative/candidate (party)	2018 election results
1	**Debra A. Haaland (D)**	**144,299**
	Janice E. Arnold-Jones (R)	89,062
	Lloyd Princeton (LB)	11,143
2	**Xochitl Torres Small (D)**	**99,441**
	Yvette Herrell (R)	96,715
3	**Ben Ray Luján* (D)**	**154,057**
	Jerald Steve McFall (R)	76,043
	Christopher Manning (LB)	13,181

New York

Dist.	Representative/candidate (party)	2018 election results
1	**Lee M. Zeldin* (R)**	**130,919**
	Perry Gershon (D)	115,795
2	**Peter T. King* (R)**	**122,103**
	Liuba Grechen Shirley (D)	106,996
3	**Thomas R. Suozzi* (D)**	**145,060**
	Dan P. DeBono (R)	103,278
4	**Kathleen M. Rice* (D)**	**149,078**
	Ameer N. Benno (R)	95,187
5	**Gregory W. Meeks* (D)**	**Unopposed**
6	**Grace Meng* (D)**	**103,823**
	Thomas J. Hillgardner (Green)	10,514
7	**Nydia M. Velázquez* (D)**	**137,444**
	Joseph Lieberman (Conservative)	8,107
8	**Hakeem S. Jeffries* (D)**	**166,981**
	Ernest C. Johnson (Conservative)	9,514
9	**Yvette D. Clarke* (D)**	**167,199**
	Lutchi Gayot (R)	19,336
10	**Jerrold Nadler* (D)**	**146,749**
	Naomi Levin (R)	33,931
11	**Max N. Rose (D)**	**95,458**
	Dan Donovan* (R)	84,665
12	**Carolyn B. Maloney* (D)**	**194,974**
	Eliot Rabin (R)	27,838
13	**Adriano Espaillat* (D)**	**167,667**
	Jineea R. Butler (R)	9,525
14	**Alexandria Ocasio-Cortez (D)**	**100,044**
	Anthony Pappas (R)	17,762
15	**José E. Serrano* (D)**	**112,798**
	Jason Gonzalez (R)	4,647
16	**Eliot L. Engel* (D)**	**Unopposed**
17	**Nita M. Lowey* (D)**	**157,275**
	Joseph J. Ciardullo (RF)	21,640
18	**Sean Patrick Maloney* (D)**	**118,342**
	James O'Donnell (R)	96,594

Dist.	Representative/candidate (party)	2018 election results
19	**Antonio Delgado (D)**	**122,644**
	John Faso* (R)	117,029
20	**Paul D. Tonko* (D)**	**163,148**
	Joe Vitollo (R)	83,788
21	**Elise Stefanik* (R)**	**122,863**
	Tedra L. Cobb (D)	90,526
22	*Anthony J. Brindisi (D)*	*117,931*
	Claudia Tenney (R)*	*116,638*
23	**Thomas W. Reed II* (R)**	**122,881**
	Tracy Mitrano (D)	100,495
24	**John M. Katko* (R)**	**129,276**
	Dana Balter (D)	114,102
25	**Joseph D. Morelle (D)**	**149,993**
	Jim Maxwell (R)	105,925
26	**Brian Higgins* (D)**	**157,086**
	Renee M. Zeno (R)	58,128
27	*Chris Collins* (R)*	*134,251*
	Nathan D. McMurray (D)	*131,341*

North Carolina

Dist.	Representative/candidate (party)	2018 election results
1	**G. K. Butterfield* (D)**	**188,060**
	Roger W. Allison (R)	81,474
2	**George Holding* (R)**	**166,035**
	Linda Coleman (D)	148,572
3	**Walter B. Jones* (R)**	**Unopposed**
4	**David Price* (D)**	**242,002**
	Steve A. Von Loor (R)	80,546
	Barbara Howe (LB)	11,947
5	**Virginia Foxx* (R)**	**158,444**
	DD Adams (D)	118,558
6	**B. Mark Walker* (R)**	**159,651**
	Ryan Watts (D)	122,323
7	**David Rouzer* (R)**	**155,705**
	Kyle Horton (D)	119,606
8	**Richard Hudson* (R)**	**140,347**
	Frank McNeill (D)	112,971
9	**Mark Harris (R)**	**138,338**
	Dan McCready (D)	136,478
10	**Patrick T. McHenry* (R)**	**164,060**
	David Wilson Brown (D)	112,386
11	**Mark Meadows* (R)**	**177,143**
	Phillip G. Price (D)	115,794
12	**Alma Adams* (D)**	**202,228**
	Paul Wright (R)	74,639
13	**Ted Budd* (R)**	**145,962**
	Kathy Manning (D)	128,764

North Dakota

Dist.	Representative/candidate (party)	2018 election results
	Kelly Armstrong (R)	**192,733**
	Mac Schneider (D-NPL)	113,891
	Charles Tuttle (Ind.)	13,004

Ohio

Dist.	Representative/candidate (party)	2018 election results
1	**Steve Chabot* (R)**	**151,107**
	Aftab Pureval (D)	135,467
2	**Brad Wenstrup* (R)**	**163,450**
	Jill Schiller (D)	115,777
3	**Joyce Beatty* (D)**	**174,421**
	Jim Burgess (R)	63,470
4	**Jim Jordan* (R)**	**164,640**
	Janet Garrett (D)	87,061
5	**Bob Latta* (R)**	**173,894**
	J. Michael Galbraith (D)	97,352
6	**Bill Johnson* (R)**	**169,668**
	Shawna Roberts (D)	75,196
7	**Bob Gibbs* (R)**	**150,317**
	Ken Harbaugh (D)	105,105
8	**Warren Davidson* (R)**	**170,561**
	Vanessa Enoch (D)	84,738
9	**Marcy Kaptur* (D)**	**152,682**
	Steven W. Kraus (R)	73,183
10	**Mike Turner* (R)**	**153,640**
	Theresa A. Gasper (D)	114,699
11	**Marcia L. Fudge* (D)**	**197,147**
	Beverly A. Goldstein (R)	43,443
12	**Troy Balderson* (R)**	**171,757**
	Danny O'Connor (D)	156,863
13	**Tim Ryan* (D)**	**149,271**
	Chris DePizzo (R)	96,225
14	**David P. Joyce* (R)**	**166,483**
	Betsy Rader (D)	134,059

Dist.	Representative/candidate (party)	2018 election results
15	**Steve Stivers* (R)**	**166,632**
	Rick Neal (D)	112,546
16	**Anthony Gonzalez (R)**	**166,933**
	Susan Moran Palmer (D)	126,736

Oklahoma

Dist.	Representative/candidate (party)	2018 election results
1	**Kevin Hern (R)**	**149,938**
	Tim Gilpin (D)	102,878
2	**Markwayne Mullin* (R)**	**140,305**
	Jason Nichols (D)	64,958
3	**Frank Lucas* (R)**	**172,757**
	Frankie Robbins (D)	61,095
4	**Tom Cole* (R)**	**149,127**
	Mary Brannon (D)	78,022
5	**Kendra Horn (D)**	**121,013**
	Steve Russell* (R)	117,725

Oregon

Dist.	Representative/candidate (party)	2018 election results
1	**Suzanne Bonamici* (D)**	**184,293**
	John Verbeek (R)	94,784
	Drew A. Layda (LB)	10,906
2	**Greg Walden* (R)**	**203,216**
	Jamie McLeod-Skinner (D)	140,954
	Mark Roberts (Ind.)	15,073
3	**Earl Blumenauer* (D)**	**244,154**
	Tom Harrison (R)	68,105
	Marc W. Koller (Ind.)	17,200
4	**Peter DeFazio* (D)**	**204,046**
	Art Robinson (R)	149,616
5	**Kurt Schrader* (D)**	**176,469**
	Mark Callahan (R)	134,720

Pennsylvania

Dist.	Representative/candidate (party)	2018 election results
1	**Brian Fitzpatrick** (R)**	**168,841**
	Scott Wallace (D)	160,098
2	**Brendan F. Boyle** (D)**	**154,384**
	David Torres (R)	41,416
3	**Dwight Evans** (D)**	**275,062**
	Bryan E. Leib (R)	19,549
4	**Madeleine Dean (D)**	**210,216**
	Dan David (R)	121,117
5	**Mary Gay Scanlon (D)**	**189,957**
	Pearl Kim (R)	101,861
6	**Chrissy Houlahan (D)**	**175,516**
	Greg McCauley (R)	122,896
7	**Susan Wild (D)**	**137,122**
	Marty Nothstein (R)	111,862
8	**Matt Cartwright** (D)**	**134,519**
	John Chrin (R)	111,640
9	**Dan Meuser (R)**	**146,675**
	Denny Wolff (D)	98,232
10	**Scott Perry** (R)**	**148,790**
	George Scott (D)	140,956
11	**Lloyd K. Smucker** (R)**	**162,227**
	Jess King (D)	112,605
12	**Tom Marino** (R)**	**159,251**
	Marc Friedenberg (D)	81,390
13	**John Joyce (R)**	**175,046**
	Brent Ottaway (D)	73,494
14	**Guy Reschenthaler (R)**	**149,147**
	Bibiana Boerio (D)	108,179
15	**Glenn W. Thompson Jr.** (R)**	**161,990**
	Susan Boser (D)	76,502
16	**Mike Kelly** (R)**	**130,580**
	Ron DiNicola (D)	119,412
17	**Conor Lamb** (D)**	**176,293**
	Keith Rothfus** (R)	137,906
18	**Mike Doyle** (D)**	**Unopposed**

Rhode Island

Dist.	Representative/candidate (party)	2018 election results
1	**David N. Cicilline* (D)**	**114,604**
	Patrick J. Donovan (R)	57,115
2	**Jim Langevin* (D)**	**125,090**
	Salvatore G. Caiozzo (R)	71,716

South Carolina

Dist.	Representative/candidate (party)	2018 election results
1	**Joe Cunningham (D)**	**144,828**
	Katie Arrington (R)	140,792
2	**Joe Wilson* (R)**	**141,577**
	Sean Carrigan (D)	104,272
3	**Jeff Duncan* (R)**	**152,417**
	Mary Geren (D)	69,662
4	**William Timmons (R)**	**144,990**
	Brandon P. Brown (D)	88,849
5	**Ralph Norman* (R)**	**140,417**
	Archie Parnell (D)	102,167
6	**Jim Clyburn* (D)**	**139,006**
	Gerhard R. Gressmann (R)	56,377
7	**Tom Rice* (R)**	**140,938**
	Robert Williams (D)	95,438

South Dakota

Dist.	Representative/candidate (party)	2018 election results
	Dustin "Dusty" Johnson (R)	**202,673**
	Tim Bjorkman (D)	121,002

Tennessee

Dist.	Representative/candidate (party)	2018 election results
1	**Phil Roe* (R)**	**172,708**
	Marty Olsen (D)	47,087
2	**Tim Burchett (R)**	**171,994**
	Renee Hoyos (D)	86,635
3	**Chuck Fleischmann* (R)**	**156,385**
	Danielle Mitchell (D)	84,632
4	**Scott DesJarlais* (R)**	**147,196**
	Mariah Phillips (D)	77,955
5	**Jim Cooper* (D)**	**177,661**
	Jody M. Ball (R)	84,196
6	**John Rose (R)**	**172,682**
	Dawn Barlow (D)	70,298
7	**Mark E. Green (R)**	**169,769**
	Justin Kanew (D)	81,574
8	**David Kustoff* (R)**	**166,400**
	Erika Stotts Pearson (D)	74,126
9	**Steve Cohen* (D)**	**143,690**
	Charlotte Bergmann (R)	34,710

Texas

Dist.	Representative/candidate (party)	2018 election results
1	**Louie Gohmert* (R)**	**167,734**
	Shirley J. McKellar (D)	60,957
2	**Dan Crenshaw (R)**	**138,502**
	Todd Litton (D)	118,570
3	**Van Taylor (R)**	**168,775**
	Lorie Burch (D)	137,547
4	**John Ratcliffe* (R)**	**188,003**
	Catherine Krantz (D)	57,209
5	**Lance Gooden (R)**	**130,404**
	Dan Wood (D)	78,394
6	**Ron Wright (R)**	**135,779**
	Jana Lynne Sanchez (D)	116,040
7	**Lizzie Pannill Fletcher (D)**	**126,168**
	John Culberson* (R)	114,859
8	**Kevin Brady* (R)**	**200,320**
	Steven David (D)	67,691
9	**Al Green* (D)**	**135,427**
	Phil Kurtz (LB)	5,898
10	**Michael T. McCaul* (R)**	**154,652**
	Mike Siegel (D)	142,511
11	**Mike Conaway* (R)**	**174,749**
	Jennie Lou Leeder (D)	40,028
12	**Kay Granger* (R)**	**172,205**
	Vanessa Adia (D)	90,676
13	**Mac Thornberry* (R)**	**168,090**
	Greg Sagan (D)	34,859
14	**Randy Weber* (R)**	**137,582**
	Adrienne Bell (D)	90,937
15	**Vicente Gonzalez* (D)**	**98,089**
	Tim Westley (R)	63,593
16	**Veronica Escobar (D)**	**122,676**
	Rick Seeberger (R)	48,495
17	**Bill Flores* (R)**	**134,375**
	Rick Kennedy (D)	97,574
18	**Sheila Jackson Lee* (D)**	**137,567**
	Ava Reynero Pate (R)	38,081
19	**Jodey Arrington* (R)**	**152,012**
	Miguel Levario (D)	49,941
20	**Joaquin Castro* (D)**	**138,249**
	Jeffrey Blunt (LB)	32,727
21	**Chip Roy (R)**	**176,913**
	Joseph Kopser (D)	167,020
22	**Pete Olson* (R)**	**152,318**
	Sri Preston Kulkarni (D)	137,500

Dist.	Representative/candidate (party)	2018 election results
23	Will Hurd* (R)	102,903
	Gina Ortiz Jones (D)	101,753
24	Kenny E. Marchant* (R)	132,992
	Jan McDowell (D)	124,580
25	Roger Williams* (R)	162,288
	Julie Oliver (D)	135,288
26	Michael C. Burgess* (R)	185,268
	Linsey Fagan (D)	121,584
27	Michael Cloud* (R)	124,958
	Eric Holguin (D)	75,761
28	Henry Cuellar* (D)	117,178
	Arthur M. Thomas IV (LB)	21,647
29	Sylvia R. Garcia (D)	87,679
	Phillip Aronoff (R)	27,945
30	Eddie Bernice Johnson* (D)	166,102
	Shawn Jones (LB)	16,318
31	John Carter* (R)	143,330
	Mary Jennings "MJ" Hegar (D)	134,675
32	Colin Allred (D)	142,885
	Pete Sessions* (R)	125,600
33	Marc Veasey* (D)	90,311
	Willie Billups (R)	26,007
34	Filemon Vela* (D)	85,647
	Rey Gonzalez Jr. (R)	57,157
35	Lloyd Doggett* (D)	137,325
	David Smalling (R)	50,276
36	Brian Babin* (R)	160,592
	Dayna Steele (D)	60,486

Utah

Dist.	Representative/candidate (party)	2018 election results
1	Rob Bishop* (R)	124,377
	Lee Castillo (D)	48,372
	Eric Eliason (United Utah)	21,872
2	Chris Stewart* (R)	122,540
	Shireen Ghorbani (D)	79,510
3	John Curtis* (R)	108,476
	James Courage Singer (D)	46,477
4	Ben McAdams (D)	104,266
	Mia Love* (R)	97,510

Vermont

Dist.	Representative/candidate (party)	2018 election results
	Peter Welch* (D)	188,146
	Anya Tynio (R)	70,490

Virginia

Dist.	Representative/candidate (party)	2018 election results
1	Robert J. Wittman* (R)	179,296
	Vangie A. Williams (D)	142,508
2	Elaine G. Luria (D)	139,328
	Scott W. Taylor* (R)	133,319
3	Robert C. "Bobby" Scott* (D)	Unopposed
4	A. Donald McEachin* (D)	184,250
	Ryan A. McAdams (R)	105,446
5	Denver L. Riggleman III (R)	165,107
	Leslie C. Cockburn (D)	144,493
6	Ben L. Cline (R)	168,334
	Jennifer Lynn Lewis (D)	112,438
7	Abigail A. Spanberger (D)	170,737
	Dave A. Brat* (R)	165,962

Dist.	Representative/candidate (party)	2018 election results
8	Donald S. Beyer Jr.* (D)	246,831
	Thomas S. Oh (R)	76,492
9	H. Morgan Griffith* (R)	160,888
	Anthony J. Flaccavento (D)	85,658
10	Jennifer T. Wexton (D)	202,557
	Barbara J. Comstock* (R)	157,561
11	Gerry Connolly* (D)	213,587
	Jeff A. Dove Jr. (R)	81,375

Washington

Dist.	Representative/candidate (party)	2018 election results
1	Suzan DelBene* (D)	129,442
	Jeffrey Beeler (R)	91,454
2	Rick Larsen* (D)	135,831
	Brian Luke (LB)	51,709
3	Jaime Herrera Beutler* (R)	115,616
	Carolyn Long (D)	105,654
4	Dan Newhouse* (R)	85,149
	Christine Brown (D)	45,040
5	Cathy McMorris Rodgers* (R)	103,238
	Lisa Brown (D)	81,295
6	Derek Kilmer* (D)	124,292
	Douglas Dightman (R)	73,561
7	Pramila Jayapal* (D)	224,351
	Craig Keller (R)	44,732
8	Kim Schrier (D)	104,520
	Dino Rossi (R)	92,900
9	Adam Smith* (D)	111,449
	Sarah Smith (D)	47,502
10	Denny Heck* (D)	89,137
	Joseph Brumbles (R)	57,272

West Virginia

Dist.	Representative/candidate (party)	2018 election results
1	David B. McKinley* (R)	128,725
	Kendra Fershee (D)	70,402
2	Alex Mooney* (R)	109,018
	Talley Sergent (D)	86,678
3	Carol Miller (R)	98,048
	Richard Ojeda II (D)	75,776

Wisconsin

Dist.	Representative/candidate (party)	2018 election results
1	Bryan Steil (R)	177,490
	Randy Bryce (D)	137,507
	Ken Yorgan (Ind.)	10,006
2	Mark Pocan* (D)	Unopposed
3	Ron Kind* (D)	187,615
	Steve Toft (R)	126,897
4	Gwen Moore* (D)	208,127
	Tim Rogers (R)	60,240
5	Jim Sensenbrenner* (R)	223,989
	Tom Palzewicz (D)	136,995
6	Glenn Grothman* (R)	180,314
	Dan Kohl (D)	144,530
7	Sean P. Duffy* (R)	193,126
	Margaret Engebretson (D)	123,548
8	Mike Gallagher* (R)	209,400
	Beau Liegeois (D)	119,263

Wyoming

Dist.	Representative/candidate (party)	2018 election results
	Liz Cheney* (R)	127,882
	Greg Hunter (D)	59,929

(1) Nominee April Freeman died Sept. 23, 2018. Votes for her on the official ballot were counted for Allen Ellison. (2) John Conyers resigned Dec. 5, 2017. Brenda Jones won a separate Nov. 6, 2018, special election to fill the seat for the remainder of his term expiring Jan. 3, 2019, and was expected to be sworn in immediately following the election.

Nonvoting Members of Congress

Source: World Almanac research

Delegate/candidate (party)	2018 election results
American Samoa	
Aumua Amata Coleman Radewagen* (R)	7,194
Meleagi Suitonu-Chapman (D)	659
Tuika Tuika (Ind.)	785
District of Columbia	
Eleanor Holmes Norton* (D)	188,316
Nelson F. Rimensnyder (R)	9,098
Natale "Lino" Stracuzzi (DC Statehood Green)	8,287
Guam	
Michael F.Q. San Nicolas (D)	19,053
Doris Flores Brooks (R)	15,263

Delegate/candidate (party)	2018 election results
Northern Mariana Islands	
Gregorio Kilili Camacho Sablan* (Ind.)	—
Angel Aldan Demapan (R)	—
Puerto Rico—Resident Commissioner (4-year term began in Jan. 2017.)	
Jenniffer González-Colón (New Progressive)	
Virgin Islands	
Stacey E. Plaskett* (D)	Unopposed

— = Election scheduled for Nov. 13, 2018.

Governors of U.S. States, Commonwealths, and Territories

Source: © Associated Press; all rights reserved. 2018 results are preliminary as of Nov. 7-10, 2018.

Not including territories and commonwealths, governors include 25 Republicans, 23 Democrats. Results in pending races are set in italics. Boldface denotes the 2018 election winner. Third-party or independent candidates receiving fewer than 50,000 votes are not necessarily listed. Governors of states not holding elections in Nov. 2018 are shown for reference with date of term end in place of results.

Terms are for four years, with the exception of two-year terms for governors of New Hampshire and Vermont.

* = Incumbent. D = Democrat; R = Republican; DFL = Dem.-Farmer-Labor; Ind. = Independent; LB = Libertarian; PNP = New Progressive Party.

State	Governor/ candidate (party)	2018 election results
Alabama	**Kay Ivey* (R)**	**1,014,821**
	Walt Maddox (D)	686,774
Alaska	**Mike Dunleavy (R)**	**123,447**
	Mark Begich (D)	102,654
	Billy Toien (LB)	43,227
American Samoa	Lolo Matalasi Moliga (Ind.)	NA (Jan. 2021)
Arizona	**Doug Ducey* (R)**	**993,573**
	David Garcia (D)	690,259
Arkansas	**Asa Hutchinson* (R)**	**576,755**
	Jared Henderson (D)	280,035
California	**Gavin Newsom (D)**	**4,158,682**
	John Cox (R)	2,840,837
Colorado	**Jared Polis (D)**	**1,000,016**
	Walker Stapleton (R)	871,534
	Scott Helker (LB)	48,248
Connecticut	**Ned Lamont (D)**	**650,420**
	Bob Stefanowski (R)	632,164
	Oz Griebel (Ind.)	53,052
Delaware	John Carney Jr. (D)	NA (Jan. 2021)
Florida	*Ron DeSantis (R)*	*4,075,879*
	Andrew Gillum (D)	*4,042,195*
Georgia	*Brian Kemp (R)*	*1,973,910*
	Stacey Abrams (D)	*1,910,745*
	Ted Metz (LB)	*37,094*
Guam	**Lou Leon Guerrero (D)**	**18,081**
	Ray Tenorio (R)	9,419
Hawaii	**David Ige* (D)**	**244,814**
	Andria Tupola (R)	131,604
Idaho	**Brad Little (R)**	**357,707**
	Paulette Jordan (D)	226,669
Illinois	**J.B. Pritzker (D)**	**2,356,991**
	Bruce Rauner* (R)	1,716,331
	Sam McCann (Conservative)	188,015
	Kash Jackson (LB)	104,673
Indiana	Eric Holcomb (R)	NA (Jan. 2021)
Iowa	**Kim Reynolds* (R)**	**662,634**
	Fred Hubbell (D)	623,105
Kansas	**Laura Kelly (D)**	**489,337**
	Kris Kobach (R)	443,346
	Greg Orman (Ind.)	66,163
Kentucky	Matt Bevin (R)	NA (Dec. 2019)
Louisiana	John Bel Edwards (D)	NA (Jan. 2020)
Maine	**Janet Mills (D)**	**295,344**
	Shawn Moody (R)	246,791
Maryland	**Larry Hogan* (R)**	**1,196,352**
	Ben Jealous (D)	909,923
Massachusetts	**Charlie Baker* (R)**	**1,668,774**
	Jay Gonzalez (D)	836,527
Michigan	**Gretchen Whitmer (D)**	**2,169,788**
	Bill Schuette (R)	1,812,673
	Bill Gelineau (LB)	55,432
Minnesota	**Tim Walz (DFL)**	**1,392,913**
	Jeff Johnson (R)	1,097,683
	Chris Wright (Grassroots)	68,726
Mississippi	Phil Bryant (R)	NA (Jan. 2020)
Missouri	Mike Parson (R)	NA (Jan. 2021)

— = Election scheduled for Nov. 13, 2018. NA = Not applicable.

State	Governor/ candidate (party)	2018 election results
Montana	Steve Bullock (D)	NA (Jan. 2021)
Nebraska	**Pete Ricketts* (R)**	**402,262**
	Bob Krist (D)	275,318
Nevada	**Steve Sisolak (D)**	**477,000**
	Adam Laxalt (R)	437,690
New Hampshire	**Chris Sununu* (R)**	**299,359**
	Molly Kelly (D)	259,831
New Jersey	Phil Murphy (D)	NA (Jan. 2022)
New Mexico	**Michelle Lujan Grisham (D)**	**385,689**
	Steve Pearce (R)	292,045
New York	**Andrew Cuomo* (D)**	**3,349,999**
	Marc Molinaro (R)	2,088,176
	Howie Hawkins (Green)	95,652
	Larry Sharpe (LB)	90,664
	Stephanie Miner (Ind.)	51,274
North Carolina	Roy Cooper (D)	NA (Jan. 2021)
North Dakota	Doug Burgum (R)	NA (Dec. 2020)
Northern Mariana Isls.	Ralph Deleon Guerrero Torres* (R)	—
	Joseph S. Inos (D)	—
	Juan Babauta (Ind.)	—
Ohio	**Mike DeWine (R)**	**2,187,619**
	Richard Cordray (D)	2,005,627
	Travis Irvine (LB)	77,184
Oklahoma	**Kevin Stitt (R)**	**643,987**
	Drew Edmondson (D)	500,430
	Chris Powell (LB)	40,768
Oregon	**Kate Brown* (D)**	**832,673**
	Knute Buehler (R)	749,499
Pennsylvania	**Tom Wolf* (D)**	**2,829,155**
	Scott Wagner (R)	2,005,380
Puerto Rico	Ricardo Rosselló (PNP)	NA (Jan. 2021)
Rhode Island	**Gina Raimondo* (D)**	**196,046**
	Allan Fung (R)	138,858
South Carolina	**Henry McMaster* (R)**	**912,045**
	James Smith (D)	769,768
South Dakota	**Kristi Noem (R)**	**172,894**
	Billie Sutton (D)	161,416
Tennessee	**Bill Lee (R)**	**1,297,658**
	Karl Dean (D)	846,186
Texas	**Greg Abbott* (R)**	**4,634,885**
	Lupe Valdez (D)	3,523,210
	Mark Tippetts (LB)	139,983
Utah	Gary Herbert (R)	NA (Jan. 2021)
Vermont	**Phil Scott* (R)**	**150,761**
	Christine Hallquist (D)	110,136
Virgin Islands	*Kenneth Mapp* (Ind.)*	*9,265*
	Albert Bryan (D)	*8,271*
Virginia	Ralph Northam (D)	NA (Jan. 2022)
Washington	Jay Inslee (D)	NA (Jan. 2021)
West Virginia	Jim Justice (R)	NA (Jan. 2021)
Wisconsin	**Tony Evers (D)**	**1,324,648**
	Scott Walker* (R)	1,293,799
Wyoming	**Mark Gordon (R)**	**136,339**
	Mary Throne (D)	55,984

Balance of Power: State Government

Source: National Conference of State Legislatures

After 2018 election results, for the first time since 1914, only one state (Minnesota) had a divided legislature.

Controlling party	Chambers		Legislatures		State control (legislature and governor)	
	Before	After	Before	After	Before	After[1]
Democrats	31	37	14	18	7	14
Republicans	65	61	31	30	25	20
Tied/divided	2	0	4	1	17	13

Note: Nebraska's unicameral legislature is considered nonpartisan, so it is not shown. (1) Florida and Georgia races for governor were pending.

Nov. 1, 2017, to Oct. 31, 2018

The Chronology of Events reports the top National, International, and General news stories, month by month.

November 2017

National

Army Deserter Bergdahl Receives Dishonorable Discharge, Avoids Prison Time—U.S. Army Sgt. Bowe Bergdahl, who left his base in eastern Afghanistan in June 2009, received a dishonorable discharge but no prison time from a military judge Nov. 3 after pleading guilty to desertion and misbehavior before the enemy in Oct. After his departure, which set off a search during which several military personnel were badly injured, Bergdahl was held by the Taliban for nearly five years before the Obama administration traded five Taliban detainees for his release in 2014. Bergdahl, who was diagnosed with a severe personality disorder after his release, said he suffered torture and extreme isolation in Taliban captivity. The sentence, which Pres. Donald J. Trump called a "total disgrace," also included a demotion in rank to private. Trump had repeatedly denounced Bergdahl during the presidential campaign, calling for his execution. Bergdahl's defense argued that Trump's public comments had prejudiced the military justice system against him.

Texas Church Shooting Leaves More Than Two Dozen Dead—Armed with a semi-automatic assault rifle and wearing a bulletproof vest, a gunman killed 26 people and injured at least 20 others at a Baptist church Nov. 5 in Sutherland Springs, TX, about 30 mi southeast of San Antonio. A local resident shot the 26-year-old suspected shooter, Devin Patrick Kelley, twice before a high-speed chase ended in Kelley's death from a self-inflicted gunshot. The shooter, who had been court-martialed and received a bad conduct discharge from the U.S. Air Force over domestic abuse, should have been legally barred from purchasing or possessing a firearm, but the Air Force had neglected to report his convictions to a national crime database.

Justice Dept. Seeks to Block AT&T-Time Warner Merger; Dow Jones Surpasses 24,000; Other Economic News—The U.S. Dept. of Justice Nov. 20 sued to block telecommunications company AT&T's proposed $85-bil buyout of multimedia giant Time Warner. The Justice Dept. said the deal would stifle competition and innovation and raise cable TV rates, but defenders of the merger pointed to successful similar "vertical mergers" and questioned whether Pres. Trump, a frequent critic of news coverage by CNN (owned by Time Warner), had influenced the Justice Dept.'s antitrust review.

The U.S. unemployment rate dipped to a 17-year-low of 4.1% in Oct. and added 261,000 new jobs, according to a Nov. 3 report by the U.S. Dept. of Labor. The numbers were the strongest yet for the Trump administration and marked a record 85 straight months of job growth. The Dow Jones industrial average closed Nov. at 24,272.35, the index's first closing over 24,000, and up 3.8% from Oct. The Nasdaq composite index finished the month at 6,873.97, up 2.2%, while the S&P 500 closed Nov. at 2,647.58, up 2.8%.

Trump Administration Ends Protected Status for Haitians, Others; Other White House News—U.S. Dept. of Homeland Security officials announced Nov. 20 it was ending deportation protections for some 46,000 Haitians living in the U.S. under Temporary Protected Status (TPS) since a 2010 earthquake devastated Haiti, requiring those under TPS to leave by July 22, 2019. TPS is extended to certain people in the U.S. from countries where natural disasters or armed conflict preclude safe repatriation. Homeland Security officials said Haiti was ready for the returning Haitians, but some lawmakers in both parties expressed doubts about Haiti's readiness and criticized the move. The Trump administration Nov. 6 had said it was revoking TPS in Jan. 2019 from 2,800 Nicaraguans living in the U.S. since a 1998 hurricane, and the TPS of 57,000 Hondurans and 195,000 El Salvadorans remained in limbo.

Pres. Trump Nov. 13 announced his nomination of former Eli Lilly pharmaceuticals executive Alex Azar as secretary of health and human services, replacing Tom Price, who resigned in late Sept. amid reports of his use of charter jets at the public's expense.

Trump Nov. 29 retweeted three anti-Muslim videos from a far-right British group, drawing criticism from many, including an unusual condemnation from British Prime Min. Theresa May.

International

Saudi Crown Prince Purges Elites—An anticorruption panel led by 32-year-old Saudi Crown Prince Mohammed bin Salman by Nov. 9 arrested more than 200 prominent Saudis including 11 princes, 4 government ministers, and influential business leaders in what many observers labeled an outright power grab. According to Saudi Arabia's attorney general, the kingdom had lost $100 bil over several decades through corruption and embezzlement; the detainees were reportedly pressed to turn over their assets. Along with consolidating his power, some speculated Mohammed bin Salman was demonstrating his commitment to freeing Saudi Arabia of graft to better attract foreign investment and diversify the kingdom's oil-dominated economy.

Trump Visits Asia, Makes Bid for Unity in Opposition to North Korea—Pres. Donald J. Trump visited Asia Nov. 3-14 in his longest foreign trip to date and first to the continent as president. Throughout his five-nation tour, Trump pressed China and others to work together in opposition to a nuclear North Korea, but he struck a more isolationist note on trade. At a joint airbase outside of Tokyo Nov. 5, Trump hailed the U.S and Japan's military alliance while refraining from inflammatory remarks against North Korea. But he reverted to a more incendiary tone during a speech in South Korea Nov. 8, saying that a North Korean strike against the U.S. or its allies would be a "fatal miscalculation." The U.S. State Dept. Nov. 20 rebranded North Korea as a state sponsor of terrorism—after being off the list since 2008—in hopes of increasing pressure on the totalitarian regime.

Speaking at the Asia-Pacific Economic Cooperation (APEC) summit in Da Nang, Vietnam, Trump Nov. 10 criticized the Trans-Pacific Partnership (TPP) trade agreement in a speech emphasizing "America first." Representatives for the remaining 11 countries in the TPP (including Australia, Canada, and Japan) signed the Comprehensive and Progressive Agreement for Trans-Pacific Partnership as a replacement for TPP without U.S. participation that same day.

After speaking with Russian Pres. Vladimir Putin Nov. 11, Trump told reporters he believed Putin was being sincere when he said Russia did not meddle in the 2016 U.S. elections. Unlike previous U.S. presidents, Trump did not publicly voice concern over human rights in China nor Philippine Pres. Rodrigo Duterte's widely condemned extrajudicial drug war.

Coalition Nears Defeat of ISIS in Iraq, Syria; Civilian Cost Probed—Iraqi security forces liberated Rawa, the last major town in Iraq under the control of the Sunni extremist group Islamic State of Iraq and Syria (ISIS), Nov. 17. Rawa's liberation scattered the remaining militants and signaled the nearly complete defeat of a unified ISIS force, which had declared a caliphate in 2014 and had at its peak controlled major swaths of territory, including Raqqa in Syria and Fallujah, Ramadi, and Mosul in Iraq. The Syrian army Nov. 19 retook the eastern city of Abu Kamal, ISIS's last urban stronghold in Syria. After losing Abu Kamal and a nearby border crossing it had used to transport fighters and arms, ISIS in Syria appeared to be relegated to remote desert and several villages on the Euphrates River.

After three years of combat against ISIS extremists, Prime Min. Haider al-Abadi announced Iraq's total liberation from ISIS Dec. 9, but the U.S. State Dept. and Pentagon officials stressed ISIS's continuing threat in the Middle East and elsewhere. A Dec. 28 suicide bombing claimed by ISIS killed at least 41 people at a Shiite cultural center in Kabul, Afghanistan.

Bolstering human rights groups' critiques of the U.S.-led coalition effort against ISIS, the *New York Times* Nov. 16 reported that airstrikes over an 18-month period had killed Iraqi civilians at a rate 31 times greater than acknowledged by the Pentagon, which claimed 89 civilian deaths in 14,000 airstrikes in Iraq since 2014. The UN Assistance Mission for Iraq

(UNAMI) Jan. 2 reported a low-end estimate of 3,298 civilian deaths in 2017. An Associated Press report Dec. 20 found the civilian death toll in the battle to liberate Mosul was 10 times greater than previously reported.

Mugabe Ends 37-Year Reign in Zimbabwe—Facing likely impeachment, autocratic Zimbabwean president Robert Mugabe resigned Nov. 21, a week after a military takeover. The physically ailing 93-year-old Mugabe, in power since Zimbabwe's independence from Britain in 1980, was put under house arrest as the military seized control. Mugabe earlier in the month had fired Vice Pres. Emmerson Mnangagwa, a move critics said was intended to clear the way for Grace Mugabe, the president's 52-year-old wife, to succeed him. Mnangagwa was sworn in as interim president Nov. 24, ahead of 2018 elections. Mugabe—last reelected in 2013 in a race riddled by fraud reports—orchestrated a land redistribution campaign in 2000 that triggered food insecurity and massive inflation.

Serbian Warlord Sentenced in Srebrenica Massacre—A United Nations-backed tribunal sentenced former Bosnian Serb commander Ratko Mladic to life in prison Nov. 22 after the tribunal found him guilty of genocide, war crimes, and crimes against humanity during the 1992-95 conflict in the former Yugoslavia that killed some 100,000 people. Known as the "Butcher of Bosnia," Mladic orchestrated the deaths of some 8,000 Bosnian Muslim men and boys in Srebrenica after Bosnian Serbian troops overran the UN-declared "safe area" there in 1995. Mladic was arrested in 2011 after years in hiding; the trial began in The Hague, Netherlands, in 2012 and lasted 530 days with testimony from hundreds of witnesses.

Slobodan Praljak, a convicted Bosnian Croat war criminal, committed suicide by drinking potassium cyanide in The Hague immediately after the tribunal upheld his 20-year war crimes sentence Nov. 29.

Terror Assault on Egyptian Mosque Kills Hundreds—A bomb and gun attack on a crowded Sufi mosque in a village near Bir al-Abed, Egypt, killed at least 305 people and injured more than 120 others Nov. 24, in what officials said was the country's deadliest act of terrorism in modern history. Some 30 militants reportedly detonated at least one bomb inside the mosque, then blocked escape routes and shot worshippers attempting to flee. It was the latest in a string of terror incidents on non-Sunni religious groups in the region blamed on an ISIS affiliate; previous attacks in Egypt had targeted Coptic Christians.

General

Houston Astros Win First World Series—For the first time in the franchise's 56-year history, the Houston Astros won Major League Baseball's World Series, defeating the L.A. Dodgers at Dodger Stadium in Los Angeles, CA, in Game 7, 5-1, on Nov. 1. The Astros won both Games 2 and 5, 7-6 and 13-12, respectively, in extra innings. (Houston twice came back from a three-run deficit in Game 5, which—at 5 hr., 17 min.—was the second-longest World Series game ever.) The teams hit a combined World Series-record 25 home runs, with a new Series single-game record eight home runs in Game 2. Houston outfielder George Springer, with five home runs, was named the World Series MVP.

Gun Runner Takes Breeders' Cup Classic—Four-year-old colt Gun Runner pulled away from Collected down the final stretch of Del Mar Racetrack in Del Mar, CA, to win thoroughbred racing's 34th Breeders' Cup Classic by 2¼ lengths, Nov. 4. Capturing his fourth straight victory, Gun Runner finished the 1¼-mi, $6-mil contest in 2:01.29. Arrogate, the 2016 Classic winner and highest-earning horse in North American racing history, placed fifth.

Iran-Iraq Earthquake Kills Hundreds—A 7.3 magnitude earthquake struck the Iran-Iraq border region Nov. 12, killing over 600 and injuring thousands in western Iran's hardest-hit province of Kermanshah. The quake, the deadliest in 2017, was estimated by officials to have destroyed 12,000 houses and damaged 15,000 others.

Da Vinci Painting Sells for Record $450 Mil—A new record high price for a work of art sold at auction was set Nov. 15, as Leonardo da Vinci's *Salvator Mundi* (Savior of the World) fetched $450.3 mil, including fees, at Christie's in New York, NY. The sale of the long-lost piece to an anonymous buyer shattered the previous record of $179.4 mil established in 2015 by Pablo Picasso's *Les Femmes d'Alger*

(Women of Algiers). The Saudi government disputed reports in Dec. that Saudi crown prince Mohammed bin Salman had purchased the painting through a distant cousin. The painting was expected to be displayed at the recently opened Louvre Abu Dhabi.

Prince Harry to Wed American Actress—The UK's 33-year-old Prince Harry, fifth in succession to the British throne, Nov. 27 announced his engagement to 36-year-old actress Meghan Markle. Markle, who identifies as half black and half white, would be the first American to marry into the royal family since 1937. The wedding was expected to be held in May 2018.

Women Continue to Come Forward With #MeToo Accusations—Allegations against high-profile men accused of sexual assault or misconduct—commonly associated with the #MeToo movement that grew prominent on social media in the wake of allegations against producer Harvey Weinstein in Oct. 2017—continued to draw media attention and to have consequences for those accused. CBS Nov. 21 fired *CBS This Morning* co-host and *60 Minutes* correspondent Charlie Rose after eight women who had worked with Rose accused him of misconduct, including groping and unwanted advances. PBS, home to Rose's longtime self-titled interview show, also cut ties. Matt Lauer, co-host of NBC's *Today* show for 20 years, was terminated Nov. 29 following a report of "inappropriate sexual behavior" from a junior colleague. *Variety* and the *New York Times* that same day reported accusations against Lauer by several anonymous women, who told *Variety* that NBC executives had previously ignored their complaints, a charge NBC denied. Other prominent figures accused of sexual assault, harassment, or misconduct in late 2017 included radio host Garrison Keillor, comedian Louis C.K., and music producer and business mogul Russell Simmons.

Argentine Submarine Crew Lost at Sea—Argentina's navy Nov. 30 called off a rescue mission for the 44-person crew of a missing submarine, *San Juan*, 15 days after an explosion was detected in the area of the craft's last known position in the Atlantic off the coast of Patagonia. Officials said the submarine's crew had sufficient air for only 7-10 days.

December 2017
National

Flynn Agrees to Cooperate in Russia Investigation Guilty Plea—Pres. Donald Trump's former national security adviser Michael Flynn pleaded guilty Dec. 1 to lying to the FBI about his communications with a Russian official in the waning days of the Obama administration. Flynn was the first senior White House official to be indicted—and the fourth person to be charged—as part of special counsel Robert S. Mueller III's probe into Russian interference with the U.S. election in 2016. According to court documents filed with the plea, Flynn admitted to lying to FBI investigators about two conversations with Russia's ambassador to the U.S., Sergey Kislyak.

In the first, Dec. 22, 2016, Flynn asked that Russia delay or reject a UN Security Council vote condemning new Israeli settlements in the West Bank and Jerusalem. The next week, Flynn called Kislyak to discuss new Obama administration sanctions on Russia for election meddling and to request that Russia not escalate the situation with its response, to which Kislyak agreed. Flynn, whose plea was conditioned on his full cooperation with investigators, was reportedly urged to contact Kislyak by an unconfirmed member of the Trump transition team (believed to be either Trump's son-in-law and adviser Jared Kushner or former deputy national security adviser K. T. McFarland).

CVS, Disney Announce Megamergers; Bitcoin Crashes After All-Time High; Other Economic News—Drugstore chain CVS Health Dec. 3 announced an agreement to acquire health insurer Aetna in a $69-bil deal, and Walt Disney Co. Dec. 14 made public a planned $52.4-bil takeover of most of 21st Century Fox. Both deals required approval from federal antitrust regulators.

Signaling the widening acceptance of Bitcoin and other cryptocurrencies, the U.S. Commodity Futures Trading Commission Dec. 1 approved Bitcoin futures trading on three major markets. But the nine-year-old digital currency fell from an all-time trading high of $20,089 to a low of $11,833, Dec. 17-22. Bitcoin boosters noted that the currency—

unbacked by any governmental authority, central bank, or administrator—was still trading far above its price of less than $1,000 a year earlier.

Wall Street wrapped up a year of strong growth, with the Dow Jones industrial average finishing the month and year on Dec. 29 at 24,719.22, up 1.8% from Nov. and 25.1% over the close of 2016. The Nasdaq composite index was somewhat flat in Dec., ending at 6,903.39, up 0.4% over Nov., but still gaining 28.2% on the year. The S&P 500 closed at 2,673.61, up 1.0% from Nov. and 19.4% from 2016. The U.S. Labor Dept. monthly numbers reported Dec. 8 that the economy added 228,000 jobs in Nov., as unemployment held steady at 4.1%. The Bureau of Economic Analysis's revised figures for the third quarter of 2017 showed that real GDP grew by a healthy 3.2%—the highest rate since first quarter 2015.

Trump Scales Back Utah National Monuments—Visiting Utah Dec. 4, Pres. Trump announced that the amount of land covered by two federally protected national monuments in the southern part of the state would be drastically cut. The protected areas encompassed by Bears Ears National Monument and Grand Staircase-Escalante National Monument would respectively shrink from about 1.35 mil to 220,000 acres and 1.86 mil to 1 mil acres. Trump argued that public lands should be subject to fewer federal restrictions, in favor of local control that maintained the possibility of resource and commercial development. Conservationists and environmental groups vowed to file legal challenges, as did those who view Bears Ears as sacred, including the Navajo Nation and other tribes.

#MeToo Allegations Force Resignations in Congress—U.S. Rep. John Conyers Jr. (D, MI) Dec. 5 became the first federal lawmaker to resign amid heightened public scrutiny of sexual misconduct sparked by a wave of high-profile allegations against film producer Harvey Weinstein in Oct. 2017. The 88-year-old Conyers, who was first elected in 1964, was accused by multiple former female staffers of misconduct. Under pressure from Democratic colleagues, Sen. Al Franken (D, MN) announced Dec. 7 that he would step down following allegations he inappropriately kissed and groped several women before he was elected. That same day, Rep. Trent Franks (R, AZ) said he would resign after admitting he asked two former female staffers to carry his child as a surrogate mother.

Alabama Senate Candidate Defeated Amid Sexual Assault Allegations—Alabama Dec. 12 elected attorney Doug Jones (D) to the U.S. Senate over former state Supreme Court chief justice Roy Moore (R), 50.0%-48.3%, in a contentious, widely watched special election to fill the seat vacated by Attorney Gen. Jeff Sessions (R). The race was reconfigured following reporting in the *Washington Post* Nov. 9 that Moore had initiated sexual contact with a 14-year-old girl when he was a 32-year-old assistant district attorney, and that he had pursued three other teenagers; five more women claiming misconduct by Moore came forward by mid-Nov. The 70-year-old Moore, a controversial conservative who was not endorsed by GOP leadership until after his primary victory in Sept., did not withdraw his candidacy despite many intraparty calls that he do so, and the Republican National Committee reinstated its support in early Dec. Jones's election marked the first time since 1992 that a Republican lost a U.S. Senate race in Alabama; it narrowed GOP control of the Senate to 51-49.

FCC Revokes Net Neutrality Rules—Led by Trump appointee Ajit Pai, the Federal Communications Commission (FCC) voted 3-2 Dec. 14 to scrap so-called net neutrality regulations passed by the FCC in 2015. Under net neutrality rules, internet service providers (ISPs) were mandated to provide equal access to all internet applications and sites without favoring, slowing down, or blocking any. Pai argued—in agreement with many telecom companies and ISPs—that the Obama-era regulations stifled competition and investment in infrastructure. But net neutrality was strongly embraced by consumer groups and much of the tech industry, who said scrapping the regulations posed a threat to consumers, as well as to startups and small businesses who might not be able to compete with established industry giants.

Some 22 mil public comments were filed with the FCC leading up to the vote. While several organized campaigns sought comments for and against net neutrality, FCC Commissioner Jessica Rosenworcel, an Obama appointee, said

8 mil comments could be attributed to domains linked to Fake MailGenerator.com, and nearly 500,000 others could be linked to Russian email addresses.

Congress Passes Major Tax Overhaul, Temporarily Averts Shutdown—Pres. Donald Trump signed the most comprehensive federal tax legislation in 30-plus years Dec. 22, achieving his first major legislative milestone as president. The divisive Tax Cuts and Jobs Act (TCJA) was passed Dec. 19 by the Senate, 51-48 in a party-line vote, and Dec. 20 by the House, 224-201, with no Democratic support and without backing from 12 GOP members. The final legislation, projected to cost $1.5 tril over 10 years, permanently cut the top corporate tax rate from 35% to 21%, abolished the corporate alternative minimum tax, and allowed a large deduction for so-called pass-through businesses. For personal income tax payers, tax rates were cut across nearly all income levels until 2025, and exemptions for estate and gift taxes were doubled. The standard deduction was increased, but many personal exemptions and deductions were eliminated or limited, including those for state and local taxes and mortgage interest.

First introduced in the House just seven weeks earlier, the bill was consistently criticized by Democratic lawmakers as a giveaway to corporations and the wealthy. According to Congress's Joint Committee on Taxation, most households earning less than $75,000 per year would face a tax increase after the individual tax breaks expire. The nonpartisan Tax Policy Center reported the wealthiest 1% of taxpayers would receive 83% of the bill's benefits by 2027.

The tax bill also achieved two long-standing GOP policy goals by permitting oil drilling in Alaska's Arctic National Wildlife Refuge and repealing Obamacare's controversial individual mandate. The Congressional Budget Office projected repeal of the mandate would save the government $338 bil and lead to 13 mil more uninsured people by 2027.

At a stalemate on immigration reform and other issues, lawmakers in the House and Senate avoided a partial government shutdown Dec. 21, voting 231-188 and 66-32, respectively, to pass a temporary stopgap bill funding the government through Jan. 19, 2018.

Pentagon Confirms Short-Lived UFO Unit—In 2007-12, the U.S. Dept. of Defense spent $22 mil investigating unidentified flying objects (UFOs), the Pentagon conceded in reports published Dec. 16 by *Politico* and the *New York Times*. Initiated by then-Senate Majority Leader Harry Reid (D, NV), the Advanced Aerospace Threat Identification Program was led by Pentagon intelligence official Luis Elizondo, who claimed that the existence of advanced UFOs had been proved "beyond reasonable doubt."

International

Roadside Attack Kills Yemen's Former President—Yemen's Houthi rebels reportedly killed their onetime ally, former Yemeni Pres. Ali Abdullah Saleh, Dec. 4, dimming hopes of an end to Yemen's nearly three-year-old conflict that had led to what the United Nations called the world's worst current humanitarian crisis in 2017. Saleh Dec. 2 had publicly dissolved his alliance with the Iran-supported Houthi rebels when he indicated he would be open to peace talks if the Saudi-led coalition battling the rebels agreed to a cease-fire and lifted the blockade on the country, firmly in place since at least Oct. 2017. A Houthi representative called Saleh's comments "a coup," and Saleh was killed as he attempted to flee the capital of Sanaa, where fighting between Houthis and Saleh loyalist militias resulted in dozens of deaths.

The UN had recorded at least 13,800 civilian casualties in Yemen since the conflict began in 2015, when Houthi rebels expelled Yemeni Pres. Abd Rabbuh Mansur Hadi, and said that more than 22 mil people there were in need of urgent aid, including 8 mil at risk of starvation, 17.8 mil food insecure, and 1 mil suspected of having cholera.

White House Recognizes Jerusalem as Israel's Capital—Overturning nearly seven decades of U.S. foreign policy, Pres. Donald Trump in a televised White House address Dec. 6 formally recognized Jerusalem as the capital of Israel and announced plans to move the U.S. Embassy in Israel there. The development, which Trump described as a "recognition of reality," was embraced by Israeli officials but immediately condemned by Palestinian leaders, who said it threatened the

U.S.'s ability to act as an impartial moderator, and many traditional U.S. allies. Roman Catholic leader Pope Francis and the European Union's top diplomatic representative likewise argued it jeopardized peace prospects.

Demonstrations against the move turned violent, with at least six killed and hundreds injured, mostly on the Gaza border. The UN General Assembly, voting 128-9 in a nonbinding resolution Dec. 21, called for the U.S. to rescind its Jerusalem recognition.

Chile Returns Conservative President to Power—Chileans steered their government back to the right when they elected billionaire former Pres. Sebastián Piñera in a presidential runoff Dec. 17. Of the 48.5% of eligible voters who cast ballots, 54.6% chose Piñera over center-left Sen. Alejandro Guillier, who was backed by incumbent Pres. Michelle Bachelet. (The constitution prohibited Bachelet from another consecutive term; she both preceded and succeeded Piñera's 2010-14 term as president.) Piñera while campaigning had vowed to revive Chile's flagging economy by slashing corporate taxes. A corruption scandal involving Bachelet's daughter-in-law along with the nation's economic woes had caused Bachelet's popularity to wane, but she had managed to achieve parts of her reform agenda, including free higher education for low-income students, an end to a decades-old blanket ban on abortion, and introducing same-sex marriage legislation. Piñera had pledged to halt the marriage bill, but his Chile Vamos coalition failed to win a majority of seats in Nov. elections.

South Africa's ANC Rejects Zuma Successor—South Africa's ruling African National Congress (ANC) appeared to chart a new direction for itself ahead of 2019 elections Dec. 18, narrowly choosing South African Deputy Pres. Cyril Ramaphosa to lead the party over the candidate supported by two-term Pres. Jacob Zuma. Ramaphosa, who defeated former African Union Commission head Nkosazana Dlamini-Zuma (former wife of Jacob Zuma) by just 179 ballots among 4,708 cast, had promised to improve services to South Africa's impoverished, recruit foreign investment to revitalize the economy, and address the corruption that had badly damaged the ANC, the party associated with South Africa's first black president, Nelson Mandela. Jacob Zuma's faction won three of five other top ANC posts contested that same day.

Liberia Ushers in First Democratic Power Transfer Since 1944—Former professional soccer star and current senator George Weah won a Dec. 26 presidential runoff against Liberian Vice Pres. Joseph Boakai of the Unity Party, ushering in that country's first democratic transition of power in over seven decades. Winning 61.5% support in a vote with a 56% participation rate, Weah and his Coalition for Democratic Change charged two-term president Ellen Johnson Sirleaf with failing to adequately address poverty and corruption following successive civil wars that killed an estimated 250,000 Liberians in 1989-2003. The runoff was assessed by international observers as largely free and fair, although Johnson Sirleaf was expelled from her Unity Party in Jan. 2018 amid charges she had meddled in the first round of voting by failing to support her party's candidate in favor of Weah. Weah was inaugurated Jan. 22, 2018.

General

Another Record Fire Scorches Southern California—Capping a year that had already set wildfire records, California's largest fire in modern history ignited Dec. 4 north of Santa Paula, in Ventura County, burning more than 280,000 acres and destroying at least 1,060 structures. Dubbed the Thomas Fire, the blaze spread quickly, aided by strong Santa Ana winds that gusted 60-70 mph, and forced the evacuation of over 104,000 Ventura and Santa Barbara County residents. More than 8,500 firefighters, the largest mobilization in state history, fought the fire before it was fully extinguished Jan. 12, 2018; one firefighter was killed.

According to a Jan. 2018 report from the National Centers for Environmental Information, Western wildfires in 2017 cost an estimated $18 bil and killed 54.

Toronto FC Wins MLS Championship—Avenging their 2016 Major League Soccer (MLS) Cup loss, Toronto FC defeated the defending champion Seattle Sounders, 2-0, in a Dec. 9 rematch at BMO Field in Toronto, ON, Canada, claiming the team's first MLS Cup since joining the league in 2007.

The first Canadian club to win the MLS Cup greatly outshot the Sounders 22-7 (11-2 on target) and appeared to outplay them nearly the entire match despite failing to score until the 67th minute. Forward Jozy Altidore, who scored that goal, was named the Cup's MVP.

Amtrak Route Debut Crash Kills Three—An Amtrak passenger train derailed Dec. 18 on an interstate overpass near DuPont, WA, killing three passengers and injuring about 100, including several interstate motorists. According to federal investigators, the southbound Cascades train, which was on its inaugural run of a new route between Seattle and Portland, OR, was traveling at 80 mph in a 30-mph zone when it derailed. Safety advocates once again called for the installation of the positive train control (PTC) system, which could prevent some accidents, including derailments caused by excessive speed and train-on-train collisions.

January 2018
National

Court Blocks DACA Phase-Out; Alleged Trump Slur Draws Rebuke—A California federal district judge Jan. 9 ordered a nationwide injunction against Pres. Donald Trump's plan to allow the expiration of an Obama-era program that had protected nearly 700,000 immigrants from deportation and allowed them to work legally. Though the injunction required the Trump administration to allow so-called Dreamers brought to the U.S. illegally as children to renew their existing Deferred Action for Childhood Arrivals (DACA) status after the Mar. 5 deadline set by the administration, the court did not mandate the acceptance of new DACA applicants. The U.S. Supreme Court Feb. 26 declined the Justice Dept. request that the nation's highest court step in before the appellate court ruled on the district court's injunction.

During a White House meeting on immigration reform attended by bipartisan legislators, Pres. Trump Jan. 11 reportedly referred to Haiti, El Salvador, and African nations as "shithole countries," from which immigration was undesirable, drawing a firestorm of criticism; Trump denied that he made the comment.

Missile Alert Error Strikes Fear in Hawaii—A false alert Jan. 13 warned Hawaiian residents of an inbound ballistic missile threat via mobile devices, radio, and TV. Though the state's Emergency Management Agency (EMA) used Facebook and Twitter to report "NO missile threat" less than 15 min. later, a new message rescinding the warning, which occurred mistakenly during a test of the state's emergency systems, was not sent until 38 min. had passed. The EMA head resigned amid federal and state investigations into the incident.

Dow Jones Surge Continues; Senate Confirms New Fed Chair; Other Economic, Business Developments—Less than two weeks after closing above 25,000 for the first time, the Dow Jones industrial average Jan. 17 climbed above 26,000, closing at 26,115.65, and finished the month strong Jan. 31 at 26,149.39, up 5.8% from Dec. The Nasdaq composite index ended Jan. at 7,411.48, up 7.4%, and the S&P 500 closed at 2,823.81, up 5.6% from Dec.

The U.S. Senate Jan. 23 confirmed Jerome H. Powell, 84-13, to replace Federal Reserve chair Janet Yellen on Feb. 3. Powell, who had served on the Fed's board since 2012, said he was not planning major monetary or regulatory changes. The value of the U.S. dollar fell to a three-year-low the next day, after Treasury Sec. Steve Mnuchin said publicly that a weaker dollar would benefit U.S. trade.

The U.S. Labor Dept. reported Jan. 5 that the unemployment rate held steady at 4.1% in Dec. as 148,000 jobs were created. More than 2 mil new jobs were created in 2017, including 196,000 in manufacturing. Walmart, the nation's largest private employer, announced it was raising its starting U.S. hourly wage to $11 in Feb. 2018, citing the tax overhaul passed by Congress in Dec. 2017. That same day, the company said it was closing 63 Sam's Club warehouse stores, affecting up to 11,000 jobs.

Brief Government Shutdown Ends in Budget Deal—Congress ended a three-day federal government shutdown Jan. 22 after enough Senate-minority Democrats agreed to a three-week spending bill. The stopgap measure, which passed 81-18, did not include a resolution to questions surrounding so-called Dreamers or other undocumented immigrants Democrats had sought, but Majority Leader Mitch McConnell (R, KY) pledged to hold a vote on immigration reform in the coming weeks. The House voted, 266-150, later that same day in favor of the bill, which also renewed the Children's Health Insurance Program (CHIP) for six years. Pres. Donald Trump signed the measure, the fourth short-term funding measure passed since Sept.

Trump Calls for Unity in State of the Union Address; Voter Fraud Commission Dissolved; Other White House Developments—In his first State of the Union Address Jan. 30, Pres. Donald Trump called for unity and celebrated the "extraordinary success" of his first year in office, counting among his achievements 200,000 new manufacturing jobs, a booming stock market, and $1.5 tril in tax cuts passed in Dec. 2017. He also called on Congress to support a nationwide infrastructure plan that Democrats criticized as relying almost completely on state/local funding. Trump struck a darker tone on immigration, which he sought to link to increased crime. After voicing support for a pathway to citizenship for so-called Dreamers brought to the U.S. illegally as children, Trump drew boos from Democrats over his call to end family-sponsored "chain migration."

In an executive order, Trump Jan. 3 dissolved a voter fraud commission established in May 2017 to investigate what he claimed was massive election fraud that cost him the popular vote win. Trump gave no evidence for his claims and numerous states had refused to provide the voter data requested by the commission on privacy or other legal grounds. Attorney Gen. Jeff Sessions Jan. 4 rescinded Obama-era legal guidance that had established a federal policy of non-interference with states that legalized or decriminalized marijuana. Also on Jan. 4, the administration made public a proposal to allow oil drilling in nearly all U.S. coastal waters.

A cease-and-desist letter from Trump counsel Charles J. Harder to the publishers was unsuccessful in preventing the publication on Jan. 5 of journalist Michael Wolff's *Fire and Fury*. The book portrayed the Trump administration in a chaotic state, led by an incompetent and narcissistic president. Though some questioned the book's credibility, citing factual and grammatical errors in the text, it was an immediate best-seller.

International

Widespread Protests Turn Deadly in Iran—Rare nationwide protests in Iran continued to claim lives Jan. 1-2, including those of six allegedly attempting to break into a police station in Qahdarijan. Three more people, including a Revolutionary Guard member, were killed that same day in nearby towns, bringing the number killed to at least 21 since mass protests began Dec. 28. Originating in Iran's second largest city of Mashhad, where hundreds demonstrated against high food and gas prices, unemployment, and corruption, protests spread to more than 80 cities and soon included calls for the resignation or death of theocratic leader Ayatollah Ali Khamenei and for Iran to end its support of the Syrian regime of Bashar al-Assad. According to an Iranian lawmaker, about 3,700 protesters were arrested before security forces quashed the last of the protests by Jan. 7.

Trump and North Korea Exchange Threats; Other Korean Developments—Pres. Donald Trump Jan. 3 said via Twitter that his "nuclear button" was "much bigger & more powerful" than that of autocratic North Korean leader Kim Jong Un. Trump, who often deprecatingly referred to Kim as "Little Rocket Man" was responding to Kim's threat that his "nuclear button is always on the desk of my office." Several U.S. lawmakers and diplomats associated with both parties publicly criticized Trump's taunt as irresponsible and juvenile.

In the first direct talks between North and South Korea since Dec. 2015, representatives met Jan. 9 and agreed to hold future meetings aimed at alleviating tensions. In response to a Nov. 29 intercontinental missile ballistic missile test, the United Nations Security Council in late Dec. had imposed stringent new sanctions on North Korean international trade.

Turkey Expands Attacks on Kurds in Syria—Turkey's military fired at Kurdish militia (YPG) targets in the Afrin region of northwestern Syria Jan. 19, opening a new front in Syria's already multisided seven-year-old civil war. Turkish Pres. Recep Tayyip Erdogan said the offensive would push eastwards in YPG-controlled Syria toward Manbij, which threatened to provoke direct confrontation with U.S. troops, who had been training and supplying YPG forces there. U.S. Pres. Donald Trump reportedly warned Erdogan Jan. 24 against coming into conflict with U.S. forces in the region, while Erdogan continued to demand that Trump cut off supplies to YPG, who were essential to U.S. strategic and territorial victories over ISIS in 2017. A Syrian-rebel commander said that 25,000 anti-Assad rebels from the Turkish-backed Free Syrian Army had joined the operation against YPG with the goal of recapturing formerly Arab-held Syrian towns.

Kabul Ambulance Bombing Kills Dozens; U.S. Suspends Pakistan's Security Aid; Other Regional Developments—Suicide bombers detonated an ambulance packed with explosives at a police checkpoint in a supposedly secure zone of Kabul, Afghanistan, Jan. 27, killing at least 103 people and injuring more than 230. The Taliban claimed the attack was in retaliation for the U.S.'s increased troop presence and airstrikes in 2017. Only a week earlier, a 14-hour siege by the Taliban on a large luxury hotel in Kabul killed at least 22 people including 4 Americans. The UK-based charity Save the Children suspended its operations in Afghanistan after an attack on its offices in Jalalabad, claimed by ISIS, killed at least four people. ISIS, which had been fighting the Taliban for territory, claimed at least three other deadly attacks in Kabul from late Dec. through Jan. that killed at least 72 people, including 11 Afghan soldiers.

According to a BBC study released Jan. 30, the Taliban was in control of or an open presence in about 70% of Afghanistan. (The U.S.-led NATO coalition estimated the Taliban controlled or contested 45% of the country, as of Jan. 2018.) The United Nations reported Feb. 15, 2018, more than 10,000 civilian casualties—mostly in bombings—in the ongoing conflict there in 2017; in 2009-17, about 28,300 civilians had been killed.

In early Jan., the Trump administration announced its suspension of most military security assistance—totaling at least $900 mil—to Pakistan until it "takes decisive action" against Afghan Taliban and al-Qaeda and Taliban-affiliated Haqqani militants the White House said were taking refuge within its borders.

General

Golden Globes and Oprah Spotlight #MeToo—Honored by the Hollywood Foreign Press Assn. with the Cecil B. DeMille Award for lifetime achievement, actress, TV host, and mogul Oprah Winfrey delivered a rousing speech at the Golden Globes ceremony in Beverly Hills, CA, Jan. 7, during which she honored women who thrived in spite of sexual abuse or misconduct. Winfrey also warned perpetrators that "their time is up," a nod to the newly developed "Time's Up" initiative to find solutions to the problems made prominent by #MeToo revelations. Many nominees and others in attendance at the ceremony wore all-black ensembles in support of #MeToo and other movements against sexual violence.

The night's honorees included the murder drama *Three Billboards Outside Ebbing, Missouri* and coming-of-age comedy *Lady Bird*, which each won best picture in their respective categories.

Alabama Captures College Football Championship; Mayfield Wins Heisman—The Univ. of Alabama Crimson Tide claimed their second title in three years, edging the Univ. of Georgia Bulldogs, 26-23 in overtime, at Mercedes-Benz Stadium in Atlanta, GA, Jan. 8. Scoreless at halftime, Alabama pulled its quarterback and came back to win on a 41-yard pass to DeVonta Smith from freshman backup quarterback Tua Tagovailoa. Tagovailoa, the game's offensive MVP, passed for 166 yards and three touchdowns. Alabama head coach Nick Saban won his sixth career collegiate championship, matching iconic Alabama coach Bear Bryant's record.

Oklahoma Sooners quarterback Baker Mayfield Dec. 9, 2017, became the first walk-on to win college football's Heisman Trophy.

California Mudslides Turn Deadly—At least 21 people were killed by landslides in the wealthy Southern California community of Montecito early Jan. 9 after a burst of rain fell on areas affected by the Thomas Fire—the largest on state record—the month before. Repelled by hardened, burned soil, the rain drove mud, debris, and boulders from mountains above into Montecito, destroying dozens of homes and damaging hundreds more.

California Couple Charged With Abusing 13 Children—Law enforcement Jan. 14 arrested David and Louise Turpin for allegedly holding captive, torturing, and starving their 13 children, ages 2-29, in their Perris, CA, home. Allowed to shower only once yearly and frequently shackled to beds, the siblings were liberated only after one escaped and sought help.

Scores of Abuse Survivors Rebuke Olympic Gymnastics Doctor—During a seven-day sentencing hearing that began Jan. 16, 156 women, including six-time Olympic medalist Aly Raisman, provided emotional testimony regarding sexual abuse by former USA Gymnastics team doctor Larry Nassar. The hearing ended Jan. 24 in Lansing, MI, with Nassar sentenced to up to 175 years in prison after he pleaded guilty to seven counts of criminal sexual conduct. The tally of Nassar's self-identified abuse victims grew to 265 by the end of the month and included Olympic gold medalists Simone Biles and Gabby Douglas and students from Michigan State (MSU), where Nassar practiced medicine.

The Detroit News in Jan. reported that at least 14 MSU officials were aware of but failed to act on accusations against Nassar; by Jan. 31, about 140 victims sued USA Gymnastics and MSU over claims they had ignored abuse allegations. MSU's president and athletic director resigned, as did the entire USA Gymnastics board of directors.

Primate Cloning Milestone Reached—Scientists in Shanghai, China, became the first to successfully clone primates using the complex technique that created Dolly the sheep 22 years earlier, according to research published Jan. 24 in the journal *Cell*. The cloning birth of two long-tailed macaques was lauded by researchers for its potential to boost disease research but drew immediate concerns from ethicists.

Six Elected to Baseball Hall of Fame—The Baseball Writers' Assn. of America (BBWAA) elected Vladimir Guerrero, Trevor Hoffman, Chipper Jones, and Jim Thome to the Baseball Hall of Fame Jan. 24. Thome, who slugged 612 home runs over 22 seasons, and switch-hitting 8-time All-Star Jones were both selected in their first year of eligibility. Guerrero, an outfielder who was the first Dominican position player to achieve Hall status, was elected in his second year of eligibility, and longtime closer Hoffman—with 601 saves, the second highest in league history—was selected in his third. Pitcher Jack Morris and shortstop Alan Trammell were elected Dec. 10 by the Hall's Modern Era Committee.

Wozniacki, Federer Take Australian Open—Denmark's Caroline Wozniacki defeated Simona Halep of Romania (7-6, 3-6, 6-4) in the women's finals match at a steamy Rod Laver Arena in Melbourne, Jan. 27. It was her first Grand Slam title in 43 attempts since 2008. The next night, 36-year-old Roger Federer of Switzerland secured his 20th Grand Slam title, the most ever for a man, after holding off Croatian Marin Cilic in a 3 hr., 3 min. match (6-2, 6-7, 6-3, 3-6, 6-1).

Bruno Mars, Kendrick Lamar Dominate Grammys—Singer-songwriter Bruno Mars won six Grammy Awards at the 60th annual awards ceremony held Jan. 28 in New York City. His *24K Magic* received both album and R&B album of the year awards and its title song won record of the year. Mars's "That's What I Like" claimed song of the year and best R&B song, as well as best R&B performance. Rapper Kendrick Lamar's five awards included best rap album for *DAMN.*, plus best rap song, rap performance, and music video for "Humble."

February 2018
National

Dow Drops Nearly 1,200 Points Over One Day; Other Economic News—Ending a record-setting rally, the Dow Jones industrial average suffered its largest-ever one-day point loss Feb. 5, shedding 1,175 points (–4.6%) to close at 24,345.75. Analysts linked the plunge to spiking bond rates and wage growth in Jan., which sparked investors' concerns of possible inflation and interest rate increases. That same day, the S&P 500 also fell 4.1%, or 113 points, while the Nasdaq composite index dropped 273 points, or 3.8%. The Dow closed the month at 25,029.20, a 4.3% fall from Jan., and the Nasdaq

ended Feb. at 7,273.01, down 1.9%; the S&P 500 closed at 2,713.83, down 3.9% from Jan.

The U.S. Dept. of Labor reported Feb. 2 that the U.S. economy added 200,000 jobs in Jan. as unemployment held at 4.1% for the fourth straight month.

Trump Aide Resigns Amid Abuse Accusations; Other White House Developments—White House Staff Sec. Rob Porter resigned Feb. 7 after his two ex-wives made public accusations that he had physically and emotionally abused them. Porter denied the allegations, first published in the UK tabloid *Daily Mail* Feb. 6. White House spokesman Raj Shah said Feb. 8 that White House chief of staff John Kelly had just become "fully aware" of the allegations and that the FBI background check of Porter was still ongoing. But FBI Dir. Christopher Wray in Senate Intelligence Committee testimony Feb. 13 contradicted the White House stance, testifying that the FBI had completed the background check in late July 2017 and closed the investigation in Jan. 2018. In a letter to the House Oversight Committee in Apr. 2018, the FBI confirmed it had informed the White House of its concerns regarding Porter and the violent abuse allegations in Mar. 2017. Kelly, who was quoted in the Feb. 6 *Daily Mail* article calling Porter "a man of true integrity and honor," revamped the administration's security clearance processes amid revelations that Porter had access to highly classified material through interim security clearance only. The new procedures resulted in the downgrading Feb. 23 of the highest-level interim clearances held by some Trump aides, including most notably son-in-law and senior adviser Jared Kushner.

White House Communications Dir. Hope Hicks announced her resignation Feb. 28, a day after she testified before a House committee investigating Russia's interference in the 2016 election and said that she told "white lies" for Trump. The 29-year-old Hicks was one of Trump's longest serving staffers, having joined his presidential campaign in 2015.

Congress Passes Budget, Ending Hours-Long Shutdown—Ending a second government shutdown in just three weeks, the House of Representatives in the early morning hours Feb. 9 approved (240-186) a six-week stopgap bill that raised spending caps through Sept. 2019 for both military and domestic programs by $165 bil and $131 bil, respectively. The bill, signed that same day by Pres. Trump, provided nearly $90 bil in disaster relief for multiple hurricanes and wildfires that occurred in 2017, raised the nation's debt limit, and extended the Children's Health Insurance Program (CHIP) for four more years. The shutdown began midnight Feb. 9 when Sen. Rand Paul (R, KY) delayed the vote over objections that it would result in trillion-dollar annual deficit increases, but the Senate passed the bill, 71-28, ahead of the House. Trump signed the measure 8 hr., 45 min. after the shutdown began.

House Minority Leader Nancy Pelosi (D, CA) Feb. 7 spoke for 8 hr., 7 min.—the longest House floor speech on record—in protest of House Speaker Paul Ryan's (R, WI) refusal to commit to holding a vote on immigration legislation.

Florida High School Shooting Kills 17, Revives Gun Law Debate—A former student killed 17 people—including three staff—and wounded 17 others at Marjory Stoneman Douglas High School in Parkland, FL, on Feb. 14. The shooter fired for roughly 6 min. after pulling a fire alarm, then allegedly dropped his legally purchased AR-15 semiautomatic rifle and blended in with other students. He was apprehended on foot by police less than 90 min. later and identified as 19-year-old Nikolas Cruz, who had been expelled from the school in 2017. The Broward County Sheriff's Office drew criticism after media reported it had received tips in both 2016 and 2017 specifically warning about Cruz in relation to a school shooting. The FBI received similar tips in Sept. 2017 and Jan. 2018, but it did not forward the tips to the agency's local office. An armed sheriff's deputy stationed at the school was also criticized for failing to enter the building as the shooting progressed; he resigned Feb. 22.

Calls for stricter gun control measures—in this instance led by the student-survivors themselves—commanded widespread and continued attention after the incident. Florida's House Feb. 20 voted 71-36 to reject a motion to debate a bill that would ban sale or possession of assault weapons. Pres. Trump in a televised meeting Feb. 21 with students and parents affected by the Parkland and other mass school shootings pledged tougher background checks and mental health screenings for gun purchases, advocated arming some teachers, and appeared open to raising the minimum gun purchase age, a move opposed by the powerful gun lobby led by the National Rifle Association. By the end of Feb., both Dick's Sporting Goods and Walmart increased the age of gun-purchase eligibility to 21.

Mueller Probe Indicts Russians, Adds to Manafort Charges; Nunes Memo Released—The Robert Mueller-led investigation into Russia's interference in the 2016 U.S. presidential race indicted of 13 Russian nationals and three Russian entities, including a so-called troll farm, on Feb. 16. The probe brought conspiracy charges against all of the defendants; some were also charged with identity theft. Pres. Trump said, via Twitter, that the indictments indicated his campaign had not colluded with Russia, a fact neither proven nor disproven by the probe's developments thus far. All of the indicted defendants, along with six other Russian individuals and entities accused of cyberattacks, were included in White House sanctions enacted the next month. The congressionally mandated sanctions represented the administration's toughest response yet related to Russian election interference.

Mueller on Feb. 22 leveled 32 new counts of money laundering and bank- and tax-fraud charges against former Trump campaign head Paul Manafort and adviser Rick Gates. Gates pleaded guilty the following day to conspiracy and lying to the FBI and agreed to cooperate with the investigation.

The Republican-led House Intelligence Committee, separately investigating the Russia election matter, Feb. 2 released a four-page memo by Devin Nunes (R, CA) alleging a Foreign Intelligence Surveillance Act (FISA) warrant on Trump adviser Carter Page abused the FISA process and showed bias by the FBI. The memo alleged the FBI had failed to disclose in its FISA application that the work of former British spy Christopher Steele—who provided the U.S. with intelligence pertinent to the warrant—was partly financed by the Democratic Natl. Committee and lawyers for Hillary Clinton's campaign. The FBI and Justice Dept. said that the Nunes memo, which was released with the approval of Pres. Trump on the heels of a social media campaign, excluded key facts and could reveal classified information. Democrats on the committee authored a rebuttal memo, and while its release was initially blocked by committee Republicans and then by Trump, a redacted version made public Feb. 24 argued the FBI had not omitted material information about Steele and reiterated that improper contacts between Trump adviser George Papadopoulos and Russians had triggered the FBI to open its Russia investigation in July 2016.

West Virginia Teachers Strike Statewide—Teachers throughout West Virginia walked off the job Feb. 22 in a protest over pay and benefits, the day after Gov. Jim Justice (R) signed a bill providing a 2% raise, the first across-the-board pay increase in four years. The striking teachers, many of whom demonstrated at the Capitol in Charleston, drew attention to West Virginia's average teacher salary of $45,622 in 2016 (ranked 48th nationally) compared to the $58,353 national average. The strike ended Mar. 6 after the state legislature unanimously approved a 5% pay increase for teachers and all other state workers.

International

South African President Resigns in Disgrace—South African Pres. Jacob Zuma resigned Feb. 14 following a public standoff with his African National Congress (ANC) party. The 75-year-old Zuma had ruled the country for nearly nine years, during which both he and the ANC—the party of anti-apartheid leader Nelson Mandela—were increasingly marred by charges of financial mismanagement and an ongoing string of corruption scandals. Zuma, an anti-apartheid fighter imprisoned with Mandela in 1963-73, was dealt a blow in Dec. 2017 when his chosen successor to lead the ANC—his ex-wife Nkosazana Dlamini-Zuma—was rejected in favor of then-Deputy Pres. Cyril Ramaphosa. Ramaphosa was sworn in as the nation's president Feb. 15.

Zuma Apr. 6 was charged with 16 counts of corruption, racketeering, fraud, and money laundering related to a $2.5-bil arms deal in the late 1990s.

Syrian Forces Target Damascus Suburb; U.S. Strikes Kill Scores of Syrian Troops—Military forces under Pres. Bashar al-Assad launched a Russian-backed air offensive Feb. 18 against Eastern Ghouta, a suburban area near Damascus and one of the last rebel-held strongholds in the country. Within hours of a UN Security Council resolution calling for a 30-day cease-fire across Syria, in a state of civil war since Mar. 2011, Syrian government ground forces Feb. 25 attacked rebel fighters on multiple fronts in Eastern Ghouta. Accurate casualty tallies were impossible to ascertain, but estimates put the number of civilian deaths at more than 500; some 400,000 people were believed to be living in the territory when the offensive began.

U.S. airstrikes Feb. 7 targeted Assad forces, killing more than 100 in the eastern province of Deir al-Zour in what U.S. officials said was a defensive move following an unprovoked assault against a base used by U.S.-backed Syrian Democratic Forces (SDF) and coalition military advisers in the fight against Islamic State of Iraq and Syria (ISIS) militants.

Boko Haram Kidnaps Dozens More Girls—The Nigeria-based radical Islamist group Boko Haram kidnapped up to 110 girls from a secondary school in Dapchi, a town in NE Nigeria, Feb. 19. Four years earlier, the group gained global infamy for kidnapping 276 girls—more than 100 of whom were still being held or otherwise unaccounted for—from a boarding school in Chibok. The attack reportedly came within weeks of the withdrawal of Nigerian army troops from Dapchi. Nigerian officials said Boko Haram returned 104 of the Dapchi girls Mar. 21; five others apparently died and one remained captive. The Council on Foreign Relations estimated Boko Haram had killed more than 20,000 people since May 2011 and displaced some 2.3 mil others.

General

Amtrak Accident Kills Two—An Amtrak passenger train Feb. 4 collided with an empty, stationary freight train in Cayce, SC, killing two crew members and injuring 116 people. Investigators attributed the accident to an incorrectly set switch that diverted the Amtrak train to a side track. It was the third fatal Amtrak accident in as many months, following a Dec. derailment in Washington state and a Jan. 31 incident in which a chartered Amtrak train struck a garbage truck. Safety advocates once again called for the installation of the positive train control system, which could prevent some accidents.

Eagles Defeat the Perennial Patriots for First-Ever Super Bowl Win—The Philadelphia Eagles overcame the defending champion New England Patriots, 41-33, at U.S. Bank Stadium in Minneapolis, MN, to win Super Bowl LII on Feb. 4. The offense-heavy matchup set a single-game record for most combined yards gained at 1,151. Named Super Bowl MVP with 28 of 43 pass completions for 373 yards and three touchdowns, Eagles QB Nick Foles was the first player ever to both throw and catch a touchdown pass in one Super Bowl. The broadcast, which included a halftime show headlined by Justin Timberlake, was watched by an average 103.4 mil viewers, down nearly 8 mil from 2017.

SpaceX Launches Largest Rocket Yet—The private aerospace company SpaceX on Feb. 6 launched its highly anticipated Falcon Heavy rocket, the most powerful rocket since the Saturn V used by NASA in its Moon missions. Blasting off from Florida's Kennedy Space Center, the partially reusable Falcon Heavy was capable of carrying nearly 141,000 lbs, roughly twice the capacity of competitor United Launch Alliance's Delta IV Heavy. The rocket released a Tesla Roadster (manufactured by SpaceX CEO Elon Musk's electric car company) as a test payload; SpaceX livestreamed the Roadster and its spacesuit-clad mannequin "driver" drifting into space. Two of the rocket's three reusable boosters set down on land; the third crashed into the ocean near the drone ship on which it was meant to land.

Norway Wins Big at Winter Olympics—More than 2,900 athletes from 92 countries competed in 102 events at the XXIII Winter Olympic Games Feb. 9-25 in Pyeongchang, South Korea. South Korea and North Korea, still technically at war though formal hostilities ended in 1953, entered the opening ceremony under one flag; the two nations likewise participated as a unified team in women's hockey. Russia's Olympic delegation was officially banned following state-sponsored doping allegations, but dozens of athletes were allowed to participate neutrally as "Olympic Athletes from Russia" (OAR).

Germany and Norway tied for most gold medals with 14. Norway also led the overall medal count with 39 (14 gold, 14 silver, 11 bronze), followed by Germany with 31 (14-10-7), Canada with 29 (11-8-10), and the U.S. with 23 (9-8-6).

Norwegian cross-country skier Marit Bjoergen won five medals, which brought her Olympic career total to 15, the most of any Winter Games athlete. The Czech Republic's Ester Ledecká became the first woman to earn gold medals in two different sports at the same Winter Games—Alpine skiing's super-G and snowboarding's parallel giant slalom. American snowboarder Shaun White claimed his third career gold, and the U.S. women's hockey team won gold in a 3-2 shootout with Canada.

Pyeongchang's Olympic venues also hosted the Paralympic Games, Mar. 9-18, at which 48 countries—along with "Neutral Paralympic Athletes" (NPA) from Russia—were represented by some 570 athletes with disabilities. The U.S. team finished first with 36 medals (13 gold, 15 silver, 8 bronze), followed by Canada with 28 (8-4-16) and NPA with 24 (8, 10, 6).

Two Plane Crashes Kill All Onboard—Saratov Airlines Flight 703 crashed Feb. 11 some 50 mi southeast of departure city Moscow, killing all 71 passengers and crew. The jet, an Antonov An-148, lost communication minutes into its flight and appeared to be on fire as it descended. A week later, all 65 passengers and crew aboard Iran's Aseman Airlines Flight 3704 were believed dead after the twin-engine turboprop ATR 72 crashed Feb. 18 into a mountain in southwest Iran, an hour after departing Tehran.

Dillon Triumphs at Daytona 500—Austin Dillon won his first Daytona 500 in Daytona Beach, FL, Feb. 18, in a two-lap overtime finish forced by a 13-car pileup. The 27-year-old Dillon bumped Aric Almirola out of the lead on the final lap—the only lap Dillon led—and held off Darrell Wallace Jr. and Denny Hamlin, who finished in second and third, respectively. Wallace's finish was the highest ever in the race by an African-American driver.

March 2018

National

Adult Film Actress Sues President Over Nondisclosure Agreement—Pornographic film actress Stormy Daniels (a.k.a. Stephanie Clifford) sued Pres. Donald Trump Mar. 6, claiming a nondisclosure agreement—arranged by Trump's personal attorney Michael Cohen in Oct. 2016 to prevent Daniels from revealing details of an alleged affair with Trump in 2006-07—was invalid because Trump did not sign it. Cohen in Feb. 2018 said he facilitated a $130,000 payment to Daniels using his own money, saying it was "not a campaign contribution or a campaign expenditure." Daniels shared details about the alleged affair and pressure to conceal it on CBS's *60 Minutes* Mar. 25 in a highly promoted interview.

Trump denied the affair or knowledge of the transaction through White House spokesperson Sarah Huckabee Sanders Mar. 7.

Florida Strengthens Gun Control Laws After School Shooting; Student Activists Organize to Push for Action—Florida Gov. Rick Scott (R) signed a gun safety bill Mar. 9 that instituted a three-day waiting period for firearm purchases and raised the minimum age of purchasers from 18 to 21 years. The Republican-controlled state legislature took the action in the wake of the Feb. mass shooting that killed 17 at a Parkland, FL, high school, defying the powerful gun lobby led by the National Rifle Assn. The measure, passed by Florida's House, 67-50, and Senate, 20-18, also allowed police to petition to seize firearms from their owners and permitted schools to arm certain personnel. Florida's Senate Mar. 3 had rejected an assault rifle ban called for by student activists.

Tens of thousands of students across the U.S. Mar. 14 participated in a 17-min. school walkout to memorialize those killed in the Parkland shooting and to protest gun violence. More than 750 student-led March for Our Lives events took place Mar. 24, with the main march, in Washington, DC, drawing some 200,000 attendees.

Trump Ousts Key Administration Personnel—Pres. Trump Mar. 13 fired Sec. of State Rex Tillerson, the highest ranking White House official of several to have retired or been dismissed in the past two weeks. The dismissal, announced via Twitter, followed months of public tension between Trump and the former ExxonMobil CEO, which included both Tillerson's failure in Oct. 2017 to deny an NBC News report that

he had called the president a "moron," and more substantive differences, such as Tillerson's support for the Paris climate accord and Iran nuclear deal. Trump's nominee to replace Tillerson, hawkish CIA Dir. Mike Pompeo, was confirmed by the Senate, 57-42, in Apr.

Trump Mar. 22 ousted his national security adviser, Lt. Gen. H. R. McMaster, and replaced him with George W. Bush-era U.N. Ambassador John Bolton. A longtime Fox News commentator, Bolton, who began serving in the post Apr. 9, had previously backed preemptive military strikes against Iran and North Korea.

Trump fired Veterans Affairs Sec. David Shulkin Mar. 28 following a scandal over his travel spending; an underlying issue reportedly was Shulkin's lack of action toward privatizing some veterans' health care services. FBI Deputy Dir. Andrew McCabe was formally fired Mar. 16, two days after agency officials recommended his dismissal over claims he permitted details of an investigation into the Clinton Foundation to be given to the media. McCabe argued that his termination—which took place 26 hours before he was set to retire—was politically motivated to discredit the FBI amid its special investigation into Russian efforts to influence the 2016 election.

Democrat Wins Pennsylvania House Seat—Federal prosecutor Conor Lamb (D) narrowly won a closely watched special election Mar. 13 in southwestern Pennsylvania's 18th Congressional District, where Donald Trump had defeated Hillary Clinton in the 2016 presidential election by 20 points. The 33-year-old Lamb edged out veteran state representative Rick Saccone, 49.9%-49.5%, amid more than $12 mil in spending from outside groups ($10.7 mil of it in favor of Saccone).

Toys R Us and Other Bankruptcies Cost Jobs; Trump Blocks Major Tech Merger; Other Economic News—Seventy-year-old retailer Toys R Us, which had struggled with $5 bil in debt after a 2005 leveraged buyout and had filed for bankruptcy in Sept. 2017, announced Mar. 15 it would need to sell or close all 730 of its U.S. stores, affecting over 30,000 employees. Several more well-known companies filed for bankruptcy protection in Mar., including iHeartMedia, the largest U.S. radio station operator; The Weinstein Company film studio, tainted by the sexual assault allegations against former studio head Harvey Weinstein; and jewelry retailer Claire's.

Pres. Donald Trump Mar. 12 blocked Singapore-based microchip-maker Broadcom's proposed $117-bil merger with mobile technologies provider Qualcomm, citing potential threats to national security.

The U.S. Labor Dept. reported Mar. 9 that the U.S. economy added 313,000 jobs in Feb. as the unemployment rate held steady at 4.1% for the fifth straight month. Stocks indexes declined in Mar., with the Dow Jones industrial average closing at 24,103.11, a 3.7% fall from Feb. The Nasdaq composite index ended Mar. at 7,063.45, down 2.9%, and the S&P 500 closed at 2,640.87, down 2.7%. The Bureau of Economic Analysis reported Mar. 28 that U.S. real gross domestic product in the fourth quarter of 2017 increased at a healthy annual rate of 2.9%, down only slightly from 3.2% the previous quarter.

Fitness company Under Armour Mar. 29 announced that hackers stole personal details, including user names and email addresses, from some 150 mil users of its MyFitnessPal app.

Fatal Uber Accident Halts Self-Driving Test Fleet—Rideshare app company Uber temporarily suspended its self-driving cars from four North American test cities after one of its vehicles killed a woman who was walking a bicycle across a street in Tempe, AZ, Mar. 18. Thought to be the first pedestrian fatality involving a self-driving car, the accident occurred as the vehicle was traveling at about 40 mph and failed to brake (as did the person behind the wheel) for the woman, who was not in a crosswalk. Automaker Toyota also suspended its autonomous test fleet from public roads.

A Tesla Model X in "autopilot" mode crashed into a highway barrier and caught fire Mar. 23, killing the 38-year-old behind the wheel.

Congress Passes 2018 Budget, Boosting Military Spending—Despite making a same-day veto threat via Twitter, Pres. Donald Trump Mar. 23 signed Congress's $1.3-tril omnibus spending bill, averting a federal shutdown and funding the government through Sept. 2018. The legislation—passed in a 256-167 vote by the House and 65-32 by the Senate—boosted defense spending by $60 bil and border security funds by $1.6 bil. It also included over $21 bil for infrastructure projects and provided nearly $4 bil to fight the nationwide opioid-abuse epidemic, a $3 bil increase.

Trump criticized lawmakers and the legislation for failing to fully fund his long-promised border wall with Mexico nor to resolve the fate of undocumented Dreamers brought to the U.S. as children. He said that the increase in military spending—which included a 2.4% troop pay raise—swayed him to sign.

International

Targeting China, U.S. Announces Tariffs on Steel, Aluminum—U.S. Pres. Donald Trump Mar. 1 announced plans to impose new import tariffs of 25% and 10%, respectively, on steel and aluminum products. Key trading partners Canada and Mexico would initially be exempted from the tariffs, which were authorized a week later. Trump made the order in accordance with provisions that allow the president to act with broad discretion where national security is concerned, removing the need for approval from a majority in Congress, which along with most of Trump's cabinet had opposed the move. (National Economic Council Dir. Gary Cohn resigned, at least partially in protest, Mar. 6.)

While campaigning Trump had heavily criticized U.S. trade policy, which he saw as responsible for killing U.S. jobs and depleting domestic revenue, and repeatedly indicated he believed the U.S. was at a disadvantage due to "unfair" trade policies adopted by its international partners. The president later temporarily exempted the European Union and four more countries (along with Mexico and Canada) before the tariffs took effect Mar. 23.

Trump Mar. 22 accused China of "tremendous intellectual property theft" and announced additional tariffs on up to $60 bil of Chinese-made products. China responded by proposing tariffs on U.S. products valued at $3 bil. The actions raised fears of a global trade war.

Russian Spy Poisoned in Britain; Putin Wins Election—A former Russian military intelligence officer-turned-British-spy and his 33-year-old daughter were poisoned Mar. 4, allegedly by Russian agents, in Salisbury, England, UK. Investigators said Sergei Skripal and Yulia Skripal had been exposed to the nerve agent Novichok at their home; both were found unresponsive on a public park bench and hospitalized. Yulia regained consciousness after almost four weeks. Sergei—who had been convicted and imprisoned in 2006 on charges related to providing Russian secret agent identities to the UK but released in a 2010 spy exchange with the U.S.—began to recover after about five weeks. Prime Min. Theresa May expelled 23 Russian diplomats from the UK, saying in a House of Commons statement Mar. 14 that it was "highly likely that Russia was responsible for this reckless and despicable act." More than 20 other mostly Western countries, including the U.S., announced plans to expel more than 115 Russian envoys by Mar. 27. Russia denied involvement in the attack, and in tit-for-tat retaliation expelled equivalent numbers of diplomats back to the UK, U.S., and other nations.

As expected, Russian Pres. Vladimir Putin won a fourth six-year term in office Mar. 18, claiming 76.6% support in voting participated in by 67.5% of the electorate but marred by reports of irregularities. Opposition leader Alexei Navalny was barred from running.

U.S. Plans Nuclear Talks With North Korea—In a surprise announcement, Pres. Donald Trump Mar. 8 accepted an invitation from North Korean leader Kim Jong Un to meet in the first-ever direct talks between a sitting U.S. president and North Korean leader. The historic summit was reportedly suggested by Kim himself Mar. 5 as he took part in his first face-to-face talks with South Korean officials since assuming power in 2011. A day after Trump accepted the North Korean invitation, White House Press Sec. Sarah Huckabee Sanders said that the president, who in past months had used highly charged rhetoric in speaking about Kim and North Korea's nuclear program, would expect "concrete and verifiable steps" toward denuclearization before the meeting.

China Removes Presidential Term Limits—China's National People's Congress passed a constitutional amendment Mar. 11 that eliminated presidential term limits and cleared the way for current Pres. Xi Jinping to remain in power indefinitely. Out of 2,964 delegates, just two voted against the constitutional changes (three abstained; one ballot was invalidated). The next week, 64-year-old Xi was reappointed to a second five-year term. Since taking office as general secretary of the Chinese Communist Party (CCP) in 2012 and president in 2013, Xi had consolidated his control over the CCP, increased censorship of the media, and promoted a more assertive foreign policy, while also reasserting the CCP's authority over the government and policymaking.

Peru's President Steps Down in Corruption Scandal—Peruvian Pres. Pedro Pablo Kuczynski (commonly known as PPK) resigned Mar. 21, the day before an impeachment vote was scheduled to be held over illegal payments he allegedly received from Brazilian construction firm Odebrecht beginning in 2004, while serving as Peru's finance minister. PPK had survived a Dec. 2017 impeachment vote over the continent-spanning Odebrecht scandal. But some PPK supporters were alienated when he pardoned former Pres. Alberto Fujimori—convicted of human rights abuses in 2009—later that same month in a move viewed as payback for support from Fujimori's congressman son, Kenji Fujimori. Videos made public Mar. 20 showed key PPK allies trying to buy the support of other lawmakers.

Vice Pres. Martín Vizcarra, a former regional governor and ambassador to Canada, was sworn in as president Mar. 23.

Israeli Forces Shoot Gaza Protesters; Corruption Investigations Ensnare PM Netanyahu—Israeli forces shot into crowds of protesters, killing at least 15 Palestinians and injuring hundreds more in the Gaza Strip Mar. 30 at several locations along the self-governing Palestinian territory's 40 mi-long border with Israel. An estimated 30,000 Palestinians had massed along the border fence as part of a Hamas-backed, six-week-long demonstration for the right to return (to land from which they or their ancestors fled or were evicted upon Israel's creation in 1948). Israeli officials said troops were justified in "firing towards the main instigators" to prevent a breach of the border, at which some protesters were throwing rocks or rolling burning tires. At least 42 Palestinians were reported killed at the Gaza border in the demonstrations by Apr. 27.

A string of recent investigations by Israeli police implicated Prime Min. Benjamin Netanyahu in bribery, fraud, corruption, and other alleged criminal activities. According to the *NY Times* as of Mar. 2, Netanyahu had been questioned by the police 8 times in the past 14 months. Charges were recommended in at least one case, but the prosecutors' decision was pending.

Syrian Rebels Surrender Most of Eastern Ghouta; Forces Seize Major Kurdish City—The Syrian military declared itself in control of the region of Eastern Ghouta (minus the town of Douma), Mar. 31, nearly six weeks after the government and its allied forces launched an offensive to seize what was reportedly the last rebel stronghold around Damascus. The offensive, which included Russian and Syrian airstrikes, by Mar. 20 had killed nearly 1,500 civilians in Eastern Ghouta. That same week, Russia agreed to cease-fire deals with rebel groups that would allow tens of thousands of fighters and civilians to evacuate to the rebel-dominated northwestern province of Idlib. The largest evacuation convoy—100 buses carrying over 6,700 people—left Mar. 27.

Syrian rebels backed by Turkey Mar. 18 took control of the Kurdish-controlled northern Syrian city of Afrin, achieving the main objective of a two-month-long offensive to rid the border region of Kurdish YPG militants linked by Turkish officials to their country's separatist Kurdistan Workers' Party (PKK).

General

Package Bomber Repeatedly Strikes Texas—A serial bomber put Texas on high alert Mar. 2-21, setting off explosions that killed two victims and injured six others. The first three package bombings, which detonated at Austin-area residential targets on Mar. 2 and Mar. 12, killed two black men and injured one black woman and one Hispanic woman, leading to speculation that targets were chosen according to the bomber's racial bias. A trip-wired roadside package bomb injured two white men Mar. 18, and an explosion at a FedEx facility outside San Antonio injured one person Mar. 20. The suspected bomber, 23-year-old Mark Anthony Conditt, detonated explosives that killed himself and injured an officer as police closed in on his vehicle. Investigators reported finding a 25-min. confession to the bombings on the suspect's phone.

The Shape of Water Wins Big at Oscars—Mexican filmmaker Guillermo del Toro's fantasy fable *The Shape of Water* picked up the best picture prize, as well as best director for del Toro, at the 90th Academy Awards held Mar. 4 at the Dolby Theatre in Los Angeles. Frances McDormand and Sam Rockwell claimed best actress and best supporting actor, respectively, for *Three Billboards Outside Ebbing, Missouri*. Allison Janney won best supporting actress for her portrayal of figure skater Tonya Harding's estranged mother in the biopic *I, Tonya*. Jordan Peele became the first black screenwriter to win best original screenplay, for *Get Out*. Hosting for the second straight year, late-night TV host Jimmy Kimmel drew mixed reviews and an all-time low 26.5 mil viewers.

Russian Mall Fire Kills Dozens—A fire in a shopping mall in the Siberian city of Kemerovo Mar. 25 killed at least 64 people, including 41 children. The cause of the blaze was not immediately determined, but investigators found that the building's fire exits were inaccessible and fire alarms were not functioning. Four people associated with the mall's management faced criminal charges within two days of the disaster.

April 2018
National

Trump Calls National Guard to Border, Decries Asylum "Caravan"; Other White House Developments—Acting to block migrants from entering the U.S. while awaiting approval and funding for his proposed border wall, Pres. Donald Trump Apr. 4 directed the Pentagon and the Dept. of Homeland Security to coordinate the deployment of National Guard troops along the U.S. border with Mexico. (National Guard troops are commanded by the governors of their respective states.) Trump via Twitter also continued to advocate for tougher asylum laws. By the end of Apr., hundreds of Central American migrants seeking asylum, traveling in a size-diminished but much-publicized caravan, reached the Mexico-California border despite Trump's denouncements.

Pres. Trump Apr. 13 pardoned former Vice Pres. Dick Cheney's chief of staff, I. Lewis "Scooter" Libby, whose prison sentence for perjury, lying to the FBI, and obstruction of justice was commuted in 2007 by then-Pres. George W. Bush.

Former FBI Dir. James Comey, fired by Trump in May 2017 and on an extensive media tour promoting his book *A Higher Loyalty*, heavily criticized the president, calling him "untethered to truth" and "morally unfit" to be president. White House physician Rear Adm. Ronny Jackson withdrew himself from consideration as Trump's nominee to lead the Dept. of Veterans Affairs amid allegations of personal and professional misconduct.

FBI Conducts Search of Trump Personal Attorney's Office; Other Russia Probe Developments—FBI agents raided the Manhattan office and hotel room of Pres. Donald Trump's longtime personal lawyer Michael Cohen Apr. 9, seizing a wide array of documents—including those relating to Cohen's payment of $130,000 to adult-film star Stormy Daniels that she claimed was hush money for an alleged affair with Trump. (On May 3, Trump confirmed the payment—for which he said he reimbursed Cohen using his own funds—but continued to deny the affair.) The FBI obtained a warrant for the search via a federal prosecutor, who was apparently advised of Cohen's possible criminal activities by Robert Mueller, the special counsel in the probe on Russian interference in the 2016 presidential election. In Twitter messages Apr. 9, Trump declared the raid a "witch hunt" and a "disgrace."

The *New York Times* Apr. 30 published dozens of questions Mueller submitted to Trump's attorneys, many of which related to Trump's mindset regarding possible obstruction and the probe itself.

Facebook Head Testifies on Privacy, Post-Cambridge Analytica Revelations—In nearly 10 hours of committee testimony before the Senate and House, Apr. 10-11, Facebook founder and CEO Mark Zuckerberg apologized for revelations related to the Cambridge Analytica scandal. Lawmakers on both sides of the political aisle grilled Zuckerberg, who admitted that his company should have alerted authorities and affected users after it discovered the violation in 2015. A week earlier, Zuckerberg had said Facebook users worldwide would have the same level of privacy controls required by the European Union's General Data Protection Regulation, scheduled to go into effect in May 2018. But even as he emphasized user awareness and control of available privacy settings, he stopped short of pledging Facebook's support for any specific U.S. privacy legislation.

First reported in Mar. 2018 and criticized as major data privacy violation, the Cambridge Analytica scandal involved a British political consulting firm by that name, which in 2014 obtained data from 270,000 Facebook users, who completed an app-based survey and consented to its academic use. Cambridge Analytica accessed the data and that of up to 87 mil other affiliated users—the wider group's information obtained without knowledge or consent of any party—and is alleged to have leveraged the data in services it provided to several political campaigns, including that of then-presidential candidate Donald Trump.

Teacher Strikes in Oklahoma, Kentucky, Arizona Bring Concessions—Following a successful statewide strike in West Virginia earlier in the year, Oklahoma public school teachers ended a nine-day strike Apr. 12 after receiving a pay raise—the same pledged prior to the strike—along with several concessions on school funding demands. More than 30 Kentucky school districts closed Apr. 13, the same day the state's GOP-led legislature overrode a gubernatorial veto of state budget legislation that would increase education spending. Kentucky Gov. Matt Bevin (R) apologized Apr. 15 after his remarks that the strike left children vulnerable to sexual assault were met with bipartisan criticism. Arizona Gov. Doug Ducey (R) signed a 20% pay raise for teachers May 3 ending a six-day walkout that kept some 800,000 students out of classrooms.

Wells Fargo Penalized for Auto Loan, Mortgage Abuse; T-Mobile to Acquire Sprint; Other Economic News—Federal regulators announced $1 bil in combined fines Apr. 20 against Wells Fargo—the largest penalty levied by the Trump administration against a major bank—for forcing unsolicited insurance on 570,000 car loan customers and inappropriately fining home mortgage clients. The bank had also paid a $185 mil fine in Sept. 2016 for opening millions of bank and credit card accounts without customer approval.

Capping years of negotiations, T-Mobile agreed to acquire Sprint in a nearly $27-bil merger of the nation's third- and fourth-largest wireless carriers, respectively. The deal required regulatory approval.

The Labor Dept. reported that the economy added 103,000 jobs in Mar., far less than predicted. Nevertheless, the unemployment rate held at 4.1% for a sixth straight month. The Dow Jones industrial average closed the month at 24,163.15, a 0.3% increase from Mar., while the Nasdaq composite index ended Apr. flat at 7,066.27, up less than 0.1%; the S&P 500 closed at 2,648.05, up 0.3% from Mar.

House Committee Releases Russia Report—The Republican-led House Intelligence Committee Apr. 27 released a redacted version of their final report on the committee's year-long investigation into Russian interference in the 2016 election (unrelated to that led by Robert Mueller). The report said they the committee had found no evidence of collusion with the Trump campaign and suggested that the intelligence community's consensus—that Russia's election meddling was intended to elect Trump—was not Russia's primary goal. Democrats on the committee rejected the report and released a redacted dissent, which declared the majority assessment "misleading and unsupported by the facts."

International

Former Brazilian President Surrenders—Ending an overnight standoff, former Brazilian Pres. Luiz Inácio Lula da Silva surrendered to authorities Apr. 7 to begin a 12-year prison term. Lula had taken refuge in a metal workers' union headquarters near São Paulo after Brazil's highest court rejected his petition to remain free pending appeal on his July 2017 conviction on corruption and bribery charges; dozens of his supporters initially physically blocked the building exits. In spite of the conviction and six additional pending corruption trials, Lula remained popular with tens of millions of Brazilians who supported his antipoverty social programs, and he led in many polls for upcoming Oct. presidential election.

Far-Right Hungarian Coalition Strengthens Control—The coalition led by the anti-immigrant Fidesz party won big in parliamentary elections in Hungary, Apr. 8, securing a two-thirds majority (133 out of 199 seats with ally the Christian Democrats) that would allow it to carry out constitutional changes unopposed. Participated in by 68.1% of eligible voters, a relatively high turnout historically, the election handed Prime Min. Viktor Orban a third straight four-year term. Long known for his vows to secure borders, particularly against Middle Eastern and African migrants, Orban also campaigned against intrusion by the EU and United Nations.

U.S., Allies Bomb Syria Over Suspected Chemical Weapons Strike; Assad Forces Claim Eastern Ghouta—In response to reports that chemical weapons attacks by the regime of Syrian Pres. Bashar al-Assad had killed at least 40 civilians in the rebel-held Damascus suburb of Douma, the U.S., UK, and France launched airstrikes against Syria late Apr. 13. The airstrikes, greenlit by Pres. Trump without congressional approval, targeted three sites thought to be vital to chemical weapons production and constituted the strongest military action to date by the coalition against Assad in seven years of civil war there. But the U.S. role in Syria remained unclear, given Trump's repeated calls for withdrawing the roughly 2,000 U.S. troops stationed there.

The Assad regime's takeover of Douma Apr. 12 gave it complete control over Eastern Ghouta, which had recently suffered heavy bombing as the regime, supported by its allies, launched an offensive to retake the region long held by the rebels. According to the Syrian Observatory for Human Rights, a UK-based monitoring group, 1,600 people had been killed in Eastern Ghouta since the offensive began in Feb.

Nicaraguan Austerity Protests Kill Dozens—Protests erupted Apr. 18 in the Nicaraguan capital of Managua and at least 10 other cities in response to increasingly authoritarian Pres. Daniel Ortega's plan to reduce pensions and increase workers' social security contributions. Police fired both tear-gas and rubber bullets at rock-throwing protesters in Managua, where there were also reports of firebombs, arson, and looting. Nicaragua's Permanent Commission on Human Rights reported Apr. 26 that the violence had killed up to 63 people.

After Ortega publicly revoked the reforms Apr. 22, largely more peaceful demonstrations followed, with up to tens of thousands marching in Managua Apr. 28.

Cuba Elects First Non-Castro President—Miguel Díaz-Canel Bermúdez was sworn in as Cuba's president Apr. 19, taking the reins from 86-year-old Raúl Castro and marking the first time a non-Castro led the country since 1959. Raúl, who had succeeded his brother Fidel as president in 2008 and handpicked Díaz-Canel as his successor, retained his position as first secretary of Cuba's Communist Party, a role he said would also pass to Díaz-Canel in 2021. The 57-year-old Díaz-Canel had voiced his commitment to maintaining the island nation's single-party political system and government-planned economy.

Afghanistan Bombings Target Would-Be Voters—An Apr. 22 suicide bombing claimed by ISIS struck a voter registration center in Kabul, Afghanistan, killing 60 people and injuring 138. Six more people were killed that same day by a roadside bomb near a voter registration center in the northern province of Baghlan. Within the first three weeks of the voter registration period that began Apr. 14 for Oct. 2018 elections, the UN Assistance Mission in Afghanistan (UNAMA) reported 23 election-related incidents resulting in 86 deaths.

ISIS also took credit for at least 25 people killed in Kabul Apr. 30, including several journalists who were killed by a second blast that occurred when they arrived at the scene of the earlier detonation.

Korea's Leaders Agree to End War in Historic Meeting; Other Korean Developments—North Korean ruler Kim Jong Un walked across the Korean Demilitarized Zone (DMZ) Apr. 27 to meet with South Korean Pres. Moon Jae-in, becoming North Korea's first leader to set foot in South Korea since the de facto end of the Korean War 65 years earlier. Following historic talks at the DMZ's Peace House, Kim and Moon in a press conference agreed to work toward transforming the

Korean War armistice into a formal peace agreement. The two leaders also pledged to rid the Korean Peninsula of nuclear weapons, though that pledge lacked a timetable. Kim and Moon met in advance of a planned denuclearization summit between Kim and U.S. Pres. Donald Trump. Kim Apr. 20 had said that North Korea was ending further nuclear and long-range missile testing, and that he would shut down its test site.

Former South Korean Pres. Park Geun-hye, removed from office in Mar. 2017 over extortion, corruption, and abuse of power allegations, was convicted of 16 of 18 charges Apr. 6 and sentenced to 24 years in prison.

U.S.-Led Coalition Ends Anti-ISIS Combat Operations in Iraq—Though the Sunni extremist group ISIS continued to carry out bombings in Iraq and remained active in Syria, the U.S.-led coalition against ISIS Apr. 30 marked the end of major combat operations against ISIS in Iraq by closing its land forces command headquarters. Iraqi Prime Min. Haider al-Abadi had declared victory over ISIS there in late 2017. NATO troops—which include U.S. forces in their numbers—had agreed in Feb. to "train and advise" Iraqi security forces to prevent an ISIS resurgence.

General

Notre Dame, Villanova Win NCAA Basketball Tournaments—The Univ. of Notre Dame Fighting Irish edged the Mississippi State Bulldogs, 61-58, on a buzzer-beater to win the school's second women's NCAA basketball championship at Nationwide Arena in Columbus, OH, Apr. 1. With 0.1 seconds remaining, guard Arike Ogunbowale swished a three-pointer that clinched Notre Dame's victory, less than 48 hours after making a similar last-second shot to defeat UConn. Ogunbowale was named the most outstanding player of the Final Four. Head coach Muffet McGraw claimed her 800th Notre Dame win in the final.

The Villanova Univ. Wildcats defeated the Univ. of Michigan Wolverines, 79-62, at the Alamodome in San Antonio, TX, on Apr. 2 to claim the men's NCAA tournament final and the school's second title in three years. The Pennsylvania-based Wildcats brought sophomore guard Donte DiVincenzo in off the bench to score 31 points; he was named the Final Four's most outstanding player.

Bus Accident Kills Canadian Hockey Players—Sixteen people were killed and 13 injured Apr. 6 in rural Saskatchewan, Canada, after a hockey team's bus was involved in a crash with a semi-trailer truck. Ten of those killed were 16-to-21-year-old members of the Saskatchewan Junior Hockey League's Humboldt Broncos, drawing condolences from NHL teams and across Canada. A crowdfunding campaign for the victims' families raised more than $15 mil, a Canadian record for GoFundMe. The truck's driver was arrested and charged in causing the fatalities July 6.

Reed Wins Masters Tournament—Patrick Reed held off fellow American golfer Rickie Fowler by one stroke at Augusta Natl. Golf Club in Augusta, GA, Apr. 8 to win the Masters Tournament and his first major title. The 27-year-old Reed entered the last round with a three-shot lead before sinking two birdie putts on the back nine to finish 15-under-273. Four-time green-jacket winner Tiger Woods, playing in his first Masters in three years, tied for 32nd.

Algerian Military Plane Crashes, Kills All Onboard—An Algerian military plane crashed southwest of Algiers Apr. 11, killing all 257 onboard, including 10 crew. The crash was the deadliest since 2014, when a Malaysian Airlines flight was shot down over Ukraine, killing 298 people.

American Woman Wins Boston Marathon—Two-time Olympian Desiree Linden finished the Boston Marathon in pouring rain Apr. 16 in 2 hr., 39 min., 54 sec. to become the first American to win the women's race in Boston since 1985. Amateur Japanese marathoner Yuki Kawauchi claimed the men's title in 2:15:58, marking the first win at Boston for a Japanese runner since 1987.

Southwest Airlines Engine Explodes Midflight, Kills Passenger—A passenger died Apr. 17 on Southwest Airlines Flight 1380 after fragments from an exploding engine broke through a window, causing her to be partially ejected from a Boeing 737 en route from New York City to Dallas, TX. Battling rapid depressurization, pilot Tammie Jo Shults made an emergency landing with the unstable aircraft in Philadelphia. It was the first accidental death on a U.S. commercial airline since 2009.

Canadian Vehicle Assault Kills Pedestrians—A van-ramming attack killed 10 people and injured 16 in Toronto, ON, Canada, Apr. 23. The 25-year-old suspect drove a rented vehicle on sidewalks, plowing into pedestrians for multiple city blocks; he was apprehended without gunfire. Authorities after accessing his social media suggested a motive based on hatred of women.

Cosby Found Guilty of Sexual Assault—A Pennsylvania jury found 80-year-old comedy legend Bill Cosby guilty Apr. 26 of all three counts of aggravated indecent assault against Andrea Constand. A previous trial ended with a deadlocked jury in June 2017. Constand said Cosby had drugged her prior to the 2004 assault, a tactic described by five other alleged victims who testified in the retrial.

Cosby was sentenced Sept. 25 to 3-10 years in prison; he had been accused by about 60 women of sexual misconduct dating back to the mid-1960s.

May 2018

National

EPA Chief Faces Ethics Questions—Embattled Environmental Protection Agency administrator Scott Pruitt was questioned at a Senate appropriation subcommittee hearing May 16 over agency expenses and allegations of ethics violations. During the hearing, Pruitt's third before Congress in less than a month, he largely deflected the allegations or blamed subordinates and agency policy while admitting that in some cases, he "would not make the same decisions again." Pruitt was the subject of about a dozen ongoing investigations (conducted by, among others, Congress, the EPA's Office of Inspector General, and the Government Accountability Office), including one into a Capitol Hill apartment that he rented at a below-market rate from a lobbyist's wife and another into improperly spending public funds on first-class travel and 24-hour security.

Shooter Kills 10 at Texas School—A 17-year-old student May 18 fatally shot eight students and two teachers and wounded at least 10 others at a public high school in Santa Fe, TX, about 30 mi southeast of Houston. Armed with what authorities believed were his father's legally purchased shotgun and handgun, the confessed shooter, Dimitrios Pagourtzis, then exchanged gunfire with two armed school officers and other police before negotiating a surrender. One officer was critically injured.

Weinstein Faces Criminal Charges; MSU Settles Sex Abuse Suits—Disgraced movie mogul Harvey Weinstein, who more than 80 women, mostly in the entertainment industry, accused of sexual misconduct, was charged with rape and sexual abuse, May 25, in New York, NY. Released on $1 mil bail, the 66-year-old Weinstein, whose high-profile downfall in 2017 contributed to the watershed #MeToo movement, also faced criminal investigations in Los Angeles and London.

Michigan State Univ. May 16 announced it had agreed to pay $500 mil to settle lawsuits by 332 women over their abuse—disguised as medical treatment—by convicted MSU physician Larry Nassar.

New EU Data Regulations Echo in U.S.; Starbucks Addresses Bias Claims; Other Business News—The European Union's General Data Protection Regulation (GDPR)—aimed at providing EU residents with greater control over their digital personal data and how it is used—went into effect May 25. Several U.S.-based companies, including Facebook and Google, were subject to official complaints that same day, and some news outlets, including the *L.A. Times* and *Chicago Tribune*, blocked access to European users due to known issues with their own company compliance.

Starbucks closed all of its approximately 8,000 U.S. stores the afternoon of May 29 so that some 175,000 employees could attend anti-bias training. The training was scheduled in response to an Apr. 2018 incident in which a Philadelphia Starbucks manager called police, who arrested two black Starbucks patrons waiting in the store for a business meeting.

Iconic 124-year-old guitar maker Gibson Brands filed for bankruptcy May 1. Wells Fargo announced May 4 that it had agreed to pay $480 mil to settle a class action suit from investors that said the bank misled them about its fraudulent creation of millions of customer accounts. Walmart announced

May 9 that it was acquiring a controlling stake of India's leading online retailer, Flipkart, for $16 bil.

Unemployment hit a 17-year low 3.9% in Apr., according to the May 4 Labor Dept report. The Dow Jones industrial index closed the month at 24,415.84, a 1.0% increase from Apr., while the Nasdaq composite index ended May at 7,442.12, up 5.3%; the S&P 500 closed at 2,705.27, up 2.2% from Apr.

Rising GOP Star Resigns Missouri Governorship—Facing possible impeachment over sex and corruption scandals, first-term Missouri Gov. Eric Greitens (R) announced his resignation May 29 (effective June 1). Greitens, a former Navy SEAL, had admitted in Jan. to having had an affair with his hairstylist in 2015, but he denied blackmailing her with a compromising photo, which he allegedly took without her permission. By mid-Apr., a Missouri House committee report alleged Greitens also engaged in non-consensual sexual activity with the woman.

Study Estimates Thousands Died in Puerto Rico Hurricane; PR National Guard Plane Crashes—A Harvard Univ.-led study published May 29 in the *New England Journal of Medicine* estimated that more than 4,600 people died in Puerto Rico due to Hurricane Maria—far more than the 64 deaths officially acknowledged by Puerto Rican officials. Multiple news organizations had already released their own estimates of more than 1,000 dead in the storm's aftermath, and Puerto Rican government mortality data released June 1 showed at least 1,400 more dead compared with the same period in 2016.

All nine people onboard a Puerto Rico Air Natl. Guard C-130 were killed May 2 when it crashed and burst into flames on a roadway near Savannah, GA.

International

Trump Pulls U.S. Out of Iran Nuclear Deal—Against the advice of U.S. allies, Pres. Trump declared May 8 that he was withdrawing the U.S. from the 2015 Iran nuclear deal (Joint Comprehensive Plan of Action, or JCPOA) negotiated by the U.S., Iran, and five other nations to curb Iran's nuclear weapons development. The terms of the deal, a signature achievement of Pres. Barack Obama's foreign policy, lifted international sanctions in return for restrictions on Iran's nuclear program through 2030. While international monitors had repeatedly declared Iran in compliance with the terms of JCPOA, Trump said that Iran had violated the spirit of the agreement spirit by testing ballistic missiles and by supporting Houthi rebels in Yemen and the Lebanon-based militant group Hezbollah.

Leaders of Germany, France, and the UK vowed to remain in JCPOA, though companies doing business in Iran faced a return of the stringent economic sanctions previously ended by the deal.

Protests Topple Armenian Strongman—Opposition lawmaker Nikol Pashinyan was elected prime minister of Armenia May 8, less than six weeks after he launched a 120-mi march from Gyumri to Yerevan to protest what he saw as a power grab extending then-Pres. Serzh Sargsyan's rule. Pashinyan, who was joined in that protest (if not the march itself) by thousands of supporters, overcame initial parliamentary resistance to his bid for prime minister by publicly calling for a nationwide strike May 2, and his supporters brought much of the country to a standstill. The parliament, long dominated by Sargsyan's Republican Party, had changed the constitution to shift most presidential powers to the prime minister in 2015, and the term-limited Sargsyan had reneged on a pledge not to run for that post. Sargsyan was elected Apr. 17 but resigned less than one week later.

Malaysian Parliament Shifts for First Time in 60 Years; MA Flight 17 Crash Cause Revealed—The opposition Pakatan Harapan (Alliance of Hope, or PH) bloc decisively defeated the ruling Barisan Nasional (National Front, or BN) coalition in Malaysia's parliamentary voting May 9, marking the country's first major change in government control since it gained independence from Britain in 1957. Despite gerrymandering, vote-buying allegations, and nomination controversies that all allegedly favored BN, PH secured a simple majority with 121 (up from 53) of 222 seats in voting participated in by 82.3% of the electorate. The 92-year-old Mahathir Mohamad, who had served as prime minister in 1981-2003, became the world's oldest elected leader when he was sworn in May 10.

A Dutch-led team investigating Malaysia Airlines Flight 17, which crashed in 2014 and killed all 298 onboard, said May 24 that a Russian military missile was involved.

Populist Cleric's Bloc Wins Iraq Election—A coalition led by anti-American populist cleric Muqtada al-Sadr (not himself a candidate for office) won the largest bloc of seats in Iraqi parliamentary elections May 12. Still far from an outright majority, Sadr's Saairun Alliance emerged with 54 of 329 seats in Iraq's unicameral legislature, 7 seats ahead of the Iranian-supported Fatah Alliance and 12 seats ahead of Prime Min. Haider al-Abadi's Victory Alliance, preferred by the U.S. Campaigning against corruption with an "Iraq First" theme, Saairun formed an unlikely governing coalition in June with the Fatah and Victory Alliances. Election turnout was a record low 44.5% even as no bombings were reported at polling sites, a first since the U.S. invasion in 2003.

U.S. Opens Jerusalem Embassy as Dozens Are Killed in Gaza Protest; Hamas Fires Rockets at Israel—The U.S. Embassy in Israel officially relocated to Jerusalem from Tel Aviv May 14, formalizing Pres. Donald Trump's controversial announcement in late 2017 that the U.S. would recognize Jerusalem as Israel's capital. The opening—attended by Ivanka Trump and Jared Kushner, the president's daughter and son-in-law, who were also presidential advisers—was simultaneously celebrated by Israeli officials and condemned by Palestinians, who claim the contested city as their own capital. The relocation also upended decades of U.S. policy to withhold official recognition of Jerusalem until its status was worked out as part of a final peace agreement.

Some 60 mi away that same day, Israeli forces killed at least 60 protesters and injured more than 2,700 (according to Gaza's health ministry), marking the bloodiest day in Gaza since 2014. Thousands of largely (but not exclusively) unarmed Palestinians were gathered at the Gaza Strip's border with Israel as Hamas-organized "right of return" demonstrations continued. By May 20, 112 Gaza protestors had been killed and more than 13,000 injured, according to the ministry, since the demonstrations began Mar. 30. Israel's high court rejected petitions from human rights groups that Israel discontinue the use of live ammunition and snipers against the protestors on May 24.

Hamas and another militant Islamic group claimed responsibility for more than 70 rockets and mortars fired from Gaza into southern Israel, May 29, in the most forceful attack since 2014. In response, Israeli aircraft attacked some 35 militant targets in Gaza.

Ireland Referendum Repeals Abortion Ban—Irish citizens voted decisively, 66.4%-33.6%, to eliminate the country's constitutional prohibition on abortion May 25. The 64.1% turnout for the referendum was the third-highest since Ireland's constitution was enacted in 1937, and the result marked the declining influence of the Catholic Church and its traditional anti-abortion stance there. An amendment to the constitution had blocked the procedure in all circumstances (with narrow exceptions for abortions that would save a woman's life) since 1983. Irish Prime Min. Leo Varadkar said parliament would work quickly to pass new abortion legislation.

General

Hawaiian Volcano Erupts Violently—Hawaii's Kilauea volcano began to erupt May 3 on the state's Big Island, with lava flowing into the eastern Puna district and forcing the evacuation of some 1,700 residents. The flow evaporated Hawaii's largest freshwater lake, Green Lake, by June 2. A magnitude 6.9 earthquake struck near Kilauea's south flank May 4, and hundreds of lesser quakes followed over the next month. By late June, state officials reported about 10 sq mi and over 650 homes were destroyed.

Probing Lander Heads for Mars; Other Mars News—NASA launched *InSight* (short for Interior Exploration using Seismic Investigations, Geodesy and Heat Transport) May 5 from Vandenberg Air Force Base near Lompoc, CA. The InSight mission was scheduled to touch down on Mars in late Nov., and dig 10-16 ft below the surface to investigate the planet's interior. The nearly 800-lb, solar-powered stationary lander was also capable of detecting seismic activity and "marsquakes."

According to a study published June 8 in *Science*, NASA's *Curiosity* rover, which landed on Mars in 2012, identified organic matter in 3-bil-year-old mudstones found in Mars's Gale crater. Though it was not necessarily evidence of life itself, the discovery demonstrated that organic material could be preserved in Mars's harsh surface environment.

Justify Takes Kentucky Derby and Preakness Stakes—Undefeated three-year-old colt and race-favorite Justify claimed the lead entering the final turn to win the 144th Kentucky Derby May 5 in 2:04.20 at Churchill Downs in Louisville, KY. Running the 1¼ mi contest on a sloppy track inundated with a record 3+ in. of race-day rain, Justify became the first horse since 1882 to win the Derby without racing as a two-year-old. It was the second Derby victory for jockey Mike Smith, who also edged victorious with Justify at the 143rd Preakness Stakes in Baltimore, MD, May 19. Justify edged Bravazo by half a length in mud and fog to finish in 1:55.93.

Cuban Airliner Crashes, Killing Over 100—A Boeing 737 operated on behalf of the state-run airline Cubana de Aviación crashed shortly after taking off from Havana May 18, killing all but one of the 113 passengers and crew on board. The 39-year-old jet, owned by Global Air of Mexico, was bound for Holguín in eastern Cuba. Witnesses reported seeing the aircraft on fire before it plummeted into a field just six mi from the airport.

British Royal Marries American Actress—Prince Harry, the second-born son of Prince Charles and Princess Diana and sixth in succession to the British throne, and American actress Meghan Markle were married May 19 at St. George's Chapel in Windsor Castle. The 36-year-old Markle became the first known biracial person to officially join the British royal family. Departing from a number of traditions, the highly anticipated ceremony was reportedly watched by 22 mil viewers in the UK and 29 mil in the U.S. Prince Henry of Wales—as Harry was formally known—and Markle assumed the titles of the Duke and Duchess of Sussex.

NFL Announces National Anthem Protest Policy—Seeking to end controversy over players protesting police brutality and racial inequality by kneeling during the pregame national anthem, NFL team owners May 23 announced a new policy that would require players and other team personnel to either stand during "The Star Spangled Banner" or remain in the locker room. Teams whose players or other personnel knelt or sat during the anthem would face fines. The practice of protesting during the pregame anthem became more widespread as an act of protest in 2017 after Pres. Donald Trump encouraged NFL team owners to fire kneeling players and fans to boycott.

In early June, Pres. Trump disinvited the Super Bowl-winning Philadelphia Eagles from a White House ceremony in their honor after many among the invited delegation said they would not attend.

Power Victorious at Indy 500—Veteran Australian driver Will Power won the 102nd Indy 500 at a scorching hot Indianapolis Motor Speedway May 27, becoming the first ever to win both the Indy 500 and the IndyCar Grand Prix in the same year. Leading 59 of 200 total laps, Power captured and held onto the top spot with four laps remaining after the two frontrunners pitted for fuel. Ed Carpenter finished more than three seconds behind, followed by Scott Dixon. Seven crashes waylaid numerous drivers, including defending Indy winner Takuma Sato and Danica Patrick, the most successful woman driver ever, who was competing in her last professional race.

June 2018
National

AT&T, Time Warner Complete Merger; Unemployment Rate Dips to 3.8%—Telecom giant AT&T completed its $85.4 bil acquisition of Time Warner June 14, two days after a federal judge ruled against the U.S. Justice Dept. in its antitrust suit to block the merger, saying the Justice Dept. had not provided enough evidence that customers and competition would be harmed by the deal. The closely watched decision appeared to signal that other so-called vertical mergers in the media industry could go forward. In late June, regulators approved Walt Disney's proposed $71.3-bil buyout of 21st Century Fox, provided it sell off 22 local sports networks.

The U.S. Labor Dept. reported June 1 that the U.S. economy added 223,000 jobs in May as unemployment fell to an 18-year-low of 3.8%. The Bureau of Economic Analysis reported June 28 that U.S. real gross domestic product in the first quarter of 2018 grew at an annual rate of 2.0% compared to 2.9% the previous quarter. The Dow Jones industrial average closed the month at 24,271.41, down 0.6% from May, and the Nasdaq composite index ended June at 7,510.30, up 0.9%; the S&P 500 closed at 2,718.37, up 0.5%.

Justice Dept. Report Criticizes Comey Actions—A report by the U.S. Justice Dept. into former FBI Dir. James Comey's handling of the investigation into Hillary Clinton's use of a private email server as secretary of state, released June 14, concluded Comey broke agency protocol but was not politically biased. The inspector general said Comey made a "serious error of judgment" in announcing his reopening of the Clinton inquiry a week before the presidential election but did not find fault with Comey's decision not to charge her. Pres. Donald Trump, who frequently dismissed the investigation into his campaign's possible collusion with Russia as a "witch hunt," focused his response on the report's publication of text messages between two FBI officials that reflected anti-Trump sentiments. But the report did not conclude that bias had affected the investigations.

Family Separation Crisis Peaks; Other Immigration Policy News—Public criticism of the separation of undocumented parents and children at the U.S. border with Mexico reached a fever pitch in June, two months after the Justice Dept. declared a "zero-tolerance" policy of prosecuting all caught crossing the border illegally. The Dept. of Homeland Security (DHS) acknowledged June 15 that 1,995 children had been separated from parents or guardians Apr. 19-May 31 and placed in facilities around the country. (Within days, a count for May 5-June 9 reported the number at more than 2,300.) Pres. Trump falsely said that DHS was legally bound to carry out the separations and repeatedly faulted Democrats for U.S. immigration policy and the need for zero-tolerance. Video footage of cage-like conditions at a children's detention facility was distributed broadly online and via broadcast and cable news, drawing widespread condemnation. Trump June 20 signed an executive order ending family separations and temporarily halting prosecutions of noncriminals, though he said that zero-tolerance was still in effect. A federal judge June 26 temporarily halted separations and ordered the families be reunited within 30 days, though some of the parents/guardians involved had already been deported.

The House June 21 failed in a 193-231 vote to pass a hardline immigration bill. The rejected measure would have funded a border wall, cut legal immigration levels, and eliminated the diversity visa lottery program. The House also voted down, 121-301, a more moderate reform bill that included a citizenship pathway for so-called Dreamers.

Black Teen's Shooting Triggers Pittsburgh Protests—A newly sworn-in police officer shot and killed 17-year-old Antwon Rose Jr., an unarmed African-American student, in East Pittsburgh, PA, June 19 as he ran away from the officer on foot following a traffic stop. The incident sparked Pittsburgh-area protests that extended into early July. The rookie officer, Michael Rosfeld, was charged with criminal homicide in the shooting.

Supreme Court Ends Term with Rulings on Labor Unions, Trump Travel Ban; Justice Kennedy Announces Retirement—The U.S. Supreme Court concluded its 2017-18 term June 27 with a landmark 5-4 decision in *Janus v. AFSCME* that overturned precedent permitting public sector labor unions to collect mandatory fees from nonconsenting employees whom it nonetheless represented during collective bargaining. Associate Justice Samuel Alito's majority opinion said that the 1977 ruling that had established the precedent violated non-members' First Amendment rights by forcing them to support political messages advocated by the unions with which they may not agree. Justices Roberts, Kennedy, Thomas, and Gorsuch joined Alito's opinion.

The same 5-4 majority June 26 upheld the Trump Administration's controversial travel ban that chiefly affected several Muslim-majority countries. Writing the majority opinion in *Trump v. Hawaii*, Chief Justice John Roberts dismissed the argument that Trump's incendiary campaign statements about Muslims and the ban's focus on Muslim-majority countries violated the First Amendment's guarantee of religious freedom. Citing the order's neutral tone, Roberts's opinion upheld the president's authority to enforce the nation's borders as delegated by Congress. In a notably scathing dissent, Associate

Justice Sonia Sotomayor compared the decision to the Court's 1944 decision regarding the legality of Japanese internment.

In a decision with wide-ranging privacy and criminal justice ramifications, the Court held in *Carpenter v. United States* June 22, 5-4, that authorities must obtain a search warrant to track locations through an individual's cellphone. The Court June 18 disappointed critics of gerrymandering by unanimously declining in two separate cases to address the constitutionality of legislative districts intentionally drawn to diminish one political party's power.

Associate Justice Anthony Kennedy, appointed in 1988, announced his retirement after the Court's term ended June 27. A frequent majority-swaying "swing vote," the 81-year-old had aligned with conservatives on issues including campaign finance and gun and voting rights, but voted outside of conservative orthodoxy on other issues, authoring several key LGBT rights decisions during his tenure. Trump's eventual nominee for the seat could place the Court on a firmly conservative track for decades.

Maryland Shooter Targets Newspaper Staff—A man fatally shot five employees and injured two others at the *Capital Gazette* offices in Annapolis, MD, June 28. The suspect, 38-year-old Jarrod Ramos, unsuccessfully sued the *Gazette* in 2012 for defamation over its reporting of a criminal harassment case against him and posted frequent Twitter threats. He was arrested at the scene.

International

Corruption Scandal Unseats Spanish Prime Minister; New Government in Catalonia—Spain's center-right, two-term Prime Min. Mariano Rajoy was removed June 1 in a no-confidence vote in parliament. The 180-169 vote came a week after Spain's high court ordered Rajoy's Popular Party to repay 245,000 euro ($285,000) for a massive corruption scheme, involving kickbacks for public contracts, which led to the convictions of 29 businessmen and former party officials. Pedro Sánchez of the opposition Socialist Workers' Party was sworn in as prime minister June 2.

That same day, Spain relinquished direct control of its northeastern region of Catalonia—which pushed unsuccessfully for independence in 2017—after a regional government amenable to the national leadership was sworn in. (In May, Spain rejected a Catalan government assembled by hardline separatist leader Quim Torra that also included four ministers still facing legal action for their role in the secession attempt.)

The Basque separatist group ETA, which killed more than 800 people in northern Spain between 1968 and 2010, formally dissolved itself May 2 after apologizing to victims' families.

Italy Forms Populist Government—Italy's new right-wing populist government was sworn in June 1, ending almost three months of political stalemate following early Mar. general elections. Led by new Prime Min. Giuseppe Conte, a law professor without political experience who ran as an independent, the government was an alliance of the anti-immigrant League and the anti-establishment Five Star Movement (M5S) and included dual deputy prime minister posts filled by either party. In Mar. elections, the center-right coalition, including the League, captured 265 lower-house seats to 226 for M5S. Incumbent Prime Min. Matteo Renzi's center-left Democratic Party won just 122 seats, losing 227. The M5S and the League, which blamed high unemployment on Renzi's government, promised tax cuts and new social welfare spending.

Trump Upends G7 Conference as Canada, EU, Mexico, Respond to New U.S. Tariffs; Other Trade Developments—U.S. Pres. Donald Trump appeared to reject diplomatic protocol and traditional U.S. alliances following the G7 summit held June 8-9 in La Malbaie, QC, Canada, by refusing to endorse a joint statement for the summit. Trump had previously pledged to support the statement, though contentious talks on U.S. trade policy had dominated the meetings. Trump labeled Canadian Prime Min. Justin Trudeau "dishonest and weak" via Twitter as he departed the conference, after Trudeau said that Canada would retaliate against new U.S. tariffs on steel and aluminum from Canada that went into effect June 1 (along with similar metals duties on imports from the EU and Mexico). All three parties responded with their own tariffs against U.S. goods: Mexican levies of $3 bil, EU duties of $3.2 bil, and Canadian tariffs of $12.5 bil went into effect June 5, June 22, and July 1, respectively.

Responding to alleged intellectual property theft by China, the White House in mid-June announced a 25% tariff totaling some $34 bil on Chinese industrial goods to take effect July 6, immediately after which China declared equivalent duties on U.S. automobiles, boat parts, and agriculture products, including pork and soybeans. China, which has had multibillion trade surpluses with the U.S. since the 1990s, had been subject to increased aluminum and steel tariffs since Mar. 23.

Trump Meets North Korean Leader in Historic Summit—U.S. Pres. Donald Trump met one-on-one with North Korean leader Kim Jong Un in Singapore June 12, marking the first-ever meeting between sitting leaders of the two countries and a possible first step towards ending the autocratic Kim's nuclear weapons program. Following the roughly 40-min. meeting, Trump, Kim, and officials from both countries held bilateral talks after which the two leaders signed a joint statement with the goal of "complete denuclearization of the Korean Peninsula." Sanctions relief and security guarantees would be discussed in further negotiations, led by U.S. Sec. of State Mike Pompeo. Though the White House said it would maintain economic sanctions until Kim took further steps, Trump said he was suspending the U.S.'s standard annual joint military exercises with South Korea, a shift that apparently took U.S. and South Korean military officials by surprise. While Trump hailed the agreement as "very, very comprehensive," many noted its lack of timetable or verification requirements and questioned Trump's effusive praise of Kim, who by most definitions was a ruthless dictator.

The summit nonetheless represented a drastic de-escalation. Over the past year, North Korea tested missiles capable of reaching U.S. cities, and the two leaders exchanged frequent threats, including one by Trump in Aug. 2017 to unleash "fire and fury like the world has never seen" at Kim's regime. The status of the summit itself had also repeatedly been in question: though North Korea on May 9 released three Americans and said it destroyed its nuclear test site, Trump May 24 temporarily canceled the summit, and Kim had expressed anger over Vice Pres. Mike Pence's statement that North Korea "could end like the Libyan model" if it did not denuclearize. (Libya gave up its nascent nuclear weapons program in 2003 in exchange for sanctions relief and reintegration with the international community. The longtime Libyan regime of Muammar al-Qaddafi was toppled by a domestic uprising, aided by NATO, in 2011.)

President of Turkey Wins Reelection and New Powers—Turkey's autocratic Pres. Recep Tayyip Erdogan secured a second five-year term June 24, winning nearly 53% support in general election voting, the first under a new constitution. Approved by 51% of voters in 2017, the constitutional changes abolished the prime minister post (occupied by Erdogan from 2003-14), reduced the power of parliament, and made the president head of state and government. Erdogan's ruling AKP party also won 295 of 600 parliamentary seats. While no major irregularities were reported, Amnesty International said voting, participated in by 86.2% of the electorate, was held under a "climate of fear." Erdogan was said to have jailed some 160,000 people since a failed coup attempt in July 2016.

Saudi Arabia Lifts Women's Driving Ban—Women in Saudi Arabia gained the right to drive automobiles starting June 24. Nevertheless, Saudi women faced numerous restrictions, including the guardianship system under which women required consent of a male "guardian" to get married or divorced, travel, file for a passport, and sign contracts.

General

Capitals Win First-Ever Stanley Cup—The Washington Capitals defeated the Vegas Golden Knights, 4-3, June 7 in Game 5 at T-Mobile Arena in Las Vegas, NV, to win the Caps' first Stanley Cup in 44 years as a franchise. Capitals forward Alex Ovechkin won the Conn Smythe Trophy as the most valuable player in the playoffs, scoring 15 goals and 12 assists in 24 games. The Golden Knights were the first NHL team ever to make it to the Stanley Cup finals in their debut season.

Golden State Warriors Win NBA Championship—The Golden State Warriors won Game 4, 108-85, over the Cleveland Cavaliers June 8 at Quicken Loans Arena in Cleveland,

OH, to claim the NBA championship. The Warriors' 2018 sweep marked the two teams' fourth straight Finals face-off, of which Golden State won three. Warrior forward Kevin Durant was named Finals MVP for a second straight year, averaging 28.8 points.

Cleveland star LeBron James announced July 1 that he was leaving the Cavaliers to sign with the L.A. Lakers, in a four-year, $153.3-mil contract.

Halep and Nadal Take French Open Titles—Top-ranked Simona Halep of Romania beat No. 10-ranked American Sloane Stephens (3-6, 6-4, 6-1) to win the French Open women's singles title June 9 at Roland Garros in Paris, France. It was the first Grand Slam victory for the 26-year-old Halep, who lost in the French Open final last year. The next day, defending champion Rafael Nadal of Spain overcame Austrian Dominic Thiem (6-4, 6-3, 6-2) to win his 11th French Open title.

Justify Wins Triple Crown—Justify became the 13th horse overall and the second in four years to claim thoroughbred racing's coveted Triple Crown after winning the 150th Belmont Stakes June 9 at Belmont Park in Elmont, NY. Ridden by jockey Mike Smith, Justify charged out of the post position to claim an early lead, finishing 1¾ lengths ahead of Gronkowski in 2:28.18. Justify trainer Bob Babbert became the first trainer to win two Triple Crowns, having won with American Pharoah in 2015.

Koepka Claims Second Straight U.S. Open—Defending champion Brooks Koepka won the 118th U.S. Open golf tournament June 17 at Shinnecock Hills Golf Club in Shinnecock Hills, NY. Beginning the final round in a four-way tie, Koepka outlasted the trio to finish atop the leaderboard with a 1-over-281, one shot ahead of British golfer Tommy Fleetwood. Koepka's winning back-to-back Open titles was a first since 1988-89.

Indonesian Ferry Capsizes, Killing Nearly 200—A heavily overloaded ferry capsized and sank in Sumatra's Lake Toba in Indonesia June 18, killing almost 200 people. The ship was said to be carrying some five times the legal passenger capacity along with dozens of motorcycles. Though a search drone located the wreckage in about 1,500 ft of water, technical difficulties and dangerous conditions caused officials to call off the effort to retrieve victims; only four deaths were confirmed. Eighteen survived, including the captain.

Vatican Removes U.S. Cardinal Over Abuse—The Vatican removed influential emeritus archbishop of Washington, Cardinal Theodore McCarrick, from public ministry June 20 amid credible allegations that he sexually abused a teen 47 years earlier in New York. The 87-year-old McCarrick, who himself developed church policies regarding sexual abuse, had been accused earlier by three different people. McCarrick officially resigned from the College of Cardinals July 28.

July 2018
National

Scandal-Besieged EPA Head Resigns; Former Fox News Executive Joins White House Staff—Environmental Protection Agency (EPA) administrator Scott Pruitt resigned July 5 amid ongoing ethics scandals and spending controversies that prompted about a dozen federal investigations by Congress, the EPA Inspector General, and the Government Accountability Office. These inquiries were looking into Pruitt's below-market rental of a condo co-owned by an energy lobbyist's wife, his spending public funds on 24-hour security and frequent first-class travel, and his asking a government employee to help his wife find a high-paying job. CNN reported July 3 that Pruitt and aides had used a secret calendar to keep track of and conceal meetings with industry representatives or other potentially controversial figures. Deputy EPA administrator Andrew Wheeler, a former coal lobbyist who shared Pruitt's commitment to industry deregulation, became acting agency chief.

Trump July 5 named former Fox News co-Pres. Bill Shine as his deputy chief of staff for communications. Shine was forced out at Fox News over his handling of the network's sexual abuse scandals, and there were accusations that Shine was aware that private detectives were used to intimidate those who made allegations of abuse.

Trump Nominates Kavanaugh to U.S. Supreme Court—Pres. Donald Trump July 9 nominated 53-year-old U.S. Court of Appeals for the DC Circuit Judge Brett Kavanaugh to replace retiring Supreme Court Justice Anthony Kennedy. Kavanaugh, Trump's second nominee for the high court, served in the executive branch during both Bush administrations and was part of the independent investigation into Pres. Bill Clinton led by Kenneth Starr.

Deadlines to Reunite Hundreds of Undocumented Children and Parents Pass—The Trump administration failed to meet a federal court-imposed deadline of July 10 to reunify at least 102 undocumented migrant children under the age of 5 with parents from whom they were separated under its now-suspended zero-tolerance immigration policy, in place from late Apr. to mid June. As of July 10, only four children and their parents had been reunited; by July 12, officials said 57 more were with parents (at least a dozen parents had reportedly been deported and officials were seeking to locate them). By July 26, the deadline to reunite children over the age of 5, the administration said 1,820 of 2,531 had rejoined parents, been placed with a guardian, or simply released if they had turned 18. Parents of at least 431 of the still-detained older children had been deported. (By Aug. 23, 2,126 children out of 2,654 had been reunited or released.) A federal judge Aug. 3 castigated the administration's lack of action on locating deported parents and rejected the government's request to make the ACLU and other rights organizations shoulder that responsibility.

Russians Officially Charged With DNC Hack; Another Russian National Indicted on Spy Charges—The Justice Dept. charged 12 Russian intelligence officers July 13 with hacking the Hillary Clinton campaign and Democratic National Committee and releasing emails and data prior to the 2016 presidential election. The indictments represented special counsel Robert Mueller's strongest evidence thus far of official Russian government interference in the election. According to the indictments, Russians first tried to access Clinton's servers on July 27, 2016, the same day Trump publicly urged Russia to hack her emails.

Separately, the Justice Dept. July 17 charged Maria Butina, a 29-year-old Russian national, with spying within the U.S. for Russia by infiltrating political groups and establishing back-channel communications with politicians.

Facebook Suffers Record Stock Loss; EU Fines Google; Other Economic News—Facebook stock July 26 lost approximately $119 bil in value, the largest one-day drop ever on the U.S. stock market. (Intel in 2000 shed more than $90 bil.) The Nasdaq-traded company's 19% loss in value came the day after Facebook reported weaker-than-anticipated second quarter profits and forecast slower growth in the second half of 2018.

The European Union levied a record-setting antitrust penalty of $5 bil on Google July 18 for, among other things, requiring manufacturers to pre-install Google Search and the Chrome browser on Android mobile devices, preventing them from using rival systems.

The Labor Dept. reported July 6 that the economy added 213,000 jobs in June, exceeding expectations. The unemployment rate rose slightly to 4.0% from 3.8% in May as some 600,000 additional workers entered the labor force. On Wall Street, the Dow Jones industrial average closed July at 25,415.19, a 4.7% increase from June, while the Nasdaq composite index ended the month at 7,671.79, up 2.2%; the S&P 500 closed at 2,816.29, up 3.6%.

International

Populist Wins Mexico's Presidency After Violent Campaign Season—Mexican voters soundly rejected the incumbent Institutional Revolutionary Party (PRI) July 1, electing leftist Andrés Manuel López Obrador as president with 53.2% of the first-round vote over PAN candidate Ricardo Anaya (22.3%) and PRI candidate José Antonio Meade (16.4%). The first Mexican president to win an outright majority in first-round voting in three decades, López Obrador had promised to reduce violence and corruption and boost social services, including old-age pensions, educational grants, and farm aid. He also railed against U.S. Pres. Donald Trump's proposed border wall and argued that outgoing Pres. Enrique Peña Nieto (prevented from running due to term limits) had failed to take a stand.

A report from July 1 found that 145 candidates and party workers had been killed in the nine months ahead of Mexico's election, which saw a 63.4% voter turnout in spite of the violence.

North Korean Talks Hit Snag; War Dead Remains Returned to U.S.—In the wake of the Singapore summit between U.S. Pres. Donald Trump and North Korean leader Kim Jong Un, further talks between U.S. Sec. of State Mike Pompeo and a top North Korean official July 6-7 drew mixed reactions. A North Korean official said the U.S. had a "gangster-like mindset" and that it would not denuclearize without simultaneous concessions from the U.S., but Pompeo said progress was made on most issues.

The remains of 55 U.S. servicemen killed during the 1950-53 Korean War were transferred to a U.S. Air Force transport plane from North Korea, July 27, and formally repatriated Aug. 1 during a ceremony at the Osan Air Force base near Seoul, South Korea, and also at a ceremony attended Aug. 1 by Vice Pres. Mike Pence at Hawaii's Joint Base Pearl Harbor-Hickam. Detailed analysis and identification of the remains was expected to begin upon the remains' arrival in Hawaii. The remains of some 5,300 U.S. service members who died during the Korean War were never returned to the U.S.

The *Washington Post* July 30 reported unnamed U.S. intelligence officials had concluded that North Korea was producing new intercontinental ballistic missiles.

Bombings Target Pakistan Political Rallies, Mar Voting; Cricket Star Elected PM—Both the Taliban and the Sunni extremist group known as ISIS claimed responsibility for a suicide bombing that killed more than 150 people July 13 at a political rally about 20 mi south of Quetta, a provincial capital in Pakistan. The second deadliest terror attack in the country's history, the explosion killed a candidate for a local assembly seat. Three days earlier, an attack claimed by the Taliban on a campaign event in the northwestern city of Peshawar killed a candidate and some 19 others. A suicide bomber detonated explosives outside a polling station in Quetta July 25, killing at least 31, as voters headed to polls to elect Pakistan's third successive civilian government.

The July 25 election, participated in by 51.6% of eligible voters, ousted the ruling Pakistan Muslim League-Nawaz (PML-N) party. Led by the brother of convicted ex-Prime Min. Nawaz Sharif, the PML-N won just 64 of 270 contested seats—giving it control of 82 of 342 total seats—to 116 claimed by the centrist Pakistan Tehreek-e-Insaf (PTI) party (in control of 158 seats total). Pakistan's parliament Aug. 17 elected former professional cricket star and PTI founder Imran Khan as prime minister.

Haitian PM Leaves Office Amid Unrest—Facing a no-confidence vote, Haiti's Prime Min. Jack Guy Lafontant resigned July 14 following violent protests over sharp and sudden proposed fuel price hikes. Lafontant July 7 temporarily suspended subsidies that resulted in price increases of 38% on gasoline and 47% on diesel the day after they were announced. During the subsequent unrest, July 6-11, at least two people including a police officer were killed, and rioters looted businesses and shut down roads with burning tires.

Trump-Putin Summit Draws Bipartisan Criticism; Other Russia News—Pres. Donald Trump and Russian Pres. Vladimir Putin held their first official summit in Helsinki, Finland, July 16. During the joint press conference following their one-on-one sit-down, Trump drew bipartisan criticism when he refused to directly support the consensus finding of U.S. intelligence officials that Russia interfered in the 2016 U.S. presidential election, saying that he did not "see any reason why" Russia would have meddled in U.S. polling. Though he asserted that he had "great confidence in my intelligence people," Trump lauded Putin's strong denial of election meddling and touted Russia's offer to interrogate the 12 Russian intelligence officers indicted three days earlier by the U.S. Justice Dept. for allegedly hacking the DNC. Reading a prepared statement the next day, Trump said he misspoke and meant to say he did not see why Russia would not be responsible.

Though no synopsis of Trump and Putin's direct talks was made public, the two reportedly discussed the Syrian conflict at length, as well as extending the START nuclear weapons treaty, set to expire in 2021, and Crimea, which Putin was expected to ask the U.S. to recognize as Russian territory.

A 44-year-old woman in Amesbury, England, died July 8 from exposure to the nerve agent Novichok, the same toxin used in the Mar. 2018 attack (blamed by the UK on Russia) that poisoned former Russian spy Sergei Skripal and his daughter. The Amesbury woman's boyfriend, who was poisoned but regained consciousness, reportedly picked up a discarded perfume bottle containing the agent, which authorities suspected was from the same batch used to poison the Skripals.

ISIS Assault Kills Hundreds in Southern Syria; Israel Rescues Syrian White Hats; Other Developments—The Sunni extremist Islamic State in Iraq and Syria (ISIS) carried out suicide bomb and shooting attacks on Sweida, Syria, and nearby villages July 25, killing more than 220 people, including 139 civilians. The ambush on mostly government-held Sweida, the capital of a southern province of the same name, also killed a number of Syrian pro-government fighters. In the course of the attack, militants also kidnapped several dozen women and children belonging to the minority Druze sect, which ISIS considers heretical.

Syrian military aircraft in retaliation struck ISIS's desert stronghold of Karaa, northeast of Sweida. By July 31, the Syrian army and its allies claimed control of the Yarmouk Basin bordering Israel and Jordan.

Ahead of advancing Syrian government forces, Israel July 22 at the request of the U.S. and other allies evacuated some 400 so-called White Helmet Syrian volunteer rescue workers and family members from the last anti-government stronghold bordering the Golan Heights.

General

Thai Boys Trapped in Cave, Freed—Twelve Thai boys and their assistant soccer coach were rescued from a flooded cave complex in northern Thailand July 8-10, capping an international effort involving more than 10,000 people. While exploring Tham Luang Nang Non cave in Chiang Rai Province, June 23, the team was trapped by heavy rains. By July 2, a pair of British divers located the group in a chamber 2.5 mi from the still-flooded cave entrance and about 0.3 mi below ground level. Teams of divers retrieved the team through narrow passageways in three waves. One former Thai Navy SEAL died in the effort after delivering oxygen supplies.

Djokovic and Kerber Take Wimbledon Championships—No. 11-seed Angelique Kerber of Germany defeated No. 25-seed and 7-time Wimbledon champion Serena Williams in just 65 min. in straight sets (6-3, 6-3) to win her first Wimbledon Championship in London July 14. It was only the American superstar's fourth tournament since giving birth in Sept. 2017. The next day, No. 12-ranked Novak Djokovic of Serbia bested South Africa's No. 8-ranked Kevin Anderson (6-2, 6-2, 7-6) in a 2 hr., 19 min. match that brought Djokovic his fourth Wimbledon title and 13th Grand Slam singles win.

Climate-Related Disasters Kill Hundreds—Multiple weather-related disasters claimed lives around the globe in July. In western Japan, torrential rains resulted in flooding and landslides that killed at least 220 people by July 14; another 116 were killed in a heat wave there. A heat wave in early July killed up to 70 people in Québec, Canada; about half died in Montréal. At least 91 people were killed by a fast-moving wildfire east of Athens, Greece, July 23-24; it was Europe's deadliest wildfire since 1900. Seventeen wildfires raged in California by the end of the month, killing at least eight people and burning 375 sq mi and over 1,000 structures.

France Triumphs in Men's World Cup Soccer—France's national soccer team won its second FIFA men's World Cup title July 15, defeating Croatia, 4-2, at Russia's Luzhniki Stadium in Moscow. France's 19-year-old Kylian Mbappé became the first teen since Brazil's Pelé in 1958 to score in a Cup final; he earned him the best young player award of the tournament, while Croatian Luka Modric was given the Golden Ball award for best player.

Halted briefly by four anti-Putin protestors, the final match capped a month-long, 64-game tournament. Four-time champion Italy had failed to qualify for the Cup for the first time in 60 years, as did the U.S., but both Panama and Iceland made debut appearances. Defending men's World Cup champion Germany did not advance beyond the first round.

In June, FIFA agreed to hold the 2026 tournament jointly in Canada, Mexico, and the U.S.

Missouri Duck Boat Sinks, Killing Tourists—An amphibious tourist duck boat sank in high winds and rain on Table Rock Lake near Branson, MO, July 19, killing 17 of 31 people onboard and drawing attention to the wheeled craft's regulation and possible design flaws, including a continuous canopy that may have prevented escape. Thirteen people had drowned in an Arkansas duck boat accident in 1999 that also involved a continuous canopy; a private safety inspector in 2017 told the Branson tour boat operator, Ride the Ducks, that the pumps that pull water out of the vessel's hull could malfunction in stormy weather. The boat's captain, who survived, was said to have told passengers they didn't need life jackets; reportedly, none of the victims wore one.

Molinari Takes British Open—Italian Francesco Molinari won the 147th Open Championship at Carnoustie Golf Links in Angus, Scotland, UK, July 22. Three strokes behind at the start of the final round, Molinari scored two birdies and par on the remaining 16 holes to finish at 8-under-276, two ahead of a four-way tie for second place. Tiger Woods, who hadn't won a major tournament in 10 years and began the day four strokes back, gained the lead in the final round before double bogeying on the 11th.

Scientists Find Lake on Mars—Italian research scientists July 25 announced evidence of a 12-mi-long, salty Martian lake located below a mile of ice near the planet's South Pole. Detected by the European spacecraft *Mars Express*, the lake marked the first discovery of permanent (non-seasonal), liquid-state water on Mars.

Welsh Racer Thomas Wins Tour de France—Geraint Thomas of Wales won the 105th Tour de France July 29, his first Tour victory and the sixth in seven years by a UK rider. The 32-year-old double Olympic gold medalist completed the 2,081-mi, 21-stage course in 83 hr., 17 min., 13 sec., ahead of Dutch rider Tom Dumoulin by 1 min., 51 sec. Defending champion Chris Froome finished third, 2 min., 24 sec. behind Thomas.

August 2018
National

Apple Hits $1 Tril Market Cap; Monsanto Ordered to Pay Cancer Settlement; Other Business, Economic News—Two decades after it nearly went bankrupt, tech giant Apple Aug. 2 became the first publicly traded U.S. company to be worth more than $1 tril when its shares reached $207.05. The iPhone-maker ended the month trading at $227.63. Facebook Aug. 28 announced that hackers had accessed the accounts—including personal information—of almost 50 mil of its users.

Missouri-based Monsanto, acquired in June by Germany's Bayer, was ordered by a California jury Aug. 10 to pay $289 mil to a 46-year-old former groundskeeper, Dewayne Johnson, after the jury found that the chemical giant's weed killers caused his terminal cancer, and that the company had knowingly neglected to alert consumers. The suit was the first to go to trial over claims that glyphosate-based weed killers cause cancer, and Monsanto was expected to appeal the verdict. (The World Health Organization in 2015 declared glyphosate as "probably carcinogenic," but the U.S. EPA said it was safe with careful use.)

The Labor Dept. reported Aug. 3 that 157,000 jobs were added to the U.S. economy in July, as the unemployment rate ticked down from 4.0% to 3.9%. On Wall St., the Dow Jones industrial average closed Aug. at 25,964.82, a 2.2% increase from July, while the Nasdaq composite index ended the month at 8,109.54, up 5.7%, and the S&P 500 closed Aug. at 2,901.52, up 3.0% from July.

Trump Pulls Former CIA Director's Security Clearance, Feuds With Fired Staffer—Pres. Donald Trump Aug. 15 revoked the security clearance of former CIA Dir. John Brennan (2013-17), citing concern over Brennan's "objectivity and credibility." An outspoken critic of Trump, Brennan had notably characterized the president's July meeting with Russian Pres. Vladimir Putin as "nothing short of treasonous." By the next week, some 175 former intelligence officials denounced the revoked security clearance as retaliation against a private citizen making unclassified public comments.

Omarosa Manigault Newman, a former reality TV star and communications staffer fired from the White House in Dec. 2017, released a tell-all book, *Unhinged*, Aug. 14, that presented an unflattering image of the president. Manigault Newman also released a number of audio recordings, one of which included Trump advisers discussing the possible existence of a recording of the president using the N-word. Trump referred to Manigault Newman via Twitter as a "dog" and "lowlife," garnering criticism.

Trump Lawyer Accepts Guilty Plea, Former Trump Campaign Head Convicted; Other Developments—Pres. Donald Trump's former personal attorney Michael Cohen pleaded guilty Aug. 21 to eight federal criminal charges, including two campaign contribution violations originating from $280,000 of so-called hush money Cohen said he paid to cover up the president's alleged extramarital affairs. The 51-year-old Cohen said in his plea that he paid both adult film star Stormy Daniels and former *Playboy* model Karen McDougal at the specific direction of a "federal candidate" (known to be Trump) to influence the election. According to the Justice Dept., the payments were arranged with the Trump campaign, and were thus illegal, unreported expenditures in support of the campaign. The president accused Cohen of lying to reach a better deal with prosecutors and said that the money in question came from him, not his campaign. Other charges against Cohen included tax evasion and bank fraud; his plea agreement did not require that he cooperate with Robert Mueller's investigation into Russian interference in the 2016 election, but Cohen was reportedly willing to do so.

At almost the same time on Aug. 21, a Virginia federal jury convicted Trump's former campaign chair, Paul Manafort, of eight financial crimes unrelated to Cohen's charges, including laundering $30 mil earned consulting for pro-Russian Ukrainian politicians, defrauding banks to receive more than $4 mil in loans, and concealing foreign bank accounts. The jury was deadlocked on the remaining 10 charges, including bank fraud. The not-yet-sentenced Manafort Sept. 14 admitted guilt on these and other charges, including witness tampering, and agreed to cooperate with Mueller's investigation. With Cohen and Manafort, a total of five Trump associates had pleaded guilty or been criminally charged since Jan. 2017.

NSA contractor Reality Winner, who pleaded guilty to leaking a classified report on U.S. election hacking by Russia to news media, was sentenced Aug. 23 to more than five years in prison.

Presidential Nominee and Influential Senator McCain Dies—Longtime Sen. John S. McCain (R, AZ) died in office Aug. 25, at age 81, from brain cancer diagnosed the previous year. A naval aviator shot down and held hostage for five-and-a-half years during the Vietnam War, McCain began his Senate service in 1987 after two House terms and was the GOP's 2008 presidential nominee. Though he was a reliable conservative vote on most issues, he leaned into his reputation as a maverick, willing to reach across the political aisle on multiple issues, as in the 2002 campaign finance reform legislation he championed with Sen. Russ Feingold (D, WI). McCain also criticized Pres. Donald Trump on numerous occasions and cast a memorable vote against the Republicans' signature Obamacare repeal effort in 2017. Ahead of his death, McCain requested that Trump not attend his funeral service, at which former presidents George W. Bush and Barack Obama were asked to speak.

Hurricane Death Toll in Puerto Rico Revised—The results of a public health study by George Washington Univ., released Aug. 28, increased the estimated number of deaths in Puerto Rico as a result of Hurricane Maria in Sept. 2017 to 2,975 from the previous, much questioned official government tally of 64. The Puerto Rican government, which had commissioned the study, accepted the results that same day. Pres. Trump continued to insist the federal government's response to the disaster was an "unsung success," and in Sept. dismissed the new estimate, which he said Democrats fabricated to "make me look as bad as possible." The Federal Emergency Management Agency (FEMA) in a July report said it was understaffed and unprepared for the Category 4 storm.

International

Saudi-Led Airstrikes Target Civilians in Yemen—Saudi-led coalition airstrikes hit a bus in Dahyan in the northern province of Saada, Yemen, Aug. 9, killing over 50, 40 of them children. UN Sec.-Gen. António Guterres condemned the attack, which the U.S.-backed coalition initially justified as a "legitimate military operation." The coalition also accused the Iran-aligned, opposition Houthi rebels of deliberately using children as human shields. (The coalition's Joint Forces Command expressed "regret over the mistakes" related to the strike Sept. 1, and pledged to hold those who committed the mistakes responsible with legal proceedings.) A Saudi spokesperson also denied the coalition had carried out Aug. 2 airstrikes on a fish market and hospital in the rebel-held Yemeni port city of Hodeidah that killed some 55 people, blaming the attacks instead on Houthi rebels.

From the start of Yemen's conflict in Mar. 2015 through Aug. 9, 2018, the UN documented 17,062 total civilian casualties including 6,592 deaths, with 10,471 casualties attributed to coalition airstrikes. (Experts believe the total number of casualties is likely vastly higher.) More than 22 mil people in Yemen (out of 30 mil total) were in need of humanitarian assistance.

Taliban, ISIS Violence Kills Scores in Afghanistan—Taliban fighters launched a surprise offensive against the strategic Afghan provincial capital of Ghazni early Aug. 10, killing around 30 civilians and over 100 Afghan troops and police before retreating four days later amid a government counter-assault supported by U.S. airstrikes. The attack, which also left some 200 Taliban fighters dead, was one of several by the group in Aug.-Sept. On Aug. 13, militants killed at least 17 troops and captured dozens more in the northern province of Faryab; hundreds of militants killed more than 40 at an army base and a checkpoint in the northern province of Baghlan Aug. 15. In four separate attacks Sept. 10, about six weeks before scheduled parliamentary elections, Taliban militants killed more than 50 police and soldiers in the northern provinces of Kunduz, Samangan, and Sar-i-Pul.

The Sunni extremist group Islamic State of Iraq and Syria (ISIS) was widely blamed for an Aug. 15 suicide bombing in western Kabul that killed at least 48 young people preparing for university exams at an education center in a Shiite neighborhood. A coalition airstrike in Nangarhar province reportedly killed ISIS's head in Afghanistan, Abu Sayed Orakzai, and 10 other fighters Aug. 26.

Turkish Currency Crisis Worsens Amid Rift With Trump—The Turkish lira fell to a record low against the U.S. dollar Aug. 13, having lost more than 40% of its value since 2018 began. The currency freefall alarmed European banks with stakes in Turkey and sparked warnings of an imminent recession. Despite an inflation rate of 17.9% in Aug., Turkey's president, Recep Tayyip Erdogan, continued to resist calls for Turkey's central bank to raise interest rates, and called on Turks to exchange any dollars or euros for lira.

Erdogan had angered U.S. Pres. Donald Trump by failing to respond to his efforts in late July to secure the release of U.S. pastor Andrew Brunson, who was being tried in Turkey on espionage and terrorism-related charges. Trump on Aug. 10 mandated the doubling of tariffs on steel and aluminum imports from Turkey to 50% and 20%, respectively.

Venezuelan Inflation Crisis Deepens; Migration Overwhelms Neighbors; Other Developments—Attempting to curb runaway hyperinflation in Venezuela that surpassed 60,000% by Aug. 19, socialist Pres. Nicolás Maduro Moros Aug. 20 redenominated the national currency, the bolívar, as the "sovereign bolívar" by eliminating five zeros. Monetary analysts criticized the strategy, which also included anchoring the new currency to the country's dubious "petro" or oil-backed cryptocurrency (not yet in circulation), as failing to address the root causes of the oil-rich nation's ongoing economic crisis.

Increasingly unable to purchase food, medicine, and household goods amid shortages and inflation, more than 2.3 mil Venezuelans (about 7% of the population) left the country between 2014—when oil prices began to slump—and June 2018. Most migrated to Colombia, Ecuador, Peru, or Brazil. Ecuador declared a state of emergency over some 4,200 migrants arriving daily in Aug., and Brazil temporarily shut its northern border in early Aug. and sent troops Aug. 29 to respond to clashes between residents and migrants there. On Aug. 2, Colombia granted 440,000 Venezuelans there two-year access to medical and social service aid.

Maduro was uninjured by what he claimed was a bombing assassination attempt via two drones in Caracas, Aug. 4. Maduro critics suggested the bombing was staged to justify repression of opponents.

Conservative Shift Ousts Australian Prime Minister—Australian Prime Min. Malcolm Turnbull was turned out of office Aug. 24 amid a party leadership challenge ("spill") vote, won that same day by Scott Morrison, a more conservative MP of Turnbull's center-right Liberal Party. Turnbull had been criticized by right-leaning colleagues for proposing a bill capping greenhouse gas emissions and sat out of the second-round leadership vote won by Morrison, 45-40, against the Liberal Party's far-right MP Peter Dutton, an advocate of pulling Australia out of the Paris climate accord. The socially conservative Morrison was Australia's fifth prime minister in as many years, with elections to be held by May 2019.

General

Exoplanet Called Suitable for Sustaining Life—An exoplanet about 1.5 times the size of Earth and located some 1,400 light years away is the most likely to support life outside of Earth's solar system, according to a study published Aug. 1 in *Science Advances*. According to the Univ. of Cambridge and the Medical Research Council Laboratory of Molecular Biology (MRC LMB), the exoplanet Kepler-452b is thought to orbit its star inside both the habitable or "Goldilocks" zone—with temperatures that could allow for liquid surface water—and in an "abiogenesis" zone, allowing the planet to receive ideal levels and types of radiation to activate life-generating chemical reactions.

Indonesian Earthquake Kills Hundreds—A series of earthquakes and aftershocks struck the eastern Indonesian island of Lombok, beginning with a magnitude 6.9 earthquake Aug. 5, killing approximately 555 people and injuring nearly 8,000 by the end of the month. The quake displaced nearly 400,000 residents—about 10% of Lombok's population—and was followed by at least 1,000 aftershocks over the course of the month. A 6.4 magnitude quake had killed 16 at the end of July.

Koepka Takes PGA Championship—Brooks Koepka won the 100th PGA Championship and his third victory in a major at Bellerive Country Club in Town and Country, MO, Aug. 12. The 28-year-old American finished with a 16-under-264, two shots ahead of 42-year-old legend Tiger Woods, who delivered his best result in a major since 2009.

Nearly 800 Die in Indian Flooding—Up to 1,000 people drowned or died in accidents related to seasonal monsoon flooding in seven states in India by mid-Aug., with most of the deaths occurring in Kerala, Uttar Pradesh, and West Bengal, according to India's Home Ministry. Kerala saw its worst flooding since 1924, according to officials, with some 1.2 mil people displaced to relief camps.

Italian Bridge Collapse Kills Dozens—A heavily trafficked concrete bridge collapsed in Genoa, Italy, shortly before noon Aug. 14, killing at least 43 people. The more-than-650-ft section gave way during heavy rainfall, causing up to 35 cars to plummet into a swollen stream about 150 ft below. The bridge's operator had reportedly been doing maintenance work to strengthen its road foundations at the time of the collapse.

Pennsylvania Grand Jury Holds Catholic Church Responsible for Decades of Abuse—A Pennsylvania grand jury Aug. 14 released a 900-page report detailing seven decades of clerical sexual abuse and its methodical cover-up in six Roman Catholic Church dioceses—Allentown, Erie, Greensburg, Harrisburg, Pittsburgh, and Scranton. The investigation identified more than 1,000 child victims and 300 offending priests, though thousands more victims were considered likely to exist. The abuse survivors included boys and girls, including five girls from the same family, one of whom reportedly was first abused at just 18 months old.

Missing Iowa College Student Found Dead—A highly publicized, month-long search for 20-year-old missing Univ. of Iowa student Mollie Tibbetts ended Aug. 21 after police found her body near her hometown of Brooklyn, IA. Police arrested 24-year-old suspect Cristhian Bahena Rivera, who according to authorities admitted he pursued Tibbetts while she was jogging and abducted her. Pres. Donald Trump cited Rivera's status as an undocumented migrant to renew his call for a southern border wall with Mexico—where Rivera was born—and stricter immigration laws.

California Firefighters Contain Largest Fire in State History—Northern California's Mendocino Complex fire, the largest ever recorded in the state, was 90% contained by firefighters by Aug. 27, a full month after it was first reported. Comprised of the River and much larger Ranch Fires burning in close proximity roughly 100 mi northwest of Sacramento, the complex killed one firefighter and burned over 459,000 acres (715 sq mi) in Mendocino, Lake, Colusa, and Glenn Counties. The previous largest California fire on record, at nearly 282,000 acres burned, was set by the Thomas Fire in Santa Barbara and Ventura Counties less than a year ago.

September 2018
National

Woodward Book, Anonymous Essay Roil White House—Widely respected journalist Bob Woodward's book *Fear: Trump in the White House*, released Sept. 11, portrayed numerous aspects of Pres. Donald Trump's presidency in a negative light. Damaging details included top aides physically removing trade orders from Trump's desk to prevent his signature, Chief of Staff John Kelly referring to Trump as "unhinged" and an "idiot," and Trump calling on Defense Sec. James Mattis to assassinate Syrian Pres. Bashar al-Assad in 2017. In the first week, the book sold 1.1 mil copies, but prior to its release Trump said it would be "another bad book" and Woodward lacked credibility.

The *NY Times* Sept. 5 published an anonymous essay by a person, described as a White House official, in which the author claimed that they, along with others in the administration, were working to oppose Trump and that his cabinet had previously discussed using the 25th Amendment to remove Trump from power. Trump said that the *Times* needed to reveal the author's identity due to national security concerns.

Hurricane Florence Inundates Carolinas—Hurricane Florence made landfall as a Category 1 hurricane near Wrightsville Beach, NC, Sept. 14, unleashing wind gusts up to 105 mph and heavy rainfall that caused at least 48 deaths in the Carolinas and Virginia. Though the 400-mi-wide Florence weakened considerably before reaching shore, it nevertheless caused extensive flooding along the North Carolina coast. Elizabethtown, NC, recorded 35.9 in. of rain, and the Cape Fear River, one of many that flooded, rose to over 61 ft, well above the 35-ft flood stage, Sept. 19 near Fayetteville, NC. South Carolina also experienced torrential rain levels. Though under mandatory evacuation orders, numerous coastal residents who chose to remain required rescuing; as of Sept. 27, over 1,500 people were staying in shelters. An early estimate of the storm's property damage, released Sept. 21 while rivers were still rising, projected a cost of $38-$50 bil.

Supreme Court Nomination Mired in Sexual Abuse Allegations—A *Washington Post* report published Sept. 16 alleged U.S. Supreme Court nominee Brett Kavanaugh had sexually assaulted psychology professor Christine Blasey Ford when the two were teenagers. (*The New Yorker* published her account two days earlier without naming Ford.) Nominated by Pres. Donald Trump in July, Kavanaugh had appeared before the Senate Judiciary Committee for confirmation hearings Sept. 4-7. Committee Democrats objected to the withholding of more than 100,000 pages of documents from his work in former Pres. George W. Bush's administration, and Kavanaugh refused to answer questions as to whether Trump could legally pardon himself and whether *Roe v. Wade*, the basis of abortion rights in the U.S., was correctly decided, but the committee appeared likely to pass the nomination easily along party lines until Ford's allegations surfaced.

Both Ford and Kavanaugh testified separately before the same committee over her allegations Sept. 27, after accusations against Kavanaugh had surfaced from two additional women. In her testimony, Ford said that at about age 15 she attended a house party in Maryland at which she was pushed into a bedroom, where an intoxicated Kavanaugh, in the presence of his friend Mark Judge, held her down on a bed, tried to remove her clothes, and held his hand over her mouth to prevent her calling for help. Ford was questioned by Democratic committee members and by an Arizona sex crimes prosecutor, to whom Republican members initially ceded their time. Following her testimony, which Trump reportedly called credible,

Kavanaugh opened his portion of the hearing with an emotional statement in which he denied the allegations, calling the process a "national disgrace" and notably treading into partisan conspiracy theory—unusual for a Supreme Court nominee—by saying he was a victim of "revenge on behalf of the Clintons."

Sen. Dick Durbin (D, IL) and Sen. Kamala Harris (D, CA) both pressed Kavanagh to request the White House initiate an FBI investigation into the allegations. In a heated follow-up to Durbin, Sen. Lindsey Graham (R, SC) called Democrats' questioning an "unethical sham," and Graham and other Republicans accused Sen. Dianne Feinstein (D, CA) of intentionally withholding the allegations to keep the Court seat open. Feinstein, who had received a letter July 30 outlining Ford's accusation, said she was respecting Ford's stated desire for confidentiality.

While voting to pass the nomination out of committee, frequent Trump critic Sen. Jeff Flake (R, AZ) Sept. 28 forced a one-week delay in the floor vote to allow the FBI to investigate. Trump instructed the FBI to perform a limited probe that same day.

Tesla CEO Settles SEC Fraud Charges; U.S. GDP Growth Continues; Other Economic, Business News—The SEC charged Tesla CEO Elon Musk with fraud Sept. 27, claiming he issued "false and misleading" Twitter statements regarding privatizing Tesla; settling two days later, Musk agreed to withdraw as chairman for at least three years and pay a $20 mil fine. Tesla also agreed to settle related SEC charges and pay an equivalent fine. Musk remained in place as CEO of both Tesla and SpaceX. Earlier in Sept., Musk had appeared in a video recorded when he was a guest on comedian Joe Rogan's podcast, during which he seemed to smoke marijuana. Two of Tesla's executives resigned, and the company's stock lost 9% of its value in trading Sept. 7.

On Sept. 17, the U.S. Dept. of Justice antitrust division approved health insurer Cigna Corp.'s $52-bil acquisition of pharmacy benefit management company Express Scripts.

The Labor Dept. reported Sept. 7 that 201,000 new jobs were added in Aug., as unemployment held steady at 3.9%. The Bureau of Economic Analysis reported Sept. 27 that the U.S. real gross domestic product (GDP) in the second quarter of 2018 rose at an annual rate of 4.2%, an increase from 2.2% the previous quarter. On Wall Street, the Dow Jones industrial average closed Sept. at 26,458.31, a 1.9% increase from Aug., while the Nasdaq composite index ended the month at 8,046.35, down 0.8%; the S&P 500 finished Sept. at 2,913.98, up 0.4% from Aug.

International

Ethiopia, Eritrea End Border Conflict; Ethnic Clashes Kill Dozens in Addis Ababa—Ethiopia and Eritrea opened border crossing points between their two countries for the first time in 20 years Sept. 11, after a peace deal was reached in July, effectively ending a border dispute that had killed some 80,000 people in 1998-2000. (Eritrea declared independence from Ethiopia in 1993.) The development, which secured Ethiopia direct access to Eritrea's ports on the Red Sea, came five days before Eritrean Pres. Isaias Afwerki and Ethiopian Prime Min. Abiy Ahmed signed their second peace agreement since July. Earlier in Sept., Ethiopia reopened its embassy in Eritrea; Eritrea had done the same in July.

At least 58 people were killed in unrelated ethnic violence Sept. 15-16 in the outskirts of the Ethiopian capital Addis Ababa. Reportedly, the Dorze, Gamo, and Wolaita victims were attacked by neighboring Oromos.

South Sudanese Celebrate Peace Deal—The international community cautiously embraced a peace agreement signed Sept. 12 by South Sudan Pres. Salva Kiir and the country's main rebel leader Riek Machar that would end five years of civil war that killed tens of thousands of South Sudanese and displaced 4 mil. Arbitrated by Sudan over a 15-month period and signed in Ethiopia's capital, Addis Ababa, the deal followed at least 10 prior cease-fire attempts and was similar to a 2015 agreement. It called for a power-sharing transitional government to be in place within the next eight months under which Kiir would serve as president and Machar would hold one of five vice-presidential posts, with elections to be held after three years. Unlike the prior accord, the country would have a unified army.

Maldives Voters Oust Strongman Leader—Maldives' autocratic president Abdulla Yameen conceded to opposition candidate Ibrahim Mohamed Solih Sept. 24, the day after Solih won a decisive surprise victory in the Indian Ocean island nation's third democratic election since gaining independence from Britain in 1965. Pledging via Twitter to investigate abuses against journalists and work towards a free press, Solih won, 58.3%-41.7%, in voting participated in by almost 90% of eligible voters. In Feb. 2018, Yameen had imposed a 45-day state of emergency following the Supreme Court decision to release several political opponents, which resulted in the jailing of the former president and two Supreme Court justices.

Swedish Anti-Immigrant Party Surges in Election, Topples PM—Sweden's Prime Min. Stefan Löfven lost a confidence vote in parliament Sept. 25, more than two weeks after the governing center-left coalition—including his Social Democratic Party—lost 15 seats (down from 159) in general elections for 349 parliamentary seats. The opposition center-right alliance won 143 seats and the unaligned far-right, strongly anti-immigrant Sweden Democrats captured 62 seats (up from 49). Though both nearly equal blocs lacked a majority, neither appeared willing to form a coalition with the Sweden Democrats, complicating efforts to form a government.

Deadly Clashes Escalate in Libyan Capital Before Cease-Fire—Fighting between rival militias vying for power in Tripoli killed at least 115 people between late Aug. and Sept. 25, when a fragile cease-fire, initially brokered in early Sept., went into effect. The clashes between the two sides, composed of multiple militia groups, which operate with official status under the Libya's UN-recognized Government of National Accord (GNA), also displaced some 25,000 residents. Since 2011, the country has remained split between the GNA in Tripoli and an opposing government in the east, allowing terror groups to proliferate. A United Nations envoy in late Sept. questioned Libya's ability to hold elections in Dec. as agreed to by the competing administrations, citing violence and undrafted parliamentary electoral legislation.

Canada Accepts U.S.-Revised NAFTA Deal; U.S. Imposes More Tariffs on China—Facing a U.S.-imposed deadline, Canada Sept. 30 ended its holdout and joined the U.S. and Mexico in a trade deal intended to replace the 24-year-old North American Free Trade Agreement (NAFTA). The United States-Mexico-Canada Agreement (USMCA), pending ratification and formal signature, would open more of Canada's dairy market to U.S. producers, initially an issue for Canada, along with the U.S.'s desire to eliminate a special dispute process, which the USMCA retained. The USMCA required that 75% of an automobile's parts (up from 62.5%) be made in the U.S., Canada, or Mexico by 2020 to be eligible for zero tariffs, and mandated that 40% of a vehicle be produced by workers earning $16 per hour or more by 2023. Other major provisions included increased labor and environmental rules and intellectual property protection. Subject to review after six years, the 16-year deal did not affect Trump's 25% tariffs on steel from Canada or Mexico.

The White House ratcheted up the stakes on its trade fight with China, imposing a 10% tariff on $200 bil worth of imported Chinese goods that went into effect Sept. 24, covering thousands of products. Retaliatory tariffs by China on $60 bil worth of U.S. exports took effect that same day. Major U.S. companies, including General Motors, Walmart, and Coca-Cola, said the White House action, which extended the total amount of Chinese products under Trump's tariffs to $250 bil (about half of goods imported from China), could force them to increase prices.

General

Mass Grave Found in Mexico—A state prosecutor announced Sept. 6 that a mass grave was discovered in Veracruz, Mexico, containing at least 166 skulls and further skeletal remains. Located by drones and radar, the remains were presumed to be the victims of drug cartels. Investigators in 2016 and 2017 found 253 skulls and other remains in a similar site near the state capital, Xalapa. A record 31,174 people were murdered in Mexico in 2017.

CBS President Resigns Amid Sexual Misconduct Accusations; Soccer Superstar Faces Rape-Related Lawsuit—CBS chairman, CEO, and president Les Moonves resigned Sept. 9, hours after *The New Yorker* reported new accusations of sexual misconduct—including assault—by six women. The new allegations were separate from an investigation the same magazine published in late July detailing allegations by six others.

German magazine *Der Spiegel* reported Sept. 29 that Portuguese soccer superstar Cristiano Ronaldo was being sued by a woman who had previously settled a claim that he raped her in a Las Vegas hotel room in 2009. According to the suit, Ronaldo admitted that "she said 'no' and 'stop' several times" and he had apologized for his actions. Las Vegas police confirmed Oct. 1 that it had reopened a criminal investigation into the matter.

Storm Win WNBA Championship—The Seattle Storm won Game 3 over the Washington Mystics, 98-82, at EagleBank Arena in Fairfax, VA, to claim the franchise's third WNBA Championship Sept. 12. Breanna Stewart of the Storm scored a series-high 30 points in Game 3 and averaged 25.6 points throughout the sweep to earn Finals MVP. Sue Bird, a veteran of Seattle's 2004 and 2010 championship teams, had 10 assists.

***Game of Thrones*, *The Marvelous Mrs. Maisel* Win Big at Emmys**—HBO's epic fantasy *Game of Thrones* reclaimed the Emmy for outstanding TV drama series—its third in four years—at the 70th Primetime Emmy Awards Sept. 17 in Los Angeles. The series won nine awards in 2018, including outstanding supporting actor in a drama for Peter Dinklage, and increased its trophy count to 47 over seven seasons. Amazon's *The Marvelous Mrs. Maisel* captured outstanding comedy series, with Rachel Brosnahan winning lead actress in a comedy, along with six other awards. Outstanding lead actor in a comedy series went to Bill Hader for HBO's *Barry*, while Matthew Rhys and Claire Foy won outstanding dramatic series lead actor and actress for FX's spy thriller *The Americans* and Netflix's royal drama *The Crown*, respectively.

Lake Victoria Ferry Disaster Kills 200—A Tanzanian ferry capsized on Lake Victoria approximately 650 ft from its destination, Ukara Island, killing at least 224 people Sept. 20. Officials said *MV Nyerere* was heavily overloaded—carrying some 400 passengers though it was rated for 100—and was thought to have tipped when passengers shifted sides as it approached the dock.

Woods Pulls Off First PGA Tour Victory Since 2013—Golf legend Tiger Woods won the Tour Championship at East Lake Golf Club in Atlanta, GA, Sept. 23, capping a comeback following years of injuries, personal crises, and four back surgeries. The 42-year-old Woods started the last round with a three-shot advantage and finished atop the leaderboard with an 11-under-269, two shots ahead of Billy Horschel. It was his first PGA Tour win in more than five years.

Earthquake, Tsunami Devastate Indonesian Island—A magnitude 7.5 earthquake struck Indonesia's central island of Sulawesi Sept. 28, triggering a tsunami up to 20 ft high that crashed into the provincial capital of Palu, where most of the 2,045 deaths (as of Oct. 10) occurred. Centered about 50 mi north of the city, the quake was followed over the next few days by more than 200 aftershocks, complicating efforts by rescuers to search for survivors. The city quickly turned into a humanitarian disaster as over 65,000 homes were destroyed, and more than 191,000 people were in need of urgent aid. Though a tsunami detection system was in place, officials said it was not fully functional; a more advanced warning system was not installed due to its $69,000 cost.

October 2018

National

Jury Delivers Guilty Verdict in Chicago Police Shooting of Black Teen—Chicago police officer Jason Van Dyke was found guilty Oct. 5 of second-degree murder in the Oct. 2014 shooting of black 17-year-old Laquan McDonald. The incident was caught on police dashcam video made public in Nov. 2015, leading to protests across the city. The first Chicago officer convicted of on-duty murder in over 50 years, Van Dyke, who is white, said he feared for his life as McDonald lunged at him with a knife, despite the video appearing to show McDonald walking away as Van Dyke shot him 16 times.

Supreme Court Nominee Kavanaugh Sworn in Following Contentious Confirmation—The Senate voted largely along party lines, 50-48, to confirm Pres. Donald Trump's Supreme Court nominee Brett Kavanaugh Oct. 6. The vote capped nearly three weeks of heated rhetoric on Capitol Hill

and from the White House, as Kavanaugh faced allegations of sexual assault or misconduct by at least three women, including Christine Blasey Ford, who had testified at a Sept. confirmation hearing. As a condition of voting to pass the nomination out of committee, Sen. Jeff Flake (R, AZ) had forced a supplemental FBI investigation, ordered by Trump with strict parameters Sept. 28, to address the accusations. Judiciary Committee ranking member Sen. Dianne Feinstein (D, CA) and others criticized the probe for its failure to question Kavanaugh, Ford, and other material witnesses. Senate leadership said the resulting non-public FBI report, made available in one shared copy to all senators Oct. 4, failed to corroborate Ford's allegations and quickly moved to end debate. Sen. Joe Manchin (D, WV) was the sole Democrat to vote in favor of the nomination, and Sen. Lisa Murkowski (R, AK), voted "present" during the Oct. 6 vote. Kavanaugh was sworn in hours later by Chief Justice John Roberts Jr. and Justice Anthony Kennedy, whom the 53-year-old judge replaced.

Public outcry, including protests at the Supreme Court building, continued post-confirmation, fortified in part by earlier public statements by at least four of Kavanaugh's Yale Univ. classmates that he had lied under oath when denying ever drinking to the point of a blackout. Trump, who branded critics of the nomination as an "angry left-wing mob," said Kavanaugh's confirmation would energize Republican voters to turn out for midterm elections in Nov.

UN Ambassador Haley Resigns; Trump Orders Troops to Southern Border; Other White House Developments—U.S. Ambassador to the UN Nikki Haley said Oct. 9 that she would resign by the end of 2018. The announcement drew speculation of a presidential run by the former South Carolina governor in 2020. Though Haley wrote in a *Washington Post* op-ed in Sept. that she "does not agree with the president on everything," she in practice had advocated or defended many of Pres. Donald Trump's policies, including moving the U.S. embassy from Tel Aviv to Jerusalem, and she praised his blunt diplomatic approach to North Korea. On Oct. 20, Trump announced the U.S. would pull out of the 1987 Intermediate-range Nuclear Forces (INF) treaty, saying that Russia had been violating the INF for many years.

The *NY Times* Oct. 21 reported that a draft memo from the U.S. Dept. of Health and Human Services proposed strictly defining a person's gender by their sex at birth, which would reverse an Obama administration policy allowing individuals to claim another gender identity and cause some 1.4 mil transgender people to lose certain civil rights protections under Title IX.

Trump Oct. 29 ordered 5,200 active-duty troops to the southern border to halt a caravan of Central American migrants that was some 1,000 mi away from home in the U.S. Lambasted by critics as pandering to his base ahead of midterm elections, Trump also said the White House was preparing an executive order to end birthright citizenship of children born to undocumented migrants, a move that most constitutional experts said would exceed the president's authority.

Hurricane Michael Slams Florida Panhandle—Category 4 Hurricane Michael made landfall Oct. 10 near Mexico Beach, FL, with peak winds of 155 mph, killing at least 45 people in the U.S. including 35 in Florida. Michael caught forecasters by surprise as it intensified in less than two days from a Category 1 storm to the most powerful hurricane to strike the continental U.S. since Andrew in 1992 and the strongest ever on record in Florida's Panhandle. As the storm progressed northeast, it weakened but still caused heavy damages. High winds in southern Georgia severely damaged crops, and floodwaters killed at least five people in Virginia. Early estimates projected $8-$11 bil in damages.

Sears Declares Bankruptcy; Jobless Rate Drops Near 50-Year Low—The 132-year-old Sears Holdings, at one time the largest U.S. retailer, filed for bankruptcy protection Oct. 15 and said it would close at least 142 unprofitable stores in the U.S. (of about 700). Though its creditors could reorganize rather than liquidate the company originally known through its mail-order catalog, analysts said Sears, which merged with K-Mart in 2005, faced an uphill battle for survival. Sears had shuttered more than 1,000 stores over the past decade and lost some $5.8 bil since 2013.

The Labor Dept. reported Oct. 5 that the unemployment rate in Sept. fell to 3.7%, its lowest point since 1969, as the economy added 134,000 jobs. In a losing month on Wall Street, the Dow Jones industrial average closed Oct. at 25,115.76, a 5.1% decrease from Sept., while the Nasdaq composite index ended the month at 7,305.9, falling 9.2%; the S&P 500 finished Oct. at 2,711.74, down 6.9% from Sept.

Multiple Explosive Devices Sent to Political Targets—Authorities intercepted more than a dozen package bombs addressed to prominent critics and targets of Pres. Donald Trump—including former Pres. Barack Obama and 2016 Democratic presidential nominee Hillary Clinton—before arresting the alleged would-be bomber, 56-year-old Cesar Sayoc, near Miami, FL, Oct. 26. No one was harmed by the devices. After the first was detected Oct. 22 at a residence of billionaire political donor George Soros, devices targeting former Vice Pres. Joe Biden, Sen. Cory Booker (D, NJ), Sen. Kamala Harris (D, CA), Rep. Maxine Waters (D, CA), CNN's New York office, and others were also seized. Authorities detected Sayoc's fingerprint on Waters's package and also found his DNA on two of the devices. He faced up to 48 years in prison if convicted.

Shooter Kills Pittsburgh Synagogue Congregants—A gunman opened fire in a synagogue in Pittsburgh, PA, Oct. 27, killing 11 mostly elderly victims and injuring six, including four police officers. Armed with an assault rifle and at least three handguns, the suspected shooter, 46-year-old Robert Bowers, reportedly screamed anti-Semitic threats and epithets during his 20-min. attack at the Tree of Life synagogue in the city's historically Jewish Squirrel Hill neighborhood. Shortly before the shooting, he posted without proof on the social media site Gab that the Hebrew Immigrant Aid Society (HIAS) worked to assist violent refugee "invaders." Bowers, shot multiple times by police, pleaded not guilty Nov. 1 to 44 federal charges.

Pres. Donald Trump said an armed guard could have stopped the tragedy, thought to be the deadliest single attack on Jews in the U.S. Thousands protested Trump's visit to Squirrel Hill Oct. 30, with some critics citing his frequent anti-immigrant rhetoric as Bower's motivation. Trump via Twitter blamed the media—especially CNN—for what he said was inaccurate "fake news" reporting that generated anger.

International

Saudi Dissident Apparently Murdered in Istanbul's Saudi Consulate—Saudi dissident and *Washington Post* contributor Jamal Khashoggi, a U.S. resident, was apparently killed and dismembered inside the Saudi consulate in Istanbul, Turkey, Oct. 2, sparking outrage and straining relations between Saudi Arabia and the U.S. and other allies. Saudi officials first claimed Khashoggi left the consulate unharmed before they alleged that he was accidentally killed in a fistfight. By Oct. 25, Saudi Arabia's attorney general admitted that evidence from Turkish officials indicated his murder was premeditated.

Turkish officials had quickly disputed Saudi Arabia's earlier claims, citing security video footage of the building; among other evidence, video of a 15-member alleged Saudi hit squad arriving in Istanbul was later released, and the Turkish government Oct. 17 leaked details of a grisly 7-min. audio recording reportedly taken during Khashoggi's torture, beheading, and death. Saudi diplomat Mohammad al-Otaibi, who was said to have witnessed the incident, fled to Riyadh Oct. 16.

Saudi officials repeatedly denied the involvement of Crown Prince Mohammed bin Salman, a claim U.S. intelligence officials reportedly found dubious. Though Pres. Donald Trump called the killing the "worst cover-up ever," he drew criticism for his public opposition Oct. 13 to canceling a $110-bil arms deal with Saudi Arabia.

Major UN Climate Report Calls for Swift Action to Forestall Catastrophe—The United Nations Intergovernmental Panel on Climate Change (IPCC) delivered a grim report Oct. 8 on the world's ability to curb climate change and its effects, warning that Earth's average global temperature would increase 2.7°F (1.5°C) over pre-industrial levels by as early as 2030. (By 2018, Earth's temperature had already warmed 1.8°F.) Failing to make "far-reaching and unprecedented changes" to limit warming would boost risk of drought, sea-level rise, extreme weather, and species loss. Pres. Donald Trump, who had pulled the U.S.—the world's second largest producer of greenhouse gases after China—out

of the Paris Climate Agreement in June 2017, said during a *60 Minutes* interview Oct. 14 that he was not convinced climate change was man-made and claimed scientists have a "very big political agenda."

Canada Legalizes Recreational Marijuana—Legalization of recreational marijuana took effect Oct. 17 throughout Canada, making it the first industrialized nation to do so and only the second country in the world after Uruguay (2013) to permit possession for non-medicinal purposes (medical use had been legal since 2001). Prime Min. Justin Trudeau had pledged to legalize pot ahead of his 2015 election, arguing it would cut criminals' profits and reduce use among minors. The measure passed in June 2018 by the House of Commons (205-82) and Senate (52-29) made it legal to possess up to 30 g (1.06 oz.), grow more than four plants per household, and buy from unlicensed dealers.

Brazil Elects Far-Right President After More Than a Decade of Leftist Government—Far-right candidate Jair Bolsonaro easily won Brazil's presidential runoff election Oct. 28 over leftist Fernando Haddad, former mayor of São Paulo. The outspoken populist, a retired military officer and seven-term congressman, won 55.13% support in voting participated in by 71% of about 147 mil eligible voters. Bolsonaro's rise was partially attributed to the country's worst-ever recession and to voters' disdain for previous leaders' embroilment in corruption and graft scandals. But Bolsonaro alarmed opponents with his outspoken rhetoric against gays and women and his approval of torture, dictatorship, and ending protection of indigenous lands and the Amazon rainforest; he also pledged to jail or exile political opponents. Bolsonaro, who survived a severe stabbing he sustained while campaigning in Sept., nevertheless vowed during his victory speech to defend freedom.

General

Limo Accident Kills 20 in Upstate New York—A limousine crash Oct. 6 in Schoharie, NY, killed two pedestrians and all 18 people in the vehicle, a modified Ford Excursion. The limo did not stop at a stop sign before a three-way intersection, causing the deadliest roadway accident in the U.S. since 2005. The crash drew attention to safety issues concerning stretch limos, which are not always required to install more seat belts.

Boston Red Sox Win World Series—The Boston Red Sox won the World Series over the Los Angeles Dodgers in a decisive Game 5 victory Oct. 28 at Dodger Stadium in Los Angeles. The Sox, who finished the regular season with a 108-54 record—the most wins of any MLB team since 2001—racked up four home runs from Steve Pearce (2), Mookie Betts, and J. D. Martinez to secure a 5-1 win, as David Price allowed only three hits in seven innings. It was the ninth World Series win in Boston's franchise history. Los Angeles's sole victory came, 3-2, in an 18-inning Game 3 played over 7 hr. and 20 min., making it the longest-ever Series game by both time and innings. With three home runs and 8 RBIs over five games, Pearce was named the World Series MVP.

Airline Crash Kills Nearly 200 in Indonesia—All 189 people aboard Indonesian airline Lion Air Flight 610 were killed Oct. 29 after the aircraft, a Boeing 737 Max 8, crashed into the Java Sea 13 min. after departing Jakarta. The pilot had requested permission to return, and preliminary flight information showed the jet losing and gaining altitude before it plunged into the ocean at almost 400 mph. The crash was the first accident involving the new Boeing design released about 17 months earlier. Of yet unknown cause, the tragedy renewed concerns over the safety of Indonesia's quickly expanding airline industry.

NASA Retires Planet-Finding Kepler Probe, Breaks Sun-Proximity Record—NASA announced Oct. 30 that it was retiring its Kepler space telescope, which had discovered more than 2,600 planets outside the Earth's solar system since its launch in 2009. Kepler over the course of its mission—twice as long as scheduled—showed the Milky Way galaxy to hold far more planets than stars and revealed that possibly habitable exoplanets were much more common than previously thought. Out of fuel some 94 mil mi from the Earth, the craft would drift in orbit around the Sun indefinitely.

NASA's Parker Solar Probe Oct. 29 achieved a record-closest distance from the Sun by a spacecraft (26.55 mil mi) previously set by the German-American Helios 2 in 1976.

OBITUARIES
(Nov. 1, 2017-Oct. 31, 2018)

A

Abel, Alan, 94, prankster whose hoaxes included the Society for Indecency to Naked Animals (1958), faking his own death (1980), and impersonating Howard Hughes; Southbury, CT, Sept. 14, 2018.

Akaka, Daniel, 93, U.S. rep. (D, HI, 1977-90) and sen. (1990-2013) who advocated recognition of Asian-American World War II veterans; Honolulu, HI, Apr. 6, 2018.

Alberts, Alfred, 87, biochemist who helped develop the first widely used statin for treating high cholesterol; Fort Collins, CO, June 16, 2018.

Allen, Marty, 95, comedian known as half of the comedy team Allen & (Steve) Rossi; Las Vegas, NV, Feb. 12, 2018.

Allen, Paul, 65, Microsoft cofounder who became a philanthropist and owner of the Seattle Seahawks and Portland Trail Blazers; Seattle, WA, Oct. 15, 2018.

Alsop, Will, 70, British architect known for playful designs and bright colors in urban designs, including London's Peckham Library; London, Eng., UK, May 12, 2018.

Anderson, Harry, 65, actor and magician known as Judge Harry Stone on TV sitcom *Night Court* (1984-92); Asheville, NC, Apr. 16, 2018.

Anderson, John, 95, U.S. rep. (R, IL, 1961-81) who ran for president in 1980 as an independent, winning 6.6% of the popular vote; Washington, DC, Dec. 3, 2017.

Anderson, Michael, 98, British director known for *Around the World in 80 Days* (1956) and *Logan's Run* (1976); Vancouver, BC, Can., Apr. 25, 2018.

Annan, Kofi, 80, Nobel Peace Prize-winning Ghanaian diplomat who served as UN sec.-gen. (1997-2006); Bern, Switz., Aug. 18, 2018.

Avicii (Tim Bergling), 28, Swedish DJ and music producer whose hits included "Levels" (2011) and "Wake Me Up" (2013); Muscat, Oman, Apr. 20, 2018.

Ayres, Gillian, 88, British abstract artist known for large colorful works; North Devon, Eng., UK, Apr. 11, 2018.

Aznavour, Charles, 94, French-Armenian singer and actor whose 70-year career included songs "Yesterday, When I Was Young" (1964) and "She" (1974); Mouriès, France, Oct. 1, 2018.

B

Bakken, Earl, 94, Medtronic founder who helped develop the first wearable battery-powered artificial pacemaker (1957); North Kona District, HI, Oct. 21, 2018.

Balin, Marty, 76, Rock & Roll Hall of Fame musician who cofounded Jefferson Airplane (1965); Tampa, FL, Sept. 27, 2018.

Bannister, Roger, 88, British athlete and physician who in 1954 was the first to run a sub-4-min. mile; Oxford, Eng., UK, Mar. 3, 2018.

Barlow, John Perry, 70, Grateful Dead lyricist who became a digital rights activist and cofounded the Electronic Frontier Foundation (1990); San Francisco, CA, Feb. 7, 2018.

Bata, Sonja, 91, Swiss-Canadian businesswoman and philanthropist whose personal collection of shoes led to the creation of Toronto's Bata Shoe Museum; Toronto, ON, Can., Feb. 20, 2018.

Baylis, Trevor, 80, British inventor of the windup portable radio; Eel Pie Island, Eng., UK, Mar. 5, 2018.

Beach, Gary, 70, Tony Award-winning actor known for Broadway's *Beauty and the Beast* (1994) and *The Producers* (2001); Palm Springs, CA, July 17, 2018.

Bean, Alan, 86, *Apollo 12* astronaut who in 1969 was the fourth person to walk on the Moon; Houston, TX, May 26, 2018.

Bell, Anne Olivier, 102, English editor and scholar who edited Virginia Woolf's diaries and was a member of the so-called Monuments Men following World War II; Firle, Eng., UK, July 18, 2018.

Bell, Art, 72, radio host known for paranormal-themed show *Coast to Coast AM*; Pahrump, NV, Apr. 13, 2018.

Benshoof, Janet, 70, lawyer and activist who founded the Center for Reproductive Rights (1992) and Global Justice Center (2005); New York, NY, Dec. 18, 2017.

Benson, Tom, 90, colorful owner of the NFL's New Orleans Saints (1985-2018) and NBA's New Orleans Pelicans (2012-18); Jefferson, LA, Mar. 15, 2018.

Blobel, Günter, 81, Nobel Prize-winning German-born biologist whose "signal hypothesis" found how cells direct proteins; New York, NY, Feb. 18, 2018.

Bochco, Steven, 74, Emmy Award-winning TV producer and writer who created *Hill Street Blues* (1981-87), *L.A. Law* (1986-94), and *NYPD Blue* (1993-2005); Pacific Palisades, CA, Apr. 1, 2018.

Bocuse, Paul, 91, French chef and innovator of *nouvelle cuisine*, helping to modernize French food in the 1960s and '70s; Collonges-au-Mont-d'Or, France, Jan. 20, 2018.

Bol, Todd, 62, teacher who created the Little Free Library; Oakdale, MN, Oct. 18, 2018.

Booker, Simeon, 99, journalist known for reporting on the Emmett Till trial and civil rights movement for *Ebony*, *Jet*, and *Washington Post*; Solomons, MD, Dec. 10, 2017.

Bopp, Thomas, 68, amateur astronomer who with Alan Hale discovered the Hale-Bopp comet (1995); Phoenix, AZ, Jan. 5, 2018.

Bourdain, Anthony, 61, Emmy Award-winning chef, TV personality, and writer (*Kitchen Confidential*, 2000) who documented travels through food and culture; Kaysersberg-Vignoble, Haut-Rhin, France, June 8, 2018.

Bower, Johnny, 93, Canadian Hall of Fame goaltender who won four Stanley Cup titles with the Toronto Maple Leafs; Mississauga, ON, Can., Dec. 26, 2017.

Boyer, Paul D., 99, Nobel Prize-winning biochemist who explained the process by which organisms' cells create and exchange energy; Los Angeles, CA, June 2, 2018.

Brazelton, T(homas) Berry, 99, pediatrician and author who studied early child development; Barnstable, MA, Mar. 13, 2018.

Brown, Linda, 75, symbolic center of the landmark civil rights case *Brown v. Board of Education* (1954), which ended legal racial segregation in public schools; Topeka, KS, Mar. 25, 2018.

Bueno, Maria, 78, Brazilian tennis player who won seven Grand Slam singles titles; São Paulo, Brazil, June 8, 2018.

Bulger, James "Whitey", 89, organized crime boss who became an FBI informant then fled; arrested in 2011 and sentenced to life in prison; died as a result of an apparent beating; Bruceton Mills, WV, Oct. 30, 2018.

Burrows, Edwin G., 74, Pulitzer Prize-winning historian as co-author of *Gotham: A History of New York City to 1898* (1998); Huntington, NY, May 4, 2018.

Bush, Barbara, 92, former first lady known for personal candor who campaigned to improve literacy during husband George H. W. Bush's presidency; also mother of Pres. George W. Bush; Houston, TX, Apr. 17, 2018.

Byrne, Brendan, 93, New Jersey gov. (D, 1974-82) who instituted the state's first income tax; Livingston, NJ, Jan. 4, 2018.

C

Caballé, Monserrat, 85, Spanish opera soprano known for bel canto roles; Barcelona, Spain, Oct. 6, 2018.

Campanella, Joseph, 93, character actor remembered for *Mannix* (1967-68), *The Bold Ones* (1969-72), and numerous guest roles; Sherman Oaks, CA, May 16, 2018.

Carlsson, Arvid, 95, Nobel Prize-winning Swedish neuropharmacologist whose research led to a standard treatment for Parkinson's disease; Gothenburg, Sweden, June 29, 2018.

Carlucci, Frank, 87, national security adviser (1986-87) and defense sec. (1987-89) under Pres. Ronald Reagan; McLean, VA, June 3, 2018.

Cassidy, David, 67, actor, singer-songwriter, and teen idol known best for TV musical sitcom *The Partridge Family* (1970-74); Fort Lauderdale, FL, Nov. 21, 2017.

Cathey, Reg E., 59, Emmy Award-winning actor known for roles on *The Wire* (2006-08) and *House of Cards* (2013-16); New York, NY, Feb. 9, 2018.

Chermayeff, Ivan, 85, British-born graphic designer whose firm produced iconic logo iterations, including for Chase, Mobil, and Showtime; New York, NY, Dec. 2, 2017.

Coates, Anne V., 92, Academy Award-winning British film editor best known for *Lawrence of Arabia* (1962) and *The Elephant Man* (1980); Woodland Hills, CA, May 8, 2018.

Cole, Olivia, 75, Emmy Award-winning actress best known for miniseries *Roots* (1977); San Miguel de Allende, Mexico, Jan. 19, 2018.

Cone, James, H., 79, theologian and racial-justice advocate known for writing *Black Theology & Black Power* (1969); New York, NY, Apr. 28, 2018.

Coors, William, 102, Coors Brewing Co. executive who developed the recyclable aluminum can; also known for conservative views and racist comments; Golden, CO, Oct. 13, 2018.

Cotton, Dorothy, 88, civil rights activist with the Southern Christian Leadership Conference; Ithaca, NY, June 10, 2018.

Cozza, Carmen, 87, College Football Hall of Fame coach at Yale (1965-96); New Haven, CT, Jan. 4, 2018.

D

Dabney, Ted, 81, electrical engineer who cofounded Atari and helped create early video game *Pong*; Clearlake, CA, May 26, 2018.

Daily, Bill, 91, actor known for TV sitcoms *I Dream of Jeannie* (1965-70) and *The Bob Newhart Show* (1972-78); Santa Fe, NM, Sept. 4, 2018.

Damone, Vic, 89, singer whose 50+-year career included hits "You're Breaking My Heart" (1949) and "On the Street Where You Live" (1956); Miami Beach, FL, Feb. 11, 2018.

Dellums, Ron, 82, U.S. rep. (D, CA, 1971-98) who fought against apartheid and opposed military projects; founding member of the Congressional Black Caucus; Washington, DC, July 30, 2018.

Desfor, Max, 104, Pulitzer Prize-winning AP photographer known for coverage of the Korean War; Silver Spring, MD, Feb. 19, 2018.

Deukmejian, George, 89, California gov. (R, 1983-91) known as a fiscal conservative and crime fighter; Long Beach, CA, May 8, 2018.

DeVos, Richard, 92, Amway cofounder and owner of NBA's Orlando Magic; Ada, MI, Sept. 6, 2018.

Diaz, Alan, 71, Pulitzer Prize-winning photographer best known for image of the Miami raid to seize 6-year-old Elián González, a Cuban refugee, in 2000; July 3, 2018.

Ditko, Steve, 90, comic book writer and artist who with Stan Lee created Marvel

Comics characters Spider-Man and Doctor Strange; New York, NY, June 29, 2018.

Doerr, Bobby, 99, Hall of Fame Boston Red Sox second baseman; Junction City, OR, Nov. 13, 2017.

Donovan, Anne, 56, Hall of Fame basketball player and coach; first woman to win a WNBA championship as head coach (2004); Wilmington, NC, June 13, 2018.

Dorough, Bob, 94, jazz pianist and singer who created songs for the animated series *Schoolhouse Rock!*; Mount Bethel, PA, Apr. 23, 2018.

Duerk, Alene, 98, first woman U.S. Navy rear admiral (1972); Lake Mary, FL, July 21, 2018.

Duncan, David Douglas, 102, photojournalist known for wartime combat photographs and images of Pablo Picasso; Grasse, France, June 7, 2018.

E

Edgerton, David, 90, Burger King cofounder who helped invent the continuous-chain broiler; Miami, FL, Apr. 3, 2018.

Edwards, Dennis, 74, R&B singer whose hits with the Temptations included "Cloud Nine" (1968) and "Papa Was a Rollin' Stone" (1972); Chicago, IL, Feb. 1, 2018.

Ellison, Harlan, 84, prolific writer known for science-fiction short stories and screenplays; filed notorious lawsuits against those he believed plagiarized his work; Los Angeles, CA, June 27, 2018.

Emerick, Geoff, 72, British Grammy Award-winning recording engineer for The Beatles on *Revolver* (1966), *Sgt. Pepper's Lonely Hearts Club Band* (1967), and *Abbey Road* (1969); Los Angeles, CA, Oct. 2, 2018.

Enberg, Dick, 82, Emmy Award-winning sportscaster in a 60-year career for NBC, CBS, and ESPN; La Jolla, CA, Dec. 21, 2017.

F

Fabray, Nanette, 97, Tony and Emmy Award-winning actress known for *Caesar's Hour* (1954-55) and *One Day at a Time* (1979-84); Palos Verdes, CA, Feb. 22, 2018.

Felsher, Howard, 90, Emmy Award-winning game show producer associated with quiz-show scandals of the 1950s who made a comeback with *Family Feud* (1976-85); Tarzana, CA, July 23, 2018.

Ferrell, Robert H., 97, historian known for books on U.S. presidents and diplomacy; Chelsea, MI, Aug. 8, 2018.

Flach, Ken, 54, tennis player who won six Grand Slam doubles titles and Olympic gold (1988); San Francisco, CA, Mar. 12, 2018.

Forman, Milos, 86, Czech-born Academy Award-winning director whose films included *One Flew Over the Cuckoo's Nest* (1975) and *Amadeus* (1984); Danbury, CT, Apr. 13, 2018.

Fornés, María Irene, 88, Cuban-American Obie Award-winning playwright known for experimental works including *Fefu and Her Friends* (1977); New York, NY, Oct. 30, 2018.

Franklin, Aretha, 76, Grammy Award-winning gospel and R&B singer-songwriter known as the "Queen of Soul"; hits included 1967's "Respect" and "Chain of Fools"; Detroit, MI, Aug. 16, 2018.

Freeman, Frankie Muse, 101, civil rights attorney who fought to end housing segregation; St. Louis, MO, Jan. 12, 2018.

G

Gagliardi, John, 91, Hall of Fame college football coach who claimed the all-time wins record (489) with Div. III St. John's (1953-2012); Collegeville, MN, Oct. 7, 2018.

Gallagher, Tom, 77, U.S. foreign service officer, recognized as the first one to come out publicly as gay, in 1975; Tinton Falls, NJ, July 8, 2018.

Garner, Erica, 27, police reform activist whose father's 2014 death, following a NYPD officer's use of a banned chokehold, inspired protest; Brooklyn, NY, Dec. 30, 2017.

Gavin, John, 86, actor known for *Imitation of Life* (1959) and *Psycho* (1960); later served as ambassador to Mexico (1981-86); Beverly Hills, CA, Feb. 9, 2018.

Gerron Rackman, Peggy Sue, 78, inspiration of Buddy Holly songs "Peggy Sue" (1957) and "Peggy Sue Got Married" (1959); Lubbock, TX, Oct. 1, 2018.

de Givenchy, Hubert, 91, French fashion designer known for chic elegance in designs worn by Jacqueline Kennedy and muse Audrey Hepburn; Paris, France, Mar. 10, 2018.

Gold, Bill, 97, graphic designer whose iconic movie posters included *Casablanca* (1942), *A Streetcar Named Desire* (1951), and *The Exorcist* (1973); Greenwich, CT, May 20, 2018.

Gold, Jonathan, 57, Pulitzer Prize-winning restaurant critic who celebrated the culinary diversity of Los Angeles; Los Angeles, CA, July 21, 2018.

González, Jerry, 69, Latin jazz percussionist and trumpeter; bandleader of the Fort Apache Band; Madrid, Spain, Oct. 1, 2018.

González de Recabarren, Ana, 93, Chilean human rights activist who protested the disappearance of alleged dissenters during Chile's military dictatorship; Santiago, Chile, Oct. 26, 2018.

Grafton, Sue, 77, writer of the well-known Kinsey Millhone mystery series, beginning with *A Is for Alibi* (1982) and ending with *Y Is for Yesterday* (2017); Santa Barbara, CA, Dec. 28, 2017.

Graham, Billy, 99, world-renowned Southern Baptist televangelist; religious adviser to U.S. presidents; Montreat, NC, Feb. 21, 2018.

Grossman, Robert, 78, illustrator known for lampooning politicians and for the *Airplane!* (1980) movie poster; New York, NY, Mar. 15, 2018.

Grünberg, Peter, 78, Nobel Prize-winning German physicist, whose co-discovery of the giant magnetoresistance effect allowed data storage to be miniaturized; Jülich, Ger., Apr. 7, 2018.

Gurney, Dan, 86, race car driver and designer who was first to win in all four major motor sports (Grand Prix, Indy, Nascar, sports cars); Newport Beach, CA, Jan. 14, 2018.

H

Hall, Donald, 89, U.S. poet laureate known for reflections on nature and rural New England; Wilmot, NH, June 23, 2018.

Halladay, Roy, 40, two-time Cy Young Award-winning pitcher for Toronto and Philadelphia; near Holiday, FL, Nov. 7, 2017.

Hallyday, Johnny, 74, French singer, known as the "French Elvis" for popularizing rock music there; Marnes-la-Coquette, France, Dec. 6, 2017.

Harris, Barbara, 83, Tony Award-winning actress known for film roles in *Nashville* (1975) and *Freaky Friday* (1976); Scottsdale, AZ, Aug. 21, 2018.

Harvey, Anthony, 87, British director and editor known for *The Lion in Winter* (1968) and collaborations with Stanley Kubrick; Water Mill, NY, Nov. 23, 2017.

Harvey, Doug, 87, Hall of Fame MLB umpire nicknamed "God"; Visalia, CA, Jan. 13, 2018.

Harvey, Larry, 70, cofounder of the countercultural Burning Man festival (1986); San Francisco, CA, Apr. 28, 2018.

Hashimoto, Shinobu, 100, Japanese screenwriter of Akira Kurosawa's classic films *Rashomon* (1950) and *Seven Samurai* (1954); Tokyo, Japan, July 19, 2018.

Hawking, Stephen, 76, British theoretical physicist known for work with black holes and relativity and the bestseller *A Brief History of Time* (1988); Cambridge, Eng., UK, Mar. 14, 2018.

Hays, Anna Mae, 97, U.S. Army nurse who was first woman promoted to brigadier general (1970); Washington, DC, Jan. 7, 2018.

Heart, Frank, 89, computer engineer who helped design the first routing computer for ARPANET, the forerunner of the internet; Lexington, MA, June 24, 2018.

Heckler, Margaret, 87, U.S. rep. (R, MA, 1967-83) and Health and Human Services sec. (1983-85); Arlington, VA, Aug. 6, 2018.

Hillerman, John, 84, Emmy Award-winning actor best known as the stuffy British caretaker on *Magnum, P.I.* (1980-88); Houston, TX, Nov. 9, 2017.

Howard, Elbert "Big Man," 80, founding member of the Black Panther Party (1966) who served as its communications director; Santa Rosa, CA, July 23, 2018.

Huizenga, H. Wayne, 80, entrepreneur and former owner of the Florida Panthers, Miami Dolphins, and then-Florida Marlins; Fort Lauderdale, FL, Mar. 22, 2018.

Hunter, Tab, 86, actor and singer known for *Damn Yankees!* (1958) whose career received new life in John Waters's *Polyester* (1981); Santa Barbara, CA, July 8, 2018.

Huntsman, Jon, Sr., 80, founder of chemical company Huntsman Corp.; donated some $1.4 bil to cancer research; Salt Lake City, UT, Feb. 2, 2018.

Hyman, Earle, 91, actor best known for *The Cosby Show* (1984-92); Englewood, NJ, Nov. 17, 2017.

I

Indiana, Robert, 89, pop artist whose iconic *LOVE* print (1966) and sculpture (1970) were widely reproduced; Vinalhaven, ME, May 19, 2018.

Irving, Clifford, 87, author known for concocting an allegedly authorized autobiography of billionaire recluse Howard Hughes (a hoax revealed in 1972); Sarasota, FL, Dec. 19, 2017.

Ishizaka, Kimishige, 92, Japanese immunologist who with wife Teruko Ishizaka identified the class of antibodies that cause allergic reactions; Yamagata, Japan, July 6, 2018.

J

Jackson, Joe, 89, patriarch who launched his children's hugely successful musical careers starting with the Jackson 5; Las Vegas, NV, June 27, 2018.

Jackson, Keith, 89, sportscaster who covered college football for over 50 years; Los Angeles, CA, Jan. 12, 2018.

Jago, Tom, 93, British liquor executive who helped develop Baileys Irish Cream, Malibu rum, and Johnnie Walker Blue Label scotch; London, Eng., UK, Oct. 12, 2018.

Jean, Gloria, 92, actress and singer known for *Never Give a Sucker an Even Break* (1941) with W.C. Fields; Mountain View, HI, Aug. 31, 2018.

Jin Yong (Louis Cha), 94, Hong Kong writer known as "China's Tolkien" for his martial arts novels; Happy Valley, Hong Kong, Oct. 30, 2018.

Johnson, Mamie, 82, pitcher who was one of three women to play baseball in the 1950s Negro Leagues; Washington, DC, Dec. 19, 2017.

K

Kamman, Madeleine, 87, French chef and restaurateur who hosted PBS's *Madeleine Cooks* (1984-91); Middlebury, VT, July 16, 2018.

Kamprad, Ingvar, 91, Swedish founder of furnishings retailer IKEA, known for ready-to-assemble furniture; Smaland, Sweden, Jan. 27, 2018.

Kao, Charles, 84, Chinese-born Nobel Prize-winning physicist and engineer considered the "father of fiber optic communications"; Hong Kong, Sept. 23, 2018.

Kasell, Carl, 84, NPR newscaster who also judged its news quiz show *Wait Wait... Don't Tell Me!*; Potomac, MD, Apr. 17, 2018.

Kashio, Kazuo, 89, Japanese businessman who introduced compact calculators and helped make Casio Computer Co. an international business; Tokyo, Japan, June 18, 2018.

Kidder, Margot, 69, Canadian-American actress best known as Lois Lane in four *Superman* films (1978-87); Livingston, MT, May 13, 2018.

Killen, Edgar Ray, 92, Ku Klux Klan leader found guilty in 2005 for directing the notorious 1964 murders of three civil rights workers in Mississippi; Parchman, MS, Jan. 11, 2018.

Knox, Chuck, 86, NFL coach for L.A. Rams, Buffalo Bills, and Seattle Seahawks; Chula Vista, CA, May 12, 2018.

Koko, 46, American-bred Western lowland gorilla who was taught sign language; Woodside, CA, June 19, 2018.

Krauthammer, Charles, 68, Pulitzer Prize-winning columnist and TV commentator who advocated hawkish foreign policy; Atlanta, GA, June 21, 2018.

Krim, Mathilde, 91, Italian-born medical researcher who raised awareness and money to combat AIDS; Kings Point, NY, Jan. 15, 2018.

Kurtz, Connie, 81, LGBT rights activist whose lawsuit with partner Ruthie Berman resulted in domestic-partner benefits for NYC public school employees; West Palm Beach, FL, May 27, 2018.

Kurtz, Gary, 78, film producer who collaborated with George Lucas on *American Graffiti* (1973), *Star Wars* (1977), and *The Empire Strikes Back* (1980); London, Eng., UK, Sept. 23, 2018.

L

Lanzmann, Claude, 92, French filmmaker known for Holocaust documentary *Shoah* (1985); Paris, France, July 5, 2018.

Law, Bernard F., 86, Roman Catholic archbishop of Boston (1984-2002); forced to resign over his role in cover-up of clergy sex abuse; Rome, Italy, Dec. 20, 2017.

Laxalt, Paul, 96, Nevada gov. (1967-71) and sen. (R, 1974-87) who also served as campaign chairman for Ronald Reagan; McLean, VA, Aug. 6, 2018.

Le Guin, Ursula K., 88, novelist and poet known for science-fiction and fantasy works including *The Left Hand of Darkness* (1969) and the Earthsea series; Portland, OR, Jan. 22, 2018.

Leach, Robin, 76, British journalist best known as host of TV series *Lifestyles of the Rich and Famous* (1984-95); Las Vegas, NV, Aug. 24, 2018.

Lederman, Leon, 96, Nobel Prize-winning physicist who discovered and studied subatomic particles; Rexburg, ID, Oct. 3, 2018.

Lee, Ed, 65, first Asian-American mayor of San Francisco (2011-17); San Francisco, CA, Dec. 12, 2017.

Leiber, Judith, 97, Hungarian-born designer who created uniquely shaped and embellished handbags; Springs, NY, Apr. 28, 2018.

Leitsch, Dick, 83, LGBT rights activist who led "sip-ins" in 1960s New York City bars; New York, NY, June 22, 2018.

Lester, Julius, 78, Newbery Honor-winning writer known for *To Be a Slave* (1968) and other works about the black experience; Palmer, MA, Jan. 18, 2018.

Loud, Bill, 97, patriarch featured in the TV documentary series *An American Family* (1973); Los Angeles, CA, July 26, 2018.

Lynne, Dame Gillian, 92, British dancer and choreographer known for *Cats* (1981) and *The Phantom of the Opera* (1986); London, Eng., UK, July 1, 2018.

M

Madikizela-Mandela, Winnie, 81, South African anti-apartheid activist and politician who was married (1958-96) to ANC leader Nelson Mandela; Johannesburg, South Africa, Apr. 2, 2018.

Mahoney, John, 77, English-born actor best known as down-to-earth father Martin Crane on TV sitcom *Frasier* (1993-2004); Chicago, IL, Feb. 4, 2018.

Malone, Dorothy, 93, Academy Award-winning actress best known for TV series *Peyton Place* (1964-68); Dallas, TX, Jan. 19, 2018.

Manson, Charles, 83, notorious leader of the so-called Manson Family; convicted of nine 1969 murders, including that of actress Sharon Tate; Kern County, CA, Nov. 19, 2017.

Maren, Jerry, 98, diminutive actor who played a Munchkin member of the Lollipop Guild in *The Wizard of Oz* (1939); La Jolla, CA, May 24, 2018.

de Mariani, Maria Isabel Chorobik "Chicha," 94, Argentine activist and founder of Grandmothers of the Plaza de Mayo, devoted to finding children kidnapped during the country's military dictatorship; La Plata, Argentina, Aug. 20, 2018.

Masteroff, Joe, 98, Tony Award-winning playwright of *She Loves Me* (1963) and *Cabaret* (1966); Englewood, NJ, Sept. 28, 2018.

Mayle, Peter, 78, British writer whose *A Year in Provence* (1989) inspired many in the travel memoir genre; France, Jan. 18, 2018.

Mazzie, Marin, 57, Broadway actress and singer best known for *Passion* (1994-95), *Ragtime* (1998-2000), and *Kiss Me, Kate* (1999-2001); New York, NY, Sept. 13, 2018.

McCain, John, 81, Navy officer, U.S. rep. (R, AZ, 1983-87), and sen. (1987-2018) who was the 2008 Republican nominee for president; known as a war hero POW in Vietnam and as a "maverick" in Congress; Cornville, AZ, Aug. 25, 2018.

McCann, Chuck, 83, actor best known for children's TV, such as *DuckTales* (1987-90); Los Angeles, CA, Apr. 8, 2018.

McCovey, Willie, 80, Hall of Fame baseball player mainly for the San Francisco Giants; Stanford, CA, Oct. 31, 2018.

McFaddin, Jean, 75, Emmy Award-winning event planner who expanded and popularized the Macy's Thanksgiving Day Parade; New York, NY, Apr. 18, 2018.

McKayle, Donald, 87, modern dance pioneer who was the first black man to direct and choreograph a Broadway musical (*Raisin*, 1973); Irvine, CA, Apr. 6, 2018.

Meglin, Nick, 82, longtime editor and writer at *Mad* magazine (1956-2004); Durham, NC, June 2, 2018.

Melcher, John, 93, U.S. rep. (D, MT, 1969-77) and sen. (1977-89) who advocated for environmental protections; Missoula, MT, Apr. 12, 2018.

Michael I, 96, Romanian king (1927-30, 1940-47) known for having the nation's pro-Hitler prime minister arrested in 1944; Aubonne, Switz., Dec. 5, 2017.

Midgley, Mary, 99, British moral philosopher who made ideas accessible to a wide audience; Jesmond, Newcastle upon Tyne, Eng., UK, Oct. 10, 2018.

Mikita, Stan, 78, Slovak-born Canadian Hall of Fame center who helped the Chicago Blackhawks win the 1961 Stanley Cup; Chicago, IL, Aug. 7, 2018.

Miller, Mac, 26, rapper and producer whose first studio album, *Blue Side Park*, debuted at No. 1 on the Billboard 200 (2011); Los Angeles, CA, Sept. 7, 2018.

Miller, Zell, 86, Georgia gov. (1991-99) and U.S. sen. (D, 2000-05), who often sided with Republicans; Young Harris, GA, Mar. 23, 2018.

Mischel, Walter, 88, Austrian-born psychologist whose "marshmallow test" studies with 1960s preschoolers helped develop theories on self-control; New York, NY, Sept. 12, 2018.

Mitchell, Arthur, 84, dancer and choreographer who cofounded the Dance Theatre of Harlem (1969); New York, NY, Sept. 19, 2018.

Monson, Thomas, 90, president of the Church of Jesus Christ of Latter-day Saints (2008-18); Salt Lake City, UT, Jan. 2, 2018.

Montevecchi, Liliane, 85, French Tony Award-winning dancer and actress known for *Nine* (1982-84) and *Grand Hotel* (1989-92); New York, NY, June 29, 2018.

Moon, Wally, 87, L.A. Dodgers outfielder known for home runs nicknamed "Moon shots"; Bryan, TX, Feb. 9, 2018.

Morison, Patricia, 103, actress known for originating starring role in Broadway's *Kiss Me, Kate* (1948); West Hollywood, CA, May 20, 2018.

Mumford, Thad, 67, Emmy Award-winning writer and producer known for TV show *M*A*S*H* (1979-83); Silver Spring, MD, Sept. 6, 2018.

N

Nabors, Jim, 87, actor and singer known for TV sitcoms *The Andy Griffith Show* (1962-64) and *Gomer Pyle, U.S.M.C.* (1964-69); Honolulu, HI, Nov. 30, 2017.

Naipaul, V. S., 85, Trinidadian-born Nobel Prize-winning British writer best known for *A House for Mr. Biswas* (1961); London, Eng., UK, Aug. 11, 2018.

Nuriddin, Jalal Mansur, 73, poet often referred to as the "Grandfather of Rap"; Atlanta, GA, June 4, 2018.

O

O'Riordan, Dolores, 46, Irish singer-songwriter who led rock group the Cranberries; London, Eng., UK, Jan. 15, 2018.

Oversteegen, Freddie, 92, Dutch woman resistance fighter who as a teenager killed Nazis and collaborators; Driehuis, Netherlands, Sept. 5, 2018.

P

Pacheco, Ferdie, 89, physician best known as "fight doctor" to boxer Muhammad Ali; Miami, FL, Nov. 16, 2017.

Parker Fraley, Naomi, 96, 1940s U.S. Navy machinist who may have inspired "Rosie the Riveter" icon on World War II-era "We Can Do It!" posters; Longview, WA, Jan. 20, 2018.

Parra, Nicanor, 103, Chilean physicist and mathematician who won fame as a non-traditional poet; Santiago, Chile, Jan. 23, 2018.

Parry, Robert, 68, investigative journalist who exposed the Reagan-era Iran-Contra affair; Arlington, VA, Jan. 27, 2018.

Paul, Art, 93, graphic designer who created the iconic *Playboy* logo of a debonair rabbit; Chicago, IL, Apr. 28, 2018.

Peck, Richard, 84, Newbery Medal-winning writer who interpreted adult subjects for a young audience; New York, NY, May 23, 2018.

Polchinski, Joseph, 63, theoretical physicist known for work on string theory; Santa Barbara, CA, Feb. 2, 2018.

R

Rae, Charlotte, 92, actress known as Edna Garrett on TV sitcoms *Diff'rent Strokes* (1978-79) and *The Facts of Life* (1979-86); Los Angeles, CA, Aug. 5, 2018.

Ramsey, Frank, 86, Hall of Fame Boston Celtics guard who helped win seven NBA championships as pioneering "sixth man"; Evansville, IN, July 8, 2018.

Reese, Della, 86, jazz and gospel singer also known for TV drama *Touched by an Angel* (1994-2003); Encino, CA, Nov. 19, 2017.

Regula, Mary, 91, founder of the National First Ladies' Library (1994) in Canton, OH; Navarre, OH, Apr. 5, 2018.

Reilly, Dorcas, 92, Campbell Soup Co. recipe developer who created the Thanksgiving favorite green bean casserole; Camden, NJ, Oct. 15, 2018.

Reinhardt, Stephen, 87, federal appellate judge whose opinions overturned bans on same-sex marriage and physician-assisted suicide; Los Angeles, CA, Mar. 29, 2018.

Reynolds, Burt, 82, Emmy Award-winning actor known for *Deliverance* (1972), *Smokey and the Bandit* (1977), and *Boogie Nights* (1997); Jupiter, FL, Sept. 6, 2018.

Richter, Burton, 87, Nobel Prize-winning physicist who discovered a subatomic particle that helped inform a greater understanding of matter; Palo Alto, CA, July 18, 2018.

Robuchon, Joël, 73, inventive French chef and acclaimed restaurateur; Geneva, Switz., Aug. 6, 2018.

Romero, Juan, 68, hotel busboy who aided Sen. Robert F. Kennedy (D, NY) when he was fatally shot in Los Angeles; Modesto, CA, Oct. 1, 2018.

Rose Marie, 94, actress who was a vaudeville child star; best known as wisecracking Sally Rogers on *The Dick Van Dyke Show* (1961-66); Van Nuys, CA, Dec. 28, 2017.

Roth, Philip, 85, Pulitzer Prize-winning writer whose novels included *Goodbye, Columbus* (1959), *Portnoy's Complaint* (1969), and *American Pastoral* (1997); New York, NY, May 22, 2018.

Roundtree, Dovey Johnson, 104, civil rights activist and lawyer who helped ban segregated interstate bus travel; Charlotte, NC, May 21, 2018.

Rush, Otis, 84, Grammy Award-winning blues guitarist and singer acclaimed for "I Can't Quit You Baby" (1956) and "Double Trouble" (1958); Sept. 29, 2018.

S

Saleh, Ali Abdullah, 75?, Yemeni leader for more than three decades who was killed by rebel forces; Sanaa, Yemen, Dec. 4, 2017.

Sammartino, Bruno, 82, Italian-born pro wrestler who was WWE heavyweight champ for a record 11 years; Pittsburgh, PA, Apr. 18, 2018.

Schoendienst, Red, 95, Hall of Fame second baseman, manager, and coach, mostly with St. Louis Cardinals; Town and Country, MO, June 6, 2018.

Schultz, Ed, 64, radio/TV host and political commentator; Washington, DC, July 5, 2018.

Severin, Marie, 89, Marvel Comics artist who co-created Spider-Woman; Amityville, NY, Aug. 29, 2018.

Shange, Ntozake, 70, Obie Award-winning playwright and poet best known for *for colored girls who have considered suicide / when the rainbow is enuf* (1975); Bowie, MD, Oct. 27, 2018.

Shay, Art, 96, photographer known for Chicago street-life photos and portraits of celebrities; Deerfield, IL, Apr. 28, 2018.

Shimomura, Osamu, 90, Nobel Prize-winning Japanese chemist who helped develop a fluorescent protein that aided cancer research; Nagasaki, Japan, Oct. 19, 2018.

Shore, Mitzi, 87, cofounder of L.A.'s Comedy Store who fostered careers of stand-up comedians, including David Letterman, Richard Pryor, and Robin Williams; West Hollywood, CA, Apr. 11, 2018.

Shreve, Anita, 71, author whose novels included *The Weight of Water* (1997) and *The Pilot's Wife* (1998); Newfields, NH, Mar. 29, 2018.

Simon, Neil, 91, Pulitzer Prize and Tony Award-winning playwright known for comedies including *The Odd Couple* (1965), *Brighton Beach Memoirs* (1983), and *Lost in Yonkers* (1991); New York, NY, Aug. 26, 2018.

Slaughter, Louise, 88, U.S. rep. (D, NY, 1987-2018) who advocated for women's rights and manufacturing jobs; Washington, DC, Mar. 16, 2018.

Smith, Bob, 59, comedian and writer who in 1994 was the first openly gay comic to appear on *The Tonight Show*; New York, NY, Jan. 20, 2018.

Smith, Keely, 89, Grammy Award-winning jazz singer whose hits with then husband Louis Prima included "That Old Black Magic" (1958); Palm Springs, CA, Dec. 16, 2017.

Smith, Liz, 94, syndicated gossip columnist known for reporting on celebrities she befriended; New York, NY, Nov. 12, 2017.

Snoddy, Glenn, 96, recording engineer who unintentionally invented the "fuzz tone," a distortion made by guitars on a mixing board; Murfreesboro, TN, May 21, 2018.

Spade, Kate, 55, fashion designer who cofounded her eponymous handbag company in 1993 and grew it into a clothing and home-goods empire; New York, NY, June 5, 2018.

Spanos, Alex, 95, real estate developer and San Diego/L.A. Chargers owner; Stockton, CA, Oct. 9, 2018.

Sridevi (Kapoor), 54, Indian actress who made hundreds of films as Bollywood's first female superstar; Dubai, UAE, Feb. 24, 2018.

Staub, Rusty, 73, NY Mets and Montréal Expos player who became known for charitable efforts; West Palm Beach, FL, Mar. 29, 2018.

Steitz, Thomas, 78, Nobel Prize-winning biochemist who determined the atomic structure of the ribosome; Branford, CT, Oct. 9, 2018.

Stiers, David Ogden, 75, actor known as Maj. Charles Winchester on the TV series *M*A*S*H* (1977-83); Newport, OR, Mar. 3, 2018.

T

Taylor, Cecil, 89, avant-garde jazz pianist and poet known for unique style; Brooklyn, NY, Apr. 5, 2018.

Taylor, Jim, 83, Hall of Fame football player who scored the first rushing Super Bowl touchdown (1967); Baton Rouge, LA, Oct. 13, 2018.

Taylor, Paul, 88, modern dancer and choreographer who founded eponymous dance company (1954); New York, NY, Aug. 29, 2018.

Taylor, Richard E., 88, Canadian-born Nobel Prize-winning atomic physicist who helped discover subatomic particles known as quarks; Stanford, CA, Feb. 22, 2018.

Thomson, Peter, 88, Australian golfer who was a five-time British Open winner; Melbourne, Vict., Austral., June 20, 2018.

Tillis, Mel, 85, Country Music Hall of Fame singer-songwriter who overcame a stutter; Ocala, FL, Nov. 19, 2017.

Tisch, Joan, 90, philanthropist who was a benefactor of the arts and an early supporter of HIV/AIDS organizations; New York, NY, Nov. 2, 2017.

Troyer, Verne, 49, diminutive actor and stunt man best known as Mini-Me in the Austin Powers film series; Los Angeles, CA, Apr. 21, 2018.

Tsvangirai, Morgan, 65, Zimbabwean opposition party leader; Johannesburg, South Africa, Feb. 14, 2018.

Tuck, Dick, 94, Democratic prankster best known for tormenting Richard Nixon; Tucson, AZ, May 28, 2018.

Turner, Stansfield, 94, U.S. Navy admiral who served as CIA director (1977-81); Seattle, WA, Jan. 18, 2018.

V

Vajpayee, Atal Bihari, 93, Indian prime min. (1996, 1998-2004) who improved relations with Pakistan and ended a moratorium on nuclear weapons; New Delhi, India, Aug. 16, 2018.

Valiant, Johnny, 71, WWE Hall of Fame pro wrestler and manager; Ross Township, PA, Apr. 4, 2018.

Van Dyke, Jerry, 86, actor best known for TV sitcoms *My Mother the Car* (1965-66) and *Coach* (1989-97); Malvern, AR, Jan. 5, 2018.

van Hulst, Johan, 107, Dutch school director who helped save 600 Jewish children during the Holocaust; Amsterdam, Netherlands, Mar. 22, 2018.

Venturi, Robert, 93, Pritzker Prize-winning architect whose landmark works include the National Gallery Sainsbury Wing (London, Eng., 1991); Philadelphia, PA, Sept. 18, 2018.

Vinton, Will, 70, Academy Award-winning animator who developed the "Claymation" stop-motion animation technique; Portland, OR, Oct. 4, 2018.

Voinovich, Vladimir, 85, Russian writer and dissident who was stripped of his Soviet citizenship in 1981; Moscow, Russia, July 27, 2018.

W

Walker, Clint, 90, actor known for roles in Westerns, including TV series *Cheyenne* (1955-62); Grass Valley, CA, May 21, 2018.

Walker, George, 96, composer who was the first African American to win a Pulitzer Prize for Music (1996); Montclair, NJ, Aug. 23, 2018.

Walker, Mort, 94, cartoonist known for creating *Beetle Bailey* (syndicated since 1950) and *Hi and Lois* (1954); Stamford, CT, Jan. 27, 2018.

Watson, W(illiam) Marvin, Jr., 93, de facto White House chief of staff (1965-69) to Pres. Lyndon B. Johnson; The Woodlands, TX, Nov. 26, 2017.

Wessel, Henry, Jr., 76, photographer known for images of life in the American West; Point Richmond, CA, Sept. 21, 2018.

Weston, Randy, 92, pianist inspired by the African roots of jazz; Brooklyn, NY, Sept. 1, 2018.

White, Jo Jo, 71, Hall of Fame basketball player who led the Boston Celtics to two national championships; Jan. 16, 2018.

Wolfe, Tom, 88, writer and pioneer of "New Journalism"; best known for *The Right Stuff* (1979) and *The Bonfire of the Vanities* (1987); New York, NY, May 14, 2018.

Y

Young, John, 87, NASA astronaut who walked on the Moon (1972) and commanded the first shuttle mission (1981); Houston, TX, Jan. 5, 2018.

Young, Malcolm, 64, Scottish-born guitarist and songwriter who cofounded hard rock band AC/DC in 1973; Sydney, NSW, Australia, Nov. 18, 2017.

Z

Zieman, Nancy, 64, author and designer known for TV's long-running *Sewing With Nancy* (1982-2017); Beaver Dam, WI, Nov. 14, 2017.

CONGRESS

Key Information on the 115th Congress

The 115th Congress convened Jan. 3, 2017, with Republicans maintaining control of both the Senate (52-46, 2 ind.) and the House (240-197, 4 vacancies). A record 109 women were serving at the start of Congress, of whom 21 were in the Senate and 88 (including 4 nonvoting delegates and Puerto Rico's Resident Commissioner) were in the House. The 115th Congress also had record minority representation, including five Hispanic lawmakers serving in the Senate and 40 (including 1 nonvoting delegate and the resident commissioner) in the House. The Senate membership also included three African Americans and three senators of Asian, South Asian, or Pacific Islander heritage. The House had 49 African-American members (including 2 nonvoting delegates); 15 Asian/South Asian/Pac. Isl. Americans (including 2 nonvoting delegates); and 2 American Indians. Two lawmakers died during the 115th Congress: 16-term Rep. Louise Slaughter (D, NY)—the oldest member of Congress, at 88—on Mar. 16, 2018, and six-term Sen. John S. McCain (R, AZ), on Aug. 25, 2018.

Vice Pres. Mike Pence cast a tie-breaking vote Feb. 7, 2017, to confirm Betsy DeVos as secretary of education, a Senate first for a cabinet-level confirmation. Republican Senators lowered the threshold for ending debate on U.S. Supreme Court justice nominees from 60 votes to a simple majority, thereby allowing confirmation of Neil Gorsuch Apr. 7, 2017.

Leadership. Paul Ryan (R, WI) continued as Speaker of the House when the 115th Congress convened; he announced in Apr. 2018 that he would not seek reelection. Majority Leader Kevin McCarthy (R, CA), Majority Whip Steve Scalise (R, LA), Minority Leader Nancy Pelosi (D, CA) and Minority Whip Steny Hoyer (D, MD) all retained their House roles. Scalise was shot and critically injured June 14, 2017, and his role was filled temporarily by Patrick McHenry (R, NC).

In the Senate, Mitch McConnell (R, KY) continued to serve as majority leader, and Charles Schumer (D, NY) took over minority leadership from the retiring Harry Reid (D, NV). Majority Whip John Cornyn (R, TX) and Minority Whip Richard Durbin (D, IL) both retained their posts.

Ethics. Amid a widespread backlash against sexual harassment and misconduct, eight lawmakers facing accusations either resigned or announced they would not seek reelection. (Another, 8-term Rep. Tim Murphy (R, PA), resigned effective Oct. 21, 2017, amid reports of an extramarital affair and of his having pressured his partner to have an abortion.) Congress's longest serving member, 88-year-old Rep. John Conyers (D, MI), resigned in his 27th term Dec. 5, 2017, following allegations he harassed female staff and used taxpayer money to settle a claim against him. Three days later, Rep. Trent Franks (R, AZ) left office after reports that he asked two former staffers to serve as pregnancy surrogates. Sen. Al Franken (D, MN) resigned Jan. 2, 2018, amid multiple allegations of harassment dating mostly to before his election. GOP Reps. Blake Farenthold (TX) and Patrick Meehan (PA) resigned Apr. 6 and 27, 2018, respectively, amid accusations from former staff; both settled complaints using taxpayer funds. Rep. Ruben Kihuen (D, NV), alleged to have harassed at least two women; Rep. Joe Barton (R, TX), who sent lewd text messages and nude images to women; and Rep. Elizabeth Esty, (D, CT), who admitted to mishandling allegations against her former chief of staff, all announced they would not seek reelection.

Defeated in the 2016 Democratic primary, 12-term Rep. Corrine Brown (D, FL) was sentenced Dec. 4, 2017, to five years in prison after she was found guilty of federal corruption charges related to her pocketing of some $800,000 from a charity for impoverished students. Rep. Chris Collins (R, NY) was arrested Aug. 8, 2018, on federal securities fraud charges related to an Australian biotech company. Rep. Duncan Hunter (R, CA) and his wife were indicted Aug. 21, 2018, on federal charges stemming from their alleged use of $250,000 in campaign money for personal expenses.

Unfinished Business. The House, Sept. 28, 2018, and Senate, Oct. 11, 2018, adjourned for the election campaign season, leaving multiple measures unpassed or unfunded. Congress's inability to resolve the fate of undocumented "Dreamers" brought to the U.S. as children—as well as broader immigration issues—brought bipartisan criticism. Congress also failed to either repeal or stabilize the Affordable Care Act (Obamacare) or reauthorize the Temporary Assistance for Needy Families (TANF) program.

For Further Information. Detailed legislative information can be accessed at www.congress.gov.

Major Actions of the 115th Congress

Major actions taken by the 115th Congress through Sept. 30, 2018. Laws are identified by their Public Law (PL) number.

Veterans Affairs. Department of Veterans Affairs Accountability and Whistleblower Protection Act of 2017 gives VA more power to discipline/fire employees and curtails previously lengthy employee appeals process. Also sets up internal whistleblower office and prohibits retaliation against those filing complaints. Passed by the Senate, June 6, voice vote; passed by the House, June 13, 368-55; signed by Pres. Trump, June 23, 2017 (PL 115-41).

Economic Sanctions. Countering America's Adversaries Through Sanctions Act (CAATSA) imposes new and codifies existing sanctions on Russia over its ongoing involvement in Ukraine and Syria and its interference in the 2016 U.S. elections; a condition of the act blocks the president from unilaterally easing or lifting sanctions on Russia. Sanctions North Korean cargo and shipping, as well as goods produced by employers of North Korean forced labor. Passed by the House, July 25, 2017, 419-3; passed by the Senate, July 27, 98-2; signed by Pres. Trump, Aug. 2, 2017 (PL 115-44).

Tax Revision. Tax Cuts and Jobs Act of 2017 provides largest overhaul of U.S. tax code in more than 30 years. Reduces taxes by about $1.5 tril over 10 years, with long-term benefits going primarily to corporations. Top corporate tax rate cut from 35% to 21% and overall personal income tax rates cut by 8% in 2019, though individuals' breaks expire in 2025. Repeals Obamacare's individual mandate, doubles child tax credit and estate tax exemptions, caps the state and local income tax deduction at $10,000, and lowers the limit for home mortgage interest deduction. Passed by the Senate (as amended), Dec. 20, 51-48; passed by the House (as amended), Dec. 20, 224-201; signed into law by Pres. Trump, Dec. 22, 2017 (PL 115-97).

Government Spending. Bipartisan Budget Act of 2018 funds government for two years and raises debt limit, ending 9-hour government shutdown. Increases military spending cap by $80 bil in FY2018 and $85 bil in FY2019, and non-defense domestic discretionary limit by $63 bil in 2018 and $68 bil in 2019. Funds Children's Health Insurance Program (CHIP) for full decade (up from six years) and provides $90 bil for disaster relief. Passed by the Senate (as amended) Feb. 9, 71-28; passed by the House (as amended), Feb. 9, 240-186; signed by Pres. Trump, Feb. 9, 2018 (PL 115-123).

Sex Trafficking. Allow States and Victims to Fight Online Sex Trafficking Act (FOSTA) amends the Communications Decency Act to make internet companies such as Craigslist, Facebook, and Twitter liable for sex trafficking facilitated through their sites. Passed by the House, Feb. 27, 388-25; passed by the Senate, Mar. 21, 97-2; signed by Pres. Trump, Apr. 11, 2018 (PL 115-164).

Leadership of Selected Congressional Committees

Congressional leadership as of Sept. 30, 2018.

House

Appropriations: Rodney P. Frelinghuysen (R, NJ)
Armed Services: Mac Thornberry (R, TX)
Budget: Steve Womack (R, AR)
Education and the Workforce: Virginia Foxx (R, NC)
Energy and Commerce: Greg Walden (R, OR)
Ethics: Susan W. Brooks (R, IN)
Financial Services: Jeb Hensarling (R, TX)
Foreign Affairs: Ed Royce (R, CA)
Intelligence: Devin Nunes (R, CA)
Judiciary: Bob Goodlatte (R, VA)
Natural Resources: Rob Bishop (R, UT)
Oversight and Government Reform: Trey Gowdy (R, SC)
Transportation and Infrastructure: Bill Shuster (R, PA)
Ways and Means: Kevin Brady (R, TX)

Senate

Appropriations: Richard Shelby (R, AL)
Armed Services: James M. Inhofe (R, OK)
Banking, Housing, and Urban Affairs: Mike Crapo (R, ID)
Budget: Michael B. Enzi (R, WY)
Commerce, Science, and Transportation: John Thune (R, SD)
Energy and Natural Resources: Lisa Murkowski (R, AK)
Environment and Public Works: John R. Barrasso (R, WY)
Finance: Orrin G. Hatch (R, UT)
Foreign Relations: Bob Corker (R, TN)
Health, Education, Labor, and Pensions: Lamar Alexander (R, TN)
Judiciary: Chuck Grassley (R, IA)

Joint Committees

Economic: Rep. Erik Paulsen (R, MN), Sen. Mike Lee (R, UT)
Taxation: Sen. Orrin G. Hatch (R, UT), Rep. Kevin Brady (R, TX)

U.S. SUPREME COURT

The U.S. Supreme Court's 2017-18 term began Oct. 2, 2017, and concluded June 27, 2018. The justices decided 72 cases (59 of which carried signed opinions). Chief Justice John G. Roberts Jr. presided over his 13th full term. The seven associate justices in Oct. 2017, by order of seniority, were Anthony M. Kennedy, Clarence Thomas, Ruth Bader Ginsburg, Stephen G. Breyer, Samuel A. Alito Jr., Sonia Sotomayor, Elena Kagan, and Neil M. Gorsuch.

Justice Kennedy notified Pres. Trump June 27, 2018, that he would be retiring at the end of July. Kennedy had an outsized role as the primary swing voter in the court's current configuration, though he most frequently sided with the conservative bloc (along with Roberts, Thomas, Alito, and Gorsuch). Trump July 9 nominated Judge Brett M. Kavanaugh of the U.S. Court of Appeals for the DC Circuit to replace Kennedy. Following a contentious process during which Kavanaugh faced accusations of sexual assault dating back to his adolescence, the Senate Oct. 6, 2018, voted, 50-48, to confirm Kavanaugh to the Supreme Court.

Notable Supreme Court Decisions, 2017-18

Note: The columns on the right provide information on how each justice voted. Gray shading indicates a justice who was part of the majority; black, a justice who did not participate in the decision. MO = justice authored majority opinion; CO = justice authored concurring opinion; COJ = justice authored opinion concurring in judgment but not its reasoning; COP = justice authored opinion concurring in part of the judgment; DO = justice authored dissenting opinion.

Abortion
The Supreme Court June 26 ruled, 5-4, in favor of anti-abortion pregnancy centers and clinics (a.k.a. "crisis pregnancy centers") that aimed to convince women to carry their pregnancies to term; the centers had argued that they could not be compelled by states to provide information about state-sponsored reproductive health services, including abortion. The case was *National Institute of Family and Life Advocates v. Becerra*.

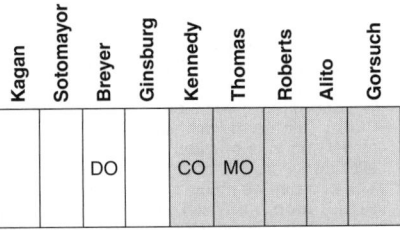

Kagan	Sotomayor	Breyer	Ginsburg	Kennedy	Thomas	Roberts	Alito	Gorsuch
		DO		CO	MO			

Civil Rights
The court June 4 ruled, 7-2, in *Masterpiece Cakeshop v. Colorado Civil Rights Commission* that the commission had not given a fair hearing to a baker when it determined in 2014 that he had violated Colorado law by refusing to make a wedding cake for a same-sex couple. The high court's ruling sidestepped ruling on the major constitutional claim made by the baker, who argued that he had the right to refuse service based on the First Amendment rights to freedom of speech and religion.

Kagan	Sotomayor	Breyer	Ginsburg	Kennedy	Thomas	Roberts	Alito	Gorsuch
CO			DO	MO	COJ/COP			CO

Commerce
In *South Dakota v. Wayfair*, the court June 21 ruled, 5-4, that a state could impose sales taxes on online retailers even if they had no physical stores or warehouses in the state. The ruling, which overturned 1967 and 1992 Supreme Court precedents that dealt with states' attempts to tax mail-order businesses, could have a significant impact on e-commerce and on state budgets.

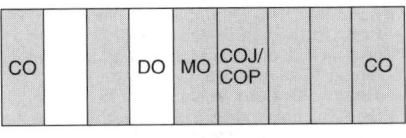

Kagan	Sotomayor	Breyer	Ginsburg	Kennedy	Thomas	Roberts	Alito	Gorsuch
				MO	CO	DO		CO

Criminal Justice
The Supreme Court June 22 ruled in *Carpenter v. U.S.*, 5-4, that police needed to obtain a warrant before accessing seven or more days' worth of a person's location data as tracked by a mobile phone. The data in question was collected by cellular companies based on the location of a phone with respect to individual cell towers over time.

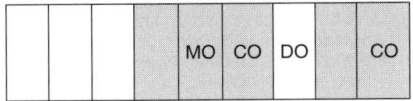

Kagan	Sotomayor	Breyer	Ginsburg	Kennedy	Thomas	Roberts	Alito	Gorsuch
				DO	DO	MO	DO	DO

Immigration and Travel Bans
The court Apr. 17 ruled, 5-4, in *Sessions v. Dimaya* to strike down a section of federal immigration law used to deport noncitizens who had committed "crimes of violence," calling the clause that classified those crimes unconstitutionally vague.

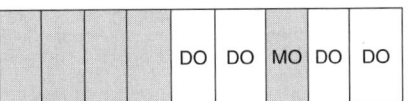

Kagan	Sotomayor	Breyer	Ginsburg	Kennedy	Thomas	Roberts	Alito	Gorsuch
MO					DO	DO		COJ/COP

In *Trump v. Hawaii*, the Supreme Court June 26 ruled, 5-4, to uphold a Sept. 2017 executive order from Pres. Donald Trump that temporarily banned travelers from North Korea, Venezuela, and five Muslim-majority countries—Iran, Libya, Somalia, Syria, and Yemen—from entering the U.S. The court said the wide powers related to immigration regulation afforded the president by Congress and the Constitution superseded the main challenge to the travel ban, which was on the grounds that derogatory statements by Trump about Muslim people suggested the ban was motivated by unconstitutional religious animus.

Kagan	Sotomayor	Breyer	Ginsburg	Kennedy	Thomas	Roberts	Alito	Gorsuch
		DO	DO	CO	CO	MO		

The court Feb. 27 ruled, 5-3, in *Jennings v. Rodriguez* that federal immigration law did not require the government to provide regular bail hearings to detained immigrants facing deportation. The court sent the case back to a lower court to consider whether the U.S. Constitution required such hearings. The ruling applied to a class-action suit that had begun under the Obama administration.

Kagan	Sotomayor	Breyer	Ginsburg	Kennedy	Thomas	Roberts	Alito	Gorsuch
(did not participate)		DO			COJ/COP		MO	

Labor
The Supreme Court June 27, 5-4, overturned a 40-year precedent and struck down rules in more than 20 states that compelled public employees who opted not to join a union to nonetheless pay fees to the union in support of its collective-bargaining efforts. The ruling held that those fees amounted to forced subsidization of political speech in violation of the First Amendment's free-speech protections. The case was *Janus v. American Federation of State, County and Municipal Employees (AFSCME)*.

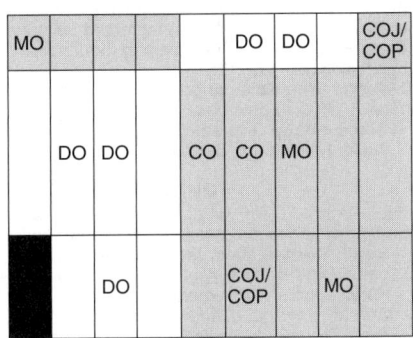

Kagan	Sotomayor	Breyer	Ginsburg	Kennedy	Thomas	Roberts	Alito	Gorsuch
DO	DO						MO	

The court May 21 ruled, 5-4, that employers could require employees to address complaints through individual arbitration proceedings rather than through collective legal action. Some 25 million U.S. workers whose contracts required them to use individual arbitration could be affected by the ruling, which came in three consolidated cases collectively referred to as *EPIC Systems Corp. v. Lewis*.

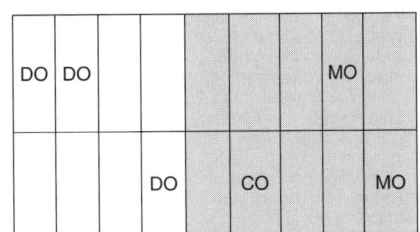

Kagan	Sotomayor	Breyer	Ginsburg	Kennedy	Thomas	Roberts	Alito	Gorsuch
			DO		CO			MO

Voting Rights and Elections
The court June 11 ruled, 5-4, to uphold a system used by the state of Ohio to purge the names of certain voters from its voter rolls. Voters who had had their voter registrations revoked said that the system violated a provision of federal electoral law, but the decision held in *Husted v. A. Philip Randolph Institute* that Ohio's process was legal and could be used to cull the state's voter rolls ahead of the 2018 midterm elections.

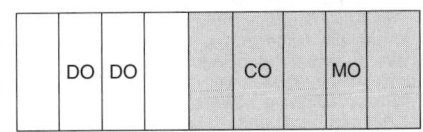

Kagan	Sotomayor	Breyer	Ginsburg	Kennedy	Thomas	Roberts	Alito	Gorsuch
	DO	DO			CO		MO	

NOTABLE QUOTES, 2018

National News

"[M]y two greatest assets have been mental stability and being, like, really smart. … I went from VERY successful businessman, to top T.V. Star … to President of the United States (on my first try). I think that would qualify as not smart, but genius … and a very stable genius at that!"
—**Pres. Donald Trump**, Jan. 6, in Twitter messages denouncing critics who questioned his mental stability.

"We will not stop until every man, every woman, every child, and every American can live without fear of gun violence."
—**David Hogg**, survivor of the Feb. 14 shooting at a Parkland, FL, high school; at the March for Our Lives rally against gun violence in Washington, DC, Mar. 24.

"I actually really like Sarah. I think she's very resourceful. She burns facts, and then she uses that ash to create a perfect smoky eye. Like maybe she's born with it, maybe it's lies. It's probably lies."
—Comedian **Michelle Wolf** on White House Press Sec. Sarah Huckabee Sanders in her controversial monologue at White House Correspondents' Assn. dinner, Apr. 28.

"I thought I'd never see them again."
—**Ludin** [last name withheld], an asylum seeker from Guatemala, who was reunited with her children, June 28, 40 days after they were separated by U.S. border officials.

"Much of our news media is indeed the enemy of the people."
—**Pres. Trump**, via Twitter, July 15.

"There is No Collusion! The Robert Mueller Rigged Witch Hunt … was started by a fraudulent Dossier, paid for by Crooked Hillary and the DNC. Therefore, the Witch Hunt is an illegal Scam!"
—**Pres. Trump**, via Twitter, July 29.

"The America of John McCain has no need to be made great again because America was always great."
—**Meghan McCain**, in eulogy for her father, Sen. John McCain (R, AZ), at his memorial service Sept. 1 in Washington, DC.

"[M]any of the senior officials in [Trump's] own administration are working diligently from within to frustrate parts of his agenda and his worst inclinations. I would know. I am one of them."
—**Anonymous** author of an op-ed essay published Sept. 5 in the *NY Times*, attributed to an unnamed "senior official in the Trump administration."

"I am here today not because I want to be. I am terrified. I am here because I believe it is my civic duty to tell you what happened to me while Brett Kavanaugh and I were in high school."
—**Dr. Christine Blasey Ford**, at Senate Judiciary Committee confirmation hearing for Supreme Court nominee Brett Kavanaugh, Sept. 27.

"This whole two-week effort has been a calculated and orchestrated political hit, fueled with apparent pent-up anger about President Trump and the 2016 election, fear that has been unfairly stoked about my judicial record, revenge on behalf of the Clintons, and millions of dollars in money from outside left-wing opposition groups."
—**Judge Brett Kavanaugh**, at confirmation hearing, Sept. 27.

"This is not a job interview. This is hell."
—**Sen. Lindsey Graham** (R, SC), at Senate confirmation hearing for Kavanaugh, Sept. 27.

Around the World

"Here in Korea, we will continue our endeavor to broaden the horizon of peace that began in Pyeongchang."
—**South Korean Pres. Moon Jae-in**, Feb. 25, at closing ceremony for the 2018 Winter Olympics, where North and South Korea appeared ceremonially under the same flag.

"Trade wars are good, and easy to win."
—**Pres. Trump**, via Twitter Mar. 2, after announcing Mar. 1 that he intended to impose tariffs on steel and aluminum.

"I no longer have a family. The ruling regime is guilty. Every bureaucrat dreams of stealing like Putin. Every state functionary treats people like garbage."
—**Igor Vostrikov**, who lost his family in a mall fire in Kemerovo, Siberia, Russia, Mar. 25, amid protests blaming officials for taking bribes to overlook safety concerns.

"We're like the piggy bank that everybody's robbing—and that ends."
—**Pres. Trump**, speaking after a G7 summit meeting, June 9.

"Twelve wild boars and coach are out of the cave. Everyone safe. … Hooyah."
—**Thai Navy SEALs'** July 10 Facebook post after rescuing 12 youth soccer players and their coach, who were trapped 17 days in a flooded cave in Thailand.

"My people came to me. … They said they think it's Russia. I have President Putin; he just said it's not Russia. I will say this: I don't see any reason why it would be."
—**Pres. Trump** at news conference following summit with the Russian president in Helsinki, Finland, July 16, in reference to interference in the 2016 U.S. election; he later said he had meant to say "wouldn't be."

"No prior president has ever abased himself more abjectly before a tyrant."
—**Sen. John McCain** (R, AZ), in tweet following Trump's press conference in Helsinki, July 16.

"We showed no care for the little ones; we abandoned them."
—**Pope Francis**, in an open letter to "the People of God," Aug. 20, after the Aug. 14 release of a grand jury report on sex abuse and its cover-up in six Pennsylvania Roman Catholic dioceses.

"I didn't expect that reaction, but that's okay."
—**Pres. Trump**, Sept. 25, when his claim that his presidency had "accomplished more than almost any administration in the history of our country" generated a ripple of laughter at the UN General Assembly.

"I was really being tough and so was he. And we would go back and forth. And then we fell in love, OK? No really. He wrote me beautiful letters."
—**Pres. Trump** speaking about his relationship with North Korean leader Kim Jong Un, Sept. 29.

"Let's make Brazil Great! Let's be proud of our homeland once again!"
—**Jair Bolsonaro**, right-wing populist candidate for president of Brazil, via Facebook Live, a day before first-round voting, Oct. 7.

"It's a line in the sand and what it says to our species is that this is the moment and we must act now."
—**Debra Roberts**, co-chair of a working group that helped prepare dramatic climate change report released Oct. 8 by UN Intergovernmental Panel on Climate Change (IPCC).

"You can hear his voice and the voices of men speaking Arabic … You can hear how he was interrogated, tortured, and then murdered."
—**Unnamed officials**, quoted in *Washington Post* Oct. 11, on covert audio recording that documented the disappearance of Saudi-born journalist Jamal Khashoggi in Saudi Arabia's consulate in Istanbul.

People and Culture

"[W]hen that new day finally dawns, it will be because of a lot of magnificent women … fighting hard to … take us to the time when nobody ever has to say 'Me too' again."
—**Oprah Winfrey** at the Golden Globe Awards, Jan. 7.

"People didn't believe me, even people I thought were my friends. They called me a liar, a whore, and even accused me of making all of this up just to get attention. … Well, who do they believe now, Larry?"
—**Olympic gymnast Jamie Dantzscher**, at Jan. 18 sentencing hearing for former USA Gymnastics doctor Larry Nassar, who pleaded guilty to many charges of criminal sexual abuse.

"I am an immigrant."
—**Guillermo del Toro**, accepting the Oscar for best director, Mar. 4.

"It's not just the guy who's never worked a day in his life. … It's Joe Citizen that is dying."
—**Gust Andrew Teague II**, deputy sheriff in Montgomery County, OH, on the opioid addiction crisis in *Time* magazine, Mar. 5.

"You look amazing."
—**Prince Harry**, greeting his bride, Meghan Markle, at the British royal wedding at St. George's Chapel, Windsor Castle, May 19.

"While all pharmaceutical treatments have side effects, racism is not a known side effect of any Sanofi medication."
—**Sanofi**, manufacturer of the sleep aid Ambien, in a tweet after Roseanne Barr, May 29, blamed the drug for the racist post that led ABC to cancel her TV sitcom.

"She's the superhero we need right now."
—**Nicole Maines**, July 21, after it was announced Maines, a transgender actress, would play a trans superhero in TV's *Supergirl*.

"Every job is worthwhile and valuable, and if we have a kind of a rethinking about that because of what's happened to me, that would be great, but no one should feel sorry for me. … I've had a great life."
—**Geoffrey Owens**, on *Good Morning America* Sept. 4, after a photo taken of the former actor on *The Cosby Show* working at a Trader Joe's grocery store sparked widespread publicity.

"You stole a point from me. You're a thief, too."
—**Serena Williams**, in dispute with the chair umpire over alleged discrimination against women tennis players, during her U.S. Open final against Naomi Osaka, Sept 8.

"What is yes?"
—**Maria Shafer**, *Jeopardy!* audience member, accepting a marriage proposal from contestant Michael Pascuzzi, using the prescribed answer-as-question format, in Sept. 27 episode of the quiz show.

Good Grief, Cleveland Browns

When the local team wins a championship or has a perfect season, it's traditional to hold a parade. In Jan. 2018, fans of the Cleveland Browns showed that could apply even when a season is perfectly awful. The idea arose in 2016: the Browns were on a winless streak, and season-ticket holder Chris McNeil sarcastically suggested via Twitter that a parade would be in order. He got a permit, raised money, and started making arrangements, but the team won its second-to-last game of the season. McNeil donated the parade funds to a local food bank, the team matched them, and he figured that was the end of it. But the team went 0-16 in 2017, and suddenly the parade was back on. An estimated 2,500-3,200 fans came out in 8-degree-Fahrenheit weather and heavy wind Jan. 6 to put the season to rest. Floats included a toilet, a coffin draped with a Browns flag, and a "sad Santa." T-shirt vendors offered fake jerseys with the name "Owen" over the number 16, and shirts reading "2017 CLEVELAND BRO NS: A team without a W."

Special Delivery

Suppose you're a pregnant American woman flying to a vacation in Germany. You arrive at your 17-hour layover in Istanbul, Turkey, with what feels like food poisoning. As you go through customs, you realize that, actually, you might be in labor. You don't know anybody in Turkey. You don't know how Turkish hospitals work. What do you do? For Tia Freeman, a 22-year-old Air Force member from Nashville, TN, the answer was simple: she went to a hotel, looked up some YouTube videos about childbirth, filled the bathtub, and followed the instructions for a water birth. She later noted on Twitter that this was a much messier process than YouTube would lead one to believe, but "it happened pretty quickly," and her son was born on Mar. 7, 2018.

She returned to the airport the following day with an undocumented newborn, whom she named Xavier Ata Freeman. "I was bombarded with questions (naturally) but finally I proved that I wasn't a trafficker," she said. Mother and son were taken to the U.S. embassy, where she applied for a birth certificate and passport, and then to the hospital, where Xavier was checked out and found to be healthy. Turkish Airlines paid for their hotel stay for the next two weeks, while they recuperated. Freeman told *USA Today* her story shows "there's nothing you can't do as long as you have the internet."

A Bird in the Hand

In Mar. 2018, after just 17 years, the Fairmont Empress hotel in Victoria, BC, Canada, agreed to lift a lifetime ban against Nova Scotia resident Nick Burchill.

Back in Apr. 2001, Burchill was in Victoria on a business trip and took the opportunity to visit some Navy buddies, bringing them an entire suitcase filled with pepperoni from a Halifax deli, Brothers Meats. His room didn't have a refrigerator, so he decided to keep the pepperoni cool by opening the window and spreading it on the sill and a nearby table. When he returned from a long walk, Burchill found "an entire flock of seagulls" eating his pepperoni, and learned that it "does NASTY things to a seagull's digestive system." Spooked by his entrance, the gulls started flying around and knocking over lamps in "a tornado of seagull excrement, feathers, pepperoni chunks, and fairly large birds." He shooed most of the birds out, but ensuing complications involving one last gull, Burchill's shoe, a sink full of water, and a hairdryer led to his knocking out power to part of the hotel. Eventually, he left the mess in the hands of the housekeeping service and ran off to his business dinner. His belongings were moved to another room, but his company later received a letter banning him from the hotel.

In 2018, Burchill posted a full apology on Facebook, and the hotel agreed to allow him back. He also gave the hotel a pound of Brothers Meats pepperoni as a peace offering.

"The Man With the Golden Arm"

James Harrison, of New South Wales, Australia, donated blood for the first time when he turned 18, then the legal minimum age, and continued giving blood and plasma regularly for more than six decades, for a total of 1,173 times. He started because he had a lung removed when he was 14 and received blood transfusions from numerous strangers during the operation, but another reason followed. A representative of the Australian Red Cross explained to CNN that "up until about 1967, there were literally thousands of babies dying each year, [and] doctors didn't know why." The infants, it turns out, were suffering from a disease caused when mothers with Rh-negative blood gave birth to children with Rh-positive blood, and the mothers' bodies developed antibodies that attacked the fetal blood cells, with dire consequences. Scientists discovered that—perhaps because of the transfusions he got—Harrison's blood contained an unusually high concentration of an antibody that could be used to create a treatment to prevent the disease.

The Australian Red Cross estimated that Harrison's donations helped save the lives of around 2.4 million babies, with 17% of Australian pregnant women needing the treatment. He made his final donation on May 11, 2018, at age 81, now over the age limit.

This Suit Is Bananas: B-A-N-A-N-A-S

In 2010, the Rasta Imposta costume company copyrighted the design of a banana costume, which it began selling in 2011. In 2017, it found out that Kangaroo Manufacturing was making a competing costume, and sued. Kangaroo contended that there was nothing original about the costume design, making it ineligible for copyright. Ripe bananas are yellow, and their ends are black; all banana costumes are going to look about the same. Rasta Imposta argued otherwise, and in May 2018, a U.S. District Court judge agreed, citing eight examples of identifiable features making Rasta Imposta's costume distinctive: overall length; curvature; length above and below the torso; shape, size, and color of the ends; locations of head and arm cutouts; "the soft, smooth, almost shiny look of the chosen synthetic fabric"; parallel lines mimicking ridges; and bright, uniform, golden yellow color. Rasta Imposta gave examples of 21 other banana costumes for sale that did not look like theirs; by contrast, Kangaroo's version was, the judge found, "nearly identical." Technically, the lawsuit was a split decision: Rasta Imposta got its preliminary injunction—as it was found likely to succeed in the forthcoming trial—but it had to put down a $100,000 bond in case it loses.

I Saw the Sign

In May 2018, Diane Turton, Realtors in New Jersey received this email: "Hi, Just wanted to let you know that I found part of one of your signposts washed up on the beach near Bordeaux France pictures available if wanted. Not in best shape after that crossing." The recipients were understandably skeptical at first, but they determined that the sign had been lost from a waterfront house in Brielle, NJ, when Hurricane Sandy hit in Oct. 2012. The real estate agents proudly posted the photos to Facebook and on their website as proof that they were "a global real estate company," and traveled to France to retrieve the sign.

Oceanographer Curtis Ebbesmeyer explained to the *NY Times* that the sign had likely completed its third trip across the Atlantic. "There is a great gyre of water that runs from New Jersey to northern Europe down to Spain and back to New Jersey … and it takes about a year and a half to drift across the North Atlantic one way from New Jersey to France. … So five and a half years is just about right." He described the find as "good scientific data" into the drift of floating objects.

Birds of a Feather Collect Trash Together

What do you do when you want people to pick up after themselves in public spaces? Post signs? Impose fines? The Puy du Fou historical theme park, located about four hours from Paris, France, decided to try setting a good example. This wouldn't be noteworthy, except that the people setting the example aren't people at all. They're six crows—Baco, Bamboo, Bill, Black, Boubou, and Bricole—trained to collect bits of trash in exchange for treats. NPR reported in Aug. 2018 that one of the park's falconers, Christophe Gaborit, began training the birds in a variation on an existing act, where the crows would pick up roses and bring them to an actress playing a princess. This is not a serious attempt to have the crows clean the park—they do their act four days a week, supervised by a falconer—but rather an attempt to educate human visitors. If birds can pick up cigarette butts, why can't people?

HISTORICAL ANNIVERSARIES

1919 — 100 Years Ago

The 18th Amendment, providing for prohibition of the "manufacture, sale, or transportation of intoxicating liquors," is ratified Jan. 16 (to take effect on Jan. 16, 1920).

Congress approves legislation that establishes Grand Canyon National Park in Arizona and Lafayette (later Acadia) National Park in Maine Feb. 26.

Major work stoppages—including a general strike in Seattle in Feb. and by Boston police and some 300,000 U.S. steelworkers in Sept.—are used to stoke fears of labor radicalism.

The Communist International (a.k.a. Third International, or Comintern) is founded Mar. 2 in Moscow.

Mexican revolutionary leader Emiliano Zapata is murdered in an ambush Apr. 10.

British troops Apr. 13 open fire on unarmed civilians in Amritsar, Punjab, India, killing hundreds, in an incident that marked a turning point for Indian nationalism.

Anarchists are blamed for a series of bombings, some successful, targeting U.S. government officials and businessmen Apr.-June.

The first nonstop transatlantic flight travels from Newfoundland to Ireland, June 14-15.

Following the Paris Peace Conference, the Treaty of Versailles is signed in France June 28, bringing World War I to a formal end.

A riot in Chicago, touched off when a black teenager was stoned and drowned in Lake Michigan July 27, ultimately kills 38 people and leaves 1,000 black families homeless. About 25 similar racially charged riots take place throughout the U.S.—including Knoxville, TN; Omaha, NE; and Washington, DC—in what becomes known as the "Red Summer."

In rural Elaine, AR, an estimated 100-250 people are killed Sept. 30-Oct. 2 as white vigilantes escalated violence in response to black sharecroppers' attempts to organize.

After returning to Washington from a national speaking tour, Pres. Woodrow Wilson suffers a debilitating stroke Oct. 2.

Congress passes the Volstead Act Oct. 27-28, overriding a veto by Pres. Wilson, to enforce alcohol prohibition.

About 249 foreign-born "radicals" are deported Dec. 21 to Soviet Russia on a ship nicknamed the "Soviet ark."

Art. Walter Gropius founds the Bauhaus school. John Covert's *Ex Act*, Marcel Duchamp's *L.H.O.O.Q.*, Man Ray's *Aerograph*, John Singer Sargent's *Gassed*.

Film. Charlie Chaplin, Douglas Fairbanks, D. W. Griffith, and Mary Pickford launch United Artists film studio to exercise control of their work. Felix the Cat makes his film debut. Griffith's *Broken Blossoms*, Oscar Micheaux's *The Homesteader*, Cecil B. DeMille's *Male and Female*.

Health and medicine. The outbreak commonly known as the Spanish flu begins to abate.

Literature. Sherwood Anderson's *Winesburg, Ohio*; Amy Lowell's *Pictures of the Floating World*.

Music. Sergei Prokofiev's comic opera *The Love for Three Oranges*, Jean Sibelius's *Symphony No. 5*.

Nonfiction. John Maynard Keynes's *The Economic Consequences of the Peace*.

Pop music. Irving Berlin's "A Pretty Girl Is Like a Melody," Irving Caesar and George Gershwin's "Swanee."

Science and technology. Ernest Rutherford discovers that radioactive particles could be used to "disintegrate" nuclei and provoke a nuclear reaction.

Sports. The Cincinnati Reds beat the Chicago White Sox in what becomes known as the rigged "Black Sox" World Series. Sir Barton is first to win horse racing's Triple Crown. Jack Dempsey wins the world heavyweight boxing title, which he'll hold for seven years.

Theater. An Actors' Equity strike closes many Broadway productions and wins concessions.

Miscellaneous. Molasses floods Boston, killing 21 people.

1969 — 50 Years Ago

Pres. Richard M. Nixon is inaugurated Jan. 20.

Soviet and Chinese troops skirmish along their shared border beginning in Mar., threatening larger military action.

U.S. bombers are diverted from Vietnam to Cambodia in a then-secret bombing campaign, starting Mar. 18.

U.S. Supreme Court Chief Justice Earl Warren retires upon swearing in his replacement, Warren Burger, June 23.

Patrons of the Stonewall Inn, a gay bar in New York City, resist a police raid June 28, leading to riots and sparking the formation of many LGBT rights groups.

Sen. Ted Kennedy (D, MA) July 18 drives his car off a bridge on Chappaquiddick Island, MA, and passenger Mary Jo Kopechne dies in the submerged vehicle.

U.S. astronaut Neil Armstrong, commander of the *Apollo 11* mission, becomes the first person to set foot on the Moon, July 20, followed by Edwin "Buzz" Aldrin.

Several members of a small cult known as the Manson Family kill five people, including actress Sharon Tate, Aug. 8-9, in Los Angeles.

WORLD ALMANAC EDITORS' PICKS
2018 Time Capsule

The editors of *The World Almanac* have selected the following items as representative of the year 2018.

- Two emergency alerts: Hawaii's mistaken message to residents Jan. 13 that a ballistic missile was inbound, and the first-ever presidential (test) alert sent Oct. 3.
- The Vikings-purple U.S. Bank Stadium seat smuggled home from Minnesota by a Philadelphia Eagles fan after the team's first Super Bowl win, over the Patriots, Feb. 4.
- Elon Musk's Tesla Roadster and spaceman mannequin, launched into space as the first payload on the Falcon Heavy rocket Feb. 6.
- A unified Korea flag, which North and South Korean athletes carried together at the 2018 Winter Olympic Games opening ceremonies in Pyeongchang, Feb. 9.
- Three rings: 1) from Arie Luyendyk's retracted proposal on *The Bachelor* finale in Mar.; 2) the one Prince Harry gave to Meghan Markle on a more permanent basis prior to the British royal wedding in May; and 3) the $93,000 ring singer Ariana Grande returned to *SNL*'s Pete Davidson after their engagement was broken in Oct.
- A sign from the student-led March for Our Lives demonstrations in favor of gun control Mar. 24.
- Stormy Daniels's nondisclosure agreement—regarding Pres. Donald Trump—about which the adult film star spoke repeatedly beginning in Mar. 2018.

- Diving equipment used to rescue 12 boys and their soccer coach July 8-10 from a flooded cave in Thailand, where the team had been trapped since June 23.
- Single-use plastic straws, which Starbucks July 9 announced it was eliminating from its stores by 2020.
- Design plans for a 3D-printed plastic gun, which gun rights activists hoped to distribute online beginning Aug. 1.
- Shares of Apple and Amazon, which in Aug.-Sept. became the first publicly traded U.S. companies with $1-trillion valuations.
- Philadelphia Flyers new furry orange mascot Gritty, introduced Sept. 24, and Cleveland Indians mascot Chief Wahoo, who was officially retired when the team's season ended Oct. 8.
- The 1982 calendar pages submitted to the Senate Judiciary Committee Sept. 26 by Judge Brett Kavanaugh after he was accused of sexual assault as a teenager during his U.S. Supreme Court confirmation process.
- Banksy's self-destructing artwork *Girl With Balloon*, which partially fed through a shredder built into its frame a short time after the piece sold for $1.4 million at Sotheby's Oct. 5.
- The Intergovernmental Panel on Climate Change's alarming special report, "Global Warming of 1.5°C," released Oct. 8, which ramped up warnings on the risk of an imminent crisis.

The British Army is deployed Aug. 14 to restore order in Londonderry and Belfast, Northern Ireland, marking the first military escalation of a 30-year period of conflict known as the Troubles.

The Woodstock music festival in Bethel, NY, draws about 400,000 people, Aug. 15-18.

Hurricane Camille Aug. 17-18 leaves 256 dead and causes $1.4 billion in damages.

A military junta led by Muammar al-Qaddafi seizes power in Libya Sept. 1.

Anti-Vietnam War demonstrations are held in cities across the U.S., marking Vietnam Moratorium day, Oct. 15; on Nov. 15, some 500,000 marched in Washington, DC.

In TV address Nov. 3, Pres. Nixon appeals to "silent majority" in U.S. to support his Vietnam policies.

The 1968 massacre of hundreds of civilians by U.S. troops at My Lai, South Vietnam, is made public Nov. 12.

American Indian activists take over and occupy Alcatraz Island, CA, for 19 months beginning Nov. 20.

The Altamont music festival in northern California draws about 300,000 people, Dec. 6, but the festival is marred by violence; several attendees die.

Congress passes legislation creating the Alternative Minimum Tax for high-income taxpayers Dec. 30.

Art. Group exhibition *January 5-31, 1969* draws focus to conceptual art. Francis Bacon's *Three Studies of Lucian Freud*.

Film. *Butch Cassidy and the Sundance Kid*; *Easy Rider*; *Hello, Dolly!* starring Barbra Streisand; *The Italian Job*; *The Love Bug*; *Midnight Cowboy*; *Paint Your Wagon*; *The Prime of Miss Jean Brodie* starring Maggie Smith; *They Shoot Horses, Don't They?*; *True Grit* starring John Wayne; *The Wild Bunch*.

Health and medicine. Dorothy Hodgkin determines structure of insulin. Denton Cooley performs first human transplant of a totally artificial heart.

Literature. A literary hoax intended to illustrate vulgarity and bad writing in popular fiction made *Naked Came the Stranger* a bestseller. Michael Crichton's *The Andromeda Strain*, John Fowles's *The French Lieutenant's Woman*, Ursula K. Le Guin's *The Left Hand of Darkness*, Mario Puzo's *The Godfather*, Philip Roth's *Portnoy's Complaint*, Kurt Vonnegut's *Slaughterhouse-Five*.

Music. Karlheinz Stockhausen's *Fresco*.

Nonfiction. *The American Heritage Dictionary of the English Language* is released. Maya Angelou's *I Know Why the Caged Bird Sings*, Elisabeth Kübler-Ross's *On Death and Dying*, Joe McGinniss's *The Selling of the President 1968*.

Pop music. The Archies' "Sugar, Sugar"; The Beatles' *Abbey Road*; Creedence Clearwater Revival's "Fortunate Son"; The 5th Dimension's "Aquarius/Let the Sunshine In"; Marvin Gaye's "I Heard It Through the Grapevine"; Jackson 5's "I Want You Back"; Led Zeppelin and *Led Zeppelin II*; Elvis Presley's "Suspicious Minds"; Rolling Stones' "Gimme Shelter"; The Temptations' "I Can't Get Next to You."

Science and technology. First U.S. automated teller machine (ATM) is installed at Chemical Bank branch in Rockville Centre, NY. Sony demonstrates video cassette prototype.

Sports. Joe Namath and the NY Jets upset the Baltimore Colts in Super Bowl III. NY Mets win World Series over the Baltimore Orioles. Australian Rod Laver wins all four Grand Slam men's singles tennis titles.

Television. *The Brady Bunch*, *Hee Haw*, and *Sesame Street* premiere; *Monty Python's Flying Circus* is first broadcast on BBC. *The Smothers Brothers Comedy Hour* is canceled.

Theater. *The Great White Hope* and *1776* win Tony Awards. *Coco* starring Katharine Hepburn; *Oh! Calcutta!*

Miscellaneous. Cleveland's polluted Cuyahoga River catches fire. "Zodiac killer" letters arrive at San Francisco-area newspapers, claiming responsibility for several killings.

1994 — 25 Years Ago

The North American Free Trade Agreement officially takes effect on Jan. 1.

A predawn earthquake Jan. 17 in the Los Angeles area kills 61.

White supremacist Byron De La Beckwith is convicted Feb. 5 of the 1963 murder of civil rights leader Medgar Evers in Jackson, MS.

CIA officer Aldrich Ames and wife Rosario Ames are charged, Feb. 21, with espionage on behalf of Russia.

U.S. troops in Mar. complete withdrawal from Somalia.

A federal jury in New York City Mar. 4 finds four defendants guilty of bombing the World Trade Center in 1993.

Leading Mexican presidential candidate Luis Donaldo Colosio is assassinated Mar. 23 at a campaign rally in Tijuana.

South Africa, emerging from apartheid, elects Nelson Mandela as the country's first black president in Apr.-May.

An estimated 800,000 Rwandans are killed, Apr.-June, in a genocidal campaign against the minority Tutsi ethnic group.

Several days after his ex-wife and her friend were found murdered, football star and actor O.J. Simpson leads police on a low-speed pursuit June 17, marking the beginning of a lengthy legal battle.

North Korean dictator Kim Il Sung dies July 8 and is succeeded by his son, Kim Jong Il.

Terrorists July 18 bomb a Jewish community center in Buenos Aires, Argentina, killing 85 people.

UN Security Council votes July 31 to authorize a U.S.-led invasion of Haiti to depose a military junta.

Kenneth Starr takes over as the independent counsel leading the Whitewater probe into Pres. Clinton, Aug. 5.

Clinton signs a major crime bill into law Sept. 13, incentivizing states to enact tougher mandatory minimum sentences.

Senate Majority Leader George Mitchell (D, ME), Sept. 26, declared Congress was ending its efforts to pass Clinton's health-care reform package.

Republicans gained control of both House and Senate in Nov. 8 elections.

Russian troops enter Chechnya in Dec. to end independence movement there, beginning a 20-month conflict.

Art. Edvard Munch's *The Scream* is stolen from Oslo museum (and recovered three months later). Kara Walker's *Gone: An Historical Romance of a Civil War as It Occurred b'tween the Dusky Thighs of One Young Negress and Her Heart*; Ai Weiwei's *Han Dynasty Urn With Coca-Cola Logo*.

Film. Jim Carrey stars in *Ace Ventura: Pet Detective*, *Dumb and Dumber*, and *The Mask*; *The Crow* starring Brandon Lee (who died in an accidental shooting on set); *Forrest Gump*; *Four Weddings and a Funeral*; *The Lion King*; *The Professional*; Quentin Tarantino's *Pulp Fiction*; *Reality Bites*; *The Shawshank Redemption*; *Speed*; *True Lies*.

Health and medicine. Former Pres. Ronald Reagan discloses his diagnosis of Alzheimer's disease.

Literature. Sharon Creech's *Walk Two Moons*; Michael Crichton's *Disclosure*; John Grisham's *The Chamber*; Rick Moody's *The Ice Storm*.

Music. Peter Maxwell Davies's *Symphony No. 5*.

Nonfiction. Three different "Magic Eye" books appeared on best-seller lists. George Chauncey's *Gay New York*, Richard Feynman's *Six Easy Pieces*, Doris Kearns Goodwin's *No Ordinary Time*, Charles Murray's *The Bell Curve*, Elizabeth Wurtzel's *Prozac Nation*.

Pop music. Nirvana's Kurt Cobain dies from suicide. All-4-One's "I Swear," Beastie Boys' "Sabotage," Beck's "Loser," Boyz II Men's "I'll Make Love to You," Jeff Buckley's "Hallelujah," Celine Dion's "The Power of Love," Green Day's *Dookie*, Lisa Loeb and Nine Stories' "Stay (I Missed You)," Notorious B.I.G.'s *Ready to Die*, Rednex's "Cotton Eye Joe," Salt-N-Pepa's "Whatta Man," Snoop Dogg's "Gin and Juice," Weezer's so-called *Blue Album*.

Science and technology. Netscape Navigator web browser debuts. Yahoo (originally "Jerry and David's Guide to the World Wide Web") is launched.

Sports. Buffalo Bills lose fourth straight Super Bowl. U.S. Olympic figure skater Tonya Harding is accused of involvement in an attack on fellow skater Nancy Kerrigan. World Series is canceled due to a players' strike.

Television. HGTV launches. NBC sitcom *Seinfeld* is among highest-rated programs; NBC's future ratings blockbusters *Friends* and *ER* premiere.

Theater. Disney's *Beauty and the Beast* begins a 13-year Broadway run.

Miscellaneous. Lorena Bobbitt is found not guilty for notorious 1993 attack on her husband. Michael Jackson and Lisa Marie Presley are married.

ECONOMICS

U.S. Gross Domestic Product, 1930-2017

Source: Bureau of Economic Analysis, U.S. Dept. of Commerce
(in billions of current dollars)

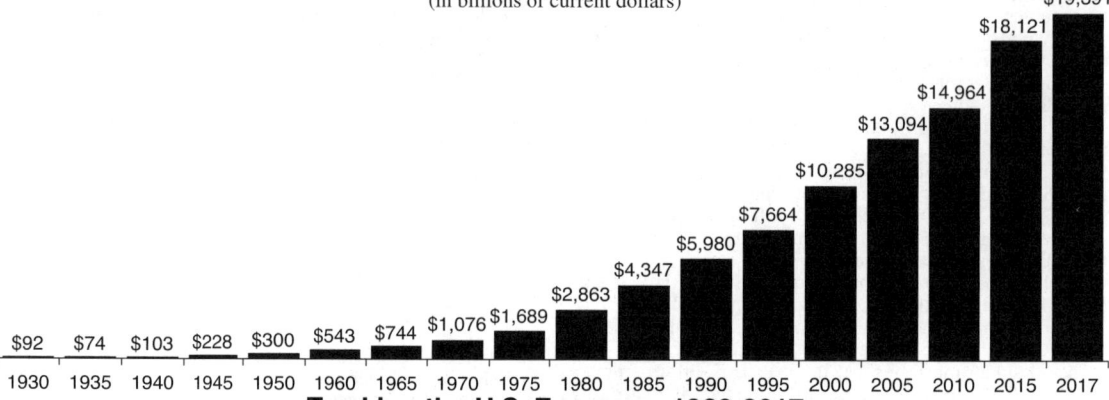

Tracking the U.S. Economy, 1960-2017

Source: Bureau of Economic Analysis, U.S. Dept. of Commerce
(in billions of current dollars, revised)

	1960	1970	1980	1990	2000	2010	2016	2017
Gross domestic product	$543.3	$1,075.9	$2,862.5	$5,979.6	$10,284.8	$14,964.4	$18,624.5	$19,390.6
Gross national product	546.4	1,082.3	2,896.7	6,014.3	10,321.8	15,170.3	18,821.6	19,607.4
Less: Consumption of fixed capital. . .	67.9	136.8	426.0	886.8	1,514.2	2,381.6	2,916.7	3,034.7
Equals: Net national product.	478.5	945.5	2,470.7	5,127.5	8,807.5	12,788.8	15,904.8	16,572.7
Less: Statistical discrepancy	−1.4	5.3	43.9	91.4	−99.5	49.2	−147.2	−37.1
Equals: National income	479.9	940.1	2,426.8	5,036.1	8,907.0	12,739.5	16,052.0	16,609.8
Less: Corporate profits with inventory valuation and capital consumption adjustments.	54.7	86.2	223.6	417.2	781.2	1,746.4	2,073.5	2,164.6
Less: Taxes on production and imports less subsidies[1]	43.4	86.6	190.5	398.0	662.7	1,001.2	1,226.2	1,268.8
Less: Contributions for government social insurance	16.4	46.4	166.2	410.1	705.8	984.1	1,245.3	1,302.6
Less: Net interest and miscellaneous payments on assets	10.7	40.5	186.2	450.1	565.0	489.4	570.6	586.4
Less: Business current transfer payments (net)	1.7	4.4	14.0	39.2	85.3	128.5	164.0	161.8
Less: Current surplus of government enterprises	0.5	−1.2	−5.1	3.2	10.7	−22.9	−10.1	−11.0
Plus: Personal income receipts on assets	44.3	112.7	386.0	991.2	1,453.5	1,739.6	2,377.8	2,442.4
Plus: Personal current transfer receipts	25.7	74.7	280.1	596.9	1,087.3	2,324.7	2,768.4	2,850.1
Equals: Personal income.	422.5	864.6	2,317.5	4,906.4	8,637.1	12,477.1	15,928.7	16,429.1
Addenda:								
Gross domestic income	544.6	1,070.5	2,818.6	5,888.2	10,384.3	14,915.2	18,771.6	19,427.7
Gross national income	547.8	1,076.9	2,852.8	5,922.9	10,421.3	15,121.1	18,968.7	19,644.5

Note: Numbers may not add up to totals due to rounding. (1) Subsidies are included net of the current surplus of government enterprises.

U.S. Gross Domestic Product, 2000-17

Source: Bureau of Economic Analysis, U.S. Dept. of Commerce

	Billions of current dollars				Billions of constant (2009) dollars			
	2000	2005	2016	2017	2000	2005	2016	2017
Gross domestic product . . .	$10,284.8	$13,093.7	$18,624.5	$19,390.6	$12,559.7	$14,234.2	$16,716.2	$17,096.2
Personal consumption expenditures	6,792.4	8,794.1	12,820.7	13,395.5	8,170.7	9,531.8	11,572.1	11,890.7
Goods.	2,452.9	3,080.3	4,121.4	4,295.3	2,588.3	3,177.2	4,072.2	4,229.4
Durable goods	912.6	1,127.2	1,411.0	1,473.8	758.3	1,046.9	1,595.1	1,701.6
Nondurable goods	1,540.3	1,953.1	2,710.4	2,821.5	1,863.6	2,132.3	2,514.3	2,575.0
Services	4,339.5	5,713.8	8,699.3	9,100.2	5,599.3	6,353.4	7,507.3	7,675.2
Gross private domestic investment.	2,033.8	2,527.1	3,057.2	3,212.8	2,375.5	2,672.6	2,858.3	2,952.3
Fixed investment.	1,979.2	2,467.5	3,022.1	3,197.2	2,316.2	2,611.0	2,803.4	2,915.9
Nonresidential	1,493.8	1,611.5	2,316.3	2,449.6	1,647.7	1,717.4	2,210.4	2,314.2
Structures	318.1	345.6	516.2	560.2	533.5	421.2	446.4	471.5
Equipment.	766.1	790.7	1,043.9	1,098.4	726.9	801.6	1,047.8	1,098.1
Intellectual property products.	409.5	475.1	756.2	791.0	426.1	495.0	720.4	748.8
Residential	485.4	856.1	705.9	747.6	637.9	872.6	587.4	597.9
Change in inventories.	54.5	59.6	35.1	15.7	66.2	64.3	33.4	15.2
Net exports of goods and services.	−375.8	−721.2	−521.2	−571.6	−477.8	−782.3	−586.3	−621.8
Exports.	1,096.8	1,308.9	2,214.6	2,344.0	1,258.4	1,381.9	2,120.1	2,191.4
Goods.	797.3	926.6	1,446.0	1,546.8	902.2	970.6	1,447.5	1,512.3
Services	299.6	382.3	768.5	797.1	354.3	410.3	672.8	681.3
Imports	1,472.6	2,030.1	2,735.8	2,915.6	1,736.2	2,164.2	2,706.3	2,813.2
Goods.	1,251.5	1,719.4	2,224.2	2,381.8	1,455.4	1,817.9	2,220.0	2,315.0
Services	221.2	310.7	511.6	533.8	276.4	341.1	484.0	496.2
Government consumption expenditures and gross investment.	1,834.4	2,493.7	3,267.8	3,353.8	2,498.2	2,826.2	2,900.2	2,903.3
Federal	632.4	946.3	1,231.5	1,260.7	817.7	1,034.8	1,114.6	1,116.4
National defense.	391.7	608.3	728.9	744.4	512.3	665.5	667.0	668.6
Nondefense	240.7	338.1	502.6	516.2	305.4	369.4	447.0	447.2
State and local	1,202.0	1,547.4	2,036.3	2,093.2	1,689.1	1,792.3	1,783.6	1,785.0

U.S. National Income by Type, 1930-2017

Source: Bureau of Economic Analysis, U.S. Dept. of Commerce
(in billions of current dollars)

	1930	1940	1950	1970	1980	1990	2000	2010	2016	2017
NATIONAL INCOME[1]	$83.1	$91.6	$267.0	$940.1	$2,426.8	$5,036.1	$8,907.0	$12,739.5	$16,052.0	$16,609.8
Employee compensation	47.2	52.8	158.5	625.1	1,626.2	3,342.7	5,856.6	7,961.4	9,978.6	10,309.3
Wages and salaries	46.2	49.9	147.3	551.6	1,373.4	2,741.2	4,825.9	6,377.5	8,085.2	8,353.2
Government	5.2	8.5	22.6	117.2	261.5	519.0	779.8	1,191.1	1,307.5	1,341.2
Other.	41.0	41.4	124.6	434.3	1,112.0	2,222.2	4,046.1	5,186.4	6,777.8	7,012.0
Supplements to wages and salaries. .	1.0	2.9	11.2	73.6	252.8	601.5	1,030.7	1,583.9	1,893.4	1,956.1
Employer contributions for employee pension and insurance funds. . . .	1.0	1.6	7.8	49.7	163.9	395.0	685.5	1,114.6	1,309.8	1,345.8
Employer contributions for government social insurance . . .	0.0	1.4	3.4	23.8	88.9	206.5	345.2	469.4	583.6	610.3
Proprietors' income with inventory valuation and capital consumption adjustments	10.9	12.2	37.5	77.8	171.6	354.4	757.8	1,032.7	1,341.9	1,386.0
Farm.	3.9	4.1	12.9	12.9	11.7	32.2	31.5	46.0	43.2	35.1
Nonfarm	7.0	8.2	24.6	64.9	159.9	322.3	726.3	986.7	1,298.7	1,350.9
Rental income of persons with capital consumption adjustments.	5.4	3.8	8.8	20.7	19.7	31.4	187.7	402.8	707.3	743.9
Corporate profits with inventory valuation and capital consumption adjustments	7.5	9.9	36.1	86.2	223.6	417.2	781.2	1,746.4	2,073.5	2,164.6
Taxes on corporate income	0.8	2.8	17.9	34.8	87.2	145.4	265.1	370.6	471.0	466.7
Profits after tax with inventory valuation and capital consumption adjustments.	6.7	7.0	18.1	51.5	136.4	271.7	516.1	1,375.9	1,602.4	1,697.9
Net dividends	5.5	4.0	8.8	24.3	64.1	169.1	384.7	564.0	981.9	990.2
Undistributed profits with inventory valuation and capital consumption adjustments	1.2	3.0	9.3	27.2	72.3	102.7	131.4	811.9	620.6	707.7
Net interest and miscellaneous payments.	4.8	3.3	3.2	40.5	186.2	450.1	565.0	489.4	570.6	586.4

Note: Numbers may not add up to totals because of rounding and incomplete enumeration. (1) National income is the aggregate of labor and property earnings that arise in the production of goods and services. It is the sum of employee compensation, proprietors' income, rental income, adjusted corporate profits, and net interest. It measures the total factor costs of goods and services produced by the economy. Income is measured before deduction of taxes. Total national income figures include adjustments not itemized.

U.S. National Income by Industry, 2000-17

Source: Bureau of Economic Analysis, U.S. Dept. of Commerce
(in billions of current dollars)

	2000	2005	2010	2014	2015	2016	2017
National income without capital consumption adjustment	$8,817.5	$11,338.8	$12,662.6	$15,081.9	$15,639.6	$15,941.7	$16,423.5
Domestic industries	8,780.5	11,246.3	12,456.7	14,847.4	15,435.1	15,744.6	16,206.7
Private industries	7,729.4	9,865.5	10,776.9	13,086.3	13,612.6	13,870.9	14,280.4
Agriculture, forestry, fishing, and hunting . . .	73.8	94.0	123.1	166.0	150.7	138.7	123.7
Mining.	90.7	175.0	184.7	272.8	180.1	110.6	144.4
Utilities	137.3	162.1	188.2	190.4	181.9	183.8	193.9
Construction	470.7	648.9	523.4	677.0	739.1	791.9	833.3
Manufacturing.	1,243.1	1,326.7	1,350.2	1,655.3	1,679.4	1,636.3	1,653.3
Durable goods	758.2	753.2	752.8	942.7	961.0	955.7	973.7
Nondurable goods	485.0	573.5	597.5	712.6	718.4	680.6	679.6
Wholesale trade	570.6	685.2	737.3	917.2	945.1	929.7	921.8
Retail trade	666.7	857.0	872.2	1,029.7	1,080.2	1,112.1	1,138.8
Transportation and warehousing	268.5	333.4	368.4	454.1	475.9	487.5	507.0
Information	306.8	423.0	442.7	543.5	585.3	596.6	611.2
Finance, insurance, real estate, rental, and leasing	1,472.6	1,969.1	2,142.5	2,609.8	2,766.6	2,832.7	2,919.2
Professional and business services[1]	1,115.7	1,428.1	1,697.4	2,040.9	2,170.0	2,268.4	2,360.5
Educational services, health care, and social assistance.	689.4	988.4	1,294.8	1,471.9	1,546.3	1,620.6	1,663.8
Arts, entertainment, recreation, accommodation, and food services	340.1	437.2	483.3	619.9	656.1	692.6	725.5
Other services, except government	283.3	337.4	368.4	437.7	455.9	469.5	483.8
Government	1,051.0	1,380.8	1,679.8	1,761.1	1,822.5	1,873.7	1,926.4
Rest of the world.	37.0	92.6	206.0	234.5	204.5	197.1	216.8

Note: Estimates based on the 2002 North American Industry Classification System (NAICS). (1) Consists of professional, scientific, and technical services; management of companies and enterprises; and administrative and waste management services.

Consumer Price Index

The Consumer Price Index (CPI) is a measure of the change in prices over time of one or more kinds of basic consumer goods and services. The overall CPI is based on the price of food, clothing, shelter, and fuels; transportation fares; charges for doctors' and dentists' services; drug prices; and the cost of other goods and services bought for day-to-day living. Since Jan. 1988, the base period for comparison has been 1982-84, which equals 100.0. The price of apparel, entertainment and recreation, and education and communication have not risen significantly, while the cost of medical care has more than quadrupled since 1982-84. The Consumer Price Index for all urban consumers (CPI-U) covers about 87% of the total U.S. population. The Bureau of Labor Statistics also publishes a separate Consumer Price Index for urban wage earners and clerical workers (CPI-W), which covers about 32% of the total U.S. population.

Distribution of U.S. Total Personal Income, 1930-2017

Source: Bureau of Economic Analysis, U.S. Dept. of Commerce
(in billions of current dollars, except for per capita figures)

Year	Personal income	Personal current taxes	Disposable personal income	Personal outlays	Personal savings	Savings as % of income[1]	Disposable personal income per capita Current dollars	Constant (2009) dollars
1930	$76.5	$1.6	$74.9	$71.6	$3.3	4.4%	$608	$6,411
1940	79.4	1.7	77.7	72.4	5.3	6.8	588	7,464
1950	233.9	18.9	215.0	195.0	20.0	9.3	1,417	10,033
1960	422.5	46.1	376.5	338.6	37.8	10.0	2,083	11,877
1970	864.6	103.1	761.5	665.5	96.1	12.6	3,713	16,643
1980	2,317.5	299.5	2,018.0	1,804.8	213.2	10.6	8,861	20,158
1990	4,906.4	594.7	4,311.8	3,976.3	335.4	7.8	17,235	25,555
2000	8,637.1	1,236.6	7,400.5	7,092.8	307.7	4.2	26,206	31,524
2005	10,614.0	1,213.2	9,400.8	9,157.7	243.1	2.6	31,760	34,424
2010	12,477.1	1,239.3	11,237.9	10,607.9	630.0	5.6	36,275	35,685
2011	13,254.5	1,453.2	11,801.4	11,091.2	710.1	6.0	37,813	36,307
2012	13,915.1	1,511.4	12,403.7	11,457.0	946.7	7.6	39,455	37,180
2013	14,073.7	1,677.8	12,395.8	11,775.7	620.1	5.0	39,153	36,411
2014	14,818.2	1,785.6	13,032.6	12,293.8	738.8	5.7	40,861	37,433
2015	15,553.0	1,937.9	13,615.0	12,786.7	828.4	6.1	42,372	38,702
2016	15,928.7	1,960.1	13,968.6	13,288.0	680.6	4.9	43,157	38,954
2017	16,429.1	2,048.6	14,380.4	13,893.0	487.4	3.4	44,114	39,158

Note: Personal income minus current taxes equals disposable income; disposable income minus outlays equals savings. Figures may not add up to totals because of rounding. (1) Personal savings as a percentage of disposable personal income.

U.S. Consumer Price Index, 1915-2017

Source: Bureau of Labor Statistics, U.S. Dept. of Labor

Excluding 2009, prices as measured by the U.S. Consumer Price Index have risen steadily since World War II. What cost $1.00 in 1982-84 cost about $0.10 in 1913, $0.18 in 1945, and $2.45 in 2017.

(Annual averages of monthly figures, for all urban consumers. **1982-84 = 100.**)

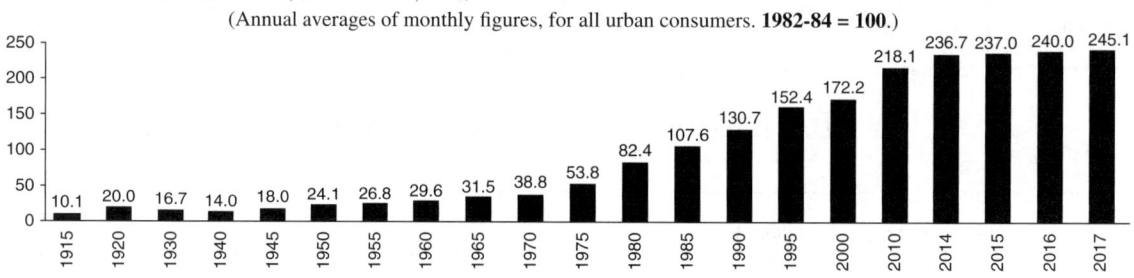

U.S. Consumer Price Index by Major Group, 1915-2017

Source: Bureau of Labor Statistics, U.S. Dept. of Labor
For all urban consumers. **1982-84 = 100**, unless otherwise noted.

Year	All items	Apparel	Food & beverages	Housing	Transpor- tation	Medical care	Entertainment & recreation[1]	Educ. & communi- cation[1]	Other goods & services
1915	10.1	15.3	—	—	—	—	—	—	—
1920	20.0	43.1	—	—	—	—	—	—	—
1930	16.7	24.2	—	—	—	—	—	—	—
1940	14.0	21.8	—	—	14.2	10.4	—	—	—
1945	18.0	31.4	—	—	15.9	11.9	—	—	—
1950	24.1	40.3	—	—	22.7	15.1	—	—	—
1955	26.8	42.9	—	—	25.8	18.2	—	—	—
1960	29.6	45.7	—	—	29.8	22.3	—	—	—
1965	31.5	47.8	—	—	31.9	25.2	—	—	—
1970	38.8	59.2	40.1	36.4	37.5	34.0	—	—	40.9
1975	53.8	72.5	60.2	50.7	50.1	47.5	—	—	53.9
1980	82.4	90.9	86.7	81.1	83.1	74.9	—	—	75.2
1985	107.6	105.0	105.6	107.7	106.4	113.5	—	—	114.5
1990	130.7	124.1	132.1	128.5	120.5	162.8	—	—	159.0
1995	152.4	132.0	148.9	148.5	139.1	220.5	94.5	92.2	206.9
2000	172.2	129.6	168.4	169.6	153.3	260.8	103.3	102.5	271.1
2005	195.3	119.5	191.2	195.7	173.9	323.2	109.4	113.7	313.4
2010	218.1	119.5	220.0	216.3	193.4	388.4	113.3	129.9	381.3
2012	229.6	126.3	233.7	222.7	217.3	414.9	114.7	133.8	394.4
2013	233.0	127.4	237.0	227.4	217.4	425.1	115.3	135.9	401.0
2014	236.7	127.5	242.4	233.2	215.9	435.3	115.5	137.5	408.1
2015	237.0	125.9	246.8	238.1	199.1	446.8	115.9	138.2	414.9
2016	240.0	126.0	247.7	244.0	194.9	463.7	117.0	139.1	423.1
2017	245.1	125.6	249.8	251.2	201.6	475.3	118.5	136.5	432.6

— = Comparable data not available. (1) Dec. 1997 = 100. Entertainment was reclassified as Recreation in 1997. Data is not seasonally adjusted.

Consumer Price Indexes by Region and Major Cities, 1990-2017

Source: Bureau of Labor Statistics, U.S. Dept. of Labor
For all urban consumers; % change not annualized. **1982-84 = 100**, unless otherwise noted.

Region and city	1990	1995	2000	2005	2010	2014	2015	2016	2017
U.S. city average	**130.7**	**152.4**	**172.2**	**195.3**	**218.1**	**236.7**	**237.0**	**240.0**	**245.1**
Northeast urban	**136.3**	**159.1**	**179.4**	**207.5**	**233.9**	**252.5**	**252.2**	**254.9**	**259.5**
Boston-Cambridge-Newton, MA-NH	138.9	158.6	183.6	216.4	237.4	255.2	256.7	260.5	267.0
New York-Newark-Jersey City, NY-NJ-PA	138.5	162.2	182.5	212.7	240.9	260.2	260.6	263.4	268.5
Philadelphia-Camden-Wilmington, PA-NJ-DE-MD	135.8	158.7	176.5	204.2	227.7	244.1	243.9	245.3	248.4
Pittsburgh, PA	126.2	149.2	168.0	189.8	215.4	239.0	240.6	244.6	250.1
Midwest urban	**127.4**	**148.4**	**168.3**	**188.4**	**208.0**	**225.4**	**224.2**	**226.1**	**229.9**
Chicago-Naperville-Elgin, IL-IN-WI	131.7	153.3	173.8	194.3	212.9	228.5	227.8	229.3	233.6
Cincinnati-Hamilton, OH-KY-IN.	126.5	146.2	164.8	181.6	204.7	224.1	223.3	226.4	229.9
Cleveland-Akron, OH	129.0	147.9	168.0	187.9	204.6	220.6	220.5	220.9	223.4
Detroit-Warren-Dearborn, MI	128.6	148.6	169.8	190.8	205.1	221.8	218.7	222.2	226.9
Kansas City, MO-KS	126.0	145.3	166.6	185.3	205.4	222.7	222.3	224.1	228.2
Milwaukee-Racine, WI	126.2	151.0	168.6	185.2	209.6	227.8	226.6	227.9	232.4
Minneapolis-St. Paul, MN-WI	127.0	147.0	170.1	193.1	211.7	232.0	230.6	234.1	239.2
St. Louis, MO-IL	128.1	145.2	163.1	186.2	203.2	220.2	219.3	221.1	224.7
South urban	**127.9**	**149.0**	**167.2**	**188.3**	**211.3**	**230.6**	**230.1**	**232.7**	**237.5**
Atlanta-Sandy Springs-Roswell, GA	131.7	150.9	170.6	188.9	203.5	221.0	221.6	225.5	232.9
Dallas-Fort Worth-Arlington, TX	125.1	144.9	164.7	184.7	201.6	218.4	217.5	220.7	226.1
Houston-The Woodlands-Sugar Land, TX	120.6	139.8	154.2	175.6	194.2	213.4	213.0	216.4	220.7
Miami-Fort Lauderdale-W. Palm Beach, FL	128.0	148.9	167.8	194.3	223.1	243.1	245.4	249.8	256.7
Tampa-St. Petersburg-Clearwater, FL[1]	111.7	129.7	145.7	168.5	193.5	210.8	211.6	214.0	219.5
Washington-Baltimore, DC-MD-VA-WV[2]	NA	NA	107.6	124.3	142.2	154.8	155.4	157.2	159.2
West urban	**131.5**	**153.5**	**174.8**	**198.9**	**221.2**	**240.2**	**243.0**	**247.7**	**254.7**
Anchorage, AK	118.6	138.9	150.9	171.8	195.1	215.8	216.9	217.8	218.9
Denver-Aurora-Lakewood, CO	120.9	147.9	173.2	190.9	212.4	237.2	240.0	246.6	255.0
Honolulu, HI	138.1	168.1	176.3	197.8	234.9	257.6	260.2	265.3	272.0
Los Angeles-Riverside-Orange County, CA	135.9	154.6	171.6	201.8	225.9	242.4	244.6	249.2	256.2
Phoenix-Mesa-Scottsdale, AZ[3]	NA	NA	NA	108.3	118.2	127.8	128.0	130.1	133.3
Portland-Salem, OR-WA	127.4	153.2	178.0	196.0	218.3	241.2	244.2	249.4	259.8
San Diego-Carlsbad, CA	138.4	156.8	182.8	220.6	245.5	265.1	269.4	274.7	283.0
San Francisco-Oakland-Hayward, CA	132.1	151.6	180.2	202.7	227.5	252.0	258.6	266.3	274.9
Seattle-Tacoma-Bellevue, WA	126.8	152.3	179.2	200.2	226.7	246.0	249.4	254.9	262.7

NA = Not available. **Note:** Data is not seasonally adjusted. (1) 1987 = 100. (2) Nov. 1996 = 100. (3) Dec. 2001 = 100.

World's Wealthiest Individuals, 2018

Source: *Forbes* magazine, Mar. 6, 2018

Rank	Name, country	Source of wealth	Net worth (bil)
1.	Jeff Bezos, U.S.	Amazon.com	$112.0
2.	Bill Gates, U.S.	Microsoft	90.0
3.	Warren Buffett, U.S.	Berkshire Hathaway	84.0
4.	Bernard Arnault, France	Louis Vuitton-Moët Hennessy	72.0
5.	Mark Zuckerberg, U.S.	Facebook	71.1
6.	Amancio Ortega, Spain	Zara	70.0
7.	Carlos Slim Helú, Mexico	Telecom	67.1
8.	Charles Koch, U.S.	Manufacturing, energy	60.0
8.	David Koch, U.S.	Manufacturing, energy	60.0
10.	Larry Ellison, U.S.	Oracle	58.5
11.	Michael Bloomberg, U.S.	Bloomberg, LP	50.0
12.	Larry Page, U.S.	Google	48.8
13.	Sergey Brin, U.S.	Google	47.5
14.	Jim Walton, U.S.	Walmart	46.4
15.	S. Robson Walton, U.S.	Walmart	46.2
16.	Alice Walton, U.S.	Walmart	46.0
17.	Ma Huateng, China	Internet media	45.3
18.	Françoise Bettencourt Meyers, France	L'Oréal cosmetics	42.2
19.	Mukesh Ambani, India	Petrochemicals, oil and gas	40.1
20.	Jack Ma, China	Alibaba	39.0
21.	Sheldon Adelson, U.S.	Casinos	38.5
22.	Steve Ballmer, U.S.	Microsoft	38.4
23.	Li Ka-shing, Hong Kong	Diversified	34.9
24.	Hui Ka Yan, China	Real estate	30.3
25.	Lee Shau Kee, Hong Kong	Real estate	30.3
26.	Wang Jianlin, China	Real estate	30.0
27.	Beate Heister and Karl Albrecht Jr., Germany	Aldi supermarkets	29.8
28.	Phil Knight, U.S.	Nike	29.6
29.	Jorge Paulo Lemann, Brazil	Beer	27.4
30.	François Pinault, France	Luxury goods	27.0
31.	Georg Schaeffler, Germany	Auto parts	$25.3
32.	Susanne Klatten, Germany	BMW, pharmaceuticals	25.0
32.	David Thomson, Canada	Media	25.0
34.	Jacqueline Mars, U.S.	Candy, pet food	23.6
34.	John Mars, U.S.	Candy, pet food	23.6
36.	Joseph Safra, Brazil	Banking	23.5
37.	Giovanni Ferrero, Italy	Nutella, chocolates	23.0
37.	Dietrich Mateschitz, Austria	Red Bull	23.0
39.	Michael Dell, U.S.	Dell computers	22.7
39.	Masayoshi Son, Japan	Internet, telecom	22.7
41.	Serge Dassault, France	Diversified	22.6
42.	Stefan Quandt, Germany	BMW	22.0
43.	Yang Huiyan, China	Real estate	21.9
44.	Paul Allen, U.S.	Microsoft, investments	21.7
45.	Leonardo Del Vecchio, Italy	Eyeglasses	21.2
46.	Dieter Schwarz, Germany	Retail	20.9
47.	Thomas Peterffy, U.S.	Discount brokerage	20.3
48.	Theo Albrecht Jr., Germany	Aldi, Trader Joe's	20.2
48.	Len Blavatnik, U.S.	Diversified	20.2
50.	He Xiangjian, China	Home appliances	20.1
50.	Lui Che Woo, Hong Kong	Casinos	20.1
52.	James Simons, U.S.	Hedge funds	20.0
52.	Henry Sy, Philippines	Diversified	20.0
54.	Elon Musk, U.S.	Tesla Motors	19.9
55.	Hinduja family, United Kingdom	Diversified	19.5
55.	Tadashi Yanai, Japan	Fashion retail	19.5
57.	Vladimir Lisin, Russia	Steel, transport	19.1
58.	Laurene Powell Jobs, U.S.	Apple, Disney	18.8
58.	Azim Premji, India	Software services	18.8
60.	Alexey Mordashov, Russia	Steel, investments	18.7

Median Income by Race, Hispanic Origin, and Sex, 1948-2017
Source: Current Population Survey, U.S. Census Bureau, U.S. Dept. of Commerce

Race, Hispanic origin, and year		Male			Female		
		Number with income (thous.)	Median income Current dollars	2017 dollars	Number with income (thous.)	Median income Current dollars	2017 dollars
All races	2017	114,849	$40,396	$40,396	116,618	$25,486	$25,486
	2016	113,158	38,869	39,705	115,371	24,892	25,427
	2010	105,191	32,205	36,286	107,220	20,775	23,408
	2000	98,504	28,343	40,458	101,704	16,063	22,929
	1990	88,220	20,293	37,018	92,245	10,070	18,369
	1980	78,661	12,530	35,589	80,826	4,920	13,974
	1970	65,008	6,670	37,682	51,647	2,237	12,638
	1960	55,172	4,080	29,635	36,526	1,261	9,159
	1950	47,585	2,570	22,908	24,651	953	8,495
	1948	47,370	2,396	21,357	22,725	1,009	8,994
White	2017	91,659	41,578	41,578	90,690	25,793	25,793
	2016	90,590	40,632	41,506	90,052	25,221	25,763
	2010	86,368	34,374	38,730	85,486	20,896	23,544
	2000	83,372	29,797	42,533	84,123	16,079	22,952
	1990	76,480	21,170	38,617	78,566	10,317	18,820
	1980	69,420	13,328	37,855	70,573	4,947	14,051
	1970	58,447	7,011	39,608	45,288	2,266	12,802
	1960	49,788	4,296	31,204	32,001	1,352	9,820
	1950	NA	2,709	24,147	NA	1,060	9,448
	1948	NA	2,510	22,373	NA	1,133	10,099
White, not Hispanic	2017	74,985	45,836	45,836	76,232	27,116	27,116
	2016	74,620	43,400	44,333	76,213	26,495	27,065
	2010	72,723	37,154	41,862	73,995	21,715	24,467
	2000	72,530	31,508	44,976	75,206	16,665	23,788
	1990	69,987	21,958	40,055	72,939	10,581	19,301
	1980	65,564	13,681	38,858	67,084	4,980	14,145
Black	2017	13,640	29,962	29,962	16,246	23,499	23,499
	2016	13,295	29,376	30,008	15,923	22,690	23,178
	2010	11,433	23,086	26,011	14,212	19,548	22,025
	2000	9,905	21,343	30,466	12,461	15,881	22,669
	1990	8,820	12,868	23,473	10,687	8,328	15,192
	1980	7,387	8,009	22,748	8,596	4,580	13,008
	1970	5,844	4,157	23,485	5,844	2,063	11,655
	1960	5,384	2,260	16,416	4,525	837	6,080
	1950	NA	1,471	13,112	NA	474	4,225
	1948	NA	1,363	12,149	NA	492	4,385
Asian	2017	7,190	47,213	47,213	7,239	28,324	28,324
	2016	6,901	45,829	46,815	6,996	26,548	27,119
	2010	5,406	35,121	39,571	5,604	23,552	26,536
	2000	4,303	30,833	44,012	4,192	17,356	24,775
	1990	2,235	19,394	35,378	2,333	11,086	20,223
Hispanic	2017	18,607	30,691	30,691	16,455	20,312	20,312
	2016	17,879	30,512	31,168	15,768	19,906	20,334
	2010	15,106	22,420	25,261	12,947	16,292	18,356
	2000	11,343	19,498	27,832	9,431	12,248	17,483
	1990	6,767	13,470	24,571	5,903	7,532	13,740
	1980	3,996	9,659	27,434	3,617	4,405	12,511

NA = Not available. **Note:** Income for persons 15 years of age and over beginning in Mar. 1980; 14 years of age and over as of Mar. of the following year for previous years. Beginning in 2010, totals for black and Asian include those who identified themselves as being that race in combination with some other race; totals for white are for those who identified as white alone. Before 2010, Asian category includes Pacific Islanders. Hispanic persons may be of any race.

Consumer Credit Outstanding, 2010-17
Source: Federal Reserve System
(in billions of dollars, not seasonally adjusted)

	2010	2016	2017		2010	2016	2017
TOTAL	$2,647.2	$3,643.7	$3,831.0	Credit unions	$36.3	$53.1	$58.4
Major holders				Nonfinancial business	25.5	23.1	22.2
Depository institutions	1,185.5	1,532.1	1,616.5	Pools of securitized assets[3] . . .	31.4	22.5	13.4
Finance companies	705.0	547.9	539.9	**Nonrevolving**	1,807.8	2,674.2	2,802.4
Credit unions	226.5	380.3	418.4	Depository institutions	520.8	686.9	708.5
Federal government[1]	363.8	1,049.3	1,145.6	Finance companies	623.5	522.4	513.4
Nonprofit and				Credit unions	190.1	327.2	360.0
educational institutions[2]	71.3	41.3	34.8	Federal government[1]	363.8	1,049.3	1,145.6
Nonfinancial business	44.8	42.8	41.8	Nonprofit and			
Pools of securitized assets[3] . . .	50.3	50.0	33.9	educational institutions[2]	71.3	41.3	34.8
Major types of credit, by holder				Nonfinancial business	19.3	19.7	19.7
Revolving	839.4	969.4	1,028.5	Pools of securitized assets[3] . . .	19.0	27.5	20.5
Depository institutions	664.7	845.2	908.0				
Finance companies	81.5	25.5	26.6				

(1) Includes student loans originated by the Dept. of Education under the Federal Direct Loan Program and the Perkins Loan Program, as well as Federal Family Education Program loans that the government purchased under the Ensuring Continued Access to Student Loans Act. (2) Includes student loans originated under the Federal Family Education Loan Program and held by educational institutions and nonprofit organizations. (3) Outstanding balances of pools upon which securities have been issued; these balances are no longer carried on the balance sheets of the loan originators.

Poverty Thresholds by Family Size, 1980-2017
Source: U.S. Census Bureau, U.S. Dept. of Commerce

	1980	1990	2000	2010	2017		1980	1990	2000	2010	2017
1 person	$4,190	$6,652	$8,791	$11,137	$12,488	3 people	$6,565	$10,419	$13,740	$17,373	$19,515
Under age 65. . . .	4,290	6,800	8,959	11,344	12,752	4 people	8,414	13,359	17,604	22,315	25,094
Age 65 or older . .	3,949	6,268	8,259	10,458	11,756	5 people	9,966	15,792	20,815	26,442	29,714
2 people	5,363	8,509	11,235	14,216	15,877	6 people	11,269	17,839	23,533	29,904	33,618
Householder						7 people	12,761	20,241	26,750	34,019	38,173
under age 65 . .	5,537	8,794	11,589	14,676	16,493	8 people	14,199	22,582	29,701	37,953	42,684
Householder age						9 or more people . .	16,896	26,848	35,150	45,224	50,081
65 or older.	4,983	7,905	10,418	13,194	14,828						

Note: Weighted averages; not used for computing poverty data.

Persons Below Poverty Level by Race and Hispanic Origin, 1960-2017
Source: U.S. Census Bureau, U.S. Dept. of Commerce

	Number below poverty level (mil)					% of subgroup below poverty level					Avg. income cutoff, family of 4 at poverty level[4]
Year	All races[1]	Asian[2]	White	Black[2]	Hispanic[3]	All races[1]	Asian[2]	White	Black[2]	Hispanic[3]	
1960	39.9	NA	28.3	NA	NA	22.2%	NA	17.8%	NA	NA	$3,022
1970	25.4	NA	17.5	7.5	NA	12.6	NA	9.9	33.5%	NA	3,968
1980	29.3	NA	19.7	8.6	3.5	13.0	NA	10.2	32.5	25.7%	8,414
1990	33.6	0.9	22.3	9.8	6.0	13.5	12.2%	10.7	31.9	28.1	13,359
1995	36.4	1.4	24.4	9.9	8.6	13.8	14.6	11.2	29.3	30.3	15,569
2000	31.6	1.3	21.6	8.0	7.7	11.3	9.9	9.5	22.5	21.5	17,604
2005	37.0	1.5	24.9	9.5	9.4	12.6	10.9	10.6	24.7	21.8	19,971
2010	46.3	2.1	31.1	11.6	13.5	15.1	12.0	13.0	27.4	26.5	22,315
2011	46.2	2.2	30.8	11.7	13.2	15.0	12.3	12.8	27.5	25.3	23,021
2012	46.5	2.1	30.8	11.8	13.6	15.0	11.4	12.7	27.1	25.6	23,492
2013	46.3	2.4	31.3	11.1	13.4	14.8	12.5	12.9	25.3	24.7	23,834
2014	46.7	2.3	31.1	11.6	13.1	14.8	11.5	12.7	26.0	23.6	24,230
2015	43.1	2.2	28.6	10.8	12.1	13.5	11.1	11.6	23.9	21.4	24,257
2016	40.6	2.1	27.1	10.0	11.1	12.7	9.9	11.0	21.8	19.4	24,563
2017	39.7	2.1	26.4	9.8	10.8	12.3	9.8	10.7	21.2	18.3	25,094

NA = Not available. **Note:** Because of a change in the definition of poverty, data prior to 1980 are not directly comparable to data since 1980. (1) Includes other races not shown separately. (2) Beginning in 2002, numbers include those who identified themselves as being Asian or black in combination with some other race. For 1990-2000, Asian includes Pacific Islanders. (3) Persons of Hispanic origin may be of any race. (4) Figures for 1960-80 for nonfarm families only.

Families Below Poverty Level by Status, Race, and Sex, 1980-2017
Source: U.S. Census Bureau, U.S. Dept. of Commerce
(numbers in thousands)

	All families			Married-couple families			Male householder, no wife present			Female householder, no husband present		
		Below poverty level			Below poverty level			Below poverty level			Below poverty level	
Year and race	Total	Number	Percent	Total	Number	Percent	Total	Number	Percent	Total	Number	Percent
All races												
1980	60,309	6,217	10.3%	49,294	3,032	6.2%	1,933	213	11.0%	9,082	2,972	32.7%
1990	66,322	7,098	10.7	52,147	2,981	5.7	2,907	349	12.0	11,268	3,768	33.4
2000	73,778	6,400	8.7	56,598	2,637	4.7	4,277	485	11.3	12,903	3,278	25.4
2010	79,559	9,400	11.8	58,667	3,681	6.3	5,649	892	15.8	15,243	4,827	31.7
2015	82,199	8,589	10.4	60,258	3,245	5.4	6,311	939	14.9	15,630	4,404	28.2
2016	82,854	8,081	9.8	60,821	3,096	5.1	6,452	847	13.1	15,581	4,138	26.6
2017	83,103	7,758	9.3	61,254	3,005	4.9	6,424	793	12.4	15,425	3,959	25.7
White[1]												
1980	52,710	4,195	8.0	44,860	2,437	5.4	1,584	149	9.4	6,266	1,609	25.7
1990	56,803	4,622	8.1	47,014	2,386	5.1	2,277	226	9.9	7,512	2,010	26.8
2000	61,330	4,333	7.1	49,473	2,181	4.4	3,283	332	10.1	8,574	1,820	21.2
2010	63,976	6,305	9.9	50,016	2,921	5.8	4,176	563	13.5	9,784	2,822	28.8
2015	65,272	5,743	8.8	50,588	2,539	5.0	4,643	610	13.1	10,042	2,594	25.8
2016	65,750	5,433	8.3	50,834	2,397	4.7	4,773	547	11.5	10,143	2,489	24.5
2017	65,678	5,170	7.9	51,039	2,287	4.5	4,740	520	11.0	9,898	2,363	23.9
Black[1]												
1980	6,317	1,826	28.9	3,392	474	14.0	291	52	17.7	2,634	1,301	49.4
1990	7,471	2,193	29.3	3,569	448	12.6	472	97	20.6	3,430	1,648	48.1
2000	8,731	1,686	19.3	4,214	266	6.3	732	120	16.3	3,785	1,300	34.3
2010	9,982	2,403	24.1	4,473	407	9.1	979	257	26.3	4,531	1,738	38.4
2015	10,342	2,175	21.0	4,670	369	7.9	1,099	256	23.3	4,573	1,551	33.9
2016	10,441	1,976	18.9	4,986	373	7.5	1,068	217	20.3	4,387	1,386	31.6
2017	10,543	1,912	18.1	5,015	351	7.0	1,097	201	18.3	4,432	1,361	30.7
Hispanic[2]												
1980	3,235	751	23.2	2,365	363	15.3	164	26	16.0	706	362	51.3
1990	4,981	1,244	25.0	3,454	605	17.5	341	66	19.4	1,186	573	48.3
2000	8,017	1,540	19.2	5,426	772	14.2	765	104	13.6	1,826	664	36.4
2010	11,284	2,739	24.3	7,065	1,221	17.3	1,241	248	20.0	2,978	1,270	42.6
2015	12,761	2,502	19.6	8,003	1,077	13.5	1,473	259	17.6	3,284	1,166	35.5
2016	13,017	2,253	17.3	8,250	970	11.8	1,539	229	14.9	3,228	1,055	32.7
2017	13,201	2,156	16.3	8,370	861	10.3	1,497	206	13.8	3,335	1,089	32.7

Note: The Census Bureau revised race categories in 2002, so data after 2002 are not directly comparable with data for previous years. (1) Beginning in 2010, totals for white include only those who identified themselves as white alone; totals for black include those who identified themselves as black alone or in combination with some other race. (2) Persons of Hispanic origin may be of any race.

Poverty Rates by State, 1990-2017

Source: U.S. Census Bureau, U.S. Dept. of Commerce

The poverty rate is the proportion of the population with income below the government's official poverty level, which is the same nationwide but is adjusted each year for inflation. As the U.S. economy recovered from the 2008 global recession, the poverty rate ticked down nationally, but still remains higher than it was in 2000, when just 11.3% of the population lived below the poverty line.

State	1990	2000	2010	2016	2017	State	1990	2000	2010	2016	2017
Alabama.......	19.2%	13.3%	17.2%	16.2%	15.0%	Montana	16.3%	14.1%	14.5%	11.7%	9.7%
Alaska........	11.4	7.6	12.5	12.6	14.4	Nebraska	10.3	8.6	10.2	9.6	10.4
Arizona........	13.7	11.7	18.8	16.1	13.2	Nevada........	9.8	8.8	16.6	10.1	13.7
Arkansas.......	19.6	16.5	15.3	16.0	14.8	New Hampshire..	6.3	4.5	6.5	6.4	6.6
California	13.9	12.7	16.3	13.9	12.4	New Jersey.....	9.2	7.3	11.1	9.4	8.6
Colorado.......	13.7	9.8	12.3	8.5	7.7	New Mexico	20.9	17.5	18.3	17.8	18.6
Connecticut.....	6.0	7.7	8.6	9.8	10.9	New York	14.3	13.9	16.0	11.9	13.4
Delaware	6.9	8.4	12.2	11.6	9.2	North Carolina ..	13.0	12.5	17.4	13.6	14.5
Dist. of Columbia	21.1	15.2	19.5	16.3	13.6	North Dakota ...	13.7	10.4	12.6	11.1	11.3
Florida.........	14.4	11.0	16.0	13.0	13.7	Ohio	11.5	10.0	15.4	13.7	12.7
Georgia........	15.8	12.1	18.8	15.4	13.3	Oklahoma......	15.6	14.9	16.3	14.6	12.6
Hawaii.........	11.0	8.9	12.4	9.3	10.3	Oregon	9.2	10.9	14.3	11.8	10.2
Idaho..........	14.9	12.5	13.8	11.1	11.7	Pennsylvania ...	11.0	8.6	12.2	11.1	11.2
Illinois	13.7	10.7	14.1	12.1	10.9	Rhode Island ...	7.5	10.2	14.0	11.4	12.2
Indiana	13.0	8.5	16.3	11.8	11.4	South Carolina ..	16.2	11.1	16.9	14.1	15.6
Iowa	10.4	8.3	10.3	9.8	9.1	South Dakota ...	13.3	10.7	13.6	14.5	10.4
Kansas........	10.3	8.0	14.5	11.2	14.7	Tennessee	16.9	13.5	16.7	14.9	11.5
Kentucky.......	17.3	12.6	17.7	15.2	14.4	Texas	15.9	15.5	18.4	13.8	13.4
Louisiana	23.6	17.2	21.5	20.2	21.4	Utah	8.2	7.6	10.0	8.6	8.6
Maine	13.1	10.1	12.6	12.7	12.0	Vermont	10.9	10.0	10.8	9.6	10.2
Maryland.......	9.9	7.4	10.9	7.1	7.8	Virginia	11.1	8.3	10.7	11.4	10.3
Massachusetts ..	10.7	9.8	10.9	9.6	10.6	Washington.....	8.9	10.8	11.6	11.0	9.9
Michigan.......	14.3	9.9	15.7	11.1	12.7	West Virginia ...	18.1	14.7	16.8	18.0	17.3
Minnesota......	12.0	5.7	10.8	8.7	9.2	Wisconsin......	9.3	9.3	10.1	10.7	9.5
Mississippi	25.7	14.9	22.5	21.1	18.3	Wyoming.......	11.0	10.8	9.6	10.9	12.4
Missouri	13.4	9.2	15.0	13.0	11.1	**United States...**	**13.5**	**11.3**	**15.1**	**12.7**	**12.3**

Income Inequality in the U.S., 1970-2017

Source: U.S. Census Bureau, U.S. Dept. of Commerce

Top earners' share of income has grown considerably over the past half century. In 1970, the richest 5% of Americans earned 16.6% percent of all income while the share earned by the poorest 20% was 4.1%. By 2017, the top 5% took home 22.3% of income and the poorest 20% earned just 3.1% of the total. The middle class's share declined from 17.4% to 14.3% over the same period.

Income group	Income in 2017[1]	Percentage of income earned by each quintile											
		1970	1975	1980	1985	1990	1995	2000	2005	2010	2015	2016	2017
Lowest 20%	$13,258	4.1%	4.3%	4.2%	3.9%	3.8%	3.7%	3.6%	3.4%	3.3%	3.1%	3.1%	3.1%
Second quintile..	35,401	10.8	10.4	10.2	9.8	9.6	9.1	8.9	8.6	8.5	8.2	8.3	8.2
Middle 20%	61,564	17.4	17.0	16.8	16.2	15.9	15.2	14.8	14.6	14.6	14.3	14.2	14.3
Fourth quintile...	99,030	24.5	24.7	24.7	24.4	24.0	23.3	23.0	23.0	23.4	23.2	22.9	23.0
Highest 20%....	221,846	43.3	43.6	44.1	45.6	46.6	48.7	49.8	50.4	50.3	51.1	51.5	51.5
Top 5%	385,289	16.6	16.5	16.5	17.6	18.5	21.0	22.1	22.2	21.3	22.1	22.6	22.3

(1) Mean household income in 2017.

Temporary Assistance for Needy Families (TANF), 1997-2016

Source: Office of Family Assistance, Admin. for Children and Families, U.S. Dept. of Health and Human Services

Year	Total TANF expenditures (mil)	Average number of monthly cash beneficiaries			Year	Total TANF expenditures (mil)	Average number of monthly cash beneficiaries		
		Families	Recipients	Children			Families	Recipients	Children
1997	$19,010.2	3,936,610	10,935,125	NA	2007	$26,922.0	1,697,432	3,957,330	3,047,043
1998	22,036.4	3,199,720	8,700,149	NA	2008	28,129.7	1,726,799	4,041,292	3,084,413
1999	23,114.6	2,673,610	7,187,658	NA	2009	30,577.8	1,847,152	4,364,979	3,280,150
2000	24,780.7	2,229,315	5,833,043	4,303,943	2010	33,255.5	1,847,152	4,364,979	3,280,150
2001	25,667.4	2,087,646	5,335,891	3,968,499	2011	30,264.1	1,921,243	4,599,846	3,435,218
2002	25,414.4	2,038,373	5,067,963	3,791,560	2012	28,867.3	1,876,426	4,476,476	3,351,971
2003	26,340.0	2,009,666	4,900,889	3,693,056	2013	29,147.1	1,751,067	4,102,491	3,091,076
2004	25,821.2	1,965,960	4,722,588	3,581,448	2014	29,350.9	1,652,996	3,894,213	2,934,582
2005	25,580.1	1,901,810	4,495,175	3,428,885	2015	29,295.9	1,333,707	4,176,387	2,370,198
2006	25,593.8	1,789,460	4,179,295	3,207,216	2016	28,321.2	1,206,820	3,886,868	2,144,955

NA = Not available.

Adults Receiving TANF Funds by Employment Status, 2016

Source: Office of Family Assistance, Admin. for Children and Families, U.S. Dept. of Health and Human Services

State	Adults	Employed	State	Adults	Employed	State	Adults	Employed	State	Adults	Employed
AL.......	5,531	38.6%	IL........	5,482	63.5%	NE.......	1,530	61.2%	SC.......	3,308	35.8%
AK.......	2,590	31.5	IN........	1,628	26.4	NV.......	5,392	41.1	SD.......	602	15.1
AZ.......	3,939	18.9	IA	6,672	41.4	NH	1,091	26.8	TN.......	16,915	29.4
AR.......	2,178	34.5	KS.......	2,899	45.0	NJ.......	10,545	17.0	TX.......	7,772	29.9
CA......	241,725	29.3	KY.......	7,739	28.8	NM	7,179	28.4	UT.......	1,708	16.2
CO	12,958	52.4	LA	2,043	19.2	NY.......	66,676	33.1	VT.......	1,454	19.6
CT.......	6,217	29.6	ME	2,434	24.6	NC	4,321	34.3	Virgin Isls.	228	3.4
DE.......	1,272	27.8	MD	12,970	12.7	ND	466	51.1	VA........	11,168	31.3
DC	3,294	29.1	MA	19,081	11.0	OH	13,298	23.3	WA.......	18,377	19.5
FL.......	12,162	12.3	MI	7,100	40.6	OK	2,280	10.5	WV.......	2,359	20.5
GA	2,453	15.9	MN	9,894	42.7	OR	10,602	11.1	WI.......	8,338	35.0
Guam	352	6.2	MS	2,651	21.0	PA.......	38,079	24.7	WY.......	200	22.4
HI	5,730	38.7	MO	10,117	19.7	Puerto Rico	8,168	3.3	**U.S. total**	**637,472**	**28.2**
ID	62	6.4	MT	1,642	26.6	RI	2,602	18.3			

TANF = Temporary Assistance for Needy Families.

Selected Personal Consumption Expenditures in the U.S., 1990-2017

Source: Bureau of Economic Analysis, U.S. Dept. of Commerce
(in billions of dollars)

	1990	2000	2005	2010	2015	2016	2017
Personal consumption expenditures	$3,809.0	$6,762.1	$8,747.1	$10,185.8	$12,294.5	$12,766.9	$13,321.4
GOODS	1,491.3	2,453.2	3,082.9	3,317.8	3,919.7	3,996.3	4,156.1
Durable goods	497.1	912.6	1,128.6	1,049.0	1,306.6	1,346.6	1,406.5
Motor vehicles and parts	205.1	363.2	410.0	344.5	473.9	483.7	498.2
New motor vehicles	134.7	210.7	248.9	182.3	276.2	273.5	280.1
Net purchases of used motor vehicles	42.2	110.7	110.5	105.6	127.9	138.6	145.3
Motor vehicle parts and accessories	28.3	41.8	50.6	56.6	69.8	71.6	72.9
Furnishings, durable household equipment	120.9	208.1	271.3	240.9	288.1	301.3	315.4
Furniture and furnishings	69.2	121.7	160.6	140.5	171.1	180.0	189.6
Household appliances	23.7	34.1	45.1	44.1	52.7	54.3	55.3
Glassware, tableware, and household utensils	18.4	35.3	44.6	36.4	37.0	38.4	39.8
Recreational goods and vehicles	105.6	230.9	306.4	298.6	343.6	357.3	378.1
Video, audio, photo, and info-processing equip.	56.1	127.7	174.1	182.8	202.1	207.4	217.8
Sporting equipment, guns, ammunition	19.9	39.1	50.9	52.8	64.8	67.8	69.0
Sports and recreational vehicles	16.6	34.9	49.1	35.8	52.0	56.4	64.8
Recreational books	10.9	24.4	27.0	22.6	19.2	20.0	20.8
Other durable goods	65.5	110.4	141.0	165.0	201.0	204.3	214.7
Jewelry and watches	30.3	49.1	59.8	60.9	72.8	73.2	76.9
Therapeutic appliances and equipment	18.4	32.2	43.2	52.4	61.7	64.5	68.8
Nondurable goods	994.2	1,540.6	1,954.3	2,268.9	2,613.1	2,649.7	2,749.6
Food and beverages purchased for off-premises consumption	391.2	540.6	668.2	786.9	921.0	944.2	965.8
Food and nonalcoholic beverages	341.2	463.1	575.3	678.6	795.0	812.1	829.5
Alcoholic beverages	49.3	77.1	92.6	107.9	125.4	131.6	135.8
Clothing and footwear	195.2	280.8	310.5	316.6	366.3	373.0	379.7
Women's and girls' clothing	94.5	132.7	149.6	149.2	170.6	173.3	176.2
Men's and boys' clothing	57.4	85.9	86.3	83.7	97.4	98.4	100.9
Children's and infants' clothing	8.1	11.4	15.4	18.0	18.1	18.3	18.6
Other clothing materials and footwear	35.3	50.8	59.1	65.8	80.2	83.1	83.9
Gasoline and other energy goods	124.2	184.5	283.8	336.7	309.2	274.9	307.0
Other nondurable goods	283.6	534.7	691.8	828.7	1,016.6	1,057.6	1,097.2
Pharmaceutical and other medical products	59.1	159.0	248.5	326.1	445.8	467.9	489.1
Recreational items	50.9	91.9	112.6	129.9	156.4	162.3	169.2
Household supplies	54.2	86.7	102.0	108.2	126.4	130.9	135.8
Personal care products	39.3	68.5	88.0	106.0	125.2	129.5	133.0
Tobacco	41.0	68.5	76.7	97.9	94.4	93.8	92.1
Magazines, newspapers, and stationery	36.5	56.6	58.0	52.2	61.5	66.5	71.4
SERVICES	2,317.7	4,309.0	5,664.2	6,868.0	8,374.8	8,770.6	9,165.3
Housing and utilities	696.5	1,198.6	1,583.6	1,903.9	2,257.9	2,353.0	2,447.8
Housing	570.6	1,010.5	1,332.5	1,604.0	1,940.6	2,038.3	2,123.8
Rental of tenant-occupied nonfarm housing	150.8	227.9	268.3	372.6	515.9	546.5	563.3
Imputed rental of owner-occupied nonfarm housing	412.8	768.9	1,044.3	1,214.2	1,405.7	1,473.2	1,540.9
Household utilities	125.9	188.1	251.1	299.9	317.2	314.7	324.0
Water supply and sanitation	27.1	50.4	61.3	78.5	91.6	93.8	97.4
Electricity	71.8	98.4	128.5	166.8	177.6	177.0	177.8
Natural gas	27.0	39.3	61.3	54.6	48.1	43.8	48.8
Health care	506.2	918.4	1,320.5	1,699.6	2,062.5	2,171.6	2,271.2
Outpatient services	232.1	436.6	624.4	774.6	936.3	984.8	1,029.2
Physician services	134.8	229.2	333.9	410.5	498.5	526.3	549.1
Dental services	32.4	63.6	87.9	104.5	117.0	122.8	126.7
Paramedical services	64.9	143.8	202.6	259.6	320.8	335.7	353.4
Hospitals	228.8	393.9	577.2	769.9	953.1	1,006.9	1,055.2
Nursing homes	45.3	87.9	119.0	155.1	173.1	179.8	186.8
Transportation services	126.4	261.3	283.9	305.2	399.3	417.8	437.0
Motor vehicle services	87.2	174.4	193.6	201.0	256.2	274.4	287.6
Motor vehicle maintenance and repair	73.9	112.5	136.9	136.7	163.3	173.5	181.0
Public transportation	39.2	86.9	90.2	104.2	143.1	143.4	149.4
Recreation services	121.8	254.4	328.1	403.7	493.5	516.1	541.8
Membership clubs, sports centers, parks, theaters, museums	49.7	91.9	117.9	146.1	178.5	189.2	201.8
Audio-video, photographic, and information processing equipment services	37.9	70.1	81.1	106.4	135.0	138.2	140.8
Gambling	23.7	67.6	96.1	109.4	125.8	130.1	136.0
Food services and accommodations	262.7	408.8	533.6	635.7	832.7	873.5	897.3
Purchased meals and beverages	228.3	344.9	446.0	521.8	677.5	711.9	732.3
Accommodations	27.6	55.0	75.5	98.6	136.2	141.4	144.3
Financial services and insurance	230.8	543.0	659.0	754.4	963.1	989.1	1,060.4
Financial services	119.0	336.7	386.9	465.5	610.0	624.9	679.7
Insurance	111.7	206.3	272.2	289.0	353.1	364.3	380.7
Other services	297.5	566.5	745.1	871.1	998.8	1,057.4	1,106.5
Telecommunication services	60.7	126.4	137.7	147.6	152.7	157.3	157.3
Internet access	0.1	12.0	19.1	40.5	65.2	73.3	76.1
Higher education	34.7	76.8	110.9	155.0	172.4	176.2	181.5
Nursery, elementary, and secondary schools	14.8	24.1	29.6	35.6	41.4	45.0	47.7
Commercial and vocational schools	11.1	24.3	30.3	39.9	47.3	48.8	51.6
Professional and other services	67.7	113.0	148.4	158.9	179.9	186.2	193.9
Personal care and clothing services	44.5	80.4	103.3	115.8	141.4	148.3	156.1
Social services and religious activities	41.2	81.1	110.2	139.0	171.5	181.6	194.8
Household maintenance	25.4	49.2	56.9	61.6	79.4	81.0	80.4

Note: Subtotals may not add up to totals due to rounding or incomplete enumeration.

Leading U.S. Businesses, 2017

Source: *Fortune* magazine, June 2018

(ranked by revenues, in millions of dollars)

Industry/company (rank)	Revenues
Advertising, Marketing	
Omnicom Group (188)	$15,274
Interpublic Group (359)	7,882
Aerospace	
Boeing (27)	$93,392
United Technologies (51)	59,837
Lockheed Martin (59)	51,048
General Dynamics (99)	30,973
Northrop Grumman (118)	25,803
Raytheon (119)	25,348
Textron (208)	14,198
Arconic (225)	12,960
L3 Technologies (276)	11,002
Huntington Ingalls Industries (381)	7,441
Spirit AeroSystems Holdings (405)	6,983
Harris (407)	6,939
Rockwell Collins (415)	6,822
Airlines	
American Airlines Group (71)	$42,207
Delta Air Lines (75)	41,244
United Continental Holdings (81)	37,736
Southwest Airlines (142)	21,171
Alaska Air Group (355)	7,933
JetBlue Airways (402)	7,015
Apparel	
Nike (89)	$34,350
VF (242)	12,400
PVH (332)	8,915
Ralph Lauren (421)	6,653
Hanesbrands (433)	6,478
Automotive Retailing, Services	
AutoNation (138)	$21,535
Penske Automotive Group (139)	21,389
CarMax (174)	16,637
Group 1 Automotive (273)	11,124
Lithia Motors (294)	10,087
Sonic Automotive (298)	9,867
Avis Budget Group (333)	8,848
Hertz Global Holdings (335)	8,803
Asbury Automotive Group (434)	6,457
Beverages	
Coca-Cola (87)	$35,410
Molson Coors Brewing (275)	11,003
Constellation Brands (386)	7,332
Dr Pepper Snapple Group (418)	6,690
Building Materials, Glass	
Builders FirstSource (400)	$7,034
Owens Corning (442)	6,384
Chemicals	
DowDuPont (47)	$62,683
Sherwin-Williams (190)	14,984
PPG Industries (191)	14,967
Monsanto (199)	14,640
Ecolab (215)	13,838
Praxair (264)	11,437
Huntsman (282)	10,592
Eastman Chemical (310)	9,549
Air Products & Chemicals (345)	8,442
Westlake Chemical (352)	8,041
Mosaic (382)	7,409
Olin (448)	6,268
Chemours (451)	6,183
Celanese (455)	6,140
Commercial Banks	
JPMorgan Chase (20)	$113,899
Bank of America Corp. (24)	100,264
Wells Fargo (26)	97,741
Citigroup (32)	87,966
Morgan Stanley (67)	43,642
Goldman Sachs Group (70)	42,254
Capital One Financial (101)	29,999
U.S. Bancorp (122)	23,996
PNC Financial Services (165)	18,035
Bank of New York Mellon (175)	16,621
BB&T Corp. (250)	12,156
State Street Corp. (259)	11,774
Discover Financial Services (263)	11,545
SunTrust Banks (303)	9,741
Fifth Third Bancorp (366)	7,713
KeyCorp (412)	6,868
Citizens Financial Group (435)	6,454
Regions Financial (460)	6,093

Industry/company (rank)	Revenues
M&T Bank Corp. (467)	$6,019
Northern Trust (486)	5,716
Computer Software	
Microsoft (30)	$89,950
Oracle (82)	37,728
salesforce.com (285)	10,480
Adobe Systems (389)	7,302
Computers, Office Equipment	
Apple (4)	$229,234
Dell Technologies (35)	78,660
HP (58)	52,056
Hewlett-Packard Enterprise (107)	28,871
Western Digital (158)	19,093
Xerox (291)	10,265
NCR (432)	6,516
NetApp (495)	5,519
Construction, Farm Machinery	
Caterpillar (65)	$45,462
Deere (102)	29,738
Paccar (155)	19,456
Navistar International (342)	8,570
AGCO (347)	8,307
Oshkosh (414)	6,830
Diversified Financials	
Fannie Mae (21)	$112,394
Freddie Mac (38)	74,676
American Express (86)	35,583
INTL FCStone (103)	29,424
Icahn Enterprises (136)	21,744
Synchrony Financial (173)	16,695
Marsh & McLennan (212)	14,024
Jefferies Financial Group (241)	12,408
Ameriprise Financial (252)	12,075
Ally Financial (299)	9,866
Voya Financial (307)	9,660
Blackstone Group (398)	7,119
Arthur J. Gallagher (454)	6,160
Diversified Outsourcing Services	
Aramark (200)	$14,604
ADP (243)	12,380
Conduent (466)	6,022
ABM Industries (498)	5,454
Cintas (500)	5,429
Electronics, Electrical Equipment	
Honeywell (77)	$40,534
Whirlpool (140)	21,253
Corning (293)	10,116
Rockwell Automation (445)	6,311
Energy	
World Fuel Services (91)	$33,696
NGL Energy Partners (223)	13,022
NRG Energy (269)	11,275
Calpine (336)	8,752
Williams (353)	8,031
UGI (457)	6,121
Cheniere Energy (489)	5,601
Vistra Energy (499)	5,430
Engineering, Construction	
Fluor (153)	$19,521
AECOM (164)	18,203
Jacobs Engineering Group (297)	10,023
Quanta Services (316)	9,467
Peter Kiewit Sons' (339)	8,678
EMCOR Group (368)	7,688
MasTec (428)	6,607
Entertainment	
Disney (55)	$55,137
Time Warner (98)	31,271
Twenty-First Century Fox (109)	28,500
CBS (197)	14,710
Viacom (221)	13,263
Live Nation Entertainment (290)	10,337
Liberty Media (377)	7,594
Activision Blizzard (401)	7,017
Discovery (409)	6,873
iHeartMedia (452)	6,178
Financial Data Services	
Visa (161)	$18,358
PayPal Holdings (222)	13,094
Mastercard (236)	12,497

Industry/company (rank)	Revenues
First Data (254)	$12,052
Fidelity National Information Services (326)	9,123
Alliance Data Systems (365)	7,719
S&P Global (463)	6,063
Fiserv (487)	5,696
Western Union (494)	5,524
Food Consumer Products	
PepsiCo (45)	$63,525
Kraft Heinz (114)	26,232
Mondelēz International (117)	25,896
General Mills (182)	15,620
Land O'Lakes (216)	13,740
Kellogg (226)	12,923
Conagra Brands (321)	9,235
Hormel Foods (323)	9,168
Campbell Soup (358)	7,890
Dean Foods (362)	7,795
Hershey (379)	7,515
J.M. Smucker (383)	7,392
TreeHouse Foods (446)	6,307
Food & Drug Stores	
Kroger (17)	$122,662
Walgreens Boots Alliance (19)	118,214
Albertsons Cos. (53)	59,678
Publix Super Markets (88)	34,837
Rite Aid (94)	32,845
Supervalu (180)	16,009
Food Production	
Archer Daniels Midland (48)	$60,828
Tyson Foods (80)	38,260
CHS (96)	31,935
Ingredion (478)	5,832
Seaboard (481)	5,809
Food Services	
McDonald's (131)	$22,820
Starbucks (132)	22,387
Darden Restaurants (396)	7,170
Yum China Holdings (397)	7,144
Yum Brands (472)	5,878
Forest & Paper Products	
Weyerhaeuser (394)	$7,196
General Merchandisers	
Walmart (1)	$500,343
Costco (15)	129,025
Target (39)	71,879
Macy's (120)	24,837
Kohl's (157)	19,095
Sears Holdings (172)	16,702
Nordstrom (183)	15,478
J.C. Penney (235)	12,506
Dillard's (439)	6,423
Health Care: Insurance & Managed Care	
UnitedHealth Group (5)	$201,159
Anthem (29)	90,039
Aetna (49)	60,535
Humana (56)	53,767
Centene (61)	48,572
Cigna (73)	41,616
Molina Healthcare (152)	19,883
WellCare Health Plans (170)	17,007
Magellan Health (475)	5,839
Health Care: Medical Facilities	
HCA Healthcare (63)	$47,653
Tenet Healthcare (147)	20,613
Community Health Systems (160)	18,477
DaVita (179)	16,038
Universal Health Services (268)	11,279
LifePoint Health (390)	7,263
Kindred Healthcare (416)	6,768
Health Care: Pharmacy & Other Services	
CVS Health (7)	$184,765
Express Scripts Holding (25)	100,065
Envision Healthcare (198)	14,701
Laboratory Corp. of America (286)	10,441
IQVIA Holdings (304)	9,739
Quest Diagnostics (367)	7,709
Home Equipment, Furnishings	
Newell Brands (196)	$14,742
Stanley Black & Decker (228)	12,747
Mohawk Industries (315)	9,491

Industry/company (rank)	Revenues	Industry/company (rank)	Revenues	Industry/company (rank)	Revenues
Masco (373)	$7,644	Loews (217)	$13,735	Owens-Illinois (410)	$6,869
Homebuilders		Fidelity National Financial (302)	9,769	Avery Dennison (427)	6,614
D.R. Horton (211)	$14,091	American Family Insurance Group		Packaging Corp. of America (436)	6,445
Lennar (230)	12,646	(311)	9,545	Sealed Air (456)	6,131
PulteGroup (341)	8,573	W.R. Berkley (369)	7,685	**Petroleum Refining**	
NVR (444)	6,322	American Financial Group (413)	6,865	Exxon Mobil (2)	$244,363
Toll Brothers (480)	5,815	Alleghany (437)	6,425	Chevron (13)	134,533
Hotels, Casinos, Resorts		Assurant (440)	6,415	Phillips 66 (28)	91,568
Marriott International (127)	$22,894	Old Republic International (450)	6,263	Valero Energy (31)	88,407
Las Vegas Sands (227)	12,882	Markel (464)	6,062	Marathon Petroleum (41)	67,610
MGM Resorts International (280)	10,774	AmTrust Financial Services (469)	5,959	Andeavor (90)	34,204
Hilton Worldwide Holdings (324)	9,140	First American Financial (483)	5,772	PBF Energy (135)	21,787
Wynn Resorts (447)	6,306	Cincinnati Financial (484)	5,732	HollyFrontier (206)	14,251
Wyndham Destinations (479)	5,821	**Internet Services & Retailing**		Delek US Holdings (384)	7,350
Household & Personal Products		Amazon.com (8)	$177,866	**Pharmaceuticals**	
Procter & Gamble (42)	$66,217	Alphabet (22)	110,855	Johnson & Johnson (37)	$76,450
Kimberly-Clark (163)	18,259	Facebook (76)	40,653	Pfizer (57)	52,546
Colgate-Palmolive (184)	15,454	Booking Holdings (229)	12,681	Merck (78)	40,122
Estée Lauder (258)	11,824	Netflix (261)	11,693	AbbVie (110)	28,216
Coty (371)	7,650	Qurate Retail (288)	10,404	Gilead Sciences (116)	26,107
HRG Group (422)	6,650	Expedia Group (295)	10,060	Eli Lilly (129)	22,871
Clorox (66)	5,973	eBay (309)	9,567	Amgen (130)	22,849
Avon Products (485)	5,716	**Mail, Package, & Freight Delivery**		Bristol-Myers Squibb (145)	20,776
Industrial Machinery		UPS (44)	$65,872	Celgene (224)	13,003
General Electric (18)	$122,274	FedEx (50)	60,319	Biogen (245)	12,274
Cummins (149)	20,428	**Medical Products & Equipment**		Regeneron Pharmaceuticals (473)	5,872
Emerson Electric (178)	16,301	Abbott Laboratories (111)	$27,390	**Pipelines**	
Illinois Tool Works (204)	14,314	Danaher (162)	18,330	Energy Transfer Equity (64)	$47,487
Parker-Hannifin (256)	12,029	Stryker (240)	12,444	Enterprise Products Partners (105)	29,242
Dover (360)	7,830	Becton Dickinson (251)	12,093	Plains GP Holdings (115)	26,223
Fortive (420)	6,656	Baxter International (283)	10,561	Kinder Morgan (218)	13,705
Information Technology Services		Boston Scientific (328)	9,048	Oneok (249)	12,174
IBM (34)	$79,139	Zimmer Biomet Holdings (361)	7,824	Targa Resources (334)	8,815
CDW (189)	15,192	**Metals**		DCP Midstream (344)	8,462
Cognizant Technology Solutions		Nucor (151)	$20,252	**Publishing, Printing**	
(195)	14,810	United States Steel (246)	12,250	News Corp. (350)	$8,139
Leidos Holdings (292)	10,170	Alcoa (262)	11,652	R.R. Donnelley & Sons (406)	6,940
DXC Technology (374)	7,607	Reliance Steel & Aluminum (305)	9,721	**Railroads**	
Insight Enterprises (417)	6,704	Steel Dynamics (312)	9,539	Union Pacific (141)	$21,240
Booz Allen Hamilton (482)	5,804	AK Steel Holding (461)	6,081	CSX (265)	11,408
Insurance: Life, Health (Mutual)		**Mining, Crude Oil Production**		Norfolk Southern (284)	10,551
New York Life Insurance (69)	$42,296	ConocoPhillips (95)	$32,584	**Real Estate**	
TIAA (84)	36,025	Freeport-McMoRan (176)	16,416	CBRE Group (207)	$14,210
Massachusetts Mutual Life		Devon Energy (213)	13,949	Jones Lang LaSalle (356)	7,932
Insurance (93)	33,495	Occidental Petroleum (220)	13,274	American Tower (419)	6,664
Northwestern Mutual (104)	29,331	Anadarko Petroleum (257)	11,908	Realogy Holdings (458)	6,114
Guardian Life Ins. Co. of America		EOG Resources (270)	11,228	Simon Property Group (493)	5,539
(239)	12,455	Chesapeake Energy (314)	9,496	**Scientific, Photographic, &**	
Thrivent Financial for Lutherans		Newmont Mining (385)	7,348	**Control Equipment**	
(343)	8,528	Apache (438)	6,423	Thermo Fisher Scientific (144)	$20,918
Western & Southern Financial		Peabody Energy (491)	5,579	**Securities**	
Group (476)	5,836	Pioneer Natural Resources (497)	5,455	BlackRock (237)	$12,491
Insurance: Life, Health (Stock)		**Miscellaneous**		Charles Schwab (330)	8,960
MetLife (43)	$66,153	3M (97)	$31,657	Jones Financial (Edward Jones)	
Prudential Financial (52)	59,689	A-Mark Precious Metals (404)	6,990	(376)	7,597
Aflac (137)	21,667	United Rentals (424)	6,641	Raymond James Financial (431)	6,525
Lincoln National (205)	14,257	**Motor Vehicles & Parts**		Franklin Resources (441)	6,392
Principal Financial (210)	14,093	General Motors (10)	$157,311	KKR (470)	5,930
Reinsurance Group of America		Ford Motor (11)	156,776	Intercontinental Exchange (477)	5,834
(234)	12,516	Lear (148)	20,467	**Semiconductors & Other**	
Unum Group (267)	11,287	Goodyear Tire & Rubber (187)	15,377	**Electronic Components**	
Pacific Life (313)	9,510	Tesla (260)	11,759	Intel (46)	$62,761
Mutual of Omaha Insurance (337)	8,732	Autoliv (289)	10,383	Qualcomm (133)	22,291
Genworth Financial (348)	8,295	BorgWarner (301)	9,799	Micron Technology (150)	20,322
Securian Financial Group (462)	6,067	Tenneco (320)	9,274	Jabil (159)	19,063
Insurance: Property & Casualty		Thor Industries (392)	7,247	Texas Instruments (192)	14,961
(Mutual)		Dana (393)	7,209	Applied Materials (201)	14,537
State Farm Insurance Cos. (36)	$78,331	American Axle & Manufacturing		Nvidia (306)	9,714
Nationwide (66)	43,940	(449)	6,266	Lam Research (354)	8,014
Farmers Insurance Exchange		**Network & Other**		Sanmina (411)	6,869
(253)	12,072	**Communications Equipment**		ON Semiconductor (492)	5,543
Auto-Owners Insurance (375)	7,604	Cisco Systems (62)	$48,005	**Specialty Retailers: Apparel**	
Erie Insurance Group (378)	7,535	Amphenol (403)	7,011	TJX (85)	$35,865
Insurance: Property & Casualty		Motorola Solutions (443)	6,380	Gap (181)	15,855
(Stock)		**Oil and Gas Equipment &**		Ross Stores (209)	14,135
Berkshire Hathaway (3)	$242,137	**Services**		L Brands (231)	12,632
AIG (60)	49,520	Halliburton (146)	$20,620	Foot Locker (363)	7,782
Liberty Mutual Insurance Group		National Oilwell Varco (388)	7,304	Ascena Retail Group (423)	6,650
(68)	42,687	**Packaging, Containers**		Burlington Stores (459)	6,110
Allstate (79)	38,524	International Paper (124)	$23,302	**Specialty Retailers: Other**	
USAA (100)	30,016	WestRock (194)	14,860	Home Depot (23)	$100,904
Travelers Cos. (106)	28,902	Ball (277)	10,983	Lowe's (40)	68,619
Progressive (112)	26,839	Crown Holdings (338)	8,698	Best Buy (72)	42,151
Hartford Financial Services (156)	19,228	Berry Global Group (399)	7,095	Dollar General (123)	23,471
				Dollar Tree (134)	22,246
				Bed Bath & Beyond (248)	12,216
				Toys R Us (272)	11,146

Industry/company (rank)	Revenues
AutoZone (278)	$10,889
Murphy USA (279)	10,853
Office Depot (281)	10,752
Advance Auto Parts (317)	9,374
GameStop (322)	9,225
O'Reilly Automotive (329)	8,978
Dick's Sporting Goods (340)	8,591
Tractor Supply (391)	7,256
Casey's General Stores (425)	6,641
TravelCenters of America (465)	6,052
Ulta Beauty (471)	5,885
Telecommunications	
AT&T (9)	$160,546
Verizon (16)	126,034
Comcast (33)	84,526
Charter Communications (74)	41,581
CenturyLink (166)	17,656
DISH Network (203)	14,391
Frontier Communications (325)	9,128
Windstream Holdings (474)	5,853
Temporary Help	
ManpowerGroup (143)	$21,034
Tobacco	
Philip Morris International (108)	$28,748
Altria Group (154)	19,494
Transportation Equipment	
Harley-Davidson (488)	$5,647
Polaris Industries (496)	5,505
Transportation & Logistics	
XPO Logistics (186)	$15,381
C.H. Robinson Worldwide (193)	14,869

Industry/company (rank)	Revenues
Expeditors International of Washington (408)	$6,921
Trucking, Truck Leasing	
Ryder System (387)	$7,330
J.B. Hunt Transport Services (395)	7,190
Utilities: Gas & Electric	
Exelon (92)	$33,531
Duke Energy (125)	23,189
Southern (126)	23,031
NextEra Energy (167)	17,195
PG&E Corp. (168)	17,135
American Electric Power (185)	15,425
AES (214)	13,850
FirstEnergy (219)	13,627
DTE Energy (232)	12,607
Dominion Energy (233)	12,586
Edison International (244)	12,320
Consolidated Edison (255)	12,033
Xcel Energy (266)	11,404
Sempra Energy (271)	11,207
Entergy (274)	11,075
CenterPoint Energy (308)	9,614
Public Service Enterprise Group (327)	9,084
Eversource Energy (364)	7,752
WEC Energy Group (372)	7,649
PPL (380)	7,447
CMS Energy (429)	6,583
Ameren (453)	6,177
Waste Management	
Waste Management (202)	$14,485

Industry/company (rank)	Revenues
Republic Services (296)	$10,042
Wholesalers, Diversified	
Genuine Parts (177)	$16,309
W.W. Grainger (287)	10,425
LKQ (300)	9,848
Global Partners (331)	8,921
Veritiv (346)	8,365
Univar (349)	8,254
WESCO International (370)	7,679
Graybar Electric (426)	6,631
HD Supply Holdings (430)	6,534
Wholesalers: Electronics & Office Equipment	
Tech Data (83)	$36,775
Arrow Electronics (113)	26,813
Avnet (128)	22,872
Synnex (169)	17,046
Anixter International (357)	7,927
Wholesalers: Food & Grocery	
Sysco (54)	$55,371
US Foods Holding (121)	24,147
Performance Food Group (171)	16,762
Core-Mark Holding (247)	12,225
United Natural Foods (319)	9,275
SpartanNash (351)	8,128
Wholesalers: Health Care	
McKesson (6)	$198,533
AmerisourceBergen (12)	153,144
Cardinal Health (14)	129,976
Henry Schein (238)	12,462
Owens & Minor (318)	9,318
Patterson (490)	5,593

World's Largest Companies, 2017

Source: *Fortune* magazine, July 2018
(ranked by 2017 revenues, in millions of dollars)

Rank	Company (2016 rank), country	Revenue	Rank	Company (2016 rank), country	Revenue
1.	Walmart (1), U.S.	$500,343	51.	BMW Group (52), Germany	$111,231
2.	State Grid (2), China	348,903	52.	Alphabet (65), U.S.	110,855
3.	Sinopec Group (3), China	326,953	53.	China Mobile Communications (47), China	110,159
4.	China National Petroleum (4), China	326,008	54.	Nissan Motor (44), Japan	107,868
5.	Royal Dutch Shell (7), Netherlands	311,870	55.	Nippon Telegraph & Telephone (50), Japan	106,500
6.	Toyota Motor (5), Japan	265,172	56.	China Railway Engineering (55), China	102,767
7.	Volkswagen (6), Germany	260,028	57.	Home Depot (59), U.S.	100,904
8.	BP (12), UK	244,582	58.	China Railway Construction (58), China	100,855
9.	Exxon Mobil (10), U.S.	244,363	59.	Assicurazioni Generali (57), Italy	100,552
10.	Berkshire Hathaway (8), U.S.	242,137	60.	Bank of America Corp. (62), U.S.	100,264
11.	Apple (9), U.S.	229,234	61.	Express Scripts Holding (53), U.S.	100,065
12.	Samsung Electronics (15), South Korea	211,940	62.	Wells Fargo (61), U.S.	97,741
13.	McKesson (11), U.S.	208,357	63.	Lukoil (102), Russia	93,897
14.	Glencore (16), Switzerland	205,476	64.	Boeing (60), U.S.	93,392
15.	UnitedHealth Group (13), U.S.	201,159	65.	Dongfeng Motor (68), China	93,294
16.	Daimler (17), Germany	185,235	66.	Siemens (66), Germany	91,585
17.	CVS Health (14), U.S.	184,765	67.	Phillips 66 (96), U.S.	91,568
18.	Amazon.com (26), U.S.	177,866	68.	Carrefour (67), France	91,276
19.	EXOR Group (20), Italy	161,677	69.	Nestlé (64), Switzerland	91,222
20.	AT&T (19), U.S.	160,546	70.	Anthem (70), U.S.	90,039
21.	General Motors (18), U.S.	157,311	71.	Microsoft (69), U.S.	89,950
22.	Ford Motor (21), U.S.	156,776	72.	Huawei Investment & Holding (83), China	89,311
23.	China State Construction Engineering (24), China	156,071	73.	Petrobras (75), Brazil	88,827
24.	Hon Hai Precision Industry (27), Taiwan	154,699	74.	Valero Energy (106), U.S.	88,407
25.	AmerisourceBergen (23), U.S.	153,144	75.	Bosch Group (76), Germany	87,997
26.	Industrial & Commercial Bank of China (22), China	153,021	76.	Citigroup (74), U.S.	87,966
27.	AXA (25), France	149,461	77.	Banco Santander (73), Spain	87,401
28.	Total (30), France	149,099	78.	Hyundai Motor (78), South Korea	85,259
29.	Ping An Insurance (39), China	144,197	79.	Hitachi (71), Japan	84,559
30.	Honda Motor (29), Japan	138,646	80.	Comcast (79), U.S.	84,526
31.	China Construction Bank (28), China	138,594	81.	Deutsche Telekom (77), Germany	84,481
32.	Trafigura Group (54), Singapore	136,421	82.	Crédit Agricole (80), France	84,222
33.	Chevron (45), U.S.	134,533	83.	Enel (84), Italy	84,134
34.	Cardinal Health (35), U.S.	129,976	84.	SK Holdings (95), South Korea	83,544
35.	Costco (36), U.S.	129,025	85.	SoftBank Group (72), Japan	82,665
36.	SAIC Motor (41), China	128,819	86.	China Resources (86), China	82,184
37.	Verizon (32), U.S.	126,034	87.	China National Offshore Oil (115), China	81,482
38.	Allianz (34), Germany	123,532	88.	Uniper (91), Germany	81,428
39.	Kroger (40), U.S.	122,662	89.	ENI (132), Italy	80,006
40.	Agricultural Bank of China (38), China	122,366	90.	HSBC Holdings (88), UK	79,637
41.	General Electric (31), U.S.	122,274	91.	China Communications Construction (103), China	79,417
42.	China Life Insurance (51), China	120,224	92.	IBM (81), U.S.	79,139
43.	Walgreens Boots Alliance (37), U.S.	118,214	93.	Dell Technologies (124), U.S.	78,660
44.	BNP Paribas (43), France	117,375	94.	Électricité de France (82), France	78,490
45.	Japan Post Holdings (33), Japan	116,616	95.	State Farm Insurance Cos. (85), U.S.	78,331
46.	Bank of China (42), China	115,423	96.	Pacific Construction Group (89), China	77,205
47.	JPMorgan Chase (48), U.S.	113,899	97.	Sony (105), Japan	77,116
48.	Fannie Mae (46), U.S.	112,394	98.	Sinochem Group (143), China	76,765
49.	Gazprom (63), Russia	111,983	99.	JXTG Holdings (127), China	76,629
50.	Prudential (56), U.S.	111,458	100.	Johnson & Johnson (97), U.S.	76,450

Top U.S. Franchises, 2018

Source: *Entrepreneur* magazine

Rank	Company (2017 rank)	Type of business	Locations[1]	Startup costs[2]
1.	McDonald's (2)	Burgers, chicken, salads, beverages	37,406	$1 mil-2.2 mil
2.	7-Eleven Inc. (1)	Convenience stores	66,193	$38,000-1.1 mil
3.	Dunkin' Donuts (3)	Coffee, doughnuts, baked goods	12,676	$229,000-1.7 mil
4.	The UPS Store (4)	Business support centers	5,071	$169,000-398,000
5.	RE/MAX LLC (10)	Real estate services	7,985	$38,000-225,000
6.	Sonic Drive-in Restaurants (39)	Burgers, hot dogs, chicken sandwiches	3,953	$1.1 mil-2.4 mil
7.	Great Clips (27)	Hair salons	4,261	$137,000-258,000
8.	Taco Bell (12)	Mexican fast food	6,905	$525,000-2.6 mil
9.	Hardee's (16)	Burgers, chicken, biscuits	2,247	$1.5 mil-1.9 mil
10.	Sport Clips (9)	Men's sports-themed hair salons	1,776	$189,000-355,000
11.	Jimmy John's Gourmet Sandwiches (5)	Sandwiches	2,793	$330,000-558,000
12.	Servpro (48)	Disaster restoration and cleaning	1,687	$158,000-212,000
13.	Culver Franchising System Inc. (20)	Frozen custard, specialty burgers	667	$1.8 mil-4.3 mil
14.	Supercuts (13)	Hair salons	2,665[3]	$144,000-297,000
15.	Carl's Jr. Restaurants (29)	Burgers	1,636	$1.4 mil-2 mil
16.	Papa John's Intl. (55)	Pizza	5,247	$130,000-844,000
17.	Anytime Fitness (14)	Fitness centers	4,081	$89,000-678,000
18.	uBreakiFix (93)	Electronics repairs	421	$60,000-221,000
19.	Ace Hardware Corp. (7)	Hardware and home improvement stores	5,068	$273,000-1.6 mil
20.	Kumon Math & Reading Centers (11)	Education programs	25,881	$70,000-149,000
21.	Planet Fitness (32)	Fitness centers	1,608	$857,000-4.2 mil
22.	Keller Williams (77)	Real estate	973	$184,000-337,000
23.	Budget Blinds (68)	Window coverings, rugs, accessories	1,154	$110,000-236,000
24.	Jersey Mike's Subs (21)	Sandwiches	1,431	$179,000-746,000
25.	Marco's Pizza (38)	Pizza, subs, wings, cheese bread	905	$290,000-763,000

Note: Franchises are ranked by a combination of factors, including financial strength and stability, growth rate, number of locations, startup costs, and whether the company provides financing. (1) Includes locations outside the U.S. and company-owned franchises as of Oct. 2018 unless noted. (2) Does not include franchise fees, which vary. (3) As of 2017.

Small Businesses in the U.S. Economy, 1977-2015

Source: Business Dynamics Statistics, U.S. Census Bureau; Small Business Administration

Year	Total businesses	Small businesses	Small businesses as % of private nonfarm GDP	Total employed	Small business employees	% employed by small business
1977	3,432,013	3,421,875	52.0%	66,091,813	34,519,673	52.2%
1980	3,608,883	3,597,797	51.0	74,749,926	39,441,701	52.8
1985	3,977,854	3,965,106	50.0	80,896,890	44,020,000	54.4
1990	4,312,888	4,297,295	51.0	92,553,401	49,405,250	53.4
1995	4,617,160	4,600,494	50.0	98,485,465	52,017,989	52.8
2000	4,840,136	4,821,350	50.3	112,607,042	56,925,603	50.6
2001	4,884,934	4,865,778	50.3	114,009,997	57,132,852	50.1
2002	4,923,438	4,904,152	48.3	111,827,416	56,576,798	50.6
2003	4,965,328	4,946,995	48.1	112,409,112	57,701,058	51.3
2004	5,041,791	5,023,270	47.5	113,707,630	58,647,695	51.6
2005	5,141,900	5,123,273	46.3	115,140,083	59,011,437	51.3
2006	5,185,814	5,166,701	46.1	118,614,800	60,480,334	51.0
2007	5,253,216	5,232,786	46.2	119,627,021	60,201,946	50.3
2008	5,204,140	5,184,058	45.8	119,780,685	59,688,492	49.8
2009	5,030,089	5,010,001	46.0	113,333,976	56,056,768	49.5
2010	4,956,460	4,937,934	44.6	110,792,627	54,863,184	49.5
2011	4,915,209	4,896,614	NA	112,121,688	54,908,981	49.0
2012	4,991,078	4,971,340	NA	114,761,137	56,024,730	48.8
2013	5,025,673	5,005,505	NA	117,194,376	56,678,331	48.4
2014	5,060,326	5,039,793	NA	119,102,910	57,525,365	48.3
2015	5,108,544	5,087,860	NA	121,637,451	58,583,432	48.2

NA = Not available. **Note:** Small businesses are firms employing fewer than 500 people. Figures include only businesses with paid employees.

Denominations of U.S. Currency

Since 1969 the largest denomination of U.S. currency that has been issued is the $100 bill. As larger-denomination bills reach the Federal Reserve Bank, they are removed from circulation. Because some discontinued currency is expected to be in the hands of holders for many years, the description of the various denominations below is continued.

Note	Portrait	Embellishment on back	Note	Portrait	Embellishment on back
$1	George Washington	Great Seal of U.S.	$500[1]	William McKinley	Ornate denominational marking
2	Thomas Jefferson	Signers of Declaration	1,000[2]	Grover Cleveland	Ornate denominational marking
5	Abraham Lincoln	Lincoln Memorial	5,000	James Madison	Washington resigning as Army commander
10	Alexander Hamilton	U.S. Treasury			
20	Andrew Jackson	White House	10,000	Salmon Chase	Embarkation of the Pilgrims
50	Ulysses S. Grant	U.S. Capitol	100,000[3]	Woodrow Wilson	Ornate denominational marking
100	Benjamin Franklin	Independence Hall			

(1) John Marshall appeared on the earliest version of the $500 bill. (2) Alexander Hamilton appeared on the earliest version of the $1,000 bill, but these were discontinued to avoid confusion with the $10 bill. (3) For use only in transactions between Federal Reserve System and Treasury Department.

The U.S. $1 Bill

Plate position: Shows where on the 32-note plate this bill was printed.

Serial number: Each bill has its own.

Federal Reserve Bank number: Shows which district issued the bill.

Federal Reserve seal: The name of the Federal Reserve Bank that issued the bill is printed in the seal. The letter also tells you which bank distributed the bill. Here are the number and letter codes for the 12 Federal Reserve Banks:

1/A: Boston
2/B: New York
3/C: Philadelphia
4/D: Cleveland
5/E: Richmond
6/F: Atlanta
7/G: Chicago
8/H: St. Louis
9/I: Minneapolis
10/J: Kansas City
11/K: Dallas
12/L: San Francisco

Treasurer of the U.S. signature

Series indicator: Year note's design was first used.

Secretary of the Treasury signature

Treasury Department seal: The balancing scales represent justice. The pointed stripe across the middle has 13 stars for the original 13 colonies. The key represents authority.

Plate serial number: Shows which printing plate was used for the face of the bill.

Plate serial number: Shows which plate was used for the back.

Front of the Great Seal of the United States: The bald eagle is the national bird. The shield has 13 stripes for the 13 original colonies. The eagle holds 13 arrows (symbol of war) and an olive branch with 13 olives and leaves (symbol of peace). Above the eagle is the motto "E Pluribus Unum," Latin for "out of many, one," and a constellation of 13 stars.

Reverse of the Great Seal of the United States: The pyramid symbolizes something that endures for ages. The eye, known as the Eye of Providence, probably comes from an ancient Egyptian symbol. The pyramid has 13 levels; at its base are the Roman numerals for 1776, the year of American independence. "Annuit Coeptis" is Latin for "God has favored our undertaking." "Novus Ordo Seclorum" is Latin for "a new order of the ages." Both phrases are from the works of the Roman poet Virgil.

U.S. Currency and Coin

Source: Bureau of the Fiscal Service, U.S. Dept. of the Treasury

Total Money in Circulation, 1955-2018

Date	Dollars (mil)	Per capita[1]	Date	Dollars (mil)	Per capita[1]	Date	Dollars (mil)	Per capita[1]
June 30, 1955	$30,229	$183	Sept. 30, 1990	$278,903	$1,105	June 30, 2013	$1,193,771	$3,774
June 30, 1960	32,064	177	Sept. 30, 1995	409,272	1,553	June 30, 2014	1,282,431	4,027
June 30, 1965	39,719	204	Sept. 30, 2000	568,614	2,061	June 30, 2015	1,368,622	4,260
June 30, 1970	54,351	265	Sept. 30, 2005	766,487	2,578	June 30, 2016	1,463,923	4,520
June 30, 1975	81,196	380	June 30, 2010	945,138	3,051	June 30, 2017	1,561,808	4,800
Sept. 30, 1980	129,916	581	June 30, 2011	1,028,910	3,302	June 30, 2018	1,666,817	5,081
Sept. 30, 1985	187,337	782	June 30, 2012	1,111,901	3,540			

(1) Based on U.S. Census Bureau population estimates.

Money in Circulation by Denomination, 2018

Denomination	Amount in circulation	Denomination	Amount in circulation	Denomination	Amount in circulation
$1	$12,173,717,483	$50	$86,648,265,100	$10,000	$3,450,000
$2	2,464,974,612	$100	1,300,711,680,600	Fractional notes[1]	600
$5	14,791,004,735	$500	141,744,500	**Total currency**	**$1,619,651,043,350**
$10	19,394,249,030	$1,000	165,122,000	**Total coins**	**$47,166,243,709**
$20	183,155,069,690	$5,000	1,765,000	**Total currency and coins**	**$1,666,817,287,059**

(1) Represents the value of certain partial denominations not presented for redemption.

U.S. Budget Receipts and Outlays, 1789-1940

Source: U.S. Dept. of the Treasury

(in thousands of dollars; annual statements for years ending June 30, unless otherwise noted)

Yearly average	Receipts	Outlays	Yearly average	Receipts	Outlays	Yearly average	Receipts	Outlays
1789-1800[1]	$5,717	$5,776	1866-1870	$447,301	$377,642	1906-1910	$628,507	$639,178
1801-1810[2]	13,056	9,086	1871-1875	336,830	287,460	1911-1915	710,227	720,252
1811-1820[2]	21,032	23,943	1876-1880	288,124	255,598	1916-1920	3,483,652	8,065,333
1821-1830[2]	21,928	16,162	1881-1885	366,961	257,691	1921-1925	4,306,673	3,578,989
1831-1840[2]	30,461	24,495	1886-1890	375,448	279,134	1926-1930	4,069,138	3,182,807
1841-1850[2]	28,545	34,097	1891-1895	352,891	363,599	1931-1935	2,770,973	5,214,874
1851-1860	60,237	60,163	1896-1900	434,877	457,451	1936-1940	4,960,614	10,192,367
1861-1865	160,907	683,785	1901-1905	559,481	535,559			

(1) Average for period Mar. 4, 1789, to Dec. 31, 1800. (2) Years 1801-42 end Dec. 31; average for 1841-50 is for the period Jan. 1, 1841, to June 30, 1850.

U.S. Budget Receipts and Outlays, Fiscal Years 2000-17

Source: Congressional Budget Office; *Budget of the U.S. Government*, Office of Mgmt. and Budget, Exec. Office of the President

A $236 bil government surplus in 2000 ballooned into a $1.4 tril deficit by 2009. The deficit was reduced by nearly $1 tril during the two-term Obama administration, but the deficit began rising again in 2016.

(in millions of current dollars; numbers may not add up to totals because of independent rounding or omitted subcategories, including some subcategories with negative values)

Function and subfunction	2000	2005	2010	2015	2016	2017
NET RECEIPTS	**$2,025,191**	**$2,153,611**	**$2,162,706**	**$3,249,887**	**$3,267,961**	**$3,316,182**
Individual income taxes	1,004,462	927,222	898,549	1,540,802	1,546,075	1,587,120
Corporation income taxes	207,289	278,282	191,437	343,797	299,571	297,048
Social insurance and retirement receipts	652,852	794,125	864,814	1,065,257	1,115,065	1,161,897
Employment and general retirement	620,451	747,664	815,894	1,010,427	1,062,305	1,111,897
Old-age and survivors insurance (off-budget)	411,677	493,646	539,996	658,543	665,672	688,048
Disability insurance (off-budget)	68,907	83,830	91,691	111,829	144,508	162,570
Hospital insurance	135,529	166,068	180,068	234,189	246,812	255,930
Railroad retirement/pension fund	2,688	2,284	2,285	3,336	3,128	3,136
Railroad social security equivalent account . . .	1,650	1,836	1,854	2,530	2,185	2,213
Unemployment insurance	27,640	42,002	44,823	51,178	48,856	45,808
Other retirement	4,761	4,459	4,097	3,652	3,875	4,158
Excise taxes	68,865	73,094	66,909	98,279	95,026	83,823
Federal funds	22,692	22,547	18,256	37,759	33,991	21,191
Alcohol	8,140	8,111	9,229	9,639	9,799	9,924
Tobacco	7,221	7,920	17,160	14,453	14,103	13,804
Telephone	5,670	6,047	993	607	548	558
Transportation fuels	819	−770	−11,030	−3,394	−4,755	−3,400
Trust funds	46,173	50,547	48,653	60,520	61,035	62,632
Transportation	34,972	37,892	34,992	40,813	41,344	41,020
Airport and airway	9,739	10,314	10,612	14,268	14,406	15,055
Black lung disability	518	610	595	552	440	429
Inland waterway	101	91	74	98	111	114
Oil spill liability	182	—	476	496	508	516
Aquatic resources	342	429	580	574	561	559
Leaking underground storage tank	184	189	169	179	202	225
Tobacco assessments	—	899	937	49	4	3
Vaccine injury compensation	133	123	218	275	291	270
Other receipts	91,723	80,888	140,997	201,752	212,224	186,294
OUTLAYS	**1,788,950**	**2,471,957**	**3,457,079**	**3,688,383**	**3,852,612**	**3,981,554**
National defense	294,363	495,294	693,485	589,659	593,372	598,722
Department of Defense—Military	281,029	474,071	666,703	562,499	565,370	568,896
Military personnel	75,950	127,463	155,690	145,206	147,905	144,701
Operation and maintenance	105,812	188,118	275,988	247,239	243,198	245,184
Procurement	51,696	82,294	133,603	101,342	102,656	104,127
Research, development, test, and evaluation . .	37,602	65,694	76,990	64,124	64,873	68,127
Military construction	5,109	5,331	21,169	8,114	6,677	6,671
Family housing	3,413	3,720	3,173	1,198	1,304	1,207
Atomic energy defense activities	12,138	18,031	19,308	18,692	19,387	20,482
Defense-related activities	1,196	3,192	7,474	8,468	8,615	9,344
International affairs	17,213	34,565	45,195	48,576	45,306	46,309
International development and humanitarian assistance	6,516	17,696	19,014	24,087	24,129	24,542
International security assistance	6,387	7,895	11,363	12,907	11,305	12,240
Conduct of foreign affairs	4,708	9,148	13,557	13,246	13,874	12,888
Foreign information and exchange activities	817	1,129	1,485	1,531	1,546	1,595
International financial programs	−1,215	−1,303	−224	−3,195	−5,548	−4,956
General science, space, and technology	18,594	23,597	30,100	29,412	30,174	30,394
General science and basic research	6,167	8,819	11,730	11,719	11,950	12,320
Space flight, research, and supporting activities	12,427	14,778	18,370	17,693	18,224	18,074
Energy	−761	440	11,618	6,838	3,719	3,856
Energy supply	−1,818	−929	5,801	4,707	2,019	2,827
Energy conservation	666	883	4,997	1,187	967	1,048
Emergency energy preparedness	162	162	199	449	234	−536
Energy information, policy, and regulation	229	324	621	495	499	517
Natural resources and environment	25,003	27,983	43,667	36,034	39,082	37,896
Water resources	5,078	5,724	11,662	7,760	7,379	7,527
Conservation and land management	6,762	6,226	10,783	10,519	12,305	12,244
Recreational resources	2,540	2,990	3,911	3,501	3,688	3,874
Pollution control and abatement	7,395	8,065	10,841	7,241	8,619	8,089
Agriculture	36,458	26,565	21,356	18,500	18,342	18,870
Farm income stabilization	33,446	22,048	16,604	13,424	13,418	14,204
Agricultural research and services	3,012	4,517	4,752	5,076	4,924	4,666
Commerce and housing credit	3,207	7,566	−82,316	−37,905	−34,077	−26,834
Mortgage credit	−3,335	−862	35,804	−35,658	−34,721	−30,230
Postal service	2,129	−1,223	−682	−1,610	−1,265	−2,238
Deposit insurance	−3,053	−1,371	−32,033	−12,812	−13,052	−12,098
Transportation	46,853	67,894	91,972	89,533	92,566	93,522
Ground transportation	31,697	42,317	60,784	59,126	62,136	62,854
Air transportation	10,571	18,807	21,431	20,033	20,028	20,251
Water transportation	4,394	6,439	9,351	9,994	10,064	10,056
Community and regional development	10,623	26,262	23,894	20,669	20,140	24,907
Community development	5,480	5,861	9,901	7,817	7,095	6,718
Area and regional development	2,538	2,745	3,249	3,861	2,451	3,082
Disaster relief and insurance	2,605	17,656	10,744	8,991	10,594	15,107
Education, training, employment, and social services	53,764	97,555	128,598	122,061	109,737	143,976
Elementary, secondary, and vocational education	20,578	38,271	73,261	40,022	39,779	40,631
Higher education	10,115	31,442	20,908	51,341	38,764	71,801
Research and general education aids	2,543	3,124	3,631	3,493	3,529	3,691

Function and subfunction	2000	2005	2010	2015	2016	2017
Training and employment	$6,777	$6,852	$9,854	$7,103	$7,027	$7,018
Social services	12,557	16,251	19,179	18,303	18,760	18,935
Health.	**154,504**	**250,548**	**369,068**	**482,230**	**511,297**	**533,129**
Health care services.	136,201	219,559	330,710	446,367	474,779	492,835
Health research and training.	15,979	28,050	34,214	31,400	31,831	34,875
Consumer and occupational health and safety . .	2,324	2,939	4,144	4,463	4,687	5,419
Medicare	**197,113**	**298,638**	**451,636**	**546,202**	**594,536**	**597,307**
Income security	**253,724**	**345,847**	**622,210**	**508,843**	**514,139**	**503,484**
General retirement and disability insurance (excl. social security).	5,189	6,976	6,564	7,805	3,777	4,528
Federal employee retirement and disability	77,152	93,351	119,867	139,166	144,757	142,202
Unemployment compensation	23,012	35,435	160,145	34,978	35,159	33,320
Housing assistance	28,949	37,899	58,651	47,823	49,076	50,011
Food and nutrition assistance.	32,483	50,833	95,110	104,797	102,300	99,702
Social security	**409,423**	**523,305**	**706,737**	**887,753**	**916,067**	**944,878**
Veterans benefits and services	**46,989**	**70,120**	**108,384**	**159,738**	**174,516**	**176,543**
Income security for veterans.	24,907	35,767	49,163	76,360	86,796	86,093
Veterans education, training, and rehabilitation . .	1,285	2,790	8,089	13,383	14,354	13,320
Hospital and medical care for veterans.	19,516	28,754	45,714	61,897	65,248	69,732
Veterans housing	364	860	540	743	804	−546
Administration of justice	**28,499**	**40,019**	**54,383**	**51,906**	**55,768**	**57,944**
Federal law enforcement activities	12,121	19,912	28,713	26,937	28,886	29,818
Federal litigative and judicial activities	7,762	9,641	13,073	14,717	14,892	15,105
Federal correctional activities	3,707	5,862	7,748	7,049	6,952	6,977
Criminal justice assistance	4,909	4,604	4,849	3,203	5,038	6,044
General government.	**13,013**	**16,997**	**23,014**	**20,956**	**23,146**	**23,896**
Legislative functions	2,227	3,460	4,100	3,751	3,831	3,914
Executive direction and management.	456	569	528	510	418	610
Central fiscal operations	8,285	9,515	11,906	11,096	11,795	11,827
General property and records management.	−32	472	1,194	−490	−325	−241
Central personnel management	184	101	338	81	−362	−47
General purpose fiscal assistance	2,084	3,333	5,082	7,266	7,092	7,010
Deductions for offsetting receipts	−2,383	−2,841	−1,721	−4,786	−4,046	−3,463
Net interest	**222,949**	**183,986**	**196,194**	**223,181**	**240,033**	**262,551**
Undistributed offsetting receipts.	**−42,581**	**−65,224**	**−82,116**	**−115,803**	**−95,251**	**−89,826**
TOTAL SURPLUS/DEFICIT	**236,241**	**−318,346**	**−1,294,373**	**−438,496**	**−584,651**	**−665,372**

Federal Receipts, Outlays, and Surpluses or Deficits, 1901-2018

Source: *Budget of the U.S. Government, Fiscal Year 2018*, Office of Management and Budget, Exec. Office of the President
(in millions of current dollars)

Fiscal year	Receipts	Outlays	Surplus or deficit (−)	Fiscal year	Receipts	Outlays	Surplus or deficit (−)	Fiscal year	Receipts	Outlays	Surplus or deficit (−)
1901	$588	$525	**$63**	1941	$8,712	$13,653	−$4,941	1980	$517,112	$590,941	−$73,830
1902	562	485	**77**	1942	14,634	35,137	−20,503	1981	599,272	678,241	−78,968
1903	562	517	**45**	1943	24,001	78,555	−54,554	1982	617,766	745,743	−127,977
1904	541	584	−43	1944	43,747	91,304	−47,557	1983	600,562	808,364	−207,802
1905	544	567	−23	1945	45,159	92,712	−47,553	1984	666,438	851,805	−185,367
1906	595	570	**25**	1946	39,296	55,232	−15,936	1985	734,037	946,344	−212,308
1907	666	579	**87**	1947	38,514	34,496	**4,018**	1986	769,155	990,382	−221,227
1908	602	659	−57	1948	41,560	29,764	**11,796**	1987	854,288	1,004,017	−149,730
1909	604	694	−89	1949	39,415	38,835	**580**	1988	909,238	1,064,416	−155,178
1910	676	694	−18	1950	39,443	42,562	−3,119	1989	991,105	1,143,744	−152,639
1911	702	691	**11**	1951	51,616	45,514	**6,102**	1990	1,031,958	1,252,994	−221,036
1912	693	690	**3**	1952	66,167	67,686	−1,519	1991	1,054,988	1,324,226	−269,238
1913	714	715	—	1953	69,608	76,101	−6,493	1992	1,091,208	1,381,529	−290,321
1914	725	726	—	1954	69,701	70,855	−1,154	1993	1,154,335	1,409,386	−255,051
1915	683	746	−63	1955	65,451	68,444	−2,993	1994	1,258,566	1,461,753	−203,186
1916	761	713	**48**	1956	74,587	70,640	**3,947**	1995	1,351,790	1,515,742	−163,952
1917	1,101	1,954	−853	1957	79,990	76,578	**3,412**	1996	1,453,053	1,560,484	−107,431
1918	3,645	12,677	−9,032	1958	79,636	82,405	−2,769	1997	1,579,232	1,601,116	−21,884
1919	5,130	18,493	−13,363	1959	79,249	92,098	−12,849	1998	1,721,728	1,652,458	**69,270**
1920	6,649	6,358	**291**	1960	92,492	92,191	**301**	1999	1,827,452	1,701,842	**125,610**
1921	5,571	5,062	**509**	1961	94,388	97,723	−3,335	2000	2,025,191	1,788,950	**236,241**
1922	4,026	3,289	**736**	1962	99,676	106,821	−7,146	2001	1,991,082	1,862,846	**128,236**
1923	3,853	3,140	**713**	1963	106,560	111,316	−4,756	2002	1,853,136	2,010,894	−157,758
1924	3,871	2,908	**963**	1964	112,613	118,528	−5,915	2003	1,782,314	2,159,899	−377,585
1925	3,641	2,924	**717**	1965	116,817	118,228	−1,411	2004	1,880,114	2,292,841	−412,727
1926	3,795	2,930	**865**	1966	130,835	134,532	−3,698	2005	2,153,611	2,471,957	−318,346
1927	4,013	2,857	**1,155**	1967	148,822	157,464	−8,643	2006	2,406,869	2,655,050	−248,181
1928	3,900	2,961	**939**	1968	152,973	178,134	−25,161	2007	2,567,985	2,728,686	−160,701
1929	3,862	3,127	**734**	1969	186,882	183,640	**3,242**	2008	2,523,991	2,982,544	−458,553
1930	4,058	3,320	**738**	1970	192,807	195,649	−2,842	2009	2,104,989	3,517,677	−1,412,688
1931	3,116	3,577	−462	1971	187,139	210,172	−23,033	2010	2,162,706	3,457,079	−1,294,373
1932	1,924	4,659	−2,735	1972	207,309	230,681	−23,373	2011	2,303,466	3,603,059	−1,299,593
1933	1,997	4,598	−2,602	1973	230,799	245,707	−14,908	2012	2,449,988	3,536,951	−1,086,963
1934	2,955	6,541	−3,586	1974	263,224	269,359	−6,135	2013	2,775,103	3,454,647	−679,544
1935	3,609	6,412	−2,803	1975	279,090	332,332	−53,242	2014	3,021,491	3,506,091	−484,600
1936	3,923	8,228	−4,304	1976	298,060	371,792	−73,732	2015	3,249,887	3,688,383	−438,496
1937	5,387	7,580	−2,193	1977	355,559	409,218	−53,659	2016	3,267,961	3,852,612	−584,651
1938	6,751	6,840	−89	1978	399,561	458,746	−59,185	2017	3,316,182	3,981,554	−665,372
1939	6,295	9,141	−2,846	1979	463,302	504,028	−40,726	2018[1]	3,340,360	4,172,992	−832,632
1940	6,548	9,468	−2,920								

— = $500,000 or less. Figures in **bold** denote annual surplus. **Note:** Budget figures prior to 1933 are based on administrative budget concepts rather than unified budget concepts. Through 1976, fiscal year ends June 30; after 1976, fiscal year ends Sept. 30. Surplus or deficit column may not equal difference between figures because of rounding. (1) Estimate as of Feb. 2018.

Public Debt of the U.S., 1946-2026

Source: *Budget of the U.S. Government*, Office of Management and Budget, Exec. Office of the President

Year	Debt held by public — Current dollars (bil)	Debt held by public — FY2017 dollars (bil)	As % of GDP	Interest on public debt as % of — Total federal outlays	Interest on public debt as % of — GDP	Year	Debt held by public — Current dollars (bil)	Debt held by public — FY2017 dollars (bil)	As % of GDP	Interest on public debt as % of — Total federal outlays	Interest on public debt as % of — GDP
1946	$241.9	$2,492.6	106.1%	7.6%	1.8%	2010	$9,018.9	$10,103.9	60.9%	6.6%	1.5%
1950	219.0	1,826.1	78.5	11.4	1.7	2015	13,116.7	13,497.0	72.9	7.1	1.4
1955	226.6	1,660.5	55.7	7.6	1.3	2016	14,167.6	14,411.2	76.7	7.4	1.5
1960	236.8	1,537.6	44.3	8.5	1.5	2017	14,665.5	14,665.5	76.5	7.8	1.6
1965	260.8	1,585.7	36.7	8.1	1.3	2018[1]	15,789.7	15,546.5	78.8	8.6	1.8
1970	283.2	1,434.8	27.0	7.9	1.5	2019[1]	16,871.7	16,338.7	80.3	9.4	2.0
1975	394.7	1,473.8	24.5	7.5	1.6	2020[1]	17,946.8	17,063.7	81.3	10.8	2.3
1980	711.9	1,850.0	25.5	10.6	2.2	2021[1]	18,950.5	17,669.3	81.7	11.9	2.4
1985	1,507.3	2,989.5	35.3	16.2	3.6	2022[1]	19,946.3	18,232.1	81.9	12.6	2.6
1990	2,411.6	4,112.4	40.8	16.2	3.4	2023[1]	20,808.6	18,644.9	81.3	13.2	2.7
1995	3,604.4	5,424.2	47.5	15.8	3.2	2024[1]	21,495.3	18,882.7	79.9	13.7	2.7
2000	3,409.8	4,730.3	33.6	13.0	2.3	2025[1]	22,137.0	19,063.5	78.4	13.7	2.7
2005	4,592.2	5,683.6	35.6	7.7	1.5	2026[1]	22,703.3	19,165.6	76.6	13.7	2.6

Note: As of end of fiscal year. Through 1976, the fiscal year ended June 30. For 1977 on, the fiscal year ended Sept. 30. (1) Estimate.

State Finances: Revenues, Taxes, Expenditures, and Debt, 2016

Source: U.S. Census Bureau, U.S. Dept. of Commerce

(in thousands of dollars)

State	Revenues — Total revenue	Revenues — General revenue	Revenues — Intergovernmental revenue	Taxes	Total expenditure	Debt at end of fiscal year
Alabama	$30,502,706	$25,619,102	$9,746,605	$9,919,794	$30,434,595	$8,667,105
Alaska	8,071,737	7,628,656	2,853,202	1,042,164	12,452,033	5,953,933
Arizona	38,338,699	34,689,284	14,629,239	14,693,921	42,204,155	14,400,191
Arkansas	21,439,227	20,346,096	7,431,541	9,452,883	22,910,901	4,828,756
California	322,332,341	282,907,926	94,336,283	155,231,252	326,837,836	151,307,658
Colorado	31,399,864	27,529,600	8,703,745	12,795,318	34,596,327	16,686,588
Connecticut	28,139,072	26,171,704	7,320,793	15,244,947	32,202,351	37,024,731
Delaware	8,083,659	7,962,885	2,231,253	3,522,301	9,378,888	5,045,161
Florida	85,575,636	80,261,324	27,390,107	37,640,420	88,220,438	33,469,117
Georgia	45,859,181	42,278,966	14,571,741	21,454,446	47,867,768	13,130,551
Hawaii	13,417,610	12,919,339	2,943,377	6,919,035	12,425,875	9,216,583
Idaho	9,405,581	8,154,365	2,721,813	4,209,359	9,377,948	3,542,856
Illinois	75,492,133	68,847,197	20,264,895	38,907,220	78,334,318	65,791,900
Indiana	38,687,720	36,259,733	13,041,760	17,587,958	39,557,565	22,470,543
Iowa	23,715,865	21,074,247	6,645,648	9,559,058	23,731,772	5,956,424
Kansas	17,609,012	16,459,697	3,828,203	8,058,949	18,748,723	9,537,833
Kentucky	29,941,369	28,222,220	11,579,669	11,778,866	35,347,118	14,453,423
Louisiana	26,842,105	24,110,397	10,361,925	9,309,673	31,444,186	17,913,229
Maine	9,003,011	8,326,381	2,893,679	4,130,242	9,403,020	4,845,408
Maryland	42,037,052	39,159,671	12,290,258	20,894,199	44,089,713	27,871,287
Massachusetts	60,312,959	54,702,779	16,401,221	27,277,284	63,562,063	76,861,071
Michigan	71,188,554	61,246,103	20,908,261	27,436,607	70,811,041	33,744,508
Minnesota	44,247,753	41,213,212	11,321,336	25,189,128	46,694,801	16,213,046
Mississippi	20,880,790	18,953,934	8,299,349	7,660,391	22,247,200	7,283,371
Missouri	33,039,255	28,850,421	10,987,857	12,245,169	32,778,347	19,103,212
Montana	6,878,900	6,027,319	2,455,420	2,627,943	7,316,671	3,052,423
Nebraska	10,881,575	10,129,757	3,162,157	5,117,133	11,026,935	1,950,506
Nevada	16,808,682	13,904,474	4,558,408	8,025,043	15,315,276	3,222,367
New Hampshire	8,343,685	6,996,686	2,609,075	2,641,946	7,687,843	7,869,122
New Jersey	65,689,159	60,952,881	17,976,242	31,546,720	72,617,584	66,721,791
New Mexico	18,602,071	16,536,739	7,030,082	5,462,105	20,158,082	6,951,535
New York	185,619,993	164,398,893	56,822,852	81,353,963	195,571,229	137,479,990
North Carolina	55,216,582	51,110,192	15,908,501	26,201,576	53,857,036	16,919,235
North Dakota	7,330,392	6,705,492	1,647,517	3,709,105	8,287,006	2,355,700
Ohio	78,331,623	67,466,442	24,257,560	28,694,883	87,016,871	33,164,507
Oklahoma	22,862,875	20,920,581	7,246,312	8,491,187	24,950,729	8,702,914
Oregon	32,781,473	28,126,200	10,044,740	11,043,311	34,331,929	13,355,878
Pennsylvania	90,792,145	79,737,894	26,240,030	37,394,589	96,439,652	47,099,314
Rhode Island	8,201,456	7,430,240	2,518,206	3,265,727	8,625,101	9,052,017
South Carolina	28,937,828	24,904,905	8,272,305	9,555,900	31,630,447	16,228,097
South Dakota	4,537,220	4,250,719	1,475,385	1,747,550	5,059,935	3,366,459
Tennessee	31,427,933	28,984,418	11,238,782	13,386,169	32,459,124	6,075,745
Texas	144,218,813	122,794,738	43,750,542	52,132,817	148,449,673	49,357,183
Utah	18,164,518	16,441,022	4,233,941	7,082,961	19,630,299	7,013,698
Vermont	6,488,122	6,121,318	2,139,158	3,085,865	6,763,948	2,492,083
Virginia	51,655,912	45,425,587	10,227,735	21,219,757	53,747,025	28,628,254
Washington	50,774,856	43,629,247	13,704,988	22,280,088	53,463,325	33,059,765
West Virginia	13,928,479	12,867,298	4,868,024	5,127,970	14,562,503	7,223,531
Wisconsin	36,854,453	34,643,763	9,319,175	17,607,733	39,241,416	23,052,389
Wyoming	5,914,028	5,090,453	2,143,281	1,913,607	6,351,534	775,568
United States	**2,136,805,664**	**1,909,492,497**	**637,554,178**	**922,876,232**	**2,240,220,155**	**1,160,488,556**

Note: Figures may not add up to totals because of rounding.

State and Local Government Receipts and Current Expenditures, 1960-2017

Source: Bureau of Economic Analysis, U.S. Dept. of Commerce
(in billions of current dollars; as of Aug. 2018)

	1960	1970	1980	1990	2000	2010	2015	2016	2017
Current receipts	$44.2	$119.1	$335.9	$730.1	$1,304.1	$1,994.4	$2,368.6	$2,421.9	$2,484.2
Current tax receipts	37.0	91.3	230.0	519.1	893.2	1,306.4	1,592.8	1,628.5	1,689.9
Personal current taxes	4.2	14.2	48.9	122.6	236.7	294.1	406.9	408.6	421.2
Income taxes	2.5	10.9	42.6	109.6	217.4	265.8	374.3	375.1	386.7
Other	1.7	3.3	6.3	13.0	19.4	28.3	32.7	33.5	34.5
Taxes on production and imports	31.5	73.3	166.7	374.1	621.3	966.3	1,129.5	1,166.1	1,215.7
Sales taxes	5.3	17.0	53.6	125.6	221.4	295.1	372.3	380.9	395.7
Excise taxes	6.8	14.7	29.2	58.7	95.5	154.8	180.5	185.3	190.7
Property taxes	16.2	36.7	68.8	161.5	254.7	438.6	487.8	508.4	532.2
Other	3.1	5.0	15.0	28.2	49.8	77.8	89.0	91.5	97.1
Taxes on corporate income	1.2	3.7	14.5	22.5	35.2	46.1	56.3	53.9	52.9
Contributions for government social insurance	0.5	1.1	3.6	10.0	10.8	17.8	19.2	20.0	20.6
Income receipts on assets	1.3	5.2	26.3	68.5	94.2	83.5	85.2	85.0	86.0
Interest receipts	1.0	4.3	23.1	64.1	86.6	69.0	68.3	68.2	68.8
Dividends	—	—	0.1	0.2	1.4	3.0	5.2	5.5	5.9
Rents and royalties	0.3	0.8	3.1	4.2	6.3	11.4	11.7	11.2	11.3
Current transfer receipts	4.3	20.1	76.9	126.4	299.7	604.4	673.7	689.0	690.7
Federal grants-in-aid	3.8	18.3	69.7	104.4	233.1	505.2	533.4	557.1	559.3
From business (net)	0.2	0.6	2.5	7.1	28.6	40.3	65.0	55.1	51.5
From persons	0.3	1.2	4.7	14.9	38.0	58.8	74.9	76.8	80.0
Current surplus of government enterprises	1.2	1.4	−0.8	6.1	6.1	−17.7	−2.2	−0.6	−2.9
Current expenditures	41.7	117.6	341.8	766.3	1,344.8	2,301.8	2,592.2	2,667.8	2,743.3
Consumption expenditures	33.5	90.4	249.0	544.0	961.7	1,509.5	1,656.9	1,691.9	1,744.5
Government social benefit payments to persons	4.6	16.1	51.2	127.7	271.4	523.9	665.6	693.3	712.3
Interest payments	3.6	11.1	41.2	94.3	111.1	266.9	269.2	281.9	286.0
Subsidies	0.0	0.0	0.4	0.4	0.5	1.6	0.5	0.5	0.6
Net state and local government saving	2.5	1.4	−5.9	−36.2	−40.6	−307.5	−223.6	−245.8	−259.1
Social insurance funds	0.0	0.2	1.3	2.0	2.0	0.9	3.4	3.8	4.0
Other	2.5	1.3	−7.2	−38.2	−42.6	−308.4	−227.0	−249.7	−263.1
Addenda:									
Total receipts	47.2	125.3	354.5	755.1	1,348.3	2,071.3	2,437.6	2,494.2	2,558.3
Current receipts	44.2	119.1	335.9	730.1	1,304.1	1,994.4	2,368.6	2,421.9	2,484.2
Capital transfer receipts	3.0	6.2	18.6	25.0	44.2	76.9	69.0	72.3	74.0
Total expenditures	52.1	137.1	376.6	837.6	1,468.2	2,447.7	2,709.3	2,791.2	2,857.3
Current expenditures	41.7	117.6	341.8	766.3	1,344.8	2,301.8	2,592.2	2,667.8	2,743.3
Gross government investment	14.1	29.3	65.7	132.2	231.5	347.3	356.5	366.8	364.8
Net purchases of nonproduced assets	0.9	1.1	2.2	5.7	8.6	12.0	11.9	13.0	13.5
Less: Consumption of fixed capital	4.5	10.9	33.1	66.6	116.6	213.4	251.3	256.3	265.6
Net lending or net borrowing (–)	−4.9	−11.8	−22.1	−82.5	−119.9	−376.4	−271.7	−297.0	−299.0

Federal Deposit Insurance Corporation (FDIC)

The Federal Deposit Insurance Corporation (FDIC) was created by Congress during the height of the Depression to maintain stability and public confidence in the nation's banking system. It covered depositors for up to $2,500 in case of bank failure in 1934; the limit today is 100 times that much, or $250,000. In its unique role as deposit insurer of banks and savings associations, and in cooperation with other federal and state regulatory agencies, the FDIC seeks to promote the safety and soundness of insured depository institutions in the U.S. financial system.

The quarterly premiums on deposit insurance are paid by the banks rather than by consumers. The amount of the premium is based on the institution's balance of insured deposits for the preceding quarter and the institution's risk to the insurance fund. In 2009, Congress permanently increased the limit that the FDIC may borrow from the U.S. Treasury from $30 bil to $100 bil.

U.S. Banks, 1935-2018

Source: *Summary of Deposits*, Federal Deposit Insurance Corp (FDIC)
Comprises all FDIC-insured commercial and savings banks, including savings and loan institutions (S&Ls).

	Number of banks					Deposits (in mil dollars)				
		Commercial banks[2]			Savings		Commercial banks[2]			Savings
Year	All banks[1]	National charter	State charter	Non-members	banks, total	All deposits[1]	National charter	State charter	Non-members	banks, total
1935[3]	15,295	5,386	1,001	7,735	1,173	$45,102	$24,802	$13,653	$5,669	$978
1940	15,772	5,144	1,342	6,956	2,330	67,494	35,787	20,642	7,040	4,025
1950	16,500	4,958	1,912	6,576	3,054	171,963	84,941	41,602	19,726	25,694
1960	17,549	4,530	1,641	6,955	4,423	310,262	120,242	65,487	34,369	90,164
1970	18,205	4,621	1,147	7,743	4,694	686,901	285,436	101,512	95,566	204,367
1980	18,763	4,425	997	9,013	4,328	1,832,716	656,752	191,183	344,311	640,470
1990	15,158	3,979	1,009	7,355	2,815	3,637,292	1,558,915	397,797	693,438	987,142
1995	12,289	2,941	995	6,230	2,082	3,214,678	1,337,105	439,430	696,108	735,856
2000	10,119	2,302	996	5,180	1,622	4,003,744	1,792,773	707,562	793,275	706,461
2005	8,855	1,864	906	4,779	1,293	5,933,742	2,946,589	765,673	1,191,977	1,023,620
2010	7,821	1,427	836	4,413	1,135	7,676,878	4,305,697	1,002,425	1,464,022	891,159
2011	7,523	1,349	824	4,240	1,100	8,249,233	4,708,210	1,120,747	1,491,112	909,912
2012	7,255	1,285	836	4,101	1,023	8,947,239	5,250,842	1,220,930	1,576,616	874,850
2013	6,950	1,194	849	3,937	960	9,433,525	5,667,790	1,281,662	1,648,153	806,933
2014	6,669	1,110	860	3,789	900	10,112,716	6,089,894	1,445,246	1,729,783	807,157
2015	6,358	1,027	816	3,629	876	10,657,721	6,393,433	1,573,880	1,823,558	823,906
2016	6,068	962	794	3,482	820	11,280,518	6,786,562	1,713,434	1,873,530	867,643
2017	5,797	897	783	3,331	776	11,859,860	7,153,816	1,776,419	1,949,135	933,174
2018	5,551	850	763	3,219	709	12,307,919	7,420,588	1,910,259	2,006,686	924,864

Note: Figures are for the end of the year shown through 1990 and for June 30 thereafter. (1) Includes U.S. branches of foreign banks not listed separately. (2) Nonmembers are banks that are not members of the Federal Reserve System; national charter and state charter institutions are Federal Reserve members. (3) Figures for 1935 do not include S&Ls, the data for which are not available.

U.S. Bank Failures, 1934-2018

Source: Federal Deposit Insurance Corp. (FDIC)

Covers all FDIC-insured commercial and savings banks, including savings and loan institutions (S&Ls) 1980 and after. As of Oct. 10, 2018.

Year	Closed or assisted	Year	Closed or assisted	Year	Closed or assisted	Year	Closed or assisted	Year	Closed or assisted
1934	9	1960-69	44	1989	534	2000	7	2010	157
1935	25	1970-79	79	1990	382	2001	4	2011	92
1936	69	1980	22	1991	271	2002	11	2012	51
1937	75	1981	40	1992	181	2003	3	2013	24
1938	74	1982	119	1993	50	2004	4	2014	18
1939	60	1983	99	1994	15	2005	0	2015	8
1940	43	1984	106	1995	8	2006	0	2016	5
1941	15	1985	180	1996	6	2007	3	2017	8
1942	20	1986	204	1997	1	2008	30	2018	0
1943-49	21	1987	262	1998	3	2009	148	**Total,**	
1950-59	28	1988	470	1999	8			**1934-2018**	**4,096**

Largest U.S. Bank Holding Companies, 2018

Source: National Information Center, Federal Financial Institutions Examination Council

(ranked by total assets, in millions of dollars; as of Mar. 31, 2018)

Rank	Institution, location	Assets	Rank	Institution, location	Assets
1.	JPMorgan Chase & Co., New York, NY	$2,609,785	19.	Ally Financial Inc., Detroit, MI	$170,021
2.	Bank of America Corp., Charlotte, NC	2,338,754	20.	Barclays U.S. LLC, New York, NY	166,157
3.	Citigroup Inc., New York, NY	1,922,104	21.	State Farm Mutual Automobile Insurance	
4.	Wells Fargo & Company, San Francisco, CA	1,915,388		Company, Bloomington, IL	158,976
5.	Goldman Sachs Group, Inc., New York, NY	973,546	22.	United Services Automobile Association, San	
6.	Morgan Stanley, New York, NY	858,495		Antonio, TX	157,945
7.	U.S. Bancorp, Minneapolis, MN	460,119	23.	MUFG Americas Holdings Corp., New York, NY	157,310
8.	TD Group U.S. Holdings LLC, Wilmington, DE	382,198	24.	Citizens Financial Group, Inc., Providence, RI	153,851
9.	PNC Financial Services Group, Inc.,		25.	BNP Paribas USA, Inc., New York, NY	146,266
	Pittsburgh, PA	379,754	26.	Fifth Third Bancorp, Cincinnati, OH.	141,500
10.	Bank of New York Mellon Corp., New York, NY	373,597	27.	UBS Americas Holding LLC, New York, NY	140,921
11.	Capital One Financial Corp., McLean, VA.	362,857	28.	Credit Suisse Holdings (USA), Inc., New York,	
12.	Teachers Insurance & Annuity Association of			NY.	139,637
	America, New York, NY.	298,107	29.	BMO Financial Corp., Wilmington, DE	138,860
13.	HSBC North America Holdings Inc., New York,		30.	KeyCorp, Cleveland, OH.	137,486
	NY.	289,643	31.	DB USA Corp., New York, NY.	133,302
14.	State Street Corp., Boston, MA	250,286	32.	Northern Trust Corp., Chicago, IL.	129,672
15.	Charles Schwab Corp., San Francisco, CA	248,320	33.	Santander Holdings USA, Inc., Boston, MA	129,228
16.	BB&T Corp., Winston-Salem, NC	220,729	34.	Regions Financial Corp., Birmingham, AL	123,042
17.	SunTrust Banks, Inc., Atlanta, GA	205,430	35.	M&T Bank Corp., Buffalo, NY.	118,623
18.	American Express Company, New York, NY.	179,944			

Note: Includes foreign-owned banks with a strong presence in the U.S.

Status of Top Recipients of Treasury Department "Bailout" Funds, 2018

Source: ProPublica

Since Oct. 2008, the federal government has spent $632 bil to bail out more than 900 institutions severely affected by the financial crisis. As of Oct. 1, 2018, the government had recouped $390 bil in loans and $323 bil in dividends, interest, and other returns, leading to an overall profit of more than $97 bil. Companies that have failed to repay the government, resulting in a loss to the taxpayers, are listed in bold italics.

(in billions of dollars, ranked by amount disbursed; as of Oct. 10, 2018)

Recipient	Disbursed	Repaid[1]	Net profit or amount outstanding	Recipient	Disbursed	Repaid[1]	Net profit or amount outstanding
Fannie Mae	$119.8	$171.7	$51.9	BB&T	$3.1	$3.3	$0.2
Freddie Mac	71.6	114.0	42.3	*Wells Fargo Bank, NA*	*3.1*	*0.0*	*−3.1*
AIG	67.8	72.9	5.0	JPMorgan Chase			
General Motors	*50.7*	*39.4*	*−11.4*	*subsidiaries*	*3.0*	*0.0*	*−3.0*
Bank of America	45.0	49.6	4.6	Bank of New York Mellon	3.0	3.2	0.2
Citigroup	45.0	58.4	13.4	KeyCorp	2.5	2.9	0.4
JPMorgan Chase	25.0	26.7	1.7	*CalHFA Mortgage*			
Wells Fargo	25.0	27.3	2.3	*Assistance Corp.*	*2.3*	*0.0*	*−2.3*
GMAC (now Ally Financial)	16.3	19.3	3.1	*CIT Group*	*2.3*	*—*	*−2.3*
Chrysler	*10.7*	*9.5*	*−1.2*	Comerica Incorporated	2.3	2.6	0.3
Goldman Sachs	10.0	11.4	1.4	*Bank of America subsids.*			
Morgan Stanley	10.0	11.3	1.3	*(incl. Countrywide)*	*2.2*	*0.0*	*−2.2*
PNC Financial Services	7.6	8.3	0.7	State Street	2.0	2.1	0.1
U.S. Bancorp	6.6	6.9	0.3	RLJ Western Asset Public/			
SunTrust	4.9	5.4	0.5	Private Master Fund, L.P.	1.9	2.3	0.5
Ocwen Loan Servicing, LLC	*4.3*	*0.0*	*−4.3*	Invesco Legacy Securities			
Capital One Financial Corp.	3.6	3.8	0.3	Master Fund, L.P.	1.7	2.3	0.6
Regions Financial Corp.	3.5	4.1	0.6	Marshall and Ilsley	1.7	1.9	0.2
Wellington Management				Oaktree PPIP Fund, L.P.	1.7	2.0	0.3
Legacy Securities PPIF				Blackrock PPIF, L.P.	1.6	2.0	0.4
Master Fund, LP	3.4	4.2	0.7	Northern Trust	1.6	1.7	0.1
Fifth Third Bancorp	3.4	4.0	0.6	Chrysler Financial Services	1.5	1.5	—
Hartford Financial Services	3.4	4.2	0.8	Marathon Legacy Securities			
American Express	3.4	3.8	0.4	Public-Private Investment			
AG GECC PPIF Master				Partnership, L.P.	1.4	1.8	0.4
Fund, L.P.	3.4	4.3	0.9	Zions Bancorp	1.4	1.7	0.3
AllianceBernstein Legacy				Huntington Bancshares	1.4	1.6	0.2
Securities Master Fund, L.P.	3.2	3.8	0.6	*Select Portfolio Servicing*	*1.4*	*0.0*	*−1.4*
				Total	**631.4**	**728.4**	**97.1**

— = less than $0.1 bil. **Note:** Total includes other disbursements not shown. Figures may not add up to totals due to rounding. (1) Amounts repaid include principal, dividends, interest, warrants, and other proceeds.

Federal Reserve System

The Federal Reserve System is the central bank for the U.S. The system was established on Dec. 23, 1913, originally to give the country an elastic currency, provide facilities for discounting commercial paper, and improve the supervision of banking. Since then, the system's responsibilities have been broadened. Over the years, stability and growth of the economy, a high level of employment, stability in the purchasing power of the dollar, and reasonable balance in transactions with other countries have come to be recognized as primary objectives of governmental economic policy.

The Federal Reserve System consists of the Board of Governors, the 12 District Reserve Banks and their branch offices, and the Federal Open Market Committee. Several advisory councils help the board meet its varied responsibilities.

The hub of the system is the seven-member **Board of Governors** in Washington, DC. The members of the board are appointed by the president and confirmed by the Senate to 14-year terms. The president also appoints the chairman and vice chairman of the board from among the board members for four-year terms. As of Oct. 2018, the board members were Jerome H. Powell, chair; Richard H. Clarida, vice chair; Randal K. Quarles, vice chair for supervision; and Lael Brainard. Three seats were vacant.

The 12 **District Reserve Banks** and their branch offices serve as the decentralized portion of the system, carrying out day-to-day operations such as circulating currency and coin and providing fiscal agency functions and payments mechanism services. The 12 are in Boston, New York, Philadelphia, Cleveland, Richmond, Atlanta, Chicago, St. Louis, Minneapolis, Kansas City, Dallas, and San Francisco.

The system's principal function is monetary policy, which it controls using three tools: reserve requirements, the discount rate, and open market operations.

Uniform **reserve requirements**, set by the board, are applied to the transaction accounts and nonpersonal time deposits of all depository institutions. Responsibility for setting the **discount rate** (the interest rate at which depository institutions can borrow money from the Reserve Banks) is shared by the Board of Governors and the Reserve Banks. Changes in the discount rate are recommended by the individual boards of directors of the Reserve Banks and are subject to approval by the Board of Governors.

The most important tool of monetary policy is **open market operations**, or the purchase and sale of government securities. Responsibility for influencing the cost and availability of money and credit through the purchase and sale of government securities lies with the **Federal Open Market Committee** (FOMC), which comprises the seven members of the Board of Governors, the president of the Federal Reserve Bank of New York, and four other Federal Reserve Bank presidents, who each serve one-year terms on a rotating basis. The committee bases its decisions on economic and financial developments and outlook, setting yearly growth objectives for key measures of money supply and credit. The decisions of the committee are carried out by the domestic trading desk of the Federal Reserve Bank of New York.

A Federal Advisory Council of banking industry representatives meets with the Federal Reserve Board four times a year to discuss business and financial conditions, as well as to make recommendations.

Website: www.federalreserve.gov

Federal Reserve Board Benchmark Interest Rates, 1955-2018

The interest rate that the Federal Reserve charges its member banks to borrow money overnight, the discount rate, was divided into two categories in 2003: primary credit, for banks in sound financial condition, and secondary credit, for banks that do not qualify for primary credit. The secondary credit rate is ½ a percentage point higher than the primary credit rate shown here for Jan. 9, 2003, and thereafter. Banks typically raise or lower the rates they extend to customers in accordance with changes in these rates.

Effective date	Rate	Effective date	Rate	Effective date	Rate	Effective date	Rate	Effective date	Rate
1955		**1971**		**1980**		**1992**		**2005**	
Jan. 3	1½	Jan. 8	5¼	Feb. 15	13	July 2	3	Feb. 2	3½
Apr. 15	1¾	Jan. 22	5	May 30	12	**1994**		Mar. 22	3¾
Aug. 5	2	Feb. 19	4¾	June 13	11	May 17	3½	May 3	4
Sept. 9	2¼	July 16	5	July 28	10	Aug. 16	4	June 30	4¼
Nov. 18	2½	Nov. 19	4¾	Sept. 26	11	Nov. 15	4¾	Aug. 9	4½
1956		Dec. 17	4½	Nov. 17	12	**1995**		Sept. 20	4¾
Apr. 13	2¾	**1973**		Dec. 5	13	Feb. 1	5	Nov. 1	5
Aug. 24	3	Jan. 15	5	**1981**		**1996**		Dec. 13	5¼
1957		Feb. 26	5½	May 5	14	Jan. 31	5	**2006**	
Aug. 23	3½	May 4	5¾	Nov. 2	13	**1998**		Jan. 31	5½
Nov. 15	3	May 11	6	Dec. 4	12	Oct. 15	4¾	Mar. 28	5¾
1958		June 11	6½	**1982**		Nov. 17	4½	May 10	6
Jan. 24	2¾	July 2	7	July 20	11½	**1999**		June 29	6¼
Mar. 7	2¼	Aug. 14	7½	Aug. 2	11	Aug. 24	4¾	**2007**	
Apr. 18	1¾	**1974**		Aug. 16	10	Nov. 16	5	Aug. 17	5¾
Sept. 12	2	Apr. 25	8	Aug. 27	10	**2000**		Sept. 18	5¼
Nov. 7	2½	Dec. 9	7¾	Oct. 12	9½	Feb. 2	5¼	Nov. 1	5
1959		**1975**		Dec. 15	8½	Mar. 21	5½	Dec. 12	4¾
Mar. 6	3	Jan. 10	7¼	**1984**		May 16	6	**2008**	
May 29	3½	Feb. 5	6¾	Apr. 9	9	**2001**		Jan. 22	4
Sept. 11	4	Mar. 10	6¼	Nov. 21	8½	Jan. 3	5¾	Jan. 30	3½
1960		May 16	6	Dec. 24	8	Jan. 31	5	Mar. 17	3¼
June 10	3½	**1976**		**1985**		Mar. 20	4½	Mar. 18	2½
Aug. 12	3	Jan. 19	5½	May 20	7½	Apr. 18	4	Apr. 30	2¼
1963		Nov. 22	5¼	**1986**		May 15	3½	Oct. 8	1¾
July 17	3½	**1977**		Mar. 7	7	June 27	3¼	Oct. 29	1¼
1964		Aug. 31	5¾	Apr. 21	6½	Aug. 21	3	Dec. 16	½
Nov. 24	4	Oct. 26	6	July 11	6	Sept. 17	2½	**2010**	
1965		**1978**		Aug. 21	5½	Oct. 2	2	Feb. 19	¾
Dec. 6	4½	Jan. 9	6½	**1987**		Dec. 11	1¼	**2015**	
1967		May 11	7	Sept. 4	6	**2002**		Dec. 17	1
Apr. 7	4	July 3	7¼	**1988**		Nov. 6	¾	**2016**	
Nov. 20	4½	Aug. 21	7¾	Aug. 9	6½	**2003**		Dec. 15	1¼
1968		Sept. 22	8	**1989**		Jan. 9	2¼	**2017**	
Mar. 22	5	Oct. 16	8½	Feb. 24	7	June 25	2	Mar. 16	1½
Apr. 19	5½	Nov. 1	9½	**1990**		**2004**		June 15	1¾
Aug. 30	5¼	**1979**		Dec. 18	6½	June 30	2¼	Dec. 14	2
Dec. 18	5½	July 20	10	**1991**		Aug. 10	2½	**2018**	
1969		Aug. 17	10½	Apr. 30	5½	Sept. 21	2¾	Mar. 22	2¼
Apr. 4	6	Sept. 19	11	Sept. 13	5	Nov. 10	3	June 14	2½
1970		Oct. 8	12	Nov. 6	4½	Dec. 14	3¼	Sept. 27	2¾
Nov. 13	5¾			Dec. 20	3½				
Dec. 4	5½								

Note: As of Oct. 15, 2018, rate effective Sept. 27, 2018, was unchanged.

Standard & Poor's 500 Index, 1965-2018

Source: S&P Dow Jones Indices

(as of Oct. 10, 2018)

Year	Highest close		Lowest close		Year	Highest close		Lowest close	
1965	Nov. 15	92.63	June 28	81.60	2006	Dec. 15	1,427.09	June 13	1,223.69
1970	Jan. 5	93.46	May 26	69.29	2007	Oct. 9	1,565.15	Mar. 5	1,374.12
1975	July 15	95.61	Jan. 8	70.04	2008	Jan. 2	1,447.16	Nov. 20	752.44
1980	Nov. 28	140.52	Mar. 27	98.22	2009	Dec. 28	1,127.78	Mar. 9	676.53
1985	Dec. 16	212.02	Jan. 4	163.68	2010	Dec. 29	1,259.78	July 2	1,022.58
1990	July 16	368.95	Oct. 11	295.46	2011	Apr. 29	1,363.61	Oct. 3	1,099.23
1995	Dec. 13	621.69	Jan. 3	459.11	2012	Sept. 14	1,465.77	Jan. 3	1,277.06
2000	Mar. 24	1,527.46	Dec. 20	1,264.74	2013	Dec. 31	1,848.36	Jan. 8	1,457.15
2001	Jan. 30	1,373.73	Sept. 21	965.80	2014	Dec. 29	2,090.57	Feb. 3	1,741.89
2002	Jan. 4	1,172.51	Oct. 9	776.76	2015	May 21	2,130.82	Aug. 25	1,867.61
2003	Dec. 31	1,111.92	Mar. 11	800.73	2016	Dec. 13	2,271.72	Feb. 11	1,829.08
2004	Dec. 30	1,213.55	Aug. 12	1,063.23	2017	Dec. 18	2,690.16	Jan. 3	2,257.83
2005	Dec. 14	1,272.74	Apr. 20	1,137.50	2018	Sept. 20	2,930.75	Feb. 8	2,581.00

U.S. Holdings of Foreign Securities, 2005-16

Source: *U.S. Portfolio Holdings of Foreign Securities*, U.S. Dept. of the Treasury

(in billions of dollars; countries within each region ranked by 2016 holdings)

Country	2005	2010	2014	2015	2016	Country	2005	2010	2014	2015	2016
Europe	$2,297	$3,154	$4,847	$4,472	$4,433	Latin America and					
United Kingdom . .	815	1,001	1,300	1,240	1,196	Caribbean	$739	$1,064	$2,007	$1,959	$2,214
France	274	366	485	474	496	Cayman Islands . .	249	366	1,112	1,217	1,369
Ireland	75	132	387	498	462	Bermuda[1]	187	160	227	217	247
Netherlands	192	233	388	404	436	Brazil	90	235	166	116	151
Switzerland	196	327	424	420	421	Mexico	86	109	166	148	145
Germany	217	299	375	378	373	Curaçao[2]	47	83	82	70	91
Sweden	75	122	165	138	134	British Virgin					
Luxembourg	46	100	133	128	132	Islands[1]	8	16	77	63	64
Spain	70	87	133	115	112	Asia	940	1,342	1,757	1,817	1,888
Jersey[1]	19	42	91	92	102	Japan	531	519	689	822	854
Italy	79	66	109	107	92	South Korea	119	148	178	171	177
Denmark	25	49	69	90	75	China	28	102	133	108	101
Canada	419	695	844	705	831	India	33	91	129	130	133
Australia	128	323	311	296	296	Taiwan	58	95	114	108	130
Africa	46	99	121	104	119	Hong Kong	46	135	151	136	124
South Africa	34	78	83	63	79	Singapore	36	64	98	99	115
Israel	44	64	75	80	65	Total	4,609	6,763	9,604	9,455	9,891

Note: Regional totals include countries not shown here. (1) Not included in UK totals. (2) Figures are for Netherlands Antilles prior to 2012.

Record One-Day Gains and Losses of the Dow Jones Industrial Average

Source: S&P Dow Jones Indices

(ranked by largest one-day losses and gains for two terms; as of Oct. 10, 2018)

	Greatest % gains					Greatest point gains			
Rank	Date	Close	Net chg.	% chg.	Rank	Date	Close	Net chg.	% chg.
1.	3/15/1933	62.10	8.26	15.34%	1.	10/13/2008	9,387.61	936.42	11.08%
2.	10/6/1931	99.34	12.86	14.87	2.	10/28/2008	9,065.12	889.35	10.88
3.	10/30/1929	258.47	28.40	12.34	3.	11/13/2008	8,835.25	552.59	6.67
4.	9/21/1932	75.16	7.67	11.36	4.	3/16/2000	10,630.60	499.19	4.93
5.	10/13/2008	9,387.61	936.42	11.08	5.	3/23/2009	7,775.86	497.48	6.84

	Greatest % losses					Greatest point losses			
Rank	Date	Close	Net chg.	% chg.	Rank	Date	Close	Net chg.	% chg.
1.	10/19/1987	1,738.74	−508.00	−22.61%	1.	9/29/2008	10,365.45	−777.68	−6.98%
2.	10/28/1929	260.64	−38.33	−12.82	2.	10/15/2008	8,577.91	−733.08	−7.87
3.	10/29/1929	230.07	−30.57	−11.73	3.	9/17/2001	8,920.70	−684.81	−7.13
4.	11/6/1929	232.13	−25.55	−9.92	4.	12/1/2008	8,149.09	−679.95	−7.70
5.	12/18/1899	58.27	−5.57	−8.72	5.	10/9/2008	8,579.19	−678.91	−7.33

Dow Jones Industrial Average, 1965-2018

Source: S&P Dow Jones Indices

(as of Oct. 10, 2018)

Year	Highest close		Lowest close		Year	Highest close		Lowest close	
1965	Dec. 31	969.26	June 28	840.59	2002	Mar. 19	10,635.25	Oct. 9	7,286.27
1970	Dec. 29	842.00	May 6	631.16	2003	Dec. 31	10,453.90	Mar. 11	7,524.06
1975	July 15	881.81	Jan. 2	632.04	2004	Dec. 28	10,854.54	Oct. 25	9,749.99
1980	Nov. 20	1,000.17	Apr. 21	759.13	2005	Mar. 4	10,940.50	Apr. 20	10,012.36
1985	Dec. 16	1,553.10	Jan. 4	1,184.96	2006	Dec. 27	12,510.57	Jan. 20	10,667.39
1990	July 16	2,999.75	Oct. 11	2,365.10	2007	Oct. 9	14,164.53	Mar. 5	12,050.41
1991	Dec. 31	3,168.83	Jan. 9	2,470.30	2008	Jan. 3	13,056.72	Nov. 20	7,552.29
1992	June 1	3,413.21	Oct. 9	3,136.58	2009	Dec. 30	10,548.51	Mar. 9	6,547.05
1993	Dec. 29	3,794.33	Jan. 20	3,241.95	2010	Dec. 29	11,585.38	July 2	9,686.48
1994	Jan. 31	3,978.36	Apr. 4	3,593.35	2011	Apr. 29	12,810.54	Oct. 3	10,655.30
1995	Dec. 13	5,216.47	Jan. 30	3,832.08	2012	Oct. 5	13,610.15	June 4	12,101.46
1996	Dec. 27	6,560.91	Jan. 10	5,032.94	2013	Dec. 31	16,576.66	Jan. 8	13,328.85
1997	Aug. 6	8,259.31	Apr. 11	6,391.69	2014	Dec. 26	18,053.71	Feb. 3	15,372.80
1998	Nov. 23	9,374.27	Aug. 31	7,539.07	2015	May 19	18,312.39	Aug. 25	15,666.44
1999	Dec. 31	11,497.12	Jan. 22	9,120.67	2016	Dec. 20	19,974.62	Feb. 11	15,660.18
2000	Jan. 14	11,722.98	Mar. 7	9,796.03	2017	Dec. 28	24,837.51	Jan. 19	19,732.40
2001	May 21	11,337.92	Sept. 21	8,235.81	2018	Oct. 3	26,828.39	Mar. 23	23,533.20

Milestones of the Dow Jones Industrial Average

(as of Oct. 10, 2018)

First close over—		First close over—		First close over—		First close over—		First close over—	
100	Jan. 12, 1906	3,500	May 19, 1993	7,000	Feb. 13, 1997	13,000	Apr. 25, 2007	20,000	Jan. 25. 2017
500	Mar. 12, 1956	4,000	Feb. 23, 1995	8,000	July 16, 1997	14,000	July 19, 2007	21,000	Mar. 1, 2017
1,000	Nov. 14, 1972	4,500	June 16, 1995	9,000	Apr. 6, 1998	15,000	June 27, 2013	22,000	Aug. 2, 2017
1,500	Dec. 11, 1985	5,000	Nov. 21, 1995	10,000	Mar. 29, 1999	16,000	Nov. 21, 2013	23,000	Oct. 17, 2017
2,000	Jan. 8, 1987	5,500	Feb. 8, 1996	10,500	Apr. 21, 1999	17,000	July 3, 2014	24,000	Nov. 30, 2017
2,500	July 17, 1987	6,000	Oct. 14, 1996	11,000	May 3, 1999	18,000	Dec. 23, 2014	25,000	Jan. 4, 2018
3,000	Apr. 17, 1991	6,500	Nov. 25, 1996	12,000	Oct. 19, 2006	19,000	Nov. 22, 2016	26,000	Jan. 16, 2018

Components of the Dow Jones Averages

(as of Oct. 1, 2018)

Dow Jones Industrial Average

- 3M Co. (MMM)
- American Express Co. (AXP)
- Apple Inc. (AAPL)
- Boeing Co. (BA)
- Caterpillar Inc. (CAT)
- Chevron Corp. (CVX)
- Cisco Systems Inc. (CSCO)
- Coca-Cola Co. (KO)
- DowDuPont (DWDP)
- Exxon Mobil Corp. (XOM)
- Goldman Sachs Group Inc. (GS)
- Home Depot Inc. (HD)
- Intel Corp. (INTC)
- International Business Machines Corp. (IBM)
- Johnson & Johnson (JNJ)
- JPMorgan Chase & Co. (JPM)
- McDonald's Corp. (MCD)
- Merck & Co. Inc. (MRK)
- Microsoft Corp. (MSFT)
- Nike Inc. (NKE)
- Pfizer Inc. (PFE)
- Procter & Gamble Co. (PG)
- Travelers Companies Inc. (TRV)
- United Technologies Corp. (UTX)
- UnitedHealth Group Inc. (UNH)
- Verizon Communications Inc. (VZ)
- Visa Inc. (V)
- Walgreens Boots Alliance (WBA)
- Walmart Inc. (WMT)
- Walt Disney Co. (DIS)

Note: In June 2018, General Electric, the last company remaining from the original 1896 Dow Jones industrial average, was replaced by Walgreens Boots Alliance.

Dow Jones Utility Average

- AES Corp. (AES)
- American Electric Power Co. Inc. (AEP)
- American Water Works Co. Inc. (AWK)
- CenterPoint Energy Inc. (CNP)
- Consolidated Edison Inc. (ED)
- Dominion Resources Inc. (D)
- Duke Energy Corp. (DUK)
- Edison International (EIX)
- Exelon Corp. (EXC)
- FirstEnergy Corp. (FE)
- NextEra Energy Inc. (NEE)
- NiSource Inc. (NI)
- PG&E Corp. (PCG)
- Public Service Enterprise Group Inc. (PEG)
- Southern Co. (SO)

Dow Jones Transportation Average

- Alaska Air Group Inc. (ALK)
- American Airlines Group Inc. (AAL)
- Avis Budget Group Inc. (CAR)
- C.H. Robinson Worldwide Inc. (CHRW)
- CSX Corp. (CSX)
- Delta Air Lines Inc. (DAL)
- Expeditors International of Washington Inc. (EXPD)
- FedEx Corp. (FDX)
- J.B. Hunt Transport Services Inc. (JBHT)
- JetBlue Airways Corp. (JBLU)
- Kansas City Southern (KSU)
- Kirby Corp. (KEX)
- Landstar System Inc. (LSTR)
- Matson Inc. (MATX)
- Norfolk Southern Corp. (NSC)
- Ryder System Inc. (R)
- Southwest Airlines Co. (LUV)
- Union Pacific Corp. (UNP)
- United Continental Holdings (UAL)
- United Parcel Service Inc. (UPS)

Record One-Day Gains and Losses of the Nasdaq Composite Index

Source: Nasdaq, Inc.

(ranked by largest one-day losses and gains for two terms; as of Oct. 10, 2018)

Greatest point gains			Greatest % gains			Greatest point losses			Greatest % losses		
Rank	Date	Change	Rank	Date	% change	Rank	Date	Change	Rank	Date	% change
1.	1/3/2001	324.83	1.	1/3/2001	14.17%	1.	4/14/2000	−355.49	1.	10/19/1987	−11.35%
2.	12/5/2000	274.05	2.	10/13/2008	11.81	2.	4/3/2000	−349.15	2.	4/14/2000	−9.67
3.	4/18/2000	254.41	3.	12/5/2000	10.48	3.	4/12/2000	−286.27	3.	9/29/2008	−9.14
4.	5/30/2000	254.37	4.	10/28/2008	9.53	4.	2/8/2018	−274.82	4.	10/20/1987	−9.00
5.	10/19/2000	247.04	5.	4/5/2001	8.92	5.	2/5/2018	−273.42	5.	10/26/1987	−9.00
6.	10/13/2000	242.09	6.	4/18/2001	8.12	6.	4/10/2000	−258.25	6.	12/1/2008	−8.95
7.	6/2/2000	230.88	7.	5/30/2000	7.94	7.	1/4/2000	−229.46	7.	8/31/1998	−8.56
8.	4/25/2000	228.75	8.	10/13/2000	7.87	8.	3/27/2018	−211.73	8.	10/15/2008	−8.47
9.	3/26/2018	227.87	9.	10/19/2000	7.79	9.	6/24/2016	−202.06	9.	4/3/2000	−7.64
10.	4/17/2000	217.87	10.	5/8/2002	7.78	10.	3/14/2000	−200.61	10.	1/2/2001	−7.23

Nasdaq Composite Index Closing Prices, 1971-2018

Source: Nasdaq, Inc.; as of Oct. 10, 2018

Year	High	Low	Year	High	Low	Year	High	Low	Year	High	Low
1971	114.12	99.68	1983	329.11	229.88	1995	1,072.82	740.53	2007	2,811.61	2,340.68
1972	135.15	113.65	1984	288.41	223.91	1996	1,328.45	978.17	2008	2,609.63	1,505.90
1973	136.84	88.67	1985	325.53	245.82	1997	1,748.62	1,194.39	2009	2,167.70	1,265.52
1974	96.53	54.87	1986	411.21	322.14	1998	2,200.63	1,357.09	2010	2,671.48	2,091.79
1975	88.00	60.70	1987	456.27	288.49	1999	4,090.61	2,193.13	2011	2,873.54	2,335.83
1976	97.88	78.06	1988	397.54	329.00	2000	5,048.62	2,332.78	2012	3,183.95	2,648.36
1977	105.05	93.66	1989	487.60	376.87	2001	2,892.36	1,387.06	2013	4,176.59	3,091.81
1978	139.25	99.09	1990	470.30	322.93	2002	2,059.38	1,114.11	2014	4,806.91	3,996.96
1979	152.29	117.84	1991	586.35	352.85	2003	2,009.88	1,271.47	2015	5,218.86	4,506.49
1980	208.29	124.09	1992	676.95	545.85	2004	2,178.00	1,752.00	2016	5,487.44	4,266.84
1981	223.96	170.80	1993	790.56	645.02	2005	2,273.37	1,904.18	2017	6,965.36	5,429.09
1982	241.63	158.92	1994	803.93	691.23	2006	2,465.98	2,020.39	2018	8,109.69	6,777.16

Average Yields of Treasury, Corporate, and State and Local Bonds, 1977-2018

Source: Office of Market Finance, U.S. Dept. of the Treasury; Federal Reserve System

Year	Treasury 30-year bonds[1]	New Aa corporate bonds[2]	State and local bonds[3]	Year	Treasury 30-year bonds[1]	New Aa corporate bonds[2]	State and local bonds[3]	Year	Treasury 30-year bonds[1]	New Aa corporate bonds[2]	State and local bonds[3]
1977	7.75%	8.02%	5.68%	1991	8.14%	8.77%	6.92%	2005	4.64%	5.24%	4.40%
1978	8.49	8.73	6.03	1992	7.67	8.14	6.44	2006	4.91	5.59	4.40
1979	9.28	9.63	6.52	1993	6.59	7.22	5.59	2007	4.84	5.56	4.40
1980	11.27	11.94	8.55	1994	7.37	7.96	6.19	2008	4.28	5.63	4.85
1981	13.45	14.17	11.34	1995	6.88	7.59	5.95	2009	4.08	5.31	4.62
1982	12.76	13.79	11.64	1996	6.71	7.37	5.76	2010	4.25	4.94	4.30
1983	11.18	12.04	9.51	1997	6.61	7.26	5.52	2011	3.91	4.64	4.50
1984	12.41	12.71	10.10	1998	5.58	6.53	5.09	2012	2.92	3.67	3.73
1985	10.79	11.37	9.11	1999	5.87	7.04	5.43	2013	3.45	4.24	4.26
1986	7.78	9.02	7.34	2000	5.94	7.62	5.71	2014	3.34	4.16	4.24
1987	8.59	9.38	7.65	2001	5.49	7.08	5.15	2015	2.84	3.89	3.65
1988	8.96	9.71	7.68	2002	5.43	6.49	5.04	2016	2.59	3.67	3.14
1989	8.45	9.26	7.23	2003	4.96	5.67	4.75	2017	2.89	3.74	NA
1990	8.61	9.32	7.27	2004	5.04	5.63	4.68	2018[4]	3.05	3.96	NA

NA = Not available. (1) On Feb. 18, 2002, the U.S. Treasury discontinued the 30-year constant maturity yield and reintroduced it on Feb. 9, 2006; rates in the interim are for 20-year yields. (2) Treasury series based on 3-week moving average of reoffering yields of new corporate bonds rated Aa by Moody's Investors Service with an original maturity of at least 20 years. Treasury discontinued yield index after Jan. 31, 2003. Rates thereafter are for Moody's seasoned Aaa corporate bonds as listed by Federal Reserve. (3) Index of new reoffering yields on 20-year general obligations rated Aa by Moody's Investors Service; discontinued by Treasury Jan. 31, 2003; rates thereafter are from Bond Buyer Index of general obligation, 20 years to maturity, mixed quality state and local bonds. (4) Rates are for June 2018.

Ownership of U.S. Treasury Securities, 1990-2017

Source: *Treasury Bulletin, Sept. 2018*, Financial Management Service, U.S. Dept. of the Treasury

In 1990, just over 14% of U.S. treasury securities were held by foreign and international investors. By 2016, the total public debt had sextupled, while the portion held by investors outside the U.S. had more than doubled, to 31%.

(in billions of dollars)

	1990	1995	2000	2005	2010	2015	2016	2017
Total public debt	$3,365	$4,989	$5,662	$8,170	$14,025	$18,922	$19,977	$20,493
Federal Reserve and intra-governmental holdings...	1,060	1,681	2,782	4,200	5,656	7,711	8,006	8,132
Total privately held	2,305	3,308	2,880	3,971	8,369	11,211	11,971	12,361
Depository institutions	207	315	261	129	319	547	652	634
U.S. savings bonds	126	185	185	205	188	172	166	160
Private pension funds[1]	130	142	182	184	207	505	527	387
Pension funds of state and local governments	145	192	206	154	154	174	190	228
Insurance companies	138	242	117	202	248	304	328	371
Mutual funds	163	287	338	254	722	1,315	1,703	1,803
State and local governments	411	290	246	512	596	651	714	723
Foreign and international	487	835	1,201	2,034	4,436	6,146	6,006	6,285
Other investors[2]	500	821	145	295	1,500	1,396	1,687	1,770

(1) Includes securities held by the Federal Employees Retirement System Thrift Savings Plan "G Fund." (2) Includes individuals, government-sponsored enterprises, brokers and dealers, bank personal trusts and estates, corporate and noncorporate businesses, and other investors.

Financial Assets of U.S. Families, 1989-2016

Source: Survey of Consumer Finances (triennial), Federal Reserve System

Category	1989	1992	1995	1998	2001	2004	2007	2010	2013	2016
Median net worth (thous.)	$47.2	$61.3	$66.4	$78.0	$106.1	$107.2	$126.4	$77.3	$83.7	$97.3
Average net worth (thous.)	183.7	230.5	244.8	307.4	487.0	517.1	584.6	498.8	551.3	692.1
Percent of families holding asset										
Any asset	NA	NA	96.3%	96.8%	96.7%	97.9%	97.7%	97.4%	97.9%	99.4%
Any financial asset	88.4%	90.7%	91.0	92.9	93.1	93.8	93.9	94.0	94.5	98.5
Transaction accounts	85.1	87.5	87.0	90.5	90.9	91.3	92.1	92.5	93.2	98.0
Certificates of deposit	19.4	16.6	14.3	15.3	15.7	12.7	16.1	12.2	7.8	6.5
Savings bonds	23.8	22.7	22.8	19.3	16.7	17.6	14.9	12.0	10.0	8.6
Bonds	5.3	4.7	3.1	3.0	3.0	1.8	1.6	1.6	1.4	1.2
Stocks	16.2	17.8	15.2	19.2	21.3	20.7	17.9	15.1	13.8	13.9
Pooled investment funds (mutual funds)	7.1	11.2	12.3	16.5	17.7	15.0	11.4	8.7	8.2	10.0
Retirement accounts	35.4	39.3	45.2	48.8	52.2	49.7	52.6	50.4	49.2	52.1
Cash value life insurance	34.7	35.3	32.0	29.6	28.0	24.2	23.0	19.7	19.2	19.4
Other managed assets	3.5	4.3	3.9	5.9	6.6	7.3	5.8	5.7	5.2	5.5
Other	13.4	11.4	11.1	9.4	9.3	10.0	9.3	8.0	6.9	8.1
Any nonfinancial asset	89.1	91.3	90.9	89.9	90.7	92.5	92.0	91.3	91.0	90.8
Vehicles	83.6	86.4	84.1	82.8	84.8	86.3	87.0	86.7	86.3	85.2
Primary residence	63.8	63.8	64.7	66.2	67.7	69.1	68.6	67.3	65.2	63.7
Other residential property	20.0	20.0	11.8	12.8	11.3	12.5	13.7	14.3	13.2	13.8
Equity in nonresidential property	NA	NA	9.4	8.6	8.3	8.3	8.1	7.7	7.2	6.2
Business equity	13.2	14.9	11.1	11.5	11.8	11.5	12.0	13.3	11.7	13.0
Other	11.9	8.5	9.0	8.5	7.6	7.8	7.2	7.0	7.3	6.5

NA = Not available.

Characteristics of Mutual Fund Investors, 2017

Source: *The Investment Company Fact Book 2018*, Investment Company Institute

Median age of head of household	51	Married or living with a partner	72%
Median annual household income	$100,000	Four-year college degree or more	51%
Median household financial assets	$200,000	Own Individual Retirement Accounts (IRAs)	64%
Median mutual fund assets	$120,000	Hold more than half their financial assets in	
Median number of funds owned	3	mutual funds	65%
Employed	74%		

Performance of Mutual Funds by Type, 2018

Source: *Kiplinger's Personal Finance* magazine analysis of Morningstar data
(as of Aug. 31, 2018)

Fund type/fund objective	Average annual return 1-year	3-year	5-year	Fund type/fund objective	Average annual return 1-year	3-year	5-year
Large-Company				**Sector**			
Growth	24.40%	16.28%	15.05%	Equity Precious Metals	15.37%	13.49%	12.06%
Blend	17.70	13.95	12.62	Financial	−23.93	9.43	−6.57
Value	14.18	12.23	10.73	Health	21.05	9.45	15.54
Midsize-Company				Natural Resources	9.95	9.60	2.30
Growth	24.45	14.33	12.99	Real Estate	5.75	8.88	9.81
Blend	16.69	11.75	11.07	Technology	28.51	24.26	19.82
Value	13.57	11.42	10.43	Utilities	2.35	11.00	10.00
Small-Company				**Multialternative**			
Growth	32.89	16.87	13.48	Multialternative Funds	2.02	2.06	2.23
Blend	21.89	13.96	11.48	**International**			
Value	18.68	13.10	10.06	Diversified Emerging Markets	−2.79	9.40	4.06
Taxable Government Bond				World Bond	−1.61	2.44	1.46
Short-Term	−0.23	0.35	0.58	World Stock	11.01	11.16	9.34
Intermediate-Term	−1.44	0.62	1.58	**Corporate Bond**			
Long-Term	−3.13	2.04	5.10	High Yield	2.67	5.45	4.44
Tax-Free Government Bond				Short-Term	0.40	1.40	1.35
Short-Term Municipal	0.18	0.92	1.11	Intermediate-Term	−0.95	1.88	2.44
Intermediate-Term Municipal	0.14	2.21	3.40	Long-Term	−0.96	4.55	5.65
Long-Term Municipal	0.54	2.82	4.53				

Mutual Fund Ownership, 1940-2017

Source: *The Investment Company Fact Book 2018*, Investment Company Institute

Year	Mutual funds	Mutual fund accounts (thous.)	Total net assets (bil)	Households owning mutual funds Number (thous.)	Percent of all households	Exchange-traded funds (ETFs) Number of funds	Total net assets (bil)
1940	68	296	$0.45	NA	NA	NA	NA
1950	98	939	2.53	NA	NA	NA	NA
1960	161	4,898	17.03	NA	NA	NA	NA
1970	361	10,690	47.62	NA	NA	NA	NA
1980	564	12,088	134.76	4,600	5.7%	NA	NA
1990	3,079	61,948	1,065.19	23,400	25.1	NA	NA
2000	8,154	244,705	6,964.31	48,600	45.7	80	$65.59
2001	8,304	248,701	6,974.63	54,800	52.0	102	82.99
2002	8,242	251,125	6,382.92	54,200	49.6	113	102.14
2003	8,126	260,701	7,401.85	53,300	47.9	119	150.98
2004	8,044	269,479	8,095.50	53,900	48.1	152	227.54
2005	7,976	277,713	8,891.01	50,300	44.4	204	300.82
2006	8,122	288,596	10,397.75	49,900	43.6	359	422.55
2007	8,040	292,555	11,999.71	50,600	43.6	629	608.42
2008	8,039	264,599	9,620.27	52,500	45.0	728	531.29
2009	7,663	269,224	11,111.16	50,400	43.0	797	777.13
2010	7,555	291,299	11,833.09	53,200	45.3	923	991.99
2011	7,590	279,715	11,632.59	52,900	44.1	1,135	1,048.14
2012	7,590	257,074	13,054.49	53,800	44.4	1,195	1,337.12
2013	7,715	264,848	15,048.98	56,700	46.3	1,295	1,674.71
2014	7,927	NA	15,873.40	53,200	43.3	1,412	1,974.55
2015	8,115	NA	15,652.06	53,600	43.0	1,595	2,100.66
2016	8,066	NA	16,343.72	54,900	43.6	1,716	2,524.39
2017	7,956	NA	18,746.29	56,200	44.5	1,832	3,400.70

NA = Not available. **Note:** Does not include data for funds that invest primarily in other mutual funds. Mutual fund accounts data include both individual and omnibus accounts.

Gold Owned by the U.S., 2018

Source: *Status Report of U.S. Treasury-Owned Gold*, Bureau of the Fiscal Service, U.S. Dept. of the Treasury
(as of July 31, 2018; numbers may not add to totals due to rounding)

	Fine troy ounces	Book value		Fine troy ounces	Book value
Total Treasury-owned gold	**261,498,926**	**$11,041,059,958**	**Held by the Federal Reserve**		
Gold bullion	258,641,878	10,920,429,099	**Bank**	**13,452,811**	**$568,007,257**
Gold coins, blanks,			Gold bullion	13,378,981	564,890,013
miscellaneous	2,857,048	120,630,859	Federal Reserve Banks–		
Held by the U.S. Mint	**248,046,116**	**10,473,052,701**	NY vault	13,376,988	564,805,851
Denver, CO, deep storage	43,853,707	1,851,599,996	Federal Reserve Banks–display	1,993	84,162
Fort Knox, KY, deep storage	147,341,858	6,221,097,413	Gold coins	73,830	3,117,244
West Point, NY, deep storage	54,067,331	2,282,841,677	Federal Reserve Banks–		
Gold coins, blanks,			NY vault	73,452	3,101,308
miscellaneous	2,783,219	117,513,615	Federal Reserve Banks–display	377	15,936

World's Leading Gold Producers, 1980-2017

Source: *Mineral Commodity Summaries 2018*, U.S. Geological Survey, U.S. Dept. of the Interior
(ranked by 2017 production; in thousands of troy ounces)

Country	1980	1990	2000	2005	2010	2012	2013	2014	2015	2016	2017[1]
China	225	3,215	5,787	7,234	11,092	12,957	13,825	14,468	14,468	14,564	14,146
Australia	548	7,845	9,530	8,423	8,391	8,038	8,520	8,809	8,938	9,324	9,645
Russia[2]	8,300	9,710	4,598	5,279	6,173	7,009	7,395	7,941	8,102	8,134	8,198
United States . .	970	9,452	11,349	8,231	7,427	7,555	7,395	6,752	6,880	7,137	7,877
Canada	1,627	5,433	5,022	3,844	2,926	3,344	3,987	4,887	4,919	5,305	5,787
Peru	134	293	4,263	6,682	5,273	5,176	4,855	4,501	4,662	4,919	4,983
South Africa . . .	21,669	19,451	13,767	9,474	6,076	5,144	5,144	4,887	4,662	4,662	4,662
Mexico	196	311	848	976	2,347	3,119	3,151	3,794	4,340	3,569	3,537
Uzbekistan	NA	NA	2,733	2,894	2,894	2,990	3,151	3,215	3,279	3,279	3,215
Brazil	NA	NA	NA	NA	1,865	2,090	2,283	2,572	2,604	2,733	2,733
Ghana	353	540	2,318	2,149	2,637	2,797	2,894	2,926	2,829	2,540	2,572
Indonesia	60	360	4,006	4,200	3,858	1,897	1,961	2,218	3,119	2,572	2,572
World	**39,197**	**70,089**	**82,949**	**79,412**	**82,306**	**86,485**	**90,022**	**96,131**	**99,667**	**99,989**	**101,275**

NA = Not available. **Note:** One metric ton is equal to 32,150.7 troy ounces. (1) Estimated. (2) Figures for 1980-90 refer to the former USSR. Includes gold recovered as a byproduct but excludes secondary production.

Prices of Precious Metals, 1990-2017

Source: *Mineral Commodity Summaries 2018*, U.S. Geological Survey, U.S. Dept. of the Interior

Year	Dollars per troy ounce			Dollars per pound			
	Platinum[1]	Gold	Silver	Copper[2]	Lead[3]	Tin[4]	Zinc[5]
1990	$467	$385	$4.82	$1.23	$0.46	$3.86	$0.75
1995	425	386	5.15	1.38	0.42	4.16	0.56
2000	549	280	5.00	0.88	0.44	3.70	0.56
2001	533	272	4.39	0.77	0.44	3.15	0.44
2002	543	311	4.62	0.76	0.44	2.92	0.39
2003	694	365	4.91	0.85	0.44	3.40	0.41
2004	849	411	6.69	1.34	0.55	5.47	0.52
2005	900	446	7.34	1.74	0.61	4.83	0.67
2006	1,144	606	11.57	3.15	0.77	5.65	1.59
2007	1,308	699	13.41	3.28	1.24	8.99	1.54
2008	1,578	874	15.00	3.19	1.20	11.29	0.89
2009	1,208	975	14.69	2.41	0.87	8.37	0.78
2010	1,616	1,228	20.20	3.48	1.09	12.40	1.02
2011	1,725	1,572	35.28	4.06	1.22	15.75	1.06
2012	1,555	1,673	31.22	3.67	1.14	12.83	0.96
2013	1,490	1,415	23.87	3.40	1.10	13.52	0.96
2014	1,388	1,269	19.37	3.18	1.06	10.23	1.07
2015	1,056	1,163	15.72	2.56	0.91	7.56	0.96
2016	990	1,252	17.20	2.25	0.94	8.38	1.01
2017[E]	960	1,260	17.20	2.85	1.13	9.50	1.34

E = Estimated. (1) Average annual dealer prices. (2) U.S. producer price for cathode copper. (3) North American producer price through 2012; North American market price thereafter. (4) *Platts Metals Week* composite price through 2013, New York dealer prices thereafter. (5) *Platts Metals Week* price for North American special high grade zinc except for 1990, which shows average price for high grade zinc.

Top Brands in Selected Categories, 2017-18

Source: Information Resources, Inc., a Chicago-based marketing research company

Data, for the 52-week period ending Aug. 12, 2018, represent "Total U.S. Multi-Outlet Sales," which includes grocery, drug, mass market, and select club, military, and dollar retailers. Percent change represents dollar sales change in 2017-18 over same period in 2016-17.

Product	Sales	% change	Market share
Beer, domestic, total	**$12,217,247,554**	**0.8%**	
Bud Light	1,903,471,167	−4.0	15.58%
Coors Light	1,023,752,988	−2.9	8.38
Miller Lite	902,575,747	0.1	7.39
Michelob Ultra	845,214,418	18.9	6.92
Budweiser	662,333,175	−4.6	5.42
Bottled water, total	**$8,319,509,389**	**6.0%**	
Private label	2,426,186,295	8.7	29.16%
Dasani	698,076,556	1.4	8.39
Nestlé Pure Life	689,066,467	−3.9	8.28
Aquafina	652,880,530	−0.7	7.85
Poland Spring	502,228,445	2.9	6.04
Cat food (dry), total	**$2,350,669,811**	**1.5%**	
Private label	226,034,052	14.5	9.62%
Purina Kit & Kaboodle	198,874,146	−2.3	8.46
Meow Mix Original Choice	191,730,505	1.2	8.16
Purina Cat Chow Naturals	122,798,638	3.1	5.22
Purina Cat Chow Indoor . .	111,107,447	−2.7	4.73
Cereal (ready-to-eat), total	**$8,458,859,013**	**−1.4%**	
Private label	604,275,550	−6.0	7.14%
General Mills Cheerios . . .	419,690,559	26.6	4.96
General Mills Honey Nut Cheerios	412,562,409	−16.4	4.88
Kellogg's Frosted Flakes . .	400,004,912	−0.2	4.73
Post Honey Bunches of Oats	374,644,263	−4.8	4.43

Product	Sales	% change	Market share
Chocolate candy, total	**$4,862,010,306**	**0.2%**	
M&M's	816,446,009	11.7	16.79%
Hershey's	414,370,266	0.9	8.52
Reese's	282,962,362	5.5	5.82
Hershey's Kisses	216,122,928	1.6	4.45
Lindt Lindor	184,422,838	12.4	3.79
Coffee (ground), total	**$3,996,262,261**	**−0.1%**	
Folger's	1,072,734,611	−5.3	26.84%
Maxwell House	509,767,878	−6.7	12.76
Starbucks	448,915,622	5.7	11.23
Private label	428,360,316	12.2	10.72
Dunkin' Donuts	291,622,366	2.7	7.30
Cookies, total	**$7,846,139,016**	**3.7%**	
Private label	1,321,650,287	10.1	16.84%
Nabisco Oreo	681,179,093	2.4	8.68
Nabisco Chips Ahoy!	610,841,812	−1.1	7.79
Nabisco belVita	329,926,791	7.9	4.20
Nabisco Oreo Double Stuf	262,990,988	7.2	3.35
Disposable diapers, total . .	**$3,626,647,668**	**−2.7%**	
Private label	679,499,234	0.3	18.74%
Pampers Swaddlers Sesame Beginnings	410,984,950	−1.8	11.33

Product	Sales	% change	Market share		Product	Sales	% change	Market share
Luvs Ultra Leakguards. . . .	$337,430,647	24.9%	9.3%		Herdez.	$75,250,593	21.1%	6.36%
Huggies Snug & Dry					Chi-Chi's	43,150,107	−3.0	3.65
Disney Baby.	330,982,265	10.1	9.13		**Soft drinks (regular), total**	**13,339,355,686**	**1.1%**	
Huggies Little Movers					Coca-Cola	3,200,850,467	1.4	24.00%
Disney Baby.	296,866,978	1.6	8.19		Pepsi	1,760,434,088	−2.9	13.20
					Mountain Dew	1,352,978,518	−1.0	10.14
Dog food (dry), total	**$5,156,684,190**	**1.7%**			Dr Pepper	1,259,853,121	2.5	9.44
Private label.	738,916,898	−4.6	14.33%		Sprite.	1,153,670,469	4.5	8.65
Pedigree	606,235,859	5.7	11.76		**Soft drinks (low-calorie),**			
Purina Dog Chow	455,530,929	1.8	8.83		**total**	**$5,388,316,802**	**1.6%**	
Purina One Smart Blend . .	344,734,149	−1.8	6.69		Diet Coke.	1,436,478,935	2.7	26.66%
Rachael Ray Nutrish	259,614,182	8.1	5.03		Diet Pepsi	740,687,372	2.3	13.75
					Coca-Cola Zero	587,177,727	16.8	10.90
Ice cream, total	**$5,653,340,371**	**1.3%**			Diet Mountain Dew	506,183,576	−0.5	9.39
Private label.	1,036,725,655	−2.9	18.34%		Diet Dr Pepper.	444,651,050	2.8	8.25
Blue Bell	498,969,758	9.4	8.83					
Häagen-Dazs.	485,948,189	2.4	8.60		**Toilet tissue, total**	**$8,555,410,463**	**0.3%**	
Ben & Jerry's	461,125,955	4.6	8.16		Private label.	1,870,053,155	7.0	21.86%
Breyers	412,468,711	0.3	7.30		Angel Soft	1,159,700,031	−3.2	13.56
					Charmin Ultra Strong.	1,013,110,005	0.3	11.84
Pasta, total.	**$1,883,298,308**	**−1.0%**			Charmin Ultra Soft.	1,008,816,592	−6.2	11.79
Barilla	569,550,290	1.9	30.24%		Scott	920,241,138	−1.7	10.76
Private label.	531,071,608	0.0	28.20					
Ronzoni	105,884,418	−0.7	5.62		**Toothpaste, total**	**$2,882,280,757**	**2.8%**	
Mueller's	70,467,358	0.8	3.74		Crest 3D White.	258,939,945	8.4	8.98%
Creamette	54,266,856	−1.6	2.88		Sensodyne.	213,655,921	12.6	7.41
					Sensodyne ProNamel	188,338,345	5.0	6.53
Potato chips, total.	**$5,846,624,902**	**2.3%**			Colgate Total	178,460,695	3.4	6.19
Lay's	1,699,992,340	0.6	29.08%		Colgate Optic White.	167,873,418	7.5	5.82
Ruffles	692,486,185	15.2	11.84					
Pringles	589,315,772	9.1	10.08		**Yogurt, total**.	**$6,442,328,145**	**−4.1%**	
Private label.	509,347,090	8.6	8.71		Chobani.	855,429,931	−4.2	13.28%
Wavy Lay's.	465,644,095	−5.4	7.96		Dannon Light & Fit.	621,983,619	−4.2	9.65
					Private label.	555,825,958	−1.9	8.63
Salsa, total.	**$1,182,437,586**	**2.3%**			Yoplait Original.	482,626,036	−5.4	7.49
Tostitos	464,159,962	2.0	39.25%		Chobani Flip	360,845,651	6.0	5.60
Private label.	166,028,438	3.0	14.04					
Pace	130,928,960	3.2	11.07					

Note: "Private label" represents the aggregated sales figures for store-branded products in that category. Total category sales include other brands not listed here.

Who Owns What: Familiar Consumer Products and Services

The following is a partial list of well-known consumer brands with their (U.S.) parent companies as of Sept. 2018. Among brands not listed are many whose parent companies have the same or a similar name (e.g., Colgate is owned by Colgate-Palmolive Co.).

ABC broadcasting: Walt Disney
Ace bandages: 3M
Advil: Pfizer
Ajax cleanser: Colgate-Palmolive
Altoids mints: Mars
Amana appliances: Whirlpool
American Girl: Mattel
Aquafina water: PepsiCo
Arm & Hammer: Church & Dwight
Band-Aid bandages: Johnson & Johnson
Barbie dolls: Mattel
Ben & Jerry's ice cream: Unilever
Betty Crocker products: General Mills
Bounty paper towels: Procter & Gamble
Braun appliances: Procter & Gamble
Brita water systems: Clorox
Cadbury chocolates: Mondelēz International
Calphalon cookware: Newell Rubbermaid
Canada Dry ginger ale: Dr Pepper Snapple Group
ChapStick: Pfizer
Charmin toilet tissue: Procter & Gamble
Cheer detergent: Procter & Gamble
Chips Ahoy!: Mondelēz International
Claritin allergy products: Bayer
Contadina tomatoes: Del Monte
Coppertone sunscreen: Bayer
Crest toothpaste: Procter & Gamble
Crisco shortening: J.M. Smucker
Dasani water: Coca-Cola
Depends adult diapers: Kimberly-Clark
Doritos chips: PepsiCo
Dove soap: Unilever
Dreyer's ice cream: Nestlé

ESPN networks: Walt Disney
Febreze: Procter & Gamble
Fisher-Price toys: Mattel
Folgers coffee: J.M. Smucker
Frito-Lay's snacks: PepsiCo
Fruit of the Loom apparel: Berkshire Hathaway
Gatorade sports drinks: PepsiCo
GEICO auto insurance: Berkshire Hathaway
Gerber baby food: Nestlé
Gillette: Procter & Gamble
Glad products: Clorox
Glade air fresheners: S.C. Johnson
Green Giant vegetables: General Mills
Grey Poupon mustard: Kraft Heinz
Halls cough drops: Mondelēz International
Head & Shoulders shampoo: Procter & Gamble
Healthy Choice meals: ConAgra
Hebrew National meats: ConAgra
Hellmann's mayonnaise: Unilever
Hidden Valley Salad dressings: Clorox
Hillshire Farm: Tyson Foods
Hot Wheels/Matchbox cars: Mattel
Hot Pockets: Nestlé
Huggies diapers: Kimberly-Clark
Hunt's tomatoes: ConAgra
Iams pet food: Mars
Irish Spring soap: Colgate-Palmolive
Ivory soap: Procter & Gamble
Jell-O: Kraft Heinz
Jennie-O turkey: Hormel
Jif peanut butter: J.M. Smucker
Jimmy Dean sausages: Tyson Foods

Jolly Rancher candy: Hershey
Keebler cookies: Kellogg Co.
KFC restaurants: Yum! Brands
Kibbles 'n Bits pet food: J.M. Smucker
Kingsford charcoal: Clorox
Kit Kat candy: Hershey
KitchenAid appliances: Whirlpool
Kiwi shoe products: S.C. Johnson
Kleenex: Kimberly-Clark
Knorr soups: Unilever
Kool-Aid: Kraft Heinz
Lea & Perrins Worcestershire sauce: Kraft Heinz
Lipton tea: Unilever
Listerine mouthwash: Johnson & Johnson
Maxwell House coffee: Kraft Heinz
Maytag appliances: Whirlpool
Minute Maid juices: Coca-Cola
Mr. Clean: Procter & Gamble
Monopoly board game: Hasbro
Mountain Dew soda: PepsiCo
Neosporin: Johnson & Johnson
Neutrogena soap: Johnson & Johnson
9Lives cat food: J.M. Smucker
o.b. tampons: Edgewell Personal Care
OFF! insect repellents: S.C. Johnson
Olay: Procter & Gamble
Old Navy clothing: Gap
Old Spice: Procter & Gamble
Oral-B toothbrushes: Procter & Gamble
Oreo cookies: Mondelēz International
Oscar Mayer meats: Kraft Heinz
Pampers diapers: Procter & Gamble
Pantene shampoo: Procter & Gamble
Paper Mate pens: Newell Rubbermaid

Pedigree pet food: Mars
Pepperidge Farm prods.: Campbell Soup
Pepto-Bismol: Procter & Gamble
Perrier water: Nestlé
Philadelphia cream cheese: Kraft Heinz
Pine-Sol cleaner: Clorox
Pizza Hut restaurants: Yum! Brands
Planters nuts: Kraft Heinz
Post-it notes: 3M
Prego pasta sauce: Campbell Soup
Pringles snacks: Kellogg Co.
Promise spread: Unilever
Purina pet foods: Nestlé
Q-tips: Unilever
Quaker Oats: PepsiCo
Raid insecticide: S.C. Johnson
Reese's candy: Hershey
Rice-A-Roni: PepsiCo
Right Guard deodorant: Henkel

Ritz crackers: Mondelēz International
Robitussin: Pfizer
Rogaine hair regrowth treatment: Johnson & Johnson
Saran wrap: S.C. Johnson
Schick razors: Edgewell Personal Care
Scope mouthwash: Procter & Gamble
Scotch tape: 3M
Skippy peanut butter: Hormel
Splenda artificial sweetener: Heartland Food Products
Sprite soda: Coca-Cola
Sudafed: Johnson & Johnson
Swanson broth: Campbell Soup
Taco Bell restaurants: Yum! Brands
Tampax tampons: Procter & Gamble
Tide detergent: Procter & Gamble
Timberland apparel: V.F. Corp.

Trident gum: Mondelēz International
Trojan condoms: Church & Dwight
Tropicana juice: PepsiCo
Twizzlers candy: Hershey
Tylenol: Johnson & Johnson
Uncle Ben's Rice: Mars
V8 vegetable juice: Campbell Soup
Vans apparel: V.F. Corp.
Vaseline: Unilever
Velveeta cheese products: Kraft Heinz
Viagra: Pfizer
Vicks cold medicines: Procter & Gamble
Visine eye drops: Johnson & Johnson
Windex cleaning products: S.C. Johnson
Wrigley's candy and gum: Mars
Xanax: Pfizer
Yoplait yogurt: General Mills
Ziploc storage bags: S.C. Johnson

U.S. Home Ownership Rates by Selected Characteristics 1970-2018

Source: U.S. Census Bureau, U.S. Dept. of Commerce

	1970	1980	1990	1995	2000	2005	2010	2015	2017	2018
Region										
Northeast	58.2%	60.8%	62.2%	62.3%	63.4%	64.7%	64.2%	60.2%	60.4%	61.3%
Midwest	69.3	69.4	67.4	68.5	72.2	73.4	70.8	68.4	68.0	68.3
South	66.3	68.6	65.8	66.5	69.2	70.4	69.1	64.9	65.5	65.9
West	59.4	60.2	57.3	59.8	61.9	63.8	61.4	58.5	58.9	59.7
Age										
Under 35 years	—	—	—	38.7	40.2	42.8	39.0	34.8	35.3	36.5
35-44 years	—	—	—	65.1	67.5	68.7	65.6	58.0	58.8	60.0
45-54 years	—	—	—	75.2	76.7	76.3	73.6	69.9	69.3	70.6
55-64 years	—	—	—	79.9	80.3	81.3	78.7	75.4	75.4	75.1
65+ years	—	—	—	78.1	80.3	80.3	80.4	78.5	78.2	78.0
Race/ethnicity[1]										
White alone, non-Hispanic	—	—	—	70.2	73.7	75.6	74.4	71.6	72.2	72.9
Black alone	—	—	—	42.6	46.7	48.0	46.2	43.0	42.3	41.6
Hispanic	—	—	—	42.2	45.4	49.2	47.8	45.4	45.5	46.6
Other	—	—	—	47.6	54.4	58.0	55.7	52.6	54.3	55.7
Income[2]										
Median family income or more	—	—	—	79.5	81.8	84.0	81.9	78.3	77.9	78.3
Below median family income	—	—	—	48.6	50.8	52.7	51.9	48.6	49.6	50.2
Total U.S.	64.0	65.5	63.7	64.7	67.2	68.6	66.9	63.4	63.7	64.3

Note: Figures are for 2nd quarter of year shown. Not seasonally adjusted. (1) Hispanic householders may be of any race. "Other" includes householders self-identifying as Asian, Native Hawaiian/Pacific Islander, and American Indian/Alaska Native, as well as combinations of two or more races/ethnicities. (2) Due to a change in survey methodology, data from 2010 forward are not directly comparable with prior years.

U.S. Housing Affordability, 1990-2018

Source: National Association of REALTORS®

Year[1]	Median-priced existing home	Avg. mortgage rate[2]	Monthly principal & interest payment	Payment as % of median monthly income	Year[1]	Median-priced existing home	Avg. mortgage rate[2]	Monthly principal & interest payment	Payment as % of median monthly income
1990	$92,000	10.04%	$648	22.0%	2011	$166,200	4.67%	$687	13.4%
1995	110,500	7.85	639	18.9	2012	177,200	3.83	663	12.7
2000	139,000	8.03	818	19.3	2013	197,400	4.00	754	14.1
2005	219,000	5.91	1,040	22.4	2014	208,900	4.31	828	15.1
2008	196,600	6.15	958	18.1	2015	223,900	4.03	858	15.1
2009	172,100	5.14	751	14.8	2016	235,500	3.88	886	15.2
2010	173,100	4.89	734	14.5	2017	248,800	4.20	973	15.9
					2018	279,300	4.74	1,164	18.5

(1) 2018 figures are for June, the latest available. All other figures are annual averages. (2) All figures assume a down payment of 20% of the home price. Based on effective rate on loans closed on existing homes for the period shown.

S&P/Case-Shiller National Home Price Index, 1975-2018

Source: S&P Dow Jones Indices

This index compares the median price of existing U.S. homes over time. The baseline for comparison is Jan. 2000; all numbers before or after reflect home prices in relation to it. For example, the Jan. 2018 index of 196.4 means that home prices were nearly double what they were 18 years earlier, while the Jan. 1975 index of 25.2 means prices then were 25.2% of what they were in 2000.

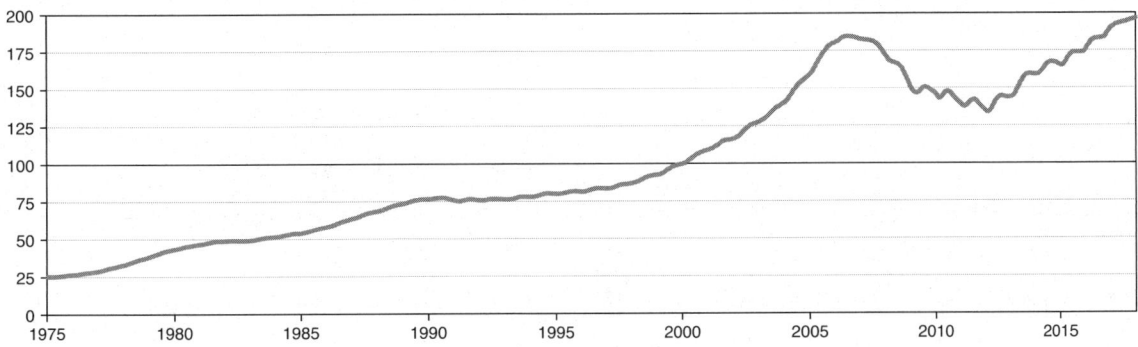

Median Price of Existing Single-Family Homes, by Metropolitan Area, 2010-18

Source: National Association of REALTORS®

Median prices are in thousands of dollars and based on all transactions within time period shown.

Metropolitan area	2010	2017	2018[1]	Metropolitan area	2010	2017	2018[1]
Akron, OH	$108.9	$135.1	$148.6	Little Rock-N. Little Rock-Conway, AR	$132.5	$141.7	$151.5
Albany-Schenectady-Troy, NY	195.7	205.3	212.6	Los Angeles-Long Beach-Glendale, CA	323.3	550.8	557.2
Albuquerque, NM	178.7	196.6	210.6	Louisville/Jefferson County, KY-IN	134.6	171.6	183.9
Allentown-Bethlehem-Easton, PA-NJ	224.0	190.3	200.0	Madison, WI	217.7	267.9	289.5
Amarillo, TX	124.7	157.7	158.1	Manchester-Nashua, NH	232.0	281.9	304.3
Anaheim-Santa Ana-Irvine, CA	546.4	780.0	830.0	Memphis, TN-MS-AR	120.2	166.7	189.1
Atlanta-Sandy Springs-Marietta, GA	114.8	198.5	228.8	Miami-Fort Lauderdale-West Palm			
Atlantic City-Hammonton, NJ	226.4	187.1	193.2	Beach, FL	201.9	330.0	353.0
Austin-Round Rock, TX	193.6	295.8	330.2	Milwaukee-Waukesha-West Allis, WI	205.9	239.6	256.9
Baltimore-Columbia-Towson, MD	246.1	262.9	297.2	Minneapolis-St. Paul-Bloomington,			
Barnstable Town, MA	326.0	385.5	406.8	MN-WI	170.6	252.1	280.2
Baton Rouge, LA	169.6	198.6	212.2	Mobile, AL	121.0	136.8	143.0
Beaumont-Port Arthur, TX	125.1	150.3	153.6	Montgomery, AL	129.0	137.7	145.7
Birmingham-Hoover, AL	143.0	197.0	214.8	Nashville-Davidson—Murfreesboro—			
Bismarck, ND	163.4	242.2	263.2	Franklin, TN	153.8	241.7	263.2
Bloomington, IL	157.9	156.2	157.9	New Haven-Milford, CT	231.0	221.1	238.8
Boise City-Nampa, ID	136.2	226.7	262.8	New Orleans-Metairie, LA	159.7	198.4	216.1
Boston-Cambridge-Newton, MA-NH	357.3	452.9	495.9	New York-Newark-Jersey City,			
Boulder, CO	358.1	566.1	631.1	NY-NJ-PA	393.7	404.3	410.5
Bridgeport-Stamford-Norwalk, CT	408.6	455.9	473.1	North Port-Sarasota-Bradenton, FL	164.6	280.0	295.0
Buffalo-Cheektowaga-Niagara				Norwich-New London, CT	204.7	220.2	231.5
Falls, NY	121.2	142.7	149.1	Oklahoma City, OK	145.7	154.3	164.5
Burlington-South Burlington, VT	261.2	280.1	292.8	Omaha-Council Bluffs, NE-IA	137.3	175.9	195.8
Canton-Massillon, OH	90.9	129.8	136.8	Orlando-Kissimmee-Sanford, FL	134.7	244.9	269.0
Cape Coral-Fort Myers, FL	88.9	243.5	259.3	Palm Bay-Melbourne-Titusville, FL	103.0	210.0	226.4
Cedar Rapids, IA	144.7	152.6	163.2	Pensacola-Ferry Pass-Brent, FL	141.0	185.0	205.0
Champaign-Urbana, IL	141.9	148.8	157.7	Peoria, IL	116.9	122.6	129.4
Charleston-North Charleston, SC	200.5	268.8	291.0	Philadelphia-Camden-Wilmington,			
Charleston, WV	129.1	135.7	141.6	PA-NJ-DE-MD	214.9	230.0	236.1
Charlotte-Concord-Gastonia, NC-SC	143.3	226.9	252.4	Phoenix-Mesa-Scottsdale, AZ	139.2	246.7	272.0
Chattanooga, TN-GA	121.4	176.1	188.6	Pittsfield, MA	195.5	207.9	205.6
Chicago-Naperville-Elgin, IL-IN-WI	191.4	248.5	275.1	Portland-South Portland, ME	NA	268.1	294.2
Cincinnati, OH-KY-IN	128.0	162.0	183.9	Portland-Vancouver-Hillsboro, OR-WA	237.3	381.8	407.1
Cleveland-Elyria, OH	114.5	140.4	153.2	Providence-Warwick, RI-MA	228.5	278.5	294.7
Colorado Springs, CO	195.5	281.6	323.6	Raleigh, NC	190.4	266.8	290.6
Columbia, MO	146.3	179.7	186.3	Reading, PA	153.3	164.6	162.5
Columbia, SC	142.6	162.3	171.6	Reno, NV	179.5	345.1	386.4
Columbus, OH	136.4	189.9	208.6	Richmond, VA	NA	250.5	267.0
Corpus Christi, TX	135.1	186.3	197.8	Riverside-San Bernardino-Ontario, CA	179.3	336.0	360.0
Cumberland, MD-WV	100.3	90.7	94.9	Rochester, NY	118.9	137.7	151.9
Dallas-Fort Worth-Arlington, TX	143.8	247.4	268.2	Rockford, IL	NA	117.8	128.8
Davenport-Moline-Rock Island, IA-IL	112.2	126.3	130.3	Sacramento—Roseville—Arden-Arcade,			
Dayton, OH	103.6	138.7	154.0	CA	184.2	340.0	374.0
Deltona-Daytona Beach-Ormond				St. Louis, MO-IL	131.1	169.4	185.7
Beach, FL	115.6	190.0	209.5	Salem, OR	173.5	265.5	295.8
Denver-Aurora-Lakewood, CO	232.4	414.7	462.9	Salt Lake City, UT	206.5	308.9	331.6
Des Moines-West Des Moines, IA	150.9	194.0	211.6	San Antonio-New Braunfels, TX	151.0	217.2	230.3
Detroit-Warren-Dearborn, MI	NA	NA	NA	San Diego-Carlsbad, CA	385.7	599.0	645.0
Dover, DE	193.3	200.2	202.6	San Francisco-Oakland-Hayward, CA	525.6	900.0	1,070.0
Durham-Chapel Hill, NC	158.3	254.7	288.5	San Jose-Sunnyvale-Santa Clara, CA	595.0	1,180.0	1,405.0
El Paso, TX	134.3	151.5	155.9	Seattle-Tacoma-Bellevue, WA	295.7	465.8	530.3
Erie, PA	107.7	115.7	121.7	Shreveport-Bossier City, LA	156.6	166.7	172.0
Eugene, OR	196.3	264.6	293.5	Sioux Falls, SD	143.3	194.4	219.2
Fargo, ND-MN	NA	208.5	219.8	Spartanburg, SC	118.2	158.2	175.1
Gainesville, FL	161.6	210.0	232.9	Spokane-Spokane Valley, WA	172.2	223.4	242.9
Gary-Hammond, IN	122.9	160.5	171.5	Springfield, IL	124.0	132.4	138.2
Grand Rapids-Wyoming, MI	91.5	177.5	200.1	Springfield, MA	190.0	206.8	221.6
Green Bay, WI	130.4	163.2	181.8	Springfield, MO	109.1	134.3	145.2
Greensboro-High Point, NC	129.8	157.2	166.7	Syracuse, NY	125.1	130.5	140.4
Greenville-Anderson-Mauldin, SC	145.3	195.7	216.8	Tallahassee, FL	152.8	204.9	218.0
Gulfport-Biloxi-Pascagoulia, MS	125.0	133.5	140.7	Tampa-St. Petersburg-Clearwater, FL	134.2	220.0	238.7
Hartford-W. Hartford-E. Hartford, CT	235.8	230.1	239.4	Toledo, OH	81.5	118.2	128.6
Honolulu, HI	607.6	757.3	795.2	Topeka, KS	107.2	128.6	139.3
Houston-The Woodlands-Sugar Land,				Trenton, NJ	250.7	251.8	259.4
TX	155.0	231.1	244.4	Tucson, AZ	156.6	210.3	227.3
Indianapolis-Carmel-Anderson, IN	123.3	171.5	194.1	Tulsa, OK	132.3	160.2	170.3
Jackson, MS	133.2	174.7	180.7	Virginia Beach-Norfolk-Newport News,			
Jacksonville, FL	137.7	228.9	250.0	VA-NC	205.0	225.0	235.0
Kansas City, MO-KS	141.6	194.8	215.0	Washington-Arlington-Alexandria,			
Knoxville, TN	140.9	175.9	190.1	DC-VA-MD-WV	325.3	406.7	443.1
Lansing-East Lansing, MI	84.4	139.7	152.9	Wichita, KS	118.7	132.9	148.9
Las Vegas-Henderson-Paradise, NV	138.0	256.5	291.4	Wilmington, NC	NA	237.7	259.6
Lexington-Fayette, KY	143.2	162.7	174.7	Winston-Salem, NC	NA	155.0	168.4
Lincoln, NE	133.6	175.4	192.1	Worcester, MA-CT	223.3	252.7	277.4

NA = Not available. (1) Preliminary figures for second quarter, 2018.

Characteristics of American Housing Units, 2017

Source: *American Housing Survey, 2017*, U.S. Census Bureau, U.S. Dept. of Commerce

Characteristic	Number of homes (thous.)	% of all homes	Characteristic	Number of homes (thous.)	% of all homes
Total housing units	137,000	100.0%	**Number of bedrooms**		
Units in structure			None	1,187	0.9%
1, detached.................	84,530	61.7%	1	15,970	11.7
1, attached	10,050	7.3	2	35,640	26.0
2-4..........................	9,721	7.1	3	54,400	39.7
5-9..........................	6,629	4.8	4 or more...................	29,810	21.8
10-19........................	6,168	4.5	**Number of complete bathrooms**		
20-49........................	4,885	3.6	1	46,320	33.8
50 or more...................	6,593	4.8	1-1/2	15,990	11.7
Manufactured/mobile home/trailer	8,355	6.1	2	41,520	30.3
Cooperatives.................	1,139	0.8	2-1/2	17,320	12.6
Condominiums	8,751	6.4	3 or more....................	15,513	11.3
Year built			**Mortgage characteristics[1]**		
2016-17......................	1,006	0.7	None, owned free and clear	31,250	40.4
2010-15......................	5,772	4.2	One regular mortgage only........	39,980	51.7
2005-09......................	9,026	6.6	Two or more regular mortgages ...	1,899	2.5
2000-04......................	10,500	7.7	*Median outstanding principal*		
1995-99......................	9,988	7.3	*amount*	*$127,000*	NA
1990-94......................	7,258	5.3	**Lot size[2]**		
1985-89......................	10,100	7.4	Less than 1/8 acre	14,690	14.8
1980-84......................	8,826	6.4	1/8-1/4 acre..................	33,350	33.5
1970-79......................	20,370	14.9	1/4-1/2 acre..................	19,850	20.0
1960-69......................	14,240	10.4	1/2-1 acre	9,403	9.5
1950-59......................	14,200	10.4	1-5 acres....................	15,050	15.1
1940-49......................	6,598	4.8	5-10 acres...................	3,058	3.1
1930-39......................	4,182	3.1	10+ acres	4,000	4.0
1920-29......................	5,407	3.9	**Equipment**		
1919 or earlier................	9,524	7.0	Washing machine	110,200	80.4
Median year built	*1977*	NA	Clothes dryer.................	108,300	79.1
Square footage of unit			Dishwasher...................	95,460	69.7
Less than 500	3,402	2.5	Central air conditioning	93,500	68.2
500-749......................	9,508	6.9	Lacking full kitchen facilities	4,420	3.2
750-999......................	16,470	12.0	**Main heating fuel[3]**		
1,000-1,499..................	31,480	23.0	Piped gas	58,500	43.2
1,500-1,999..................	24,250	17.7	Electricity	60,190	44.4
2,000-2,499..................	15,600	11.4	Fuel oil......................	6,605	4.9
2,500-2,999..................	8,310	6.1	Bottled gas	6,484	4.8
3,000-3,999..................	7,868	5.7	Wood.......................	2,544	1.9
4,000 or more	3,918	2.9	Solar	33	<0.1
Not reported	16,200	11.8			
Median square footage.........	*1,470*	NA			

NA = Not applicable. (1) Percentages based on 77,310 homes. (2) Percentages based on 99,420 1-unit structures; does not include cooperatives or condominiums. (3) Percentages based on 135,500 homes with heat. Not all heating fuels are shown here.

Fair Market Rents for Select Metropolitan Areas, 2019

Source: *Fair Market Rents FY 2019*, U.S. Dept. of Housing and Urban Development (HUD)

Metropolitan area	0	1	2	3	4	Metropolitan area	0	1	2	3	4
Atlanta, GA	$942	$966	$1,106	$1,427	$1,752	Milwaukee, WI	$621	$753	$918	$1,167	$1,302
Austin, TX	931	1,086	1,315	1,734	2,099	Minneapolis, MN.......	763	915	1,151	1,636	1,923
Baltimore, MD..........	862	1,074	1,342	1,732	1,992	Nashville, TN	830	911	1,103	1,455	1,738
Birmingham, AL	706	763	873	1,154	1,282	New Orleans, LA	723	844	1,008	1,304	1,492
Boston, MA	1,394	1,561	1,902	2,383	2,571	New York, NY	1,559	1,599	1,831	2,324	2,475
Buffalo, NY	671	695	838	1,050	1,204	Oklahoma City, OK......	637	689	867	1,184	1,463
Charlotte, NC	875	897	1,028	1,388	1,779	Orlando, FL.............	932	1,004	1,190	1,576	1,879
Chicago, IL	915	1,044	1,212	1,542	1,844	Philadelphia, PA	840	992	1,200	1,503	1,715
Cincinnati, OH	584	670	884	1,223	1,414	Phoenix, AZ	744	868	1,073	1,551	1,776
Cleveland, OH	569	678	836	1,102	1,158	Pittsburgh, PA	647	725	896	1,137	1,248
Columbus, OH	643	761	957	1,225	1,424	Portland, OR...........	1,040	1,134	1,325	1,916	2,327
Dallas, TX	836	989	1,201	1,600	2,080	Providence, RI	786	889	1,060	1,328	1,565
Denver, CO.............	1,029	1,204	1,508	2,119	2,461	Richmond, VA..........	889	932	1,067	1,421	1,713
Detroit, MI	621	753	967	1,261	1,371	Riverside, CA	826	986	1,232	1,717	2,132
Hartford, CT	768	960	1,194	1,496	1,674	Sacramento, CA	853	968	1,220	1,764	2,143
Honolulu, HI	1,390	1,563	2,067	2,989	3,631	St. Louis, MO	635	713	924	1,215	1,430
Houston, TX	812	907	1,104	1,509	1,897	Salt Lake City, UT.......	708	870	1,075	1,518	1,727
Indianapolis, IN.........	651	751	918	1,226	1,389	San Antonio, TX	688	844	1,050	1,379	1,689
Jacksonville, FL	632	798	973	1,280	1,647	San Diego, CA	1,333	1,490	1,938	2,776	3,404
Kansas City, MO........	640	786	953	1,286	1,457	San Francisco, CA	1,822	2,255	2,809	3,663	3,912
Las Vegas, NV	652	791	979	1,416	1,717	San Jose, CA	1,865	2,212	2,712	3,658	4,198
Los Angeles, CA........	1,158	1,384	1,791	2,401	2,641	San Juan, PR	431	459	549	728	913
Louisville, KY	602	688	853	1,158	1,307	Seattle, WA	1,416	1,557	1,899	2,733	3,228
Memphis, TN	658	742	875	1,194	1,372	Tampa, FL.............	860	916	1,133	1,485	1,794
Miami, FL	951	1,147	1,454	1,934	2,354	Washington, DC	1,415	1,454	1,665	2,176	2,678

Note: Figures are projections made in the previous fiscal year. Metropolitan areas include adjacent cities not shown here. Fair market rents are primarily used by HUD to determine payment standard amounts for the Housing Choice Voucher program.

TRADE

U.S. Trade in Goods With Selected Countries and Major Areas, 2017

Source: U.S. Census Bureau and U.S. Bureau of Economic Analysis, U.S. Dept. of Commerce; *World Development Indicators 2017*, The World Bank

Weighted mean tariff rate is the average of tariffs applied to all products weighted by the product's share of the country's imports. A low tariff on a heavily imported product, therefore, has more impact on the weighted mean tariff rate than a high tariff on a product that is rarely imported.

(trade in millions of dollars; top 25 countries as ranked by amount of total trade with U.S.)

Rank	Country	Total trade with U.S.	U.S. exports to (rank)	U.S. imports from (rank)	U.S. trade balance with (rank[1])	Weighted mean tariff rate
1.	China[2]	$635,364	$129,894 (3)	$505,470 (1)	−$375,576 (1)	3.5%
2.	Canada	581,584	282,265 (1)	299,319 (3)	−17,054 (12)	1.6
3.	Mexico	557,582	243,314 (2)	314,267 (2)	−70,953 (2)	4.4
4.	Japan	204,086	67,605 (4)	136,481 (4)	−68,876 (3)	2.6
5.	Germany	171,472	53,897 (6)	117,575 (5)	−63,678 (4)	2.0
6.	South Korea	119,771	48,326 (7)	71,444 (6)	−23,118 (9)	8.7
7.	United Kingdom	109,318	56,258 (5)	53,060 (7)	3,198 (225)	2.0
8.	France	82,494	33,596 (11)	48,899 (9)	−15,303 (14)	2.0
9.	India	74,292	25,689 (15)	48,603 (11)	−22,914 (10)	6.4
10.	Italy	68,322	18,405 (19)	49,918 (8)	−31,513 (7)	2.0
11.	Taiwan	68,191	25,730 (14)	42,462 (13)	−16,732 (13)	NA
12.	Brazil	66,673	37,222 (10)	29,452 (17)	7,770 (228)	8.0
13.	Ireland	59,504	10,708 (27)	48,797 (10)	−38,089 (6)	2.0
14.	Netherlands	59,295	41,510 (8)	17,785 (22)	23,726 (233)	2.0
15.	Switzerland	57,682	21,685 (17)	35,997 (15)	−14,312 (15)	1.3
16.	Vietnam	54,622	8,133 (32)	46,489 (12)	−38,355 (5)	2.9
17.	Malaysia	50,360	12,964 (23)	37,396 (14)	−24,431 (8)	4.0
18.	Singapore	49,173	29,806 (13)	19,368 (20)	10,438 (229)	0.1
19.	Hong Kong	47,315	39,939 (9)	7,376 (37)	32,563 (234)	0.0
20.	Belgium	44,921	29,924 (12)	14,998 (25)	14,926 (231)	2.0
21.	Thailand	42,144	10,992 (26)	31,152 (16)	−20,160 (11)	3.5
22.	Saudi Arabia	35,228	16,348 (20)	18,880 (21)	−2,532 (35)	4.5
23.	Australia	34,572	24,527 (16)	10,045 (33)	14,482 (230)	1.2
24.	Israel	34,495	12,550 (24)	21,945 (18)	−9,394 (19)	2.8
25.	Indonesia	27,073	6,864 (36)	20,209 (19)	−13,346 (16)	2.6

Major area/group

North America...........	$1,139,166	$525,580	$613,587	−$88,007	
Europe	839,012	332,714	506,298	−173,584	
Euro Area	553,665	210,597	343,068	−132,471	
EU....................	717,902	283,269	434,633	−151,363	
Africa	55,473	22,062	33,411	−11,350	
OECD.................	2,361,780	1,013,516	1,348,264	−334,748	
Pacific Rim Countries.....	1,265,036	398,759	866,277	−467,517	
Asia-Near East..........	128,696	64,760	63,936	825	
Asia-South	92,153	31,324	60,829	−29,504	
ASEAN................	247,759	77,968	169,790	−91,822	
APEC	2,564,492	972,228	1,592,264	−620,035	
South/Central America....	266,193	150,194	115,999	34,195	
Twenty Latin Amer. Reps...	803,074	378,192	424,883	−46,691	
CAFTA-DR	54,258	30,619	23,639	6,980	
Central Amer. Common Market................	41,685	22,792	18,893	3,899	
NATO Allies.............	1,231,086	560,053	671,033	−110,980	
OPEC	131,498	59,305	72,193	−12,888	
WORLD TOTAL	**3,914,260**	**1,553,383**	**2,360,878**	**−807,495**	

NA = Not available. **Note:** Figures shown are on Census Bureau basis and are not seasonally adjusted. Figures may not equal totals due to rounding. Country grouping data reflect groups at the time of reporting. Rankings include territories as well as nations. (1) Rank by size of U.S. trade deficit. (2) Not incl. Hong Kong, Macau, and Taiwan.

Countries With Highest and Lowest Mean Tariff Rates, 2017

Source: *World Development Indicators 2017*, The World Bank

	HIGHEST TARIFF RATES				LOWEST TARIFF RATES	
Rank	Country	Weighted mean tariff rate		Rank	Country	Weighted mean tariff rate
1.	The Bahamas..............	18.6%		1.	Hong Kong	0.0%
2.	Djibouti	17.6			Macau....................	0.0
3.	Gabon...................	16.9			Libya....................	0.0
4.	Chad....................	16.4		4.	Singapore	0.1
5.	Equatorial Guinea..........	15.6		5.	Brunei	0.5
6.	Iran.....................	15.2		6.	Botswana	0.6
7.	Central African Republic......	14.5		7.	Georgia...................	0.7
8.	Barbados	14.2		8.	Mauritius..................	0.8
	Syria	14.2		9.	Namibia	1.0
10.	Solomon Islands...........	14.1		10.	Albania	1.1
11.	Cameroon................	12.7		11.	Australia	1.2
	The Gambia	12.7			Bosnia and Herzegovina	1.2
13.	Grenada	12.4			Eswatini	1.2
	Nepal	12.4		14.	New Zealand	1.3
15.	Kenya	12.3			Switzerland................	1.3
	St. Kitts and Nevis...........	12.3		16.	Guatemala	1.4
17.	Liberia...................	12.2		17.	Iceland	1.5
18.	Ethiopia..................	12.1			Oman	1.5
19.	Sudan...................	12.0		19.	Canada...................	1.6
20.	Antigua and Barbuda	11.9			Tuvalu....................	1.6
	Guinea	11.9		21.	Laos	1.7
22.	Benin	11.6			United States	1.7
	Congo Republic	11.6		23.	Belarus	1.8
24.	Nigeria	11.3			Costa Rica	1.8
25.	Maldives.................	11.2			El Salvador................	1.8
					Peru	1.8

U.S. Exports and Imports by Principal Commodities, 2017
Source: U.S. Census Bureau and U.S. Bureau of Economic Analysis, U.S. Dept. of Commerce
(in millions of dollars)

Item	Exports	Imports	Item	Exports	Imports
Total[1]	$1,546,273	$2,341,963	Essential oil and reinoids	$16,271	$15,424
Manufactured goods	1,095,425	2,021,560	Fertilizers	3,011	5,593
Agricultural commodities	138,166	120,984	Plastics in primary forms	32,853	15,495
			Plastics in nonprimary forms	13,254	10,489
Food and live animals	99,072	105,866	Chemical materials and products	31,302	16,402
Live animals other than fish	906	2,812	Manufactured goods by material	106,553	255,841
Meat and preparations	18,026	8,870	Leather and leather manufactures	1,026	1,431
Dairy products and birds	4,599	2,005	Rubber manufactures	8,973	20,876
Fish and preparations	5,436	21,403	Cork and wood manufactures	2,007	11,573
Cereals and preparations	22,463	9,599	Paper and paperboard	15,477	16,168
Vegetables and fruits	22,514	34,518	Textile yarn, fabrics	12,181	28,414
Sugar, preparations, and honey	1,967	4,670	Nonmetallic mineral manufactures	13,179	45,661
Coffee, tea, cocoa, and spices	3,025	14,043	Iron and steel	14,732	36,892
Feeding stuff for animals	11,038	2,889	Nonferrous metals	14,289	41,998
Miscellaneous edible products	9,098	5,057	Manufactures of metals	24,690	52,827
Beverages and tobacco	6,359	24,973	Machinery and transport		
Beverages	5,151	22,840	equipment	501,998	1,014,628
Tobacco and manufactures	1,208	2,133	Power-generating machinery	34,816	68,424
Crude materials except fuels	76,496	33,880	Specialized industrial machinery	44,958	49,170
Hides, skins, and furskins (raw)	1,888	100	Metalworking machinery	4,878	10,397
Oil seeds and oleaginous fruits	23,265	1,047	General industrial machinery	59,325	98,224
Crude rubber	2,727	3,321	Office machinery	19,634	123,995
Cork and wood	7,536	8,666	Telecommunications equipment	21,559	167,722
Pulp and waste paper	8,606	3,160	Electrical machinery	78,380	175,981
Textile fibers including waste	7,712	1,285	Road vehicles	116,719	286,315
Crude fertilizers	2,753	2,595	Transport equipment	121,729	34,399
Metalliferous ores and metal scrap	18,866	7,981	Miscellaneous manufactured		
Crude animal and vegetable			articles	119,728	381,105
materials	3,141	5,725	Prefabricated buildings	2,357	13,891
Mineral fuels and lubricants	137,374	194,784	Furniture	6,296	50,143
Coal, coke, and briquettes	10,188	966	Travel goods	634	10,865
Petroleum products and preparations	104,525	181,662	Apparel and clothing accessories	3,008	88,245
Gas, natural and manufactured	22,475	9,890	Footwear	859	25,640
Electric current	187	2,266	Scientific and controlling equipment	47,166	56,751
Animal and vegetable oils	2,743	6,807	Photographic equipment	6,387	14,475
Animal oil and fat	687	269	Miscellaneous manufactured articles	53,021	121,095
Fixed vegetable fats and oil, crude	1,814	6,335	Miscellaneous commodities	62,555	102,840
Animal or vegetable fats, processed	242	203	Special transactions	9,347	72,823
Chemicals and related products	194,668	221,239	Coin, including gold coin	135	1,059
Organic chemicals	34,073	43,748	Coin, other than gold	6	17
Inorganic chemicals	11,299	10,550	Gold, nonmonetary	20,392	11,484
Dyeing, tanning, and coloring			Low value estimate	32,674	17,457
materials	7,565	4,023	Re-exports	238,727	NA
Medicinal and pharmaceutical			Agricultural commodities	4,706	NA
products	45,040	99,514	Manufactured goods	227,847	NA

NA = Not applicable. **Note:** Numbers may not add up to totals due to rounding. (1) Total on Census Bureau basis; includes re-exports.

Trends in U.S. Foreign Trade, 1790-2017
Source: U.S. Census Bureau and U.S. Bureau of Economic Analysis, U.S. Dept. of Commerce
In 1790, U.S. exports and imports combined came to $43 mil, and there was a $3 mil trade deficit. The trade balance was positive for much of the 20th century, but the U.S. has had a trade deficit in every year since 1975.
(in millions of dollars)

Year	Exports	Imports	Trade balance	Year	Exports	Imports	Trade balance	Year	Exports	Imports	Trade balance
1790	$20	$23	–$3	1890	$858	$789	$69	1990	$535,233	$616,097	–$80,864
1795	48	70	–22	1895	808	732	76	1995	794,387	890,771	–96,384
1800	71	91	–20	1900	1,394	850	545	2000	1,075,321	1,447,837	–372,517
1805	96	121	–25	1905	1,519	1,118	401	2001	1,005,654	1,367,165	–361,511
1810	67	85	–19	1910	1,745	1,557	188	2002	978,706	1,397,660	–418,955
1815	53	113	–60	1915	2,769	1,674	1,094	2003	1,020,418	1,514,308	–493,890
1820	70	74	–5	1920	8,228	5,278	2,950	2004	1,161,549	1,771,433	–609,883
1825	91	90	1	1925	4,910	4,227	683	2005	1,286,022	2,000,267	–714,245
1830	72	63	9	1930	3,843	3,061	782	2006	1,457,642	2,219,358	–761,716
1835	115	137	–22	1935	2,283	2,047	235	2007	1,653,548	2,358,922	–705,375
1840	124	98	25	1940	4,021	2,625	1,396	2008	1,841,612	2,550,339	–708,726
1845	106	113	–7	1945	9,806	4,159	5,646	2009	1,583,053	1,966,827	–383,774
1850	144	174	–29	1950	9,997	8,954	1,043	2010	1,853,038	2,348,263	–495,225
1855	219	258	–39	1955	14,298	11,566	2,732	2011	2,125,947	2,675,646	–549,699
1860	334	354	–20	1960	25,940	22,432	3,508	2012	2,218,354	2,755,762	–537,408
1865	166	239	–73	1965	35,285	30,621	4,664	2013	2,294,199	2,755,334	–461,135
1870	393	436	–43	1970	56,640	54,386	2,254	2014	2,376,657	2,866,241	–489,584
1875	513	533	–20	1975	132,585	120,181	12,404	2015	2,266,691	2,765,216	–498,525
1880	836	668	168	1980	271,834	291,241	–19,407	2016	2,215,844	2,717,846	–502,001
1885	742	578	165	1985	289,070	410,950	–121,880	2017	2,351,072	2,903,349	–552,277

Note: Figures shown using balance of payments basis.

World Trade Organization (WTO)

The World Trade Organization is an international body that seeks to promote free trade by eliminating barriers to trade. Founded in 1995, the WTO had grown to 164 member countries as of Oct. 2018, with 23 others, including Belarus and Iran, granted observer status. International intergovernmental organizations, such as the International Monetary Fund and the World Bank, may also be granted observer status. With the exception of Vatican City, observers must start accession negotiations within five years of becoming observers.

U.S. Trade in Goods and Services, 2017
Source: U.S. Census Bureau and U.S. Bureau of Economic Analysis, U.S. Dept. of Commerce
(top countries as ranked by amount of total trade with U.S.; in millions of dollars)

Country and category	Food and live animals	Beverages and tobacco	Crude materials, except fuels	Mineral fuels, lubricants	Chemicals	Manu- factured goods	Machinery and transport equip- ment	Misc. manu- factured articles	Commo- dities and transac- tions[1]	Total
China										
U.S. exports to	$5,581	$273	$26,907	$8,571	$15,748	$5,496	$55,296	$10,184	$1,787	**$129,894**
U.S. imports fr.	6,195	106	2,288	680	18,723	57,853	274,732	159,161	6,266	**526,059**
Trade balance	−614	167	24,619	7,892	−2,976	−52,356	−219,436	−148,977	−4,479	**−396,165**
Canada										
U.S. exports to	21,431	2,501	6,611	19,560	31,856	34,174	128,708	28,483	8,504	**282,265**
U.S. imports fr.	22,136	922	13,129	77,274	24,621	40,030	91,046	14,577	20,677	**306,465**
Trade balance	−705	1,579	−6,518	−57,714	7,235	−5,856	37,662	13,906	−12,173	**−24,200**
Mexico										
U.S. exports to	14,913	436	6,821	26,493	27,240	31,769	109,458	18,456	7,129	**243,314**
U.S. imports fr.	21,672	5,282	1,699	11,606	6,465	20,747	202,622	34,992	12,002	**317,216**
Trade balance	−6,760	−4,846	5,122	14,887	20,776	11,023	−93,164	−16,536	−4,873	**−73,901**
Japan										
U.S. exports to	11,206	334	3,742	5,535	11,514	3,531	21,218	9,270	1,222	**67,605**
U.S. imports fr.	727	150	592	582	9,059	9,212	105,140	10,872	3,411	**139,797**
Trade balance	10,478	183	3,150	4,953	2,455	−5,681	−83,923	−1,602	−2,189	**−72,192**
Germany										
U.S. exports to	1,132	255	1,983	758	8,582	4,145	27,434	7,363	2,202	**53,897**
U.S. imports fr.	1,555	516	1,261	259	21,912	10,448	66,430	11,509	6,097	**120,004**
Trade balance	−423	−261	722	499	−13,329	−6,303	−38,996	−4,145	−3,896	**−66,108**
South Korea										
U.S. exports to	5,996	116	2,500	4,029	7,012	2,249	20,990	4,476	716	**48,326**
U.S. imports fr.	633	196	500	2,961	5,428	9,090	48,979	4,273	1,389	**73,452**
Trade balance	5,363	−79	2,000	1,067	1,584	−6,841	−27,989	203	−673	**−25,125**
United Kingdom										
U.S. exports to	1,254	470	1,556	3,525	7,034	3,637	22,343	8,996	7,365	**56,258**
U.S. imports fr.	760	2,080	476	3,082	9,190	3,399	21,970	7,440	5,665	**54,076**
Trade balance	495	−1,610	1,079	442	−2,156	238	373	1,555	1,700	**2,182**

Note: Figures for exports are "free alongside ship" values; figures for imports are "cost, insurance, and freight" values. Neither is directly comparable with the Census Bureau basis shown in other tables in this section. Trade balance is with U.S. and may not sum from export/import numbers due to rounding. Total includes categories not shown here. (1) Not classified elsewhere.

Exchange Rates for Foreign Currencies, 1970-2017
Source: Federal Reserve Board
One U.S. dollar was worth the following amounts in each country's national currency; exchange rates are annual averages.

Country (currency)	1970	1980	1990	2000	2005	2010	2014	2015	2016	2017
Australia (dollar)	0.90	0.88	1.28	1.72	1.31	1.09	1.11	1.33	1.34	1.30
Austria (schilling; euro)	25.88	12.95	11.37	1.08	0.80	0.75	0.75	0.90	0.90	0.89
Belgium (franc; euro)	49.68	29.24	33.42	1.08	0.80	0.75	0.75	0.90	0.90	0.89
Brazil (real)	NA	NA	NA	1.83	2.44	1.76	2.35	3.34	3.48	3.19
Canada (dollar)	1.01	1.17	1.17	1.49	1.21	1.03	1.10	1.28	1.32	1.30
China (yuan)	NA	NA	4.79	8.28	8.19	6.77	6.16	6.28	6.64	6.76
Denmark (krone)	7.49	5.63	6.19	8.10	6.00	5.63	5.62	6.73	6.73	6.60
France (franc; euro)	5.52	4.22	5.45	1.08	0.80	0.75	0.75	0.90	0.90	0.89
Germany[1] (mark; euro)	3.65	1.82	1.62	1.08	0.80	0.75	0.75	0.90	0.90	0.89
Greece (drachma; euro)	30.00	42.62	158.51	365.92	0.80	0.75	0.75	0.90	0.90	0.89
Hong Kong (dollar)	NA	NA	7.79	7.79	7.78	7.77	7.75	7.75	7.76	7.79
India (rupee)	7.58	7.89	17.50	45.00	44.00	45.65	61.00	64.11	67.16	65.07
Ireland (pound; euro)	2.40	2.06	1.66	1.08	0.80	0.75	0.75	0.90	0.90	0.89
Italy (lira; euro)	623.00	856.00	1,198.00	1.08	0.80	0.75	0.75	0.90	0.90	0.89
Japan (yen)	357.60	226.63	144.79	107.80	110.11	87.78	105.74	121.05	108.66	112.10
Malaysia (ringgit)	3.09	2.18	2.71	3.80	3.79	3.22	3.27	3.90	4.14	4.30
Mexico (peso[2])	NA	NA	NA	9.46	10.89	12.62	13.30	15.87	18.67	18.88
Netherlands (guilder; euro)	3.60	2.0	1.82	1.08	0.80	0.75	0.75	0.90	0.90	0.89
Norway (krone)	7.14	4.94	6.26	8.81	6.44	6.05	6.30	8.07	8.39	8.27
Portugal (escudo; euro)	28.75	50.08	142.55	1.08	0.80	0.75	0.75	0.90	0.90	0.89
Singapore (dollar)	3.08	2.14	1.81	1.73	1.66	1.36	1.26	1.37	1.38	1.38
South Korea (won)	310.57	607.43	707.76	1,130.90	1,023.75	1,155.74	1,052.29	1,130.96	1,159.34	1,129.04
Spain (peseta; euro)	69.72	71.76	101.93	1.08	0.80	0.75	0.75	0.90	0.90	0.89
Sweden (krona)	5.17	4.23	5.92	9.17	7.47	7.20	6.86	8.44	8.55	8.54
Switzerland (franc)	4.32	1.68	1.39	1.69	1.25	1.04	0.91	0.96	0.98	0.98
Taiwan (dollar)	NA	NA	26.92	31.26	32.13	31.50	30.30	31.74	32.23	30.40
Thailand (baht)	21.00	20.48	25.58	40.21	40.25	31.70	32.46	34.24	35.26	33.91
United Kingdom (pound)	0.42	0.43	0.56	0.66	0.55	0.65	0.61	0.65	0.74	0.78

NA = Not available. **Note:** The euro, the European Union's single currency, replaced the national currencies in the EU nations shown above. Since 1999 (or 2001 in the case of Greece), the euro has been fixed at the following conversion rates: 13.7603 Austrian schillings, 40.3399 Belgian francs, 6.55957 French francs, 1.95583 German marks, 340.750 Greek drachmas, 0.787564 Irish pounds, 1,936.27 Italian lire, 2.20371 Netherlands guilders, 200.482 Portuguese escudos, and 166.386 Spanish pesetas. (1) West Germany before 1991. (2) Mexico re-based its currency in 1993; earlier values are not comparable.

Top U.S. Trading Partners, 1985-2017

Source: U.S. Census Bureau, U.S. Dept. of Commerce
(in millions of dollars; top five countries as ranked by amount of total trade with U.S. in 2017)

Country/category	1985	1990	1995	2000	2005	2010	2014	2015	2016	2017
China										
U.S. exports	$3,856	$4,806	$11,754	$16,185	$41,192	$91,911	$123,657	$115,873	$115,546	$129,894
U.S. imports from	3,862	15,237	45,543	100,018	243,470	364,953	468,475	483,202	462,542	505,470
Trade balance	−6	−10,431	−33,790	−83,833	−202,278	−273,042	−344,818	−367,328	−346,997	−375,576
Canada										
U.S. exports to	47,251	83,674	127,226	178,941	211,899	249,257	312,817	280,855	266,735	282,265
U.S. imports from	69,006	91,380	144,370	230,838	290,384	277,637	349,286	296,305	277,782	299,319
Trade balance	−21,755	−7,706	−17,144	−51,897	−78,486	−28,380	−36,469	−15,450	−11,048	−17,054
Mexico										
U.S. exports to	13,635	28,279	46,292	111,349	120,248	163,665	241,007	236,460	230,051	243,314
U.S. imports from	19,132	30,157	62,100	135,926	170,109	229,986	295,730	296,433	293,924	314,267
Trade balance	−5,497	−1,878	−15,808	−24,577	−49,861	−66,321	−54,723	−59,973	−63,873	−70,953
Japan										
U.S. exports to	22,631	48,580	64,343	64,924	54,681	60,472	66,892	62,388	63,226	67,605
U.S. imports from	68,783	89,684	123,479	146,479	138,004	120,552	134,505	131,446	132,030	136,481
Trade balance	−46,152	−41,105	−59,137	−81,555	−83,323	−60,080	67,613	−69,058	−68,804	−68,876
Germany										
U.S. exports to	9,050	18,760	22,394	29,448	34,184	48,155	49,419	49,979	49,432	53,897
U.S. imports from	20,239	28,162	36,844	58,513	84,751	82,450	124,182	124,888	114,107	117,575
Trade balance	−11,189	−9,402	−14,450	−29,065	−50,567	−34,295	−74,763	−74,909	−64,675	−63,679

Note: Figures shown are on Census Bureau basis.

Busiest U.S. Ports, 2016

Source: U.S. Army Corps of Engineers, Dept. of the Army, U.S. Dept. of Defense
(figures in millions of short tons; ranked by total tonnage handled)

Rank	Port	Domestic	Foreign	Total	Rank	Port	Domestic	Foreign	Total
1.	South Louisiana, LA	137.6	124.3	261.9	26.	Richmond, CA	9.0	15.6	24.7
2.	Houston, TX	84.0	164.0	248.0	27.	Port Everglades, FL	12.1	12.1	24.2
3.	New York, NY-NJ	47.3	86.1	133.4	28.	Seattle, WA	6.3	17.9	24.2
4.	New Orleans, LA	48.9	41.3	90.3	29.	Charleston, SC	2.1	21.0	23.0
5.	Beaumont, TX	36.3	48.3	84.5	30.	Philadelphia, PA	11.2	11.8	23.0
6.	Corpus Christi, TX	32.6	49.4	82.0	31.	Pittsburgh, PA	22.5	0.0	22.5
7.	Long Beach, CA	10.4	67.4	77.8	32.	Portland, OR	7.9	12.6	20.5
8.	Baton Rouge, LA	43.4	29.6	73.0	33.	Freeport, TX	4.8	14.8	19.6
9.	Los Angeles, CA	6.3	56.3	62.6	34.	Oakland, CA	2.0	17.1	19.1
10.	Mobile, AL	22.8	35.2	58.0	35.	Jacksonville, FL	7.6	10.9	18.5
11.	Plaquemines, LA	33.3	23.5	56.8	36.	Paulsboro, NJ	7.3	11.2	18.5
12.	Lake Charles, LA	26.6	29.5	56.0	37.	Boston, MA	5.0	12.2	17.2
13.	Virginia, VA	5.4	48.7	54.0	38.	Chicago, IL	14.7	1.8	16.4
14.	Cincinnati-N. Kentucky,				39.	Marcus Hook, PA	9.4	6.3	15.7
	OH-KY	43.1	0.0	43.1	40.	Two Harbors, MN	15.1	0.4	15.4
15.	Texas City, TX	14.4	26.8	41.3	41.	Kalama, WA	1.2	14.2	15.4
16.	Baltimore, MD	7.0	31.9	38.8	42.	Honolulu, HI	12.4	1.3	13.7
17.	Huntington-Tristate, WV . .	37.4	0.0	37.4	43.	Detroit, MI	10.5	2.7	13.3
18.	Savannah, GA	1.2	35.3	36.4	44.	Longview, WA	1.3	11.8	13.1
19.	Tampa, FL	21.8	13.5	35.3	45.	Cleveland, OH	10.8	1.6	12.4
20.	Port Arthur, TX	8.7	26.5	35.2	46.	Indiana Harbor, IN	12.0	0.2	12.2
21.	St. Louis, MO and IL	32.2	0.0	32.2	47.	Memphis, TN	12.2	0.0	12.2
22.	Duluth-Superior, MN-WI . .	22.6	7.6	30.3	48.	San Juan, PR	4.8	5.9	10.7
23.	Valdez, AK	27.2	0.5	27.7	49.	Anacortes, WA	8.3	2.4	10.7
24.	Pascagoula, MS	9.5	17.3	26.9	50.	New Castle, DE	5.2	5.4	10.6
25.	Tacoma, WA	4.5	21.2	25.7					

World's Busiest Ports, 2013-16

Source: *Review of Maritime Transport, 2017*, United Nations Conference on Trade and Development
(ranked by throughput volume in 2016 as measured in thousands of twenty-ft equivalent units (TEUs))

Rank	Port	Volume (TEUs)				Percent change		
		2013	2014	2015	2016	2013-14	2014-15	2015-16
1.	Shanghai, China	33,617	35,290	36,537	37,135	4.98%	3.54%	1.6%
2.	Singapore	32,579	33,869	30,962	30,930	3.96	−8.70	−0.1
3.	Shenzhen, China	23,279	24,040	24,204	23,980	3.27	0.67	−0.9
4.	Ningbo and Zhoushan, China	17,351	19,450	20,593	21,565	12.10	6.07	4.7
5.	Hong Kong, China	22,352	22,200	20,114	19,580	−0.68	−9.46	−2.7
6.	Busan, South Korea	17,686	18,683	19,296	19,378	5.64	4.20	0.4
7.	Guangzhou, China	15,309	16,610	17,457	18,859	8.50	5.90	8.0
8.	Qingdao, China	15,520	16,580	17,465	18,050	6.83	5.13	3.3
9.	Dubai, United Arab Emirates	13,641	15,200	15,592	14,772	11.43	2.57	−5.3
10.	Tianjin, China	13,000	14,060	14,109	14,523	8.15	0.36	2.9
11.	Port Klang, Malaysia	10,350	10,946	11,891	13,167	5.76	8.60	10.7
12.	Rotterdam, Netherlands	11,621	12,298	12,235	12,385	5.83	−0.51	1.2
13.	Kaohsiung, Taiwan	9,938	10,593	10,264	10,460	6.59	−3.14	1.9
14.	Antwerp, Belgium	8,578	8,978	9,650	10,037	4.66	7.53	4.0
15.	Xiamen, China	8,008	8,572	9,179	9,614	7.04	7.09	4.7
16.	Dalian, China	10,015	10,130	9,449	9,584	1.15	−6.71	1.4
17.	Hamburg, Germany	7,868	8,340	8,825	8,900	6.00	−2.16	0.8
18.	Los Angeles, CA, U.S.	9,257	9,720	8,160	8,857	5.00	−9.25	8.5
19.	Tanjung Pelepas, Malaysia	7,628	8,500	8,799	8,029	11.43	7.41	−8.8
20.	Cat Lai, Vietnam	NA	NA	6,863	7,547	2.56	5.46	10.0

NA = Not available. **Note:** A TEU is the size of a typical shipping container.

Value of Freight Shipments by Transportation Mode, 2012-16

Source: *Freight Analysis Framework 2016*, U.S. Dept. of Transportation

(value in billions of 2012 dollars)

Mode of transportation	2012 Total	2012 Domestic	2012 Exports	2012 Imports	2016 Total	2016 Domestic	2016 Exports	2016 Imports
Truck	$10,929	$10,251	$366	$311	$11,225	$10,532	$347	$347
Rail	582	411	63	109	621	445	65	111
Water	631	270	73	288	527	279	98	151
Air, air and truck	1,067	135	461	472	1,081	132	447	502
Multiple modes and mail	3,246	1,746	552	947	3,315	1,784	487	1,044
Pipeline	1,233	1,150	13	70	1,282	1,169	31	81
Other and unknown	40	1	17	22	91	1	67	23
Total	**17,729**	**13,965**	**1,545**	**2,219**	**18,142**	**14,341**	**1,542**	**2,259**

Note: Imports and exports that pass through the U.S. from a foreign origin to a foreign destination by any mode not included. 2016 data are provisional estimates. All truck, rail, water, and pipeline movements that involve more than one mode, including exports and imports that change mode at international gateways, are included in multiple modes and mail to avoid double counting.

Merchant Fleets of the World, 2017

Source: *Review of Maritime Transport, 2017*, United Nations Conference on Trade and Development

(ranked by dead-weight tonnage under flag of registration as of Jan. 1, 2017)

Flag of registration	Number of ships	Percent of total world ships	Dead-weight tonnage	Percent of total world tonnage	Average vessel size (dead-weight tons)	Tonnage change, 2016-17
Panama	8,052	8.64%	343,397,556	18.44%	45,237	2.75%
Liberia	3,296	3.54	219,397,222	11.78	66,706	5.66
Marshall Islands	3,199	3.43	216,616,351	11.63	67,968	7.76
Hong Kong (China)	2,576	2.77	173,318,337	9.31	68,695	6.23
Singapore	3,558	3.82	124,237,959	6.67	36,942	0.21
Malta	2,170	2.33	99,216,495	5.33	46,297	5.14
The Bahamas	1,440	1.55	79,842,485	4.29	56,625	0.79
China	4,287	4.60	78,400,273	4.21	20,555	2.12
Greece	1,364	1.46	74,637,988	4.01	66,999	1.60
United Kingdom	1,551	1.66	40,985,692	2.20	30,495	10.42
Japan	5,289	5.68	34,529,405	1.85	8,574	6.60
Cyprus	1,022	1.10	33,764,669	1.81	33,798	1.82
Norway	1,585	1.70	21,900,458	1.18	16,319	6.89
Indonesia	8,782	9.43	20,143,854	1.08	4,269	7.58
India	1,674	1.80	17,253,564	0.93	10,899	5.34
Denmark	654	0.70	16,893,333	0.91	28,344	−1.73
Italy	1,430	1.53	15,944,268	0.86	13,477	−2.32
South Korea	1,907	2.05	15,171,035	0.81	9,008	−10.80
Portugal	466	0.50	13,752,758	0.74	32,744	54.97
United States	3,611	3.88	11,798,309	0.63	6,329	0.75
Bermuda	160	0.17	10,957,895	0.59	69,795	2.44
Germany	614	0.66	10,443,699	0.56	20,084	−6.15
Antigua and Barbuda	964	1.03	10,153,044	0.55	10,609	−9.68
Malaysia	1,690	1.81	10,058,653	0.54	7,412	4.70
Russia	2,572	2.76	8,277,175	0.44	3,292	−2.95
Turkey	1,285	1.38	8,200,982	0.44	8,055	−3.83
Belgium	185	0.20	8,039,665	0.43	50,883	−3.57
Vietnam	1,818	1.95	7,991,039	0.43	4,745	2.96
Netherlands	1,244	1.34	7,619,143	0.41	7,263	−5.31
France	547	0.59	6,966,582	0.37	17,033	0.90
Iran	739	0.79	6,583,064	0.35	11,253	34.49
Philippines	1,508	1.62	6,135,144	0.33	5,203	−3.63
Cayman Islands	161	0.17	5,549,056	0.30	36,268	28.52
Thailand	781	0.84	5,374,875	0.29	8,269	0.13
Kuwait	161	0.17	5,155,256	0.28	38,761	−3.85
World total	**93,161**	**100.00**	**1,861,851,750**	**100.00**	**24,062**	**2.94**

Note: World total includes flags of registration not shown.

U.S. International Transactions, 1970-2017

Source: U.S. Bureau of Economic Analysis, U.S. Dept. of Commerce

(in millions of dollars)

CURRENT ACCOUNT	1970	1980	1990	2000	2010	2015	2016	2017
Exports of goods and services and income payments (credits)	$68,388	$344,440	$712,128	$1,469,648	$2,623,991	$3,207,288	$3,183,783	$3,433,239
Goods	42,469	224,250	387,401	784,940	1,290,279	1,511,381	1,456,957	1,553,383
Services	14,171	47,585	147,833	290,381	562,759	755,310	758,888	797,690
Primary income receipts	11,748	72,605	176,894	356,706	680,169	810,073	830,174	928,118
Imports of goods and services and income payments (debits)	66,055	342,124	791,097	1,873,098	3,055,256	3,615,053	3,616,656	3,882,380
Goods	39,866	249,750	498,438	1,231,722	1,938,950	2,273,249	2,208,008	2,360,878
Services	14,519	41,492	117,660	216,115	409,313	491,966	509,838	542,471
Primary income payments	5,514	42,533	148,345	338,637	511,948	606,464	637,151	706,386
Secondary income payments (current transfers)[1]	6,156	8,349	26,654	86,624	195,045	243,372	261,659	272,645
CAPITAL ACCOUNT								
Capital transfer receipts, other credits	NA	NA	0	35	0	0	0	24,788
Capital transfer payments, other debits	NA	NA	7,220	36	157	42	59	42
Net U.S. acquisition of financial assets[2]	9,336	86,968	103,985	587,682	958,703	202,208	348,625	1,182,749
Net U.S. incurrence of liabilities[2]	7,226	62,036	162,109	1,066,074	1,391,042	501,121	741,529	1,537,683
Balance on current account	**2,331**	**2,318**	**−78,969**	**−403,450**	**−431,265**	**−407,764**	**−432,873**	**−449,142**
Balance on capital account	**NA**	**NA**	**−7,221**	**−1**	**−157**	**−42**	**−59**	**24,746**
Net lending (+) or net borrowing (−) from financial-acct. transactions[3]	2,331	2,318	−86,190	−403,451	−431,422	−407,807	−432,932	−424,395

NA = Not available or applicable. (1) Includes U.S. government and private transfers, such as U.S. government grants and pensions, fines and penalties, withholding taxes, personal transfers (remittances), insurance-related transfers, and other current transfers. (2) Excludes financial derivatives. (3) Net lending means that U.S. residents are net suppliers of funds to foreign residents, and net borrowing means the opposite. Net lending or net borrowing can be computed from current- and capital-account transactions or from financial-account transactions.

U.S. International Direct Investments, 1990-2017
Source: U.S. Bureau of Economic Analysis, U.S. Dept. of Commerce
(in millions of dollars)

	U.S. direct investment abroad					Foreign direct investment in U.S.				
	1990	2000	2010	2016	2017	1990	2000	2010	2016	2017
All countries[1]	$430,521	$1,316,247	$3,741,910	$5,586,030	$6,013,335	$394,911	$1,256,867	$2,280,044	$3,765,114	$4,025,492
Canada	69,508	132,472	295,206	365,375	391,208	29,544	114,309	192,463	380,730	453,127
Europe[1]	**214,739**	**687,320**	**2,034,559**	**3,309,782**	**3,553,429**	**247,320**	**887,014**	**1,659,774**	**2,603,054**	**2,731,290**
Austria	1,113	2,872	11,485	6,871	7,819	625	3,007	4,532	10,516	12,303
Belgium	9,464	17,973	43,975	51,589	54,954	3,900	14,787	69,565	104,007	103,451
Czech Rep.	NA	1,228	5,268	4,888	5,406	NA	NA	65	112	NA
Denmark	1,726	5,270	11,802	17,018	13,873	819	4,025	7,772	18,004	17,974
Finland	544	1,342	1,597	3,200	3,318	1,504	8,875	4,943	5,686	6,507
France	19,164	42,628	78,320	80,739	85,572	18,650	125,740	189,763	256,011	275,470
Germany	27,609	55,508	103,319	133,696	136,128	28,232	122,412	203,077	294,257	310,190
Greece	282	795	1,775	1,042	1,224	94	659	−41	682	NA
Hungary	NA	1,920	4,237	7,223	7,131	NA	5,287	39,266	11,308	12,938
Ireland	5,894	35,903	158,851	391,264	446,383	1,340	25,523	24,097	105,756	147,834
Italy	14,063	23,484	27,137	30,922	30,708	1,524	6,576	20,142	29,898	29,285
Luxembourg	1,697	27,849	272,206	640,646	676,418	2,195	58,930	170,309	424,109	410,729
Netherlands	19,120	115,429	514,689	898,495	936,728	64,671	138,894	234,408	345,899	367,145
Norway	4,209	4,379	28,541	29,230	29,187	773	2,665	10,478	25,201	26,035
Poland	NA	3,884	13,152	11,863	12,604	29	57	4,386	NA	NA
Portugal	897	2,664	2,612	1,985	2,060	−19	−68	204	932	1,066
Russia	NA	1,147	10,040	14,520	13,881	NA	118	5,689	4,499	4,466
Spain	7,868	21,236	52,390	33,484	33,128	792	5,068	43,095	68,897	74,571
Sweden	1,787	25,959	23,275	31,723	34,622	5,484	21,991	38,780	48,780	50,902
Switzerland	25,099	55,377	119,891	187,048	249,968	17,674	64,719	180,642	283,212	309,363
Turkey	522	1,826	4,155	3,852	4,266	20	188	749	1,673	1,975
UK	72,707	230,762	501,247	686,048	747,571	98,676	277,613	400,435	535,083	540,922
Latin America[1]	**71,413**	**266,576**	**752,788**	**929,459**	**1,008,080**	**20,168**	**53,691**	**62,130**	**124,568**	**124,862**
Argentina	2,531	17,488	11,747	14,057	14,907	420	364	464	873	1,020
The Bahamas	4,004	NA	NA	NA	NA	1,535	1,254	1,753	301	297
Barbados	252	2,141	7,524	20,194	20,368	191	1,560	706	1,132	2,069
Bermuda	20,169	60,114	265,524	314,853	346,804	1,550	18,336	365	9,070	6,697
Brazil	14,384	36,717	66,963	66,418	68,272	377	882	1,357	−2,445	−2,025
Chile	1,896	10,052	30,747	28,959	25,884	5	24	391	2,057	2,097
Colombia	1,677	3,693	6,181	7,467	7,222	55	2	382	−21	−84
Costa Rica	251	1,716	1,827	1,349	1,567	−2	2	−48	−2	−112
Curaçao[2]	−4,501	NA	NA	5,608	17,242	12,974	3,807	2,819	1,509	1,339
Dominican Rep.	529	1,143	1,432	1,226	2,140	0	79	−142	NA	2
Ecuador	280	832	1,283	1,036	779	6	29	77	−4	14
Honduras	262	399	936	1,283	1,405	8	−3	7	1	−62
Mexico	10,313	39,352	85,751	100,734	109,671	575	7,462	10,970	17,209	18,011
Panama	9,289	30,758	5,156	4,301	4,706	4,188	3,819	952	2,723	2,443
Peru	599	3,130	7,196	5,742	6,370	NA	−13	182	145	164
UK isls. in Caribbean	5,929	33,451	191,680	306,512	331,391	−2,979	15,191	38,477	86,857	87,409
Venezuela	1,087	10,531	10,255	7,364	6,632	496	792	3,122	4,469	4,519
Africa[1]	**3,650**	**11,891**	**54,816**	**51,689**	**50,285**	**505**	**2,700**	**2,265**	**4,466**	**5,591**
Egypt	1,231	1,998	12,599	12,561	9,352	1	−4	−277	−112	−12
Nigeria	−401	470	5,058	4,349	5,774	−17	NA	23	41	61
South Africa	775	3,562	6,017	6,659	7,334	10	704	699	2,985	4,117
Middle East[1]	**3,959**	**10,863**	**34,431**	**48,593**	**69,132**	**4,425**	**6,506**	**16,808**	**24,406**	**26,025**
Israel	746	3,735	9,464	10,325	26,667	640	3,012	8,714	12,289	11,940
Saudi Arabia	1,899	3,661	7,436	10,585	11,085	1,811	NA	NA	NA	NA
UAE	409	683	4,935	13,568	16,785	99	64	747	3,194	4,837
Asia and Pacific[1]	**64,718**	**207,125**	**570,111**	**881,132**	**941,202**	**92,948**	**192,647**	**346,605**	**627,889**	**684,598**
Australia	15,110	34,838	125,421	166,430	168,855	6,542	18,775	35,632	69,276	66,736
China	354	11,140	58,996	97,287	107,556	NA	277	3,300	40,447	39,518
Hong Kong	6,055	27,447	41,264	68,944	81,234	1,511	1,493	4,440	11,210	11,022
India	372	2,379	24,666	38,634	44,458	NA	96	4,102	8,805	9,819
Indonesia	3,207	8,904	10,558	14,944	15,171	25	16	138	538	311
Japan	22,599	57,091	113,523	124,550	129,064	83,091	159,690	255,012	418,331	469,047
Korea, South	2,695	8,968	26,233	38,493	41,602	−1,009	3,110	15,746	42,508	51,770
Malaysia	1,466	7,910	11,791	14,606	15,080	56	310	338	1,134	1,101
New Zealand	3,156	4,271	6,724	11,948	11,938	157	395	584	209	164
Philippines	1,355	3,638	5,399	6,325	7,116	77	47	103	740	750
Singapore	3,975	24,133	102,778	255,344	274,260	1,289	5,087	21,517	23,579	22,360
Taiwan	2,226	7,836	22,188	15,935	17,031	836	3,174	4,642	7,573	8,058
Thailand	1,790	5,824	12,999	18,021	15,006	150	132	158	2,887	2,929

NA = Not available. **Note:** On a historical cost basis for comparison purposes. Direct investment in all industries. Book value of foreign direct investors' equity in, and net outstanding loans to, their U.S. affiliates. A U.S. affiliate is a U.S. business enterprise in which a single foreign direct investor owns at least 10% of the voting securities, or the equivalent. (1) Totals and subtotals include countries or territories not shown in table. (2) Curaçao figures before 2010 are for the entire Netherlands Antilles, a confederation that ended in 2010.

TRANSPORTATION AND TRAVEL

Top Motor Vehicle Producing Nations, 2017

Source: International Organization of Motor Vehicle Manufacturers (OICA)
(in thousands of units; ranked by total production)

Nation	Total motor vehicles	Cars	Light commercial vehicles[1]	% change, 2016-17[2]	Nation	Total motor vehicles	Cars	Light commercial vehicles[1]	% change, 2016-17[2]
China[3]	29,015	24,807	4,209	3.2%	Hungary	505	502	3	−4.0%
U.S.	11,190	3,033	8,157	−8.1	Argentina . . .	472	204	268	−0.1
Japan	9,694	8,348	1,346	5.3	Malaysia	460	425	35	−15.6
Germany. . . .	5,646	5,646	0	−1.8	Belgium.	379	336	43	−5.1
India	4,783	3,953	830	5.8	Morocco	377	342	34	9.0
South Korea	4,115	3,735	380	−2.7	Romania	359	359	0	0.0
Mexico	4,068	1,900	2,168	13.0	Taiwan	292	230	61	−5.8
Spain	2,848	2,291	557	−1.3	Sweden.	226	226	0	10.0
Brazil.	2,700	2,269	430	25.2	Slovenia	190	190	0	42.0
France.	2,227	1,748	479	6.5	Portugal	176	126	49	22.7
Canada.	2,200	749	1,450	−7.2	Netherlands . .	157	155	2	75.0
Thailand	1,989	818	1,170	2.3	Uzbekistan . .	140	140	0	59.1
UK.	1,749	1,671	78	−3.7	Austria	100	81	19	−9.0
Turkey.	1,696	1,143	553	14.1	Australia	99	88	10	−38.9
Russia.	1,551	1,348	203	19.0	Finland	92	92	0	90.8
Iran	1,515	1,419	97	18.2	Serbia	80	79	1	−0.5
Czech Rep.	1,420	1,414	6	0.0	Egypt	37	10	27	1.1
Indonesia . . .	1,217	982	234	3.3	Ukraine.	10	7	2	81.3
Italy.	1,142	743	400	3.5	Others.	759	537	222	16.0
Slovakia	1,002	1,002	0	−3.7	**NAFTA**	**17,458**	**5,683**	**11,775**	**−3.8**
Poland.	690	515	175	1.2	**Total**	**97,303**	**73,457**	**23,846**	**2.4**
South Africa	590	321	269	−1.5					

NAFTA = North American Free Trade Agreement. **Note:** Numbers may not add up to totals due to rounding. (1) Also includes heavy trucks, coaches, and buses. (2) Percent change in number of total motor vehicles. (3) Not including Taiwan.

World Motor Vehicle Production, 1950-2017

Source: For 1950-90, American Automobile Manufacturers Assn.; 2000-12, Automotive News Data Center and R.L. Polk; 2013-17, OICA
(in thousands of units)

Year	U.S.	Canada	Europe[1]	Japan	Other	World total	U.S. % of world total
1950	8,006	388	1,991	32	160	10,577	75.7%
1960	7,905	398	6,837	482	866	16,488	47.9
1970	8,284	1,160	13,049	5,289	1,637	29,419	28.2
1980	8,010	1,324	15,496	11,043	2,692	38,565	20.8
1990	9,783	1,928	18,866	13,487	4,496	48,554	20.1
2000	12,832	2,952	17,678	10,145	16,098	59,704	21.5
2004	12,021	2,698	20,850	10,512	16,573	65,654	18.3
2005	12,018	2,665	20,855	10,800	20,691	67,892	17.7
2006	11,351	2,545	21,490	11,486	23,180	70,992	16.0
2007	10,611	2,602	22,858	11,596	26,019	74,647	14.2
2008	8,503	2,046	21,608	10,969	31,224	67,602	12.6
2009	5,591	1,476	17,075	7,648	32,374	59,096	9.5
2010	7,632	2,074	19,371	9,197	35,036	73,311	10.4
2011	8,462	2,127	20,709	7,901	36,828	76,027	11.1
2012	10,142	2,454	22,324	9,448	36,714	81,082	12.5
2013	11,066	2,380	19,923	9,630	44,508	87,507	12.6
2014	11,661	2,394	20,430	9,775	45,536	89,776	12.9
2015	12,100	2,283	21,096	9,278	46,024	90,781	13.3
2016	12,198	2,370	21,700	9,205	49,504	94,977	12.8
2017	11,190	2,200	22,161	9,694	52,058	97,303	11.5

Note: Data may not be fully comparable across all years because they are derived from different sources. Number of units may not add up to totals due to rounding. (1) Prior to 2004, numbers exclude Eastern European production.

New and Used Passenger Cars Imported Into the U.S. by Country of Origin, 1970-2017

Source: Economic Indicators Division, U.S. Census Bureau, U.S. Dept. of Commerce
(in number of units)

Year	Canada	Japan	Mexico	S. Korea	Germany[1]	UK	Italy	Sweden	France	Total[2]
1970	692,783	381,338	NA	NA	674,945	76,257	42,523	57,844	37,114	2,013,420
1975	733,766	695,573	0	NA	370,012	67,106	102,344	51,993	15,647	2,074,653
1980	594,770	1,991,502	1	NA	338,711	32,517	46,899	61,496	47,386	3,116,448
1985	1,144,805	2,527,467	13,647	NA	473,110	24,474	8,689	142,640	42,882	4,397,679
1990	1,220,221	1,867,794	215,986	201,475	245,286	27,271	11,045	93,084	1,976	3,944,602
1995	1,552,691	1,114,360	462,800	131,718	204,932	42,450	1,031	82,593	14	3,624,428
2000	2,138,825	1,837,631	933,948	568,153	491,704	81,079	3,129	86,707	28,024	6,326,013
2005	1,967,985	1,832,534	693,149	730,500	547,191	184,716	5,377	93,736	412	6,564,844
2008	1,609,005	2,190,013	928,273	612,300	502,971	110,737	5,783	59,638	28,198	6,525,836
2009	1,164,849	1,238,773	649,740	476,912	348,093	78,999	3,067	27,017	16,900	4,276,163
2010	1,741,493	1,569,220	902,565	515,601	506,053	96,689	4,298	38,749	4,153	5,668,111
2011	1,835,819	1,421,750	953,514	587,574	537,158	95,742	5,372	26,884	3,580	5,673,139
2012	2,094,793	1,723,014	1,052,212	705,089	629,579	114,073	11,767	24,653	10,949	6,590,863
2013	2,009,140	1,722,119	1,127,375	759,964	657,832	115,326	14,289	21,617	12,694	6,682,557
2014	2,022,449	1,530,386	1,290,183	895,141	624,891	105,135	21,607	26,443	25,292	6,813,003
2015	1,969,502	1,609,709	1,438,840	1,065,972	639,879	134,413	132,340	37,789	28,034	7,420,613
2016	2,010,907	1,714,368	1,417,622	1,001,021	555,578	199,612	133,002	47,769	16,497	7,482,325
2017	1,850,685	1,731,913	1,723,456	929,531	501,359	217,344	159,846	58,492	9,800	7,659,716

NA = Not available. **Note:** Excludes cars assembled in U.S. foreign trade zones. (1) Figures prior to 1991 are for West Germany. (2) Includes units imported from countries not shown in table.

Passenger Car Production in U.S. Plants, 2015-17

Source: Wards Intelligence
(in number of units)

	2017	2016	2015		2017	2016	2015
FCA TOTAL[1]	531	72,493	287,114	**HONDA TOTAL**	526,818	686,378	678,828
Chrysler 200 Series	—	43,116	190,439	Acura ILX	9,808	15,297	28,017
Chrysler Total	—	43,116	190,439	Acura NSX	925	712	—
Dodge Dart	—	28,766	96,150	Acura TLX	42,080	43,156	53,224
Dodge Viper	531	611	525	**Acura Total**	52,813	59,165	81,241
Dodge Total	531	29,377	96,675	Honda Accord	327,425	378,393	379,385
				Honda Civic	146,580	248,820	218,202
FORD TOTAL	396,736	408,637	550,008	**Honda Total**.	474,005	627,213	597,587
Ford C-Max	19,672	18,801	23,619				
Ford Focus	179,110	162,426	237,921	**HYUNDAI TOTAL**	269,919	342,845	384,519
Ford Fusion	—	7,864	41,453	Hyundai Elantra	131,753	173,926	172,244
Ford Mustang.	120,780	142,382	165,138	Hyundai Sonata	138,166	168,919	212,275
Ford Taurus.	51,375	59,125	74,358	**KIA TOTAL**	96,444	112,488	109,522
Ford Total	370,937	390,598	542,489	Kia Optima	96,444	112,488	109,522
Lincoln Continental	25,799	14,925	20				
Lincoln MKS.	—	3,114	7,499	**MERCEDES-BENZ TOTAL** . . .	53,628	72,040	93,505
Lincoln Total.	25,799	18,039	7,519	Mercedes C-Class	53,628	72,040	93,505
				NISSAN TOTAL	340,554	412,149	421,110
GENERAL MOTORS TOTAL . .	490,629	864,779	725,535	Nissan Altima	261,872	327,541	346,530
Buick LaCrosse	12,208	38,266	34,399	Nissan Leaf	8,719	13,863	19,340
Buick Verano	—	28,395	41,929	Nissan Maxima	69,963	70,745	55,240
Buick Total	12,208	66,661	76,328				
Cadillac ATS.	13,335	24,017	23,411	**SUBARU TOTAL**[2]	158,484	123,993	145,845
Cadillac CT6	9,914	17,676	—	Subaru Impreza	109,038	13,399	—
Cadillac CTS	8,929	16,658	17,813	Subaru Legacy.	49,446	74,649	66,002
Cadillac ELR	—	212	375	**Subaru Total**	158,484	88,048	66,002
Cadillac Total	32,178	58,563	41,599	Toyota Camry.	—	35,945	79,843
Chevrolet Camaro	59,869	100,188	10,251				
Chevrolet Corvette	21,999	38,030	40,403	**TESLA TOTAL**	53,846	50,478	50,578
Chevrolet Cruze.	131,617	211,929	269,437	Tesla Model 3	2,685	—	—
Chevrolet Impala	14,747	30,137	29,584	Tesla Model S	51,161	50,478	50,578
Chevrolet Malibu	161,816	277,904	181,443	**TOYOTA TOTAL**	584,421	676,970	629,088
Chevrolet Sonic	34,324	48,879	60,748	Lexus ES	41,657	43,588	4,088
Chevrolet Volt.	21,871	32,488	15,741	Toyota Avalon.	39,635	50,898	69,087
Chevrolet Total	446,243	739,555	607,607	Toyota Camry.	339,297	400,459	365,399
Opel Ampera	—	—	1	Toyota Corolla	163,832	182,025	190,514
				Toyota Total	542,764	633,382	625,000
				VOLKSWAGEN TOTAL	61,206	93,334	87,156
				Volkswagen Passat	61,206	93,334	87,156
				TOTAL CARS	3,033,216	3,916,584	4,162,808

— = No production. (1) Fiat Chrysler Automobiles, or FCA, was formed in 2014 when Fiat acquired the remaining shares of Chrysler Group that it did not already own. (2) SIA (Subaru of Indiana Automotive) built the Toyota Camry in collaboration with Toyota from 2007-16.

Domestic and Imported Retail Car Sales in the U.S., 1980-2017

Source: Wards Intelligence
(in number of units)

	Cars			Light trucks			All vehicles		
Year	Domestic[1]	Imports	Total cars	Domestic[1]	Imports	Total light trucks	Domestic[1]	Imports	Total vehicles
1980	6,579,778	2,369,457	8,949,235	1,750,735	478,887	2,229,622	8,330,513	2,848,344	11,178,857
1985	8,204,670	2,774,517	10,979,187	3,629,080	832,186	4,461,266	12,109,999	3,615,292	15,725,291
1990	6,916,860	2,384,346	9,301,206	3,956,756	611,941	4,568,697	11,133,504	3,013,865	14,147,369
1995	7,113,902	1,506,257	8,620,159	5,705,708	402,181	6,107,889	13,192,861	1,923,464	15,116,325
1996	7,206,349	1,272,196	8,478,545	6,179,881	438,757	6,618,638	13,732,379	1,723,733	15,456,112
1997	6,862,175	1,355,305	8,217,480	6,324,758	579,483	6,904,241	13,549,251	1,948,609	15,497,860
1998	6,705,208	1,379,781	8,084,989	6,802,016	656,002	7,458,018	13,913,028	2,054,259	15,967,287
1999	6,918,781	1,718,927	8,637,708	7,480,607	775,223	8,255,830	14,901,266	2,513,462	17,414,728
2000	6,761,603	2,016,120	8,777,723	7,719,707	852,325	8,572,032	14,922,648	2,889,025	17,811,673
2001	6,254,371	2,097,629	8,352,000	7,789,089	981,280	8,770,369	14,372,624	3,099,754	17,472,378
2002	5,816,671	2,225,584	8,042,255	7,707,738	1,066,375	8,774,113	13,829,568	3,309,084	17,138,652
2003	5,472,500	2,083,051	7,555,551	7,856,322	1,227,180	9,083,502	13,638,351	3,329,091	16,967,442
2004	5,333,496	2,149,059	7,482,555	8,138,107	1,246,258	9,384,365	13,880,251	3,418,322	17,298,573
2005	5,473,450	2,186,533	7,659,983	8,072,456	1,215,315	9,287,771	14,020,528	3,423,801	17,444,329
2006	5,416,828	2,344,764	7,761,592	7,396,058	1,346,750	8,742,808	13,334,843	3,714,138	17,048,981
2007	5,197,271	2,365,063	7,562,334	7,138,803	1,388,085	8,526,888	12,687,016	3,773,299	16,460,315
2008	4,490,863	2,278,271	6,769,134	5,329,165	1,096,469	6,425,634	10,107,753	3,385,439	13,493,192
2009	3,558,283	1,843,282	5,401,565	4,116,550	884,242	5,000,792	7,867,766	2,734,277	10,602,043
2010	3,791,499	1,844,240	5,635,739	5,020,441	898,644	5,919,085	9,020,088	2,752,438	11,772,526
2011	4,145,964	1,946,897	6,092,861	5,666,512	982,443	6,648,955	10,108,762	2,939,624	13,048,386
2012	5,119,844	2,125,325	7,245,169	6,127,314	1,060,720	7,188,034	11,581,776	3,197,708	14,779,484
2013	5,433,158	2,153,176	7,586,334	6,704,499	1,239,268	7,943,767	12,479,306	3,403,406	15,882,712
2014	5,609,878	2,098,122	7,708,000	7,384,280	1,359,910	8,744,190	13,388,628	3,471,215	16,859,843
2015	5,595,123	1,921,703	7,516,826	8,097,387	1,782,078	9,879,465	14,127,526	3,718,098	17,845,624
2016	5,152,055	1,720,674	6,872,729	8,436,243	2,155,805	10,592,048	13,975,597	3,890,176	17,865,773
2017	4,607,665	1,472,564	6,080,229	8,651,622	2,403,628	11,055,250	13,658,985	3,891,536	17,550,521

Note: Vehicles are cars and light trucks belonging to gross vehicle weight (GVW) classes 1-3 (under 14,001 lbs). (1) Includes the U.S., Canada, and Mexico.

U.S. Vehicle Sales, 1980-2017
Source: Wards Intelligence
(in millions)

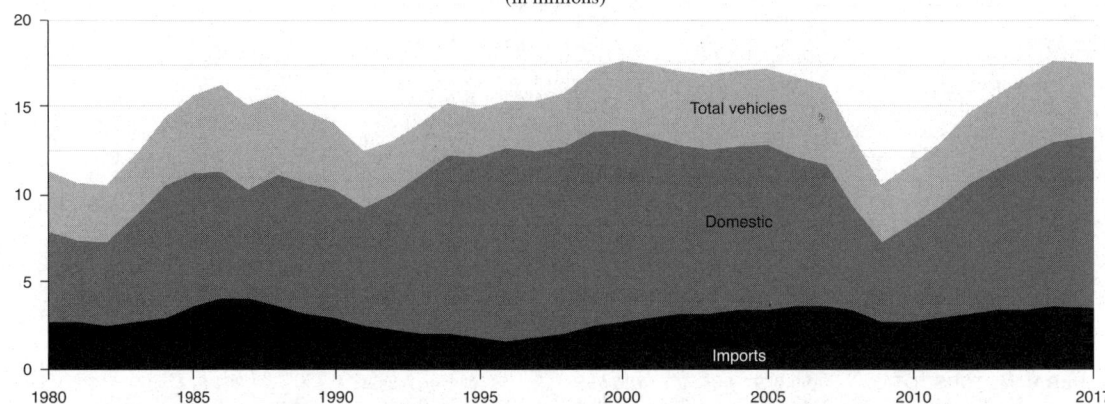

Note: Vehicles are cars and light trucks belonging to gross vehicle weight (GVW) classes 1-3 (under 14,001 lbs). Domestic sales include the U.S., Canada, and Mexico.

U.S. Sales of Hybrid and Electric Vehicles, 2000-17
Source: Wards Intelligence; in number of units sold

Power type	2000	2005	2010	2011	2012	2013	2014	2015	2016	2017
Hybrid car............	9,350	151,253	231,819	229,150	393,054	468,005	416,944	350,753	276,995	252,366
Hybrid light truck.........	0	54,575	42,286	30,432	24,170	20,023	26,872	22,606	64,797	111,363
Total hybrid............	**9,350**	**205,828**	**274,105**	**259,582**	**417,224**	**488,028**	**443,816**	**373,359**	**341,792**	**363,729**
Electric car.............	463	0	326	10,447	14,534	47,424	67,067	72,313	64,307	61,488
Electric light truck.........	0	0	0	0	192	1,096	1,184	61	16,067	40,012
Total electric..........	**463**	**0**	**326**	**10,447**	**14,726**	**48,520**	**68,251**	**72,374**	**80,374**	**101,500**
Plug-in hybrid car.........	0	0	326	7,671	38,585	49,043	55,341	41,739	60,972	76,420
Plug-in hybrid light truck....	0	0	0	0	0	0	100	2,076	10,357	14,607
Total plug-in hybrid	**0**	**0**	**326**	**7,671**	**38,585**	**49,043**	**55,441**	**43,815**	**71,329**	**91,027**

Top-Selling Passenger Cars in the U.S., 2014-17
Source: Wards Intelligence
(ranked by number of vehicles sold)

Car	2017 sales	Car	2017 sales	Car	2017 sales
1. Toyota Camry..........	387,081	8. Hyundai Elantra........	198,210	15. Kia Soul...............	115,712
2. Honda Civic...........	377,286	9. Chevrolet Malibu........	185,857	16. Kia Optima.............	107,493
3. Honda Accord..........	322,655	10. Chevrolet Cruze........	184,751	17. Nissan Versa...........	106,772
4. Toyota Corolla..........	308,695	11. Ford Focus............	158,385	18. Toyota Prius...........	96,247
5. Nissan Altima..........	254,996	12. Hyundai Sonata........	131,803	19. Dodge Charger.........	88,351
6. Nissan Sentra..........	218,451	13. Kia Forte..............	117,596	20. Subaru Impreza........	86,043
7. Ford Fusion............	209,623	14. Volkswagen Jetta.......	115,807		

Car	2016 sales	Car	2015 sales	Car	2014 sales
1. Toyota Camry..........	388,618	1. Toyota Camry..........	429,355	1. Toyota Camry..........	428,606
2. Honda Civic...........	366,927	2. Toyota Corolla..........	363,332	2. Honda Accord..........	388,374
3. Toyota Corolla..........	360,483	3. Honda Accord..........	355,557	3. Toyota Corolla..........	339,498
4. Honda Accord..........	345,225	4. Honda Civic...........	335,384	4. Nissan Altima..........	335,644
5. Nissan Altima..........	307,380	5. Nissan Altima..........	333,398	5. Honda Civic...........	325,981
6. Ford Fusion............	265,840	6. Ford Fusion............	300,170	6. Ford Fusion............	306,860
7. Chevrolet Malibu........	227,881	7. Hyundai Elantra........	241,706	7. Chevrolet Cruze........	273,060
8. Nissan Sentra..........	214,709	8. Chevrolet Cruze........	226,602	8. Hyundai Elantra........	222,023
9. Hyundai Elantra........	208,319	9. Hyundai Sonata........	213,303	9. Ford Focus............	219,634
10. Hyundai Sonata........	199,416	10. Nissan Sentra..........	203,509	10. Hyundai Sonata........	216,936

U.S. Retail Car Sales by Vehicle Size, 1985-2017
Source: Wards Intelligence
(as percent of total U.S. sales)

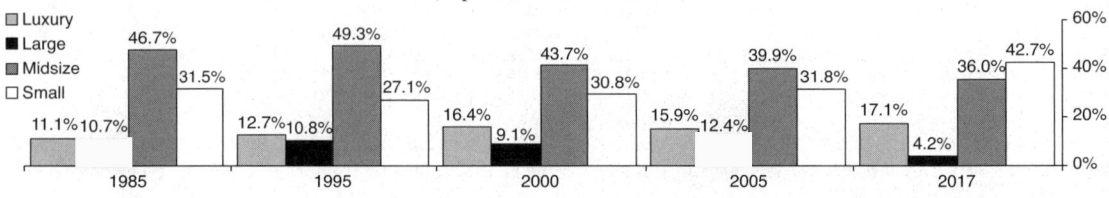

U.S. Light Truck Sales by Type, 1985-2017

Source: Wards Intelligence

(as percent of total U.S. sales)

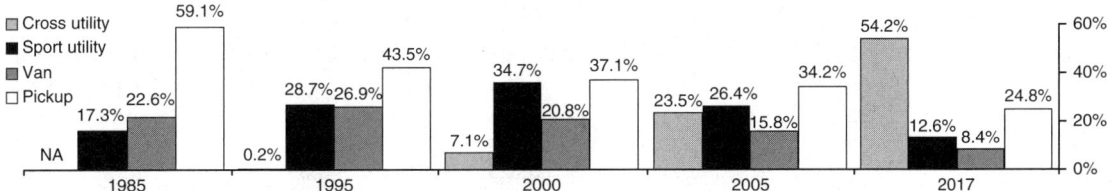

- ▨ Cross utility
- ■ Sport utility
- ▨ Van
- ☐ Pickup

NA = Not applicable. **Note:** Comm. chassis sales (not shown) were 1.0% (for 1985), 0.7% (1995), 0.2% (2000), 0.1% (2005), 0.04% (2017).

Top-Selling Light Trucks in the U.S., 2015-17

Source: Wards Intelligence

(ranked by number of vehicles sold)

Truck	2017 sales	Truck	2016 sales	Truck	2015 sales
1. Ford F-Series	834,445	1. Ford F-Series	763,887	1. Ford F-Series	725,726
2. Chevrolet Silverado	585,864	2. Chevrolet Silverado	574,876	2. Chevrolet Silverado	600,544
3. Ram Pickup	483,520	3. Ram Pickup	473,681	3. Ram Pickup	434,435
4. Toyota RAV4	407,594	4. Honda CR-V	357,335	4. Honda CR-V	345,647
5. Nissan Rogue	403,465	5. Toyota RAV4	352,154	5. Toyota RAV4	315,412
6. Honda CR-V	377,895	6. Nissan Rogue	329,904	6. Ford Escape	306,492
7. Ford Escape	308,296	7. Ford Escape	307,069	7. Nissan Rogue	287,190
8. Chevrolet Equinox	290,458	8. Ford Explorer	248,507	8. Chevrolet Equinox	277,589
9. Ford Explorer	271,131	9. Chevrolet Equinox	242,195	9. Ford Explorer	249,251
10. Jeep Grand Cherokee	240,696	10. GMC Sierra	221,680	10. GMC Sierra	224,139

Most Popular Colors by Vehicle Type, 2017

Source: Axalta Coating Systems; for 2017 model year

Luxury cars/SUVs		Intermediate cars/CUVs		Compact/sports cars		Light trucks	
Color	Percent	Color	Percent	Color	Percent	Color	Percent
White/white pearl	29%	White/white pearl	23%	White/white pearl	21%	White/white pearl	33%
Black/black effect	24	Black/black effect	20	Black/black effect	18	Black/black effect	21
Gray	18	Gray	20	Blue	16	Gray	13
Silver	10	Silver	13	Gray	14	Silver	11
Blue	7	Red	11	Silver	11	Red	8
Red	7	Blue	9	Red	10	Blue	7
Beige/brown	3	Beige/brown	1	Green	4	Beige/brown	3
Yellow/gold	2	Yellow/gold	1	Yellow/gold	3	Yellow/gold	2
Green	<1	Green	1	Other	3	Green	1
Other	<1	Other	1	Beige/brown	<1	Other	1

U.S. Light-Duty Vehicle Fuel Efficiency, 1975-2017

Source: Natl. Vehicle and Fuel Emissions Laboratory, Office of Transportation and Air Quality, U.S. Environmental Protection Agency

Cars and light-duty trucks (SUVs, minivans, passenger vans, and pickup trucks) showed significant fuel-efficiency improvements from 1975 through 1987, when the fuel economy for both combined reached a high of 22 miles per gallon (mpg). The fuel economy value mainly declined, 1988-2004, but since 2005, fuel economy has generally increased, reaching a new all-time high of 25.2 mpg in 2017.

Year[1]	Cars (mpg)	Light-duty trucks (mpg)	All light-duty vehicles (mpg)	Year[1]	Cars (mpg)	Light-duty trucks (mpg)	All light-duty vehicles (mpg)
1975	13.5	11.6	13.1	2006	23.0	17.2	20.1
1980	20.0	15.8	19.2	2007	23.7	17.4	20.6
1985	23.0	17.5	21.3	2008	23.9	17.8	21.0
1990	23.3	17.4	21.2	2009	25.0	18.5	22.4
1995	23.3	17.0	20.5	2010	25.7	18.8	22.6
1999	22.7	16.6	19.7	2011	25.4	19.1	22.3
2000	22.5	16.8	19.8	2012	26.9	19.3	23.6
2001	22.6	16.5	19.6	2013	27.7	19.8	24.2
2002	22.8	16.5	19.5	2014	27.6	20.3	24.1
2003	23.0	16.7	19.6	2015	28.2	21.1	24.6
2004	22.9	16.5	19.3	2016	28.5	21.2	24.7
2005	23.1	16.9	19.9	2017[2]	29.1	21.2	25.2

Note: Adjusted mpg composite values (city and highway fuel efficiency combined in a 55%/45% ratio) are used for all vehicles and are intended to reflect real-world use. (1) Because of changes in methodology, mpg figures prior to 1986 are not entirely comparable with later values. (2) Preliminary.

Registered Cars in the U.S., 1900-2016

Source: Office of Highway Policy Information, Federal Highway Administration, U.S. Dept. of Transportation

(number of automobiles for public and private use)

Year	Reg. cars	Year	Reg. cars	Year	Reg. cars	Year	Reg. cars	Year	Reg. cars
1900	8,000	1945	25,796,985	1990	133,700,497	1999	132,432,044	2008	137,079,843
1905	77,400	1950	40,339,077	1991	128,299,601	2000	133,621,420	2009	134,879,600
1910	458,377	1955	52,144,739	1992	126,581,148	2001	137,633,467	2010	130,892,240
1915	2,332,426	1960	61,671,390	1993	127,327,189	2002	135,920,677	2011	125,656,528
1920	8,131,522	1965	75,257,588	1994	127,883,469	2003	135,669,897	2012	111,289,906
1925	17,481,001	1970	89,243,557	1995	128,386,775	2004	136,430,651	2013	113,676,345
1930	23,034,753	1975	106,705,934	1996	129,728,311	2005	136,568,083	2014	113,898,845
1935	22,567,827	1980	121,600,843	1997	129,748,704	2006	135,399,945	2015	112,864,228
1940	27,465,826	1985	127,885,193	1998	131,838,538	2007	135,932,930	2016	112,961,266

Note: There were no publicly owned vehicles before 1925; statistics also exclude military vehicles for all years. Alaska and Hawaii data included since 1960.

Licensed Drivers by Age and Sex, 1980-2016

Source: Office of Highway Policy Information, Federal Highway Administration, U.S. Dept. of Transportation
(numbers in thousands)

Age (years)	1980 Total	1990 Total	2000 Total	2010 Male	2010 Female	2010 Total	2016 Male	2016 Female	2016 Total	% total drivers
Under 16	93	43	27	199	198	398	32	32	63	0.0%
16	1,823	1,443	1,470	608	605	1,213	555	566	1,121	0.5
17	2,790	2,132	2,331	1,025	1,004	2,028	991	982	1,973	0.9
18	3,247	2,595	2,839	1,408	1,323	2,731	1,338	1,282	2,619	1.2
19	3,542	3,037	3,077	1,641	1,546	3,187	1,556	1,484	3,040	1.4
19 and under	**11,496**	**9,249**	**9,744**	**4,880**	**4,676**	**9,556**	**4,470**	**4,346**	**8,816**	**4.0**
20	3,636	3,229	3,140	1,744	1,682	3,426	1,654	1,596	3,250	1.5
21	3,733	3,249	3,172	1,756	1,717	3,474	1,722	1,668	3,390	1.5
22	3,811	3,262	3,182	1,757	1,725	3,483	1,794	1,753	3,547	1.6
23	3,938	3,398	3,247	1,767	1,748	3,515	1,867	1,825	3,691	1.7
24	3,915	3,758	3,225	1,792	1,779	3,571	1,927	1,905	3,832	1.7
20-24	**19,032**	**16,897**	**15,966**	**8,817**	**8,651**	**17,469**	**8,963**	**8,747**	**17,710**	**8.0**
25-29	18,925	19,895	17,586	9,179	9,253	18,431	9,847	9,875	19,723	8.9
30-34	17,369	20,578	19,155	8,934	8,915	17,849	9,682	9,789	19,472	8.8
35-39	13,696	19,055	21,059	9,079	9,082	18,161	9,238	9,411	18,649	8.4
40-44	11,134	16,905	21,093	9,613	9,565	19,178	8,856	8,996	17,852	8.1
45-49	10,076	13,020	19,154	10,381	10,433	20,814	9,560	9,661	19,221	8.7
50-54	10,090	10,484	16,868	10,241	10,388	20,628	9,996	10,191	20,186	9.1
55-59	9,770	9,438	12,760	9,127	9,313	18,440	9,990	10,314	20,304	9.2
60-64	8,232	9,235	9,915	7,847	8,011	15,858	8,843	9,232	18,076	8.2
65-69	6,580	8,375	8,386	5,652	5,816	11,468	7,522	7,895	15,417	7.0
70-74	NA	NA	7,468	4,029	4,202	8,231	5,190	5,463	10,653	4.8
75-79	NA	NA	5,911	2,966	3,192	6,158	3,441	3,710	7,151	3.2
80-84	NA	NA	3,511	2,090	2,373	4,464	2,195	2,410	4,606	2.1
85 and over	**NA**	**NA**	**2,050**	**1,541**	**1,870**	**3,411**	**1,792**	**2,085**	**3,877**	**1.7**
Total	**145,295**	**167,015**	**190,625**	**104,374**	**105,740**	**210,115**	**109,587**	**112,125**	**221,712**	**100.0**

NA = Not available. **Note:** Numbers may not add up to totals due to rounding.

Mobile Device Handheld Phone and Texting Laws for Drivers, 2018

Source: Insurance Institute for Highway Safety; as of July 2018

State	Handheld ban	Texting ban	Enforcement	State	Handheld ban	Texting ban	Enforcement	State	Handheld ban	Texting ban	Enforcement
AL	No[1]	Yes	P	KY	No[5]	Yes	P	ND	No[5]	Yes	P
AK	No	Yes	P	LA	No[5,6,7]	Yes	P[8]	OH	No[5]	Yes	P[12]
AZ	No[2]	No[2]	S	ME	No[6]	Yes	P	OK	No[6]	Yes	P
AR	No[3]	Yes	P[4]	MD	Yes	Yes	P	OR	Yes	Yes	P
CA	Yes	Yes	P[4]	MA	No[5]	Yes	P	PA	No	Yes	P
CO	No[5]	Yes	P	MI	No[6]	Yes	P	RI	Yes	Yes	P
CT	Yes	Yes	P	MN	No[9]	Yes	P	SC	No	Yes	P
DE	Yes	Yes	P	MS	No	Yes	P	SD	No[6]	Yes	S
DC	Yes	Yes	P	MO	No	No[10]	P	TN	No[6]	Yes	P
FL	No	Yes	S	MT	No	No	NA	TX	No[5]	Yes	P
GA	Yes	Yes	P	NE	No[11]	Yes	S	UT	No[5]	Yes	P
HI	Yes	Yes	P	NV	Yes	Yes	P	VT	Yes	Yes	P
ID	No	Yes	P	NH	Yes	Yes	P	VA	No[5]	Yes	P[4]
IL	Yes	Yes	P	NJ	Yes	Yes	P	WA	Yes	Yes	P
IN	No[3]	Yes	P	NM	No[6]	Yes	P	WV	Yes	Yes	P
IA	No[6]	Yes	P	NY	Yes	Yes	P	WI	No[6]	Yes	P
KS	No[6]	Yes	P	NC	No[5]	Yes	P	WY	No	Yes	P

NA = Not applicable. P = Officer may stop vehicle for violation (primary); S = Officer may issue citation only when vehicle is stopped for another moving violation (secondary). **Note:** Laws shown for licensed passenger car drivers. Different laws and regulations apply to school bus, municipal transit, and other mass transit operators. Different laws may apply in school zones, construction zones, or other such areas. (1) Yes for 16-year-old drivers and for 17-year-old drivers who have held an intermediate license for fewer than 6 months. (2) Yes for learner's permit and intermediate license holders during the first 6 months after licensing. (3) Yes for drivers under 21 years of age. (4) Secondary for cellphone use by young drivers. (5) Yes for drivers under 18. (6) Yes for learner's permit and intermediate license holders. (7) Yes for drivers in the year after getting their first license. (8) Secondary for cellphone use by novice drivers age 18 and older. (9) Yes for learner's permit and provisional license holders in their first year after licensing. (10) Yes for drivers 21 and younger. (11) Yes for learner's permit and intermediate license holders under 18. (12) Primary for drivers younger than 18, and secondary for texting.

Selected Motor Vehicle Statistics

Source: Federal Highway Admin., U.S. Dept. of Transportation; Insurance Inst. for Highway Safety; American Petroleum Inst.

Driver's license age requirements, state gas tax, and safety belt use laws (incl. laws passed, but not in effect) as of 2018. Other figures are for 2016.

STATE	Driver's license age requirements Learner's permit	Regular[1]	Gas taxes (cents/ gal)[5]	Safety belt use law[6]	Licensed drivers Per 1,000 resident pop.	Per reg. motor vehicle	Reg. motor vehicles per 1,000 pop.	Fuel use per reg. motor vehicle (gal)	Annual miles driven Per gal used	Per reg. vehicle	Per lic. driver
Alabama	15	17	39.3	P	811	0.74	1,124	687	18.43	12,660	17,557
Alaska	14	16y, 6m	32.8	P	721	0.69	1,071	520	12.73	6,618	9,837
Arizona	15y, 6m	16y, 6m	37.4	S	733	0.89	835	653	17.40	11,368	12,944
Arkansas	14	18	40.2	P	800	0.86	940	776	16.41	12,733	14,953
California	15y, 6m	17[2]	73.1	P	668	0.88	770	618	18.20	11,254	12,982
Colorado	15	17	40.4	S	734	0.80	923	590	17.26	10,193	12,824
Connecticut	16	18[2,3,4]	57.7	P	730	0.92	795	630	17.68	11,133	12,117
Delaware	16	17[2]	41.4	P	794	0.76	1,054	573	17.71	10,139	13,457
Dist. of Columbia	16	18[4]	41.9	P	719	1.62	495	390	27.53	10,744	7,394
Florida	15	18	59.8	P	712	0.90	805	645	20.12	12,985	14,688
Georgia	15	18[2]	50.0	P	677	0.86	799	750	19.88	14,904	17,604
Hawaii	15y, 6m	17[2]	65.3	P	652	0.77	862	427	20.22	8,635	11,415
Idaho	14y, 6m	16[2]	51.4	S	690	0.63	1,095	597	15.63	9,336	14,815
Illinois	15	18[2]	54.2	P	665	0.84	803	631	16.55	10,442	12,603
Indiana	15	18	60.3	P	686	0.74	926	730	18.56	13,547	18,269
Iowa	14	17[2]	48.9	P	716	0.62	1,173	663	13.67	9,068	14,845
Kansas	14	16y, 6m	42.4	P(a)	698	0.77	911	699	17.32	12,115	15,814
Kentucky	16	17[2]	44.4	P	683	0.73	952	718	16.25	11,672	16,267
Louisiana	15	17[2]	38.4	P	725	0.89	834	768	16.40	12,588	14,478
Maine	15	16y, 9m[2]	48.4	P	767	0.94	832	920	14.56	13,396	14,528
Maryland	15y, 9m	18	52.2	P(a)	709	1.04	695	789	17.93	14,152	13,866
Massachusetts	16	18[2]	44.9	S	740	1.01	744	651	18.74	12,195	12,265
Michigan	14y, 9m	17[2]	60.8	P	713	0.86	839	697	17.13	11,933	14,055
Minnesota	15	16y, 6m[2]	47.0	P	612	0.64	971	656	16.78	11,016	17,475
Mississippi	15	16y, 6m	37.2	P	675	0.98	692	1,190	16.57	19,715	20,187
Missouri	15	17y, 11m	35.8	S(b)	697	0.75	933	661	19.70	13,021	17,418
Montana	14y, 6m	16[2]	50.7	S	765	0.45	1,722	456	15.38	7,020	15,805
Nebraska	15	17	47.7	S	736	0.74	1,023	710	14.94	10,606	14,739
Nevada	15y, 6m	18[2]	52.2	S	637	0.79	816	637	17.53	11,168	14,307
New Hampshire	15y, 6m	18[2]	42.2	None	821	0.84	991	622	16.43	10,216	12,326
New Jersey	16	18[2]	55.5	P(a)	697	1.06	664	866	14.98	12,976	12,358
New Mexico	15	16y, 6m[2]	37.3	P	731	0.85	876	830	18.41	15,288	18,324
New York	16	17[2]	63.1	P	605	1.08	563	650	16.99	11,052	10,289
North Carolina	15	16y, 6m[2]	53.8	P(a)	716	0.89	815	711	19.86	14,116	16,066
North Dakota	14	16[2]	41.4	S	733	0.64	1,181	829	13.12	10,882	17,519
Ohio	15y, 6m	18[2]	46.4	S	687	0.75	920	634	17.51	11,099	14,873
Oklahoma	15y, 6m	16y, 6m	35.4	P	637	0.67	953	772	16.99	13,114	19,620
Oregon	15	17[2,3]	55.2	P	698	0.77	931	572	16.85	9,633	12,858
Pennsylvania	16	17	77.1	S(b)	704	0.85	841	605	15.59	9,430	11,266
Rhode Island	16	17y, 6m[2]	52.4	P	713	0.88	829	497	18.19	9,047	10,525
South Carolina	15	16y, 6m	39.2	P	755	0.91	872	862	14.63	12,615	14,560
South Dakota	14	16	48.4	S	719	0.51	1,440	580	13.16	7,627	15,268
Tennessee	15	17	43.8	P	781	0.94	858	778	17.31	13,465	14,791
Texas	15	18	38.4	P	570	0.74	781	904	13.78	12,463	17,082
Utah	15	17[2]	47.8	P	642	0.86	759	731	18.56	13,571	16,042
Vermont	15	16y, 6m[2]	49.2	S	886	0.92	986	628	19.08	11,985	13,333
Virginia	15y, 6m	18[2]	40.8	S	703	0.83	868	706	16.38	11,569	14,287
Washington	15	17[2]	67.8	P	773	0.82	967	502	17.24	8,658	10,827
West Virginia	15	17	54.1	P	633	0.70	931	658	17.41	11,461	16,854
Wisconsin	15y, 6m	16y, 9m[2]	51.3	P	728	0.77	963	624	18.45	11,510	15,225
Wyoming	15	16y, 6m[2]	42.4	S	719	0.50	1,461	836	13.04	10,901	22,139
U.S. AVERAGE			**52.1**		**686**	**0.84**	**832**	**691**	**17.09**	**11,810**	**14,318**

Note: Most states have graduated licensing systems that phase in full driving privileges. During the learner's stage, driving generally is not permitted without adult supervision. In an intermediate stage, young licensees may be allowed to drive unsupervised under certain conditions. (1) Min. age at which all restrictions may be lifted on private passenger car operation. (2) Applicants under a specified age (typically between 17 and 19) must complete driver education. (3) Home training (CT) or more hours of supervised driving (OR) may be substituted for driver ed. (4) Learner's stage mandatory for all license applicants regardless of age. (5) Some values rounded. Includes 18.4 cents per gallon in federal excise taxes. (6) P = Officer may stop vehicle for violation (primary); S = Officer may issue seat belt citation only when vehicle is stopped for another moving violation (secondary). (a) Secondary enforcement for rear seat occupants; (b) Primary enforcement for children under a specified age.

International Tourism Receipts, 2000-17

Source: World Tourism Organization (UNWTO), © UNWTO
(in billions of U.S. dollars; ranked by most recent figures available)

Rank	Country	2000	2005	2010	2015	2016	2017*	Rank	Country	2000	2005	2010	2015	2016	2017*
1.	U.S.	$100.2	$101.5	$137.0	$206.9	$206.9	$210.7	26.	South Korea	$6.8	$5.8	$10.3	$15.2	$17.3	$13.4
2.	Spain	30.9	49.7	54.6	56.6	60.5	68.0	27.	Poland.	5.7	6.3	9.6	10.5	11.0	12.8
3.	France.	33.0	44.0	57.1	58.3	54.5	60.7	28.	Indonesia . .	5.0	4.5	7.0	10.8	11.2	12.5
4.	Thailand . .	7.5	9.6	20.1	44.9	48.8	57.5	29.	Taiwan . . .	3.7	5.0	8.7	14.4	13.4	12.3
5.	Italy	27.5	35.4	38.8	39.4	40.2	44.2	30.	Belgium. . . .	6.6	9.9	11.4	12.0	11.6	12.2
6.	UK.	22.2	32.1	34.9	45.5	41.5	43.9	31.	Saudi Arabia	NA	4.6	6.7	10.1	11.1	12.1
7.	Australia . . .	9.4	18.4	32.6	34.2	37.0	41.7	32.	Croatia . . .	2.8	7.4	8.1	8.8	9.6	10.9
8.	Germany. . .	18.7	29.2	34.7	36.9	37.5	39.8	33.	New Zealand	2.9	6.5	6.5	9.0	9.5	10.3
9.	Macau.	3.2	6.9	22.3	31.0	30.4	35.6	34.	Russia.	3.4	5.9	8.8	8.4	7.8	8.9
10.	Japan	3.4	6.6	13.2	25.0	30.7	34.1	35.	Vietnam . . .	NA	2.3	4.5	7.4	8.3	8.9
11.	Hong Kong	5.9	10.3	22.2	36.2	32.8	33.2	36.	South Africa	2.7	7.5	9.1	8.2	7.9	8.8
12.	China[1].	16.2	29.3	45.8	45.0	44.4	32.6	37.	Egypt	4.3	6.9	12.5	6.1	2.6	7.8
13.	India	3.5	7.5	14.5	21.0	22.4	27.4	38.	Morocco . . .	2.0	4.6	6.7	6.3	6.5	7.4
14.	Turkey.	7.6	19.2	22.6	26.6	18.7	22.5	39.	Denmark. . .	3.7	5.3	5.9	6.7	7.0	7.4
15.	Mexico	8.3	11.8	12.0	17.7	19.6	21.3	40.	Dom. Rep...	2.9	3.5	4.2	6.1	6.7	7.2
16.	United Arab							41.	Lebanon . . .	NA	5.5	8.0	6.9	7.0	NA
	Emirates	1.1	3.2	8.6	17.5	19.5	21.0	42.	Philippines	2.2	2.3	2.6	5.3	5.1	7.0
17.	Austria	9.8	16.1	18.6	18.2	19.3	20.4	43.	Czechia. . . .	3.0	4.8	7.2	6.1	6.3	6.9
18.	Canada. . . .	10.8	13.7	15.8	16.5	18.0	20.3	44.	Israel.	4.4	3.2	4.8	5.9	5.9	6.8
19.	Singapore . .	5.1	6.2	14.2	16.6	18.9	19.7	45.	Hungary . . .	3.8	4.1	5.6	5.3	5.7	6.2
20.	Malaysia . .	5.0	8.8	18.1	17.6	18.1	18.3	46.	Qatar.	0.1	0.8	0.6	5.0	5.4	6.0
21.	Portugal . . .	5.2	7.7	10.1	12.7	14.0	17.1	47.	Brazil.	1.8	3.9	5.3	5.8	6.0	5.8
22.	Switzerland	6.6	10.0	14.7	16.4	16.3	17.0	48.	Ireland.	2.6	4.8	4.1	4.8	5.2	5.6
23.	Greece . . .	9.2	13.3	12.7	15.7	14.6	16.5	49.	Norway	2.2	3.5	4.7	4.9	5.2	5.4
24.	Netherlands	7.2	9.1	11.7	13.2	14.1	15.9	50.	Argentina . .	2.9	2.7	4.9	4.9	4.7	5.1
25.	Sweden. . . .	4.1	6.6	8.4	11.3	12.8	14.1		**World**	**495**	**704**	**977**	**1,217**	**1,239**	**1,332**

NA = Not available. * = Preliminary. (1) Not including Hong Kong and Macau.

International Tourist Arrivals by Country of Destination, 2000-17

Source: World Tourism Organization (UNWTO), © UNWTO
(visitors in millions; 2017 ranks as per UNWTO [some 2017 data was pending])

Rank	Country	2000	2005	2010	2015	2016	2017*	% change, 2016-17	Rank	Country	2000	2005	2010	2015	2016	2017*	% change, 2016-17
1.	France. . . .	77.2	75.0	77.6	84.5	82.6	NA	NA	26.	India	2.6	3.9	5.8	13.3	14.6	15.5	6.2%
2.	U.S.	51.2	49.2	60.0	77.5	75.9	NA	NA	27.	Croatia . . .	5.3	7.7	9.1	12.7	13.8	15.6	13.0
3.	Spain	46.4	55.9	52.7	68.2	75.3	81.8	8.6%	28.	Ukraine . . .	6.4	17.6	21.2	12.4	13.3	14.2	6.8
4.	China[1]. . . .	31.2	46.8	55.7	56.9	59.3	60.7	2.4	29.	Singapore .	6.1	7.1	9.2	12.1	12.9	13.9	7.8
5.	Italy	41.2	36.5	43.6	50.7	52.4	58.3	11.3	30.	Czechia. . .	4.8	9.4	8.6	11.6	12.1	NA	NA
6.	UK.	23.2	28.0	28.3	34.4	35.8	NA	NA	31.	Indonesia . .	NA	5.0	7.0	10.0	11.1	NA	NA
7.	Germany. . .	19.0	21.5	26.9	35.0	35.6	37.5	5.3	32.	Denmark. .	3.5	9.2	8.7	10.4	10.8	NA	NA
8.	Mexico . . .	20.6	21.9	23.3	32.1	35.1	39.3	12.0	33.	Taiwan . . .	2.6	3.4	5.6	10.4	10.7	10.7	0.0
9.	Thailand . .	9.6	11.6	15.9	29.9	32.6	35.4	8.6	34.	Switzerland	7.8	7.2	8.6	9.3	10.4	NA	NA
10.	Turkey. . . .	9.6	24.2	31.4	39.5	30.3	37.6	24.1	35.	Morocco . .	4.3	5.8	9.3	10.2	10.3	11.3	9.7
11.	Austria	18.0	20.0	22.0	26.7	28.1	29.5	5.0	36.	Ireland. . . .	6.6	7.3	7.1	9.5	10.1	NA	NA
12.	Malaysia . .	10.2	16.4	24.6	25.7	26.8	25.9	–3.4	37.	South Africa	5.9	7.4	8.1	8.9	10.0	10.3	3.0
13.	Hong Kong	8.8	14.8	20.1	26.7	26.6	27.9	4.9	38.	Vietnam . . .	2.1	3.5	5.0	7.9	10.0	12.9	29.0
14.	Greece . . .	13.1	14.8	15.0	23.6	24.8	27.2	9.7	39.	Australia . .	4.9	5.5	5.9	7.4	8.3	8.8	6.0
15.	Russia. . . .	21.2	22.2	22.3	26.9	24.6	24.4	–0.8	40.	Bulgaria . .	2.8	4.8	6.0	7.1	8.3	NA	NA
16.	Japan	4.8	6.7	8.6	19.7	24.0	28.7	19.6	41.	Belgium. . .	6.5	6.7	7.2	8.4	7.5	8.4	12.0
17.	Canada. . .	19.6	18.8	16.2	18.0	20.0	20.8	4.0	42.	Slovakia . .	1.1	6.2	5.4	7.0	NA	NA	NA
18.	Portugal . .	5.7	10.6	6.8	10.1	18.2	NA	NA	43.	Argentina .	2.9	3.8	5.3	5.7	6.6	6.7	1.5
19.	Saudi								44.	Sweden. . .	3.8	4.9	5.0	6.1	6.6	6.9	4.5
	Arabia . .	6.6	8.0	10.9	18.0	18.0	16.1	–10.6	45.	Brazil.	5.3	5.4	5.2	6.3	6.5	6.6	1.5
20.	Poland. . . .	17.4	15.2	12.5	16.7	17.5	18.4	5.1	46.	Philippines	2.0	2.6	3.5	5.4	6.0	6.6	10.0
21.	S. Korea . .	5.3	6.0	8.8	13.2	17.2	13.3	–22.7	47.	Norway . . .	3.1	3.8	4.8	5.4	6.0	6.3	5.0
22.	Netherlands	10.0	10.0	10.9	15.0	15.8	17.9	13.3	48.	Dominican							
23.	Macau. . . .	5.2	9.0	11.9	14.3	15.7	17.3	10.2		Republic	3.0	3.7	4.1	5.6	6.0	6.2	3.3
24.	Hungary . .	3.0	10.0	9.5	14.3	15.3	15.8	3.3	49.	Tunisia . . .	5.1	6.4	7.8	5.4	5.7	7.1	24.6
25.	United Arab								50.	Chile	1.7	2.0	2.8	4.5	5.6	6.4	14.3
	Emirates[2]	3.1	5.8	7.4	14.2	14.9	15.8	6.0		**World**	**674**	**809**	**952**	**1,195**	**1,239**	**1,323**	**6.8**

NA = Not available or not applicable. * = Preliminary. (1) Not including Hong Kong and Macau. (2) Dubai only.

World Tourism Receipts, 1990-2017

Source: World Tourism Organization (UNWTO), © UNWTO
(in billions of U.S. dollars)

Year	Receipts[1]	Year	Receipts[1]	Year	Receipts[1]	Year	Receipts[1]	Year	Receipts[1]	Year	Receipts[1]
1990	$271	1998	$457	2002	$501	2006	$766	2010	$977	2014	$1,252
1995	415	1999	475	2003	549	2007	883	2011	1,073	2015	1,217
1996	449	2000	495	2004	652	2008	968	2012	1,110	2016	1,239
1997	449	2001	481	2005	704	2009	881	2013	1,197	2017	1,332*

* = Provisional. (1) Total of all transactions made by or on behalf of visitors for the duration of their visit. Does not include receipts from international passenger transport contracted from companies outside a traveler's country of residence.

International Travel to the U.S., 1990-2017

Source: National Travel and Tourism Office, Intl. Trade Admin., U.S. Dept. of Commerce
(number of visitors in millions)

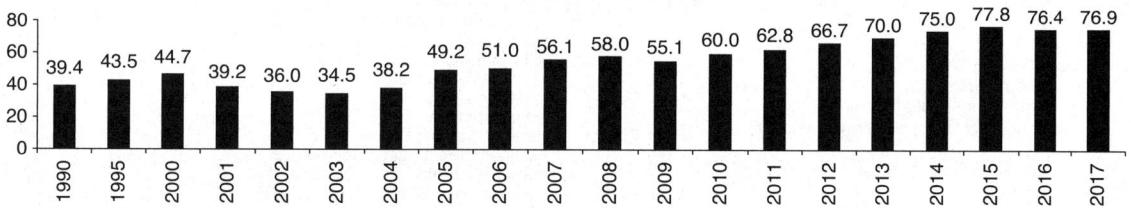

U.S. Domestic Leisure Travel Volume, 2000-17

Source: U.S. Travel Assn.
(in billions of person-trips of 50 mi or more, one-way)

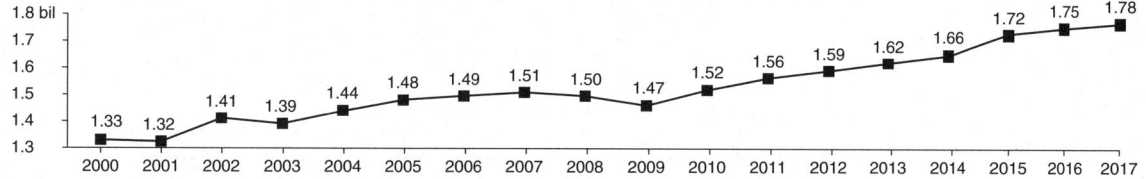

Note: Method of collecting travel data has been revised; data for earlier years have been adjusted to maintain comparability.

Top 10 U.S. States by Traveler Spending, 2016

Source: U.S. Travel Assn.
(domestic and international traveler spending within state, in billions of dollars)

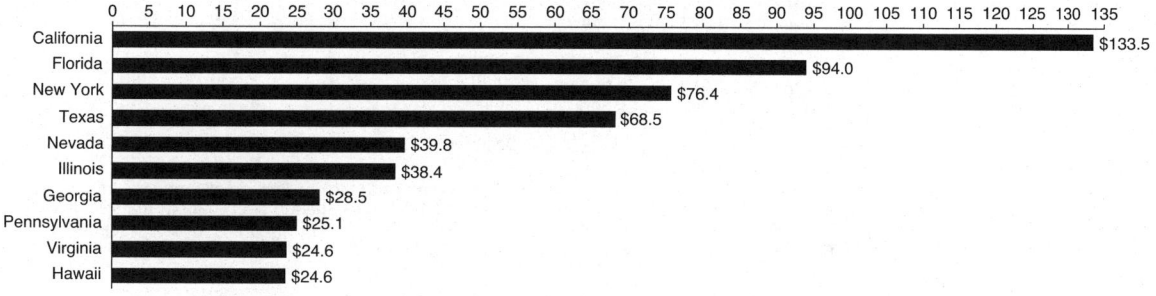

State	Spending
California	$133.5
Florida	$94.0
New York	$76.4
Texas	$68.5
Nevada	$39.8
Illinois	$38.4
Georgia	$28.5
Pennsylvania	$25.1
Virginia	$24.6
Hawaii	$24.6

International Visitors to the U.S. by Top Countries of Origin, 2016

Source: National Travel and Tourism Office, Intl. Trade Admin., U.S. Dept. of Commerce
(ranked by number of visitors)

Country of origin	Visitors	Expenditures (mil)	Expenditures per visitor	Country of origin	Visitors	Expenditures (mil)	Expenditures per visitor
1. Canada	19,301,507	$19,083	$989	12. Italy	982,841	$4,020	$4,090
2. Mexico	18,730,015	20,334	1,086	13. Argentina	906,496	4,601	5,076
3. United Kingdom	4,573,708	16,060	3,511	14. Colombia	835,915	NA	NA
4. Japan	3,576,955	16,613	4,644	15. Spain	800,697	2,954	3,689
5. China[1]	2,972,264	33,172	11,161	16. Netherlands	672,046	2,555	3,802
6. Germany	2,034,866	8,064	3,963	17. Venezuela	579,948	3,870	6,673
7. South Korea	1,973,936	8,626	4,370	18. Sweden	558,624	1,899	3,399
8. Brazil	1,693,328	11,378	6,719	19. Switzerland	469,381	2,614	5,569
9. France	1,628,069	5,983	3,675	20. Taiwan	463,225	2,221	4,795
10. Australia	1,346,487	8,727	6,481	**All countries**	**75,620,836**	**244,710**	**3,236**
11. India	1,172,256	13,384	11,417				

NA = Not available. **Note:** Expenditures include passenger fares. (1) Not including Hong Kong, Macau, and Taiwan.

Traveler Spending in the U.S., 1987-2017

Source: National Travel and Tourism Office, Intl. Trade Admin., U.S. Dept. of Commerce; U.S. Travel Assn.
(in billions of dollars by origin of traveler)

Year	Domestic	International	Year	Domestic	International	Year	Domestic	International
1987	$235	$31	1999	$458	$75	2009	$606	$94
1990	291	43	2000	503	82	2010	644	104
1991	296	48	2001	484	72	2011	694	119
1992	306	55	2002	478	67	2012	728	127
1993	323	58	2003	496	65	2013	751	135
1994	340	58	2004	532	75	2014	792	136
1995	360	63	2005	572	82	2015	814	157
1996	385	70	2006	610	86	2016	837	156
1997	406	73	2007	641	97	2017	880	156
1998	425	71	2008	662	110			

Characteristics of U.S. Travelers Visiting Overseas Destinations, 2016

Source: Survey of Intl. Air Travelers, National Travel and Tourism Office, Intl. Trade Admin., U.S. Dept. of Commerce

Total U.S. resident travelers	35,137,000
Males (adults)............................	49%
Females (adults).........................	51%
Avg. age of males (yrs.)	45.2
Avg. age of females (yrs.)	43.9
Median annual household income	$100,000
Avg. total trip expend. per visitor (incl. airfare) ..	$2,581
Avg. international airfare..................	$1,117
Avg. expend. outside the U.S. per visitor per day	$85
Pre-booked lodging......................	55%
Median number of nights	10

Main purpose of trip	% of travelers
Vacation/holiday	55%
Visit friends/relatives.....................	27
Business	8
Education	4
Convention/conference/trade show	3
Religion/pilgrimages	2
Health treatment.........................	1

Leisure/recreational activities[1]	% of travelers
Sightseeing.............................	81%
Shopping	75
Small towns/countryside.................	45
Historical locations	40
Fine dining	39
Guided tours	38
Art galleries/museums	33
Cultural/ethnic heritage sights	33
National parks/monuments...............	30
Nightclubbing/dancing	24
Water sports	20
Concert/play/musical	13
Amusement/theme parks	10
Casino/gamble	9
Camping/hiking	8
Environmental/ecological excursions	8
Sporting event	7
Golfing/tennis	3
Hunting/fishing	3
Snow sports	1

(1) Percentages based on multiple responses.

U.S. Resident Travel Abroad, 1997-2016

Source: National Travel and Tourism Office, Intl. Trade Admin., U.S. Dept. of Commerce
(numbers in thousands)

Region/country[1]	2016	2000	1997
Total outbound[2]	80,226	61,327	52,735
Mexico	31,194	19,285	17,909
Canada...............	13,895	15,189	13,401
Overseas subtotal[3].......	35,137	26,853	21,634
Europe	12,544	13,373	NA
United Kingdom	3,197	4,189	3,570
Italy.................	2,214	2,148	1,471
France	2,178	2,927	2,098
Germany.............	1,968	2,309	1,796
Spain	1,405	1,262	714
Central America	2,776	886	NA
Costa Rica	1,124	NA	303

Region/country[1]	2016	2000	1997
Caribbean..............	8,152	3,867	NA
Dominican Republic	2,706	779	195
Jamaica	1,476	886	1,341
Bahamas	1,054	913	1,017
Asia...................	6,606	4,914	NA
China[4].................	1,300	644	476
India	1,195	457	368
South America	2,530	2,095	NA
Middle East.............	1,757	1,370	NA
Africa	984	483	NA
Oceania	703	1,047	NA

NA = Not available. **Note:** Visits of one or more nights. Visitation estimates for Canada and Mexico include all modes of transportation used. Estimates for all other countries are available only for air travel to that country and are based upon data from the airlines that voluntarily provided it. (1) Only individual countries that received more than 1 mil visitors in 2016 are shown. Region figures include U.S. resident travelers to all countries in region. (2) To Canada, Mexico, and overseas. (3) To all countries except Canada and Mexico. (4) Not including Hong Kong, Macau, and Taiwan.

U.S. Commercial Airline Safety, 1985-2016

Source: National Transportation Safety Board; Federal Aviation Administration, U.S. Dept. of Transportation

Year	Departures (mil)	Fatal accidents	Fatalities[1]	Rate of fatal accidents[2]	Year	Departures (mil)	Fatal accidents	Fatalities[1]	Rate of fatal accidents[2]
1985	6.1	4	197	0.066	2007	10.7	0	0	—
1990	7.8	4	11	0.051	2008	10.3	0	0	—
1995	8.1	1	160	0.012	2009	9.6	1	50	0.010
2000	11.1	2	89	0.018	2010	9.5	0	0	—
2001[3]	10.6	6	531	0.019	2011	9.4	0	0	—
2002	10.3	0	0	—	2012	9.2	0	0	—
2003	10.2	2	22	0.020	2013	9.2	0	0	—
2004	10.8	1	13	0.009	2014	9.1	0	0	—
2005	10.9	3	22	0.027	2015	9.0	0	0	—
2006	10.6	2	50	0.019	2016*	9.1	0	0	—

— = Not applicable. * = Preliminary. **Note:** Statistics are for scheduled commercial carriers. (1) Includes deaths that occurred on the ground as a result of an accident, except for fatalities resulting from the Sept. 11, 2001, terrorist attacks. (2) Per 100,000 departures. (3) The Sept. 11, 2001, terrorist attacks have been included among the number of fatal accidents but have been excluded when calculating the fatal accident rate.

U.S. Airline Statistics, 1995-2017

Source: Airlines for America

	1995	2000	2005	2010	2013	2014	2015	2016	2017
Passengers enplaned (mil)[1]	547.8	666.1	738.6	720.5	743.2	762.7	798.2	823.0	849.4
Revenue passenger miles (bil)[1,2]	540.7	692.8	779.0	798.0	840.4	862.5	902.2	933.5	964.3
Available seat miles (bil)[1,3]	807.1	957.0	1,003.4	972.6	1,011.2	1,034.3	1,077.0	1,118.9	1,154.9
Cargo revenue ton miles (mil)[1,2]	16,921	23,888	28,039	27,885	26,441	27,236	26,619	27,009	29,684
% of seating utilized[1]	67.0%	72.4%	77.6%	82.1%	83.1%	83.4%	83.8%	83.4%	83.5%
Passenger revenue (mil)[4] ..	$70,132	$94,307	$94,340	$104,431	$121,332	$127,455	$126,880	$125,213	$130,086
Net profit (mil)[4]	$2,001	$2,238	−$28,647	$2,245	$12,183	$7,383	$24,794	$14,224	$15,679
Total employment (thous.)[5]	595.6	739.6	619.6	564.4	584.0	589.1	605.3	660.8	697.2

(1) Scheduled service only. (2) One fare-paying passenger or one ton of revenue cargo transported one mile. (3) One seat transported one mile. (4) Passenger carriers only. (5) Figures are of the sum of full-time and part-time employees.

Top 25 U.S. Passenger Airlines, 2017

Source: Airlines for America

In 2017, 99.2% of all passengers enplaned flew on the top 25 U.S. passenger airlines.
(in millions; ranked by number of passengers enplaned in scheduled service in 2017)

Airline	Passengers	Airline	Passengers	Airline	Passengers	Airline	Passengers
1. Southwest Airlines	157.7	8. Spirit Airlines....	23.8	14. Allegiant Air.....	12.2	21. GoJet Airlines...	5.3
2. Delta Air Lines ..	145.6	9. Republic Airlines	16.9	15. Envoy Air.......	11.8	22. Air Wisconsin	
3. American Airlines	144.9	10. Frontier Airlines..	16.8	16. Endeavor Air....	11.8	Airlines	3.6
4. United Air Lines	107.2	11. ExpressJet		17. Hawaiian Airlines	11.3	23. Trans States	
5. JetBlue Airways..	40.0	Airlines	15.5	18. Virgin America ..	8.4	Airlines	3.5
6. SkyWest Airlines	35.8	12. Mesa Airlines....	13.4	19. Horizon Air.....	7.0	24. Piedmont Airlines	3.1
7. Alaska Airlines ..	26.1	13. PSA Airlines	12.6	20. Compass Airlines	6.1	25. Sun Country....	2.4

Note: Includes domestic and international passengers on U.S. airlines.

Top North American Airports by Passenger Traffic, 2017

Source: *2017 World Annual Traffic Report*, Airports Council Intl.

City/airport name (airport code)	Total passengers[1]
1. Hartsfield-Jackson Atlanta Intl. (ATL)	103,902,992
2. Los Angeles Intl. (LAX)....................	84,557,968
3. Chicago O'Hare Intl. (ORD)	79,828,183
4. Dallas/Ft. Worth Intl. (DFW)	67,092,194
5. Denver Intl. (DEN).......................	61,379,396
6. New York John F. Kennedy Intl. (JFK)	59,392,500
7. San Francisco Intl. (SFO)	55,822,129
8. Las Vegas McCarran Intl. (LAS)	48,565,117
9. Toronto Pearson Intl. (YYZ)...............	47,130,358
10. Seattle-Tacoma Intl. (SEA)...............	46,934,194
11. Charlotte Douglas Intl. (CLT).............	45,909,899
12. Orlando Intl. (MCO)	44,611,265
13. Miami Intl. (MIA)	44,071,313
14. Phoenix Sky Harbor Intl. (PHX)	43,921,670
15. Newark Liberty Intl. (EWR)...............	43,234,161
16. Houston George Bush Intercontinental (IAH) ...	40,696,189
17. Boston Logan Intl. (BOS)	38,454,539
18. Minneapolis/St. Paul Intl. (MSP)	38,034,341
19. Detroit Metropolitan Wayne County (DTW)....	34,701,497
20. Ft. Lauderdale-Hollywood Intl. (FLL)........	32,511,053

Top World Airports by Passenger Traffic, 2017

Source: *2017 World Annual Traffic Report*, Airports Council Intl.

City/airport name (country; airport code)	Total passengers[1]
1. Beijing Capital Intl. (China; PEK)	95,786,442
2. Dubai Intl. (United Arab Emirates; DXB).......	88,242,099
3. Tokyo Haneda Intl. (Japan; HND).............	85,408,975
4. London Heathrow (UK; LHR).................	78,014,598
5. Hong Kong Intl. (China; HKG)...............	72,664,075
6. Shanghai Pudong Intl. (China; PVG).........	70,001,237
7. Paris Charles de Gaulle (France; CDG).......	69,471,442
8. Amsterdam Schiphol (Netherlands; AMS)	68,515,425
9. Guangzhou Baiyun Intl. (China; CAN).......	65,887,473
10. Frankfurt (Germany; FRA)	64,500,386
11. Istanbul Atatürk Intl. (Turkey; IST)...........	64,119,374
12. Delhi Indira Gandhi Intl. (India; DEL)	63,451,503
13. Jakarta Soekarno-Hatta Intl. (Indonesia; CGK)..	63,015,620
14. Singapore Changi (Singapore; SIN)	62,220,000
15. Seoul Incheon Intl. (South Korea; ICN).......	62,157,834
16. Bangkok Suvarnabhumi Intl. (Thailand; BKK)..	60,860,557
17. Kuala Lumpur KL Intl. (Malaysia; KUL).......	58,554,627
18. Adolfo Suárez Madrid-Barajas (Spain; MAD) ...	53,386,075
19. Chengdu Shuangliu Intl. (China; CTU)	49,801,693
20. Barcelona-El Prat (Spain; BCN)	47,262,826

Note: World list excludes North American airports and airports that do not participate in Airports Council Intl.'s Airport Traffic Statistics collection. (1) Arriving and departing passengers and direct transit passengers counted once.

Busiest Amtrak Stations, 2017

Source: Amtrak; ranked by total ridership

Station	Tickets from	Tickets to	Total ridership	Station	Tickets from	Tickets to	Total ridership
New York, NY	5,204,417	5,193,312	10,397,729	Wilmington, DE......	344,863	343,569	688,432
Washington, DC	2,610,311	2,615,149	5,225,460	Newark, NJ.........	340,491	341,529	682,020
Philadelphia, PA	2,210,760	2,200,902	4,411,662	Seattle, WA.........	337,120	330,355	667,475
Chicago, IL	1,698,648	1,689,403	3,388,051	New Haven, CT	318,030	309,035	627,065
Los Angeles, CA	884,218	832,174	1,716,392	Boston-Back Bay, MA	315,661	310,342	626,003
Boston-South, MA ...	803,376	764,251	1,567,627	Milwaukee, WI.......	304,786	300,565	605,351
Sacramento, CA	543,340	530,244	1,073,584	Portland, OR........	294,768	302,359	597,127
Baltimore, MD.......	532,152	531,476	1,063,628	Emeryville, CA	290,391	290,747	581,138
Albany-Rensselaer, NY..........	403,408	399,940	803,348	Lancaster, PA	278,691	278,145	556,836
San Diego, CA	394,352	383,609	777,961	Harrisburg, PA......	253,223	250,969	504,192
Providence, RI	361,278	384,425	745,703	Bakersfield, CA	238,666	243,610	482,276
BWI Airport, MD	358,311	366,554	724,865	Route 128, MA	227,716	221,068	448,784
				Boston-North, MA....	227,890	220,593	448,483

U.S. Public Transportation Usage, 1996-2016

Source: Federal Transit Administration, U.S. Dept. of Transportation

Public transportation usage is measured in unlinked passenger trips (UPT), which counts the number of passengers who board public transportation vehicles each time they board.

(in millions)

Number of passengers by year					
Year	UPT	Year	UPT	Year	UPT
1996.....	7,565	2003.....	8,876	2010.....	9,960
1997.....	7,982	2004.....	8,937	2011.....	10,085
1998.....	8,115	2005.....	9,175	2012.....	10,352
1999.....	8,522	2006.....	9,379	2013.....	10,408
2000.....	8,720	2007.....	9,948	2014.....	10,505
2001.....	9,008	2008.....	10,257	2015.....	10,365
2002.....	9,018	2009.....	10,134	2016.....	10,240

Number of passengers by mode of transportation			
Mode	2007 UPT	2016 UPT	% change, 2007-16
Bus	5,279	4,966	−5.9%
Heavy rail[1]	3,460	3,848	11.2
Commuter rail[2].............	458	499	9.0
Light rail[3]	418	498	19.1
Other	220	282	28.2
Demand response[4]	91	111	22.5
Vanpool..................	23	36	59.3

(1) An electric railway that operates on exclusive track with the ability to carry a heavy volume of passengers and is typically powered by an electrified third rail. (2) An electric- or diesel-propelled railway for urban passenger travel on the general railroad system between a central city and adjacent suburbs. (3) An electric railway that intersects vehicular traffic at grade crossings and is typically powered by overhead wires. (4) Includes automobiles, vans, or small buses dispatched by request to pick up passengers and transport them to their destinations.

Public Spending on Transportation Infrastructure, 1960-2017
Source: *Public Spending on Transportation and Water Infrastructure, 1956 to 2017*, Congressional Budget Office

Year	Federal spending[1]			State and local spending[2]		
	Highways	Mass transit and rail	Aviation	Highways	Mass transit and rail	Aviation
1960	60.33%	0.20%	11.59%	61.45%	6.47%	2.70%
1970	55.81	1.89	17.30	59.98	7.47	4.42
1980	32.83	19.45	12.68	51.99	9.84	4.20
1990	42.17	12.69	20.92	43.15	13.25	4.92
2000	46.61	11.38	19.16	41.84	13.77	6.55
2005	45.03	14.00	20.42	40.27	14.86	6.30
2010	45.13	15.79	16.69	37.09	15.10	6.68
2015	46.73	15.71	17.36	38.10	71.01	5.86
2016	47.32	16.94	17.00	38.40	16.84	5.71
2017	46.59	17.30	17.05	38.31	16.83	5.94
PERCENT CHANGE						
1960-2017	−22.77	8,550.00	47.11	−37.66	160.12	120.00
2000-17	−0.04	52.02	−11.01	−8.44	22.22	−9.31

Note: State and local spending is net of federal grants and loan subsidies. (1) Figures represent percentage of total federal infrastructure spending for the year, including categories not shown. (2) Figures represent percentage of total state and local infrastructure spending for the year, including categories not shown.

Top Travel Websites, 2018
Source: comScore, Inc.; ranked by number of visitors

Rank	Website	Visitors[1]	Rank	Website	Visitors[1]
1.	TripAdvisor Inc.	90,272	12.	American Airlines	12,472
2.	Expedia Inc.	68,206	13.	Delta Airlines.	11,911
3.	Uber	53,210	14.	USA Today Travel	11,562
4.	Priceline.com Inc.	43,958	15.	Fareportal Media Group	11,497
5.	Lyft, Inc.	27,559	16.	InterContinental Hotels Group	10,795
6.	Airbnb Sites	23,941	17.	United Airlines.	10,400
7.	Southwest Airlines Co.	20,180	18.	Conde Nast Traveler & Mediavine Travel . . .	10,161
8.	Marriott	15,396	19.	TheCultureTrip.com	10,090
9.	Kayak.com Network	15,337	20.	Disney Parks & Travel.	9,327
10.	Hilton Worldwide.	14,279		**Total travel audience[2].**	**190,051**
11.	Choice Hotels International	13,393		**Total internet audience[2].**	**255,713**

(1) Number of unique visitors, in thousands, who visited website at least once in June 2018. (2) Audience comprises all desktop users older than 2 years of age and all mobile users older than 18.

Record-Breaking Roller Coasters
Source: Roller Coaster DataBase; World Almanac research

Steel-Tracked Roller Coasters

Fastest

	Roller coaster	Theme park, location
149.1 mph	Formula Rossa	Ferrari World Abu Dhabi, United Arab Emirates
128	Kingda Ka	Six Flags Great Adventure, Jackson, NJ
120	Top Thrill Dragster	Cedar Point, Sandusky, OH
111.8	Red Force	Ferrari Land, Salou, Spain
111.8	Dododonpa	Fuji-Q Highland, Fujiyoshida-shi, Japan
100	Tower of Terror II . .	Dreamworld, Coomera, Australia
100	Superman: Escape From Krypton . . .	Six Flags Magic Mountain, Valencia, CA

Tallest

	Roller coaster	Theme park, location
456 ft	Kingda Ka	Six Flags Great Adventure, Jackson, NJ
420	Top Thrill Dragster	Cedar Point, Sandusky, OH
415	Superman: Escape From Krypton . . .	Six Flags Magic Mountain, Valencia, CA
377.3	Tower of Terror II . .	Dreamworld, Coomera, Australia
367.5	Red Force	Ferrari Land, Salou, Spain

Largest drop

	Roller coaster	Theme park, location
418 ft	Kingda Ka	Six Flags Great Adventure, Jackson, NJ
400	Top Thrill Dragster	Cedar Point, Sandusky, OH
328.1	Superman: Escape From Krypton . . .	Six Flags Magic Mountain, Valencia, CA
328.1	Tower of Terror II . .	Dreamworld, Coomera, Australia

Longest

	Roller coaster	Theme park, location
8,133.2 ft. .	Steel Dragon 2000	Nagashima Spa Land, Mie, Japan
7,442	The Ultimate	Lightwater Valley, Ripon, UK
6,708.7 . . .	Fujiyama	Fuji-Q Highland, Fujiyoshida-shi, Japan
6,602	Fury 325	Carowinds, Charlotte, NC

Wood-Tracked Roller Coasters

Fastest

	Roller coaster	Theme park, location
73 mph	Lightning Rod	Dollywood, Pigeon Forge, TN
72	Goliath	Six Flags Great America, Gurnee, IL
71.5	Wildfire	Kolmården Wildlife Park, Norrköping, Sweden
70	El Toro	Six Flags Great Adventure, Jackson, NJ
68	Outlaw Run.	Silver Dollar City, Branson, MO

Tallest

	Roller coaster	Theme park, location
187 ft	Wildfire	Kolmarden Wildlife Park, Norrköping, Sweden
183.8	T Express	Everland, Yongin-si, S. Korea
181	El Toro	Six Flags Great Adventure, Jackson, NJ
173	The Voyage	Holiday World, Santa Claus, IN
165	Goliath	Six Flags Great America, Gurnee, IL

Largest drop

	Roller coaster	Theme park, location
180 ft	Goliath.	Six Flags Great America, Gurnee, IL
176	El Toro.	Six Flags Great Adventure, Jackson, NJ
165	Lightning Rod	Dollywood, Pigeon Forge, TN
162	Outlaw Run	Silver Dollar City, Branson, MO
160.8	Wildfire	Kolmården Wildlife Park, Norrköping, Sweden

Longest

	Roller coaster	Theme park, location
7,359 ft	The Beast	Kings Island, Mason, OH
6,442	The Voyage	Holiday World, Santa Claus, IN
5,383.8	T Express	Everland, Yongin-si, S. Korea
5,383	Shivering Timbers . .	Michigan's Adventure, Muskegon, MI
5,249.3	Jupiter	Kijima Kogen, Beppu, Japan

Most Visited Amusement/Theme Parks, 2017

Source: Themed Entertainment Association

(visitors in thousands)

Rank	North America Park, location	Visitors	Rank	World Park, location	Visitors
1.	Magic Kingdom[1], Lake Buena Vista, FL	20,450	1.	Tokyo Disneyland, Tokyo, Japan	16,600
2.	Disneyland, Anaheim, CA	18,300	2.	Universal Studios Japan, Osaka, Japan	14,935
3.	Disney's Animal Kingdom[1], Lake Buena Vista, FL	12,500	3.	Tokyo DisneySea, Tokyo, Japan	13,500
			4.	Shanghai Disneyland, Shanghai, China	11,000
4.	Epcot[1], Lake Buena Vista, FL	12,200	5.	Chimelong Ocean Kingdom, Hengqin, China	9,788
5.	Disney's Hollywood Studios[1], Lake Buena Vista, FL	10,722	6.	Disneyland Park at Disneyland Paris, Marne-la-Vallée, France	9,660
6.	Universal Studios[2], Orlando, FL	10,198	7.	Lotte World, Seoul, South Korea	6,714
7.	Disney California Adventure, Anaheim, CA	9,574	8.	Everland, Gyeonggi-do, South Korea	6,310
8.	Islands of Adventure[2], Orlando, FL	9,549	9.	Hong Kong Disneyland, Hong Kong, China	6,200
9.	Universal Studios Hollywood, Universal City, CA	9,056	10.	Nagashima Spa Land, Kuwana, Japan	5,930
10.	Knott's Berry Farm, Buena Park, CA	4,034			

Note: World list excludes North American parks. (1) Located at Walt Disney World. (2) Located at Universal Orlando.

Passports, Travel Warnings, and Regulations for Foreign Travel

Source: Bureau of Consular Affairs, U.S. Dept. of State; Centers for Disease Control and Prevention (CDC), U.S. Dept. of Health and Human Services; World Health Organization (WHO); Transportation Security Administration (TSA), U.S. Dept. of Homeland Security

Passports, Visas

Passports are issued by the Dept. of State to U.S. citizens and nationals to provide documentation for foreign travel. As of Oct. 2018, the fees for a new passport book and passport card for persons ages 16 and over total $175; provided certain criteria are met, these can be renewed for $140. For a passport book alone, fees are $145 for a new passport and $110 for passport renewal.

In 2008, the U.S. government began issuing passport cards. Travelers arriving by land or sea from Canada, Mexico, the Caribbean, and Bermuda may present a passport card to enter the U.S. Passport cards may not be used for air travel, however. The fees for a new passport card for persons ages 16 and over total $65 ($30 with a valid passport book).

A U.S. passport is often sufficient for U.S. citizens to gain admission for a limited stay in another country. Some countries also require an entry visa. Each country has its own specific guidelines concerning length and purpose of visit, among other considerations. Visitors may need to provide proof of sufficient funds for their intended stay, onward/return tickets, and/or at least six months remaining validity on their U.S. passports.

All persons traveling by air outside of the U.S. (excluding direct travel to and from a U.S. territory) are required to present a passport or other valid document upon reentering the U.S.

For up-to-date passport and international travel information, visit the Consular Affairs website (travel.state.gov) or call the National Passport Information Center at 1-877-4USA-PPT (1-877-487-2778).

Travel Advisories and Alerts

The State Dept. issues travel advisories as recommendations to Americans traveling outside the country. Under a new system announced in Jan. 2018, the department issues an advisory for every country, providing levels of advice ranging from 1 to 4. Level 1 indicates "exercise normal precautions"; level 2, "exercise increased caution"; level 3, "reconsider travel"; and level 4, "do not travel." Travel advisory levels are based on many factors, including crime, terrorist activity, civil unrest, health, natural disaster/weather, and other current events. As of Oct. 2018, level 3 travel advisories were issued for Burkina Faso, Burundi, Chad, Dem. Rep. of the Congo, El Salvador, Guinea-Bissau, Haiti, Honduras, Lebanon, Mauritania, Nicaragua, Niger, Nigeria, Pakistan, Russia, Sudan, Turkey, and Venezuela; level 4 travel advisories were issued for Afghanistan, Central African Republic, Iran, Iraq, North Korea, Libya, Mali, Somalia, South Sudan, Syria, and Yemen.

For the latest travel advisories and alerts, see travel.state.gov.

Summary of TSA Regulations

Airplane carry-ons. TSA promotes the liquids (or "3-1-1") rule regarding carry-on items. Containers with liquids, gels, aerosols, creams, or pastes must hold **3.4** oz or less; these containers should be packed inside a single **1**-quart, clear plastic, resealable bag; and this **1** bag must be X-rayed when going through security. Exceptions to the liquids rule include medication, baby formula and food, and breast milk. Travelers must declare any exceptions at security.

Security checkpoint identification. Adult travelers (18 years of age and over) must present a photo ID. Acceptable documents include a U.S. passport or passport card; foreign government-issued passport; state-issued driver's license; permanent resident card; or U.S. military ID, among others.

Screening process. Travelers may wear loose fitting or religious garments (incl. head coverings) through security. They may be subject to additional screening if clothing could conceal prohibited items. Travelers may request a private area if selected for personal screening. Travelers will be screened by someone of the same gender.

Disability-related permitted carry-on items:

- Wheelchairs, scooters
- Crutches, canes, and walkers
- Portable oxygen concentrators (though not permitted by all airlines)
- Medications and associated supplies
- Service animals

Permitted carry-on items:

- Disposable razors
- Eye drops and saline solution (amounts greater than 3.4 oz must be declared)
- Nail clippers, tweezers
- Strollers, baby carriers, child car seats
- Beverages (any size) purchased after security screening

Prohibited carry-on items:

- Knives (except for plastic or round-bladed butter knives), incl. pocket knives and knives that are religious objects
- Baseball bats, golf clubs, hockey sticks
- Firearms or realistic firearm replicas, ammunition, firearm parts
- Hammers, screwdrivers, wrenches, pliers, and other tools more than 7 in. in length
- Lighter fluid
- Self-defense sprays

For complete travel information, visit www.tsa.gov/travel

AGRICULTURE

Number and Acreage of Farms by State, 2000, 2017

Source: National Agricultural Statistics Service, U.S. Dept. of Agriculture

State	No. of farms (thous.) 2017	2000	Acreage in farms (mil) 2017	2000	Acreage per farm 2017	2000	State	No. of farms (thous.) 2017	2000	Acreage in farms (mil) 2017	2000	Acreage per farm 2017	2000
AL.....	43.6	47.0	8.9	9.0	204	191	NE....	47.4	46.1	45.2	46.1	954	887
AK.....	0.8	0.6	0.8	0.9	1,092	1,569	NV....	4.0	3.1	6.0	6.4	1,493	2,065
AZ.....	19.6	10.7	25.9	26.9	1,321	2,518	NH....	4.4	3.3	0.5	0.4	107	133
AR.....	42.3	48.0	13.6	14.6	322	304	NJ.....	9.1	9.7	0.7	0.8	79	86
CA.....	77.1	83.1	25.3	28.0	328	337	NM....	24.7	18.0	43.3	44.9	1,753	2,494
CO.....	33.8	30.0	31.8	31.6	941	1,060	NY....	35.5	37.5	7.2	7.7	203	205
CT.....	6.0	4.2	0.4	0.4	73	86	NC....	47.8	55.5	8.1	9.2	169	166
DE.....	2.5	2.6	0.5	0.6	200	215	ND....	29.9	30.8	39.1	39.4	1,308	1,279
FL.....	47.0	44.0	9.5	10.4	201	238	OH....	73.6	79.0	14.0	14.8	190	187
GA....	40.9	49.1	9.3	10.9	227	223	OK....	77.2	84.5	34.0	33.8	440	401
HI.....	7.0	5.5	1.1	1.4	160	251	OR....	34.2	40.0	16.3	17.3	477	433
ID.....	24.3	24.5	11.9	11.9	490	486	PA....	58.0	59.0	7.6	7.7	132	130
IL.....	71.0	77.0	26.6	27.5	375	357	RI.....	1.2	0.8	0.1	0.1	56	75
IN.....	56.8	63.4	14.7	15.2	259	240	SC....	24.3	24.2	5.0	4.9	206	203
IA.....	86.9	94.0	30.5	32.5	351	346	SD....	31.0	32.4	43.3	44.0	1,397	1,358
KS.....	59.6	64.5	45.9	47.5	770	736	TN....	65.9	88.0	10.8	11.8	164	134
KY.....	75.8	90.0	12.8	13.7	169	152	TX....	240.0	228.3	129.6	130.9	540	573
LA.....	26.5	29.0	7.7	8.0	291	277	UT....	18.2	15.5	11.0	11.6	604	747
ME....	8.2	7.1	1.5	1.4	177	190	VT....	7.3	6.6	1.3	1.3	171	192
MD....	12.2	12.4	2.0	2.1	166	172	VA....	44.3	48.5	8.1	8.7	183	180
MA....	7.8	6.1	0.5	0.5	67	89	WA....	35.7	37.0	14.7	15.6	412	420
MI.....	50.9	53.0	10.0	10.2	195	192	WV....	20.4	20.8	3.6	3.6	176	173
MN....	73.2	81.0	25.9	27.9	354	344	WI....	68.5	77.5	14.3	16.0	209	206
MS....	35.8	42.0	10.7	11.2	299	266	WY....	11.4	9.2	30.2	34.5	2,649	3,750
MO....	97.3	109.0	28.5	30.2	293	277	**U.S.**	**2,048.0**	**2,166.8**	**910.0**	**945.1**	**444**	**436**
MT....	27.1	27.8	59.8	59.3	2,207	2,133							

Supplemental Nutrition Assistance Program (SNAP), 1969-2017

Source: Food and Nutrition Service (FNS), U.S. Dept. of Agriculture

Fiscal year	Avg. participation (thous.)	Avg. monthly benefit per person	Total benefits (mil)	All other costs (mil)[1]	Total costs (mil)	Fiscal year	Avg. participation (thous.)	Avg. monthly benefit per person	Total benefits (mil)	All other costs (mil)[1]	Total costs (mil)
1969	2,878	$6.63	$228.8	$21.7	$250.5	2004	23,811	$86.16	$24,618.9	$2,480.1	$27,099.0
1970	4,340	10.55	549.7	27.2	576.9	2005	25,628	92.89	28,567.9	2,504.1	31,072.0
1975	17,064	21.40	4,385.5	233.2	4,618.7	2006	26,549	94.75	30,187.4	2,715.7	32,903.1
1980	21,082	34.47	8,720.9	485.6	9,206.5	2007	26,316	96.18	30,373.3	2,800.3	33,173.5
1985	19,899	44.99	10,743.6	959.6	11,703.2	2008	28,223	102.19	34,608.4	3,031.3	37,639.6
1990	20,049	58.78	14,142.8	1,304.5	15,447.3	2009	33,490	125.31	50,359.9	3,260.0	53,619.9
1995	26,619	71.27	22,764.1	1,856.3	24,620.4	2010	40,302	133.79	64,702.2	3,581.3	68,283.5
1997	22,858	71.27	19,548.9	1,958.7	21,507.6	2011	44,709	133.85	71,810.9	3,875.6	75,686.5
1998	19,791	71.12	16,890.5	2,097.8	18,988.3	2012	46,609	133.41	74,619.3	3,791.8	78,411.1
1999	18,183	72.27	15,769.4	2,051.5	17,820.9	2013	47,636	133.07	76,066.3	3,792.7	79,859.1
2000	17,194	72.62	14,983.3	2,070.7	17,054.0	2014	46,664	125.01	69,998.8	4,062.5	74,061.4
2001	17,318	74.81	15,547.4	2,242.0	17,789.4	2015	45,767	126.81	69,645.1	4,302.1	73,947.2
2002	19,096	79.67	18,256.2	2,380.8	20,637.0	2016	44,219	125.40	66,539.4	4,384.3	70,923.7
2003	21,250	83.94	21,404.3	2,412.0	23,816.3	2017	44,203	125.80	63,708.3	4,392.5	68,100.7

(1) Includes the federal share of state administrative expenses, nutrition education, and employment and training programs, in addition to other federal costs (e.g., benefit and retailer redemption and monitoring, payment accuracy, EBT [electronic benefit transfer] systems, program evaluation and modernization, program access, health and nutrition pilot projects).

U.S. Federal Food Assistance Programs, 1990-2017

Source: Food and Nutrition Service (FNS), U.S. Dept. of Agriculture

(in millions of dollars; for fiscal years ending on Sept. 30)

Program	1990	1995	2000	2005	2010	2014	2015	2016	2017
Supplemental Nutrition Assistance Program (SNAP)[1].................	$15,491	$24,620	$17,054	$31,073	$68,284	$74,061	$73,947	$70,910	$68,108
Puerto Rico nutrition assistance[2]......	937	1,131	1,268	1,495	2,001	1,903	1,951	1,959	1,449
Natl. school lunch[3].................	3,834	5,160	6,149	8,031	10,880	12,658	13,004	13,568	13,643
School breakfast[3,4].................	596	1,048	1,393	1,927	2,859	3,685	3,892	4,212	4,252
WIC (Women, Infants, and Children)[5]..	2,122	3,440	3,982	4,994	6,690	6,355	6,230	6,000	5,635
Summer food service[6]..............	164	237	267	267	359	466	488	478	483
Child and adult care[7]...............	813	1,464	1,683	2,111	2,638	3,131	3,307	3,519	3,534
Special milk[4]......................	19	17	15	16	12	10	11	9	8
Nutrition for the elderly (NSIP)[8].......	142	148	137	4	3	2	3	3	3
Food distrib. to Indian reserv.[9]......	66	65	76	76	95	110	120	123	122
Commodity supplemental food prog.[9]...	85	99	98	156	165	198	193	187	204
Food distrib. to charitable insts.[10]......	104	64	2	4	1	0	0	0	0
Emergency food assistance (TEFAP)[11]..	334	135	225	373	631	629	525	664	661
Total[12]........................	**24,707**	**37,628**	**32,349**	**50,527**	**94,618**	**103,208**	**103,671**	**101,632**	**98,102**

Note: 2017 data are preliminary. All data subject to revision by the FNS. (1) Formerly known as the Food Stamp Program. Includes benefits and admin. expenses. (2) Provides benefits analogous to SNAP. (3) Nine-month averages (summer months excluded). (4) Cash payments based on federal reimbursement rates to states. (5) Includes food benefits, nutrition services and admin. funds, Farmers' Market Nutrition Program, infrastructure, breastfeeding promotion and peer counseling, program evaluation, and technical assistance. (6) Includes cash payments, commodity costs, and admin. costs for services similar to natl. school lunch and breakfast programs. (7) Includes cash payments, entitlement and bonus commodities, cash-in-lieu of commodities, sponsor admin. costs, start-up costs, and audits. (8) For 2003 and on, program administered by the Agency on Aging, Dept. of Health and Human Services; FNS costs limited to value of commodities distributed. (9) Includes cost of commodity distrib. and admin. expenses. (10) Includes summer camps. (11) Includes cost of commodities to hunger relief orgs. (e.g., food banks, soup kitchens) and admin. expenses. (12) Does not include federal share of state admin. costs for some programs shown.

U.S. Cost of Food, 2018

Source: Center for Nutrition Policy and Promotion (CNPP), U.S. Dept. of Agriculture (USDA)

Age-gender group	Weekly cost[1]				Monthly cost[1]			
	Thrifty plan	Low-cost plan	Mod.-cost plan	Liberal plan	Thrifty plan	Low-cost plan	Mod.-cost plan	Liberal plan
Individual child[1]								
1 year	$21.60	$28.80	$32.70	$40.10	$93.70	$124.80	$141.80	$173.60
2-3 years.	23.70	30.50	36.70	44.60	102.90	132.20	159.10	193.20
4-5 years.	25.00	31.40	39.10	47.70	108.40	135.90	169.30	206.90
6-8 years.	31.70	44.20	53.40	63.40	137.50	191.40	231.20	274.60
9-11 years.	35.80	47.90	61.90	72.10	155.10	207.50	268.10	312.50
Individual male[1]								
12-13 years	38.60	54.90	68.90	80.80	167.40	237.70	298.30	350.20
14-18 years.	39.80	55.70	70.80	81.50	172.70	241.30	306.70	353.00
19-50 years.	42.70	55.30	69.20	84.90	185.20	239.50	299.90	367.90
51-70 years	39.00	52.20	65.00	78.50	168.80	226.10	281.50	340.20
71+ years	39.20	51.30	63.70	78.90	169.90	222.30	275.90	341.70
Individual female[1]								
12-13 years	38.60	47.30	57.00	69.90	167.10	204.80	246.80	302.70
14-18 years	37.90	47.10	56.70	70.10	164.20	204.00	245.50	303.80
19-50 years	37.90	47.90	58.90	75.40	164.30	207.60	255.20	326.60
51-70 years	37.60	46.70	58.20	70.50	162.80	202.20	252.30	305.40
71+ years	36.40	46.00	57.20	69.10	157.70	199.30	248.00	299.60
2-person family								
19-50 years	88.70	113.50	140.90	176.30	384.50	491.80	610.60	763.90
51-70 years	84.20	108.70	135.50	163.90	364.80	471.20	587.20	710.20
4-person family[2] with 2 children ages—								
2-3 and 4-5 years	129.40	165.10	203.90	252.60	560.80	715.30	883.50	1,094.50
6-8 and 9-11 years. . . .	148.20	195.20	243.40	295.80	642.10	846.00	1,054.40	1,281.60

Note: As of June 2018. The official USDA food plans represent a nutritious diet at four different cost levels. The nutritional bases are the 1997-2005 Dietary Reference Intakes, 2005 Dietary Guidelines for Americans, and 2005 MyPyramid food intake recommendations. In addition to cost, differences among plans are in specific foods and quantities of foods. Another basis of the food plans is that all meals and snacks are prepared at home. For specific foods and quantities, see *Thrifty Food Plan, 2006* and *The Low-Cost, Moderate-Cost, and Liberal Food Plans, 2007* from the CNPP. All four plans are based on 2001-02 data and updated to current dollars using the consumer price index for specific food items. All costs are rounded to nearest 10 cents. (1) The costs given are for individuals in 4-person families. (2) Defined as a couple, 19-50 years old, and two children.

U.S. Household Food Security by Selected Characteristics, 2017

Source: Economic Research Service, U.S. Dept. of Agriculture

(in thousands of households)

	Total[1]	Food secure		With low food security		With very low food security	
		No.	%	No.	%	No.	%
All households	127,272	112,254	88.2%	9,261	7.3%	5,757	4.5%
Household composition							
With children under 18 years old	37,942	31,976	84.3	4,421	11.6	1,545	4.1
With children under 6 years old	16,200	13,551	83.6	2,008	12.4	641	4.0
Married-couple families	24,744	22,383	90.5	1,876	7.5	485	2.0
Female head, no spouse	9,561	6,663	69.7	2,038	21.3	860	9.0
Male head, no spouse	3,057	2,455	80.3	429	14.0	173	5.7
Other household with child[2].	581	476	81.9	NA	NA	NA	NA
With no children under 18 years old	89,330	80,278	89.9	4,840	5.4	4,212	4.7
More than one adult.	53,107	48,997	92.3	2,357	4.4	1,753	3.3
Women living alone	19,963	17,195	86.1	1,362	6.9	1,406	7.0
Men living alone.	16,260	14,087	86.6	1,120	6.9	1,053	6.5
With elderly person age 65 and older.	37,805	34,814	92.1	1,833	4.8	1,158	3.1
Elderly living alone.	14,312	13,078	91.4	710	4.9	524	3.7
Race/ethnicity							
White, non-Hispanic	84,548	77,083	91.2	4,389	5.2	3,076	3.6
Black, non-Hispanic	16,358	12,799	78.2	2,164	13.3	1,395	8.5
Other, non-Hispanic	9,169	8,263	90.1	572	6.3	334	3.6
Hispanic[3]	17,197	14,108	82.0	2,137	12.5	952	5.5
Area of residence[4]							
Inside metropolitan area	108,977	96,401	88.5	7,807	7.1	4,769	4.4
In principal cities[5]	37,365	32,194	86.2	3,132	8.4	2,034	5.4
Not in principal cities	55,330	50,152	90.6	3,204	5.8	1,974	3.6
Outside metropolitan area	18,295	15,853	86.7	1,454	7.9	988	5.4

NA = Not reported. **Note:** Low food security households report food acquisition problems and reduced diet quality but typically few, if any, indications of reduced food intake. The very low food security category identifies households in which the food intake of one or more members was reduced and eating patterns disrupted because of insufficient money and resources for food. (1) Totals exclude households of unknown food security status. Exclusions represented 0.3% of all households in 2017. (2) Households with children in complex living arrangements, e.g., children of other relatives or unrelated roommate or boarder. (3) Hispanics may be of any race. (4) Based on 2013 Office of Management and Budget delineations of metropolitan areas. (5) Households within incorporated areas of the largest cities in each metropolitan area. Residence in or out of principal cities unknown for about 15% of households in metropolitan statistical areas.

U.S. Adoption of Genetically Modified Crops, 2000-18

Source: Economic Research Service, U.S. Dept of Agriculture

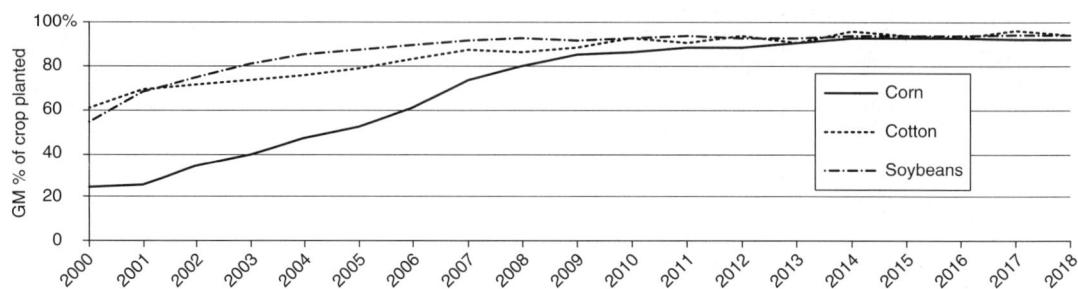

U.S. Annual Per Capita Consumption of Selected Foods, 1970-2015

Source: Economic Research Service, U.S. Dept. of Agriculture; Distilled Spirits Council of the U.S.; Beer Institute; Wine Institute
(fruits and vegetables in pounds, beverages in gallons)

	1970	1990	2015	% change, 1970-2015		1970	1990	2015	% change, 1970-2015
Fresh fruit	100.9	117.0	135.4	34.2%	**Fresh vegetables**	144.4	163.9	172.2	19.3%
Apples.	17.2	19.8	17.4	0.7	Bell peppers	2.0	5.4	10.2	415.0
Avocados	0.5	1.4	7.0	1,448.7	Broccoli.	0.5	3.1	6.8	1,289.5
Bananas	17.4	24.3	28.0	61.3	Cabbage	8.1	7.8	5.8	−27.6
Grapes	2.9	7.9	7.9	170.9	Carrots	5.8	8.0	8.5	47.3
Melons	21.4	24.6	23.1	8.1	Celery	6.8	6.7	5.0	−25.3
Oranges	16.2	12.4	8.5	−47.5	Cucumbers	2.6	4.3	6.9	167.0
Peaches/nectarines	5.8	5.5	3.0	−49.0	Garlic	0.4	1.1	1.9	432.7
Pears	1.9	3.3	2.8	43.7	Head lettuce	20.8	25.8	12.6	−39.5
Pineapples	0.7	2.1	7.0	898.0	Onions	9.5	14.2	17.8	86.4
Strawberries	1.7	3.2	7.8	349.0	Potatoes	59.3	44.9	32.8	−44.8
Canned vegetables	93.0	110.3	82.1	−11.6	Sweet corn	7.2	6.2	7.9	10.7
Green peas.	0.9	1.9	0.8	−10.0	Tomatoes	10.3	13.2	17.4	68.8
Snap beans	1.1	3.7	2.9	164.7	**Beverages**				
Sweet corn	14.3	10.9	5.3	−62.6	Coffee	33.4	26.8	26.2	−21.5
Tomatoes	62.1	75.3	56.3	−9.4	Fruit juice	5.5	7.5	5.7	3.0
Frozen vegetables	43.7	66.7	70.1	60.4	Beer	18.5	23.9	20.0	8.0
Broccoli.	1.0	2.2	2.6	168.0	Wine	1.3	2.1	2.9	119.1
Carrots	1.4	2.3	1.4	−2.8	Distilled spirits.	1.8	1.5	1.7	−8.1
Green peas.	1.9	2.2	1.5	−23.1	**Sweeteners**	119.1	132.3	129.0	8.2
Potatoes	28.5	46.4	49.7	74.1	Sugar	101.8	64.4	69.1	−32.1
Sweet corn	5.7	8.6	8.0	39.3	Honey	1.0	0.7	1.3	25.2
					High fructose corn syrup	0.5	49.6	42.5	7,655.6

Note: All figures are rounded; percent change is calculated based on unrounded original data. Per capita consumption based on total population. Alcoholic beverage consumption would be higher if based on legal drinking age population.

U.S. Meat Production and Consumption, 1940-2018

Source: Economic Research Service, U.S. Dept. of Agriculture
(in millions of pounds)

Year	Beef Prod.	Beef Cons.	Veal Prod.	Veal Cons.	Lamb and mutton Prod.	Lamb and mutton Cons.	Pork Prod.	Pork Cons.	All red meats[1] Prod.	All red meats[1] Cons.	All poultry[2] Prod.	All poultry[2] Cons.
1940	7,175	7,257	981	981	876	873	10,044	9,701	19,076	18,812	NA	NA
1950	9,534	9,825	1,230	1,206	597	602	10,714	10,612	22,075	22,279	3,174	3,097
1960	14,753	15,490	1,109	1,118	768	856	13,905	14,057	30,535	31,521	6,310	6,168
1970	21,684	23,451	588	613	551	669	14,699	14,957	37,522	39,689	10,193	9,981
1980	21,643	23,560	400	420	318	351	16,617	16,838	38,978	41,170	14,173	13,525
1990	22,743	24,030	327	325	363	397	15,354	16,025	38,787	40,778	23,468	22,152
2000	26,888	27,338	225	225	234	354	18,952	18,643	46,299	46,560	36,073	30,508
2010	26,412	26,392	145	150	168	317	22,437	19,072	49,180	45,931	43,058	35,201
2011	26,281	25,545	136	137	153	295	22,758	18,384	49,346	44,363	43,513	35,548
2012	25,995	25,752	125	123	161	299	23,253	18,604	49,549	44,779	43,523	34,870
2013	25,790	25,483	117	119	161	324	23,187	19,095	49,273	45,020	44,159	35,630
2014	24,316	24,686	100	98	161	340	22,843	19,069	47,345	44,192	44,827	36,379
2015	23,760	24,771	88	88	155	357	24,517	20,656	48,520	45,872	45,769	38,785
2016	25,221	25,673	81	73	155	381	24,941	20,891	50,388	47,019	47,225	39,577
2017	26,187	26,492	80	78	150	395	25,584	21,035	51,991	48,000	48,178	40,236
2018*	27,150	27,163	NA	NA	NA	NA	26,745	21,891	54,118	49,529	48,972	40,998

NA = Not available. * = July projection. (1) Includes beef, veal, lamb and mutton, and pork. May not add up to totals because of rounding. (2) Includes broilers, turkeys, and mature chicken.

U.S. Annual Per Capita Consumption of Meat and Dairy, 1910-2015

Source: Economic Research Service, U.S. Dept. of Agriculture

(in pounds per capita per year, unless otherwise noted)

Meat	1910	1930	1950	1970	1990	2000	2010	2013	2014	2015	% change, 1910-2015
Beef.	48.5	33.7	44.6	79.6	63.9	64.5	56.7	53.6	51.5	51.4	5.9%
Chicken	11.0	11.1	14.3	27.4	42.4	54.2	58.0	57.7	58.7	62.6	469.9
Fish/shellfish	11.2	10.2	11.9	11.7	14.9	15.2	15.8	14.3	14.5	15.5	38.2
Pork.	38.2	41.1	43.0	48.1	46.4	47.8	44.4	43.5	42.6	46.3	21.0
Red meat.	96.0	83.6	95.8	131.9	112.2	113.7	102.1	97.9	95.0	98.6	2.7
Dairy											
Butter.	18.4	17.6	10.9	5.4	4.3	4.5	4.9	5.5	5.5	5.6	−69.5
Cheese, American.	2.8	3.2	5.5	7.0	11.1	12.7	13.3	13.3	13.7	14.0	408.6
Cheese, other	1.5	1.5	2.2	4.4	13.5	16.9	19.4	20.1	20.5	21.1	1,291.1
Ice cream.	1.9	9.3	16.4	16.7	14.8	15.6	13.5	12.8	12.2	12.6	549.4
Milk, skim/lower fat (gallons)	7.1	5.0	2.9	5.8	15.2	14.6	14.8	13.8	13.1	12.5	77.4
Milk, whole (gallons)	25.2	28.2	34.2	25.3	10.5	8.2	5.7	5.4	5.3	5.5	−78.0

U.S. Organic Farmland and Animals, 1995-2011

Source: Economic Research Service, U.S. Dept. of Agriculture

Crop	1995	2000	Organic acreage[1] 2004	2005	2008	2011	% change, 1995-2011	% change, 2005-11	Total U.S. farmland[2]
Total cropland	638,500	1,218,905	1,452,353	1,723,271	2,655,382	3,084,989	383.2%	79.0%	370,653,755
Grains									
Corn.	32,650	77,912	99,111	130,672	194,637	234,470	618.1	79.4	93,600,000
Wheat	120,820	206,474	214,244	293,824	415,902	344,644	185.3	17.3	60,433,000
Oats.	13,250	29,771	42,616	46,465	57,374	62,015	368.0	33.5	3,760,000
Barley	17,150	41,904	26,629	39,271	46,954	63,903	272.6	62.7	4,020,000
Rice.	8,400	26,870	22,173	26,428	49,638	48,533	477.8	83.6	2,761,000
Beans									
Soybeans	47,200	136,071	114,239	122,217	125,621	132,411	180.5	8.3	63,631,000
Dry beans	NA	14,010	7,642	10,561	16,465	28,656	NA	171.3	1,526,900
Dry peas & lentils	5,900	10,144	15,893	17,757	16,987	17,887	203.2	0.7	571,000
Hay & silage	84,100	231,207	356,590	411,342	793,442	785,970	834.6	91.1	61,625,000
All vegetables	NA	62,342	86,822	98,525	177,049	147,446	NA	49.7	2,045,020
All fruits.	NA	43,481	80,707	97,277	121,066	131,498	NA	35.2	3,839,300
Other crops									
Cotton	32,850	15,027	9,213	9,537	15,377	12,030	−63.4	26.1	10,830,300
Peanuts	NA	2,085	9,514	11,940	16,776	13,258	NA	11.0	1,230,000
Potatoes	NA	5,433	7,300	6,581	8,273	13,258	NA	101.5	1,148,800
Trees for maple syrup	10,200	11,965	13,357	12,247	31,340	43,831	329.7	257.9	NA
Fallow land	NA	57,688	116,582	198,650	194,428	271,644	NA	36.7	37,968,749
Total pasture & rangeland.	276,300	557,167	1,592,756	2,331,158	2,160,577	2,298,130	731.8	−1.4	473,212,960
Total farmland	914,800	1,776,073	3,045,109	4,054,429	4,815,959	5,383,119	488.4	32.8	843,866,715

Animal	1995	2000	Number of organic animals[1] 2004	2005	2008	2011	% change, 2000-11	% change, 2005-11	Total U.S. animals
Total livestock	NA	56,028	157,253	196,506	475,829	492,353	778.8%	150.6%	167,512,858
Beef cows	NA	13,829	36,662	36,113	63,680	106,181	667.8	194.0	32,834,801
Milk cows	NA	38,196	74,840	87,082	249,766	254,771	567.0	192.6	9,266,574
Other cows[3].	NA	NA	36,598	58,822	144,817	113,114	NA	92.3	54,246,483
Hogs & pigs.	NA	1,724	4,883	10,018	10,111	12,373	617.7	23.5	65,110,000
Sheep & lambs.	NA	2,279	4,270	4,471	7,455	5,914	159.5	32.3	6,055,000
Total poultry	NA	3,159,050	7,304,566	13,757,270	15,518,075	37,028,242	1,072.1	169.2	9,632,362,000
Layer hens	NA	1,113,746	1,787,901	2,415,056	5,538,011	6,663,278	498.3	175.9	377,492,000
Broilers	NA	1,924,807	4,769,104	10,405,879	9,015,984	28,644,354	1,388.2	175.3	8,882,000,000
Turkeys	NA	9,138	164,292	144,086	398,531	504,315	5,418.9	250.0	262,460,000
Other/ unclassified	NA	111,359	583,269	792,249	565,549	1,216,295	992.2	53.5	110,410,000

NA = Not available. (1) Based on information from USDA-accredited state and private organic certifiers. (2) Total acreage of organic and nonorganic land used for agricultural purposes. (3) Includes breeding stock, replacement heifers, and unclassified cows.

Livestock on Farms in the U.S., 1900-2018

Source: National Agricultural Statistics Service, U.S. Dept. of Agriculture

(in thousands as of Jan. 1, unless otherwise noted)

Year	All cattle[1]	Milk cows	Sheep and lambs	Hogs and pigs[2]	Year	All cattle[1]	Milk cows	Sheep and lambs	Hogs and pigs[2]
1900.	59,739	16,544	48,105	51,055	2000.	98,199	9,183	7,036	59,335
1910.	58,993	19,450	50,239	48,072	2005.	95,018	9,004	6,135	60,975
1920.	70,400	21,455	40,743	60,159	2007.	96,573	9,145	6,165	62,490
1930.	61,003	23,032	51,565	55,705	2008.	96,035	9,257	5,950	66,963
1940.	68,309	24,940	52,107	61,165	2009.	94,721	9,332	5,747	66,768
1950.	77,963	23,853	29,826	58,937	2010.	93,881	9,086	5,620	65,327
1960.	96,236	19,527	33,170	59,026	2011.	100,000	9,200	5,480	64,625
1965.	109,000	16,981	25,127	56,106	2012.	90,769	9,230	5,365	66,361
1970.	112,369	12,091	20,423	57,046	2013.	89,300	9,218	5,335	66,373
1975.	132,028	11,220	14,515	54,693	2014.	88,526	9,208	5,245	64,775
1980.	111,242	10,758	12,699	67,318	2015.	89,143	9,307	5,280	66,145
1985.	109,582	10,777	10,716	54,073	2016.	91,918	9,310	5,300	68,919
1990.	95,816	10,015	11,358	53,788	2017.	93,705	9,346	5,250	71,545
1995.	102,785	9,482	8,886	57,150	2018.	94,399	9,400	5,230	73,230

(1) For 1970 and on, includes milk cows and heifers that have calved. (2) As of Dec. 1 of preceding year.

Production of Principal U.S. Crops, 1990-2017

Source: National Agricultural Statistics Service, U.S. Dept. of Agriculture

Year	Corn for grain (1,000 bu)	Oats (1,000 bu)	Barley (1,000 bu)	Sorghum for grain (1,000 bu)	All wheat (1,000 bu)	Rye (1,000 bu)	Canola (1,000 lb)	Cotton (upland) (1,000 b)	Cottonseed (1,000 t)
1990	7,934,028	357,654	422,196	573,303	2,729,778	10,176	NA	15,505.4	5,968.5
1995	7,373,876	162,027	359,562	460,373	2,182,591	10,064	548,447	17,532.2	6,848.7
2000	9,915,051	149,545	318,728	470,526	2,232,460	8,386	1,998,310	16,799.2	6,435.6
2005	11,114,082	114,878	211,896	392,933	2,104,690	7,537	1,580,985	23,259.7	8,172.1
2007	13,037,875	90,430	210,110	497,445	2,051,088	6,311	1,430,734	18,355.1	6,588.7
2008	12,091,648	89,135	240,193	472,342	2,499,164	7,979	1,445,064	12,384.5	4,300.3
2009	13,091,862	93,081	227,323	382,983	2,218,061	6,993	1,464,780	11,787.6	4,148.8
2010	12,446,865	81,190	180,268	345,625	2,206,916	7,431	2,447,628	17,600.0	6,098.1
2011	12,359,612	53,649	155,780	214,443	1,999,347	6,326	1,528,010	14,722.0	5,370.0
2012	10,755,111	61,486	218,990	247,742	2,252,307	6,542	2,391,610	16,534.0	5,666.0
2013	13,828,964	64,642	216,745	392,331	2,134,979	7,626	2,210,505	12,275.0	4,203.0
2014	14,215,532	70,232	181,542	432,575	2,026,310	7,189	2,512,645	15,753.0	5,125.0
2015	13,601,964	89,535	218,187	596,751	2,061,939	11,616	2,878,470	12,455.0	4,043.0
2016	15,148,038	64,770	199,914	480,261	2,308,723	13,451	3,086,340	16,601.0	5,369.0
2017	14,604,067	49,391	141,923	363,832	1,740,582	9,696	3,118,680	20,570.0	6,725.0

Year	Tobacco (1,000 lb)	All hay (1,000 t)	Beans, dry edible (1,000 cwt)	Peas, dry edible (1,000 cwt)	Peanuts[1] (1,000 lb)	Soybeans[2] (1,000 bu)	Potatoes (1,000 cwt)	Sweet potatoes (1,000 cwt)
1990	1,626,380	146,212	32,379	2,372	3,602,770	1,925,947	402,110	12,594
1995	1,268,538	154,166	30,812	4,765	4,247,455	2,176,814	443,606	12,906
2000	1,052,999	151,921	26,409	3,474	3,265,505	2,757,810	513,621	13,794
2005	645,015	151,017	26,772	14,003	4,869,860	3,063,237	423,926	15,730
2007	787,653	146,901	25,586	16,287	3,672,250	2,667,117	444,875	18,070
2008	800,504	146,270	25,558	12,270	5,162,400	2,967,007	415,055	18,443
2009	822,581	147,700	25,427	17,137	3,691,650	3,359,011	432,601	19,469
2010	718,190	145,624	31,801	14,221	4,156,840	3,329,181	404,273	23,845
2011	598,252	131,216	19,890	5,625	3,658,590	3,093,524	429,647	26,964
2012	762,709	117,072	31,925	11,002	6,753,880	3,042,044	464,970	26,482
2013	723,579	135,002	24,576	15,620	4,173,170	3,357,984	434,652	24,785
2014	876,415	139,923	28,910	17,155	5,188,665	3,927,090	442,170	29,584
2015	719,171	134,502	30,057	18,283	6,001,357	3,926,339	441,205	31,016
2016	628,720	134,995	28,703	27,762	5,581,570	4,296,086	441,411	31,546
2017	710,161	131,455	35,845	14,177	7,233,600	4,391,553	441,307	35,646

Year	Rice (1,000 cwt)	Sugarcane (1,000 t)	Sugar beets (1,000 t)	Pecans[3] (1,000 lb)	Apples (1,000 t)	Grapes (1,000 t)	Peaches (1,000 t)	Oranges[4] (1,000 bx)	Grapefruit[4] (1,000 bx)
1990	156,088	28,136	27,513	205,000	4,828	5,660	1,121	184,415	49,300
1995	173,871	30,944	27,954	268,000	5,293	5,922	1,150	263,605	71,050
2000	190,872	36,114	32,541	209,850	5,291	7,688	1,276	299,760	66,980
2005	223,235	26,606	27,433	280,250	4,853	7,814	1,185	216,500	25,640
2007	198,388	29,969	31,834	387,305	4,545	7,057	1,127	177,280	39,900
2008	203,733	27,603	26,881	202,080	4,817	7,319	1,135	234,376	37,900
2009	219,850	30,432	29,783	302,020	4,853	7,307	1,104	210,709	32,025
2010	243,104	27,360	32,034	293,740	4,646	7,471	1,150	192,835	30,400
2011	184,941	29,224	28,896	269,700	4,713	7,448	1,072	204,949	30,360
2012	199,939	32,227	35,224	302,300	4,496	7,531	968	206,119	27,650
2013	189,953	30,761	32,789	266,330	5,216	8,632	904	189,893	28,950
2014	222,215	30,424	31,285	264,150	5,907	7,884	853	155,977	25,200
2015	193,148	32,122	35,371	254,290	5,023	7,621	847	146,602	21,950
2016	224,145	32,118	36,920	268,770	5,689	7,697	796	141,891	19,400
2017	178,228	32,243	35,325	293,850	5,703	7,363	697	120,420	16,560

b = bale; bu = bushel; bx = box; cwt = hundred weight; lb = pound; t = ton. **Note:** Some 2017 figures are preliminary estimates. (1) Harvested for nuts. (2) Harvested for beans. (3) Utilized production only. (4) Crop year ending in year cited.

Animal Products: Average Prices Received by U.S. Farmers, 1940-2017

Source: National Agricultural Statistics Service, U.S. Dept. of Agriculture

Figures represent dollars per 100 lb for veal calves, beef cattle, hogs, lambs, milk (wholesale), and sheep; dollars per head for milk cows; cents per lb for broilers, chickens, turkeys, and wool; and cents per dozen for eggs. Weighted calendar year prices for livestock and livestock products other than wool. For 1943-63, wool prices were weighted on marketing year basis. The marketing year was changed in 1964 from a calendar year to a Dec.-Nov. basis for broilers, chickens, eggs, and hogs.

Year	Broilers	Calves (veal)	Cattle (beef)	Chickens (excl. broilers)	Eggs	Hogs	Lambs[1]	Milk	Milk cows	Sheep[1]	Turkeys	Wool
1940	17.3	8.83	7.56	13.0	18.0	5.39	8.10	1.82	61	3.95	15.2	28.4
1950	27.4	26.30	23.30	22.2	36.3	18.00	25.10	3.89	198	11.60	32.8	62.1
1960	16.9	22.90	20.40	12.2	36.1	15.30	17.90	4.21	223	5.61	25.4	42.0
1970	13.6	34.50	27.10	9.1	39.1	22.70	26.40	5.71	332	7.51	22.6	35.4
1980	27.7	76.80	62.40	11.0	56.3	38.00	63.60	13.05	1,190	21.30	41.3	88.1
1990	32.6	95.60	74.60	9.3	70.9	53.70	55.50	13.74	1,160	23.20	39.4	80.0
2000	33.6	104.00	68.60	5.7	61.8	42.30	79.80	12.40	1,340	34.30	40.7	33.0
2005	43.6	135.00	89.70	6.5	54.0	50.20	110.00	15.19	1,770	45.10	44.9	71.0
2006	36.3	133.00	87.20	5.8	58.2	46.00	95.50	12.96	1,730	35.20	47.9	68.0
2007	43.6	119.00	89.90	5.6	88.5	46.60	98.50	19.21	1,830	31.00	52.3	87.0
2008	45.8	110.00	89.10	6.6	109.0	47.00	99.60	18.45	1,950	27.20	56.5	99.0
2009	45.7	105.00	80.30	7.2	81.7	41.60	99.60	12.93	1,390	32.50	50.0	79.0
2010	48.2	117.00	92.20	8.1	85.7	54.10	125.00	16.35	1,330	49.70	61.5	115.0
2011	46.6	142.00	113.00	8.7	95.6	65.30	NA	20.25	1,420	NA	68.2	167.0

Year	Broilers	Calves (veal)	Cattle (beef)	Chickens (excl. broilers)	Eggs	Hogs	Lambs[1]	Milk	Milk cows	Sheep[1]	Turkeys	Wool
2012	50.0	168.00	122.00	8.8	101.1	64.20	NA	18.56	1,430	NA	72.1	153.0
2013	60.6	181.00	125.00	9.5	107.2	67.20	NA	20.12	1,380	NA	66.5	145.0
2014	63.7	261.00	152.00	10.1	122.1	76.50	NA	24.07	1,830	NA	73.5	146.0
2015	53.8	247.00	147.00	10.3	168.0	55.30	NA	17.21	1,990	NA	81.1	145.0
2016	47.8	158.00	119.00	8.1	76.3	49.30	NA	16.34	1,760	NA	82.6	145.0
2017	54.4	168.00	118.00	4.7	85.7	53.10	NA	17.69	1,620	NA	64.6	147.0

NA = Not available. (1) Prices not calculated after 2010.

Crops: Average Prices Received by U.S. Farmers, 1940-2017

Source: National Agricultural Statistics Service, U.S. Dept. of Agriculture

Figures represent cents per lb for apples, cotton, and peanuts; dollars per bushel for barley, corn, oats, soybeans, and wheat; dollars per 100 lb for potatoes, rice, and sorghum; and dollars per ton for cottonseed and baled hay. Weighted crop year prices. The marketing year is described as follows: apples, June-May; barley, hay, oats, potatoes, and wheat, July-June; cotton, cottonseed, peanuts, and rice, Aug.-July; soybeans, Sept.-Aug.; and corn and sorghum grain, Oct.-Sept.

Year	Apples	Barley	Corn	Cotton-seed	Cotton (upland)*	Hay	Oats	Peanuts	Pota-toes	Rice	Sor-ghum	Soy-beans	Wheat
1940	NA	0.39	0.62	21.70	9.8	9.78	0.30	3.7	0.85	1.80	0.87	0.89	0.67
1950	NA	1.19	1.52	86.60	39.9	21.10	0.79	10.9	1.50	5.09	1.88	2.47	2.00
1960	2.7	0.84	1.00	42.50	30.1	21.70	0.60	10.0	2.00	4.55	1.49	2.13	1.74
1970	6.5	0.97	1.33	56.40	21.9	26.10	0.62	12.8	2.21	5.17	2.04	2.85	1.33
1980	12.1	2.86	3.11	129.00	74.4	71.00	1.79	25.1	6.55	12.80	5.25	7.57	3.91
1990	20.9	2.14	2.28	121.00	67.1	80.60	1.14	34.7	6.08	6.68	3.79	5.74	2.61
2000	17.8	2.11	1.85	105.00	49.8	84.60	1.10	27.4	5.08	5.61	3.37	4.54	2.62
2005	24.4	2.53	2.00	96.00	47.7	98.20	1.63	17.3	7.06	7.65	3.33	5.66	3.42
2006	31.7	2.85	3.04	111.00	46.5	110.00	1.87	17.7	7.33	9.96	5.88	6.43	4.26
2007	28.8	4.02	4.20	162.00	59.3	128.00	2.63	20.5	7.51	12.80	7.28	10.10	6.48
2008	23.2	5.37	4.06	223.00	47.8	152.00	3.15	23.0	9.09	16.80	5.72	9.97	6.78
2009	23.1	4.66	3.55	158.00	62.9	108.00	2.02	21.7	8.25	14.40	5.75	9.59	4.87
2010	25.1	3.86	5.18	161.00	81.5	114.00	2.52	22.5	9.20	12.70	8.96	11.30	5.70
2011	30.3	5.35	6.22	260.00	88.3	178.00	3.49	31.8	9.41	14.50	10.70	12.50	7.24
2012	37.1	6.43	6.89	252.00	72.5	191.00	3.89	30.1	8.63	15.10	11.30	14.40	7.77
2013	30.3	6.06	4.46	246.00	77.9	176.00	3.75	24.9	9.71	16.30	7.64	13.00	6.87
2014	25.7	5.30	3.70	194.00	61.3	172.00	3.21	22.0	8.88	13.40	7.20	10.10	5.99
2015	33.6	5.52	3.61	227.00	61.2	145.00	2.12	19.3	8.76	12.20	5.91	8.95	4.89
2016	31.7	4.96	3.36	195.00	68.0	129.00	2.06	19.7	9.08	10.40	4.98	9.47	3.89
2017[1]	32.1	4.45	3.30	139.00	67.4	140.00	2.60	23.0	10.30	12.50	5.65	9.30	4.60

* = Beginning in 1964, 480-lb net weight bales. NA = Not available. (1) Preliminary.

World Meat Production, 2000, 2016

Source: UN Food and Agriculture Organization; in thousands of metric tons; ranked by top producers in 2016

Rank	Top beef producers Country	2000	2016	Rank	Top pork producers Country	2000	2016	Rank	Top poultry producers Country	2000	2016
1.	U.S.	12,017	11,470	1.	China[1]	39,660	54,130	1.	U.S.	16,575	21,483
2.	Brazil	6,579	9,284	2.	U.S.	8,597	11,320	2.	China[1]	11,890	18,080
3.	China[1]	4,988	7,351	3.	Germany	3,982	5,590	3.	Brazil	6,125	14,498
4.	Argentina	2,718	2,644	4.	Spain	2,905	3,947	4.	Russia	775	4,141
5.	India	2,242	2,522	5.	Vietnam	1,418	3,665	5.	India	904	3,426
6.	Australia	1,988	2,361	6.	Brazil	2,600	3,514	6.	Mexico	1,869	3,116
7.	Mexico	1,409	1,879	7.	Russia	1,578	3,368	7.	Japan	1,195	2,345
8.	Pakistan	886	1,815	8.	France	2,312	2,185	8.	Poland	589	2,253
9.	Russia	1,898	1,619	9.	Canada	1,640	2,048	9.	Indonesia	818	2,147
10.	France	1,528	1,458	10.	Poland	1,923	2,009	10.	Iran	815	2,138
11.	Germany	1,304	1,155	11.	Philippines	1,213	1,790	11.	Argentina	1,000	1,973
12.	Canada	1,263	1,133	12.	Denmark	1,625	1,579	12.	Turkey	668	1,933
13.	South Africa	582	1,109	13.	Italy	1,479	1,544	13.	South Africa	821	1,840
14.	Turkey	359	989	14.	Netherlands	1,623	1,453	14.	UK	1,513	1,792
15.	UK	705	912	15.	Mexico	1,030	1,376	15.	France	2,148	1,770
16.	Uzbekistan	390	895	16.	Japan	1,256	1,279	16.	Malaysia	714	1,671
17.	Egypt	570	849	17.	South Korea	916	1,216	17.	Thailand	1,149	1,670
18.	Colombia	745	828	18.	Belgium	1,042	1,061	18.	Myanmar	244	1,663
19.	Italy	1,153	810	19.	Thailand	693	945	19.	Germany	790	1,550
20.	New Zealand	587	673	20.	UK	899	919	20.	Peru	510	1,514
21.	Spain	651	635	21.	Myanmar	118	874	21.	Colombia	504	1,488
22.	Ireland	577	588	22.	Taiwan	921	797	22.	Spain	990	1,427
23.	Iran	289	572	23.	Ukraine	676	748	23.	Canada	1,065	1,357
24.	Indonesia	386	561	24.	Argentina	214	522	24.	Italy	1,092	1,354
25.	Uruguay	453	550	25.	Austria	505	515	25.	Philippines	557	1,238
	Africa	4,298	6,700		Africa	784	1,457		Africa	2,955	5,913
	Asia	12,898	19,104		Asia	47,959	66,282		Asia	22,907	42,992
	Central America	1,766	2,407		Central America	1,140	1,572		Central America	2,371	4,187
	Europe	11,771	10,594		Europe	25,283	28,906		Europe	11,825	20,688
	North America	13,280	12,603		North America	10,237	13,368		North America	17,640	22,840
	Oceania	2,591	3,048		Oceania	488	522		Oceania	767	1,455
	South America	11,846	15,104		South America	3,774	5,699		South America	9,697	21,627
	World total	**58,674**	**69,800**		**World total**	**89,873**	**118,169**		**World total**	**68,638**	**120,302**

(1) Not including Hong Kong or Macao.

World Corn, Rice, and Wheat Production, 2000, 2016

Source: UN Food and Agriculture Organization; in millions of metric tons; ranked by top producers in 2016

Rank	Top corn producers Country	2000	2016	Rank	Top rice producers Country	2000	2016	Rank	Top wheat producers Country	2000	2016
1.	U.S.	251.9	384.8	1.	China	189.8	211.1	1.	China	99.6	131.7
2.	China	106.2	231.8	2.	India	127.5	158.8	2.	India	76.4	93.5
3.	Brazil	32.3	64.1	3.	Indonesia	51.9	77.3	3.	Russia	34.5	73.3
4.	Argentina	16.8	39.8	4.	Bangladesh	37.6	52.6	4.	U.S.	60.6	62.9
5.	Mexico	17.6	28.3	5.	Vietnam	32.5	43.4	5.	Canada	26.5	30.5
6.	Ukraine	3.8	28.1	6.	Myanmar	21.0	25.7	6.	France	37.4	29.5
7.	India	12.0	26.3	7.	Thailand	25.8	25.3	7.	Ukraine	10.2	26.1
8.	Indonesia	9.7	20.4	8.	Philippines	12.4	17.6	8.	Pakistan	21.1	26.0
9.	Russia	1.5	15.3	9.	Brazil	11.1	10.6	9.	Germany	21.6	24.5
10.	Canada	7.0	12.3	10.	Pakistan	7.2	10.4	10.	Australia	22.1	22.3
11.	France	16.0	12.1	11.	U.S.	8.7	10.2	11.	Turkey	21.0	20.6
12.	Romania	4.9	10.7	12.	Cambodia	4.0	9.8	12.	Argentina	15.5	18.6
13.	Nigeria	4.1	10.4	13.	Japan	11.9	8.0	13.	Kazakhstan	9.1	15.0
14.	Egypt	6.5	8.0	14.	Egypt	6.0	6.3	14.	United Kingdom	16.7	14.4
15.	Ethiopia	2.7	7.8	15.	Nigeria	3.3	6.1	15.	Iran	8.1	11.1
16.	South Africa	11.4	7.8	16.	South Korea	7.2	5.6	16.	Poland	8.5	10.8
17.	Hungary	5.0	7.4	17.	Nepal	4.2	4.3	17.	Egypt	6.6	9.0
18.	Serbia	NA	7.4	18.	Laos	2.2	4.1	18.	Romania	4.4	8.4
19.	Philippines	4.5	7.2	19.	Sri Lanka	2.9	4.1	19.	Italy	7.5	8.0
20.	Italy	10.1	6.8	20.	Madagascar	2.5	3.8	20.	Uzbekistan	3.7	6.9
21.	Turkey	2.3	6.4	21.	Peru	1.9	3.2	21.	Brazil	1.7	6.8
22.	Pakistan	1.6	6.1	22.	Tanzania	0.8	3.0	22.	Spain	7.3	6.4
23.	Tanzania	2.0	5.9	23.	Mali	0.7	2.8	23.	Bulgaria	2.8	5.7
24.	Vietnam	2.0	5.2	24.	North Korea	1.7	2.5	24.	Czech Republic	4.1	5.5
25.	Paraguay	0.6	5.2	25.	Colombia	2.2	2.5	25.	Hungary	3.7	4.8
	Africa	43.8	70.6		Africa	17.5	32.5		Africa	14.3	23.1
	Asia	149.1	324.1		Asia	545.2	667.9		Asia	254.7	326.8
	Central America	20.3	32.3		Central America	1.3	1.2		Central America	3.5	3.9
	Europe	63.1	117.4		Europe	3.2	4.2		Europe	183.4	250.1
	North America	258.8	397.1		North America	8.7	10.2		North America	87.2	93.3
	Oceania	0.6	0.6		Oceania	1.1	0.3		Oceania	22.4	22.7
	South America	55.8	117.2		South America	20.5	23.1		South America	19.6	29.6
	World total	**592.0**	**1,060.1**		**World total**	**598.7**	**741.0**		**World total**	**585.0**	**749.5**

NA = Not available.

Value of U.S. Agricultural Exports and Imports, 1978-2017

Source: Economic Research Service, U.S. Dept. of Agriculture

(in billions of dollars, unless otherwise noted)

Year[1]	Agric. trade surplus	Agric. exports	% of all exports	Agric. imports	% of all imports	Year[1]	Agric. trade surplus	Agric. exports	% of all exports	Agric. imports	% of all imports
1978	$13.4	$27.3	21%	$13.9	8%	2000	$11.9	$50.8	7%	$38.9	3%
1980	23.2	40.5	19	17.3	7	2001	13.7	52.7	8	39.0	3
1984	19.1	38.0	18	18.9	6	2002	12.4	53.3	8	41.0	4
1985	11.5	31.2	15	19.7	6	2003	10.3	56.0	9	45.7	4
1986	5.4	26.3	13	20.9	6	2004	9.7	62.4	9	52.7	4
1987	7.2	27.9	12	20.7	5	2005	4.8	62.5	8	57.7	4
1988	14.3	35.3	12	21.0	5	2006	4.6	68.6	8	64.0	3
1989	18.1	39.7	12	21.6	5	2007	12.2	82.2	8	70.1	4
1990	16.6	39.5	11	22.9	5	2008	35.6	114.9	10	79.3	4
1991	16.4	39.3	10	22.9	5	2009	22.9	96.3	10	73.4	5
1992	18.3	43.1	10	24.8	5	2010	29.6	108.5	10	79.0	4
1993	17.7	42.9	10	25.1	4	2011	43.0	137.5	11	94.5	4
1994	19.2	46.2	10	27.0	4	2012	32.5	135.9	10	103.4	5
1995	26.0	56.3	10	30.3	4	2013	37.3	141.1	10	103.9	5
1996	26.8	60.3	10	33.5	4	2014	43.1	152.3	11	109.3	5
1997	21.7	57.3	9	35.7	4	2015	25.5	139.8	11	114.2	5
1998	16.8	53.7	8	36.8	4	2016	16.6	129.6	11	113.0	5
1999	11.8	49.1	8	37.3	4	2017	21.3	140.5	11	119.1	5

(1) Fiscal year (Oct.-Sept.).

Crop Consumption Per Capita in Selected Nations, 1980-2013

Source: UN Food and Agriculture Organization

(in kilograms per capita per year, unless otherwise noted)

Country	Corn 1980	1990	2013	% change, 1980-2013	Rice 1980	1990	2013	% change, 1980-2013	Wheat 1980	1990	2013	% change, 1980-2013
Afghanistan	33	24	3	−92.5%	20	17	14	−29.6%	162	140	160	−0.8%
Argentina	6	5	10	75.5	2	6	9	253.6	115	114	103	−10.0
Australia	2	4	5	117.6	8	8	11	45.3	81	70	70	−12.6
Bangladesh	0	0	1	7,900.0	144	159	172	19.1	29	21	17	−39.0
Brazil	22	22	28	26.0	39	41	32	−18.1	50	44	53	6.9
Canada	4	3	19	416.3	3	5	13	277.6	76	78	85	11.3
China	5	4	7	40.0	76	81	77	2.3	58	77	63	7.9
Congo Republic	5	3	4	−21.8	2	5	17	882.7	33	33	40	20.8
Cuba	0	0	28	NA	51	47	68	33.1	78	74	55	−29.8
Egypt	49	57	62	28.4	26	31	40	50.5	129	151	147	13.6
France	2	13	11	503.8	4	4	5	39.4	95	92	108	13.6
Germany	3	6	12	291.3	2	2	3	74.0	69	67	83	21.6
India	8	8	6	−21.7	64	78	69	8.9	45	41	61	35.0
Indonesia	24	29	35	49.3	125	131	135	7.7	10	9	25	161.8
Iran	1	1	2	330.9	30	30	30	0.9	154	164	153	−0.4
Iraq	0	3	0	150.0	31	37	41	29.5	144	185	136	−5.5
Israel	12	23	15	27.9	6	8	17	178.8	138	124	111	−19.5

Country	Corn 1980	Corn 1990	Corn 2013	Corn % change, 1980-2013	Rice 1980	Rice 1990	Rice 2013	Rice % change, 1980-2013	Wheat 1980	Wheat 1990	Wheat 2013	Wheat % change, 1980-2013
Italy.................	5	3	4	-15.1%	5	5	6	25.6%	174	149	146	-15.7%
Japan................	15	19	9	-36.7	73	65	60	-18.4	44	44	45	2.7
Kenya................	114	88	76	-33.2	2	2	13	439.2	20	23	35	73.2
Korea, North..........	43	56	46	7.2	71	70	74	4.2	32	22	21	-32.2
Korea, South..........	2	13	12	678.8	138	97	85	-38.1	49	48	51	3.3
Mexico...............	118	124	116	-1.3	5	4	6	20.5	42	42	35	-16.5
New Zealand..........	1	3	4	233.1	2	4	9	288.1	78	69	77	-1.6
Nigeria..............	6	33	33	438.2	15	21	28	92.6	16	3	21	33.8
Pakistan.............	7	6	15	117.0	23	14	12	-45.6	114	128	114	-0.2
Philippines..........	22	19	20	-8.6	97	94	119	23.4	17	20	23	37.6
Russia...............	NA	NA	0	NA	NA	NA	5	NA	NA	NA	131	NA
Saudi Arabia..........	12	13	21	80.8	33	18	36	8.3	88	104	89	2.1
South Africa.........	120	108	100	-16.6	4	8	17	295.7	56	56	60	7.0
Thailand.............	5	5	10	121.8	137	114	115	-16.6	4	4	11	170.5
Turkey...............	8	21	24	187.6	3	6	11	210.4	210	223	170	-19.0
Ukraine..............	NA	NA	11	NA	NA	NA	3	NA	NA	NA	105	NA
United Arab Emirates	1	1	1	22.6	43	34	56	30.4	63	65	101	61.3
UK...................	3	3	3	-7.9	2	2	6	239.9	82	82	99	19.9
U.S..................	8	13	12	55.5	4	7	7	78.2	70	81	80	14.6
Venezuela............	55	54	55	-0.2	21	13	23	12.1	50	51	49	-2.5
Vietnam..............	7	7	10	45.6	128	133	145	12.6	17	3	10	-37.4
Africa...............	38	41	44	18.4	15	17	24	60.7	45	47	48	5.9
Asia.................	8	9	10	23.0	77	82	78	0.8	53	60	63	18.2
Central America........	107	113	103	-4.1	8	7	10	31.8	38	38	35	-7.0
Europe...............	4	5	7	94.3	5	4	5	-6.3	118	117	109	-7.5
North America.........	7	12	13	72.7	4	7	7	95.5	71	81	81	14.3
Oceania..............	2	4	4	130.9	9	10	13	57.7	79	69	71	-10.6
South America.........	22	23	28	27.1	29	32	29	-2.5	58	53	57	-1.6
World per capita consumption........	13	15	18	37.3	50	54	54	8.5	64	68	65	1.5

NA = Not available or not applicable. **Note:** All figures are rounded. Percent change based on unrounded raw data.

Meat Consumption Per Capita in Selected Nations, 1980-2013

Source: UN Food and Agriculture Organization

(in kilograms per capita per year, unless otherwise noted)

Country	Beef 1980	Beef 1990	Beef 2013	Beef % change, 1980-2013	Pork 1980	Pork 1990	Pork 2013	Pork % change, 1980-2013	Poultry 1980	Poultry 1990	Poultry 2013	Poultry % change, 1980-2013
Afghanistan...........	5	7	5	-9.6%	NA	NA	NA	NA	1	1	2	169.2%
Argentina............	85	64	55	-34.8	9	4	11	10.9%	11	11	39	245.2
Australia.............	53	47	34	-35.6	15	18	24	65.2	21	24	46	122.2
Bangladesh...........	1	1	1	-14.1	0	0	0	NA	1	1	1	118.8
Brazil................	22	28	39	74.6	8	7	13	58.5	10	14	45	346.9
Canada...............	40	36	30	-24.9	35	28	23	-34.1	22	28	37	66.1
China................	0	1	5	1,352.8	12	20	39	223.6	2	3	14	722.2
Congo Republic........	4	1	4	19.8	1	2	2	227.4	2	5	13	557.6
Cuba.................	15	13	6	-57.1	5	10	20	322.6	9	12	20	113.7
Egypt................	7	8	13	84.8	10	11	5	-50.5	4	4	14	279.7
France...............	33	33	24	-27.2	0	0	0	-66.7	16	21	23	43.0
Germany..............	23	22	13	-42.9	37	34	33	-11.8	10	11	18	83.7
India................	2	2	1	-65.2	60	60	52	-13.7	0	0	2	889.5
Indonesia............	2	2	3	43.9	0	0	0	-24.3	1	3	8	514.8
Iran.................	6	6	4	-42.1	1	3	3	146.3	6	7	25	341.4
Iraq.................	5	7	3	-35.9	0	0	0	NA	9	11	15	73.5
Israel................	13	14	29	120.2	0	0	0	NA	35	39	63	76.9
Italy.................	26	27	19	-29.1	25	32	40	62.1	18	20	19	2.6
Japan................	5	8	9	84.1	13	15	21	53.2	10	14	19	92.1
Kenya................	12	9	10	-18.9	0	0	0	38.1	2	1	0	-76.3
Korea, North..........	2	2	1	-50.3	18	9	15	-14.3	2	3	2	-15.4
Korea, South..........	3	6	15	469.8	12	14	22	93.7	2	6	16	547.8
Mexico...............	11	14	15	45.0	1	1	1	182.7	6	10	30	375.8
New Zealand..........	57	39	22	-60.8	0	0	0	NA	10	17	35	262.9
Nigeria..............	5	2	2	-56.5	9	12	18	111.0	2	2	2	-3.9
Pakistan.............	5	6	9	85.7	8	13	33	318.4	1	1	5	763.8
Philippines..........	3	2	4	45.0	NA	NA	26	NA	5	4	12	149.7
Russia...............	NA	NA	17	NA	NA	NA	26	NA	NA	NA	28	NA
Saudi Arabia..........	6	4	6	2.5	3	4	4	38.7	24	29	49	105.5
South Africa.........	20	17	18	-8.2	6	9	13	130.5	8	15	38	383.5
Thailand.............	6	6	3	-55.9	0	0	0	0.0	7	9	14	98.1
Turkey...............	3	7	12	262.6	NA	NA	21	NA	6	8	19	230.1
Ukraine..............	NA	NA	9	NA	26	25	26	NA	NA	NA	24	NA
United Arab Emirates	14	13	6	-60.0	NA	NA	NA	NA	43	39	41	-5.4
UK...................	23	21	18	-20.3	26	25	26	-2.4	14	19	32	132.0
U.S..................	47	43	36	-23.4	33	28	28	-16.1	26	39	50	89.6
Venezuela............	22	18	26	17.4	6	5	7	20.1	17	13	39	125.7
Vietnam..............	2	2	7	297.7	5	10	35	559.1	2	2	12	606.3
Africa...............	7	6	6	-10.8	1	1	1	104.2	2	3	7	177.0
Asia.................	2	3	4	125.6	6	9	16	158.1	2	3	10	357.5
Central America........	10	12	13	29.4	14	8	13	-10.3	6	9	28	373.7
Europe...............	23	25	15	-36.3	32	35	35	7.5	12	15	23	99.7
North America.........	47	43	36	-23.6	33	28	27	-17.9	26	38	49	87.6
Oceania..............	50	43	30	-39.7	14	17	23	68.1	18	22	43	137.7
South America.........	28	27	32	13.7	7	6	11	57.4	9	12	37	303.9
World per capita consumption........	11	10	9	-12.2	12	13	16	35.1	6	8	15	160.2

NA = Not available or not applicable. **Note:** All figures are rounded. Percent change based on unrounded raw data.

World Capture of Fish, Crustaceans, and Mollusks, 2006-15

Source: UN Food and Agriculture Organization

(in thousands of metric tons; ranked by 2015 captures)

Country	2006	2008	2010	2014	2015	Country	2006	2008	2010	2014	2015
China	14,725	14,791	15,415	17,107	17,591	Myanmar	1,823	1,907	1,961	1,971	1,954
Indonesia	4,785	4,994	5,374	6,437	6,485	Chile	4,161	3,555	2,680	2,175	1,787
U.S.	4,852	4,353	4,387	4,976	5,039	Thailand	2,699	1,873	1,811	1,670	1,693
India	3,845	4,099	4,689	4,982	4,843	South Korea	1,759	1,957	1,722	1,736	1,649
Peru	7,017	7,395	4,302	3,573	4,824	Bangladesh	1,436	1,558	1,727	1,591	1,624
Russia	3,284	3,384	4,070	4,259	4,457	Malaysia	1,286	1,398	1,433	1,465	1,492
Japan	4,338	4,337	4,091	3,641	3,460	Mexico	1,363	1,582	1,527	1,520	1,467
Vietnam	2,027	2,055	2,250	2,695	2,757	Morocco	877	997	1,136	1,365	1,365
Norway	2,256	2,431	2,680	2,302	2,294	Iceland	1,327	1,284	1,061	1,077	1,317
Philippines	2,296	2,489	2,500	2,246	2,152	Taiwan	968	1,016	853	1,068	988

(1) Includes nations not shown.

World Aquaculture Production, 2006-15

Source: UN Food and Agriculture Organization; ranked by 2015 production volume

Country	Metric tons (thous.)					Value (mil)				
	2006	2008	2010	2014	2015	2006	2008	2010	2014	2015
China	29,821	32,730	36,734	45,469	47,610	$34,219	$51,074	$58,822	$73,286	$76,793
India	3,181	3,851	3,786	4,881	5,235	4,184	6,240	7,339	10,768	10,457
Indonesia	1,293	1,690	2,305	4,254	4,342	2,255	2,814	4,895	8,888	7,911
Vietnam	1,658	2,462	2,683	3,340	3,438	3,316	4,606	5,980	7,902	8,511
Bangladesh	892	1,006	1,309	1,957	2,060	1,359	1,766	2,840	4,853	5,150
Norway	712	848	1,020	1,332	1,381	2,749	3,139	5,087	7,060	5,823
Egypt	595	694	920	1,137	1,175	951	1,251	1,680	2,025	1,831
Chile	794	843	701	1,215	1,046	4,350	4,503	3,753	10,276	6,834
Myanmar	575	675	851	962	997	1,119	817	956	1,868	1,645
Thailand	1,354	1,331	1,286	898	897	1,996	2,346	2,817	2,557	2,350
Philippines	623	741	745	788	782	982	1,576	1,563	1,880	1,870
Japan	734	730	718	648	704	3,036	3,347	4,091	3,760	3,461
Brazil	272	331	411	563	575	469	851	1,307	1,535	1,218
South Korea	514	474	476	480	479	1,419	1,287	1,482	1,660	1,720
Ecuador	170	173	273	368	426	758	768	1,250	1,961	2,303
U.S.	520	501	497	421	426	1,002	984	1,023	1,108	1,150
Iran	129	155	220	320	346	379	447	638	967	1,029
Nigeria	85	143	201	313	317	239	410	576	894	904
Taiwan	310	324	310	340	313	880	1,069	1,116	1,378	1,205
Spain	293	250	252	282	290	355	557	520	562	508
World total[1]	47,257	52,915	58,964	73,681	76,600	75,082	100,940	119,537	160,892	157,920

Note: Does not include production of aquatic plants or marine mammals. (1) Includes nations not shown.

U.S. Commercial Landings of Fish and Shellfish, 1990-2015

Source: Natl. Marine Fisheries Service, Natl. Oceanic and Atmospheric Admin., U.S. Dept. of Commerce

Year	Landings for human food		Landings for industrial purposes[1]		Total	
	Weight (mil lbs)	Value (mil)	Weight (mil lbs)	Value (mil)	Weight (mil lbs)	Value (mil)
1990	7,041	$3,366	2,363	$156	9,404	$3,522
1995	7,667	3,625	2,121	145	9,788	3,770
2000	6,912	3,398	2,157	152	9,069	3,550
2003	7,521	3,185	1,986	157	9,507	3,347
2004	7,794	3,611	1,889	145	9,683	3,756
2005	7,997	3,825	1,710	117	9,707	3,933
2006	7,842	3,911	1,641	113	9,483	4,024
2007	7,490	4,015	1,819	177	9,309	4,192
2008	6,633	4,231	1,692	152	8,325	4,383
2009	6,198	3,733	1,833	158	8,031	3,891
2010	6,526	4,356	1,705	164	8,231	4,520
2011	7,909	5,108	1,949	181	9,858	5,289
2012	7,477	4,923	2,157	180	9,634	5,103
2013	8,043	5,268	1,827	198	9,870	5,466
2014	7,828	5,256	1,658	192	9,486	5,448
2015[2]	7,750	4,972	1,968	231	9,718	5,203

Note: Does not include products of aquaculture, except oysters and clams. Landings reported in round (live) weight for all items except univalve and bivalve mollusks (e.g., clams, oysters, and scallops), which are reported in weight of meats (excluding the shell). (1) Processed into meal, oil, solubles, and shell products or used as bait or animal food. (2) Preliminary.

U.S. Domestic Landings by Region, 2005, 2015

Source: Natl. Marine Fisheries Service, Natl. Oceanic and Atmospheric Admin., U.S. Dept. of Commerce

Region	2005		2015[1]	
	Weight (thous. lbs)	Value (thous.)	Weight (thous. lbs)	Value (thous.)
New England	684,090	$971,663	590,982	$1,238,588
Middle Atlantic[2]	199,937	221,505	641,560	511,425
Chesapeake[2]	508,953	218,933	NA	NA
South Atlantic	122,422	125,117	109,298	214,397
Gulf	1,196,355	620,987	1,534,739	816,487
Pacific Coast (incl. Alaska)	6,950,647	1,700,927	6,791,476	2,296,363
Great Lakes[3]	16,732	12,434	14,949	22,345
Hawaii	28,159	70,811	34,623	103,399
Total	9,707,275	3,942,376	9,717,627	5,203,004

NA = Not available. **Note:** Landings reported in round (live) weight for all items except univalve and bivalve mollusks (e.g., clams, oysters, scallops), which are reported in weight of meats (excluding the shell). (1) Preliminary. (2) Chesapeake Region states (Maryland and Virginia) included with Middle Atlantic in 2015. (3) Data for the Great Lakes states lag by one year (i.e., figures are for 2004 and 2014).

EMPLOYMENT

Employment and Unemployment in the U.S., 1900-2017
Source: Bureau of Labor Statistics, U.S. Dept. of Labor

(civilian labor force, persons 16 years of age and older unless otherwise noted; annual averages, in thousands)

Year	Employed	Unemployed Number	Unemployed Rate	Year	Employed	Unemployed Number	Unemployed Rate	Year	Employed	Unemployed Number	Unemployed Rate
1900[1]	26,956	1,420	5.0%	1988	114,968	6,701	5.5%	2003	137,736	8,774	6.0%
1910[1]	34,599	2,150	5.9	1989	117,342	6,528	5.3	2004	139,252	8,149	5.5
1920[1]	39,208	2,132	5.2	1990	118,793	7,047	5.6	2005	141,730	7,591	5.1
1930[1]	44,183	4,340	8.9	1991	117,718	8,628	6.8	2006	144,427	7,001	4.6
1940[1]	47,520	8,120	14.6	1992	118,492	9,613	7.5	2007	146,047	7,078	4.6
1950	58,918	3,288	5.3	1993	120,259	8,940	6.9	2008	145,362	8,924	5.8
1955	62,170	2,852	4.4	1994	123,060	7,996	6.1	2009	139,877	14,265	9.3
1960	65,778	3,852	5.5	1995	124,900	7,404	5.6	2010	139,064	14,825	9.6
1965	71,088	3,366	4.5	1996	126,708	7,236	5.4	2011	139,869	13,747	8.9
1970	78,678	4,093	4.9	1997	129,558	6,739	4.9	2012	142,469	12,506	8.1
1975	85,846	7,929	8.5	1998	131,463	6,210	4.5	2013	143,929	11,460	7.4
1980	99,303	7,637	7.1	1999	133,488	5,880	4.2	2014	146,305	9,617	6.2
1985	107,150	8,312	7.2	2000	136,891	5,692	4.0	2015	148,834	8,296	5.3
1986	109,597	8,237	7.0	2001	136,933	6,801	4.7	2016	151,436	7,751	4.9
1987	112,440	7,425	6.2	2002	136,485	8,378	5.8	2017	153,337	6,982	4.4

Note: Because of revisions in population controls, data for a given year may not be strictly comparable to other years. **Other unemployment rates (1905-45)**, persons 14 years of age and older: 1905, 4.3%; 1915, 8.5%; 1925, 3.2%; 1935, 20.3%; 1936, 16.9%; 1937, 14.3%; 1938, 19.0%; 1939, 17.2%; 1945, 1.9%. (1) Persons 14 years of age and older.

Unemployment Rate and Benefits Data by State, 2017
Source: Employment and Training Admin., U.S. Dept. of Labor; state programs only

State/terr.	Unemployment rate	Monetarily eligible claimants	Number of first payments	Number of final payments	Initial claims	Benefits paid	Average weekly benefit	Employers subject to state law
AL	4.4%	90,687	54,127	17,967	149,907	$158,331,196	$221.13	88,333
AK	7.2	39,055	23,561	11,311	60,641	101,099,871	274.09	18,143
AZ	4.9	122,319	70,334	29,650	219,017	241,567,815	227.89	132,848
AR	3.7	69,398	42,484	13,488	103,845	119,541,069	267.39	69,675
CA	4.8	893,038	942,090	464,195	2,250,004	5,100,862,774	324.44	1,377,907
CO	2.8	92,119	72,780	32,616	109,642	425,037,640	421.17	172,376
CT	4.7	125,540	110,262	36,803	192,987	624,880,931	391.69	102,807
DE	4.6	23,696	15,878	5,288	34,328	63,663,112	260.98	29,216
DC	6.1	25,010	20,746	8,945	18,116	115,123,676	347.11	33,625
FL	4.2	284,903	172,846	82,566	399,379	381,350,831	245.76	537,212
GA	4.7	208,095	138,618	50,883	325,597	308,928,220	287.86	234,453
HI	2.4	29,587	22,547	6,648	64,896	159,579,342	495.31	31,936
ID	3.2	31,062	29,079	8,611	68,162	90,153,437	317.98	52,854
IL	5.0	307,955	290,780	102,529	532,495	1,711,770,138	376.08	322,646
IN	3.5	112,598	74,213	16,236	155,123	254,356,838	281.67	129,411
IA	3.1	96,525	79,125	21,605	139,103	398,341,312	392.43	78,345
KS	3.6	66,143	42,678	17,353	110,786	130,277,995	380.56	73,933
KY	4.9	102,875	47,890	16,882	159,486	273,914,308	326.16	93,123
LA	5.1	77,809	48,075	19,480	116,574	206,391,416	213.26	99,626
ME	3.3	28,170	21,415	5,932	40,939	84,039,116	323.88	46,090
MD	4.1	130,522	80,856	31,889	194,335	466,031,419	340.39	146,656
MA	3.7	206,708	176,843	57,647	308,168	1,367,359,036	507.41	220,746
MI	4.6	322,437	224,068	70,618	471,478	801,511,455	307.69	215,502
MN	3.5	148,735	111,130	37,054	202,820	696,666,617	446.45	131,998
MS	5.1	46,529	28,422	8,307	73,486	76,191,893	206.13	55,868
MO	3.8	132,996	92,635	31,097	231,195	296,579,797	260.58	159,612
MT	4.0	31,032	21,729	7,765	49,010	97,936,343	339.95	40,563
NE	2.9	31,725	18,480	5,129	46,021	73,232,101	327.94	57,746
NV	5.0	88,541	62,663	22,101	134,011	293,950,246	339.05	68,854
NH	2.7	20,639	13,194	2,470	31,131	52,685,596	326.84	42,456
NJ	4.6	310,559	260,765	113,030	529,665	1,877,324,148	439.84	234,375
NM	6.2	35,847	26,813	11,832	50,628	135,875,861	330.25	47,321
NY	4.7	577,910	414,937	136,087	936,868	2,053,772,823	338.50	525,905
NC	4.6	143,208	83,486	41,981	153,684	178,892,344	256.80	217,404
ND	2.6	24,191	18,599	8,190	29,122	118,560,952	482.03	25,324
OH	5.0	244,083	174,679	45,507	376,202	852,382,004	362.65	223,780
OK	4.3	6,829	40,900	19,744	77,452	231,178,698	362.85	89,039
OR	4.1	126,861	83,801	25,887	217,872	481,096,445	383.47	127,952
PA	4.9	392,285	337,228	94,426	821,851	1,744,414,070	381.99	301,039
PR	10.8	104,273	81,475	26,686	133,815	144,551,919	118.38	49,835
RI	4.5	35,861	28,741	8,453	59,125	148,684,039	354.68	34,260
SC	4.3	97,897	57,542	21,261	139,352	162,572,923	257.10	112,351
SD	3.3	9,943	5,962	935	12,190	28,809,176	325.53	27,657
TN	3.7	108,189	67,480	18,994	139,721	214,784,504	236.57	123,086
TX	4.3	635,665	431,975	186,660	859,735	2,271,049,802	399.44	535,035
UT	3.2	49,046	32,297	9,200	60,869	145,717,094	392.01	79,982
VT	3.0	18,646	15,296	2,317	30,938	60,532,052	355.04	22,706
VA	3.8	125,262	71,801	29,254	158,809	320,107,341	308.51	219,043
VI	NA	5,435	3,905	647	6,355	4,076,487	307.11	3,601
WA	4.8	192,273	146,685	41,003	320,377	925,980,994	495.16	238,701
WV	5.2	46,017	35,779	10,720	55,672	141,296,191	284.99	35,803
WI	3.3	158,898	115,199	19,826	306,474	399,620,045	317.14	141,306
WY	4.2	15,672	11,223	4,163	19,833	60,150,361	381.85	22,705
U.S.	4.4	7,451,298	5,696,116	2,119,868	12,489,291	27,872,785,813	351.25	8,280,056

NA = Not available.

Unemployment, Underemployment, and Gross Domestic Product, 1995-2018

Source: Current Population Survey, Bureau of Labor Statistics, U.S. Dept. of Labor; Bureau of Economic Analysis, U.S. Dept. of Commerce, via Federal Reserve Bank of St. Louis

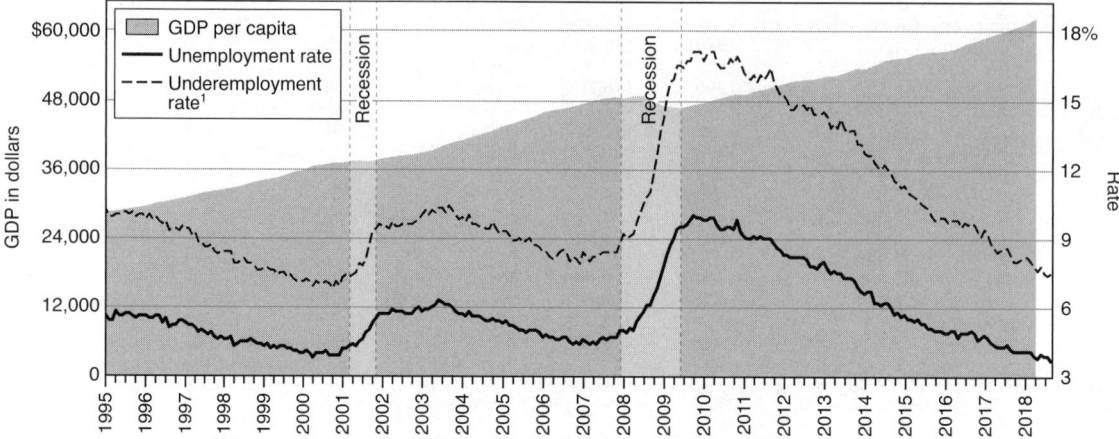

(1) Unemployment rate combined with a) those who currently are neither working nor looking for work but indicate that they want and are available for a job and have looked for work sometime in the past 12 months and b) those employed part time who want and are available for full-time work but have had to settle for a part-time schedule.

U.S. Unemployment Duration by Industry and Occupation, 2017

Source: Bureau of Labor Statistics, U.S. Dept. of Labor

	Total	Number of unemployed persons (thous.)				Weeks of unemployment	
Occupation	Total	Less than 5 weeks	5 to 14 weeks	15 to 26 weeks	27 weeks and over	Average (mean) duration	Median duration
Management, professional, and related...............	1,383	415	402	196	370	27.7	10.6
Management, business, and financial operations..........	558	141	155	94	169	31.6	13.3
Professional and related	825	274	247	102	201	25.1	9.3
Service...	1,530	521	427	222	360	23.5	9.8
Sales and office..	1,443	452	400	216	375	25.9	10.5
Sales and related..........................	699	220	191	105	184	25.2	10.5
Office and administrative support.....................	744	232	210	111	191	26.5	10.5
Natural resources, construction, and maintenance...........	903	310	269	131	194	23.2	9.3
Farming, fishing, and forestry..........................	113	42	40	17	14	14.0	8.0
Construction and extraction..........................	611	214	183	89	125	22.3	8.9
Installation, maintenance, and repair...................	179	53	46	25	55	31.7	12.1
Production, transportation, and material moving.............	1,014	339	302	152	221	23.0	9.4
Production	435	138	128	71	99	25.0	10.0
Transportation and material moving	579	201	174	81	122	21.5	9.0
Industry[1]							
Agriculture and related industries.......................	128	48	45	19	16	16.3	8.0
Mining, quarrying, and oil and gas extraction	32	9	6	6	11	—	—
Construction..	572	191	175	97	109	21.3	9.5
Manufacturing...	569	173	167	90	139	27.2	10.4
Wholesale and retail trade.............................	953	295	276	143	240	25.7	10.3
Transportation and utilities............................	295	98	80	40	78	25.4	10.2
Information	124	34	34	20	36	30.6	12.5
Financial activities	247	66	67	38	77	33.5	13.0
Professional and business services.....................	796	247	234	111	204	24.4	10.5
Education and health services.........................	953	314	289	135	216	23.6	9.4
Leisure and hospitality................................	888	331	248	131	178	20.5	8.6
Other services	256	82	65	32	77	27.8	10.6
Public administration	141	39	34	26	43	30.9	13.8
No previous work experience..........................	690	227	201	98	164	25.7	9.8
Total unemployed[2].................................	**6,982**	**2,270**	**2,008**	**1,017**	**1,687**	**25.0**	**10.0**

Note: Persons 16 years of age and older. (1) Includes wage and salary workers only. (2) Includes persons whose last job was in the U.S. Armed Forces.

U.S. Displaced Workers, 2018

Source: Bureau of Labor Statistics, U.S. Dept. of Labor

	Number (thous.)	Reason for job loss (% distrib.)		
	Number (thous.)	Plant or company closed down or moved	Insufficient work	Position or shift abolished
Total displaced workers............	**2,981**	**36.7%**	**26.3%**	**37.0%**
Age: 20 to 24 years................	73	NA	NA	NA
25 to 54 years................	1,759	36.4	28.6	35.0
55 to 64 years................	798	35.9	20.3	43.8
65 years and over.............	351	37.1	28.9	33.9
Sex: Men	1,681	33.0	31.8	35.2
Women.....................	1,301	41.4	19.4	39.3
Race: White	2,435	36.4	26.6	37.0
Black.......................	285	33.2	30.3	36.4
Asian.......................	157	46.5	14.2	39.3
Hispanic or Latino.............	404	52.0	28.0	20.0

NA = Not available. **Note:** As of Jan. 2018. Displaced workers are persons age 20 or older who lost or left jobs they had held for at least three years. Workers in this table were displaced between Jan. 2015 and Dec. 2017. Hispanic or Latino persons may be of any race.

U.S. Unemployment Rates by Selected Characteristics, 1995-2018

Source: Bureau of Labor Statistics, U.S. Dept. of Labor

	1995	2000	2005	2010	2014	2015	2016	2017 Jan.	2017 June	2017 Yr.	2018 Jan.	2018 June
Total (all civilian workers)	5.6%	4.0%	5.1%	9.6%	6.2%	5.3%	4.9%	5.1%	4.5%	4.4%	4.5%	4.2%
Men, 20 years and older	4.8	3.3	4.4	9.8	5.7	4.9	4.5	5.1	3.8	4.0	4.5	3.6
Women, 20 years and older	4.9	3.6	4.6	8.0	5.6	4.8	4.4	4.5	4.2	4.0	3.8	3.8
Both sexes, 16 to 19 years	17.3	13.1	16.6	25.9	19.6	16.9	15.7	15.4	16.0	14.0	14.6	14.9
White	4.9	3.5	4.4	8.7	5.3	4.6	4.3	4.7	4.0	3.8	3.9	3.7
Black	10.4	7.6	10.0	16.0	11.3	9.6	8.4	7.9	7.2	7.5	8.0	6.6
Asian	—	3.6	4.0	7.5	5.0	3.8	3.6	3.8	3.8	3.4	3.1	3.4
Hispanic or Latino (any race)	9.3	5.7	6.0	12.5	7.4	6.6	5.8	6.6	4.9	5.1	5.8	4.6
Married men, spouse present[1]	3.3	—	—	6.8	3.4	2.8	2.7	2.7	2.2	2.4	2.3	2.1
Married women, spouse present[1]	3.9	—	—	5.9	3.8	3.1	3.0	3.0	2.8	2.7	2.4	2.5
Women who maintain families, spouse absent	8.0	5.9	7.8	12.3	8.6	7.4	6.8	6.3	6.9	6.2	6.5	5.5
Occupation												
Management, professional, and related	2.4	1.8	2.3	4.7	3.1	2.5	2.5	2.3	2.3	2.2	2.2	2.5
Service	7.5	5.2	6.4	10.3	7.3	6.7	5.8	6.3	5.3	5.4	5.9	5.0
Sales and office	5.0	3.8	4.8	9.0	6.0	5.1	4.6	5.0	4.3	4.1	4.3	3.8
Natural resources, constr., and maintenance	—	5.3	6.5	16.1	8.0	7.2	6.4	8.3	4.9	6.0	7.1	4.8
Production, transp., and material moving	—	5.1	6.5	12.8	7.4	6.3	6.1	6.7	5.4	5.4	5.7	4.4
Industry												
Nonagricultural private wage and salary workers	5.8	4.1	5.2	9.9	5.9	5.1	4.6	5.1	4.1	4.2	4.5	3.8
Mining	5.2	4.4	3.1	9.4	4.7	8.6	8.0	6.8	2.6	4.1	4.1	2.9
Construction	11.5	6.2	7.4	20.6	8.9	7.3	6.3	9.4	4.5	6.0	7.3	4.7
Manufacturing	4.9	3.5	4.9	10.6	4.9	4.3	4.3	4.2	3.4	3.6	3.4	3.1
Durable goods	4.4	3.2	4.6	11.2	4.7	4.1	4.2	4.5	3.4	3.7	3.3	2.8
Nondurable goods	5.7	4.0	5.3	9.6	5.2	4.6	4.4	3.6	3.3	3.5	3.7	3.7
Wholesale and retail trade	6.5	4.3	5.4	9.5	6.1	5.5	5.0	5.5	5.0	4.6	5.3	4.2
Transportation and utilities	4.5	3.4	4.1	8.4	5.7	4.4	4.2	4.7	3.6	4.1	3.5	3.2
Information	—	3.2	5.0	9.7	5.2	3.9	4.6	4.9	4.8	4.5	5.3	4.6
Financial activities	3.3	2.4	2.9	6.9	4.0	2.6	2.7	3.3	2.5	2.4	2.2	2.1
Professional and business services	—	4.8	6.2	10.8	6.9	5.6	5.1	5.7	4.1	4.5	5.0	3.3
Education and health services	—	2.5	3.4	5.8	4.2	3.6	3.3	2.7	3.1	3.0	2.7	3.2
Leisure and hospitality	—	6.6	7.8	12.2	8.6	7.9	6.8	7.9	6.1	6.1	6.8	5.7
Other services	8.4	3.9	4.8	8.5	5.7	5.2	4.4	4.0	4.0	3.8	4.4	3.9
Agricultural and related private wage and salary workers	11.1	9.0	8.3	13.9	9.4	9.4	8.3	12.4	5.9	7.2	10.0	7.2
Government workers	2.9	2.1	2.6	4.4	3.2	2.7	2.7	2.2	3.3	2.5	2.2	3.2
Self-employed and unpaid family workers	—	2.1	2.7	5.9	4.4	3.9	3.8	3.8	2.8	3.2	3.5	3.0

— = Not available. **Note:** All monthly rates are unadjusted, except for married men and women, which are seasonally adjusted. (1) Refers to persons in opposite-sex married couples only.

U.S. Workers by Industry and Type, 2007, 2017

Source: Bureau of Labor Statistics, U.S. Dept. of Labor
(in thousands)

Industry	2007 Total employed	2007 Private industry workers	2007 Govt. workers	2007 Self-employed workers	2017 Total employed	2017 Private industry workers[1]	2017 Govt. workers	2017 Self-employed workers
Mining[2]	736	710	6	19	748	735	2	11
Construction	11,856	9,511	440	1,890	10,692	8,767	352	1,567
Manufacturing	16,302	15,850	98	348	15,408	15,014	106	280
Durable goods	10,363	10,066	80	213	9,698	9,436	89	167
Nondurable goods	5,938	5,784	18	134	5,710	5,578	17	113
Wholesale and retail trade	20,937	19,697	102	1,116	20,314	19,368	93	842
Wholesale trade	4,367	4,162	10	192	3,594	3,455	12	126
Retail trade	16,570	15,535	92	924	16,720	15,914	81	716
Transportation and utilities	7,650	5,707	1,534	405	8,159	6,393	1,310	453
Transportation and warehousing	6,457	4,855	1,192	405	6,810	5,361	994	453
Utilities	1,193	851	342	—	1,349	1,033	317	—
Information	3,566	3,237	194	135	2,903	2,559	200	143
Financial activities	10,488	9,417	239	829	10,482	9,615	200	666
Finance and insurance	7,306	6,819	145	341	7,288	6,942	119	226
Real estate and rental and leasing	3,182	2,599	94	488	3,194	2,673	81	440
Professional and business services	15,621	13,190	403	2,009	18,835	16,269	458	2,102
Professional and technical services	9,208	7,825	223	1,152	11,764	10,397	254	1,112
Management, administrative, and waste services	6,412	5,364	180	857	7,072	5,872	205	990
Education and health services	30,662	18,790	10,759	1,102	34,483	22,889	10,602	985
Educational services	12,828	3,621	9,020	187	13,763	4,716	8,844	203
Health care and social assistance	17,834	15,169	1,739	915	20,720	18,173	1,757	782
Hospitals	5,955	5,154	786	15	7,042	6,277	750	15
Health services, except hospitals	8,733	7,856	463	405	10,359	9,478	491	387
Social assistance	3,147	2,159	490	495	3,319	2,419	517	380
Leisure and hospitality	12,415	11,273	443	679	14,291	13,216	385	682
Arts, entertainment, and recreation	2,833	2,041	383	407	3,399	2,632	316	451
Accommodation and food services	9,582	9,232	60	272	10,891	10,584	69	232
Other services	6,972	5,898	38	1,026	7,485	6,435	42	1,005
Other services, except private households	6,159	5,085	38	1,026	6,828	5,778	42	1,005
Private households	813	813	—	—	657	657	—	—
Public administration	6,746	—	6,746	—	7,083	—	7,083	—

— = No data or data that do not meet publication criteria. (1) Includes self-employed workers whose businesses are incorporated. (2) For 2017, includes quarrying and oil and gas extraction.

Persons Not in the U.S. Labor Force, 2017

Source: Bureau of Labor Statistics, U.S. Dept. of Labor

The Labor Dept.'s unemployment rate, based on its household survey, shows the number of people out of work as a percentage of adults age 16 and older in the labor force. That rate excludes the millions of adults considered to be not in the labor force.

(in thousands)

	Number	Age in years			Sex	
		16 to 24	25 to 54	55 and over	Men	Women
Total not in the labor force	**94,759**	**16,989**	**23,014**	**54,756**	**38,130**	**56,629**
Do not want a job now[1]...............	89,242	15,335	20,732	53,175	35,591	53,650
Want a job[1]......................	5,518	1,655	2,282	1,581	2,539	2,979
Did not search for work in previous year	3,320	953	1,281	1,086	1,450	1,870
Searched in previous year but not previous four weeks[2]	2,198	702	1,001	495	1,089	1,109
Not available to work now	610	263	258	90	254	357
Available to work now	1,587	439	743	405	835	752
Reason not currently looking[3]						
Discouraged over job prospects[4].......	476	115	223	138	299	177
Reasons other than discouragement.....	1,112	324	519	268	536	575
Family responsibilities	188	23	121	44	53	135
In school or training	187	141	41	6	103	84
Ill health or disability..............	139	13	54	71	68	71
Other[5]........................	598	147	304	147	312	286

(1) Includes some persons who are not asked if they want a job. (2) Persons who had a job in the prior 12 months must have searched since the end of that job to be considered unemployed. (3) Of those available to work now. (4) Includes believing no work is available, not being able to find work, lacking necessary schooling or training, thought of as too young or old by employers, and other types of discrimination. (5) Includes those who did not actively look for work in the prior four weeks for such reasons as child-care and transportation problems, as well as a small number for which reason for nonparticipation was not ascertained.

U.S. Small Business Employment by Industry, 2015

Source: U.S. Small Business Administration

Industry	Small business employment	Total private employment	% small business employment
Health care and social assistance	8,687,568	19,221,864	45.2%
Accommodation and food services...........................	7,997,654	13,196,892	60.6
Retail trade...	5,514,378	15,704,167	35.1
Manufacturing...	5,155,086	11,605,501	44.4
Professional, scientific, and technical services...................	5,075,601	8,798,260	57.7
Construction	4,944,116	6,008,286	82.3
Other services (excl. public administration)	4,626,826	5,401,233	85.7
Administrative, support, and waste management................	3,625,057	11,112,465	32.6
Wholesale trade	3,486,807	6,076,109	57.4
Finance and insurance	1,920,066	6,135,914	31.3
Transportation and warehousing	1,650,009	4,616,568	35.7
Educational services	1,603,707	3,642,170	44.0
Real estate, rental and leasing.............................	1,410,530	2,065,427	68.3
Arts, entertainment, and recreation	1,370,194	2,230,822	61.4
Information	897,225	3,394,317	26.4
Management of companies and enterprises	404,386	3,308,759	12.2
Mining, quarrying, and oil and gas extraction	296,005	743,660	39.8
Agriculture, forestry, and fishing and hunting	136,254	160,144	85.1
Utilities	112,523	639,234	17.6
Industries not classified	24,155	24,155	100.0
Total employed	**58,938,147**	**124,085,947**	**47.5**

Note: A small business is defined here as an independent business with fewer than 500 employees.

U.S. Occupations Projected to Grow Most, 2016-26

Source: Employment Projections Program, Bureau of Labor Statistics, U.S. Dept. of Labor

(numbers in thousands)

Occupation	Employment		Change, 2016-26		Median annual wage, 2016
	2016	2026	Number	Percent	
Total, all occupations...................	**156,063.8**	**167,582.3**	**11,518.6**	**7.4%**	**$37,040**
Personal care aides	2,016.1	2,793.8	777.6	38.6	21,920
Food preparation/serving, including fast food............	3,452.2	4,032.1	579.9	16.8	19,440
Registered nurses	2,955.2	3,393.2	438.1	14.8	68,450
Home health aides	911.5	1,342.7	431.2	47.3	22,600
Software developers, applications	831.3	1,086.6	255.4	30.7	100,080
Janitors and cleaners, except maids and housekeepers	2,384.6	2,621.2	236.5	9.9	24,190
General and operations managers......................	2,263.1	2,468.3	205.2	9.1	99,310
Laborers and freight, stock, and material movers, hand......	2,628.4	2,828.1	199.7	7.6	25,980
Medical assistants	634.4	818.4	183.9	29.0	31,540
Waiters and waitresses....................	2,600.5	2,783.0	182.5	7.0	19,990
Nursing assistants	1,510.3	1,683.7	173.4	11.5	26,590
Construction laborers	1,216.7	1,367.1	150.4	12.4	33,430
Cooks, restaurant.......................	1,231.9	1,377.2	145.3	11.8	24,140
Accountants and auditors..................	1,397.7	1,537.6	139.9	10.0	68,150
Market research analysts and marketing specialists	595.4	733.7	138.3	23.2	62,560
Customer service representatives	2,784.5	2,920.8	136.3	4.9	32,300
Landscaping and groundskeeping workers	1,197.9	1,333.1	135.2	11.3	26,320
Medical secretaries......................	574.2	703.2	129.0	22.5	33,730
Management analysts	806.4	921.6	115.2	14.3	81,330
Maintenance and repair workers, general.	1,432.6	1,545.1	112.5	7.9	36,940
Teacher assistants	1,308.1	1,417.6	109.5	8.4	25,410
Financial managers	580.4	689.0	108.6	18.7	121,750
Heavy and tractor-trailer truck drivers...................	1,871.7	1,980.1	108.4	5.8	41,340
Elementary school teachers, except special education	1,410.9	1,514.9	104.1	7.4	55,800
Stock clerks and order fillers.................	2,008.6	2,109.6	100.9	5.0	23,840

U.S. Occupations Projected to Decline Most, 2016-26

Source: Employment Projections Program, Bureau of Labor Statistics, U.S. Dept. of Labor

(numbers in thousands)

Occupation	Employment 2016	Employment 2026	Change, 2016-26 Number	Change, 2016-26 Percent	Median annual wage, 2016
Total, all occupations..............................	156,063.8	167,582.3	11,518.6	7.4%	$37,040
Secretaries and administrative assistants, except legal, medical, and executive..........................	2,536.2	2,371.3	−164.9	−6.5	34,820
Team assemblers.................................	1,130.9	985.9	−145.0	−12.8	30,060
Executive secretaries and executive administrative assistants	685.3	566.2	−119.2	−17.4	55,860
Inspectors, testers, sorters, samplers, and weighers	520.7	465.2	−55.5	−10.7	36,780
Electrical and electronic equipment assemblers............	218.9	173.3	−45.6	−20.8	31,310
Data entry keyers.................................	203.8	160.6	−43.3	−21.2	30,100
Tellers..	502.7	460.9	−41.8	−8.3	27,260
Postal service mail carriers..........................	316.7	278.5	−38.2	−12.1	58,110
Legal secretaries.................................	194.7	157.5	−37.1	−19.1	44,180
Correctional officers and jailers.......................	450.0	415.5	−34.5	−7.7	42,820
Assemblers and fabricators, all other	232.4	199.8	−32.6	−14.0	28,550
Office clerks, general	3,117.7	3,086.0	−31.8	−1.0	30,580
Cashiers.......................................	3,555.5	3,524.9	−30.6	−0.9	20,180

Projected Employment by Typical Entry-Level Education, 2016-26

Source: Employment Projections Program, Bureau of Labor Statistics, U.S. Dept. of Labor

Typical entry-level education	Employment, 2016 Number (thous.)	Employment, 2016 Percent distribution	% change in employment, 2016-26	Median annual wage, 2016
Total, all occupations......................	156,063.8	100.0%	7.4%	$37,040
Doctoral or professional degree	4,230.9	2.7	13.1	102,230
Master's degree	2,670.6	1.7	16.7	68,090
Bachelor's degree.........................	33,372.4	21.4	10.1	71,550
Associate's degree	3,617.9	2.3	11.0	51,270
Postsecondary nondegree award	9,582.9	6.1	11.1	36,860
Some college, no degree	3,858.4	2.5	4.2	34,520
High school diploma or equivalent	61,504.1	39.4	5.1	35,540
No formal educational credential	37,226.7	23.9	6.4	22,410

Note: The occupational employment and growth rates shown in this table include projected growth in all jobs from 2016-26, not just entry-level jobs. Entry-level education reflects 2016 requirements—BLS does not project educational requirements.

Highest Average Weekly Wages by County, 2017

Source: Bureau of Labor Statistics, U.S. Dept. of Labor

County	Avg. weekly wage	% change, 2016-17	County	Avg. weekly wage	% change, 2016-17
Santa Clara, CA	$2,576	8.9%	Fairfax, VA...................	$1,646	2.0%
New York, NY	2,439	10.4	Middlesex, MA	1,613	5.1
San Mateo, CA	2,341	11.5	King, WA...................	1,583	7.0
San Francisco, CA	2,232	7.4	Morris, NJ..................	1,582	3.9
Suffolk, MA.................	1,986	5.4	Somerset, NJ	1,568	0.3
Washington, DC.............	1,812	2.7	Alexandria City, VA	1,531	2.5
Arlington, VA...............	1,727	2.8	Montgomery, MD	1,482	4.2
Fairfield, CT	1,688	0.7			

Note: Figures shown are for the 4th quarter, from among the 346 largest U.S. counties, which comprise 73.0% of total covered workers. Cameron County, TX, recorded the lowest average weekly earnings among the largest counties, with an average of $652. It was followed by Hidalgo, TX ($664); Horry, SC ($674); Webb, TX ($706); Lake, FL ($740); Osceola, FL ($740); El Paso, TX ($748); Harrison, MS ($749); Marion, FL ($756); Pasco, FL ($760); and Cleveland, OK ($769). Data include all workers covered by state and federal unemployment insurance programs.

Fatal Occupational Injuries, 2016

Source: Census of Fatal Occupational Injuries, Bureau of Labor Statistics, U.S. Dept. of Labor, in cooperation with other agencies

Event or exposure	Fatalities Number	%	Event or exposure	Fatalities Number	%
Total......................	5,190	100%	Nonroadway incident involving motorized land vehicle............................	245	5%
Violence and other injuries by persons or animals	866	17	Nonroadway noncollision incident.........	182	4
Intentional injury by person................	792	15	Jack-knifed or overturned, nonroadway...	120	2
Homicides..............................	500	10	**Fire or explosion**	88	2
Shooting by other person—intentional....	394	8	**Fall, slip, trip**	849	16
Stabbing, cutting, slashing, piercing	38	1	Fall on same level	134	3
Suicides...............................	291	6	Fall to lower level	697	13
Transportation incidents	2,083	40	Fall from collapsing structure or equipment	65	1
Aircraft incidents	130	3	Fall through surface or existing opening....	87	2
Rail vehicle incidents	50	1	**Exposure to harmful substances or environments**	518	10
Pedestrian vehicular incident	342	7	Exposure to electricity...................	154	3
Pedestrian struck by vehicle in work zone ..	58	1	Exposure to temperature extremes..........	48	1
Water vehicle incident.....................	48	1	Exposure to other harmful substances	268	5
Roadway incident involving motorized land vehicle................................	1,252	24	Nonmedical use of drugs or alcohol, unintentional overdose.................	217	4
Roadway collision with other vehicle......	628	12	Inhalation of harmful substance	39	1
Roadway collision moving in same direction......................	168	3	**Contact with objects and equipment**	761	15
Roadway collision moving in opposite directions, oncoming	199	4	Struck by object or equipment...........	553	11
Roadway collision moving perpendicularly	150	3	Struck by powered vehicle, nontransport ...	232	4
Roadway collision with object other than vehicle..............................	342	7	Struck by falling object or equipment	255	5
Vehicle struck object or animal on side of roadway...........................	321	6	Caught in or compressed by equipment or objects............................	117	2
Roadway noncollision incident	278	5	Caught in running equipment or machinery	103	2
Jack-knifed or overturned, roadway......	238	5	Struck, caught, or crushed in collapsing structure, equipment, or material	82	2

Note: Category totals may include subcategories not shown. Percentages show incidence rate per total fatalities.

U.S. Occupational Injuries and Illnesses Involving Days Away From Work, 2016

Source: Bureau of Labor Statistics, U.S. Dept. of Labor

| Characteristic | Illnesses/injuries[2] | Percent of days-away-from-work cases[1] involving— | | | | | | | Median days away from work |
		1 day	2 days	3-5 days	6-10 days	11-20 days	21-30 days	31 days or more	
Total	892,270	14.3%	11.0%	17.3%	11.8%	11.0%	6.5%	28.2%	8
Occupation(s)									
Management	20,760	23.7	9.5	16.5	12.1	10.7	6.4	21.1	6
Business, financial operations	5,500	16.5	12.9	22.5	10.5	9.5	8.2	19.8	5
Computer, mathematical	1,580	17.7	10.8	20.3	9.5	12.7	3.8	25.3	6
Architecture, engineering	2,570	15.6	11.3	17.1	9.7	13.2	10.1	23.7	8
Life, physical, social science	1,470	14.3	17.0	11.6	6.1	8.8	28.6	13.6	13
Community, social services	9,320	16.6	12.1	25.0	12.3	7.8	4.3	21.9	5
Legal	1,000	9.0	7.0	9.0	5.0	—	2.0	67.0	88
Education, training, library	10,050	20.7	18.7	19.5	12.7	7.2	3.8	17.4	5
Arts, design, entertainment, sports, media	6,470	11.7	9.3	24.1	15.5	13.9	7.1	18.4	7
Health-care practitioners	46,830	15.5	11.4	19.8	13.6	10.5	6.2	23.1	6
Health-care support	48,960	15.1	13.2	21.5	12.2	10.7	5.1	22.2	6
Protective service	9,450	13.0	14.8	17.2	11.9	10.4	5.9	26.8	7
Food preparation, serving	71,700	16.4	14.7	19.4	13.4	10.4	5.6	20.1	5
Building and grounds cleaning, maintenance	59,630	13.2	12.4	19.0	12.8	12.3	6.4	23.7	7
Personal care, service	26,100	15.2	11.5	17.3	11.6	10.8	7.8	25.8	7
Sales	56,070	16.3	11.8	16.3	12.3	10.6	5.9	26.8	7
Office and administrative support . .	64,580	16.6	10.3	17.1	11.4	11.4	6.5	26.7	8
Farming, fishing, forestry	14,380	12.8	12.4	17.9	13.6	10.8	7.4	25.0	7
Construction, extraction	77,780	13.5	10.8	15.5	10.4	10.1	6.5	33.1	10
Installation, maintenance, repair . . .	78,670	13.7	10.5	15.2	10.6	12.0	7.0	31.0	10
Production	99,070	15.6	10.5	16.9	10.9	11.1	6.3	28.8	8
Transportation, material moving . . .	178,620	10.2	8.1	15.4	11.9	11.3	7.3	35.9	14

(1) Cases include those that resulted in days away from work. (2) Number of nonfatal occupational injuries and illnesses involving days away from work for private industry workers; excludes farms with fewer than 11 employees.

Federal Minimum Hourly Wage Rates

Source: Bureau of Labor Statistics, U.S. Dept. of Labor; as of Mar. 2018

Effective date	Minimum wage	% avg. earnings[1]	In 2018 dollars	Effective date	Minimum wage	% avg. earnings[1]	In 2018 dollars
Oct. 24, 1938	$0.25	40%	$4.46	Jan. 1, 1978	$2.65	43%	$10.58
Oct. 24, 1939	0.30	48	5.35	Jan. 1, 1979	2.90	43	10.60
Oct. 24, 1945	0.40	39	5.52	Jan. 1, 1980	3.10	43	9.94
Jan. 25, 1950	0.75	52	7.96	Jan. 1, 1981	3.35	42	9.61
Mar. 1, 1956	1.00	51	9.31	Apr. 1, 1990	3.80	35	7.36
Sept. 3, 1961	1.15	50	9.57	Apr. 1, 1991	4.25	38	7.84
Sept. 3, 1963	1.25	51	10.16	Oct. 1, 1996	4.75	37	7.49
Feb. 1, 1967	1.40	49	10.62	Sept. 1, 1997	5.15	39	7.97
Feb. 1, 1968	1.60	53	11.68	July 24, 2007	5.85	34	7.01
May 1, 1974	2.00	45	10.27	July 24, 2008	6.55	37	7.43
Jan. 1, 1975	2.10	43	10.06	July 24, 2009	7.25	40	8.40
Jan. 1, 1976	2.30	44	10.32				

Note: Before 1961, the minimum wage applied primarily to employees engaged in, or producing goods for, interstate commerce. Coverage was added 1961-64 primarily to employees in large retail and service enterprises and to local transit, construction, and gas station employees. Coverage was added 1966-77 (at reduced rates) to farm workers; government employees; workers in various retail and service trades; and certain domestic workers. Starting in 1978, minimum wage applied equally to all covered, nonexempt workers. Exceptions apply to certain workers with disabilities, full-time students, persons under age 20 in their first 90 days of employment, tipped employees, and student-learners. (1) Percent of gross hourly earnings of production workers in manufacturing.

Civilian Employment of the Federal Government, 1940-2019

Source: U.S. Office of Personnel Management; Office of Management and Budget

(numbers in thousands)

| Year | Total executive branch | Dept. of Defense | Total employees | Civilian agencies/depts. | | | | | | | | |
				Agriculture	HHS, Education, Social Sec.[1]	Homeland Sec.	Interior	Justice	Transportation	Treasury	Veterans Affairs	Other
1940	699	256	443	98	9	18	46	11	NA	45	40	176
1945	3,370	2,635	736	82	11	20	45	19	NA	84	65	409
1950	1,439	753	686	84	13	20	66	20	NA	76	188	219
1955	1,860	1,187	673	86	40	21	54	24	NA	65	178	206
1960	1,808	1,047	761	99	62	21	56	24	NA	62	172	265
1965	1,901	1,034	867	113	87	21	71	27	NA	74	167	307
1970	2,203	1,219	983	118	112	23	75	33	62	84	169	308
1975	2,149	1,042	1,107	121	147	31	80	47	69	101	213	297
1980	2,161	960	1,201	129	163	40	77	48	66	102	228	346
1985	2,252	1,107	1,145	122	147	40	80	55	56	110	247	286
1990	2,250	1,034	1,216	123	129	49	78	71	61	132	248	326
1995	1,970	822	1,148	104	129	54	72	82	57	129	228	292
2000	1,814	660	1,153	95	128	67	67	95	57	113	203	328
2005	1,830	653	1,177	100	128	143	70	103	56	110	222	244
2010	2,128	741	1,386	96	137	173	71	113	57	112	285	342
2015	2,042	725	1,317	86	139	179	64	114	54	95	335	251
2017	2,062	726	1,336	87	140	182	65	118	55	92	352	245
2018[2]	2,085	741	1,344	89	141	182	64	117	55	90	359	246
2019[2]	2,095	744	1,351	81	140	195	60	117	55	88	366	249

NA = Not available. HHS = Health and Human Services. **Note:** End-of-fiscal-year count; U.S. Postal Service excluded. All years are not directly comparable, as 1940-90 is civilian employment of full-time permanent, temporary, part-time, and intermittent employees; 1995-2019 is full-time equivalent employees. (1) Estimated, 1940-50. (2) Estimated.

Unemployment Rates and Earnings by Education, 2017

Source: Bureau of Labor Statistics, U.S. Dept. of Labor

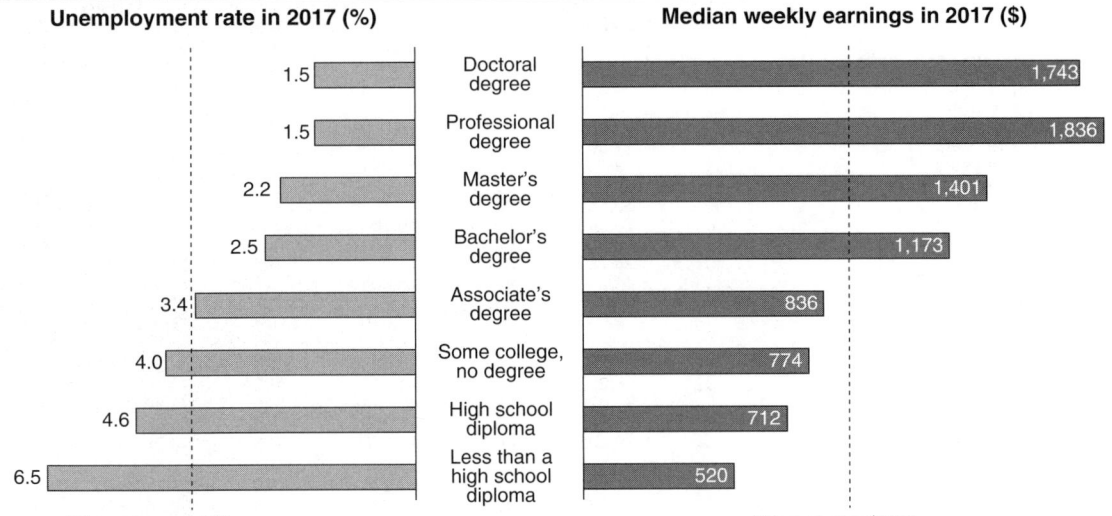

Unemployment rate in 2017 (%)

Education	Rate
Doctoral degree	1.5
Professional degree	1.5
Master's degree	2.2
Bachelor's degree	2.5
Associate's degree	3.4
Some college, no degree	4.0
High school diploma	4.6
Less than a high school diploma	6.5

All workers: 3.6%

Median weekly earnings in 2017 ($)

Education	Earnings
Doctoral degree	1,743
Professional degree	1,836
Master's degree	1,401
Bachelor's degree	1,173
Associate's degree	836
Some college, no degree	774
High school diploma	712
Less than a high school diploma	520

All workers: $907

Note: Data are for persons age 25 and over. Earnings are for full-time wage and salary workers.

Median Earnings by Industry and Sex, 2017

Source: American Community Survey, U.S. Census Bureau, U.S. Dept. of Commerce

Industry	Employed			Median earnings			
	Total	% men	% women	Total	Men	Women	Women's as % of men's
Total..................................	155,058,331	52.5%	47.5%	$36,693	$42,184	$31,174	73.9%
Agriculture, forestry, fishing and hunting, mining	2,637,326	79.2	20.8	34,330	37,335	22,098	59.2
Arts, entertainment, and recreation; accommodation and food services..........................	15,071,444	48.7	51.3	17,473	20,713	15,644	75.5
Construction.................................	10,292,425	90.3	9.7	40,039	40,244	36,453	90.6
Educational services, health care, social assistance ...	35,805,182	25.6	74.4	37,279	46,893	35,206	75.1
Finance and insurance; real estate, rental, leasing.....	10,227,159	46.7	53.3	51,414	65,347	44,154	67.6
Information.................................	3,135,019	59.5	40.5	51,733	60,656	41,939	69.1
Manufacturing..............................	15,631,115	71.1	28.9	45,624	50,338	36,054	71.6
Professional, scientific, and management; administrative, waste management services	17,865,131	58.1	41.9	46,924	54,899	38,038	69.3
Public administration........................	7,127,010	55.5	44.5	54,543	61,563	47,265	76.8
Other services, except public administration	7,596,464	45.9	54.1	25,622	32,549	20,554	63.1
Retail trade................................	17,342,338	51.1	48.9	23,357	27,797	20,344	73.2
Transportation and warehousing; utilities	8,343,526	75.2	24.8	43,014	46,779	35,607	76.1
Wholesale trade.............................	3,984,192	70.5	29.5	45,749	49,504	38,841	78.5

Note: For the civilian employed population 16 years of age and over including workers not employed full-time.

Net Productivity and Workers' Hourly Compensation, 1948-2016

Source: Economic Policy Institute (EPI), based on U.S. Bureau of Economic Analysis and U.S. Bureau of Labor Statistics data

This graph shows the cumulative percent change since 1948 in net productivity and hourly compensation in the U.S. Net productivity is the growth of goods and services produced minus depreciation per hour worked. Hourly compensation is average wages and benefits for private-sector production and nonsupervisory workers, who make up around 80% of private payroll employment. The two data series began to diverge in the 1970s, with productivity increasing more rapidly than compensation.

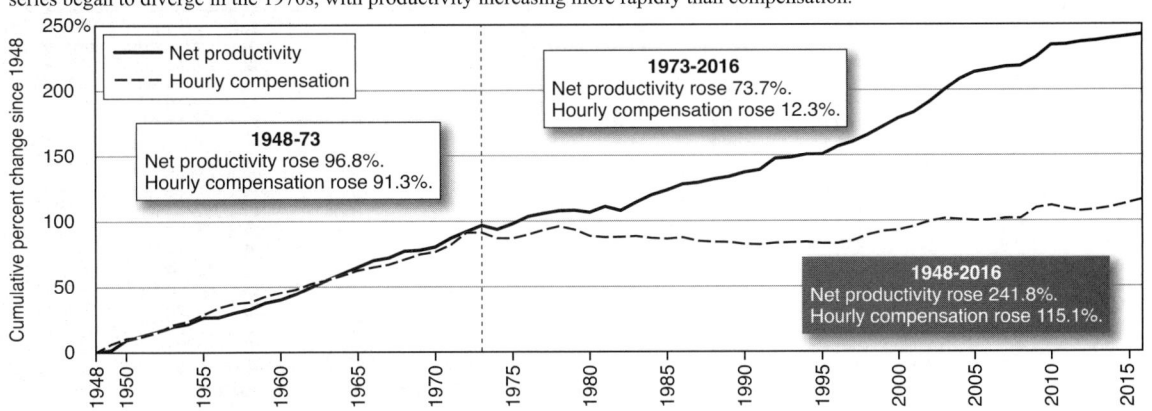

1948-73
Net productivity rose 96.8%.
Hourly compensation rose 91.3%.

1973-2016
Net productivity rose 73.7%.
Hourly compensation rose 12.3%.

1948-2016
Net productivity rose 241.8%.
Hourly compensation rose 115.1%.

U.S. Median Weekly Earnings, 2018
Source: Bureau of Labor Statistics, U.S. Dept. of Labor

AGE, RACE, AND ETHNICITY	Total Number of workers (thous.)	Total Median weekly earnings	Men Number of workers (thous.)	Men Median weekly earnings	Women Number of workers (thous.)	Women Median weekly earnings
All workers, by age						
16 years and over	115,758	$876	64,437	$959	51,321	$780
16 to 24 years	10,665	519	6,009	528	4,656	511
16 to 19 years	1,503	450	918	465	585	424
20 to 24 years	9,162	540	5,091	561	4,071	523
25 years and over	105,093	928	58,428	1,015	46,665	824
25 to 54 years	80,864	907	45,101	991	35,763	811
25 to 34 years	28,842	794	16,163	857	12,679	738
35 to 44 years	26,292	971	14,874	1,085	11,418	866
45 to 54 years	25,730	986	14,064	1,108	11,666	854
55 years and over	24,230	994	13,328	1,117	10,902	868
55 to 64 years	19,537	993	10,711	1,127	8,826	856
65 years and over	4,692	996	2,616	1,074	2,076	925
White						
16 years and over	89,250	907	50,883	985	38,367	815
16 to 24 years	8,222	527	4,739	556	3,483	513
25 years and over	81,028	961	46,144	1,044	34,884	857
25 to 54 years	61,396	934	35,089	1,008	26,307	839
55 years and over	19,632	1,042	11,055	1,165	8,577	919
Black						
16 years and over	14,951	683	7,234	720	7,717	644
16 to 24 years	1,488	462	783	438	705	483
25 years and over	13,463	715	6,451	768	7,012	676
25 to 54 years	10,674	711	5,099	753	5,575	681
55 years and over	2,789	743	1,352	841	1,436	640
Asian						
16 years and over	7,635	1,083	4,196	1,245	3,439	918
16 to 24 years	388	598	177	546	211	688
25 years and over	7,247	1,130	4,019	1,270	3,228	943
25 to 54 years	5,928	1,175	3,321	1,331	2,607	964
55 years and over	1,319	962	698	1,014	621	744
Hispanic[1]						
16 years and over	20,422	674	12,321	704	8,101	621
16 to 24 years	2,315	504	1,401	516	914	483
25 years and over	18,108	704	10,920	734	7,187	652
25 to 54 years	15,447	699	9,345	725	6,102	647
55 years and over	2,661	751	1,576	805	1,085	690
OCCUPATION						
Managerial, professional, and related	48,615	1,242	23,713	1,463	24,902	1,080
Management, business, and financial	19,679	1,346	10,524	1,515	9,155	1,170
Professional and related	28,936	1,176	13,189	1,428	15,747	1,019
Service	16,603	558	7,966	615	8,637	512
Sales and office	23,330	734	9,353	813	13,977	693
Sales and related	9,927	781	5,408	941	4,519	630
Office and administrative support	13,403	711	3,945	705	9,458	713
Natural resources, construction, and maintenance	11,451	836	10,990	840	462	741
Farming, fishing, and forestry	788	612	622	634	166	472
Construction and extraction	6,390	802	6,200	802	191	797
Installation, maintenance, and repair	4,273	955	4,168	950	105	1,148
Production, transportation, and material moving	15,758	703	12,414	757	3,344	555
Production	7,847	739	5,865	812	1,982	583
Transportation and material moving	7,911	670	6,550	704	1,362	522

Note: Not seasonally adjusted; figures are median usual weekly earnings of full-time wage and salary workers for second quarter 2018. Total includes races not shown here. (1) May be of any race.

Average Hours and Earnings of U.S. Production Workers, 1969-2017
Source: Bureau of Labor Statistics, U.S. Dept. of Labor
(annual averages)

Year	Weekly hours	Hourly earnings	Weekly earnings	Year	Weekly hours	Hourly earnings	Weekly earnings	Year	Weekly hours	Hourly earnings	Weekly earnings
1969	37.5	$3.22	$120.70	1985	34.9	$8.74	$304.62	2001	33.9	$14.54	$493.61
1970	37.0	3.40	125.79	1986	34.7	8.93	309.78	2002	33.9	14.96	506.57
1971	36.7	3.63	133.22	1987	34.7	9.14	317.39	2003	33.7	15.37	517.76
1972	36.9	3.90	143.87	1988	34.6	9.44	326.48	2004	33.7	15.68	528.84
1973	36.9	4.14	152.59	1989	34.5	9.80	338.34	2005	33.8	16.12	544.00
1974	36.4	4.43	161.61	1990	34.3	10.20	349.63	2006	33.9	16.75	567.09
1975	36.0	4.73	170.29	1991	34.1	10.51	358.46	2007	33.8	17.42	589.18
1976	36.1	5.06	182.65	1992	34.2	10.77	368.20	2008	33.6	18.06	607.42
1977	35.9	5.44	195.58	1993	34.3	11.05	378.89	2009	33.1	18.61	615.96
1978	35.8	5.88	210.29	1994	34.5	11.34	391.19	2010	33.4	19.05	636.19
1979	35.6	6.34	225.69	1995	34.3	11.65	400.04	2011	33.6	19.44	652.89
1980	35.2	6.85	241.07	1996	34.3	12.04	413.25	2012	33.7	19.74	665.65
1981	35.2	7.44	261.53	1997	34.5	12.51	431.86	2013	33.7	20.13	677.70
1982	34.7	7.87	273.10	1998	34.5	13.01	448.59	2014	33.7	20.61	694.85
1983	34.9	8.20	286.43	1999	34.3	13.49	463.15	2015	33.7	21.03	708.90
1984	35.1	8.49	298.26	2000	34.3	14.02	480.99	2016	33.6	21.54	723.31
								2017	33.7	22.05	742.56

Note: Data refer to production workers in natural resources, mining, and manufacturing; construction workers; and nonsupervisory workers in the service industries.

Elderly in U.S. Labor Force, 1890-2017

Source: U.S. Census Bureau, U.S. Dept. of Commerce

(percent of persons age 65 and older who participated in the labor force; 1910 figures not available)

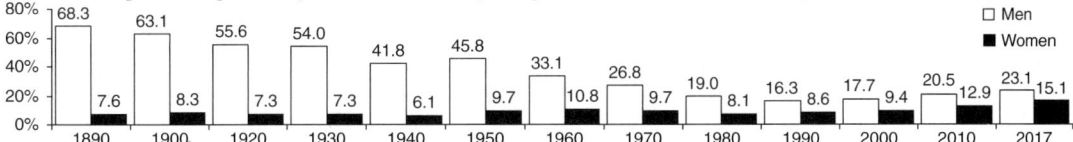

☐ Men
■ Women

Year	Men	Women
1890	68.3	7.6
1900	63.1	8.3
1920	55.6	7.3
1930	54.0	7.3
1940	41.8	6.1
1950	45.8	9.7
1960	33.1	10.8
1970	26.8	9.7
1980	19.0	8.1
1990	16.3	8.6
2000	17.7	9.4
2010	20.5	12.9
2017	23.1	15.1

U.S. Union Membership, 1930-2017

Source: Bureau of Labor Statistics, U.S. Dept. of Labor

(numbers in thousands)

Year	Total employed[1]	% in union	Union members[2]	Year	Total employed[1]	% in union	Union members[2]	Year	Total employed[1]	% in union	Union members[2]
1930	29,424	11.6%	3,401	1975	76,945	25.5%	19,611	2009	124,490	12.3%	15,327
1935	27,053	13.2	3,584	1980	90,564	21.9	19,843	2010	124,073	11.9	14,715
1940	32,376	26.9	8,717	1985	94,521	18.0	16,996	2011	125,187	11.8	14,764
1945	40,394	35.5	14,322	1990	103,905	16.1	16,740	2012	127,577	11.3	14,366
1950	45,222	31.5	14,267	1995	110,038	14.9	16,360	2013	129,110	11.3	14,528
1955	50,675	33.2	16,802	2000	120,786	13.5	16,258	2014	131,431	11.1	14,576
1960	54,234	31.4	17,049	2005	125,889	12.5	15,685	2015	133,743	11.1	14,795
1965	60,815	28.4	17,299	2007	129,767	12.1	15,670	2016	136,101	10.7	14,555
1970	70,920	27.3	19,381	2008	129,377	12.4	16,098	2017	137,890	10.7	14,817

(1) Prior to 1985, total labor force figure, which includes unemployed persons. From 1985 on, does not include self-employed workers. (2) From 1930 to 1980, includes dues-paying members of traditional trade unions, regardless of employment status; after 1980, includes employed only. From 1985 on, includes members of employee associations similar to a union.

Median Weekly Earnings of U.S. Workers by Union Affiliation, 2000, 2017

Source: Bureau of Labor Statistics, U.S. Dept. of Labor

Sex and age	2000				2017			
	Total	Union members[1]	Represented by unions[2]	Non-union	Total	Union members[1]	Represented by unions[2]	Non-union
Total, 16 years and older	**$576**	**$696**	**$691**	**$542**	**$860**	**$1,041**	**$1,028**	**$829**
16 to 24 years	361	437	436	355	519	663	652	514
25 years and older	611	709	705	592	907	1,065	1,054	883
25 to 34 years	550	627	624	529	773	921	909	756
35 to 44 years	631	716	712	614	964	1,122	1,111	935
45 to 54 years	671	755	752	639	977	1,113	1,103	953
55 to 64 years	617	727	723	592	974	1,112	1,106	947
65 years and older	442	577	565	422	909	1,058	1,054	888
Men, 16 years and older	**646**	**739**	**737**	**620**	**941**	**1,102**	**1,094**	**914**
16 to 24 years	376	458	457	370	547	701	683	533
25 years and older	700	753	752	682	996	1,128	1,124	976
25 to 34 years	603	678	675	591	821	964	953	803
35 to 44 years	731	776	774	718	1,062	1,195	1,183	1,038
45 to 54 years	777	801	799	769	1,103	1,184	1,180	1,080
55 to 64 years	738	755	757	729	1,098	1,160	1,166	1,073
65 years and older	537	613	613	514	1,016	1,140	1,132	1,004
Women, 16 years and older	**491**	**616**	**613**	**472**	**770**	**970**	**954**	**746**
16 to 24 years	342	406	405	339	499	606	600	496
25 years and older	515	627	623	497	810	988	974	784
25 to 34 years	493	579	578	483	724	864	854	705
35 to 44 years	520	605	604	506	860	1,037	1,026	831
45 to 54 years	565	697	692	522	855	1,018	1,002	827
55 to 64 years	505	659	647	481	856	1,025	1,011	831
65 years and older	378	485	484	365	782	991	986	751

Note: Data refer to the sole or principal job of full-time wage and salary workers. Excludes self-employed workers regardless of whether or not their businesses are incorporated. (1) Includes members of an employee association similar to a union. (2) Includes members of a labor union as well as those whose jobs are covered by a union or an employee-association contract.

Work Stoppages (Strikes and Lockouts) in the U.S., 1950-2017

Source: Bureau of Labor Statistics, U.S. Dept. of Labor; involving 1,000 workers or more

Year	No.	Workers (thous.)	Days idle (thous.)	Year	No.	Workers (thous.)	Days idle (thous.)	Year	No.	Workers (thous.)	Days idle (thous.)
1950	424	1,698	30,390	1986	69	533	11,861	2002	19	46	660
1955	363	2,055	21,180	1987	46	174	4,481	2003	14	129	4,091
1960	222	896	13,260	1988	40	118	4,381	2004	17	171	3,344
1965	268	999	15,140	1989	51	452	16,996	2005	22	100	1,736
1970	381	2,468	52,761	1990	44	185	5,926	2006	20	70	2,688
1975	235	965	17,563	1991	40	392	4,584	2007	21	189	1,265
1976	231	1,519	23,962	1992	35	364	3,989	2008	15	72	1,954
1977	298	1,212	21,258	1993	35	182	3,981	2009	5	13	124
1978	219	1,006	23,774	1994	45	322	5,021	2010	11	45	302
1979	235	1,021	20,409	1995	31	192	5,771	2011	19	113	1,020
1980	187	795	20,844	1996	37	273	4,889	2012	19	148	1,131
1981	145	729	16,908	1997	29	339	4,497	2013	15	55	290
1982	96	656	9,061	1998	34	387	5,116	2014	11	34	200
1983	81	909	17,461	1999	17	73	1,996	2015	12	47	740
1984	62	376	8,499	2000	39	394	20,419	2016	15	99	1,543
1985	54	324	7,079	2001	29	99	1,151	2017	7	25	440

Note: Numbers cover stoppages that began in the year indicated. Workers are counted more than once if they are involved in more than one stoppage during the year. For work stoppages ongoing at the end of a calendar year, days idle include only the days for the calendar year.

ENERGY

U.S. Energy Overview, 1960-2017

Source: *Monthly Energy Review*, Aug. 2018, Energy Information Administration (EIA), U.S. Dept. of Energy; in quadrillion Btu

	1960	1970	1980	1990	1995	2000	2005	2010	2015	2016	2017
Production	42.80	63.50	67.23	70.70	71.17	71.33	69.43	74.86	88.20	84.35	87.64
Fossil fuels	39.87	59.19	59.01	58.56	57.54	57.37	55.05	58.22	70.21	65.60	68.08
Coal[1]	10.82	14.61	18.60	22.49	22.13	22.74	23.19	22.04	17.95	14.67	15.62
Natural gas (dry)	12.66	21.67	19.91	18.33	19.08	19.66	18.56	21.81	28.07	27.65	27.85[E]
Crude oil[2]	14.93	20.40	18.25	15.57	13.89	12.36	10.97	11.59	19.63	18.51	19.56[E]
Natural gas plant liquids (NGPL)	1.46	2.51	2.25	2.17	2.44	2.61	2.33	2.78	4.57	4.77	5.05
Nuclear electric power	0.01	0.24	2.74	6.10	7.08	7.86	8.16	8.43	8.34	8.43	8.42
Renewable energy	2.93	4.08	5.49	6.04	6.56	6.10	6.22	8.21	9.65	10.33	11.14
Conventional hydroelectric power[3]	1.61	2.63	2.90	3.05	3.21	2.81	2.70	2.54	2.32	2.47	2.77
Biomass[4]	1.32	1.43	2.48	2.74	3.10	3.01	3.10	4.45	4.91	4.98	5.04
Geothermal energy	—	0.01	0.11	0.17	0.15	0.16	0.18	0.21	0.21	0.21	0.21
Solar	NA	NA	NA	0.06	0.07	0.06	0.06	0.09	0.43	0.57	0.77
Wind	NA	NA	NA	0.03	0.03	0.06	0.18	0.92	1.78	2.10	2.35
Imports	4.19	8.34	15.80	18.82	22.18	28.87	34.66	29.87	23.79	25.38	25.35
Coal	0.01	—	0.03	0.07	0.24	0.31	0.76	0.48	0.26	0.22	0.17
Natural gas	0.16	0.85	1.01	1.55	2.90	3.87	4.45	3.83	2.79	3.08	3.12
All petroleum prods.[5]	4.00	7.47	14.66	17.12	18.80	24.42	29.20	25.36	20.41	21.70	21.76
Electricity[6]	0.02	0.02	0.09	0.06	0.15	0.17	0.15	0.15	0.26	0.25	0.22
Exports	1.48	2.63	3.69	4.75	4.50	3.96	4.46	8.18	12.90	14.12	17.90
Coal	1.02	1.94	2.42	2.77	2.32	1.53	1.27	2.10	1.85	1.55	2.39
Natural gas	0.01	0.07	0.05	0.09	0.16	0.25	0.74	1.15	1.80	2.36	3.20
All petroleum prods.[5]	0.43	0.55	1.16	1.82	1.98	2.11	2.34	4.78	9.12	9.99	12.04
Electricity[6]	—	0.01	0.01	0.06	0.01	0.05	0.07	0.07	0.03	0.02	0.03
Consumption	45.09	67.84	78.12	84.49	91.03	98.82	100.19	97.58	97.53	97.58	97.74
Fossil fuels	42.14	63.52	69.83	72.33	77.26	84.74	85.71	80.89	79.33	78.67	78.11
Coal	9.84	12.26	15.42	19.17	20.09	22.58	22.80	20.83	15.55	14.23	13.86
Natural gas[7]	12.39	21.80	20.24	19.60	22.67	23.82	22.57	24.58	28.19	28.45	28.03
Petroleum[8]	19.92	29.52	34.20	33.55	34.44	38.27	40.30	35.49	35.61	36.02	36.24
Nuclear electric power	0.01	0.24	2.74	6.10	7.08	7.86	8.16	8.43	8.34	8.43	8.42
Renewable energy	2.93	4.08	5.49	6.04	6.56	6.10	6.23	8.17	9.63	10.26	11.02
Conventional hydroelectric power[3]	1.61	2.63	2.90	3.05	3.21	2.81	2.70	2.54	2.32	2.47	2.77
Biomass[4]	1.32	1.43	2.48	2.74	3.10	3.01	3.11	4.41	4.90	4.91	4.91
Geothermal energy	—	0.01	0.11	0.17	0.15	0.16	0.18	0.21	0.21	0.21	0.21
Solar	NA	NA	NA	0.06	0.07	0.06	0.06	0.09	0.43	0.57	0.77
Wind	NA	NA	NA	0.03	0.03	0.06	0.18	0.92	1.78	2.10	2.35

NA = Not available. — = Less than 0.005 quadrillion Btu. E = Estimate. **Note:** Numbers may not add up to totals because of rounding. (1) Incl. waste coal supplied beginning in 1989 and refuse recovery beginning in 2001. (2) Incl. lease condensate. (3) Starting in 1990, pumped storage was removed and expanded coverage of industrial use of hydroelectric power was included. (4) Category known as "wood, waste, and alcohol" for years prior to 2000. Includes wood, waste, and alcohol fuels (ethanol blended into motor gasoline). Ethanol is included in both Petroleum and Biomass categories but is only counted once in totals. (5) Imports incl. crude oil for the Strategic Petroleum Reserve, which began in 1977. Imports/exports excl. biofuels. (6) Small amts. transmitted across borders with Canada and Mexico. (7) Excl. supplemental gaseous fuels. (8) Petroleum products supplied, incl. natural gas plant liquids and crude oil burned as fuel.

World's Largest Energy Producers and Consumers, 1980-2015

Source: Energy Information Administration (EIA), U.S. Dept. of Energy

(primary energy in quadrillion Btu; ranked by 2015 data)

Production	1980	1990	2000	2005	2010	2011	2012	2013	2014	2015
1. China	18.12	29.37	38.48	61.44	88.27	94.58	98.89	103.91	104.18	103.13
2. United States	67.14	70.30	70.87	69.05	74.33	77.49	78.66	81.09	87.03	83.54
3. Russia	NA	NA	41.70	51.05	52.83	54.32	55.07	55.88	55.33	55.94
4. Saudi Arabia	22.43	15.92	21.59	26.13	25.30	26.67	27.87	27.52	27.52	28.54
5. Canada	10.28	13.41	18.13	18.88	18.37	18.78	19.18	19.75	20.63	20.55
6. Australia	3.25	6.16	9.66	10.95	12.93	12.79	13.34	13.36	14.32	14.45
7. Iran	3.94	7.67	10.40	13.12	14.61	14.79	13.63	13.05	13.90	14.42
8. India	3.14	6.68	9.88	11.94	15.72	16.11	16.10	14.77	14.23	14.24
9. Indonesia	4.23	5.30	7.76	8.99	12.56	14.16	15.52	15.13	14.55	13.10
10. Brazil	1.90	3.76	6.36	7.66	9.47	9.91	9.76	9.71	10.10	10.39
Consumption	**1980**	**1990**	**2000**	**2005**	**2010**	**2011**	**2012**	**2013**	**2014**	**2015**
1. China	17.94	28.29	40.62	71.27	103.52	112.87	118.36	118.69	119.60	119.61
2. United States	78.03	84.08	98.36	99.72	97.07	96.43	93.95	96.69	97.77	92.90
3. Russia	NA	NA	26.12	27.95	29.69	30.69	31.22	30.33	30.09	29.63
4. India	3.97	7.80	13.28	16.58	23.58	24.78	26.07	23.79	24.73	25.27
5. Japan	15.55	18.78	22.04	22.33	21.44	20.76	20.27	19.54	19.07	18.74
6. Canada	9.88	10.96	13.00	13.85	13.88	14.39	14.38	14.44	14.55	14.36
7. Germany	NA	NA	14.17	14.15	14.01	13.44	13.57	13.44	13.05	13.20
8. Brazil	4.00	5.75	8.50	9.24	11.42	11.84	12.21	12.63	12.80	12.69
9. South Korea	1.73	3.80	7.89	9.34	10.98	11.39	11.54	10.94	11.12	11.40
10. Iran	1.61	3.10	5.28	7.58	9.32	9.72	9.91	10.15	10.60	10.84

NA = Not applicable or not available.

U.S. Energy Consumption by Source, 1949-2017

Source: *Monthly Energy Review*, Aug. 2018, Energy Information Administration (EIA), U.S. Dept. of Energy

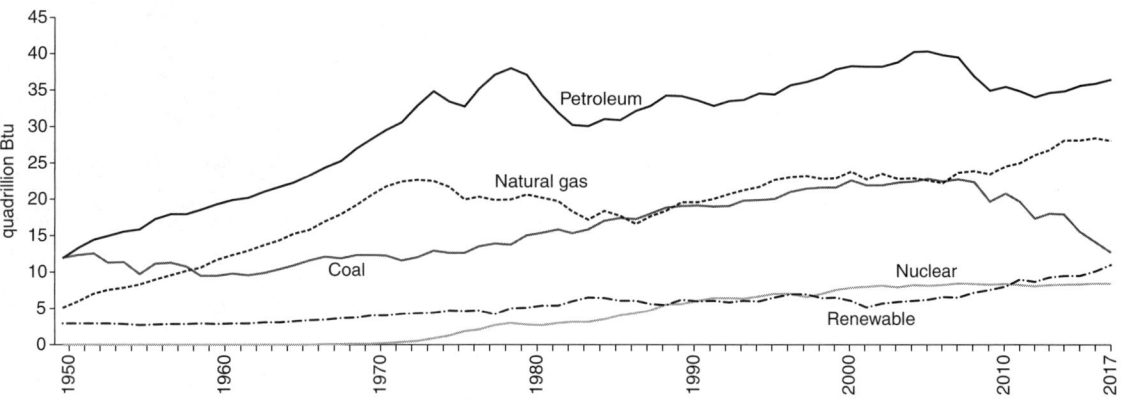

Gasoline Retail Prices in Selected Countries, 1990-2017

Source: *World Energy Prices 2018*, International Energy Agency
(average price in dollars per gallon, including taxes)

Country	1990	1995	2000	2005	2007	2008	2009	2010	2011	2012	2013	2014	2015	2016	2017
					Regular unleaded										
Australia	NA	$1.93	$1.93	$3.22	$3.82	$4.43	$3.79	$4.39	$5.56	$5.60	$5.30	$5.00	$3.63	$3.29	$3.75
Canada	$1.85	1.51	1.82	2.88	3.60	4.05	3.14	3.79	4.73	4.85	4.69	4.43	3.22	2.91	3.33
China	NA	NA	NA	NA	NA	NA	NA	NA	NA	NA	4.24	4.32	3.41	3.14	3.29
Germany	2.65	3.97	3.44	5.64	6.89	7.80	6.81	7.04	NA	NA	NA	NA	NA	NA	NA
Japan	3.14	4.43	3.63	4.28	4.50	5.75	4.85	5.72	6.93	6.97	6.06	5.83	4.32	4.20	4.50
South Korea	2.04	2.95	4.16	5.30	6.21	5.83	4.77	5.60	6.59	6.66	6.66	6.59	5.07	4.58	5.00
Mexico	1.02	1.10	2.01	2.23	2.42	2.46	2.12	2.46	2.80	2.95	3.37	3.60	3.14	2.73	3.18
Taiwan	2.46	2.23	2.16	2.76	3.22	3.52	3.03	3.56	4.05	4.16	4.24	4.01	2.84	2.61	3.03
United States	1.17	1.10	1.48	2.27	2.80	3.26	2.35	2.80	3.52	3.63	3.52	3.37	2.42	2.16	2.42
					Premium unleaded										
France	$3.63	$4.28	$3.79	$5.41	$6.59	$7.53	$6.36	$6.70	$7.87	$7.61	$7.76	$7.50	$5.68	$5.49	$5.87
Germany	2.76	4.13	3.52	5.72	6.97	7.80	6.81	7.04	8.21	8.03	8.06	7.76	5.91	5.49	5.83
Italy	4.58	4.01	3.75	5.72	6.74	7.68	6.47	6.78	8.18	8.67	8.82	8.63	6.47	6.06	6.51
Mexico	NA	NA	2.23	2.57	2.95	3.03	2.65	2.95	3.14	3.14	3.56	3.79	3.37	2.88	3.56
South Africa	NA	NA	1.78	3.07	3.63	4.13	3.22	4.16	5.22	5.15	5.07	4.73	3.67	3.26	3.86
Spain	NA	3.26	2.84	4.47	5.38	6.17	5.26	5.79	6.93	6.93	7.23	7.00	5.15	4.85	5.19
Thailand	NA	NA	1.48	2.23	3.22	4.01	4.13	4.92	5.53	5.64	5.75	5.45	3.79	3.41	3.86
United Kingdom	2.84	3.22	4.58	5.98	7.15	7.38	5.87	6.81	8.14	8.14	7.95	7.91	6.47	5.56	5.72
United States	NA	1.21	1.59	2.38	2.91	3.37	2.46	2.91	3.63	3.75	3.67	3.56	2.65	2.38	2.69

NA = Not available. **Note:** Premium unleaded refers to fuels with a research octane number of 95.

Average U.S. Gasoline Prices, 1980-2017

Source: *Monthly Energy Review*, Aug. 2018; *Short-Term Energy Outlook*, Aug. 2018; Energy Information Administration (EIA), U.S. Dept. of Energy

(in dollars per gallon, including taxes; constant dollars is price in Aug. 2018 dollars)

Year	Current dollars Unleaded regular	Diesel	Constant dollars, unleaded regular[1]	Year	Current dollars Unleaded regular	Diesel	Constant dollars, unleaded regular[1]
1980	$1.25	NA	$3.81	2009	$2.35	$2.47	$2.76
1985	1.20	NA	2.73	2010	2.79	2.99	3.22
1990	1.16	NA	2.18	2011	3.53	3.84	3.95
1995	1.15	$1.11	1.84	2012	3.64	3.97	3.98
2000	1.51	1.49	2.18	2013	3.53	3.92	3.79
2005	2.30	2.40	2.93	2014	3.37	3.83	3.58
2006	2.59	2.71	3.22	2015	2.45	2.71	2.58
2007	2.80	2.89	3.41	2016	2.14	2.30	2.26
2008	3.27	3.80	3.81	2017	2.41	2.65	2.49

NA = Not applicable. (1) Base prices vary slightly from unleaded regular column at left.

Fracking in the U.S.

Hydraulic fracturing, more commonly known as fracking, is a process by which water, sand, and chemicals are injected at high pressure to create fractures in shale rock, releasing the oil and/or natural gas within. Enormous shale deposits in Pennsylvania, California, and other parts of North America have inspired predictions that the U.S. could become a net energy exporting nation. However, more recent estimates from the U.S. Dept. of Energy have significantly reduced the amount of oil that can realistically be derived from some of those shale deposits. Fracking also involves numerous environmental concerns, including pollution of groundwater, massive use of freshwater in drought-prone areas, and effects on seismicity in earthquake-prone areas. Maryland, New York, and Vermont have all banned fracking within their borders, while Connecticut has prohibited the storage or handling of fracking waste.

Energy Consumption by State, 2016

Source: State Energy Data System, Energy Information Administration (EIA), U.S. Dept. of Energy

Total Consumption

Rank, state	Btu (tril)	Rank, state	Btu (tril)
1. Texas	13,183.5	27. Massachusetts	1,422.8
2. California	7,830.3	28. Maryland	1,359.3
3. Florida	4,240.2	29. Mississippi	1,166.3
4. Louisiana	4,205.3	30. Kansas	1,093.0
5. Illinois	3,907.1	31. Arkansas	1,056.5
6. Pennsylvania	3,755.3	32. Oregon	977.5
7. Ohio	3,684.8	33. Nebraska	868.3
8. New York	3,661.5	34. Utah	810.1
9. Georgia	2,838.9	35. West Virginia	766.2
10. Indiana	2,802.3	36. Connecticut	723.9
11. Michigan	2,751.6	37. Nevada	679.1
12. North Carolina	2,553.8	38. New Mexico	667.8
13. Virginia	2,332.0	39. Alaska	600.0
14. New Jersey	2,219.4	40. North Dakota	586.4
15. Tennessee	2,211.3	41. Idaho	528.5
16. Washington	2,058.2	42. Wyoming	502.9
17. Alabama	1,933.6	43. Montana	394.5
18. Minnesota	1,806.9	44. Maine	387.8
19. Wisconsin	1,781.1	45. South Dakota	383.2
20. Missouri	1,780.0	46. New Hampshire	300.9
21. Kentucky	1,702.4	47. Hawaii	282.9
22. South Carolina	1,653.3	48. Delaware	273.5
23. Oklahoma	1,636.0	49. Rhode Island	186.2
24. Iowa	1,529.8	50. Wash., DC	174.2
25. Colorado	1,484.6	51. Vermont	128.7
26. Arizona	1,470.6	**United States**	**97,314.7**

Consumption per Capita

Rank, state	Btu (mil)	Rank, state	Btu (mil)
1. Louisiana	897.4	27. Missouri	292.2
2. Wyoming	859.8	28. Maine	291.6
3. Alaska	809.1	29. Delaware	287.0
4. North Dakota	776.2	30. Washington	282.7
5. Iowa	488.6	31. Virginia	277.1
6. Texas	472.4	32. Michigan	277.0
7. Nebraska	455.2	33. Georgia	275.3
8. South Dakota	444.8	34. Colorado	268.5
9. Indiana	422.4	35. Utah	266.1
10. West Virginia	419.0	36. Wash., DC	254.5
11. Oklahoma	417.2	37. North Carolina	251.4
12. Alabama	397.8	38. New Jersey	247.2
13. Mississippi	390.7	39. Oregon	239.2
14. Kentucky	383.8	40. Nevada	231.1
15. Montana	379.8	41. Maryland	225.6
16. Kansas	375.9	42. New Hampshire	225.4
17. Arkansas	353.6	43. Arizona	212.9
18. South Carolina	333.3	44. Massachusetts	208.5
19. Tennessee	332.6	45. Vermont	206.4
20. Minnesota	327.0	46. Florida	205.3
21. New Mexico	320.2	47. Connecticut	201.8
22. Ohio	317.0	48. California	199.3
23. Idaho	314.6	49. Hawaii	198.0
24. Wisconsin	308.5	50. New York	184.6
25. Illinois	304.4	51. Rhode Island	176.0
26. Pennsylvania	293.7	**United States**	**300.9**

Note: U.S. total includes 19.1 trillion Btu of net exports of coal coke that is not allocated to the states.

U.S. Production of Crude Oil by State, 2000-17

Source: *Petroleum Supply Annual 2017*, Energy Information Administration (EIA), U.S. Dept. of Energy

Oil production in North Dakota more than tripled between 2010 and 2017 through the use of hydraulic fracturing, or fracking, a process by which water, sand, and chemicals are injected at high pressure to create fractures in shale rock, releasing the oil or natural gas within. Fracking accounted for just 2% of U.S. oil production in 2000 but grew to 50% by 2017.

(in thousands of barrels; ranked by 2017 production)

Rank, state	2000	2010	2016	2017	Rank, state	2000	2010	2016	2017
1. Texas	443,397	426,725	1,166,540	1,282,692	18. Pennsylvania	1,500	3,238	6,306	6,573
2. North Dakota	32,719	112,530	377,803	392,127	19. Michigan	7,907	6,976	5,675	5,356
3. Alaska	355,199	218,904	179,169	180,467	20. Arkansas	7,154	5,415	5,519	5,288
4. California	271,132	200,370	186,079	174,107	21. Kentucky	3,465	2,519	2,595	2,477
5. New Mexico	67,198	65,569	146,389	171,440	22. Nebraska	2,957	2,331	2,288	2,125
6. Oklahoma	69,976	67,512	155,679	161,678	23. Florida	4,626	1,777	1,934	1,923
7. Colorado	18,481	32,996	116,481	130,732	24. Indiana	2,098	1,835	1,817	1,779
8. Wyoming	60,726	53,891	72,553	75,669	25. South Dakota	1,170	1,607	1,407	1,305
9. Louisiana	105,425	67,274	56,820	52,024	26. Nevada	621	426	277	286
10. Kansas	34,463	40,468	37,938	35,822	27. Tennessee	346	257	257	271
11. Utah	15,636	24,664	30,529	34,205	28. New York	210	381	225	184
12. Montana	15,428	25,332	23,178	20,706	29. Missouri	94	146	123	113
13. Ohio	6,575	4,769	21,559	18,942	30. Idaho	0	0	215	91
14. Mississippi	19,844	24,080	20,385	17,781	31. Arizona	59	40	8	13
15. West Virginia	1,400	1,842	7,636	9,136	32. Virginia	9	12	7	7
16. Illinois	12,206	9,067	8,639	8,314	**Federal offshore**	**558,242**	**588,335**	**591,212**	**618,494**
17. Alabama	10,457	7,155	8,107	6,827	**U.S. total**	**2,130,707**	**1,998,444**	**3,235,352**	**3,418,954**

Note: One barrel is equal to 42 U.S. gallons.

Shale Dry Gas Production in the U.S., 2000-18

Source: *Shale in the U.S.*, Energy Information Administration (EIA), U.S. Dept. of Energy

(production in billions of cubic ft per day; ranked by 2018 production)

Site name (primary location)	2000	2005	2010	2012	2013	2014	2015	2016	2017	2018
Marcellus (PA, WV, OH, NY)	—	—	0.6	5.1	8.1	11.8	15.0	16.2	16.5	18.4
Utica (OH, PA, WV)	0	0	0	—	0.1	0.7	2.0	3.6	4.2	5.8
Permian (TX, NM)	0.5	0.6	0.8	1.2	1.6	2.3	2.7	3.4	4.2	5.7
Haynesville (LA, TX)	0.1	0.1	2.5	7.4	6.0	4.1	3.8	3.7	3.7	5.3
Eagle Ford (TX)	0	0	0.1	1.7	2.8	3.6	4.7	4.6	3.9	4.2
Barnett (TX)	0.1	1.0	4.1	5.1	4.8	4.4	3.9	3.3	2.9	2.6
Woodford (OK)	—	—	1.0	1.4	1.7	1.6	2.0	2.4	2.4	2.6
Fayetteville (AR)	0	—	1.8	2.7	2.8	2.8	2.6	2.2	1.8	1.4
Bakken (ND, MT)	—	—	0.1	0.3	0.5	0.6	0.9	1.1	1.1	1.4
Antrim (MI, IN, OH)	0.5	0.4	0.3	0.3	0.3	0.3	0.2	0.2	0.2	0.2
Other U.S. shale locations	0.8	0.8	0.9	1.1	1.2	1.3	1.7	2.1	2.1	2.3
Total	**2.0**	**2.9**	**12.3**	**26.4**	**29.7**	**33.3**	**39.7**	**42.9**	**42.8**	**49.9**

— = Less than 100 million cubic feet per day. **Note:** Figures are monthly averages of production per day estimates as of Jan. 1 of year shown.

U.S. Petroleum Trade, 1955-2017

Source: *Monthly Energy Review*, Aug. 2018, Energy Information Administration (EIA), U.S. Dept. of Energy

(in thousands of barrels per day; average for the year)

Year	Imports from Persian Gulf[1]	Total imports	Total exports	Net imports[2]	Petroleum products supplied[3]	Year	Imports from Persian Gulf[1]	Total imports	Total exports	Net imports[2]	Petroleum products supplied[3]
1955	NA	1,248	368	880	8,455	2007	2,163	13,468	1,433	12,036	20,680
1960	326	1,815	202	1,613	9,797	2008	2,370	12,915	1,802	11,114	19,498
1965	359	2,468	187	2,281	11,512	2009	1,689	11,691	2,024	9,667	18,771
1970	184	3,419	259	3,161	14,697	2010	1,711	11,793	2,353	9,441	19,180
1975	1,165	6,056	209	5,846	16,322	2011	1,861	11,436	2,986	8,450	18,887
1980	1,519	6,909	544	6,365	17,056	2012	2,156	10,598	3,205	7,393	18,487
1985	311	5,067	781	4,286	15,726	2013	2,009	9,859	3,621	6,237	18,967
1990	1,966	8,018	857	7,161	16,988	2014	1,875	9,241	4,176	5,065	19,100
1995	1,573	8,835	949	7,886	17,725	2015	1,507	9,449	4,738	4,711	19,534
2000	2,488	11,459	1,040	10,419	19,701	2016	1,766	10,055	5,261	4,795	19,687
2005	2,334	13,714	1,165	12,549	20,802	2017	1,741	10,075	6,343	3,732	19,877
2006	2,211	13,707	1,317	12,390	20,687						

NA = Not available. **Note:** U.S. exports include shipments to U.S. territories; imports include receipts from U.S. territories. Numbers may not add up to totals because of rounding. (1) Bahrain, Iran, Iraq, Kuwait, Qatar, Saudi Arabia, United Arab Emirates, and the Neutral Zone between Kuwait and Saudi Arabia. (2) Total imports minus total exports. (3) Includes domestic production and imports minus change in stocks, refinery imports, and exports.

World Fossil Fuel Reserves

Source: International Energy Statistics Database, Energy Information Administration (EIA), U.S. Dept. of Energy

	Crude oil (bil barrels), 2018	Natural gas (tril cu ft), 2018	Coal (mil short tons), 2015		Crude oil (bil barrels), 2018	Natural gas (tril cu ft), 2018	Coal (mil short tons), 2015
North America. . .	**212.2[1]**	**411.4[1]**	**263,688**	Middle East	807.7	2,816.4	1,326
Canada	170.5	72.6	7,255	Bahrain	0.1	3.3	0
Greenland	0.0	0.0	202	Iran	157.2	1,190.8	1,326
Mexico.	6.6	9.9	1,335	Iraq	148.8	134.9	0
United States. . .	35.2[1]	322.2[1]	254,896	Israel	0.0	6.2	0
Central & South				Kuwait	101.5	63.0	0
America	**328.3**	**280.6**	**15,450**	Oman.	5.4	23.0	0
Argentina.	2.2	11.9	551	Qatar	25.2	850.1	0
Bolivia	0.2	10.5	1	Saudi Arabia . . .	266.2	304.4	0
Brazil	12.6	13.3	7,271	Syria	2.5	8.5	0
Chile	0.2	3.5	1,302	UAE.	97.8	215.1	0
Colombia	1.7	4.0	5,380	Yemen	3.0	16.9	0
Cuba	0.1	2.5	0	**Africa . . . .**	**127.4**	**618.1**	**39,048**
Ecuador.	8.3	0.4	26	Algeria.	12.2	159.1	65
Peru.	0.4	16.1	112	Angola	9.5	10.9	0
Trinidad &				Congo, Dem.			
Tobago.	0.2	15.8	0	Rep. of	0.2	0.0	97
Venezuela	302.3	202.7	806	Congo Rep.	1.6	3.2	0
Europe	**11.3**	**112.1**	**108,591**	Egypt	4.4	77.2	18
Albania	0.2	0.0	575	Eswatini			
Bosnia & Herz.	0.0	0.0	2,496	(Swaziland) . .	0.0	0.0	159
Bulgaria	0.0	0.2	2,608	Libya	48.4	53.1	0
Czechia	0.0	0.1	4,052	Mozambique . . .	0.0	100.0	1,975
Germany	0.1	1.4	39,917	Namibia.	0.0	2.2	0
Greece.	0.0	0.0	3,170	Niger	0.2	NA	7
Hungary.	0.0	0.2	3,207	Nigeria.	37.5	193.4	379
Italy	0.5	1.3	19	South Africa. . . .	0.0	NA	35,384
Macedonia.	0.0	0.0	366	Sudan[2].	5.0	3.0	0
Montenegro	0.0	0.0	157	Tanzania	0.0	0.2	297
Netherlands. . . .	0.1	28.3	548	Zimbabwe	0.0	0.0	553
Norway	6.4	62.9	2	**Asia & Oceania . .**	**46.1[1]**	**556.5**	**461,936**
Poland.	0.1	2.8	26,633	Afghanistan	0.0	1.8	73
Romania	0.6	3.7	321	Australia	1.8	70.2	159,634
Serbia	0.1	1.7	8,283	Bangladesh	0.0	6.6	323
Slovakia.	0.0	0.5	149	Brunei	1.1	9.2	0
Slovenia.	0.0	0.0	409	China	25.6	192.1	147,352
Spain	0.2	0.1	1,308	India.	4.5	45.5	104,465
Turkey	0.3	0.2	12,515	Indonesia.	3.3	101.2	28,189
United Kingdom	2.1	6.2	77	Japan.	0.0	0.7	386
Eurasia.	**118.9**	**2,178.0**	**246,288**	Korea, North . . .	0.0	0.0	661
Armenia.	0.0	0.0	180	Korea, South . . .	NA	0.3	359
Azerbaijan	7.0	35.0	0	Laos.	0.0	0.0	554
Belarus	0.2	0.1	0	Malaysia	3.6	41.8	198
Georgia	0.0	0.3	222	Mongolia	NA	0.0	2,778
Kazakhstan	30.0	85.0	28,225	Myanmar.	0.1	22.5	7
Kyrgyzstan.	0.0	0.2	1,070	New Zealand . . .	0.1	1.2	8,350
Russia	80.0	1,688.2	176,771	Pakistan.	0.3	20.8	3,377
Tajikistan	0.0	0.2	413	Philippines.	0.1	3.5	348
Turkmenistan. . .	0.6	265.0	0	Thailand.	0.3	6.8	1,172
Ukraine	0.4	39.0	37,892	Vietnam.	4.4	24.7	3,704
Uzbekistan.	0.6	65.0	1,516	**World[1] . . . .**	**1,645.7**	**6,922.9**	**1,136,327**

NA = Not available. **Note:** Regional and world totals may include countries not shown. Proved reserves only. Some countries omitted for lack of appreciable reserves. (1) As of 2017, the latest year available. (2) Includes South Sudan.

U.S. Crude Oil Imports by Selected Countries, 1975-2017

Source: *Petroleum Supply Annual*, Energy Information Administration (EIA), U.S. Dept. of Energy

The United States' dependence on foreign oil continues to decline as a consequence of increased U.S. production of crude oil, natural gas, and domestic biofuels like ethanol and biodiesel. Imports stood at just 7.9 mil barrels a day in 2017, down from more than 10.1 mil barrels per day in 2005. However, from 2015 to 2017, imports from the Oil Producing and Exporting Countries (OPEC) jumped from 2.7 to 3.1 mil barrels daily, in large part because of increased imports from Algeria, Angola, Iraq, and Nigeria. In 2017, approximately 19% of the petroleum consumed by the United States was imported from foreign countries, the lowest percentage since 1967. Since 2005, Canada has been the largest supplier of U.S. oil, responsible for about 40% of all U.S. oil imports. Imports from Canada exceeded those from all OPEC countries combined in 2017. Since 1995, sanctions have prohibited the U.S. from importing oil from Iran.

(in thousands of barrels per day; ranked by 2017 imports)

Country	1975	1980	1990	1995	2000	2005	2010	2015	2016	2017
Canada.............	600	199	643	1,040	1,348	1,633	1,970	3,169	3,227	3,421
*Saudi Arabia...........	701	1,250	1,195	1,260	1,523	1,445	1,082	1,052	1,099	943
*Venezuela.............	395	156	666	1,151	1,223	1,241	912	776	741	618
Mexico	70	507	689	1,027	1,313	1,556	1,152	688	582	608
*Iraq	2	28	514	0	620	527	415	229	419	602
Colombia	0	0	140	207	318	156	338	373	442	333
*Nigeria...............	746	841	784	621	875	1,077	983	54	207	309
*Ecuador[1].............	0	0	0	96	125	276	210	225	237	207
Brazil.................	0	1	0	0	5	94	255	190	145	198
*Kuwait...............	4	27	79	213	263	227	195	204	209	144
*Angola[2].............	71	37	236	360	295	456	383	124	159	129
*Algeria...............	264	456	63	27	1	228	328	3	51	66
*Libya	223	548	0	0	0	44	43	3	12	57
Russia[3]..............	0	0	1	14	7	199	269	38	38	49
Norway	12	144	96	258	302	119	25	9	35	37
Chad.................	NA	NA	NA	NA	NA	74	18	72	67	29
United Kingdom	0	173	155	341	291	224	120	11	19	24
*United Arab Emirates	117	172	9	5	3	9	2	2	11	20
*Indonesia[4].............	379	314	98	64	36	19	33	36	34	18
Oman	NA	NA	NA	20	2	22	12	NA	30	14
*Equatorial Guinea[5]	NA	NA	NA	NA	6	68	50	5	6	12
Trinidad and Tobago	115	115	76	62	56	64	45	7	9	8
Guatemala	NA	NA	NA	8	18	11	11	8	7	8
Azerbaijan..............	NA	NA	NA	NA	NA	NA	55	13	10	7
*Gabon[6]	NA	NA	NA	229	143	127	47	10	1	4
*Congo Republic[7]	NA	NA	NA	20	42	25	70	9	3	4
Australia	0	0	47	16	49	10	10	10	4	2
Vietnam	NA	NA	NA	1	9	31	12	9	4	2
Argentina	NA	NA	NA	44	53	56	29	18	12	NA
**Non-OPEC countries.....	NA	NA	NA	3,660	4,526	5,310	4,661	4,690	4,670	4,800**
**OPEC countries	3,211	3,864	3,514	3,570	4,544	4,816	4,553	2,673	3,180	3,112**
**Persian Gulf countries[8]...	1,121	1,508	1,801	1,479	2,409	2,207	1,694	1,487	1,738	1,710**
**TOTAL	4,105	5,263	5,894	7,230	9,071	10,126	9,213	7,363	7,850	7,912**

* = OPEC member. NA = Not available. **Note:** Subtotals and totals include countries not shown here. For years of OPEC membership, see footnotes on individual countries. (1) Ecuador suspended its OPEC membership Dec. 1992-Nov. 2007. Imports from Ecuador in 1993-2007 appear in non-OPEC totals. (2) Angola became a member of OPEC as of 2007 and is not included in OPEC totals from before that year. (3) May include oil from USSR states before 1992. (4) Indonesia withdrew from OPEC, 2009-15, rejoined in Jan. 2016, but "suspended" its membership in Nov. 2016. Imports from Indonesia for 2010-15 appear in non-OPEC totals. (5) Equatorial Guinea joined OPEC in Jan. 2017 and is not included in OPEC totals from before that year. (6) Gabon withdrew from OPEC as of Dec. 31, 1994, but rejoined in July 2016. Imports for 1995-2015 appear in non-OPEC totals. (7) Congo Republic joined OPEC in June 2018 but was not a member in years shown. (8) Bahrain, Iran, Iraq, Kuwait, Qatar, Saudi Arabia, and United Arab Emirates.

U.S. Coal Production and Consumption, 1950-2017

Source: *Monthly Energy Review*, Aug. 2018; *Annual Coal Report, 2016*; Energy Information Administration (EIA); U.S. Dept. of Energy

(in thousand short tons)

	Coal production[1]			Coal consumption				
Year	Surface mining	Underground mining	Total production	Residential	Commercial	Industrial	Electric power[2]	Total consumption
1950	139,388	421,000	560,388	51,562	63,021	224,637	91,871	494,102
1960	141,745	292,584	434,329	24,159	16,789	177,402	176,685	398,081
1970	272,131	340,530	612,661	9,024	7,090	186,637	320,182	523,231
1975	361,174	293,467	654,641	2,823	6,587	147,244	405,962	562,640
1980	492,192	337,508	829,700	1,355	5,097	127,004	569,274	702,730
1985	532,838	350,800	883,638	1,711	6,068	116,429	693,841	818,049
1990	604,529	424,546	1,029,076	1,345	5,379	115,207	782,567	904,498
1995	636,725	396,249	1,032,974	755	5,052	106,067	850,230	962,104
2000	699,953	373,659	1,073,612	454	3,673	94,147	985,821	1,084,095
2005	762,887	368,612	1,131,498	378	4,342	83,774	1,037,485	1,125,978
2010	745,357	337,155	1,084,368	339	3,081	70,381	975,052	1,048,514
2013	641,191	341,685	984,482	NA	1,951	64,529	857,962	924,442
2014	643,721	354,704	1,000,049	NA	1,887	64,243	851,602	917,731
2015	588,736	306,821	896,941	NA	1,503	58,167	738,444	798,115
2016	475,407	252,106	728,364	NA	1,183	51,333	678,554	731,071
2017	NA	NA	NA	NA	1,061	51,151	664,749	716,961

NA = Not available. (1) A small amount of refuse recovery has been included in coal production figures since 2001. (2) Electricity-only and combined-heat-and-power (CHP) plants whose primary business is to sell electricity or electricity and heat to the public. Through 1988, data are for electric utilities only; beginning in 1989, data are for electric utilities and independent power producers.

World Nuclear Power Summary, 2017

Source: *Nuclear Power Reactors in the World*, International Atomic Energy Agency (IAEA); as of Dec. 31, 2017

Country	Reactors in operation No. of units	Reactors in operation Total MW(e)	Reactors under construction[1] No. of units	Reactors under construction[1] Total MW(e)	Nuclear electricity supplied in 2017 TW(e).h[2]	Nuclear electricity supplied in 2017 % of nation's total	Total operating experience[3] Years	Total operating experience[3] Months
Argentina	3	1,633	1	25	5.7	4.5%	82	2
Armenia	1	375	—	—	2.4	32.5	43	8
Belgium	7	5,918	—	—	40.2	49.9	289	7
Brazil	2	1,884	1	1,340	14.9	2.7	53	3
Bulgaria	2	1,926	—	—	14.9	34.3	163	3
Canada	19	13,554	—	—	95.1	14.6	731	6
China	39	34,514	18	19,016	232.8	3.9	280	9
Czechia	6	3,930	—	—	26.8	33.1	158	10
Finland	4	2,769	1	1,600	21.6	33.2	155	4
France	58	63,130	1	1,630	381.8	71.6	2,164	4
Germany	7	9,515	—	—	72.2	11.6	832	7
Hungary	4	1,889	—	—	15.2	50.0	130	2
India	22	6,255	7	4,824	34.9	3.2	482	11
Iran	1	915	—	—	6.4	2.2	6	4
Japan	42	39,752	2	2,653	29.3	3.6	1,823	5
Korea, South	24	22,494	4	5,360	141.3	27.1	523	5
Mexico	2	1,552	—	—	10.6	6.0	51	11
Netherlands	1	482	—	—	3.3	2.9	73	0
Pakistan	5	1,318	2	2,028	8.1	6.2	72	5
Romania	2	1,300	—	—	10.6	17.7	31	11
Russia	35	26,142	7	5,520	190.1	17.8	1,261	9
Slovakia	4	1,814	2	880	14.0	54.0	164	7
Slovenia	1	688	—	—	6.0	39.1	36	3
South Africa	2	1,860	—	—	15.1	6.7	66	3
Spain	7	7,121	—	—	55.6	21.2	329	1
Sweden	8	8,629	—	—	63.1	39.6	451	0
Switzerland	5	3,333	—	—	19.6	33.4	214	11
Taiwan	6	502	2	2,600	21.6	9.3	218	1
Ukraine	15	13,107	2	2,070	80.4	55.1	488	6
United Kingdom	15	8,918	—	—	63.9	19.3	1,589	7
United States	99	99,952	2	2,234	805.6	20.0	4,309	9
TOTAL	**448**	**391,721**	**59**	**60,460**	**2,502.9**	**NA**	**17,430**	**6**

— = Not applicable. MW(e) = Megawatt electricity. (1) Bangladesh, Belarus, and United Arab Emirates have reactors under construction, which are included in totals but not listed separately. (2) 1 terawatt-hour [TW(e).h] = 106 megawatt-hour [MW(e).h]. For an average power plant, 1 TW(e).h = 0.39 megaton of coal equivalent (input) and 0.23 megaton of oil equivalent (input). (3) Total includes shutdown plants for countries not listed here: Italy (80 years, 8 months), Kazakhstan (25 years, 10 months), and Lithuania (43 years, 6 months).

Nuclear Reliance by Nation, 2017

Source: *Nuclear Power Reactors in the World*, International Atomic Energy Agency (IAEA)

(nuclear electricity generation as % of total electricity generated within country; as of Dec. 31, 2017)

Rank	Country	Nuclear share	Rank	Country	Nuclear share	Rank	Country	Nuclear share	Rank	Country	Nuclear share
1.	France	71.6%	9.	Switzerland	33.4%	17.	Russia	17.8%	25.	Argentina	4.5%
2.	Ukraine	55.1	10.	Finland	33.2	18.	Romania	17.7	26.	China	3.9
3.	Slovakia	54.0	11.	Czechia	33.1	19.	Canada	14.6	27.	Japan	3.6
4.	Hungary	50.0	12.	Armenia	32.5	20.	Germany	11.6	28.	India	3.2
5.	Belgium	49.9	13.	South Korea	27.1	21.	Taiwan	9.3	29.	Netherlands	2.9
6.	Sweden	39.6	14.	Spain	21.2	22.	South Africa	6.7	30.	Brazil	2.7
7.	Slovenia	39.1	15.	United States	20.1	23.	Pakistan	6.2	31.	Iran	2.2
8.	Bulgaria	34.3	16.	United Kingdom	19.3	24.	Mexico	6.0			

U.S. Nuclear Reactors and Power Plant Operations, 1953-2017

Source: *Monthly Energy Review*, Aug. 2018, Energy Information Administration (EIA), U.S. Dept. of Energy

Years	Ordered[1]	Canceled	Construction permits issued[2]	Low-power licenses issued[3]	Full-power licenses issued[4]	Shutdown[5]	Operable units[6]	Capacity factor[6,7]	Nuclear electricity generation (bil net kWh)[6]	Nuclear share of domestic electricity generation[6]
1953-59	14	0	8	2	2	0	2	NA	0.2	NA
1960-64	7	0	12	13	12	2	13	NA	3.3	0.3%
1965-69	81	0	50	8	9	4	17	NA	13.9	1.0
1970-74	143	16	59	41	41	5	55	47.8%	114.0	6.1
1975-79	13	43	48	17	17	3	69	58.4	255.2	11.3
1980-84	0	54	0	24	19	1	87	56.3	327.6	13.5
1985-89	0	7	0	24	28	4	111	62.2	529.4	17.8
1990-94	0	2	0	2	3	3	109	73.8	640.4	19.7
1995-99	0	2	0	1	1	6	104	85.3	728.3	19.7
2000-04	0	0	0	0	0	0	104	90.1	788.5	19.9
2005-09	0	0	0	0	0	0	104	90.3	798.9	20.2
2010-17	0	0	0	0	0	6	99	92.2	805.0	20.0
Total	**259**	**124**	**177**	**132**	**132**	**34**	**NA**	**NA**	**NA**	**NA**

NA = Not applicable. **Note:** The permit/license categories shown here are historic. (1) Order placed by a utility or government agency for a nuclear steam supply system. (2) Permits issued in a given period, not extant permits. (3) Permission to conduct testing but not operate at full power. (4) Permission to operate at full power. (5) Permanently ceased operation. (6) As of the end of the designated period. (7) The ratio of electric energy produced to the amount that could be produced at continuous full-power operation.

U.S. Nuclear Reactors Generating the Most Electricity, 2017

Source: U.S. Nuclear Statistics Database, Energy Information Administration (EIA), U.S. Dept. of Energy

(in thousand net megawatt-hours)

Rank	Reactor, location	Electricity generated	Capacity[1]	Rank	Reactor, location	Electricity generated	Capacity[1]
1.	South Texas-2, Bay City, TX	11,498,337	102.5%	14.	South Texas-1, Bay City, TX	10,083,139	89.9%
2.	Peach Bottom-2, Delta, PA	11,310,279	105.5	15.	Limerick-1, Limerick, PA	9,992,846	101.9
3.	Palo Verde-3, Wintersburg, AZ	11,273,581	98.1	16.	Seabrook-1, Seabrook, NH.	9,990,704	91.3
4.	Nine Mile Point-2, Scriba, NY	11,107,751	98.5	17.	LaSalle-1, Marseilles, IL	9,856,322	99.1
5.	Susquehanna-1, Salem Township, PA	10,990,505	100.6	18.	Perry-1, Perry, OH	9,812,376	90.3
6.	Wolf Creek-1, Burlington, KS	10,647,987	99.2	19.	Browns Ferry-1, Athens, AL	9,801,351	101.6
7.	Hope Creek-1, Hancock Bridge, NJ	10,627,333	103.5	20.	Vogtle-2, Waynesboro, GA	9,769,210	96.8
8.	Palo Verde-2, Wintersburg, AZ	10,588,602	92.0	21.	Susquehanna-2, Salem Township, PA	9,762,060	89.4
9.	Braidwood-1, Braceville, IL	10,537,328	101.7	22.	Comanche Peak-1, Glen Rose, TX	9,736,838	92.2
10.	Palo Verde-1, Wintersburg, AZ	10,477,955	91.2	23.	Millstone-3, Waterford, CT	9,717,817	90.9
11.	Peach Bottom-3, Delta, PA	10,412,264	96.9	24.	Diablo Canyon-2, Avila Beach, CA.	9,708,398	99.1
12.	Donald C. Cook-2, Bridgman, MI	10,330,862	101.0	25.	Browns Ferry-3, Athens, AL	9,651,063	99.7
13.	Catawba-2, York, SC.	10,177,378	101.0				

(1) The ratio of power generated to the maximum potential generation expressed as a percentage.

Renewable Energy Sources

Source: U.S. Dept. of Energy

Concern over the environmental impact of burning fossil fuels has helped spur interest in alternative fuels that are less polluting. And because the supply of fossil fuels is finite and diminishing, there is interest in "renewable" sources that do not deplete existing supplies. However, renewable energy sources still make up only a small share of U.S. domestic energy production (about 13% in 2017). The main reason for this is their relatively higher cost (in some cases two to four times that of power obtained from traditional fuels). The following are the major renewable energy sources available.

Biomass is plant-derived material usable as an energy source. It includes wood energy crops such as hybrid poplars and willow trees, agricultural crops including soybeans and corn, and animal and other wastes. Biomass is one of the two most common renewable energy sources in the U.S. today, along with hydropower. Biomass such as wood can be burned to produce heat and generate electricity. Agricultural crops can be chemically converted into fuels such as ethanol and biodiesel, the two most common biofuels; these are typically blended with petroleum fuels when used in practical applications. Bringing ethanol and biodiesel into wide use would require more energy-efficient methods of production and transportation. Second-generation biofuels made from other materials are in development. Overall, biomass fuels burn much cleaner than fossil fuels, though biomass fuels still produce carbon dioxide and other pollutants.

Geothermal energy is generated from heat inside of the Earth. This form of energy is both clean and renewable. The technology has caught on in countries with substantial geothermal activity such as Iceland, where it accounts for approximately two-thirds of primary energy use. In the U.S., the best sources for geothermal power are in the West and in Hawaii, where there are many heated underground lakes. Large-scale access would require drilling. A major goal in this field is to find a way to harness energy directly from magma (molten rock material), which has great potential because of its high temperatures.

Hydrogen is the third most abundant element on Earth. It does not naturally occur on Earth as a pure gas or liquid but is always combined with other elements (such as oxygen, to form water, or carbon, to form methane). If hydrogen is to be used for energy, it must be separated from these other elements. That can be achieved through methods involving heat, photosynthesis, sunlight, or electricity.

Hydrogen batteries, or fuel cells, were used by NASA's space shuttles. Within a fuel cell, a chemical reaction occurs in which electrons are released from hydrogen atoms. These electrons flow through an external circuit as electricity. The hydrogen atoms' protons combine with oxygen (and some of the electrons in the electric current) to produce heat and water suitable for drinking. Fuel cells do not run down but work as long as hydrogen is supplied. Some experts think hydrogen will be the power source of the future. An infrastructure would need to be created for safe and cost-effective transportation and storage of hydrogen.

Hydropower, or hydroelectric power, is generated by water flowing through turbines. Along with biomass fuels, it is one of the two most common renewable energy sources in the U.S. today by amount of energy produced. A dam on a river is a common hydropower producer. No harmful greenhouse gases are produced, but the dams needed to generate power can harm river ecosystems. Researchers are working on turbine technologies to maximize use of hydropower and reduce adverse environmental effects.

Ocean energy can be generated in two ways. Thermal ocean energy uses heat that the ocean absorbs from the sun to power generators, sometimes producing drinkable desalinated water as a byproduct. Mechanical ocean energy is generated by the movement of tides and waves through turbines. In both cases, power generation is not very efficient with current technology. Much more research is needed. Mechanical ocean energy requires the building of large dams or breakwater-type structures called tidal barrages, which could harm coastal ecosystems.

Solar energy is generated using heat and light from the sun. Solar energy is an increasingly common source of electricity. Photovoltaic (PV) solar cells are made of semiconducting materials that can directly convert sunlight to electricity without producing any harmful waste. Arrays of mirrors can concentrate the sun's rays onto PV panels, making solar collectors more efficient. Solar thermal systems can use sunlight to heat water. According to the Dept. of Energy, homes incorporating solar heating designs can save as much as 50% on heating bills. Solar energy is limited by its dependence on a range of factors, including location, time of year, and weather, as well as the efficiency of solar batteries.

Wind energy uses wind turbines to produce energy. They are perched on high towers, usually 100 ft tall or higher, and often placed in large groups ("farms"). Farmers and homeowners sometimes use standalone turbines to generate supplemental electricity. Tax credits for wind energy producers and government incentives for homeowners have significantly lowered the price of wind power. But some object to wind farms because of their appearance or the noise the turbines make. Wind power raises few other environmental problems, but the turbines can pose a danger to birds. In addition, because weather is involved, consistent energy generation can be a challenge.

CRIME

Crime in the U.S., 1990-2016

Source: *Crime in the United States, 2016*, Federal Bureau of Investigation (FBI), U.S. Dept. of Justice; Natl. Archive of Criminal Justice Data

Reported offenses are classified as **violent crimes** if they involve force or the threat of force: murder and nonnegligent manslaughter, rape, robbery, and aggravated assault. The following offenses are considered **property crimes**: burglary, larceny-theft, motor vehicle theft, and arson (excluded from this table because of insufficient data to make estimates).

Year(s)	Violent crime					Property crime			
	All violent crimes	Murder and nonnegligent manslaughter	Rape[1]	Robbery	Aggravated assault[2]	All property crimes	Burglary	Larceny-theft[3]	Motor vehicle theft
NUMBER OF OFFENSES									
1990	1,820,127	23,438	102,555	639,271	1,054,863	12,655,486	3,073,909	7,945,670	1,635,907
1995	1,798,792	21,606	97,470	580,509	1,099,207	12,063,935	2,593,784	7,997,710	1,472,441
2000	1,425,486	15,586	90,178	408,016	911,706	10,182,584	2,050,992	6,971,590	1,160,002
2005	1,390,745	16,740	94,347	417,438	862,220	10,174,754	2,155,448	6,783,447	1,235,859
2007	1,422,970	17,128	92,160	447,324	866,358	9,882,212	2,190,198	6,591,542	1,100,472
2010	1,251,248	14,722	85,593	369,089	781,844	9,112,625	2,168,459	6,204,601	739,565
2011	1,206,005	14,661	84,175	354,746	752,423	9,052,743	2,185,140	6,151,095	716,508
2012	1,217,057	14,856	85,141	355,051	762,009	9,001,992	2,109,932	6,168,874	723,186
2013	1,168,298	14,319	82,109	345,093	726,777	8,651,892	1,932,139	6,019,465	700,288
2014	1,153,022	14,164	84,864	322,905	731,089	8,209,010	1,713,153	5,809,054	686,803
2015	1,199,310	15,883	91,261	328,109	764,057	8,024,115	1,587,564	5,723,488	713,063
2016	1,248,185	17,250	95,730	332,198	803,007	7,919,035	1,515,096	5,638,455	765,484
PERCENT CHANGE: NUMBER OF OFFENSES									
2015-16	4.1%	8.6%	4.9%	1.2%	5.1%	−1.3%	−4.6%	−1.5%	7.4%
2012-16	2.6	16.1	12.4	−6.4	5.4	−12.0	−28.2	−8.6	5.8
2007-16	−12.3	0.7	3.9	−25.7	−7.3	−19.9	−30.8	−14.5	−30.4
CRIME RATE PER 100,000 RESIDENTS									
1990	729.6	9.4	41.1	256.3	422.9	5,073.1	1,232.2	3,185.1	655.8
1995	684.5	8.2	37.1	220.9	418.3	4,590.5	987.0	3,043.2	560.3
2000	506.5	5.5	32.0	145.0	324.0	3,618.3	728.8	2,477.3	412.2
2005	469.0	5.6	31.8	140.8	290.8	3,431.5	726.9	2,287.8	416.8
2007	471.8	5.7	30.6	148.3	287.2	3,276.4	726.1	2,185.4	364.9
2010	404.5	4.8	27.7	119.3	252.8	2,945.9	701.0	2,005.8	239.1
2011	387.1	4.7	27.0	113.9	241.5	2,905.4	701.3	1,974.1	230.0
2012	387.8	4.7	27.1	113.1	242.8	2,868.0	672.2	1,965.4	230.4
2013	369.1	4.5	25.9	109.0	229.6	2,733.6	610.5	1,901.9	221.3
2014	361.6	4.4	26.6	101.3	229.2	2,574.1	537.2	1,821.5	215.4
2015	373.7	4.9	28.4	102.2	238.1	2,500.5	494.7	1,783.6	222.2
2016	386.3	5.3	29.6	102.8	248.5	2,450.7	468.9	1,745.0	236.9
PERCENT CHANGE: CRIME RATE PER 100,000 RESIDENTS									
2015-16	3.4%	7.9%	4.2%	0.5%	4.4%	−2.0%	−5.2%	−2.2%	6.6%
2012-16	−0.4	12.8	9.2	−9.1	2.4	−14.5	−30.2	−11.2	2.8
2007-16	−18.1	−6.0	−3.0	−30.7	−13.5	−25.2	−35.4	−20.2	−35.1

(1) In 2013, the FBI began collecting rape data under a revised definition. For comparison purposes, this table presents data under the legacy definition of rape: "carnal knowledge of a female forcibly and against her will." That definition does not include statutory rape, other types of sexual offenses, or attacks with male victims. (2) Attack or attempted attack upon another with the intent of doing serious bodily harm; usually accompanied by the use of a weapon or other means likely to produce death or great bodily harm. (3) The unlawful taking of another's property not involving force or fraud (e.g., theft of motor vehicle parts, shoplifting). Excludes crimes such as embezzlement and check fraud.

Violent Crime Rates in the U.S., 1970-2016

Source: *Crime in the United States, 2016*, Federal Bureau of Investigation (FBI), U.S. Dept. of Justice; Natl. Archive of Criminal Justice Data

After rising during much of the 1970s and 1980s, the violent crime rate dropped sharply. The 2015 overall rate (372.6) was half its historic high in 1991 (758.2), and the rates of aggravated assault and robbery dropped even more precipitously over that same time period. In 2016, however, the violent crime rate rose slightly across all four offenses. Crime rate is the number of reported offenses per 100,000 population. Rape data are based on the Uniform Crime Reporting Program's legacy definition of rape.

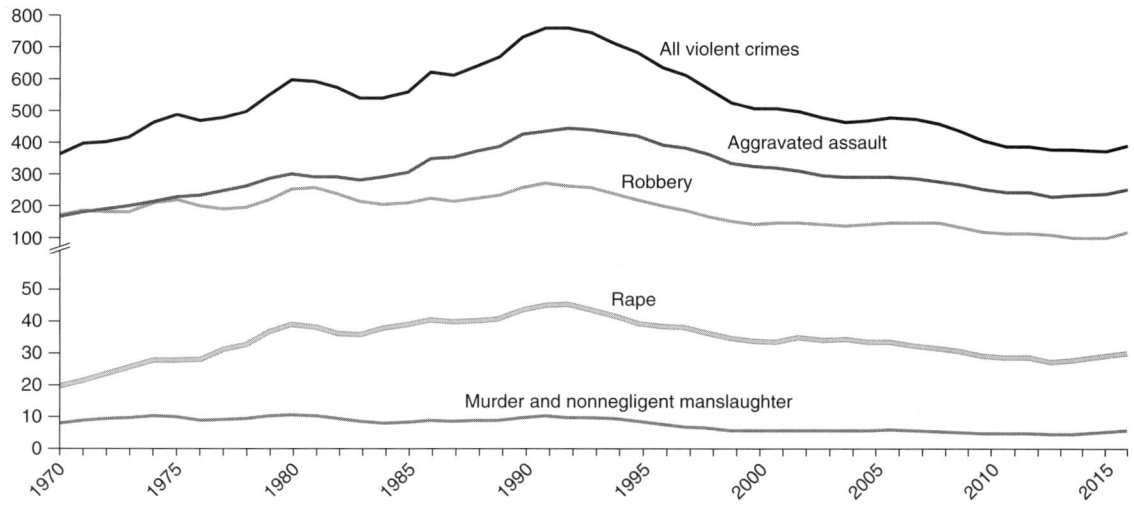

U.S. Crime Rates by Region and State, 2016

Source: *Crime in the United States, 2016*, Federal Bureau of Investigation (FBI), U.S. Dept. of Justice

(per 100,000 population, based on U.S. Census Bureau estimates for July 1)

Area	Violent crime					Property crime[1]			
	All violent crimes	Murder and nonnegligent manslaughter	Rape[2]	Robbery	Aggravated assault[3]	All property crimes	Burglary	Larceny-theft[4]	Motor vehicle theft
Total U.S.[5]	397.1	5.3	40.4	102.8	248.5	2,450.7	468.9	1,745.0	236.9
Northeast.	317.1	3.5	29.6	94.3	189.7	1,618.8	253.9	1,262.6	102.2
New England	282.3	2.0	30.6	63.8	185.9	1,654.3	285.7	1,241.8	126.8
Connecticut.	227.1	2.2	21.3	75.6	128.0	1,808.0	280.9	1,328.5	198.7
Maine	123.8	1.5	30.9	20.0	71.3	1,645.7	300.6	1,286.8	58.2
Massachusetts	376.9	2.0	31.2	78.8	265.0	1,561.1	281.8	1,161.0	118.3
New Hampshire.	197.6	1.3	43.6	32.0	120.7	1,512.9	222.0	1,225.7	65.3
Rhode Island.	238.9	2.7	41.8	51.1	143.2	1,898.7	358.6	1,389.0	151.1
Vermont.	158.3	2.2	28.5	17.0	110.6	1,697.4	336.7	1,315.6	45.1
Middle Atlantic.	329.5	4.0	29.3	105.2	191.0	1,606.1	242.6	1,270.0	93.5
New Jersey	245.0	4.2	16.2	100.4	124.2	1,544.6	282.7	1,135.2	126.6
New York.	376.2	3.2	31.7	113.0	228.3	1,545.6	201.7	1,271.0	72.9
Pennsylvania.	316.4	5.2	34.7	96.4	180.1	1,742.7	277.8	1,362.8	102.1
Midwest	378.4	5.7	46.2	94.2	232.3	2,273.3	442.1	1,637.6	193.7
East North Central	386.7	6.4	47.3	105.9	227.2	2,213.1	444.8	1,587.7	180.6
Illinois	436.3	8.2	38.3	139.3	250.5	2,049.0	374.9	1,518.6	155.5
Indiana	404.7	6.6	37.7	110.5	249.9	2,589.4	514.0	1,853.3	222.1
Michigan	459.0	6.0	71.8	71.7	309.5	1,909.9	398.5	1,308.1	203.2
Ohio	300.3	5.6	48.1	107.8	138.7	2,577.5	575.9	1,832.3	169.3
Wisconsin	305.9	4.0	34.2	81.4	186.3	1,933.3	336.1	1,424.8	172.3
West North Central	360.1	4.3	43.9	68.5	243.3	2,406.2	436.1	1,747.6	222.5
Iowa	290.6	2.3	39.8	36.6	212.0	2,086.0	479.5	1,447.6	159.0
Kansas	380.4	3.8	45.1	57.5	274.0	2,695.5	494.1	1,962.9	238.6
Minnesota	242.6	1.8	42.5	67.5	130.7	2,133.3	337.1	1,638.1	158.1
Missouri.	519.4	8.8	41.9	107.8	360.8	2,799.1	520.4	1,978.4	300.3
Nebraska.	291.0	2.6	52.1	49.6	186.7	2,263.3	337.9	1,677.6	247.8
North Dakota.	251.1	2.0	45.1	23.9	180.1	2,295.9	427.9	1,608.9	259.1
South Dakota	418.4	3.1	58.8	31.4	325.0	1,980.6	346.6	1,460.4	173.6
South[5]	430.8	6.5	40.3	105.3	278.7	2,733.7	560.0	1,955.0	218.7
South Atlantic[5]	404.7	6.4	34.9	103.9	259.5	2,648.0	516.4	1,931.6	199.9
Delaware.	508.8	5.9	32.4	142.7	327.8	2,766.0	527.6	2,078.7	159.7
District of Columbia[5]	1,205.9	20.4	78.1	510.9	596.5	4,802.9	346.6	4,019.8	436.5
Florida.	430.3	5.4	36.9	97.9	290.2	2,686.8	486.7	1,990.8	209.3
Georgia	397.6	6.6	34.0	118.4	238.5	3,004.5	614.4	2,130.1	259.9
Maryland.	472.0	8.0	29.2	171.0	263.8	2,284.5	410.4	1,677.4	196.7
North Carolina.	372.2	6.7	28.1	92.0	245.5	2,737.5	710.4	1,876.2	150.8
South Carolina	501.8	7.4	48.1	81.3	365.0	3,243.8	664.7	2,298.5	280.6
Virginia	217.6	5.8	32.5	57.1	122.2	1,859.4	238.0	1,505.1	116.4
West Virginia	358.1	4.4	35.9	39.3	278.5	2,047.2	507.9	1,402.3	137.0
East South Central	457.6	7.3	39.9	96.4	314.0	2,709.0	626.0	1,866.2	216.7
Alabama.	532.3	8.4	39.4	96.4	388.2	2,947.8	700.5	2,006.3	241.1
Kentucky.	232.3	5.9	37.0	75.9	113.5	2,189.7	469.6	1,497.4	222.8
Mississippi.	280.5	8.0	42.7	80.2	149.6	2,768.1	781.4	1,842.1	144.7
Tennessee.	632.9	7.3	40.8	117.5	467.3	2,854.1	606.1	2,020.7	227.3
West South Central	460.4	6.3	49.1	112.0	293.0	2,884.3	598.8	2,035.3	250.2
Arkansas.	550.9	7.2	71.7	70.9	401.0	3,268.6	795.5	2,233.6	239.4
Louisiana.	566.1	11.8	38.8	119.1	396.4	3,297.7	740.5	2,336.3	220.8
Oklahoma	449.8	6.2	52.0	80.6	311.0	2,982.9	741.7	1,931.4	309.8
Texas.	434.4	5.3	48.0	119.6	261.6	2,759.8	533.8	1,978.1	247.8
West	418.4	4.5	43.4	112.6	257.8	2,766.6	504.9	1,858.7	403.0
Mountain	430.4	4.7	55.0	91.1	279.5	2,830.1	514.1	1,989.2	326.8
Arizona	470.1	5.5	47.5	101.8	315.4	2,978.4	544.4	2,168.1	265.8
Colorado	342.6	3.7	64.2	63.7	211.1	2,740.7	431.4	1,955.3	354.0
Idaho.	230.3	2.9	42.7	12.7	172.0	1,744.2	375.4	1,245.4	123.4
Montana	368.3	3.5	55.4	25.5	283.9	2,683.5	377.4	2,043.0	263.1
Nevada	678.1	7.6	58.9	215.6	395.9	2,586.6	641.1	1,497.1	448.3
New Mexico.	702.5	6.7	73.3	131.5	491.0	3,937.1	830.4	2,542.4	564.3
Utah	242.8	2.4	49.8	50.5	140.1	2,951.5	420.7	2,223.2	307.7
Wyoming	244.2	3.4	35.0	10.1	195.7	1,957.3	302.5	1,518.2	136.6
Pacific	412.9	4.4	38.2	122.3	248.0	2,738.0	500.8	1,799.8	437.4
Alaska	804.2	7.0	141.9	114.6	540.6	3,353.0	546.3	2,394.7	412.1
California.	445.3	4.9	34.9	139.6	265.9	2,553.0	479.8	1,623.0	450.3
Hawaii	309.2	2.5	43.3	69.6	193.8	2,992.7	421.2	2,175.8	395.8
Oregon	264.6	2.8	42.0	55.6	164.1	2,964.4	412.0	2,230.0	322.3
Washington	302.2	2.7	42.2	77.5	179.7	3,494.1	674.8	2,376.3	443.0
Puerto Rico	224.0	19.9	5.0	93.8	105.4	1,031.9	241.9	679.0	111.0

Note: Offense totals are based on all agencies in the Uniform Crime Reporting (UCR) Program and include estimates for agencies that submitted less than 12 months of data. Only the most serious offense in a multiple-offense incident is used in calculating crime rates. (1) Excludes arson because of insufficient data to make estimates. (2) Figures were estimated using the FBI's definition of rape (revised in 2013): "penetration, no matter how slight, of the vagina or anus with any body part or object, or oral penetration by a sex organ of another person, without the consent of the victim." The legacy definition of rape (dating to 1929) was "carnal knowledge of a female forcibly and against her will." (3) Attack or attempted attack upon another with the intent of doing serious bodily harm; usually accompanied by the use of a weapon or other means likely to produce death or great bodily harm. (4) The unlawful taking of another's property not involving force or fraud (e.g., theft of motor vehicle parts, shoplifting). Excludes crimes such as embezzlement and check fraud. (5) Includes offenses reported by Metro Transit Police and DC Fire and Emergency Medical Services Arson Investigation Unit.

Crime Rates in the Largest U.S. Metropolitan Areas, 2016

Source: *Crime in the United States, 2016*, Federal Bureau of Investigation (FBI), U.S. Dept. of Justice
(per 100,000 population, based on U.S. Census Bureau estimates for July 1)

Data includes metropolitan statistical areas (MSAs) with sufficient law enforcement agency participation and 12 months of data from the principal city/cities. (MSAs not meeting the FBI's reporting threshold in 2016 included Charlotte-Concord-Gastonia, NC-SC, and Kansas City, MO-KS.)

Monroe, LA, was the MSA with the highest rate of violent crime in 2016, with 1,186.9 per 100,000 residents. Guayama, PR, had the highest rate of murder and nonnegligent manslaughter (24.4). Among MSAs with populations over 2 mil, Cincinnati, OH, had the lowest violent crime rate (257.3), while Portland-Vancouver-Hillsboro, OR-WA, had the lowest murder rate (1.7).

Metropolitan statistical area (MSA)	MSA pop. (mil)	Violent crime					Property crimes[3]
		Total	Murder[1]	Rape[2]	Robbery	Aggravated assault	
Atlanta-Sandy Springs-Roswell, GA	5.8	403.2	6.8	24.0	144.1	228.2	2,998.3
Austin-Round Rock, TX	2.1	316.9	3.4	57.4	68.7	187.4	2,555.2
Baltimore-Columbia-Towson, MD	2.8	710.3	14.1	32.5	276.7	386.9	2,790.4
Boston-Cambridge-Newton, MA-NH	4.8	NA	1.9	26.9	71.8	NA	1,399.4
Chicago-Naperville-Elgin, IL-IN-WI	9.5	443.0	10.2	33.2	166.8	232.8	2,081.6
Cincinnati, OH-KY-IN	2.2	257.3	4.7	41.1	102.3	109.2	2,616.6
Cleveland-Elyria, OH	2.1	445.5	9.2	43.8	195.1	197.4	2,383.8
Columbus, OH	2.0	284.9	5.2	59.7	125.1	94.9	2,911.2
Dallas-Fort Worth-Arlington, TX	7.2	359.7	5.1	43.8	124.2	186.6	2,476.2
Denver-Aurora-Lakewood, CO	2.9	389.0	4.3	67.0	86.2	231.5	2,954.0
Detroit-Warren-Dearborn, MI	4.3	555.6	9.0	49.8	108.2	388.6	2,085.1
Houston-The Woodlands-Sugar Land, TX	6.8	578.2	7.2	39.9	215.5	315.6	2,923.8
Indianapolis-Carmel-Anderson, IN	2.0	713.4	9.2	46.8	218.9	438.5	3,206.9
Las Vegas-Henderson-Paradise, NV	2.2	771.0	9.0	65.9	268.1	428.0	2,727.9
Los Angeles-Long Beach-Anaheim, CA	13.4	476.7	5.1	37.2	166.9	267.5	2,386.2
Miami-Fort Lauderdale-West Palm Beach, FL	6.1	486.1	5.8	30.5	152.1	297.7	3,214.6
Minneapolis-St. Paul-Bloomington, MN-WI	3.6	287.7	2.2	43.1	94.9	147.5	2,315.6
New York-Newark-Jersey City, NY-NJ-PA	20.2	354.9	3.3	19.6	121.2	210.9	1,356.7
Orlando-Kissimmee-Sanford, FL[4]	2.4	504.3	8.1	50.1	99.3	346.8	2,963.5
Philadelphia-Camden-Wilmington, PA-NJ-DE-MD	6.1	446.5	7.9	33.7	162.8	242.1	2,172.1
Phoenix-Mesa-Scottsdale, AZ	4.7	426.9	5.5	46.1	112.7	262.6	2,870.1
Pittsburgh, PA	2.3	289.0	5.1	22.9	82.9	178.1	1,746.5
Portland-Vancouver-Hillsboro, OR-WA	2.4	276.1	1.7	49.2	68.4	156.8	2,794.2
Riverside-San Bernardino-Ontario, CA	4.5	397.3	5.1	26.7	115.0	250.6	2,667.3
Sacramento—Roseville—Arden-Arcade, CA	2.3	411.0	4.2	26.1	120.1	260.7	2,391.0
St. Louis, MO-IL	2.8	NA	11.1	38.1	122.5	NA	2,490.2
San Antonio-New Braunfels, TX	2.4	526.4	7.7	65.8	104.9	348.0	4,081.9
San Diego-Carlsbad, CA	3.3	330.4	3.0	32.8	83.7	210.8	1,850.1
San Francisco-Oakland-Hayward, CA	4.7	477.7	5.1	33.9	223.2	215.5	3,348.1
San Jose-Sunnyvale-Santa Clara, CA	2.0	280.1	2.9	33.0	82.6	161.6	2,176.5
Seattle-Tacoma-Bellevue, WA	3.8	353.2	2.7	39.5	109.2	201.7	3,890.0
Tampa-St. Petersburg-Clearwater, FL	3.0	340.8	3.9	32.7	75.6	228.7	2,333.9
Washington-Arlington-Alexandria, DC-VA-MD-WV	6.2	301.3	4.5	30.7	108.3	157.8	1,842.9

NA = Not available because FBI determined agency data were overreported. (1) Data in category includes nonnegligent manslaughter. (2) Data submitted using both the revised and legacy definitions of rape. (3) Includes burglary, larceny-theft, and motor vehicle theft but not arson because of insufficient data to make estimates. (4) Murder offenses include victims of Pulse nightclub mass shooting.

Criminal Victimization, 1993-2016

Source: National Crime Victimization Survey, Bureau of Justice Statistics (BJS), U.S. Dept. of Justice

A crime committed against an individual or single household counts as one **victimization**. Because more than one person may be victimized during a criminal incident, the number of victimizations may be greater than the number of personal crime incidents. **Victimization rates** measure the frequency with which victimizations occurred.

Crime type	1993	1997	2001	2005	2009	2012	2015	2016
	Number of victimizations							
VIOLENT VICTIMIZATION	16,822,618	13,425,406	7,476,599	6,947,795	5,669,237	6,842,593	5,006,615	5,749,330
Serious violent victimization	6,131,961	4,637,783	2,527,981	2,258,400	1,969,921	2,084,691	1,827,171	1,908,473
Rape/sexual assault	898,239	553,523	476,578	207,760	305,574	346,830	431,837	323,449
Robbery	1,752,667	1,188,879	667,736	769,148	635,073	741,756	578,578	500,682
Aggravated assault	3,481,055	2,895,381	1,383,667	1,281,491	1,029,273	996,106	816,757	1,084,342
Simple assault	10,690,657	8,787,623	4,948,619	4,689,395	3,699,316	4,757,902	3,179,444	3,840,857
Personal theft/larceny	481,384	369,860	188,368	229,459	133,210	153,583	88,857	111,110
PROPERTY VICTIMIZATION	35,093,887	27,771,423	19,473,197	18,673,357	16,222,976	19,622,977	14,611,043	15,917,429
Household burglary	6,378,721	5,036,240	3,404,382	3,584,847	3,411,298	3,764,539	2,904,554	3,291,490
Motor vehicle theft	1,921,179	1,460,748	1,034,419	1,003,150	735,765	633,742	564,158	585,500
Theft	26,793,987	21,274,435	15,034,396	14,085,360	12,075,913	15,224,695	11,142,310	12,040,438
	Rates of victimization per 1,000 persons age 12 or older							
VIOLENT VICTIMIZATION	79.8	61.1	32.6	28.4	22.3	26.1	18.6	21.1
Serious violent victimization	29.1	21.1	11.0	9.2	7.8	8.0	6.8	7.0
Rape/sexual assault	4.3	2.5	2.1	0.8	1.2	1.3	1.6	1.2
Robbery	8.3	5.4	2.9	3.1	2.5	2.8	2.1	1.8
Aggravated assault	16.5	13.2	6.0	5.2	4.1	3.8	3.0	4.0
Simple assault	50.7	40.0	21.6	19.2	14.6	18.2	11.8	14.1
Personal theft/larceny	2.3	1.7	0.8	0.9	0.5	0.6	0.3	0.4
	Rates of victimization per 1,000 households							
PROPERTY VICTIMIZATION	351.8	267.1	177.7	159.5	132.6	155.8	110.7	119.4
Household burglary	63.9	48.4	31.1	30.6	27.9	29.9	22.0	24.7
Motor vehicle theft	19.3	14.0	9.4	8.6	6.0	5.0	4.3	4.4
Theft	268.6	204.6	137.2	120.3	98.7	120.9	84.4	90.3

Note: Details may not sum to totals due to rounding and/or missing data. Because of methodological changes in the survey, use caution when comparing 2016 ests. to those for other years. Among counties that remained in the survey sample, there was no statistically significant change in the violent and property crime rates from 2015 to 2016.

Prison Population by State, 2000-16

Source: National Prisoner Statistics Program, Bureau of Justice Statistics (BJS), U.S. Dept. of Justice

As of Dec. 31, 2016, 1,506,757 prisoners were under the jurisdiction, or legal authority, of state (87.4%) or federal (12.6%) correctional authorities, the smallest U.S. prison population since 2004. Despite the decline, some states saw an increase from 2015 to 2016, led by South Dakota (7.5%), Kentucky (6.1%), and Maine (5.5%). Jails, which are locally operated, typically hold persons awaiting trial or sentencing as well as those sentenced to one year or less.

Jurisdiction	2000	2015	2016	% change, 2015-16	Jurisdiction	2000	2015	2016	% change, 2015-16
U.S. total[1]	1,394,231	1,526,603	1,506,757	−1.3%	Mississippi	20,241	18,911	19,192	1.5%
Federal[2,3]	145,416	196,455	189,192	−3.7	Missouri	27,543	32,330	32,461	0.4
State[1]	1,248,815	1,330,148	1,317,565	−0.9	Montana	3,105	3,685	3,814	3.5
Alabama	26,406	30,810	28,883	−6.3	Nebraska	3,895	5,372	5,302	−1.3
Alaska[4]	4,173	5,338	4,434	−16.9	Nevada	10,063	13,071	13,757	—
Arizona	26,510	42,719	42,320	−0.9	New Hampshire	2,257	2,897	2,818	−2.7
Arkansas	11,915	17,707	17,537	−1.0	New Jersey	29,784	20,489	19,786	−3.4
California	163,001	129,593	130,390	0.6	New Mexico	5,342	7,104	7,055	−0.7
Colorado	16,833	20,041	19,981	−0.3	New York	70,199	51,727	50,716	−2.0
Connecticut[4]	18,355	15,816	14,957	−5.4	North Carolina	31,266	36,617	35,697	−2.5
Delaware[4]	6,921	6,654	6,585	−1.0	North Dakota	1,076	1,795	1,791	−0.2
Dist. of Columbia[3]	10,352	—	—	—	Ohio	45,833	52,233	52,175	−0.1
Florida	71,319	101,424	99,974	−1.4	Oklahoma	23,181	28,547	28,231	−1.1
Georgia	44,232	52,193	53,627	2.7	Oregon	10,580	15,245	15,166	—
Hawaii[4]	5,053	5,879	5,602	−4.7	Pennsylvania	36,847	49,858	49,244	−1.2
Idaho	5,535	8,052	8,252	2.5	Rhode Island[4]	3,286	3,248	3,103	−4.5
Illinois[5]	45,281	46,240	43,657	—	South Carolina	21,778	20,929	20,858	−0.3
Indiana	20,125	27,355	25,546	−6.6	South Dakota	2,616	3,564	3,831	7.5
Iowa	7,955	8,849	9,031	2.1	Tennessee	22,166	28,172	28,203	0.1
Kansas	8,344	9,857	9,920	0.6	Texas	166,719	163,909	163,703	−0.1
Kentucky	14,919	21,701	23,022	6.1	Utah	5,637	6,495	6,182	−4.8
Louisiana	35,207	36,377	35,682	−1.9	Vermont[4]	1,697	1,750	1,735	−0.9
Maine	1,679	2,279	2,404	5.5	Virginia	30,168	38,403	37,813	−1.5
Maryland	23,538	20,764	19,994	−3.7	Washington	14,915	18,284	19,104	4.5
Massachusetts	10,722	9,922	9,403	−5.2	West Virginia	3,856	7,118	7,162	0.6
Michigan	47,718	42,628	41,122	−3.5	Wisconsin	20,754	22,975	23,377	1.7
Minnesota	6,238	10,798	10,592	−1.9	Wyoming	1,680	2,424	2,374	−2.1

— = Not calculated or not applicable. (1) Includes BJS-imputed counts for states that did not submit prisoner data: Nevada (2015), North Dakota (2016), Oregon (2015, 2016). (2) Includes prisoners held in nonsecure privately operated community corrections facilities and juveniles held in contract facilities. (3) DC has not operated a prison system since year-end 2001. 2000 figure includes jail and prison population. Felons sentenced under DC's criminal code are currently housed in federal facilities. (4) Prisons and jails form one integrated system. Data include total jail and prison populations. (5) State changed reporting methodology in 2016; counts from earlier years are not directly comparable.

Death Penalty by State, 1930-2017

Source: *Capital Punishment, 2016*, National Prisoner Statistics Program, Bureau of Justice Statistics (BJS), U.S. Dept. of Justice

In 2017, eight states executed 23 inmates according to an advance count by the BJS. In 2016, there were 20 executions, the lowest number executed in a year since 1991. The death row population has decreased every year since 2000, but the demographic composition has changed little: as of year-end 2016, the most recent year for which data are available, 98.2% of prisoners under sentence of death were male, 55.4% were white, and 42.3% were black.

At year-end 2017, 31 states and the federal government authorized the death penalty. Of the 19 states without the death penalty, Alaska, Hawaii, Maine, Michigan, Minnesota, North Dakota, Rhode Island, and Wisconsin are not shown here; they did not execute anyone after 1930. Several states have changed their laws more recently. Capital punishment was abolished in Maryland (for offenses committed after May 2, 2013), Connecticut (for crimes after Apr. 25, 2012), Illinois (on July 1, 2011), and New Mexico (for crimes after July 1, 2009). Delaware's Supreme Court ruled in Aug. 2016 that the state's death penalty law was unconstitutional; those on death row subsequently had their sentences commuted to life in prison. The Nebraska legislature outlawed capital punishment in 2015, but Nebraska voters, in a 2016 referendum, overturned the ban.

All death penalty states authorized lethal injection as their primary method of execution in 2017. Some states also permitted execution by electrocution, lethal gas, hanging, firing squad, and nitrogen hypoxia.

Jurisdiction	Prisoners under sentence of death, year-end 2016[1]	Executions[2,3] 2017	Executions[2,3] 1930-2017	Executions[2,3] 1977-2017	Jurisdiction	Prisoners under sentence of death, year-end 2016[1]	Executions[2,3] 2017	Executions[2,3] 1930-2017	Executions[2,3] 1977-2017
U.S. total	2,814	23	5,324	1,465	Missouri	25	1	150	88
Federal[1]	58	0	36	3	Montana	2	0	9	3
State	2,756	23	5,288	1,462	Nebraska	10	0	7	3
Alabama	183	3	196	61	Nevada	83	0	41	12
Arizona	118	0	75	37	New Hampshire	1	0	1	0
Arkansas	35	4	149	31	New Jersey	—	—	74	0
California	742	0	305	13	New Mexico[4]	2	0	9	1
Colorado	3	0	48	1	New York	0	—	329	0
Connecticut[3]	0	—	22	1	North Carolina	150	0	306	43
Delaware	13	—	28	16	Ohio	140	2	227	55
Dist. of Columbia	—	—	40	0	Oklahoma	46	0	172	112
Florida	382	3	265	93	Oregon	33	0	21	2
Georgia	58	1	436	70	Pennsylvania	174	0	155	3
Idaho	9	0	6	3	South Carolina	37	0	205	43
Illinois	—	—	102	12	South Dakota	3	0	4	3
Indiana	13	0	61	20	Tennessee	63	0	99	6
Iowa	—	—	18	0	Texas	244	7	842	545
Kansas	10	0	15	0	Utah	9	0	20	7
Kentucky	32	0	106	3	Vermont	—	—	4	0
Louisiana	73	0	161	28	Virginia	7	2	205	113
Maryland	—	—	73	5	Washington	9	0	52	5
Massachusetts	—	—	27	0	West Virginia	—	—	40	0
Mississippi	47	0	175	21	Wyoming	0	0	8	1

— = Not available or applicable. **Note:** 2017 data are preliminary. (1) Excludes persons held under Armed Forces jurisdiction with a military death sentence for murder. (2) Does not include 160 executions carried out by military authorities between 1930 and 1961. (3) CT Supreme Court ruling extended repeal of capital statute to prisoners under sentence of death, who will be resentenced to life in prison without possibility of parole. (4) NM continued to hold prisoners on death row for crimes committed before state repealed capital punishment.

U.S. Prison Population, 1925-2016

Source: National Prisoner Statistics Program, Bureau of Justice Statistics (BJS), U.S. Dept. of Justice

As recently as 1970, the U.S. had fewer than 200,000 people behind bars nationwide, or less than 1 in 1,000 residents. That number rose steadily from the 1970s on, reaching an all-time high of more than 1.6 mil prisoners in 2009. The imprisonment rate has declined since its high of 506 prisoners per 100,000 residents in 2008.

Year	Prisoners	Imprison-ment rate	Year	Prisoners	Imprison-ment rate	Year	Prisoners	Imprison-ment rate
1925	91,669	79	1980	329,821	138	2011	1,598,968	492
1930	129,453	104	1990	773,919	295	2012	1,570,397	480
1940	173,706	131	1995	1,125,874	411	2013	1,576,950	477
1950	166,165	109	2000	1,394,231	470	2014	1,562,319	471
1960	212,953	117	2005	1,525,910	492	2015	1,526,603	459
1970	196,441	96	2010	1,613,803	500	2016	1,506,757	450

Note: Imprisonment rate is per 100,000 U.S. residents based on U.S. Census Bureau pop. ests. Since 1971, the rate is of prisoners sentenced to more than one year. Data for 1940-70 include all adult felons serving sentences in state and federal institutions. In 1977, the BJS began to include persons under state jurisdiction but not in a state's physical custody, such as persons in private prisons, local jails, and other facilities. Figures may not be directly comparable over time.

Prison Situation Under Correctional Authorities' Jurisdiction, 2016

Source: *Prisoners in 2016*, Bureau of Justice Statistics (BJS), U.S. Dept. of Justice

Largest prison populations		% increase in prison population, 2015-16		Imprisonment rate of sentenced prisoners		Prison population as % of maximum estimated capacity	
Jurisdiction	Number	Jurisdiction	% change[1]	Jurisdiction	Rate[2]	Jurisdiction	% max. capacity[3]
U.S. total	1,506,757	U.S. total	−1.30%	U.S. total	450	U.S. total	NA
Federal[4,5]	189,192	Federal[4,5]	−3.70	Federal[4]	53	Federal	114.0%
State	1,317,565	State	−0.95	State	397	State	NA
1. Texas	163,703	1. South Dakota	7.49	1. Louisiana	760	1. Illinois[7]	137.8
2. California	130,390	2. Kentucky	6.09	2. Oklahoma	708	2. Nebraska[7]	126.2
3. Florida	99,974	3. Maine	5.48	3. Mississippi	624	3. Iowa	115.0
4. Georgia	53,627	4. Washington	4.48	4. Arizona	585	4. Delaware[7]	113.8
5. Ohio	52,175	5. Montana	3.50	5. Arkansas	583	5. Colorado	109.2
6. New York	50,716	6. Georgia	2.75	6. Alabama	571	6. Virginia	108.5
7. Pennsylvania	49,244	7. Idaho	2.48	7. Texas	563	7. Idaho[8]	103.1
8. Illinois	43,657	8. Iowa	2.06	8. Missouri	532	8. Washington	102.8
9. Arizona	42,320	9. Wisconsin	1.75	9. Kentucky	518	9. North Dakota	101.9
10. Michigan	41,122	10. Mississippi	1.49	10. Georgia	512	10. Montana	101.7
11. Virginia	37,813	11. Kansas	0.64	11. Florida	481	11. Pennsylvania[8]	101.4
12. North Carolina	35,697	12. West Virginia	0.62	12. Nevada	460	12. Wisconsin	100.7
13. Louisiana	35,682	13. California	0.62	13. Ohio	449	13. Missouri[7]	100.6
14. Missouri	32,461	14. Missouri	0.41	14. Virginia	448	14. Minnesota	100.1
15. Alabama	28,883	15. Tennessee	0.11	15. South Dakota	440	15. Hawaii	100.0
16. Oklahoma	28,231	16. Ohio	−0.11	16. Idaho	435	16. Kansas	100.0
17. Tennessee	28,203	17. Texas	−0.13	17. Delaware[6]	428	17. South Dakota[7,8]	99.3
18. Indiana	25,546	18. North Dakota	−0.22	18. Tennessee	422	18. Kentucky	99.3
19. Wisconsin	23,377	19. Colorado	−0.30	19. Michigan	414	19. Louisiana[9]	99.0
20. Kentucky	23,022	20. South Carolina	−0.34	20. South Carolina	408	20. Nevada	98.7

NA = Not applicable. **Note:** Jurisdiction refers to the legal authority of state or federal correctional officials over a prisoner, regardless of where the prisoner is held. Nevada (2015), North Dakota (2016), and Oregon (2015, 2016) did not submit prisoner data for one or both years. BJS imputed counts are included in state and U.S. totals. (1) Rankings do not include Illinois, which changed reporting methodology; Nevada; or Oregon. (2) Prisoners sentenced to more than one year per 100,000 U.S. residents based on U.S. Census Bureau pop. estimates. (3) Based on custody population. Does not include inmates held in local jails, other states, or private facilities unless otherwise noted. Rankings do not include Connecticut or Ohio, which did not report capacity data. (4) Includes prisoners held in nonsecure privately operated community corrections facilities and juveniles held in contract facilities. (5) Includes felons sentenced under DC's criminal code and housed in federal facilities. (6) Prisons and jails form one integrated system. Data include total jail and prison populations. (7) State defines capacity differently than BJS. (8) Includes prisoners in private facilities. (9) Includes prisoners in local facilities.

Imprisonment Rate by Gender, Race, Hispanic Origin, and Age, 2016

Source: *Prisoners in 2016*, Bureau of Justice Statistics (BJS), U.S. Dept. of Justice

(number of prisoners with a sentence of more than one year, under the jurisdiction of state or federal correctional officials, per 100,000 U.S. residents in each group)

Age	All prisoners	Male					Female				
		Total	White	Black	Hispanic	Other[1]	Total	White	Black	Hispanic	Other[1]
Total[2]	450	848	401	2,417	1,093	1,307	64	49	97	67	118
18-19	130	244	72	853	298	338	11	8	25	11	21
20-24	653	1,191	453	3,371	1,417	1,831	85	61	141	85	168
25-29	998	1,801	803	4,725	2,249	2,485	167	136	216	170	271
30-34	1,091	1,981	960	5,334	2,450	3,006	186	155	232	193	312
35-39	1,053	1,944	934	5,435	2,359	2,791	164	136	214	161	263
40-44	886	1,655	820	4,645	1,975	2,430	129	108	181	114	213
45-49	710	1,333	688	3,781	1,611	2,106	100	79	158	90	150
50-54	575	1,093	572	3,087	1,359	1,756	75	56	124	69	133
55-59	377	733	376	2,142	1,016	1,208	40	28	72	41	79
60-64	220	439	229	1,246	739	683	19	13	33	22	35
65 or older	76	165	97	430	319	321	5	4	8	8	9

Note: Rates are based on U.S. Census Bureau population estimates. Includes imputed counts for states that did not submit prisoner data. Hispanics may be of any race, but white, black, and "other" rates shown exclude persons of Hispanic or Latino origin. (1) Includes American Indians and Alaska Natives; Asians, Native Hawaiians, and other Pacific Islanders; and persons of two or more races. (2) Includes persons under age 18.

Prisoners and Incarceration Rates by Country, 2005-15

Source: UN Survey on Crime Trends and Operations of Criminal Justice Systems, United Nations (UN) Office on Drugs and Crime

The U.S. prison population is the largest of any nation, and its incarceration rate is the world's highest. The following table ranks the countries with the most persons aged 18 or over incarcerated per 100,000 resident adults in 2015. Non-criminals held for administrative purposes, e.g., persons held pending immigration status investigation, not included.

Country	Total number of prisoners					Incarceration rate				
	2005	2008	2011	2014	2015	2005	2008	2011	2014	2015
United States	2,179,600	2,289,500	2,244,800	2,219,900	2,168,600	978.45	994.18	942.09	901.49	872.31
El Salvador	12,525	19,814	25,367	28,334	32,645	352.40	536.27	658.60	703.02	798.63
Trinidad and Tobago	3,566	3,304	4,074	3,228	7,299	379.27	338.22	406.25	316.04	711.38
Grenada	—	—	439	513	502	—	—	626.11	710.71	689.73
Panama*	11,571	9,651	13,207	14,876	17,811	543.23	422.69	542.18	572.61	671.05
Russia	804,489	876,015	751,209	668,425	643,024	701.04	751.89	641.51	574.88	555.42
Thailand	162,293	—	—	244,513	257,107	337.38	—	—	462.24	482.34
Barbados	—	1,046	1,060	864	954	—	498.57	495.62	397.76	437.44
Brazil*	—	451,219	514,582	—	622,202	—	337.80	366.23	—	416.43
Guyana	1,439	2,083	2,019	—	1,998	334.17	474.38	443.12	—	409.75
Costa Rica	8,271	8,225	12,154	13,620	13,168	291.59	270.06	374.56	396.10	376.20
Peru	33,010	43,286	—	71,961	77,242	192.59	237.07	—	349.65	368.53
Kazakhstan	43,572	47,836	49,153	43,095	42,019	407.96	428.30	420.50	354.33	342.48
Chile	38,586	53,539	59,261	47,683	46,235	339.16	444.92	466.93	357.48	341.21
Honduras	—	—	12,006	14,882	16,158	—	—	271.77	308.27	325.35
Turkey	55,293	100,489	126,270	156,728	175,695	123.90	212.79	252.03	293.55	322.81
Lithuania	7,958	7,800	9,790	8,552	7,270	303.13	302.35	391.64	356.42	306.66
Paraguay	6,281	5,824	7,161	10,847	12,896	186.87	161.28	185.57	262.33	305.07
Mongolia	6,948	7,958	7,929	7,619	5,455	433.65	456.98	426.67	388.51	274.03
Singapore*	14,453	11,807	12,405	12,349	12,196	418.89	313.50	302.84	279.35	269.66
Latvia	7,342	6,349	6,493	4,707	4,367	408.53	361.45	380.71	285.00	267.64
Albania*	2,576	4,832	4,538	5,602	5,892	124.33	230.48	213.95	256.26	266.64
New Zealand	7,324	7,765	8,370	8,571	9,075	239.52	242.96	252.78	252.09	264.50
Mexico*	205,621	219,754	230,943	223,656	217,595	304.27	302.95	295.79	269.41	256.68
Estonia*	3,349	3,414	3,371	3,001	2,644	307.38	313.17	310.87	279.08	247.18

— = Not available. * = Country's data may not be comparable over time because of changes in definitions and/or counting rules. **Note:** Data not available for all nations in all years. Use caution when making comparisons because of differences in each country's legal definitions and in methods of offense counting and reporting.

Law Enforcement Officers and Civilian Employees, 2016

Source: *Crime in the United States, 2016* and *Law Enforcement Officers Killed and Assaulted, 2016*; Federal Bureau of Investigation (FBI); U.S. Dept. of Justice

As of Oct. 31, 2016, 13,217 city, county, state, college and university, and tribal agencies around the country collectively employed 933,142 full-time law enforcement workers. About 70% of these employees were sworn officers. The FBI defines a sworn law enforcement officer as a person who ordinarily carries a firearm and badge, has full arrest powers, and is paid from government funds specifically dedicated to sworn law enforcement personnel. Civilians (e.g., clerks, radio dispatchers, correctional officers) made up the remainder.

Altogether, they provided service to an estimated 277.6 mil people around the country, meaning there were 3.4 full-time law enforcement employees and 2.4 sworn officers per 1,000 residents.

The great majority of sworn officers (87.9%) were men, while women made up 60.0% of civilian employees. The most

populous state, California, employed the greatest number of full-time law enforcement workers (119,190). Washington, DC, had the highest rate, with 7.1 full-time law enforcement employees per 1,000 residents, followed by New Jersey (4.7) and Louisiana (4.6).

Nationwide, 66 law enforcement officers were killed feloniously (that is, willfully and intentionally by the offender) in the line of duty in 2016, compared to 41 officers in 2015 and a 10-year high of 72 in 2011. Of the 66 officers, 17 were killed in ambush situations and 13 in responding to disturbance calls; 62 were killed by firearms. On average, the officers were 40 years of age and had served in law enforcement for 13 years when killed. An additional 52 officers were killed accidentally in 2016 while performing their duties, the majority (26) in auto accidents; 57,180 officers were assaulted in the line of duty.

Sentenced State Prisoners by Offense and Selected Characteristics, 2015

Source: *Prisoners in 2016*, Bureau of Justice Statistics (BJS), U.S. Dept. of Justice

	All prisoners[1]	Male	Female	White[2]	Black[2]	Hispanic
Total number of sentenced inmates	1,298,159	1,204,799	93,360	403,600	429,000	278,600
	Percent of total in category by most serious offense					
Violent	54.5%	55.9%	37.0%	47.1%	58.8%	60.2%
Murder and nonnegligent manslaughter	13.7	13.8	11.6	10.2	15.6	15.3
Manslaughter	1.3	1.3	2.4	1.4	0.8	1.0
Rape or sexual assault	12.5	13.3	2.4	16.0	8.2	13.6
Robbery	13.2	13.6	8.1	7.5	19.3	12.9
Aggravated or simple assault	10.5	10.6	8.6	8.9	11.6	13.3
Other	3.4	3.3	3.9	3.1	3.4	4.1
Property	18.0	17.3	26.9	24.0	15.2	12.8
Burglary	9.7	9.9	7.3	11.6	9.2	7.6
Larceny-theft	3.7	3.3	8.8	5.2	2.8	2.2
Motor vehicle theft	0.7	0.7	0.8	1.0	0.5	0.9
Fraud	1.9	1.5	7.1	3.1	1.4	1.0
Other	2.0	1.9	3.0	3.1	1.2	1.1
Drug[3]	15.2	14.4	24.9	15.1	14.4	13.9
Public order[4]	11.6	11.7	10.2	12.9	11.2	12.7
Other/unspecified[5]	0.7	0.7	1.0	0.9	0.4	0.4

Note: Counts based on prisoners with a sentence of more than one year under the jurisdiction, or legal authority, of state correctional officials. Details may not add up to totals due to rounding and missing offense data. Hispanics may be of any race. (1) Includes race categories not shown here. (2) Excludes persons of Hispanic or Latino origin and persons of two or more races. (3) Includes possession, trafficking, and other drug offenses. (4) Includes weapons, driving under the influence, and court offenses; commercialized vice, morals, and decency offenses; liquor law violations; and other public-order offenses. (5) Includes juvenile offenses and other unspecified offense categories.

Arrests by Race and Hispanic Origin, 2016

Source: *Crime in the United States, 2016*, Federal Bureau of Investigation (FBI), U.S. Dept. of Justice

Each instance in which a person is arrested, cited, or summoned for an offense is counted as one arrest. Arrest data therefore do not show the number of individuals arrested but the number of times persons were arrested, as an individual may be arrested multiple times in one year. Arrest estimates are based on statistics from law enforcement agencies that reported 12 months of arrest data.

Offense charged	Total[2]	White	Black/ African Amer.	Amer. Indian/ Alaska Native	Asian	Hawaiian/ other Pacific Isl.	Total[2]	Hispanic/ Latino
			Arrests by race[1]				Arrests by Hispanic origin	
Total arrests	8,421,481	69.6%	26.9%	2.0%	1.2%	0.3%	6,647,012	18.4%
Violent crime	408,873	59.0	37.5	1.8	1.4	0.3	331,656	23.8
Murder and nonnegligent manslaughter	9,374	44.7	52.6	1.2	1.2	0.3	6,882	20.0
Rape[3]	18,606	67.6	29.1	1.3	1.7	0.4	13,896	27.0
Robbery	76,267	43.4	54.5	0.9	0.9	0.4	60,116	21.1
Aggravated assault	304,626	62.8	33.3	2.1	1.5	0.3	250,762	24.4
Property crime	1,074,136	68.7	28.1	1.7	1.2	0.3	813,260	16.4
Burglary	164,641	68.4	29.1	1.0	1.2	0.3	130,179	20.8
Larceny-theft	833,558	69.0	27.7	1.8	1.2	0.2	624,800	14.6
Motor vehicle theft	68,170	66.0	30.7	1.5	1.3	0.5	52,786	26.8
Arson	7,767	72.0	23.3	2.8	1.5	0.3	5,495	16.6
Other assaults[4]	853,493	65.2	31.4	1.8	1.2	0.3	665,711	18.2
Forgery and counterfeiting	44,831	65.5	31.9	0.6	1.7	0.2	35,180	15.9
Fraud	101,301	67.0	30.5	1.2	1.1	0.1	79,089	11.5
Embezzlement	12,592	61.4	35.8	0.8	1.7	0.3	10,178	12.0
Stolen property; buying, receiving, possessing	74,492	64.2	33.4	1.2	1.1	0.2	56,243	19.7
Vandalism	154,958	68.4	28.1	2.2	1.1	0.3	121,519	18.5
Weapons; carrying, possessing, etc.	124,150	55.9	41.8	0.9	1.1	0.2	97,279	23.4
Prostitution and commercialized vice	30,322	55.5	37.9	0.4	6.0	0.2	25,718	19.9
Sex offenses (except rape and prostitution)	40,292	71.6	24.7	1.6	1.9	0.3	32,402	25.1
Drug abuse violations	1,242,630	71.0	26.7	1.0	1.1	0.2	991,426	20.3
Gambling	2,905	45.0	48.4	0.3	5.7	0.6	1,958	25.6
Offenses against the family and children	69,546	67.1	29.1	3.0	0.7	0.1	55,805	11.4
Driving under the influence	798,012	82.2	13.6	1.8	2.0	0.4	657,336	22.6
Liquor laws	183,514	79.2	14.5	4.6	1.5	0.2	134,376	14.5
Drunkenness	299,248	76.5	14.7	7.7	1.0	0.1	266,894	24.1
Disorderly conduct	291,951	63.3	32.2	3.5	0.8	0.2	207,010	12.9
Vagrancy	19,755	66.0	30.7	2.1	1.2	0.1	16,265	16.1
All other offenses (except traffic)	2,567,092	69.2	27.4	2.0	1.0	0.4	2,024,802	16.2
Suspicion	440	35.0	30.7	32.5	1.1	0.7	239	7.1
Curfew and loitering law violations	26,948	56.3	40.7	1.6	1.1	0.3	22,666	21.8

(1) Percentages may not add up to 100 because of rounding. (2) Not all agencies provide data by ethnicity so total arrests by race will not equal total arrests by Hispanic origin. Hispanic or Latino persons may be of any race. (3) Aggregate totals based on both the legacy and revised Uniform Crime Reporting definition of rape. (4) Simple assaults or attempted simple assaults, in which no weapons were used and the victim did not sustain serious injury (e.g., stalking).

Foreign Nationals Removed From the U.S. by Criminal Status and Nationality, 2007-16

Source: *Immigration Enforcement Actions: 2016*, Office of Immigration Statistics, U.S. Dept. of Homeland Security

(countries ranked by total foreign nationals removed in 2016)

Country of nationality	2007[1] Total removed	% criminal[2]	2009 Total removed	% criminal[2]	2011 Total removed	% criminal[2]	2013 Total removed	% criminal[2]	2015 Total removed	% criminal[2]	2016 Total removed	% criminal[2]
Total	319,382	32.1%	391,283	33.7%	385,778	49.0%	433,034	46.0%	326,962	42.7%	340,056	39.9%
Mexico	208,996	36.8	276,537	36.0	286,731	50.6	308,828	47.5	235,087	44.9	245,306	41.7
Guatemala	25,898	15.1	29,641	22.1	30,343	38.6	46,948	32.7	33,398	31.6	33,729	31.3
Honduras	29,737	17.6	27,283	25.6	22,027	49.1	36,591	45.4	20,334	42.2	21,891	39.0
El Salvador	20,045	24.7	20,884	30.4	17,379	48.9	20,921	45.2	21,610	33.1	20,127	33.2
Colombia	2,993	39.8	2,714	41.4	1,899	55.2	1,440	66.7	1,571	49.7	2,052	36.4
Dominican Rep.	2,990	68.4	3,576	61.7	2,892	74.1	2,297	78.8	1,897	81.0	1,949	75.0
Brazil	4,210	8.4	3,724	10.4	3,350	16.4	1,449	25.4	1,008	28.9	1,485	21.6
Ecuador	1,564	25.1	2,383	25.3	1,716	41.0	1,510	38.7	1,441	33.9	1,399	32.8
Jamaica	1,490	76.4	1,662	75.0	1,473	83.2	1,108	90.0	866	74.0	1,069	57.0
Nicaragua	2,307	22.0	2,172	28.5	1,502	46.3	1,346	51.6	922	47.9	872	44.3
All other countries	19,147	29.6	20,740	29.5	16,466	39.0	10,596	50.5	8,828	41.2	10,177	34.2

Note: Fiscal year (Oct. 1-Sept. 30) data. Numbers may not add up to totals because of removals of persons of unknown nationality. (1) Data includes criminals removed by Customs and Border Protection. (2) Persons who had a prior criminal conviction.

Gun Violence Incidents and Deaths, 2014-18

Source: Gun Violence Archive

The Gun Violence Archive is an independent data collection and research group with no affiliation with any advocacy organization. Since 2013, it has maintained an online archive of gun violence incidents, which it collects daily from more than 2,500 media, law enforcement, government, and commercial sources.

(data are number of actual deaths and injuries or number of incidents reported and verified as of Oct. 17, 2018)

	2014	2015	2016	2017	2018
Total gun violence incidents	44,827	53,759	58,953	61,854	45,806
Deaths	12,477	13,535	15,109	15,641	11,608
Injuries	22,888	27,051	30,636	31,251	22,682
Children killed or injured	610	695	671	732	535
Teens killed or injured	2,321	2,698	3,135	3,248	2,259
Mass shootings[1]	270	335	382	346	289

	2014	2015	2016	2017	2018
Home invasions	2,604	2,397	2,579	2,572	1,603
Defensive uses	1,560	1,381	1,993	2,111	1,438
Unintentional shootings	1,600	1,962	2,203	2,036	1,271
Officer-involved incidents					
Officer shot or killed	261	320	327	315	238
Subject-suspect shot or killed	1,751	1,916	1,907	2,081	1,712

Note: Children are age 11 or under; teens are age 12-17. Table does not include deaths from suicide. (1) Four or more people shot and/or killed in a single event, not including the shooter.

Hate Crimes by Offense Type and Bias Motivation, 2016
Source: *Hate Crime Statistics, 2016*, Federal Bureau of Investigation (FBI), U.S. Dept. of Justice

Hate crimes are defined as crimes motivated in whole or in part by the offender's bias against a characteristic such as race, ethnicity, or religion. The Hate Crime Statistics Act of 1990 led to the collection of hate crime data as part of the FBI's Uniform Crime Reporting (UCR) program. Not all agencies that participate in the UCR program submit hate crime data, so the data presented is not representative of the nation as a whole.

Bias motivation	Total offenses	Crimes against persons				Crimes against property					Crimes against society[3]
		Aggravated assault	Simple assault	Intimidation	Other[1]	Robbery	Burglary	Larceny-theft	Destruction/ damage/ vandalism	Other[2]	
Total	7,321	873	1,687	2,109	51	134	123	231	1,913	118	82
Single-bias incidents	7,227	866	1,677	2,074	49	131	122	227	1,882	117	82
Race/ethnicity/ancestry	4,229	548	1,002	1,320	22	71	75	149	916	73	53
Anti-white	876	120	241	188	12	30	22	78	122	32	31
Anti-black or African American	2,122	273	455	782	6	14	17	14	537	14	10
Anti-American Indian or Alaska Native	161	8	17	36	1	0	18	31	29	16	5
Anti-Asian, Native Hawaiian, or other Pac. Isl.	140	15	44	48	0	2	4	5	20	0	2
Anti-multiple races, group	178	17	36	49	0	4	5	0	62	5	0
Anti-Arab	56	8	16	17	0	1	0	0	13	1	0
Anti-Hispanic or Latino	449	91	129	140	2	19	2	5	57	0	4
Anti-other race/ethnicity/ancestry	247	16	64	60	1	1	7	16	76	5	1
Religion	1,538	85	168	433	2	10	29	47	720	28	16
Anti-Jewish	834	12	61	238	0	3	9	15	489	6	1
Anti-Catholic	63	1	5	6	0	0	3	10	31	3	4
Anti-Protestant	20	1	3	1	0	0	1	4	8	1	1
Anti-Islamic (Muslim)	381	52	75	144	0	4	2	3	92	5	4
Anti-other religion[4]	186	17	20	23	1	2	13	13	83	8	6
Anti-multiple religions, group	48	2	4	21	0	1	1	1	15	3	0
Anti-atheism/agnosticism/etc.	6	0	0	0	1	0	0	1	2	2	0
Sexual orientation	1,218	197	414	289	14	38	10	17	221	12	6
Anti-gay (male)	765	126	281	183	5	28	6	6	126	1	3
Anti-lesbian	141	23	46	37	4	0	2	3	23	3	0
Anti-LGBT (mixed group)	262	45	71	59	5	10	1	1	64	5	1
Anti-heterosexual	23	1	2	7	0	0	0	5	6	0	2
Anti-bisexual	27	2	14	3	0	0	1	2	2	3	0
Gender	36	6	11	7	1	0	3	0	7	1	0
Anti-male	10	0	7	1	1	0	1	0	0	0	0
Anti-female	26	6	4	6	0	0	2	0	7	1	0
Gender identity	130	25	49	16	6	11	2	6	12	1	2
Anti-transgender	111	24	47	14	6	11	1	2	5	1	0
Anti-gender non-conforming	19	1	2	2	0	0	1	4	7	0	2
Disability	76	5	33	9	4	1	3	8	6	2	5
Anti-physical	29	2	15	4	1	0	2	2	1	1	1
Anti-mental	47	3	18	5	3	1	1	6	5	1	4
Multiple-bias incidents[5]	94	7	10	35	2	3	1	4	31	1	0

(1) Includes murder, nonnegligent manslaughter, rape (revised and legacy definitions), and additional offenses not shown here in detail. (2) Includes arson, motor vehicle theft, and additional offenses not shown here in detail. (3) Includes drug or narcotic offenses, gambling and prostitution offenses, and weapon law violations where society as a whole is considered the victim. (4) Includes offenses against religions not shown. (5) Incidents in which one or more offense types are motivated by two or more biases.

Federal Sentence Length by Criminal Offense, 2017
Source: 2017 Sourcebook of Federal Sentencing Statistics, U.S. Sentencing Commission

Data based on court documentation for federal cases involving felonies and misdemeanors (excluding petty misdemeanors punishable by a maximum of 30 days of imprisonment) in which the offender was sentenced in fiscal year 2017 (Oct. 1, 2016-Sept. 30, 2017). Excludes cases where no imprisonment was ordered (e.g., probation sentences) or where data was missing or incomplete.

Primary offense[1]	Mean months	Median months	Number of cases	Primary offense[1]	Mean months	Median months	Number of cases
Total	45	21	66,871	Forgery/counterfeiting	18	13	371
Murder	224	180	72	Bribery	20	15	155
Manslaughter	68	56	62	Tax	13	10	433
Kidnapping/hostage taking	230	210	62	Money laundering	33	18	679
Sexual abuse	137	120	649	Racketeering/extortion	99	60	940
Assault	29	18	788	Gambling/lottery	4	0	47
Robbery	74	60	650	Civil rights	36	10	56
Arson	63	60	40	Immigration	12	8	20,420
Drugs—trafficking	70	55	19,043	Child pornography	147	97	1,810
Drugs—communication facility	28	24	263	Prison offenses	12	10	522
Drugs—simple possession	4	6	1,301	Admin. of justice offenses[2]	19	12	1,064
Firearms	71	48	8,064	Environmental/wildlife	3	0	109
Burglary/breaking and entering	19	15	33	National defense[3]	56	27	89
Auto theft	72	44	64	Antitrust	13	8	31
Larceny	10	1	808	Food and drug	6	0	86
Fraud	26	15	6,029	Other misc. offenses[4]	16	0	1,735
Embezzlement	7	3	396				

(1) Applicable offense with the highest statutory maximum. (2) For example, contempt, obstruction of justice, or perjury. (3) Includes evasion of export controls and exportation of arms without license. (4) Includes interference with flight crew aboard aircraft, criminal infringement of copyright/trademark, trespass, and destruction of property among other offenses not within any of the other categories.

American Deaths in Terrorist Attacks, 1995-2016

Source: Global Terrorism Database, National Consortium for the Study of Terrorism and Responses to Terrorism (START)

Year	Total attacks in U.S.	Total fatalities in U.S.	U.S. fatalities in U.S.	U.S. fatalities worldwide	Year	Total attacks in U.S.	Total fatalities in U.S.	U.S. fatalities in U.S.	U.S. fatalities worldwide
1995	60	170	170	188	2007	9	0	0	1
1996	35	2	2	36	2008	18	2	2	14
1997	40	2	1	14	2009	10	18	18	19
1998	30	4	3	135	2010	17	4	4	6
1999	53	20	20	25	2011	10	0	0	3
2000	32	0	0	36	2012	19	7	6	12
2001	41	3,005	2,908	2,910	2013	20	23	21	29
2002	33	4	0	30	2014	26	19	19	34
2003	32	0	0	17	2015	39	44	43	58
2004	9	0	0	5	2016	61	68	59	79
2005	20	0	0	3	**Total**	**620**	**3,393**	**3,277**	**3,658**
2006	6	1	1	4					

Note: Number of fatalities includes those of perpetrators. Fatalities worldwide do not include deaths in Afghanistan and Iraq.

Notable Terrorist Incidents Worldwide Since 1971

Source: U.S. Dept. of State; *Facts On File World News Digest*; World Almanac research

Selected noteworthy incidents, excluding most assassinations, kidnappings, and military targets. Does not include all incidents in Iraq or Afghanistan, 2001-present; see also Chronology of the Year's Events.

1971—Mar. 1: Senate wing of U.S. Capitol Building in Wash., DC, bombed by Weather Underground; no deaths.

1972—July 21: "Bloody Friday." Provisional IRA exploded 20+ bombs across Belfast, N. Ireland; 9 killed, hundreds injured. **Sept. 5:** Palestinian group Black September killed 2 Israeli athletes and seized 9 others at Olympic Village in Munich, W. Germany, during Summer Olympics; 9 hostages, 5 militants, 1 Ger. officer died in botched rescue.

1973—Dec. 17: Palestinian gunmen attacked Rome airport and bombed plane on tarmac; hijacked Lufthansa plane with 5 Italian hostages to Athens, Greece, then to Kuwait; 31 killed in all.

1974—June 17: Houses of Parliament in London, England, bombed by Provisional IRA; 11 injured.

1975—Jan. 27: Puerto Rican FALN nationalists bombed Fraunces Tavern in New York City; 4 killed, 53 injured. **Jan. 29:** U.S. State Dept. building in Wash., DC, bombed by Weather Underground; no deaths.

1976—June 27: Palestinian and Baader-Meinhof militants forced Air France jet to land in Entebbe, Uganda. Israeli army rescued 103 hostages from airport terminal in battle with terrorists and Ugandan troops, July 3-4; 32 killed in all.

1978—Mar. 11: Palestinian militants shot civilians and hijacked bus with hostages from Haifa to Tel Aviv, Israel. Bus exploded during firefight with police at a roadblock; 38 killed.

1979—Nov. 4: Iranian radicals seized U.S. embassy in Tehran, taking 66 Americans hostage. 52 were held until Jan. 20, 1981. **Nov. 20:** Around 200 Islamic fundamentalists opposed to the Saudi monarchy seized Grand Mosque in Mecca, Saudi Arabia, and held hundreds of pilgrims hostage. Saudi forces retook mosque Dec. 4; about 270 died.

1980—Feb. 27: Members of leftist guerrilla group April 19 Movement (M-19) seized Dominican Republic embassy in Bogota, Colombia; 80 hostages taken, 18 held until Apr. 27.

1983—Apr. 18: Hezbollah suicide truck bomb at U.S. embassy in Beirut, Lebanon, killed 63. **Oct. 9:** N. Korean agents ambushed a S. Korean govt. delegation in Rangoon, Burma, killing 21. **Oct. 23:** Hezbollah suicide truck bombings of U.S. and French military bases, Beirut, Lebanon; 242 Americans, 58 French killed.

1984—Sept. 20: U.S. embassy annex nr. Beirut, Lebanon, bombed, killing approx. 20. **Sept. 20:** In worst bioterrorism attack in U.S. history, members of Rajneesh cult contaminated an Oregon salsa bar with salmonella, sickening 751.

1985—Apr. 12: Bomb blast at restaurant nr. U.S. air base in Torrejon, Spain; 18 killed. **June 14:** Hezbollah members hijacked TWA Flight 847 with 153 passengers and crew to Beirut, Lebanon; 39 held for 17 days, 1 U.S. Navy sailor killed. **June 23:** Air India Flight 182 destroyed by bomb off coast of Ireland; 329 killed. Blamed on Sikh terrorists. **Oct. 7:** Four Palestinians hijacked Italian cruise ship *Achille Lauro*; 1 passenger killed. **Nov. 23:** EgyptAir Flight 648 from Athens, Greece, to Cairo hijacked to Malta by Palestinian group Abu Nidal; 60 killed in rescue. **Dec. 27:** Palestinian militants opened fire at El-Al (Isr.) airline counters at Rome and Vienna airports; 19 killed.

1986—Apr. 5: Nightclub in Berlin, W. Germany, bombed; 3 killed, incl. 2 U.S. service personnel, 200+ hurt. 3 Libyan embassy workers in Germany convicted.

1987—Apr. 17: Bomb in Sri Lankan capital killed 100+; blamed on Tamil rebels who, 4 days later, attacked Sinhalese travelers on highway, killing 127. **June 19:** Basque group ETA bombed supermarket garage in Barcelona, Spain; 21 killed. **Nov. 29:** Bomb planted by N. Korean agents exploded on Korean Air Lines Flight 858 over Indian Ocean; 115 killed.

1988—Dec. 21: Pan Am Flight 103 exploded over Lockerbie, Scotland, killing all 259 aboard and 11 on ground; Libya took responsibility for bombing in Aug. 2003.

1989—Sept. 19: French UTA Flight 722 from Congo Republic to Paris destroyed by bomb in midair over Niger; 170 killed.

1992—Mar. 17: Israeli embassy in Buenos Aires, Argentina, bombed; 28 killed, 200+ injured. Hezbollah suspected.

1993—Feb. 26: Truck bomb exploded in World Trade Center garage in New York City; 6 killed. Blast later linked to al-Qaeda. **Mar. 12-19:** At least 11 bombs ripped through Bombay and Calcutta, India; 300+ killed.

1994—Feb. 25: U.S.-born Israeli settler Baruch Goldstein opened fire in mosque in Hebron, West Bank; about 30 Muslim worshippers killed. **July 18:** Buenos Aires, Argentina, Jewish center bombed; 87 killed. Blamed on Hezbollah.

1995—Mar. 20: Twelve killed and over 5,000 injured when Japanese cult members released sarin nerve gas in Tokyo subway cars. **Apr. 19:** Murrah Federal Building in Oklahoma City bombed, killing 168. Timothy McVeigh and Terry Nichols convicted. McVeigh executed in 2001; Nichols sentenced to life in prison. **Nov. 13:** U.S. military compound in Riyadh, Saudi Arabia, bombed by Islamic Movement of Change; 7 killed.

1996—Jan. 31: Tamil Tigers drove explosives-laden truck into Central Bank in Colombo, Sri Lanka; 90 killed. **June 25:** Fuel truck exploded outside Khobar Towers, U.S. military complex in Dhahran, Saudi Arabia; killed 19. **July 27:** Bomb exploded in Atlanta, GA, during Olympic Games; killed 2, injured 100+. Extremist Eric Robert Rudolph sentenced to life in prison, 2005. **Dec. 3:** Bomb exploded on subway in Paris; 4 killed, 86 injured. Algerian Islamic extremist group suspected.

1997—Nov. 17: Gamaa al-Islamiya militants killed 58 tourists and 4 Egyptians in Valley of the Kings nr. Luxor, Egypt.

1998—Aug. 7: U.S. embassies in Nairobi, Kenya, and Dar-es-Salaam, Tanzania, bombed; 257 people killed. Al-Qaeda claimed responsibility. **Aug. 15:** IRA car bomb outside courthouse in Omagh, N. Ireland, killed 29. **Oct. 18:** National Liberation Army of Colombia blew up Ocensa oil pipeline; about 71 killed.

1999—Sept. 9-16: Three buildings bombed in Moscow and Volgodonsk, Russia; about 300 killed. Chechen rebels blamed.

2000—Oct. 12: Small boat assisting in docking of USS *Cole* exploded alongside it in Aden, Yemen; 17 U.S. sailors killed. Blamed on al-Qaeda.

2001—Sept. 11: 19 al-Qaeda terrorists hijacked 4 U.S. domestic flights, including 2 planes that crashed into New York City's World Trade Center towers and 1 into Pentagon. Total dead minus hijackers: 2,977; deadliest terrorist attack yet on U.S. soil. **Sept.-Nov. 7:** Letters tainted with deadly anthrax bacteria mailed through U.S. postal system killed 5, sickened 17; investigation concluded in 2010 that government-employed microbiologist Bruce Ivins, who committed suicide in 2008, was responsible.

2002—Mar. 27: Suicide bombing at hotel in Netanya, Israel, during Passover celebration; 27 killed. **Oct. 12:** Resort in Bali, Indonesia, bombed; 202 dead. Jemaah Islamiah blamed. **Oct. 23:** Chechen guerrillas seized theater in Moscow, held 700+ hostages. Russian authorities gassed theater; most guerrillas and about 128 hostages killed. **Dec. 27:** Chechen rebels plowed truck bomb into pro-Russian govt. headquarters in Grozny, Chechnya; 80 killed, 152 injured.

2003—May 12-13: Al-Qaeda militants detonated car bombs at 3 residential complexes used by Westerners in Riyadh, Saudi Arabia; 34 killed. **May 16:** Five explosions in Casablanca, Morocco; 44 killed. Blamed on al-Qaeda. **Aug. 19:** UN headquarters in Baghdad bombed by truck; 22 killed, incl. UN envoy to Iraq. **Aug. 25:** 2 bombs exploded in taxis in Mumbai, India; 46 killed. Islamic militants suspected. **Nov. 15:** Two synagogues in Istanbul, Turkey, bombed; 25 killed. **Nov. 20:** British consulate and offices of HSBC bombed in Istanbul, Turkey; 27 killed. Blamed on al-Qaeda. **Dec. 5:** Suicide bombing on commuter train in Yessentuki, Russia; 44 killed. Blamed on Chechen rebels.

2004—Feb. 6: Bomb exploded in Moscow subway; 39 killed, 130 injured. Chechen rebels blamed. **Mar. 11:** Al-Qaeda cell bombed 4 commuter trains during morning rush hour in Madrid, Spain; 191 killed, about 1,200 injured. **May 29:** Al-Qaeda militants stormed foreigner compound in Khobar, Saudi Arabia, taking hostages; 22 killed. **Aug. 24:** Chechen suicide bombers caused crash of two Russian passenger planes in diff. parts of Russia; 90 killed. **Sept. 1:** Chechen militants seized school in Beslan, in North Ossetia, Russia; held 1,000+ hostage for 3 days before Russian troops stormed school. About 330 killed, incl. 27 hostage-takers.

2005—July 7: Four bombs exploded on 3 separate subways and 1 bus in London, Eng.; 52 killed, about 700 injured. **July 23:** Three car bombs explode nr. Sharm el-Sheik, Egypt, resorts; about 90 killed. **Nov. 9:** 3 suicide bombings targeted hotels in Amman, Jordan; killed 56. Al-Qaeda in Iraq took responsibility.

2006—July 11: 8 explosions struck 7 different trains and 1 station of public commuter rail system in Mumbai, India; 207 killed. Lashkar-e-Qahhar (Army of Terror) claimed responsibility.

2007—Feb. 19: Train traveling between New Delhi and border with Pakistan caught fire, 68 killed; Indian ministers blamed Muslim militants for trying to disrupt peace talks between India and Pakistan. **Dec. 11:** Two coordinated car bombs went off outside govt. building and UN office building in Algiers, Algeria; 41 killed, incl. 17 UN employees, 170 wounded.

2008—Sept. 20: Suicide bomber in truck set off explosion outside of Marriott Hotel in Islamabad, Pakistan; 53 killed, 271 wounded. **Nov. 26-29:** Series of attacks and bombings on luxury hotels and high-profile targets in Mumbai, India; 171 killed, 300 injured.

2009—Feb. 20: Suicide bomber targeted Shiite funeral in Dera Ismail Khan, Pakistan; 30 killed. **Dec. 25:** A Nigerian man failed to blow up a flight from Amsterdam to Detroit with bomb hidden in his underpants.

2010—Jan. 1: Taliban suicide bomber killed more than 100 on playground in NW Pakistan. **Mar. 29:** Two female Chechen separatists detonated suicide bombs at two landmark Moscow subway stations, killing at least 40. **July 9:** Suicide bombers targeted tribal elders in Mohmand, Pakistan, killing more than 100. **July 11:** Several bombs claimed by al-Shabab exploded simultaneously in Kampala, Uganda, killing more than 70 people who had gathered to watch the World Cup final broadcast.

2011—Jan. 24: Suicide bomber killed 35 in Moscow's Domodedovo Airport, location chosen to maximize deaths of foreigners. **July 22:** Anders Behring Breivik, right-wing Norwegian extremist, set off a bomb in van outside govt. buildings in Oslo, then massacred dozens of young people at a summer camp on Tyrifjorden Lake, bringing death toll to 77.

2012—Jan. 21: Series of attacks by Islamist extremist group Boko Haram killed more than 185 in Kano, Nigeria. **May 21:** Suicide bomber claimed by al-Qaeda in the Arabian Peninsula (AQAP) killed more than 100 soldiers during military parade rehearsal nr. Yemeni presidential palace. **Sept. 11:** Terrorists stormed U.S. embassy in Benghazi, Libya, killing 4 Americans, including U.S. Amb. J. Christopher Stevens.

2013—Apr. 15: Two bombs exploded nr. Boston Marathon finish line, killing 3 and injuring 264; 4-day search ended in death of suspect Tamerlan Tsarnaev and capture of his brother, Dzhokhar, a naturalized Chechen immigrant. **Sept. 21:** Al-Shabab, a Somali militant group, killed up to 70 people and wounded at least 175 at a Nairobi, Kenya, shopping mall.

2014—Apr.-May: Islamist extremist group Boko Haram kidnapped more than 250 girls from schools in Nigeria; killed more than 150 villagers in Gamboru. **Dec. 15:** Nine Taliban gunmen attacked military-affiliated school in Peshawar, Pakistan, executing about 150, including 132 children.

2015—Jan. 7: Gunmen stormed Paris offices of *Charlie Hebdo*, a satirical newspaper, killing 12. Two days later, French police killed suspects, brothers who identified themselves as belonging to AQAP. **Mar. 18:** Gunmen killed 21 tourists and a police officer at Tunisia's National Bardo Museum. Several terrorist groups claimed credit. **Apr. 2:** Al-Shabab militants killed 147 students at Kenya's Garissa Univ. after separating Christian and Muslim students. **June 17:** Lone white-supremacist gunman killed 9, incl. a state senator, in a historically black church in Charleston, SC. **Oct. 31:** Terrorists downed a Russian charter flight shortly after takeoff from Egyptian resort, killing all 224 onboard. Egyptian affiliate of the Sunni extremist group the Islamic State in Iraq and Syria (ISIS) said it smuggled a soda-can bomb onto plane. **Nov. 13:** Series of coordinated suicide bombings and other attacks by ISIS on Paris cafes, a soccer stadium, and a concert hall killed 137 (incl. 7 attackers); wounded 350+. **Dec. 2:** A heavily armed married couple opened fire on the husband's coworkers at a holiday party for San Bernardino (CA) County Health Dept., killing 14 wounding 21.

2016—Mar. 22: Three explosions in Brussels, two at the airport and one at a busy subway station, killed 35 people (incl. 3 bombers) and injured 300+. ISIS claimed credit; investigators linked perpetrators to 2015 Paris attacks. **June 12:** Lone gunman killed 49 people and wounded 53 at a gay nightclub in Orlando, FL. **July 7:** A heavily armed man shot and killed five police officers and wounded seven other officers and two civilians in downtown Dallas, TX, during peaceful protest. **July 14:** Tunisian-born man drove rented truck into Bastille Day crowds in Nice, France, killing 86 and injuring 400+. **Dec. 19:** Tunisian man on Germany's terror watch list drove hijacked truck through outdoor market in Berlin, killing 12; 56+ injured.

2017—May 22: Suicide bomber detonated in entrance hall of Manchester, England, arena as fans left a concert by U.S. singer Ariana Grande, killing 22; 800 injured. ISIS claimed responsibility. **June 3:** Three assailants in a van hit pedestrians on London Bridge before exiting vehicle and attacking people with knives; 8 killed and 48+ injured. **Aug. 18:** A Moroccan man killed 2 and injured 8 with a knife in Turku, Finland; country's first terror attack. **Oct. 14:** Two truck bombs detonated in Mogadishu, Somalia, leaving 512 dead, 300+ injured. Blamed on al-Shabab. **Nov. 24:** Attack on Sufi mosque in Bir al-Abed, Egypt, by extremists affiliated with ISIS, killed 311 people and injured 100+ others.

Notable Assassinations Since 1865

1865—Apr. 14: U.S. Pres. Abraham Lincoln shot by John Wilkes Booth, well-known actor with Confederate sympathies, at Ford's Theater in Washington, DC; died Apr. 15.

1881—Mar. 13: Alexander II of Russia. **July 2:** U.S. Pres. James A. Garfield shot by Charles J. Guiteau, disappointed office seeker, in Washington, DC; died Sept. 19.

1894—June 24: French Pres. Sadi Carnot by Sante Caserio, Italian anarchist, in Lyon.

1898—Sept. 10: Empress Elizabeth of Austria stabbed by Luigi Luccheni, Italian anarchist.

1900—July 29: Umberto I, king of Italy, by an anarchist.

1901—Sept. 6: U.S. Pres. William McKinley shot by Leon Czolgosz, anarchist, in Buffalo, NY; died Sept. 14.

1908—Feb. 1: King Carlos I of Portugal and his son Luís Filipe, in Lisbon.

1913—Feb. 23: Mexican Pres. Francisco I. Madero and Vice Pres. José María Pino Suárez. **Mar. 18:** King George of Greece, by an anarchist.

1914—June 28: Archduke Franz Ferdinand of Austria-Hungary and his wife shot by Gavrilo Princip, Serb nationalist, in Sarajevo, Bosnia.

1916—Dec. 30: Grigory Rasputin, Russian mystic and court figure, by group of aristocrats.

1918—July 12: Grand Duke Michael of Russia, at Perm. **July 16:** Nicholas II, former (abdicated) czar of Russia; his wife, Czarina Alexandra; their son, Czarevitch Alexis; their daughters, Grand Duchesses Olga, Tatiana, Marie, Anastasia; and 4 members of household executed by Bolsheviks at Ekaterinburg.

1920—May 20: Mexican Pres. Gen. Venustiano Carranza, in Tlaxcalantongo.

1922—Aug. 22: Michael Collins, Irish revolutionary, in West Cork. **Dec. 16:** Polish Pres. Gabriel Narutowicz in Warsaw.
1923—July 20: Gen. Francisco "Pancho" Villa, ex-rebel leader, in Parral, Mexico.
1928—July 17: Gen. Alvaro Obregon, president-elect of Mexico, in San Angel.
1932—May 6: French Pres. Paul Doumer shot by Russian émigré, Pavel Gorgulov, in Paris.
1934—July 25: Austrian Chancellor Engelbert Dollfuss by Nazis, in Vienna.
1935—Sept. 8: Sen. Huey P. Long, former Louisiana governor, shot by Dr. Carl Austin Weiss, son-in-law of political opponent, in Baton Rouge; died Sept. 10.
1940—Aug. 20: Leon Trotsky (Lev Bronstein), exiled Soviet commissar of war, fatally wounded with ice ax by Soviet agent nr. Mexico City.
1948—Jan. 30: Leader of movement for Indian independence Mohandas K. Gandhi (Mahatma) shot by Hindu fanatic in New Delhi. **Sept. 17:** Count Folke Bernadotte, UN mediator for Palestine, by Jewish extremists in Jerusalem.
1951—July 20: Jordanian King Abdullah ibn Hussein. **Oct. 16:** Prime Min. Liaquat Ali Khan of Pakistan shot, in Rawalpindi.
1956—Sept. 21: Pres. Anastasio Somoza of Nicaragua shot in Leon by a young poet; died Sept. 29.
1957—July 26: Guatemalan Pres. Carlos Castillo Armas, in Guatemala City by one of his guards.
1958—July 14: King Faisal of Iraq, Crown Prince Abdullah, and **July 15**, Prem. Nuri as-Said, by rebels in Baghdad.
1959—Sept. 25: Prime Min. Solomon Bandaranaike of Ceylon (Sri Lanka), by Buddhist monk in Colombo.
1961—Jan. 17: First elected prime min. of Dem. Rep. of the Congo, Patrice Lumumba, in Katanga Prov. by political rivals. **May 30:** Dominican dictator Rafael Leónidas Trujillo Molina, nr. Ciudad Trujillo.
1963—June 12: Medgar Evers, NAACP's Mississippi field secretary, shot by Byron De La Beckwith in Jackson, MS. **Nov. 2:** Pres. Ngo Dinh Diem of South Vietnam and his brother, Ngo Dinh Nhu, in military coup. **Nov. 22:** U.S. Pres. John F. Kennedy shot while riding in motorcade through downtown Dallas, TX; accused gunman Lee Harvey Oswald murdered by nightclub owner Jack Ruby while awaiting trial.
1965—Jan. 21: Iranian Prem. Hassan Ali Mansour, in Tehran. **Feb. 21:** Malcolm X, black nationalist leader, shot by 3 men linked to Nation of Islam at New York City rally.
1966—Sept. 6: Prime Min. Hendrik F. Verwoerd of South Africa stabbed to death in parliament at Cape Town.
1968—Apr. 4: Rev. Martin Luther King Jr. fatally shot in Memphis, TN; James Earl Ray convicted of crime. **June 5:** Sen. Robert F. Kennedy (D, NY) shot in Los Angeles; died June 6. Sirhan Sirhan convicted of crime.
1971—Nov. 28: Jordanian Prime Min. Wasfi Tal by Palestinian guerrillas, in Cairo, Egypt.
1973—Mar. 2: U.S. Amb. Cleo A. Noel Jr., U.S. Charge d'Affaires George C. Moore, and Belgian Charge d'Affaires Guy Eid by Palestinian guerrillas, in Khartoum, Sudan. **Dec. 20:** Spanish Prem. Luis Carrero Blanco in car bombing by Basque separatist group ETA, in Madrid.
1974—Aug. 19: U.S. Amb. to Cyprus, Rodger P. Davies, by sniper's bullet in Nicosia.
1975—Feb. 11: Pres. Richard Ratsimandrava of Madagascar shot in Antananarivo. **Mar. 25:** Saudi Arabian King Faisal shot by nephew Prince Musad Abdel Aziz, in Riyadh. **Aug. 15:** Bangladesh Pres. Sheik Mujibur Rahman killed in coup.
1976—Feb. 13: Nigerian head of state, Gen. Murtala Ramat Mohammed, by self-styled young revolutionaries.
1977—Mar. 16: Kamal Jumblat, Lebanese Druse chieftain, shot nr. Beirut. **Mar. 18:** Rep. of the Congo Pres. Marien Ngouabi shot in Brazzaville.
1978—May 9: Former Italian Prem. Aldo Moro killed by Red Brigades terrorists who had abducted him Mar. 16 in Rome and held him hostage. **July 9:** Former Iraqi Prem. Abdul Razzak al-Naif shot in London.
1979—Aug. 27: Lord Mountbatten, WWII hero, and 2 others when a bomb exploded on his fishing boat off coast of Co. Sligo, Ireland. IRA claimed responsibility. **Oct. 26:** S. Korean Pres. Park Chung Hee and 6 bodyguards fatally shot by Kim Jae Kyu, head of S. Korean intelligence agency.
1980—Apr. 12: Liberian Pres. William R. Tolbert, in military coup. **Sept. 17:** Former Nicaraguan Pres. Anastasio Somoza Debayle shot in Paraguay.
1981—Oct. 6: Egyptian Pres. Anwar al-Sadat shot by commandos while reviewing military parade in Cairo; 7 others killed, 28 wounded.
1982—Sept. 14: Lebanese Pres.-elect Bashir Gemayel killed by bomb in east Beirut.
1983—Aug. 21: Philippine opposition leader Benigno Aquino Jr. shot at Manila Intl. Airport.

1984—Oct. 31: Indian Prime Min. Indira Gandhi shot by 2 Sikh bodyguards in New Delhi.
1986—Feb. 28: Swedish Prime Min. Olof Palme shot on Stockholm street; case still unsolved.
1987—June 1: Lebanese Prem. Rashid Karami killed when bomb exploded aboard helicopter.
1988—Apr. 16: PLO military chief Khalil Wazir (Abu Jihad) gunned down by Israeli commandos in Tunisia.
1989—Aug. 18: Colombian pres. candidate Luis Carlos Galán killed by Medellín cartel drug traffickers at campaign rally in Bogotá. **Nov. 22:** Lebanese Pres. Rene Moawad killed when bomb exploded next to his motorcade.
1990—Mar. 22: Colombian pres. candidate Bernardo Jaramillo Ossa shot at airport in Bogotá.
1991—May 21: Former Indian Prime Min. Rajiv Gandhi killed by bomb during election rally in Madras.
1992—June 29: Algerian Pres. Mohammed Boudiaf shot in Annaba.
1993—May 1: Sri Lankan Pres. Ranasinghe Premadasa killed by suicide bomber in Colombo.
1994—Apr. 6: Burundian Pres. Cyprien Ntaryamira and Rwandan Pres. Juvénal Habyarimana killed with 8 others when their plane was shot down, precipitating Rwandan genocide.
1995—Nov. 4: Israeli Prime Min. Yitzhak Rabin shot by Jewish extremist at peace rally in Tel Aviv.
1996—Oct. 2: Andrei Lukanov, former Bulgarian prime min., shot outside home by unidentified assailant.
1998—Apr. 26: Guatemalan Roman Catholic Bishop Juan Gerardi Conedera, human rights champion, found beaten to death in Guatemala City.
1999—Apr. 9: Niger Pres. Ibrahim Bare Mainassara ambushed and killed by dissident soldiers. **Oct. 27:** Armenian Prime Min. Vazgen Sarkissian, along with 7 others, shot during session of parliament.
2001—Jan. 16: Dem. Rep. of the Congo Pres. Laurent Kabila shot to death by bodyguard at pres. palace in Kinshasa. **June 1:** Nepal's King Birendra, Queen Aiswarya, and 7 other royals fatally shot by Crown Prince Dipendra, who also killed himself.
2002—July 6: Afghan Vice Pres. Haji Abdul Qadir shot outside his office in Kabul.
2003—Mar. 12: Serbian Prime Min. Zoran Djindjic shot by paramilitary snipers outside govt. headquarters in Belgrade.
2004—Feb. 13: Former Chechen Pres. Zelimkhan Yandarbiyev killed after car exploded in Qatar. **Mar. 22:** Sheik Ahmed Yassin, spiritual leader of Hamas, by Israeli missile attack in Gaza City. **May 9:** Chechen Pres. Akhmad Kadyrov by bomb at WWII memorial service in Grozny. **Nov. 2:** Filmmaker Theo van Gogh, critic of Islam and great-grandnephew of painter Vincent van Gogh, shot and stabbed by Muslim militant in Amsterdam.
2005—Jan. 4: Baghdad Gov. Ali al-Haidari gunned down by insurgents in Baghdad, Iraq.
2007—Aug. 2: *Oakland Post* editor Chauncey Bailey, who was investigating financial status of Your Black Muslim Bakery, shot in Oakland, CA. **Dec. 27:** Benazir Bhutto, former Pakistani prime min. and first female elected leader of a Muslim state, by bomb and gunman later linked to then-Pres. Pervez Musharraf.
2008—Feb. 12: Imad Mughniyeh, top Hezbollah commander and reputed mastermind of the 1983 bombing of U.S. embassy in Beirut, by car bomb in Damascus, Syria. Mughniyeh had been on FBI's Most Wanted Terrorist list. **Oct. 23:** Ivo Pukanic, editor-in-chief of Croatian political newspaper *Nacional*, killed in Zagreb when bomb exploded nr. his car.
2009—Mar. 2: Guinea-Bissau's longtime Pres. João Bernardo Vieira shot by army troops outside his home in Bissau. **May 31:** Dr. George Tiller, one of the few doctors in the U.S. to perform abortions late in pregnancy, shot to death in his Wichita, KS, church by anti-abortion extremist.
2011—Sept. 20: Burhanuddin Rabbani, leader of Afghanistan's High Peace Council and a former pres., killed in his Kabul home by assassin with explosives hidden in his turban.
2012—Jan. 11: Iranian nuclear scientist Mostafa Ahmadi Roshan killed by car bomb.
2014—Sept. 1: U.S. airstrikes killed Ahmed Abdi Godane, leader of Somalia-based Islamist militant group al-Shabab.
2015—Feb. 27: Boris Y. Nemtsov, Russian opposition leader and former first deputy prime minister, shot near Red Square.
2016—June 16: UK Labour MP Jo Cox shot and stabbed in West Yorkshire by far-right assailant. **Dec. 20:** Turkish police officer shot Russian ambassador to Turkey, Andrei Karlov, in Ankara. Apparently motivated by Russian military involvement in Syria, the attack was caught on widely distributed video.
2017—Feb. 13: Kim Jong Nam, half-brother to N. Korean leader Kim Jong Un, killed in chemical nerve agent attack at Kuala Lumpur airport. Two women, charged in attack by Malaysian authorities, blamed coercion under false pretenses by N. Korean agents.

Notable U.S. Kidnappings Since 1924

Bobby Franks, 14, in Chicago, May 21, 1924, by 2 youths from wealthy families—Richard Loeb, 18, and Nathan Leopold, 19—who killed boy. Demand for $10,000 ignored. Loeb killed in prison; Leopold paroled 1958.

Charles A. Lindbergh Jr., 20 months old, nr. Hopewell, NJ, Mar. 1, 1932; found dead May 12. Ransom of $50,000 paid to man identified as Bruno Richard Hauptmann, 35, paroled German convict who entered U.S. illegally. Hauptmann convicted, electrocuted in Trenton, NJ, prison, Apr. 3, 1936.

William A. Hamm Jr., 39, brewing company pres. in St. Paul, MN, June 15, 1933, by Karpis-Barker gang. $100,000 paid. Alvin Karpis given life sentence, paroled in 1969.

Charles F. Urschel, in Oklahoma City, July 22, 1933. Released July 31 after $200,000 paid. George "Machine Gun" Kelly and 5 others sentenced to life.

Brooke L. Hart, 22, in San Jose, CA. Thomas Thurmond and John Holmes arrested after demanding $40,000. When Hart's body was found in San Francisco Bay, Nov. 26, 1933, a mob forced its way into jail and lynched the 2 kidnappers.

June Robles, 6, abducted in Tucson, AZ, Apr. 25, 1934. Missing for 19 days after ransom notes sent to family. Found alive in cage buried in desert after authorities received anonymous letter. No one was ever convicted.

George Weyerhaeuser, 9, of Weyerhaeuser lumber company, in Tacoma, WA, May 24, 1935. Returned home June 1 after $200,000 paid. Kidnappers given 20 to 60 years.

Robert C. Greenlease, 6, son of wealthy car dealer, taken from Kansas City, MO, school Sept. 28, 1953; held for $600,000. Body found Oct. 7. Bonnie Brown Heady and Carl A. Hall pleaded guilty, were executed.

Adolph Coors III, 45, brewing company heir, near Morrison, CO, Feb. 9, 1960. Wife received ransom note but no further word. Body found Sept. 11. Kidnapper caught, convicted, sentenced to life in prison.

Frank Sinatra Jr., 19, from hotel room in Lake Tahoe, CA, Dec. 8, 1963. Released Dec. 11 after his father paid $240,000 ransom. Three men sentenced to prison.

Barbara Jane Mackle, 20, abducted Dec. 17, 1968, from Atlanta, GA, motel; found unharmed 3 days later, buried in coffin-like box 18 in. underground, after her father paid $500,000 ransom. Gary Steven Krist sentenced to life, Ruth Eisenmann-Schier to 7 years.

Virginia Piper, 49, abducted July 27, 1972, from her home in suburban Minneapolis, MN; found unharmed nr. Duluth 2 days later after husband, retired banker, paid $1 mil ransom.

J. Paul Getty III, 17, grandson of the oil billionaire, disappeared July 10, 1973, in Rome, Italy. Ransom of $3 mil paid after abductors, with links to organized crime, sent one of Getty's ears to an Italian newspaper with a warning that other parts of his body would be mutilated. Released Dec. 15.

Patricia "Patty" Hearst, 19, taken from her Berkeley, CA, apartment Feb. 4, 1974; "Symbionese Liberation Army" captors demanded her father, publisher Randolph Hearst, give millions to area poor. Patty implicated in San Francisco bank holdup, Apr. 15. The FBI, Sept. 18, 1975, captured her and others. She was convicted of bank robbery, Mar. 20, 1976; released from prison under executive clemency, Feb. 1, 1979. In 1978, William and Emily Harris were sentenced to 10 years to life for the kidnapping; both were paroled in 1983.

J. Reginald Murphy, 40, an editor of *Atlanta Constitution* (GA), kidnapped Feb. 20, 1974; freed Feb. 22 after newspaper paid $700,000 ransom. William A. H. Williams later convicted.

Jack Teich, Kings Point, NY, steel executive, seized Nov. 12, 1974; released Nov. 19 after ransom payment of $750,000.

Adam Walsh, 6, abducted from Hollywood, FL, dept. store, July 27, 1981. Severed head found 2 weeks later. Case officially closed in 2008; drifter who had died in prison while serving life sentences for murder found responsible.

Terry Anderson, 37, Middle East bureau chief for Associated Press, in Beirut, Lebanon, by Islamic fundamentalist group Hezbollah, Mar. 16, 1985. Freed Dec. 4, 1991. Anderson had been held hostage with **William Buckley**, 55, CIA station chief in Beirut who was kidnapped Mar. 16, 1984, and died in captivity.

Jacob Wetterling, 11, kidnapped Oct. 22, 1989, nr. his home in St. Joseph, MN, by armed man. Federal legislation named for Wetterling passed in 1994, requiring states to set up registries of offenders convicted of sexually violent crimes or crimes against children. Wetterling's remains found in 2016 after his kidnapper confessed (as part of a plea) to having killed the boy.

Jaycee Dugard, 11, kidnapped nr. her home in South Lake Tahoe, CA, June 10, 1991; held for 18 years by Nancy and Philip Garrido, who fathered 2 girls with Dugard during her captivity. Dugard, along with her 11- and 15-year-old daughters, was reunited with her family Aug. 27, 2009, after police arrested the Garridos.

Sidney J. Reso, oil company exec., seized Apr. 29, 1992; died May 3. Arthur D. Seale—former security official at oil company—and his wife, Irene, arrested June 19. Arthur sentenced to life in prison; Irene sentenced to 20-year prison term.

Polly Klaas, 12, Petaluma, CA, abducted at knife point, Oct. 1, 1993, during slumber party at her home. Police arrested Richard Allen Davis on Nov. 30; he led them to her body, found Dec. 4 in wooded area of Cloverdale, CA. Davis found guilty June 18, 1996, and sentenced to death Sept. 26.

Amber Hagerman, 9, abducted Jan. 13, 1996, while riding her bicycle in Arlington, TX, found dead five days later. Her murder, which remains unsolved, led to the creation of the AMBER Alert, used to broadcast child abductions over the nation's Emergency Alert System.

Kamiyah Mobley, newborn, kidnapped July 10, 1998, from Jacksonville, FL, hospital by woman posing as nurse. Investigators confirmed, Jan. 2017, that Mobley was alive and raised in SC as abductor's biological daughter.

Tionda Z. Bradley, 10, and sister **Diamond Yvette Bradley**, 3, went missing July 6, 2001, in Chicago. Note left by Tionda at home stated the 2 girls were going to the store and playground. Disappearance still unsolved.

Daniel Pearl, 38, *Wall Street Journal* reporter, abducted Jan. 23, 2002, while investigating links between al-Qaeda and British-born "shoe-bomber" Richard Reid. Beheaded Feb. 1, 2002; act captured on videotape. British-born militant Ahmad Omar Saeed Sheikh and 3 others convicted July 15, 2002, of kidnapping and murder by a judge in Hyderabad, India. In 2007, while in captivity at Guantanamo Bay, Cuba, Khalid Sheikh Mohammed, mastermind of the Sept. 11 attacks, admitted to murdering Pearl.

Elizabeth Smart, 14, abducted from her home in Salt Lake City, UT, June 5, 2002, by Brian D. Mitchell, and forced to live with Mitchell and wife Wanda for 9 months in various U.S. cities; found walking down street with captors in Sandy, UT, 15 mi from Smart family home, Mar. 12, 2003.

Michelle Knight, 21, abducted Aug. 23, 2002; **Amanda Berry**, 17, seized Apr. 21, 2003; and **Gina DeJesus**, 14, kidnapped Apr. 2, 2004. All 3 women escaped from the Cleveland, OH, home of Ariel Castro, May 6, 2013, after a decade in captivity during which Berry gave birth to a daughter.

Jill Carroll, 28, freelance journalist on assignment for *Christian Science Monitor*, seized in Baghdad by group called the Revenge Brigade, Jan. 7, 2006. She was released Mar. 30; 4 Iraqis arrested in connection with her kidnapping.

Steve Centanni, 60, Fox News reporter released Aug. 26, 2006 (along with a colleague), after being held hostage for 13 days by Palestinian militant group Holy Jihad Brigades. The group had demanded U.S. release of all Muslims in its prisons.

Reigh Storrow Mills, 7, abducted July 27, 2008, by her father, Christian Gerhartsreiter (alias Clark Rockefeller); reunited with her mother Aug. 2. Gerhartsreiter sentenced to 4-5 years.

Felix Batista, 55, Cuban-American security expert who negotiated the release of numerous kidnapping victims, abducted in Mexico, Dec. 10, 2008. Still missing with no communication from kidnappers.

Jessica Buchanan, 32, aid worker for Danish Refugee Council, taken hostage by Somali pirates Oct. 25, 2011; rescued by U.S. Navy SEALs Jan. 25, 2012.

James Foley, 39, freelance journalist, taken hostage during civil war in Syria's Idlib province, Nov. 22, 2012. Sunni extremist group the Islamic State in Iraq and Syria (ISIS) released video Aug. 19, 2014, showing execution of Foley.

Richard Engel, 39, NBC News foreign correspondent in Syria and his crew held captive, Dec. 13, 2012; freed by rebel militia 5 days later.

Hannah Anderson, 16, abducted Aug. 3, 2013, by James DiMaggio, a family friend who killed her mother and brother at his California home before fleeing with her to Idaho; freed Aug. 10 when FBI agents shot and killed DiMaggio.

Madyson Middleton, 8, reported missing July 26, 2015, from Santa Cruz, CA, arts center; found dead July 27. A 15-year-old neighbor was charged with her rape and murder.

Long Ma, 71, cabdriver kidnapped Jan. 22, 2016, by three escapees from an Orange County (CA) jail who forced him, at gunpoint, to drive to San Jose and enable them to obtain motel rooms and cash. Released Jan. 29 when one escapee surrendered.

MILITARY AFFAIRS

Chairmen of the Joint Chiefs of Staff, 1949-2018

Chairman	Service
Gen. of the Army Omar N. Bradley, USA	8/16/1949-8/15/1953
Adm. Arthur W. Radford, USN.	8/15/1953-8/15/1957
Gen. Nathan F. Twining, USAF.	8/15/1957-9/30/1960
Gen. Lyman L. Lemnitzer, USA.	10/1/1960-9/30/1962
Gen. Maxwell D. Taylor, USA	10/1/1962-7/1/1964
Gen. Earle G. Wheeler, USA.	7/3/1964-7/2/1970
Adm. Thomas H. Moorer, USN	7/2/1970-7/1/1974
Gen. George S. Brown, USAF.	7/1/1974-6/20/1978
Gen. David C. Jones, USAF	6/21/1978-6/18/1982
Gen. John W. Vessey Jr., USA	6/18/1982-9/30/1985

Chairman	Service
Adm. William J. Crowe Jr., USN	10/1/1985-9/30/1989
Gen. Colin L. Powell, USA.	10/1/1989-9/30/1993
Gen. John M. Shalikashvili, USA.	10/25/1993-9/30/1997
Gen. Henry H. Shelton, USA.	10/1/1997-9/30/2001
Gen. Richard B. Myers, USAF.	10/1/2001-9/30/2005
Gen. Peter Pace, USMC.	10/1/2005-9/30/2007
Adm. Michael G. Mullen, USN.	10/1/2007-9/30/2011
Gen. Martin E. Dempsey, USA	10/1/2011-9/30/2015
Gen. Joseph F. Dunford Jr., USMC.	10/1/2015-

Chief Commanding Officers of the U.S. Military

Chairman, Joint Chiefs of Staff: Gen. Joseph F. Dunford Jr. (USMC)
Vice Chairman: Gen. Paul J. Selva (USAF)

Date of rank is date when the individual achieved his or her current rank. While serving in any of these positions, or as commander of a unified or specified combatant command, basic pay is $15,800.10 per month. Officers hold positions listed as of Sept. 1, 2018.

Army

Chief of Staff (CSA)	Date of rank
Milley, Mark A.	Aug. 14, 2014

Other Generals	
Abrams, Robert B.	Aug. 10, 2015
Brooks, Vincent K.	July 2, 2013
Brown, Robert B.	May 4, 2016
Lyons, Stephen R.	Aug. 24, 2018
McConville, James C.	June 16, 2017
Murray, John M.	Aug. 24, 2018
Nakasone, Paul M.	May 4, 2018
Nicholson, John W., Jr.	Mar. 3, 2016
Perna, Gustave F.	Sept. 30, 2016
Scaparrotti, Curtis M.	Oct. 2, 2013
Thomas, Raymond A., III	Mar. 30, 2016
Townsend, Stephen J.	Mar. 2, 2018
Votel, Joseph L.	Aug. 28, 2014

Air Force

Chief of Staff (CSAF or AF/CC)	Date of rank
Goldfein, David L.	July 1, 2016

Other Generals	
Brown, Charles Q., Jr.	July 26, 2018
Everhart, Carlton D., II	Aug. 11, 2015
Holmes, James M.	Mar. 10, 2017
Hyten, John E.	Aug. 15, 2014
Lengyel, Joseph L.	Aug. 3, 2016
O'Shaughnessy, Terrence J.	July 12, 2016
Pawlikowski, Ellen M.	June 8, 2015
Ray, Timothy M.	Aug. 21, 2018
Raymond, John W.	Oct. 25, 2016
Selva, Paul J.	Nov. 29, 2012
Wilson, Stephen W.	July 22, 2016
Wolters, Tod D.	Aug. 11, 2016

Navy

Chief of Naval Operations (CNO)	Date of rank
Richardson, John M. (submariner)	July 26, 2012

Other Admirals	
Aquilino, John C. (aviator)	May 17, 2018
Caldwell, James F., Jr. (submariner)	Aug. 14, 2015
Davidson, Philip S. (surface warfare)	Dec. 19, 2014
Foggo, James G., III (submariner)	Oct. 20, 2017
Grady, Christopher W. (surface warfare)	May 4, 2018
Moran, William F. (aviator)	May 31, 2016
Rogers, Michael S. (information warfare)	Mar. 31, 2014
Tidd, Kurt W. (surface warfare)	Jan. 14, 2016

Marine Corps

Commandant of the Marine Corps (CMC)	Date of rank
Neller, Robert B.	Sept. 24, 2015

Other Generals	
Dunford, Joseph F.	Oct. 23, 2010
Waldhauser, Thomas D.	July 18, 2016
Walters, Glenn M.	Aug. 2, 2016

Coast Guard

Commandant, with rank of Admiral	Date of rank
Schultz, Karl L.	June 1, 2018

Vice Commandant, with rank of Admiral	
Ray, Charles W.	May 24, 2018

Commanders of the Unified Combatant Commands

U.S. European Command, Stuttgart-Vaihingen, Germany:
Gen. Curtis M. Scaparrotti (U.S. Army)
U.S. Indo-Pacific Command, Honolulu, Hawaii:
Adm. Philip S. Davidson (USN)
U.S. Special Operations Command, MacDill AFB, Florida:
Gen. Raymond A. Thomas III (U.S. Army)
U.S. Transportation Command, Scott AFB, Illinois:
Gen. Stephen R. Lyons (U.S. Army)
U.S. Central Command, MacDill AFB, Florida:
Gen. Joseph L. Votel (U.S. Army)

U.S. Southern Command, Doral, Florida:
Adm. Kurt W. Tidd (USN)
U.S. Northern Command, Peterson AFB, Colorado:
Gen. Terrence J. O'Shaughnessy (USAF)
U.S. Strategic Command, Offutt AFB, Nebraska:
Gen. John E. Hyten (USAF)
U.S. Africa Command, Kelley Barracks, Stuttgart, Germany:
Gen. Thomas D. Waldhauser (USMC)
U.S. Cyber Command, Fort George G. Meade, Maryland:
Gen. Paul M. Nakasone, (U.S. Army)

North Atlantic Treaty Organization (NATO) International Commands

NATO Headquarters: Chairman, NATO Military Committee:
Air Chief Marshal Stuart Peach (British Armed Forces)
ACO Operational Level Commands:
Joint Force Command Brunssum (JFC Brunssum):
Gen. Riccardo Marchiò (Italian Army), Commander
Joint Force Command Naples (JFC Naples):
Adm. James G. Foggo III (USN), Commander

Strategic Commands:
Allied Command Operations (ACO): Gen. Curtis M. Scaparrotti (U.S. Army), Supreme Allied Commander, Europe
Allied Command Transformation (ACT): Gen. Denis Mercier (French Air Force), Supreme Allied Commander Transformation

Directors of the Central Intelligence Agency, 1946-2018

In 1942, Pres. Franklin D. Roosevelt established the Office of Strategic Services (OSS); it was disbanded in 1945. In 1946, Pres. Harry Truman established the Central Intelligence Group (CIG) to operate under the National Intelligence Authority (NIA). A 1947 law replaced the NIA with the National Security Council (NSC) and the CIG with the Central Intelligence Agency (CIA).

Director	Served	Appointed by President
Adm. Sidney W. Souers	1946	Truman
Gen. Hoyt S. Vandenberg	1946-1947	Truman
Adm. Roscoe H. Hillenkoetter	1947-1950	Truman
Gen. Walter Bedell Smith	1950-1953	Truman
Allen W. Dulles	1953-1961	Eisenhower
John A. McCone	1961-1965	Kennedy
Adm. William F. Raborn Jr.	1965-1966	Johnson, L. B.
Richard Helms	1966-1973	Johnson, L. B.
James R. Schlesinger	1973	Nixon
William E. Colby	1973-1976	Nixon
George H. W. Bush	1976-1977	Ford
Adm. Stansfield Turner	1977-1981	Carter
William J. Casey	1981-1987	Reagan

Director	Served	Appointed by President
William H. Webster	1987-1991	Reagan
Robert M. Gates	1991-1993	Bush, G. H. W.
R. James Woolsey	1993-1995	Clinton
John M. Deutch	1995-1996	Clinton
George J. Tenet	1997-2004	Clinton
Porter Goss	2004-2006	Bush, G. W.
Gen. Michael V. Hayden	2006-2009	Bush, G. W.
Leon E. Panetta	2009-2011	Obama
Gen. David H. Petraeus	2011-2012	Obama
John O. Brennan	2013-2017	Obama
Michael R. Pompeo	2017-2018	Trump
Gina Haspel	2018-	Trump

U.S. Military Personnel Strength on Active Duty Worldwide, 2018

Source: U.S. Dept. of Defense

(as of Mar. 31, 2018)

Area	Personnel	Area	Personnel	Area	Personnel
TOTAL WORLDWIDE[1]	1,330,832	Somalia	60	Kuwait	2,036
		Regional total[2]	767	Qatar	548
U.S., TERRITORIES, AND		**FORMER SOVIET UNION**		Saudi Arabia	305
SPEC. LOCATIONS		Regional total[2]	106	United Arab Emirates	403
Regional total[2]	1,154,369			Regional total[2,3]	8,318
		EAST ASIA AND PACIFIC			
OTHER WESTERN		Australia	228	**EUROPE**	
HEMISPHERE		British Indian Ocean Territory . . .	292	Belgium	896
Brazil	57	Japan	55,043	Germany	34,821
Canada	135	South Korea	24,915	Greece	388
Colombia	67	Philippines	110	Greenland	149
Cuba (Guantánamo)	831	Singapore	196	Hungary	208
El Salvador	53	Thailand	461	Italy	12,766
Honduras	366	Regional total[2]	81,386	Netherlands	402
Mexico	64			Norway	330
Regional total[2]	2,013	**NORTH AFRICA, NEAR EAST, AND**		Poland	147
		SOUTH ASIA		Portugal	227
SUB-SAHARAN AFRICA		Bahrain	4,173	Romania	257
Djibouti	52	Egypt	274	Spain	3,680
Niger	194	Israel	348	Turkey	1,623
				United Kingdom	9,184
				Regional total[2]	65,283

(1) Includes undistributed personnel. (2) Most countries and areas with fewer than 100 assigned U.S. military members not listed; regional totals include personnel stationed in countries and areas not shown. (3) Does not include troops deployed to Afghanistan/Iraq/Syria.

U.S. Military Personnel in U.S. States and Territories, 2018

Source: U.S. Dept. of Defense

(as of Mar. 31, 2018)

State/area	Active personnel	Reserve personnel	State/area	Active personnel	Reserve personnel	State/area	Active personnel	Reserve personnel
Alabama	8,813	19,577	Michigan	2,129	15,221	Texas	119,272	53,632
Alaska	19,907	4,635	Minnesota	585	18,526	Utah	4,228	11,865
Arizona	19,470	14,990	Mississippi	11,833	16,390	Vermont	165	3,614
Arkansas	3,621	10,971	Missouri	15,084	19,213	Virginia	123,341	26,432
California	157,583	56,288	Montana	3,310	4,368	Washington	60,794	18,268
Colorado	35,557	13,291	Nebraska	6,306	6,223	West Virginia	196	8,415
Connecticut	6,242	6,636	Nevada	11,052	7,677	Wisconsin	991	14,467
Delaware	3,490	5,002	New Hampshire	1,321	4,085	Wyoming	3,148	2,876
Florida	63,456	36,268	New Jersey	7,808	17,071	District of		
Georgia	63,645	26,465	New Mexico	12,489	5,059	Columbia	3,490	4,288
Hawaii	43,540	9,517	New York	21,427	29,067	**U.S. total[1]**	**1,143,990[1]**	**779,378**
Idaho	3,498	5,458	North Carolina . .	100,606	21,276	American Samoa	2	0
Illinois	20,038	24,054	North Dakota . . .	7,396	4,416	Guam	5,451	1,750
Indiana	959	18,825	Ohio	6,958	28,128	Northern Mariana		
Iowa	246	10,836	Oklahoma	20,274	13,575	Islands	1	0
Kansas	22,012	10,286	Oregon	1,636	9,495	Puerto Rico	162	7,345
Kentucky	32,081	12,847	Pennsylvania	2,526	30,453	U.S. Virgin		
Louisiana	15,690	17,239	Rhode Island . . .	3,417	4,243	Islands	4	729
Maine	1,173	3,794	South Carolina . .	32,822	17,720	Wake Island	5	0
Maryland	29,118	18,491	South Dakota . . .	3,414	4,670	**Territorial total** . .	**5,625**	**9,824**
Massachusetts . .	3,664	15,191	Tennessee	2,169	17,984			

Note: Armed Forces (AF) Europe, AF Pacific, and AF the Americas personnel—deployed primarily at sea or not at fixed-duty stations (4,754 active, 9 reserve)—are not shown. (1) Includes undistributed/other personnel.

U.S. Army Personnel on Active Duty, 1940-2018

Source: Dept. of the Army, U.S. Dept. of Defense

(as of midyear, except where noted)

Date	Total strength[1]	Commissioned officers			Warrant officers[3]		Enlisted personnel		
		Total	Male	Female[2]	Male	Female	Total	Male	Female
1940	267,767	17,563	16,624	939	763	—	249,441	249,441	—
1942	3,074,184	203,137	190,662	12,475	3,285	—	2,867,762	2,867,762	—
1943	6,993,102	557,657	521,435	36,222	21,919	—	6,413,526	6,358,200	55,325
1944	7,992,868	740,077	692,351	47,726	36,893	10	7,215,688	7,144,601	71,287
1945	8,266,373	835,403	772,511	62,892	56,216	44	7,374,710	7,283,930	90,780
1946	1,889,690	257,300	240,658	16,642	9,826	18	1,622,546	1,605,847	16,699
1950	591,487	67,784	63,375	4,409	4,760	22	518,921	512,370	6,551
1955	1,107,606	111,347	106,196	5,151	10,552	48	985,659	977,943	7,716
1960	871,348	91,056	86,832	4,224	10,141	39	770,112	761,833	8,279
1965	967,049	101,812	98,029	3,783	10,285	23	854,929	846,409	8,520
1970	1,319,735	143,704	138,469	5,235	23,005	13	1,153,013	1,141,537	11,476
1975	781,316	89,756	85,184	4,572	13,214	22	678,324	640,621	37,703
1980 (Sept. 30)	772,661	85,339	77,843	7,496	13,265	113	673,944	612,593	61,351
1990 (Mar. 31)	746,220	91,330	79,520	11,810	15,177	470	639,713	567,015	72,698
2000	471,633	66,344	56,391	9,953	10,608	781	393,900	333,947	59,953
2005 (Sept. 30)	492,728	69,174	57,675	11,499	11,506	976	406,923	346,194	57,354
2010 (Sept. 30)	566,045	78,588	64,952	13,636	14,106	1,434	467,248	406,871	60,377
2015 (Dec. 31)	482,264	78,586	64,223	14,363	13,577	1,421	384,301	331,620	52,681
2016	474,472	78,742	64,253	14,489	13,323	1,391	376,432	324,117	52,315
2017	466,990	77,040	62,735	14,305	13,088	1,361	372,082	319,313	52,769
2018	468,331	77,850	63,184	14,666	12,987	1,378	372,667	319,270	53,397

— = Not applicable. **Note:** Represents strength of active Army, including Philippine Scouts (1940-46), ret. Regular Army personnel on extended active duty, and National Guard and Reserve personnel on extended active duty; excl. those (e.g. U.S. Military Academy cadets, contract surgeons, and National Guard and Reserve personnel) not on extended active duty. (1) Includes categories not listed, e.g., West Point cadets. Data for 1940-46 include personnel in the Army Air Forces and its predecessors (Air Service and Air Corps). (2) Includes Army Nurse Corps for all years, Women's Army Corps (1942-78), and Medical Specialists Corps (1949 and after). (3) Act of Congress approved Apr. 27, 1926, directed the appointment as warrant officers of field clerks still in active service. Includes flight officers as follows: 1943, 5,700; 1944, 13,615; 1945, 31,117; 1946, 2,580.

U.S. Navy Personnel on Active Duty, 1940-2018

Source: U.S. Dept. of Defense

(as of midyear, except where noted)

Year	Officers	Nurses[1]	Enlisted	Officer candi-dates[1]	Total[2]	Year	Officers	Nurses[1]	Enlisted	Officer candi-dates[1]	Total[2]
1940	13,162	442	144,824	2,569	160,997	2000 (Oct.)	53,698	—	320,212	—	373,910
1945	320,293	11,086	2,988,207	61,231	3,380,817	2005	54,039	—	305,368	—	363,858
1950	42,687	1,964	331,860	5,037	381,538	2010	53,071	—	273,609	—	330,065
1960	67,456	2,103	544,040	4,385	617,984	2011	53,620	—	270,425	—	328,648
1970	78,488	2,273	605,899	6,000	692,660	2012 (Mar.)	52,558	—	263,928	—	320,961
1980	63,100	—	464,100	—	527,200	2013 (Feb.)	52,450	—	260,581	—	317,464
1990 (Sept.)	74,429	—	530,133	—	604,562	2014	54,852	—	265,622	—	323,792
1995 (May)	61,075	—	402,626	—	463,701	2015	54,770	—	268,408	—	326,504
1997	57,341	—	340,616	—	397,957	2016	54,973	—	271,100	—	330,556
1998 (Sept.)	55,007	—	326,196	—	381,203	2017	55,047	—	264,404	—	323,938
1999	55,726	—	322,372	—	378,098	2018	55,401	—	268,340	—	328,244

— = Not applicable. (1) Starting in 1980, "Nurses" are included with "Officers," and "Officer candidates" are included with "Enlisted."
(2) May include categories not shown, e.g., midshipmen.

U.S. Air Force Personnel on Active Duty, 1918-2018

Source: U.S. Dept. of Defense

(as of midyear, except where noted)

Year[1]	Total	Year[1]	Total	Year[1]	Total	Year[1]	Total	Year[1]	Total	Year[1]	Total
1918 . . .	195,023	1943 . . .	2,197,114	1980 . . .	557,969	1994 . . .	426,327	2000 . . .	357,777	2014 . . .	328,791
1920 . . .	9,050	1944 . . .	2,372,292	1986 . . .	608,200	1995 . . .	400,051	2005 . . .	358,705	2015 . . .	312,195
1930 . . .	13,531	1945 . . .	2,282,259	1990 . . .	535,233	1996 . . .	389,400	2010 . . .	337,505	2016 . . .	315,786
1940 . . .	51,165	1950 . . .	411,277	1991 . . .	510,432	1997 . . .	378,681	2011 . . .	333,729	2017 . . .	322,559
1941 . . .	152,125	1960 . . .	814,213	1992 . . .	470,315	1998 . . .	363,479	2012[2] . .	332,709	2018 . . .	325,222
1942 . . .	764,415	1970 . . .	791,078	1993 . . .	444,351	1999 . . .	357,929	2013[3] . .	334,157		

(1) Prior to 1950, data are for U.S. Army Air Corps and Air Service of the Signal Corps. (2) In Mar. (3) In Feb.

U.S. Marine Corps Personnel on Active Duty, 1940-2018

Source: U.S. Dept. of Defense

(as of midyear, except where noted)

Year	Officers	Enlisted	Total	Year	Officers	Enlisted	Total	Year	Officers	Enlisted	Total
1940	1,800	26,545	28,345	1994	18,430	159,949	178,379	2010	21,680	179,446	201,126
1945	37,067	437,613	474,680	1995	18,017	153,929	171,946	2011	22,281	178,546	200,827
1950	7,254	67,025	74,279	1996	18,146	154,141	172,287	2012 (Mar.) . .	22,253	176,174	198,427
1960	16,203	154,418	170,621	1997	18,089	154,240	172,329	2013 (Feb.) . .	21,907	173,222	195,129
1970	24,941	234,796	259,737	1998	17,984	154,648	172,632	2014	21,507	169,327	190,834
1980	18,198	170,271	188,469	1999	17,892	155,250	173,142	2015	21,144	163,144	184,587
1990	19,958	176,694	196,652	2000	17,897	154,744	172,641	2016	20,827	162,543	183,370
1993	18,878	161,205	180,083	2005	19,118	159,113	178,231	2017	21,296	163,234	184,530
								2018	21,582	163,637	185,219

U.S. Coast Guard Personnel on Active Duty, 1970-2018

Source: U.S. Dept. of Defense

(as of midyear, except where noted)

Year	Officers	Cadets	Enlisted	Total	Year	Officers	Cadets	Enlisted	Total
1970	5,512	653	31,524	37,689	2011	8,659	1,053	33,615	43,327
1980	6,463	877	32,041	39,381	2012 (Mar.)	8,316	988	33,758	43,062
1985	6,775	733	31,087	38,595	2013 (Jan.)	8,376	1,010	32,971	42,357
1990	6,475	820	29,860	37,308	2014	8,572	676	31,233	40,481
1995	7,489	841	28,401	36,731	2015	8,550	623	30,896	40,069
2000	7,154	863	27,695	35,712	2016	8,550	623	30,896	40,069
2005	7,908	1,006	31,900	40,814	2017	8,483	623	32,015	41,121
2010	8,678	744	33,713	43,135	2018	8,578	807	32,719	42,104

Women in the U.S. Armed Forces

Source: U.S. Dept. of Defense; U.S. Census Bureau, U.S. Dept. of Commerce; U.S. Coast Guard, U.S. Dept. of Homeland Security

Women in the Army, Navy, Air Force, Marines, and Coast Guard are fully integrated with male personnel. All enlisted jobs were opened to women when the draft ended June 30, 1973. Admission to service academies began in 1976. Under rules instituted in 1993, women began to fly combat aircraft and serve aboard warships. By the mid-1990s, 80% of all jobs and more than 90% of all career fields had been opened to women. A woman first achieved the rank of four-star general in 2009. In 2010, the Navy removed its ban on women serving on submarine crews. The Pentagon in 2013 lifted its ban on women serving in direct ground combat units. In Aug. 2015, the first two women graduated from the Army's Ranger School. In Sept. 2017, the first female Marine graduated the Infantry Officer Course.

Women Active Duty Troops, 2018

Service	% women
Army	15.0%
Navy	19.6
Marines	8.6
Air Force	20.2
Coast Guard	14.5

Women on Active Duty, All DOD[1] Services, 1973-2018

Year	% women	Year	% women
1973	2.5%	2005	14.6%
1975	4.6	2010	14.5
1981	8.9	2012	14.6
1987	10.2	2015	15.6
1993	11.6	2017	16.3
2000	14.4	2018	16.3

Women Veterans by Period of Service, 2018

Period of service	% of women vets[2]
Gulf War era[3]	64.0%
Vietnam era	12.0
Korean War	2.1
World War II	1.2
Peacetime only	21.9

NA = Not available. **Note:** Numbers on active duty are as of Sept. 30 in previous years and June 30 in 2018. (1) Does not include Coast Guard. (2) Some women served in multiple periods. (3) Includes women who served both pre- and post-9/11 but not in peacetime only.

Average Age and Length of Service of Active Enlisted Personnel, 1973-2016

Source: U.S. Dept. of Defense

Year	Avg. age	Avg. months of service	Year	Avg. age	Avg. months of service	Year	Avg. age	Avg. months of service
1973	25.0	69.8	1988	26.3	76.7	2002	27.1	84.1
1974	25.0	69.6	1989	26.4	78.0	2003	27.0	83.3
1975	24.9	68.2	1990	26.7	81.8	2004	27.0	82.6
1976	24.9	67.6	1991	27.0	84.8	2005	27.1	83.2
1977	24.9	66.5	1992	27.1	86.4	2006	27.1	82.0
1978	25.0	67.3	1992	27.1	86.4	2007	27.1	81.0
1979	25.1	67.7	1993	27.2	87.7	2008	27.1	80.3
1980	25.0	66.5	1994	27.3	89.6	2009	27.2	80.4
1981	25.1	67.1	1995	27.4	89.3	2010	27.3	80.9
1982	25.4	68.6	1996	27.4	89.6	2011	27.4	81.1
1983	25.6	70.0	1997	27.4	89.2	2012	27.4	NA
1984	25.7	71.1	1998	27.3	88.4	2013	27.3	NA
1985	25.8	72.3	1999	27.3	87.3	2014	27.3	NA
1986	25.9	73.1	2000	27.1	85.5	2015	27.2	NA
1987	26.1	74.8	2001	27.0	84.4	2016	27.1	NA

NA = Not available.

Monthly Military Pay Scale, 2018

Source: U.S. Dept. of Defense
(effective Jan. 1, 2018; salaries rounded to nearest dollar)

	≤2	2	3	4	6	8	10	12	14	16	18	20	22	24	26
Commissioned officers															
O-10	NA	NA	NA	NA	NA	NA	NA	NA	NA	NA	NA	15,800	15,800	15,800	15,800
O-9	NA	NA	NA	NA	NA	NA	NA	NA	NA	NA	NA	14,696	14,909	15,215	15,748
O-8	10,399	10,739	10,966	11,029	11,311	11,782	11,891	12,339	12,467	12,853	13,411	13,925	14,268	14,268	14,268
O-7	8,641	9,042	9,228	9,375	9,643	9,907	10,212	10,517	10,822	11,782	12,592	12,592	12,592	12,592	12,656
O-6	6,552	7,199	7,671	7,671	7,700	8,030	8,074	8,074	8,533	9,344	9,820	10,296	10,567	10,841	11,372
O-5	5,462	6,154	6,579	6,659	6,926	7,084	7,434	7,691	8,022	8,530	8,771	9,009	9,280	9,280	9,280
O-4	4,713	5,456	5,820	5,901	6,239	6,601	7,053	7,404	7,648	7,788	7,869	7,869	7,869	7,869	7,869
O-3	4,144	4,697	5,070	5,528	5,793	6,083	6,271	6,580	6,742	6,742	6,742	6,742	6,742	6,742	6,742
O-2	3,581	4,078	4,696	4,855	4,955	4,955	4,955	4,955	4,955	4,955	4,955	4,955	4,955	4,955	4,955
O-1	3,108	3,235	3,910	3,910	3,910	3,910	3,910	3,910	3,910	3,910	3,910	3,910	3,910	3,910	3,910
Commisioned officers with over 4 years of active duty service as enlisted member or warrant officer															
O-3E	NA	NA	NA	5,528	5,793	6,083	6,271	6,580	6,841	6,991	7,195	7,195	7,195	7,195	7,195
O-2E	NA	NA	NA	4,855	4,955	5,113	5,379	5,585	5,738	5,738	5,738	5,738	5,738	5,738	5,738
O-1E	NA	NA	NA	3,910	4,175	4,330	4,488	4,643	4,855	4,855	4,855	4,855	4,855	4,855	4,855
Warrant officers															
W-5	NA	NA	NA	NA	NA	NA	NA	NA	NA	NA	NA	7,615	8,001	8,288	8,607
W-4	4,283	4,607	4,739	4,869	5,093	5,315	5,539	5,876	6,173	6,454	6,685	6,910	7,240	7,511	7,821
W-3	3,911	4,074	4,241	4,296	4,471	4,815	5,174	5,343	5,539	5,740	6,102	6,347	6,493	6,648	6,860
W-2	3,461	3,788	3,889	3,958	4,182	4,531	4,704	4,874	5,082	5,245	5,392	5,568	5,684	5,776	5,776
W-1	3,038	3,365	3,452	3,638	3,858	4,182	4,333	4,544	4,752	4,916	5,066	5,249	5,249	5,249	5,249
Enlisted members															
E-9	NA	NA	NA	NA	NA	NA	5,174	5,291	5,439	5,612	5,788	6,069	6,307	6,556	6,939
E-8	NA	NA	NA	NA	NA	4,235	4,423	4,539	4,677	4,828	5,100	5,237	5,472	5,602	5,922
E-7	2,944	3,213	3,337	3,499	3,627	3,845	3,968	4,187	4,369	4,493	4,625	4,676	4,848	4,940	5,291
E-6	2,546	2,802	2,926	3,046	3,172	3,454	3,564	3,777	3,842	3,889	3,944	3,944	3,944	3,944	3,944
E-5	2,333	2,490	2,610	2,733	2,925	3,126	3,291	3,311	3,311	3,311	3,311	3,311	3,311	3,311	3,311
E-4	2,139	2,249	2,370	2,491	2,597	2,597	2,597	2,597	2,597	2,597	2,597	2,597	2,597	2,597	2,597
E-3	1,931	2,052	2,177	2,177	2,177	2,177	2,177	2,177	2,177	2,177	2,177	2,177	2,177	2,177	2,177
E-2	1,836	1,836	1,836	1,836	1,836	1,836	1,836	1,836	1,836	1,836	1,836	1,836	1,836	1,836	1,836
E-1[1]	1,638	1,638	1,638	1,638	1,638	1,638	1,638	1,638	1,638	1,638	1,638	1,638	1,638	1,638	1,638

NA = Not applicable. **Note:** Basic pay rate for Academy cadets/midshipmen and ROTC members/applicants is $1,088. See Dept. of Defense Financial Management Regulations for details on pay-scale limitations and eligibility requirements. **Over 30 years**—O-10: $15,800; O-9: 15,800; O-8: 14,626; O-7: 12,910; O-6: 11,600; W-5: 9,038; W-4: 7,977; E-9: 7,286; E-8: 6,041. **Over 34 years**—O-10: $15,800; O-9: 15,800; O-8: 14,991; W-5: 9,489; E-9: 7,650. **Over 38 years**—O-10: $15,800; O-9: 15,800; W-5: 9,964; E-9: 8,033. (1) Applicable to E-1 with 4 months or more of active duty. Basic pay for an E-1 with less than 4 months of active duty is $1,515.

U.S. Veteran Population, 2018

Source: U.S. Dept. of Veterans Affairs
(projected population, in thousands, as of Sept. 30)

Period of service	Vet. pop.	Period of service	Vet. pop.
Total peacetime veterans[1]	**4,422**	Total Vietnam War era[3]	6,460
Service between Vietnam War era and Gulf War era	2,932	Vietnam War era with no other wartime service	5,978
Service between Korean War and Vietnam War era	1,424	Vietnam War era with service in Korea	115
Service between WWII and Korean War	61	Vietnam War era with service in Korea and WWII	16
Pre-WWII service	5	Total Gulf War era[3]	7,442
Total wartime veterans[2]	**15,181**	Gulf War era pre-9/11 with service in Vietnam era	287
Total World War II[3]	497	Gulf War era pre-9/11, post-9/11, and with service	
WWII only	444	in Vietnam War era	63
Total Korean War[3]	1,317	Gulf War era pre-9/11	2,584
Korean War with no other wartime service	1,149	Gulf War era pre-9/11 and post-9/11	1,391
Korean War with service in WWII	37	Gulf War era post-9/11	3,118
		TOTAL VETERANS IN CIVILIAN LIFE	**19,602**

Note: Figures are for U.S. veterans worldwide. Includes those who served on active duty in Army, Navy, Air Force, Marines, Coast Guard, uniformed Public Health Service and NOAA, and reservists called to federal active duty. Excludes those dishonorably discharged, those whose only active duty was training, and those currently on active duty. (1) Veterans with both wartime and peacetime service are counted only as "wartime veterans." (2) Veterans serving in more than one period are counted only once in total. (3) Total includes veterans who also served in other periods.

African American Service in U.S. Wars
Source: U.S. Dept. of Defense; U.S. Census Bureau, U.S. Dept. of Commerce

American Revolution. About 5,000 served in the Continental Army, mostly in integrated units, some in all-black combat units.

Civil War. Some 180,000 served in 163 units of the Union Army's U.S. Colored Troops, and 200,000 worked in service units—10% of the Union Army in all; about 37,000 died, 31,000 wounded.

World War I. 350,000-400,000 served in the armed forces, 100,000 in France. Some 40,000 fought.

World War II. Some 1 mil served in the armed forces—8% of all troops—mostly in Army service units; all-black fighter and bomber Army Air Force units and infantry divisions gave distinguished service.

Korean War. More than 600,000 served in the military; 3,075 lost their lives in combat. By 1954, armed forces were completely desegregated.

Vietnam War. 274,937 served in the armed forces (1965-74)—9.8% of all troops; 7,243 were killed in combat.

Persian Gulf War. About 104,000 served in the Kuwaiti theater—20% of all U.S. troops; 66 died in combat.

Operation Enduring Freedom/Freedom's Sentinel. 198 military deaths and 1,437 wounded in Afghanistan and elsewhere.

Operation Iraqi Freedom/Operation New Dawn/Operation Inherent Resolve. 458 military deaths and 2,767 wounded.

Outlays for Individual Payments to Veterans, 1940-2019
Source: White House Office of Management and Budget
(in millions of dollars)

Year	Total	Compensation	Pensions	Hospital, medical	Education	Insurance & burial	Year	Total	Compensation	Pensions	Hospital, medical	Education	Insurance & burial
1940	$574	$244	$185	$69	—	$76	2007	$73,726	$31,064	$3,376	$34,485	$3,456	$1,345
1950	8,613	1,533	476	764	$2,739	3,101	2008	84,463	36,266	3,790	39,409	3,634	1,364
1960	5,300	2,049	1,263	931	392	665	2009	94,985	40,490	4,161	44,637	4,328	1,369
1970	8,883	2,980	2,255	1,798	1,002	848	2010	106,454	43,498	4,359	48,506	8,773	1,318
1980	21,063	7,446	3,585	6,423	2,421	1,188	2011	122,524	52,780	4,664	52,681	11,112	1,287
1990	28,801	10,735	3,594	12,281	791	1,400	2012	119,544	50,058	4,537	52,972	10,734	1,243
2000	46,835	20,777	2,969	20,090	1,636	1,363	2013	134,083	59,393	5,173	55,067	13,220	1,230
2001	46,187	18,587	2,760	21,730	1,763	1,347	2014	143,412	64,360	5,251	58,906	13,729	1,166
2002	52,621	22,429	3,166	23,465	2,241	1,320	2015	153,506	69,725	5,299	63,652	13,605	1,225
2003	57,407	24,705	3,229	25,568	2,574	1,331	2016	167,046	79,907	5,824	65,810	14,579	926
2004	62,567	26,307	3,334	28,556	2,978	1,392	2017	167,399	79,839	5,505	67,949	13,520	586
2005	69,824	30,888	3,663	30,650	3,254	1,369	2018*	170,103	79,011	4,990	71,079	13,969	1,054
2006	71,139	31,000	3,547	31,888	3,354	1,350	2019*	189,918	92,409	5,521	75,587	15,439	962

— = Not available. * = Estimate. **Note:** Compensation is service-connected; pension is not.

Veterans Health Administration Characteristics, 2002-15
Source: U.S. Dept. of Veterans Affairs

Fiscal year	Total enrollees[1] (mil)	Outpatient visits[2] (mil)	Inpatient admissions (thous.)	Fiscal year	Total enrollees[1] (mil)	Outpatient visits[2] (mil)	Inpatient admissions (thous.)
2002	6.8	46.5	564.7	2009	8.1	74.9	662.0
2003	7.1	49.8	567.3	2010	8.3	80.2	682.3
2004	7.3	54.0	589.8	2011	8.6	79.8	692.1
2005	7.7	57.5	585.8	2012	8.8	83.6	703.5
2006	7.9	59.1	568.9	2013	8.9	86.4	694.7
2007	7.8	62.3	589.0	2014	9.1	92.4	707.4
2008	7.8	67.7	641.4	2015	9.0	95.2	699.1

(1) Includes non-enrolled veteran patients. (2) Includes fee visits.

Employment Status of Veterans With Service-Connected Disabilities, 2017
Source: Bureau of Labor Statistics, U.S. Dept. of Labor; as of Aug. 2017

Veteran status, presence of disability, and period of service	Employed (thous.) Total	Men	Women	Unemployed (thous.) Total	Men	Women	Unemployment rate (%) Total	Men	Women	Not in labor force (thous.) Total	Men	Women
Total veterans	9,618	8,452	1,166	448	369	78	4.4%	4.2%	6.3%	10,497	9,709	788
With service-connected disability	2,287	1,995	292	103	92	11	4.3	4.4	3.6	2,549	2,304	245
Without service-connected disability	7,005	6,173	832	333	274	59	4.5	4.2	6.6	7,567	7,072	494
Gulf War era, total	5,769	4,930	839	232	169	64	3.9	3.3	7.0	1,489	1,155	334
With service-connected disability	1,809	1,535	274	76	65	11	4.0	4.1	3.9	728	570	159
Without service-connected disability	3,732	3,202	530	146	102	44	3.8	3.1	7.7	648	508	140
Gulf War era II	3,150	2,659	491	147	102	46	4.5	3.7	8.5	788	578	209
With service-connected disability	1,215	1,054	160	50	43	7	3.9	3.9	4.1	403	295	108
Without service-connected disability	1,791	1,483	308	90	59	31	4.8	3.8	9.1	319	234	85
Gulf War era I	2,619	2,271	348	85	67	18	3.1	2.9	4.9	701	577	124
With service-connected disability	594	480	114	26	22	4	4.3	4.4	3.5	326	275	51
Without service-connected disability	1,941	1,719	222	57	43	14	2.8	2.4	5.8	329	273	55
WWII, Korean War, and Vietnam era	1,582	1,520	62	124	120	4	7.3	7.3	NA	6,343	6,120	223
With service-connected disability	250	250	NA	10	10	NA	3.9	3.9	NA	1,432	1,389	43
Without service-connected disability	1,309	1,247	62	112	108	4	7.9	8.0	NA	4,736	4,562	173
Other service periods	2,267	2,002	265	91	80	11	3.9	3.8	3.9	2,664	2,434	231
With service-connected disability	228	210	18	16	16	NA	6.7	7.3	NA	389	345	44
Without service-connected disability	1,965	1,725	240	74	64	11	3.6	3.6	4.3	2,183	2,002	181

NA = Not available. **Note:** Veterans in survey were on active duty in the U.S. Armed Forces during these periods of service: Gulf War era II (Sept. 2001-present), Gulf War era I (Aug. 1990-Aug. 2001), Vietnam era (Aug. 1964-Apr. 1975), Korean War (July 1950-Jan. 1955), World War II (Dec. 1941-Dec. 1946), and other service periods. Veterans who served in more than one wartime period are classified in the most recent period only. A service-connected disability is a health condition or impairment caused or made worse by military service.

Nations With Largest Armed Forces, 2018

Source: *The Military Balance 2018*, International Institute for Strategic Studies, published by Routledge Journals, Taylor & Francis, UK
(ranked by active-duty troop strength as of 2018; all other data as of Nov. 2017 unless otherwise noted)

Rank	Country	Active troops (thous.)	Reserve troops (thous.)	Defense expend. (mil)	Tanks (MBT) (army only)	Cruisers/ frigates/ destroyers	Sub-marines	Combat aircraft (air force only) FGA	Combat aircraft (air force only) FTR
1.	China	2,035	510	$150,458	6,740+	59F/23D*	62	566	819
2.	India	1,395	1,155	52,494	3,097+	13F/14D*	14	561	62
3.	United States	1,348	858	602,783	2,384	23C/9F/64D*	68	903	265
4.	North Korea	1,280	600	—	3,500+	2F	73	30	401+
5.	Russia	900	2,000	45,600	2,780	5C/13F/15D*	62	378	222
6.	Pakistan	654	0	9,720	2,467+	10F	8	224	153
7.	South Korea	625	3,100	35,674	2,514	3C/16F/6D	24	333	174
8.	Iran	523	350	16,035	1,513+	0	21	85	184+
9.	Vietnam	482	5,000	4,319	1,270	2F	8	74	0
10.	Egypt	439	479	2,669	2,460	9F/1D	6	298+	62
11.	Myanmar	406	0	2,095	185+	5F	0	0	66
12.	Indonesia	396	400	8,981	79	13F	3	33	9
13.	Thailand	361	200	6,163	318	8F*	0	11	78
14.	Turkey	355	379	7,983	2,485	18F	12	280	53
15.	Brazil	335	1,340	29,408	393	9F/2D	5	49	47
16.	Colombia	293	35	9,999	0	4F	4	22	0
17.	Mexico	277	82	4,532	0	5F	0	0	0
18.	Japan	247	56	46,004	690	2C/9F/32D*	19	143	189
19.	Saudi Arabia	227	0	76,678	900	4F/3D	0	161	81
20.	Taiwan	215	1,657	10,429	565	4C/20F	4	128	286
21.	Ukraine	204	900	2,734	832	1F	0	14	71
22.	France	203	32	48,640	200	11F/11D*	10	189	41
23.	Sri Lanka	243	6	1,704	62	0	0	15	8
24.	Eritrea	202	120	78[1]	270	0	0	2	8
25.	Morocco	196	150	3,487	407	5F/1D	0	49	22
26.	South Sudan	185	0	97	80+	0	0	0	0
27.	Germany	179	28	41,734	236	7F/7D	6	0	123
28.	Israel	177	465	18,547	460	0	5	259	58
29.	Italy	175	18	22,859	160	8F/10D*	8	78	86
30.	Afghanistan	174	0	2,166	20	0	0	0	0

— = Not available. * = Navy with aircraft carrier(s), as follows: China 1, France 1, India 1, Italy 2, Japan 3, Russia 1, Thailand 1, U.S. 11.
FGA = Fighter, ground attack. FTR = Fighter. MBT = Main battle tank. (1) As of 2013.

Budget for Global War on Terror Operations, 2001-14

Source: Congressional Research Service, Library of Congress
(in billions of dollars)

	2001/02[1]	2003	2004	2005	2007	2008	2010	2012	2013	2014	Total 2001-14
Total: war designated funding	$35.8	$74.4	$96.0	$108.4	$169.7	$195.2	$165.4	$129.7	$99.9	$95.2	$1,608.9
Dept. of Defense.	35.0	70.7	74.3	103.6	164.0	188.7	154.6	115.3	87.5	85.4	1,498.7
Foreign aid and diplomacy[2]	0.8	3.8	21.7	4.8	5.0	5.4	8.9	11.5	9.2	6.0	92.7
Veterans Affairs medical. . . .	0.0	0.0	0.0	0.0	0.7	1.0	1.9	2.9	3.2	3.7	17.6
Total: war designated funding not war-related	0.0	0.0	0.0	6.6	7.3	12.1	6.4	8.6	6.6	12.8	81.3
Dept. of Defense.	0.0	0.0	0.0	6.6	7.3	12.1	6.4	5.4	1.9	10.2	70.9
Foreign aid and diplomacy[2]	0.0	0.0	0.0	0.0	0.0	0.0	0.0	3.2	4.6	2.6	10.4
Op. Iraqi Freedom/New Dawn	0.0	51.0	76.7	79.1	130.8	143.9	64.8	20.3	7.7	4.8	814.6
Dept. of Defense.	0.0	48.0	57.1	77.1	127.1	140.3	59.9	13.5	4.9	1.1	753.1
Foreign aid and diplomacy[2]	0.0	3.0	19.5	2.0	3.2	2.7	3.3	4.7	0.7	1.4	48.6
Veterans Affairs medical. . . .	0.0	0.0	0.0	0.0	0.6	0.9	1.6	2.1	2.1	2.3	12.9
Op. Enduring Freedom[3]	22.8	17.4	15.4	20.7	31.1	39.0	94.1	100.6	85.6	77.4	685.6
Dept. of Defense.	22.0	16.7	13.2	17.9	29.2	36.1	88.2	96.3	80.6	74.0	647.3
Foreign aid and diplomacy[2]	0.8	0.7	2.2	2.8	1.9	2.7	5.6	3.5	3.9	2.0	33.6
Veterans Affairs medical. . . .	0.0	0.0	0.0	0.0	0.1	0.1	0.3	0.8	1.1	1.4	4.7
Op. Noble Eagle[4].	13.0	6.0	4.0	2.0	0.5	0.2	0.1	0.2	0.1	0.1	27.4

(1) Fiscal year (FY) 2001 and FY2002 funds combined because most were obligated in FY2002 after the Sept. 11, 2001, attacks at the end of FY2001, on Sept. 30, 2001. (2) Includes monies for reconstruction, development and humanitarian aid, embassy operations, counternarcotics, initial training of the Afghan and Iraqi armies, foreign military sales credits, and Economic Support Funds. (3) Covers Afghanistan (officially ended Dec. 2014) and other Global War on Terror operations, ranging from the Philippines to Djibouti, that began immediately after the Sept. 11, 2001, attacks. (4) Dept. of Defense funds that rebuilt the Pentagon and provided higher security at U.S. military bases and other homeland security, including combat air patrol.

Arms Transfer Agreements With the World by Supplier, 2008-15

Source: Congressional Research Service, Library of Congress
(in millions of current U.S. dollars)

Supplier	2008	2009	2010	2011	2012	2013	2014	2015	2008-15
United States	$34,987	$20,385	$19,285	$64,780	$23,851	$25,903	$36,123	$40,157	$265,471
Russia.	5,600	15,200	8,200	7,000	19,400	10,800	11,200	11,100	88,500
France	6,600	9,900	2,000	4,700	3,200	5,000	5,700	15,300	52,400
United Kingdom	200	1,500	1,600	700	5,700	3,900	500	700	14,800
China	2,200	3,100	2,000	3,200	3,500	4,300	3,300	6,000	27,600
Germany.	3,900	5,300	200	200	5,100	9,200	700	900	25,500
Italy.	4,000	1,700	1,600	1,600	1,900	1,000	1,600	1,000	14,400
All other European	5,100	6,900	4,600	3,800	8,600	5,200	25,300	3,100	62,600
All others.	3,300	5,400	2,400	3,500	6,600	5,000	4,600	1,600	32,400
Total.	65,887	69,385	41,885	89,480	77,851	70,303	89,023	79,857	583,671

Note: All data are for the calendar year given except for U.S. MAP (Military Assistance Program), IMET (International Military Education, and Training), and Excess Defense Article data, which are included with the particular fiscal year. All amounts given include the values of all categories of weapons, spare parts, construction, all associated services, military assistance, excess defense articles, and training programs. Statistics for foreign countries are based upon estimated selling prices.

U.S. Foreign Military Financing, 2010-17

Source: Defense Security Cooperation Agency, U.S. Dept. of Defense

Listed are grants extended to foreign governments in a fiscal year to pay for military equipment and services. May be from the U.S. Dept. of Defense (DOD) or, for specific countries, negotiated directly with U.S. commercial suppliers with DOD approval.

(in thousands of U.S. dollars)

	2010	2015	2017		2010	2015	2017
Western Hemisphere	**$89,720**	**$48,550**	**$74,897**	**Europe**	**$151,696**	**$146,150**	**$170,080**
Colombia	55,000	27,000	38,525	Bosnia and			
Costa Rica	325	1,200	7,000	Herzegovina	4,000	4,000	4,000
Guatemala	1,375	1,000	2,427	Bulgaria	9,000	5,000	7,450
Honduras	1,514	3,100	5,000	Croatia	2,500	3,500	3,000
Mexico	5,250	4,675	5,000	Czech Republic	6,000	2,127	3,000
Panama	1,800	1,800	4,375	Estonia	2,500	1,600	20,000
Near East and				Georgia	16,000	30,000	37,000
South Asia	**4,666,797**	**4,886,776**	**4,668,408**	Latvia	2,500	2,535	10,000
Bahrain	19,000	7,500	0	Lithuania	2,700	2,400	19,680
Egypt	1,300,000	1,300,000	195,000	Moldova	750	11,250	12,750
Iraq	0	0	107,378	Poland	47,000	9,000	8,150
Israel	2,775,000	3,100,000	3,760,000	Romania	12,999	5,400	8,350
Jordan	300,000	385,000	470,000	Ukraine	11,000	47,000	14,000
Lebanon	0	84,117	132,330	**Africa**	**45,370**	**52,950**	**129,500**
Oman	8,847	4,000	0	Chad	500	0	4,090
Pakistan	248,000	0	0	Djibouti	2,000	710	500
East Asia and				Kenya	1,500	1,810	4,200
Pacific	**59,100**	**77,250**	**93,600**	Liberia	6,000	2,500	2,500
Indonesia	20,000	14,000	14,000	Morocco	9,000	12,000	10,000
Mongolia	4,500	2,000	2,600	Niger	0	500	6,535
Philippines	29,000	50,000	50,250	Tunisia	18,000	30,000	95,000
Vietnam	2,000	10,750	26,750	**World total**	**5,015,952**	**5,211,901**	**5,144,253**

NA = Not available. **Note:** Regional subtotals include countries not listed. (1) World total includes funding for global security, peacekeeping, and other activities.

Leading Defense Contract Recipients, 2017

Source: U.S. Dept. of Defense; Federal Procurement Data System

Listed are the 50 companies or organizations receiving the largest dollar volume of prime contract awards from the U.S. Dept. of Defense during fiscal year 2017 (Oct. 1, 2016-Sept. 30, 2017).

(in millions of U.S. dollars)

Rank	Recipient	Funds awarded	Rank	Recipient	Funds awarded
1.	Lockheed Martin Corp.	$48,167.8	26.	CACI International Inc.	$1,534.1
2.	The Boeing Co.	21,332.8	27.	Oshkosh Corp.	1,519.8
3.	Raytheon Co.	13,961.9	28.	Textron Inc.	1,460.1
4.	General Dynamics Corp.	13,687.2	29.	AECOM	1,440.2
5.	Northrop Grumman Corp.	9,968.6	30.	Cerberus Capital Management L.P.	1,350.8
6.	Huntington Ingalls Industries Inc.	6,745.3	31.	Health Net Inc.	1,316.8
7.	BAE Systems PLC	5,440.7	32.	KBR Inc.	1,213.6
8.	L3 Technologies Inc.	4,912.4	33.	Leonardo S.p.A.	1,122.4
9.	Humana Inc.	3,645.4	34.	Honeywell International Inc.	1,064.4
10.	Bechtel Group Inc.	3,515.8	35.	Massachusetts Institute of Tech.	1,035.8
11.	UnitedHealth Group Inc.	2,904.1	36.	Sierra Nevada Corp.	1,034.8
12.	McKesson Corp.	2,838.7	37.	Vectrus Systems Corp.	1,009.9
13.	United Technologies Corp.	2,630.0	38.	BP Products North America Inc.	1,006.5
14.	General Atomic Technologies Corp.	2,563.3	39.	The Aerospace Corp.	886.1
15.	Bell Boeing Joint Project Office.	2,509.7	40.	MacAndrews & Forbes Holdings Inc.	864.8
16.	Science Applications Intl. Corp. (SAIC)	2,358.2	41.	Rockwell Collins Inc.	841.8
17.	General Electric Co.	2,297.1	42.	The MITRE Corp.	810.7
18.	AmerisourceBergen Corp.	2,219.0	43.	Johns Hopkins University	783.1
19.	Harris Corp.	2,035.4	44.	Rolls-Royce Corp.	759.8
20.	United Launch Alliance LLC	1,951.4	45.	Royal Dutch Shell PLC	735.6
21.	Booz Allen Hamilton Holding Corp.	1,934.3	46.	Fluor Corp.	731.8
22.	Leidos Holdings, Inc.	1,762.3	47.	Alion Science and Tech. Corp.	688.9
23.	Centene Corp.	1,583.1	48.	Express Scripts Holding Co.	640.4
24.	Atlantic Diving Supply Inc.	1,570.2	49.	Insight Enterprises Inc.	639.2
25.	Alliant Techsystems Inc.	1,540.3	50.	Austal Ltd.	603.0

U.S. Army and Air Force Units

Army Units. Squad: In infantry, usually 8-16 enlisted personnel under a sergeant or staff sergeant. **Platoon:** In infantry, 3 squads under a lieutenant. **Company:** Headquarters and 3-5 platoons under a captain. (Company-size unit in the artillery is a battery; in the cavalry, a troop.) **Battalion:** 3-6 companies under a lieutenant colonel. (Battalion-size unit in the cavalry is a squadron.) **Brigade:** Three or more battalions under a colonel. (Brigade-size unit in the cavalry and rangers is a regiment; in the special forces, a group.) **Division:** 3 brigades with combat support and combat service support units under a major general. **Corps:** 2-5 divisions with corps troops under a lieutenant general. **Army:** 2-5 corps with operational and support responsibilities under a general.

Air Force Units. Flight: Numerically designated flights are the lowest level unit. They are used primarily where there is a need for small mission elements to be incorporated into an organized unit. **Squadron:** The basic unit. Designates specific operational or support capability like mission units in operational commands. **Group:** Flexible unit composed of 2 or more squadrons whose functions may be operational, support, or administrative in nature. **Wing:** Primary group with supporting groups on a distinct mission with significant scope such as combat, flying training, or airlift. **Numbered Air Force (NAF):** Normally operationally oriented, the numbered air force is designed for the control of subordinate units with the same mission and/or geographical location. **Major Command (MAJCOM):** A major subdivision with full staff that manages a major segment of the USAF mission. Major command is composed of 3 or more numbered air forces.

Personal Salutes and Honors

The U.S. **national salute**, 21 guns, is also the salute to a national flag. U.S. independence is commemorated by the salute to the Union—one gun for each state—fired at noon July 4, at all military posts provided with suitable artillery.

A 21-gun salute on arrival and departure, with 4 ruffles and flourishes, is rendered to the **president**, to a former president, and to a president-elect. The national anthem or "Hail to the Chief," as appropriate, is played for the president, and the national anthem for the others. A 21-gun salute on arrival and departure, with 4 ruffles and flourishes, also is rendered to the **sovereign or chief of state of a foreign country** or a member of a reigning royal family, and the national anthem of his or her country is played. The music is considered an inseparable part of the salute and immediately follows the ruffles and flourishes without pause. For the Honors March, generals receive the "General's March," admirals receive the "Flag Officer's March," and all others receive the 32-bar medley of "The Stars and Stripes Forever."

GRADE, TITLE, OR OFFICE	SALUTE (IN GUNS) Arriving	SALUTE (IN GUNS) Leaving	Ruffles and flourishes	Music
Vice President of U.S.	19	—	4	Hail, Columbia
Speaker of the House.	19	—	4	Honors March
U.S. or foreign ambassador in country to which accredited	19	—	4	Natl. anthem of official
Premier or prime minister	19	—	4	Natl. anthem of official
Secretary of Defense, Army, Navy, or Air Force	19	19	4	Honors March
Other cabinet members, Senate president pro tempore, governor, or chief justice of U.S.	19	—	4	Honors March
Chairman, Joint Chiefs of Staff.	19	19	4	Honors March
Army chief of staff, chief of naval operations, Air Force chief of staff, Marine commandant.	19	19	4	Honors March
General of the Army, general of the Air Force, fleet admiral	19	19	4	Honors March
Generals, admirals.	17	17	4	Honors March
Assistant secretaries of Defense, Army, Navy, or Air Force.	17	17	4	Honors March
Chair of a committee of Congress	17	—	4	Honors March

Medal of Honor

Source: Congressional Medal of Honor Society; U.S. Army, U.S. Dept. of Defense
(as of Aug. 31, 2018)

The Medal of Honor is the highest military award for individual bravery in the U.S. On Dec. 21, 1861, Pres. Abraham Lincoln signed a bill to create the Navy Medal of Honor. Lincoln, on July 14, 1862, approved a resolution providing for the presentation of Medals of Honor to enlisted men of the Army and Voluntary Forces. The law was amended on Mar. 3, 1863, so that officers as well as enlisted men were eligible. The first Army Medals of Honor were awarded on Mar. 25, 1863; the first Navy medals went to sailors and Marines on Apr. 3, 1863.

The Medal of Honor is awarded in the name of Congress to a person who, while a member of the armed forces, distinguishes himself or herself conspicuously by gallantry and intrepidity at the risk of life above and beyond the call of duty while engaged in an action against any enemy of the U.S.; while engaged in military operations involving conflict with an opposing foreign force; or while serving with friendly foreign forces engaged in an armed conflict against an opposing armed force in which the U.S. is not a belligerent party.

The deed performed must have been one of personal bravery or self-sacrifice so conspicuous as to clearly distinguish the individual above his or her comrades and must have involved risk of life. Incontestable proof of the performance of service is required, and each recommendation for award of this decoration is considered on the standard of extraordinary merit.

Prior to World War I, the 2,625 Army Medal of Honor awards up to that time were reviewed to determine which met new stringent criteria. The Army removed 911 names from the list, most of them former members of a Civil War volunteer infantry group who had been induced to extend their enlistments when they were promised the medal; the medal was restored to Dr. Mary Walker in 1977 and to Buffalo Bill Cody and seven other Indian scouts in 1989.

Seven African American soldiers were awarded Medals of Honor for service in World War II (six of them posthumously) in Jan. 1997. Previously, no black soldier had received the medal for World War II service; an Army inquiry begun in 1993 concluded that the prevailing political climate and Army practices of the time had prevented proper recognition of heroism on the part of black soldiers in that war. In 1996, Congress authorized a review of Asian American and Pacific Islander recipients of the Distinguished Service Cross whose award should be upgraded. Twenty-two Asian Americans received the Medal of Honor for World War II service in June 2000.

In one of the largest Medal of Honor ceremonies in U.S. history, Pres. Barack Obama Mar. 18, 2014, awarded 24 mostly Hispanic, Jewish, and African-American veterans with the nation's highest military decoration for valor displayed in World War II, the Korean War, and Vietnam. The recipients, three of whom were alive to receive the award, had been found deserving following a congressionally mandated review of the records of service members who may have been overlooked due to discrimination.

Medal of Honor Recipients From Recent Conflicts

Honoree	Rank	Branch of service	Date of action	Date of award
Somalia Campaign				
Gordon, Gary I.*	Master Sgt.	U.S. Army	10/3/1993	5/23/1994
Shughart, Randall D.*	Sgt. First Class	U.S. Army	10/3/1993	5/23/1994
War in Iraq				
Dunham, Jason L.*	Corporal	USMC	4/14/2004	1/11/2007
McGinnis, Ross A.*	Pvt. First Class/Specialist*	U.S. Army	12/4/2006	6/5/2008
Monsoor, Michael A.*	Petty Officer Second Class	U.S. Navy	9/29/2006	4/8/2008
Smith, Paul R.*	Sgt. First Class	U.S. Army	4/4/2003	4/5/2005
War in Afghanistan				
Byers, Edward C., Jr.	Chief	U.S. Navy	12/8-9/2012	2/29/2016
Carpenter, William Kyle	Lance Cpl.	USMC	11/21/2010	6/19/2014
Carter, Ty M.	Specialist	U.S. Army	10/3/2009	8/26/2013
Chapman, John A.*	Technical Sgt.	USAF	3/4/2002	8/22/2018
Giunta, Salvatore A.	Staff Sgt.	U.S. Army	10/25/2007	11/16/2010
Groberg, Florent A.	Capt.	U.S. Army	8/8/2012	11/12/2015
Meyer, Dakota	Sgt.	USMC	9/8/2009	9/15/2011
Miller, Robert J.*	Staff Sgt.	U.S. Army	1/25/2008	10/6/2010
Monti, Jared C.*	Sgt. First Class	U.S. Army	6/21/2006	9/17/2009
Murphy, Michael P.*	Lt.	U.S. Navy	6/28/2005	10/22/2007
Petry, Leroy A.	Staff Sgt.	U.S. Army	5/26/2008	7/12/2011
Pitts, Ryan M.	Sgt.	U.S. Army	7/13/2008	7/21/2014
Romesha, Clinton L.	Staff Sgt.	U.S. Army	10/3/2009	2/11/2013
Slabinski, Britt K.	Senior Chief	U.S. Navy	3/4/2002	5/24/2018
Swenson, William D.	Capt.	U.S. Army	9/8/2009	10/15/2013
White, Kyle J.	Sgt.	U.S. Army	11/9/2007	5/13/2014

* = Awarded posthumously.

Other Selected Awards

Source: The Institute of Heraldry, U.S. Army; Navy Department Awards Web Service; Air Force Personnel Center

Distinguished Service Cross

Established by Congress July 9, 1918, on recommendation of Gen. John J. "Black Jack" Pershing, and awarded for extraordinary heroism not justifying the award of a Medal of Honor. The act or acts of heroism must have been so notable and have involved risk of life so extraordinary as to set the individual apart from his or her comrades. The Navy Cross and Air Force Cross are equivalent.

Silver Star

Third-highest military combat honor. An earlier version of this award, the Citation Star, was established by Congress on July 19, 1918, and retroactively awarded to soldiers for "gallantry in action," back to the Spanish-American War. The Silver Star medal replaced the Citation Star in 1932 and is awarded for gallantry in action which, while of a lesser degree than that required for award of the Distinguished Service Cross, must nevertheless have been performed with marked distinction.

Legion of Merit

Established by Congress on July 20, 1942, and awarded to individuals who have distinguished themselves by exceptionally meritorious conduct in the performance of outstanding services. There are different designs depending on the level of command of the award recipient.

Distinguished Flying Cross

Established by Congress July 2, 1926, and awarded for heroism or extraordinary achievement while participating in aerial flight. Awards are made only to recognize single acts of heroism or extraordinary achievement, not sustained operational activities against an armed enemy. Initial awards were given to persons who made record-breaking long-distance and endurance flights or who set altitude records. The first DFC was awarded to Cpt. Charles A. Lindbergh on May 31, 1927. DFCs were awarded retroactively to Orville and Wilbur Wright.

Soldier's Medal

Established by Congress July 2, 1926, to recognize acts of heroism not involving actual conflict with an enemy. The same degree of heroism is required as for the award of the Distinguished Flying Cross. The performance must have involved personal hazard or danger and the voluntary risk of life under conditions not involving conflict with an armed enemy. Awards are not made solely on the basis of having saved a life.

Bronze Star

Established by executive order Feb. 4, 1944, largely to raise the morale of ground troops in WWII, on the recommendation of Gen. George C. Marshall. It is awarded to any person who, while serving in any capacity in or with the U.S. military, distinguishes himself or herself by heroic or meritorious achievement or service not involving participation in aerial flight.

Purple Heart

The original Purple Heart, designated as the Badge of Military Merit, was established by Gen. George Washington on Aug. 7, 1782. Following the American Revolution, the badge fell into disuse until 1932, the 200th anniversary of Washington's birth. During WWII, the Order of the Purple Heart was awarded for both wounds received in action and for meritorious service. Following the introduction of the Legion of Merit, the Purple Heart was awarded only for combat wounds. Today, it is awarded to any armed forces member who, while serving with the U.S. Armed Services, has been wounded or killed, or who has died or may hereafter die after being wounded in action against an enemy of the U.S. or in an armed conflict in which the U.S. or friendly foreign forces are engaged; as the result of an act of any hostile foreign force; as a result of an international terrorist attack against the U.S. or a friendly foreign nation; or as a result of military operations outside the U.S. as part of a peacekeeping force. Wounds must be inflicted directly by enemy action, including while held as a prisoner of war or while being taken captive.

Air Medal

Authorized by Pres. Franklin D. Roosevelt on May 11, 1942, and awarded for heroism or meritorious achievement while participating in aerial flight. Awards may be made to recognize single acts of merit or heroism or for meritorious service. Awards are not made to individuals who use air transportation solely for the purpose of moving between points in a combat zone.

Army Commendation

Established Dec. 18, 1945, and awarded for heroism, meritorious achievement, or meritorious service. It may also be awarded to a member of the armed forces of a friendly foreign nation who distinguishes him- or herself by an act of heroism, extraordinary achievement, or meritorious service.

U.S. Military Awards in Selected Wars and Conflicts

Source: U.S. Army Human Resources Command, U.S. Dept. of Defense; Congressional Medal of Honor Society

Award	Civil War	WWI	WWII	Korea	Vietnam	Gulf War	Afghanistan[1]	Iraq[2]
Medal of Honor	1,522	127	473	146	262	0	16	4
Distinguished Service Cross	NA	6,428	4,710	734	1,066	0	26	15
Silver Star	NA	NA	73,654	10,061	21,634	75	403	372
Legion of Merit	NA	NA	20,273	NA	10,356	158	231	163
Distinguished Flying Cross	NA	NA	126,318	NA	21,697	108	216	121
Soldier's Medal	NA	NA	12,485	581	5,402	43	64	111
Bronze Star (total)	NA	NA	395,408	30,359	719,971	28,857	69,931	114,172
Purple Heart	NA	NA	NA	NA	220,527	504	9,273	22,815
Air Medal (total)	NA	NA	1,166,471	0	1,039,125	6,399	19,150	22,643
Army Commendation (total)	NA	NA	0	0	837,040	81,979	180,847	399,549

NA = Not available or applicable. **Note:** Numbers for the individual decorations shown here represent only those awards that were properly processed and reported to Dept. of the Army Headquarters. The actual number of individual decorations awarded under combat conditions, when award approval authority is delegated to field commanders, cannot be stated with absolute certainty. Numbers here reflect the current statistics recorded by the Military Awards Branch, as of July 13, 2018, except for MOH, which was reported by the Congressional Medal of Honor Society as of Aug. 27, 2018. (1) Operation Enduring Freedom and Operation Freedom's Sentinel. May include awards for actions related to operations but occurring outside of Afghanistan. (2) Operation Iraqi Freedom, Operation New Dawn, and Operation Inherent Resolve. May include awards for actions related to operations but occurring in other nations, including Syria.

Federal Service Academies

U.S. Military Academy, West Point, NY. Founded 1802. Awards B.S. degree and Army commission for a 5-year service obligation. **Website:** www.usma.edu

U.S. Naval Academy, Annapolis, MD. Founded 1845. Awards B.S. degree and Navy or Marine Corps commission for a 5-year service obligation. **Website:** www.usna.edu

U.S. Air Force Academy, Colorado Springs, CO. Founded 1954. Awards B.S. degree and Air Force commission for a 6-year service obligation. **Website:** www.usafa.af.mil

U.S. Coast Guard Academy, New London, CT. Founded 1876. Awards B.S. degree and Coast Guard commission for a 5-year service obligation. **Website:** www.cga.edu

U.S. Merchant Marine Academy, Kings Point, NY. Founded 1943. Awards B.S. degree; a license as a deck, engineer, or dual officer; and a U.S. Naval Reserve commission. Service obligations vary according to options taken by the graduate. **Website:** www.usmma.edu

U.S. Army, Navy, Air Force, Marine Corps, and Coast Guard Insignia

Source: Dept. of the Army, Dept. of the Navy, Dept. of the Air Force, U.S. Dept. of Defense; U.S. Coast Guard, U.S. Dept. of Homeland Security

Army

General of the Armies—Gen. John J. Pershing (1860-1948), the only person to have held this rank while living, was authorized to prescribe his own insignia but never wore in excess of four stars. Congress established the rank in 1799 to be bestowed on George Washington; Washington was finally promoted to the rank by joint resolution of Congress, approved by Pres. Gerald Ford, Oct. 19, 1976.

General of the Army—Five silver stars fastened together in a circle and the coat of arms of the U.S. in gold color metal with shield and crest enameled. Reserved for wartime use only.

Rank	Insignia
General of the Army*	Five silver stars
General	Four silver stars
Lieutenant General	Three silver stars
Major General	Two silver stars
Brigadier General	One silver star
Colonel	Silver eagle
Lieutenant Colonel	Silver oak leaf
Major	Gold oak leaf
Captain	Two silver bars
First Lieutenant	One silver bar
Second Lieutenant	One gold bar

Warrant Officers

Grade Five—Silver bar with enamel black line.
Grade Four—Silver bar with 4 enamel black squares.
Grade Three—Silver bar with 3 enamel black squares.
Grade Two—Silver bar with 2 enamel black squares.
Grade One—Silver bar with 1 enamel black square.

Noncommissioned Officers

Sergeant Major of the Army (E-9)—Three chevrons above 3 arcs, with a U.S. coat of arms centered on the chevrons, flanked by 2 stars—1 star on each side of the eagle. Also distinctive red-and-white shield collar insignia.
Command Sergeant Major (E-9)—Three chevrons above 3 arcs with a 5-pointed star with a wreath around the star between the chevrons and arcs.
Sergeant Major (E-9)—Three chevrons above 3 arcs with a 5-pointed star between the chevrons and arcs.
First Sergeant (E-8)—Three chevrons above 3 arcs with a lozenge between the chevrons and arcs.
Master Sergeant (E-8)—Three chevrons above 3 arcs.
Sergeant First Class (E-7)—Three chevrons above 2 arcs.
Staff Sergeant (E-6)—Three chevrons above 1 arc.
Sergeant (E-5)—Three chevrons.
Corporal (E-4)—Two chevrons.

Specialists

Specialist (E-4)—Eagle device only.

Other Enlisted

Private First Class (E-3)—One chevron above 1 arc.
Private (E-2)—One chevron.
Private (E-1)—None.
*Rank reserved for wartime use only.

Air Force

Insignia for Air Force officers are identical to those of the Army. Insignia for enlisted personnel are worn on both sleeves and consist of 1 star and an appropriate number of rockers. Chevrons appear above 5 rockers for the top three noncommissioned officer ranks, as follows (in ascending order): Master Sergeant, 1 chevron; Senior Master Sergeant, 2 chevrons; Chief Master Sergeant, 3 chevrons. The insignia of the Chief Master Sergeant of the Air Force has 3 chevrons and a wreath around the star design, while the Command Chief Master Sergeant insignia features an additional star. General of the Air Force is reserved for wartime use only.

Navy

The following stripes are worn on the lower sleeves of the Service Dress Blue uniform. They are of gold embroidery.

Rank	Insignia
Fleet Admiral*	1 two inch with 4 one-half inch
Admiral	1 two inch with 3 one-half inch
Vice Admiral	1 two inch with 2 one-half inch
Rear Admiral (upper half)	1 two inch with 1 one-half inch
Rear Admiral (lower half)	1 two inch
Captain	4 one-half inch
Commander	3 one-half inch
Lieutenant Commander	2 one-half inch with 1 one-quarter inch between
Lieutenant	2 one-half inch
Lieutenant (jr. grade)	1 one-half inch with 1 one-quarter inch above
Ensign	1 one-half inch
Warrant Officer W-5	½" stripe under ⅛" blue strip with 1 break
Warrant Officer W-4	½" stripe with 1 break
Warrant Officer W-3	½" stripe with 2 breaks, 2" apart
Warrant Officer W-2	½" stripe with 3 breaks, 2" apart

Enlisted personnel (noncommissioned petty officers)—Rating badge worn on the upper left sleeve consisting of a spread eagle, appropriate number of chevrons, and centered specialty mark.

* = Rank reserved for wartime use only.

Marine Corps

Marine Corps' distinctive cap and collar ornament is the Marine Corps emblem—a combination of the American eagle, a globe, and an anchor. Marine Corps and Army officer insignia are similar. Marine Corps enlisted insignia, although basically similar to the Army's, feature crossed rifles beneath the chevrons. Marine Corps enlisted rank insignia are as follows:

Sergeant Major of the Marine Corps (E-9)—Same as Sergeant Major (below) but with Marine Corps emblem in the center with a 5-pointed star on both sides of the emblem.
Sergeant Major (E-9)—Three chevrons above 4 rockers with a 5-pointed star in the center.
Master Gunnery Sergeant (E-9)—Three chevrons above 4 rockers with a bursting bomb insignia in the center.
First Sergeant (E-8)—Three chevrons above 3 rockers with a diamond in the middle.
Master Sergeant (E-8)—Three chevrons above 3 rockers with crossed rifles in the middle.
Gunnery Sergeant (E-7)—Three chevrons above 2 rockers with crossed rifles in the middle.
Staff Sergeant (E-6)—Three chevrons above 1 rocker with crossed rifles in the middle.
Sergeant (E-5)—Three chevrons above crossed rifles.
Corporal (E-4)—Two chevrons above crossed rifles.
Lance Corporal (E-3)—One chevron above crossed rifles.
Private First Class (E-2)—One chevron.
Private (E-1)—None.

Coast Guard

Coast Guard insignia follow Navy custom, with certain minor changes such as the officer cap insignia. The Coast Guard shield is worn on both sleeves of officers and on the right sleeve of all enlisted personnel.

U.S. Armed Forces Contact Information

Additional information on all the U.S. Armed Forces branches, as well as many other related organizations, can be accessed through the Dept. of Defense. **Website:** www.defense.gov

Army—Office of the Chief of Public Affairs, Media Relations Division—MRD, 1500 Army Pentagon, Washington, DC 20310-1500. **Website:** www.army.mil

Navy—Chief of Information, 1200 Navy Pentagon, Washington, DC 20350-1200. **Website:** www.navy.mil

Air Force—Office of Public Affairs, 1690 Air Force Pentagon, Washington, DC 20330-1690. **Website:** www.af.mil

Marine Corps—Marine Corps Headquarters, Division of Public Affairs, 3000 Marine Corps, Pentagon, Washington, DC 20350-3000. **Website:** www.usmc.mil

Coast Guard—Office of Governmental & Public Affairs (CG-0922), 2703 Martin Luther King Jr. Ave. SE, Washington, DC 20593-0007. **Website:** www.uscg.mil

Casualties in Principal Wars of the U.S.

Source: U.S. Dept. of Defense; U.S. Coast Guard, U.S. Dept. of Homeland Security

Data prior to World War I are based on incomplete records in many cases. Casualty data are confined to dead and wounded personnel and, therefore, exclude personnel captured or missing in action who were subsequently returned to military control.

	Branch of service	Number serving	CASUALTIES			
			Battle deaths	Other deaths	Wounds not mortal[1]	Total[2]
Revolutionary War	Total	184,000 to 250,000[13]	4,435	—	6,188	10,623
1775-83						
War of 1812	Total	286,730[14]	2,260	—	4,505	6,765
1812-15	Army	—	1,950	—	4,000	5,950
	Navy	—	265	—	439	704
	Marines	—	45	—	66	111
Mexican War	Total	78,718[14]	1,733	11,550	4,152	17,435
1846-48	Army	—	1,721	11,550	4,102	17,373
	Navy	—	1	—	3	4
	Marines	—	11	—	47	58
	Coast Guard[8] . .	71 off.	—	—	—	—
Civil War						
1861-65						
Union forces[3]	Total	2,213,363	140,414	224,097	281,881	646,392
	Army	2,128,948[14]	138,154	221,374	280,040	639,568
	Navy	84,415	2,112	2,411	1,710	6,233
	Marines	(in Navy total)	148	312	131	591
	Coast Guard[8] . .	219 off.	1	—	—	1
Confederate forces (estimate)[3]	Total	600,000 to 1.5 mil	74,524	59,297	—	133,821
Spanish-American War	Total	306,760	385	2,061	1,662	4,108
1898	Army[9]	280,564	369	2,061	1,594	4,024
	Navy	22,875	10	—	47	57
	Marines	3,321	6	—	21	27
	Coast Guard[8] . .	660	0	—	—	—
World War I	Total	4,734,991	53,402	63,114	204,002	320,518
Apr. 6, 1917-Nov. 11, 1918	Army[10]	4,057,101	50,510	55,868	193,663	300,041
	Navy	599,051	431	6,856	819	8,106
	Marines	78,839	2,461	390	9,520	12,371
	Coast Guard . . .	8,835	111	81	—	192
World War II[4]	Total	16,112,566	291,557	113,842	670,846	1,076,245
Dec. 7, 1941-Dec. 31, 1946	Army[11]	11,260,000	234,874	83,400	565,861	884,135
	Navy[12]	4,183,466	36,950	25,664	37,778	100,392
	Marines	669,100	19,733	4,778	67,207	91,718
	Coast Guard . . .	241,093	574	1,343	—	1,917
Korean War[5]	Total	5,720,000	33,739	2,835	103,284	139,858
June 25, 1950-July 27, 1953	Army	2,834,000	27,731	2,125	77,596	107,452
	Navy	1,177,000	503	154	1,576	2,233
	Marines	424,000	4,267	242	23,744	28,253
	Air Force	1,285,000	1,238	314	368	1,920
	Coast Guard . . .	44,143	—	—	—	—
Vietnam War[6]	Total	8,744,000	47,434	10,786	153,303	211,523
Aug. 4, 1964-Jan. 27, 1973	Army	4,368,000	30,963	7,261	96,802	135,026
	Navy	1,842,000	1,631	935	4,178	6,744
	Marines	794,000	13,095	1,749	51,392	66,236
	Air Force	1,740,000	1,745	841	931	3,517
	Coast Guard . . .	8,000	7	2	60	69
Persian Gulf War	Total	2,225,000	147	235	467	849
1991	Army	782,000	98	126	354	578
	Navy	669,000	5	50	12	67
	Marines	213,000	24	44	92	160
	Air Force	561,000	20	15	9	44
	Coast Guard . . .	400	—	—	—	—
Iraq War[7]	Total	269,363[15]	3,519	964	32,253	36,736
Mar. 19, 2003-Dec. 15, 2011	Army	99,664[15]	2,574	722	22,523	25,819
	Navy	61,018[15]	63	45	651	759
	Marines	66,166[15]	852	171	8,626	9,649
	Air Force	42,515[15]	29	26	452	507
	Coast Guard . . .	1,250[15]	1	—	1	2

— = Not available. Off. = Officers. **Note:** As of Aug. 2018, there were 1,844 battle deaths, 503 non-hostile deaths, and 20,094 wounded in Op. Enduring Freedom (Oct. 7, 2001-Dec. 31, 2014), mostly in Afghanistan and the Persian Gulf area; 37 battle deaths, 15 non-hostile deaths, and 318 wounded in Operation Freedom's Sentinel (Jan. 1, 2015-) in Afghanistan; 14 battle deaths, 53 non-hostile deaths, and 72 wounded in Operation Inherent Resolve (Aug. 8, 2014-) against ISIS in Iraq and Syria. (1) Marine Corps data for Iraq War, World War II, Spanish-American War, and prior wars represent the number of individuals wounded, whereas all other data in this column represent the total number (incidence) of wounds. (2) Totals for all branches do not include categories for which no data are listed. (3) From the final report of the Provost Marshal General, 1863-66. Authoritative statistics for the Confederate forces are not available. In addition, an estimated 26,000-31,000 Confederate personnel died in Union prisons. New estimates published in *Civil War History* in 2012 recalculated the death toll for both sides and determined that it was 20% higher than previously thought, at 750,000. (4) Data are for Dec. 1, 1941, through Dec. 31, 1946, when hostilities were officially terminated by presidential proclamation; few battle deaths or wounds not mortal were incurred after Japanese acceptance of Allied peace terms on Aug. 14, 1945. Numbers serving Dec. 1, 1941-Aug. 31, 1945: Total—14,903,213; Army—10,420,000; Navy—3,883,520; Marine Corps—599,693. (5) As a result of an ongoing Dept. of Defense review of available Korean War casualty record information, updates have been made to previously reported figures for battle deaths and other deaths. (6) Number serving Aug. 5, 1964-Jan. 27, 1973 (date of cease-fire). Includes casualties incurred in Mayaguez incident. Wounds not mortal exclude 150,341 persons not requiring hospital care. (7) Military deaths during the invasion phase, which ended Apr. 30, 2003, totaled 115 combat-related and 23 other. (8) Then known as the U.S. Revenue Cutter Services, predecessor to the U.S. Coast Guard. (9) Number serving Apr. 21-Aug. 13, 1898, while dead and wounded data are for May 1-Aug. 31, 1898. Active hostilities ceased on Aug. 13, 1898, but the U.S. and Spain did not exchange ratifications of the treaty of peace until Apr. 11, 1899. (10) Includes Army Air Forces battle deaths and wounds not mortal, as well as casualties suffered by American forces in northern Russia to Aug. 25, 1919, and in Siberia to Apr. 1, 1920. Other deaths cover Apr. 1, 1917-Dec. 31, 1918. (11) Includes Army Air Forces. (12) Battle deaths and wounds not mortal include casualties incurred in Oct. 1941 due to hostile action. (13) Estimated. (14) As reported by Commissioner of Pensions in his Annual Report for Fiscal Year 1903. (15) Number serving as of Mar. 31, 2003, i.e., does not include numbers of troops deployed since then.

Timeline of Major Wars Since 1066

Norman Conquest
1066-71

William I, duke of Normandy, landed on the English coast near Hastings on Sept. 28, 1066, and defeated Harold II, Saxon king of England, at Battle of Hastings Oct. 14. William crowned king Dec. 25 in Westminster Abbey. Most revolts were suppressed by 1071. **Conquest linked England's interests with those of the continent and led to its rise as a powerful monarchy.**

Crusades
1095-1270/1291

Military expeditions undertaken by **Western European Christians**, usually at the behest of the **papacy**, to recover **Jerusalem** and other Biblical places of pilgrimage from **Muslim** control. In the long term, stimulated trade and flow of ideas between East and West. Pope Urban II called Nov. 27, 1095, for the **First Crusade**; Crusaders took Jerusalem on July 15, 1099, massacred inhabitants, and founded four temporary states: Antioch, Edessa, Jerusalem, and Tripoli. The failed **Second Crusade** was prompted by Muslims' capture of Edessa in 1144. Jerusalem was captured by Ayyubid sultan Saladin on Oct. 2, 1187, leading to the **Third Crusade**, which involved the Holy Roman emperor, Frederick I (Barbarossa); the French king, Philip II (Augustus); and the English king, Richard I (Lion-Heart) but did not lead to a Crusader victory. The **Fourth Crusade** sacked Constantinople on Apr. 13, 1204. The **Fifth Crusade** began with capture of Damietta in Egypt (1219) but failed at Cairo. A **Sixth Crusade** led to the Treaty of Jaffa in 1229, giving Jerusalem to the Crusaders until 1244, when its seizure by the Khwarezmians led to the launch of a **Seventh Crusade**. The last crusade abruptly ended when its leader, French King Louis IX, died in 1270. The last major Crusader stronghold, Acre, was lost on May 18, 1291.

Hundred Years War
1337-1453

Series of armed conflicts over rival claims to the French throne, broken by a number of truces and peace treaties. Edward III declared self king of France in 1338 and invaded, with victories at Crécy (1346) and Poitiers (1356). **Treaty of Brétigny** signed May 8, 1360, but French king Charles V renewed fighting in 1369. Truce from 1396 until **Henry V** of England invaded in 1415 and **defeated French army at Agincourt**, capturing land north of Loire River, including Paris. **Treaty of Troyes** in 1420 made Henry VI heir of both thrones. The siege of French stronghold Orléans, lifted in 1429 with help from **Joan of Arc**, turned tide in favor of French, who won last battle (1453). **War ended English claims to France, paved way for French absolute monarchy.**

Wars of the Roses
1455-85

Series of dynastic civil wars for the throne in England fought by the **rival houses of Lancaster and York**. Richard, third duke of York, in conflict with the Lancastrian King **Henry VI**, won victories at St. Albans (1455) and Northampton (1460); Richard died at Battle of Wakefield on Dec. 30, 1460, before coronation, leaving his son to become King Edward IV. Henry VI imprisoned in Tower of London, 1465. Edward died in 1483; his brother became **Richard III** after usurping throne from Edward V, nephew. Henry Tudor defeated Richard III at the Battle of Bosworth Field (1485). As Henry VII, he married Edward IV's daughter Elizabeth, 1486, **uniting the houses**.

Thirty Years' War
1618-48

A series of religious and political conflicts involving **most countries of Western Europe**; majority of fighting in Germany, devastating it. Protestants stormed Habsburg palace in the "Defenestration of Prague" (May 23, 1618). Major conflicts included defeat of King Christian IV of Denmark and Norway by Catholic League (1626); victories by Lutheran King Gustav II Adolph of Sweden at Breitenfeld (1631) and Lützen (1632). France, under cardinal and statesman **Richelieu**, chief minister of King Louis XIII, declared war on the Habsburgs in May 1635; defeated Austro-Bavarian army (Aug. 3, 1645), leading to Truce of Ulm. **Peace of Westphalia** signed at Münster on Oct. 24, 1648, bringing peace by recognizing the rulers' sovereignty within their lands and their right to determine the religious beliefs of their subjects.

English Civil Wars
1638-60

Series of conflicts between followers of King Charles (Cavaliers) and of Parliament (Roundheads), over divine right of king versus Parliament's right to control national finances. Presbyterian Scots, allied with Parliament, rioted and in 1640 occupied the northern counties of England. **Oliver Cromwell**, second in command of Parliament's New Model Army, destroyed the king's army at Battle of Naseby (June 14, 1645); first civil war ended May 1646 when Charles surrendered to the Scots. Charles later allied with Scots but was defeated by Cromwell at Preston Aug. 17-19, 1648, and executed Jan. 30, 1649. Parliament abolished monarchy and House of Lords. Cromwell suppressed Irish and Scottish rebellions, was briefly succeeded by son Richard after death (1658). **Charles II restored to the throne** by the "Long Parliament," May 1660.

War of the Spanish Succession
1701-14

War fought by the Grand Alliance (originally England, Netherlands, Denmark, and Austria; later also Portugal), against coalition of France, Spain, and a number of small Italian and German principalities to preserve balance of power after death of Spanish king Charles II. Opened with invasion of Italy, via Venice, by an Austrian army under Prince Eugène of Savoy in May 1701. French forced to withdraw from Netherlands and Italy in 1706 and were finally defeated in 1709 in bloodiest battle of the war at French village of Malplaquet. Treaties of Rastatt and Baden signed in 1714; **Austria given control of Spanish Netherlands, and peace settled between Austria and France.**

War of the Austrian Succession
1740-48

Conflict over rival claims for the **hereditary dominions of the Habsburg family**, following death (1740) of Charles VI, Holy Roman emperor and archduke of Austria. An alliance of Bavaria, France, Spain, Sardinia, Prussia, and Saxony fought against Austria, allied with Holland and Great Britain. King Frederick the Great of Prussia captured Silesia from Austria in the First (1740-42) and Second (1744-45) Silesian Wars. British king George II defeated French army at Battle of Dettingen am Main (June 27, 1743). French conquered Austrian Netherlands (1745-46). Treaty of Aix-la-Chapelle Oct. 18, 1748, **restored most original borders; Prussia became significant force.**

Seven Years' War
1756-63

Worldwide conflicts fought for **control of Germany** and for **supremacy in colonial N America and India**. French defeated British Gen. Edward Braddock in Battle of Monongahela in 1754, leading to formal declaration of **French-Indian War**, May 1756. Frederick II of Prussia invaded Saxony on Aug. 29, 1756; defeated French at Rossbach (1757), Austrians at Leuthen (1757), Russians at Zorndorf (1758). By 1760, British conquered French Canada. Peter III of Russia signed armistice with Prussia, 1762. Treaty of Paris signed Feb. 10, 1763; Peace of Hubertusburg Feb. 15, 1763, between Prussia and Austria. **England emerged as leading world naval power.**

American Revolution
1775-83

Conflict between Great Britain and 13 British colonies in eastern N America. George Washington took command of the Continental Army, July 3, 1775, and King George III declared colonies traitors on Aug. 23. **Declaration of Independence of colonies adopted July 4, 1776.** France recognized the colonies' independence Feb. 6, 1778, followed by Spain on June 21, 1779; both pledged support. French fleet drove British fleet under Adm. Thomas Graves from Chesapeake Bay on Sept. 5, 1781. French and Americans laid siege to Yorktown, VA, Sept. 28-Oct. 19, forcing British Gen. Cornwallis to surrender. **Treaty of Paris** (Sept. 3, 1783) recognized U.S. independence.

Wars of French Revolution and Napoleonic Wars
1792-1815

Large-scale wars fought between France and two multinational coalitions. France declared war on the Austrian part of the Holy Roman Empire, Apr. 20, 1792. Newly created French Republic declared war on monarchs of Britain and Holland, Feb. 1, 1793, and of Spain, Mar. 7. **Napoleon Bonaparte** defeated Austria in N Italy (1796-97), captured Egypt from Britain (1798-99; Battle of the Pyramids, July 21, 1798), and became First Consul after coup d'état of Nov. 9-10, 1799. French Grande Armée later swept through Europe using innovative and aggressive tactics. French navy defeated by British under Adm. Horatio Nelson at **Trafalgar** (Oct. 21, 1805), but Napoleon defeated Austro-Russian forces at Austerlitz (Dec. 2) and controlled most of Europe except Russia and Great Britain by 1808. France suffered its first major defeat by Austria at Aspern-Essling, May 21-22, 1809. **Napoleon invaded Russia**, captured Moscow Sept. 14, 1812, but fled the bitter Russian winter and abandoned Germany after defeat at Leipzig, Oct. 16-19, 1813. Paris captured by Allied armies Mar. 30-31, 1814. Napoleon exiled to Elba May 4 but returned for "Hundred Days" reign, Mar. 20-June 28, 1815; **final defeat at Waterloo** by British and Prussian troops (June 18). The **Bourbon monarchy was restored under Louis XVIII**, and Britain, Prussia, Russia, and Austria maintained European peace.

Crimean War 1853-56	Conflict between **Russia** and coalition of **Great Britain, France, Sardinia, and Turkey for influence over Balkans** and the straits between the Black Sea and Mediterranean. Russia destroyed Turkish fleet at Sinope on Nov. 30, 1853. Britain and France declared war in Mar. 1854 and with Turkish troops defeated Russians at Battle of Alma River, Sept. 20. Lord Lucan of Britain prevented Russia from capturing Balaklava on Oct. 25 ("Charge of the Light Brigade" led by Lord Cardigan). Siege of Sevastopol ended when Russia evacuated Sept. 8, 1855. Treaty of Paris signed Mar. 30, 1856; **curbed Russian expansion and loosened European power alignments**.
American Civil War 1861-65	Conflict between the U.S. (the Union) and 11 secessionist Southern states (the Confederate States of America). Union garrison at Fort Sumter in harbor of Charleston, SC, surrendered to Brig. Gen. P.G.T. Beauregard (Apr. 12-13, 1861). Under Beauregard, 22,000 Confederates repelled 35,000 Union troops under Gen. Irvin McDowell along Bull Run stream near Manassas, VA (July 21). The *Merrimack* (renamed *Virginia*) battled the *Monitor* Mar. 9, 1862. In **Battle of Antietam**, MD (Sept. 17), some 12,000 Northerners and 12,700 Southerners were killed or wounded. Pres. Abraham Lincoln announced **Emancipation Proclamation** Sept. 22. Confederate Gen. Robert E. Lee's 75,000 forces battled 88,000 Union troops under Gen. George Meade at **Gettysburg**, PA, July 1-3, 1863; Lee's army forced across the Potomac R. Lee surrendered to Ulysses S. Grant at **Appomattox Court House** in Virginia (Apr. 9, 1865). **The Union was preserved and slavery subsequently abolished**.
Franco-Prussian War 1870-71	German states led by Prussia defeated France, seizing Alsace and part of Lorraine. French defeated in several major battles, culminating at **Sedan** Sept. 1, 1870, when Prussian forces decisively defeated the French army and captured emperor Napoleon III. Prussian king William I was made emperor of unified Germany, Jan 18, 1871. **France surrendered** Jan. 28. Final treaty signed May 10; set the stage for later **German imperialistic expansion**.
Spanish-American War 1898	War waged by the U.S. to **liberate Cuba from Spanish rule**. A mysterious explosion, blamed on Spain by American newspapers, sank the U.S. battleship *Maine* in Havana's harbor (Feb. 15, 1898), killing 260. The U.S. called for Spain's withdrawal from Cuba, and Spain declared war (Apr. 24). William Rufus Shafter led 17,000 U.S. troops from Daiquirí to Santiago de Cuba, taking **San Juan Hill** with help of the Rough Riders under Teddy Roosevelt. Santiago de Cuba surrendered July 17. The Treaty of Paris (Dec. 10, 1898) provided for the **independence of Cuba** and the cession by Spain to the U.S. of **Puerto Rico, Guam, and for a $20 mil payment, the Philippine Islands**.
World War I 1914-18	Local European war that grew into a global war involving 32 nations: the Allies and the Associated Powers—28 nations including Great Britain, France, Russia, Italy, and the U.S.—versus the Central Powers of Germany, Austria-Hungary, Turkey, and Bulgaria. Archduke Francis Ferdinand of Austria assassinated in Sarajevo, Bosnia (June 28, 1914). Germany invaded France through Belgium; advance on Paris halted by the French under Gen. Joseph Jacques Césaire Joffre at the **First Battle of the Marne**, Sept. 5-12. Germany checked the Russian army at the Battle of Tannenberg, Aug. 26-30. The British suffered 57,470 casualties (19,240 dead) in the opening day of the **First Battle of the Somme** (July 1-Nov. 18, 1916), first of 12 battles that forced Germany back to Hindenburg Line. **U.S. declared war on Germany Apr. 6, 1917.** Russian involvement ended when Bolshevik party seized power on Nov. 7; signed armistice Dec. 15. German offensive halted by U.S. and French troops at **Second Battle of the Marne** (July 15-Aug. 5, 1918), turning point of the war. Allied counteroffensive broke the fortified defensive Hindenburg Line, and an armistice was signed Nov. 11.
World War II 1939-45	Global military conflict stemming from European unrest after World War I and Japan's aggressive expansion into Asia and the Pacific. **War in Europe:** Nazi-Soviet nonaggression pact (Aug. 23, 1939) freed Germany and the Soviet Union to attack Poland in Sept. **Britain and France declared war on Germany** Sept. 3. German forces raced through Europe (Apr.-June 1940), captured Paris June 14. **Italy declared war on France and Britain** June 10. German-Italian campaigns won the Balkans and N Africa by June 1941. U.S. entered war Dec. 1941. Three million Axis troops invaded Russia June 22, 1941, but Russian counterthrusts stopped the German advance (**Stalingrad**, Aug. 20, 1942-Feb. 2, 1943), and Allies took N Africa (Nov. 8, 1942-May 13, 1943), Italy (July 10, 1943-May 2, 1945). Normandy invaded on **D-Day**, June 6, 1944; Paris liberated Aug. 25. Leaders at Yalta Conference (Feb. 4-11, 1945) discussed defeat and division of Germany into four. Adolf Hitler committed suicide Apr. 30. **Germany surrendered unconditionally** May 7. **War in the Pacific:** Japan invaded China (July 7, 1937), joined alliance with Germany and Italy (Sept. 27, 1940), and signed nonaggression pact with Russia (Apr. 13, 1941); attacked Hawaii's Pearl Harbor, Dec. 7, 1941. U.S. declared war on Japan Dec. 8. **Battle of Midway** (June 4-7, 1942) repulsed Japanese advance. Marines landed on Guadalcanal Aug. 7. Navy defeated Japanese fleet at **Leyte Gulf**, Oct. 23-26, 1944. B-29 bombing raids on Japan began in Nov. Marines invaded Iwo Jima (Feb. 19-Mar. 16, 1945) with heavy casualties, then Okinawa (Apr. 1-June 21). **U.S. atom bombs dropped** on Hiroshima (Aug. 6) and Nagasaki (Aug. 9) and Soviet invasion of Manchuria (Aug. 8) **forced Japan to agree, on Aug. 14, to surrender**; formal surrender on Sept. 2.
Korean War 1950-53	Military struggle fought on the Korean Peninsula between the Democratic Peoples' Republic of Korea (N Korea) and the Republic of Korea (S Korea) that developed into an international war involving China allied with N Korea against the U.S. and other nations under the UN flag. DPRK army crossed the 38th parallel and invaded S Korea (June 25, 1950), entering Seoul (June 26). Amphibious assault launched at **Inchon** by Gen. Douglas MacArthur (Sept. 15) helped U.S. forces rout DPRK close to Yalu River by Nov. 24. The Chinese, in counterattack, retook Seoul (Jan. 4, 1951) but were forced back to the 38th parallel by Apr. 22. Armistice was signed (July 27, 1953) by the UN, DPRK, and China, but not ROK, **leaving the peninsula partitioned at about the 38th parallel**.
Vietnam War 1959-75	Struggle primarily in S Vietnam that widened into a war between S Vietnam supported mainly by the U.S. and N Vietnam supported by the USSR and China. Viet Minh, led by Communist leader Ho Chi Minh, formed the Democratic Republic of Vietnam (Sept. 2, 1945). Colonial power France withdrew after fortress at Dien Bien Phu fell (May 8, 1954). Pres. John F. Kennedy pledged U.S. commitment to S Vietnamese independence Dec. 14, 1961. USS *Maddox* destroyer damaged in **Gulf of Tonkin** (Aug. 2, 1964), prompting Congress to increase involvement. Regular bombing of N Vietnam began (Feb. 24, 1965), and the first U.S. combat ground forces arrived (Mar. 6). N Vietnamese Army siege of **Khe Sanh** (Jan. 21-Apr. 7, 1968) and the **"Tet"** offensive (Jan. 30) aimed to cause insurrection in the S. **My Lai Massacre** by U.S. soldiers of civilians (Mar. 16, 1968) created scandal, fueled U.S. disaffection with war. U.S. forces peaked at 543,400 in Apr. 1969. NVA **"Easter Offensive"** (Mar. 30, 1972) rebuffed, and U.S. responded with aerial bombings in May and Dec. U.S. withdrew after cease-fire, Jan. 1973. **NVA offensive captured Saigon, Apr. 30, 1975, and unified Vietnam under Communist rule**.
Persian Gulf Wars 1991, 2003-10	Conflicts fought principally between Iraq and the U.S. concerning Iraq's influence in the Middle East and its development of weapons of mass destruction. **First Gulf War:** Iraq under dictator Saddam Hussein invaded Kuwait Aug. 2, 1990, and annexed it; UN Security Council ordered Iraqi forces to withdraw by Jan. 15, 1991. Beginning Jan. 17, a U.S.-led multinational force (**Operation Desert Storm**) bombed military targets in Iraq and Kuwait. A coordinated air-land offensive (**Operation Desert Sabre**, begun Feb. 24) retook Kuwait City Feb. 26, and permanent cease-fire was signed on Apr. 6. Iraq was ordered to pay reparations to Kuwait, reveal locations of biological and chemical weapons, and eliminate weapons of mass destruction. **Second Gulf War:** The U.S. and UK mistakenly asserted that Iraq was still producing WMDs and posed an imminent threat. The UN passed Resolution 1441, Nov. 8, 2002, warning Iraq of "serious consequences" if it failed to cooperate fully and unconditionally with UN weapons inspectors. Iraq rejected a Mar. 17, 2003, U.S. ultimatum demanding Hussein and his sons leave Iraq. U.S. launched **Operation Iraqi Freedom** Mar. 19, 2003, with support from UK and other allies, but without full UN Security Council support. Baghdad fell Apr. 9, and major combat operations declared over May 1. Hussein was captured Dec. 13, 2003, but guerrilla opposition to U.S. troops and insurgent violence continued. U.S. combat operations in Iraq formally ended Aug. 31, 2010.

HEALTH

U.S. Health Expenditures, 1960-2016

Source: *Health, United States, 2017*, National Center for Health Statistics, CDC, U.S. Dept. of Health and Human Services

Type of national health expenditure	1960	1970	1980	1990	2000	2009	2015	2016
			Amount in billions					
National health expenditures (total)	$27.2	$74.6	$255.3	$721.4	$1,369.7	$2,495.4	$3,200.8	$3,337.2
			Percent distribution					
Health consumption expenditures	90.8%	89.9%	92.2%	93.4%	93.9%	94.4%	95.2%	95.3%
Personal health care.	85.5	84.6	85.0	85.3	84.8	84.7	84.8	84.9
Hospital care	33.0	36.4	39.4	34.7	30.4	31.2	32.3	32.4
Professional services	29.1	26.5	25.3	28.7	28.3	26.8	26.2	26.4
Physician and clinical services	20.4	19.2	18.7	22.0	21.0	19.9	19.7	19.9
Other professional services	1.4	1.0	1.4	2.4	2.7	2.7	2.7	2.8
Dental services	7.3	6.3	5.2	4.4	4.5	4.1	3.7	3.7
Other health, residential, personal care	1.6	1.7	3.3	3.3	4.7	4.9	5.1	5.2
Home health care[1]	0.2	0.3	0.9	1.7	2.4	2.7	2.8	2.8
Nursing care facilities and continuing care retirement communities[1]	3.0	5.4	6.0	6.2	6.2	5.4	4.9	4.9
Retail outlet sales of medical products . .	18.5	14.2	10.1	10.6	13.0	13.7	13.5	13.2
Prescription drugs	9.8	7.4	4.7	5.6	8.8	10.1	10.1	9.8
Durable medical equipment	2.7	2.3	1.6	1.9	1.8	1.5	1.5	1.5
Other nondurable medical products . .	6.0	4.5	3.8	3.1	2.3	2.0	1.9	1.9
Government administration	0.2	1.0	1.1	1.0	1.2	1.2	1.3	1.3
Net cost of health insurance	3.7	2.5	3.6	4.4	4.7	5.5	6.5	6.6
Government public health activities[2]	1.4	1.8	2.5	2.8	3.1	3.0	2.6	2.5
Investment	9.2	10.1	7.8	6.6	6.1	5.6	4.8	4.7
Research[3]	2.6	2.6	2.1	1.8	1.9	1.8	1.5	1.4
Structures and equipment	6.7	7.5	5.7	4.8	4.2	3.8	3.4	3.3
			Average annual percent change from previous year shown					
National health expenditures	—	10.6%	13.9%	10.9%	6.6%	6.9%	4.2%	4.3%
Health consumption expenditures	—	10.5	14.2	11.1	6.7	7.0	4.4	4.4
Personal health care.	—	10.5	13.9	11.0	6.6	6.9	4.3	4.4
Hospital care	—	11.7	14.4	9.6	5.2	7.2	4.8	4.7
Professional services	—	9.6	13.2	12.4	6.4	6.3	3.9	5.2
Physician and clinical services	—	9.9	13.5	12.7	6.2	6.3	4.0	5.4
Other professional services	—	6.3	21.1	17.4	7.8	6.9	4.6	4.7
Dental services	—	9.0	10.7	9.0	7.0	5.8	2.4	4.6
Other health, residential, personal care	—	11.5	23.9	11.0	10.4	7.6	4.9	5.3
Home health care[1]	—	14.5	30.7	18.1	9.9	8.6	4.6	4.0
Nursing care facilities and continuing care retirement communities[1]	—	17.4	13.7	11.4	6.6	5.3	2.6	2.9
Retail outlet sales of medical products . .	—	7.7	10.4	11.4	8.8	7.5	4.1	2.1
Prescription drugs	—	7.5	8.4	12.8	11.6	8.5	4.3	1.3
Durable medical equipment	—	9.0	7.7	13.0	6.2	4.6	4.3	4.9
Other nondurable medical products . .	—	7.4	14.6	8.6	3.5	5.3	2.9	4.4
Government administration	—	30.0	13.2	10.0	9.0	6.3	6.1	4.0
Net cost of health insurance	—	6.4	22.0	13.0	7.4	8.9	7.0	5.8
Government public health activities[2]	—	13.8	16.8	12.0	8.0	6.2	1.6	0.6
Investment	—	11.6	10.3	9.1	5.8	5.8	1.7	2.4
Research[3]	—	10.9	10.0	8.9	7.2	6.6	0.4	2.6
Structures and equipment	—	11.9	10.4	9.2	5.3	5.5	2.3	2.3

— = Not applicable. **Note:** Numbers may not add up to totals because of rounding. (1) In freestanding facilities only. Additional services of this type provided in hospital-based facilities are considered hospital care. (2) Includes health care services delivered by government public health agencies. (3) Excludes research and development expenditures of drug companies and other mfrs. and providers of medical equipment and supplies. They are included in the expenditure class in which a product falls.

Health Coverage for Persons Under 65, 1984-2016

Source: *Health, United States, 2017*, National Center for Health Statistics, CDC, U.S. Dept. of Health and Human Services
(percent of population)

	Private insurance[1]				Medicaid[1,2]				Not covered[3]			
	1984[4]	2000	2010	2016	1984[4]	2000	2010	2016	1984[4]	2000	2010	2016
Total	76.8%	71.5%	61.7%	65.7%	6.8%	9.5%	16.9%	21.1%	14.5%	17.0%	18.2%	10.3%
Age												
Under 18 years	72.6	66.6	54.1	54.3	11.9	19.6	36.4	39.6	13.9	12.6	7.8	5.2
18-44 years	76.5	70.5	60.0	67.2	5.1	5.6	10.9	16.0	17.1	22.4	27.1	14.8
45-64 years	83.3	78.7	71.3	73.6	3.4	4.5	6.8	11.6	9.6	12.6	15.7	8.8
Race and Hispanic origin												
White only, non-Hispanic	82.4	79.5	72.0	75.2	3.7	6.1	11.0	14.2	11.9	12.5	13.7	7.3
Black only, non-Hispanic	58.2	56.0	45.1	51.2	20.7	21.0	30.0	33.5	19.7	19.5	20.7	11.3
Hispanic or Latino, any race . . .	55.7	47.8	36.8	45.3	13.3	15.5	28.6	33.6	29.5	35.6	32.0	19.6
Percent of poverty level												
Below 100%	32.2	25.2	16.0	19.8	33.0	38.4	50.8	59.4	33.9	34.2	30.3	18.5
100%-199%	70.3	50.1	34.8	36.6	5.3	16.2	28.5	41.4	21.8	31.0	32.4	18.0
200%-399%	89.3	78.1	70.7	73.7	0.8	4.0	8.4	12.8	7.6	15.4	17.4	10.1
400% or more	95.4	91.9	89.9	91.3	0.2	0.9	2.0	2.7	3.2	5.9	5.6	3.7
Geographic region												
Northeast	80.5	76.3	68.2	69.5	8.6	10.6	17.9	22.7	10.2	12.2	12.4	6.7
Midwest	80.6	78.8	66.7	70.8	7.4	8.0	17.3	19.3	11.3	12.3	14.1	7.8
South	74.3	66.8	57.5	61.8	5.1	9.4	16.0	19.3	17.7	20.5	22.5	14.3
West	71.9	66.5	58.9	63.9	7.0	10.4	17.1	24.0	18.2	20.7	20.6	9.3

Note: Data based on household interviews of a sample of the civilian noninstitutionalized population. Totals incl. groups not shown separately. (1) Incl. persons who also had another type of coverage in addition. (2) Incl. other public assistance, such as a state-sponsored health plan or Children's Health Insurance Program (CHIP). (3) Incl. persons not covered by private insurance, Medicaid or other public assistance, Medicare, or military plans. (4) Because of questionnaire redesign, data for 1984 are not strictly comparable with data for later years.

Spending on Health in the 50 Most Populous Countries, 2015

Source: Global Health Expenditure Database, World Health Organization (WHO)

Country	As % of GDP	Per capita[1]	Country	As % of GDP	Per capita[1]	Country	As % of GDP	Per capita[1]	Country	As % of GDP	Per capita[1]
Afghanistan...	10.3%	$60	France......	11.1%	$4,026	Morocco	5.5%	$160	Sudan........	6.3%	$152
Algeria	7.1	292	Germany.....	11.2	4,592	Mozambique..	5.4	28	Tanzania.....	6.1	32
Angola	2.9	109	Ghana.......	5.9	80	Myanmar.....	4.9	59	Thailand	3.8	219
Argentina	6.8	998	India	3.9	63	Nepal	6.1	44	Turkey.......	4.1	455
Bangladesh...	2.6	32	Indonesia	3.4	114	Nigeria	3.6	98	Uganda	7.3	46
Brazil........	8.9	780	Iran	7.6	366	Pakistan	2.7	38	Ukraine......	6.1	125
Canada......	10.4	4,508	Iraq	3.4	154	Peru	5.3	323	UK..........	9.9	4,356
China	5.3	426	Italy........	9.0	2,700	Philippines ...	4.4	127	U.S.	16.8	9,536
Colombia	6.2	374	Japan	10.9	3,733	Poland.......	6.3	797	Uzbekistan ...	6.2	134
Congo, Dem.			Kenya	5.2	70	Russia.......	5.6	524	Venezuela....	3.2	973
Rep. of the..	4.3	20	Korea, South..	7.4	2,013	Saudi Arabia ..	5.8	1,194	Vietnam	5.7	117
Egypt	4.2	157	Malaysia	3.9	377	South Africa ..	8.2	471	Yemen.......	6.0	72
Ethiopia......	4.0	24	Mexico	5.9	535	Spain	9.2	2,354	**World[2]**	**6.3**	**822**

(1) At average exchange rate. (2) Includes other nations not shown.

Population Not Covered by Health Insurance by State, 1990-2017

Source: American Community Survey and Current Population Survey, U.S. Census Bureau, U.S. Dept. of Commerce
(numbers in thousands)

	1990 No. not covered	1990 % pop. not covered	2000 No. not covered	2000 % pop. not covered	2017 No. not covered	2017 % pop. not covered		1990 No. not covered	1990 % pop. not covered	2000 No. not covered	2000 % pop. not covered	2017 No. not covered	2017 % pop. not covered
AL	710	17.4%	547	12.5%	449	9.4%	MT	115	14.0%	144	16.1%	88	8.5%
AK	77	15.4	108	17.4	98	13.7	NE	138	8.5	134	7.9	157	8.3
AZ	547	15.5	853	16.4	695	10.1	NV	201	16.5	321	15.7	333	11.2
AR	421	17.4	373	14.1	232	7.9	NH	107	9.9	97	7.9	77	5.8
CA	5,683	19.1	5,956	17.5	2,797	7.2	NJ	773	10.0	857	10.2	688	7.7
CO	495	14.7	559	12.9	414	7.5	NM	339	22.2	415	23.0	187	9.1
CT	226	6.9	300	8.9	194	5.5	NY	2,176	12.1	2,730	14.5	1,113	5.7
DE	96	13.9	66	8.5	51	5.4	NC	883	13.8	964	12.1	1,076	10.7
DC	109	19.2	71	12.8	26	3.8	ND	40	6.3	61	9.8	56	7.5
FL	2,376	18.0	2,591	16.2	2,676	12.9	OH	1,123	10.3	1,101	9.8	686	6.0
GA	971	15.3	1,126	13.9	1,375	13.4	OK	574	18.6	587	17.4	545	14.2
HI	81	7.3	95	7.9	53	3.8	OR	360	12.4	398	11.6	281	6.8
ID	159	15.2	198	15.4	172	10.1	PA	1,218	10.1	915	7.6	692	5.5
IL	1,272	10.9	1,474	12.0	859	6.8	RI	105	11.1	71	6.9	48	4.6
IN	587	10.7	608	10.1	536	8.2	SC	550	16.2	426	10.7	542	11.0
IA	225	8.1	233	8.1	146	4.7	SD	81	11.6	80	10.8	77	9.1
KS	272	10.8	256	9.6	249	8.7	TN	673	13.7	603	10.7	629	9.5
KY	480	13.2	509	12.7	235	5.4	TX	3,569	21.1	4,555	22.0	4,817	17.3
LA	797	19.7	736	16.8	383	8.4	UT	156	9.0	243	10.8	282	9.2
ME	139	11.2	131	10.4	107	8.1	VT	54	9.5	44	7.4	28	4.6
MD	601	12.7	473	9.0	366	6.1	VA	996	15.7	670	9.6	729	8.8
MA	530	9.1	450	7.1	190	2.8	WA	557	11.4	767	13.1	446	6.1
MI	865	9.4	767	7.8	510	5.2	WV	249	13.8	239	13.4	109	6.1
MN	389	8.9	393	8.0	243	4.4	WI	321	6.7	378	7.1	309	5.4
MS	531	19.9	368	13.2	352	12.0	WY	58	12.5	71	14.7	70	12.3
MO	665	12.7	474	8.6	548	9.1	**U.S.**	**34,719**	**13.9**	**36,586**	**13.1**	**28,019**	**8.7**

Persons Not Covered by Health Insurance by Selected Characteristics, 2017

Source: Annual Social and Economic Supplement, Current Population Survey, U.S. Census Bureau, U.S. Dept. of Commerce
(numbers in thousands)

	Number not covered	% of pop. specified at left		Number not covered	% of pop. specified at left
Total.........................	**28,543**	**8.8%**	**Nativity**		
Race and Hispanic origin[1]			Native....................	20,921	7.5%
White......................	21,075	8.5	Foreign born...............	7,622	16.8
White, not Hispanic	12,362	6.3	Naturalized citizen..........	1,936	8.9
Black......................	4,512	10.6	Not a citizen	5,687	24.1
Asian......................	1,413	7.3	**Household income**		
Hispanic (any race)...........	9,508	16.1	Less than $25,000	6,482	13.9
Age			$25,000 to $49,999.........	7,618	12.3
Under 65 years	27,865	10.2	$50,000 to $74,999..........	5,570	10.4
Under 18 years	3,930	5.3	$75,000 and over	8,873	5.5
Under 6 years	1,424	6.0	**Work experience[2]**		
6 to 11 years	1,247	5.1	All workers	17,194	11.3
12 to 17 years	1,259	5.0	Full-time, year round	10,776	9.8
18 to 24 years	3,782	12.9	Less than full-time, year round..	6,418	15.1
25 to 34 years	6,981	15.6	Did not work at least one week...	6,742	14.7
35 to 44 years	5,407	13.3	**Marital status[3]**		
45 to 54 years	4,252	10.2	Married....................	9,262	9.1
55 to 64 years	3,513	8.4	Widowed...................	479	13.4
65 years and older	678	1.3	Divorced...................	2,652	13.6
			Separated..................	886	20.3
			Never married...............	10,365	16.0

(1) Numbers are for one race alone unless otherwise noted. (2) Persons age 18 to 64 only. (3) Persons age 19 to 64 only.

Health Insurance Marketplace Plan Enrollment by Selected Characteristics

Source: Centers for Medicare & Medicaid Services (CMS), U.S. Dept. of Health and Human Services
(cumulative enrollment-related activity for Nov. 1, 2017-Feb. 5, 2018 [exact end date varies by state])

	Marketplace total		Federal marketplaces[1]		State marketplace[2]	
	Number	Percent	Number	Percent	Number	Percent
Number who have selected a plan	11,750,175	100.0%	8,743,642	100.0%	3,006,533	100.0%
Number receiving financial assistance[3].....	9,781,207	83.2	7,463,080	85.4	2,318,127	77.1
With cost-sharing reduction........	6,302,193	53.6	4,758,871	54.4	1,543,322	51.3
With advance premium tax credit	9,762,104	83.1	7,447,615	85.2	2,314,489	77.0
Number who have selected a plan by known age[4]						
0 to 34 years of age	4,077,541	34.7	3,087,215	35.3	990,326	32.9
Under 18 years of age................	1,003,825	8.5	803,649	9.2	200,176	6.7
18 to 34 years of age................	3,073,716	26.2	2,283,566	26.1	790,150	26.3
35 to 44 years of age	1,843,037	15.7	1,378,238	15.8	464,799	15.5
45 to 54 years of age	2,388,266	20.3	1,773,445	20.3	614,821	20.4
55 to 64 years of age	3,227,927	27.5	2,409,107	27.6	818,820	27.2
65 years of age and older..............	131,611	1.1	95,637	1.1	35,974	1.2

NA = Not available (not reported). **Note:** Figures may not add up to totals due to rounding. (1) For states with marketplaces supported or fully run by the Dept. of Health and Human Services, or the federally facilitated marketplace. (2) For states implementing their own marketplaces, known as state-based marketplaces. (3) Advance premium tax credit with or without cost-sharing reduction. (4) Except for those under 18 years of age who have selected a plan, marketplace total and state marketplace subtotals exclude Idaho, which reports plan selections by different age ranges.

Health Insurance Marketplace Average Monthly Premiums, 2018

Source: Centers for Medicare & Medicaid Services, U.S. Dept. of Health and Human Services
In the 39 states with health insurance marketplaces supported or fully run by the federal government, 85.2% of those who selected a plan chose one with advance premium tax credits based on projected income compared to 77.0% of those who used one of the 12 state-based exchanges. States using the HealthCare.gov platform unless otherwise noted.
(based on enrollment-related activity for Nov. 1, 2017-Feb. 5, 2018 [exact end date varies by state])

State	Avg. premium after tax credits	Avg. premium before tax credits	Avg. tax credit	Avg. % reduction in premium after tax credits	State	Avg. premium after tax credits	Avg. premium before tax credits	Avg. tax credit	Avg. % reduction in premium after tax credits
Alabama	$120.52	$677.07	$622.28	82.2%	Montana	$182.94	$643.25	$550.89	71.6%
Alaska........	163.53	803.87	724.44	79.7	Nebraska	118.79	857.15	804.52	86.1
Arizona.......	179.06	633.80	553.93	71.7	Nevada[1]	151.07	515.39	443.95	70.7
Arkansas[1]	189.97	512.34	381.41	62.9	New Hampshire	274.78	639.52	513.96	57.0
California[2]	154.00	540.00	440.00	71.5	New Jersey ...	234.02	574.52	442.09	59.3
Colorado[2]	256.00	626.00	531.00	59.1	New Mexico[1]...	164.28	537.56	475.56	69.4
Connecticut[2]...	236.00	682.00	613.00	65.4	New York[2]	241.59	568.33	296.28	57.5
Delaware	223.14	749.82	643.90	70.2	North Carolina	134.04	767.66	703.43	82.5
Dist. of Columbia[2]	399.00	414.00	268.00	3.6	North Dakota ..	183.93	455.53	325.56	59.6
Florida	110.29	595.23	531.32	81.5	Ohio	220.42	509.52	391.99	56.7
Georgia.......	145.91	609.05	544.65	76.0	Oklahoma.....	95.11	698.51	670.67	86.4
Hawaii	239.18	631.14	498.40	62.1	Oregon[1]	214.30	526.87	421.04	59.3
Idaho[2]........	233.00	556.00	568.00	58.1	Pennsylvania...	165.98	700.04	631.34	76.3
Illinois	207.32	644.05	533.20	67.8	Rhode Island[2]..	190.36	417.82	289.66	54.4
Indiana.......	251.91	484.97	345.42	48.1	South Carolina	138.60	658.13	586.08	78.9
Iowa	226.66	978.64	883.51	76.8	South Dakota ..	152.76	635.19	531.54	75.9
Kansas	163.59	623.91	554.86	73.8	Tennessee	131.07	801.42	796.71	83.6
Kentucky[1]	200.99	543.69	455.28	63.0	Texas	136.38	543.47	476.65	74.9
Louisiana	200.63	648.39	524.82	69.1	Utah	98.13	483.52	436.55	79.7
Maine	151.51	711.31	656.60	78.7	Vermont[2]......	176.00	514.00	325.00	65.8
Maryland[2]	226.00	629.00	545.00	64.1	Virginia	171.82	648.21	585.69	73.5
Massachusetts[2]	207.18	385.46	232.81	46.3	Washington[2]...	294.00	525.00	372.00	44.0
Michigan......	178.64	498.71	388.94	64.2	West Virginia...	262.75	855.33	689.92	69.3
Minnesota[2]	298.00	531.00	385.00	43.9	Wisconsin	189.75	749.54	667.10	74.7
Mississippi	101.23	672.97	620.44	85.0	Wyoming......	137.65	982.60	925.92	86.0
Missouri	148.94	645.52	595.61	76.9	**Total ....**	**153.05**	**621.40**	**549.86**	**75.4**

(1) State-based marketplace using the HealthCare.gov platform. (2) State-based exchange.

Health Care Visits by Selected Characteristics, 1997-2016

Source: *Health, United States, 2017*, National Center for Health Statistics, CDC, U.S. Dept. of Health and Human Services

	Zero visits			1-3 visits			4-9 visits			10 or more visits		
Characteristic	1997	2010	2016	1997	2010	2016	1997	2010	2016	1997	2010	2016
						Percent distribution						
All persons[1]...............	16.5%	15.6%	14.6%	46.2%	45.4%	49.5%	23.6%	25.8%	23.2%	13.7%	13.2%	12.7%
Age												
Under 6 years	5.0	3.7	4.9	44.9	48.9	52.5	37.0	36.8	34.6	13.0	10.6	7.9
6-17 years	15.3	10.4	10.0	58.7	59.1	64.3	19.3	23.6	19.1	6.8	6.9	6.6
18-44 years	21.7	24.2	22.0	46.7	43.9	48.6	19.0	20.6	17.9	12.6	11.3	11.5
45-64 years	16.9	14.8	12.8	42.9	42.8	45.6	24.7	26.1	25.1	15.5	16.4	16.5
65-74 years	9.8	6.3	6.8	36.9	36.1	39.7	31.6	35.7	34.6	21.6	21.9	18.9
75 years and over	7.7	4.1	5.8	31.8	31.0	33.6	33.8	38.0	35.7	26.6	27.0	25.0
Sex												
Male...................	21.3	20.4	18.6	47.1	46.4	50.1	20.6	22.7	21.1	11.0	10.5	10.3
Female.................	11.8	10.9	10.6	45.4	44.4	49.1	26.5	28.8	25.2	16.3	15.9	15.1
Health insurance status[2]												
Insured continuously	14.1	12.1	12.5	49.2	48.6	52.8	23.6	26.2	22.5	13.0	13.0	12.2
Uninsured, up to 12 mos. ..	18.9	18.5	24.2	46.0	47.8	47.2	20.8	22.0	18.0	14.4	11.6	10.5
Uninsured 12+ mos........	39.0	43.8	49.9	41.4	39.7	38.0	13.2	12.6	9.1	6.4	3.9	3.0

Note: Totals include visits to hospital emergency departments, doctor offices, and clinics as well as home visits by a health care professional. (1) Includes persons of unknown health insurance status. (2) In 12 months prior to interview, for persons under age 65 only.

Reasons Given by Patients for Physician Office Visits, 2015

Source: National Ambulatory Medical Care Survey, National Center for Health Statistics, Centers for Disease Control and Prevention, U.S. Dept. of Health and Human Services

Rank	Reason	Number of visits (thous.)	% of all visits	Rank	Reason	Number of visits (thous.)	% of all visits
1.	Progress visit, not otherwise specified	140,842	14.2%	12.	For other and unspecified test results	15,159	1.5%
2.	General medical examination	75,412	7.6	13.	Stomach and abdominal pain, cramps, and spasms	15,026	1.5
3.	Medication, other and unspecified kinds	35,232	3.6	14.	Well-baby examination	13,217	1.3
4.	Counseling, not otherwise specified	26,528	2.7	15.	Shoulder symptoms	12,619*	1.3*
5.	Postoperative visit	25,441	2.6	16.	Diabetes mellitus	12,432	1.3
6.	Cough	20,984	2.1	17.	Skin rash	9,464	1.0
7.	Gynecological examination	20,735	2.1	18.	Preoperative visit	9,443	1.0
8.	Prenatal examination, routine	18,152	1.8	19.	Symptoms referable to throat	9,346	0.9
9.	Knee sympoms	16,241	1.6	20.	Other special examination	9,092	0.9
10.	Back symptoms	15,875	1.6		**All other reasons**	473,807	47.8
11.	Hypertension	15,762*	1.6		**All visits**	990,808	100.0

* = Figure does not meet source's standards of reliability or precision. **Note:** Numbers of visits to nonfederal office-based patient care physicians may not add to totals because of rounding.

Visits to Physician Offices and Hospital Outpatient and Emergency Departments, 1995-2015

Source: National Ambulatory Medical Care Survey and National Hospital Ambulatory Medical Care Survey, National Center for Health Statistics, Centers for Disease Control and Prevention, U.S. Dept. of Health and Human Services

(number of visits per 100 persons)

Sex and age	All places[1]			Physician offices[2]				Hospital outpatient depts.			Hospital emergency depts.			
	1995	2000	2011	1995	2000	2010	2015	1995	2000	2011	1995	2000	2010	2015
Total	334	374	400	271	304	325	297	26	31	40	37	40	43	44
Male	290	325	354	232	261	283	252	21	26	32	37	38	40	40
Under 18	273	302	372	209	231	262	203	25	29	37	40	41	43	44
18-44	190	203	208	139	148	151	122	14	17	20	37	38	38	39
45-54	275	316	322	229	260	265	251	20	26	34	26	30	35	36
55-64	351	428	430	300	367	396	378	26	32	45	25	30	32	31
65-74	508	614	655	445	539	597	560	29	38	52	34	36	37	34
75 and over	711	771	869	616	670	760	799	34	42	49	61	59	60	60
Female	377	420	444	309	345	367	342	31	35	48	37	41	47	48
Under 18	277	285	341	217	221	252	204	25	29	38	35	35	37	43
18-44	336	377	393	265	298	323	285	31	33	47	40	46	57	57
45-54	400	451	459	339	384	372	411	32	36	53	29	31	40	39
55-64	446	529	520	382	453	469	424	38	45	54	26	31	31	33
65-74	603	692	707	534	609	647	607	36	46	60	32	37	40	38
75 and over	666	763	790	571	645	685	736	34	49	61	61	69	66	61

Note: Data based on reporting by a sample of survey respondents. (1) Incl. visits to physician offices and hospital outpatient and emergency departments. Prior to 2006, visits to community health centers were not included in survey. (2) 2010 data incl. visits to community health centers.

Most Frequently Mentioned Drugs at Office Visits, 2014

Source: National Ambulatory Medical Care Survey, National Center for Health Statistics, Centers for Disease Control and Prevention, U.S. Dept. of Health and Human Services

Rank	Therapeutic drug category[1]	No. of mentions (thous.)	% of total[2]	Rank	Therapeutic drug category[1]	No. of mentions (thous.)	% of total[2]
1.	Analgesics[3]	366,555	11.6%	11.	Dermatological agents	98,116	3.1%
2.	Antihyperlipidemic agents	162,139	5.1	12.	Proton pump inhibitors	94,122	3.0
3.	Antidepressants	142,674	4.5	13.	Vitamin and mineral combinations	84,640	2.7
4.	Anxiolytics, sedatives, and hypnotics	122,258	3.9	14.	Immunostimulants	81,257	2.6
5.	Vitamins	121,595	3.9	15.	Diuretics	73,421	2.3
6.	Antidiabetic agents	119,441	3.8	16.	Antihistamines	72,022	2.3
7.	Antiplatelet agents	116,943	3.7	17.	ACE[4] inhibitors	71,426	2.3
8.	Anticonvulsants	103,950	3.3	18.	Thyroid hormones	60,441	1.9
9.	Beta-adrenergic blocking agents	102,055	3.2	19.	Minerals and electrolytes	60,410	1.9
10.	Bronchodilators	99,519	3.2	20.	Antiemetic or antivertigo agents	59,534	1.9

Note: A mention is a documentation in a patient's record of a drug provided, prescribed, or continued at a visit to a nonfederal office-based patient care physician. (1) Based on the Multum Lexicon second-level therapeutic drug category. (2) Based on an estimated 3,150,461,000 drug mentions at office visits in 2014. (3) Incl. narcotic and nonnarcotic analgesics and nonsteriodal anti-inflammatory drugs. (4) Angiotensin-converting enzyme.

U.S. Organ Transplants

Source: Organ Procurement and Transplantation Network (OPTN), United Network for Organ Sharing (UNOS)

Waiting List, Aug. 2018

Type of transplant	Registered candidates	% of total
Any organ	114,362	100.0%
Kidney	94,954	83.0
Liver	13,773	12.0
Heart	3,951	3.5
Kidney-pancreas	1,628	1.4
Lung	1,465	1.3
Pancreas	876	0.8
Intestine	254	0.2
Heart-lung	48	0.04

Transplants Performed, 2017

Type of transplant	Number	% of total
Any organ	34,770	—
Kidney	19,849	57.1%
Liver	8,082	23.2
Heart	3,244	9.3
Lung	2,449	7.0
Kidney-pancreas	789	2.3
Pancreas	213	0.6
Intestine	109	0.3
Heart-lung	29	0.1

Note: Waiting list as of Aug. 16, 2018. Total transplants performed include organs not shown separately.

Illicit Drug Use Among Persons Age 12 or Older, 2002-16

Source: National Survey on Drug Use and Health, SAMHSA, U.S. Dept. of Health and Human Services

Of all those age 12 or older who used an illicit drug in the past month, approximately 2.0 mil were adolescents aged 12-17 (making 7.9% of that age group current drug users). About 8.0 mil current users were young adults aged 18-25 (or 23.2% of that age group).

(numbers in thousands)

Drug	2002 No.	%	2005 No.	%	2010 No.	%	2014 No.	%	2015 No.	%	2016 No.	%
Used in lifetime												
Illicit drugs[1]	—	—	—	—	—	—	—	—	130,610	48.8	130,628	48.5
Marijuana	94,946	40.4	97,545	40.1	106,613	42.0	117,213	44.2	117,865	44.0	118,524	44.0
Cocaine	33,910	14.4	33,673	13.8	37,361	14.7	39,200	14.8	38,744	14.5	38,880	14.4
Crack	8,402	3.6	7,928	3.3	9,208	3.6	9,424	3.6	9,035	3.4	8,776	3.3
Heroin	3,668	1.6	3,534	1.5	4,144	1.6	4,813	1.8	5,099	1.9	4,981	1.8
Hallucinogens	—	—	—	—	—	—	—	—	40,915	15.3	41,490	15.4
LSD	24,516	10.4	22,433	9.2	23,375	9.2	25,035	9.4	25,324	9.5	25,861	9.6
PCP	7,418	3.2	6,603	2.7	6,255	2.5	6,388	2.4	6,323	2.4	6,450	2.4
Inhalants	—	—	—	—	—	—	—	—	25,765	9.6	24,404	9.1
Used in past year												
Illicit drugs[1]	—	—	—	—	—	—	—	—	47,730	17.8	48,501	18.0
Marijuana	25,755	11.0	25,375	10.4	29,301	11.6	35,124	13.2	36,043	13.5	37,570	13.9
Cocaine	5,902	2.5	5,523	2.3	4,533	1.8	4,553	1.7	4,828	1.8	5,071	1.9
Crack	1,554	0.7	1,381	0.6	885	0.3	773	0.3	833	0.3	882	0.3
Heroin	404	0.2	379	0.2	621	0.2	914	0.3	828	0.3	948	0.4
Hallucinogens	—	—	—	—	—	—	—	—	4,692	1.8	4,903	1.8
LSD	999	0.4	563	0.2	881	0.3	1,290	0.5	1,535	0.6	1,896	0.7
PCP	235	0.1	164	0.1	96	0.0	90	0.0	120	0.0	103	0.0
Inhalants	—	—	—	—	—	—	—	—	1,759	0.7	1,660	0.6
Methamphetamine	—	—	—	—	—	—	—	—	1,713	0.6	1,391	0.5
Misuse of psychotherapeutics[2]	—	—	—	—	—	—	—	—	18,942	7.1	18,671	6.9
Opioids[3]	—	—	—	—	—	—	—	—	12,693	4.7	11,824	4.4
Used in past month												
Illicit drugs[1]	—	—	—	—	—	—	—	—	27,080	10.1	28,564	10.6
Marijuana	14,584	6.2	14,626	6.0	17,409	6.9	22,188	8.4	22,226	8.3	23,981	8.9
Cocaine	2,020	0.9	2,397	1.0	1,472	0.6	1,530	0.6	1,876	0.7	1,874	0.7
Crack	567	0.2	682	0.3	378	0.1	354	0.1	394	0.1	432	0.2
Heroin	166	0.1	136	0.1	239	0.1	435	0.2	329	0.1	475	0.2
Hallucinogens	—	—	—	—	—	—	—	—	1,240	0.5	1,390	0.5
LSD	112	0.0	104	0.0	155	0.1	287	0.1	352	0.1	374	0.1
PCP	58	0.0	48	0.0	36	0.0	*	*	25	0.0	21	0.0
Inhalants	—	—	—	—	—	—	—	—	527	0.2	600	0.2
Methamphetamine	—	—	—	—	—	—	—	—	897	0.3	667	0.2
Misuse of psychotherapeutics[2]	—	—	—	—	—	—	—	—	6,365	2.4	6,207	2.3
Opioids[3]	—	—	—	—	—	—	—	—	3,963	1.5	3,649	1.4

— = Not comparable due to methodological changes or not reported due to measurement issues. * = Low precision. **Note:** Misuse is defined as use in any way not directed by a doctor, including use without a prescription or use in greater amounts, more often, or for a longer period of time. (1) Includes marijuana, cocaine (including crack), heroin, hallucinogens, inhalants, or methamphetamine or the misuse of prescription psychotherapeutics. (2) Includes four categories of prescription drugs (pain relievers, tranquilizers, stimulants, sedatives) but not over-the-counter drugs. (3) Includes the misuse of prescription opioid pain relievers and the use of heroin.

Lifetime Prevalence of Drug Use in 12th Graders, 1975-2017

Source: Monitoring the Future study, Univ. of Michigan Inst. for Social Research; Natl. Inst. on Drug Abuse, Natl. Insts. of Health

(percent who have ever used)

Drug	1975	1980	1985	1990	1995	2000	2005	2010	2013	2014	2015	2016	2017	2016-17 change
Any illicit drug[1]	55.2%	65.4%	60.6%	47.9%	48.4%	54.0%	50.4%	48.2%	49.8%	49.1%	48.9%	48.3%	48.9%	0.6%
Marijuana/hashish	47.3	60.3	54.2	40.7	41.7	48.8	44.8	43.8	45.5	44.4	44.7	44.5	45.0	0.5
Inhalants[2]	—	17.3	18.1	18.5	17.4	14.2	11.4	9.0	6.9	6.5	5.7	5.0	4.9	−0.2
Nitrites	—	11.1	7.9	2.1	1.5	0.8	1.1	—	—	—	—	—	—	—
Hallucinogens[3]	—	15.6	12.1	9.7	12.7	13.0	8.8	8.6	7.6	6.3	6.4	6.7	6.7	0.0
LSD	11.3	9.3	7.5	8.7	11.7	11.1	8.8	4.0	3.9	3.7	4.3	4.9	5.0	0.1
PCP	—	9.6	4.9	2.8	2.7	3.4	2.4	1.8	1.3	—	—	—	—	—
Ecstasy (MDMA)	—	—	—	—	—	11.0	5.4	7.3	7.1	7.9	5.9	4.9	4.9	0.0
Cocaine	9.0	15.7	17.3	9.4	6.0	8.6	8.0	5.5	4.5	4.6	4.0	3.7	4.2	0.5
Crack	—	—	—	3.5	3.0	3.9	3.5	2.4	1.8	1.8	1.7	1.4	1.7	0.3
Heroin	2.2	1.1	1.2	1.3	1.6	2.4	1.5	1.6	1.0	1.0	0.8	0.7	0.7	0.0
Narcotics other than heroin[4]	9.0	9.8	10.2	8.3	7.2	10.6	12.8	13.0	11.1	9.5	8.4	7.8	6.8	−1.0
Amphetamines[4]	22.3	26.4	26.2	17.5	15.3	15.6	13.1	11.1	13.8	12.1	10.8	10.0	9.2	−0.8
Methamphetamine	—	—	—	—	—	7.9	4.5	2.3	1.5	1.9	1.0	1.2	1.1	−0.1
Crystal meth	—	—	—	2.7	3.9	4.0	4.0	1.8	2.0	1.3	1.2	1.4	1.5	0.1
Sedatives (barbiturates)[4]	18.2	14.9	11.8	7.5	7.4	9.2	10.5	7.5	7.5	6.8	5.9	5.2	4.5	−0.7
Methaqualone[4]	8.1	9.5	6.7	2.3	1.2	0.8	1.3	0.4	—	—	—	—	—	—
Tranquilizers[4]	17.0	15.2	11.9	7.2	7.1	8.9	9.9	8.5	7.7	7.4	6.9	7.6	7.5	−0.1
Alcohol	90.4	93.2	92.2	89.5	80.7	80.3	75.1	71.0	68.2	66.0	64.0	61.2	61.5	0.3
Cigarettes	73.6	71.0	68.8	64.4	64.2	62.5	50.0	42.2	38.1	34.4	31.1	28.3	26.6	−1.7
Any vaping[5]	—	—	—	—	—	—	—	—	—	—	35.5	33.8	35.8	—
Smokeless tobacco	—	—	—	—	30.9	23.1	17.5	17.6	17.2	15.1	13.2	14.2	11.0	−3.2
Steroids[4]	—	—	—	2.9	2.3	2.5	2.6	2.0	2.1	1.9	2.3	1.6	1.6	0.0

— = Not available. **Note:** Because of changes to question wording, some data may not be directly comparable across years. (1) Includes marijuana, LSD, other hallucinogens, crack, other cocaine, or heroin; or any use of narcotics other than heroin, amphetamines, sedatives (barbiturates), or tranquilizers not under a doctor's orders. (2) Not adjusted for underreporting of amyl and butyl nitrites. (3) Not adjusted for underreporting of PCP. (4) Includes only drug use not under a doctor's orders. (5) Survey question was changed in 2017 from asking about vaping in general to vaping specific substances.

Cigarette Use in the U.S., 1985-2016

Source: National Survey on Drug Use and Health, Substance Abuse and Mental Health Services Admin. (SAMHSA), U.S. Dept. of Health and Human Services

(percentage of persons age 12 or older, unless otherwise noted, reporting use in the month prior to the survey)

	1985	2000	2005	2010	2014	2015	2016		1985	2000	2005	2010	2014	2015	2016
Total	38.7	24.9	24.9	23.0	20.8	19.4	19.1	**Race/Hispanic origin**							
Sex								White, not Hispanic. . .	38.9	25.9	26.0	24.3	22.3	20.7	20.7
								Black, not Hispanic. . .	38.0	23.3	24.5	22.6	22.5	21.3	19.3
Male	43.4	26.9	27.4	25.4	23.2	21.8	21.2	Hispanic, any race . . .	40.0	20.7	22.1	20.1	16.7	15.3	14.7
Female	34.5	23.1	22.5	20.7	18.6	17.1	17.1	**Education[2]**							
Age								Non-HS graduate	37.3	32.4	34.8	34.3	31.2	28.1	27.9
12-17 years.	29.4	13.4	10.8	8.4	4.9	4.2	3.4	HS graduate	37.0	31.1	31.8	29.6	28.6	27.4	28.3
18-25 years.	47.4	38.3	39.0	34.3	28.4	26.7	23.5	Some college	32.6	27.7	28.1	25.8	24.8	23.5	22.3
26 years or older[1]	45.7	24.2	24.3	22.8	21.5	20.0	20.2	College graduate	23.0	13.9	13.8	12.8	10.9	9.6	9.6

HS = High school. **Note:** Because of methodological changes in 2002 and 2015, data may not be comparable across years. (1) Persons age 26 to 34 only in 1985. (2) Persons age 18 or older.

Daily Use of Cigarettes by 8th, 10th, and 12th Graders, 1995-2017

Source: Monitoring the Future study, Univ. of Michigan Inst. for Social Research; Natl. Inst. on Drug Abuse, Natl. Insts. of Health

(percent who smoked daily in last 30 days)

	8th grade				% change, 2005-17	10th grade				% change, 2005-17	12th grade				% change, 2005-17
	1995	2000	2005	2017		1995	2000	2005	2017		1995	2000	2005	2017	
Total	9.3	7.4	4.0	0.6	−85.0%	16.3	14.0	7.5	2.2	−70.7%	21.6	20.6	13.6	4.2	−69.1%
Sex															
Male	9.2	7.0	3.9	0.6	−84.6	16.3	13.7	7.2	2.3	−68.1	21.7	20.9	14.6	4.3	−70.5
Female	9.2	7.5	4.0	0.5	−87.5	16.1	14.1	7.7	1.9	−75.3	20.8	19.7	11.9	3.8	−68.1
College plans															
None/ under 4 yrs. . . .	22.5	21.7	14.4	1.8	−87.5	32.7	28.8	19.2	8.9	−53.6	33.7	31.7	24.9	8.7	−65.1
Complete 4 yrs.	7.5	5.6	2.9	0.4	−86.2	13.3	11.6	5.9	1.4	−76.3	17.4	16.6	10.5	3.1	−70.5
Region															
Northeast	9.2	6.9	3.2	0.2	−93.8	15.8	14.1	7.6	2.2	−71.1	22.5	22.8	13.3	4.1	−69.2
Midwest	11.0	9.0	4.8	0.8	−83.3	17.6	16.3	8.6	2.8	−67.4	25.7	23.6	16.3	4.3	−73.6
South	9.4	7.8	5.0	0.6	−88.0	19.3	15.7	8.8	2.1	−76.1	21.7	19.4	15.4	5.2	−66.2
West	7.0	4.9	2.4	0.6	−75.0	9.4	7.8	4.0	2.1	−47.5	14.5	16.9	7.6	2.7	−64.5
Parental education[1]															
Some HS/less. . .	15.8	13.1	7.8	1.1	−85.9	20.0	18.9	9.9	3.8	−61.6	21.3	22.8	11.7	3.8	−67.5
Some/completed HS.	11.3	11.3	6.3	0.7	−88.9	21.6	17.6	11.1	3.5	−68.5	24.6	22.9	18.3	5.3	−71.0
Completed HS/ some coll.	9.4	6.7	4.3	0.6	−86.0	17.0	14.2	7.9	2.5	−68.4	21.6	21.2	14.4	4.6	−68.1
Some/completed coll.	7.2	3.9	2.2	0.3	−86.4	12.6	11.5	5.2	1.1	−78.8	19.7	18.6	11.7	3.6	−69.2
Completed coll./higher. . . .	5.7	4.1	1.4	0.3	−78.6	10.3	9.8	4.4	1.0	−77.3	18.5	15.2	8.1	2.6	−67.9
Race/Hispanic origin[2]															
White	10.5	9.0	4.6	0.9	−80.4	17.6	17.7	9.1	2.5	−72.5	23.9	25.7	17.1	5.8	−66.1
Black.	2.8	3.2	2.1	0.4	−81.0	4.7	5.2	3.9	0.9	−76.9	6.1	8.0	5.6	2.5	−55.4
Hispanic	9.2	7.1	3.1	0.6	−80.6	9.9	8.8	5.9	1.6	−72.9	11.6	15.7	7.7	1.9	−75.3

Coll. = college; HS = high school. **Note:** Figures may not add up to totals because of rounding. (1) Avg. highest level of education attained by respondent's mother and father. (2) For each of these groups, data for the specified year and previous year have been combined to increase sample size and thus provide more stable estimates.

Tobacco Use by High School and Middle School Students, 2017

Source: National Youth Tobacco Survey, Centers for Disease Control and Prevention (CDC), U.S. Dept. of Health and Human Services

Between 2011 and 2017, tobacco use declined among high school students (from 24.2% using to 19.6%) and middle school students (7.5% to 5.6%). Electronic cigarettes (e-cigarettes) have been the most commonly used tobacco product by both groups since 2014. Use is defined as use of any product on at least one day in the past 30 days.

	High school students using tobacco				Middle school students using tobacco			
Tobacco product	Female	Male	All students	Estimated no. of users[1]	Female	Male	All students	Estimated no. of users[1]
E-cigarettes.	9.9%	13.3%	11.7%	1,730,000	2.9%	3.7%	3.3%	390,000
Cigarettes	7.5	7.6	7.6	1,120,000	2.2	2.0	2.1	250,000
Cigars	6.3	9.0	7.7	1,130,000	1.4	1.6	1.5	170,000
Smokeless tobacco	3.0	7.7	5.5	810,000	1.2	2.4	1.9	210,000
Hookah.	3.2	3.3	3.3	480,000	1.1	1.6	1.4	150,000
Pipe tobacco.	0.5	1.0	0.8	120,000	—	—	0.4	40,000
Bidis[2]	0.6	0.7	0.7	100,000	—	—	0.3	30,000
Any tobacco product use. . .	**17.5**	**21.5**	**19.6**	**2,950,000**	**4.8**	**6.4**	**5.6**	**670,000**
2+ tobacco product use	7.6	10.7	9.2	1,380,000	2.0	2.7	2.4	280,000
Any combustible tobacco product[3].	12.2	13.5	12.9	1,940,000	3.2	3.5	3.4	390,000

— = Not available. (1) Rounded down to nearest 10,000. (2) Small brown cigarettes wrapped in a leaf. (3) Excludes e-cigarettes and smokeless tobacco (i.e., chewing or dissolvable tobacco, snuff, dip, snus).

Alcohol Use by 8th and 12th Graders, 1980-2017

Source: Monitoring the Future study, Univ. of Michigan Inst. for Social Research; Natl. Inst. on Drug Abuse, Natl. Insts. of Health

	1980	1990	1995	2000	2005	2010	2013	2015	2016	2017	% change, 2016-17
Alcohol use[1]					Percent using in the 30 days before the survey						
All 8th graders	—	—	24.6%	22.4%	17.1%	13.8%	10.2%	9.7%	7.3%	8.0%	0.7%
Male	—	—	25.0	22.5	16.2	13.2	9.3	9.1	6.7	6.8	0.2
Female	—	—	24.0	22.0	17.9	14.3	11.2	9.9	7.8	9.1	1.3
White...........	—	—	25.4	24.7	17.9	13.9	9.5	8.9	8.2	7.2	−1.0
Black...........	—	—	18.7	16.0	14.9	11.8	9.7	8.2	6.9	6.0	−0.9
Hispanic	—	—	32.4	26.7	20.6	18.1	14.3	10.4	9.5	9.0	−0.5
All 12th graders ...	72.0%	57.1%	51.3	50.0	47.0	41.2	39.2	35.3	33.2	33.2	−0.1
Male	77.4	61.3	55.7	54.0	50.7	44.2	41.8	36.0	34.5	34.1	−0.4
Female	66.8	52.3	47.0	46.1	43.3	37.9	36.3	35.0	32.0	32.3	0.3
White...........	75.4	63.8	54.5	55.1	52.3	45.4	43.6	40.9	39.0	39.0	0.0
Black...........	47.6	35.8	35.2	30.0	29.0	31.4	28.4	24.0	21.8	20.3	−1.5
Hispanic	63.6	49.1	48.7	51.2	43.3	40.1	39.0	36.3	34.9	30.9	−4.0
Heavy alcohol use[2]					Percent heavily using in the two weeks before the survey						
All 8th graders	—	—	12.3%	11.7%	8.4%	7.2%	5.1%	4.6%	3.4%	3.7%	0.3%
Male	—	—	12.5	11.7	8.2	6.5	4.5	4.6	3.2	3.1	0.0
Female	—	—	12.1	11.3	8.6	7.8	5.7	4.6	3.6	4.2	0.6
White...........	—	—	12.1	13.0	9.0	7.1	4.2	4.0	3.6	3.0	−0.6
Black...........	—	—	8.3	7.3	6.1	5.3	4.5	4.1	3.4	2.9	−0.5
Hispanic	—	—	18.4	16.0	12.1	10.8	7.8	5.4	5.3	4.9	−0.4
All 12th graders ...	41.2%	32.2%	29.8	30.0	27.1	23.2	22.1	17.2	15.5	16.6	1.1
Male	52.1	39.1	36.9	36.7	32.6	28.0	26.1	19.3	17.2	18.5	1.4
Female	30.5	24.4	23.0	23.5	21.6	18.4	18.1	14.9	13.5	14.6	1.1
White...........	44.3	36.6	32.3	34.6	32.5	27.6	25.6	21.2	19.1	19.6	0.5
Black...........	17.7	14.4	14.9	11.5	11.3	13.1	12.5	9.8	8.3	7.7	−0.6
Hispanic	33.1	25.6	26.6	31.0	23.9	22.1	22.4	18.5	16.7	14.4	−2.3

— = Not available. **Note:** To derive percentages for each race/ethnicity subgroup, data for the specified year and previous year have been combined to increase sample size and thus provide more stable estimates. (1) In 1993, the alcohol question was changed slightly to indicate that a "drink" is defined as "more than a few sips." (2) Five or more drinks in a row on one or more occasions.

Acquired Immune Deficiency Syndrome (AIDS)

Source: Centers for Disease Control and Prevention (CDC), U.S. Dept. of Health and Human Services

AIDS (Acquired Immune Deficiency Syndrome) is caused by the human immunodeficiency virus (HIV). HIV disables or kills crucial immune cells, progressively destroying the body's ability to fight disease.

HIV is commonly spread through unprotected sexual contact with an infected partner's semen or vaginal fluids. It is also spread through contact with infected blood. Where modern screening techniques are used, it is rare to contract HIV from transfusion or organ/tissue transplants. But it can be contracted when intravenous drug users share syringes and similar equipment. A woman can also transmit HIV to her child during pregnancy or delivery or through breastfeeding. With treatment, a woman can reduce her transmission rate from about 20% to less than 1%. There is no evidence HIV can spread through saliva or casual contact such as shaking hands or the sharing of food utensils, towels and bedding, or toilet seats.

Some people experience flu-like symptoms within a few weeks of being infected with HIV. Even when symptoms are not present, HIV is active in the body, multiplying, infecting, and killing crucial CD4+ T cells, also known as T-lymphocytes or T-helper cells, which signal other immune cells to perform their functions.

The term AIDS applies to the final stage of HIV infection. According to the official case definition issued by the CDC, an HIV-infected person 6 years of age or older with fewer than 200 CD4+ T cells per cubic millimeter of blood can be said to have AIDS. (Healthy adults usually have 500-1,600 per cubic millimeter.) An HIV-infected person, regardless of T cell count, can also be diagnosed with AIDS if he or she develops one of 20+ opportunistic illnesses, such as invasive cervical cancer, Kaposi sarcoma, or lymphoma, that can occur when the immune system is so ravaged by HIV that the body cannot fight off certain bacteria, viruses, and microbes.

Months or years prior to the onset of AIDS, people may experience such symptoms as swollen glands, lack of energy, fevers and sweats, and skin rashes. People diagnosed with AIDS may develop infections of the intestinal tract, lungs, brain, eyes, and other organs. Children with AIDS may have delayed development or fail to thrive.

HIV is primarily detected by testing blood for the presence of antibodies (disease-fighting proteins of the immune system) to HIV. HIV antibodies can usually be detected within three months of infection although it can take up to six months after exposure for antibodies to reach detectable levels. Combination HIV tests look for both HIV antibodies and parts of the virus called antigens. There are currently two home HIV tests available.

Antiretroviral therapy (ART) extends the period between HIV infection and the development of serious illness as well as lowers the risk of HIV transmission. Patients typically take a combination of drugs to reduce the chance of the virus developing a resistance.

In 1987, a drug called zidovudine (commonly known as AZT) became the first approved HIV medicine. Since then, the U.S. Food and Drug Administration has approved approximately 40 drugs to treat people living with HIV/AIDS. These drugs are grouped into classes: nucleoside reverse transcriptase inhibitors (NRTIs), non-nucleoside reverse transcriptase inhibitors (NNRTIs), protease inhibitors (PIs), fusion inhibitors, CCR5 antagonists, integrase inhibitors (INSTIs), post-attachment inhibitors (PAIs), and pharmacokinetic enhancers. Each class of drug attacks the virus at a different point in its life cycle. Patients generally take three different HIV medicines from at least two different classes. Fixed-dose combinations of two or more medications in a single pill are also available.

Since there is no vaccine or cure for AIDS, the best way to prevent HIV infection is to avoid activities that carry a risk. The CDC recommends abstinence, mutual monogamy with an uninfected partner, limiting the number of sexual partners, never sharing needles, and using condoms correctly and consistently. People who do not have HIV but are at high risk of exposure can choose to take medication daily to prevent HIV infection, called pre-exposure prophylaxis (PrEP). Post-exposure prophylaxis (PEP) is the emergency use of HIV medicines after a single high-risk event to stop HIV from making copies of itself and spreading throughout the body. PEP must be started no more than 72 hours after exposure to HIV, and it is not always effective.

New AIDS Diagnoses in the U.S., by Transmission Category, 1985-2016

Source: *HIV Surveillance Report, 2016*; National Center for HIV/AIDS, Viral Hepatitis, STD, and TB Prevention; CDC

Transmission category	All years[1]	1985	1990	2000	2005	2010	2014	2015	2016[2]
All males 13 years of age and older	971,120	7,504	36,193	28,796	25,836	20,636	14,591	13,951	13,851
Male-to-male sexual contact	599,230	5,348	23,658	15,884	15,895	14,096	10,413	10,067	10,075
Injection drug use	185,414	1,103	6,923	6,214	3,755	1,966	1,159	1,010	952
Male-to-male sexual contact and injection drug use	87,872	661	2,943	2,704	2,355	1,432	782	786	751
Heterosexual contact[3]	86,911	32	715	3,809	3,686	3,026	2,157	1,989	1,992
Other[4]	11,694	—	—	185	145	116	80	99	81
All females 13 years of age and older	251,653	524	4,547	10,120	9,310	6,922	4,747	4,489	4,271
Injection drug use	91,021	287	2,347	3,510	2,527	1,415	840	786	728
Heterosexual contact[3]	154,584	119	1,538	6,480	6,654	5,378	3,820	3,625	3,434
Other[4]	6,048	—	—	130	129	129	87	78	109
All children, under 13 years of age	9,573	—	—	135	55	22	71	40	38
Perinatal	8,697	—	—	—	—	—	61	31	31
Other[4]	876	—	—	—	—	—	10	9	7

— = Not available. **Note:** Table shows number of persons diagnosed with an HIV infection at stage 3 (AIDS). The definition of AIDS cases for reporting purposes has expanded over time. (1) Includes number of diagnoses for years not shown, from the beginning of the epidemic (1981) through 2016. (2) Preliminary. (3) Heterosexual contact with a person known to have or be at high risk for HIV infection. (4) Includes hemophilia, blood transfusion, perinatal exposure (for persons 13 and older), and risk factor not reported or not identified.

New HIV Diagnoses in the U.S., 2011-16

Source: *HIV Surveillance Report, 2016*; National Center for HIV/AIDS, Viral Hepatitis, STD, and TB Prevention; CDC

Characteristic	Number of diagnoses						Diagnoses per 100,000 resident pop.					
	2011	2012	2013	2014	2015	2016[1]	2011	2012	2013	2014	2015	2016[1]
All persons	41,984	41,168	39,652	40,276	39,876	39,782	13.5	13.1	12.5	12.6	12.4	12.3
Male, 13 years and over	32,964	32,671	31,772	32,476	32,306	32,131	26.1	25.6	24.7	25.0	24.7	24.3
Female, 13 years and over	8,822	8,257	7,694	7,620	7,435	7,529	6.7	6.2	5.7	5.6	5.4	5.4
Age at diagnosis												
Under 13 years	198	240	186	180	135	122	0.4	0.5	0.4	0.3	0.3	0.2
13-14 years	42	47	41	35	26	23	0.5	0.6	0.5	0.4	0.3	0.3
15-19 years	1,999	1,882	1,692	1,731	1,721	1,652	9.2	8.8	8.0	8.2	8.2	7.8
20-24 years	7,072	7,141	7,058	7,349	7,228	6,776	31.9	31.6	30.9	32.1	31.9	30.3
25-29 years	6,364	6,469	6,661	7,188	7,600	7,964	29.9	30.2	30.9	32.7	33.9	34.8
30-34 years	5,251	5,468	5,214	5,460	5,461	5,701	25.6	26.1	24.5	25.4	25.3	26.2
35-39 years	4,463	4,158	3,985	4,266	4,253	4,242	22.8	21.3	20.3	21.5	20.9	20.4
40-44 years	4,791	4,449	3,945	3,789	3,416	3,334	22.8	21.1	18.9	18.4	16.9	16.9
45-49 years	4,573	4,302	3,934	3,627	3,319	3,156	20.6	19.8	18.5	17.4	16.0	15.1
50-54 years	3,350	3,199	2,982	2,907	2,987	2,959	14.8	14.2	13.2	12.9	13.4	13.5
55-59 years	1,990	1,928	2,022	1,938	1,886	1,923	9.8	9.3	9.5	9.0	8.7	8.7
60-64 years	1,068	1,059	1,074	975	997	1,089	6.0	5.9	5.9	5.3	5.2	5.6
65 years and over	823	826	858	831	847	841	2.0	1.9	1.9	1.8	1.8	1.7
Race/ethnicity												
Not Hispanic/Latino												
White	11,146	11,039	10,636	10,618	10,465	10,345	5.6	5.6	5.4	5.4	5.3	5.2
Black	18,992	18,258	17,470	17,530	17,432	17,528	49.5	47.1	44.6	44.4	43.7	43.6
Amer. Ind./Alaska Native	143	176	154	187	197	243	6.2	7.6	6.6	8.0	8.3	10.2
Asian	744	784	810	938	947	977	4.9	5.0	5.0	5.6	5.5	5.5
Native Hawaiian/other Pacific Islander	55	54	49	44	80	48	10.8	10.4	9.2	8.1	14.4	8.5
Multiple races	1,612	1,566	1,436	1,249	1,060	875	27.7	26.1	23.2	19.6	16.1	12.9
Hispanic/Latino, any race	9,292	9,291	9,097	9,710	9,695	9,766	17.9	17.5	16.8	17.6	17.2	17.0

Note: Data shown are for the 50 states and DC. They are estimates of the min. number of persons for whom HIV infection has been diagnosed (during 2011-16) and reported to the CDC as of June 30, 2017. Sums of subpopulations may not equal totals. Because of a change in case definition, HIV diagnoses prior to 2014 are not strictly comparable to those in 2014 or later. (1) Preliminary.

U.S. Deaths of Persons With HIV Ever Classified as AIDS, 1981-2015

Source: *HIV Surveillance Report, 2016*; National Center for HIV/AIDS, Viral Hepatitis, STD, and TB Prevention; CDC

	Number	% of total
Age at death		
Under 13 years	4,968	0.7%
13-14 years	296	0.04
15-19 years	1,313	0.2
20-24 years	10,077	1.5
25-29 years	47,563	6.9
30-34 years	102,737	14.8
35-39 years	129,420	18.7
40-44 years	124,221	17.9
45-49 years	98,819	14.3
50-54 years	70,633	10.2
55-59 years	46,000	6.6
60-64 years	27,909	4.0
65 years and over	28,833	4.2
Race/ethnicity		
American Indian/Alaska Native	1,988	0.3
Asian[1]	3,542	0.5
Black/African American	285,744	41.2
Hispanic/Latino (any race)	106,644	15.4
Native Hawaiian/other Pac. Islander	369	0.1
White	279,807	40.4
Multiple races	14,647	2.1

	Number	% of total
Transmission category		
Male adult or adolescent	561,296	81.0%
Male-to-male sexual contact	325,330	47.0
Injection drug use	134,466	19.4
Male-to-male sexual contact and injection drug use	53,521	7.7
Heterosexual contact[2]	38,727	5.6
Perinatal	463	0.1
Other[3]	8,789	1.3
Female adult or adolescent	126,525	18.3
Injection drug use	59,438	8.6
Heterosexual contact[2]	62,839	9.1
Perinatal	592	0.1
Other[3]	3,655	0.5
Child (under 13 years old at death)	4,968	0.7
Perinatal	4,507	0.7
Other[3]	461	0.1
Region of residence		
Northeast	213,084	30.8
Midwest	73,965	10.7
South	272,756	39.4
West	132,984	19.2
Total	692,789	100.0

Note: Deaths of persons with diagnosed HIV infection may be due to any cause. Number of deaths are cumulative from the beginning of the epidemic, in 1981. Figures are estimated and calculated independently, so they may not add up to totals. (1) Includes "Asian/Pacific Islander" legacy cases. (2) Heterosexual contact with a person known to have or to be at high risk for HIV infection. (3) Includes hemophilia, blood transfusion, and risk factor not reported or not identified.

Allergies and Asthma

Source: Asthma and Allergy Foundation of America, Centers for Disease Control and Prevention (CDC)

An estimated one in six Americans suffers from allergies each year. People with allergies have immune systems that overreact to a normally harmless substance, called an allergen. Common allergens include plant pollens, dust mites, or animal dander; plants such as poison ivy; certain drugs, such as penicillin; and foods such as eggs, milk, wheat, nuts, or seafood.

The tendency to develop allergies is usually inherited. Though allergies typically manifest in childhood, they can show up at any age. Food allergies and eczema (inflamed or irritated skin) are common allergies among infants. Older children and adults may develop allergic rhinitis, or hay fever, in reaction to an inhaled allergen. Allergic rhinitis symptoms include nasal congestion, runny nose, and sneezing.

People with allergies should avoid contact with an allergen, if feasible. Medications, such as antihistamines and nasal corticosteroids, may be used to decrease an allergic reaction. Other effective allergy treatments include decongestants, eye drops, and ointments. There are also treatments aimed at gradually desensitizing a patient to an allergen.

Some allergy sufferers also have asthma. About 26.5 mil Americans have asthma, which can develop at any age. Asthma is a chronic inflammation disease affecting the passageways that carry air into and out of the lungs. During an asthma attack, these airways become inflamed and fill with mucus. A person may experience wheezing, difficulty breathing, tightening of the chest, and coughing. Exposure to an allergen can set off an attack. Asthma can become life-threatening if not controlled in its early stages. The following symptoms may be indicative of an emergency: the patient shows no improvement minutes after initial treatment; struggles to breathe while hunched over with chest and neck pulled in; has trouble walking or talking; and develops gray or blue lips or fingernails.

Tobacco smoke, cold air, and expressing strong emotion can also trigger an asthma attack, as can respiratory infections or physical exercise. An accurate diagnosis by a physician is important. Although there is no cure for asthma or allergies, they can be controlled through lifestyle changes and quick-relief and long-term medications.

Website: www.aafa.org

Persons With Asthma, 2016

Source: National Health Interview Survey, NCHS, CDC, U.S. Dept. of Health and Human Services

	Number (thous.)	Percent
Total	26,515	8.3%
Child (under age 18)	6,132	8.3
Adult	20,383	8.3
Age		
0-4 years	767	3.8
5-14 years	4,141	10.1
15-19 years	2,085	10.0
20-24 years	1,993	9.5
25-34 years	3,087	7.1
35-64 years	10,914	8.8
65+ years.	3,529	7.4
Sex		
Males.	10,728	6.9
Under age 18	3,461	9.2
Age 18 and over	7,268	6.2
Females	15,787	9.7
Under age 18	2,671	7.4
Age 18 and over	13,116	10.4
Race/ethnicity		
White non-Hispanic	16,107	8.3
Black non-Hispanic	4,480	11.6
Other non-Hispanic	2,194	8.0
Hispanic (any race)	3,735	6.6
Puerto Rican.	847	14.3
Mexican/Mexican American	1,982	5.7

Note: Includes only those with a current diagnosis of asthma. Numbers may not add up to totals due to rounding.

Alzheimer's Disease

Source: Alzheimer's Association

Alzheimer's disease is a degenerative brain disease in which nerve cells deteriorate and die. It is the most common cause of dementia. Early symptoms include forgetting newly learned information and apathy or depression. As the disease advances, a person may exhibit disorientation and behavior changes; confusion about events, time, and place; suspicion towards family, friends, and caregivers; and ultimately, difficulty speaking, swallowing, and walking.

The rate of the disease's progression varies, with changes to the brain possibly beginning 20 or more years before symptoms occur in a stage researchers call preclinical Alzheimer's disease. In the next stage—mild cognitive impairment (MCI) due to Alzheimer's disease—a person can still perform everyday activities without significant trouble. The average length of time from diagnosis of Alzheimer's dementia, the third stage of the disease, until death is 4-8 years for those age 65 and older. As they become progressively debilitated, affected individuals grow increasingly susceptible to infections of the lungs, urinary tract, and other organs.

Alzheimer's dementia affected an estimated 5.7 mil Americans in 2018. Within the U.S. population, about 10% of persons age 65 and older and 32% of those age 85 and older have Alzheimer's dementia. Approximately 200,000 persons under age 65 have younger-onset, or early-onset, Alzheimer's dementia. Almost two-thirds of Americans with Alzheimer's are women.

Diagnosis involves a comprehensive evaluation that may include a complete health history, physical examination, neurological and mental status assessments, and other tests. Depression, drug interactions, nutritional imbalances, and infections such as AIDS, meningitis, and syphilis can cause similar symptoms. Other forms of dementia, such as those associated with Parkinson's disease, frontotemporal lobar dementia, and vascular disease, can also appear to be Alzheimer's. Absolute confirmation of a diagnosis requires a brain biopsy or autopsy, though scientists are researching possible biological markers for Alzheimer's disease.

Treatments for cognitive and behavioral symptoms are available, and clinical trials are ongoing for ways to prevent Alzheimer's or reverse its course. The FDA has approved six drugs that temporarily improve symptoms, but their effectiveness varies. Age is the greatest risk factor for Alzheimer's disease, followed by a family history of the disease and having the e4 form of the APOE (Apolipoprotein E) gene. Staying physically and mentally active and socially connected may be associated with a lower risk for the disease. In the disease's advanced stages, many individuals require long-term residential care.

The U.S. cost of diagnosing, treating, and providing long-term care for persons with Alzheimer's or other dementias is estimated to be $277 bil in 2018. The unpaid care that family members, friends, and others provided persons with Alzheimer's or other dementias was valued at around $232.1 bil in 2017; the lifetime cost of caring for a person with dementia was estimated to be $341,840. People with Alzheimer's need a safe, stable, and secure environment with a regular schedule offering appropriate stimulation. An identification bracelet with the person's name, address, and condition can help ensure the safety of an individual who wanders.

Website: www.alz.org

Warning Signs of Alzheimer's Disease

- Memory loss that disrupts daily life
- Challenges in planning or solving problems
- Difficulty completing familiar tasks at home, at work, or at leisure
- Confusion with time or place
- Trouble understanding visual images and spatial relationships
- New problems with words in speaking or writing
- Misplacing things and losing the ability to retrace steps
- Decreased or poor judgment
- Withdrawal from work or social activities
- Changes in mood and personality

Arthritis

Source: Arthritis Foundation; Centers for Disease Control and Prevention (CDC), U.S. Dept. of Health and Human Services

The term arthritis refers to more than 100 different diseases that cause pain, aching, stiffness, and swelling in or around the joints. An estimated 54.4 mil U.S. adults (22.7%) reported having doctor-diagnosed arthritis in 2013-15. The cause for most types of arthritis is unknown; scientists are studying the roles played by genetics, lifestyle, and environment.

Symptoms may develop gradually or suddenly. A visit to the doctor should be made when a person experiences—for three days or more—pain, stiffness, swelling in a joint, or difficulty in moving a joint. To diagnose arthritis, the doctor will record a patient's symptoms and perform a physical exam, looking for any swelling or limited movement. In addition, the doctor will check for other signs often seen with arthritis, such as rashes, mouth sores, or eye involvement. The doctor may test blood, urine, or joint fluid, or take X-rays of the joints.

Of the three most prevalent forms of arthritis, **osteoarthritis** (OA) is the most common, affecting approximately 30.8 mil Americans. It becomes more prevalent with age, especially among those 45 and over. In patients with OA, also called degenerative arthritis, the protective cartilage of joints is lost and changes occur in the bone, leading to pain and stiffness. The joints most commonly affected are the lower back, hips, knees, hands, and feet.

Fibromyalgia, another common arthritis condition, affects about 4 mil Americans. People suffering from fibromyalgia experience widespread pain, abnormal pain processing, sleep disturbance, fatigue, and psychological distress. Other symptoms include morning stiffness, tingling or numbness in hands and feet, headaches, or problems with thinking and memory. Twice as many women as men are afflicted with this type of arthritis.

Rheumatoid arthritis (RA) is an autoimmune disease that affects an estimated 1.5 mil in the U.S. It is one of the most serious and disabling forms of arthritis, which women experience at 2-3 times the rate of men. With RA, the body's immune system attacks healthy cells in the joints, causing inflammation that can lead to cartilage and bone damage.

Other forms of arthritis and related conditions include lupus, gout, scleroderma, and Sjögren's syndrome. Bursitis and tendinitis, which may result from injuring or overusing a joint, are also related.

Medications that relieve pain and swelling, such as analgesics, anti-inflammatory drugs, biologic response modifiers, glucocorticoids, and antirheumatic drugs, can be used to treat arthritis. They also tend to slow the disease process. Most treatment programs call for exercise, use of heat or cold, and joint-protection techniques, such as avoidance of excess stress on the joints, the use of assistive devices, and weight loss and control. In some cases, surgery may help.

Website: www.arthritis.org

Attention Deficit Hyperactivity Disorder (ADHD)

Source: Centers for Disease Control and Prevention; Natl. Institute of Mental Health; Children and Adults with Attention-Deficit/Hyperactivity Disorder (CHADD)

Attention deficit hyperactivity disorder, or ADHD, is one of the most common neurodevelopmental disorders of childhood, when it is usually first diagnosed. Individuals with ADHD may have trouble paying attention and controlling impulsive behaviors.

Signs and Symptoms of ADHD

- Daydreaming a lot
- Forgetting or losing things frequently
- Squirming or fidgeting
- Talking too much
- Making careless mistakes or taking unnecessary risks
- Having a hard time resisting temptation
- Having trouble taking turns
- Having difficulty getting along with others

There are three different types of ADHD. A person who is **predominantly inattentive** is easily distracted or forgets details of daily routines. Someone who is **predominantly hyperactive-impulsive** may feel restless and impulsive. In the third type, **combined presentation**, an individual displays symptoms of the first two types. The cause of ADHD is unknown, but current research shows that genetics plays a significant role. Scientists are also looking into possible risk factors such as alcohol, tobacco, or drug use during pregnancy and low birth weight.

ADHD affects about 4.4% of American adults age 18-44 years. According to a 2016 survey, about 9.4% of American children age 2 to 17 years have ever been diagnosed with ADHD. Boys were more likely to have been diagnosed than girls. Two out of three children (63.8%) with a current diagnosis of ADHD had at least one co-occurring condition, including oppositional defiant disorder, conduct disorder, anxiety or depression, or a learning disorder.

In most cases, ADHD is treated with a combination of medication and behavior therapy. Stimulants are the most widely used medication. Nonstimulants do not work as quickly as stimulants but have fewer side effects and can last up to 24 hours.

Breast Cancer

Source: American Cancer Society, Inc.; National Cancer Institute, National Institutes of Health

In 2018, an estimated 266,120 women and 2,550 men in the U.S. will be newly diagnosed with breast cancer, and about 40,920 women and 480 men will die from it. More than 3.5 mil women live with a history of breast cancer, but mortality rates have been declining, especially among younger women, probably because of earlier detection and improved treatment.

The risk for breast cancer increases with age. It is higher for women with a personal or family history of cancer (particularly breast cancer), a longer menstrual history (menstrual periods that started early and ended later in life), recent use of birth control pills, use of menopausal hormone therapy containing estrogen and progestin, and in those who have no children or had no live birth until after age 30. Other risk factors include alcohol consumption, physical inactivity, and being overweight or obese. Inherited mutations such as in the BRCA1 and BRCA2 genes greatly increase risk, but these probably account for 5%-10% of all female breast cancers and 15%-20% of all familial breast cancers. Most women who develop breast cancer have no family history of it.

Breast cancer often manifests first as a new lump or mass. Other symptoms include swelling, distortion, tenderness, skin irritation, redness, scaliness, or nipple abnormalities, such as ulceration, retraction, or spontaneous discharge.

Studies show that early detection increases survival and treatment options. Although most detected breast lumps are noncancerous, any suspicious lump should be biopsied.

Treatment for breast cancer may involve breast-conserving surgery (removal of the tumor and surrounding tissue), mastectomy (surgical removal of the breast), radiation therapy, chemotherapy, hormone therapy, and/or targeted therapy. The five-year survival rate for female invasive breast cancer patients has improved from 75% in 1975-77 to 91% in 2008-14. The five-year survival for women diagnosed with localized breast cancer (cancer that has not spread to lymph nodes or other locations outside the breast) is 100%.

Website: www.cancer.org

Prostate Cancer

Source: Prostate Cancer Foundation; American Cancer Society, Inc.

The prostate is a male gland located between the bladder and scrotum that secretes seminal fluid. Among men in the U.S., prostate cancer is the most commonly diagnosed non-skin cancer and the second-most common cause, after lung cancer, of cancer deaths. In 2018, an estimated 164,690 men will be newly diagnosed with prostate cancer, and about 29,430 will die from the disease. An estimated 3.3 mil men in the U.S. are living with a history of prostate cancer today.

The most identifiable risk factors for prostate cancer are age, family history, and African ancestry. The median age at diagnosis is 66, and the chances of developing the disease rise dramatically with age. Black men in the U.S. and Caribbean have the world's highest documented incidence rate of prostate cancer. The cause for this disparity remains unclear.

Usually, the disease has no symptoms in its early stages. As the disease advances, a man may experience weak or interrupted urine flow; inability to urinate or difficulty starting or stopping the urine flow; the need to urinate frequently, especially at night; blood in the urine; or pain or burning with urination. Advanced prostate cancer commonly spreads to the bones, causing pain in areas such as the hips, spine, or ribs.

The American Cancer Society recommends that once they reach 50, men at average risk of prostate cancer should speak with their health care provider about the benefits and limitations of prostate-specific antigen (PSA) testing. Black men or those with a family history of the disease (a close relative who was diagnosed before age 65) should be aware of their screening options beginning at age 45. Men with more than one close relative with prostate cancer should discuss screening at 40. Men under 40 seldom get prostate cancer.

Prostate cancer treatment may include surgery, radiation, hormonal therapy, chemotherapy, or some combination. If caught early on, while tumor cells are localized within the prostate, the five-year relative survival rate approaches 100%.

Websites: www.pcf.org; www.cancer.org

Skin Cancer

Source: American Cancer Society, Inc.

Skin cancer—the most common cancer diagnosed in the U.S.—is generally divided into **nonmelanomas** and **melanomas**, which affect different types of skin cells. Invasive melanoma accounts for only about 1% of all skin cancers but the majority of skin cancer deaths. Risk factors include heavy exposure to UV light, multiple moles (more than 50), fair skin, family or personal history of skin cancers, a history of sunburns, and occupational exposure to certain compounds.

Melanomas generally look like abnormal moles on the surface of the skin. Abnormal moles differ from regular skin cells and may be a sign of skin cancer. An irregular mole should be examined by a doctor as soon as possible.

If caught early, melanoma is highly curable. The five-year relative survival rate for melanoma at the localized stage is 99%; at the regional stage, 63%; and 20% at the distant stage.

Treatment may include simple removal of the melanoma; amputation if the cancer is found on a finger or toe; or chemotherapy, immunotherapy, and/or radiation if the melanoma has spread to other parts of the body.

Warning Signs of Abnormal Moles

- **A**symmetry: one half does not match the other half
- **B**order: edges are irregular, ragged, notched, or blurred
- **C**olor: not uniform; may be shades of brown or black, and patches of pink, red, blue, or white
- **D**iameter: moles wider than ¼ inch are abnormal (however, melanomas can be smaller)
- **E**volving: mole changes size, shape, or color over time

Website: www.cancer.org

Cancer Risk Factors

Source: American Cancer Society, Inc., www.cancer.org; National Cancer Institute, National Institutes of Health

Alcohol: Alcohol consumption increases the risk of cancers of the mouth, pharynx, larynx, esophagus, liver, colorectum, breast, and possibly pancreas. Alcohol consumption combined with tobacco use increases the risk of cancers of the mouth, pharynx, larynx, and esophagus far more than either drinking or smoking alone.

Diet and physical activity: Overweight and obesity are associated with increased risk for developing many cancers, including cancers of the breast in postmenopausal women, colorectum, kidney, pancreas, and esophagus. Overweight and obesity may also be associated with increased risk of fatal prostate cancer, non-Hodgkin lymphoma, and male breast cancer. It's not yet known for certain how diet, nutrition intake, and the amount and distribution of body fat factor into the development of certain cancers.

Environmental hazards: Exposure to certain substances, called carcinogens, can increase the risk of various cancers. Carcinogens like arsenic or radon may occur naturally, or they may be manufactured, like vinyl chloride. The risk of lung cancer from asbestos exposure is greatly increased among smokers.

Estrogen: Menopausal hormone therapy (MHT, formerly called hormone replacement therapy) without the use of progestin can increase the risk of endometrial and ovarian cancer. Combining progestin with estrogen MHT may help minimize that risk. Studies, however, suggest that use of MHT increases the risk of breast cancer. The benefits and risks of the use of estrogen should be discussed carefully with one's doctor.

HPV infection: Although most HPV infections do not cause cancer, almost all cervical cancers are caused by a persistent HPV infection. Persistent HPV infections also cause about 90% of anal cancers, 70% of oropharyngeal cancers, and 60%-70% of vaginal, vulvar, and penile cancers. The Centers for Disease Control and Prevention (CDC) estimates that most people in the U.S. will acquire HPV at some point in their lives. There are three vaccines approved for use against HPV, although only one was available in the U.S. as of 2017. The CDC recommends routine vaccination of both sexes at age 11-12.

Radiation: Excessive exposure to ionizing radiation can increase cancer risk. Medical and dental X-rays are adjusted to deliver the lowest dose possible without sacrificing image quality. Excessive radon exposure in the home may increase lung cancer risk, especially in cigarette smokers.

Smokeless tobacco: Use of chewing tobacco, snuff, snus, and other tobacco products that are not smoked increase the risk of oral, esophageal, and pancreatic cancers. The excess risk of cancer of the cheek and gum is especially high among long-term snuff users.

Smoking: Smoking is responsible for about 3 in 10 cancer deaths and about 80% of lung, bronchus, and trachea cancer deaths in the U.S. Cigarette smoking also increases the risk of the following types of cancer: larynx, oral cavity and pharynx, esophagus, stomach, pancreas, uterine cervix, kidney, bladder, stomach, colorectum, and acute myeloid leukemia. Cigar smoking causes many of the same cancers. While electronic cigarettes generally have lower carcinogen levels than combustible tobacco products, they still present a cardiovascular and lung risk because of nicotine.

Sunlight: Many of the 5.4 mil skin cancers diagnosed annually in the U.S. could have been prevented by protection from the sun's rays and avoiding indoor tanning. Epidemiological evidence shows that sun exposure is a major factor in the development of melanoma and that incidence rates are increasing.

Screening Guidelines for Early Detection of Cancer

Cancer site	Population	Test or procedure	Frequency
Breast	Women, age 40+	Mammography	The American Cancer Society no longer recommends regular breast self-exams or clinical breast exams; research has not found that they reduce the risk of dying from breast cancer. Women should be familiar with how their breasts look and feel and report any changes to a health care professional. For women at average risk (e.g., lack of strong family history of breast cancer), at age 40: begin annual mammography if desired; for ages 45-54: annual mammograms; for ages 55+: mammograms yearly or every two years for those in good health with a life expectancy of 10 or more years. Women at high risk for breast cancer, such as a BRCA1 or BRCA2 gene mutation, should get an MRI and mammogram yearly.
Cervix	Women, ages 21+	Pap test, HPV test	All women should begin screening at age 21. For ages 21-29: Pap test every 3 years; HPV testing may be done after an abnormal test result. For ages 30-65, the preferred screening method is a Pap test combined with an HPV test every 5 years. Another option is to get a Pap test alone every 3 years. For ages 65+: women who have had regular screenings with normal results in the previous 10 years should no longer be tested; women with a history of serious cervical precancers should continue to be tested for at least 20 years after diagnosis. Women who have had a total hysterectomy for reasons unrelated to cervical cancer should not be screened. Women should not be screened annually by any method at any age.
Colorectal	Men and women, ages 45-75 or 50-75	Guaiac-based fecal occult blood test (gFOBT) **or** fecal immunochemical test (FIT) **or**	The U.S. Preventive Services Task Force recommends screening beginning at age 50, though the American Cancer Society recommends starting at age 45. Annual, for people with average risk. Testing at home with adherence to manufacturer's recommendation for collection techniques and number of samples is recommended. An FOBT or FIT done with a stool sample collected during a digital rectal examination in a health care setting is not sufficient for screening.
		Stool DNA test (sDNA), **or**	Every 3 years, starting at age 45 or 50.
		Flexible sigmoidoscopy (FSIG), **or**	Every 5 years, starting at age 45 or 50. Can be performed every 10 years if an FIT is done yearly.
		CT, or virtual, colonography, **or**	Every 5 years, starting at age 45 or 50.
		Colonoscopy	Every 10 years, starting at age 45 or 50. A colonoscopy should also be done if any of the above tests is positive.
Endometrial	Women, at menopause		Women at average risk should be informed about risks and symptoms of endometrial cancer and strongly encouraged to report any unexpected bleeding or spotting to their physicians.
Lung	Current or former smokers, ages 55-74	Low-dose CT scan (LDCT)	Apparently healthy patients with a history of heavy smoking (at least one pack per day over 30 years, or two packs per day over 15 years, etc.), whether they currently smoke or have quit within the past 15 years, should discuss with a clinician the potential benefits, limitations, and harms associated with lung-cancer screening.
Prostate	Men, age 50+	Digital rectal examination (DRE) and prostate-specific antigen test (PSA)	Men with an average risk and an expected life span of 10+ years should talk with their health care provider at age 50 about whether the benefits of screening surpass the risks. African Americans—who have a higher rate of prostate cancer—and men with a first-degree relative diagnosed with prostate cancer before age 65 should have this talk at age 45. Men with more than one first-degree relative diagnosed at an early age should have the talk at age 40.

New U.S. Cancer Cases and Deaths for Leading Sites, 2018

Source: *Cancer Facts & Figures 2018*, American Cancer Society

The following estimates exclude basal cell and squamous cell skin cancers, also referred to as nonmelanoma skin cancers, and in situ carcinomas (i.e., noninvasive cancers) except of the urinary bladder. In 2018, an estimated 63,960 cases of carcinoma in situ of the female breast and 87,290 cases of melanoma in situ are expected to be diagnosed. An est. 5.4 mil cases of basal cell and squamous cell skin cancer were diagnosed among 3.3 mil people in 2012 according to the most recent study available.

Estimated New Cases

Both sexes		Male		Female	
Breast	268,670	Prostate	164,690	Breast	266,120
Lung and bronchus	234,030	Lung and bronchus	121,680	Lung and bronchus	112,350
Prostate	164,690	Colon and rectum	75,610	Colon and rectum	64,640
Colon and rectum	140,250	Urinary bladder	62,380	Uterine corpus	63,230
Melanoma—skin	91,270	Melanoma—skin	55,150	Thyroid	40,900
Urinary bladder	81,190	Kidney and renal pelvis	42,680	Melanoma—skin	36,120
Non-Hodgkin lymphoma	74,680	Non-Hodgkin lymphoma	41,730	Non-Hodgkin lymphoma	32,950
Kidney and renal pelvis	65,340	Oral cavity and pharynx	37,160	Pancreas	26,240
Uterine corpus	63,230	Leukemia	35,030	Leukemia	25,270
Leukemia	60,300	Liver and intrahepatic bile duct	30,610	Kidney and renal pelvis	22,660
All sites	**1,735,350**	**All sites**	**856,370**	**All sites**	**878,980**

Estimated Deaths

Both sexes		Male		Female	
Lung and bronchus	154,050	Lung and bronchus	83,550	Lung and bronchus	70,500
Colon and rectum	50,630	Prostate	29,430	Breast	40,920
Pancreas	44,330	Colon and rectum	27,390	Colon and rectum	23,240
Breast	41,400	Pancreas	23,020	Pancreas	21,310
Liver and intrahepatic bile duct	30,200	Liver and intrahepatic bile duct	20,540	Ovary	14,070
Prostate	29,430	Leukemia	14,270	Uterine corpus	11,350
Leukemia	24,370	Esophagus	12,850	Leukemia	10,100
Non-Hodgkin lymphoma	19,910	Urinary bladder	12,520	Liver and intrahepatic bile duct	9,660
Urinary bladder	17,240	Non-Hodgkin lymphoma	11,510	Non-Hodgkin lymphoma	8,400
Brain and other nervous system	16,830	Kidney and renal pelvis	10,010	Brain and other nervous system	7,340
All sites	**609,640**	**All sites**	**323,630**	**All sites**	**286,010**

U.S. Cancer Survival Rates by Year of Diagnosis, 1960-2014

Source: SEER (Surveillance, Epidemiology, and End Results) Cancer Statistics Review 1975-2015, National Cancer Institute, National Institutes of Health

	All races			White			Black		
Year of diagnosis	% total	% male	% female	% total	% male	% female	% total	% male	% female
1960-63	—	—	—	39%	—	—	27%	—	—
1970-73	—	—	—	43	—	—	31	—	—
1975-77	48.9%	41.7%	55.9%	49.8	42.7%	56.5%	39.1	32.7%	46.2%
1978-80	49.0	43.1	55.0	50.0	44.3	55.6	39.0	33.3	45.6
1981-83	50.2	45.2	55.1	51.3	46.6	56.0	38.8	34.2	44.4
1984-86	52.4	47.2	57.6	53.6	48.6	58.6	40.2	35.5	45.5
1987-89	55.3	51.1	59.6	56.7	52.8	60.6	43.0	38.9	47.7
1990-92	59.9	59.1	60.9	61.4	60.8	62.1	47.9	47.7	48.2
1993-95	61.3	60.9	61.8	62.4	62.1	62.8	52.9	54.6	50.6
1996-98	63.3	63.0	63.7	64.4	64.1	64.7	55.3	58.0	52.2
1999-2001	66.0	66.3	65.7	67.2	67.6	66.8	58.1	61.2	54.4
2002-04	67.1	67.7	66.5	68.4	69.0	67.7	59.6	63.4	55.4
2005-07	68.6	69.3	67.8	69.7	70.4	69.0	61.4	64.9	57.6
2008-14	69.2	68.9	69.5	70.1	69.8	70.5	63.3	65.7	60.7

— = Statistic could not be calculated. **Note:** The geographic areas of surveillance may vary for different years. Rates are five-year relative (estimated) survival rates for all invasive cancer sites; based on follow-up of patients into 2015.

U.S. Cancer Survival Rates by Age at Diagnosis, 2008-14

Source: SEER (Surveillance, Epidemiology, and End Results) Cancer Statistics Review, 1975-2015, National Cancer Institute, National Institutes of Health

	All races			White			Black		
Age at diagnosis	% total	% male	% female	% total	% male	% female	% total	% male	% female
Under age 45..........	82.7%	78.3%	85.4%	84.0%	79.9%	86.6%	72.9%	67.9%	75.9%
Ages 45-54	74.3	68.9	78.6	75.3	69.5	79.9	66.5	65.4	67.4
Ages 55-64	70.1	69.1	71.3	70.9	69.7	72.5	63.4	65.2	60.5
Under age 65..........	73.9	70.5	77.1	74.8	71.2	78.2	66.0	65.6	66.4
Ages 65-74	66.9	68.9	64.1	67.3	68.9	65.0	61.7	66.3	55.1
Ages 65 and older	59.3	62.3	55.9	59.7	62.1	56.8	54.5	60.5	47.7
Ages 75 and older	50.5	53.0	48.1	51.0	53.0	49.2	43.1	48.4	38.9

Note: Rates are five-year relative (estimated) survival rates for all invasive cancer sites; based on follow-up of patients into 2015.

Depression

Source: National Institute of Mental Health (NIMH), National Institutes of Health, U.S. Dept. of Health and Human Services

Depression is a serious illness that affects thoughts, feelings, and the ability to function in everyday life. It is one of the most common mental disorders in the U.S., affecting all age groups. The NIMH estimates that in 2016, about 16.2 mil adults age 18 and older (or 6.7% of the adult population) in the U.S. had at least one major depressive episode. Over the same 12-month period, 10.9% of persons aged 18 to 25 years experienced at least one major depressive episode versus 4.8% of those 50 or older. More women (8.5%) than men (4.8%) reported suffering at least one major depressive episode in 2016.

Available treatments can alleviate symptoms. But many depressed people—and those around them—still fail to realize that they have an illness or could benefit from medical help.

Symptoms and Types of Depression

• Persistent sad, anxious, or "empty" feelings
• Feelings of hopelessness or pessimism
• Feelings of guilt, worthlessness, or helplessness
• Irritability, restlessness
• Loss of interest in activities or hobbies once pleasurable, including sex
• Fatigue and decreased energy
• Difficulty concentrating, remembering, or making decisions
• Insomnia, early-morning wakefulness, or excessive sleeping
• Appetite and/or weight changes
• Thoughts of death or suicide, or suicide attempts
• Aches or pains, headaches, cramps, or digestive problems that do not ease even with treatment

A diagnosis of **major depressive disorder** (or **clinical depression**) is made if an individual reports experiencing five or more of these symptoms in the same two-week period.

Bipolar disorder (or **manic-depressive illness**), while distinct from depression, is characterized by periods of depression alternating with episodes of mania, when a person experiences a an abnormally elevated mood, less need for sleep, increased talkativeness, racing thoughts, distractibility,

agitation, and engaging in risky activities (e.g., spending a lot of money, reckless sex). Depression in women who are pregnant or who recently gave birth; psychotic depression, where a person also suffers some psychosis; and seasonal affective disorder are some other forms of depression.

Treatments for Depression

Depression can be treated by medication, psychotherapy, or a combination of the two. Antidepressants influence the functioning of certain neurotransmitters in the brain. The most popular antidepressants are selective serotonin reuptake inhibitors (SSRIs). Serotonin and norepinephrine reuptake inhibitors (SNRIs) and bupropion are also commonly prescribed as they have fewer side effects than drugs from older classes, such as tricyclics, tetracyclics, and monoamine oxidase inhibitors (MAOIs). Some people respond better, however, to the older antidepressants.

NIMH research has shown that certain types of psychotherapy, particularly cognitive-behavioral therapy (CBT) and interpersonal therapy (IPT), can help relieve depression. CBT helps patients change the negative thinking and behaving patterns often associated with depression. IPT focuses patients on working through personal relationships that may contribute to depression. Studies of adults have shown that a combination of psychotherapy and antidepressant medication is most effective in treating moderate-to-severe depression.

Electroconvulsive therapy (ECT) has been found effective in treating some cases of severe depression, particularly those that have not responded to other treatment. ECT involves producing a seizure in the brain of a patient under general anesthesia by applying electrical stimulation through electrodes placed on the scalp. Memory loss and other cognitive problems, though common side effects, are typically short-lived. Other types of treatment involving brain stimulation are currently being studied.

Website: www.nimh.nih.gov

Diabetes

Source: American Diabetes Association; Centers for Disease Control and Prevention (CDC), U.S. Dept. of Health and Human Services

Diabetes is a chronic disease in which the body does not produce or properly use the hormone **insulin**. Insulin is needed to convert sugar, starches, and other foods into energy. Both genetics and environment appear to play roles in the onset of diabetes. This disease, which has no cure, was the seventh leading cause of death in the U.S. in 2016, with 80,058 deaths. In 2015, an est. 30.3 mil Americans (9.4% of the population) had diabetes. Of that number, 7.2 mil had undiagnosed diabetes. Diagnosed diabetes in the U.S. cost an estimated $327 bil in direct medical costs and in reduced productivity in 2017.

The American Diabetes Association supports studies proving that detection at an earlier stage and modest lifestyle changes, such as eating better and exercising more, will help prevent or delay complications.

There are two major types of diabetes:

Type 1 (formerly known as insulin-dependent or juvenile diabetes). The body does not produce insulin; the disease is usually diagnosed in children and young adults. People with type 1 diabetes must take daily insulin to stay alive.

Type 2 (formerly known as non-insulin dependent or adult-onset diabetes). The body does not produce enough or cannot properly use insulin. It is the most common form of the disease (90%-95% of all diabetes cases) and often begins later in life.

Prediabetes

In 2015, 84.1 mil Americans age 18 and older (33.9% of that population) had prediabetes, the state that occurs when a person's blood glucose levels are higher than normal but not high enough for a diagnosis of diabetes. People with prediabetes are at increased risk of developing type 2 diabetes unless lifestyle changes are made.

Complications From Diabetes

People often have diabetes for many years before it is diagnosed. During that time, serious complications may develop. Potential complications include the following:

Diabetic eye disease. High blood glucose can damage blood vessels to the eyes. About one in three people with diabetes over 40 years of age have some signs of diabetic retinopathy, the most common cause of vision loss among those with diabetes. People with diabetes are also about twice as likely to develop glaucoma or cataracts.

Kidney disease. One in three adults with diabetes may have chronic kidney disease. In 2014, a total of 52,159 people in the U.S. developed end-stage renal disease due to diabetes.

Amputations. Diabetes is the most frequent cause for nontraumatic lower-limb amputations. The risk of a leg amputation is about eight times greater for a person with diabetes than for the average American. Approximately 108,000 hospitalizations among adults aged 18 and over in 2014 were for a lower-limb amputation in persons with diagnosed diabetes.

Heart disease and stroke. People with diabetes are about twice as likely to have heart disease or a stroke.

Common Diabetes Symptoms

- Frequent urination
- Thirst
- Hunger
- Fatigue
- Blurry vision
- Cuts and bruises that are slow to heal
- Weight loss, nausea, vomiting (type 1)
- Tingling or numbness in hands or feet (type 2)

Gestational Diabetes

Gestational diabetes is a form of diabetes that develops during or is first diagnosed during pregnancy. Hormones released during pregnancy can cause insulin resistance, allowing blood glucose levels to rise. The condition affects up to 9.2% of pregnant women. Usually there are no symptoms, or the symptoms are mild. Because gestational diabetes usually starts around the 24th week, pregnant women should receive a glucose tolerance test between the 24th and 28th week of pregnancy. Diet and exercise can help keep blood glucose levels within normal limits. Treatment may also include daily blood glucose testing and insulin injections. Women with gestational diabetes tend to have larger babies at birth, which can complicate delivery. Glucose levels usually return to normal after delivery, but the odds of recurrence in future pregnancies and development of type 2 diabetes later in life increase.

Website: www.diabetes.org

Eating Disorders

Source: National Institute of Mental Health (NIMH), National Institutes of Health, U.S. Dept. of Health and Human Services

Eating disorders are medical illnesses that involve serious disturbances in eating behavior, usually in the forms of extreme and unhealthy reduction of food intake or severe overeating. The main types are anorexia nervosa, bulimia nervosa, and binge-eating disorder (technically categorized with "eating disorders not otherwise specified"). These disorders usually develop in adolescence or early adulthood, possibly as a result of multiple risk factors, including genetics, social history, and trauma. They often occur with other illnesses such as depression, substance abuse, and anxiety disorders. If not treated, eating disorders can lead to serious complications, including heart conditions and kidney failure, which may result in death.

Anorexia nervosa affects an estimated 0.6% of the U.S. adult population and three times as many women as men. It has the highest mortality rate of any mental disorder in the U.S. Symptoms include resistance to maintaining weight at minimally healthy levels, intense fear of gaining weight, exaggerated importance of body weight or shape in one's self image, and infrequent or absent menstrual periods. Anorexics see themselves as overweight even when they are dangerously thin. In response, they avoid food and take other extreme measures to lose weight, such as exercising compulsively or purging by means of vomiting or laxatives and enemas. While some anorexics fully recover after a single episode, others may relapse frequently or experience chronic deterioration.

Bulimia nervosa affects an estimated 1.0% of the U.S. adult population. It is five times more prevalent in women than men. It is characterized by recurrent uncontrolled binge-eating episodes followed by what is believed to be compensatory behavior to prevent weight gain, such as self-induced vomiting, use of laxatives or diuretics, exercising excessively, or fasting. Persons with bulimia can weigh within the normal range for their age and height, but they still fear gaining weight and are intensely dissatisfied with their bodies. They often perform their behaviors in secret, feeling shame when they binge and relief when they purge.

Binge-eating disorder affects an estimated 2.8% of the U.S. adult population, with women twice as likely than men to have it. As with bulimia, a binge-eating disorder involves episodes of excessive eating during which the sufferer may feel a complete lack of control. But individuals with this disorder do not compensate by purging, exercising, or fasting. Many are thus overweight or obese, and the shame they feel can lead to further binge-eating.

Early diagnosis and a comprehensive treatment program are essential to recovery. Some patients may need immediate hospitalization. For anorexia, treatment usually follows three established steps: weight restoration, usually in an inpatient hospital setting; treatment of any accompanying psychological disturbances, including the use of medications; and achieving long-term remission or recovery by reducing or eliminating negative thoughts and behaviors.

Heart and Blood Vessel Disease

Source: American Heart Assn.; American Stroke Assn.; Natl. Ctr. for Chronic Disease Prevention and Health Promotion, Centers for Disease Control and Prevention; Natl. Heart, Blood, and Lung Inst., Natl. Insts. of Health (NIH), U.S. Dept. of Health and Human Services

Warning Signs of Heart Attack

- Discomfort in chest. Most heart attacks involve discomfort, such as pressure, squeezing, or pain, in the center of the chest that lasts more than a few minutes or occurs intermittently. Most common symptom in men and women.
- Discomfort in other upper body areas, including one or both arms, the back, neck, jaw, or stomach.
- Shortness of breath, with or without chest discomfort.
- Breaking out in a cold sweat, nausea, or lightheadedness, among other signs.

While chest discomfort is the most common symptom of a heart attack, women are more likely to experience the other symptoms, such as abdominal pain, shortness of breath, dizziness, fainting, and extreme fatigue, without having any chest pain. The American Heart Association advises calling 911 at onset of symptoms so that emergency medical services can begin treatment on the way to the hospital.

Warning Signs of Stroke

- **F**ace drooping
- **A**rm weakness
- **S**peech difficulty
- **T**ime to call 911
  Other stroke symptoms, which may appear separately or in combination with F.A.S.T.:
- Sudden numbness or weakness of the face, arm, or leg, especially on one side of the body.
- Sudden confusion or trouble speaking or comprehending.
- Sudden vision difficulty in one or both eyes.
- Sudden trouble walking, dizziness, or loss of coordination.
- Sudden severe headache with no known cause.

If someone has one or more stroke symptoms lasting more than a few minutes, call 911 or the emergency medical service number immediately so an ambulance, ideally one with advanced life support, can be sent. Prompt treatment of a stroke can prevent death or lessen the long-term effects.

Major Modifiable Risk Factors

Major risk factors for heart and blood vessel (cardiovascular) disease that can't be changed include age, gender, and heredity. People 65 years of age or older are more likely to die of coronary heart disease. Men are at greater risk, as well as African Americans and those with a family history of heart disease. Major risk factors that can be modified include the following:

High blood pressure. High blood pressure, or hypertension, increases the risk of stroke, heart attack, kidney failure, and congestive heart failure. It affects men and women of all races, ethnic origins, and ages. But obesity, physical inactivity, and an unhealthy diet can contribute to this often symptomless disease. Everyone 3 years of age and older should have a blood pressure reading at least once a year.

A blood pressure reading consists of two measurements written one above the other, such as 122/78 mmHg (millimeters of mercury). The upper number (systolic pressure) represents the amount of pressure in the arteries when the heart contracts (beats) and pushes blood through the circulatory system. The lower number (diastolic pressure) represents the pressure in the arteries between beats, when the heart is resting. According to revised guidelines, a blood pressure reading below 120/80 is considered normal, while a reading of 130/80 or higher indicates hypertension, of which there are two stages:

Stage 1 is 130-139 (systolic) over 80-89 (diastolic);
Stage 2 is 140+ (systolic) over 90+ (diastolic).

The diagnosis can be based on either the systolic or the diastolic reading. Any reading of 180/120 or higher is a hypertensive crisis that must be addressed by a doctor immediately.

High blood pressure usually cannot be cured, but it can be controlled in a variety of ways, including through diet, exercise, quitting smoking (where applicable), and medication. Treatment should be at the direction and under the supervision of a physician.

High blood cholesterol. Cholesterol is a waxy fat-like substance found in all cells of the body. It is produced by the body and also comes in some foods. The body needs some cholesterol, but excess levels increase the risk of heart disease. High cholesterol in itself usually does not cause symptoms, so many people are unaware that they have a problem.

There are two major kinds of cholesterol: LDL (low-density lipoprotein), often called "bad" cholesterol, leads to narrowing of the arteries. HDL (high-density lipoprotein), known as "good" cholesterol, helps reduce that risk.

NIH guidelines classify healthy total cholesterol levels (determined by a blood test) as less than 170 mg/dL for those age 19 or younger and 125 to 200 mg/dL for persons age 20 or older. About 27.1% of Americans age 20 and over in 2013-16 had a cholesterol level of 240 mg/dL or higher. LDL levels of less than 100 mg/dL are considered healthy. Healthy levels of HDL are more than 45 mg/dL for those age 19 or younger, 40 mg/dL or higher for men ages 20+, and 50 mg/dL or higher for women ages 20+.

As with high blood pressure, high blood cholesterol can be controlled by lifestyle changes and medication and should be treated by a physician.

Triglycerides, another form of fat in the blood, can also raise the risk of heart disease. Levels that are borderline high (150-199 mg/dL) or high (200 or more) may need treatment.

Diabetes. Even with glucose levels under control, at least 68% of people age 65 or older with diabetes mellitus die of some form of heart disease; 16% die of stroke.

Tobacco smoke. Cigarette smokers and nonsmokers exposed to secondhand smoke are more likely to develop coronary heart disease (CHD).

Obesity. People with excess body fat, especially around the waist, are more likely to develop heart and blood vessel disease even without any other risk factors.

Physical inactivity. A sedentary lifestyle is a risk factor for CHD. The risk increase is comparable to that observed for high blood cholesterol, high blood pressure, or cigarette smoking.

Women and Cardiovascular Disease

Heart disease was the number one cause of death for women in the United States in 2016, accounting for 22.0% of all female deaths. (Stroke was the third leading cause.) Because heart disease was long viewed as a "man's" disease, many of the major cardiovascular studies were conducted only on men. Researchers are now trying to understand the influence of gender on cardiovascular disease risk and prevention, but important gaps in knowledge remain.

One problem in **diagnosis** is that women tend to have heart attacks later in life than men, so symptoms may be masked by other age-related diseases such as arthritis or osteoporosis. Even certain diagnostic tests and procedures such as the exercise stress test may not be as accurate in women, with the result that the disease process leading to heart attack or stroke may not be detected early on, with potentially serious consequences.

Website: www.heart.org

Common Infectious Diseases

Source: Centers for Disease Control and Prevention (CDC), U.S. Dept. of Health and Human Services; World Health Organization

State and local officials, in connection with the CDC, monitor certain diseases in the interests of public health. Some diseases must be confirmed in a laboratory while others may be diagnosed based on epidemiologic data (e.g., exposure to a foodborne pathogen linked to confirmed cases of illness in other patients). Statistics may thus appear uneven because of different reporting methods for each disease. This list is meant to be used for reference purposes only and not as a diagnostic tool.

Chicken pox

(*Varicella simplex*) Usually nonthreatening viral disease commonly associated with children. In adults, the disease can be serious. **Transmission:** highly contagious. Transmitted by direct contact with rash, coughing, or sneezing of infected persons. **Symptoms:** blister-like rash, discomfort, high fever. Infected people may develop shingles later in life. **Vaccine:** available since 1995. **Treatment:** none; antibiotics in some severe cases. **Annual U.S. cases:** before 1995, about 4 mil, mostly children; 8,953 cases, 3 deaths reported in 2016.

Chlamydia

(*Chlamydia trachomatis*) One of the most widely spread sexually transmitted diseases (STDs), and the most common condition reported to the CDC of the diseases that it tracks. **Transmission:** sexually transmitted. Infants can be infected during delivery. **Symptoms:** Most of those infected show no symptoms. In women, vaginal discharge, infection of the cervix and urinary tract; can cause pelvic inflammatory disease. In men, infection of urinary tract and epididymitis (inflammation of testicular duct); can also infect the throat, rectum, and eyes. **Treatment:** curable with antibiotics. **Annual U.S. cases:** 1,598,354 in 2016.

Common cold

(More than 200 different viruses, rhinoviruses being most common) An upper respiratory viral infection. **Transmission:** touching one's nose, eyes, or mouth after touching something contaminated by the virus; inhalation of airborne virus. **Symptoms:** irritated nose or scratchy throat, sneezing and watery green or yellow nasal discharge, coughing, muscle aches, headaches, postnasal drip, decreased appetite. **Treatment:** no cure. Over-the-counter remedies can relieve symptoms; effectiveness of antiviral drugs uncertain. **Annual U.S. cases:** about 1 bil.

Gonorrhea

(*Neisseria gonorrhoeae*) Common bacterial STD. **Transmission:** sexually transmitted. Can pass from mother to infant during delivery. **Symptoms:** in men, white, yellow, or green discharge; burning during urination. In women, pain or burning during urination, increased vaginal discharge, vaginal bleeding between periods. Most women do not present symptoms. **Treatment:** highly curable with antibiotics, although disease has become increasingly resistant. **Annual U.S. cases:** 468,514 in 2016.

Hepatitis

A viral disease that causes inflammation of the liver. In the U.S., five forms are endemic: A, B, C, D, and E. Forms A, B, and C are the most common. HBV and HCV can cause chronic disease. **Symptoms:** all forms have generally similar symptoms including jaundice, fatigue, abdominal pain, loss of appetite, nausea, mild flu-like symptoms. Many cases cause no symptoms. In extreme cases, infected persons may develop end-stage liver disease.

Hepatitis A (*Hepatovirus picornaviridae*). **Transmission:** consuming food or water contaminated with feces from infected persons. **Vaccine:** effective; travelers are advised to not drink tap water in countries where disease is common. **Treatment:** disease usually resolves on its own; alcohol consumption should be avoided. **Annual U.S. cases:** in 2016, 2,007 cases reported to the CDC, which estimated there to be 4,000 actual acute cases.

Hepatitis B (*Orthohepadnavirus hepadnaviridae*). **Transmission:** unsterilized needle sharing; contaminated blood transfusions; sexual contact; infants during childbirth. **Vaccine:** highly effective. **Treatment:** for chronic cases, drug treatment is necessary. For acute cases, disease usually resolves itself. **Annual U.S. cases:** in 2016, 3,218 acute cases reported to the CDC; 20,900 acute cases estimated.

Hepatitis C (*Hepacivirus flavinviridae*). **Transmission:** unsterilized needle sharing; contaminated blood transfusions;

sexual contact; infants during childbirth. **Vaccine:** none. **Treatment:** chronic cases treated with drugs, which can eliminate the virus in more than 90% of patients. For acute cases, the CDC recommends monitoring by a doctor and starting treatment if the infection becomes chronic. **Annual U.S. cases:** in 2016, 2,967 acute cases were reported to the CDC; est. 41,200 acute cases.

HPV

(More than 200 related human papillomaviruses) Most common sexually transmitted infection in U.S.; causes virtually all cases of cervical cancer, about 95% of anal cancers. **Transmission:** sexually transmitted. **Symptoms:** most of those infected have no symptoms but can still transmit virus. In some cases, genital warts and precancerous bumps on anus, cervix or vulva, or penis. **Vaccine:** 3 approved for use with routine vaccination recommended at ages 11 or 12. **Treatment:** while there is no cure, a healthy immune system can usually fight off HPV on its own. Women with a normal Pap test result but a positive HPV test should repeat the screening in one year. Follow up with a colposcopy may be suggested if a woman has an abnormal Pap test result, regardless of the outcome of the HPV test. **Annual U.S. cases:** est. 14 mil new cases; approximately 79 mil currently infected with HPV.

Influenza

(Various influenza viruses) Highly contagious viral respiratory infection. **Transmission:** airborne; contact with face after touching infected surface. **Symptoms:** chills, fatigue, fever, headaches, sore throat, sinus congestion, coughing. ("Stomach flu" is not influenza.) **Vaccine:** yearly vaccinations recommended; available as injection or nasal spray. **Treatment:** antiviral drugs; disease normally runs its course in a matter of days. **Annual U.S. cases:** about 30.9 mil illnesses, 600,000 hospitalizations in the 2016-17 influenza season; 12,000-56,000 deaths since 2010.

Lyme disease

(*Borrelia burgdorferi*) Bacterial inflammatory disease, first identified 1975 in Old Lyme, CT. Concentrated heavily in the Northeast and upper Midwest U.S., usually in areas with large deer populations. **Transmission:** bite from infected blacklegged (or deer) tick. Mice and deer are most common tick hosts. **Symptoms:** mimic those of other diseases. Flu-like symptoms: fatigue, stiff neck, joints. Skin rash may appear at site of tick bite. **Treatment:** antibiotics in early stages; anti-inflammatory drugs to relieve symptoms. Without treatment, long-term complications (some fatal) involving joints, heart, and nervous system. **Annual U.S. cases:** from 9,895 reported cases in 1992 to 26,203 confirmed and 10,226 probable cases in 2016. Up to 300,000 people are diagnosed with Lyme disease each year according to CDC estimates.

Malaria

(*Plasmodium* parasite) Infectious disease virtually eradicated in developed countries; still a major killer in tropical regions. **Transmission:** bite from infected mosquito. **Symptoms:** high fever, shaking chills, heavy sweating, headaches, fatigue, enlarged spleen. If left untreated, organ damage and death. **Treatment:** antimalarial drugs, including chloroquine, for treatment and prevention. **Annual cases:** 1,517 (1 congenital) in the U.S. in 2015; worldwide in 2016, est. 216 mil cases and 445,000 deaths, with 15 countries (all in sub-Saharan Africa with the exception of India) accounting for 80% of the global malaria burden.

Measles

(*Rubeola* virus) Once-common viral infection; occurs sporadically in U.S. **Transmission:** airborne transmission by infected persons. **Symptoms:** itchy and raised rash, sore throat, cough, pink eye, high fever. In rare cases, encephalitis, seizures, permanent deafness, death. **Vaccine:** highly effective. **Treatment:** no specific treatment; symptoms relieved with bed rest, acetaminophen, humidified air. **Annual U.S. cases:** 120 in 2017.

Mumps

(Mumps virus) Acute and contagious viral infection. **Transmission:** direct contact with mucus or saliva of infected persons. **Symptoms:** painful, visible swelling of the salivary or parotid glands in the face. Chills, headaches, fever, painful swallowing. In some cases, inflammation of testes, pancreas, ovaries. In severe cases, brain swelling and symptoms ranging from nausea and drowsiness to seizures and permanent deafness. **Vaccine:** MMR (measles, mumps, and rubella) vaccine is effective. **Treatment:** no specific treatment; symptoms may be relieved by applying ice or heat to swollen glands. **Annual U.S. cases:** 5,629 provisional cases in 2017.

Peptic ulcer

(Most from *Helicobacter pylori* [*H. pylori*] bacteria; also overuse of aspirin or other anti-inflammatory drugs) Weakening of the stomach's protective mucous coating, allowing stomach acid and bacteria to irritate stomach lining. **Transmission:** *H. pylori* may be transmitted through food and water; possibly through close contact between infected persons. **Symptoms:** indigestion; bloating; dull, transient abdominal pain or discomfort; nausea; vomiting. **Treatment:** antibiotics, acid-suppressing drugs. **Annual U.S. cases:** more than 6 mil people.

Pertussis or Whooping cough

(*Bordetella pertussis* or *B. parepertussis*) Upper respiratory bacterial infection. **Transmission:** airborne transmission by infected persons; highly contagious. **Symptoms:** initially, mild cold-like symptoms, fever, diarrhea, difficulty breathing; later, violent coughing with characteristic "whooping" sound when patient tries to breathe between coughs, vomiting. In severe cases, apnea, pneumonia, seizures, encephalopathy. **Vaccine:** available as part of Tdap (tetanus, diphtheria, pertussis) combination vaccine. **Treatment:** antibiotics in early cases; otherwise, disease must run its course. **Annual U.S. cases:** 17,972 in 2016; 15,808 (provisional) in 2017.

Salmonella or Salmonellosis

(*Salmonella*) Bacterial infection. **Transmission:** eating foods contaminated by feces carrying the bacteria or eating undercooked meats or raw eggs contaminated by bacteria. Contact with feces of infected wild and domestic animals. **Symptoms:** fever, diarrhea, abdominal cramps 12 to 72 hours after infection. **Treatment:** no standard treatment. Runs its course in four to seven days. Antibiotics in severe cases. **Annual U.S. cases:** 46,623 lab-confirmed infections in 2016.

Shigellosis

(Four species of *Shigella*: *boydii, dysenteriae, flexneri,* and *sonnei*) Bacterial infection and a form of dysentery, an intestinal disease. **Transmission:** consuming food contaminated by infected feces or eating vegetables grown in fields containing contaminated sewage. Swimming in contaminated water. **Symptoms:** watery or bloody diarrhea one to four days after infection, high fever, vomiting, painful bowel movements. In extreme cases, seizures in children, intestinal perforation. **Treatment:** mild infection allowed to run its course; replacement of fluids and salts lost through excessive diarrhea. Antibiotics in severe cases. Although severe diarrhea is symptomatic, antidiarrheal medicines may make illness worse. **Annual U.S. cases:** 11,795 provisional cases in 2017.

Syphilis

(*Treponema pallidum*) Bacterial infection that can cause significant health problems if left untreated. **Transmission:** sexually transmitted; pregnant women can transmit during fetal development or at birth. **Symptoms:** primary stage: painless sore, called a chancre, where bacteria enters the body; usually heals in 3-6 weeks with or without treatment. Without treatment, disease enters secondary stage: skin rash as chancre is healing or weeks after it has healed. Without treatment, enters latent stage (no visible symptoms). Very rarely, can move into tertiary stage 10-30 years after infection and cause death. Syphilis can spread to the brain and nervous system (neurosyphilis) or eyes (ocular syphilis) at any stage; symptoms include fever, fatigue, dementia, vision changes. **Treatment:** curable with antibiotics (mostly penicillin). **Annual U.S. cases:** 88,042 (27,814 primary and secondary) in 2016.

Tetanus or Lockjaw

(*Clostridium tetani*) Bacterial infection. **Transmission:** bacteria, found in soil, entering body through broken skin. **Symptoms:** muscle stiffness and spasms or "locking" of muscles of the jaw, neck, and limbs. **Vaccine:** four forms of immunization. **Treatment:** tetanus immune globulin to fight infection. With treatment, less than 10% of cases are fatal. **Annual U.S. cases:** 31 provisional cases in 2017.

Tuberculosis

(*Mycobacterium tuberculosis*) Bacterial infection that primarily affects the lungs. **Transmission:** airborne transmission by persons with active TB infection. **Symptoms:** weight loss, fever, cough with discharge (sometimes with bloody sputum), night sweats, growing shortness of breath over time, chest pains. **Vaccine/treatment:** BCG (Bacille Calmette Guerin) vaccine only effective in protecting young children and used where TB is prevalent. Not recommended by health experts for use in the U.S. because of the low risk of infection and its variable effectiveness. **Annual U.S. cases:** 9,093 provisional cases in 2017.

Yellow fever

(Yellow fever virus, in *flavivirus* group) Viral infection endemic in tropical areas of Africa and Central and South America. **Transmission:** bite from mosquito carrying the virus. **Symptoms:** headaches, muscle aches, fever, jaundice (yellowing skin), nausea and vomiting, kidney failure, severe generalized pain. In severe cases, shock, coma, and death. **Vaccine:** available, safe, and effective. **Treatment:** symptoms treated until disease runs its course. **Annual cases:** none in the U.S.; an estimated 84,000-170,000 severe cases and 29,000-60,000 deaths worldwide in 2013.

U.S. Reported Cases and Deaths From Vaccine-Preventable Diseases, 1950-2016

Source: Centers for Disease Control and Prevention (CDC), U.S. Dept. of Health and Human Services

Year	Diphtheria Cases	Diphtheria Deaths	Tetanus Cases	Tetanus Deaths	Pertussis Cases	Pertussis Deaths	Polio (paralytic) Cases	Polio (paralytic) Deaths	Measles Cases	Measles Deaths	Mumps Cases	Mumps Deaths	Rubella Cases	Rubella Deaths
1950	5,796	410	486	336	120,718	1,118	33,300	1,904	319,124	468	NR	NA	NR	NA
1960	918	69	368	231	14,809	118	3,190	230	441,703	380	NR	42	NR	12
1970	435	30	148	79	4,249	12	33	7	47,351	89	104,953	16	56,552	31
1980	3	1	95	28	1,730	11	9	2	13,506	11	8,576	2	3,904	1
1990	4	1	64	11	4,570	12	6	0	27,786	64	5,292	1	1,125	8
2000	1	0	35	5	7,867	12	0	0	86	1	338	2	176	0
2003	1	1	20	4	11,647	11	0	0	56	1	231	0	7	0
2004	0	0	34	4	25,827	16	0	0	37	0	258	0	10	1
2005	0	0	27	1	25,616	31	1[1]	0	66	NA	314	0	11	0
2006	0	0	41	4	15,632	9	0	0	55	0	6,584	1	11	0
2007	0	0	28	5	10,454	9	0	0	43	0	800	0	11	1
2008	0	0	19	3	13,278	6	0	0	140	0	454	2	16	0
2009	0	0	18	6	16,858	1	1[1]	0	71	2	1,991	2	3	1
2010	0	0	26	3	27,550	5	0	0	63	2	2,612	1	5	1
2011	0	0	36	6	18,719	1	0	0	220	1	404	0	4	1
2012	1	0	37	4	48,277	4	0	0	55	2	229	0	9	0
2013	0	0	26	3	28,639	2	1[1]	0	187	0	584	1	9	0
2014	1	0	25	1	32,971	7	0	0	667	0	1,223	0	6	0
2015	0	NA	29	NA	20,762	NA	0	NA	188	NA	1,329	NA	5	NA
2016	0	NA	34	NA	17,972	NA	0	NA	85	NA	6,369	NA	1	NA

NA = Not applicable or available. NR = Not nationally reportable. (1) Vaccine-associated/derived paralytic polio.

Effectiveness of the Seasonal Flu Vaccine, 2004-18

Source: National Center for Immunization and Respiratory Diseases, Centers for Disease Control and Prevention (CDC)

The CDC conducts studies to determine how effective each season's flu vaccine was in preventing the flu among a nationwide sample of patients.

Flu season	Vaccine effectiveness (%)	Flu season	Vaccine effectiveness (%)
2004-05	10%	2011-12	47%
2005-06	21	2012-13	49
2006-07	52	2013-14	52
2007-08	37	2014-15	19
2008-09	41	2015-16	48
2009-10	56	2016-17	40
2010-11	60	2017-18*	40

* = Preliminary.

Estimated Calorie Requirements

Source: *2015-2020 Dietary Guidelines for Americans*, U.S. Dept. of Agriculture and U.S. Dept. of Health and Human Services

Estimated amount of calories, rounded to the nearest 200, needed to maintain energy balance by sex, for various age groups and levels of physical activity. In adults, calorie needs generally decrease with age.

	Age (years)	Sedentary[1]	Moderately active[2]	Active[3]		Age (years)	Sedentary[1]	Moderately active[2]	Active[3]
Female[4]	2-3	1,000	1,000-1,200	1,000-1,400	**Male**	2-3	1,000	1,000-1,400	1,000-1,400
	4-8	1,200-1,400	1,400-1,600	1,400-1,800		4-8	1,200-1,400	1,400-1,600	1,600-2,000
	9-13	1,400-1,600	1,600-2,000	1,800-2,200		9-13	1,600-2,000	1,800-2,200	2,000-2,600
	14-18	1,800	2,000	2,400		14-18	2,000-2,400	2,400-2,800	2,800-3,200
	19-30	1,800-2,000	2,000-2,200	2,400		19-30	2,400-2,600	2,600-2,800	3,000
	31-50	1,800	2,000	2,200		31-50	2,200-2,400	2,400-2,600	2,800-3,000
	51+	1,600	1,800	2,000-2,200		51+	2,000-2,200	2,200-2,400	2,400-2,800

Note: Based on Estimated Energy Requirements (EER) equations, using reference heights (average) and reference weights (healthy) for each age-sex group. For children and adolescents, reference height and weight vary. For adults, the reference man is 5 ft 10 in. tall and weighs 154 lbs. The reference woman is 5 ft 4 in. tall and weighs 126 lbs. (1) Engaging only in the light activities associated with ordinary day-to-day life. (2) Includes physical activity equivalent to walking 1.5-3 mi per day at 3-4 mph. (3) Includes physical activity equivalent to walking more than 3 mi per day at 3-4 mph. (4) Excludes women who are pregnant or breastfeeding.

Understanding Food Components

The National Academies of Sciences, Engineering, and Medicine developed the Dietary Reference Intakes (DRIs), daily consumption values for vitamins and elements (often called minerals) for optimal health. DRIs include the Recommended Dietary Allowance (RDA), which meets the nutrient requirements of 97%-98% of healthy individuals in a group.

Water dissolves and transports other nutrients throughout the body, aiding in the processes of digestion, absorption, circulation, and excretion. It helps regulate body temperature.

Macronutrients

Carbohydrates, of which starches and sugars are the major types, are the most important source of energy for the body. The digestive system changes carbohydrates into glucose, which the body uses for energy for cells, tissues, and organs. The body stores extra sugar in the liver and muscles. Best sources: grains, legumes, vegetables, fruits.

Fats provide energy by furnishing calories to the body. They also help the body absorb vitamins A, D, E, and K. Best sources of polyunsaturated and monounsaturated fats: vegetable/plant oils, nuts. Concentrated sources of saturated fats: meats, cheeses, butter, cream, egg yolks, lard.

Fiber is the portion of plant foods that our bodies cannot digest. There are two basic types: insoluble and soluble. Insoluble fibers help move food materials through the digestive tract; soluble fibers tend to slow them down. Both types absorb water, thus preventing constipation. Soluble fibers may also be helpful in reducing blood cholesterol levels. Best sources: beans, bran, fruits, whole grains, vegetables.

Proteins, composed of amino acids, are essential to good nutrition. They build, maintain, and repair the body. Proteins from animal sources (eggs, meat, fish, milk) supply adequate amounts of all indispensable amino acids and are thus called complete. Proteins from plants, legumes, nuts, seeds, and vegetables are considered incomplete but can be combined to meet protein needs.

Vitamins

Vitamin A promotes good eyesight; helps keep skin and mucous membranes resistant to infection. Best sources: liver, sweet potatoes, carrots, kale, cantaloupe, fortified milk.

Vitamin B$_1$ (thiamine) is essential to carbohydrate metabolism and nervous system health. Best sources: enriched bread and flour, whole grains, nuts, seeds, pork.

Vitamin B$_2$ (riboflavin) protects the skin, mouth, eyes, and mucous membranes. Essential to growth, red blood cell production, and energy metabolism. Best sources: dairy products, organ meats, bread products.

Vitamin B$_6$ (pyridoxine) is important in the regulation of the central nervous system and in protein metabolism. Best sources: whole grains, meat, fish, nuts, avocado, bananas.

Vitamin B$_{12}$ (cobalamin) is needed to form red blood cells. Best sources: meat, shellfish, poultry.

Folate (folic acid, or vitamin B$_9$) is required for new cell formation, growth, and reproduction and for important chemical reactions in body cells. Best sources: dark leafy vegetables, enriched and whole-grain breads, fortified cereals.

Niacin (vitamin B$_3$) maintains health of skin, nerves, and the digestive system. Best sources: poultry, nuts, fish, eggs.

Other B vitamins include biotin and pantothenic acid.

Vitamin C (ascorbic acid) maintains collagen, a protein necessary for the formation of skin, ligaments, and bones. Helps heal wounds and mend fractures. Best sources: citrus fruits, broccoli, Brussels sprouts, potatoes, tomatoes, cabbage.

Vitamin D is important for bone development. Best sources: sunlight, fortified dairy products, tuna, salmon, oysters.

Vitamin E (tocopherol) helps protect red blood cells. Best sources: vegetable oils, wheat germ, whole grains, eggs, peanuts, green leafy vegetables.

Vitamin K is necessary for formation of prothrombin, which helps blood to clot. Also made by intestinal bacteria. Best dietary sources: green leafy vegetables, plant oils.

Minerals

Calcium works with phosphorus to build and maintain bones and teeth. Best sources: dairy, leafy green vegetables.

Iron is a component of myoglobin, a reservoir of oxygen for muscle tissue, and hemoglobin, which transports oxygen within blood. Best sources: lean meats, beans, green leafy vegetables, shellfish, whole grains.

Phosphorus performs more functions than any other mineral and plays a part in nearly every chemical reaction in the body. Best sources: cheese, milk, meats, poultry, fish, tofu.

Other minerals include chromium, copper, fluoride, iodine, magnesium, manganese, molybdenum, potassium, selenium, zinc.

Understanding Food Label Claims

Source: Center for Food Safety and Applied Nutrition, U.S. Food and Drug Admin. (FDA), U.S. Dept. of Health and Human Services; Food Safety and Inspection Service, Agricultural Marketing Service, U.S. Dept. of Agriculture (USDA)

Nutrition Packaging Terms

Manufacturers can make certain claims on processed food labels only if they meet the definitions specified here.

SUGAR. Sugar free: less than 0.5 g per serving; **No added sugars; Without added sugars:** no sugars or sugar-containing ingredients added during processing; must state if food is not "low calorie" or "reduced calorie"; **Unsweetened; No added sweeteners:** factual statements; **Reduced sugar:** at least 25% less sugar per serving than reference food.

FAT. Fat free: less than 0.5 g of total fat per serving; **Saturated fat free:** less than 0.5 g of saturated fat and less than 0.5 g of trans fatty acids per serving; **Low fat:** 3 g or less of total fat per serving (and per 50 g if the serving size is small, i.e., 30 g or less, 2 tbs or less); **Low saturated fat:** 1 g or less per serving and not more than 15% of calories from saturated fat; **Reduced fat; Less fat:** at least 25% less total fat per serving than reference food.

FIBER. High fiber: 20% or more of the daily value per serving; **Good source of fiber:** 10%-19% of the daily value per serving; **More fiber; Added fiber:** 10% or more of the daily value per serving than reference food.

SODIUM. Sodium free: less than 5 mg per serving; **Low sodium:** 140 mg or less per serving (and per 50 g if the serving size is small, i.e., 30 g or less, 2 tbs or less); **Very low sodium:** 35 mg or less per serving (and per 50 g if the serving size is small); **Reduced sodium; Less sodium:** at least 25% less per serving than reference food.

CALORIES. Calorie free: less than 5 calories per serving; **Low calorie:** 40 calories or less per serving (and per 50 g if the serving size is small, i.e., 30 g or less, 2 tbs or less); **Reduced calories; Fewer calories:** at least 25% fewer calories per serving than reference food.

CHOLESTEROL. Cholesterol claims are only permitted when food contains 2 g or less saturated fat per serving. **Cholesterol free:** less than 2 mg of cholesterol; **Low cholesterol:** 20 mg or less of cholesterol (and per 50 g of food if the serving size is small, i.e., 30 g or less, 2 tbs or less); **Reduced cholesterol; Less cholesterol:** at least 25% less per serving than reference food.

Other Packaging Terms

The FDA allows food producers and marketers to use language on their packaging that advertises the health benefits and production methods of their products. Products marked "certified" have been formally evaluated for class, grade, or other quality characteristics by a USDA National Organic Program-authorized certifying agent. Below are some common packaging terms and their meanings.

Organic: Produced using environmentally friendly approved methods. Before a product can be labeled organic, a farm or business must pass a site inspection by a USDA-accredited certifying agent. Organic foods must be produced without irradiation, sewage sludge, synthetic fertilizers, prohibited pesticides, and genetic engineering.

Foods that contain all organic ingredients may advertise "100 percent certified organic" on the "principal display panel" (generally the front of the packaging) along with the USDA organic seal. Foods with at least 95% organic ingredients may be called "organic" and may place the official seal on their packaging. Products with at least 70% organic ingredients may display "made with organic—" but may not use the organic seal. Products with less than 70% organic ingredients may not make any organic claims on the principal display panel but may list organic ingredients on the information panel.

Natural: The FDA has not established a definition for the term "natural" or its derivatives. It has not objected to use of the term for food that does not contain added color, artificial flavors, or synthetic substances.

Free range or **free roaming:** Producers must demonstrate that poultry has been allowed access to the outside.

Fresh poultry: Whole poultry and cuts that have never been below 26°F.

Frozen poultry: Temperature of raw, frozen poultry is 0°F or below.

Gluten free: Products with a gluten limit of 20 parts per million.

Halal and **Zabiah Halal:** Produced in federally inspected meat packing plants and handled in accordance with Islamic law and under Islamic authority.

Kosher: Meat and poultry products prepared under rabbinical supervision.

No hormones: Hormones are not allowed in the raising of hogs or poultry, so those products may not make this claim. If sufficient documentation is provided to the USDA, this term may appear on packages of beef.

No antibiotics: Claim may be made on a package (red meat and poultry) if sufficient documentation is provided to the USDA showing that the animals were raised without antibiotics.

Dietary Guidelines for Americans, 2015-20: Key Recommendations

Source: *2015-2020 Dietary Guidelines for Americans,* U.S. Dept. of Agriculture and U.S. Dept. of Health and Human Services

The federal government revises its dietary guidelines every five years. The most recent edition aims to help Americans establish a healthy eating pattern that meets nutrient needs over time at an appropriate calorie level. All foods and beverages consumed should be accounted for.

Healthy eating patterns include a variety from the following food groups:

- **Vegetables** from the five subgroups: dark green, red and orange, legumes (beans and peas), starchy, and other.
- **Fruits**, especially whole fruits.
- **Grains**, at least half of which should be whole grains. Choose refined grains that are enriched.
- Fat-free or low-fat **dairy**, including milk, yogurt, and cheese. Those who cannot or choose not to consume dairy should eat foods, such as fortified soy beverages, that provide the same nutrients.
- A variety of **protein foods**, including seafood, lean meats and poultry, eggs, nuts, seeds, and soy products. Legumes (beans and peas) can be considered vegetables or proteins but should be counted in one group only.
- **Oils**, such as corn oil and olive oil, are fats that are usually liquid at room temperature because of their higher percentage of unsaturated fatty acids. Oils should replace solid fats where possible.
- Potassium, dietary fiber, calcium, and vitamin D are among the nutrients underconsumed in American diets, which affects public health. The underconsumption of iron by young children and women who could become or are pregnant is also of concern.

Dietary components to limit:

- Less than 2,300 mg per day of **sodium**. Adults with prehypertension and hypertension may benefit from consuming less than 1,500 mg of sodium per day.
- Less than 10% of daily calories from **saturated fats**; replace with monounsaturated and polyunsaturated fats.
- Less than 10% of daily calories from **added sugars**.
- As little as possible of **trans fats** and **dietary cholesterol**.
- **Alcohol** in moderation, if at all—up to one drink per day for women and two drinks per day for men.

Top 10 Calorie Sources in American Diets

Source: National Health and Nutrition Examination Survey, 2005-06, National Center for Health Statistics, CDC, U.S. Dept. of Health and Human Services

Rank	All Americans (ages 2+)	Rank	Children and adolescents (ages 2-18)	Rank	All adults (ages 19+)
1.	Grain-based desserts	1.	Grain-based desserts	1.	Grain-based desserts
2.	Yeast breads	2.	Pizza	2.	Yeast breads
3.	Chicken dishes	3.	Soda/energy/sports drinks	3.	Chicken dishes
4.	Soda/energy/sports drinks	4.	Yeast breads	4.	Soda/energy/sports drinks
5.	Pizza	5.	Chicken dishes	5.	Alcoholic beverages
6.	Alcoholic beverages	6.	Pasta dishes	6.	Pizza
7.	Pasta dishes	7.	Reduced-fat milk	7.	Tortillas, burritos, tacos
8.	Tortillas, burritos, tacos	8.	Dairy desserts	8.	Pasta dishes
9.	Beef dishes	9.	Potato/corn/other chips	9.	Beef dishes
10.	Dairy desserts	10.	Ready-to-eat cereals	10.	Dairy desserts

Note: Data are drawn from analyses of usual dietary intakes conducted by the Natl. Cancer Institute. Foods and beverages consumed were divided into 97 categories and ranked according to calorie contribution to the diet. Average total daily calorie intake was 2,157 overall, 2,027 for children and adolescents (ages 2-18), and 2,199 for adults (ages 19+).

Weight Guidelines for Adults

Source: National Center for Health Statistics, CDC, U.S. Dept. of Health and Human Services

Clinical guidelines on the identification, evaluation, and treatment of overweight and obesity in adults were released in 1998 by the National Heart, Lung, and Blood Institute (NHLBI) in cooperation with the National Institute of Diabetes and Digestive and Kidney Diseases (NIDDK). The guidelines define overweight and obese in terms of **body mass index (BMI)**. BMI, based on a person's weight and height, can be an indicator of total body fat. A BMI of 25.0-29.9 is said to indicate **overweight**; a BMI of 30.0 or higher indicates **obesity**. BMI can be calculated at www.nhlbi.nih.gov/health/educational/lose_wt/BMI/bmicalc.htm.

Waist circumference should be evaluated along with BMI. Men with a waist circumference of more than 40 inches and non-pregnant women with a waist circumference of more than 35 inches may be at higher risk for disease because of excess abdominal fat. BMI and waist circumference are screening tools, not diagnostics. A health-care provider should also perform other assessments to evaluate risk and diagnose disease, taking into consideration such factors as high blood pressure, cholesterol levels, and family medical history.

The National Center for Health Statistics notes that in 2015-16, 39.8% of American adults (ages 20 and over) and 18.5% of youth (ages 2-19) were obese. The prevalence of obesity has increased over time, from 30.5% of adults and 13.9% of youth in 1999-2000 to its current levels. Among all age groups, obesity was more prevalent in the non-Hispanic black and Hispanic population than among non-Hispanic whites and non-Hispanic Asians.

A high prevalence of overweight and obesity is a public health concern because higher body weights increase a person's risk of developing type 2 diabetes, hypertension, dyslipidemia, cardiovascular disease, stroke, gallbladder disease, sleep and respiratory problems, osteoarthritis, and certain cancers.

Adults Meeting U.S. Fitness Guidelines, 1998-2016

Source: National Health Interview Survey, National Center for Health Statistics, CDC, U.S. Dept. of Health and Human Services

Characteristic	% meeting aerobic activity guidelines					% meeting muscle-strengthening guidelines				
	1998	2000	2005	2010	2016	1998	2000	2005	2010	2016
Sex and age										
Male, 18-44 years........	51.5%	53.6%	50.0%	59.0%	63.2%	27.2%	26.3%	28.7%	35.6%	37.2%
Male, 45-54 years........	44.3	45.2	42.6	50.7	53.6	18.8	18.0	19.2	24.8	26.4
Male, 55-64 years........	38.3	38.9	38.4	46.0	49.8	12.9	13.8	15.7	22.9	22.9
Male, 65-74 years........	38.5	41.8	38.3	40.7	49.0	12.0	12.2	14.5	20.6	23.2
Male, 75 years and over..	26.1	30.7	28.6	32.3	35.3	9.5	10.1	12.4	14.5	15.8
Female, 18-44 years.....	40.0	42.0	43.1	48.5	55.2	17.9	17.9	19.8	22.1	24.8
Female, 45-54 years.....	36.1	39.1	38.1	44.7	48.9	13.7	16.1	19.8	20.4	22.3
Female, 55-64 years.....	32.5	33.5	34.1	38.6	46.9	10.3	12.4	15.9	17.5	19.5
Female, 65-74 years.....	26.2	32.6	30.2	31.8	41.0	7.8	10.5	13.3	15.6	17.5
Female, 75 years and over	14.0	16.8	18.8	18.3	25.3	5.7	6.7	6.7	10.8	11.9
Race or Hispanic origin[1]										
White, not Hispanic......	43.1	45.7	45.7	51.5	56.7	18.7	19.3	22.5	26.3	28.6
Black, not Hispanic......	30.4	31.7	29.1	37.3	44.4	15.6	16.0	15.7	21.6	24.8
Amer. Indian or AK Native..	39.7	29.7	41.6	42.0	41.8	18.2	13.9	20.5	16.7	18.2
Asian..................	37.1	41.7	37.5	44.2	52.1	17.2	17.2	16.9	21.9	20.7
Two or more races	—	43.9	41.1	50.2	55.3	—	22.2	23.6	30.4	31.1
Hispanic or Latino.......	29.1	30.8	28.5	36.2	44.5	12.7	11.9	12.9	18.1	20.1
Geographic region										
Northeast	39.6	45.3	43.3	46.9	52.3	17.5	20.0	21.6	24.3	27.6
Midwest	42.0	43.5	43.5	46.1	53.9	18.2	19.3	21.9	24.7	27.4
South	35.3	37.3	36.5	45.0	48.8	15.0	15.1	17.6	22.0	23.5
West	46.7	46.9	44.4	52.0	57.8	22.3	19.7	21.3	27.5	28.0
Total, 18 years and over	**40.0**	**42.2**	**41.1**	**47.3**	**52.7**	**17.7**	**18.0**	**20.2**	**24.4**	**26.2**

— = Not available. **Note:** Measures of physical activity reflect the federal 2008 Physical Activity Guidelines for Americans, which recommend that for substantial health benefits, adults each week perform at least 150 min. of moderate-intensity, 75 min. of vigorous-intensity, or an equivalent combination of moderate- and vigorous-intensity aerobic activity. Aerobic activity should be performed in episodes of at least 10 min., preferably spread throughout the week. The guidelines also recommend that adults perform muscle-strengthening activities that are moderate or high intensity and involve all major muscle groups on two or more days a week. (1) Persons reporting only one race, unless otherwise noted. Persons of Hispanic origin may be of any race.

Obesity Among Adults in the U.S., 2017

Source: National Health Interview Survey, National Center for Health Statistics, CDC, U.S. Dept. of Health and Human Services

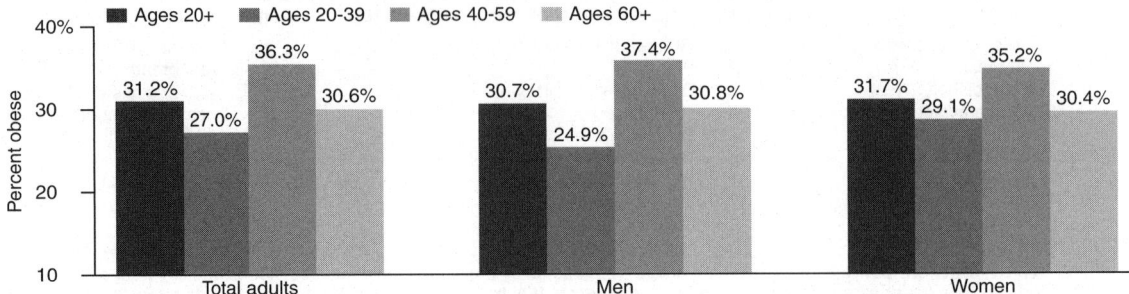

Overweight and Obesity Among U.S. Adults, 1960-2016

Source: National Health and Nutrition Examination Survey, NCHS, CDC, U.S. Dept. of Health and Human Services
(as percent of adults age 20-74 in 1960-80 and age 20 and over for all other years shown here)

Survey period	Total			Men			Women		
	Overweight	Obesity	Severe obesity	Overweight	Obesity	Severe obesity	Overweight	Obesity	Severe obesity
1960-62	31.5%	13.4%	0.9%	38.7%	10.7%	0.3%	24.7%	15.8%	1.4%
1971-74	32.7	14.5	1.3	41.7	12.1	0.6	24.3	16.6	2.0
1976-80	32.1	15.0	1.4	39.9	12.7	0.4	24.9	17.0	2.2
1988-94	33.1	22.9	2.8	40.7	20.2	1.7	25.9	25.4	3.9
1999-2000	34.0	30.5	4.7	39.7	27.5	3.1	28.6	33.4	6.2
2001-02	35.1	30.5	5.1	42.2	27.7	3.6	28.2	33.2	6.5
2003-04	34.1	32.2	4.8	39.7	31.1	2.8	28.6	33.2	6.9
2005-06	32.6	34.3	5.9	39.9	33.3	4.2	25.5	35.3	7.4
2007-08	34.3	33.7	5.7	40.1	32.2	4.2	28.6	35.4	7.3
2009-10	33.0	35.7	6.3	38.4	35.5	4.4	27.9	35.8	8.1
2011-12	33.6	34.9	6.4	37.8	33.5	4.4	29.7	36.1	8.3
2013-14	32.5	37.7	7.7	38.7	35.0	5.5	26.5	40.4	9.9
2015-16	31.6	39.6	7.7	36.5	37.9	5.6	26.9	41.1	9.7

Note: Overweight is body mass index (BMI) of 25 or greater but less than 30; obesity is BMI greater than or equal to 30; extreme obesity is BMI greater than or equal to 40. Does not include pregnant women.

Obesity Among Children and Adolescents in the U.S., 1988-2016

Source: National Health and Nutrition Examination Survey, NCHS, CDC, U.S. Dept. of Health and Human Services
(percent of population)

Age/sex/poverty level	1988-94	1999-2002	2003-06	2005-08	2007-10	2009-12	2011-14	2013-16
2-5 years								
Both sexes	7.2%	10.3%	12.5%	10.5%	11.1%	10.2%	8.9%	11.6%
Boys	6.2	10.0	12.8	9.8	11.9	12.0	9.2	11.5
Girls	8.2	10.6	12.2	11.2	10.2	8.4	8.6	11.7
Percent of poverty level[1]								
Below 100%	9.7	10.9	14.3	12.3	13.2	12.3	11.6	13.5
100%-199%	7.3	13.8*	12.7	10.0	11.8	11.6	10.2	12.6
200%-399%	5.6	7.6*	11.9	11.6	13.9	11.0	7.7*	10.4
400% or more	—	—	10.0*	—	5.8*	5.0*	—	8.2
6-11 years								
Both sexes	11.3	15.9	17.0	17.4	18.8	17.9	17.5	17.9
Boys	11.6	16.9	18.0	18.7	20.7	18.3	17.6	19.6
Girls.	11.0	14.7	15.8	16.0	16.9	17.4	17.5	16.1
Percent of poverty level[1]								
Below 100%	11.4	19.1	22.0	21.5	22.2	24.6	21.5	20.8
100%-199%	11.1	16.4	19.2	22.2	20.7	18.5	20.4	20.8
200%-399%	11.7	15.3	16.7	16.8	18.9	15.8	15.7	17.1
400% or more	—	12.9*	9.2*	9.5*	12.5*	12.2*	12.2*	12.2
12-19 years								
Both sexes	10.5	16.0	17.6	17.9	18.2	19.4	20.5	20.6
Boys	11.3	16.7	18.2	18.7	19.4	20.0	20.1	20.0
Girls	9.7	15.3	16.8	17.0	16.9	18.9	21.0	21.2
Percent of poverty level[1]								
Below 100%	15.8	19.8	19.3	23.1	24.3	23.2	22.4	25.7
100%-199%	11.2	15.1	18.4	19.8	20.1	22.5	25.7	24.3
200%-399%	9.4	15.7	19.3	17.2	16.3	17.9	19.7	19.3
400% or more	—	13.9	12.6	14.0	14.0	13.8	13.7*	13.7

* = Estimate is considered unreliable. — = Estimate not given as it is considered unreliable. **Note:** Obesity is defined as body mass index (BMI) at or above the sex- and age-specific 95th percentile of the 2000 CDC growth charts. (1) Ratio of family's household income to contemporary federal poverty guidelines.

Basic First Aid

Source: Courtesy of the American National Red Cross, www.redcross.org. All rights reserved in all countries.

Note: This information is not intended to be a substitute for formal training. It is recommended that you contact your local American Red Cross chapter to sign up for a First Aid/CPR/AED (automated external defibrillator) course.

In an emergency, it is important to get medical assistance as soon as possible, but knowing what to do until a doctor or other trained person gets to the scene can save a life, especially in cases of severe bleeding, choking, poisoning, and shock. The "Stop the Bleed" initiative provides free training in bleeding control techniques to the general public. **Website:** www.bleedingcontrol.org

People with special medical problems, such as diabetes, cardiovascular disease, epilepsy, or allergies, are urged to wear some sort of emblem identifying the problem as a safeguard against receiving medication that might be harmful or even fatal. Emblems can be purchased from MedicAlert Foundation, 5226 Pirrone Ct., Salida, CA 95368; (800) 432-5378; www.medicalert.org.

Allergic reaction and anaphylaxis: If you know the person has a severe allergy or is having difficulty breathing, call 911 or the local emergency number. Have the person use any medication he or she might carry to use in an emergency, such as epinephrine.

Animal bite: Call 911 or the local emergency number if the wound is bleeding seriously or if the animal was wild or a stray or you suspect it of having rabies. Control any bleeding. Wash minor wounds with soap under running water and apply antibiotic ointment and a dressing. When possible, proper authorities should test the animal for rabies.

Bleeding: Use a barrier between your hand and the wound to help prevent infection. Cover wound with a sterile dressing. Apply direct pressure until bleeding stops. Cover compress with a bandage. Call 911 or the local emergency number if bleeding is severe.

Burn: Check for life-threatening conditions. If the burn is mild, with skin unbroken and no blisters, flush with cold running water for at least 10 minutes (at least 15 minutes if the burn was caused by a chemical). Gently wash with soap and water and pat dry. Apply a thin layer of antibiotic ointment and then a loose, sterile dry dressing to prevent infection. If the burn is severe, call 911 or the local emergency number. Care for shock (see separate entry). Keep the person from getting chilled or overheated until advanced medical assistance arrives. Do not try to clean a severe burn or break blisters.

Chemical in eye: Call 911 or the local emergency number. Turn the person's head to the side so that the affected eye is lower than the unaffected eye. Flush the affected eye with large amounts of water for at least 20 minutes.

Choking: See **First Aid for Choking** below.

Convulsions (seizures): Remove nearby objects that might cause injury. Protect the person's head by placing a thin folded towel or item of clothing under it. Roll him or her on one side to drain fluids from the mouth. Do not place anything between the person's teeth. Stay with the person until he or she is fully conscious. If convulsions do not stop, get medical attention immediately.

Cut (minor): Use a clean barrier between your hand and the wound to prevent infection. Apply direct pressure for a few minutes to control any bleeding. Wash the wound thoroughly with soap and water and apply a thin layer of antibiotic ointment or a microthin film dressing. Cover the wound with a sterile dressing and a bandage.

Diabetic emergency: A person experiencing a diabetic emergency might have a headache or even appear intoxicated, slurring his or her speech and moving with difficulty. Offer the person some form of sugar only if he or she is conscious and able to swallow. Call 911 if the person is unresponsive.

Foreign object in eye: If an object is embedded in someone's eye, do not remove it. If the object is not embedded, have the person blink several times. If the object doesn't come out, gently flush the eye with saline solution or water. Do not rub the eye. Seek medical attention if the foreign object remains.

Frostbite: Handle the frostbitten area gently. Do not rub. If there is no danger of the affected area refreezing, soak it in warm water (not warmer than 105°F). Do not allow the frostbitten area to touch the side of the water container. Keep the frostbitten part in the water until normal color returns and it feels warm. Loosely bandage the area with dry, sterile dressings. If fingers or toes are frostbitten, put cotton or gauze between them. Do not break any blisters. Call 911 or seek emergency help as soon as possible.

Heart attack and stroke: See **Heart and Blood Vessel Disease** earlier in chapter.

Heat stroke: Remove the person from the heat. Loosen any tight clothing. Immerse person in cold water until he or she becomes alert. If a large enough source of water is not available, drench the person with cold water and fan constantly. If the person is conscious, have him or her slowly drink some cool water. Call 911 if the person's condition does not improve.

Hypothermia: Call 911 or the local emergency number. For mild hypothermia, cover all exposed skin. Replace wet clothes with something dry. If the person is alert, give him or her simple carbohydrates to eat and warm, nonalcoholic and decaffeinated liquids to drink. Apply heat pads or other heat sources if available but do not place against bare skin.

Loss of limb: Call 911 or the local emergency number and care for any life-threatening conditions. If a limb is severed, it is important to properly protect the limb so that it can possibly be reattached. After the victim is cared for, the limb should be wrapped in sterile gauze and placed in a plastic bag. Place bag in a larger bag or container of an ice and water slurry, not ice alone. Be sure the limb is taken to the hospital with the person.

Poisoning: Care for any life-threatening conditions. Call the National Capital Poison Center (800-222-1222), 911, or the local emergency number. Do not give the person any food or drink or induce vomiting unless specified to do so by medical professionals. In cases of **alcohol poisoning**, place the person in a position that keeps his or her airway clear. In cases of **carbon monoxide poisoning**, remove the person from the area if you can do so safely.

Shock (injury-related): Monitor breathing and consciousness. Have the person lie down and keep him or her as comfortable as possible. Do not give the person anything to eat or drink as it increases the risk of vomiting or aspiration. If the weather is cold or damp, place blankets or extra clothing over and under the person; if the weather is hot, provide shade.

Snakebite: Call 911 or the local emergency number immediately if you're not sure whether or not the snake was venomous. Do not wait for symptoms to appear. Gently wash the injury with soap and water and keep the area below the level of the heart. Have the person remain still if possible. Do not cut, suck at, or apply a tourniquet or ice to a snakebite. Applying an elastic roller bandage may help slow the spread of venom.

Sprains and strains: Splint any injured bone or joint that the person cannot use.

Sting from bee or wasp: If possible, remove the stinger by scraping it away with your finger or a plastic card (like a credit card) or using tweezers. If you use tweezers, grasp the stinger, not the venom sac. Wash the area with soap and water and cover it with a bandage. Apply cold to the area to reduce swelling and pain. Call 911 or the local emergency number immediately if the wound does not stop swelling, the person collapses, or he or she is known to be allergic to the sting.

Tick bite: Promptly remove any ticks to lower the chance of infection. Use tweezers to grasp it at its head as close to the skin as possible. Pull it slowly and steadily out. Do not use a match or petroleum jelly to remove an embedded tick. Wash and dress the bite area.

Unconsciousness: Call 911 or the local emergency number immediately. Do not move the person if a spinal injury is suspected.

First Aid for Choking

The recommended first aid for a conscious choking victim who is unable to speak, cough, or breathe is to deliver a series of five blows to the back followed by five thrusts to the abdomen. Have another person call 911 or the local emergency number. Obtain consent from the victim to treat him or her. Apply the back blows by leaning the victim forward and striking his or her back between the shoulder blades with the heel of your hand. If the victim is still choking, stand or kneel behind the victim and wrap your arms around his or her waist. Make a fist with one hand and place the thumb side against the middle of the person's abdomen, just above the navel and well below the lower tip of the breastbone. Grasp your fist in your other hand and quickly thrust upwards into the abdomen. Continue back blows and abdominal thrusts until the object is dislodged, and the person can breathe or cough forcefully, or the person loses consciousness.

VITAL STATISTICS
Births and Deaths in the U.S., 1960-2017
Source: National Center for Health Statistics (NCHS), CDC, U.S. Dept. of Health and Human Services

Year	BIRTHS Total number	Rate	DEATHS Total number	Rate	Year	BIRTHS Total number	Rate	DEATHS Total number	Rate
1960	4,257,850	23.7	1,711,982	9.5	2007	4,316,233	14.3	2,423,712	8.0
1970	3,731,386	18.4	1,921,031	9.5	2008	4,247,694	14.0	2,471,984	8.1
1980	3,612,258	15.9	1,989,841	8.8	2009	4,130,665	13.5	2,437,163	7.9
1990	4,092,994	16.7	2,148,463	8.6	2010	3,999,386	13.0	2,468,435	8.0
1995	3,899,589	14.6	2,312,132	8.7	2011	3,953,590	12.7	2,515,458	8.1
2000	4,058,814	14.4	2,403,351	8.5	2012	3,952,841	12.6	2,543,279	8.1
2001	4,025,933	14.1	2,416,425	8.5	2013	3,932,181	12.4	2,596,993	8.2
2002	4,021,726	13.9	2,443,387	8.5	2014	3,988,076	12.5	2,626,418	8.2
2003	4,089,950	14.1	2,448,288	8.4	2015	3,978,497	12.4	2,712,630	8.4
2004	4,112,052	14.0	2,397,615	8.2	2016	3,945,875	12.2	2,744,248	8.5
2005	4,138,349	14.0	2,448,017	8.3	2017[1]	3,853,472	11.8[2]	2,806,000	8.7
2006	4,265,555	14.2	2,426,264	8.1					

Note: Rates are per 1,000 population; population counts are enumerated as of Apr. 1 for decennial census years and estimated as of July 1 for all other years. Beginning in 1970, statistics exclude births and deaths among nonresidents of the U.S. (1) Provisional. (2) Not directly comparable to previous years due to difference in calculation.

Marriage and Divorce Rates in the U.S., 1920-2016
Source: National Center for Health Statistics (NCHS), CDC, U.S. Dept. of Health and Human Services
(Per 1,000 total population. Rates for 2000-16 may exclude data and populations from nonreporting states. Some data are provisional.)

The U.S. marriage rate dipped during the Depression and peaked sharply just after World War II; the trend after that has been more gradual. The divorce rate generally rose from the 1920s through 1981, when it peaked at 5.3 per 1,000 population, before declining somewhat. The graph below shows marriage and divorce rates since 1920.

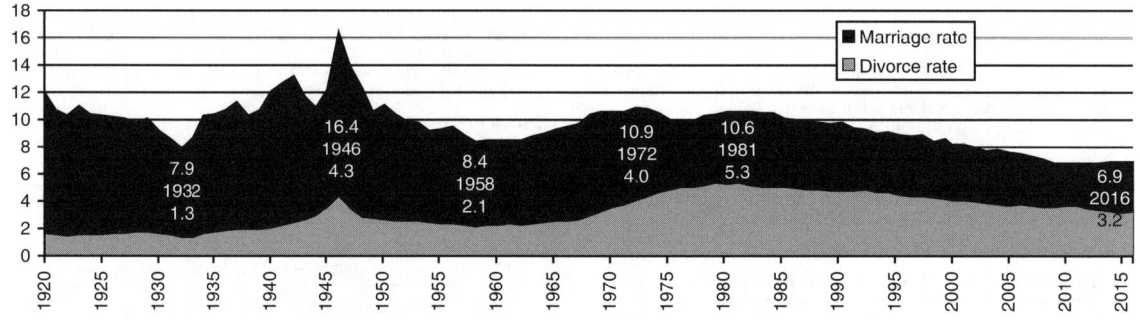

U.S. Median Age at First Marriage, 1890-2017
Source: U.S. Census Bureau, U.S. Dept. of Commerce

Year[1]	Men	Women	Year[1]	Men	Women	Year[1]	Men	Women	Year[1]	Men	Women
1890	26.1	22.0	1950	22.8	20.3	1990	26.1	23.9	2012	28.6	26.6
1900	25.9	21.9	1960	22.8	20.3	1995	26.9	24.5	2013	29.0	26.6
1910	25.1	21.6	1970	23.2	20.8	2000	26.8	25.1	2014	29.3	27.0
1920	24.6	21.2	1975	23.5	21.1	2005	27.1	25.3	2015	29.2	27.1
1930	24.3	21.3	1980	24.7	22.0	2010	28.2	26.1	2016	29.5	27.4
1940	24.3	21.5	1985	25.5	23.3	2011	28.4	26.4	2017	29.5	27.4

(1) Figures for 1947 and on are based on Current Population Survey data; earlier figures based on decennial censuses.

Divorce Rates by State, 2016
Source: National Center for Health Statistics (NCHS), CDC, U.S. Dept. of Health and Human Services
(per 1,000 population, estimated as of July 1)

State	Divorce rate	State	Divorce rate	State	Divorce rate
Alabama	3.8	Louisiana	2.0	Ohio	3.0
Alaska	3.9	Maine	3.4	Oklahoma	4.4
Arizona	3.4	Maryland	2.7	Oregon	3.4
Arkansas	3.9	Massachusetts	2.3	Pennsylvania	2.6
California	NA	Michigan	2.9	Rhode Island	2.8
Colorado	3.6	Minnesota	NA	South Carolina	2.5
Connecticut	3.2	Mississippi	3.2	South Dakota	2.8
Delaware	3.1	Missouri	3.3	Tennessee	3.8
District of Columbia	2.7	Montana	3.1	Texas	4.2
Florida	3.9	Nebraska	3.1	Utah	3.6
Georgia	NA	Nevada	4.3	Vermont	3.1
Hawaii	NA	New Hampshire	3.4	Virginia	3.4
Idaho	4.0	New Jersey	2.7	Washington	3.5
Illinois	2.0	New Mexico	NA	West Virginia	3.8
Indiana	NA	New York	2.7	Wisconsin	2.6
Iowa	1.3	North Carolina	3.2	Wyoming	4.2
Kansas	2.7	North Dakota	2.6	**United States**	**3.2**
Kentucky	3.8				

NA = Not available. **Note:** Rates based on provisional counts of divorce including annulments and, for certain areas, divorce petitions filed or legal separations.

Birth Rates and Fertility Rates by Age of Mother, 1950-2017

Source: National Center for Health Statistics (NCHS), CDC, U.S. Dept. of Health and Human Services

Live births per 1,000 women by age of mother

Year	Birth rate[1]	Fertility rate[2]	10-14 years	15-19 years	15-17 years	18-19 years	20-24 years	25-29 years	30-34 years	35-39 years	40-44 years	45-49 years[3]
1950	24.1	106.2	1.0	81.6	40.7	132.7	196.6	166.1	103.7	52.9	15.1	1.2
1960	23.7	118.0	0.8	89.1	43.9	166.7	258.1	197.4	112.7	56.2	15.5	0.9
1970	18.4	87.9	1.2	68.3	38.8	114.7	167.8	145.1	73.3	31.7	8.1	0.5
1980	15.9	68.4	1.1	53.0	32.5	82.1	115.1	112.9	61.9	19.8	3.9	0.2
1990	16.7	70.9	1.4	59.9	37.5	88.6	116.5	120.2	80.8	31.7	5.5	0.2
1995	14.6	64.6	1.3	56.0	35.5	87.7	107.5	108.8	81.1	34.0	6.6	0.3
2000	14.4	65.9	0.9	47.7	26.9	78.1	109.7	113.5	91.2	39.7	8.0	0.5
2005	14.0	66.7	0.7	40.5	21.4	69.9	102.2	115.5	95.8	46.3	9.1	0.6
2006	14.2	68.5	0.6	41.9	22.0	73.0	105.9	116.7	97.7	47.3	9.4	0.6
2007	14.3	69.5	0.6	42.5	22.1	73.9	106.3	117.5	99.9	47.5	9.5	0.6
2008	14.0	68.6	0.6	41.5	21.7	70.6	103.0	115.1	99.3	46.9	9.8	0.7
2009	13.5	66.2	0.5	37.9	19.6	64.0	96.2	111.5	97.5	46.1	10.0	0.7
2010	13.0	64.1	0.4	34.2	17.3	58.2	90.0	108.3	96.5	45.9	10.2	0.7
2011	12.7	63.2	0.4	31.3	15.4	54.1	85.3	107.2	96.5	47.2	10.3	0.7
2012	12.6	63.0	0.4	29.4	14.1	51.4	83.1	106.5	97.3	48.3	10.4	0.7
2013	12.4	62.5	0.3	26.5	12.3	47.1	80.7	105.5	98.0	49.3	10.4	0.8
2014	12.5	62.9	0.3	24.2	10.9	43.8	79.0	105.8	100.8	51.0	10.6	0.8
2015	12.4	62.5	0.2	22.3	9.9	40.7	76.8	104.3	101.5	51.8	11.0	0.8
2016	12.2	62.0	0.2	20.3	8.8	37.5	73.8	102.1	102.7	52.7	11.4	0.9
2017[4]	11.8[5]	60.2	0.2	18.8	7.8	35.1	71.0	97.9	100.3	52.2	11.6	0.9

(1) Live births per 1,000 population. (2) Live births per 1,000 women 15-44 years of age. (3) Beginning in 1997, rate computed by relating the number of births to women age 45 and over to women 45-49 years of age. (4) Provisional. (5) Not directly comparable to previous years due to difference in calculation.

Cesarean Delivery Rates by State, 2000-17

Source: National Center for Health Statistics (NCHS), CDC, U.S. Dept. of Health and Human Services

State	2000	2010	2013	2017[1]	Percent change, 2000-17	State	2000	2010	2013	2017[1]	Percent change, 2000-17
Alabama	26.3%	35.3%	35.8%	35.1%	33.5%	Montana	19.0%	30.3%	29.7%	28.5%	50.0%
Alaska	17.0	21.5	24.0	22.5	32.4	Nebraska	22.5	31.1	30.3	30.4	35.1
Arizona	18.6	27.0	27.4	26.9	44.6	Nevada	21.7	34.8	34.9	34.2	57.6
Arkansas	26.3	34.8	34.4	33.5	27.4	New Hampshire	21.0	30.4	30.1	31.0	47.6
California	23.4	33.0	33.2	31.4	34.2	New Jersey	27.3	38.4	38.4	35.9	31.5
Colorado	18.3	25.9	26.0	26.5	44.8	New Mexico	17.1	22.8	24.3	24.7	44.4
Connecticut	21.6	35.1	34.8	34.8	61.1	New York	24.6	34.5	34.3	34.1	38.6
Delaware	24.8	33.9	31.5	31.8	28.2	North Carolina	23.0	30.8	30.4	29.4	27.8
District of Columbia	22.6	33.0	34.2	32.2	42.5	North Dakota	20.6	27.7	28.6	28.3	37.4
Florida	24.9	37.8	37.7	37.2	49.4	Ohio	20.0	30.7	31.1	30.3	51.5
Georgia	22.5	33.8	34.2	34.2	52.0	Oklahoma	21.0	34.7	33.8	32.2	53.3
Hawaii	14.6	27.2	25.2	25.9	77.4	Oregon	19.4	29.4	28.0	28.1	44.8
Idaho	18.3	24.8	24.9	23.7	29.5	Pennsylvania	21.7	31.3	31.3	30.5	40.6
Illinois	20.9	31.1	31.7	31.1	48.8	Rhode Island	21.9	33.0	31.3	31.5	43.8
Indiana	21.5	30.3	30.5	29.7	38.1	South Carolina	25.2	35.0	35.0	33.6	33.3
Iowa	20.8	30.3	30.8	29.7	42.8	South Dakota	22.8	26.6	25.5	24.5	7.5
Kansas	22.2	30.5	30.2	30.0	35.1	Tennessee	24.8	34.2	33.4	32.3	30.2
Kentucky	23.6	35.4	36.6	35.2	49.2	Texas	24.7	35.1	35.2	35.0	41.7
Louisiana	26.6	39.6	38.9	37.5	41.0	Utah	16.8	23.1	22.4	22.8	35.7
Maine	22.8	29.8	30.0	29.9	31.1	Vermont	17.3	27.5	27.3	25.7	48.6
Maryland	24.1	34.5	35.1	33.9	40.7	Virginia	23.1	34.3	33.7	32.6	41.1
Massachusetts	23.3	33.0	31.5	31.5	35.2	Washington	20.6	29.5	28.3	27.7	34.5
Michigan	21.9	32.6	32.6	32.1	46.6	West Virginia	25.4	36.0	35.9	35.2	38.6
Minnesota	19.4	27.1	26.9	27.4	41.2	Wisconsin	17.5	26.0	26.2	26.4	50.9
Mississippi	28.2	37.0	38.5	37.8	34.0	Wyoming	19.4	27.9	28.9	26.4	36.1
Missouri	22.3	31.9	31.1	30.1	35.0	**United States**	**22.8**	**32.7**	**32.7**	**32.0**	**40.4**

Note: The cesarean rate is the percentage of all live births by cesarean delivery. (1) Provisional.

Infertility and Use of Infertility Services by Age, 2002-15

Source: National Survey of Family Growth, National Center for Health Statistics (NCHS), U.S. Dept. of Health and Human Services

A special tabulation in 2011-15 found 7.3 mil women, or 12.0% of women ages 15-44, had ever received any type of infertility services, including advice (6.3%), medical help to prevent miscarriage (5.4%), tests on woman or man (5.2%), ovulation drugs (4.2%), and/or artificial insemination (1.4%).

Age	% of all married women who are infertile			% of all married, childless women who are infertile			% of childless women who have ever received any infertility service		
	2002	2006-10	2011-15	2002	2006-10	2011-15	2002	2006-10	2011-15
15-29 years	6.3%	5.0%	5.8%	11.0%	8.1%	8.7%	2.9%	3.2%	3.6%
30-34 years	8.1	4.6	6.3	16.9	9.1	11.0	17.3	15.3	13.4
35-39 years	5.7	7.8	6.5	22.6	24.7	23.0	15.2	20.1	21.5
40-44 years	9.4	6.2	8.0	27.4	29.7	26.2	29.1	24.0	23.7
Total 15-44 years	**7.4**	**6.0**	**6.7**	**16.6**	**14.0**	**14.2**	**7.1**	**6.5**	**6.9**

Note: Infertility here applies to women who are not surgically sterile and have had at least 12 consecutive months of unprotected sexual intercourse without becoming pregnant.

Numbers of Multiple Births in the U.S., 1990-2016

Source: National Center for Health Statistics (NCHS), CDC, U.S. Dept. of Health and Human Services

Year	Twins	Triplets	Quadruplets	Quintuplets[1]	Year	Twins	Triplets	Quadruplets	Quintuplets[1]
1990	93,865	2,830	185	13	2008	138,660	5,877	345	46
1995	96,736	4,551	365	57	2009	137,217	5,905	355	80
2000	118,916	6,742	506	77	2010	132,562	5,153	313	37
2002	125,134	6,898	434	69	2011	131,269	5,137	239	41
2003	128,665	7,110	468	85	2012	131,024	4,598	276	45
2004	132,219	6,750	439	86	2013	132,324	4,364	270	66
2005	133,122	6,208	418	68	2014	135,336	4,233	246	47
2006	137,085	6,118	355	67	2015	133,155	3,871	228	24
2007	138,961	5,967	369	91	2016	131,723	3,755	217	31

(1) Quintuplets and other multiple births of five or more.

Origin Countries for U.S. Foreign Adoptions, 2000-17

Source: Annual Report on Intercountry Adoption, Bureau of Consular Affairs, U.S. Dept. of State; Office of Immigration Statistics, U.S. Dept. of Homeland Security

(ranked by fiscal year 2017 adoptions)

Country	2017	2016	2015	2014	2013	2012	2011	2010	2009	2005	2000
China[1]	1,905	2,231	2,354	2,040	2,306	2,697	2,589	3,401	2,990	7,906	5,053
Ethiopia	313	183	335	716	993	1,568	1,727	2,513	2,221	441	95
South Korea	276	260	318	370	138	627	736	863	1,106	1,630	1,794
Haiti	227	178	143	464	388	154	33	133[2]	336	234	131
India	221	194	138	136	119	159	228	243	297	323	503
Ukraine	215	303	303	521	438	395	632	445	605	821	659
Colombia	181	131	153	172	159	195	216	235	238	291	246
Nigeria	176	121	154	130	183	197	148	189	110	65	4
Bulgaria	147	201	185	183	159	125	75	40	15	30	214
Philippines	111	156	150	172	178	125	230	214	292	271	173
Total[3]	4,714	5,372	5,648	6,441	7,094	8,668	9,320	11,059[2]	12,782	22,710	18,120

(1) Not incl. adoptions from Hong Kong. (2) Does not reflect approx. 1,090 Haitian children admitted as part of the Special Humanitarian Parole following the 2010 earthquake in Haiti. (3) Includes countries not shown.

Leading Causes of Infant Death in the U.S., 2016

Source: National Vital Statistics System, National Center for Health Statistics (NCHS), CDC, U.S. Dept. of Health and Human Services

Cause of death	Number	Percent of total deaths	Mortality rate[1]
Congenital malformations, deformations, and chromosomal abnormalities (congenital malformations)	4,816	20.8%	122.1
Disorders related to short gestation and low birth weight, not elsewhere classified	3,927	17.0	99.5
Sudden infant death syndrome	1,500	6.5	38.0
Newborn affected by maternal complications of pregnancy	1,402	6.1	35.5
Accidents (unintentional injuries)	1,219	5.3	30.9
Newborn affected by complications of placenta, cord, and membranes	841	3.6	21.3
Bacterial sepsis[2] of newborn	583	2.5	14.8
Respiratory distress of newborn	488	2.1	12.4
Diseases of the circulatory system	460	2.0	11.7
Neonatal hemorrhage	398	1.7	10.1
All other causes	7,527	32.5	—
All causes	**23,161**	**100.0**	**587.0**

— = Not available. (1) Deaths of infants under 1 year of age per 100,000 live births. (2) Toxic condition resulting from the spread of bacteria.

Nonmarital Childbearing in the U.S., 1970-2016

Source: National Center for Health Statistics (NCHS), CDC, U.S. Dept. of Health and Human Services

	1970	1975	1980	1985	1990	1995	2000	2005	2010	2014	2015	2016
Live births to unmarried mothers (thous.)	399	448	666	828	1,165	1,254	1,347	1,527	1,633	1,605	1,602	1,570
Race/Hispanic origin of mother						Percent of live births to unmarried women						
All races and origins	10.7%	14.3%	18.4%	22.0%	28.0%	32.2%	33.2%	36.9%	40.8%	40.2%	40.3%	39.8%
White	5.5	7.1	11.2	14.7	20.4	25.3	27.1	31.7	35.9	35.7	35.8	28.5
Black	37.5	49.5	56.1	61.2	66.5	69.9	68.5	69.3	72.1	70.4	70.1	69.8
American Indian or Alaska Native	22.4	32.7	39.2	46.8	53.6	57.2	58.4	63.5	65.6	65.7	65.8	68.1
Asian or Pacific Islander[1]	—	—	7.3	9.5	13.2	16.3	14.8	16.2	17.0	16.4	16.4	13.3
Hispanic origin (select states)[2,3]	—	—	23.6	29.5	36.7	40.8	42.7	48.0	53.4	52.9	53.0	52.6
Maternal age						Percent distribution of live births to unmarried women						
Under 20 years	50.1%	52.1%	40.8%	33.8%	30.9%	30.9%	28.0%	23.1%	20.1%	13.9%	12.9%	12.1%
20-24 years	31.8	29.9	35.6	36.3	34.7	34.5	37.4	38.3	36.8	36.1	35.0	33.7
25 years and over	18.1	18.0	23.5	29.9	34.4	34.7	34.6	38.7	43.1	50.0	52.1	54.2
Race/Hispanic origin of mother						Live births per 1,000 unmarried women 15-44 years of age[4]						
All races and origins	26.4	24.5	29.4	32.8	43.8	44.3	44.0	47.2	47.5	43.9	43.4	42.4
White[5]	13.9	12.4	18.1	22.5	32.9	37.0	38.2	43.2	44.5	40.6	40.4	30.3
Black[5]	95.5	84.2	81.1	77.0	90.5	74.5	70.5	67.2	65.3	61.5	59.6	57.9
Hispanic origin (select states)[2,3]	—	—	—	—	89.6	88.7	87.2	96.2	80.6	68.5	67.4	66.0

— = Not available. (1) For 2016, data is for Asian and Native Hawaiian or Other Pacific Islander combined. (2) Hispanic origin data prior to 1995 is not directly comparable with data for more recent years due to differences in reporting area. (3) Hispanics may be of any race. (4) Rates computed by dividing births to unmarried mothers, regardless of mother's age, by the pop. of unmarried women 15-44 years of age. (5) For 1970 and 1975, birth rates are by race of child.

Number, Ratio, and Rate of Legal Abortions in U.S., 1970-2014

Source: *Abortion Surveillance—United States, 2014*, Centers for Disease Control and Prevention, U.S. Dept. of Health and Human Services

Year	Legal abortions	Ratio[1]	Rate[2]	Year	Legal abortions	Ratio[1]	Rate[2]	Year	Legal abortions	Ratio[1]	Rate[2]
1970	193,491	52	5	1995	1,210,883	311	20	2005	820,151	235	16
1971	485,816	137	11	1996	1,225,937	315	21	2006	852,385	236	16
1972	586,760	180	13	1997	1,186,039	306	20	2007	827,609	229	16
1973	615,831	196	14	1998	884,273	270	17	2008	825,564	231	16
1974	763,476	242	17	1999	861,789	261	17	2009	789,217	226	15
1975	854,853	272	18	2000	857,475	251	16	2010	765,651	227	15
1980	1,297,606	359	25	2001	853,485	249	16	2011	730,322	218	14
1990	1,429,247	344	24	2002	854,122	250	16	2012	699,202	209	13
1993	1,330,414	333	23	2003	848,163	245	16	2013	664,435	199	12
1994	1,267,415	321	21	2004	839,226	241	16	2014	652,639	186	12

Note: After 1998, reporting area varies. (1) Number of abortions per 1,000 live births. (2) Number of abortions per 1,000 women aged 15-44 years.

Reported U.S. Abortions by Age, Race, and Marital Status, 2014

Source: *Abortion Surveillance—United States, 2014*, Centers for Disease Control and Prevention, U.S. Dept. of Health and Human Services

Characteristic	White No.	White %	Black No.	Black %	Other No.	Other %	Total, all races No.	Total, all races %
Age[1]								
Under 15 years.	354	0.3%	408	0.4%	69	0.2%	831	0.3%
15-19 years.	14,802	10.6	10,848	10.0	2,599	9.3	28,249	10.2
20-24 years.	45,405	32.4	37,028	34.3	8,008	28.7	90,441	32.8
25-29 years.	36,610	26.1	30,106	27.9	7,137	25.6	73,853	26.8
30-34 years.	23,541	16.8	17,996	16.7	5,119	18.3	46,656	16.9
35-39 years.	13,802	9.9	8,963	8.3	3,443	12.3	26,208	9.5
40 years and over.	5,582	4.0	2,623	2.4	1,548	5.5	9,753	3.5
Total	140,096	100.0	107,972	100.0	27,923	100.0	275,991	100.0
Marital status[2]								
Married.	19,366	15.8	6,827	7.5	6,648	26.1	32,841	13.7
Unmarried.	103,068	84.2	84,383	92.5	18,785	73.9	206,236	86.3
Total	122,434	100.0	91,210	100.0	25,433	100.0	239,077	100.0

Note: The CDC requests data annually from the central health agencies of 52 reporting areas (all states, DC, and NYC). Reporting is voluntary. Data exclude areas that did not report, did not report by characteristic, or did not meet reporting standards. (1) Data from 35 reporting areas; excludes 17 (CA, CT, FL, IL, KY, MD, MA, NV, NH, NM, NY, NYC, PA, TX, UT, WA, WY). (2) Data from 32 reporting areas; excludes 20 (CA, CT, DC, FL, IL, KY, MD, MA, NV, NH, NM, NY, NYC, NC, PA, TX, UT, WA, WI, WY).

Adult Transgender Population by State

Source: "How Many Adults Identify as Transgender in the United States?" (2016), The Williams Institute, UCLA School of Law

State	Population	Percent	State	Population	Percent	State	Population	Percent
Alabama	22,500	0.61%	Maine	5,350	0.50%	Oklahoma	18,350	0.64%
Alaska	2,700	0.49	Maryland.	22,300	0.49	Oregon	19,750	0.65
Arizona	30,550	0.62	Massachusetts . .	29,900	0.57	Pennsylvania. . . .	43,800	0.44
Arkansas.	13,400	0.60	Michigan	32,900	0.43	Rhode Island . . .	4,250	0.51
California	218,400	0.76	Minnesota	24,250	0.59	South Carolina . .	21,000	0.58
Colorado	20,850	0.53	Mississippi	13,650	0.61	South Dakota . . .	2,150	0.34
Connecticut.	12,400	0.44	Missouri	25,050	0.54	Tennessee	31,200	0.63
Delaware.	4,550	0.64	Montana	2,700	0.34	Texas	125,350	0.66
Florida	100,300	0.66	Nebraska	5,400	0.39	Utah	7,200	0.36
Georgia.	55,650	0.75	Nevada	12,700	0.61	Vermont	3,000	0.59
Hawaii.	8,450	0.78	New Hampshire	4,500	0.43	Virginia	34,500	0.55
Idaho.	4,750	0.41	New Jersey	30,100	0.44	Washington.	32,850	0.62
Illinois	49,750	0.51	New Mexico	11,750	0.75	Washington, DC	14,550	2.77
Indiana	27,600	0.56	New York.	78,600	0.51	West Virginia . . .	6,100	0.42
Iowa	7,400	0.31	North Carolina . .	44,750	0.60	Wisconsin	19,150	0.43
Kansas	9,300	0.43	North Dakota . . .	1,650	0.30	Wyoming.	1,400	0.32
Kentucky.	17,700	0.53	Ohio	39,950	0.45	**United States. . .**	**1,397,150**	**0.58**
Louisiana	20,900	0.60						

Self-Identification of U.S. Transgender Persons by Age, 2015

Source: *The Report of the 2015 U.S. Transgender Survey*, National Center for Transgender Equality
(percent of all respondents who identified as trans)

Age	Crossdressers[1]	Nonbinary[2]	Trans men	Trans women
18-24 years.	8%	61%	43%	24%
25-44 years.	29	35	47	46
45-64 years.	43	4	9	26
65 years and over.	20	1	<1	5
Total	**3**	**35**	**29**	**33**

(1) Individuals who dress in a way that is typically associated with a gender different from the one they were thought to be at birth, but who may not identify with that gender or intend to live full-time as that gender. (2) Individuals whose gender is not exclusively male or female, including those who identify as no gender, as a gender other than male or female, or as more than one gender.

Sexual Orientation Among U.S. Adults, 2015

Source: *National Health Interview Survey, 2015*, National Center for Health Statistics (NCHS), U.S. Dept. of Health and Human Services

	Gay or lesbian[1]		Straight[2]		Bisexual	
	Number (thous.)	% of group	Number (thous.)	% of group	Number (thous.)	% of group
Total	3,770	1.6%	226,684	97.6%	1,870	0.8%
Sex						
Men.	2,046	1.8	109,487	97.7	559	0.5
Women	1,724	1.4	117,197	97.5	1,311	1.1
Age						
18-44 years.	2,110	2.0	104,298	96.7	1,455	1.3
45-64 years.	1,258	1.6	78,033	98.0	328	0.4
65 years and older	403	0.9	44,353	98.9	87	0.2[3]

Note: Percent distributions may not equal 100 due to rounding. (1) Response option provided was "gay" for men and "gay or lesbian" for women. (2) Response option provided was "straight, that is, not gay" for men and "straight, that is, not gay or lesbian" for women. (3) Does not meet standards of reliability or precision.

Sexual Behavior With Opposite-Sex and Same-Sex Partners, 2011-13

Source: National Survey of Family Growth, National Center for Health Statistics (NCHS), U.S. Dept. of Health and Human Services

Characteristic	Number (thous.)	Percent of selected pop. at left who have had any—				
		Opposite-sex sexual contact[1]	Vaginal intercourse with opposite-sex partner	Oral sex with opposite-sex partner	Anal sex with opposite-sex partner	Same-sex sexual contact[2]
All women aged 18-44	55,271	95.3%	94.2%	86.2%	35.9%	17.4%
Age						
18-24 years.	14,269	85.6	81.7	77.3	28.4	19.4
25-34 years.	20,790	98.3	98.0	89.8	39.0	20.0
35-44 years.	20,212	99.1	99.1	88.7	38.0	13.1
Marital/cohabiting status						
Currently married	23,191	100.0	100.0	91.2	37.5	10.9
Currently cohabiting	9,032	100.0	100.0	90.3	42.2	23.9
Never married, not cohabiting.	17,499	85.2	81.5	76.4	27.8	20.1
Formerly married, not cohabiting . . .	5,549	100.0	100.0	89.0	44.4	25.0
All men aged 18-44	54,685	93.5	92.0	87.4	42.3	6.2
Age						
18-24 years.	14,718	83.5	79.9	77.6	29.3	6.6
25-34 years.	20,453	95.6	94.6	90.1	49.3	6.0
35-44 years.	19,514	98.9	98.5	92.0	44.8	6.0
Marital/cohabiting status						
Currently married	21,298	100.0	100.0	93.4	45.4	3.9
Currently cohabiting	8,157	100.0	100.0	94.7	57.0	5.4
Never married, not cohabiting.	21,793	83.7	79.9	77.4	30.8	8.9
Formerly married, not cohabiting . . .	3,438	100.0	100.0	97.3	60.4	5.2

Note: Totals include those of other or multiple race and origin groups not shown separately. (1) Includes vaginal, oral, or anal sex. (2) For women, includes oral sex or any sexual experience with same-sex (female) partners. For men, includes oral or anal sex with male partners.

Contraceptive Use in the U.S., 2002-15

Source: National Survey of Family Growth, National Center for Health Statistics (NCHS), U.S. Dept. of Health and Human Services

Method	2002	2006-10	2011-15	2002	2006-10	2011-15
	Ever used[1]			Currently using[2]		
Any method of contraception	98.2%	99.1%	99.3%	61.9%	62.2%	61.6%
Male condom	89.7	93.4	95.0	14.7	10.2	9.2
Pill.	82.3	81.9	79.3	19.2	17.1	15.9
Withdrawal	56.1	59.6	64.8	5.4	3.2	3.9
3-month injectable (Depo-Provera).	16.8	23.2	25.4	3.3	2.3	2.6
Female sterilization.	20.7	19.5	17.1	16.7	16.5	14.3
Calendar rhythm method	16.2	18.1	15.9	NA	NA	NA
Male sterilization.	13.0	13.3	11.4	6.3	6.2	4.5
Emergency contraception.	4.2	10.8	20.0	NA	NA	NA
Contraceptive patch	0.9	10.4	10.6	NA	NA	NA
Intrauterine device (IUD).	5.8	7.7	15.0	1.3	3.5	6.8
Not currently using contraception[3]	NA	NA	NA	38.1	37.8	38.4

NA = Not available/not applicable. (1) Among women ages 15-44 who have ever had intercourse. (2) Percentage of women ages 15-44 using specified contraception in month of interview. Women could be using more than one method. Women are classified here according to the one most effective contraceptive method they are using. Additional methods women may be using are not shown. (3) Currently pregnant or postpartum, trying to get pregnant, not having sex, etc.

Child Care Arrangements of Young Children, 2016

Source: *Digest of Education Statistics*, National Center for Education Statistics, U.S. Dept. of Education

Child's characteristic	Pop. under 6 years old (thous.)	% in center-based programs[1]	Hours per week in nonparental care[2]	Type of care (% distrib.)					
				Parental care only	Center-based care	Non-relative's home	Non-relative in child's home	Relative	Multiple arrange-ments[3]
Total	21,362	35.9%	30.6	40.3%	29.4%	6.9%	3.2%	18.5%	1.8%
Age									
Under 1 year	4,724	13.2	33.0	52.6	10.7	8.0	3.7	23.2	1.6
1-2 years	8,552	24.7	30.8	46.0	21.4	7.9	3.5	19.9	1.3
3-5 years	8,087	60.9	29.5	27.1	48.7	5.1	2.5	14.4	2.3
Race/ethnicity									
White	10,731	38.5	30.5	37.8	31.4	8.5	3.9	16.4	2.0
Black	2,837	40.3	33.5	32.5	31.6	6.6	2.2	24.9	2.3
Hispanic	5,418	28.3	28.1	48.5	23.1	4.9	2.3	19.7	1.5
Asian/Pacific Islander	1,009	36.1	30.0	43.2	30.9	2.3	3.5	19.6	NA
Two or more races . .	1,235	37.3	33.6	39.2	33.7	6.9	2.1	17.7	NA

NA = Not applicable. **Note:** Detail may not sum to totals because of rounding and because children in multiple care arrangements are included under the category in which the child spent the most time. (1) Includes day care centers, Head Start programs, preschools, prekindergartens, and other early childhood programs. (2) Mean hours per week per child, among preschool children enrolled in any type of nonparental care arrangement. For children with more than one arrangement, the hours of each weekly arrangement were summed to calculate the total amount of time in child care per week. (3) Children who spent an equal number of hours per week in multiple nonparental care arrangements. (4) Race categories exclude persons of Hispanic ethnicity (Hispanic persons can be of any race).

Sexual Activity of U.S. High School Students, 2017

Source: *Youth Risk Behavior Surveillance—United States, 2017*, Centers for Disease Control and Prevention, U.S. Dept. of Health and Human Services

(percent of selected population to have engaged in activity)

Race/ethnicity	Ever had sexual intercourse			First sexual intercourse before age 13			Currently sexually active[1]			Condom use during last sexual intercourse[2]		
	Female	Male	Total	Female	Male	Total	Female	Male	Total	Female	Male	Total
White, non-Hispanic . . .	38.7%	38.5%	38.6%	1.8%	2.3%	2.1%	30.0%	27.6%	28.8%	47.0%	61.9%	54.1%
Black, non-Hispanic . . .	39.4	52.7	45.8	2.5	12.8	7.5	28.4	34.6	31.3	45.8	57.9	52.1
Hispanic, any race	37.9	44.1	41.1	1.9	6.0	4.0	28.2	30.0	29.2	47.1	62.4	54.9
Grade												
9	17.2	23.3	20.4	2.2	5.7	4.1	11.7	14.1	12.9	46.8	61.1	54.5
10	34.4	38.0	36.2	2.2	4.6	3.4	24.6	25.3	24.9	52.4	63.2	57.8
11	45.8	48.8	47.3	1.2	3.5	2.3	35.8	34.7	35.3	50.0	63.1	56.3
12	55.8	58.9	57.3	1.9	5.1	3.5	45.1	43.5	44.3	41.3	59.1	49.9
Sexual identity												
Heterosexual (straight)	36.3	41.6	39.1	1.3	4.6	3.0	28.0	29.1	28.5	49.6	61.8	56.1
Gay, lesbian, or bisexual	50.1	42.5	48.4	5.2	8.1	6.1	36.5	26.0	33.7	37.3	52.9	39.9
Not sure	25.7	30.8	28.4	2.5	4.6	4.1	18.6	19.1	19.8	39.2	NA	44.1
Sex of sexual contacts[3]												
Opposite sex only	76.6	79.6	78.2	2.8	8.4	5.8	57.7	55.8	56.7	50.3	61.6	56.3
Same sex only or both sexes	74.0	76.1	74.5	8.2	17.5	10.5	58.0	48.0	55.6	36.1	52.0	39.7
All students	**37.7**	**41.4**	**39.5**	**2.0**	**4.8**	**3.4**	**28.8**	**28.6**	**28.7**	**46.9**	**61.3**	**53.8**

NA = Not available. (1) Sexual intercourse with at least 1 person during the 3 months before the survey. (2) Among the 28.7% of students who were currently sexually active. (3) Students who had no sexual contact are excluded from the analyses by sex of sexual contacts.

Sexual Violence Against U.S. High School Students, 2017

Source: *Youth Risk Behavior Surveillance—United States, 2017*, CDC, U.S. Dept. of Health and Human Services

(as percent of selected population)

Race/ethnicity	Ever physically forced to have sexual intercourse[1]			Experienced sexual violence by anyone[2]			Experienced sexual dating violence[3]		
	Female	Male	Total	Female	Male	Total	Female	Male	Total
White, non-Hispanic	11.2%	3.3%	7.3%	16.6%	3.5%	10.0%	11.1%	2.6%	6.9%
Black, non-Hispanic	11.7	3.4	7.6	11.0	5.8	8.5	6.8	2.7	4.8
Hispanic, any race	11.2	3.6	7.3	15.1	4.2	9.5	11.4	2.5	6.9
Grade									
9	8.1	2.7	5.4	14.7	3.8	9.1	11.0	2.2	6.6
10	11.2	3.5	7.4	15.3	4.4	9.8	10.6	2.9	6.9
11	12.1	2.8	7.5	16.1	4.1	10.1	11.5	1.8	6.7
12	13.9	4.8	9.4	14.4	4.7	9.6	9.4	4.0	6.8
Sexual identity									
Heterosexual (straight)	8.8	2.5	5.4	13.4	3.1	7.9	9.3	2.1	5.5
Gay, lesbian, or bisexual	23.7	15.6	21.9	22.8	19.6	22.2	16.3	13.5	15.8
Not sure	12.7	11.8	13.1	18.9	11.3	16.7	15.5	9.2	14.1
Total	**11.3**	**3.5**	**7.4**	**15.2**	**4.3**	**9.7**	**10.7**	**2.8**	**6.9**

(1) When they did not want to. (2) Being forced to do "sexual things" (e.g., kissing, touching, or being physically forced to have sexual intercourse) they did not want to by anyone, one or more times during the 12 months before the survey. (3) Being forced to do "sexual things" by someone they were dating or going out with, one or more times, among the 68.3% of students nationwide who dated or went out with someone during the 12 months before the survey.

Risky Vehicular Behaviors by U.S. High School Students, 2017

Source: *Youth Risk Behavior Surveillance—United States, 2017*, Centers for Disease Control and Prevention, U.S. Dept. of Health and Human Services

(percent of selected population to have engaged in activity)

Race/ethnicity	Rarely or never wore a seat belt[1]			Rode with a driver who had been drinking alcohol[2]			Drove when drinking alcohol[3]			Texted or emailed while driving[4]		
	Female	Male	Total	Female	Male	Total	Female	Male	Total	Female	Male	Total
White, non-Hispanic . . .	3.4%	5.3%	4.3%	15.7%	14.2%	15.0%	3.8%	6.3%	5.0%	46.0%	41.7%	43.9%
Black, non-Hispanic . . .	8.1	11.3	9.8	19.1	14.8	17.0	4.2	4.1	4.1	27.4	26.3	26.9
Hispanic, any race	7.6	7.0	7.3	21.9	19.5	20.7	5.4	8.5	7.0	36.8	36.5	36.6
Grade												
9	6.5	5.9	6.2	17.8	16.0	16.9	2.4	4.0	3.2	11.3	14.4	12.9
10	4.5	5.9	5.2	18.2	16.2	17.2	2.4	4.0	3.2	25.1	24.0	24.5
11	4.6	6.9	5.8	16.3	14.3	15.4	4.1	6.9	5.5	47.9	43.2	45.5
12	4.0	7.9	5.9	15.8	16.1	16.0	5.9	10.4	8.1	60.3	58.5	59.3
Total	5.1	6.6	5.9	17.1	15.7	16.5	4.1	6.8	5.5	40.2	38.2	39.2

(1) When riding in a car driven by someone else. (2) In a car or other vehicle, one or more times during the 30 days before the survey. (3) Among the 62.6% of students who had driven a car or other vehicle one or more times during the 30 days before the survey. (4) Among the 62.8% of students who had driven a car or other vehicle on at least one day during the 30 days before the survey.

U.S. Motor Vehicle Crashes, 2016

Source: National Safety Council website: injuryfacts.nsc.org; Natl. Highway Traffic Safety Admin. (NHTSA)

An estimated 40,327 people in the U.S. were killed in motor vehicle crashes in 2016, up 6.8% from the total for 2015. The number of licensed drivers (222.0 mil) and vehicle miles driven (3.17 tril) increased in 2016; the death rate per 100 mil vehicle miles increased 4% to 1.27.

Motor vehicle deaths per 10,000 registered vehicles was 1.5 in 2016. In comparison, the death rate was 1.43 in 2015 and 1.81 in 2006, which represents a 17% decrease over 10 years. The number of fatalities per 100,000 population declined 18% between 2006 and 2016 but increased 6% from 2015 to 2016.

In 2015 (the most recent year for which data is available), male drivers were involved in about 6.4 mil crashes, whereas female drivers were in 4.9 mil. In 2016, male drivers were involved in 72% of fatal crashes, or about 37,564, compared with 13,279 incidents involving female drivers.

In 2016, 10,497 motor vehicle traffic fatalities (28%) involved an alcohol-impaired (blood alcohol concentration of 0.08% or greater) driver or motorcycle operator.

Seat belt use was 90% in 2017. The least likely seat belt users were occupants of pickup trucks (83%) and those traveling in light traffic (82%). In 2016, the most recent year for which data was available, seat belts and child restraints saved an estimated 14,996 lives among passenger vehicle occupants; frontal air bags saved an estimated 2,756 more lives.

Crashes	Deaths	Injuries
All motor vehicle crashes	40,327	4,600,000
Collision between motor vehicles	16,500	3,590,000
Collision with fixed object	11,300	570,000
Collision with pedestrian	7,400	164,000
Noncollision accidents (e.g., rollovers)	3,800	155,000
Collision with pedalcycle	1,100	110,000
Collision with railroad train	127	1,000
Other (mostly collisions with animals). .	100	10,000

Note: NSC numbers are rounded and preliminary.

U.S. Passenger Deaths and Death Rates, 1999-2015

Source: National Safety Council website: injuryfacts.nsc.org

Year	Light duty vehicles[1]		Vans, SUVs, pickup trucks[1]		Buses[2]		Railroad passenger trains		Scheduled airlines[3]	
	Deaths	Rate[4]	Deaths	Rate[4]	Deaths	Rate[4]	Deaths	Rate[4]	Deaths	Rate[4]
1999	20,851	0.84	11,295	0.76	40	0.07	14	0.10	23	0.005
2000	20,689	0.81	11,545	0.76	3	0.01	4	0.03	94	0.02
2002	20,564	0.78	12,278	0.78	36	0.06	7	0.05	0	0.00
2003	19,723	0.74	12,551	0.78	30	0.05	3	0.02	23	0.005
2004	19,183	0.71	12,678	0.75	27	0.05	3	0.02	13	0.002
2005	18,509	0.68	13,043	0.76	43	0.07	16	0.10	20	0.003
2006	17,792	0.66	12,723	0.72	15	0.02	2	0.01	51	0.01
2007	29,075	0.66	NA	NA	18	0.03	5	0.03	0	0.00
2008	25,457	0.59	NA	NA	50	0.08	24	0.13	0	0.00
2009	23,441	0.53	NA	NA	21	0.04	3	0.02	49	0.01
2010	22,271	0.50	NA	NA	28	0.05	3	0.02	0	0.00
2011	21,221	0.48	NA	NA	35	0.06	6	0.03	0	0.00
2012	21,669	0.49	NA	NA	25	0.05	5	0.02	0	0.00
2013	21,127	0.47	NA	NA	29	0.05	6	0.03	5	0.001
2014	21,014	0.46	NA	NA	28	0.04	5	0.02	0	0.00
2015	22,435	0.48	NA	NA	28	0.04	15	0.07	0	0.00

NA = Not available. (1) From 2007 on, light duty vehicles include passenger cars and vans, SUVs, pickup trucks, and other light trucks, which were classified separately in previous years. Drivers of light duty vehicles (except taxis) are considered passengers. Includes taxi passengers. (2) Excludes school buses. (3) Excludes charter, cargo, and on-demand services and deaths due to suicide/sabotage. (4) Deaths per 100 mil passenger miles.

Related Factors in Fatal Crashes, 1995-2016

Source: National Highway Traffic Safety Admin. (NHTSA)

Factor	2016 Number	%	2010 Number	%	2005 Number	%	1995 Number	%
Driving too fast for conditions or in excess of posted speed limit.	9,234	17.8%	9,532	21.4%	11,803	20.0%	11,656	20.8%
Under the influence of alcohol, drugs, or medication	5,592	10.8	7,052	15.9	7,441	12.6	—	—
Failure to keep in proper lane or running off road	3,890	7.5	7,436	16.7	16,551	28.0	15,873	28.3
Failure to yield right of way	3,659	7.0	3,196	7.2	4,306	6.3	4,868	8.7
Distracted (phone, talking, eating, etc.)[1]	3,210	6.2	2,912	6.6	3,415	5.8	3,323	5.9
Operating vehicle in a careless manner[2]	2,696	5.2	—	—	2,712	4.6	2,850	5.1
Failure to obey traffic signs, signals, or officer	2,064	4.0	1,912	4.3	2,354	4.0	3,189	5.7
Operating vehicle in erratic, reckless, or negligent manner[2]	2,002	3.9	2,438	5.5	—	—	—	—
Overcorrecting/oversteering	1,967	3.8	2,034	4.6	2,319	3.9	1,328	2.4
Vision obscured (rain, snow, glare, etc.)	1,566	3.0	1,426	3.2	1,496	2.5	1,309	2.3
Drowsy, asleep, fatigued, ill, or blackout	1,310	2.5	1,218	2.7	1,552	2.6	1,816	3.2
Swerving or avoiding due to wind, slippery surface, etc.	1,307	2.5	1,687	3.8	2,301	3.9	1,926	3.4
Driving wrong way on one-way or on wrong side of road	1,169	2.3	1,356	3.1	858	1.5	1,387	2.5
Making improper turn	348	0.7	970	2.2	1,590	2.7	1,253	2.2
Other factors	6,130	11.8	5,971	13.4	9,304	15.7	9,096	16.2
None reported	15,970	30.8	13,521	30.4	21,265	36.0	20,443	36.4
Unknown	8,479	16.3	3,408	7.7	1,187	2.0	990	1.8
Total drivers	**51,914**	**100.0**	**44,440**	**100.0**	**59,104**	**100.0**	**56,155**	**100.0**

— = Not available or not applicable. **Note:** For each year, the sum of the numbers and percentages is greater than total drivers as more than one factor may be present for the same driver. (1) "Inattentive (talking, eating, etc.)" in 1995, 2005. (2) In 1995 and 2005, the two categories were combined; "careless" not mentioned in factor in 2010.

U.S. Death Rates for Suicide at Selected Ages, 1960-2016

Source: *Health, United States, 2016*, National Center for Health Statistics (NCHS), CDC, U.S. Dept. of Health and Human Services

(deaths per 100,000 resident population)

Age	2016 Both sexes	Male	Female	2000 Both sexes	Male	Female	1980 Both sexes	Male	Female	1960 Both sexes	Male	Female
15-24 years	13.2	20.5	5.4	10.2	17.1	3.0	12.3	20.2	4.3	5.2	8.2	2.2
25-44 years	16.9	26.2	7.6	13.4	21.3	5.4	15.6	24.0	7.7	12.2	17.9	6.6
45-64 years	19.2	29.1	9.9	13.5	21.3	6.2	15.9	23.7	8.9	22.0	34.4	10.2
65 years and older	16.7	31.0	5.3	15.2	31.1	4.0	17.6	35.0	6.1	24.5	44.0	8.4
All ages[1]	**13.5**	**21.4**	**6.0**	**10.4**	**17.7**	**4.0**	**12.2**	**19.9**	**5.7**	**12.5**	**20.0**	**5.6**

(1) Incl. ages not shown separately here.

Leading Causes of Death in the U.S., 2016

Source: National Vital Statistics System, National Center for Health Statistics, CDC, U.S. Dept. of Health and Human Services

Cause of death	Number	% of total deaths	Death rate[1]	Cause of death	Number	% of total deaths	Death rate[1]
All causes	2,744,248	100.0%	728.8	6. Alzheimer's disease	116,103	4.2%	30.3
1. Heart disease	635,260	23.1	165.5	7. Diabetes	80,058	2.9	21.0
2. Cancer	598,038	21.8	155.8	8. Influenza and pneumonia	51,537	1.9	13.5
3. Unintentional injuries	161,374	5.9	47.4	9. Kidney disease	50,046	1.8	13.1
4. Chronic lower respiratory diseases	154,596	5.6	40.6	10. Suicide	44,965	1.6	13.5
5. Stroke	142,142	5.2	37.3	All other causes (residual)	710,129	25.9	—

— = Not available. (1) Per 100,000 U.S. population.

Overdose Deaths From Selected Drugs in the U.S., 1999-2016

Source: National Center on Health Statistics (NCHS), CDC WONDER, U.S. Dept. of Health and Human Services

	1999	2000	2003	2005	2007	2010	2012	2015	2016	Percent change, 1999-2016	Percent change, 2015-16
Total overdose deaths	16,849	17,415	25,785	29,813	36,010	38,329	41,502	52,404	63,632	277.7%	21.4%
Female	5,591	5,852	9,386	11,089	13,712	15,323	16,390	19,447	22,074	294.8	13.5
Male	11,258	11,563	16,399	18,724	22,298	23,006	25,112	32,957	41,558	269.1	26.1
Any opioid	8,048	8,407	12,939	14,917	18,515	21,088	23,164	33,091	42,249	425.0	27.7
Female	2,057	2,264	4,137	5,161	6,581	7,733	8,431	11,420	13,751	568.5	20.4
Male	5,991	6,143	8,802	9,756	11,934	13,355	14,733	21,671	28,498	375.7	31.5
Prescription opioids	3,442	3,785	7,461	9,612	12,796	14,583	14,240	15,281	17,087	396.4	11.8
Other synthetic narcotics[1]	730	782	1,400	1,742	2,213	3,007	2,628	9,580	19,413	2,559.3	102.6
Heroin	1,960	1,842	2,080	2,009	2,399	3,036	5,925	12,989	15,469	689.2	19.1
Cocaine	3,822	3,544	5,199	6,208	6,512	4,183	4,404	6,784	10,375	171.5	52.9
Benzodiazepines . .	1,135	1,298	2,248	3,084	4,500	6,497	6,524	8,791	10,684	841.3	21.5
Psychostimulants[2]	547	578	1,179	1,608	1,378	1,854	2,635	5,716	7,542	1,278.8	31.9
Antidepressants . . .	1,749	1,798	2,512	2,861	3,425	3,889	4,259	4,894	4,812	175.1	−1.7

Note: Numbers include all deaths with underlying causes of drug poisoning, regardless of intent. (1) Synthetic narcotics other than methadone. This category is dominated by fentanyl-related overdoses. (2) This category, "Psychostimulants with abuse potential" is dominated by methamphetamine-related overdoses.

Drug-Induced Deaths in the U.S., 2016

Source: National Vital Statistics System, National Center for Health Statistics, CDC, U.S. Dept. of Health and Human Services

Numbers include deaths from poisoning and medical conditions caused by use of legal or illegal drugs regardless of intent (accident, suicide, homicide, or undetermined).

State	Number	Rate[1]	State	Number	Rate[1]	State	Number	Rate[1]	State	Number	Rate[1]
Alabama	855	17.6	Indiana	1,574	23.7	Nebraska	146	7.7	South Carolina	927	18.7
Alaska	138	18.6	Iowa	338	10.8	Nevada	678	23.1	South Dakota	75	8.7
Arizona	1,500	21.6	Kansas	333	11.5	New Hampshire	495	37.1	Tennessee	1,740	26.2
Arkansas	423	14.2	Kentucky	1,525	34.4	New Jersey	2,132	23.8	Texas	2,965	10.6
California	5,094	13.0	Louisiana	1,036	22.1	New Mexico	525	25.2	Utah	685	22.5
Colorado	973	17.6	Maine	369	27.7	New York	3,894	19.7	Vermont	131	21.0
Connecticut	997	27.9	Maryland	2,089	34.7	North Carolina	2,040	20.1	Virginia	1,444	17.2
Delaware	288	30.3	Massachusetts	2,379	34.9	North Dakota	86	11.3	Washington	1,212	16.6
Florida	4,963	24.1	Michigan	2,701	27.2	Ohio	4,477	38.5	West Virginia	912	49.8
Georgia	1,461	14.2	Minnesota	750	13.6	Oklahoma	840	21.4	Wisconsin	1,103	19.1
Hawaii	207	14.5	Mississippi	374	12.5	Oregon	651	15.9	Wyoming	103	17.6
Idaho	260	16.3	Missouri	1,418	23.3	Pennsylvania	4,762	37.2	Washington, DC	276	40.5
Illinois	2,455	19.2	Montana	136	13.0	Rhode Island	330	31.2	**U.S.**	**67,265**	**20.8**

(1) Number of deaths due to drug-induced causes per 100,000 population.

Principal Types of Accidental Deaths in the U.S., 1970-2016

Source: National Safety Council website: injuryfacts.nsc.org; National Center for Health Statistics, U.S. Dept. of Health and Human Services

Year[1]	Total[2]	Motor vehicle	Falls	Poisoning	Choking: Inhalation of food, object	Drowning	Fires, flames, smoke	Mechanical suffocation	Firearms
1970	114,638	54,633	16,926	5,299	2,753	7,860	6,718	NA	2,406
1980	105,718	53,172	13,294	4,331	3,249	7,257	5,822	NA	1,955
1985	93,457	45,901	12,001	5,170	3,551	5,316	4,938	NA	1,649
1990	91,983	46,814	12,313	5,803	3,303	4,685	4,175	NA	1,416
1995	93,320	43,363	13,986	9,072	3,185	4,350	3,761	NA	1,225
2000	97,900	43,354	13,322	12,757	4,313	3,482	3,377	1,335	776
2005	117,809	45,343	19,656	23,617	4,386	3,582	3,197	1,514	789
2009	118,046	36,216	24,792	31,758	4,370	3,517	2,756	1,569	554
2010	120,859	35,332	26,009	33,041	4,570	3,782	2,782	1,595	606
2011	126,438	35,303	27,483	36,280	4,708	3,556	2,746	1,534	591
2012	127,792	36,415	28,756	36,332	4,634	3,551	2,464	1,604	548
2013	130,557	35,369	30,208	38,851	4,864	3,391	2,760	1,737	505
2014	135,928	35,398	31,959	42,032	4,816	3,406	2,701	1,764	461
2015	146,571	37,757	33,381	47,478	5,051	3,602	2,646	1,863	489
2016	161,374	40,327	34,673	58,335	4,829	3,789	2,730	1,781	495
Deaths per 100,000 population									
1970	56.2	26.8	8.3	2.6	1.4	3.9	3.3	NA	1.2
1980	46.5	23.4	5.9	1.9	1.4	3.2	2.6	NA	0.9
1985	39.3	19.3	5.0	2.2	1.5	2.2	2.1	NA	0.7
1990	36.9	18.8	4.9	2.3	1.3	1.9	1.7	NA	0.6
1995	35.5	16.5	5.3	3.4	1.2	1.7	1.4	NA	0.5
2000	35.6	15.7	4.8	4.6	1.6	1.3	1.2	0.5	0.3
2005	39.7	15.3	6.6	8.0	1.5	1.2	1.1	0.5	0.3
2009	38.5	11.8	8.1	10.3	1.4	1.1	0.9	0.5	0.2
2010	39.0	11.4	8.4	10.7	1.5	1.2	0.9	0.5	0.2
2011	40.6	11.3	8.8	11.6	1.5	1.1	0.9	0.5	0.2
2012	40.7	11.6	9.2	11.6	1.5	1.1	0.8	0.5	0.2
2013	41.3	11.2	9.6	12.3	1.5	1.1	0.9	0.5	0.2
2014	42.6	11.1	10.0	13.2	1.5	1.1	0.8	0.6	0.1
2015	45.6	11.7	10.4	14.8	1.6	1.1	0.8	0.6	0.2
2016	49.9	12.5	10.7	18.1	1.5	1.2	0.8	0.6	0.2

NA = Not available. **Note:** All figures include on-the-job deaths. (1) Data after 1999 are not comparable with earlier data because of classification changes. (2) Total incl. other accidental deaths not shown in detail here.

Deaths in the U.S. Involving Firearms by Age and Sex, 2016

Source: National Safety Council website: injuryfacts.nsc.org

Type and sex	All ages	Under 5	5-14	15-24	25-44	45-54	55-64	65-74	75 or older
Total firearms deaths	38,654	113	377	7,503	13,995	5,458	4,942	3,259	3,007
Male	32,990	68	271	6,630	11,933	4,452	4,071	2,802	2,763
Female	5,664	45	106	873	2,062	1,006	871	457	244
Unintentional	495	35	39	121	113	67	63	32	25
Male	424	29	30	110	99	57	48	29	22
Female	71	6	9	11	14	10	15	3	3
Suicide	22,936	—	160	2,683	6,397	3,873	4,067	2,932	2,824
Male	19,645	—	126	2,348	5,362	3,161	3,418	2,574	2,656
Female	3,291	—	34	335	1,035	712	649	358	168
Homicide	14,414	75	163	4,553	7,065	1,420	738	263	137
Male	12,212	36	104	4,040	6,098	1,146	549	172	67
Female	2,202	39	59	513	967	274	189	91	70
Legal intervention	510	0	2	76	303	71	43	10	5
Male	488	0	1	74	290	67	42	9	5
Female	22	0	1	2	13	4	1	1	0
Undetermined[1]	299	3	13	70	117	27	31	22	16
Male	221	3	10	58	84	21	14	18	13
Female	78	0	3	12	33	6	17	4	3

— = Not applicable. (1) The intention of the death (unintentional, suicide, or homicide) could not be determined.

U.S. Infant Mortality Rates by Race and Sex, 1960-2016

Source: National Center for Health Statistics (NCHS), CDC, U.S. Dept. of Health and Human Services
(deaths of infants under 1 year old per 1,000 live births)

Year	All races[1] Both sexes	Male	Female	White[2] Both sexes	Male	Female	Black[2] Both sexes	Male	Female
1960	26.0	29.3	22.6	22.9	26.0	19.6	44.3	49.1	39.4
1970	20.0	22.4	17.5	17.8	20.0	15.4	32.7	36.2	29.0
1980	12.6	13.9	11.2	10.9	12.1	9.5	22.2	24.2	20.2
1990	9.2	10.3	8.1	7.6	8.5	6.6	18.0	19.6	16.3
1995	7.6	8.3	6.8	6.3	7.0	5.6	15.1	16.3	13.9
2000	6.9	7.6	6.2	5.7	6.3	5.1	14.1	15.5	12.7
2001	6.9	7.5	6.1	5.7	6.3	5.1	14.0	15.5	12.5
2002	7.0	7.6	6.3	5.9	6.5	5.1	14.3	15.4	13.2
2003	6.9	7.6	6.1	5.7	6.4	5.0	14.2	15.7	12.6
2004	6.8	7.5	6.1	5.7	6.3	5.1	14.2	15.7	12.7
2005	6.9	7.6	6.2	5.7	6.7	4.8	14.3	15.8	12.8
2006	6.7	7.3	6.0	5.6	6.2	5.0	13.8	15.0	12.5
2007	6.8	7.4	6.1	5.6	6.2	5.0	13.8	15.0	12.4
2008	6.6	7.2	6.0	5.5	6.0	5.0	13.1	14.4	11.9
2009	6.4	7.0	5.8	5.3	5.8	4.7	13.1	14.6	11.5
2010	6.2	6.7	5.6	5.1	5.5	4.6	12.0	13.1	10.9
2011	6.1	6.6	5.5	5.1	5.5	4.6	12.0	13.1	10.8
2012	6.0	6.5	5.4	5.0	5.4	4.5	11.6	12.8	10.4
2013	6.0	6.5	5.4	5.0	5.5	4.4	11.6	12.5	10.7
2014	5.8	6.3	5.3	4.8	5.3	4.3	11.4	12.3	10.4
2015	5.9	6.4	5.4	4.8	5.3	4.4	11.7	12.8	10.7
2016	5.9	6.4	5.3	4.8	5.2	4.3	11.8	12.7	10.8

Note: Number of live births is tabulated according to mother's race (1980 and on) or parents' race (before 1980) stated on birth certificate. (1) Incl. races not shown. (2) Non-Hispanic.

Years of Life Expected at Birth in U.S., 1900-2016

Source: National Center for Health Statistics (NCHS), CDC, U.S. Dept. of Health and Human Services

Year	All races[1] Both sexes	Male	Female	White[2] Both sexes	Male	Female	Black[2,3] Both sexes	Male	Female
1900[4]	47.3	46.3	48.3	47.6	46.6	48.7	33.0	32.5	33.5
1950	68.2	65.6	71.1	69.1	66.5	72.2	60.8	59.1	62.9
1960	69.7	66.6	73.1	70.6	67.4	74.1	63.6	61.1	66.3
1970	70.8	67.1	74.7	71.7	68.0	75.6	64.1	60.0	68.3
1980	73.7	70.0	77.4	74.4	70.7	78.1	68.1	63.8	72.5
1990	75.4	71.8	78.8	76.1	72.7	79.4	69.1	64.5	73.6
2000	76.8	74.1	79.3	77.3	74.7	79.9	71.8	68.2	75.1
2005	77.6	75.0	80.1	78.0	75.5	80.5	73.0	69.5	76.2
2006	77.8	75.2	80.3	78.2	75.7	80.6	73.1	69.5	76.4
2007	78.1	75.5	80.6	78.4	75.9	80.8	73.5	69.9	76.7
2008	78.2	75.6	80.6	78.4	76.0	80.7	73.9	70.5	77.0
2009	78.5	76.0	80.9	78.7	76.3	81.0	74.4	71.0	77.4
2010	78.7	76.2	81.0	78.8	76.4	81.1	74.7	71.5	77.7
2011	78.7	76.3	81.1	78.7	76.4	81.1	75.0	71.8	77.8
2012	78.8	76.4	81.2	78.9	76.5	81.2	75.1	71.9	78.1
2013	78.8	76.4	81.2	78.8	76.5	81.2	75.1	71.9	78.1
2014	78.9	76.5	81.3	78.8	76.5	81.2	75.3	72.2	78.2
2015	78.7	76.3	81.1	78.7	76.3	81.0	75.1	71.9	78.1
2016	78.6	76.1	81.1	78.5	76.1	81.0	74.8	71.5	77.9

(1) Includes races not shown. (2) Non-Hispanic. (3) Data for 1900-60 are for the nonwhite pop. (4) Data prior to 1950 does not include all states.

U.S. Life Expectancy at Selected Ages, 2016

Source: National Center for Health Statistics (NCHS), CDC, U.S. Dept. of Health and Human Services

Exact age in years	All races[1] Both sexes	Male	Female	White[2] Both sexes	Male	Female	Black[2] Both sexes	Male	Female
0	78.6	76.1	81.1	78.5	76.1	81.0	74.8	71.5	77.9
1	78.1	75.6	80.5	77.9	75.5	80.3	74.7	71.4	77.7
5	74.1	71.7	76.6	74.0	71.6	76.4	70.8	67.6	73.8
10	69.2	66.7	71.6	69.0	66.6	71.4	65.9	62.6	68.9
15	64.2	61.8	66.6	64.1	61.7	66.5	60.9	57.7	64.0
20	59.4	57.0	61.7	59.2	56.9	61.5	56.2	53.0	59.1
25	54.7	52.4	56.9	54.5	52.3	56.7	51.6	48.6	54.3
30	50.0	47.8	52.1	49.8	47.7	51.9	47.0	44.2	49.5
35	45.3	43.2	47.3	45.2	43.2	47.1	42.4	39.7	44.8
40	40.7	38.7	42.6	40.6	38.6	42.4	37.9	35.4	40.2
45	36.1	34.2	37.9	36.0	34.1	37.8	33.5	31.1	35.7
50	31.6	29.8	33.3	31.5	29.8	33.2	29.2	26.9	31.3
55	27.3	25.6	28.9	27.3	25.6	28.8	25.2	22.9	27.1
60	23.3	21.7	24.7	23.2	21.7	24.6	21.5	19.4	23.2
65	19.4	18.0	20.6	19.3	18.0	20.5	18.0	16.2	19.5
70	15.7	14.5	16.6	15.6	14.4	16.5	14.8	13.2	15.9
75	12.2	11.3	13.0	12.1	11.2	12.9	11.8	10.5	12.7
80	9.2	8.4	9.7	9.1	8.3	9.7	9.1	8.1	9.7
85	6.6	5.9	7.0	6.5	5.9	6.9	6.9	6.1	7.2
90	4.6	4.1	4.8	4.5	4.0	4.7	5.0	4.5	5.2
95	3.2	2.8	3.3	3.1	2.7	3.2	3.7	3.3	3.8
100	2.2	2.0	2.3	2.2	2.0	2.2	2.7	2.5	2.7

(1) Includes races not shown. (2) Non-Hispanic.

NOTED PERSONALITIES

Widely Known Americans of the Present

Political leaders, journalists, other prominent living persons. As of Oct. 2018. Excludes most who fall in categories listed elsewhere in Noted Personalities, such as Writers of the Present and Entertainment Personalities of the Present. Includes some figures who are active in American life but are not U.S. citizens.

Sheldon Adelson, b 8/4/1933 (Dorchester, MA), Las Vegas Sands founder, CEO.

Madeleine K. Albright, b 5/15/1937 (Prague, Czech.), former sec. of state.

Edwin "Buzz" Aldrin, b 1/20/1930 (Montclair, NJ), former astronaut, second person to walk on the Moon.

Samuel A. Alito Jr., b 4/1/1950 (Trenton, NJ), U.S. Supreme Court justice.

Marin Alsop, b 10/16/1956 (New York, NY), Baltimore Symphony musical dir.

Christiane Amanpour, b 1/12/1958 (London, Eng., UK), TV journalist.

Marc Andreessen, b 7/9/1971 (New Lisbon, IA), co-author of web browser Mosaic, cofounder of Netscape.

David Axelrod, b 2/22/1955 (New York, NY), political strategist; former sr. adviser to Pres. Obama.

F. Lee Bailey, b 6/10/1933 (Waltham, MA), attorney.

James Baker, b 4/28/1930 (Houston, TX), former sec. of state.

Russell Baker, b 8/14/1925 (Morrisonville, VA), columnist.

Steve Ballmer, b 3/24/1956 (Detroit, MI), former Microsoft CEO; L.A. Clippers owner.

Steve Bannon, b 11/27/1953 (Norfolk, VA), former chief strategist to Pres. Trump, Breitbart News exec.

Mike Barnicle, b 8/24/1944 (Fitchburg, MA), columnist.

Mary Barra, b 12/24/1961 (Waterford, MI), General Motors CEO.

Dave Barry, b 7/3/1947 (Armonk, NY), humorist.

Mario Batali, b 9/19/1960 (Yakima, WA), chef, TV personality.

Gary Bauer, b 5/4/1946 (Covington, KY), domestic policy adviser to Pres. Reagan; founder, Campaign for Working Families.

Glenn Beck, b 2/10/1964 (Mount Vernon, WA), political commentator.

Chris Berman, b 5/10/1955 (Greenwich, CT), sportscaster.

Ben Bernanke, b 12/13/1953 (Augusta, GA), former Federal Reserve chair.

Carl Bernstein, b 2/14/1944 (Washington, DC), journalist; with Bob Woodward cracked Watergate scandal.

Jeff Bezos, b 1/12/1964 (Albuquerque, NM), founder and CEO of Amazon.

Jill Biden, b 6/5/1951 (Hammonton, NJ), professor, wife of former U.S. vice pres. Joe Biden.

Joseph R. Biden Jr., b 11/20/1942 (Scranton, PA), former U.S. vice pres., sen. (D, DE).

Wolf Blitzer, b 3/22/1948 (Augsburg, Germany), TV journalist.

Harold Bloom, b 7/11/1930 (New York, NY), literary critic.

Michael R. Bloomberg, b 2/14/1942 (Brighton, MA), former NYC mayor, financial information/media entrepreneur.

Charles M. Blow, b 8/11/1970 (Gibsland, LA), columnist.

John Boehner, b 11/17/1949 (Cincinnati, OH), former U.S. rep. (R, OH) and speaker of the House.

Cory Booker, b 4/27/1969 (Washington, DC), U.S. sen. (D, NJ), former Newark mayor.

Andy Borowitz, b 1/4/1958 (Cleveland, OH), humorist.

Barbara Boxer, b 11/11/1940 (Brooklyn, NY), U.S. senator (D, CA).

Donna Brazile, b 12/15/1959 (Kenner, LA), political analyst.

Stephen Breyer, b 8/15/1938 (San Francisco, CA), U.S. Supreme Court justice.

Sergey Brin, b 8/21/1973 (Moscow, Russia), cofounder of Google.

Tom Brokaw, b 2/6/1940 (Webster, SD), TV journalist, retired anchor.

David Brooks, b 8/11/1961 (Toronto, ON, Can.), columnist, political commentator.

Aaron Brown, b 11/10/1948 (Hopkins, MN), broadcast journalist.

Jerry (Edmund G.) Brown Jr., b 4/7/1938 (San Francisco, CA), CA gov. (D, 1975-83, 2011-), former pres. candidate.

Frank Bruni, b 10/31/1964 (White Plains, NY), columnist.

Pat Buchanan, b 11/2/1938 (Washington, DC), journalist, former pres. candidate (R).

Warren Buffett, b 8/30/1930 (Omaha, NE), investor, leading philanthropist.

Barbara Bush, b 11/25/1981 (Dallas, TX), daughter of former pres. George W. Bush.

George H. W. Bush, b 6/12/1924 (Milton, MA), 41st U.S. president.

George W. Bush, b 7/6/1946 (New Haven, CT), 43rd U.S. president.

Jeb Bush, b 2/11/1953 (Midland, TX), FL gov. (R); 2016 pres. contender.

Laura Bush, b 11/4/1946 (Midland, TX), former first lady.

Gretchen Carlson, b 6/21/1966 (Anoka, MN), TV journalist.

Tucker Carlson, b 5/16/1969 (San Francisco, CA), journalist, TV commentator.

Jimmy Carter, b 10/1/1924 (Plains, GA), 39th U.S. president; 2002 Nobel Peace Prize winner.

Rosalynn Carter, b 8/18/1927 (Plains, GA), former first lady.

James Carville Jr., b 10/25/1944 (Fort Benning, GA), political analyst.

Steve Case, b 8/21/1958 (Honolulu, HI), former AOL Time Warner chair.

Joaquin Castro, b 9/16/1974 (San Antonio, TX), U.S. rep. (D, TX).

Dick Cheney, b 1/30/1941 (Lincoln, NE), former U.S. vice president.

Lynne Cheney, b 8/14/1941 (Casper, WY), political commentator, wife of former U.S. vice pres. Dick Cheney.

Brian Chesky, b 8/29/1981 (Niskayuna, NY), Airbnb founder, CEO.

Judy Chicago, b 7/20/1939 (Chicago, IL), artist.

Dale Chihuly, b 9/20/1941 (Tacoma, WA), glass sculptor.

Noam Chomsky, b 12/7/1928 (Philadelphia, PA), linguist, activist.

Chris Christie, b 9/6/1962 (Newark, NJ), former NJ gov. (R); 2016 pres. contender.

Connie Chung, b 8/20/1946 (Washington, DC), former TV journalist.

Bill Clinton, b 8/19/1946 (Hope, AR), 42nd U.S. president.

Chelsea Clinton, b 2/27/1980 (Little Rock, AR), daughter of former pres. Bill Clinton and Hillary Clinton.

Hillary Rodham Clinton, b 10/26/1947 (Chicago, IL), former sec. of state, U.S. sen. (D, NY), first lady; 2016 presidential nominee (D).

Kate Clinton, b 11/9/1947 (Buffalo, NY), political humorist.

Dan Coats, b 5/16/1943 (Jackson, MI), director of national intelligence.

Michael Cohen, b 8/25/1966 (Lawrence, NY), former personal atty. to Pres. Trump.

Kenneth Cole, b 3/23/1954 (Brooklyn, NY), fashion designer.

Gail Collins, b 11/25/1945 (Cincinnati, OH), newspaper columnist, writer.

Jason Collins, b 12/2/1978 (Northridge, CA), first openly active gay active NBA player.

James Comey, b 12/14/1960 (Yonkers, NY), former FBI director.

Kellyanne Conway, b 1/20/1967 (Camden, NJ), counselor to Pres. Trump.

Tim Cook, b 11/1/1960 (Robertdale, AZ), CEO of Apple, Inc.

Anderson Cooper, b 6/3/1967 (New York, NY), TV news anchor.

Bob Corker, b 8/24/52 (Orangeburg, SC), U.S. sen. (R, TN).

John Cornyn, b 2/2/1952 (Houston, TX), U.S. sen. (R, TX), majority whip.

Bob Costas, b 3/22/1952 (Astoria, Queens, NY), TV sports journalist.

Ann Coulter, b 12/8/1961 (New Canaan, CT), political commentator, author.

Katie Couric, b 1/7/1957 (Arlington, VA), TV and online journalist.

Candy Crowley, b 12/12/1948 (Kalamazoo, MI), TV journalist.

Ted Cruz, b 12/22/1970 (Calgary, AB, Can.), U.S. sen. (R, TX); 2016 pres. contender.

Mark Cuban, b 7/31/1958 (Pittsburgh, PA), entrepreneur, Dallas Mavericks owner.

Andrew Cuomo, b 12/6/1957 (New York, NY), NY gov. (D); former state atty. gen.

Ann Curry, b 11/19/1956 (Guam), TV journalist.

Bill de Blasio, b 5/8/1961 (New York, NY), NYC mayor (D).

Michael Dell, b 2/23/1965 (Houston, TX), founder, chair, and CEO of Dell computers.

Alan Dershowitz, b 9/1/1938 (Brooklyn, NY), attorney, political commentator.

Betsy DeVos, b 1/8/1958 (Holland, MI), education sec., philanthropist.

Barry Diller, b 2/2/1942 (San Francisco, CA), media exec.

Jamie Dimon, b 3/13/1956 (New York, NY), chair, CEO of JPMorgan Chase.

Lou Dobbs, b 9/24/1945 (Childress, TX), TV journalist.

James Dobson, b 4/21/1936 (Shreveport, LA), evangelical Christian leader, founder of Focus on the Family.

Timothy Dolan, b 2/6/1950 (St. Louis, MO), Rom. Cath. cardinal, archbishop of NY.

Robert Dole, b 7/22/1923 (Russell, KS), former U.S. Senate majority leader (R, KS), 1996 pres. nominee.

Jack Dorsey, b 11/19/1976 (St. Louis, MO), Twitter cofounder.

Maureen Dowd, b 1/14/1952 (Washington, DC), columnist.

Elizabeth Drew, b 11/16/1935 (Cincinnati, OH), journalist.

Matt Drudge, b 10/27/1966 (Takoma Park, MD), Drudge Report founder/editor.

Michael S. Dukakis, b 11/3/1933 (Brookline, MA), former MA gov. (D), 1988 pres. nominee.

David Duke, b 7/1/1950 (Tulsa, OK), white nationalist activist; politician.

Dick Durbin, b 11/21/1944 (East St. Louis, IL), U.S. Senate minority whip (D, IL).

Sylvia Earle, b 8/30/1935 (Gibbstown, NJ), marine biologist.

Marian Wright Edelman, b 6/6/1939 (Bennettsville, SC), pres. and founder of Children's Defense Fund.

John Edwards, b 6/10/1953 (Seneca, SC), former U.S. sen. (D, NC), 2004 vice-pres. nominee, 2008 pres. contender.

Michael Eisner, b 3/7/1942 (Mt. Kisco, NY), former Disney Co. CEO.

Lawrence J. Ellison, b 8/17/1944 (New York, NY), Oracle Corp. cofounder.

Rahm Emanuel, b 11/29/1959 (Chicago, IL), Chicago mayor; former Obama chief of staff, U.S. rep. (D, IL).

Myrlie Evers-Williams, b 3/17/1933 (Vicksburg, MS), civil rights activist.

Louis Farrakhan, b 5/11/1933 (Roxbury, MA), Nation of Islam leader.

Dianne Feinstein, b 6/22/1933 (San Francisco, CA), U.S. sen. (D, CA).

Larry Fink, b 11/2/1952 (Los Angeles, CA), BlackRock CEO.

Carly (Carleton) S. Fiorina, b 9/6/1954 (Austin, TX), former Hewlett-Packard CEO, 2016 pres. contender (R).

Michael Flynn, b 12/1/1958 (Middletown, RI), U.S. Army gen. (ret.); briefly Pres. Trump's natl. security adviser.

Larry Flynt, b 11/1/1942 (Lakeville, KY), publisher.

Steve (Malcolm) Forbes Jr., b 7/18/1947 (Morristown, NJ), publisher, former pres. contender.

Tom Ford, b 8/27/1961 (Austin, TX), fashion designer.

Barney Frank, b 3/31/1940 (Bayonne, NJ), attorney, former U.S. rep. (D, MA).

Thomas Friedman, b 7/20/1953 (Minneapolis, MN), columnist, author.

Bill Gates, b 10/28/1955 (Seattle, WA), software pioneer; Microsoft exec.

Henry Louis Gates Jr., b 9/16/1950 (Keyser, WV), African American studies scholar.

Melinda Gates, b 8/15/1964 (Dallas, TX), philanthropist.

Robert M. Gates, b 9/25/1943 (Wichita, KS), former sec. of defense.

David Geffen, b 2/21/1943 (Brooklyn, NY), entertainment exec.

Charles Gibson, b 3/4/1943 (Evanston, IL), TV journalist.

Gabrielle Giffords, b 6/8/1970 (Tucson, AZ), former U.S. rep. (D, AZ); shot in 2011 assassination attempt.

Kirsten Gillibrand, b 12/9/1966 (Albany, NY), U.S. sen. (D, NY), attorney.

Newt Gingrich, b 6/17/1943 (Harrisburg, PA), former House speaker (R, GA), 2012 pres. contender.

Ruth Bader Ginsburg, b 3/15/1933 (Brooklyn, NY), U.S. Supreme Court justice.

Rudolph Giuliani, b 5/28/1944 (Brooklyn, NY), atty. for Pres. Trump, former NYC mayor (R).

Ira Glass, b 3/3/1959 (Baltimore, MD), radio host.

Roger Goodell, b 2/19/1959 (Jamestown, NY), NFL commissioner.

Ellen Goodman, b 4/11/1941 (Newton, MA), columnist.

Doris Kearns Goodwin, b 1/4/1943 (Brooklyn, NY), historian, TV commentator.

Berry Gordy, b 11/28/1929 (Detroit, MI), Motown record label founder.

Al Gore Jr., b 3/31/1948 (Washington, DC), former U.S. sen. (D, TN), vice pres., pres. nominee; 2007 Nobel Peace Prize winner.

Lindsey Graham, b 7/9/1955 (Central, SC), U.S. sen. (R, SC); 2016 pres. contender.

Temple Grandin, b 8/29/1947 (Boston, MA), animal behavioral scientist, autism activist.

Jeff Greenfield, b 6/10/1943 (New York, NY), TV journalist.

Alan Greenspan, b 3/6/1926 (New York, NY), former Federal Reserve chair.

Savannah Guthrie, b 12/27/1971 (Melbourne, Vic., Australia), TV journalist.

Jenna Bush Hager, b 11/25/1981 (Dallas, TX), daughter of former pres. George W. Bush.

Nikki Haley, b 1/20/1972 (Bamberg, SC), U.S. ambassador to UN, 2017-18; former SC gov. (R).

Pete Hamill, b 6/24/1935 (Brooklyn, NY), journalist, author.

Sean Hannity, b 12/30/1961 (New York, NY), radio and TV host, author, political commentator.

Kamala Harris, b 10/20/1964 (Oakland, CA), U.S. sen. (D, CA).

Reed Hastings, b 10/8/1960 (Boston, MA), founder, pres., CEO and board chair, Netflix, Inc.

Orrin Hatch, b 3/22/1934 (Homestead Park, PA), U.S. sen. (R, UT) and Senate pres. pro tempore.

Carla Hayden, b 8/10/1952 (Tallahassee, FL), librarian of U.S. Congress.

Tommy Hilfiger, b 3/24/1951 (Elmira, NY), fashion designer.

Anita Hill, b 7/30/1956 (Morris, OK), legal scholar; complainant against U.S. Supreme Court justice Clarence Thomas.

Paris Hilton, b 2/17/1981 (New York, NY), heiress, actress.

Perez Hilton, b 3/23/1978 (Miami, FL), gossip columnist.

James P. Hoffa, b 5/19/1941 (Detroit, MI), Teamsters Union head.

Eric Holder Jr., b 1/21/1951 (Bronx, NY), former U.S. atty. gen.

Lester Holt, b 3/8/1959 (San Francisco, CA), TV journalist.

David Horowitz, b 1/10/1939 (New York, NY), consumer advocate, columnist, author.

Steny H. Hoyer, b 6/14/1939 (New York, NY), House minority whip (D, MD).

Mike Huckabee, b 8/24/1955 (Hope, AR), former AR gov. (R), TV host, pres. contender (2008, '16).

Dolores Huerta, b 4/10/1930 (Dawson, NM), labor activist.

Arianna Huffington, b 7/15/1950 (Athens, Greece), political commentator.

H. Wayne Huizenga, b 12/29/1939 (Evergreen Park, IL), entrepreneur, sports exec.

Brit Hume, b 6/22/1943 (Washington, DC), TV journalist.

Lee Iacocca, b 10/15/1924 (Allentown, PA), former auto exec. (Ford, Chrysler).

Carl Icahn, b 2/16/1936 (Brooklyn, NY), financier.

Bob Iger, b 2/10/1951 (Oceanside, NY), Walt Disney Co. CEO.

Don Imus, b 7/23/1940 (Riverside, CA), talk-show host.

Patricia Ireland, b 10/19/1945 (Oak Park, IL), feminist leader.

Jesse Jackson, b 10/8/1941 (Greenville, SC), civil rights leader, former pres. contender (D).

Marc Jacobs, b 4/9/1964 (New York, NY), fashion designer.

Valerie Jarrett, b 11/14/1956 (Shiraz, Iran), former sr. adviser to Pres. Obama.

Bobby Jindal, b 6/10/1971 (Baton Rouge, LA), former LA gov. (R); 2016 pres. contender.

Jasper Johns, b 5/15/1930 (Augusta, GA), painter, printmaker.

Katherine Johnson, b 8/26/1918 (White Sulphur Springs, WV), NASA scientist.

Robert L. Johnson, b 4/8/1946 (Hickory, MS), Black Entertainment Television founder.

Alex Jones, b 2/11/1974 (Dallas, TX), InfoWars creator, radio host.

Vernon E. Jordan Jr., b 8/15/1935 (Atlanta, GA), attorney, former pres. adviser, civil rights leader.

Colin Kaepernick, b 11/3/1987 (Milwaukee, WI), football player, activist.

Elena Kagan, b 4/28/1960 (New York, NY), U.S. Supreme Court justice.

Tim Kaine, b 2/26/1958 (St. Paul, MN), U.S. sen. (D, VA), 2016 vice-pres. nominee.

Travis Kalanick, b 8/6/1976 (Los Angeles, CA), Uber cofounder and former CEO.

Donna Karan, b 10/2/1948 (Forest Hills, Queens, NY), fashion designer.

John Kasich, b 5/13/1952 (McKees Rocks, PA), OH gov. (R); 2016 pres. contender.

Jeffrey Katzenberg, b 12/21/1950 (New York, NY), entertainment exec.

Brett Kavanaugh, b 2/12/1965 (Washington, DC), U.S. Supreme Court justice.

Garrison Keillor, b 8/7/1942 (Anoka, MN), author, broadcaster.

John F. Kelly, b 5/11/1950 (Boston, MA), Trump White House chief of staff; U.S. Marine gen. (ret.).

Mark Kelly, b 2/21/1964 (Orange, NJ), U.S. Navy capt., former NASA shuttle commander.

Megyn Kelly, b 11/18/1970 (Syracuse, NY), TV commentator, host.

Anthony M. Kennedy, b 7/23/1936 (Sacramento, CA), former U.S. Supreme Court justice.

John Kerry, b 12/11/1943 (Aurora, CO), former sec. of state, U.S. sen. (D, MA); 2004 pres. nominee.

Larry King, b 11/19/1933 (Brooklyn, NY), TV talk-show host.

Michael Kinsley, b 3/9/1951 (Detroit, MI), editor, political commentator.

Henry Kissinger, b 5/27/1923 (Furth, Germany), former sec. of state.

Calvin Klein, b 11/19/1942 (Bronx, NY), fashion designer.

Philip H. Knight, b 2/24/1938 (Portland, OR), founder and chair emeritus of Nike.

Charles G. Koch, b 5/3/1940 (Wichita, KS), Koch Industries exec., philanthropist.

David H. Koch, b 11/1/1935 (Wichita, KS), Koch Industries exec., philanthropist.

Sarah Koenig, b 7/9/1969 (New York, NY), radio journalist.

Jeff Koons, b 1/21/1955 (York, PA), artist.

Ted Koppel, b 2/8/1940 (Lancashire, Eng., UK), former TV journalist.

Michael Kors, b 8/9/1959 (Merrick, NY), fashion designer.

Hoda Kotb, b 8/9/1964 (Norman, OK), TV journalist.

Larry Kramer, b 6/25/1935 (Bridgeport, CT), AIDS activist, writer.

Nicholas D. Kristof, b 4/27/1959 (Chicago, IL), columnist, author.

William Kristol, b 12/23/1952 (New York, NY), editor, columnist.

Steve Kroft, b 8/22/1945 (Kokomo, IN), TV journalist.

Paul Krugman, b 2/28/1953 (Albany, NY), economist, columnist.

Jared Kushner, b 1/10/1981 (Livingston, NJ), Trump senior adviser; real estate developer.

Brian Lamb, b 10/9/1941 (Lafayette, IN), cable TV exec., journalist.

Wayne LaPierre Jr., b 11/8/1949 (Schenectady, NY), National Rifle Assn. exec. VP.

Matt Lauer, b 12/30/1957 (New York, NY), TV journalist.

Ralph Lauren, b 10/14/1939 (Bronx, NY), fashion designer.

Patrick Leahy, b 3/31/1940 (Montpelier, VT), U.S. sen. (D, VT).

Norman Lear, b 7/27/1922 (New Haven, CT), TV producer, political activist.

Jim Lehrer, b 5/19/1934 (Wichita, KS), TV journalist, author.

Annie Leibovitz, b 10/2/1949 (Waterbury, CT), photographer.

Monica Lewinsky, b 7/23/1973 (San Francisco, CA), former White House intern.

John Lewis, b 2/21/1940 (Troy, AL), U.S. rep. (D, AL); civil rights activist.

Joseph Lieberman, b 2/24/1942 (Stamford, CT), former U.S. sen. (I, CT), 2000 vice-pres. nominee (D).

Rush Limbaugh, b 1/12/1951 (Cape Girardeau, MO), radio talk-show host.

Shannon Lucid, b 1/14/1943 (Shanghai, China), NASA scientist, astronaut.

Loretta Lynch, b 5/21/1959 (Greensboro, NC), former U.S. atty. gen.

Rachel Maddow, b 4/1/1973 (Castro Valley, CA), TV/radio host, political commentator.

Bernie Madoff, b 4/29/1938 (Queens, NY), financier who swindled investors; sentenced to 150 years in prison.

Michelle Malkin, b 10/20/1980 (Philadelphia, PA), political commentator.

Rob Manfred, b 9/28/1958 (Rome, NY), MLB commissioner.

Chelsea (fmr. Bradley) Manning, b 12/17/1987 (Crescent, OK), Army pvt. convicted on espionage charges.

Susana Martinez, b 7/14/1959 (El Paso, TX), NM gov. (R).

Mary Matalin, b 8/19/1953 (Chicago, IL), political commentator.

Chris Matthews, b 12/17/1945 (Philadelphia, PA), TV journalist.

James Mattis, b 9/8/1950 (Pullman, WA), sec. of defense; U.S. Marine gen. (ret.).

Peter Max, b 10/19/1937 (Berlin, Germany), artist.

Marissa Mayer, b 5/30/1975 (Wausau, WI), former Yahoo! CEO.

Kevin McCarthy, b 1/26/1965 (Bakersfield, CA), U.S. rep. (R, CA), House majority leader.

Mitch McConnell, b 2/20/1942 (Tuscumbia, AL), U.S. sen. (R, KY) majority leader.

David McCullough, b 7/7/1933 (Pittsburgh, PA), historian, biographer.

Ronna Romney McDaniel, b 1973 (Austin, TX), Rep. Natl. Committee chair.

Dr. Phil McGraw, b 9/1/1950 (Vinita, OK), talk-show host, motivational speaker, author.

Lorne Michaels, b 11/17/44 (Toronto, ON, Canada), creator and producer of *Saturday Night Live*.

Kate Michelman, b 8/4/1942 (NJ), activist.

George Mitchell, b 8/20/1933, (Waterville, ME), former U.S. Sen. majority leader (D, ME), diplomat, Disney Co. chair.

Steven Mnuchin, b 12/21/1962 (New York, NY), Treasury sec.

Walter Mondale, b 1/5/1928 (Ceylon, MN), former vice-pres., U.S. sen. (D, MN), 1984 pres. nominee.

Michael Moore, b 4/23/1954 (Davison, MI), activist, documentary filmmaker, author.

Bill Moyers, b 6/5/1934 (Hugo, OK), TV journalist, author.

Robert S. Mueller III, b 8/7/1944 (New York, NY), special counsel investigating Russian interference in 2016 U.S. elections; former FBI director.

David Muir, b 11/8/1973 (Syracuse, NY), TV news anchor.

Rupert Murdoch, b 3/11/1931 (Melbourne, Vic., Austral.), media exec.

Bobby Murphy, b 7/19/1988 (Berkeley, CA), Snapchat cofounder.

Elon Musk, b 6/28/1971 (Pretoria, S. Afr.), SpaceX and Tesla CEO.

Satya Nadella, b 8/19/1967 (Hyderabad, India), Microsoft CEO.

Ralph Nader, b 2/27/1934 (Winsted, CT), consumer advocate, independent pres. cand. (1996, 2000, '04, '08).

Janet Napolitano, b 11/29/1957 (New York, NY), Univ. of Calif. pres.; former homeland security sec., AZ gov. (D).

Craig Newmark, b 12/6/1952 (Morristown, NJ), founder of Craigslist.com.

Peggy Noonan, b 9/7/1950 (Brooklyn, NY), columnist, speechwriter.

Oliver North, b 10/7/1943 (San Antonio, TX), NRA pres., former Natl. Sec. Council aide, figure in Iran-contra scandal.

Eleanor Holmes Norton, b 6/13/1937 (Washington, DC), DC delegate to U.S. House (D).

Barack Obama, b 8/4/1961 (Honolulu, HI), 44th U.S. president, former U.S. sen. (D, IL).

Michelle Obama, b 1/17/1964 (Chicago, IL), former first lady, lawyer.

Soledad O'Brien, b 9/19/1966 (Smithtown, NY), TV journalist.

Sandra Day O'Connor, b 3/26/1930 (El Paso, TX), former Supreme Court justice.

Keith Olbermann, b 1/27/1959 (New York, NY), political commentator, former ESPN/MSNBC host.

Todd Oldham, b 11/22/1961 (Corpus Christi, TX), fashion designer.

Martin O'Malley, b 1/18/63 (Bethesda, MD), former MD gov. (D); 2016 pres. contender.

Bill O'Reilly, b 9/10/1949 (New York, NY), TV personality.

Suze Orman, b 5/5/1951 (Chicago, IL), financial adviser; TV host.

Joel Osteen, b 3/5/1963 (Houston, TX), televangelist, author.

Michael Ovitz, b 12/14/1946 (Encino, CA), entertainment exec.

Clarence Page, b 6/2/1947 (Dayton, OH), journalist, TV commentator.

Lawrence Page, b 3/26/1973 (East Lansing, MI), cofounder of Google.

Camille Paglia, b 4/2/1947 (Endicott, NY), scholar, author.

Sarah Palin, b 2/11/1964 (Sandpoint, ID), former AK gov. (R), 2008 vice-pres. nominee.

Leon E. Panetta, b 6/28/1938 (Monterey, CA), former sec. of defense, CIA director, Obama chief of staff, U.S. rep. (D, CA).

Sean Parker, b 12/3/1979 (Herndon, VA), cofounder of Napster, Facebook.

George Pataki, b 6/24/1945 (Peekskill, NY), former NY gov. (R); 2016 pres. contender.

Rand Paul, b 1/7/1963 (Pittsburgh, PA), U.S. sen. (R, KY); 2016 pres. contender.

Ron Paul, b 8/20/1935 (Pittsburgh, PA), physician, former U.S. rep. (R, TX), pres. contender (2008, '12).

Jane Pauley, b 10/31/1950 (Indianapolis, IN), TV journalist.

Nancy Pelosi, b 3/26/1940 (Baltimore, MD), U.S. rep. (D, CA), House minority leader, former House speaker.

Karen Pence, b 1/1/1957 (Indianapolis, IN), wife of U.S. vice pres. Mike Pence.

Mike Pence, b 6/7/1959 (Columbus, IN), U.S. vice pres., former IN gov. (R).

Tom Perez, b 10/7/1961 (Buffalo, NY), Dem. Natl. Committee chair; former sec. of labor.

Ross Perot, b 6/27/1930 (Texarkana, TX), entrepreneur, independent and Reform pres. contender (1992, '96).

David Petraeus, b 11/7/1952 (Cornwall-on-Hudson, NY), former CIA director, U.S. Forces Afghanistan cmdr., CENTCOM cmdr.

Mike Pompeo, b 12/30/1963 (Orange, CA), sec. of state; former CIA director.

Colin Powell, b 4/5/1937 (New York, NY), former sec. of state, natl. security adviser, Joint Chiefs of Staff chair.

Reince Priebus, b 3/18/1972 (Kenosha, WI), former White House chief of staff, Rep. Natl. Committee chair.

Scott Pruitt, b 5/9/1968 (Danville, KY), former EPA admin.

Dan Quayle, b 2/4/1947 (Indianapolis, IN), former U.S. vice pres., U.S. sen. (R, IN).

Anna Quindlen, b 7/8/1953 (Philadelphia, PA), author, columnist.

Martha Raddatz, b 1953 (Idaho Falls, ID), TV journalist.

Jorge Ramos, b 3/15/1958 (Mexico City, Mex.), TV journalist.

Dan Rather, b 10/31/1931 (Wharton, TX), TV journalist, retired anchor.

Sumner Redstone, b 5/27/1923 (Boston, MA), media executive.

Ralph Reed Jr., b 6/24/1961 (Portsmouth, VA), political adviser.

Robert B. Reich, b 6/24/1946 (Scranton, PA), economist, author, former labor sec.

Harry Reid, b 12/2/1939 (Searchlight, NV), former U.S. Sen. minority leader (D, NV).

Condoleezza Rice, b 11/14/1954 (Birmingham, AL), former sec. of state, natl. security adviser.

Frank Rich, b 6/2/1949 (Washington, DC), essayist, columnist.

Cecile Richards, b 7/15/1957 (Waco, TX), former pres. of Planned Parenthood.

Geraldo Rivera, b 7/4/1943 (New York, NY), TV journalist.

Cokie Roberts, b 12/27/1943 (New Orleans, LA), TV journalist.

John G. Roberts, b 1/27/1955 (Buffalo, NY), U.S. Supreme Court chief justice.

Robin Roberts, b 11/23/1960 (Tuskegee, AL), *Good Morning America* co-host.

Pat Robertson, b 3/22/1930 (Lexington, VA), religious broadcasting exec., former pres. contender (R).

Eugene Robinson, b 3/12/1954 (Orangeburg, SC), columnist.

V. Gene Robinson, b 5/29/1947 (Lexington, KY), first openly gay Episcopal bishop (retired).

Al Roker, b 8/20/1954 (Queens, NY), TV weather person.

Mitt Romney, b 3/12/1947 (Detroit, MI), 2012 pres. nominee, former MA gov. (R).

Charlie Rose, b 1/5/1942 (Henderson, NC), TV journalist.

Rod Rosenstein, b 1/13/65 (Philadelphia, PA), U.S. deputy atty. gen.

Karl Rove, b 12/25/1950 (Denver, CO), former adviser to Pres. G. W. Bush, political commentator.

Marco Rubio, b 5/28/1971 (Miami, FL), U.S. sen. (R, FL), 2016 pres. contender.

Donald Rumsfeld, b 7/9/1932 (Chicago, IL), former sec. of defense.

Edward Ruscha, b 12/16/1937 (Omaha, NE), artist.

Paul Ryan, b 1/29/1970 (Janesville, WI), 2012 vice-pres. nominee, U.S. rep. (R, WI) and speaker of the House.

Sheryl Sandberg, b 8/28/1969 (Washington, DC), Facebook exec.; author.

Bernie Sanders, b 9/8/1941 (New York, NY), U.S. sen. (I, VT); 2016 Dem. pres. contender.

Sarah Huckabee Sanders, b 8/13/1982 (Hope, AR), White House press sec.

Diane Sawyer, b 12/22/1945 (Glasgow, KY), TV journalist.

Stephen Scalise, b 10/6/1965 (New Orleans, LA), U.S. rep. (R, LA), House majority whip.

Bob Schieffer, b 2/25/1937 (Austin, TX), TV journalist.

Caroline Kennedy Schlossberg, b 11/27/1957 (New York, NY), author, daughter of Pres. Kennedy.

Eric Schmidt, b 4/27/1955 (Washington, DC), former Google CEO.

Charles Schumer, b 11/23/1950 (Brooklyn, NY), U.S. Sen. minority leader (D, NY).

Arnold Schwarzenegger, b 7/30/1947 (Thal, Styria, Austria), actor, former CA gov. (R).

Willard Scott, b 3/7/1934 (Alexandria, VA), former TV weather person.

Richard Serra, b 11/2/1939 (San Francisco, CA), sculptor.

Jeff Sessions, b 12/24/1946 (Selma, AL), U.S. atty. gen., former U.S. sen. (R, AL).

Al Sharpton, b 10/3/1954 (Brooklyn, NY), activist, civil rights leader, TV personality.

Will Shortz, b 8/26/1952 (Crawfordsville, IN), puzzle editor.

Maria Shriver, b 11/6/1955 (Chicago, IL), TV journalist, former CA first lady.

George P. Shultz, b 12/13/1920 (New York, NY), economist; former sec. of state.

Michelangelo Signorile, b 12/19/1960 (Brooklyn, NY), journalist, author.

Adam Silver, b 4/25/1962 (Rye, NY), NBA commissioner.

Nate Silver, b 1/13/1978 (E. Lansing, MI), statistician.

Russell Simmons, b 10/4/1957 (Queens, NY), music producer.

O. J. Simpson, b 7/9/1947 (San Francisco, CA), former NFL star, murder defendant.

Harry Smith, b 8/21/1951 (Lansing, IL), TV journalist.

Edward Snowden, b 6/21/1983 (Elizabeth City, NC), computer specialist accused of leaking classified information about U.S. and UK govt. surveillance.

George Soros, b 8/12/1930 (Budapest, Hung.), financier, philanthropist.

Sonia Sotomayor, b 6/25/1954 (Bronx, NY), U.S. Supreme Court justice.

Sean Spicer, b 9/23/1971 (Manhasset, NY), former Trump White House press sec.

Evan Spiegel, b 6/4/1990 (Los Angeles, CA), Snapchat cofounder.

Steven Spielberg, b 12/18/1946 (Cincinnati, OH), movie director, producer.

Eliot Spitzer, b 6/10/1959 (Bronx, NY), former NY gov. (D); resigned after involvement with prostitutes exposed.

Lesley Stahl, b 12/16/1941 (Swampscott, MA), TV journalist.

Shelby Steele, b 1/1/1946 (Chicago, IL), scholar, critic.

Ben Stein, b 11/25/1944 (Washington, DC), attorney, columnist, TV personality.

Gloria Steinem, b 3/25/1934 (Toledo, OH), author, feminist.

Frank Stella, b 5/12/1936 (Malden, MA), painter.

George Stephanopoulos, b 2/10/1961 (Fall River, MA), TV journalist, *Good Morning America* co-host; former pres. adviser.

Howard Stern, b 1/12/1954 (Jackson Heights, NY), radio host.

John Paul Stevens, b 4/20/1920 (Chicago, IL), former U.S. Supreme Court justice.

Martha Stewart, b 8/3/1941 (Nutley, NJ), homemaking adviser, entrepreneur, TV personality.

Biz Stone, b 3/10/1974 (Boston, MA), cofounder of Twitter.

Roger Stone, b 8/27/1952 (Norwalk, CT), political consultant.

Chesley Sullenberger III, b 1/23/1951 (Denison, TX), pilot who safely landed a passenger jet in the Hudson River.

Andrew Sullivan, b 8/10/1963 (S. Godstone, Eng., UK), political commentator.

A(rthur) G(regg) Sulzberger, b 8/5/1980 (Washington, DC), *NY Times* publisher

Arthur Ochs Sulzberger Jr., b 9/22/1951 (Mt. Kisco, NY), NY Times Co. chairman.

Lawrence H. Summers, b 11/30/1954 (New Haven, CT), economist; former Natl. Economic Council dir., Harvard Univ. pres., sec. of treasury.

Jake Tapper, b 3/12/1969 (New York, NY), TV journalist.

George Tenet, b 1/5/1953 (Flushing, Queens, NY), former CIA director.

Clarence Thomas, b 6/23/1948 (Savannah, GA), U.S. Supreme Court justice.

Rex Tillerson, b 3/23/1952 (Wichita Falls, KS), former sec. of state, ExxonMobil CEO.

Joseph Tobin, b 5/3/1952 (Detroit, MI), Rom. Cath. cardinal, archbishop of Newark, NJ.

Chuck Todd, b 4/8/1972 (Miami, FL), TV journalist, *Meet the Press* moderator.

Richard Trumka, b 7/24/1949 (Waynesburg, PA), pres. of AFL-CIO.

Donald Trump, b 6/14/1946 (Jamaica, Queens, NY), 45th U.S. president; real estate exec., TV personality.

Ivanka Trump, b 10/30/1981 (New York, NY), daughter of and adviser to Pres. Trump.

Melania Trump, b 4/26/1970 (Novo Mesto, [now] Slovenia), first lady; former model.

Ted Turner, b 11/19/1938 (Cincinnati, OH), TV exec., philanthropist.

Neil deGrasse Tyson, b 10/5/1958 (New York, NY), astrophysicist, director of NYC's Hayden Planetarium, author, TV host.

Hamdi Ulukaya, b 10/26/1972 (Erzincan, Turkey), Chobani CEO.

Urvashi Vaid, b 10/8/1958 (New Delhi, India), LGBT rights activist.

Gloria Vanderbilt, b 2/20/1924 (New York, NY), fashion designer, heiress.

Greta Van Susteren, b 6/11/1954 (Appleton, WI), attorney, TV journalist.

Jesse Ventura, b 7/15/1951 (Minneapolis, MN), former wrestler, MN gov. (I).

Meredith Vieira, b 12/30/1953 (Providence, RI), TV journalist/host.

Paul Volcker, b 9/5/1927 (Cape May, NJ), economist, former Federal Reserve chair.

Diane von Fürstenberg, b 12/31/1946 (Brussels, Belgium), fashion designer.

Jimmy Wales, b 8/8/1966 (Huntsville, AL), cofounder of Wikipedia.

Scott Walker, b 11/2/1967 (Colorado Springs, CO), WI gov. (R), 2016 pres. contender.

Barbara Walters, b 9/25/1929 (Boston, MA), TV journalist.

Alexander Wang, b 5/17/1984 (San Francisco, CA), fashion designer.

Vera Wang, b 6/27/1949 (New York, NY), fashion designer.

Elizabeth Warren, b 6/22/1949 (Oklahoma City, OK), U.S. sen. (D, MA).

Rick Warren, b 1/28/1954 (San Jose, CA), evangelical Christian pastor, founder of Saddleback Church, author.

Maxine Waters, b 8/15/1938 (St. Louis, MO), U.S. rep. (D, CA).

James Watson, b 4/6/1928 (Chicago, IL), biochemist, DNA pioneer, co-winner of the 1962 Nobel Prize in Physiology/Medicine.

Andrew Weil, b 6/8/1942 (Philadelphia, PA), health adviser.

Harvey Weinstein, b 3/19/1952 (Flushing, Queens, NY), movie exec.

Jack Welch, b 11/19/1935 (Peabody, MA), former General Electric CEO.

Leana Wen, b 1/27/1988 (Shanghai, China), pres. of Planned Parenthood.

Jann Wenner, b 1/7/1946 (New York, NY), founder of *Rolling Stone*.

Cornel West, b 6/23/1953 (Tulsa, OK), academic, critic.

Ruth Westheimer, b 6/4/1928 (Frankfurt am Main, Germany), human sexuality expert.

Meg Whitman, b 8/4/1956 (Cold Spring Harbor, NY), former eBay, HPE CEO.

Kehinde Wiley, b 2/28/1977 (Los Angeles, CA), artist.

George Will, b 5/4/1941 (Champaign, IL), journalist, author.

Brian Williams, b 5/5/1959 (Ridgewood, NJ), TV journalist.

Evan Williams, b 3/31/1972 (Clarks, NE), Twitter cofounder.

Jody Williams, b 10/9/1950 (Brattleboro, VT), peace activist, 1997 Nobel Peace Prize winner.

Oprah Winfrey, b 1/29/1954 (Kosciusko, MS), TV and media personality, entrepreneur, actress.

Anna Wintour, b 11/3/1949 (London, Eng., UK), *Vogue* editor.

Susan Wojcicki, b 7/5/1968 (Santa Clara, CA), CEO of YouTube.

Judy Woodruff, b 11/20/1946 (Tulsa, OK), TV journalist.

Bob Woodward, b 3/26/1943 (Geneva, IL), journalist; with Carl Bernstein cracked Watergate scandal.

Steve Wozniak, b 8/11/1950 (Sunnyvale, CA), inventor, cofounder of Apple.

Steve Wynn, b 1/27/1942 (New Haven, CT), casino developer.

Chuck Yeager, b 2/13/1923 (Myra, WV), test pilot, first to break sound barrier.

Janet Yellen, b 8/13/1946 (New York, NY), former Federal Reserve chair.

Mark Zuckerberg, b 5/14/1984 (Dobbs Ferry, NY), founder of Facebook.

Mortimer Zuckerman, b 6/4/1937 (Montréal, QC, Can.), publisher, columnist.

Widely Known World Personalities of the Present

Living non-Americans only. Generally excludes current heads of state or government (see Nations of the World) and excludes most others covered elsewhere, such as in Widely Known Americans, Writers, and Entertainment or Sports Personalities.

Mahmoud Abbas (Abu Mazen), b 3/26/1935 (Safed, Palestine [now Israel]), president of the Palestinian National Authority.

Gerry Adams, b 10/6/1948 (Belfast, N. Ireland, UK), Sinn Fein leader.

Mahmoud Ahmadinejad, b 10/28/1956 (Garmsar, Iran), former Iranian pres.

Ai Weiwei, b 1957 (Beijing, China), visual artist, activist.

Albert II, b 6/6/1934 (Brussels, Belgium), former king of Belgium (1993-2013).

Prince Andrew (Duke of York), b 2/19/1960 (London, Eng., UK), second son of Queen Elizabeth II.

Princess Anne (Princess Royal), b 8/15/1950 (London, Eng., UK), daughter of Queen Elizabeth II.

Oscar Arias Sánchez, b 9/13/1941 (Heredia, Costa Rica), former Costa Rican pres., 1987 Nobel Peace Prize laureate.

Giorgio Armani, b 7/30/1934 (Piacenza, Italy), fashion designer.

Hanan Ashrawi, b 10/8/1946 (Nablus, Israel), Palestinian activist.

Julian Assange, b 7/3/1971 (Townsville, Qld., Austral.), founder of WikiLeaks media org.

Ban Ki-moon, b 6/13/1944 (Umsong, [now] South Korea), former UN sec.-gen.

Ehud Barak, b 2/12/1942 (Mishmar HaSharon Kibbutz, Israel), former Israeli min. of defense, prime min.

Beatrix, b 1/31/1938 (Baarn, Netherlands), former Dutch queen (2013-2013).

Jocelyn Bell Burnell, b 7/15/1943 (Belfast, N. Ire.), astrophysicist.

Benedict XVI (Joseph Ratzinger), b 4/16/1927 (Marktl am Inn, Germany), pope emeritus of Rom. Cath. Church, elected 2005, resigned 2013.

Tim Berners-Lee, b 6/8/1955 (London, Eng., UK), World Wide Web inventor.

Tony Blair, b 5/6/1953 (Edinburgh, Scot., UK), former British prime min.

Hans Blix, b 6/28/1928 (Uppsala, Swed.), former UN weapons inspector.

Bono (Paul David Hewson), b 5/20/1960 (Glasnevin, Dublin, Ire.), musician, social activist, philanthropist.

Fernando Botero, b 4/19/1932 (Medellín, Colombia), artist.

Richard Branson, b 7/18/1950 (S. London, Eng., UK), British Virgin Records and Airways founder.

Gordon Brown, b 2/20/1951 (Glasgow, Scot., UK), former British prime min.

Tina Brown, b 11/21/1953 (Maidenhead, Eng., UK), journalist, author.

Gisele Bündchen, b 7/20/1980 (Horizontina, Rio Grande do Sul, Braz.), model.

Mark Burnett, b 7/17/1960 (Myland, Eng., UK), reality TV producer.

Rhonda Byrne, b 3/12/1951 (Australia), author, TV writer and producer.

David Cameron, b 10/9/1966 (London, Eng., UK), former British prime min.

Kim Campbell, b 3/10/1947 (Port Alberni, BC, Can.), former Canadian prime min.

Pierre Cardin, b 7/7/1922 (San Biaggio di Callalta, Italy), fashion designer.

Magnus Carlsen, b 11/30/1990 (Tonsberg, Norway), world chess champion.

Princess Caroline, b 1/23/1957 (Monte Carlo, Monaco), Monaco royal (eldest daughter of Prince Rainier and Princess Grace).

Raúl Castro Ruz, b 6/3/1931 (Birán, Cuba), former pres. of Cuba.

Catherine (Kate) Middleton (Duchess of Cambridge), b 1/9/1982 (Reading, Eng., UK), wife of Prince William.

Prince Charles (of Wales), b 11/14/1948 (London, Eng., UK), eldest son of Queen Elizabeth II; heir to British throne.

Princess Charlotte Elizabeth Diana (of Cambridge), b 5/2/2015 (London, Eng.,

UK), daughter of Prince William and Catherine.

Chen Guangcheng, b 11/12/1971 (Dongshigu, China), civil rights activist.

Yao Chen, b 10/5/1979 (Nanping, Fujian, China), actress, microblogger.

Jacques Chirac, b 11/29/1932 (Paris, France), former French pres.

Deepak Chopra, b 1946 (New Delhi, India), writer, alternative medicine advocate.

Jean Chrétien, b 1/11/1934 (Shawinigan, QC, Can.), former Canadian prime min.

Christo (Javacheff), b 6/13/1935 (Gabrovo, Bulg.), artist.

Joe (Charles Joseph) Clark, b 6/5/1939 (High River, AB, Can.), former Canadian prime min.

King Constantine II, b 6/2/1940 (Psychiko, Greece), former king of Greece.

Simon Cowell, b 10/7/1959 (Brighton, East Sussex, Eng., UK), music exec., TV producer, former *American Idol* host.

Dalai Lama, 14th (Tenzin Gyatso), b 7/6/1935 (Taktser, Amdo, Tibet), Buddhist leader; 1989 Nobel Peace Prize winner.

Richard Dawkins, b 3/26/1941 (Nairobi, Kenya), ethologist, evolutionary biologist, author.

F. W. (Frederik Willem) de Klerk, b 3/18/1936 (Johannesburg, S. Afr.), former S. African pres.; 1993 Nobel Peace Prize winner.

Mario Draghi, b 9/3/1947 (Rome, Italy), European Central Bank pres.

Shirin Ebadi, b 6/21/1947 (Hamadan, Iran), human rights activist, 2003 Nobel Peace Prize winner.

Prince Edward (Earl of Essex), b 3/10/1964 (London, Eng., UK), third son of Queen Elizabeth II.

Daniel Ek, b 2/21/1983 (Stockholm, Sweden), Spotify cofounder/CEO.

Mohamed ElBaradei, b 6/17/1942 (Cairo, Egypt), former director general of the International Atomic Energy Agency (IAEA); 2005 Nobel Peace Prize winner.

Sarah Ferguson, b 10/15/1958 (London, Eng., UK), Duchess of York, ex-wife of Prince Andrew.

Francis (Jorge Mario Bergoglio), b 12/17/1936 (Buenos Aires, Argentina), pope of Rom. Cath. Church.

John Galliano, b 11/28/1960 (Gibraltar, UK), fashion designer.

Prince George Alexander Louis (of Cambridge), b 7/22/2013 (London, Eng., UK), son of Prince William and Catherine.

Wael Ghonim, b 12/23/1980 (Cairo, Egypt), computer engineer and internet activist.

Valery Giscard d'Estaing, b 2/2/1926 (Koblenz, Ger.), former French pres.

Jane Goodall, b 4/3/1934 (London, Eng., UK), anthropologist, primatologist.

Mikhail Gorbachev, b 3/2/1931 (Privolnoye, USSR), former Soviet pres.; 1990 Nobel Peace Prize winner.

António Guterres, b 4/30/1949 (Lisbon, Portugal), UN sec.-gen.

Jürgen Habermas, b 6/18/1929 (Dusseldorf, Ger.), philosopher.

Stephen Harper, b 4/30/1959 (Toronto, ON, Can.), former Canadian prime min.

Prince Henry (Harry) (Duke of Sussex), b 9/15/1984 (London, Eng., UK), son of Prince Charles and Diana.

Damien Hirst, b 6/7/1965 (Bristol, Eng., UK), artist.

David Hockney, b 7/9/1937 (Bradford, Eng., UK), artist.

Hu Jintao, b 12/21/1942 (Shanghai, China), former pres. of China.

Jiang Zemin, b 8/17/1926 (Yangzhou, Jiangsu Prov., China), former pres. of China.

Boris Johnson, b 6/19/1964 (New York, NY), former British foreign minister.

Juan Carlos I, b 1/5/1938 (Rome, Italy), former king of Spain (1975-2014).

Hamid Karzai, b 12/24/1957 (Kandahar, Afghanistan), former pres. of Afghanistan.

Garry Kasparov, b 4/13/1963 (Baku, Azerbaijan, USSR), former world chess champion; Russian pro-democracy leader.

Ayatollah Ali Khamenei, b 7/17/1939 (Mashhad, Iran), Supreme Leader, cleric; former president of Iran.

Hans Küng, b 3/19/1928 (Sursee, Switz.), Rom. Cath. theologian.

Christine Lagarde, b 1/1/1956 (Paris, Fr.), Intl. Monetary Fund managing dir.

Karl Lagerfeld, b 9/10/1938 (Hamburg, Ger.), fashion designer.

Richard Leakey, b 12/19/1944 (Nairobi, Kenya), anthropologist, paleontologist, conservationist.

Jean-Marie Le Pen, b 6/20/1928 (La Trinité-sur-Mer, Fr.), French right-wing politician.

Marine Le Pen, b 8/5/1968 (Neuilly-sur-Seine, Fr.), head of France's National Front.

Tzipi Livni, b 7/5/1958 (Tel Aviv, Isr.), attorney, Israeli politician.

Prince Louis Arthur Charles (of Cambridge), b 4/23/2018 (London, Eng., UK), son of Prince William and Catherine.

John Major, b 3/29/1943 (Wimbledon, Eng., UK), former British prime min.

Nouri al-Malaki, b 7/1/1950 (Iraq), former prime min. of Iraq.

Imelda Marcos, b 7/2/1929 (Manila, Philip.), former first lady of the Philippines.

Meghan Markle (Duchess of Sussex), b 8/4/1981 (Los Angeles, CA), wife of Prince Harry, actress.

Paul Martin, b 8/28/1938 (Windsor, ON, Can.), former prime min. of Canada.

Stella McCartney, b 9/13/1971 (London, Eng., UK), fashion designer.

Rigoberta Menchú, b 1959 (Aldea Chimel, Guatemala), human rights activist, 1992 Nobel Peace Prize winner.

Angela Merkel, b 7/17/1954 (Hamburg, Ger.), first woman chancellor of Germany.

Jean-Marie Messier, b 12/13/1956 (Grenoble, Fr.), former CEO of Vivendi Universal.

Empress Michiko, b 10/20/1934 (Tokyo, Japan), empress of Japan.

Mohammed Morsi, b 8/8/1951 (Edwa, Egypt), first democratically elected pres. of Egypt; deposed July 2013.

Kate Moss, b 1/16/1974 (Addiscombe, Surrey, Eng., UK), model.

Hosni Mubarak, b 5/4/1928 (Kafre al-Musailha, Egypt), deposed Egyptian president.

Brian Mulroney, b 3/20/1939 (Baie-Comeau, QC, Can.), former Canadian prime min.

Renhō Murata, b 11/28/1968 (Tokyo, Japan), first woman leader of Japan's Democratic Party.

Prince Naruhito, b 2/23/1960 (Tokyo, Japan), crown prince of Japan.

Hassan Nasrallah, b 8/31/1960 (Qarantina, Lebanon), sec.-gen. of Hezbollah.

Queen Noor (Lisa Halaby), b 8/23/1951 (Washington, DC), American-born widow of Jordan's King Hussein.

Ehud Olmert, b 9/30/1945 (Binyamina, Palestine), former prime min. of Israel.

Daniel Ortega Saavedra, b 11/11/1945 (La Libertad, Nicar.), Nicaraguan pres., Sandinista leader.

Camilla Parker-Bowles (Duchess of Cornwall), b 7/17/1947 (London, Eng., UK), wife of Prince Charles.

Javier Pérez de Cuéllar, b 1/19/1920 (Lima, Peru), former UN sec.-gen.

Prince Philip (Duke of Edinburgh), b 6/10/1921 (Corfu, Greece), husband of Queen Elizabeth II.

Gerhard Richter, b 2/9/1932 (Dresden, Ger.), artist.

Mary Robinson, b 5/21/1944 (Ballina, Co. Mayo, Ire.), former Irish pres., former UN High Commissioner for Human Rights.

Arundhati Roy, b 11/24/1961 (Shillong, Meghalaya, India), author, political activist.

Ségolène Royal, b 9/22/1953 (Dakar, Senegal), French socialist politician.

Muqtada al-Sadr, b 8/12/1973? (Najaf, Iraq), extremist Shiite cleric.

Mohammad bin Salman, b 8/31/1985 (Riyadh, Saudi Arabia), Saudi crown prince.

Nicolas Sarkozy, b 1/28/1955 (Paris, France), former French pres.

Gerhard Schröder, b 4/7/1944 (Mossenburg, Ger.), former German chancellor.

Ayatollah Ali al-Sistani, b 8/4/1930 (Mashhad, Iran), major Iraqi Shiite religious leader.

Carlos Slim Helú, b 1/28/1940 (Mexico City, Mex.), founder of Grupo Carso; former chair of Telmex, América Móvil.

Princess Stephanie, b 2/1/1965 (Monte Carlo, Monaco), youngest child of Prince Rainier and Princess Grace.

Dominique Strauss-Kahn, b 4/25/1949 (Neuilly-sur-Seine, France), former Intl. Monetary Fund managing dir.

Aung San Suu Kyi, b 6/19/1945 (Rangoon, Myanmar), political activist, 1991 Nobel Peace Prize winner; de facto Myanmar govt. leader.

Valentina Tereshkova, b 3/6/1937 (Maslennikovo, Russia, USSR), first woman in space.

John Napier Turner, b 6/7/1929 (Richmond, Surrey, Eng., UK), former Canadian prime min.

Desmond Tutu, b 10/7/1931 (Klerksdorp, Transvaal, S. Afr.), former S. African archbishop; 1984 Nobel Peace Prize winner.

Lech Walesa, b 9/29/1943 (Popowo, Pol.), Solidarity leader, former pres. of Poland; 1983 Nobel Peace Prize winner.

Justin Welby, b 1/6/1956 (London, Eng., UK), archbishop of Canterbury.

Prince William (Duke of Cambridge), b 6/21/1982 (London, Eng., UK), eldest son of Prince Charles and Diana; 2nd in line to British throne.

Betty Williams, b 5/22/1944 (Belfast, N. Ire.), civil rights activist, 1977 Nobel Peace Prize winner.

Rowan Williams, b 6/14/1950 (Ystradgynlais, Wales, UK), former archbishop of Canterbury.

Malala Yousafzai, b 7/12/1997 (Mingora, Pakistan), activist for girls' education, 2014 Nobel Peace Prize winner.

Muhammad Yunus, b 6/28/1940 (Chittagong, Bangladesh), economist, 2006 Nobel Peace Prize winner.

Mohammad Javad Zarif, b 1/8/1960 (Tehran, Iran), Irani minister of foreign affairs.

Ayman al-Zawahiri, b 6/19/1951 (Cairo, Egypt), reputed high-ranking al-Qaeda leader.

Architects

Alvar Aalto, 1898-1976, Säynätsalo Town Hall, Vuoksenniska Church, Finland.

Max Abramovitz, 1908-2004, Avery Fisher Hall, New York, NY; U.S. Steel Tower (Bldg.), Pittsburgh, PA.

Tadao Ando, b 1941, Modern Art Museum, Ft. Worth, TX; Stone Hill Center, MA.

Michael Arad, b 1969, Natl. 9/11 Memorial, New York, NY.

Henry Bacon, 1866-1924, Lincoln Memorial, Washington, DC.

Benjamin Banneker, 1731-1806, African-American inventor, astronomer, mathematician; helped design and lay out Washington, DC.

Pietro Belluschi, 1899-1994, Juilliard School, Lincoln Center, Pan Am Bldg. (now MetLife Bldg.) with Walter Gropius, New York, NY.

Marcel Breuer, 1902-81, Whitney Museum of American Art [now Met Breuer] (with Hamilton Smith), New York, NY.

Filippo Brunelleschi, 1377-1446, Santa Maria del Fiore Cathedral, Florence, Italy.

Charles Bulfinch, 1763-1844, State House, Boston, MA; Capitol (part), Wash., DC.

Gordon Bunshaft, 1909-90, Lever House, New York, NY; Hirshhorn Museum, Washington, DC.

Daniel H. Burnham, 1846-1912, Union Station, Washington, DC; Flatiron Bldg., New York, NY.

Irwin Chanin, 1892-1988, theaters, skyscrapers, New York, NY.

David Childs, b 1941, Washington Mall Master Plan/Constitution Gardens, Washington, DC; One World Trade Center, New York, NY.

Lucio Costa, 1902-98, master plan for city of Brasilia, Brazil (with Oscar Niemeyer).

Ralph Adams Cram, 1863-1942, Cath. of St. John the Divine, New York, NY; U.S. Military Acad. (part), West Point, NY.

Norman Foster, b 1935, Commerzbank Headquarters, Frankfurt-am-Main, Ger.;

London Millennium Bridge, 30 St. Mary Axe ("The Gherkin"), London, Eng., UK.

James Ingo Freed, 1930-2005, Holocaust Memorial Museum, Washington, DC; Jacob K. Javits Center, New York, NY.

R. Buckminster Fuller, 1895-1983, U.S. Pavilion (geodesic domes), Expo 67, Montréal, QC, Can.

Antoni Gaudí, 1852-1926, Basilica and Expiatory Temple of the Sagrada Familia, Barcelona, Spain.

Frank O. Gehry, b 1929, Guggenheim Museum, Bilbao, Spain; Walt Disney Concert Hall, Los Angeles, CA.

Cass Gilbert, 1859-1934, Custom House, Woolworth Bldg., New York, NY; Supreme Court Bldg., Washington, DC.

Bertram G. Goodhue, 1869-1924, Capitol, Lincoln, NE; St. Thomas's Church, St. Bartholomew's Church, New York, NY.

Michael Graves, 1934-2015, Portland Bldg., Portland, OR; Humana Bldg., Louisville, KY.

Walter Gropius, 1883-1969, Pan Am Bldg. (now MetLife Bldg.) (with Pietro Belluschi), New York, NY.

Zaha Hadid, 1950-2016, Rosenthal Center for Contemporary Art, Cincinnati, OH; London Aquatics Centre, Eng., UK.

Lawrence Halprin, 1916-2009, Ghirardelli Sq., San Francisco, CA; Nicollet Mall, Minneapolis, MN; FDR Memorial, Wash., DC.

Peter Harrison, 1716-75, Touro Synagogue, Redwood Library, Newport, RI.

Wallace K. Harrison, 1895-1981, Metropolitan Opera House, Lincoln Center, New York, NY.

Thomas Hastings, 1860-1929, NY Public Library (with John Carrère), Frick Mansion, New York, NY.

James Hoban, 1762-1831, White House, Washington, DC.

Raymond Hood, 1881-1934, Rockefeller Center (part), Daily News Bldg., New York, NY; Tribune Tower, Chicago, IL.

Richard M. Hunt, 1827-95, Metropolitan Museum (part), New York, NY; Biltmore Estate, Asheville, NC.

Toyo Ito, b 1941, Sendai Mediatheque, Sendai, Japan; Tower of Winds, Yokohama, Japan.

Helmut Jahn, b 1940, United Airlines Terminal, O'Hare Airport, Chicago, IL.

William Le Baron Jenney, 1832-1907, Home Insurance Bldg. (demolished 1931), Chicago, IL.

Philip C. Johnson, 1906-2005, AT&T Bldg. (now 550 Madison Ave.), New York, NY; Transco (now Williams) Tower, Houston, TX.

Albert Kahn, 1869-1942, General Motors Bldg. (now Cadillac Place), Detroit, MI.

Louis Kahn, 1901-74, Salk Laboratory, La Jolla, CA; Yale Art Gallery, New Haven, CT.

Rem Koolhaas, b 1944, Seattle Central Library, Seattle, WA.

Christopher Grant LaFarge, 1862-1938, Roman Catholic Chapel, West Point, NY.

Benjamin H. Latrobe, 1764-1820, Capitol (part), Washington, DC; State Capitol Bldg., Richmond, VA.

Le Corbusier (Charles-Edouard Jeanneret), 1887-1965, Salvation Army Hostel, Swiss Dormitory, Paris, France; master plan for cities of Algiers and Buenos Aires.

William Lescaze, 1896-1969, Philadelphia Savings Fund Society, PA; Borg-Warner Bldg., Chicago, IL.

Daniel Libeskind, b 1946, developed master plan for the rebuilding of World Trade Center site, New York, NY.

Maya Lin, b 1959, Vietnam Veterans Mem., Washington, DC.

Charles Rennie Mackintosh, 1868-1928, Glasgow School of Art; Hill House, Helensburgh, Scot., UK.

Bernard R. Maybeck, 1862-1957, Hearst Hall, Univ. of CA, Berkeley; First Church of Christ Scientist, Berkeley, CA.

Charles F. McKim, 1847-1909, Boston Public Library; Columbia Univ. (part), New York, NY.

Charles M. McKim, 1920-2017, KUHT-TV Transmitter Bldg., Lutheran Church of the Redeemer, Houston, TX.

Richard Meier, b 1934, Getty Center, Los Angeles, CA; High Museum of Art, Atlanta, GA.

Ludwig Mies van der Rohe, 1886-1969, Seagram Bldg. (with Philip C. Johnson), New York, NY; National Gallery, Berlin, Ger.

Robert Mills, 1781-1855, Washington Monument, Washington, DC.

Charles Moore, 1925-93, Sea Ranch, nr. San Francisco, CA; Piazza d'Italia, New Orleans, LA.

Julia Morgan, 1872-1957, Hearst Castle, San Simeon, CA.

John Nash, 1752-1835, Buckingham Palace, London, Eng., UK.

Richard J. Neutra, 1892-1970, Orange Co. Courthouse, Santa Ana, CA.

Oscar Niemeyer, 1907-2012, government buildings, Brasilia Palace Hotel, Brasilia, Braz.

Gyo Obata, b 1923, Natl. Air and Space Museum, Smithsonian Inst., Washington, DC; Dallas-Ft. Worth Airport, TX.

Frederick L. Olmsted, 1822-1903, Central Park, New York, NY; Fairmount Park, Philadelphia, PA.

I(eoh) M(ing) Pei, b 1917, East Wing, Natl. Gallery of Art, Washington, DC; Pyramid, The Louvre, Paris, Fr.; Rock & Roll Hall of Fame and Museum, Cleveland, OH.

Cesar Pelli, b 1926, World Financial Center, Carnegie Hall Tower, New York, NY; Petronas Twin Towers, Malaysia.

William Pereira, 1909-85, Cape Canaveral, FL; Transamerica Pyramid, San Francisco.

Renzo Piano, b 1937, Pompidou Centre, Paris, Fr.; New York Times Bldg., New York, NY; The Shard, London, Eng., UK.

John Russell Pope, 1874-1937, National Gallery, Jefferson Memorial, Wash., DC.

John Portman, 1924-2017, Peachtree Center, Atlanta, GA.

George Browne Post, 1837-1913, NY Stock Exchange, New York, NY; Capitol, Madison, WI.

James Renwick Jr., 1818-95, Grace Church, St. Patrick's Cathedral, New York, NY; Smithsonian Institution (Castle), Washington, DC.

Henry H. Richardson, 1838-86, Trinity Church, Boston, MA.

Kevin Roche, b 1922, Oakland Museum, Oakland, CA; Fine Arts Center, Univ. of Massachusetts, Amherst, MA.

James Gamble Rogers, 1867-1947, Columbia-Presbyterian Medical Ctr., New York, NY; Northwestern Univ., Evanston, IL.

John Wellborn Root, 1887-1963, Palmolive Bldg., Chicago, IL; Hotel Statler (now Capital Hilton), Washington, DC.

Paul Rudolph, 1918-97, Jewitt Art Center, Wellesley College, MA; Art & Architecture Bldg., Yale Univ., New Haven, CT.

Eero Saarinen, 1910-61, Gateway to the West Arch, St. Louis, MO; TWA Flight Center, JFK Airport, New York, NY.

Kazuyo Sejima, b 1956, 21st Century Museum of Contemporary Art (with Ryue Nishizawa), Kanazawa, Japan.

Kodja Mimar Sinan, 1489-1588, chief court architect of Ottoman dynasty.

Louis Skidmore, 1897-1962, Atomic Energy Commission town site, Oak Ridge, TN; Terrace Plaza Hotel, Cincinnati, OH.

Norma Merrick Sklarek, 1928-2012, Terminal One, Los Angeles International Airport, CA.

Clarence S. Stein, 1882-1975, Temple Emanu-El, New York, NY.

Edward Durell Stone, 1902-78, interior of Radio City Music Hall, Museum of Modern Art, New York, NY.

Louis H. Sullivan, 1856-1924, Auditorium Bldg., Chicago, IL.

Kenzo Tange, 1913-2005, Hiroshima Peace Park, 1964 Tokyo Olympic stadiums, Japan.

Richard Upjohn, 1802-78, Trinity Church, New York, NY.

Max O. Urbahn, 1912-95, Vehicle Assembly Bldg., Cape Canaveral, FL.

Joern Utzon, 1918-2008, Sydney Opera House, NSW, Australia.

William Van Alen, 1883-1954, Chrysler Building, New York, NY.

Robert Venturi, 1925-2018, Gordon Wu Hall, Princeton, NJ; Mielparque Nikko Kirifuri Resort, Japan.

Ralph T. Walker, 1889-1973, NY Telephone (now Verizon) Bldg., Irving Trust Bldg. (now 1 Wall St.), New York, NY.

Wang Shu, b 1963, Ningbo Museum, China.

Roland A. Wank, 1898-1970, Cincinnati Union Terminal, OH; head architect, 1933-44, Tennessee Valley Authority.

Stanford White, 1853-1906, Washington Arch in Washington Square Park, first Madison Square Garden, New York, NY.

Christopher Wren, 1632-1723, St. Paul's Cathedral, London, Eng., UK.

Frank Lloyd Wright, 1867-1959, Imperial Hotel, Tokyo, Jpn.; Guggenheim Museum, New York, NY; Kaufmann "Fallingwater" house, Mill Run, PA; Taliesin West, Scottsdale, AZ.

Thomas Wright, b 1957, Burj Al Arab hotel, Dubai, UAE.

William Wurster, 1895-1973, Ghirardelli Sq., San Francisco, CA.

Minoru Yamasaki, 1912-86, World Trade Center (destroyed 2001), New York, NY.

Artists, Photographers, and Sculptors of the Past

Artists are painters unless otherwise indicated.

Berenice Abbott, 1898-1991, (U.S.) photographer. Documentary of New York City, *Changing New York* (1939).

Ansel Easton Adams, 1902-84, (U.S.) photographer. Landscapes of the American Southwest.

Washington Allston, 1779-1843, (U.S.) landscapist. *Belshazzar's Feast*.

Albrecht Altdorfer, 1480-1538, (Ger.) landscapist.

Fra Angelico, c. 1400-55, (It.) Renaissance muralist. *Madonna of the Linen Drapers' Guild*.

Diane Arbus, 1923-71, (U.S.) photographer. Disturbing images.

Alexsandr Archipenko, 1887-1964, (U.S.) sculptor. *Boxing Match*, *Medranos*.

Jean Arp, 1887-1966, (Fr.) sculptor and painter. Founder of Dada movement.

Richard Artschwager, 1923-2013, (U.S.) painter and sculptor. *Table With Pink Tablecloth*.

Eugène Atget, 1856-1927, (Fr.) photographer. Paris life.

John James Audubon, 1785-1851, (U.S.) *Birds of America*.

Richard Avedon, 1923-2004, (U.S.) fashion and celebrity photographer.

Hans Baldung-Grien, 1484-1545, (Ger.) *Todentanz*.

Ernst Barlach, 1870-1938, (Ger.) Expressionist sculptor. *Man Drawing a Sword*.

Frédéric-Auguste Bartholdi, 1834-1904, (Fr.) sculptor. *Liberty Enlightening the World* (Statue of Liberty).

Fra Bartolommeo, 1472-1517, (It.) *Vision of St. Bernard*.

Romare Bearden, 1911-88, (U.S.) collage and other media. *The Visitation*.

Aubrey Beardsley, 1872-98, (Br.) illustrator. *Salome*, *Lysistrata*, *Morte d'Arthur*, *Volpone*.

Cecil Beaton, 1904-80, (Br.) fashion and celebrity photographer.

Max Beckmann, 1884-1950, (Ger.) Expressionist. *The Descent From the Cross*.

Gentile Bellini, 1426-1507, (It.) Renaissance. *Procession in St. Mark's Square*.

Giovanni Bellini, 1428-1516, (It.) Renaissance. *St. Francis in Ecstasy*.

Jacopo Bellini, 1400-70, (It.) Renaissance. *Crucifixion*.

George Wesley Bellows, 1882-1925, (U.S.) sports artist, portraitist, landscapist. *Stag at Sharkey's, Edith Clavell*.

Thomas Hart Benton, 1889-1975, (U.S.) American regionalist. *Threshing Wheat, Arts of the West*.

Ruth Bernhard, 1905-2006, (Ger.-U.S.) photographer. Black-and-white studies of female nudes.

Gianlorenzo Bernini, 1598-1680, (It.) Baroque sculptor. *The Assumption*.

Albert Bierstadt, 1830-1902, (U.S.) landscapist. *The Rocky Mountains, Mount Corcoran*.

George Caleb Bingham, 1811-79, (U.S.) American frontier. *Fur Traders Descending the Missouri*.

William Blake, 1757-1827, (Br.) engraver. *Book of Job, Songs of Innocence, Songs of Experience*.

Rosa Bonheur, 1822-99, (Fr.) Realist. *The Horse Fair*.

Pierre Bonnard, 1867-1947, (Fr.) Intimist. *The Breakfast Room, Girl in a Straw Hat*.

Gutzon Borglum, 1867-1941, (U.S.) sculptor. Mt. Rushmore Memorial.

Hieronymus Bosch, 1450-1516, (Flem.) religious allegories. *The Crowning With Thorns*.

Sandro Botticelli, 1444-1510, (It.) Renaissance. *Birth of Venus, Adoration of the Magi, Guiliano de' Medici*.

Louise Bourgeois, 1911-2010, (Fr.) sculptor. *Maman*.

Margaret Bourke-White, 1904-71, (U.S.) photographer, photojournalist. WWII, USSR, rural South during the Depression.

Mathew Brady, c. 1823-96, (U.S.) photographer. Civil War.

Constantin Brancusi, 1876-1957, (Romania-Fr.) Nonobjective sculptor. *Flying Turtle, The Kiss*.

Georges Braque, 1882-1963, (Fr.) Cubist. *Violin and Palette*.

Pieter Bruegel the Elder, c. 1525-69, (Flem.) Renaissance. *The Peasant Dance, Hunters in the Snow, Magpie on the Gallows*.

Pieter Bruegel the Younger, 1564-1638, (Flem.) Baroque. *Village Fair, The Crucifixion*.

Edward Burne-Jones, 1833-98, (Br.) Pre-Raphaelite artist-craftsman. *The Mirror of Venus*.

Alexander Calder, 1898-1976, (U.S.) sculptor. *Lobster Trap and Fish Tail*.

Julia Margaret Cameron, 1815-79, (Br.) photographer, prominent portraitist.

Robert Capa (Endre Friedmann), 1913-54, (Hung.-U.S.) photographer, war photojournalist. Invasion of Normandy.

Michelangelo Merisi da Caravaggio, 1573-1610, (It.) Baroque. *The Supper at Emmaus*.

Emily Carr, 1871-1945, (Can.) landscapist. *Blunden Harbour, Big Raven, Rushing Sea of Undergrowth*.

Carlo Carrà, 1881-1966, (It.) Metaphysical school. *Lot's Daughters, The Enchanted Room*.

Leonora Carrington, 1917-2011, (Br.) Surrealist. *The Inn of the Dawn Horse (Self-Portrait)*.

Henri Cartier-Bresson, 1908-2004, (Fr.) photographer. *Imagenes à la sauvette*.

Mary Cassatt, 1844-1926, (U.S.) Impressionist. *The Cup of Tea, Woman Bathing, The Boating Party*.

George Catlin, 1796-1872, (U.S.) American Indian life. *Gallery of Indians, Buffalo Dance*.

Benvenuto Cellini, 1500-71, (It.) Mannerist sculptor, goldsmith. *Perseus and Medusa*.

Paul Cézanne, 1839-1906, (Fr.) Post-Impressionist. *Card Players, Mont-Sainte-Victoire With Large Pine Trees*.

Marc Chagall, 1887-1985, (Russ.) Jewish life and folklore. *I and the Village, The Praying Jew*.

John Chamberlain, 1927-2011, (U.S.) sculptor of automobile metal.

Jean Simeon Chardin, 1699-1779, (Fr.) still lifes. *The Kiss, The Grace*.

Giorgio de Chirico, 1888-1978, (It.) founded the Metaphysical school. *Enigma of an Autumn Night*.

Frederick Church, 1826-1900, (U.S.) Hudson River school. *Niagara, Andes of Ecuador*.

Giovanni Cimabue, 1240-1302, (It.) Byzantine mosaicist. *Madonna Enthroned With St. Francis*.

Claude (Lorrain) (Claude Gellée), 1600-82, (Fr.) Ideal-landscapist. *The Enchanted Castle*.

Thomas Cole, 1801-48, (U.S.) Hudson River school. *The Ox-Bow, In the Catskills*.

John Constable, 1776-1837, (Br.) landscapist. *Salisbury Cathedral From the Bishop's Grounds*.

John Singleton Copley, 1738-1815, (U.S.) portraitist. *Samuel Adams, Watson and the Shark*.

Lovis Corinth, 1858-1925, (Ger.) Expressionist. *Apocalypse*.

Jean-Baptiste-Camille Corot, 1796-1875, (Fr.) landscapist. *Souvenir de Mortefontaine, Pastorale*.

Correggio, 1494-1534, (It.) Renaissance muralist. *Mystic Marriages of St. Catherine*.

Gustave Courbet, 1819-77, (Fr.) Realist. *The Artist's Studio*.

Lucas Cranach the Elder, 1472-1553, (Ger.) Protestant Reformation portraitist. *Luther*.

Bill Cunningham, 1929-2016, (U.S.) fashion photographer.

Imogen Cunningham, 1883-1976, (U.S.) photographer, portraitist. Plants.

Nathaniel Currier, 1813-88, and **James M. Ives**, 1824-95, (both U.S.) lithographers. *A Midnight Race on the Mississippi, American Forest Scene—Maple Sugaring*.

John Steuart Curry, 1897-1946, (U.S.) Americana, murals. *Baptism in Kansas*.

Edward S. Curtis, 1868-1952, (U.S.) photographer. *The North American Indian*.

Louis Daguerre, 1787-1851, (Fr.) photographer. Invented daguerreotype process.

Salvador Dalí, 1904-89, (Sp.) Surrealist. *Persistence of Memory, The Crucifixion*.

Honoré Daumier, 1808-79, (Fr.) caricaturist. *The Third-Class Carriage*.

Jacques-Louis David, 1748-1825, (Fr.) Neoclassicist. *The Oath of the Horatii*.

Arthur Davies, 1862-1928, (U.S.) Romantic landscapist. *Unicorns, Leda and the Dioscuri*.

Edgar Degas, 1834-1917, (Fr.) Realist/Impressionist. *The Ballet Class*.

Willem de Kooning, 1904-97, (Neth.-U.S.) Abstract Expressionist. *Excavation, Woman I, Door to the River*.

Eugène Delacroix, 1798-1863, (Fr.) Romantic. *Massacre at Chios, Liberty Leading the People*.

Paul Delaroche, 1797-1856, (Fr.) historical themes. *Children of Edward IV*.

Luca Della Robbia, 1400-82, (It.) Renaissance terra-cotta. *Cantoria* (singing gallery), Florence cathedral.

Donatello, 1386-1466, (It.) Renaissance sculptor. *David, Gattamelata*.

Aaron Douglas, 1899-79, (U.S.) Harlem Renaissance illustrator and muralist.

Jean Dubuffet, 1902-85, (Fr.) painter, sculptor, printmaker. *Group of Four Trees*.

Marcel Duchamp, 1887-1968, (Fr.) Dadaist. *Nude Descending a Staircase, No. 2*.

Raoul Dufy, 1877-1953, (Fr.) Fauvist. *Chateau and Horses*.

Asher Brown Durand, 1796-1886, (U.S.) Hudson River school. *Kindred Spirits*.

Albrecht Dürer, 1471-1528, (Ger.) Renaissance painter, engraver, woodcuts. *St. Jerome in His Study, Melencolia I*.

Anthony van Dyck, 1599-1641, (Flem.) Baroque portraitist. *Portrait of Charles I Hunting*.

Thomas Eakins, 1844-1916, (U.S.) Realist. *The Gross Clinic*.

Alfred Eisenstaedt, 1898-1995, (Ger.-U.S.) photographer, photojournalist. Famous photo, V-J Day, Aug. 14, 1945.

Peter Henry Emerson, 1856-1936, (Br.) photographer. Promoted photography as an independent art form.

Jacob Epstein, 1880-1959, (Br.) religious and allegorical sculptor. *Genesis, Ecce Homo*.

Erté (Romain de Tiertoff), 1892-1990, (Fr.) painter, fashion and stage designer.

Walker Evans, 1903-75, (U.S.) photographer. Documented Great Depression.

Jan van Eyck, c. 1390-1441, (Flem.) naturalistic panels. *Adoration of the Lamb*.

Horst Faas, 1933-2012, (Ger.) Vietnam War photographer.

Roger Fenton, 1819-69, (Br.) photographer. Crimean War.

Anselm Feuerbach, 1829-80, (Ger.) Romantic Classicist. *Judgment of Paris, Iphigenia*.

John Bernard Flannagan, 1895-1942, (U.S.) animal sculptor. *Triumph of the Egg*.

Jean-Honoré Fragonard, 1732-1806, (Fr.) Rococo. *The Swing*.

Helen Frankenthaler, 1928-2011, (U.S.) Abstract Expressionist. *Mountains and Sea*.

Daniel Chester French, 1850-1931, (U.S.) sculptor. *The Minute Man of Concord*; seated *Lincoln*, Lincoln Memorial, Washington, DC.

Lucian Freud, 1922-2011, (Ger.-Br.) portraitist. *Girl With Roses*.

Caspar David Friedrich, 1774-1840, (Ger.) Romantic landscapist. *Man and Woman Gazing at the Moon*.

Thomas Gainsborough, 1727-88, (Br.) portraitist. *The Blue Boy, The Watering Place, The Parish Clerk*.

Alexander Gardner, 1821-82, (U.S.) photographer. Civil War, railroad construction, Great Plains Indians.

Paul Gauguin, 1848-1903, (Fr.) Post-Impressionist. *The Tahitians, Spirit of the Dead Watching*.

Lorenzo Ghiberti, 1378-1455, (It.) Renaissance sculptor. "Gates of Paradise" baptistery doors, Florence, It.

Alberto Giacometti, 1901-66, (Switz.) attenuated sculptures of solitary figures. *Man Pointing*.

Giorgione, c. 1477-1510, (It.) Renaissance. *The Tempest*.

Giotto di Bondone, 1267-1337, (It.) Renaissance. *Presentation of Christ in the Temple*.

François Girardon, 1628-1715, (Fr.) Baroque sculptor of classical themes. *Apollo Tended by the Nymphs*.

Edward Gorey, 1925-2000, (U.S.) illustrator. *The Doubtful Guest*.

Arshile Gorky, 1905-48, (U.S.) Surrealist. *The Liver Is the Cock's Comb*.

Francisco de Goya y Lucientes, 1746-1828, (Sp.) painter, printmaker. *The Naked Maja, The Disasters of War* (etchings).

El Greco (Domenikos Theotokopoulos), 1541-1614, (Gr.-Sp.) painter, sculptor. *View of Toledo, Assumption of the Virgin*.

Horatio Greenough, 1805-52, (U.S.) Neoclassical sculptor.

Matthias Grünewald, 1480-1528, (Ger.) mystical religious themes. *The Resurrection*.

Frans Hals, c. 1580-1666, (Neth.) portraitist. *Laughing Cavalier, Gypsy Girl*.

Richard Hamilton, 1922-2011, (Br.) Pop Art. *Just What Is It That Makes Today's Homes So Different, So Appealing?*

Austin Hansen, 1910-96, (U.S.) photographer. Harlem, NY, life.

Keith Haring, 1958-90, (U.S.) painter, muralist. *Crack is Wack*.

Childe Hassam, 1859-1935, (U.S.) Impressionist. *Southwest Wind, July 14 Rue Daunon*.

Edward Hicks, 1780-1849, (U.S.) folk. *The Peaceable Kingdom*.

Lewis Wickes Hine, 1874-1940, (U.S.) photographer. Studies of immigrants, children in industry.

Hans Hofmann, 1880-1966, (U.S.) early Abstract Expressionist. *Spring, The Gate*.

William Hogarth, 1697-1764, (Br.) caricaturist. *The Rake's Progress*.

Katsushika Hokusai, 1760-1849, (Jpn.) printmaker. *Crabs*.

Hans Holbein the Elder, 1460-1524, (Ger.) late Gothic. *Presentation of Christ in the Temple*.

Hans Holbein the Younger, 1497-1543, (Ger.) portraitist. *Henry VIII, The French Ambassadors*.

Winslow Homer, 1836-1910, (U.S.) naturalist, marine themes. *Marine Coast, High Cliff*.

Edward Hopper, 1882-1967, (U.S.) realistic urban scenes. *Nighthawks, House by the Railroad*.

Horst P. Horst, 1906-99, (Ger.) fashion, celebrity photographer.

Jean-Auguste-Dominique Ingres, 1780-1867, (Fr.) Classicist. *Valpincon Bather*.

George Inness, 1825-94, (U.S.) luminous landscapist. *Delaware Water Gap*.

William Henry Jackson, 1843-1942, (U.S.) photographer. American West, building of Union Pacific Railroad.

Jeanne-Claude (Javacheff), 1935-2009, (Moroc.), created large-scale, temporary installations in public places with her husband, Christo.

Frances Benjamin Johnston, 1864-1952, (U.S.) photographer. Historic homes.

Donald Judd, 1928-94, (U.S.) sculptor, major Minimalist.

Frida Kahlo, 1907-54, (Mex.) folkloric stylist. *Self-Portrait With Monkey*.

Wassily Kandinsky, 1866-1944, (Russ.) Abstractionist. *Capricious Forms, Improvisation 28 (second version)*.

Ellsworth Kelly, 1923-2015, (U.S.) painter, sculptor. *Red Blue Green*.

Paul Klee, 1879-1940, (Switz.) Abstractionist. *Twittering Machine, Pastoral, Death and Fire*.

Gustav Klimt, 1862-1918, (Austria) cofounder of Vienna Secession Movement. *The Kiss*.

Oskar Kokoschka, 1886-1980, (Austria) Expressionist. *View of Prague, Harbor of Marseilles*.

Käthe Kollwitz, 1867-1945, (Ger.) printmaker, social justice themes. *The Peasant War*.

Gaston Lachaise, 1882-1935, (U.S.) figurative sculptor. *Standing Woman*.

John La Farge, 1835-1910, (U.S.) muralist. *Red and White Peonies, The Ascension*.

Sir Edwin (Henry) Landseer, 1802-73, (Br.) painter, sculptor. *Shoeing, Rout of Comus*.

Dorothea Lange, 1895-1965, (U.S.) photographer. Great Depression, migrant farm workers.

Fernand Léger, 1881-1955, (Fr.) Machine art. *The Cyclists*.

Saul Leiter, 1923-2013, (U.S) photographer.

Leonardo da Vinci, 1452-1519, (It.) Renaissance. *Mona Lisa, Last Supper, The Annunciation*.

Emanuel Leutze, 1816-68, (U.S.) historical themes. *Washington Crossing the Delaware*.

Edmonia Lewis, 1844?-1907, (U.S.) sculptor. *The Death of Cleopatra*.

Roy Lichtenstein, 1923-97, (U.S.) Pop Art.

Jacques Lipchitz, 1891-1973, (Fr.) Cubist sculptor. *Harpist*.

Filippino Lippi, 1457-1504, (It.) Renaissance. *Adoration of the Magi*.

Fra Filippo Lippi, 1406-69, (It.) Renaissance. *Coronation of the Virgin, Madonna and Child With Angels*.

Morris Louis, 1912-62, (U.S.) Abstract Expressionist. *Signa, Stripes, Alpha-Phi*.

René Magritte, 1898-1967, (Belg.) Surrealist. *The Descent of Man, The Betrayal of Images*.

Aristide Maillol, 1861-1944, (Fr.) sculptor. *L'Harmonie*.

Édouard Manet, 1832-83, (Fr.) forerunner of Impressionism. *Luncheon on the Grass, Olympia*.

Andrea Mantegna, 1431-1506, (It.) Renaissance frescoes. *Triumph of Caesar*.

Robert Mapplethorpe, 1946-89, (U.S.) photographer.

Franz Marc, 1880-1916, (Ger.) Expressionist. *Blue Horses*.

John Marin, 1870-1953, (U.S.) Expressionist seascapes. *Maine Island*.

Reginald Marsh, 1898-1954, (U.S.) satire. *Tattoo and Haircut*.

Agnes Martin, 1912-2004, (U.S.) abstract artist. *Night Sea*.

Masaccio, 1401-28, (It.) Renaissance. *The Tribute Money*.

Henri Matisse, 1869-1954, (Fr.) Fauvist. *Woman With the Hat*.

John McCracken, 1934-2011, (U.S.) Minimalist sculptor.

Michelangelo Buonarroti, 1475-1564, (It.) Renaissance. *Pietà, David, Moses, The Last Judgment*, Sistine Chapel ceiling.

Jean-Francois Millet, 1814-75, (Fr.) peasants. *The Gleaners, The Man With a Hoe*.

Joan Miró, 1893-1983, (Sp.) exuberant colors, playful images. *Catalan landscape, Dutch Interior*.

Amedeo Modigliani, 1884-1920, (It.) figurative paintings, sculptures. *Reclining Nude*.

Piet Mondrian, 1872-1944, (Neth.) Abstractionist. *Composition With Red, Yellow and Blue*.

Claude Monet, 1840-1926, (Fr.) Impressionist. *The Bridge at Argenteuil, Haystacks, Bridge Over a Pond of Water Lillies*.

Henry Moore, 1898-1986, (Br.) sculptor of large-scale, abstract works. *Reclining Figure* (several).

Gustave Moreau, 1826-98, (Fr.) Symbolist. *The Apparition (Dance of Salome)*.

James Wilson Morrice, 1865-1924, (Can.) landscapist. *The Ferry, Quebec, Venice, Looking Over the Lagoon*.

William Morris, 1834-96, (Br.) decorative artist, leader of Arts and Crafts movement.

Grandma Moses (Anna Mary Robertson Moses), 1860-1961, (U.S.) folk. *Out for the Christmas Tree, Catching the Thanksgiving Turkey*.

Samuel Morse, 1791-1872, (U.S.) portraitist. *Gallery of the Louvre*.

Edvard Munch, 1863-1944, (Nor.) Expressionist. *The Cry*.

Bartolome Murillo, 1618-82, (Sp.) Baroque religious artist. *Vision of St. Anthony, The Two Trinities*.

Elizabeth Murray, 1940-2007, (U.S.) abstract colors. *Kitchen Party*.

Eadweard Muybridge, 1830-1904, (Br.-U.S.) photographer. Studies of motion, *Animal Locomotion*.

Nadar (Gaspar-Félix Tournachon), 1820-1910, (Fr.) photographer, caricaturist, portraitist. Invented photo-essay.

LeRoy Neiman, 1921-2012, (U.S.) sports expressionist painter.

Arnold Newman, 1918-2006, (U.S.) portrait photographer.

Barnett Newman, 1905-70, (U.S.) Abstract Expressionist. *Stations of the Cross*.

Isamu Noguchi, 1904-88, (U.S.) abstract sculptor, designer. *Kouros, BirdC(MU)*, sculptural gardens.

Kenneth Noland, 1924-2010, (U.S.) Color Field, abstract.

Georgia O'Keeffe, 1887-1986, (U.S.) Southwest motifs. *Cow's Skull: Red, White, and Blue; The Shelton With Sunspots*.

José Clemente Orozco, 1883-1949, (Mex.) frescoes. *House of Tears, Pre-Columbian Golden Age*.

Timothy H. O'Sullivan, 1840-82, (U.S.) Civil War photographer.

Gordon Parks, 1912-2006, (U.S.) African American photographer, filmmaker. *Life* photographer, 1948-68.

Charles Willson Peale, 1741-1827, (U.S.) Amer. Revolutionary portraitist. *The Staircase Group*, U.S. presidents.

Rembrandt Peale, 1778-1860, (U.S.) portraitist. *Thomas Jefferson*.

Irving Penn, 1917-2009, (U.S.) portraitist, fashion photographer.

Pietro Perugino, 1446-1523, (It.) Renaissance. *Delivery of the Keys to St. Peter*.

Pablo Picasso, 1881-1973, (Sp.) painter, sculptor. *Guernica, Dove, Head of a Woman, Head of a Bull, Metamorphosis*.

Piero della Francesca, c. 1415-92, (It.) Renaissance. *Duke of Urbino, Flagellation of Christ*.

Camille Pissarro, 1830-1903, (Fr.) Impressionist. *Boulevard des Italiens, Morning, Sunlight; Bather in the Woods*.

Jackson Pollock, 1912-56, (U.S.) Abstract Expressionist. *Autumn Rhythm*.

Nicolas Poussin, 1594-1665, (Fr.) Baroque pictorial classicism. *St. John on Patmos*.

Maurice B. Prendergast, c. 1860-1924, (U.S.) Postimpressionist watercolorist. *Umbrellas in the Rain*.

Pierre-Paul Prud'hon, 1758-1823, (Fr.) Romanticist. *Crime Pursued by Vengeance and Justice*.

Pierre Cecile Puvis de Chavannes, 1824-98, (Fr.) muralist. *The Poor Fisherman*.

Raphael Sanzio, 1483-1520, (It.) Renaissance. *Disputa, School of Athens, Sistine Madonna*.

Robert Rauschenberg, 1925-2008, (U.S.) printmaker. *Combine, Bed, Revolvers, Outpost*.

Man Ray (Emmanuel Radnitsky), 1890-1976, (U.S.) Dadaist and Surrealist. *Observing Time, The Lovers, Marquis de Sade*.

Odilon Redon, 1840-1916, (Fr.) Symbolist painter, lithographer. *In the Dream, Vase of Flowers*.

Rembrandt van Rijn, 1606-69, (Neth.) painter, printmaker. *The Bridal Couple, The Night Watch*.

Frederic Remington, 1861-1909, (U.S.) painter, sculptor. Portrayer of the American West, *Bronco Buster*.

Pierre-Auguste Renoir, 1841-1919, (Fr.) Impressionist. *The Luncheon of the Boating Party, Dance in the Country*.

Joshua Reynolds, 1723-92, (Br.) portraitist. *Mrs. Siddons as the Tragic Muse*.

Herb Ritts, 1952-2002, (U.S.) photographer. Nudes, celebrities.

Diego Rivera, 1886-1957, (Mex.) frescoes. *The Fecund Earth*.

Larry Rivers, 1923-2002, (U.S.) painter, sculptor, often realistic. Dutch Masters series.

Henry Peach Robinson, 1830-1901, (Br.) a leader of "high art" photography.

Norman Rockwell, 1894-1978, (U.S.) painter, illustrator. *Saturday Evening Post* covers.

Auguste Rodin, 1840-1917, (Fr.) sculptor. *The Thinker*.

Milton Rogovin, 1909-2011, (U.S.) documentary photographer.

Willy Ronis, 1910-2009, (Fr.) photographer. Postwar Paris.

Joe Rosenthal, 1911-2006, (U.S.) photojournalist; photographed six Marines raising the U.S. flag over Iwo Jima in WWII.

Mark Rothko, 1903-70, (U.S.) Abstract Expressionist. *Light, Earth and Blue*.

Georges Rouault, 1871-1958, (Fr.) Expressionist. *Three Judges*.

Henri Rousseau, 1844-1910, (Fr.) primitive exotic themes. *The Snake Charmer*.

Theodore Rousseau, 1812-67, (Switz.-Fr.) landscapist. *Under the Birches, Evening*.

Peter Paul Rubens, 1577-1640, (Flem.) Baroque. *Mystic Marriage of St. Catherine*.

Jacob van Ruisdael, c. 1628-82, (Neth.) landscapist. *Jewish Cemetery*.

Charles M. Russell, 1866-1926, (U.S.) Western life.

Salomon van Ruysdael, c. 1600-70, (Neth.) landscapist. *River With Ferry-Boat*.

Albert Pinkham Ryder, 1847-1917, (U.S.) seascapes, allegories. *Toilers of the Sea*.

Augustus Saint-Gaudens, 1848-1907, (U.S.) memorial statues. *Farragut, Mrs. Henry Adams (Grief)*.

Niki de Saint Phalle, 1930-2002, (Fr.) paintings, sculptures, prints, large public installations.

Andrea Sansovino, 1460-1529, (It.) Renaissance sculptor. *Baptism of Christ*.

Jacopo Sansovino, 1486-1570, (It.) Renaissance sculptor. *St. John the Baptist*.

John Singer Sargent, 1856-1925, (U.S.) Edwardian society portraitist. *The Wyndham Sisters, Madame X*.

Andrea del Sarto, 1486-1530, (It.) frescoes. *Madonna of the Harpies*.

George Segal, 1924-2000, (U.S.) sculptor. Life-sized figures realistically depicting daily life.

Georges Seurat, 1859-91, (Fr.) Pointillist. *Sunday Afternoon on the Island of La Grande Jatte*.

Gino Severini, 1883-1966, (It.) Futurist and Cubist. *Dynamic Hieroglyph of the Bal Tabarin*.

Ben Shahn, 1898-1969, (U.S.) social and political themes. Sacco and Vanzetti series, *Seurat's Lunch, Handball*.

Charles Sheeler, 1883-1965, (U.S.) abstractionist.

David Alfaro Siqueiros, 1896-1974, (Mex.) political muralist. *March of Humanity*.

David Smith, 1906-65, (U.S.) welded metal sculpture. *Hudson River Landscape, Zig, Cubi* series.

Edward Steichen, 1879-1973, (U.S.) photographer. Credited with transforming photography into an art form.

Alfred Stieglitz, 1864-1946, (U.S.) photographer, editor. Helped create acceptance of photography as art.

Paul Strand, 1890-1976, (U.S.) photographer. People, nature, landscapes.

Gilbert Stuart, 1755-1828, (U.S.) portraitist. George Washington, Thomas Jefferson, James Madison.

Thomas Sully, 1783-1872, (U.S.) portraitist. *Col. Thomas Handasyd Perkins*, *The Passage of the Delaware*.

William Henry Fox Talbot, 1800-77, (Br.) photographer. *Pencil of Nature*, early photographically illustrated book.

George Tames, 1919-94, (U.S.) photographer. Presidents, political leaders.

Yves Tanguy, 1900-55, (Fr.) Surrealist. *Rose of the Four Winds*; *Mama, Papa Is Wounded!*

Giovanni Battista Tiepolo, 1696-1770, (It.) Rococo frescoes. *The Crucifixion*.

Louis Comfort Tiffany, 1848-1933, (U.S.) stained glass; decorative arts.

Jacopo Tintoretto, 1518-94, (It.) Mannerist. *The Last Supper*.

Titian (Tiziano Vecellio), c. 1488-1576, (It.) Renaissance. *Venus and the Lute Player*, *The Bacchanal*.

Jose Rey Toledo, 1916-94, (U.S.) Native American life. Tribal dances.

George Tooker, 1920-2011, (U.S.) Magic Realist. *Subway*.

Henri de Toulouse-Lautrec, 1864-1901, (Fr.) Postimpressionist. *At the Moulin Rouge*.

John Trumbull, 1756-1843, (U.S.) historical themes. *The Declaration of Independence*.

Deborah Turbeville, 1937-2013, (U.S.) fashion photographer.

J(oseph) M(allord) W(illiam) Turner, 1775-1851, (Br.) Romantic landscapist. *Snow Storm*.

Cy Twombly, 1928-2011, (U.S.) painter and sculptor. *Leda and the Swan*.

Paolo Uccello, 1397-1475, (It.) Gothic-Renaissance. *The Rout of San Romano*.

Maurice Utrillo, 1883-1955, (Fr.) Impressionist. *Sacré-Coeur de Montmartre*.

Vincent van Gogh, 1853-90, (Neth.) *The Starry Night*, *L'Arlesienne*, *Bedroom at Arles*, *Self-Portrait*.

John Vanderlyn, 1775-1852, (U.S.) Neoclassicist. *Ariadne Asleep on the Island of Naxos*.

Diego Velázquez, 1599-1660, (Sp.) Baroque. *Las Meninas*, *Portrait of Juan de Pareja*.

Jan Vermeer, 1632-75, (Neth.) interior genre subjects. *Young Woman With a Water Jug*.

Paolo Veronese, 1528-88, (It.) devotional themes, vastly peopled canvases. *The Temptation of St. Anthony*.

Andrea del Verrocchio, 1435-88, (It.) sculptor. *Colleoni*.

Maurice de Vlaminck, 1876-1958, (Fr.) Fauvist landscapist. *Red Trees*.

Andy Warhol, 1928-87, (U.S.) Pop Art. *Campbell's Soup Cans*, *Marilyn Diptych*.

Antoine Watteau, 1684-1721, (Fr.) Rococo "scenes of gallantry." *The Embarkation for Cythera*.

George Frederic Watts, 1817-1904, (Br.) painter and sculptor. Grandiose allegorical themes. *Hope*.

Benjamin West, 1738-1820, (U.S.) realistic historical themes. *Death of General Wolfe*.

Edward Weston, 1886-1958, (U.S.) photographer. Landscapes of American West.

James Abbott McNeill Whistler, 1834-1903, (U.S.) *Arrangement in Grey and Black No. 1 (Portrait of the Artist's Mother)*.

Archibald M. Willard, 1836-1918, (U.S.) murals. *The Spirit of '76*.

Grant Wood, 1891-1942, (U.S.) Midwestern regionalist. *American Gothic*, *Daughters of Revolution*.

Andrew Wyeth, 1917-2009, (U.S.), regionalist. *Christina's World*.

Ossip Zadkine, 1890-1967, (Russ.) School of Paris sculptor. *The Destroyed City*, *Musicians*, *Christ*.

Business Leaders and Philanthropists of the Past

Giovanni Agnelli, 1921-2003, (It.) industrialist; principal shareholder of Fiat.

Karl Albrecht, 1920-2014, and **Theo Albrecht**, 1922-2010, (both Ger.) cofounders of Aldi supermarkets.

Paul Allen, 1953-2018, (U.S.) Microsoft cofounder; philanthropist.

Walter Annenberg, 1908-2002, (U.S.) publisher, founder of *TV Guide*, philanthropist.

Elizabeth Arden (F. N. Graham), 1884-1966, (U.S.) Canadian-born founder of cosmetics empire.

Philip D. Armour, 1832-1901, (U.S.) industrialist; streamlined meatpacking.

Brooke Astor, 1902-2007, (U.S.) philanthropist; pres. of Vincent Astor Foundation.

John Jacob Astor, 1763-1848, (U.S.) German-born fur trader, banker, real estate magnate; at death, richest in U.S.

Francis W. Ayer, 1848-1923, (U.S.) ad industry pioneer.

August Belmont, 1816-90, (U.S.) German-born financier.

Liliane Bettencourt, 1922-2017, (Fr.) L'Oreal heiress, philanthropist.

James B. (Diamond Jim) Brady, 1856-1917, (U.S.) financier, philanthropist, legendary bon vivant.

Adolphus Busch, 1839-1913, (U.S.) German-born brewery founder.

Asa Candler, 1851-1929, (U.S.) founded Coca-Cola Co.

Andrew Carnegie, 1835-1919, (U.S.) Scottish-born industrialist, philanthropist; founded Carnegie Steel Co.

Tom Carvel, 1908-89, (Gr.-U.S.) founded ice cream chain.

William Colgate, 1783-1857, (Br.-U.S.) businessman, philanthropist; founded soap-making empire.

Jay Cooke, 1821-1905, (U.S.) financier.

Peter Cooper, 1791-1883, (U.S.) industrialist, inventor, philanthropist; founded Cooper Union college (1859).

Ezra Cornell, 1807-74, (U.S.) businessman, philanthropist; headed Western Union.

Erastus Corning, 1794-1872, (U.S.) financier; headed New York Central Railroad.

Charles Crocker, 1822-88, (U.S.) railroad builder, financier.

Samuel Cunard, 1787-1865, (Can.) pioneered transatlantic steam navigation.

Marcus Daly, 1841-1900, (U.S.) Irish-born copper magnate.

W. Edwards Deming, 1900-93, (U.S.) quality-control expert who revolutionized Japanese manufacturing.

Walt Disney, 1901-66, (U.S.) pioneer in cinema animation; built entertainment empire.

Herbert H. Dow, 1866-1930, (U.S.) founder of chemical co.

Anthony Drexel, 1826-93, (U.S.) banker, philanthropist, university founder.

James Duke, 1856-1925, (U.S.) founded American Tobacco, Duke Univ.

Eleuthere I. du Pont, 1771-1834, (Fr.-U.S.) gunpowder manufacturer.

Thomas C. Durant, 1820-85, (U.S.) railroad official, financier.

William C. Durant, 1861-1947, (U.S.) industrialist; formed General Motors.

George Eastman, 1854-1932, (U.S.) inventor; manufacturer of photographic equipment.

Marshall Field, 1834-1906, (U.S.) founded Chicago's largest department store.

Harvey Firestone, 1868-1938, (U.S.) founded tire company.

Avery Fisher, 1906-94, (U.S.) industrialist, philanthropist; founded Fisher Electronics.

Henry M. Flagler, 1830-1913, (U.S.) financier; helped form Standard Oil, developed FL as resort state.

Malcolm Forbes, 1919-90, (U.S.) magazine publisher.

Henry Ford, 1863-1947, (U.S.) automaker; developed first popular low-priced car.

Henry Ford II, 1917-87, (U.S.) headed auto company founded by grandfather.

Henry C. Frick, 1849-1919, (U.S.) steel and coke magnate; had prominent role in development of U.S. Steel.

Jakob Fugger (Jakob the Rich), 1459-1525, (Ger.) headed leading banking, trading house in 16th-cent. Europe.

Alfred C. Fuller, 1885-1973, (U.S.) Canadian-born businessman; founded brush company.

Elbert H. Gary, 1846-1927, (U.S.) chaired board of U.S. Steel, 1903-27.

Jean Paul Getty, 1892-1976, (U.S.) founded oil empire.

Amadeo Giannini, 1870-1949, (U.S.) founded Bank of America.

Stephen Girard, 1750-1831, (U.S.) French-born financier, philanthropist; richest man in U.S. at time of death.

Leonard H. Goldenson, 1905-99, (U.S.) turned ABC into major TV network.

Jay Gould, 1836-92, (U.S.) railroad magnate, financier.

Hetty Green, 1834-1916, (U.S.) financier, the "witch of Wall St."; richest woman in U.S. in her day.

William Gregg, 1800-67, (U.S.) launched textile industry in the South.

Meyer Guggenheim, 1828-1905, (U.S.) Swiss-born merchant, philanthropist; built merchandising, mining empires.

Armand Hammer, 1898-1990, (U.S.) headed Occidental Petroleum, promoted U.S.-Soviet ties.

Elliot Handler, 1916-2011, (U.S.) cofounder of Mattel; introduced the Barbie doll.

Edward H. Harriman, 1848-1909, (U.S.) railroad financier; headed Union Pacific.

Hugh Hefner, 1926-2017, (U.S.) founded Playboy Enterprises.

Henry J. Heinz, 1844-1919, (U.S.) founded food company.

Harry, 1909-97, and **Leona Helmsley**, 1920-2007, (U.S.) real estate magnates, philanthropists.

Milton Snavely Hershey, 1857-1945, (U.S.) chocolate co. founder, philanthropist.

James J. Hill, 1838-1916, (U.S.) Canadian-born railroad magnate, financier; founded Great Northern Railway.

Conrad N. Hilton, 1888-1979, (U.S.) hotel chain founder.

Howard Hughes, 1905-76, (U.S.) industrialist, aviator, filmmaker.

H. L. Hunt, 1889-1974, (U.S.) oil magnate.

Collis P. Huntington, 1821-1900, (U.S.) railroad magnate.

Henry E. Huntington, 1850-1927, (U.S.) railroad builder, philanthropist.

Walter L. Jacobs, 1898-1985, (U.S.) founder of the first rental car agency.

Steve Jobs, 1955-2011, (U.S.) Apple cofounder and exec.; Pixar exec.

Howard Johnson, 1896-1972, (U.S.) founded restaurants.

John H. Johnson, 1918-2005, (U.S.) built publishing empire based on *Ebony* and *Jet*.

Samuel Curtis Johnson, 1928-2004, (U.S.) headed S.C. Johnson & Sons.

Henry J. Kaiser, 1882-1967, (U.S.) industrialist; built empire in steel, aluminum.

Ingvar Kamprad, 1926-2018, (Swed.) Ikea founder.

Minor C. Keith, 1848-1929, (U.S.) railroad magnate; founded United Fruit Co.

Will K. Kellogg, 1860-1951, (U.S.) businessman, philanthropist; founded breakfast food co.

Kirk Kerkorian, 1917-2015, (U.S.) private equity magnate; real estate developer.

Richard King, 1825-85, (U.S.) cattle farmer; founded King Ranch in Texas.

John W. Kluge, 1914-2010, (Ger.-U.S.) Metromedia chair; philanthropist.

William S. Knudsen, 1879-1948, (U.S.) Danish-born auto industry executive.

Samuel H. Kress, 1863-1955, (U.S.) businessman, art collector, philanthropist; founded "dime store" chain.

Ray A. Kroc, 1902-84, (U.S.) original CEO of McDonald's Corp.; oversaw company's vast expansion.

Alfred Krupp, 1812-87, (Ger.) armaments magnate.

Estée Lauder, 1908-2004, (U.S.) cofounder of Estée Lauder companies.

Kenneth L. Lay, 1942-2006, (U.S.), former CEO of Enron; indicted on fraud charges.

William Levitt, 1907-94, (U.S.) industrialist; "suburb maker."

Thomas Lipton, 1850-1931, (Scot.) merchant; tea empire.

James McGill, 1744-1813, (Scot.-Can.) funded Montréal's McGill Univ.

Andrew W. Mellon, 1855-1937, (U.S.) financier, industrialist, philanthropist.

Charles E. Merrill, 1885-1956, (U.S.) financier; developed firm of Merrill Lynch.

J(ohn) P(ierpont) Morgan, 1837-1913, (U.S.) most powerful figure in finance and industry at turn of 20th cent.

Akio Morita, 1921-99, (Jpn.) cofounded Sony Corp.

Malcolm Muir, 1885-1979, (U.S.) created *Business Week* magazine; headed *Newsweek*, 1937-61.

Roy Neuberger, 1903-2010, (U.S.) financier, art patron.

Samuel Newhouse, 1895-1979, (U.S.) publishing and broadcasting magnate.

Jean Nidetch, 1923-2015, (U.S.) Weight Watchers cofounder.

Aristotle Onassis, 1906-75, (Gr.) shipping magnate.

William S. Paley, 1901-90, (U.S.) built CBS communications empire.

Frederick D. Patterson, 1901-88, (U.S.) founder of United Negro College Fund, 1944.

George Peabody, 1795-1869, (U.S.) merchant, financier, philanthropist.

James C. Penney, 1875-1971, (U.S.) businessman; developed department store.

Frank Perdue, 1920-2005, (U.S.) founder of Perdue Farms, chicken-processing co.

William C. Procter, 1862-1934, (U.S.) headed soap co.

David Rockefeller, 1915-2017, (U.S.) banker, philanthropist.

John D. Rockefeller, 1839-1937, (U.S.) industrialist; established Standard Oil.

John D. Rockefeller Jr., 1874-1960, (U.S.) philanthropist; provided land for UN.

Laurance S. Rockefeller, 1910-2004, (U.S.) philanthropist, conservationist.

Meyer A. Rothschild, 1743-1812, (Ger.) founded international banking house.

Thomas Fortune Ryan, 1851-1928, (U.S.) financier; a founder of American Tobacco.

Edmond J. Safra, 1932-99, (U.S.) banker.

David Sarnoff, 1891-1971, (U.S.) broadcasting pioneer; established first radio network, NBC.

Richard Sears, 1863-1914, (U.S.) founded mail-order co.

Werner von Siemens, 1816-92, (Ger.) industrialist, inventor.

Alfred P. Sloan, 1875-1966, (U.S.) industrialist, philanthropist; headed General Motors.

A. Leland Stanford, 1824-93, (U.S.) railroad official, philanthropist; founded university.

Frank Stanton, 1908-2006, (U.S.) president of CBS network, 1946-71.

Nathan Straus, 1848-1931, (U.S.) German-born merchant, philanthropist; headed Macy's dept. stores.

Levi Strauss, c. 1829-1902, (U.S.) pants manufacturer.

Clement Studebaker, 1831-1901, (U.S.) wagon, carriage maker.

Gustavus Swift, 1839-1903, (U.S.) pioneer meatpacker.

Gerard Swope, 1872-1957, (U.S.) industrialist, economist; headed General Electric.

Dave Thomas, 1932-2002, (U.S.) Wendy's restaurant chain founder.

James Walter Thompson, 1847-1928, (U.S.) ad exec., founder of ad agency.

Alice Tully, 1902-93, (U.S.) arts patron.

Theodore N. Vail, 1845-1920, (U.S.) organized Bell Telephone system, headed AT&T.

Cornelius Vanderbilt, 1794-1877, (U.S.) financier; established steamship, railroad empires.

Lillian Vernon, 1927-2015, (Ger.-U.S.) catalog merchant, philanthropist.

Henry Villard, 1835-1900, (U.S.) German-born railroad executive, financier.

Charles R. Walgreen, 1873-1939, (U.S.) founded drugstore chain.

Madame C. J. Walker, 1867-1919, (U.S.) African-American hair care entrepreneur, philanthropist.

DeWitt Wallace, 1889-1981, and **Lila Wallace**, 1889-1984, (both U.S.) cofounders of *Reader's Digest* magazine.

Sam Walton, 1918-92, (U.S.) founder of Wal-Mart stores.

John Wanamaker, 1838-1922, (U.S.) department-store merchandising pioneer.

Aaron Montgomery Ward, 1843-1913, (U.S.) established first mail-order firm.

Thomas J. Watson, 1874-1956, (U.S.) IBM head, 1914-56.

George Westinghouse, 1846-1914, (U.S.) inventor, manufacturer; organized Westinghouse Electric Co., 1886.

John Hay Whitney, 1905-82, (U.S.) publisher, sportsman, philanthropist.

Chuck Williams, 1915-2015, (U.S.) Williams-Sonoma founder.

Charles E. Wilson, 1890-1961, (U.S.) auto exec., public official.

Frank W. Woolworth, 1852-1919, (U.S.) created five-and-dime chain.

William Wrigley Jr., 1861-1932, (U.S.) founded Wrigley chewing gum co.

American Cartoonists

Reviewed by Lucy Shelton Caswell, Professor and Curator, Cartoon Research Library, Ohio State University.

Scott Adams, b 1957, Dilbert.

Charles Addams, 1912-88, macabre cartoons.

Brad Anderson, 1924-2015, Marmaduke.

Sergio Aragonés, b 1937, (Span.-Mex.) *Mad* magazine.

Peter Arno, 1904-68, *The New Yorker*.

Tex Avery, 1908-80, animator; Bugs Bunny, Porky Pig.

George Baker, 1915-75, The Sad Sack.

Carl Barks, 1901-2000, Donald Duck comic books.

Alison Bechdel, b 1960, graphic novelist.

C. C. Beck, 1910-89, Captain Marvel.

Dave Berg, 1920-2002, *Mad* magazine.

Jim Berry, 1932-2015, Berry's World.

Herb Block (Herblock), 1909-2001, political cartoonist.

George Booth, b 1926, *The New Yorker*.

Berkeley Breathed, b 1957, Bloom County.

Dik Browne, 1917-89, Hi & Lois, Hagar the Horrible.

Marjorie Buell, 1904-93, Little Lulu.

Ernie Bushmiller, 1905-82, Nancy.

Milton Caniff, 1907-88, Terry & the Pirates, Steve Canyon.

Al Capp, 1909-79, Li'l Abner.

Roz Chast, b 1954, *The New Yorker*.

Gene Colan, 1926-2011, Daredevil.

Paul Conrad, 1924-2010, political cartoonist.

Roy Crane, 1901-77, Captain Easy, Buz Sawyer.

R(obert) Crumb, b 1943, underground cartoonist.

Shamus Culhane, 1908-96, animator.

Jay N. "Ding" Darling, 1876-1962, political cartoonist.

Jack Davis, 1924-2016, *Mad* magazine.

Jim Davis, b 1945, Garfield.

Billy DeBeck, 1890-1942, Barney Google.

Rudolph Dirks, 1877-1968, The Katzenjammer Kids.

Walt Disney, 1901-66, produced animated cartoons; created Mickey Mouse, Donald Duck.

Steve Ditko, 1927-2018, Spider-Man.

Mort Drucker, b 1929, *Mad* magazine.

Will Eisner, 1917-2005, The Spirit.

Jules Feiffer, b 1929, political cartoonist.

Bud Fisher, 1885-1954, Mutt & Jeff.

Ham Fisher, 1900-55, Joe Palooka.

Max Fleischer, 1883-1972, Betty Boop.

Hal Foster, 1892-1982, Tarzan, Prince Valiant.

Fontaine Fox, 1884-1964, Toonerville Folks.

Isadore "Friz" Freleng, 1905-95, animator; Yosemite Sam, Porky Pig, Sylvester and Tweety Bird.

Rube Goldberg, 1883-1970, Boob McNutt.

Chester Gould, 1900-85, Dick Tracy.

Harold Gray, 1894-1968, Little Orphan Annie.

Matt Groening, b 1954, Life in Hell, The Simpsons.

Cathy Guisewite, b 1950, Cathy.

Bill Hanna, 1910-2001, and **Joe Barbera**, 1911-2006, animators; Tom & Jerry, Yogi Bear, Flintstones.

Oliver Harrington, 1912-95, Bootsie.

Johnny Hart, 1931-2007, B.C., Wizard of Id.

Alfred Harvey, 1913-94, created Casper the Friendly Ghost.

Jimmy Hatlo, 1898-1963, Little Iodine.

John Held Jr., 1889-1958, Jazz Age.

George Herriman, 1881-1944, Krazy Kat.

Harry Hershfield, 1885-1974, Abie the Agent.

Stephen Hillenburg, b 1961, SpongeBob SquarePants.

Al Hirschfeld, 1903-2003, *NY Times* theater caricaturist.

Burne Hogarth, 1911-96, Tarzan.

Helen Hokinson, 1900-49, *The New Yorker*.

Nicole Hollander, b 1939, Sylvia.

Al Jaffee, b 1921, *Mad* magazine.

Lynn Johnston, b 1947, (Can.) For Better or For Worse.

Oliver Johnston, 1912-2008, Disney animator.

Chuck Jones, 1912-2002, animator; Bugs Bunny, Porky Pig; created Road Runner, Wile E. Coyote.

Mike Judge, b 1962, Beavis and Butt-Head, King of the Hill.

Bob Kane, 1916-98, Batman.

Bil Keane, 1922-2011, The Family Circus.

Walt Kelly, 1913-73, Pogo.

Hank Ketcham, 1920-2001, Dennis the Menace.

Ted Key, 1912-2008, Hazel.

Frank King, 1883-1969, Gasoline Alley.

Jack Kirby, 1917-94, Fantastic Four, The Incredible Hulk.

Rollin Kirby, 1875-1952, political cartoonist.

B(ernard) Kliban, 1935-90, cat books.

Edward Koren, b 1935, *The New Yorker*.

John Kricfalusi, b 1955, Ren & Stimpy.

Joe Kubert, 1926-2012, Sgt. Rock.

Harvey Kurtzman, 1921-93, *Mad* magazine.

Walter Lantz, 1900-94, Woody Woodpecker.

Gary Larson, b 1950, The Far Side.

Mell Lazarus, 1927-2016, Momma, Miss Peach.

Stan Lee, b 1922, Marvel Comics.

David Levine, 1926-2009, *NY Review of Books* caricatures.

Seth MacFarlane, b 1973, Family Guy.

Jeff MacNelly, 1947-2000, political cartoonist; Shoe.

Doug Marlette, 1949-2007, political cartoonist; Kudzu.

Don Martin, 1931-2000, *Mad* magazine.

Bill Mauldin, 1921-2003, political cartoonist.

Winsor McCay, 1872-1934, Little Nemo.

John T. McCutcheon, 1870-1949, political cartoonist.

Patrick McDonnell, b 1956, Mutts.

Dwayne McDuffie, 1962-2011, *Justice League*.

Aaron McGruder, b 1974, The Boondocks.

George McManus, 1884-1954, Bringing Up Father.

Dale Messick, 1906-2005, Brenda Starr.

Wiley Miller, b 1951, Non Sequitur.

Norman Mingo, 1896-1980, Alfred E. Neuman.

Bob Montana, 1920-75, Archie.

Dick Moores, 1909-86, Gasoline Alley.

Willard Mullin, 1902-78, sports cartoonist; Dodgers' "Brooklyn Bum," "Mets Kid."

Randall Munroe, b 1984, xkcd.

Russell Myers, b 1938, Broom Hilda.

Thomas Nast, 1840-1902, political cartoonist; Republican elephant, Democratic donkey.

Pat Oliphant, b 1935, political cartoonist.

Frederick Burr Opper, 1857-1937, Happy Hooligan.

Richard Outcault, 1863-1928, Yellow Kid, Buster Brown.

Brant Parker, 1920-2007, Wizard of Id.

Trey Parker, b 1969, animator, co-creator of South Park.

Harvey Pekar, 1939-2010, American Splendor.

Mike Peters, b 1943, Mother Goose & Grimm.

George Price, 1901-95, *The New Yorker*.

Antonio Prohias, 1921-98, Spy vs. Spy.

Alex Raymond, 1909-56, Flash Gordon, Jungle Jim.

Forrest (Bud) Sagendorf, 1915-94, Popeye.

Art Sansom, 1920-91, The Born Loser.

Charles Schulz, 1922-2000, Peanuts.

Elzie C. Segar, 1894-1938, Popeye.

Marie Severin, 1929-2018, Marvel Comics.

Joe Shuster, 1914-92, and **Jerry Siegel**, 1914-96, Superman.

Sidney Smith, 1887-1935, The Gumps.

Otto Soglow, 1900-75, Little King.

Art Spiegelman, b 1948, Raw, Maus.

William Steig, 1907-2003, *The New Yorker*.

Matt Stone, b 1971, animator, co-creator of South Park.

James Swinnerton, 1875-1974, Little Jimmy, Canyon Kiddies.

Paul Szep, b 1941, political cartoonist.

Paul Terry, 1887-1971, animator of Mighty Mouse.

Bob Thaves, 1924-2006, Frank and Ernest.

James Thurber, 1894-61, *The New Yorker*.

Garry Trudeau, b 1948, Doonesbury.

Jim Unger, 1937-2012, Herman.

Mort Walker, 1923-2018, Beetle Bailey.

Bill Watterson, b 1958, Calvin and Hobbes.

Russ Westover, 1887-1966, Tillie the Toiler.

Signe Wilkinson, b 1950, political cartoonist.

Frank Willard, 1893-1958, Moon Mullins.

J. R. Williams, 1888-1957, The Willets Family, Out Our Way.

Gahan Wilson, b 1930, *The New Yorker*.

Tom Wilson, 1931-2011, Ziggy.

Art Young, 1866-1943, political cartoonist.

Chic Young, 1901-73, Blondie.

Economists, Educators, Historians, and Social Scientists of the Past

For psychologists, see Scientists of the Past.

Brooks Adams, 1848-1927, (U.S.) historian, political theoretician; *The Law of Civilization and Decay*.

Henry Adams, 1838-1918, (U.S.) historian, autobiographer; *The Education of Henry Adams*.

Stephen Ambrose, 1936-2002, (U.S.) historian; *Eisenhower*.

Hannah Arendt, 1906-75, (Ger.) political philosopher; *The Origins of Totalitarianism*.

Francis Bacon, 1561-1626, (Eng.) philosopher, essayist, statesman; championed observation and induction.

George Bancroft, 1800-91, (U.S.) historian; 10-volume *History of the United States*.

Jack Barbash, 1910-94, (U.S.) labor economist; helped create the AFL-CIO.

Henry Barnard, 1811-1900, (U.S.) public school reformer.

Charles A. Beard, 1874-1948, (U.S.) historian; *The Economic Basis of Politics*.

(St.) Bede (the Venerable), c. 673-735, (Br.) scholar, historian; *Ecclesiastical History of the English People*.

Daniel Bell, 1919-2011, (U.S.) sociologist; *The End of Ideology*.

Ruth Benedict, 1887-1948, (U.S.) anthropologist; studied Indian tribes of the Southwest.

Sir Isaiah Berlin, 1909-97, (Br.) philosopher, historian; *The Age of Enlightenment*.

Leonard Bloomfield, 1887-1949, (U.S.) linguist; *Language*.

Franz Boas, 1858-1942, (U.S.) German-born anthropologist; studied American Indians.

Van Wyck Brooks, 1886-1963, (U.S.) historian; critic of New England culture, especially literature.

Edmund Burke, 1729-97, (Ire.) British parliamentarian and political philosopher; *Reflections on the Revolution in France*.

James MacGregor Burns, 1918-2014, (U.S.) historian, political scientist.

Nicholas Murray Butler, 1862-1947, (U.S.) educator; headed Columbia Univ., 1902-45; 1931 Nobel Peace Prize winner.

Joseph Campbell, 1904-87, (U.S.) author, editor, teacher; wrote books on mythology, folklore.

Thomas Carlyle, 1795-1881, (Scot.) historian, critic; *Sartor Resartus*, *Past and Present*, *The French Revolution*.

(Charles) Bruce Catton, 1899-1978, (U.S.) historian; *A Stillness at Appomattox*.

Edward Channing, 1856-1931, (U.S.) historian; 6-volume *History of the United States*.

Henry Steele Commager, 1902-98, (U.S.) historian, educator; *The Growth of the American Republic*.

John R. Commons, 1862-1945, (U.S.) economist, labor historian; *Legal Foundations of Capitalism*.

James B. Conant, 1893-1978, (U.S.) educator, diplomat; *The American High School Today*.

Benedetto Croce, 1866-1952, (It.) philosopher, statesman, historian; *Philosophy of the Spirit*.

Bernard A. De Voto, 1897-1955, (U.S.) historian; wrote trilogy on American West, edited Mark Twain manuscripts.

Melvil Dewey, 1851-1931, (U.S.) devised decimal system of library-book classification.

Donald Herbert Donald, 1920-2009, (U.S.) Pulitzer Prize-winning Civil War and Lincoln historian.

St. Clair Drake, 1911-90, (U.S.) sociologist, black studies pioneer; *Black Metropolis* (1945), with Horace R. Cayton.

W(illiam) E(dward) B(urghardt) Du Bois, 1868-1963, (U.S.) historian, sociologist; NAACP founder, 1909.

Will(iam), 1885-1981, (U.S.) and **Ariel Durant**, 1898-1981, (Ukraine) historians; *The Story of Civilization*.

Emile Durkheim, 1858-1917, (Fr.) a founder of modern sociology; *The Rules of Sociological Method*.

Charles Eliot, 1834-1926, (U.S.) educator, Harvard president.

Friedrich Engels, 1820-95, (Ger.) political writer; with Karl Marx wrote the *Communist Manifesto*.

Irving Fisher, 1867-1947, (U.S.) economist; contributed to the development of modern monetary theory.

John Fiske, 1842-1901, (U.S.) historian and lecturer; popularized Darwinian theory of evolution.

Charles Fourier, 1772-1837, (Fr.) utopian socialist.

John Hope Franklin, 1915-2009, (U.S.) historian; *From Slavery to Freedom: A History of African Americans*.

Sir James George Frazer, 1854-1941, (Br.) anthropologist; studied myth in religion; *The Golden Bough*.

Milton Friedman, 1912-2006, (U.S.) economist; advocate for free markets.

Paul Fussell, 1924-2012, (U.S.) literary historian; *The Great War and Modern Memory*.

John Kenneth Galbraith, 1908-2006, (Can.-U.S.) economist, author, professor, former amb. to India.

Peter Gay, 1923-2015, (Ger.-U.S.) cultural historian; *The Enlightenment: An Interpretation*.

Giovanni Gentile, 1875-1944, (It.) philosopher, educator; reformed Italian educational system.

Henry George, 1839-97, (U.S.) economist, reformer; led single-tax movement.

Edward Gibbon, 1737-94, (Br.) historian; *The History of the Decline and Fall of the Roman Empire*.

Andrew Greeley, 1928-2013, (U.S.) Rom. Cath. priest; sociologist.

Francesco Guicciardini, 1483-1540, (It.) historian; *Storia d'Italia*, principal historical work of the 16th cent.

Thomas Hobbes, 1588-1679, (Eng.) philosopher, political theorist; *Leviathan*.

Richard Hofstadter, 1916-70, (U.S.) historian; *The Age of Reform*.

Charles Hamilton Houston, 1895-1950, (U.S.) African-American lawyer, Howard Univ. instructor; champion of minority rights.

Samuel Huntington, 1927-2008, (U.S.), political scientist, Harvard University professor; *The Clash of Civilizations*.

Alfred Kahn, 1917-2010, (U.S.) economist; deregulated the U.S. airline industry.

John Keegan, 1934-2012, (Br.) war historian; *The Face of Battle*.

George F. Kennan, 1904-2005, (U.S.) diplomat, historian; main architect of U.S. Cold War "containment" strategy.

John Maynard Keynes, 1883-1946, (Br.) economist; principal advocate of deficit spending.

Alfred Kinsey, 1894-1956, (U.S.) zoologist; pioneering human sex researcher.

Russell Kirk, 1918-94, (U.S.) social philosopher; *The Conservative Mind*.

Alfred L. Kroeber, 1876-1960, (U.S.) cultural anthropologist; studied Indians of North and South America.

Elisabeth Kubler-Ross, 1926-2004, (Switz.) psychiatrist, author; *On Death and Dying*.

Christopher Lasch, 1932-94, (U.S.) social critic, historian; *The Culture of Narcissism*.

James L. Laughlin, 1850-1933, (U.S.) economist; helped establish Federal Reserve System.

Margaret Leech, 1893-1974, (U.S.) historian; *Reveille in Washington, 1860-1865*.

Lucien Lévy-Bruhl, 1857-1939, (Fr.) philosopher; studied the psychology of primitive societies; *Primitive Mentality*.

John Locke, 1632-1704, (Eng.) philosopher, political theorist; *Two Treatises of Government*.

Thomas B. Macaulay, 1800-59, (Br.) historian, statesman.

Niccolò Machiavelli, 1469-1527, (It.) writer, statesman; *The Prince*.

Bronislaw Malinowski, 1884-1942, (Pol.) considered the father of social anthropology.

Thomas R. Malthus, 1766-1834, (Br.) economist; *Essay on the Principle of Population*.

Horace Mann, 1796-1859, (U.S.) pioneered modern public school system.

Karl Mannheim, 1893-1947, (Hung.) sociologist, historian; *Ideology and Utopia*.

Harriet Martineau, 1802-76, (Eng.) writer, feminist; *Society in America*.

Karl Marx, 1818-83, (Ger.) political theorist, proponent of Communism; *Communist Manifesto*, *Das Kapital*.

Benjamin Mays, 1895-1984, (U.S.) minister, educator, civil rights leader; headed Morehouse College, 1940-67.

Giuseppe Mazzini, 1805-72, (It.) political philosopher.

William H. McGuffey, 1800-73, (U.S.) his *Reader* was a mainstay of 19th-cent. U.S. public education.

George H. Mead, 1863-1931, (U.S.) philosopher, social psychologist.

Margaret Mead, 1901-78, (U.S.) cultural anthropologist; popularized field; *Coming of Age in Samoa*.

Alexander Meiklejohn, 1872-1964, (U.S.) Br.-born educator; championed academic freedom and experimental curricula.

James Mill, 1773-1836, (Scot.) philosopher, historian, economist; a proponent of utilitarianism.

John Stuart Mill, 1806-73, (Eng.) philosopher, economist; *Utilitarianism*. Eldest son of James Mill.

Perry G. Miller, 1905-63, (U.S.) historian; interpreted 17th-cent. New England.

Theodor Mommsen, 1817-1903, (Ger.) historian; *The History of Rome*.

Ashley Montagu, 1905-99, (Eng.) anthropologist; *The Natural Superiority of Women*.

Charles-Louis Montesquieu, 1689-1755, (Fr.) social philosopher; *The Spirit of Laws*.

Maria Montessori, 1870-1952, (It.) educator, physician; started Montessori method of student self-motivation.

Samuel Eliot Morison, 1887-1976, (U.S.) historian; chronicled voyages of early explorers.

Lewis Mumford, 1895-1990, (U.S.) sociologist, critic; *The Culture of Cities*.

Gunnar Myrdal, 1898-1987, (Swed.) economist, social scientist; *Asian Drama: An Inquiry Into the Poverty of Nations*.

Allan Nevins, 1890-1971, (U.S.) historian, biographer; *The Ordeal of the Union*.

José Ortega y Gasset, 1883-1955, (Sp.) philosopher; advocated control by elite; *The Revolt of the Masses*.

Elinor Ostrom, 1933-2012, (U.S.) political economist.

Robert Owen, 1771-1858, (Br.) political philosopher, reformer; pioneer in cooperative movement.

Thomas Paine, 1737-1809, (Br.-U.S.) political theorist, writer; *Common Sense*.

Vilfredo Pareto, 1848-1923, (It.) economist, sociologist.

Francis Parkman, 1823-93, (U.S.) historian; *France and England in North America*.

Elizabeth P. Peabody, 1804-94, (U.S.) education pioneer; founded first kindergarten in U.S., 1860.

William Prescott, 1796-1859, (U.S.) early American historian; *The Conquest of Peru*.

Pierre Joseph Proudhon, 1809-65, (Fr.) social theorist; father of anarchism; *The Philosophy of Property*.

François Quesnay, 1694-1774, (Fr.) economic theorist.

Robert V. Remini, 1921-2013, (U.S.) historian; *The Life of Andrew Jackson*.

David Ricardo, 1772-1823, (Br.) economic theorist; advocated free international trade.

David Riesman, 1909-2002, (U.S.) sociologist; co-author, *The Lonely Crowd*.

Jacqueline de Romilly, 1913-2010, (Fr.) scholar of Greek civilization and language.

Theodore Roszak, 1933-2011, (U.S.) historian; *The Making of a Counter Culture*.

Jean-Jacques Rousseau, 1712-78, (Fr.) social philosopher; the father of romantic sensibility; *Confessions*.

Paul Samuelson, 1915-2009, (U.S.) economist, famed for modern mathematical approach to economics.

Edward Sapir, 1884-1939, (Ger.-U.S.) anthropologist; studied ethnology and linguistics of American Indian groups.

Ferdinand de Saussure, 1857-1913, (Switz.) a founder of modern linguistics.

Arthur Schlesinger Jr., 1917-2007, (U.S.) historian, author; *The Imperial Presidency*.

Joseph Schumpeter, 1883-1950, (Czech.-U.S.) economist, sociologist.

Elizabeth Seton, 1774-1821, (U.S.) nun; est. parochial school education in U.S., first native-born American saint.

Georg Simmel, 1858-1918, (Ger.) sociologist, philosopher; helped establish German sociology.

Robert Sklar, 1936-2011, (U.S.) film scholar.

Adam Smith, 1723-90, (Br.) economist; advocated laissez-faire economy, free trade; *The Wealth of Nations*.

Jared Sparks, 1789-1866, (U.S.) historian, educator, editor; *The Library of American Biography*.

Oswald Spengler, 1880-1936, (Ger.) philosopher, historian; *The Decline of the West*.

Leo Steinberg, 1920-2011, (Russ.-U.S.) art historian.

William G. Sumner, 1840-1910, (U.S.) social scientist, economist; laissez-faire economy, Social Darwinism.

Hippolyte Taine, 1828-93, (Fr.) historian, basis of naturalistic school; *The Origins of Contemporary France*.

A(lan) J(ohn) P(ercivale) Taylor, 1906-90, (Br.) historian; *The Origins of the Second World War*.

Nikolaas Tinbergen, 1907-88, (Neth.-Br.) ethologist; pioneer in study of animal behavior.

Alexis de Tocqueville, 1805-59, (Fr.) political scientist, historian; *Democracy in America*.

Francis E. Townsend, 1867-1960, (U.S.) led old-age pension movement, 1933.

Arnold Toynbee, 1889-1975, (Br.) historian; *A Study of History*, sweeping analysis of hist. of civilizations.

George Trevelyan, 1876-1962, (Br.) historian, statesman. Favored "literary" over "scientific" history; *History of England*.

Henri Troyat, 1911-2007, (Russ.-Fr.), biographies of major figures in Russian history.

Frederick J. Turner, 1861-1932, (U.S.) historian, educator; *The Frontier in American History*.

Thorstein B. Veblen, 1857-1929, (U.S.) economist, social philosopher; *The Theory of the Leisure Class*.

Giovanni Vico, 1668-1744, (It.) historian, biographer; regarded by many as first modern historian; *New Science*.

Izaak Walton, 1593-1683, (Eng.) biographer; political-philosophical study of fishing, *The Compleat Angler*.

Booker T. Washington, 1856-1915, (U.S.) founder, 1881, and first pres. of Tuskegee Institute; *Up From Slavery*.

Sidney J., 1859-1947, and **Beatrice Webb**, 1858-1943, (both Br.) leading figures in Fabian Society and Labor Party.

Max Weber, 1864-1920, (Ger.) sociologist; *The Protestant Ethic and the Spirit of Capitalism*.

Walter White, 1893-1955, (U.S.) exec. sec., NAACP, 1931-55.

Roy Wilkins, 1901-81, (U.S.) exec. director, NAACP, 1955-77.

Emma Hart Willard, 1787-1870, (U.S.) pioneered higher education for women.

James Q. Wilson, 1931-2012, (U.S.) political scientist; co-authored broken windows theory.

Carter G. Woodson, 1875-1950, (U.S.) historian; founded Assn. for the Study of Negro Life and History.

C. Vann Woodward, 1908-99, (U.S.) historian; *The Strange Career of Jim Crow*.

Howard Zinn, 1922-2010, (U.S.) historian; *A People's History of the United States*.

American Journalists of the Past

Reviewed by Dean Mills, Dean, Missouri School of Journalism.

See also Business Leaders and Philanthropists, American Cartoonists, and Writers of the Past.

Franklin P. Adams (F.P.A.), 1881-1960, humorist; wrote column "The Conning Tower."

Roger Ailes, 1940-2017, Fox News cofounder and CEO.

Joseph W. Alsop, 1910-89, and **Stewart Alsop**, 1914-74, Washington-based political analysts, columnists.

Jack Anderson, 1922-2006, muckraking Washington, DC, syndicated columnist.

Brooks Atkinson, 1894-1984, theater critic.

Robert L. Bartley, 1937-2003, editorial-page editor for *Wall Street Journal*.

Jessie Tarbox Beals, 1870-1942, photojournalist.

James Gordon Bennett, 1795-1872, editor and publisher; founded *NY Herald*.

James Gordon Bennett Jr., 1841-1918, succeeded father, financed expeditions, founded afternoon paper.

Nellie Bly (Elizabeth Cochrane), 1864?-1922, pioneer woman journalist, investigative reporter; noted for series on trip around the world.

Elias Boudinot, c. 1803-39, founding editor of first Native American newspaper in U.S., *Cherokee Phoenix* (1828-34).

Benjamin Bradlee, 1921-2014, (U.S.) *Washington Post* exec. editor.

Ed Bradley, 1941-2006, TV journalist (*60 Minutes*).

Andrew Breitbart, 1969-2012, conservative commentator and blogger.

Jimmy Breslin, 1928-2017, *NY Daily News* columnist.

David Brinkley, 1920-2003, co-anchor of NBC's *Huntley-Brinkley Report*, host of ABC's *This Week With David Brinkley*.

Arthur Brisbane, 1864-1936, editor; helped introduce "yellow journalism" with sensational, simply written articles.

David Broder, 1929-2011, political journalist for *Washington Post*.

Joyce Brothers, 1927-2013, psychologist, columnist.

Heywood Broun, 1888-1939, author, columnist; founded American Newspaper Guild.

Helen Gurley Brown, 1922-2012, author; editor-in-chief of *Cosmopolitan* magazine (1965-97).

Art Buchwald, 1925-2007, journalist, humorist, syndicated columnist.

William F. Buckley Jr., 1925-2008, columnist and commentator; founder of *National Review*.

Herb Caen, 1916-97, longtime columnist for *San Francisco Chronicle* and *Examiner*.

John Campbell, 1653-1728, published *Boston News-Letter*, first continuing newspaper in the American colonies.

Jimmy Cannon, 1909-73, syndicated sports columnist.

John Chancellor, 1927-96, NBC reporter, anchor.

Harry Chandler, 1864-1944, *L.A. Times* publisher (1917-41).

Otis Chandler, 1928-2006, *Los Angeles Times* publisher (1960-80).

Marquis Childs, 1903-90, reporter and columnist for *St. Louis Post-Dispatch* and United Feature syndicate.

Craig Claiborne, 1920-2000, *NY Times* food editor and critic; key in internationalizing American tastes.

Alexander Cockburn, 1941-2012, left-wing journalist.

Charles Collingwood, 1917-85, CBS news correspondent.

Alistair Cooke, 1908-2004, Brit. journalist, TV narrator; naturalized American citizen, "Letter From America" series.

Howard Cosell, 1920-95, TV and radio sportscaster.

Gardner Cowles, 1861-1946, founded newspaper chain.

Judith Crist, 1922-2012, film critic.

Walter Cronkite, 1916-2009, CBS evening news anchor, TV journalist.

Evelyn Cunningham, 1916-2010, African-American civil rights reporter.

Cyrus Curtis, 1850-1933, publisher of *Saturday Evening Post*, *Ladies' Home Journal*, *Country Gentleman*.

John Charles Daly, 1914-91, war correspondent, TV journalist; Voice of America head.

Charles Anderson Dana, 1819-97, editor, publisher; made *NY Sun* famous for its news reporting.

Elmer (Holmes) Davis, 1890-1958, *NY Times* editorial writer, radio commentator.

Richard Harding Davis, 1864-1916, war correspondent, travel writer, fiction writer.

Benjamin Day, 1810-89, published *NY Sun* beginning in 1833, introducing penny press to the U.S.

Dorothy Dix (Elizabeth Meriwether Gilmer), 1861-1951, reporter; pioneer of the advice column genre.

Finley Peter Dunne, 1867-1936, humorist, social critic; wrote "Mr. Dooley" columns.

Roger Ebert, 1942-2013, film critic.

Mary Baker Eddy, 1821-1910, founded Christian Science movement and *Christian Science Monitor*.

Rowland Evans Jr., 1921-2001, Washington columnist.

Fanny Fern (Sara Willis Parton), 1811-72, newspaper columnist, author.

Marshall Field III, 1893-1956, retail magnate, *Chicago Sun* founder.

Doris Fleeson, 1901-70, war correspondent, columnist.

Benjamin Franklin, 1706-90, publisher of *Poor Richard's Almanack*.

James Franklin, 1697-1735, printer, pioneer journalist; publisher of *New England Courant* and *Rhode Island Gazette*.

Fred W. Friendly, 1915-98, radio, TV reporter, producer, executive; collaborator with Edward R. Murrow.

Margaret Fuller, 1810-50, social reformer, transcendentalist, critic and foreign correspondent for *NY Tribune*.

Frank E. Gannett, 1876-1957, founded newspaper chain.

Mary Ellen Garber, 1916-2008, sports journalist.

William Lloyd Garrison, 1805-79, abolitionist; publisher of *The Liberator*.

Jack Germond, 1928-2013, political reporter.

Edwin Lawrence Godkin, 1831-1902, founder of *The Nation*, editor of *NY Evening Post*.

Katharine Graham, 1917-2001, *Washington Post* publisher.

Sheilah Graham, 1904-89, Hollywood gossip columnist.

Horace Greeley, 1811-72, editor, politician; founded *NY Tribune*.

Meg Greenfield, 1930-99, *Newsweek* columnist, *Washington Post* editorial page editor.

Gilbert Hovey Grosvenor, 1875-1966, longtime editor of *National Geographic* magazine.

John Gunther, 1901-70, *Chicago Daily News* foreign correspondent, author.

David Halberstam, 1934-2007, journalist, sports reporter, author; *The Best and the Brightest*, *Summer of '49*.

Sarah Josepha Buell Hale, 1788-1879, first female magazine editor; *Ladies' Magazine*, later *Godey's Lady's Book*.

Paul Harvey, 1918-2009, radio broadcaster and commentator.

William Randolph Hearst, 1863-1951, founder of Hearst newspaper chain, one of the pioneers of yellow journalism.

Gabriel Heatter, 1890-1972, radio commentator.

John Hersey, 1914-98, foreign correspondent for *Time*, *Life*, and *The New Yorker*; author.

Marguerite Higgins, 1920-66, reporter, war correspondent.

Christopher Hitchens, 1949-2011, columnist and literary critic.

Hedda Hopper, 1885-1966, Hollywood gossip columnist.

Roy Howard, 1883-1964, editor, executive; Scripps-Howard papers and United Press (later United Press International).

Chet (Chester Robert) Huntley, 1911-74, co-anchor of NBC's *Huntley-Brinkley Report*.

Ada Louise Huxtable, 1921-2013, architecture critic.

Gwen Ifill, 1955-2016, TV journalist.

Ralph Ingersoll, 1900-85, editor; *Fortune*, *Time*, *Life* exec.

Molly Ivins, 1944-2007, author, syndicated political columnist.

Peter Jennings, 1938-2005, ABC correspondent, anchor.

Pauline Kael, 1919-2001, film critic.

H. V. (Hans von) Kaltenborn, 1878-1965, radio commentator, reporter.

Murray Kempton, 1917-97, reporter, columnist for magazines and newspapers, including *NY Post*.

Dorothy Kilgallen, 1913-65, crime reporter, columnist.

James J. Kilpatrick, 1920-2010, political columnist, author and television personality.

John S. Knight, 1894-1981, editor, publisher; founded Knight newspaper group, which merged into Knight-Ridder.

Joseph Kraft, 1942-86, foreign policy columnist.

Irving Kristol, 1920-2009, columnist, commentator.

Arthur Krock, 1886-1974, *NY Times* political writer, Washington bureau chief.

Charles Kuralt, 1934-97, TV anchor; host of CBS "On the Road" featuring stories about life in the U.S.

Ann Landers (Eppie Lederer), 1918-2002, advice columnist.

David Lawrence, 1888-1973, reporter, columnist, publisher; founded *U.S. News & World Report*.

Frank Leslie, 1821-80, engraver, publisher of newspapers and magazines, notably *Leslie's Illustrated Newspaper*.

Anthony Lewis, 1927-2013, legal journalist.

Alexander Liberman, 1912-99, editorial director for Condé Nast magazines.

A(bbott) J(oseph) Liebling, 1904-63, foreign correspondent, critic; principally with *The New Yorker*.

Walter Lippmann, 1889-1974, political analyst, social critic, columnist, author.

Peter Lisagor, 1915-76, Washington bureau chief, *Chicago Daily News*; broadcast commentator.

David Ross Locke, 1833-88, humorist, satirist under pseudonym P.V. Nasby; owned *Toledo (Ohio) Blade*.

Elijah Parish Lovejoy, 1802-37, abolitionist editor in St. Louis and in Alton, IL; killed by proslavery mob.

Clare Booth Luce, 1903-87, war correspondent for *Life*, diplomat, playwright.

Henry R. Luce, 1898-1967, founded *Time*, *Fortune*, *Life*, *Sports Illustrated*.

Dwight Macdonald, 1906-82, reporter, social critic.

Don Marquis, 1878-1937, humor columnist for *NY Sun* and *NY Tribune*; wrote "Archy and Mehitabel" stories.

Nancy Hicks Maynard, 1946-2008, African American publisher, journalist.

Robert Maynard, 1937-97, first African-American editor and then owner of major U.S. paper, the *Oakland Tribune*.

C(harles) K(enny) McClatchy, 1858-1936, founder of McClatchy newspaper chain.

Sarah McClendon, 1910-2003, veteran White House correspondent.

Samuel McClure, 1857-1949, founder (1893) of *McClure's Magazine*, famous for its investigative reporting.

Anne O'Hare McCormick, 1889-1954, foreign correspondent; first woman on *NY Times* editorial board.

Robert R. McCormick, 1880-1955, editor, publisher, executive of *Chicago Tribune* and *NY Daily News*.

Ralph McGill, 1893-1969, crusading editor, publisher of *Atlanta Constitution*.

Mary McGrory, 1918-2004, Washington columnist.

O(scar) O(dd) McIntyre, 1884-1938, feature writer, syndicated columnist on every-day life in New York City.

John McLaughlin, 1927-2016, TV journalist.

Joseph Medill, 1823-99, longtime editor of the *Chicago Tribune*.

H(enry) L(ouis) Mencken, 1880-1956, reporter, editor, columnist with *Baltimore Sun* papers; anti-establishment viewpoint.

Edwin Meredith, 1876-1928, founder of magazine company.

Frank A. Munsey, 1854-1925, owner, editor, and publisher of newspapers and magazines, including *Munsey's Magazine*.

Edward R. Murrow, 1908-65, broadcast reporter, exec.; reported from Britain in WWII; hosted *See It Now*, *Person to Person*.

Allen Neuharth, 1924-2013, *USA Today* founder.

Edwin Newman, 1919-2010, NBC news correspondent.

Louella Parsons, 1881-1972, Hollywood gossip columnist.

Ethel L. Payne, 1911-91, African American civil rights reporter.

Daniel Pearl, 1963-2002, American journalist; kidnapped and murdered in Pakistan.

Drew (Andrew Russell) Pearson, 1897-1969, investigative reporter, columnist.

(James) Westbrook Pegler, 1894-1969, reporter, columnist.

Shirley Povich, 1905-98, sports columnist.

Joseph Pulitzer, 1847-1911, *NY World* publisher; founded Columbia Journalism School, Pulitzer Prizes.

Joseph Pulitzer II, 1885-1955, longtime *St. Louis Post-Dispatch* editor, publisher; built it into major paper.

Ernie Pyle, 1900-45, reporter, war correspondent; killed in WWII.

William Raspberry, 1935-2012, public affairs columnist.

Henry Raymond, 1820-69, cofounder, editor, *NY Times*.

Harry Reasoner, 1923-91, ABC and CBS news reporter, anchor.

John Reed, 1887-1920, reporter; foreign correspondent famous for coverage of Bolshevik Revolution; buried at the Kremlin.

Whitelaw Reid, 1837-1912, longtime editor, *NY Tribune*.

James Reston, 1909-95, *NY Times* political reporter, columnist.

Frank Reynolds, 1923-83, ABC reporter, anchor.

(Henry) Grantland Rice, 1880-1954, sportswriter.

Jacob Riis, 1849-1914, reporter, photographer; exposed slum conditions in *How the Other Half Lives*.

Max Robinson, 1939-88, first African American to anchor network news (ABC), 1978.

Andy Rooney, 1919-2011, radio and TV commentator (*60 Minutes*).

A. M. Rosenthal, 1922-2006, reporter, editor for *NY Times* (1943-99).

Harold Ross, 1892-1951, founder, editor, *The New Yorker*.

Carl T. Rowan, 1925-2000, reporter, columnist, author.

Mike Royko, 1932-97, Chicago newspaper columnist; wrote *Boss*, biography of Mayor Richard J. Daley (1902-76).

Louis Rukeyser, 1933-2006, TV journalist, financial analyst; hosted *Wall Street Week* on public television.

(Alfred) Damon Runyon, 1884-1946, sportswriter, columnist; stories collected in *Guys and Dolls*.

Tim Russert, 1950-2008, TV journalist; moderator of *Meet the Press* (NBC).

John B. Russwurm, 1799-1851, cofounded (1827) nation's first black newspaper, *Freedom's Journal*, in New York, NY.

Morley Safer, 1931-2016, TV journalist (*60 Minutes*).

William Safire, 1929-2009, Pulitzer Prize-winning columnist, *NY Times*.

Adela Rogers St. Johns, 1894-1988, reporter, sportswriter for Hearst newspapers.

Pierre Salinger, 1925-2004, press sec. under Pres. Kennedy and Johnson, foreign correspondent.

Harrison Salisbury, 1908-93, reporter, foreign correspondent; Soviet specialist.

Andrew Sarris, 1928-2012, film critic, *Village Voice*.

Daniel Schorr, 1916-2010, broadcast and print journalist.

E(dward) W(illis) Scripps, 1854-1926, founded first large U.S. newspaper chain, pioneered syndication.

Eric Sevareid, 1912-92, war correspondent, radio newscaster, CBS commentator.

Anthony Shadid, 1968-2012, foreign correspondent.

Randy Shilts, 1951-94, journalist; author of *And the Band Played On*.

William L. Shirer, 1904-93, broadcaster, foreign correspondent; wrote *The Rise and Fall of the Third Reich*.

Howard K. Smith, 1914-2002, ABC news reporter, anchor.

Liz Smith, 1923-2017, gossip columnist.

Red (Walter) Smith, 1905-82, sportswriter.

Edgar P. Snow, 1905-71, correspondent; expert on Chinese Communist movement.

Tony Snow, 1955-2008, columnist, radio/TV journalist, White House press sec.

Tom Snyder, 1936-2007, television journalist.

Lawrence Spivak, 1900-94, co-creator, moderator, producer of *Meet the Press*.

(Joseph) Lincoln Steffens, 1866-1936, muckraking journalist.

I(sidor) F(einstein) Stone, 1907-89, one-man editor of *I. F. Stone's Weekly*.

Arthur Hays Sulzberger, 1891-1968, longtime publisher of *NY Times* (1935-61).

Arthur Ochs "Punch" Sulzberger, 1926-2012, longtime publisher of *NY Times* (1963-92).

C(yrus) L(eo) Sulzberger, 1912-93, *NY Times* foreign correspondent, columnist.

David Susskind, 1920-87, TV producer, public affairs talk-show host (*Open End*).

John Cameron Swayze, 1906-95, early TV newscaster (NBC).

Herbert Bayard Swope, 1882-1958, war correspondent, editor of *NY World*.

Ida Tarbell, 1857-1944, muckraking journalist.

Helen Thomas, 1920-2013, White House correspondent, 1959-2010.

Isaiah Thomas, 1750-1831, printer, publisher; cofounder of revolutionary journal, *Massachusetts Spy*.

Lowell Thomas, 1892-1981, radio newscaster, world traveler.

Dorothy Thompson, 1894-1961, foreign correspondent, columnist, radio commentator.

Hunter S. Thompson, 1937-2005, political journalist, author; *Fear and Loathing on the Campaign Trail* (1972).

Kenneth Thompson, 1923-2006, Canadian media magnate; owned Toronto *Globe and Mail* newspaper.

Abigail Van Buren (Pauline Phllips), 1918-2013, advice columnist.

Mike Wallace, 1918-2012, TV journalist (*60 Minutes*).

Ida Bell Wells-Barnett, 1862-1931, African-American reporter, editor, anti-lynching crusader.

William Allen White, 1868-1944, newspaper editor, publisher.

Tom Wicker, 1926-2011, *NY Times* political reporter, columnist.

Walter Winchell, 1897-1972, reporter, columnist, broadcaster of celebrity news.

John Peter Zenger, 1697-1746, printer, journalist; acquitted in precedent-setting libel suit (1735).

YEAR *in* PICTURES | 2018

WORLD

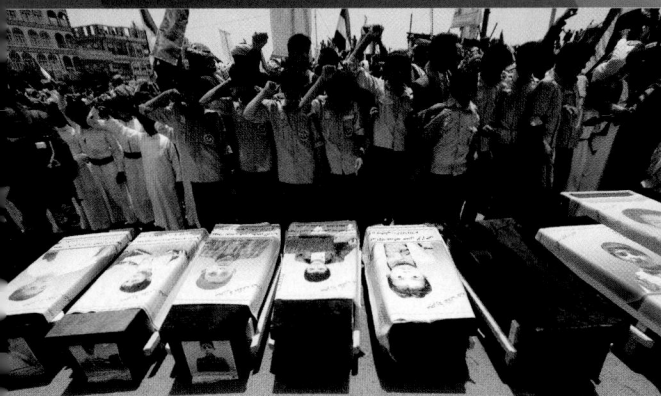

AFGHAN AMBULANCE ATTACK In an attack claimed by the Taliban, more than 100 were killed when a bomb disguised in an ambulance was detonated in a secure zone in Kabul, Afghanistan, Jan. 27, 2018.

CASUALTIES OF WAR Yemen's war and concurrent humanitarian crisis continued well into 2018, with an unknown number of dead, more than 2 million people internally displaced, and about 280,000 Yemeni refugees.

VIOLENCE FLARES IN GAZA
Demonstrations expanded at the Gaza border in Mar.-May 2018 and violence ensued, with Israeli soldiers firing on protesters.

ONGOING TRAGEDY An apparent chemical attack killed dozens in residential areas of Syria's then-rebel-held Douma Apr. 7, 2018.

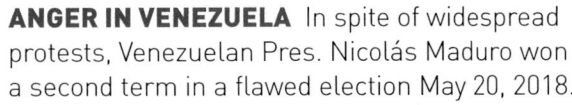

ANGER IN VENEZUELA In spite of widespread protests, Venezuelan Pres. Nicolás Maduro won a second term in a flawed election May 20, 2018.

SPY VS. SPY Investigations into the nerve-agent poisoning of Russian double agent Sergei Skripal and daughter Yulia in Salisbury, England, on Mar. 4, 2018, led the UK to charge two Russian men in the attack.

LEFT BEHIND The U.S. decision in May 2018 to pull out of the joint nuclear deal between Iran, the U.S., and other world powers, was greeted by protests in Iran and elsewhere.

65 YEARS LATER North Korean leader Kim Jong Un met South Korean Pres. Moon Jae-in at the demilitarized zone between the two nations Apr. 27, 2018, and Kim became the first North Korean leader to cross into the South since the Korean War.

WORLD

WOMEN TAKE THE WHEEL The ban on women driving in Saudi Arabia was officially lifted June 24, 2018, but the country's strict male guardianship laws remained a major obstacle to women's equality.

CAVE ESCAPE A Thai boys soccer team and their coach trapped in a partially flooded cave in Chiang Rai, Thailand, held the world's attention and drew a daring rescue operation in July 2018.

OLD FRIENDS The June 2018 G7 summit with traditional allies like German Chancellor Angela Merkel proved contentious, as U.S. Pres. Donald Trump rejected the summit's joint communiqué.

NEW MEXICO Mexican Pres.-elect Andrés Manuel López Obrador and Pres. Enrique Peña Nieto made preparations for López Obrador to take office Dec. 1, 2018, after winning July 2018 elections.

TWIN DISASTERS A 7.5 magnitude earthquake and 20-ft tsunami left more than 2,000 dead and 70,000 displaced from their homes on the Indonesian island of Sulawesi.

CHURCH CHALLENGED Amid a renewed deluge of clerical sex abuse charges against the Roman Catholic Church, Pope Francis visited Ireland Aug. 25-26, 2018, and was greeted by protesters as well as devotees.

A NEW DAY IN ZIMBABWE? Zimbabwe held its first presidential elections since the ousting of longtime ruler Robert Mugabe in late 2017; former Vice Pres. Emmerson Mnangagwa was inaugurated Aug. 26, 2018, after a disputed July 2018 election.

HEAD TO HEAD U.S. Pres. Donald Trump and Russian Pres. Vladimir Putin appeared at a joint press conference July 16, 2018, to face questions about Russian interference in the 2016 U.S. election and other subjects discussed during their summit in Helsinki, Finland.

NATIONAL

CHANGING OF THE GUARD Republicans in Congress celebrated the successful passage of the biggest tax overhaul in 30 years Dec. 20, 2017, but a wave of long-serving members announced their retirements, including House Speaker Paul Ryan (R, WI) and Sen. Orrin Hatch (R, UT).

SCHOOL'S OUT Teachers in Arizona, Kentucky, West Virginia, and elsewhere organized statewide strikes in 2018, seeking better pay and benefits and increased funding for public schools.

LEADING THE CHARGE The "March for Our Lives" gun control rallies held Mar. 24, 2018, were organized by student activists like Emma González, a survivor of the mass shooting that killed 17 at Marjory Stoneman Douglas High School in Parkland, FL, on Feb. 14.

STRANGE BEDFELLOWS Adult film actress Stormy Daniels drew attention in Mar. 2018 when she said she had received a $130,000 payment—in exchange for not disclosing a 2006 affair with Pres. Trump—from Trump personal attorney Michael Cohen.

NEVER FORGOTTEN The National Memorial for Peace and Justice opened in Montgomery, AL, Apr. 26, 2018, to commemorate the thousands of Americans killed in racially motivated lynchings.

BIG ISLAND ERUPTION Hawaii's Kilauea volcano began to erupt May 3, 2018, spilling lava over parts of the Big Island and destroying hundreds of homes.

BROKEN FAMILIES The Trump administration's policy of separating undocumented children and families drew widespread, bipartisan criticism in May-June 2018.

UNDER FIRE California and other Western states faced another record-setting fire season in 2018, with thousands of homes damaged or destroyed.

CRIME AND PUNISHMENT Former Trump presidential campaign manager Paul Manafort was found guilty of financial crimes Aug. 21, 2018, in the first trial related to special counsel Robert Mueller's investigation into the 2016 campaign.

NATIONAL

JUSTICE FOR ALL? Supreme Court nominee Brett Kavanaugh and Dr. Christine Blasey Ford, who said the DC Circuit judge had sexually assaulted her when they were teenagers, both gave emotional testimony to the Senate Judiciary Committee Sept. 27, 2018. Kavanaugh was confirmed, 50-48, Oct. 6.

COUNTING THE COST Many protested the Puerto Rican government's statistics on those killed in 2017's Hurricane Maria and its aftermath; the number was officially revised upward Aug. 28, 2018, from 64 to 2,975.

IN WITH THE NEW Alexandria Ocasio-Cortez and Ayanna Pressley won Democratic congressional primaries ahead of Nov. 2018 midterm elections and were cited as part of a wave of new representation for women and diverse voices.

RAINED OUT Hurricane Florence targeted North and South Carolina in mid-Sept. 2018, with dozens of inches of rain in some areas.

Military and Naval Leaders of the Past
Reviewed by Alan C. Aimone, U.S. Military Academy Library.

Alexander the Great, 356-323 BCE, (Maced.) conquered Persia and much of the world known to Europeans.

Harold Alexander, 1891-1969, (Br.) led Allied invasion of Italy, 1943, WWII.

Ethan Allen, 1738-89, (U.S.) headed Green Mountain Boys; captured Ft. Ticonderoga, 1775, Amer. Rev.

Edmund Allenby, 1861-1936, (Br.) in Boer War, WWI; led Egyptian expeditionary force, 1917-18.

Benedict Arnold, 1741-1801, (U.S.) victorious at Saratoga; tried to betray West Point to British, Amer. Rev.

Henry "Hap" Arnold, 1886-1950, (U.S.) commanded Army Air Force in WWII.

Ashurnasirpal II, 884-859 BCE, (Assyria) king; began Assyrian conquest of Middle East.

John Barry, 1745-1803, (U.S.) won numerous sea battles during Amer. Rev.

Pierre Beauregard, 1818-93, (U.S.) Confed. general; ordered bombardment of Ft. Sumter that began Civil War.

Belisarius, c. 505-565, (Byzant.) won remarkable victories for Byzantine emperor Justinian I.

Gebhard von Blücher, 1742-1819, (Ger.) helped defeat Napoleon at Waterloo.

Simón Bolívar, 1783-1830, (Venez.) S. Amer. revolutionary who liberated much of the continent from Spanish rule.

Napoleon Bonaparte, 1769-1821, (Fr.) defeated Russia and Austria at Austerlitz, 1805; invaded Russia, 1812; defeated at Waterloo, 1815.

Edward Braddock, 1695-1755, (Br.) commanded forces in French and Indian War.

Omar N. Bradley, 1893-1981, (U.S.) headed U.S. ground troops in Normandy invasion, 1944, WWII.

John Burgoyne, 1722-92, (Br.) general; defeated at Saratoga, Amer. Rev.

Julius Caesar, 100-44 BCE, (Rom.) general and politician; conquered northern Gaul, overthrew Roman Republic.

Charlemagne, 742-814, (Fr.) king of the Franks, Holy Roman Emperor; conquered most of Western Europe.

Claire Lee Chennault, 1893-1958, (U.S.) headed Flying Tigers in WWII.

El Cid (Rodrigo Diaz de Vivar), 1040-99, (Sp.) renowned knight; captured Valencia (1094), hero of "Song of Cid" epic.

Mark W. Clark, 1896-1984, (U.S.) helped plan N African invasion in WWII; commander of UN forces, Korean War.

Karl von Clausewitz, 1780-1831, (Prus.) military theorist.

Lucius D. Clay, 1897-1978, (U.S.) led Berlin airlift, 1948-49.

Henry Clinton, 1738-95, (Br.) commander of forces in Amer. Rev., 1778-81.

Cochise, c. 1815-74, (Amer. Ind.) chief of Chiricahua band of Apache Indians in Southwest U.S.

Charles Cornwallis, 1738-1805, (Br.) victorious at Brandywine, 1777; surrendered at Yorktown, Amer. Rev.

Hernán Cortés, 1485-1547, (Sp.) led Spanish conquistadors in the defeat of the Aztec empire, 1519-28.

Crazy Horse, 1849-77, (Amer. Ind.) Sioux war chief victorious at Battle of Little Bighorn.

George Armstrong Custer, 1839-76, (U.S.) army officer defeated and killed at Battle of Little Bighorn.

Benjamin O. Davis Jr., 1912-2002, (U.S.) leader of WWII black aviators; first African-American general in U.S. Air Force.

Benjamin O. Davis Sr., 1877-1970, (U.S.) first African-American general in U.S. Army, 1940.

Moshe Dayan, 1915-81, (Isr.) directed campaigns in the 1967, 1973 Arab-Israeli wars.

Stephen Decatur, 1779-1820, (U.S.) naval hero of Barbary wars, War of 1812.

Anton Denikin, 1872-1947, (Russ.) led White forces in Russian civil war.

George Dewey, 1837-1917, (U.S.) destroyed Spanish fleet at Manila, 1898, Span.-Amer. War.

Karl Doenitz, 1891-1980, (Ger.) submarine cmdr. in chief and naval cmdr., WWII; last pres. of Third Reich.

Jimmy Doolittle, 1896-1993, (U.S.) led 1942 air raid on Tokyo and other Japanese cities in WWII.

Hugh Dowding, 1882-1970, (Br.) headed RAF Fighter Command, 1936-40, WWII.

Jubal Early, 1816-94, (U.S.) Confed. general; led raid on Washington, DC, 1864, Civil War.

Dwight D. Eisenhower, 1890-1969, (U.S.) commanded Allied forces in Europe, WWII.

Erich von Falkenhayn, 1861-1922, (Ger.) minister of war, general, commander at Verdun in WWI.

David Farragut, 1801-70, (U.S.) Union admiral; captured New Orleans, Mobile Bay, Civil War.

John Arbuthnot Fisher, 1841-1920, (Br.) WWI admiral; naval reformer.

Ferdinand Foch, 1851-1929, (Fr.) headed victorious Allied armies, 1918, WWI.

Nathan Bedford Forrest, 1821-77, (U.S.) Confed. general; led raids against Union supply lines, Civil War.

Frederick the Great, 1712-86, (Prus.) led Prussia in Seven Years' War.

Horatio Gates, 1728-1806, (U.S.) commanded army at Saratoga, Amer. Rev.

Genghis Khan, 1162-1227, (Mongol) unified Mongol tribes, subjugated much of Asia, 1206-21.

Geronimo, 1829-1909, (Amer. Ind.) leader of Chiricahua band of Apache Indians.

Vo Nguyen Giap, 1911?-2013, (Viet.) commanded People's Army of Vietnam against U.S.

Charles G. Gordon, 1833-85, (Br.) led forces in China; Crimean War; killed at Khartoum, Sudan.

Ulysses S. Grant, 1822-85, (U.S.) headed Union army, Civil War, 1864-65; forced Robert E. Lee's surrender, 1865.

Nathanael Greene, 1742-86, (U.S.) defeated British in Southern campaign, 1780-81, Amer. Rev.

Heinz Guderian, 1888-1954, (Ger.) tank theorist; led panzer tank forces in Poland, France, Russia, WWII.

Gustavus Adolphus, 1594-1632, (Swed.) king, military tactician, reformer; led forces in Thirty Years' War.

Douglas Haig, 1861-1928, (Br.) led British armies in France, 1915-18, WWI.

William F. Halsey, 1882-1959, (U.S.) defeated Japanese fleet at Leyte Gulf, 1944, WWII.

Hannibal, 247-183 BCE, (Carthage) invaded Rome, crossing Alps, in Second Punic War, 218-201 BCE.

Sir Arthur Travers Harris, 1895-1984, (Br.) led Britain's WWII bomber command.

Paul von Hindenburg, 1847-1934, (Ger.) chief of general staff, WWI; second pres. of Weimar Republic.

Richard Howe, 1726-99, (Br.) commanded navy in Amer. Rev., 1776-78; June 1 victory against French, 1794.

William Howe, 1729-1814, (Br.) commanded forces in Amer. Rev., 1776-78.

Isaac Hull, 1773-1843, (U.S.) sunk British frigate *Guerriere*, War of 1812.

Thomas "Stonewall" Jackson, 1824-63, (U.S.) Confed. general; led Shenandoah Valley campaign, Civil War.

Daniel James Jr., 1920-78, (U.S.) first black 4-star general, 1975; commander, N. American Air Defense Command.

Joseph Joffre, 1852-1931, (Fr.) headed Allied armies in WWI; won Battle of the Marne, 1914, WWI.

John Paul Jones, 1747-92, (U.S.) commanded *Bonhomme Richard* in victory over *Serapis*, Amer. Rev., 1779.

Chief Joseph, c. 1840-1904, (Amer. Ind.) chief of the Nez Percé; forced by U.S. army to retreat and surrender.

Stephen Kearny, 1794-1848, (U.S.) headed Army of the West in Mexican War.

Albert Kesselring, 1885-1960, (Ger.) field marshal who led the defense of Italy in WWII.

Ernest J. King, 1878-1956, (U.S.) key WWII naval strategist.

Horatio H. Kitchener, 1850-1916, (Br.) led forces in Boer War, victorious at Khartoum, organized army in WWI.

Henry Knox, 1750-1806, (U.S.) general in Amer. Rev.; first sec. of war under U.S. Constitution.

Lavrenti Kornilov, 1870-1918, (Russ.) commander-in-chief, 1917; led counter-revolutionary march on Petrograd.

Thaddeus Kosciuszko, 1746-1817, (Pol.) aided Amer. Rev.

Walter Krueger, 1881-1967, (U.S.) led Sixth Army in WWII in Southwest Pacific.

Mikhail Kutuzov, 1745-1813, (Russ.) fought at Borodino, Napol. Wars, 1812; abandoned Moscow, forced French retreat.

Marquis de Lafayette, 1757-1834, (Fr.) fought in, secured French aid for Amer. Rev.

T(homas) E. Lawrence (of Arabia), 1888-1935, (Br.) organized revolt of Arabs against Turks in WWI.

William Daniel Leahy, 1875-1959, (U.S.) chief of staff to Pres. Roosevelt in WWII, Fleet Admiral.

Henry (Light-Horse Harry) Lee, 1756-1818, (U.S.) cavalry officer in Amer. Rev.

Robert E. Lee, 1807-70, (U.S.) Confed. general; defeated at Gettysburg, Civil War; surrendered to Grant, 1865.

Curtis LeMay, 1906-90, (U.S.) Air Force cmdr. in WWII, Korean War, Vietnam War.

Lyman Lemnitzer, 1899-1988, (U.S.) WWII hero; later general, chairman of Joint Chiefs of Staff.

James Longstreet, 1821-1904, (U.S.) aided Lee at Gettysburg, Civil War.

Erich Ludendorff, 1865-1937, (Ger.) general; victor at Tannenberg, WWI.

Douglas MacArthur, 1880-1964, (U.S.) commanded forces in SW Pacific in WWII; headed occupation forces in Japan, 1945-51; UN commander in Korean War.

Carl Gustaf Mannerheim, 1867-1951, (Fin.) army officer and pres. of Finland, 1944-46.

Erich von Manstein, 1887-1973, (Ger.) served WWI, WWII; planned invasion of France (1940); convicted of war crimes.

Francis Marion, 1733-95, (U.S.) led guerrilla actions in South Carolina during Amer. Rev.

Duke of Marlborough, 1650-1722, (Br.) led forces against Louis XIV in War of the Spanish Succession.

George C. Marshall, 1880-1959, (U.S.) chief of staff in WWII; authored Marshall Plan.

Maurice, Count of Nassau, 1567-1625, (Neth.) military innovator; led forces in Thirty Years' War.

George B. McClellan, 1826-85, (U.S.) Union general; commanded Army of the Potomac, 1861-62, Civil War.

George Meade, 1815-72, (U.S.) commanded Union forces at Gettysburg, Civil War.

Doris "Dorie" Miller, 1919-43, (U.S.) Navy hero of Pearl Harbor attack; first African American awarded Navy Cross.

Billy Mitchell, 1879-1936, (U.S.) WWI air-power advocate; court-martialed for insubordination, later vindicated.

Helmuth von Moltke, 1800-91, (Ger.) victorious in Austro-Prussian, Franco-Prussian wars.

Louis de Montcalm, 1712-59, (Fr.) headed troops in Canada, French and Indian War; defeated at Quebec, 1759.

Bernard Law Montgomery, 1887-1976, (Br.) stopped German offensive at Alamein, 1942, WWII; helped plan Normandy invasion.

Daniel Morgan, 1736-1802, (U.S.) victorious at Cowpens, 1781, Amer. Rev.

Louis Mountbatten, 1900-79, (Br.) Supreme Allied Commander of SE Asia, 1943-46, WWII.

Joachim Murat, 1767-1815, (Fr.) led cavalry at Marengo, Austerlitz, and Jena, Napoleonic Wars.

Horatio Nelson, 1758-1805, (Br.) naval cmdr.; destroyed French fleet at Trafalgar.

Michel Ney, 1769-1815, (Fr.) commanded forces in Switz., Austria, Russ., Napoleonic Wars; defeated at Waterloo.

Chester Nimitz, 1885-1966, (U.S.) cmdr. of naval forces in Pacific in WWII.

George S. Patton, 1885-1945, (U.S.) led assault on Sicily, 1943, Third Army invasion of Europe, WWII.

Oliver Perry, 1785-1819, (U.S.) won Battle of Lake Erie in War of 1812.

John Pershing, 1860-1948, (U.S.) commanded Mexican border campaign, 1916; Amer. Expeditionary Force, WWI.

Henri Philippe Pétain, 1856-1951, (Fr.) defended Verdun, 1916; headed Vichy government in WWII.

George E. Pickett, 1825-75, (U.S.) Confed. general famed for "charge" at Gettysburg, Civil War.

Charles Portal, 1893-1971, (Br.) chief of staff, Royal Air Force, 1940-45; led in Battle of Britain.

Manfred Freiherr von Richthofen (Red Baron), 1892-1918, (Ger.) WWI flying ace, led elite fighter squadron.

Hyman Rickover, 1900-86, (U.S.) father of nuclear navy.

Matthew Bunker Ridgway, 1895-1993, (U.S.) commanded Allied ground forces in Korean War.

Erwin Rommel, 1891-1944, (Ger.) headed Afrika Korps, WWII.

Gerd von Rundstedt, 1875-1953, (Ger.) supreme cmdr. in West, 1942-45, WWII.

Saladin, 1138-93, (Kurdish Muslim) recaptured Jerusalem from Crusaders.

Aleksandr Samsonov, 1859-1914, (Russ.) led invasion of E Prussia, WWI; defeated at Tannenberg, 1914.

Antonio López de Santa Anna, 1794-1876, (Mex.) defeated Texans at the Alamo; defeated in Mexican War.

Maurice, Count of Saxe, 1696-1750, (Fr.) general, noted tactician; War of Austrian Succession, War of Pol. Succession.

H. Norman Schwarzkopf, 1934-2012, (U.S.) army general; led Persian Gulf War, 1991.

Scipio Africanus the Elder, 234?-183 BCE, (Roman) hero of Second Punic War; defeated Hannibal, invaded N Africa.

Winfield Scott, 1786-1866, (U.S.) hero of War of 1812; headed forces in Mexican War, took Mexico City.

Philip Sheridan, 1831-88, (U.S.) Union cavalry officer; headed Army of the Shenandoah, 1864-65, Civil War.

William T. Sherman, 1820-91, (U.S.) Union general; sacked Atlanta during "march to the sea," 1864, Civil War.

Sitting Bull, c. 1831-90, (Amer. Ind.) Hunkpapa Sioux chief; victorious at Battle of the Little Big Horn.

Carl Spaatz, 1891-1974, (U.S.) directed strategic bombing against Germany, later Japan, in WWII.

Raymond Spruance, 1886-1969, (U.S.) victorious at Midway Island, 1942, WWII.

Joseph W. Stilwell, 1883-1946, (U.S.) headed forces in the China, Burma, India theater in WWII.

J.E.B. Stuart, 1833-64, (U.S.) Confed. cavalry commander, Civil War.

Sun Tzu, 6th? cent. BCE, (China) general; author of *The Art of War*.

Aleksandr Suvorov, 1729-1800, (Russ.) commanded Allied Russian and Austrian armies, Russo-Turkish War.

Tamerlane, 1336-1405, (Turkoman Mongol) conqueror; established empire from India to Mediterranean Sea.

Tecumseh, 1768-1813, (Amer. Ind.) Shawnee chief; led Indian confederation opposing colonists.

George H. Thomas, 1816-70, (U.S.) saved Union army at Chattanooga, 1863; won at Nashville, 1864, Civil War.

Semyon Timoshenko, 1895-1970, (USSR) defended Moscow, Stalingrad, WWII; led winter offensive, 1942-43.

Alfred von Tirpitz, 1849-1930, (Ger.) responsible for submarine blockade in WWI.

Henri de la Tour d'Auvergne, Viscount of Turenne, 1611-75, (Fr.) marshal; Thirty Years' War, Fronde, War of Devolution.

Sebastien Le Prestre de Vauban, 1633-1707, (Fr.) innovative military engineer, theorist.

Jonathan M. Wainwright, 1883-1953, (U.S.) forced to surrender on Corregidor, Philippines, 1942, WWII.

George Washington, 1732-99, (U.S.) led Continental army, 1775-83, Amer. Rev.

Archibald Wavell, 1883-1950, (Br.) commanded forces in N and E Africa, SE Asia in WWII.

Anthony Wayne, 1745-96, (U.S.) captured Stony Point, NY, 1779, Amer. Rev.

Duke of Wellington, 1769-1852, (Br.) defeated Napoleon at Waterloo, 1815.

William Westmoreland, 1914-2005, (U.S.) commanded forces in Vietnam, 1964-68.

William I (The Conqueror), 1027-87, (Br.) victor, Battle of Hastings, 1066; became first Norman king of England.

James Wolfe, 1727-59, (Br.) captured Quebec from French, 1759, French and Indian War.

Isoroku Yamamoto, 1884-1943, (Jpn.) cmdr. in chief of Japanese fleet, naval planner before and during WWII.

Georgi Zhukov, 1895-1974, (Russ.) defended Moscow, 1941; led assault on Berlin, 1945, WWII.

Philosophers and Religious Figures of the Past

Excludes biblical figures and popes (see Religion chapter). For Greeks and Romans, see also Historical Figures chapter.

Lyman Abbott, 1835-1922, (U.S.) clergyman, reformer; advocate of Christian Socialism.

Pierre Abelard, 1079-1142, (Fr.) philosopher, theologian, teacher; used dialectic method to support Christian beliefs.

Felix Adler, 1851-1933, (U.S.) German-born founder of the Ethical Culture Soc.

Mortimer Adler, 1902-2001, (U.S.) philosopher; helped create "Great Books" program.

(St.) Anselm, c. 1033-1109, (It.) philosopher-theologian, church leader; "ontological argument" for God's existence.

(St.) Thomas Aquinas, 1225-74, (It.) preeminent medieval philosopher-theologian; *Summa Theologica*.

Aristotle, 384-322 BCE, (Gr.) pioneering wide-ranging philosopher, logician, ethician, naturalist.

(St.) Augustine, 354-430, (N Africa) philosopher, theologian, bishop; *Confessions*, *City of God*, *On the Trinity*.

J. L. Austin, 1911-60, (Br.) ordinary-language philosopher.

Averroes (Ibn Rushd), 1126-98, (Sp.) Islamic philosopher, physician.

Avicenna (Ibn Sina), 980-1037, (Iran) Islamic philosopher, scientist.

A(lfred) J(ules) Ayer, 1910-89, (Br.) philosopher, logical positivist; *Language, Truth, and Logic*.

Roger Bacon, c. 1214-94, (Eng.) philosopher, scientist.

Bahá'u'lláh (Mirza Husayn Ali), 1817-92, (Pers.) founder of Bahá'í faith.

Karl Barth, 1886-1968, (Switz.) theologian; a leading force in 20th-cent. Protestantism.

Thomas à Becket, 1118-70, (Eng.) archbishop of Canterbury; opposed Henry II, murdered by king's men.

(St.) Benedict, c. 480-547, (It.) founded the Benedictines.

Jeremy Bentham, 1748-1832, (Br.) philosopher, reformer; enunciated utilitarianism.

Henri Bergson, 1859-1941, (Fr.) philosopher of evolution.

George Berkeley, 1685-1753, (Ire.) idealist philosopher, bishop.

John Biddle, 1615-62, (Eng.) founder of English Unitarianism.

Jakob Boehme, 1575-1624, (Ger.) theosophist, mystic.

Dietrich Bonhoeffer, 1906-45, (Ger.) Lutheran theologian, pastor; executed as opponent of Nazis.

William Brewster, 1567-1644, (Eng.) *Mayflower* passenger, Plymouth Colony leader.

Emil Brunner, 1889-1966, (Switz.) Protestant theologian.

Giordano Bruno, 1548-1600, (It.) philosopher, pantheist.

Martin Buber, 1878-1965, (Ger.) Jewish philosopher, theologian; *I and Thou*.

Buddha (Siddhartha Gautama), c. 563-c. 483 BCE, (India) philosopher; founded Buddhism.

John Calvin, 1509-64, (Fr.) theologian; a key figure in the Protestant Reformation.

Rudolph Carnap, 1891-1970, (U.S.) German-born analytic philosopher; a founder of logical positivism.

William Ellery Channing, 1780-1842, (U.S.) clergyman; early spokesman for Unitarianism.

Auguste Comte, 1798-1857, (Fr.) philosopher; originated positivism.

Confucius, 551-479 BCE, (China) founder of Confucianism.

John Cotton, 1584-1652, (Eng.) Puritan theologian.

Thomas Cranmer, 1489-1556, (Eng.) Anglican churchman; wrote much of *Book of Common Prayer*.

Jacques Derrida, 1930-2004, (Fr.) deconstructionist philosopher.

René Descartes, 1596-1650, (Fr.) philosopher, mathematician; "father of modern philosophy"; *Discourse on Method*, *Meditations on First Philosophy*.

John Dewey, 1859-1952, (U.S.) philosopher, educator; instrumentalist theory of knowledge, progressive education.

Denis Diderot, 1713-84, (Fr.) philosopher, encyclopedist.

John Duns Scotus, c. 1266-1308, (Scot.) Franciscan philosopher, theologian.

Mary Baker Eddy, 1821-1910, (U.S.) founder of Christian Science; *Science and Health*.

Jonathan Edwards, 1703-58, (U.S.) preacher, theologian; "Sinners in the Hands of an Angry God."

(Desiderius) Erasmus, c. 1466-1536, (Neth.) Renaissance humanist; *On the Freedom of the Will*.

Jerry Falwell, 1933-2007, (U.S.) TV evangelist, religious commentator.

Johann Fichte, 1762-1814, (Ger.) idealist philosopher.

Michel Foucault, 1926-84, (Fr.) structuralist philosopher, historian.

George Fox, 1624-91, (Br.) founder of Society of Friends (Quakers).

(St.) Francis of Assisi, 1182-1226, (It.) espoused voluntary poverty, founded Franciscans order.

al-Ghazali, 1058-1111, (Iran) Islamic philosopher.

Billy Graham, 1918-2018, (U.S.) evangelist, adviser to presidents.

Billy James Hargis, 1925-2004, (U.S.) anti-Communist televangelist; founder of the Church of the Christian Crusade.

Georg W. F. Hegel, 1770-1831, (Ger.) idealist philosopher; *Phenomenology of Mind*.

Martin Heidegger, 1889-1976, (Ger.) existentialist philosopher; affected many fields; *Being and Time*.

Johann G. Herder, 1744-1803, (Ger.) philosopher, cultural historian; a founder of German Romanticism.

Thomas Hobbes, 1588-1679, (Eng.) philosopher, political theorist; *Leviathan*.

David Hume, 1711-76, (Scot.) empiricist philosopher; *Enquiry Concerning Human Understanding*.

Jan Hus, 1369-1415, (Czech.) religious reformer.

Edmund Husserl, 1859-1938, (Ger.) philosopher; founded the phenomenological movement.

Thomas Huxley, 1825-95, (Br.) philosopher, educator.

William Ralph Inge, 1860-1954, (Br.) theologian; explored mystic aspects of Christianity.

William James, 1842-1910, (U.S.) philosopher, psychologist, pragmatist; studied religious experience.

Karl Jaspers, 1883-1969, (Ger.) existentialist philosopher.

Joan of Arc, 1412-31, (Fr.) national heroine, a patron saint of France; key figure in the Hundred Years War.

Immanuel Kant, 1724-1804, (Ger.) philosopher; founder of modern critical philosophy; *Critique of Pure Reason*.

Thomas à Kempis, c. 1380-1471, (Ger.) monk, devotional writer; *Imitation of Christ* attributed to him.

Soren Kierkegaard, 1813-55, (Den.) religious philosopher, pre-existentialist; *Either/Or*, *The Sickness Unto Death*.

John Knox, 1505-72, (Scot.) leader of Protestant Reformation in Scotland.

Lao-Tzu, 604-531 BCE, (China) philosopher; considered the founder of the Taoist religion.

Gottfried von Leibniz, 1646-1716, (Ger.) rationalistic philosopher, logician, mathematician.

John Locke, 1632-1704, (Eng.) political theorist, empiricist philosopher; *Essay Concerning Human Understanding*.

(St.) Ignatius Loyola, 1491-1556, (Sp.) founder of the Jesuits; *Spiritual Exercises*.

Martin Luther, 1483-1546, (Ger.) leader of the Protestant Reformation; founded Lutheran church.

Jean-Francois Lyotard, 1924-98, (Fr.) postmodern philosopher, lecturer; *The Post-Modern Condition*.

Maimonides, 1135-1204, (Sp.) major Jewish philosopher.

Gabriel Marcel, 1889-1973, (Fr.) Rom. Cath. existentialist philosopher, dramatist.

Jacques Maritain, 1882-1973, (Fr.) neo-Thomist philosopher.

Cotton Mather, 1663-1728, (U.S.) defender of orthodox Puritanism; founded Yale, 1701.

Aimee Semple McPherson, 1890-1944, (Can.) Pentecostal evangelist.

Philipp Melanchthon, 1497-1560, (Ger.) theologian, humanist; an important voice in the Reformation.

Maurice Merleau-Ponty, 1908-61, (Fr.) existentialist philosopher; *Phenomenology of Perception*.

Thomas Merton, 1915-68, (U.S.) Trappist monk, spiritual writer; *The Seven Storey Mountain*.

Dwight Moody, 1837-99, (U.S.) evangelist.

Rev. Sun Myung Moon, 1920-2012, (N. Kor.) Unification Church founder.

G(eorge) E(dward) Moore, 1873-1958, (Br.) philosopher; *Principia Ethica*, "A Defense of Common Sense."

Muhammad, c. 570-632, (Arab.) prophet of Islam.

Elijah Muhammad, 1897-1975, (U.S.) founder of Black Muslim group, Nation of Islam.

Heinrich Muhlenberg, 1711-87, (Ger.) organized the Lutheran Church in America.

John H. Newman, 1801-90, (Br.) Rom. Cath. convert, cardinal; led Oxford Movement; *Apologia pro Vita Sua*.

Reinhold Niebuhr, 1892-1971, (U.S.) Protestant theologian.

Richard Niebuhr, 1894-1962, (U.S.) Protestant theologian.

Friedrich Nietzsche, 1844-1900, (Ger.) philosopher; *The Birth of Tragedy*, *Beyond Good and Evil*, *Thus Spake Zarathustra*.

Robert Nozick, 1938-2002, (U.S.) political philosopher; *Anarchy, State, and Utopia*.

Blaise Pascal, 1623-62, (Fr.) philosopher, mathematician; *Pensées* (Thoughts).

(St.) Patrick, c. 389-c. 461, (Br.) brought Christianity to Ireland.

Norman Vincent Peale, 1898-1993, (U.S.) minister, author; *The Power of Positive Thinking*.

C(harles) S. Peirce, 1839-1914, (U.S.) philosopher, logician; originated concept of pragmatism, 1878.

Plato, c. 428-347 BCE, (Gr.) philosopher; wrote Socratic dialogues; argued for immortality of soul, indep. reality of ideas or forms; *Republic*, *Meno*, *Phaedo*, *Apology*.

Plotinus, 205-70, (Rom.) a founder of neo-Platonism; *Enneads*.

W(illard) V(an) O(rman) Quine, 1908-2001, (U.S.) philosopher, logician; "On What There Is."

John Rawls, 1922-2002, (U.S.) political philosopher; *A Theory of Justice*.

Oral Roberts, 1918-2009, (U.S.) televangelist, university founder.

Moishe Rosen, 1932-2010, (U.S.) Jews for Jesus founder.

Josiah Royce, 1855-1916, (U.S.) idealist philosopher.

Bertrand Russell, 1872-1970, (Br.) philosopher, logician; one of the founders of modern logic; prolific popular writer.

Charles T. Russell, 1852-1916, (U.S.) founder of Jehovah's Witnesses.

Gilbert Ryle, 1900-76, (Br.) analytic philosopher; *The Concept of Mind*.

George Santayana, 1863-1952, (U.S.) philosopher, writer, critic; *The Sense of Beauty*, *The Realms of Being*.

Jean-Paul Sartre, 1905-80, (Fr.) philosopher, novelist, playwright; *Nausea*, *No Exit*, *Being and Nothingness*.

Friedrich von Schelling, 1775-1854, (Ger.) philosopher of romantic movement.

Friedrich Schleiermacher, 1768-1834, (Ger.) theologian; a founder of modern Protestant theology.

Arthur Schopenhauer, 1788-1860, (Ger.) philosopher; *The World as Will and Idea*.

Robert Schuller, 1926-2015, (U.S.) evangelist; Crystal Cathedral founder.

Albert Schweitzer, 1875-1965, (Ger.) theologian, social philosopher, medical missionary.

Joseph Smith, 1805-44, (U.S.) founded Latter-Day Saints (Mormon) movement, 1830.

Socrates, 469-399 BCE, (Gr.) philosopher immortalized by Plato.

Herbert Spencer, 1820-1903, (Br.) philosopher of evolution.

Herbert Spiegel, 1914-2009, (U.S.) psychiatrist who popularized hypnosis.

Baruch de Spinoza, 1632-77, (Neth.) rationalist philosopher; *Ethics*.

John Stott, 1921-2011, (Br.) evangelical Anglican cleric.

Billy Sunday, 1862-1935, (U.S.) evangelist.

Daisetz Teitaro Suzuki, 1870-1966, (Jpn.) Buddhist scholar.

Emanuel Swedenborg, 1688-1772, (Swed.) philosopher, mystic; *Principia*.

Pierre Teilhard de Chardin, 1881-1955, (Fr.) Jesuit priest, paleontologist, philosopher-theologian; *The Divine Milieu*.

(St.) Therese of Lisieux, 1873-97, (Fr.) Carmelite nun ("Little Flower"), revered for everyday sanctity; *The Story of a Soul*.

Paul Tillich, 1886-1965, (U.S.) German-born philosopher, theologian; brought depth psychology to Protestantism.

John Wesley, 1703-91, (Br.) theologian, evangelist; founded Methodism.

Alfred North Whitehead, 1861-1947, (Br.) philosopher, mathematician; *Process and Reality*.

William of Occam, c. 1285-c. 1349, (Eng.) medieval scholastic philosopher, nominalist.

Roger Williams, c. 1603-83, (U.S.) clergyman; championed religious freedom and separation of church and state.

Ludwig Wittgenstein, 1889-1951, (Austria) philosopher; major influence on contemporary language philosophy; *Tractatus Logico-Philosophicus*, *Philosophical Investigations*.

John Woolman, 1720-72, (U.S.) Quaker social reformer, abolitionist, writer; *The Journal*.

John Wycliffe, 1320-84, (Eng.) theologian, reformer.

(St.) Francis Xavier, 1506-52, (Sp.) Jesuit missionary; "Apostle of the Indies."

Brigham Young, 1801-77, (U.S.) Mormon leader after Joseph Smith's death; colonized Utah.

Huldrych Zwingli, 1484-1531, (Switz.) theologian; led Swiss Protestant Reformation.

Political Leaders of the Past

U.S. presidents, vice presidents, Supreme Court justices, and signers of the Declaration of Independence listed elsewhere. See also Historical Figures.

Abu Bakr, 573-634, (Arab.) Muslim leader, first caliph, chosen successor to Muhammad.

Dean Acheson, 1893-1971, (U.S.) sec. of state; architect of Cold War foreign policy.

Samuel Adams, 1722-1803, (U.S.) patriot; Boston Tea Party firebrand.

Konrad Adenauer, 1876-1967, (Ger.) first West German chancellor.

Emilio Aguinaldo, 1869-1964, (Philip.) revolutionary; fought against Spain and the U.S.

Akbar, 1542-1605, Mogul emperor of India.

Carl Albert, 1908-2000, (U.S.) House rep. (D, OK), Speaker, 1971-76.

Salvador Allende Gossens, 1908-73, (Chile) Marxist pres., 1970-73; ousted and died in coup.

Idi Amin, 1925-2003, (Uganda) Ugandan ruler, 1971-79; blamed for hundreds of thousands of deaths.

Kofi Annan, 1938-2018, (Ghana) UN sec. gen.

Corazon Aquino, 1933-2009, (Philip.) pres. of the Philippines, 1986-92.

Yasir Arafat, 1929-2004, (Egypt) leader of the Palestine Liberation Organization (PLO).

Herbert H. Asquith, 1852-1928, (Br.) Liberal prime min.; instituted major social reforms.

Hafez al Assad, 1930-2000, (Syr.) pres. of Syria, 1970-2000.

Atahualpa, 1500?-33, (Inca) last ruling chief of Incan empire (in present-day Peru).

Kemal Atatürk, 1881-1938, (Turk.) founded modern Turkey.

Clement Attlee, 1883-1967, (Br.) Labour leader, prime min.; enacted natl. health service, nationalized many industries.

Stephen F. Austin, 1793-1836, (U.S.) led Texas colonization.

Mikhail Bakunin, 1814-76, (Russ.) revolutionary; leading exponent of anarchism.

Arthur J. Balfour, 1848-1930, (Br.) foreign sec. under Lloyd George; issued Balfour Declaration backing Zionism.

Bernard M. Baruch, 1870-1965, (U.S.) financier, govt. adviser.

Fulgencio Batista y Zaldívar, 1901-73, (Cuba) Cuban pres., 1940-44, 1952-59; overthrown by Castro.

Lord Beaverbrook, 1879-1964, (Br.) financier, statesman, newspaper owner.

Menachem Begin, 1913-92, (Isr.) Israeli prime min.; shared 1978 Nobel Peace Prize.

Ahmed Ben Bella, 1918-2012, (Alg.) first Algerian pres., 1963-65.

Eduard Benes, 1884-1948, (Czech.) pres. during interwar and post-WWII eras.

David Ben-Gurion, 1886-1973, (Isr.) first prime min. of Israel, 1948-53, 1955-63.

Thomas Hart Benton, 1782-1858, (U.S.) MO senator; championed agrarian interests and westward expansion.

Aneurin Bevan, 1897-1960, (Br.) Labour party leader.

Ernest Bevin, 1881-1951, (Br.) Labour party leader, foreign minister; helped lay foundation for NATO.

King Bhumibol Adulyadej, 1927-2016, (Thai.) monarch (1946-2016).

Benazir Bhutto, 1953-2007, (Pak.) Pakistan prime min.; first elected woman leader of a majority-Muslim country.

Otto von Bismarck, 1815-98, (Ger.) statesman known as the Iron Chancellor; uniter of Germany, 1870.

James G. Blaine, 1830-93, (U.S.) Republican politician, diplomat; influential in Pan-American movement.

Léon Blum, 1872-1950, (Fr.) socialist leader, writer; headed first Popular Front government.

William E. Borah, 1865-1940, (U.S.) isolationist senator (R, ID); helped block U.S. membership in League of Nations.

Cesare Borgia, 1476-1507, (It.) soldier, politician; Italian Renaissance figure who partly inspired Machiavelli's *The Prince*.

P. W. Botha, 1916-2006, (S. Afr.) S. African president, prime min.

Boutros Boutros-Ghali, 1922-2016, (Egypt), UN sec.-gen.

Tom Bradley, 1917-98, (U.S.) first African-American mayor of L.A.

Willy Brandt, 1913-92, (Ger.) statesman, chancellor of West Germany, 1969-74; promoted East/West peace, *Ostpolitik*.

Leonid Brezhnev, 1906-82, (USSR) Soviet leader, 1964-82.

Aristide Briand, 1862-1932, (Fr.) foreign min.; chief architect of Locarno Pact and anti-war Kellogg-Briand Pact.

William Jennings Bryan, 1860-1925, (U.S.) Democratic, populist leader, orator; three times lost race for presidency.

Ralph Bunche, 1904-71, (U.S.) first black person to win the Nobel Peace Prize, 1950; undersecretary of the UN, 1950.

Robert Byrd, 1917-2010, (U.S.) longest serving U.S. senator (D, WV), 1959-2010.

John C. Calhoun, 1782-1850, (U.S.) political leader; champion of states' rights and a symbol of the Old South.

James Callaghan (Baron Callaghan), 1912-2005, (Br.) Labour party politician, prime min., 1976-79.

Robert Castlereagh, 1769-1822, (Br.) foreign sec.; guided Grand Alliance against Napoleon.

Fidel Castro, 1926-2016, (Cuba) prime min./pres., 1959-2008; led Communist revolution.

Camillo Benso Cavour, 1810-61, (It.) statesman; largely responsible for uniting Italy under the House of Savoy.

Nicolae Ceausescu, 1918-89, (Rom.) Communist leader, head of state, 1967-89; executed.

Austen Chamberlain, 1863-1937, (Br.) statesman; helped finalize Locarno Treaties, both 1925.

Neville Chamberlain, 1869-1940, (Br.) Conservative prime min. whose appeasement of Hitler led to Munich Pact.

Hugo Chávez, 1954-2013, (Venez.) socialist Venezuelan pres., 1999-2013.

Chiang Kai-shek, 1887-1975, (China) Nationalist Chinese pres. whose govt. was driven from mainland to Taiwan.

Madame Chiang Kai-shek (Mayling Soong), 1898-2003, (China) highly influential wife of Nationalist Chinese leader Chiang Kai-shek.

Shirley Chisholm, 1924-2005, (U.S.) first black woman elected to U.S. House (1968, D, NY); pres. contender, 1972.

Warren Christopher, 1925-2011, (U.S.) secretary of state, diplomat.

Winston Churchill, 1874-1965, (Br.) prime min., soldier, author; guided Britain through WWII.

Galeazzo Ciano, 1903-44, (It.) Fascist foreign minister; helped create Rome-Berlin Axis; executed by Benito Mussolini.

Henry Clay, 1777-1852, (U.S.) "The Great Compromiser"; one of the most influential pre-Civil War political leaders.

Georges Clemenceau, 1841-1929, (Fr.) twice prem.; Woodrow Wilson's antagonist at Paris Peace Conference after WWI.

DeWitt Clinton, 1769-1828, (U.S.) political leader; promoted Erie Canal.

Robert Clive, 1725-74, (Br.) first administrator of Bengal; laid foundation for British Empire in India.

Jean Baptiste Colbert, 1619-83, (Fr.) statesman; influential under Louis XIV; created the French navy.

Bettino Craxi, 1934-2000, (It.) Italy's first post-WWII Socialist prem.

David Crockett, 1786-1836, (U.S.) frontiersman, congressman; died defending the Alamo.

Oliver Cromwell, 1599-1658, (Br.) Lord Protector of England; led parliamentary forces during Civil War.

Mario Cuomo, 1932-2015, NY governor (D), 1983-94.

Curzon of Kedleston, 1859-1925, (Br.) viceroy of India, foreign sec.; major force in post-WWI world.

Édouard Daladier, 1884-1970, (Fr.) Radical Socialist politician, arrested by Vichy, interned by Germans until 1945.

Richard J. Daley, 1902-76, (U.S.) Chicago mayor, 1955-76.

Georges Danton, 1759-94, (Fr.) leading French Rev. figure.

Jefferson Davis, 1808-89, (U.S.) pres. of the Confederacy.

Charles G. Dawes, 1865-1951, (U.S.) statesman, banker; advanced plan to stabilize post-WWI German finances.

William L. Dawson, 1886-1970, (U.S.) U.S. rep. (D, IL); first black chair of a standing U.S. House committee.

Alcide De Gasperi, 1881-1954, (It.) prime min.; founder of Christian Democratic party.

Charles De Gaulle, 1890-1970, (Fr.) general, statesman; first pres. of the Fifth Republic.

Deng Xiaoping, 1904-97, (China) "paramount leader" of China; backed economic modernization.

Eamon De Valera, 1882-1975, (Ire.-U.S.) statesman; led fight for Irish independence.

Thomas E. Dewey, 1902-71, (U.S.) NY governor (R); twice lost in try for presidency.

Ngo Dinh Diem, 1901-63, (Viet.) South Vietnamese pres.; assassinated in government takeover.

Everett M. Dirksen, 1896-1969, (U.S.) Senate Republican minority leader, orator.

Benjamin Disraeli, 1804-81, (Br.) prime min.; considered founder of modern Conservative party.

Anatoly Dobrynin, 1919-2010, (Russ.) diplomat and Soviet amb. to U.S. (1962-86).

Engelbert Dollfuss, 1892-1934, (Austria) chancellor; assassinated by Nazis.

Andrea Doria, 1466-1560, (It.) Genoese admiral, statesman; called "Father of Peace" and "Liberator of Genoa."

Stephen A. Douglas, 1813-61, (U.S.) Democratic leader, orator; ran against Lincoln for IL sen. seat, presidency.

Alexander Dubcek, 1921-92, (Czech.) statesman whose attempted liberalization was crushed, 1968.

John Foster Dulles, 1888-1959, (U.S.) sec. of state under Eisenhower; Cold War policy maker.

Lawrence Eagleburger, 1930-2011, (U.S.) diplomat and foreign policy adviser.

Abba Eban, 1915-2002, (Isr.) diplomat; foreign min., 1966-74.

Friedrich Ebert, 1871-1925, (Ger.) Social Democratic movement leader; first pres., Weimar Republic, 1919-25.

Sir Anthony Eden, 1897-1977, (Br.) foreign sec., prime min. during Suez invasion of 1956.

Ludwig Erhard, 1897-1977, (Ger.) economist, West German chancellor; led nation's economic rise after WWII.

King Fahd, 1923-2005, (Saudi Arabia) monarch from 1982 but inactive after 1995 stroke; encouraged U.S. relations.

Geraldine Ferraro, 1935-2011, (U.S.) U.S. rep. (D, NY), vice-pres. nominee.

João Baptista de Figueiredo, 1918-99, (Braz.) pres. of Brazil; restored nation's democracy after military rule.

Hamilton Fish, 1808-93, (U.S.) sec. of state; successfully mediated disputes with Great Britain, Latin America.

James V. Forrestal, 1892-1949, (U.S.) sec. of navy, first sec. of defense.

Francisco Franco, 1892-1975, (Sp.) leader of rebel forces during Spanish Civil War, longtime ruler of Spain.

Benjamin Franklin, 1706-90, (U.S.) printer, publisher, author, inventor, scientist, diplomat.

Louis de Frontenac, 1620-98, (Fr.) governor of New France (Canada).

J. William Fulbright, 1905-95, (U.S.) U.S. senator (D, AR); leading figure in U.S. foreign policy during Cold War years.

Hugh Gaitskell, 1906-63, (Br.) Labour party leader; major force in reversing its stand for unilateral disarmament.

Albert Gallatin, 1761-1849, (U.S.) sec. of treasury; instrumental in negotiating end of War of 1812.

Léon Gambetta, 1838-82, (Fr.) statesman, politician; one of the founders of the Third Republic.

Indira Gandhi, 1917-84, (India) daughter of Jawaharlal Nehru; prime min. of India, 1966-77, 1980-84; assassinated.

Mohandas K. Gandhi, 1869-1948, (India) political leader, ascetic; led movement against British rule; assassinated.

Giuseppe Garibaldi, 1807-82, (It.) patriot, soldier; a leader in the Risorgimento, Italian unification movement.

William E. Gladstone, 1809-98, (Br.) prime min.; dominant force of Liberal party 1868-94.

Paul Joseph Goebbels, 1897-1945, (Ger.) Nazi propagandist; master of mass psychology.

Barry Goldwater, 1909-98, (U.S.) conservative U.S. senator (R, AZ), 1964 pres. nominee.

Klement Gottwald, 1896-1953, (Czech.) Communist leader.

Haile Selassie (Tafari Makonnen), 1892-1975, (Ethiopia) emperor of Ethiopia.

Alexander Hamilton, 1755-1804, (U.S.) first treasury sec.; champion of strong central government.

Dag Hammarskjöld, 1905-61, (Swed.) statesman; UN sec.-general.

King Hassan II, 1929-99, (Moroc.) ruler of Morocco, 1962-99.

Vaclav Havel, 1936-2011, (Czech.) first president of Czech Republic, 1989-92.

John Hay, 1838-1905, (U.S.) sec. of state; primarily associated with Open Door Policy toward China.

Sir Edward Heath, 1916-2005, (Br.) Conservative prime min., 1970-74; promoted European unity.

Jesse Helms, 1921-2008, (U.S.) conservative U.S. senator (R, NC).

Patrick Henry, 1736-99, (U.S.) major Revolutionary War figure, orator.

Édouard Herriot, 1872-1957, (Fr.) Radical Socialist leader; twice prem., pres. of National Assembly.

Theodor Herzl, 1860-1904, (Hung.) founded modern Zionism.

Heinrich Himmler, 1900-45, (Ger.) head of Nazi SS and Gestapo.

Paul von Hindenburg, 1847-1934, (Ger.) field marshal, WWI; second pres. of Weimar Republic, 1925-34.

Adolf Hitler, 1889-1945, (Ger.) dictator; built Nazism, launched WWII, presided over the Holocaust.

Ho Chi Minh, 1890-1969, (Viet.) N. Vietnamese pres., Communist leader.

Harry L. Hopkins, 1890-1946, (U.S.) New Deal administrator; closest adviser to Franklin D. Roosevelt during WWII.

Edward M. House, 1858-1938, (U.S.) diplomat; confidential adviser to Woodrow Wilson.

Samuel Houston, 1793-1863, (U.S.) leader of struggle for Texas independence.

Cordell Hull, 1871-1955, (U.S.) sec. of state, 1933-44; initiated reciprocal trade to lower tariffs, helped organize UN.

Hubert H. Humphrey, 1911-78, (U.S.) U.S. senator (D, MN), vice pres., pres. nominee.

King Hussein, 1935-99, (Jordan) peacemaker; ruler of Jordan, 1952-99.

Saddam Hussein, 1937-2006, (Iraq) Iraqi ruler; put to death for crimes against humanity.

Muhammad Ali Jinnah, 1876-1948, (Pak.) founder, first gov.-gen. of Pakistan.

Barbara Jordan, 1936-96, (U.S.) U.S. rep. (D, TX), orator, educator; first black woman to win a seat in the TX state senate, 1966.

Benito Juarez, 1806-72, (Mex.) rallied his country against foreign threats; sought to create democratic, federal republic.

Constantine Karamanlis, 1907-98, (Gr.) Greek prime min.; restored democracy, later president.

Frank B. Kellogg, 1856-1937, (U.S.) sec. of state; negotiated Kellogg-Briand Pact to outlaw war.

Jack Kemp, 1935-2009, (U.S.) sec. of HUD, U.S. rep. (R, NY), football player.

Edward M. Kennedy, 1932-2009, (U.S.) senator (D, MA); championed progressive causes.

Robert F. Kennedy, 1925-68, (U.S.) attorney general, U.S. sen. (D, NY); assassinated while seeking presidency.

Aleksandr Kerensky, 1881-1970, (Russ.) headed provisional government after Feb. 1917 revolution.

Ayatollah Ruhollah Khomeini, 1900-89, (Iran), religious-political leader; spearheaded overthrow of Shah, 1979.

Nikita Khrushchev, 1894-1971, (USSR) prem., first sec. of Communist party; initiated de-Stalinization.

Kim Dae-jung, 1925-2009, (Korea) S. Korean dissident, opposition leader, pres.; 2000 Nobel Peace Prize winner.

Kim Il Sung, 1912-94, (Korea) N. Korean dictator, 1948-94.

Kim Jong Il, 1942-2011, (Korea) N. Korean dictator, 1994-2011.

Edward I. Koch, 1924-2013, (U.S.) New York City mayor, 1978-89.

Helmut Kohl, 1930-2017, (Ger.) chancellor, 1982-98; reunified Germany.

Lajos Kossuth, 1802-94, (Hung.) principal figure in 1848 Hungarian revolution.

Pyotr Kropotkin, 1842-1921, (Russ.) anarchist; championed the peasants but opposed Bolshevism.

Kublai Khan, c. 1215-94, (Mongol) emperor; founder of Yuan dynasty in China.

Béla Kun, 1886-c. 1939, (Hung.) member of Third Communist International; tried to foment worldwide revolution.

Robert M. LaFollette, 1855-1925, (U.S.) WI public official; leader of progressive movement.

Fiorello La Guardia, 1882-1947, (U.S.) New York City reform mayor, 1933-45.

Pierre Laval, 1883-1945, (Fr.) politician, Vichy foreign min.; executed for treason.

Andrew Bonar Law, 1858-1923, (Can.) Conservative party politician, British prime min.; led opposition to Irish home rule.

Vladimir Ilyich Lenin (Ulyanov), 1870-1924, (Russ.) revolutionary; founded Bolshevism; Soviet leader, 1917-24.

Ferdinand de Lesseps, 1805-94, (Fr.) diplomat, engineer; conceived idea of Suez Canal.

René Lévesque, 1922-87, (Can.) prem. of Quebec, 1976-85; led unsuccessful separatist campaign.

Trygve Lie, 1896-1968, (Nor.) first UN sec.-gen.

Maxim Litvinov, 1876-1951, (Pol.-Russ.) revolutionary, commissar of foreign affairs; favored cooperation with West.

Liu Shaoqi, c. 1898-1969, (China) Communist leader; fell from grace during Cultural Revolution.

David Lloyd George, 1863-1945, (Br.) Liberal party prime min.; laid foundations for modern welfare state.

Henry Cabot Lodge, 1850-1924, (U.S.) U.S. senator (R, MA); led opposition to participation in League of Nations.

Huey P. Long, 1893-1935, (U.S.) Louisiana political demagogue, governor, U.S. senator (D); assassinated.

Rosa Luxemburg, 1871-1919, (Ger.) revolutionary; leader of the German Social Democratic party and Spartacus party.

J. Ramsay MacDonald, 1866-1937, (Br.) first Labour party prime min. of Great Britain.

Harold Macmillan, 1895-1986, (Br.) prime min. of Great Britain, 1957-63.

Makarios III, 1913-77, (Cyprus) Greek Orthodox archbishop; first pres. of Cyprus.

Nelson Mandela, 1918-2013, (S. Afr.) anti-apartheid leader; first black pres. of S. Africa, 1994-99.

Wilma Mankiller, 1945-2010, (U.S.) first female chief of the Cherokee Nation.

Mao Zedong, 1893-1976, (China) chief Chinese Marxist theorist, revolutionary, political leader; led revolution establishing his nation as Communist state.

Jean Paul Marat, 1743-93, (Fr.) revolutionary, politician; identified with radical Jacobins; assassinated.

Thurgood Marshall, 1908-93, (U.S.) first black U.S. solicitor general, 1965; first black justice of U.S. Supreme Court, 1967-91.

José Martí, 1853-95, (Cuba) patriot, poet; independence leader.

Jan Masaryk, 1886-1948, (Czech.) foreign min.; died under mysterious circumstances, allegedly committed suicide following Communist coup.

Thomas G. Masaryk, 1850-1937, (Czech.) statesman, philosopher; first pres. of Czechoslovakia.

Jules Mazarin, 1602-61, (Fr.) cardinal, statesman; prime min. under Louis XIII and queen regent Anne of Austria.

Giuseppe Mazzini, 1805-72, (It.) reformer dedicated to Risorgimento movement for renewal of Italy.

Tom Mboya, 1930-69, (Kenya) political leader; instrumental in securing independence for Kenya.

John McCain, 1936-2018, (U.S.) U.S. sen. (R, AZ), 2008 pres. nominee.

Eugene McCarthy, 1916-2005, (U.S.) political leader, author; 1968 Dem. presidential contender.

Joseph R. McCarthy, 1908-57, (U.S.) senator (R, WI); extremist in searching out alleged Communists and pro-Communists.

George McGovern, 1922-2012, (U.S.) liberal senator (D, SD), 1972 pres. nominee.

Cosimo I de' Medici, 1519-74, (It.) Duke of Florence, grand duke of Tuscany.

Lorenzo de' Medici (the Magnificent), 1449-92, (It.) merchant prince; a towering figure in Italian Renaissance.

Catherine de Médicis, 1519-89, (Fr.) queen consort of Henry II, regent of France; influential in Catholic-Huguenot wars.

Golda Meir, 1898-1978, (Ukr.-Isr.) a founder of the state of Israel; prime min., 1969-74.

Klemens W. N. L. Metternich, 1773-1859, (Austria) statesman; arbiter of post-Napoleonic Europe.

Slobodan Milosevic, 1941-2006, (Serb./Yugo.) former Yugoslav pres.; tried for genocide, crimes against humanity.

François Mitterrand, 1916-96, (Fr.) pres. of France, 1981-95.

Mobutu Sese Seko, 1930-97, (Zaire) longtime ruler of Zaire (now Dem. Rep. of Congo), 1965-97; exiled after rebellion.

Guy Mollet, 1905-75, (Fr.) socialist politician, resistance leader.

Henry Morgenthau Jr., 1891-1967, (U.S.) sec. of treasury; fundraiser for New Deal and U.S. WWII activities.

Gouverneur Morris, 1752-1816, (U.S.) statesman, diplomat, financial expert; helped plan decimal coinage.

Daniel Patrick Moynihan, 1927-2003, (U.S.) senator (D, NY), diplomat, social scientist, author.

Benito Mussolini, 1883-1945, (It.) leader of the Italian fascist state; assassinated.

Imre Nagy, c. 1896-1958, (Hung.) Communist prem.; assassinated after Soviets crushed 1956 uprising.

Gamal Abdel Nasser, 1918-70, (Egypt) leader of Arab unification, second Egyptian pres.

Jawaharlal Nehru, 1889-1964, (India) prime min.; guided India through its early years of independence.

Kwame Nkrumah, 1909-72, (Ghana) first prime min., 1957-60; pres., 1960-66, of Ghana.

Manuel Noriega, 1934-2017, (Pan.) dictator, 1983-89; military officer, CIA informant.

Frederick North, 1732-92, (Br.) prime min.; his policies led to loss of American colonies.

Julius K. Nyerere, 1922-99, (Tanz.) founding father; first pres., 1962-85, of Tanzania.

Daniel O'Connell, 1775-1847, (Ire.) nationalist political leader; known as The Liberator.

Omar, c. 581-644, (Arab.) Muslim leader; second caliph, led Islam to become an imperial power.

Thomas P. (Tip) O'Neill Jr., 1912-94, (U.S.) U.S. rep. (D, MA), speaker of the House, 1977-86.

Ignace Paderewski, 1860-1941, (Pol.) statesman, pianist, composer, briefly prime min.; ardent patriot.

Ian Paisley, 1926-2014, (Ire.) Unionist Party leader who agreed to power sharing in N. Ireland.

Viscount Palmerston, 1784-1865, (Br.) Whig-Liberal prime min., foreign min.; embodied British nationalism.

Andreas George Papandreou, 1919-96, (Gr.) leftist politician; served as prem., 1981-89, 1993-96.

Georgios Papandreou, 1888-1968, (Gr.) Republican politician; served three times as prime min.

Franz von Papen, 1879-1969, (Ger.) politician; major role in overthrow of Weimar Republic and rise of Hitler.

Charles Stewart Parnell, 1846-1891, (Ire.) nationalist leader; "uncrowned king of Ireland."

Lester Pearson, 1897-1972, (Can.) diplomat, Liberal party leader, prime min.

Robert Peel, 1788-1850, (Br.) reformist prime min.; founder of Conservative party.

Shimon Peres, 1922-2016, (Bela.-Isr.) Israel prime min., 1984-86, 1995-96; president, 2007-14.

Frances Perkins, 1882-1965, (U.S.) first female cabinet member (sec. of labor).

Eva (Evita) Perón, 1919-52, (Arg.) highly influential second wife of Juan Perón.

Juan Perón, 1895-1974, (Arg.) dynamic pres. of Argentina, 1946-55, 1973-74.

Joseph Pilsudski, 1867-1935, (Pol.) statesman; instrumental in reestablishing Polish state in the 20th cent.

Charles Pinckney, 1757-1824, (U.S.) founding father; his Pinckney plan largely incorporated into Constitution.

Christian Pineau, 1905-95, (Fr.) leader of French Resistance during WWII; foreign min., 1956-58.

Augusto Pinochet (Ugarte), 1915-2006, (Chile) former Chilean ruler; indicted for human rights abuses while in office.

William Pitt the Elder, 1708-78, (Br.) statesman; the "Great Commoner," transformed Britain into imperial power.

William Pitt the Younger, 1759-1806, (Br.) prime min. during French Revolutionary wars.

Georgi Plekhanov, 1857-1918, (Russ.) revolutionary, social philosopher; called "father of Russian Marxism."

Raymond Poincaré, 1860-1934, (Fr.) French pres.; advocated harsh punishment of Germany after WWI.

Pol Pot, 1925-98, (Camb.) leader of Khmer Rouge; ruled Cambodia, 1975-79; responsible for mass deaths.

Georges Pompidou, 1911-74, (Fr.) Gaullist political leader; pres., 1969-74.

Grigori Potemkin, 1739-91, (Russ.) field marshal; favorite of empress Catherine II.

Adam Clayton Powell Jr., 1908-72, (U.S.) civil rights leader; U.S. rep. (D, NY), 1945-69.

Muammar al-Qaddafi, 1942-2011, (Libya) Libyan ruler, 1969-2011.

Yitzhak Rabin, 1922-95, (Isr.) military, political leader; prime min. of Israel, 1974-77, 1992-95; assassinated.

Joseph H. Rainey, 1832-87, (U.S.) first black person elected to U.S. House (1869), from SC.

Edmund Randolph, 1753-1813, (U.S.) attorney; prominent in drafting, ratification of Constitution.

John Randolph, 1773-1833, (U.S.) Southern planter; strong advocate of states' rights.

Jeannette Rankin, 1880-1973, (U.S.) pacifist; first woman member of U.S. Congress (R, MT).

Walter Rathenau, 1867-1922, (Ger.) industrialist, statesman.

Sam Rayburn, 1882-1961, (U.S.) U.S. rep. (D, TX) for 47 years, House speaker for 17.

Janet Reno, 1938-2016, (U.S.) first woman attorney general.

Hiram R. Revels, 1822-1901, (U.S.) first African-American U.S. senator (R); elected in MS, served 1870-71.

Paul Reynaud, 1878-1966, (Fr.) statesman; prem. in 1940 at time of France's defeat by Germany.

Syngman Rhee, 1875-1965, (Korea) first pres. of S. Korea.

Cecil Rhodes, 1853-1902, (Br.) imperialist, industrial magnate; established Rhodes scholarships in his will.

Ann Richards, 1933-2006, (U.S.) former TX gov.

Cardinal de Richelieu, 1585-1642, (Fr.) statesman, known as "red eminence"; chief minister to Louis XIII.

Maximilien Robespierre, 1758-94, (Fr.) leading figure in French Revolution and Reign of Terror.

Nelson Rockefeller, 1908-79, (U.S.) Republican governor of NY, 1959-73; U.S. vice pres., 1974-77.

Eleanor Roosevelt, 1884-1962, (U.S.) influential first lady, humanitarian, UN diplomat.

Elihu Root, 1845-1937, (U.S.) lawyer, statesman, diplomat; leading Republican supporter of the League of Nations.

Dean Rusk, 1909-95, (U.S.) statesman; sec. of state, 1961-69.

John Russell, 1792-1878, (Br.) Liberal prime min. during the Irish potato famine.

Anwar al-Sadat, 1918-81, (Egypt) pres., 1970-81; promoted peace with Israel; Nobel laureate; assassinated.

António de Oliveira Salazar, 1889-1970, (Port.) longtime dictator of Portugal.

José de San Martin, 1778-1850, ([now] Arg.) S. Amer. revolutionary; protector of Peru.

Eisaku Sato, 1901-75, (Jpn.) prime min.; presided over Japan's post-WWII emergence as major world power.

Abdul Aziz Ibn Saud, c. 1880-1953, (Saudi Arabia) king of Saudi Arabia, 1932-53.

Helmut Schmidt, 1918-2015, (Ger.) German chancellor, 1974-82.

Robert Schuman, 1886-1963, (Fr.) statesman; founded European Coal and Steel Community.

Carl Schurz, 1829-1906, (U.S.) German-American political leader, journalist, orator, dedicated reformer.

Kurt Schuschnigg, 1897-1977, (Austria) chancellor; unsuccessful in stopping Austria's annexation by Germany.

William H. Seward, 1801-72, (U.S.) anti-slavery activist; as U.S. sec. of state purchased Alaska.

Carlo Sforza, 1872-1952, (It.) foreign min., anti-Fascist.

Yitzhak Shamir, 1915-2012, (Russ.-Isr.) prime min. of Israel, 1983-84, 1986-92.

Ariel Sharon, 1928-2014, (Isr.) prime min. of Israel, 2001-06.

Eduard Shevardnadze, 1928-2014, (Geo.) Georgian pres., 1995-2003.

Norodom Sihanouk, 1922-2012, (Camb.) king of Cambodia (1941-55, 1993-2004).

Sitting Bull, c. 1831-90, (Amer. Ind.) Sioux leader in Battle of Little Bighorn against George A. Custer, 1876.

Alfred E. Smith, 1873-1944, (U.S.) NY Democratic governor; first Roman Catholic to run for president.

Margaret Chase Smith, 1897-1995, (U.S.) U.S. rep., senator (R, ME); first woman elected to both houses of Congress.

Jan C. Smuts, 1870-1950, (S. Afr.) statesman, philosopher, soldier, prime min.

Paul Henri Spaak, 1899-1972, (Belg.) statesman, socialist leader.

Joseph Stalin, 1879-1953, (USSR) Soviet dictator, 1924-53; instituted forced collectivization, massive purges, and labor camps, causing millions of deaths.

Edwin M. Stanton, 1814-69, (U.S.) sec. of war, 1862-68.

Alexander Stephens, 1812-83, (U.S.) vice pres. of the Confederacy.

Edward R. Stettinius Jr., 1900-49, (U.S.) industrialist; sec. of state who coordinated aid to WWII allies.

Adlai E. Stevenson, 1900-65, (U.S.) Democratic leader, diplomat, governor (IL), presidential nominee.

Henry L. Stimson, 1867-1950, (U.S.) statesman; served in five administrations, foreign policy adviser in 1930s and 1940s.

Carl Stokes, 1927-96, (U.S.) first black mayor of a major American city (Cleveland, 1967-72).

Suharto, 1921-2008, (Indon.) former longtime Indonesian ruler.

Sukarno, 1901-70, (Indon.) dictatorial first pres. of the Indonesian republic.

Sun Yat-sen, 1866-1925, (China) revolutionary; leader of Kuomintang political party, regarded as father of modern China.

Robert A. Taft, 1889-1953, (U.S.) conservative Senate leader (OH); called "Mr. Republican."

Charles de Talleyrand, 1754-1838, (Fr.) statesman, diplomat; the major force of the Congress of Vienna of 1814-15.

U Thant, 1909-74, (Burma) statesman, UN sec.-general.

Margaret Thatcher, 1925-2013, (Br.) conservative British prime min., 1979-90; first woman UK prime min.

Norman M. Thomas, 1884-1968, (U.S.) social reformer; six times Socialist party presidential candidate.

Josip Broz Tito, 1892-1980, (Yugo.) pres. of Yugoslavia from 1953; WWII guerrilla chief, postwar rival of Stalin.

Palmiro Togliatti, 1893-1964, (It.) major Italian Communist leader.

Hideki Tojo, 1885-1948, (Jpn.) statesman, soldier; prime min. during most of WWII.

François Toussaint L'Ouverture, c. 1744-1803, (Haiti) patriot, martyr; thwarted French colonial aims.

Leon Trotsky, 1879-1940, (Russ.) revolutionary; founded Red Army, expelled from party in conflict with Stalin; assassinated.

Pierre Elliott Trudeau, 1919-2000, (Can.) longtime liberal prime min. of Canada, 1968-79, 1980-84; achieved native Canadian constitution.

Rafael L. Trujillo Molina, 1891-1961, (Dom. Rep.) dictator of Dominican Republic, 1930-61; assassinated.

Moise K. Tshombe, 1919-69, (Congo) pres. of secessionist Katanga prov., prem. of Congo (now Dem. Rep. of the Congo).

William M. Tweed, 1823-78, (U.S.) political boss of Tammany Hall, New York City's Democratic political machine.

Walter Ulbricht, 1893-1973, (Ger.) Communist leader of German Democratic Republic.

Arthur H. Vandenberg, 1884-1951, (U.S.) senator (R, MI); proponent of bipartisan anti-Communist foreign policy.

Eleutherios Venizelos, 1864-1936, (Gr.) most prominent Greek statesman of early 20th cent.

Hendrik F. Verwoerd, 1901-66, (S. Afr.) prime min.; rigorously applied apartheid policy despite protest.

Kurt Waldheim, 1918-2007, (Austria) UN sec.-gen., Austrian pres.

George Wallace, 1919-98, (U.S.) former segregationist governor of Alabama, pres. candidate.

Robert Walpole, 1676-1745, (Br.) statesman; generally considered Britain's first prime min.

Harold Washington, 1922-87, (U.S.) first black mayor of Chicago.

Robert C. Weaver, 1907-97, (U.S.) first African American appointed to cabinet; sec. of Housing and Urban Development.

Daniel Webster, 1782-1852, (U.S.) orator, politician; advocate of business interests during Jacksonian agrarianism.

Caspar Weinberger, 1917-2006, (U.S.) business exec., former defense sec., other cabinet posts.

Chaim Weizmann, 1874-1952, (Russ.-Isr.) Zionist leader, scientist; first Israeli pres.

Kevin White, 1929-2012, (U.S.) Boston mayor, 1967-84.

Wendell L. Willkie, 1892-1944, (U.S.) Republican who tried to unseat Franklin D. Roosevelt when he ran for his third term.

Harold Wilson, 1916-95, (Br.) Labour party leader; prime min., 1964-70, 1974-76.

Boris Yeltsin, 1931-2007, (Russ.) first freely elected pres. of post-Soviet Russia.

Coleman A. Young, 1918-97, (U.S.) first African-American mayor of Detroit, 1974-93.

Emiliano Zapata, c. 1879-1919, (Mex.) revolutionary; major influence on modern Mexico.

Todor Zhivkov, 1911-98, (Bulg.) Communist ruler of Bulgaria from 1954 until ousted in a 1989 coup.

Zhou Enlai, 1898-1976, (China) diplomat, prime min.; a leading figure of the Chinese Communist party.

Scientists of the Past

Revised by Peter Barker, Prof. and Chair, Dept. of the History of Science, Univ. of Oklahoma.

For pre-modern scientists, see also Philosophers and Religious Figures of the Past and the Historical Figures chapter.

Albertus Magnus, c. 1200-80, (Ger.) theologian, philosopher; helped found medieval study of natural science.

Alhazen (Ibn al-Haytham), c. 965-c. 1040, (Arab.) mathematician, astronomer, optical theorist.

Andre-Marie Ampère, 1775-1836, (Fr.) mathematician, chemist; founder of electrodynamics.

Mary Anning, 1799-1847, (Br.) paleontologist.

Neil Armstrong, 1930-2012, (U.S.) astronaut, first man to walk on the Moon.

John V. Atanasoff, 1903-95, (U.S.) physicist; co-invented Atanasoff-Berry electronic digital computer (1939-41).

Amedeo Avogadro, 1776-1856, (It.) chemist, physicist; proposed that equal volumes of gas contain equal numbers of molecules, permitting determination of molecular weights.

John Bardeen, 1908-91, (U.S.) double Nobel laureate in physics (transistor, 1956; superconductivity, 1972).

A. H. Becquerel, 1852-1908, (Fr.) physicist; discovered radioactivity in uranium (1896).

Alexander Graham Bell, 1847-1922, (U.S.) inventor; first to patent and commercially exploit the telephone (1876).

Daniel Bernoulli, 1700-82, (Switz.) mathematician; developed fluid dynamics and kinetic theory of gases.

Clifford Berry, 1918-63, (U.S.) collaborated with John V. Atanasoff on the ABC electronic digital computer (1939-41).

Jöns Jakob Berzelius, 1779-1848, (Swed.) chemist; developed modern chemical symbols and formulas.

Henry Bessemer, 1813-98, (Br.) engineer; invented Bessemer steel-making process.

Hans Bethe, 1906-2005, (Ger.-U.S.) physicist; won Nobel Prize in 1967 for describing how stars generate energy.

Bruno Bettelheim, 1903-90, (Austria-U.S.) psychoanalyst; studied disturbed children; *Uses of Enchantment* (1976).

Louis Blériot, 1872-1936, (Fr.) engineer; monoplane pioneer.

Franz Boas, 1858-1942, (Ger.-U.S.) founded modern anthropology; studied Pacific Coast tribes.

Niels Bohr, 1885-1962, (Den.) atomic and nuclear physicist; founded quantum mechanics.

Norman Borlaug, 1914-2009, (U.S.) plant pathologist and geneticist; father of "green" (agricultural) revolution.

Max Born, 1882-1970, (Ger.) atomic and nuclear physicist; helped develop quantum mechanics.

Satyendranath Bose, 1894-1974, (India) physicist; forerunner of modern quantum theory for integral-spin particles.

Louis de Broglie, 1892-1987, (Fr.) physicist; proposed quantum wave-particle duality.

Robert Bunsen, 1811-99, (Ger.) chemist; pioneered spectroscopic analysis; discovered rubidium, caesium.

Luther Burbank, 1849-1926, (U.S.) naturalist; developed plant breeding into a modern science.

Vannevar Bush, 1890-1974, (U.S.) electrical engineer; developed differential analyzer, an early analogue computer; headed WWII Office of Scientific Res. and Dev.

Marvin Camras, 1916-95, (U.S.) inventor, electrical engineer; invented magnetic tape recording.

Alexis Carrel, 1873-1944, (Fr.) surgeon, biologist; developed methods of suturing blood vessels, transplanting organs.

Rachel Carson, 1907-64, (U.S.) marine biologist, environmentalist; *Silent Spring* (1962).

George Washington Carver, 1864-1943, (U.S.) chemist and botanist; promoted alternative crops.

James Chadwick, 1891-1974, (Br.) physicist; discovered the neutron (1932); led Brit. team on Manhattan Project in U.S.

Eugenie Clark, 1922-2015, (U.S.) ichthyologist and oceanographer.

Albert Claude, 1898-1983, (Belg.-U.S.) a founder of modern cell biology; determined role of mitochondria.

Samuel Cohen, 1921-2010, (U.S.) physicist who invented the neutron bomb.

Barry Commoner, 1917-2012, biologist; noted environmentalist.

Nicolaus Copernicus, 1473-1543, (Pol.) first modern astronomer to propose Sun as center of the planets' motions.

Jacques Yves Cousteau, 1910-97, (Fr.) oceanographer; co-inventor, with Emile Gagnan (Fr.), of the Aqualung (1943).

Seymour Cray, 1925-96, (U.S.) computer industry pioneer; developed supercomputers.

Francis Crick, 1916-2004, (Br.) biophysicist; co-discoverer of genetic code; shared 1962 Nobel Prize in Physiology/Medicine.

Marie, 1867-1934, (Pol.-Fr.) and **Pierre Curie**, 1859-1906, (Fr.) physical chemists; pioneer investigators of radioactivity; discovered radium and polonium (1898).

Gottlieb Daimler, 1834-1900, (Ger.) engineer, inventor; pioneer automobile manufacturer.

John Dalton, 1766-1844, (Br.) chemist, physicist; formulated atomic theory, made first table of atomic weights.

Charles Darwin, 1809-82, (Br.) naturalist; established theory of organic evolution; *Origin of Species* (1859).

Lee De Forest, 1873-1961, (U.S.) inventor of triode; pioneer in wireless telegraphy, sound pictures, television.

Pierre-Gilles de Gennes, 1932-2007, (Fr.) physicist whose research aided development of liquid-crystal display (LCD); awarded 1991 Nobel Prize for Physics.

Max Delbrück, 1906-81, (Fr.-Ger.-U.S.) a founder of molecular biology.

Rudolf Diesel, 1858-1913, (Ger.) mechanical engineer; patented Diesel engine (1892).

Theodosius Dobzhansky, 1900-75, (Russ.-U.S.) biologist; reconciled genetics and natural selection.

Christian Doppler, 1803-53, (Austria) physicist; showed change in wave frequency caused by motion of source, now known as Doppler effect.

J. Presper Eckert Jr., 1919-95, (U.S.) co-inventor, with John W. Mauchly, of the ENIAC computer (1943-45).

Thomas A. Edison, 1847-1931, (U.S.) inventor; held more than 1,000 patents, including incandescent electric lamp.

Robert Edwards, 1925-2013, (Br.) physiologist; pioneered in vitro fertilization.

Paul Ehrlich, 1854-1915, (Ger.) medical researcher in immunology and bacteriology; pioneered antitoxin production.

Albert Einstein, 1879-1955, (Ger.-U.S.) theoretical physicist; founded relativity theory.

John F. Enders, 1897-1985, (U.S.) virologist; helped discover vaccines against polio, measles, mumps, and chicken pox.

Erik Erikson, 1902-94, (U.S.) psychoanalyst, author; theory of developmental stages of life; *Childhood and Society* (1950).

Leonhard Euler, 1707-83, (Switz.) mathematician, physicist; pioneer of calculus, revived ideas of Fermat.

Gabriel Fahrenheit, 1686-1736, (Ger.) physicist; improved thermometers and introduced Fahrenheit temperature scale.

Michael Faraday, 1791-1867, (Br.) chemist, physicist; discovered electrical induction and invented dynamo (1831).

Philo T. Farnsworth, 1906-71, (U.S.) inventor; built first television system (San Francisco, 1928).

Pierre de Fermat, 1601-65, (Fr.) mathematician; founded modern theory of numbers.

Enrico Fermi, 1901-54, (It.-U.S.) nuclear physicist; demonstrated first controlled chain reaction (Chicago, 1942).

Richard Feynman, 1918-88, (U.S.) theoretical physicist, author; founder of Quantum Electrodynamics (QED).

Alexander Fleming, 1881-1955, (Br.) bacteriologist; discovered penicillin (1928).

Dian Fossey, 1932-85, (U.S.) primatologist.

Jean B. J. Fourier, 1768-1830, (Fr.) introduced Fourier Series, method of analysis in math and physics.

Sigmund Freud, 1856-1939, (Austria) psychiatrist; founder of psychoanalysis; *Interpretation of Dreams* (1901).

Erich Fromm, 1900-80, (U.S.) psychoanalyst; *Man for Himself* (1947).

Galileo Galilei, 1564-1642, (It.) physicist; used telescope to vindicate Copernicus, founded modern science of motion.

Carl Friedrich Gauss, 1777-1855, (Ger.) mathematician; completed work of Fermat and Euler in number theory.

Josiah W. Gibbs, 1839-1903, (U.S.) theoretical physicist, chemist; founded chemical thermodynamics.

John Glenn, 1921-2016, (U.S.) astronaut, first American to orbit Earth (1962).

Robert H. Goddard, 1882-1945, (U.S.) physicist; invented liquid fuel rocket (1926).

George W. Goethals, 1858-1928, (U.S.) chief engineer who completed Panama Canal (1907-14).

William C. Gorgas, 1854-1920, (U.S.) physician; pioneer in prevention of yellow fever and malaria.

Stephen Jay Gould, 1941-2002, (U.S.) paleontologist, evolutionary biologist, writer.

Ernest Haeckel, 1834-1919, (Ger.) zoologist, evolutionist; early Darwinist, introduced concept of "ecology."

Otto Hahn, 1879-1968, (Ger.) chemist; with Lise Meitner discovered nuclear fission (1938).

Edmund Halley, 1656-1742, (Br.) astronomer; predicted return of 1682 comet (Halley's Comet) in 1759.

William Harvey, 1578-1657, (Br.) physician, anatomist; discovered circulation of the blood (1628).

Stephen Hawking, 1942-2018, (Br.) physicist; explored gravity, black holes; *A Brief History of Time* (1988).

Werner Heisenberg, 1901-76, (Ger.) physicist; developed matrix mechanics and uncertainty principle (1927).

Hermann von Helmholtz, 1821-94, (Ger.) physicist, physiologist; formulated principle of conservation of energy.

Caroline Herschel, 1750-1848, (Ger.-Br.) astronomer.

William Herschel, 1738-1822, (Ger.-Br.) astronomer; discovered Uranus (1781).

Heinrich Hertz, 1857-94, (Ger.) physicist; discovered radio waves and photo-electric effect (1886-87).

David Hilbert, 1862-1943, (Ger.) mathematician; contributed to algebra, calculus, and foundational studies (formalism).

Albert Hofmann, 1906-2008, (Switz.) chemist; inventor of LSD.

Edwin P. Hubble, 1889-1953, (U.S.) astronomer; discovered observational evidence of expanding universe.

Alexander von Humboldt, 1769-1859, (Ger.) naturalist; explored Central, S. America, ideated ecology.

Edward Jenner, 1749-1823, (Br.) physician; pioneered vaccination, introduced term "virus."

James Joule, 1818-89, (Br.) physicist; found relation between heat and mechanical energy (conservation of energy).

Carl Jung, 1875-1961, (Switz.) psychiatrist; founder of analytical psychology.

Ernest Everett Just, 1883-1941, (U.S.) marine biologist; studied egg development; *Biology of Cell Surfaces* (1941).

Johannes Kepler, 1571-1630, (Ger.) astronomer; discovered laws of planetary motion.

Al-Khwarizmi, early 9th cent., (Arab.) mathematician; regarded as founder of algebra.

Robert Koch, 1843-1910, (Ger.) bacteriologist; isolated bacterial causes of tuberculosis and other diseases.

Georges Köhler, 1946-95, (Ger.) immunologist; with Cesar Milstein, developed monoclonal antibody technique.

Willem Kolff, 1911-2009, (Neth.-U.S.) physician, biomedical engineer; developed first practical kidney dialysis machine; considered the "father of artificial organs."

Jacques Lacan, 1901-81, (Fr.) influential psychoanalyst.

Joseph Lagrange, 1736-1813, (Fr.) geometer, astronomer; showed that gravity of Earth and Moon cancel, creating stable points in space around them.

Jean B. Lamarck, 1744-1829, (Fr.) naturalist; forerunner of Darwin in evolutionary theory.

Pierre Simon de Laplace, 1749-1827, (Fr.) astronomer, physicist; proposed nebular origin for solar system.

Lewis H. Latimer, 1848-1928, (U.S.) African American scientist; associate of Edison; supervised installation of first electric street lighting in New York City.

Antoine Lavoisier, 1743-94, (Fr.) a founder of modern chemistry.

Ernest O. Lawrence, 1901-58, (U.S.) physicist; invented the cyclotron.

Louis, 1903-72, and **Mary Leakey**, 1913-96, (both Br.) early hominid paleoanthropologists; discovered remains in Africa.

Anton van Leeuwenhoek, 1632-1723, (Neth.) founder of microscopy.

Jerome Lejeune, 1927-94, (Fr.) geneticist; discovered chromosomal cause of Down syndrome (1959).

Claude Lévi-Strauss, 1908-2009, (Belg.-Fr.) cultural anthropologist, sociologist, philosopher.

Kurt Lewin, 1890-1947, (Ger.-U.S.) social psychologist; studied human motivation and group dynamics.

Justus von Liebig, 1803-73, (Ger.) founded quantitative organic chemistry.

Joseph Lister, 1827-1912, (Br.) physician; pioneered antiseptic surgery.

Hendrik Lorentz, 1853-1928, (Neth.) physicist; developed electron theory of matter, contributed to relativity theory.

Konrad Lorenz, 1903-89, (Austria) ethologist; pioneer in study of animal behavior.

Bernard Lovell, 1913-2012, (Br.) physicist and radio astronomer.

Percival Lowell, 1855-1916, (U.S.) astronomer; predicted the existence of Pluto.

Louis, 1864-1948, and **Auguste Lumière**, 1862-1954, (both Fr.) invented cinematograph, made first motion picture (1895).

Theodore H. Maiman, 1927-2007, (U.S.) physicist; invented the first workable laser, which he displayed in 1960.

Guglielmo Marconi, 1874-1937, (It.) physicist; developed wireless telegraphy.

John W. Mauchly, 1907-80, (U.S.) co-inventor, with J. Presper Eckert Jr., of computer ENIAC (1943-45).

James Clerk Maxwell, 1831-79, (Br.) physicist; unified electricity and magnetism, electromagnetic theory of light.

Maria Goeppert Mayer, 1906-72, (Ger.-U.S.) physicist; developed shell model of atomic nuclei.

Barbara McClintock, 1902-92, (U.S.) geneticist; showed that some genetic elements are mobile.

Lise Meitner, 1878-1968, (Austria) co-discoverer, with Otto Hahn, of nuclear fission (1938).

Gregor J. Mendel, 1822-84, (Austria) botanist, monk; his experiments became the foundation of modern genetics.

Dmitri Mendeleyev, 1834-1907, (Russ.) chemist; established Periodic Table of the Elements.

Bruce R. Merrifield, 1921-2006, (U.S.) chemist; discovered how to synthesize proteins quickly and efficiently.

Franz Mesmer, 1734-1815, (Ger.) physician; introduced hypnotherapy.

Albert A. Michelson, 1852-1931, (U.S.) physicist; invented interferometer.

Robert A. Millikan, 1868-1953, (U.S.) physicist; measured electronic charge.

Thomas Hunt Morgan, 1866-1945, (U.S.) geneticist, embryologist; established role of chromosomes in heredity.

John F. Nash Jr., 1928-2015, (U.S.) mathematician; Nobel Prize winner (1994) in economics for work on game theory.

Isaac Newton, 1642-1727, (Br.) natural philosopher; discovered laws of gravitation, motion; with Gottfried Wilhelm von Leibniz, founded calculus.

Robert N. Noyce, 1927-90, (U.S.) invented microchip.

J. Robert Oppenheimer, 1904-67, (U.S.) physicist; scientific director of Manhattan Project.

Wilhelm Ostwald, 1853-1932, (Ger.) chemist, philosopher; main founder of modern physical chemistry.

Louis Pasteur, 1822-95, (Fr.) chemist; showed that germs cause disease and fermentation; originated pasteurization.

Linus C. Pauling, 1901-94, (U.S.) chemist; studied chemical bonds; campaigned for nuclear disarmament.

Jean Piaget, 1896-1980, (Switz.) psychologist; four-stage theory of intellectual development in children.

Max Planck, 1858-1947, (Ger.) physicist; introduced quantum hypothesis (1900).

Jules Henri Poincaré, 1854-1912, (Fr.) mathematician; founded algebraic topology, many other discoveries.

Walter S. Reed, 1851-1902, (U.S.) Army physician; proved mosquitoes transmit yellow fever.

Theodor Reik, 1888-1969, (Austria-U.S.) psychoanalyst; major Freudian disciple.

Sally Ride, 1951-2012, (U.S.) astronaut, 1st U.S. woman in space.

Bernhard Riemann, 1826-66, (Ger.) mathematician; developed non-Euclidean geometry used by Einstein.

Norbert Rillieux, 1806-94, (U.S.) African American inventor of a vacuum pan evaporator (1846); revolutionized sugar-refining industry.

Wilhelm Roentgen, 1845-1923, (Ger.) physicist; discovered X-rays (1895).

Carl Rogers, 1902-87, (U.S.) psychotherapist, author; originated nondirective therapy.

Ernest Rutherford, 1871-1937, (Br.) physicist; pioneer investigator of radioactivity, identified the atomic nucleus.

Albert B. Sabin, 1906-93, (Russ.-U.S.) developed oral polio live-virus vaccine.

Carl Sagan, 1934-96, (U.S.) astronomer, author.

Jonas Salk, 1914-95, (U.S.) developed first successful polio vaccine, widely used in U.S. after 1955.

Allan Sandage, 1926-2010, (U.S.) astronomer; refined the Hubble Constant, a measure of the universe's expansion.

Frederick Sanger, 1918-2013, (Br.) biochemist; detailed molecular structure of insulin.

Giovanni Schiaparelli, 1835-1910, (It.) astronomer; reported canals on Mars.

Erwin Schrödinger, 1887-1961, (Austria) physicist; developed wave equation for quantum systems.

Glenn T. Seaborg, 1912-99, (U.S.) chemist; Nobel Prize winner (1951); co-discoverer of plutonium.

Harlow Shapley, 1885-1972, (U.S.) astronomer; mapped galactic clusters and position of Sun in Milky Way Galaxy.

Norman E. Shumway, 1923-2006, (U.S.) surgeon; performed world's first successful heart-lung transplant.

B. F. Skinner, 1904-90, (U.S.) psychologist; leading advocate of behaviorism.

Richard E. Smalley, 1943-2005, (U.S.) chemist; with three other scientists, discovered buckminsterfullerenes, a previously unknown class of carbon molecules.

Roger W. Sperry, 1913-94, (U.S.) neurobiologist; established different functions of right and left sides of brain.

Benjamin Spock, 1903-98, (U.S.) pediatrician, child care expert; *Common Sense Book of Baby and Child Care*.

Charles P. Steinmetz, 1865-1923, (Ger.-U.S.) electrical engineer; developed basic ideas on alternating current.

Ernst Stuhlinger, 1913-2008, (Ger.) rocket scientist; electric propulsion for NASA in early space age.

Leo Szilard, 1898-1964, (Hung.-U.S.) physicist; helped on Manhattan Project, later opposed nuclear weapons.

Edward Teller, 1908-2003, (Hung.-U.S.) physicist; aided on Manhattan Project, had key role in development of H-bomb.

Nikola Tesla, 1856-1943, (Serb.-U.S.) invented electrical devices including AC dynamos, transformers, and motors.

William Thomson (Lord Kelvin), 1824-1907, (Br.) physicist; aided in success of transatlantic telegraph cable (1865); proposed Kelvin absolute temperature scale.

Alan Turing, 1912-54, (Br.) mathematician; helped develop basis for computers.

James Van Allen, 1914-2006, (U.S.) physicist; discovered the presence of radiation belts around Earth (Van Allen belts).

Rudolf Virchow, 1821-1902, (Ger.) pathologist; pioneered the modern theory that diseases affect the body through cells.

Alessandro Volta, 1745-1827, (It.) physicist; electricity pioneer.

Wernher von Braun, 1912-77, (Ger.-U.S.) developed rockets for warfare and space exploration.

John von Neumann, 1903-57, (Hung.-U.S.) mathematician; originated game theory; basic design for modern computers.

Alfred Russell Wallace, 1823-1913, (Br.) naturalist; proposed concept of evolution independently of Darwin.

John B. Watson, 1878-1958, (U.S.) psychologist; a founder of behaviorism.

James E. Watt, 1736-1819, (Br.) mechanical engineer, inventor; invented modern steam engine (1765).

Alfred L. Wegener, 1880-1930, (Ger.) meteorologist, geophysicist; postulated continental drift.

Norbert Wiener, 1894-1964, (U.S.) mathematician; founder of cybernetics.

Daniel Hale Williams, 1858-1931, (U.S.) African American surgeon; performed one of first two open-heart operations (1893).

Sewall Wright, 1889-1988, (U.S.) evolutionary theorist; helped found population genetics.

Wilhelm Wundt, 1832-1920, (Ger.) founder of experimental psychology.

Qian Xuesen, 1911-2009, (China) rocket scientist; helped found Jet Propulsion Lab, father of China's space program.

Rosalyn Yalow, 1921-2011, (U.S.) physicist; co-developer of radioimmunoassay.

Ferdinand von Zeppelin, 1838-1917, (Ger.) soldier, aeronaut; airship designer.

Social Reformers, Activists, and Humanitarians of the Past

Ralph David Abernathy, 1926-90, (U.S.) black civil rights activist; pres., 1968, Southern Christian Leadership Conf.

Jane Addams, 1860-1935, (U.S.) cofounder of Hull House; won Nobel Peace Prize, 1931.

Susan B. Anthony, 1820-1906, (U.S.) a leader in temperance, antislavery, and woman suffrage movements.

Thomas Barnardo, 1845-1905, (Br.) social reformer; pioneer in care of destitute children.

Clara Barton, 1821-1912, (U.S.) organized American Red Cross.

Daisy Bates, 1914-99, (U.S.) black civil rights leader who fought for integration; advocate for the "Little Rock 9" during Arkansas desegregation crisis in 1957.

Henry Ward Beecher, 1813-87, (U.S.) clergyman, abolitionist.

Peter Benenson, 1921-2005, (Br.) activist; founded Amnesty International, 1961.

Mary McLeod Bethune, 1875-1955, (U.S.) black educator, civil rights activist; adviser to FDR and Truman; founder, pres., Bethune-Cookman College.

Elizabeth Blackwell, 1821-1910, (Br.) first female physician in the U.S.

Amelia Bloomer, 1818-94, (U.S.) suffragette, social reformer.

Julian Bond, 1940-2015, (U.S.) civil rights leader, NAACP chair, 1998-2015.

Yelena Bonner, 1923-2011, (Russ.) human rights activist in former Soviet Union.

William Booth, 1829-1912, (Br.) founded Salvation Army.

James Brady, 1940-2014, (U.S.) gun control advocate; Reagan press sec.

John Brown, 1800-59, (U.S.) abolitionist who led murder of five pro-slavery men; hanged.

Frances Xavier (Mother) Cabrini, 1850-1917, (It.-U.S.) nun; founded charitable institutions; first American canonized as a saint, 1946.

Stokely Carmichael (Kwame Ture), 1941-98, (Trinidad-U.S.) black power activist; major proponent of Pan-Africanism; prime min. of Black Panthers.

Carrie Chapman Catt, 1859-1947, (U.S.) suffragette.

Cesar Chavez, 1927-93, (U.S.) labor leader; helped establish United Farm Workers of America.

Eldridge Cleaver, 1935-98, (U.S.) revolutionary social critic; former minister of information for Black Panthers; *Soul on Ice*.

Clarence Darrow, 1857-1938, (U.S.) lawyer; defender of underdog, opponent of capital punishment.

Ossie Davis, 1917-2005, (U.S.) black civil rights activist, actor, director.

Dorothy Day, 1897-1980, (U.S.) founder of Catholic Worker movement.

Eugene V. Debs, 1855-1926, (U.S.) labor leader; led Pullman Strike, 1894; four-time Socialist presidential candidate.

Vine Deloria Jr., 1933-2005, (U.S.) Native American activist, author; *Custer Died for Your Sins*.

Dorothea Dix, 1802-87, (U.S.) crusader for mentally ill.

Thomas Dooley, 1927-61, (U.S.) "jungle doctor"; noted for efforts to supply medical aid to developing countries.

Marjory Stoneman Douglas, 1890-1998, (U.S.) writer, environmentalist; campaigned to save Florida Everglades.

Frederick Douglass, 1817-95, (U.S.) author, editor, orator, diplomat; edited abolitionist weekly *The North Star*.

Andrea Dworkin, 1946-2005, (U.S.) radical feminist, antipornography crusader.

Medgar Evers, 1925-63, (U.S.) black civil rights leader; campaigned to register black voters; assassinated.

James Farmer, 1920-99, (U.S.) black civil rights leader; founded Congress of Racial Equality (CORE).

Betty Friedan, 1921-2006, (U.S.) author, feminist; *The Feminine Mystique*.

Millard Fuller, 1935-2009, (U.S.) founder of Habitat for Humanity.

William Lloyd Garrison, 1805-79, (U.S.) abolitionist.

Miep Gies, 1909-2010, (Neth.) protector of Anne Frank and her family during WWII.

Emma Goldman, 1869-1940, (Russ.-U.S.) published anarchist *Mother Earth*; birth-control advocate.

Samuel Gompers, 1850-1924, (U.S.) labor leader; first pres. of the American Federation of Labor (AFL).

Juliette Gordon Low, 1860-1927, (U.S.) Girl Scouts founder.

Prince Hall, 1735-1807, (U.S.) activist; founded black Freemasonry; served in American Revolutionary War.

Michael Harrington, 1928-89, (U.S.) exposed poverty in affluent U.S. in *The Other America*, 1963.

Dorothy Height, 1912-2010, (U.S.) civil rights activist; pres. of the National Council of Negro Women, 1957-97.

Sidney Hillman, 1887-1946, Lith.- (U.S.) labor leader; helped organize CIO.

Benjamin Hooks, 1925-2010, (U.S.) civil rights activist; exec. dir. NAACP, 1977-92.

Samuel G. Howe, 1801-76, (U.S.) social reformer; changed public attitudes toward the blind, deaf, mentally challenged.

Franklin Kameny, 1925-2011, (U.S.) gay rights activist.

Helen Keller, 1880-1968, (U.S.) crusader for better treatment for the disabled; deaf and blind herself.

Jack Kevorkian 1928-2011, (U.S.) pathologist; assisted-suicide activist.

Coretta Scott King, 1927-2006, (U.S.) black civil rights leader; wife of Rev. Martin Luther King Jr.

Rev. Martin Luther King Jr., 1929-68, (U.S.) civil rights leader; led 1955-56 Montgomery, AL, boycott; founder, pres., Southern Christian Leadership Conference, 1957; Nobel peace laureate, 1964; assassinated.

Maggie Kuhn, 1905-95, (U.S.) founded Gray Panthers, 1970.

William Kunstler, 1919-95, (U.S.) civil liberties attorney.

John L. Lewis, 1880-1969, (U.S.) labor leader; headed United Mine Workers, 1920-60.

Belva Lockwood, 1830-1917, (U.S.) lawyer; first woman to argue before U.S. Supreme Court.

Almena Lomax, 1915-2011, (U.S.) civil rights activist; journalist who founded *The Los Angeles Tribune*.

Clara Luper, 1923-2011, (U.S.) civil rights activist.

Wangari Maathai, 1940-2011, (Kenya), environmental activist; 2004 Nobel Peace Prize winner.

Robert Macauley, 1923-2010, (U.S.) founder of AmeriCares.

Malcolm X (Little), 1925-65, (U.S.) Black Muslim, black nationalist leader; promoted black pride; assassinated.

Russell Means, 1939-2012, (U.S.) American Indian activist.

Karl Menninger, 1893-1990, (U.S.) with brother William, founded Menninger Clinic and Menninger Foundation.

Kate Millett, 1934-2017, (U.S.) writer, feminist; *Sexual Politics*.

Lucretia Mott, 1793-1880, (U.S.) reformer, pioneer feminist.

Philip Murray, 1886-1952, (U.S.) Scottish-born labor leader.

Huey P. Newton, 1942-89, (U.S.) co-founded Black Panther Party, 1966.

Florence Nightingale, 1820-1910, (Br.) founder of modern nursing.

Emmeline Pankhurst, 1858-1928, (Br.) suffragette.

Rosa Parks,1913-2005, (U.S.) black civil rights activist; her actions sparked 1955-56 Montgomery, AL, bus boycott.

A. Philip Randolph, 1889-1979, (U.S.) organized Brotherhood of Sleeping Car Porters, 1925; an organizer of 1941 and 1963 March on Washington movements.

Walter Reuther, 1907-70, (U.S.) labor leader; headed United Auto Workers.

Jacob Riis, 1849-1914, (U.S.) crusader for urban reforms.

Paul Robeson, 1898-1976, (U.S.) actor, singer, black civil rights activist.

Bayard Rustin, 1910-87, (U.S.) black and LGBT civil rights activist; an organizer of the 1963 March on Washington.

Margaret Sanger, 1883-1966, (U.S.) social reformer; pioneered the birth-control movement.

Phyllis Schlafly, 1924-2016, (U.S.) anti-Equal Rights Amendment activist.

Earl of Shaftesbury (A. A. Cooper), 1801-85, (Br.) social reformer.

Eunice Kennedy Shriver, 1921-2009, (U.S.) cofounder of Special Olympics for athletes with intellectual disabilities.

Sargent Shriver, 1915-2011, (U.S.) founding director of Peace Corps; founder of Job Corps, Head Start.

Fred Shuttlesworth, 1922-2011, (U.S.) civil rights activist.

Albertina Sisulu, 1918-2011, (S. Africa), anti-apartheid activist.

Elizabeth Cady Stanton, 1815-1902, (U.S.) woman suffrage pioneer.

Lucy Stone, 1818-93, (U.S.) feminist, abolitionist.

Mother Teresa of Calcutta, 1910-97, (Alban.) nun; founded order to care for sick, dying poor; 1979 Nobel Peace Prize winner; canonized 2016.

Willard Townsend, 1895-1957, (U.S.) organized the United Transport Service Employees (Red Caps), 1935.

Sojourner Truth (Isabella Baumfree), 1797-1883, (U.S.) preacher, abolitionist; worked for black educ. opportunity.

Harriet Tubman, 1823-1913, (U.S.) prominent figure in the Underground Railroad; nurse, spy for Union Army in the Civil War.

Nat Turner, 1800-31, (U.S.) slave who led the most significant of more than 200 slave revolts in U.S., in Southampton, VA; hanged.

Philip Vera Cruz, 1905-94, (Philip.-U.S.) helped found the United Farm Workers Union.

Edgar Wayburn, 1906-2010, (U.S.) conservationist; Sierra Club pres.

Elie Wiesel, 1928-2016, (Rom.-U.S.) Holocaust survivor, author, and activist; 1986 Nobel Peace Prize winner.

William Wilberforce, 1759-1833, (Br.) social reformer; prominent in struggle to abolish slave trade.

Frances E. Willard, 1839-98, (U.S.) temperance, women's rights leader.

Edith Windsor, 1929-2007, (U.S.) LGBT civil rights activist.

Mary Wollstonecraft, 1759-97, (Br.) *Vindication of the Rights of Women*.

Victoria Woodhull, 1838-1927, (U.S.) suffragist, first woman to run for president (1872).

Sports Personalities of the Past and Present

Henry (Hank) Aaron, b 1934, Milwaukee-Atlanta outfielder; hit then-record 755 home runs, record 2,297 RBI.

Kareem Abdul-Jabbar, b 1947, Milwaukee, L.A. Lakers center; MVP 6 times; all-time leading NBA scorer, 38,387 pts.

Andre Agassi, b 1970, tennis player; won Wimbledon (1992); U.S. Open ('94, '99), Austral. Open ('95, 2000-01, '03), French Open ('99).

Troy Aikman, b 1966, quarterback; led Dallas Cowboys to Super Bowl wins in 1993-94, '96; Super Bowl MVP, 1993.

Ben Ainslie, b 1977, (Br.) most decorated Olympic sailor; gold, 2000, '04, '08, '12, silver, 1996.

Michelle Akers, b 1966, soccer player; led U.S. to victory in World Cup (1991, '99).

Amy Alcott, b 1956, golfer; 33 career wins (5 majors); inducted into Hall of Fame, 1999.

Grover Cleveland "Pete" Alexander, 1887-1950, pitcher; won 373 NL games; pitched 16 shutouts, 1916.

Muhammad Ali, 1942-2016, 3-time heavyweight champion, activist.

Fernando Alonso, b 1981, (Sp.) Formula 1 racer; youngest ever to win a World Grand Prix championship, 2005; defended title, 2006.

Morten Andersen, b 1960, (Den.) kicker; NFL's career points leader, with 2,544 (1982-2007).

Gary Anderson, b 1959, (S. Afr.) kicker; NFL's 2nd in career points, with 2,434.

Sparky Anderson, 1934-2010, first manager to win World Series in the NL (Cincinnati, 1975-76) and AL (Detroit, 1984).

Mario Andretti, b 1940, (It.) race-car driver; won Daytona 500 (1967), Indy 500 (1969); Formula 1 world title (1978).

Earl Anthony, 1938-2001, bowler; won record 6 PBA Championships (1973-75, '81-'83), 43 career PBA tournaments.

Eddie Arcaro, 1916-97, only jockey to win racing's Triple Crown twice, 1941, '48; rode to 4,779 wins in his career.

Lance Armstrong, b 1971, cyclist; record 7-time winner of Tour de France (1999-2005); stripped of victories in 2012 for use of performance-enhancing drugs.

Arthur Ashe, 1943-93, tennis player; won U.S. Open (1968), Wimbledon (1975).

Evelyn Ashford, b 1957, sprinter; won 100m gold (1984) and silver (1988); member of 5 U.S. Olympic teams.

Red Auerbach, 1917-2006, coached Boston to 9 NBA titles.

Geno Auriemma, b 1954, (It.) UConn women's basketball coach; record-11 NCAA women's basketball titles.

Tracy Austin, b 1962, tennis player; youngest to win U.S. Open (age 16 in 1979).

Victoria Azarenka, b 1989, (Belarus) tennis player; won Austral. Open (2012-13).

Ernie Banks, 1931-2015, Chicago Cubs slugger; hit 512 NL homers; twice MVP.

Roger Bannister, 1929-2018, (Br.) physician; ran 1st sub-4-min. mile, May 6, 1954 (3 min., 59.4 sec.).

Charles Barkley, b 1963, NBA MVP, 1993; 4th player ever to surpass 20,000 pts., 10,000 rebounds, 4,000 assists.

Rick Barry, b 1944, NBA scoring leader, 1967; ABA scoring leader, 1969.

Sammy Baugh, 1914-2008, Washington Redskins quarterback, punter, defensive back.

Elgin Baylor, b 1934, L.A. Lakers forward; 11-time all-star.

Bob Beamon, b 1946, Olympic long jump gold medalist, 1968; world record jump of 29 ft 2½ in. stood until 1991.

Boris Becker, b 1967, (Ger.) tennis star; won U.S. Open 1989; Wimbledon champ 1985-86, '89.

David Beckham, b 1975, (Br.) soccer star; joined L.A. Galaxy, 2007-12, with record-breaking $250-mil contract.

Bill Belichick, b 1952, NFL coach; led New England to 5 Super Bowl wins; best all-time post-season coaching record.

Jean Béliveau, 1931-2014, (Can.) Montréal Canadiens center; scored 507 career goals; twice MVP.

Johnny Bench, b 1947, Cincinnati Reds catcher; twice MVP; led league in home runs twice, RBIs 3 times.

Patty Berg, 1918-2006, 80+ golf tournament wins; AP Woman Athlete of the Year 3 times.

Chris Berman, b 1955, sportscaster.

Yogi Berra, 1925-2015, Yankee catcher (1946-63); 3-time MVP.

Abebe Bikila, 1932-73, (Eth.) runner; won consecutive Olympic marathon gold medals in 1960 (barefoot), '64.

Simone Biles, b 1997, gymnast; won 4 Olympic gold medals, including all-around and team (2016).

Matt Biondi, b 1965, swimmer; won 5 golds, 1988 Olympics.

Larry Bird, b 1956, Boston Celtics forward (1979-92); NBA MVP, 1984-86; 1998 coach of the year with Indiana Pacers.

Bonnie Blair, b 1964, speed skater; won 5 individual gold medals in 3 Olympics (1988, '92, '94).

George Blanda, 1927-2010, quarterback, kicker; 26 years as active player, scored 2,002 career points.

Fanny Blankers-Koen, 1918-2004, (Neth.) track star; won 4 golds in 1948 Olympics.

Wade Boggs, b 1958, AL batting champ, 1983, '85-'88; reached 3,000 career hits, 1999 (3,010).

Usain Bolt, b 1986, (Jam.) Olympic sprinter, gold medalist, 2008, '12, '16; world record for men's 100-m, 200-m runs.

Barry Bonds, b 1964, outfielder; hit record 73 homers, 2001; NL MVP, 1990, '92-'93, 2001-04; 1st all-time in HRs (762); indicted in steroid scandal, 2007.

Björn Borg, b 1956, (Swed.) led Sweden to first Davis Cup, 1975; 6-time French Open, 5-time Wimbledon champion.

Ray Bourque, b 1960, (Can.) Boston defenseman,1979-2000; 5-time Norris

Trophy winner; won Stanley Cup with Colorado, 2001.

Bill Bradley, b 1943, led NY Knicks to 2 NBA titles (1970, '73); U.S. senator (NJ), 1979-97.

Donald Bradman, 1908-2001, (Austral.) widely regarded as greatest cricketer ever; set several batting records.

Terry Bradshaw, b 1948, quarterback; led Pittsburgh to 4 Super Bowl wins, 1975-76, '79-'80; NFL MVP, 1978.

Tom Brady, b 1977, quarterback; led New England to 5 Super Bowl titles, 2002, '04-'05, '15, '17; Super Bowl MVP, 2002, '04, '15, '17; NFL MVP, 2007, '10, '17.

Drew Brees, b 1979, New Orleans Saints quarterback; Super Bowl MVP, 2010.

Christine Brennan, b 1958, sports journalist for *USA Today*, radio and TV commentator specializing in figure skating.

George Brett, b 1953, Kansas City Royals infielder; led AL in batting, 1976, '80, '90; MVP, 1980.

Lou Brock, b 1939, St. Louis Cardinals outfielder; stole NL single-season record 118 bases, 1974; led NL 8 times.

Jim Brown, b 1936, Cleveland fullback; 12,312 career yds; NFL MVP 1957-58, '65.

Paul Brown, 1908-91, football team owner, coach; led eponymous Cleveland Browns to 3 NFL championships.

Bob Bryan and **Mike Bryan**, b 1978, doubles tennis players; won 16 Grand Slam doubles titles (2003-14); Olympic gold, 2012.

Kobe Bryant, b 1978, NBA guard; won 3 titles with Lakers (2000-02); leading NBA scorer, 2006, '07; NBA MVP, 2008; NBA Finals MVP, 2010; Olympic gold medal winner (2008, '12).

Paul "Bear" Bryant, 1913-83, college football coach with 323 wins; led Alabama to 6 national titles (1961, '64-'65, '73, '78-'79).

Sergei Bubka, b 1963, (Ukr.) pole vaulter; first to clear 20 ft; gold medal, 1988 Olympics.

Don Budge, 1915-2000, won numerous amateur and pro tennis titles; Grand Slam, 1938.

Reggie Bush, b 1985, NFL running back; helped USC to 2 national titles (2003-04; '04 vacated).

Dick Butkus, b 1942, Chicago Bears linebacker; NFL defensive player of the year (1969-70).

Dick Button, b 1929, figure skater; won 1948, '52 Olympic gold medals; world titleholder, 1948-52.

Miguel Cabrera, b 1983, (Venez.) 11-time MLB All-Star; won AL triple crown (2012); AL MVP 2012, 2013.

Walter Camp, 1859-1925, Yale football player, coach, athletic director; established many rules for modern football.

Roy Campanella, 1921-93, Hall of Fame catcher for the Brooklyn Dodgers (1948-57); 3-time NL MVP.

Earl Campbell, b 1955, NFL running back; MVP 1978-79.

Jose Canseco, b 1964, outfielder; led Oakland A's to the World Series, 1988; wrote book about steroids in baseball, 2005.

Eric Cantona, b 1966, (Fr.) soccer star; Manchester United (1992-97).

Rod Carew, b 1945, AL infielder; 7 batting titles, 1977 MVP.

Steve Carlton, b 1944, NL pitcher; won 20 games 6 times, 4-time Cy Young winner; 4,136 career strikeouts.

Pete Carroll, b 1951, football coach; NCAA champion (2003, '04); won Super Bowl XLVIII.

Billy Casper, 1931-2015, PGA Player of the Year 2 times; U.S. Open champ twice.

Tamika Catchings, b 1979, basketball forward, WNBA MVP, 2011; 4-time Olympic gold medalist.

Tracy Caulkins, b 1963, swimmer; 3-time Olympic gold medalist.

Wilt Chamberlain, 1936-99, center; 7-time NBA leading scorer, 4-time MVP; scored 100 pts. in a game, 1962.

Bobby Clarke, b 1949, (Can.) Philadelphia Flyers center; led team to 2 Stanley Cup championships; MVP 3 times.

Roger Clemens, b 1962, pitcher; 1986 AL MVP; only 7-time Cy Young winner; 354 wins, 4,672 Ks (3rd all-time); accused of lying to Congress about steroids, 2010.

Roberto Clemente, 1934-72, Pittsburgh Pirates outfielder; won 4 batting titles; MVP, 1966; 3,000 career hits; killed in plane crash.

Kim Clijsters, b 1983, (Belg.) tennis player; U.S. Open winner (2005, '09-'10); Austral. Open (2011).

Ty Cobb, 1886-1961, Detroit Tigers outfielder; record .367 lifetime batting average, 12 batting titles.

Sebastian Coe, b 1956, (Br.) runner; won Olympic 1,500m gold medal and 800m silver medal in both 1980, '84.

Nadia Comaneci, b 1961, (Rom.) gymnast; won 3 gold medals, achieved 7 perfect scores, 1976 Olympics; 9 Olympic medals overall.

Maureen Connolly, 1934-69, won tennis Grand Slam, 1953; AP Woman Athlete of the Year 3 times.

Jimmy Connors, b 1952, tennis player; 8 Grand Slam singles titles.

Alberto Contador, b 1982, (Sp.) cyclist; won Tour de France 2007, '09; stripped of 2010 title because of doping offense.

Cynthia Cooper, b 1963, WNBA player; 4-time finals MVP; 2-time league MVP.

James J. Corbett, 1866-1933, heavyweight champion, 1892-97; credited with being the first "scientific" boxer.

Angel Cordero Jr., b 1942, jockey; leading money winner, 1976, '82-'83; rode 3 Kentucky Derby winners.

Margaret Smith Court, b 1942, (Austral.) tennis great; won 24 Grand Slam events.

Bob Cousy, b 1928, Boston guard; 6 NBA titles, 1957 MVP.

Sidney Crosby, b 1987, (Can.) hockey player; Art Ross, Hart Trophies (2007, '14), Olympic gold medal (2010, '14).

Mark Cuban, b 1958, Dallas Mavericks owner; known for outspokenness.

Stephen Curry, b 1988, NBA point guard; NBA MVP, 2015, '16.

Bjoern Daehlie, b 1967, (Nor.) cross-country skier; won record 8 Winter Olympic gold medals.

Lindsay Davenport, b 1976, tennis player; won Olympic gold, 1996; U.S. Open, 1998; Wimbledon, 1999; Austral. Open, 2000.

Al Davis, 1929-2011, Oakland Raiders owner, former coach.

Oscar De La Hoya, b 1973, won IBF lightweight (1995); WBC super lightweight (1996); welterweight (1997-99, 2000) titles.

Donna de Varona, b 1947, swimmer; won 2 Olympic golds, 1964; 1st female sportscaster at a major network, 1965.

Dizzy Dean, 1910-74, pitcher; St. Louis Cardinals' "Gashouse Gang" in the '30s.

Mary Decker Slaney, b 1958, runner; has held 6 separate American records from the 800m to 10,000m.

Frank Deford, 1938-2017, writer for *Sports Illustrated*; author, commentator.

Jack Dempsey, 1895-1983, heavyweight champ, 1919-26.

Gail Devers, b 1966, Olympic 100m gold medalist (1992, '96).

Joe DiMaggio, 1914-99, NY Yankees outfielder; hit safely in record 56 consecutive games, 1941; AL MVP 3 times.

Novak Djokovic, b 1987, (Serb.) tennis player; 14 Grand Slam singles titles.

Landon Donovan, b 1982, soccer forward.

Tony Dorsett, b 1954, Heisman winner who led the Dallas Cowboys to an NFL title in his rookie year, 1977.

Gabrielle Douglas, b 1995, gymnast; Olympic gold in all-around (2012), team (2012, '16).

Tim Duncan, b 1976, San Antonio center; 3-time NBA Finals MVP, 1999, 2003, '05; NBA MVP, 2002, '03.

Margaret Osborne duPont, 1918-2012, tennis player; 6-time Grand Slam singles champion.

Roberto Duran, b 1951, (Pan.) boxer; held titles at 3 weights; lost 1980 "no mas" fight to Sugar Ray Leonard.

Kevin Durant, b 1988, NBA forward; NBA MVP, 2014; Finals MVP, 2017, '18; Olympic gold medalist, 2012, '16.

Leo Durocher, 1905-91, manager; won 3 NL pennants (Brooklyn, 1941; NY Giants, 1951, '54), 1954 World Series.

Dale Earnhardt Jr., b 1974, stock car racer; Daytona 500 winner (2004, '14).

Dale Earnhardt Sr., 1951-2001, 7-time NASCAR Winston Cup champ; died in a last-lap crash at 2001 Daytona 500.

Ashton Eaton, b 1988, Olympic decathlon gold medalist, 2012, '16.

Stefan Edberg, b 1966, (Swed.) tennis player; U.S. Open (1991-92), Wimbledon (1988, '90), Austral. Open (1985, '87).

Gertrude Ederle, 1905-2003, first woman to swim English Channel; broke existing men's record, 1926.

Teresa Edwards, b 1964, 5-time basketball Olympian; gold medalist, 1984, '88, '96, 2000; bronze medalist, 1992.

Hicham El Guerrouj, b 1974, (Morocco) runner; holds world records in mile (3:43.13) and 1,500m (3:26); won gold medals in 1,500m and 5,000m, 2004 Olympics.

John Elway, b 1960, quarterback; led Denver Broncos to 2 Super Bowl wins, 1998-99; NFL MVP, 1987; Super Bowl MVP, 1999.

Roy Emerson, b 1936 (Austral.), tennis player; 12-time Grand Slam singles and 16-time Grand Slam doubles champion.

Julius "Dr. J" Erving, b 1950, 3-time ABA MVP, 1981 NBA MVP.

Phil Esposito, b 1942, (Can.) NHL scoring leader 5 times.

Janet Evans, b 1971, 4 Olympic swimming golds, 1988, '92.

Lee Evans, b 1947, Olympic 400m gold medalist in 1968 with 43.86-sec. world record not broken until 1988.

Chris Evert, b 1954, 6-time U.S. Open tennis champ; 3-time Wimbledon champ.

Ray Ewry, 1873-1937, track-and-field star; won 8 Olympic gold medals (1900, '04, '08).

Nick Faldo, b 1957, (Br.) golfer; won Masters, British Open 3 times each.

Juan Manuel Fangio, 1911-95 (Arg.), 5-time World Grand Prix driving champ (1951, '54-'57).

Marshall Faulk, b 1973, 2000 NFL MVP; scored then-record 26 TDs, 2001; 3-time Off. Player of the Year (1999-2001).

Brett Favre, b 1969, quarterback; led Green Bay to Super Bowl win, 1997; NFL MVP, 1995-97.

Roger Federer, b 1981, (Switz.) tennis player; 20 Grand Slam singles titles (1st all-time).

Bob Feller, 1918-2010, Cleveland Indians pitcher; won 266 games; pitched 3 no-hitters, 12 one-hitters.

Rollie Fingers, b 1946, pitcher; 341 career saves; AL MVP, Cy Young, 1981; World Series MVP, 1974.

Peggy Fleming, b 1948, world figure skating champion, 1966-68; gold medalist, 1968 Olympics.

Whitey Ford, b 1928, NY Yankees pitcher; won record 10 World Series games.

George Foreman, b 1949, heavyweight champion, 1973-74, '94-'95; at 45, oldest to win a heavyweight title; gold medalist, 1968 Olympics.

Dick Fosbury, b 1947, high jumper; won 1968 Olympic gold medal; developed the "Fosbury Flop."

Jimmie Foxx, 1907-67, Red Sox, Athletics slugger; MVP 3 times; triple crown, 1933.

A.J. Foyt, b 1935, won Indy 500 4 times; U.S. Auto Club champ 7 times.

Dario Franchitti, b 1973, (Scot.) 3-time Indy 500 winner, 2007, '10, '12.

Missy Franklin, b 1995, swimmer; 5-time Olympic gold medalist (2012, '16).

Joe Frazier, 1944-2011, heavyweight champion, 1970-73; gold medalist, 1964 Olympics.

Walt Frazier, b 1945, Hall of Fame guard for NY Knicks' NBA championship teams (1970, '73).

Chris Froome, b 1985, (Kenya) 4-time Tour de France winner (2013, '15-'17).

Peter Gammons, b 1945, sportswriter, broadcaster.

Lou Gehrig, 1903-41, NY Yankees 1st baseman; MVP, 1927, '36; triple crown, 1934; played 2,130 straight games (1925-39).

Althea Gibson, 1927-2003, 2-time U.S. Nationals and Wimbledon champ.

Bob Gibson, b 1935, St. Louis Cardinals pitcher; won Cy Young twice; struck out 3,117 batters.

Josh Gibson, 1911-47, Negro Leagues Hall of Fame catcher; hit as many as 84 home runs in one season and 800 in career.

Marc Girardelli, b 1963, (Lux.) skier; won 5 World Cup titles.

Raúl González, b 1977, (Sp.) soccer player; led Real Madrid to 3 Champions League titles (1998, 2000, '02).

Jeff Gordon, b 1971, race-car driver; youngest to win NASCAR title 4 times (1995, '97-'98, 2001).

Steffi Graf, b 1969, (Ger.) tennis player; 22 Grand Slam singles titles (3rd all-time).

Otto Graham, 1921-2003, Cleveland quarterback; 4-time all-pro.

Red Grange, 1903-91, All-American at Univ. of Illinois, 1923-25; played for Chicago Bears, 1925-35.

"Mean" Joe Greene, b 1946, Pittsburgh Steelers lineman; twice NFL outstanding defensive player.

Wayne Gretzky, b 1961, (Can.) top scorer in NHL history with record 894 goals, 1,963 assists, 2,857 pts.; MVP, 1980-87, '89.

Bob Griese, b 1945, All-Pro quarterback; led Miami Dolphins to 17-0 season, 1972, 2 Super Bowl titles, 1973-74.

Ken Griffey Jr., b 1969, Hall of Fame outfielder; led AL in homers 1994, '97-'99; 1997 AL MVP; 10 gold gloves.

Archie Griffin, b 1954, Ohio State running back; only 2-time winner of the Heisman Trophy (1974-75).

Florence Griffith Joyner, 1959-98, sprinter; won 3 gold medals at 1988 Olympics; world and Olympic record for 100m.

Lefty Grove, 1900-75, pitcher; won 300 AL games.

Vladimir Guerrero, b 1975, (Dom. Rep.) right fielder; 2004 AL MVP award.

Janet Guthrie, b 1938, 1st woman driver in Indy 500 (1977).

Tony Gwynn, 1960-2014, 8-time NL batting champ (1984, '87-'89, '94-'97); 3,141 career hits.

Walter Hagen, 1892-1969, golfer; 5 PGA, 4 British Open titles.

Mika Hakkinen, b 1968, (Fin.) Formula One racing driver; Formula One champion, 1998-99.

George Halas, 1895-1983, founder/player/coach of Chicago Bears; won 6 NFL championships as coach.

Roy Halladay, 1977-2017, pitcher; Cy Young, 2003, '10; pitched perfect game, 2010.

Dorothy Hamill, b 1956, figure skater; Olympic gold medalist, 1976.

Scott Hamilton, b 1958, U.S. and world figure skating champion, 1981-84; Olympic gold medalist, 1984.

Mia Hamm, b 1972, soccer player; led U.S. teams to World Cup victories (1991, '99) and Olympic gold (1996, 2004).

James Harden, b 1989, shooting guard for Houston Rockets; NBA MVP, 2018.

Franco Harris, b 1950, running back; 4 Super Bowls with Steelers (1975-76, '79-'80); 1,000+ yds in a season 8 times.

Marvin Harrison, b 1972, Indianapolis Colts wide receiver; NFL record for single-season receptions (143), 2002.

Bill Hartack, 1932-2007, jockey; rode 5 Kentucky Derby winners.

Dominik Hasek, b 1965, (Czech.) NHL goaltender; won Vezina Trophy, 1994-95, '97-'99, 2001; NHL MVP, 1997-98.

John Havlicek, b 1940, Boston Celtics forward; scored 26,395 career pts.

Elvin Hayes, b 1945, 12-time NBA All-Star; scored 27,313 career pts.

Eric Heiden, b 1958, speed skater; won 5 Olympic golds, 1980.

Rickey Henderson, b 1958, outfielder; 1990 AL MVP; record 130 stolen bases, 1982; all-time leader in steals, runs.

Sonja Henie, 1912-69, (Nor.) world champion figure skater, 1927-36; Olympic gold medalist, 1928, '32, '36.

Martina Hingis, b 1980, (Switz.) won Austral. and U.S. Opens, Wimbledon; youngest number-one player (16 yrs., 6 mos.), 1997.

Ben Hogan, 1912-97, golfer; won 4 U.S. Open titles, 2 PGA Championships, 2 Masters.

Larry Holmes, b 1949, World Heavyweight Champion, 1978-85.

Santonio Holmes, b 1984, wide receiver; Super Bowl MVP, 2009.

Evander Holyfield, b 1962, 4-time heavyweight champion.

Rogers Hornsby, 1896-1963, NL 2nd baseman; batted record .424, 1924; twice won triple crown.

Paul Hornung, b 1935, Green Bay Packers running back, placekicker; scored record 176 pts., 1960.

Gordie Howe, 1928-2016, (Can.) hockey forward; NHL MVP 6 times; scored 801 goals in 26 NHL seasons.

Carl Hubbell, 1903-88, NY Giants pitcher; 20-game winner 5 consecutive seasons, 1933-37.

Bobby Hull, b 1939, (Can.) NHL all-star 10 times; MVP, 1965-66.

Brett Hull, b 1964, (Can.) St. Louis Blues forward; led NHL in goals, 1990-92; MVP, 1991.

Catfish Hunter, 1946-99, pitched perfect game, 1968; 20-game winner 5 times.

Don Hutson, 1913-97, Packers receiver; caught 99 TD passes; 2-time NFL MVP.

Juli Inkster, b 1960, Hall of Fame golfer; won 7 career major titles.

Bo Jackson, b 1962, NFL running back (1987-90) and MLB outfielder (1986-91, '93-'94); 1985 Heisman Trophy winner.

Phil Jackson, b 1945, won 11 NBA titles as coach of Bulls and Lakers; 1970, '73 title as player with NY Knicks.

Reggie Jackson, b 1946, slugger; led AL in home runs 4 times; MVP, 1973; hit 5 World Series home runs, 1977.

"Shoeless" Joe Jackson, 1889-1951, outfielder; 3rd highest career batting average (.356); one of the "Black Sox" banned for allegedly throwing 1919 World Series.

Jaromír Jágr, b 1972, (Czech.) hockey player; NHL MVP, 1999; Art Ross Trophy (leading scorer), 1995, 1998-2001.

LeBron James, b 1984, NBA forward; Olympic gold medalist (2008, '12); NBA MVP, 2009, '10, '12, '13.

Ron Jaworski, b 1951, NFL quarterback (1974-89), analyst.

Sally Jenkins, b 1960, sports journalist and writer for Washington Post.

Caitlyn (fmr. Bruce) Jenner, b 1949, Olympic decathlon gold medalist, 1976; came out as transgender woman, 2015.

Lynn Jennings, b 1960, runner; 3-time World, 9-time U.S. cross country champ; bronze (10,000m), 1992 Olympics.

Derek Jeter, b 1974, shortstop; led NY Yankees to 5 World Series titles; World Series MVP, 2000.

Earvin "Magic" Johnson, b 1959, NBA MVP, 1987, '89, '90; playoff MVP, 1980, '82, '87.

Jack Johnson, 1878-1946, heavyweight champion, 1908-15.

Jimmie Johnson, b 1975, 7-time NASCAR Sprint Cup Series champ.

Michael Johnson, b 1967, sprinter; 4-time Olympic gold medalist (1992,

'96, 2000); longtime world and Olympic record-holder.

Randy Johnson, b 1963, MLB pitcher with 4,875 strikeouts (2nd all-time), perfect game, 2004; 5-time Cy Young winner.

Walter Johnson, 1887-1946, Washington Senators pitcher; won 417 games; record 110 shutouts.

Bobby Jones, 1902-71, won golf's Grand Slam, 1930; U.S. amateur champ 5 times, U.S. Open champ 4 times.

Cobi Jones, b 1970, soccer player; most U.S. national team appearances with 164.

David "Deacon" Jones, 1938-2013, 5-time All-Pro with L.A. Rams (1965-69); "sack" specialist credited with inventing the term.

Marion Jones, b 1975, multi-event Olympic medalist; stripped of medals in 2007 after admitting use of PEDs.

Roy Jones Jr., b 1969, light heavyweight champ, 1999-2004.

Michael Jordan, b 1963, guard; leading NBA scorer, 1987-93, '96-'98; MVP, 1988, '91-'92, '96, '98; playoff MVP, 1991-93, '96-'98; ESPN Athlete of the Century.

Jackie Joyner-Kersee, b 1962, Olympic gold medalist in heptathlon (1988, '92), long jump (1988).

Dorothy Kamenshek, 1925-2010, led Rockford (IL) Peaches to 4 All-American Girls Baseball League titles in the 1940s.

Mary Keitany, b 1982, (Ken.) distance runner; 3-time NYC marathon winner.

Clayton Kershaw, b 1988, pitcher; NL Cy Young winner (2011, '13, '14).

Harmon Killebrew, 1936-2011, Minnesota Twins slugger; led AL in home runs 6 times; 573 career home runs.

Jean Claude Killy, b 1943, (Fr.) skier; 3 Olympic golds, 1968.

Kim Yu-na, b 1990, (S. Kor.) figure skater; Olympic medal winner (gold, 2010; silver, 2014); world champion, 2009, '13.

Ralph Kiner, 1922-2014, Pittsburgh Pirates slugger; led NL in home runs 7 consecutive years, 1946-52.

Billie Jean King, b 1943, U.S. singles champ 4 times; Wimbledon champ 6 times; beat Bobby Riggs, 1973.

Peter King, b 1957, sportswriter.

Bob Knight, b 1940, NCAA basketball coach; led Indiana to men's title in 1976, '81, '87.

Brooks Koepka, b 1990, golfer; won U.S. Open, 2017-18.

Olga Korbut, b 1955, (Belarus) gymnast; 4 Olympic gold medals, 1972, '76.

Sandy Koufax, b 1935, 3-time Cy Young winner; lowest ERA in NL, 1962-66; pitched 4 no-hitters, 1 perfect game.

Jack Kramer, 1921-2009, world's number one tennis player, 1946-53; first at Wimbledon to compete in shorts.

Ingrid Kristiansen, b 1956, (Nor.) only runner to have held simultaneous world records in 5,000m, 10,000m, and marathon.

Julie Krone, b 1963, winningest female jockey; first woman to ride a winner in a Triple Crown race (Belmont, 1993).

Mike Krzyzewski, b 1947, basketball coach; 5 NCAA championships with Duke; led 3 Olympic gold medal teams (2008, '12, '16).

Petra Kvitová, b 1990, (Czech.) tennis player; won Wimbledon, 2011, '14.

Michelle Kwan, b 1980, figure skater; 9 U.S., 5 World titles; silver medalist at 1998 Olympics, bronze in 2002.

Guy Lafleur, b 1951, (Can.) 3-time NHL scoring leader; 1977-78 MVP.

Alexi Lalas, b 1970, soccer player; first modern-era American to play in Italian League Serie A.

Kenesaw Mountain Landis, 1866-1944, 1st commissioner of baseball (1920-44); banned the 8 "Black Sox" involved in fixing 1919 World Series.

Tom Landry, 1924-2000, Dallas Cowboys head coach, 1960-88; won 2 Super Bowls (1972, '78); 3rd in career wins (270).

Dick "Night Train" Lane, 1928-2002, Hall of Fame defensive back; intercepted an NFL season record 14 passes (1952).

Don Larsen, b 1929, as NY Yankee, pitched only World Series perfect game, Oct. 8, 1956—2-0 win over Brooklyn.

Rod Laver, b 1938, (Austral.) tennis player; 11-time Grand Slam singles champ.

Katie Ledecky, b 1997, swimmer; Olympic medalist, incl. 5 gold (2012, '16).

Mario Lemieux, b 1965, (Can.) 6-time NHL leading scorer; MVP, 1988, '93, '96; playoff MVP, 1991-92.

Greg Lemond, b 1961, cyclist; 3-time Tour de France winner (1986, '89-'90); first American to win the event.

Ivan Lendl, b 1960, (Czech.) 8 Grand Slam tennis titles, including U.S. Open, 1985-87.

Sugar Ray Leonard, b 1956, boxer; held titles in 5 different weight classes.

Lisa Leslie, b 1972, L.A. Sparks center; 3-time WNBA MVP (2001, '04, '06).

Carl Lewis, b 1961, track-and-field star; won 9 Olympic gold medals in sprinting and long jump.

Lennox Lewis, b 1965, (Br.) heavyweight champ, 1994, 1997-2004; Olympic gold medalist, 1988.

Ray Lewis, b 1975, linebacker for the Baltimore Ravens; Super Bowl MVP, 2001.

Li Na, b 1982, (China) tennis player; won French Open, 2011, Austral. Open 2014.

Tim Lincecum, b 1984, pitcher; NL Cy Young winner, 2008-09.

Tara Lipinski, b 1982, youngest figure skater to win in U.S., world championships, 1997, and Winter Olympic gold, 1998.

Carli Lloyd, b 1982, soccer midfielder; Olympic gold medalist (2008, '12); World Cup champion (2015).

Ryan Lochte, b 1984, swimmer; 12-time Olympic medalist, incl. 6 gold (2004, '08, '12, '16).

Vince Lombardi, 1913-70, Green Bay Packers coach; led team to 5 NFL championships, 2 Super Bowl victories.

Nancy Lopez, b 1957, Hall of Fame golfer; 4-time LPGA Player of the Year, 3-time winner of the LPGA Championship.

Greg Louganis, b 1960, won Olympic gold medals in both springboard and platform diving, 1984, '88.

Joe Louis, 1914-81, heavyweight champion, 1937-49.

Sid Luckman, 1916-98, Chicago Bears quarterback; led team to 4 NFL championships; MVP, 1943.

Evan Lysacek, b 1985, figure skater; world champion, 2009; Olympic gold winner, 2010.

Connie Mack, 1862-1956, Philadelphia Athletics manager, 1901-50; won 9 pennants, 5 championships.

John Madden, b 1936, won Super Bowl as coach of Oakland Raiders (1977); former NFL TV analyst.

Greg Maddux, b 1966, Hall of Fame pitcher; won 4 Cy Young awards, 1992-95; 355 career wins.

Karl Malone, b 1963, Utah Jazz, L.A. Lakers forward; MVP, 1997, '99; 14-time All-Star; 36,928 career pts. (2nd all-time).

Moses Malone, 1955-2015, NBA center; MVP, 1979, '82, '83.

Eli Manning, b 1981, NY Giants quarterback; Super Bowl MVP, 2008, '12.

Peyton Manning, b 1976, quarterback; most NFL MVP awards, 2003-04, '08-'09, '13; Super Bowl MVP, 2007; single-season passing yards record (5,477), 2013.

Mickey Mantle, 1931-95, NY Yankees outfielder; triple crown, 1956; 18 World Series home runs; MVP 3 times.

Diego Maradona, b 1960, (Arg.) soccer player; led Argentina to World Cup, 1986.

Pete Maravich, 1947-88, guard; scored NCAA record 44.2 ppg during collegiate career; led NBA in scoring, 1977.

Rocky Marciano, 1923-69, heavyweight champion, 1952-56; retired undefeated.

Dan Marino, b 1961, Miami quarterback; NFL record single-season yards passing (5,084), 1984.

Roger Maris, 1934-85, NY Yankees outfielder; hit AL record 61 home runs, 1961, record held 37 years; MVP, 1960-61.

Marta (Marta Vieira da Silva), b 1986, (Braz.) soccer forward; FIFA World Player of the Year, 2006-10.

Curtis Martin, b 1973, Jets running back; 5-time Pro-Bowler; 4th in all-time rushing yards with 14,101.

Eddie Mathews, 1931-2001, Milwaukee-Atlanta Braves 3rd baseman; hit 512 career home runs.

Christy Mathewson, 1880-1925, pitcher; won 373 games.

Bob Mathias, 1930-2006, decathlon gold, 1948, '52 Olympics.

Misty May-Treanor, b 1977, beach volleyball player; 3-time Olympic gold medalist with Kerri Walsh Jennings (2004, '08, '12).

Willie Mays, b 1931, NY-S.F. Giants center fielder; hit 660 home runs, led NL 4 times; had 3,283 hits; twice MVP.

Willie McCovey, b 1938, S.F. Giants slugger; hit 521 home runs; led NL 3 times; MVP, 1969.

John McEnroe, b 1959, U.S. Open tennis champ (1979-81, '84); Wimbledon champ (1981, '83-'84).

John McGraw, 1873-1934, NY Giants manager; led team to 10 pennants, 3 championships.

Conor McGregor, b 1988, (Ire.) mixed martial artist.

Mark McGwire, b 1963, hit then-record 70 home runs in 1998; 583 career home runs; admitted PED use, 2010.

Rory McIlroy, b 1989, (N. Ire.) golfer; won U.S. Open, 2011; won PGA Championship, 2012, '14; British Open, 2014.

Tamara McKinney, b 1962, 1st U.S. skier to win overall Alpine World Cup championship (1983).

Andrea Mead Lawrence, 1932-2009, skier; first woman to win 2 gold medals in alpine skiing at one Olympics (1952).

Lionel Messi, b 1987, (Arg.) forward for FC Barcelona; FIFA World Player of the Year, 2009-10.

Mark Messier, b 1961, (Can.) center; NHL MVP, 1990, '92; Conn Smythe Trophy, 1984.

Debbie Meyer, b 1952, 1st swimmer to win 3 individual Olympic golds (1968).

Al Michaels, b 1944, *NBC Sunday Night Football* announcer.

Phil Mickelson, b 1970, golfer; 5 career major titles.

George Mikan, 1924-2005, Minn. Lakers center; considered the best basketball player of first half of 20th cent.

Stan Mikita, 1940-2018, (Czech.) Chicago Blackhawks center; led NHL in scoring 4 times; MVP twice.

Billy Mills, b 1938, runner; upset winner of the 1964 Olympic 10,000m; only American man ever to win the event.

Joe Montana, b 1956, S.F. 49ers quarterback; Super Bowl MVP, 1982, '85, '90.

Archie Moore, 1913-98, light-heavyweight champ, 1952-62.

Howie Morenz, 1902-37, (Can.) Montréal Canadiens forward; considered best hockey player of first half of 20th cent.

Edwin Moses, b 1955, undefeated in 122 consecutive 400m hurdles races, 1977-87; Olympic gold medalist, 1976, '84.

Shirley Muldowney, b 1940, 1st woman to race Natl. Hot Rod Assn. Top Fuel dragsters; 3-time NHRA points champ.

Andy Murray, b 1987, (Br.) tennis player; 3-time Grand Slam singles champion; Olympic gold medal in men's singles (2012, '16).

Eddie Murray, b 1956, 3rd player with both 3,000+ hits and 500+ home runs.

Stan Musial, 1920-2013, St. Louis Cardinals star; won 7 NL batting titles; MVP 3 times.

Rafael Nadal, b 1986, (Sp.) tennis player; 17-time Grand Slam singles champion; Olympic gold medal in men's singles (2008).

Bronko Nagurski, 1908-90, (Can.) Chicago Bears fullback and tackle; gained more than 4,000 yds rushing.

Joe Namath, b 1943, Jets quarterback; 1969 Super Bowl MVP.

Rosie Napravnik, b 1988, jockey.

Steve Nash, b 1974, (Can.) Phoenix Suns point guard; NBA MVP, 2005, '06.

Martina Navratilova, b 1956, (Czech.) tennis player; won 18 Grand Slam singles titles.

Byron Nelson, 1912-2006, won 11 consecutive golf tournaments in 1945; twice Masters and PGA titlist.

Ernie Nevers, 1903-76, Stanford football star; selected as best college fullback to play between 1919 and 1969.

Paula Newby-Fraser, b 1962, ([now] Zimbabwe) 8-time Ironman Triathlon world champ.

John Newcombe, b 1944, (Austral.) tennis player; 7 Grand Slam singles and 17 Grand Slam men's doubles titles.

Neymar (Neymar da Silva Santos Júnior), b 1992, (Braz.) soccer forward; led Brazil to Olympic gold, 2016.

Jack Nicklaus, b 1940, PGA Player of the Year, 1967, '72; leading money winner 8 times; won 18 majors (6 Masters).

Chuck Noll, 1932-2014, Pittsburgh Steelers coach; won 4 Super Bowls.

Dirk Nowitzki, b 1978, (Ger.) NBA forward; led Mavericks to NBA title, 2011; NBA MVP, 2007.

Paavo Nurmi, 1897-1973, (Fin.) distance runner; won 9 Olympic gold medals, 1920, '24, '28.

Lorena Ochoa, b 1981, (Mex.) LPGA Player of the Year, 2006-09, money leader 2006-08.

Al Oerter, 1936-2007, discus thrower; won gold medal at 4 consecutive Olympics, 1956, '60, '64, '68.

Apolo Ohno, b 1982, short-track speed skater; most decorated U.S. Winter Olympic athlete with 2 gold, 2 silver, 4 bronze (2002, '06, '10).

Hakeem Olajuwon, b 1963, (Nigeria) Houston center; NBA MVP, 1994, playoff MVP, 1994-95; career blocked shots leader (3,830).

Barney Oldfield, 1878-1946, pioneer auto racer; was first to drive a car 60 mph, 1903.

Shaquille O'Neal, b 1972, center; led L.A. Lakers to NBA titles, 2000-02, and Miami Heat to NBA title, 2006; Finals MVP 2000-02; NBA MVP 2000.

Bobby Orr, b 1948, (Can.) Boston Bruins defenseman; 8-time Norris Trophy winner; led NHL in scoring twice, assists 5 times.

Mel Ott, 1909-58, NY Giants right fielder; hit 511 home runs; led NL 6 times.

Alexander Ovechkin, b 1985, (Russ.) hockey player; NHL MVP, 2008, '09, '13.

Jesse Owens, 1913-80, track-and-field athlete; won 4 1936 Olympic golds.

Terrell Owens, b 1973, wide receiver.

Satchel Paige, 1906-82, pitcher; starred in Negro Leagues, 1924-48; entered major leagues at age 42.

Arnold Palmer, 1929-2016, golf's first $1 mil winner; won 4 Masters, 2 British Opens.

Jim Palmer, b 1945, Baltimore Orioles pitcher; won Cy Young award 3 times; 20-game winner 8 times.

Inbee Park, b 1988, (S. Kor.) golfer; 2nd woman ever to win first 3 majors of season (2013).

Candace Parker, b 1986, L.A. Sparks forward; WNBA MVP (2008, '13); Olympic gold medalist (2008, '12).

Joe Paterno, 1926-2012, Penn St. football coach; national title-winner, 1982, '86; most wins in NCAA Div. I coaching history (409); legacy complicated by child sex abuse scandal at Penn St.

Danica Patrick, b 1982, race car driver; 1st woman to lead Indy 500 and to win NASCAR Sprint Cup series pole.

Floyd Patterson, 1935-2006, 2-time heavyweight champion; first to ever regain the title after losing it.

Walter Payton, 1954-99, Chicago Bears running back; 2nd most rushing yards in NFL history; top NFC rusher, 1976-80.

Pelé (Edson Arantes do Nascimento), b 1940, (Braz.) soccer player; led Brazil to 3 World Cups (1958, '62, '70); scored 1,281 goals.

Bob Pettit, b 1932, first NBA player to score 20,000 pts.; twice NBA scoring leader.

Richard Petty, b 1937, NASCAR national champ 7 times; 7-time Daytona 500 winner.

Michael Phelps, b 1985, Olympic swimmer; record-holder, most Olympic medals (28) and gold medals (23) won by a single athlete.

Oscar Pistorius, b 1986, (S. Afr.) sprinter; 1st double-leg amputee to compete in Olympics, 2012; convicted (2015) of murder in girlfriend's death.

Jacques Plante, 1929-86, (Can.) NHL goaltender; 7 Vezina trophies; first goalie to wear mask in a game.

Gary Player, b 1935, (S. Afr.) golfer; won 3 Masters, 3 British Opens, 2 PGA Championships, and U.S. Open.

Mike Powell, b 1963, track-and-field athlete; holds world record for long jump (29 ft 4.5 in.)

Steve Prefontaine, 1951-75, runner; 1st to win 4 NCAA titles in same event (5,000m, 1970-73).

Kirby Puckett, 1960-2006, Minnesota Twins center fielder (1984-95); led team to World Series titles in 1987, '91.

Albert Pujols, b 1980, MLB slugger; NL MVP, 2005, '08-'09.

Paula Radcliffe, b 1973, British runner; set marathon world record of 2:15:25 in London, 2003.

Manny Ramirez, b 1972, (Dom. Rep.) outfielder; 2004 World Series MVP; suspended for violating MLB performance-enhancing drug policy, 2009, '11.

Willis Reed, b 1942, NY Knicks center; MVP, 1970; playoff MVP, 1970, '73.

Mary Lou Retton, b 1968, gymnast; won all-around gold medal at 1984 Olympics; also won 2 silvers, 2 bronzes.

Jerry Rice, b 1962, receiver; 1989 Super Bowl MVP; NFL record for career touchdowns (208), receptions (1,549).

Maurice Richard, 1921-2000, (Can.) Montréal Canadiens forward; scored 544 regular season goals, 82 playoff goals.

Branch Rickey, 1881-1965, MLB exec. helped break baseball's color barrier, 1947; initiated farm system, 1919.

Cal Ripken Jr., b 1960, Baltimore shortstop; AL MVP, 1983, '91; most consecutive games played (2,632).

Mariano Rivera, b 1969, (Pan.) relief pitcher; helped NY Yankees to 5 World Series titles; World Series MVP, 1999; all-time MLB leader in regular season and postseason saves.

Oscar Robertson, b 1938, NBA guard; averaged career 25.7 pts. per game; MVP, 1964.

Brooks Robinson, b 1937, Baltimore Orioles 3rd baseman; played in 4 World Series; MVP, 1964; 16 gold gloves.

Frank Robinson, b 1935, MVP in both NL and AL; triple crown, 1966; 586 career home runs; first black manager in majors.

Jackie Robinson, 1919-72, broke baseball's color barrier with Brooklyn Dodgers, 1947; NL MVP, 1949.

Sugar Ray Robinson, 1921-89, boxer; middleweight champion 5 times; welterweight champion, 1946-51.

Knute Rockne, 1888-1931, Notre Dame football coach, 1918-31; revolutionized game by stressing forward pass.

Aaron Rodgers, b 1983, Green Bay quarterback; led Packers to victory in Super Bowl XLV; Super Bowl MVP, 2011; NFL MVP, 2011, '14.

Bill Rodgers, b 1947, runner; won Boston and New York City marathons 4 times each between 1975 and 1980.

Alex Rodriguez, b 1975, MLB infielder; AL MVP in 2003, '05, '07; 14-time All Star; admitted steroid use 2001-03;

suspended 162 games for PED use, 2013-14.

Juan "Chi Chi" Rodriguez, b 1935, champion golfer; 8 PGA tour wins, 22 Champions tour wins.

Ben Roethlisberger, b 1982, Pittsburgh Steelers quarterback; youngest QB to win Super Bowl, 2005.

Ronaldinho (Ronaldo de Assis Moreira), b 1980, (Braz.) soccer midfielder; FIFA World Player of the Year, 2004, '05.

Ronaldo (Ronaldo Luiz Nazario de Lima), b 1976, (Braz.) soccer forward; led Brazil to 2002 World Cup title; 3-time FIFA world player of the year, 1996-97.

Cristiano Ronaldo, b 1985, (Port.) soccer forward; FIFA player of the year, 2008; UEFA career scoring leader (120).

Art Rooney, 1901-88, NFL owner; bought Pittsburgh Pirates in 1933, renamed Steelers, 1940.

Pete Rose, b 1941, won 3 NL batting titles; hit in 44 consecutive games, 1978; most career hits, 4,256; banned for gambling, 1989; admitted betting on his team, 2004.

Ken Rosewall, b 1934, (Austral.) tennis player; 8 Grand Slam singles titles.

Ronda Rousey, b 1987, judoka and mixed martial arts fighter.

Patrick Roy, b 1965, (Can.) Montréal-Colorado goalie; only 3-time NHL playoffs MVP, 1986, '93, 2001.

Wilma Rudolph, 1940-94, sprinter; won 3 1960 Olympic golds.

Adolph Rupp, 1901-77, NCAA basketball coach; led Kentucky to 4 national titles, 1948-49, '51, '58.

Bill Russell, b 1934, Boston Celtics center; led team to 11 NBA titles; MVP 5 times; first black coach of major pro sports team.

Babe Ruth, 1895-1948, NY Yankees outfielder; hit 60 home runs, 1927, 714 lifetime (3rd all-time); led AL 12 times.

Johnny Rutherford, b 1938, auto racer; won 3 Indy 500s.

Nolan Ryan, b 1947, pitcher; holds season (383), career (5,714) strikeout records; won 324 games (7 no-hitters).

Pete Sampras, b 1971, tennis player; 14 Grand Slam singles wins.

Joan Benoit Samuelson, b 1957, won 1st Olympic women's marathon (1984), Boston Marathon (1979, '83).

Barry Sanders, b 1968, running back; won Heisman Trophy, 1988; NFL MVP, 1997.

Deion Sanders, b 1967, NFL cornerback (1989-2000, '04-'05) and MLB outfielder (1989-95, '97, 2005).

Gale Sayers, b 1943, Chicago running back; twice led NFL in rushing.

Mike Schmidt, b 1949, Phillies 3rd baseman; led NL in home runs 8 times; 548 lifetime; NL MVP, 1980-81, '86.

Michael Schumacher, b 1969, (Ger.) race-car driver; 7-time Formula 1 world champ (1994-95, 2000-04).

Tom Seaver, b 1944, pitcher; won NL Cy Young award 3 times; won 311 major league games.

Monica Seles, b 1973, (Yugo.) tennis player; won 9 Grand Slam singles titles; stabbed on court by spectator, 1993.

Maria Sharapova, b 1987, (Russ.) tennis player; won Wimbledon (2004), U.S. Open (2006), Austral. Open (2008), French Open (2012, '14); Olympic silver, 2012.

Patty Sheehan, b 1956, Hall of Fame golfer; 3 LPGA Championships (1983-84, '93).

Willie Shoemaker, 1931-2003, jockey; rode 4 Kentucky Derby, 5 Belmont Stakes winners.

Frank Shorter, b 1947, runner; only American to win men's Olympic marathon (1972) since 1908; silver medalist (1976).

Don Shula, b 1930, all-time winningest NFL coach (347 games).

Bill Simmons, b 1969, columnist; podcast, TV host; Grantland and theringer.com founder.

O. J. Simpson, b 1947, running back; rushed for 2,003 yds, 1973; AFC leading rusher 4 times; acquitted of murder, 1995; found guilty of robbery and kidnapping, imprisoned 2008-17.

Dean Smith, 1931-2015, retired basketball coach; 879 Division I wins; led North Carolina to 2 NCAA titles (1982, '93).

Emmitt Smith, b 1969, running back; NFL and Super Bowl MVP, 1993; rushed for career record 18,355 yds.

Conn Smythe, 1895-1980, (Can.) won 7 Stanley Cups as Toronto GM (1929-61); playoff MVP award named in his honor.

Sam Snead, 1912-2002, PGA and Masters champ 3 times each; record 82 PGA tournament victories.

Annika Sorenstam, b 1970, (Swed.) golfer; set LPGA 18-hole record of 59 (−13), 72-hole record of 27-under-par, 2001; won 10 LPGA majors, including career Grand Slam.

Sammy Sosa, b 1968, (Dom. Rep.) MLB slugger; NL MVP, 1998; 1st to hit 60+ HR 3 times (1998-99, 2001).

Warren Spahn, 1921-2003, pitcher; won 363 NL games; 20-game winner 13 times; Cy Young winner, 1957.

Tris Speaker, 1888-1958, AL outfielder; batted .345 over 22 seasons; hit record 792 career doubles.

Jordan Spieth, b 1993, golfer; won Masters, 2015; U.S. Open, 2015.

Mark Spitz, b 1950, swimmer; won 7 golds at 1972 Olympics.

Amos Alonzo Stagg, 1862-1965, football innovator; Univ. of Chicago football coach for 41 years, 5 undefeated seasons.

Bart Starr, b 1934, Green Bay Packers quarterback; led team to 5 NFL titles, 2 Super Bowl victories.

Roger Staubach, b 1942, Dallas Cowboys quarterback; leading NFC passer 5 times.

George Steinbrenner, 1930-2010, NY Yankees owner.

Casey Stengel, 1890-1975, managed Yankees to 10 pennants, 7 World Series wins between 1949 and 1960.

Jackie Stewart, b 1939, (Scot.) auto racer; 27 Grand Prix wins.

John Stockton, b 1962, Utah Jazz guard; NBA career leader in assists, steals; NBA assists leader, 1988-96.

Picabo Street, b 1971, skier; 2-time World Cup downhill champion (1995-96); Olympic super G gold medalist, 1998.

Louise Suggs, 1923-2015, golfer; U.S. Women's Open champ, 1949, '52; 11 major victories.

John L. Sullivan, 1858-1918, last bareknuckle heavyweight champion, 1882-92.

Pat Summerall, 1930-2013, NFL kicker, radio and TV sportscaster who announced 26 Super Bowls.

Pat Summitt, 1952-2016, women's basketball coach; led Tennessee to 8 NCAA titles; NCAA-record 1,098 career wins.

Ichiro Suzuki, b 1973, (Jpn.) outfielder; AL MVP, 2001; single-season hits record (262), 2004; career (Japan-U.S.) hits leader since 2013; 3,000th U.S. hit, 2016.

Sheryl Swoopes, b 1971, guard/forward; 1st 3-time WNBA MVP (2000, '02, '05); Olympic gold medalist (1996, 2000, '04).

Fran Tarkenton, b 1940, Minnesota, NY Giants quarterback; 342 career TD passes; 1975 Player of the Year.

Diana Taurasi, b 1982, WNBA guard; 4-time Olympic gold medalist; WNBA MVP, 2009.

Lawrence Taylor, b 1959, linebacker; led NY Giants to 2 Super Bowl titles; played in 10 Pro Bowls.

Daley Thompson, b 1958, (Br.) decathlete; Olympic gold medalist in 1980, '84.

Jenny Thompson, b 1973, swimmer; 12 Olympic medals (8 gold) in 1992, '96, 2000, '04.

Bobby Thomson, 1923-2010, MLB utility player known for pennant-clinching "Shot

Heard 'Round the World" for the NY Giants, 1951.

Jim Thorpe, 1888-1953, football All-American, 1911-12; won pentathlon and decathlon, 1912 Olympics.

Bill Tilden, 1893-1953, won 7 U.S. tennis titles, 3 Wimbledon.

Y. A. Tittle, 1926-2017, NY Giants quarterback; MVP, 1961, '63.

Alberto Tomba, b 1966, (It.) skier; 5 Olympic alpine medals (3 golds, 2 silver) in 1988, '92, '94.

LaDainian "L.T." Tomlinson, b 1979, running back; NFL single-season record for rushing touchdowns (28).

Joe Torre, b 1940, MLB player, manager; NL MVP, 1971; won 4 World Series in 5 years as NY Yankees manager.

Lee Trevino, b 1939, golfer; won U.S., British Open twice.

Bryan Trottier, b 1956, (Can.) Islanders, Penguins center for 6 Stanley Cup champs.

Mike Trout, b 1991, MLB player; 2-time AL MVP, 2014, '16.

Gene Tunney, 1897-1978, heavyweight champion, 1926-28.

Mike Tyson, b 1966, undisputed heavyweight champ, 1987-90; at 20, youngest to win a heavyweight title (WBC, 1986).

Wyomia Tyus, b 1945, Olympic 100m gold medalist, 1964, '68.

Johnny Unitas, 1933-2002, Baltimore Colts quarterback; passed for more than 40,000 yds; MVP, 1957, '67.

Al Unser, b 1939, Indy 500 winner 4 times.

Bobby Unser, b 1934, Indy 500 winner 3 times.

Norm Van Brocklin, 1926-83, quarterback; passed for game record 554 yds, 1951; MVP, 1960.

Amy Van Dyken, b 1973, swimmer; first American woman to win 4 gold medals in one Olympics (1996).

Justin Verlander, b 1983, pitcher; won AL MVP and Cy Young, 2011.

Michael Vick, b 1980, quarterback; suspended and convicted (2007) of illegal dog fighting, gambling activities.

Lasse Viren, b 1949, (Fin.) runner; Olympic 5,000m and 10,000m gold medalist in 1972, '76.

Lindsey Vonn, b 1984; skier, Olympic gold, 2010; 4 World Cup titles 2008-10, '12.

Dwyane Wade, b 1982, guard; led Miami Heat to NBA title, 2006, '12-'13; finals MVP, 2006; NBA scoring title, 2009.

Honus Wagner, 1874-1955, Pittsburgh Pirates shortstop; 8 NL batting titles.

Grete Waitz, 1953-2011, (Nor.) distance runner; 9-time winner of the New York City Marathon (1978-80, '82-'86, '88).

"Jersey" Joe Walcott, 1914-94, boxer; became heavyweight champion at age 37, 1951-52.

Kerri Walsh Jennings, b 1978, beach volleyball player; 3-time Olympic gold medalist with Misty May-Treanor (2004, '08, '12).

Bill Walton, b 1952, center; led Portland Trail Blazers to 1977 NBA title; MVP, 1978; NBA TV commentator.

Abby Wambach, b 1980, soccer player; 2 gold medals in Olympics (2004, '12); all-time intl.-competition goal scorer.

Kurt Warner, b 1971, quarterback; NFL MVP, 1999, 2001; Super Bowl MVP, 2000.

Gerry "Bubba" Watson, b 1978, golfer; won Masters, 2012, '14.

Tom Watson, b 1949, golfer; 6-time PGA Player of the Year; won 5 British Opens, 2 Masters, U.S. Open.

Stan Wawrinka, b 1985, (Switz.) tennis player; won Austral. Open (2014), French Open (2015); U.S. Open (2016).

Karrie Webb, b 1974, (Austral.) golfer; youngest woman (26 yrs., 6 mos.) to win career Grand Slam, 1999-2001.

Johnny Weissmuller, 1903-84, swimmer; won 52 national

championships, 5 Olympic gold medals; set 67 world records.

Jerry West, b 1938, L.A. Lakers guard; had career average 27 pts. per game; first team all-star 10 times.

Dan Wheldon, 1978-2011, (Br.) race-car driver; 2-time Indy 500 winner (2005, '11).

Byron "Whizzer" White, 1917-2002, running back; led NCAA in scoring and rushing at Colorado, 1937; led NFL in rushing twice, 1938, '40; Supreme Court justice, 1962-93.

Shaun White, b 1986, snowboarder/skateboarder, Olympic gold medalist in halfpipe (2006, '10, '18).

Kathy Whitworth, b 1939, 7-time LPGA Player of the Year (1966-69, '71-'73); 88 tour wins, most on LPGA or PGA tour.

Michelle Wie, b 1989, golfer; in 2002 became youngest-ever qualifier for LPGA event; turned pro at age 15.

Bradley Wiggins, b 1980, (Br.) cyclist; Tour de France winner, 2012; 8 Olympic medals (5 gold) over 5 Games.

Michael Wilbon, b 1958, commentator/analyst for ESPN.

Lenny Wilkens, b 1937, 2nd winningest coach in NBA history; Hall of Fame player and coach.

Serena Williams, b 1981, tennis player; 23-time Grand Slam singles champion; Olympic gold medals in singles (2012) and doubles (2000, '08, '12) with sister Venus.

Ted Williams, 1918-2002, Boston Red Sox outfielder; won 6 batting titles, 2 triple crowns; hit .406 in 1941.

Venus Williams, b 1980, tennis player; 7-time Grand Slam singles champion; Olympic gold medals in singles (2000) and doubles with sister Serena (2000, '08, '12).

Helen Wills Moody, 1905-98, tennis star; won U.S. Open 7 times, Wimbledon 8 times.

Katarina Witt, b 1965, (Ger.) figure skater; won Olympic gold medal, 1984, '88; world champ, 1984-85, '87-'88.

John Wooden, 1910-2010, UCLA basketball coach; 10 NCAA titles.

Tiger Woods, b 1975, golfer; youngest to win career Grand Slam, at age 24 (1997-2000); 14 career major titles.

Mickey Wright, b 1935, golfer; won LPGA and U.S. Open championship 4 times; 82 career wins, including 13 majors.

Eric Wynalda, b 1969, soccer; scored 1st goal in major league soccer history (1996).

Kristi Yamaguchi, b 1971, figure skater; won national, world, Olympic titles, in 1992.

Yao Ming, b 1980, (China) center for Houston Rockets; 8-time NBA All-Star.

Carl Yastrzemski, b 1939, Boston Red Sox slugger; won 3 batting titles; triple crown, 1967.

Cy Young, 1867-1955, pitcher; won record 511 games.

Steve Young, b 1961, 49ers quarterback; led NFL in passing, 1991-94, '96-'97; NFL MVP, 1992, '94; Super Bowl MVP, 1995.

Babe Didrikson Zaharias, 1911-56, all-around athlete; 3 track-and-field medals (2 golds), 1932 Olympics; won 10 golf majors; also played baseball; 6-time AP Female Athlete of the Year.

Emil Zátopek, 1922-2000, (Czech.) runner; won 3 gold medals at 1952 Olympics (5,000m, 10,000m, marathon).

Zinedine Zidane, b 1972, (Fr.) soccer midfielder; led France to 1998 World Cup title; named top player in 2006; 3-time FIFA world player of the year (1998, 2000, '03).

Writers of the Present

Name	Birthplace	Birthdate
Chimamanda Ngozi Adichie	Enugu, Nigeria	9/15/1977
Mitch Albom	Passaic, NJ	5/23/1958
Elizabeth Alexander	New York, NY	5/30/1962
Sherman Alexie	Wellpinit, WA	10/7/1966
Isabel Allende	Lima, Peru	8/2/1942
Dorothy Allison	Greenville, SC	4/11/1949
Martin Amis	Oxford, England, UK	8/25/1949
Piers Anthony	Oxford, England, UK	8/6/1934
Jeffrey Archer	Somerset, England, UK	4/15/1940
Margaret Atwood	Ottawa, ON, Canada	11/18/1939
David Auburn	Chicago, IL	11/30/1969
Jean Auel	Chicago, IL	2/18/1936
Paul Auster	Newark, NJ	2/3/1947
Alan Ayckbourn	Hampstead, England, UK	4/12/1939
Fredrik Backman	Stockholm, Sweden	6/2/1981
Nicholson Baker	New York, NY	1/7/1957
David Baldacci	Richmond, VA	8/5/1960
Russell Banks	Newton, MA	3/28/1940
Sebastian Barry	Dublin, Ireland	7/5/1955
John Barth	Cambridge, MD	5/27/1930
Ann Beattie	Washington, DC	9/8/1947
Alan Bennett	Leeds, England, UK	5/9/1934
John Berendt	Syracuse, NY	12/5/1939
Elizabeth Berg	St. Paul, MN	12/2/1948
Judy Blume	Elizabeth, NJ	2/12/1938
T. Coraghessan Boyle	Peekskill, NY	12/2/1948
Barbara Taylor Bradford	Leeds, England, UK	5/10/1933
Christopher Bram	Buffalo, NY	2/22/1952
Geraldine Brooks	Sydney, NSW, Australia	9/14/1955
Dan Brown	Exeter, NH	6/22/1964
Rita Mae Brown	Hanover, PA	11/28/1944
Christopher Buckley	New York, NY	9/28/1952
James Lee Burke	Houston, TX	12/5/1936
Augusten Burroughs	Pittsburgh, PA	10/23/1965
Robert Olen Butler	Granite City, IL	1/20/1945
A. S. Byatt	Sheffield, England, UK	8/24/1936
Ethan Canin	Ann Arbor, MI	7/19/1960
Peter Carey	Bacchus-Marsh, Vic., Australia	5/7/1943
Robert A. Caro	New York, NY	10/30/1935
Caleb Carr	New York, NY	8/2/1955
Michael Chabon	Washington, DC	5/24/1963
Tracy Chevalier	Washington, DC	10/19/1962
Lee Child	Coventry, England, UK	10/29/1954
Sandra Cisneros	Chicago, IL	12/20/1954
Mary Higgins Clark	Bronx, NY	12/24/1927
Beverly Cleary	McMinnville, OR	4/12/1916
Ta-Nehisi Coates	Baltimore, MD	9/30/1975
Harlan Coben	Newark, NJ	1/4/1962
Paulo Coelho	Rio de Janeiro, Brazil	8/24/1947
J(ohn) M(axwell) Coetzee	Capetown, South Africa	2/9/1940
Billy Collins	New York, NY	3/22/1941
Suzanne Collins	Hartford, CT	8/10/1962
Robin Cook	New York, NY	5/4/1940
Patricia Cornwell	Miami, FL	6/9/1956
Michael Cunningham	Cincinnati, OH	11/6/1952
Clive Cussler	Aurora, IL	7/15/1931
Don DeLillo	Bronx, NY	11/20/1936
Nelson DeMille	Jamaica, Queens, NY	8/23/1943
Junot Díaz	Santo Domingo, Dominican Republic	12/31/1968
Joan Didion	Sacramento, CA	12/5/1934
Annie Dillard	Pittsburgh, PA	4/30/1945
Anthony Doerr	Cleveland, OH	10/27/1973
Emma Donoghue	Dublin, Ireland	10/24/1969
Rita Dove	Akron, OH	8/28/1952
Roddy Doyle	Dublin, Ireland	5/8/1958
Carol Ann Duffy	Glasgow, Scotland, UK	12/23/1955
Jennifer Egan	Chicago, IL	9/7/1962
Dave Eggers	Boston, MA	3/12/1970
Bret Easton Ellis	Los Angeles, CA	3/7/1964
James Ellroy	Los Angeles, CA	3/4/1948
Louise Erdrich	Little Falls, MN	6/7/1954
Laura Esquivel	Mexico City, Mexico	9/30/1950
Jeffrey Eugenides	Detroit, MI	3/8/1960
Janet Evanovich	South River, NJ	4/22/1943
Lawrence Ferlinghetti	Yonkers, NY	3/24/1919
Helen Fielding	Morley, Yorkshire, Eng., UK	2/19/1958
Fannie Flagg	Birmingham, AL	9/21/1944
Gillian Flynn	Kansas City, MO	2/24/1971
Jonathan Safran Foer	Washington, DC	2/21/1977
Ken Follett	Cardiff, Wales, UK	6/5/1949
Richard Ford	Jackson, MS	2/16/1944
Frederick Forsyth	Ashford, England, UK	8/25/1938
Jonathan Franzen	Western Springs, IL	8/17/1959
Michael Frayn	London, England, UK	9/8/1933
Charles Frazier	Asheville, NC	11/4/1950
Neil Gaiman	Portchester, England, UK	11/10/1960
Ernest J. Gaines	Oscar, LA	1/15/1933
Roxane Gay	Omaha, NE	10/15/1974
Malcolm Gladwell	Fareham, Hampshire, Eng., UK	9/3/1963
Robert Goddard	Fareham, Hampshire, Eng., UK	11/13/1954
Gail Godwin	Birmingham, AL	6/18/1937
William Goldman	Highland Park, IL	8/12/1931
Mary Gordon	Far Rockaway, NY	12/8/1949
Shirley Ann Grau	New Orleans, LA	7/8/1929
John Green	Indianapolis, IN	8/24/1977
John Grisham	Jonesboro, AR	2/8/1955
John Guare	New York, NY	2/5/1938
Pete Hamill	Brooklyn, NY	6/24/1935
David Handler	Los Angeles, CA	9/14/1952
Paul Harding	Wenham, MA	12/19/1967
David Hare	St. Leonards, Sussex, Eng., UK	6/5/1947
Robert Hass	San Francisco, CA	3/1/1941
Paula Hawkins	Harare, Zimbabwe	8/28/1972
Mark Helprin	New York, NY	6/28/1947
Carl Hiaasen	Plantation, FL	3/12/1953
Laura Hillenbrand	Fairfax, VA	5/15/1967
S. E. Hinton	Tulsa, OK	7/22/1948
Alice Hoffman	New York, NY	3/16/1952
Alan Hollinghurst	Stroud, Gloucestershire, England, UK	5/26/1954
Khaled Hosseini	Kabul, Afghanistan	3/4/1965
John Irving	Exeter, NH	3/2/1942
Walter Isaacson	New Orleans, LA	5/20/1952
Kazuo Ishiguro	Nagasaki, Japan	11/8/1954
John Jakes	Chicago, IL	3/31/1932
E. L. James	London, England, UK	7/3/1963
Elfriede Jelinek	Müzzuschlag, Austria	10/20/1946
Ha Jin	Liaoning, China	2/21/1956
Adam Johnson	South Dakota	7/12/1967
Edward P. Jones	Washington, DC	10/5/1950
Erica Jong	New York, NY	3/26/1942
Sebastian Junger	Boston, MA	1/17/1962
Jan Karon	Lenoir, NC	3/14/1937
Garrison Keillor	Anoka, MN	8/7/1942
Thomas Keneally	Sydney, NSW, Australia	10/7/1935
William Kennedy	Albany, NY	1/16/1928
Sue Monk Kidd	Sylvester, GA	8/12/1948
Jamaica Kincaid	St. John's, Antigua and Barbuda	5/25/1949
Stephen King	Portland, ME	9/21/1947
Barbara Kingsolver	Annapolis, MD	4/8/1955
Maxine Hong Kingston	Stockton, CA	10/27/1940
Dean Koontz	Everett, PA	7/9/1945
Ted Kooser	Ames, IA	4/25/1939
Jon Krakauer	Brookline, MA	4/12/1954
Larry Kramer	Bridgeport, CT	6/25/1935
Judith Krantz	New York, NY	1/9/1928
Milan Kundera	Brno, Czechoslovakia	4/1/1929
Tony Kushner	New York, NY	7/16/1956
Jhumpa Lahiri	London, England, UK	7/11/1967
Erik Larson	Brooklyn, NY	1/3/1954
John Le Carré	Poole, England, UK	10/19/1931
Jean Marie Gustave Le Clézio	Nice, France	4/13/1940
David Leavitt	Pittsburgh, PA	6/23/1961
Jonathan Lethem	Brooklyn, NY	2/19/1964
David Lodge	South London, England, UK	1/28/1935
Alison Lurie	Chicago, IL	9/3/1926
Gregory Maguire	Albany, NY	6/9/1954
David Malouf	Brisbane, Qld., Australia	3/20/1934
Thomas Mallon	Glen Cove, NY	11/2/1951
David Mamet	Chicago, IL	11/30/1947
Hilary Mantel	Derbyshire, England, UK	7/6/1952
Yann Martel	Salamanca, Spain	6/25/1963
George R. R. Martin	Bayonne, NJ	9/20/1948
Bobbie Ann Mason	nr. Mayfield, KY	5/1/1940
Armistead Maupin	Washington, DC	4/13/1944
Colum McCann	Dublin, Ireland	2/28/1965
Cormac McCarthy	Providence, RI	7/20/1933
David McCullough	Pittsburgh, PA	7/7/1933
Alice McDermott	Brooklyn, NY	6/27/1953
Ian McEwan	Aldershot, England, UK	6/21/1948
Thomas McGuane	Wyandotte, MI	12/11/1939
Jay McInerney	Hartford, CT	1/13/1955
Terry McMillan	Port Huron, MI	10/18/1951
Larry McMurtry	Wichita Falls, TX	6/3/1936
Terrence McNally	St. Petersburg, FL	11/3/1939
John McPhee	Princeton, NJ	3/8/1931
W(illiam) S(tanley) Merwin	New York, NY	9/30/1927
Stephenie Meyer	Hartford, CT	12/24/1973
Steven Millhauser	New York, NY	8/3/1943
Toni Morrison	Lorain, OH	2/18/1931

Name	Birthplace	Birthdate	Name	Birthplace	Birthdate
Walter Mosley	Los Angeles, CA	1/12/1952	Norman Rush	San Francisco, CA	10/24/1933
Andrew Motion	London, England, UK	10/26/1952	Salman Rushdie	Bombay, India	6/19/1947
Jojo Moyes	Maidstone, England, UK	8/4/1969	Richard Russo	Johnstown, NY	7/15/1949
Herta Müller	Nitzkydorf, Banat, Romania	8/17/1953	George Saunders	Amarillo, TX	12/2/1958
Alice Munro	Wingham, ON, Canada	7/10/1931	Alice Sebold	Madison, WI	9/6/1963
Haruki Murakami	Kyoto, Japan	1/12/1949	David Sedaris	Johnson City, NY	12/26/1956
Celeste Ng	Pittsburgh, PA	1980?	Vikram Seth	Calcutta, India	6/20/1952
Viet Thanh Nguyen	Buon Me Thuot, Vietnam	3/13/1971	John Patrick Shanley	Bronx, NY	10/13/1950
Lynn Nottage	Brooklyn, NY	11/2/1964	Lionel Shriver	Gastonia, NC	5/18/1957
Joyce Carol Oates	Lockport, NY	6/16/1938	Anne Rivers Siddons	Atlanta, GA	1/9/1936
Edna O'Brien	Tuamgraney, Ireland	12/15/1930	Jane Smiley	Los Angeles, CA	9/26/1949
Tim O'Brien	Austin, MN	10/1/1946	Zadie Smith	London, Eng., UK	10/25/1975
Kenzaburō Ōe	Uchiko, Japan	1/31/1935	Wole Soyinka	Abeokuta, Nigeria	7/13/1934
Michael Ondaatje	Colombo, Sri Lanka	9/12/1943	Nicholas Sparks	Omaha, NE	12/31/1965
Cynthia Ozick	New York, NY	4/17/1928	Danielle Steel	New York, NY	8/14/1947
Orhan Pamuk	Istanbul, Turkey	6/7/1952	R(obert) L(awrence)		
Suzan-Lori Parks	Fort Knox, KY	5/10/1963	Stine	Columbus, OH	10/8/1943
Ann Patchett	Los Angeles, CA	12/2/1963	Kathryn Stockett	Jackson, MS	1969
James Patterson	Newburgh, NY	3/22/1947	Tom Stoppard	Zlin, Czechoslovakia	7/3/1937
Jodi Picoult	New York, NY	5/19/1966	Elizabeth Strout	Portland, ME	1/6/1956
Marge Piercy	Detroit, MI	3/31/1936	Amy Tan	Oakland, CA	2/19/1952
Robert Pinsky	Long Branch, NJ	10/20/1940	Donna Tartt	Greenwood, MS	12/23/1963
Michael Pollan	New York, NY	2/6/1955	Paul Theroux	Medford, MA	4/10/1941
Richard Powers	Evanston, IL	6/18/1957	Calvin Trillin	Kansas City, MO	12/5/1935
Richard Price	Bronx, NY	10/12/1949	Scott F. Turow	Chicago, IL	4/12/1949
E. Annie Proulx	Norwich, CT	8/22/1935	Anne Tyler	Minneapolis, MN	10/25/1941
Philip Pullman	Norwich, England, UK	10/19/1946	Mario Vargas Llosa	Arequipa, Peru	3/28/1936
Thomas Pynchon	Glen Cove, NY	5/8/1937	Paula Vogel	Washington, DC	11/16/1951
David Rabe	Dubuque, IA	3/10/1940	Sarah Vowell	Muskogee, OK	12/27/1969
Ishmael Reed	Chattanooga, TN	2/22/1938	Alice Walker	Eatonton, GA	2/9/1944
Anne Rice	New Orleans, LA	10/4/1941	Joseph Wambaugh	East Pittsburgh, PA	1/22/1937
Mary Roach	Etna, NH	3/20/1959	Jesmyn Ward	DeLisle, MS	4/1/1977
Nora Roberts	Silver Spring, MD	10/10/1950	Edmund White	Cincinnati, OH	1/13/1940
Marilynne Robinson	Sandpoint, IL	11/26/1943	Colson Whitehead	New York, NY	11/6/1969
Veronica Roth	New York, NY	8/19/1988	Tobias Wolff	Birmingham, AL	6/19/1945
J. K. Rowling	Chipping Sodbury, Eng., UK	7/31/1965	Herman Wouk	New York, NY	5/27/1915

Writers of the Past

See also Journalists, and Greeks and Romans in Historical Figures chapter.

Chinua Achebe, 1930-2013, (Nigeria) novelist. *Things Fall Apart.*

Alice Adams, 1926-99, (U.S.) novelist, short-story writer. *Superior Woman.*

Richard Adams, 1920-2016, (Br.) novelist. *Watership Down.*

James Agee, 1909-55, (U.S.) novelist. *A Death in the Family.*

S(hmuel) Y(osef) Agnon, 1888-1970, (Isr.) Hebrew novelist. *Only Yesterday.*

Conrad Aiken, 1889-1973, (U.S.) poet, critic. *Ushant.*

Anna Akhmatova, 1889-1966, (Russ.) poet. *Requiem.*

Edward Albee, 1928-2016, (U.S.) playwright. *Who's Afraid of Virginia Woolf?*

Louisa May Alcott, 1832-88, (U.S.) novelist. *Little Women.*

Sholom Aleichem, 1859-1916, (Russ.) Yiddish writer. *Tevye's Daughters, The Old Country.*

Vicente Aleixandre, 1898-1984, (Sp.) poet. *La destrucción o el amor, Dialogo- los del conocimiento.*

Horatio Alger, 1832-99, (U.S.) "rags-to- riches" books.

Jorge Amado, 1912-2001, (Brazil) novelist. *Dona Flor and Her Two Husbands, The Violent Land.*

Eric Ambler, 1909-98, (Br.) suspense novelist. *A Coffin for Dimitrios.*

Kingsley Amis, 1922-95, (Br.) novelist, critic. *Lucky Jim.*

Hans Christian Andersen, 1805-75, (Den.) author of fairy tales. *The Ugly Duckling.*

Maxwell Anderson, 1888-1959, (U.S.) playwright. *What Price Glory?, High Tor, Winterset, Key Largo.*

Sherwood Anderson, 1876-1941, (U.S.) short-story writer. "Death in the Woods," *Winesburg, Ohio.*

Maya Angelou, 1928-2014, (U.S.) poet, memoirist. *I Know Why the Caged Bird Sings.*

Reinaldo Arenas, 1943-90, (Cuba) short- story writer, novelist. *Before Night Falls.*

Ludovico Ariosto, 1474-1533, (It.) poet. *Orlando Furioso.*

Matthew Arnold, 1822-88, (Br.) poet, critic. "Thrysis," "Dover Beach," "Culture and Anarchy."

John Ashbery, 1927-2007, (U.S.) poet. *Self-Portrait in a Convex Mirror.*

Isaac Asimov, 1920-92, (U.S.) versatile writer, espec. of science fiction. *I Robot.*

Miguel Angel Asturias, 1899-1974, (Guat.) novelist. *El Señor Presidente.*

Louis Auchincloss, 1917-2010, (U.S.) novelist, memoirist, short-story writer. *The Rector of Justin.*

W(ystan) H(ugh) Auden, 1907-73, (Br.) poet, playwright, literary critic. "The Age of Anxiety."

Jane Austen, 1775-1817, (Br.) novelist. *Pride and Prejudice, Sense and Sensi- bility, Emma, Mansfield Park.*

Ba Jin (Li Yaotang), 1904-2005, (China) novelist of pre-revolutionary China.

Isaac Babel, 1894-1941, (Russ.) short- story writer, playwright. *Odessa Tales, Red Cavalry.*

James Baldwin, 1924-87, (U.S.) author, playwright. *The Fire Next Time, Blues for Mister Charlie.*

Honoré de Balzac, 1799-1850, (Fr.) novelist. *Le Père Goriot, Cousine Bette, Eugénie Grandet.*

James M. Barrie, 1860-1937, (Br.) play- wright, novelist. *Peter Pan, Dear Brutus, What Every Woman Knows.*

Charles Baudelaire, 1821-67, (Fr.) poet. *Les Fleurs du Mal.*

L(yman) Frank Baum, 1856-1919, (U.S.) Wizard of Oz series.

Simone de Beauvoir, 1908-86, (Fr.) nov- elist, essayist. *The Second Sex, Mem- oirs of a Dutiful Daughter.*

Samuel Beckett, 1906-89, (Ire.) novelist, playwright. *Waiting for Godot, Endgame* (plays); *Murphy, Watt, Molloy* (novels).

Brendan Behan, 1923-64, (Ire.) play- wright. *The Quare Fellow, The Hostage, Borstal Boy.*

Saul Bellow, 1915-2005, (U.S.) novelist. *The Adventures of Augie March, Hum- boldt's Gift.*

Robert Benchley, 1889-1945, (U.S.) humorist.

Stephen Vincent Benét, 1898-1943, (U.S.) poet, novelist. *John Brown's Body.*

Jan Berenstain, 1923-2012, and **Stan Berenstain**, 1923-2005, (both U.S.) co-writers and illustrators of Berenstain Bears series of children's books.

Thomas Berger, 1924-2014, (U.S.) novel- ist. *Little Big Man.*

John Berryman, 1914-72, (U.S.) poet. *Homage to Mistress Bradstreet.*

Ambrose Bierce, 1842-1914, (U.S.) short-story writer, journalist. *In the Midst of Life, The Devil's Dictionary.*

Maeve Binchy, 1940-2012, (Ire.) novelist, short-story writer. *Circle of Friends, Tara Road.*

Elizabeth Bishop, 1911-79, (U.S.) poet. *North and South—A Cold Spring.*

William Blake, 1757-1827, (Br.) poet, artist. *Songs of Innocence, Songs of Experience.*

Aleksandr Blok, 1880-1921, (Russ.) poet. "The Twelve," "The Scythians."

Enid Blyton, 1897-1968, (Br.) children's writer. Famous Five series.

Giovanni Boccaccio, 1313-75, (It.) poet. *Decameron.*

Heinrich Böll, 1917-85, (Ger.) novelist, short-story writer. *Group Portrait With Lady.*

Jorge Luis Borges, 1900-86, (Arg.) short-story writer, poet, essayist. *Labyrinths.*

James Boswell, 1740-95, (Scot.) biogra- pher. *The Life of Samuel Johnson.*

Pierre Boulle, 1913-94, (Fr.) novelist. *The Bridge Over the River Kwai, Planet of the Apes.*

Paul Bowles, 1910-99, (U.S.) novelist, short-story writer. *The Sheltering Sky.*

Ray Bradbury, 1920-2012, (U.S.) novel- ist, short-story writer. *Fahrenheit 451, The Martian Chronicles.*

Anne Bradstreet, c. 1612-72, (U.S.) poet. *The Tenth Muse Lately Sprung Up in America.*

Bertolt Brecht, 1898-1956, (Ger.) dra- matist, poet. *The Threepenny Opera, Mother Courage and Her Children.*

Joseph Brodsky, 1940-96, (Russ.-U.S.) poet. *A Part of Speech, Less Than One, To Urania.*

Charlotte Brontë, 1816-55, (Br.) novelist. *Jane Eyre.*

Emily Brontë, 1818-48, (Br.) novelist. *Wuthering Heights.*

Sterling A. Brown, 1901-89, (U.S.) poet, literature professor. *Southern Road.*

William Wells Brown, 1815-84, (U.S.) writer, memoirist; first novel by an African American, *Clotel*, 1853.

Elizabeth Barrett Browning, 1806-61, (Br.) poet. *Sonnets From the Portuguese, Aurora Leigh.*

Robert Browning, 1812-89, (Br.) poet. "My Last Duchess," "Fra Lippo Lippi," *The Ring and the Book.*

Pearl S. Buck, 1892-1973, (U.S.) novelist. *The Good Earth.*

Charles Bukowski, 1920-94, (U.S.) novelist, poet. *Ham on Rye, Women.*

Mikhail Bulgakov, 1891-1940, (Russ.) novelist, playwright. *The Heart of a Dog, The Master and Margarita.*

John Bunyan, 1628-88, (Br.) writer. *Pilgrim's Progress.*

Anthony Burgess, 1917-93, (Br.) author. *A Clockwork Orange.*

Frances Hodgson Burnett, 1849-1924, (Br.-U.S.) novelist. *The Secret Garden.*

Robert Burns, 1759-96, (Scot.) poet. "Flow Gently, Sweet Afton," "My Heart's in the Highlands," "Auld Lang Syne."

Edgar Rice Burroughs, 1875-1950, (U.S.) writer; created Tarzan, John Carter.

William S. Burroughs, 1914-97, (U.S.) novelist. *Naked Lunch.*

Octavia Butler, 1947-2006, (U.S.) science-fiction writer. *Kindred.*

George Gordon, Lord Byron, 1788-1824, (Br.) poet. *Don Juan, Childe Harold, Manfred, Cain.*

Pedro Calderon de la Barca, 1600-81, (Sp.) playwright. *Life Is a Dream.*

Hortense Calisher, 1911-2009, (U.S.) novelist, short-story writer. *False Entry.*

Italo Calvino, 1923-85, (It.) novelist, short-story writer. *If on a Winter's Night a Traveler.*

Luís Vaz de Camões, 1524?-80 (Port.) poet. *The Lusiads.*

Albert Camus, 1913-60, (Fr.) writer. *The Stranger, The Fall.*

Elias Canetti, 1905-94, (Bulg.) novelist, essayist. *Auto-Da-Fe.*

Karel Capek, 1890-1938, (Czech.) playwright, novelist, essayist. *R.U.R. (Rossum's Universal Robots).*

Truman Capote, 1924-84, (U.S.) author. *Other Voices, Other Rooms; Breakfast at Tiffany's; In Cold Blood.*

Lewis Carroll (Charles Dodgson), 1832-98, (Br.) writer, mathematician. *Alice's Adventures in Wonderland.*

Barbara Cartland 1901-2000, (Br.) romance novelist.

Giacomo Casanova, 1725-98, (It.) adventurer, memoirist.

Willa Cather, 1873-1947, (U.S.) novelist. *O Pioneers!, My Ántonia, Death Comes for the Archbishop.*

Constantine Cavafy, 1863-1933, (Gr.) poet. "Ithaka," "Sensual Pleasures."

Camilo Jose Cela, 1916-2001, (Sp.) novelist. *The Family of Pascual Duarte, The Hive.*

Miguel de Cervantes Saavedra, 1547-1616, (Sp.) novelist, dramatist, poet. *Don Quixote.*

Raymond Chandler, 1888-1959, (U.S.) writer of detective fiction. Philip Marlowe series.

Geoffrey Chaucer, c. 1340-1400, (Br.) poet. *The Canterbury Tales, Troilus and Criseyde.*

John Cheever, 1912-82, (U.S.) novelist, short-story writer. *The Wapshot Scandal*, "The Country Husband."

Anton Chekhov, 1860-1904, (Russ.) short-story writer, dramatist. *Uncle Vanya, The Cherry Orchard, The Three Sisters.*

Charles Waddell Chesnutt, 1858-1932, (U.S.) known for his short stories. *The Conjure Woman.*

G(ilbert) K(eith) Chesterton, 1874-1936, (Br.) critic, novelist, relig. apologist. Father Brown series of mysteries.

Kate Chopin, 1851-1904, (U.S.) writer. *The Awakening.*

Agatha Christie, 1890-1976, (Br.) mystery writer; created Miss Marple, Hercule Poirot. *Murder on the Orient Express, Murder of Roger Ackroyd.*

Tom Clancy, 1947-2013, novelist. *The Hunt for Red October.*

Arthur C. Clarke, 1917-2008, (Br.) science-fiction writer. *2001: A Space Odyssey.*

James Clavell, 1924-94, (Br.-U.S.) novelist. *Shogun, King Rat.*

Jean Cocteau, 1889-1963, (Fr.) writer, visual artist, filmmaker. *The Beauty and the Beast, Les Enfants Terribles.*

Samuel Taylor Coleridge, 1772-1834, (Br.) poet, critic. "Kubla Khan," "The Rime of the Ancient Mariner."

(Sidonie) Colette, 1873-1954, (Fr.) novelist. *Claudine, Gigi.*

Wilkie Collins, 1824-89, (Br.) novelist. *The Moonstone.*

Evan S. Connell, 1924-2013, (Br.) novelist, short-story writer. *Mrs. Bridge.*

Joseph Conrad, 1857-1924, (Br.) novelist. *Lord Jim, Heart of Darkness, The Secret Agent.*

Pat Conroy, 1945-2016, (U.S.) novelist. *The Prince of Tides, The Great Santini.*

James Fenimore Cooper, 1789-1851, (U.S.) novelist. *Leatherstocking Tales, The Last of the Mohicans.*

Pierre Corneille, 1606-84, (Fr.) dramatist. *Medeé, Le Cid.*

Hart Crane, 1899-1932, (U.S.) poet. "The Bridge."

Stephen Crane, 1871-1900, (U.S.) novelist, short-story writer. *The Red Badge of Courage*, "The Open Boat."

Harry Crews, 1935-2012, (U.S.) novelist. *A Feast of Snakes.*

Michael Crichton, 1942-2008, (U.S.) writer. *The Andromeda Strain, Jurassic Park.*

Countee Cullen, 1903-46, (U.S.) poet, prominent in the Harlem Renaissance of the 1920s. *The Black Christ.*

E. E. Cummings, 1894-1962, (U.S.) poet. *Tulips and Chimneys.*

Roald Dahl, 1916-90, (Br.-U.S.) writer. *Charlie and the Chocolate Factory, James and the Giant Peach.*

Gabriele D'Annunzio, 1863-1938, (It.) poet, novelist, dramatist. *The Child of Pleasure, The Intruder, The Victim.*

Dante Alighieri, 1265-1321, (It.) poet. *The Divine Comedy.*

Robertson Davies, 1913-95, (Can.) novelist, playwright, essayist. Salterton, Deptford, and Cornish trilogies.

Daniel Defoe, 1660-1731, (Br.) writer. *Robinson Crusoe, Moll Flanders, Journal of the Plague Year.*

Philip K. Dick, 1928-82, (U.S.) science-fiction writer. *Do Androids Dream of Electric Sheep?*

Charles Dickens, 1812-70, (Br.) novelist. *David Copperfield, Oliver Twist, Great Expectations, A Tale of Two Cities.*

James Dickey, 1923-97, (U.S.) poet, novelist. *Deliverance.*

Emily Dickinson, 1830-86, (U.S.) poet. "Because I could not stop for Death ...," "Success is counted sweetest ..."

Isak Dinesen (Karen Blixen), 1885-1962, (Den.) author. *Out of Africa, Seven Gothic Tales, Winter's Tales.*

E(dgar) L(awrence) Doctorow, 1931-2015, (U.S.) novelist. *Ragtime, Billy Bathgate.*

John Donne, 1573-1631, (Br.) poet. *Songs and Sonnets.*

José Donoso, 1924-96, (Chile) surreal novelist and short-story writer. *The Obscene Bird of Night.*

John Dos Passos, 1896-1970, (U.S.) novelist. *U.S.A.*

Fyodor Dostoyevsky, 1821-81, (Russ.) novelist. *Crime and Punishment, The Brothers Karamazov, The Possessed.*

Arthur Conan Doyle, 1859-1930, (Br.) novelist. Sherlock Holmes mystery stories.

Theodore Dreiser, 1871-1945, (U.S.) novelist. *An American Tragedy, Sister Carrie.*

John Dryden, 1631-1700, (Br.) poet, dramatist, critic. *All for Love, Mac Flecknoe, Absalom and Achitophel.*

Alexandre Dumas (père), 1802-70, (Fr.) novelist, dramatist. *The Three Musketeers, The Count of Monte Cristo.*

Alexandre Dumas (fils), 1824-95, (Fr.) dramatist, novelist. *La Dame aux Camélias, Le Demi-Monde.*

Paul Laurence Dunbar, 1872-1906, (U.S.) poet, novelist. *Lyrics of Lowly Life.*

Lawrence Durrell, 1912-90, (Br.) novelist, poet. *Alexandria Quartet.*

Umberto Eco, 1932-2016, (It.) novelist. *The Name of the Rose.*

Ilya G. Ehrenburg, 1891-1967, (Russ.) writer. *The Thaw.*

George Eliot (Mary Ann or Marian Evans), 1819-80, (Br.) novelist. *Silas Marner, Middlemarch.*

T(homas) S(tearns) Eliot, 1888-1965, (Br.) poet, critic. *The Waste Land*, "The Love Song of J. Alfred Prufrock."

Stanley Elkin, 1930-95, (U.S.) novelist, short-story writer. *George Mills.*

Ralph Ellison, 1914-94, (U.S.) writer. *Invisible Man.*

Ralph Waldo Emerson, 1803-82, (U.S.) poet, essayist. "Brahma," "Nature," "The Over-Soul," "Self-Reliance."

James T. Farrell, 1904-79, (U.S.) novelist. *Studs Lonigan.*

Howard Fast, 1914-2003, (U.S.) novelist. *Spartacus, The Immigrants.*

William Faulkner, 1897-1962, (U.S.) novelist. *Sanctuary; Light in August; The Sound and the Fury; Absalom, Absalom!*

Edna Ferber, 1887-1968, (U.S.) novelist, short-story writer, playwright. *So Big, Cimarron, Show Boat.*

Henry Fielding, 1707-54, (Br.) novelist. *Tom Jones.*

F(rancis) Scott Fitzgerald, 1896-1940, (U.S.) short-story writer, novelist. *The Great Gatsby, Tender Is the Night.*

Gustave Flaubert, 1821-80, (Fr.) novelist. *Madame Bovary.*

Ian Fleming, 1908-64, (Br.) novelist. James Bond spy thrillers: *Dr. No, Goldfinger.*

Horton Foote, 1916-2009, (U.S.) playwright, screenwriter. *The Trip to Bountiful.*

Ford Madox Ford, 1873-1939, (Br.) novelist, critic, poet. *The Good Soldier.*

C(ecil) S(cott) Forester, 1899-1966, (Br.) writer. Horatio Hornblower books.

E(dward) M(organ) Forster, 1879-1970, (Br.) novelist. *A Passage to India, Howards End.*

Anatole France, 1844-1924, (Fr.) writer. *Penguin Island, My Friend's Book, The Crime of Sylvestre Bonnard.*

Dick Francis, 1920-2010, (Br.) crime novelist.

Marilyn French, 1929-2009, (U.S.) novelist. *The Women's Room.*

Brian Friel, 1929-2015, (N. Ire.) playwright. *Dancing at Lughnasa.*

Robert Frost, 1874-1963, (U.S.) poet. "Birches," "Fire and Ice," "Stopping by Woods on a Snowy Evening."

Carlos Fuentes, 1928-2012, (Pan.) novelist, essayist. *The Old Gringo.*

William Gaddis, 1922-98, (U.S.) novelist. *The Recognitions.*

John Galsworthy, 1867-1933, (Br.) novelist, dramatist. *The Forsyte Saga.*

Federico García Lorca, 1898-1936, (Sp.) poet, dramatist. *Blood Wedding.*

Gabriel García Márquez, 1927-2014, (Col.) novelist. *One Hundred Years of Solitude.*

Erle Stanley Gardner, 1889-1970, (U.S.) mystery writer; created Perry Mason.

Jean Genet, 1911-86, (Fr.) playwright, novelist. *The Maids.*

Kahlil Gibran, 1883-1931, (Leban.-U.S.) mystical novelist, essayist, poet. *The Prophet.*

André Gide, 1869-1951, (Fr.) writer. *The Immoralist, The Pastoral Symphony, Strait Is the Gate.*

Allen Ginsberg, 1926-97, (U.S.) Beat poet. "Howl."

Jean Giraudoux, 1882-1944, (Fr.) novelist, dramatist. *Electra, The Madwoman of Chaillot, Ondine, Tiger at the Gate.*

Johann Wolfgang von Goethe, 1749-1832, (Ger.) poet, dramatist, novelist. *Faust, Sorrows of Young Werther.*

Nikolai Gogol, 1809-52, (Russ.) short-story writer, dramatist, novelist. *Dead Souls, The Inspector General.*

William Golding, 1911-93, (Br.) novelist. *Lord of the Flies.*

Oliver Goldsmith, 1728-74, (Br.-Ire.) dramatist, novelist. *The Vicar of Wakefield, She Stoops to Conquer.*

Nadine Gordimer, 1923-2014, (S. Afr.) novelist. *Burger's Daughter.*

Maxim Gorky, 1868-1936, (Russ.) dramatist, novelist. *The Lower Depths.*

Sue Grafton, 1940-2017, (U.S.) crime novelist; created Kinsey Millhone "alphabet mysteries."

Günter Grass, 1927-2015, (Ger.) novelist, poet. *The Tin Drum.*

Robert Graves, 1895-1985, (Br.) poet, classical scholar, novelist. *I, Claudius; The White Goddess.*

Thomas Gray, 1716-71, (Br.) poet. "Elegy Written in a Country Churchyard," "The Progress of Poesy."

Julien Green, 1900-98, (U.S.-Fr.) expatriate American novelist. *Moira, Each Man in His Darkness.*

Graham Greene, 1904-91, (Br.) novelist. *The Power and the Glory, The Heart of the Matter, The Ministry of Fear.*

Zane Grey, 1872-1939, (U.S.) writer of Western stories.

Jakob Grimm, 1785-1863, philologist, folklorist; with brother **Wilhelm Grimm**, 1786-1859, (both Ger.) collected *Grimm's Fairy Tales.*

Alex Haley, 1921-92, (U.S.) author. *Roots.*

Dashiell Hammett, 1894-1961, (U.S.) detective-story writer; created Sam Spade. *The Maltese Falcon.*

Jupiter Hammon, c. 1720-1800, (U.S.) poet; first African American to have his works published, 1761.

Knut Hamsun, 1859-1952, (Nor.) novelist. *Hunger.*

Lorraine Hansberry, 1930-65, (U.S.) playwright. *A Raisin in the Sun.*

Thomas Hardy, 1840-1928, (Br.) novelist, poet. *The Return of the Native, Tess of the D'Urbervilles, Jude the Obscure.*

E. Lynn Harris, 1955-2009, (U.S.) novelist. *Invisible Life, Basketball Jones.*

Joel Chandler Harris, 1848-1908, (U.S.) writer. Uncle Remus stories.

Jim Harrison, 1937-2016, (U.S.) novelist and essayist. *Legends of the Fall.*

Moss Hart, 1904-61, (U.S.) playwright. *Once in a Lifetime, You Can't Take It With You, The Man Who Came to Dinner.*

Bret Harte, 1836-1902, (U.S.) short-story writer, poet. *The Luck of Roaring Camp.*

Jaroslav Hasek, 1883-1923, (Czech.) writer, playwright. *The Good Soldier Schweik.*

Vaclav Havel, 1936-2011, (Czech.) essayist, poet, playwright. *The Power of the Powerless.*

John Hawkes, 1925-98, (U.S.) experimental fiction writer. *The Goose on the Grave, Blood Oranges.*

Nathaniel Hawthorne, 1804-64, (U.S.) novelist, short-story writer. *The Scarlet Letter*, "Young Goodman Brown."

Seamus Heaney, 1939-2013, (Ire.) poet. *Death of a Naturalist.*

Heinrich Heine, 1797-1856, (Ger.) poet. *Book of Songs.*

Robert Heinlein, 1907-88, (U.S.) science-fiction writer. *Stranger in a Strange Land.*

Joseph Heller, 1923-99, (U.S.) novelist. *Catch-22.*

Lillian Hellman, 1905-84, (U.S.) playwright, memoirist. *The Little Foxes, An Unfinished Woman, Pentimento.*

Ernest Hemingway, 1899-1961, (U.S.) novelist, short-story writer. *A Farewell to Arms, For Whom the Bell Tolls.*

O. Henry (W. S. Porter), 1862-1910, (U.S.) short-story writer. "The Gift of the Magi."

George Herbert, 1593-1633, (Br.) poet. "The Altar," "Easter Wings."

Zbigniew Herbert, 1924-98, (Pol.) poet. "Apollo and Marsyas."

Robert Herrick, 1591-1674, (Br.) poet. "To the Virgins to Make Much of Time."

John Hersey, 1914-93, (U.S.) novelist, journalist. *Hiroshima, A Bell for Adano.*

Hermann Hesse, 1877-1962, (Ger.) novelist, poet. *Death and the Lover, Steppenwolf, Siddhartha.*

Georgette Heyer, 1902-74, (Br.) Regency romance novelist.

Oscar Hijuelos, 1951-2013, (U.S.) novelist. *The Mambo Kings Play Songs of Love.*

Tony Hillerman, 1925-2008, (U.S.) novelist. *Dance Hall of the Dead.*

James Hilton, 1900-54, (Br.) novelist. *Lost Horizon.*

Chester Himes, 1909-84, (U.S.) novelist. *Cotton Comes to Harlem.*

Oliver Wendell Holmes, 1809-94, (U.S.) poet, novelist. *The Autocrat of the Breakfast-Table.*

Gerard Manley Hopkins, 1844-89, (Br.) poet. "Pied Beauty," "God's Grandeur."

A(lfred) E. Housman, 1859-1936, (Br.) poet. *A Shropshire Lad.*

William Dean Howells, 1837-1920, (U.S.) novelist, critic. *The Rise of Silas Lapham.*

Langston Hughes, 1902-67, (U.S.) poet, lyric writer, author; a major influence in 1920s Harlem Renaissance.

Ted Hughes, 1930-98, (Br.) British poet laureate, 1984-98. *Crow, The Hawk in the Rain.*

Victor Hugo, 1802-85, (Fr.) poet, dramatist, novelist. *Notre Dame de Paris, Les Misérables.*

Zora Neale Hurston, 1891-1960, (U.S.) novelist, folklorist. *Their Eyes Were Watching God, Mules and Men.*

Aldous Huxley, 1894-1963, (Br.) writer. *Brave New World.*

Henrik Ibsen, 1828-1906, (Nor.) dramatist, poet. *A Doll's House, Ghosts, The Wild Duck, Hedda Gabler.*

William Inge, 1913-73, (U.S.) playwright. *Picnic; Come Back, Little Sheba; Bus Stop.*

Eugene Ionesco, 1910-94, (Fr.) surrealist dramatist. *The Bald Soprano, The Chairs.*

Washington Irving, 1783-1859, (U.S.) writer. "Rip Van Winkle," "The Legend of Sleepy Hollow."

Christopher Isherwood, 1904-86, (Br.) novelist, playwright. *The Berlin Stories.*

Shirley Jackson, 1916-65, (U.S.) short-story writer. "The Lottery."

Henry James, 1843-1916, (U.S.) novelist, short-story writer, critic. *The Portrait of a Lady, The Ambassadors, Daisy Miller.*

P(hyllis) D(orothy) James, 1920-2014, (Br.) mystery novelist.

Robinson Jeffers, 1887-1962, (U.S.) poet, dramatist. *Tamar and Other Poems, Medea.*

James Weldon Johnson, 1871-1938, (U.S.) poet, novelist, diplomat; lyricist for *Lift Every Voice and Sing.*

Samuel Johnson, 1709-84, (Br.) author, scholar, critic. *Dictionary of the English Language, Vanity of Human Wishes.*

Ben Jonson, 1572-1637, (Br.) dramatist, poet. *Volpone.*

James Joyce, 1882-1941, (Ire.) writer. *Ulysses, Dubliners, A Portrait of the Artist as a Young Man, Finnegans Wake.*

Ernst Junger, 1895-1998, (Ger.) novelist, essayist. *The Peace, On the Marble Cliff.*

Franz Kafka, 1883-1924, (Austria-Hung./Czech.) novelist, short-story writer. *The Trial, The Castle,* "The Metamorphosis."

George S. Kaufman, 1889-1961, (U.S.) playwright. *The Man Who Came to Dinner, You Can't Take It With You.*

Yasunari Kawabata, 1899-1972, (Jpn.) novelist. *The Sound of the Mountains.*

Nikos Kazantzakis, 1883-1957, (Gr.) novelist. *Zorba the Greek, A Greek Passion.*

Alfred Kazin, 1915-98 (U.S.) author, critic, teacher. *On Native Grounds.*

John Keats, 1795-1821, (Br.) poet. "Ode on a Grecian Urn," "Ode to a Nightingale," "La Belle Dame Sans Merci."

Jack Kerouac, 1922-69, (U.S.) author, Beat poet. *On the Road, The Dharma Bums,* "Mexico City Blues."

Joyce Kilmer, 1886-1918, (U.S.) poet. "Trees."

Galway Kinnell, 1927-2014, (U.S.) poet.

Rudyard Kipling, 1865-1936, (Br.) author, poet. "The White Man's Burden," "Gunga Din," *The Jungle Book.*

Maxine Kumin, 1925-2014, (U.S.) poet, author. *Up Country: Poems of New England.*

Jean de la Fontaine, 1621-95, (Fr.) poet. *Fables choisies* (Selected Fables).

Pär Lagerkvist, 1891-1974, (Swed.) poet, dramatist, novelist. *Barabbas, The Sybil.*

Selma Lagerlöf, 1858-1940, (Swed.) novelist. *Jerusalem, The Ring of the Lowenskolds.*

Alphonse de Lamartine, 1790-1869, (Fr.) poet, novelist, statesman. *Méditations poétiques.*

Charles Lamb, 1775-1834, (Br.) essayist. *Specimens of English Dramatic Poets, Essays of Elia.*

Louis L'Amour, 1908-88, (U.S.) Western author, screenwriter. *Hondo, The Cherokee Trail.*

Giuseppe di Lampedusa, 1896-1957, (It.) novelist. *The Leopard.*

William Langland, c. 1332-1400, (Br.) poet. *Piers Plowman.*

Ring Lardner, 1885-1933, (U.S.) short-story writer, humorist.

Steig Larsson, 1954-2004, (Swed.) novelist. *The Girl With the Dragon Tattoo.*

Arthur Laurents, 1917-2011, (U.S.) playwright and director. *West Side Story.*

D(avid) H(erbert) Lawrence, 1885-1930, (Br.) novelist. *Sons and Lovers, Women in Love, Lady Chatterley's Lover.*

Halldór Laxness, 1902-98, (Iceland) novelist. *Iceland's Bell.*

Harper Lee, 1926-2016, (U.S.) novelist. *To Kill a Mockingbird.*

Ursula K. Le Guin, 1929-2018, (U.S.) science-fiction writer. *The Left Hand of Darkness.*

Madeleine L'Engle, 1918-2007, (U.S.) novelist of young adult fiction. *A Wrinkle in Time.*

Elmore Leonard, 1925-2013, (U.S.) novelist. *Get Shorty.*

Mikhail Lermontov, 1814-41, (Russ.) novelist, poet. "Demon," *Hero of Our Time.*

Alain-René Lesage, 1668-1747, (Fr.) novelist. *Gil Blas de Santillane.*

Doris Lessing, 1919-2013, (Br.) writer. *The Golden Notebook.*

Gotthold Lessing, 1729-81, (Ger.) dramatist, philosopher, critic. *Miss Sara Sampson, Minna von Barnhelm.*

Ira Levin, 1929-2007, (U.S.) novelist, playwright. *Deathtrap, Rosemary's Baby.*

C(live) S(taples) Lewis, 1898-1963, (Br.) critic, novelist, religious writer. *Allegory of Love; The Lion, the Witch and the Wardrobe; Out of the Silent Planet.*

Sinclair Lewis, 1885-1951, (U.S.) novelist. *Babbitt, Main Street, Arrowsmith, Dodsworth.*

Li Po, 701-762, (China) poet. "Song Before Drinking," "She Spins Silk."

Vachel Lindsay, 1879-1931, (U.S.) poet. *General William Booth Enters Into Heaven, The Congo.*

Hugh Lofting, 1886-1947, (Br.) writer. Dr. Doolittle series.

Jack London, 1876-1916, (U.S.) novelist, journalist. *Call of the Wild, The Sea-Wolf, White Fang.*

Henry Wadsworth Longfellow, 1807-82, (U.S.) poet. *Evangeline, The Song of Hiawatha.*

Lope de Vega, 1562-1635, (Sp.) playwright. *Noche de San Juan, Maestro de Danzar.*

H(oward) P(hillips) Lovecraft, 1890-1937, (U.S.) novelist, short-story writer. "At the Mountains of Madness."

Amy Lowell, 1874-1925, (U.S.) poet, critic. "Lilacs."

James Russell Lowell, 1819-91, (U.S.) poet, editor. *Poems, The Biglow Papers*.

Robert Lowell, 1917-77, (U.S.) poet. "Lord Weary's Castle."

Joaquim Maria Machado de Assis, 1839-1908, (Brazil) novelist, poet. *The Posthumous Memoirs of Bras Cubas*.

Archibald MacLeish, 1892-1982, (U.S.) poet. *Conquistador*.

Naguib Mahfouz, 1911-2006, (Egypt) novelist; first Arabic-language writer to win the Nobel Prize for Literature. *Cairo Trilogy*.

Norman Mailer, 1923-2007, (U.S.) novelist, essayist, journalist. *The Naked and the Dead*.

Bernard Malamud, 1914-86, (U.S.) short-story writer, novelist. "The Magic Barrel," *The Assistant, The Fixer*.

Stéphane Mallarmé, 1842-98, (Fr.) poet. *Poésies*.

Sir Thomas Malory, c. 1410-71, (Br.) writer. *Morte d'Arthur*.

Andre Malraux, 1901-76, (Fr.) novelist. *Man's Fate*.

Osip Mandelstam, 1891-1938, (Russ.) poet. *Stone, Tristia*.

Thomas Mann, 1875-1955, (Ger.) novelist, essayist. *Buddenbrooks, The Magic Mountain*, "Death in Venice."

Katherine Mansfield, 1888-1923, (Br.) short-story writer. "Bliss."

Christopher Marlowe, 1564-93, (Br.) dramatist, poet. *Tamburlaine the Great, Dr. Faustus, The Jew of Malta*.

Andrew Marvell, 1621-78, (Br.) poet. "To His Coy Mistress."

John Masefield, 1878-1967, (Br.) poet. "Sea Fever," "Cargoes," *Salt Water Ballads*.

Edgar Lee Masters, 1869-1950, (U.S.) poet, biographer. *Spoon River Anthology*.

Peter Matthiessen, 1927-2014, (U.S.) novelist. *The Snow Leopard*.

W(illiam) Somerset Maugham, 1874-1965, (Br.) author. *Of Human Bondage, The Moon and Sixpence*.

Guy de Maupassant, 1850-93, (Fr.) novelist, short-story writer. "A Life," "Bel-Ami," "The Necklace."

François Mauriac, 1885-1970, (Fr.) novelist, dramatist. *Viper's Tangle, The Kiss to the Leper*.

Vladimir Mayakovsky, 1893-1930, (Russ.) poet, dramatist. *The Cloud in Trousers*.

Mary McCarthy, 1912-89, (U.S.) critic, novelist, memoirist. *Memories of a Catholic Girlhood*.

Frank McCourt, 1930-2009, (U.S.) memoirist. *Angela's Ashes, 'Tis*.

Carson McCullers, 1917-67, (U.S.) novelist. *The Heart Is a Lonely Hunter, Member of the Wedding*.

Colleen McCullough, 1937-2015, (Austral.) novelist. *The Thorn Birds*.

Herman Melville, 1819-91, (U.S.) novelist, poet. *Moby-Dick, Typee, Billy Budd, Omoo*.

George Meredith, 1828-1909, (Br.) novelist, poet. *The Ordeal of Richard Feverel, The Egoist*.

Prosper Mérimée, 1803-70, (Fr.) author. *Carmen*.

James Merrill, 1926-95, (U.S.) poet. *Divine Comedies*.

James Michener, 1907-97, (U.S.) novelist. *Tales of the South Pacific*.

Edna St. Vincent Millay, 1892-1950, (U.S.) poet. *The Harp Weaver and Other Poems*.

Arthur Miller,1915-2005, (U.S.) playwright. *The Crucible, After the Fall, Death of a Salesman*.

Henry Miller, 1891-1980, (U.S.) novelist. *Tropic of Cancer*.

A(lan) A(lexander) Milne, 1882-1956, (Br.) author. *Winnie-the-Pooh*.

Czeslaw Milosz, 1911-2004, (Pol.) essayist, poet. "Esse," "Encounter."

John Milton, 1608-74, (Br.) poet, writer. *Paradise Lost, Comus, Lycidas, Areopagitica*.

Mishima Yukio (Hiraoka Kimitake) 1925-70, (Jpn.) writer. *Confessions of a Mask*.

Gabriela Mistral, 1889-1957, (Chile) poet. *Sonnets of Death*.

Margaret Mitchell, 1900-49, (U.S.) novelist. *Gone With the Wind*.

Jean Baptiste Molière, 1622-73, (Fr.) dramatist. *Tartuffe, Le Misanthrope, Le Bourgeois Gentilhomme*.

Ferenc Molnár, 1878-1952, (Hung.) dramatist, novelist. *Liliom, The Guardsman, The Swan*.

Michel de Montaigne, 1533-92, (Fr.) essayist. *Essais*.

Eugenio Montale, 1896-1981, (It.) poet.

Brian Moore, 1921-99, (Ire.-U.S.) novelist. *The Lonely Passion of Judith Hearne*.

Clement C. Moore, 1779-1863, (U.S.) poet, educator. "A Visit From Saint Nicholas."

Marianne Moore, 1887-1972, (U.S.) poet.

Alberto Moravia, 1907-90, (It.) novelist, short-story writer. *The Time of Indifference*.

Sir Thomas More, 1478-1535, (Br.) writer, statesman, saint. *Utopia*.

Wright Morris, 1910-98, (U.S.) novelist. *My Uncle Dudley*.

Bharati Mukherjee, 1940-2017, (India-U.S.) novelist, short-story writer. *Jasmine*.

Murasaki Shikibu, c. 978-1026, (Jpn.) novelist. *The Tale of Genji*.

Iris Murdoch, 1919-99, (Br.) novelist, philosopher. *The Sea, the Sea*.

Alfred de Musset, 1810-57, (Fr.) poet, dramatist. *La Confession d'un Enfant du Siècle*.

Vladimir Nabokov, 1899-1977, (Russ.-U.S.) novelist. *Lolita, Pale Fire*.

V. S. Naipaul, 1932-2018, (Trinidad) novelist, travel writer. *A House for Mr. Biswas*.

R. K. Narayan, 1906-2001, (India) novelist. *The Guide*.

Ogden Nash, 1902-71, (U.S.) poet of light verse.

Irène Némirovsky, 1903-42, (Ukraine) novelist. *David Golder, Suite Française*.

Pablo Neruda, 1904-73, (Chile) poet. *Twenty Love Poems and One Song of Despair, Toward the Splendid City*.

Patrick O'Brian, 1914-2000, (Br.) historical novelist. *Master and Commander, Blue at the Mizzen*.

Sean O'Casey, 1884-1964, (Ire.) dramatist. *Juno and the Paycock, The Plough and the Stars*.

Flannery O'Connor, 1925-64, (U.S.) novelist, short-story writer. *Wise Blood*, "A Good Man Is Hard to Find."

Frank O'Connor (Michael Donovan), 1903-66, (Ire.) short-story writer. "Guests of a Nation."

Clifford Odets, 1906-63, (U.S.) playwright. *Waiting for Lefty, Awake and Sing, Golden Boy, The Country Girl*.

John O'Hara, 1905-70, (U.S.) novelist, short-story writer. *From the Terrace, Appointment in Samarra, Pal Joey*.

Omar Khayyam, c. 1028-1122, (Per.) poet. *Rubaiyat*.

Eugene O'Neill, 1888-1953, (U.S.) playwright. *Emperor Jones, Anna Christie, Long Day's Journey Into Night*.

George Orwell (Eric Arthur Blair), 1903-50, (Br.) novelist, essayist. *Animal Farm, Nineteen Eighty-Four*.

John Osborne, 1929-95, (Br.) dramatist, novelist. *Look Back in Anger, The Entertainer*.

Wilfred Owen, 1893-1918, (Br.) poet. "Dulce et Décorum Est."

Grace Paley, 1922-2007, (U.S.) short-story writer, poet. *The Little Disturbances of Man*.

Dorothy Parker, 1893-1967, (U.S.) poet, short-story writer. *Enough Rope, Laments for the Living*.

Robert B. Parker, 1932-2010, (U.S.) crime novelist. "Spenser" novels.

Boris Pasternak, 1890-1960, (Russ.) poet, novelist. *Doctor Zhivago*.

Alan Paton, 1903-88, (S. Africa) novelist. *Cry, the Beloved Country*.

Octavio Paz, 1914-98, (Mex.) poet, essayist. *The Labyrinth of Solitude, They Shall Not Pass!, The Sun Stone*.

Samuel Pepys, 1633-1703, (Br.) public official, diarist.

S(idney) J(oseph) Perelman, 1904-79, (U.S.) humorist. *The Road to Miltown, Under the Spreading Atrophy*.

Charles Perrault, 1628-1703, (Fr.) writer. *Tales From Mother Goose* (*Sleeping Beauty, Cinderella*).

Petrarch (Francesco Petrarca), 1304-74, (It.) poet. *Africa, Trionfi, Canzoniere*.

Harold Pinter, 1930-2008, (Br.) playwright. *The Birthday Party, The Caretaker, The Homecoming*.

Luigi Pirandello, 1867-1936, (It.) novelist, dramatist. *Six Characters in Search of an Author*.

Sylvia Plath, 1932-63, (U.S.) author, poet. *The Bell Jar, The Colossus*.

Edgar Allan Poe, 1809-49, (U.S.) poet, short-story writer, critic. "Annabel Lee," "The Raven," "The Purloined Letter."

Alexander Pope, 1688-1744, (Br.) poet. *The Rape of the Lock, The Dunciad, An Essay on Man*.

Katherine Anne Porter, 1890-1980, (U.S.) novelist, short-story writer. *Ship of Fools*.

Chaim Potok, 1929-2002, (U.S.) novelist. *The Chosen*.

Ezra Pound, 1885-1972, (U.S.) poet. *Cantos*.

Anthony Powell, 1905-2000, (Br.) novelist. *A Dance to the Music of Time* series.

Terry Pratchett, 1948-2015 (Br.) fantasy novelist. *Discworld* series.

Reynolds Price, 1933-2011, (U.S.) novelist, short-story writer, poet. *A Long and Happy Life*.

J(ohn) B(oynton) Priestley, 1894-1984, (Br.) novelist, dramatist. *The Good Companions*.

Marcel Proust, 1871-1922, (Fr.) novelist. *Remembrance of Things Past*.

Aleksandr Pushkin, 1799-1837, (Russ.) poet, novelist. *Boris Godunov, Eugene Onegin*.

Mario Puzo, 1920-99, (U.S.) novelist. *The Godfather*.

François Rabelais, 1495-1553, (Fr.) writer. *Gargantua*.

Jean Racine, 1639-99, (Fr.) dramatist. *Andromaque, Phèdre, Bérénice, Britannicus*.

David Rakoff, 1964-2012, (Can.-U.S.) essayist. *Fraud, Don't Get Too Comfortable*.

Ayn Rand, 1905-82, (Russ.-U.S.) novelist, moral theorist. *The Fountainhead, Atlas Shrugged*.

Terence Rattigan, 1911-77, (Br.) playwright. *Separate Tables, The Browning Version*.

Erich Maria Remarque, 1898-1970, (Ger.-U.S.) novelist. *All Quiet on the Western Front*.

Mary Renault, 1905-83, (Br.) novelist. *The Last of the Wine*.

Ruth Rendell, 1930-2015, (Br.) novelist. Chief Inspector Reginald Wexford mysteries.

Adrienne Rich, 1929-2012, (U.S.) poet. *Diving Into the Wreck: Poems, 1971-1972*.

Samuel Richardson, 1689-1761, (Br.) novelist. *Pamela; or Virtue Rewarded*.

Rainer Maria Rilke, 1875-1926, (Ger.) poet. *Life and Songs, Duino Elegies, Poems From the Book of Hours*.

Arthur Rimbaud, 1854-91, (Fr.) poet. *A Season in Hell*.

Harold Robbins, 1916-97, (U.S.) novelist, *The Carpetbaggers*.

Edwin Arlington Robinson, 1869-1935, (U.S.) poet. "Richard Cory," "Miniver Cheevy," *Merlin*.

Theodore Roethke, 1908-63, (U.S.) poet. *Open House, The Waking, The Far Field*.

Romain Rolland, 1866-1944, (Fr.) novelist, biographer. *Jean-Christophe*.

Pierre de Ronsard, 1524-85, (Fr.) poet. *Sonnets pour Hélène, La Franciade*.

Christina Rossetti, 1830-94, (Br.) poet. "When I Am Dead, My Dearest."

Dante Gabriel Rossetti, 1828-82, (Br.) poet, painter. "The Blessed Damozel."

Edmond Rostand, 1868-1918, (Fr.) poet, dramatist. *Cyrano de Bergerac*.

Philip Roth, 1933-2018, (U.S.) novelist. *Portnoy's Complaint*.

Damon Runyon, 1880-1946, (U.S.) short-story writer, journalist. *Guys and Dolls, Blue Plate Special*.

John Ruskin, 1819-1900, (Br.) critic, social theorist. *Modern Painters, The Seven Lamps of Architecture*.

Oliver Sacks, 1933-2015, (Br.) neurologist, writer. *The Man Who Mistook His Wife for a Hat*.

François Sagan (Françoise Quoirez), 1935-2004, (Fr.) novelist. *Bonjour Tristesse*.

Antoine de Saint-Exupéry, 1900-44, (Fr.) writer. *Wind, Sand and Stars; The Little Prince*.

Saki (or H[ector] H[ugh] Munro), 1870-1916, (Br.) writer. *The Chronicles of Clovis*.

J. D. Salinger, 1919-2010, (U.S.) novelist. *The Catcher in the Rye*.

George Sand (Amandine Lucie Aurore Dupin), 1804-76, (Fr.) novelist. *Indiana, Consuelo*.

Carl Sandburg, 1878-1967, (U.S.) poet. *The People, Yes; Chicago Poems; Smoke and Steel; Harvest Poems*.

José Saramago, 1922-2010, (Port.) novelist. *Blindness*.

William Saroyan, 1908-81, (U.S.) playwright, novelist. *The Time of Your Life, The Human Comedy*.

Nathalie Sarraute, 1900-99, (Fr.) Nouveau Roman novelist. *Tropismes*.

May Sarton, 1914-95, (Belg.-U.S.) poet, novelist. *Encounter in April, Anger*.

Dorothy L. Sayers, 1893-1957, (Br.) mystery writer; created Lord Peter Wimsey.

Richard Scarry, 1920-94, (U.S.) author of children's books. *Richard Scarry's Best Story Book Ever*.

Friedrich von Schiller, 1759-1805, (Ger.) dramatist, poet, historian. *Don Carlos, Maria Stuart, Wilhelm Tell*.

Sir Walter Scott, 1771-1832, (Scot.) novelist, poet. *Ivanhoe*.

Gil Scott-Heron, 1949-2011, (U.S.) poet. "The Revolution Will Not Be Televised."

Jaroslav Seifert, 1902-86, (Czech.) poet.

Maurice Sendak, 1928-2012, (U.S.) children's book author and illustrator. *Where the Wild Things Are*.

Dr. Seuss (Theodor Seuss Geisel), 1904-91, (U.S.) children's book author and illustrator. *The Cat in the Hat*.

William Shakespeare, 1564-1616, (Br.) dramatist, poet. *Romeo and Juliet, Hamlet, King Lear, Julius Caesar*, sonnets.

Karl Shapiro, 1913-2000, (U.S.) poet. "Elegy for a Dead Soldier."

George Bernard Shaw, 1856-1950, (Ire.-Br.) playwright, critic. *St. Joan, Pygmalion, Major Barbara, Man and Superman*.

Sidney Sheldon, 1917-2007, (U.S.) screenwriter, novelist. *Rage of Angels, Memories of Midnight*.

Mary Wollstonecraft Shelley, 1797-1851, (Br.) novelist, feminist. *Frankenstein, The Last Man*.

Percy Bysshe Shelley, 1792-1822, (Br.) poet. *Prometheus Unbound, Adonais*, "Ode to the West Wind," "To a Skylark."

Sam Shepard, 1943-2017, (U.S.) playwright. *Buried Child, True West*.

Richard B. Sheridan, 1751-1816, (Br.) dramatist. *The Rivals, School for Scandal*.

Robert Sherwood, 1896-1955, (U.S.) playwright, biographer. *The Petrified Forest, Abe Lincoln in Illinois*.

Mikhail Sholokhov, 1906-84, (Russ.) writer. *The Silent Don*.

Shel Silverstein, 1932-99, (U.S.) poet, writer. *The Giving Tree, Where the Sidewalk Ends*.

Georges Simenon (Georges Sims), 1903-89, (Belg.-Fr.) mystery writer; created Inspector Maigret.

Neil Simon, 1927-2018, (U.S.) playwright. *The Odd Couple, Brighton Beach Memoirs*.

Upton Sinclair, 1878-1968, (U.S.) novelist. *The Jungle*.

Isaac Bashevis Singer, 1904-91, (Pol.-U.S.) novelist, short-story writer, in Yiddish. *The Magician of Lublin*.

C(harles) P(ercy) Snow, 1905-80, (Br.) novelist, scientist. *Strangers and Brothers, Corridors of Power*.

Aleksandr Solzhenitsyn, 1918-2008, (Russ.) novelist, dramatist. *One Day in the Life of Ivan Denisovich*.

Susan Sontag, 1933-2004, (U.S.) critic, essayist, novelist. *Notes on Camp, The Volcano Lover, In America*.

Stephen Spender, 1909-95, (Br.) poet, critic, novelist. *Twenty Poems*, "Elegy for Margaret."

Edmund Spenser, 1552-99, (Br.) poet. *The Faerie Queene*.

Mickey Spillane, 1918-2006, (U.S.) novelist; Mike Hammer detective novels. *The Killing Man*.

Johanna Spyri, 1827-1901, (Switz.) children's author. *Heidi*.

Christina Stead, 1903-83, (Austral.) novelist, short-story writer. *The Man Who Loved Children*.

Richard Steele, 1672-1729, (Br.) essayist, playwright; began the *Tatler* and *Spectator*. *The Conscious Lovers*.

Gertrude Stein, 1874-1946, (U.S.) writer. *Three Lives*.

John Steinbeck, 1902-68, (U.S.) novelist. *The Grapes of Wrath, Of Mice and Men, The Winter of Our Discontent*.

Stendhal (Marie Henri Beyle), 1783-1842, (Fr.) novelist. *The Red and the Black, The Charterhouse of Parma*.

Laurence Sterne, 1713-68, (Br.) novelist. *Tristram Shandy*.

Wallace Stevens, 1879-1955, (U.S.) poet. *Harmonium, The Man With the Blue Guitar, Notes Toward a Supreme Fiction*.

Robert Louis Stevenson, 1850-94, (Br.) novelist, poet, essayist. *Treasure Island, A Child's Garden of Verses*.

Mary Stewart, 1916-2014, (Br.) novelist. *Merlin* trilogy.

Bram Stoker, 1847-1912, (Br.) writer. *Dracula*.

Rex Stout, 1886-1975, (U.S.) mystery writer; created Nero Wolfe.

Harriet Beecher Stowe, 1811-96, (U.S.) novelist. *Uncle Tom's Cabin*.

Lytton Strachey, 1880-1932, (Br.) biographer, critic. *Eminent Victorians, Queen Victoria, Elizabeth and Essex*.

Mark Strand, 1934-2014, (Can.-U.S.) poet. *Blizzard of One*.

August Strindberg, 1849-1912, (Swed.) dramatist, novelist. *The Father, Miss Julie, The Creditors*.

William Styron, 1925-2006, (U.S.) novelist, essayist. *The Confessions of Nat Turner, Sophie's Choice, Darkness Visible: A Memoir of Madness*.

Jonathan Swift, 1667-1745, (Br.) satirist, poet. *Gulliver's Travels*, "A Modest Proposal."

Algernon C. Swinburne, 1837-1909, (Br.) poet, dramatist. *Atalanta in Calydon*.

John M. Synge, 1871-1909, (Ire.) poet, dramatist. *Riders to the Sea, The Playboy of the Western World*.

Wisława Szymborska, 1923-2012, (Pol.) poet. "Cat in an Empty Apartment."

Rabindranath Tagore, 1861-1941, (India) author, poet. *Sadhana, The Realization of Life, Gitanjali*.

Booth Tarkington, 1869-1946, (U.S.) novelist. *The Magnificent Ambersons*.

Peter Taylor, 1917-94, (U.S.) novelist. *A Summons to Memphis*.

Sara Teasdale, 1884-1933, (U.S.) poet. *Helen of Troy and Other Poems, Rivers to the Sea*.

Alfred, Lord Tennyson, 1809-92, (Br.) poet. *Idylls of the King, In Memoriam*, "The Charge of the Light Brigade."

William Makepeace Thackeray, 1811-63, (Br.) novelist. *Vanity Fair, Henry Esmond, Pendennis*.

Dylan Thomas, 1914-53, (Wales) poet. *Under Milk Wood, A Child's Christmas in Wales*.

Hunter S. Thompson, 1937-2005, (U.S.) author, journalist. *Hell's Angels, Fear and Loathing in Las Vegas*.

Henry David Thoreau, 1817-62, (U.S.) writer, philosopher, naturalist. *Walden*, "Civil Disobedience."

James Thurber, 1894-1961, (U.S.) humorist. "The Secret Life of Walter Mitty," *My Life and Hard Times*.

J(ohn) R(onald) R(euel) Tolkien, 1892-1973, (Br.) writer. *The Hobbit, Lord of the Rings* trilogy.

Leo Tolstoy, 1828-1910, (Russ.) novelist, short-story writer. *War and Peace, Anna Karenina*, "The Death of Ivan Ilyich."

Lionel Trilling, 1905-75, (U.S.) critic, author, teacher. *The Liberal Imagination*.

Anthony Trollope, 1815-82, (Br.) novelist. *The Warden, Barchester Towers*, the Palliser novels.

Ivan Turgenev, 1818-83, (Russ.) novelist, short-story writer. *Fathers and Sons, First Love, A Month in the Country*.

Amos Tutuola, 1920-97, (Nigeria) novelist. *The Palm-Wine Drunkard, My Life in the Bush of Ghosts*.

Mark Twain (Samuel Clemens), 1835-1910, (U.S.) novelist, humorist. *The Adventures of Huckleberry Finn*.

Sigrid Undset, 1881-1949, (Nor.) novelist. *Kristin Lavransdatter*.

John Updike, 1932-2009, (U.S.) novelist, literary critic. *Rabbit is Rich, The Witches of Eastwick*.

Paul Valéry, 1871-1945, (Fr.) poet, critic. *La Jeune Parque, The Graveyard by the Sea*.

Paul Verlaine, 1844-96, (Fr.) Symbolist poet. *Songs Without Words*.

Jules Verne, 1828-1905, (Fr.) novelist. *Twenty Thousand Leagues Under the Sea*.

Gore Vidal, 1925-2012, (U.S.) novelist. *The City and the Pillar*.

François Villon, 1431-c. 1463, (Fr.) poet. *The Lays, The Grand Testament*.

Voltaire (F. M. Arouet), 1694-1778, (Fr.) writer of "philosophical romances"; philosopher, historian. *Candide*.

Kurt Vonnegut Jr., 1922-2007, (U.S.) novelist, essayist. *Cat's Cradle, Slaughterhouse-Five, Breakfast of Champions*.

Derek Walcott, 1930-2016, (St. Lucia) poet. "Omeros."

David Foster Wallace, 1962-2008, (U.S.) novelist, essayist. *Infinite Jest, A Supposedly Fun Thing I'll Never Do Again*.

Robert Penn Warren, 1905-89, (U.S.) novelist, poet, critic. *All the King's Men*.

Wendy Wasserstein, 1950-2006, (U.S.) playwright. *The Heidi Chronicles*.

Evelyn Waugh, 1903-66, (Br.) novelist. *The Loved One, Brideshead Revisited, A Handful of Dust*.

H(erbert) G(eorge) Wells, 1866-1946, (Br.) novelist. *The Time Machine, The Invisible Man, The War of the Worlds*.

Eudora Welty, 1909-2001, (U.S.) Southern short-story writer, novelist. "Why I Live at the P.O.," "The Ponder Heart."

Rebecca West, 1893-1983, (Br.) novelist, critic, journalist. *Black Lamb and Grey Falcon*.

Edith Wharton, 1862-1937, (U.S.) novelist. *The Age of Innocence, The House of Mirth, Ethan Frome*.

Phillis Wheatley, c. 1753-84, (U.S.) poet; 2nd American woman and first black woman to be published, 1770.

E(lwyn) B(rooks) White, 1899-1985, (U.S.) essayist, novelist. *Charlotte's Web, Stuart Little*.

Patrick White, 1912-90, (Austral.) novelist. *The Tree of Man*.

T(erence) H(anbury) White, 1906-64, (Br.) author. *The Once and Future King, A Book of Beasts*.

Walt Whitman, 1819-92, (U.S.) poet. *Leaves of Grass*.

John Greenleaf Whittier, 1807-92, (U.S.) poet, journalist. *Snow-Bound*.

Elie Wiesel, 1928-2016, (Rom.) memoirist, novelist. *Night*.

Oscar Wilde, 1854-1900, (Ire.) novelist, playwright. *The Picture of Dorian Gray, The Importance of Being Earnest*.

Laura Ingalls Wilder, 1867-1957, (U.S.) novelist. Little House on the Prairie series of children's books.

Thornton Wilder, 1897-1975, (U.S.) playwright. Our Town, The Skin of Our Teeth, The Matchmaker.

Tennessee Williams, 1911-83, (U.S.) playwright. A Streetcar Named Desire, Cat on a Hot Tin Roof, The Glass Menagerie.

William Carlos Williams, 1883-1963, (U.S.) poet, physician. The Tempers, Al Que Quiere! Paterson, "This Is Just to Say."

Edmund Wilson, 1895-1972, (U.S.) critic, novelist. Axel's Castle, To the Finland Station.

Lanford Wilson, 1937-2011, (U.S.) playwright. Talley's Folly, Fifth of July.

P(elham) G(renville) Wodehouse, 1881-1975, (Br.-U.S.) humorist. Jeeves novels, Anything Goes.

Thomas Wolfe, 1900-38, (U.S.) novelist, journalist. Look Homeward, Angel; You Can't Go Home Again.

Tom Wolfe, 1930-2018, (U.S.) novelist, journalist. Bonfire of the Vanities, The Right Stuff.

Virginia Woolf, 1882-1941, (Br.) novelist, essayist. Mrs. Dalloway, To the Lighthouse, A Room of One's Own.

William Wordsworth, 1770-1850, (Br.) poet. "Tintern Abbey," "Ode: Intimations of Immortality," The Prelude.

Richard Wright, 1908-60, (U.S.) novelist, short-story writer. Native Son, Black Boy, Uncle Tom's Children.

Elinor Wylie, 1885-1928, (U.S.) poet. Nets to Catch the Wind.

William Butler Yeats, 1865-1939, (Ire.) poet, playwright. "The Second Coming," The Wild Swans at Coole.

Frank Yerby, 1916-91, (U.S.) first best-selling African American novelist. The Foxes of Harrow.

Yevgeny Yevtushenko, 1933-2017, (Russ.) poet. "Babi Yar."

Émile Zola, 1840-1902, (Fr.) novelist. Nana, Thérèse Raquin.

Poets Laureate

There is no record of the origin of the office of Poet Laureate of England. Henry III (1216-72) reportedly had a Versificator Regis, or King's Poet, paid 100 shillings per year. Other poets said to have filled the role include Geoffrey Chaucer (d 1400), Edmund Spenser (d 1599), Ben Jonson (d 1637), and Sir William d'Avenant (d 1668). The first official English poet laureate was John Dryden, appointed 1668, for life (as was customary). Then came Thomas Shadwell, in 1689; Nahum Tate, 1692; Nicholas Rowe, 1715; Rev. Laurence Eusden, 1718; Colley Cibber, 1730; William Whitehead, 1757; Rev. Thomas Warton, 1785; Henry James Pye, 1790; Robert Southey, 1813; William Wordsworth, 1843; Alfred, Lord Tennyson, 1850; Alfred Austin, 1896; Robert Bridges, 1913; John Masefield, 1930; C. Day Lewis, 1968; Sir John Betjeman, 1972; Ted Hughes, 1984; Andrew Motion, 1999; and Carol Ann Duffy, 2009.

In the U.S., appointment is by the Librarian of Congress to a term of one year, which may be renewed: Robert Penn Warren, appointed 1986; Richard Wilbur, 1987; Howard Nemerov, 1988; Mark Strand, 1990; Joseph Brodsky, 1991; Mona Van Duyn, 1992; Rita Dove, 1993; Robert Hass, 1995; Robert Pinsky, 1997; Stanley Kunitz, 2000; Billy Collins, 2001; Louise Glück, 2003; Ted Kooser, 2004; Donald Hall, 2006; Charles Simic, 2007; Kay Ryan, 2008; W. S. Merwin, 2010; Philip Levine, 2011; Natasha Trethewey, 2012; Charles Wright, 2014; Juan Felipe Herrera, 2015; Tracy K. Smith, 2017.

Composers of Classical and Avant-Garde Music

John Adams, b 1947, (U.S.) Nixon in China, The Death of Klinghoffer.

Milton Babbitt, 1916-2011, (U.S.) serial and electronic music.

Carl Philipp Emanuel Bach, 1714-88, (Ger.) cantatas, passions, numerous keyboard and instrumental works.

Johann Christian Bach, 1735-82, (Ger.) concertos, operas, sonatas. Known as the "English" Bach.

Johann Sebastian Bach, 1685-1750, (Ger.) St. Matthew Passion, The Well-Tempered Clavier.

Samuel Barber, 1910-81, (U.S.) Adagio for Strings, Vanessa.

Béla Bartók, 1881-1945, (Hung.) Concerto for Orchestra, The Miraculous Mandarin.

Amy Beach (Mrs. H. H. A. Beach), 1867-1944, (U.S.) The Year's at the Spring, Fireflies, The Chambered Nautilus.

Ludwig van Beethoven, 1770-1827, (Ger.) concertos (Emperor), sonatas (Moonlight, Pathétique), 9 symphonies.

Vincenzo Bellini, 1801-35, (It.) I Puritani, La Sonnambula, Norma.

Alban Berg, 1885-1935, (Austria) Wozzeck, Lulu.

Hector Berlioz, 1803-69, (Fr.) Damnation of Faust, Symphonie Fantastique, Requiem.

Leonard Bernstein, 1918-90, (U.S.) Chichester Psalms, Jeremiah Symphony, Mass.

Georges Bizet, 1838-75, (Fr.) Carmen, Pearl Fishers.

Ernest Bloch, 1880-1959, (Switz.-U.S.) Macbeth (opera), Schelomo, Voice in the Wilderness.

Luigi Boccherini, 1743-1805, (It.) chamber music and guitar pieces.

Alexander Borodin, 1833-87, (Russ.) Prince Igor, In the Steppes of Central Asia, Polovtzian Dances.

Pierre Boulez, 1925-2016, (Fr.) Le Visage nuptial, Éclat/Multiples, Domaines.

Johannes Brahms, 1833-97, (Ger.) Liebeslieder Waltzes, Academic Festival Overture, chamber music, 4 symphonies.

Henry Brant, 1913-2008, (Can.) spatial music.

Benjamin Britten, 1913-76, (Br.) Peter Grimes, Turn of the Screw, A Ceremony of Carols, War Requiem.

Anton Bruckner, 1824-96, (Austria) 9 symphonies.

Dietrich Buxtehude, 1637-1707, (Den.) organ works, vocal music.

William Byrd, 1543-1623, (Br.) masses, motets.

John Cage, 1912-92, (U.S.) Winter Music, Fontana Mix.

Elliott Carter, 1908-2012, (U.S.) Second String Quartet, Third String Quartet.

Emmanuel Chabrier, 1841-94, (Fr.) Le Roi Malgré Lui, España.

Gustave Charpentier, 1860-1956, (Fr.) Louise.

Frédéric Chopin, 1810-49, (Pol.) mazurkas, waltzes, etudes, nocturnes, polonaises, sonatas.

Aaron Copland, 1900-90, (U.S.) Appalachian Spring, Fanfare for the Common Man, Lincoln Portrait.

John Corigliano, b 1938, (U.S.) Symphony No. 2.

Paul Creston, 1906-85, (U.S.) Walt Whitman.

Claude Debussy, 1862-1918, (Fr.) Pelleas et Melisande, La Mer, Prelude to the Afternoon of a Faun.

David Del Tredici, b 1937, (U.S.) Child Alice, In Memory of a Summer Day.

Gaetano Donizetti, 1797-1848, (It.) Elixir of Love, Lucia di Lammermoor, Daughter of the Regiment.

Paul Dukas, 1865-1935, (Fr.) Sorcerer's Apprentice.

Antonín Dvořák, 1841-1904, (Czech.) Songs My Mother Taught Me, Symphony in E Minor (From the New World).

Edward Elgar, 1857-1934, (Br.) Enigma Variations, Pomp and Circumstance.

Manuel de Falla, 1876-1946, (Sp.) El Amor Brujo, La Vida Breve, The Three-Cornered Hat.

Gabriel Fauré, 1845-1924, (Fr.) Requiem, Elègie for Cello and Piano.

Cesar Franck, 1822-90, (Belg.) Symphony in D minor, Violin Sonata.

George Gershwin, 1898-1937, (U.S.) Rhapsody in Blue, An American in Paris, Porgy and Bess.

Philip Glass, b 1937, (U.S.) Einstein on the Beach, The Voyage.

Mikhail Glinka, 1804-57, (Russ.) A Life for the Tsar, Ruslan and Ludmilla.

Christoph W. Gluck, 1714-87, (Ger.) Alceste, Iphigènie en Tauride.

Henryk Gorecki, 1933-2010, (Pol.) Symphony no. 3 (Symphony of Sorrowing Songs).

Charles Gounod, 1818-93, (Fr.) Faust, Romeo and Juliet.

Percy Grainger, 1882-1961, (Austral.) Country Gardens.

Edvard Grieg, 1843-1907, (Nor.) Peer Gynt Suite, Concerto in A minor for piano.

George Frideric Handel, 1685-1759, (Ger.-Br.) Messiah, Water Music.

Howard Hanson, 1896-1981, (U.S.) Symphonies No. 1 (Nordic) and No. 2 (Romantic).

Roy Harris, 1898-1979, (U.S.) symphonies.

(Franz) Joseph Haydn, 1732-1809, (Austria) symphonies (Clock, London, Toy), chamber music, oratorios.

Hildegard von Bingen, 1098-1179, (Ger.) Ordo virtutum.

Paul Hindemith, 1895-1963, (U.S.) Mathis der Maler.

Gustav Holst, 1874-1934, (Br.) The Planets.

Arthur Honegger, 1892-1955, (Fr.) Judith, Le Roi David, Pacific 231.

Alan Hovhaness, 1911-2000, (U.S.) symphonies, Magnificat.

Engelbert Humperdinck, 1854-1921, (Ger.) Hansel and Gretel.

Charles Ives, 1874-1954, (U.S.) Concord Sonata, symphonies.

Aram Khachaturian, 1903-78, (Russ.) ballets, piano pieces, Sabre Dance.

Zoltán Kodaly, 1882-1967, (Hung.) Háry János, Psalmus Hungaricus.

Fritz Kreisler, 1875-1962, (Austria) Caprice Viennois, Tambourin Chinois.

Edouard Lalo, 1823-92, (Fr.) Symphonie Espagnole.

David Lang, b 1957, (U.S.) The Little Match Girl Passion.

Morten Lauridsen, b 1943, (U.S.) Lux Aeterna.

Ruggero Leoncavallo, 1857-1919, (It.) Pagliacci.

György Ligeti, 1923-2006, (Rom.) Atmosphères, Requiem.

Franz Liszt, 1811-86, (Hung.) 20 Hungarian rhapsodies, symphonic poems.

Edward MacDowell, 1861-1908, (U.S.) To a Wild Rose.

Gustav Mahler, 1860-1911, (Austria) Das Lied von der Erde; 9 complete symphonies.

Pietro Mascagni, 1863-1945, (It.) Cavalleria Rusticana.

Jules Massenet, 1842-1912, (Fr.) *Manon, Le Cid, Thaïs.*

Felix Mendelssohn, 1809-47, (Ger.) *A Midsummer Night's Dream, Songs Without Words,* violin concerto.

Gian Carlo Menotti, 1911-2007, (It.-U.S.) *The Medium, The Consul, Amahl and the Night Visitors.*

Olivier Messiaen, 1908-1992, (Fr.) *Apparition de l'Église Éternelle.*

Claudio Monteverdi, 1567-1643, (It.) opera, masses, madrigals.

Wolfgang Amadeus Mozart, 1756-91, (Austria) chamber music, concertos, operas (*Magic Flute, Marriage of Figaro*), 41 symphonies.

Modest Mussorgsky, 1839-81, (Russ.) *Boris Godunov, Pictures at an Exhibition.*

Carl Nielsen, 1865-1931, (Den.) *Saul og David.*

Jacques Offenbach, 1819-80, (Fr.) *Tales of Hoffmann.*

Carl Orff, 1895-1982, (Ger.) *Carmina Burana.*

Johann Pachelbel, 1653-1706, (Ger.) Canon and Fugue in D major.

Ignacy Paderewski, 1860-1941, (Pol.) Minuet in G.

Niccolò Paganini, 1782-1840, (It.) Caprices for violin solo.

Giovanni Palestrina, c. 1525-94, (It.) masses, madrigals.

Arvo Pärt, b 1935, (Eston.) sacred music. *Fratres, Cantus in memoriam Benjamin Britten, Tabula Rasa.*

Krzysztof Penderecki, b 1933, (Pol.) *Psalmus, Polymorphia, De natura sonoris.*

Francis Poulenc, 1899-1963, (Fr.) *Dialogues des Carmélites.*

Mel Powell, 1923-98, (U.S.) *Duplicates: A Concerto for Two Pianos and Orchestra, Cantilena Concertante.*

Sergei Prokofiev, 1891-1953, (Russ.) *Classical Symphony, Love for Three Oranges, Peter and the Wolf.*

Giacomo Puccini, 1858-1924, (It.) *La Boheme, Manon Lescaut, Tosca, Madama Butterfly.*

Henry Purcell, 1659-95, (Br.) *Dido and Aeneas.*

Sergei Rachmaninoff, 1873-1943, (Russ.) concertos, preludes (Prelude in C sharp minor), symphonies.

Maurice Ravel, 1875-1937, (Fr.) *Boléro, Daphnis et Chloë,* Piano Concerto in D for Left Hand Alone.

Steve Reich, b 1936, (U.S.) *Double Sextet, Three Tales.*

Nikolai Rimsky-Korsakov, 1844-1908, (Russ.) *Golden Cockerel, Scheherazade, Flight of the Bumblebee.*

Gioachino Rossini, 1792-1868, (It.) *Barber of Seville, Otello, William Tell.*

John Rutter, b 1945, (Br.) *Magnificat, Requiem.*

Camille Saint-Saëns, 1835-1921, (Fr.) *Carnival of Animals (The Swan), Samson and Delilah, Danse Macabre.*

Alessandro Scarlatti, 1660-1725, (It.) cantatas, oratorios, operas.

Domenico Scarlatti, 1685-1757, (It.) harpsichord works.

Alfred Schnittke, 1934-98 (Russ.-Ger.) *Life With an Idiot.*

Arnold Schoenberg, 1874-1951, (Austria) *Pelleas and Melisande, Pierrot Lunaire, Verklärte Nacht.*

Franz Schubert, 1797-1828, (Austria) chamber music (*Trout Quintet*), lieder, symphonies ("Unfinished").

Robert Schumann, 1810-56, (Ger.) *Die Frauenliebe und Leben, Träumerei.*

Dmitri Shostakovich, 1906-75, (Russ.) symphonies, *Lady Macbeth of the District Mzensk.*

Jean Sibelius, 1865-1957, (Fin.) *Finlandia.*

Bedrich Smetana, 1824-84, (Czech.) *The Bartered Bride.*

Karlheinz Stockhausen, 1928-2008, (Ger.) *Kontra-Punkte, Kontakte for Electronic Instruments.*

Richard Strauss, 1864-1949, (Ger.) *Salome, Elektra, Der Rosenkavalier, Thus Spake Zarathustra.*

Igor Stravinsky, 1882-1971, (Russ.) *Noah and the Flood, The Rake's Progress, The Rite of Spring.*

Toru Takemitsu, 1930-96, (Jpn.) *Requiem for Strings, Dorian Horizon.*

Thomas Tallis, c. 1505-85, (Br.) anthems, motets.

Peter I. Tchaikovsky, 1840-93, (Russ.) *Nutcracker, Swan Lake, The Sleeping Beauty.*

Georg Philipp Telemann, 1681-1767, (Ger.) church music, orchestral suites, chamber music.

Virgil Thomson, 1896-1989, (U.S.) opera, film music, *Four Saints in Three Acts.*

Dmitri Tiomkin, 1894-1979, (Russ.-U.S.) film scores, including *High Noon.*

Sir Michael Tippett, 1905-98, (Br.) *A Child of Our Time, The Midsummer Marriage, The Knot Garden.*

Michael Torke, b 1961, (U.S.) *Bright Blue Music, Ecstatic Orange.*

Eric Whitacre, b 1970, (U.S.) *Cloudburst.*

Ralph Vaughan Williams, 1872-1958, (Br.) *Fantasia on a Theme by Thomas Tallis,* symphonies, vocal music.

Giuseppe Verdi, 1813-1901, (It.) *Aida, Rigoletto, Don Carlo, Il Trovatore, La Traviata, Falstaff, Macbeth.*

Heitor Villa-Lobos, 1887-1959, (Braz.) *Bachianas Brasileiras.*

Antonio Vivaldi, 1678-1741, (It.) Concerto grossos (*The Four Seasons*).

Richard Wagner, 1813-83, (Ger.) *Rienzi, Tannhäuser, Lohengrin, Tristan und Isolde.*

William Walton, 1902-83, (Br.) *Façade, Belshazzar's Feast.*

Carl Maria von Weber, 1786-1826, (Ger.) *Der Freischutz.*

Composers of Operettas, Musicals, and Popular Music

Richard Adler, 1921-2012, (U.S.) *Pajama Game; Damn Yankees.*

Milton Ager, 1893-1979, (U.S.) "I Wonder What's Become of Sally"; "Hard-Hearted Hannah"; "Ain't She Sweet?"

Leroy Anderson, 1908-75, (U.S.) "Sleigh Ride"; "Blue Tango"; "Syncopated Clock."

Paul Anka, b 1941, (Can.) "My Way"; *Tonight Show* theme.

Harold Arlen, 1905-86, (U.S.) "Stormy Weather"; "Over the Rainbow"; "Blues in the Night"; "That Old Black Magic."

Burt Bacharach, b 1928, (U.S.) "Raindrops Keep Fallin' on My Head"; "Walk on By"; "What the World Needs Now Is Love."

Ernest Ball, 1878-1927, (U.S.) "Mother Machree"; "When Irish Eyes Are Smiling."

John Barry, 1933-2011, (U.S.) *Born Free; Lion in Winter; Out of Africa.*

Irving Berlin, 1888-1989, (U.S.) *Annie Get Your Gun; Call Me Madam;* "God Bless America"; "White Christmas."

Leonard Bernstein, 1918-90, (U.S.) *On the Town; Wonderful Town; Candide; West Side Story.*

Eubie Blake, 1883-1983, (U.S.) *Shuffle Along;* "I'm Just Wild About Harry."

Jerry Bock, 1928-2010, (U.S.) *Mr. Wonderful; Fiorello; Fiddler on the Roof; The Rothschilds.*

Carrie Jacobs Bond, 1862-1946, (U.S.) "I Love You Truly."

Nacio Herb Brown, 1896-1964, (U.S.) "Singing in the Rain"; "You Were Meant for Me"; "All I Do Is Dream of You."

Hoagy Carmichael, 1899-1981, (U.S.) "Stardust"; "Georgia on My Mind"; "Old Buttermilk Sky."

James Cleveland, 1931-91, (U.S.) composer, musician, singer; first black gospel artist to appear at Carnegie Hall.

George M. Cohan, 1878-1942, (U.S.) "Give My Regards to Broadway"; "You're a Grand Old Flag"; "Over There."

Cy Coleman, 1929-2004, (U.S.) *Sweet Charity;* "Witchcraft."

John Frederick Coots, 1895-1985, (U.S.) "Santa Claus Is Coming to Town"; "You Go to My Head"; "For All We Know."

Noël Coward, 1899-1973, (Br.) *Bitter Sweet;* "Mad Dogs and Englishmen"; "Mad About the Boy."

Neil Diamond, b 1941, (U.S.) "I'm a Believer"; "Sweet Caroline."

Walter Donaldson, 1893-1947, (U.S.) "My Buddy"; "Carolina in the Morning"; "Makin' Whoopee."

Vernon Duke, 1903-69, (U.S.) "April in Paris."

Bob Dylan, b 1941, (U.S.) "Blowin' in the Wind"; "Like a Rolling Stone."

Gus Edwards, 1879-1945, (U.S.) "School Days"; "By the Light of the Silvery Moon"; "In My Merry Oldsmobile."

Sherman Edwards, 1919-81, (U.S.) "See You in September"; "Wonderful! Wonderful!"

Duke Ellington, 1899-1974, (U.S.) "Sophisticated Lady"; "Satin Doll"; "It Don't Mean a Thing"; "Solitude."

Sammy Fain, 1902-89, (U.S.) "I'll Be Seeing You"; "Love Is a Many-Splendored Thing."

Fred Fisher, 1875-1942, (U.S.) "Peg O' My Heart"; "Chicago."

Stephen Collins Foster, 1826-64, (U.S.) "My Old Kentucky Home"; "Old Folks at Home"; "Beautiful Dreamer."

Rudolf Friml, 1879-1972, (Czech.-U.S.) *The Firefly; Rose Marie; Vagabond King; Bird of Paradise.*

John Gay, 1685-1732, (Br.) *The Beggar's Opera.*

George Gershwin, 1898-1937, (U.S.) "Someone to Watch Over Me"; "I've Got a Crush on You"; "Embraceable You."

Morton Gould, 1913-96, (U.S.) "Fall River Suite"; "Holocaust Suite"; "Spirituals for Orchestra"; "Stringmusic."

Ferde Grofe, 1892-1972, (U.S.) "Grand Canyon Suite."

Marvin Hamlisch, 1944-2012, (U.S.) "The Way We Were"; "Nobody Does It Better"; *A Chorus Line.*

Ray Henderson, 1896-1970, (U.S.) *George White's Scandals;* "That Old Gang of Mine"; "Five Foot Two, Eyes of Blue."

Victor Herbert, 1859-1924, (Ire.-U.S.) *Mlle. Modiste; Babes in Toyland; The Red Mill; Naughty Marietta; Sweethearts.*

Jerry Herman, b 1931, (U.S.) *Hello, Dolly!; Mame.*

Brian Holland, b 1941, **Lamont Dozier**, b 1941, **Eddie Holland**, b 1939, (all U.S.) "Heat Wave"; "Stop! In the Name of Love"; "Baby, I Need Your Loving."

Rupert Holmes, b 1947, (Br.-U.S.) *The Mystery of Edwin Drood; Curtains.*

James Horner, 1953-2015, (U.S.) *Titanic;* "Somewhere Out There"; "My Heart Will Go On."

Antonio Carlos Jobim, 1927-94, (Brazil) "The Girl From Ipanema"; "Desafinado"; "One Note Samba."

Billy Joel (William Martin), b 1949, (U.S.) "Just the Way You Are"; "Honesty"; "Piano Man."

Elton John, b 1947, (Br.) *The Lion King;* "Candle in the Wind"; "Your Song."

Scott Joplin, 1868-1917, (U.S.) Maple Leaf Rag; *Treemonisha.*

John Kander, b 1927, (U.S.) *Cabaret; Chicago; Funny Lady.*

Jerome Kern, 1885-1945, (U.S.) *Sally; Sunny; Show Boat.*

Carole King, b 1942, (U.S.) "Will You Love Me Tomorrow?"; "Natural Woman"; "One Fine Day"; "Up on the Roof."

Burton Lane, 1912-97, (U.S.) *Finian's Rainbow.*

Jonathan Larson, 1960-96, (U.S.) *tick, tick... BOOM!; Rent.*

Franz Lehar, 1870-1948, (Hung.) *Merry Widow*.

Jerry Leiber, 1933-2011, and **Mike Stoller**, b 1933, (both U.S.) "Hound Dog"; "Searchin'"; "Yakety Yak"; "Love Me Tender."

Mitch Leigh, 1928-2014, (U.S.) *Man of La Mancha*.

John Lennon, 1940-80, and **Paul McCartney**, b 1942, (both Br.) "I Want to Hold Your Hand"; "She Loves You."

Jay Livingston, 1915-2001, (U.S.) "Mona Lisa"; "Que Sera, Sera."

Andrew Lloyd Webber, b 1948, (Br.) *Jesus Christ Superstar*; *Evita*; *Cats*; *The Phantom of the Opera*.

Frank Loesser, 1910-69, (U.S.) *Guys and Dolls*; *Where's Charley?*; *The Most Happy Fella*; *How to Succeed in Business….*

Frederick Loewe, 1901-88, (Austria-U.S.) *Brigadoon*; *Paint Your Wagon*; *My Fair Lady*; *Camelot*.

Robert Lopez, b 1975, (U.S.) *Avenue Q*; *The Book of Mormon*; *Frozen*.

Henry Mancini, 1924-94, (U.S.) "Moon River"; "Days of Wine and Roses"; "Pink Panther Theme."

Barry Mann, b 1939, and **Cynthia Weil**, b 1937, (both U.S.) "You've Lost That Loving Feeling."

Hugh Martin, 1914-2011, (U.S.) "Have Yourself a Merry Little Christmas"; "The Trolley Song."

Jimmy McHugh, 1894-1969, (U.S.) "Don't Blame Me"; "I'm in the Mood for Love"; "I Feel a Song Coming On."

Alan Menken, b 1949, (U.S.) *Little Shop of Horrors*; *Beauty and the Beast*.

Joseph Meyer, 1894-1987, (U.S.) "If You Knew Susie"; "California, Here I Come"; "Crazy Rhythm."

Lin-Manuel Miranda, b 1980, (U.S.) *In the Heights*; *Hamilton*.

Willie Nelson, b 1933, (U.S.) "Crazy"; "On the Road Again."

Chauncey Olcott, 1858-1932, (U.S.) "Mother Machree."

Jerome "Doc" Pomus, 1925-91, (U.S.) "Save the Last Dance for Me"; "A Teenager in Love."

Cole Porter, 1891-1964, (U.S.) *Anything Goes*; *Kiss Me Kate*; *Can Can*; *Silk Stockings*.

Smokey Robinson, b 1940, (U.S.) "Shop Around"; "My Guy"; "My Girl"; "Get Ready."

Richard Rodgers, 1902-79, (U.S.) *Oklahoma!*; *Carousel*; *South Pacific*; *The King and I*; *The Sound of Music*.

Sigmund Romberg, 1887-1951, (Hung.) *Maytime*; *The Student Prince*; *Desert Song*; *Blossom Time*.

Harold Rome, 1908-93, (U.S.) *Pins and Needles*; *Call Me Mister*; *Wish You Were Here*; *Fanny*; *Destry Rides Again*.

Vincent Rose, 1880-1944, (U.S.) "Avalon"; "Whispering"; "Blueberry Hill."

Harry Ruby, 1895-1974, (U.S.) "Three Little Words"; "Who's Sorry Now?"

Arthur Schwartz, 1900-84, (U.S.) *The Band Wagon*; "Dancing in the Dark"; "By Myself"; "That's Entertainment."

Steven Schwartz, b 1948, (U.S.) *Godspell*; *Pippin*; *Wicked*.

Neil Sedaka, b 1939, (U.S.) "Breaking Up Is Hard to Do."

Marc Shaiman, b 1959, (U.S.) *Hairspray*.

Paul Simon, b 1942, (U.S.) "Sounds of Silence"; "I Am a Rock"; "Mrs. Robinson"; "Bridge Over Troubled Waters."

Stephen Sondheim, b 1930, (U.S.) *A Little Night Music*; *Company*; *Sweeney Todd*; *Sunday in the Park With George*.

John Philip Sousa, 1854-1932, (U.S.) *El Capitan*; "Stars and Stripes Forever."

Oskar Straus, 1870-1954, (Austrian) *Chocolate Soldier*.

Johann Strauss, 1825-99, (Austrian) *Gypsy Baron*; *Die Fledermaus*; waltzes: Blue Danube; Artist's Life.

Charles Strouse, b 1928, (U.S.) *Bye Bye, Birdie*; *Annie*.

Jule Styne, 1905-94, (Br.-U.S.) *Gentlemen Prefer Blondes*; *Bells Are Ringing*; *Gypsy*; *Funny Girl*.

Arthur S. Sullivan, 1842-1900, (Br.) *H.M.S. Pinafore*; *Pirates of Penzance*; *The Mikado*.

Deems Taylor, 1885-1966, (U.S.) *Peter Ibbetson*.

Jeanine Tesori, 1971, (U.S.) *Fun Home*, *Shrek the Musical*.

Harry Tobias, 1905-94, (U.S.) *I'll Keep the Lovelight Burning*.

Egbert van Alstyne, 1882-1951, (U.S.) "In the Shade of the Old Apple Tree"; "Memories"; "Pretty Baby."

Jimmy Van Heusen, 1913-90, (U.S.) "Moonlight Becomes You"; "Swinging on a Star"; "All the Way"; "Love and Marriage."

Albert von Tilzer, 1878-1956, (U.S.) "I'll Be With You in Apple Blossom Time"; "Take Me Out to the Ball Game."

Harry von Tilzer, 1872-1946, (U.S.) "Only a Bird in a Gilded Cage"; "Wait 'til the Sun Shines, Nellie."

Fats Waller, 1904-43, (U.S.) "Honeysuckle Rose"; "Ain't Misbehavin'."

Harry Warren, 1893-1981, (U.S.) "You're My Everything"; "We're in the Money"; "I Only Have Eyes for You."

Jimmy Webb, b 1946, (U.S.) "Up, Up and Away"; "By the Time I Get to Phoenix"; "Didn't We?"; "Wichita Lineman."

Kurt Weill, 1900-50, (Ger.-U.S.) *Threepenny Opera*; *Lady in the Dark*; *Knickerbocker Holiday*; *One Touch of Venus*.

Percy Wenrich, 1887-1952, (U.S.) "When You Wore a Tulip"; "Moonlight Bay"; "Put On Your Old Gray Bonnet."

Richard A. Whiting, 1891-1938, (U.S.) "Till We Meet Again"; "Sleepytime Gal"; "Beyond the Blue Horizon"; "My Ideal."

Frank Wildhorn, b 1959, (U.S.) *Jekyll and Hyde*; *Victor/Victoria*; *The Civil War*.

John Williams, b 1932, (U.S.) *Jaws*; *E.T.*; *Star Wars* series; *Raiders of the Lost Ark* series.

Meredith Willson, 1902-84, (U.S.) *The Music Man*.

Stevie Wonder, b 1950, (U.S.) "You Are the Sunshine of My Life"; "Signed, Sealed, Delivered, I'm Yours."

Vincent Youmans, 1898-1946, (U.S.) *Two Little Girls in Blue*; *Wildflower*; *No, No, Nanette*; *Hit the Deck*; *Rainbow*; *Smiles*.

Lyricists

Howard Ashman, 1950-91, (U.S.) *Little Shop of Horrors*; *The Little Mermaid*.

Johnny Burke, 1908-84, (U.S.) "Misty"; "Imagination."

Irving Caesar, 1895-1996, (U.S.) "Swanee"; "Tea for Two"; "Just a Gigolo."

Sammy Cahn, 1913-93, (U.S.) "High Hopes"; "Love and Marriage"; "The Second Time Around"; "It's Magic."

Leonard Cohen, 1934-2016, (Can.) "Suzanne"; "Hallelujah."

Betty Comden, 1917-2006, and **Adolph Green**, 1915-2002, (both U.S.) "The Party's Over"; "New York, New York."

Hal David, 1921-2012, (U.S.) "What the World Needs Now Is Love."

Buddy De Sylva, 1895-1950, (U.S.) "When Day Is Done"; "Look for the Silver Lining"; "April Showers."

Howard Dietz, 1896-1983, (U.S.) "Dancing in the Dark"; "That's Entertainment."

Al Dubin, 1891-1945, (U.S.) "Tiptoe Through the Tulips"; "Lullaby of Broadway."

Fred Ebb, 1936-2004, (U.S.) *Cabaret*; *Zorba*; *Woman of the Year*; *Chicago*.

Ray Evans, 1915-2007, (U.S.) "Mona Lisa"; "Que Sera, Sera."

Dorothy Fields, 1905-74, (U.S.) "On the Sunny Side of the Street"; "Don't Blame Me"; "The Way You Look Tonight."

Ira Gershwin, 1896-1983, (U.S.) "The Man I Love"; "S'Wonderful"; "Embraceable You."

William S. Gilbert, 1836-1911, (Br.) *H.M.S. Pinafore*; *Pirates of Penzance*.

Gerry Goffin, 1939-2014, (U.S.) "Will You Love Me Tomorrow"; "Take Good Care of My Baby"; "Up on the Roof."

Mack Gordon, 1905-59, (Pol.-U.S.) "You'll Never Know"; "The More I See You"; "Chattanooga Choo-Choo."

Oscar Hammerstein II, 1895-1960, (U.S.) *Show Boat*; *Oklahoma!*; *Carousel*.

E. Y. (Yip) Harburg, 1898-1981, (U.S.) "Brother, Can You Spare a Dime"; "April in Paris"; "Over the Rainbow."

Sheldon Harnick, b 1924, (U.S.) *Fiddler on the Roof*; *She Loves Me*.

Lorenz Hart, 1895-1943, (U.S.) "Isn't It Romantic"; "Blue Moon"; "Lover"; "Manhattan"; "My Funny Valentine."

DuBose Heyward, 1885-1940, (U.S.) "Summertime."

Gus Kahn, 1886-1941, (U.S.) "Memories"; "Ain't We Got Fun."

Alan J. Lerner, 1918-86, (U.S.) *Brigadoon*; *My Fair Lady*; *Camelot*; *Gigi*; *On a Clear Day You Can See Forever*.

Johnny Mercer, 1909-76, (U.S.) "Blues in the Night"; "Come Rain or Come Shine"; "Laura"; "That Old Black Magic."

Bob Merrill, 1921-98, (U.S.) "People"; "(How Much Is That) Doggie in the Window."

Jack Norworth, 1879-1959, (U.S.) "Take Me Out to the Ball Game"; "Shine On Harvest Moon."

Mitchell Parish, 1901-93, (U.S.) "Stardust"; "Stairway to the Stars."

Andy Razaf, 1895-1973, (U.S.) "Honeysuckle Rose"; "Ain't Misbehavin."

Leo Robin, 1900-84, (U.S.) "Thanks for the Memory"; "Diamonds Are a Girl's Best Friend."

Robert Sherman, 1925-2012, (U.S.) *Mary Poppins*; *The Jungle Book*.

Bernie Taupin, b 1947 (Br.) "Rocket Man"; "Your Song."

Paul Francis Webster, 1907-84, (U.S.) "Secret Love"; "The Shadow of Your Smile"; "Love Is a Many-Splendored Thing."

Jack Yellen, 1892-1991, (U.S.) "Ain't She Sweet"; "Happy Days Are Here Again."

Blues and Jazz Artists of the Past

Julian "Cannonball" Adderley, 1928-75, alto sax.

Nat Adderley, 1931-2000, cornet.

Henry "Red" Allen, 1908-67, trumpet.

Mose Allison, 1927-2016, piano.

Louis "Satchmo" Armstrong, 1901-71, trumpet, singer, bandleader.

Albert Ayler, 1936-70, tenor sax, alto sax.

Mildred Bailey, 1907-51, singer.

Chet Baker, 1929-88, trumpet, singer.

Ray Barretto, 1930-2006, conga drummer.

William "Count" Basie, 1904-84, bandleader, piano, composer.

Sidney Bechet, 1897-1959, soprano sax, clarinet.

Bix Beiderbecke, 1903-31, cornet, composer, piano.

Rowland "Bunny" Berigan, 1908-42, trumpet.

Barney Bigard, 1906-80, clarinet.

Eubie Blake, 1883-1983, composer, piano.

Art Blakey, 1919-90, drums, bandleader.

Jimmy Blanton, 1921-42, bass.

Charles "Buddy" Bolden, 1877-1931, cornet, pioneer bandleader.

Lester Bowie, 1941-99, trumpet, composer, bandleader.

Michael Brecker, 1949-2007, saxophone.

Big Bill Broonzy, 1893-1958, blues singer, guitar.

Clarence "Gatemouth" Brown, 1924-2005, guitar, singer.

Clifford Brown, 1930-56, trumpet.

Ray Brown, 1926-2002, bass.

Dave Brubeck, 1920-2012, piano, bandleader.

Don Byas, 1912-72, tenor sax.

Charlie Byrd, 1925-99, guitar; popularized bossa nova.

Cab Calloway, 1907-94, bandleader, singer.

Harry Carney, 1910-74, baritone sax, clarinet.

Benny Carter, 1907-2003, alto sax.

Betty Carter, 1930-98, jazz singer.
Sidney "Big Sid" Catlett, 1910-51, drums.
Adolphus Anthony "Doc" Cheatham, 1905-97, trumpet.
Don Cherry, 1936-95, trumpet.
Charlie Christian, 1916-42, guitar.
Kenny "Klook" Clarke, 1914-85, drums.
Buck Clayton, 1911-91, trumpet.
Al Cohn, 1925-88, tenor sax.
Nat "King" Cole, 1919-65, piano, singer.
William "Cozy" Cole, 1909-81, drums.
Ornette Coleman, 1930-2015, alto sax, composer.
Alice Coltrane, 1937-2007, piano, composer.
John Coltrane, 1926-67, tenor sax, soprano sax, composer.
Eddie Condon, 1905-73, guitar, bandleader.
Tadd Dameron, 1917-65, piano, composer.
Eddie "Lockjaw" Davis, 1921-86, tenor sax.
Miles Davis, 1926-91, trumpet, composer.
Wild Bill Davison, 1906-89, cornet.
Blossom Dearie, 1924-2009, singer.
Paul Desmond, 1924-77, alto sax.
Vic Dickenson, 1906-84, trombone.
Willie Dixon, 1915-92, composer, bass.
Johnny Dodds, 1892-1940, clarinet.
Warren "Baby" Dodds, 1898-1959, drums.
Eric Dolphy, 1928-64, alto sax, bass clarinet, flute.
Jimmy Dorsey, 1904-57, alto sax, bandleader.
Tommy Dorsey, 1905-56, trombone, bandleader.
Billy Eckstine, 1914-93, singer, bandleader.
Harry "Sweets" Edison, 1915-99, trumpet.
David "Honeyboy" Edwards, 1915-2011, guitar, singer.
Roy Eldridge, 1911-89, trumpet, singer.
Duke Ellington, 1899-1974, piano, bandleader, composer.
Bill Evans, 1929-80, piano.
Gil Evans, 1912-88, composer, arranger, piano.
Art Farmer, 1928-99, trumpet, flugelhorn.
Maynard Ferguson, 1926-2006, trumpet, bandleader.
Ella Fitzgerald, 1917-96, singer.
Tommy Flanagan, 1930-2001, piano.
Pete Fountain, 1930-2016, clarinetist.
Erroll Garner, 1921-77, piano, composer.
Stan Getz, 1927-91, tenor sax.
Dizzy Gillespie, 1917-93, trumpet, composer, singer.
Jimmy Giuffre, 1921-2008, clarinetist, composer.
Benny Goodman, 1909-86, clarinet, bandleader.
Dexter Gordon, 1923-90, tenor sax.
Stéphane Grappelli, 1908-97, violin.
Bobby Hackett, 1915-76, trumpet, cornet.
Lionel Hampton, 1908-2002, vibraphone, bandleader.
W. C. Handy, 1873-1958, composer.
Jimmy Harrison, 1900-31, trombone.
Coleman Hawkins, 1904-69, tenor sax.
Percy Heath, 1923-2005, bass.
Fletcher Henderson, 1898-1952, bandleader, arranger.
Woody Herman, 1913-87, clarinet, alto sax, bandleader.
Jay C. Higginbotham, 1906-73, trombone.
Ruiz Hilton, 1952-2006, piano, composer.
Earl "Fatha" Hines, 1903-83, piano.
Milt Hinton, 1910-2000, bass.
Al Hirt, 1922-99, trumpet.
Johnny Hodges, 1906-70, alto sax.
Billie Holiday, 1915-59, singer.
John Lee Hooker, 1917-2001, blues guitar, singer.
Sam "Lightnin'" Hopkins, 1912-82, blues singer, guitar.
Shirley Horn, 1934-2005, piano, singer.
Howlin' Wolf (Chester Burnett), 1910-76, blues singer, harmonica, guitar.
Alberta Hunter, 1895-1984, singer.
Mahalia Jackson, 1911-72, gospel singer.

Milt Jackson, 1923-99, vibraphone.
Elmore James, 1918-63, blues singer, guitar.
Etta James, 1938-2012, blues singer.
Al Jarreau, 1940-2017, jazz singer.
"Blind" Lemon Jefferson, 1897-1929, blues singer, guitar.
J. J. Johnson, 1924-2001, trombone.
James P. Johnson, 1891-1955, piano, composer.
Robert Johnson, 1912-38, blues singer, guitar.
William "Bunk" Johnson, 1879-1949, trumpet.
Elvin Jones, 1927-2004, drums.
Jo Jones, 1911-85, drums.
Philly Joe Jones, 1923-85, drums.
Thad Jones, 1923-86, cornet, bandleader, composer.
Scott Joplin, 1868-1917, ragtime composer.
Louis Jordan, 1908-75, singer, alto sax.
Stan Kenton, 1911-79, bandleader, composer, piano.
Barney Kessel, 1923-2004, guitar.
Albert King, 1923-92, blues guitar.
B. B. King, 1925-2015, blues guitar, singer.
John Kirby, 1908-52, bandleader, bass.
Rahsaan Roland Kirk, 1936-77, saxophone, composer.
Gene Krupa, 1909-73, drums, bandleader.
Scott LaFaro, 1936-61, bass.
Lead Belly (Huddie Ledbetter), 1888-1949, folk and blues singer, guitar.
Peggy Lee, 1920-2002, singer.
John Lewis, 1920-2001, piano, Modern Jazz Quartet founder.
Mel Lewis, 1929-90, drums, bandleader.
Jimmie Lunceford, 1902-47, bandleader.
Machito (Frank Grillo), 1908-84, Latin percussion, singer, bandleader.
Shelly Manne, 1920-84, drums, bandleader.
Jackie McLean, 1931-2006, saxophone, composer.
Jimmy McPartland, 1907-91, trumpet.
Marian McPartland, 1918-2013, pianist.
Carmen McRae, 1920-94, singer.
Glenn Miller, 1904-44, trombone, bandleader.
Charles Mingus, 1922-79, bass, composer, bandleader.
Thelonious Monk, 1917-82, piano, composer.
Wes Montgomery, 1925-68, guitar.
James Moody, 1925-2010, saxophone.
Ferdinand "Jelly Roll" Morton, 1885-1941, composer, piano.
Bennie Moten, 1894-1935, piano, bandleader.
Gerry Mulligan, 1927-96, baritone sax, composer.
Theodore "Fats" Navarro, 1923-50, trumpet.
Red Nichols, 1905-65, cornet, bandleader.
Red Norvo, 1908-99, vibraphone, xylophone, bandleader.
Anita O'Day, 1919-2006, singer.
Arturo "Chico" O'Farrill, 1921-2001, Latin composer, arranger.
King Oliver, 1885-1938, cornet, bandleader.
Sy Oliver, 1910-88, arranger, composer.
Edward "Kid" Ory, 1886-1973, trombone, bandleader.
Johnny Otis, 1921-2012, blues singer.
Oran "Hot Lips" Page, 1908-54, trumpet, singer.
Charlie "Bird" Parker, 1920-55, alto sax, composer.
Joe Pass, 1929-94, guitar.
Jaco Pastorius, 1951-87, bass guitarist.
Art Pepper, 1925-82, alto sax.
Pinetop Perkins, 1913-2011, piano.
Oscar Peterson, 1925-2007, piano.
Oscar Pettiford, 1922-60, bass.
Earl "Bud" Powell, 1924-66, piano.
Chano Pozo, 1915-48, percussionist, singer.

Louis Prima, 1911-78, singer, bandleader.
Tito Puente, 1923-2000, Latin percussion, bandleader.
Gertrude "Ma" Rainey, 1886-1939, blues singer.
Lou Rawls, 1933-2006, singer.
Dewey Redman, 1931-2006, tenor sax.
Don Redman (Robert Rodney Chudnick), 1900-64, composer, arranger.
Django Reinhardt, 1910-53, guitar.
Buddy Rich, 1917-87, drums.
Max Roach, 1924-2007, drums, composer.
Red Rodney (Robert Chudnick), 1927-94, trumpet.
Jimmy Rowles, 1918-96, piano.
Jimmy Rushing, 1903-72, blues and jazz singer.
Charles "Pee Wee" Russell, 1906-69, clarinet.
Artie Shaw, 1910-2004, swing-era bandleader, clarinet.
George Shearing, 1919-2011, piano.
Nina Simone (Eunice Waymon), 1933-2003, singer.
John "Zoot" Sims, 1925-85, tenor sax.
Zutty Singleton, 1898-1975, drums.
Bessie Smith, 1894-1937, blues singer.
Clarence "Pinetop" Smith, 1904-29, piano, singer, boogie woogie pioneer.
Willie "The Lion" Smith, 1897-1973, piano, composer.
Francis "Muggsy" Spanier, 1906-67, cornet.
Edward "Sonny" Stitt, 1924-82, tenor sax, alto sax.
Billy Strayhorn, 1915-67, composer, piano, Duke Ellington collaborator.
Sun Ra (Herman Blount), 1915?-93, bandleader, piano, composer.
Art Tatum, 1910-56, piano.
Art Taylor, 1929-95, drums.
Billy Taylor, 1921-2010, piano.
Jack Teagarden, 1905-64, trombone, singer.
Clark Terry, 1920-2015, trumpet.
Mel Tormé, 1925-99, singer ("The Velvet Fog").
Dave Tough, 1908-48, drums.
Lennie Tristano, 1919-78, piano, composer.
Joe Turner, 1911-85, blues singer.
Sarah Vaughan, 1924-90, singer.
Joe Venuti, 1903-78, violin.
Aaron "T-Bone" Walker, 1910-75, blues guitar.
Thomas "Fats" Waller, 1904-43, piano, singer, composer.
Dinah Washington (Ruth Jones), 1924-63, singer.
Grover Washington Jr., 1943-99, pop-jazz sax, composer.
Ethel Waters, 1896-1977, jazz and blues singer.
Muddy Waters (McKinley Morganfield), 1915-83, blues singer, songwriter.
Julius Watkins, 1921-77, French horn.
William "Chick" Webb, 1902-39, bandleader, drums.
Ben Webster, 1909-73, tenor sax.
Junior Wells (Amos Blackmore), 1934-98, blues singer, harmonica.
Paul Whiteman, 1890-1967, bandleader.
Margaret Whiting, 1924-2011, singer.
Charles "Cootie" Williams, 1910-85, trumpet, bandleader.
Joe Williams, 1918-99, singer.
Mary Lou Williams, 1910-81, piano, composer.
Tony Williams, 1945-97, drums.
John Lee "Sonny Boy" Williamson, 1914-48, blues singer, harmonica.
Sonny Boy Williamson (Aleck "Rice" Miller), 1900?-65, blues singer, harmonica.
Teddy Wilson, 1912-86, piano.
Kai Winding, 1922-83, trombone.
Jimmy Yancey, 1894-1951, piano.
Lester "Pres" Young, 1909-59, tenor sax.

Country Music Artists of the Past and Present

* = Inducted into Country Music Hall of Fame (Nashville, TN) as performer between 1961 and 2018.

*Roy Acuff, 1903-92, fiddler, singer, songwriter; "Wabash Cannon Ball."

*Alabama (Jeff Cook, b 1949; Teddy Gentry, b 1952; Mark Herndon, b 1955; Randy Owen, b 1949); "Feels So Right."

Jason Aldean, b 1977, singer; "Don't You Wanna Stay."

James "Whispering Bill" Anderson, b 1937, singer, songwriter; "Make Mine Night Time."

*Eddy Arnold, 1918-2008, singer, guitarist, known as the Tennessee Plowboy.

*Chet Atkins, 1924-2001, guitarist, composer, producer; helped create the "Nashville sound."

*Gene Autry, 1907-98, singing movie cowboy; "Back in the Saddle Again."

Clint Black, b 1962, singer, songwriter; "Killin' Time."

*Garth Brooks, b 1962, singer, songwriter; "Friends in Low Places."

Brooks & Dunn (Kix Brooks, b 1955; Ronnie Dunn, b 1953); "Hard Workin' Man."

Luke Bryan, b 1976, singer, songwriter; "Someone Else Calling You Baby."

*Boudleaux, 1920-87, and **Felice Bryant**, 1925-2003, songwriting team; "Hey Joe."

*Glen Campbell, 1936-2017, singer, guitarist; "Gentle on My Mind."

Mary Chapin Carpenter, b 1958, singer, songwriter; "I Feel Lucky."

*Carter Family (original members A. P., 1891-1960; "Mother" Maybelle, 1909-78; Sara, 1898-1979); "Wildwood Flower."

*Johnny Cash, 1932-2003, singer, songwriter; "I Walk the Line," "Ring of Fire," "Folsom Prison Blues."

Kenny Chesney, b 1968, guitarist, singer, songwriter; "You Had Me From Hello."

*Roy Clark, b 1933, guitarist, banjoist, singer, co-host of *Hee Haw*; "Yesterday, When I Was Young."

*Patsy Cline, 1932-63, singer; "Walkin' After Midnight," "Crazy," "Sweet Dreams."

Billy Ray Cyrus, b 1961, singer, songwriter; "Achy Breaky Heart."

*Charlie Daniels, b 1936, guitarist, fiddler; "The Devil Went Down to Georgia."

*Jimmy Dean, 1928-2010, singer; "Big Bad John."

John Denver, 1943-97, singer, songwriter; "Rocky Mountain High."

Dixie Chicks (Natalie Maines, b 1974; Emily Erwin Robison, b 1972; Martie Seidel, b 1969); *Wide Open Spaces*.

Dale Evans, 1912-2001, singer, actress, married Roy Rogers.

Sara Evans, b 1971, singer, songwriter; "Born to Fly."

*Flatt & Scruggs (Lester Flatt, 1914-79; Earl Scruggs, 1924-2012), guitar-banjo duo and soloists; "Foggy Mountain Breakdown."

*Red Foley, 1910-68, singer; "Chattanoogie Shoe Shine Boy."

*Tennessee Ernie Ford, 1919-91, singer, TV host; "Sixteen Tons."

*William "Lefty" Frizzell, 1928-75, singer, guitarist; "Long Black Veil."

*Vince Gill, b 1957, singer, songwriter; "When I Call Your Name."

*Merle Haggard, 1937-2016, singer, songwriter; "Okie From Muskogee."

*Emmylou Harris, b 1947, singer, songwriter, folk-country crossover artist; "If I Could Only Win Your Love."

Hunter Hayes, b 1991, singer; "Wanted."

Faith Hill, b 1967, singer, songwriter; "Breathe."

*Alan Jackson, b 1958, singer, songwriter; "Where Were You (When the World Stopped Turning)."

*Waylon Jennings, 1937-2002, singer, songwriter, outlaw country pioneer; "Luckenbach, Texas."

*George Jones, 1931-2013, singer; "He Stopped Loving Her Today."

The Judds (Naomi, b 1946; Wynonna, b 1964), mother-daughter duo; Wynonna also a solo act.

Toby Keith, b 1961, singer, songwriter, guitarist; "Should've Been a Cowboy."

Alison Krauss, b 1971, bluegrass fiddler, singer, bandleader; "When You Say Nothing at All."

*Kris Kristofferson, b 1936, singer, songwriter, actor; "Me and Bobby McGee."

Lady Antebellum (Dave Haywood, b 1982; Charles Kelley, b 1981; Hillary Scott, b 1984); *Need You Now*.

Miranda Lambert, b 1983, singer, guitarist; "The House That Built Me."

*Louvin Brothers (Charlie, 1927-2011; Ira, 1924-65), singers; "If I Could Only Win Your Love."

Patty Loveless, b 1957, singer, songwriter; "How Can I Help You Say Goodbye."

Lyle Lovett, b 1957, singer, songwriter, bandleader, actor; "Cowboy Man."

*Loretta Lynn, b 1932, singer; "Coal Miner's Daughter."

*Barbara Mandrell, b 1948, singer; "I Was Country When Country Wasn't Cool."

Kathy Mattea, b 1959, singer, songwriter; "Eighteen Wheels and a Dozen Roses."

Martina McBride, b 1966, singer, songwriter; "Independence Day."

*Reba McEntire, b 1955, singer, songwriter, actress; "Whoever's in New England."

Tim McGraw, b 1967, singer; "It's Your Love," "I Like It, I Love It."

*Roger Miller, 1936-92, singer, songwriter; "King of the Road."

*Ronnie Milsap, b 1944, singer, songwriter; "There's No Gettin' Over Me."

*Bill Monroe, 1911-96, singer, songwriter, mandolin player; "father of bluegrass music"; "Mule Skinner Blues."

Anne Murray, b 1945, singer; "You Needed Me."

*Willie Nelson, b 1933, singer, songwriter, actor; "On the Road Again."

Mark O'Connor, b 1961, fiddler, country-classical crossover composer.

*Buck Owens, 1929-2006, singer, guitarist; "Act Naturally."

Brad Paisley, b 1972, singer, songwriter; "Whiskey Lullaby," "When I Get Where I'm Going."

*Dolly Parton, b 1946, singer, songwriter, actress; "Here You Come Again," "9 to 5."

Johnny Paycheck (Don Lytle), 1938-2003, singer, guitarist; "Take This Job and Shove It."

*Minnie Pearl, 1912-96, comedian, Grand Ole Opry star.

Kellie Pickler, b 1986, singer, songwriter.

*Ray Price, 1926-2013, country singer, guitarist, songwriter; "Crazy Arms."

*Charley Pride, b 1938, singer, first African American country star; "Kiss an Angel Good Mornin'."

Eddie Rabbit, 1941-98, singer, songwriter; "I Love a Rainy Night."

Rascal Flatts (Jay DeMarcus, b 1971; Gary LeVox, b 1970; Joe Don Rooney, b 1975); "Life Is a Highway"; "Rewind."

*Jim Reeves, 1923-64, singer, songwriter; "Four Walls."

Charlie Rich, 1932-95, singer, songwriter called the "Silver Fox"; "The Most Beautiful Girl."

LeAnn Rimes, b 1982, singer; *Blue*.

*Tex Ritter, 1905-74, singer, songwriter; "Jingle, Jangle, Jingle."

*Marty Robbins, 1925-82, singer, songwriter; "A White Sport Coat and a Pink Carnation."

*Jimmie Rodgers, 1897-1933, singer, songwriter; "T for Texas."

*Kenny Rogers, b 1938, singer, songwriter; "The Gambler."

*Roy Rogers (Leonard Slye), 1911-98, singer, actor, "King of the Cowboys," sang with Sons of the Pioneers.

*Fred Rose, 1898-1954, songwriter, singer, producer; "Blue Eyes Cryin' in the Rain."

Blake Shelton, b 1976, singer; "Home."

*Ricky Skaggs, b 1954, singer, songwriter, bandleader; "Don't Cheat in Our Hometown."

Ralph Stanley, 1927-2016, singer, banjo player; "Man of Constant Sorrow."

Chris Stapleton, b 1978, singer, songwriter; *Traveller*.

*George Strait, b 1952, singer, bandleader; "Ace in the Hole."

Sugarland (Kristian Bush, b 1970; Jennifer Nettles, b 1974); "Stay."

Taylor Swift, b 1989, singer, songwriter; "You Belong With Me."

*Lonnie "Mel" Tillis, b 1932, singer, songwriter, bandleader; "I Ain't Never."

*Merle Travis, 1917-83, singer, guitarist, songwriter; "Divorce Me C.O.D."

*Randy Travis, b 1959, singer, songwriter; "Forever and Ever, Amen."

*Ernest Tubb, 1914-84, singer, songwriter, guitarist; "Walking the Floor Over You."

Josh Turner, b 1977, singer; "Why Don't We Just Dance."

Shania Twain, b 1965, singer, songwriter; "You're Still the One."

*Conway Twitty, 1933-93, singer, songwriter; "Hello Darlin'."

Carrie Underwood, b 1983, singer, songwriter; *American Idol* winner.

Keith Urban, b 1967, guitarist, singer, songwriter; "Somebody Like You."

*Porter Wagoner, 1927-2007, singer, songwriter, guitarist; "Soul of a Convict."

*Kitty Wells (Ellen Deason), 1919-2012, singer, songwriter; "It Wasn't God Who Made Honky-Tonk Angels."

*Dottie West, 1932-91, singer, songwriter; "Here Comes My Baby."

Hank Williams Jr., b 1949, singer, songwriter; "Bocephus"; "All My Rowdy Friends (Have Settled Down)."

*Hank Williams Sr., 1923-53, singer, songwriter; "Your Cheatin' Heart."

*Bob Wills, 1905-75, Western Swing fiddler, singer, bandleader, songwriter; "New San Antonio Rose."

Lee Ann Womack, b 1966, singer, songwriter; "I Hope You Dance."

*Tammy Wynette, 1942-98, singer; "Stand By Your Man."

Trisha Yearwood, b 1964, singer, songwriter; "How Do I Live."

Dwight Yoakam, b 1957, singer, songwriter, actor; "Ain't That Lonely Yet."

Zac Brown Band (Coy Bowles, b 1979; Zac Brown, b 1978; Clay Cook, Jimmy De Martini, Chris Fryar, b 1970; John Driskell Hopkins, b 1971); "Chicken Fried."

Dance Figures of the Past

Alvin Ailey, 1931-89, (U.S.) modern dancer, choreographer; melded modern dance and Afro-Caribbean techniques.

Frederick Ashton, 1904-88, (Br.) ballet choreographer; director of Great Britain's Royal Ballet, 1963-70.

Fred Astaire, 1899-1987, dancer, actor; teamed with dancer/actress **Ginger Rogers**, 1911-95, (both U.S.) in movie musicals.

George Balanchine, 1904-83, (Russ.-U.S.) ballet choreographer, teacher; most influential exponent of neoclassical style; founded, with Lincoln Kirstein, School of American Ballet and New York City Ballet.

Pina Bausch, 1940-2009, (Ger.) modern dance choreographer influencing the Tanztheater style of dance.

Carlo Blasis, 1795-1878, (It.) ballet dancer, choreographer, writer; his teaching methods are standards of classical dance.

August Bournonville, 1805-79, (Den.) ballet dancer, choreographer, teacher; exuberant, light style.

Fernando Bujones, 1955-2005, (Cuba-U.S.) ballet dancer.

Gisella Caccialanza, 1914-98, (U.S.) ballerina; charter member of Balanchine's American Ballet.

Irene, 1893-1969, (U.S.) and **Vernon Castle**, 1887-1918, (Br.) husband-and-wife ballroom dancers.

Enrico Cecchetti, 1850-1928, (It.) ballet dancer, leading dancer of Russia's Imperial Ballet; his technique was basis for Britain's Imperial Soc. of Teachers of Dancing.

Gower, 1921-80, dancer, choreographer, director; with wife **Marge Champion**, b 1923, (both U.S.) choreographed, danced in Broadway musicals and films.

John Cranko, 1927-73, (S. Afr.) choreographer; created narrative ballets based on literary works.

Merce Cunningham, 1919-2009, (U.S.) dancer, choreographer of avant-garde dance.

Alexandra Danilova, 1903-97, (Russ.) ballerina; noted teacher at the School of American Ballet.

Agnes de Mille, 1905-93, (U.S.) ballerina, choreographer; known for using American themes, she choreographed the ballet *Rodeo* and the musical *Oklahoma!*

Dame Ninette De Valois, 1898-2001, (Br.) choreographer, founding director of London's Royal Ballet; *The Rake's Progress*.

Sergei Diaghilev, 1872-1929, (Russ.) impresario; founded Les Ballet Russes; saw ballet as art unifying dance, drama, music, and decor.

Isadora Duncan, 1877-1927, (U.S.) expressive dancer who united free movement with serious music; one of the founders of modern dance.

Katherine Dunham, 1910-2006, (U.S.) dancer, choreographer; internationally known for African, Caribbean, and African American dance forms.

Fanny Elssler, 1810-84, (Austria) ballerina of the Romantic era; known for dramatic skill, sensual style.

Michel Fokine, 1880-1942, (Russ.) ballet dancer, choreographer, teacher; rejected strict classicism in favor of dramatically expressive style.

Margot Fonteyn, 1919-91, (Br.) prima ballerina, Royal Ballet of Great Britain; famed performance partner of Rudolf Nureyev.

Bob Fosse, 1927-87, (U.S.) jazz dancer, choreographer, director; Broadway musicals and film.

Serge Golovine, 1924-98, (Fr.) ballet dancer with Grand Ballet du Marquis de Cuevas, choreographer.

Martha Graham, 1894-1991, (U.S.) modern dancer, choreographer; created and codified her own dramatic technique.

Melissa Hayden, 1923-2006, (Can.) ballet dancer.

Martha Hill, 1900-95, (U.S.) educator; leading figure in modern dance. Founded American Dance Festival.

Gregory Hines, 1946-2003, (U.S.) tap-dance innovator; master of improvisation.

Doris Humphrey, 1895-1958, (U.S.) modern dancer, choreographer, writer, teacher.

Michael Jackson, 1958-2009, (U.S.) singer and dancer who perfected the "moonwalk."

Robert Joffrey, 1930-88, ballet dancer, choreographer; cofounded with **Gerald Arpino**, 1928-2008, (both U.S.) the Joffrey Ballet.

Kurt Jooss, 1901-79, (Ger.) choreographer, teacher; created expressionist works using modern and classical techniques.

Tamara Karsavina, 1885-1978, (Russ.) prima ballerina of Russia's Imperial Ballet and Diaghilev's Ballets Russes; partner of Nijinsky.

Nora Kaye, 1920-87, (U.S.) ballerina with Metropolitan Opera Ballet and Ballet Theater (now American Ballet Theatre).

Gene Kelly, 1912-96, (U.S.) dancer, actor in movie musicals.

Michael Kidd, 1915-2003, (U.S.) dancer, film and theater choreographer.

Lincoln Kirstein, 1907-96 (U.S.) brought ballet as an art form to U.S.; founded, with George Balanchine, School of American Ballet and New York City Ballet.

Serge Lifar, 1905-86, (Russ.-Fr.) prem. danseur, choreographer; director of dance at Paris Opera, 1930-45, 1947-58.

José Limón, 1908-72, (Mex.-U.S.) modern dancer, choreographer, teacher; developed technique based on Humphrey.

Catherine Littlefield, 1908-51, (U.S.) ballerina, choreographer, teacher; pioneer of American ballet.

Kenneth MacMillan, 1929-92, (Br.) dancer, choreographer; directed Royal Ballet of Great Britain, 1970-77.

Dame Alicia Markova, 1910-2004, (Br.) ballerina known for title role in *Giselle*; helped popularize ballet in U.S. and Britain.

Léonide Massine, 1896-1979, (Russ.-U.S.) ballet dancer, choreographer; known for his "symphonic ballet."

Arthur Mitchell, 1934-2018, (U.S.) dancer, choreographer; cofounded Dance Theatre of Harlem.

Fayard Nicholas, 1914-2006, tap dancer, choreographer, actor; together with brother **Harold Nicholas**, 1921-2000, (both U.S.) formed the Nicholas Brothers.

Vaslav Nijinsky, 1890-50, (Russ.) prem. danseur, choreographer; leading member of Diaghilev's Ballets Russes. His ballets were revolutionary for their time.

Alwin Nikolais, 1910-93, (U.S.) modern choreographer; created dance theater utilizing mixed media effects.

Jean-George Noverre, 1727-1810, (Fr.) ballet choreographer, teacher, writer; "Shakespeare of the Dance."

Rudolf Nureyev, 1938-93, (Russ.) prem. danseur, choreographer; leading male dancer of his generation; director of dance at Paris Opera, 1983-89.

Ruth Page, 1899-1991, (U.S.) ballerina, choreographer; danced, directed ballet at Chicago Lyric Opera.

Anna Pavlova, 1881-1931, (Russ.) prima ballerina; toured with her own company to world acclaim.

Marius Petipa, 1818-1910, (Fr.) ballet dancer, choreographer; ballet master of the Imperial Ballet; established Russian classicism as leading style of late 19th cent.

Roland Petit, 1924-2011, (Fr.) dancer, choreographer; founder of Les Ballets de Paris.

Pearl Primus, 1919-95, (Trinidad-U.S.) modern dancer, choreographer, scholar; combined African, Caribbean, and African American styles.

Jerome Robbins, 1918-98, (U.S.) choreographer, director, dancer; *The King and I*, *West Side Story*, *Fiddler on the Roof*.

Bill "Bojangles" Robinson, 1878-1949, (U.S.) famed tap dancer; called "King of Tapology" on stage and screen.

Ruth St. Denis, 1877-1968, (U.S.) influential interpretive dancer, choreographer, teacher.

Ted Shawn, 1891-1972, (U.S.) modern dancer, choreographer; formed dance company and school with Ruth St. Denis; established Jacob's Pillow Dance Festival.

Marie Taglioni, 1804-84, (It.) ballerina, teacher; in title role of *La Sylphide* established image of the ethereal ballerina.

Maria Tallchief, 1925-2013, (U.S.) prima ballerina, 1st of Amer. Indian descent.

Paul Taylor, 1930-2018, (U.S.) dancer, choreographer, teacher.

Glen Tetley, 1926-2007, (U.S.) dancer, choreographer, ballet director; fused elements of modern dance with ballet.

Antony Tudor, 1908-87, (Br.) choreographer, teacher; exponent of the "psychological ballet."

Galina Ulanova, 1910-98, (Russ.) revered ballerina with Bolshoi Ballet.

Agrippina Vaganova, 1879-1951, (Russ.) ballet teacher, director called "queen of variations"; codified Soviet ballet technique.

Mary Wigman, 1886-1973, (Ger.) modern dancer, choreographer, teacher; influenced European expressionist dance.

Opera Singers of the Past

Licia Albanese, 1909-2014, (It.) soprano.

Frances Alda, 1879-1952, (N.Z.) soprano.

Pasquale Amato, 1878-1942, (It.) baritone.

Marian Anderson, 1897-1993, (U.S.) contralto.

Charles Anthony, 1929-2012, (U.S.) tenor.

Jussi Björling, 1911-60, (Swed.) tenor.

Lucrezia Bori, 1887-1960, (It.) soprano.

Montserrat Caballé, 1933-2018, (Sp.) soprano.

Maria Callas, 1923-77, (U.S.) soprano.

Emma Calvé, 1858-1942, (Fr.) soprano.

Enrico Caruso, 1873-1921, (It.) tenor.

Feodor Chaliapin, 1873-1938, (Russ.) bass.

Lili Chookasian, 1921-2012, (U.S.) contralto.

Boris Christoff, 1914-93, (Bulg.) bass.

Franco Corelli, 1921-2003, (It.) tenor.

Hughes Cuenod, 1902-2010, (Switz.) tenor.

Victoria De Los Angeles, 1923-2005, (Sp.) soprano.

Giuseppe De Luca, 1876-1950, (It.) baritone.

Fernando De Lucia, 1860-1925, (It.) tenor.

Edouard De Reszke, 1853-1917, (Pol.) bass.

Jean De Reszke, 1850-1925, (Pol.) tenor.

Emmy Destinn, 1878-1930, (Czech.) soprano.

Mattiwilda Dobbs, 1925-2015, (U.S.) coloratura soprano.

Emma Eames, 1865-1952, (U.S.) soprano.

(Carlo Broschi) Farinelli, 1705-82, (It.) castrato.

Geraldine Farrar, 1882-1967, (U.S.) soprano.

Eileen Farrell, 1920-2002, (U.S.) soprano.

Kathleen Ferrier, 1912-53, (Eng.) contralto.

Dietrich Fischer-Dieskau, 1925-2012, (Ger.) baritone.
Kirsten Flagstad, 1895-1962, (Nor.) soprano.
Olive Fremstad, 1871-1951, (Swed.-U.S.) soprano.
Amelita Galli-Curci, 1882-1963, (It.) soprano.
Mary Garden, 1874-1967, (Br.) soprano.
Nicolai Gedda, 1925-2017, (Swed.) tenor.
Nicolai Ghiaurov, 1929-2004, (Bulg.) bass.
Beniamino Gigli, 1890-1957, (It.) tenor.
Tito Gobbi, 1913-84, (It.) baritone.
Giulia Grisi, 1811-69, (It.) soprano.
Frieda Hempel, 1885-1955, (Ger.) soprano.
Jerome Hines, 1921-2003, (U.S.) bass.
Hans Hotter, 1909-2003, (Ger.) bass-baritone.
Maria Jeritza, 1887-1982, (Czech.) soprano.
Sena Jurinac, 1921-2011, (Yugo.) soprano.
Alexander Kipnis, 1891-1978, (Russ.-U.S.) bass.
Dorothy Kirsten, 1910-92, (U.S.) soprano.
Alfredo Kraus, 1927-99, (Sp.) tenor.
Luigi Lablache, 1794-1858, (It.) bass.
Lilli Lehmann, 1848-1929, (Ger.) soprano.
Lotte Lehmann, 1888-1976, (Ger.-U.S.) soprano.
Jenny Lind, 1820-87, (Swed.) soprano.
Cornell MacNeil, 1922-2011, (U.S.) baritone.
Maria Malibran, 1808-36, (Sp.) mezzo-soprano.
Giovanni Martinelli, 1885-1969, (It.) tenor.
John McCormack, 1884-1945, (Ire.) tenor.

Nellie Melba, 1861-1931, (Austral.) soprano.
Lauritz Melchior, 1890-1973, (Den.) tenor.
Robert Merrill, 1919-2004, (U.S.) baritone.
Zinka Milanov, 1906-89, (Yugo.) soprano.
Patrice Munsel, 1925-2015, (U.S.) coloratura soprano.
Patricia Neway, 1919-2012, (U.S.) soprano.
Birgit Nilsson, 1918-2005, (Swed.) soprano.
Lillian Nordica, 1857-1914, (U.S.) soprano.
Magda Olivero, 1910-2014, (It.) soprano.
Giuditta Pasta, 1797-1865, (It.) soprano.
Adelina Patti, 1843-1919, (It.) soprano.
Luciano Pavarotti, 1935-2007, (It.) tenor.
Peter Pears, 1910-86, (Eng.) tenor.
Jan Peerce, 1904-84, (U.S.) tenor.
Roberta Peters, 1930-2017, (U.S.) soprano.
Ezio Pinza, 1892-1957, (It.) bass.
Lily Pons, 1898-1976, (Fr.) soprano.
Rosa Ponselle, 1897-1981, (U.S.) soprano.
Hermann Prey, 1929-98, (Ger.) baritone.
Margaret Price, 1941-2011, (U.K.) soprano.
Regina Resnik, 1922-2013, (U.S.) soprano turned mezzo-soprano.
Elisabeth Rethberg, 1894-1976, (Ger.) soprano.
Giovanni Battista Rubini, 1794-1854, (It.) tenor.
Leonie Rysanek, 1926-98, (Austria) soprano.
Dorothy Sarnoff, 1914-2008, (U.S.) soprano.
Bidú Sayão, 1902-99, (Braz.) soprano.
Friedrich Schorr, 1888-1953, (Hung.) bass-baritone.
Elisabeth Schwarzkopf, 1915-2006, (Ger.) soprano.

Marcella Sembrich, 1858-1935, (Pol.) soprano.
Cesare Siepi, 1923-2010, (It.) bass.
Beverly Sills, 1929-2007, (U.S.) soprano.
Elisabeth Söderström, 1927-2009, (Swed.) soprano.
Eleanor Steber, 1914-90, (U.S.) soprano.
Risë Stevens, 1913-2013, (U.S.) mezzo-soprano.
Joan Sutherland, 1926-2010, (Austral.) soprano.
Ferrucio Tagliavini, 1913-95, (It.) tenor.
Renata Tebaldi, 1922-2004 (It.) soprano.
Luisa Tetrazzini, 1871-1940, (It.) soprano.
Lawrence Tibbett, 1896-1960, (U.S.) baritone.
Giorgio Tozzi, 1923-2011, (U.S.) bass-baritone.
Tatiana Troyanos, 1938-93, (U.S.) mezzo-soprano.
Richard Tucker, 1913-75, (U.S.) tenor.
Shirley Verrett, 1931-2010, (U.S.) mezzo-soprano.
Pauline Viardot, 1821-1910, (Fr.) mezzo-soprano.
Jon Vickers, 1926-2015, (Can.) tenor.
William Warfield, 1920-2002, (U.S.) bass-baritone.
Leonard Warren, 1911-60, (U.S.) baritone.
Ljuba Welitsch, 1913-96, (Bulg.) soprano.
Camilla Williams, 1919-2012, (U.S.) soprano.
Wolfgang Windgassen, 1914-74, (Ger.) tenor.

Rock 'n' Roll, Rhythm and Blues, and Rap Artists

Titles in quotation marks are singles; others are albums. * = Inducted into Rock & Roll Hall of Fame as performer between 1986 and 2018; year is in parentheses.

*ABBA (2010): "Dancing Queen"
Paula Abdul: "Straight Up"
*AC/DC (2003): "Back in Black"
Bryan Adams: "Cuts Like a Knife"
Adele: "Rolling in the Deep"
*Aerosmith (2001): "Sweet Emotion"
Christina Aguilera: "What a Girl Wants"
Alice in Chains: "Heaven Beside You"
*The Allman Brothers Band (1995): "Ramblin' Man"
*The Animals (1994): "House of the Rising Sun"
Paul Anka: "Lonely Boy"
Fiona Apple: "Criminal"
Frankie Avalon: "Venus"
Iggy Azalea: "Fancy"
The B-52s: "Love Shack"
Bachman Turner Overdrive: "Takin' Care of Business"
Backstreet Boys: "I Want It That Way"
Bad Company: "Can't Get Enough"
Erykah Badu: "On and On"
*Joan Baez (2017): "The Night They Drove Old Dixie Down"
*La Vern Baker (1991): "I Cried a Tear"
*Hank Ballard[1] and the Midnighters (1990): "Work With Me, Annie"
*The Band (1994): "The Weight"
Barenaked Ladies: "One Week"
*The Beach Boys (1988): "Good Vibrations"
*Beastie Boys (2012): "(You Gotta) Fight for Your Right (to Party)"
*The Beatles (1988): Sgt. Pepper's Lonely Hearts Club Band
Beck: "Loser"
*Jeff Beck (2009): "Escape"
*The Bee Gees (1997): "Stayin' Alive"
Pat Benatar: "Hit Me With Your Best Shot"
*Chuck Berry (1986): "Johnny B. Goode"
Beyoncé: "Crazy in Love"
The Big Bopper: "Chantilly Lace"
Björk: "Human Behavior"
The Black Crowes: "Hard to Handle"
Black Eyed Peas: Elephunk
*Black Sabbath (2006): "Paranoid"
*Bobby "Blue" Bland (1992): "Turn On Your Love Light"
Mary J. Blige: My Life
Blind Faith: "Can't Find My Way Home"
Blink-182: "All the Small Things"
*Blondie (2006): "Heart of Glass"
Blood, Sweat, and Tears: "Spinning Wheel"
Blues Traveler: "Run-Around"
Gary "U.S." Bonds: "Quarter to Three"
*Bon Jovi (2018): "Livin' on a Prayer"
*Booker T. and the M.G.'s (1992): "Green Onions"
Boston: "More Than a Feeling"

*David Bowie (1996): "Space Oddity"
Boyz II Men: "I'll Make Love to You"
Toni Braxton: "Un-Break My Heart"
Chris Brown: "Kiss Kiss"
*James Brown (1986): "Papa's Got a Brand New Bag"
*Ruth Brown (1993): "Lucky Lips"
*Jackson Browne (2004): "Doctor My Eyes"
*Buffalo Springfield (1997): "For What It's Worth"
Jimmy Buffett: "Margaritaville"
*Solomon Burke (2001): "Over and Over (Huggin' and Lovin')"
*The Paul Butterfield Blues Band (2015): "Born in Chicago"
*The Byrds (1991): "Turn! Turn! Turn!"
Mariah Carey: "Vision of Love"
The Carpenters: "(They Long to Be) Close to You"
*The Cars (2018): "Shake It Up"
*Johnny Cash (1992): "I Walk the Line"
*Ray Charles (1986): "Georgia on My Mind"
*Cheap Trick (2016): "Surrender"
Chubby Checker: "The Twist"
*Chicago (2016): "Saturday in the Park"
*Eric Clapton (2000): "Layla"
Kelly Clarkson: "Since U Been Gone"
*The Clash (2003): "Rock the Casbah"
*Jimmy Cliff (2010): "I Can See Clearly Now"
*The Coasters (1987): "Yakety Yak"
*Eddie Cochran (1987): "Summertime Blues"
Joe Cocker: "With a Little Help From My Friends"
*Leonard Cohen (2008): "Suzanne"
Coldplay: "Clocks"
Collective Soul: "The World I Know"
Phil Collins: "Against All Odds"
*Sam Cooke (1986): "You Send Me"
Coolio: "Gangsta's Paradise"
*Alice Cooper (2011): "School's Out"
*Elvis Costello and the Attractions (2003): "Alison"
Counting Crows: "Mr. Jones"
*Cream (1993): "Sunshine of Your Love"
Creed: "Arms Wide Open"
*Creedence Clearwater Revival (1993): "Proud Mary"
*Crosby, Stills, and Nash (1997): "Suite: Judy Blue Eyes"
Sheryl Crow: "All I Want to Do"
The Crystals: "Da Doo Ron Ron"
The Cure: "Boys Don't Cry"
Daft Punk: "Get Lucky"
Danny and the Juniors: "At the Hop"
*Bobby Darin (1990): "Splish Splash"

Daughtry: "It's Not Over"
*The Dave Clark Five (2008): "Glad All Over"
Dave Matthews Band: "Don't Drink the Water"
*Miles Davis (2006): Bitches Brew
Spencer Davis Group: "Gimme Some Lovin'"
*Deep Purple (2016): "Smoke on the Water"
Def Leppard: "Photograph"
*The Dells (2004): "Oh, What a Night"
Depeche Mode: "Strange Love"
Destiny's Child: "Survivor"
*Neil Diamond (2011): "Cracklin' Rosie"
*Bo Diddley (1987): "Who Do You Love?"
*Dion[1] and the Belmonts (1989): "A Teenager in Love"
Celine Dion: "Because You Loved Me"
*Dire Straits (2018): "Money for Nothing"
DMX: "What's My Name"
*Fats Domino (1986): "Blueberry Hill"
*Donovan (2012): "Mellow Yellow"
The Doobie Brothers: "What a Fool Believes"
*The Doors (1993): "Light My Fire"
Dr. Dre: "Nothin' But a 'G' Thang"
*Dr. John (2011): "Right Place, Wrong Time"
Drake: "Hotline Bling"
*The Drifters (1988): "Save the Last Dance for Me"
Duran Duran: "Hungry Like the Wolf"
*Bob Dylan (1988): "Like a Rolling Stone"
*The Eagles (1998): "Hotel California"
*Earth, Wind, and Fire (2000): "Shining Star"
*Duane Eddy (1994): "Rebel-Rouser"
*Electric Light Orchestra (2017): "Don't Bring Me Down"
Missy Elliott: "Sock It 2 Me"
Eminem: "The Real Slim Shady"
En Vogue: "Hold On"
The Eurythmics: "Sweet Dreams (Are Made of This)"
Everclear: "Father Of Mine"
*The Everly Brothers (1986): "Wake Up, Little Susie"
50 Cent (Curtis Jackson): Get Rich or Die Tryin'
The Five Satins: "In the Still of the Night"
Roberta Flack: "The First Time Ever I Saw Your Face"
*The Flamingos (2001): "I Only Have Eyes for You"
*Fleetwood Mac (1998): Rumours
The Foo Fighters: "I'll Stick Around"
Foreigner: "Double Vision"
*The Four Seasons (1990): "Sherry"
*The Four Tops (1990): "I Can't Help Myself (Sugar Pie, Honey Bunch)"

*Aretha Franklin (1987): "Respect"
fun.: "We Are Young"
Nelly Furtado: "I'm Like a Bird"
*Peter Gabriel (2014): "Shock the Monkey"
*Gamble (Kenny) and Huff (Leon) (2008): "If You Don't Know Me by Now"
*Marvin Gaye (1987): "I Heard It Through the Grapevine"
*Genesis (2010): "No Reply at All"
Goo Goo Dolls: "Iris"
Grand Funk Railroad: "We're an American Band"
*Grandmaster Flash and the Furious Five (2007): "The Message"
*The Grateful Dead (1994): "Uncle John's Band"
*Al Green (1995): "Let's Stay Together"
*Green Day (2015): "Boulevard of Broken Dreams"
The Guess Who: "American Woman"
*Guns N' Roses (2012): "Sweet Child o' Mine"
*Buddy Guy (2005): A Man and His Blues
*Bill Haley[1] and His Comets (1987): "Rock Around the Clock"
*Hall (Darryl) and Oates (John) (2014): "Kiss on My List"
*George Harrison (2004): "My Sweet Lord"
*Isaac Hayes (2002): "Theme From 'Shaft'"
*Heart (2013): "Barracuda"
*Jimi Hendrix (1992): "Purple Haze"
Lauryn Hill: "Doo-Wop (That Thing)"
*The Hollies (2010): "Long Cool Woman (In a Black Dress)"
*Buddy Holly (1986): "Peggy Sue"
*John Lee Hooker (1991): "Boogie Chillen"
Hootie and the Blowfish: Cracked Rear View
Whitney Houston: "I Will Always Love You"
*The Impressions (1991): "For Your Precious Love"
Indigo Girls: "Closer to Fine"
INXS: "Need You Tonight"
*The Isley Brothers (1992): "It's Your Thing"
Ja Rule: Venni, Vetti, Vecci
*The Jackson Five (1997): "ABC"
Janet Jackson: Rhythm Nation
*Michael Jackson (2001): Thriller
*Etta James (1993): "At Last"
Tommy James and the Shondells: "Crimson and Clover"
Jane's Addiction: "Jane Says"
Jay and the Americans: "This Magic Moment"
Jay Z: "99 Problems"
*Jefferson Airplane (1996): "White Rabbit"
Jethro Tull: Aqualung
*Joan Jett and the Blackhearts (2015): "I Love Rock 'n' Roll"
Jewel: "You Were Meant for Me"
*Billy Joel (1999): "Piano Man"
*Elton John (1994): "Candle in the Wind"
*Little Willie John (1996): "Sleep"
Norah Jones: Come Away With Me
*Janis Joplin (1995): "Me and Bobby McGee"
*Journey (2017): "Don't Stop Believin'"
K.C. and the Sunshine Band: "Get Down Tonight"
R. Kelly: "I Can't Sleep Baby (If I)"
Alicia Keys: "Fallin'"
Kid Rock: "Cowboy"
*B. B. King (1987): "The Thrill Is Gone"
Carole King: Tapestry
*The Kinks (1990): "You Really Got Me"
*Kiss (2014): "Rock 'n' Roll All Night"
*Gladys Knight and the Pips (1996): "Midnight Train to Georgia"
Korn: "Blind"
Lenny Kravitz: "Are You Gonna Go My Way?"
Lady Gaga: "Poker Face"
Kendrick Lamar: DAMN.
*Led Zeppelin (1995): "Stairway to Heaven"
*Brenda Lee (2002): "I'm Sorry"
John Legend: "Ordinary People"
*John Lennon (1994): "Imagine"
*Jerry Lee Lewis (1986): "Whole Lotta Shakin' Going On"
Lil' Kim: "No Matter What They Say"
Lil Wayne: Tha Block Is Hot
Limp Bizkit: "Break Stuff"
Linkin Park: "One Step Closer"
*Little Anthony and the Imperials (2009): "Tears on My Pillow"
*Little Richard (1986): "Tutti Frutti"
*Little Walter (2008): "Juke"

LL Cool J: "Mama Said Knock You Out"
Jennifer Lopez: "Love Don't Cost a Thing"
*Darlene Love (2011): "He's a Rebel"
*The Lovin' Spoonful (2000): "Summer in the City"
Ludacris: "Money Maker"
*Frankie Lymon and the Teenagers (1993): "Why Do Fools Fall in Love?"
*Lynyrd Skynyrd (2006): "Free Bird"
*Madonna (2008): "Material Girl"
*The Mamas and the Papas (1998): "Monday, Monday"
Marilyn Manson: "Beautiful People"
*Bob Marley (1994): Exodus
Maroon 5: "Moves Like Jagger"
Bruno Mars: "Just the Way You Are"
*Martha and the Vandellas (1995): "Dancin' in the Streets"
The Marvelettes: "Please, Mr. Postman"
Matchbox 20: "Push"
John Mayer: "Daughters"
*Curtis Mayfield (1999): "Superfly"
*Paul McCartney (1999): "Band on the Run"
Don McLean: "American Pie"
*Clyde McPhatter (1987): "A Lover's Question"
Meat Loaf: "Paradise by the Dashboard Light"
*John (Cougar) Mellencamp (2008): "Jack and Diane"
Men at Work: "Who Can It Be Now?"
*Metallica (2009): "Enter Sandman"
George Michael: "Faith"
*Steve Miller (2016): "Take the Money and Run"
Nicki Minaj: Pink Friday.
*Joni Mitchell (1997): "Both Sides Now"
Moby: "Bodyrock"
Janelle Monáe: "Make Me Feel"
The Monkees: "I'm a Believer"
*Moody Blues (2018): "Nights in White Satin"
*The Moonglows (2000): "Blue Velvet"
Alanis Morissette: "Ironic"
*Van Morrison (1993): "Brown-Eyed Girl"
Mötley Crüe: "Live Wire"
Motörhead: "Ace of Spades"
Jason Mraz: "I'm Yours"
Mumford & Sons: "Little Lion Man"
Nelly: Country Grammar
*Ricky Nelson (1987): "Hello, Mary Lou"
Nine Inch Nails: "Closer"
*Nirvana (2014): Nevermind
No Doubt: Rock Steady
The Notorious B.I.G.: "Mo Money Mo Problems"
NSYNC: "Bye, Bye, Bye"
Ted Nugent: "Stranglehold"
*N.W.A. (2016): "Straight Outta Compton"
*The O'Jays (2005): "Back Stabbers"
One Direction: "What Makes You Beautiful"
*Roy Orbison (1987): "Oh, Pretty Woman"
Ozzy Osbourne: "Crazy Train"
OutKast: Speakerboxxx/The Love Below
*Parliament/Funkadelic (1997): "One Nation Under a Groove"
*Pearl Jam (2017): Ten
*Carl Perkins (1987): "Blue Suede Shoes"
Katy Perry: "Firework"
Peter, Paul, and Mary: "Leaving on a Jet Plane"
*Tom Petty and the Heartbreakers (2002): "Refugee"
Liz Phair: Exile in Guyville
Phish: "Sample in a Jar"
*Wilson Pickett (1991): "Land of 1,000 Dances"
Pink: Missundaztood
*Pink Floyd (1996): The Wall
*Gene Pitney (2002): "Only Love Can Break a Heart"
*The Platters (1990): "The Great Pretender"
The Pointer Sisters: "I'm So Excited"
*The Police (2003): "Every Breath You Take"
Iggy Pop: "Lust for Life"
*Elvis Presley (1986): "Love Me Tender"
*The Pretenders (2005): "Back on the Chain Gang"
*Lloyd Price (1998): "Stagger Lee"
*Prince (2004): "Purple Rain"
*Public Enemy (2013): "Fight the Power"
Puff Daddy and the Family: No Way Out
*Queen (2001): "Bohemian Rhapsody"
Radiohead: OK Computer
Rage Against the Machine: "Bulls on Parade"
*Bonnie Raitt (2000): "Something to Talk About"

*The Ramones (2002): "I Wanna Be Sedated"
*Red Hot Chili Peppers (2012): "Under the Bridge"
*Otis Redding (1989): "(Sittin' on) The Dock of the Bay"
*Jimmy Reed (1991): "Ain't That Loving You, Baby?"
*Lou Reed (2015): "Walk on the Wild Side"
*R.E.M. (2007): "Losing My Religion"
REO Speedwagon: "Can't Fight This Feeling"
Busta Rhymes: "What's It Gonna Be?"
*The Righteous Brothers (2003): "You've Lost That Lovin' Feelin'"
Rihanna: "Umbrella"
Johnny Rivers: "Poor Side of Town"
*Smokey Robinson[1] and the Miracles (1987): "Shop Around"
*The Rolling Stones (1989): "Satisfaction"
*The Ronettes (2007): "Be My Baby"
*Linda Ronstadt (2014): "You're No Good"
Diana Ross: "I'm Coming Out"
*Run-D.M.C. (2009): "Raisin' Hell"
*Rush (2013): "Tom Sawyer"
Sade: "Smooth Operator"
Salt-N-Pepa: "Shoop"
*Sam and Dave (1992): "Soul Man"
*Santana (1998): "Black Magic Woman"
Seal: "Kiss From a Rose"
Neil Sedaka: "Breaking Up Is Hard to Do"
*Bob Seger (2004): "Old Time Rock & Roll"
*Sex Pistols (2006): "Anarchy in the UK"
Shakira: "Whenever, Wherever"
*Tupac Shakur (2017): "How Do U Want It"
*Del Shannon (1999): "Runaway"
Ed Sheeran: "Thinking Out Loud"
*The Shirelles (1996): "Soldier Boy"
Carly Simon: "You're So Vain"
*Paul Simon (2001): "50 Ways to Leave Your Lover"
*Simon and Garfunkel (1990): "Bridge Over Troubled Water"
*Nina Simone (2018): "Mississippi Goddamn"
*Percy Sledge (2005): "When a Man Loves a Woman"
*Sly and the Family Stone (1993): "Everyday People"
Smashing Pumpkins: "Today"
*Patti Smith (2007): "Because the Night"
Sam Smith: "Stay With Me"
Will Smith: "Gettin' Jiggy With It"
The Smiths: "This Charming Man"
Snoop Dogg (a.k.a. Snoop Lion, Snoopzilla): "Gin and Juice"
Sonic Youth: "Bull in the Heather"
Soundgarden: "Black Hole Sun"
Britney Spears: "Hit Me Baby One More Time"
Spice Girls: "Wannabe"
*Dusty Springfield (1999): "I Only Want to Be With You"
*Bruce Springsteen (1999): "Born to Run"
*Staple Singers (1999): "I'll Take You There"
*Steely Dan (2001): "Rikki Don't Lose That Number"
Gwen Stefani: "Hollaback Girl"
Steppenwolf: "Born to Be Wild"
*Cat Stevens (2014): "Wild World"
*Rod Stewart (1994): "Maggie Mae"
Sting: "If You Love Somebody, Set Them Free"
Stone Temple Pilots: "Plush"
*The Stooges (2010): "I Wanna Be Your Dog"
Styx: "Come Sail Away"
The Sugar Hill Gang: "Rapper's Delight"
*Donna Summer (2013): "Bad Girls"
*The Supremes (1988): "Stop! In the Name of Love"
*Talking Heads (2002): "Once in a Lifetime"
*James Taylor (2001): "You've Got a Friend"
*The Temptations (2001): "My Girl"
Robin Thicke: "Blurred Lines"
Three Dog Night: "Joy to the World"
Justin Timberlake: "SexyBack"
TLC: "Waterfalls"
*Traffic (2004): Traffic
*Big Joe Turner (1987): "Shake, Rattle & Roll"
*Ike and Tina Turner (1991): "Proud Mary"
The Turtles: "Happy Together"
*U2 (2005): "With or Without You"
Usher: "You Make Me Wanna"
*Ritchie Valens (2001): "La Bamba"
*Van Halen (2007): "Running With the Devil"
*Stevie Ray Vaughan & Double Trouble (2015): "Change It"
*The Velvet Underground (1996): "Sweet Jane"

*The Ventures (2008): "Walk, Don't Run"
*Gene Vincent (1998): "Be-Bop-A-Lula"
*Tom Waits (2011): "Downtown Train"
The Wallflowers: "One Headlight"
Dionne Warwick: "I Say a Little Prayer"
*Muddy Waters (1987): "I Can't Be Satisfied"
Mary Wells: "My Guy"
Kanye West: "Gold Digger"
The White Stripes: "Seven Nation Army"

Whitesnake: "Here I Go Again"
*The Who (1990): Tommy
Pharrell Williams: "Happy"
*Jackie Wilson (1987): "That's Why"
*Bill Withers (2015): "Lean on Me"
*Bobby Womack (2009): "Lookin' for a Love"
*Stevie Wonder (1989): "You Are the Sunshine of My Life"

Wu-Tang Clan: "Protect Ya Neck"
*The Yardbirds (1992): "For Your Love"
*Yes (2017): "Owner of a Lonely Heart"
*Neil Young (1995): "Down by the River"
*The Young Rascals/The Rascals (1997): "Good Lovin'"
*Frank Zappa[1]/Mothers of Invention (1995): Hot Rats
*ZZ Top (2004): "Legs"

(1) Only individual performer is in Rock and Roll Hall of Fame.

Entertainment Personalities of the Present
Living actors, musicians, dancers, singers, producers, directors, and radio-TV performers.

Name	Birthplace	Birthdate
Abdul, Paula	San Fernando, CA	6/19/1962
Abraham, F. Murray	Pittsburgh, PA	10/24/1939
Abrams, J(effrey) J(acob)	New York, NY	6/27/1966
Adams, Amy	Vicenza, Italy	8/20/1974
Adams, Bryan	Kingston, ON, Canada	11/5/1959
Adams, Yolanda	Houston, TX	8/27/1961
Adele	London, England, UK	5/5/1988
Adjani, Isabelle	Paris, France	6/27/1955
Ad-Rock	South Orange, NJ	10/31/1966
Aduba, Uzo	Boston, MA	2/10/1981
Affleck, Ben	Berkeley, CA	8/15/1972
Affleck, Casey	Falmouth, MA	8/12/1975
Aghdashloo, Shohreh	Tehran, Iran	5/11/1952
Aguilera, Christina	Staten Island, NY	12/18/1980
Ahmed, Riz	Wembley, Eng., UK	12/1/1982
Aiello, Danny	New York, NY	6/20/1933
Aiken, Clay	Raleigh, NC	11/30/1978
Aimée, Anouk	Paris, France	4/27/1932
Alba, Jessica	Pomona, CA	4/28/1981
Alberghetti, Anna Maria	Pesaro, Italy	5/15/1936
Albert, Marv	Brooklyn, NY	6/12/1941
Alda, Alan	New York, NY	1/28/1936
Alexander, Jane	Boston, MA	10/28/1939
Alexander, Jason	Newark, NJ	9/23/1959
Ali, Mahershala	Oakland, CA	2/16/1974
Allen, Debbie	Houston, TX	1/16/1950
Allen, Joan	Rochelle, IL	8/20/1956
Allen, Karen	Carrollton, IL	10/5/1951
Allen, Kris	Jacksonville, AR	6/21/1985
Allen, Tim	Denver, CO	6/13/1953
Allen, Woody	Bronx, NY	12/1/1935
Alley, Kirstie	Wichita, KS	1/12/1951
Alpert, Herb	Los Angeles, CA	3/31/1935
Almodóvar, Pedro	Calzada de Calatrava, Spain	9/24/1949
Ambrose, Lauren	New Haven, CT	2/20/1978
Ames, Ed	Malden, MA	7/9/1927
Amos, John	Newark, NJ	12/27/1939
Amos, Tori	Newton, NC	8/22/1963
Anderson, Anthony	Los Angeles, CA	8/15/1970
Anderson, Gillian	Chicago, IL	8/9/1968
Anderson, Ian	Dunfermline, Scotland, UK	8/10/1947
Anderson, Loni	St. Paul, MN	8/5/1945
Anderson, Louie	St. Paul, MN	3/24/1953
Anderson, Melissa Sue	Berkeley, CA	9/26/1962
Anderson, Pamela	Ladysmith, BC, Canada	7/1/1967
Anderson, Richard Dean	Minneapolis, MN	1/23/1950
Anderson, Wes	Houston, TX	5/1/1969
Andersson, Bibi	Stockholm, Sweden	11/11/1935
André 3000	Atlanta, GA	5/27/1975
Andress, Ursula	Bern, Switzerland	3/19/1936
Andrews, Julie	Walton-on-Thames, Surrey, England, UK	10/1/1935
Andrews, Naveen	London, England, UK	1/17/1969
Aniston, Jennifer	Sherman Oaks, CA	2/11/1969
Anka, Paul	Ottawa, ON, Canada	7/30/1941
Ann-Margret	Stockholm, Sweden	4/28/1941
Ansari, Aziz	Columbia, SC	2/23/1983
Anthony, Marc	New York, NY	9/16/1968
Apatow, Judd	Syosset, NY	12/6/1967
Apple, Fiona	New York, NY	9/13/1977
Applegate, Christina	Los Angeles, CA	11/25/1971
Archer, Anne	Los Angeles, CA	8/24/1947
Arkin, Adam	Brooklyn, NY	8/19/1956
Arkin, Alan	New York, NY	3/26/1934
Armisen, Fred	Hattiesburg, MS	12/4/1966
Arnaz, Desi, Jr.	Hollywood, CA	1/19/1953
Arnaz, Lucie	Hollywood, CA	7/17/1951
Arnett, Will	Toronto, ON, Canada	5/4/1970
Arnold, Tom	Ottumwa, IA	3/6/1959
Arquette, David	Winchester, VA	9/8/1971
Arquette, Patricia	Chicago, IL	4/8/1968
Arquette, Rosanna	New York, NY	8/10/1959
Arroyo, Martina	New York, NY	2/2/1937
Ashanti (Douglas)	Glen Cove, NY	10/13/1980
Ashley, Elizabeth	Ocala, FL	8/30/1939

Name	Birthplace	Birthdate
Asner, Ed	Kansas City, KS	11/15/1929
Assante, Armand	New York, NY	10/4/1949
Astin, John	Baltimore, MD	3/30/1930
Astin, Sean	Santa Monica, CA	2/25/1971
Atkins, Eileen	London, England, UK	6/16/1934
Atkins, Sharif	Pittsburgh, PA	1/29/1975
Atkinson, Rowan	Newcastle upon Tyne, Eng., UK	1/6/1955
Auberjonois, Rene	New York, NY	6/1/1940
Austin, Patti	New York, NY	8/10/1948
Avalon, Frankie	Philadelphia, PA	9/18/1940
Aykroyd, Dan	Ottawa, ON, Canada	7/1/1952
Azalea, Iggy	Sydney, NSW, Australia	6/7/1990
Azaria, Hank	Forest Hills, Queens, NY	4/25/1964
Babyface	Indianapolis, IN	4/10/1959
Baccarin, Morena	Rio de Janeiro, Brazil	6/2/1979
Bacon, Kevin	Philadelphia, PA	7/8/1958
Badalucco, Michael	Brooklyn, NY	12/20/1954
Bader, Diedrich	Alexandria, VA	12/24/1966
Badu, Erykah	Dallas, TX	2/26/1971
Baez, Joan	Staten Island, NY	1/9/1941
Baio, Scott	Brooklyn, NY	9/22/1960
Baker, Anita	Toledo, OH	1/26/1958
Baker, Carroll	Johnstown, PA	5/28/1931
Baker, Diane	Hollywood, CA	2/25/1938
Baker, Joe Don	Groesbeck, TX	2/12/1936
Baker, Kathy	Midland, TX	6/8/1950
Baker, Simon	Launceston, Tas., Australia	7/30/1969
Bakula, Scott	St. Louis, MO	10/9/1954
Baldwin, Alec	Massapequa, NY	4/3/1958
Baldwin, Daniel	Massapequa, NY	10/5/1960
Baldwin, Stephen	Massapequa, NY	5/12/1966
Baldwin, William	Massapequa, NY	2/21/1963
Bale, Christian	Pembrokeshire, Wales, UK	1/30/1974
Ballard, Kaye	Cleveland, OH	11/20/1926
Ballas, Mark	Houston, TX	5/24/1986
Bana, Eric	Melbourne, Vic., Australia	8/9/1968
Banderas, Antonio	Málaga, Spain	8/10/1960
Banks, Elizabeth	Pittsfield, MA	2/10/1974
Banks, Jonathan	Washington, DC	1/31/1947
Banks, Tyra	Los Angeles, CA	12/4/1973
Baranski, Christine	Buffalo, NY	5/2/1952
Barbeau, Adrienne	Sacramento, CA	6/11/1945
Bardem, Javier	Las Palmas, Canary Islands, Spain	3/1/1969
Bardot, Brigitte	Paris, France	9/28/1934
Barker, Bob	Darrington, WA	12/12/1923
Barkin, Ellen	Bronx, NY	4/16/1955
Barrie, Barbara	Chicago, IL	5/23/1931
Barrino, Fantasia	High Point, NC	6/30/1984
Barrymore, Drew	Los Angeles, CA	2/22/1975
Bartoli, Cecilia	Rome, Italy	6/4/1966
Barton, Misha	London, England, UK	1/24/1986
Baryshnikov, Mikhail	Riga, Latvia	1/28/1948
Basinger, Kim	Athens, GA	12/8/1953
Bass, Lance	Laurel, MS	5/4/1979
Bassett, Angela	New York, NY	8/16/1958
Bassey, Shirley	Cardiff, Wales, UK	1/8/1937
Bateman, Jason	Rye, NY	1/14/1969
Bateman, Justine	Rye, NY	2/19/1966
Bates, Kathy	Memphis, TN	6/28/1948
Batt, Bryan	New Orleans, LA	3/1/1963
Battle, Kathleen	Portsmouth, OH	8/13/1948
Baxter, Meredith	South Pasadena, CA	6/21/1947
Bean, Orson	Burlington, VT	7/22/1928
Bean, Sean	Sheffield, England, UK	4/17/1959
Beatty, Ned	Louisville, KY	7/6/1937
Beatty, Warren	Richmond, VA	3/30/1937
Beauvais, Garcelle	St. Marc, Haiti	11/26/1966
Beck	Los Angeles, CA	7/8/1970
Beck, Jeff	Wallington, Surrey, Eng., UK	6/24/1944
Beckham, Victoria	Hertfordshire, England, UK	4/17/1974
Beckinsale, Kate	London, England, UK	7/26/1973
Bedelia, Bonnie	New York, NY	3/25/1948
Bee, Samantha	Toronto, ON, Canada	10/25/1969

Name	Birthplace	Birthdate
Begley, Ed, Jr.	Los Angeles, CA	9/16/1949
Behar, Joy	Brooklyn, NY	10/7/1942
Belafonte, Harry	New York, NY	3/1/1927
Bell, Kristen	Huntington Woods, MI	7/18/1980
Bello, Maria	Norristown, PA	4/18/1967
Belmondo, Jean-Paul	Neuilly-sur-Seine, France	4/9/1933
Belushi, Jim	Chicago, IL	6/15/1954
Belzer, Richard	Bridgeport, CT	8/4/1944
Benanti, Laura	Kinnelon, NJ	7/15/1979
Benatar, Pat	Brooklyn, NY	1/10/1953
Benedict, Dirk	Helena, MT	3/1/1945
Benigni, Roberto	Misericordia, Italy	10/27/1952
Bening, Annette	Topeka, KS	5/29/1958
Benjamin, Richard	New York, NY	5/22/1938
Bennett, Alan	Leeds, England, UK	5/9/1934
Bennett, Tony	Astoria, Queens, NY	8/3/1926
Benson, George	Pittsburgh, PA	3/22/1943
Benson, Robby	Dallas, TX	1/21/1956
Berenger, Tom	Chicago, IL	5/31/1950
Bergen, Candice	Beverly Hills, CA	5/9/1946
Bergeron, Tom	Haverhill, MA	5/6/1955
Bernard, Crystal	Garland, TX	9/30/1961
Bernhard, Sandra	Flint, MI	6/6/1955
Bernsen, Corbin	North Hollywood, CA	9/7/1954
Berry, Halle	Cleveland, OH	8/14/1966
Berry, Ken	Moline, IL	11/3/1933
Bertinelli, Valerie	Wilmington, DE	4/23/1960
Bertolucci, Bernardo	Parma, Italy	3/16/1940
Best, Eve	London, England, UK	7/31/1971
Bettany, Paul	London, England, UK	5/27/1971
Bialik, Mayim	San Diego, CA	12/12/1975
Bichir, Demián	Mexico City, Mexico	8/1/1963
Bieber, Justin	Stratford, ON, Canada	3/1/1994
Biel, Jessica	Ely, MN	3/3/1982
Big Boi	Savannah, GA	2/1/1975
Bigelow, Kathryn	San Carlos, CA	11/27/1951
Biggs, Jason	Pompton Plains, NJ	5/12/1978
Bilson, Rachel	Los Angeles, CA	8/25/1981
Binoche, Juliette	Paris, France	3/9/1964
Birch, Thora	Beverly Hills, CA	3/11/1982
Birney, David	Washington, DC	4/23/1939
Bisset, Jacqueline	Weybridge, England, UK	9/13/1944
Björk (Gudmundsdottir)	Reykjavik, Iceland	11/21/1965
Black, Clint	Long Branch, NJ	2/4/1962
Black, Jack	Santa Monica, CA	8/28/1969
Black, Lewis	Washington, DC	8/30/1948
Blades, Ruben	Panama City, Panama	7/16/1948
Blair, Linda	St. Louis, MO	1/22/1959
Blake, Robert	Nutley, NJ	9/18/1933
Blanchett, Cate	Melbourne, Vic., Australia	5/14/1969
Bledsoe, Tempestt	Chicago, IL	8/1/1973
Bleeth, Yasmine	New York, NY	6/14/1968
Blethyn, Brenda	Ramsgate, Kent, Eng., UK	2/20/1946
Blige, Mary J.	Bronx, NY	1/11/1971
Bloom, Claire	London, England, UK	2/15/1931
Bloom, Orlando	Canterbury, England, UK	1/13/1977
Bloom, Rachel	Manhattan Beach, CA	4/3/1987
Blunt, Emily	London, England, UK	2/23/1983
Blyth, Ann	Mt. Kisco, NY	8/16/1928
Bocelli, Andrea	Lajatico, Italy	9/22/1958
Bogdanovich, Peter	Kingston, NY	7/30/1939
Bogosian, Eric	Woburn, MA	4/24/1953
Bolton, Michael	New Haven, CT	2/26/1953
Bomer, Matt	Spring, TX	10/11/1977
Bon Jovi, Jon	Sayreville, NJ	3/2/1962
Bonaduce, Danny	Broomall, PA	8/13/1959
Bonet, Lisa	San Francisco, CA	11/16/1967
Bonham Carter, Helena	London, England, UK	5/26/1966
Bonneville, Hugh	London, England, UK	11/10/1963
Bono	Dublin, Ireland	5/10/1960
Boone, Debby	Hackensack, NJ	9/22/1956
Boone, Pat	Jacksonville, FL	6/1/1934
Boreanaz, David	Buffalo, NY	5/16/1969
Bosco, Philip	Jersey City, NJ	9/26/1930
Boseman, Chadwick	Anderson, SC	11/29/1976
Bostwick, Barry	San Mateo, CA	2/24/1945
Bosworth, Kate	Los Angeles, CA	1/2/1983
Bottoms, Timothy	Santa Barbara, CA	8/30/1951
Bow Wow	Columbus, OH	3/9/1987
Bowen, Julie	Baltimore, MD	3/3/1970
Bowles, Peter	London, England, UK	10/16/1936
Boxleitner, Bruce	Elgin, IL	5/12/1950
Boy George	Bexleyheath, England, UK	6/14/1961
Boyle, Danny	Manchester, England, UK	10/20/1956
Boyle, Lara Flynn	Davenport, IA	3/24/1970
Boyle, Susan	Blackburn, Scotland, UK	4/1/1961
Bracco, Lorraine	Brooklyn, NY	10/2/1955
Brady, Wayne	Orlando, FL	6/2/1972
Braff, Zach	South Orange, NJ	4/6/1975
Branagh, Kenneth	Belfast, N. Ireland, UK	12/10/1960
Brand, Russell	Grays, Essex, UK	6/4/1975
Brandauer, Klaus Maria	Steiermark, Austria	6/22/1944
Brandy (Norwood)	McComb, MS	2/11/1979
Bratt, Benjamin	San Francisco, CA	12/16/1963
Braugher, Andre	Chicago, IL	7/1/1962

Name	Birthplace	Birthdate
Braxton, Toni	Severn, MD	10/7/1966
Bremner, Ewen	Edinburgh, Scotland, UK	1/23/1972
Brendon, Nicholas	Los Angeles, CA	4/12/1971
Brenneman, Amy	Glastonbury, CT	6/22/1964
Bridges, Beau	Los Angeles, CA	12/9/1941
Bridges, Jeff	Los Angeles, CA	12/4/1949
Brightman, Sarah	Berkhamsted, England, UK	8/14/1960
Brimley, Wilford	Salt Lake City, UT	9/27/1934
Brinkley, Christie	Monroe, MI	2/2/1954
Britton, Connie	Boston, MA	3/6/1967
Broadbent, Jim	Lincolnshire, England, UK	5/24/1949
Broderick, Matthew	New York, NY	3/21/1962
Brody, Adam	San Diego, CA	12/15/1979
Brody, Adrien	New York, NY	4/14/1973
Brolin, James	Los Angeles, CA	7/18/1940
Brolin, Josh	Los Angeles, CA	2/12/1968
Brooks, Albert	Beverly Hills, CA	7/22/1947
Brooks, Garth	Tulsa, OK	2/7/1962
Brooks, James L.	North Bergen, NJ	5/9/1940
Brooks, Mel	Brooklyn, NY	6/28/1926
Brosnahan, Rachel	Milwaukee, WI	12/15/1990
Brosnan, Pierce	Navan, Co. Meath, Ireland	5/16/1953
Brown, Blair	Washington, DC	4/23/1946
Brown, Bobby	Roxbury, MA	2/5/1969
Brown, Bryan	Panania, NSW, Australia	6/23/1947
Brown, Chris	Tappahannock, VA	5/5/1989
Brown, Foxy	Brooklyn, NY	9/6/1979
Brown, Sterling K.	St. Louis, MO.	4/5/1976
Browne, Jackson	Heidelberg, Germany	10/9/1948
Bruckheimer, Jerry	Detroit, MI	9/21/1943
Bryan, Luke	Leesburg, GA	7/17/1976
Bryson, Peabo	Greenville, SC	4/13/1951
Bublé, Michael	Burnaby, BC, Canada	9/9/1975
Buckley, Betty	Big Spring, TX	7/3/1947
Buffett, Jimmy	Pascagoula, MS	12/25/1946
Bujold, Geneviève	Montréal, QC, Canada	7/1/1942
Bullock, Sandra	Arlington, VA	7/26/1964
Bumbry, Grace	St. Louis, MO.	1/4/1937
Bündchen, Gisele	Horizontina, Brazil	7/20/1980
Burgess, Tituss	Athens, GA	2/21/1979
Burghoff, Gary	Bristol, CT	5/24/1943
Burke, Cheryl	San Francisco, CA	5/3/1984
Burke, Delta	Orlando, FL	7/30/1956
Burnett, Carol	San Antonio, TX	4/26/1933
Burns, Edward	Woodside, Queens, NY	1/29/1968
Burns, Ken	New York, NY	7/29/1953
Burrell, Ty	Grants Pass, OR	8/22/1967
Burstyn, Ellen	Detroit, MI	12/7/1932
Burton, LeVar	Landstuhl, Germany	2/16/1957
Burton, Tim	Burbank, CA	8/25/1958
Buscemi, Steve	Brooklyn, NY	12/13/1957
Busey, Gary	Goose Creek, TX	6/29/1944
Busfield, Timothy	Lansing, MI	6/12/1957
Butler, Brett	Montgomery, AL	1/30/1958
Butler, Dan	Fort Wayne, IN	12/2/1954
Butler, Gerard	Glasgow, Scotland, UK	11/13/1969
Butz, Norbert Leo	St. Louis, MO.	1/30/1967
Buzzi, Ruth	Westerly, RI	7/24/1936
Bynes, Amanda	Thousand Oaks, CA	4/3/1986
Byrne, David	Dumbarton, Scotland, UK	5/14/1952
Byrne, Gabriel	Dublin, Ireland	5/12/1950
Byrne, Rose	Sydney, NSW, Australia	7/24/1979
Caan, James	Bronx, NY	3/26/1940
Cage, Nicolas	Long Beach, CA	1/7/1964
Cain, Dean	Mt. Clemens, MI	7/31/1966
Caine, Michael	London, England, UK	3/14/1933
Caldwell, Zoe	Hawthorn, Vic., Australia	9/14/1933
Callies, Sarah Wayne	LaGrange, IL	6/1/1977
Callow, Simon	London, England, UK	6/15/1949
Cameron, James	Kapuskasing, ON, Canada	8/16/1954
Cameron, Kirk	Panorama City, CA	10/12/1970
Campbell, Bruce	Royal Oak, MI	6/22/1958
Campbell, Naomi	South London, Eng., UK	5/22/1970
Campbell, Neve	Guelph, ON, Canada	10/3/1973
Campion, Jane	Waikanae, New Zealand	4/30/1954
Cannavale, Bobby	Union City, NJ	5/3/1971
Cannon, Dyan	Tacoma, WA	1/4/1937
Cannon, Nick	San Diego, CA	10/8/1980
Caplan, Lizzy	Los Angeles, CA	6/30/1982
Capshaw, Kate	Ft. Worth, TX	11/3/1953
Cara, Irene	New York, NY	3/18/1959
Cardellini, Linda	Redwood City, CA	6/25/1975
Cardi B	New York, NY	10/11/1992
Cardinale, Claudia	Tunis, Tunisia	4/15/1938
Carell, Steve	Concord, MA	8/16/1962
Carey, Drew	Cleveland, OH	5/23/1958
Carey, Mariah	Huntington, NY	3/27/1970
Cariou, Len	St. Boniface, MB, Canada	9/30/1939
Carlton, Vanessa	Milford, PA	8/16/1980
Carlyle, Robert	Glasgow, Scotland, UK	4/14/1961
Carmen, Eric	Cleveland, OH	8/11/1949
Caron, Leslie	Boulogne, France	7/1/1931
Carpenter, John	Carthage, NY	1/16/1948
Carpenter, Mary Chapin	Princeton, NJ	2/21/1958
Carr, Vikki	El Paso, TX	7/19/1941

Name	Birthplace	Birthdate	Name	Birthplace	Birthdate
Carreras, Jose	Barcelona, Spain	12/5/1946	Conway, Tim	Willoughby, OH	12/15/1933
Carrere, Tia	Honolulu, HI	1/2/1967	Coogler, Ryan	Oakland, CA	5/23/1986
Carrey, Jim	Newmarket, ON, Canada	1/17/1962	Cook, David	Houston, TX	12/20/1982
Carroll, Diahann	Bronx, NY	7/17/1935	Coolidge, Rita	Nashville, TN	5/1/1945
Carroll, Pat	Shreveport, LA	5/5/1927	Coolio	Compton, CA	8/1/1963
Carter, Jim	Harrogate, Yorkshire, England, UK	8/19/1948	Coon, Carrie	Copley, OH	1/24/1981
			Cooper, Alice	Detroit, MI	2/4/1948
Carter, Lynda	Phoenix, AZ	7/24/1951	Cooper, Bradley	Philadelphia, PA	1/5/1975
Carter, Nick	Jamestown, NY	1/28/1980	Cooper, Chris	Kansas City, MO	7/9/1951
Carter, Ron	Ferndale, MI	5/4/1937	Copeland, Misty	Kansas City, MO	9/10/1982
Cartwright, Nancy	Kettering, OH	10/25/1957	Copperfield, David	Metuchen, NJ	9/16/1956
Caruso, David	Forest Hills, Queens, NY	1/17/1956	Coppola, Francis Ford	Detroit, MI	4/7/1939
Carvey, Dana	Missoula, MT	6/2/1955	Coppola, Sofia	New York, NY	5/14/1971
Cash, Rosanne	Memphis, TN	5/24/1955	Corbett, John	Wheeling, WV	5/9/1961
Castellaneta, Dan	Chicago, IL	10/29/1957	Corbin, Barry	Lamesa, TX	10/16/1940
Castle-Hughes, Keisha	Donnybrook, WA, Australia	3/24/1990	Corden, James	Hillingdon, England, UK	8/22/1978
Cates, Phoebe	New York, NY	7/16/1963	Corea, Chick	Chelsea, MA	6/12/1941
Cattrall, Kim	Liverpool, England, UK	8/21/1956	Corgan, Billy	Elk Grove, IL	3/17/1967
Cavanagh, Tom	Ottawa, ON, Canada	10/26/1963	Corwin, Jeff	Norwell, MA	7/11/1967
Cavett, Dick	Gibbon, NE	11/19/1936	Cosby, Bill	Philadelphia, PA	7/12/1937
Caviezel, Jim	Mount Vernon, WA	9/26/1968	Cosgrove, Miranda	Los Angeles, CA	5/14/1993
Cavill, Henry	Jersey, Channel Isls., UK	5/5/1983	Costas, Bob	Astoria, Queens, NY	3/22/1952
Cedric the Entertainer	Jefferson City, MO	4/24/1964	Costello, Elvis	London, England, UK	8/25/1954
Cera, Michael	Brampton, ON, Canada	6/7/1988	Costner, Kevin	Compton, CA	1/18/1955
Chalamet, Timothée	New York, NY	12/27/1995	Cotillard, Marion	Paris, France	9/30/1975
Chalke, Sarah	Ottawa, ON, Canada	8/27/1976	Cowell, Simon	London, England, UK	10/7/1959
Chamberlain, Richard	Beverly Hills, CA	3/31/1934	Cox, Brian	Dundee, Scotland, UK	6/1/1946
Chambers, Justin	Springfield, OH	7/11/1970	Cox, Courteney	Birmingham, AL	6/15/1964
Chan, Jackie	Hong Kong	4/7/1954	Cox, Laverne	Mobile, AL	5/29/1972
Chance the Rapper	Chicago, IL	4/16/1993	Cox, Ronny	Cloudcroft, NM	7/23/1938
Chandler, Kyle	Buffalo, NY	9/17/1965	Coyote, Peter	New York, NY	10/10/1941
Channing, Carol	Seattle, WA	1/31/1921	Craig, Daniel	Chester, England, UK	3/2/1968
Channing, Stockard	New York, NY	2/13/1944	Cranston, Bryan	San Fernando Valley, CA	3/7/1956
Chaplin, Geraldine	Santa Monica, CA	7/31/1944	Crawford, Cindy	DeKalb, IL	2/20/1966
Chapman, Tracy	Cleveland, OH	3/30/1964	Crawford, Michael	Salisbury, England, UK	1/19/1942
Chappelle, Dave	Washington, DC	8/24/1973	Criss, Darren	San Francisco, CA	2/5/1987
Charles, Josh	Baltimore, MD	9/15/1971	Cromwell, James	Los Angeles, CA	1/27/1940
Charo	Murcia, Spain	1/15/1951?	Crosby, David	Los Angeles, CA	8/14/1941
Chase, Chevy	New York, NY	10/8/1943	Cross, Ben	London, England, UK	12/16/1947
Chasez, JC (Joshua)	Washington, DC	8/8/1976	Cross, Marcia	Marlborough, MA	3/25/1962
Chastain, Jessica	Sacramento, CA	3/29/1977	Crouse, Lindsay	New York, NY	5/12/1948
Cheadle, Don	Kansas City, MO	11/29/1964	Crow, Sheryl	Kennett, MO	2/11/1962
Checker, Chubby	Spring Gulley, SC	10/3/1941	Crowe, Cameron	Palm Springs, CA	7/13/1957
Chen, Julie	New York, NY	1/6/1970	Crowe, Russell	Wellington, New Zealand	4/7/1964
Chenoweth, Kristin	Broken Arrow, OK	7/24/1968	Crudup, Billy	Manhasset, NY	7/8/1948
Cher	El Centro, CA	5/20/1946	Cruise, Tom	Syracuse, NY	7/3/1962
Chesney, Kenny	Lutrelle, TN	3/26/1968	Cruz, Penelope	Madrid, Spain	4/28/1974
Chianese, Dominic	Bronx, NY	2/24/1931	Cryer, Jon	New York, NY	4/16/1965
Chiba, Sonny	Fukuoka, Kyushu, Japan	1/23/1939	Crystal, Billy	Long Beach, NY	3/14/1948
Chiklis, Michael	Lowell, MA	8/30/1963	Cuarón, Alfonso	Mexico City, Mexico	11/28/1961
Chlumsky, Anna	Chicago, IL	12/3/1980	Culkin, Macaulay	New York, NY	8/26/1980
Chmerkovskiy, Maksim	Odessa, Ukraine	1/17/1980	Cullum, John	Knoxville, TN	3/2/1930
Cho, Margaret	San Francisco, CA	12/5/1968	Cumberbatch, Benedict	London, England, UK	7/19/1976
Chong, Thomas	Edmonton, AB, Canada	5/24/1938	Cumming, Alan	Aberfeldy, Perthshire, Scotland, UK	1/27/1965
Chopra, Priyanka	Jamshedpur, India	7/18/1982			
Chow Yun-Fat	Lamma Island, Hong Kong	5/18/1955	Cuoco, Kaley	Camarillo, CA	11/30/1985
Christensen, Hayden	Vancouver, BC, Canada	4/19/1981	Curry, Tim	Grappenhall, Cheshire, England, UK	4/19/1946
Christie, Julie	Chukua, Assam, India	4/14/1940			
Chuck D	Roosevelt, NY	8/1/1960	Curtin, Jane	Cambridge, MA	9/6/1947
Church, Charlotte	Llandaff, Cardiff, Wales, UK	2/21/1986	Curtis, Jamie Lee	Los Angeles, CA	11/22/1958
Church, Thomas Haden	El Paso, TX	6/17/1960	Cusack, Joan	New York, NY	10/11/1962
Clapp, Gordon	North Conway, NH	9/24/1948	Cusack, John	Evanston, IL	6/28/1966
Clapton, Eric	Ripley, Surrey, Eng., UK	3/30/1945	Cyrus, Billy Ray	Flatwoods, KY	8/25/1961
Clark, Petula	Epson, Surrey, Eng., UK	11/15/1932	Cyrus, Miley	Nashville, TN	11/23/1992
Clark, Roy	Meherrin, VA	4/15/1933	Dafoe, Willem	Appleton, WI	7/22/1955
Clarkson, Kelly	Burleson, TX	4/24/1982	Dahl, Arlene	Minneapolis, MN	8/11/1925
Clarkson, Patricia	New Orleans, LA	12/29/1959	Dale, Jim	Rothwell, England, UK	8/15/1935
Clay, Andrew Dice	Brooklyn, NY	9/29/1957	Dalton, Timothy	Colwyn Bay, Wales, UK	3/21/1946
Cleese, John	Weston-super-Mare, Eng., UK	10/27/1939	Daltrey, Roger	London, England, UK	3/1/1944
Clooney, George	Lexington, KY	5/6/1961	Daly, Carson	Santa Monica, CA	6/22/1973
Close, Glenn	Greenwich, CT	3/19/1947	Daly, Timothy	New York, NY	3/1/1956
Coen, Ethan	St. Louis Park, MN	9/21/1957	Daly, Tyne	Madison, WI	2/21/1946
Coen, Joel	St. Louis Park, MN	11/29/1954	Damon, Matt	Cambridge, MA	10/8/1970
Cohen, Andy	St. Louis, MO	6/2/1968	Dane, Eric	San Francisco, CA	11/9/1972
Cohen, Sacha Baron	London, England, UK	10/13/1971	Danes, Claire	New York, NY	4/12/1979
Colbert, Stephen	Washington, DC	5/13/1964	D'Angelo	Richmond, VA	2/11/1974
Cole, Gary	Park Ridge, IL	9/20/1956	D'Angelo, Beverly	Columbus, OH	11/15/1954
Coleman, Dabney	Austin, TX	1/3/1932	Daniels, Anthony	Salisbury, England, UK	2/21/1946
Colfer, Chris	Fresno, CA	5/27/1990	Daniels, Charlie	Wilmington, NC	10/28/1936
Collette, Toni	Blacktown, NSW, Australia	11/1/1972	Daniels, Jeff	Athens, GA	2/19/1955
Collins, Joan	London, England, UK	5/23/1933	Daniels, Lee	Philadelphia, PA	12/24/1959
Collins, Judy	Seattle, WA	5/1/1939	Daniels, William	Brooklyn, NY	3/31/1927
Collins, Pauline	Exmouth, England, UK	9/3/1940	Danner, Blythe	Rosemont, PA	2/3/1943
Collins, Phil	London, England, UK	1/30/1951	Danson, Ted	San Diego, CA	12/29/1947
Collins, Stephen	Des Moines, IA	10/1/1947	Danza, Tony	Brooklyn, NY	4/21/1951
Columbus, Chris	Spangler, PA	9/10/1958	Darby, Kim	Hollywood, CA	7/8/1948
Colvin, Shawn	Vermillion, SD	1/10/1956	Daughtry, Chris	Roanoke Rapids, NC	12/26/1979
Combs, Sean	New York, NY	11/4/1969	David, Larry	Brooklyn, NY	7/2/1947
Connelly, Jennifer	Round Top, NY	12/12/1970	Davidson, John	Pittsburgh, PA	12/13/1941
Connery, Sean	Edinburgh, Scotland, UK	8/25/1930	Davis, Clifton	Chicago, IL	10/4/1945
Connick, Harry, Jr.	New Orleans, LA	9/11/1967	Davis, Geena	Wareham, MA	1/21/1956
Connolly, Kevin	Patchogue, NY	3/5/1974	Davis, Hope	Englewood, NJ	3/23/1964
Conrad, Robert	Chicago, IL	3/1/1935	Davis, Judy	Perth, WA, Australia	4/23/1955
Conroy, Frances	Monroe, GA	11/13/1953	Davis, Kristin	Boulder, CO	2/24/1965
Constantine, Michael	Reading, PA	5/22/1927	Davis, Mac	Lubbock, TX	1/21/1942
Conti, Tom	Paisley, Scotland, UK	11/22/1941	Davis, Viola	Saint Matthews, SC	8/11/1965

Name	Birthplace	Birthdate
Dawber, Pam	Farmington Hills, MI	10/18/1951
Dawson, Rosario	New York, NY	5/9/1979
Day, Doris	Cincinnati, OH	4/3/1922
Day-Lewis, Daniel	London, England, UK	4/29/1957
De Havilland, Olivia	Tokyo, Japan	7/1/1916
De Mornay, Rebecca	Santa Rosa, CA	8/29/1962
De Niro, Robert	New York, NY	8/17/1943
De Rossi, Portia	Melbourne, Vic., Australia	1/31/1973
DeGeneres, Ellen	Metairie, LA	1/26/1958
DeGraw, Gavin	Middletown, NY	2/4/1977
Del Toro, Benicio	Santurce, Puerto Rico	2/19/1967
Del Toro, Guillermo	Guadalajara, Jalisco, Mexico	10/9/1964
Delaney, Kim	Philadelphia, PA	11/29/1961
Delany, Dana	New York, NY	3/13/1956
Delon, Alain	Sceaux, France	11/8/1935
Dempsey, Patrick	Lewiston, ME	1/13/1966
Dench, Judi	York, England, UK	12/9/1934
Deneuve, Catherine	Paris, France	10/22/1943
Dennehy, Brian	Bridgeport, CT	7/9/1938
DePalma, Brian	Newark, NJ	9/11/1940
Depardieu, Gerard	Chateauroux, France	12/27/1948
Depp, Johnny	Owensboro, KY	6/9/1963
Derek, Bo	Long Beach, CA	11/20/1956
Dern, Bruce	Winnetka, IL	6/4/1936
Dern, Laura	Santa Monica, CA	2/10/1967
Deschanel, Zooey	Los Angeles, CA	1/17/1980
Devine, Loretta	Houston, TX	8/21/1949
DeVito, Danny	Neptune, NJ	11/17/1944
DeWitt, Joyce	Wheeling, WV	4/23/1949
Dey, Susan	Pekin, IL	12/10/1952
Diamond, Neil	Brooklyn, NY	1/24/1941
Diaz, Cameron	San Diego, CA	8/30/1972
Diaz, Guillermo	New Jersey	3/22/1975
DiCaprio, Leonardo	Hollywood, CA	11/11/1974
Dick, Andy	Charleston, SC	12/21/1965
Dickens, Kim	Huntsville, AL	6/18/1965
Dickinson, Angie	Kulm, ND	9/30/1931
Diesel, Vin	New York, NY	7/18/1967
Diggs, Taye	Newark, NJ	1/2/1972
Dillahunt, Garret	Castro Valley, CA	11/24/1964
Dillon, Kevin	Mamaroneck, NY	8/19/1965
Dillon, Matt	New Rochelle, NY	2/18/1964
Dinklage, Peter	Morristown, NJ	6/11/1969
DioGuardi, Kara	Scarsdale, NY	12/9/1970
Dion (DiMucci)	Bronx, NY	7/18/1939
Dion, Celine	Charlemagne, QC, Canada	3/30/1968
Djalili, Omid	London, England, UK	9/30/1965
Dobrev, Nina	Sofia, Bulgaria	1/9/1989
Dobson, Kevin	Jackson Heights, Queens, NY	3/18/1943
Dockery, Michelle	Barking, Essex, Eng., UK	12/15/1981
Doherty, Shannen	Memphis, TN	4/12/1971
Dolenz, Micky	Los Angeles, CA	3/8/1945
Domingo, Placido	Madrid, Spain	1/21/1941
Donahue, Phil	Cleveland, OH	12/21/1935
Donen, Stanley	Columbia, SC	4/13/1924
D'Onofrio, Vincent	Brooklyn, NY	6/30/1959
Donovan (Leitch)	Glasgow, Scotland, UK	5/10/1946
Donovan, Tate	New York, NY	9/25/1963
Dorn, Michael	Luling, TX	12/9/1952
Douglas, Kirk	Amsterdam, NY	12/9/1916
Douglas, Michael	New Brunswick, NJ	9/25/1944
Dourdan, Gary	Philadelphia, PA	12/11/1966
Dovolani, Tony	Pristina, Kosovo	7/17/1973
Dow, Tony	Hollywood, CA	4/13/1945
Dowd, Ann	Holyoke, MA	1/30/1956
Down, Lesley-Anne	London, England, UK	3/17/1954
Downey, Robert, Jr.	New York, NY	4/4/1965
Downey, Roma	Derry, N. Ireland, UK	5/6/1960
Downs, Hugh	Akron, OH	2/14/1921
Drake	Toronto, ON, Canada	10/24/1986
Drescher, Fran	Flushing, Queens, NY	9/30/1957
Dreyfuss, Richard	Brooklyn, NY	10/29/1947
Driver, Adam	San Bernardino, CA	11/19/1983
Driver, Minnie	London, England, UK	1/31/1970
Dryer, Fred	Hawthorne, CA	7/6/1946
Duchovny, David	New York, NY	8/7/1960
Duff, Hilary	Houston, TX	9/28/1987
Duffy (Aimee Anne)	Bangor, Gwynedd, Wales, UK	6/23/1984
Duffy, Julia	Minneapolis, MN	6/27/1951
Duffy, Patrick	Townsend, MT	3/17/1949
Duhamel, Josh	Minot, ND	11/14/1972
Dujardin, Jean	Rueil-Malmaison, France	6/19/1972
Dukakis, Olympia	Lowell, MA	6/20/1931
Dullea, Keir	Cleveland, OH	5/30/1936
Dunaway, Faye	Bascom, FL	1/14/1941
Duncan, Lindsay	Edinburgh, Scotland, UK	11/7/1950
Duncan, Sandy	Henderson, TX	2/20/1946
Dunham, Lena	New York, NY	5/13/1986
Dunne, Griffin	New York, NY	6/8/1955
Dunst, Kirsten	Point Pleasant, NJ	4/30/1982
Dussault, Nancy	Pensacola, FL	6/30/1936

Name	Birthplace	Birthdate
Dutton, Charles S.	Baltimore, MD	1/30/1951
Duvall, Robert	San Diego, CA	1/5/1931
Duvall, Shelley	Houston, TX	7/7/1949
DuVernay, Ava	Los Angeles, CA	8/24/1972
Dylan, Bob	Duluth, MN	5/24/1941
Dylan, Jakob	New York, NY	12/9/1969
Dzundza, George	Rosenheim, Germany	7/19/1945
Eads, George	Fort Worth, TX	3/1/1967
Easton, Sheena	Bellshill, Scotland, UK	4/27/1959
Eastwood, Clint	San Francisco, CA	5/31/1930
Ebersole, Christine	Chicago, IL	2/21/1953
Eckhart, Aaron	Cupertino, CA	3/12/1968
Eden, Barbara	Tucson, AZ	8/23/1931
Edwards, Anthony	Santa Barbara, CA	7/19/1962
Efron, Zac	San Luis Obispo, CA	10/18/1987
Ehle, Jennifer	Winston-Salem, NC	12/29/1969
Eikenberry, Jill	New Haven, CT	1/21/1947
Eisenberg, Jesse	Bayside, NY	10/5/1983
Ejiofor, Chiwetel	London, England, UK	7/10/1974
Ekland, Britt	Stockholm, Sweden	10/6/1942
Elba, Idris	London, England, UK	9/6/1972
Electra, Carmen	Cincinnati, OH	4/20/1972
Elfman, Jenna	Los Angeles, CA	9/30/1971
Elgort, Ansel	New York, NY	3/14/1994
Elizondo, Hector	New York, NY	12/22/1936
Elliott, Chris	New York, NY	5/31/1960
Elliott, Missy	Portsmouth, VA	7/1/1971
Elliott, Sam	Sacramento, CA	8/9/1944
Elvira	Manhattan, KS	9/17/1951
Emerson, Michael	Cedar Rapids, IA	9/7/1954
Eminem	St. Joseph, MO	10/17/1972
Enberg, Dick	Mt. Clemens, MI	1/9/1935
Englund, Robert	Glendale, CA	6/6/1949
Enya	Gweedore, Ireland	5/17/1961
Epps, Omar	Brooklyn, NY	7/23/1973
Estefan, Gloria	Havana, Cuba	9/1/1957
Estevez, Emilio	New York, NY	5/12/1962
Estrada, Erik	New York, NY	3/16/1949
Etheridge, Melissa	Leavenworth, KS	5/29/1961
Evans, Chris	Framingham, MA	6/13/1981
Evans, Linda	Hartford, CT	11/18/1942
Evans, Luke	Pontypool, Wales, UK	4/15/1979
Evans, Robert	New York, NY	6/29/1930
Everett, Rupert	Norfolk, England, UK	5/29/1959
Everly, Don	Brownie, KY	2/1/1937
Evigan, Greg	South Amboy, NJ	10/14/1953
Fabares, Shelley	Santa Monica, CA	1/19/1944
Fabian	Philadelphia, PA	2/6/1943
Fabio (Lanzoni)	Milan, Italy	3/15/1959
Fabolous	Brooklyn, NY	11/18/1977
Facinelli, Peter	Queens, NY	11/26/1973
Fairchild, Morgan	Dallas, TX	2/3/1950
Faison, Donald	New York, NY	6/22/1974
Falana, Lola	Philadelphia, PA	9/11/1942
Falco, Edie	Brooklyn, NY	7/5/1963
Fallon, Jimmy	Brooklyn, NY	9/19/1974
Fanning, Dakota	Conyers, GA	2/23/1994
Fanning, Elle	Conyers, GA	4/9/1998
Fargo, Donna	Mt. Airy, NC	11/10/1949
Faris, Anna	Baltimore, MD	11/29/1976
Farmiga, Vera	Clifton, NJ	8/6/1973
Farr, Jamie	Toledo, OH	7/1/1934
Farrell, Colin	Dublin, Ireland	5/31/1976
Farrell, Mike	St. Paul, MN	2/6/1939
Farrell, Perry	Bayside, Queens, NY	3/29/1959
Farrell, Suzanne	Cincinnati, OH	8/16/1945
Farrelly, Bobby	Cumberland, RI	6/17/1958
Farrelly, Peter	Phoenixville, PA	12/17/1956
Farrow, Mia	Los Angeles, CA	2/9/1945
Fassbender, Michael	Heidelberg, Germany	4/2/1977
Fatone, Joey	Brooklyn, NY	1/28/1977
Feinstein, Michael	Columbus, OH	9/7/1956
Feldman, Corey	Los Angeles, CA	7/16/1971
Feldon, Barbara	Bethel Park, PA	3/12/1933
Feldshuh, Tovah	New York, NY	12/27/1952
Feliciano, Jose	Lares, Puerto Rico	9/10/1945
Fenn, Sherilyn	Detroit, MI	2/1/1965
Fergie	Hacienda Heights, CA	3/27/1975
Ferguson, Craig	Glasgow, Scotland, UK	5/17/1962
Ferguson, Jesse Tyler	Missoula, MT	10/22/1975
Ferrara, Jerry	Brooklyn, NY	11/29/1979
Ferrell, Conchata	Charleston, WV	3/28/1943
Ferrell, Will	Irvine, CA	7/16/1967
Ferrera, America	Los Angeles, CA	4/18/1984
Feuerstein, Mark	New York, NY	6/8/1971
Fey, Tina	Upper Darby, PA	5/18/1970
Field, Sally	Pasadena, CA	11/6/1946
Fiennes, Joseph	Salisbury, England, UK	5/27/1970
Fiennes, Ralph	Suffolk, England, UK	12/22/1962
Fierstein, Harvey	Brooklyn, NY	6/6/1954
50 Cent	Jamaica, Queens, NY	7/6/1976
Fillion, Nathan	Edmonton, AB, Canada	3/27/1971
Fincher, David	Denver, CO	8/28/1962
Finney, Albert	Salford, England, UK	5/9/1936
Fiorentino, Linda	Philadelphia, PA	3/9/1960
Firth, Colin	Grayshott, England, UK	9/10/1960

Name	Birthplace	Birthdate
Firth, Peter	Bradford, Yorkshire, Eng., UK.	10/27/1953
Fischer, Jenna	Ft. Wayne, IN.	3/7/1974
Fishburne, Laurence	Augusta, GA	7/30/1961
Flack, Roberta	Black Mountain, NC	2/10/1939
Flanagan, Fionnula	Dublin, Ireland	12/10/1941
Flavor Flav	Roosevelt, NY	3/16/1959
Fleetwood, Mick	Redruth, Cornwall, Eng., UK	6/24/1942
Fleming, Renée	Indiana, PA	2/14/1959
Fleming, Rhonda	Hollywood, CA.	8/10/1923
Fletcher, Louise	Birmingham, AL.	7/22/1934
Flockhart, Calista	Freeport, IL	11/11/1964
Florek, Dann	Flat Rock, MI	5/1/1950
Fogerty, John	Berkeley, CA	5/28/1945
Foley, Dave	Etobicoke, ON, Canada	1/4/1963
Foley, Scott	Kansas City, KS.	7/15/1972
Fonda, Bridget	Los Angeles, CA	1/27/1964
Fonda, Jane	New York, NY	12/21/1937
Fonda, Peter	New York, NY	2/23/1940
Ford, Faith	Alexandria, LA.	9/14/1964
Ford, Harrison	Chicago, IL	7/13/1942
Forte, Will	Alameda Co., CA.	6/17/1970
Foster, Jodie	Los Angeles, CA	11/19/1962
Foster, Sutton	Statesboro, GA	3/18/1975
Fox, James	London, England, UK	5/19/1939
Fox, Jorja	New York, NY	7/7/1968
Fox, Matthew	Abington, PA	7/14/1966
Fox, Megan	Rockwood, TN.	5/16/1986
Fox, Michael J.	Edmonton, AB, Canada	6/9/1961
Fox, Vivica A.	South Bend, IN	7/30/1964
Foxworth, Robert	Houston, TX	11/1/1941
Foxworthy, Jeff	Atlanta, GA	9/6/1958
Foxx, Jamie	Terrell, TX	12/13/1967
Foy, Claire	Stockport, England, UK	4/16/1984
Frampton, Peter	Kent, England, UK	4/22/1950
Francis, Connie	Newark, NJ	12/12/1938
Franco, Dave	Palo Alto, CA	6/12/1985
Franco, James	Palo Alto, CA	4/19/1978
Franken, Al	New York, NY	5/21/1951
Franz, Dennis	Maywood, IL	10/28/1944
Fraser, Brendan	Indianapolis, IN	12/3/1968
Freeman, Martin	Aldershot, Hampshire, Eng., UK	9/8/1971
Freeman, Morgan	Memphis, TN.	6/1/1937
French, Dawn	Holyhead, Wales, UK.	10/11/1957
Fricker, Brenda	Dublin, Ireland	2/17/1945
Friedkin, William	Chicago, IL	8/29/1939
Froggatt, Joanne	Littlebeck, North Yorkshire, England, UK	8/21/1980
Fry, Stephen	London, England, UK	8/24/1957
Fuentes, Daisy	Havana, Cuba	11/17/1966
Fuller, Robert	Troy, NY	7/29/1933
Furlong, Edward	Pasadena, CA	8/2/1977
Furtado, Nelly	Victoria, BC, Canada	12/2/1978
Gabriel, Peter	Surrey, England, UK	2/13/1950
Gaines, Boyd	Atlanta, GA	5/11/1953
Galecki, Johnny	Bree, Belgium	4/30/1975
Galifianakis, Zach	Wilkesboro, NC	10/1/1969
Gallagher, Peter	Armonk, NY.	8/19/1955
Gallo, Vincent	Buffalo, NY	4/11/1961
Galway, James	Belfast, N. Ireland, UK	12/8/1939
Garber, Victor	London, ON, Canada.	3/16/1949
Garcia, Andy	Havana, Cuba	4/12/1956
Garfield, Andrew	Los Angeles, CA	8/20/1983
Garfunkel, Art	Forest Hills, Queens, NY	11/5/1941
Garlin, Jeff	Chicago, IL	6/5/1962
Garner, Jennifer	Houston, TX	4/17/1972
Garofalo, Janeane	Newton, NJ	9/28/1964
Garr, Teri	Lakewood, OH.	12/11/1944
Garrett, Brad	Woodland Hills, CA	4/14/1960
Garth, Jennie	Urbana, IL	4/3/1972
Gatlin, Larry	Seminole, TX	5/2/1948
Gayle, Crystal	Paintsville, KY	1/9/1951
Gaynor, Mitzi	Chicago, IL	9/4/1931
Geary, Anthony	Coalville, UT	5/29/1947
Gellar, Sarah Michelle	New York, NY	4/14/1977
Gere, Richard	Philadelphia, PA	8/31/1949
Gervais, Ricky	Reading, England, UK	6/25/1961
Gerwig, Greta	Sacramento, CA	8/4/1983
Giamatti, Paul	New Haven, CT.	6/6/1967
Giannini, Giancarlo	La Spezia, Italy	8/1/1942
Gibb, Barry	Isle of Man, England, UK	9/1/1946
Gibbons, Leeza	Hartsville, SC	3/26/1957
Gibbs, Marla	Chicago, IL	6/14/1931
Gibson, Debbie	Brooklyn, NY	8/31/1970
Gibson, Mel	Peekskill, NY.	1/3/1956
Gibson, Thomas	Charleston, SC	7/3/1962
Gifford, Kathie Lee	Neuilly-sur-Seine, France.	8/16/1953
Gilbert, Melissa	Los Angeles, CA	5/8/1964
Gilbert, Sara	Santa Monica, CA	1/29/1975
Gilberto, Astrud	Salvador, Brazil	3/30/1940
Gill, Vince	Norman, OK	4/12/1957
Gillette, Anita	Baltimore, MD	8/16/1936
Gilley, Mickey	Natchez, MS	3/9/1936
Gilliam, Terry	Minneapolis, MN	11/22/1940
Gilmour, David	Cambridge, England, UK	3/6/1946

Name	Birthplace	Birthdate
Gilpin, Peri	Waco, TX	5/27/1961
Gilsig, Jessalyn	Montréal, QC, Canada	11/30/1971
Givens, Robin	New York, NY	11/27/1964
Glaser, Paul Michael	Cambridge, MA.	3/25/1943
Gleeson, Brendan	Belfast, N. Ireland, UK	3/29/1955?
Glenn, Scott	Pittsburgh, PA	1/26/1941
Gless, Sharon	Los Angeles, CA	5/31/1943
Glover, Crispin	New York, NY	4/20/1964
Glover, Danny	San Francisco, CA	7/22/1947
Glover, Donald	Edwards Air Force Base, CA	9/25/1983
Glover, Julian	London, England, UK	3/27/1935
Glover, Savion	Newark, NJ.	11/19/1973
Godard, Jean-Luc	Paris, France	12/3/1930
Goldberg, Whoopi	New York, NY	11/13/1955
Goldblum, Jeff	Pittsburgh, PA	10/22/1952
Goldthwait, Bobcat	Syracuse, NY	5/26/1962
Goldwyn, Tony	Los Angeles, CA	5/20/1960
Gomez, Selena	Grand Prairie, TX	7/22/1992
Gooding, Cuba, Jr.	Bronx, NY	1/2/1968
Goodman, John	Affton, MO.	6/20/1952
Goodman, Len	London, England, UK	4/25/1944
Gordon-Levitt, Joseph	Los Angeles, CA	2/17/1981
Gosling, Ryan	London, ON, Canada	11/12/1980
Gosselaar, Mark-Paul	Panorama City, CA	3/1/1974
Gossett, Louis, Jr.	Brooklyn, NY.	5/27/1936
Gottfried, Gilbert	Brooklyn, NY.	2/28/1955
Gould, Elliott	Brooklyn, NY.	8/29/1938
Grace, Topher	New York, NY	7/12/1978
Graham, Heather	Milwaukee, WI.	1/29/1970
Grammer, Kelsey	St. Thomas, U.S. Virgin Isls.	2/21/1955
Grande, Ariana	Boca Raton, FL	6/26/1993
Grant, Amy	Augusta, GA	11/25/1960
Grant, Hugh	London, England, UK	9/9/1960
Grant, Lee	Bronx, NY	10/31/1925
Gray, Linda	Santa Monica, CA	9/12/1940
Gray, Macy	Canton, OH.	9/6/1969
Green, Al	Forrest City, AR.	4/13/1946
Green, Cee Lo	Atlanta, GA	5/30/1974
Green, Seth	Philadelphia, PA	2/8/1974
Green, Tom	Pembroke, ON, Canada	7/30/1971
Greene, Graham	Six Nations Reserve, ON, Canada	6/22/1952
Greene, Shecky	Chicago, IL	4/8/1926
Greenfield, Max	Dobbs Ferry, NY	9/4/1980
Greenwood, Bruce	Noranda, QC, Canada	8/12/1956
Gregory, Cynthia	Los Angeles, CA	7/8/1946
Grenier, Adrian	Santa Fe, NM	7/10/1976
Grey, Jennifer	New York, NY	3/26/1960
Grey, Joel	Cleveland, OH	4/11/1932
Grier, David Alan	Detroit, MI.	6/30/1955
Grier, Pam	Winston-Salem, NC	5/26/1949
Gries, Jon	Glendale, CA	6/17/1957
Griffin, Kathy	Oak Park, IL	11/4/1961
Griffith, Melanie	New York, NY	8/9/1957
Griffiths, Rachel	Melbourne, Vic., Australia	12/18/1968
Grint, Rupert	Walton-at-Stone, Hertfordshire, Eng., UK	8/24/1988
Groban, Josh	Los Angeles, CA	2/27/1981
Grodin, Charles	Pittsburgh, PA	4/21/1935
Groff, Jonathan	Lancaster, PA	3/26/1985
Grohl, Dave	Warren, OH.	1/14/1969
Gross, Michael	Chicago, IL	6/21/1947
Guest, Christopher	New York, NY	2/5/1948
Gumbel, Bryant	New Orleans, LA	9/29/1948
Gumbel, Greg	New Orleans, LA	5/3/1946
Gunn, Anna	Santa Fe, NM	8/11/1968
Gunn, Tim	Washington, DC	7/29/1953
Guthrie, Arlo	Brooklyn, NY.	7/10/1947
Guttenberg, Steve	Brooklyn, NY.	8/24/1958
Guy, Buddy	Lettsworth, LA.	7/30/1936
Guy, Jasmine	Boston, MA.	3/10/1964
Gyllenhaal, Jake	Los Angeles, CA.	12/19/1980
Gyllenhaal, Maggie	New York, NY.	11/16/1977
Hackman, Gene	San Bernardino, CA	1/30/1930
Haddish, Tiffany	Los Angeles, CA	12/3/1979
Hader, Bill	Tulsa, OK	6/7/1978
Hagerty, Julie	Cincinnati, OH	6/15/1955
Haid, Charles	San Francisco, CA	6/2/1943
Hale, Tony	West Point, NY	9/30/1970
Hall, Anthony Michael	West Roxbury, MA	4/14/1968
Hall, Arsenio	Cleveland, OH	2/12/1955
Hall, Daryl	Pottstown, PA	10/11/1946
Hall, Deidre	Milwaukee, WI.	10/31/1947
Hall, Michael C.	Raleigh, NC	2/1/1971
Hall, Tom T.	Olive Hill, KY.	5/25/1936
Halliwell, Geri	Watford, England, UK.	8/6/1972
Hamill, Mark	Oakland, CA.	9/25/1951
Hamilton, George	Memphis, TN.	8/12/1939
Hamilton, Linda.	Salisbury, MD	9/26/1956
Hamlin, Harry	Pasadena, CA.	10/30/1951
Hamm, Jon	St. Louis, MO	3/10/1971
Hammer, Armie	Los Angeles, CA.	8/28/1986
Hammer (M.C.)	Oakland, CA.	3/30/1963
Hammond, Darrell	Melbourne, FL	10/8/1955
Hancock, Herbie	Chicago, IL	4/12/1940
Handler, Chelsea	Livingston, NJ.	2/25/1975

Name	Birthplace	Birthdate
Hanks, Colin	Sacramento, CA	11/24/1977
Hanks, Tom	Concord, CA	7/9/1956
Hannah, Daryl	Chicago, IL	12/3/1960
Hannigan, Alyson	Washington, DC	3/24/1974
Hanson, Isaac	Tulsa, OK	11/17/1980
Hanson, Taylor	Tulsa, OK	3/14/1983
Hanson, Zac	Tulsa, OK	10/22/1985
Harden, Marcia Gay	La Jolla, CA	8/14/1959
Hardy, Tom	London, England, UK	9/15/1977
Harewood, Dorian	Dayton, OH	8/6/1950
Hargitay, Mariska	Los Angeles, CA	1/23/1964
Harmon, Angie	Highland Park, TX.	8/10/1972
Harmon, Mark	Burbank, CA	9/2/1951
Harper, Ben	Claremont, CA	10/28/1969
Harper, Tess	Mammoth Spring, AR	8/15/1950
Harper, Valerie	Suffern, NY	8/22/1939
Harrelson, Woody	Midland, TX.	7/23/1961
Harris, Ed	Tenafly, NJ	11/28/1950
Harris, Emmylou	Birmingham, AL	4/2/1947
Harris, Neil Patrick	Albuquerque, NM	6/15/1973
Harris, Rosemary	Ashby, England, UK	9/19/1927?
Harris, Steve	Chicago, IL	12/3/1965
Harrison, Gregory	Avalon, CA	5/31/1950
Harry, Deborah	Miami, FL	7/1/1945
Hart, Kevin	Philadelphia, PA	7/3/1980
Hart, Mary	Madison, SD	11/8/1950
Hart, Melissa Joan	Smithtown, NY	4/18/1976
Hartley, Mariette	New York, NY	6/21/1940
Hartman, David	Pawtucket, RI	5/19/1935
Hartman Black, Lisa	Houston, TX	6/1/1956
Hartnett, Josh	San Francisco, CA	7/21/1978
Harvey, P. J.	Yeovil, Somerset, Eng., UK	10/9/1969
Harvey, Steve	Welch, WV	1/17/1956
Hasselbeck, Elisabeth	Cranston, RI	5/28/1977
Hasselhoff, David	Baltimore, MD	7/17/1952
Hatcher, Teri	Sunnyvale, CA	12/8/1964
Hatfield, Juliana	Wiscasset, ME	7/27/1967
Hathaway, Anne	Brooklyn, NY.	11/12/1982
Hauer, Rutger	Breukelen, Netherlands	1/23/1944
Hawke, Ethan	Austin, TX.	11/6/1970
Hawn, Goldie	Washington, DC	11/21/1945
Hayek, Salma	Coatzacoalcos, Mexico	9/2/1966
Hayes, Hunter	Breaux Bridge, LA	9/9/1991
Hayes, Sean	Glen Ellyn, IL	6/26/1970
Hays, Robert	Bethesda, MD	7/24/1947
Haysbert, Dennis	San Mateo, CA	6/2/1955
Head, Anthony	Camden Town, Eng., UK	2/20/1954
Hearn, George	St. Louis, MO	6/18/1934
Heaton, Patricia	Bay Village, OH	3/4/1958
Heche, Anne	Aurora, OH	5/25/1969
Heder, Jon	Fort Collins, CO	10/26/1977
Hedren, Tippi	New Ulm, MN	1/19/1930
Heigl, Katherine	Washington, DC	11/24/1978
Helberg, Simon	Los Angeles, CA	12/9/1980
Helfgott, David	Melbourne, Vic., Australia	5/19/1947
Helgenberger, Marg	Fremont, NE	11/16/1958
Helmond, Katherine	Galveston, TX	7/5/1929
Helms, Ed	Atlanta, GA	1/24/1974
Hemingway, Mariel	Mill Valley, CA	11/22/1961
Hemsworth, Chris	Melbourne, Vic., Australia	8/11/1983
Hemsworth, Liam	Melbourne, Vic., Australia	1/13/1990
Hemsworth, Luke	Melbourne, Vic., Australia	11/5/1980
Hendricks, Christina	Knoxville, TN.	5/3/1975
Henley, Don	Gilmer, TX.	7/22/1947
Henner, Marilu	Chicago, IL	4/6/1952
Hennessy, Jill	Edmonton, AB, Canada	11/25/1968
Henry, Buck	New York, NY	12/9/1930
Henson, Taraji P.	Washington, DC	9/11/1970
Herman, Pee-Wee	Peekskill, NY.	8/27/1952
Hershey, Barbara	Hollywood, CA	2/5/1948
Hesseman, Howard	Lebanon, OR	2/27/1940
Hetfield, James	Downey, CA	8/3/1963
Hewitt, Jennifer Love	Waco, TX	2/21/1979
Hicks, Catherine	Scottsdale, AZ.	8/6/1951
Hiddleston, Tom	London, England, UK	2/9/1981
Higgins, John Michael	Boston, MA.	2/12/1963
Hightower, Chelsie	Las Vegas, NV	7/21/1989
Hill, Dulé	Orange, NJ	5/3/1975
Hill, Faith	Jackson, MS	9/21/1967
Hill, Jonah	Los Angeles, CA	12/20/1983
Hill, Lauryn	South Orange, NJ	5/26/1975
Hines, Cheryl	Miami Beach, FL.	9/21/1965
Hirsch, Emile	Palms, CA	3/13/1985
Hirsch, Judd	Bronx, NY	3/15/1935
Hodgman, John	Cambridge, MA.	6/3/1971
Hoffman, Dustin	Los Angeles, CA	8/8/1937
Hogan, Hulk	Augusta, GA	8/11/1953
Hogan, Paul	Lightning Ridge, NSW, Australia	10/8/1939
Holbrook, Hal	Cleveland, OH	2/17/1925
Holliday, Polly	Jasper, AL.	7/2/1937
Holloway, Josh	San Jose, CA	7/20/1969
Holly, Lauren	Bristol, PA	10/28/1963

Name	Birthplace	Birthdate
Holm, Ian	Ilford, England, UK	9/12/1931
Holmes, Katie	Toledo, OH	12/18/1978
Hopkins, Anthony	Port Talbot, South Wales, UK	12/31/1937
Hopkins, Bo	Greenville, SC	2/2/1942
Hopkins, Telma	Louisville, KY.	10/28/1948
Horne, Marilyn	Bradford, PA	1/16/1934
Hornsby, Bruce	Williamsburg, VA	11/23/1954
Horsley, Lee	Muleshoe, TX	5/15/1955
Hough, Derek	Salt Lake City, UT	5/17/1985
Hough, Julianne	Salt Lake City, UT	7/20/1988
Hounsou, Djimon	Cotonou, Benin	4/24/1964
Howard, Clint	Burbank, CA	4/20/1959
Howard, Ron	Duncan, OK.	3/1/1954
Howard, Terrence	Chicago, IL	3/11/1969
Howell, C. Thomas	Van Nuys, CA	12/7/1966
Howes, Sally Ann	St. John's Wood, London, England, UK	7/20/1930
Hudgens, Vanessa	Salinas, CA	12/14/1988
Hudson, Jennifer	Chicago, IL	9/12/1981
Hudson, Kate	Los Angeles, CA	4/19/1979
Huffman, Felicity	Bedford, NY.	12/9/1962
Hughley, D. L.	Los Angeles, CA	3/6/1963
Hulce, Tom	Detroit, MI	12/6/1953
Humperdinck, Engelbert	Madras, India.	5/2/1936
Humphries, Barry	Melbourne, Vic., Australia.	2/17/1934
Hunt, Bonnie	Chicago, IL	9/22/1964
Hunt, Helen	Culver City, CA	6/15/1963
Hunt, Linda	Morristown, NJ	4/2/1945
Hunter, Holly	Conyers, GA	3/20/1958
Hurley, Elizabeth	Hampshire, England, UK.	6/10/1965
Hurt, Mary Beth	Marshalltown, IA	9/26/1948
Hurt, William	Washington, DC	3/20/1950
Huston, Anjelica	Santa Monica, CA	7/8/1951
Hutcherson, Josh	Union, KY.	10/12/1992
Hutton, Lauren	Charleston, SC	11/17/1943
Hutton, Timothy	Malibu, CA.	8/16/1960
Ian, Janis	Bronx, NY	4/7/1951
Ice Cube	Los Angeles, CA	6/15/1969
Ice-T	Newark, NJ	2/16/1958
Idle, Eric	S. Shields, England, UK.	3/29/1943
Idol, Billy	Middlesex, England, UK	11/30/1955
Iglesias, Enrique	Madrid, Spain	5/8/1975
Iglesias, Julio	Madrid, Spain	9/23/1943
Iler, Robert	New York, NY	3/2/1985
Iman	Mogadishu, Somalia	7/25/1955
Imbruglia, Natalie	Sydney, NSW, Australia	2/4/1975
Imperioli, Michael	Mount Vernon, NY	3/26/1966
Imus, Don	Riverside, CA.	7/23/1940
Iñárritu, Alejandro G.	Mexico City, Mexico.	8/15/1963
Ingram, James	Akron, OH	2/16/1952
Innes, Laura	Pontiac, MI	8/16/1957?
Ireland, Kathy	Glendale, CA.	3/20/1963
Irons, Jeremy	Cowes, Isle of Wight, Eng., UK	9/19/1948
Irving, Amy	Palo Alto, CA	9/10/1953
Irwin, Bill	Santa Monica, CA	4/11/1950
Isaac, Oscar	Guatemala.	1/5/1980
Ivanek, Željko	Ljubljana, Yugo. (Slovenia)	8/15/1957
Ivey, Judith	El Paso, TX	9/4/1951
Ivory, James	Berkeley, CA	6/7/1928
Izzard, Eddie	Aden, Yemen.	2/7/1962
Ja Rule	Hollis, Queens, NY	2/29/1976
Jackée (Harry)	Winston-Salem, NC	8/14/1956
Jackman, Hugh	Sydney, NSW, Australia	10/12/1968
Jackson, Cheyenne	Newport, WA.	7/12/1975
Jackson, Glenda	Birkenhead, England, UK.	5/9/1936
Jackson, Janet	Gary, IN.	5/16/1966
Jackson, Jermaine	Gary, IN.	12/11/1954
Jackson, Jonathan	Orlando, FL	5/11/1982
Jackson, Joshua	Vancouver, BC, Canada.	6/11/1978
Jackson, Kate	Birmingham, AL.	10/29/1948
Jackson, La Toya	Gary, IN.	5/29/1956
Jackson, Peter	Wellington, New Zealand.	10/31/1961
Jackson, Samuel L.	Washington, DC	12/21/1948
Jacobi, Derek	London, England, UK	10/22/1938
Jagger, Mick	Dartford, England, UK	7/26/1943
James, Kevin	Mineola, NY.	4/26/1965
Jamison, Judith	Philadelphia, PA	5/10/1943
Janis, Conrad	New York, NY	2/11/1928
Janney, Allison	Dayton, OH	11/19/1959
Janssen, Famke	Amsterdam, Netherlands.	11/5/1965
Jardine, Al.	Lima, OH.	9/3/1942
Jarmusch, Jim	Akron, OH.	1/22/1953
Jarrett, Keith	Allentown, PA	5/8/1945
Jay Z	Brooklyn, NY.	12/4/1969
Jenkins, Richard	DeKalb, IL	5/4/1947
Jenner, Caitlyn	Mount Kisco, NY	10/28/1949
Jenner, Kendall	Los Angeles, CA	9/3/1995
Jenner, Kris	San Diego, CA.	11/5/1955
Jenner, Kylie	Los Angeles, CA	8/10/1997
Jepsen, Carly Rae	Mission, BC, Canada.	11/21/1985
Jett, Joan	Philadelphia, PA	9/22/1958
Jewel (Kilcher)	Payson, UT	5/23/1974

Name	Birthplace	Birthdate
Jewison, Norman	Toronto, ON, Canada	7/21/1926
Jillette, Penn	Greenfield, MA	3/5/1955
Jillian, Ann	Cambridge, MA	1/29/1950
Joel, Billy	Bronx, NY	5/9/1949
Johansson, Scarlett	New York, NY	11/22/1984
John, Elton	Pinner, Middlesex, Eng., UK	3/25/1947
Johns, Glynis	Durban, South Africa	10/5/1923
Johnson, Arte	Benton Harbor, MI	1/20/1929
Johnson, Beverly	Buffalo, NY	10/13/1952
Johnson, Don	Flatt Creek, MO	12/15/1949
Johnson, Dwayne "The Rock"	Hayward, CA	5/2/1972
Johnston, Bruce	Los Angeles, CA	6/24/1942
Johnston, Kristen	Washington, DC	9/20/1967
Jolie, Angelina	Los Angeles, CA	6/4/1975
Jonas, Joe	Casa Grande, AZ	8/15/1989
Jonas, Kevin	Teaneck, NJ	11/5/1987
Jonas, Nick	Dallas, TX	9/16/1992
Jones, Angus T.	Austin, TX	10/8/1993
Jones, Bill T.	Bunnell, FL	2/15/1952
Jones, Cherry	Paris, TN	11/21/1956
Jones, Gemma	London, England, UK	12/4/1942
Jones, Grace	Spanish Town, Jamaica	5/19/1948
Jones, Jack	Hollywood, CA	1/14/1938
Jones, James Earl	Arkabutla, MS	1/17/1931
Jones, John Paul	Sidcup, England, UK	1/3/1946
Jones, January	Sioux Falls, SD	1/5/1978
Jones, Leslie	Memphis, TN	9/7/1967
Jones, Mick	London, England, UK	6/26/1955
Jones, Norah	New York, NY	3/30/1979
Jones, Quincy	Chicago, IL	3/14/1933
Jones, Shirley	Charleroi, PA	3/31/1934
Jones, Star	Badin, NC	3/24/1962
Jones, Tom	Pontypridd, Wales, UK	6/7/1940
Jones, Tommy Lee	San Saba, TX	9/15/1946
Jonze, Spike	Rockville, MD	10/22/1969
Jordan, Michael B.	Santa Ana, CA	2/9/1987
Jovovich, Milla	Kiev, Ukraine	12/17/1975
Judd, Ashley	Granada Hills, CA	4/19/1968
Judd, Naomi	Ashland, KY	1/11/1946
Judd, Wynonna	Ashland, KY	5/30/1964
Kaczmarek, Jane	Milwaukee, WI	12/21/1955
Kaling, Mindy	Cambridge, MA	6/24/1979
Kaluuya, Daniel	London, Eng., UK	2/24/1989
Kanaly, Steve	Burbank, CA	3/14/1946
Kane, Carol	Cleveland, OH	6/18/1952
Kaplan, Gabe	Brooklyn, NY	3/31/1945
Kardashian, Khloe	Los Angeles, CA	6/27/1984
Kardashian, Kim	Los Angeles, CA	10/21/1980
Kardashian, Kourtney	Los Angeles, CA	4/18/1979
Karlen, John	New York, NY	5/28/1940
Karn, Richard	Seattle, WA	2/17/1956
Katic, Stana	Hamilton, ON, Canada	4/26/1978
Kattan, Chris	Sherman Oaks, CA	10/19/1970
Kaufmann, Jonas	Munich, Germany	1/10/1969
Kavner, Julie	Burbank, CA	9/7/1951
Kaye, Judy	Phoenix, AZ	12/11/1948
Kazan, Lainie	New York, NY	5/15/1940
Keach, Stacy	Savannah, GA	6/2/1941
Keaton, Diane	Santa Ana, CA	1/5/1946
Keaton, Michael	Coraopolis, PA	9/5/1951
Keener, Catherine	Miami, FL	3/23/1959
Keillor, Garrison	Anoka, MN	8/7/1942
Keitel, Harvey	Brooklyn, NY	5/13/1939
Keith, David	Knoxville, TN	5/8/1954
Keith, Penelope	Sutton, Surrey, Eng., UK	4/2/1940
Kellerman, Sally	Long Beach, CA	6/2/1937
Kelly, Minka	Los Angeles, CA	6/24/1980
Kelly, R(obert)	Chicago, IL	1/8/1967
Kemper, Ellie	Kansas City, MO	5/2/1980
Kendrick, Anna	Portland, ME	8/9/1985
Kennedy, Jamie	Upper Darby, PA	5/25/1970
Kenny G	Seattle, WA	6/5/1956
Kent, Allegra	Santa Monica, CA	8/11/1937
Keoghan, Phil	Christchurch, New Zealand	5/31/1967
Kercheval, Ken	Wolcottville, IN	7/15/1935
Kerns, Joanna	San Francisco, CA	2/12/1953
Kesha	Los Angeles, CA	3/1/1987
Keys, Alicia	New York, NY	1/25/1981
Khalifa, Wiz	Minot, ND	9/8/1987
Khan, Chaka	Great Lakes, IL	3/23/1953
Kid Rock	Romeo, MI	1/17/1971
Kidman, Nicole	Honolulu, HI	6/20/1967
Kilborn, Craig	Kansas City, KS	8/24/1962
Kilmer, Val	Los Angeles, CA	12/31/1959
Kim, Daniel Dae	Pusan, South Korea	8/4/1968
Kimmel, Jimmy	Brooklyn, NY	11/13/1967
King, Carole	Brooklyn, NY	2/9/1942
King, Gayle	Chevy Chase, MD	12/28/1954?
King, Larry	Brooklyn, NY	11/19/1933
King, Perry	Alliance, OH	4/30/1948
King, Regina	Los Angeles, CA	1/15/1971
Kingsley, Ben	Scarborough, England, UK	12/31/1943
Kingston, Alex	London, England, UK	3/11/1963
Kinnear, Greg	Logansport, IN	6/17/1963
Kinney, Kathy	Stevens Point, WI	11/3/1954
Kinski, Nastassja	Berlin, W. Germany	1/24/1960
Kirkland, Gelsey	Bethlehem, PA	12/29/1952
Kirkpatrick, Chris	Clarion, PA	10/17/1971
Kirshner, Mia	Toronto, ON, Canada	1/25/1975
Kitsch, Taylor	Kelowna, BC, Canada	4/8/1981
Klein, Robert	Bronx, NY	2/8/1942
Kline, Kevin	St. Louis, MO	10/24/1947
Klum, Heidi	Bergish-Gladbach, Germany	6/1/1973
Knight, Gladys	Atlanta, GA	5/28/1944
Knight, Shirley	Goessel, KS	7/5/1936
Knight, T. R.	Minneapolis, MN	3/26/1973
Knight, Wayne	New York, NY	8/7/1955
Knightley, Keira	Teddington, England, UK	3/26/1985
Knopfler, Mark	Glasgow, Scotland, UK	8/12/1949
Knowles, Beyoncé	Houston, TX	9/4/1981
Knoxville, Johnny	Knoxville, TN	3/11/1971
Konitz, Lee	Chicago, IL	10/13/1927
Kopell, Bernie	Brooklyn, NY	6/21/1933
Kotto, Yaphet	New York, NY	11/15/1937
Krakowski, Jane	Parsippany, NJ	10/11/1968
Krasinski, John	Newton, MA	10/20/1979
Krause, Peter	Alexandria, MN	8/12/1965
Kressley, Carson	Allentown, PA	11/11/1969
Kretschmann, Thomas	Dessau, E. Germany	9/8/1962
Kristofferson, Kris	Brownsville, TX	6/22/1936
Kudrow, Lisa	Encino, CA	7/30/1963
Kunis, Mila	Kiev, Ukraine	8/14/1983
Kurtz, Swoosie	Omaha, NE	9/6/1944
Kutcher, Ashton	Cedar Rapids, IA	2/7/1978
Kwan, Nancy	Hong Kong	5/19/1939
LaBelle, Patti	Philadelphia, PA	5/24/1944
LaBeouf, Shia	Los Angeles, CA	6/11/1986
Lachey, Nick	Harlan, KY	11/9/1973
Ladd, Cheryl	Huron, SD	7/12/1951
Ladd, Diane	Meridian, MS	11/29/1932
Lady Gaga	New York, NY	3/28/1986
Lagasse, Emeril	Fall River, MA	10/15/1959
Lahti, Christine	Birmingham, MI	4/4/1950
Laine, Cleo	Southall, England, UK	10/28/1927
Lake, Ricki	Hastings-on-Hudson, NY	9/21/1968
Lamar, Kendrick	Compton, CA	6/17/1987
Lamas, Lorenzo	Santa Monica, CA	1/20/1958
Lambert, Adam	Indianapolis, IN	1/29/1982
Lambert, Christopher	Great Neck, NY	3/29/1957
Lambert, Miranda	Longview, TX	11/10/1983
Landis, John	Chicago, IL	8/3/1950
Lane, Diane	New York, NY	1/22/1965
Lane, Nathan	Jersey City, NJ	2/3/1956
lang, k.d.	Consort, AB, Canada	11/2/1961
Lang, Stephen	Jamaica Estates, Queens, NY	7/11/1952
Lange, Jessica	Cloquet, MN	4/20/1949
Langella, Frank	Bayonne, NJ	1/1/1938
Lansbury, Angela	London, England, UK	10/16/1925
LaPaglia, Anthony	Adelaide, SA, Australia	1/31/1959
Larroquette, John	New Orleans, LA	11/25/1947
Larson, Brie	Sacramento, CA	10/1/1989
LaSalle, Eriq	Hartford, CT	6/23/1962
Lauper, Cyndi	Ozone Park, Queens, NY	6/22/1953
Laurie, Hugh	Oxford, England, UK	6/11/1959
Laurie, Piper	Detroit, MI	1/22/1932
Lautner, Taylor	Grand Rapids, MI	2/11/1992
Lavigne, Avril	Belleville, ON, Canada	9/27/1984
Lavin, Linda	Portland, ME	10/15/1937
Law, Jude	London, England, UK	12/29/1972
Lawless, Lucy	Mount Albert, New Zealand	3/29/1968
Lawrence, Carol	Melrose Park, IL	9/5/1934
Lawrence, Jennifer	Louisville, KY	8/15/1990
Lawrence, Joey	Montgomery, PA	4/20/1976
Lawrence, Martin	Frankfurt, Germany	4/16/1965
Lawrence, Steve	Brooklyn, NY	7/8/1935
Lawrence, Vicki	Inglewood, CA	3/26/1949
Leachman, Cloris	Des Moines, IA	4/30/1926
Lear, Norman	New Haven, CT	7/27/1922
Learned, Michael	Washington, DC	4/9/1939
Leary, Denis	Worcester, MA	8/18/1957
LeBlanc, Matt	Newton, MA	7/25/1967
LeBon, Simon	Bushey, England, UK	10/27/1958
Lee, Ang	Pingtung, Taiwan	10/23/1954
Lee, Brenda	Lithonia, GA	12/11/1944
Lee, Jason	Huntington Beach, CA	4/25/1970
Lee, Michele	Los Angeles, CA	6/24/1942
Lee, Spike	Atlanta, GA	3/20/1957
Leeves, Jane	Ilford, England, UK	4/18/1961
Legend, John	Springfield, OH	12/28/1978
Legrand, Michel	Paris, France	2/24/1932
Leguizamo, John	Bogotá, Colombia	7/22/1964
Leibman, Ron	New York, NY	10/11/1937
Leigh, Jennifer Jason	Hollywood, CA	2/5/1962
Leighton, Laura	Iowa City, IA	7/24/1968
Lennox, Annie	Aberdeen, Scotland, UK	12/25/1954
Leno, Jay	New Rochelle, NY	4/28/1950
Leo, Melissa	New York, NY	9/14/1960
Leonard, Robert Sean	Westwood, NJ	2/28/1969
Leoni, Tea	New York, NY	2/25/1966
Leto, Jared	Bossier City, LA	12/26/1971

Name	Birthplace	Birthdate
Letterman, David	Indianapolis, IN	4/12/1947
Levin, Harvey	Los Angeles, CA	9/2/1960
Levine, Adam	Los Angeles, CA	3/18/1979
Levine, James	Cincinnati, OH	6/23/1943
Levine, Ted	Bellaire, OH	5/29/1957
Levinson, Barry	Baltimore, MD	4/6/1942
Levy, Eugene	Hamilton, ON, Canada	12/17/1946
Lewis, Damian	London, Eng., UK	2/11/1971
Lewis, Huey	New York, NY	7/5/1950
Lewis, Jason	Newport Beach, CA	6/25/1971
Lewis, Jerry Lee	Ferriday, LA	9/29/1935
Lewis, Juliette	Los Angeles, CA	6/21/1973
Lewis, Leona	London, England, UK	4/3/1985
Lewis, Richard	Brooklyn, NY	6/29/1947
Li, Jet	Beijing, China	4/26/1963
Light, Judith	Trenton, NJ	2/9/1949
Lightfoot, Gordon	Orillia, ON, Canada	11/17/1938
Lil' Kim	Brooklyn, NY	7/11/1975
Lil' Romeo	New Orleans, LA	8/19/1989
Lil Wayne	New Orleans, LA	9/27/1982
Lilly, Evangeline	Fort Saskatchewan, AB, Can.	8/3/1979
Lincoln, Andrew	London, England, UK	9/14/1973
Linden, Hal	Bronx, NY	3/20/1931
Ling, Lisa	Sacramento, CA	8/30/1973
Linn-Baker, Mark	St. Louis, MO.	6/17/1954
Linney, Laura	New York, NY	2/5/1964
Liotta, Ray	Newark, NJ	12/18/1954
Lithgow, John	Rochester, NY	10/19/1945
Little, Rich	Ottawa, ON, Canada	11/26/1938
Little Richard	Macon, GA	12/5/1932
Littrell, Brian	Lexington, KY	2/20/1975
Liu, Lucy	Jackson Heights, Queens, NY	12/2/1968
Lively, Blake	Tarzana, CA.	8/25/1987
LL Cool J	St. Albans, Queens, NY	1/14/1968
Lloyd, Christopher.	Stamford, CT	10/22/1938
Lloyd Webber, Andrew	London, England, UK	3/22/1948
Locke, Sondra	Shelbyville, TN	5/28/1944
Lockhart, June	New York, NY	6/25/1925
Locklear, Heather	Westwood, CA.	9/25/1961
Loggins, Kenny	Everett, WA	1/7/1948
Lohan, Lindsay	New York, NY	7/2/1986
Lollobrigida, Gina	Subiaco, Italy	7/4/1927
Lonergan, Kenneth	New York, NY	10/16/1962
Long, Nia	Brooklyn, NY	10/30/1970
Long, Shelley	Ft. Wayne, IN.	8/23/1949
Longoria, Eva	Corpus Christi, TX	3/15/1975
Lopez, George	Mission Hills, CA	4/23/1961
Lopez, Jennifer	Bronx, NY	7/24/1969
Lopez, Mario	San Diego, CA.	10/10/1973
Lorde	Takapuna, New Zealand	11/7/1996
Loren, Sophia	Rome, Italy	9/20/1934
Loring, Gloria	New York, NY	12/10/1946
Louis C.K.	Washington, DC	9/12/1967
Louis-Dreyfus, Julia	New York, NY	1/13/1961
Lovato, Demi	Dallas, TX	8/20/1992
Love, Courtney	San Francisco, CA.	7/9/1964
Love, Mike	Baldwin Hills, CA	3/15/1941
Loveless, Patty	Pikeville, KY	1/4/1957
Lovett, Lyle	Klein, TX	11/1/1957
Lovitz, Jon	Tarzana, CA.	7/21/1957
Lowe, Rob.	Charlottesville, VA	3/17/1964
Lucas, George	Modesto, CA.	5/14/1944
Lucci, Susan	Scarsdale, NY	12/23/1946
Luckinbill, Laurence	Ft. Smith, AR	11/21/1934
Ludacris	Champaign, IL	9/11/1977
Ludwig, Christa	Berlin, Germany	3/16/1924
Luhrmann, Baz	Sydney, NSW, Australia	9/17/1962
LuPone, Patti	Northport, NY	4/21/1949
Lynch, David	Missoula, MT.	1/20/1946
Lynch, Jane	Dolton, IL.	7/14/1960
Lynley, Carol	New York, NY	2/13/1942
Lynn, Loretta	Butcher Hollow, KY	4/14/1932
Lynn, Vera.	London, England, UK	3/20/1917
Lynne, Shelby	Quantico, VA	10/22/1968
Ma, Yo-Yo	Paris, France	10/7/1955
Macchio, Ralph.	Huntington, NY	11/4/1961
MacDonald, Kelly	Glasgow, Scotland, UK	2/23/1976
MacDowell, Andie	Gaffney, SC.	4/21/1958
MacFarlane, Seth	Kent, CT	10/26/1973
MacGowan, Shane	Tunbridge, Kent, Eng., UK	12/25/1957
MacGraw, Ali.	Pound Ridge, NY	4/1/1939
Macklemore	Seattle, WA	6/19/1983
MacLachlan, Kyle	Yakima, WA.	2/22/1959
MacLaine, Shirley	Richmond, VA	4/24/1934
MacLeod, Gavin	Mt. Kisco, NY	2/28/1931
MacNicol, Peter	Dallas, TX	4/10/1954
MacPherson, Elle	Sydney, NSW, Australia	3/29/1964
Macy, Bill.	Revere, MA	5/18/1922
Macy, William H.	Miami, FL	3/13/1950
Madden, John.	Austin, MN.	4/10/1936
Madigan, Amy	Chicago, IL	9/11/1950
Madonna (Ciccone)	Bay City, MI.	8/16/1958
Madsen, Michael	Chicago, IL	9/25/1959
Maguire, Tobey	Santa Monica, CA	6/27/1975

Name	Birthplace	Birthdate
Maher, Bill.	New York, NY	1/20/1956
Majors, Lee.	Wyandotte, MI	4/23/1939
Makarova, Natalia	Leningrad, Russia	11/21/1940
Malek, Rami	Los Angeles, CA	5/12/1981
Malick, Terrence	Ottawa, IL	11/30/1943
Malick, Wendie	Buffalo, NY	12/13/1950
Malina, Joshua	New York, NY	1/17/1966
Malkovich, John	Christopher, IL.	12/9/1953
Mamet, David	Chicago, IL	11/30/1947
Manchester, Melissa	Bronx, NY	2/15/1951
Mandel, Howie	Toronto, ON, Canada.	11/29/1955
Mandrell, Barbara	Houston, TX	12/25/1948
Mangione, Chuck	Rochester, NY	11/29/1940
Manheim, Camryn	Caldwell, NJ	3/8/1961
Manilow, Barry	Brooklyn, NY	6/17/1943
Mann, Aimee.	Richmond, VA	8/9/1960
Manoff, Dinah	New York, NY	1/25/1958
Manson, Marilyn	Canton, OH	1/5/1969
Mantegna, Joe	Chicago, IL	11/13/1947
Mantello, Joe	Rockford, IL.	12/27/1962
Mara, Kate	Bedford, NY.	2/27/1983
Mara, Rooney	Bedford, NY.	4/17/1985
Marcil, Vanessa	Indio, CA	10/15/1969
Margulies, Julianna	Spring Valley, NY.	6/8/1966
Marie, Constance	Hollywood, CA.	9/9/1965
Marin, Cheech	Los Angeles, CA	7/13/1946
Marinaro, Ed	New York, NY	3/31/1950
Mars, Bruno	Honolulu, HI	10/8/1985
Marsalis, Branford	Breaux Bridge, LA	8/26/1960
Marsalis, Wynton	New Orleans, LA	10/18/1961
Marsh, Jean	London, England, UK	7/1/1934
Marshall, Penny	Bronx, NY	10/15/1942
Marshall, Peter	Huntington, WV	3/30/1926
Martin, Chris.	Devon, England, UK	3/2/1977
Martin, Jesse L.	Rocky Mount, VA.	1/18/1969
Martin, Kellie.	Riverside, CA.	10/16/1975
Martin, Ricky	San Juan, Puerto Rico	12/24/1971
Martin, Steve	Waco, TX.	8/14/1945
Martindale, Margo	Jacksonville, TX.	7/18/1951
Martins, Peter	Copenhagen, Denmark	10/27/1946
Maslany, Tatiana	Regina, SK, Canada	9/22/1985
Mason, Jackie.	Sheboygan, WI	6/9/1931
Mason, Marsha.	St. Louis, MO.	4/3/1942
Masterson, Christopher	Long Island, NY.	1/22/1980
Masterson, Mary Stuart	New York, NY	6/28/1966
Mastrantonio, Mary Elizabeth	Lombard, IL.	11/17/1958
Masur, Richard	New York, NY	11/20/1948
Mathers, Jerry	Sioux City, IA.	6/2/1948
Matheson, Tim	Glendale, CA.	12/31/1947
Mathis, Johnny	Gilmer, TX.	9/30/1935
Matlin, Marlee	Morton Grove, IL	8/24/1965
Matthews, Dave	Johannesburg, South Africa	1/9/1967
May, Elaine	Philadelphia, PA	4/21/1932
Mayer, John	Bridgeport, CT.	10/16/1977
Mays, Jayma	Bristol, TN	7/16/1979
Mazar, Debi	Jamaica, Queens, NY	8/13/1964
McAdams, Rachel.	London, ON, Canada.	11/17/1978
McArdle, Andrea	Abington, PA	11/5/1963
McAvoy, James.	Glasgow, Scotland, UK	4/21/1979
McBride, Patricia	Teaneck, NJ	8/23/1942
McCallum, David.	Glasgow, Scotland, UK	9/19/1933
McCarthy, Andrew.	Westfield, NJ	11/29/1962
McCarthy, Jenny.	Chicago, IL	11/1/1972
McCarthy, Melissa	Plainfield, IL.	8/26/1970
McCartney, Paul	Liverpool, England, UK	6/18/1942
McCarver, Tim	Memphis, TN.	10/16/1941
McConaughey, Matthew	Uvalde, TX.	11/4/1969
McCoo, Marilyn.	Jersey City, NJ.	9/30/1943
McCormack, Eric	Toronto, ON, Canada.	4/18/1963
McCormack, Mary	Plainsfield, NJ	2/8/1969
McCrane, Paul	Philadelphia, PA	1/19/1961
McCreery, Scotty	Garner, NC	10/9/1993
McDaniel, James	Washington, DC	3/25/1958
McDermott, Dylan.	Waterbury, CT	10/26/1961
McDiarmid, Ian	Carnoustie, Tayside, Scot., UK	4/17/1944?
McDonald, Audra	Berlin, Germany	7/3/1970
McDonnell, Mary	Wilkes-Barre, PA	4/28/1952
McDormand, Frances	Chicago, IL	6/23/1957
McDowell, Malcolm.	Leeds, England, UK.	6/13/1943
McEntire, Reba.	McAlester, OK	3/28/1955
McFerrin, Bobby	New York, NY	3/11/1950
McGillis, Kelly	Newport Beach, CA.	7/9/1957
McGovern, Elizabeth	Evanston, IL	7/18/1961
McGovern, Maureen.	Youngstown, OH	7/27/1949
McGraw, Tim.	Delhi, LA	5/1/1967
McGregor, Ewan.	Crieff, Scotland, UK.	3/31/1971
McHale, Joel.	Rome, Italy	11/20/1971
McHale, Kevin.	Plano, TX.	6/14/1988
McKean, Michael	New York, NY	10/17/1947
McKechnie, Donna	Pontiac, MI	11/16/1942
McKellen, Ian	Burnley, England, UK.	5/25/1939
McKenzie, Ben	Austin, TX	9/12/1978
McKidd, Kevin.	Elgin, Scotland, UK	8/9/1973
McKinnon, Kate	Sea Cliff, NY	1/6/1984

Name	Birthplace	Birthdate
McLachlan, Sarah	Halifax, NS, Canada	1/28/1968
McLean, A. J.	West Palm Beach, FL	1/9/1978
McNichol, Kristy	Los Angeles, CA	9/11/1962
McRaney, Gerald	Collins, MS	8/19/1947
McQueen, Steve	London, England, UK	10/9/1969
McQueen, Steven R.	Los Angeles, CA	7/13/1988
McShane, Ian	Blackburn, England, UK	9/29/1942
Meat Loaf	Dallas, TX	9/27/1947
Meester, Leighton	Marco Island, FL	4/9/1986
Mehta, Zubin	Bombay, India	4/29/1936
Mellencamp, John	Seymour, IN	10/7/1951
Meloni, Christopher	Washington, DC	4/2/1961
Mendes, Sam	Redding, England, UK	8/1/1965
Mendes, Sergio	Niteroi, Brazil	2/11/1941
Mendes, Shawn	Toronto, ON, Canada	8/8/1998
Menzel, Idina	Syosset, NY	5/30/1971
Merchant, Natalie	Jamestown, NY	10/26/1963
Merkerson, S. Epatha	Saginaw, MI	11/28/1952
Messing, Debra	Brooklyn, NY	8/15/1968
Metcalf, Laurie	Carbondale, IL	6/16/1955
Meyers, Seth	Bedford, NH	12/28/1973
Michaels, Al	Brooklyn, NY	11/12/1944
Michaels, Bret	Butler, PA	3/15/1963
Michaels, Lorne	Toronto, ON, Canada	11/17/1944
Michele, Lea	Bronx, NY	8/29/1986
Midler, Bette	Honolulu, HI	12/1/1945
Midori (Goto)	Osaka, Japan	10/25/1971
Mike D	Brooklyn, NY	11/20/1965
Milano, Alyssa	Brooklyn, NY	12/19/1972
Miles, Sarah	Ingatestone, England, UK	12/31/1941
Miles, Vera	nr. Boise City, OK	8/23/1930
Miller, Dennis	Pittsburgh, PA	11/3/1953
Miller, Jonny Lee	Kingston Upon Thames, England, UK	11/15/1972
Miller, Penelope Ann	Santa Monica, CA	1/13/1964
Mills, Donna	Chicago, IL	12/11/1943
Mills, Hayley	London, England, UK	4/18/1946
Milnes, Sherrill	Downers Grove, IL	1/10/1935
Milsap, Ronnie	Robinsville, NC	1/16/1944
Mimieux, Yvette	Hollywood, CA	1/8/1942
Minaj, Nicki	St. James, Trinidad and Tobago	12/8/1982
Ming-Na (Wen)	Coloane Island, Macao	11/20/1963
Minnelli, Liza	Los Angeles, CA	3/12/1946
Minogue, Kylie	Melbourne, Vic., Australia	5/28/1968
Miranda, Lin-Manuel	New York, NY	1/16/1980
Mirren, Helen	London, England, UK	7/26/1945
Mitchell, Brian Stokes	Seattle, WA	10/31/1957
Mitchell, Elizabeth	Los Angeles, CA	3/27/1970
Mitchell, Jerry	Paw Paw, MI	1/15/1960
Mitchell, Joni	Fort McLeod, AB, Canada	11/7/1943
Moby	New York, NY	9/11/1965
Modine, Matthew	Loma Linda, CA	3/22/1959
Moffat, Donald	Plymouth, England, UK	12/26/1930
Molina, Alfred	London, England, UK	5/24/1953
Moll, Richard	Pasadena, CA	1/13/1943
Moloney, Janel	Woodland Hills, CA	10/3/1969
Monáe, Janelle	Kansas City, KS	12/1/1985
Monaghan, Dominic	Berlin, Germany	12/8/1976
Monica (Arnold)	College Park, GA	10/24/1980
Mo'Nique	Woodlawn, MD	12/11/1967
Moore, Demi	Roswell, NM	11/11/1962
Moore, Julianne	Fort Bragg, NC	12/3/1960
Moore, Mandy	Nashua, NH	4/10/1984
Moore, Melba	New York, NY	10/29/1945
Moore, Michael	Flint, MI	4/23/1954
Moore, Terry	Los Angeles, CA	1/7/1929
Morales, Esai	Brooklyn, NY	10/1/1962
Moranis, Rick	Toronto, ON, Canada	4/18/1953
Moreno, Rita	Humacao, Puerto Rico	12/11/1931
Morgan, Jeffrey Dean	Seattle, WA	4/22/1966
Morgan, Piers	Guildford, Surrey, UK	3/30/1965
Morgan, Tracy	Bronx, NY	11/10/1968
Moriarty, Michael	Detroit, MI	4/5/1941
Morris, Garrett	New Orleans, LA	2/1/1937
Morissette, Alanis	Ottawa, ON, Canada	6/1/1974
Morrison, Matthew	Fort Ord, CA	10/30/1978
Morrison, Van	Belfast, N. Ireland, UK	8/31/1945
Morrissey (Steven Patrick)	Manchester, England, UK	5/22/1959
Morrow, Rob	New Rochelle, NY	9/21/1962
Morse, David	Beverly, MA	10/11/1953
Morse, Robert	Newton, MA	5/18/1931
Mortensen, Viggo	New York, NY	10/20/1958
Mortimer, Emily	London, England, UK	12/1/1971
Morton, Joe	New York, NY	10/18/1947
Morton, Samantha	Nottingham, England, UK	5/13/1977
Moses, William	Los Angeles, CA	11/17/1959
Moss, Carrie-Anne	Vancouver, BC, Canada	8/21/1967
Moss, Elisabeth	Los Angeles, CA	7/24/1982
Moss, Kate	Croydon, Surrey, Eng., UK	1/16/1974
Moyer, Stephen	Brentwood, UK	10/11/1969
Moynahan, Bridget	Binghamton, NY	4/28/1971
Mueller-Stahl, Armin	Tilsit, E. Prussia	12/17/1930
Muldaur, Diana	Brooklyn, NY	8/19/1938
Mulgrew, Kate	Dubuque, IA	4/29/1955
Mull, Martin	Chicago, IL	8/18/1943
Mullally, Megan	Los Angeles, CA	11/12/1958
Mullan, Peter	Peterhead, Scotland, UK	11/2/1959
Mulligan, Carey	London, England, UK	5/28/1985
Mulroney, Dermot	Alexandria, VA	10/31/1963
Muniz, Frankie	Wood-Ridge, NJ	12/5/1985
Murphy, Ben	Jonesboro, AR	3/6/1942
Murphy, Donna	Corona, Queens, NY	3/7/1958
Murphy, Eddie	Brooklyn, NY	4/3/1961
Murphy, Michael	Los Angeles, CA	5/5/1938
Murray, Anne	Springhill, NS, Canada	6/20/1945
Murray, Bill	Wilmette, IL	9/21/1950
Murray, Don	Hollywood, CA	7/31/1929
Musburger, Brent	Portland, OR	5/26/1939
Muti, Riccardo	Naples, Italy	7/28/1941
Myers, Mike	Scarborough, ON, Canada	5/25/1963
Nagra, Parminder	Leicester, England, UK	10/5/1975
Nanjiani, Kumail	Karachi, Pakistan	2/21/1978
Nash, Graham	Blackpool, England, UK	2/2/1942
Nash, Niecy	Palmdale, CA	2/23/1970
Naughton, James	Middletown, CT	12/6/1945
Navarro, Dave	Santa Monica, CA	6/7/1967
Nealon, Kevin	St. Louis, MO	11/18/1953
Neeson, Liam	Ballymena, N. Ireland, UK	6/7/1952
Neff, Lucas	Chicago, IL	11/7/1985
Neill, Sam	Ulster, N. Ireland, UK	9/14/1947
Nelligan, Kate	London, ON, Canada	3/16/1951
Nelly	Austin, TX	11/2/1974
Nelson, Craig T.	Spokane, WA	4/4/1944
Nelson, Judd	Portland, ME	11/28/1959
Nelson, Tracy	Santa Monica, CA	10/25/1963
Nelson, Willie	Abbott, TX	4/30/1933
Nero, Peter	Brooklyn, NY	5/22/1934
Nesmith, Michael	Houston, TX	12/30/1942
Neuwirth, Bebe	Newark, NJ	12/31/1958
Neville, Aaron	New Orleans, LA	1/24/1941
Newhart, Bob	Oak Park, IL	9/5/1929
Newman, Randy	New Orleans, LA	11/28/1943
Newton, Thandie	London, Eng., UK	11/6/1972
Newton, Wayne	Norfolk, VA	4/3/1942
Newton-John, Olivia	Cambridge, England, UK	9/26/1948
Nicholas, Denise	Detroit, MI	7/12/1944
Nicholson, Jack	Neptune, NJ	4/22/1937
Nicks, Stevie	Phoenix, AZ	5/26/1948
Nighy, Bill	Caterham, Surrey, Eng., UK	12/12/1949
Nixon, Cynthia	New York, NY	4/9/1966
Noah, Trevor	Soweto, South Africa	2/20/1984
Noble, John	Port Pirie, S. Austral., Australia	8/20/1948
Nolan, Christopher	London, England, UK	7/30/1970
Nolte, Nick	Omaha, NE	2/8/1941
Noone, Peter	Manchester, England, UK	11/5/1947
Norman, Jessye	Augusta, GA	9/15/1945
Norris, Chuck	Ryan, OK	3/10/1940
Northam, Jeremy	Cambridge, England, UK	12/1/1961
Norton, Edward	Boston, MA	8/18/1969
Noth, Christopher	Madison, WI	11/13/1954
Novak, Kim	Chicago, IL	2/13/1933
Nuyen, France	Marseilles, France	7/31/1939
Nyong'o, Lupita	Mexico City, Mexico	3/1/1983
Oates, John	New York, NY	4/7/1949
O'Brien, Conan	Brookline, MA	4/18/1963
O'Brien, Margaret	San Diego, CA	1/15/1937
Ocean, Billy	Fyzabad, Trinidad and Tobago	1/21/1950
Ocean, Frank	Long Beach, CA	10/28/1987
O'Connor, Sinead	Glenageary, Ireland	12/8/1966
Odenkirk, Bob	Berwyn, IL	10/22/1962
O'Donnell, Chris	Winnetka, IL	6/26/1970
O'Donnell, Rosie	Commack, NY	3/21/1962
O'Grady, Gail	Detroit, MI	1/23/1963
Oh, Sandra	Nepean, ON, Canada	7/20/1971
O'Hara, Catherine	Toronto, ON, Canada	3/4/1954
O'Hare, Denis	Kansas City, MO	1/17/1962
Oka, Masi	Tokyo, Japan	12/27/1974
Oldman, Gary	South London, Eng., UK	3/21/1958
Olin, Ken	Chicago, IL	7/30/1954
Olin, Lena	Stockholm, Sweden	3/22/1955
Oliver, Jamie	Clavering, England, UK	5/27/1975
Oliver, John	Birmingham, England, UK	4/23/1977
Olmos, Edward James	E. Los Angeles, CA	2/24/1947
Olsen, Ashley	Sherman Oaks, CA	6/13/1986
Olsen, Mary-Kate	Sherman Oaks, CA	6/13/1986
Olson, Nancy	Milwaukee, WI	7/14/1928
Olyphant, Timothy	Honolulu, HI	5/20/1968
O'Malley, Mike	Boston, MA	10/31/1966
O'Neal, Ryan	Los Angeles, CA	4/20/1941
O'Neal, Tatum	Los Angeles, CA	11/5/1963
O'Neill, Ed	Youngstown, OH	4/12/1946
Ontkean, Michael	Vancouver, BC, Canada	1/24/1946
O'Quinn, Terry	Newbury, MI	7/15/1952
Orlando, Tony	New York, NY	4/3/1944
Ormond, Julia	Epsom, England, UK	1/4/1965
Osbourne, Jack	London, England, UK	11/8/1985
Osbourne, Kelly	London, England, UK	10/27/1984
Osbourne, Ozzy	Birmingham, England, UK	12/3/1948
Osbourne, Sharon	London, England, UK	10/9/1952

Name	Birthplace	Birthdate
Osment, Haley Joel	Los Angeles, CA	4/10/1988
Osmond, Donny	Ogden, UT	12/9/1957
Osmond, Marie	Ogden, UT	10/13/1959
O'Toole, Annette	Houston, TX	4/1/1951
Owen, Clive	Keresley, England, UK	10/3/1964
Oyelowo, David	Oxford, England, UK	4/1/1976
Oz, Frank	Herford, England, UK	5/25/1944
Ozawa, Seiji	Shenyang, China	9/1/1935
Pacino, Al	New York, NY	4/25/1940
Packer, Billy	Wellsville, NY	2/25/1940
Page, Ellen	Halifax, NS, Canada	2/21/1987
Page, Jimmy	Heston, England, UK	1/9/1944
Paget, Debra	Denver, CO	8/19/1933
Paige, Janis	Tacoma, WA	9/16/1922
Paisley, Brad	Glen Dale, WV	10/28/1972
Palin, Michael	Sheffield, England, UK	5/5/1943
Palmer, Geoffrey	London, England, UK	6/4/1927
Palminteri, Chazz	Bronx, NY	5/15/1951
Paltrow, Gwyneth	Los Angeles, CA	9/27/1972
Panettiere, Hayden	Palisades, NY	8/21/1989
Panjabi, Archie	Edgware, England, UK	5/31/1972
Pantoliano, Joe	Hoboken, NJ	9/12/1951
Papas, Irene	Chiliomodi, Greece	9/3/1926
Paquin, Anna	Winnipeg, MB, Canada	7/24/1982
Parker, Alan	Islington, England, UK	2/14/1944
Parker, Jameson	Baltimore, MD	11/18/1947
Parker, Mary-Louise	Fort Jackson, SC	8/2/1964
Parker, Sarah Jessica	Nelsonville, OH	3/25/1965
Parsons, Estelle	Marblehead, MA	11/20/1927
Parsons, Jim	Houston, TX	3/24/1973
Parton, Dolly	Sevierville, TN	1/19/1946
Pasdar, Adrian	Pittsfield, MA	4/30/1965
Patinkin, Mandy	Chicago, IL	11/30/1952
Patric, Jason	Flushing, Queens, NY	6/17/1966
Pattinson, Robert	London, England, UK	5/13/1986
Patton, Will	Charleston, SC	6/14/1954
Paul, Aaron	Emmett, ID	8/27/1979
Paul, Adrian	London, England, UK	5/29/1959
Paulson, Sarah	Tampa, FL	12/17/1975
Pearce, Guy	Ely, England, UK	10/5/1967
Peele, Jordan	New York, NY	2/21/1979
Peet, Amanda	New York, NY	1/11/1972
Penn, Kal	Montclair, NJ	4/23/1977
Penn, Sean	Burbank, CA	8/17/1960
Pepper, Barry	Campbell River, BC, Can.	4/4/1970
Perez, Rosie	Brooklyn, NY	9/6/1964
Perkins, Elizabeth	Flushing, Queens, NY	11/18/1960
Perlman, Itzhak	Tel Aviv, Israel	8/31/1945
Perlman, Rhea	Brooklyn, NY	3/31/1948
Perlman, Ron	New York, NY	4/13/1950
Perrine, Valerie	Galveston, TX	9/3/1943
Perry, Katy	Santa Barbara, CA	10/25/1984
Perry, Luke	Mansfield, OH	10/11/1965
Perry, Matthew	Williamstown, MA	8/19/1969
Perry, Tyler	New Orleans, LA	9/13/1969
Persoff, Nehemiah	Jerusalem, Israel	8/2/1919
Pesci, Joe	Newark, NJ	2/9/1943
Peters, Bernadette	Ozone Park, Queens, NY	2/28/1948
Peters, Evan	St. Louis, MO	1/20/1987
Petersen, Wolfgang	Emden, Germany	3/14/1941
Petty, Lori	Chattanooga, TN	3/23/1963
Pfeiffer, Michelle	Santa Ana, CA	4/29/1958
Phair, Liz	New Haven, CT	4/17/1967
Philbin, Regis	New York, NY	8/25/1931
Phillippe, Ryan	New Castle, DE	9/10/1974
Phillips, Lou Diamond	Subic Bay, Philippines	2/17/1962
Phillips, Mackenzie	Alexandria, VA	11/10/1959
Phillips, Michelle	Long Beach, CA	6/4/1944
Phillips, Phillip	Leesburg, GA	9/20/1990
Phillips, Sian	Bettws, Wales, UK	5/14/1934
Phoenix, Joaquin	San Juan, Puerto Rico	10/28/1974
Pierce, David Hyde	Albany, NY	4/3/1959
Pike, Rosamund	London, England, UK	1/27/1979
Pinchot, Bronson	New York, NY	5/20/1959
Pink	Doylestown, PA	9/8/1979
Pinkett Smith, Jada	Baltimore, MD	9/18/1971
Pirner, Dave	Green Bay, WI	4/16/1964
Piscopo, Joe	Passaic, NJ	6/17/1951
Pitbull	Miami, FL	1/15/1981
Pitt, Brad	Shawnee, OK	12/18/1963
Piven, Jeremy	New York, NY	7/26/1965
Plant, Robert	W. Bromwich, England, UK	8/20/1948
Plimpton, Martha	New York, NY	11/16/1970
Plowright, Joan	Brigg, England, UK	10/28/1929
Plummer, Amanda	New York, NY	3/23/1957
Plummer, Christopher	Toronto, ON, Canada	12/13/1927
Poehler, Amy	Newton, MA	9/16/1971
Poitier, Sidney	Miami, FL	2/20/1927
Polanski, Roman	Paris, France	8/18/1933
Pompeo, Ellen	Everett, MA	11/10/1969
Pop, Iggy	Muskegon, MI	4/21/1947
Portman, Natalie	Jerusalem, Israel	6/9/1981
Posey, Parker	Baltimore, MD	11/8/1968
Post, Markie	Palo Alto, CA	11/4/1950
Potente, Franka	Dulmen bei Munster, Germany	7/22/1974

Name	Birthplace	Birthdate
Potts, Annie	Nashville, TN	10/28/1952
Povich, Maury	Washington, DC	1/17/1939
Powell, Jane	Portland, OR	4/1/1929
Powers, Stefanie	Hollywood, CA	11/2/1942
Pratt, Chris	Virginia, MN	6/21/1979
Prentiss, Paula	San Antonio, TX	3/4/1939
Prepon, Laura	Watchung, NJ	3/7/1980
Presley, Priscilla	Brooklyn, NY	5/24/1945
Pressly, Jaime	Kinston, NC	7/30/1977
Previn, Andre	Berlin, Germany	4/6/1929
Price, Leontyne	Laurel, MS	2/10/1927
Price, Molly	North Plainfield, NJ	12/15/1966
Pride, Charley	Sledge, MS	3/18/1938
Priestley, Jason	Vancouver, BC, Canada	8/28/1969
Prince, Faith	Augusta, GA	8/5/1957
Principal, Victoria	Fukuoka, Japan	1/3/1950
Probst, Jeff	Wichita, KS	11/4/1962
Proctor, Emily	Raleigh, NC	10/8/1968
Pryce, Jonathan	Holywell, N. Wales, UK	6/1/1947
Puck, Wolfgang	St. Veit, Austria	1/8/1949
Pulliam, Keshia Knight	Newark, NJ	4/9/1979
Pullman, Bill	Hornell, NY	12/17/1953
Purcell, Sarah	Richmond, IN	10/8/1948
Purefoy, James	Taunton, England, UK	6/3/1964
Quaid, Dennis	Houston, TX	4/9/1954
Quaid, Randy	Houston, TX	10/1/1950
Queen Latifah	Newark, NJ	3/18/1970
Quinn, Aidan	Chicago, IL	3/8/1959
Quinn, Colin	Brooklyn, NY	6/6/1959
Quinn, Martha	Albany, NY	5/11/1959
Quinto, Zachary	Pittsburgh, PA	6/2/1977
Rachins, Alan	Cambridge, MA	10/3/1942
Radcliffe, Daniel	London, England, UK	7/23/1989
Radnor, Josh	Columbus, OH	7/29/1974
Raffi (Cavoukian)	Cairo, Egypt	7/8/1948
Raitt, Bonnie	Burbank, CA	11/8/1949
Ramey, Samuel	Colby, KS	3/28/1942
Ramirez, Efren	Los Angeles, CA	10/2/1973
Ramirez, Sara	Mazatlan, Mexico	8/31/1975
Rampling, Charlotte	Sturmer, MA	2/5/1946
Ramsay, Gordon	Elderslie, Scotland, UK	11/8/1966
Rancic, Giuliana	Naples, Italy	8/17/1975
Randolph, Joyce	Detroit, MI	10/21/1924
Raphael, Sally Jessy	Easton, PA	2/25/1935
Rashad, Phylicia	Houston, TX	6/19/1948
Ratzenberger, John	Bridgeport, CT	4/6/1947
Raver, Kim	New York, NY	3/15/1969
Ray, Rachael	Glen Falls, NY	8/25/1968
Reddy, Helen	Melbourne, Vic., Australia	10/25/1941
Redford, Robert	Santa Monica, CA	8/18/1936
Redgrave, Vanessa	London, England, UK	1/30/1937
Redmayne, Eddie	London, England, UK	1/6/1982
Reed, Rex	Ft. Worth, TX	10/2/1938
Reeves, Keanu	Beirut, Lebanon	9/2/1964
Reeves, Martha	Eufaula, AL	7/18/1941
Regalbuto, Joe	New York, NY	8/24/1949
Reid, Tara	Wyckoff, NJ	11/8/1975
Reid, Tim	Norfolk, VA	12/19/1944
Reid, Vernon	London, England, UK	8/22/1958
Reilly, John C.	Chicago, IL	5/24/1965
Reiner, Carl	Bronx, NY	3/20/1922
Reiner, Rob	Bronx, NY	3/6/1947
Reinhold, Judge	Wilmington, DE	5/21/1957
Reinking, Ann	Seattle, WA	11/10/1949
Reiser, Paul	New York, NY	3/30/1957
Reitman, Ivan	Komarno, Czechoslovakia	10/26/1946
Remini, Leah	Brooklyn, NY	6/15/1970
Renner, Jeremy	Modesto, CA	1/7/1971
Reynolds, Ryan	Vancouver, BC, Canada	10/23/1976
Reznor, Trent	Mercer, PA	5/17/1965
Rhames, Ving	New York, NY	5/12/1959
Rhimes, Shonda	Chicago, IL	1/13/1970
Rhymes, Busta	Brooklyn, NY	5/20/1972
Rhys, Matthew	Cardiff, Wales, UK	11/4/1974
Rhys Meyers, Jonathan	Dublin, Ireland	7/27/1977
Ribisi, Giovanni	Los Angeles, CA	12/17/1974
Ricci, Christina	Santa Monica, CA	2/12/1980
Richards, Denise	Downers Grove, IL	2/17/1971
Richards, Keith	Dartford, Kent, Eng., UK	12/18/1943
Richards, Michael	Culver City, CA	7/24/1949
Richardson, Kevin	Lexington, KY	10/3/1971
Richardson, Miranda	Lancashire, England, UK	3/3/1958
Richardson, Patricia	Bethesda, MD	2/23/1951
Richie, Lionel	Tuskegee, AL	6/20/1949
Richie, Nicole	Berkeley, CA	9/21/1981
Richter, Andy	Grand Rapids, MI	10/28/1966
Riegert, Peter	New York, NY	4/11/1947
Rigg, Diana	Doncaster, England, UK	7/20/1938
Rihanna	St. Michael, Barbados	2/20/1988
Riley, Amber	Long Beach, CA	2/15/1986
Rimes, LeAnn	Jackson, MS	8/28/1982
Ringwald, Molly	Roseville, CA	2/18/1968
Ripa, Kelly	Stratford, NJ	10/2/1970
Rivera, Chita	Washington, DC	1/23/1933
Rivera, Geraldo	New York, NY	7/4/1943
Robbie, Margot	Dalby, Qld., Australia	7/2/1990

Name	Birthplace	Birthdate
Robbins, Tim	W. Covina, CA	10/16/1958
Roberts, Eric	Biloxi, MS	4/18/1956
Roberts, Julia	Smyrna, GA.	10/28/1967
Roberts, Tony	New York, NY	10/22/1939
Robinson, Smokey	Detroit, MI	2/19/1940
Rock, Chris	Andrews, SC	2/7/1965
Rockwell, Sam	Daly City, CA	11/5/1968
Rodgers, Jimmie	Camas, WA	9/18/1933
Rodriguez, Johnny	Sabinal, TX	12/10/1951
Rodriguez, Michelle	Bexar County, TX.	7/12/1978
Rogan, Joe	Newark, NJ	8/11/1967
Rogen, Seth	Vancouver, BC, Canada.	4/15/1982
Rogers, Kenny	Houston, TX	8/21/1938
Rogers, Mimi	Coral Gables, FL	1/27/1956
Rohm, Elisabeth	Dusseldorf, Germany.	4/28/1973
Rollins, Henry	Washington, DC	2/13/1961
Rollins, Sonny	New York, NY	9/7/1930
Romano, Ray	Forest Hills, Queens, NY	12/21/1957
Romijn, Rebecca	Berkeley, CA	11/6/1972
Ronan, Saoirse	New York, NY	4/12/1994
Ronson, Mark	London, England, UK	9/4/1975
Ronstadt, Linda	Tucson, AZ	7/15/1946
Root, Stephen	Sarasota, FL	11/17/1951
Rose, Axl	Lafayette, IN	2/6/1962
Roseanne	Salt Lake City, UT	11/3/1952
Ross, Charlotte	Winnetka, IL	1/21/1968
Ross, Diana	Detroit, MI	3/26/1944
Ross, Katharine	Hollywood, CA.	1/29/1940
Ross, Marion	Albert Lea, MN	10/25/1928
Ross, Tracee Ellis	Los Angeles, CA	10/29/1972
Rossdale, Gavin	London, England, UK	10/30/1965
Rossellini, Isabella	Rome, Italy	6/18/1952
Rossum, Emmy	New York, NY	9/12/1986
Roth, David Lee	Bloomington, IN.	10/10/1955
Roth, Tim	London, England, UK	5/14/1961
Rotten, Johnny	London, England, UK	1/31/1956
Roundtree, Richard	New Rochelle, NY	7/9/1942
Rourke, Mickey	Schenectady, NY	9/16/1952
Routh, Brandon	Des Moines, IA	10/9/1979
Routledge, Patricia	Birkenhead, England, UK.	2/17/1929
Rowan, Kelly	Ottawa, ON, Canada	10/26/1965
Rowlands, Gena	Cambria, WI	6/19/1930
Rubinstein, John	Beverly Hills, CA	12/8/1946
Rudd, Paul	Passaic, NJ	4/6/1969
Rudner, Rita	Miami, FL	9/17/1955?
Rudolph, Maya	Gainesville, FL.	7/27/1972
Ruehl, Mercedes	Jackson Heights, Queens, NY	2/28/1948
Ruffalo, Mark	Kenosha, WI	11/22/1967
RuPaul	San Diego, CA	11/17/1960
Rupp, Debra Jo	Glendale, CA	2/24/1951
Rush, Barbara	Denver, CO	1/4/1927
Rush, Geoffrey	Toowoomba, Qld., Australia	7/6/1951
Russell, Keri	Fountain Valley, CA	3/23/1976
Russell, Kurt	Springfield, MA	3/17/1951
Russell, Mark	Buffalo, NY	8/23/1932
Russell, Theresa	San Diego, CA.	3/20/1957
Russo, Rene	Burbank, CA	2/17/1954
Ruttan, Susan	Oregon City, OR	9/16/1950
Ryan, Meg	Fairfield, CT.	11/19/1961
Ryan, Roz	Detroit, MI	7/7/1951
Rydell, Bobby	Philadelphia, PA	4/26/1942
Ryder, Winona	Winona, MN	10/29/1971
Rylance, Mark	Ashford, England, UK	1/18/1960
Sabato, Antonio, Jr.	Rome, Italy	2/29/1972
Sade (Adu)	Ibadan, Nigeria	1/16/1959
Sagal, Katey	Hollywood, CA.	1/19/1954
Saget, Bob	Philadelphia, PA	5/17/1956
Sagnier, Ludivine	La Celle-St.-Cloud, France	7/3/1979
Sahl, Mort	Montréal, QC, Canada.	5/11/1927
Saint, Eva Marie	Newark, NJ	7/4/1924
St. James, Susan	Hollywood, CA.	8/14/1946
St. John, Jill	Los Angeles, CA	8/19/1940
St. Patrick, Mathew	Philadelphia, PA	3/17/1968
Sajak, Pat	Chicago, IL	10/26/1946
Saldana, Zoë	Passaic, NJ	6/19/1978
Salonga, Lea	Manila, Philippines	2/22/1971
Samberg, Andy	Berkeley, CA	8/18/1978
Samms, Emma	London, England, UK	8/28/1960
San Giacomo, Laura	Hoboken, NJ	11/14/1962
Sandler, Adam	Brooklyn, NY	9/9/1966
Sands, Julian	West Yorkshire, Eng., UK.	1/15/1958
Santana, Carlos	Autlan, Mexico	7/20/1947
Sara, Mia	Brooklyn, NY	6/19/1967
Sarandon, Susan	New York, NY	10/4/1946
Sartain, Gailard	Tulsa, OK	9/18/1946
Savage, Ben	Highland Park, IL.	9/13/1980
Savage, Fred	Highland Park, IL.	7/9/1976
Sawa, Devon	Vancouver, BC, Canada.	9/7/1978
Saxon, John	Brooklyn, NY	8/5/1936
Sayles, John	Schenectady, NY	9/28/1950
Scacchi, Greta	Milan, Italy	2/18/1960
Scaggs, Boz	Canton, OH	6/8/1944
Scales, Prunella	Sutton Abinger, Eng., UK.	6/22/1932

Name	Birthplace	Birthdate
Scalia, Jack	Brooklyn, NY	11/10/1951
Schiff, Richard	Bethesda, MD	5/27/1955
Schiffer, Claudia	Rheinbach, Germany.	8/25/1970
Schneider, John	Mt. Kisco, NY.	4/8/1960
Schneider, Rob	San Francisco, CA.	10/31/1963
Schreiber, Liev	San Francisco, CA.	10/4/1967
Schroder, Rick	Staten Island, NY.	4/13/1970
Schumer, Amy	New York, NY	6/1/1981
Schwarzenegger, Arnold	Thal, Austria	7/30/1947
Schwimmer, David	Astoria, Queens, NY	11/2/1966
Sciorra, Annabella	Wethersfield, CT	3/24/1964
Scolari, Peter	New Rochelle, NY	9/12/1954
Scorsese, Martin	Flushing, Queens, NY	11/17/1942
Scott, Ridley	South Shields, England, UK	11/30/1937
Scott, Seann William	Cottage Grove, MN	10/3/1976
Scott Thomas, Kristin	Redruth, England, UK	5/24/1960
Scotto, Renata	Savona, Italy	2/24/1934
Scully, Vin	Bronx, NY	11/29/1927
Seacrest, Ryan	Atlanta, GA	12/24/1974
Seagal, Steven	Lansing, MI	4/10/1951
Secor, Kyle	Tacoma, WA	5/31/1957
Sedaka, Neil	Brooklyn, NY	3/13/1939
Sedgwick, Kyra	New York, NY	8/19/1965
Segal, George	Great Neck, NY	2/13/1934
Segel, Jason	Los Angeles, CA	1/18/1980
Seidelman, Susan	Abington, PA	12/11/1952
Seinfeld, Jerry	Brooklyn, NY	4/29/1954
Sellecca, Connie	Bronx, NY	5/25/1955
Selleck, Tom	Detroit, MI	1/29/1945
Severinsen, Doc	Arlington, OR.	7/7/1927
Sevigny, Chloë	Springfield, MA	11/18/1974
Sewell, Rufus	Twickenham, Middlesex, England, UK	10/29/1967
Seyfried, Amanda	Allentown, PA	12/3/1985
Seymour, Jane	Hillingdon, England, UK.	2/15/1951
Shackelford, Ted	Oklahoma City, OK	6/23/1946
Shaffer, Paul	Thunder Bay, ON, Canada	11/28/1949
Shakira (Mebarak Ripoll)	Barranquilla, Colombia	2/2/1977
Shalhoub, Tony	Green Bay, WI	10/9/1953
Shannon, Molly	Shaker Heights, OH.	9/16/1964
Shatner, William	Montréal, QC, Canada.	3/22/1931
Shaughnessy, Charles	London, England, UK	2/9/1955
Shaver, Helen	St. Thomas, ON, Canada.	2/24/1951
Shawkat, Alia	Riverside, CA.	4/18/1989
Shea, John	North Conway, NH.	4/14/1949
Shearer, Harry	Los Angeles, CA	12/23/1943
Sheedy, Ally	New York, NY	6/13/1962
Sheen, Charlie	Los Angeles, CA	9/3/1965
Sheen, Martin	Dayton, OH	8/3/1940
Sheen, Michael	Newport, Wales, UK	2/5/1969
Sheeran, Ed	Hebden Bridge, West Yorkshire, Eng., UK	2/17/1991
Sheindlin, Judy	Brooklyn, NY	10/21/1942
Shelton, Blake	Ada, OK	6/18/1976
Shepherd, Cybill	Memphis, TN	2/18/1950
Shepherd, Sherri	Chicago, IL	4/22/1967
Sheridan, Nicollette	Worthing, England, UK	11/21/1963
Shields, Brooke	New York, NY	5/31/1965
Shire, Talia	Lake Success, NY	4/25/1946
Short, Martin	Hamilton, ON, Canada.	3/26/1950
Shortz, Will	Crawfordsville, IN.	8/26/1952
Show, Grant	Detroit, MI	2/27/1962
Shue, Andrew	South Orange, NJ	2/20/1967
Shue, Elisabeth	Wilmington, DE	10/6/1963
Shyamalan, M. Night.	Pondicherry, India	8/6/1970
Sidibe, Gabourey	Brooklyn, NY	5/6/1983
Sigler, Jamie-Lynn	Jericho, NY	5/15/1981
Sikking, James B.	Los Angeles, CA	3/5/1934
Silverman, Jonathan	Beverly Hills, CA	8/5/1966
Silverman, Sarah	Bedford, NH.	12/1/1970
Silverstone, Alicia	San Francisco, CA.	10/4/1976
Simmons, Gene	Haifa, Israel	8/25/1949
Simmons, Henry	Stamford, CT.	7/1/1970
Simmons, Richard	New Orleans, LA.	7/12/1948
Simon, Carly	New York, NY	6/25/1945
Simon, Paul	Newark, NJ	10/13/1941
Simpson, Ashlee	Waco, TX.	10/3/1984
Simpson, Jessica	Abilene, TX.	7/10/1980
Sinatra, Nancy	Jersey City, NJ.	6/8/1940
Sinbad	Benton Harbor, MI	11/10/1956
Singleton, John	Los Angeles, CA	1/6/1968
Sinise, Gary	Blue Island, IL	3/17/1955
Sirico, Tony	Brooklyn, NY	7/29/1942
Sisto, Jeremy	Grass Valley, CA	10/6/1974
Sizemore, Tom	Detroit, MI	9/29/1961
Skarsgard, Alexander	Stockholm, Sweden.	8/25/1976
Skarsgard, Stellan	Gothenburg, Sweden.	6/13/1951
Skerritt, Tom	Detroit, MI	8/25/1933
Slater, Christian	New York, NY	8/18/1969
Slater, Helen	Massapequa, NY.	12/15/1963
Slattery, John	Boston, MA	8/13/1962
Slezak, Erika	Hollywood, CA.	8/5/1946
Slick, Grace	Evanston, IL	10/30/1939
Smirnoff, Karina	Kharkiv, Ukraine	1/2/1978

Name	Birthplace	Birthdate
Smirnoff, Yakov	Odessa, Ukraine	1/24/1951
Smith, Allison	New York, NY	12/9/1969
Smith, Jaclyn	Houston, TX	10/26/1945
Smith, Jaden	Malibu, CA	7/8/1998
Smith, Kevin	Red Bank, NJ	8/2/1970
Smith, Maggie	Ilford, England, UK	12/28/1934
Smith, Patti	Chicago, IL	12/30/1946
Smith, Robert	Blackpool, England, UK	4/21/1959
Smith, Sam	London, England, UK	5/19/1992
Smith, Will	Philadelphia, PA	9/25/1968
Smith, Willow	Los Angeles, CA	10/31/2000
Smits, Jimmy	Brooklyn, NY	7/9/1955
Smothers, Dick	Governor's Island, NY	11/20/1938
Smothers, Tom	Governor's Island, NY	2/2/1937
Smulders, Cobie	Vancouver, BC, Canada	4/3/1982
Snipes, Wesley	Orlando, FL	7/31/1962
Snooki (Nicole Polizzi)	Santiago, Chile	11/23/1987
Snoop Dogg	Long Beach, CA	10/20/1971
Soderbergh, Steven	Atlanta, GA	1/14/1963
Soloway, Jill	Chicago, IL	9/26/1965
Somerhalder, Ian	Covington, LA	12/8/1978
Somers, Suzanne	San Bruno, CA	10/16/1946
Sommer, Elke	Berlin, Germany	11/5/1940
Sorbo, Kevin	Mound, MN	9/24/1958
Sorvino, Mira	Tenafly, NJ	9/28/1967
Sorvino, Paul	Brooklyn, NY	4/13/1939
Soul, David	Chicago, IL	8/28/1943
Spacek, Sissy	Quitman, TX	12/25/1949
Spacey, Kevin	South Orange, NJ	7/26/1959
Spade, David	Birmingham, MI	7/22/1964
Spader, James	Boston, MA	2/7/1960
Spalding, Esperanza	Portland, OR	10/18/1984
Spano, Joe	San Francisco, CA	7/7/1946
Sparks, Jordin	Phoenix, AZ	12/22/1989
Spears, Britney	Kentwood, LA	12/2/1981
Spears, Jamie-Lynn	McComb, MS	4/4/1991
Spector, Phil	Bronx, NY	12/26/1940
Spelling, Tori	Los Angeles, CA	5/16/1973
Spencer, Octavia	Montgomery, AL	5/25/1972
Spielberg, Steven	Cincinnati, OH	12/18/1946
Spiner, Brent	Houston, TX	2/2/1949
Springer, Jerry	London, England, UK	2/13/1944
Springfield, Rick	Sydney, NSW, Australia	8/23/1949
Springsteen, Bruce	Long Branch, NJ	9/23/1949
Spurlock, Morgan	Parksburg, WV	11/7/1970
Stahl, Nick	Harlingen, TX	12/5/1979
Stallone, Sylvester	New York, NY	7/6/1946
Stamos, John	Cypress, CA	8/19/1963
Stamp, Terence	Stepney, England, UK	7/22/1938
Stapleton, Chris	Lexington, KY	4/15/1978
Starr, Ringo	Liverpool, England, UK	7/7/1940
Statham, Jason	Shirebrook, England, UK	7/26/1967
Steenburgen, Mary	Newport, AR	2/8/1953
Stefani, Gwen	Fullerton, CA	10/3/1969
Stein, Ben	Washington, DC	11/25/1944
Stern, Daniel	Bethesda, MD	8/28/1957
Stern, Howard	Roosevelt, NY	1/12/1954
Sternhagen, Frances	Washington, DC	1/13/1930
Stevens, Andrew	Memphis, TN	6/10/1955
Stevens, Cat (Yusef Islam)	London, England, UK	7/21/1948
Stevens, Connie	Brooklyn, NY	8/8/1938
Stevens, Stella	Yazoo City, MS	10/1/1936
Stevenson, Parker	Philadelphia, PA	6/4/1952
Stewart, French	Albuquerque, NM	2/20/1964
Stewart, Jon	New York, NY	11/28/1962
Stewart, Kristen	Los Angeles, CA	4/9/1990
Stewart, Patrick	Mirfield, England, UK	7/13/1940
Stewart, Rod	London, England, UK	1/10/1945
Stiles, Julia	New York, NY	3/28/1981
Stiller, Ben	New York, NY	11/30/1965
Stiller, Jerry	Brooklyn, NY	6/8/1927
Stills, Stephen	Dallas, TX	1/3/1945
Sting	Newcastle upon Tyne, England, UK	10/2/1951
Stipe, Michael	Decatur, GA	1/4/1960
Stockwell, Dean	North Hollywood, CA	3/5/1936
Stoltz, Eric	Whittier, CA	9/30/1961
Stone, Dee Wallace	Kansas City, KS	12/14/1948
Stone, Emma	Scottsdale, AZ	11/6/1988
Stone, Oliver	New York, NY	9/15/1946
Stone, Sharon	Meadville, PA	3/10/1958
Stonestreet, Eric	Kansas City, KS	9/9/1971
Stookey, Paul	Baltimore, MD	12/30/1937
Storch, Larry	New York, NY	1/8/1923
Stowe, Madeleine	Eagle Rock, CA	8/18/1958
Strahan, Michael	Houston, TX	11/21/1971
Strait, George	Pearsall, TX	5/18/1952
Strasser, Robin	New York, NY	5/7/1945
Strathairn, David	San Francisco, CA	1/26/1949
Strauss, Peter	Croton-on-Hudson, NY	2/20/1947
Streep, Meryl	Summit, NJ	6/22/1949
Streisand, Barbra	Brooklyn, NY	4/24/1942
Stringfield, Sherry	Colorado Springs, CO	6/24/1967

Name	Birthplace	Birthdate
Stroman, Susan	Wilmington, DE	10/17/1954
Struthers, Sally	Portland, OR	7/28/1948
Studdard, Ruben	Frankfurt, Germany	9/12/1978
Styles, Harry	Holmes Chapel, Cheshire, Eng., UK	2/1/1994
Suchet, David	London, England, UK	5/2/1946
Sudeikis, Jason	Fairfax, VA	9/18/1975
Sullivan, Erik Per	Worcester, MA	7/12/1991
Sullivan, Susan	New York, NY	11/18/1942
Sunjata, Daniel	Evanston, IL	12/30/1971
Sutherland, Donald	St. John, NB, Canada	7/17/1934
Sutherland, Kiefer	London, England, UK	12/21/1966
Suvari, Mena	Newport, RI	2/9/1979
Swank, Hilary	Lincoln, NE	7/30/1974
Swift, Taylor	Wyomissing, PA	12/13/1989
Swinton, Tilda	London, England, UK	11/5/1960
Swit, Loretta	Passaic, NJ	11/4/1937
Sykes, Wanda	Portsmouth, VA	3/7/1964
Szmanda, Eric	Milwaukee, WI	7/24/1975
T, Mr.	Chicago, IL	5/21/1952
Takei, George	Los Angeles, CA	4/20/1937
Tamblyn, Amber	Santa Monica, CA	5/14/1983
Tamblyn, Russ	Los Angeles, CA	12/30/1934
Tambor, Jeffrey	San Francisco, CA	7/8/1944
Tarantino, Quentin	Knoxville, TN	3/27/1963
Tatum, Channing	Cullman, AL	4/26/1980
Tautou, Audrey	Beaumont, France	8/9/1976?
Taylor, Buck	Hollywood, CA	5/13/1938
Taylor, James	Boston, MA	3/12/1948
Taylor, Lili	Glencoe, IL	2/20/1967
Taylor, Rip	Washington, DC	1/13/1934
Taymor, Julie	Newton, MA	12/15/1952
Te Kanawa, Kiri	Gisborne, New Zealand	3/6/1944
Teller	Philadelphia, PA	2/14/1948
Tennant, David	Bathgate, West Lothian, Scotland, UK	4/18/1971
Tennant, Victoria	London, England, UK	9/30/1950
Tennille, Toni	Montgomery, AL	5/8/1940
Tesh, John	Garden City, NY	7/9/1952
Tharp, Twyla	Portland, IN	7/1/1941
The Weeknd	Toronto, ON, Canada	2/16/1990
Theron, Charlize	Benoni, South Africa	8/7/1975
Thicke, Robin	Los Angeles, CA	3/10/1977
Thiessen, Tiffani	Long Beach, CA	1/23/1974
Thomas, Jonathan Taylor	Bethlehem, PA	9/8/1981
Thomas, Marlo	Deerfield, MI	11/21/1937
Thomas, Michael Tilson	Hollywood, CA	12/21/1944
Thomas, Philip Michael	Columbus, OH	5/26/1949
Thomas, Richard	New York, NY	6/13/1951
Thomas, Sean Patrick	Wilmington, DE	12/17/1970
Thompson, Emma	London, England, UK	4/15/1959
Thompson, Jack	Sydney, NSW, Australia	8/31/1940
Thompson, Kenan	Atlanta, GA	5/10/1978
Thompson, Lea	Rochester, MN	5/31/1961
Thorne-Smith, Courtney	San Francisco, CA	11/8/1967
Thornton, Billy Bob	Hot Springs, AR	8/4/1955
Thurman, Uma	Boston, MA	4/29/1970
Tiegs, Cheryl	Breckenridge, MN	9/25/1947
Tierney, Maura	Boston, MA	2/3/1965
Tilly, Jennifer	Harbor City, CA	9/16/1958
Tilly, Meg	Long Beach, CA	2/14/1960
Timberlake, Justin	Memphis, TN	1/31/1981
Tisdale, Ashley	West Deal, NJ	7/2/1985
Tomei, Marisa	Brooklyn, NY	12/4/1964
Tomlin, Lily	Detroit, MI	9/1/1939
Tonioli, Bruno	Ferrara, Italy	11/25/1955
Tork, Peter	Washington, DC	2/13/1942
Torn, Rip	Temple, TX	2/6/1931
Townsend, Robert	Chicago, IL	2/6/1957
Townshend, Peter	Chiswick, England, UK	5/19/1945
Travanti, Daniel J.	Kenosha, WI	3/7/1940
Travis, Nancy	Astoria, Queens, NY	9/21/1961
Travis, Randy	Marshville, NC	5/4/1959
Travolta, John	Englewood, NJ	2/18/1954
Trebek, Alex	Sudbury, ON, Canada	7/22/1940
Tripplehorn, Jean	Tulsa, OK	6/10/1963
Tritt, Travis	Marietta, GA	2/9/1963
Tucci, Stanley	Peekskill, NY	1/11/1960
Tucker, Chris	Decatur, GA	8/31/1972
Tucker, Michael	Baltimore, MD	2/6/1944
Tucker, Tanya	Seminole, TX	10/10/1958
Tune, Tommy	Wichita Falls, TX	2/28/1939
Turlington, Christy	Walnut Creek, CA	1/2/1969
Turner, Janine	Lincoln, NE	12/6/1962
Turner, Kathleen	Springfield, MO	6/19/1954
Turner, Tina	Nutbush, TN	11/26/1939
Turturro, John	Brooklyn, NY	2/28/1957
Tveit, Aaron	Middletown, NY	10/21/1983
Twain, Shania	Windsor, ON, Canada	8/28/1965
Twiggy (Lawson)	London, England, UK	9/19/1949
Tyler, Liv	New York, NY	7/1/1977
Tyler, Steven	Yonkers, NY	3/26/1948
Tyson, Cicely	New York, NY	12/19/1924
Uecker, Bob	Milwaukee, WI	1/26/1934

Name	Birthplace	Birthdate
Uggams, Leslie	New York, NY	5/25/1943
Ullman, Tracey	Slough, England, UK	12/30/1959
Ullmann, Liv	Tokyo, Japan	12/16/1938
Ulrich, Skeet	Lynchburg, VA	1/20/1970
Underwood, Blair	Tacoma, WA	8/25/1964
Underwood, Carrie	Muskogee, OK	3/10/1983
Urban, Keith	Whangarei, North Island, New Zealand	10/26/1967
Urie, Michael	Dallas, TX	8/8/1980
Usher (Raymond IV)	Dallas, TX	10/14/1978
Vaccaro, Brenda	Brooklyn, NY	11/18/1939
Valley, Mark	Ogdensburg, NY	12/24/1964
Valli, Frankie	Newark, NJ	5/3/1934
Van Ark, Joan	New York, NY	6/16/1943
Van Damme, Jean-Claude	Brussels, Belgium	10/18/1960
Van Der Beek, James	Cheshire, CT	3/8/1977
Van Doren, Mamie	Rowena, SD	2/6/1931
Van Dyke, Dick	West Plains, MO	12/13/1925
Van Halen, Eddie	Nijmegen, Netherlands	1/26/1955
Van Peebles, Mario	Mexico City, Mexico	1/15/1957
Van Sant, Gus	Louisville, KY	7/24/1952
Van Zandt, Steven	Winthrop, MA	11/22/1950
VanCamp, Emily	Port Perry, ON, Canada	5/12/1986
Vance, Courtney B.	Detroit, MI	3/12/1960
Vardalos, Nia	Winnipeg, MB, Canada	9/24/1962
Vaughn, Vince	Minneapolis, MN	3/28/1970
Vedder, Eddie	Evanston, IL	12/23/1964
Vega, Alexa	Miami, FL	8/27/1988
Ventimiglia, Milo	Anaheim, CA	7/8/1977
Vereen, Ben	Miami, FL	10/10/1946
Vergara, Sofia	Barranquilla, Colombia	7/10/1972
Vieira, Meredith	Providence, RI	12/30/1953
Vikander, Alicia	Gothenburg, Sweden	10/3/1988
Villella, Edward	Long Island, NY	10/1/1936
Vincent, Jan-Michael	Denver, CO	7/15/1944
Vinton, Bobby	Canonsburg, PA	4/16/1935
Visnjic, Goran	Sibenik, Yugo. (Croatia)	9/9/1972
Vitale, Dick	East Rutherford, NJ	6/9/1939
Voight, Jon	Yonkers, NY	12/29/1938
Von Stade, Frederica	Somerville, NJ	6/1/1945
Von Sydow, Max	Lund, Sweden	4/10/1929
Von Trier, Lars	Copenhagen, Denmark	4/30/1956
Wagner, Jack	Washington, MO	10/3/1959
Wagner, Lindsay	Los Angeles, CA	6/22/1949
Wagner, Robert	Detroit, MI	2/10/1930
Wahl, Ken	Chicago, IL	10/31/1954
Wahlberg, Donnie	Dorchester, MA	8/17/1969
Wahlberg, Mark	Dorchester, MA	6/5/1971
Waits, Tom	Pomona, CA	12/7/1949
Walden, Robert	New York, NY	9/25/1943
Walken, Christopher	Astoria, Queens, NY	3/31/1943
Wallis, Quvenzhané	Houma, LA	8/23/2008
Walsh, Kate	San Jose, CA	10/13/1967
Walter, Jessica	Brooklyn, NY	1/31/1941
Waltz, Christoph	Vienna, Austria	10/4/1956
Warburton, Patrick	Paterson, NJ	11/14/1964
Ward, Fred	San Diego, CA	12/30/1942
Ward, Sela	Meridian, MS	7/11/1956
Warfield, Marsha	Chicago, IL	3/5/1954
Warner, Malcolm-Jamal	Jersey City, NJ	8/18/1970
Warren, Lesley Ann	New York, NY	8/16/1946
Warwick, Dionne	East Orange, NJ	12/12/1940
Washington, Denzel	Mt. Vernon, NY	12/28/1954
Washington, Isaiah	Houston, TX	8/3/1963
Washington, Kerry	Bronx, NY	1/31/1977
Wasikowska, Mia	Canberra, Australia	10/14/1989
Watanabe, Ken	Koide, Niigata, Japan	10/21/1959
Waters, John	Baltimore, MD	4/22/1946
Waters, Roger	Great Bookham, Eng., UK	9/6/1943
Waterston, Sam	Cambridge, MA	11/15/1940
Watson, Emily	London, England, UK	1/14/1967
Watson, Emma	Paris, France	4/15/1990
Watts, Naomi	Shoreham, England, UK	9/28/1968
Wayans, Damon	New York, NY	9/4/1960
Wayans, Keenen Ivory	Brooklyn, NY	6/8/1958
Wayans, Marlon	New York, NY	7/23/1972
Wayans, Shawn	New York, NY	1/19/1971
Weathers, Carl	New Orleans, LA	1/14/1948
Weaver, Sigourney	New York, NY	10/8/1949
Weir, Peter	Sydney, NSW, Australia	8/21/1944
Weisz, Rachel	London, England, UK	3/7/1971
Weitz, Bruce	Norwalk, CT	5/27/1943
Welch, Raquel	Chicago, IL	9/5/1940
Weld, Tuesday	New York, NY	8/27/1943
Weller, Peter	Stevens Point, WI	6/24/1947
Welling, Tom	Putnam Valley, NY	4/26/1977
Wendt, George	Chicago, IL	10/17/1948
Wentz, Pete	Wilmette, IL	6/5/1979
West, Kanye	Atlanta, GA	6/8/1977
West, Shane	Baton Rouge, LA	6/10/1978
Wettig, Patricia	Cincinnati, OH	12/4/1951
Whalley, Joanne	Manchester, England, UK	8/25/1964
Wheaton, Wil	Burbank, CA	7/29/1972
Whitaker, Forest	Longview, TX	7/15/1961
White, Betty	Oak Park, IL	1/17/1922
White, Jack	Detroit, MI	7/9/1975
White, Jaleel	Pasadena, CA	11/27/1976
White, Vanna	N. Myrtle Beach, SC	2/18/1957
Whitford, Bradley	Madison, WI	10/10/1959
Wiest, Dianne	Kansas City, MO	3/28/1948
Wiig, Kristen	Canandaigua, NY	8/22/1973
Wilde, Olivia	New York, NY	3/10/1984
Wilkinson, Tom	Leeds, England, UK	12/12/1948
Williams, Armstrong	Marion, SC	2/5/1959
Williams, Barry	Santa Monica, CA	9/30/1954
Williams, Billy Dee	New York, NY	4/6/1937
Williams, Cindy	Van Nuys, CA	8/22/1947
Williams, Hal	Columbus, OH	12/14/1938
Williams, Hank, Jr.	Shreveport, LA	5/26/1949
Williams, JoBeth	Houston, TX	12/6/1948
Williams, Lucinda	Lake Charles, LA	1/26/1953
Williams, Michelle	Kalispell, MT	9/9/1980
Williams, Montel	Baltimore, MD	7/3/1956
Williams, Paul	Omaha, NE	9/19/1940
Williams, Pharrell	Virginia Beach, VA	4/5/1973
Williams, Treat	Rowayton, CT	12/1/1951
Williams, Vanessa	Millwood, NY	3/18/1963
Williams-Paisley, Kimberly	Rye, NY	9/14/1971
Williamson, Kevin	New Bern, NC	3/14/1965
Willis, Bruce	Idar-Oberstein, W. Germany	3/19/1955
Wilmore, Larry	Los Angeles, CA	10/30/1961
Wilson, Brian	Inglewood, CA	6/20/1942
Wilson, Cassandra	Jackson, MS	12/4/1955
Wilson, Chandra	Houston, TX	8/27/1969
Wilson, Demond	Valdosta, GA	10/13/1946
Wilson, Luke	Dallas, TX	9/21/1971
Wilson, Nancy	Chillicothe, OH	2/20/1937
Wilson, Owen	Dallas, TX	11/18/1968
Wilson, Rainn	Seattle, WA	1/20/1966
Wilson, Rebel	Sydney, NSW, Australia	2/3/1980
Winfrey, Oprah	Kosciusko, MS	1/29/1954
Winger, Debra	Cleveland, OH	5/16/1955
Winkler, Henry	New York, NY	10/30/1945
Winningham, Mare	Phoenix, AZ	5/16/1959
Winslet, Kate	Reading, England, UK	10/5/1975
Winwood, Steve	Birmingham, England, UK	5/12/1948
Withers, Jane	Atlanta, GA	4/12/1926
Witherspoon, Reese	New Orleans, LA	3/22/1976
Witt, Alicia	Worcester, MA	8/21/1975
Wolf, Scott	Boston, MA	6/4/1968
Wonder, Stevie	Saginaw, MI	5/13/1950
Wong, B. D.	San Francisco, CA	10/24/1962
Wong, Faye	Beijing, China	8/8/1969
Woo, John	Guangzhou, China	5/1/1946
Wood, Elijah	Cedar Rapids, IA	1/28/1981
Wood, Evan Rachel	Raleigh, NC	9/7/1987
Woodard, Alfre	Tulsa, OK	11/8/1952
Woodley, Shailene	Simi Valley, CA	11/15/1991
Woods, James	Vernal, UT	4/18/1947
Woodward, Joanne	Thomasville, GA	2/27/1930
Wopat, Tom	Lodi, WI	9/9/1951
Worthington, Sam	Godalming, Surrey, Eng., UK	8/2/1976
Wright, Jeffrey	Washington, DC	12/7/1965
Wright, Max	Detroit, MI	8/2/1943
Wright, Robin	Dallas, TX	4/8/1966
Wright, Steven	New York, NY	12/6/1955
Wyle, Noah	Hollywood, CA	6/4/1971
Wyman, Bill	London, England, UK	10/24/1936
Yankovic, Weird Al	Lynwood, CA	10/23/1959
Yanni (Chrysomallis)	Kalamata, Greece	11/14/1954
Yarrow, Peter	New York, NY	5/31/1938
Yearwood, Trisha	Monticello, GA	9/19/1964
Yeoh, Michelle	Ipoh, Malaysia	8/6/1962
Yoakam, Dwight	Pikesville, KY	10/23/1956
York, Michael	Fulmer, England, UK	3/27/1942
Young, Burt	New York, NY	4/30/1940
Young, Neil	Toronto, ON, Canada	11/12/1945
Young, Sean	Louisville, KY	11/20/1959
Zane, Billy	Chicago, IL	2/24/1966
Zeffirelli, Franco	Florence, Italy	2/12/1923
Zellweger, Renée	Katy, TX	4/25/1969
Zemeckis, Robert	Chicago, IL	5/14/1952
Zerbe, Anthony	Long Beach, CA	5/20/1936
Zeta-Jones, Catherine	Swansea, Wales, UK	9/25/1969
Zhang Ziyi	Beijing, China	2/9/1979
Zimbalist, Stephanie	New York, NY	10/8/1956
Zimmer, Constance	Seattle, WA	10/11/1970
Zimmer, Kim	Grand Rapids, MI	2/2/1955
Zukerman, Pinchas	Tel Aviv, Israel	7/16/1948
Zuniga, Daphne	Berkeley, CA	10/28/1962

Entertainment Personalities of the Past

See also other lists for some deceased entertainers not included here.

Name	Born	Died
Aaliyah (Haughton)	1979	2001
Abbado, Claudio	1933	2014
Abbott, Bud	1895	1974
Abbott, George	1887	1995
Acuff, Roy	1903	1992
Adams, Don	1923	2005
Adams, Edie	1927	2008
Adams, Joey	1911	1999
Adams, Maude	1872	1953
Adler, Jacob P.	1855	1926
Adler, Stella	1902	1992
Adoree, Renee	1898	1933
Agar, John	1921	2002
Aherne, Brian	1902	1986
Ailey, Alvin	1931	1989
Akins, Claude	1918	1994
Albert, Eddie	1906	2005
Albertson, Jack	1907	1981
Alda, Robert	1914	1986
Allen, Fred	1894	1956
Allen, Gracie	1906	1964
Allen, Mel	1913	1996
Allen, Peter	1944	1992
Allen, Steve	1921	2000
Allgood, Sara	1883	1950
Allman, Gregg	1947	2017
Allyson, June	1917	2006
Altman, Robert	1925	2006
Ameche, Don	1908	1993
Ames, Leon	1903	1993
Amsterdam, Morey	1908	1996
Anderson, G. M. "Bronco Billy"	1882	1971
Anderson, Harry	1952	2018
Anderson, Judith	1897	1992
Anderson, Marian	1897	1993
Anderson, Richard	1926	2017
Andre the Giant	1946	1993
Andrews, Dana	1909	1992
Andrews, Laverne	1913	1967
Andrews, Maxene	1916	1995
Andrews, Patty	1918	2013
Angeli, Pier	1932	1971
Antonioni, Michelangelo	1912	2007
Arbuckle, Fatty (Roscoe)	1887	1933
Archerd, Army	1922	2009
Arden, Eve	1908	1990
Arlen, Richard	1900	1976
Arliss, George	1868	1946
Armstrong, Louis	1901	1971
Arnaz, Desi	1917	1986
Arness, James	1923	2011
Arnold, Eddy	1918	2008
Arnold, Edward	1890	1956
Arquette, Cliff	1905	1974
Arthur, Beatrice	1922	2009
Arthur, Jean	1900	1991
Arzner, Dorothy	1897	1979
Ashcroft, Peggy	1907	1991
Astaire, Fred	1899	1987
Astor, Mary	1906	1987
Atkins, Chet	1924	2001
Attenborough, Richard	1923	2014
Atwill, Lionel	1885	1946
Autry, Gene	1907	1998
Avildsen, John	1935	2017
Ayres, Lew	1908	1996
Aznavour, Charles	1924	2018
Bacall, Lauren	1924	2014
Backus, Jim	1913	1989
Bailey, Pearl	1918	1990
Bain, Conrad	1923	2013
Bainter, Fay	1892	1968
Baker, Josephine	1906	1975
Balanchine, George	1904	1983
Ball, Lucille	1911	1989
Balsam, Martin	1919	1996
Bancroft, Anne	1931	2005
Bankhead, Tallulah	1902	1968
Bara, Theda	1885?	1955
Barnum, Phineas T.	1810	1891
Barrett, Syd	1946	2006
Barry, Gene	1919	2009
Barrymore, Ethel	1879	1959
Barrymore, John	1882	1942
Barrymore, Lionel	1878	1954
Barrymore, Maurice	1848	1905
Barthelmess, Richard	1895	1963
Bartholomew, Freddie	1924	1992
Barty, Billy	1924	2000
Basehart, Richard	1914	1984
Basie, Count	1904	1984
Bates, Alan	1934	2003
Bavier, Frances	1902	1989
Baxter, Anne	1923	1985
Baxter, Warner	1889	1951
Beaumont, Hugh	1909	1982
Beavers, Louise	1902	1962
Beery, Noah, Jr.	1913	1994
Beery, Noah, Sr.	1884	1946
Beery, Wallace	1885	1949
Begley, Ed	1901	1970
Bel Geddes, Barbara	1922	2005
Bell, Art	1945	2018
Bellamy, Ralph	1904	1991
Belushi, John	1949	1982
Benaderet, Bea	1906	1968
Bendix, William	1906	1964
Bennett, Constance	1904	1965
Bennett, Joan	1910	1990
Bennett, Michael	1943	1987
Benny, Jack	1894	1974
Berg, Gertrude	1899	1966
Bergen, Edgar	1903	1978
Bergen, Polly	1930	2014
Bergman, Ingmar	1918	2007
Bergman, Ingrid	1915	1982
Berkeley, Busby	1895	1976
Berle, Milton	1908	2002
Berlin, Irving	1888	1989
Berman, Shelley	1925	2017
Bernardi, Herschel	1923	1986
Bernhardt, Sarah	1844	1923
Bernstein, Leonard	1918	1990
Berry, Chuck	1926	2017
Bessell, Ted	1939	1996
Bickford, Charles	1889	1967
Big Bopper, The	1930	1959
Bikel, Theodore	1924	2015
Billingsley, Barbara	1915	2010
Bing, Rudolf	1902	1997
Bishop, Joey	1918	2007
Bitzer, Billy	1872	1944
Bixby, Bill	1934	1993
Black, Karen	1939	2013
Blackstone, Harry, Jr.	1934	1997
Blackstone, Harry, Sr.	1885	1965
Blaine, Vivian	1921	1995
Blake, Amanda	1931	1989
Blake, Eubie	1887	1983
Blanc, Mel	1908	1989
Blocker, Dan	1928	1972
Blondell, Joan	1909	1979
Blondin, Charles	1824	1897
Blyden, Larry	1925	1975
Bogarde, Dirk	1921	1999
Bogart, Humphrey	1899	1957
Boland, Mary	1880	1965
Boles, John	1895	1969
Bolger, Ray	1904	1987
Bologna, Joseph	1934	2017
Bond, Ward	1903	1960
Bondi, Beulah	1888	1981
Bono, Sonny	1935	1998
Boone, Richard	1917	1981
Booth, Edwin	1833	1893
Booth, John Wilkes	1838	1865
Booth, Junius Brutus	1796	1852
Booth, Shirley	1898	1992
Borge, Victor	1909	2000
Borgnine, Ernest	1917	2012
Borzage, Frank	1893	1962
Bosley, Tom	1927	2010
Bourdain, Anthony	1956	2018
Bow, Clara	1905	1965
Bowes, Maj. Edward	1874	1946
Bowie, David	1947	2016
Bowman, Lee	1914	1979
Boxcar Willie	1931	1999
Boyd, Stephen	1928	1977
Boyd, William	1898	1972
Boyer, Charles	1899	1978
Boyle, Peter	1935	2006
Bracken, Eddie	1915	2002
Brady, Alice	1892	1939
Brando, Marlon	1924	2004
Branigan, Laura	1957	2004
Brazzi, Rossano	1916	1994
Brennan, Eileen	1932	2013
Brennan, Walter	1894	1974
Brenner, David	1936	2014
Brent, George	1904	1979
Brett, Jeremy	1935	1995
Brewer, Teresa	1931	2007
Brice, Fanny	1891	1951
Bridges, Lloyd	1913	1998
Broderick, Helen	1891	1959
Bronson, Charles	1921	2003
Brooks, Foster	1912	2001
Brooks, Louise	1906	1985
Brown, Clarence	1890	1987
Brown, James	1933	2006
Brown, Joe E.	1892	1973
Brown, Johnny Mack	1904	1974
Brown, Les	1912	2001
Browne, Roscoe Lee	1925	2007
Browning, Tod	1882	1962
Brubeck, Dave	1920	2012
Bruce, Lenny	1925	1966
Bruce, Nigel	1895	1953
Bruce, Virginia	1910	1982
Brynner, Yul	1915	1985
Buchanan, Edgar	1903	1979
Buñuel, Luis	1900	1983
Buono, Victor	1938	1982
Burke, Billie	1885	1970
Burnette, Smiley	1911	1967
Burns, George	1896	1996
Burr, Raymond	1917	1993
Burton, Richard	1925	1984
Busch, Mae	1897	1946
Bushman, Francis X.	1883	1966
Buttons, Red	1919	2006
Byington, Spring	1893	1971
Caballé, Montserrat	1933	2018
Cabot, Bruce	1904	1972
Cabot, Sebastian	1918	1977
Caesar, Sid	1922	2014
Cagney, James	1899	1986
Caldwell, Sarah	1924	2006
Calhern, Louis	1895	1956
Calhoun, Rory	1922	1999
Callas, Charlie	1927	2011
Callas, Maria	1923	1977
Calloway, Cab	1907	1994
Cambridge, Godfrey	1933	1976
Campanella, Joseph	1924	2018
Campbell, Glen	1936	2017
Campbell, Mrs. Patrick	1865	1940
Candy, John	1950	1994
Canova, Judy	1916	1983
Cantinflas	1911	1993
Cantor, Eddie	1892	1964
Capra, Frank	1897	1991
Carey, Harry	1878	1947
Carey, Harry, Jr.	1921	2012
Carle, Frankie	1903	2001
Carlin, George	1937	2008
Carlisle Hart, Kitty	1910	2007
Carney, Art	1918	2003
Carpenter, Karen	1950	1983
Carradine, David	1936	2009
Carradine, John	1906	1988
Carrillo, Leo	1880	1961
Carroll, Leo G.	1892	1972
Carroll, Madeleine	1906	1987
Carson, Jack	1910	1963
Carson, Johnny	1925	2005
Carter, Benny	1907	2003
Carter, Dixie	1939	2010
Carter, Jack	1923	2015
Carter, Nell	1948	2003
Caruso, Enrico	1873	1921
Casals, Pablo	1876	1973
Cash, Johnny	1932	2003
Cash, June Carter	1929	2003
Cass, Peggy	1924	1999
Cassavetes, John	1929	1989
Cassidy, David	1950	2017
Cassidy, Jack	1927	1976
Castle, Irene	1893	1969
Castle, Vernon	1887	1918
Champion, Gower	1919	1980
Chandler, Jeff	1918	1961

Name	Born	Died	Name	Born	Died	Name	Born	Died
Chaney, Lon	1883	1930	Crosby, Bing	1903	1977	Dumbrille, Douglass	1890	1974
Chaney, Lon, Jr.	1905	1973	Crothers, Scatman	1910	1986	Dumont, Margaret	1889	1965
Chapin, Harry	1942	1981	Cruz, Celia	1925	2003	Duncan, Isadora	1878	1927
Chaplin, Charles	1889	1977	Cugat, Xavier	1900	1990	Duncan, Michael Clarke	1957	2012
Chapman, Graham	1941	1989	Cukor, George	1899	1983	Dunham, Katherine	1910	2006
Charisse, Cyd	1922	2008	Cullen, Bill	1920	1990	Dunn, James	1905	1967
Charles, Ray	1930	2004	Culp, Robert	1930	2010	Dunne, Irene	1898	1990
Chase, Ilka	1905	1978	Cummings, Constance	1910	2005	Dunnock, Mildred	1901	1991
Chatterton, Ruth	1893	1961	Cummings, Robert	1908	1990	Durante, Jimmy	1893	1980
Cherrill, Virginia	1908	1996	Curtis, Tony	1925	2010	Durbin, Deanna	1921	2013
Chevalier, Maurice	1888	1972	Curtiz, Michael	1888	1962	Durning, Charles	1923	2012
Child, Julia	1912	2004	Cushing, Peter	1913	1994	Duryea, Dan	1907	1968
Christopher, William	1932	2016	Da Silva, Howard	1909	1986	Duse, Eleanora	1858	1924
Cimino, Michael	1939	2016	Dailey, Dan	1915	1978	Dvorak, Ann	1912	1979
Clair, René	1898	1981	Damone, Vic	1928	2018	Dysart, Richard	1929	2015
Clark, Dick	1929	2012	Dandridge, Dorothy	1923	1965	Eagels, Jeanne	1894	1929
Clayburgh, Jill	1944	2010	Dangerfield, Rodney	1921	2004	Ebert, Roger	1942	2013
Clayton, Jan	1917	1983	Daniell, Henry	1894	1963	Ebsen, Buddy	1908	2003
Clemons, Clarence	1942	2011	Daniels, Bebe	1901	1971	Eckstine, Billy	1914	1993
Cliburn, Van	1934	2013	Darin, Bobby	1936	1973	Eddy, Nelson	1901	1967
Clift, Montgomery	1920	1966	Darnell, Linda	1923	1965	Edelman, Herb	1933	1996
Cline, Patsy	1932	1963	Darwell, Jane	1879	1967	Edwards, Blake	1922	2010
Clooney, Rosemary	1928	2002	Davenport, Harry	1866	1949	Edwards, Cliff	1895	1971
Cobain, Kurt	1967	1994	Davies, Marion	1897	1961	Edwards, Ralph	1913	2005
Cobb, Lee J.	1911	1976	Davis, Ann B.	1926	2014	Edwards, Vince	1928	1996
Coburn, Charles	1877	1961	Davis, Bette	1908	1989	Egan, Richard	1923	1987
Coburn, James	1928	2002	Davis, Joan	1907	1961	Eisenstein, Sergei	1898	1948
Coca, Imogene	1908	2001	Davis, Ossie	1917	2005	Ekberg, Anita	1931	2015
Cocker, Joe	1944	2014	Davis, Sammy, Jr.	1925	1990	Elam, Jack	1916	2003
Coco, James	1930	1987	Dawson, Richard	1932	2012	Ellington, Duke	1899	1974
Cody, Buffalo Bill	1846	1917	Day, Dennis	1917	1988	Elliot, Cass	1941	1974
Cody, Iron Eyes	1907	1999	Day, Laraine	1920	2007	Elliott, Bob	1923	2016
Cohan, George M.	1878	1942	De Carlo, Yvonne	1922	2007	Elliott, Denholm	1922	1992
Cohen, Leonard	1934	2016	De Laurentiis, Dino	1919	2010	Ellis, Mary	1897	2003
Cohen, Myron	1902	1986	de Mille, Agnes	1905	1993	Elman, Mischa	1891	1967
Colbert, Claudette	1903	1996	De Mille, Cecil B.	1881	1959	Ephron, Nora	1941	2012
Cole, Nat "King"	1919	1965	De Wilde, Brandon	1942	1972	Evans, Dale	1912	2001
Cole, Natalie	1950	2015	De Wolfe, Billy	1907	1974	Evans, Edith	1888	1976
Coleman, Gary	1968	2010	Dean, James	1931	1955	Evans, Maurice	1901	1989
Coleman, Ornette	1930	2015	Dean, Jimmy	1928	2010	Everett, Chad	1937	2012
Collins, Gary	1938	2012	Dearie, Blossom	1924	2009	Everly, Phil	1939	2014
Collins, Ray	1890	1965	Dee, Frances	1907	2004	Ewell, Tom	1909	1994
Colman, Ronald	1891	1958	Dee, Ruby	1922	2014	Fabray, Nanette	1920	2018
Columbo, Russ	1908	1934	Dee, Sandra	1942	2005	Fairbanks, Douglas	1883	1939
Comden, Betty	1917	2006	Defore, Don	1917	1993	Fairbanks, Douglas, Jr.	1909	2000
Como, Perry	1912	2001	DeFranco, Buddy	1923	2014	Falk, Peter	1927	2011
Conklin, Chester	1888	1971	DeHaven, Gloria	1925	2016	Farentino, James	1938	2012
Conniff, Ray	1916	2002	Dekker, Albert	1905	1968	Farina, Dennis	1944	2013
Connors, Chuck	1921	1992	Del Rio, Dolores	1905	1983	Farley, Chris	1964	1997
Connors, Mike	1925	2017	DeLuise, Dom	1933	2009	Farmer, Frances	1913	1970
Conrad, William	1920	1994	Demarest, William	1892	1983	Farnsworth, Richard	1920	2000
Conried, Hans	1917	1982	Demme, Jonathan	1944	2017	Farnum, Dustin	1874	1929
Conte, Richard	1911	1975	Dennis, Sandy	1937	1992	Farnum, William	1876	1953
Convy, Bert	1933	1991	Denny, Reginald	1891	1967	Farrar, Geraldine	1882	1967
Coogan, Jackie	1914	1984	Denver, Bob	1935	2005	Farrell, Charles	1901	1990
Cook, Barbara	1927	2017	Denver, John	1943	1997	Farrell, Eileen	1920	2002
Cook, Elisha, Jr.	1904	1995	Derek, John	1926	1998	Fassbinder, Rainer Werner	1946	1982
Cooke, Alistair	1908	2004	DeSica, Vittorio	1901	1974	Fawcett, Farrah	1947	2009
Cooke, Sam	1931	1964	Devine, Andy	1905	1977	Faye, Alice	1915	1998
Cooper, Gary	1901	1961	Dewhurst, Colleen	1924	1991	Fazenda, Louise	1895	1962
Cooper, Gladys	1888	1971	Diamond, Selma	1920	1985	Feld, Fritz	1900	1993
Cooper, Jackie	1922	2011	Diddley, Bo	1928	2008	Feldman, Marty	1933	1982
Copland, Aaron	1900	1990	Dietrich, Marlene	1901	1992	Fell, Norman	1924	1998
Corby, Ellen	1913	1999	Diller, Phyllis	1917	2012	Fellini, Federico	1920	1993
Corelli, Franco	1921	2003	Disney, Walt	1901	1966	Fenneman, George	1919	1997
Corey, Jeff	1914	2002	Dix, Richard	1894	1949	Ferrer, Jose	1912	1992
Corio, Ann	1914	1999	Dmytryk, Edward	1908	1999	Ferrer, Mel	1917	2008
Corley, Pat	1930	2006	Domino, Fats	1928	2017	Fetchit, Stepin	1898	1985
Cornelius, Don	1936	2012	Donahue, Troy	1936	2001	Fiedler, Arthur	1894	1979
Cornell, Chris	1964	2017	Donat, Robert	1905	1958	Fiedler, John	1925	2005
Cornell, Katharine	1893	1974	Donlevy, Brian	1901	1972	Fields, Gracie	1898	1979
Correll, Charles	1890	1972	Dors, Diana	1931	1984	Fields, Totie	1930	1978
Costello, Dolores	1905	1979	Dorsey, Jimmy	1904	1957	Fields, W. C.	1879	1946
Costello, Lou	1906	1959	Dorsey, Tommy	1905	1956	Finch, Peter	1916	1977
Cotten, Joseph	1905	1994	Dotrice, Roy	1923	2017	Fine, Larry	1902	1975
Coward, Noel	1899	1973	Douglas, Melvyn	1901	1981	Fisher, Carrie	1956	2016
Cox, Wally	1924	1973	Dove, Billie	1900	1998	Fisher, Eddie	1928	2010
Crabbe, Buster	1908	1983	Downey, Morton, Jr.	1933	2001	Fiske, Minnie Maddern	1865	1932
Crain, Jeanne	1925	2003	Doyle, David	1929	1997	Fitzgerald, Barry	1888	1961
Crane, Bob	1928	1978	Drake, Alfred	1914	1992	Fitzgerald, Ella	1917	1996
Craven, Wes	1939	2015	Draper, Ruth	1884	1956	Fitzgerald, Geraldine	1913	2005
Crawford, Broderick	1911	1986	Dressler, Marie	1869	1934	Fleming, Art	1924	1995
Crawford, Joan	1904	1977	Drew, Ellen	1915	2003	Fleming, Victor	1889	1949
Crenna, Richard	1926	2003	Drew, Mrs. John	1820	1897	Flynn, Errol	1909	1959
Crews, Laura Hope	1880	1942	Dru, Joanne	1923	1996	Flynn, Joe	1925	1974
Crisp, Donald	1880	1974	Duchin, Eddy	1909	1951	Foch, Nina	1924	2008
Crisp, Quentin	1908	1999	Duff, Howard	1917	1990	Fogelberg, Dan	1951	2007
Croce, Jim	1942	1973	Duggan, Andrew	1923	1988	Foley, Red	1910	1968
Cronyn, Hume	1911	2003	Duke, Patty	1946	2016	Fonda, Henry	1905	1982

Name	Born	Died	Name	Born	Died	Name	Born	Died
Fontaine, Joan	1917	2013	Gordon, Ruth	1896	1985	Hayward, Louis	1909	1985
Fontanne, Lynn	1887	1983	Gorme, Eydie	1932	2013	Hayward, Susan	1917	1975
Fonteyn, Margot	1919	1991	Gorshin, Frank	1934	2005	Hayworth, Rita	1918	1987
Ford, Glenn	1916	2006	Gosden, Freeman	1899	1982	Head, Edith	1897	1981
Ford, John	1894	1973	Gottschalk, Louis	1829	1869	Healy, Ted	1896	1937
Ford, Paul	1901	1976	Gould, Glenn	1932	1982	Heard, John	1945	2017
Ford, Tennessee Ernie	1919	1991	Gould, Harold	1923	2010	Heckart, Eileen	1919	2001
Forman, Milos	1932	2018	Gould, Morton	1913	1996	Heflin, Van	1910	1971
Forrest, Edwin	1806	1872	Goulet, Robert	1933	2007	Heifetz, Jascha	1901	1987
Forrest, Helen	1917	1999	Grable, Betty	1916	1973	Held, Anna	1873	1918
Forsythe, John	1918	2010	Graham, Martha	1894	1991	Helm, Levon	1940	2012
Fosse, Bob	1927	1987	Graham, Virginia	1912	1998	Hemingway, Margaux	1955	1996
Foster, Preston	1901	1970	Grahame, Gloria	1925	1981	Hemsley, Sherman	1938	2012
Foxx, Redd	1922	1991	Granger, Farley	1925	2011	Henderson, Florence	1934	2016
Foy, Eddie	1856	1928	Granger, Stewart	1913	1993	Henderson, Skitch	1918	2005
Franchi, Sergio	1926	1990	Grant, Cary	1904	1986	Hendrix, Jimi	1942	1970
Franciosa, Anthony	1928	2006	Granville, Bonita	1923	1988	Henie, Sonja	1912	1969
Francis, Anne	1930	2011	Grapewin, Charley	1869	1956	Henreid, Paul	1908	1992
Francis, Arlene	1907	2001	Graves, Peter	1926	2010	Henson, Jim	1936	1990
Francis, Kay	1905	1968	Gray, Dolores	1924	2002	Hepburn, Audrey	1929	1993
Franciscus, James	1934	1991	Gray, Spalding	1941	2004	Hepburn, Katharine	1907	2003
Frankenheimer, John	1930	2002	Grayson, Kathryn	1922	2010	Herrmann, Edward	1943	2014
Franklin, Aretha	1942	2018	Greco, Jose	1918	2000	Hersholt, Jean	1886	1956
Franklin, Bonnie	1944	2013	Green, Adolph	1915	2002	Heston, Charlton	1923	2008
Frawley, William	1887	1966	Greene, Lorne	1915	1987	Hickey, William	1928	1997
Frederick, Pauline	1885	1938	Greenstreet, Sydney	1879	1954	Hickson, Joan	1906	1998
Freed, Alan	1921	1965	Greenwood, Charlotte	1890	1978	Hildegarde	1906	2005
Freeman, Al, Jr.	1934	2012	Gregory, Dick	1932	2017	Hill, Arthur	1922	2006
Freeman, Mona	1926	2014	Gregory, James	1911	2002	Hill, Benny	1925	1992
French, Victor	1934	1989	Griffin, Merv	1925	2007	Hill, George Roy	1921	2002
Friganza, Trixie	1870	1955	Griffith, Andy	1926	2012	Hiller, Wendy	1912	2003
Froman, Jane	1907	1980	Griffith, D. W.	1874	1948	Hillerman, John	1932	2017
Frost, David	1939	2013	Griffith, Hugh	1912	1980	Hines, Gregory	1946	2003
Funicello, Annette	1942	2013	Griffiths, Richard	1947	2013	Hingle, Pat	1924	2009
Funt, Allen	1914	1999	Grimes, Tammy	1934	2016	Hirt, Al	1922	1999
Furness, Betty	1916	1994	Grizzard, George	1928	2007	Hitchcock, Alfred	1899	1980
Gabin, Jean	1904	1976	Guardino, Harry	1925	1995	Ho, Don	1930	2007
Gable, Clark	1901	1960	Guillaume, Robert	1927	2017	Hodiak, John	1914	1955
Gabor, Eva	1920	1995	Guinness, Sir Alec	1914	2000	Hoffman, Philip Seymour	1967	2014
Gabor, Zsa Zsa	1917	2016	Guthrie, Woody	1912	1967	Holden, William	1918	1981
Gandolfini, James	1961	2013	Gwenn, Edmund	1875	1959	Holder, Geoffrey	1930	2014
Garagiola, Joe	1926	2016	Gwynne, Fred	1926	1993	Holiday, Billie	1915	1959
Garbo, Greta	1905	1990	Hackett, Buddy	1924	2003	Holliday, Judy	1921	1965
Garcia, Jerry	1942	1995	Hackett, Joan	1934	1983	Holloway, Sterling	1905	1992
Gardenia, Vincent	1922	1992	Hagen, Jean	1923	1977	Holly, Buddy	1936	1959
Gardner, Ava	1922	1990	Hagen, Uta	1919	2004	Holm, Celeste	1919	2012
Garfield, John	1913	1952	Haggard, Merle	1937	2016	Holt, Jack	1888	1951
Garland, Beverly	1926	2008	Hagman, Larry	1931	2012	Holt, Tim	1918	1973
Garland, Judy	1922	1969	Haines, William	1900	1973	Homolka, Oscar	1898	1978
Garner, James	1928	2014	Hale, Alan, Jr.	1918	1990	Hooker, John Lee	1917	2001
Garrett, Betty	1919	2011	Hale, Alan, Sr.	1892	1950	Hope, Bob	1903	2003
Garson, Greer	1904	1996	Hale, Barbara	1922	2017	Hopkins, Miriam	1902	1972
Gassman, Vittorio	1922	2000	Haley, Bill	1925	1981	Hopper, Dennis	1936	2010
Gavin, John	1931	2018	Haley, Jack	1899	1979	Hopper, DeWolf	1858	1935
Gaye, Marvin	1939	1984	Hall, Huntz	1919	1999	Hopper, Hedda	1885	1966
Gaynor, Janet	1906	1984	Hall, Jon	1915	1979	Horowitz, Vladimir	1904	1989
Gazzara, Ben	1930	2012	Hall, Monty	1921	2017	Horne, Lena	1917	2010
Gebel-Williams, Gunther	1934	2001	Hamilton, Margaret	1902	1985	Horton, Edward Everett	1886	1970
Geer, Will	1902	1978	Hammerstein, Oscar	1847	1919	Hoskins, Bob	1942	2014
George, Gladys	1904	1954	Hammerstein, Oscar, II	1895	1960	Houdini, Harry	1874	1926
Gershwin, George	1898	1937	Hampton, Lionel	1908	2002	Houseman, John	1902	1988
Getty, Estelle	1923	2008	Hardwicke, Cedric	1893	1964	Houston, Whitney	1963	2012
Ghostley, Alice	1926	2007	Hardy, Oliver	1892	1957	Howard (Horwitz), Curly	1903	1952
Gibb, Andy	1958	1988	Harlow, Jean	1911	1937	Howard, Ken	1944	2016
Gibb, Maurice	1949	2003	Harrington, Pat, Jr.	1929	2016	Howard, Leslie	1890	1943
Gibb, Robin	1949	2012	Harris, Julie	1925	2013	Howard (Horwitz), Moe	1897	1975
Gibson, Henry	1935	2009	Harris, Phil	1904	1995	Howard (Horwitz), Shemp	1895	1955
Gibson, Hoot	1892	1962	Harris, Richard	1930	2002	Howard, Trevor	1916	1988
Gielgud, John	1904	2000	Harrison, George	1943	2001	Hudson, Rock	1925	1985
Gifford, Frank	1930	2015	Harrison, Rex	1908	1990	Hughes, Bernard	1915	2006
Gilbert, Billy	1894	1971	Hart, William S.	1864	1946	Hughes, John	1950	2009
Gilbert, John	1895	1936	Hartman, Phil	1948	1998	Hull, Henry	1890	1977
Gilford, Jack	1907	1990	Harvey, Laurence	1928	1973	Hull, Josephine	1886	1957
Gillespie, Dizzy	1917	1993	Harvey, Paul	1918	2009	Hunter, Jeffrey	1926	1969
Gillette, William	1853	1937	Harwell, Ernie	1918	2010	Hunter, Kim	1922	2002
Gingold, Hermione	1897	1987	Hatfield, Bobby	1940	2003	Hunter, Ross	1920	1996
Gish, Dorothy	1898	1968	Havens, Richie	1941	2013	Hunter, Tab	1931	2018
Gish, Lillian	1893	1993	Havoc, June	1912	2010	Hurt, John	1940	2017
Gleason, Jackie	1916	1987	Hawkins, Jack	1910	1973	Hussey, Ruth	1911	2005
Gleason, James	1886	1959	Hawkins, Screamin' Jay	1929	2000	Huston, John	1906	1987
Gluck, Alma	1884	1938	Hawks, Howard	1896	1977	Huston, Walter	1884	1950
Gobel, George	1919	1991	Hawthorne, Nigel	1929	2001	Hutton, Betty	1921	2007
Goddard, Paulette	1905?	1990	Hayakawa, Sessue	1890	1973	Hutton, Jim	1934	1979
Godfrey, Arthur	1903	1983	Hayden, Sterling	1916	1986	Hyde-White, Wilfrid	1903	1991
Godunov, Alexander	1949	1995	Hayes, Gabby	1885	1969	Hyman, Earle	1926	2017
Goldwyn, Samuel	1882	1974	Hayes, Helen	1900	1993	Ingram, Rex	1895	1969
Goodman, Benny	1909	1986	Hayes, Isaac	1942	2008	Ireland, Jill	1936	1990
Gorcey, Leo	1917	1969	Haymes, Dick	1917	1980	Ireland, John	1915	1992
Gordon, Gale	1906	1995	Hayward, Leland	1902	1971	Irving, George S.	1922	2016

Name	Born	Died	Name	Born	Died	Name	Born	Died
Irving, Henry	1838	1905	Kirby, Bruno	1949	2006	Lombard, Carole	1908	1942
Ives, Burl	1909	1995	Kirby, George	1923	1995	Lombardo, Guy	1902	1977
Irwin, Steve	1962	2006	Kirby, Durward	1912	2000	Long, Richard	1927	1974
Iturbi, Jose	1895	1980	Kitt, Eartha	1927	2008	Lopes, Lisa	1971	2002
Jackson, Anne	1926	2016	Klemperer, Werner	1920	2000	Lopez, Vincent	1895	1975
Jackson, Mahalia	1911	1972	Klugman, Jack	1922	2012	Lord, Jack	1920	1998
Jackson, Michael	1958	2009	Knievel, Evel	1938	2007	Lorne, Marion	1888	1968
Jackson, Milt	1923	1999	Knight, Ted	1923	1986	Lorre, Peter	1904	1964
Jaeckel, Richard	1926	1997	Knotts, Don	1924	2006	Loudon, Dorothy	1925	2003
Jaffe, Sam	1891	1984	Korman, Harvey	1927	2008	Lowe, Edmund	1890	1971
Jagger, Dean	1903	1991	Kostelanetz, Andre	1901	1980	Loy, Myrna	1905	1993
Jam Master Jay	1965	2002	Kovacs, Ernie	1919	1962	Lubitsch, Ernst	1892	1947
James, Dennis	1917	1997	Kramer, Stanley	1913	2001	Ludden, Allen	1918	1981
James, Etta	1938	2012	Kruger, Otto	1885	1974	Lugosi, Bela	1882	1956
James, Harry	1916	1983	Kubrick, Stanley	1928	1999	Lukas, Paul	1894	1971
James, Rick	1948	2004	Kulp, Nancy	1921	1991	Lumet, Sidney	1924	2011
Janis, Elsie	1889	1956	Kurosawa, Akira	1910	1998	Lunt, Alfred	1892	1977
Jannings, Emil	1886	1950	Kyser, Kay	1906	1985	Lupino, Ida	1918	1995
Janssen, David	1930	1980	Ladd, Alan	1913	1964	Lymon, Frankie	1942	1968
Jarreau, Al	1940	2017	Lahr, Bert	1895	1967	Lynde, Paul	1926	1982
Jeffreys, Anne	1923	2017	Laine, Frankie	1913	2007	Maazel, Lorin	1930	2014
Jenkins, Allen	1900	1974	Lake, Arthur	1905	1987	Mabley, Jackie "Moms"	1894	1975
Jennings, Waylon	1937	2002	Lake, Veronica	1919	1973	Mac, Bernie	1957	2008
Jessel, George	1898	1981	LaLanne, Jack	1914	2011	MacArthur, James	1937	2010
Jeter, Michael	1952	2003	Lamarr, Hedy	1913	2000	MacCorkindale, Simon	1952	2010
Johnson, Ben	1918	1996	Lamas, Fernando	1915	1982	MacDonald, Jeanette	1903	1965
Johnson, Celia	1908	1982	Lamour, Dorothy	1914	1996	Mack, Ted	1904	1976
Johnson, Chic	1892	1962	Lancaster, Burt	1913	1994	MacKenzie, Gisele	1927	2003
Johnson, J.J.	1924	2001	Lanchester, Elsa	1902	1986	MacLane, Barton	1902	1969
Johnson, Robert	1911	1938	Landau, Martin	1928	2017	MacMurray, Fred	1908	1991
Johnson, Van	1916	2008	Landis, Carole	1919	1948	MacNee, Patrick	1922	2015
Jolson, Al	1886	1950	Landon, Michael	1936	1991	MacRae, Gordon	1921	1986
Jones, Brian	1942	1969	Lane, Priscilla	1917	1995	Macready, George	1909	1973
Jones, Buck	1889	1942	Lang, Fritz	1890	1976	Madison, Guy	1922	1996
Jones, Carolyn	1933	1983	Langdon, Harry	1884	1944	Magnani, Anna	1908	1973
Jones, Davy	1945	2012	Lange, Hope	1931	2003	Mahoney, John	1940	2018
Jones, Dean	1931	2015	Langford, Frances	1914	2005	Mancini, Henry	1924	1994
Jones, Elvin	1927	2004	Langtry, Lillie	1853	1929	Main, Marjorie	1890	1975
Jones, George	1931	2013	Lanza, Mario	1921	1959	Malden, Karl	1912	2009
Jones, Henry	1912	1999	LaRue, Lash (Alfred)	1917	1996	Malle, Louis	1932	1995
Jones, Jennifer	1919	2009	Lauder, Harry	1870	1950	Malone, Dorothy	1925?	2018
Jones, Spike	1911	1965	Laughton, Charles	1899	1962	Mamoulian, Rouben	1897	1987
Joplin, Janis	1943	1970	Laurel, Stan	1890	1965	Mankiewicz, Joseph	1909	1993
Joplin, Scott	1868	1917	Lawford, Peter	1923	1984	Mann, Herbie	1930	2003
Jordan, Richard	1937	1993	Lawrence, Florence	1886	1938	Mansfield, Jayne	1932	1967
Jory, Victor	1902	1982	Lawrence, Gertrude	1898	1952	Mantovani, Annunzio	1905	1980
Jourdan, Louis	1921	2015	Leach, Robin	1941	2018	Marais, Jean	1913	1998
Julia, Raul	1940	1994	Lean, David	1908	1991	March, Fredric	1897	1975
Jump, Gordon	1932	2003	Ledger, Heath	1979	2008	March, Hal	1920	1970
Jurado, Katy	1924	2002	Lee, Anna	1913	2004	Marchand, Nancy	1928	2000
Jurgens, Curt	1915	1982	Lee, Bernard	1908	1981	Markova, Alicia	1910	2004
Kahn, Madeline	1942	1999	Lee, Bruce	1940	1973	Marley, Bob	1945	1981
Kane, Helen	1904	1966	Lee, Canada	1907	1952	Marriner, Neville	1924	2016
Kanin, Garson	1912	1999	Lee, Christopher	1922	2015	Marsh, Mae	1895	1968
Karloff, Boris	1887	1969	Lee, Gypsy Rose	1914	1970	Marshall, E. G.	1914	1998
Karras, Alex	1935	2012	Lee, Peggy	1920	2002	Marshall, Garry	1934	2016
Kasem, Casey	1932	2014	LeGallienne, Eva	1899	1991	Marshall, Herbert	1890	1966
Kaufman, Andy	1949	1984	Leigh, Janet	1927	2004	Martin, Dean	1917	1995
Kaye, Danny	1911	1987	Leigh, Vivien	1913	1967	Martin, Dick	1922	2008
Kaye, Stubby	1918	1997	Leighton, Margaret	1922	1976	Martin, Mary	1913	1990
Kazan, Elia	1909	2003	Lemmon, Jack	1925	2001	Martin, Ross	1920	1981
Kean, Charles	1811	1868	Lennon, John	1940	1980	Martin, Tony	1913	2012
Kean, Mrs. Charles	1806	1880	Lenya, Lotte	1898	1981	Marvin, Lee	1924	1987
Kean, Edmund	1787	1833	Leonard, Eddie	1870	1941	Marx, Harpo (Arthur)	1888	1964
Keaton, Buster	1895	1966	Leonard, Sheldon	1907	1997	Marx, Zeppo (Herbert)	1901	1979
Keel, Howard	1919	2004	Leone, Sergio	1929	1989	Marx, Groucho (Julius)	1890	1977
Keeler, Ruby	1910	1993	LeRoy, Mervyn	1900	1987	Marx, Chico (Leonard)	1887	1961
Keeshan, Bob (Captain Kangaroo)	1927	2004	Leslie, Joan	1925	2015	Marx, Gummo (Milton)	1893	1977
Keith, Brian	1921	1997	Levant, Oscar	1906	1972	Mason, James	1909	1984
Kellaway, Cecil	1893	1973	Levene, Sam	1905	1980	Massey, Raymond	1896	1983
Kelley, DeForest	1920	1999	Lewis, Al	1923	2006	Mastroianni, Marcello	1924	1996
Kelly, Emmett	1898	1979	Lewis, Jerry	1926	2017	Masur, Kurt	1927	2015
Kelly, Gene	1912	1996	Lewis, Joe E.	1902	1971	Matthau, Walter	1920	2000
Kelly, Grace	1929	1982	Lewis, Shari	1934	1998	Mature, Victor	1913	1999
Kelly, Jack	1927	1992	Lewis, Ted	1892	1971	Maxwell, Marilyn	1921	1972
Kelly, Patsy	1910	1981	Liberace	1919	1987	Mayer, Louis B.	1885	1957
Kennedy, Arthur	1914	1990	Lillie, Beatrice	1894	1989	Mayfield, Curtis	1942	1999
Kennedy, Edgar	1890	1948	Lincoln, Elmo	1889	1952	Mayo, Virginia	1920	2005
Kennedy, George	1925	2016	Lind, Jenny	1820	1887	Mazurki, Mike	1909	1990
Kerr, Deborah	1921	2007	Lindfors, Viveca	1920	1995	Mazursky, Paul	1930	2014
Kibbee, Guy	1886	1956	Lindley, Audra	1918	1997	MCA (Adam Yauch)	1964	2012
Kidder, Margot	1948	2018	Linkletter, Art	1912	2010	McCambridge, Mercedes	1916	2004
Kiel, Richard	1939	2014	Linville, Larry	1939	2000	McCarey, Leo	1898	1969
Kilbride, Percy	1888	1964	Little, Cleavon	1939	1992	McCarthy, Kevin	1914	2010
Kiley, Richard	1922	1999	Llewelyn, Desmond	1914	1999	McCartney, Linda	1941	1998
King, Alan	1927	2004	Lloyd, Harold	1893	1971	McClanahan, Rue	1934	2010
King, B. B.	1925	2015	Lloyd, Marie	1870	1922	McClure, Doug	1935	1995
King, Henry	1896	1982	Lockhart, Gene	1891	1957	McCormack, John	1884	1945
Kinski, Klaus	1926	1991	Loggia, Robert	1930	2015	McCrea, Joel	1905	1990
			Lom, Herbert	1917	2012	McDaniel, Hattie	1895	1952

Name	Born	Died	Name	Born	Died	Name	Born	Died
McDowall, Roddy	1928	1998	Muni, Paul	1895	1967	Parker, Fess	1925	2010
McFarland, Spanky (George)	1928	1993	Munshin, Jules	1915	1970	Parker, Jean	1915	2005
McGoohan, Patrick	1928	2009	Murnau, F. W.	1888	1931	Parks, Bert	1914	1992
McGuire, Al	1931	2001	Murphy, Audie	1924	1971	Parks, Larry	1914	1975
McGuire, Dorothy	1916	2001	Murphy, Brittany	1977	2009	Pasternack, Josef A.	1881	1940
McHugh, Frank	1898	1981	Murphy, George	1902	1992	Pastor, Tony (vaudevillian)	1837	1908
McIntire, John	1907	1991	Murray, Arthur	1895	1991	Pastor, Tony (bandleader)	1907	1969
McLaglen, Victor	1886	1959	Murray, Kathryn	1906	1999	Patrick, Gail	1911	1980
McMahon, Ed	1923	2009	Murray, Mae	1889	1965	Patti, Adelina	1843	1919
McNeill, Don	1907	1996	Nabors, Jim	1930	2017	Patti, Carlotta	1840	1889
McPartland, Marian	1918	2013	Nagel, Conrad	1897	1970	Paul, Les	1915	2009
McQueen, Butterfly	1911	1995	Naish, J. Carroll	1900	1973	Pavarotti, Luciano	1935	2007
McQueen, Steve	1930	1980	Naldi, Nita	1898	1961	Pavlova, Anna	1885	1931
Meader, Vaughn	1936	2004	Nance, Jack	1943	1996	Paxton, Bill	1955	2017
Meadows, Audrey	1924	1996	Natwick, Mildred	1908	1994	Paycheck, Johnny	1938	2003
Meadows, Jayne	1919	2015	Nazimova, Alla	1879	1945	Payne, John	1912	1989
Meara, Anne	1929	2015	Neal, Patricia	1926	2010	Pearl, Minnie	1912	1996
Meek, Donald	1880	1946	Negri, Pola	1897	1987	Peck, Gregory	1916	2003
Meeker, Ralph	1920	1988	Nelson, David	1936	2011	Peckinpah, Sam	1925	1984
Méliès, Georges	1861	1938	Nelson, Ed	1928	2014	Peerce, Jan	1904	1984
Menjou, Adolphe	1890	1963	Nelson, Harriet (Hilliard)	1909	1994	Pendergrass, Teddy	1950	2010
Menuhin, Yehudi	1916	1999	Nelson, Ozzie	1906	1975	Penn, Arthur	1922	2010
Mercer, Marian	1935	2011	Nelson, Rick	1940	1985	Penner, Joe	1905	1941
Mercouri, Melina	1925	1994	Nesbit, Evelyn	1884	1967	Peppard, George	1928	1994
Mercury, Freddie	1946	1991	Nettleton, Lois	1927	2008	Perkins, Anthony	1932	1992
Meredith, Burgess	1909	1997	Newley, Anthony	1931	1999	Perkins, Carl	1932	1998
Merman, Ethel	1908	1984	Newman, Edwin	1919	2010	Perkins, Marlin	1905	1986
Merrick, David	1911	2000	Newman, Paul	1925	2008	Peters, Brock	1927	2005
Merrill, Dina	1925	2017	Nicholas, Fayard	1914	2006	Peters, Jean	1926	2000
Merrill, Gary	1915	1990	Nicholas, Harold	1924	2000	Peters, Roberta	1930	2017
Michael, George	1963	2016	Nichols, Mike	1931	2014	Peters, Susan	1921	1952
Milestone, Lewis	1895	1980	Nielsen, Leslie	1926	2010	Peterson, Oscar	1925	2007
Mifune, Toshiro	1920	1997	Nijinsky, Vaslav	1890	1950	Petty, Tom	1950	2017
Milland, Ray	1905	1986	Nilsson, Anna Q.	1888	1974	Phillips, John	1935	2001
Miller, Ann	1923	2004	Nimoy, Leonard	1931	2015	Phoenix, River	1970	1993
Miller, Glenn	1904	1944	Niven, David	1910	1983	Piaf, Edith	1915	1963
Miller, Marilyn	1898	1936	Nolan, Lloyd	1902	1985	Pickens, Slim	1919	1983
Miller, Mitch	1911	2010	Normand, Mabel	1894	1930	Pickett, Wilson	1941	2006
Miller, Roger	1936	1992	North, Sheree	1933	2005	Pickford, Mary	1892	1979
Mills, Donald	1915	1999	Notorious B.I.G.	1972	1997	Picon, Molly	1898	1992
Mills, Harry	1913	1982	Novarro, Ramon	1899	1968	Pidgeon, Walter	1897	1984
Mills, Herbert	1912	1989	Nureyev, Rudolf	1938	1993	Pinza, Ezio	1892	1957
Mills, John	1889	1967	Oakie, Jack	1903	1978	Pitney, Gene	1941	2006
Mills, Sir John	1908	2005	Oakley, Annie	1860	1926	Pitts, Zasu	1898	1963
Milner, Martin	1931	2015	Oates, Warren	1928	1982	Plato, Dana	1964	1999
Mineo, Sal	1939	1976	Oberon, Merle	1911	1979	Pleasence, Donald	1919	1995
Miner, Jan	1917	2004	O'Brian, Hugh	1925	2016	Pleshette, Suzanne	1937	2008
Minghella, Anthony	1954	2008	O'Brien, Edmond	1915	1985	Pollack, Sydney	1934	2008
Mingus, Charles	1922	1979	O'Brien, George	1900	1985	Pons, Lily	1904	1976
Minnelli, Vincente	1903	1986	O'Brien, Pat	1899	1983	Ponselle, Rosa	1897	1981
Miranda, Carmen	1909	1955	O'Connell, Arthur	1908	1981	Ponti, Carlo	1912	2007
Mitchell, Thomas	1892	1962	O'Connell, Helen	1921	1993	Porter, Edwin S.	1870	1941
Mitchum, Robert	1917	1997	O'Connor, Carroll	1924	2001	Postlethwaite, Pete	1946	2011
Mix, Tom	1880	1940	O'Connor, Donald	1925	2003	Poston, Tom	1921	2007
Molinaro, Al	1919	2015	O'Connor, Una	1880	1959	Powell, Dick	1904	1963
Monroe, Marilyn	1926	1962	Odetta (Holmes)	1930	2008	Powell, Eleanor	1912	1982
Monroe, Vaughn	1911	1973	O'Hara, Maureen	1920	2015	Powell, William	1892	1984
Montalban, Ricardo	1920	2009	O'Herlihy, Daniel	1919	2005	Power, Tyrone	1914	1958
Montand, Yves	1921	1991	O'Keefe, Dennis	1908	1968	Preminger, Otto	1905	1986
Monteith, Cory	1982	2013	Oland, Warner	1880	1938	Presley, Elvis	1935	1977
Montez, Maria	1917	1951	Olcott, Chauncey	1860	1932	Preston, Billy	1946	2006
Montgomery, Elizabeth	1933	1995	Oliveira, Manoel de	1908	2015	Preston, Robert	1918	1987
Montgomery, George	1916	2000	Oliver, Edna May	1883	1942	Price, Ray	1926	2013
Montgomery, Robert	1904	1981	Olivier, Laurence	1907	1989	Price, Vincent	1911	1993
Moody, Ron	1924	2015	Olsen, Merlin	1940	2010	Prima, Louis	1911	1978
Moore, Clayton	1914	1999	O'Neal, Ron	1937	2004	Prince	1958	2016
Moore, Colleen	1900	1988	O'Neill, James	1849	1920	Prinze, Freddie	1954	1977
Moore, Dudley	1935	2002	Ophüls, Max	1902	1957	Prosky, Robert	1930	2008
Moore, Garry	1915	1993	Orbach, Jerry	1935	2004	Provine, Dorothy	1937	2010
Moore, Grace	1898	1947	Orbison, Roy	1936	1988	Prowse, Juliet	1936	1996
Moore, Mary Tyler	1936	2017	Ormandy, Eugene	1899	1985	Pryor, Richard	1940	2005
Moore, Roger	1927	2017	O'Shea, Milo	1926	2013	Puente, Tito	1923	2000
Moorehead, Agnes	1906	1974	O'Sullivan, Maureen	1911	1998	Pyle, Denver	1920	1997
Moreau, Jeanne	1928	2017	O'Toole, Peter	1932	2013	Quayle, Anthony	1913	1989
Morgan, Dennis	1910	1994	Ouspenskaya, Maria	1876	1949	Questel, Mae	1908	1998
Morgan, Frank	1890	1949	Owen, Reginald	1887	1972	Quinn, Anthony	1915	2001
Morgan, Harry	1915	2011	Owens, Buck	1929	2006	Quintero, José	1924	1999
Morgan, Helen	1900	1941	Paar, Jack	1918	2004	Rabb, Ellis	1930	1998
Morgan, Henry	1915	1994	Paderewski, Ignace	1860	1941	Rabbit, Eddie	1941	1998
Morita, Pat	1932	2005	Page, Bettie	1923	2008	Radner, Gilda	1946	1989
Morley, Robert	1908	1992	Page, Geraldine	1924	1987	Rae, Charlotte	1926	2018
Morris, Chester	1901	1970	Page, Patti	1927	2013	Rafferty, Gerry	1947	2011
Morris, Greg	1934	1996	Pakula, Alan	1928	1998	Raft, George	1895	1980
Morrison, Jim	1943	1971	Palance, Jack	1919	2006	Rainer, Luise	1910	2014
Morrow, Vic	1929	1982	Pallette, Eugene	1889	1954	Rains, Claude	1889	1967
Morton, Jelly Roll	1885	1941	Palmer, Betsy	1926	2015	Raitt, John	1917	2005
Mostel, Zero	1915	1977	Palmer, Lilli	1914	1986	Ralston, Esther	1902	1994
Mowbray, Alan	1897	1969	Palmer, Robert	1949	2003	Ramis, Harold	1944	2014
Mulhare, Edward	1923	1997	Pangborn, Franklin	1894	1958	Ramone, Dee Dee	1952	2002
Mulligan, Gerry	1927	1996	Pardo, Don	1918	2014	Ramone, Joey	1951	2001
Mulligan, Richard	1932	2000	Parker, Eleanor	1922	2013	Ramone, Johnny	1948	2004

Name	Born	Died	Name	Born	Died	Name	Born	Died
Ramone, Tommy	1949	2014	Rowan, Dan	1922	1987	Simmons, Jean	1929	2010
Rampal, Jean-Pierre	1922	2000	Rubinstein, Artur	1887	1982	Simone, Nina	1933	2003
Randall, Tony	1920	2004	Rubenstein, Zelda	1933	2010	Sinatra, Frank	1915	1998
Randolph, John	1915	2004	Ruggles, Charles	1886	1970	Sinclair, Madge	1938	1995
Rathbone, Basil	1892	1967	Russell, Harold	1914	2002	Singleton, Penny	1908	2003
Ratoff, Gregory	1897	1960	Russell, Jane	1921	2011	Sirk, Douglas	1900	1987
Rawls, Lou	1933	2006	Russell, Ken	1927	2011	Siskel, Gene	1946	1999
Ray, Aldo	1926	1991	Russell, Leon	1942	2016	Sjostrom, Victor	1879	1960
Ray, Johnnie	1927	1990	Russell, Lillian	1861	1922	Skelton, Red	1913	1997
Ray, Nicholas	1911	1979	Russell, Nipsey	1923	2005	Skinner, Otis	1858	1942
Rayburn, Gene	1917	1999	Russell, Rosalind	1911	1976	Sledge, Percy	1940	2015
Raye, Martha	1916	1994	Rutherford, Ann	1917	2012	Smith, Alexis	1921	1993
Raymond, Gene	1908	1998	Rutherford, Margaret	1892	1972	Smith, Bessie	1894?	1937
Reagan, Ronald	1911	2004	Ryan, Irene	1903	1973	Smith, Buffalo Bob	1917	1998
Redding, Otis	1941	1967	Ryan, Robert	1909	1973	Smith, C. Aubrey	1863	1948
Redgrave, Corin	1939	2010	Sabu (Dastagir)	1924	1963	Smith, Elliott	1969	2003
Redgrave, Lynn	1943	2010	St. Cyr, Lili	1917	1999	Smith, Kate	1907	1986
Redgrave, Michael	1908	1985	St. Denis, Ruth	1877	1968	Smith, Keely	1928	2017
Reed, Donna	1921	1986	Sakall, S. Z.	1883	1955	Snodgress, Carrie	1946	2004
Reed, Jerry	1937	2008	Saks, Gene	1921	2015	Snow, Hank	1914	1999
Reed, Lou	1942	2013	Sale (Chic), Charles	1885	1936	Snyder, Tom	1936	2007
Reed, Oliver	1938	1999	Sales, Soupy	1926	2009	Solti, George	1912	1997
Reed, Robert	1932	1992	Sanders, George	1906	1972	Sondergaard, Gale	1899	1985
Rees, Roger	1944	2015	Sanford, Isabel	1917	2004	Sothern, Ann	1909	2001
Reese, Della	1931	2017	Sargent, Dick	1933	1994	Sousa, John Philip	1854	1932
Reeve, Christopher	1952	2004	Sarrazin, Michael	1940	2011	Sparks, Ned	1884	1957
Reeves, George	1914	1959	Savalas, Telly	1922	1994	Spelling, Aaron	1923	2006
Reeves, Steve	1926	2000	Schallert, William	1922	2016	Spencer, John	1946	2005
Reid, Wallace	1891	1923	Scheider, Roy	1935	2008	Sperber, Wendie Jo	1958	2005
Reilly, Charles Nelson	1931	2007	Schell, Maria	1926	2005	Springfield, Dusty	1939	1999
Reinhardt, Max	1873	1943	Schell, Maximilian	1930	2014	Stack, Robert	1919	2003
Remick, Lee	1935	1991	Schenkel, Chris	1923	2005	Stafford, Jo	1917	2008
Renaldo, Duncan	1904	1980	Schiavelli, Vincent	1948	2005	Stander, Lionel	1908	1994
Rennie, Michael	1909	1971	Schildkraut, Joseph	1896	1964	Stang, Arnold	1918	2009
Renoir, Jean	1894	1979	Schipa, Tito	1888	1965	Stanley, Kim	1925	2001
Rettig, Tommy	1941	1996	Schlesinger, John	1926	2003	Stanton, Harry Dean	1926	2017
Reynolds, Burt	1936	2018	Schnabel, Artur	1882	1951	Stanwyck, Barbara	1907	1990
Reynolds, Debbie	1932	2016	Schneider, Maria	1952	2011	Stapleton, Jean	1923	2013
Reynolds, Marjorie	1921	1997	Schneider, Romy	1938	1982	Stapleton, Maureen	1925	2006
Rich, Charlie	1932	1995	Schwartzkopf, Elizabeth	1915	2006	Steiger, Rod	1925	2002
Richardson, Ian	1934	2007	Scofield, Paul	1922	2008	Sterling, Jan	1921	2004
Richardson, Natasha	1963	2009	Scott, George C.	1927	1999	Stern, Isaac	1920	2001
Richardson, Ralph	1902	1983	Scott, Gordon	1926	2007	Stevens, Craig	1918	2000
Rickles, Don	1926	2017	Scott, Hazel	1920	1981	Stevens, George	1904	1975
Rickman, Alan	1946	2016	Scott, Lizabeth	1922	2015	Stevens, Inger	1934	1970
Riddle, Nelson	1921	1985	Scott, Martha	1914	2003	Stevens, Mark	1916	1994
Riefenstahl, Leni	1902	2003	Scott, Randolph	1898	1987	Stevens, Risë	1913	2013
Ripperton, Minnie	1947	1979	Scott, Stuart	1965	2015	Stevenson, McLean	1929	1996
Ritchard, Cyril	1898	1977	Scott, Zachary	1914	1965	Stewart, James	1908	1997
Ritter, John	1948	2003	Scott-Heron, Gil	1949	2011	Stickney, Dorothy	1896	1998
Ritter, Tex	1905	1974	Scott-Siddons, Mrs.	1843	1896	Stiers, David Ogden	1942	2018
Ritter, Thelma	1905	1969	Seberg, Jean	1938	1979	Stokowski, Leopold	1882	1977
Ritz, Al	1901	1965	Seeger, Pete	1919	2014	Stone, Fred	1873	1959
Ritz, Harry	1906	1986	Seeley, Blossom	1892	1974	Stone, Lewis	1879	1953
Ritz, Jimmy	1903	1985	Segovia, Andres	1893	1987	Stone, Milburn	1904	1980
Rivers, Joan	1933	2014	Seldes, Marian	1928	2014	Storm, Gale	1922	2009
Roach, Hal	1892	1992	Selena (Quintanilla)	1971	1995	Straight, Beatrice	1918	2001
Roach, Max	1924	2007	Sellers, Peter	1925	1980	Strasberg, Lee	1901	1982
Robards, Jason	1922	2000	Selznick, David O.	1902	1965	Strasberg, Susan	1938	1999
Robbins, Jerome	1918	1998	Sennett, Mack	1880	1960	Stritch, Elaine	1925	2014
Robbins, Marty	1925	1982	Señor Wences	1896	1999	Strode, Woody	1914	1994
Roberts, Doris	1925	2016	Serling, Rod	1924	1975	Strummer, Joe	1952	2002
Roberts, Pernell	1928	2010	Shakur, Tupac	1971	1996	Stuart, Gloria	1910	2010
Roberts, Rachel	1927	1980	Shandling, Garry	1949	2016	Stuarti, Enzo	1919	2005
Robertson, Cliff	1925	2011	Shankar, Ravi	1920	2012	Sturges, Preston	1898	1959
Robertson, Dale	1923	2013	Sharif, Omar	1932	2015	Sullavan, Margaret	1911	1960
Robeson, Paul	1898	1976	Shaw, Artie	1910	2004	Sullivan, Barry	1912	1994
Robinson, Bill	1878	1949	Shaw, Robert (actor)	1927	1978	Sullivan, Ed	1902	1974
Robinson, Edward G.	1893	1973	Shaw, Robert (conductor)	1916	1999	Sumac, Yma	1922	2008
Robson, Flora	1902	1984	Shawn, Ted	1891	1972	Summer, Donna	1948	2012
Roche, Eugene	1928	2004	Shean, Al	1868	1949	Summerville, Slim	1892	1946
Rochester (Eddie Anderson)	1905	1977	Shearer, Moira	1926	2006	Sutherland, Joan	1926	2010
Roddenberry, Gene	1921	1991	Shearer, Norma	1902	1983	Swanson, Gloria	1899	1983
Rodgers, Jimmie	1897	1933	Shearing, George	1919	2011	Swarthout, Gladys	1904	1969
Rogers, Buddy	1904	1999	Shelley, Carole	1939	2018	Swayze, Patrick	1952	2009
Rogers, Fred	1928	2003	Shepard, Sam	1943	2017	Sweet, Blanche	1896	1986
Rogers, Ginger	1911	1995	Sheppard, Bob	1910	2010	Switzer, Carl "Alfalfa"	1927	1959
Rogers, Roy	1911	1998	Sheridan, Ann	1915	1967	Talbot, Lyle	1902	1996
Rogers, Wayne	1933	2015	Shore, Dinah	1917	1994	Tallchief, Maria	1925	2013
Rogers, Will	1879	1935	Short, Bobby	1924	2005	Talmadge, Constance	1900	1973
Rohmer, Éric	1920	2010	Shubert, Lee	1875	1953	Talmadge, Norma	1893	1957
Roland, Gilbert	1905	1994	Shull, Richard B.	1929	1999	Tamiroff, Akim	1899	1972
Rolle, Esther	1920	1998	Siddons, Sarah	1755	1831	Tandy, Jessica	1909	1994
Rollins, Howard	1950	1996	Sidney, Sylvia	1910	1999	Tanguay, Eva	1878	1947
Roman, Ruth	1924	1999	Siegel, Don	1912	1991	Tati, Jacques	1908	1982
Romero, Cesar	1907	1994	Signoret, Simone	1921	1985	Taylor, Billy	1921	2010
Rooney, Mickey	1920	2014	Sills, Beverly	1929	2007	Taylor, Deems	1885	1966
Rose Marie	1923	2017	Silver, Ron	1946	2009	Taylor, Dub	1907	1994
Rose, Billy	1899	1966	Silverheels, Jay	1912	1980	Taylor, Elizabeth	1932	2011
Rossellini, Roberto	1906	1977	Silvers, Phil	1912	1985	Taylor, Estelle	1899	1958
Rostropovich, Mstislav	1927	2007	Sim, Alastair	1900	1976	Taylor, Laurette	1887	1946

Name	Born	Died	Name	Born	Died	Name	Born	Died
Taylor, Paul	1930	2018	Vidor, King	1094	1982	Wilding, Michael	1912	1979
Taylor, Robert	1911	1969	Vigoda, Abe	1921	2016	Williams, Andy	1927	2012
Taylor, Rod	1930	2015	Villechaize, Herve	1943	1993	Williams, Bert	1874	1922
Temple Black, Shirley	1928	2014	Vincent, Gene	1935	1971	Williams, Esther	1921	2013
Terry, Ellen	1847	1928	Vicious, Sid	1957	1979	Williams, Guy	1924	1989
Thalberg, Irving	1899	1936	Von Stroheim, Erich	1885	1957	Williams, Hank, Sr.	1923	1953
Thaw, John	1942	2002	Von Zell, Harry	1906	1981	Williams, Robin	1951	2014
Thaxter, Phyllis	1919	2012	Wain, Bea	1917	2017	Williamson, Nicol	1936	2011
Thicke, Alan	1947	2016	Waite, Ralph	1928	2014	Wills, Bob	1905	1975
Thigpen, Lynne	1948	2003	Walker, Clint	1927	2018	Wills, Chill	1902	1978
Thomas, Danny	1912	1991	Walker, Junior	1942	1995	Wilson, Carl	1946	1998
Thomas, Jay	1948	2017	Walker, Nancy	1922	1992	Wilson, Dennis	1944	1983
Thompson, Sada	1927	2011	Walker, Paul	1973	2013	Wilson, Dooley	1894	1953
Thorndike, Sybil	1882	1976	Walker, Robert	1918	1951	Wilson, Elizabeth	1921	2015
Thulin, Ingrid	1926	2004	Wallace, Marcia	1942	2013	Wilson, Flip	1933	1998
Tierney, Gene	1920	1991	Wallach, Eli	1915	2014	Wilson, Jackie	1934	1984
Tillis, Mel	1932	2017	Wallenda, Karl	1905	1978	Wilson, Marie	1917	1972
Tiny Tim	1932	1996	Walsh, J. T.	1943	1998	Windom, William	1923	2012
Todd, Michael	1909	1958	Walsh, Raoul	1887	1980	Windsor, Marie	1919	2000
Todd, Richard	1919	2009	Walston, Ray	1914	2001	Winehouse, Amy	1983	2011
Tomlinson, David	1917	2000	Walter, Bruno	1876	1962	Winfield, Paul	1941	2004
Tone, Franchot	1905	1968	Ward, Simon	1941	2012	Winter, Johnny	1944	2014
Torme, Mel	1925	1999	Warden, Jack	1920	2006	Winters, Jonathan	1925	2013
Toscanini, Arturo	1867	1957	Waring, Fred	1900	1984	Winters, Shelley	1920	2006
Tracy, Lee	1898	1968	Warner, H. B.	1876	1958	Wise, Robert	1914	2005
Tracy, Spencer	1900	1967	Warrick, Ruth	1915	2005	Wiseman, Joseph	1918	2009
Travers, Henry	1874	1965	Washington, Dinah	1924	1963	Wolfman Jack	1938	1995
Travers, Mary	1936	2009	Waters, Ethel	1896	1977	Wong, Anna May	1907	1961
Treacher, Arthur	1894	1975	Waters, Muddy	1913?	1983	Wood, Ed	1924	1978
Tree, Herbert Beerbohm	1853	1917	Waxman, Al	1935	2001	Wood, Natalie	1938	1981
Trevor, Claire	1909	2000	Wayne, David	1914	1995	Wood, Peggy	1892	1978
Truex, Ernest	1890	1973	Wayne, John	1907	1979	Wood, Sam	1884	1949
Truffaut, Francois	1932	1984	Weaver, Dennis	1924	2006	Woodard, Edward	1930	2009
Tucker, Forrest	1919	1986	Weaver, Fritz	1926	2016	Wooley, Sheb	1921	2003
Tucker, Richard	1913	1975	Webb, Clifton	1891	1966	Woolley, Monty	1888	1963
Tucker, Sophie	1884	1966	Webb, Jack	1920	1982	Worth, Irene	1916	2002
Turner, Big Joe	1911	1985	Weems, Ted	1901	1963	Wray, Fay	1907	2004
Turner, Ike	1931	2008	Weiland, Scott	1967	2015	Wright, Teresa	1918	2005
Turner, Lana	1920?	1995	Weissmuller, Johnny	1904	1984	Wyatt, Jane	1910	2006
Turpin, Ben	1869	1940	Welk, Lawrence	1903	1992	Wyler, William	1902	1981
Twitty, Conway	1933	1993	Welles, Orson	1915	1985	Wyman, Jane	1917	2007
Urich, Robert	1946	2002	Wellman, William	1896	1975	Wynette, Tammy	1942	1998
Ustinov, Peter	1921	2004	Wells, Kitty	1919	2012	Wynn, Ed.	1886	1966
Valens, Ritchie	1941	1959	Werner, Oskar	1922	1984	Wynn, Keenan	1916	1986
Valentino, Rudolph	1895	1926	West, Adam	1928	2017	York, Dick	1928	1992
Vallee, Rudy	1901	1986	West, Mae	1893	1980	York, Susannah	1939	2011
Van, Bobby	1928	1980	Weston, Jack	1924	1996	Young, Alan	1919	2016
Van Cleef, Lee	1925	1989	Whale, James	1889	1957	Young, Clara Kimball	1890	1960
Van Fleet, Jo	1922	1996	White, Barry	1944	2003	Young, Gig	1913	1978
Van Patten, Dick	1928	2015	White, Jesse	1919	1997	Young, Loretta	1913	2000
Vance, Vivian	1912	1979	White, Pearl	1889	1938	Young, Robert	1907	1998
Vandross, Luther	1951	2005	Whiteman, Paul	1891	1967	Young, Roland	1887	1953
Varney, Jim	1949	2000	Whiting, Margaret	1924	2011	Youngman, Henny	1906	1998
Vaughan, Sarah	1924	1990	Whitmore, James	1921	2009	Zanuck, Darryl F.	1902	1979
Vaughn, Robert	1932	2016	Whitty, May	1865	1948	Zappa, Frank	1940	1993
Veidt, Conrad	1893	1943	Wickes, Mary	1910	1995	Zevon, Warren	1947	2003
Velez, Lupe	1908	1944	Widmark, Richard	1914	2008	Ziegfeld, Florenz	1869	1932
Vera-Ellen (Rohe)	1926	1981	Wilde, Cornel	1915	1989	Zimbalist, Efrem, Jr.	1918	2014
Verdon, Gwen	1925	2000	Wilder, Billy	1906	2002	Zinneman, Fred	1907	1997
Verrett, Shirley	1931	2010	Wilder, Gene	1933	2016	Zukor, Adolph	1873	1976
Vickers, Jon	1926	2015						

Original Names of Selected Entertainers

Adele: Adele Laurie Blue Adkins
Ad-Rock: Adam Horovitz
Clay Aiken: Clayton Grissom
Alan Alda: Alphonso D'Abruzzo
Jason Alexander: Jay Greenspan
Woody Allen: Allen Konigsberg
André 3000: Andre Benjamin
Julie Andrews: Julia Wells
Criss Angel: Christopher Sarantakos
Beatrice Arthur: Bernice Frankel
Fred Astaire: Frederick Austerlitz
Babyface: Kenneth Edmonds
Lauren Bacall: Betty Joan Perske
Erykah Badu: Erica Wright
Eric Bana: Eric Banadinovich
Anne Bancroft: Anna Maria Italiano
Theda Bara: Theodosia Goodman
Beck: Bek David Campbell
Pat Benatar: Patricia Andrejewski
Tony Bennett: Anthony Benedetto
Jack Benny: Benjamin Kubelsky
Milton Berle: Mendel Berlinger
Irving Berlin: Israel Baline
Sarah Bernhardt: Henriette-Rosine Bernard

Jello Biafra: Eric Reed Boucher
Big Boi: Antwan Patton
The Big Bopper: Jiles Perry "J.P." Richardson
Robert Blake: Michael James Vijencio Gubitosi
Jon Bon Jovi: John Francis Bongiovi
Bono: Paul Hewson
David Bowie: David Robert Jones
Boy George: George Alan O'Dowd
Fanny Brice: Fanny Borach
Charles Bronson: Charles Buchinski
Albert Brooks: Albert Einstein
Mel Brooks: Melvin Kaminsky
Foxy Brown: Inga Marchand
George Burns: Nathan Birnbaum
Ellen Burstyn: Edna Gilhooley
Richard Burton: Richard Jenkins
Red Buttons: Aaron Chwatt
Nicolas Cage: Nicholas Coppola
Michael Caine: Maurice Micklewhite
Maria Callas: Maria Kalogeropoulos
Cardi B: Belcalis Marlenis Almánza
Jackie Chan: Chan Kwong-Sung
Cyd Charisse: Tula Finklea

Ray Charles: Ray Charles Robinson
Charo: María Rosario Pilar Martínez Molina Baeza
Chubby Checker: Ernest Evans
Cher: Cherilyn Sarkisian
Chuck D: Carlton Ridenhour
Patsy Cline: Virginia Patterson Hensley
Claudette Colbert: Lily Chauchoin
Coolio: Artis Leon Ivey Jr.
Alice Cooper: Vincent Furnier
David Copperfield: David Kotkin
Howard Cosell: Howard Cohen
Elvis Costello: Declan McManus
Lou Costello: Louis Cristillo
Peter Coyote: Peter Cohon
Joan Crawford: Lucille LeSueur
Quentin Crisp: Denis Pratt
Tom Cruise: Thomas Cruise Mapother IV
Tony Curtis: Bernard Schwartz
Miley Cyrus: Destiny Hope Cyrus
D'Angelo: Michael D'Angelo Archer
Rodney Dangerfield: Jacob Cohen
Bobby Darin: Walden Robert Cassotto
Doris Day: Doris von Kappelhoff

Yvonne De Carlo: Peggy Middleton
Portia de Rossi: Amanda Lee Rogers
Sandra Dee: Alexandra Zuck
John Denver: Henry John Deutschendorf Jr.
Bo Derek: Mary Cathleen Collins
Danny DeVito: Daniel Michaeli
Angie Dickinson: Angeline Brown
Bo Diddley: Elias Bates
Vin Diesel: Mark Vincent
Phyllis Diller: Phyllis Driver
Divine: Harris Glenn Milstead
DMX: Earl Simmons
Troy Donahue: Merle Johnson Jr.
Kirk Douglas: Issur Danielovitch
Drake: Aubrey Drake Graham
Bob Dylan: Robert Zimmerman
Barbara Eden: Barbara Huffman
Elvira: Cassandra Peterson
Eminem: Marshall Mathers
Enya: Eithne Ni Bhraonain
Dale Evans: Frances Smith
Chad Everett: Raymon Cramton
Fabian: Fabian Anthony Forte
Fabolous: John David Jackson
Douglas Fairbanks: Douglas Ullman
Morgan Fairchild: Patsy McClenny
Jamie Farr: Jameel Farah
Fergie: Stacy Ferguson
Stepin Fetchit: Lincoln Perry
W. C. Fields: William Claude Dukenfield
50 Cent: Curtis Jackson
Flavor Flav: William Drayton
Joan Fontaine: Joan de Havilland
Jodie Foster: Alicia Christian Foster
Jamie Foxx: Eric Bishop
Redd Foxx: John Sanford
Arlene Francis: Arlene Kazanjian
Connie Francis: Concetta Franconero
Greta Garbo: Greta Gustafsson
Judy Garland: Frances Gumm
James Garner: James Bumgarner
Crystal Gayle: Brenda Gail Webb
George Gershwin: Jacob Gershowitz
Kathie Lee Gifford: Kathie Epstein
Whoopi Goldberg: Caryn Johnson
Cary Grant: Archibald Leach
Lee Grant: Lyova Rosenthal
Robert Guillaume: Robert Williams
Buddy Hackett: Leonard Hacker
Hammer: Stanley Kirk Burrell
Jean Harlow: Harlean Carpenter
Helen Hayes: Helen Brown
Susan Hayward: Edythe Marrener
Rita Hayworth: Margarita Cansino
Pee-Wee Herman: Paul Reubenfeld
Charlton Heston: John Charles Carter
Perez Hilton: Mario Lavandeira Jr.
Hulk Hogan: Terry Gene Bollea
Billie Holiday: Eleanora Fagan
Judy Holliday: Judith Tuvim
Bob Hope: Leslie Townes Hope
Harry Houdini: Erik Weisz
Howlin' Wolf: Chester Burnett
Rock Hudson: Roy Scherer Jr. (later Fitzgerald)
Engelbert Humperdinck: Arnold Dorsey
Kim Hunter: Janet Cole
Ice Cube: O'Shea Jackson
Ice-T: Tracy Morrow
Billy Idol: William Broad
Etta James: Jamesetta Hawkins
Ja Rule: Jeffrey Atkins
Jay-Z: Shawn Carter
Elton John: Reginald Dwight
Al Jolson: Asa Yoelson
Jennifer Jones: Phylis Isley
Tom Jones: Thomas Woodward
Spike Jonze: Adam Spiegel
Wynonna Judd: Christina Ciminella
Boris Karloff: William Henry Pratt
Diane Keaton: Diane Hall

Michael Keaton: Michael Douglas
Kesha: Kesha Rose Sebert
Alicia Keys: Alicia Augello Cook
Chaka Khan: Yvette Stevens
Kid Rock: Robert Ritchie
Carole King: Carole Klein
Larry King: Larry Zeiger
Ben Kingsley: Krishna Banji
Ted Knight: Tadewurz Wladziu Konopka
Cheryl Ladd: Cheryl Stoppelmoor
Lady Gaga: Stefani Germanotta
Veronica Lake: Constance Ockleman
Kendrick Lamar: Kendrick Lamar Duckworth
Hedy Lamarr: Hedwig Kiesler
Dorothy Lamour: Mary Leta Dorothy Slaton
Michael Landon: Eugene Orowitz
Mario Lanza: Alfredo Cocozza
Queen Latifah: Dana Owens
Stan Laurel: Arthur Jefferson
Brenda Lee: Brenda Mae Tarpley
Gypsy Rose Lee: Rose Louise Hovick
Peggy Lee: Norma Egstrom
Janet Leigh: Jeanette Morrison
Vivien Leigh: Vivian Hartley
Huey Lewis: Hugh Cregg
Jerry Lewis: Joseph Levitch
Lil' Kim: Kimberly Denise Jones
Little Richard: Richard Penniman
LL Cool J: James Todd Smith
Carole Lombard: Jane Peters
Lorde: Ella Yelich-O'Connor
Sophia Loren: Sophia Scicolone
Peter Lorre: Laszlo Lowenstein
Louis C.K.: Louis Szekely
Myrna Loy: Myrna Williams
Bela Lugosi: Bela Ferenc Blasko
Moms Mabley: Loretta Mary Aiken
Macklemore: Ben Haggerty
Shirley MacLaine: Shirley Beaty
Elle Macpherson: Eleanor Gow
Madonna: Madonna Louise Veronica Ciccone
Lee Majors: Harvey Lee Yeary
Karl Malden: Mladen Sekulovich
Barry Manilow: Barry Alan Pincus
Jayne Mansfield: Vera Jane Palmer
Marilyn Manson: Brian Warner
Bruno Mars: Peter Gene Hernandez
Dean Martin: Dino Crocetti
Ricky Martin: Enrique Jose Martin Morales
MCA: Adam Yauch
Meat Loaf: Marvin Lee Aday
Freddie Mercury: Farrokh Bulsara
Ethel Merman: Ethel Zimmermann
George Michael: Georgios Panayiotou
Mike D: Michael Diamond
Nicki Minaj: Onika Tanya Maraj
Helen Mirren: Ilynea Lydia Mironoff
Joni Mitchell: Roberta Joan Anderson
Moby: Richard Melville Hall
Mo'Nique: Monique Imes
Marilyn Monroe: Norma Jean Mortenson (later Baker)
Yves Montand: Ivo Livi
Demi Moore: Demetria Guynes
Rita Moreno: Rosita Alverio
Harry Morgan: Harry Bratsburg
Morrissey: Steven Patrick Morrissey
Mr. T: Lawrence Tureaud
Paul Muni: Mehilem Weisenfreund
Nelly: Cornell Haynes Jr.
Mike Nichols: Michael Igor Peschowsky
Chuck Norris: Carlos Ray Norris
Notorious B.I.G.: Christopher Wallace
Hugh O'Brian: Hugh Krampke
Maureen O'Hara: Maureen FitzSimons
Jack Palance: Vladimir Palanuik
Minnie Pearl: Sarah Ophelia Cannon
Katy Perry: Kathryn Hudson
Bernadette Peters: Bernadette Lazzara

Joaquin Phoenix: Joaquin Bottom
Edith Piaf: Edith Gassion
Slim Pickens: Louis Lindley
Mary Pickford: Gladys Smith
Pink: Alecia Moore
Pitbull: Armando Christian Pérez
Iggy Pop: James Newell Osterberg
Natalie Portman: Natalie Hershlag
Prince: Prince Rogers Nelson
Dee Dee Ramone: Douglas Colvin
Joey Ramone: Jeffrey Hyman
Johnny Ramone: John Cummings
Tommy Ramone: Tom Erdelyi
Tony Randall: Leonard Rosenberg
Della Reese: Delloreese Patricia Early
Busta Rhymes: Trevor Smith Jr.
Joan Rivers: Joan Sandra Molinsky
Edward G. Robinson: Emmanuel Goldenberg
The Rock: Dwayne Johnson
Ginger Rogers: Virginia McMath
Roy Rogers: Leonard Franklin Slye
Mickey Rooney: Joe Yule Jr.
Johnny Rotten: John Lydon
Lillian Russell: Helen Leonard
Meg Ryan: Margaret Hyra
Winona Ryder: Winona Horowitz
Sade: Helen Folsade Abu
Soupy Sales: Milton Supman
Susan Sarandon: Susan Tomaling
Seal: Seal Henry Olusegun Olumide Adeola Samuel
Jane Seymour: Joyce Frankenberg
Omar Sharif: Michael Shalhoub
Charlie Sheen: Carlos Irwin Estevez
Martin Sheen: Ramon Estevez
Talia Shire: Talia Coppola
Beverly Sills: Belle Silverman
Phil Silvers: Philip Silversmith
Gene Simmons: Chaim Witz
Sinbad: David Adkins
Anna Nicole Smith: Vickie Lynn Hogan
Snoop Dogg: Calvin Broadus
Barbara Stanwyck: Ruby Stevens
Jean Stapleton: Jeanne Murray
Ringo Starr: Richard Starkey
Cat Stevens: Stephen Demetre Georgiou
Connie Stevens: Concetta Ingolia
Jon Stewart: Jonathan Stuart Leibowitz
Sting: Gordon Sumner
Joe Strummer: John Graham Mellor
Donna Summer: La Donna Gaines
Rip Taylor: Charles Elmer Taylor Jr.
Robert Taylor: Spangler Brugh
The Weeknd: Abel Makkonen Tesfaye
Danny Thomas: Muzyad Yakhoob (later Amos Jacobs)
Tiny Tim: Herbert Khaury
Rip Torn: Elmore Rual Torn Jr.
Randy Travis: Randy Traywick
Tina Turner: Annie Mae Bullock
Shania Twain: Eileen Regina Edwards
Twiggy: Lesley Hornby
Conway Twitty: Harold Lloyd Jenkins
Steven Tyler: Stephen Tallarico
Rudolph Valentino: Rudolpho D'Antonguolla
Frankie Valli: Frank Castelluccio
Eddie Vedder: Edward Louis Seversen III
Sid Vicious: John Simon Ritchie
John Wayne: Marion Morrison
Raquel Welch: Raquel Tejada
Gene Wilder: Jerome Silberman
Shelley Winters: Shirley Schrift
Stevie Wonder: Stevland Morris
Jane Wyman: Sarah Jane Mayfield
Loretta Young: Gretchen Michaels Young
Buckwheat Zydeco: Stanley Dural Jr.

ARTS AND MEDIA

Notable New Movies, Sept. 2017-Aug. 2018

Film (rating)	Stars	Director(s)
Adrift (PG-13)	Shailene Woodley, Sam Claflin	Baltasar Kormákur
All the Money in the World (R)	Michelle Williams, Christopher Plummer, Mark Wahlberg	Ridley Scott
American Assassin (R)	Michael Keaton, Dylan O'Brien, Taylor Kitsch, Sanaa Lathan	Michael Cuesta
American Made (R)	Tom Cruise, Jesse Plemons, Domhnall Gleeson	Doug Liman
Annihilation (R)	Tessa Thompson, Natalie Portman, Jennifer Jason Leigh, Oscar Isaac	Alex Garland
Ant-Man and the Wasp (PG-13)	Paul Rudd, Evangeline Lilly, Michael Peña, Walton Goggins	Peyton Reed
Avengers: Infinity War (PG-13)	Robert Downey Jr., Chris Hemsworth, Mark Ruffalo, Chris Evans	Anthony Russo, Joe Russo
A Bad Moms Christmas (R)	Mila Kunis, Kristen Bell, Kathryn Hahn, Christine Baranski, Susan Sarandon	Jon Lucas, Scott Moore
Battle of the Sexes (PG-13)	Emma Stone, Steve Carell	Jonathan Dayton, Valerie Faris
Black Panther (PG-13)	Chadwick Boseman, Lupita Nyong'o, Michael B. Jordan, Angela Bassett	Ryan Coogler
BlacKkKlansman (R)	John David Washington, Adam Driver, Topher Grace	Spike Lee
Blade Runner 2049 (R)	Ryan Gosling, Harrison Ford, Barkhad Abdi, Robin Wright, Jared Leto	Denis Villeneuve
Blockers (R)	Leslie Mann, Kathryn Newton, John Cena	Kay Cannon
Book Club (PG-13)	Jane Fonda, Diane Keaton, Candice Bergen, Mary Steenburgen	Bill Holderman
Call Me by Your Name (R)	Armie Hammer, Timothée Chalamet, Michael Stuhlbarg	Luca Guadagnino
Christopher Robin (PG)	Ewan McGregor, Hayley Atwell	Marc Foster
Coco (PG)	Animated. Anthony Gonzalez, Gael García Bernal, Benjamin Bratt	Lee Unkrich
The Commuter (PG-13)	Liam Neeson, Vera Farmiga, Patrick Wilson, Jonathan Banks	Jaume Collet-Serra
Crazy Rich Asians (PG-13)	Constance Wu, Henry Golding, Michelle Yeoh, Awkwafina	Jon M. Chu
Darkest Hour (PG-13)	Gary Oldman, Lily James, Ben Mendelsohn, Kristin Scott Thomas	Joe Wright
Deadpool 2 (R)	Ryan Reynolds, Josh Brolin, Morena Baccarin	David Leitch
Den of Thieves (R)	Gerard Butler, O'Shea Jackson Jr., Pablo Schreiber	Christian Gudegast
The Disaster Artist (R)	James Franco, Seth Rogen, Dave Franco, Ari Graynor	James Franco
Downsizing (R)	Matt Damon, Christoph Waltz, Kristen Wiig, Hong Chau	Alexander Payne
Eighth Grade (R)	Elsie Fisher, Josh Hamilton	Bo Burnham
Ferdinand (PG)	Animated. John Cena, Kate McKinnon, Bobby Cannavale, Jeremy Sisto	Carlos Saldanha
The 15:17 to Paris (PG-13)	Ray Corasani, Alek Skarlatos, Anthony Sadler, Spencer Stone	Clint Eastwood
Fifty Shades Freed (R)	Dakota Johnson, Jamie Dornan	James Foley
The Foreigner (R)	Jackie Chan, Pierce Brosnan	Martin Campbell
Game Night (R)	Rachel McAdams, Jason Bateman, Kyle Chandler, Jesse Plemons, Michael C. Hall	John Francis Daley, Jonathan Goldstein
The Greatest Showman (PG)	Hugh Jackman, Michelle Williams, Zac Efron, Zendaya	Michael Gracey
I Feel Pretty (PG-13)	Amy Schumer, Michelle Williams, Emily Ratajkowski	Abby Kohn, Marc Silverstein
Incredibles 2 (PG)	Animated. Craig T. Nelson, Holly Hunter, Samuel L. Jackson, Bob Odenkirk	Brad Bird
Isle of Dogs (PG-13)	Animated. Bryan Cranston, Jeff Goldblum, Scarlett Johansson	Wes Anderson
It (R)	Bill Skarsgard, Jaeden Lieberher	Andrés Muschietti
I, Tonya (R)	Margot Robbie, Allison Janney, Sebastian Stan	Craig Gillespie
Jane (PG)	Documentary. Jane Goodall	Brett Morgen
Jumanji: Welcome to the Jungle (PG-13)	Dwayne Johnson, Jack Black, Kevin Hart	Jake Kasdan
Jurassic World: Fallen Kingdom (PG-13)	Chris Pratt, Bryce Dallas Howard, Jeff Goldblum, James Cromwell	J.A. Bayona
Justice League (PG-13)	Ben Affleck, Henry Cavill, Gal Gadot, Amy Adams	Zack Snyder
Kingsman: The Golden Circle (R)	Channing Tatum, Taron Egerton, Colin Firth, Julianne Moore	Matthew Vaughn
Lady Bird (R)	Saoirse Ronan, Laurie Metcalf, Timothée Chalamet, Tracy Letts	Greta Gerwig
The Lego Ninjago Movie (PG)	Animated. Jackie Chan, Dave Franco, Michael Peña	Charlie Bean, Paul Fisher, Bob Logan
Love, Simon (PG-13)	Nick Robinson, Josh Duhamel, Jennifer Garner	Greg Berlanti
Loving Vincent (PG-13)	Animated. Douglas Booth, Jerome Flynn, Robert Gulaczyk, Saoirse Ronan	Dorota Kobiela, Hugh Welchman
Mamma Mia! Here We Go Again (PG-13)	Christine Baranski, Pierce Brosnan, Cher, Dominic Cooper, Colin Firth, Andy Garcia, Lily James, Amanda Seyfried, Meryl Streep	Ol Parker
Marshall (PG-13)	Chadwick Boseman, Josh Gad, Kate Hudson, Dan Stevens, James Cromwell	Reginald Hudlin
Mission Impossible: Fallout (PG-13)	Tom Cruise, Henry Cavill, Simon Pegg	Christopher McQuarrie
Molly's Game (R)	Jessica Chastain, Idris Elba, Kevin Costner, Michael Cera, Chris O'Dowd	Aaron Sorkin
mother! (R)	Jennifer Lawrence, Michelle Pfeiffer, Javier Bardem, Ed Harris	Darren Aronofsky
Murder on the Orient Express (PG-13)	Kenneth Branagh, Penélope Cruz, Willem Dafoe, Judi Dench	Kenneth Branagh
Ocean's 8 (PG-13)	Sandra Bullock, Cate Blanchett, Anne Hathaway, Rihanna, Helena Bonham Carter, Sarah Paulson, Awkwafina, Mindy Kaling	Gary Ross
Overboard (PG-13)	Anna Faris, Eva Longaria, Eugenio Derbez, Swoozie Kurtz	Rob Greenberg
Pacific Rim Uprising (PG-13)	John Boyega, Scott Eastwood, Rinko Kikuchi, Charlie Day	Steven S. DeKnight
Paddington 2 (PG)	Hugh Grant, Brendan Gleeson, Hugh Bonneville, Sally Hawkins	Paul King
Peter Rabbit (PG)	Animated. Daisy Ridley, Margot Robbie, Rose Byrne, James Corden	Will Gluck
Phantom Thread (R)	Daniel Day-Lewis, Lesley Manville	Paul Thomas Anderson
Pitch Perfect 3 (PG-13)	Anna Kendrick, Rebel Wilson	Trish Sie
Pope Francis: A Man of His Word (PG)	Documentary. Pope Francis, Joe Biden, Paul Ryan	Wim Wenders
The Post (PG-13)	Tom Hanks, Meryl Streep, Sarah Paulson, Bradley Whitford	Steven Spielberg
A Quiet Place (PG-13)	Emily Blunt, John Krasinski	John Krasinski
RBG (PG)	Documentary. Ruth Bader Ginsburg	Julie Cohen, Betsy West
Ready Player One (PG-13)	Tye Sheridan, Olivia Cooke, Simon Pegg, Lena Waithe	Steven Spielberg
Roman J. Israel, Esq. (PG-13)	Denzel Washington, Colin Farrell, Carmen Ejogo	Dan Gilroy
The Shape of Water (R)	Sally Hawkins, Michael Shannon, Richard Jenkins, Octavia Spencer	Guillermo del Toro
Sicario: Day of the Soldado (R)	Benicio Del Toro, Josh Brolin, Isabela Moner, Jeffrey Donovan	Stefano Sollima
Skyscraper (PG-13)	Dwayne Johnson, Neve Campbell	Rawson Marshall Thurber
Solo: A Star Wars Story (PG-13)	Alden Ehrenreich, Donald Glover, Emilia Clarke, Woody Harrelson	Ron Howard
The Spy Who Dumped Me (R)	Mila Kunis, Kate McKinnon, Justin Theroux, Gillian Anderson	Susanna Fogel
Star Wars: The Last Jedi (PG-13)	Daisy Ridley, John Boyega, Adam Driver, Oscar Isaac	Rian Johnson
Tag (R)	Ed Helms, Lil Rey Howery, John Hamm, Annabelle Wallis	Jeff Tomsic
Thor: Ragnarok (PG-13)	Chris Hemsworth, Tom Hiddleston, Cate Blanchett, Idris Elba	Taika Waititi
Three Billboards Outside Ebbing, Missouri (R)	Frances McDormand, Woody Harrelson, Sam Rockwell, Peter Dinklage	Martin McDonagh
Three Identical Strangers (PG-13)	Documentary. David Kellman, Robert Shafran	Tim Wardle
Tomb Raider (PG-13)	Alicia Vikander, Dominic West, Walton Goggins	Roar Uthaug
12 Strong (R)	Chris Hemsworth, Michael Shannon, Michael Peña	Nicolai Fuglsig
Victoria & Abdul (PG-13)	Judi Dench, Ali Fazal, Tim Pigott-Smith, Eddie Izzard	Stephen Frears
Whitney (R)	Documentary. Whitney Houston, Bobbi Kristina Brown, Bobby Brown	Kevin Macdonald
Wonder (PG)	Julia Roberts, Jacob Tremblay, Owen Wilson	Stephen Chbosky
Won't You Be My Neighbor? (PG-13)	Documentary. Fred Rogers	Morgan Neville
A Wrinkle in Time (PG)	Storm Reid, Oprah Winfrey, Reese Witherspoon, Mindy Kaling	Ava DuVernay

50 Top-Grossing Movies, 2017

Source: comScore, Inc.

Rank	Title	Gross (mil)	Rank	Title	Gross (mil)
1.	Star Wars: The Last Jedi	$549.0	26.	Girls Trip	$115.2
2.	Beauty and the Beast	504.0	27.	Fifty Shades Darker	114.6
3.	Wonder Woman	412.6	28.	La La Land	109.4
4.	Guardians of the Galaxy Vol. 2	389.8	29.	Baby Driver	107.8
5.	Spider-Man: Homecoming	334.2	30.	Daddy's Home 2	102.5
6.	It	327.5	31.	Annabelle: Creation	102.1
7.	Thor: Ragnarok	311.9	32.	Murder on the Orient Express	101.1
8.	Despicable Me 3	264.6	33.	Kingsman: The Golden Circle	100.2
9.	Justice League	226.5	34.	John Wick: Chapter Two	92.0
10.	Logan	226.3	35.	Blade Runner 2049	91.7
11.	The Fate of the Furious	226.0	36.	The Emoji Movie	86.1
12.	Jumanji: Welcome to the Jungle	206.5	37.	Power Rangers	85.4
13.	Dunkirk	188.4	38.	The Mummy	80.2
14.	Coco	186.5	39.	Rogue One: A Star Wars Story	76.9
15.	The Lego Batman Movie	175.8	40.	Sing	76.6
16.	Get Out	175.7	41.	Pitch Perfect 3	75.8
17.	The Boss Baby	175.0	42.	The Hitman's Bodyguard	75.5
18.	Pirates of the Caribbean: Dead Men Tell No Tales	172.6	43.	Alien: Covenant	74.3
19.	Kong: Skull Island	168.1	44.	Captain Underpants: The First Epic Movie	73.9
20.	Hidden Figures	166.7	45.	A Bad Moms Christmas	72.0
21.	Cars 3	152.9	46.	A Dog's Purpose	64.5
22.	War for the Planet of the Apes	146.9	47.	The Greatest Showman	63.1
23.	Split	138.3	48.	Ferdinand	62.8
24.	Transformers: The Last Knight	130.2	49.	The Lego Ninjago Movie	59.3
25.	Wonder	124.3	50.	Baywatch	58.1

Note: Box-office grosses in the U.S. and Canada Jan. 6, 2017-Jan. 4, 2018; some films had 2016 release dates.

All-Time Top-Grossing American Movies

Source: comScore, Inc.

Rank	Title (original release date)	Gross (mil)	Rank	Title (original release date)	Gross (mil)
1.	Star Wars: The Force Awakens (2015)	$936.7	26.	Captain America: Civil War (2016)	$408.1
2.	Avatar (2009)	760.5	27.	The Hunger Games (2012)	408.0
3.	Black Panther (2018)	700.0	28.	Jumanji: Welcome to the Jungle (2017)	404.5
4.	Avengers: Infinity War (2018)	678.8	29.	Spider-Man (2002)	403.7
5.	Jurassic World (2015)	652.3	30.	Jurassic Park (1993)	402.5
6.	The Avengers (2012)	623.4	31.	Transformers: Revenge of the Fallen (2009)	402.1
7.	Star Wars: The Last Jedi (2017)	620.2	32.	Frozen (2013)	400.7
8.	Incredibles 2 (2018)	602.6	33.	Guardians of the Galaxy Vol. 2 (2017)	389.8
9.	Titanic (1997)	600.8	34.	Harry Potter and the Deathly Hallows: Part 2 (2011)	381.0
10.	The Dark Knight (2008)	533.3	35.	Star Wars: Episode III—Revenge of the Sith (2005)	380.3
11.	Rogue One: A Star Wars Story (2016)	532.2	36.	Lord of the Rings: The Return of the King (2003)	377.0
12.	Beauty and the Beast (2017)	504.0	37.	Spider-Man 2 (2004)	373.4
13.	Finding Dory (2016)	486.3	38.	The Passion of the Christ (2004)	370.3
14.	Star Wars: Episode 1—Phantom Menace (1999)	474.5	39.	The Secret Life of Pets (2016)	368.4
15.	Star Wars (1977)	461.0	40.	Despicable Me 2 (2013)	368.1
16.	Avengers: Age of Ultron (2015)	459.0	41.	The Jungle Book (2016)	364.0
17.	The Dark Knight Rises (2012)	448.1	42.	Deadpool (2016)	363.1
18.	Shrek 2 (2004)	436.7	43.	Inside Out (2015)	356.5
19.	E.T. the Extra-Terrestrial (1982)	435.0	44.	Furious 7 (2015)	353.0
20.	The Hunger Games: Catching Fire (2013)	424.7	45.	Transformers: Dark of the Moon (2011)	352.4
21.	Pirates of the Caribbean: Dead Man's Chest (2006)	423.3	46.	American Sniper (2014)	350.1
22.	Jurassic World: Fallen Kingdom (2018)	415.2	47.	Lord of the Rings: The Two Towers (2002)	341.7
23.	Toy Story 3 (2010)	415.0	48.	Zootopia (2016)	341.3
24.	Wonder Woman (2017)	412.6	49.	Finding Nemo (2003)	339.7
25.	Iron Man 3 (2013)	409.0	50.	The Hunger Games: Mockingjay, Part 1 (2014)	337.1

Note: Box-office grosses in the U.S. and Canada through Aug. 31, 2018, in absolute dollars. Rising ticket prices favor newer films. Revenues from re-releases are included.

National Film Registry, 2017

Source: National Film Registry, Library of Congress

The National Film Registry adds 25 "culturally, historically, or aesthetically significant" American films annually.

Ace in the Hole (aka Big Carnival) (1951)
Boulevard Nights (1979)
Die Hard (1988)
Dumbo (1941)
Field of Dreams (1989)
4 Little Girls (1997)
Fuentes Family Home Movies Collection (1920s and 1930s)
Gentleman's Agreement (1947)

The Goonies (1985)
Guess Who's Coming to Dinner (1967)
He Who Gets Slapped (1924)
Interior New York Subway, 14th Street to 42nd Street (1905)
La Bamba (1987)
Lives of Performers (1972)
Memento (2000)
Only Angels Have Wings (1939)
The Sinking of the Lusitania (1918)

Spartacus (1960)
Superman (1978)
Thelonius Monk: Straight, No Chaser (1988)
Time and Dreams (1976)
Titanic (1997)
To Sleep With Anger (1990)
Wanda (1971)
With the Abraham Lincoln Brigade in Spain (1937-38)

Best American Movies of All Time

Source: American Film Institute

First unveiled in 1998 based on ballots sent to 1,500 individuals, mostly from the film world, in 1997. Updated in 2007 (the version shown here) to include newly eligible films and reflect shifting cultural perspectives. Criteria for judging included historical significance, cultural impact, critical recognition and awards, and popularity. The year each film was first released is in parentheses.

1. Citizen Kane (1941)
2. The Godfather (1972)
3. Casablanca (1942)
4. Raging Bull (1980)
5. Singin' in the Rain (1952)
6. Gone With the Wind (1939)
7. Lawrence of Arabia (1962)
8. Schindler's List (1993)
9. Vertigo (1958)
10. The Wizard of Oz (1939)
11. City Lights (1931)
12. The Searchers (1956)
13. Star Wars (1977)
14. Psycho (1960)
15. 2001: A Space Odyssey (1968)
16. Sunset Boulevard (1950)
17. The Graduate (1967)
18. The General (1927)
19. On the Waterfront (1954)
20. It's a Wonderful Life (1946)
21. Chinatown (1974)
22. Some Like It Hot (1959)
23. The Grapes of Wrath (1940)
24. E.T. the Extra-Terrestrial (1982)
25. To Kill a Mockingbird (1962)
26. Mr. Smith Goes to Washington (1939)
27. High Noon (1952)
28. All About Eve (1950)
29. Double Indemnity (1944)
30. Apocalypse Now (1979)
31. The Maltese Falcon (1941)
32. The Godfather Part II (1974)
33. One Flew Over the Cuckoo's Nest (1975)
34. Snow White and the Seven Dwarfs (1937)
35. Annie Hall (1977)
36. The Bridge on the River Kwai (1957)
37. The Best Years of Our Lives (1946)
38. The Treasure of the Sierra Madre (1948)
39. Dr. Strangelove (1964)
40. The Sound of Music (1965)
41. King Kong (1933)
42. Bonnie and Clyde (1967)
43. Midnight Cowboy (1969)
44. The Philadelphia Story (1940)
45. Shane (1953)
46. It Happened One Night (1934)
47. A Streetcar Named Desire (1951)
48. Rear Window (1954)
49. Intolerance (1916)
50. The Lord of the Rings: The Fellowship of the Ring (2001)
51. West Side Story (1961)
52. Taxi Driver (1976)
53. The Deer Hunter (1978)
54. M*A*S*H (1970)
55. North by Northwest (1959)
56. Jaws (1975)
57. Rocky (1976)
58. The Gold Rush (1925)
59. Nashville (1975)
60. Duck Soup (1933)
61. Sullivan's Travels (1941)
62. American Graffiti (1973)
63. Cabaret (1972)
64. Network (1976)
65. The African Queen (1951)
66. Raiders of the Lost Ark (1981)
67. Who's Afraid of Virginia Woolf? (1966)
68. Unforgiven (1992)
69. Tootsie (1982)
70. A Clockwork Orange (1971)
71. Saving Private Ryan (1998)
72. The Shawshank Redemption (1994)
73. Butch Cassidy and the Sundance Kid (1969)
74. The Silence of the Lambs (1991)
75. In the Heat of the Night (1967)

Movie Theaters, 1946-2017

Source: Motion Picture Association of America (MPAA); Rentrak Corporation

Year	Box office (mil)	Admissions (mil)	Admissions per week (mil)	Screens	Avg. ticket price	Films produced	Films released
1946	$1,692.0	4,067.3	78.2	NA	$0.42	NA	400
1950	1,379.0	3,017.5	58.0	NA	0.46	NA	483
1955	1,204.0	2,072.3	39.9	NA	0.58	NA	319
1960	984.4	1,304.5	25.1	NA	0.76	NA	248
1965	1,041.8	1,031.5	19.8	NA	1.01	NA	279
1970	1,429.2	920.6	17.7	NA	1.55	279	306
1975	2,114.8	1,032.8	19.9	15,030	2.03	258	233
1980	2,748.5	1,021.5	19.6	17,590	2.69	214	233
1985	3,749.4	1,056.1	20.3	21,147	3.55	264	470
1990	5,021.8	1,188.6	22.9	23,689	4.22	346	410
1995	5,269.0	1,211.0	23.3	27,805	4.35	631	411
2000	7,468.0	1,383.0	26.6	37,396	5.39	683	475
2005	8,832.0	1,376.0	26.5	38,852	6.41	920	507
2010	10,741.0	1,341.0	25.8	39,547	7.89	795	563
2011	10,186.1	1,285.0	24.7	39,641	7.93	818	609
2012	10,774.5	1,358.0	26.0	39,918	7.96	476[1]	678
2013	10,919.7	1,340.0	25.8	42,814	8.13	455[1]	661
2014	10,357.4	1,267.6	24.4	43,265	8.17	481[1]	709
2015	11,097.7	1,321.0	25.4	43,661	8.43	501[1]	708
2016	11,372.1	1,315.0	25.3	43,531	8.65	510	718
2017	11,122.7	1,240.0	23.8	43,216	8.97	544	777

NA = Not available. (1) Non-MPAA members with est. budget under $1 mil were not tracked.

Most Popular Movie Digital Sales and Rentals, 2017

Source: comScore Dynamic Studio Share and Digital Download Essentials Industry Services

U.S. home entertainment spending totaled $20.5 bil in 2017. Spending on physical formats fell to $6.8 bil from $11.6 bil in 2013, but digital spending increased from $6.5 bil in 2013 to $13.7 bil in 2017.

Digital Sales, 2017

Rank	Movie	Rank	Movie
1.	Moana (2016)	11.	The Boss Baby
2.	Wonder Woman	12.	John Wick: Chapter 2
3.	Rogue One: A Star Wars Story (2016)	13.	The Lego Batman Movie
4.	Trolls (2016)	14.	Arrival (2016)
5.	Guardians of the Galaxy Vol. 2	15.	Fifty Shades Darker
6.	Sing (2016)	16.	Beauty and the Beast
7.	Spider-Man: Homecoming	17.	Kong: Skull Island
8.	Logan	18.	The Fate of the Furious
9.	Fantastic Beasts and Where to Find Them (2016)	19.	The Accountant (2016)
10.	Doctor Strange (2016)	20.	Hacksaw Ridge (2016)

Digital Rentals, 2017

Rank	Movie	Rank	Movie
1.	The Accountant (2016)	12.	The Boss Baby
2.	Moana (2016)	13.	Hacksaw Ridge (2016)
3.	Wonder Woman	14.	Passengers (2016)
4.	Arrival (2016)	15.	Get Out
5.	Sing (2016)	16.	Sully (2016)
6.	Guardians of the Galaxy (2014)	17.	Kong: Skull Island
7.	Trolls (2016)	18.	John Wick: Chapter 2
8.	Logan	19.	Fantastic Beasts and Where to Find Them (2016)
9.	Hidden Figures (2016)	20.	Split (2016)
10.	Beauty and the Beast		
11.	The Girl on the Train (2016)		

Note: Includes electronic sell-through (EST), video-on-demand (VOD), and subscription streaming (paid subscribers only). Movies released in 2017 unless otherwise noted.

Top-Selling Video Games, 2017

Source: The NPD Group/Retail Tracking Service

U.S. consumers spent $29.1 bil on video game content in 2017: $6.2 bil on physical software and other physical formats (including rental/used content) and $22.9 bil on content in digital formats. Spending decreased 2% on physical content, but digital content spending grew 27%. Ranked by combined sales of game in physical/digital formats.

Rank	Game (console)	Rank	Game (console)
1.	Call of Duty: WWII (PC, PS4, XBO)	6.	Grand Theft Auto V (360, PC, PS3, PS4, XBO)
2.	NBA 2K18 (360, PC, PS3, PS4, Switch, XBO)	7.	Tom Clancy's Ghost Recon: Wildlands (PC, PS4, XBO)
3.	Destiny 2 (PC, PS4, XBO)	8.	Star Wars: Battlefront II 2017 (PC, PS4, XBO)
4.	Madden NFL 18 (PS4, XBO)	9.	Super Mario Odyssey (Switch)
5.	The Legend of Zelda: Breath of the Wild (Switch, Wii)	10.	Mario Kart 8 (Switch, Wii)

Note: Includes bundled, collector's, or game-of-the-year editions, except those bundled with hardware. 360 = Microsoft Xbox 360; PC = personal computer; PS3 = PlayStation 3; PS4 = PlayStation 4; XBO = Microsoft Xbox One.

Video Game Sales, 2017

Source: Entertainment Software Assn.; The NPD Group/Retail Tracking Service/Digital Games Tracking Service

Game sales by type	% of units sold	Deciding factors of game sales	% of sales affected
Shooter	25.9%	Quality of the graphics	66%
Action	21.9	Price	63
Sports	11.6	Interesting story	61
Role-playing	11.3	Continuation of previous game	51
Adventure	9.1	Online game capability	50
Racing	6.4	Product is familiar	47
Fighting	6.0		
Strategy	4.2		
All others	3.6		

Most Pirated Video Games, 2017

Source: Excipio

(ranked by number of P2P [peer-to-peer] transactions worldwide)

Rank	Game	Transactions	Rank	Game	Transactions
1.	The Sims 4	153,635,178	6.	Minecraft	62,537,045
2.	Grand Theft Auto: San Andreas	117,616,008	7.	Grand Theft Auto V	54,501,738
3.	Counter-Strike: Global Offensive	76,475,091	8.	Counter-Strike 1.6	43,481,503
4.	Grand Theft Auto	72,797,849	9.	Pro Evolution Soccer	41,643,571
5.	Euro Truck Simulator 2	64,382,037	10.	The Sims 3	36,743,933

Film and TV Content Ratings

The Motion Picture Association of America (MPAA) established a ratings system in 1968. It was revised in 1984 and in 1990. The MPAA, Natl. Cable Television Assn., and Natl. Assn. of Broadcasters developed the TV ratings system in 1997, in accordance with the Telecommunications Act of 1996; it was implemented in Oct. 1997.

Film Ratings

G: General Audience. All ages admitted. Does not contain themes, language, nudity, sex, or violence that the MPAA ratings board believes would offend parents whose younger children see the film. Does not necessarily denote a certificate of approval nor children's movie. No nudity, sex scenes, or drug use depicted.

PG: Parental Guidance Suggested. Some material may not be suited for children. The MPAA ratings board recommends that parents determine whether the content of the film is appropriate for their children. The film may contain more mature themes, some profanity, violence, or brief nudity. No drug use depicted.

PG-13: Parents Strongly Cautioned. Some material may be inappropriate for children under 13. Any movie depicting drug use or more than brief nudity is automatically rated at least PG-13. Violence is permitted, though it is generally not both realistic or extreme and persistent violence. The single use of one sexually-derived expletive rates a PG-13; more than one use requires at least an R rating.

R: Restricted. Under 17 requires accompanying parent or adult guardian. Movies given R ratings contain some adult material, defined as adult themes or activity, hard language, intense or persistent violence, sexually-oriented nudity, or drug abuse.

NC-17: No One 17 and Under Admitted. Those films that most parents would consider too adult for children under 17. An NC-17 rating does not mean the film is obscene or pornographic. The rating can be based on violence, sex, aberrational behavior, drug abuse, or any other element.

TV Ratings

TV-Y: All Children. Program designed to be acceptable for children of all ages. Its themes and elements are designed for a very young audience.

TV-Y7: Directed to Older Children. Program designed for children ages 7 and older, and more appropriate for those who have the skills to distinguish between make-believe and reality. May include mild fantasy/comedic violence. Programs with more than mild fantasy violence are denoted TV-Y7-FV.

TV-G: General Audience. Program not necessarily designed for children, but most parents would find it suitable for all ages. Little or no violence, no strong language, and little or no sexual dialogue or situations.

TV-PG: Parental Guidance Suggested. Program might contain material that parents would consider inappropriate for children, such as an adult theme or one or more of the following: suggestive dialogue (D), infrequent coarse language (L), some sexual situations (S), or moderate violence (V).

TV-14: Parents Strongly Cautioned. Program contains material that many parents would consider inappropriate for children under 14, such as one or more of the following: intensely suggestive dialogue (D), strong coarse language (L), intense sexual situations (S), or intense violence (V).

TV-MA: Mature Audience Only. Program specifically designed for adults and may be unsuitable for children under 17. Contains one or more of the following: crude indecent language (L), explicit sexual activity (S), or graphic violence (V).

Opera: Most Produced Works, 2017-18

Source: OPERA America

Work, composer	Productions	Work, composer	Productions	Work, composer	Productions
The Barber of Seville, Gioachino Rossini	16	*The Marriage of Figaro*, Wolfgang Amadeus Mozart	11	*Don Giovanni*, Wolfgang Amadeus Mozart	9
La traviata, Giuseppe Verdi	14	*Madama Butterfly*, Giacomo Puccini	11	*As One*, Laura Kaminsky	9
Tosca, Giacomo Puccini	13	*Turandot*, Giacomo Puccini	10	*Candide*, Leonard Bernstein	8
Carmen, Georges Bizet	13	*The Magic Flute*, Wolfgang Amadeus Mozart	9	*Maria de Buenos Aires*, Astor Piazzolla	7
Rigoletto, Giuseppe Verdi	12			*L'elisir d'amore*, Gaetano Donizetti	7
La bohème, Giacomo Puccini	12				

Note: Scheduled productions of a given work (not individual performances) during the 2017-18 season (generally Oct.-Sept.) by members of OPERA America and Opera.ca.

Longest-Running Broadway Shows
Source: The Broadway League

Rank	Title (run)[1]	Performances[2]	Rank	Title (run)[1]	Performances[2]	Rank	Title (run)[1]	Performances[2]
1.	*The Phantom of the Opera (1988-)	12,622	17.	Life With Father (1939-47)	3,224	34.	Pippin (1972-77)	1,944
2.	*Chicago (revival) (1996-)	8,947	18.	Tobacco Road (1933-41)	3,182	35.	South Pacific (1949-54)	1,925
3.	*The Lion King (1997-)	8,549	19.	*The Book of Mormon (2011-)	3,002	36.	The Magic Show (1974-78)	1,920
4.	Cats (1982-2000)	7,485	20.	Hello, Dolly! (1964-70)	2,844	37.	Aida (2000-04)	1,852
5.	Les Misérables (1987-2003)	6,680	21.	My Fair Lady (1956-62)	2,717	38.	*Beautiful: The Carole King Musical (2014-)	1,824
6.	A Chorus Line (1975-90)	6,137	22.	Hairspray (2002-09)	2,642	39.	Gemini (1977-81)	1,819
7.	*Wicked (2003-)	6,085	23.	Mary Poppins (2006-13)	2,619	40.	Deathtrap (1978-82)	1,793
8.	Oh! Calcutta! (revival) (1976-89)	5,959	24.	Avenue Q (2003-09)	2,534	41.	Harvey (1944-49)	1,775
9.	Mamma Mia! (2001-15)	5,758	25.	The Producers (2001-07)	2,502	42.	Dancin' (1978-82)	1,774
10.	Beauty and the Beast (1994-2007)	5,461	26.	Cabaret (revival) (1998-2004)	2,377	43.	La Cage aux Folles (1983-87)	1,761
11.	Rent (1996-2008)	5,123	27.	Annie (1977-83)	2,377	44.	*Aladdin (2014-)	1,755
12.	Jersey Boys (2005-17)	4,642	28.	Rock of Ages (2009-15)	2,328	45.	Hair (1968-72)	1,750
13.	Miss Saigon (1991-2001)	4,092	29.	Man of La Mancha (1965-71)	2,328	46.	The Wiz (1975-79)	1,672
14.	42nd Street (1980-89)	3,486	30.	Abie's Irish Rose (1922-27)	2,327	47.	Born Yesterday (1946-49)	1,642
15.	Grease (1972-80)	3,388	31.	Oklahoma! (1943-48)	2,212	48.	Crazy for You (1992-96)	1,622
16.	Fiddler on the Roof (1964-72)	3,242	32.	*Kinky Boots (2013-)	2,146	49.	Ain't Misbehavin' (1978-82)	1,604
			33.	Smokey Joe's Café (1995-2000)	2,036	50.	The Best Little Whorehouse in Texas (1978-82)	1,584

* = Still running as of Sept. 1, 2018. (1) Unless noted, listings reflect a play's first run on Broadway. (2) Number of performances through May 27, 2018.

Broadway Season Statistics, 1959-2018
Source: The Broadway League

Season	Gross (mil $)	Attendance (mil)	Playing weeks	New produc- tions	Avg. ticket price	Season	Gross (mil $)	Attendance (mil)	Playing weeks	New produc- tions	Avg. ticket price
1959-1960	$46	7.9	1,156	58	$5.82	2007-2008	$938	12.3	1,560	36	$76.45
1964-1965	51	8.2	1,250	67	6.20	2008-2009	943	12.2	1,548	43	77.61
1969-1970	53	7.1	1,047	62	7.46	2009-2010	1,020	11.9	1,464	39	85.79
1974-1975	57	6.6	1,101	54	8.64	2010-2011	1,081	12.5	1,588	42	86.27
1979-1980	146	9.6	1,540	61	15.21	2011-2012	1,139	12.3	1,522	41	92.38
1984-1985	209	7.3	1,078	33	28.47	2012-2013	1,139	11.6	1,430	46	98.42
1989-1990	282	8.0	1,070	39	35.07	2013-2014	1,269	12.2	1,496	44*	103.88
1994-1995	406	9.0	1,120	33	44.91	2014-2015	1,365	13.1	1,626	37	104.18
1999-2000	603	11.4	1,460	37	52.99	2015-2016	1,373	13.3	1,648	39	103.11
2004-2005	769	11.5	1,494	39	66.70	2016-2017	1,449	13.3	1,580	45**	109.21
2005-2006	862	12.0	1,501	39	71.83	2017-2018	1,697	13.8	1,624	33	123.07
2006-2007	939	12.3	1,509	35	76.28						

* = Includes one return engagement. ** = Includes two return engagements.

Notable U.S. Museums

This unofficial list of some of the largest museums in the U.S., by budget, was compiled with the assistance of the American Association of Museums (AAM). Zoos, aquariums, arboretums, botanical gardens, and planetariums may be AAM members but are not included here.

Museum	City	State	Museum	City	State
American Museum of Natural History	New York	NY	Franklin Institute	Philadelphia	PA
Amon Carter Museum of Western Art	Ft. Worth	TX	The Frick Collection	New York	NY
The Art Institute of Chicago	Chicago	IL	J. Paul Getty Museum	Los Angeles	CA
Boston Children's Museum	Boston	MA	Solomon R. Guggenheim Museum of Art	New York	NY
Brooklyn Museum of Art	Brooklyn	NY	Harvard University Art Museums	Cambridge	MA
Busch-Reisinger Museum	Cambridge	MA	Henry F. DuPont Winterthur Museum	Winterthur	DE
California Academy of Sciences	San Francisco	CA	Henry Ford Museum/Greenfield Village	Dearborn	MI
California Science Center	Los Angeles	CA	High Museum of Art	Atlanta	GA
Carnegie Museums of Pittsburgh	Pittsburgh	PA	Houston Museum of Natural Science	Houston	TX
Children's Museum of Indianapolis	Indianapolis	IN	Jamestown-Yorktown Foundation	Williamsburg	VA
Cincinnati Art Museum	Cincinnati	OH	Jewish Museum	New York	NY
Cincinnati Museum Center	Cincinnati	OH	L.A. County Museum of Art	Los Angeles	CA
Cleveland Museum of Art	Cleveland	OH	Liberty Science Center, Liberty State Park	Jersey City	NJ
Colonial Williamsburg	Williamsburg	VA	Maryland Science Center	Baltimore	MD
Corning Museum of Glass	Corning	NY	Mashantucket Pequot Museum and Research Center	Mashantucket	CT
Crystal Bridges Museum of American Art	Bentonville	AR	Metropolitan Museum of Art	New York	NY
Dallas Museum of Art	Dallas	TX	Milwaukee Public Museum	Milwaukee	WI
Denver Art Museum	Denver	CO	Minneapolis Institute of Arts	Minneapolis	MN
Denver Museum of Nature and Science	Denver	CO	Museum of African American History	Detroit	MI
Detroit Institute of Arts	Detroit	MI	Museum of the American West	Los Angeles	CA
Exploratorium	San Francisco	CA	Museum of Contemporary Art	Los Angeles	CA
The Field Museum	Chicago	IL	Museum of Fine Arts	Boston	MA
Fine Arts Museums of San Francisco	San Francisco	CA			

Museum	City	State
Museum of Fine Arts	Houston	TX
Museum of Modern Art	New York	NY
Museum of New Mexico	Santa Fe	NM
Museum of Science	Boston	MA
Museum of Science and Industry	Chicago	IL
Musical Instrument Museum	Phoenix	AZ
Mystic Seaport Museum	Mystic	CT
National Air and Space Museum	Washington	DC
National Baseball Hall of Fame and Museum, Inc.	Cooperstown	NY
National Civil Rights Museum	Memphis	TN
National Constitution Center	Philadelphia	PA
National Gallery of Art	Washington	DC
National Museum of African American History and Culture	Washington	DC
National Museum of American History	Washington	DC
National Museum of the American Indian	Washington	DC
National Museum of Natural History	Washington	DC
National 9/11 Memorial & Museum	New York	NY
National World War II Museum	New Orleans	LA
Nelson-Atkins Museum of Art	Kansas City	MO
New-York Historical Society	New York	NY
New York State Museum	Albany	NY
Newseum	Washington	DC
Peabody Essex Museum	Salem	MA
Philadelphia Museum of Art	Philadelphia	PA
Rock and Roll Hall of Fame and Museum, Inc.	Cleveland	OH
St. Louis Science Center	St. Louis	MO
San Diego Museum of Art	San Diego	CA
San Francisco Museum of Modern Art	San Francisco	CA
Science Museum of Minnesota	St. Paul	MN
Toledo Museum of Art	Toledo	OH
U.S. Holocaust Memorial Museum	Washington	DC
Univ. of Pennsylvania Museum of Archaeology and Anthropology	Philadelphia	PA
Virginia Museum of Fine Arts	Richmond	VA
Wadsworth Atheneum	Hartford	CT
Walker Art Center	Minneapolis	MN
Whitney Museum of American Art	New York	NY

Characteristics of Public Libraries by State, 2016

Source: Public Libraries Survey, Institute of Museum and Library Services

State	Libraries[1]	Operating revenue[2] (thous.)	Library visits		Circulation[3]		Internet use[4]	
			Total (thous.)	Per capita	Total (thous.)	Per capita	Total (thous.)	Per capita
AL	219	$103,361	15,440	3.4	19,820	4.3	3,897	0.8
AK	71	38,219	3,452	5.4	4,756	7.4	597	0.9
AZ	90	185,284	25,321	3.7	44,492	6.6	6,626	1.0
AR	59	77,092	10,236	4.0	13,214	5.2	1,636	0.6
CA	184	1,495,977	155,615	4.0	208,699	5.4	29,310	0.8
CO	114	339,695	32,014	6.0	63,275	11.8	6,591	1.2
CT	182	196,082	20,585	6.0	26,317	8.1	4,090	1.2
DE	21	26,088	4,126	4.4	6,234	6.6	620	0.7
DC	1	57,158	3,931	5.8	4,440	6.5	981	1.4
FL	80	577,714	70,991	3.5	110,441	5.5	15,367	0.8
GA	63	194,629	27,987	2.7	38,233	3.7	11,927	1.2
HI	1	35,692	4,490	3.1	6,282	4.4	845	0.6
ID	102	57,157	8,597	6.2	15,140	10.9	1,618	1.2
IL	621	806,718	67,336	5.7	107,433	9.1	12,490	1.1
IN	236	341,749	33,364	5.5	74,510	12.2	6,581	1.1
IA	534	127,877	17,733	5.9	26,425	8.8	2,996	1.0
KS	321	134,552	13,697	5.5	24,845	9.9	2,889	1.2
KY	119	185,263	18,028	4.1	29,846	6.8	4,164	1.0
LA	68	247,410	20,263	4.3	21,456	4.6	5,292	1.1
ME	227	45,539	6,787	5.9	8,656	7.6	999	0.9
MD	24	290,432	27,482	4.6	58,187	9.8	5,724	0.9
MA	368	300,655	40,431	6.1	61,813	9.3	5,983	0.9
MI	396	428,623	46,732	4.7	77,196	7.9	9,359	1.0
MN	137	226,837	24,063	4.4	50,473	9.3	4,772	0.9
MS	52	56,234	8,915	3.0	7,468	2.5	2,331	0.8
MO	147	256,777	27,066	4.9	53,630	9.8	5,398	1.0
MT	82	29,717	4,298	4.4	5,992	6.1	1,225	1.2
NE	237	58,240	7,865	5.1	12,516	8.2	1,839	1.2
NV	22	96,985	9,733	3.4	20,050	6.9	2,676	0.9
NH	222	61,085	7,217	5.5	10,359	7.9	783	0.6
NJ	282	477,833	42,002	4.9	53,348	6.3	8,679	1.0
NM	88	52,107	7,163	4.4	9,322	5.7	1,860	1.1
NY	756	1,403,148	103,081	5.3	131,093	6.8	18,013	0.9
NC	81	225,135	33,605	3.3	50,179	5.0	6,576	0.7
ND	74	19,782	2,204	3.3	4,290	6.3	579	0.9
OH	251	803,744	74,120	6.4	184,417	16.0	16,002	1.4
OK	119	122,650	13,113	4.1	22,504	7.0	3,595	1.1
OR	131	225,689	20,613	5.8	55,068	15.5	3,390	1.0
PA	454	286,980	44,145	3.6	63,560	5.1	7,011	0.6
RI	48	50,607	5,778	5.5	6,490	6.1	1,054	1.0
SC	42	141,862	15,803	3.4	25,129	5.4	3,918	0.8
SD	112	27,377	3,727	4.9	5,914	7.8	1,038	1.4
TN	186	123,028	18,702	2.9	26,620	4.1	4,671	0.7
TX	544	530,421	70,891	2.8	116,374	4.6	15,176	0.6
UT	72	108,470	16,137	5.4	35,254	12.0	2,697	0.9
VT	162	24,523	3,636	6.3	4,136	7.6	557	1.0
VA	92	290,548	35,650	4.3	67,729	8.2	7,524	0.9
WA	62	433,466	38,703	5.5	85,552	12.1	7,882	1.1
WV	97	40,569	5,231	2.8	6,501	3.5	914	0.5
WI	381	248,315	31,443	5.5	57,085	9.9	5,148	0.9
WY	23	34,109	3,537	6.0	4,821	8.2	849	1.5
U.S.	**9,057**	**12,749,201**	**1,353,081**	**4.4**	**2,227,583**	**7.2**	**276,439**	**1.0**

(1) Includes central libraries only. (2) Some operating revenues may be estimated. (3) The total annual circulation of all library materials of all types, including renewals. (4) Total number of sessions accessing the internet using the library's devices.

Top 25 Public Libraries in the U.S by Holdings, 2016

Source: American Library Association (ALA)

Rank Library name	Print materials	Electronic books	Audio and video	Total holdings
1. New York Public Library, The Branch Libraries, NY	21,935,221	1,788,493	1,547,509	25,271,223
2. Public Library of Cincinnati and Hamilton County, OH	4,936,677	5,889,477	895,276	11,721,430
3. Boston Public Library, MA.	7,997,591	95,927	103,492	8,197,010
4. Los Angeles Public Library, CA.	5,922,133	171,493	641,935	6,735,561
5. Chicago Public Library, IL.	5,451,914	46,195	451,142	5,949,251
6. County of Los Angeles Public Library, CA	4,734,248	40,403	1,005,192	5,779,843
7. Queens Borough Public Library, NY	4,972,997	85,829	611,737	5,670,563
8. San Diego Public Library, CA	4,715,696	96,457	460,626	5,272,779
9. Dallas Public Library, TX.	4,563,199	68,076	524,372	5,155,647
10. Hennepin County Library, MN	4,366,003	253,743	275,566	4,895,312
11. Dayton Metro Library, OH.	871,785	3,670,432	177,457	4,719,674
12. Detroit Public Library, MI.	4,083,856	6,517	303,820	4,394,193
13. King County Library System, WA	3,091,198	232,684	643,990	3,967,872
14. Cleveland Public Library, OH	3,219,589	373,194	353,633	3,946,416
15. Cuyahoga County Public Library, OH.	1,551,993	1,376,514	732,757	3,661,264
16. Brooklyn Public Library, NY	3,175,967	131,448	353,117	3,660,532
17. Miami-Dade Public Library System, FL.	3,160,588	156,845	308,720	3,626,153
18. Allen County Public Library, IN	3,048,427	220,412	299,603	3,568,442
19. Hawaii State Public Library System, HI.	2,967,198	58,452	377,927	3,403,577
20. City of St. Louis Municipal Library District, MO	2,894,428	222,614	164,338	3,281,380
21. Broward County Libraries Division, FL.	2,408,899	92,815	692,631	3,194,345
22. San Francisco Public Library, CA	2,618,747	159,602	343,910	3,122,259
23. Houston Public Library, TX	2,597,505	217,319	269,809	3,084,633
24. Las Vegas-Clark County Library District, NV	2,246,053	109,257	685,709	3,041,019
25. Atlanta Fulton Public Library System, GA	2,619,417	232,772	99,225	2,951,414

Most Challenged Books, 2017

Source: Office for Intellectual Freedom, American Library Association (ALA)

A challenge is a formal, written complaint filed with a library or school requesting that materials be removed because of content or appropriateness. The common reasons given for challenges follow each book's title and author.

1. *Thirteen Reasons Why*, Jay Asher. Suicide.
2. *The Absolutely True Diary of a Part-Time Indian*, Sherman Alexie. Alcohol use, profanity, sexually explicit.
3. *Drama*, Raina Telgemeier. LGBT characters, sexually explicit, offensive political viewpoint.
4. *The Kite Runner*, Khaled Hosseini. Offensive language, unsuited to age group, violence.
5. *George*, Alex Gino. LGBT character.
6. *Sex Is a Funny Word*, Cory Silberberg. Sex education, may lead children to "want to have sex or ask questions about sex."
7. *To Kill a Mockingbird*, Harper Lee. Violence, profanity.
8. *The Hate U Give*, Angie Thomas. Drug use, profanity, "pervasively vulgar."
9. *And Tango Makes Three*, Peter Parnell and Justin Richardson. LGBT characters.
10. *I Am Jazz*, Jessica Herthel and Jazz Jennings. Transgender child; language, sex education, and offensive viewpoints.

Best-Selling U.S. Magazines, 2018

Source: Alliance for Audited Media (AAM)

General magazines, exclusive of comics; also excludes magazines that failed to file reports to AAM. Based on total average paid and verified circulation during the six months ending June 30, 2018; ranked by paid circulation size.

Publication	Paid circ.	Publication	Paid circ.	Publication	Paid circ.
1. AARP The Magazine	24,099,602	18. ESPN The Magazine.	2,144,483	34. Golf Digest.	1,642,049
2. AARP Bulletin	23,475,727	19. Redbook.	2,109,366	35. Money	1,606,113
3. Better Homes and		20. Taste of Home	2,080,735	36. Women's Health	1,543,222
Gardens	7,645,902	21. Martha Stewart Living	2,064,993	37. Bon Appetit	1,513,658
4. Game Informer Magazine	7,137,476	22. Parents.	2,064,665	38. Entertainment Weekly	1,511,269
5. Good Housekeeping	4,311,679	23. Real Simple	1,984,532	39. Allrecipes	1,417,529
6. Family Circle	4,018,288	24. Us Weekly	1,964,332	40. Golf Magazine	1,413,862
7. People	3,423,322	25. Seventeen	1,901,924	41. Country Living	1,378,889
8. Woman's Day.	3,255,790	26. American Rifleman.	1,891,046	42. Health.	1,361,089
9. Cosmopolitan.	3,040,285	27. American Legion		43. HGTV Magazine	1,328,334
10. Southern Living	2,823,644	Magazine	1,859,529	44. Guideposts.	1,303,145
11. Sports Illustrated	2,763,966	28. Men's Health	1,825,164	45. TV Guide Magazine.	1,283,701
12. National Geographic	2,720,313	29. Smithsonian.	1,808,770	46. Magnolia Journal	1,282,352
13. Reader's Digest.	2,701,972	30. Cooking Light.	1,780,148	47. Rolling Stone	1,272,976
14. Shape.	2,544,949	31. Food Network Magazine . .	1,760,721	48. The New Yorker.	1,269,055
15. O, The Oprah Magazine . .	2,381,944	32. Rachael Ray Every Day . .	1,718,511	49. Sunset	1,268,196
16. Time	2,348,566	33. InStyle	1,708,509	50. Men's Journal	1,237,599
17. Glamour.	2,303,374				

Best-Selling Digital Replica U.S. Magazines, 2018

Source: Alliance for Audited Media (AAM)

General magazines, exclusive of comics; also excludes magazines that failed to file reports to AAM. Based on total average paid and verified circulation during the six months ending June 30, 2018; ranked by paid circulation size.

Publication	Paid circ.	Publication	Paid circ.	Publication	Paid circ.
1. Game Informer Magazine	2,073,057	17. ESPN The Magazine . . .	108,194	34. Woman's World.	69,850
2. Star Magazine.	353,371	18. Good Housekeeping. . . .	99,241	35. Taste of Home	69,607
3. Better Homes and		19. Backpacker.	97,140	36. Redbook.	66,080
Gardens	351,934	20. Yoga Journal	95,299	37. EatingWell	65,644
4. OK! Weekly.	241,131	21. Clean Eating.	92,652	38. Marie Claire	65,353
5. Rolling Stone	232,011	22. ABA Journal	91,107	39. Military Times	64,940
6. Cosmopolitan	222,522	23. Allrecipes	87,840	40. Woman's Day	64,599
7. Shape.	197,707	24. Food Network Magazine	86,936	41. Motor Trend.	62,998
8. Family Circle	171,607	25. Men's Health	86,009	42. Ski.	61,316
9. The New Yorker.	167,602	26. Outside	85,868	43. Popular Mechanics	61,262
10. Martha Stewart Living. . .	165,574	27. Traditional Home.	83,969	44. Women's Health	61,089
11. Parents	158,441	28. Us Weekly.	83,119	45. Esquire	60,119
12. O, The Oprah Magazine	134,510	29. HGTV Magazine	76,460	46. Car and Driver	60,092
13. Men's Journal	128,806	30. The Family Handyman . .	72,996	47. Vanity Fair.	59,020
14. National Geographic. . . .	126,850	31. The Knot	72,515	48. In Touch Weekly	58,175
15. Rachael Ray Every Day	114,698	32. Reader's Digest	70,311	49. Hot Rod Magazine	55,875
16. First For Women	112,078	33. Elle	70,302	50. Wired	54,451

Some Notable New Books, 2018

Source: Reference and User Services Association, American Library Association (ALA)

Fiction

Stay With Me, Ayobami Adebayo
Days Without End, Sebastian Barry
The Last Ballad, Wiley Cash
American War, Omar El Akkad
Here in Berlin, Cristina Garcia
Less, Andrew Sean Greer
Exit West, Mohsin Hamid
Human Acts, Han Kang
Pachinko, Min Jin Lee
Solar Bones, Mike McCormack
Lincoln in the Bardo, George Saunders
Sing, Unburied, Sing, Jesmyn Ward

Poetry

I Know Your Kind, William Brewer
Virginia State Colony for Epileptics and Feebleminded,
    Molly McCully Brown

Nonfiction

You Don't Have to Say You Love Me: A Memoir, Sherman Alexie
Hue 1968: A Turning Point of the American War in Vietnam,
    Mark Bowden
The Best We Could Do: An Illustrated Memoir, Thi Bui
Grant, Ron Chernow
*The Woman Who Smashed Codes: A True Story of Love, Spies,
    and the Unlikely Heroine Who Outwitted America's Enemies*,
    Jason Fagone
*The Butchering Art: Joseph Lister's Quest to Transform the
    Grisly World of Victorian Medicine*, Lindsey Fitzharris
Hunger: A Memoir of (My) Body, Roxane Gay
*Killers of the Flower Moon: The Osage Murders and the Birth of
    the FBI*, David Grann
*Robert Lowell, Setting the River on Fire: A Study of Genius,
    Mania, and Character*, Kay Redfield Jamison
Radium Girls: The Dark Story of America's Shining Women, Kate
    Moore
*Bellevue: Three Centuries of Medicine and Mayhem at
    America's Most Storied Hospital*, David Oshinsky
The Blood of Emmett Till, Timothy Tyson

Best-Selling Books, 2017

Source: Nielsen BookScan

Hardcover Fiction

1. *Origin*, Dan Brown
2. *The Rooster Bar*, John Grisham
3. *Camino Island*, John Grisham
4. *Into the Water*, Paula Hawkins
5. *The Midnight Line*, Lee Child
6. *Sleeping Beauties*, Stephen King
7. *Norse Mythology*, Neil Gaiman
8. *A Column of Fire*, Ken Follett
9. *Lincoln in the Bardo*, George Saunders
10. *Hardcore Twenty-Four*, Janet Evanovich

Hardcover Nonfiction

1. *Astrophysics for People in a Hurry*, Neil deGrasse Tyson
2. *What Happened*, Hillary Rodham Clinton
3. *The Pioneer Woman Cooks: Come and Get It!* Ree
    Drummond
4. *Make Your Bed: Little Things That Can Change Your Life...
    and Maybe the World*, William H. McRaven
5. *Killing England: The Brutal Struggle for American
    Independence*, Bill O'Reilly and Martin Dugard
6. *Leonardo da Vinci*, Walter Isaacson
7. *Obama: An Intimate Portrait*, Pete Souza
8. *Grant*, Ron Chernow
9. *Killers of the Flower Moon: The Osage Murders and the
    Birth of the FBI*, David Grann
10. *Guinness World Records 2018*

Trade Paperback

1. *Milk and Honey*, Rupi Kaur
2. *You Are a Badass: How to Stop Doubting Your Greatness
    and Start Living an Awesome Life*, Jen Sincero
3. *A Man Called Ove*, Fredrik Backman
4. *The Woman in Cabin 10*, Ruth Ware
5. *The Sun and Her Flowers*, Rupi Kaur

6. *The Handmaid's Tale*, Margaret Atwood
7. *Lilac Girls*, Martha Hall Kelly
8. *Everything, Everything*, Nicola Yoon
9. *The 5 Love Languages: The Secret to Love That Lasts*,
    Gary Chapman
10. *All the Light We Cannot See*, Anthony Doerr

Mass Market Fiction

1. *The Whistler*, John Grisham
2. *Cross the Line*, James Patterson
3. *The Wrong Side of Goodbye*, Michael Connelly
4. *Wyoming Winter: A Small-Town Christmas Romance*, Diana
    Palmer
5. *Dangerous Games*, Danielle Steel
6. *The Silent Corner: A Novel of Suspense*, Dean Koontz
7. *The Games*, James Patterson
8. *Odessa Sea*, Clive Cussler and Dirk Cussler
9. *The Crush*, Sandra Brown
10. *Dragon Teeth*, Michael Crichton

Children's and Young Adult Hardcover

1. *The Getaway (Diary of a Wimpy Kid #12)*, Jeff Kinney
2. *Dog Man Unleashed*, Dav Pilkey
3. *Everything, Everything*, Nicola Yoon
4. *Harry Potter and the Prisoner of Azkaban: The Illustrated
    Edition (Harry Potter, Book 3)*, J. K. Rowling
5. *Turtles All the Way Down*, John Green
6. *Dog Man: A Tale of Two Kitties*, Dav Pilkey
7. *Dork Diaries 12: Tales From a Not-So-Secret Crush
    Catastrophe*, Rachel Renée Russell
8. *The Hate U Give*, Angie Thomas
9. *Pete the Cat: 5-Minute Pete the Cat Stories: Includes 12
    Groovy Stories!* James Dean
10. *The Trials of Apollo, Book 2: The Dark Prophecy*, Rick
    Riordan

Note: Hardcover and mass market bestsellers include frontlist/2017 releases only. Trade paperback bestsellers are for overall 2017 sales of paperback editions for titles first published in any year.

U.S. Daily Newspapers, 2016

Source: *Editor & Publisher International Data Book*
(ranked by circulation as of Sept. 30, 2016)

Rank	Newspaper	Circulation	Rank	Newspaper	Circulation
1.	McLean (VA) *USA Today*	3,981,877	27.	Pittsburgh (PA) *Post-Gazette*	161,385
2.	New York (NY) *Wall Street Journal*	2,285,084	28.	Sacramento (CA) *Bee*	160,344
3.	New York (NY) *Times*	2,100,822	29.	Honolulu (HI) *Star-Advertiser*	153,351
4.	Los Angeles (CA) *Times*	571,403	30.	Woodland Park (NJ) *Herald News*	152,167
5.	New York (NY) *Post*	487,762	31.	St. Louis (MO) *Post-Dispatch*	151,086
6.	Melville (NY) *Newsday*	460,149	32.	Washington (DC) *Post Express*	150,634
7.	New York (NY) *Daily News*	441,618	33.	Atlanta (GA) *Journal-Constitution*	141,003
8.	Chicago (IL) *Tribune*	418,999	34.	Cleveland (OH) *Plain Dealer*	139,971
9.	Washington (DC) *Post*	386,285	35.	St. Paul (MN) *Pioneer Press*	139,403
10.	Las Vegas (NV) *Review-Journal*	364,326	36.	Santa Ana (CA) *Orange County Register*	135,609
11.	Minneapolis (MN) *Star Tribune*	288,315	37.	Little Rock (AR) *Democrat-Gazette*	130,625
12.	Denver (CO) *Post*	285,027	38.	Indianapolis (IN) *Star*	128,326
13.	St. Petersburg (FL) *Tampa Bay Times*	276,681	39.	Las Vegas (NV) *Sun*	127,648
14.	Philadelphia (PA) *Inquirer*	249,921	40.	Buffalo (NY) *News*	127,502
15.	Boston (MA) *Globe*	243,986	41.	Milwaukee (WI) *Journal Sentinel*	127,367
16.	Dallas (TX) *Morning News*	237,928	42.	Hartford (CT) *Courant*	125,094
17.	Houston (TX) *Chronicle*	237,549	43.	Ft. Lauderdale (FL) *South Florida Sun-Sentinel*	123,378
18.	Austin (TX) *American-Statesman*	226,049	44.	Miami (FL) *Herald*	121,620
19.	Newark (NJ) *Star-Ledger*	213,890	45.	Norfolk (VA) *Virginian-Pilot*	120,091
20.	Phoenix (AZ) *Republic*	210,682	46.	Orlando (FL) *Sentinel*	119,823
21.	Springfield (MA) *Republican*	194,292	47.	Vancouver (WA) *Columbian*	113,571
22.	San Francisco (CA) *Chronicle*	185,048	48.	Baltimore (MD) *Sun*	113,557
23.	Chicago (IL) *Sun-Times*	183,604	49.	Walnut Creek (CA) *East Bay Times*	113,068
24.	San Diego (CA) *Union-Tribune*	179,104	50.	Gettysburg (PA) *Tribune-Review*	108,810
25.	Seattle (WA) *Times*	167,995			
26.	Kansas City (MO) *Star*	165,646			

Note: Excludes newspapers for which no average weekday circulation number was available.

Paid U.S. Newspaper Circulation, 1940-2016

Source: *Editor & Publisher International Data Book*
(circulation figures in thousands, as of Sept. 30, 2016)

Year	Number of daily newspapers			Circulation of daily newspapers			Sunday newspapers	
	Morning	Evening	Total	Morning	Evening	Total	Number	Circulation
1940	380	1,498	1,878	16,114	25,018	41,132	525	32,371
1950	322	1,450	1,772	21,266	32,563	53,829	549	46,582
1960	312	1,459	1,763	24,029	34,853	58,882	563	47,699
1970	334	1,429	1,748	25,934	36,174	62,108	586	49,217
1980	387	1,388	1,745	29,414	32,787	62,202	736	54,676
1990	559	1,084	1,611	41,311	21,017	62,328	863	62,635
2000	766	727	1,480	46,772	9,000	55,773	917	59,421
2005	817	645	1,452	46,122	7,222	53,345	914	55,270
2006	833	614	1,437	45,441	6,888	52,329	907	53,179
2007	867	565	1,422	44,548	6,194	50,742	907	51,246
2008	872	546	1,408	42,758	5,840	48,598	902	49,115
2009	869	528	1,397	40,796	5,482	46,278	919	46,850
2011	931	451	1,382	40,321	4,100	44,421	900	48,510
2012	985	442	1,427	38,723	4,709	43,432	981	48,821
2013	980	444	1,395	36,795	3,737	40,712	934	43,292
2014	953	402	1,331	36,765	3,655	40,420	923	42,751
2015	972	389	1,350	31,620	3,280	34,900	904	40,013
2016	939	369	1,286	30,357	3,063	33,419	869	37,998

Note: Data for 2010 was not available.

Canadian Daily Newspapers, 2016

Source: *Editor & Publisher International Data Book*
(ranked by circulation as of Sept. 30, 2016)

Rank	Newspaper	Circulation	Rank	Newspaper	Circulation
1.	Toronto (ON) *Globe and Mail*	222,575	6.	Vancouver (BC) *Province*	96,810
2.	Toronto (ON) *National Post*	186,225	7.	Montréal (QC) *La Presse*	91,762
3.	Toronto (ON) *Star*	171,674	8.	Calgary (AB) *Herald*	89,304
4.	Montréal (QC) *Le Journal de Montréal*	171,560	9.	Halifax (NS) *Chronicle Herald*	88,893
5.	Vancouver (BC) *Sun*	120,494	10.	Edmonton (AB) *Journal*	88,037

Top Newspaper Websites, 2018

Source: comScore, Inc.
(ranked by number of visitors, in thousands)

Rank	Website	Visitors[1]	Rank	Website	Visitors[1]
1.	The New York Times	87,342	11.	Telegraph Media Group	15,643
2.	WashingtonPost.com	80,824	12.	Berkshire Hathaway Media Group	14,408
3.	Tronc (formerly Tribune Newspapers)	72,675	13.	Express.co.uk	14,018
4.	NY Post Network	66,336	14.	Lee Enterprises, Inc.	13,203
5.	Mail Online/Daily Mail	50,396	15.	KiwiReport.com	10,812
6.	Hearst Newspapers	45,546	16.	Epoch Digital Network	10,586
7.	The Guardian	35,007	17.	Miami Herald Sites	9,403
8.	MediaNews Group	27,978	18.	Cox Media Group-Newspaper	8,587
9.	Independent & Evening Standard (ESi Media)	24,294	19.	A. H. Belo	7,918
10.	The Sun Online	18,053	20.	Michigan.com Sites	7,866

(1) Number of persons age 2 and older, in thousands, who visited the media property (including website/apps) at least once from any U.S. location in June 2018. Mobile visitors under age 18 are not measured.

Top News/Information Websites, 2018

Source: comScore, Inc.

(ranked by number of visitors, in thousands)

Rank Website	Visitors[1]	Rank Website	Visitors[1]
1. CNN Network	146,917	11. Tronc (formerly Tribune Newspapers)	72,675
2. Yahoo-HuffPost News Network	139,399	12. ABC News Digital	66,828
3. USA Today Network	123,348	13. NY Post Network	66,336
4. The Weather Company	120,453	14. BBC Sites	57,259
5. NBC News Digital	116,799	15. AccuWeather Sites	55,926
6. CBS News	102,792	16. Buzzfeed.com	54,329
7. Fox News Digital Network	93,055	17. Mail Online/Daily Mail	50,396
8. New York Times Digital	87,478	18. Tribune Media	49,707
9. WashingtonPost.com	80,824	19. Hearst Newspapers	45,546
10. Insider Inc.	78,803	20. Advance Digital	44,421

(1) Number of persons age 2 and older, in thousands, who visited the media property (including website/apps) at least once from any U.S. location in June 2018. Mobile visitors under age 18 are not measured.

National Recording Registry, 2017

Source: Library of Congress

Each year since 2002, the National Recording Registry at the Library of Congress adds 25 recordings showcasing the "range and diversity of American recorded sound heritage."

"Dream Melody Intermezzo: Naughty Marietta" (single), Victor Herbert and His Orchestra (1911)
Standing Rock Preservation Recordings, George Herzog and Members of the Yanktoni Tribe (1928)
"Lamento Borincano" (single), Canario y Su Grupo (1930)
"Sitting on Top of the World" (single), Mississippi Sheiks (1930)
The Complete Beethoven Piano Sonatas, Artur Schnabel (1932-35)
"If I Didn't Care" (single), The Ink Spots (1939)
Proceedings of the United Nations Conference on International Organization (Apr. 25-June 26, 1945)
Folk Songs of the Hills, Merle Travis (1946)
"How I Got Over" (single), Clara Ward and the Ward Singers (1950)
"(We're Gonna) Rock Around the Clock" (single), Bill Haley and His Comets (1954)
Calypso, Harry Belafonte (1956)
"I Left My Heart in San Francisco" (single), Tony Bennett (1962)

"My Girl" (single), The Temptations (1964)
King Biscuit Time (radio show), Sonny Boy Williamson II and others (1965)
The Sound of Music, film soundtrack (1965)
"Alice's Restaurant Massacree" (single), Arlo Guthrie (1967)
New Sounds in Electronic Music, Steve Reich, Richard Maxfield, Pauline Oliveros (1967)
An Evening with Groucho, Groucho Marx (1972)
Rumours, Fleetwood Mac (1977)
"Le Freak" (single), Chic (1978)
"The Gambler" (single), Kenny Rogers (1978)
"Footloose" (single), Kenny Loggins (1984)
Raising Hell, Run-DMC (1986)
"Rhythm Is Gonna Get You" (single), Gloria Estefan and the Miami Sound Machine (1987)
Yo-Yo Ma Premieres: Concertos for Violoncello and Orchestra (1996)

U.S. Commercial Radio Stations by Format, 2008-18

Source: Inside Radio (www.insideradio.com)

(as of July 2018; ranked by 2018 numbers)

Primary format	2008	2009	2010	2011	2012	2013	2014	2015	2016	2017	2018
1. Country	2,018	1,995	1,997	1,987	2,020	2,042	2,053	2,112	2,132	2,121	2,143
2. News/Talk	1,365	1,416	1,437	1,455	1,503	1,453	1,409	1,360	1,350	1,330	1,296
3. Classic Hits	524	582	637	657	657	678	754	805	859	965	1,001
4. Spanish	799	803	806	818	816	835	844	862	872	858	865
5. Sports	595	634	665	670	692	740	788	788	776	752	726
6. Top 40	472	484	495	523	559	573	577	579	585	594	595
7. Adult Contemporary	670	626	634	607	597	605	597	609	606	592	581
8. Classic Rock	474	477	481	477	477	486	486	486	482	519	522
9. Hot Adult Contemporary	373	409	417	435	420	428	465	462	462	451	452
10. Religion (Teaching, Variety)	299	324	322	332	342	336	324	318	322	332	351
11. Oldies	708	649	637	628	597	566	476	413	361	293	295
12. Rock	287	298	294	301	295	299	302	304	309	291	285
13. Black Gospel	244	242	235	225	214	212	211	218	211	206	198
14. Contemporary Christian	136	162	166	166	171	172	157	168	171	193	172
15. Urban Adult Contemporary	161	162	159	155	152	158	167	166	162	170	170
Total stations	**11,095**	**11,083**	**11,112**	**11,094**	**11,170**	**11,165**	**11,170**	**11,126**	**11,168**	**11,207**	**11,160**

Note: Totals include stations that are changing or did not report format, as well as formats not listed here.

Top-Selling Albums of All Time

Source: Recording Industry Assn. of America (RIAA)

Sales figures represent RIAA multi-platinum certifications; albums ranked by latest sales certification. As of Aug. 22, 2018.

Rank	Title, artist	Unit sales (mil)	Rank	Title, artist	Unit sales (mil)
1.	*Their Greatest Hits (1971-1975)*, Eagles	38.0	15.	*Boston*, Boston	17.0
2.	*Thriller*, Michael Jackson	33.0	16.	*Greatest Hits*, Elton John	17.0
3.	*Hotel California*, Eagles	26.0	17.	*No Fences*, Garth Brooks	17.0
4.	*Greatest Hits Volume I & Volume II*, Billy Joel	23.0	18.	*The Beatles 1967-1970*, The Beatles	17.0
5.	*Led Zeppelin IV*, Led Zeppelin	23.0	19.	*Jagged Little Pill*, Alanis Morissette	16.0
6.	*The Wall*, Pink Floyd	23.0	20.	*Saturday Night Fever* (soundtrack), Bee Gees	16.0
7.	*Back in Black*, AC/DC	22.0	21.	*Physical Graffiti*, Led Zeppelin	16.0
8.	*Double Live*, Garth Brooks	21.0	22.	*Metallica*, Metallica	16.0
9.	*Cracked Rear View*, Hootie & the Blowfish	21.0	23.	*Legend*, Bob Marley and the Wailers	15.0
10.	*Rumours*, Fleetwood Mac	20.0	24.	*Born in the U.S.A.*, Bruce Springsteen	15.0
11.	*Come on Over*, Shania Twain	20.0	25.	*Greatest Hits*, Journey	15.0
12.	*The Beatles*, The Beatles	19.0	26.	*Dark Side of the Moon*, Pink Floyd	15.0
13.	*Appetite for Destruction*, Guns N' Roses	18.0	27.	*Supernatural*, Santana	15.0
14.	*The Bodyguard* (soundtrack), Whitney Houston	18.0	28.	*The Beatles 1962-1966*, The Beatles	15.0

Top Artists by Digital Singles

Source: Recording Industry Assn. of America (RIAA)

Units represent digital singles certified as sold, including streaming-equivalent, as of Aug. 22, 2018.

Artist	Units (mil)	Artist	Units (mil)	Artist	Units (mil)	Artist	Units (mil)
Drake	142.0	Luke Bryan	43.5	Nicki Minaj	29.5	Imagine Dragons	25.0
Rihanna	125.0	Flo Rida	43.0	Linkin Park	29.5	Fall Out Boy	24.5
Taylor Swift	120.0	The Weeknd	42.0	Wiz Khalifa	29.0	The Black Eyed Peas	24.0
Eminem	107.5	Kendrick Lamar	41.0	Jason Aldean	28.5	Jay-Z	23.0
Katy Perry	98.0	Post Malone	34.0	Jason Derulo	27.0	DJ Khaled	23.0
Justin Bieber	69.5	Florida Georgia Line	34.0	Meghan Trainor	26.5	Future	22.5
Kanye West	64.0	Lil Wayne	32.0	Blake Shelton	26.0	Macklemore & Ryan Lewis	22.5
Lady Gaga	61.0	Adele	31.5	Beyoncé	26.0	Zac Brown Band	22.0
Bruno Mars	54.5	Twenty One Pilots	31.5	Maroon 5	25.5	Queen	21.5
Chris Brown	50.0	Ariana Grande	30.5	Sam Smith	25.5	Big Sean	21.5
Ed Sheeran	45.5	Carrie Underwood	30.5	Miley Cyrus	25.0		

Most Pirated Artists, 2017

Source: Excipio

(ranked by number of P2P [peer-to-peer] transactions worldwide)

Rank	Artist	Total transactions	Rank	Artist	Total transactions
1.	Drake	21,619,030	6.	Major Lazer	14,116,949
2.	Ed Sheeran	19,763,486	7.	Pink Floyd	13,647,670
3.	Kendrick Lamar	16,973,060	8.	Coldplay	12,312,742
4.	Metallica	16,325,650	9.	Armin van Buuren	11,939,592
5.	The Weeknd	14,390,530	10.	Adele	11,641,671

Multi-Platinum Awards for Recorded Music, 2017-18

Source: Recording Industry Assn. of America (RIAA)

To be certified platinum, an **album** must sell 1 mil units (LPs, CDs, or digital) with a manufacturer's dollar volume of at least $2 mil based on one-third of the suggested retail list price for each copy sold. To achieve multi-platinum status, an album must reach minimum total sales of at least 2 mil units with a manufacturer's dollar volume of at least $4 mil based on one-third of the list price. RIAA began including streaming in their award formulas in 2017; 1,500 streams count as the equivalent of ten track sales or one album sale. **Digital singles** must sell 2 mil to achieve a multi-platinum award. For digital singles award formulas, 150 streams equal one download sold.

Awards listed here are for albums and digital singles (released Sept. 2016-Aug. 2018) that were certified Sept. 2017-Aug. 2018. Number in parentheses represents millions sold. Alphabetized by artist name.

Albums

DAMN. Kendrick Lamar (3)
Beerbongs & Bentleys, Post Malone (2)
Stoney, Post Malone (3)
÷, Ed Sheeran (3)
Reputation, Taylor Swift (3)
Moana soundtrack, various artists (2)
Trolls soundtrack, various artist (2)

Digital Singles

"Drowning" (3), A Boogie Wit Da Hoodie feat. Kodak Black
"Plain Jane" (2), A$AP Ferg
"Rolex" (2), Ayo & Teo
"Bounce Back" (4), Big Sean
"Prblms" (2), 6LACK
"Do Re Mi" (2), Blackbear
"Look Alive" (2), BlocBoy JB feat. Drake
"Heaven" (2), Kane Brown
"What Ifs" (3), Kane Brown feat. Lauren Alaina
"Never Be the Same" (2), Camila Cabello
"Havana" (5), Camila Cabello feat. Young Thug
"Bartier Cardi" (2), "Bodak Yellow" (6), Cardi B
"I Like It" (2), Cardi B feat. J. Balvin & Bad Bunny
"Something Just Like This" (4), The Chainsmokers & Coldplay
"Redbone" (4), Childish Gambino
"Hurricane" (2), Luke Combs
"How Far I'll Go" (3), Auli'i Cravalho
"Swalla" (2), Jason Derulo
"I'm the One" (6), DJ Khaled feat. Justin Bieber, Quavo, Chance the Rapper & Lil Wayne
"Wild Thoughts" (4), DJ Khaled feat. Rihanna & Bryson Tiller
"Fake Love" (4), "God's Plan" (8), "Nice for What" (3), "Passionfruit" (3), "Portland" (2), Drake
"Despacito" (10), Luis Fonsi & Daddy Yankee

"Unforgettable" (5), French Montana feat. Swae Lee
"Mask Off" (5), Future
"No Limit" (3), G-Eazy feat. A$AP Rocky & Cardi B
"Crew" (2), GoldLink feat. Brent Faiyaz & Shy Glizzy
"I Get the Bag" (3), Gucci Mane feat. Migos
"Bad at Love" (3), "Now or Never" (2), Halsey
"Feels" (2), "Slide" (2), Calvin Harris
"Slow Hands" (3), Niall Horan
"Body Like a Back Road" (5), Sam Hunt
"Believer" (5), Imagine Dragons
"Mi Gente" (2), J Balvin & Willy William
"You're Welcome" (2), Dwayne Johnson
"Young Dumb & Broke" (3), Khalid
"iSpy" (4), Kyle feat. Lil Yachty
"DNA." (3), "HUMBLE." (7), Kendrick Lamar
"LOYALTY." (2), Kendrick Lamar feat. Rihanna
"All the Stars" (2), Kendrick Lamar and SZA
"LOVE." (4), Kendrick Lamar feat. Zacari
"Freaky Friday" (2), Lil Dicky feat. Chris Brown
"Gucci Gang" (3), Lil Pump
"XO Tour Llif3" (6), Lil Uzi Vert
"New Rules" (3), Dua Lipa
"1-800-273-8255" (4), Logic
"Sorry Not Sorry" (4), Demi Lovato
"Bad Things" (2), Machine Gun Kelly & Camila Cabello
"Boo'd Up" (2), Ella Mai
"Cold Water" (4), Major Lazer feat. Justin Bieber & MØ
"Don't Wanna Know" (2), Maroon 5 feat. Kendrick Lamar
"What Lovers Do" (2), Maroon 5 feat. SZA
"That's What I Like" (7), "24K Magic" (5), Bruno Mars
"Finesse" (3), Bruno Mars & Cardi B
"Silence" (2), Marshmello feat. Khalid

"There's Nothing Holdin' Me Back" (3), Shawn Mendes
"Issues" (3), Julia Michaels
"Motorsport" (3), "Stir Fry" (2), "Walk It Talk It" (2), Migos
"Let You Down" (3), NF
"Probablemente" (5), Christian Nodal
"Ric Flair Drip" (2), Offset & Metro Boomin
"Strip That Down" (3), Liam Payne
"Magnolia" (2), Playboi Carti
"Feel It Still" (3), Portugal. The Man
"Congratulations" (8), "I Fall Apart" (3), "Psycho" (3), "Rockstar" (7), Post Malone
"Attention" (3), Charlie Puth
"Meant to Be" (3), Bebe Rexha feat. Florida Georgia Line
"Plug Walk" (3), Rich the Kid
"King's Dead" (2), Jay Rock feat. Kendrick Lamar, Future, James Blake
"Imitadora" (7), Romeo Santos
"Butterfly Effect" (2), "Goosebumps" (4), Travis Scott
"Castle on the Hill" (2), "Perfect" (4), "Shape of You" (8), Ed Sheeran
"Too Good at Goodbyes" (4), Sam Smith
"Sign of the Times" (2), Harry Styles
"Look What You Made Me Do" (4), "...Ready for It" (2), Taylor Swift
"Love Galore" (2), "The Weekend" (2), SZA
"I Feel It Coming" (3), The Weeknd
"Bank Account" (3), 21 Savage
"It's a Vibe" (2), 2 Chainz
"Jocelyn Flores" (2), "Love" (2), "Sad!" (2), XXXTentacion
"Rake It Up" (2), Yo Gotti feat. Nicki Minaj
"In Case You Didn't Know" (3), Brett Young
"I Don't Wanna Live Forever" (4), Zayn & Taylor Swift

Top-Grossing North American Concert Tours, 1985-2017
Source: Pollstar

Rank Artist (year)	Total gross[1]	Cities/ shows	Rank Artist (year)	Total gross[1]	Cities/ shows
1. Taylor Swift (2015)	$199.4	41/62	14. The Rolling Stones (1994)	$121.2	43/60
2. U2 (2017)	176.1	26/30	15. Kenny Chesney (2015)	116.4	56/59
3. Beyoncé (2016)	169.4	30/32	16. Bruce Springsteen & The E Street		
4. The Rolling Stones (2005)	162.0	38/42	Band (2003)	115.9	30/47
5. U2 (2011)	156.0	21/25	17. Garth Brooks (2015)	114.9	23/120
6. U2 (2005)	138.9	43/78	18. Taylor Swift (2013)	112.7	47/66
7. The Rolling Stones (2006)	138.5	35/39	19. Bruno Mars (2017)	112.4	50/67
8. Madonna (2012)	133.7	31/45	20. Metallica (2017)	110.3	24/26
9. The Police (2007)	133.2	41/54	21. The Rolling Stones (2015)	109.7	14/14
10. Guns N' Roses (2016)	130.8	24/31	22. U2 (2001)	109.7	56/80
11. One Direction (2014)	127.2	21/31	23. Bon Jovi (2010)	108.2	38/51
12. U2 (2009)	123.0	16/20	24. Bon Jovi (2013)	107.3	58/62
13. Bruce Springsteen & The E Street			25. Madonna (2008)	105.3	19/30
Band (2016)	122.4	42/48			

(1) In millions. Not adjusted for inflation.

Music Sales by Format and Value, 2000-17
Source: Recording Industry Assn. of America
(in millions, net after returns)

	2000	2005	2010	2012	2013	2014	2015	2016	2017	% change, 2016-17
Physical units shipped	1,079.2	748.8	267.7	212.7	188.8	161.3	141.1	115.5	105.6	−8.6%
Dollar value	$14,323.7	11,195.0	3,663.7	2,772.3	2,463.8	2,245.6	1,981.9	1,552.3	1,495.5	−3.7
Compact discs (CDs)	942.5	705.4	253.0	198.2	173.8	142.5	119.9	97.6	87.6	−10.3
Dollar value	$13,214.5	10,520.2	3,389.4	2,485.6	2,140.9	1,829.1	1,482.5	1,130.8	1,057.3	−6.5
LPs/EPs	2.2	1.0	4.2	6.9	9.4	13.1	16.9	14.8	15.6	5.3
Dollar value	$27.7	14.2	88.9	160.7	210.7	313.0	414.5	355.4	388.5	9.3
Music videos	18.2	33.8	9.1	6.0	4.8	4.1	3.2	2.5	1.9	−24.8
Dollar value	$281.9	602.2	177.6	116.6	106.3	90.9	71.2	56.9	38.6	−32.2
Other physical[1]	116.3	8.6	1.4	1.6	0.8	1.6	1.2	0.7	0.6	−4.9
Dollar value	$799.6	58.4	7.8	9.4	5.9	12.6	13.7	9.2	11.0	19.7
Digital formats: number downloaded	—	553.1	1,471.8	1,590.7	1,502.2	1,319.6	1,131.1	984.5	636.9	−35.3
Digital formats: dollar value	—	$925.3	2,699.8	3,019.8	2,926.3	2,602.8	2,349.8	1,767.0	1,330.7	−24.7
Albums downloaded	—	13.6	85.8	116.7	118.0	117.5	109.3	85.1	66.4	−22.0
Dollar value	—	$135.7	872.4	1,204.8	1,232.1	1,150.0	1,090.0	818.8	623.7	−23.8
Singles downloaded	—	366.9	1,177.4	1,392.2	1,332.8	1,167.1	994.5	743.0	553.5	−25.5
Dollar value	—	$363.3	1,336.4	1,623.6	1,573.4	1,370.3	1,195.1	872.9	650.8	−25.4
Ringtones & ringbacks	—	170.0	188.5	69.3	39.3	26.6	21.9	22.6	14.3	−37.0
Dollar value	—	$421.6	448.0	166.9	97.9	66.3	54.6	51.1	34.2	−33.0
Other digital downloads[2]	—	2.6	20.1	12.5	12.1	8.4	5.4	3.9	2.7	−30.1
Dollar value	—	$4.7	43.0	24.5	22.9	16.2	10.1	24.2	22.0	−9.0
Other digital licensing	—	—	—	—	—	—	—	17.1	16.9	−1.5
Subscription & streaming dollar value	—	$169.60	461.6	1,032.8	1,454.6	1,839.1	2,334.1	3,962.1	5,664.5	43.0
Subscription formats[3]	—	1.3	1.5	3.4	6.2	7.7	10.8	22.7	35.3	55.5
Dollar value	—	$149.2	212.4	399.9	643.3	778.8	1,158.9	2,244.2	3,500.5	56.0
Limited tier paid subscriptions	—	—	—	—	—	—	—	263.4	591.6	124.6
SoundExchange distribution[4]	—	$20.4	249.2	462.0	590.4	773.4	802.6	883.9	652.0	−26.2
On-demand streaming (ad supported)[5]	—	—	—	170.9	220.9	286.9	372.7	489.4	658.6	34.6
Other ad-supported streaming[6]	—	—	—	—	—	—	—	81.3	261.8	222.2
Synchronization royalties[7]	—	—	$188.7	190.6	189.7	189.7	202.9	204.4	232.1	13.5
Total physical and digital[8]	1,079.2	1,301.9	1,739.5	1,803.4	1,691.0	1,480.9	1,272.3	970.1	742.5	−23.5
Total value physical and digital	$14,323.7	12,289.9	7,013.8	7,015.5	7,034.4	6,877.2	6,868.7	7,485.7	8,722.8	16.5

— = Not available or not applicable. (1) Includes CD singles, cassettes, vinyl singles, DVD audio, and SACD. (2) Includes kiosk and music video downloads. (3) Streaming, tethered, and other paid subscription services not operating under statutory licenses. Subscription volume is annual average number of subscriptions (excluding limited tier). (4) Estimated payments to performers/copyright holders for digital radio services under statutory licenses. (5) Ad-supported audio and music video services not operating under statutory licenses. (6) Revenues from services paid directly that are not distributed by SoundExchange or included in other streaming categories. (7) Includes fees and royalties from sound recordings used in other media. (8) Units total includes physical and downloaded albums and singles but not streaming, subscriptions, or royalties.

Top Basic Cable TV Networks, 2017
Source: Kagan, the media research group within S&P Global Market Intelligence

Rank	Network (year began)	Subscribers (mil)	Rank	Network (year began)	Subscribers (mil)
1.	C-SPAN (1979)	96.1	11.	HSN (1982)	90.9
2.	Food Network (1993)	93.1	12.	AMC (1984)	90.8
3.	TBS (1976)	92.0	13.	HLN (1982)	90.8
4.	CNN (1980)	91.9	14.	TNT (1988)	90.7
5.	USA (1980)	91.8	15.	FX (1994)	90.4
6.	Discovery Channel (1985)	91.5	16.	Lifetime Television (1994)	90.4
7.	Disney Channel (1983)	91.4	17.	A&E (1994)	90.4
8.	HGTV (1994)	91.2	18.	TLC (1980)	89.9
9.	Cartoon Network (1992)/Adult Swim (2001)	91.1	19.	National Geographic Channel (2001)	89.9
10.	History (1995)	91.1	20.	E! (1987)	89.8

U.S. Television Owners, 2018
Source: Nielsen Media Research, July 2018

Of the 119.6 mil U.S. households that owned at least one TV in 2018—

83.3% had 2 or more TV sets	0.8% had a VCR	80.9% received basic cable
30.7% had 4 or more TV sets	70.3% had a DVD player	46.6% received premium cable
	54.0% had a DVR	

U.S. Households With Cable Television, 1980-2018
Source: Nielsen Media Research

Year[1]	Subscribers[2] (mil)	As % of households with TVs	Year[1]	Subscribers[2] (mil)	As % of households with TVs	Year[1]	Subscribers[2] (mil)	As % of households with TVs
1980	17.7	22.6%	2001	81.5	79.8%	2010	104.1	90.6%
1985	38.7	45.3	2002	87.8	83.8	2011	104.8	90.4
1990	53.9	58.6	2003	88.4	82.9	2012	103.6	90.3
1990	62.1	65.1	2004	92.4	85.3	2013	103.3	90.5
1996	63.6	66.3	2005	94.0	85.7	2014	103.7	89.6
1997	65.1	67.2	2006	95.0	86.2	2015	100.2	86.0
1998	65.9	67.2	2007	94.5	83.8	2016	97.8	84.0
1999	76.4	76.9	2008	99.7	88.2	2017	96.0	81.0
2000	78.6	77.9	2009	103.0	89.7	2018	96.7	80.9

(1) After 1998, figures include wired-cable households as well as households that receive TV programming via alternate delivery systems (including satellite receivers, SMATV, and MMDS). (2) Households that subscribe to basic cable service.

Selected Reality TV Show Winners, 2000-18
Numbers in parentheses represent the season, edition, or cycle of the show. As of Sept. 2018.

The Amazing Race. Debuted Aug. 2001 on CBS. Rob Frisbee & Brennan Swain (1); Chris Luca & Alex Boylan (2); Flo Pesenti & Zach Behr (3); Reichen Lehmkuhl & Chip Arndt (4); Chip & Kim McAllister (5); Freddy Holliday & Kendra Bentley (6); Uchenna & Joyce Agu (7); The Linz Family (8); B. J. Averell & Tyler Mac-Niven (9); Tyler Denk & James Branaman (10); Eric Sanchez & Danielle Turner (All Stars, 11); TK Erwin & Rachel Morales (12); Nick & Starr Spangler (13); Tammy & Victor Jih (14); Meghan Rickey & Cheyne Whitney (15); Dan & Jordan Pious (16); Natalie Strand & Katherine Chang (17); LaKisha & Jennifer Hoffman (18); Ernie Halvorsen & Cindy Chiang (19); Rachel Brown & Dave Brown Jr. (20); Josh Kilmer-Purcell & Brent Ridge (21); Bates & Anthony Battaglia (22); Jason Case & Amy Diaz (23); David & Connor O'Leary (All Stars, 24); Amy DeJong & Maya Warren (25); Laura Pierson & Tyler Adams (26); Kelsey Gerckens & Joey Buttitta (27); Dana Borriello & Matt Steffanina (28); Brooke Camhi & Scott Flanary (29); Jessica Graf & Cody Nickson (30).

American Idol. Debuted July 2002 on FOX. Kelly Clarkson (1); Ruben Studdard (2); Fantasia Barrino (3); Carrie Underwood (4); Taylor Hicks (5); Jordin Sparks (6); David Cook (7); Kris Allen (8); Lee DeWyze (9); Scotty McCreery (10); Phillip Phillips (11); Candice Glover (12); Caleb Johnson (13); Nick Fradiani (14); Trent Harmon (15); Maddie Poppe (16).

America's Got Talent. Debuted June 2006 on NBC. Bianca Ryan (1); Terry Fator (2); Neil E. Boyd (3); Kevin Skinner (4); Michael Grimm (5); Landau Eugene Murphy Jr. (6); Olate Dogs (7); Kenichi Ebina (8); Mat Franco (9); Paul Zerdin (10); Grace VanderWaal (11); Darci Lynne Farmer (12); Shin Lim (13).

America's Next Top Model. Debuted May 2003 on UPN. Adrianne Curry (1); Yoanna House (2); Eva Pigford (3); Naima Mora (4); Nicole Linkletter (5); Danielle Evans (6); CariDee English (7); Jaslene Gonzalez (8); Saleisha Stowers (9); Whitney Thompson (10); McKey Sullivan (11); Teyona Anderson (12); Nicole Fox (13); Krista White (14); Ann Ward (15); Brittani Kline (16); D'Amato (17); Sophie Sumner (18); Laura James (19); Jourdan Miller (20); Keith Carlos (21); Nyle DiMarco (22); India Gants (23); Kyla Coleman (24).

The Apprentice. Debuted Jan. 2004 on NBC. Bill Rancic (1); Kelly Perdew (2); Kendra Todd (3); Randal Pinkett (4); Sean Yazbeck (5); Stefani Schaeffer (6); Brandy Kuentzel (7). *Celebrity Apprentice:* Piers Morgan (1); Joan Rivers (2); Bret Michaels (3); John Rich (4); Arsenio Hall (5); Trace Adkins (All Stars, 6); Leeza Gibbons (7); Matt Iseman (8).

The Bachelor. Debuted Mar. 2002 on ABC. Alex Michel chose Amanda Marsh (1); Aaron Buerge, Helene Eksterowicz (2); Andrew Firestone, Jen Schefft (3); Bob Guiney, Estella Gardinier (4); Jesse Palmer, Jessica Bowlin (5); Byron Velvick, Mary Delgado (6); Charlie O'Connell, Sarah Brice (7); Travis Stork, Sarah Stone (8); Lorenzo Borghese, Jennifer Wilson (9); Andy Baldwin, Tessa Horst (10); Brad Womack, no one (11); Matt Grant, Shayne Lamas (12); Jason Mesnick, Melissa Rycroft (13); Jake Pavelka, Vienna Girardi (14); Brad Womack, Emily Maynard (15); Ben Flajnik, Courtney Robertson (16); Sean Lowe, Catherine Giudici (17); Juan Pablo Galavis, Nikki Ferrell (18); Chris Soules, Whitney Bischoff (19); Ben Higgins, Lauren Bushnell (20); Nick Viall, Vanessa Grimaldi (21); Arie Luyendyk Jr., Becca Kufrin (22).

The Bachelorette. Debuted Jan. 2003 on ABC. Trista Rehn chose Ryan Sutter (1); Meredith Phillips, Ian McKee (2); Jen Schefft, Jerry Ferris (3); DeAnna Pappas, Jesse Csincsak (4); Jillian Harris, Ed Swiderski (5); Ali Fedotowsky, Roberto Martinez (6); Ashley Hebert, J. P. Rosenbaum (7); Emily Maynard, Jef Holm (8); Desiree Hartsock, Chris Siegfried (9); Andi Dorfman, Josh Murray (10); Kaitlyn Bristowe, Shawn Booth (11); JoJo Fletcher, Jordan Rodgers (12); Rachel Lindsay, Bryan Abasolo (13); Becca Kufrin, Garrett Yrigoyen (14).

Big Brother. Debuted July 2000 on CBS. Eddie McGee (1); Will Kirby (2); Lisa Donahue (3); Jun Song (4); Drew Daniel (5); Maggie Ausburn (6); Mike Malinto (7); Dick Donato (8); Adam Jasinski (9); Dan Gheesling (10); Jordan Lloyd (11); Hayden Moss (12); Rachel Reilly (13); Ian Terry (14); Andy Herren (15);

Derrick Levasseur (16); Steve Moses (17); Nicole Franzel (18); Josh Martinez (19); Kaycee Clark (20).

Dancing With the Stars. Debuted June 2005 on ABC. Kelly Monaco & Alex Mazo (1); Drew Lachey & Cheryl Burke (2); Emmitt Smith & Cheryl Burke (3); Apolo Anton Ohno & Julianne Hough (4); Helio Castroneves & Julianne Hough (5); Kristi Yamaguchi & Mark Ballas (6); Brooke Burke & Derek Hough (7); Shawn Johnson & Mark Ballas (8); Donny Osmond & Kym Johnson (9); Nicole Scherzinger & Derek Hough (10); Jennifer Grey & Derek Hough (11); Hines Ward & Kym Johnson (12); J.R. Martinez & Karina Smirnoff (13); Donald Driver & Peta Murgatroyd (14); Melissa Rycroft & Tony Dovolani (All Stars, 15); Kellie Pickler & Derek Hough (16); Amber Riley & Derek Hough (17); Meryl Davis & Maksim Chmerkovskiy (18); Alfonso Ribeiro & Witney Carson (19); Rumer Willis & Val Chmerkovskiy (20); Bindi Irwin & Derek Hough (21); Nyle DiMarco & Peta Murgatroyd (22); Laurie Hernandez & Val Chmerkovskiy (23); Rashad Jennings & Emma Slater (24); Jordan Fisher & Lindsay Arnold (25); Adam Rippon & Jenna Johnson (26).

Hell's Kitchen. Debuted Mar. 2005 on FOX. Michael Wray (1); Heather West (2); Rock Harper (3); Christina Machamer (4); Danny Veltri (5); Dave Levey (6); Holli Ugalde (7); Nona Sivley (8); Paul Niedermann (9); Christina Wilson (10); Ja'Nel Witt (11); Scott Commings (12); La Tasha McCutchen (13); Meghan Gill (14); Ariel Malone (15); Kimberly Ann Ryan (16); Michelle Tribble (All Stars, 17).

Project Runway. Debuted Dec. 2004 on Bravo. Jay McCarroll (1); Chloe Dao (2); Jeffrey Sebelia (3); Christian Siriano (4); Leanne Marshall (5); Irina Shabayeva (6); Seth Aaron Henderson (7); Gretchen Jones (8); Anya Ayoung-Chee (9); Dmitry Sholokhov (10); Michelle Lesniak Franklin (11); Dom Streater (12); Sean Kelly (13); Ashley Nell Tipton (14); Erin Robertson (15); Kentaro Kameyama (16). *All-Stars:* Mondo Guerra (1); Anthony Ryan Auld (2); Seth Aaron Henderson (3); Dmitry Sholokhov (4); Dom Streater (5); Anthony Williams (6).

RuPaul's Drag Race. Debuted Feb. 2009 on Logo. Bebe Zahara Benet (1); Tyra Sanchez (2); Raja (3); Sharon Needles (4); Jinkx Monsoon (5); Bianca Del Rio (6); Violet Chachki (7); Bob the Drag Queen (8); Sasha Velour (9); Aquaria (10).

So You Think You Can Dance. Debuted July 2005 on FOX. Nick Lazzarini (1); Benji Schwimmer (2); Sabra Johnson (3); Joshua Allen (4); Jeanine Mason (5); Russell Ferguson (6); Lauren Froderman (7); Melanie Moore (8); Eliana Girard & Chehon Wespi-Tschopp (9); DuShaunt "Fik-Shun" Stegall & Amy Yakima (10); Ricky Ubeda (11); Gaby Diaz (12); Leon "Kida" Burns (13); Lex Ishimoto (14); Hannahlei Cabanilla (15).

Survivor. Debuted May 2000 on CBS. Richard Hatch (1); Tina Wesson (2); Ethan Zohn (3); Vecepia Towery (4); Brian Heidik (5); Jenna Morasca (6); Sandra Diaz-Twine (7); Amber Brkich (8); Chris Daugherty (9); Tom Westman (10); Danni Boatwright (11); Aras Baskauskas (12); Yul Kwon (13); Earl Cole (14); Todd Herzog (15); Parvati Shallow (16); Robert Crowley (17); James "JT" Thomas (18); Natalie White (19); Sandra Diaz-Twine (20); Jud Birza (21); Rob Mariano (22); Sophie Clarke (23); Kim Spradlin (24); Denise Stapley (25); John Cochran (26); Tyson Apostol (27); Tony Vlachos (28); Natalie Anderson (29); Mike Holloway (30); Jeremy Collins (31); Michele Fitzgerald (32); Adam Klein (33); Sarah Lacina (34); Wendell Holland (35).

Top Chef. Debuted Mar. 2006 on Bravo. Harold Dieterle (1); Ilan Hall (2); Hung Huynh (3); Stephanie Izard (4); Hosea Rosenberg (5); Michael Voltaggio (6); Kevin Sbraga (7); Richard Blais (8); Paul Qui (9); Kristen Kish (10); Nicholas Elmi (11); Mei Lin (12); Jeremy Ford (13); Brooke Williamson (14); Joseph Flamm (15). *Top Chef Masters:* Rick Bayless (1); Marcus Samuelsson (2); Floyd Cardoz (3); Chris Cosentino (4); Douglas Keane (5).

The Voice. Debuted Apr. 2011 on NBC. Javier Colon (1); Jermaine Paul (2); Cassadee Pope (3); Danielle Bradbery (4); Tessanne Chin (5); Josh Kaufman (6); Craig Wayne Boyd (7); Sawyer Fredericks (8); Jordan Smith (9); Alisan Porter (10); Sundance Head (11); Chris Blue (12); Chloe Kohanski (13); Brynn Cartelli (14).

Average U.S. Television Viewing Time, 2017-18

Source: Nielsen Media Research; viewing time given in hours:minutes

Group	Age	Total per week	M-F 7-10 AM	M-F 10 AM-4 PM	M-Sun. 8-11 PM	M-F 11:30 PM-1 AM	Sat. 7 AM-1 PM	Sun. 1-7 PM
Men	18+	31:26	1:56	4:20	7:20	1:27	0:59	1:45
	18-24	12:30	0:35	1:41	2:48	0:42	0:20	0:43
	25-54	25:43	1:26	3:05	6:12	1:20	0:49	1:30
	55+	46:11	3:06	7:03	10:31	1:52	1:26	2:28
Women	18+	35:49	2:23	5:36	8:03	1:38	1:05	1:42
	18-24	14:07	0:43	2:11	3:08	0:45	0:23	0:42
	25-54	29:09	1:53	4:10	6:41	1:27	0:54	1:26
	55+	50:34	3:31	8:23	11:14	2:08	1:32	2:21
Children	2-11	16:36	1:06	2:30	3:26	0:33	0:45	0:58
Teens	12-17	11:05	0:29	1:08	2:42	0:31	0:23	0:40
All viewers[1]		29:39	1:54	4:21	6:45	1:20	0:57	1:33

Note: For viewing period Sept. 25, 2017-May 27, 2018. Includes DVR playback. (1) Ages 2+.

Highest-Rated Prime-Time Television Programs, 2017-18

Source: Nielsen Media Research

Data are for regularly scheduled network programs Sept. 25, 2017-May 23, 2018 (unless otherwise noted). Ranked by average audience percentages, or ratings, which are estimates of the percentage of all TV-owning households watching a particular program live or on DVR within seven days of broadcast. Audience share percentages are estimates of the percentage of those watching TV at a certain time that are tuned in to a particular program.

Rank	Program, network	Avg. audience	Audience share	Rank	Program, network	Avg. audience	Audience share
1.	The Big Bang Theory, CBS	11.3%	20.4%	26.	Dancing With the Stars: Athletes[3], ABC	6.1%	11.0%
2.	Roseanne, ABC	11.3	20.8	27.	S.W.A.T., CBS	6.0	11.8
3.	This Is Us, NBC	10.9	19.0	28.	Survivor[4], CBS	6.0	11.0
4.	NCIS, CBS	10.5	18.5	29.	American Idol[5]-Monday, ABC	5.8	10.1
5.	The Good Doctor, ABC	9.9	18.7	30.	Law and Order: SVU, NBC	5.8	10.3
6.	Young Sheldon, CBS	9.8	17.3	31.	Madam Secretary, CBS	5.8	11.8
7.	Bull, CBS	9.0	15.6	32.	Will & Grace, NBC	5.7	9.9
8.	Blue Bloods, CBS	8.4	16.8	33.	American Idol[5]-Sunday, ABC	5.6	10.1
9.	NCIS: New Orleans, CBS	8.0	15.3	34.	Code Black, CBS	5.5	10.9
10.	Grey's Anatomy, ABC	7.4	13.4	35.	Blacklist, NBC	5.4	9.8
11.	60 Minutes, CBS	7.2	13.0	36.	Wisdom of the Crowd, CBS	5.4	9.0
12.	Dancing With the Stars[1], ABC	7.2	12.1	37.	Ellen's Games of Games	5.3	9.2
13.	The Voice[2], NBC	7.2	12.4	38.	MacGyver, CBS	5.3	10.4
14.	Hawaii Five-0, CBS	6.9	13.3	39.	Scorpion, CBS	5.3	10.1
15.	The Voice[2]-Tuesday, NBC	6.9	12.2	40.	Designated Survivor, ABC	5.2	10.2
16.	Mom, CBS	6.8	12.1	41.	Station 19, ABC	5.2	9.5
17.	Chicago Med, NBC	6.7	13.1	42.	The Bachelor[6], ABC	5.1	8.8
18.	Chicago P.D., NBC	6.7	13.1	43.	Life in Pieces, CBS	5.1	9.2
19.	NCIS: Los Angeles, CBS	6.7	11.8	44.	Scandal, ABC	5.1	9.2
20.	911, FOX	6.5	11.6	45.	Empire, FOX	5.0	9.1
21.	The O.T., FOX	6.5	12.7	46.	The Brave, NBC	4.8	9.0
22.	Chicago Fire, NBC	6.4	12.4	47.	Kevin Can Wait, CBS	4.8	8.2
23.	Instinct, CBS	6.3	11.3	48.	The Middle, ABC	4.7	8.2
24.	Seal Team, CBS	6.3	11.1	49.	The Resident, FOX	4.7	8.3
25.	Criminal Minds, CBS	6.2	12.0	50.	Amazing Race[7], CBS	4.6	8.2

(1) Sept. 18-Nov. 21, 2017. (2) Sept. 25-Dec. 19, 2017. (3) Apr. 30-May 21, 2018. (4) Sept. 27-Dec. 20, 2017. (5) Mar. 11-May 21, 2018. (6) Jan. 1-Mar. 6, 2018. (7) Jan. 3-Feb. 21, 2018.

Highest-Rated Syndicated Programs, 2017-18

Source: Nielsen Media Research

Average audience percentages, or ratings, are estimates of the percentage of all TV-owning households watching a program live or on DVR within seven days of broadcast, Sept. 25, 2017-Aug. 14, 2018.

Rank	Program	Avg. audience	Rank	Program	Avg. audience
1.	Judge Judy	7.2%	14.	Modern Family (weekend)	2.6%
2.	Family Feud	6.6	15.	Wheel of Fortune (weekend)	2.4
3.	Jeopardy	6.3	16.	Hot Bench	2.3
4.	Litton's Weekend Adventure	6.0	17.	Modern Family	2.3
5.	Wheel of Fortune	6.0	18.	Live Olympic Coverage	2.3
6.	The Big Bang Theory	4.9	19.	Live With Kelly and Ryan	2.2
7.	Law & Order: Special Victims Unit (weekend)	3.5	20.	The Ellen DeGeneres Show	2.2
8.	Dateline	3.5	21.	Last Man Standing	1.9
9.	Family Feud (weekend)	3.4	22.	Access Hollywood (weekend)	1.9
10.	Dr. Phil Show	3.3	23.	Blue Bloods	1.9
11.	Inside Edition	3.0	24.	Relationship Court	1.8
12.	Entertainment Tonight	3.0	25.	Jeopardy (weekend)	1.8
13.	The Big Bang Theory (weekend)	3.0			

Highest-Rated Basic Cable Programs, 2017-18

Source: Nielsen Media Research

Data are for regularly scheduled basic cable programs Sept. 25, 2017-Aug. 14, 2018; excludes children's series, miniseries, movies, and news events. Average audience percentages, or ratings, are estimates of the percentage of all TV-owning households watching a program live or on DVR within seven days of broadcast.

Rank	Program, channel	Avg. audience	Rank	Program, channel	Avg. audience
1.	The Walking Dead, AMC	6.7%	17.	The Real Housewives of Beverly Hills, Bravo	2.1%
2.	Rick & Morty, Adult Swim	3.1	18.	Good Witch, Hallmark	2.1
3.	Yellowstone, Paramount	3.0	19.	Project Runway, Lifetime	2.1
4.	American Horror Story, FX	2.8	20.	The Real Housewives of Orange County, Bravo	2.0
5.	Fixer Upper, HGTV	2.7	21.	The Sinner, USA	2.0
6.	Major Crimes, TNT	2.7	22.	Love & Hip Hop Atlanta, VH1	2.0
7.	The Curse of Oak Island, History	2.6	23.	Rachel Maddow Show, MSNBC	2.0
8.	Gold Rush, Discovery	2.5	24.	American Crime Story: The Assassination of	
9.	Fear the Walking Dead, AMC	2.5		Gianni Versace, FX	2.0
10.	Vikings, History	2.3	25.	Jersey Shore: Family Vacation, MTV	1.9
11.	When Calls the Heart, Hallmark	2.3	26.	Tucker Carlson Tonight, Fox News Channel	1.9
12.	The Real Housewives of Atlanta, Bravo	2.2	27.	The Haves and the Have Nots, OWN	1.9
13.	The Alienist, TNT	2.2	28.	Jodi Arias: An American Murder Mystery,	
14.	Hannity, Fox News Channel	2.2		Investigation Discovery	1.9
15.	Talking Dead, AMC	2.2	29.	Love & Hip Hop Hollywood 4	1.8
16.	Better Call Saul, AMC	2.1	30.	Love & Hip Hop Hollywood 5	1.8

Highest-Rated Premium Cable Programs, 2017-18

Source: Nielsen Media Research

Average audience percentages, or ratings, are estimates of the percentage of all TV-owning households watching a program live or on DVR within seven days of broadcast, Sept. 25, 2017-Aug. 14, 2018.

Highest-Rated Series		Highest-Rated Movies	
Rank Program, channel	Avg. audience	Rank Program, channel	Avg. audience
1. Real Time With Bill Maher, HBO	1.7%	1. Murder on the Orient Express, HBO	0.6%
2. Shameless, Showtime	1.7	2. Justice League, HBO	0.5
3. Westworld, HBO	1.6	3. Office Christmas Party, Showtime	0.5
4. Last Week Tonight With John Oliver, HBO	1.6	4. Three Billboards Outside Ebbing, Missouri, HBO	0.4
5. Outlander, Starz	1.4	5. The Girl on the Train, Showtime	0.4
6. Homeland, Showtime	1.4	6. Wonder Woman, HBO	0.4
7. Ray Donovan, Showtime	1.4	7. Baby Driver, Showtime	0.4
8. Power, Starz	1.3	8. Kingsman: The Golden Circle, HBO	0.4
9. Sharp Objects, HBO	1.2	9. Patriots Day, Showtime	0.3
10. Ballers, HBO	1.2	10. Kong: Skull Island, HBO	0.3
11. Curb Your Enthusiasm, HBO	1.1	11. It, HBO	0.3
12. Billions, Showtime	1.1	12. John Wick: Chapter 2, HBO	0.3
13. The Deuce, HBO	0.9	13. American Made, HBO	0.3
14. The Chi, Showtime	0.8	14. Harry Potter and the Sorcerer's Stone,	
15. Silicon Valley, HBO	0.8	HBO	0.3
		15. Harry Potter and the Prisoner of Azkaban,	
		HBO	0.3

All-Time Most Watched Television Programs

Source: Nielsen Media Research, Jan. 1961-Aug. 2018

Estimates exclude unsponsored or joint network telecasts (e.g., presidential addresses) and programs under 30 minutes long. Ranked by number of TV-owning households tuned in to the program. (Rating is percentage of all TV-owning households tuned in.)

Rank	Program	Telecast date	Network	Rating	Avg. audience (thous.)
1.	Super Bowl XLIX	2/1/2015	NBC	48.1%	55,948
2.	Super Bowl 50	2/7/2016	CBS	47.1	54,775
3.	Super Bowl XLVIII	2/2/2014	FOX	47.1	54,585
4.	Super Bowl LI	2/5/2017	FOX	45.8	54,180
5.	Super Bowl XLVI	2/5/2012	NBC	47.0	53,910
6.	Super Bowl XLV	2/6/2011	FOX	46.1	53,435
7.	Super Bowl XLVII	2/3/2013	CBS	46.7	53,363
8.	Super Bowl LII	2/4/2018	NBC	43.5	52,017
9.	Super Bowl XLIV	2/7/2010	CBS	45.2	51,873
10.	Super Bowl XLVII Delay	2/3/2013	CBS	44.5	50,861
11.	M*A*S*H (last episode)	2/28/1983	CBS	60.2	50,150
12.	Super Bowl XLII	2/3/2008	FOX	43.2	48,721
13.	Super Bowl XLIII	2/1/2009	NBC	42.0	48,139
14.	Super Bowl XLI	2/4/2007	CBS	42.7	47,535
15.	Super Bowl XL	2/5/2006	ABC	41.6	45,869
16.	XVII Winter Olympics (Women's figure skating)	2/23/1994	CBS	48.5	45,690
17.	Super Bowl XXXIX	2/6/2005	FOX	41.1	45,080
18.	Super Bowl XXXVIII	2/1/2004	CBS	41.4	44,910
19.	Super Bowl XXX	1/28/1996	NBC	46.0	44,150
20.	Super Bowl XXXII	1/25/1998	NBC	44.5	43,630
21.	Super Bowl XXXIV	1/30/2000	ABC	43.3	43,620
22.	Super Bowl XXXVII	1/26/2003	ABC	40.7	43,430
23.	Super Bowl XXVIII	1/30/1994	NBC	45.5	42,860
24.	Super Bowl XXXVI	2/3/2002	FOX	40.4	42,660
25.	Cheers (last episode)	5/20/1993	NBC	45.5	42,360
26.	Super Bowl XXXI	1/26/1997	FOX	43.3	42,000
27.	Super Bowl XXVII	1/31/1993	NBC	45.1	41,990
28.	XVII Winter Olympics (Women's figure skating)	2/25/1994	CBS	44.1	41,540
29.	Super Bowl XX	1/26/1986	NBC	48.3	41,490
30.	Dallas ("Who Shot J.R.?" episode)	11/21/1980	CBS	53.3	41,470

Highest-Rated Television Programs by Season, 1950-2018

Source: Nielsen Media Research; regular series programs, Sept.-May season

Rating is percentage of all TV-owning households tuned in to the program. Data prior to 1988-89 exclude Alaska and Hawaii.

Season	Program	Rating	TV-owning households (thous.)	Season	Program	Rating	TV-owning households (thous.)
1950-51	Texaco Star Theatre	61.6%	10,320	1983-84	Dallas	25.7%	83,800
1951-52	Godfrey's Talent Scouts	53.8	15,300	1984-85	Dynasty	25.0	84,900
1952-53	I Love Lucy	67.3	20,400	1985-86	The Cosby Show	33.8	85,900
1953-54	I Love Lucy	58.8	26,000	1986-87	The Cosby Show	34.9	87,400
1954-55	I Love Lucy	49.3	30,700	1987-88	The Cosby Show	27.8	88,600
1955-56	$64,000 Question	47.5	34,900	1988-89	Roseanne	25.5	90,400
1956-57	I Love Lucy	43.7	38,900	1989-90	Roseanne	23.4	92,100
1957-58	Gunsmoke	43.1	41,920	1990-91	Cheers	21.6	93,100
1958-59	Gunsmoke	39.6	43,950	1991-92	60 Minutes	21.7	92,100
1959-60	Gunsmoke	40.3	45,750	1992-93	60 Minutes	21.6	93,100
1960-61	Gunsmoke	37.3	47,200	1993-94	Home Improvement	21.9	94,200
1961-62	Wagon Train	32.1	48,555	1994-95	Seinfeld	20.5	95,400
1962-63	Beverly Hillbillies	36.0	50,300	1995-96	E.R.	22.0	95,900
1963-64	Beverly Hillbillies	39.1	51,600	1996-97	E.R.	21.2	97,000
1964-65	Bonanza	36.3	52,700	1997-98	Seinfeld	22.0	98,000
1965-66	Bonanza	31.8	53,850	1998-99	E.R.	17.8	99,400
1966-67	Bonanza	29.1	55,130	1999-2000	Who Wants to Be a Millionaire	18.6	100,800
1967-68	The Andy Griffith Show	27.6	56,670	2000-01	Survivor II	17.4	102,200
1968-69	Rowan & Martin's Laugh-In	31.8	58,250	2001-02	Friends	15.3	105,500
1969-70	Rowan & Martin's Laugh-In	26.3	58,500	2002-03	CSI	16.3	106,700
1970-71	Marcus Welby, M.D.	29.6	60,100	2003-04	CSI	15.9	108,400
1971-72	All in the Family	34.0	62,100	2004-05	CSI	16.5	106,900
1972-73	All in the Family	33.3	64,800	2005-06	American Idol-Tuesday	17.6	110,200
1973-74	All in the Family	31.2	66,200	2006-07	American Idol-Wednesday	17.3	112,800
1974-75	All in the Family	30.2	68,500	2007-08	American Idol-Tuesday	15.5	113,050
1975-76	All in the Family	30.1	69,600	2008-09	American Idol-Wednesday	14.4	114,900
1976-77	Happy Days	31.5	71,200	2009-10	American Idol-Tuesday	13.7	114,900
1977-78	Laverne & Shirley	31.6	72,900	2010-11	American Idol-Wednesday	14.5	115,900
1978-79	Laverne & Shirley	30.5	74,500	2011-12	NCIS	12.3	114,700
1979-80	60 Minutes	28.2	76,300	2012-13	NCIS	13.5	114,200
1980-81	Dallas	31.2	79,900	2013-14	NCIS	12.6	115,800
1981-82	Dallas	28.4	81,500	2014-15	The Big Bang Theory	11.6	116,400
				2015-16	NCIS	12.8	116,400
1982-83	60 Minutes	25.5	83,300	2016-17	The Big Bang Theory	11.5	118,400
				2017-18	The Big Bang Theory	11.3	119,600

All-Time Highest-Rated Television Programs

Source: Nielsen Media Research, Jan. 1961-Aug. 2018

Estimates exclude unsponsored or joint network telecasts (e.g., presidential addresses) and programs under 30 minutes long. Ranked only by rating (percentage of all TV-owning households tuned in to the program). Average audience is number of TV-owning households tuned in.

Rank	Program	Telecast date	Network	Rating	Avg. audience (thous.)
1.	M*A*S*H (last episode)	2/28/1983	CBS	60.2%	50,150
2.	Dallas ("Who Shot J.R.?" episode)	11/21/1980	CBS	53.3	41,470
3.	Roots-Pt. 8	1/30/1977	ABC	51.1	36,380
4.	Super Bowl XVI	1/24/1982	CBS	49.1	40,020
5.	Super Bowl XVII	1/30/1983	NBC	48.6	40,480
6.	XVII Winter Olympics (Women's figure skating)	2/23/1994	CBS	48.5	45,690
7.	Super Bowl XX	1/26/1986	NBC	48.3	41,490
8.	Super Bowl XLIX	2/1/2015	NBC	48.1	55,948
9.	Gone With the Wind-Pt. 1	11/7/1976	NBC	47.7	33,960
10.	Gone With the Wind-Pt. 2	11/8/1976	NBC	47.4	33,750
11.	Super Bowl XII	1/15/1978	CBS	47.2	34,410
12.	Super Bowl XLVIII	2/2/2014	FOX	47.1	54,585
12.	Super Bowl XIII	1/21/1979	NBC	47.1	35,090
12.	Super Bowl 50	2/7/2016	CBS	47.1	54,775
15.	Super Bowl XLVI	2/5/2012	NBC	47.0	53,910
16.	Super Bowl XLVII	2/3/2013	CBS	46.7	53,363
17.	Bob Hope Christmas Show	1/15/1970	NBC	46.6	27,260
18.	Super Bowl XVIII	1/22/1984	CBS	46.4	38,880
18.	Super Bowl XIX	1/20/1985	ABC	46.4	39,390
20.	Super Bowl XIV	1/20/1980	CBS	46.3	35,330
21.	Super Bowl XLV	2/6/2011	FOX	46.1	53,435
22.	Super Bowl XXX	1/28/1996	NBC	46.0	44,150
22.	ABC Sunday Night Movie (*The Day After*)	11/20/1983	ABC	46.0	38,550
24.	Roots-Pt. 6	1/28/1977	ABC	45.9	32,680
24.	The Fugitive (last episode)	8/29/1967	ABC	45.9	25,700
26.	Super Bowl LI	2/5/2017	FOX	45.8	54,180
26.	Super Bowl XXI	1/25/1987	CBS	45.8	40,030
28.	Roots-Pt. 5	1/27/1977	ABC	45.7	32,540
29.	Super Bowl XXVIII	1/30/1994	NBC	45.5	42,860
30.	Cheers (last episode)	5/20/1993	NBC	45.5	42,360
31.	The Ed Sullivan Show (first live U.S. TV appearance of The Beatles)	2/9/1964	CBS	45.3	23,240

AWARDS — MEDALS — PRIZES

Alfred B. Nobel Prizes, 1901-2018

Alfred B. Nobel (1833-96) bequeathed $9 mil, the interest on which was to be distributed yearly to those judged to have most benefited humankind in chemistry, literature, promotion of peace, physics, and physiology or medicine. Prizes were first awarded in 1901. The prize in economics, funded by Sweden's central bank, was first awarded in 1969. Each prize is now worth 9 mil Swedish kronor (about $1.0 mil). If year is omitted, no award was given. The Royal Swedish Academy selects prize winners for chemistry, economics, and physics; the Nobel Assembly at Karolinska Institutet, physiology or medicine; the Swedish Academy, literature; and the Norwegian Nobel Committee, the peace prize. The 2018 Nobel Prizes were announced Oct. 1-8. Winners sharing a prize are generally listed in alphabetical order, except when the awarding body has given a larger proportion of a shared prize to one or more recipients.

Nobel Prizes, 2018

Chemistry: Frances H. Arnold, U.S., was awarded half the prize "for the directed evolution of enzymes" and George P. Smith, U.S., and Gregory P. Winter, UK, shared the other half "for the phage display of peptides and antibodies."

Economics: William D. Nordhaus, U.S., was awarded half the prize "for integrating climate change into long-run macroeconomic analysis," and Paul M. Romer, U.S., the other half "for integrating technological innovations into long-run macroeconomic analysis."

Literature: No award. The Swedish Academy announced it would name two laureates in 2019 as it regrouped in the wake of a wide-ranging crisis that included multiple resignations, accusations of sexual misconduct, financial mismanagement, and repeated leaks.

Medicine: James P. Allison, U.S. and Tasuku Honjo, Jpn., shared the prize for separate work on developing immunotherapy as a course of treatment for cancer.

Peace: Congolese surgeon Denis Mukwege and Nadia Murad, an Iraq-born Yazidi who survived sexual enslavement, were awarded the prize for working "to end the use of sexual violence as a weapon of war."

Physics: For "groundbreaking inventions in the field of laser physics," Arthur Ashkin, U.S., was awarded half the prize; Gérard Mourou, Fr., and Donna Strickland, Can., shared the other half.

Physics

1901 Wilhelm C. Röntgen, Ger.	**1958** Pavel Cherenkov, Il'ja Frank, Igor Y. Tamm, USSR	**1990** Jerome I. Friedman, Henry W. Kendall, U.S.; Richard E. Taylor, Can.
1902 Hendrik A. Lorentz, Pieter Zeeman, Neth.	**1959** Owen Chamberlain, Emilio G. Segre, U.S.	**1991** Pierre-Gilles de Gennes, Fr.
1903 Antoine Henri Becquerel, Pierre Curie, Fr.; Marie Curie, Pol.-Fr.	**1960** Donald A. Glaser, U.S.	**1992** Georges Charpak, Pol.-Fr.
1904 Lord Rayleigh (John W. Strutt), UK	**1961** Robert Hofstadter, U.S.; Rudolf L. Mossbauer, Ger.	**1993** Russell A. Hulse, Joseph H. Taylor, U.S.
1905 Philipp E. A. von Lenard, Ger.	**1962** Lev D. Landau, USSR	**1994** Bertram N. Brockhouse, Can.; Clifford G. Shull, U.S.
1906 Joseph J. Thomson, UK	**1963** Maria Goeppert-Mayer, Eugene P. Wigner, U.S.; J. Hans D. Jensen, Ger.	**1995** Martin Perl, Frederick Reines, U.S.
1907 Albert A. Michelson, U.S.		**1996** David M. Lee, Douglas D. Osheroff, Robert C. Richardson, U.S.
1908 Gabriel Lippmann, Fr.	**1964** Nicolay G. Basov, Aleksandr M. Prokhorov, USSR; Charles H. Townes, U.S.	**1997** Steven Chu, William D. Phillips, U.S.; Claude Cohen-Tannoudji, Fr.
1909 Carl F. Braun, Ger.; Guglielmo Marconi, Ital.		**1998** Robert B. Laughlin, U.S.; Horst L. Störmer, Ger.-U.S; Daniel C. Tsui, China-U.S.
1910 Johannes D. van der Waals, Neth.	**1965** Sin-Itiro Tomonaga, Jpn.; Julian S. Schwinger, Richard P. Feynman, U.S.	
1911 Wilhelm Wien, Ger.		**1999** Gerardus 't Hooft, Martinus J. G. Veltman, Neth.
1912 Nils G. Dalén, Swed.	**1966** Alfred Kastler, Fr.	
1913 Heike Kamerlingh Onnes, Neth.	**1967** Hans A. Bethe, U.S.	**2000** Jack S. Kilby, U.S.; Herbert Kroemer, Ger.-U.S.; Zhores I. Alferov, Russ.
1914 Max von Laue, Ger.	**1968** Luis W. Alvarez, U.S.	
1915 William H. Bragg, William L. Bragg, UK	**1969** Murray Gell-Mann, U.S.	**2001** Eric A. Cornell, Carl E. Wieman, U.S.; Wolfgang Ketterle, Ger.
1917 Charles G. Barkla, UK	**1970** Hannes Alfvén, Swed.; Louis Néel, Fr.	
1918 Max K. E. L. Planck, Ger.		**2002** Raymond Davis Jr., Riccardo Giacconi, U.S.; Masatoshi Koshiba, Jpn.
1919 Johannes Stark, Ger.	**1971** Dennis Gabor, UK	
1920 Charles E. Guillaume, Fr.-Switz.	**1972** John Bardeen, Leon N. Cooper, John R. Schrieffer, U.S.	**2003** Alexei A. Abrikosov, Vitaly L. Ginzburg, Russ.; Anthony J. Leggett, UK
1921 Albert Einstein, Ger.-U.S.		
1922 Niels Bohr, Den.	**1973** Brian D. Josephson, UK; Leo Esaki, Jpn.; Ivar Giaever, U.S.	
1923 Robert A. Millikan, U.S.		**2004** David J. Gross, H. David Politzer, Frank Wilczek, U.S.
1924 Karl M. G. Siegbahn, Swed.	**1974** Antony Hewish, Martin Ryle, UK	
1925 James Franck, Gustav Hertz, Ger.		**2005** Roy J. Glauber, John L. Hall, U.S.; Theodor W. Hänsch, Ger.
1926 Jean B. Perrin, Fr.	**1975** Aage Bohr, Den.; Ben Mottelson, U.S.-Den.; Leo James Rainwater, U.S.	
1927 Arthur H. Compton, U.S.; Charles T. R. Wilson, UK		**2006** John C. Mather, George F. Smoot, U.S.
1928 Owen W. Richardson, UK	**1976** Burton Richter, Samuel C. C. Ting, U.S.	
1929 Prince Louis-Victor de Broglie, Fr.		**2007** Albert Fert, Fr.; Peter Grünberg, Ger.
1930 Chandrasekhara V. Raman, India	**1977** Philip W. Anderson, John H. van Vleck, U.S.; Nevill F. Mott, UK	**2008** Yoichiro Nambu, U.S.; Makoto Kobayashi, Toshihide Maskawa, Jpn.
1932 Werner Heisenberg, Ger.		
1933 Paul A. M. Dirac, UK; Erwin Schrödinger, Austria	**1978** Pyotr Kapitsa, USSR; Arno Penzias, Robert Wilson, U.S.	**2009** Charles K. Kao, U.S.-UK; Willard S. Boyle, U.S.-Can.; George E. Smith, U.S.
1935 James Chadwick, UK	**1979** Sheldon L. Glashow, Steven Weinberg, U.S.; Abdus Salam, Pakistan	
1936 Carl D. Anderson, U.S.; Victor F. Hess, Austria		**2010** Andre Geim, Russ.-Neth.; Konstantin Novoselov, Russ.-UK
1937 Clinton J. Davisson, U.S.; George P. Thomson, UK	**1980** James W. Cronin, Val L. Fitch, U.S.	**2011** Saul Perlmutter, Adam G. Riess, U.S.; Brian P. Schmidt, Austral.-U.S.
1938 Enrico Fermi, Ital.-U.S.	**1981** Nicolaas Bloembergen, Arthur Schawlow, U.S.; Kai M. Siegbahn, Swed.	
1939 Ernest O. Lawrence, U.S.		**2012** Serge Haroche, Fr.; David J. Wineland, U.S.
1943 Otto Stern, U.S.	**1982** Kenneth G. Wilson, U.S.	
1944 Isidor Isaac Rabi, U.S.	**1983** Subramanyan Chandrasekhar, William A. Fowler, U.S.	**2013** François Englert, Belg.; Peter W. Higgs, UK
1945 Wolfgang Pauli, U.S.-Austria		
1946 Percy W. Bridgman, U.S.	**1984** Carlo Rubbia, Ital.; Simon van der Meer, Neth.	**2014** Isamu Akasaki, Hiroshi Amano, Jpn.; Shuji Nakamura, Jpn.-U.S.
1947 Edward V. Appleton, UK		
1948 Patrick M. S. Blackett, UK	**1985** Klaus von Klitzing, Ger.	**2015** Takaaki Kajita, Jpn.; Arthur B. McDonald, Can.
1949 Hideki Yukawa, Jpn.	**1986** Ernest Ruska, Gerd Binnig, Ger.; Heinrich Rohrer, Switz.	
1950 Cecil F. Powell, UK		**2016** David J. Thouless, UK-U.S.; F. Duncan M. Haldane, J. Michael Kosterlitz, UK-U.S.
1951 John D. Cockcroft, UK; Ernest T. S. Walton, Ire.	**1987** J. Georg Bednorz, Ger.; K. Alex Müller, Switz.	
1952 Felix Bloch, Edward M. Purcell, U.S.	**1988** Leon M. Lederman, Melvin Schwartz, Jack Steinberger, U.S.	**2017** Rainer Weiss, Ger.-U.S.; Barry C. Barish, Kip S. Thorne, U.S.
1953 Frits Zernike, Neth.		
1954 Max Born, UK; Walter Bothe, Ger.	**1989** Norman F. Ramsey, U.S.; Hans G. Dehmelt, Ger.-U.S.; Wolfgang Paul, Ger.	**2018** Arthur Ashkin, U.S.; Gérard Mourou, Fr.; Donna Strickland, Can.
1955 Polykarp Kusch, Willis E. Lamb, U.S.		
1956 John Bardeen, Walter H. Brattain, William Shockley, U.S.		
1957 Tsung-Dao Lee, Chen Ning Yang, U.S.-China		

Chemistry

1901	Jacobus H. van 't Hoff, Neth.	
1902	Emil Fischer, Ger.	
1903	Svante A. Arrhenius, Swed.	
1904	William Ramsay, UK	
1905	Adolf von Baeyer, Ger.	
1906	Henri Moissan, Fr.	
1907	Eduard Buchner, Ger.	
1908	Ernest Rutherford, UK	
1909	Wilhelm Ostwald, Ger.	
1910	Otto Wallach, Ger.	
1911	Marie Curie, Pol.-Fr.	
1912	Victor Grignard, Paul Sabatier, Fr.	
1913	Alfred Werner, Switz.	
1914	Theodore W. Richards, U.S.	
1915	Richard M. Willstätter, Ger.	
1918	Fritz Haber, Ger.	
1920	Walther H. Nernst, Ger.	
1921	Frederick Soddy, UK	
1922	Francis W. Aston, UK	
1923	Fritz Pregl, Austria	
1925	Richard A. Zsigmondy, Ger.	
1926	Theodor Svedberg, Swed.	
1927	Heinrich O. Wieland, Ger.	
1928	Adolf O. R. Windaus, Ger.	
1929	Arthur Harden, UK;	
	Hans von Euler-Chelpin, Swed.	
1930	Hans Fischer, Ger.	
1931	Friedrich Bergius, Carl Bosch, Ger.	
1932	Irving Langmuir, U.S.	
1934	Harold C. Urey, U.S.	
1935	Frédéric Joliot, Irène Joliot-Curie, Fr.	
1936	Peter J. W. Debye, Neth.	
1937	Walter N. Haworth, UK;	
	Paul Karrer, Switz.	
1938	Richard Kuhn, Ger.	
1939	Adolf F. J. Butenandt, Ger.;	
	Leopold Ruzicka, Switz.	
1943	George de Hevesy, Hung.	
1944	Otto Hahn, Ger.	
1945	Artturi I. Virtanen, Fin.	
1946	James B. Sumner, John H.	
	Northrop, Wendell M. Stanley, U.S.	
1947	Robert Robinson, UK	
1948	Arne W. K. Tiselius, Swed.	
1949	William F. Giauque, U.S.	
1950	Kurt Alder, Otto P. H. Diels, Ger.	
1951	Edwin M. McMillan,	
	Glenn T. Seaborg, U.S.	
1952	Archer J. P. Martin,	
	Richard L. M. Synge, UK	
1953	Hermann Staudinger, Ger.	
1954	Linus C. Pauling, U.S.	
1955	Vincent du Vigneaud, U.S.	
1956	Cyril N. Hinshelwood, UK;	
	Nikolay N. Semenov, USSR	

1957	Lord (Alexander R.) Todd, UK	
1958	Frederick Sanger, UK	
1959	Jaroslav Heyrovsky, Czech.	
1960	Willard F. Libby, U.S.	
1961	Melvin Calvin, U.S.	
1962	John C. Kendrew, Max F. Perutz, UK	
1963	Giulio Natta, Ital.; Karl Ziegler, Ger.	
1964	Dorothy C. Hodgkin, UK	
1965	Robert B. Woodward, U.S.	
1966	Robert S. Mulliken, U.S.	
1967	Manfred Eigen, Ger.; Ronald G. W.	
	Norrish, George Porter, UK	
1968	Lars Onsager, U.S.	
1969	Derek H. R. Barton, UK;	
	Odd Hassel, Nor.	
1970	Luis F. Leloir, Arg.	
1971	Gerhard Herzberg, Can.	
1972	Christian B. Anfinsen, Stanford	
	Moore, William H. Stein, U.S.	
1973	Ernst Otto Fischer, Ger.;	
	Geoffrey Wilkinson, UK	
1974	Paul J. Flory, U.S.	
1975	John Cornforth, Austral.-UK;	
	Vladimir Prelog, Bosnia-Switz.	
1976	William N. Lipscomb, U.S.	
1977	Ilya Prigogine, Belg.	
1978	Peter Mitchell, UK	
1979	Herbert C. Brown, U.S.;	
	Georg Wittig, Ger.	
1980	Paul Berg, Walter Gilbert, U.S.;	
	Frederick Sanger, UK	
1981	Kenichi Fukui, Jpn.;	
	Roald Hoffmann, U.S.	
1982	Aaron Klug, UK-Lith.	
1983	Henry Taube, Can.	
1984	Robert Bruce Merrifield, U.S.	
1985	Herbert A. Hauptman,	
	Jerome Karle, U.S.	
1986	Dudley Herschbach, Yuan T. Lee,	
	U.S.; John C. Polanyi, Can.	
1987	Donald J. Cram,	
	Charles J. Pedersen, U.S.;	
	Jean-Marie Lehn, Fr.	
1988	Johann Deisenhofer, Robert Huber,	
	Hartmut Michel, Ger.	
1989	Sidney Altman,	
	Thomas R. Cech, U.S.	
1990	Elias James Corey, U.S.	
1991	Richard R. Ernst, Switz.	
1992	Rudolph A. Marcus, Can.-U.S.	
1993	Kary B. Mullis, U.S.;	
	Michael Smith, UK-Can.	
1994	George A. Olah, U.S.	
1995	Paul Crutzen, Neth.;	
	Mario Molina, Mex.-U.S.;	
	Sherwood Rowland, U.S.	

1996	Robert F. Curl Jr.,	
	Richard E. Smalley, U.S.;	
	Harold W. Kroto, UK	
1997	Paul D. Boyer, U.S.; John E. Walker,	
	UK; Jens C. Skou, Den.	
1998	Walter Kohn, U.S.;	
	John A. Pople, UK	
1999	Ahmed H. Zewail, U.S.	
2000	Alan J. Heeger, U.S.;	
	Alan G. MacDiarmid, N.Z.-U.S.;	
	Hideki Shirakawa, Jpn.	
2001	K. Barry Sharpless,	
	William S. Knowles, U.S.;	
	Ryoji Noyori, Jpn.	
2002	John B. Fenn, U.S.;	
	Koichi Tanaka, Jpn.;	
	Kurt Wüthrich, Switz.	
2003	Peter Agre,	
	Roderick MacKinnon, U.S.	
2004	Aaron Ciechanover, Avram Hershko,	
	Isr.; Irwin Rose, U.S.	
2005	Yves Chauvin, Fr.; Robert H.	
	Grubbs, Richard R. Schrock, U.S.	
2006	Roger D. Kornberg, U.S.	
2007	Gerhard Ertl, Ger.	
2008	Martin Chalfie, Osamu Shimomura,	
	Roger Y. Tsien, U.S.	
2009	Venkatraman Ramakrishnan, UK;	
	Thomas A. Steitz, U.S.;	
	Ada E. Yonath, Isr.	
2010	Richard F. Heck, U.S.;	
	Ei-ichi Negishi, Jpn.-U.S.;	
	Akira Suzuki, Jpn.	
2011	Dan Shechtman, Isr.	
2012	Brian K. Kobilka,	
	Robert J. Lefkowitz, U.S.	
2013	Martin Karplus, Austria-U.S.;	
	Michael Levitt, S. Afr.-U.S.;	
	Arieh Warshel, Isr.-U.S.	
2014	Eric Betzig, William E. Moerner,	
	U.S.; Stefan W. Hell, Ger.	
2015	Tomas Lindahl, Swed.-UK;	
	Paul Modrich, U.S.;	
	Aziz Sancar, Turk.-U.S.	
2016	Bernard L. Feringa, Neth.;	
	Jean-Pierre Sauvage, France;	
	J. Fraser Stoddart, UK-U.S.	
2017	Jacques Dubochet, Switz.;	
	Joachim Frank, Ger.-U.S.;	
	Richard Henderson, UK	
2018	Frances H. Arnold, U.S.;	
	George P. Smith, U.S.;	
	Gregory P. Winter, UK	

Physiology or Medicine

1901	Emil A. von Behring, Ger.	
1902	Ronald Ross, UK	
1903	Niels R. Finsen, Den.	
1904	Ivan P. Pavlov, Russ.	
1905	Robert Koch, Ger.	
1906	Camillo Golgi, Ital.;	
	Santiago Ramón y Cajal, Spain	
1907	Charles L. A. Laveran, Fr.	
1908	Paul Ehrlich, Ger.;	
	Ilya Mechnikov, Fr.	
1909	Emil T. Kocher, Switz.	
1910	Albrecht Kossel, Ger.	
1911	Allvar Gullstrand, Swed.	
1912	Alexis Carrel, Fr.	
1913	Charles R. Richet, Fr.	
1914	Robert Bárány, Austria	
1919	Jules Bordet, Belg.	
1920	Schack A. S. Krogh, Den.	
1922	Archibald V. Hill, UK;	
	Otto F. Meyerhof, Ger.	
1923	Frederick G. Banting, Can.;	
	John J. R. Macleod, UK	
1924	Willem Einthoven, Neth.	
1926	Johannes A. G. Fibiger, Den.	
1927	Julius Wagner-Jauregg, Austria	
1928	Charles J. H. Nicolle, Fr.	
1929	Christiaan Eijkman, Neth.;	
	Frederick G. Hopkins, UK	
1930	Karl Landsteiner, Ger.	
1931	Otto H. Warburg, Ger.	
1932	Edgar D. Adrian,	
	Charles S. Sherrington, UK	
1933	Thomas H. Morgan, U.S.	

1934	George R. Minot, William P. Murphy,	
	G. H. Whipple, U.S.	
1935	Hans Spemann, Ger.	
1936	Henry H. Dale, UK;	
	Otto Loewi, U.S.	
1937	Albert Szent-Gyorgyi, Hung.-U.S.	
1938	Corneille J. F. Heymans, Belg.	
1939	Gerhard Domagk, Ger.	
1943	Henrik C. P. Dam, Den.;	
	Edward A. Doisy, U.S.	
1944	Joseph Erlanger,	
	Herbert S. Gasser, U.S.	
1945	Ernst B. Chain, Alexander	
	Fleming, Howard W. Florey, UK	
1946	Hermann J. Muller, U.S.	
1947	Carl F. Cori, Gerty T. Cori, U.S.;	
	Bernardo A. Houssay, Arg.	
1948	Paul H. Müller, Switz.	
1949	Walter R. Hess, Switz.;	
	Antonio Egas Moniz, Port.	
1950	Philip S. Hench, Edward C. Kendall,	
	U.S.; Tadeus Reichstein, Switz.	
1951	Max Theiler, U.S.	
1952	Selman A. Waksman, U.S.	
1953	Hans A. Krebs, UK;	
	Fritz A. Lipmann, U.S.	
1954	John F. Enders, Frederick C.	
	Robbins, Thomas H. Weller, U.S.	
1955	Alex H. T. Theorell, Swed.	
1956	André F. Cournand,	
	Dickinson W. Richards, U.S.;	
	Werner Forssmann, Ger.	
1957	Daniel Bovet, Ital.	

1958	George W. Beadle, Edward L.	
	Tatum, Joshua Lederberg, U.S.	
1959	Arthur Kornberg,	
	Severo Ochoa, U.S.	
1960	Frank Macfarlane Burnet,	
	Austral.; Peter B. Medawar, UK	
1961	Georg von Békésy, U.S.	
1962	Francis H. C. Crick,	
	Maurice H. F. Wilkins, UK;	
	James D. Watson, U.S.	
1963	John C. Eccles, Austral.;	
	Alan L. Hodgkin,	
	Andrew F. Huxley, UK	
1964	Konrad E. Bloch, U.S.;	
	Feodor Lynen, Ger.	
1965	François Jacob, André Lwoff,	
	Jacques Monod, Fr.	
1966	Charles B. Huggins,	
	Peyton Rous, U.S.	
1967	Ragnar Granit, Swed.;	
	Haldan Keffer Hartline,	
	George Wald, U.S.	
1968	Robert W. Holley,	
	H. Gobind Khorana,	
	Marshall W. Nirenberg, U.S.	
1969	Max Delbrück, Alfred D. Hershey,	
	Salvador Luria, U.S.	
1970	Julius Axelrod, U.S.;	
	Bernard Katz, UK;	
	Ulf von Euler, Swed.	
1971	Earl W. Sutherland Jr., U.S.	
1972	Gerald M. Edelman, U.S.;	
	Rodney R. Porter, UK	

1973 Konrad Lorenz, Austria; Nikolaas Tinbergen, UK; Karl von Frisch, Ger.	1987 Susumu Tonegawa, Jpn.	2004 Richard Axel, Linda B. Buck, U.S.
1974 Albert Claude, Lux.-U.S.; Christian de Duve, Belg.; George Emil Palade, Rom.-U.S.	1988 James W. Black, UK; Gertrude B. Elion, George H. Hitchings, U.S.	2005 Barry J. Marshall, J. Robin Warren, Austral. 2006 Andrew Z. Fire, Craig C. Mello, U.S.
1975 David Baltimore, Howard Temin, U.S.; Renato Dulbecco, Ital.-U.S.	1989 J. Michael Bishop, Harold E. Varmus, U.S.	2007 Mario R. Capecchi, Oliver Smithies, U.S.;
1976 Baruch S. Blumberg, Daniel Carleton Gajdusek, U.S.	1990 Joseph E. Murray, E. Donnall Thomas, U.S.	Martin J. Evans, UK 2008 Harald zur Hausen, Ger.;
1977 Rosalyn S. Yalow, Roger Guillemin, Andrew V. Schally, U.S.	1991 Edwin Neher, Bert Sakmann, Ger. 1992 Edmond H. Fisher, Edwin G. Krebs, U.S.	Françoise Barré-Sinoussi, Luc Montagnier, Fr. 2009 Elizabeth H. Blackburn,
1978 Werner Arber, Switz.; Daniel Nathans, Hamilton O. Smith, U.S.	1993 Richard J. Roberts, UK; Phillip A. Sharp, U.S.	Carol W. Greider, Jack W. Szostak, U.S. 2010 Robert G. Edwards, UK
1979 Allan M. Cormack, U.S.; Godfrey N. Hounsfield, UK	1994 Alfred G. Gilman, Martin Rodbell, U.S.	2011 Bruce A. Beutler, U.S.; Jules A. Hoffmann, Fr.;
1980 Baruj Benacerraf, George Snell, U.S.; Jean Dausset, Fr.	1995 Edward B. Lewis, Eric F. Wieschaus, U.S.; Christiane Nüsslein-Volhard, Ger.	Ralph M. Steinman, Can.-U.S. 2012 John B. Gurdon, UK; Shinya Yamanaka, Jpn.-U.S.
1981 Roger W. Sperry, David H. Hubel, Torsten N. Wiesel, U.S.	1996 Peter C. Doherty, Austral.; Rolf M. Zinkernagel, Switz.	2013 James E. Rothman, Randy W. Schekman, U.S.;
1982 Sune K. Bergström, Bengt I. Samuelsson, Swed.; John R. Vane, UK	1997 Stanley B. Prusiner, U.S. 1998 Robert F. Furchgott, Louis J. Ignarro, Ferid Murad, U.S.	Thomas C. Südhof, Ger.-U.S. 2014 John O'Keefe, U.S.-UK; May-Britt Moser, Edvard I. Moser, Nor.
1983 Barbara McClintock, U.S.	1999 Günter Blobel, U.S.	2015 William C. Campbell, Ire.-U.S.;
1984 Niels K. Jerne, UK-Den.; Georges J. F. Köhler, Ger.; César Milstein, UK-Arg.	2000 Arvid Carlsson, Swed.; Paul Greengard, U.S.; Eric R. Kandel, Austria-U.S.	Satoshi Omura, Jpn.; Youyou Tu, China 2016 Yoshinori Ohsumi, Jpn.
1985 Michael S. Brown, Joseph L. Goldstein, U.S.	2001 Leland H. Hartwell, U.S.; R. Timothy (Tim) Hunt, Paul M. Nurse, UK	2017 Jeffrey C. Hall, Michael Rosbash, Michael W. Young, U.S.
1986 Stanley Cohen, U.S.; Rita Levi-Montalcini, Ital.-U.S.	2002 Sydney Brenner, John E. Sulston, UK; H. Robert Horvitz, U.S. 2003 Paul C. Lauterbur, U.S.; Peter Mansfield, UK	2018 James P. Allison, U.S.; Tasuku Honjo, Jpn.

Literature

1901 Rene F. A. Sully Prudhomme, Fr.	1945 Gabriela Mistral, Chile	1981 Elias Canetti, Bulg.-UK
1902 Theodor Mommsen, Ger.	1946 Hermann Hesse, Ger.-Switz.	1982 Gabriel García Márquez, Colombia
1903 Bjørnstjerne Bjørnson, Nor.	1947 André Gide, Fr.	1983 William Golding, UK
1904 José Echegaray y Eizaguirre, Spain; Fréderic Mistral, Fr.	1948 T. S. Eliot, UK	1984 Jaroslav Siefert, Czech.
1905 Henryk Sienkiewicz, Pol.	1949 William Faulkner, U.S.	1985 Claude Simon, Fr.
1906 Giosuè Carducci, Ital.	1950 Bertrand Russell, UK	1986 Wole Soyinka, Nigeria
1907 Rudyard Kipling, UK	1951 Pär F. Lagerkvist, Swed.	1987 Joseph Brodsky, USSR-U.S.
1908 Rudolf C. Eucken, Ger.	1952 François Mauriac, Fr.	1988 Naguib Mahfouz, Egypt
1909 Selma Lagerlöf, Swed.	1953 Winston Churchill, UK	1989 Camilo José Cela, Spain
1910 Paul J. L. Heyse, Ger.	1954 Ernest Hemingway, U.S.	1990 Octavio Paz, Mex.
1911 Maurice Maeterlinck, Belg.	1955 Halldór K. Laxness, Ice.	1991 Nadine Gordimer, S. Afr.
1912 Gerhart Hauptmann, Ger.	1956 Juan Ramón Jiménez, Spain	1992 Derek Walcott, St. Lucia
1913 Rabindranath Tagore, India	1957 Albert Camus, Fr.	1993 Toni Morrison, U.S.
1915 Romain Rolland, Fr.	1958 Boris L. Pasternak, USSR (declined)	1994 Kenzaburō Oe, Jpn.
1916 Verner von Heidenstam, Swed.	1959 Salvatore Quasimodo, Ital.	1995 Seamus Heaney, Ire.
1917 Karl A. Gjellerup, Henrik Pontoppidan, Den.	1960 Saint-John Perse, Fr.	1996 Wislawa Szymborska, Pol.
1919 Carl F. G. Spitteler, Switz.	1961 Ivo Andric, Yugo.	1997 Dario Fo, Ital.
1920 Knut Hamsun, Nor.	1962 John Steinbeck, U.S.	1998 José Saramago, Por.
1921 Anatole France, Fr.	1963 Giorgos Seferis, Greece	1999 Günter Grass, Ger.
1922 Jacinto Benavente, Spain	1964 Jean-Paul Sartre, Fr. (declined)	2000 Gao Xingjian, China-Fr.
1923 William Butler Yeats, Ire.	1965 Mikhail Sholokhov, USSR	2001 V. S. Naipaul, UK
1924 Wladyslaw S. Reymont, Pol.	1966 Shmuel Yosef Agnon, Isr.; Nelly Sachs, Swed.	2002 Imre Kertész, Hung.
1925 George Bernard Shaw, Ire.-UK	1967 Miguel Angel Asturias, Guat.	2003 J. M. Coetzee, S. Afr.
1926 Grazia Deledda, Ital.	1968 Yasunari Kawabata, Jpn.	2004 Elfriede Jelinek, Austria
1927 Henri Bergson, Fr.	1969 Samuel Beckett, Ire.	2005 Harold Pinter, UK
1928 Sigrid Undset, Nor.	1970 Aleksandr I. Solzhenitsyn, USSR	2006 Orhan Pamuk, Turk.
1929 Thomas Mann, Ger.	1971 Pablo Neruda, Chile	2007 Doris Lessing, UK
1930 Sinclair Lewis, U.S.	1972 Heinrich Böll, Ger.	2008 Jean-Marie Gustave Le Clézio, Fr.
1931 Erik A. Karlfeldt, Swed.	1973 Patrick White, Austral.	2009 Herta Müller, Ger.
1932 John Galsworthy, UK	1974 Eyvind Johnson, Harry Edmund Martinson, Swed.	2010 Mario Vargas Llosa, Peru
1933 Ivan A. Bunin, USSR	1975 Eugenio Montale, Ital.	2011 Tomas Tranströmer, Swed.
1934 Luigi Pirandello, Ital.	1976 Saul Bellow, U.S.	2012 Mo Yan, China
1936 Eugene O'Neill, U.S.	1977 Vicente Aleixandre, Spain	2013 Alice Munro, Can.
1937 Roger Martin du Gard, Fr.	1978 Isaac Bashevis Singer, U.S.	2014 Patrick Modiano, Fr.
1938 Pearl S. Buck, U.S.	1979 Odysseus Elytis, Greece	2015 Svetlana Alexievich, Belarus
1939 Frans E. Sillanpää, Fin.	1980 Czeslaw Milosz, Pol.-U.S.	2016 Bob Dylan, U.S.
1944 Johannes V. Jensen, Den.		2017 Kazuo Ishiguro, Jpn.-UK
		2018 No award

Peace

1901 Jean H. Dunant, Switz.; Frédéric Passy, Fr.	1909 Auguste M. F. Beernaert, Belg.; Paul H. B. B. d'Estournelles de Constant, Fr.	1922 Fridtjof Nansen, Nor. 1925 Austen Chamberlain, UK;
1902 Élie Ducommun, Charles A. Gobat, Switz.	1910 Permanent Intl. Peace Bureau	Charles G. Dawes, U.S. 1926 Aristide Briand, Fr.;
1903 William R. Cremer, UK	1911 Tobias M. C. Asser, Neth.; Alfred H. Fried, Austria	Gustav Stresemann, Ger. 1927 Ferdinand E. Buisson, Fr.;
1904 Institute of International Law, Belg.	1912 Elihu Root, U.S.	Ludwig Quidde, Ger.
1905 Baroness Bertha von Suttner, Austria	1913 Henri La Fontaine, Belg.	1929 Frank B. Kellogg, U.S.
1906 Theodore Roosevelt, U.S.	1917 Intl. Committee of the Red Cross	1930 Nathan Söderblom, Swed.
1907 Ernesto T. Moneta, Ital.; Louis Renault, Fr.	1919 Woodrow Wilson, U.S.	1931 Jane Addams, Nicholas Murray Butler, U.S.
1908 Klas P. Arnoldson, Swed.; Fredrik Bajer, Den.	1920 Léon V. A. Bourgeois, Fr. 1921 Karl H. Branting, Swed.; Christian L. Lange, Nor.	1933 Norman Angell, UK 1934 Arthur Henderson, UK

1935	Carl von Ossietzky, Ger.	1975	Andrei Sakharov, USSR	
1936	Carlos Saavedra Lamas, Arg.	1976	Mairead Corrigan,	
1937	Lord Robert Cecil, UK		Betty Williams, N. Ire.	
1938	Nansen Intl. Office for Refugees	1977	Amnesty International, UK	
1944	Intl. Committee of the Red Cross	1978	Anwar al-Sadat, Egypt;	
1945	Cordell Hull, U.S.		Menachem Begin, Isr.	
1946	Emily G. Balch, John R. Mott, U.S.	1979	Mother Teresa of Calcutta,	
1947	Friends Service Council, UK; Amer.		Alb.-India	

1935 Carl von Ossietzky, Ger.
1936 Carlos Saavedra Lamas, Arg.
1937 Lord Robert Cecil, UK
1938 Nansen Intl. Office for Refugees
1944 Intl. Committee of the Red Cross
1945 Cordell Hull, U.S.
1946 Emily G. Balch, John R. Mott, U.S.
1947 Friends Service Council, UK; Amer.
       Friends Service Committee, U.S.
1949 Lord John Boyd Orr of Brechin, UK
1950 Ralph J. Bunche, U.S.
1951 Léon Jouhaux, Fr.
1952 Albert Schweitzer, Fr.
1953 George C. Marshall, U.S.
1954 Office of UN High Commissioner
       for Refugees
1957 Lester B. Pearson, Can.
1958 Georges Pire, Belg.
1959 Philip J. Noel-Baker, UK
1960 Albert J. Lutuli, S. Afr.
1961 Dag Hammarskjöld, Swed.
1962 Linus C. Pauling, U.S.
1963 Intl. Committee of the Red Cross,
       League of Red Cross Societies
1964 Martin Luther King Jr., U.S.
1965 UN Children's Fund (UNICEF)
1968 René Cassin, Fr.
1969 Intl. Labor Organization, Switz.
1970 Norman E. Borlaug, U.S.
1971 Willy Brandt, Ger.
1973 Henry Kissinger, U.S.;
       Le Duc Tho, N. Viet. (Tho declined)
1974 Seán MacBride, Ire.;
       Eisaku Sato, Jpn.

1975 Andrei Sakharov, USSR
1976 Mairead Corrigan,
       Betty Williams, N. Ire.
1977 Amnesty International, UK
1978 Anwar al-Sadat, Egypt;
       Menachem Begin, Isr.
1979 Mother Teresa of Calcutta,
       Alb.-India
1980 Adolfo Pérez Esquivel, Arg.
1981 Office of UN High Commissioner
       for Refugees
1982 Alfonso García Robles, Mex.;
       Alva Myrdal, Swed.
1983 Lech Walesa, Pol.
1984 Bishop Desmond Tutu, S. Afr.
1985 Intl. Physicians for the Prevention
       of Nuclear War, U.S.
1986 Elie Wiesel, Rom.-U.S.
1987 Oscar Arias Sánchez, Costa Rica
1988 UN Peacekeeping Forces
1989 Dalai Lama (Tenzin Gyatso), Tibet
1990 Mikhail S. Gorbachev, USSR
1991 Aung San Suu Kyi, Burma
1992 Rigoberta Menchú Tum, Guat.
1993 Frederik W. de Klerk,
       Nelson Mandela, S. Afr.
1994 Yasser Arafat, Pal.; Shimon Peres,
       Yitzhak Rabin, Isr.
1995 Joseph Rotblat, Pol.-UK;
       Pugwash Conferences, Can.
1996 Bishop Carlos Ximenes Belo,
       José Ramos-Horta, Timor-Leste
1997 Jody Williams, U.S.;
       Intl. Campaign to Ban Landmines

1998 John Hume, David Trimble, N. Ire.
1999 Médecins Sans Frontières
       (Doctors Without Borders), Fr.
2000 Kim Dae Jung, S. Kor.
2001 UN; Kofi Annan, Ghana
2002 Jimmy Carter, U.S.
2003 Shirin Ebadi, Iran
2004 Wangari Maathai, Kenya
2005 Mohamed ElBaradei, Egypt;
       Intl. Atomic Energy Agency, Austria
2006 Muhammad Yunus,
       Grameen Bank, Bangl.
2007 Intergovernmental Panel on Climate
       Change, Switz.;
       Albert Arnold Gore Jr., U.S.
2008 Martti Ahtisaari, Fin.
2009 Barack H. Obama, U.S.
2010 Liu Xiaobo, China
2011 Leymah Gbowee,
       Ellen Johnson Sirleaf, Liberia;
       Tawakkol Karman, Yemen
2012 European Union
2013 Organization for the Prohibition of
       Chemical Weapons (OPCW)
2014 Kailash Satyarthi, India;
       Malala Yousafzai, Pakistan
2015 National Dialogue Quartet, Tunisia
2016 Juan Manuel Santos, Colombia
2017 Intl. Campaign to Abolish Nuclear
       Weapons
2018 Denis Mukwege, Congo;
       Nadia Murad, Iraq

Nobel Memorial Prize in Economic Sciences

1969 Ragnar Frisch, Nor.;
       Jan Tinbergen, Neth.
1970 Paul A. Samuelson, U.S.
1971 Simon Kuznets, U.S.
1972 Kenneth J. Arrow, U.S.;
       John R. Hicks, UK
1973 Wassily Leontief, U.S.
1974 Gunnar Myrdal, Swed.;
       Friedrich A. von Hayek, Austria
1975 Leonid Kantorovich, USSR;
       Tjalling C. Koopmans, Neth.-U.S.
1976 Milton Friedman, U.S.
1977 James E. Meade, UK;
       Bertil Ohlin, Swed.
1978 Herbert A. Simon, U.S.
1979 Arthur Lewis, UK;
       Theodore W. Schultz, U.S.
1980 Lawrence R. Klein, U.S.
1981 James Tobin, U.S.
1982 George J. Stigler, U.S.
1983 Gerard Debreu, Fr.-U.S.
1984 Richard Stone, UK
1985 Franco Modigliani, Ital.-U.S.
1986 James M. Buchanan, U.S.
1987 Robert M. Solow, U.S.

1988 Maurice Allais, Fr.
1989 Trygve Haavelmo, Nor.
1990 Harry M. Markowitz, Merton H.
       Miller, William F. Sharpe, U.S.
1991 Ronald H. Coase, UK-U.S.
1992 Gary S. Becker, U.S.
1993 Robert W. Fogel,
       Douglass C. North, U.S.
1994 John C. Harsanyi, John F. Nash,
       U.S.; Reinhard Selten, Ger.
1995 Robert E. Lucas Jr., U.S.
1996 James A. Mirrlees, UK;
       William Vickrey, Can.-U.S.
1997 Robert C. Merton, U.S.;
       Myron S. Scholes, Can.-U.S.
1998 Amartya Sen, India
1999 Robert A. Mundell, Can.
2000 James J. Heckman,
       Daniel L. McFadden, U.S.
2001 George A. Akerlof, A. Michael
       Spence, Joseph E. Stiglitz, U.S.
2002 Daniel Kahneman, U.S.-Isr.;
       Vernon L. Smith, U.S.
2003 Robert F. Engle, U.S.;
       Clive W. J. Granger, UK

2004 Finn E. Kydland, Nor.;
       Edward C. Prescott, U.S.
2005 Robert J. Aumann, Isr.-U.S.;
       Thomas C. Schelling, U.S.
2006 Edmund S. Phelps, U.S.
2007 Leonid Hurwicz, Eric S. Maskin,
       Roger B. Myerson, U.S.
2008 Paul Krugman, U.S.
2009 Elinor Ostrom,
       Oliver E. Williamson, U.S.
2010 Peter A. Diamond, Dale T.
       Mortensen, U.S.; Christopher A.
       Pissarides, Cyprus-UK
2011 Thomas J. Sargent,
       Christopher A. Sims, U.S.
2012 Alvin E. Roth, Lloyd S. Shapley, U.S.
2013 Eugene F. Fama, Lars Peter
       Hansen, Robert J. Shiller, U.S.
2014 Jean Tirole, Fr.
2015 Angus Deaton, UK-U.S.
2016 Oliver Hart, U.S.;
       Bengt Holmström, Fin.-U.S.
2017 Richard H. Thaler, U.S.
2018 William D. Nordhaus,
       Paul M. Romer, U.S.

Pulitzer Prizes in Journalism, Letters, and Music, 1917-2018

Endowed by Joseph Pulitzer (1847-1911), publisher of the *New York World*, in a bequest to Columbia Univ. and awarded annually, in years shown, for work published the previous year. Prizes are currently $10,000 in each category except Public Service (in Journalism), for which a gold medal is given. The prize board began considering submissions from online-only publications in 2009.

Pulitzer Prizes in Journalism, 2018

Public Service: *NY Times*, led by Jodi Kantor and Megan Twohey, and Ronan Farrow, *The New Yorker*, for exposing powerful, wealthy sexual predators—including publicizing allegations against film producer Harvey Weinstein—and spurring a worldwide reckoning about sexual abuse.

Breaking News Reporting: *Press Democrat* (Santa Rosa, CA) staff, for reporting on historic wildfires in Sonoma County.

Investigative Reporting: *Washington Post* staff, for relentless reporting that changed the course of a U.S. Senate race in Alabama by revealing the alleged sexual harassment of teenage girls by a leading candidate.

Explanatory Reporting: *Arizona Republic* (Phoenix, AZ) and USA Today Network staffs, for multimedia efforts to examine the difficulties and consequences of fulfilling Pres. Trump's pledge to build a wall along the U.S.-Mexico border.

Local Reporting: *Cincinnati Enquirer* (OH) staff, for narrative and video documenting seven days in the area's heroin epidemic.

National Reporting: *NY Times* and *Washington Post* staffs, for coverage that furthered understanding of Russian interference in the 2016 presidential election and its possible connections to the Trump campaign, transition team, and eventual administration.

International Reporting: Clare Baldwin, Andrew R.C. Marshall, and Manuel Mogato, Reuters, for reporting on Philippines

Pres. Rodrigo Duterte's war on drugs and associated killing campaign.

Feature Writing: Rachel Kaadzi Ghansah, freelance reporter for *GQ*, for portrait of Dylann Roof, the confessed killer of nine inside a historically black church in Charleston, SC, and her analysis of the historical and cultural forces behind his crimes.

Commentary: John Archibald, Alabama Media Group (Birmingham, AL), for locally rooted commentary with a national resonance on topics such as corrupt politicians, women's rights, and hypocrisy.

Criticism: Jerry Saltz, *New York*, for visual art reviews that conveyed a canny and often daring perspective.

Editorial Writing: Andie Dominick, *Des Moines Register* (IA), for editorials examining the damaging consequences for poor Iowans of privatizing the state's Medicaid administration.

Editorial Cartooning: Jake Halpern (writer) and Michael Sloan (cartoonist), freelancers for *NY Times*, for series chronicling daily struggles of a real-life refugee family and its fear of deportation.

Breaking News Photography: Ryan Kelly, *Daily Progress* (Charlottesville, VA), for documenting the moment of impact of a car attack during a racially charged protest in Charlottesville.

Feature Photography: Reuters staff, for exposing violence faced by Rohingya refugees fleeing Myanmar.

Pulitzer Prizes in Letters, 1918-2018

Other Pulitzer Prize Winners, 2018: Biography/autobiography: Caroline Fraser, *Prairie Fires: The American Dreams of Laura Ingalls Wilder*. History (U.S.): Jack E. Davis, *The Gulf: The Making of an American Sea*. Poetry: Frank Bidart, *Half-light: Collected Poems 1965-2016*.

Fiction

1918 Ernest Poole, *His Family*
1919 Booth Tarkington, *The Magnificent Ambersons*
1921 Edith Wharton, *The Age of Innocence*
1922 Booth Tarkington, *Alice Adams*
1923 Willa Cather, *One of Ours*
1924 Margaret Wilson, *The Able McLaughlins*
1925 Edna Ferber, *So Big*
1926 Sinclair Lewis, *Arrowsmith* (refused)
1927 Louis Bromfield, *Early Autumn*
1928 Thornton Wilder, *The Bridge of San Luis Rey*
1929 Julia Peterkin, *Scarlet Sister Mary*
1930 Oliver La Farge, *Laughing Boy*
1931 Margaret Ayer Barnes, *Years of Grace*
1932 Pearl S. Buck, *The Good Earth*
1933 T. S. Stribling, *The Store*
1934 Caroline Miller, *Lamb in His Bosom*
1935 Josephine W. Johnson, *Now in November*
1936 Harold L. Davis, *Honey in the Horn*
1937 Margaret Mitchell, *Gone With the Wind*
1938 John P. Marquand, *The Late George Apley*
1939 Marjorie Kinnan Rawlings, *The Yearling*
1940 John Steinbeck, *The Grapes of Wrath*
1942 Ellen Glasgow, *In This Our Life*
1943 Upton Sinclair, *Dragon's Teeth*
1944 Martin Flavin, *Journey in the Dark*
1945 John Hersey, *A Bell for Adano*
1947 Robert Penn Warren, *All the King's Men*
1948 James A. Michener, *Tales of the South Pacific*
1949 James Gould Cozzens, *Guard of Honor*
1950 A. B. Guthrie Jr., *The Way West*
1951 Conrad Richter, *The Town*
1952 Herman Wouk, *The Caine Mutiny*
1953 Ernest Hemingway, *The Old Man and the Sea*
1955 William Faulkner, *A Fable*
1956 MacKinlay Kantor, *Andersonville*
1958 James Agee, *A Death in the Family*
1959 Robert Lewis Taylor, *The Travels of Jaimie McPheeters*
1960 Allen Drury, *Advise and Consent*
1961 Harper Lee, *To Kill a Mockingbird*
1962 Edwin O'Connor, *The Edge of Sadness*
1963 William Faulkner, *The Reivers*
1965 Shirley Ann Grau, *The Keepers of the House*
1966 Katherine Anne Porter, *Collected Stories*
1967 Bernard Malamud, *The Fixer*
1968 William Styron, *The Confessions of Nat Turner*
1969 N. Scott Momaday, *House Made of Dawn*
1970 Jean Stafford, *Collected Stories*
1972 Wallace Stegner, *Angle of Repose*
1973 Eudora Welty, *The Optimist's Daughter*
1975 Michael Shaara, *The Killer Angels*
1976 Saul Bellow, *Humboldt's Gift*
1978 James Alan McPherson, *Elbow Room*
1979 John Cheever, *The Stories of John Cheever*
1980 Norman Mailer, *The Executioner's Song*
1981 John Kennedy Toole, *A Confederacy of Dunces*
1982 John Updike, *Rabbit Is Rich*
1983 Alice Walker, *The Color Purple*
1984 William Kennedy, *Ironweed*
1985 Alison Lurie, *Foreign Affairs*
1986 Larry McMurtry, *Lonesome Dove*
1987 Peter Taylor, *A Summons to Memphis*
1988 Toni Morrison, *Beloved*
1989 Anne Tyler, *Breathing Lessons*
1990 Oscar Hijuelos, *The Mambo Kings Play Songs of Love*
1991 John Updike, *Rabbit at Rest*
1992 Jane Smiley, *A Thousand Acres*
1993 Robert Olen Butler, *A Good Scent From a Strange Mountain*
1994 E. Annie Proulx, *The Shipping News*
1995 Carol Shields, *The Stone Diaries*
1996 Richard Ford, *Independence Day*
1997 Steven Millhauser, *Martin Dressler: The Tale of an American Dreamer*
1998 Philip Roth, *American Pastoral*
1999 Michael Cunningham, *The Hours*
2000 Jhumpa Lahiri, *Interpreter of Maladies*
2001 Michael Chabon, *The Amazing Adventures of Kavalier & Clay*

2002 Richard Russo, *Empire Falls*
2003 Jeffrey Eugenides, *Middlesex*
2004 Edward P. Jones, *The Known World*
2005 Marilynne Robinson, *Gilead*
2006 Geraldine Brooks, *March*
2007 Cormac McCarthy, *The Road*
2008 Junot Díaz, *The Brief Wondrous Life of Oscar Wao*
2009 Elizabeth Strout, *Olive Kitteridge*
2010 Paul Harding, *Tinkers*
2011 Jennifer Egan, *A Visit From the Goon Squad*
2013 Adam Johnson, *The Orphan Master's Son*
2014 Donna Tartt, *The Goldfinch*
2015 Anthony Doerr, *All the Light We Cannot See*
2016 Viet Thanh Nguyen, *The Sympathizer*
2017 Colson Whitehead, *The Underground Railroad*
2018 Andrew Sean Greer, *Less*

Drama

1918 Jesse Lynch Williams, *Why Marry?*
1920 Eugene O'Neill, *Beyond the Horizon*
1921 Zona Gale, *Miss Lulu Bett*
1922 Eugene O'Neill, *Anna Christie*
1923 Owen Davis, *Icebound*
1924 Hatcher Hughes, *Hell-Bent Fer Heaven*
1925 Sidney Howard, *They Knew What They Wanted*
1926 George Kelly, *Craig's Wife*
1927 Paul Green, *In Abraham's Bosom*
1928 Eugene O'Neill, *Strange Interlude*
1929 Elmer Rice, *Street Scene*
1930 Marc Connelly, *The Green Pastures*
1931 Susan Glaspell, *Alison's House*
1932 George S. Kaufman, Morrie Ryskind, and Ira Gershwin, *Of Thee I Sing*
1933 Maxwell Anderson, *Both Your Houses*
1934 Sidney Kingsley, *Men in White*
1935 Zoe Akins, *The Old Maid*
1936 Robert E. Sherwood, *Idiot's Delight*
1937 George S. Kaufman and Moss Hart, *You Can't Take It With You*
1938 Thornton Wilder, *Our Town*
1939 Robert E. Sherwood, *Abe Lincoln in Illinois*
1940 William Saroyan, *The Time of Your Life*
1941 Robert E. Sherwood, *There Shall Be No Night*
1943 Thornton Wilder, *The Skin of Our Teeth*
1945 Mary Chase, *Harvey*
1946 Russel Crouse and Howard Lindsay, *State of the Union*
1948 Tennessee Williams, *A Streetcar Named Desire*
1949 Arthur Miller, *Death of a Salesman*
1950 Richard Rodgers, Oscar Hammerstein II, and Joshua Logan, *South Pacific*
1952 Joseph Kramm, *The Shrike*
1953 William Inge, *Picnic*
1954 John Patrick, *The Teahouse of the August Moon*
1955 Tennessee Williams, *Cat on a Hot Tin Roof*
1956 Frances Goodrich and Albert Hackett, *The Diary of Anne Frank*
1957 Eugene O'Neill, *Long Day's Journey Into Night*
1958 Ketti Frings, *Look Homeward, Angel*
1959 Archibald MacLeish, *J.B.*
1960 George Abbott, Jerome Weidman, Sheldon Harnick, and Jerry Bock, *Fiorello!*
1961 Tad Mosel, *All the Way Home*
1962 Frank Loesser and Abe Burrows, *How to Succeed in Business Without Really Trying*
1965 Frank D. Gilroy, *The Subject Was Roses*
1967 Edward Albee, *A Delicate Balance*
1969 Howard Sackler, *The Great White Hope*
1970 Charles Gordone, *No Place to Be Somebody*
1971 Paul Zindel, *The Effect of Gamma Rays on Man-in-the-Moon Marigolds*
1973 Jason Miller, *That Championship Season*
1975 Edward Albee, *Seascape*
1976 Michael Bennett, James Kirkwood, Nicholas Dante, Marvin Hamlisch, and Edward Kleban, *A Chorus Line*
1977 Michael Cristofer, *The Shadow Box*
1978 Donald L. Coburn, *The Gin Game*
1979 Sam Shepard, *Buried Child*
1980 Lanford Wilson, *Talley's Folly*

1981 Beth Henley, *Crimes of the Heart*
1982 Charles Fuller, *A Soldier's Play*
1983 Marsha Norman, *'night, Mother*
1984 David Mamet, *Glengarry Glen Ross*
1985 Stephen Sondheim and James Lapine, *Sunday in the Park With George*
1987 August Wilson, *Fences*
1988 Alfred Uhry, *Driving Miss Daisy*
1989 Wendy Wasserstein, *The Heidi Chronicles*
1990 August Wilson, *The Piano Lesson*
1991 Neil Simon, *Lost in Yonkers*
1992 Robert Schenkkan, *The Kentucky Cycle*
1993 Tony Kushner, *Angels in America: Millennium Approaches*
1994 Edward Albee, *Three Tall Women*
1995 Horton Foote, *The Young Man From Atlanta*
1996 Jonathan Larson, *Rent*
1998 Paula Vogel, *How I Learned to Drive*
1999 Margaret Edson, *Wit*
2000 Donald Margulies, *Dinner With Friends*
2001 David Auburn, *Proof*
2002 Suzan-Lori Parks, *Topdog/Underdog*
2003 Nilo Cruz, *Anna in the Tropics*
2004 Doug Wright, *I Am My Own Wife*
2005 John Patrick Shanley, *Doubt, a parable*
2007 David Lindsay-Abaire, *Rabbit Hole*
2008 Tracy Letts, *August: Osage County*
2009 Lynn Nottage, *Ruined*
2010 Tom Kitt and Brian Yorkey, *Next to Normal*
2011 Bruce Norris, *Clybourne Park*
2012 Quiara Alegría Hudes, *Water by the Spoonful*
2013 Ayad Akhtar, *Disgraced*
2014 Annie Baker, *The Flick*
2015 Stephen Adly Guirgis, *Between Riverside and Crazy*
2016 Lin-Manuel Miranda, *Hamilton*
2017 Lynn Nottage, *Sweat*
2018 Martyna Majok, *Cost of Living*

General Nonfiction

1962 Theodore H. White, *The Making of the President 1960*
1963 Barbara W. Tuchman, *The Guns of August*
1964 Richard Hofstadter, *Anti-Intellectualism in American Life*
1965 Howard Mumford Jones, *O Strange New World*
1966 Edwin Way Teale, *Wandering Through Winter*
1967 David Brion Davis, *The Problem of Slavery in Western Culture*
1968 Will and Ariel Durant, *Rousseau and Revolution*
1969 Norman Mailer, *The Armies of the Night*; Rene Jules Dubos, *So Human an Animal: How We Are Shaped by Surroundings and Events*
1970 Eric H. Erikson, *Gandhi's Truth*
1971 John Toland, *The Rising Sun*
1972 Barbara W. Tuchman, *Stilwell and the American Experience in China, 1911-1945*
1973 Frances FitzGerald, *Fire in the Lake: The Vietnamese and the Americans in Vietnam*; Robert Coles, *Children of Crisis, Vols. II and III*
1974 Ernest Becker, *The Denial of Death*
1975 Annie Dillard, *Pilgrim at Tinker Creek*
1976 Robert N. Butler, *Why Survive? Being Old in America*
1977 William W. Warner, *Beautiful Swimmers*
1978 Carl Sagan, *The Dragons of Eden*
1979 Edward O. Wilson, *On Human Nature*
1980 Douglas R. Hofstadter, *Gödel, Escher, Bach: An Eternal Golden Braid*
1981 Carl E. Schorske, *Fin-de-Siècle Vienna: Politics and Culture*
1982 Tracy Kidder, *The Soul of a New Machine*
1983 Susan Sheehan, *Is There No Place on Earth for Me?*
1984 Paul Starr, *Social Transformation of American Medicine*
1985 Studs Terkel, *The Good War*
1986 Joseph Lelyveld, *Move Your Shadow*; J. Anthony Lukas, *Common Ground*

1987 David K. Shipler, *Arab and Jew: Wounded Spirits in a Promised Land*
1988 Richard Rhodes, *The Making of the Atomic Bomb*
1989 Neil Sheehan, *A Bright Shining Lie: John Paul Vann and America in Vietnam*
1990 Dale Maharidge and Michael Williamson, *And Their Children After Them*
1991 Bert Holldobler and Edward O. Wilson, *The Ants*
1992 Daniel Yergin, *The Prize: The Epic Quest for Oil, Money, and Power*
1993 Garry Wills, *Lincoln at Gettysburg*
1994 David Remnick, *Lenin's Tomb: The Last Days of the Soviet Empire*
1995 Jonathan Weiner, *The Beak of the Finch: A Story of Evolution in Our Time*
1996 Tina Rosenberg, *The Haunted Land: Facing Europe's Ghosts After Communism*
1997 Richard Kluger, *Ashes to Ashes: America's Hundred-Year Cigarette War, the Public Health, and the Unabashed Triumph of Philip Morris*
1998 Jared Diamond, *Guns, Germs, and Steel: The Fates of Human Societies*
1999 John McPhee, *Annals of the Former World*
2000 John W. Dower, *Embracing Defeat: Japan in the Wake of World War II*
2001 Herbert P. Bix, *Hirohito and the Making of Modern Japan*
2002 Diane McWhorter, *Carry Me Home: Birmingham, Alabama: The Climactic Battle of the Civil Rights Revolution*
2003 Samantha Power, *A Problem From Hell: America and the Age of Genocide*
2004 Anne Applebaum, *Gulag: A History*
2005 Steve Coll, *Ghost Wars*
2006 Caroline Elkins, *Imperial Reckoning: The Untold Story of Britain's Gulag in Kenya*
2007 Lawrence Wright, *The Looming Tower: Al-Qaeda and the Road to 9/11*
2008 Saul Friedländer, *The Years of Extermination: Nazi Germany and the Jews, 1939-1945*
2009 Douglas A. Blackmon, *Slavery by Another Name: The Re-Enslavement of Black Americans From the Civil War to World War II*
2010 David E. Hoffman, *The Dead Hand: The Untold Story of the Cold War Arms Race and Its Dangerous Legacy*
2011 Siddhartha Mukherjee, *The Emperor of All Maladies: A Biography of Cancer*
2012 Stephen Greenblatt, *The Swerve: How the World Became Modern*
2013 Gilbert King, *Devil in the Grove: Thurgood Marshall, the Groveland Boys, and the Dawn of a New America*
2014 Dan Fagin, *Toms River: A Story of Science and Salvation*
2015 Elizabeth Kolbert, *The Sixth Extinction: An Unnatural History*
2016 Joby Warrick, *Black Flags: The Rise of ISIS*
2017 Matthew Desmond, *Evicted: Poverty and Profit in the American City*
2018 James Forman Jr., *Locking up Our Own: Crime and Punishment in Black America*

Special Citation in Letters

1944 Richard Rodgers and Oscar Hammerstein II, for *Oklahoma!*
1957 Kenneth Roberts, for his historical novels
1960 *The Armada*, by Garrett Mattingly
1961 *American Heritage Picture History of the Civil War*
1973 *George Washington, Vols. I-IV*, by James Thomas Flexner
1977 Alex Haley, for *Roots*
1978 E. B. White
1984 Theodor Seuss Geisel (Dr. Seuss)
1992 Art Spiegelman, for *Maus*
2006 Edmund S. Morgan
2007 Ray Bradbury

Pulitzer Prizes in Music, 1943-2018

1943 William Schuman, *Secular Cantata No. 2, A Free Song*
1944 Howard Hanson, *Symphony No. 4, Op. 34*
1945 Aaron Copland, *Appalachian Spring*
1946 Leo Sowerby, *The Canticle of the Sun*
1947 Charles Ives, *Symphony No. 3*
1948 Walter Piston, *Symphony No. 3*
1949 Virgil Thomson, *Louisiana Story*
1950 Gian-Carlo Menotti, *The Consul*
1951 Douglas Moore, *Giants in the Earth*
1952 Gail Kubik, *Symphony Concertante*
1954 Quincy Porter, *Concerto for Two Pianos and Orchestra*
1955 Gian-Carlo Menotti, *The Saint of Bleecker Street*

1956 Ernest Toch, *Symphony No. 3*
1957 Norman Dello Joio, *Meditations on Ecclesiastes*
1958 Samuel Barber, *Vanessa*
1959 John LaMontaine, *Concerto for Piano and Orchestra*
1960 Elliott Carter, *Second String Quartet*
1961 Walter Piston, *Symphony No. 7*
1962 Robert Ward, *The Crucible*
1963 Samuel Barber, *Piano Concerto No. 1*
1966 Leslie Bassett, *Variations for Orchestra*
1967 Leon Kirchner, *Quartet No. 3*
1968 George Crumb, *Echoes of Time and the River*
1969 Karel Husa, *String Quartet No. 3*

1970 Charles Wuorinen, *Time's Encomium*
1971 Mario Davidovsky, *Synchronisms No. 6*
1972 Jacob Druckman, *Windows*
1973 Elliott Carter, *String Quartet No. 3*
1974 Donald Martino, *Notturno*
1975 Dominick Argento, *From the Diary of Virginia Woolf*
1976 Ned Rorem, *Air Music*
1977 Richard Wernick, *Visions of Terror and Wonder*
1978 Michael Colgrass, *Deja Vu for Percussion and Orchestra*
1979 Joseph Schwantner, *Aftertones of Infinity*
1980 David Del Tredici, *In Memory of a Summer Day*
1982 Roger Sessions, *Concerto for Orchestra*
1983 Ellen Taaffe Zwilich, *Symphony No. 1*
1984 Bernard Rands, *Canti del Sole*
1985 Stephen Albert, *Symphony, RiverRun*
1986 George Perle, *Wind Quintet IV*
1987 John Harbison, *The Flight Into Egypt*
1988 William Bolcom, *12 New Etudes for Piano*
1989 Roger Reynolds, *Whispers Out of Time*
1990 Mel Powell, *Duplicates: A Concerto for Two Pianos and Orchestra*
1991 Shulamit Ran, *Symphony*
1992 Wayne Peterson, *The Face of the Night, The Heart[2] of the Dark*
1993 Christopher Rouse, *Trombone Concerto*
1994 Gunther Schuller, *Of Reminiscences and Reflections*
1995 Morton Gould, *Stringmusic*
1996 George Walker, *Lilacs for Voice and Orchestra*
1997 Wynton Marsalis, *Blood on the Fields*
1998 Aaron Jay Kernis, *String Quartet No. 2 (musica instrumentalis)*

1999 Melinda Wagner, *Concerto for Flute, Strings, and Percussion*
2000 Lewis Spratlan, *Life is a Dream, Opera in Three Acts: Act II, Concert Version*
2001 John Corigliano, *Symphony No. 2 for String Orchestra*
2002 Henry Brant, *Ice Field*
2003 John Adams, *On the Transmigration of Souls*
2004 Paul Moravec, *Tempest Fantasy*
2005 Steven Stucky, *Second Concerto for Orchestra*
2006 Yehudi Wyner, *Piano Concerto: "Chiavi in Mano"*
2007 Ornette Coleman, *Sound Grammar*
2008 David Lang, *The Little Match Girl Passion*
2009 Steve Reich, *Double Sextet*
2010 Jennifer Higdon, *Violin Concerto*
2011 Zhou Long, *Madame White Snake*
2012 Kevin Puts, *Silent Night: Opera in Two Acts*
2013 Caroline Shaw, *Partita for 8 Voices*
2014 John Luther Adams, *Become Ocean*
2015 Julia Wolfe, *Anthracite Fields*
2016 Henry Threadgill, *In for a Penny, In for a Pound*
2017 Du Yun, *Angel's Bone*
2018 Kendrick Lamar, *DAMN.*

Special Citation in Music

1974 Roger Sessions
1976 Scott Joplin
1982 Milton Babbitt
1985 William Schuman
1998 George Gershwin
1999 Edward Kennedy "Duke" Ellington
2006 Thelonious Monk
2007 John Coltrane
2008 Bob Dylan
2010 Hank Williams

Man Booker Prize for Fiction, 1969-2018

The Booker Prize for fiction, established in 1968 and renamed the Man Booker Prize in 2002, is £50,000, awarded annually to the author of the best new full-length novel written in English. Award-winning authors were required to be a citizen of the UK, the Commonwealth, or Ireland until 2014, the first year in which all English-language novels published in Britain were considered.

Year Author, book
1969 P. H. Newby, *Something to Answer For*
1970 Bernice Rubens, *The Elected Member*
1971 V. S. Naipaul, *In a Free State*
1972 John Berger, *G*
1973 J. G. Farrell, *The Siege of Krishnapur*
1974 Nadine Gordimer, *The Conservationist*; Stanley Middleton, *Holiday*
1975 Ruth Prawer Jhabvala, *Heat and Dust*
1976 David Storey, *Saville*
1977 Paul Scott, *Staying On*
1978 Iris Murdoch, *The Sea, the Sea*
1979 Penelope Fitzgerald, *Offshore*
1980 William Golding, *Rites of Passage*
1981 Salman Rushdie, *Midnight's Children[1]*
1982 Thomas Keneally, *Schindler's Ark*
1983 J. M. Coetzee, *Life and Times of Michael K*
1984 Anita Brookner, *Hotel du Lac*
1985 Keri Hulme, *The Bone People*
1986 Kingsley Amis, *The Old Devils*
1987 Penelope Lively, *Moon Tiger*
1988 Peter Carey, *Oscar and Lucinda*
1989 Kazuo Ishiguro, *The Remains of the Day*
1990 A. S. Byatt, *Possession*
1991 Ben Okri, *The Famished Road*
1992 Michael Ondaatje, *The English Patient[2]*; Barry Unsworth, *Sacred Hunger*

Year Author, book
1993 Roddy Doyle, *Paddy Clarke Ha Ha Ha*
1994 James Kelman, *How Late It Was, How Late*
1995 Pat Barker, *The Ghost Road*
1996 Graham Swift, *Last Orders*
1997 Arundhati Roy, *The God of Small Things*
1998 Ian McEwan, *Amsterdam*
1999 J. M. Coetzee, *Disgrace*
2000 Margaret Atwood, *The Blind Assassin*
2001 Peter Carey, *True History of the Kelly Gang*
2002 Yann Martel, *Life of Pi*
2003 DBC Pierre, *Vernon God Little*
2004 Alan Hollinghurst, *The Line of Beauty*
2005 John Banville, *The Sea*
2006 Kiran Desai, *The Inheritance of Loss*
2007 Anne Enright, *The Gathering*
2008 Aravind Adiga, *The White Tiger*
2009 Hilary Mantel, *Wolf Hall*
2010 Howard Jacobson, *The Finkler Question*
2011 Julian Barnes, *The Sense of an Ending*
2012 Hilary Mantel, *Bring up the Bodies*
2013 Eleanor Catton, *The Luminaries*
2014 Richard Flanagan, *The Narrow Road to the Deep North*
2015 Marlon James, *A Brief History of Seven Killings*
2016 Paul Beatty, *The Sellout*
2017 George Saunders, *Lincoln in the Bardo*
2018 Anna Burns, *Milkman*

(1) Rushdie's *Midnight's Children* also won the Booker of Bookers prize in 1993 and the Best of the Booker prize in 2008.
(2) Ondaatje's *The English Patient* also won the Golden Man Booker prize in 2018.

Newbery Medal, 1922-2018

The Newbery Medal is awarded annually by the Association for Library Service to Children, a division of the American Library Association, to the most distinguished contribution to American children's literature published in the previous year.

Year Book, author
1922 *The Story of Mankind*, Hendrik Willem van Loon
1923 *The Voyages of Dr. Dolittle*, Hugh Lofting
1924 *The Dark Frigate*, Charles Boardman Hawes
1925 *Tales From Silver Lands*, Charles J. Finger
1926 *Shen of the Sea*, Arthur Bowie Chrisman
1927 *Smoky, the Cowhorse*, Will James
1928 *Gay-Neck: The Story of a Pigeon*, Dhan Gopal Mukerji
1929 *The Trumpeter of Krakow*, Eric P. Kelly
1930 *Hitty, Her First Hundred Years*, Rachel Field
1931 *The Cat Who Went to Heaven*, Elizabeth Coatsworth
1932 *Waterless Mountain*, Laura Adams Armer
1933 *Young Fu of the Upper Yangtze*, Elizabeth Foreman Lewis
1934 *Invincible Louisa*, Cornelia Meigs

Year Book, author
1935 *Dobry*, Monica Shannon
1936 *Caddie Woodlawn*, Carol Ryrie Brink
1937 *Roller Skates*, Ruth Sawyer
1938 *The White Stag*, Kate Seredy
1939 *Thimble Summer*, Elizabeth Enright
1940 *Daniel Boone*, James Daugherty
1941 *Call It Courage*, Armstrong Sperry
1942 *The Matchlock Gun*, Walter D. Edmonds
1943 *Adam of the Road*, Elizabeth Janet Gray
1944 *Johnny Tremain*, Esther Forbes
1945 *Rabbit Hill*, Robert Lawson
1946 *Strawberry Girl*, Lois Lenski
1947 *Miss Hickory*, Carolyn Sherwin Bailey

Year	Book, author
1948	*The Twenty-One Balloons*, William Pène du Bois
1949	*King of the Wind*, Marguerite Henry
1950	*The Door in the Wall*, Marguerite de Angeli
1951	*Amos Fortune, Free Man*, Elizabeth Yates
1952	*Ginger Pye*, Eleanor Estes
1953	*Secret of the Andes*, Ann Nolan Clark
1954	*... And Now Miguel*, Joseph Krumgold
1955	*The Wheel on the School*, Meindert DeJong
1956	*Carry On, Mr. Bowditch*, Jean Lee Latham
1957	*Miracles on Maple Hill*, Virginia Sorensen
1958	*Rifles for Watie*, Harold Keith
1959	*The Witch of Blackbird Pond*, Elizabeth George Speare
1960	*Onion John*, Joseph Krumgold
1961	*Island of the Blue Dolphins*, Scott O'Dell
1962	*The Bronze Bow*, Elizabeth George Speare
1963	*A Wrinkle in Time*, Madeleine L'Engle
1964	*It's Like This, Cat*, Emily Cheney Neville
1965	*Shadow of a Bull*, Maia Wojciechowska
1966	*I, Juan de Pareja*, Elizabeth Borton de Trevino
1967	*Up a Road Slowly*, Irene Hunt
1968	*From the Mixed-Up Files of Mrs. Basil E. Frankweiler*, E. L. Konigsburg
1969	*The High King*, Lloyd Alexander
1970	*Sounder*, William H. Armstrong
1971	*The Summer of the Swans*, Betsy Byars
1972	*Mrs. Frisby and the Rats of NIMH*, Robert C. O'Brien
1973	*Julie of the Wolves*, Jean Craighead George
1974	*The Slave Dancer*, Paula Fox
1975	*M. C. Higgins, the Great*, Virginia Hamilton
1976	*The Grey King*, Susan Cooper
1977	*Roll of Thunder, Hear My Cry*, Mildred D. Taylor
1978	*Bridge to Terabithia*, Katherine Paterson
1979	*The Westing Game*, Ellen Raskin
1980	*A Gathering of Days*, Joan Blos
1981	*Jacob Have I Loved*, Katherine Paterson
1982	*A Visit to William Blake's Inn: Poems for Innocent and Experienced Travelers*, Nancy Willard

Year	Book, author
1983	*Dicey's Song*, Cynthia Voigt
1984	*Dear Mr. Henshaw*, Beverly Cleary
1985	*The Hero and the Crown*, Robin McKinley
1986	*Sarah, Plain and Tall*, Patricia MacLachlan
1987	*The Whipping Boy*, Sid Fleischman
1988	*Lincoln: A Photobiography*, Russell Freedman
1989	*Joyful Noise: Poems for Two Voices*, Paul Fleischman
1990	*Number the Stars*, Lois Lowry
1991	*Maniac Magee*, Jerry Spinelli
1992	*Shiloh*, Phyllis Reynolds Naylor
1993	*Missing May*, Cynthia Rylant
1994	*The Giver*, Lois Lowry
1995	*Walk Two Moons*, Sharon Creech
1996	*The Midwife's Apprentice*, Karen Cushman
1997	*The View From Saturday*, E. L. Konigsburg
1998	*Out of the Dust*, Karen Hesse
1999	*Holes*, Louis Sachar
2000	*Bud, Not Buddy*, Christopher Paul Curtis
2001	*A Year Down Yonder*, Richard Peck
2002	*A Single Shard*, Linda Sue Park
2003	*Crispin: The Cross of Lead*, Avi
2004	*The Tale of Despereaux*, Kate DiCamillo
2005	*Kira-Kira*, Cynthia Kadohata
2006	*Criss Cross*, Lynne Rae Perkins
2007	*The Higher Power of Lucky*, Susan Patron
2008	*Good Masters! Sweet Ladies! Voices From a Medieval Village*, Laura Amy Schlitz
2009	*The Graveyard Book*, Neil Gaiman
2010	*When You Reach Me*, Rebecca Stead
2011	*Moon Over Manifest*, Clare Vanderpool
2012	*Dead End in Norvelt*, Jack Gantos
2013	*The One and Only Ivan*, Katherine Applegate
2014	*Flora & Ulysses: The Illuminated Adventures*, Kate DiCamillo
2015	*The Crossover*, Kwame Alexander
2016	*Last Stop on Market Street*, Matt de la Peña
2017	*The Girl Who Drank the Moon*, Kelly Barnhill
2018	*Hello, Universe*, Erin Entrada Kelly

Caldecott Medal, 1938-2018

The Caldecott Medal is awarded annually by the Association for Library Service to Children, a division of the American Library Association, to the illustrator of the most distinguished American picture book for children.

Year	Book, illustrator
1938	*Animals of the Bible*, Dorothy P. Lathrop
1939	*Mei Li*, Thomas Handforth
1940	*Abraham Lincoln*, Ingri and Edgar Parin d'Aulaire
1941	*They Were Strong and Good*, Robert Lawson
1942	*Make Way for Ducklings*, Robert McCloskey
1943	*The Little House*, Virginia Lee Burton
1944	*Many Moons*, Louis Slobodkin
1945	*Prayer for a Child*, Elizabeth Orton Jones
1946	*The Rooster Crows*, Maude and Miska Petersham
1947	*The Little Island*, Leonard Weisgard
1948	*White Snow, Bright Snow*, Roger Duvoisin
1949	*The Big Snow*, Berta and Elmer Hader
1950	*Song of the Swallows*, Leo Politi
1951	*The Egg Tree*, Katherine Milhous
1952	*Finders Keepers*, Nicolas, pseud. (Nicholas Mordvinoff)
1953	*The Biggest Bear*, Lynd Ward
1954	*Madeline's Rescue*, Ludwig Bemelmans
1955	*Cinderella, or the Little Glass Slipper*, Marcia Brown
1956	*Frog Went A-Courtin'*, Feodor Rojankovsky
1957	*A Tree Is Nice*, Marc Simont
1958	*Time of Wonder*, Robert McCloskey
1959	*Chanticleer and the Fox*, Barbara Cooney
1960	*Nine Days to Christmas*, Marie Hall Ets
1961	*Baboushka and the Three Kings*, Nicolas Sidjakov
1962	*Once a Mouse*, Marcia Brown
1963	*The Snowy Day*, Ezra Jack Keats
1964	*Where the Wild Things Are*, Maurice Sendak
1965	*May I Bring a Friend?*, Beni Montresor
1966	*Always Room for One More*, Nonny Hogrogian
1967	*Sam, Bangs, and Moonshine*, Evaline Ness
1968	*Drummer Hoff*, Ed Emberley
1969	*The Fool of the World and the Flying Ship*, Uri Shulevitz
1970	*Sylvester and the Magic Pebble*, William Steig
1971	*A Story A Story*, Gail E. Haley
1972	*One Fine Day*, Nonny Hogrogian
1973	*The Funny Little Woman*, Blair Lent
1974	*Duffy and the Devil*, Margot Zemach
1975	*Arrow to the Sun*, Gerald McDermott
1976	*Why Mosquitoes Buzz in People's Ears*, Leo and Diane Dillon
1977	*Ashanti to Zulu: African Traditions*, Leo and Diane Dillon
1978	*Noah's Ark*, Peter Spier
1979	*The Girl Who Loved Wild Horses*, Paul Goble
1980	*Ox-Cart Man*, Barbara Cooney
1981	*Fables*, Arnold Lobel

Year	Book, illustrator
1982	*Jumanji*, Chris Van Allsburg
1983	*Shadow*, Marcia Brown
1984	*The Glorious Flight: Across the Channel With Louis Bleriot*, Alice and Martin Provensen
1985	*Saint George and the Dragon*, Trina Schart Hyman
1986	*The Polar Express*, Chris Van Allsburg
1987	*Hey, Al*, Richard Egielski
1988	*Owl Moon*, John Schoenherr
1989	*Song and Dance Man*, Stephen Grammell
1990	*Lon Po Po: A Red-Riding Hood Story From China*, Ed Young
1991	*Black and White*, David Macaulay
1992	*Tuesday*, David Wiesner
1993	*Mirette on the High Wire*, Emily Arnold McCully
1994	*Grandfather's Journey*, Allen Say
1995	*Smoky Night*, David Diaz
1996	*Officer Buckle and Gloria*, Peggy Rathmann
1997	*Golem*, David Wisniewski
1998	*Rapunzel*, Paul O. Zelinsky
1999	*Snowflake Bentley*, Mary Azarian
2000	*Joseph Had a Little Overcoat*, Simms Taback
2001	*So You Want to be President?*, David Small
2002	*The Three Pigs*, David Wiesner
2003	*My Friend Rabbit*, Eric Rohmann
2004	*The Man Who Walked Between the Towers*, Mordicai Gerstein
2005	*Kitten's First Full Moon*, Kevin Henkes
2006	*The Hello, Goodbye Window*, Chris Raschka
2007	*Flotsam*, David Wiesner
2008	*The Invention of Hugo Cabret*, Brian Selznick
2009	*The House in the Night*, Beth Krommes
2010	*The Lion & the Mouse*, Jerry Pinkney
2011	*A Sick Day for Amos McGee*, Erin E. Stead
2012	*A Ball for Daisy*, Chris Raschka
2013	*This Is Not My Hat*, Jon Klassen
2014	*Locomotive*, Brian Floca
2015	*The Adventures of Beekle: The Unimaginary Friend*, Dan Santat
2016	*Finding Winnie: The True Story of the World's Most Famous Bear*, Sophie Blackall
2017	*Radiant Child: The Story of Young Artist Jean-Michel Basquiat*, Javaka Steptoe
2018	*Wolf in the Snow*, Matthew Cordell

National Book Awards, 1950-2017

The National Book Awards (known as American Book Awards 1980-86) are administered by the National Book Foundation and have been given annually since 1950. The prizes, each valued at $10,000, are awarded to U.S. citizens for works published in the U.S. In some years, multiple awards were given for nonfiction in various categories; in such cases, the history and biography (if any) or biography winner is listed. Selected additional awards in nonfiction are listed in footnotes.

Other National Book Awards, 2017: Poetry: Frank Bidart, *Half-light: Collected Poems 1965-2016*. Young People's Literature: Robin Benway, *Far From the Tree*. Distinguished Contribution to American Letters: Annie Proulx. Literarian Award: Dick Robinson.

Fiction

Year	Author, book	Year	Author, book
1950	Nelson Algren, *The Man With the Golden Arm*	1983	Alice Walker, *The Color Purple*
1951	William Faulkner, *The Collected Stories*	1984	Ellen Gilchrist, *Victory Over Japan*
1952	James Jones, *From Here to Eternity*	1985	Don DeLillo, *White Noise*
1953	Ralph Ellison, *Invisible Man*	1986	E. L. Doctorow, *World's Fair*
1954	Saul Bellow, *The Adventures of Augie March*	1987	Larry Heinemann, *Paco's Story*
1955	William Faulkner, *A Fable*	1988	Pete Dexter, *Paris Trout*
1956	John O'Hara, *Ten North Frederick*	1989	John Casey, *Spartina*
1957	Wright Morris, *The Field of Vision*	1990	Charles Johnson, *Middle Passage*
1958	John Cheever, *The Wapshot Chronicle*	1991	Norman Rush, *Mating*
1959	Bernard Malamud, *The Magic Barrel*	1992	Cormac McCarthy, *All the Pretty Horses*
1960	Philip Roth, *Goodbye, Columbus*	1993	E. Annie Proulx, *The Shipping News*
1961	Conrad Richter, *The Waters of Kronos*	1994	William Gaddis, *A Frolic of His Own*
1962	Walker Percy, *The Moviegoer*	1995	Philip Roth, *Sabbath's Theater*
1963	J. F. Powers, *Morte d'Urban*	1996	Andrea Barrett, *Ship Fever and Other Stories*
1964	John Updike, *The Centaur*	1997	Charles Frazier, *Cold Mountain*
1965	Saul Bellow, *Herzog*	1998	Alice McDermott, *Charming Billy*
1966	Katherine Anne Porter, *The Collected Stories*	1999	Ha Jin, *Waiting*
1967	Bernard Malamud, *The Fixer*	2000	Susan Sontag, *In America*
1968	Thornton Wilder, *The Eighth Day*	2001	Jonathan Franzen, *The Corrections*
1969	Jerzy Kosinski, *Steps*	2002	Julia Glass, *Three Junes*
1970	Joyce Carol Oates, *Them*	2003	Shirley Hazzard, *The Great Fire*
1971	Saul Bellow, *Mr. Sammler's Planet*	2004	Lily Tuck, *The News From Paraguay*
1972	Flannery O'Connor, *The Complete Stories*	2005	William T. Vollmann, *Europe Central*
1973	John Barth, *Chimera*	2006	Richard Powers, *The Echo Maker*
1974	Thomas Pynchon, *Gravity's Rainbow*	2007	Denis Johnson, *Tree of Smoke*
1974	Isaac Bashevis Singer, *A Crown of Feathers*	2008	Peter Matthiessen, *Shadow Country*
1975	Robert Stone, *Dog Soldiers*	2009	Colum McCann, *Let the Great World Spin*
1976	William Gaddis, *JR*	2010	Jaimy Gordon, *Lord of Misrule*
1977	Wallace Stegner, *The Spectator Bird*	2011	Jesmyn Ward, *Salvage the Bones*
1978	Mary Lee Settle, *Blood Ties*	2012	Louise Erdrich, *The Round House*
1979	Tim O'Brien, *Going After Cacciato*	2013	James McBride, *The Good Lord Bird*
1980	William Styron, *Sophie's Choice*	2014	Phil Klay, *Redeployment*
1981	Wright Morris, *Plains Song*	2015	Adam Johnson, *Fortune Smiles: Stories*
1982	John Updike, *Rabbit Is Rich*	2016	Colson Whitehead, *The Underground Railroad*
		2017	Jesmyn Ward, *Sing, Unburied, Sing*

Nonfiction

Year	Author, book	Year	Author, book
1950	Ralph L. Rusk, *Ralph Waldo Emerson*	1975	Richard B. Sewall, *The Life of Emily Dickinson*[6]
1951	Newton Arvin, *Herman Melville*	1976	David Brion Davis, *The Problem of Slavery in the Age of Revolution, 1770-1823*
1952	Rachel Carson, *The Sea Around Us*		
1953	Bernard A. De Voto, *The Course of an Empire*	1977	W. A. Swanberg, *Norman Thomas: The Last Idealist*[7]
1954	Bruce Catton, *A Stillness at Appomattox*	1978	W. Jackson Bate, *Samuel Johnson*
1955	Joseph Wood Krutch, *The Measure of Man*	1979	Arthur M. Schlesinger Jr., *Robert Kennedy and His Times*
1956	Herbert Kubly, *An American in Italy*	1980	Tom Wolfe, *The Right Stuff*
1957	George F. Kennan, *Russia Leaves the War*	1981	Maxine Hong Kingston, *China Men*
1958	Catherine Drinker Bowen, *The Lion and the Throne*	1982	Tracy Kidder, *The Soul of a New Machine*
1959	J. Christopher Herold, *Mistress to an Age: A Life of Madame De Stael*	1983	Fox Butterfield, *China: Alive in the Bitter Sea*
		1984	Robert V. Remini, *Andrew Jackson and the Course of American Democracy, 1833-1845*
1960	Richard Ellman, *James Joyce*		
1961	William L. Shirer, *The Rise and Fall of the Third Reich*	1985	J. Anthony Lukas, *Common Ground: A Turbulent Decade in the Lives of Three American Families*
1962	Lewis Mumford, *The City in History: Its Origins, Its Transformations, and Its Prospects*		
		1986	Barry Lopez, *Arctic Dreams*
1963	Leon Edel, *Henry James, Vol. II: The Conquest of London* and *Vol. III: The Middle Years*	1987	Richard Rhodes, *The Making of the Atom Bomb*
		1988	Neil Sheehan, *A Bright Shining Lie: John Paul Vann and America in Vietnam*
1964	William H. McNeill, *The Rise of the West: A History of the Human Community*		
		1989	Thomas L. Friedman, *From Beirut to Jerusalem*
1965	Louis Fisher, *The Life of Lenin*	1990	Ron Chernow, *The House of Morgan: An American Banking Dynasty and the Rise of Modern Finance*
1966	Arthur M. Schlesinger Jr., *A Thousand Days: John F. Kennedy in the White House*		
		1991	Orlando Patterson, *Freedom*
1967	Peter Gay, *The Enlightenment, An Interpretation, Vol. I: The Rise of Modern Paganism*	1992	Paul Monette, *Becoming a Man: Half a Life Story*
		1993	Gore Vidal, *United States: Essays 1952-1992*
1968	George F. Kennan, *Memoirs: 1925-1950*[1]	1994	Sherwin B. Nuland, *How We Die: Reflections on Life's Final Chapter*
1969	Winthrop D. Jordan, *White Over Black: American Attitudes Toward the Negro, 1550-1812*[2]		
		1995	Tina Rosenberg, *The Haunted Land: Facing Europe's Ghosts After Communism*
1970	T. Harry Williams, *Huey Long*[3]		
1971	James MacGregor Burns, *Roosevelt: The Soldier of Freedom*	1996	James Carroll, *An American Requiem: God, My Father, and the War That Came Between Us*
1972	Joseph P. Lash, *Eleanor and Franklin: The Story of Their Relationship, Based on Eleanor Roosevelt's Private Papers*	1997	Joseph J. Ellis, *American Sphinx: The Character of Thomas Jefferson*
		1998	Edward Ball, *Slaves in the Family*
1973	James Thomas Flexner, *George Washington, Vol. IV: Anguish and Farewell, 1793-1799*[4]	1999	John W. Dower, *Embracing Defeat: Japan in the Wake of World War II*
1974	John Clive, *Macaulay, The Shaping of the Historian*; Douglas Day, *Malcolm Lowry: A Biography*[5]	2000	Nathaniel Philbrick, *In the Heart of the Sea: The Tragedy of the Whaleship Essex*

Year	Author, book
2001	Andrew Solomon, *The Noonday Demon: An Atlas of Depression*
2002	Robert A. Caro, *Master of the Senate: The Years of Lyndon Johnson*
2003	Carlos Eire, *Waiting for Snow in Havana: Confessions of a Cuban Boy*
2004	Kevin Boyle, *Arc of Justice: A Saga of Race, Civil Rights, and Murder in the Jazz Age*
2005	Joan Didion, *The Year of Magical Thinking*
2006	Timothy Egan, *The Worst Hard Time: The Untold Story of Those Who Survived the Great American Dust Bowl*
2007	Tim Weiner, *Legacy of Ashes: The History of the CIA*
2008	Annette Gordon-Reed, *The Hemingses of Monticello: An American Family*

Year	Author, book
2009	T. J. Stiles, *The First Tycoon: The Epic Life of Cornelius Vanderbilt*
2010	Patti Smith, *Just Kids*
2011	Stephen Greenblatt, *The Swerve: How the World Became Modern*
2012	Katherine Boo, *Behind the Beautiful Forevers: Life, Death, and Hope in a Mumbai Undercity*
2013	George Packer, *The Unwinding: An Inner History of the New America*
2014	Evan Osnos, *Age of Ambition: Chasing Fortune, Truth, and Faith in the New China*
2015	Ta-Nehisi Coates, *Between the World and Me*
2016	Ibram X. Kendi, *Stamped From the Beginning: The Definitive History of Racist Ideas in America*
2017	Masha Gessen, *The Future Is History: How Totalitarianism Reclaimed Russia*

(1) Science, Philosophy, & Religion: Jonathan Kozol, *Death at an Early Age*. (2) Arts & Letters: Norman Mailer, *The Armies of the Night: History as a Novel, the Novel as History*. (3) Arts & Letters: Lillian Hellman, *An Unfinished Woman: A Memoir*. (4) Contemp. Affairs: Frances FitzGerald, *Fire in the Lake: The Vietnamese and the Americans in Vietnam*. (5) Arts & Letters: Pauline Kael, *Deeper Into the Movies*. (6) Arts & Letters: Roger Shattuck, *Marcel Proust*; Lewis Thomas, *The Lives of a Cell: Notes of a Biology Watcher*. (7) Contemp. Thought: Bruno Bettelheim, *The Uses of Enchantment: The Meaning and Importance of Fairy Tales*.

Journalism Awards, 2018

National Magazine Awards, by American Society of Magazine Editors and Columbia Univ. Graduate School of Journalism, honoring excellence in print and on digital platforms. General Excellence—News, Sports, and Entertainment: *The New Yorker*; Literature, Science, and Politics: *Aperture*; Service and Lifestyle: *T, The NY Times Style Magazine*; Special Interest: *San Francisco*. ASME Award for Fiction: *Zoetrope: All-Story*. Columns and Commentary: *New York*. Design: *GQ*. Digital Innovation: SB Nation. Essays and Criticism: *The Atlantic*. Feature Photography: *The New Yorker*. Feature Writing: *GQ*. Leisure Interests: *Texas Monthly*. Magazine Section: *New York*. Personal Service: *Cosmopolitan*. Photography: *W*. Public Interest: *The New Yorker*. Reporting: *The NY Times Magazine*. Single-Topic Issue: *National Geographic*. Social Media: *SELF*. Video: *Time* and Mic. Website: *New York*.

George Foster Peabody Awards, by Univ. of Georgia, awarded to the best in electronic media. Career achievement: Carol Burnett. Institutional award: The Fred Rogers Company, *60 Minutes*. Others alphabetically by media outlet. *The Cut: Exploring FGM*, Al Jazeera. *The Marvelous Mrs. Maisel*, Amazon. *Better Call Saul*, AMC. *Plight of Rohingya Refugees*, BBC World News. "The Whistleblower," *60 Minutes*, CBS. *Fall of ISIS in Iraq and Syria*, CNN. *Indivisible: Love Knows No Borders*, Fuse. "The Raid," *Uncivil*, Gimlet Media. *Insecure*; *Last Week Tonight With John Oliver*; "Charlottesville: Race and Terror," *VICE News Tonight*; HBO. *The Handmaid's Tale*, Hulu. "Deej," *America ReFramed*, ITVS/WORLD Channel. "Big Buses, Bigger Problems: Taxpayers Taken for a Ride," KXAS-TV, Dallas-Ft. Worth. *The Pope's Long Con*, Louisville Public Media/Kentucky Center for Investigative Reporting. "Political Satire 2017," *Saturday Night Live*, NBC. *74 Seconds*, Minnesota Public Radio/American Public Media. *American Vandal, Chasing Coral, Hasan Minhaj: Homecoming King, A Series of Unfortunate Events*, Netflix. *Lost Mothers: Maternal Mortality in the U.S.*, NPR/ProPublica. "Newtown," *Independent Lens*; "The Islands and the Whales," "Last Men in Aleppo," *POV*; PBS. "Inside Putin's Russia," *PBS NewsHour*, PBS/WETA. "Oklahoma City," *American Experience*, PBS/WGBH. "Maya Angelou: And Still I Rise," *American Masters*, PBS/WNET. *S-Town*, Serial/This American Life. *TIME: The Kalief Browder Story*, Spike.

Scripps Howard Awards, by Scripps Howard Foundation. Breaking News: *San Francisco Chronicle* staff (CA). Broadcast, Local Coverage: Brendan Keefe, WXIA 11Alive Atlanta. Broadcast Natl. and Intl. Coverage: Debora Patta, Sarah Carter, Meshack Dube, CBS News. Business/Financial Reporting: Brian Grow, John Shiffman, and team, Reuters. Community Journalism: *Bristol Herald Courier* staff (Bristol, VA). Distinguished Service to the First Amendment: *Kansas City Star* staff (MO). Environmental Reporting: Kale Williams, *The Oregonian/OregonLive*. Human Interest Storytelling: John Woodrow Cox, *Washington Post*. Innovation: *Arizona Republic* staff. Investigative Reporting: *NY Times* staff. Multimedia: *Washington Post* staff. Opinion: Melinda Henneberger, *Kansas City Star*. Visual journalism: Leah Millis, *San Francisco Chronicle*. Radio/Podcast: Gregory Warner, Marianne McCune, Jess Jiang, Laura Heaton, Michael May, NPR. Topic of the Year: Elle Reeve, Vice News.

Miscellaneous Book Awards, 2018

Coretta Scott King Awards, by American Library Assn., for African American authors and illustrators of outstanding books for children and young adults. Author: Renée Watson, *Piecing Me Together*. Illustrator: Ekua Holmes, *Out of Wonder: Poems Celebrating Poets*. New talent: David Barclay Moore, *The Stars Beneath Our Feet*.

Costa Book Awards. Book of the Year (formerly Whitbread Award): *Inside the Wave*, Helen Dunmore.

Edgar Awards, by the Mystery Writers of America. Novel: *Bluebird, Bluebird*, Attica Locke. First Novel: *She Rides Shotgun*, Jordan Harper. Paperback Original: *The Unseeing*, Anna Mazzola. Fact Crime: *Killers of the Flower Moon: The Osage Murders and the Birth of the FBI*, David Grann. Critical/Biographical: *Chester B. Himes: A Biography*, Lawrence P. Jackson. Short Story: "Spring Break," *New Haven Noir*, John Crowley. Juvenile: *Vanished!*, James Ponti. Young Adult: *Long Way Down*, Jason Reynolds. TV Episode: "Somebody to Love," *Fargo*, Noah Hawley. Robert L. Fish Award: "The Queen of Secrets," *New Haven Noir*, Lisa D. Gray. Grand Master: Jane Langton, William Link, Peter Lovesey. Raven Award: Kristopher Zgorski, BOLO Books; The Raven Bookstore, Lawrence, KS. Ellery Queen Award: Robert Pépin. Simon & Schuster-Mary Higgins Clark Award: *The Widow's House*, Carol Goodman.

Golden Kite Awards, by the Society of Children's Book Writers and Illustrators. Middle Grade: *See You in the Cosmos*, Jack Cheng. Nonfiction (older readers): *Vincent and Theo*, Deborah Heiligman. Nonfiction (younger readers): *Schomburg: The Man Who Built a Library*, Carole Boston Weatherford. YA: *What Girls Are Made Of*, Elana K. Arnold. Picture Book Text: *There Might Be Lobsters*, Carolyn Crimi. Picture Book Illustration: *Goodbye Autumn, Hello Winter*, Kenard Pak. Sid Fleischman Humor Award: *The Magnificent Mya Tibbs: The Wall of Fame Game*, Crystal Allen.

Hugo Awards, by the World Science Fiction Society (WSFS). Novel: *The Stone Sky*, N. K. Jemisin. Novella: *All Systems Red*, Martha Wells. Novelette: "The Secret Life of Bots," Suzanne Palmer. Short Story: "Welcome to your Authentic Indian Experience™," by Rebecca Roanhorse. Related Work: *No Time to Spare: Thinking About What Matters*, Ursula K. Le Guin. Series: World of the Five Gods, Lois McMaster Bujold. Graphic Story: *Monstress, Volume 2: The Blood*, Marjorie M. Liu, illus. by Sana Takeda. Dramatic Presentation, long form: *Wonder Woman*, Allan Heinberg. Dramatic Presentation, short form: "The Trolley Problem," *The Good Place*, Josh Siegal and Dylan Morgan.

National Book Critics Circle Awards. Fiction: Joan Silber, *Improvement*. Nonfiction: Frances FitzGerald, *The Evangelicals: The Struggle to Shape America*. Autobiography: Xiaolu Guo, *Nine Continents: A Memoir In and Out of China*. Biography: Caroline Fraser, *Prairie Fires: The American Dreams of Laura Ingalls Wilder*. Criticism: Carina Chocano, *You Play the Girl: On Playboy Bunnies, Stepford Wives, Trainwrecks, & Other Mixed Messages*. Poetry: Layli Long Soldier, *Whereas*. John Leonard Prize: Carmen Maria Machado, *Her Body and Other Parties*. Ivan Sandrof Lifetime Achievement Award: John McPhee. Nona Balakian Citation for Excellence in Reviewing: Charles Finch.

Nebula Awards, by the Science Fiction and Fantasy Writers of America. Novel: *The Stone Sky*, N. K. Jemisin. Novella: *All Systems Red*, Martha Wells. Novelette: "A Human Stain," Kelly Robson. Short Story: "Welcome to Your Authentic Indian Experience™," Rebecca Roanhorse. Ray Bradbury Award: *Get Out*, Jordan Peele. Andre Norton Award: *The Art of Starving*, Sam J. Miller.

PEN/Faulkner Award, for fiction: Joan Silber, *Improvement*.

Printz Award, for young adult literature: *We Are Okay*, Nina LaCour.

Spingarn Medal, 1915-2018

The Spingarn Medal has been awarded annually in most years since 1915 by the National Assn. for the Advancement of Colored People for outstanding achievement by an African American.

1915 Ernest E. Just	1942 A. Philip Randolph	1967 Edward W. Brooke	1993 Dorothy I. Height
1916 Charles Young	1943 William H. Hastie	1968 Sammy Davis Jr.	1994 Maya Angelou
1917 Harry T. Burleigh	1944 Charles Drew	1969 Clarence M. Mitchell Jr.	1995 John Hope Franklin
1918 William S. Braithwaite	1945 Paul Robeson	1970 Jacob Lawrence	1996 A. Leon Higginbotham Jr.
1919 Archibald H. Grimké	1946 Thurgood Marshall	1971 Leon H. Sullivan	1997 Carl T. Rowan
1920 W. E. B. Du Bois	1947 Dr. Percy L. Julian	1972 Gordon Parks	1998 Myrlie Evers-Williams
1921 Charles S. Gilpin	1948 Channing H. Tobias	1973 Wilson C. Riles	1999 Earl G. Graves Sr.
1922 Mary B. Talbert	1949 Ralph J. Bunche	1974 Damon Keith	2000 Oprah Winfrey
1923 George W. Carver	1950 Charles H. Houston	1976 Henry (Hank) Aaron	2001 Vernon E. Jordan Jr.
1924 Roland Hayes	1951 Mabel K. Staupers	1977 Alvin Ailey	2002 John Lewis
1925 James W. Johnson	1952 Harry T. Moore	1977 Alex Haley	2003 Constance Baker Motley
1926 Carter G. Woodson	1953 Paul R. Williams	1979 Andrew Young	2004 Robert L. Carter
1927 Anthony Overton	1954 Theodore K. Lawless	1979 Rosa L. Parks	2005 Oliver W. Hill
1928 Charles W. Chesnutt	1955 Carl Murphy	1980 Dr. Rayford W. Logan	2006 Dr. Benjamin S. Carson
1929 Mordecai W. Johnson	1956 Jack R. Robinson	1981 Coleman Young	2007 John Conyers Jr.
1930 Henry A. Hunt	1957 Martin Luther King Jr.	1982 Dr. Benjamin E. Mays	2008 Ruby Dee
1931 Richard B. Harrison	1958 Daisy Bates and the	1983 Lena Horne	2009 Julian Bond
1932 Robert R. Moton	Little Rock Nine	1985 Thomas Bradley	2010 Cicely Tyson
1933 Max Yergan	1959 Duke Ellington	1985 Bill Cosby	2011 Frankie Muse Freeman
1934 William T. B. Williams	1960 Langston Hughes	1986 Dr. Benjamin L. Hooks	2012 Harry Belafonte
1935 Mary McLeod Bethune	1961 Kenneth B. Clark	1987 Percy E. Sutton	2013 Jessye Norman
1936 John Hope	1962 Robert C. Weaver	1988 Frederick D. Patterson	2014 Quincy Jones
1937 Walter White	1963 Medgar W. Evers	1989 Jesse Jackson	2015 Sidney Poitier
1939 Marian Anderson	1964 Roy Wilkins	1990 L. Douglas Wilder	2016 Nathaniel R. Jones
1940 Louis T. Wright	1965 Leontyne Price	1991 Gen. Colin L. Powell	2018 Willie L. Brown Jr.
1941 Richard Wright	1966 John H. Johnson	1992 Barbara Jordan	

Miss America Winners, 1921-2019

Year	Winner, hometown	Year	Winner, hometown
1921	Margaret Gorman, Washington, DC	1974	Rebecca Ann King, Denver, Colorado
1922-23	Mary Campbell, Columbus, Ohio	1975	Shirley Cothran, Denton, Texas
1924	Ruth Malcolmson, Philadelphia, Pennsylvania	1976	Tawney Elaine Godin, Saratoga Springs, New York
1925	Fay Lamphier, Oakland, California	1977	Dorothy Kathleen Benham, Edina, Minnesota
1926	Norma Smallwood, Tulsa, Oklahoma	1978	Susan Perkins, Columbus, Ohio
1927	Lois Delander, Joliet, Illinois	1979	Kylene Barker, Roanoke, Virginia
1933	Marion Bergeron, West Haven, Connecticut	1980	Cheryl Prewitt, Ackerman, Mississippi
1935	Henrietta Leaver, Pittsburgh, Pennsylvania	1981	Susan Powell, Elk City, Oklahoma
1936	Rose Coyle, Philadelphia, Pennsylvania	1982	Elizabeth Ward, Russellville, Arkansas
1937	Bette Cooper, Bertrand Island, New Jersey	1983	Debra Maffett, Anaheim, California
1938	Marilyn Meseke, Marion, Ohio	1984[1]	Suzette Charles, Mays Landing, New Jersey
1939	Patricia Donnelly, Detroit, Michigan	1985	Sharlene Wells, Salt Lake City, Utah
1940	Frances Marie Burke, Philadelphia, Pennsylvania	1986	Susan Akin, Meridian, Mississippi
1941	Rosemary LaPlanche, Los Angeles, California	1987	Kellye Cash, Memphis, Tennessee
1942	Jo-Caroll Dennison, Tyler, Texas	1988	Kaye Lani Rae Rafko, Monroe, Michigan
1943	Jean Bartel, Los Angeles, California	1989	Gretchen Carlson, Anoka, Minnesota
1944	Venus Ramey, Washington, DC	1990	Debbye Turner, Columbia, Missouri
1945	Bess Myerson, New York, New York	1991	Marjorie Vincent, Oak Park, Illinois
1946	Marilyn Buferd, Los Angeles, California	1992	Carolyn Suzanne Sapp, Honolulu, Hawaii
1947	Barbara Walker, Memphis, Tennessee	1993	Leanza Cornett, Jacksonville, Florida
1948	BeBe Shopp, Hopkins, Minnesota	1994	Kimberly Aiken, Columbia, South Carolina
1949	Jacque Mercer, Litchfield, Arizona	1995	Heather Whitestone, Birmingham, Alabama
1951	Yolande Betbeze, Mobile, Alabama	1996	Shawntel Smith, Muldrow, Oklahoma
1952	Coleen Kay Hutchins, Salt Lake City, Utah	1997	Tara Dawn Holland, Overland Park, Kansas
1953	Neva Jane Langley, Macon, Georgia	1998	Kate Shindle, Evanston, Illinois
1954	Evelyn Margaret Ay, Ephrata, Pennsylvania	1999	Nicole Johnson, Roanoke, Virginia
1955	Lee Meriwether, San Francisco, California	2000	Heather Renee French, Maysville, Kentucky
1956	Sharon Ritchie, Denver, Colorado	2001	Angela Perez Baraquio, Honolulu, Hawaii
1957	Marian McKnight, Manning, South Carolina	2002	Katie Harman, Gresham, Oregon
1958	Marilyn Van Derbur, Denver, Colorado	2003	Erika Harold, Urbana, Illinois
1959	Mary Ann Mobley, Brandon, Mississippi	2004	Ericka Dunlap, Orlando, Florida
1960	Lynda Lee Mead, Natchez, Mississippi	2005	Deidre Downs, Birmingham, Alabama
1961	Nancy Fleming, Montague, Michigan	2006	Jennifer Berry, Tulsa, Oklahoma
1962	Maria Fletcher, Asheville, North Carolina	2007	Lauren Nelson, Lawton, Oklahoma
1963	Jacquelyn Mayer, Sandusky, Ohio	2008	Kirsten Haglund, Farmington Hills, Michigan
1964	Donna Axum, El Dorado, Arkansas	2009	Katie Stam, Seymour, Indiana
1965	Vonda Kay Van Dyke, Phoenix, Arizona	2010	Caressa Cameron, Fredricksburg, Virginia
1966	Deborah Irene Bryant, Overland Park, Kansas	2011	Teresa Scanlan, Gering, Nebraska
1967	Jane Anne Jayroe, Laverne, Oklahoma	2012	Laura Kaeppeler, Kenosha, Wisconsin
1968	Debra Dene Barnes, Moran, Kansas	2013	Mallory Hytes Hagen, Brooklyn, New York
1969	Judith Anne Ford, Belvidere, Illinois	2014	Nina Davuluri, Syracuse, New York
1970	Pamela Anne Eldred, Birmingham, Michigan	2015	Kira Kazantsev, New York, New York
1971	Phyllis Ann George, Denton, Texas	2016	Betty Cantrell, Warner Robins, Georgia
1972	Laurie Lea Schaefer, Bexley, Ohio	2017	Savvy Shields, Fayetteville, Arkansas
1973	Terry Anne Meeuwsen, DePere, Wisconsin	2018	Cara Mund, Bismarck, North Dakota
		2019	Nia Franklin, Brooklyn, New York

Note: Since the 1950 pageant, winners have been crowned Miss America of the following year (e.g., Miss America 1951 competed in 1950). (1) Miss New York, Vanessa Williams, resigned July 23, 1984.

Tony (Antoinette Perry) Awards, 2018

Play: *Harry Potter and the Cursed Child, Parts One and Two*
Musical: *The Band's Visit*
Book of a musical: *The Band's Visit*, Itamar Moses
Original score: *The Band's Visit*, David Yazbek
Play revival: *Angels in America*
Musical revival: *Once on This Island*
Actor, play: Andrew Garfield, *Angels in America*
Actress, play: Glenda Jackson, *Edward Albee's Three Tall Women*
Actor, musical: Tony Shalhoub, *The Band's Visit*
Actress, musical: Katrina Lenk, *The Band's Visit*
Featured actor, play: Nathan Lane, *Angels in America*
Featured actress, play: Laurie Metcalf, *Edward Albee's Three Tall Women*
Featured actor, musical: Ari'el Stachel, *The Band's Visit*
Featured actress, musical: Lindsay Mendez, *Rodgers & Hammerstein's Carousel*
Direction, play: John Tiffany, *Harry Potter and the Cursed Child, Parts One and Two*
Direction, musical: David Cromer, *The Band's Visit*
Choreography: Justin Peck, *Rodgers & Hammerstein's Carousel*
Orchestrations: Jamshied Sharifi, *The Band's Visit*

Costume design, play: Katrina Lindsay, *Harry Potter and the Cursed Child, Parts One and Two*
Costume design, musical: Catherine Zuber, *My Fair Lady*
Lighting design, play: Neil Austin, *Harry Potter and the Cursed Child, Parts One and Two*
Lighting design, musical: Tyler Micoleau, *The Band's Visit*
Scenic design, play: Christine Jones, *Harry Potter and the Cursed Child, Parts One and Two*
Scenic design, musical: David Zinn, *SpongeBob SquarePants: The Musical*
Sound design, play: Gareth Fry, *Harry Potter and the Cursed Child, Parts One and Two*
Sound design, musical: Kai Harada, *The Band's Visit*
Regional theatre: La MaMa Experimental Theatre Club, New York, NY
Special Tony Award: John Leguizamo, Bruce Springsteen
Special Tony Award, lifetime achievement: Chita Rivera, Andrew Lloyd Webber
Isabelle Stevenson Award: Nick Scandalios
Tony Honors for Excellence in the Theatre: Sara Krulwich, Bessie Nelson, Ernest Winzer Cleaners

Tony Awards, 1948-2018

Year	Play	Musical
1948	*Mister Roberts*	No award
1949	*Death of a Salesman*	*Kiss Me Kate*
1950	*The Cocktail Party*	*South Pacific*
1951	*The Rose Tattoo*	*Guys and Dolls*
1952	*The Fourposter*	*The King and I*
1953	*The Crucible*	*Wonderful Town*
1954	*The Teahouse of the August Moon*	*Kismet*
1955	*The Desperate Hours*	*The Pajama Game*
1956	*The Diary of Anne Frank*	*Damn Yankees*
1957	*Long Day's Journey Into Night*	*My Fair Lady*
1958	*Sunrise at Campobello*	*The Music Man*
1959	*J.B.*	*Redhead*
1960	*The Miracle Worker*	*Fiorello!* and *The Sound of Music*
1961	*Becket*	*Bye, Bye Birdie*
1962	*A Man for All Seasons*	*How to Succeed in Business Without Really Trying*
1963	*Who's Afraid of Virginia Woolf?*	*A Funny Thing Happened on the Way to the Forum*
1964	*Luther*	*Hello, Dolly!*
1965	*The Subject Was Roses*	*Fiddler on the Roof*
1966	*Marat/Sade*	*Man of La Mancha*
1967	*The Homecoming*	*Cabaret*
1968	*Rosencrantz and Guildenstern Are Dead*	*Hallelujah, Baby!*
1969	*The Great White Hope*	*1776*
1970	*Borstal Boy*	*Applause*
1971	*Sleuth*	*Company*
1972	*Sticks and Bones*	*Two Gentlemen of Verona*
1973	*That Championship Season*	*A Little Night Music*
1974	*The River Niger*	*Raisin*
1975	*Equus*	*The Wiz*
1976	*Travesties*	*A Chorus Line*
1977	*The Shadow Box*	*Annie*
1978	*Da*	*Ain't Misbehavin'*
1979	*The Elephant Man*	*Sweeney Todd*
1980	*Children of a Lesser God*	*Evita*
1981	*Amadeus*	*42nd Street*
1982	*The Life and Adventures of Nicholas Nickelby*	*Nine*
1983	*Torch Song Trilogy*	*Cats*
1984	*The Real Thing*	*La Cage aux Folles*
1985	*Biloxi Blues*	*Big River*
1986	*I'm Not Rappaport*	*The Mystery of Edwin Drood*
1987	*Fences*	*Les Misérables*
1988	*M. Butterfly*	*Phantom of the Opera*
1989	*The Heidi Chronicles*	*Jerome Robbins' Broadway*
1990	*The Grapes of Wrath*	*City of Angels*
1991	*Lost in Yonkers*	*The Will Rogers Follies*
1992	*Dancing at Lughnasa*	*Crazy for You*
1993	*Angels in America: Millennium Approaches*	*Kiss of the Spider Woman*
1994	*Angels in America: Perestroika*	*Passion*
1995	*Love! Valour! Compassion!*	*Sunset Boulevard*
1996	*Master Class*	*Rent*
1997	*The Last Night of Ballyhoo*	*Titanic*
1998	*Art*	*The Lion King*
1999	*Side Man*	*Fosse*
2000	*Copenhagen*	*Contact*
2001	*Proof*	*The Producers*
2002	*Edward Albee's The Goat or Who Is Sylvia?*	*Thoroughly Modern Millie*
2003	*Take Me Out*	*Hairspray*
2004	*I Am My Own Wife*	*Avenue Q*
2005	*Doubt*	*Monty Python's Spamalot*
2006	*The History Boys*	*Jersey Boys*
2007	*The Coast of Utopia*	*Spring Awakening*
2008	*August: Osage County*	*In the Heights*
2009	*God of Carnage*	*Billy Elliot, The Musical*
2010	*Red*	*Memphis*
2011	*War Horse*	*The Book of Mormon*
2012	*Clybourne Park*	*Once*
2013	*Vanya and Sonia and Masha and Spike*	*Kinky Boots*
2014	*All the Way*	*A Gentleman's Guide to Love & Murder*
2015	*The Curious Incident of the Dog in the Night-Time*	*Fun Home*
2016	*The Humans*	*Hamilton*
2017	*Oslo*	*Dear Evan Hansen*
2018	*Harry Potter and the Cursed Child, Parts One and Two*	*The Band's Visit*

Selected Prime-Time Emmy Awards, 2018

Drama series: *Game of Thrones*, HBO
Comedy series: *The Marvelous Mrs. Maisel*, Amazon
Limited series: *The Assassination of Gianni Versace: American Crime Story*, FX
TV movie: *Black Mirror: USS Callister*, Netflix
Variety talk series: *Last Week Tonight With John Oliver*, HBO
Variety sketch series: *Saturday Night Live*, NBC
Lead actor, drama: Matthew Rhys, *The Americans*, FX
Lead actress, drama: Claire Foy, *The Crown*, Netflix
Lead actor, comedy: Bill Hader, *Barry*, HBO
Lead actress, comedy: Rachel Brosnahan, *The Marvelous Mrs. Maisel*, Amazon
Lead actor, limited series: Darren Criss, *The Assassination of Gianni Versace: American Crime Story*, FX
Lead actress, limited series: Regina King, *Seven Seconds*, Netflix
Sup. actor, drama: Peter Dinklage, *Game of Thrones*, HBO
Sup. actress, drama: Thandie Newton, *Westworld*, HBO
Sup. actor, comedy: Henry Winkler, *Barry*, HBO
Sup. actress, comedy: Alex Borstein, *The Marvelous Mrs. Maisel*, Amazon
Sup. actor, limited series: Jeff Daniels, *Godless*, Netflix
Sup. actress, limited series: Merritt Wever, *Godless*, Netflix
Reality-competition program: *RuPaul's Drag Race*, VH1

Prime-Time Emmy Awards, 1952-2018

The Academy of Television Arts and Sciences presented the first Emmy Awards in 1949. Through the years, award categories have changed, but since 1952, the Academy has given out an outstanding comedy and drama award annually.

Year	Comedy	Drama	Year	Comedy	Drama
1952	Red Skelton Show, NBC	Studio One, CBS	1982	Barney Miller, ABC	Hill Street Blues, NBC
1953	I Love Lucy, CBS	Robert Montgomery Presents, NBC	1983	Cheers, NBC	Hill Street Blues, NBC
1954	I Love Lucy, CBS	The U.S. Steel Hour, ABC	1984	Cheers, NBC	Hill Street Blues, NBC
1955	Make Room for Daddy, ABC	The U.S. Steel Hour, ABC	1985	The Cosby Show, NBC	Cagney & Lacey, CBS
1956	Phil Silvers Show, CBS	Producers' Showcase, NBC	1986	Golden Girls, NBC	Cagney & Lacey, CBS
1957	Phil Silvers Show, CBS	"Requiem for a Heavyweight," CBS[1]	1987	Golden Girls, NBC	L.A. Law, NBC
			1988	The Wonder Years, ABC	thirtysomething, ABC
1958	Phil Silvers Show, CBS	Gunsmoke, CBS	1989	Cheers, NBC	L.A. Law, NBC
1959[2]	Jack Benny Show, CBS	2 awards[3]	1990	Murphy Brown, CBS	L.A. Law, NBC
1960	Art Carney Special, NBC	Playhouse 90, CBS	1991	Cheers, NBC	L.A. Law, NBC
1961	Jack Benny Show, CBS	Hallmark Hall of Fame: Macbeth, NBC	1992	Murphy Brown, CBS	Northern Exposure, CBS
			1993	Seinfeld, NBC	Picket Fences, CBS
1962	Bob Newhart Show, CBS	The Defenders, CBS	1994	Frasier, NBC	Picket Fences, CBS
1963	Dick Van Dyke Show, CBS	The Defenders, CBS	1995	Frasier, NBC	NYPD Blue, ABC
1964	Dick Van Dyke Show, CBS	The Defenders, CBS	1996	Frasier, NBC	ER, NBC
1965	Dick Van Dyke Show, CBS	Hallmark Hall of Fame: The Magnificent Yankee, NBC	1997	Frasier, NBC	Law & Order, NBC
			1998	Frasier, NBC	The Practice, ABC
1966	Dick Van Dyke Show, CBS	The Fugitive, ABC	1999	Ally McBeal, FOX	The Practice, ABC
1967	The Monkees, NBC	Mission: Impossible, CBS	2000	Will & Grace, NBC	The West Wing, NBC
1968	Get Smart, NBC	Mission: Impossible, CBS	2001	Sex and the City, HBO	The West Wing, NBC
1969	Get Smart, NBC	NET Playhouse, NET	2002	Friends, NBC	The West Wing, NBC
1970	My World and Welcome to It, NBC	Marcus Welby, M.D., ABC	2003	Everybody Loves Raymond, CBS	The West Wing, NBC
1971	All in the Family, CBS	The Bold Ones: The Senator, NBC	2004	Arrested Development, FOX	The Sopranos, HBO
			2005	Everybody Loves Raymond, CBS	Lost, ABC
1972	All in the Family, CBS	Masterpiece Theatre: Elizabeth R, PBS	2006	The Office, NBC	24, FOX
1973	All in the Family, CBS	The Waltons, CBS	2007	30 Rock, NBC	The Sopranos, HBO
1974	M*A*S*H, CBS	Masterpiece Theatre: Upstairs, Downstairs; PBS	2008	30 Rock, NBC	Mad Men, AMC
			2009	30 Rock, NBC	Mad Men, AMC
1975	Mary Tyler Moore Show, CBS	Masterpiece Theatre: Upstairs, Downstairs; PBS	2010	Modern Family, ABC	Mad Men, AMC
			2011	Modern Family, ABC	Mad Men, AMC
1976	Mary Tyler Moore Show, CBS	Police Story, NBC	2012	Modern Family, ABC	Homeland, Showtime
1977	Mary Tyler Moore Show, CBS	Masterpiece Theatre: Upstairs, Downstairs; PBS	2013	Modern Family, ABC	Breaking Bad, AMC
			2014	Modern Family, ABC	Breaking Bad, AMC
1978	All in the Family, CBS	The Rockford Files, NBC	2015	Veep, HBO	Game of Thrones, HBO
1979	Taxi, ABC	Lou Grant, CBS	2016	Veep, HBO	Game of Thrones, HBO
1980	Taxi, ABC	Lou Grant, CBS	2017	Veep, HBO	The Handmaid's Tale, Hulu
1981	Taxi, ABC	Hill Street Blues, NBC	2018	The Marvelous Mrs. Maisel, Amazon	Game of Thrones, HBO

(1) Best single program of the year; shown on Playhouse 90, which was named best new series. (2) Beginning in 1959, Emmys were awarded for work in the season encompassing the previous and current year. (3) Playhouse 90 (CBS) was best dramatic series of one hour or longer, Alcoa-Goodyear Theatre (NBC) of less than one hour.

Selected Daytime Emmy Awards, 2018

Children's/family viewing series: Free Rein, Netflix
Children's series, animated: SpongeBob SquarePants, Nickelodeon
Culinary program: A Chef's Life, PBS
Drama series: Days of Our Lives, NBC
Drama series, digital: The Bay, Amazon
Education/informational series: Giver, ION
Entertainment news program: Entertainment Tonight, CBS
Entertainment program, Spanish language: Destinos, CNN en Español
Game show: The Price Is Right, CBS
Legal/courtroom program: Judge Mathis, synd.
Morning program: Good Morning America, ABC
Morning program, Spanish language: Despiérta America, Univision

Talk show, entertainment: The Talk, CBS
Talk show, informative: The Dr. Oz Show, synd.
Lead actress: Eileen Davidson, The Young and the Restless, CBS
Lead actor: James Reynolds, Days of Our Lives, NBC
Culinary host: Lidia Bastianich, Lidia's Kitchen, PBS
Game show host: Wayne Brady, Let's Make a Deal, CBS
Guest performer: Vernee Watson, General Hospital, ABC
Supporting actress: Camryn Grimes, The Young and the Restless, CBS
Supporting actor: Greg Vaughan, Days of Our Lives, NBC
Talk show host, entertainment: Adrienne Houghton, Loni Love, Jeannie Mai, Tamera Mowry-Housley, The Real, synd.
Talk show host, informative: Steve Harvey, Steve, synd.
Directing team: Days of Our Lives, NBC
Writing team: Days of Our Lives, NBC

Golden Globe Awards, 2018

The Hollywood Foreign Press Association (then the Hollywood Foreign Correspondents Association) presented its first awards for achievement in film in 1944; television was considered for the first time in 1955. **Cecil B. DeMille Award, 2018:** Oprah Winfrey.

Film

Drama: Three Billboards Outside Ebbing, Missouri
Comedy/musical: Lady Bird
Actress, drama: Frances McDormand, Three Billboards Outside Ebbing, Missouri
Actor, drama: Gary Oldman, Darkest Hour
Actress, comedy/musical: Saoirse Ronan, Lady Bird
Actor, comedy/musical: James Franco, The Disaster Artist
Supporting actress: Allison Janney, I, Tonya
Supporting actor: Sam Rockwell, Three Billboards Outside Ebbing, Missouri
Director: Guillermo del Toro, The Shape of Water
Screenplay: Martin McDonagh, Three Billboards Outside Ebbing, Missouri
Animated film: Coco
Foreign-language film: In the Fade, Germany/France
Original score: Alexandre Desplat, The Shape of Water
Original song: "This Is Me," The Greatest Showman, Benj Pasek and Justin Paul

Television

Series, drama: The Handmaid's Tale, Hulu
Series, comedy/musical: The Marvelous Mrs. Maisel, Amazon
Limited series or made-for-TV movie: Big Little Lies, HBO
Actress, drama: Elisabeth Moss, The Handmaid's Tale, Hulu
Actor, drama: Sterling K. Brown, This Is Us, NBC
Actress, comedy/musical: Rachel Brosnahan, The Marvelous Mrs. Maisel, Amazon
Actor, comedy/musical: Aziz Ansari, Master of None, Netflix
Actress, limited series/TV movie: Nicole Kidman, Big Little Lies, HBO
Actor, limited series/TV movie: Ewan McGregor, Fargo, FX
Supporting actress: Laura Dern, Big Little Lies, HBO
Supporting actor: Alexander Skarsgård, Big Little Lies, HBO

Academy Awards (Oscars), 1927-2017

Year	Picture	Actor	Actress	Supporting actor[1]	Supporting actress[1]	Director
1927 -28	*Wings*	Emil Jannings *The Way of All Flesh*	Janet Gaynor *Seventh Heaven*	NA	NA	Frank Borzage *Seventh Heaven;* Lewis Milestone *Two Arabian Knights*
1928 -29	*Broadway Melody*	Warner Baxter *In Old Arizona*	Mary Pickford *Coquette*	NA	NA	Frank Lloyd *The Divine Lady*
1929 -30	*All Quiet on the Western Front*	George Arliss *Disraeli*	Norma Shearer *The Divorcee*	NA	NA	Lewis Milestone *All Quiet on the Western Front*
1930 -31	*Cimarron*	Lionel Barrymore *Free Soul*	Marie Dressler *Min and Bill*	NA	NA	Norman Taurog *Skippy*
1931 -32	*Grand Hotel*	Fredric March *Dr. Jekyll and Mr. Hyde;* Wallace Beery *The Champ*	Helen Hayes *The Sin of Madelon Claudet*	NA	NA	Frank Borzage *Bad Girl*
1932 -33	*Cavalcade*	Charles Laughton *The Private Life of Henry VIII*	Katharine Hepburn *Morning Glory*	NA	NA	Frank Lloyd *Cavalcade*
1934	*It Happened One Night*	Clark Gable *It Happened One Night*	Claudette Colbert *It Happened One Night*	NA	NA	Frank Capra *It Happened One Night*
1935	*Mutiny on the Bounty*	Victor McLaglen *The Informer*	Bette Davis *Dangerous*	NA	NA	John Ford *The Informer*
1936	*The Great Ziegfeld*	Paul Muni *The Story of Louis Pasteur*	Luise Rainer *The Great Ziegfeld*	Walter Brennan *Come and Get It*	Gale Sondergaard *Anthony Adverse*	Frank Capra *Mr. Deeds Goes to Town*
1937	*The Life of Emile Zola*	Spencer Tracy *Captains Courageous*	Luise Rainer *The Good Earth*	Joseph Schildkraut *The Life of Emile Zola*	Alice Brady *In Old Chicago*	Leo McCarey *The Awful Truth*
1938	*You Can't Take It With You*	Spencer Tracy *Boys Town*	Bette Davis *Jezebel*	Walter Brennan *Kentucky*	Fay Bainter *Jezebel*	Frank Capra *You Can't Take It With You*
1939	*Gone With the Wind*	Robert Donat *Goodbye, Mr. Chips*	Vivien Leigh *Gone With the Wind*	Thomas Mitchell *Stage Coach*	Hattie McDaniel *Gone With the Wind*	Victor Fleming *Gone With the Wind*
1940	*Rebecca*	James Stewart *The Philadelphia Story*	Ginger Rogers *Kitty Foyle*	Walter Brennan *The Westerner*	Jane Darwell *The Grapes of Wrath*	John Ford *The Grapes of Wrath*
1941	*How Green Was My Valley*	Gary Cooper *Sergeant York*	Joan Fontaine *Suspicion*	Donald Crisp *How Green Was My Valley*	Mary Astor *The Great Lie*	John Ford *How Green Was My Valley*
1942	*Mrs. Miniver*	James Cagney *Yankee Doodle Dandy*	Greer Garson *Mrs. Miniver*	Van Heflin *Johnny Eager*	Teresa Wright *Mrs. Miniver*	William Wyler *Mrs. Miniver*
1943	*Casablanca*	Paul Lukas *Watch on the Rhine*	Jennifer Jones *The Song of Bernadette*	Charles Coburn *The More the Merrier*	Katina Paxinou *For Whom the Bell Tolls*	Michael Curtiz *Casablanca*
1944	*Going My Way*	Bing Crosby *Going My Way*	Ingrid Bergman *Gaslight*	Barry Fitzgerald *Going My Way*	Ethel Barrymore *None But the Lonely Heart*	Leo McCarey *Going My Way*
1945	*The Lost Weekend*	Ray Milland *The Lost Weekend*	Joan Crawford *Mildred Pierce*	James Dunn *A Tree Grows in Brooklyn*	Anne Revere *National Velvet*	Billy Wilder *The Lost Weekend*
1946	*The Best Years of Our Lives*	Fredric March *The Best Years of Our Lives*	Olivia de Havilland *To Each His Own*	Harold Russell *The Best Years of Our Lives*	Anne Baxter *The Razor's Edge*	William Wyler *The Best Years of Our Lives*
1947	*Gentleman's Agreement*	Ronald Colman *A Double Life*	Loretta Young *The Farmer's Daughter*	Edmund Gwenn *Miracle on 34th Street*	Celeste Holm *Gentleman's Agreement*	Elia Kazan *Gentleman's Agreement*
1948	*Hamlet*	Laurence Olivier *Hamlet*	Jane Wyman *Johnny Belinda*	Walter Huston *The Treasure of the Sierra Madre*	Claire Trevor *Key Largo*	John Huston *The Treasure of the Sierra Madre*
1949	*All the King's Men*	Broderick Crawford *All the King's Men*	Olivia de Havilland *The Heiress*	Dean Jagger *Twelve O'Clock High*	Mercedes McCambridge *All the King's Men*	Joseph L. Mankiewicz *Letter to Three Wives*
1950	*All About Eve*	José Ferrer *Cyrano de Bergerac*	Judy Holliday *Born Yesterday*	George Sanders *All About Eve*	Josephine Hull *Harvey*	Joseph L. Mankiewicz *All About Eve*
1951	*An American in Paris*	Humphrey Bogart *The African Queen*	Vivien Leigh *A Streetcar Named Desire*	Karl Malden *A Streetcar Named Desire*	Kim Hunter *A Streetcar Named Desire*	George Stevens *A Place in the Sun*
1952	*The Greatest Show on Earth*	Gary Cooper *High Noon*	Shirley Booth *Come Back, Little Sheba*	Anthony Quinn *Viva Zapata!*	Gloria Grahame *The Bad and the Beautiful*	John Ford *The Quiet Man*
1953	*From Here to Eternity*	William Holden *Stalag 17*	Audrey Hepburn *Roman Holiday*	Frank Sinatra *From Here to Eternity*	Donna Reed *From Here to Eternity*	Fred Zinnemann *From Here to Eternity*

Year	Picture	Actor	Actress	Supporting actor[1]	Supporting actress[1]	Director
1954	*On the Waterfront*	Marlon Brando *On the Waterfront*	Grace Kelly *The Country Girl*	Edmond O'Brien *The Barefoot Contessa*	Eva Marie Saint *On the Waterfront*	Elia Kazan *On the Waterfront*
1955	*Marty*	Ernest Borgnine *Marty*	Anna Magnani *The Rose Tattoo*	Jack Lemmon *Mister Roberts*	Jo Van Fleet *East of Eden*	Delbert Mann *Marty*
1956	*Around the World in 80 Days*	Yul Brynner *The King and I*	Ingrid Bergman *Anastasia*	Anthony Quinn *Lust for Life*	Dorothy Malone *Written on the Wind*	George Stevens *Giant*
1957	*The Bridge on the River Kwai*	Alec Guinness *The Bridge on the River Kwai*	Joanne Woodward *The Three Faces of Eve*	Red Buttons *Sayonara*	Miyoshi Umeki *Sayonara*	David Lean *The Bridge on the River Kwai*
1958	*Gigi*	David Niven *Separate Tables*	Susan Hayward *I Want to Live*	Burl Ives *The Big Country*	Wendy Hiller *Separate Tables*	Vincente Minnelli *Gigi*
1959	*Ben-Hur*	Charlton Heston *Ben-Hur*	Simone Signoret *Room at the Top*	Hugh Griffith *Ben-Hur*	Shelley Winters *Diary of Anne Frank*	William Wyler *Ben-Hur*
1960	*The Apartment*	Burt Lancaster *Elmer Gantry*	Elizabeth Taylor *Butterfield 8*	Peter Ustinov *Spartacus*	Shirley Jones *Elmer Gantry*	Billy Wilder *The Apartment*
1961	*West Side Story*	Maximilian Schell *Judgment at Nuremberg*	Sophia Loren *Two Women*	George Chakiris *West Side Story*	Rita Moreno *West Side Story*	Jerome Robbins and Robert Wise *West Side Story*
1962	*Lawrence of Arabia*	Gregory Peck *To Kill a Mockingbird*	Anne Bancroft *The Miracle Worker*	Ed Begley *Sweet Bird of Youth*	Patty Duke *The Miracle Worker*	David Lean *Lawrence of Arabia*
1963	*Tom Jones*	Sidney Poitier *Lilies of the Field*	Patricia Neal *Hud*	Melvyn Douglas *Hud*	Margaret Rutherford *The V.I.P.s*	Tony Richardson *Tom Jones*
1964	*My Fair Lady*	Rex Harrison *My Fair Lady*	Julie Andrews *Mary Poppins*	Peter Ustinov *Topkapi*	Lila Kedrova *Zorba the Greek*	George Cukor *My Fair Lady*
1965	*The Sound of Music*	Lee Marvin *Cat Ballou*	Julie Christie *Darling*	Martin Balsam *A Thousand Clowns*	Shelley Winters *A Patch of Blue*	Robert Wise *The Sound of Music*
1966	*A Man for All Seasons*	Paul Scofield *A Man for All Seasons*	Elizabeth Taylor *Who's Afraid of Virginia Woolf?*	Walter Matthau *The Fortune Cookie*	Sandy Dennis *Who's Afraid of Virginia Woolf?*	Fred Zinnemann *A Man for All Seasons*
1967	*In the Heat of the Night*	Rod Steiger *In the Heat of the Night*	Katharine Hepburn *Guess Who's Coming to Dinner*	George Kennedy *Cool Hand Luke*	Estelle Parsons *Bonnie and Clyde*	Mike Nichols *The Graduate*
1968	*Oliver!*	Cliff Robertson *Charly*	Katharine Hepburn *The Lion in Winter*; Barbra Streisand *Funny Girl*	Jack Albertson *The Subject Was Roses*	Ruth Gordon *Rosemary's Baby*	Carol Reed *Oliver!*
1969	*Midnight Cowboy*	John Wayne *True Grit*	Maggie Smith *The Prime of Miss Jean Brodie*	Gig Young *They Shoot Horses, Don't They?*	Goldie Hawn *Cactus Flower*	John Schlesinger *Midnight Cowboy*
1970	*Patton*	George C. Scott *Patton* (refused)	Glenda Jackson *Women in Love*	John Mills *Ryan's Daughter*	Helen Hayes *Airport*	Franklin Schaffner *Patton*
1971	*The French Connection*	Gene Hackman *The French Connection*	Jane Fonda *Klute*	Ben Johnson *The Last Picture Show*	Cloris Leachman *The Last Picture Show*	William Friedkin *The French Connection*
1972	*The Godfather*	Marlon Brando *The Godfather* (refused)	Liza Minnelli *Cabaret*	Joel Grey *Cabaret*	Eileen Heckart *Butterflies Are Free*	Bob Fosse *Cabaret*
1973	*The Sting*	Jack Lemmon *Save the Tiger*	Glenda Jackson *A Touch of Class*	John Houseman *The Paper Chase*	Tatum O'Neal *Paper Moon*	George Roy Hill *The Sting*
1974	*The Godfather Part II*	Art Carney *Harry and Tonto*	Ellen Burstyn *Alice Doesn't Live Here Anymore*	Robert DeNiro *The Godfather Part II*	Ingrid Bergman *Murder on the Orient Express*	Francis Ford Coppola *The Godfather Part II*
1975	*One Flew Over the Cuckoo's Nest*	Jack Nicholson *One Flew Over the Cuckoo's Nest*	Louise Fletcher *One Flew Over the Cuckoo's Nest*	George Burns *The Sunshine Boys*	Lee Grant *Shampoo*	Milos Forman *One Flew Over the Cuckoo's Nest*
1976	*Rocky*	Peter Finch *Network*	Faye Dunaway *Network*	Jason Robards *All the President's Men*	Beatrice Straight *Network*	John G. Avildsen *Rocky*
1977	*Annie Hall*	Richard Dreyfuss *The Goodbye Girl*	Diane Keaton *Annie Hall*	Jason Robards *Julia*	Vanessa Redgrave *Julia*	Woody Allen *Annie Hall*
1978	*The Deer Hunter*	Jon Voight *Coming Home*	Jane Fonda *Coming Home*	Christopher Walken *The Deer Hunter*	Maggie Smith *California Suite*	Michael Cimino *The Deer Hunter*
1979	*Kramer vs. Kramer*	Dustin Hoffman *Kramer vs. Kramer*	Sally Field *Norma Rae*	Melvyn Douglas *Being There*	Meryl Streep *Kramer vs. Kramer*	Robert Benton *Kramer vs. Kramer*
1980	*Ordinary People*	Robert DeNiro *Raging Bull*	Sissy Spacek *Coal Miner's Daughter*	Timothy Hutton *Ordinary People*	Mary Steenburgen *Melvin and Howard*	Robert Redford *Ordinary People*
1981	*Chariots of Fire*	Henry Fonda *On Golden Pond*	Katharine Hepburn *On Golden Pond*	John Gielgud *Arthur*	Maureen Stapleton *Reds*	Warren Beatty *Reds*
1982	*Gandhi*	Ben Kingsley *Gandhi*	Meryl Streep *Sophie's Choice*	Louis Gossett Jr. *An Officer and a Gentleman*	Jessica Lange *Tootsie*	Richard Attenborough *Gandhi*
1983	*Terms of Endearment*	Robert Duvall *Tender Mercies*	Shirley MacLaine *Terms of Endearment*	Jack Nicholson *Terms of Endearment*	Linda Hunt *The Year of Living Dangerously*	James L. Brooks *Terms of Endearment*
1984	*Amadeus*	F. Murray Abraham *Amadeus*	Sally Field *Places in the Heart*	Haing S. Ngor *The Killing Fields*	Peggy Ashcroft *A Passage to India*	Milos Forman *Amadeus*

Year	Picture	Actor	Actress	Supporting actor[1]	Supporting actress[1]	Director
1985	Out of Africa	William Hurt *Kiss of the Spider Woman*	Geraldine Page *The Trip to Bountiful*	Don Ameche *Cocoon*	Anjelica Huston *Prizzi's Honor*	Sydney Pollack *Out of Africa*
1986	Platoon	Paul Newman *The Color of Money*	Marlee Matlin *Children of a Lesser God*	Michael Caine *Hannah and Her Sisters*	Dianne Wiest *Hannah and Her Sisters*	Oliver Stone *Platoon*
1987	The Last Emperor	Michael Douglas *Wall Street*	Cher *Moonstruck*	Sean Connery *The Untouchables*	Olympia Dukakis *Moonstruck*	Bernardo Bertolucci *The Last Emperor*
1988	Rain Man	Dustin Hoffman *Rain Man*	Jodie Foster *The Accused*	Kevin Kline *A Fish Called Wanda*	Geena Davis *The Accidental Tourist*	Barry Levinson *Rain Man*
1989	Driving Miss Daisy	Daniel Day-Lewis *My Left Foot*	Jessica Tandy *Driving Miss Daisy*	Denzel Washington *Glory*	Brenda Fricker *My Left Foot*	Oliver Stone, *Born on the Fourth of July*
1990	Dances With Wolves	Jeremy Irons *Reversal of Fortune*	Kathy Bates *Misery*	Joe Pesci *Goodfellas*	Whoopi Goldberg *Ghost*	Kevin Costner *Dances With Wolves*
1991	The Silence of the Lambs	Anthony Hopkins *The Silence of the Lambs*	Jodie Foster *The Silence of the Lambs*	Jack Palance *City Slickers*	Mercedes Ruehl *The Fisher King*	Jonathan Demme *The Silence of the Lambs*
1992	Unforgiven	Al Pacino *Scent of a Woman*	Emma Thompson *Howards End*	Gene Hackman *Unforgiven*	Marisa Tomei *My Cousin Vinny*	Clint Eastwood *Unforgiven*
1993	Schindler's List	Tom Hanks *Philadelphia*	Holly Hunter *The Piano*	Tommy Lee Jones *The Fugitive*	Anna Paquin *The Piano*	Steven Spielberg *Schindler's List*
1994	Forrest Gump	Tom Hanks *Forrest Gump*	Jessica Lange *Blue Sky*	Martin Landau *Ed Wood*	Dianne Wiest, *Bullets Over Broadway*	Robert Zemeckis *Forrest Gump*
1995	Braveheart	Nicolas Cage *Leaving Las Vegas*	Susan Sarandon *Dead Man Walking*	Kevin Spacey *The Usual Suspects*	Mira Sorvino *Mighty Aphrodite*	Mel Gibson *Braveheart*
1996	The English Patient	Geoffrey Rush *Shine*	Frances McDormand *Fargo*	Cuba Gooding Jr. *Jerry Maguire*	Juliette Binoche *The English Patient*	Anthony Minghella *The English Patient*
1997	Titanic	Jack Nicholson *As Good As It Gets*	Helen Hunt *As Good As It Gets*	Robin Williams *Good Will Hunting*	Kim Basinger *L.A. Confidential*	James Cameron *Titanic*
1998	Shakespeare in Love	Roberto Benigni *Life Is Beautiful*	Gwyneth Paltrow *Shakespeare in Love*	James Coburn *Affliction*	Judi Dench *Shakespeare in Love*	Steven Spielberg *Saving Private Ryan*
1999	American Beauty	Kevin Spacey *American Beauty*	Hilary Swank *Boys Don't Cry*	Michael Caine, *The Cider House Rules*	Angelina Jolie *Girl, Interrupted*	Sam Mendes *American Beauty*
2000	Gladiator	Russell Crowe *Gladiator*	Julia Roberts *Erin Brockovich*	Benicio Del Toro *Traffic*	Marcia Gay Harden *Pollock*	Steven Soderbergh *Traffic*
2001	A Beautiful Mind	Denzel Washington *Training Day*	Halle Berry *Monster's Ball*	Jim Broadbent *Iris*	Jennifer Connelly *A Beautiful Mind*	Ron Howard *A Beautiful Mind*
2002	Chicago	Adrien Brody *The Pianist*	Nicole Kidman *The Hours*	Chris Cooper *Adaptation*	Catherine Zeta-Jones, *Chicago*	Roman Polanski *The Pianist*
2003	The Lord of the Rings: The Return of the King	Sean Penn *Mystic River*	Charlize Theron *Monster*	Tim Robbins *Mystic River*	Renée Zellweger *Cold Mountain*	Peter Jackson *The Lord of the Rings: The Return of the King*
2004	Million Dollar Baby	Jamie Foxx *Ray*	Hilary Swank *Million Dollar Baby*	Morgan Freeman *Million Dollar Baby*	Cate Blanchett *The Aviator*	Clint Eastwood *Million Dollar Baby*
2005	Crash	Philip Seymour Hoffman *Capote*	Reese Witherspoon *Walk the Line*	George Clooney *Syriana*	Rachel Weisz *The Constant Gardener*	Ang Lee *Brokeback Mountain*
2006	The Departed	Forest Whitaker, *The Last King of Scotland*	Helen Mirren *The Queen*	Alan Arkin *Little Miss Sunshine*	Jennifer Hudson *Dreamgirls*	Martin Scorsese *The Departed*
2007	No Country for Old Men	Daniel Day-Lewis *There Will Be Blood*	Marion Cotillard *La Vie en Rose*	Javier Bardem *No Country for Old Men*	Tilda Swinton *Michael Clayton*	Joel Coen and Ethan Coen, *No Country for Old Men*
2008	Slumdog Millionaire	Sean Penn *Milk*	Kate Winslet *The Reader*	Heath Ledger *The Dark Knight*	Penelope Cruz, *Vicky Cristina Barcelona*	Danny Boyle *Slumdog Millionaire*
2009	The Hurt Locker	Jeff Bridges *Crazy Heart*	Sandra Bullock *The Blind Side*	Christoph Waltz *Inglourious Basterds*	Mo'Nique *Precious*	Kathryn Bigelow *The Hurt Locker*
2010	The King's Speech	Colin Firth *The King's Speech*	Natalie Portman *Black Swan*	Christian Bale *The Fighter*	Melissa Leo *The Fighter*	Tom Hooper *The King's Speech*
2011	The Artist	Jean Dujardin *The Artist*	Meryl Streep *The Iron Lady*	Christopher Plummer, *Beginners*	Octavia Spencer *The Help*	Michel Hazanavicius *The Artist*
2012	Argo	Daniel Day-Lewis *Lincoln*	Jennifer Lawrence *Silver Linings Playbook*	Christoph Waltz *Django Unchained*	Anne Hathaway *Les Misérables*	Ang Lee *Life of Pi*
2013	12 Years a Slave	Matthew McConaughey *Dallas Buyers Club*	Cate Blanchett *Blue Jasmine*	Jared Leto *Dallas Buyers Club*	Lupita Nyong'o *12 Years a Slave*	Alfonso Cuarón *Gravity*
2014	Birdman	Eddie Redmayne *The Theory of Everything*	Julianne Moore *Still Alice*	J. K. Simmons *Whiplash*	Patricia Arquette *Boyhood*	Alejandro G. Iñárritu *Birdman*
2015	Spotlight	Leonardo DiCaprio *The Revenant*	Brie Larson *Room*	Mark Rylance *Bridge of Spies*	Alicia Vikander *The Danish Girl*	Alejandro G. Iñárritu *The Revenant*
2016	Moonlight	Casey Affleck *Manchester by the Sea*	Emma Stone *La La Land*	Mahershala Ali *Moonlight*	Viola Davis *Fences*	Damien Chazelle *La La Land*
2017	The Shape of Water	Gary Oldman *Darkest Hour*	Frances McDormand *Three Billboards Outside Ebbing, Missouri*	Sam Rockwell *Three Billboards Outside Ebbing, Missouri*	Allison Janney *I, Tonya*	Guillermo del Toro *The Shape of Water*

NA = Not applicable. (1) Award not given until 1936.

Other Academy Award Winners, 2017

Animated film: *Coco*
Cinematography: *Blade Runner 2049*
Costume design: *Phantom Thread*
Documentary feature: *Icarus*
Film editing: *Dunkirk*
Foreign language film: *A Fantastic Woman*, Chile
Makeup and hairstyling: *Darkest Hour*
Original score: *The Shape of Water*, Alexandre Desplat
Original song: "Remember Me," *Coco*, Kristen Anderson-Lopez and Robert Lopez

Production design: *The Shape of Water*
Screenplay, adapted: *Call Me by Your Name*, James Ivory
Screenplay, original: *Get Out*, Jordan Peele
Short films: *Dear Basketball* (animated), *Heaven Is a Traffic Jam on the 405* (documentary), *The Silent Child* (live action)
Sound editing: *Dunkirk*
Sound mixing: *Dunkirk*
Visual effects: *Blade Runner 2049*

Other Film Awards, 2018

British Academy of Film and Television Awards (BAFTAs)

Awarded in 2018 to films released in the UK in 2017.
Best film: *Three Billboards Outside Ebbing, Missouri*
Outstanding British film: *Three Billboards Outside Ebbing, Missouri*
Director: Guillermo del Toro, *The Shape of Water*
Original screenplay: Martin McDonagh, *Three Billboards Outside Ebbing, Missouri*
Adapted screenplay: James Ivory, *Call Me by Your Name*
Animated film: *Coco*
Documentary: *I Am Not Your Negro*
Film not in the English language: *The Handmaiden*, South Korea
Actor: Gary Oldman, *Darkest Hour*
Actress: Frances McDormand, *Three Billboards Outside Ebbing, Missouri*
Supporting actor: Sam Rockwell, *Three Billboards Outside Ebbing, Missouri*
Supporting actress: Allison Janney, *I, Tonya*

Canadian Screen Awards

Motion picture: *Maudie*
Actor: Nabil Rajo, *Boost*
Actress: Sally Hawkins, *Maudie*
Screenplay: Sherry White, *Maudie*
Director: Aisling Walsh, *Maudie*
Comedy series: *Kim's Convenience*
Drama series: *Anne*

Cannes International Film Festival Awards

Palme d'Or: *Manbiki Kazoku [Shoplifters]*, Japan
Grand Prix: *BlacKkKlansman*, U.S.
Best director: Pawel Pawlikowski, *Zimna Wojna [Cold War]*, Poland/UK/France
Best screenplay: Alice Rohrwacher, *Lazzaro Felice [Happy as Lazzaro]*, Italy/Switzerland/France/Germany; Jafar Panahi, *Se Rokh [Three Faces]*, Iran
Best actress: Samal Yeslyamova, *Ayka*, Russia/Germany/Poland/Kazakhstan
Best actor: Marcello Fonte, *Dogman*, Italy/France
Jury prize: *Capharnaüm*, Lebanon
Special palme d'or: *Le Livre D'Image [Image Book]*, Switzerland
Palme d'Or, short film: *All These Creatures*, Australia

Directors Guild of America Awards

Feature film: Guillermo del Toro, *The Shape of Water*
First-time feature film: Jordan Peele, *Get Out*
Documentary: Matthew Heineman, *City of Ghosts*
TV movie/miniseries: Jean-Marc Vallée, *Big Little Lies*
TV series (drama): Reed Morano, *The Handmaid's Tale*, "Offred"
TV series (comedy): Beth McCarthy-Miller, *Veep*, "Chicklet"

Screen Actors Guild Awards

Motion picture cast: *Three Billboards Outside Ebbing, Missouri*
Female actor in a lead role: Frances McDormand, *Three Billboards Outside Ebbing, Missouri*
Male actor in a lead role: Gary Oldman, *Darkest Hour*
Female actor in a supporting role: Allison Janney, *I, Tonya*
Male actor in a supporting role: Sam Rockwell, *Three Billboards Outside Ebbing, Missouri*
Drama series ensemble: *This Is Us*
Female actor in a drama series: Claire Foy, *The Crown*
Male actor in a drama series: Sterling K. Brown, *This Is Us*
Comedy series ensemble: *Veep*
Female actor in a comedy series: Julia Louis-Dreyfus, *Veep*
Male actor in a comedy series: William H. Macy, *Shameless*
Female actor in a TV movie/limited series: Nicole Kidman, *Big Little Lies*
Male actor in a TV movie/limited series: Alexander Skarsgård, *Big Little Lies*

Sundance Film Festival Awards

U.S. Grand Jury Prize: *The Miseducation of Cameron Post* (drama); *Kailash* (doc.)
World Cinema Jury Prize: *Butterflies*, Turkey (drama); *Of Fathers and Sons*, Germany/Syria/Lebanon/Qatar (doc.)
U.S. Audience Award: *Burden* (drama); *The Sentence* (doc.)
World Cinema Audience Award: *The Guilty*, Denmark (drama); *This Is Home*, U.S./Jordan (doc.)
NEXT Audience Award: *Search*
U.S. Directing: Sara Colangelo, *The Kindergarten Teacher* (drama); Alexandria Bombach, *On Her Shoulders* (doc.)
World Cinema Directing: Ísold Uggadóttir, *And Breathe Normally*, Iceland/Sweden/Belgium (drama); Sandi Tan, *Shirkers*, U.S. (doc.)
Waldo Salt Screenwriting Award: Christina Choe, *NANCY*
Alfred P. Sloan Feature Prize: *Search*

Academy of Country Music Awards, 2018

Entertainer: Jason Aldean
Male vocalist: Chris Stapleton
Female vocalist: Miranda Lambert
Vocal duo: Brothers Osborne
Vocal group: Old Dominion

Album: *From a Room: Volume. 1*, Chris Stapleton
Single: "Body Like a Back Road," Sam Hunt
Song: "Tin Man," Miranda Lambert

Video: "It Ain't My Fault," Brothers Osborne
Vocal event: "The Fighter," Keith Urban
New female vocalist: Lauren Alaina
New male vocalist: Brett Young
New vocal duo or group: Midland
Songwriter: Rhett Akins

Selected Grammy Awards, 2017

Source: National Academy of Recording Arts and Sciences
For albums released Oct. 1, 2016-Sept. 30, 2017, awarded in Jan. 2018.

Record of the year (single): "24K Magic," Bruno Mars
Album of the year: *24K Magic*, Bruno Mars
Song of the year: "That's What I Like," Bruno Mars (Christopher Brody Brown, James Fauntleroy, Philip Lawrence, Bruno Mars, Ray Charles McCullough II, Jeremy Reeves, Ray Romulus, and Jonathan Yip, songwriters)
New artist: Alessia Cara
Pop performance, solo: "Shape of You," Ed Sheeran
Pop performance, duo/group: "Feel It Still," Portugal. The Man
Pop album, traditional vocal: *Tony Bennett Celebrates 90*, various artists
Pop album, vocal: ÷, Ed Sheeran
Dance recording: "Tonite," LCD Soundsystem
Dance/electronic album: *3-D The Catalogue*, Kraftwerk
Contemporary instrumental album: *Prototype*, Jeff Lorber Fusion
Rock performance: "You Want It Darker," Leonard Cohen
Metal performance: "Sultan's Curse," Mastodon
Rock song: "Run," Foo Fighters (Foo Fighters, songwriters)
Rock album: *A Deeper Understanding*, The War on Drugs
Alternative music album: *Sleep Well Beast*, The National
R&B performance: "That's What I Like," Bruno Mars
R&B performance, traditional: "Redbone," Childish Gambino
R&B song: "That's What I Like," Bruno Mars (Christopher Brody Brown, James Fauntleroy, Philip Lawrence, Bruno Mars, Ray Charles McCullough II, Jeremy Reeves, Ray Romulus, and Jonathan Yip, songwriters)
R&B album: *24K Magic*, Bruno Mars
Urban contemporary album: *Starboy*, The Weeknd
Rap performance: "HUMBLE.," Kendrick Lamar
Rap/sung performance: "LOYALTY.," Kendrick Lamar feat. Rihanna

Rap song: "HUMBLE.," Kendrick Lamar (K. Duckworth, Asheton Hogan, and M. Williams II, songwriters)
Rap album: *DAMN.*, Kendrick Lamar
Country performance, solo: "Either Way," Chris Stapleton
Country performance, duo/group: "Better Man," Little Big Town
Country song: "Broken Halos," Chris Stapleton (Mike Henderson and Chris Stapleton, songwriters)
Country album: *From a Room: Volume 1*, Chris Stapleton
Jazz album, instrumental: *Rebirth*, Billy Childs
Jazz album, vocal: *Dreams and Daggers*, Cécile McLorin Salvant
Americana album: *The Nashville Sound*, Jason Isbell and the 400 Unit
Blues album, traditional: *Blue & Lonesome*, The Rolling Stones
Folk album: *Mental Illness*, Aimee Mann
Gospel album: *Let Them Fall in Love*, CeCe Winans
Latin pop album: *El Dorado*, Shakira
New age album: *Dancing on Water*, Peter Kater
Comedy album: *The Age of Spin & Deep in the Heart of Texas*, Dave Chappelle
Spoken word album: *The Princess Diarist*, Carrie Fisher
Soundtrack album, compilation: *La La Land*, various artists (Marius de Vries and Justin Hurwitz, compilation producers)
Soundtrack album, score: *La La Land*, Justin Hurwitz
Song, visual media: "How Far I'll Go," *Moana*, Auli'i Cravalho (Lin-Manuel Miranda, songwriter)
Music video: "HUMBLE.," Kendrick Lamar
Music film: *The Defiant Ones*, various artists

Grammy Awards, 1958-2017

Record of the Year (single)	Year	Album of the Year
Domenico Modugno, "Nel Blu Dipinto Di Blu (Volare)"	1958	Henry Mancini, *The Music From Peter Gunn*
Bobby Darin, "Mack the Knife"	1959	Frank Sinatra, *Come Dance With Me*
Percy Faith, "Theme From a Summer Place"	1960	Bob Newhart, *Button Down Mind*
Henry Mancini, "Moon River"	1961	Judy Garland, *Judy at Carnegie Hall*
Tony Bennett, "I Left My Heart in San Francisco"	1962	Vaughn Meader, *The First Family*
Henry Mancini, "The Days of Wine and Roses"	1963	Barbra Streisand, *The Barbra Streisand Album*
Stan Getz and Astrud Gilberto, "The Girl From Ipanema"	1964	Stan Getz and João Gilberto, *Getz/Gilberto*
Herb Alpert, "A Taste of Honey"	1965	Frank Sinatra, *September of My Years*
Frank Sinatra, "Strangers in the Night"	1966	Frank Sinatra, *A Man and His Music*
5th Dimension, "Up, Up and Away"	1967	The Beatles, *Sgt. Pepper's Lonely Hearts Club Band*
Simon and Garfunkel, "Mrs. Robinson"	1968	Glen Campbell, *By the Time I Get to Phoenix*
5th Dimension, "Aquarius/Let the Sunshine In"	1969	Blood, Sweat & Tears, *Blood, Sweat & Tears*
Simon and Garfunkel, "Bridge Over Troubled Water"	1970	Simon and Garfunkel, *Bridge Over Troubled Water*
Carole King, "It's Too Late"	1971	Carole King, *Tapestry*
Roberta Flack, "The First Time Ever I Saw Your Face"	1972	George Harrison and Friends, *The Concert for Bangla Desh*
Roberta Flack, "Killing Me Softly With His Song"	1973	Stevie Wonder, *Innervisions*
Olivia Newton-John, "I Honestly Love You"	1974	Stevie Wonder, *Fulfillingness' First Finale*
Captain & Tennille, "Love Will Keep Us Together"	1975	Paul Simon, *Still Crazy After All These Years*
George Benson, "This Masquerade"	1976	Stevie Wonder, *Songs in the Key of Life*
Eagles, "Hotel California"	1977	Fleetwood Mac, *Rumours*
Billy Joel, "Just the Way You Are"	1978	Bee Gees, *Saturday Night Fever*
The Doobie Brothers, "What a Fool Believes"	1979	Billy Joel, *52nd Street*
Christopher Cross, "Sailing"	1980	Christopher Cross, *Christopher Cross*
Kim Carnes, "Bette Davis Eyes"	1981	John Lennon and Yoko Ono, *Double Fantasy*
Toto, "Rosanna"	1982	Toto, *Toto IV*
Michael Jackson, "Beat It"	1983	Michael Jackson, *Thriller*
Tina Turner, "What's Love Got to Do With It"	1984	Lionel Richie, *Can't Slow Down*
USA for Africa, "We Are the World"	1985	Phil Collins, *No Jacket Required*
Steve Winwood, "Higher Love"	1986	Paul Simon, *Graceland*
Paul Simon, "Graceland"	1987	U2, *The Joshua Tree*
Bobby McFerrin, "Don't Worry, Be Happy"	1988	George Michael, *Faith*
Bette Midler, "Wind Beneath My Wings"	1989	Bonnie Raitt, *Nick of Time*
Phil Collins, "Another Day in Paradise"	1990	Quincy Jones, *Back on the Block*
Natalie Cole, with Nat "King" Cole, "Unforgettable"	1991	Natalie Cole, with Nat "King" Cole, *Unforgettable*
Eric Clapton, "Tears in Heaven"	1992	Eric Clapton, *Unplugged*
Whitney Houston, "I Will Always Love You"	1993	Whitney Houston, *The Bodyguard*
Sheryl Crow, "All I Wanna Do"	1994	Tony Bennett, *MTV Unplugged*
Seal, "Kiss From a Rose"	1995	Alanis Morissette, *Jagged Little Pill*
Eric Clapton, "Change the World"	1996	Celine Dion, *Falling Into You*
Shawn Colvin, "Sunny Came Home"	1997	Bob Dylan, *Time Out of Mind*
Celine Dion, "My Heart Will Go On"	1998	Lauryn Hill, *The Miseducation of Lauryn Hill*
Santana feat. Rob Thomas, "Smooth"	1999	Santana, *Supernatural*
U2, "Beautiful Day"	2000	Steely Dan, *Two Against Nature*
U2, "Walk On"	2001	Various artists, *O Brother, Where Art Thou?*
Norah Jones, "Don't Know Why"	2002	Norah Jones, *Come Away With Me*
Coldplay, "Clocks"	2003	OutKast, *Speakerboxxx/The Love Below*
Ray Charles and Norah Jones, "Here We Go Again"	2004	Ray Charles and various artists, *Genius Loves Company*
Green Day, "Boulevard of Broken Dreams"	2005	U2, *How to Dismantle an Atomic Bomb*
Dixie Chicks, "Not Ready to Make Nice"	2006	Dixie Chicks, *Taking the Long Way*
Amy Winehouse, "Rehab"	2007	Herbie Hancock, *River: The Joni Letters*
Robert Plant and Alison Krauss, "Please Read the Letter"	2008	Robert Plant and Alison Krauss, *Raising Sand*
Kings of Leon, "Use Somebody"	2009	Taylor Swift, *Fearless*
Lady Antebellum, "Need You Now"	2010	Arcade Fire, *The Suburbs*
Adele, "Rolling in the Deep"	2011	Adele, *21*
Gotye, "Somebody That I Used to Know"	2012	Mumford & Sons, *Babel*
Daft Punk feat. Pharrell Williams and Nile Rodgers, "Get Lucky"	2013	Daft Punk, *Random Access Memories*
Sam Smith, "Stay With Me"	2014	Beck, *Morning Phase*
Mark Ronson feat. Bruno Mars, "Uptown Funk"	2015	Taylor Swift, *1989*
Adele, "Hello"	2016	Adele, *25*
Bruno Mars, "24K Magic"	2017	Bruno Mars, *24K Magic*

MTV Video Music Awards, 2018

Video of the year: "Havana," Camila Cabello feat. Young Thug
Artist of the year: Camila Cabello
Song of the year: "rockstar," Post Malone feat. 21 Savage
Best new artist: Cardi B
Push artist of the year: Hayley Kiyoko
Collaboration: "Dinero," Jennifer Lopez feat. DJ Khaled and Cardi B
Video With a Message: "This Is America," Childish Gambino
Dance video: "Lonely Together," Avicii feat. Rita Ora
Hip-hop video: "Chun-Li," Nicki Minaj

Latin video: "Mi Gente," J Balvin, Willy William
Pop video: "No Tears Left to Cry," Ariana Grande
Rock video: "Whatever It Takes," Imagine Dragons
Song of the summer: "I Like It," Cardi B, Bad Bunny, and J Balvin
Art direction: "APES**T," The Carters
Choreography: "This Is America," Childish Gambino
Direction: "This Is America," Childish Gambino
Editing: "Lemon," N.E.R.D. feat. Rihanna
Visual effects: "All the Stars," Kendrick Lamar and SZA

SCIENCE

Science and Technology News

The following were some of the more newsworthy developments in science and technology in the previous year, as of Sept. 2018.

Gene Therapy Milestones

The prospect of fighting disease by replacing or modifying defective genes has long fascinated scientists. But progress toward this goal has been slow. The pace picked up in 2017, however, with a couple of significant milestones by year's end.

A paper in the Nov. 2, 2017, issue of the *New England Journal of Medicine*, reported on a successful gene-replacement treatment for a generally fatal form of spinal muscular atrophy (SMA) in children. SMA1, or Werdnig-Hoffmann disease, which results from a mutated gene that causes a shortage of a protein required for neuron function in the spinal cord, ranks as the most common genetic cause of death in infants. It is a progressive disorder that affects motor neurons, causing muscle atrophy, and symptoms, including trouble breathing and swallowing, typically begin showing up soon after birth. For those diagnosed, mechanical feeding support is commonly required by the age of 1, and many die or require mechanical ventilation by age 2.

The new treatment uses a single intravenous injection to introduce into the body a harmless virus carrying the gene for this protein. The virus ferries the gene to target nerve cells. Researchers gave the treatment to 15 infant patients just a few months after birth. All 15 were still alive and did not need mechanical breathing support at the end of the study, at an age of 20 months or more. Most showed notable improvement in motor function.

On Dec. 19, 2017, the FDA issued its first approval of a gene therapy for a disorder caused by mutations in a single gene. The therapy, known as Luxturna, targets a mutation that gives rise to various retinal conditions gradually leading to loss of vision and potentially resulting in blindness.

Thinnest Mirror in the World

As described in papers in the Jan. 19, 2018, issue of the journal *Physical Review Letters*, two separate research groups developed mirrors just one atom thick. The reflectivity of the mirrors was electronically switchable, meaning they might find application in circuits using electricity to produce and transmit light signals. Such optoelectronic devices with extremely small sensors or chips that use light to transfer information, could make good use of lightweight mirrors with controllable reflectivity. Both research teams used ultrathin sheets of molybdenum diselenide ($MoSe_2$) to make their mirrors. The material is naturally highly reflective for a particular light frequency. The researchers found that by applying a voltage they could tune the reflectivity, which they measured with laser light. Switching the voltage on and off caused a more than twofold difference in reflectivity.

Human Prehistory Outside Africa

Based on known evidence, *Homo sapiens*, or modern humans, are believed to have originated in Africa and then spread throughout the world. In Eurasia they encountered two archaic types of humans (viewed sometimes as separate species, sometimes as subspecies) that are now extinct: Neanderthals in the west, and Denisovans in the east. Two fossil reports in 2018 added striking new details to this generally accepted narrative. One indicated that *Homo sapiens* crossed out of Africa at least some 50,000 years earlier than widely believed. The other described a first-generation Neanderthal-Denisovan hybrid, documenting the first concrete evidence of an individual whose parents represented different species (or subspecies) of humans.

The first report, in the journal *Science* on Jan. 26, 2018, described an ancient jawbone found in a cave in Israel. Careful analyses showed that the bone belonged to *Homo sapiens* and dated to 177,000-194,000 years ago. The oldest previously known *Homo sapiens* fossils not discovered in Africa—also found in caves in Israel—dated to approximately 90,000-120,000 years ago. Analysis of ancient DNA had suggested the possibility of an earlier migration from Africa, but fossil evidence had been lacking.

The second report was initially published in *Nature* online Aug. 22, 2018. The fossil, a bone fragment found in Siberia's Denisova cave, came from a female who was at least 13 when she died, some 90,000 years ago. DNA analysis showed that she had a Neanderthal mother and a Denisovan father.

Cloning Breakthrough

In the Feb. 8, 2018, issue of the journal *Cell*, Chinese scientists reported the successful creation via cloning of two genetically identical macaque monkeys. It was the first time any primates—the mammal order that includes human beings—had been cloned by means of the complex technique known as somatic cell nuclear transfer (SCNT). This basically involves placing the DNA-carrying nucleus of a body-tissue cell into an animal egg whose own nucleus has been removed, then applying enzymes to transform the egg into a productive embryonic state, and finally implanting the egg into a surrogate mother. The first successful SCNT clone of a mammal was the sheep Dolly in 1996. Since then, the method has been successfully used with over 20 other species, but prior attempts with primates always had failed—until macaques Zhong Zhong and Hua Hua were respectively born in China on Nov. 27 and Dec. 5, 2017.

U.S. scientists cloned a rhesus monkey in 1999 using a simpler procedure—splitting an embryo, similarly to what happens in the natural development of identical twins. However, SCNT is a more customizable technology and should be capable of producing larger numbers of clones. The ability to clone non-human primates was seen to have potential benefits for disease research and other purposes, though that and the looming possibility of human cloning pose serious ethical questions.

SCNT still requires substantial refinement before it can be regarded as a practical means of cloning primates. While Dolly was cloned from an adult cell, the Chinese met success only by using a fetal cell. And, according to their paper, out of 79 well-developed embryos implanted in 21 surrogate mothers, Hua Hua and Zhong Zhong were the only successful results.

Close Encounters

A study published in *Monthly Notices of the Royal Astronomical Society: Letters* on May 1, 2018, provided support for the notion that a star skimmed the solar system roughly 70,000 years ago. "Scholz's star" (actually a small binary system) had been thought by some astronomers, based on its observed motion, to have passed through the outer portion of the Oort cloud—the large collection of small icy bodies in the remote outer reaches of our solar system. The 2018 research, focusing on orbits of Oort cloud bodies that travel toward the inner solar system, found several orbits that could be explained by the gravitational effects of the "Scholz's star" flyby.

Scientists have long speculated that the uncommon features of the planet Uranus—for example, it spins on its side, has an oddly shaped magnetic field, and is remarkably cold—may be due to a gigantic collision eons ago. A study in the July 1, 2018, issue of the *Astrophysical Journal* bolstered this view through supercomputer simulations. These indicated that the impacting body probably had about twice the mass of Earth.

The sighting of a tumbling, cigar-shaped object in our solar system in Oct. 2017 prompted the International Astronomical Union to establish a new category of small bodies: the interstellar asteroid (designation I) in Nov. 2017. The object was perhaps as long as a quarter-mile and moving so fast, and in such a path, that it had to be from outside the solar system. The first such object of its kind ever observed, it is now classified as 1I/2017 U1, and dubbed 'Oumuamua ("scout" in Hawaiian).

Crowd-Sourcing Quantum Theory

In the universe as understood by quantum mechanics, particles that are "entangled," or linked, can communicate faster than the speed of light—in fact, instantaneously, even when they are far apart. Albert Einstein didn't like this idea of "spooky action-at-a-distance," which contradicts traditional physics, but experiments satisfying the authoritative "Bell test" have shown repeatedly that entanglement does exist. The Bell test requires randomized measurements, creating potential loopholes. For example, the experimental procedure might not be exactly random: the results might be shaped by some hidden variable. An innovative study that was reported in the May 10, 2018, issue of the journal *Nature* seemed to dispel the concern of the "freedom-of-choice loophole", the chance that hidden variables might give the false appearance of entanglement. On Nov. 30, 2016, some 100,000 volunteers located around the globe played an online video game, called the "BIG Bell Quest," which involved fast, continuous input of unpredictable choices. The millions of bits of data thus randomly generated were sent to a dozen labs on five continents, where they were used to establish the measurement settings of 13 different Bell test experiments, and the results contradicted the traditional physics views of Einstein. The result: another win for quantum theory.

Science Glossary

This glossary covers some concepts that come up frequently in the news, in biology, chemistry, geology, and physics.

Biology

Amino acid: one of about 20 similar small molecules that are the building blocks of proteins.

Antibiotic: a substance produced by or derived from a bacterium, fungus, or other organism that battles infections and diseases caused by microorganisms, especially bacteria; it works by killing the microorganism or halting its growth.

Archaeon (plural, archaea): one of a group of single-celled microorganisms; archaea are prokaryotes, like bacteria, but they share some similarities with eukaryotes.

Autoimmunity: a condition in which an individual's immune system reacts against his or her own tissues; leads to diseases such as lupus, some forms of diabetes, inflammatory bowel disease, and rheumatoid arthritis.

Bacterium (plural, bacteria): one of a large, varied class of microscopic and simple, single-celled organisms. Bacteria live almost everywhere; some forms cause disease, while others are useful in digestion and other natural processes.

Biodiversity (biological diversity): richness of variety of life-forms—including plants, animals, and other types—in a given environment.

Cell: the smallest unit of life capable of living independently, or with other cells; usually bounded by a membrane. May include a nucleus and other specialized parts.

Cholesterol: a fatty substance in animal tissues. It is produced by the liver in humans; is found in foods such as butter, eggs, and meat; and is an essential body constituent.

Chromosome: one of the rod-like structures in cell nuclei that carry genetic material (DNA).

Cloning: the process of copying a particular piece of DNA to allow it to be sequenced, studied, or used in some other way; can also refer to producing a genetic copy of an organism.

DNA (deoxyribonucleic acid): a usually double-stranded molecule that carries genetic information, which determines the form and functioning of all living things.

Ecosystem: an interdependent community of living organisms and their climatic and geographical habitat.

Enzyme: a protein that promotes a particular chemical reaction in the body.

Estrogen: one of a group of hormones that promote development of female secondary sex characteristics and the growth and health of the female reproductive system; males also produce small amounts of estrogen.

Eukaryote: any of the group of single- or multi-celled organisms whose cells have distinct nuclei.

Evolution: the process of gradual change that can occur in a species as it adapts to its environment; natural selection is the process by which evolution occurs.

Gene: a portion of a DNA molecule that provides the blueprint for the assembly of a protein.

Gene pool: the collection and total diversity of genes in an interbreeding population.

Gene therapy: a treatment in which scientists try to implant functioning genes into a person's cells so the genes can produce proteins that the person lacks or that help the person fight disease.

Genetic sequencing: the process of finding the order of subunits in a gene or the order of all an organism's genes.

Genome: the complete set of an organism's genetic material.

Hormone: a substance secreted in one part of an organism that regulates the functioning of other tissues or organs.

Meiosis: the process of cell division that results in gametes (sperm or egg cells), all of which contain half the number of chromosomes as their precursor.

Metabolism: the sum total of the body's chemical processes providing energy for vital functions and enabling new material to be synthesized.

Mitosis: the process by which a cell divides its nucleus and other cell materials into two duplicate daughter cells with the same DNA.

Neuron or **nerve cell:** any of the cells in the nervous system that send electrical and chemical messages to other cells.

Nucleus (plural, nuclei): the center of an atom; or the portion of a eukaryotic cell that contains most of the cell's genetic material.

Organism: a living entity, capable of growth, metabolism, and usually reproduction.

Phenotype: the observable properties and characteristics of an organism arising at least in part from its genetic makeup.

Pheromone: a chemical secreted by an organism to influence the behavior of other members of its species.

Placebo effect: a phenomenon in which patients show improvements even though they have taken a medically inactive substance, called a placebo.

Prokaryote: a single-celled organism that does not have a distinct nucleus, such as a bacterium or archaeon.

Protein: a complex molecule made up of one or more chains of amino acids; essential to the structure and function of all cells.

RNA (ribonucleic acid): a complex molecule similar to the genetic material DNA but usually single-stranded; several forms of RNA translate the genetic code of DNA and use that code to assemble proteins for structural and biological functions in the body. RNA also serves as the genetic material of some viruses.

Species: a population of organisms that breed with each other in nature and produce fertile offspring; other definitions of species exist to accommodate the diversity of life on Earth.

Stem cell: a cell that can develop into other types of cells; for instance, stem cells in bone marrow can differentiate into different types of blood cells.

Steroid: a type of chemical substance with a certain molecular structure. Some steroids are hormones that can suppress immune response or influence stress reaction, blood pressure, or sexual development.

Testosterone: a steroid hormone that stimulates the development and maintenance of male sexual characteristics and the production of sperm; women also produce small amounts of testosterone.

Virus: a microscopic, often disease-causing, agent made of genetic material surrounded by a protein shell; can only reproduce inside a living cell. There also exist "subviral" infectious agents, such as **viroids** (which consist of a short, circular strand of RNA without a protein coat) and **prions** (consisting of protein material).

Chemistry

Acid: a class of compounds that contrasts with bases. Acids taste sour, turn litmus red/pink, and often produce hydrogen gas in contact with some metals. Acids donate protons (hydrogen atoms minus the electron) in chemical reactions.

Base: a substance that yields hydroxyl ions (OH-) when dissolved in water; any of a class of compounds whose aqueous solutions taste bitter, feel slippery, turn litmus blue, and react with acids to form salts; also known as **alkaline**.

Carbon fiber: an extremely strong, thin fiber made by pyrolyzing (decomposing by heat) synthetic fibers, such as rayon, until charred; used to make high-strength composites.

Chlorofluorocarbon (CFC): one of a group of industrial chemicals that contain chlorine, fluorine, and carbon and can damage Earth's ozone layer.

Element: a substance that cannot be chemically decomposed into simpler substances; all the atoms of an element have the same number of protons.

Isotope: an atom of a chemical element with the same number of protons in its nucleus as other atoms of that element, but with a different number of neutrons.

Molecule: the basic unit of a chemical compound, composed of two or more atoms bound together.

Noble gases or **inert gases:** a group of gases including helium, neon, argon, krypton, xenon, and radon that are not reactive except in rare and limited instances.

Osmosis: the transfer of a fluid across a semipermeable membrane, usually from an area of higher concentration to one of lower concentration.

Polymer: a huge molecule containing hundreds or thousands of smaller molecules arranged in repeating units.

Salt: a neutral compound produced by the reaction of an acid and a base.

Geology

Fault, tectonic: a crack or break in Earth's crust, often due to the slippage of tectonic plates past or over one another; usually geologically unstable.

Igneous: a type of rock formed by solidification from a molten state, especially from molten magma.

Magma: hot liquid rock material under Earth's surface, from which igneous rock is formed by cooling.

Metamorphic: in geology, the name given to rocks or minerals that have recrystallized under the influence of heat and pressure since their original formation.

Pangaea: a single supercontinent that scientists believe began to break apart at least 200 mil years ago to form the current continents.

Plate tectonics: theory that Earth's lithosphere—the uppermost layer that includes the crust—is made up of many separate rigid plates of rock that float on top of hot semi-liquid rock.

Sedimentary: a type of rock formed by the buildup of material at the bottoms of bodies of water.

Physics

Absolute zero: the theoretical temperature at which all motion within a molecule stops, corresponding to −273.15°C (−459.67°F).

Antimatter: matter that consists of antiparticles, such as antiprotons, that have an opposite charge from normal particles; when matter meets antimatter, both are destroyed, and their combined mass is converted to energy. Antimatter is created in certain radioactive decay processes but appears to be present in only small amounts in the universe.

Atom: the basic unit of a chemical element.

Atomic mass: the total mass of an atom of a given element; atoms of the same element with different atomic masses (different numbers of neutrons but not protons) are called **isotopes**.

Atomic number: the number of protons in an atom of a given element of the periodic table; the characteristic that sets atoms of different elements apart.

Axion: a hypothetical subatomic particle with low mass and energy that has been proposed to exist because of the properties of the strong nuclear force.

Bose-Einstein condensate (BEC): a "super-atom" comprising thousands of atoms super-cooled to within a few hundred millionths of a degree of absolute zero and thus condensed into the lowest energy state. Atoms bound in the BEC behave synchronously, giving the BEC wavelike properties.

Boson: one of the two primary categories of particles in the Standard Model; bosons include the Higgs boson and force-carrying particles such as photons, gluons, and the W and Z particles.

Dark energy: a mysterious, undefined energy leading to a repulsive force pervading all of space-time; proposed by cosmologists as counteracting gravity and accelerating the expansion of the universe; predicted to make up 68.3% of the universe's composition.

Dark matter: hypothetical, invisible matter that some scientists believe makes up 26.8% of the universe (dark matter and ordinary matter together make up 31.7% of the universe). Its existence was proposed to account for otherwise inexplicable gravitational forces observed in space.

Doppler effect: a change in the frequency of sound, light, or radio waves caused by the motion of the source emitting the waves or the motion of the person or instrument perceiving the waves.

Electron: negatively charged particle that (along with its positively charged counterpart, the **positron**) is the least massive electrically charged fundamental particle; one of six **leptons**.

Energy: capacity to perform work. Energy can take various forms, such as potential energy, kinetic energy, and chemical energy.

Entropy: a measure of disorder in a system.

Fermion: any one of a number of matter particles including electrons, protons, neutrons, neutrinos, leptons, and quarks; one of the two primary categories of particles in the Standard Model, the other being bosons.

Field: the existence of physical effects such as forces (gravitational, electric, etc.) is visualized and described mathematically by physicists in terms of fields, which show the strength and direction of a force at a given position.

Fission: a nuclear reaction that occurs when the nuclei of large, unstable atoms break apart, releasing large amounts of energy.

Fluorescence: luminescence that is caused by the absorption of radiation at one wavelength followed by an almost immediate re-radiation, usually at a different wavelength, that stops almost immediately when the causative radiation stops.

Force: in classical physics, something that causes acceleration in a body; can be thought of as a push or pull.

Fusion: a nuclear reaction occurring when atomic nuclei collide at high temperatures and combine to form one heavier atomic nucleus, releasing enormous energy in the process.

Gravity: an attractive force between any two objects or particles, proportional to the mass (or energy) of the objects; strength of the force decreases with greater distance; the only fundamental force still unaccounted for by the Standard Model.

Half-life: the time it takes for half of a given amount of a radioactive element to decay.

Hertz (Hz): a measure of frequency, or how many times a given event occurs per second; applied to sound waves, electrical current, and microchip clock speeds.

Higgs boson: a boson associated with a field accounting for the existence of mass in many particles.

Laser: light consisting of a cascade of photons all having the same wavelength; stands for Light Amplification by Stimulated Emission of Radiation.

Light-emitting diode (LED): a semiconductor that emits light when an electrical current is passed through it. The color of the light depends on the material used in making the diode.

Neutrino: a tiny fundamental particle, or fermion, with no electrical charge and very small mass that moves very quickly through the universe; comes in three varieties, or flavors, called electron, muon, and tau.

Neutron: a neutral particle found in the nuclei of atoms.

Particle accelerator: a large machine with a circular or long, straight tunnel in which charged particles are accelerated to extremely high speeds.

Phosphorescence: luminescence that is caused by the absorption of radiation at one wavelength followed by a delayed re-radiation, usually at a different wavelength, that continues for a time after the causative radiation stops.

Photon: the elementary unit, or quantum, of electromagnetic radiation, such as light. It has no mass or electrical charge and is one of the fundamental force-carrying particles described by the Standard Model.

Plasma: a high-energy state of matter different from solid, liquid, or gas in which atomic nuclei and the electrons orbiting them separate from each other.

Proton: a positively charged subatomic particle, made up of quarks, found in the nuclei of atoms.

Quantum: a natural unit of some physically measurable property, such as energy or electrical charge.

Quark: a fermion and a fundamental matter particle that makes up neutrons and protons, forming atomic nuclei; there are six different varieties, or flavors, of quarks grouped in pairs: up and down, charm and strange, top and bottom.

Radiation: energy emitted as rays or particles. Radiation includes heat, light, ultraviolet rays, gamma rays, X-rays, cosmic rays, alpha particles, and beta particles.

Relativity, general theory of: a theory of space-time proposed by Albert Einstein in 1915; it links gravity to the curvature of space-time.

Relativity, special theory of: Albert Einstein's theory of space and time: all laws of physics are valid in all uniformly moving frames of reference, and the speed of light in a vacuum is always the same, so long as the source and the observer are moving uniformly (not accelerating).

Standard Model: prevailing theory of the interaction of subatomic particles. Particles are either fermions—such as electrons, neutrinos, and quarks—or bosons—such as Higgs bosons, gluons, W or Z bosons, and photons; successfully explains three of the four elementary forces acting on particles (strong, weak, electromagnetic) but thus far has not incorporated gravity.

String theory: a theory that seeks to unify quantum mechanics and general relativity, positing that the basic constituents of matter can best be understood not as pointlike particles but as tiny oscillating "strings."

Subatomic particle: a particle that makes up an atom; includes electrons (elementary particles) and neutrons and protons (composite particles).

Superconductivity: the property of certain materials, usually metals and chemically complex ceramics, to conduct electricity without resistance, generally at very cold temperatures.

Thermodynamics: the branch of physics that describes how energy, heat, and temperature flow in physical systems.

Ultraviolet radiation: a form of light, invisible to the human eye, that has a shorter wavelength and greater energy than visible light but a longer wavelength and less energy than X-rays.

Virtual particle: subatomic particles that rapidly pop into and out of existence and can exert real forces; usually occur in particle-antiparticle pairs and are rapidly annihilated.

Mohs Scale of Hardness

Hardness is the ability of a solid substance to resist abrasion or deformation on its surface. Soft minerals scratch more easily than hard ones. For example, a diamond will scratch graphite because graphite is softer. In 1812, German mineralogist Frederich Mohs (1773-1839) created the arbitrary scale shown below to measure relative hardness using 10 minerals that were readily available at that time. The numbers in the Mohs scale are arranged in order of increasing hardness. An item's hardness is obtained by determining which mineral in the Mohs scale can scratch it.

Mohs scale		Selected items and their relative hardness	
1 . . . . . . Talc	6 . . . . . Orthoclase feldspar	2.5 . . . . . .Fingernail	5.5 . . . . . .Steel knife blade
2 . . . . . . Gypsum	7 . . . . . . Quartz	2.5-3 . . . .Gold, silver	6-7 . . . . . .Glass
3 . . . . . . Calcite	8 . . . . . . Topaz	3 . . . . . . .Copper penny	6.5 . . . . . .Iron pyrite
4 . . . . . . Fluorite	9 . . . . . Corundum	4-4.5 . . . .Platinum	7+. . . . . .Hardened steel file
5 . . . . . . Apatite	10 . . . . . . Diamond	4-5 . . . . . .Iron	

Chemical Elements, Atomic Numbers, Year Discovered

Source: International Union of Pure and Applied Chemistry (IUPAC)

See Periodic Table of the Elements on the following page for atomic weights.

Element	Symbol	Atomic number	Year discov.	Element	Symbol	Atomic number	Year discov.	Element	Symbol	Atomic number	Year discov.
Actinium	Ac	89	1899	Gold	Au	79	BCE	Potassium	K	19	1807
Aluminum	Al	13	1825	Hafnium	Hf	72	1923	Praseodymium	Pr	59	1885
Americium	Am	95	1944	Hassium	Hs	108	1984	Promethium	Pm	61	1945
Antimony	Sb	51	1450	Helium	He	2	1868	Protactinium	Pa	91	1917
Argon	Ar	18	1894	Holmium	Ho	67	1878	Radium	Ra	88	1898
Arsenic	As	33	13th cent.	Hydrogen	H	1	1766	Radon	Rn	86	1900
Astatine	At	85	1940	Indium	In	49	1863	Rhenium	Re	75	1925
Barium	Ba	56	1808	Iodine	I	53	1811	Rhodium	Rh	45	1803
Berkelium	Bk	97	1949	Iridium	Ir	77	1804	Roentgenium	Rg	111	1995
Beryllium	Be	4	1798	Iron	Fe	26	BCE	Rubidium	Rb	37	1861
Bismuth	Bi	83	15th cent.	Krypton	Kr	36	1898	Ruthenium	Ru	44	1845
Bohrium	Bh	107	1981	Lanthanum	La	57	1839	Rutherfordium	Rf	104	1969
Boron	B	5	1808	Lawrencium	Lr	103	1961	Samarium	Sm	62	1879
Bromine	Br	35	1826	Lead	Pb	82	BCE	Scandium	Sc	21	1879
Cadmium	Cd	48	1817	Lithium	Li	3	1817	Seaborgium	Sg	106	1974
Calcium	Ca	20	1808	Livermorium	Lv	116	2000	Selenium	Se	34	1817
Californium	Cf	98	1950	Lutetium	Lu	71	1907	Silicon	Si	14	1823
Carbon	C	6	BCE	Magnesium	Mg	12	1829	Silver	Ag	47	BCE
Cerium	Ce	58	1803	Manganese	Mn	25	1774	Sodium	Na	11	1807
Cesium	Cs	55	1860	Meitnerium	Mt	109	1982	Strontium	Sr	38	1790
Chlorine	Cl	17	1774	Mendelevium	Md	101	1955	Sulfur	S	16	BCE
Chromium	Cr	24	1797	Mercury	Hg	80	BCE	Tantalum	Ta	73	1802
Cobalt	Co	27	1735	Molybdenum	Mo	42	1782	Technetium	Tc	43	1937
Copernicium	Cn	112	1996	Moscovium	Mc	115	2004	Tellurium	Te	52	1782
Copper	Cu	29	BCE	Neodymium	Nd	60	1885	Tennessine	Ts	117	2010
Curium	Cm	96	1944	Neon	Ne	10	1898	Terbium	Tb	65	1843
Darmstadtium	Ds	110	1995	Neptunium	Np	93	1940	Thallium	Tl	81	1861
				Nickel	Ni	28	1751	Thorium	Th	90	1828
Dubnium (Hahnium)[1]	Db (Ha)	105	1970	Nihonium	Nh	113	2004	Thulium	Tm	69	1879
Dysprosium	Dy	66	1886	Niobium[2]	Nb	41	1801	Tin	Sn	50	BCE
Einsteinium	Es	99	1952	Nitrogen	N	7	1772	Titanium	Ti	22	1791
Erbium	Er	68	1843	Nobelium	No	102	1958	Tungsten (Wolfram)	W	74	1783
Europium	Eu	63	1901	Oganesson	Og	118	2006				
Fermium	Fm	100	1953	Osmium	Os	76	1804	Uranium	U	92	1789
Flerovium	Fl	114	1999	Oxygen	O	8	1774	Vanadium	V	23	1830
Fluorine	F	9	1771	Palladium	Pd	46	1803	Xenon	Xe	54	1898
Francium	Fr	87	1939	Phosphorus	P	15	1669	Ytterbium	Yb	70	1878
Gadolinium	Gd	64	1886	Platinum	Pt	78	1735	Yttrium	Y	39	1794
Gallium	Ga	31	1875	Plutonium	Pu	94	1941	Zinc	Zn	30	BCE
Germanium	Ge	32	1886	Polonium	Po	84	1898	Zirconium	Zr	40	1789

(1) The name Dubnium (Db) was approved by IUPAC for element 105, but the name Hahnium (Ha) was used in most of the scientific literature before 1998 and is still sometimes used in the U.S. (2) Formerly Columbium.

Periodic Table of the Elements

Source: Los Alamos National Laboratory Chemistry Division; International Union of Pure and Applied Chemistry (IUPAC)

Shaded elements are commonly regarded as metals.

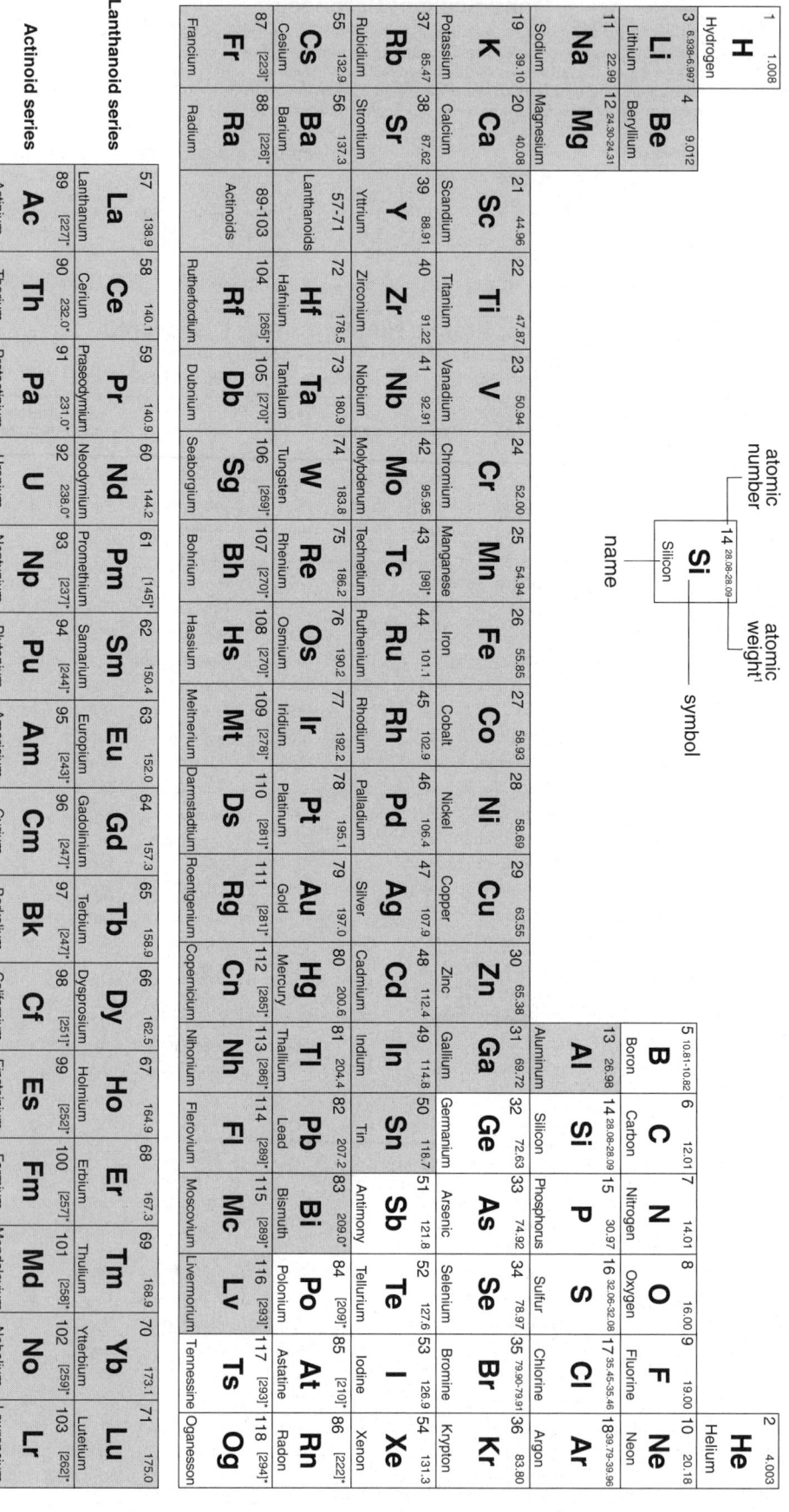

Note: Atomic weight shown is a weighted average of the atomic masses of normally found isotopes. * = Element has no stable nuclides. A value enclosed in brackets, e.g. [209], indicates the mass number of the longest-lived isotope of the element. However, four such elements (Bi, Th, Pa, and U) do have a characteristic terrestrial isotopic composition, and for these an atomic weight is tabulated. (1) For elements having two or more stable isotopes with a notable variation in atomic-weight values, a range is shown.

Basic Laws of Physics

Newton's Laws of Motion

1. An object in motion moves at a constant velocity in a straight line unless acted upon by a force. Likewise, an object at rest will stay at rest. These two properties are known as inertia.

2. The acceleration of an object is proportional to the force acting on it and inversely proportional to the mass of the object. Force (F) equals mass (m) times acceleration (a):

$$F = ma$$

3. For every action, there is an equal and opposite reaction. For example, if a force of one ton pushes down on an object, the object pushes up with an equal force. As per the second law, the amount of movement (acceleration) produced in the object will depend on the object's mass.

Law of Gravity

In common usage, gravity refers to the gravitational force between planets and objects on or near them. But in scientific parlance, gravitation is one of four basic forces controlling the interactions of matter. (The others are the strong and weak forces, which act on the subatomic level, and electromagnetic force.) The gravitational force (F) between objects is proportional to the product of their masses (m_1 and m_2) and inversely proportional to the square of the distance (d) between them. G represents the gravitational constant in Newton's law of gravity, a fixed ratio of approximately 6.67408×10^{-11} newton m^2/kg^2.

The basic law of gravity is:

$$F = G \frac{m_1 m_2}{d^2}$$

Near Earth's surface, Earth's gravitational force pulls objects downward at a constant acceleration of 9.8 m/s^2 (g). This allows calculation of the vertical velocity (v) of an object with an initial vertical velocity of v_0 in free fall at a given point in time (t) and calculation of the distance (d) of an object from Earth at any given time with a given initial velocity (v_0) and a known initial height (a) via the following equations (here, the effects of air resistance are ignored, and downward velocities and directions are negative):

$$v = v_0 - gt$$

$$d = -\tfrac{1}{2}g(t^2) + v_0 t + a$$

Assuming that height is measured in feet and speeds in feet per second, the maximum height (H) reached by an object with a positive (upward) initial velocity is expressed as:

$$H = a + \frac{v_0^2}{64}$$

For motion not near Earth's surface, more complicated equations are required. Also, if the object's upward velocity is very great, the object may escape Earth's gravity. Even near Earth's surface, there are slight complications. Gravity is lessened by the centrifugal force of the Earth's rotation. At the poles, where centrifugal force is absent, acceleration due to gravity is greater.

Gravity is weaker on a mountaintop than at sea level because the mountaintop is farther from Earth's center.

Conservation Laws

In physics, laws of conservation state that in a closed system, where neither mass nor energy is added or subtracted, certain measurable quantities remain constant.

Conservation of Mass: Mass is neither created nor destroyed within a closed system except when converted from or to energy.

Conservation of Momentum: All moving objects have momentum, and in a closed system, total momentum is always conserved. Linear momentum is the product of the mass of an object and its velocity. In the following equation, M and V represent the initial total mass and velocity of objects within a closed system. After a collision between those objects, the mass and velocity of individual objects may change (for example, one object breaks into smaller pieces, each traveling at a different velocity), but the product of the total mass and velocity in the system after the collision (mv) will remain the same.

$$MV = mv$$

Any object moving in a circle has another kind of momentum—angular momentum. This is because circular motion requires acceleration toward the center of the circle. The amount of acceleration depends on the speed of the object and the square of the radius of the circle. (Angular momentum is the product of this speed, the mass of the object, and the square of the radius.)

Conservation of Energy: The total amount of energy in a closed system will not change except when converted to mass.

Conservation of Mass-Energy: Although mass and energy can be converted into one another, the total amount of mass and energy together must be conserved. This is reflected in Einstein's famous equation, where m is mass, E is energy, and c is the speed of light in a vacuum (which is constant):

$$E = mc^2$$

Relativistic mass can describe how mass increases with velocity. The following equation—where m is the mass of a moving object, m_0 is the object's mass when not moving, v is the object's velocity in relation to a stationary observer, and c is the speed of light—shows the relationship:

$$m = \frac{m_0}{\sqrt{1 - \dfrac{v^2}{c^2}}}$$

The theory that no object can travel faster than the speed of light is based in this equation. As an object approaches c, so much energy is converted to mass that it no longer accelerates.

Laws of Thermodynamics

1. Heat is a form of energy. Within a closed system energy must be conserved except in nuclear reactions or other extreme conditions. It is neither created nor destroyed.

2. Within a self-sustaining system, heat can never go from an area of low temperature to an area of high temperature, for that would require added energy. Without added energy, disorder, or entropy, can only increase.

3. Absolute zero cannot be attained by any procedure in a finite number of steps. Although it can be approached asymptotically, it can never be reached.

Laws of Current Electricity

Electric current generally represents the flow of electrons through a conductor. The rate at which electrons flow can be measured in amperes, defined as the number of electrons (measured in a unit called the coulomb, equal to about 6.24 quintillion or 6.24×10^{18} electrons) moving past a particular point every second. One ampere is equal to 1 coulomb of charge passing each second. Like water, electrons tend to move from areas of high pressure to low pressure. The difference between these two pressures, known as potential difference, is measured in volts.

Certain substances, such as copper and carbon, allow electric currents to pass more readily than others—that is, they have greater conductivity. Resistance to conductivity is measured in ohms.

Ohm's Law: Electric current is directly proportional to the potential difference and inversely proportional to the total resistance of the circuit. I is electric current (measured in amperes), V is the potential difference (measured in volts), and R is resistance (measured in ohms):

$$I = \frac{V}{R}$$

Law of Electric Power: Electric power (P), measured in watts, represents the rate at which electricity is converted into some other form of energy (such as light, in the case of a lightbulb). For a direct-current circuit, P is the product of current and potential difference:

$$P = IV$$

Two Basic Laws of Quantum Physics

1. Heisenberg's uncertainty principle: Certain pairs of observable quantities like energy and time or position and momentum cannot be measured with complete accuracy simultaneously. Also known as the indeterminacy principle.

2. Pauli's exclusion principle: Two electrons in an atom cannot simultaneously occupy the same quantum or energy state. This has since been shown to be true for many subatomic particles.

Breaking the Sound Barrier; Speed of Sound

The prefix **Mach** is used to describe supersonic speed. It was named for Ernst Mach (1838-1916), a Czech-born Austrian physicist. Mach may be defined as the ratio of the velocity of an object to the velocity of sound in a particular medium. A plane moving at the speed of sound moves at Mach 1. At twice the speed of sound, it moves at Mach 2.

When a plane passes the sound barrier—that is, flies faster than the speed at which sound travels—people in the area, though not the people on the plane, hear what seem to be thunderclaps. These sounds are sometimes called sonic booms.

Sound is produced by vibrations of an object. It is transmitted by the alternating increase and decrease in pressure that radiates outward from a source through a material medium of molecules, like waves spreading out on a pond after a rock has been tossed in.

The **frequency of sound** is determined by the number of times the vibrating waves undulate per second. It is measured in cycles per second. The slower the cycle of waves, the lower the frequency. As the frequency increases, the sound becomes higher in pitch. The human ear is sensitive to frequencies between 20 and 20,000 vibrations per second, although this range varies among individuals and decreases with age.

Intensity, or loudness, is the strength of the pressure of these radiating waves and is measured in decibels (dB).

The **speed of sound** varies depending on temperature and the medium through which it travels. It moves faster in water than in air, for example. At sea level and a temperature of 59°F (15°C), the speed of sound is approximately 761 mph, or 1,100 ft per sec.

Light and Colors of the Spectrum

Light, a form of electromagnetic radiation similar to radiant heat, radio waves, and X-rays, is emitted from a source in straight lines and spreads in area as it travels. For emission from a point source, light per unit area diminishes in proportion to the square of the distance.

The English mathematician and physicist Isaac Newton (1642-1727) described light as an **emission of particles**; the Dutch astronomer, mathematician, and physicist Christiaan Huygens (1629-95) and others developed the theory that light travels in a **wave motion**. It is now believed that these two theories are essentially complementary. The development of quantum theory has led to results where light acts like a series of particles in some experiments and like a wave in others.

The first relatively accurate measurement of the **speed of light** was made by French physicist Armand Hippolyte Louis Fizeau (1819-96). Today the speed of light is known precisely as 299,792.458 km per sec (or 186,282.397 mi/sec) in a vacuum. In water the speed of light is about 25% less, and in glass, 33% less.

Color sensations are produced through the excitation of the retina of the eye by light vibrating at different frequencies. The different colors of the visible spectrum may be seen by viewing light refracted by passage through a prism, which separates light into its component wavelengths.

Customarily, the basic colors are taken to be the six monochromatic (single) colors that occupy relatively large areas of the spectrum: red, orange, yellow, green, blue, and violet. So-called primary colors can be combined to produce the sensation of other colors. However, scientists disagree about how many and what primary colors to recognize. The color sensation of **black** is due to complete lack of stimulation of the retina, that of **white** to complete stimulation.

Infrared and **ultraviolet rays**, which are below the red (long) end and above the violet (short) end of the visible spectrum, respectively, are invisible to the naked human eye. Heat is the principal effect of infrared rays, and chemical action that of ultraviolet rays. Some animals can see infrared or ultraviolet light.

Life Cycles of Selected Animals

Information reviewed by Ronald M. Nowak, author of *Walker's Mammals of the World* (6th ed., Johns Hopkins University Press, 1999). Average longevity figures supplied by Ronald T. Reuther. These apply to animals in captivity; the potential life span of animals is rarely attained in nature. Figures on gestation and incubation are averages based on estimates.

Animal	Gestation (days)	Average longevity (yrs.)	Maximum longevity (yrs.-mos.)	Animal	Gestation (days)	Average longevity (yrs.)	Maximum longevity (yrs.-mos.)
Ass	365	12	47	Leopard	98	12	23
Baboon	187	20	45	Lion	100	15	30
Bear (black)	219	18	36-10	Monkey (rhesus)	166	15	37
Bear (grizzly)	225	25	50	Moose	240	12	27
Bear (polar)	240	20	45	Mouse (domestic white)	19	3	6
Beaver	105	5	50	Mouse (meadow)	21	3	4
Bison	285	15	40	Opossum (American)	13	1	5
Camel	406	12	50	Pig (domestic)	112	10	27
Cat (domestic)	63	12	38	Puma	90	12	20
Chimpanzee	230	20	60	Rabbit (domestic)	31	5	18-10
Chipmunk	31	6	10	Rhinoceros (black)	450	15	45-10
Cow	284	15	30	Rhinoceros (white)	480	20	50
Deer (white-tailed)	201	8	20	Sea lion (California)	350	12	34
Dog (domestic)	61	12	21	Sheep (domestic)	154	12	23
Elephant (African)	660	35	70	Squirrel (gray)	44	10	23-6
Elephant (Asian)	645	40	77	Tiger	105	16	26-3
Elk	250	15	26-8	Wolf (maned)	63	5	15-8
Fox (red)	52	7	14	Zebra (Grant's)	365	15	50
Giraffe	457	10	36-2				
Goat (domestic)	151	8	18	**Animal**		**Incubation time (days)**	
Gorilla	258	20	54	Chicken			21
Guinea pig	68	4	8	Duck			30
Hippopotamus	238	41	61	Goose			30
Horse	330	20	50	Pigeon			18
Kangaroo (gray)	36	7	24	Turkey			26

Geologic Time Scale

Our understanding of Earth's ancient history is largely a result of geoscientists' study of climate, rock strata, ice samples, mineral deposits, and fossils from around the world; clues to the planet's origin have also been found through the study of extraterrestrial bodies. Geologists divide Earth's history into the following units (MYA = million years ago):

PRECAMBRIAN TIME (4,600-541 MYA)

HADEAN EON (4,600-4,000 MYA) Earth has no continents, oceans, or life; surface conditions are defined by intense volcanic activity and widespread meteorite impact. Oldest known minerals and rocks, many of meteoric origin, date to this eon, which may also have seen the first appearance of life.

ARCHEAN EON (4,000-2,500 MYA) Earth's surface cools and water vapor in atmosphere condenses to form early oceans, which define small protocontinents; there is substantial evidence for the existence of single-celled organisms, bacteria and archaea, in these oceans.

PROTEROZOIC EON (2,500-541 MYA) Protocontinents merge into larger landmasses as Earth's crust continues to shift. Atmospheric oxygen levels increase, and first known multicellular life appears. Later, soft-bodied marine animals emerge.

PHANEROZOIC EON (541 MYA-present)

Paleozoic Era (541-252 MYA)

Cambrian Period (541-485 MYA). The supercontinent known as Gondwana, or Gondwanaland, dominates the Southern Hemisphere. Seas experience an explosion of invertebrate animal life, including thousands of species of trilobites; the first known vertebrates appear. There is no life on land.

Ordovician Period (485-444 MYA). Gondwanaland extends from South Pole to tropic regions; Northern Hemisphere is mostly open ocean. Average global temperatures are warmer than in the current era. First primitive land plants, early ancestors of starfish and mollusks, and first armored, jawless fishes appear. The period ends in mass extinction of a majority of species, possibly a result of a global drop in sea level due to glaciation.

Silurian Period (444-419 MYA). South Pole remains covered by supercontinent, but precursors of present-day N America, Europe, and Asia coalesce around the equator and middle latitudes. Appearance of first known vascular land plants, first freshwater fish, first jawed fish, first coral reefs, and first air-breathing animals (certain eurypterids, also called sea scorpions, largest known arthropods).

Devonian Period (419-359 MYA). Collisions between Gondwanaland and ancestral landmasses of N America and Eurasia produce mountains visible today as northern Appalachians. Newly-formed ozone layer offers protection from sun's rays, allowing first air-breathing spiders and mites to appear on dry land. Fish with fins and scales and first amphibians emerge. Late Devonian mass extinction.

Carboniferous Period (359-299 MYA). Precursors of modern N America and Northern Europe lie in tropical latitudes N of the equator; warm and humid conditions there facilitate spread of lush forests and peat swamps that later form most of the world's coal and limestone. Later period sees emergence of first true conifers, Lepidodendrales ("scale trees") as tall as 100 ft, and first true reptiles.

Permian Period (299-252 MYA). All major landmasses collide to form the supercontinent Pangaea, surrounded by the world ocean Panthalassa. Gradual warming through much of the Permian allows for initial flourishing of species, including dinosaur precursors (up to 10 ft long) and marine species in shallow inland seas. The period ended with the largest of Earth's five mass extinctions. As much as 95% of all marine species and most land species went extinct in the event, which was likely caused by increased greenhouse gases in atmosphere.

Mesozoic Era (252-66 MYA)

Triassic Period (252-201 MYA). Pangaea separates into supercontinents of Laurasia and Gondwana; subtropical conditions extend as far N as present-day Wyoming and New England. Emergence of icthyosaurs and plesiosaurs (large marine reptiles), several species of dinosaurs (up to 15 ft long), first true mammals, and first insects to undergo metamorphosis from larva to pupa to adult. Triassic-Jurassic mass extinction.

Jurassic Period (201-145 MYA). N American continent drifts westward, opening Gulf of Mexico; rift forms between S America and Africa. Warm, moist climate contributes to flourishing of coral reefs and temperate and subtropical forests. Appearance of first angiosperms (flowering plants), pterosaurs (winged reptiles), the earliest known birds (offshoots of a dinosaur group), and huge dinosaurs such as the carnivorous *Allosaurus* and herbivorous *Apatosaurus*.

Cretaceous Period (145-66 MYA). African continental plate drifts N, creating roots of European Alps; gap between S America and Africa broadens; western movement of N America drives formation of Sierra Nevada and Rocky Mountains, turning the western interior of continent into a vast swamp. Later, sea levels rise and cover about one-third of Earth's present land area. The global climate is warm and mild. The period ends in a mass extinction of plant and animal species (including dinosaurs). Likely causes include an asteroid impact and increased volcanic activity.

Cenozoic Era (66 MYA-present)

Paleogene Period (66-23 MYA)

• Paleocene Epoch (66-56 MYA). Australia begins to separate from Antarctica; N America and Greenland begin to spread apart. Mammalian life predominates, including early marsupials, insectivores, creodonts (carnivorous relatives of cats and dogs), and primitive hoofed mammals.

• Eocene Epoch (56-33.9 MYA). Australia drifts farther from Antarctica; the Indian subcontinent becomes welded to Asia, and tectonic forces drive the upheaval of the Alpine-Himalayan system. Climate in N America and Europe is subtropical and moist, with temperate forests as far N as Greenland and Siberia. Ancestors of modern horses, elephants, rhinoceroses, camels, bats, primates, and squirrel-like rodents emerge; earliest known marine mammals appear in later Eocene.

• Oligocene Epoch (33.9-23 MYA). San Andreas fault develops between N American and Pacific plates. Mammalian species continue to diversify, producing modern horse and multiple rodent, camel, and rhinoceros-like species, as well as first known species of great ape. Long-term cooling trend begins that would later cause Pleistocene ice ages.

Neogene Period (23 MYA-2.6 MYA)

• Miocene Epoch (23-5.3 MYA). Crustal plate collisions continue to drive uplift of Alps, Himalayas, and Cordilleran Ranges in Americas; eroded sediment is deposited in shallow marine basins, forming reservoirs for oil fields of California, Romania, and Caspian Sea. Ocean currents prevent Antarctica from receiving warmer waters, fostering growth of Antarctic ice sheet. Northern forests become grassy prairies. Large apes related to the orangutan live in Asia and southern Europe. Oldest hominin fossils from Africa date to this epoch.

• Pliocene Epoch (5.3-2.6 MYA). Alps continue to rise in Europe, and subduction of the Pacific tectonic plate elevates the Sierra Nevada and volcanic Cascade Range. Climate becomes cooler and drier, driving formation of permanent Arctic ice cap. Rapid primate evolution produces *Ardipithecus* and *Australopithecus*, two of the earliest known direct ancestors of *Homo sapiens*.

Quarternary Period (2.6 MYA-present)

• Pleistocene Epoch (2.6 MYA-11,700 years ago). Glacier ice covers as much as 25% or more of Earth's land surface, carving numerous present-day features including the Great Lakes; increased rainfall in lower latitudes allows plant and animal life to flourish in northern and eastern Africa. Late Pleistocene brings worldwide extinction of many large mammals, including the mastodon, saber-toothed tiger, and ground sloth. Evidence of Neanderthals and Denisovans dates from the latter part of the Pleistocene.

• Holocene Epoch (11,700 years ago-present). Melting ice caused sea levels to rise 100 ft or more in early Holocene, covering large areas of land and extending continental shelf of N America. Humans proliferate, and civilization begins.

Biological Classification

In biology, classification is the identification, naming, and grouping of organisms into a formal system. The two fields that are most directly concerned with classification are taxonomy and systematics. Although they overlap, taxonomy is more concerned with nomenclature (naming) and with constructing hierarchical systems, and systematics with uncovering evolutionary relationships. Two kingdoms of living forms, Plantae and Animalia, have been recognized since Aristotle established the first taxonomy in the 4th century BCE. Plants and animals are examples of eukaryotes; their cells have nuclei bound by membranes. Two other kingdoms of eukaryotes that have been identified are Protista (mostly one-celled organisms) and Fungi. Single-celled bacteria and archaea lack such nuclei. They are referred to as prokaryotes (or procaryotes) and are commonly placed in separate kingdoms. The seven basic categories of classification (from most general to most specific) are kingdom, phylum (or division), class, order, family, genus, and species. (In addition, many scientists group all eukaryotes in a single "domain," and treat bacteria and archaea as two other domains.) Below are two examples of classification:

ZOOLOGICAL HIERARCHY

Kingdom	Phylum	Class	Order	Family	Genus	Species name	Common name
Animalia	Chordata	Mammalia	Primates	Hominidae	*Homo*	*Homo sapiens*	Human

BOTANICAL HIERARCHY

Kingdom	Division*	Class	Order	Family	Genus	Species name	Common name
Plantae	Magnoliophyta	Magnoliopsida	Magnoliales	Magnoliaceae	*Magnolia*	*M. virginiana*	Sweet bay

*In botany, the division is generally used in place of the phylum.

Major Venomous Animals

Snakes

Asian pit viper—2 ft to 5 ft long; throughout Asia; reactions and mortality vary, but most bites cause tissue damage; mortality generally low.

Australian brown snake—4 ft to 7 ft long; very slow onset of cardiac or respiratory distress; moderate mortality, but because death can be sudden and unexpected, it is the most dangerous of the Australian snakes; antivenom.

Barba amarilla or fer-de-lance—up to 7 ft long; from tropical Mexico to Brazil; severe tissue damage common; moderate mortality; antivenom.

Black mamba—up to 14 ft long; southern and central Africa; rapid onset of dizziness, difficulty breathing, erratic heartbeat; mortality high, nears 100% without antivenom.

Boomslang—less than 6 ft long; African savannahs; rapid onset of nausea and dizziness, often followed by slight recovery and then sudden death from internal hemorrhaging; bites rare, mortality high; antivenom.

Bushmaster—up to 12 ft long; tropical forests of Central and S America; few bites occur, but mortality high.

Common, or Asian, cobra—4 ft to 8 ft long; throughout S Asia; considerable tissue damage, sometimes paralysis; mortality probably not more than 10%; antivenom.

Copperhead—less than 4 ft long; New England to Texas; pain and swelling; very seldom fatal; antivenom seldom needed.

Coral snake—2 ft to 5 ft long; in Americas S of Canada; bite may be painless; slow onset of paralysis, impaired breathing; mortalities rare but high without antivenom and mechanical respiration.

Cottonmouth water moccasin—up to 5 ft long; wetlands of southern U.S. from Virginia to Texas; rapid onset of severe pain, swelling, tissue destruction can be extensive; mortality low; antivenom.

Death adder—less than 3 ft long; Australia; rapid onset of faintness, cardiac and respiratory distress; at least 50% mortality without antivenom.

Desert horned viper—up to 2 ft long; dry areas of Africa and western Asia; swelling and tissue damage; mortality low; antivenom.

European viper—1 ft to 3 ft long; throughout Europe; bleeding and tissue damage; mortality low; antivenom.

Gaboon viper—more than 6 ft long; S of the Sahara; massive tissue damage, internal bleeding; few recorded bites.

King cobra—up to 16 ft long; throughout S Asia; rapid swelling, dizziness, loss of consciousness, difficulty breathing, erratic heartbeat; mortality varies with amount of venom involved, but most bites involve nonfatal amounts; antivenom.

Krait—up to 5 ft long; SE Asia; rapid onset of sleepiness, numbness; up to 50% mortality even with use of antivenom.

Puff adder—up to 5 ft long, thick; S of the Sahara, throughout the Middle East; rapid large swelling, great pain, dizziness; moderate mortality, often from internal bleeding; antivenom.

Rattlesnake—2 ft to 6 ft long; throughout Western Hemisphere; rapid onset of severe pain, swelling; mortality low, but amputation of affected digits is sometimes necessary; antivenom. Mojave rattler may produce temporary paralysis.

Ringhals, or spitting, cobra—5 ft to 7 ft long; southern Africa; squirts venom through holes in front of fangs as a defense; venom severely irritating and can cause blindness.

Russell's viper or tic-polonga—more than 5 ft long; throughout Asia; internal bleeding; bite reports common; moderate mortality rate; antivenom.

Saw-scaled, or carpet, viper—up to 2 ft long; dry areas from India to Africa; severe bleeding, fever; high mortality, causes more human fatalities than any other snake; antivenom.

Sea snake—3 ft to 10 ft long; throughout Pacific, Indian Oceans except NE Pacific; almost painless bite; variety of muscle pain, paralysis; mortality low, many bites not envenomed; some antivenoms.

Sharp-nosed pit viper or hundred-pace snake—up to 5 ft long; S Vietnam, Taiwan, and China; the most toxic of Asian pit vipers; very rapid onset of swelling and tissue damage, internal bleeding; moderate mortality; antivenom.

Taipan—up to 11 ft long; Australia and New Guinea; rapid paralysis with severe breathing difficulty; mortality nears 100% without antivenom.

Tiger snake—2 ft to 6 ft long; southern Australia; pain, numbness, mental disturbances with rapid paralysis; may be deadliest of all land snakes, but antivenom is quite effective.

Yellow, or cape, cobra—7 ft long; southern Africa; most toxic venom of any cobra; rapid onset of swelling, breathing and cardiac difficulties; mortality is high without treatment; antivenom.

Note: Not all bites by venomous snakes are actually envenomed. Any animal bite, however, carries the danger of tetanus, and anyone suffering a venomous snake bite should seek medical attention. Antivenoms do not cure; they are only an aid in the treatment of bites. Mortality rates above are for envenomed bites: low mortality, c. 2% or less; moderate, 2%-5%; high, 5%-15%.

Lizards

Gila monster—up to 24 in. long, with heavy body and tail; high desert in SW U.S. and northern Mexico; immediate severe pain, transient low blood pressure; no recent mortality.

Mexican beaded lizard—similar to Gila monster; W coast of Mexico; reaction and mortality similar to Gila monster.

Insects

Ants, bees, hornets, wasps—global distribution; usual reaction is piercing pain in area of sting, though many people suffer allergic reactions (swelling, rashes); not directly fatal, except in cases of massive multiple stings, and a few may die within minutes from severe sensitivity to the venom (anaphylactic shock).

Spiders, scorpions

Black widow—small, round-bodied with red hourglass marking; the widow and its relatives are found in tropical and temperate zones; severe musculoskeletal pain, weakness, breathing difficulty, convulsions, which may be more serious in small children; low mortality; antivenom. The **redback** spider of Australia has the hourglass marking on its back, rather than on its front, but otherwise looks almost identical to the black widow.

Brown recluse, or fiddleback, spider—small, oblong body; throughout U.S.; pain with later ulceration, which may last months, at place of bite; fever, nausea, and stomach cramps in severe cases; very low mortality.

Funnel web spider—several varieties, often large; Australia; slow onset of breathing, circulation difficulties; low mortality; antivenom.

Scorpion—crablike body with stinger in tail, various sizes; many varieties throughout tropical and subtropical areas; severe pain spreading from the wound, numbness, severe agitation, cramps, and even respiratory failure; low mortality, usually in children; antivenoms.

Tarantula—large, hairy spider; worldwide; the American tarantula, and probably all other tarantulas, are harmless to humans, though their bite may cause some pain and swelling.

Sea life

Cone-shell—mollusk in small shell; S Pacific and Indian Oceans; shoots barbs into victims; paralysis; low mortality.

Octopus—global distribution, usually in warm waters; rapid onset of paralysis with breathing difficulty; all varieties produce venom, but only a few can cause death.

Portuguese man-of-war—jellyfish-like siphonophore with tentacles up to 100 ft long; in most warm water areas; immediate severe pain; not directly fatal, though shock may cause death in rare cases.

Sea wasp or box jellyfish—tentacles up to 30 ft long; S Pacific; very rapid onset of circulatory problems; high mortality because of speed of toxic reaction; antivenom.

Stingray—several varieties of differing sizes; tropical and temperate seas and some freshwater; severe pain, rapid onset of nausea, vomiting, breathing difficulties; wound area may ulcerate, gangrene may occur; seldom fatal.

Stonefish—brownish fish that lies motionless on bottom of shallow waters; throughout S Pacific and Indian Oceans; extraordinary pain, rapid paralysis; low mortality; antivenom, warm water relieves pain.

Speeds of Selected Animals

Source: *Natural History* magazine. © American Museum of Natural History

Animal	Speed (mph)	Animal	Speed (mph)	Animal	Speed (mph)
Cheetah	70	Mongolian wild ass	40	Human	27.89
Pronghorn antelope	61	Greyhound	39.35	Elephant	25
Wildebeest	50	Whippet	35.50	Black mamba snake	20
Lion	50	Rabbit (domestic)	35	Six-lined race runner (lizard)	18
Thomson's gazelle	50	Mule deer	35	Wild turkey	15
Quarterhorse	47.5	Jackal	35	Squirrel	12
Elk	45	Reindeer	32	Pig (domestic)	11
Cape hunting dog	45	Giraffe	32	Chicken	9
Coyote	43	White-tailed deer	30	Spider (*Tegenaria atrica*)	1.17
Gray fox	42	Warthog	30	Giant tortoise	0.17
Hyena	40	Grizzly bear	30	Three-toed sloth	0.15
Zebra	40	Cat (domestic)	30	Garden snail	0.03

Note: Most of these measurements are for maximum speeds over approximate quarter-mile distances. Exceptions are the lion and elephant, whose speeds were clocked in the act of charging; the whippet, which was timed over a 200-yd course; the cheetah, timed over a 100-yd distance; a human, timed over a 15-yd segment of a 100-yd run; and the black mamba, six-lined race runner, spider, giant tortoise, three-toed sloth, and garden snail, which were measured over various small distances.

Most Popular Breeds of Cats, 2017

Source: The Cat Fanciers' Association
(ranked by total registrations)

Rank	Breed	Rank	Breed	Rank	Breed	Rank	Breed	Rank	Breed
1.	Exotic	10.	Abyssinian	18.	Bengal	27.	Somali	34.	American Bobtail
2.	Ragdoll	11.	Oriental	19.	Tonkinese	28.	Balinese/	35.	European Burmese
3.	British Shorthair	12.	Siamese	20.	Burmese		Javanese	36.	Chartreux
4.	Persian	13.	Cornish Rex	21.	Ocicat	29.	Manx	37.	Korat
5.	Maine Coon Cat	14.	Norwegian Forest	22.	American Curl	30.	Singapura	38.	Havana Brown
6.	American Shorthair		Cat	23.	Selkirk Rex	31.	Bombay	39.	Burmilla
7.	Scottish Fold	15.	Siberian	24.	Japanese Bobtail	32.	Colorpoint	40.	LaPerm
8.	Sphynx	16.	Birman	25.	Egyptian Mau		Shorthair	41.	Turkish Van
9.	Devon Rex	17.	Russian Blue	26.	RagaMuffin	33.	Turkish Angora	42.	American Wirehair

Most Popular American Kennel Club Dog Breed Registrations, 2014-17

Source: American Kennel Club (AKC)
(ranked by 2017 registrations)

Breed	Rank 2017	2016	2015	2014	Breed	Rank 2017	2016	2015	2014
Labrador Retrievers	1	1	1	1	Doberman Pinschers	16	15	14	14
German Shepherds	2	2	2	2	Australian Shepherds	17	16	17	18
Golden Retrievers	3	3	3	3	Miniature Schnauzers	18	17	16	16
French Bulldogs	4	6	6	9	Cavalier King Charles				
Bulldogs	5	4	4	4	Spaniels	19	19	18	19
Beagles	6	5	5	5	Shih Tzu	20	20	19	17
Poodles	7	7	8	7	Boston Terriers	21	21	22	23
Rottweilers	8	8	9	10	Pomeranians	22	22	21	20
Yorkshire Terriers	9	9	7	6	Havanese	23	23	24	25
German Shorthaired					Shetland Sheepdogs	24	24	23	21
Pointers	10	11	11	12	Bernese Mountain Dogs	25	27	29	32
Boxers	11	10	10	8	Brittanys	26	25	26	27
Siberian Huskies	12	12	12	13	English Springer Spaniels	27	26	27	28
Dachshunds	13	13	13	11	Mastiffs	28	28	25	26
Great Danes	14	14	15	15	Cocker Spaniels	29	29	30	30
Pembroke Welsh Corgis	15	18	20	22	Vizslas	30	31	32	34

Dog Breeds by Type

Source: American Kennel Club (AKC)

As of mid-2018, the AKC recognized 190 registered breeds and used the following seven groups to classify them, according to functions and other distinctive traits.

Herding Group: Australian Cattle Dog, Australian Shepherd, Bearded Collie, Beauceron, Belgian Malinois, Belgian Sheepdog, Belgian Tervuren, Bergamasco Sheepdog, Berger Picard, Border Collie, Bouvier des Flandres, Briard, Canaan Dog, Cardigan Welsh Corgi, Collie, Entlebucher Mountain Dog, Finnish Lapphund, German Shepherd Dog, Icelandic Sheepdog, Miniature American Shepherd, Norwegian Buhund, Old English Sheepdog, Pembroke Welsh Corgi, Polish Lowland Sheepdog, Puli, Pumi, Pyrenean Shepherd, Shetland Sheepdog, Spanish Water Dog, Swedish Vallhund.

Hound Group: Afghan Hound, American English Coonhound, American Foxhound, Basenji, Basset Hound, Beagle, Black and Tan Coonhound, Bloodhound, Bluetick Coonhound, Borzoi, Cirneco dell'Etna, Dachshund, English Foxhound, Grand Basset Griffon Vendéen, Greyhound, Harrier, Ibizan Hound, Irish Wolfhound, Norwegian Elkhound, Otterhound, Petit Basset Griffon Vendéen, Pharaoh Hound, Plott, Portuguese Podengo Pequeno, Redbone Coonhound, Rhodesian Ridgeback, Saluki, Scottish Deerhound, Sloughi, Treeing Walker Coonhound, Whippet.

Non-Sporting Group: American Eskimo Dog, Bichon Frise, Boston Terrier, Bulldog, Chinese Shar-Pei, Chow Chow, Coton de Tulear, Dalmatian, Finnish Spitz, French Bulldog, Keeshond, Lhasa Apso, Löwchen, Norwegian Lundehund, Poodle (standard and miniature), Schipperke, Shiba Inu, Tibetan Spaniel, Tibetan Terrier, Xoloitzcuintli.

Sporting Group: American Water Spaniel, Boykin Spaniel, Brittany, Chesapeake Bay Retriever, Clumber Spaniel, Cocker Spaniel, Curly-Coated Retriever, English Cocker Spaniel, English Setter, English Springer Spaniel, Field Spaniel, Flat-Coated Retriever, German Shorthaired Pointer, German Wirehaired Pointer, Golden Retriever, Gordon Setter, Irish Red and White Setter, Irish Setter, Irish Water Spaniel, Labrador Retriever, Lagotto Romagnolo, Nederlandse Kooikerhondje, Nova Scotia Duck Tolling Retriever, Pointer, Spinone Italiano, Sussex Spaniel, Vizsla, Weimaraner, Welsh Springer Spaniel, Wirehaired Pointing Griffon, Wirehaired Vizsla.

Terrier Group: Airedale Terrier, American Hairless Terrier, American Staffordshire Terrier, Australian Terrier, Bedlington Terrier, Border Terrier, Bull Terrier, Cairn Terrier, Cesky Terrier, Dandie Dinmont Terrier, Glen of Imaal Terrier, Irish Terrier, Kerry Blue Terrier, Lakeland Terrier, Manchester Terrier (standard), Miniature Bull Terrier, Miniature Schnauzer, Norfolk Terrier, Norwich Terrier, Parson Russell Terrier, Rat Terrier, Russell Terrier, Scottish Terrier, Sealyham Terrier, Skye Terrier, Smooth Fox Terrier, Soft Coated Wheaten Terrier, Staffordshire Bull Terrier, Welsh Terrier, West Highland White Terrier, Wire Fox Terrier.

Toy Group: Affenpinscher, Brussels Griffon, Cavalier King Charles Spaniel, Chihuahua, Chinese Crested, English Toy Spaniel, Havanese, Italian Greyhound, Japanese Chin, Maltese, Manchester Terrier (toy), Miniature Pinscher, Papillon, Pekingese, Pomeranian, Poodle (toy), Pug, Shih Tzu, Silky Terrier, Toy Fox Terrier, Yorkshire Terrier.

Working Group: Akita, Alaskan Malamute, Anatolian Shepherd Dog, Bernese Mountain Dog, Black Russian Terrier, Boerboel, Boxer, Bullmastiff, Cane Corso, Chinook, Doberman Pinscher, Dogue de Bordeaux, German Pinscher, Giant Schnauzer, Great Dane, Great Pyrenees, Greater Swiss Mountain Dog, Komondor, Kuvasz, Leonberger, Mastiff, Neapolitan Mastiff, Newfoundland, Portuguese Water Dog, Rottweiler, Saint Bernard, Samoyed, Siberian Husky, Standard Schnauzer, Tibetan Mastiff.

Discoveries and Innovations: Biology, Chemistry, Medicine, Physics

Discovery	Date	Discoverer(s)	Nationality
Acetylene gas	1862	Berthelot	French
ACTH	1927	Evans, Long	U.S.
Adrenaline	1901	Takamine	Japanese
Aluminum, electrolytic process	1886	Hall	U.S.
Aluminum, isolated	1825	Oersted	Danish
Anesthesia, ether	1842	Long	U.S.
Anesthesia, local	1885	Koller	Austrian
Anesthesia, spinal	1898	Bier	German
Aniline dye	1856	Perkin	English
Anti-rabies	1885	Pasteur	French
Antiseptic surgery	1867	Lister	English
Antitoxin, diphtheria	1891	Von Behring	German
Argyrol	1897	Bayer	German
Arsphenamine	1910	Ehrlich	German
Aspirin	1853	Gerhardt	French
Atabrine	1932	Mietzsch, et al.	German
Atomic numbers	1913	Moseley	English
Atomic theory	1803	Dalton	English
Atomic time clock	1948	Lyons	U.S.
Atom-smashing theory	1919	Rutherford	English
Bacitracin	1943	Johnson, Meleneyl	U.S.
Bacteria, description	1676	Leeuwenhoek	Dutch
Bacterial genome, synthetic	2010	Venter	U.S.
Bleaching powder	1798	Tennant	English
Blood, circulation	1628	Harvey	English
Bordeaux mixture	1885	Millardet	French
Bromine from the sea	1826	Balard	French
Calcium carbide	1888	Wilson	U.S.
Calculus	1670	Newton	English
Camphor synthetic	1896	Haller	French
Canning (food)	1804	Appert	French
Carbon oxides	1925	Fisher	German
Chemotherapy	1909	Ehrlich	German
Chloamphenicol	1947	Burkholder	U.S.
Chlorine	1774	Scheele	Swedish
Chloroform	1831	Guthrie	U.S.
Chlortetracycline	1948	Duggen	U.S.
Classification of plants and animals	1735	Linnaeus	Swedish
Cloning, DNA	1973	Boyer, Cohen	U.S.
Cloning, mammal	1996	Wilmut, et al.	Scottish
Cocaine	1860	Niermann	German
Combustion explained	1777	Lavoisier	French
Conditioned reflex	1914	Pavlov	Russian
Cortisone	1936	Kendall	U.S.
Cortisone, synthesis	1946	Sarett	U.S.
Cosmic rays	1910	Gockel	Swiss
Cyclotron	1930	Lawrence	U.S.
DDT (not applied as insecticide until 1939)	1874	Zeidler	German
Denisovan humans (DNA analysis)	2010	Krause, et al. Pääbo	German Swedish
Deuterium	1932	Urey, Brickwedde, Murphy	U.S.
DNA (as carrier of heredity)	1943	Avery, MacLeod, McCarty	U.S.
DNA (structure)	1953	Crick, Wilkins Watson	English U.S.
Electric resistance, law of	1827	Ohm	German
Electric waves	1888	Hertz	German
Electrolysis	1852	Faraday	English
Electromagnetism	1819	Oersted	Danish
Electron	1897	Thomson, J.	English
Electron diffraction	1936	Thomson, G. Davisson	English U.S.
Electroshock treatment	1938	Cerletti, Bini	Italian
Erythromycin	1952	McGuire	U.S.
Evolution, natural selection	1858	Darwin	English
Falling bodies, law of	1590	Galileo	Italian
Gases, law of combining volumes	1808	Gay-Lussac	French
Geometry, analytic	1619	Descartes	French
Gold, cyanide process for extraction	1887	MacArthur, R.Forrest, W. Forrest	Scottish
Gravitation, law	1687	Newton	English
Gravitational waves (detection)	2015	LIGO	U.S.-Intl.
Higgs boson	2012	CERN	International
HIV (human immuno-deficiency virus)	1984	Montagnier Gallo	French U.S.
Holograph	1948	Gabor	Hung.-British
Homo floresiensis ("hobbit" humans)	2003	Morwood, et al.	New Zea.
Human genome sequence (first draft)	2001	Human Genome Project, Celera Genomics Corp.	U.S.-Intl.
Human heart transplant	1967	Barnard	S. African
In vitro fertilization	1978	Steptoe, Edwards	English
Indigo, synthesis of	1880	Baeyer	German
Induction, electric	1830	Henry	U.S.
Insulin	1922	Banting, Best Macleod	Canadian Scottish
Intelligence testing	1905	Binet, Simon	French
Isotopes, theory	1912	Soddy	English
Laser	1957	Gould	U.S.

Discovery	Date	Discoverer(s)	Nationality
Light, velocity	1675	Roemer	Danish
Light, wave theory	1690	Huygens	Dutch
Lithography	1796	Senefelder	Bohemian
Logarithms	1614	Napier	Scottish
LSD-25	1943	Hoffman	Swiss
Mendelian laws	1866	Mendel	Austrian
Mercator projection (map)	1568	Mercator (Kremer)	Flemish
Methanol	1661	Boyle	Irish
Milk condensation	1853	Borden	U.S.
Molecular hypothesis	1811	Avogadro	Italian
Motion, laws of	1687	Newton	English
Neomycin	1949	Waksman, Lechevalier	U.S.
Neutrino	1956	Reines, Cowan	U.S.
Neutron	1932	Chadwick	English
Nitric acid	1648	Glauber	German
Nitric oxide	1772	Priestley	English
Nitroglycerin	1846	Sobrero	Italian
Oil cracking process	1891	Dewar	U.S.
Oxygen	1774	Priestley	English
Oxytetracycline	1950	Finlay, et al.	U.S.
Ozone	1840	Schonbein	German
Paper, sulfite process	1867	Tilghman	U.S.
Paper, wood pulp, sulfate process	1884	Dahl	German
Penicillin	1928	Fleming	Scottish
Penicillin, practical use	1941	Florey, Chain	English
Periodic law and table of elements	1869	Mendeleyev	Russian
Physostigmine synthesis	1935	Julian	U.S.
Pill, birth-control	1954	Pincus, Rock	U.S.
Planetary motion, laws	1609	Kepler	German
Plutonium fission	1940	Kennedy, Wahl, Seaborg, Segre	U.S.
Polymyxin	1947	Ainsworth	English
Positron	1932	Anderson	U.S.
Proton	1919	Rutherford	New Zea.
Psychoanalysis	1900	Freud	Austrian
Pulsars	1967	Bell	English
Quantum theory	1900	Planck	German
Quasars	1963	Matthews, Sandage	U.S.
Quinine synthetic	1946	Woodward, Doering	U.S.
Radioactivity	1896	Becquerel	French
Radiocarbon dating	1947	Libby	U.S.
Radium	1898	Curie, Pierre	French
		Curie, Marie	Pol.-Fr.
Relativity theory	1905	Einstein	German

Discovery	Date	Discoverer(s)	Nationality
Reserpine	1949	Jal Vakil	Indian
Schick test	1913	Schick	U.S.
Silicon	1823	Berzelius	Swedish
Smallpox eradication	1979	World Health Org.	UN
Streptomycin	1944	Waksman, et al.	U.S.
Sulfanilamide	1935	Bovet, Trefouel	French
Sulfanilamide theory	1908	Gelmo	German
Sulfapyridine	1938	Ewins, Phelps	English
Sulfathiazole	1939	Fosbinder, Walter	U.S.
Sulfuric acid	1831	Phillips	English
Sulfuric acid, lead	1746	Roebuck	English
Superconductivity	1911	Onnes	Dutch
Superconductivity theory	1957	Bardeen, Cooper, Schreiffer	U.S.
Superconductors, high-temp.	1986	Bednorz, Muller	Ger., Swiss
Syphilis test	1906	Wassermann	German
Transplant, heart	1967	Barnard	S. African
Tuberculin	1890	Koch	German
Uranium fission, atomic reactor	1942	Fermi, Szilard	U.S.
Uranium fission theory	1939	Hahn, Meitner, Strassmann	German
		Bohr	Danish
		Fermi	Italian
		Einstein, Pegram, Wheeler	U.S.
Vaccine, measles	1963	Enders	U.S.
Vaccine, MMR	1971	Hilleman	U.S.
Vaccine, meningitis (first conjugate)	1987	Gordon, et al., Connaught Labs	U.S.
Vaccine, polio	1954	Salk	U.S.
Vaccine, polio, oral	1960	Sabin	U.S.
Vaccine, rabies	1885	Pasteur	French
Vaccine, smallpox	1796	Jenner	English
Vaccine, typhus	1909	Nicolle	French
Vaccine, varicella	1974	Takahashi	Japanese
Van Allen belts, radiation	1958	Van Allen	U.S.
Vitamin A	1913	McCollum, Davis	U.S.
Vitamin B	1916	McCollum	U.S.
Vitamin C	1928	Szent-Gyorgyi	Hungarian
		King	U.S.
Vitamin D	1922	McCollum	U.S.
Xerography	1938	Carlson	U.S.
X-ray	1895	Roentgen	German

Inventions

Invention	Date	Inventor(s)	Nationality
Adding machine	1642	Pascal	French
Adding machine	1885	Burroughs	U.S.
Aerosol spray	1926	Rotheim	Norwegian
Air brake	1869	Westinghouse	U.S.
Air conditioning	1902	Carrier	U.S.
Air pump	1654	Guericke	German
Airbag	1952	Hetrick	U.S.
Airplane, automatic pilot	1912	Sperry	U.S.
Airplane, experimental	1896	Langley	U.S.
Airplane, hydro	1911	Curtiss	U.S.
Airplane jet engine	1939	Ohain	German
Airplane with motor	1903	Wright Bros.	U.S.
Airship	1852	Giffard	French
Aqua-Lung	1943	Cousteau, Gagnan	French
Arc welder	1919	Thomson	U.S.
Aspartame	1965	Schlatter	U.S.
Autogyro	1920	de la Cierva	Spanish
Automobile, diff. gear	1885	Benz	German
Automobile, electric	1892	Morrison	U.S.
Automobile, exp'mtl	1864	Marcus	Austrian
Automobile, gasoline	1889	Daimler	German
Automobile, gasoline	1892	Duryea	U.S.
Automobile magneto	1897	Bosch	German
Automobile muffler	1904	Pope	U.S.
Automobile self-starter	1911	Kettering	U.S.
Bakelite	1907	Baekeland	Belg., U.S.
Bar code	1952	Woodland, Silver	U.S.
Barometer	1643	Torricelli	Italian
Bicycle, modern	1885	Starley	English
Bifocal lens	1780	Franklin	U.S.
Bottle machine	1895	Owens	U.S.
Bluetooth	1994	Haartsen	Dutch
Braille printing	1829	Braille	French
Brassiere, modern	1913	Jacob	U.S
Bubble gum	1928	Diemer	U.S.
Burner, gas	1855	Bunsen	German
Calculator, electronic pocket	1972	Merryman, Van Tassel	U.S.
Calculator, mechanical	1623	Schickard	German
Camera, digital	1977	Lloyd, Sasson	U.S.
Camera, Kodak	1888	Eastman, Walker	U.S.
Camera, Polaroid Land	1948	Land	U.S.

Invention	Date	Inventor(s)	Nationality
Can, pop-top	1959	Fraze	U.S.
Car coupler	1873	Janney	U.S.
Carburetor, gasoline	1893	Maybach	German
Carding machine	1797	Whittemore	U.S.
Carpet sweeper	1876	Bissell	U.S.
Cash register	1879	Ritty	U.S.
Cassette, audio	1963	Philips Co.	Dutch
Cassette, videotape	1969	Sony	Japanese
CAT, or CT, scan	1973	Hounsfield	English
Cathode-ray tube	1897	Braun	German
Cellophane	1908	Brandenberger	Swiss
Celluloid	1870	Hyatt	U.S.
Cement, Portland	1824	Aspdin	English
Chronometer	1735	Harrison	English
Circuit breaker	1925	Hilliard	U.S.
Circuit, integrated	1959	Kilby, Noyce, Texas Instr.	U.S.
Clock, pendulum	1657	Huygens	Dutch
Coaxial cable system	1929	Affel, Espensched.	U.S.
Coca-Cola	1885	Pemberton	U.S.
Coffeemaker, auto drip	1963	Bunn Corp.	U.S.
Compressed air rock drill	1871	Ingersoll	U.S.
Comptometer	1887	Felt	U.S.
Computer, electronic	1942	Atanasoff, Berry	U.S.
Computer, laptop	1987	Sinclair	English
Computer, large-scale automatic digital	1943	Aiken, et al.	U.S.
Computer, mini	1960	Digital Corp.	U.S.
Condenser microphone (telephone)	1916	Wente	U.S.
Contact lens, corneal	1948	Tuohy	U.S.
Contraceptive, oral	1954	Pincus, Rock	U.S.
Corn, hybrid	1917	Jones	U.S.
Cotton gin	1793	Whitney	U.S.
Cream separator	1878	DeLaval	Swedish
Cultivator, disc	1878	Mallon	U.S.
Cyclotron	1931	Lawrence	U.S.
Cystoscope	1878	Nitze	German
Diapers, disposable	1950	Donovan	U.S.
Diesel engine	1895	Diesel	German

Invention	Date	Inventor(s)	Nationality
Disc, compact	1972	RCA	U.S.
Disc player, compact	1979	Sony, Philips Co.	Japanese, Dutch
Dishwasher	1893	Cochrane	U.S.
Disk, floppy	1970	IBM	U.S.
Disk, video	1972	Philips Co.	Dutch
Dynamite	1866	Nobel	Swedish
Dynamo, contin. current	1871	Gramme	Belgian
Electric battery	1800	Volta	Italian
Electric fan	1882	Wheeler	U.S.
Electrocardiograph	1903	Einthoven	Dutch
Electroencephalograph	1929	Berger	German
Electromagnet	1824	Sturgeon	English
Electron microscope	1931	Ruska, Knoll	German
Electron spectrometer	1944	Deutsch, Elliott, Evans	U.S.
Electron tube multigrid	1913	Langmuir	U.S.
Electronic cigarette (nicotine-based)	2003	Hon (Han)	Chinese
Electronic paper (e-ink)	1974	Sheridon	U.S.
Electroplating	1805	Brugnatelli	Italian
Electrostatic generator	1929	Van de Graaff	U.S.
Elevator brake	1852	Otis	U.S.
Elevator, push button	1922	Larson	U.S.
Engine, automatic transmission	1910	Fottinger	German
Engine, coal-gas 4-cycle	1876	Otto	German
Engine, compression ignition	1883	Daimler	German
Engine, electric ignition	1883	Benz	German
Engine, gas, compound	1926	Eickemeyer	U.S.
Engine, gasoline	1872	Brayton	U.S.
Engine, gasoline	1889	Daimler	German
Engine, jet	1930	Whittle	English
Engine, steam, piston	1705	Newcomen	English
Engine, steam, piston	1769	Watt	Scottish
Engraving, half-tone	1852	Talbot	U.S.
Ferris wheel	1893	Ferris	U.S.
Fiber optic wire	1970	Keck, Maurer, Schultz	U.S.
Fiber optics	1955	Kapany	English
Fiberglass	1938	Owens-Corning	U.S.
Filament, tungsten	1913	Coolidge	U.S.
Flanged rail	1831	Stevens	U.S.
Flatiron, electric	1882	Seely	U.S.
Food, frozen	1923	Birdseye	U.S.
Freon	1930	Midgley, et al.	U.S.
Furnace (for steel)	1858	Siemens	German
Galvanometer	1820	Sweigger	German
Garbage bag, polyethylene	1950	Wasylyk	Canadian
Gas discharge tube	1922	Hull	U.S.
Gas lighting	1792	Murdoch	Scottish
Gas mantle	1885	Welsbach	Austrian
Gasoline, cracked	1913	Burton	U.S.
Gasoline, high octane	1930	Ipatieff	Russian
Gasoline (lead ethyl)	1922	Midgley	U.S.
Geiger counter	1913	Geiger	German
Geodesic dome	1948	Fuller	U.S.
Glass, laminated safety	1909	Benedictus	French
Glider	1853	Cayley	English
Google search software	1996	Brin, Page	U.S.
Gun, breechloader	1811	Thornton	U.S.
Gun, Browning	1897	Browning	U.S.
Gun, magazine	1875	Hotchkiss	U.S.
Gun, silencer	1908	Maxim, H. P.	U.S.
Guncotton (nitrocellulose)	1847	Schoenbein	German
Gyrocompass	1911	Sperry	U.S.
Gyroscope	1852	Foucault	French
Hard drive, computer	1955	Johnson	U.S.
Harvester-thresher	1818	Lane	U.S.
Heart, artificial	1982	Jarvik	U.S.
Helicopter	1939	Sikorsky	U.S.
Hovercraft	1955	Cockerell	English
Hydrometer	1768	Baume	French
Iron lung	1928	Drinker, Slaw	U.S.
Jet Ski	1973	Jacobsen	U.S.
Kaleidoscope	1817	Brewster	Scottish
Kevlar	1965	Kwolek, Blades	U.S.
Kidney dialysis machine	1941	Kolff	Dutch
Kinetoscope	1889	Edison	U.S.
Lamp, arc	1847	Staite	English
Lamp, fluorescent	1938	General Electric, Westinghouse	U.S.
Lamp, incandescent	1879	Edison	U.S.
Lamp, incand., gas	1913	Langmuir	U.S.
Lamp, klieg	1911	Kliegl, A. and J.	U.S.
Lamp, mercury vapor	1912	Hewitt	U.S.

Invention	Date	Inventor(s)	Nationality
Lamp, miner's safety	1816	Davy	English
Lamp, neon	1909	Claude	French
Lathe, turret	1845	Fitch	U.S.
Launderette	1934	Cantrell	U.S.
Lens, achromatic	1758	Dollond	English
Lens, fused bifocal	1908	Borsch	U.S.
Leyden jar (condenser)	1745	von Kleist	German
Lightning rod	1752	Franklin	U.S.
Linoleum	1860	Walton	English
Linotype	1884	Mergenthaler	U.S.
Linux	1991	Torvalds	Finnish
Liquid Paper	c.1951	Graham	U.S.
Lock, cylinder	1851	Yale	U.S.
Locomotive, electric	1851	Vail	U.S.
Locomotive, exp'mtl	1802	Trevithick	English
Locomotive, exp'mtl	1812	Fenton, et al.	English
Locomotive, exp'mtl	1814	Stephenson	English
Locomotive, 1st U.S.	1830	Cooper	U.S.
Locomotive, practical	1829	Stephenson	English
Loom, power	1785	Cartwright	English
Loudspeaker, dynamic	1924	Rice, Kellogg	U.S.
Machine gun	1862	Gatling	U.S.
Machine gun, improved	1872	Hotchkiss	U.S.
Machine gun (Maxim)	1883	Maxim, H. S.	U.S.-Eng.
Magnet, electro	1828	Henry	U.S.
Magnetic Resonance Imaging (MRI)	1971	Damadian	U.S.
Maser	1953	Townes	U.S.
Mason jar	1858	Mason	U.S.
Match, friction	1827	Walker	English
Mercerized textiles	1843	Mercer	English
Meter, induction	1888	Shallenberger	U.S.
Metronome	1816	Malezel	German
Microcomputer	1973	Truong, et al.	French
Micrometer	1636	Gascoigne	English
Microphone	1877	Berliner	U.S.
Microprocessor	1971	Intel Corp.	U.S.
Microscope, compound	1590	Janssen	Dutch
Microscope, electronic	1931	Knoll, Ruska	German
Microscope, field ion	1951	Mueller	German
Microwave oven	1947	Spencer	U.S.
Monitor, warship	1861	Ericsson	U.S.
Monotype	1887	Lanston	U.S.
Motor, AC	1892	Tesla	U.S.
Motor, DC	1837	Davenport	U.S.
Motor, induction	1887	Tesla	U.S.
Motorcycle	1885	Daimler	German
Mouse, computer	1967	Engelbart	U.S.
Movie machine	1894	Jenkins	U.S.
Movie, panoramic	1952	Waller	U.S.
Movie, talking	1927	Warner Bros.	U.S.
Mower, lawn	1831	Budding, Ferrabee	English
Mowing machine	1822	Bailey	U.S.
Neoprene	1930	Carothers	U.S.
Nylon	1937	Carothers, DuPont	U.S.
Oil cracking furnace	1891	Gavrilov	Russian
Oil filled power cable	1921	Emanueli	Italian
Oleomargarine	1869	Mege-Mouries	French
Ophthalmoscope	1851	Helmholtz	German
Pacemaker	1952	Zoll	U.S.
Pacemaker, implantable cardiac	1958	Greatbatch	U.S.
Paper	105	Ts'ai	Chinese
Paper clip	1900	Waaler	Norwegian
Paper machine	1809	Dickinson	U.S.
Parachute	1785	Blanchard	French
Pen, ballpoint	1888	Loud	U.S.
Pen, fountain	1884	Waterman	U.S.
Pen, steel	1780	Harrison	English
Pendulum	1583	Galileo	Italian
Percussion cap	1807	Forsythe	Scottish
Phonograph	1877	Edison	U.S.
Photo, color	1892	Ives	U.S.
Photo film, celluloid	1893	Reichenbach	U.S.
Photo film, transparent	1884	Eastman, Goodwin	U.S.
Photocopier	1938	Carlson	U.S.
Photoelectric cell	1895	Elster	German
Photographic paper	1835	Talbot	English
Photography	1816	Niepce	French
Photography	1835	Daguerre	French
Photography	1835	Talbot	English
Photophone	1880	Bell	U.S.-Scot.
Phototelegraphy	1925	Bell Labs	U.S.
Piano	1709	Cristofori	Italian
Piano, player	1863	Fourneaux	French

Invention	Date	Inventor(s)	Nationality
Pin, safety	1849	Hunt	U.S.
Pistol (revolver)	1836	Colt	U.S.
Plow, cast iron	1785	Ransome	English
Plow, disc	1896	Hardy	U.S.
Pneumatic hammer	1890	King	U.S.
Post-it note	1980	Fry, Silver	U.S.
Powder, smokeless	1884	Vieille	French
Printing press, rotary	1845	Hoe	U.S.
Printing press, web	1865	Bullock	U.S.
Propeller, screw	1804	Stevens	U.S.
Propeller, screw	1837	Ericsson	Swedish
Punch card accounting	1889	Hollerith	U.S.
Radar	1940	Watson-Watt	Scottish
Radio amplifier	1906	De Forest	U.S.
Radio beacon	1928	Donovan	U.S.
Radio crystal oscillator	1918	Nicolson	U.S.
Radio FM, 2-path	1933	Armstrong	U.S.
Radio, magnetic detector	1902	Marconi	Italian
Radio receiver, cascade tuning	1913	Alexanderson	U.S.
Radio receiver, heterodyne	1913	Fessenden	Canadian
Radio, signals	1895	Marconi	Italian
Radio transmitter triode modulation	1914	Alexanderson	U.S.
Radio tube diode	1904	Fleming	English
Radio tube oscillator	1915	De Forest	U.S.
Radio tube triode	1906	De Forest	U.S.
Rayon (acetate)	1895	Cross	English
Rayon (cuprammonium)	1890	Despeissis	French
Rayon (nitrocellulose)	1884	Chardonnet	French
Razor, electric	1928	Schick	U.S.
Razor, safety	1895	Gillette	U.S.
Reading machine for the blind	1976	Kurzweil	U.S.
Reaper	1834	McCormick	U.S.
Record, cylinder	1887	Bell, Tainter	U.S.
Record, disc	1887	Berliner	U.S.
Record, long playing	1947	Goldmark	U.S.
Record, wax cylinder	1888	Edison	U.S.
Refrigerator car	1868	David	U.S.
Remote control	1898	Tesla	U.S.
Resin, synthetic	1931	Hill	English
Richter scale	1935	Richter	U.S.
Rifle, repeating	1860	Henry	U.S.
Rocket, liquid fuel	1926	Goddard	U.S.
Rollerblades	1980	Olson	U.S.
Rubber, vulcanized	1839	Goodyear	U.S.
Saccharin	1879	Remsen, Fahlberg	U.S.
Saw, circular	1777	Miller	English
Scotch tape	1930	Drew	U.S.
Seat belt	1959	Volvo	Swedish
Segway human transporter	2001	Kamen	U.S.
Seismograph	1880	Milne, Ewing, Gray	Eng.-Scot.
Sewing machine	1790	Saint	English
Shoe-lasting machine	1883	Matzeliger	U.S.
Shoe-sewing machine	1860	McKay	U.S.
Shrapnel shell	1784	Shrapnel	English
Shuttle, flying	1733	Kay	English
Skates, in-line	1759	Merlin	Belgian
Sleeping-car	1865	Pullman	U.S.
Slide rule	1620	Oughtred	English
Slinky	1943	James	U.S.
Smoke detector	1969	Smith, House	U.S.
Soap, hardware	1928	Bertsch	German
Spectroscope	1859	Kirchoff, Bunsen	German
Spectroscope (mass)	1918	Dempster	U.S.
Spinning jenny	c.1764	Hargreaves	English
Spinning mule	1779	Crompton	English
Steam car	1770	Cugnot	French
Steam turbine	1884	Parsons	English
Steamboat, exp'mtl	1778	Jouffroy	French
Steamboat, exp'mtl	1785	Fitch	U.S.
Steamboat, exp'mtl	1787	Rumsey	U.S.
Steamboat, exp'mtl	1803	Fulton	U.S.
Steamboat, exp'mtl	1804	Stevens	U.S.
Steamboat, practical	1802	Symington	Scottish
Steamboat, practical	1807	Fulton	U.S.
Steel alloy, high-speed	1901	Taylor, White	U.S.
Steel (converter)	1856	Bessemer	English
Steel, manganese	1884	Hadfield	English
Steel, stainless	1916	Brearley	English
Stereoscope	1838	Wheatstone	English
Stethoscope	1819	Laennec	French
Stethoscope, binaural	1840	Cammann	U.S.
Stock ticker	1870	Edison	U.S.
Storage battery, rechargeable	1859	Plante	French
Stove, electric	1896	Hadaway	U.S.
Submarine	1891	Holland	U.S.
Submarine, even keel	1894	Lake	U.S.
Submarine, torpedo	1776	Bushnell	U.S.
Synthesizer	1964	Moog	U.S.
Tank, military	1914	Swinton	English
Tape recorder, magnetic	1899	Poulsen	Danish
Taser	1974	Cover	U.S.
Teflon	1938	Du Pont	U.S.
Telegraph, magnetic	1837	Morse	U.S.
Telegraph, quadruplex	1864	Edison	U.S.
Telegraph, railroad	1887	Woods	U.S.
Telegraph, wireless high frequency	1895	Marconi	Italian
Telephone[1]	1871	Meucci	U.S.-Italian
Telephone[1]	1876	Bell	U.S.-Scot.
Telephone amplifier	1912	De Forest	U.S.
Telephone answering machine (1st practical)	1954	Hashimoto	Japanese
Telephone, automatic	1891	Strowger	U.S.
Telephone, cellular	1947	Bell Labs	U.S.
Telephone, cordless[2]	1950	Gross	U.S.
Telephone, radio	1900	Poulsen	Danish
		Fessenden	Canadian
Telephone, radio	1906	De Forest	U.S.
Telephone, radio, long distance	1915	AT&T	U.S.
Telephone, recording	1898	Poulsen	Danish
Telescope	1608	Lippershey	Dutch
Telescope	1609	Galileo	Italian
Telescope, astronomical	1611	Kepler	German
Telescope, reflecting	1668	Newton	English
Teletype	1928	Morkrum, Kleinschmidt	U.S.
Television, color	1928	Baird	Scottish
Television, electronic	1927	Farnsworth	U.S.
Television, iconoscope	1923	Zworykin	U.S.
Television, mech. scanner	1923	Baird	Scottish
Tesla coil	1891	Tesla	U.S.
Thermometer	1593	Galileo	Italian
Thermometer	1730	Reaumur	French
Thermometer, mercury	1714	Fahrenheit	German
3D printing (stereolithography)	1984	Hull	U.S.
Time recorder	1890	Bundy	U.S.
Tire, double-tube	1845	Thomson	Scottish
Tire, pneumatic	1888	Dunlop	Scottish
Toaster, automatic	1921	Strite	U.S.
Toilet, flush	1589	Harington	English
Torpedo, marine	1804	Fulton	U.S.
Tractor, crawler	1904	Holt	U.S.
Transformer, AC	1885	Stanley	U.S.
Transistor	1947	Shockley, Brattain, Bardeen	U.S.
Trolley car, electric	1884-87	Van DePoele, Sprague	U.S.
Tungsten, ductile	1912	Coolidge	U.S.
Tupperware®	1945	Tupper	U.S.
Turbine, gas	1849	Bourdin	French
Turbine, hydraulic	1849	Francis	U.S.
Turbine, steam	1884	Parsons	English
Type, movable	1447	Gutenberg	German
Typewriter	1867	Sholes, Soule, Glidden	U.S.
Universal Serial Bus (USB)	1994	Bhatt, et al.	U.S.
Vacuum cleaner, electric	1907	Spangler	U.S.
Vacuum evaporating pan	1846	Rillieux	U.S.
Velcro	1948	de Mestral	Swiss
Video game ("Pong")	1972	Bushnell	U.S.
Video home system (VHS)	1975	Matsushita, JVC	Japanese
Vinyl	1926	Semon	U.S.

Invention	Date	Inventor(s)	Nationality	Invention	Date	Inventor(s)	Nationality
Washer, electric	1901	Fisher	U.S.	Windshield wiper	1903	Anderson	U.S.
Welding, atomic hydrogen	1924	Langmuir, Palmer	U.S.	Wire, barbed	1874	Glidden	U.S.
				World Wide Web	1989	Berners-Lee	English
Welding, electric	1877	Thomson	U.S.	Wrench, double-acting	1913	Owen	U.S.
Wheelchair, multiterrain	1986	Twitchell	U.S.	X-ray tube	1913	Coolidge	U.S.
Wheelchair, stair-climbing	1962	Blanco	U.S.	Zamboni	1949	Zamboni	U.S.
				Zeppelin	1900	Zeppelin	German
Wiki software	1995	Cunningham	U.S.	Zipper, early model	1893	Judson	U.S.
Wind tunnel	1912	Eiffel	French	Zipper, improved	1913	Sundback	Canadian

(1) While Alexander Graham Bell has traditionally been credited with invention of the telephone, which he patented, Antonio Meucci developed a working model before Bell. (2) Al Gross held a number of important early patents in the field of wireless communication; other people were also involved in the development of practical cordless telephones.

Corporations Receiving U.S. Patents, 2015

Source: U.S. Patent and Trademark Office, U.S. Dept. of Commerce
(ranked by number of U.S. utility patents, or patents for inventions, granted)

Rank	Company	No. of patents	Rank	Company	No. of patents
1.	International Business Machines Corp.	7,309	14.	General Electric Co.	1,756
2.	Samsung Electronics Co., Ltd.	5,059	15.	Ricoh Co., Ltd.	1,618
3.	Canon Kabushiki Kaisha	4,127		Seiko Epson Corp.	1,618
4.	Qualcomm, Inc.	2,900	17.	Panasonic Intellectual Property Mgmt. Co., Ltd.	1,474
5.	Google, Inc.	2,835	18.	Toyota Jidosha K.K.	1,463
6.	Toshiba Corp.	2,582	19.	Fujitsu Limited	1,455
7.	Sony Corp.	2,448	20.	Telefonaktiebolaget LM Ericsson (Publ.)	1,406
8.	LG Electronics Inc.	2,241	21.	GM Global Technology Operations LLC	1,309
9.	Intel Corp.	2,046	22.	Hewlett-Packard Development Co.	1,304
10.	Microsoft Technology Licensing, LLC	1,955	23.	Brother Kogyo Kabushiki Kaisha	1,187
11.	Apple, Inc.	1,937	24.	Ford Global Technologies, LLC	1,184
12.	Samsung Display Co., Ltd.	1,825	25.	Amazon Technologies, Inc.	1,136
13.	Taiwan Semiconductor Manufacturing Co., Ltd.	1,758			

Note: Reflects patent ownership at time of patent granting. Changes may occur after patent is granted. Where more than one assignee exists, patents are attributed to first-named assignee.

U.S. Utility Patents, 1790-2015

Source: U.S. Patent and Trademark Office, U.S. Dept. of Commerce

Year	Patent applications	Patents granted	Year	Patent applications	Patents granted
1790	NA	3	2001	326,508	166,035
1805	NA	57	2002	334,445	167,331
1820	NA	155	2003	342,441	169,023
1835	NA	752	2004	356,943	164,290
1850	2,193	884	2005	390,733	143,806
1865	10,664	6,099	2006	425,967	173,772
1880	21,761	12,926	2007	456,154	157,282
1895	39,145	20,855	2008	456,321	157,772
1910	63,293	35,130	2009	456,106	167,349
1925	80,208	46,432	2010	490,226	219,614
1940	60,863	42,237	2011	503,582	224,505
1955	77,188	30,432	2012	542,815	253,155
1970	103,175	64,429	2013	571,612	277,835
1985	117,006	71,661	2014	578,802	300,678
2000	295,926	157,494	2015	589,410	298,407

NA = Not available. **Note:** Utility patents are, essentially, patents for the function of the invention.

Patent Offices Granting Most Patents, 2010-16

Source: World Intellectual Property Organization statistics database
(ranked by 2016 figures; as of May 2018)

National or regional office	2010	2011	2012	2013	2014	2015	2016
China	135,110	172,113	217,105	207,688	233,228	359,316	404,208
United States	219,614	224,505	253,155	277,835	300,678	298,407	303,049
Japan	222,693	238,323	274,791	277,079	227,142	189,358	203,087
South Korea	68,843	94,720	113,467	127,330	129,786	101,873	108,875
European Patent Office	58,108	62,112	65,665	66,696	64,608	68,431	95,956
Russia	30,322	29,999	32,880	31,638	33,950	34,706	33,536
Canada	19,120	20,762	21,819	23,833	23,749	22,201	26,424
Australia	14,557	17,877	17,724	17,112	19,304	23,098	23,744
Germany	13,678	11,719	11,332	13,858	15,030	14,795	15,652
France	9,899	10,213	12,913	11,405	11,889	12,699	12,374
Mexico	9,399	11,485	12,358	10,368	9,819	9,338	8,652
India	7,138	5,168	4,328	3,377	6,153	6,022	8,248
World	**915,500**	**1,002,600**	**1,138,700**	**1,175,400**	**1,179,900**	**1,241,000**	**1,351,600**

TECHNOLOGY

Computer Milestones

1623: German mathematician Wilhelm Schickard developed the first mechanical calculator, capable of adding, subtracting, multiplying, and dividing.

1642: French mathematician Blaise Pascal built the first of more than four dozen copies of an adding and subtracting machine that he invented.

1801: French inventor Joseph Marie Jacquard demonstrated a new control system for looms. He "programmed" the loom, communicating desired weaving operations to the machine via patterns of holes in paper cards.

1833-71: British mathematician and scientist Charles Babbage used the Jacquard punch-card system in his design for a sophisticated, programmable "Analytical Engine" that foreshadowed basic features of today's computers. Babbage's concept was beyond the capabilities of the technology of his time, and the machine remained unfinished at his death in 1871.

1889: American engineer Herman Hollerith patented an electromechanical punch-card tabulating system that facilitated the handling of large amounts of statistical data and quickly found use in censuses in the U.S. and other countries.

1911: Hollerith's Tabulating Machine Company merged with two other enterprises to form the Computing-Tabulating-Recording Company, which was renamed the International Business Machines Corporation (IBM) in 1924.

1941: German engineer Konrad Züse completed the Z3, the first fully functional digital computer to be controlled by a program; the Z3 was not electronic—it was based on electrical switches called relays.

1942: Iowa State Coll. physicist John Vincent Atanasoff and assistant Clifford Berry completed a working model of the first fully electronic computer using vacuum tubes, which could operate much more quickly than relays; the rudimentary machine was not programmable.

1943: IBM and Harvard professor Howard Aiken completed the first large-scale automatic digital computer, the Mark I, a relay-based machine 55-ft long and 8-ft high. British scientists built their first Colossus machine, an electronic computer for breaking German codes during World War II.

1946: ENIAC (Electronic Numerical Integrator and Computer), a 30-ton room-sized electronic computer with more than 18,000 vacuum tubes, was completed by physicist John Mauchly and engineer J. Presper Eckert at the Univ. of Pennsylvania for the U.S. Army. ENIAC could be programmed to do different tasks, but cables had to be plugged in, and switches had to be set by hand.

1951: Eckert and Mauchly's UNIVAC (Universal Automatic Computer) became the first commercially available computer in the U.S. Its first customer was the Census Bureau. CBS-TV used a UNIVAC in 1952 to predict presidential election results.

1959: COBOL, a computer programming language designed for business use, first appeared, based on programming language innovations of American mathematician Grace Hopper.

1967: American computer pioneer Doug Engelbart applied for a patent on the mouse.

1969-71: The powerful Unix operating system was developed at Bell Laboratories; later versions became widely used on large computers and formed the basis for the Macintosh OS X operating system.

1971: Intel released the 4004, the first commercial microprocessor (an entire computer processing unit on a chip).

1973: The Alto computer, developed at Xerox's Palo Alto Research Center, became operational, implementing many features of modern commercial personal computers, including a graphical user interface (GUI) featuring windows, icons, and pointers that could be manipulated by a mouse.

1975: The first widely marketed personal computer (PC), the MITS Altair 8800, was introduced in kit form, with no keyboard, video display, or printer, for under $400. Microsoft was founded by Americans Bill Gates and Paul Allen.

1976: The first word-processing program for personal computers, Electric Pencil, was written. Apple Computer Company was founded by Americans Steven Jobs and Stephen Wozniak.

1977: Apple introduced the Apple II; capable of displaying text and graphics in color, the machine enjoyed phenomenal success.

1981: IBM unveiled its Personal Computer (IBM 5150), which used an operating system from Microsoft known as MS-DOS (Disk Operating System).

1984: Apple introduced the first Macintosh. The easy-to-use Macintosh came with a proprietary operating system and was the first popular computer to have a GUI and a mouse.

1990: Microsoft released Windows 3.0, the first workable version of its own GUI.

1991: The Unix-like Linux operating system was invented by Helsinki Univ. student Linus Torvalds and made available for free.

1996: The Palm Pilot, the first widely successful handheld computer and personal information manager, arrived.

1997: The IBM supercomputer Deep Blue beat Russian world chess champion Garry Kasparov in a 6-game match, 2-1, with 3 draws.

2001: Apple introduced the Unix-based operating system OS X for the Macintosh.

2002: The total number of personal computers, including desktop and laptop machines of all types, shipped by manufacturers since 1975 reached 1 bil.

2007: Amazon launched the Kindle, a hardware/software system for displaying books electronically.

2008: Google released the Linux-based Android operating system for mobile devices.

2010: Apple released the iPad tablet computer and sold more than 3 mil devices in the first 80 days.

2012: Microsoft released Windows 8, featuring enhanced support for touchscreens and an interface with a grid of tiles displaying actively updated content and apps.

2015: Microsoft released Windows 10, promising faster startup and improved security, along with features like a personal digital assistant and a new web browser, Microsoft Edge.

2016: Univ. of Maryland scientists developed the first reprogrammable quantum computer; it used lasers to manipulate its five qubits, or bits of quantum information.

2018: Apple became the world's first company to achieve a stock market value of $1 tril.

Nations With the Most Personal Computers in Use, 2017

Source: Computer Industry Almanac, year-end 2017

Rank	Nation	PCs in use (mil)	% of world total	Rank	Nation	PCs in use (mil)	% of world total
1.	China	482.4	18.05%	10.	Italy	59.8	2.24%
2.	U.S.	391.9	14.67	11.	South Korea	51.4	1.92
3.	India	159.7	5.97	12.	Mexico	50.9	1.91
4.	Japan	123.7	4.63	13.	Spain	41.1	1.54
5.	Russia	101.7	3.80	14.	Canada	38.0	1.42
6.	Germany	87.0	3.25	15.	Indonesia	32.3	1.21
7.	Brazil	77.7	2.91		**Other countries**	839.3	31.41
8.	United Kingdom	68.0	2.54		**Worldwide**	**2,672.5**	**100.00**
9.	France	67.6	2.53				

World's Fastest Supercomputers, 2018

Source: Top500.org, as of midyear 2018

Rank	Name	Location	Manufacturer/ vendor	Processors (cores)	Top speed[1]
1.	Summit.............	Oak Ridge National Laboratory, TN, U.S. ....IBM	IBM	2,282,544	122.30
2.	Sunway TaihuLight	National Supercomputing Center, Wuxi, China...........	NRCPC[2]	10,649,600	93.01
3.	Sierra..............	Lawrence Livermore National Laboratory, CA, U.S.	IBM	1,572,480	71.61
4.	Tianhe-2A (Milky Way-2A)	National Supercomputing Center, Guangzhou, China	NUDT[3]	4,981,760	61.44
5.	AI Bridging Cloud Infrastructure.......	National Institute of Advanced Industrial Science and Technology, Japan	Fujitsu	391,680	19.88
6.	Piz Daint............	Swiss National Supercomputing Centre, Switzerland......	Cray	361,760	19.59
7.	Titan...............	Oak Ridge National Laboratory, TN, U.S.	Cray	560,640	17.59
8.	Sequoia	Lawrence Livermore National Laboratory, CA, U.S.	IBM	1,572,864	17.17
9.	Trinity	Los Alamos National Laboratory, NM, U.S.	Cray	979,968	14.14
10.	Cori...............	National Energy Research Computing Center, CA, U.S. ...Cray	Cray	622,336	14.01

Note: The 500 fastest supercomputers use a version of the Linux operating system. (1) Top speed, in petaflops, achieved as measured according to the Linpack Benchmark. 1 petaflop = 1 quadrillion floating-point operations per sec. (2) NRCPC = National Research Center of Parallel Computer Engineering and Technology. (3) NUDT = National University of Defense Technology.

U.S. Sales and Household Penetration of Selected Hardware, 2015-17

Source: Consumer Technology Association (fmr. Consumer Electronics Association)

(factory sales to dealers in thousands of units and millions of dollars; percent of all households for Jan. of year shown)

Hardware	2015			2016			2017		
	Units	Sales	%	Units	Sales	%	Units	Sales	%
Desktop computers[1,2].............	19,472	$11,780	55%	18,109	$10,684	52%	16,745	$9,746	51%
Laptop/notebook/netbook PCs[2]	45,606	28,732	67	46,974	28,114	68	48,778	28,318	69
Tablet computers	66,315	20,425	54	61,673	17,856	59	51,688	14,454	62
E-readers	7,534	527	32	6,630	477	29	5,923	430	30
Smartphones	174,641	52,916	72	179,880	54,504	74	186,121	60,861	87
Digital video recorders (DVRs)	16,750	2,337	47	14,040	1,916	46	NA	NA	NA
Digital cameras.................	8,336	2,684	64	5,171	2,174	61	5,339	2,186	53
Camcorders	777	187	28	513	126	27	378	109	23
Smart watches	10,598	3,052	NA	9,008	2,465	NA	12,120	3,091	12

NA = Not available. **Note:** Based on sales data tracking and consumer surveys conducted by CEA/CTA. (1) Includes all-in-one computers. (2) Includes commercial and consumer shipments.

About the Internet

The internet is not owned or funded by any one institution, organization, or government. It has no CEO and is not a commercial service. Its development is guided by the Internet Society (ISOC), a nonprofit formed in 1992. The Internet Society helps fund the Internet Engineering Task Force (IETF), which deals with short-term issues of standards and the internet's architecture. The Internet Architecture Board (IAB), a committee of the IETF, oversees the latter's work and appoints the chair of the Internet Research Task Force (IRTF). The IAB and IRTF focus on long-term issues.

Major Historical Highlights

1969: ARPANET, an experimental four-computer network, was established by the Advanced Research Projects Agency (ARPA) of the U.S. Defense Dept. Two years later, ARPANET linked about 23 computers ("hosts") at 15 sites, including MIT and Harvard.

1971: Engineer Bob Thomas created Creeper, generally considered the first worm, a virus able to self-replicate over a network.

1978: The first spam, or junk email, was sent over ARPANET.

1982: Author William Gibson coined the term "cyberspace" in the story "Burning Chrome."

1983: The set of communications rules (protocol) known as TCP/IP became the main networking protocol of ARPANET. Its adoption was tantamount to the birth of the internet. The military portion of ARPANET was moved onto MILNET.

1986: The U.S. National Science Foundation (NSF) launched NSFNET, the first large-scale network using internet technology.

1988: Internet Relay Chat (IRC) was developed by Finnish student Jarkko Oikarinen, enabling people to communicate via the internet in "real time."

1988: A worm crafted by Cornell Univ. computer science graduate student Robert Morris Jr. infected thousands of computers, shutting many down and causing millions of dollars of damage—the first known case of large-scale damage caused by a computer virus spread via the internet.

1989: Massachusetts-based The World—the first commercial internet service provider supplying dial-up access—debuted.

1989-90: English scientist Tim Berners-Lee invented the World Wide Web. Created as an environment in which scientists at the European Center for Nuclear Research in Switzerland could share information, it gradually evolved into a medium with text, graphics, audio, animation, and video.

1990: ARPANET was disbanded.

1991: NSFNET was opened to commercial traffic. Berners-Lee introduced the first browser, or software for accessing the web.

1993: The National Center for Supercomputing Applications (U.S.) released versions of Mosaic, the first web browser able to present both text and images on a single page.

1994: Netscape Communications released the Netscape Navigator browser.

1995: Microsoft released its Internet Explorer browser. It initially failed to make a dent in Netscape's dominance of the browser market, but Internet Explorer surpassed Netscape by 1999.

1998: Under a contract with the U.S. Dept. of Commerce, the nonprofit Internet Corporation for Assigned Names and Numbers (ICANN) took over the management of assigning domain names and internet protocol (IP) addresses.

1999: Release of the free Napster file-sharing service enabled users to easily exchange files containing music or other content without regard to copyright restrictions.

2000: Estonia became the first country to pass a law declaring internet access a fundamental human right of its citizens.

2004: A group of Harvard students founded social network TheFacebook (later just Facebook).

2004: The Mozilla Foundation released the first official version of the open-source browser Mozilla Firefox.

2006: The microblogging and social networking service Twitter was introduced.

2008: Google introduced its Chrome browser. By 2012, Chrome ranked as the most widely used browser in the world, according to StatCounter.com.

2009: The software for Bitcoin, the world's first "cryptocurrency," was released. It relied on cryptography and a complex decentralized public ledger to secure transactions.

2011: ICANN decided to allow the use of almost any characters in any language for the names of generic top-level domains.

2012: The number of Facebook users surpassed 1 bil.

2014: The number of internet hosts (websites) passed 1 bil.

2014: Estonia became the first country in the world to offer noncitizens "e-residency"—a government-issued transnational digital identity.

2016: The leak of more than 11.5 mil documents from Panamanian law firm Mossack Fonseca, which said it was the victim of a hack, exposed large-scale offshore tax evasion.

2016: Global internet traffic surpassed 1 zettabyte (1 tril gigabytes), according to networking giant Cisco.

2017: The number of Facebook users surpassed 2 bil.

2018: Amid growing concern over the misuse of individuals' personal data, the European Union's General Data Protection Regulation (GDPR) went into effect, providing strong safeguards governing personal data held by any organization worldwide that conducts business in Europe.

Safety and Security on the Internet

Common sense dictates some basic security rules:

- Avoid using the same password for multiple websites. A password manager can generate passwords and then save them.

- Do not give out your phone number, address, credit card number, or other personal information unless needed for a transaction at a site you trust.

- If you feel someone is being threatening or dangerous, inform your internet service provider.

- Use protective firewall, antivirus, and antispyware software to guard your system against attacks by hackers.

- Be careful about opening email and file attachments from unknown correspondents.

- To avoid falling victim to **phishing**—which uses a forged email message, purportedly from a respectable organization, to elicit personal data—do not click on hyperlinks in emails from companies with which you do business. Phishing emails typically contain a link leading to a fabricated website resembling the site of the ostensible sender. If you want to visit a company's website, open your browser and manually enter the site's address.

- Users of so-called **peer-to-peer** (P2P) file-sharing networks or protocols should open up only part of their computer system, not their entire hard drive, to sharing.

- When manufacturers provide **patches** to solve security flaws or other problems with operating systems, web browsers, or other software, it is usually advisable to install these fixes. If a fix is not available for a serious security problem, consider switching to an alternative program.

Internet Addresses

The fundamental part of an address on the internet is called the domain. The final part of a domain name, known as the **top-level domain (TLD)**, is its most basic part. For example, .com is the top-level domain of *The World Almanac*'s web address (www.worldalmanac.com). So-called generic top-level domains (gTLDs) consist of three or more letters. Domain names with two letters are generally for countries or regions. Country-code TLDs (ccTLDs) are usually managed by an organization within a certain country.

Cybersecurity Threats, 2015-17

Source: Symantec™ Global Intelligence Network; Symantec Internet Security Threat Report, vol. 23

	2015	2016	2017
Total vulnerabilities reported in software and hardware	8,077	7,692	8,718
Vulnerabilities disclosed in industrial control systems.	200	165	212
Ramsomware detections per day[1]	933	1,271	1,242[2]
New ransomware families.	30	98	28
Average ransom demand	$294	$1,071	$522
New malware variants	355,419,881	357,019,453	669,947,865
Email malware rate.	1 in every 220	1 in every 131	1 in every 412
Phishing rate.	1 in every 1,846	1 in every 2,596	1 in every 2,995
Spam rate[3]	52.7%	53.4%	54.6%

(1) Ransomware is malware that prevents victims from accessing their data until a ransom is paid. (2) Excluding attacks involving WannaCry and Petya/NotPetya; WannaCry is a worm that delivers a ransomware payload, and Petya/NotPetya is a disk wiper. (3) Percentage of email determined to be spam.

Internet Crime Victims and Losses, 2017

Source: Internet Crime Complaint Center, Federal Bureau of Investigation

Rank	Type of crime	Victims	Rank	Type of crime	Loss amount
1.	Nonpayment/nondelivery	84,079	1.	Business email compromise/email account compromise.	$676,151,185
2.	Personal data breach	30,904	2.	Confidence fraud/romance	211,382,989
3.	Phishing/vishing/smishing/pharming	25,344	3.	Nonpayment/nondelivery	141,110,441
4.	Overpayment[1]	23,135	4.	Investment	96,844,144
5.	No lead value	20,241	5.	Personal data breach	77,134,865
6.	Identity theft	17,636	6.	Identity theft	66,815,298
7.	Advanced fee	16,368	7.	Corporate data breach	60,942,306
8.	Harassment/threats of violence	16,194	8.	Advanced fee	57,861,324
9.	Employment	15,784	9.	Credit card fraud	57,207,248
10.	Business email compromise/email account compromise.	15,690	10.	Real estate/rental	56,231,333

(1) In overpayment, the scammer typically makes a payment via fake check or credit card for more than the agreed upon amount, and then asks that the victim return the excess amount by wire or other form of direct payment.

Fixed Broadband Penetration in Selected Countries, 2002-17

Source: Organisation for Economic Cooperation and Development (OECD)
(nonmobile broadband subscriptions per 100 inhabitants, for fourth quarter of given year; ranked by 2017 figures)

Country	2002	2004	2006	2008	2010	2012	2014	2016	2017
France.	2.7	10.5	20.1	27.6	32.7	36.6	39.2	41.4	42.8
Germany.	3.9	8.4	18.2	27.4	32.6	34.7	36.5	38.7	40.2
United Kingdom	2.3	10.4	21.5	28.1	31.3	34.1	36.7	38.8	39.4
Canada	12.1	17.6	24.3	28.2	31.8	33.6	35.4	36.9	37.8
United States	6.7	12.8	20.3	25.5	27.3	29.4	30.7	32.7	33.7[1]
Japan	6.2	15.0	20.7	23.5	26.6	27.7	28.7	30.5	31.0
Italy.	1.7	8.1	14.2	18.9	21.8	22.8	23.6	25.7	27.4

Note: Includes internet connections with speeds greater than 256 kilobits per second (256 kbps). (1) Estimate.

Nations With Highest Percentage of Population Using the Internet, 2000-17

Source: © International Telecommunication Union; ranked by 2016 figures

Rank	Nation	2000	2005	2010	2012	2013	2014	2015	2016	2017
1.	Iceland	44.47%	87.00%	93.39%	96.21%	96.55%	98.16%	98.20%	98.24%	NA
2.	Luxembourg	22.89	70.00	90.62	91.95	93.78	94.67	96.38	98.14	97.83%
3.	Liechtenstein.	36.52	63.37	80.00	89.41	93.80	95.21	96.64	98.09	NA
4.	Bahrain.	6.15	21.30	55.00	88.00	90.00	90.50	93.48	98.00	95.88
5.	Andorra.	10.54	37.61	81.00	86.43	94.00	95.90	96.91	97.93	NA
6.	Norway	52.00	81.99	93.39	94.65	95.05	96.30	96.81	97.30	96.51
7.	Denmark.	39.17	82.74	88.72	92.26	94.63	95.99	96.33	96.97	97.10
8.	Monaco.	42.18	55.46	75.00	87.00	90.70	92.40	93.36	95.21	NA
9.	United Kingdom	26.82	70.00	85.00	87.48	89.84	91.61	92.00	94.78	NA
10.	Qatar.	4.86	24.73	69.00	69.30	85.30	91.49	92.88	94.29	NA
11.	Japan	29.99	66.92	78.21	79.50	88.22	89.11	91.06	93.18	90.87
12.	South Korea	44.70	73.50	83.70	84.07	84.77	87.56	89.90	92.84	95.10
13.	Canada.	51.30	71.66	80.30	83.00	85.80	87.12	88.47	91.16	NA
14.	United Arab Emirates . .	23.63	40.00	68.00	85.00	88.00	90.40	90.50	90.60	94.82
15.	Netherlands	43.98	81.00	90.72	92.86	93.96	91.67	91.72	90.41	93.20
16.	Brunei.	9.00	36.47	53.00	60.27	64.50	68.77	71.20	90.00	NA
17.	Sweden.	45.69	84.83	90.00	93.18	94.78	92.52	90.61	89.65	96.41
18.	Germany.	30.22	68.71	82.00	82.35	84.17	86.19	87.59	89.65	84.40
19.	Switzerland.	47.10	70.10	83.90	85.20	86.34	87.40	87.48	89.13	93.71
20.	New Zealand	47.38	62.72	80.46	81.64	82.78	85.50	88.22	88.47	NA

NA = Not available.

Nations With the Most Internet Users, 2017

Source: Computer Industry Almanac, year-end 2017

Rank	Nation	Internet users (mil)	% of worldwide users	Rank	Nation	Internet users (mil)	% of worldwide users
1.	China	700.0	19.83%	10.	France.	55.3	1.57%
2.	India	371.2	10.51	11.	Mexico	55.1	1.56
3.	United States	292.4	8.28	12.	Italy.	51.5	1.46
4.	Brazil.	134.4	3.81	13.	Turkey.	47.6	1.35
5.	Japan	112.4	3.18	14.	Philippines	45.8	1.30
6.	Indonesia	97.2	2.75	15.	Egypt	45.4	1.28
7.	Russia.	97.0	2.75		**Other countries**.	**1,299.0**	**36.79**
8.	Germany.	71.1	2.01				
9.	United Kingdom	55.5	1.57		**World total**.	**3,530.9**	**100.00**

Most-Visited World Websites, 2018

Source: comScore, Inc.

Some websites represent an aggregation of commonly owned domain names; examples of popular domains within a group added in parentheses by World Almanac editors.

Rank	Website	Visitors[1]	Rank	Website	Visitors[1]
1.	Google sites (YouTube, Blogger)	1,485,064	11.	Qihoo.com sites	455,485
2.	Facebook (Instagram).	1,064,183	12.	Twitter.	424,076
3.	Microsoft sites (Bing, Xbox Live).	929,570	13.	360buy Corp.	383,217
4.	Alibaba.com Corp.	775,902	14.	SINA Corp.	340,004
5.	Tencent Inc. (QQ)	772,931	15.	Apple Inc. (iTunes)	337,170
6.	Amazon sites (Zappos, Audible, IMDb).	677,488	16.	Iqiyi sites	336,455
7.	Oath (AOL, HuffPost, Yahoo, Tumblr)	622,575	17.	CBS Interactive (CNET, ZDNet)	332,163
8.	Baidu.com Inc.	586,315	18.	LinkedIn	297,457
9.	Sohu.com Inc.	557,682	19.	PayPal.	295,353
10.	Wikimedia Foundation sites (Wikipedia)	462,470	20.	Youku & Tudou.	294,163

(1) Number of persons, in thousands, who visited a website at least once in June 2018.

Top Web Browsers Worldwide, 2009-18

Source: StatCounter Global Stats, gs.statcounter.com

Browser	% of browser market				
	2009	2012	2015	2017	2018
Chrome.	3.01%	33.81%	55.39%	63.48%	67.60%
Firefox.	30.50	23.73	17.24	13.82	11.23
Internet Explorer . .	60.11	32.04	18.86	9.03	6.97
Safari	3.02	7.12	4.70	5.04	5.01
Edge.	—	—	0.05	3.95	4.19
Opera	2.64	1.72	1.91	2.25	2.48

— = Not available. **Note:** Percent of desktop (and laptop) computer users accessing the web via a particular browser, for July of year shown.

Top Operating Systems Worldwide, 2009-18

Source: StatCounter Global Stats, gs.statcounter.com

Operating system	% of OS market				
	2009	2012	2015	2017	2018
Android.	0.02%	3.29%	25.62%	41.24%	42.26%
Windows.	93.85	79.14	50.85	35.24	35.93
iOS	0.36	5.16	11.37	13.20	12.82
OS X.	4.07	6.16	4.90	4.66	5.39
Unknown.	0.37	0.55	2.28	2.99	1.94
Linux.	0.76	0.75	1.12	0.77	0.77
Series 40	0.00	0.55	1.38	0.31	0.12
Symbian OS	0.25	1.63	0.43	0.10	0.04

Note: Percent of users accessing the web with a particular operating system (OS), for July of year shown. Includes desktop, laptop, tablet, and mobile devices' operating systems.

U.S. Internet Use by Selected Characteristics, 2013-18

Source: Pew Research Center

	% who are users			% who are users			% who are users	
	2013	2018		2013	2018		2013	2018
All adults	84%	89%	**Race/ethnicity**			**Annual household income**		
Gender			White, non-Hispanic. . .	85%	89%	Less than $30,000 . . .	72%	81%
Male	84	89	Black, non-Hispanic. . .	79	87	$30,000-$49,999	86	93
Female	84	88	Hispanic	80	88	$50,000-$74,999	93	97
Age			**Education**			$75,000 or more	97	98
18-29	97	98	No high school diploma	54	65	**Geography**		
30-49	92	97	High school graduate. .	75	84	Urban	86	92
50-64	81	87	Some college	92	93	Suburban	85	90
65+	56	66	College graduate.	96	97	Rural.	78	78

Note: Percent of U.S. adults, age 18 and over, who use the internet, email, or access the internet via a mobile device. Data for each year based on a pooled analysis of all surveys conducted during that year. Hispanic data includes only those surveys incorporating Spanish-language interviews.

Most-Visited U.S. Websites, 2018

Source: comScore, Inc.; comScore qSearch

Some websites represent an aggregation of commonly owned domain names; examples of popular domains within a group as of June 2018 added in parentheses by World Almanac editors.

All U.S. Sites

Rank	Website	Visitors[1]
1.	Google sites (Blogger, YouTube).	246,738
2.	Oath sites (AOL, HuffPost, Tumblr, Yahoo)	211,267
3.	Microsoft sites (Bing, Xbox Live).	211,031
4.	Facebook (Instagram).	209,441
5.	Amazon sites	202,054
6.	Comcast NBCUniversal	171,000
7.	CBS Interactive (CNET, ZDNet)	161,629
8.	Twitter	151,952
9.	Apple Inc. (iTunes)	151,374
10.	Turner Digital (CNN)	150,582
11.	PayPal.	139,588
12.	The Walt Disney Company (ABC, ESPN).	139,462
13.	Hearst	134,626
14.	Snapchat	134,208
15.	Meredith Digital.	133,784

Email

Rank	Website	Visitors[1]
1.	Google (Gmail).	162,194
2.	Oath Mail network (AOL Mail, Yahoo Mail)	84,517
3.	Outlook (Outlook.com)	38,479
4.	Outlook Web.	14,645
5.	Xfinity.com WebMail	1,860

Social Networking Sites

Rank	Website	Visitors[1]
1.	Facebook and Messenger	207,254
2.	Twitter	151,952
3.	Instagram	141,256
4.	Snapchat	134,208
5.	Pinterest	111,022
6.	LinkedIn	95,782
7.	Reddit	72,202
8.	Tumblr.	37,408
9.	Google+	36,559
10.	Goodreads	15,930

Blog Sites

Rank	Website	Visitors[1]
1.	Blogger.	45,131
2.	Wordpress.com.	25,633
3.	Twentytwowords.com	18,049
4.	Thepennyhoarder.com	15,770
5.	Trend-chaser.com	14,276

Video Sites

Rank	Website	Visitors[2]
1.	Google sites (YouTube).	149,801
2.	Facebook	61,643
3.	Oath	53,049
4.	Microsoft sites.	46,182
5.	The Walt Disney Company	41,695
6.	CBS Interactive.	40,047
7.	BroadbandTV	37,766
8.	Comcast NBCUniversal	35,716
9.	Warner Music	35,437
10.	Amazon sites	34,993

Search and Navigation

Rank	Website	Searches (mil)	% of searches
1.	Google sites	11,537	63.4%
2.	Microsoft sites (Bing)	4,387	24.1
3.	Oath (AOL, Yahoo)	2,071	11.4
4.	Ask Network	195	1.1

Note: Search and navigation data are for desktop computer users only for searches from the properties' core search engines (as opposed to searches within, for example, YouTube or Gmail). (1) Number of persons in thousands, who visited the media property (including website/apps) at least once from any U.S. location in June 2018. Mobile users under age 18 are not measured. (2) Number of persons, in thousands, who visited the media property from a desktop in June 2018. Excludes advertisement videos.

Most Popular U.S. Mobile Apps, 2018

Source: comScore, Inc.

Rank	App	Reach	Rank	App	Reach
1.	YouTube	79.2%	9.	Instagram	52.0%
2.	Facebook	78.6	10.	Amazon Mobile.	43.6
3.	Google Search	71.4	11.	Pandora Radio	39.4
4.	Google Maps	68.0	12.	Google Drive	38.1
5.	Facebook Messenger	67.6	13.	Google Photos	33.6
6.	Snapchat	59.8	14.	Apple News	30.0
7.	Gmail	56.0	15.	Pinterest	29.6
8.	Google Play	54.6			

Note: Reach is percentage of all U.S. smartphone mobile media users on iOS and Android platforms, age 18 or over, in June 2018.

U.S. Fixed Broadband Internet Connections by Technology, 2012-16

Source: Federal Communications Commission
(internet connections in thousands, as of Dec. of given year)

Connection type	2012	2013	2014	2015	2016
aDSL (asymmetric digital subscriber line)	13,108	18,540	18,557	20,741	21,042
sDSL (symmetric digital subscriber line)	33	36	28	20	20
Other wireline[1]	276	308	308	330	347
Cable modem	44,133	50,236	53,853	58,423	62,881
Fiber optic[2]	6,430	7,486	8,974	10,384	11,942
Satellite	394	1,181	1,558	1,744	1,609
Fixed wireless	284	388	594	710	939
Total	**64,657**	**78,175**	**83,872**	**92,352**	**98,781**

Note: Numbers may not add up to totals due to rounding. Includes connections with transmission speeds of at least 3 megabits per second (3 mbps) downstream (internet to user) and 768 kilobits per second (768 kbps) upstream (user to internet). (1) Includes power line. (2) Fiber to the premises (FTTP).

Internet Use in the U.S., 2000-16

Source: The 2017 Digital Future Report, USC Annenberg Center for the Digital Future

	2000	2002	2005	2007	2008	2009	2010	2012	2013	2014	2015	2016
Weekly time online[1]	9.4	11.1	13.3	15.3	17.3	19	18.3	20.4	20.5	21.5	23.5	23.6
Weekly time online, at home[1]	3.3	6.8	7.8	10	10.1	10.6	12.3	14.1	14.1	16.1	17.2	17.6
Weekly time online, at work[2].........	NA	NA	5.6	7.4	8.3	9.0	9.2	13.4	10.4	10.2	10.9	10.1
% of internet users aged 18 and above who make purchases online ...	45%	40%	46%	67%	65%	65%	68%	76%	79%	78%	80%	83%
Average monthly spending by internet purchasers aged 18 and above.....	NA	$101	$113	$66	$85	$88	$73	$91	$106	$115	$109	$117

NA = Not available. (1) Average number of active-use hours per week among internet users. (2) Average number of active-use hours per week among internet users who access the internet at work.

U.S. Internet Use by Race and Ethnicity, 2003-17

Source: U.S. Census Bureau survey for National Telecommunications and Information Administration, U.S. Dept. of Commerce
(number in thousands of civilian individuals, age 3 and older)

Survey date	Total U.S.[1] Number	% with internet use	White, non-Hispanic Number	% with internet use	African-American, non-Hispanic Number	% with internet use	Asian-American, non-Hispanic Number	% with internet use	American Indian or Alaska Native, non-Hispanic Number	% with internet use	Hispanic Number	% with internet use
Oct. 2003	161,636	58.7%	122,243	65.1%	14,898	45.2%	7,043	63.0%	676	48.1%	14,038	37.2%
Oct. 2007	177,987	62.4	130,432	68.9	17,223	50.1	8,686	68.4	793	47.1	17,760	41.6
Oct. 2009	197,941	68.4	141,213	74.3	20,848	59.5	9,243	72.3	1,017	54.9	22,186	49.3
Oct. 2010	209,472	71.7	145,989	76.7	22,389	63.7	9,949	74.2	1,094	62.5	26,246	56.6
July 2011	204,596	69.7	142,827	75.0	21,287	60.2	10,010	73.6	1,142	59.7	25,648	54.4
Oct. 2012	222,038	74.7	149,231	79.1	24,290	68.3	11,643	78.4	1,350	62.5	30,960	62.1
July 2013	213,708	71.4	142,313	75.4	22,996	64.0	11,739	75.3	1,424	61.5	30,771	61.0
July 2015	226,747	74.6	147,408	78.0	25,025	67.8	12,919	77.4	1,423	70.2	34,772	65.8
Nov. 2017	240,270	77.7	151,594	80.2	27,949	73.4	13,993	79.4	1,497	62.7	39,826	72.1

(1) Includes other race categories not shown.

Popular U.S. Online Purchases, 2002-16

Source: The 2017 Digital Future Report, USC Annenberg Center for the Digital Future
(percent of internet users who buy item(s) online; ranked by 2016 figures)

Item	2002	2006	2008	2010	2012	2013	2014	2015	2016
Clothes	39%	42%	61%	59%	66%	68%	65%	67%	67%
Gifts	10	12	61	63	60	64	61	67	64
Electronic goods/appliances..........	14	11	47	50	51	54	55	57	54
Travel	16	17	57	57	66	58	50	54	51
Books	29	34	60	63	66	61	52	52	51
Products for hobbies.................	NA	NA	NA	NA	NA	41	39	44	43
Software/games	12	11	43	44	37	43	36	39	37
Videos/DVDs	6	13	48	47	42	43	36	37	37
Computers/peripherals	10	11	43	44	40	38	36	39	35

NA = Not available.

Frequency of Selected Internet Activities in the U.S., 2016

Source: The 2017 Digital Future Report, USC Annenberg Center for the Digital Future
(as % of all internet users age 12 and older)

Online activity	Several times a day	Daily	Weekly	Monthly	Less than monthly	Never
Check email	56%	33%	5%	3%	2%	2%
Browse the web	35	35	15	4	6	5
Visit social networking sites	31	29	11	5	4	19
Instant message.........................	29	26	16	5	12	13
Download or listen to music	19	20	17	10	15	20
Look for news	15	38	20	8	13	7
Play games............................	14	17	13	5	12	39
Download or watch videos	13	23	24	8	14	19
Find or check a fact	12	25	32	11	13	8
Listen to online radio......................	8	14	14	7	19	38
Post on discussion boards	7	8	10	9	24	41
Look up a definition	7	18	30	17	19	9

Telecommunications Milestones

1753: Scottish surgeon Charles Morrison proposed using 26 electric lines, one for each letter of the alphabet, to make an electric telegraph. A letter would be indicated by charging the corresponding line, causing movement of a light object at the receiving end. Swiss scientist Georges-Louis Lesage built such a 26-line "electrostatic" system in 1774.

1837: In England, Charles Wheatstone and William Fothergill Cooke patented an electromagnetic telegraph. To indicate letters, their system used the magnetic field generated by a current to deflect compass needles. In 1839, they built the first commercial electric telegraph along a 13-mi (21-km) route.

1837: American inventor Samuel Morse filed a provisional patent application for a different type of electric telegraph that indicated letters by making marks of various lengths on paper. In 1844, he completed a 30-mi telegraph line from Washington, DC, to Baltimore, MD.

1866: The first successful transatlantic telegraph cable was laid.

1876: Alexander Graham Bell applied for a U.S. patent on the telephone. In his first successful experiment, on Mar. 10, he used the device to call his assistant.

1901: Italian inventor Guglielmo Marconi successfully transmitted the first transatlantic radio signal—from Cornwall, England, to Newfoundland, Canada.

1927: Commercial transatlantic telephone service (via radio) began between New York and London.

1946: The first commercial mobile phone service was launched, in St. Louis, MO.

1947: U.S. scientists invented the transistor, thereby giving birth to a revolution in telecommunications and electronics.

1948: U.S. mathematician/engineer Claude Shannon's epochal paper "A Mathematical Theory of Communication" laid the foundation for modern information theory. Its treatment of such crucial concepts as data compression and error detection and correction opened the way to digital communication.

1951: The mayors of Englewood, NJ, and Alameda, CA, made the first customer-dialed long-distance telephone call, facilitated by the introduction of area codes.

1956: The first transoceanic telephone cable went into service.

1962: NASA launched the world's first active communications satellite, AT&T's *Telstar 1*.

1978: Trials were conducted in Chicago and Newark, NJ, on a cellular approach to mobile telephony. This divided a region into a multitude of small overlapping areas, or cells, and made possible a significant increase in quality of calls and quantity of callers. Callers could be switched from one cell to another as they moved about.

1983: The first commercial cellular system in the U.S. went into operation in Chicago. A similar system was also launched in the Baltimore, MD-Washington, DC, area.

1984: As a result of a 1982 antitrust settlement with the U.S. government, AT&T, which handled most telephone service in the U.S., was broken up into several separate entities.

1994: The first smartphone, IBM's Simon Personal Communicator, went on the market. A bricklike touchscreen device, it combined a cellular phone with such features as an address book, calendar, calculator, email and faxing capability, and games.

2007: Apple released the iPhone, inaugurating an era of multifunctional smartphones.

2012: By late in the year more than 1 bil smartphones of all types were in use worldwide.

2016: Users of Facebook's messaging app Messenger passed the 1 bil mark.

2016: Total sales of Apple's iPhone reached 1 bil units.

Global Communications Technology Developments, 2001-17

Source: ITU World Telecommunication/Information and Communication Technology (ICT) Indicators Database
(per 100 inhabitants; 2017 data is estimated)

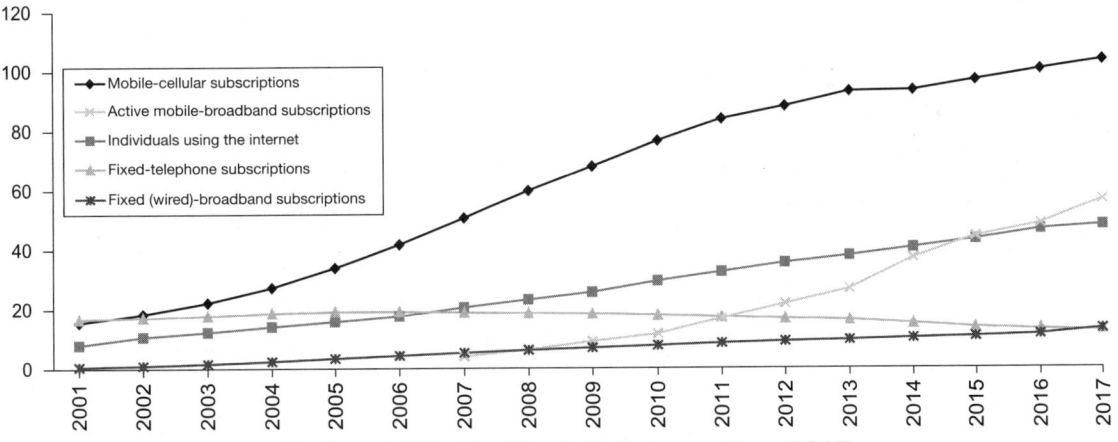

Nations With the Most Cellphone Use, 2017

Source: © International Telecommunication Union, estimated; ranked by countries with most cellphone subscriptions

Rank	Country	Subscriptions (thous.)	Per 100 pop.	Rank	Country	Subscriptions (thous.)	Per 100 pop.
1.	China	1,474,097	104.58	14.	Mexico	114,327	88.51
2.	India	1,168,902	87.28	15.	Germany	106,000	129.09
3.	Indonesia	458,923	173.84	16.	Egypt	102,958	105.54
4.	United States	395,881	122.01	17.	South Africa	91,878	161.99
5.	Brazil	236,489	113.00	18.	Iran	87,107	107.32
6.	Russia	227,342	157.89	19.	Italy	83,872	141.29
7.	Japan	170,128	133.45	20.	United Kingdom	79,174	119.63
8.	Bangladesh	145,114	88.12	21.	Turkey	77,800	96.35
9.	Nigeria	144,920	75.92	22.	France	69,017	106.21
10.	Pakistan	144,526	73.36	23.	South Korea	63,659	124.86
11.	Thailand	121,530	176.03	24.	Ethiopia	62,617	59.66
12.	Vietnam	120,016	125.62	25.	Colombia	62,222	126.81
13.	Philippines	115,825	110.40		**World**	**7,740,000**	**103.51**

U.S. Wireless Industry, 1985-2017

Source: CTIA Semi-Annual Industry Survey, used with permission of CTIA. As of Dec. of year shown.

Year	Est. total subscribers	Total service revenues (thous.)	Cellphone antennas	Avg. monthly revenue per subscriber unit	Avg. local call length (min.)
1985	340,213	$482,428	913	NA	NA
1987	1,230,855	1,151,519	2,305	NA	2.33
1989	3,508,944	3,340,595	4,169	NA	2.48
1991	7,557,148	5,708,522	7,847	NA	2.38
1993	16,009,461	10,892,175	12,824	$76.55	2.41
1995	33,785,661	19,081,239	22,663	59.43	2.15
1997	55,312,293	27,485,633	51,600	49.39	2.31
1999	86,047,003	40,018,489	81,698	46.39	2.38
2000	109,478,031	52,466,020	104,288	48.55	2.56
2001	128,374,512	65,316,235	127,540	49.79	2.74
2003	158,721,981	87,624,093	162,986	51.55	3.07
2004	182,140,362	102,121,210	175,725	52.54	3.05
2005	207,896,198	113,538,221	183,689	50.65	3.00
2006	233,040,781	125,456,825	195,613	49.07	3.03
2007	255,395,599	138,869,304	213,299	49.26	NA
2008	270,333,881	148,084,170	242,130	48.87	2.27
2009	285,646,191	152,551,854	247,081	47.97	1.81
2010	296,285,629	159,929,649	253,086	47.53	1.79
2012	326,475,248	185,013,935	301,779	48.99	1.80
2013	335,652,171	189,192,812	304,360	48.79	NA
2014	355,445,472	187,848,447	298,055	46.64	NA
2015	377,921,241	191,949,025	307,626	44.65	NA
2016	395,881,497	188,524,256	308,334	41.50	NA
2017	400,205,829	179,091,135	323,448	38.66	NA

NA = Not available. **Note:** Survey conducted annually beginning 2013.

U.S. Use of Selected Mobile Phone Functions, 2007-16

Source: The 2017 Digital Future Report, USC Annenberg School Center for the Digital Future
(as % of mobile phone users age 12 and older; ranked by percent use in 2016)

Function	2007	2008	2009	2010	2012	2013	2014	2015	2016
Text message	31%	45%	54%	62%	82%	77%	83%	87%	93%
Take pictures	33	47	52	60	79	70	76	83	89
Access the internet	8	13	18	23	59	59	73	79	84
Play games	17	22	20	23	43	43	51	54	58

U.S. Use of Selected Mobile Phone Functions, 2016

Source: The 2017 Digital Future Report, USC Annenberg School Center for the Digital Future
(% of mobile phone users age 12 and older who used function)

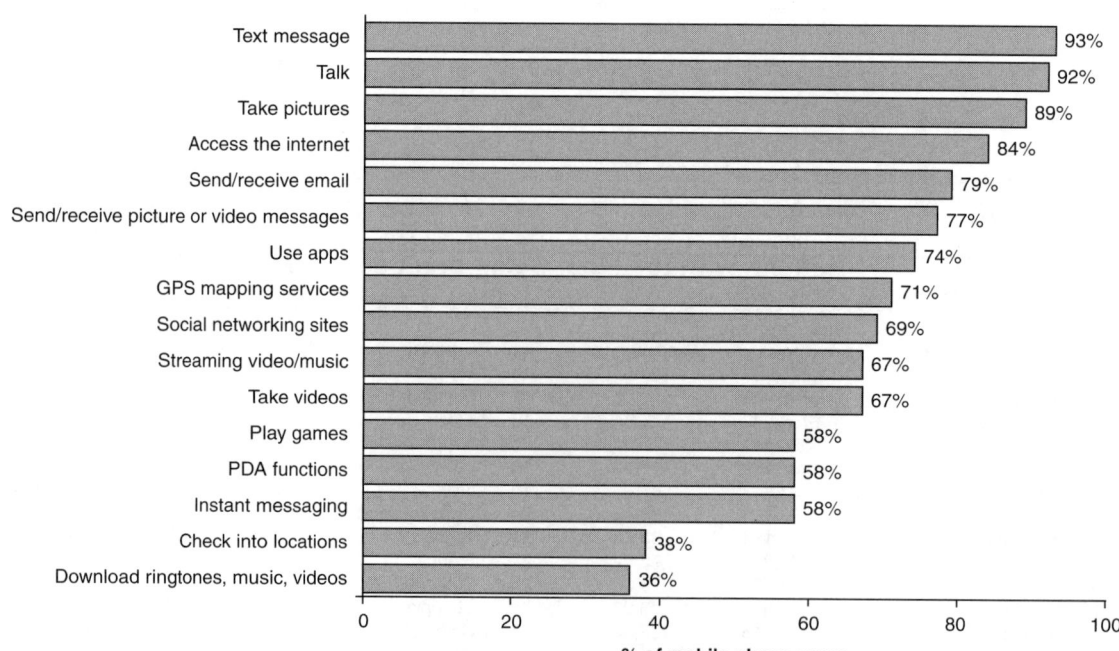

Function	%
Text message	93%
Talk	92%
Take pictures	89%
Access the internet	84%
Send/receive email	79%
Send/receive picture or video messages	77%
Use apps	74%
GPS mapping services	71%
Social networking sites	69%
Streaming video/music	67%
Take videos	67%
Play games	58%
PDA functions	58%
Instant messaging	58%
Check into locations	38%
Download ringtones, music, videos	36%

% of mobile phone users

U.S. Greenhouse Gas Emissions From Human Activities, 1990-2016

Source: U.S. Environmental Protection Agency

Gas and major source(s)	1990	2005	2012	2013	2014	2015	2016	% change, 1990-2016
Carbon dioxide (CO_2)	5,121.3	6,132.0	5,366.7	5,519.6	5,568.8	5,420.8	5,310.9	3.7%
Fossil fuel combustion	4,740.3	5,746.9	5,024.4	5,156.9	5,200.3	5,049.3	4,966.0	4.8
Methane (CH_4)	779.9	688.6	662.5	662.6	664.0	665.4	657.4	−15.7
Enteric fermentation	164.2	168.9	166.7	165.5	164.2	166.5	170.1	3.6
Natural gas systems[1]	195.2	169.1	159.6	163.8	164.3	166.3	163.5	−16.2
Landfills	179.6	132.7	117.0	113.3	112.7	111.7	107.7	−40.0
Manure management	37.2	56.3	65.6	63.3	62.9	66.3	67.7	82.0
Nitrous oxide (N_2O)	354.8	357.8	335.8	363.2	361.2	379.6	369.5	4.1
Agricultural soil management	250.5	253.5	247.9	276.6	274.0	295.0	283.6	13.2
Hydrofluorocarbons (HFCs), etc.[2]	99.7	142.0	163.7	163.8	169.2	172.4	173.4	73.9
Total U.S. emissions	6,355.6	7,320.3	6,528.8	6,709.1	6,763.1	6,638.1	6,511.3	2.4
Net U.S. emissions[3]	5,536.0	6,589.1	5,775.3	5,973.3	6,022.8	5,942.9	5,794.5	4.7

Note: Emissions given in terms of equivalent emissions of carbon dioxide (CO_2), using units of million metric tons of carbon dioxide equivalent (MMT CO_2 eq.). (1) Digestive process of ruminant animals, such as cattle and sheep, producing methane as a byproduct. (2) Includes HFCs, PFCs (perfluorocarbons), SF_6 (sulfur hexafluoride), and NF_3 (nitrogen trifluoride). (3) Total emissions minus the net sum of all emissions (i.e., sources) of greenhouse gases to the atmosphere plus removals of CO_2 (i.e., sinks or negative emissions) from the atmosphere.

U.S. Greenhouse Gas Emissions, 2016

Source: U.S. Environmental Protection Agency

World Carbon Dioxide Emissions From the Use of Fossil Fuels, 2015

Source: U.S. Energy Information Administration

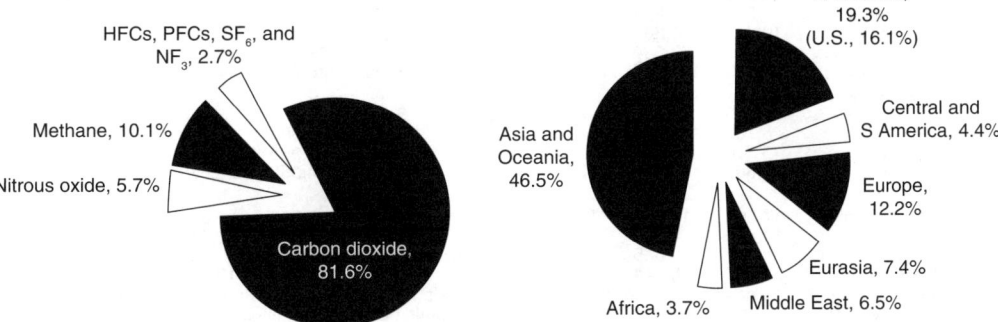

U.S. Greenhouse Gas Emissions, 2016:
HFCs, PFCs, SF_6, and NF_3, 2.7%
Methane, 10.1%
Nitrous oxide, 5.7%
Carbon dioxide, 81.6%

World Carbon Dioxide Emissions From the Use of Fossil Fuels, 2015:
N America, 19.3% (U.S., 16.1%)
Central and S America, 4.4%
Europe, 12.2%
Eurasia, 7.4%
Middle East, 6.5%
Africa, 3.7%
Asia and Oceania, 46.5%

HFC = hydrofluorocarbon; PFC = perfluorocarbon; SF_6 = sulfur hexafluoride; NF_3 = nitrogen trifluoride. **Note:** Emissions sources are independently rounded; percentages may not add up to 100.

Top 20 Nations Producing Carbon Dioxide Emissions, 1980-2015

Source: Energy Information Administration, U.S. Dept. of Energy

(in million metric tons of carbon dioxide emitted from the consumption of energy; ranked by 2015 totals)

Country	1980	1990	2000	2005	2010	2014	2015	% change, 1980-2015	% change, 1990-2015
China	1,486	2,363	3,163	5,738	8,111	9,014	8,866	496.8%	275.2%
United States	4,680	4,981	5,829	6,000	5,580	5,417	5,269	12.6	5.8
India	263	529	874	1,191	1,779	1,856	1,894	621.4	257.8
Russia[1]	3,247	3,975	1,484	1,593	1,660	1,701	1,687	−48.1	−57.6
Japan	939	1,044	1,157	1,247	1,156	1,157	1,126	19.9	7.9
Germany[2]	739	648	813	833	795	741	743	0.5	14.6
Iran	118	201	320	450	565	647	654	454.9	226.1
Korea, South	138	245	435	506	598	632	644	368.5	162.7
Saudi Arabia	177	208	291	405	510	575	606	242.2	190.7
Canada	430	438	525	609	586	603	600	39.6	37.0
Brazil	185	238	347	367	458	541	541	192.6	127.4
Indonesia	85	158	264	327	448	493	502	492.3	218.2
Mexico	239	300	379	402	446	442	453	89.8	50.9
United Kingdom	597	575	555	583	532	443	430	−28.1	−25.2
South Africa	225	324	386	428	464	455	406	80.0	25.3
Australia	191	261	335	402	422	370	371	94.0	42.2
Italy	371	410	442	470	421	341	351	−5.3	−14.5
France	482	364	399	415	381	327	331	−31.3	−9.0
Turkey	75	152	231	230	268	318	329	338.8	117.0
Thailand	34	91	165	242	286	316	316	818.7	247.6
World[3]	18,430	21,689	24,098	28,479	31,943	32,929	32,722	77.6	50.9

(1) Numbers for 1980-90 are for the former Soviet Union. (2) Numbers for 1980-90 are for former West Germany. (3) Includes nations not listed.

Atmospheric Concentration of Carbon Dioxide, 1744-2017

Source: Carbon Dioxide Information Analysis Center, U.S. Dept. of Energy; Earth System Research Laboratory, Natl. Oceanic and Atmospheric Admin., U.S. Dept. of Commerce

Year[1]	CO₂ in ppm	Year[1]	CO₂ in ppm	Year[1]	CO₂ in ppm	Year[1]	CO₂ in ppm	Year[1]	CO₂ in ppm
1744	277	1878	290	1960	317	2005	380	2013	397
1791	280	1903	295	1970	326	2009	387	2014	399
1816	284	1915	301	1980	339	2010	390	2015	401
1843	287	1927	306	1990	354	2011	392	2016	404
1869	289	1943	308	2000	370	2012	394	2017	407

ppm = Parts per million. (1) Measurements for 1744-1943 were derived from a 200-m-deep ice core sample drilled near Siple Station in Antarctica in 1983-84. Measurements for 1960-2017 were taken directly from the atmosphere at Mauna Loa Observatory in Hawaii.

Emissions of Principal Air Pollutants in the U.S., 1970-2017

Source: Office of Air Quality Planning and Standards, U.S. Environmental Protection Agency; in million tons

Pollutant	1970	1975	1980	1985	1990	1995	2000	2005	2010	2017
Carbon monoxide	204.0	188.4	185.4	176.8	154.2	126.8	114.5	88.5	73.8	60.1
Nitrogen oxides[1]	26.9	26.4	27.1	25.8	25.5	25.0	22.6	20.4	14.8	10.8
Particulate matter[2]										
PM10	13.0	7.6	7.0	41.3	27.8	25.8	23.7	21.3	20.8	18.2
PM2.5	NA	NA	NA	NA	7.6	6.9	7.3	5.6	6.0	5.3
Sulfur dioxide	31.2	28.0	25.9	23.3	23.1	18.6	16.3	14.5	7.7	2.8
Volatile org. compounds[1]	34.7	30.8	31.1	27.4	24.1	22.0	17.5	17.8	17.8	16.2
Ammonia	NA	NA	NA	NA	4.3	4.7	4.9	3.9	4.3	3.6
Total[3]	309.8	281.2	276.5	294.6	266.6	229.8	206.8	172.0	145.2	117.0

NA = Not available. (1) Ozone, a major air pollutant and the primary constituent of smog, is not emitted directly to the air but is formed by sunlight acting on emissions of nitrogen oxides and volatile organic compounds. (2) PM10 = particulates 10 microns or smaller in diameter. PM2.5 = particulates 2.5 microns or smaller in diameter. (3) Totals are rounded, as are components of totals.

Sources of Air Pollutants in the U.S., 1970-2017

Source: Office of Air Quality Planning and Standards, U.S. Environmental Protection Agency; in thousand tons

Carbon monoxide sources	1970	1975	1980	1985	1990	1995	2000	2005	2010	2017
Fuel combustion, elec. util.	237	276	322	291	363	372	484	643	766	731
Industrial processes[1]	10,610	8,304	7,700	5,894	5,572	5,631	3,628	3,074	2,807	2,951
Transportation[2]	174,602	167,884	160,512	153,216	131,702	107,755	92,239	64,729	43,596	32,162
Total carbon monoxide[3]	**204,042**	**188,398**	**185,408**	**176,845**	**154,188**	**126,778**	**114,467**	**88,546**	**73,771**	**60,109**
Nitrogen oxide sources										
Fuel combustion, elec. util.	4,900	5,694	7,024	6,127	6,663	6,384	5,330	3,792	2,458	1,155
Industrial processes[1]	5,100	4,546	4,110	4,009	3,831	3,909	3,518	2,783	2,406	2,308
Transportation[2]	15,276	15,029	14,846	14,508	13,373	12,989	12,560	12,612	9,017	6,355
Total nitrogen oxide[3]	**26,882**	**26,378**	**27,080**	**25,757**	**25,527**	**24,955**	**22,598**	**20,355**	**14,846**	**10,776**
Sulfur dioxide sources										
Fuel combustion, elec. util.	17,398	18,268	17,469	16,272	15,909	12,080	11,396	10,404	5,696	1,385
Industrial processes[1]	11,661	7,993	6,725	5,597	5,402	4,945	3,515	2,721	1,447	1,033
Transportation[2]	551	635	717	809	874	741	697	682	158	96
Total sulfur dioxide[3]	**31,218**	**28,044**	**25,926**	**23,307**	**23,077**	**18,619**	**16,347**	**14,546**	**7,732**	**2,815**

(1) Industrial fuel combustion, chemical and allied manufacturing, metals processing, and petroleum and other industrial sectors. (2) Highway and off-highway vehicles. (3) Numbers may not add up to totals because not all categories are listed.

Average Global Temperature and Atmospheric Carbon Dioxide, 1880-2017

Source: Goddard Institute for Space Studies, National Aeronautics and Space Administration, via Earth Policy Institute; National Centers for Environmental Information, National Oceanic and Atmospheric Admin. (NOAA), U.S. Dept. of Commerce

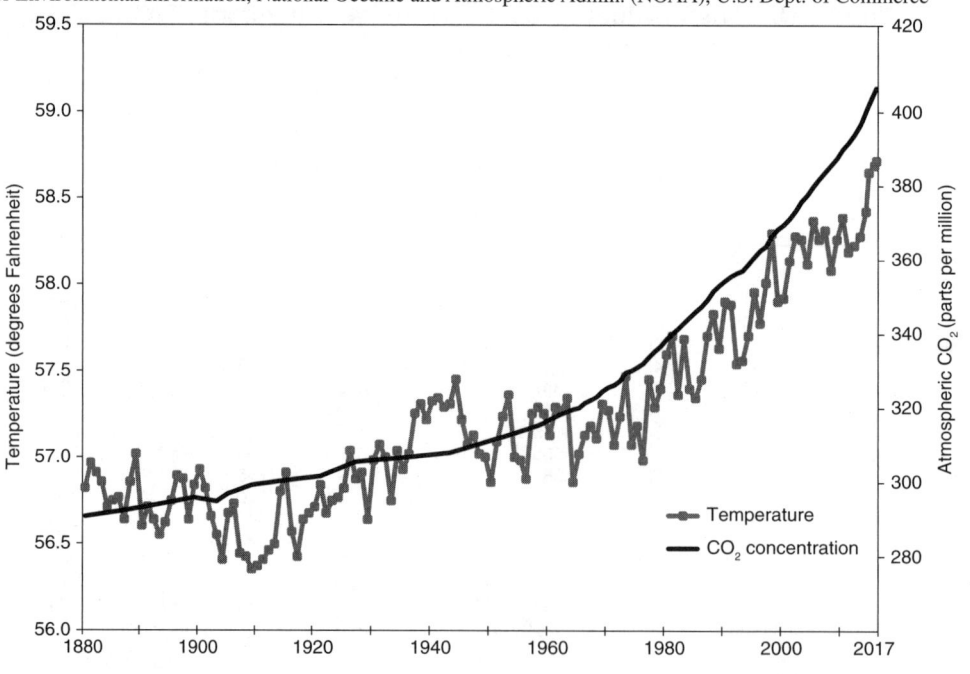

Air Pollution in Selected World Cities

Source: World Health Organization (WHO); *World Development Indicators 2015*, The World Bank

Particulate matter in the following table refers to smoke, soot, dust, and liquid droplets from combustion that are in the air—specifically, to particulates less than 10 microns in diameter (PM10) capable of reaching deep into the respiratory tract. The level of particulates, an important indicator of air quality, is significantly affected by the state of technology and pollution controls. WHO estimated that outdoor air pollution caused 4.2 mil premature deaths worldwide in 2016 due to exposure to particulates less than 2.5 microns in diameter (PM2.5). **Sulfur dioxide** is a pollutant formed when fossil fuels containing sulfur are burned. **Nitrogen dioxide** is a poisonous, pungent gas formed when nitric oxide combines with hydrocarbons in sunlight, producing photochemical smog. Nitrogen oxides are emitted by bacteria, nitrogenous fertilizers, aerobic decomposition of organic matter, biomass combustion, and, especially, burning fuel for vehicles and industrial activities. Emissions of sulfur dioxide and nitrogen oxides lead to acid rain.

Data in the table represent the annual average of outdoor particulates, in micrograms per cubic meter (mpcm), that a resident of a city is exposed to. They are based on reports from urban monitoring sites. The figures give a general indication of air quality, but results should be interpreted with caution. WHO standards for acceptable air quality are annual mean concentrations of 20 mpcm for particulate matter less than 10 microns in diameter and 40 mpcm for nitrogen dioxide and daily mean concentrations of 20 mpcm for sulfur dioxide.

City, country	Particulate matter[1]	Sulfur dioxide[2]	Nitrogen dioxide[2]	City, country	Particulate matter[1]	Sulfur dioxide[2]	Nitrogen dioxide[2]
Accra, Ghana	98[3]	NA	NA	Moscow, Russia	33	109	NA
Amsterdam, Netherlands	23	10	58	Mumbai, India	117	33	39
Bangkok, Thailand	42	11	23	New York, NY, U.S.	16	26	79
Barcelona, Spain	24	11	43	Oslo, Norway	22	8	43
Beijing, China	108	90	122	Paris, France	28	14	57
Berlin, Germany	24	18	26	Prague, Czech Republic	27	14	33
Cairo, Egypt	135[3]	69	NA	Quito, Ecuador	36	22	NA
Cape Town, South Africa	30[3]	21	72	Rio de Janeiro, Brazil	49	129	NA
Caracas, Venezuela	47	33	57	Rome, Italy	28	NA	NA
Chicago, IL, U.S.	22	14	57	São Paulo, Brazil	35	43	83
Delhi, India	229	24	41	Seoul, South Korea	46	44	60
Jakarta, Indonesia	48[3]	NA	NA	Shanghai, China	84	53	73
Kolkata, India	135	49	34	Sofia, Bulgaria	43	39	122
London, England, UK	22	25	77	Sydney, Australia	17	28	81
Los Angeles, CA, U.S.	20	9	74	Tehran, Iran	77	209	NA
Manila, Philippines	55	33	NA	Tokyo, Japan	28	18	68
Mexico City, Mexico	42	74	130	Toronto, ON, Canada	14	17	43
Milan, Italy	37	31	248	Warsaw, Poland	33	16	32
Montréal, QC, Canada	16	10	42				

NA = Not available. (1) WHO data is most recent available, as of 2009-14, unless noted. (2) World Bank data as of 2001. (3) As of 2008-12.

Air Quality of Selected U.S. Urban Areas, 1980-2017

Source: Office of Air Quality Planning and Standards, U.S. Environmental Protection Agency

Data indicate the number of days metropolitan statistical areas or corresponding core-based statistical areas failed to meet acceptable air-quality standards based on monitoring of six common pollutants.

Urban area	1980	1990	2000	2005	2010	2013	2014	2015	2016	2017
Atlanta-Sandy Springs-Roswell, GA	32	58	48	17	7	1	1	2	4	0
Bakersfield, CA	73	91	109	79	40	32	42	29	14	0
Baltimore-Columbia-Towson, MD	64	29	17	20	20	0	0	1	5	2
Baton Rouge, LA	27	30	35	22	3	2	1	2	0	0
Boston-Cambridge-Newton, MA-NH	27	8	2	8	1	0	0	1	0	0
Chicago-Naperville-Elgin, IL-IN-WI	96	47	10	26	2	1	1	3	5	1
Cincinnati, OH-KY-IN	80	51	14	22	4	0	0	1	0	0
Cleveland-Elyria, OH	37	19	9	21	5	1	2	1	5	0
Dallas-Fort Worth-Arlington, TX	43	26	35	40	5	5	3	5	1	0
Denver-Aurora-Lakewood, CO	28	3	1	2	2	8	1	2	4	1
Detroit-Warren-Dearborn, MI	48	16	5	18	2	0	0	1	0	1
Fresno, CA	89	55	106	45	22	25	33	23	25	4
Houston-The Woodlands-Sugar Land, TX	82	57	53	44	17	5	1	15	1	1
Indianapolis-Carmel-Anderson, IN	59	11	21	8	1	0	1	1	0	0
Kansas City, MO-KS	57	6	12	17	0	1	0	0	0	0
Las Vegas-Henderson-Paradise, NV	24	10	1	9	0	4	2	1	1	1
Los Angeles-Long Beach-Anaheim, CA	203	146	66	61	15	25	28	38	25	15
Memphis, TN-MS-AR	73	22	23	14	2	0	0	0	1	1
Miami-Fort Lauderdale-West Palm Beach, FL	19	2	1	1	0	0	0	0	1	0
Minneapolis-St. Paul-Bloomington, MN-WI	67	15	1	7	0	0	0	0	1	0
Nashville-Davidson–Murfreesboro–Franklin, TN	69	70	18	6	1	0	0	0	1	0
New Orleans-Metairie, LA	11	4	13	3	19	4	1	0	0	0
New York-Newark-Jersey City, NY-NJ-PA	90	45	18	22	12	3	2	3	2	2
Philadelphia-Camden-Wilmington, PA-NJ-DE-MD	90	39	20	26	12	0	3	2	2	2
Phoenix-Mesa-Scottsdale, AZ	113	29	19	11	2	25	22	3	7	5
Pittsburgh, PA	121	93	30	33	18	1	1	2	1	0
Riverside-San Bernardino-Ontario, CA	170	154	114	93	71	60	54	51	67	44
Sacramento–Roseville–Arden-Arcade, CA	52	42	42	42	9	6	7	6	16	1
Salt Lake City, UT	77	45	13	8	7	8	2	2	5	0
San Francisco-Oakland-Hayward, CA	11	6	4	2	1	0	0	0	2	1
Seattle-Tacoma-Bellevue, WA	35	8	5	1	0	0	0	3	1	2
Tucson, AZ	50	1	0	2	0	2	0	0	0	0
Washington-Arlington-Alexandria, DC-VA-MD-WV	53	23	12	18	13	0	1	1	0	0
Winston-Salem, NC	0	7	18	3	3	0	0	0	0	0

Municipal Solid Waste, 2015

Source: U.S. Environmental Protection Agency

In 2015, Americans generated about 262 mil tons of refuse collected as municipal solid waste (MSW). Of that MSW, paper represented 25.9%; food 15.1%; yard trimmings 13.3%; plastics 13.1%; rubber, leather, and textiles 9.3%; metals 9.1%; wood 6.2%; glass 4.4%; and other material 3.6%. About 34.7%, or 91 mil tons, was recycled or composted; nearly half of recycled/composted materials consisted of paper and paperboard.

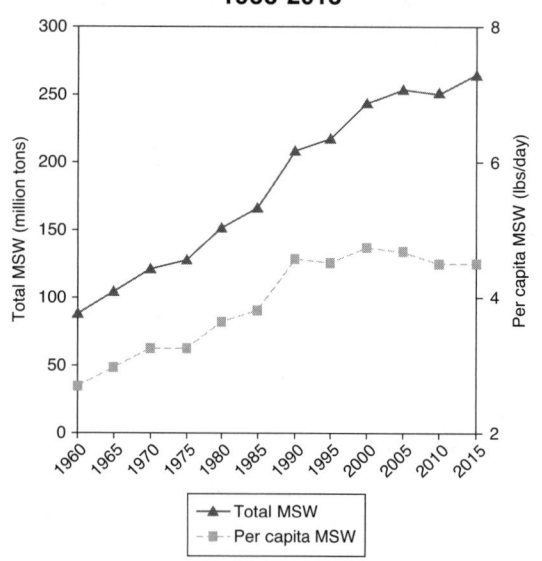

Municipal Solid Waste Generation, 1960-2015

- ▲ Total MSW
- ■ Per capita MSW

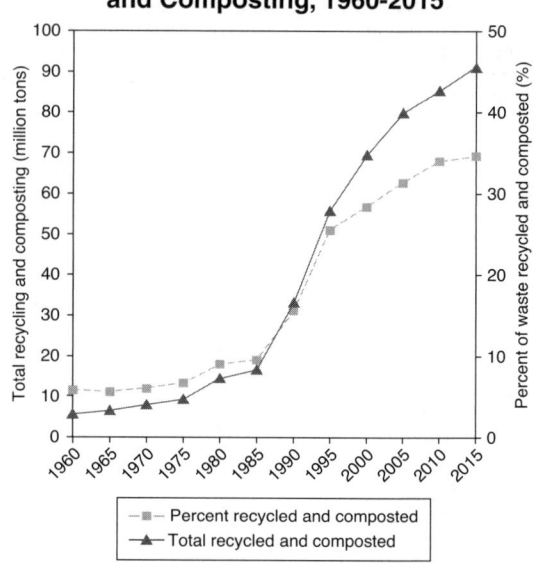

Municipal Solid Waste Recycling and Composting, 1960-2015

- ■ Percent recycled and composted
- ▲ Total recycled and composted

Hazardous Waste Sites in the U.S., 2018

Source: National Priorities List, U.S. Environmental Protection Agency; as of Apr. 2018

State/territory	Proposed Gen.	Proposed Fed.	Final Gen.	Final Fed.	Total	State/territory	Proposed Gen.	Proposed Fed.	Final Gen.	Final Fed.	Total
Alabama	2	0	9	3	14	Nebraska	0	0	16	1	17
Alaska	0	0	1	5	6	Nevada	1	0	1	0	2
Arizona	0	0	7	2	9	New Hampshire	1	0	19	1	21
Arkansas	0	0	9	0	9	New Jersey	1	0	108	6	115
California	2	0	74	24	100	New Mexico	0	0	15	1	16
Colorado	1	0	17	3	21	New York	1	0	82	4	87
Connecticut	1	0	13	1	15	North Carolina	0	0	37	2	39
Delaware	2	0	13	1	16	North Dakota	0	0	0	0	0
District of Columbia	0	0	0	1	1	Ohio	4	1	35	3	43
Florida	1	0	48	6	55	Oklahoma	1	0	7	1	9
Georgia	1	0	14	2	17	Oregon	1	0	11	2	14
Guam	0	0	1	1	2	Pennsylvania	2	0	88	6	96
Hawaii	0	0	1	2	3	Puerto Rico	0	0	17	1	18
Idaho	3	0	4	2	9	Rhode Island	0	0	10	2	12
Illinois	3	1	41	4	49	South Carolina	1	0	23	2	26
Indiana	3	0	39	0	42	South Dakota	0	0	1	1	2
Iowa	1	0	11	1	13	Tennessee	1	0	15	3	19
Kansas	1	0	11	1	13	Texas	3	0	49	4	56
Kentucky	0	0	12	1	13	Utah	3	0	10	5	18
Louisiana	3	0	12	1	16	Vermont	0	0	12	0	12
Maine	0	0	10	3	13	Virgin Islands	0	0	1	0	1
Maryland	1	0	10	10	21	Virginia	0	0	20	11	31
Massachusetts	1	0	25	6	32	Washington	0	0	36	13	49
Michigan	1	1	65	0	67	West Virginia	0	0	8	2	10
Minnesota	1	0	22	2	25	Wisconsin	1	0	37	0	38
Mississippi	2	0	9	0	11	Wyoming	0	0	1	1	2
Missouri	0	0	30	3	33	**Total**	**52**	**3**	**1,184**	**157**	**1,396**
Montana	1	0	17	0	18						

Gen. = Non-federal sites; Fed. = Hazardous waste produced by federal agency. **Note:** Sites that have been proposed for federal Superfund financing are listed under Proposed; sites that have qualified for Superfund financing are under Final.

Renewable Water Resources, 2015

Source: Food and Agriculture Organization (FAO), United Nations

Globally, water supplies are abundant, but they are unevenly distributed among and within countries. In some areas, water withdrawals are so high, relative to supply, that surface water supplies are shrinking, and groundwater reserves are being depleted faster than they can be replenished by precipitation. According to the FAO, the U.S. (including Alaska and Hawaii) has 8,758 cubic meters per capita and 2,818 cubic kilometers of internal renewable water resources total.

The tables below take into account only countries for which data are available, draw upon studies done over a number of years, and use 2015 population data. Numbers represent each country's internal resources. Countries ranked by per capita figures.

Countries With Greatest Internal Water Resources

Country	Cubic m per capita	Total cubic km
Iceland	516,090	170.0
Guyana.	314,170	241.0
Suriname	182,320	99.0
Papua New Guinea	105,132	801.0
Bhutan	100,671	78.0
Gabon	95,072	164.0
Canada.	79,299	2,850.0
Solomon Islands.	76,594	44.7
Norway.	73,306	382.0
New Zealand	72,201	327.0

Countries With Lowest Internal Water Resources

Country	Cubic m per capita	Total cubic km
Kuwait.	0.0	0.0
Bahrain.	2.905	0.004
United Arab Emirates . . .	16.38	0.15
Egypt	19.67	1.8
Qatar	25.06	0.056
Saudi Arabia.	76.09	2.4
Yemen	78.26	2.1
Maldives.	82.49	0.03
Jordan	89.8	0.682
Israel.	93.01	0.75

Top Countries by Forest Area, 1990-2015

Source: Food and Agriculture Organization, United Nations

(in square kilometers; ranked by 2015 area)

Country	Forest area, 1990	Forest area, 2015	% change, 1990-2015	% of land area covered by forest in 2015	Country	Forest area, 1990	Forest area, 2015	% change, 1990-2015	% of land area covered by forest in 2015
Russia.	NA	8,149,305	NA	49.8%	Argentina	347,930	271,120	−22.1%	9.9%
Brazil.	5,467,050	4,935,380	−9.7%	59.0	Japan	249,500	249,580	0.0	68.5
Canada.	3,482,730	3,470,690	−0.3	38.2	Gabon	220,000	230,000	4.5	89.3
United States	3,024,500	3,100,950	2.5	33.9	Congo Rep.	227,260	223,340	−1.7	65.4
China	1,571,406	2,083,213	32.6	22.2	Finland	218,750	222,180	1.6	73.1
Congo.	1,603,630	1,525,780	−4.9	67.3	Malaysia	223,760	221,950	−0.8	67.6
Australia	1,285,410	1,247,510	−2.9	16.2	Central African				
Indonesia	1,185,450	910,100	−23.2	50.2	Republic	225,600	221,700	−1.7	35.6
Peru	779,210	739,730	−5.1	57.8	Sudan	NA	192,099	NA	NA
India	639,390	706,820	10.5	23.8	Cameroon.	243,160	188,160	−22.6	39.8
Mexico	697,600	660,400	−5.3	34.0	Laos	176,449	187,614	6.3	81.3
Colombia	644,170	585,017	−9.2	52.7	Spain	138,095	184,179	33.4	36.8
Angola	609,760	578,560	−5.1	46.4	Chile	152,630	177,350	16.2	23.9
Bolivia	627,950	547,640	−12.8	50.6	France.	144,360	169,890	17.7	31.0
Zambia	528,000	486,350	−7.9	65.4	Guyana.	166,600	165,260	−0.8	84.0
Venezuela	520,260	466,830	−10.3	52.9	Thailand	140,050	163,990	17.1	32.1
Tanzania.	559,200	460,600	−17.6	52.0	Suriname	154,300	153,320	−0.6	98.3
Mozambique.	433,780	379,400	−12.5	48.2	Paraguay	211,570	153,230	−27.6	38.6
Papua New Guinea	336,270	335,590	−0.2	74.1	Vietnam	221,640	147,730	−33.3	47.6
Myanmar.	392,180	290,410	−25.9	44.5	Zimbabwe.	93,630	140,620	50.2	36.4
Sweden.	280,630	280,730	0.0	68.9	**World**	**41,282,695**	**39,991,336**	**−3.1**	**30.7**

NA = Not available.

Largest Trees in the U.S.

Source: American Forests

Nearly 900 native and naturalized species of trees grow in the U.S. The trunk of the world's largest known living tree, the General Sherman giant sequoia in California, weighs almost 1,400 tons—about as much as 15 adult blue whales. To determine the country's largest trees (or "national champions"), American Forests uses a point system whereby trunk circumference, or girth at 4.5 ft above ground level (in inches) + height (in feet) + ¼ average crown spread (in feet) = total points. As of June 27, 2018.

Tree type	Girth at 4.5 ft (in.)	Height (ft)	Crown spread (ft)	Total points	Location
Giant sequoia (Gen. Sherman tree) . .	1,020	274	107	1,321	Sequoia National Park, CA
Coast redwood	950	321	75	1,290	Jedediah Smith Redwoods State Park, CA
Coast redwood	895	307	83	1,223	Jedediah Smith Redwoods State Park, CA
Coast redwood	845	349	89	1,216	Redwood National Park, CA
Coast redwood	867	299	101	1,191	Prairie Creek Redwoods State Park, CA
Western redcedar.	761	159	45	931	Olympic National Park, WA
Sitka spruce	668	191	96	883	Olympic National Park, WA
Coast Douglas-fir	599	200	37	808	Olympic National Park, WA
Coast Douglas-fir	505	281	71	804	Olympic National Forest, WA
Coast Douglas-fir	444	327	82	792	Coos County, OR

Selected Endangered Animal Species

Source: Fish and Wildlife Service, U.S. Dept. of the Interior

As of Feb. 2018, the Fish and Wildlife Service determined that the eastern puma (*Puma concolor couguar*) was extinct and removed it from the Federal List of Endangered and Threatened Wildlife. It was originally listed as an endangered species in 1973.

Common name	Scientific name	Range
Albatross, Amsterdam	Diomedia amsterdamensis	Amsterdam Island, Indian Ocean
Antelope, giant sable	Hippotragus niger variani	Angola
Armadillo, giant	Priodontes maximus	Venezuela, Guyana, Argentina
Bandicoot, desert	Perameles eremiana	Australia
Bat, gray	Myotis grisescens	Central, southeastern U.S.
Bear, Mexican grizzly	Ursus arctos	Mexico
Bobcat, Mexican	Lynx rufus escuinapae	Mexico
Bumble bee, rusty patched	Bombus affinis	Canada; Eastern, midwestern U.S.
Camel, Bactrian	Camelus bactrianus	Mongolia, China
Caribou, woodland	Rangifer tarandus caribou	Canada, U.S. (ID, WA)
Cheetah	Acinonyx jubatus	India
Chimpanzee, pygmy	Pan paniscus	Dem. Rep. of the Congo
Condor, California	Gymnogyps californianus	U.S. (AZ, CA, NV, UT)
Crane, whooping	Grus americana	Canada, central U.S.
Crocodile, American	Crocodylus acutus	Caribbean (except for FL pop.); Central, S America
Dolphin, Chinese river	Lipotes vexillifer	China
Duck, Hawaiian	Anas wyvilliana	U.S. (HI)
Elephant, Asian	Elephas maximus	South-central and southeastern Asia
Fox, northern swift	Vulpes velox hebes	Canada
Frog, mountain yellow-legged	Rana muscosa	U.S. (CA)
Gorilla	Gorilla gorilla	Central and western Africa
Hawk, Hawaiian	Buteo solitarius	U.S. (HI)
Hyena, brown	Parahyaena brunnea	Southern Africa
Impala, black-faced	Aepyceros melampus petersi	Angola, Namibia
Kangaroo, Tasmanian forester	Macropus giganteus tasmaniensis	Australia (Tasmania)
Leopard	Panthera pardus	Central and Southern Africa
Monkey, spider	Ateles geoffroyi frontatus	Costa Rica, Nicaragua
Ocelot	Leopardus pardalis	U.S. (AZ, TX), Mexico
Orangutan	Pongo pygmaeus	Indonesia
Ostrich, West African	Struthio camelus spatzi	Western Sahara
Otter, marine	Lontra felina	Peru
Panda, giant	Ailuropoda melanoleuca	China
Panther, Florida	Puma concolor coryi	U.S. (FL)
Parakeet, golden	Aratinga guarouba	Brazil
Parrot, imperial	Amazona imperialis	Dominica
Penguin, Galapagos	Spheniscus mendiculus	Ecuador (Galapagos Islands)
Rhinoceros, black	Diceros bicornis	Sub-Saharan Africa
Salamander, Chinese giant	Andrias davidianus	China
Salmon, sockeye	Oncorhynchus nerka	U.S. (OR, WA)
Sea lion, Steller (Western pop.)	Eumetopias jubatus	U.S. (AK), Russia
Squirrel, Carolina northern flying	Glaucomys sabrinus coloratus	U.S. (NC, TN, VA)
Tiger	Panthera tigris	Asia
Tortoise, Galapagos	Geochelone nigra	Ecuador (Galapagos Islands)
Whale, gray (Western North Pacific pop.)	Eschrichtius robustus	NW Pacific Ocean
Whale, humpback	Megaptera novaeangliae	W North Pacific, Arabian Sea, Cape Verde Island, Central America
Wolf, red	Canis rufus	U.S. (FL)
Woodpecker, ivory-billed	Campephilus principalis	U.S. (AR)
Yak, wild	Bos mutus	China (Tibet), India
Zebra, mountain	Equus zebra zebra	South Africa

Status of Endangered and Threatened Species, 2018

Source: Fish and Wildlife Service, U.S. Dept. of the Interior; as of Apr. 2018

Group	Endangered		Threatened		Total species[1]	U.S. species with recovery plans
	U.S.	Foreign	U.S.	Foreign		
Mammals	66	260	27	23	376	57
Birds	80	217	21	18	336	85
Fishes	92	22	73	6	193	106
Reptiles	17	71	29	24	141	40
Clams	76	2	15	0	93	71
Insects	74	4	11	0	89	41
Snails	40	1	12	0	53	33
Amphibians	21	8	15	1	45	22
Crustaceans	24	0	4	0	28	19
Corals	0	3	7	15	25	0
Arachnids	12	0	0	0	12	12
Animal subtotals	**502**	**588**	**214**	**87**	**1,391**	**486**
Flowering Plants	735	1	167	0	903	644
Ferns and Allies	36	0	2	0	38	26
Conifers and Cycads	1	0	3	2	6	3
Lichens	2	0	0	0	2	2
Plant subtotals	**774**	**1**	**172**	**2**	**949**	**675**
Grand total	**1,276**	**589**	**386**	**89**	**2,340**	**1,161**

(1) 21 animal species are counted more than once in this table, primarily because these animals have distinct population segments, each with its own individual listing status. The U.S. dual-status species, all tallied as endangered, are Atlantic sturgeon, California tiger salamander, Chinook salmon, chum salmon, coho salmon, gray wolf, loggerhead sea turtle, mountain yellow-legged frog, roseate tern, piping plover, sockeye salmon, and steelhead. The foreign dual-status species are argali, broad-snouted caiman, humpback whale, leopard, loggerhead sea turtle, scalloped hammerhead shark, and vicuña. Green sea turtles appear on both U.S. and foreign lists.

METEOROLOGY

National Weather Service Watches and Warnings

Source: National Weather Service, National Oceanic and Atmospheric Admin. (NOAA), U.S. Dept. of Commerce; *Glossary of Meteorology*, American Meteorological Society

The National Weather Service issues watches, warnings, and advisories for specific geographic areas to alert people to the possibility or imminent arrival of severe weather or of flooding. Often the weather hazard is a convective storm (a storm involving upward and downward movement of heat and moisture). A severe thunderstorm or tornado watch is issued when a severe convective storm, covering a relatively small geographic area or moving in a narrow path, is sufficiently intense to threaten life and property. Excessive localized convective rains are not classified as severe storms but are often the product of severe local storms. Such rainfall may result in phenomena, such as flash floods, that threaten life and property. Lightning occurs with all thunderstorms and, along with flash floods, is a leading cause of storm deaths and injuries.

Cyclone: Atmospheric circulation of winds rotating counterclockwise in the Northern Hemisphere and clockwise in the Southern Hemisphere. Tornadoes, hurricanes/typhoons, and the lows shown on weather maps are all examples of cyclones. Cyclones are usually accompanied by precipitation or stormy weather.

Severe thunderstorm: Thunderstorm (any local atmospheric disturbance) that produces a tornado, winds of at least 50 knots (58 mph), and/or hail at least 1 in. in diameter. A severe thunderstorm watch indicates conditions are favorable for the development of a severe thunderstorm within 4 to 8 hours. A severe thunderstorm warning indicates a severe thunderstorm has been sighted by radar or reported by a spotter.

Tornado: Violently rotating column of air that extends from the base of a thunderstorm to the ground. On a local scale, it is the most destructive of all atmospheric phenomena. Tornado paths range from a few feet to more than 100 mi long (avg. 5 mi) and from a few feet to more than 1 mi in diameter (avg. 220 yds). The average forward speed is 30 mph, and wind speeds can exceed 200 mph. A rotating column of air over water is called a **waterspout**.

Tropical storm: Cyclone that develops over tropical or subtropical waters with 1-min. sustained surface winds between 34 and 63 knots (39-73 mph). A tropical storm watch is issued when tropical storm conditions pose a threat to specified coastal areas within 48 hours. A tropical storm warning is issued when such conditions are expected in a specified coastal area within 36 hours.

Hurricane: Tropical cyclone having 1-min. sustained surface winds of 64 knots (74 mph) or more. (In the western North Pacific Ocean, west of the International Date Line, such storms are known as **typhoons**.) The hurricane-force winds form a circle or oval, sometimes as wide as 300 mi in diameter. In the lower latitudes, hurricanes usually move W or NW at 10-15 mph. When the center approaches 25° to 30° N, the direction of motion often changes to the NE, with increased forward speed. In the Atlantic, hurricane season is June 1-Nov. 30.

Hurricane season is May 15-Nov. 30 in the eastern Pacific. A hurricane warning is issued when a hurricane is forecast for an area within 36 hours.

Winter storm and **blizzard:** A winter storm watch is issued when there is a potential for heavy snow or significant ice accumulations, usually at least 24-36 hours in advance. A winter storm warning is issued when a winter storm is producing or is forecast to produce heavy snow or significant ice accumulations. A blizzard warning is issued for winter storm conditions where winds are 35 mph or more, there is sufficient falling and/or blowing snow to frequently reduce visibility to less than ¼ mi, and the conditions are expected to prevail for at least 3 hours.

River flooding: Occurs when rains, sometimes coupled with melting snow, quickly fill river basins with an excess of water. Torrential rains from decaying hurricanes or tropical systems are also a major cause. **Coastal flooding:** Tropical storm and hurricane winds or intense offshore low-pressure systems can drive ocean water inland. Coastal floods can also be produced by sea waves called **tsunamis**, produced by earthquakes or underwater volcanic eruptions or landslides. **Flash flooding:** Usually due to copious amounts of rain falling in a short time. Ice can also cause flash flooding. When ice accumulates at natural or artificial obstructions, it can stop the flow of water. The resulting buildup of water can lead to flooding upstream. If the jam suddenly gives way, a flash flood can happen downstream. Flash flooding typically occurs within 6 hours of the causative event.

Flash floods account for the majority of flood deaths in the U.S. and are the leading cause of deaths associated with thunderstorms. Urbanization significantly increases runoff because less rain is absorbed by the terrain, making flash flooding in urban areas extremely dangerous. Streets can become swift-moving rivers, and basements can fill with water.

A flood watch indicates flooding or flash flooding is possible within a designated area. A flood warning indicates flooding is in progress, imminent, or highly likely.

National Weather Service Marine Warnings and Advisories

Primary sources of dissemination are mobile apps and push notifications, commercial radio, TV, U.S. Coast Guard radio, and National Oceanic and Atmospheric Admin. (NOAA) VHF radio broadcasts. The NOAA Weather Radio All Hazards (NWR) network broadcasts on seven frequencies between 162.40 and 162.55 MHz. These broadcasts can usually be received within about 40 mi of the transmission site using a special radio receiver. The following are examples of the warnings and advisories that may be addressed to mariners.

Small craft advisory: Alerts mariners to sustained weather and/or sea conditions, present or forecast, potentially hazardous to small boats, including winds 20-33 knots (23-38 mph) and/or dangerous wave conditions. The advisory is also issued when sea or lake ice exists that could be hazardous to small boats. Criteria vary depending on region and type of marine environment.

Special marine warning: Indicates potentially hazardous weather conditions not covered by existing marine warnings.

The conditions are usually of short duration (2 hr. or less) and involve wind speeds of 34 knots (39 mph) or more, and/or hail at least ¾ in. in diameter or waterspouts.

Gale warning: Indicates winds of 34-47 knots (39-54 mph) not directly associated with a tropical storm are forecast for the area.

Storm warning: Indicates winds 48-63 knots (55-73 mph) not directly associated with a tropical storm are forecast for the area.

Hurricane and Tornado Classifications

Source: National Weather Service, NOAA, U.S. Dept. of Commerce

The Saffir-Simpson Hurricane Wind Scale, created by Herbert Saffir and expanded upon by Robert Simpson, rates a hurricane's intensity from 1 to 5. The scale, updated in 2012, provides examples of the type of damage and impacts associated with winds of the indicated intensity. The Fujita (or F) Scale was created by T. Theodore Fujita in 1971 to classify tornadoes. The Enhanced Fujita Scale, an update, was implemented in the U.S. in 2007. It uses 3-sec. gusts estimated at the point of damage based on a judgment of eight levels of damage to 28 indicators.

Saffir-Simpson Hurricane Wind Scale			Enhanced Fujita Scale (Tornadoes)	
Category	Wind speed[1]	Summary of damage	Rank	3-sec. gust
1	74-95 mph	Very dangerous winds will produce some damage.	EF-0	65-85 mph
2	96-110 mph	Extremely dangerous winds will cause extensive damage.	EF-1	86-110 mph
3	111-129 mph	Devastating damage will occur.	EF-2	111-135 mph
4	130-156 mph	Catastrophic damage will occur.	EF-3	136-165 mph
5	Over 156 mph	Catastrophic damage will occur.	EF-4	166-200 mph
(1) 1-min. sustained winds.			EF-5	Over 200 mph

Monthly Normal Mean Temperatures, Precipitation in U.S. Cities

Source: National Climatic Data Center, NESDIS, NOAA, U.S. Dept. of Commerce

Normals are averages covering a 30-year period. The temperature and precipitation normals given here are based on records for 1981-2010. Temperatures listed below represent means of the normal daily maximum and normal daily minimum temperatures for each month. For stations that did not have continuous records from the same site for the entire 30 years, the means have been adjusted to the record at the present site. (*) = City station. Other figures are for airport stations. T = Temperature in Fahrenheit; P = Precipitation in inches.

	Jan.		Feb.		Mar.		Apr.		May		June		July		Aug.		Sept.		Oct.		Nov.		Dec.	
Station	T	P	T	P	T	P	T	P	T	P	T	P	T	P	T	P	T	P	T	P	T	P	T	P
Albany, NY	23	2.6	26	2.2	35	3.2	48	3.2	58	3.6	67	3.8	72	4.1	70	3.5	62	3.3	50	3.7	40	3.3	29	2.9
Albuquerque, NM	36	0.4	41	0.5	48	0.5	56	0.6	66	0.5	75	0.7	78	1.5	76	1.6	69	1.1	58	1.0	45	0.6	36	0.5
Anchorage, AK	17	0.7	20	0.7	27	0.6	37	0.5	48	0.7	55	1.0	59	1.8	57	3.3	49	3.0	35	2.0	22	1.2	19	1.1
Asheville, NC	37	3.7	40	3.8	47	3.8	55	3.3	63	3.7	71	4.7	74	4.3	73	4.4	66	3.8	56	2.9	47	3.7	39	3.6
Atlanta, GA	43	4.2	47	4.7	54	4.8	62	3.4	70	3.7	77	4.0	80	5.3	79	3.9	74	4.5	63	3.4	54	4.1	45	3.9
Atlantic City, NJ	33	3.2	35	2.9	42	4.2	52	3.6	61	3.4	71	3.1	76	3.7	74	4.1	67	3.2	56	3.4	47	3.3	37	3.7
Baltimore, MD	33	3.1	36	2.9	44	3.9	54	3.2	54	4.0	72	3.5	77	4.1	75	3.3	68	4.0	56	3.3	47	3.3	37	3.4
Barrow, AK	–13	0.1	–14	0.1	–13	0.1	2	0.2	21	0.2	36	0.3	41	1.0	39	1.1	32	0.1	17	0.4	–2	0.2	–8	0.1
Birmingham, AL	44	4.8	48	4.5	55	5.2	63	4.4	71	5.0	78	4.4	81	4.8	81	3.9	75	3.9	64	3.4	54	4.9	46	4.5
Bismarck, ND	13	0.4	18	0.5	30	0.9	44	1.3	56	2.4	65	3.2	71	2.9	70	2.3	59	1.6	45	1.3	29	0.7	16	0.5
Boise, ID	31	1.2	37	1.0	45	1.4	51	1.2	59	1.4	68	0.7	76	0.3	75	0.2	65	0.6	53	0.8	40	1.4	31	1.6
Boston, MA	29	3.4	32	3.3	38	4.3	48	3.7	58	3.5	68	3.7	73	3.4	72	3.4	65	3.4	54	3.9	45	4.0	35	3.8
Buffalo, NY	25	3.2	26	2.5	34	2.9	46	3.0	57	3.5	66	3.7	71	3.2	70	3.3	62	3.9	51	3.5	41	4.0	30	3.9
Burlington, VT	19	2.1	22	1.8	31	2.2	45	2.8	56	3.5	66	3.7	71	4.2	69	3.9	61	3.6	48	3.6	38	3.1	26	2.4
Caribou, ME	10	2.7	14	2.2	25	2.5	39	2.7	52	3.3	61	3.5	66	4.1	64	3.8	55	3.3	43	3.5	32	3.6	18	3.3
Charleston, SC	48	3.7	52	3.0	58	3.7	65	2.9	73	3.0	79	5.7	82	6.5	81	7.2	76	6.1	67	3.8	59	2.4	51	3.1
Charleston, WV	34	3.0	38	3.2	46	3.9	56	3.2	64	4.8	72	4.3	75	4.9	74	3.7	67	3.3	57	2.7	47	3.7	37	3.3
Chicago, IL	24	1.7	28	1.8	38	2.5	49	3.4	59	3.7	69	3.5	74	3.7	72	4.9	65	3.2	53	3.2	40	3.2	28	2.3
Cleveland, OH	28	2.7	31	2.3	38	2.9	50	3.5	60	3.7	69	3.4	74	3.5	72	3.5	65	3.8	54	3.1	44	3.6	32	3.1
Columbus, OH	30	2.7	33	2.3	42	3.0	53	3.4	63	4.2	72	4.0	75	4.8	74	3.3	67	2.8	55	2.6	44	3.2	34	3.0
Dallas-Ft. Worth, TX	46	2.1	50	2.7	58	3.5	66	3.1	74	4.9	81	3.8	85	2.2	86	1.9	78	2.6	68	4.2	57	2.7	47	2.6
Denver, CO	31	0.4	33	0.3	40	0.9	47	1.7	57	2.2	67	2.0	74	3.0	73	1.6	63	1.0	51	1.0	38	0.6	30	0.3
Des Moines, IA	23	1.0	27	1.3	39	2.3	52	3.9	62	4.7	72	4.9	76	4.5	74	4.1	66	3.1	53	2.6	39	2.2	26	1.4
Detroit, MI	26	2.0	28	2.0	37	2.3	49	2.9	60	3.4	69	3.5	74	3.4	72	3.0	64	3.3	52	2.5	42	2.8	30	2.4
Dodge City, KS	32	0.6	36	0.7	44	1.6	54	1.8	64	2.9	74	3.2	80	3.1	78	2.8	69	1.7	57	1.7	43	0.8	33	0.8
Duluth, MN	10	1.0	15	0.8	26	1.5	40	2.4	51	3.2	60	4.2	66	3.9	64	3.7	56	4.1	43	2.9	29	2.1	15	1.2
Fairbanks, AK	–8	0.6	–1	0.4	11	0.3	33	0.3	49	0.6	60	1.4	63	2.2	56	1.9	45	1.1	24	0.8	3	0.7	–4	0.6
Fresno, CA	47	2.2	52	2.0	57	2.0	62	1.0	70	0.4	77	0.2	83	0.0	82	0.0	76	0.2	66	0.6	54	1.1	47	1.8
Galveston, TX*	53	3.7	55	3.0	61	2.9	68	2.2	76	3.0	82	4.8	84	3.9	84	3.4	80	5.4	73	4.2	64	3.4	56	3.4
Grand Rapids, MI	24	2.1	27	1.8	36	2.4	48	3.4	59	4.0	68	3.8	73	3.8	71	3.6	63	4.3	51	3.3	40	3.5	29	2.5
Helena, MT	23	0.4	28	0.3	36	0.6	45	1.0	54	1.9	62	2.1	70	1.2	68	1.2	58	1.1	46	0.7	33	0.5	22	0.4
Honolulu, HI	73	2.3	73	2.0	75	2.0	76	0.6	78	0.6	80	0.3	81	0.5	82	0.6	82	0.7	80	1.8	78	2.4	75	3.2
Houston, TX	53	3.4	56	3.2	63	3.4	70	3.3	77	5.1	82	5.9	84	3.8	85	3.8	80	4.1	72	5.7	62	4.3	54	3.7
Huron, SD	17	0.5	22	0.6	33	1.5	47	2.3	58	3.1	68	3.9	74	2.9	72	2.4	62	2.5	48	1.8	33	0.9	19	0.5
Indianapolis, IN	28	2.7	32	2.3	42	3.6	53	3.8	63	5.1	72	4.3	75	4.6	74	3.1	67	3.1	55	3.1	44	3.7	32	3.2
Jackson, MS	46	5.0	50	4.8	57	5.0	64	5.0	72	4.4	79	4.1	82	4.8	81	4.2	76	3.0	65	3.9	56	4.8	48	5.2
Jacksonville, FL	53	3.3	56	3.2	62	4.0	67	2.6	74	2.5	80	6.5	82	6.6	82	6.8	78	8.2	70	3.9	62	2.1	55	2.8
Juneau, AK	28	5.4	30	4.1	34	3.8	41	2.9	49	3.4	55	3.2	57	4.6	56	5.7	50	8.6	42	8.6	33	6.0	30	5.8
Kansas City, MO	29	1.1	34	1.5	44	2.4	55	3.7	65	5.2	74	5.2	78	4.5	77	3.9	68	4.6	56	3.2	44	2.2	32	1.5
Knoxville, TN	38	4.3	42	4.3	50	4.3	59	4.0	67	4.5	75	3.8	78	5.1	78	3.3	71	3.2	60	2.5	50	4.0	41	4.5
Lander, WY	22	0.4	25	0.6	36	1.2	44	1.9	53	2.2	63	1.3	71	0.8	70	0.6	59	1.1	46	1.3	31	0.9	21	0.6
Lexington, KY	33	3.2	37	3.2	46	4.1	55	3.6	64	5.3	73	4.4	76	4.7	75	3.3	68	2.9	57	3.1	46	3.5	36	3.9
Little Rock, AR	41	3.6	45	3.7	53	4.7	62	5.1	71	4.9	79	3.7	83	3.3	83	2.6	75	3.2	64	4.9	53	5.3	43	5.0
Los Angeles, CA*	58	3.1	59	3.8	61	2.4	63	0.9	66	0.3	69	0.1	73	0.0	74	0.0	73	0.2	69	0.7	62	1.0	58	2.3
Louisville, KY	35	3.2	39	3.2	48	4.2	58	4.0	67	5.3	76	3.8	79	4.2	78	3.3	71	3.1	60	3.2	49	3.6	38	3.8
Marquette, MI*	19	1.8	21	1.3	29	2.0	40	2.5	51	2.5	60	2.7	67	2.8	67	2.6	59	3.2	47	3.1	35	2.6	24	2.0
Memphis, TN	41	4.0	46	4.4	54	5.2	63	5.5	72	5.3	80	3.6	83	4.6	82	2.9	75	3.1	64	4.0	53	5.5	44	5.7
Miami, FL	68	1.6	70	2.3	73	3.0	76	3.1	80	5.3	83	9.7	84	6.5	84	8.9	83	9.9	80	6.3	75	3.3	71	2.0
Milwaukee, WI	22	1.8	26	1.7	35	2.3	46	3.6	56	3.4	66	3.9	72	3.7	71	4.0	63	3.2	51	2.7	39	2.7	27	2.0
Minneapolis, MN	16	0.9	21	0.8	33	1.9	48	2.7	59	3.4	69	4.2	74	4.0	71	4.3	62	3.1	49	2.4	34	1.8	20	1.2
Mobile, AL	50	5.7	54	5.1	60	6.1	66	4.8	74	5.1	80	6.1	82	7.2	82	7.0	78	5.1	68	3.7	60	5.1	52	5.1
Moline, IL	23	1.5	27	1.6	39	2.9	51	3.6	62	4.3	72	4.5	75	4.3	74	4.5	65	3.1	53	3.0	40	2.6	27	2.2
Nashua, NH	24	3.7	27	3.2	35	4.3	46	4.0	57	2.9	66	4.3	71	3.7	70	4.5	62	3.4	50	4.7	40	4.1	30	3.7
Nashville, TN	38	3.8	42	3.9	50	4.1	59	4.0	68	5.5	76	4.1	79	3.6	79	3.2	72	3.4	60	3.0	50	4.3	40	4.2
New Orleans, LA	53	5.2	57	5.3	63	4.6	69	4.6	77	4.6	82	8.1	83	5.9	83	6.0	80	5.1	71	3.6	63	4.5	56	5.3
New York, NY*	33	3.7	35	3.1	43	4.4	53	4.5	62	4.2	71	4.4	77	4.6	75	4.4	68	4.3	57	4.4	48	4.0	38	4.0
Newark, NJ	32	3.5	35	2.9	42	4.2	53	4.2	63	4.1	72	4.0	77	4.8	76	3.7	68	3.8	57	3.6	47	3.7	37	3.8
Norfolk, VA	40	3.4	43	3.1	49	3.7	58	3.4	67	3.4	75	4.3	80	5.1	78	5.5	72	4.8	62	3.4	53	3.2	44	3.3
Oklahoma City, OK	39	1.4	44	1.6	52	3.1	61	3.1	70	4.7	78	4.9	83	2.9	82	3.3	74	4.1	63	3.7	51	2.0	41	1.9
Omaha, NE	24	0.7	28	0.9	40	2.0	52	3.0	62	4.8	72	4.2	77	3.8	75	3.8	66	2.7	53	2.2	39	1.6	26	1.0
Philadelphia, PA	33	3.0	36	2.7	44	3.8	54	3.6	64	3.7	73	3.4	78	4.4	77	3.5	69	3.8	58	3.2	48	3.0	38	3.6
Phoenix, AZ	56	0.9	60	0.9	65	1.0	73	0.3	82	0.1	91	0.0	95	1.1	94	1.0	88	0.6	77	0.6	64	0.7	55	0.9
Pittsburgh, PA	29	2.7	32	2.7	40	3.1	52	3.2	61	4.2	69	4.0	73	3.8	72	3.5	65	3.4	53	2.5	43	3.4	33	2.9
Portland, ME	22	3.4	26	3.3	34	4.2	44	4.3	54	4.0	63	3.8	69	3.6	68	3.1	60	3.7	49	4.9	39	4.9	29	4.0
Portland, OR	41	4.9	44	3.7	48	3.7	52	2.7	58	2.5	64	1.7	69	0.7	70	0.7	65	1.5	55	3.0	47	5.6	40	5.5
Providence, RI	29	3.9	32	3.3	39	5.0	49	4.4	59	3.6	68	3.6	74	3.3	72	3.6	65	3.9	54	3.9	45	4.5	34	4.2
Raleigh, NC	41	3.5	45	3.2	52	4.1	60	2.9	68	3.3	76	3.5	80	4.7	79	4.3	72	4.4	61	3.3	52	3.1	44	3.1
Rapid City, SD	25	0.3	27	0.4	35	0.9	45	1.8	55	3.2	65	2.5	73	1.9	72	1.6	61	1.3	48	1.4	35	0.5	25	0.4
Reno, NV	36	1.0	40	1.0	46	0.8	51	0.5	60	0.5	68	0.5	75	0.2	73	0.2	65	0.4	54	0.5	43	0.8	35	1.0
Richmond, VA	38	3.0	41	2.8	49	4.0	58	3.3	66	3.8	75	3.9	79	4.5	78	4.7	71	4.1	60	3.0	50	3.2	41	3.3
St. Louis, MO	32	2.4	36	2.2	46	3.3	57	3.7	67	4.7	76	4.3	80	4.1	79	3.0	70	3.1	59	3.3	47	3.9	35	2.8
Salt Lake City, UT	30	1.3	34	1.3	44	1.8	51	2.0	60	2.0	70	1.0	79	0.6	77	0.7	66	1.2	53	1.5	40	1.5	30	1.4
San Antonio, TX	52	1.8	56	1.8	62	2.3	69	2.1	77	4.0	82	4.1	85	2.7	85	2.1	80	3.0	71	4.1	61	2.3	53	1.9
San Diego, CA	57	2.0	58	2.3	59	1.8	62	0.8	64	0.1	66	0.1	70	0.0	72	0.0	71	0.2	67	0.6	61	1.0	57	1.5
San Francisco, CA	50	4.2	53	4.1	55	3.0	57	1.3	60	0.5	62	0.1	64	0.0	65	0.0	65	0.2	62	1.0	56	2.4	51	4.0
San Juan, PR	78	3.8	78	2.4	79	2.0	80	4.7	82	5.9	83	4.4	83	5.1	84	5.5	84	5.8	83	5.6	81	6.4	79	5.0
Santa Fe, NM	32	0.6	36	0.5	43	0.8	50	0.7	60	0.9	69	1.1	73	1.8	71	2.6	64	1.6	53	1.4	40	0.7	31	0.8
Savannah, GA	50	3.7	53	2.8	59	3.7	66	3.1	73	3.0	80	6.0	83	5.6	82	6.6	77	4.6	68	3.7	59	2.4	52	3.0
Seattle, WA	42	5.6	43	3.5	47	3.7	50	2.7	56	1.9	61	1.6	66	0.7	66	0.9	61	1.5	53	3.5	45	6.6	41	5.4
Spokane, WA	30	1.8	33	1.3	40	1.6	47	1.3	55	1.6	62	1.3	70	0.6	69	0.6	60	0.7	48	1.2	36	2.3	27	2.3
Springfield, MO	33	2.5	37	2.5	46	3.6	56	4.3	65	5.1	73	4.9	78	3.7	78	3.6	69	4.6	58	3.6	46	4.2	35	3.0
Tampa, FL	61	2.2	63	2.8	67	3.0	72	2.0	78	2.1	82	6.7	83	7.1	83	7.8	82	6.3	76	2.3	69	1.6	63	2.5
Washington, DC	36	2.8	39	2.6	47	3.5	57	3.1	66	4.0	75	3.8	80	3.7	78	2.9	71	3.7	60	3.4	50	3.2	40	3.1
Wilmington, DE	32	3.0	35	2.7	43	3.9	53	3.5	63	4.0	72	3.9	77	4.6	75	3.2	68	4.3	56	3.4	47	3.1	37	3.5
Windsor Locks, CT	26	3.2	30	2.9	38	3.6	49	3.7	60	4.4	69	4.4	74	4.2	72	3.9	64	3.9	52	4.4	42	3.9	32	3.4

Normal High and Low Temperatures, Precipitation in U.S. Cities

Source: National Climatic Data Center, NESDIS, NOAA, U.S. Dept. of Commerce

The normal temperatures and precipitation data given here are based on records for the period 1981-2010. The extreme temperatures are based on records from the time of each station's installation. (*) = City station. Other figures are for airport stations.

State	Station	NORMAL TEMPERATURE (°F) January Max.	January Min.	July Max.	July Min.	EXTREME TEMPERATURE (°F) Highest	Lowest	AVG. ANNUAL PRECIPITATION (in.)
Alabama	Mobile	61	40	91	73	105	3	66.15
Alaska	Anchorage	23	11	65	52	85	−34	16.58
Alaska	Barrow	−7	−20	47	35	79	−56	4.53
Alaska	Juneau	33	24	64	50	90	−22	62.27
Arizona	Phoenix	67	46	106	78	122	17	8.03
Arkansas	North Little Rock	50	33	92	73	111	−6	50.03
California	Los Angeles	65	49	74	64	110	23	12.82
California	San Francisco	56	44	72	55	106	20	20.65
Colorado	Denver	44	17	89	59	105	−19	14.92
Connecticut	Windsor Locks	35	18	85	63	102	−26	45.85
Delaware	Wilmington	40	25	86	68	103	11	43.08
District of Columbia	Washington–Reagan	43	29	88	71	105	−5	39.74
Florida	Jacksonville	65	41	92	73	105	7	52.39
Florida	Miami	76	60	91	77	98	30	61.90
Georgia	Atlanta	52	34	89	71	105	−8	49.71
Georgia	Savannah	60	39	92	73	105	3	47.96
Hawaii	Honolulu	80	66	88	75	95	53	17.10
Idaho	Boise	38	25	91	60	111	−25	11.73
Illinois	Chicago	31	17	84	64	104	−27	36.89
Indiana	Indianapolis	36	21	85	66	104	−27	42.44
Iowa	Des Moines	31	14	86	67	108	−26	36.01
Kansas	Dodge City	44	20	93	66	110	−21	21.60
Kentucky	Lexington	41	25	86	66	103	−21	45.17
Kentucky	Louisville	43	27	89	70	106	−22	44.91
Louisiana	New Orleans	62	45	91	75	102	11	62.66
Maine	Caribou	20	1	76	55	96	−41	38.49
Maine	Portland	31	13	79	59	103	−39	47.25
Maryland	Baltimore	41	24	87	67	105	−7	41.88
Massachusetts	Boston	36	22	81	65	102	−12	43.77
Michigan	Detroit	32	19	83	64	104	−21	33.47
Michigan	Grand Rapids	31	18	83	62	100	−22	38.27
Michigan	Sault Ste. Marie	23	8	76	54	98	−36	32.95
Minnesota	Duluth	19	2	76	55	97	−39	30.96
Minnesota	Minneapolis	24	8	83	64	105	−34	30.61
Mississippi	Jackson	56	35	92	72	107	2	54.14
Missouri	Kansas City	38	20	88	68	109	−23	38.86
Missouri	St. Louis	40	24	89	71	107	−18	40.96
Montana	Helena	33	13	86	54	105	−42	11.22
Nebraska	Omaha	33	14	87	66	114	−23	30.62
Nevada	Reno	46	25	92	58	108	−16	7.40
New Hampshire	Concord	31	10	82	58	102	−37	40.61
New Jersey	Atlantic City	42	25	86	67	106	−11	41.75
New Mexico	Albuquerque	47	26	90	66	107	−17	9.45
New York	Albany	31	15	82	61	100	−28	39.35
New York	Buffalo	31	19	80	62	99	−20	40.48
New York	New York–Central Park*	38	27	84	69	106	−15	49.94
North Carolina	Raleigh	51	31	90	70	105	−9	43.34
North Dakota	Bismarck	23	2	85	57	112	−44	17.85
Ohio	Cleveland	34	22	83	64	104	−20	39.14
Ohio	Columbus	37	23	85	66	102	−22	39.31
Oklahoma	Oklahoma City	50	29	94	72	110	−8	36.52
Oregon	Portland	47	36	81	58	107	−3	36.03
Pennsylvania	Philadelphia	40	26	87	69	104	−7	41.53
Pennsylvania	Pittsburgh	36	21	83	63	103	−22	38.19
Puerto Rico	San Juan	83	72	89	78	98	60	56.35
Rhode Island	Providence	37	21	83	64	104	−13	47.18
South Carolina	Charleston	59	38	91	73	105	6	51.03
South Dakota	Huron	27	7	86	61	112	−41	22.90
South Dakota	Rapid City	37	13	87	58	111	−31	16.29
Tennessee	Memphis	50	33	92	74	108	−13	53.68
Tennessee	Nashville	47	28	89	68	107	−17	47.25
Texas	Dallas-Fort Worth	56	36	96	75	113	−1	36.14
Texas	Houston	63	43	94	75	109	7	49.77
Utah	Salt Lake City	37	22	93	65	107	−30	16.10
Vermont	Burlington	27	10	81	60	101	−30	36.82
Virginia	Norfolk	48	33	87	72	105	−3	46.53
Virginia	Richmond	47	28	90	69	105	−12	43.60
Washington	Seattle-Tacoma	47	37	76	56	103	0	37.49
Washington	Spokane	34	25	83	56	108	−25	16.56
West Virginia	Charleston	43	26	85	66	104	−16	44.03
Wisconsin	Milwaukee	29	16	80	64	103	−26	34.76
Wyoming	Lander	33	10	87	56	101	−37	12.66

Mean annual snowfall (in.), selected cities: Based on climate normals 1981-2010: Albany, NY, 59.1; Anchorage, AK, 74.5; Boston, MA, 43.8; Burlington, VT, 81.2; Lander, WY, 91.4; Sault Ste. Marie, MI, 123.4.

Wettest spot: Mt. Waialeale in Kauai, HI, may be the rainiest place in the U.S. It has a recorded average annual rainfall of 460 in.

Temperature extremes: The highest temperature ever recorded under standard conditions in the U.S. was 134°F in Death Valley, CA, on July 10, 1913. The record low in the U.S. was −80°F at Prospect Creek, AK, Jan. 23, 1971.

Annual Climatological Data for U.S. Cities, 2017

Source: National Climatic Data Center, NESDIS, NOAA, U.S. Dept. of Commerce

Station	Elev. (ft)	TEMPERATURE (°F) Highest	Date	Lowest	Date	PRECIPITATION Total (in.)	Greatest in 24 hrs. (in.)	Date	Snowfall[1] Total snowfall (in.)	Greatest in 24 hrs. (in.)	Date	FASTEST WIND[2] MPH	Date	NO. OF DAYS Prec. 0.01 in. or more	Snow, sleet 1 in. or more
Albany, NY	281	95	6/12	−5	12/28	40.16	1.72	8/18	58.5	17.0	3/14	43	11/19	143	12
Albuquerque, NM	5,308	103	6/22	14	1/6	7.67	0.86	9/28-29	3.4	1.1	2/12	52	5/9	48	1
Anchorage, AK	222	76	7/23	−15	1/19+	18.66	0.95	8/12-13	72.0	10.3	1/21	31	10/25	123	19
Asheville, NC	2,174	91	7/22+	8	1/8	54.10	3.54	10/22-23	18.1	7.5	12/8	38	2/9	142	5
Atlanta, GA	974	94	7/26+	15	1/8	52.48	4.27	4/5	2.3	1.5	12/9	45	9/11	121	1
Atlantic City, NJ	117	97	7/13	0	1/9	50.48	5.81	7/28-29	17.7	6.0	1/7	43	1/23	118	5
Baltimore, MD	196	98	7/20	8	12/31	38.28	3.84	7/28-29	7.3	2.8	12/9	41	4/6	121	2
Barrow, AK	38	68	7/29	−36	1/19	8.52	0.64	7/23	47.0	4.2	5/25	45	1/5	132	10
Birmingham, AL	630	96	7/21	13	1/8	69.04	3.86	7/23-24	4.3	4.0	12/8	52	1/22	118	1
Bismarck, ND	1,654	103	7/5	−30	1/7	13.79	2.82	8/12-13	35.0	7.8	1/2	48	3/7	81	11
Boise, ID	2,861	104	7/8	−11	1/6	15.37	1.74	3/29-30	34.9	6.5	1/4	41	8/24	106	12
Boston, MA	180	95	6/13+	2	12/29	43.45	2.15	6/16-17	50.9	10.9	2/9	46	10/30	138	11
Buffalo, NY	717	91	9/25	−1	12/28	48.48	2.57	7/12-13	79.0	13.2	3/14	46	1/11	167	25
Burlington, VT	348	95	6/11	−10	12/30	39.90	2.14	6/29-30	105.9	17.8	3/14	41	10/30	171	25
Caribou, ME	626	91	6/11	−19	2/12	43.01	3.00	10/25-26	106.3	11.7	3/14	39	5/18	174	31
Charleston, SC	48	98	8/16	22	1/8	52.87	5.51	9/11	T	T	7/19	43	9/11	101	0
Cheyenne, WY	6,128	97	7/19	−17	1/6	15.16	1.65	5/18	70.2	11.0	5/18	58	1/10	103	17
Chicago, IL	658	95	9/23	−4	12/27	43.10	4.21	10/14-15	13.8	3.9	3/13	41	3/8	122	4
Cleveland, OH	805	94	9/25	3	12/31	43.80	2.60	6/30	44.8	3.6	3/2	47	3/8	165	18
Columbus, OH	812	93	6/16+	2	12/31	46.61	3.12	7/13-14	12.0	2.1	12/30	44	6/19	142	4
Dallas-Ft. Worth, TX	562	102	7/28	14	1/7	36.62	3.98	6/23-24	0.1	0.1	1/6	44	1/15	79	0
Denver, CO	5,382	100	7/19+	−7	1/6	11.69	1.62	5/17-18	17.2	2.8	10/9	49	8/4	74	7
Des Moines, IA	971	101	7/21	−15	12/31	30.25	1.71	8/21-22	17.2	2.6	2/8	44	5/17	107	8
Detroit, MI	631	93	9/26	−4	12/27	35.46	2.00	11/17-18	43.5	6.3	12/13	49	3/8	144	12
Duluth, MN	1,429	88	6/10	−26	12/31	36.78	2.13	6/29	72.6	10.6	10/27	47	9/22	147	24
Fairbanks, AK	464	90	6/9	−51	1/18	14.47	1.54	10/9-10	81.8	7.0	2/25	32	1/5	119	28
Fresno, CA	375	110	6/20	29	12/22	13.21	2.04	4/13	T	T	4/13	36	3/30	49	0
Grand Rapids, MI	788	96	9/23	−12	12/27	39.43	2.95	10/23-24	55.8	7.0	12/25	51	3/8	158	20
Helena, MT	3,867	102	7/8	−16	2/3	10.52	1.04	9/14-15	58.4	9.0	12/29	43	10/22	91	23
Honolulu, HI	18	91	9/6	58	10/24+	22.62	5.97	2/11	—	—	—	36	10/16	72	—
Houston, TX	107	100	7/29	21	1/7	79.69	18.09	8/26-27	0.7	0.6	12/8	37	8/28	107	0
Huron, SD	1,284	101	7/17	−31	12/31	20.64	3.87	9/23-24	29.4	5.7	3/12	56	7/19	88	11
Indianapolis, IN	797	93	9/22	−3	12/27	47.45	3.78	7/11	8.7	2.1	2/8	47	1/10	124	4
Jackson, MS	296	97	7/20	17	1/8+	61.77	7.17	4/2-3	—	—	—	41	6/16	124	—
Jacksonville, FL	34	96	8/16	26	1/8	70.11	9.04	9/10-11	T	T	5/31	—	—	105	0
Kansas City, MO	1,008	98	7/22+	−6	12/31	46.02	6.14	8/21-22	4.8	1.5	1/4	53	6/16	95	3
Knoxville, TN	982	96	7/22	7	1/8	51.88	2.71	4/22-23	3.2	1.3	1/7	45	5/27	134	2
Lexington, KY	984	94	7/22+	4	1/7	49.17	3.73	10/8	3.5	2.5	1/5	37	8/2	134	1
Los Angeles, CA	326	104	10/24	40	1/24	12.26	2.94	1/22	—	—	—	36	1/20	36	—
Louisville, KY	484	97	7/22+	8	12/27	44.56	3.82	9/1-2	2.8	2.3	1/5	43	3/1	111	1
Marquette, MI	1,415	88	9/24+	−18	12/28	42.71	2.27	10/24	160.7	9.1	2/24-25	—	—	193	50
Memphis, TN	286	99	7/21	13	1/8+	51.38	4.04	8/31	2.0	2.0	1/6	47	5/27	122	1
Miami, FL	29	98	5/28	47	12/14	83.12	5.61	7/12-13	—	—	—	53	9/10	130	—
Milwaukee, WI	680	95	9/22	−4	12/31+	34.09	1.86	6/28-29	23.6	8.7	3/13	44	3/8	137	7
Minneapolis, MN	874	96	7/15	−16	12/31	32.36	2.18	10/2	21.0	3.4	3/12	55	6/11	120	6
Mobile, AL	212	96	8/18	21	1/8	83.78	5.84	1/1	1.0	1.0	12/8	46	10/8	131	1
Moline, IL	607	95	6/13	−11	12/31	36.11	3.68	7/21-22	18.2	6.7	12/29	59	7/21	108	5
Nashville, TN	574	98	7/22+	8	1/8	52.92	3.31	11/6-7	1.9	1.5	3/11	37	4/30	123	1
New Orleans, LA	7	96	8/19	27	1/7	72.42	4.20	5/3-4	—	—	—	38	6/18	117	—
New York, NY	161	94	7/20	9	12/31	45.04	3.20	5/5-6	34.7	9.4	2/9	33	1/23	121	9
Newark, NJ	28	99	6/13	9	12/31	47.49	4.07	10/29-30	34.3	7.8	2/9	44	6/19	120	9
Norfolk, VA	69	100	7/14	16	1/10	49.16	3.93	8/20	5.4	5.3	1/7	38	3/1	110	1
North Little Rock, AR	565	96	7/25+	12	1/7	51.48	5.45	4/29-30	0.8	0.8	1/6	20	5/3	114	0
Oklahoma City, OK	1,284	103	7/22	−3	1/7	33.64	2.97	10/3-4	1.8	1.6	1/6	58	10/14	73	1
Philadelphia, PA	62	96	7/19	9	12/31	41.34	2.58	9/16	23.3	4.8	3/14	40	3/2	124	9
Phoenix, AZ	1,106	119	6/20	35	1/28	4.96	0.92	8/3	—	—	—	49	7/16	26	—
Pittsburgh, PA	1,175	91	9/27	0	12/31	42.15	1.71	11/18-19	37.2	3.9	12/30	41	2/12	163	15
Portland, ME	72	93	5/18	−13	12/30+	43.63	2.77	5/25-26	97.4	16.3	3/14	48	10/30	128	18
Portland, OR	223	105	8/3	11	1/13	45.80	2.45	10/21-22	—	—	—	44	4/7	160	—
Providence, RI	53	95	6/13+	4	12/31	49.00	2.55	5/5-6	46.6	11.9	2/9	46	10/29	136	10
Raleigh-Durham, NC	430	102	7/23	9	1/9	46.54	6.11	4/24-25	1.1	0.5	1/7	44	4/6	117	0
Rapid City, SD	3,153	106	7/9	−21	12/31+	11.29	1.39	8/14-15	29.6	3.5	1/24	59	6/27	98	13
Reno, NV	4,407	104	8/2	9	1/6	13.73	1.54	1/8-9	26.6	7.6	1/22	53	9/5	67	8
Richmond, VA	167	101	7/22	0	1/9	37.96	2.20	10/10-11	10.2	7.0	1/7	39	3/1	120	2
St. Louis, MO	710	108	7/22	2	12/31+	36.65	3.99	4/29-30	6.5	2.1	12/23	60	6/14	105	3
Salt Lake City, UT	4,224	105	7/5	−6	1/7	16.00	2.07	3/22-23	42.3	6.8	1/2	45	3/5	87	12
San Antonio, TX	821	105	7/30	19	1/8	27.33	3.31	8/7	1.9	1.9	12/7	39	5/30	74	1
San Diego, CA	81	98	10/25	41	12/22	7.92	2.35	2/26-27	—	—	—	40	2/17	32	—
San Francisco, CA	89	104	9/2+	38	12/22	25.24	2.21	2/19-20	—	—	—	47	1/8	70	—
San Juan, PR	10	94	9/24+	68	1/19	74.57	7.11	9/20	0.0	0.0	—	48	9/6	202	0
Sault Ste. Marie, MI	727	90	9/23	−16	12/28	43.03	3.47	8/17-18	135.5	6.2	2/10	35	1/10	191	43
Savannah, GA	143	98	8/16	26	3/16	53.24	6.97	5/22-23	T	T	5/22	44	9/11	103	0
Scottsbluff, NE	3,949	104	7/19+	−22	1/6	15.65	1.12	3/27-28	57.9	14.2	2/23	58	6/27	96	13
Seattle, WA	434	96	6/25	20	1/6	47.87	2.60	1/17-18	13.2	5.1	2/6	39	11/13	162	5
Spokane, WA	2,384	99	7/7	−4	1/14+	22.34	1.15	12/18-19	63.5	7.1	12/15	44	10/17	123	19
Springfield, MO	1,280	98	7/22	1	1/7	47.55	4.43	4/29-30	3.4	1.8	12/23	47	3/6	100	2
Tampa, FL	40	98	5/19+	34	1/8	44.32	4.50	9/10-11	0.0	0.0	—	52	10/4	104	0
Washington, DC	3	98	7/20	15	1/8	35.60	3.76	7/28-29	5.3	1.5	12/9	52	2/12	111	3
Wilmington, DE	79	95	6/13	8	12/31	39.90	2.93	7/23-24	16.8	4.1	12/9	44	2/13	121	6
Windsor Locks, CT	165	96	6/12	−3	12/31	45.58	4.63	10/24-25	60.4	15.8	3/14	43	3/2	139	10

(+) = Indicates value for extreme also occurred on an earlier date(s). (T) = Trace amount. — = Data not available or unreported. (1) Comprises all forms of frozen precipitation, including hail and sleet. (2) Sustained for at least 2 min., not peak gust.

Record Temperatures by State

Source: National Climatic Data Center, NESDIS, NOAA, U.S. Dept. of Commerce
(as of Apr. 9, 2018)

State	LOWEST TEMPERATURE °F	Date	Station	Approx. elevation (ft)	HIGHEST TEMPERATURE °F	Date	Station	Approx. elevation (ft)
Alabama	−27	Jan. 30, 1966	New Market	732	112	Sept. 6, 1925	Centreville	220
Alaska	−80	Jan. 23, 1971	Prospect Creek Camp	955	100	June 27, 1915	Fort Yukon	445
Arizona	−40	Jan. 7, 1971	Hawley Lake	8,180	128	June 29, 1994	Lake Havasu City	449
Arkansas	−29	Feb. 13, 1905	Gravette	1,260	120	Aug. 10, 1936	Ozark	390
California	−45	Jan. 20, 1937	Boca	5,575	134	July 10, 1913	Greenland Ranch	−194
Colorado	−61	Feb. 1, 1985	Maybell	5,944	114	July 11, 1954[1]	Sedgwick	3,584
Connecticut	−32	Jan. 22, 1961[1]	Coventry	480	106	July 15, 1995[1]	Danbury	405
Delaware	−17	Jan. 17, 1893	Millsboro	20	110	July 21, 1930	Millsboro	20
Florida	−2	Feb. 13, 1899	Tallahassee	192	109	June 29, 1931	Monticello	98
Georgia	−17	Jan. 27, 1940	CCC Fire Camp F-16	1,000	112	Aug. 20, 1983[1]	Greenville	960
Hawaii	12	May 17, 1979	Mauna Kea Observ.	13,773	100	Apr. 27, 1931	Pahala	840
Idaho	−60	Jan. 18, 1943	Island Park	6,290	118	July 28, 1934	Orofino	1,320
Illinois	−36	Jan. 5, 1999	Congerville	640	117	July 14, 1954	East St. Louis	410
Indiana	−36	Jan. 19, 1994	New Whiteland	785	116	July 14, 1936	Collegeville	650
Iowa	−47	Feb. 3, 1996[1]	Elkader	788	118	July 20, 1934	Keokuk	651
Kansas	−40	Feb. 13, 1905	Lebanon	1,841	121	July 24, 1936[1]	Alton	1,685
Kentucky	−37	Jan. 19, 1994	Shelbyville	730	114	July 28, 1930	Greensburg	590
Louisiana	−16	Feb. 13, 1899	Minden	185	114	Aug. 10, 1936	Plain Dealing	251
Maine	−50	Jan. 16, 2009	Big Black River	885	105	July 10, 1911[1]	North Bridgton	449
Maryland	−40	Jan. 13, 1912	Oakland	2,420	109	July 10, 1936[2]	Frederick	380
Massachusetts	−35	Jan. 12, 1981[1]	Chester	640	107	Aug. 2, 1975[3]	Chester	640
Michigan	−51	Feb. 9, 1934	Vanderbilt	905	112	July 13, 1936[3]	Stanwood	830
Minnesota	−60	Feb. 2, 1996	Tower	1,430	115	July 29, 1917	Beardsley	1,089
Mississippi	−19	Jan. 30, 1966	Corinth	385	115	July 29, 1930	Holly Springs	502
Missouri	−40	Feb. 13, 1905	Warsaw	705	118	July 14, 1954[2]	Warsaw	705
Montana	−70	Jan. 20, 1954	Rogers Pass	5,545	117	July 5, 1937[1]	Medicine Lake	1,942
Nebraska	−47	Dec. 22, 1989[1]	Oshkosh	3,390	118	July 24, 1936[1]	Minden	2,160
Nevada	−50	Jan. 8, 1937	San Jacinto	5,203	125	June 29, 1994	Laughlin	605
New Hampshire	−50	Jan. 22, 1885	Mt. Washington	6,271	106	July 4, 1911	Nashua	135
New Jersey	−34	Jan. 5, 1904	River Vale	31	110	July 10, 1936	Runyon	20
New Mexico	−50	Feb. 1, 1951	Gavilan	7,425	122	June 27, 1994	Waste Isolat. Pilot Plant	3,411
New York	−52	Feb. 18, 1979	Old Forge	1,748	108	July 22, 1926	Troy	35
North Carolina	−34	Jan. 21, 1985	Mt. Mitchell	6,240	110	Aug. 21, 1983	Fayetteville	186
North Dakota	−60	Feb. 15, 1936	Parshall	1,950	121	July 6, 1936	Steele	1,853
Ohio	−39	Feb. 10, 1899	Milligan	875	113	July 21, 1934	Gallipolis	569
Oklahoma	−31	Feb. 10, 2011	Nowata	NA	120	Aug. 12, 1936[1]	Altus Irrigation Res. Sta.	1,380
Oregon	−54	Feb. 10, 1933[1]	Seneca	4,659	119	Aug. 10, 1898[1]	Pendleton	1,040
Pennsylvania	−42	Jan. 5, 1904	Smethport	1,469	111	July 10, 1936[1]	Phoenixville	105
Rhode Island	−28	Jan. 11, 1942	Wood River Junction	49	104	Aug. 2, 1975	Providence	60
South Carolina	−19	Jan. 21, 1985	Caesars Head	3,200	113	June 29, 2012	Columbia	242
South Dakota	−58	Feb. 17, 1936	McIntosh	2,179	120	July 15, 2006[1]	Fort Pierre	1,590
Tennessee	−32	Dec. 30, 1917	Mountain City	2,503	113	Aug. 9, 1930[1]	Perryville	371
Texas	−23	Feb. 8, 1933	Seminole	3,336	120	June 28, 1994[1]	Monahans	2,547
Utah	−50	Jan. 5, 1913	East Portal	7,615	117	July 5, 1985	Saint George	2,857
Vermont	−50	Dec. 30, 1933	Bloomfield	1,040	107	July 7, 1912	Vernon	226
Virginia	−30	Jan. 21, 1985	Mountain Lake Bio. Station	3,870	110	July 15, 1954[1]	Balcony Falls	732
Washington	−48	Dec. 30, 1968	Winthrop	1,749	118	Aug. 5, 1961[1]	Ice Harbor Dam	368
West Virginia	−37	Dec. 30, 1917	Lewisburg	2,300	112	July 10, 1936[1]	Martinsburg	534
Wisconsin	−55	Feb. 4, 1996[1]	Couderay	1,300	114	July 13, 1936	Wisconsin Dells	835
Wyoming	−66	Feb. 9, 1933	Riverside Ranger Sta.	6,500	115	July 15, 1988[1]	Diversion Dam	5,590

NA = Not available. (1) Also on earlier dates at the same or other places. (2) Also at other places on the same date and on earlier dates at the same or other places. (3) Also at other places on the same date.

Tropical Cyclone Names in 2019

Source: National Weather Service, NOAA, U.S. Dept. of Commerce

NOAA's National Hurricane Center began using name lists in 1953. Presently, six lists, maintained by the World Meteorological Organization, are used in rotation. If there are more than 21 named Atlantic storms in one season, remaining storms take names from the Greek alphabet, starting with Alpha. (This was only necessary in one year: 2005.)

Atlantic: Andrea, Barry, Chantal, Dorian, Erin, Fernand, Gabrielle, Humberto, Imelda, Jerry, Karen, Lorenzo, Melissa, Nestor, Olga, Pablo, Rebekah, Sebastien, Tanya, Van, Wendy.

Eastern North Pacific: Alvin, Barbara, Cosme, Dalila, Erick, Flossie, Gil, Henriette, Ivo, Juliette, Kiko, Lorena, Mario, Narda, Octave, Priscilla, Raymond, Sonia, Tico, Velma, Wallis, Xina, York, Zelda.

World Temperature and Precipitation

Source: World Meteorological Organization (WMO)

Average daily maximum and minimum temperatures and annual precipitation based on records for the period 1961-90. Records of extreme temperatures include all available years of data for a given location and are usually for a longer period. Surface elevations are supplied by the WMO and may differ from figures in other sections of *The World Almanac*.

Station	Surface elevation (ft)	January Max.	January Min.	July Max.	July Min.	EXTREME Max.	EXTREME Min.	Avg. annual precipitation (in.)
Algiers, Algeria	82	61.7	42.6	87.1	65.3	NA	NA	27.0
Athens, Greece	49	56.1	44.6	88.9	73.0	NA	NA	14.6
Auckland, New Zealand	20	74.8	61.2	58.5	46.4	NA	NA	49.4
Bangkok, Thailand	66	89.6	69.8	90.9	77.0	104	51	59.0
Beijing, China	177	34.9	15.1	87.4	70.9	105	−17	22.7
Berlin, Germany	190	35.2	26.8	73.6	55.2	107	−4	23.3
Bogotá, Colombia	8,357	67.3	41.7	64.6	45.5	75	21	32.4
Bucharest, Romania	298	34.7	22.1	83.8	60.1	105	−18	23.4
Budapest, Hungary	456	34.2	24.8	79.7	59.7	103	−10	20.3
Buenos Aires, Argentina	82	85.8	67.3	59.7	45.7	104	22	45.2
Cairo, Egypt	243	65.8	48.2	93.9	71.1	118	34	1.0
Cape Town, South Africa	138	79.0	60.3	63.3	44.6	105	28	20.5
Caracas, Venezuela	2,739	79.9	60.8	81.3	66.0	96	45	36.1
Casablanca, Morocco	203	62.8	47.1	77.7	66.7	NA	NA	16.8
Copenhagen, Denmark	16	35.6	28.4	68.9	55.0	NA	NA	NA
Damascus, Syria	2,004	54.3	32.9	97.2	61.9	NA	NA	5.6
Dubai, United Arab Emirates[1]	16	75.2	56.7	105.1	84.0	117	45	3.7
Dublin, Ireland	279	45.7	36.5	66.0	52.5	86	8	28.8
Geneva, Switzerland	1,364	38.3	27.9	76.3	53.2	101	−3	35.6
Havana, Cuba	164	78.4	65.5	88.3	74.8	NA	NA	46.9
Hong Kong, China	203	65.5	56.5	88.7	79.9	97	32	87.2
Istanbul, Turkey	108	47.8	37.2	82.8	65.3	105	7	27.4
Jerusalem, Israel	2,483	53.4	39.4	83.8	63.0	107	26	23.2
Karachi, Pakistan	69	78.4	50.7	91.6	81.3	117	34	8.6
Lagos, Nigeria	125	90.0	72.3	82.8	72.1	NA	NA	59.3
Lima, Peru	43	79.0	66.9	66.4	59.4	NA	NA	0.2
London, England, UK	203	44.1	32.7	71.1	52.3	99	2	29.7
Manila, Philippines	79	85.8	74.8	89.1	76.8	NA	NA	49.6
Mexico City, Mexico	7,570	70.3	43.7	73.8	53.2	NA	NA	33.4
Montreal, Canada	118	21.6	5.2	79.2	59.7	100	−36	37.0
Mumbai (Bombay), India	36	85.3	66.7	86.2	77.5	110	46	85.4
Nairobi, Kenya	5,897	77.9	50.9	71.6	48.6	NA	NA	41.9
New Delhi, India[2]	709	69.8	45.7	94.5	80.2	113	34	31.3
Paris, France	213	42.8	33.6	75.2	55.2	105	−1	25.6
Prague, Czech Republic	1,197	32.7	22.5	73.9	53.2	98	−16	20.7
Reykjavik, Iceland	200	35.4	26.6	55.9	46.9	76	−3	31.5
Riyadh, Saudi Arabia	2,034	68.4	46.8	109.0	81.3	120	28	NA
Rome, Italy	79	53.8	35.4	88.2	62.1	NA	NA	33.0
San Salvador, El Salvador	2,037	86.5	61.3	86.2	66.4	105	45	68.3
São Paulo, Brazil	2,598	81.1	65.7	71.2	53.1	NA	NA	57.4
Seoul, South Korea	285	33.4	19.2	83.3	70.9	NA	NA	NA
Shanghai, China	23	45.9	32.9	88.9	76.6	104	10	43.8
Singapore	52	85.8	73.6	87.4	75.6	NA	NA	84.6
Stockholm, Sweden	171	30.7	23.0	71.4	56.1	97	−26	21.2
Sydney, Australia	10	79.5	65.5	62.4	43.9	114	32	46.4
Tehran, Iran	3,906	45.0	30.0	98.2	75.2	109	−5	9.1
Tokyo, Japan	118	49.1	34.2	83.8	72.1	NA	NA	55.4
Toronto, Canada	567	27.5	12.0	80.2	57.6	105	−26	30.8

NA = Not available. (1) Records are for 1974-91. (2) Records are for 1971-90.

Speed of Winds in the U.S.

Source: National Climatic Data Center, NESDIS, NOAA, U.S. Dept. of Commerce

Based on available records through 2017. Maximum speeds are highest 3-sec. wind speeds.

Station	Avg. mph	Max. mph	Station	Avg. mph	Max. mph	Station	Avg. mph	Max. mph
Albuquerque, NM	8.2	89	Helena, MT	6.9	68	Oklahoma City, OK	11.3	87
Anchorage, AK	6.9	71	Honolulu, HI	10.3	49	Omaha, NE	10.0	96
Atlanta, GA	8.3	71	Houston, TX	7.5	70	Philadelphia, PA	9.3	75
Baltimore, MD	7.2	72	Indianapolis, IN	9.5	85	Phoenix, AZ	6.1	77
Birmingham, AL	6.1	75	Jackson, MS	6.1	72	Pittsburgh, PA	7.8	62
Bismarck, ND	9.4	83	Jacksonville, FL	6.7	86	Portland, ME	7.9	72
Boise, ID	7.6	68	Little Rock, AR	7.0	87	Portland, OR	7.4	67
Boston, MA	11.5	76	Los Angeles, CA	7.5	53	Providence, RI	9.3	66
Buffalo, NY	10.3	75	Louisville, KY	7.8	75	Richmond, VA	7.7	72
Burlington, VT	8.3	63	Miami, FL	8.4	104	St. Louis, MO	9.1	71
Charleston, SC	7.9	69	Milwaukee, WI	10.2	70	Salt Lake City, UT	8.4	75
Chicago, IL	9.9	70	Minneapolis, MN	9.7	71	San Francisco, CA	10.5	71
Cleveland, OH	9.6	68	Mobile, AL	7.5	83	San Juan, PR	7.8	93
Dallas-Ft. Worth, TX	10.5	78	Mount Washington, NH	35.1	231	Seattle, WA	7.9	69
Denver, CO	10.0	74	Nashville, TN	7.1	67	Sioux Falls, SD	10.2	87
Des Moines, IA	9.8	77	New Orleans, LA	8.0	77	Washington, DC	8.9	74
Detroit, MI	9.4	78	New York, NY	6.5	62	Wichita, KS	11.5	101
Fairbanks, AK	4.4	59	Newark, NJ	9.8	78	Wilmington, DE	8.5	76

Wind Chill Temperature

Source: National Weather Service, NOAA, U.S. Dept. of Commerce

Temperature and wind combine to cause heat loss from body surfaces. For example, when the air temperature is 5°F, a 10-mph wind can cause body heat loss equal to that which could occur when the air temperature is –10°F with no wind. In other words, a 10-mph wind can make 5°F feel like –10°F. Wind speeds greater than 45 mph have little additional chilling effect. Direct sunlight can increase the wind chill temperature 10°F to 15°F. When the wind chill temperature falls within the shaded areas, frostbite can occur on exposed skin in the times indicated or less.

Calm	Air temperature (°F)																	
	40	35	30	25	20	15	10	5	0	–5	–10	–15	–20	–25	–30	–35	–40	–45
Wind speed (mph)	Wind chill temperature (°F)																	
5	36	31	25	19	13	7	1	–5	–11	–16	–22	–28	–34	–40	–46	–52	–57	–63
10	34	27	21	15	9	3	–4	–10	–16	–22	–28	–35	–41	–47	–53	–59	–66	–72
15	32	25	19	13	6	0	–7	–13	–19	–26	–32	–39	–45	–51	–58	–64	–71	–77
20	30	24	17	11	4	–2	–9	–15	–22	–29	–35	–42	–48	–55	–61	–68	–74	–81
25	29	23	16	9	3	–4	–11	–17	–24	–31	–37	–44	–51	–58	–64	–71	–78	–84
30	28	22	15	8	1	–5	–12	–19	–26	–33	–39	–46	–53	–60	–67	–73	–80	–87
35	28	21	14	7	0	–7	–14	–21	–27	–34	–41	–48	–55	–62	–69	–76	–82	–89
40	27	20	13	6	–1	–8	–15	–22	–29	–36	–43	–50	–57	–64	–71	–78	–84	–91
45	26	19	12	5	–2	–9	–16	–23	–30	–37	–44	–51	–58	–65	–72	–79	–86	–93

☐ 30 minutes   ☐ 10 minutes   ☐ 5 minutes

Heat Index

Source: National Weather Service, NOAA, U.S. Dept. of Commerce

The heat index, or apparent temperature, is a measure of how hot it feels when the relative humidity is factored in with the actual air temperature. For example, when air temperature is 100°F, and relative humidity is 50%, it can feel as if it's 118°F with no humidity. Full sunlight can make one feel even hotter. On the chart, the shaded areas indicate the likelihood of heat disorders with prolonged exposure or strenuous activity.

Relative humidity (%)	Air temperature (°F)																
	80	82	84	86	88	90	92	94	96	98	100	102	104	106	108	110	
	Apparent temperature (°F)																
40	80	81	83	85	88	91	94	97	101	105	109	114	119	124	130	136	
45	80	82	84	87	89	93	96	100	104	109	114	119	124	130	137		
50	81	83	85	88	91	95	99	103	108	113	118	124	131	137			
55	81	84	86	89	93	97	101	106	112	117	124	130	137				
60	82	84	88	91	95	100	105	110	116	123	129	137					
65	82	85	89	93	98	103	108	114	121	128	136						
70	83	86	90	95	100	105	112	119	126	134							
75	84	88	92	97	103	109	116	124	132								
80	84	89	94	100	106	113	121	129									
85	85	90	96	102	110	117	126	135									
90	86	91	98	105	113	122	131										
95	86	93	100	108	117	127											
100	87	95	103	112	121	132											

☐ Caution   ☐ Extreme caution   ☐ Danger   ☐ Extreme danger

Ultraviolet (UV) Index Forecast

Source: National Weather Service (NWS), NOAA, U.S. Dept. of Commerce; U.S. Environmental Protection Agency (EPA); U.S. Food and Drug Administration, U.S. Dept. of Health and Human Services

The NWS and EPA developed and began offering a UV index in 1994 in response to increasing incidences of skin cancer, cataracts, and other effects from exposure to the sun's harmful rays. In 2004, they adapted their index to the Global Solar UV Index sponsored by the World Health Organization. The UV index is now a regular element of NWS atmospheric forecasts. To see the UV index for a given location, visit www.epa.gov/enviro/uv-index-search. For questions on scientific aspects, visit the NWS Climate Prediction Center online at www.cpc.ncep.noaa.gov.

The UV index, ranging from 0 to 11+, is an indication of the expected intensity of UV radiation reaching the Earth's surface during the solar noon hour (the time of day, dependent on location and time of year, when the sun appears to have reached its highest point in the sky). The lower the UV index value, the less the expected radiation. The UV index forecast is produced daily for 58 cities by the NWS Climate Prediction Center.

UV levels are influenced by the following:

Ozone. Ozone, a form of oxygen, the molecules of which consist of three atoms rather than two, absorbs UV radiation. The more ozone, the lower the UV radiation at the surface.

Sun height. The higher the sun is in the sky, the higher the UV radiation level.

Cloudiness. UV radiation levels are highest under cloudless skies. Even with cloud cover, UV radiation levels can be high due to the scattering of UV radiation by water molecules and fine particles in the atmosphere.

Reflectivity. Reflective surfaces intensify UV exposure. White sand reflects about 15% of UV radiation that reaches it; sea foam, 25%; snow, as much as 80%; water, up to 100% depending on reflection angle.

Altitude. At higher altitudes, UV radiation travels a shorter distance to reach Earth's surface so there is less atmosphere to absorb the rays. For every 1,000 m (3,281 ft) one travels above sea level, UV levels increase by 10%-12%. Snow and lack of pollutants intensify UV exposure at higher altitudes.

Latitude. The closer a location is to the equator, the higher the UV radiation level.

Using the UV Forecast

UV index	Exposure	Protective actions
0-2	Low	UV-blocking sunglasses, SPF 30+ sunscreen; avoid bright surfaces
3-5	Moderate	Stay in shade near midday; protective clothing, hat, sunglasses
6-7	High	Reduce time in sun 10 AM-4 PM; seek shade; protective clothing, hat, sunglasses, sunscreen; avoid bright surfaces
8-10	Very high	Minimize time in sun 10 AM-4 PM; seek shade; protective clothing, hat, sunglasses, sunscreen; avoid bright surfaces
11+	Extreme	Avoid sun 10 AM-4 PM; seek shade; protective clothing, hat, sunglasses, sunscreen; avoid bright surfaces

Lightning

Source: National Weather Service, NOAA, U.S. Dept. of Commerce

Lightning is a powerful electric discharge, or spark, that can occur in the atmosphere when an imbalance of positive and negative charges develops. It can travel within a cloud, between clouds, between a cloud and clear sky, or between a cloud and the ground. Lightning generally accompanies rainstorms but it can also be seen with snowstorms, volcano eruption clouds, and violent forest fires. In a common form of cloud-to-ground lightning, a negatively charged area in a thunderstorm sends charges down toward positively charged objects. Lightning can travel miles away from the area of a storm.

The transfer of charges in lightning generates a huge amount of heat, sending the temperature in the channel to 50,000°F or more and causing the air within it to expand rapidly. The sound of that expansion is thunder. Sound travels more slowly than light, so lightning is usually observed before thunder is heard.

An estimated 25 mil cloud-to-ground lightning bolts happen in the U.S. each year. They killed an annual average of 44 people in 1988-2017. This is a small number compared to U.S. deaths from fire (about 3,400 in 2017) and motor vehicle crashes (more than 40,000 annually in recent years), but it is still significant. In comparison, tornadoes caused an average of 69 deaths a year and hurricanes an average of 47 over the same 30-year time period. According to the National Weather Service, 16 people were struck and killed by lightning in 2017; 86 more were injured.

Most lightning deaths and injuries occur in summer when people are outdoors. If outdoors, one should run to a safe building or vehicle when thunder is first heard, lightning is seen, or dark threatening clouds are observed developing overhead. Even while indoors, one is advised to stay away from windows and doors and to avoid contact with anything conducting electricity, including corded phones, computers and other electrical equipment, and tubs, showers, and other plumbing. One should stay inside until 30 min. after the last occurrence of lightning or thunder.

More information about lightning can be found online at www.lightningsafety.noaa.gov.

Global Temperature Extremes and Precipitation Records

Source: World Weather & Climate Extremes Archive, World Meteorological Organization (WMO) Commission for Climatology
(records in each category ranked from most to least extreme; as of Apr. 11, 2018)

Highest Temperature Extremes

Continent/area	Highest temp. (°F)	Place	Elevation (ft)	Date
North America	134	Death Valley, CA, U.S. (Greenland Ranch/Furnace Creek)	−179	July 10, 1913
Africa	131[1]	Kebili, Tunisia	125	July 7, 1931
Europe/Middle East/ Greenland	129	Tirat Tsvi, Israel	−722	June 21, 1942
Southwest Pacific	123	Oodnadatta, Australia	367	Jan. 2, 1960
South America	120	Rivadavia, Argentina	673	Dec. 11, 1905
Continental Europe	118.4	Athens, Greece (and Elefsina, Greece)	774	July 10, 1977
Antarctica	67.6	Signy Research Station (UK)	23	Jan. 30, 1982
Asia	NA[2]			

NA = Not available. (1) Previous record of 136.4°F set on Sept. 13, 1922, in El Azizia, Libya, was invalidated in Sept. 2012 after the WMO determined that an error had been made in recording the temperature. (2) Under investigation as of Apr. 2018.

Lowest Temperature Extremes

Continent/area	Lowest temp. (°F)	Place	Elevation (ft)	Date
Antarctica	−128.6	Vostok Station (Soviet Union/Russia)	11,220	July 21, 1983
Asia	−90	Verkhoyansk, Russia	350	Feb. 5 and 7, 1892
	−90	Oimekon, Russia	2,625	Feb. 6, 1933
Europe/Middle East/ Greenland	−87	Northice, Greenland	7,680	Jan. 9, 1954
North America	−81.4	Snag, Yukon, Canada	2,120	Feb. 3, 1947
Continental Europe	−72.6	Ust'-Shchugor, Russia	279	Dec. 31, 1978
South America	−27	Sarmiento, Argentina	879	June 1, 1907
Southwest Pacific	−14	Eweburn (now Ranfurly), New Zealand	1,388	July 17, 1903
Africa	−11	Ifrane, Morocco	5,364	Feb. 11, 1935
Australia	−9.4	Charlotte Pass, New South Wales	5,758	June 29, 1994

Highest Measured Average Annual Precipitation Extremes

Continent/area	Highest avg. (in.)[1]	Place	Elevation (ft)	Years in averaging period
Asia	467.4	Mawsynram, India	4,695	38
Southwest Pacific	460.0	Mt. Waialeale, Kauai, HI, U.S.	5,148	30
Africa	405.0	Debundscha, Cameroon	30	32
South America	354.0	Quibdo, Colombia	230	29
Australia	316.3	Bellenden Ker, Queensland	5,102	34
North America	276	Henderson Lake, British Columbia, Canada	12	15
Europe	180.8	Crkvice, Montenegro	3,461	30
Antarctica	>31.5[2]	Along coast of E and W and over the Antarctic Peninsula	...	3[3]

(1) Official greatest average annual precipitation. The frequently cited record of 523.6 in. in Lloro, Colombia (14 mi SE and at a higher elevation than Quibdo) is an estimate. (2) Water equivalent. (3) July 1996-June 1999.

Lowest Measured Average Annual Precipitation Extremes

Continent/area	Lowest avg. (in.)	Place	Elevation (ft)	Years in averaging period
South America	0.03	Arica, Chile	213	59
Antarctica	0.08	Amundsen-Scott South Pole Station (U.S.)	9,301	10
Africa	<0.1	Wadi Halfa, Sudan	590	39
North America	1.2	Batagues, Mexico	69	14
Asia	1.8	Aden, Yemen	63	50
Southwest Pacific	4.05	Troudaninna, Australia	46	42
Continental Europe	6.4	Astrakhan, Russia	66	25

OCEANOGRAPHY
Tides and Their Causes
Source: National Ocean Service, NOAA, U.S. Dept. of Commerce

The tides are natural phenomena involving the movement of waves in the Earth's large fluid bodies as a result of the gravitational attraction of the sun and moon. These two variable influences combined produce the complex recurrent cycle of the tides. Tides may occur in both oceans and seas; to a limited extent in large lakes and in the atmosphere; and, to a very minute degree, in the Earth itself. The length of time between succeeding tides can vary.

The tide-generating force represents the difference between (1) the centrifugal force produced by Earth's revolution around the common center-of-gravity of the Earth-moon system and (2) the gravitational attraction of the moon acting upon the Earth's overlying waters. The moon is about 390 times closer to Earth than is the sun. So despite its smaller mass, the moon's tide-raising force is two times greater.

The tide-generating forces of the moon and sun acting tangentially to the Earth's surface tend to cause a maximum accumulation of waters at two diametrically opposite points on the Earth's surface and to withdraw compensating amounts of water from all points 90° removed from these tidal bulges. As the Earth rotates beneath the maxima and minima of these tide-generating forces, a sequence of two high tides, separated by two low tides, is produced each lunar day (24 hr. and 50 min., the time it takes for a specific site on the Earth to rotate from an exact point under the moon to the same point under the moon) in what is called a **semidiurnal tide**. Each ocean basin reacts differently to tidal forces.

Twice each month, when the sun, moon, and Earth are directly aligned—the moon between the Earth and sun (at new moon) or on the opposite side of Earth from the sun (at full moon)—the sun and moon exert gravitational forces in a mutual or additive fashion. The highest high tides and lowest low tides, called **spring tides**, are produced at these times. At two positions 90° in between, the moon and sun's gravitational forces—imposed at right angles—counteract each other to the greatest extent, and the range between high and low tides is reduced, resulting in **neap tides**.

The inclination of the moon's monthly orbit and of the sun to the equator during Earth's yearly passage through its orbit produce a difference in the height of succeeding high and low tides, known as the diurnal inequality. In most cases, this produces a so-called **mixed tide**. In extreme cases, these phenomena may result in a **diurnal tide**, with only one high tide and one low tide each day. There are other monthly and yearly variations in the tides because of the elliptical shape of the orbits.

The range of tides in the open ocean is generally less than in the coastal regions, where the incoming tide can be augmented by the continental shelves, as well as by bays and estuaries. The largest tidal ranges in the world occur in the Bay of Fundy, Canada, where the range of tide reaches 53.5 ft. The highest tides in the U.S. occur near Anchorage, AK, with tidal ranges up to 40 ft.

In every case, actual high or low tide can vary considerably from the average as a result of weather conditions such as strong winds, abrupt barometric pressure changes, or prolonged periods of extreme high or low pressure.

Mean Ranges of Tide

Place	Ft	In.	Place	Ft	In.	Place	Ft	In.
Baltimore, MD.	1	2	Key West, FL	1	5	Provincetown, MA	9	3
Biloxi, MS	1	6	Los Angeles, CA.	3	10	St. Petersburg, FL	1	7
Boston, MA.	9	6	Miami Beach, FL	2	4	San Diego, CA	4	1
Charleston, SC.	5	3	New London, CT	2	7	San Francisco, CA	4	1
Eastport, ME.	18	4	New York, NY.	4	6	San Juan, PR.	1	1
Ft. Pulaski, GA	6	11	Newport, RI	3	6	Sandy Hook, NJ	4	8
Galveston, TX.	1	0	Philadelphia, PA.	6	1	Seattle, WA	7	8
Honolulu, HI	1	3	Portland, ME.	9	1	Washington, DC	2	9

Note: Mean range is the difference in height between mean high water and mean low water.

El Niño and La Niña
Source: National Weather Service, NOAA, U.S. Dept. of Commerce

El Niño is a climatically significant disruption of the ocean-atmosphere system characterized by large-scale weakening of trade winds and warming of surface layer waters in the central and eastern equatorial Pacific. The term *El Niño*, Spanish for "the little boy" or "the Christ Child," was originally used by fishing crews to refer to a warm ocean current that appeared around Christmas off the west coast of Ecuador and Peru lasting several months. The term has come to be reserved for exceptionally strong warm currents that bring heavy rains.

El Niño events generally occur at irregular intervals of two to seven years, at an average of once every three to four years. They typically last 12 to 18 months. The intensity of El Niño events varies depending on the area encompassed by the abnormally warm ocean temperatures. Some are strong, such as in 1982-83, 1997-98, and 2015-16. Others are considerably weaker, such as the 2009-10 event. The eastward extent of warmer-than-normal water varies from episode to episode.

El Niño influences weather around the globe, and its impacts are most clearly seen in the winter. During El Niño years, winter temperatures in the continental U.S. tend to be warmer than normal in the northern states and on the West Coast and cooler than normal in the Southeast. Conditions tend to be wetter than normal over central and southern California, the Southwest, and across much of the South, and drier than normal over the northern portions of the Rocky Mountains and in the Ohio Valley. Globally, El Niño brings wetter than normal conditions to Peru and Chile and dry conditions to Australia and Indonesia. It should be noted that El Niño is only one of a number of factors influencing seasonal variations of climate.

La Niña ("the little girl") is characterized by colder than normal sea surface temperatures in the equatorial Pacific. La Niña typically brings wetter, cooler conditions to the Pacific Northwest and drier, warmer conditions to much of the southern U.S. El Niño and La Niña are opposite phases of the El Niño-Southern Oscillation (ENSO) cycle, which involves a shift in tropical sea-level pressure between the Eastern and Western Hemispheres.

NOAA and other agencies monitor these events using satellites, weather balloons, and buoys in the Pacific Ocean. Numerical computer models of the ocean and atmosphere use these data to predict the onset and evolution of El Niño and La Niña. Following strong La Niña conditions in the Northern Hemisphere in fall and winter 2017-18, ENSO-neutral conditions returned in spring and summer 2018, with increasing chances for El Niño development by fall 2018.

DISASTERS

U.S. Weather and Climate Disasters by Type, 1980-2018

Source: National Centers for Environmental Information, National Oceanic and Atmospheric Administration, U.S. Dept. of Commerce
Does not include disasters causing under $1 billion in consumer price index-adjusted losses. As of July 9, 2018.

Disaster type	Number of events	Losses (bil)	Percent of total losses	Average cost (bil)	Deaths
Drought.................	25	$241.0	15.2%	$9.6	2,993[1]
Flooding	29	123.3	7.8	4.3	543
Freeze..................	9	29.8	1.9	3.3	162
Severe storm[2]............	99	219.0	13.8	2.2	1,612
Tropical cyclone	40	870.2	54.9	21.8	3,469
Wildfire	15	54.8	3.5	3.7	238
Winter storm..............	16	47.2	3.0	3.0	1,044
All disasters	**233**	**1,585.3**	**100.0**	**6.8**	**10,061**

Note: Tropical cyclones include hurricanes, tropical storms, tropical depressions, and associated storm surges and flooding. (1) Drought-associated deaths are the result of heat waves, which do not always occur with drought. (2) Figures do not include Texas hail storm in June 2018.

U.S. Weather and Climate Disasters, 2017

Source: National Centers for Environmental Information, National Oceanic and Atmospheric Administration, U.S. Dept. of Commerce

Does not include disasters causing under $1 billion in consumer price index-adjusted losses. The cumulative damage of billion-dollar disasters in 2017 easily surpassed the previous U.S. annual record of $214.8 billion (CPI-adjusted), established in 2005, which included Hurricanes Dennis, Katrina, Rita, and Wilma.

Date	Event and location	Losses (bil)	Deaths
Jan. 20-22	Tornado outbreak and storms, AL, southern CA, FL, GA, LA, MS, SC, TX	$1.1	24
Feb. 8-22	Flooding, northern and central CA	1.6	5
Feb. 28-Mar. 1	Tornado outbreak, AR, IN, IL, KY, MO, OH, TN..................................	1.9	6
Mar. 1-Dec. 31	Extreme drought, MT, ND, SD	2.6	0
Mar. 6-8	Tornado outbreak, AR, IL, IA, KS, MI, MN, MO, NE, NY, OH, WI	2.3	2
Mar. 14-16	Severe freeze, AL, FL, GA, KY, MS, NC, SC, TN, VA	1.0	0
Mar. 26-28	Hail, high winds, and storms, AL, KY, MS, OK, TN, TX	2.8	0
Apr. 25-May 7	Heavy rain and flooding, AR, IL, MO	1.7	20
May 8-11	Hail, high winds, and storms, CO, MO, NM, OK, TX	3.5	0
June 1-Dec. 31	Wildfires, firestorm, MT, CA, other Western states	18.4	54
June 9-11	Hail and high winds, MN, WI	2.4	0
June 12-16	Hail, high winds, and tornadoes, IL, IA, KS, MO, NE, NY, PA, TX, VA, WY	1.6	0
June 27-29	Hail, high winds, and tornadoes, IL, IA, NE	1.5	0
Aug. 25-31	Hurricane Harvey, 30-50 in. rainfall, TX	127.5	89
Sept. 6-12	Hurricane Irma, FL, SC, U.S. VI	51.0	97
Sept. 19-21	Hurricane Maria, PR, U.S. VI	91.8	65
2017 total	**16 events**	**312.6**	**362**

Note: Compiled using preliminary data, as of July 9, 2018, on damage-related losses and deaths, which are subject to revision.

Some Notable Aircraft Disasters Since 1937

Source: National Transportation Safety Board; World Almanac research

Particularly notable disasters are in bold. Asterisk (*) indicates number of deaths includes people on ground. As of Aug. 2018.

Date	Aircraft	Site of accident	Deaths
1937, May 6	**German zeppelin Hindenburg**	**Burned at mooring, Lakehurst, NJ**	**36***
1944, Aug. 23	U.S. Air Force B-24 Liberator bomber ...	Hit school, Freckleton, England, UK........................	61*
1945, July 28	U.S. Army B-25.	Hit Empire State Building after getting lost in fog, New York, NY...	14*
1952, Dec. 20	U.S. Air Force C-124	Crashed at Moses Lake, WA	87
1953, Mar. 3	**Canadian Pacific DH-106 Comet**	**Crashed on takeoff from Karachi, Pakistan; world's first fatal commercial passenger jet crash**	**11**
1953, June 18	U.S. Air Force C-124	Crashed, burned near Tokyo, Japan........................	129
1955, Oct. 6	United Airlines DC-4.................	Crashed in Medicine Bow Peak, WY	66
1955, Nov. 1	United Airlines DC-6.................	Bomb on board exploded near Longmont, CO.................	44[1]
1956, June 20	LAV (Venezuela) Super Constellation ...	Crashed into Atlantic off Asbury Park, NJ	74
1956, June 30	TWA Super Const., United DC-7	Collided over Grand Canyon, AZ..........................	128
1960, Dec. 16	United DC-8, TWA Super Const.	Collided over New York, NY, killing all 128 on planes, 6 on ground	134*
1962, Mar. 16	Flying Tiger (U.S.) Super Constellation ..	Vanished in W Pacific en route to Philippines from Guam........	107
1962, June 3	Air France Boeing 707	Crashed on takeoff from Paris, France......................	130
1962, June 22	Air France Boeing 707	Crashed in storm, Guadeloupe, French W Indies	113
1963, Feb. 1	Lebanese Middle East Airlines Vickers Viscount 754, Turkish Mil. Douglas C-47	Collided over Ankara, Turkey, killing all 17 on planes, 87 on ground.	104*
1963, Nov. 29	Trans-Canada Air Lines DC-8	Crashed after takeoff from Montreal, QC, Canada..............	118
1965, May 20	Pakistani Boeing 720	Crashed at airport in Cairo, Egypt	121
1966, Jan. 24	Air India Boeing 707	Crashed on Mont Blanc, France-Italy.......................	117
1966, Feb. 4	All-Nippon Boeing 727	Plunged into Tokyo Bay, Japan...........................	133
1966, Mar. 5	BOAC (British Overseas Airways Corp.) Boeing 707	Crashed into Mt. Fuji, Japan, after encountering severe turbulence	124
1966, Dec. 24	U.S. military-chartered CL-44..........	Crashed into village in S Vietnam.........................	129*
1967, Apr. 20	Globe Air Bristol Britannia	Crashed on approach to airport, Nicosia, Cyprus.	126
1967, July 19	Piedmont Boeing 727, Cessna 310	Collided over Hendersonville, NC.	82
1968, Apr. 20	S. African Airways Boeing 707	Crashed on takeoff from Windhoek, Namibia.................	122
1968, May 3	Braniff International Electra	Crashed in storm near Dawson, TX	85
1968, May 12	U.S. Air Force Lockheed C-130B	Hit by enemy mortar while evacuating Kham Duc Camp, S Vietnam..	155
1969, Mar. 16	VIASA DC-9	Crashed after takeoff from Maracaibo, Venezuela.............	155[2]
1970, July 3	British-chartered DH-106 Comet	Crashed near Barcelona, Spain	112
1970, July 5	Air Canada DC-8	Crashed near Toronto Intl. Airport, ON, Canada.	108
1970, Nov. 14	Southern Airways DC-9	Crashed into mountains near Huntington, WV	75[3]
1971, July 30	All-Nippon Boeing 727, Japan Air Force F-86 fighter.........	Collided over Morioka, Japan............................	162[4]

Date	Aircraft	Site of accident	Deaths
1971, Sept. 4	Alaska Airlines Boeing 727	Crashed into mountain near Juneau, AK	111
1972, May 18	Aeroflot Antonov 10A	Wings separated from fuselage; crashed on approach to Kharkov, USSR	122
1972, June 18	British European Airways Trident-1C	Crashed near Staines after takeoff from London, Eng., UK	118
1972, Aug. 14	East German Ilyushin 62	Crashed on takeoff from East Berlin, E Germany	156
1972, Aug. 31	Aeroflot Ilyushin 18V	Crashed in field near Magnitogorsk, USSR	101
1972, Oct. 1	Aeroflot Ilyushin 18V	Crashed into Black Sea, USSR	109
1972, Oct. 13	Aeroflot Ilyushin 62	Crashed near Moscow, USSR	174
1972, Dec. 3	Spanish-chartered Convair CV-990	Crashed on takeoff from Canary Islands, Spain	155
1972, Dec. 29	Eastern Airlines Lockheed L-1011 TriStar	Crashed on approach to Miami Intl. Airport, FL	99
1973, Jan. 22	Nigerian-chartered Boeing 707	Burst into flames upon landing at Kano Airport, Nigeria	176
1973, Feb. 21	**Libyan Arab Boeing 727**	**Flew off course, shot down by Israeli fighter planes over Sinai Desert**	**108**
1973, Apr. 10	Invicta Airlines (UK) Vickers Vanguard	Crashed during snowstorm on approach to Basel, Switzerland	108
1973, June 3	Soviet Supersonic Tu-144	Crashed near Goussainville, France	14[5]
1973, July 11	Varig Airlines (Brazil) Boeing 707	Crashed on approach to Orly Airport, Paris, France	123
1973, July 31	Delta Airlines DC-9	Crashed while attempting landing in fog, Logan Airport, Boston, MA	89
1973, Sept. 30	Aeroflot Tupolev 104B	Crashed after takeoff from Sverdlovsk, USSR	108
1973, Oct. 13	Aeroflot Tupolev 104B	Crashed on approach to Moscow, USSR	122
1973, Dec. 22	Royal Air Maroc SE 210 Caravelle VIN	Flew into side of a mountain near Tangier, Morocco	106
1974, Mar. 3	Turkish DC-10	Crashed in Ermenonville, near Paris, France	346
1974, Apr. 22	Pan American (U.S.) Boeing 707	Crashed in Bali, Indonesia	107
1974, Apr. 27	Aeroflot Ilyushin 18V	Crashed after takeoff from Leningrad, USSR	109
1974, Dec. 1	TWA Boeing 727	Crashed on approach in storm, Upperville, VA	92
1974, Dec. 4	Dutch-chartered DC-8	Crashed in storm near Colombo, Sri Lanka	191
1975, Apr. 4	U.S. Air Force Galaxy C-5A	Crashed on takeoff nr. Saigon, S Vietnam; carried orphans	155
1975, June 24	Eastern Airlines 727	Crashed in storm, JFK Airport, New York, NY	113
1975, Aug. 3	Alia Royal Jordanian Boeing 707	Hit mountainside in heavy fog near Agadir, Morocco	188
1975, Aug. 20	Czechoslovakian Air Ilyushin 62	Crashed on approach to Damascus, Syria	126
1976, Mar. 6	Aeroflot Ilyushin 18E	Crashed between Moscow, USSR, and Yerevan, Armenia	111
1976, Sept. 10	British Airways Trident, Inex Adria DC-9	Collided near Zagreb, Yugoslavia	176
1976, Sept. 19	Turkish Boeing 727	Hit mountain in southern Turkey	154
1976, Oct. 13	Lloyd Aero Boliviano Boeing 707	Crashed into soccer field after takeoff from Santa Cruz, Bolivia	91[6]
1977, Mar. 27	**KLM (Neth.) 747, Pan American (U.S.) 747**	**Collided on foggy runway, Tenerife, Canary Islands, Spain**	**583**
1977, Nov. 19	TAP Portugal Boeing 727	Crashed in Madeira, Portugal	131
1977, Dec. 4	Malaysian Airlines Boeing 737	Hijacked and forced to fly to Singapore, crashed near Johor Strait	100
1978, Jan. 1	Air India 747	Crashed into sea after takeoff from Bombay, India	213
1978, Sept. 25	Pacific SW Air Boeing 727, Cessna 172	Collided over San Diego, CA	144*
1978, Nov. 15	Indonesian-chartered DC-8	Crashed on approach to airport, Colombo, Sri Lanka	183
1979, May 25	**American Airlines DC-10**	**Crashed after takeoff from O'Hare Airport, Chicago, IL; highest death toll in U.S. aviation history**	**275***
1979, Aug. 11	Aeroflot/Moldova Tu-134, Aeroflot Tu-134	Collided over Ukraine	178
1979, Nov. 26	Pakistani Boeing 707	Crashed near Jidda, Saudi Arabia	156
1979, Nov. 28	Air New Zealand DC-10	Crashed into Mt. Erebus during Antarctica flyover	257
1980, Mar. 14	PLL LOT Ilyushin 62	Crashed making emergency landing, Warsaw, Poland	87[7]
1980, Apr. 25	Dan-Air Services (UK) Boeing 727	Crashed into mountain, Tenerife, Canary Islands, Spain	146
1980, July 8	Aeroflot Tupolev 154B	Crashed after takeoff from Alma-Ata, USSR	166
1980, Aug. 19	Saudi Arabian Lockheed TriStar	Returned to Riyadh airport after fire on board; evacuation delayed	301
1981, Dec. 1	Inex Adria (Yugoslavia) DC-9	Crashed into mountain on island of Corsica, France	180
1982, Jan. 13	Air Florida Boeing 737	Crashed into bridge, Potomac R. after takeoff from Washington, DC	78*
1982, June 8	VASP (Brazil) Boeing 727	Crashed into mountain near Fortaleza, Brazil	137
1982, June 28	Aeroflot Yakovlev 42	Crashed near Mozyr, USSR	132
1982, July 9	Pan Am Boeing 727	Crashed after takeoff from Kenner, LA, near New Orleans	153*
1983, July 11	Ecuadorean Boeing 737	Inexperienced pilot crashed into hill near Cuenca, Ecuador	119
1983, Sept. 1	**S. Korean Boeing 747**	**Shot down after entering restricted Soviet airspace near Sakhalin; plane apparently misidentified**	**269**
1983, Sept. 23	Gulf Air Boeing 737	Bomb exploded in cargo hold over Mina Jebel Ali, UAE	112
1983, Nov. 27	Avianca Boeing 747	Crashed near Barajas Airport, Madrid, Spain	181
1984, Oct. 11	Aeroflot/East Siberia Tu-154	Crashed into vehicles on runway while landing in poor weather, Omsk, Russia	178*
1985, Feb. 19	Spanish Boeing 727	Crashed into Mt. Oiz, Spain	148
1985, June 23	Air India Boeing 747	Crashed into Atlantic off Ireland after bomb detonated on board	329
1985, July 10	Aeroflot Tupolev 154B	Crashed after takeoff from Uzbekistan, USSR	200
1985, Aug. 2	Delta Air Lines Lockheed L-1011 TriStar	Crashed after encountering microburst near Dallas-Ft. Worth Airport, TX	135*
1985, Aug. 12	**Japan Air Lines Boeing 747**	**Crashed into Mt. Ogura, Japan; world's worst single-plane disaster**	**520**
1985, Dec. 12	Arrow Air (U.S.) DC-8	Crashed after takeoff from Gander, NL, Canada	256[8]
1986, Mar. 31	Mexican Boeing 727	Crashed NW of Mexico City, Mexico	167
1986, Aug. 31	Aeromexico DC-9, Piper PA-28	Collided over Cerritos, CA	82*
1987, May 9	Polish IL-62M	Crashed after takeoff from Warsaw, Poland	183
1987, Aug. 16	Northwest Airlines MD-82	Crashed after takeoff from Romulus, MI	156
1987, Nov. 28	S. African Boeing 747	Crashed into Indian Ocean near Mauritius	159
1987, Nov. 29	Korean Air Boeing 707	Bomb planted by 2 N. Korean agents exploded while plane over Andaman Sea off Burma	115
1988, Mar. 17	Colombian Boeing 707	Crashed into mountainside near Venezuela border	143
1988, July 3	**Iran Air Airbus A300**	**Misidentified as hostile aircraft, shot down by U.S. Navy warship *Vincennes* over Persian Gulf**	**290**
1988, Oct. 19	Indian Airlines Boeing 737	Exploded after striking trees near runway, Ahmedabad, India	131
1988, Dec. 21	**Pan Am (U.S.) Boeing 747**	**Libyan agent planted bomb on board; exploded over Lockerbie, Scotland**	**270[9]**
1989, Feb. 8	U.S.-chartered Boeing 707	Crashed into mountain on Azores Isls., off Portugal	144
1989, June 7	Surinam Airways DC-8	Crashed near Paramaribo Airport, Suriname	176
1989, July 19	United Airlines DC-10	Crashed on landing in Sioux City, IA	111

Date	Aircraft	Site of accident	Deaths
1989, Sept. 3	Cubana Aviacion Ilyushin 62M	Crashed on takeoff from Havana, Cuba	171*
1989, Sept. 19	**UTA (France) DC-10**	**Bomb exploded on board flight from Chad to France while over desert in Niger**	**170**
1989, Oct. 21	TAN-SAHSA (Honduras) Boeing 727	Crashed into mountain near Tegucigalpa, Honduras	131
1989, Nov. 27	Avianca (Colombia) Boeing 727	Bomb exploded on flight from Bogotá, Colombia	107
1990, Jan. 25	Avianca (Colombia) Boeing 707	Crashed on landing at JFK Airport, New York, NY	73
1990, Oct. 2	Xiamen Airlines Boeing 737	Hijacked after takeoff from Xiamen; collided with China Southern Airlines 757 on runway during emergency landing, Guangzhou, China	128
1991, May 26	Lauda Air (Austria) Boeing 767-300	Broke up following takeoff from Bangkok, Thailand	223
1991, July 11	Nigeria Airways DC-8	Crashed on landing at Jidda, Saudi Arabia	261
1991, Oct. 5	U.S. Air Force Lockheed C-130 Hercules	Crashed after takeoff from Jakarta, Indonesia	135*
1992, July 31	Thai Airbus A300-310	Crashed into mountain N of Kathmandu, Nepal	113
1992, Sept. 26	Nigerian Air Force LC-130 Hercules	Transport full of military officers crashed near Lagos, Nigeria	158
1992, Sept. 28	Pakistan Intl. Air Airbus A300	Crashed into hillside near Kathmandu, Nepal	167
1992, Oct. 4	**El Al (Israel) Boeing 747-200F**	**Crashed into 2 apartment bldgs., Amsterdam, Netherlands**	**120***
1992, Nov. 24	China Southern Airlines Boeing 737	Crashed on approach to Giulin, China	141
1992, Dec. 22	Libyan Arab Air Boeing 727	Collided with Libyan Air Force MiG-23 on approach to Tripoli, Libya	159
1993, Feb. 8	Iran Air Tu-154, Iranian Air Force jet	Collided after military jet took off from Tehran, Iran	131
1993, May 19	SAM Colombia Boeing 727	Crashed into mountain near Medellín, Colombia	132
1993, Nov. 20	Macedonian Yakovlev 42D	Crashed into mountain near Skopje, Macedonia	116
1994, Jan. 3	Aeroflot Tu-154	Crashed and exploded after takeoff from Irkutsk, Russia	125*
1994, Apr. 26	China Airlines Airbus A300	Crashed on approach to Nagoya Airport, Japan	264
1994, June 6	China Northwest Airlines Tu-154	Crashed near Xian, China	160
1994, Sept. 8	USAir Boeing 737-300	Crashed near Pittsburgh Intl. Airport, Aliquippa, PA.	132
1994, Oct. 31	American Eagle ATR-72-210	Crashed in field near Roselawn, IN	68
1995, Dec. 18	Zairean Lockheed L-188C Electra	Overloaded charter crashed in Lunda Norte, Angola	141
1995, Dec. 20	American Airlines Boeing 757	Crashed into mountain N of Cali, Colombia	159
1996, Jan. 8	African Air Antonov-32 cargo plane	Crashed into a market in Kinshasa, Zaire; all deaths on ground	237*
1996, Feb. 6	Alas Nacionales (Dom. Rep.) Boeing 757	Crashed into Atlantic off Dominican Republic	189
1996, Feb. 29	Faucett (Peru) Boeing 737	Crashed into hillside near Arequipa, Peru	123
1996, Apr. 3	U.S. Air Force Boeing T-43A	Crashed into mountain near Dubrovnik, Croatia	35[10]
1996, May 11	ValuJet DC-9	Crashed into Florida Everglades after improper cargo started fire.	110
1996, July 17	Trans World Airlines Boeing 747	Exploded and crashed into Atlantic off Long Island, NY.	230
1996, Aug. 29	Vnukovo Airlines (Russia) Tu-154	Crashed into mountain on Arctic island of Spitsbergen	141
1996, Nov. 7	ADC Airlines (Nigeria) Boeing 727	Crashed into lagoon SE of Lagos, Nigeria	144
1996, Nov. 12	**Saudi Arabian Boeing 747, Kazakh Ilyushin 76 cargo plane**	**Collided near New Delhi, India; world's worst midair collision**	**349**
1996, Nov. 23	Ethiopian Airlines Boeing 767	Hijacked; crashed into Indian O. off the Comoros (fuel ran out)	127
1997, Aug. 6	Korean Air Boeing 747-300	Crashed into jungle on Guam on approach to airport.	228
1997, Sept. 26	Indonesian Airbus A300	Crashed near airport, Medan, Indonesia	234
1998, Feb. 16	China Airlines Airbus A300	Crashed on approach to airport in Taipei, Taiwan	203*
1998, Sept. 2	Swissair MD-11	Crashed into Atlantic off Nova Scotia, Canada, after onboard fire.	229
1999, Oct. 31	EgyptAir Boeing 767	Crashed off Nantucket, MA; result of deliberate actions by copilot, motives unknown	217
2000, Jan. 30	Kenya Airways Airbus A310	Crashed into Atlantic after takeoff from Abidjan, Côte d'Ivoire	169
2000, Jan. 31	Alaska Airlines MD-83	Crashed into Pacific off coast of Southern CA	88
2000, Apr. 19	Air Philippines Boeing 737-200	Crashed on approach to airport, Davao, Philippines	131
2000, July 25	**Air France Concorde**	**Crashed into hotel after takeoff from Paris; world's first Concorde crash**	**113***
2000, Aug. 23	Gulf Air Airbus A320	Crashed into Persian Gulf on approach to airport in Bahrain	143
2001, July 3	Vladivostokavia Tu-154	Crashed on approach to airport, Irkutsk, Russia	145
2001, Sept. 11	**2 Boeing 767s, 2 Boeing 757s**	**September 11 terrorist attacks**	**265[11]**
2001, Oct. 8	Cessna 525A Citation, Scandinavian Airlines System (SAS) MD-87	Collided in heavy fog on takeoff from Milan, Italy	118*
2001, Nov. 12	**American Airlines Airbus A300**	**Crashed after takeoff from JFK Airport, New York, NY**	**265***
2002, Feb. 12	Iran Air Tours Tu-154	Crashed into mountain on approach to airport, Khorramabad, Iran	119
2002, Apr. 15	Air China Boeing 767	Crashed into mountainside in rain and fog on approach to airport, Pusan, S. Korea	129
2002, May 4	EAS Airlines BAC 1-11	Crashed shortly after takeoff from Kano, Nigeria	149
2002, May 7	China Northern Airlines MD-82	Plunged into sea, apparently after a passenger started fire in cabin, NE China	112
2002, May 25	China Airlines Boeing 747	Broke apart in midair, plunged into Taiwan Strait en route to Hong Kong airport	225
2002, July 27	**Ukraine Air Force Sukhoi Su-27**	**Crashed while performing, Lviv, Ukraine; world's worst air-show crash**	**77[12]**
2002, Aug. 19	Russian Mi-26 transport helicopter	Hit by Chechen missile near Grozny, Chechnya	127
2003, Jan. 8	Turkish Airlines British Aerospace RJ-100	Crashed on approach to airport in Diyarbakir, Turkey	75
2003, Feb. 19	Iranian Revolutionary Guard Ilyushin 76	Crashed into mountain near Kerman, Iran; passengers were Revolutionary Guard members.	275
2003, May 26	Ukrain.-Medit. Airlines Yak-42	Crashed into mountain in fog approaching Trabzon, Turkey; passengers incl. Spanish peacekeepers returning from Afghan.	75
2003, July 8	Sudan Airways Boeing 737-200	Mechanical problems reported shortly after takeoff; crashed upon return to Port Sudan Airport.	115
2003, Dec. 25	Union Transp. Africains Boeing 727	Overloading caused crash on takeoff from Cotonou, Benin.	141
2004, Jan. 3	Flash Airlines Boeing 737-300	Crashed into Red Sea after takeoff from Sharm el Sheikh, Egypt.	148
2004, Aug. 24	Volga-Aviaexpress Tu-134, Sibir Airlines Tu-154	2 planes that took off from Moscow crashed within minutes of each other; brought down by Chechen suicide bombers	90
2005, Aug. 14	Helios Airways Boeing 737-300	Crashed after air pressure failure on board, near Athens, Greece.	121
2005, Aug. 16	West Caribbean Airways (Colombia) MD-82	Crashed after engine failure, near Machiques, Venezuela.	160

Date	Aircraft	Site of accident	Deaths
2005, Sept. 5	Mandala Airlines Boeing 737-200	Crashed shortly after takeoff from Medan, Sumatra, Indonesia	145*
2005, Oct. 22	Bellview Airlines Boeing 737-200	Crashed during heavy electrical storm near Lagos, Nigeria	117
2005, Dec. 6	Islamic Rep. of Iran Air Force Lockheed C-130	Crashed into apartment building after reportedly attempting emergency landing back at airport, Tehran, Iran	116*
2005, Dec. 10	Sosoliso Airlines DC-9-30	Crashed during storm on approach to Port Harcourt, Nigeria	107
2006, May 3	Armavia Airbus A320	Crashed into Black Sea on approach to airport, Sochi, Russia	113
2006, July 9	S7 Airlines Airbus A310	Skidded off runway, crashed into concrete barrier after landing, Irkutsk, Russia	125
2006, Aug. 22	Pulkovo Aviation Tu-154	Crashed after encountering storm, near Donetsk, Ukraine	170
2006, Sept. 29	Gol Airlines Boeing 737	Crashed into Amazon jungle after midair collision with Embraer Legacy jet (which itself landed safely), Brazil	154
2007, May 5	Kenya Airways Boeing 737-800	Crashed shortly after takeoff from Douala, Cameroon	114
2007, July 17	TAM Airlines Airbus 320	Crashed into cargo depot, gas station after skidding off airport runway, São Paulo, Brazil	199*
2008, Aug. 20	Spanair Boeing-MD-82	Swerved off runway, caught fire on takeoff attempt, Madrid, Spain	154
2009, Feb. 12	Colgan Air Bombardier Dash 8 Q400	Crashed into house after pilot error caused stall near Buffalo, NY, airport	50*
2009, June 1	**Air France Airbus A330**	**Plunged into Atlantic Ocean en route from Rio de Janeiro, Brazil, to Paris, France**	**228**
2009, June 29	Yemenia Airbus A310-300	Fell into Indian Ocean on approach to Moroni, Comoros	152
2009, July 15	Caspian Airlines Tupolev 154	Crashed after takeoff from Tehran, Iran	168
2010, Apr. 10	Polish Air Force Tupolev 154M	Crashed on approach to Smolensk Air Base, killing Polish Pres. Lech Kaczynski, his wife, and several members of parliament	96
2010, May 12	Afriqiyah Airways Airbus A330-200	Crashed short of runway in Tripoli, Libya	103
2010, May 22	Air India Express Boeing 737-800	Overran runway on landing at Mangalore, India	158
2010, July 28	Airblue Airbus 321-231	Crashed into Margalla Hills near Islamabad, Pakistan	152
2012, Apr. 20	Bhoja Airlines Boeing 737-236	Crashed on approach to airport in Islamabad, Pakistan	127
2012, June 3	Dana Air MD-83	Crashed into residential area of Lagos, Nigeria	163*
2014, Mar. 8	Malaysia Airlines Boeing 777	Disappeared over southern Indian O. en route from Kuala Lumpur to Beijing	239
2014, July 17	Malaysia Airlines Boeing 777	Shot down by Russian missile over disputed eastern Ukraine	298
2014, July 24	Air Algérie Boeing-MD-83	Crashed in desert near Gossi, Mali	116
2014, Dec. 28	Indonesia AirAsia Airbus A320-216	Disappeared over Java Sea between Surabaya and Singapore	162
2015, Mar. 24	Germanwings Airbus A320-211	Copilot deliberately crashed aircraft into French Alps	150
2015, June 30	Indonesian Air Force Lockheed C-130B	Transport plane crashed near Medan Soewondo Air Force Base	139*
2015, Oct. 31	Metrojet Airbus A321-231	Bomb on board detonated after takeoff from Sharm el Sheikh, Egypt	224
2016, Nov. 28	LaMia (Bolivia) Avro RJ85	Ran out of fuel and crashed near Medellín, Colombia; passengers incl. Brazilian Chapecoense soccer team	71
2016, Dec. 25	Russian Air Force Tupolev 154B-2	Crashed into Black Sea after takeoff from Sochi, Russia	92
2017, June 7	Myanmar Air Force Shaanxi Y-8-200F	Crashed into Andaman Sea en route to Yangon, Myanmar	122
2018, Apr. 11	Algerian military transport Ilyushin 76	Crashed after takeoff from near Algiers; passengers included Western Sahara separatists, refugees	257
2018, May 18	Cubana de Aviación Boeing 737	Aging aircraft crashed after takeoff from Havana, Cuba	112

(1) Bomb was planted by Jack G. Graham in insurance plot to kill his mother, Daisie E. King, a passenger. (2) 84 on plane, 71 on ground killed. (3) Incl. 43 Marshall Univ. (WV) football players and coaches. (4) Fighter pilot parachuted to safety. (5) First supersonic plane crash; killed 8 on ground. (6) Crew of 3, 88 on ground killed. (7) Incl. 22 members of U.S. amateur boxing team. (8) Incl. 248 members of U.S. 101st Airborne Division. (9) Incl. 11 on ground. (10) Incl. U.S. Sec. of Commerce Ron Brown. (11) 4 planes were hijacked and crashed, with all on board killed (265, incl. 19 hijackers). American Airlines Flight 11, a Boeing 767-200, with 81 passengers, 11 crew, crashed into Tower 1 of World Trade Center (WTC); United Airlines Flight 175, a Boeing 767-200, with 56 passengers, 9 crew, crashed into Tower 2 of WTC; American Airlines Flight 77, a Boeing 757-200, with 58 passengers, 6 crew, crashed into Pentagon outside Washington, DC; United Airlines Flight 93, a Boeing 757-200, with 37 passengers, 7 crew, crashed near Shanksville, PA. The official death toll of 2,997 includes those who died on the ground at the Pentagon and the WTC, and three later victims whose deaths were caused by exposure to toxic dust created by the disaster according to NYC's chief medical examiner. Does not include those with cancers and other medical conditions related to WTC site exposure. (12) The two pilots ejected to safety. All spectator deaths.

Some Notable Shipwrecks Since 1854

Does not include most wartime disasters.

Date—vessel(s)	Incident	Est. deaths
1854, Mar. 1—City of Glasgow	British steamer left Liverpool for Philadelphia, never heard from again	480
1854, Sept. 27—Arctic and Vesta	U.S. Collins Line steamer sunk in collision with French steamer nr. Cape Race, Canada	285-351
1856, Jan. 23—Pacific	U.S. Collins Line steamer went missing in N Atlantic	186-286
1857, Sept. 12—Central America	U.S. mail steamship sank off Florida coast with $1.5 mil in gold	427
1858, Sept. 23—Austria	German steamer destroyed by fire in N Atlantic	471
1863, Apr. 27—Anglo-Saxon	British steamer wrecked at Cape Race, Canada	238
1865, Apr. 27—Sultana	Mississippi R. steamer carrying 2,400 released Union prisoners exploded nr. Memphis, TN. Worst maritime disaster in U.S. history	1,800
1869, Feb. 20—Radetzky	Austrian steam frigate exploded in Adriatic Sea	345
1869, Oct. 27—Stonewall	U.S. steamer burned, Mississippi R. below Cairo, IL	200
1872, Nov. 7—Mary Celeste	U.S. half-brig sailing from New York City to Genoa, Italy, with 10 on board found abandoned	Unknown
1873, Jan. 22—Northfleet	British steamer rammed by Spanish steamer Murillo off Dungeness, England, UK	300
1873, Apr. 1—Atlantic	British White Star steamer off Halifax, Nova Scotia, Canada	585
1873, Nov. 23—Ville du Havre and Loch Earn	French steamer sank after collision with British sailing ship	226
1874, Nov. 17—Cospatrick	En route from London to New Zealand, caught fire off Cape of Good Hope	468
1875, May 7—Schiller	German steamer off Isles of Scilly, UK	312
1875, Nov. 4—Pacific	U.S. steamer sank after collision off Cape Flattery, WA	236

Date—vessel(s)	Incident	Est. deaths
1878, Mar. 24—Eurydice	British frigate sank off Isle of Wight, England, UK	398
1878, Sept. 3—Princess Alice	British steamer sank after collision with *Bywell Castle* in Thames R.	700
1878, Dec. 18—Byzantin and Rinaldo	French and British steamers collided in Dardanelles, off Turkey	210
1883, Jan. 19—Cimbria and Sultan	German steamer sank in collision with British steamer in North Sea	389
1887, Nov. 15—Wah Yeung	Chinese steamer burned in Canton R., Hong Kong	400
1890, Feb. 17—Duburg	British steamer wrecked, China Sea	400
1890, Sept. 16—Ertugrul	Ottoman frigate in typhoon off Japan	587
1891, Mar. 17—Utopia and Anson	British steamer sank in collision with British ironclad off Gibraltar	562
1893, June 22—Victoria	British battleship sank after collision with British warship *Camperdown*, off Syrian coast	358
1895, Jan. 30—Elbe and Craithie	German steamer sank in collision with British steamer in North Sea	332
1895, Mar. 11—Reina Regenta	Spanish cruiser foundered nr. Gibraltar	400
1898, Feb. 15—USS Maine	Explosion caused battleship to sink in Havana Harbor, Cuba	260
1898, July 4—La Bourgogne and Cromartyshire	French steamer sank in collision with British sailing ship off Nova Scotia, Canada	549
1904, May 15—Yoshino	Japanese cruiser sank after collision with cruiser *Kasuga* in fog off Liao-Tung Peninsula, China	329
1904, June 15—General Slocum	Excursion steamer burned off N. Brother Isl., New York, NY	1,021
1904, June 28—Norge	Danish steamer wrecked on Rockall Isl., Scotland, UK	620
1906, Aug. 4—Sirio	Italian steamer wrecked off Cape Palos, Spain	350
1907, Feb. 11—Larchmont	U.S. steamer sank after collision with U.S. schooner *Harry Knowlton* nr. Block Island, RI	131
1908, Mar. 23—Mutsu Maru	Japanese steamer sank in collision with another steamer nr. Hakodate, Japan	300
1909, July 26—Waratah	British steamer vanished en route from Durban to Cape Town, South Africa	300
1911, Sept. 25—Liberté	French battleship exploded at Toulon	285
1912, Apr. 14-15—Titanic	British White Star steamer hit iceberg in N Atlantic	1,503
1912, Sept. 28—Kichemaru	Japanese steamer sank off Japan coast	1,000
1914, May 29—Empress of Ireland	Canadian Pacific steamer collided with Norwegian coal transporter *Storstad* in St. Lawrence R., Canada	1,014
1914, Nov. 26—Bulwark	British battleship exploded in Sheerness Harbor, England, UK	788
1915, May 7—Lusitania	British Cunard Line steamer torpedoed and sunk by German submarine off Ireland	1,198
1915, July 24—Eastland	Steamer capsized, Chicago R., IL	844
1916, Feb. 26—Provence	French cruiser sank in Mediterranean; then-worst disaster in maritime history	3,100
1916, Mar. 5—Principe de Asturias	Spanish steamer wrecked nr. Santos, Brazil	558
1917, Dec. 6—Mont Blanc and Imo	French ammunition ship and Belgian steamer collided in Halifax Harbor, Canada	1,900+
1918, Apr. 25—Kiang-Kwan	Chinese steamer sank after collision with Chinese gunboat *Chutai* off Hankow, China	500
1918, July 12—Kawachi	Japanese battleship blew up in Tokayama Bay	500
1918, Oct. 25—Princess Sophia	Canadian-Pacific steamer sank off Vanderbilt Reef, Alaska	398
1919, Jan. 17—Chaonia	French steamer lost in Straits of Messina, Italy	460
1919, Sept. 9—Valbanera	Spanish steamer lost off FL coast	500
1920, Jan. 11—Afrique	French liner sank nr. La Rochelle, France	553
1921, Mar. 18—Hong Kong	Chinese steamer wrecked, S China Sea	1,000
1922, Aug. 26—Niitaka	Japanese cruiser sank in storm off Kamchatka, USSR	300
1927, Sept. 20—Gentoku Maru	Japanese steamer capsized in Tsingtao Bay, China	278
1927, Oct. 25—Principessa Mafalda	Italian steamer blew up, sank off Porto Seguro, Brazil	314
1934, Sept. 8—Morro Castle	U.S. steamer en route from Havana to New York, burned off Asbury Park, NJ	134
1940, June 17—Lancastria	Nazi forces sank Cunard liner evacuating British troops from France	2,500-6,000
1940, July 24—Meknes	French liner torpedoed by Nazis in English Channel	350
1942, Feb. 18—USS Truxtun and USS Pollux	Destroyer and cargo ship ran aground, sank off Newfoundland, Canada	204
1942, Oct. 2—Curacao and Queen Mary	British cruiser sank off Ireland after collision with liner carrying U.S. troops	338
1944, Dec. 17-18—Spence, Monaghan, Hull	3 U.S. destroyers sank during typhoon, Philippine Sea	790
1945, Jan. 30—Wilhelm Gustloff	Liner with German refugees, soldiers sunk by Soviet submarine in Baltic	5,000-9,000
1945, Apr. 16—Goya	Cargo ship carrying German refugees, soldiers sunk by Soviet submarine in Baltic	6,000-7,000
1945, May 3—Cap Arcona and Thielbeck	German ocean liner and freighter carrying concentration camp inmates sunk by British warplanes in Lubeck Bay, Germany	7,000-8,000
1947, Jan. 19—Himera	Greek steamer hit mine off Athens, Greece	392
1947, Apr. 16—Grandcamp	Ammonium nitrate explosion aboard French freighter caused fires throughout port, Texas City, TX	576+
1948, Dec. 3—Kiangya	Chinese refugee ship wrecked in explosion S of Shanghai	1,100+
1954, Sept. 26—Toya Maru	Japanese ferry sank, Tsugaru Strait, Japan	1,172
1956, July 26—Andrea Doria and Stockholm	Italian liner and Swedish liner collided off Nantucket Isl., MA	51
1957, July 14—Eshghabad	Soviet fishing boat ran aground in Caspian Sea	270
1961, Apr. 8—Dara	British liner exploded in Persian Gulf	236
1961, July 8—Save	Portuguese ship ran aground off Mozambique	259
1965, Nov. 13—Yarmouth Castle	Cruise ship burned and sank off Nassau, The Bahamas	89
1970, Dec. 15—Namyong-Ho	S. Korean ferry sank in Korea Strait	308
1975, Nov. 10—Edmund Fitzgerald	U.S. cargo ship sank during storm on Lake Superior	29
1980, Apr. 22—Don Juan	Sank off Mindoro Isl., Philippines, after colliding with barge	1,000+
1981, Jan. 27—Tamponas II	Indonesian car ferry caught fire and sank in Java Sea	580
1983, May 25—10th of Ramadan	Nile steamer caught fire and sank in Lake Nasser, Egypt	357
1986, May 25—Shamia	Ferry capsized in storm, Meghna R., Bangladesh	500+

Date—vessel(s)	Incident	Est. deaths
1986, Sept. 1—Admiral Nakhimov and Pyotr Vasev	Soviet cruise ship collided with Soviet freighter in Black Sea	425
1987, Dec. 20—Doña Paz and Victor	Philippine ferry and oil tanker collided in Tablas Strait, Philippines	4,341
1988, Aug. 6	Indian ferry capsized on Ganges R.	400+
1988, Oct. 24—Doña Marilyn	Philippine ferry sank by typhoon near Leyte Isl.	350+
1991, Dec. 14—Salem Express	Ferry rammed coral reef nr. Safaga, Egypt	462
1993, Feb. 17—Neptune	Ferry capsized off Port-au-Prince, Haiti	500+
1993, Oct. 10—Seohae	S. Korean ferry capsized in Yellow Sea during storm	292
1994, Sept. 28—Estonia	Ferry sank in Baltic Sea off Finland	850+
1996, May 21—Bukoba	Overcrowded Tanzanian ferry sank in Lake Victoria	500+
1997, Sept. 8—Pride of la Gonâve	Haitian ferry sank off Montrouis, Haiti	200+
1999, Feb. 6—Harta Rimba	Cargo ship sank off Indonesia	280+
1999, May 1—Miss Majestic	"Duck" boat on tour sank, Lake Hamilton, AR.	13
1999, Nov. 24—Dashun	Passenger ferry capsized nr. Yantai, China.	280
2000, June 29—Cahaya Bahari	Overloaded ferry carrying refugees from religious strife capsized in storm off Sulawesi Isl., Indonesia	500+
2001, Oct. 19	Fishing boat overloaded with refugees, mainly from Middle East, sank off Indonesia	350+
2002, May 4—Salahuddin-2	Overloaded Bangladesh ferry sank in Meghna R.	300+
2002, Sept. 26—Joola	Overloaded Senegalese ferry capsized in ocean off The Gambia	1,863
2003, July 8—MV-Nasrin 1	Overcrowded ferry sank nr. Chandpur in Bangladesh R.	400
2003, Oct. 15—Andrew J. Barberi	NYC ferry crashed into dock on approach to Staten Island	11
2004, Feb. 27—Superferry 14	Philippine ferry bombed by Islamic militants; deadliest terrorist attack at sea	116
2006, Feb. 3—Al-Salam Boccaccio 98	Ferry caught fire, sank in Red Sea off Egypt	1,000+
2006, Dec. 30—Senopati Nusantara	High waves capsized ferry en route to Java, Indonesia	400+
2007, Nov. 23—Explorer	Canadian cruise ship hit Antarctic iceberg; first commercial passenger ship to sink in region	0
2008, June 23—Princess of the Stars	Philippine ferry capsized during Typhoon Fengshen nr. Manila	800
2011, Sept. 10—MV Spice Islander	Overloaded ferry sank off coast of Tanzania	240+
2012, Jan. 17—Costa Concordia	Cruise ship ran aground off Italian coast; captain abandoned ship before evacuating passengers	32
2013, Oct. 3	Boat carrying migrants fleeing Eritrea sank near Lampedusa Isl., Italy	360
2014, Apr. 16—Sewol	Ferry carrying 476 people, most students, Korea's SW coast	304
2015, June 1—Dongfangzhixing (Eastern Star)	Chinese cruise ship sank in Yangtze R. during torrential rains	442
2015, Oct. 1—El Faro	Cargo ship en route from FL to Puerto Rico sailed into hurricane	33
2018, June 18	Overloaded ferry sank in bad weather, Lake Toba, Sumatra, Indonesia	192
2018, July 19	"Duck" boat sank in a severe storm, Table Rock Lake, nr. Branson, MO.	17
2018, Sept. 20—MV Nyerere	Overloaded Tanzanian ferry capsized in Lake Victoria	227+

Note: As migration to Europe, mostly from North Africa, swelled in 2014-17, deaths of migrants and refugees in shipwrecks and other incidents while crossing the Mediterranean Sea spiked. The UN's Intl. Organization for Migration reported 3,283 deaths in 2014, 3,782 deaths in 2015, 5,143 in 2016, and 3,139 in 2017.

Some Notable Railroad Disasters Since 1925

Date	Location	Deaths	Date	Location	Deaths
1925, June 16	Hackettstown, NJ	50	1986, Aug. 6	Bihar, India	202
1933, Dec. 23	Lagny-Pomponne, France	230	1987, July 2	Kasumbalesha Shaba, Zaire	125
1937, July 16	Near Patna, India	107	1987, Aug. 7	Between Moscow and Rostov, USSR	106
1938, Dec. 25	Near Kishinev, Romania	150	1987, Oct. 19	Jakarta, Indonesia	153
1939, Dec. 22	Genthin, near Magdeburg, Germany	132	1988, June 4	Arzamas, USSR	100
1943, Sept. 6	Frankford Junction, Philadelphia, PA	79	1988, July 8	Kerala, India	108
1943, Dec. 16	Between Rennert and Buie, NC	72	1989, Jan. 15	Maizdi Khan, Bangladesh	135
1944, Jan. 16	León Province, Spain	500	1989, June 4	Ufa, USSR	645
1944, Mar. 2	Salerno, Italy	521	1989, July 11	San Rafael R., Sinaloa State, Mexico	112
1944, Dec. 31	Bagley, UT	50	1990, Jan. 4	Sindh Province, Pakistan	307
1945, July 16	Munich, Germany	102	1991, Mar. 5	Nacala, Mozambique	109
1946, Mar. 20	Aracaju, Brazil	185	1991, June 8	Ghotki, Pakistan	100
1949, Oct. 22	Near Dwor, Poland	200+	1991, Sept. 5	Pointe-Noire, Congo Republic	110
1950, Nov. 22	Richmond Hill, Queens, NY	79	1993, Jan. 30	Near Mtito Andei, Kenya	140+
1951, Feb. 6	Woodbridge, NJ	84	1993, Apr. 25	Near Karachi, Pakistan	150
1952, Mar. 4	Near Rio de Janeiro, Brazil	119	1994, Sept. 22	Lubango, Angola	300
1952, July 9	Rzepin, Poland	160	1994, Dec. 30	Near Namkham, Myanmar	102
1952, Oct. 8	Harrow, England, UK	112	1995, Jan. 13	Dinajpur, Bangladesh	150
1953, Dec. 24	Tangiwai, New Zealand	151	1995, Aug. 20	Firozabad, India	350
1953, Dec. 24	Sakvice, Czechoslovakia	103	1995, Nov. 28	Baku, Azerbaijan	337
1955, Apr. 3	Guadalajara, Mexico	300	1997, Mar. 3	Punjab Province, Pakistan	128
1957, Sept. 1	Kendal, Jamaica	178	1997, May 4	Kisangani, Zaire	100+
1957, Sept. 29	Montgomery, W Pakistan	300	1998, Feb. 19	Yaounde, Cameroon	120
1957, Dec. 4	London, England, UK	90	1998, June 3	Eschede, Germany	102
1958, May 8	Rio de Janeiro, Brazil	128	1998, Nov. 26	Khanna, India	108
1960, Nov. 14	Pardubice, Czechoslovakia	117	1999, Aug. 2	Gauhati, India	285
1962, May 3	Tokyo, Japan	163	2002, Feb. 20	S of Cairo, Egypt	377
1963, Nov. 9	Yokohama, Japan	162	2002, May 25	Muamba, Mozambique	195
1965, Feb. 27	Near Port Sudan, Sudan	124	2002, June 24	Igandu, Tanzania	281
1970, Feb. 1	Buenos Aires, Argentina	236	2002, Sept. 10	Bihar, India	112
1972, June 16	Near Soissons, France	108	2004, Feb. 18	Neyshabur, NE Iran	300
1972, Oct. 6	Near Saltillo, Mexico	204	2004, Apr. 22	Ryongchon, North Korea	161
1974, Aug. 30	Zagreb, Yugoslavia	153	2005, Apr. 25	Near Amagasaki, Japan	107
1981, June 6	Near Mansi, India	268	2005, July 13	Ghotki, Pakistan	132
1982, Jan. 27	El Asnam, Algeria	120	2005, Oct. 29	Andra Pradesh, India	110
1982, July 11	Tepic, Mexico	120	2007, Aug. 2	Nr. Benaleka, Dem. Rep. of Congo	100
1983, Feb. 19	Empalme, Mexico	100	2010, May 28	W. Bengal, India	148
1985, Jan. 13	Awash, Ethiopia	392	2011, July 23	Wenzhou, China	140
1985, Sept. 12	Viseu, Portugal	118	2016, Nov. 20	Near Kanpur, Uttar Pradesh, India	150

Notable Droughts

Source: EM-DAT: The Emergency Events Database, CRED/D. Guha-Sapir, Université catholique de Louvain, Brussels, Belgium, www.emdat.be; World Almanac research

Date	Location	Est. deaths	Date	Location	Est. deaths
1900	Bengal, India	1,250,000	1974-76	Somalia	19,000
1900	Cape Verde islands	11,000	1981-85	Mozambique	100,000
1910-14	Zinder Dept., Niger	85,000	1981-85	Chad	3,000
1920	China	500,000	1983	Swaziland	500
1920	Cape Verde islands	24,000	1983-84	Eritrea, Ethiopia	300,000
1921	S Ukraine, Volga, USSR	1,200,000	1983-85	N Sudan	150,000
1928-30	Shaanxi, Henan, Gansu, China	3,000,000	1987	Somalia, Eritrea, Ethiopia	967
1940-44	Cape Verde islands	20,000	1987	NW India	300
1942	Calcutta, Bengal, India	1,500,000	1988	Central China	1,400
1943	Bangladesh	1,900,000	1991	Jiangxi, Hunan Provinces, China	2,000
1946	Cape Verde islands	30,000	1997	Irian Jaya, Indonesia	672
1965	Ethiopia	2,000	1999-2003	Pakistan	143
1965-67	India	1,500,000	2002	Malawi	500
1966	Lombok, Indonesia	8,000	2006	SW China	134
1973-78	Ethiopia	100,000	2014	Tharparkar, Pakistan	166

Some Notable Miscellaneous Disasters Since 1950

Date	Event	Location	Details	Est. deaths
1952, Dec.	Pollution	London, England, UK	Heavy smog blanketed city; impeded breathing	4,000
1959-61	Famine	China	Govt. policies compounded by flooding and drought	15-40 mil
1980, summer	Heat wave	Central, eastern U.S.	Combined direct and indirect deaths est. at 10,000	1,260
1984, Dec. 3	Industrial accident	Bhopal, India	Toxic gas leaked from a Union Carbide factory	16,000
1986, Aug. 21	Gas	Nr. Lake Nyos, Cameroon	Volcanic lake released cloud of carbon dioxide gas	1,700
1990, July 2	Stampede	Mecca, Saudi Arabia	Pilgrims panicked in tunnel leading to the holy city	1,426
1995, June 29	Building collapse	Seoul, South Korea	Improperly built and maintained Sampoong Dept. Store failed with shoppers inside	501
2003, summer	Heat wave	Europe	France suffered most, with 14,800 dead	35,000
2005, Aug. 31	Stampede	Baghdad, Iraq	Rumors of suicide bomber caused panic among religious pilgrims on al-Aimmah Bridge	965
2013, Apr. 24	Building collapse	Savar, Bangladesh	Garment factory found to have substandard foundation	1,100+
2015, Sept. 24	Stampede	Mina, Saudi Arabia	Two groups of pilgrims collided during hajj to Mecca	2,411

Some Notable U.S. Tornadoes Since 1925

Date	Location	Deaths	Date	Location	Deaths
1925, Mar. 18	MO, IL, IN	747	1973, May 26-27	South, Midwest	47
1927, Apr. 12	Rocksprings, TX	74	1974, Apr. 3-4	AL; GA; KY; Xenia, OH; other states	315
1927, May 9	AR; Poplar Bluff, MO	92	1977, Apr. 4	AL, MS, GA	22
1927, Sept. 29	St. Louis, MO	90	1979, Apr. 10	TX, OK	60
1930, May 6	Hill, Navarro, Ellis Cos., TX	41	1984, Mar. 28	NC, SC	57
1932, Mar. 21	Alabama	268	1985, May 31	NY; PA; OH; Ontario, Can.	75
1936, Apr. 5-6	Tupelo, MS; Gainesville, GA	454	1987, May 22	Saragosa, TX	30
1938, Sept. 29	Charleston, SC	32	1989, Nov. 15	Huntsville, AL	18
1942, Mar. 16	Central to NE Mississippi	75	1990, Aug. 28	Northern IL	25
1942, Apr. 27	Rogers and Mayes Cos., OK	52	1991, Apr. 26	KS, OK	23
1944, June 23	OH, PA, WV, MD	150	1992, Nov. 21-23	South, Midwest	26
1945, Apr. 12	OK, AR	102	1994, Mar. 27-28	AL, TN, GA, NC, SC	52
1947, Apr. 9	TX; Woodward, OK; KS	181	1995, May 6-7	Southern OK, northern TX	23
1948, Mar. 19	Bunker Hill and Gillespie, IL	33	1997, Mar. 1	Central AR	26
1949, Jan. 3	LA, AR	58	1997, May 27	Jarrell, TX	27
1952, Mar. 21-22	AR, MO, TN	208	1998, Feb. 22-23	Central FL	42
1953, May 11	Waco, TX	114	1998, Apr. 8	AL, GA, MS	39
1953, June 8	Flint-Beecher, MI; OH	142	1999, May 3	OK, KS	54
1953, June 9	Worcester and vicinity, MA	90	2000, Feb. 14	SW Georgia	22+
1953, Dec. 5	Vicksburg, MS	38	2002, Nov. 10-11	AL, MS, TN, IN, OH, PA	36
1955, May 25	Udall, KS; MO; Blackwell, OK; TX	115	2003, May 4-11	TN, MO, KS, IL, OK, WV, AL	48
1957, May 20	KS, MO	48	2005, Nov. 6	KY, IN	22
1958, June 4	NW Wisconsin	30	2007, Mar. 1	AL, GA, MO, Midwest	20
1959, Feb. 10	St. Louis, MO	21	2008, Feb. 25	TN, AR, KY, AL, MO	57
1960, May 5-6	Southeastern OK, AR	30	2008, May 10	MS, OK, GA	23
1965, Apr. 11	IA, IN, IL, OH, MI, WI	271	2011, Apr. 14-16	Southeast, Midwest, OK to VA	38
1966, Mar. 3	Jackson, MS; AL	57	2011, Apr. 25-28	362 funnels from TX to NY	321
1967, Apr. 21	IL, MO, IA, MI	33	2011, May 22	Joplin, MO	161
1968, May 15	Midwest	71	2012, Mar. 2-3	IL, IN, KY, OH, AL	42
1969, Jan. 23	Mississippi	32	2013, May 20	Moore, OK	24
1970, May 11	Lubbock, TX	23	2013, May 31	El Reno, OK	21
1971, Feb. 21	Mississippi Delta: MS, LA, AR, TN	110	2017, Jan. 22	Southern GA	16

Fifty Year Storm

Date: Aug. 1969. **Location:** Mississippi, Louisiana. **Fatalities:** 256.

Hurricane Camille crossed Cuba before making landfall as a category 5 storm along the U.S. Gulf Coast near Waveland, MS, Aug. 17-18, 1969, defying forecasts that showed it turning toward the Florida Panhandle. The storm became the second most intense hurricane to hit the continental U.S. (after the 1935 Labor Day hurricane). Sustained winds were estimated at 190 mph.

Camille weakened to a tropical depression as it headed through Tennessee, Kentucky, West Virginia, and Virginia. Wind, storm surge, and flooding killed 256 and caused $1.4 bil in damages (about $9.5 bil in 2018). Nearly half of the deaths took place in Virginia flash floods.

Some Notable Hurricanes, Typhoons, Blizzards, Other Storms

C. = cyclone; H. = hurricane; TS. = tropical storm; T. = typhoon[1].

Date	Location	Est. deaths	Date	Location	Est. deaths
1881, Aug. 24-29	H., GA, SC	700	1993, Mar. 12-14	Blizzard, Eastern U.S.	270+
1888, Mar. 11-14	Blizzard, Eastern U.S.	400	1993, June	Monsoon, Bangladesh	2,000
1893, Aug. 15-Sept. 2	H., GA, SC	1,000+	1994, Nov. 8-18	TS. Gordon, Caribbean, FL	830
1893, Oct. 1	H., LA	1,100+	1995, Oct. 2-4	H. Opal, S Mexico, FL, AL	59
1900, Sept. 8	H., Galveston, TX	8,000+	1995, Nov. 2-3	T. Angela, Philippines	600+
1906, Sept. 18	T., Hong Kong	10,000+	1996, Jan. 7-8	Blizzard, NE U.S.	100
1906, Sept. 19-24	H., LA, MS	350	1996, Aug. 22	Blizzard, Himalayas, N India	239
1909, Sept. 20	H., LA	350+	1996, Aug. 29-Sept. 6	H. Fran, Carib., NC, VA, WV	30
1915, Aug. 16	H., Galveston, TX	275	1996, Sept. 9	T. Sally, S China	114
1915, Sept. 29	H., LA	275	1996, Nov. 6	C., Andhra Pradesh, India	1,000+
1919, Sept. 6-14	H., Carib., FL Keys, Gulf, TX	600+[2]	1996, Dec. 25	TS. Greg, eastern Malaysia	100+
1922, July 27	T., Swatow, China	100,000	1997, May 19	C., Bangladesh	108
1926, Sept. 11-22	H., FL, AL, MS	370+	1997, Aug. 18-21	T. Winnie, Taiwan, E China	140+
1926, Oct. 20	H., Cuba	600	1997, Oct. 8-10	H. Pauline, SW Mexico	230
1928, Sept. 6-20	H., southern FL.	2,500+	1998, June 9	C., Gujarat, India	1,320
1930, Sept. 3	H., Dominican Republic	2,000	1998, Aug.	Monsoon, Bangladesh	326
1935, Aug. 29-			1998, Sept. 21-23	H. Georges, Carib., FL, U.S. Gulf	600+
Sept. 10	H., Caribbean, SE U.S.	400+	1998, Oct. 27-29	H. Mitch, central America	14,600
1937, Sept. 2	T., Hong Kong	10,000+	1999, Sept. 4-17	H. Floyd, The Bahamas, E U.S.	56
1938, Sept. 21	H., NY, New England	682	1999, Oct. 29	C., E India	9,392
1940, Nov. 11-12	NE, Midwest U.S.	154	1999, Dec. 26-29	Gales, France, Switz., Germany	120
1942, Oct.	T., W. Sundarbans, Bangladesh	61,000	2000, Dec. 27	Winter storm, TX, OK, AR	40+
1942, Oct. 15-16	H., Bengal, India	40,000	2001, July 30	T. Toraji, Taiwan.	200
1947, Dec. 26	Blizzard, NYC, N Atl. states	55	2001, Nov. 6-12	T. Lingling, S Philip., Vietnam.	220+
1952, Oct. 22	T., Philippines	440	2002, Aug.-Sept.	T. Rusa, N. and S. Korea	115+
1954, Aug. 30	H. Carol, NE U.S.	68	2003, Feb. 15-18	Blizzard, E seaboard U.S.	59
1954, Oct. 5-18	H. Hazel, E Canada, U.S., Haiti	347	2003, Sept. 7-19	H. Isabel, NC, VA, E seaboard	40+
1955, Aug. 7-21	H. Diane, Eastern U.S.	400	2003, Sept. 12	T. Maemi, S. Korea.	130
1955, Sept. 19	H. Hilda, Mexico	200	2004, Mar. 7-19	C. Gafilo, Madagascar	198
1956, Feb. 1-29	Blizzard, W Europe	1,000	2004, May 19	C., Myanmar.	220
1957, June 25-30	H. Audrey, TX to AL	390	2004, Aug. 12-15	T. Rananim, eastern China.	164
1958, Feb. 15-16	Blizzard, NE U.S.	171	2004, Aug. 13-14	H. Charley, FL, SC.	36
1959, Sept. 17-19	T. Sarah, Japan, S. Korea	2,000	2004, Sept. 5-6	H. Frances, The Bahamas, FL	35
1959, Sept. 26-27	T. Vera, Honshu, Japan	4,466	2004, Sept. 7-16	H. Ivan, Barbados, Grenada,	
1960, Sept. 4-12	H. Donna, Caribbean, E U.S.	148		U.S. Gulf Coast.	115
1961, Oct. 31	H. Hattie, Brit. Honduras.	400	2004, Sept. 16-26	H. Jeanne, Dom. Rep., Haiti, FL	1,500+
1962, Sept. 1	T. Wanda, Hong Kong	130-200	2005, July 7-11	H. Dennis, Jamaica, Haiti,	
1963, May 28-29	Windstorm, Bangladesh	22,000		Cuba, FL.	50
1963, Oct. 4-8	H. Flora, Caribbean	6,000	2005, Aug. 25-29	H. Katrina, LA, MS, FL, AL, GA	1,833+[3]
1964, June 30	T. Winnie, N Philippines	107	2005, Aug. 31-Sept. 1	T. Talim, Taiwan, E China	129+
1964, Sept. 5	T. Ruby, Hong Kong, China	735	2005, Sept. 21-24	H. Rita, TX, LA	62[4]
1965, May 11-12	Windstorm, Bangladesh	17,000	2005, Sept. 21-28	T. Damrey, SE Asia; Philippines;	
1965, June 1-2	Windstorm, Bangladesh	30,000		Hainan, China.	145
1965, Sept. 7-12	H. Betsy, FL, MS, LA	74	2005, Oct. 4	H. Stan, Central Amer., Mex.	1,000+[5]
1965, Dec. 15	Windstorm, Bangladesh	10,000	2006, July 14	TS. Bilis, SE China	612
1966, June 4-10	H. Alma, Honduras, SE U.S.	51	2006, Aug. 10	T. Saomai, SE China	295
1966, Sept. 24-30	H. Inez, Carib., FL, Mexico.	293	2006, Nov. 30	T. Durian, Philippines	450-1,000+
1967, July 9	T. Billie, SW Japan	347	2007, June 6-7	C. Gonu, Oman, Iran	54[6]
1967, Sept. 5-23	H. Beulah, Carib., Mex., TX	54	2007, Nov. 15	C. Sidr, southern Bangladesh.	3,363
1967, Dec. 12-20	Blizzard, SW U.S.	51	2008, May 2-3	C. Nargis, southern Myanmar.	138,366
1969, Aug. 17-18	H. Camille, MS, LA	256	2008, June 20-25	T. Fengshen, Philippines, China	233
1970, Sept. 15	T. Pitang (Georgia), Philippines	300	2008, Aug. 26-Sept. 1	H. Gustav, Haiti, Dom. Rep., U.S.	138
1970, Oct. 14	T. Sening (Joan), Philippines	583	2008, Sept. 1-4	TS. Hanna, Haiti.	529
1970, Oct. 15	T. Titang (Kate), Philippines.	526	2008, Sept. 7-13	H. Ike, Haiti; Cuba; TX	164
1970, Nov. 13	C., Bay of Bengal, Bangladesh	300,000	2009, May 23-26	C. Alia, India, Bangladesh	260
1971, Aug. 1	T. Rose, Hong Kong	130	2009, Aug. 7-9	T. Morakot, mudslides, Taiwan	700+
1972, June 19-29	H. Agnes, FL to NY.	118	2009, Sept. 23-30	T. Ketsana, Philippines,	
1972, Dec. 3	T. Theresa, Philippines.	169		Vietnam, Cambodia, Laos	498+
1973, June-Aug.	Monsoon rains, India	1,217	2009, Oct. 3-10	T. Parma, Philippines	375
1974, July 11	T. Gilda, Japan, S. Korea	108	2009, Oct. 30-Nov. 3	T. Mirinae, Philippines, Vietnam	159+
1974, Sept. 19-20	H. Fifi, Honduras.	2,000	2010, May 29	TS. Agatha, Guatemala,	
1975, Sept. 13-27	H. Eloise, Caribbean, NE U.S.	71		El Salvador, Honduras.	184
1976, May 20	T. Olga, floods, Philippines.	215	2010, July 13-17	T. Conson, Philippines.	105+
1976, Sept. 25-Oct. 2	T. Liza, western Mexico	630	2011, Dec. 16	TS. Washi, Philippines	1,257
1978, Oct. 27	T. Rita, Philippines	400	2012, Jan. 24-Feb. 14	Blizzard/cold snap, E Europe	650+
1979, Aug. 30-Sept. 7	H. David, Caribbean, E U.S.	1,100	2012, Oct. 22-31	H. Sandy, Cuba, Haiti,	
1980, Aug. 4-11	H. Allen, Caribbean, TX	272		Jamaica, Eastern U.S.	245[7]
1981, Nov. 25	T. Irma, Luzon Isl., Philippines	176	2012, Dec. 4	T. Bopha, Philippines	1,146
1983, June	Monsoon, India.	900	2013, Nov. 8	T. Haiyan, Philippines.	7,986
1984, Sept. 2	T. Ike, southern Philippines	1,363	2013, Nov. 10	C., Puntland, Somalia.	162
1985, May 25	C., Bangladesh.	15,000	2014, July 15	T. Rammasun, Philippines,	
1985, Oct. 26-Nov. 6	H. Juan, SE U.S.	97		China, Vietnam.	173
1987, Nov. 25	T. Nina, Philippines.	650	2016, Oct. 4-8	H. Matthew, Haiti, Bahamas,	
1988, Sept. 10-17	H. Gilbert, Carib., Gulf of Mex.	260		FL, GA, SC, NC.	585
1989, Sept. 16-22	H. Hugo, Caribbean, SE U.S.	86	2017, Aug. 25-30	H. Harvey, South TX, LA.	93+[8]
1990, May 6-11	C. (mult.), SE India.	450	2017, Aug. 31-		
1991, Apr. 30	C., Bangladesh.	139,000	Sept. 11	H. Irma, Barbuda, Cuba, FL	134
1991, Nov. 5	TS. Thelma, central Philippines	7,000+	2017, Sept. 17-28	H. Maria, Dominica, Virgin Isls.,	
1992, Aug. 24-26	H. Andrew, Southern FL, LA.	65		Puerto Rico.	3,022[9]

(1) What hurricanes are called W of Intl. Date Line and N of equator. (2) Incl. about 500 lost at sea. (3) Official toll as of Aug. 2006 was 1,577 in LA, 238 in MS, 14 in FL, and 2 each in AL and GA. (4) Incl. 55 indirect deaths. (5) Incl. deaths from floods and landslides. (6) First documented super cyclone in Arabian Sea. (7) Incl. 87 indirect deaths in the U.S. (8) Downgraded to a tropical storm Aug. 26, Harvey nevertheless caused severe flooding. (9) Puerto Rico's government, Aug. 2018, revised its death toll from 64 to 2,975 in line with a report they commissioned from George Washington Univ. public health experts. A separate Harvard study, in May 2018, estimated the death toll to be at least 4,645.

Some Notable Floods, Tidal Waves

Source: EM-DAT: The Emergency Events Database, CRED/D. Guha-Sapir, Université catholique de Louvain, Brussels, Belgium, www.emdat.be; World Almanac research

Date	Location	Est. deaths	Date	Location	Est. deaths
1703	Awa, Japan	100,000+	1981, Apr.	N China	550
1889, May 31	Johnstown, PA	2,200+	1981, July	Sichuan, Hubei Prov., China	1,300
1903, June 15	Heppner, OR.	325	1982, Jan. 23	Near Lima, Peru	600
1911	Chang Jiang (Yangtze) R., China	100,000	1982, May 12	Guangdong, China	430
			1982, Sept. 17-21	El Salvador, Guatemala	1,300+
1913, Mar. 25-27	OH, IN.	732	1984, Aug.-Sept.	South Korea	200+
1915, Aug. 17	Galveston, TX	275	1987, July 22	Bangladesh	2,055
1927, Jan.-July	Mississippi Valley	246+	1987, Aug.-Sept.	Northern Bangladesh	1,000+
1927, Nov. 1	Mostagenem, Algeria	3,000	1988, June-Sept.	Bangladesh	2,379
1928, Mar. 13	Dam collapse, Saugus, CA	450	1988, Sept.	N India	1,000+
1928, Sept. 16	Lake Okeechobee, FL	1,770+	1989, July 14	China	2,000
1931, Aug.	Huang He R., China	3,700,000	1994, May-Oct.	Assam, India	2,001
1933	Shandong, China	18,000	1995, July	NE China	1,200
1937, Jan. 22	OH, MS valleys	250	1995, Sept. 1-20	India	1,479
1938, June 9	Huang He R., China	500,000	1996, June-July	Guizhou, Hebei, China	2,775
1946, Apr. 1	HI, AK	159	1997, Oct.-Nov.	Somalia	2,311
1947, Sept. 20	Honshu Isl., Japan	2,000	1998, July 17	Papua New Guinea	3,000
1949, July	China	57,000	1998, July-Aug.	Hunan, Sichuan, China	3,656
1949, Oct.	Guatemala	40,000	1998, July-Sept.	Bangladesh	1,441
1950	Pakistan	2,900	1998, Aug.	India	1,811
1951, Aug. 28	Manchuria	4,800	1999, Oct.-Dec.	Central Vietnam	700+
1953, Jan. 31	Storm surge, Zuiderzee, Netherlands	2,000	1999, Dec. 15-20	NW Venezuela	30,000
			2000, Feb.-Mar.	Mozambique	700
1953, June 23	Japan	2,566	2000, Sept. 19-30	India, Bangladesh	1,000+
1954, Aug.	China	30,000	2001, Aug. 1-6	Taiwan	100+
1954, Aug. 17	Farahzad, Iran	2,000	2001, Nov. 9-10	Northern Algeria	711+
1955, Oct. 7-12	India, Pakistan	1,700	2002, Apr.-Aug.	China	800+
1959, Nov. 1	Western Mexico	2,000	2002, July-Aug.	India, Nepal, Bangladesh	1,100+
1959, Dec. 2	Frejus, France	412	2004, May 23-Jun. 1	Dom. Republic, Haiti	2,665
1960, Oct. 10	Bangladesh	6,000	2004, June-Sept.	Bangladesh, India, Myanmar, Nepal	2,000+
1960, Oct. 31	Bangladesh	4,000			
1961, July	N India	2,000	2004, June-Sept.	China	500
1962, Sept. 27	Barcelona, Spain	445	2004, Nov.-Dec.	Philippines	1,060+
1963, Oct. 9	Dam collapse, Vaiont, Italy	1,800	2004, Dec. 26	Indian Ocean nations	227,898
1967, Jan. 18-24	Eastern Brazil	894	2005, July 26-Aug. 5	Western Maharashtra state, India	1,200
1967, Mar. 19	Rio de Janeiro, Brazil	436			
1967, Nov. 26	Lisbon, Portugal	464	2006, Feb. 17	Leyte Isl., Philippines	1,000
1968, July	Rajasthan, Gujarat states, India	4,892	2006, July 17	S of Java, Indonesia	530+
			2007, July 21-Aug. 3	Bangladesh	1,110
1968, Oct. 7	NE India	780	2007, July-Sept.	India	1,103
1969, Jan. 18-26	Southern CA	100	2008, June-July	India	1,063
1969, Aug. 20-22	Western VA	189	2009, July-Sept.	India	992
1969, Oct. 1-8	Tunisia	500	2010, May-Aug.	China	1,691
1970, July 22	Himalayas, India	500	2010, June 13-24	Cenxi, China	377+
1972, Feb. 26	Buffalo Creek, WV	118	2010, July-Aug.	Pakistan	1,985
1972, June 9	Rapid City, SD	238	2010, Aug. 1-4	Zhouqu County, China	1,500+
1972, Aug. 7	Luzon Isl., Philippines	454	2011, Jan. 11-12	SE Brazil	900
1972, Aug. 19-31	Pakistan	1,500	2011, Mar. 11	NE Japan	20,896
1974, Mar. 29	Tubaro, Brazil	1,000	2011, Apr.-May	Northern Colombia	425+
1974, July	Bangladesh	28,700	2011, July-Dec.	Thailand	708+
1974, Aug. 12	Monty-Long, Bangladesh	2,500	2011, July-Dec.	Philippines, Cambodia, Myanmar	2,000+
1975, Aug. 8	Dam collapse, Henan Prov., China	171,000			
			2012, July-Oct.	Nigeria	363
1976, July 31	Big Thompson Canyon, CO	140	2012, Aug.-Oct.	Pakistan	480
1978, July	N, NE India	3,800	2012, Sept.-Oct.	Nigeria	431
1979, July 17	Lomblem Isl., Indonesia	539	2013, June	Uttarakhand, India	6,054
1979, Aug. 11	Morbi, India	10,000	2015, Nov.-Dec.	S India	500
1980, June	Sichuan, China	6,200			

Some Major Earthquakes

Source: Global Volcanism Network, Smithsonian Institution; U.S. Geological Survey, U.S. Dept. of the Interior; World Almanac research
Magnitude of earthquakes (mag.) is a relative measurement of an earthquake's energy. Deaths include those in aftershocks or related events.

Date	Location	Deaths	Mag.	Date	Location	Deaths	Mag.
526, May 20	Antioch, Syria	250,000	NA	1755, Nov. 1	Lisbon, Portugal	60,000	8.75[2]
856	Corinth, Greece	45,000	NA	1783, Feb. 4	Calabria, Italy	30,000	NA
856, Dec. 22	Damghan, Iran	200,000	NA	1797, Feb. 4	Quito, Ecuador	41,000	NA
893, Mar. 23	Ardabil, Iran	150,000	NA	1822, Sept. 5	Asia Minor, Aleppo	22,000	NA
1057	Chihli, China	25,000	NA	1828, Dec. 28	Echigo, Japan	30,000	NA
1138, Aug. 9	Aleppo, Syria	230,000	NA	1868, Aug. 13-16	Peru, Ecuador	40,000	NA
1169, Feb. 11	Nr. Mt. Etna, Sicily	15,000	NA[1]	1875, May 16	Venezuela, Colombia	16,000	NA
1268	Silicia, Asia Minor	60,000	NA	1886, Aug. 31	Charleston, SC	60	6.6
1290, Sept. 27	Chihli, China	100,000	NA	1896, June 15	Sanriku, Japan (tsunami)	27,120	8.5
1293, May 20	Kamakura, Japan	30,000	NA	1902, Apr. 19	Quezaltenango and San Marcos, Guatemala	2,000	7.5
1531, Jan. 26	Lisbon, Portugal	30,000	NA				
1556, Jan. 24	Shaanxi, China	830,000	NA	1902, Dec. 16	Uzbekistan, Russia	4,700	6.4
1667, Nov.	Shemakha, Caucasia (now Azerbaijan)	80,000	NA	1903, Apr. 28	Malazgirt, Turkey	3,500	7.0
				1905, Apr. 4	Kangra, India	19,000	7.5
1693, Jan. 11	Catania, Italy	60,000	NA	1906, Jan. 31	Off coast of Esmeraldas, Ecuador	1,000	8.8
1737, Oct. 11	India, Calcutta	300,000	NA				
1755, June 7	N Persia (current-day Iran)	40,000	NA	1906, Mar. 16	Chia-i, Taiwan	1,250	6.8

Date	Location	Deaths	Mag.	Date	Location	Deaths	Mag.
1906, Apr. 18-19	San Francisco, CA	3,000+	7.7[3]	1972, Dec. 23	Managua, Nicaragua	5,000	6.2
1906, Aug. 17	Valparaiso, Chile	3,882	8.6	1974, May 10	Zhaotong, China	1,540	6.8
1907, Oct. 21	Central Asia	12,000	8.1	1974, Dec. 28	Northern Pakistan	5,300	6.2
1908, Dec. 28	Messina, Italy	72,000	7.2	1975, Feb. 4	Haicheng, China	2,000	7.0
1909, Jan. 23	Silakhor, Iran	5,000-6,000	7.3	1975, Sept. 6	Eastern Turkey	2,300	6.7
1912, Aug. 9	Murefte, Turkey	2,800	7.4	1976, Feb. 4	Guatemala	23,000	7.5
1914, Oct. 3	Burdur, Turkey	4,000	7.0	1976, May 6	NE Italy	1,000	6.5
1915, Jan. 13	Avezzano, Italy	32,610	7.0	1976, June 25	Irian Jaya, New Guinea	422	7.1
1917, July 30	Yunnan Prov., China	1,800	7.5	1976, July 28	Tangshan, China	242,769	7.5
1920, Dec. 16	Gansu, China	200,000	7.8[4]	1976, Aug. 16	Mindanao, Philippines	8,000	7.9
1923, Mar. 24	Sichuan, China	3,500	7.3	1976, Nov. 24	NW Iran-Turkey border	5,000	7.3
1923, Mar. 25	Torbat-e Heydariyeh, Iran	2,200	5.7	1977, Mar. 4	Romania	1,500	7.2
1923, Sept. 1	Yokohama, Japan	142,860	7.9	1978, Sept. 16	NE Iran	15,000	7.8
1925, Mar. 16	Yunnan Prov., China	5,800	7.0	1980, Oct. 10	NW Algeria	5,000	7.7
1927, Mar. 7	Tango, Japan	3,020	7.6	1980, Nov. 23	Southern Italy	2,735	6.5
1927, May 22	Gansu, China	40,900	7.6	1981, June 11	Southern Iran	3,000	6.9
1929, May 1	Koppeh Dagh, Iran	3,800	7.2	1981, July 28	Southern Iran	1,500	7.3
1930, May 6	Salmas, Iran	2,500	7.2	1982, Dec. 13	W Arabian Peninsula	2,800	6.0
1930, July 23	Irpinia, Italy	1,404	6.5	1983, Oct. 30	Eastern Turkey	1,342	6.9
1931, Mar. 31	Managua, Nicaragua	2,500	6.0	1985, Sept. 19	Michoacan, Mexico	9,500	8.0
1931, Apr. 27	Armenia-Azerbaijan border	2,800	5.7	1986, Oct. 10	El Salvador	1,000+	5.5
1931, Aug. 10	Xinjiang, China	10,000	8.0	1987, Mar. 6	Colombia-Ecuador	1,000	7.0
1933, Mar. 2	Sanriku, Japan (tsunami)	2,990	8.4	1988, Aug. 20	India-Nepal border	1,000	6.8
1933, Mar. 10	Long Beach, CA	115	6.2	1988, Dec. 7	Spitak, Armenia	25,000	6.8
1933, Aug. 25	Sichuan, China	9,300	7.5	1989, Oct. 17	San Francisco Bay area, CA	63	6.9
1934, Jan. 15	Bihar, India-Nepal	10,700	8.1	1990, June 20	Western Iran	40,000+	7.4
1935, Apr. 21	Miao-li, Taiwan	3,270	7.1	1990, July 16	Luzon, Philippines	1,621	7.7
1935, May 30	Quetta, Pakistan	30,000	7.6	1991, Feb. 1	Pakistan-Afgh. border	1,200	6.8
1939, Jan. 25	Chillan, Chile	28,000	7.8	1991, Oct. 19	Northern India	2,000	7.0
1939, Dec. 26	Erzincan, Turkey	32,700	7.8	1992, Dec. 12	Flores Isl., Indonesia	2,500	7.5
1943, Sept. 10	Tottori, Japan	1,190	7.4	1993, Sept. 30	Maharashtra, S India	9,748	6.2
1943, Nov. 26	Ladik, Turkey	4,000	7.6	1994, Jan. 17	Northridge, CA	61	6.7
1944, Jan. 15	San Juan, Argentina	8,000	7.4	1994, June 6	Cauca, SW Colombia	1,000	6.8
1944, Feb. 1	Gerede, Turkey	2,790	7.4	1995, Jan. 16	Kobe, Japan	5,502	6.9
1945, Jan. 12	Mikawa, Japan	1,961	7.1	1995, May 27	Sakhalin Isl., Russia	1,989	7.5
1945, Nov. 27	Makran Coast, Pakistan	4,000	8.0	1997, Feb. 28	NW Iran	1,000+	6.1
1946, May 31	Ustukran, Turkey	1,300	5.9	1997, May 10	Northern Iran	1,567	7.3
1946, Nov. 10	Ancash, Peru	1,400	7.3	1998, Feb. 4, 8	Hindu Kush, Afghanistan	2,323	5.9
1946, Dec. 20	Honshu, Japan	1,362	8.1	1998, May 30	Afgh.-Tajikistan border	4,000+	6.6
1948, June 28	Fukui, Japan	3,769	7.3	1998, July 17	Papua New Guinea	2,183	7.0
1948, Oct. 5	Ashgabat, Turkmenistan	110,000	7.3	1999, Jan. 25	Armenia, Colombia	1,185+	6.1
1949, July 10	Khait, Tajikistan	12,000	7.5	1999, Aug. 17	Izmit, western Turkey	17,118+	7.6
1949, Aug. 5	Pelileo, Ecuador	5,050	6.8	1999, Sept. 20	Taichung, Taiwan	2,400	7.6
1950, Aug. 15	Assam, India	1,526	8.6	2001, Jan. 26	Gujarat, India	20,085	7.6
1954, Sept. 9	Orleansville, Algeria	1,250	6.8	2002, Mar. 25-26	Hindu Kush, Afghanistan	1,000+	6.1
1956, June 10-17	Northern Afghanistan	2,000	7.7	2003, May 21	Northern Algeria	2,266	6.8
1957, July 2	Northern Iran	1,200	7.1	2003, Dec. 26	Bam, SE Iran	31,000	6.6
1960, Feb. 29	Agadir, Morocco	12,000	5.7	2004, Dec. 26	Sumatra-Andaman Isls., Indonesia	227,898	9.1[7]
1960, May 21-30	Southern Chile	1,655	9.5[5]	2005, Mar. 28	N Sumatra, Indonesia	1,313	8.6
1962, Sept. 1	NW Iran	12,255	7.1	2005, Oct. 8	Kashmir, Pakistan, India	86,000	7.6
1964, Mar. 27	Prince Wm. Sound, AK	131	9.2[6]	2006, May 26	Java, Indonesia	5,749	6.3
1966, Aug. 19	Eastern Turkey	2,529	6.8	2008, May 12	E Sichuan Prov., China	87,857	7.9
1968, Aug. 31	NE Iran	12,000	7.3	2009, Sept. 30	Sumatra, Indonesia	1,117	7.5
1969, July 25	Guangdong, China	3,000	5.9	2010, Jan. 12	Haiti	316,000[8]	7.0
1970, Jan. 5	Yunnan Prov., China	10,000	7.5	2010, Apr. 13	Southern Qinghai, China	2,698+	6.9
1970, May 31	Chimbote, Peru	70,000	7.9	2011, Mar. 11	NE Japan	20,896	9.0[9]
1971, Feb. 9	San Fernando Valley, CA	65	6.6	2015, Apr. 25	Nepal	8,669+	7.8
1972, Apr. 10	Southern Iran	5,054	7.1	2017, Sept. 19	Mexico City, Mexico	369	7.1
				2017, Nov. 12	NW Iran-Iraq border	530	7.3

NA = Not available. (1) Once thought to have been a volcanic eruption; evidence indicates a destructive earthquake and tsunami occurred on this date. (2) This earthquake caused the most deadly tsunami to date in the Atlantic Ocean. (3) Incl. deaths from resulting fires; revised estimates of magnitude range from 7.7 to 7.9. (4) Commonly referred to as the Gansu quake; actually located within the Ningxia autonomous region. (5) The largest recorded earthquake; caused a deadly tsunami that spread across the Pacific Ocean as far as Japan. (6) The "Good Friday" earthquake sent a tsunami that hit British Columbia, Canada, and the U.S. Pacific coast. (7) This undersea earthquake triggered devastating Indian Ocean tsunamis. (8) Official govt. death toll announced Jan. 2011; earlier estimate was 230,000. Estimates from other groups vary widely. (9) The most powerful earthquake in Japan's history set off a tsunami that inundated much of the coast and caused a partial meltdown of the Fukushima nuclear power plant.

Some Notable Fires Since 1940

See also Some Notable Explosions Since 1920.

Date	Location	Deaths	Date	Location	Deaths
1940, Apr. 23	Nightclub, Natchez, MS	198	1958, Mar. 19	Garment factory, New York, NY	24
1942, Nov. 28	Cocoanut Grove Nightclub, Boston, MA	492	1958, Dec. 1	Parochial school, Chicago, IL	95
1942, Dec. 12	Hostel, St. John's, NL, Canada	100	1958, Dec. 16	Store, Bogotá, Colombia	83
1943, Sept. 7	Gulf Hotel, Houston, TX	55	1960, Mar. 12	Chemical plant, Pusan, Korea	68
1944, July 6	Ringling Circus, Hartford, CT	168	1960, July 14	Psychiatric hospital, Guatemala City	225
1946, June 5	LaSalle Hotel, Chicago, IL	61	1960, Nov. 13	Movie theater, Amude, Syria	152
1946, Dec. 7	Winecoff Hotel, Atlanta, GA	119	1960, Dec. 19	USS Constellation, Brooklyn, NY	49
1946, Dec. 12	Ice plant, tenement, New York, NY	37	1961, Jan. 6	Thomas Hotel, San Francisco, CA	20
1949, Apr. 5	Hospital, Effingham, IL	77	1961, Dec. 17	Circus, Niteroi, Brazil	323
1950, Jan. 7	Mercy Hospital, Davenport, IA	41	1963, May 4	Theater, Diourbel, Senegal	64
1953, Mar. 22	Nursing home, Largo, FL	35	1963, Nov. 18	Surfside Hotel, Atlantic City, NJ	25
1953, Apr. 16	Metalworking plant, Chicago, IL	35	1963, Nov. 23	Nursing home, Fitchville, OH	63
1957, Feb. 17	Home for aged, Warrenton, MO	72	1963, Dec. 29	Roosevelt Hotel, Jacksonville, FL	22
			1964, Dec. 18	Nursing home, Fountaintown, IN	20

Date	Location	Deaths
1965, Aug. 11-16	Watts riot fires, Los Angeles, CA	30+
1966, Dec. 7	Barracks, Erzurum, Turkey	68
1967, Feb. 7	Restaurant, Montgomery, AL	25
1967, May 22	Dept. store, Brussels, Belgium	322
1967, July 16	State prison, Jay, FL	37
1967, July 29	USS *Forrestal*, off N Vietnam	134
1968, May 11	Wedding hall, Vijayawada, India	58
1969, Dec. 2	Nursing home, Notre Dame, QC, Can.	54
1970, Jan. 9	Nursing home, Marietta, OH	27
1970, Nov. 1	Dance hall, Grenoble, France	145
1970, Dec. 20	Hotel, Tucson, AZ	28
1971, Dec. 25	Hotel, Seoul, S. Korea	162
1972, May 13	Nightclub, Osaka, Japan	116
1973, June 24	Bar, New Orleans, LA	32
1973, Aug. 3	Amusement park, Isle of Man, UK	51
1973, Nov. 29	Dept. store, Kumamoto, Japan	107
1973, Dec. 2	Theater, Seoul, S. Korea	50
1974, Feb. 1	Bank building, São Paulo, Brazil	189
1974, June 30	Discotheque, Port Chester, NY	24
1974, Nov. 3	Hotel, disco, Seoul, S. Korea	88
1975, Dec. 12	Pilgrim camp, Mina, Saudi Arabia	138
1976, Oct. 24	Social club, Bronx, NY	25
1977, Feb. 25	Rossiya Hotel, Moscow, Russia	45
1977, May 28	Nightclub, Southgate, KY	164
1977, June 26	Jail, Columbia, TN	42
1977, Nov. 14	Hotel, Manila, Philippines	47
1978, Aug. 19	Movie theater, Abadan, Iran	425+
1979, July 14	Hotel, Saragossa, Spain	80
1979, Dec. 31	Social club, Chapais, QC, Can.	42
1980, May 20	Nursing home, Kingston, Jamaica	157
1980, Nov. 21	MGM Grand Hotel, Las Vegas, NV	84
1980, Dec. 4	Stouffer Inn, Harrison, NY	26
1981, Jan. 9	Boarding home, Keansburg, NJ	30
1981, Feb. 14	Discotheque, Dublin, Ireland	44
1982, Nov. 8	County jail, Biloxi, MS	29
1983, Feb. 13	Movie theater, Turin, Italy	64
1983, Feb. 16	"Ash Wednesday" bushfires, S Australia and Victoria, Australia	75
1983, Dec. 17	Discotheque, Madrid, Spain	83
1984, May 11	Amusement park, Jackson Twp., NJ	8
1985, Apr. 21	Movie theaters, Tabaco, Philippines	44
1985, Apr. 26	Hospital, Buenos Aires, Argentina	79
1985, May 11	Soccer stadium, Bradford, Eng., UK	53
1985, May 13	MOVE headquarters, row houses, Philadelphia, PA	11
1986, Dec. 31	Dupont Plaza Hotel, Puerto Rico	96
1987, May 6-June 2	Forest fire, Mohe, China	191
1987, Nov. 17	Subway, London, England	30
1988, Mar. 20	2,000+ buildings, Lashio, Myanmar	134
1990, Mar. 25	Happy Land social club, Bronx, NY	87
1991, Mar. 3	Munitions dump, Addis Ababa, Ethiopia	260+
1991, Aug.-Oct.	Wildfires, Sumatra, Borneo, Indonesia	57
1991, Sept. 3	Chicken-processing plant, Hamlet, NC	25
1991, Oct. 20-21	Wildfire, Oakland, Berkeley, CA	24
1993, Apr. 19	Cult compound, Waco, TX	72
1993, May 10	Toy factory, Bangkok, Thailand	213
1993, Nov. 19	Toy factory, Shenzhen, China	87
1994, Nov. 2	Burning fuel flood, Durunka, Egypt	500
1994, Nov. 27	Dance hall, Fuxin, China	233
1994, Dec. 8	Theater, Karamay, China	323
1995, Oct. 28	Subway train, Baku, Azerbaijan	300
1995, Dec. 23	School, Mandi Dabwali, India	500+
1996, Mar. 19	Nightclub, Quezon City, Philippines	150+
1996, Mar. 28	Shopping mall, Bogor, Indonesia	78
1996, Nov. 20	Garley Building, Hong Kong	39
1997, Feb. 23	Worship site, Baripada, India	164

Date	Location	Deaths
1997, Apr. 15	Encampment, Mina, Saudi Arabia	343
1997, June 7	Temple, Thanjavur, India	60+
1997, June 13	Movie theater, New Delhi, India	60
1997, July 11	Hotel, Pattaya, Thailand	90
1997, Sept.-Nov.	Drought-fueled fire, Sumatra, Indon.	240
1998, Apr.-June	Wildfire, Oaxaca, Mexico	50
1998, Dec. 3	Orphanage, Manila, Philippines	28
1999, Mar. 24	Mt. Blanc Tunnel, France, Italy	40
1999, Oct. 30	Karaoke salon, Inchon, S. Korea	55+
2000, Mar. 17	Church, Kanungu, Uganda	530
2000, Nov. 11	Cable car, Kaprun, Austria	155
2000, Dec. 25	Shopping center, Luoyang, China	309
2001, Mar. 26	School, Machakos, Kenya	64
2001, Aug. 18	Hotel, Quezon City, Philippines	73
2001, Sept. 1	Nightclub, Tokyo, Japan	44
2001, Dec. 29	Fireworks accident, Lima, Peru	291
2003, Feb. 18	Subway train, Taegu, S. Korea	198
2003, Feb. 20	Nightclub pyrotechnics, Warwick, RI	100
2003, Sept. 15	Prison, Riyadh, Saudi Arabia	94
2003, Nov. 24	Students' hostel, Moscow, Russia	36
2004, May 17	Prison, San Pedro Sula, Honduras	104
2004, July 16	Pvt. school, Kumbakonam, India	80+
2004, Aug. 1	Market, Asunción, Paraguay	400+
2004, Dec. 30	Club, Buenos Aires, Argentina	194
2005, Feb. 14	Mosque, Tehran, Iran	59
2005, Mar. 7	Prison, Higuey, Dom. Republic	159
2005, Sept. 5	Theater, Beni Suef, Egypt	32
2006, Dec. 9	Drug treatment center, Moscow, Russ.	45
2007, Mar. 20	Nursing home, Kamyshevatskaya, Russia	62
2007, Aug. 24-Sept. 2	Wildfires (arson), Greece	73
2008, Apr. 26	Factory fire, Casablanca, Morocco	55
2008, Sept.	Wildfires, Mozambique, S. Africa, Swaziland	89
2009, Jan. 1	Nightclub fire, Bangkok, Thailand	67
2009, Jan.-Feb.	Wildfires (arson), Victoria, Australia	173
2010, July	Bushfires, Nizhiny Novgorod, Russia	53
2010, Dec. 2-5	Grassland fire, Israel	44
2012, Feb. 14	Prison fire, Comayagua, Honduras	360+
2012, Nov. 24	Garment factory, Bagladesh	112
2013, Jan. 27	Nightclub, Santa Maria, Brazil	241
2014, May 2	Trade union building, Odessa, Ukraine	40+
2016, Apr. 10	Temple fireworks, Kerala, India	110+
2016, Dec. 2	"Ghost Ship" warehouse, Oakland, CA	36
2017, June 14	Grenfell Tower apts., London, Eng., UK	80
2017, June 17-18	Forest fires, central Portugal	64
2018, July 23	Wildfires, Attica region, Greece	99

U.S. Fires, 2017

Source: National Fire Protection Association

- Public fire departments responded to 1.3 mil fires in 2017, including 499,500 structure fires (357,000 in homes), 168,000 vehicle fires, and 623,000 fires outside and in other properties. An estimated 22,500 fires were intentionally set.

- An estimated 3,400 civilians died in fires in 2017, 280 in intentionally set structure fires.

- There were an estimated 14,670 civilian fire injuries reported, 10,600 of them in home structure fires.

- Direct property damage from fires amounted to an estimated $23 bil. Structure fires accounted for $10.7 bil of property damage, and property loss associated with home fires came to $7.7 bil.

Some Notable Explosions Since 1920

See also Principal U.S. Mine Disasters Since 1867. Some bombings related to political conflicts and terrorism are not included.

Date	Location	Deaths
1920, Sept. 16	Wall Street, New York, NY	30
1921, Sept. 21	Chem. storage facility, Oppau, Ger.	561
1924, Jan. 3	Food plant, Pekin, IL	42
1927, May 18	School bombing, Bath, MI	45
1928, Apr. 13	Dance hall, West Plains, MO	40
1937, Mar. 18	School, New London, TX	311
1940, Sept. 12	Hercules Powder factory, Kenvil, NJ	55
1942, Apr. 26	Honkeiko (Benxihu) colliery, China	1,549
1942, June 5	Ordnance plant, Elwood, IL	49
1944, Apr. 14	SS *Fort Stikine*, Bombay docks, India	700

Date	Location	Deaths
1944, July 17	Munitions ships, depot, Port Chicago, CA	322
1944, Oct. 20	Liquid natural gas tanks, Cleveland, OH	130
1947, Apr. 16	Freighter, chemical co. plant, Texas City, TX	576
1948, July 28	Farben works, Ludwigshafen, Ger.	184
1950, May 19	Munitions barges, S. Amboy, NJ	30
1954, May 26	USS *Bennington*, off RI	103
1956, Aug. 7	Dynamite trucks, Cali, Colombia	1,100
1958, Apr. 18	Sunken munitions ship, Okinawa, Japan	40

Date	Location	Deaths
1959, Apr. 10	WWII bomb, Philippines	38
1959, June 28	Rail tank cars, Meldrim, GA	25
1959, Aug. 7	Truck filled with explosives, Roseburg, OR	14
1959, Nov. 2	Explosives, Jamuri Bazar, India	46
1959, Dec. 13	2 apt. bldgs., Dortmund, Germany	26
1960, Mar. 4	Belgian munitions ship, Havana, Cuba	100
1962, Oct. 3	New York Telephone Co. office, New York, NY	23
1963, Jan. 2	Packing plant, Terre Haute, IN	17
1963, Mar. 9	Dynamite plant, S. Africa	45
1963, Aug. 13	Explosives dump, Gauhaiti, India	32
1963, Oct. 31	State Fair Coliseum, Indianapolis, IN	73
1963, Nov. 9	Mitsui Miike coal mine, Japan	458
1964, July 23	Harbor munitions, Bone, Algeria	100
1965, Aug. 9	Missile silo, Searcy, AR	53
1965, Oct. 21	Bridge, Tila Bund, Pakistan	80
1965, Nov. 24	Armory, Keokuk, IA	20
1968, Apr. 6	Sports store, Richmond, IN	43
1969, Mar. 31	Coal mine, nr. Barroteran, Mexico	180
1970, Apr. 8	Subway construction, Osaka, Japan	73
1971, June 24	Tunnel under construction, Sylmar, CA	17
1973, Feb. 10	Liquid gas tank, Staten Island, NY	40
1975, Dec. 27	Coal mine, Chasnala, India	431
1976, Apr. 13	Munitions works, Lapua, Finland	40
1977, Nov. 11	Freight train, Iri, S. Korea	57
1977, Dec. 22	Grain elevator, Westwego, LA	35
1978, July 11	Propylene tank truck, Tarragona, Spain	150
1980, Oct. 23	School, Ortuella, Spain	64
1982, Apr. 25	Antiques exhibition, Todi, Italy	33
1982, Nov. 2	Salang Tunnel, Afghanistan	1,000+
1984, Feb. 25	Oil pipeline, Cubatao, Brazil	508
1984, June 21	Naval supply depot, Severomorsk, USSR	200+
1984, Nov. 19	Gas storage area, NE Mexico City	334
1984, Dec. 3	Chemical plant, Bhopal, India	3,849
1984, Dec. 5	Coal mine, Taipei, Taiwan	94
1985, June 25	Fireworks factory, Hallett, OK	21
1988, Apr. 10	Army ammunitions dump nr. Rawalpindi and Islamabad, Pakistan	100
1988, July 6	Oil rig, North Sea off NE Scotland, UK	167
1989, June 3	Gas pipeline, between Ufa, Asha, USSR	650+
1992, Mar. 3	Coal mine, Kozlu, Turkey	270+
1992, Apr. 22	Gas leak in sewers, Guadalajara, Mexico	200+
1992, May 9	Coal mine, Plymouth, Nova Scotia, Can.	26
1993, Feb. 26	World Trade Center, New York, NY	6
1994, July 18	Jewish community center, Buenos Aires, Argentina	100
1995, Apr. 19	Fed. office building, Oklahoma City, OK	168
1995, Apr. 29	Subway construction, S. Korea	110
1996, Jan. 31	Bank, Colombo, Sri Lanka	53
1996, Mar. 3-4	Jerusalem and Tel Aviv, Israel	33
1996, June 25	U.S. military housing complex, nr. Dhahran, Saudi Arabia	19
1996, July 24	Train, Colombo, Sri Lanka	86
1996, Nov. 16	Military apt., Dagestan region, Russia	68
1996, Nov. 21	Propane gas leak in building, San Juan, Puerto Rico	33
1996, Nov. 27	Coal mine, Shanxi Prov., China	91+
1996, Dec. 30	Train, Assam, India	59+
1997, Dec. 2	Coal mine, Novokuznetsk, Russia	68
1998, Feb. 14	2 oil tankers, Yaounde, Cameroon	120
1998, Feb. 14	17 bombs, Coimbatore, India	50
1998, Apr. 4	Coal mine, Donetsk, Ukraine	63
1998, Aug. 7	Bomb, U.S. emb., Nairobi, Kenya	213
1998, Aug. 7	Bomb, U.S. emb., Dar-es-Salaam, Tanzania	11
1998, Sept. 8	2 buses, São Paulo, Brazil	59
1998, Oct. 17	Oil pipeline, Jesse, Nigeria	700+
1999, May 16	Fuel truck, Punjab Prov., Pakistan	75

Date	Location	Deaths
1999, Sept. 9	Apartment building, Moscow, Russia	94
1999, Sept. 13	Apartment building, Moscow, Russia	118
1999, Sept. 16	Apartment building, Moscow, Russia	18
1999, Sept. 26	Fireworks factory, Celaya, Mexico	56
2000, Feb. 25	Bombs on 2 buses, Ozamis, Philippines	41
2000, Mar. 11	Coal mine, Krasnodon, Ukraine	80
2000, Apr. 16	Airport hangar, Dem. Rep. of Congo	100+
2000, July 16	Oil pipeline, Warri, Nigeria	30
2000, Sept. 9	Truck explosion, Urumqi, China	60
2000, Oct. 12	USS Cole, Yemen	17
2001, Mar. 6	School, Jianxi Prov., China	41
2001, Apr. 21	Coal mine, Shaanxi, China	51
2001, June 1	Dance club, Tel Aviv, Israel	21
2001, July 17	Coal mine, Guanxi, China	76+
2001, Aug. 19	Coal mine, Donetsk region, Ukraine	52
2001, Sept. 21	Chem. plant, Toulouse, France	29
2002, Jan. 21	Volcanic lava caused gas station blast, Goma, Dem. Rep. of Congo	50+
2002, Jan. 27	Munitions dump, Lagos, Nigeria	1,000+
2002, May 9	Land mine at parade, Kaspiisk, Russia	34+
2002, June 14	Car bomb outside U.S. consulate, Karachi, Pakistan	12
2002, June 18	Bomb on bus, Jerusalem, Israel	20
2002, July 5	Bomb in market, Larba, Algeria	35+
2002, Aug. 9	Explosion, Jalalabad, Afghanistan	25+
2002, Sept. 5	Car bomb, Kabul, Afghanistan	30
2002, Oct. 12	Nightclub bombings, Bali, Indonesia	202
2003, Aug. 25	Bombs in 2 taxis, Mumbai, India	52
2003, Dec. 5	Bomb on train, Yessentuki, Russia	45
2003, Dec. 23	Gas well explosion, Chongqing, China	233
2004, Jan. 19	Natural gas facility, Skikda, Algeria	27
2004, Feb. 6	Bomb on subway car, Moscow, Russia	39
2004, Mar. 11	Bombs on commuter trains, Madrid, Spain	191
2005, Feb. 14	Coal mine, NE China	214
2005, Mar. 23	Oil refinery, Texas City, TX	15
2005, May 2	Arms cache, Baghlan Prov., Afghan.	34+
2005, July 7	Bombs in mass transit, London, Eng., UK	56
2005, Oct. 1	Bombings of restaurants, Bali, Indonesia	26
2005, Nov. 27	Coal mine, NE China	161+
2006, May 12	Oil pipeline, nr. Lagos, Nigeria	200
2006, July 1	Bombings of trains, station, Mumbai, India	207
2007, Mar. 19	Coal mine, Siberia, Russia	108
2007, Mar. 22	Natl. weapons depot, Maputo, Mozambique	117
2007, June 9	Oil pipeline, Pyongan Prov., N. Korea	110
2007, Nov. 18	Methane gas buildup in coal mine, E Ukraine	90
2008, May 15	Pipeline explosion in Lagos, Nigeria	100+
2008, Sept. 20	Truck bomb outside hotel, Islamabad, Pakistan	40+
2009, Feb. 22	Coal mine, N China	74
2010, May 8-9	Coal mine, Siberia, Russia	91
2010, June 17	Coal mine, Amaga, Colombia	73
2010, Nov. 19	Coal mine, Ataru, New Zealand	29
2011, Mar. 28	Munitions factory, Abyan, Yemen	150+
2011, July 13	Bombs in three locations in Mumbai, India	27
2012, Mar. 4	Arms depot, Brazzaville, Congo Rep.	250+
2013, Apr. 17	Fertilizer plant, West, TX	15
2013, June 3	Poultry plant, Mishzai, China	119+
2013, June 30	Fuel tanker, Kampala, Uganda	30+
2013, July 6	Derailed oil train, Lac-Megantic, QC, Canada	47
2013, Aug. 1	Weapons cache, Homs, Syria	40
2014, May 13	Coal mine, Soma, Turkey	301
2015, Aug. 12	Chemical warehouse, Tianjin, China	173
2017, Oct. 27	Fireworks factory, Tangerang, Indonesia	47+

The Great Molasses Flood

Date: Jan. 15, 1919. **Location:** Boston, MA. **Fatalities:** 21.

More than 2.3 mil gallons of molasses swept through the North End of Boston in the early afternoon of Jan. 15, 1919, killing 21 people and injuring more than 150. The thick, dark brown sugar syrup burst from a massive waterfront storage tank, which had been holding the molasses since its arrival two days earlier by ship from the Caribbean. Present-day engineers believe the steel tank failed because of poor design. Regardless of the exact cause, the cold temperatures made the molasses behave like tar, according to scientists who investigated the disaster. Historic accounts describe a 30-ft-high wave of molasses moving at 35 mi per hour. Within a few minutes, the molasses had trapped and suffocated people and horses over two city blocks, and vehicles and buildings in its path were destroyed.

Principal U.S. Mine Disasters Since 1867

Source: Bureau of Mines, U.S. Dept. of the Interior; Office of Mine Safety Health Research, Centers for Disease Control
All are bituminous coal mines unless otherwise noted.

Date	Location	Deaths	Date	Location	Deaths	Date	Location	Deaths
1867, Apr. 3	Winterpock, VA	69	1910, May 5	Palos, AL	84	1924, Mar. 8	Castle Gate, UT	172
1869, Sept. 6	Plymouth, PA	110	1910, Nov. 8	Delagua, CO	79	1924, Apr. 28	Benwood, WV	119
1883, Feb. 16	Braidwood, IL	69	1911, Apr. 7	Troop, PA	73	1926, Jan. 13	Wilburton, OK	91
1884, Mar. 13	Pocahontas, VA	112	1911, Apr. 8	Littleton, AL	128	1927, Apr. 30	Everettville, WV	97
1891, Jan. 27	Mt. Pleasant, PA	109	1911, Dec. 9	Briceville, TN	84	1928, May 19	Mather, PA	195
1892, Jan. 7	Krebs, OK	100	1912, Mar. 20	McCurtain, OK	73	1929, Dec. 17	McAlester, OK	61
1895, Mar. 20	Red Canyon, WY	62	1912, Mar. 26	Jed, WV	81	1930, Nov. 5	Millfield, OH	82
1900, May 1	Scofield, UT	200	1913, Apr. 23	Finleyville, PA	98	1940, Jan. 10	Bartley, WV	91
1902, May 19	Coal Creek, TN	184	1913, Oct. 22	Dawson, NM	263	1940, Mar. 16	St. Clairsville, OH	72
1902, July 10	Johnstown, PA	112	1914, Apr. 28	Eccles, WV	181	1940, July 15	Portage, PA	63
1903, June 30	Hanna, WY	169	1915, Mar. 2	Layland, WV	115	1943, Feb. 27	Washoe, MT	74
1904, Jan. 25	Cheswick, PA	179	1917, Apr. 27	Hastings, CO	121	1944, July 5	Powhatan Pt., OH	66
1905, Feb. 20	Virginia City, AL	112	1917, June 8	Butte, MT[1]	163	1947, Mar. 25	Centralia, IL	111
1907, Jan. 29	Stuart, WV	84	1917, Aug. 4	Clay, KY	62	1951, Dec. 21	West Frankfort, IL	119
1907, Dec. 6	Monongah, WV	362	1919, June 5	Wilkes-Barre, PA	92	1968, Nov. 20	Farmington, WV	78
1907, Dec. 19	Van Meter, PA	239	1922, Nov. 6	Spangler, PA	79	1970, Dec. 30	Hyden, KY	38
1908, Nov. 28	Marianna, PA	154	1922, Nov. 22	Dolomite, AL	90	1972, Feb. 26	Saunders, WV	114
1909, Jan. 12	Switchback, WV	67	1923, Feb. 8	Dawson, NM	120	1972, May 2	Kellogg, ID[2]	91
1909, Nov. 13	Cherry, IL	259	1923, Aug. 14	Kemmerer, WY	99	2010, Apr. 5	Montcoal, WV	29
1910, Jan. 31	Primero, CO	75						

Note: The world's worst mine disaster killed 1,549 workers in Manchuria, China, Apr. 26, 1942. (1) Copper mine. (2) Silver mine.

Notable Nuclear Accidents

Oct. 7, 1957: Fire in the Windscale plutonium production reactor N of Liverpool, England, UK, released radioactive material; later blamed for 39 cancer deaths.

Jan. 3, 1961: Reactor explosion at a federal installation near Idaho Falls, ID, killed 3 workers. Radiation contained.

Oct. 5, 1966: Sodium cooling system malfunction caused a partial core meltdown at the Enrico Fermi demonstration breeder reactor, near Detroit, MI. Radiation contained.

Jan. 21, 1969: Coolant malfunction from an experimental underground reactor at Lucens Vad, Switzerland, released radiation into a cavern, which was then sealed.

Mar. 22, 1975: Fire at the Brown's Ferry reactor in Decatur, AL, caused dangerous lowering of cooling water levels.

Mar. 28, 1979: Worst commercial nuclear accident in the U.S. occurred as equipment failures and human mistakes led to a loss of coolant and a partial core meltdown at the Three Mile Island reactor in Middletown, PA.

Feb. 11, 1981: Eight workers were contaminated when 100,000 gallons of radioactive coolant leaked into the containment building of TVA's Sequoyah 1 plant near Chattanooga, TN.

Apr. 25, 1981: Some 100 workers were exposed to radiation during repairs of a nuclear plant at Tsuruga, Japan.

Jan. 6, 1986: Cylinder of nuclear material burst after being improperly heated at a Kerr-McGee plant in Gore, OK. One worker died; 100 were hospitalized.

Apr. 26, 1986: Fires and resulting explosions at the Chernobyl nuclear power plant near Kiev, USSR (now in Ukraine), left at least 31 dead in the immediate aftermath and spread radioactive material over much of Europe. An estimated 135,000 people were evacuated. Tens of thousands of excess cancer deaths (as well as increased birth defects) were expected.

Sept. 1987: Cesium chloride from an improperly discarded hospital irradiation machine contaminated more than 200 people and killed at least 4 in Goiânia, Brazil. The event focused international attention on improving security and safety standards for radioactive waste.

Mar. 11, 2011: A 9.0 magnitude earthquake caused a devastating tsunami that inundated the Fukushima Daiichi nuclear power plant on Japan's NE coast. Three of the plant's reactors suffered partial meltdowns, and more than 12,000 tons of radioactive water was released into the sea. More than two years later, the plant's owners reported that 300 tons of radioactive water was still leaking into the ocean every day.

Record Oil Spills

The exact number of barrels in a ton varies with the type of oil, but a general approximation is 7 barrels per ton. By custom, 42 gallons constitute a barrel of crude oil.

Name, location	Date	Cause	Est. tons
BP *Deepwater Horizon* rig, Gulf of Mexico, U.S.	Apr. 20-July 15, 2010	Explosion	700,000[1]
Ixtoc I oil well, S Gulf of Mexico	June 3, 1979	Blowout	600,000
Nowruz oil field, Persian Gulf	Feb. 1983	Blowout	600,000
Atlantic Empress, off Trinidad and Tobago	July 19, 1979	Collision with *Aegean Captain*	276,000
ABT Summer, off Angola	May 28, 1991	Explosion	260,000
Amoco Cadiz, near Portsall, France	Mar. 16, 1978	Grounding	223,000
Castillo de Bellver, off Cape Town, South Africa	Aug. 6, 1983	Fire	150,000-160,000
Haven, off Genoa, Italy	Apr. 11, 1991	Explosion	144,000
Odyssey, off Nova Scotia, Canada	Nov. 10, 1988	Broke apart in storm	132,000
Torrey Canyon, off Land's End, England, UK	Mar. 18, 1967	Grounding	119,000
Sea Star, Gulf of Oman	Dec. 19, 1972	Collision	115,000
Urquiola, La Coruna, Spain	May 12, 1976	Grounding	100,000

(1) The Dept. of Energy estimated the spill at 4.9 mil barrels, or more than 200 mil gallons.

Other Notable Oil Spills

Name, location	Date	Cause	Gallons
Persian Gulf	Jan. 21, 1991	Intentional spillage by Iraq	130,000,000[1]
Braer, off Shetland Islands, UK	Jan. 5, 1993	Grounding	26,000,000
Prestige, off N Spain	Nov. 13-19, 2002	Ship broke in half	22,600,000
Aegean Sea, off N Spain	Dec. 3, 1992	Grounding	21,500,000
Sea Empress, off SW Wales, UK	Feb. 15, 1996	Grounding	18,000,000
Newtown Creek, Greenpoint, Brooklyn, NY	Oct. 5, 1950-present	Industrial explosion[2]	17,000,000
Hawaiian Patriot, off Hawaii in Pacific	Feb. 23-24, 1977	Hull cracked; ship exploded	14,700,000
World Glory, off South Africa	June 13, 1968	Hull failure	13,524,000
Exxon Valdez, Prince William Sound, AK	Mar. 24, 1989	Grounding	10,080,000
Ashland Oil facility, Floreffe, PA; Monongahela R.	Jan. 2, 1988	Storage tank collapse	3,850,000

(1) Est. by Saudi Arabia. Some estimates as low as 25 mil gal. (2) Legacy of refinery operations since mid-1800s and leaking storage tanks. Spill estimated at up to 30 mil gal.

AEROSPACE

Notable Human Spaceflight Missions

Source: National Aeronautics and Space Administration (NASA); Congressional Research Service; World Almanac research

The spaceflights listed are a selection of notable crewed U.S. missions by NASA, unless otherwise noted, plus crewed non-U.S. missions (shown with an asterisk). The non-U.S missions were sponsored by the USSR—later, the Commonwealth of Independent States (CIS) and, from 1997, Russia—or by China. Launch dates are Eastern Standard Time. **EVA** = extravehicular activity. **ASTP** = Apollo-Soyuz Test Project. **STS** = Space Transportation System, NASA's name for the overall shuttle program. For shuttle flights, mission name is in parentheses following name of orbiter. Duration of flight is listed in hours:minutes for 1961-Apr. 1970; days (d.), hours (hr.), and minutes (min.) thereafter. Number of total flights taken by each crew member is given in parentheses when flight listed is not the person's first.

4/12/1961: *Vostok 1*; 1:48; Yuri A. Gagarin. **1st human orbital flight.**

5/5/1961: *Mercury-Redstone 3*; 0:15; Alan B. Shepard Jr. **1st American in space.**

7/21/1961: *Mercury-Redstone 4*; 0:15; Virgil I. Grissom. Flight successful but spacecraft sank shortly after splashdown; Grissom rescued.

8/6/1961: *Vostok 2*; 25:18; Gherman S. Titov. 1st spaceflight of more than 24 hours.

2/20/1962: *Mercury-Atlas 6*; 4:55; John H. Glenn Jr. **1st American in orbit**; three orbits.

5/24/1962: *Mercury-Atlas 7*; 4:56; M. Scott Carpenter. Manual retrofire error caused 250-mi landing overshoot.

8/11/1962: *Vostok 3*; 94:22; Andrian G. Nikolayev. *Vostok 3* and *4* made 1st group flight.

8/12/1962: *Vostok 4*; 70:57; Pavel R. Popovich. On 1st orbit, it came within 3 mi of *Vostok 3*.

10/3/1962: *Mercury-Atlas 8*; 9:13; Walter M. Schirra Jr. Landed 5 mi from target; six orbits.

5/15/1963: *Mercury-Atlas 9*; 34:19; L. Gordon Cooper. 1st U.S. evaluation of effects of one day in space on a person; 22 orbits.

6/14/1963: *Vostok 5*; 119:06; Valery F. Bykovsky. *Vostok 5* and *6* made 2nd group flight.

6/16/1963: *Vostok 6*; 70:50; Valentina V. Tereshkova. **1st woman in space**; passed within 3 mi of *Vostok 5*.

10/12/1964: *Voskhod 1*; 24:17; Vladimir M. Komarov, Konstantin P. Feoktistov, Boris B. Yegorov. 1st three-person orbital flight; 1st without space suits.

3/18/1965: *Voskhod 2*; 26:02; Pavel I. Belyayev, Aleksei A. Leonov. Leonov made **1st spacewalk** (10 min.).

3/23/1965: *Gemini-Titan 3*; 4:53; Virgil I. Grissom (2), John W. Young. 1st piloted spacecraft to change its orbital path.

6/3/1965: *Gemini-Titan 4*; 97:56; James A. McDivitt, Edward H. White II. White was **1st American to "walk in space"** (23 min.).

8/21/1965: *Gemini-Titan 5*; 190:55; L. Gordon Cooper (2), Charles Conrad Jr. Longest-duration human flight to date.

12/4/1965: *Gemini-Titan 7*; 330:35; Frank Borman, James A. Lovell Jr. Longest-duration *Gemini* flight.

12/15/1965: *Gemini-Titan 6A*; 25:51; Walter M. Schirra Jr. (2), Thomas P. Stafford. Completed 1st U.S. space rendezvous, with *Gemini 7*.

3/16/1966: *Gemini-Titan 8*; 10:41; Neil A. Armstrong, David R. Scott. **1st docking of one space vehicle with another**; mission aborted, control malfunction.

6/3/1966: *Gemini-Titan 9A*; 72:21; Thomas P. Stafford (2), Eugene A. Cernan. Performed simulation of lunar module rendezvous.

7/18/1966: *Gemini-Titan 10*; 70:47; John W. Young (2), Michael Collins. 1st use of Agena target vehicle's propulsion systems; 1st orbital docking.

9/12/1966: *Gemini-Titan 11*; 71:17; Charles Conrad Jr. (2), Richard F. Gordon Jr. 1st tethered flight; highest Earth-orbit altitude (850 mi).

11/11/1966: *Gemini-Titan 12*; 94:34; James A. Lovell Jr. (2), Edwin E. "Buzz" Aldrin Jr. Final *Gemini* mission; 5-hr. EVA.

1/27/1967: *Apollo 1*; Virgil I. Grissom, Edward H. White II, and Roger B. Chaffee died in a fire on the ground at Cape Canaveral, FL.

4/23/1967: *Soyuz 1*; 26:40; Vladimir M. Komarov (2). Crashed on reentry, killing Komarov; **1st space fatality.**

10/11/1968: *Apollo-Saturn 7*; 260:09; Walter M. Schirra Jr. (3), Donn F. Eisele, R. Walter Cunningham. **1st piloted flight of *Apollo*** spacecraft command-service module only; live TV footage of crew.

12/21/1968: *Apollo-Saturn 8*; 147:00; Frank Borman (2), James A. Lovell Jr. (3), William A. Anders. **1st lunar orbit** and piloted lunar return reentry (command-service module only); views of lunar surface televised to Earth.

1/14/1969: *Soyuz 4*; 71:21; Vladimir A. Shatalov. Docked with *Soyuz 5*.

1/15/1969: *Soyuz 5*; 72:54; Boris V. Volyanov, Aleksei S. Yeliseyev, Yevgeny V. Khrunov. Docked with *Soyuz 4*; Yeliseyev and Khrunov transferred to *Soyuz 4* via a spacewalk.

3/3/1969: *Apollo-Saturn 9*; 241:00; James A. McDivitt (2), David R. Scott (2), Russell L. Schweickart. 1st piloted flight of lunar module.

5/18/1969: *Apollo-Saturn 10*; 192:03; Thomas P. Stafford (3), John W. Young (3), Eugene A. Cernan (2). 1st lunar module orbit of Moon, 50,000 ft from Moon's surface.

7/16/1969: *Apollo-Saturn 11*; 195:18; Neil A. Armstrong (2), Michael Collins (2), Edwin E. "Buzz" Aldrin Jr. (2). **1st Moon landing** made by Armstrong and Aldrin (7/20); collected 47.5 lbs of soil, rock samples; lunar stay time 21:36.

10/11/1969: *Soyuz 6*; 118:43; Georgi S. Shonin, Valery N. Kubasov. 1st welding of metals in space.

10/12/1969: *Soyuz 7*; 118:40; Anatoly V. Flipchenko, Vladislav N. Volkov, Viktor V. Gorbatko. Space lab construction test made; *Soyuz 6, 7,* and *8*: 1st time three spacecraft, seven crew members orbited the Earth at once.

10/13/1969: *Soyuz 8*; 118:51; Vladimir A. Shatalov (2), Aleksei S. Yeliseyev (2). Part of space lab construction team.

11/14/1969: *Apollo-Saturn 12*; 244:36; Charles Conrad Jr. (3), Richard F. Gordon Jr. (2), Alan L. Bean. Conrad and Bean made **2nd Moon landing** (11/18); collected 75 lbs of samples; lunar stay time 31:31.

4/11/1970: *Apollo-Saturn 13*; 142:54; James A. Lovell Jr. (4), Fred W. Haise Jr., John L. Swigert Jr. Aborted after service module oxygen tank ruptured; crew returned in lunar module.

6/1/1970: *Soyuz 9*; 17 d., 16 hr., 59 min.; Andrian G. Nikolayev (2), Vitaly I. Sevastyanov. Longest human spaceflight to date.

1/31/1971: *Apollo-Saturn 14*; 9 d., 2 min.; Alan B. Shepard Jr. (2), Stuart A. Roosa, Edgar D. Mitchell. Shepard and Mitchell made **3rd Moon landing** (2/5); collected 94 lbs of lunar samples; lunar stay 33:31.

4/19/1971: *Salyut 1*; launched without crew. **1st space station.**

4/22/1971: *Soyuz 10*; 1 d., 23 hr., 46 min.; Vladimir A. Shatalov (3), Aleksei S. Yeliseyev (3), Nikolay N. Rukavishnikov. **1st successful docking with a space station**; failed to enter space station.

6/6/1971: *Soyuz 11*; 23 d., 28 hr., 22 min.; Georgi T. Dobrovolskiy, Vladislav N. Volkov (2), Viktor I. Patsayev. Docked and entered *Salyut 1* space station; **crew died** during reentry from loss of pressurization.

7/26/1971: *Apollo-Saturn 15*; 12 d., 17 hr., 12 min.; David R. Scott (3), James B. Irwin, Alfred M. Worden. Scott and Irwin made **4th Moon landing** (7/30). 1st lunar rover use; 1st deep spacewalk; collected 170 lbs of samples; 66:55 stay.

4/16/1972: *Apollo-Saturn 16*; 11 d., 1 hr., 51 min.; John W. Young (4), Charles M. Duke Jr., Thomas K. Mattingly II. Young and Duke made 5th Moon landing (4/20); collected 209 lbs of lunar samples; lunar stay 71:02.

12/7/1972: *Apollo-Saturn 17*; 12 d., 13 hr., 52 min.; Eugene A. Cernan (3), Ronald E. Evans, Harrison H. Schmitt. Cernan and Schmitt made 6th and **final crewed lunar landing** (12/11); collected 243 lbs of samples; record lunar stay over 75 hr.

5/14/1973: *Skylab 1*; launched without crew. **1st U.S. space station**; fell out of orbit 7/11/1979.

5/25/1973: *Skylab 2*; 28 d., 49 min.; Charles Conrad Jr. (4), Joseph P. Kerwin, Paul J. Weitz. 1st U.S.-piloted orbiting space station; crew repaired damage caused in boost.

7/28/1973: *Skylab 3*; 59 d., 11 hr., 1 min.; Alan L. Bean (2), Owen K. Garriott, Jack R. Lousma. Crew systems and operational tests; scientific activities; three EVAs, 13:44.

11/16/1973: *Skylab 4*; 84 d., 1 hr., 16 min.; Gerald P. Carr, Edward G. Gibson, William R. Pogue. Final *Skylab* mission.

7/15/1975: *Soyuz 19 (ASTP)*; 6 d., 11 hr., 31 min.; Aleksei A. Leonov (2), Valery N. Kubasov (2). U.S.-USSR joint flight; crews linked up in space (7/17), conducted experiments, shared meals, held a joint news conference.

7/15/1975: *Apollo (ASTP)*; 9 d., 7 hr., 28 min.; Vance D. Brand, Thomas P. Stafford (4), Donald K. Slayton. Joint flight with *Soyuz 19*.

12/10/1977: *Soyuz 26*; 96 d., 10 hr.; Yuri V. Romanenko, Georgiy M. Grechko (2). 1st multiple docking at a space station (*Soyuz 26* and *27* docked at *Salyut 6*).

1/10/1978: *Soyuz 27*; 5 d., 22 hr., 59 min.; Vladimir A. Dzhanibekov. See *Soyuz 26.*

3/2/1978: *Soyuz 28*; 7 d., 22 hr., 16 min.; Aleksei A. Gubarev (2), Vladimir Remek. 1st international crew launch; Remek was 1st Czech in space.

4/12/1981: *Columbia (STS-1)*; 2 d., 6 hr., 21 min.; John W. Young (5), Robert L. Crippen. **1st reusable space shuttle** to fly into Earth's orbit.

11/12/1981: *Columbia (STS-2)*; 3 days; Joe H. Engle, Richard H. Truly. 1st scientific payload; 1st reuse of space shuttle.

11/11/1982: *Columbia (STS-5)*; 6 days; Vance D. Brand (2), Robert F. Overmyer, Joseph P. Allen, William B. Lenoir. 1st four-person crew.

6/18/1983: *Challenger (STS-7)*; 7 days; Robert L. Crippen (2), Frederick H. Hauck, John M. Fabian, Sally K. Ride, Norman E. Thagard. Ride was **1st U.S. woman in space**; 1st 5-person crew.

6/27/1983: *Soyuz T-9*; 150 days; Vladimir A. Lyakhov, Aleksandr Pavlovich. Docked at *Salyut 7*. 1st construction in space.

8/30/1983: *Challenger (STS-8)*; 7 days; Richard H. Truly (2), Daniel C. Brandenstein, Dale A. Gardner, Guion S. Bluford Jr., William E. Thornton. Bluford was **1st African-American in space; 1st night launch.**

11/28/1983: *Columbia (STS-9)*; 11 days; John W. Young (6), Brewster H. Shaw Jr., Owen K. Garriott (2), Robert A.R. Parker, Byron K. Lichtenberg, Ulf Merbold. 1st six-person crew; 1st Spacelab mission.

2/3/1984: *Challenger (41-B)*; 8 days; Vance Brand (3), Robert L. Gibson, Ronald E. McNair, Bruce McCandless II, Robert L. Stewart. 1st untethered EVA.

2/8/1984: *Soyuz T-10B*; 63 days; Leonid Kizim, Vladimir Solovyov, Oleg Atkov. Docked with *Salyut 7*; crew set space duration record of 237 days (since eclipsed).

4/3/1984: *Soyuz T-11*; 182 days; Yury Malyshev (2), Gennady Strekalov (3), Rakesh Sharma. Docked with *Salyut 7*; Sharma was 1st Indian in space.

4/6/1984: *Challenger (41-C)*; 7 days; Robert L. Crippen (3), Francis R. Scobee, George D. Nelson, Terry J. Hart, James D. van Hoften. 1st in-orbit satellite repair.

8/30/1984: *Discovery (41-D)*; 7 days; Henry W. Hartsfield Jr. (2), Michael L. Coats, Richard M. Mullane, Steven A. Hawley, Judith A. Resnik, Charles D. Walker. 1st flight of non-astronaut (payload specialist Walker).

10/5/1984: *Challenger (41-G)*; 9 days; Robert L. Crippen (4), Jon A. McBride, Kathryn D. Sullivan, Sally K. Ride (2), David C. Leestma, Marc Garneau, Paul D. Scully-Power. 1st seven-person crew.

11/8/1984: *Discovery (51-A)*; 8 days; Frederick H. Hauck (2), David M. Walker, Anna L. Fisher, Dale A. Gardner (2), Joseph P. Allen (2). 1st satellite retrieval/repair.

4/12/1985: *Discovery (51-D)*; 7 days; Karol J. Bobko, Donald E. Williams, Charles D. Walker (2), M. Rhea Seddon, Jeffrey A. Hoffman, S. David Griggs, E. Jake Garn. Garn (R, UT) was **1st U.S. senator in space.**

6/17/1985: *Discovery (51-G)*; 8 days; Daniel C. Brandenstein (2), John O. Creighton, Shannon W. Lucid, John M. Fabian (2), Steven R. Nagel, Prince Sultan Salman al-Saud, Patrick Baudry. Launched three satellites; Salman al-Saud was 1st Arab in space; Baudry was 1st French person on U.S. mission.

10/3/1985: *Atlantis (51-J)*; 5 days; Karol J. Bobko (3), Ronald J. Grabe, David C. Hilmers, Robert L. Stewart (2), William A. Pailes. 1st *Atlantis* flight.

10/30/1985: *Challenger (61-A)*; 8 days; Henry W. Hartsfield Jr. (3), Steven R. Nagel (2), James F. Buchli (2), Guion S. Bluford Jr. (2), Bonnie J. Dunbar, Wubbo J. Ockels, Richard Furrer, Ernst Messerschmid. 1st eight-person crew; 1st German Spacelab mission.

1/12/1986: *Columbia (61-C)*; 7 days; Robert L. Gibson (2), Charles F. Bolden Jr., Franklin R. Chang Díaz, Steven A. Hawley (2), George D. Nelson (2), Robert J. Cenker, Bill Nelson. B. Nelson (D, FL) was **1st U.S. representative in space.**

1/28/1986: *Challenger (51-L)*; 73 seconds; Francis R. Scobee (2), Michael J. Smith, Judith A. Resnik (2), Ellison S. Onizuka (2), Ronald E. McNair, Gregory B. Jarvis, Christa McAuliffe. **Exploded 73 seconds after liftoff; all aboard were killed**, including McAuliffe, a New Hampshire schoolteacher who won competition to become 1st private citizen in space.

2/20/1986: *Mir[1]*; launched without crew. **Space station** with six docking ports launched.

3/13/1986: *Soyuz T-15*; 125 days; Leonid Kizim (3), Vladimir Solovyov (2). Ferry between stations; docked at *Mir.*

9/29/1988: *Discovery (STS-26)*; 4 days; Frederick H. Hauck (3), Richard O. Covey (2), George D. Nelson (3), John M. Lounge (2), David C. Hilmers (2). **1st shuttle flight since *Challenger* explosion** 1/28/1986.

5/4/1989: *Atlantis (STS-30)*; 4 days; David M. Walker (2), Ronald J. Grabe (2), Norman E. Thagard (3), Mary L. Cleave (2), Mark C. Lee. Launched Venus orbiter *Magellan.*

10/18/1989: *Atlantis (STS-34)*; 5 days; Donald E. Williams (2), Michael J. McCulley, Shannon W. Lucid (2), Franklin R. Chang Díaz (2), Ellen S. Baker. Launched Jupiter probe and orbiter *Galileo.*

4/24/1990: *Discovery (STS-31)*; 6 days; Loren J. Shriver (2), Charles F. Bolden Jr. (2), Steven A. Hawley (3), Bruce McCandless (2), Kathryn D. Sullivan (2). **Launched Hubble Space Telescope.**

10/6/1990: *Discovery (STS-41)*; 5 days; Richard N. Richards (2), Robert D. Cabana, Bruce E. Melnick, William M. Shepherd (2), Thomas D. Akers. Launched *Ulysses* spacecraft to investigate interstellar space and the Sun.

9/12/1992: *Endeavour (STS-47)*; 8 days; Robert L. Gibson (4), Curtis L. Brown Jr., Mark C. Lee (2), N. Jan Davis, Jay Apt (2), Mae Carol Jemison, Mamoru Mohri. Jemison was **1st black woman in space**; Lee and Davis were **1st married couple to travel together in space**; 1st Japanese Spacelab.

6/21/1993: *Endeavour (STS-57)*; 10 days; Ronald J. Grabe (4), Brian J. Duffy (2), G. David Low (3), Nancy J. Sherlock, Janice E. Voss, Peter J. K. Wisoff. Carried Spacelab commercial payload module.

12/2/1993: *Endeavour (STS-61)*; 11 days; Richard O. Covey (3), Kenneth D. Bowersox (2), F. Story Musgrave (5), Kathryn Thornton (3), Claude Nicollier (2), Jeffrey A. Hoffman (4), Thomas D. Akers (3). Hubble Space Telescope repaired; Akers set new U.S. EVA duration record (29 hr., 40 min.).

3/14/1995: *Soyuz TM-21*; 112 days; Norman E. Thagard (5), Vladimir Dezhurov, Gennady Strekalov (5). Docked with *Mir* 3/16. Thagard was 1st American on board Russian spacecraft; Valery Polyakov returned to Earth, 3/22/1995, after record stay in space (439 days).

6/27/1995: *Atlantis (STS-71)*; 10 days; Robert L. Gibson (5), Charles J. Precourt (2), Ellen S. Baker (3), Bonnie J. Dunbar (4), Gregory J. Harbaugh (3), Anatoly Solovyev (4) (to *Mir*), Nikolai M. Budarin (to *Mir*), Norman E. Thagard (5) (from *Mir*), Gennady Strekalov (from *Mir*), Vladimir Dezhurov (from *Mir*). **1st shuttle-*Mir* docking**; exchanged crew members with *Mir.*

11/12/1995: *Atlantis (STS-74)*; 9 days; Kenneth D. Cameron (3), James D. Halsell Jr. (2), Jerry L. Ross (5), William S. McArthur Jr. (2), Chris A. Hadfield. 2nd shuttle-*Mir* docking (11/15-11/18); erected a 15-ft permanent docking tunnel to *Mir* for future use by U.S. orbiters.

9/16/1996: *Atlantis (STS-79)*; 11 days; William F. Readdy (3), Terry W. Wilcutt (2), Thomas D. Akers (4), John E. Blaha (5) (to *Mir*), Jay Apt (4), Carl E. Walz (2), Shannon W. Lucid (5) (from *Mir*). Docked with *Mir* 9/18; exchanged crew members; Lucid set **U.S. and women's duration in space record** (188 days).

11/19/1996: *Columbia (STS-80)*; 18 days; Kenneth D. Cockrell (3), Kent V. Rominger (2), Tamara E. Jernigan (4), Thomas D. Jones (3), F. Story Musgrave (6). Longest-duration shuttle flight; Musgrave, 61, oldest thus far to fly in space; two science satellites deployed, retrieved.

8/5/1997: *Soyuz TM-26*; 198 days; Anatoly Solovyov (5), Pavel Vinogradov. Docked with *Mir* 8/7; repaired damaged space station.

8/7/1997: *Discovery (STS-85)*; 12 days; Curtis L. Brown Jr. (4), Kent V. Rominger (3), N. Jan Davis (3), Robert L. Curbeam Jr., Stephen K. Robinson, Bjarni V. Tryggvason. Deployed and retrieved satellite designed to study Earth's middle atmosphere; demonstrated robotic arm.

4/17/1998: *Columbia (STS-90)*; 16 days; Richard A. Searfoss (3), Scott D. Altman, Richard M. Linnehan (2), Dave R. Williams, Kathryn P. Hire, Jay C. Buckey, James A. Pawelczyk. Studied effects of microgravity on the nervous systems of the crew and more than 2,000 live animals; 1st surgery in space on animals meant to survive.

6/2/1998: *Discovery (STS-91)*; 10 days; Charles J. Precourt (4), Dominic L. Gorie, Wendy B. Lawrence (3), Franklin R. Chang Díaz (6), Janet L. Kavandi, Valery V. Ryumin (4), Andrew S. W. Thomas (2) (from *Mir*). Final docking mission with *Mir*; Thomas from *Mir*, 141 days in space.

10/29/1998: *Discovery (STS-95)*; 10 days; Curtis L. Brown Jr. (5), Steven W. Lindsey (2), Scott E. Parazynski (3), Stephen K. Robinson (2), Pedro Duque, Chiaki Mukai (2), John H. Glenn Jr. (2). The 77-year-old Glenn, one of the original *Mercury* astronauts, and at that point a senator (D, OH), became **oldest person to fly in space**; Duque was 1st Spaniard in space; experiments to study aging performed on Glenn.

12/4/1998: *Endeavour (STS-88)*; 12 days; Robert D. Cabana (4), Frederick W. Sturckow, Nancy J. Currie (3), Jerry L. Ross (6), James H. Newman (3), Sergei K. Krikalev (4). **1st assembly of International Space Station (ISS)**; attached U.S.-built *Unity* connecting module to Russian-built *Zarya* control module; 1st crew to enter ISS.

7/23/1999: *Columbia (STS-93)*; 5 days; Eileen M. Collins (3), Jeffrey S. Ashby, Steven A. Hawley (5), Catherine G. Coleman (2), Michel Tognini (2). Collins was **1st woman space shuttle commander**; deployed Chandra X-ray Observatory telescope.

2/11/2000: *Endeavour (STS-99)*; 12 days; Kevin R. Kregel (4), Dominic L. Gorie (2), Janet L. Kavandi (2), Janice E. Voss (5), Mamoru Mohri (2), Gerhard P.J. Thiele. Used radar to make most complete topographic map of Earth's surface ever produced.

10/31/2000: *Soyuz TM-31*; William M. Shepherd (4), Yuri Gidzenko (2), Sergei Krikalev (5). Established **1st permanent manning of ISS** with three-person crew for a 4-month stay.

7/12/2001: *Atlantis (STS-104)*; 13 days; Steven W. Lindsey (3), Charles O. Hobaugh, Michael L. Gernhardt (4), Janet L. Kavandi (3), James F. Reilly II (2). Installed the Joint Airlock, with nitrogen and oxygen tanks to permit future spacewalks from the ISS; three EVAs.

10/30/2002: *Soyuz TMA-1*[1]; Sergei Zalyotin (2), Frank De Winne, Yuri Lonchakov (2). 1st launch of *Soyuz TMA* (crew returned 11/10/2002 on *Soyuz TM-34* already docked at ISS).

1/16/2003: *Columbia (STS 107)*; 16 days; Rick D. Husband (2), William C. McCool, Michael P. Anderson (2), David M. Brown, Kalpana Chawla (2), Laurel B. Clark, Ilan Ramon. **Entire crew lost when *Columbia* broke apart** upon reentry, 2/1, due to heat shield damage; Ramon was 1st Israeli astronaut.

10/15/2003: *Shenzhou 5*; 21 hr.; Yang Liwei. **1st Chinese manned spacecraft.**

6/21/2004: *SpaceShipOne*[2]; 90 min.; Mike Melvill. **1st privately funded manned spaceflight.**

7/26/2005: *Discovery (STS-114)*; 14 days; Eileen M. Collins (4), James M. Kelly (2), Charles J. Camarda, Wendy B. Lawrence (4), Soichi Noguchi, Stephen K. Robinson (3), Andrew S.W. Thomas (3). **1st space shuttle flight since *Columbia* disaster**; tested new safety modifications to craft.

6/8/2007: *Atlantis (STS-117)*; 14 days; Frederick W. Sturckow (3), Lee J. Archambault, Patrick G. Forrester (2), John "Danny" Olivas, James F. Reilly (3), Steven R. Swanson, Clayton C. Anderson (to ISS), Sunita L. Williams (from ISS). Delivered truss segments and solar arrays to ISS; Williams set new record for **longest spaceflight by a woman (195 days)**.

8/8/2007: *Endeavour (STS-118)*; 13 days; Scott J. Kelly (2), Charles O. Hobaugh (2), Alvin B. Drew, Barbara R. Morgan, Tracy Caldwell Dyson, Rick A. Mastracchio (2), Dave R. Williams (2). Brought **Teacher in Space** project participant Morgan to ISS; attached new truss.

10/10/2007: *Soyuz TMA-11*[1]; Yuri I. Malenchenko (3), Sheikh Muszaphar Shukor (to ISS), Peggy A. Whitson (2) (from ISS), Yi So-yeon (from ISS). Delivered and installed components of ISS; malfunctioned on return to Earth, landing short of its touchdown area but causing no fatalities.

3/11/2008: *Endeavour (STS-123)*; 16 days; Dominic L. Gorie (4), Gregory H. Johnson, Richard M. Linnehan (4), Robert L. Behnken, Michael J. Foreman, Takao Doi (2), Garrett E. Reisman (to ISS), Léopold Eyharts (from ISS). Delivered components of the Japanese Kibo science laboratory.

4/8/2008: *Soyuz TMA-12*[1]; Oleg Kononenko, Sergei Volkov, Yi So-yeon (to ISS), Richard Garriott (from ISS). Yi became **1st S. Korean in space.**

9/25/2008: *Shenzhou 7*; 68 hr.; Jing Haipeng, Liu Boming, Zhai Zhigang. Zhai completed **1st Chinese spacewalk.**

5/11/2009: *Atlantis (STS-125)*; 13 days; Scott D. Altman (4), Gregory C. Johnson, Andrew J. Feustel, Michael T. Good, John M. Grunsfeld (5), Michael J. Massimino (2), K. Megan McArthur. Final Hubble Space Telescope servicing mission.

6/15/2010: *Soyuz TMA-19*[1]; Fyodor Yurchikhin (3), Shannon Walker, Douglas H. Wheelock (2). 100th mission since launching of the International Space Station.

7/8/2011: *Atlantis (STS-135)*; 13 days; Christopher Ferguson (3), Doug Hurley (2), Sandy H. Magnus (3), Rex J. Walheim (3). **Final space shuttle mission.**

Note: Four Soviet cosmonauts have died during spaceflight: one person was killed on *Soyuz 1* (1967) when parachute lines tangled during descent; the three-person *Soyuz 11* crew (1971) was asphyxiated. Three Americans died in the *Apollo 1* (1967) fire on the ground at Cape Canaveral, FL; seven Americans died in the *Challenger* (1986) explosion; and six Americans and an Israeli astronaut died aboard *Columbia* (2003). (1) *Soyuz* crew often return from the ISS on spacecraft that launched and were docked at the station before their arrival. (2) Date of first successful flight; later, *SpaceShipOne* flew at least 100 km (62 mi) into space, 9/29/2004, piloted by Mike Melvill, and 10/4/2004, piloted by Brian Binnie, winning the $10-mil Ansari Prize for first private venture to accomplish this feat twice within two weeks.

U.S. Space Shuttles
Source: National Aeronautics and Space Administration (NASA)

After 135 launches, the United States ended its space shuttle program with the safe landing of the *Atlantis* shuttle on July 21, 2011, at Florida's Kennedy Space Center. Two shuttles—*Challenger* in 1986 and *Columbia* in 2003—were destroyed in flight. The surviving shuttles are now on display at museums. *Enterprise* performed atmospheric test flights but never flew in space.

Atlantis: Kennedy Space Center, Titusville, FL; www.kennedyspacecenter.com
Discovery: Udvar-Hazy Center, Smithsonian National Air and Space Museum, Chantilly, VA; discovery.si.edu

Endeavour: California Science Center, Los Angeles, CA; www.californiasciencecenter.org
Enterprise: Intrepid Air, Sea, and Space Museum, New York, NY; www.intrepidmuseum.org/Space_Shuttle_Pavilion

International Space Station
Source: National Aeronautics and Space Administration (NASA)

Construction on the International Space Station (ISS) began in 1998 and was completed in 2011. It has been inhabited continuously since 2000 and visited by more than 200 international crew members.
Cooperating nations: Belgium, Canada, Denmark, France, Germany, Italy, Japan, Netherlands, Norway, Russia, Spain, Sweden, Switzerland, United Kingdom, and U.S. As of July 2018, individuals from all of these countries (except Norway and Switzerland) have flown to the ISS, as have visitors from Brazil, Kazakhstan, Malaysia, South Africa, and South Korea.

About the ISS
- It has a mass of 924,739 lbs and is about as long as a football field at 357.5 ft.
- It is entirely powered by an acre of solar panels.
- It requires three people to keep it running but has room for up to 10 people to live aboard.
- Astronauts typically spend 4-6 months aboard.

ISS Research
- Effects of long-term exposure to reduced gravity on humans, plants, crystals, cells, and pathogens
- Recording large-scale long-term changes in Earth's environment by observing the planet from orbit
- Testing recycling technologies for human life support

The Future of Human Space Exploration

Source: National Aeronautics and Space Administration (NASA); SpaceX; World Almanac research

Since the end of NASA's space shuttle program, U.S. astronauts have traveled on Russian spacecraft to reach the International Space Station (ISS), at a reported cost of $81.7 mil per seat in 2018. Private companies Boeing and SpaceX contracted with NASA in 2014 to develop transportation for NASA's ISS astronauts.

SpaceX completed the first of 12 ISS cargo resupply missions in 2012. SpaceX proposed it could make spaceflight less expensive and more efficient by developing reusable rockets and spacecraft. On May 29, 2014, the company unveiled Dragon 2, a reusable spacecraft whose propulsive landing system enabled it to touch down almost anywhere with the precision of a helicopter. SpaceX achieved a space-travel milestone May 6, 2016, when a Falcon 9 rocket, having propelled a Dragon spacecraft to the ISS minutes earlier, returned to Earth, touching down vertically onto a drone ship 185 mil off the east coast of the U.S. In 2018, NASA released the results of an independent investigation into a failed Falcon 9 launch in June 2015, concluding that a design flaw, not a manufacturing defect, was at fault.

SpaceX and Boeing were both on target to launch demonstration vehicles in 2018 that could prove their worthiness to carry human passengers. Boeing's maiden voyage with crew aboard, a CST-100 Starliner launched on a United Launch Alliance Atlas V rocket, was scheduled for mid-2019. SpaceX's first crewed launch, a Dragon spacecraft propelled by a Falcon 9 rocket, was scheduled for Apr. 2019.

The Google Lunar XPrize, which offered $20 mil to the first private company to land a spacecraft on the Moon and perform certain functions, went unclaimed at its Mar. 31, 2018, deadline. The contestants closest to fulfilling the competition's requirements were Astrobotic, a spinoff of the Carnegie Mellon Univ. Robotics Institute, and Moon Express, a startup company that received FAA approval to send a robotic lander to the Moon. Astrobotic won $1.75 mil in so-called milestone prizes while Moon Express won $1.25 mil.

SpaceX abandoned its 2017 plan to send tourists to space on the Falcon Heavy in Feb. 2018, and announced in Sept. 2018 that it planned to send a Japanese billionaire and other crew around the Moon as tourists on the in-development Big Falcon Rocket no earlier than 2023.

Summary of Worldwide Successful Launches, 1957-2017

Source: National Aeronautics and Space Administration (NASA); Space Launch Report

Year	1957-59	1960-69	1970-79	1980-89	1990-99	2000-09	2010-17	Total
Russia[1]	6	399	1,028	1,132	542	246	219	3,572
U.S.	18	614	247	191	300	206	151	1,727
China	—	—	8	16	33	52	139	248
ESA[2]	—	2	5	14	55	63	57	196
Ukraine	—	—	—	—	59	57	25	141
Japan	—	—	18	26	23	18	29	114
India	—	—	1	9	11	13	30	64
France[2]	—	4	14	5	16	0	—	39
UK[2]	—	1	6	4	7	0	—	18
Germany[2]	—	—	3	7	6	0	—	16
Canada	—	—	4	5	4	0	0	13
Israel	—	—	—	—	—	3	3	6
Iran	—	—	—	—	—	1	3	4
North Korea	—	—	—	—	—	—	2	2
South Korea	—	—	—	—	—	1	0	1
New Zealand	—	—	—	—	—	—	1	1
Total	**24**	**1,020**	**1,334**	**1,409**	**1,056**	**660**	**659**	**6,162**

— = Not applicable. (1) Data for 1957-91 apply to the Soviet Union, for 1992-96 to the Commonwealth of Independent States, after 1996 to Russia. (2) ESA = European Space Agency, which includes France, Germany, and UK after 2009.

Notable Lunar and Planetary Science Missions

Source: National Aeronautics and Space Administration (NASA)

Spacecraft	Launch date[1]	Mission	Mission notes
Mariner 2	Aug. 27, 1962	Venus	Passed within 22,000 mi of Venus 12/14/1962; confirmed high surface temperature on planet; contact lost 1/3/1963 at 54 mil mi.
Ranger 7	July 28, 1964	Moon	Yielded over 4,000 photos of lunar surface.
Mariner 4	Nov. 28, 1964	Mars	1st probe to fly by Mars; passed behind planet 7/14/1965.
Ranger 8	Feb. 17, 1965	Moon	Yielded over 7,000 photos of lunar surface.
Venera 3	Nov. 16, 1965	Venus	Soviet probe; 1st artificial probe to impact on the surface of another planet, 3/1/1966; probe failed to send back data.
Surveyor 3	Apr. 17, 1967	Moon	Scooped and tested lunar soil.
Mariner 5	June 14, 1967	Venus	In solar orbit; closest Venus flyby 10/19/1967; allowed scientists to obtain accurate readings on the composition of the Venusian atmosphere.
Mariner 6	Feb. 24, 1969	Mars	Came within 2,000 mi of Mars 7/31/1969; collected data, photos.
Mariner 7	Mar. 27, 1969	Mars	Came within 2,000 mi of Mars 8/5/1969.
Venera 7	Aug. 17, 1970	Venus	Soviet probe; 1st probe to land safely on the surface of another planet.
Mariner 9	May 30, 1971	Mars	1st craft to orbit Mars 11/13/1971; sent back over 7,000 photos.
Pioneer 10	Mar. 2, 1972	Jupiter	Passed Jupiter 12/4/1973; took readings on Jupiter's composition. Exited planetary system 6/13/1983; last signal received 1/23/2003 from 7.6 bil mi.
Pioneer 11	Apr. 5, 1973	Jupiter, Saturn	Passed Jupiter 12/3/1974; Saturn 9/1/1979; discovered an additional ring and 2 moons around Saturn. Transmission ended 9/30/1995.
Mariner 10	Nov. 3, 1973	Venus, Mercury	Passed Venus 2/5/1974, arrived at Mercury 3/29/1974. 1st time gravity of a planet (Venus) used to whip spacecraft toward another (Mercury); 1st probe to visit 2 planets; took cloud and wind pattern readings in Venusian atmosphere.
Viking 1	Aug. 20, 1975	Mars	Landed on Mars 7/20/1976; 1st probe to land safely on Mars; performed chemical analysis of soil; functioned 6 years.
Viking 2	Sept. 9, 1975	Mars	Sister probe of *Viking 1*; landed on Mars 9/3/1976; functioned 3 years.
Voyager 2	Aug. 20, 1977	Jupiter, Saturn, Uranus, Neptune	Encountered Jupiter 7/9/1979, Saturn 8/25/1981, Uranus 1/24/1986, Neptune 8/25/1989. Confirmed existence of rings around Neptune. As of 9/2013 it was 11.0 bil mi from Sun and still returning data to Earth.
Voyager 1	Sept. 5, 1977	Jupiter, Saturn	Encountered Jupiter 3/5/1979; provided evidence of rings around Jupiter; passed near Saturn 11/12/1980; passed *Pioneer 10* to become most distant human-made object 2/17/1998. As of 9/2018 it was 13.4 bil mi from Sun and still returning data to Earth.
Pioneer Venus 1	May 20, 1978	Venus	Entered Venus orbit 12/4/1978; studied atmosphere, magnetic field, weather, and surface; fuel ran out; probe was destroyed in atmospheric entry, 8/1992.

Spacecraft	Launch date[1]	Mission	Mission notes
Pioneer Venus 2 (multiprobe)	Aug. 8, 1978	Venus	Consisted of a "bus" carrying 1 large and 3 small atmospheric probes. All 4 probes entered the Venus atmosphere 12/9/1978, followed by the bus; took readings of atmosphere; probes impacted surface.
Magellan	May 4, 1989	Venus	Landed on Venus 8/10/1990; monitored geological activity; mapped more than 99% of planet surface, showed that about 85% is covered by volcanic flows; ceased operating 10/11/1994.
Galileo	Oct. 18, 1989	Jupiter	Used Earth's gravity to propel itself towards Jupiter; encountered Venus 2/10/1990, Jupiter 12/7/1995; encountered moons. Released probe into Jovian atmosphere; intentionally flown into Jupiter 9/21/2003 to prevent accidental contamination of Jupiter's moon Europa.
Mars Global Surveyor	Nov. 7, 1996	Mars	Began orbiting Mars 9/11/1997; began mapping entire surface 3/9/1999; discovered a weak magnetic field on planet; observed Martian moon Phobos; found evidence of liquid water in past 6/22/2000.
Mars Pathfinder	Dec. 4, 1996	Mars	Landed on Mars 7/4/1997; rover *Sojourner* made measurements of climate and soil composition, sent thousands of surface images; ceased operating 9/27/1997.
Cassini-Huygens	Oct. 15, 1997	Saturn	Began orbiting Saturn 6/30/2004; spotted evidence of a subterranean ocean and 300-mi-wide hot spots region on moon Titan; detected an atmosphere on moon Enceladus. Intentionally destroyed 9/15/2017. *Huygens* probe landed on Titan 1/14/2005; found a muddy surface, possible water ice, channels carved by liquid methane springs.
Lunar Prospector	Jan. 6, 1998	Moon	Began orbiting Moon 1/11/1998; mapped abundance of 11 elements on Moon's surface; discovered evidence of water ice at both lunar poles; crashed into crater near Moon's south pole 7/31/1999 to end mission.
Deep Space 1	Oct. 24, 1998	Comet Borrelly	Flew within 1,500 mi of comet; sent back photos showing 6-mi-long nucleus.
Stardust	Feb. 7, 1999	Comet Wild 2	Reached comet 1/2/2004; gathered dust samples, capsule returned to Earth 1/15/2006. Spacecraft, on new mission Stardust-NExT (follow up for Deep Impact), reached comet Tempel 1, 2/14/2011.
2001 Mars Odyssey	Apr. 7, 2001	Mars	Reached Mars 10/24/2001; detected evidence of water ice near south pole; primary mission to study climate and geologic history completed 8/2004; began extended mission, aiming to identify minerals on Mars.
Genesis	Aug. 8, 2001	Sun	Orbited Sun, collected particles from solar wind; capsule containing specimens crashed to Earth 9/8/2004; some samples survived.
Mars Express/ Beagle 2 lander	June 3, 2003	Mars	1st European Space Agency probe to another planet; arrived at Mars 12/2003; performed remote sensing including photography in search of subsurface water. *Beagle 2* lander was deployed 12/19/2003, but contact was lost.
Mars Exploration Rovers	June 7 and July 10, 2003	Mars	Rovers *Spirit* and *Opportunity* landed on Mars 1/2004, found further evidence that water existed on surface; *Spirit* took 1st photo of a Martian meteor; survived severe dust storms in 2007. *Opportunity* explored massive Victoria Crater 2007-08, set record for most distance driven off-Earth (25 mi) 7/2014.
MESSENGER	Mar. 2, 2004	Mercury	Began returning images of Mercury during initial flyby 1/14/2008; entered orbit 3/17/2011; delivered 100,000th image 5/3/2012; impacted Mercury 4/30/2015.
Deep Impact	Jan. 12, 2005	Comet Tempel 1	Reached Tempel 1; deployed impact probe that slammed into comet 7/4/2005 with force roughly equivalent to 5 tons of TNT. Flyby spacecraft, on supplemental mission EPOXI, reached comet Hartley 2, 11/4/2010.
Mars Reconnaissance Orbiter	Aug. 12, 2005	Mars	Reached Mars 3/10/2006 and began taking detailed images of Martian surface; in 3/2008, found salt deposits suggesting ancient water supplies; in 6/2008, found largest known impact crater in solar system.
New Horizons (Pluto)	Jan. 19, 2006	Pluto, Charon	Flew past Jupiter 7/2007 on its way to Pluto and its largest moon, Charon. Returned first-ever photographs of Pluto 7/14/2015. Will examine other objects in the Kuiper Belt.
Phoenix Mars Lander	Aug. 4, 2007	Mars	Landed on Mars 5/25/2008; examined northern polar region, analyzed weather/minerals; water ice verified 7/31/2008; lost contact 11/2/2008.
Dawn	Sept. 27, 2007	Asteroid Belt (bet. Jupiter and Mars)	Will compare evolution of dwarf planet Ceres with Vesta, an asteroid, in an effort to shed light on formation of the solar system. Departed Vesta 8/2012; reached Ceres 3/6/2015.
Kepler/K2	Mar. 9, 2009	Extrasolar planets	Detect potentially habitable Earth-size planets around other Milky Way stars. Kepler confirmed existence of 2,327 exoplanets before a 2013 malfunction. Repaired spacecraft, renamed K2, had confirmed 300+ more exoplanets as of 7/2018.
Lunar Crater Observation and Sensing Satellite	June 18, 2009	Moon	Impacted the Cabeus crater; detected presence of water ice in Moon's surface 10/9/2009. Lunar Reconnaissance Orbiter (LRO), launched with LCROSS, mapped Moon's surface.
Juno	Aug. 5, 2011	Jupiter	Entered Jupiter's orbit, 7/4/2016; began returning data and color images that improve understanding of the formation of the planet and solar system.
Mars Science Laboratory	Nov. 26, 2011	Mars	*Curiosity* rover landed on Mars 8/6/2012 and began assessing Mars's past and present ability to support life.
Lunar Atmosphere and Dust Environment Explorer	Sept. 6, 2013	Moon	Studied the fragile lunar atmosphere from orbit for 100 days; impacted with lunar surface 4/17/2014.
Mars Atmosphere and Volatile Evolution	Nov. 18, 2013	Mars	Entered orbit 9/21/2014; exploring Mars's upper atmosphere to determine how planet's loss of atmospheric gas changed its climate from a warmer, wetter environment to a cold desert.
Osiris-REx	Sept. 8, 2016	Bennu (asteroid)	Retrieve a sample by 9/2023 to help understand the source of Earth's organic materials and water and improve understanding of potential asteroid-Earth impacts. Scheduled arrival at Bennu 12/3/2018.
Transiting Exoplanet Survey Satellite	Apr. 18, 2018	Extrasolar planets	Survey 200,000 of the brightest nearby stars in search of planets outside our solar system.
InSight	May 5, 2018	Mars	Scheduled to land 11/26/2018 and drill beneath surface to investigate how rocky planets form and develop.
Parker Solar Probe	Aug. 12, 2018	Sun	First ever mission to observe and record the Sun from within its atmosphere. Will make 24 orbits of Sun in next 7 years.
Mars 2020	July/Aug. 2020	Mars	Rover to investigate potential for human habitation; scheduled to land 2/2021.
James Webb Space Telescope	2021	Universe	Replace Hubble Space Telescope as the world's premier astronomical observatory.
Europa Clipper	2020s	Europa	Assess if Europa, Jupiter's icy, ocean-bearing moon, is suitable for life.

Note: U.S./NASA missions unless otherwise noted. (1) In Coordinated Universal Time.

General Aviation and Air Taxi Active Aircraft, 2016

Source: Federal Aviation Administration; aircraft not associated with major airlines or the military

Aircraft type	Total active	Personal	Busi-ness	Instruc-tional	Aerial-apps.	Aerial obser-vation	Other work	Sight-seeing	Air medical	Other	On-demand operations
Fixed wing	166,167	109,363	24,651	12,779	3,081	4,007	995	221	329	4,734	6,006
Piston	142,638	106,236	13,843	12,593	1,170	3,503	657	219	260	2,321	1,837
Turboprop	9,779	1,489	3,333	84	1,829	500	235	2	26	370	1,910
Turbojet	13,751	1,639	7,475	103	82	4	103	0	43	2,043	2,258
Rotorcraft	10,577	1,626	580	1,836	894	2,034	431	178	77	522	2,398
Piston	3,344	1,027	217	1,306	236	216	16	152	0	34	140
Turbine	7,232	599	363	530	657	1,818	415	27	77	488	2,258
Other aircraft	4,986	3,645	11	488	0	2	30	699	0	14	96
Gliders	1,789	1,431	0	311	0	2	2	28	0	14	0
Lighter-than-air	3,197	2,214	11	177	0	0	28	671	0	0	96
Experimental	27,585	25,473	662	376	48	43	177	27	5	750	25
Amateur	20,490	19,387	551	214	2	11	79	2	0	243	3
Exhibition	2,015	1,664	19	32	10	7	27	4	5	248	0
Experimental light-sport	4,264	3,924	25	89	0	2	56	12	0	156	0
Other	816	497	67	42	36	24	15	10	0	103	22
Special light-sport	2,478	1,998	43	346	2	14	2	0	0	66	8
ALL AIRCRAFT	211,793	142,105	25,947	15,826	4,025	6,101	1,635	1,126	411	6,086	8,532

Note: Columns may not add to totals due to rounding. **Personal**—Flying for personal reasons; **Business**—Individual or group use for business transportation with or without a professional crew (includes fractional ownership); **Instructional**—Flying under the supervision of a flight instructor; **Aerial applications**—Includes agriculture and forestry, public health sprayings, fire fighting, etc.; **Aerial observation**—Includes aerial mapping/photography, patrol, search and rescue, hunting, traffic advisory, ranching, surveillance, oil and mineral exploration, etc.; **Other work**—Construction work, parachuting, aerial advertising, towing gliders, etc.; **Sightseeing**—Commercial sightseeing; **Air medical**—Air ambulance services, rescue, human organ transportation, emergency medical services; **Other**—Positioning flights, proficiency flights, training, ferrying, sales demos, etc.; **On-demand operations**—On-demand air taxi, air tours, commuter, and air medical services.

Estimated Active Airmen Certificates Held, 2017

Source: Federal Aviation Administration, U.S. Dept. of Transportation

Category	Certificates	Category	Certificates	Category	Certificates
Pilot total	609,306	Rotorcraft (helicopters)		Nonpilot total	671,222
Student	149,121	(only)	15,355	Mechanic	286,268
Recreational (only)	153	Glider (only)	18,139	Repairmen	35,040
Sport (only)	6,097	**Flight Instructor**		Parachute Rigger	6,192
Airplane[1]		**Certificates**	106,692	Ground Instructor	66,423
Private	162,455	**Instrument**		Dispatcher	20,664
Commercial	98,161	**Ratings**	306,652	Flight Navigator	64
Airline Transport	159,825	**Remote Pilots[2]**	69,166	Flight Attendant	222,037
				Flight Engineer	34,534

Note: The term airmen includes men and women certified as pilots, mechanics, or other aviation technicians. (1) Includes pilots with an airplane-only certificate as well as those with an airplane and a helicopter and/or glider certificate. (2) Remote pilot certification began in Aug. 2016. These numbers are not included in pilot totals.

Aircraft Operating Statistics

Source: The Boeing Company; Airbus S.A.S.; Embraer SA

Manufacturer and model	Max. # of seats	Typical # of seats	Fuel capacity (gal)	Typical cruising speed (mph)[1]	Max. range (naut. mi)	Max. thrust (thous. lbs)	Manufacturer and model	Max. # of seats	Typical # of seats	Fuel capacity (gal)	Typical cruising speed (mph)[1]	Max. range (naut. mi)	Max. thrust (thous. lbs)
Airbus							767-200ER	255	216	24,140	614	6,385	62.1
A318	132	107	6,400	630	3,100	24.0	767-300ER	290	261	24,140	614	5,990	63.3
A319	156	124	6,280	630	3,750	27.0	767-400ER	409	243	24,140	614	5,625	63.5
A320	180	150	6,280	630	3,700	27.0	777-200	375	305	31,000	645	5,420	77.0
A321	236	185	6,230	630	3,700	33.0	777-200ER	440	301	45,220	645	7,725	93.7
A330-200	406	247	36,750	660	7,250	72.0	777-200LR	301	279	47,890	645	9,395	115.3
A330-300	440	277	25,765	660	6,350	72.0	777-300	451	368	44,700	645	6,005	98.0
A340-300	440	277	37,150	660	7,300	34.0	777-300ER	370	339	47,890	645	7,390	115.3
A340-500	375	293	56,870	660	9,000	53.0	787-8						
A340-600	475	326	51,750	660	7,800	60.0	Dreamliner	359	242	33,340	652	8,200	NA
A380	853	544	84,600	684	8,200	70.0	787-9						
Boeing							Dreamliner	406	290	33,384	652	8,500	NA
737-600	132	110	6,875	602	3,225	22.7	**Embraer**						
737-700	148	128	6,875	602	3,440	26.3	175	88	76	3,071	576	2,200	14.2
737-700C	148	128	6,875	599	3,285	27.3	190	114	100	4,267	599	2,450	20.0
737-800	184	160	6,875	602	3,115	27.3	**McDonnell-Douglas**						
737-900	189	177	6,875	599	3,265	27.3	DC-10 series*	380	250	36,650	600	6,220	24.0
747-400	500	416	63,460	653	7,260	63.3	MD-11*	410	285	NA	NA	7,360	NA
747-8	467	467	64,055	653	8,000	66.5	MD-80 series*	172	155	5,840	584	2,504	21.0
757-200*	224	186	11,276	614	3,900	43.5	MD-90 series*	172	153	7,620	584	3,205	28.0
757-300*	279	243	11,490	614	3,395	43.5							

* = Aircraft no longer in production. NA = Not available. **Note:** Figures are for most commonly flown passenger models. When models within a series vary, maximums are shown. (1) Figures shown are converted from Mach speeds (a.k.a. the speed of sound), which varies depending on altitude and temperature. For comparison purposes, this table uses 768 mph as equivalent to Mach 1.

Milestones in Aviation History

Source: National Aeronautics and Space Administration (NASA); Smithsonian National Air and Space Museum; Air Transport Association of America; National Museum of the U.S. Air Force (USAF); National Park Service, U.S. Dept. of the Interior

1903, Dec. 17: Brothers Wilbur and Orville Wright (U.S.) made the first human-carrying, powered flight near Kitty Hawk, NC. Each brother made two flights; the longest, about 852 ft, lasted 59 sec.

1908, May 14: Charles Furnas (U.S.), worker for Wright brothers, became first American airplane passenger.

1911, Feb.: The Burgess Company and Curtiss, Inc. receive authorization to build Wright planes, becoming the first licensed airplane manufacturer in the U.S.

1911, Sept. 23: First transportation of mail by airplane officially approved by the U.S. Postal Service.

1914, Jan. 1: First scheduled passenger airline service began.

1914, June 18: Lawrence Burst Sperry (U.S.) released the controls and stood in his airborne plane, successfully demonstrating his gyrostabilizer, the first autopilot system.

1918, Mar. 6: The Curtiss-Sperry "Flying Bomb" (U.S.) made its first successful flight. The first radio-controlled plane led to the development of cruise missiles.

1918, May 14: First scheduled airmail service began, between New York and Washington, DC, with intermediate stop in Philadelphia. In 1921, scheduled transcontinental airmail service began between New York City and San Francisco.

1919, June 14-15: Capt. John Alcock (UK) and Lt. Arthur W. Brown (U.S.) completed the first nonstop flight across the Atlantic Ocean. They traveled from Newfoundland, Canada, to Ireland in 16 hr., 12 min.

1923, Aug.: Rotating beacons enabled the first U.S. night flights.

1924, Apr. 6-Sept. 28: Two U.S. Army planes landed in Seattle, completing the first circumnavigation of the globe. They completed the 26,000-mi journey in 371 hours of flying time.

1926, May 12-13: Roald Amundsen (Norway), Umberto Nobile (Italy), Lincoln Ellsworth (U.S.), and Oscar Wisting (Norway) made the first flight over the North Pole, in a dirigible that flew between Spitsbergen, Norway, and Teller, AK. Two weeks earlier, Adm. Richard E. Byrd and Floyd Bennett (both U.S.) claimed to have made the first flight over the Pole (May 9, 1926) in a Fokker F-VII. But when Byrd's diary was released to the public in 1996, some historians began to question whether his plane had reached the Pole.

1927, May 20-21: Charles Lindbergh (U.S.) completed the first solo transatlantic flight in the *Spirit of St. Louis*. "Lucky Lindy" traveled 3,610 mi from New York to Paris in 33 hr., 29 min., 30 sec.

1929, Aug. 8-29: Hugo Eckener (Germany) piloted the *Graf Zeppelin* around the world in record time: 20,373 mi in 21 days, 5 hr., 31 min.

1929, Nov. 28: Richard E. Byrd, Harold June, Ashley McKinley (all U.S.) and Bernt Balchen (Norway) became first to fly over the South Pole, in 18 hr., 41 min. round trip from Ross Ice Shelf base.

1930, May 15: Ellen Church (U.S.) became first flight attendant.

1931, June 23-July 1: Wiley Post and Harold Gatty (both U.S.) broke the speed record for around-the-world flight, traveling 15,474 mi in 8 days, 15 hr., 51 min., in the monoplane *Winnie Mae*.

1931, Oct. 3-5: Clyde Pangborn and Hugh Herndon (both U.S.) completed the first nonstop transpacific flight. They traveled 4,558 mi from Misawa, Japan, to East Wenatchee, WA, in 41 hr., 34 min.

1932, May 20-21: Amelia Earhart (U.S.) completed first solo transoceanic flight by a woman, making the 2,026-mi journey from Newfoundland, Canada, to Ireland in 14 hr., 56 min.

1933, July 15-22: Wiley Post completed the first solo circumnavigation of the globe. His 15,596-mi trip took 7 days, 18 hr., 49 min.

1936, June 25: American Airlines began scheduled passenger service of the first Douglas DC-3 aircraft. The DC-3 was the first aircraft with a kitchen onboard and hence offered the first in-flight hot meal service.

1937, May 6: German *Hindenburg* zeppelin exploded in Lakehurst, NJ, killing 35 of the 97 people aboard (and one on the ground). The airship had made 34 transatlantic flights in 1936.

1938, July 10-13: Howard Hughes (U.S.) and four assistants established a new speed record for circumnavigating the globe: 14,824 mi in 3 days, 9 hr., 17 min.

1939, Aug. 27: The German-made Heinkel He 178 made the first successful flight powered by a jet engine.

1947, Oct. 14: Chuck Yeager (U.S.) broke the sound barrier, reaching Mach 1 in a Bell X-1 rocket-powered aircraft.

1947, Nov. 2: Howard Hughes piloted the *Spruce Goose* on its maiden and only flight. The largest airplane ever built, it could carry 750 troops or two Sherman tanks.

1949, Mar. 2: James Gallagher (U.S.) piloted the first round-the-world flight refueled in midair. The *Lucky Lady* USAF B-50 covered 23,452 mi in 94 hr., 1 min. and refueled four times.

1950, Sept. 22: Col. David Schilling (USAF) made the first non-stop transatlantic jet flight, covering 3,300 mi in 10 hr., 1 min.

1952, Aug. 26: The UK bomber Canberra made the first round-trip transatlantic crossing on the same day, from Northern Ireland to Newfoundland, Canada, and back in 7 hr., 59 min.

1953, May 18: Jacqueline Cochran (U.S.) became the first woman to fly faster than the speed of sound.

1956, Mar. 10: Britain's Fairey FD-2 aircraft set a world speed record of 1,132 mph.

1956, Nov. 11: Convair B-58 (USAF), the first supersonic bomber, was introduced.

1957, Jan. 15-18: Three USAF B-52 Stratofortresses made the first nonstop global flight by jet planes. They were refueled in flight by KC-97 aerial tankers.

1958, Oct. 24: A Mirage III-A achieved Mach 2 (twice the speed of sound) in level flight, first European plane to do so.

1962, Nov. 29: Britain and France signed an agreement to jointly develop the Concorde, a supersonic plane that could fly twice as fast as most U.S. jets.

1969, June 5: The Soviet Tupolev Tu-144 became the first passenger airliner to break the sound barrier.

1970, May 26: The Tupolev Tu-144 became first passenger airline to exceed Mach 2 with a top speed of about 1,335 mph at 53,475 ft.

1976, Aug. 23: The Concorde began the first scheduled supersonic commercial service.

1977, Aug. 23: The *Gossamer Condor*, built by aeronautical engineer Paul MacCready (U.S.), successfully demonstrated human-powered flight through pedalling, completing a figure-8 course of 1.15 mi.

1979, June 12: MacCready's human-powered *Gossamer Albatross* crossed the English Channel in 2 hr., 49 min.

1981, July 7: MacCready-developed *Solar Challenger* became first solar-powered airplane to cross the English Channel.

1995, Aug. 15-16: The Concorde set a new around-the-world speed record of 31 hr., 27 min., 49 sec.

1999, Mar. 1-21: Bertrand Piccard (Switz.) and Brian Jones (UK) completed the first around-the-world flight in a hot-air balloon. Their 29,055-mi journey began in Chateau-d'Oex, Switzerland, and ended 19 days, 21 hr., 55 min. later in the Egyptian desert.

2001, Aug. 13: Solar-powered, propeller-driven plane *Helios* (NASA) reached 96,863 ft, breaking altitude record for non-rocket-powered aircraft.

2002, June 19-July 4: Steve Fossett (U.S.) completed the first nonstop solo circumnavigation of globe in a balloon.

2003, Nov. 26: The Concorde flew its final flight.

2005, Mar. 1-3: Steve Fossett achieved the first nonstop solo circumnavigation in an airplane without refueling.

2006, Feb. 8-11: Steve Fossett flew the longest nonstop, non-refueled solo flight (25,766 mi).

2009, Dec. 15: Boeing's 787 Dreamliner, the company's most fuel-efficient plane and the first to be constructed primarily from composite materials, made its maiden voyage.

2011, Feb. 4: Northrop Grumman and the U.S. Navy reported the first successful flight for the unmanned X-47B fighter jet.

2012, May 22-31: SpaceX became the first private company to successfully launch (and later recover) a spacecraft to the International Space Station.

2015, July 3: *Solar Impulse 2* set record for longest nonstop solo flight and longest flight in a solar-powered plane (118 hr.), traveling from Japan to Hawaii.

2016, July 26: *Solar Impulse 2* became first fuel-free plane to circumnavigate the globe. The 17-leg journey began in Mar. 2015.

ASTRONOMY

Edited by Laurence A. Marschall, Prof. Emeritus, Dept. of Physics and Astronomy, Gettysburg College

Celestial Events Summary, 2019

There are five eclipses in 2019: one partial solar eclipse, one total solar eclipse, one annular solar eclipse, a total lunar eclipse, and a partial lunar eclipse. The total solar eclipse of July 2 is the most notable of the year and will be best seen from Chile and Argentina. The total lunar eclipse of Jan. 21 is the more prominent of the lunar eclipses, with far more evident darkening than the partial lunar eclipse, and will be visible to observers across North and South America, Europe, and Africa.

A rare transit of Mercury occurs Nov. 11, when the silhouette of the planet passes directly across the face of the Sun. The entire sequence of events, visible through a telescope properly equipped to reduce the intensity of the Sun, can be viewed from Eastern North America, South America, and West Africa.

The best meteor shower viewing will be the Quarantids in Jan., and to a lesser extent the low intensity Eta Aquarids in May, both of which occur near the new Moon. Other meteor showers will be hampered by unfavorably bright Moon phases in 2019. At the start of the year, Jupiter and Venus will be visible in the predawn sky and Mars is in the evening sky. Venus remains in the predawn sky until late May, when it disappears into the vicinity of the Sun, re-emerging in the evening sky by mid Nov. to be seen as an "evening star" for the rest of the year. Mars is in the evening sky into June, disappearing into twilight, and returning to the predawn sky in late Nov. Jupiter is a morning object Jan. through June, becoming visible all night long in July and then an evening object until late Nov. Saturn begins the year too close to the Sun to be visible, becoming a predawn object from Feb. to June, after which it is visible in the evening until late Dec. Mercury, frequently too close to the Sun for easy viewing, is first visible in the dusk sky in late Feb. It is back in the morning sky in mid-Apr., the evening sky in June, evening in late Oct., and the morning sky in late Nov. to finish the year. The best opportunities for seeing Mercury in the morning sky are in Apr., while the best opportunities to see it in the evening sky occur in late June and Oct.

The crescent Moon, with its subdued light, regularly pairs with the two brightest planets, Venus and Jupiter. Waxing crescent pairings are visible in the early evening soon after sunset, while waning crescent pairings are visible in the early morning before sunrise. The waxing crescent Moon pairs with Venus in Dec., while the waning crescent pairs with Venus in the early morning sky in Jan. through May. The waxing crescent Moon pairs with Jupiter in the evening in July-Nov.; the waning crescent pairs with Jupiter in the predawn sky from Jan.-June. Venus and Jupiter are paired in the morning sky on Jan. 22, and Venus and Saturn are paired in the morning sky on Feb. 18. Mercury and Mars have a very close encounter in the evening sky on June 19. Jupiter and Venus will have a close encounter on the evening of Nov. 24.

Astronomical Positions and Constants

Two celestial bodies are in **conjunction** when they are due north and south of each other, either in **right ascension** (with respect to the north celestial pole) or in **celestial longitude** (with respect to the north ecliptic pole). Celestial bodies in conjunction will rise and set at nearly the same time. For the inner planets—Mercury and Venus—**inferior conjunction** occurs when either planet passes between Earth and the Sun, while **superior conjunction** occurs when either Mercury or Venus is on the far side of the Sun. Celestial bodies are in **opposition** when their right ascensions differ by exactly 12 hours, or when their celestial longitudes differ by 180°. In this case one of the two objects in opposition will rise while the other is setting. **Quadrature** refers to the arrangement where the coordinates of two bodies differ by exactly 90°. These terms may refer to the relative positions of any two bodies as seen from Earth, but one of the bodies is so frequently the Sun that mention of the Sun is omitted in that case.

When objects are in conjunction, the alignment is not perfect, and one usually passes above or below the other. The geocentric angular separation between the Sun and an object is termed **elongation**. Elongation is limited only for Mercury and Venus; the greatest elongation for each of these bodies is approximately the time for longest observation. **Perihelion** is the point in an object's orbit when it is nearest to the Sun, and **aphelion** is the point when it is farthest from the Sun. **Perigee** is the point in an orbit where an object is nearest Earth, **apogee** the point when it is farthest from Earth. An **occultation** of a planet or a star is an eclipse of it by some other body, usually the Moon. A **transit** of the Sun occurs when Mercury or Venus passes directly between Earth and the Sun, appearing to cross the Sun's disk.

The following were adopted as part of the International Astronomical Union System of Astronomical Constants (1976/2009): **Speed of light**, 299,792.458 km per sec., or about 186,282 statute mi per sec.; **solar parallax**, 8".794143; **astronomical unit** (AU, mean distance between the Earth and Sun), 149,597,870 km, or 92,955,807 mi; **constant of nutation**, 9".2025; and **constant of aberration**, 20".49552.

Celestial Events Highlights, 2019

(In Coordinated Universal Time, or UTC, the standard time of the prime meridian.)

January

Mercury and **Saturn** are too close to the Sun to be readily observable.

Venus is in the morning sky, reaching its highest before dawn early in the month.

Mars, **Uranus**, and **Neptune** are low in the SW at sunset.

Jupiter is in the SE just before sunrise all month.

Jan. 1: Venus 1.3° S of Moon
Jan. 2: Saturn at conjunction
Jan. 3: Earth at perihelion, Jupiter 3.1° S of Moon
Jan. 4: Quarantid Meteor Shower
Jan. 6: New Moon; Partial Solar Eclipse; Venus at greatest elongation 47° W of Sun
Jan. 9: Moon at apogee
Jan. 12: Mercury at aphelion; Mars 5.3° N of Moon
Jan. 14: First Quarter Moon
Jan. 17: Aldebaran 1.6° S of Moon

Jan. 21: Full Moon; Moon at perigee; Total Lunar Eclipse; Beehive star cluster 0.6° N of Moon
Jan. 23: Regulus 2.5° S of Moon
Jan. 27: Last Quarter Moon
Jan. 30: Mercury at superior conjunction; Jupiter 2.8° S of Moon
Jan. 31: Venus 0.1° S of Moon; occultation of Venus by Moon

February

Mercury is too close to the Sun to be visible early in the month, but by the end of the month is low in the W at sunset.

Venus, **Jupiter**, and **Saturn** are in the SE before dawn.

Mars and **Uranus** are in the SW at sunset.

Neptune is too close to the Sun for easy visibility.

Feb. 2: Saturn 0.6° S of Moon
Feb. 4: New Moon

Feb. 5: Moon at apogee
Feb. 12: First Quarter Moon
Feb. 14: Aldebaran 1.7° S of Moon
Feb. 18: Beehive star cluster 0.6° N of Moon
Feb. 19: Moon at perigee; Full Moon; Regulus 2.5° S of Moon
Feb. 25: Mercury at perihelion
Feb. 26: Last Quarter Moon
Feb. 27: Mercury at greatest elongation 18° E of Sun; Jupiter 2.3° S of Moon

March

Mercury is low in the W at sunset early in the month becoming too close to the Sun for easy visibility by the middle of the month.
Venus is in the E before dawn.
Mars is in the W for several hours in the evening.
Jupiter and **Saturn** are in the SW before dawn.
Uranus is low in the W at sunset early in the month becoming too close to the Sun for easy visibility by the end of the month.
Neptune is too close to the Sun for easy visibility.

Mar. 1: Saturn 0.3° S of Moon; occultation of Saturn by Moon
Mar. 2: Venus 1.2° N of Moon
Mar. 4: Moon at apogee
Mar. 6: New Moon
Mar. 7: Neptune in conjunction with Sun
Mar. 11: Mars 5.8° N of Moon
Mar. 13: Aldebaran 1.9° S of Moon
Mar. 14: First Quarter Moon
Mar. 15: Mercury at inferior conjunction
Mar. 17: Beehive star cluster 0.5° N of Moon
Mar. 18: Regulus 2.6° S of Moon
Mar. 19: Moon at perigee
Mar. 20: Vernal Equinox, 21:58 UTC
Mar. 21: Full Moon
Mar. 27: Jupiter 1.9° S of Moon
Mar. 28: Last Quarter Moon
Mar. 29: Saturn 0.1° N of Moon; occultation of Saturn by Moon
Mar. 31: Mars 3.1° S of Pleiades

April

Mercury is too close to the Sun to be visible at the beginning the month, becoming very low in the E at dawn at mid-month.
Venus is low in the E before dawn.
Mars is low in the W in the early evening.
Jupiter and **Saturn** are in the S after midnight.
Uranus and **Neptune** are too close to the Sun for easy visibility.

Apr. 1: Moon at apogee
Apr. 2: Venus 2.7° N of Moon; Mercury 3.6° N of Moon
Apr. 5: New Moon
Apr. 9: Mars 4.7° N of Moon; Aldebaran 2.1° S of Moon
Apr. 11: Mercury at greatest elongation 28° W of Sun
Apr. 12: First Quarter Moon
Apr. 13: Beehive star cluster 0.2° N of Moon
Apr. 15: Mars 6.4° N of Aldebaran; Regulus 2.7° S of Moon
Apr. 16: Mercury 4.3° E of Venus; Moon at perigee
Apr. 18: Venus at aphelion
Apr. 19: Full Moon
Apr. 23: Lyrid meteor shower; Uranus in conjunction with Sun; Jupiter 1.6° S of Moon
Apr. 25: Saturn 0.4° N of Moon; occultation of Saturn by Moon
Apr. 26: Last Quarter Moon
Apr. 28: Moon at apogee

May

Mercury is too close to the Sun for easy visibility.
Venus is very low in the E just before dawn.
Mars is low in the SW in early evening.

Jupiter and **Saturn** rise around midnight and are visible in the S until dawn.
Uranus and **Neptune** are too close to the Sun for easy visibility.

May 2: Venus 3.6° N of Moon
May 3: Mercury 2.9° N of Moon
May 4: New Moon
May 5: Eta Aquarid meteor shower
May 6: Aldebaran 2.3° S of Moon
May 7: Mars 3.2° N of Moon
May 10: Pollux 6.3° N of Moon
May 11: Beehive star cluster 0.0° S of Moon
May 12: First Quarter Moon; Regulus 3.0° S of Moon
May 13: Moon at perigee
May 18: Full Moon
May 20: Jupiter 1.7° S of Moon
May 21: Mercury at superior conjunction
May 22: Saturn 0.5° N of moon; occultation of Saturn by Moon
May 24: Mercury at perihelion
May 26: Moon at apogee; Last Quarter Moon

June

Mercury is low in the W just before sunset.
Venus and **Mars** are too close to the Sun to be visible.
Jupiter and **Saturn** rise well before midnight and are visible in the S until dawn.
Uranus and **Neptune** are visible late in the month in the E just before dawn.

June 1: Venus 3.2° N of Moon
June 3: New Moon
June 4: Mercury 3.7° N of Moon
June 5: Mars 1.6° N of Moon
June 6: Pollux 6.2° N of Moon
June 7: Beehive star cluster 0.2° S of Moon; Moon at perigee
June 8: Regulus 3.2° S of Moon
June 9: Venus 5.0° S of Moon
June 10: First Quarter Moon; Jupiter at opposition
June 16: Jupiter 2.0° S of Moon; Venus 4.6° N of Aldebaran
June 17: Full Moon
June 18: Mercury 0.2° NW of Mars
June 19: Saturn 0.4° N of Moon; occultation of Saturn by Moon; Mercury 5.2° S of Pollux
June 21: Mars 5.4° S of Pollux; Summer Solstice, 15:54 UTC
June 23: Moon at apogee; Mercury at greatest elongation 25° E of Sun
June 25: Last Quarter Moon
June 30: Aldebaran 2.3° S of Moon

July

Mercury is very low in the W at sunset early in the month but too close to the Sun to be visible by mid-month.
Venus and **Mars** are too close to the Sun to be visible.
Jupiter and **Saturn** are visible all night long in the S.
Uranus and **Neptune** rise after midnight and are visible in the SE and S until dawn.

July 2: New Moon; Total Solar Eclipse
July 4: Mercury 3.3° S of Moon; Beehive star cluster 0.2° S of Moon; Earth at aphelion
July 5: Moon at perigee; Mercury 3.8° S of Mars
July 6: Regulus 3.2° S of Moon
July 7: Mercury at aphelion
July 9: First Quarter Moon; Saturn at opposition
July 13: Mars 0.4° S of Moon; Jupiter 2.3° S of Moon
July 16: Saturn 0.2° N of Moon; occultation of Saturn by Moon; Full Moon; Partial Lunar Eclipse
July 21: Moon at apogee; Mercury at inferior conjunction
July 25: Last Quarter Moon
July 28: Aldebaran 2.3° S of Moon; Delta Aquarid meteor shower

August

Mercury, **Venus**, and **Mars** are too close to the Sun to be visible.

Jupiter and **Saturn** are in the SW in the evening, setting shortly after midnight.

Uranus is in the SW after midnight.

Neptune is in the SE after midnight.

Aug. 1: New Moon
Aug. 2: Moon at perigee
Aug. 7: First Quarter Moon
Aug. 8: Venus at perihelion
Aug. 9: Jupiter 2.5° S of Moon; Mercury at greatest elongation, 19° W of Sun
Aug. 12: Saturn 0.0° N of Moon; occultation of Saturn by Moon; Jupiter 4.3° N of Antares
Aug. 13: Perseid meteor shower
Aug. 14: Venus at superior conjunction
Aug. 15: Full Moon
Aug. 17: Mercury 1.2° S of Beehive star cluster; Moon at apogee
Aug. 20: Mercury at perihelion
Aug. 23: Last Quarter Moon
Aug. 24: Aldebaran 2.4° S of Moon
Aug. 26: Mars at aphelion
Aug. 27: Pollux 6.1° N of Moon
Aug. 28: Beehive star cluster 0.2° S of Moon
Aug. 30: New Moon; Moon at perigee

September

Mercury, **Venus**, and **Mars** are too close to the sun to be visible.

Jupiter and **Saturn** are in the S at sunset and set before midnight.

Uranus rises around midnight and is visible in the S until dawn.

Neptune is visible all night in the S.

Sept. 2: Mars in conjunction with Sun
Sept. 4: Mercury at superior conjunction
Sept. 6: First Quarter Moon; Jupiter 2.3° S of Moon
Sept. 8: Saturn 0.0° N of Moon; occultation of Saturn by Moon
Sept. 10: Neptune at opposition
Sept. 13: Moon at apogee
Sept. 14: Full Moon
Sept. 20: Aldebaran 2.6° S of Moon
Sept. 22: Last Quarter Moon
Sept. 23: Autumnal Equinox, 07:50 UTC; Pollux 5.9° N of Moon
Sept. 24: Beehive star cluster 0.4° S of Moon
Sept. 26: Regulus 3.3° S of Moon
Sept. 28: Moon at perigee; New Moon
Sept. 29: Mercury 1.2° N of Spica

October

Mercury is too close to the Sun to be visible early in the month, but near the third week of the month is low in the evening sky at sunset.

Venus and **Mars** are too close to the Sun to be visible.

Jupiter and **Saturn** are low in the SW in the early evening.

Uranus and **Neptune** rise before midnight and are visible in the S in the early morning.

Oct. 3: Jupiter 1.9° S of moon
Oct. 5: First Quarter Moon; Saturn 0.3° N of Moon; occultation of Saturn by Moon
Oct. 8: Draconid meteor shower
Oct. 10: Moon at apogee
Oct. 13: Full Moon
Oct. 17: Aldebaran 2.9° S of Moon
Oct. 20: Mercury at greatest elongation, 24.6° E of Sun

Oct. 21: Pollux 5.7° N of Moon; Last Quarter Moon; Orionid meteor shower
Oct. 22: Beehive star cluster 0.6° S of Moon
Oct. 23: Regulus 3.5° S of Moon
Oct. 26: Moon at perigee
Oct. 28: New Moon; Uranus at opposition
Oct. 29: Venus 3.9° S of Moon
Oct. 31: Mercury 2.5° SW of Venus; Jupiter 1.3° S of Moon

November

Mercury begins the month too close to the Sun to be visible, except on Nov. 11 when it passes in front of the Sun in a rare transit; by the end of the month it is visible low in the E just before dawn.

Venus begins the month too close to the Sun to be visible, but by mid-month it is low in the SW shortly after dusk.

Mars begins the month too close to the Sun to be visible and by the end of the month is visible in the SE just before dawn.

Jupiter and **Saturn** are low in the SW after dusk.

Uranus and **Neptune** are in the S in the evening.

Nov. 2: Saturn 0.6° N of Moon; occultation of Saturn by Moon
Nov. 4: First Quarter Moon
Nov. 6: S Taurid Meteor Shower
Nov. 7: Moon at apogee
Nov. 9: Venus 3.8° N of Antares; Mars 2.6° N of Spica
Nov. 11: Mercury at inferior conjunction; transit of Mercury across the Sun
Nov. 12: Full Moon; N Taurid meteor shower
Nov. 14: Aldebaran 3.0° S of Moon
Nov. 16: Mercury at perihelion
Nov. 17: Pollux 5.4° N of Moon
Nov. 18: Leonid meteor shower; Beehive star cluster 0.9° S of Moon
Nov. 19: Last Quarter Moon; Regulus 3.7° S of Moon
Nov. 23: Moon at perigee
Nov. 24: Mars 4.3° S of Moon; Venus 1.4° S of Jupiter
Nov. 25: Mercury 1.9° S of Moon
Nov. 26: New Moon
Nov. 28: Mercury at greatest elongation 20.1° W of Sun; Jupiter 0.7° S of Moon; occultation of Jupiter by Moon; Venus 1.9° S of Moon
Nov. 29: Saturn 0.9° N of Moon; occultation of Saturn by Moon

December

Mercury begins the month low in the E just before dawn and soon moves too close to the Sun to be visible.

Venus is in the W just after sunset.

Mars is in the SE for several hours before dawn.

Jupiter is too close to the Sun to be visible.

Saturn begins the month low in the SW after sunset and ends the month too close to the Sun to be visible.

Uranus and **Neptune** are in the S for several hours after sunset.

Dec. 4: First Quarter Moon
Dec. 5: Moon at apogee
Dec. 11: Aldebaran 3.0° S of Moon
Dec. 12: Full Moon
Dec. 14: Pollux 5.3° N of Moon; Geminid meteor shower
Dec. 15: Beehive star cluster 1.0° S of Moon
Dec. 17: Regulus 3.8° S of Moon
Dec. 18: Moon at perigee
Dec. 19: Last Quarter Moon
Dec. 22: Winter Solstice, 04:19 UTC
Dec. 23: Mars 3.5° S of Moon; Ursid meteor shower
Dec. 26: New Moon; Annular Solar Eclipse
Dec. 27: Jupiter in conjunction with Sun
Dec. 29: Venus 1.0° N of Moon; occultation of Venus by Moon
Dec. 30: Mercury at aphelion

Meteorites and Meteor Showers

When a chunk of material, ice or rock, plunges into Earth's atmosphere and burns up in a fiery display, the event is a **meteor**. While the chunk of material is still in space, it is a **meteoroid**. If a portion of the material survives passage through the atmosphere and reaches the ground, the remnant on the ground is a **meteorite**.

Meteorites found on Earth are classified into types, depending on their composition: **irons**, those composed chiefly of iron, a small percentage of nickel, and traces of other metals such as cobalt; **stones**, stony meteors consisting of silicates; and **stony irons**, containing varying proportions of both iron and stone.

Serious study of meteorites as non-Earth objects began in the 20th century. Scientists use sophisticated chemical analysis, X-rays, and mass spectrography in determining their origin and composition. Although most meteorites are now believed to be fragments of asteroids or comets, geochemical studies have shown that a few Antarctic stones came from the Moon or from Mars, presumably ejected by the explosive impact of asteroids.

The largest known meteorite, estimated to weigh about 55 metric tons, is the Hoba meteorite near Grootfontein, Namibia. The Manicouagan impact crater in Quebec, Canada, with an estimated diameter of 60 mi, is one of the largest crater structures still visible on the surface of the Earth. Not obvious to the eye because of erosion, larger impact craters identified include the Vredefort crater in South Africa at 185 mi across and the Sudbury crater in Ontario, Canada, estimated at 125 mi across. The Bedout impact site off the NW coast of Australia gained attention in 2004 when scientists identified further evidence in support of the idea that it may be linked to the Permian extinction event 250 mil years ago.

Meteor showers vary in strength, but usually the three most visible meteor showers of the year are the **Perseids**, around Aug. 13, the **Orionids**, around Oct. 21, and the **Geminids**, around Dec. 14. These showers feature meteors at the rate of about 60 per hour. Best observing conditions occur in the absence of moonlight, usually when the Moon's phase is between waning crescent and waxing quarter. Bright moons can adversely affect viewing of some of the best showers of the year.

For most meteor showers the cometary debris is relatively uniformly scattered along the comet's orbit. However, in the case of the **Leonid** meteor shower, which occurs every year around Nov. 17-18, the debris from Comet Temple-Tuttle seems to be bunched up in one stretch. Hence, the meteor shower produced in most years is relatively weak. However, about every 33 years, Earth encounters the bunched-up debris when it crosses the comet's orbit. Sometimes the expected shower is a disappointment, as in 1899 and 1933; at other times, the dense debris provides a spectacular show, as in 1833 and 1866. The Leonids stormed again more recently, producing rates of 1,000-3,000 meteors per hour in 2001.

Morning and Evening "Stars," 2019

(In Coordinated Universal Time, or UTC, the standard time of the prime meridian.)

	Morning	Evening		Morning	Evening
Jan.	Mercury to Jan. 28 Venus Jupiter Saturn	Mercury from Jan. 29 Mars Uranus Neptune	**July**	Mercury from July 23 Venus Saturn to July 9 Uranus Neptune	Mercury to July 22 Mars Jupiter Saturn from July 10
Feb.	Venus Jupiter Saturn	Mercury Mars Uranus Neptune	**Aug.**	Mercury Venus to Aug. 14 Uranus Neptune	Venus from Aug. 15 Mars Jupiter Saturn
Mar.	Mercury from Mar. 16 Venus Jupiter Saturn Neptune from Mar. 8	Mercury to Mar. 15 Mars Uranus Neptune to Mar. 7	**Sept.**	Mercury to Sept. 4 Mars from Sept. 3 Uranus Neptune to Sept. 10	Mercury from Sept. 5 Venus Mars to Sept. 2 Jupiter Saturn Neptune from Sept. 11
Apr.	Mercury Venus Jupiter Saturn Uranus from Apr. 24 Neptune	Mars Uranus to Apr. 23	**Oct.**	Mars Uranus to Oct. 28	Mercury Venus Jupiter Saturn Neptune Uranus from Oct. 29
May	Mercury to May 21 Venus Jupiter Saturn Uranus Neptune	Mercury from May 22 Mars	**Nov.**	Mercury from Nov. 12 Mars	Mercury to Nov. 11 Venus Jupiter Saturn Uranus Neptune
June	Venus Jupiter to June 10 Saturn Uranus Neptune	Mercury Mars Jupiter from June 11	**Dec.**	Mercury Mars Jupiter from Dec. 28	Venus Jupiter to Dec. 27 Saturn Uranus Neptune

Greenwich Sidereal Time for 0h UTC, 2019

UTC = Coordinated Universal Time. Add 12 hours to obtain right ascension of mean sun.

Date	Hr.	Min.	Date	Hr.	Min.	Date	Hr.	Min.	Date	Hr.	Min.
Jan. 1	6	41.4	Apr. 1	12	36.3	July 10	19	10.5	Oct. 8	1	5.4
Jan. 11	7	20.9	Apr. 11	13	15.7	July 20	19	50.0	Oct. 18	1	44.8
Jan. 21	8	0.3	Apr. 21	13	55.1	July 30	20	29.4	Oct. 28	2	24.2
Jan. 31	8	39.7	May 1	14	34.6	Aug. 9	21	8.8	Nov. 7	3	3.6
Feb. 10	9	19.1	May 11	15	14.0	Aug. 19	21	48.2	Nov. 17	3	43.1
Feb. 20	9	58.6	May 21	15	53.4	Aug. 29	22	27.7	Nov. 27	4	22.5
Mar. 2	10	38.0	May 31	16	32.8	Sept. 8	23	7.1	Dec. 7	5	1.9
Mar. 12	11	17.4	June 10	17	12.3	Sept. 18	23	46.5	Dec. 17	5	41.3
Mar. 22	11	56.8	June 20	17	51.7	Sept. 28	0	25.9	Dec. 27	6	20.8
			June 30	18	31.1						

Largest Telescopes

Astronomers indicate the size of telescopes not by length or magnification but by the diameter of the primary light-gathering component, such as the lens or mirror. The larger the diameter of the mirror or lens, the fainter the objects that can be detected. In principle, larger telescopes also have better resolving power—the ability to discern small details—than smaller telescopes. However, the Earth's atmosphere limits the details that can be seen using ground-based telescopes. That is why the Hubble Space Telescope, which orbits the Earth outside of its atmosphere, can achieve higher resolutions with its 2.4-m (7.9-ft) mirror than much larger telescopes on Earth. Adaptive optics systems can compensate for the blurring effects of the Earth's atmosphere, allowing ground-based telescopes to achieve higher levels of detail. Telescopes to detect ultraviolet, X-ray, and gamma radiation must be placed in space or high-altitude balloons because the atmosphere absorbs most of these types of radiation; as a result, such telescopes are generally much smaller than optical, infrared, and radio telescopes.

Refracting (lens) telescopes are currently not made with lens diameters of more than 40 in. Because **reflecting telescopes** can be made less expensively and with more precision than refracting telescopes, all modern large optical telescopes are made with mirrors. **Radio telescopes** are larger than optical telescopes because larger diameters are required to obtain equivalent resolution of radio's longer wavelengths. A technique called interferometry, originally developed for radio telescopes, uses arrays of telescopes to achieve better resolution.

Largest refracting (lens) optical telescope: Yerkes Observatory, 1 m (40 in.), at Williams Bay, WI

Largest reflecting (mirror) optical/infrared telescope: Gran Telescopio Canarias, 10.4 m (34 ft), on La Palma, Canary Islands (segmented mirror)

Largest infrared interferometer: Four 8.2-m (27-ft) telescopes of the Very Large Telescope Interferometer (VLTI) with a 200-m (656-ft) baseline on Cerro Paranal in Chile

Largest fully steerable radio dish: Robert Byrd Green Bank Telescope (GBT), 100 m (328 ft), in Green Bank, WV

Largest single radio dish: Five-hundred-meter Aperture Spherical Telescope (FAST), 500 m (1,640 ft), in Guizhou, China

Largest baseline radio interferometer: 10 25-m (82-ft) diameter telescopes of the Very Long Baseline Array (VLBA), dispersed from Hawaii to the Virgin Islands with a resolution equal to a radio dish of 8,600 km (5,000 mi), making it the highest resolution telescope in the solar system

Largest submillimeter interferometer: 54 12-m (39-ft) and 12 7-m (23-ft) antennas of the Atacama Large Millimeter Array (ALMA), located at a site above 5,000 m (16,400 ft) in the Atacama Desert in Chile. The antennas can be spread out over a 16-km (10-mi) distance to increase the resolving power of the array.

Largest airborne telescope: Stratospheric Observatory for Infrared Astronomy (SOFIA), 2.5-m (8.2-ft) infrared telescope aboard a NASA 747

Constellations

Culturally, constellations are imagined patterns among the stars that, in some cases, have been recognized through millennia. Knowledge of constellations was once necessary in order to function as an astronomer. For today's astronomers, constellations are simply areas of the sky in which objects await observation and interpretation.

Because Western culture has dominated much of modern scientific discourse, constellations and celestial traditions of other cultures are not well known outside their regions of origin. Even the patterns with which we are most familiar today have undergone considerable change over the centuries.

Today, **88 constellations** are officially recognized. Although many have ancient origins, some are modern, devised out of unclaimed stars by astronomers a few centuries ago. Unclaimed stars were those too faint or inconveniently placed to be included in the more prominent constellations. Stars in a constellation are not necessarily near each other; they are just located in the same direction on the celestial sphere.

Common names of stars often referred to parts of the traditional figures they represented, such as Deneb, the tail of the swan, and Betelgeuse, the giant's shoulder. Astronomers may avoid traditional names by labeling stars with Greek letters, generally to denote order of brightness. The "alpha star" would typically be the brightest in a constellation. The "of" implies possession, so the genitive (possessive) form of the constellation name is used, e.g. Alpha Orionis (the first star of Orion) for Betelgeuse. (While Rigel is brighter than Betelgeuse, its designation is Beta Orionis, possibly because Betelgeuse appeared brighter when they were named.)

Asterisms are widely recognized patterns of stars. The so-called Big Dipper is a small part of the constellation Ursa Major, the big bear; the three stars of the Summer Triangle are each in a different constellation, with Vega in Lyra the lyre, Deneb in Cygnus the swan, and Altair in Aquila the eagle. The northeast star of the asterism Great Square of Pegasus is Alpha Andromedae.

Name	Abbr.	Meaning	Name	Abbr.	Meaning	Name	Abbr.	Meaning
Andromeda	And	Chained Maiden	Cygnus	Cyg	Swan	Orion	Ori	Hunter
Antlia	Ant	Air Pump	Delphinus	Del	Dolphin	Pavo	Pav	Peacock
Apus	Aps	Bird of Paradise	Dorado	Dor	Dolphinfish	Pegasus	Peg	Flying Horse
Aquarius	Aqr	Water Bearer	Draco	Dra	Dragon	Perseus	Per	Hero
Aquila	Aql	Eagle	Equuleus	Equ	Little Horse	Phoenix	Phe	Phoenix
Ara	Ara	Altar	Eridanus	Eri	River	Pictor	Pic	Painter
Aries	Ari	Ram	Fornax	For	Furnace	Pisces	Psc	Fishes
Auriga	Aur	Charioteer	Gemini	Gem	Twins	Piscis Austrinus	PsA	Southern Fish
Boötes	Boo	Herder	Grus	Gru	Crane (bird)	Puppis	Pup	Stern (deck)
Caelum	Cae	Chisel	Hercules	Her	Hercules	Pyxis	Pyx	Compass (sea)
Camelopardalis	Cam	Giraffe	Horologium	Hor	Clock	Reticulum	Ret	Reticle
Cancer	Cnc	Crab	Hydra	Hya	Water Snake (female)	Sagitta	Sge	Arrow
Canes Venatici	CVn	Hunting Dogs				Sagittarius	Sgr	Archer
Canis Major	CMa	Greater Dog	Hydrus	Hyi	Water Snake (male)	Scorpius	Sco	Scorpion
Canis Minor	CMi	Littler Dog				Sculptor	Scl	Sculptor
Capricornus	Cap	Sea-Goat	Indus	Ind	Indian	Scutum	Sct	Shield
Carina	Car	Keel	Lacerta	Lac	Lizard	Serpens	Ser	Serpent
Cassiopeia	Cas	Queen	Leo	Leo	Lion	Sextans	Sex	Sextant
Centaurus	Cen	Centaur	Leo Minor	LMi	Littler Lion	Taurus	Tau	Bull
Cepheus	Cep	King	Lepus	Lep	Hare	Telescopium	Tel	Telescope
Cetus	Cet	Whale	Libra	Lib	Balance	Triangulum	Tri	Triangle
Chamaeleon	Cha	Chameleon	Lupus	Lup	Wolf	Triangulum Australe	TrA	Southern Triangle
Circinus	Cir	Compass (drawing)	Lynx	Lyn	Lynx	Tucana	Tuc	Toucan
Columba	Col	Dove	Lyra	Lyr	Lyre	Ursa Major	UMa	Greater Bear
Coma Berenices	Com	Berenice's Hair	Mensa	Men	Table Mountain	Ursa Minor	UMi	Littler Bear
Corona Australis	CrA	Southern Crown	Microscopium	Mic	Microscope	Vela	Vel	Sail
Corona Borealis	CrB	Northern Crown	Monoceros	Mon	Unicorn	Virgo	Vir	Maiden
Corvus	Crv	Crow	Musca	Mus	Fly	Volans	Vol	Flying Fish
Crater	Crt	Cup	Norma	Nor	Square (rule)	Vulpecula	Vul	Fox
Crux	Cru	Cross (southern)	Octans	Oct	Octant			
			Ophiuchus	Oph	Serpent Bearer			

Eclipses and Transits, 2019

(In Coordinated Universal Time, or UTC, the standard time of the prime meridian.)

A relatively rare transit of Mercury will take place Nov. 11, 2019. This occurs when the planet passes between the Earth and the Sun close enough to the ecliptic to be seen in silhouette against the solar disk. On average, it occurs 13 times in a century. The transit will only be visible through telescopes, with precautions to avoid the intense light of the Sun, just as at solar eclipses.

The tables below give the times in UTC of when the Moon or Sun will reach certain phases of each event. In the case of the lunar eclipses, the times are relevant for any observer who can see the Moon. In the case of solar eclipses, the tabulated times refer to when the given event begins or ends from specific points along the eclipse path; as the Moon's shadow sweeps quickly across the Earth, the observed duration and degree of eclipse depends on the observer's precise location. Interactive maps are available on the internet to calculate times for specific locations.

I. Partial Eclipse of the Sun: Jan. 6

This eclipse will be visible only to observers in northeast Asia and the North Pacific. Times are for the midpoint of the eclipse path in far northeast Siberia.

Event	Date	Hr.	Min.
Partial eclipse begins	Jan. 5	23	34
Greatest eclipse	Jan. 6	01	41
Partial eclipse ends	Jan. 6	03	49

II. Total Eclipse of the Moon: Jan. 21

This eclipse will be visible to observers in the central Pacific, North and South America, Europe, and Africa. Even though the Moon passes north of the center of the Earth's shadow, totality will be relatively long and dark because the Moon will be near perigee (closest approach to Earth).

Event	Date	Hr.	Min.
Penumbral eclipse begins. .	Jan. 21	02	37
Partial eclipse begins	Jan. 21	03	34
Total eclipse begins	Jan. 21	04	41
Greatest eclipse	Jan. 21	05	12
Total eclipse ends.	Jan. 21	05	43
Partial eclipse ends	Jan. 21	06	51
Penumbral eclipse ends . . .	Jan. 21	07	48

III. Total Eclipse of the Sun: July 2

The path of totality is primarily across the South Pacific, with the only landfalls in Chile and Argentina. Times are for an observer near the Chile-Argentina border.

Event	Date	Hr.	Min.
Partial eclipse begins	July 2	19	24
Total eclipse begins	July 2	20	39
Greatest eclipse	July 2	20	40
Total eclipse ends.	July 2	20	41
Partial eclipse ends	July 2	21	47

IV. Partial Eclipse of the Moon: July 16-17

This eclipse will be visible to observers across most of Europe, Africa, Asia, Australia, and South America. This is a relatively shallow eclipse, and thus relatively inconspicuous, with slightly more than half of the Moon's disk passing through the Earth's umbra at maximum.

Event	Date	Hr.	Min.
Penumbral eclipse begins	July 16	18	43
Partial eclipse begins	July 16	20	01
Greatest eclipse	July 16	21	31
Partial eclipse ends	July 16	23	00
Penumbral eclipse ends . .	July 17	00	18

V. Transit of Mercury: Nov. 11

The complete transit, which lasts about 5 hr., 30 min., will be visible from Eastern North America, all of South America, and parts of West Africa, with parts of the transit visible from Western North America, Europe, and Africa.

Event	Date	Hr.	Min.
1st contact	Nov. 11	12	35
2nd contact.	Nov. 11	12	37
Transit center	Nov. 11	15	20
3rd contact	Nov. 11	18	03
4th contact	Nov. 11	18	04

VI. Annular Eclipse of the Sun: Dec. 26

Observers in Saudi Arabia, Qatar, United Arab Emirates, Oman, southern India, northern Sri Lanka, Sumatra, Malaysia, Indonesia, Singapore, parts of Borneo, and Guam will see an annular eclipse of the sun. Times are for an observer at the midpoint of the path.

Event	Date	Hr.	Min.
Partial eclipse begins	Dec. 26	03	31
Annular eclipse begins . . .	Dec. 26	05	27
Greatest eclipse	Dec. 26	05	28
Annular eclipse ends	Dec. 26	05	30
Partial eclipse ends	Dec. 26	07	22

Total Solar Eclipses, 2019-35

Total solar eclipses actually take place nearly as often as total lunar eclipses. Total lunar eclipses are visible over at least half of the Earth, while total solar eclipses can be seen only along a very narrow path up to a few hundred miles wide and a few thousand miles long. Observing a total solar eclipse is thus a rarity for most people.

Solar eclipses can be dangerous to observe. This is not because the Sun emits more potent rays, but because the Sun is always dangerous to observe directly, and people are particularly likely to stare at it during a solar eclipse.

Date	Duration[1] min.	sec.	Width (mi)	Path of totality
2019, July 2	4	33	125	S Pacific Ocean, S America
2020, Dec. 14	2	10	56	S Pacific Ocean, S America, S Atlantic Ocean
2021, Dec. 4	1	54	260	Antarctica
2024, Apr. 8	4	28	123	Mexico, midwestern U.S., E Canada
2026, Aug. 12	2	18	183	Greenland, Iceland, Spain
2027, Aug. 2	6	23	160	Spain, N Africa, Arabian peninsula
2028, July 22	5	10	143	Indian Ocean, Australia, New Zealand
2030, Nov. 25	3	44	105	Namibia, Botswana, South Africa, Indian Ocean, E Australia
2033, Mar. 30	2	37	485	Alaska, E Russia, Arctic
2034, Mar. 20	4	9	99	Central and NE Africa, Arabian Peninsula, Central and E Asia
2035, Sept. 2	2	54	72	China, Korea, Japan, Pacific Ocean

(1) Length of time at optimal viewing area.

Total Solar Eclipses in the U.S. in the 21st Century

During the 21st century, there are eight total solar eclipses visible somewhere in the continental U.S. The first came after a long gap, in 2017. The last total solar eclipse had been on Feb. 26, 1979, in the northwestern U.S.

Date	Path of totality	Date	Path of totality
Aug. 21, 2017	Oregon to South Carolina	Mar. 30, 2052	Florida to Georgia
Apr. 8, 2024	Mexico to Texas and N through Maine	May 11, 2078	Louisiana to North Carolina
Aug. 23, 2044	Montana to North Dakota	May 1, 2079	New Jersey to the lower edge of New England
Aug. 12, 2045	Northern California to Florida	Sept. 14, 2099	North Dakota to Virginia

Beginnings of the Universe

One of the dominating astronomical discoveries of the 20th century was that the galaxies of the universe all seem to be moving away from Earth. Doppler redshifts were observed for spiral nebulae around 1920 even though they were not yet known to be galaxies. By the early 1930s, Americans Edwin Hubble and M. L. Humason had established that the more distant a galaxy, the faster it was receding. It turned out that they were moving away not just from the Earth but from one another—that is, the **universe is expanding**. Scientists conclude that the universe must once, very long ago, have been extremely compact and dense, and a rapid expansion caused the energy and matter to rapidly expand. The beginning of this expansion is referred to as the **Big Bang**.

On the subatomic level, according to this theory, there were vast changes of energy and matter and the way physical laws operated during the first few minutes after the Big Bang. After those early minutes the percentages of the basic matter of the universe—hydrogen, helium, and lithium—were set. Everything was so compact and hot that radiation dominated the early universe and there were no stable, un-ionized atoms. The universe was opaque, in the sense that any energy emitted was quickly absorbed and then re-emitted. As the universe expanded, density and temperature continued to drop. A few hundred thousand years after the Big Bang, the temperature dropped far enough that electrons and nuclei could combine to form stable atoms as the universe became transparent. Once that occurred, the radiation that had been trapped was free to escape.

In the 1940s, George Gamow (Russ.-U.S.) and others predicted that remnants of this escaped radiation should be observable. They had started to search for this background radiation when physicists Arno Penzias (Ger.-U.S.) and Robert Wilson (U.S.), using a radio telescope, inadvertently found it, for which they won the 1978 Nobel Prize in Physics.

In 2003, NASA's Wilkinson Microwave Anisotropy Probe made measurements of the temperature of this **cosmic microwave background radiation** to within millionths of a degree. From these measurements, scientists were able to deduce that our universe is 13.7 bil years old and that first-generation stars began to form a mere 200 mil years after the Big Bang.

In 2014, scientists operating a telescope in Antarctica claimed to have found direct evidence for cosmic inflation, the rapid expansion of the universe during the 10-32 sec. after the Big Bang that helps explain why variations of the cosmic background radiation are so small. Follow-up observations cast doubt on this, and higher precision measurements are planned.

A related mystery is evidence suggesting hidden matter and hidden energy that cannot be directly observed. The presence of dark matter is indicated by the rotation curves of galaxies and the dynamics of clusters of galaxies. **Dark matter** may be composed of gas; large numbers of cool, compact objects like dead stars; or even subatomic particles. Evidence for **dark energy** is derived from studies of distant Type Ia supernovae indicating that the expansion of the universe is accelerating rather than slowing. Dark energy seems to work on the very fabric of the universe, acting as a force that increases the rate at which space expands. Visible matter seems to constitute only about 4% of the total mass of the universe while the rest of the universe's mass is in the form of dark matter (27%) and dark energy (68%).

Galaxies

By the 20th century, more than 10,000 **nebulae**—cloud-like luminous objects in the sky—had been discovered. Some were correctly identified as star clusters and others as clouds of gas and dust. Those nebulae that were spiral or elliptical in shape were found in regions of the sky far from the glowing band that is our own Milky Way galaxy. German philosopher Immanuel Kant had written in 1775 that some of these fuzzy objects might be **"island universes"** apart from our own. But the idea remained speculative until 1923-24, when Edwin Hubble discovered variable stars—stars whose varying brightness makes their distance from Earth calculable—in some of these nebulae. This provided conclusive evidence that these systems were far enough away to be outside our own island universe, the Milky Way galaxy.

Galaxies range in size from small dwarf elliptical ones, with perhaps 1 mil stars, to spiral galaxies containing 300 bil stars, to giant elliptical galaxies that may be home to more than 10 tril stars. The diameters of galaxies range from 3,000 light-years in dwarf elliptical galaxies to over 500,000 light-years in giant elliptical galaxies. It is estimated that the Milky Way galaxy is about 100,000 light-years in diameter with about 400 bil stars.

Galaxies also congregate into **clusters**. The smallest are poor clusters of only a few dozen galaxies, while the largest rich clusters may contain thousands. The Milky Way is part of a poor cluster of about three dozen galaxies called the **Local Group**. The largest galaxy of the Local Group is Andromeda, a spiral galaxy visible to the unaided eye in the constellation of Andromeda on a very dark night. The Milky Way is the second largest galaxy in this group; most of the others are small.

The Solar System

The major planets of the solar system, in order of mean distance from the Sun, are **Mercury**, **Venus**, **Earth**, **Mars**, **Jupiter**, **Saturn**, **Uranus**, and **Neptune**. The dwarf planets in order of average distance from the Sun are **Ceres** (located between Mars and Jupiter), **Pluto**, **Haumea**, **Makemake**, **2007 OR10**, and **Eris**. All planets orbit counterclockwise around the Sun as viewed from above the Earth's North Pole.

Because Mercury and Venus are nearer to the Sun than is Earth, their motions about the Sun appear from Earth as wide swings first to one side of the Sun then to the other, though both planets move around the Sun in almost circular orbits. When their passage takes them between Earth and the Sun or beyond the Sun in relation to Earth, they cannot be seen.

The planets that lie farther from the Sun than does Earth may be seen for longer periods. They are invisible only when so located in the sky that they rise and set at about the same time as the Sun and are thus overwhelmed by the Sun's light.

Mercury and Venus, because they are between Earth and the Sun, show phases much as the Moon does. The planets farther from the Sun are always seen as full, although Mars does occasionally present a slightly gibbous phase, like the Moon when it is not quite full.

The planets appear to move rapidly among the stars because they are relatively closer to Earth. The stars are also in motion, some at tremendous speeds, but they are so far away that their motion does not change their apparent positions in the heavens enough to be perceived. The nearest star is about 9,000 times farther away than Neptune. The count for identified **moons** in the solar system orbiting planets and dwarf planets stood at 195 as of mid-2018. Several dwarf planet candidates are also known to have moons.

Planet Superlatives			
Largest, most massive planet	Jupiter	Smallest, least massive planet	Mercury
Fastest orbiting planet	Mercury	Slowest orbiting planet	Neptune
Fastest sidereal rotation	Jupiter	Slowest sidereal rotation	Venus
Longest (synodic) day	Mercury	Shortest (synodic) day	Jupiter
Rotational pole closest to ecliptic	Uranus	Hottest planet	Venus
Most moons	Jupiter	No moons	Mercury, Venus
Planet with largest moon	Jupiter	Planet with moon with most eccentric orbit	Neptune
Greatest average density	Earth	Lowest average density	Saturn
Tallest mountain	Mars	Deepest oceans	Jupiter
Strongest magnetic fields	Jupiter	Greatest amount of liquid water on surface	Earth
Most circular orbit	Venus		

Selected Characteristics of the Sun and Planets

Object	at unit distance[1] ″	Radius— at mean least distance[2] ″	in mi mean radius	Volume[3]	Mass[3]	Density[3]	Sidereal period d.	hr.	min.	sec.	Gravity at surface[3]	Reflect-ing power[4]	Daytime surface temp. (°F)
Sun	959.5	976.0	432,500	1,304,000	333,000	0.26	25	9	7		28.00	—	9,941
Mercury	3.36	6.5	1,516	0.0562	0.0553	0.98	58	15	36		0.38	0.11	845
Venus	8.34	33.0	3,760	0.857	0.815	0.95	243		30R		0.91	0.65	867
Earth	8.78	—	3,959	1.000	1.000	1.00		23	56	4.2	1.00	0.37	59
Moon	2.40	986.2	1,079	0.0203	0.0123	0.61	27	7	43	40	0.16	0.12	260
Mars	4.67	12.8	2,106	0.151	0.107	0.71		24	37	22	0.38	0.15	−24
Jupiter	96.40	24.5	43,441	1,321.30	317.83	0.24		9	55	30	2.53	0.52	−162
Saturn	80.29	10.05	36,184	763.6	95.16	0.12		10	39	20	1.06	0.47	−218
Uranus	34.97	2.05	15,759	63.1	14.54	0.23		17	14	20R	0.90	0.51	−323
Neptune	33.95	1.2	15,301	57.7	17.15	0.3		16	6	40	1.14	0.41	−330

R = Retrograde rotation. (1) Angular radius, in seconds of arc, if object were seen at a distance of 1 astronomical unit. (2) Angular radius, in seconds of arc, when object is closest to Earth. (3) Earth = 1. (4) A value of 1 would indicate a perfect reflector.

Planets of the Solar System

The International Astronomical Union (IAU) on Aug. 24, 2006, at their General Assembly in Prague, Czech Republic, agreed on a new definition for planet, and in the process effectively removed Pluto's planet status. The ruling came after years of debate as to whether Pluto, discovered in 1930, should still be considered the ninth planet in our solar system because of its size, orbit, and other characteristics. New discoveries of other Pluto-like objects in the solar system, such as the 2003 discovery of Eris, a **Kuiper Belt object** (KBO) comparable in size to Pluto, also contributed to the debate.

Under the IAU's new definition, Mercury, Venus, Earth, Mars, Jupiter, Saturn, Uranus, and Neptune are regarded as "classical" planets. A **planet** is now defined as a celestial body that (a) is in orbit around the Sun, (b) has sufficient mass for its self-gravity to overcome rigid body forces so that it assumes a hydrostatic equilibrium (nearly round) shape, and (c) has cleared the neighborhood around its orbit.

Pluto, Eris, Ceres, Makemake, 2007 OR10, and Haumea are regarded as dwarf planets, with the status of Pluto's largest moon, Charon, still to be determined. A **dwarf planet** is a celestial body that (a) is in orbit around the Sun, (b) has sufficient mass for its self-gravity to overcome rigid body forces so that it assumes a hydrostatic equilibrium (nearly round) shape, (c) has not cleared the neighborhood around its orbit, and (d) is not a satellite.

The IAU also created a new category, **small solar system bodies**, for all other objects orbiting the Sun, including comets, asteroids, KBOs, and other small objects. It has not yet established a process by which other solar system objects will be classified.

Note: AU = astronomical unit (92.96 mil mi, mean distance of Earth from the Sun); **d.** = 1 Earth synodic (solar) day (24 hours); **synodic day** = rotation period of a planet measured with respect to the Sun (the "true" day, i.e., the time from midday to midday, or from sunrise to sunrise); **sidereal day** = rotation period of a planet with respect to the stars.

Mercury

```
Distance from the Sun
  Perihelion . . . . . . . . . . . . . . . . . . . . . . . . .28.6 mil mi
  Semi-major axis (mean distance) . . 36 mil mi (0.387 AU)
  Aphelion . . . . . . . . . . . . . . . . . . . . . . . . . . . 43.4 mil mi
Period of revolution around Sun . . . . . . . . . . . . . . .87.97 d.
Orbital eccentricity . . . . . . . . . . . . . . . . . . . . . . . . 0.2056
Orbital inclination . . . . . . . . . . . . . . . . . . . . . . . . . .7.00°
Synodic day (midday to midday) . . . . . . . . . . . . 175.94 d.
Sidereal day . . . . . . . . . . . . . . . . . . . . . . . . . . . . 58.65 d.
Rotational inclination . . . . . . . . . . . . . . . . . . . . . . . .0.01°
Mass (Earth = 1) . . . . . . . . . . . . . . . . . . . . . . . . . . 0.0553
Mean radius . . . . . . . . . . . . . . . . . . . . . . . . . . . 1,516 mi
Mean density (Earth = 1) . . . . . . . . . . . . . . . . . . . . 0.984
Natural satellites . . . . . . . . . . . . . . . . . . . . . . . . . . . . . 0
Average surface temperature . . . . . . . . . . . . . . . . 333°F
```

Mercury, named for the Roman gods' messenger, is the closest planet to the Sun and the smallest planet in the solar system. Mercury orbits so close to the Sun that it can never be observed against a dark sky; it is always seen during morning or evening twilights. In 2008, the *Messenger* spacecraft made the first flybys of Mercury since the 1970s. *Messenger* went into orbit about Mercury in Mar. 2011 for a reconnaissance mission; the original one-year science program was extended in 2012. The goals of the mission included mapping, imaging, and measuring the surface composition of Mercury, as well as probing the planet's interior structure and interactions with the Sun. Among the discoveries were that at least part of Mercury's metallic core is liquid, that there may be water ice in shadowed craters near the poles, and that the planet's magnetic field is offset from the planet's center.

Orbit and rotation. Mercury moves with great speed around the Sun, averaging about 30 mi per second to complete its orbit, which takes about 88 Earth days. Mercury takes nearly 59 days to rotate on its axis. Because its orbital period is only about 50% longer than its sidereal rotation, the time from one sunrise to the next on Mercury is about 176 days—twice as long as a Mercurial year. Oddly, Mercury has a magnetic field, albeit a very weak one. It has been held that both a fluid core and rapid rotation—neither of which Mercury was believed to have—are necessary for the generation of a planetary magnetic field. Mercury may demonstrate the contrary.

Atmosphere. Mercury's atmosphere is almost nonexistent. What very little it has is composed of 42% oxygen, 29% sodium, 22% hydrogen, 6% helium, 0.5% potassium, and 0.5% other particles. Because of Mercury's lack of atmosphere, the surface during the day may reach a temperature of about 845°F, while the temperature at night may fall as low as −300°F. Earth-based observation has provided evidence of water ice near the poles.

Surface and composition. Mercury's surface is rocky and cratered similar to that of the Earth's moon. The most imposing feature on Mercury, the Caloris Basin, is a huge impact crater more than 800 mi in diameter. Mercury has a huge iron core that extends out to about 75% of the planet's radius; it has a higher percentage of iron than any other planet in the solar system.

Venus

```
Distance from the Sun
  Perihelion . . . . . . . . . . . . . . . . . . . . . . . . .66.8 mil mi
  Semi-major axis (mean distance) . . .67.2 mil mi (0.723 AU)
  Aphelion . . . . . . . . . . . . . . . . . . . . . . . . . . . .67.7 mil mi
Period of revolution around Sun . . . . . . . . . . . . . . . 224.7 d.
Orbital eccentricity . . . . . . . . . . . . . . . . . . . . . . . . 0.0067
Orbital inclination . . . . . . . . . . . . . . . . . . . . . . . . . 3.39°
Synodic day (midday to midday) . . . . . 116.75 d. (retrograde)
Sidereal day . . . . . . . . . . . . . . . . . . . 243.02 d. (retrograde)
Rotational inclination . . . . . . . . . . . . . . . . . . . . . . . 177.4°
Mass (Earth = 1) . . . . . . . . . . . . . . . . . . . . . . . . . .0.815
Mean radius . . . . . . . . . . . . . . . . . . . . . . . . . . . 3,760 mi
Mean density (Earth = 1) . . . . . . . . . . . . . . . . . . . .0.951
Natural satellites . . . . . . . . . . . . . . . . . . . . . . . . . . . . 0
Average surface temperature . . . . . . . . . . . . . . . . 867°F
```

Venus, named for the Roman goddess of love, is the second planet out from the Sun. Because Venus is almost the same size as Earth, it is believed that the two planets were formed at the same time by the same general process and from the same mixture of chemical elements. Venus can easily be seen from Earth with the naked eye; it is the third-brightest object in the sky, exceeded only by the Sun and the Moon.

Orbit and rotation. It takes Venus 225 Earth days to complete its orbit around the Sun. Its synodic revolution—the amount of time it takes for Venus to return to the same position relative to Earth and the Sun, which is a result of the combination of its own motion with that of Earth—is 584 days. Because of this, every 19 months Venus is closer to Earth than to any other planet.

The rotation period of Venus appears to be 243 days clockwise. In other words, its rotation is counter to the rotation of the other planets and counter to its own motion around the Sun. This rate and sense of rotation make for a solar day (sunrise to sunrise) on Venus of 116.8 Earth days. Night lasts 58 days, and day lasts 58 days. Venus has no detectable magnetic field.

Atmosphere. The Venusian atmosphere is very thick and toxic. It is composed primarily of 96.5% carbon dioxide, 3.5% nitrogen, and trace concentrations of sulfur dioxide, argon, water, carbon monoxide, helium, and neon. In addition, it exerts an atmospheric pressure at the surface more than 90 times Earth's normal sea-level pressure. The planet is covered with a dense, white, cloudy atmosphere that conceals whatever is below. These clouds are believed to contain sulfuric acid, meaning that it rains sulfuric acid on Venus. Due to the thickness of the atmosphere and resulting extreme greenhouse effect, the temperature is essentially the same day and night; the planet has an average surface temperature of about 867°F, making it the hottest planet in the solar system. Winds of about 200 mph in the clouds may account for the consistency in temperature despite the low rotation speed of the planet. However, at the surface, the winds are very slow.

Surface and composition. Radar-produced maps of the planet show large craters, continent-sized highlands, and extensive dry lowlands. No tectonic activity has been found similar to Earth's moving tectonic plates, but a system of global rift zones and numerous broad, low, dome-like structures, called coronae, may have been produced by the upwelling and subsidence of magma from the mantle. Volcanic surface features, such as vast lava plains, fields of small lava domes, and large shield volcanoes, are common. About 1,600 volcanoes and volcanic features appear on the Venusian surface; more than 85% of the surface is covered by volcanic flows. Theia Mons, a huge shield volcano, has a diameter of over 600 mi and a height of over 3.5 mi. (The largest Hawaiian volcano is only about 125 mi in diameter but rises nearly 5.5 mi from the ocean floor.) Aside from volcanoes, there are highly deformed mountain belts across Venus along with a few meteor-impact craters more than 20 mi wide. Erosion is a very slow process on Venus due to the lack of water. There are indications of some wind movement of dust and sand. The few impact craters on Venus suggest that the surface is generally geologically young—less than 800 mil years old. Despite the fact that probes have landed on Venus, there are very few pictures from the surface because the probes couldn't withstand the high temperature and atmospheric pressure for more than a few hours.

Mars

Mars	
Distance from the Sun	
Perihelion	128.4 mil mi
Semi-major axis (mean distance)	141.6 mil mi (1.524 AU)
Aphelion	154.9 mil mi
Period of revolution around Sun	686.98 d. (1.88 yr.)
Orbital eccentricity	0.0935
Orbital inclination	1.85°
Synodic day (midday to midday)	24 hr., 39 min., 35 sec.
Sidereal day	24 hr., 37 min., 22 sec.
Rotational inclination	25.19°
Mass (Earth = 1)	0.107
Mean radius	2,106 mi
Mean density (Earth = 1)	0.713
Natural satellites	2
Average surface temperature	−81°F

Named for the Roman god of war, the Red Planet has some features much like Earth. Mars has climate, seasons, volcanoes, and possibly once had liquid water flowing across its surface. Mars can easily be seen with the naked eye on most clear nights, which is why it was one of the first planets to be studied by ancient astronomers. Later, when telescopes came into use, many observers claimed that canals made by Martians existed on the planet's surface, which led to speculation as to whether there was intelligent life there. Unmanned probes have since put all those theories to rest; the canals turned out to be topographic patterns and dust storms.

Mars is currently being explored by a number of robotic craft, both on the surface and in orbit. The *Curiosity*/Mars Science Laboratory, an SUV-sized robot, landed on the surface in Aug. 2012. Its mission was to understand the history of the Martian geology and climate, search for the presence of organic matter, and assess the planet's past suitability for life. An Indian orbiter is currently using remote sensing to study the Martian surface and atmosphere, while NASA's *MAVEN* spacecraft is studying the upper atmosphere of Mars and its interaction with the solar wind. The European Space Agency *Trace Gas Orbiter* (TGO) began orbiting Mars in Oct. 2016.

Orbit and rotation. Although Mars's orbital path is nearly circular, it is somewhat more eccentric than that of most other planets. Mars is more than 26 mil mi farther from the Sun at its most distant point compared to its closest approach. Its orbit and speed in relation to Earth's bring it fairly close to Earth, at opposition, about every two years. Mars was at opposition on July 27, 2018, and will be close again on Oct. 13, 2020. Every 15-17 years the close approaches are especially favorable for observation. The 2018 opposition was particularly close, and the next such favorable opposition occurs on Sept. 15, 2035.

Mars rotates in 24 hr. and 37 min., almost the same period of time as Earth. Mars's mean distance from the Sun is 142 mil mi. Because Mars's axis of rotation is inclined by about 25° from the vertical to the plane of its solar orbit about the Sun, the planet has seasons.

Unlike Earth's global magnetic field, the Martian magnetic field is small, weak, and localized and may be the remnant of a stronger field from the planet's past.

Atmosphere. The Martian atmosphere is composed primarily of 95.32% carbon dioxide, 2.7% nitrogen, 1.6% argon, 0.13% oxygen, 0.08% carbon monoxide, and, in very minor quantities, water, hydrogen oxide, and neon. The atmosphere on Mars is very thin. It has an atmospheric pressure between 1% and 2% of Earth's (if Earth's atmosphere were that thin, there would not be enough oxygen to breathe). Because the Martian atmosphere is so thin and because of the planet's weak magnetic field, its surface is bombarded by cosmic radiation about 100 times as intense as on Earth.

Martian weather systems consist mainly of huge dust storms. On the poles, white caps (believed to be both water ice and carbon dioxide ice) grow in winter and shrink in summer. It is mainly the carbon dioxide that comes and goes with the seasons. The water ice is apparently in many layers with dust between them, indicating climatic cycles.

Surface and composition. Mars is an alien world with rust-red sand and pink skies. In the planet's beginning stages when it was much hotter, Mars's surface melted to a sufficient extent to separate into dense and lighter layers. Mars later cooled enough to allow liquid water to possibly flow across its surface. NASA scientists announced in Sept. 2015 the most convincing evidence to date that liquid water flows on the present-day Martian surface. Using imaging and spectroscopy instruments on the Mars Reconnaissance Orbiter, they showed that seasonal flows on Martian slopes contain hydrated minerals that can only form in the presence of liquid water.

Natural satellites. Mars has two small satellites called Phobos and Deimos, each discovered in 1877 by American astronomer Asaph Hall. (Phobos measures about 11 by 17 mi and Deimos about 7 by 9 mi.) Deimos, the outer satellite, revolves around the planet in about 31 hours. Phobos, the inner satellite, whips around Mars in a little more than 7 hours, making three orbits each Martian day. Since it orbits Mars faster than the planet rotates, Phobos rises in the west and sets in the east, opposite to what other bodies appear to do in the Martian sky. Both moons are irregularly shaped and pitted with numerous craters. Their origins are not known; however, some astronomers consider them to be asteroid-like objects that were captured by Mars very early in its history.

Jupiter

Jupiter	
Distance from the Sun	
Perihelion	460.1 mil mi
Semi-major axis (mean distance)	483.8 mil mi (5.204 AU)
Aphelion	507.4 mil mi
Period of revolution around Sun	11.862 yr.
Orbital eccentricity	0.0489
Orbital inclination	1.304°
Synodic day (midday to midday)	9 hr., 55 min., 33 sec.
Sidereal day	9 hr., 55 min., 30 sec.
Rotational inclination	3.13°
Mass (Earth = 1)	317.8
Mean radius	43,441 mi
Mean density (Earth = 1)	0.24
Natural satellites	79
Average temperature*	−162°F
*i.e., temperature where atmospheric pressure equals 1 Earth atmosphere.	

Jupiter, named for the Roman ruler of the gods, is the largest planet in the solar system (11 times the diameter of Earth). Its mass is more than twice the mass of all the other planets, moons, and asteroids put together. Visible to the naked eye and known to the ancients, it was a focus of the Italian scientist Galileo Galilei, who viewed the planet and its four largest moons through a homemade telescope.

Orbit and rotation. Jupiter is at an average distance of 484 mil mi from the Sun and takes almost 12 Earth years to make a complete revolution. The largest of the planets, Jupiter has an equatorial diameter of 88,846 mi; its polar diameter is more than 5,700 mi shorter. This noticeable oblateness is a result of the liquidity of the planet and its extremely rapid rotation rate—a Jupiter day is less than 10 Earth hours long. A point on Jupiter's equator moves at a speed of 22,000 mph, as compared with 1,000 mph for a point on Earth's equator. Jupiter's magnetic field is by far the strongest of any planet. Electrical activity caused by this field is so strong that it discharges trillions of watts into Jupiter's environment daily. In July 2016, NASA's *Juno* spacecraft entered orbit around the planet to begin a study of Jupiter's composition, magnetic field, and auroras, including close-up view of the poles of the planet. In 2018 the mission was extended until July 2021.

Atmosphere. Jupiter's atmosphere is primarily composed of 90% molecular hydrogen and 10% helium. Minor constituents include methane, ammonia, hydrogen deuteride, ethane, and water. Jupiter has a turbulent atmosphere characterized by thick clouds, high winds, and huge lightning storms many times larger than those on Earth. The atmospheric temperature varies, but the temperature at the tops of clouds may be about −280°F. The Great Red Spot is seen prominently on Jupiter is a huge hurricane-like storm that is three times the diameter of Earth. In 2006, the Hubble Space Telescope detected the appearance of a second, smaller red spot.

Surface and composition. Gas giant planets like Jupiter, Saturn, and Neptune do not have a surface like Earth or any of the other rocky planets. The gases become denser with depth, until they may turn into a slush or slurry. Jupiter has a liquid hydrogen ocean more than 35,000 mi deep. It likely has a rocky core about the size of Earth, but 13 times more massive. There is no sharp interface between the gaseous atmosphere and the hydrogen ocean that accounts for most of Jupiter's volume. At lower depths, under enormous pressure, the liquid hydrogen takes on the properties of a metal. It is likely that this liquid metallic hydrogen is the source for both Jupiter's persistent radio noise and for its improbably strong magnetic field.

Natural satellites. Jupiter has 79 known satellites. The discovery of 10 of these, small objects only a few kilometers in diameter, was announced in July 2018. Four of the moons (in order of distance from Jupiter), Io, Europa, Ganymede, and Callisto—all discovered by Galileo in 1610—are large and bright and are close in diameter to Earth's moon and Mercury. Because they move so rapidly around Jupiter, their change in position from night to night can be seen from Earth using binoculars.

Io is one of the most volcanically active bodies in the solar system. A gaseous, doughnut-shaped ring, or torus, enveloping Io's orbit around Jupiter may have been formed by material ejected from Io's active volcanoes. (This is not to be confused with Jupiter's rings.) These volcanoes, hotter than Earth's volcanoes, erupt mainly molten sulfur and result in a constantly changing surface appearance.

Europa may have a 30-mi-deep salty, liquid ocean beneath its icy crust, perhaps a small metallic core, and a very tenuous atmosphere. Ganymede is the biggest moon in the solar system. With a diameter of 3,120 mi, it is bigger than both Mercury and Pluto. Ganymede also has its own magnetic field produced by a molten core of perhaps iron sulfide. Callisto has the oldest, most heavily cratered surface in the solar system, a very thin atmosphere of carbon dioxide, and possibly a subsurface liquid ocean.

The other satellites are much smaller, with four closer to Jupiter than Io, five between Ganymede and Callisto, and the rest farther out. Most of Jupiter's moons orbit the planet at high inclinations from the equator, unlike the innermost satellites. These moons may be captured asteroids.

Rings. Jupiter has a diffuse, dark set of rings that were discovered by the *Voyager 1* spacecraft and cannot be seen from Earth without powerful telescopes. They are composed of small dust grains blasted off the four innermost moons by meteoroid impacts.

Saturn

Saturn, named for the Roman ruler of the Titans, is the sixth planet from the Sun and most distant of the planets visible to the unaided eye. Saturn is second in size to Jupiter, but its mass is much smaller. Saturn is the only planet less dense than water, meaning that Saturn would float if there were a pool of water gigantic enough to hold it.

Orbit and rotation. Saturn's diameter is almost 74,900 mi at the equator, while its polar diameter is more than 7,300 mi shorter. Like Jupiter, its noticeable oblateness is a result of the liquidity of the planet and its extremely rapid rate of rotation; a day is little more than 10 Earth hours long.

Distance from the Sun	
Perihelion	840.44 mil mi
Semi-major axis (mean distance)	890.8 mil mi (9.582 AU)
Aphelion	941.07 mil mi
Period of revolution around Sun	29.458 yr.
Orbital eccentricity	0.0565
Orbital inclination	2.485°
Synodic day (midday to midday)	10 hr., 39 min., 23 sec.
Sidereal day	10 hr., 39 min., 22 sec.
Rotational inclination	26.73°
Mass (Earth = 1)	95.159
Mean radius	36,184 mi
Mean density (Earth = 1)	0.125
Natural satellites	62
Average temperature*	−218°F

*i.e., temperature where atmospheric pressure equals 1 Earth atmosphere.

Atmosphere. Saturn's atmosphere is composed primarily of 96.3% hydrogen, 3.3% helium, and traces of methane, ammonia, hydrogen deuteride, ethane, and water. Saturn's atmosphere is much like that of Jupiter, except that the temperature at the top of its cloud layer is at least 50°F colder.

Surface and composition. Saturn's atmosphere resembles Jupiter's; it likely has a small dense center surrounded by a deep ocean of hydrogen.

Natural satellites. Saturn has 62 known natural satellites, most of which were not discovered until space probes reached the planet. Saturn's moon Mimas has an impact crater 81 mi across (the moon itself is only 249 mi across). Enceladus has an atmosphere and shows evidence of geysers that spit water ice and vapor. Two tiny moons orbit within the rings, plowing through and making gaps in the rings along their orbits. Pan, the innermost satellite, creates the Encke Gap of Saturn's A-ring. Daphnis creates the Keeler Gap. The most intriguing Saturnian moon is Titan. The second-biggest moon in the solar system, Titan is bigger than Mercury. Its atmosphere is similar to Earth's atmosphere of long ago; it is made up of approximately 95% nitrogen with traces of methane. Titan's atmosphere extends about 360 mi into space whereas most of Earth's atmosphere lies within 37 mi of the surface. Photographs from Titan's surface, taken by the *Huygens* lander in 2005, show a muddy terrain, with possible deposits of water ice, channels carved by liquid methane springs, and an interesting boundary between light and dark material on the surface. In 2006, scientists found sand dunes on Titan's surface. The "sand" is believed to be tiny water ice crystals or organic compounds. Surface phenomena such as sand dunes are signs of erosion and wind. Unlike winds on Earth or Mars, Titan's winds are not the result of uneven solar heating on the moon's surface but rather Saturn's gravitational pull (similar to how the Moon acts on the Earth's oceans).

Rings. Saturn's ring system is the planet's most recognizable feature. It begins about 4,000 mi above the visible disk of Saturn lying above its equator and extends about 260,000 mi into space. The diameter of the ring system visible from Earth is about 170,000 mi; the rings are estimated to be about 700 ft thick. The rings are composed of rock and ice and range in size from tiny particles to large chunks of material the size of a bus. There are several divisions in the rings. The 2,920-mi Cassini division, the gap between the A and B rings, is the largest division.

Uranus

Uranus, discovered by Sir William Herschel in 1781, was the first planet discovered using a telescope. It was named for the father of the Titans in Roman mythology.

Orbit and rotation. Uranus has a diameter of over 31,000 mi and spins once in approximately 17.23 hours, according to magnetic data collected by *Voyager 2*. One of the most fascinating features of Uranus is how far over it is tipped. Its north pole lies 98° from its orbital plane. Thus, its seasons are extreme. Over its 84-year orbit, when the Sun rises at the north pole, it shines there for about 42 Earth years; then it sets, and the north pole is in darkness for 42 Earth years. In addition to its rotational tilt, Uranus's magnetic field axis is tipped 58.6° from its rotational axis and is displaced about 30% of its radius away from the planet's center.

```
Distance from the Sun
    Perihelion ..........................1,703.4 mil mi
    Semi-major axis (mean distance) ........ 1,784.8 mil mi
                                           (19.201 AU)
    Aphelion............................ 1,866.4 mil mi
Period of revolution around Sun............... 84.01 yr.
Orbital eccentricity........................... 0.0457
Orbital inclination............................0.772°
Synodic day (midday to midday) ....17 hr., 14 min., 23 sec.
                                           (retrograde)
Sidereal day.........17 hr., 14 min., 24 sec. (retrograde)
Rotational inclination .........................97.77°
Mass (Earth = 1) .......................... 14.536
Mean radius ............................. 15,759 mi
Mean density (Earth = 1)....................... 0.23
Natural satellites .............................27
Average temperature* .......................−323°F
*i.e., temperature where atmospheric pressure equals 1 Earth
atmosphere.
```

Atmosphere. The atmosphere is composed primarily of 82.5% hydrogen, 15.2% helium, and 2.3% methane, with small amounts of hydrogen deuteride, ammonia ice, water ice, ammonia hydrosulfide, and methane ice.

Surface and composition. Uranus has no solid surface, and likely no rocky core but rather a mixture of rocks and assorted ices with about 15% hydrogen and some helium.

Natural satellites. Uranus has 27 known moons, which have orbits lying in the plane of the planet's equator. Five moons are relatively large, while 22 are very small and were only discovered with the *Voyager 2* mission or in later observations. Miranda has grooved markings, reminiscent of Jupiter's Ganymede, but often arranged in a chevron pattern. Rifts and channels on Ariel provide evidence of liquid flowing over its surface in the past. Umbriel is extremely dark, prompting some observers to regard its surface as among the oldest in the system. Titania has rifts and fractures but not the evidence of flow found on Ariel. Oberon's main feature is its surface saturated with craters, unrelieved by other formations.

Rings. In the equatorial plane there is also a complex of 11 rings, 9 of which were discovered in 1978 by observers watching Uranus pass before a star.

Neptune

Named for the Roman god of the sea, Neptune was the first planet discovered through mathematical predictions before it was directly observed. Its approximate orbit and position were first calculated independently by British astronomer John Couch Adams and French astronomer Urbain Le Verrier in 1845. In 1846, German astronomer Johann Galle first observed Neptune through a telescope.

Orbit and rotation. Neptune orbits the Sun in 164.8 Earth years in a nearly circular orbit. Its mzagnetic field is considerably asymmetric to the planet's structure, similar to, but not so extreme as, Uranus's magnetic field. Neptune's magnetic field axis is tipped 46.9° from its rotational axis and is displaced more than 55% of its radius away from the planet's center.

Atmosphere. The Neptunian atmosphere is composed primarily of 80% hydrogen, 19% helium, 1.5% methane, and small amounts of hydrogen deuteride, ethane, ammonia ice, water ice, ammonia hydrosulfide, and methane ice. Neptune's atmosphere is quite blue, with quickly changing white clouds often suspended high above an apparent surface. A Great Dark Spot, reminiscent of Jupiter's Great Red Spot, was discovered in 1989 when *Voyager 2* visited the planet. Observations with the Hubble Space Telescope have shown that the Great Dark Spot originally seen by *Voyager* has apparently dissipated, but a new dark spot has since appeared. Lightning and auroras have been found on other giant planets, but only the aurora phenomenon has been seen on Neptune. As with the other giant planets, Neptune emits more energy than it receives from the Sun. The excess has been found to be 2.7 times the solar contribution.

Surface and composition. As with the other giant planets, Neptune may have no solid surface or exact diameter. However, a mean value of 30,600 mi may be assigned to a diameter between atmosphere levels where the pressure is about the same as sea level on Earth.

Natural satellites. The largest of Neptune's 14 satellites is Triton. It is the only large moon in a retrograde orbit, which suggests that it was captured rather than having formed along with the planet. Triton's large size, sufficient to raise significant tides on the planet, may one day, billions of years from now, bring Triton close enough to Neptune for Triton to be torn apart. Triton has a tenuous atmosphere of nitrogen with a trace of hydrocarbons and evidence of active geysers injecting material into it. Triton is the coldest object yet measured in the solar system with a surface temperature of −391°F. Only about half of Triton has been observed, but its terrain shows cratering and a strange regional feature described as resembling the skin of a cantaloupe. Nereid has the highest orbital eccentricity (0.75) of any moon. Its long looping orbit suggests that it was also captured. In 2003, two more moons, which orbit farther from their parent planet than any other moons in the solar system, were discovered. In July 2013, archival Hubble Space Telescope images were used to discover the existence of a 14th natural satellite of Neptune. At less than 20 km diameter, it is the smallest of Neptune's known moons. The *Voyager 2* probe in 1989 confirmed the existence of six rings around Neptune composed of very fine particles. There may be some clumps in the rings' structure. It is not known whether Neptune's satellites influence the formation or maintenance of the rings.

```
Distance from the Sun
    Perihelion ......................... 2,761.7 mil mi
    Semi-major axis (mean distance) 2,793.1 mil mi (30.047 AU)
    Aphelion........................... 2,824.5 mil mi
Period of revolution around Sun............... 164.79 yr.
Orbital eccentricity...........................0.0113
Orbital inclination........................... 1.769°
Synodic day (midday to midday) ..... 16 hr., 6 min., 37 sec.
Sidereal day..................... 16 hr., 6 min., 36 sec.
Rotational inclination ........................ 28.32°
Mass (Earth = 1) ............................17.147
Mean radius ............................. 15,301 mi
Mean density (Earth = 1)....................... 0.297
Natural satellites ............................ 14
Average temperature* .......................−330°F
*i.e., temperature where atmospheric pressure equals
1 Earth atmosphere.
```

Dwarf Planets

Ceres

```
Distance from the Sun
    Perihelion ................... 237 mil mi (2.55 AU)
    Semi-major axis (mean distance) ... 257 mil mi (2.77 AU)
Period of revolution around Sun.................. 4.6 yr.
Orbital eccentricity...........................0.0756
Orbital inclination........................... 10.59°
Sidereal day.............................. 9.074 hr.
Mass (Earth = 1) ..........................0.00015
Mean radius................................292 mi
```

Ceres was the first asteroid discovered; Italian astronomer Guiseppe Piazzi first observed it on Jan. 1, 1801. In the 1800s,

it was considered a planet but lost that designation. Ceres is the largest object in the asteroid belt, comprising nearly one third of all the mass of asteroids. In Aug. 2006, it was designated a dwarf planet by the Intl. Astronomical Union (IAU).

After a journey of over seven years, the *Dawn* spacecraft entered into orbit around Ceres in Mar. 2015, making *Dawn* the first spacecraft to visit a dwarf planet. Astronomers are particularly interested in asteroids since they are thought to be rocky protoplanets, examples of the building blocks from which planets formed early in the history of the solar system. *Dawn*'s scientific instrumentation consists of cameras for surface imaging, a spectrometer for measuring surface mineralogy, and a neutron detector for measuring elemental composition of

Ceres. *Dawn* has produced high-resolution maps of the entire surface and the most accurate measurements of Ceres's size and mass. The images show a heavily cratered surface with features such as extremely reflective spots within a crater—thought to be freshly exposed water ice—and at least one mountain several miles high.

Orbit and rotation. Ceres orbits the Sun in the asteroid belt region between Mars and Jupiter.

Surface and composition. Ceres's composition is similar to that of the stony meteorites known as carbonaceous chondrites. These are considered to be the oldest materials in the solar system, with a composition reflecting that of the primitive solar nebula. Extremely dark in color, probably because of their hydrocarbon content, they show evidence of having absorbed water. Thus, unlike the Earth and the Moon, they have never melted nor been reheated since they first formed. *Dawn* observations suggest that the surface of Ceres consists largely of water ice, though its interior is mostly rock. Up to 25% of Ceres's mass may be water ice. There is evidence for hydrothermal vents at the surface of Ceres, perhaps indicating that liquid water existed below the surface in the recent past. Further study using *Dawn* will try to confirm observations suggesting that water evaporates from the surface and produces a diffuse atmosphere.

Pluto

Distance from the Sun	
Perihelion	2,756.9 mil mi
Semi-major axis (mean distance)	3,670.1 mil mi
	(39.482 AU)
Aphelion	4,583.2 mil mi
Period of revolution around Sun	247.74 yr.
Orbital eccentricity	0.2502
Orbital inclination	17.09°
Synodic day (midday to midday)	6 d., 9 hr., 17 min. (retrograde)
Sidereal day	6 d., 9 hr., 18 min. (retrograde)
Rotational inclination	119.59°
Mass (Earth = 1)	0.0022
Mean radius	736.5 mi
Mean density (Earth = 1)	0.339
Natural satellites	5
Average surface temperature	–369°F

Pluto, named for the Roman god of the underworld, is the largest Kuiper Belt object (KBO) by radius, and the second largest by mass. It was first discovered in 1930 by American astronomer Clyde Tombaugh and classified as a planet until 2006, when the IAU changed its designation to dwarf planet. In 2008, Pluto was designated by the IAU as the prototype for a class of objects called **plutoids**, bodies that (a) have an average distance from the Sun greater than Neptune's; (b) are large enough that gravity determines their shape; and (c) have not cleared their orbit of other objects. Haumea, Makemake, and Eris are also plutoids. The *New Horizons* spacecraft, launched on a voyage to Pluto and beyond in 2006, made the first flyby of Pluto on July 14, 2015, and is on its way to a Kuiper belt object, 2014 MU69, with a scheduled flyby on New Year's Day 2019.

Orbit and rotation. Pluto's orbit is highly eccentric; although its average distance from the Sun is 3.7 bil mi, it may get as close as 2.76 bil mi and as far as 4.58 bil mi. For about 20 years of its 248-year orbit, it is closer to the Sun than Neptune. Currently, it is beyond Neptune's orbit.

Atmosphere and surface. Before the *New Horizons* flyby, all observations of Pluto had been made with telescopes nearly 3 bil mi away, so the mission brought new data to light. The mass and density of Pluto suggests that it is composed of a rocky core with an overlying water-ice mantle. *New Horizons*'s close-up observations of Pluto revealed a mixed surface, with some ancient, heavily cratered terrain and other younger, smoother plains with no craters. The smooth terrain, estimated to be no more than 100 mil years old, is much younger than scientists expected and may indicate that geologic processes continue to modify Pluto. Nitrogen ice on the smooth plains appears to be flowing, like glaciers on Earth, onto the more heavily cratered surface. Compositional evidence shows that the smooth areas contain nitrogen, methane, and carbon monoxide ices. Scientists also found several mountain ranges rising more than 2 mi above the smooth plains; they speculated that the mountains

are made of water ice thrust up from below Pluto's nitrogen-rich icy surface.

New Horizons also provided the first close-up measurements of Pluto's atmosphere, confirming earlier measurements of methane, nitrogen, and carbon monoxide, the same molecules that form ice on Pluto's surface. Scientists speculate that the atmosphere forms from evaporation of surface ices when the dwarf planet is closer to the Sun. The new measurements also revealed hydrocarbon hazes as much as 50 mi above Pluto's surface. The hazes are thought to form when Pluto's tenuous atmosphere is exposed to the Sun's ultraviolet rays. Dark regions on Pluto's surface likely result from these hydrocarbons settling. Knowledge of Pluto will continue to improve as more data is analyzed.

Natural satellites. Pluto has five known natural satellites. Charon, the biggest, has a diameter of 750 mi—about half of Pluto's diameter of 1,474 mi. No other planet or dwarf planet has a moon so close to its size. Discovered in 1978, Charon orbits Pluto at a distance of 12,200 mi and takes 6.39 days to move around the dwarf planet. In this same length of time, Pluto and Charon both rotate once on their axes, meaning that the Pluto-Charon system appears to rotate as virtually a rigid body. Both worlds are roughly spherical and have comparable densities. Because of these similarities and their peculiar relationship, there is debate as to whether Charon should one day be designated a dwarf planet. *New Horizons* provided the first detailed look at Charon, revealing a surface with less color and likely dominated by water ice. New evidence suggests Charon may have had a water ocean in the past. Much of Charon's surface is smoother than expected, with few craters, implying that Charon has an active geology capable of resurfacing. The images also reveal fractures extending hundreds of miles and a canyon around 5 mi deep.

Two other moons, discovered in 2005 and 2006, were officially named Nix and Hydra. Two additional moons, discovered in 2011 and 2012, were officially named Kerberos and Styx by the IAU in 2013. In late 2015, NASA released *New Horizons*-sourced images of Nix and Hydra, revealing irregularly shaped objects about 25 and 35 mi across, respectively. Astronomers examining *New Horizons* data have been surprised to find no additional moons, down to the roughly 1-mi-diameter limit of detectability by the spacecraft.

Haumea

Distance from the Sun	
Semi-major axis (mean distance)	43.355 AU
Period of revolution around Sun	285.48 yr.
Orbital eccentricity	0.189
Orbital inclination	28.20°
Mass (Earth = 1)	0.0007
Mean radius	420 mi
Natural satellites	2

Haumea was discovered in 2004 and was accepted as a dwarf planet by the IAU in 2008.

Orbit and rotation. Haumea has a moderately eccentric orbit and takes about 285 years to go around the Sun.

Surface and composition. Spectra of Haumea indicate the presence of almost pure crystalline water ice. The surface reflects about 60% of the sunlight that reaches it. Haumea has a very oblong shape, twice as long as it is wide.

Natural satellites. Haumea has two natural satellites, Hi'iake and Namaka.

Makemake

Distance from the Sun	
Semi-major axis (mean distance)	45.715 AU
Period of revolution around Sun	309.1 yr.
Orbital eccentricity	0.155
Orbital inclination	28.99°
Mass (Earth = 1)	0.0007
Mean radius	450 mi
Natural satellites	1

Makemake was discovered in 2005 and was accepted as a dwarf planet by the IAU in 2008.

Orbit and rotation. Makemake has a moderately eccentric orbit and takes about 310 years to go around the Sun.

Surface and composition. Spectra of Makemake indicate the presence of frozen methane, as well as several organic compounds. The surface is highly reflective and appears similar to that of Pluto.

Natural satellites. Makemake has one natural satellite.

2007 OR10

Distance from the Sun	
Semi-major axis (mean distance)	67.143 AU
Period of revolution around Sun	550.19 yr.
Orbital eccentricity	0.505
Orbital inclination	30.87°
Mass (Earth = 1)	0.0006
Mean radius	950 mi
Natural satellites	1

2007 OR10 was discovered in 2007 and has not yet received an official name from the IAU.

Orbit and rotation. 2007 OR10 has a highly elliptical orbit and takes about 550 years to go around the Sun.

Surface and composition. Spectra of 2007 OR10 indicate the presence of frozen methane and water ice. The surface is highly reflective and appears similar to that of Pluto.

Natural satellites. One natural satellite of 2007 OR10 was discovered by astronomers using the Hubble Space Telescope in 2017.

Eris

Distance from the Sun	
Semi-major axis (mean distance)	67.6497 AU
Period of revolution around Sun	556.43 yr.
Orbital eccentricity	0.44171
Orbital inclination	44.204°
Mass (Earth = 1)	0.0027
Mean radius	723 mi
Natural satellites	1

Discovered in 2003 by astronomers at the California Institute of Technology, Eris is the largest dwarf planet by mass, about 27% larger than Pluto, although Pluto has a slightly larger radius.

Orbit and rotation. Eris has a highly elliptical orbit and takes about 560 years to go around the Sun—more than twice the time it takes Pluto. Its inclination is steep, tilted at 44° to the planetary plane. It also has an extremely eccentric orbit. It will be at its closest to the Sun, actually inside part of Pluto's orbit, in about 280 years.

Surface and composition. Eris, with a surface covered in frozen methane, may be similar to Pluto and the Neptunian moon Triton. Observations made by the Hubble Space Telescope show that Eris's surface is almost white and uniform, reflecting 86% of the light that hits it. This makes it the most reflective body in the solar system. The dwarf planet's interior is likely a mixture of rock and ice.

Natural satellites. Eris has one moon, Dysnomia.

Small Solar System Bodies

Asteroids

Besides planets and moons, many smaller objects orbit the Sun. In 2006, the International Astronomical Union (IAU) officially designated these objects "small solar system bodies." Asteroids or minor planets are found mainly in a belt between the orbits of Mars and Jupiter. Within this belt there may be millions of asteroids of varying sizes. Most asteroids are very small. Ceres, which can be classified both as an asteroid and a dwarf planet, is 588 mi in diameter, about one-quarter the diameter of our Moon.

Some of these asteroids are gravitationally locked with Jupiter and the Sun so that they have roughly the same orbit as Jupiter but are either 60° ahead or behind the planet. These are the **Trojan asteroids**. Many of the smaller moons of the solar system, especially those in retrograde orbits, may be captured asteroids. Asteroids whose orbits either cross or come close to the Earth's orbit are labeled **Near Earth asteroids**, or NEAs. A handful of asteroids have actually been imaged by the Arecibo and Goldstone radio telescopes and by the NEAR Shoemaker space probe. The *Galileo* spacecraft imaged the asteroids Gaspra and Ida (including Ida's moon Dactyl) on its way to Jupiter. As of July 2018, 13 asteroids had been visited by spacecraft.

Comets

Comets are small icy bodies that orbit the Sun. When one approaches the Sun, the energy from the Sun boils off material from the comet's icy nucleus, producing an enlarged head (or **coma**), and in many cases an extended tail. Because of that, comets are brighter when near the Sun. For large comets, the head may be 100,000 mi across and the tail more than a million mi long, though both are mainly empty space.

Comets have been known since ancient times. British astronomer Edmund Halley (1656-1742) ultimately realized that a group of historical reports were just repeated visits of the same object. Comets are the only astronomical objects named after their discoverers. In 1986, the European spacecraft *Giotto* took the first close-up images of a comet's nucleus, specifically of

Comet Halley, showing it had a peanut-shaped nucleus with a longest dimension of about 10 mi.

In 1995, U.S. observers Alan Hale (1958-) and Thomas Bopp (1949-2018) independently discovered a comet that was then beyond the orbit of Jupiter. It is one of the brightest comets of all time. It also holds the record for length of time visible to the naked eye—19 months—and is the most photographed comet in history. In July 2009, an amateur astronomer discovered a large impact scar in the upper atmosphere of Jupiter, likely the result of another cometary impact. In 2014, the *Rosetta* spacecraft became the first spacecraft to orbit a comet, 67P/Churyumov-Gerasimenko. *Rosetta* also deployed a lander onto the comet surface. As of mid-2018, nine comets have been studied directly by spacecraft.

Kuiper Belt

The Kuiper Belt is a doughnut-shaped region that extends to about 50 AU (astronomical units) from the Sun and is thought to be the source of short-period comets such as Comets Halley or Swift-Tuttle. It is filled with icy bodies that are in solar orbit. The more than 1,000 objects found in this region in recent years are called Kuiper Belt objects (KBOs). It is estimated that there are more than 70,000 objects 60 mi in diameter or larger within the Kuiper Belt. Dwarf planets Pluto and Eris are considered KBO. There are at least six KBOs larger than 300 mi in diameter.

Oort Cloud

The Oort Cloud is a vast spherical region hypothesized to exist around the Sun, planets, and KBOs, populated by comets and other icy bodies. Dutch astronomer Jan Oort (1900-92) proposed its existence as the origin for long-period comets, which can take more than 200 years to orbit the Sun. Current technology is not sufficient to detect any members of the Oort Cloud other than observed comets whose orbits may reach out as far as 50,000 AU. Recent examples of such long-period comets are Comets Hale-Bopp and Hyakutake.

The Sun

Distance from Earth, mean	92.96 mil mi (1 AU)
Sidereal day (rotation period)	25.38 d.
Mass (Earth =1)	332,900
Mean radius	432,200 mi
Mean density (Earth=1)	0.255
Average surface temperature	9,941°F

The Sun is the Earth's primary source of light and heat and its closest star. The biggest object in the solar system, the Sun is 332,900 times more massive than Earth and contains 99.86% of the mass of the entire solar system. On the whole, the Sun is made up of about 92.1% hydrogen and 7.8% helium, with trace amounts of other elements. It has a mass and luminosity greater than that of 90% of the stars in the Milky Way galaxy. Although most of the stars that can be easily seen on a clear night are bigger and brighter than the Sun, its proximity to Earth makes it

appear tremendously large and bright. The Sun is 400,000 times as bright as the full moon, and it gives Earth 6 mil times as much light as do all the other stars put together. Because of the great distance between the Sun and Earth, it takes about 499 sec., or slightly more than 8 min., for light from the Sun to reach Earth.

Composition. The Sun has six regions. The first three from the inside out are the core, the radiative zone, and the convective zone. Together they form the interior. The others, which comprise the visible surface, are the photosphere, the chromosphere, and the outermost region, the corona.

The Sun's heat and energy are produced in its core. Through a series of nuclear fusion reactions, hydrogen nuclei are converted to helium nuclei, releasing energy in the process. Temperatures in the core are theorized to be 28 mil °F. In 2017 astronomers discovered that the core rotates nearly four times faster than the surface, a rapidity left over from the time when the Sun was formed. From the core, photons transport the energy outward through the radiative zone. It can take photons several million years to pass through this area. In the convective zone, gases move energy outward at a faster rate. Like a boiling pot, bubbles of gas bring energy to the surface.

The photosphere is the visible surface of the Sun, that is, the light that we see as sunlight. When sunlight is analyzed with a spectroscope, it is found to consist of a continuous spectrum composed of all the colors of the rainbow, crossed by many dark lines. The dark "absorption lines" are produced by gaseous materials in the outer layers of the Sun. More than 60 of the natural terrestrial elements have been identified in the Sun, all in gaseous form because of the Sun's intense heat.

Just above the photosphere is the chromosphere, which is visible to the naked eye only in total solar eclipses, during which it appears to be a pinkish-violet layer with occasional great prominences projecting above its general level. With proper instruments, the chromosphere can be seen or photographed whenever the Sun is visible. Above the chromosphere is the corona, also visible to the naked eye only at times of total eclipse or with instruments that permit the brighter portions of the corona to be seen. The corona surges millions of miles from the Sun; its atoms are all in a state of extreme excitation and high ionization that indicates temperatures nearly 2 mil °F.

Sunspots. These dark, irregularly shaped regions may reach diameters of thousands of miles. There is an intimate connection between sunspots and the corona. At times of low sunspot activity, the fine streamers of the corona are longer above the Sun's equator than over the polar regions of the Sun; during periods of high sunspot activity, the corona extends fairly evenly outward from all regions of the Sun but to a much greater distance in space. The average life of a sunspot group is two months, but some have lasted for more than a year. Sunspots reach a low point, on average, every 11.3 years, with a peak of activity occurring irregularly between two successive periods of minimal activity. The Sun experienced an unusually quiet period in 2008 and 2009; its latest period of maximum activity occurred in 2014, though this was among the weakest maximums ever recorded.

Solar wind and magnetic field. Magnetic arches, called prominences, may extend tens of thousands of miles into the corona and may release enormous amounts of energy heating the corona. Coronal mass ejections are enormous releases of solar energy. Coronal holes are regions where the corona appears dark in X-rays, and are associated with open magnetic field lines, where the magnetic field lines project out into space instead of back toward the Sun. It is in these regions where the high-speed solar wind originates.

The solar wind carries the Sun's magnetic field, which extends beyond the planets. This is called the interplanetary magnetic field (IMF). Far past Pluto and the Kuiper Belt, the solar wind and the IMF lose their influence. The boundary between them and interstellar space is called the heliopause. In 2013, NASA announced that the *Voyager 1* spacecraft, launched in 1977, seemed at last to have reached the heliopause, at a distance 18 bil km (11 bil mi) from the Sun.

Searching for Extrasolar Planets

The Sun is a typical star in many respects and—with over 400 bil stars in the Milky Way—it is plausible that many other stars might have planets. Since 1995, astronomers have gathered evidence of thousands of planets orbiting stars other than the Sun. Astronomers have not directly observed most of these objects but inferred their existence from observations of their parent stars.

Astronomers have used two main techniques to detect planets. The first, called the radial-velocity method, uses the Doppler effect to detect periodic changes in the motion of a star caused by the gravitational tug of an unseen planet. The magnitude of the star's motion and the time it takes to repeat can be used to infer the planet's mass and distance from its host star. This technique is most sensitive to high-mass planets orbiting close to their stars because that situation produces more noticeable changes in a star's motion.

The second technique, the transit method, relies on the dimming of a star's light as an unseen planet repeatedly passes in front of it. Astronomers are able to infer the diameter of the planet and the distance at which the planet orbits the star. When combined with the mass determined from the radial-velocity method, astronomers can determine the density of the unseen planet and begin to infer its similarity to planets in our solar system.

Astronomers have also used optical gravitational lensing to detect extrasolar planets. This technique, which detects the observed brightening of a distant background star as a planet passes in front of it, has allowed Southern Hemisphere astronomers to find the most distant planet yet detected, about halfway to the center of our own Milky Way galaxy.

The first planets to be discovered outside the solar system tended to be massive "hot Jupiters," orbiting close to their parent stars (closer than Mercury's orbit around the Sun) and comparable in mass to the gas giant Jupiter. But as detection instruments and techniques have improved, smaller and more distant planets have been discovered. The planets discovered so far seem to fall into several groups: rocky planets as massive as 1.75 times that of Earth; mini-Neptunes, 2-3.5 times as massive as Earth, with gas surrounding a rocky core; "super Earths" more massive than the mini-Neptunes; and gas giants, as massive or more massive than Jupiter.

In 2005, astronomers obtained the first direct image of an extrasolar planet, in orbit around a younger Sun-like star called GQ Lupi. The planet is about 100 AU (astronomical units) away from the star and estimated to be about twice as massive as Jupiter.

In 2006, astronomers discovered what they call a "super Earth" orbiting a red dwarf 9,000 light-years away. The planet appears to have about 13 times Earth's mass and may be composed of rock and ice, but it is believed not to have liquid on its surface. Such super Earths appear to be common in extrasolar planetary systems. In 2007, astronomers detected water in the atmosphere of an extrasolar planet for the first time.

In 2009, NASA launched Kepler, the first telescope sensitive enough to detect Earth-sized planets around other stars. Kepler's first-released data in 2010 indicated that small planets are more common than large planets. Kepler has now detected a large number of planets with diameters similar to that of Earth. Some of the planets are known to orbit within the host star's habitable zone, meaning that the conditions are such that liquid water could exist on the planetary surface. As of July 2018, astronomers had confirmed over 3,700 planets orbiting some more than 2,816 stars; 628 of those stars host more than one planet.

Planets with masses smaller than Jupiter's are now regularly discovered. A team of astronomers announced, Aug. 2016, the discovery of a possibly Earth-like planet, Proxima b, in orbit around Proxima Centauri, the star closest to the Sun. About 4.2 light-years away, it is the closest known exoplanet. In Feb. 2017, astronomers announced the discovery of at least seven Earth-sized planets orbiting a small star, Trappist-1, located about 40 light-years away. They appear similar in mass and composition to Earth, and three of the planets are in the habitable zone of the star. In June 2017, the Kepler mission announced the discovery of 10 Earth-sized planets, probably rocky in composition, that might support liquid water and could be potentially habitable.

NASA successfully launched the Transiting Exoplanet Survey Satellite (TESS) mission on Apr. 18, 2018, aboard a SpaceX Falcon 9 rocket. This landmark mission will conduct an all-sky survey of extrasolar planets, including those orbiting bright nearby stars.

Earth: Size, Computation of Time, Seasons

Distance from the Sun	
Perihelion	91.4 mil mi
Semi-major axis (mean distance)	93 mil mi (1.0000 AU)
Aphelion	94.5 mil mi
Period of revolution	365.256 d.
Orbital eccentricity	0.0167
Orbital inclination	0°
Synodic day (midday to midday)	24 hr., 0 min., 0 sec.
Sidereal day (rotation period)	23 hr., 56 min., 4.2 sec.
Rotational inclination	23.45°
Mass (Earth = 1)	1
Mean radius	3,958.8 mi
Mean density (Earth = 1)	1
Natural satellites	1
Average surface temperature	59°F

Earth is the fifth-largest planet and the third from the Sun. Its mass is 5.9736×10^{24} kg. Earth's equatorial diameter is 7,926 mi while its polar diameter is only 7,900 mi.

Size and dimensions. Earth is considered a solid mass, yet it has a large, liquid iron, **magnetic core** with a radius of about 2,160 mi. Surprisingly, it has a solid **inner core** that may be a large iron crystal, with a radius of 760 mi. Around the core is a thick shell, or **mantle**, of dense rock. This mantle is composed of materials rich in iron and magnesium. It is somewhat plastic-like, and under slow steady pressure, it can flow like a liquid. The mantle, in turn, is covered by a thin **crust** forming the solid granite and basalt base of the continents and ocean basins. Over broad areas of Earth's surface, the crust has a thin cover of sedimentary rock such as sandstone, shale, and limestone formed by weathering and by deposits of sands, clays, and plant and animal remains.

The temperature inside the Earth increases about 1°F with every 100 to 200 ft in depth, in the upper 100 km (62 mi) of Earth. It reaches nearly 8,000°F-9,000°F at the center. The heat is believed to come from radioactivity in rocks, pressures within Earth, and the original heat of formation.

Atmosphere. Earth's atmosphere is a blanket composed of 78% nitrogen, 21% oxygen, and 1% argon. Present in minute quantities are carbon dioxide, hydrogen, neon, helium, krypton, and xenon. Water vapor displaces other gases and varies from nearly zero to about 4% by volume. The atmosphere rests on Earth's surface with a weight equivalent to a layer of water 34 ft deep. For about 300,000 ft upward, the gases remain in the proportions stated. Gravity holds the gases to Earth. The weight of the air compresses it at the bottom so that the greatest density is at Earth's surface. Pressure and density decrease as height increases.

The lowest layer of the atmosphere extending up from the Earth's surface about 7.5 mi is the **troposphere**, which contains 90% of the air. This is also where most weather phenomena occur. The temperature drops with increasing height through this layer. The **stratosphere** extends about 23 mi above the troposphere; the temperature generally increases with height within this layer. The stratosphere contains **ozone**, which prevents ultraviolet rays from reaching Earth's surface. Since there is very little convection in the stratosphere, jets regularly cruise in the lower parts to provide a smoother ride for passengers.

Above the stratosphere is the **mesosphere**, where the temperature again decreases with height for another 19 mi. Extending above the mesosphere to the outer fringes of the atmosphere is the **thermosphere**, a region where temperature once more increases with height to a value measured in thousands of degrees Fahrenheit. The lower portion of this region, extending from 50 to about 400 mi in altitude, is characterized by high ion density and is thus called the **ionosphere**. Most meteors are in the lower thermosphere or the mesosphere at the time they are observed.

Longitude and latitude. Position on the globe is measured by meridians and parallels. Meridians, which are imaginary lines drawn around Earth through the poles, determine **longitude**. The meridian running through Greenwich, England, is the **prime meridian** of longitude; all others are either E or W. Parallels, which are imaginary circles parallel with the equator, determine **latitude**. The length of a degree of longitude varies as the cosine of the latitude. At the equator a degree of longitude is 69.171 statute mi; this is gradually reduced toward the poles. Value of a longitude degree at the poles is zero.

Latitude is reckoned by the number of degrees N or S of the **equator**, an imaginary circle on Earth's surface everywhere equidistant between the two poles. According to the International Astronomical Union, the length of a degree of latitude is 68.708 statute mi at the equator and varies slightly N and S because of the oblate form of the globe. At the poles, it is 69.403 statute mi.

Definitions of time. Earth rotates on its axis and follows an elliptical orbit around the Sun. The rotation makes the Sun appear to move across the sky from E to W. This rotation determines day and night, and the complete rotation, in relation to the Sun, is called the **apparent or true solar day**. A sundial thus measures **apparent solar time**. This length of time varies, but an average determines a mean solar day of 24 hours.

The mean solar day and **mean solar time** are in universal use for civil purposes. Mean solar time may be obtained from apparent solar time by correcting observations of the Sun for the **equation of time**. Mean solar time may be up to 16 min. different from apparent solar time.

Sidereal time is the measure of time defined by the diurnal motion of the vernal equinox and is determined from observation of the meridian transits of stars. One complete rotation of Earth relative to the equinox is called the **sidereal day**. The **mean sidereal day** is 23 hr., 56 min., 4.2 sec. of mean solar time.

The interval required for Earth to make one absolute revolution around the Sun is a **sidereal year**; it consisted of 365 days, 6 hr., 9 min., and 9.5 sec. of mean solar time (approximately 24 hr. per day) in 1900 and has been increasing at the rate of 0.0001 second annually.

The **tropical year**, upon which our calendar is based, is the interval between two consecutive returns of the Sun to the vernal equinox. The tropical year consisted of 365 days, 5 hr., 48 min., and 46 sec. in 1900. It has been decreasing at the rate of 0.53 sec. per century. The **calendar year** begins at midnight precisely, local clock time, on the night of Dec. 31-Jan. 1. The day and the calendar month also begin at midnight by the clock.

On Jan. 1, 1972, the Bureau International des Poids et Mesures in Paris introduced **International Atomic Time** (TAI) as the most precisely determined time scale for astronomical usage. The fundamental unit of TAI in the international system of units is the second, defined as the duration of 9,192,631,770 periods of the radiation corresponding to the transition between two hyperfine levels of the ground state of the cesium-133 atom. **Coordinated Universal Time** (UTC), which serves as the basis for civil timekeeping and is the standard time of the prime meridian, is officially defined by a formula which relates UTC to mean sidereal time in Greenwich, England. (UTC replaced Greenwich Mean Time as the basis for standard time for the world.)

Zones and seasons. The five zones of Earth's surface are the Torrid, lying between the Tropics of Cancer and Capricorn; the N Temperate, between Cancer and the Arctic Circle; the S Temperate, between Capricorn and the Antarctic Circle; and the two Frigid Zones, between the Polar Circles and the Poles.

The inclination, or tilt, of Earth's axis, 23°45′ from a line perpendicular to Earth's orbit of the Sun, determines the seasons. These are commonly marked in the N Temperate Zone, where spring begins at the vernal equinox, summer at the summer solstice, autumn at the autumnal equinox, and winter at the winter solstice. In the S Temperate Zone, the seasons are reversed. When a vernal equinox occurs in the N Temperate Zone, the S Temperate Zone has its autumnal equinox. The summer solstice coincides with the winter solstice and so on.

The points at which the Sun crosses the equator are the **equinoxes**, when day and night are most nearly equal. The points at which the Sun is at a maximum distance from the equator are the **solstices**, when days and nights are most unequal. However, at the equator, day and night are equal throughout the year.

In June, the North Pole is tilted 23°27′ toward the Sun, and the days in the Northern Hemisphere are longer than the nights, while the days in the Southern Hemisphere are shorter than the nights. In Dec., the North Pole is tilted 23°27′ away from the Sun, and the situation is reversed.

Seasons in 2019. In 2019, the four seasons begin in the Northern Hemisphere as shown. (Add 1 hour to Eastern Standard Time for Atlantic Time; subtract 1 hour for Central, 2 for Mountain, 3 for Pacific, 4 for Alaska, 5 for Hawaii-Aleutian. Also shown is Coordinated Universal Time.)

Season	Date	UTC	EST/EDT
Vernal Equinox (spring)	Mar. 20	21:58	17:58 EDT
Northern Solstice (summer). . . .	June 21	15:54	11:54 EDT
Autumnal Equinox (fall).	Sept. 23	07:50	03:50 EDT
Southern Solstice (winter)	Dec. 22	04:19	23:19 EST
			Dec. 21

Poles. The geographic (rotation) poles, or points where Earth's axis of rotation cuts the surface, are not absolutely fixed in the body of Earth. The pole of rotation describes an irregular curve about its mean position.

Two periods have been detected in this motion: (1) an annual period due to seasonal changes in barometric pressure, to load of ice and snow on the surface, and to other seasonal phenomena; (2) a period of about 14 months due to the shape and constitution of Earth. In addition, there are small but as yet unpredictable irregularities. The whole motion is so small that the actual pole at any time remains within a circle of 30 or 40 ft in radius centered at the mean position of the pole.

The pole of rotation for the time being is, of course, the pole having a latitude of 90° and an indeterminate longitude.

Magnetic poles. Although Earth's magnetic field resembles that of an ordinary bar magnet, this magnetic field is probably produced by electric currents in the liquid currents of the Earth's outer core. The **north magnetic pole** of Earth is that region where the magnetic force is downward, and the **south magnetic pole** is that region where the magnetic force is upward. A compass placed at the magnetic poles experiences no directive force in azimuth (i.e., direction).

There are slow changes in the distribution of Earth's magnetic field. This slow temporal change is referred to as the secular change of the main magnetic field, and the magnetic poles shift due to this. The location of the N magnetic pole was first measured in 1831 at Cape Adelaide on the W coast of Boothia Peninsula in Canada's Northwest Territories (about latitude 70° N and longitude 96° W). Since then it has moved over 500 mi. As of 2018 it was estimated to be at latitude 86.5° N, longitude 178.8° W, NW of Ellef Ringnes Island in northern Canada. Measurement for several decades by Canadian scientists indicates the motion of the pole has accelerated, now averaging about 25 mi per year.

The direction of the horizontal components of the magnetic field at any point is known as magnetic N at that point, and the angle by which it deviates E or W of true N is known as the magnetic declination.

A compass without error points in the direction of magnetic north. (In general, this is not the direction of the true rotational north pole.) If you follow the direction indicated by the N end of the compass, you will go along an irregular curve that eventually reaches the north magnetic pole (though not usually by a great-circle route). However, the action of the compass should not be thought of as due to any influence of the distant pole, but simply as an indication of the distribution of Earth's magnetism at the place of observation.

Rotation. The speed of Earth's rotation about its axis is slightly variable. The variations may be classified as:

(A) **Secular.** Tidal friction acts as a brake on the rotation and causes a slow secular increase in the length of the day, about 1 millisecond per century.

(B) **Irregular.** The speed of rotation may increase for a number of years (about 5 to 10) and then start decreasing. The maximum difference from the mean in the length of the day during a century is about 5 milliseconds. The accumulated difference in time has amounted to approximately 44 seconds since 1900. The cause is probably motion in the interior of Earth.

(C) **Periodic.** Seasonal variations exist with periods of 1 year and 6 months. The cumulative effect is such that each year, Earth is late about 30 milliseconds near June 1 and is ahead about 30 milliseconds near Oct. 1. The maximum seasonal variation in the length of the day is about 0.5 millisecond. It is believed that the principal cause of the annual variation is the seasonal change in the wind patterns of the Northern and Southern Hemispheres. The semiannual variation is due chiefly to tidal action of the Sun, which distorts the shape of Earth slightly.

The Moon

```
Distance from Earth
    Perigee............................ 225,744 mi
    Semi-major axis (mean distance)......... 238,855 mi
    Apogee............................ 251,966 mi
Period of revolution....................... 27.322 d.
Orbital eccentricity ....................... 0.0549
Orbital inclination ....................... 5.145°
Synodic orbital period (period of phases)........ 29.53 d.
Sidereal day (rotation period)............... 27.322 d.
Rotational inclination ..................... 6.68°
Mass (Earth = 1)......................... 0.0123
Mean radius ........................... 1,079 mi
Mean density (Earth = 1) .................. 0.607
Average surface temperature.................–100°F
```

The Moon is the second-brightest object in the sky (the Sun is the first). Earth's only natural satellite, the Moon is the force behind the rising and falling of tides, and it helps to regulate Earth's inclination as they orbit the Sun. Many probes have been sent to the Moon, and between 1969 and 1972, 12 U.S. astronauts walked on its surface. The Moon is the subject of renewed international interest. In 2007, Japan and China orbited satellites around the Moon, India orbited a spacecraft in fall 2008, and the U.S. sent an orbiter and impactor in 2009. In Sept. 2009, American scientists announced the discovery of a thin layer of water ice near the lunar poles. The *LCROSS* mission impacted the lunar south polar region in Oct. 2009. The plume of material released in the impact contained water plus a variety of other chemical species, indicating that the lunar regolith harbors a rich and active chemistry. Since 2009, NASA has been mapping and measuring the surface composition and other properties of the Moon using the Lunar Reconnaissance Orbiter. In Sept. 2013, NASA launched *LADEE*, a mission to study the ephemeral lunar atmosphere and lunar dust from a low orbit. In Dec. 2013, China became the third nation to land a spacecraft on the Moon when *Chang'e 3* set down on Mare Imbrium. *Chang'e 3* released the *Yutu* rover to study the lunar surface.

Orbit and rotation. The Moon completes a circuit around Earth in a period that averages 27 days, 7 hr., 43.2 min. This is the Moon's sidereal period. Because of the motion of the Moon in common with Earth around the Sun, the mean duration of the lunar month—the period from one new moon to the next new moon—is 29 days, 12 hr., 44.05 min. This is the Moon's synodic period.

The mean distance of the Moon from Earth is 238,855 mi, but its orbit about Earth is elliptical, and thus the actual distance varies

considerably. The maximum distance from Earth that the Moon may reach is 251,966 mi and the least distance is 225,744 mi.

The Moon rotates on its axis in a period of time that is exactly equal to its sidereal revolution about Earth—27.322 days. Thus the backside, or farside, of the Moon always faces away from Earth. But this does not mean that the backside is always dark. The farside of the Moon gets as much direct sunlight as the nearside; at new moon phase, the farside of the Moon is fully lit but not visible from Earth.

The Moon's revolution about Earth is irregular because of its elliptical orbit. The Moon's rotation, however, is regular, and this, together with the irregular revolution, produces what is called libration in longitude, which permits an observer on Earth to see first farther around the eastern side and then farther around the western side of the Moon. The Moon's variation north or south of the ecliptic permits one to see farther over first one pole of the Moon and then the other; this is called libration in latitude. These two libration effects permit observers on Earth to see a total of about 60% of the Moon's surface over a period of time.

Atmosphere and surface. The Moon, like the planet Mercury, has no real atmosphere to speak of. What little exists is variable and tenuous. With its long day and night, the daytime temperature can reach 260°F. The coldest nighttime temperature is –280°F. This day-to-night contrast is exceeded only by that on Mercury. The lunar surface has not changed much since humans began observing it. The side visible from Earth has large craters and vast dark areas called *maria* that were once lava. The farside has almost no maria but is pockmarked with craters; it was first photographed in 1959 by the Soviet space probe *Lunik III*.

Recent findings show that up to 300 mil metric tons of water ice may exist in craters at the lunar poles. In its interior, the Moon may have a small core, which supports the idea that most of the Moon's mass was ripped away from the early Earth when a Mars-sized object collided with Earth.

Harvest moon and hunter's moon. The harvest moon, the full moon nearest the autumnal equinox, ushers in a period of several days when the Moon rises soon after sunset. This phenomenon gives farmers in temperate latitudes extra hours of light in which to harvest their crops. The 2019 harvest moon falls on Sept. 14. Harvest moon in the Southern Hemisphere temperate latitudes falls on Mar. 21.

The next full moon after harvest moon is called the hunter's moon; it is accompanied by a similar but less marked phenomenon. In 2019, the hunter's moon occurs on Oct. 13 in the Northern Hemisphere and on Apr. 19 in the Southern Hemisphere.

Moon Phases, 2019
(In Coordinated Universal Time, or UTC, the standard time of the prime meridian.)

New Moon Date	Hr.	Min.	Waxing Quarter Date	Hr.	Min.	Full Moon Date	Hr.	Min.	Waning Quarter Date	Hr.	Min.
Jan. 6	1	28	Jan. 14	6	46	Jan. 21	5	16	Jan. 27	21	10
Feb. 4	21	4	Feb. 12	22	26	Feb. 19	15	54	Feb. 26	11	28
Mar. 6	16	4	Mar. 14	10	27	Mar. 21	1	43	Mar. 28	4	10
Apr. 5	8	50	Apr. 12	19	6	Apr. 19	11	12	Apr. 26	22	18
May 4	22	45	May 12	1	12	May 18	21	11	May 26	16	34
June 3	10	2	June 10	5	59	June 17	8	31	June 25	9	46
July 2	19	16	July 9	10	55	July 16	21	38	July 25	1	18
Aug. 1	3	12	Aug. 7	17	31	Aug. 15	12	29	Aug. 23	14	56
Aug. 30	10	37	Sept. 6	3	10	Sept. 14	4	33	Sept. 22	2	41
Sept. 28	18	26	Oct. 5	16	47	Oct. 13	21	8	Oct. 21	12	39
Oct. 28	3	38	Nov. 4	10	23	Nov. 12	13	34	Nov. 19	21	11
Nov. 26	15	6	Dec. 4	6	58	Dec. 12	5	12	Dec. 19	4	57
Dec. 26	5	13									

CALENDAR

Western Calendars

The **Julian calendar**, under which all Western nations measured time until 1582 CE, was authorized by Julius Caesar in 46 BCE. It called for a year of 365¼ days, starting in Jan., with every fourth year being a **leap year** of 366 days. St. Bede, an Anglo-Saxon monk also known as the Venerable Bede, announced in 730 CE that the Julian year was 11 min., 14 sec. too long, a cumulative error of about a day every 128 years, but nothing was done about this for centuries.

By 1582 the accumulated error was estimated at 10 days. In that year, Pope Gregory XIII decreed that the day following Oct. 4, 1582, should be called Oct. 15, thus dropping 10 days and initiating the **Gregorian calendar**.

The Gregorian calendar perpetuated a chronological system devised by the monk Dionysius Exiguus (fl. 6th cent.). His chronology started with the first year following the birth of Jesus Christ, which he inaccurately took to be year 753 in the Roman calendar. Leap years were continued but, to prevent further displacements, centesimal years (years ending in 00) were made common years, not leap years, unless divisible by 400. Under this plan, 1600 and 2000 were leap years; 1700, 1800, and 1900 were not.

The Gregorian calendar was adopted at once by France, Italy, Spain, Portugal, and Luxembourg. Within two years, most German Catholic states, Belgium, and parts of Switzerland and the Netherlands were brought under the new calendar, and Hungary followed in 1587. The rest of the Netherlands, along with Denmark and the German Protestant states, made the change in 1699-1700.

The British government adopted the Gregorian calendar and imposed it on all its possessions, including the American colonies, in 1752, decreeing that the day following Sept. 2, 1752, should be called Sept. 14, a loss of 11 days. All dates preceding were marked OS, for Old Style. In addition, New Year's Day was moved to Jan. 1 from Mar. 25. (Under the old reckoning, for example, Mar. 24, 1700, was followed by Mar. 25, 1701.) Thus George Washington's birth date, which was Feb. 11, 1731, OS, became Feb. 22, 1732, NS (New Style). In 1753, Sweden also went Gregorian.

In 1793, the French revolutionary government adopted a calendar of 12 months of 30 days each with five extra days in Sept. of each common year and six extra days every fourth year. Napoleon reinstated the Gregorian calendar in 1806.

The Gregorian system later spread to non-European regions, replacing traditional calendars at least for official purposes. Japan in 1873, Egypt in 1875, China in 1912, and Turkey in 1925 made the change, usually in conjunction with political upheaval. In China, the republican government began reckoning years from its 1911 founding. After 1949, the People's Republic adopted the Common (or Christian) Era year count, even for the traditional lunar calendar, which it retained. In 1918, the Soviet Union decreed that the day after Jan. 31, 1918, OS, would be Feb. 14, 1918, NS. Greece changed over in 1923. The Russian Orthodox church and some other Christian sects retained the Julian calendar. Saudi Arabia switched to the Gregorian calendar in 2016.

As of 2018, several nations officially used non-Gregorian calendars. Ethiopia used a calendar similar to the Julian system, and Afghanistan and Iran used the traditional Persian, or Solar Hijri, calendar.

To convert from the Julian to the Gregorian calendar, add 10 days to dates Oct. 5, 1582, through Feb. 28, 1700; after that date, add 11 days through Feb. 28, 1800; 12 days through Feb. 28, 1900; and 13 days through Feb. 28, 2100.

A **century** consists of 100 consecutive years. The 1st century CE may be said to have run from the years 1 through 100. The 20th century by this reckoning consisted of the years 1901 through 2000 and ended Dec. 31, 2000, as did the 2nd millennium CE. The 21st century thus technically began on Jan. 1, 2001.

For a **perpetual calendar**, see pages 360-61.

Gregorian Calendar

Choose the desired year from the table below or from the perpetual calendar (for years 1803 to 2080). The number after each year designates which calendar to use for that year, as shown in the perpetual calendar. (The Gregorian calendar was inaugurated Oct. 15, 1582. From that date through Dec. 31, 1582, use calendar 6.)

1583-1802

1583	7	1603	4	1623	1	1643	5	1663	2	1683	6	1703	2	1723	6	1743	3	1763	7	1783	4
1584	8	1604	12	1624	9	1644	13	1664	10	1684	14	1704	10	1724	14	1744	11	1764	8	1784	12
1585	3	1605	7	1625	4	1645	1	1665	5	1685	2	1705	5	1725	2	1745	6	1765	3	1785	7
1586	4	1606	1	1626	5	1646	2	1666	6	1686	3	1706	6	1726	3	1746	7	1766	4	1786	1
1587	5	1607	2	1627	6	1647	3	1667	7	1687	4	1707	7	1727	4	1747	1	1767	5	1787	2
1588	13	1608	10	1628	14	1648	11	1668	8	1688	12	1708	8	1728	12	1748	9	1768	13	1788	10
1589	1	1609	5	1629	2	1649	6	1669	3	1689	7	1709	3	1729	7	1749	4	1769	1	1789	5
1590	2	1610	6	1630	3	1650	7	1670	4	1690	1	1710	4	1730	1	1750	5	1770	2	1790	6
1591	3	1611	7	1631	4	1651	1	1671	5	1691	2	1711	5	1731	2	1751	6	1771	3	1791	7
1592	11	1612	8	1632	12	1652	9	1672	13	1692	10	1712	13	1732	10	1752	14	1772	11	1792	8
1593	6	1613	3	1633	7	1653	4	1673	1	1693	5	1713	1	1733	5	1753	2	1773	6	1793	3
1594	7	1614	4	1634	1	1654	5	1674	2	1694	6	1714	2	1734	6	1754	3	1774	7	1794	4
1595	1	1615	5	1635	2	1655	6	1675	3	1695	7	1715	3	1735	7	1755	4	1775	1	1795	5
1596	9	1616	13	1636	10	1656	14	1676	11	1696	8	1716	11	1736	8	1756	12	1776	9	1796	13
1597	4	1617	1	1637	5	1657	2	1677	6	1697	3	1717	6	1737	3	1757	7	1777	4	1797	1
1598	5	1618	2	1638	6	1658	3	1678	7	1698	4	1718	7	1738	4	1758	1	1778	5	1798	2
1599	6	1619	3	1639	7	1659	4	1679	1	1699	5	1719	1	1739	5	1759	2	1779	6	1799	3
1600	14	1620	11	1640	8	1660	12	1680	9	1700	6	1720	9	1740	13	1760	10	1780	14	1800	4
1601	2	1621	6	1641	3	1661	7	1681	4	1701	7	1721	4	1741	1	1761	5	1781	2	1801	5
1602	3	1622	7	1642	4	1662	1	1682	5	1702	1	1722	5	1742	2	1762	6	1782	3	1802	6

Julian Period

How many days have you lived? To determine this, multiply your age by 365, add the number of days since your last birthday, and account for all leap years. Chances are your calculations will go wrong somewhere. Astronomers, however, find it convenient to express dates and time intervals in days rather than in years, months, and days. This is done by placing events within the Julian period.

The Julian period was devised in 1582 by the French classical scholar Joseph Scaliger (1540-1609). Some sources postulate Scaliger named it after his father, Julius Caesar Scaliger; others cite Scaliger's references to the Julian calendar.

Scaliger began with a zero hour, or starting time, of noon on Jan. 1, 4713 BCE (on the Julian calendar). This was the most recent time that three major chronological cycles began on the same day: (1) the 28-year solar cycle, after which dates in the Julian calendar return to the same days of the week (e.g., Feb. 11 falls on a Monday); (2) the 19-year lunar cycle, after which the phases of the moon return to the same dates of the year; and (3) the 15-year indiction cycle, used in ancient Rome to regulate taxes.

It will take 7,980 years to complete the period, the product of the numbers 28, 19, and 15, which have no common factors.

Noon (Universal Time) of Jan. 1, 2019, will be Julian date (JD) 2,458,485; that many days will have passed since the start of the current Julian period. The JD at noon of any date in 2019 may be found by adding to that number the day of the year for that date and subtracting one.

Julian Calendar

To find which of the 14 calendars of the perpetual calendar (pages 360-61) applies to any year under the Julian system, find the century for the desired year in the three leftmost columns below. Locate the desired year from among the four top rows. The number at the intersection of that row and column is the calendar designation for that year. For some years and countries, the Julian new year did not start Jan. 1; to find the correct perpetual calendar for Britain and its possessions, you can generally add one year for dates from Jan. 1 to Mar. 24. For example, to look up Feb. 2, 1705, Old Style, use the year 1706.

Year (last 2 digits of desired year)

		01	02	03	04	05	06	07	08	09	10	11	12	13	14	15	16	17	18	19	20	21	22	23	24	25	26	27	28
		29	30	31	32	33	34	35	36	37	38	39	40	41	42	43	44	45	46	47	48	49	50	51	52	53	54	55	56
		57	58	59	60	61	62	63	64	65	66	67	68	69	70	71	72	73	74	75	76	77	78	79	80	81	82	83	84
Century	00	85	86	87	88	89	90	91	92	93	94	95	96	97	98	99													
0 700 1400	12	7	1	2	10	5	6	7	8	3	4	5	13	1	2	3	11	6	7	1	9	4	5	6	14	2	3	4	12
100 800 1500	11	6	7	1	9	4	5	6	14	2	3	4	12	7	1	2	10	5	6	7	8	3	4	5	13	1	2	3	11
200 900 1600	10	5	6	7	8	3	4	5	13	1	2	3	11	6	7	1	9	4	5	6	14	2	3	4	12	7	1	2	10
300 1000 1700	9	4	5	6	14	2	3	4	12	7	1	2	10	5	6	7	8	3	4	5	13	1	2	3	11	6	7	1	9
400 1100 1800	8	3	4	5	13	1	2	3	11	6	7	1	9	4	5	6	14	2	3	4	12	7	1	2	10	5	6	7	8
500 1200 1900	14	2	3	4	12	7	1	2	10	5	6	7	8	3	4	5	13	1	2	3	11	6	7	1	9	4	5	6	14
600 1300 2000	13	1	2	3	11	6	7	1	9	4	5	6	14	2	3	4	12	7	1	2	10	5	6	7	8	3	4	5	13

Signs of the Zodiac

The zodiac is the apparent yearly path of the sun among the stars as viewed from Earth and was divided by the ancients into 12 equal sections or signs, each named for the constellation situated within its limits in ancient times. Astrologers claim that the temperament and destiny of each individual depend on the zodiac sign under which the person was born and the relationships between the planets at that time and throughout the person's life.

Below are the 12 traditional signs and the traditional range of dates pertaining to each:

♈ **Aries** (Ram), March 21-April 19

♉ **Taurus** (Bull), April 20-May 20

♊ **Gemini** (Twins), May 21-June 21

♋ **Cancer** (Crab), June 22-July 22

♌ **Leo** (Lion), July 23-August 22

♍ **Virgo** (Virgin), August 23-September 22

♎ **Libra** (Scales), September 23-October 23

♏ **Scorpio** (Scorpion), October 24-November 21

♐ **Sagittarius** (Archer), November 22-December 21

♑ **Capricorn** (Goat), December 22-January 19

♒ **Aquarius** (Water Bearer), January 20-February 18

♓ **Pisces** (Fishes), February 19-March 20

Chinese Calendar and Asian Festivals

The Chinese calendar, like the Jewish and Islamic calendars (see the Religion chapter), is a lunisolar calendar. It is divided into 12 months of 29 or 30 days (compensating for the lunar month's mean duration of 29 days, 12 hr., 44.05 min.). This calendar is synchronized with the solar year by the addition of extra months at fixed intervals.

The Chinese calendar runs on a 60-year cycle. The last 36 years of the cycle 1876-1935 along with the cycles 1936-95 and 1996-2055 are shown below grouped by their association with 1 of 12 animals in the Chinese zodiac. Feb. 5, 2019, marks the beginning of the year 4717 in the Chinese calendar and is designated the Year of the Boar.

Both the Western (Gregorian) and traditional lunar calendars are used publicly in China and in North and South Korea, and two New Year's celebrations are held. In Taiwan and Vietnam and in overseas Chinese communities, the lunar calendar is used only to set the dates for traditional festivals, with the Gregorian system in general use.

The 4-day Chinese New Year; the 3-day Vietnamese New Year festival, Tet; and the 3-to-4-day Korean festival, Suhl, begin at the second new moon after the winter solstice. The new moon in East Asia, which is west of the international date line, may be a day later than the new moon in the U.S. The festivals may start, therefore, anywhere between Jan. 21 and Feb. 19 of the Gregorian calendar.

Rat	Ox	Tiger	Hare (Rabbit)	Dragon	Snake	Horse	Sheep (Goat)	Monkey	Rooster	Dog	Pig (Boar)
1900	1901	1902	1903	1904	1905	1906	1907	1908	1909	1910	1911
1912	1913	1914	1915	1916	1917	1918	1919	1920	1921	1922	1923
1924	1925	1926	1927	1928	1929	1930	1931	1932	1933	1934	1935
1936	1937	1938	1939	1940	1941	1942	1943	1944	1945	1946	1947
1948	1949	1950	1951	1952	1953	1954	1955	1956	1957	1958	1959
1960	1961	1962	1963	1964	1965	1966	1967	1968	1969	1970	1971
1972	1973	1974	1975	1976	1977	1978	1979	1980	1981	1982	1983
1984	1985	1986	1987	1988	1989	1990	1991	1992	1993	1994	1995
1996	1997	1998	1999	2000	2001	2002	2003	2004	2005	2006	2007
2008	2009	2010	2011	2012	2013	2014	2015	2016	2017	2018	2019
2020	2021	2022	2023	2024	2025	2026	2027	2028	2029	2030	2031
2032	2033	2034	2035	2036	2037	2038	2039	2040	2041	2042	2043
2044	2045	2046	2047	2048	2049	2050	2051	2052	2053	2054	2055

Note: The first 3-7 weeks of each Western year belong to the previous Chinese year.

Perpetual Calendar

The number shown for each year indicates which Gregorian calendar to use. For 1583–1802, see "Gregorian Calendar" on page 358. For 1803–20, use numbers for 1983–2000, respectively. The years in the calendar labels are the last and next occurrences of each calendar.

Year	No.	Year	No.	Year	No.	Year	No.	Year	No.	Year	No.	Year	No.	Year	No.	Year	No.	Year	No.
1821	2	1847	6	1873	4	1899	1	1925	5	1951	2	1977	7	2003	4	2029	2	2055	6
1822	3	1848	14	1874	5	1900	2	1926	6	1952	10	1978	1	2004	12	2030	3	2056	14
1823	4	1849	2	1875	6	1901	3	1927	7	1953	5	1979	2	2005	7	2031	4	2057	2
1824	12	1850	3	1876	14	1902	4	1928	8	1954	6	1980	10	2006	1	2032	12	2058	3
1825	7	1851	4	1877	2	1903	5	1929	3	1955	7	1981	5	2007	2	2033	7	2059	4
1826	1	1852	12	1878	3	1904	13	1930	4	1956	8	1982	6	2008	10	2034	1	2060	12
1827	2	1853	7	1879	4	1905	1	1931	5	1957	3	1983	7	2009	5	2035	2	2061	7
1828	10	1854	1	1880	12	1906	2	1932	13	1958	4	1984	8	2010	6	2036	10	2062	1
1829	5	1855	2	1881	7	1907	3	1933	1	1959	5	1985	3	2011	7	2037	5	2063	2
1830	6	1856	10	1882	1	1908	11	1934	2	1960	13	1986	4	2012	8	2038	6	2064	10
1831	7	1857	5	1883	2	1909	6	1935	3	1961	1	1987	5	2013	3	2039	7	2065	5
1832	8	1858	6	1884	10	1910	7	1936	11	1962	2	1988	13	2014	4	2040	8	2066	6
1833	3	1859	7	1885	5	1911	1	1937	6	1963	3	1989	1	2015	5	2041	3	2067	7
1834	4	1860	8	1886	6	1912	9	1938	7	1964	11	1990	2	2016	13	2042	4	2068	8
1835	5	1861	3	1887	7	1913	4	1939	1	1965	6	1991	3	2017	1	2043	5	2069	3
1836	13	1862	4	1888	8	1914	5	1940	9	1966	7	1992	11	2018	2	2044	13	2070	4
1837	1	1863	5	1889	3	1915	6	1941	4	1967	1	1993	6	2019	3	2045	1	2071	5
1838	2	1864	13	1890	4	1916	14	1942	5	1968	9	1994	7	2020	11	2046	2	2072	13
1839	3	1865	1	1891	5	1917	2	1943	6	1969	4	1995	1	2021	6	2047	3	2073	1
1840	11	1866	2	1892	13	1918	3	1944	14	1970	5	1996	9	2022	7	2048	11	2074	2
1841	6	1867	3	1893	1	1919	4	1945	2	1971	6	1997	4	2023	1	2049	6	2075	3
1842	7	1868	11	1894	2	1920	12	1946	3	1972	14	1998	5	2024	9	2050	7	2076	11
1843	1	1869	6	1895	3	1921	7	1947	4	1973	2	1999	6	2025	4	2051	1	2077	6
1844	9	1870	7	1896	11	1922	1	1948	12	1974	3	2000	14	2026	5	2052	9	2078	7
1845	4	1871	1	1897	6	1923	2	1949	7	1975	4	2001	2	2027	6	2053	4	2079	1
1846	5	1872	9	1898	7	1924	10	1950	1	1976	12	2002	3	2028	14	2054	5	2080	9

The fourteen reference calendars (each showing all twelve months, arranged by Sunday–Saturday weeks) are labeled as follows:

1 — 2017/2023

2 — 2018/2029

3 — 2013/2019

4 — 2014/2025

5 — 2015/2026

6 — 2010/2021

7 — 2011/2022

JANUARY · FEBRUARY · MARCH · APRIL · MAY · JUNE · JULY · AUGUST · SEPTEMBER · OCTOBER · NOVEMBER · DECEMBER

8 — 2012/2040

JANUARY · FEBRUARY · MARCH · APRIL · MAY · JUNE · JULY · AUGUST · SEPTEMBER · OCTOBER · NOVEMBER · DECEMBER

9 — 1996/2024

JANUARY · FEBRUARY · MARCH · APRIL · MAY · JUNE · JULY · AUGUST · SEPTEMBER · OCTOBER · NOVEMBER · DECEMBER

10 — 2008/2036

JANUARY · FEBRUARY · MARCH · APRIL · MAY · JUNE · JULY · AUGUST · SEPTEMBER · OCTOBER · NOVEMBER · DECEMBER

11 — 1992/2020

JANUARY · FEBRUARY · MARCH · APRIL · MAY · JUNE · JULY · AUGUST · SEPTEMBER · OCTOBER · NOVEMBER · DECEMBER

12 — 2004/2032

JANUARY · FEBRUARY · MARCH · APRIL · MAY · JUNE · JULY · AUGUST · SEPTEMBER · OCTOBER · NOVEMBER · DECEMBER

13 — 2016/2044

JANUARY · FEBRUARY · MARCH · APRIL · MAY · JUNE · JULY · AUGUST · SEPTEMBER · OCTOBER · NOVEMBER · DECEMBER

14 — 2000/2028

JANUARY · FEBRUARY · MARCH · APRIL · MAY · JUNE · JULY · AUGUST · SEPTEMBER · OCTOBER · NOVEMBER · DECEMBER

Calendar for the Year 2019

January

S	M	T	W	T	F	S
		1	2	3	4	5
6	7	8	9	10	11	12
13	14	15	16	17	18	19
20	21	22	23	24	25	26
27	28	29	30	31		

February

S	M	T	W	T	F	S
					1	2
3	4	5	6	7	8	9
10	11	12	13	14	15	16
17	18	19	20	21	22	23
24	25	26	27	28		

March

S	M	T	W	T	F	S
					1	2
3	4	5	6	7	8	9
10	11	12	13	14	15	16
17	18	19	20	21	22	23
24	25	26	27	28	29	30
31						

April

S	M	T	W	T	F	S
	1	2	3	4	5	6
7	8	9	10	11	12	13
14	15	16	17	18	19	20
21	22	23	24	25	26	27
28	29	30				

May

S	M	T	W	T	F	S
			1	2	3	4
5	6	7	8	9	10	11
12	13	14	15	16	17	18
19	20	21	22	23	24	25
26	27	28	29	30	31	

June

S	M	T	W	T	F	S
						1
2	3	4	5	6	7	8
9	10	11	12	13	14	15
16	17	18	19	20	21	22
23	24	25	26	27	28	29
30						

July

S	M	T	W	T	F	S
	1	2	3	4	5	6
7	8	9	10	11	12	13
14	15	16	17	18	19	20
21	22	23	24	25	26	27
28	29	30	31			

August

S	M	T	W	T	F	S
				1	2	3
4	5	6	7	8	9	10
11	12	13	14	15	16	17
18	19	20	21	22	23	24
25	26	27	28	29	30	31

September

S	M	T	W	T	F	S
1	2	3	4	5	6	7
8	9	10	11	12	13	14
15	16	17	18	19	20	21
22	23	24	25	26	27	28
29	30					

October

S	M	T	W	T	F	S
		1	2	3	4	5
6	7	8	9	10	11	12
13	14	15	16	17	18	19
20	21	22	23	24	25	26
27	28	29	30	31		

November

S	M	T	W	T	F	S
					1	2
3	4	5	6	7	8	9
10	11	12	13	14	15	16
17	18	19	20	21	22	23
24	25	26	27	28	29	30

December

S	M	T	W	T	F	S
1	2	3	4	5	6	7
8	9	10	11	12	13	14
15	16	17	18	19	20	21
22	23	24	25	26	27	28
29	30	31				

Federal Holidays and Other Notable Dates, 2019

Some dates may be subject to change.

The dates in bold in the calendar above and named below in italics are U.S. federal holidays, designated by the president or Congress and applicable to federal employees and in the District of Columbia. Most U.S. states also observe these holidays, and many states observe others; practices vary by state. In most states the secretary of state's office can provide details.

January
1 *New Year's Day*; Sugar Bowl; Rose Bowl; Fiesta Bowl
7 College Football Playoff national championship game (Santa Clara, CA)
14-27 Australian Open tennis tournament
21 *Martin Luther King Jr. Day*
27 NFL Pro Bowl (Orlando, FL)
28 Australia Day (observed)

February
2 Groundhog Day
3 Super Bowl LIII (Atlanta, GA)
5 Chinese New Year
11-12 Westminster Dog Show
12 Lincoln's Birthday
14 Valentine's Day
17 NBA All-Star Game (Charlotte, NC); Daytona 500
18 *Washington's Birthday* (observed), a.k.a. Presidents' Day, or Washington-Lincoln Day (3rd Mon. in Feb.)
24 Academy Awards

March
1-6 Carnival, Brazil
2 Iditarod Trail Sled Dog Race begins
5 Mardi Gras
6 Ash Wednesday
10 Daylight saving time begins in U.S.
17 St. Patrick's Day
20 First day of spring (Northern Hemisphere)
21 Purim (Feast of Lots) begins previous night; Benito Juárez's Birthday, Mexico

April
1 April Fools' Day
5, 7 NCAA Women's Basketball Final Four (Tampa, FL)
6, 8 NCAA Men's Basketball Final Four (Minneapolis, MN)
8-14 Master's golf tournament
15 Patriots' Day; Tax Day (IRS filing deadline); Boston Marathon (3rd Mon. in Apr.)
19 Good Friday
20 Passover, 1st full day
21 Easter
22 Earth Day
25 Take Our Daughters and Sons to Work Day
26 Arbor Day
28 Easter (Orthodox)

May
1 May Day (International Workers' Day)
4 Kentucky Derby
5 Cinco de Mayo (Battle of Puebla Day), Mexico
6 Ramadan (Islamic month of fasting), 1st full day
12 Mother's Day; Buddha's Birthday, Hong Kong, South Korea
13-19 PGA Championship (Farmingdale, NY)
18 Armed Forces Day; Preakness Stakes
20 Victoria Day, Canada
26-June 9 French Open tennis tournament
27 *Memorial Day*, or Decoration Day (last Mon. in May)
30-June 2 U.S. Women's Open golf tournament (Charleston, SC)

June
7 Dragon Boat Festival, China
7- July 7 FIFA Women's World Cup soccer tournament (France)
8 Belmont Stakes
13-16 U.S. Open golf tournament (Pebble Beach, CA)
14 Flag Day
16 Father's Day
21 First day of summer (Northern Hemisphere)

July
1 Canada Day
1-14 Wimbledon tennis tournament
4 *Independence Day*
7-14 Running of the Bulls (Pamplona, Spain)
14 Bastille Day, France
18-21 British Open golf tournament (Portrush, Northern Ireland, UK)

August
31 Islamic New Year (Muharram 1) begins previous night

September
2 *Labor Day*, U.S., Canada (1st Mon. in Sept.)
8 Grandparents' Day
16 Independence Day, Mexico (celebration begins previous night)
17 Constitution Day and Citizenship Day, U.S.
23 First day of autumn (Northern Hemisphere)
30 Rosh Hashanah (New Year), 1st full day

October
3 German Unity Day, Germany
7 U.S. Supreme Court session begins
9 Yom Kippur (Day of Atonement) begins previous night
12 Día de la Raza, Spain, Mexico
14 *Columbus Day* (2nd Mon. in Oct.); Thanksgiving Day, Canada
31 Halloween

November
1 All Saints' Day
3 Daylight saving time ends in U.S.; New York City Marathon
5 Election Day (1st Tues. after 1st Mon. in Nov.)
10 Remembrance Sunday, UK
11 *Veterans Day*; Remembrance Day, Canada
28 *Thanksgiving Day*

December
10 Nobel Prizes awarded (winners announced in Oct.)
12 Día de la Virgen de Guadalupe, Mexico
21 First day of winter (Northern Hemisphere)
23-30 Hanukkah (Festival of Lights) begins previous night
25 *Christmas Day*
26 Boxing Day, Australia, Canada, New Zealand, UK
26-Jan. 1 Kwanzaa
28 Peach Bowl, Fiesta Bowl
31 Cotton Bowl

Other Calendars: Year and New Year's Day, 2019

Era	Year	Begins in 2019	Era	Year	Begins in 2019
Byzantine	7528	Sept. 14	Islamic/Muslim (Hijra)	1441	Aug. 31[1]
Chinese (Year of the Pig/Boar)	4717	Feb. 5	Japanese[2]	31	Jan. 1
Diocletian	1736	Sept. 11	Jewish	5780	Sept. 30[1]
Grecian (Seleucidae)	2331	Sept. 14 or Oct. 14	Nabonassar (Babylonian)	2768	Apr. 23
Indian (Saka)	1941	Mar. 22	Roman (Ab Urbe Condita)	2772	Jan. 14

(1) Year begins the previous night. (2) Era starts at 0 with new emperor.

Chronological Cycles, 2019

Dominical Letter	F	Roman Indiction	12	Solar Cycle	12
Golden Number (lunar cycle)	VI	Epact	24	Julian Period (year of)	6732

Special Months

There are many thousands of special months, days, and weeks because of anniversaries, official proclamations, and promotional events, both trivial and serious. Here are a few of the special months:

January: Get Organized Month, National Mentoring Month, National Poverty in America Awareness Month

February: African American History Month, American Heart Month, Library Lovers' Month, Youth Leadership Month, Return Shopping Carts to the Supermarket Month

March: Irish-American Heritage Month, National Women's History Month, Red Cross Month, National Frozen Food Month, National Talk With Your Teen About Sex Month, National Colorectal Cancer Awareness Month

April: National Child Abuse Prevention Month, National Humor Month, Stress Awareness Month, Grange Month, Sexual Assault Awareness Month

May: Clean Air Month, Get Caught Reading Month, National Barbecue Month, Asian American and Pacific Islander Heritage Month, National Inventors Month, National Mental Health Awareness Month

June: Great Outdoors Month; Lesbian, Gay, Bisexual, and Transgender Pride Month; National Safety Month

July: Cell Phone Courtesy Month, National Hot Dog Month, National Make a Difference to Children Month, Women's Motorcycle Month

August: National Black Business Month, Happiness Happens Month, National Immunization Awareness Month

September: Library Card Sign-Up Month, National Hispanic Heritage Month (Sept. 15-Oct. 15), National Biscuit Month

October: National Domestic Violence Awareness Month, National Breast Cancer Awareness Month, Diversity Awareness Month, National Popcorn Poppin' Month

November: National American Indian Heritage Month, National Adoption Month, American Diabetes Month, National Peanut Butter Lovers' Month

December: Safe Toys and Gifts Month, National Impaired Driving Prevention Month, National Tie Month

Standard Time Differences: World Cities

The time indicated in the table is fixed by law and is called the legal time or, more generally, standard time. Use of daylight saving time varies widely. An asterisk (*) indicates morning of the following day. At 12:00 noon, Eastern Standard Time, the standard time (in 24-hour time) in selected cities is as shown.

Abu Dhabi	21	00	Denver	10	00	Lisbon	17	00	St. Petersburg	20	00
Addis Ababa	20	00	Dhaka	23	00	London	17	00	Santiago	13	00
Amsterdam	18	00	Dublin	17	00	Los Angeles	9	00	São Paulo	14	00
Ankara	20	00	Edinburgh	17	00	Madrid	18	00	Sarajevo	18	00
Athens	19	00	Geneva	18	00	Manila	1	00*	Seoul	2	00*
Auckland	5	00*	Helsinki	19	00	Mecca	20	00	Shanghai	1	00*
Baghdad	20	00	Ho Chi Minh City	0	00*	Melbourne	3	00*	Singapore	1	00*
Bangkok	0	00*	Hong Kong	1	00*	Montevideo	14	00	Stockholm	18	00
Beijing	1	00*	Honolulu	7	00	Moscow	20	00	Sydney	3	00*
Belfast	17	00	Houston	11	00	Mumbai (Bombay)	22	30	Taipei	1	00*
Belgrade	18	00	Islamabad	22	00	Munich	18	00	Tashkent	22	00
Berlin	18	00	Istanbul	20	00	Nagasaki	2	00*	Tehran	20	30
Bogotá	12	00	Jakarta	0	00*	Nairobi	20	00	Tel Aviv	19	00
Brussels	18	00	Jerusalem	19	00	New Delhi	22	30	Tokyo	2	00*
Bucharest	19	00	Johannesburg	19	00	New York	12	00	Toronto	12	00
Budapest	18	00	Kabul	21	30	Oslo	18	00	Vancouver	9	00
Buenos Aires	14	00	Karachi	22	00	Paris	18	00	Vienna	18	00
Cairo	19	00	Kathmandu	22	45	Prague	18	00	Vladivostok	3	00*
Cape Town	19	00	Kiev	19	00	Pyongyang	2	00*	Warsaw	18	00
Caracas	13	00	Kinshasa	18	00	Quito	12	00	Wellington	5	00*
Casablanca	17	00	Kolkata (Calcutta)	22	30	Rio de Janeiro	14	00	Yangon (Rangoon)	23	30
Chicago	11	00	Lagos	18	00	Riyadh	20	00	Yokohama	2	00*
Copenhagen	18	00	Lima	12	00	Rome	18	00	Zurich	18	00

Wedding Anniversary Gifts

The traditional names for wedding anniversaries go back many years in social usage and have been used to suggest types of appropriate anniversary gifts. Traditional products for gifts are listed here in capital letters, with allowable revisions in parentheses, followed by common modern gifts for each anniversary.

Anniversary	Gift	Anniversary	Gift	Anniversary	Gift
1st	PAPER, clocks	9th	POTTERY (CHINA), leather goods	25th	SILVER, sterling silver
2nd	COTTON, china			30th	PEARL, diamond
3rd	LEATHER, crystal, glass	10th	TIN, ALUMINUM, diamond	35th	CORAL (JADE), jade
4th	LINEN (SILK), appliances	11th	STEEL, fashion jewelry	40th	RUBY, ruby
5th	WOOD, silverware	12th	SILK, pearls, colored gems	45th	SAPPHIRE, sapphire
6th	IRON, wood objects	13th	LACE, textiles, furs	50th	GOLD, gold
7th	WOOL (COPPER), desk sets	14th	IVORY, gold jewelry	55th	EMERALD, emerald
8th	BRONZE, linens, lace	15th	CRYSTAL, watches	60th	DIAMOND, diamond
		20th	CHINA, platinum		

Birthstones

Source: American Gem Society

Birth month	Ancient[1] birthstone	Modern birthstone	Birth month	Ancient[1] birthstone	Modern birthstone
January	Garnet	Garnet	July	Onyx	Ruby
February	Amethyst	Amethyst	August	Carnelian	Sardonyx or Peridot
March	Jasper	Bloodstone or Aquamarine	September	Chrysolite	Sapphire
April	Sapphire	Diamond	October	Aquamarine	Opal or Tourmaline
May	Agate, Chalcedony, or Carnelian	Emerald	November	Topaz	Topaz
June	Emerald	Pearl, Moonstone, or Alexandrite	December	Ruby	Turquoise, Tanzanite, or Zircon

(1) Varied by region and culture. Birthstones listed here are those of ancient Hebrew tradition.

Standard Time and Daylight Saving Time

Source: National Institute of Standards and Technology, U.S. Dept. of Commerce

See also Time Zone map, page 476.

Standard Time

Standard time is reckoned from the prime meridian of longitude in Greenwich, England. The world is divided into 24 zones, each 15 deg of arc, or one hour in time apart. The Greenwich meridian (0 deg) extends through the center of the initial zone. Each zone extends 7.5 deg on either side of its central meridian. Zones to the east are numbered from 1 to 12, with the prefix "minus" indicating the number of hours to be subtracted to obtain Greenwich Time.

Westward zones are similarly numbered, but prefixed "plus," showing the number of hours that must be added to get Greenwich Time. The standard time maintained in many countries does not coincide with zone time. For example, China extends across five time zones, but the entire country is on Greenwich Time plus 8 hours.

The U.S. and possessions are divided into nine standard time zones. All places in each zone use, instead of their local time, the time counted from the transit of the mean sun across the standard time meridian that passes near the middle of that zone. These time zones are designated as Atlantic, Eastern, Central, Mountain, Pacific, Alaska, Hawaii-Aleutian, Samoa, and Chamorro (Guam and Northern Mariana Isls.); the time in these zones is reckoned from the 60th, 75th, 90th, 105th, 120th, 135th, 150th, and 165th meridians west of Greenwich and the 150th meridian east of Greenwich. The time zone line wanders to conform to local geography. The time in the various zones in the U.S. and U.S. territories west of Greenwich is earlier than Greenwich Time by 4, 5, 6, 7, 8, 9, 10, and 11 hours, respectively. However, Chamorro crosses the international date line and is 10 hours later than Greenwich Time.

24-Hour Time

With the 24-hour system, the day begins at midnight, and times are designated 00:00 through 23:59. Twenty-four-hour time is widely used in scientific work throughout the world. In the U.S., it is also used in operations of the armed forces. In Europe, it is frequently used by the transportation networks in preference to the 12-hour AM and PM system.

International Date Line

The date line, approximately coinciding with the 180th meridian, separates the calendar dates. The date must be advanced one day when crossing in a westerly direction and set back one day when crossing in an easterly direction. The date line frequently deviates from the 180th meridian because of decisions by affected nations. The line is deflected eastward through the Bering Strait and westward of the Aleutians to prevent separating the islands by date. The line is deflected eastward of the Tonga and New Zealand islands in the South Pacific. In 1995, Kiribati announced that its islands east of the date line would observe the same date as islands to the west, though most maps do not depict this deviation in the date line. In 2011, Samoa moved west of the dateline to ease its relationship with Australia and New Zealand. The line is established by international custom; there is no international authority prescribing its exact course.

Daylight Saving Time

Daylight saving time is achieved by advancing the clock one hour. Since 2007, daylight saving time has begun at 2 AM on the second Sunday in Mar. and has ended at 2 AM on the first Sunday in Nov. **In 2019, daylight saving time begins at 2 AM on Mar. 10 and ends at 2 AM on Nov. 3.** Prior to 2007, daylight saving time traditionally ran from the first Sunday in Apr. to the last Sunday in Oct.

Daylight saving time was first observed in the U.S. during World War I and again during World War II. In the intervening years, some states and communities observed daylight saving time, using whatever beginning and ending dates they chose. In 1966, Congress passed the Uniform Time Act, which provided that any state or territory choosing to observe daylight saving time must begin and end on the dates established by federal law. Any state could, by law, exempt itself; a 1972 amendment to the act authorized states in more than one time zone to exempt the entire state or one time zone only. Currently, most of Arizona, Hawaii, Puerto Rico, the U.S. Virgin Islands, Guam, American Samoa, and Northern Mariana Isls. do not observe daylight saving time. All of Indiana, which is in two time zones, observed daylight saving time for the first time in 2006.

Congress and the secretary of transportation both have authority to change time zone boundaries, which they have done on a number of occasions since 1966. In 2018, Florida passed legislation that would keep the state on daylight saving time year-round, but either Congress or the Transportation Dept. was required to act before the new law could go into effect.

Daylight Saving Time: International Usage

Adjusting clock time so as to gain daylight on summer evenings is common throughout the world.

Canada, which extends over six time zones, generally observes daylight saving time during the same period as the U.S. Most provincial governments observe the four-week extension to daylight saving time that went into effect in 2007. Most of Saskatchewan remains on standard time year-round; communities elsewhere in Canada may also exempt themselves from daylight saving time. Most of Mexico observes daylight saving time, except for the state of Sonora, which shares a border with Arizona.

Member nations of the European Union observe a "summer-time period," a version of daylight saving time, from the last Sunday of Mar. until the last Sunday in Oct.

Turkey stopped observing daylight saving time in Oct. 2016; maintaining its "summer hours," it shifted permanently to Greenwich time plus 3 hours. Russia, which uses 11 time zones, moved to permanent standard time in Oct. 2014 after a three-year experiment to maintain year-round "summer hours" proved unpopular. From Oct. 2014 on, the country observed "winter hours" year-round.

China does not observe daylight saving time. Mongolia discontinued daylight saving time in Feb. 2017, two years after it was reintroduced. Japan, which lies within one time zone, also does not modify its legal time during the summer months.

Many countries in the Southern Hemisphere maintain daylight saving time generally from Oct. to Mar. However, most countries near the equator do not deviate from standard time.

WEIGHTS AND MEASURES

Source: National Institute of Standards and Technology (NIST), U.S. Dept. of Commerce

International System of Units (SI)

Two systems of weights and measures coexist in the U.S. today: the **U.S. Customary System** and the **International System of Units** (SI, for Système International d'Unités). The SI is a more complete, coherent version of the **metric system**. Throughout U.S. history, the customary system—parts of which were inherited but are now different from the British Imperial System—has been generally used. Federal and state legislation gave it, through implication, standing as the primary weights and measures system. The metric system, however, is the only system that Congress has ever specifically sanctioned, dating back to an 1866 law. The U.S. was one of the original 17 countries to sign the International Metric Convention (or Treaty of the Meter) May 20, 1875, which established several intergovernmental organizations to oversee and refine the SI. The U.S. is represented at these organizations by the Natl. Institute of Standards and Technology (NIST).

Since that time, use of the metric system in the U.S. has slowly increased, particularly in the scientific community, the pharmaceutical industry, and the manufacturing sector—the last motivated by the predominant use of the metric system in international commerce.

On Dec. 23, 1975, Pres. Gerald R. Ford signed the Metric Conversion Act of 1975. It defined the "metric system of measurement" as the SI, as established in 1960 by the General Conference on Weights and Measures and interpreted in the U.S. by the secretary of commerce, who delegated that authority to the director of the NIST. The Trade and Competitiveness Act of 1988 declared the metric system the preferred system of weights and measures for U.S. trade and commerce, but explicitly permitted "the continued use of traditional systems of weights and measures in nonbusiness activities." The Code of Federal Regulations made the use of metric units mandatory for federal agencies in 1991. However, the metric system has not yet become the system of choice for most Americans' daily use.

The following are the seven base SI units: **length**—meter; **mass**—kilogram; **time**—second; **electric current**—ampere; **thermodynamic temperature**—kelvin; **amount of substance**—mole; and **luminous intensity**—candela.

Frequently Used Conversions

Boldface indicates exact values. For greater accuracy, use the "multiply by" number in parentheses. For weights, avoirdupois (avdp) weight is the system applied to all goods except medicines, precious metals, and precious stones.

U.S. Customary to Metric

	If you have:	Multiply by:		To get:
Length	inches	**25.4**		millimeters
	inches	**2.54**		centimeters
	inches	**0.0254**		meters
	feet	0.3	(**0.3048**)	meters
	yards	0.9	(**0.9144**)	meters
	miles[1]	1.6	(**1.609344**)	kilometers
Area	sq inches	6.5	(**6.4516**)	sq cm
	sq feet	0.09	(**0.09290304**)	sq meters
	sq yards	0.84	(**0.83612736**)	sq meters
	acres	0.4	(0.4046873)	hectares
	sq miles[1]	2.6	(2.58998811)	sq kilometers
Weight	ounces (avdp)	28	(28.34952)	grams
	pounds (avdp)	454	(**453.59237**)	grams
	pounds (avdp)	0.45	(**0.45359237**)	kilograms
	short tons[2]	0.91	(**0.90718474**)	metric tons
	long tons[3]	1	(1.016047)	metric tons
Liquid	ounces	0.03	(0.02957353)	liters
	cups	0.24	(0.23658824)	liters
	pints	0.47	(0.473176473)	liters
	quarts	0.95	(0.946352946)	liters
	gallons	3.79	(3.785412)	liters

Metric to U.S. Customary

	If you have:	Multiply by:		To get:
Length	millimeters	0.04	(0.03937)	inches
	centimeters	0.4	(0.3937)	inches
	meters	39	(39.37)	inches
	meters	3.3	(3.280840)	feet
	meters	1.1	(1.093613)	yards
	kilometers	0.6	(0.621371)	miles[1]
Area	sq cm	0.16	(0.15500)	sq inches
	sq meters	10.8	(10.76391)	sq feet
	sq meters	1.2	(1.195990)	sq yards
	hectares	2.5	(2.471044)	acres
	sq kilometers	0.39	(0.386102)	sq miles[1]
Weight	grams	0.035	(0.03527396)	ounces (avdp)
	grams	0.002	(0.00220462)	pounds (avdp)
	kilograms	2.2	(2.204623)	pounds (avdp)
	metric tons	1.1	(1.102311)	short tons[2]
	metric tons	0.98	(0.9842065)	long tons[3]
Liquid	liters	33.8	(33.81402)	ounces
	liters	4.2	(4.226752)	cups
	liters	2.1	(2.113376)	pints
	liters	1.1	(1.056688)	quarts
	liters	0.26	(0.264172)	gallons

(1) Survey mile. (2) A short ton is 2,000 pounds. (3) A long ton is 2,240 pounds.

Temperature Conversions

The left-hand column below gives a temperature according to the **Celsius** scale, and the right-hand gives the same temperature according to the **Fahrenheit** scale. The lowest number on each scale is equivalent to absolute zero, the theoretical temperature at which all molecular motion would stop.

For temperatures not shown: To convert Fahrenheit to Celsius, subtract 32 degrees and divide by 1.8; to convert Celsius to Fahrenheit, multiply by 1.8 and add 32 degrees.

Celsius	Fahrenheit	Celsius	Fahrenheit	Celsius	Fahrenheit	Celsius	Fahrenheit	Celsius	Fahrenheit
−273.15	−459.67	−45.6	−50	−1.1	30	30	86	65.6	150
−250	−418	**−40**	**−40**	**0**	**32**	32.2	90	70	158
−200	−328	−34.4	−30	4.4	40	35	95	80	176
−184.4	−300	−30	−22	10	50	**37**	**98.6**	90	194
−156.7	−250	−28.9	−20	15.6	60	37.8	100	93.3	200
−150	−238	−23.3	−10	**20**	**68**	40	104	**100**	**212**
−128.9	−200	−20	−4	21.1	70	43.3	110	121.1	250
−101.1	−150	−17.8	0	23.9	75	48.9	120	148.9	300
−100	−148	−12.2	10	25	77	50	122	150	302
−73.3	−100	−10	14	26.7	80	54.4	130	200	392
−50	−58	−6.7	20	29.4	85	60	140	300	572

Note: Although the term *centigrade* is still frequently used, the International Committee on Weights and Measures and the National Institute of Standards and Technology have recommended since 1948 that this scale be called *Celsius.*

Boiling and Freezing Points

Water boils at 212°F (100°C) at sea level. For every 550 feet above sea level, the boiling point of water is lower by about 1°F. Methyl alcohol (wood alcohol) boils at 148.5°F. Average human oral temperature is 98.6°F. **Water freezes** at 32°F (0°C).

Selected Geometric Formulas

The value of π (the Greek letter pi) is approximately 3.14159265 (equal to the ratio of the circumference of a circle to its diameter). The equivalence is typically rounded further to 3.1416 or 3.14.

Calculating Circumference

Circle: Multiply the diameter by π.

Calculating Area

Circle: Multiply the square of the radius (equal to ½ the diameter) by π.

Rectangle: Multiply the length of the base by the height.

Sphere (surface): Multiply the square of the radius by π and multiply by 4.

Square: Square the length of one side.

Trapezoid: Add the length of the two parallel sides, multiply by the height, and divide by 2.

Triangle: Multiply the base by the height and divide by 2.

Calculating Volume

Cone: Multiply the square of the radius of the base by π, multiply by the height, and divide by 3.

Cube: Cube the length of one edge.

Cylinder: Multiply the square of the radius of the base by π and multiply by the height.

Pyramid: Multiply the area of the base by the height and divide by 3.

Rectangular prism: Multiply the length by the width by the height.

Sphere: Multiply the cube of the radius by π, multiply by 4, and divide by 3.

Playing Cards and Dice Chances

5-Card Poker Hands

Hand	Number possible	Odds against
Royal flush	4	649,739 to 1
Other straight flush	36	72,192 to 1
Four of a kind	624	4,164 to 1
Full house	3,744	693 to 1
Flush	5,108	508 to 1
Straight	10,200	254 to 1
Three of a kind	54,912	46 to 1
Two pairs	123,552	20 to 1
One pair	1,098,240	4 to 3 (1.37 to 1)
Nothing	1,302,540	1 to 1
Total	**2,598,960**	

Bridge

The odds—against suit distribution in a hand of 4-4-3-2 are about 4 to 1; against 5-4-2-2 about 8 to 1; against 6-4-2-1 about 20 to 1; against 7-4-1-1 about 254 to 1; against 8-4-1-0 about 2,211 to 1; and against 13-0-0-0 about 158,753,389,899 to 1.

Dice
(probabilities on 2 dice)

Total	Odds against (single toss)	Total	Odds against (single toss)
2	35 to 1	8	31 to 5
3	17 to 1	9	8 to 1
4	11 to 1	10	11 to 1
5	8 to 1	11	17 to 1
6	31 to 5	12	35 to 1
7	5 to 1		

Large Numbers

No. of zeros	U.S. term	British[1], French, German	No. of zeros	U.S. term	British[1], French, German
6	million	million	42	tredecillion	septillion
9	billion	milliard	45	quattuordecillion	1,000 septillion
12	trillion	billion	48	quindecillion	octillion
15	quadrillion	1,000 billion	51	sexdecillion	1,000 octillion
18	quintillion	trillion	54	septendecillion	nonillion
21	sextillion	1,000 trillion	57	octodecillion	1,000 nonillion
24	septillion	quadrillion	60	novemdecillion	decillion
27	octillion	1,000 quadrillion	63	vigintillion	1,000 decillion
30	nonillion	quintillion	100	googol	googol
33	decillion	1,000 quintillion	303	centillion	NA
36	undecillion	sextillion	600	NA	centillion
39	duodecillion	1,000 sextillion	googol	googolplex	googolplex

NA = Not available. (1) In recent years, it has become more common in Britain to use U.S. terminology for large numbers.

Prime Numbers to 1,009

A prime number is any positive integer greater than 1 that is divisible only by two positive integers—1 and itself.

	2	3	5	7	11	13	17	19	23
29	31	37	41	43	47	53	59	61	67
71	73	79	83	89	97	101	103	107	109
113	127	131	137	139	149	151	157	163	167
173	179	181	191	193	197	199	211	223	227
229	233	239	241	251	257	263	269	271	277
281	283	293	307	311	313	317	331	337	347
349	353	359	367	373	379	383	389	397	401
409	419	421	431	433	439	443	449	457	461
463	467	479	487	491	499	503	509	521	523
541	547	557	563	569	571	577	587	593	599
601	607	613	617	619	631	641	643	647	653
659	661	673	677	683	691	701	709	719	727
733	739	743	751	757	761	769	773	787	797
809	811	821	823	827	829	839	853	857	859
863	877	881	883	887	907	911	919	929	937
941	947	953	967	971	977	983	991	997	1,009

Common Fractions Converted to Decimals

8ths	16ths	32nds	64ths		8ths	16ths	32nds	64ths		8ths	16ths	32nds	64ths		8ths	16ths	32nds	64ths	
			1	= 0.015625				17	= 0.265625				33	= 0.515625				49	= 0.765625
	1		2	= 0.03125		9		18	= 0.28125			17	34	= 0.53125			25	50	= 0.78125
			3	= 0.046875				19	= 0.296875				35	= 0.546875				51	= 0.796875
	1	2	4	= 0.0625		5	10	20	= 0.3125		9	18	36	= 0.5625		13	26	52	= 0.8125
			5	= 0.078125				21	= 0.328125				37	= 0.578125				53	= 0.828125
		3	6	= 0.09375			11	22	= 0.34375			19	38	= 0.59375			27	54	= 0.84375
			7	= 0.109375				23	= 0.359375				39	= 0.609375				55	= 0.859375
1	2	4	8	= 0.125	3	6	12	24	= 0.375	5	10	20	40	= 0.625	7	14	28	56	= 0.875
			9	= 0.140625				25	= 0.390625				41	= 0.640625				57	= 0.890625
	5	10	= 0.15625			13	26	= 0.40625			21	42	= 0.65625			29	58	= 0.90625
		11	= 0.171875				27	= 0.421875				43	= 0.671875				59	= 0.921875
	3	6	12	= 0.1875		7	14	28	= 0.4375		11	22	44	= 0.6875		15	30	60	= 0.9375
			13	= 0.203125				29	= 0.453125				45	= 0.703125				61	= 0.953125
	7	14	= 0.21875			15	30	= 0.46875			23	46	= 0.71875			31	62	= 0.96875
		15	= 0.234375				31	= 0.484375				47	= 0.734375				63	= 0.984375
2	4	8	16	= 0.25	4	8	16	32	= 0.5	6	12	24	48	= 0.75	8	16	32	64	= 1.0

Roman Numerals

I — 1	IV — 4	VII — 7	X — 10	XX — 20	L — 50	C — 100	D — 500
II — 2	V — 5	VIII — 8	XI — 11	XXX — 30	LX — 60	CC — 200	CM — 900
III — 3	VI — 6	IX — 9	XIX — 19	XL — 40	XC — 90	CD — 400	M — 1,000

Note: The numerals V, X, L, C, D, or M shown with a horizontal line on top denote 1,000 times the original value.

Ancient Measures

Biblical
Cubit . . . . = 21.8 inches
Omer. . . . . = 0.45 peck
. . . . = 3.964 liters
Ephah . . . . = 10 omers
Shekel. . . . . = 0.497 ounce
. . . . = 14.1 grams

Greek
Cubit . . . . = 18.3 inches
Stadion . . . . = 607.2 or 622 feet
Obolos . . . . = 715.38 milligrams
Drachma . . . . . . = 4.2923 grams
Mina . . . . = 0.9463 pound
Talent . . . . = 60 mina

Roman
Cubit . . . . = 17.5 inches
Stadium . . . . = 202 yards
As, libra,
  pondus . . . . . . = 325.971 grams
. . . . = 0.71864 pound

Metric System Prefixes

The following prefixes, in combination with the basic unit names, provide the multiples and submultiples in the metric system. For example, the unit name *meter*, with the prefix *kilo* added, produces *kilometer*, meaning "1,000 meters."

Prefix	Symbol	Multiples	Equivalent	Prefix	Symbol	Multiples	Equivalent
yotta	Y	10^{24}	septillionfold	deci	d	10^{-1}	tenth part
zetta	Z	10^{21}	sextillionfold	centi	c	10^{-2}	hundredth part
exa	E	10^{18}	quintillionfold	milli	m	10^{-3}	thousandth part
peta	P	10^{15}	quadrillionfold	micro	μ	10^{-6}	millionth part
tera	T	10^{12}	trillionfold	nano	n	10^{-9}	billionth part
giga	G	10^{9}	billionfold	pico	p	10^{-12}	trillionth part
mega	M	10^{6}	millionfold	femto	f	10^{-15}	quadrillionth part
kilo	k	10^{3}	thousandfold	atto	a	10^{-18}	quintillionth part
hecto	h	10^{2}	hundredfold	zepto	z	10^{-21}	sextillionth part
deka	da	10^{1}	tenfold	yocto	y	10^{-24}	septillionth part

Weight and Measurement Equivalents

In this table, there is a distinction between the international foot and the survey foot. The international foot, defined in 1959 as exactly equal to 0.3048 meter, is shorter than the survey foot by exactly 2 parts in 1 million. This means that an international mile is about ⅛ inch shorter than the survey mile. The survey foot is still used in the publication of some geodetic surveys within the U.S. In this table, the survey foot is indicated with capital letters, as FEET.

When the name of a unit is enclosed in brackets, e.g., [1 hand], either (1) the unit is not in general current use in the U.S. or (2) the unit is believed to be based on custom and usage rather than on formal definition.

Equivalents involving decimals are, in most instances, rounded to the third decimal place; exact equivalents are so designated.

Lengths

1 angstrom (Å) . . . . = 0.1 nanometer (exactly)
. . . . = 0.0001 micrometer (exactly)
. . . . = 0.0000001 millimeter (exactly)
. . . . = 0.000000004 inch
1 cable's length. . . . . = 120 fathoms (exactly)
. . . . = 720 FEET (exactly)
. . . . = 219 meters
1 centimeter (cm) . . . . = 0.3937 inch
1 chain (ch) (engineer's). . . . . . = 30.48 meters (exactly)
. . . . = 100 feet
1 chain (Gunter's
  or surveyor's) . . . . = 66 FEET (exactly)
. . . . = 20.1168 meters
1 decimeter (dm) . . . . = 3.937 inches
1 degree (geographical) . . . . . . = 364,566.929 feet
. . . . = 69.047 miles (avg.)
. . . . = 111.123 kilometers (avg.)
  of latitude . . . . = 68.708 miles at equator
. . . . = 69.403 miles at poles
  of longitude . . . . = 69.171 miles at equator

1 dekameter (dam) . . . . = 32.808 feet
1 fathom (fath) . . . . = 6 FEET (exactly)
. . . . = 1.8288 meters
1 foot (ft) . . . . = 12 inches (exactly)
. . . . = 0.3048 meters (exactly)
. . . . = 0.015 chains (surveyor's)
1 furlong (fur) . . . . = 660 FEET (exactly)
. . . . = ⅛ survey mile (exactly)
. . . . = 201.168 meters
[1 hand (height measure for
  horses, from ground to top
  of their shoulders)] . . . . = 4 inches
1 inch (in.). . . . . = 2.54 centimeters (exactly)
1 kilometer (km) . . . . = 0.621371 mile
. . . . = 3,280.8 feet
1 league (land) . . . . = 3 survey miles (exactly)
. . . . = 4.828 kilometers
1 link (engineer's) . . . . = 1 foot
. . . . = 0.305 meter
1 link (Gunter's or surveyor's). . = 7.92 inches (exactly)
. . . . = 0.201 meter

1 meter (m) . . . . = 39.37 inches
                         = 1.09361 yards
1 micrometer (μm) . . . . = 0.001 millimeter (exactly)
                         = 0.00003937 inch
1 mil . . . . = 0.001 inch (exactly)
                         = 0.0254 millimeter (exactly)
1 mile (mi) (statute or land). . . . = 5,280 FEET (exactly)
                         = 1.609344 kilometers (exactly)
1 mile (nmi) (international
   nautical) . . . . = 1.852 kilometers (exactly)
                         = 1.151 miles
                         = 6,076.1 feet
1 millimeter (mm) . . . . = 0.03937 inch
1 nanometer (nm) . . . . = 0.001 micrometer (exactly)
                         = 0.00000003937 inch
1 pica (typography) . . . . = 12 points
1 point (pt) (typography) . . . . . = 0.013837 inch (exactly)
                         = 0.351 millimeter
1 rod (rd), pole, or perch . . . . . = 16½ FEET (exactly)
                         = 5.029 meters
1 yard (yd) . . . . = 3 feet (exactly)
                         = 0.9144 meter (exactly)

Areas or Surfaces

1 acre (A) . . . . = 43,560 square FEET (exactly)
                         = 4,840 square yards
                         = 0.405 hectare
1 are (a) . . . . = 119.599 square yards
                         = 0.025 acre
1 bolt (cloth measure):
   length . . . . = 100 yards
   width . . . . = 45 or 60 inches
1 hectare (ha) . . . . = 2.471 acres
[1 square (building)] . . . . = 100 square feet
1 square centimeter (cm²) . . . . = 0.155 square inch
1 square decimeter (dm²) . . . . . = 15.500 square inches
1 square foot (ft²) . . . . = 929.030 square centimeters
1 square inch (in.²) . . . . = 6.4516 square centimeters
                         (exactly)
1 square kilometer (km²) . . . . = 247.104 acres
                         = 0.386102 square mile
1 square meter (m²) . . . . = 1.196 square yards
                         = 10.764 square feet
1 square mile (mi²) . . . . = 640 acres (exactly)
                         = 258.999 hectares
1 square millimeter (mm²) . . . . = 0.002 square inch
1 square rod (rd²), square
   pole, or square perch . . . . . = 25.293 square meters
1 square yard (yd²) . . . . = 0.836127 square meter

Capacities or Volumes

1 barrel (bbl), liquid . . . . = 31 to 42 gallons*

*There are a variety of "barrels" established by law or usage. For example, federal taxes on fermented liquors are based on a barrel of 31 gallons. Many state laws fix the "barrel for liquids" as 31½ gallons; one state fixes a 36-gallon barrel for cistern measurement. Federal law recognizes a 40-gallon barrel for "proof spirits." By custom, 42 gallons constitute a barrel of crude oil or petroleum products for statistical purposes, and this equivalent is recognized "for liquids" by some states.

1 barrel (bbl), standard for
   fruits, vegetables, and other
   dry commodities except dry
   cranberries . . . . = 7,056 cubic inches
                         = 105 dry quarts
                         = 3.281 bushels, struck measure
1 barrel, standard, cranberry . . = 86 45/64 dry quarts
                         = 2.709 bushels, struck measure
                         = 5,826 cubic inches
1 board foot (lumber measure) = a foot-square board 1 inch
                         thick
1 bushel (U.S.) (struck
   measure) . . . . = 2,150.42 cubic inches (exactly)
                         = 35.239 liters
[1 bushel, heaped (U.S.)] . . . . = 2,747.715 cubic inches
                         = 1.278 bushels,
                           struck measure**

**Frequently recognized as 1¼ bushels, struck measure.

[1 bushel (bu) (British Imperial)
   (struck measure)] . . . . = 1.032 U.S. bushels,
                           struck measure
                         = 2,219.36 cubic inches
1 cord (cd) (firewood) . . . . = 128 cubic feet (exactly)

1 cubic centimeter (cm³) . . . . . = 0.061 cubic inch
1 cubic decimeter (dm³) . . . . . . = 61.024 cubic inches
1 cubic foot (ft³) . . . . = 7.481 gallons
                         = 28.317 cubic decimeters
1 cubic inch (in.³) . . . . = 0.554 fluid ounce
                         = 4.433 fluid drams
                         = 16.387 cubic centimeters
1 cubic meter (m³) . . . . = 1.308 cubic yards
1 cubic yard (yd³) . . . . = 0.765 cubic meter
1 cup, measuring . . . . = 8 fluid ounces (exactly)
                         = ½ liquid pint (exactly)
1 dekaliter (daL) . . . . = 2.642 gallons
                         = 1.135 pecks
[1 dram, fluid (fl dr) (British)] . . = 0.961 U.S. fluid dram
                         = 0.217 cubic inch
                         = 3.552 milliliters
1 gallon (gal) (U.S.) . . . . = 4 quarts, liquid (exactly)
                         = 231 cubic inches (exactly)
                         = 3.785 liters
                         = 0.833 British gallon
                         = 128 U.S. fluid ounces (exactly)
[1 gallon (British Imperial)] . . . . = 277.42 cubic inches
                         = 1.201 U.S. gallons
                         = 4.546 liters
                         = 160 British fluid ounces
                           (exactly)
1 gill (gi) . . . . = 7.219 cubic inches
                         = 4 fluid ounces (exactly)
                         = 0.118 liter
1 hectoliter (hL) . . . . = 26.418 gallons
                         = 2.838 bushels
1 liter (L) (1 cubic decimeter
   exactly) . . . . = 1.057 liquid quarts
                         = 0.908 dry quart
                         = 61.024 cubic inches
1 milliliter (mL) (1 cu cm
   exactly) . . . . = 0.271 fluid dram
                         = 16.231 minims
                         = 0.061 cubic inch
1 ounce, liquid (U.S.) . . . . = 1.805 cubic inches
                         = 29.573 milliliters
                         = 1.041 British fluid ounces
[1 ounce, fluid (fl oz) (British)] = 0.961 U.S. fluid ounce
                         = 1.734 cubic inches
                         = 28.412 milliliters
1 peck (pk) . . . . = 8.810 liters
1 pint (pt), dry . . . . = 33.600 cubic inches
                         = 0.551 liter
1 pint, liquid . . . . = 28.875 cubic inches (exactly)
                         = 0.473 liter
1 quart (qt), dry (U.S.) . . . . = 67.201 cubic inches
                         = 1.101 liters
                         = 0.969 British quart
1 quart, liquid (U.S.) . . . . = 2 pints, liquid (exactly)
                         = 4 cups (exactly)
                         = 57.75 cubic inches (exactly)
                         = 0.946 liter
                         = 0.833 British quart
[1 quart (British)] . . . . = 69.354 cubic inches
                         = 1.032 U.S. dry quarts
                         = 1.201 U.S. liquid quarts
1 tablespoon (T., Tbs, tbsp.) . . = 3 teaspoons (exactly)
                         = 4 fluid drams
                         = ½ fluid ounce (exactly)
1 teaspoon (t., tsp.) . . . . = ⅓ tablespoon (exactly)
                         = 1⅓ fluid drams***

***The equivalent "1 teaspoon = 1⅓ fluid drams" has been found to correspond more closely with the actual capacities of teaspoons in use than the equivalent "1 teaspoon = 1 fluid dram" given by many dictionaries.

Weights or Masses

1 assay ton* (AT) . . . . = 29.167 grams

*Used in assaying. The assay ton bears the same relation to the milligram that a ton of 2,000 pounds avoirdupois bears to the ounce troy; hence, the weight in milligrams of precious metal obtained from one assay ton of ore gives directly the number of troy ounces to the net ton.

1 carat (c) . . . . = 200 milligrams (exactly)
                         = 3.086 grains
1 dram avoirdupois (dr avdp) . . = 27 11/32 (= 27.344) grains
                         = 1.772 grams
1 gamma (γ) . . . . = 1 microgram (exactly)
1 grain (gr) . . . . = 64.79891 milligrams (exactly)

1 gram (g) . . . . = 15.432 grains
                 = 0.035 ounce, avoirdupois
1 hundredweight, gross or
   long** (gross cwt) . . . . = 112 pounds (exactly)
                 = 50.802 kilograms
**The gross, or long, ton and hundredweight are used commercially in the U.S. to only a limited extent, usually in restricted industrial fields. These units are the same as the British ton and hundredweight.

1 hundredweight, gross or
   short (cwt or net cwt) . . . . . . = 100 pounds (exactly)
                 = 45.359 kilograms
1 kilogram (kg) . . . . = 2.20462 pounds
1 microgram (μg) . . . . = 0.000001 gram (exactly)
1 milligram (mg) . . . . = 0.015 grain
1 ounce, avoirdupois (oz avdp) = 437.5 grains (exactly)
                 = 0.911 troy ounce
                 = 28.3495 grams
1 ounce, troy (oz t) . . . . = 480 grains (exactly)
                 = 1.097 avoirdupois ounces
                 = 31.103 grams

1 pennyweight (dwt) . . . . = 1.555 grams
1 pound, avoirdupois (lb avdp) = 7,000 grains (exactly)
                 = 1.215 troy pounds
                 = 453.59237 grams (exactly)
1 pound, troy (lb t) . . . . = 5,760 grains (exactly)
                 = 0.823 avoirdupois pound
                 = 373.242 grams
1 stone (st) . . . . = 14 pounds avdp (exactly)
                 = 6.350 kilograms
1 ton, gross or long . . . . = 2,240 pounds (exactly)
                 = 1.12 net tons (exactly)
                 = 1.016 metric tons
1 ton, metric (t) . . . . = 2,204.623 pounds
                 = 0.984 gross ton
                 = 1.102 net tons
1 ton, net or short (tn) . . . . = 2,000 pounds (exactly)
                 = 0.893 gross ton
                 = 0.907 metric ton

Electrical Units

The **watt** (W) is the unit of power (electrical, mechanical, thermal). Electrical power is given by the product of the voltage and the current.

Energy is sold by the **joule** (J), but in common practice the billing of electrical energy is expressed in terms of the **kilowatt-hour** (kWh), which is 3,600,000 joules, or 3.6 megajoules.

The **horsepower** (hp) is a nonmetric unit sometimes used in mechanics. It is equal to 746 watts.

The **ohm** (Ω) is the unit of electrical resistance and represents the physical property of a conductor that offers a resistance to the flow of electricity, permitting just 1 ampere to flow at 1 volt of pressure.

Measures of Force and Pressure

Dyne (dyn) = force necessary to accelerate a 1-gram mass 1 centimeter per second squared = 0.000072 poundal

Poundal (pdl) = force necessary to accelerate a 1-pound mass 1 foot per second squared = 13,825.5 dynes = 0.138255 newton

Newton (N) = force needed to accelerate a 1-kilogram mass 1 meter per second squared = 100,000 dynes (exactly)

Pascal (pressure) (Pa) = 1 newton per square meter = 0.020885 pound per square foot

Atmosphere (air pressure at sea level) (atm) = 2,116.217 pounds per square foot = 14.6959 pounds per square inch = 1.0332 kilograms per square centimeter = 101,325 newtons per square meter

Measures of Alcohol

Pony . . . . = 1.0 fluid ounce
Shot . . . . = varies, usu. 1.0-1.5 fluid ounces
Jigger . . . . = 1.5 fluid ounces
Pint (pt) . . . . = 16 fluid ounces
               = 0.625 fifth
Fifth . . . . = 25.6 fluid ounces
               = 1.6 pints
               = 0.8 quart
               = 0.757 liter

Quart (qt) . . . . = 32 fluid ounces
               = 1.25 fifths
Wine bottle
   (standard) . . . . = 0.75 liter
               = 25.4 fluid ounces
Magnum . . . . = 1.5 liters

For champagne and brandy:
Jeroboam . . . . = 2 magnums
               = 3 liters
               = 101 fluid ounces

For champagne:
Rehoboam . . . . = 3 magnums
Methuselah . . . . = 4 magnums
Salmanazar . . . . = 6 magnums
Balthazar . . . . = 8 magnums
Nebuchadnezzar . . . = 10 magnums

Miscellaneous Measures

Caliber (cal)—the diameter of a gun bore. In the U.S., caliber is traditionally expressed in hundredths of inches, e.g., .22. In Britain, caliber is often expressed in thousandths of inches, e.g., .270. Now it is commonly expressed in millimeters, e.g., the 5.56 mm M16 rifle. The caliber of heavier weapons has long been expressed in millimeters, e.g., the 155 mm howitzer.

Naval guns' caliber refers to the barrel length as a multiple of the bore diameter. For example, a 5-inch, 50-caliber naval gun has a 5-inch bore and a barrel length of 250 inches.

Decibel (dB)—a measure of the relative intensity of sound. The threshold of hearing is given as 0 decibels. A 20-decibel sound is 10 times more intense than a 10-decibel sound; 30 decibels is 100 times more intense. (A 10-decibel increase corresponds generally to the perception of a sound being twice as loud.)

One decibel is the smallest difference between sounds detectable by the human ear. Long or repeated exposure to an 85-decibel-or-higher sound can damage hearing.

10 decibels . . .	breathing
20	rustling leaves
30	whisper
40	refrigerator humming
50	quiet conversation
60	conversation, laughter
70	vacuum cleaner
80	city traffic
90	subway, lawn mower
100	chainsaw

Em—a printer's measure designating the width of any given type size. For example, an em of 10-point type is 10 points. An en is half an em.

Gauge (ga)—the diameter of a shotgun bore. Gauge numbers originally referred to the number of lead balls—of equal diameter as the gun barrel—required to make a pound. Thus, a 16-gauge shotgun's bore was smaller than a 12-gauge shotgun's. Today, an international agreement assigns millimeter measures to each gauge.

Gauge	Bore diameter (mm)	Gauge	Bore diameter (mm)
6	23.34	14	17.60
10	19.67	16	16.81
12	18.52	20	15.90

Horsepower (hp)—the power needed to lift 550 pounds 1 foot in 1 second or to lift 33,000 pounds 1 foot in 1 minute. Equivalent to 746 watts or 2,546 British thermal units per hour.

Karat or carat (k or c)—a measure of fineness for gold equal to 1/24 part of pure gold in an alloy. 24-karat gold is pure; 18-karat gold is ¼ alloy. The carat is also used as a unit of weight for precious stones; it is equal to 200 milligrams or 3.086 grains.

Knot (kn or kt)—a measure of the speed of ships. A knot equals 1 nautical mile (about 1.151 statute miles) per hour.

Quire (qr)—25 sheets of paper of the same size and quality.

Ream (rm)—500 sheets of paper of the same size and quality.

POSTAL INFORMATION

Administration of the U.S. Postal Service

The Postal Reorganization Act, creating a government-owned postal service under the executive branch and replacing the old executive Post Office Department, was signed into law Aug. 12, 1970. The service officially came into being on July 1, 1971. The U.S. Postal Service is governed by an 11-person board. Nine members are appointed by the president, with Senate approval. These nine choose a postmaster general. The board and the postmaster general choose the 11th member, who serves as deputy postmaster general.

Congress passed the Postal Accountability and Enhancement Act, which overhauled postal service operations for the first time since 1971, on Dec. 8, 2006. New operating provisions included the ability to adjust rates annually, negotiate for contracts, and invest profits in internal improvements. (The Postal Service last received a public service subsidy, i.e., taxpayer dollars, in 1982.)

Historical Postage Rates, 1851-2018

Postage cost for a prepaid, 1-oz. letter (the first-class standard after July 1, 1885).

Effective date	Rate	2018 dollars	Effective date	Rate	2018 dollars	Effective date	Rate	2018 dollars
July 1, 1851	$0.06[1]	$1.98	Mar. 2, 1974	$0.10	$0.52	June 30, 2002	$0.37	$0.51
July 1, 1863	0.06	1.21	Dec. 31, 1975	0.13	0.58	Jan. 8, 2006	0.39	0.49
Oct. 1, 1883	0.04	1.01	May 29, 1978	0.15	0.58	May 14, 2007	0.41	0.49
July 1, 1885	0.02	0.53	Mar. 22, 1981	0.18	0.51	May 12, 2008	0.42	0.48
Nov. 2, 1917	0.03[2]	0.55	Nov. 1, 1981	0.20	0.53	May 11, 2009	0.44	0.51
July 1, 1919	0.02[2]	0.29	Feb. 17, 1985	0.22	0.52	Jan. 22, 2012	0.45	0.50
July 6, 1932	0.03	0.55	Apr. 3, 1988	0.25	0.53	Jan. 27, 2013	0.46	0.50
Aug. 1, 1958	0.04	0.35	Feb. 3, 1991	0.29	0.54	Jan. 26, 2014	0.49[3]	0.52
Jan. 7, 1963	0.05	0.41	Jan. 1, 1995	0.32	0.53	Apr. 10, 2016	0.47	0.49
Jan. 7, 1968	0.06	0.44	Jan. 10, 1999	0.33	0.50	Jan. 22, 2017	0.49	0.50
May 16, 1971	0.08	0.50	Jan. 7, 2001	0.34	0.48	Jan. 21, 2018	0.50	—

— = Not applicable. (1) For prepaid domestic letters traveling under 3,000 miles. (2) The price increased one cent during World War I; Congress restored its prewar rate in 1919. (3) The Postal Regulatory Commission approved a 6% total price increase: a 1.7% increase for inflation and an additional 4.3% temporary increase to compensate for USPS losses during the 2008-09 recession.

Status of the U.S. Postal Service, 2001-17

Source: *Postal Facts*, U.S. Postal Service

	2001	2005	2010	2011	2012	2013	2014	2015	2016	2017
Total mail items (bil)	207.5	211.7	170.9	168.3	159.8	158.2	155.5	154.3	154.3	149.5
First-class mail items (bil)	103.7	98.1	77.6	72.5	68.7	65.8	63.8	62.6	61.2	58.7
Stamped mail items (bil)	53.6	45.9	28.9	25.8	23.2	22.6	21.8	20.7	19.7	18.5
Advertising mail items (bil)	89.9	100.9	81.8	84.0	79.5	80.8	80.3	80.0	80.9	78.3
Annual revenue (bil)	$65.8	$69.9	$67.1	$65.7	$65.2	$67.3	$67.8	$68.8	$71.4	$69.6
Total retail revenue (bil).	$14.8	$17.3	$17.5	$16.9	$17.5	$18.3	$19.0	$19.2	$13.5	$12.9
Total customer visits (bil)	1.4	1.3	1.1	1.0	1.0	1.0	0.9	0.9	0.9	0.9
Delivery points (mil)	137.7	144.3	150.9	151.5	152.1	152.9	153.9	155.0	156.1	157.3
Total delivery routes	242,600	243,000	230,600	228,160	227,000	225,152	244,365	226,777	229,104	228,483
Total retail offices	38,123	37,142	36,222	35,756	35,369	35,434	35,649	35,520	35,423	34,340
Career employees	775,903	704,716	583,908	557,251	528,458	491,017	488,300	491,863	508,908	503,103

U.S. Domestic Mail Rates

Source: *Price List* (Notice 123), U.S. Postal Service. Effective Jan. 21, 2018. Rates are for retail customers unless noted. Domestic rates apply to the U.S., its territories and possessions, APOs, FPOs, and Freely Associated States.

First-Class Mail

Includes written matter such as letters, postcards, bills, account statements, and any matter sealed or closed against inspection up to 13 oz. In most cases, delivery is within 2-3 business days.

Letters measuring up to 6⅛ by 11½ in. cost 50¢ for the first oz., 21¢ for each additional oz. or fraction thereof, up to 3.5 oz. Postcard postage is 35¢. Large envelopes up to 12 by 15 in. (or letters over 3.5 oz.) cost $1.00 for the first oz. and 21¢ for each additional oz. or fraction thereof. Presort- and automation-compatible mail can qualify for lower rates if certain piece minimums, mailing permits, and other requirements are met.

Forever Stamps. The USPS introduced the "Forever" stamp Apr. 12, 2007, at an initial cost of 41¢. The Forever stamp can be purchased at the current First-Class standard rate and will always be valid as First-Class postage on standard envelopes weighing 1 oz. or less, even after rates increase.

Priority Mail

Due to expeditious handling and transportation, Priority Mail is delivered within 1-3 business days in most cases. Can be any mailable article up to 70 lbs and not over 108 in. in length and girth combined.

Priority Mail Flat Rate: $6.70, $7.00, $7.25, regardless of weight, if matter fits into designated USPS flat-rate envelope. $7.20, $13.65, $18.90 if matter fits into flat-rate box.

Priority Mail Forever Prepaid Flat Rate packaging can be purchased online at the current priority mail flat rate and remains valid for use after future price increases.

Priority Mail Express

Provides guaranteed expedited service for any mailable article up to 70 lbs and not over 108 in. in combined length and girth. Offers next-day delivery to most destinations; $12.50 additional charge for Sunday or holiday delivery. Includes insurance up to $100, mailing receipt, proof of delivery signature record, and tracking.

Priority Mail Express Flat Rate: $24.70-$25.40, regardless of weight, if matter fits into designated USPS flat-rate envelope.

Domestic Mail Services and Fees

Adult signature required: $6.10 per piece; person 21 years of age or older must sign for shipment.

Adult signature restricted delivery: $6.35 per piece; specific addressee or agent 21 years of age or older must sign for shipment.

Certificate of mailing: $1.40 per piece.

Certified mail: $3.45 per piece; provides proof of mailing and electronic verification of delivery or delivery attempt.

Collect on delivery (COD): $7.50 for amount to be collected/insurance desired up to $50; $9.30 for $50.01-$100; $1.85 for each additional $100.

Domestic money order: $1.20 for money orders $0.01 to $500; $1.65 for $500.01 to $1,000.

Pickup on demand: $22.00 per pickup; available for Priority Mail, Priority Mail Express, and USPS Retail Ground.

Restricted delivery: $5.05 per item when purchased in combination with COD, Insured Mail, or Registered Mail; higher when purchased with other services.

Return receipt: If requested at time of mailing, $2.75 for a receipt by mail, $1.50 for email receipt.

Signature confirmation: $2.55 online, $3.00 at post office.

Sunday/holiday delivery: Available for Priority Mail Express only. Fee: $12.50.

Tracking

Formerly known as Delivery Confirmation, tracking can be used with First-Class Mail parcels, Priority Mail, USPS Retail Ground, and Package Services (Bound Printed Matter, Media Mail, and Library Mail). Available free of charge at time of mailing, except USPS Marketing Mail parcels (electronic option, fee: $0.39).

Change of Address

The USPS will forward mail to another address provided a Change of Address (COA) form has been filed in person (free) or online at moversguide.usps.com ($1.00 authentication fee). The form, which can be picked up at any post office, printed off the internet, or requested by phone at (800) ASK-USPS, can also be dropped in any mailbox for free filing.

Special Handling

Provides preferential handling, but not preferential delivery, to a practical extent. Available for First-Class Mail, Priority Mail, USPS Retail Ground, and Media Mail for a $10.45 surcharge.

Registered Mail

The most secure service provided by the USPS. Full value of item must be declared at time of registration and mailing. Insurance is included in fee for articles with a declared value of $0.01 up to $50,000. Fee: $11.90 for a declared value of $0, up to $22.55 for articles with a declared value of $4,000.01 to $5,000. For each additional $1,000.00 or fraction thereof above $5,000.00, add $1.60.

International Mail Rates

Source: *Price List* (Notice 123), U.S. Postal Service. Effective Jan. 21, 2018. Refer to www.usps.com for USPS price groups not shown here and weight limits by country.

First-Class Mail International

Letter-post items weighing up to 1 oz. and single postcards can be sent airmail for $1.15 to all countries.

Priority Mail International

Delivery is in 6-10 business days in many markets. Items must not be more than 108 in. in length and girth combined; max. weight is 70 lbs, though the limit varies by country.

Priority Mail International Flat Rate: $24.95 to Canada, $31.00-$34.25 to all other countries if matter fits into designated USPS flat-rate envelope (max. weight 4 lbs). Flat-rate boxes are $25.95-$62.35 to Canada, $32.25-$97.75 to all other countries.

Priority Mail Express International

Priority Mail Express International Flat Rate: $43.00 to Canada, $59.75 to Mexico, $63.95-$65.00 to all other countries if matter fits into flat-rate envelope (max. weight 4 lbs).

Global Express Guaranteed

Provides international expedited delivery, in partnership with FedEx, to certain countries. Item to be mailed must not weigh more than 70 lbs nor measure more than 108 in. in combined length and girth. Rate: Starts at $64.50 to countries in price group 1 up to $112.25 to countries in price group 8, for items not over 0.5 lb in weight.

International Mail Services and Fees

Business reply: Card: $1.40; envelope (up to 2 oz.): $1.90.

Customs clearance and delivery: $6.25 per piece.

Insurance: Available to many countries for loss of or damage to items. Consult USPS for each country's indemnity limits.

Registered mail: Available for letter-post items only to most countries. Fee: $15.50.

Return receipt: Shows to whom and when item is delivered. Fee: $4.00 per piece (must be purchased at time of mailing).

Postal money order: $8.55 per money order. Only accepted in certain countries.

U.S. Postal Abbreviations

The abbreviations below are approved by the U.S. Postal Service for use in addresses.

Alabama	AL	Illinois	IL	Missouri	MO	Pennsylvania	PA
Alaska	AK	Indiana	IN	Montana	MT	Puerto Rico	PR
American Samoa	AS	Iowa	IA	Nebraska	NE	Rhode Island	RI
Arizona	AZ	Kansas	KS	Nevada	NV	South Carolina	SC
Arkansas	AR	Kentucky	KY	New Hampshire	NH	South Dakota	SD
California	CA	Louisiana	LA	New Jersey	NJ	Tennessee	TN
Colorado	CO	Maine	ME	New Mexico	NM	Texas	TX
Connecticut	CT	Marshall Islands[1]	MH	New York	NY	Utah	UT
Delaware	DE	Maryland	MD	North Carolina	NC	Vermont	VT
District of Columbia	DC	Massachusetts	MA	North Dakota	ND	Virgin Islands	VI
Florida	FL	Michigan	MI	Northern Mariana Isls.	MP	Virginia	VA
Georgia	GA	Micronesia,		Ohio	OH	Washington	WA
Guam	GU	Federated States of[1]	FM	Oklahoma	OK	West Virginia	WV
Hawaii	HI	Minnesota	MN	Oregon	OR	Wisconsin	WI
Idaho	ID	Mississippi	MS	Palau[1]	PW	Wyoming	WY

(1) Although an independent nation, this country is subject to domestic rates and fees.

Canadian Province and Territory Postal Abbreviations

Source: Canada Post

Alberta	AB	Newfoundland and Labrador	NL	Nunavut	NU	Quebec	QC
British Columbia	BC	Northwest Territories	NT	Ontario	ON	Saskatchewan	SK
Manitoba	MB	Nova Scotia	NS	Prince Edward Island	PE	Yukon	YT
New Brunswick	NB						

SOCIAL SECURITY AND MEDICARE

Social Security Coverage

Source: Social Security Administration; World Almanac research; provisions shown are as under current law, Aug. 2018

Social Security Benefits

Social Security's **Old-Age, Survivors, and Disability Insurance (OASDI)** program benefits are based on a worker's **primary insurance amount (PIA)**, which is related by law to the average indexed monthly earnings (AIME) on which Social Security contributions have been paid. The full PIA is payable to a worker who retires at full retirement age (FRA), which is 65-67 depending on birth year, and to an entitled disabled worker at any age. Spouses and children of retired or disabled workers and survivors of deceased workers receive set proportions of the PIA subject to a family maximum amount. The PIA is calculated by applying varying percentages to succeeding parts of the AIME. The formula is adjusted annually to reflect changes in average annual wages.

Increases in Social Security benefits are initiated for December of each year, assuming the Consumer Price Index (CPI) for the third calendar quarter of the year increased relative to the base quarter (i.e., the third calendar quarter of the year in which an increase last took effect). The size of the benefit increase is determined by the percentage rise of the CPI between the quarters measured.

The **average monthly benefit** payable to all retired workers amounted to $1,404 in Dec. 2017. The average benefit for disabled workers in that month was $1,197.

Maximum Monthly Retired-Worker Benefits Payable to Individuals Who Retired at Full Retirement Age (FRA)

Retirement year[1]	Maximum benefit— Payable at retirement	Payable effective Dec. 2017
1990	$975	$1,892
1995	1,199	1,961
2000	1,435	2,097
2005	1,939	2,510
2006	2,053	2,553
2007	2,141	2,578
2008	2,185	2,572
2009	2,323	2,585
2010	2,346	2,610
2011	2,366	2,632
2012	2,513	2,699
2013	2,533	2,675
2014	2,642	2,749
2015	2,663	2,725
2016	2,639	2,700
2017	2,687	2,741
2018	2,788	2,788

(1) Benefits in 2002 and earlier are for retirement at age 65 at beginning of a given year. Benefits in 2003-08 are for starting benefits at exact FRA during the year. Benefits in 2009 and later are for retirement at age 66 at beginning of year.

Amount of Work Required

To qualify for benefits, the worker generally must have worked a certain length of time in covered employment. Just how long depends on when the worker reaches age 62 or, if earlier, when he or she dies or becomes disabled. A person born after 1929 who dies, becomes disabled, or reaches 62 after 1991 must generally have had at least 10 years of work credit to qualify for benefits.

Contribution and Benefit Base

(annual limit on the amount of earnings subject to taxation under OASDI)

Calendar year	OASDI[1]	Calendar year	OASDI[1]	Calendar year	OASDI[1]
1995	$61,200	2003	$87,000	2011	$106,800
1996	62,700	2004	87,900	2012	110,100
1997	65,400	2005	90,000	2013	113,700
1998	68,400	2006	94,200	2014	117,000
1999	72,600	2007	97,500	2015	118,500
2000	76,200	2008	102,000	2016	118,500
2001	80,400	2009	106,800	2017	127,200
2002	84,900	2010	106,800	2018	128,400

(1) Old-Age, Survivors, and Disability Insurance.

A person is **fully insured** when he or she has one quarter of coverage for every year after age 21 is reached (or 1950, if later) up to but not including the year the worker reaches 62, dies, or becomes disabled. In 2017, a person earns one quarter of coverage for each $1,320 of annual earnings in covered employment, up to four quarters per year.

To receive **disability benefits**, the worker, in addition to being fully insured, must generally have credit for 20 quarters of coverage out of the 40 calendar quarters before he or she became

disabled. A disabled blind worker need meet only the fully insured requirement. Persons disabled before age 31 can qualify with a briefer period of coverage. Certain survivor benefits are payable if the deceased worker had 6 quarters of coverage in the 13 quarters preceding death.

Tax Rate Schedule

(percentage of covered earnings)

Year	Total	OASDI[1]	HI[2]
	(for employees and employers, each)		
1979-80	6.13%	5.08%	1.05%
1981	6.65	5.35	1.30
1982-83	6.70	5.40	1.30
1984	7.00	5.70	1.30
1985	7.05	5.70	1.35
1986-87	7.15	5.70	1.45
1988-89	7.51	6.06	1.45
1990 and after[3]	7.65	6.20	1.45
Year	(for self-employed)		
1979-80	8.10%	7.05%	1.05%
1981	9.30	8.00	1.30
1982-83	9.35	8.05	1.30
1984	14.00	11.40	2.60
1985	14.10	11.40	2.70
1986-87	14.30	11.40	2.90
1988-89	15.02	12.12	2.90
1990 and after[3]	15.30	12.40	2.90

(1) Old-Age, Survivors, and Disability Ins. (2) Hospital Ins. (Medicare). (3) Public Law (PL) 111-147 exempted most employers from paying the employer share of OASDI payroll tax on wages paid Mar. 19-Dec. 31, 2010, to certain qualified individuals hired after Feb. 3, 2010. PL 111-312 reduced the OASDI payroll tax rate for 2011 by 2 percentage points for employees and for self-employed workers. PL 112-96 extended the 2011 rate reduction through 2012. The laws require that the general fund of the Treasury reimburses the OASI and DI Trust Funds for these temporary reductions.

What Aged Workers Receive

A person may receive monthly old-age benefits when he or she has enough work in covered employment and has reached retirement age—age 62 for reduced benefits or the age below for full benefits.

Full Retirement Age (FRA) by Birth Year

Year of birth	FRA	Year of birth	FRA
1937 or earlier	65	1955	66 and 2 mos.
1938	65 and 2 mos.	1956	66 and 4 mos.
1939	65 and 4 mos.	1957	66 and 6 mos.
1940	65 and 6 mos.	1958	66 and 8 mos.
1941	65 and 8 mos.	1959	66 and 10 mos.
1942	65 and 10 mos.	1960 or later	67
1943-54	66		

Note: If born on Jan. 1, refer to the previous birth year.

In 2000, the retirement earnings test was eliminated beginning with the month when the beneficiary reaches **full retirement age (FRA)**. A person at or above FRA no longer receives reduced benefits because of earnings. However, a person's benefits are reduced $1 for every $3 of earnings above the limit allowed by law ($45,360 for 2018) if he or she retires in the same calendar year but months prior to FRA. For retirees who have not yet attained FRA, the reduction is $1 for every $2 of earnings over the exempt amount ($17,040 for 2018).

For workers who reached age 65 between 1982 and 1989, Social Security benefits are raised by 3% for each year in which the worker did not receive benefits between FRA and 70 (72 before 1984), whether because of earnings from work, because the worker did not apply for benefits, or because the worker declined benefits after entitlement. The **delayed retirement credit** is 1% per year for workers who reached age 65 before 1982. The rate for workers who reached age 65 in 1998-99 is 5.5%; 2000-01, 6.0%; 2002-03, 6.5%; 2004-05, 7.0%. For 2006-07, it is 7.5%. The delayed retirement credit rose to 8% per year for 2008 and years after.

For workers retiring early, benefits are permanently reduced 5/9 of 1% for each month before the FRA, up to 36 months. If the number of months exceeds 36, then the benefit is further reduced 5/12 of 1% per month.

For example, workers who retire at exactly age 62 have a total of 60 months of reduction if their FRA is 67. The reduction for the first 36 months is 5/9 of 36%, or 20%. The reduction for the remaining 24 months is 5/12 of 24%, or 10%. These workers would see their benefits reduced by 30% by retiring early. The nearer to FRA a person is when he or she begins collecting a benefit, the larger the monthly benefit will be.

Benefits for Worker's Spouse

The spouse of a worker who is getting Social Security retirement or disability payments may become entitled to an insurance benefit of **one-half of the worker's PIA** if claiming benefits at full retirement age. Reduced spouse's benefits are available at age 62 and are permanently reduced 25/36 of 1% for each month before FRA, up to 36 months. If the number of months exceeds 36, then the benefit is further reduced 5/12 of 1% per month. Benefits are also payable to the aged divorced spouse of an insured worker if he or she was married to the worker for at least 10 years. To qualify for divorced spouse benefits, the insured worker does not have to be receiving benefits if the divorce occurred at least two years earlier. Benefits received as a spouse are reduced by the amount of one's PIA.

Benefits for Children of Workers

If a retired or disabled worker has a child under age 18, the **child** will usually get a benefit equal to **one-half of the worker's unreduced benefit**. So will the worker's spouse, regardless of age, if he or she is **caring for an entitled child** of the worker, and the child is under 16 or became disabled before age 22. However, total benefits paid on a worker's earnings record are subject to a family maximum. Total monthly benefits paid to the family of a worker who retired in 2018 at age 66 and always had the maximum earnings creditable under Social Security cannot exceed $4,898.

Entitled children generally stop receiving benefits at age 18, though they can continue receiving benefits until age 19 if they attend elementary or secondary school full-time. A child disabled before age 22 may get a benefit as long as the disability meets the definition in the law.

Benefits may also be paid to a grandchild or step-grandchild of a worker or of his or her spouse, in special circumstances.

OASDI Beneficiaries

Beneficiaries	May 2005	May 2010	May 2015	May 2018
Total (in thous.)[1]	48,068	53,349	59,530	62,454
Age 65 and over, total	33,811	36,914	42,536	46,323
Retired workers....	27,413	30,734	36,419	40,183
Disabled workers...	112	339	465	513
Survivors/ dependents.....	6,286	5,841	5,652	5,627
Under age 65, total...	14,257	16,435	16,994	16,131
Retired workers....	2,809	3,314	3,086	2,841
Disabled workers...	6,239	7,628	8,474	8,121
Survivors/ dependents.....	5,209	5,492	5,434	5,169
Total monthly benefits (in mil) ...	$42,074	$56,966	$72,613	$80,883

OASDI = Old-Age, Survivors, and Disability Ins. (1) Numbers may not add up to totals due to rounding or incomplete enumeration.

What Disabled Workers Receive

A worker who becomes unable to work may be eligible for a monthly disability benefit. Benefits continue until it is determined that the individual is no longer disabled. When a disabled-worker beneficiary reaches FRA (66 years for workers born 1943-54), the disability benefit becomes a retired-worker benefit.

Benefits—like those for dependents of retired-worker beneficiaries generally—may be paid to dependents of disabled beneficiaries. However, the maximum family benefit in disability cases is generally lower than in retirement cases.

Survivor Benefits

If an insured worker should die, one or more types of benefits may be payable to survivors, again subject to a maximum family benefit described above.

1. If claiming benefits at FRA, the **surviving spouse** will receive a benefit equal to 100% of the deceased worker's benefit. Benefits claimed before FRA are reduced, with a maximum reduction of 28.5% at age 60. However, if the deceased worker claimed benefits before FRA, the surviving spouse's benefits are limited to the reduced amount the worker would be getting if alive, but not less than 82.5% of the worker's PIA. Remarriage after the worker's death ends the surviving spouse's benefit rights. However, if the widow(er) marries,

and the marriage later ends, he or she regains benefit rights. (A marriage after age 60, or age 50 if disabled, is deemed not to have occurred for benefit purposes.) Survivor benefits may also be paid to a divorced spouse if the marriage lasted for at least 10 years.

Disabled widows and widowers may under certain circumstances qualify for benefits after attaining age 50 at the rate of 71.5% of the deceased worker's PIA. The widow or widower must have become totally disabled before or within seven years after the spouse's death or the last month in which he or she received mother's or father's insurance benefits.

2. There is a benefit for each **child under age 18**. The monthly benefit for a child of a deceased worker is 3/4 of the PIA, subject to the family maximum. A child who became disabled before age 22 may also receive benefits. Also, a child can receive benefits until age 19 if he or she is in full-time attendance at an elementary or secondary school.

3. There is a **mother's or father's benefit** for the widow(er) if children of the worker who are under age 16 are in his or her care. The benefit is 75% of the PIA (subject to the family maximum), and it continues until the youngest child reaches age 16, at which time payments stop even if the child's benefit continues. Benefits may continue if the widow(er) has a disabled child beneficiary age 16 or over in his or her care.

4. Dependent parents may be eligible for benefits if they have been receiving at least half their support from the worker before his or her death, have reached age 62, and (except in certain circumstances) have not remarried since the worker's death. Each parent gets 75% of the worker's PIA; if only one parent survives, the benefit is 82% (could be reduced for the family maximum).

5. A **lump sum** cash payment of **$255** is made if the worker was living with a spouse or has a child who is eligible for immediate monthly survivor benefits.

Self-Employed Workers

A self-employed person who has **net earnings of $400 or more** in a year must report such earnings for Social Security tax and credit purposes. Income from real estate, savings, dividends, loans, pensions, or insurance policies are not included unless it is part of a person's business.

A self-employed person receives one quarter of coverage for each $1,320 for 2018, up to a maximum of four quarters per year.

The nonfarm self-employed have the option of reporting their earnings as 2/3 of their gross income from self-employment. This option can be used only if actual net earnings from self-employment income are less than $1,600 and less than 2/3 of their gross income. The option may be used only five times. Also, the self-employed person must have actual net earnings of $400 or more in two of the three taxable years immediately preceding the year in which he or she uses the option.

When a person has both taxable wages and earnings from self-employment, wages are credited for Social Security purposes first; only as much self-employment income as brings total earnings up to the current taxable maximum becomes subject to the self-employment tax.

Farm Owners and Workers

Self-employed farmers whose gross annual earnings from farming are **$7,800** or less may report 2/3 of their gross earnings instead of net earnings for Social Security purposes. Farmers whose gross income is over $7,800 and whose net farm profits were less than $5,631 can report the smaller of 2/3 of gross farm income and $5,200. Cash or crop shares received from a tenant or share farmer count if the owner participated materially in production or management. The self-employed farmer pays contributions at the same rate as other self-employed persons.

Agricultural employees. A worker's earnings from farm work count toward benefits if (1) the employer pays the worker $150 or more in cash during the year or (2) the employer spends $2,500 or more in the year for agricultural labor. Under these rules, a person gets credit for one calendar quarter for each $1,320 in cash pay in 2018.

Foreign farm workers admitted to the U.S. on a temporary basis are not covered.

Household Workers

If an employer pays a household worker (e.g., maid, cook, laundry worker, nurse, babysitter, chauffeur, gardener) who is age 18 or older **$2,100 or more** in wages in 2018, the wages are covered under Social Security. This includes transportation costs paid for in cash. The job need not be regular or full-time.

The employee should get a Social Security card at the Social Security office and show it to the employer. The employer deducts the amount of the employee's Social Security tax from the worker's pay, adds an identical amount as the employer's Social Security tax, and sends the total amount to the federal government.

Medicare Coverage

Source: Centers for Medicare & Medicaid Services, U.S. Dept. of Health and Human Services

The Medicare health insurance program provides acute-care coverage for Social Security and Railroad Retirement beneficiaries age 65 and over; workers and spouses age 65 and over with sufficient Medicare-only coverage in federal, state, or local government employment; certain persons entitled to receive Social Security or Railroad Retirement disability benefits; certain disabled persons with Medicare-only coverage through government employment; certain persons with end-stage kidney disease; and certain persons in the vicinity of Libby, MT, with asbestos-related conditions. What follows is a basic description that may not cover all circumstances.

The **basic Medicare plan**, available nationwide, is a fee-for-service arrangement where the beneficiary may use any provider accepting Medicare. Some services are not covered, and there are some out-of-pocket costs.

Hospital insurance (Part A). The basic hospital insurance program pays covered services for hospital and post-hospital care, including:

- All necessary inpatient hospital care for the first 60 days of each benefit period, except for a deductible ($1,340 in 2018). For days 61-90, Medicare pays for services over and above the co-insurance ($335 per day in 2018). After 90 days, the beneficiary has 60 lifetime reserve days for which Medicare helps pay. The coinsurance amount for reserve days was $670 in 2018.
- Up to 100 days of care in a skilled-nursing facility in each benefit period. Hospital insurance pays for all covered services for the first 20 days; for days 21-100, the beneficiary pays coinsurance ($167.50 per day in 2018).
- Part-time home health care provided by nurses or other health workers.
- Limited coverage of hospice care for the terminally ill.

There is a premium for this insurance in certain—but not most—cases.

Medical insurance (Part B). Eligible elderly and disabled persons can receive benefits under this supplementary program only if they sign up and agree to a monthly premium. As of 2007, the monthly premium is tied to annual income. Individuals with an income of $85,000 or less and couples with an income of $170,000 or less pay $134 per person if they sign up upon becoming eligible in 2018. Part B covers certain medical services and supplies, including:

- Physicians' and surgeons' services, as well as some services furnished by other medical professionals.
- Services in an emergency room, outpatient clinic, or ambulatory surgical center.
- Home health care not covered under Part A.
- Laboratory tests, X-rays, and other diagnostic radiology services.
- Certain preventative care services and screening tests.
- Most physical and occupational therapy and speech pathology services.
- Comprehensive outpatient rehabilitation facility services and mental health care in a partial hospitalization psychiatric program, if inpatient care would otherwise be required.
- Radiation therapy, renal (kidney) dialysis and transplants, heart, lung, heart-lung, liver, pancreas, bone marrow, and intestinal transplants.
- Approved durable medical equipment for home use.
- Drugs that are not usually self-administered.
- Certain services for diabetes.
- Ambulance services when other transportation methods are contraindicated.
- Rural health clinic and health center services, including some telemedicine.

Part B services are generally subject to a deductible ($183 in 2018), coinsurance (generally 20% of the remaining allowed charges with certain exceptions), a deductible for blood, and amounts above the allowed charge if a doctor or supplier does not accept the Medicare-approved rate as payment in full. For outpatient hospital services, coinsurance varies by service, usually falling between 20% and 50% of allowed charges. There are no deductibles or coinsurance for certain services, such as lab tests paid under the clinical lab fee schedule, home health agency services (except some durable medical equipment, which is subject to 20% coinsurance), and some preventative care services. Payments for certain physical, speech, and occupational therapy services are subject to certain limits. Dental care, hearing aids, and routine eye care are generally not covered under the basic plan.

To get medical insurance (Part B), persons approaching age 65 may enroll during the seven-month initial enrollment period, which includes the month of their 65th birthday as well as the three months before and after. Persons desiring coverage to begin in the month they reach age 65 must enroll in the three months before their birthday. Persons who enroll after their initial enrollment period may be subject to late-enrollment premiums.

The monthly premium is deducted from the cash benefit for persons receiving Social Security, Railroad Retirement, or Civil Service Retirement benefits. Income from the medical premiums and the federal matching payments are put in a Supplementary Medical Insurance Trust Fund, from which benefits and administrative expenses are paid.

Medicare Advantage (Part C) (formerly Medicare+ Choice). Persons eligible for Medicare may have the option of getting services through a Medicare-certified local coordinated care plan, such as a health maintenance organization (HMO), local preferred provider organization (PPO), provider-sponsored organization (PSO), or other local Medicare-certified **managed care** plan; a regional preferred provider organization (RPPO); a private fee-for-service plan; or, in certain cases, a special-needs plan. Any such plan must provide at least the same benefits as Parts A and B, except for hospice services. They may provide added benefits (such as vision or hearing coverage) or reduce cost sharing or premiums. Enrollees may be required to use the plan's network of participating providers or pay higher out-of-pocket costs to go outside the network.

Prescription Drug Coverage (Part D). Effective Jan. 1, 2006, an optional Medicare prescription drug plan provides insurance coverage for prescription drugs. Medicare recipients pay a monthly premium (averaging about $33.50 in 2018 for basic coverage, depending on the provider) and a portion of drug costs. As of 2011, the monthly premium was tied to annual income; individuals with an income greater than $85,000 and couples with an income greater than $170,000 pay more. The open enrollment period is Oct. 15-Dec. 7. Coverage varies depending on the drug plan selected.

Further details are available on the Internet at www.medicare.gov or by calling 1-800-MEDICARE (1-800-633-4227).

Medicare card. Persons qualifying for hospital insurance under Social Security receive a health insurance card. The card indicates whether the individual has taken out medical insurance protection. It is to be shown to the hospital, skilled-nursing facility, home health agency, doctor, or other provider of covered services.

Payments are generally made only in the 50 states, Puerto Rico, U.S. Virgin Isls., Guam, American Samoa, and Northern Mariana Isls.

Social Security Financing

Social Security is paid for by a tax on certain earnings (for 2018, on earnings up to $128,400) for **Old-Age, Survivors, and Disability Insurance (OASDI)** and on all earnings (no upper limit) for hospital insurance with the **Medicare** program; the taxable earnings base for OASDI is adjusted annually to reflect changes in average wages. The employed worker and his or her employer share Social Security taxes equally.

Employers remit amounts withheld from employee wages for Social Security and income taxes to the Internal Revenue Service; employer Social Security taxes are also payable at the same time. (Self-employed workers pay Social Security taxes when filing their regular income tax forms.) The Social Security taxes (along with revenues arising from partial taxation of the Social Security benefits of certain high-income people) are transferred to the Social Security Trust Funds; they can be used only to pay benefits, the cost of rehabilitation services, and administrative expenses. By law, money not immediately needed for those purposes is invested in obligations of the federal government, which must pay interest on the money borrowed and must repay the principal when the obligations are redeemed or mature.

On Jan. 1, 1974, the **Supplemental Security Income (SSI)** program, established by the Social Security Amendments of 1972, replaced federal grants to the states to aid the needy aged, blind, and disabled. The program provides for federal payments, based on uniform national standards and eligibility requirements, and for state supplementary payments. The Social Security Administration administers the federal payments—financed by general funds of the Treasury—as well as the state supplement for those states that choose to have it federally administered. States may supplement the federal payment of all recipients and must supplement it for persons otherwise adversely affected by the transition from the former public assistance programs. In May 2018, the number of persons receiving federally administered SSI payments was 8,187,214; the payments totaled about $4.8 bil.

The **maximum monthly federal SSI payment** for individuals without an eligible spouse and with no other countable income, living in their own household, was $750 in 2018. For couples where both members were eligible, the maximum payment was $1,125.

For further information, contact the Social Security Administration toll-free at 1-800-772-1213 or visit its website at www.ssa.gov.

Examples of Monthly Social Security Benefits Available, 2018

Benefit or beneficiary	For low earnings ($22,510)[1]	For med. earnings ($50,021)[1]	For max. earnings ($122,516)[1,2]
Primary insurance amount (worker retiring at 66 years, 0 months) . .	$1,047.30	$1,725.70	$2,788.90
Maximum family benefit (worker retiring at 66 years, 0 months).	1,571.00	3,150.70	4,882.10
Maximum family disability benefit (worker disabled at 55; in 2017) . .	1,564.80	2,742.30	4,412.30
Disabled worker (worker disabled at 55):			
Worker alone	1,108.20	1,828.20	2,941.60
Worker, spouse, and 1 child	1,564.80	2,742.20	4,412.40
Retired worker claiming benefits at age 62:			
Worker alone[3].	807.90	1,330.30	2,146.30
Worker with spouse claiming benefits at—			
NRA or over.	1,358.80	2,237.30	3,609.70
Age 62[3]	1,184.30	1,950.00	3,146.20
Widow or widower claiming benefits at—			
Age 66 or over[4].	1,047.30	1,725.70	2,788.90
Age 60[4].	752.80	1,240.50	2,004.80
Disabled widow or widower claiming benefits at age 50-59[5]	748.80	1,233.80	1,994.00
1 surviving child[4].	785.40	1,294.20	2,091.60
Widow or widower at NRA or over and 1 child[4]	1,571.00	3,019.90	4,880.50
Widowed mother or father and 1 child[4]	1,570.80	2,588.40	4,183.20
Widowed mother or father and 2 children[4].	1,570.80	3,150.60	4,881.90

NRA = Normal retirement age. **Note:** Effective Jan. 2018. (1) Career average earnings: an average of lifetime earnings indexed to the year prior to entitlement (2017 in this case). (2) Assumes work beginning at age 22. (3) Assumes maximum reduction. (4) Assumes worker lived and worked until NRA without receiving reduced benefits. (5) Effective Jan. 1984, disabled widow or widower claiming a benefit at age 50-59 receives a benefit equal to 71.5% of the primary insurance amount.

Social Security Recipients by Age, Sex, Race, and Hispanic Origin, 2017
Source: Social Security Administration

Characteristic/benefit	Total	White	Black	American Indian, Alaska Native	Asian	Native Hawaiian/ other Pacific Isl.	Hispanic
Social Security beneficiaries (thous.)[1]	**51,434**	**43,626**	**5,677**	**883**	**1,749**	**133**	**3,866**
Sex							
Male.	22,985	19,629	2,436	428	764	64	1,721
Female	28,449	23,996	3,240	455	985	68	2,146
Age							
15-54 years	4,847	3,609	1,041	184	133	18	536
55-64 years	6,438	5,128	1,047	151	185	32	543
65-74 years	22,478	19,294	2,220	341	827	50	1,641
75 years or older	17,671	15,594	1,369	207	604	33	1,146
Supplemental Security Income recipients (thous.)[1] . .	**6,433**	**4,312**	**1,689**	**237**	**340**	**24**	**1,035**
Sex							
Male.	2,814	1,863	737	120	160	10	443
Female	3,619	2,449	952	117	180	14	593
Age							
15-54 years	3,112	2,140	832	136	94	11	531
55-64 years	1,861	1,267	523	58	38	9	228
65-74 years	884	577	215	30	78	2	166
75 years or older	576	327	119	13	129	2	111
Average annual benefit in 2016 (dollars)							
Social Security	$14,956	$15,219	$13,269	$13,630	$14,085	$14,800	$12,855
Supplemental Security Income.	8,024	8,083	7,986	7,531	7,639	NA	8,112

NA = Not available. **Note:** Race categories include people who reported being of that race, alone or in combination with another race. Persons of Hispanic origin may be of any race. The sum of the individual categories may not add up to totals because of rounding and because the totals include persons who reported being of more than one race. (1) Persons 15 or older receiving Social Security benefits or Supplemental Security Income in Mar. 2017.

Old-Age, Survivors, and Disability Insurance Beneficiaries, 2017

Source: Social Security Administration

State or area	Total benefits (thous.)	Total beneficiaries	Old-Age Retired workers	Spouses	Children	Survivors Widow(er)s and parents	Children	Disability Disabled workers	Spouses	Children
Alabama	$1,400,427	1,131,359	689,297	31,913	12,217	80,509	43,060	226,922	3,173	44,268
Alaska	121,533	98,359	68,478	3,055	1,959	5,400	4,549	12,317	165	2,436
Arizona	1,746,234	1,310,666	952,601	47,880	14,278	77,435	35,842	153,257	2,158	27,215
Arkansas	830,219	692,178	429,232	17,070	7,121	45,993	25,405	137,228	1,884	28,245
California	7,491,481	5,858,780	4,178,940	294,073	79,288	368,871	155,695	663,886	11,090	106,937
Colorado	1,120,025	852,635	614,191	35,231	7,818	51,119	23,422	102,531	1,154	17,169
Connecticut	965,243	673,359	491,627	22,079	7,304	37,659	18,552	81,260	735	14,143
Delaware	292,089	206,939	149,880	5,831	1,659	11,760	5,900	27,255	230	4,424
Dist. of Columbia	100,521	82,253	55,991	2,063	809	4,316	3,142	14,284	40	1,608
Florida	5,893,710	4,531,636	3,285,889	156,378	46,010	270,505	111,325	558,750	7,621	95,158
Georgia	2,265,765	1,790,398	1,198,814	48,983	19,711	114,324	67,086	282,646	3,788	55,046
Hawaii	349,396	266,523	206,148	9,286	3,805	14,924	6,149	21,813	392	4,006
Idaho	425,395	335,551	236,546	11,811	3,749	19,624	9,644	44,432	776	8,969
Illinois	2,945,046	2,220,171	1,554,889	83,553	24,454	150,740	70,524	282,120	3,967	49,924
Indiana	1,783,599	1,335,288	898,109	40,713	13,130	89,739	46,711	205,562	2,725	38,599
Iowa	833,681	638,322	459,104	20,987	6,167	42,529	18,332	77,521	807	12,875
Kansas	724,781	544,486	380,624	17,825	5,693	34,869	17,736	73,174	770	13,795
Kentucky	1,180,750	980,991	582,792	33,522	9,606	76,625	37,634	199,178	4,039	37,595
Louisiana	1,051,210	895,826	523,785	42,042	10,647	85,355	42,498	156,107	3,334	32,058
Maine	409,151	338,770	227,434	10,443	3,274	19,983	8,723	57,062	650	11,201
Maryland	1,350,720	983,736	700,145	32,051	9,558	57,916	32,370	129,481	899	21,316
Massachusetts	1,666,537	1,260,786	857,073	43,452	13,508	69,828	34,822	199,966	1,627	40,510
Michigan	2,973,455	2,186,709	1,461,584	75,825	23,437	144,376	69,308	341,200	5,371	65,608
Minnesota	1,367,867	1,012,620	738,425	34,681	10,070	57,628	26,053	122,142	1,076	22,545
Mississippi	783,103	661,656	404,846	15,849	8,558	47,102	30,318	127,181	1,995	25,807
Missouri	1,622,354	1,281,534	852,684	36,073	12,032	83,159	44,075	213,655	2,555	37,301
Montana	284,093	228,685	165,558	7,771	2,478	14,219	6,619	27,274	432	4,334
Nebraska	441,818	340,251	243,248	11,762	3,354	22,195	10,415	41,249	348	7,680
Nevada	676,447	521,297	380,627	15,321	5,555	28,645	14,163	65,664	780	10,542
New Hampshire	410,794	300,267	206,986	8,854	2,560	14,973	7,287	47,738	360	11,509
New Jersey	2,320,979	1,613,096	1,159,770	59,221	18,569	95,826	44,042	196,663	2,452	36,553
New Mexico	515,558	427,426	286,641	16,736	4,468	27,091	15,139	64,863	935	11,553
New York	4,796,830	3,586,883	2,492,314	142,605	45,080	215,210	97,306	493,907	6,980	93,481
North Carolina	2,667,042	2,059,436	1,428,433	49,169	19,284	118,443	63,794	320,583	3,742	55,988
North Dakota	163,330	130,831	93,384	4,992	1,115	10,347	4,358	14,114	135	2,386
Ohio	2,960,684	2,337,114	1,545,251	91,232	20,661	183,442	81,236	351,027	5,037	59,228
Oklahoma	969,564	778,970	509,843	24,428	8,300	56,331	29,486	125,634	1,835	23,113
Oregon	1,121,563	853,498	619,159	30,125	9,028	50,331	19,336	107,703	1,591	16,225
Pennsylvania	3,736,283	2,795,950	1,922,759	96,591	24,932	192,678	81,091	400,818	5,191	71,890
Rhode Island	291,888	222,851	152,898	5,523	2,438	11,680	5,757	37,133	287	7,135
South Carolina	1,453,284	1,115,313	765,602	27,468	10,502	67,759	36,189	174,597	2,215	30,981
South Dakota	217,929	175,389	128,614	5,661	1,541	11,535	5,447	18,994	156	3,441
Tennessee	1,809,413	1,431,690	936,131	41,816	14,141	95,747	50,669	245,370	3,491	44,325
Texas	5,147,432	4,126,055	2,723,111	200,562	48,018	316,553	149,101	562,264	10,208	116,238
Utah	520,196	395,718	273,509	19,849	5,038	23,415	16,120	46,926	706	10,155
Vermont	191,324	147,683	102,755	4,890	1,555	8,092	3,573	22,203	205	4,410
Virginia	1,993,263	1,501,543	1,044,208	51,413	14,785	94,684	44,631	210,694	2,766	38,362
Washington	1,794,759	1,319,176	936,179	52,595	14,275	76,818	32,114	176,269	2,229	28,697
West Virginia	587,227	473,398	279,813	22,540	5,215	42,446	17,493	87,754	2,730	15,407
Wisconsin	1,620,596	1,212,439	869,996	34,385	11,766	70,345	33,176	160,916	1,629	30,226
Wyoming	145,818	109,624	79,169	3,575	993	6,775	3,485	13,320	173	2,134
American Samoa	4,508	6,214	2,456	203	246	603	777	1,281	45	603
Guam	15,271	17,724	10,992	1,071	597	1,535	1,237	1,624	68	600
Northern Mariana Islands	1,950	2,955	1,693	130	184	305	330	234	9	70
Puerto Rico	710,441	817,745	455,831	60,235	10,792	73,186	25,668	156,044	5,850	30,139
U.S. Virgin Islands	24,986	21,794	16,526	930	447	1,278	668	1,545	45	355
Foreign countries	441,331	659,454	413,428	111,194	11,473	95,593	14,151	10,027	500	3,088
Unknown	1,684	1,360	980	59	9	155	24	113	3	17
All areas	79,732,580	61,903,360	42,446,992	2,375,575	675,261	4,090,523	1,903,757	8,695,475	126,154	1,589,623

Outcomes of Applications for Disability Benefits, 2000-15

Source: Social Security Administration

Year of application	Total	Pending final decision	Technical denial[1]	Medical denials Medical	Subsequent nonmedical[2]	Medical allowances Awards	Subsequent denials[2]	Award rate[3]	Allowance rate[4]
1999	1,265,037	0	104,332	445,995	4,056	708,797	1,857	56.0%	61.3%
2000	1,364,323	0	136,054	456,467	3,817	766,047	1,938	56.1	62.6
2005	2,087,733	0	528,760	642,170	6,964	907,877	1,962	43.5	58.4
2006	2,164,394	0	611,199	653,256	7,270	890,752	1,917	41.2	57.5
2007	2,216,564	0	651,759	641,906	7,914	913,167	1,818	41.2	58.5
2008	2,358,629	0	717,160	661,044	9,024	969,623	1,778	41.1	59.2
2009	2,753,012	4,100	845,280	786,108	10,691	1,104,985	1,848	40.2	58.2
2010	2,981,613	5,980	978,727	857,269	19,112	1,118,449	2,076	37.6	56.2
2011	2,952,087	10,416	982,064	866,486	20,813	1,070,241	2,067	36.4	54.8
2012	2,955,922	26,864	1,024,683	849,946	23,956	1,028,187	2,286	35.1	54.2
2013	2,790,682	117,452	970,984	749,185	25,392	925,409	2,260	34.6	54.6
2014	2,682,401	342,623	938,339	625,139	29,154	744,849	2,297	31.8	53.4
2015	2,505,290	393,292	901,422	573,186	28,138	607,175	2,077	28.7	50.4

Note: Data as of mid-2016. Applications for more recent years may still be pending; award and allowance rates will change. Does not include Supplemental Security Income-only applications. (1) Application denied for non-medical reason. (2) Denied for non-medical reasons after medical criteria were adjudicated. (3) Percent of all applications, minus pending claims, in which benefits were awarded. (4) Percent of all medical decisions that resulted in an allowance.

OASDI Recipients and Monthly Payments, 1940-2017

Source: Social Security Administration

Year	Total recipients	Monthly benefits Total (thous.)	Avg.[1]	Avg. (2017 dollars)[2]	Year	Total recipients	Monthly benefits Total (thous.)	Avg.[1]	Avg. (2017 dollars)[2]
1940	222,488	$4,070	$18.29	$309.91	1995	43,387,259	$28,148,078	$648.76	$1,035.03
1945	1,288,107	23,801	18.48	244.06	2000	45,414,794	34,848,920	767.35	1,085.54
1950	3,477,243	126,857	36.48	360.3	2005	48,434,445	44,351,772	915.71	1,145.63
1955	7,960,616	411,613	51.71	458.45	2010	54,032,097	58,048,364	1,074.33	1,200.28
1960	14,844,589	936,321	63.07	506.51	2011	55,404,480	62,213,382	1,122.89	1,211.44
1965	20,866,767	1,516,802	72.69	547.73	2012	56,758,185	65,430,104	1,152.79	1,218.13
1970	26,228,629	2,628,326	100.21	613.53	2013	57,978,610	68,544,382	1,182.24	1,232.39
1975	32,085,372	5,727,903	178.52	787.92	2014	59,007,158	71,693,353	1,214.99	1,247.78
1980	35,618,840	10,694,022	300.23	865.01	2015	59,963,425	73,642,029	1,228.12	1,266.49
1985	37,058,353	15,901,643	429.10	958.92	2016	60,907,307	75,917,962	1,246.45	1,272.94
1990	39,832,125	21,686,763	544.45	1,008.07	2017	61,903,360	79,732,580	1,288.02	1,288.02

OASDI = Old-Age, Survivors, and Disability Insurance. **Note:** Disability insurance payments began in 1957. (1) Avg. monthly benefit does not necessarily reflect individual payments to OASDI recipients. (2) Adjusted for inflation.

Social Security Trust Funds

Source: Social Security Administration

Old-Age and Survivors Insurance (OASI) Trust Fund, 1940-2017

(in millions)

Fiscal year[1]	Total	INCOME Net payroll tax contribs.	Income from taxing benefits	General fund reimburse-ments[2]	Net interest[3]	DISBURSEMENTS Total	Benefit pymts.[4]	Admin. expenses	Transfers to Railroad Retirement program	Net increase in fund[5]	Year-end balance
1940	$592	$550	—	—	$42	$28	$16	$12	—	$564	$1,745
1950	2,367	2,106	—	$4	257	784	727	57	—	1,583	12,893
1960	10,360	9,843	—	—	517	11,073	10,270	202	$600	−713	20,829
1970	31,746	29,955	—	442	1,350	27,321	26,268	474	579	4,425	32,616
1980	100,051	97,608	—	557	1,886	103,228	100,626	1,160	1,442	−3,177	24,566
1990	278,607	260,069	$2,924	1,471	14,143	223,481	218,948	1,564	2,969	55,126	203,445
1995	326,067	289,525	5,114	11	31,417	294,456	288,607	1,797	4,052	31,611	447,946
2000	484,228	418,219	12,476	1	53,532	353,396	347,868	1,990	3,538	130,832	893,003
2005	599,992	502,998	15,332	—	81,662	436,919	430,439	2,900	3,579	163,073	1,615,623
2008	692,873	573,750	16,396	—	102,727	509,864	502,973	3,259	3,632	183,009	2,150,052
2009	697,326	571,228	18,967	—	107,131	551,542	544,484	3,369	3,690	145,784	2,295,835
2010	682,448	552,037	21,068	737	108,606	579,907	572,515	3,462	3,930	102,541	2,398,377
2011	692,510	495,031	21,174	68,886	107,419	599,232	591,477	3,645	4,110	93,278	2,491,654
2012	728,981	500,661	27,150	95,927	105,243	634,700	627,208	3,352	4,139	94,281	2,585,936
2013	739,668	589,976	23,144	26,433	100,115	670,554	663,195	3,410	3,948	69,114	2,655,049
2014	763,295	642,256	24,641	126	96,271	705,645	698,235	3,153	4,257	57,650	2,712,699
2015	795,319	672,246	29,627	211	93,235	741,464	733,711	3,496	4,258	53,855	2,766,554
2016	799,892	679,566	31,121	138	89,067	769,827	762,122	3,417	4,287	30,066	2,796,620
2017	822,442	702,123	35,416	15	84,888	798,961	791,094	3,551	4,316	23,481	2,820,101

— = Not applicable. **Note:** Numbers may not add up to totals due to rounding. (1) Fiscal years 1977 and later consist of the 12 months ending on Sept. 30 of each year. Fiscal years prior to 1977 consisted of the 12 months ending on June 30 of each year. (2) Includes reimbursements from the general fund of the Treasury to the OASI Trust Fund for certain legislated measures since 1957. (3) Includes net profits or losses on marketable investments. Beginning in 1967, the trust fund paid administrative expenses on an estimated basis, with a final adjustment including interest made in the following fiscal year. Net interest includes these interest adjustments. Beginning in Oct. 1973, figures include relatively small gifts to the fund. (4) Beginning in 1967, includes payments for vocational rehabilitation services furnished to disabled persons receiving benefits because of their disabilities; beginning in 1983, includes reimbursements paid from the general fund to the trust fund for unnegotiated benefit checks. (5) Net change in assets during fiscal year, including amounts borrowed or repaid by other funds.

Disability Insurance (DI) Trust Fund, 1960-2017

(in millions)

Fiscal year[1]	Total	INCOME Net payroll tax contribs.	Income from taxing benefits	General fund reimburse-ments[2]	Net interest[3]	DISBURSEMENTS Total	Benefit pymts.[4]	Admin. expenses	Transfers to Railroad Retirement program	Net increase in fund[5]	Year-end balance
1960	$1,034	$987	—	—	$47	$533	$528	$32	−$27	$501	$2,167
1970	4,380	4,141	—	$16	223	2,954	2,795	149	10	1,426	5,104
1980	17,376	16,805	—	118	453	15,320	14,998	334	−12	2,056	7,680
1990	28,215	27,154	$158	138	766	25,124	24,327	717	80	3,091	11,455
1995	70,209	67,986	335	—	1,888	41,374	40,234	1,072	68	28,835	35,206
2000	77,023	70,001	756	—	6,266	56,008	54,244	1,608	159	21,014	113,752
2005	96,765	85,418	1,164	—	10,183	86,360	83,721	2,301	338	10,405	193,298
2008	109,816	97,432	1,373	8	11,003	107,153	104,222	2,513	418	2,663	216,239
2009	109,681	97,008	1,841	—	10,832	118,144	115,073	2,623	448	−8,462	207,777
2010	105,513	93,739	1,745	125	9,904	126,344	122,935	2,947	462	−20,831	186,946
2011	106,225	84,031	1,878	11,745	8,571	131,489	127,990	3,034	465	−25,264	161,682
2012	108,845	85,072	383	16,234	7,156	138,546	135,114	2,920	512	−29,701	131,981
2013	111,262	100,169	1,051	4,504	5,538	142,757	139,446	2,760	551	−31,494	100,486
2014	114,105	109,060	1,022	27	3,997	144,667	141,327	2,897	444	−30,562	69,925
2015	117,965	114,156	1,036	39	2,733	146,234	142,923	2,892	419	−28,269	41,656
2016	150,293	147,577	1,181	23	1,512	146,208	143,053	2,779	376	4,084	45,740
2017	169,480	165,901	1,951	3	1,625	145,776	142,883	2,686	207	23,704	69,444

— = Not applicable. **Note:** Numbers may not add up to totals due to rounding. (1) Fiscal years 1977 and later consist of the 12 months ending on Sept. 30 of each year. Fiscal years prior to 1977 consisted of the 12 months ending on June 30 of each year. (2) Includes reimbursements from the general fund of the Treasury to the DI Trust Fund for certain legislated measures since 1957. (3) Includes net profits or losses on marketable investments. Beginning in 1967, the trust fund paid administrative expenses on an estimated basis, with a final adjustment including interest made in the following fiscal year. Net interest includes these interest adjustments. The 1970 report describes the accounting for administrative expenses for years prior to 1967. Beginning in July 1974, figures include relatively small gifts to the fund. (4) Beginning in 1967, includes payments for vocational rehabilitation services furnished to persons receiving benefits because of a disability; beginning in 1983, includes reimbursements paid from the general fund to the trust fund for unnegotiated benefit checks. (5) Net change in assets during fiscal year, including amounts borrowed or repaid by other funds.

Supplementary Medical Insurance Trust Fund (Medicare SMI), 1975-2017

Source: Centers for Medicare & Medicaid Services, U.S. Dept. of Health and Human Services

(in millions)

Fiscal year[1]	INCOME					DISBURSEMENTS			Net change	Year-end balance
	Total	Premium from participants[2]	Govt. contribs.[3]	Transfers from states[4]	Interest and other income[5,6]	Total	Benefit pymts.[6,7,8]	Admin. expenses		
1975	$4,322	$1,887	$2,330	—	$106	$4,170	$3,765	$404	$152	$1,424
1980	10,275	2,928	6,932	—	416	10,737	10,144	593	−462	4,532
1990	46,138	11,494	33,210	—	1,434	43,022	41,498	1,524	3,115	14,527
2000	89,239	20,515	65,561	—	3,164	88,992	87,212[9]	1,780	247	45,896
2005	152,505	35,939	115,200	—	1,366	152,735	149,820[10]	2,914	−230	16,885
2008	244,872	54,158[11]	180,434	7,042	3,238	224,869	221,445[11,12]	3,423	20,003	59,149
2009	262,573	57,709[11]	194,267	7,504	3,093	260,257	256,938[11]	3,318	2,317	61,466
2010	282,734	61,364[11]	213,709	4,493	3,168	272,224	268,710[11]	3,514	10,510	71,976
2011	301,523	64,502[11]	225,178	6,536	5,307	300,672	296,842[11]	3,830	851	72,827
2012	290,864	66,067[11]	210,508	8,324	5,965	291,907	287,777[11]	4,130	−1,043	71,783
2013	313,158	71,300[11]	227,208	8,666	5,985	315,123	311,367[11]	3,756	−1,965	69,818
2014	334,943	75,887[11]	244,351	8,727	5,978	333,438	329,141[11]	4,297	1,504	71,323
2015	357,531	79,399[11]	263,484	8,797	5,851	359,412	355,807[11]	3,606	−1,882	69,441
2016	400,635	86,074[11]	299,491	9,755	5,315	403,888	399,468[11]	4,421	−3,254	66,187
2017	422,439	94,791[11]	309,647	11,072	6,928	414,119	409,258[11]	4,861	8,319	74,506

— = Not applicable. **Note:** Numbers may not add up to totals because of rounding. (1) Fiscal year 1975 ended June 30, 1975; fiscal years 1980 ended on Sept. 30 of each year. (2) For Part D, premiums include both amounts withheld from Social Security benefits (and certain other federal benefit payments) and amounts paid directly to Part D plans (estimated). (3) For Part D, includes matching payments from the general fund, plus certain interest-adjustment items. For Part B, includes all federal govt. transfers. (4) As of 2006, Medicaid was no longer the primary payer for full-benefit dual eligibles; states paid 90% of estimated costs in 2006, phasing down over a 10-year period to 75% in 2015 and after. (5) Other income includes recoveries of amounts reimbursed from the trust fund that are not trust fund obligations and other miscellaneous income. In 2008, includes an adjustment of $812 mil for interest inadvertently unearned as a result of Hospital Insurance (HI) hospice costs misallocated to, and paid from, the Part B account of the SMI trust fund May 2005-Sept. 2007. (6) Values after 2005 include additional premiums for Medicare Advantage (MA) plans that are deducted from beneficiaries' Social Security benefits, transferred to HI and SMI trust funds, and then transferred to the plans. (7) Includes costs of Peer Review Organizations in 1983-2001 and costs of Quality Review Organizations beginning in 2002. (8) For Part D, includes payments to plans, subsidies to employer-sponsored retiree drug plans, payments to states for low-income eligibility determinations, and Part D drug premiums (the amount collected from beneficiaries and transferred to plans and an estimated amount for premiums paid directly by enrollees to plans). Includes amounts for transitional assistance benefits in 2004-06. (9) Benefit payments less monies transferred from the HI trust fund for home health agency costs. (10) Certain HI hospice costs were misallocated to, and paid from, the Part B account of the SMI trust fund. See also footnote 12. (11) Includes an estimated $1.804 bil (2006), $2.295 bil (2007), $2.970 bil (2008), $3.699 bil (2009), $4.221 bil (2010), $4.843 bil (2011), $5.222 bil (2012), $6.306 bil (2013), $7.450 bil (2014), $8.465 bil (2015), $9.095 bil (2016), and $10.173 bil (2017) for premiums paid directly to Part D plans. (12) Benefit payments were $229.9 bil; amount shown includes transfer of $8.5 bil from the general fund of the Treasury to the Part B account of the SMI trust fund for HI hospice costs that were misallocated to, and paid from, the Part B account from May 2005 to Sept. 2007. (The HI trust fund, in turn, transferred $8.5 bil to the general fund.)

Hospital Insurance Trust Fund (Medicare HI), 1975-2017

Source: Centers for Medicare & Medicaid Services, U.S. Dept. of Health and Human Services

(in millions)

Fiscal year[1]	INCOME								DISBURSEMENTS			Net change	Year-end balance
	Total	Payroll taxes	Taxation of benefits	Transfers from Railroad Retirement acct.	Reimb. for uninsured persons	Premiums from voluntary enrollees	Pymts. for military wage credits	Interest and other income[2,3]	Total	Benefit pymts.[3,4]	Admin. expenses[5]		
1975	$12,568	$11,291	—	$132	$481	$6	$48	$609	$10,612	$10,353	$259	$1,956	$9,870
1980	25,415	23,244	—	244	697	17	141	1,072	24,288	23,790	497	1,127	14,490
1990	79,563	70,655	—	367	413	113	107	7,908	66,687	65,912	774	12,876	95,631
2000	159,681	137,738	$8,787	465	470	1,392	2	10,827	130,284	127,934[6]	2,350	29,397	168,084
2005	196,921	168,954	8,765	445	286	2,303	0	16,168	184,142	181,292[7]	2,850	12,779	277,723
2008	229,729	197,195	11,733	526	506	2,913	0	16,856	230,240	227,008[8]	3,231	−511	319,000
2009	228,915	194,102	12,376	524	614	2,817	968[9]	17,514	238,000	234,659	3,343	−9,086	309,914
2010	218,004	183,603	13,760	535	−142	3,314	0	16,933	248,978	245,650	3,328	−30,975	278,939
2011	226,486	192,063	15,143	477	275	3,273	0	15,255	259,628	255,717	3,911	−33,142	245,797
2012	241,730	204,752	18,643	511	262	3,400	0	14,162	258,155	254,459	3,696	−16,425	229,372
2013	243,560	212,901	14,310	577	0	3,397	0	12,375	266,546	262,411	4,135	−22,986	206,386
2014	262,753	227,579	18,066	612	432	3,259	0	12,805	266,853	262,520	4,332	−4,100	202,286
2015	272,359	237,697	20,208	595	187	3,277	0	10,396	278,736	273,248	5,488	−6,377	195,909
2016	287,106	250,472	23,022	657	158	3,232	0	9,566	290,648	285,574	5,075	−3,542	192,367
2017	298,524	259,740	24,206	637	147	3,232	0	10,302	293,265	290,279	2,986	5,259	197,626

— = Not applicable. **Note:** Numbers may not add up to totals because of rounding. (1) Fiscal year 1975 ended June 30, 1975; fiscal years 1980 and later ended Sept. 30 of each year. (2) Other income includes recoveries of amounts reimbursed from the trust fund that are not trust fund obligations, receipts from the fraud and abuse control program, and other small amounts of miscellaneous income. In 2008, includes an adjustment of −$853 mil for interest inadvertently earned as a result of HI hospice costs that were misallocated to, and paid from, the Part B account of the Supplementary Medical Insurance (SMI) trust fund from May 2005 to Sept. 2007. (3) Values after 2005 include additional premiums for Medicare Advantage (MA) plans that are deducted from beneficiaries' Social Security benefits, transferred to the HI and SMI trust funds, and then transferred to the plans. (4) Includes costs of Peer Review Organizations from 1983 through 2001 (beginning with implementation of the Prospective Payment System on Oct. 1, 1983), and costs of Quality Improvement Organizations beginning in 2002. (5) Includes costs of experiments and demonstration projects. Beginning in 1997, includes fraud and abuse control expenses. (6) Includes monies transferred to the SMI trust fund for home health agency costs. (7) Certain HI hospice costs were misallocated to, and paid from, the Part B account of the SMI trust fund. (8) Benefit payments were $218.525 bil. Amount shown includes transfer of $8.484 bil to the general fund of the Treasury for HI hospice costs that were misallocated to, and paid from, the Part B account of the SMI trust fund from May 2005 to Sept. 2007. (The general fund, in turn, transferred $8.484 bil to the Part B account of the SMI trust fund.) (9) Includes the lump-sum general revenue adjustment of −$968 mil.

TAXES

Federal Personal Income Tax Return Facts, 2018

Source: George W. Smith IV, CPA, Managing Partner, George W. Smith & Company, P.C.

Deadlines. The deadline for filing a 2018 U.S. individual income tax return (1040, 1040A, or 1040EZ) is Apr. 15, 2019.

Extensions. Taxpayers who cannot file a 2018 individual income tax return by the deadline can apply for a six-month extension to Oct. 15, 2019. To qualify for an extension, Form 4868 must be filed no later than Apr. 17, 2019.

E-Filing. The electronic filing program began as a pilot program in 1986; by 2011, 1 bil individual tax returns had been e-filed. As of Aug. 31, 2018, 129.9 mil returns for income tax year 2017 had been e-filed, compared to 127.3 mil as of Sept. 1, 2017.

Penalties. The IRS can levy two potential penalties after the filing due date when there is a balance owed. One penalty is for failing to file a timely tax return; the other is for failure to pay the tax when due. In addition, interest is charged on any unpaid tax balance.

Refunds. As of Aug. 31, 2018, the average refund for the 2018 tax filing season was $2,793, up from $2,782 in the previous tax year. The IRS refunded $303.8 bil, of which $262.4 bil was refunded with direct deposit.

Statute of limitations. Taxpayers who have not yet filed their 2015 federal tax return have until three years after the deadline to file and claim their refund. After that date, any refunds for 2015 income tax or withholding tax, including the earned income tax credit, will be lost.

Federal Income Tax Rates for Taxable-Income Brackets, 2018

Tax rate	Unmarried individuals	Married filing jointly or surviving spouses	Married filing separately	Head of household other than surviving spouses
10%	$0 to $9,525	$0 to $19,050	$0 to $9,525	$0 to $13,600
12%	$9,526 to $38,700	$19,051 to $77,400	$9,526 to $38,700	$13,601 to $51,800
22%	$38,701 to $82,500	$77,401 to $165,000	$38,701 to $82,500	$51,801 to $82,500
24%	$82,501 to $157,500	$165,001 to $315,000	$82,501 to $157,500	$82,501 to $157,500
32%	$157,501 to $200,000	$315,001 to $400,000	$157,501 to $200,000	$157,501 to $200,000
35%	$200,001 to $500,000	$400,001 to $600,000	$200,001 to $300,000	$200,001 to $500,000
37%	Over $500,000	Over $600,000	Over $300,000	Over $500,000

Standard Deduction, 2018

The standard deduction is a flat amount subtracted from the adjusted gross income of taxpayers who do not itemize deductions.

Single	$12,000
Married filing jointly or qualifying widow(er)	$24,000
Married filing separately	$12,000
Head of household	$18,000

Additional standard deduction. Elderly and/or blind, single or head of household: $1,600. Elderly and/or blind, married: $1,300.

Dependents. An individual reported as a dependent on another person's tax return generally may claim the greater of (1) $1,050 or (2) the sum of $350 plus the individual's earned income, not to exceed the standard deduction.

Personal exemption. The deduction for personal exemptions was suspended until Jan. 1, 2026, under the Tax Cuts and Jobs Act of 2018. In 2017, it was $4,050 (phased out at higher incomes).

FICA and self-employment tax. For Social Security, wages are taxable up to $128,400. For Medicare, all wages are taxable.

Common Income Tax Errors

Periodically, the IRS issues a list of the most commonly made income tax errors.

1. Wrong or missing Social Security numbers.
2. Wrong names.
3. Filing status errors, such as Head of Household instead of Single.
4. Math mistakes, for example, when adding or subtracting items on a form or worksheet.
5. Errors in credits or deductions, like the Earned Income Tax Credit, Child and Dependent Care Credit, and standard deductions.
6. Wrong bank and/or account numbers for direct deposit of any tax refund.
7. Forms not signed or dated. An unsigned tax return is not valid. Both spouses must sign a joint return.
8. E-file PIN errors. E-filed returns can be signed electronically with a personal identification number (PIN). Usually, last year's PIN can be used, but if it is unknown, adjusted gross income information from last year's original return needs to be entered for verification.

Retirement Savings Plans and Income Tax

401(k) plan. The maximum amount that an individual can contribute to a 401(k) plan for 2018 is $18,500. Individuals born before 1969 can put away an additional $6,000, for a total of $24,500.

IRAs. Contributions to IRAs and Roth IRAs were limited to $5,500 in 2018. Anyone born before 1969 can contribute an extra $1,000. Funds may be deposited into a traditional IRA for 2018 until Apr. 15, 2019. Contributions after Apr. 15 will automatically be considered funds deposited for 2019.

Roth IRA. Contributions paid into a Roth IRA are not tax deductible. Distributions of funds including investment earnings held in the account for five years or longer and distributed after age 59½ are free of both income tax and the 10% early-withdrawal penalty. Withdrawals from the account in less than five years can be subject to tax and a 10% withdrawal penalty regardless of age. There are income limitations on contributions.

Distributions. There is a 10% penalty for IRA distributions before age 59½. Distributions paid to a beneficiary due to disability/death of the owner are not subject to this penalty, nor are payments used for certain unreimbursed medical expenses, higher-education expenses, or first-time homebuyer acquisition costs (up to $10,000).

The owner of a traditional IRA (or a SIMPLE plan, pension, or profit-sharing plan account) must begin receiving distributions by Apr. 1 of the calendar year following the year in which he or she reaches age 70½. Any employee who works beyond 70½ and is not a 5% or more owner of the business can continue to defer profit-sharing and pension plan distributions.

Tax Credits

A tax deduction reduces a taxpayer's taxable income whereas tax credits reduce the amount of tax owed.

Adoption credit. The adoption credit in 2018 for qualified expenses is $13,840. The credit limit is per person, not per year, and is adjusted annually for inflation. The credit is not refundable and phases out for taxpayers at higher income levels.

American Opportunity Tax Credit. This education credit provides up to $2,500 per student per year in the first four years of a student's postsecondary education.

Child and dependent care credit. This credit is for expenses for the care of taxpayers' qualifying children under age 13 or care of a disabled spouse or dependent, while the taxpayer works or looks for work.

Child tax credit. The maximum child tax credit is $2,000 for each qualifying child.

Earned Income Credit. Lower-income workers who maintain a household may be eligible for an Earned Income Credit. This credit is based on total earned income such as wages, commissions, and tips. Military personnel can include tax-free combat pay in income to compute the credit.

Energy credits. There are many energy-related credits—from the purchase of an alternative fuel vehicle and the installation of solar/fuel cell property in a residence, to the production of biodiesel or ethanol.

Alternative Minimum Tax

The Alternative Minimum Tax (AMT) was established in 1969 to prevent individuals with very high incomes from using special tax breaks to pay little or no tax. The AMT 2018 exemption for a single taxpayer is $70,300 and $109,400 for married filing jointly. For married taxpayers filing separate returns, the exemption is $54,700.

Estate and Gift Taxes

Estate tax. The Tax Relief Act of 2010 reinstated the estate tax with a 35% flat rate and increased the exemptions to $5 mil in 2011 and $5.12 mil in 2012. The estate tax rate was increased to 40% for 2013 and subsequent years. The Tax Cuts and Jobs Act of 2017 set the 2018 exemption at $11.18 mil per person, $22.36 mil for married couples.

Gifting. For 2018 U.S. citizens, residents, and nonresident aliens have an annual gift tax exclusion of up to $15,000 per individual to as many individuals as he or she chooses. For married couples the exclusion is $30,000, even if only one spouse does all the gifting.

International property. All property owned worldwide by American citizens is subject to U.S. estate tax rules and regulations.

Resident aliens. Aliens residing in the U.S. are subject to the same rules as American citizens.

Tax Rates for Estates and Trusts

If taxable income is—	The tax is—
Not over $2,550	10% of the taxable income
Over $2,550 but not over $9,150	$255.00 plus 24% of the excess over $2,550
Over $9,150 but not over $12,500	$1,839.00 plus 35% of the excess over $9,150
Over $12,500	$3,011.50 plus 37% of the excess over $12,500

Taxable Social Security Benefits

Earnings limitations. Social Security recipients who have not reached their full retirement age of 66 in 2018 will lose $1 of their benefits for every $2 of earned income over $17,040. Recipients who reached full retirement age in 2018 will not lose any benefits if they earned $45,360 or less. Recipients will have to pay back some benefits if their income exceeded that amount.

Taxable benefits. Up to 50% of Social Security benefits may be taxable if the person's total income is more than $25,000 but less than $34,000 for a single individual, head of household, qualifying widow(er), or a married person who is filing separately if spouses lived apart all year; or more than $32,000 but less than $44,000 for married individuals filing jointly. For higher incomes, 85% of Social Security benefits may become taxable.

If the only income received during the year was Social Security, these benefits are not taxable, and the recipient probably does not have to file a tax return.

Retention of Income Tax Records

Federal tax returns generally can be audited for up to three years after filing or six years if the IRS suspects underreported income, so it's wise to keep copies of an income tax return and records for at least seven years after filing a return.

Tax Audits

Audit odds. The IRS audit rate for individual income tax returns in fiscal year 2017 was 0.62%. The odds of an audit generally trend upward with higher taxpayer income, especially on certain types of income. For taxpayers with incomes of $50,000-$75,000, the audit rate was 0.48%. For taxpayers with gross income of $1 mil-$5 mil, the rate was 3.52%. The audit rate was 0.59% for all incomes under $200,000. Most taxpayers have no reason to be concerned about being audited.

The audit selection process is not random. It is based on a set of formulas that are designed to spot questionable returns. If the IRS concludes that a person owes more tax, and he or she disagrees with the findings, the taxpayer can meet with a supervisor.

If the taxpayer still does not agree, he or she can appeal to a separate Appeals Office or take it to the U.S. Tax Court, Federal District Court, or the U.S. Court of Federal Claims.

Tax Court. The U.S. Tax Court is a federal court where taxpayers can dispute tax deficiencies as determined by the Commissioner of Internal Revenue before payment of the disputed amounts. The Tax Court is composed of presidentially appointed members. Many taxpayers choose the Tax Court because they are not required to pay the contested tax up front.

Appeals. For more information about audits, call the IRS at (800) TAX-FORM (829-3676) for its free Publication 556, *Examination of Returns, Appeal Rights, and Claims for Refund* or visit www.irs.gov.

IRS Contact Information

Website: www.irs.gov
Tax questions: (800) 829-1040
Forms/publications: (800) TAX-FORM (829-3676)
Taxpayers can view and download tax forms and publications in Spanish from www.irs.gov/es/spanish/. The IRS site also offers help in Chinese, Korean, Vietnamese, and Russian.

Hearing impaired: (800) 829-4059 (TTY/TDD)
Additional services: The Volunteer Income Tax Assistance (VITA) program offers free tax help to people who generally make $54,000 or less, persons with disabilities, and taxpayers who speak limited English in preparing their own tax returns. Visit www.irs.gov/individuals/free-tax-return-preparation-for-you-by-volunteers or (800) 829-1040.

Report wrongdoing: Report misconduct, waste, fraud, or abuse by an IRS employee to the Treasury Inspector General for Tax Administration at (800) 366-4484 or complaints@tigta.treas.gov.

Working With a Tax Preparer

The following are some suggestions when using a tax preparer:

- **Choose** wisely. Regulations require all paid tax return preparers including attorneys, certified public accountants, and IRS-enrolled agents to have a Preparer Tax Identification Number. Check the preparer's qualifications and history. Ask about service fees in advance.

- **Review** last year's tax return. Make note of any changes since then such as marriage, divorce, number of dependents, retirement, job changes, additional income, or new deductions.

- **Organize** your records with income items first, followed by itemized deductions (medical, taxes, interest, and charitable and other miscellaneous deductions), followed by gains, losses, rentals, or other items.

- **Time** spent with your preparer may affect your bill. If you provide disorganized records and deductions, there may be an additional cost to have your tax preparer organize your information.

- **Prepare** a list of questions in advance. Ask about any invoices or bills that you are not sure apply.

- **Alert** your preparer if you're waiting to receive additional information. He or she can begin preparing your tax return and include the missing data later to finalize your return. Amending a return after it is completed may incur additional fees.

- **Review** your tax return before signing it. Ask questions about any item you don't understand. Even though your preparer is required to sign the return, you are responsible for its contents.

Total U.S. Tax Collections by Type of Tax, 1960-2017

Source: *Internal Revenue Service Data Book, 2017*, Internal Revenue Service, U.S. Dept. of the Treasury
(as percent of total gross collection or total income taxes)

Fiscal year	Total IRS collections (bil)[1]	Income taxes				Employment taxes[4]	Estate taxes	Gift taxes	Excise taxes[5]
		Total	Business[2]	Individual[3]	Estate and trust[3]				
1960	$92	73.1%	33.0%	67.0%	—	12.2%	1.6%	0.20%	12.9%
1965	114	69.7	32.7	67.3	—	14.9	2.1	0.25	12.9
1970	196	70.9	25.3	74.7	—	19.1	1.7	0.22	8.1
1975	294	68.8	22.6	77.4	—	23.9	1.5	0.13	5.7
1980	519	69.3	20.1	79.9	—	24.7	1.2	0.04	4.7
1985	743	63.8	16.3	83.7	—	30.3	0.8	0.04	5.0
1990	1,056	61.6	16.9	83.1	—	34.8	0.9	0.20	2.6
1995	1,376	61.8	20.5	79.5	—	33.8	1.0	0.13	3.3
2000	2,097	65.5	17.2	82.8	—	30.5	1.2	0.20	2.6
2005	2,269	62.3	21.7	78.3	—	34.0	1.0	0.09	2.5
2010	2,345	62.0	19.1	80.0	0.8%	35.1	0.7	0.12	2.0
2012	2,524	66.1	16.9	82.2	1.0	31.1	0.5	0.08	2.2
2013	2,855	65.7	16.6	82.1	1.3	31.4	0.5	0.20	2.1
2014	3,064	65.2	17.7	80.8	1.5	31.9	0.6	0.08	2.3
2015	3,303	66.1	17.9	80.6	1.5	31.0	0.5	0.06	2.3
2016	3,333	64.8	16.0	82.6	1.4	32.2	0.6	0.07	2.3
2017	3,417	64.6	15.3	83.3	1.3	32.9	0.6	0.06	1.9

— = Not available. **Note:** Numbers may not add up to totals because of rounding. (1) Credits to taxpayer accounts excluded beginning with fiscal year 2009. (2) Incl. taxes on corporation income and unrelated business income from tax-exempt organizations. (3) Income tax reported for estates and trusts is included in individual income tax in FY1960-2007. Estate and trust income tax is reported separately from FY2008 on. (4) Incl. taxes for Old-Age, Survivors, Disability, and Hospital Insurance; federal unemployment insurance; and Railroad Retirement. (5) Excl. excise taxes collected by the U.S. Customs and Border Protection and the Alcohol and Tobacco Tax and Trade Bureau. The IRS collected taxes on alcohol and tobacco until FY1988 and taxes on firearms until FY1991.

Taxes Collected by State Governments, 2017

Source: Annual Survey of State Government Tax Collections, U.S. Census Bureau, U.S. Dept. of Commerce
(as percent of total taxes collected or total sales and gross receipts taxes)

State	Total taxes collected in dollars (mil)[1]	Property taxes	Sales and gross receipts taxes			License taxes[3]	Individual income taxes	Corporation net income taxes	Other taxes[4]
			Total	General	Selective[2]				
Alabama	$10,418	3.8%	50.4%	50.6%	49.4%	5.1%	34.8%	5.0%	1.0%
Alaska	1,190	10.2	22.1	—	100.0	11.3	—	7.4	49.0
Arizona	13,889	7.2	61.5	76.9	23.1	3.6	24.8	2.7	0.3
Arkansas	9,516	12.0	49.4	72.0	28.0	4.0	29.1	4.2	1.3
California	155,632	1.7	30.8	73.8	26.2	6.8	54.1	6.5	0.1
Colorado	13,198	—	38.9	58.1	41.9	5.7	51.5	4.0	0.0
Connecticut	16,346	—	40.7	63.7	36.3	2.7	48.7	5.5	2.4
Delaware	3,589	—	15.5	—	100.0	41.9	32.9	6.9	2.8
Dist. of Columbia	7,653	33.1	24.3	76.3	23.7	2.4	25.6	7.2	7.3
Florida	40,218	—	82.9	76.0	24.0	5.1	—	5.9	6.1
Georgia	22,419	4.4	39.3	65.1	34.9	3.0	49.0	4.3	<0.1
Hawaii	7,029	—	62.1	74.2	25.8	3.8	29.8	2.6	1.6
Idaho	4,511	—	49.8	73.5	26.5	8.5	36.8	4.8	0.1
Illinois	37,979	0.2	49.1	61.0	39.0	7.4	34.9	7.6	0.9
Indiana	18,052	0.1	60.4	69.4	30.6	3.8	30.1	5.7	<0.1
Iowa	9,755	<0.1	47.3	69.5	30.5	9.7	37.5	4.4	1.1
Kansas	8,174	8.4	52.6	74.6	25.4	5.2	28.5	4.7	0.6
Kentucky	11,908	6.0	47.4	61.8	38.2	4.2	36.9	3.9	1.6
Louisiana	11,105	0.6	63.2	60.1	39.9	3.3	26.6	2.6	3.7
Maine	4,233	0.9	51.2	66.6	33.4	6.5	36.3	4.1	1.0
Maryland	21,600	3.6	42.8	49.9	50.1	4.0	42.0	4.6	3.0
Massachusetts	27,518	<0.1	32.0	70.8	29.2	4.0	53.5	8.0	2.4
Michigan	28,629	7.4	47.8	67.3	32.7	6.2	33.1	4.2	1.2
Minnesota	25,595	3.3	41.4	55.5	44.5	5.8	42.8	4.8	1.8
Mississippi	7,783	0.4	64.1	70.7	29.3	6.2	23.6	5.2	0.5
Missouri	12,496	0.3	43.2	66.7	33.3	4.7	49.2	2.5	0.1
Montana	2,654	10.3	21.7	—	100.0	12.4	44.4	4.7	6.4
Nebraska	5,103	<0.1	47.2	76.2	23.8	3.6	43.7	5.2	0.4
Nevada	8,625	3.5	80.3	68.7	31.3	7.7	—	—	8.5
New Hampshire	2,497	16.2	38.4	—	100.0	13.2	2.6	23.0	6.5
New Jersey	32,326	<0.1	41.4	71.6	28.4	4.8	43.2	6.5	4.1
New Mexico	5,776	1.4	53.1	73.6	26.4	5.3	23.2	1.6	15.3
New York	79,678	—	31.8	55.7	44.3	2.3	56.0	5.1	4.8
North Carolina	26,855	—	43.6	65.4	34.6	8.3	45.0	2.8	0.3
North Dakota	3,465	0.1	38.9	64.6	35.4	6.2	9.2	1.8	43.8
Ohio	30,306	—	64.6	68.2	31.8	7.6	27.6	<0.1	0.2
Oklahoma	8,569	—	43.9	65.5	34.5	12.4	36.4	1.8	5.4
Oregon	11,915	0.2	13.4	—	100.0	9.0	70.3	5.3	1.8
Pennsylvania	37,853	0.1	51.9	53.5	46.5	5.9	31.9	6.2	4.0
Rhode Island	3,267	0.1	51.8	58.9	41.1	3.4	37.9	4.0	2.9
South Carolina	9,829	0.4	47.2	70.8	29.2	5.3	42.1	3.8	1.2
South Dakota	1,829	—	83.0	70.2	29.8	14.7	—	1.7	0.6
Tennessee	13,894	—	72.1	72.5	27.5	11.8	1.8	12.4	2.0
Texas	53,613	—	87.5	69.3	30.7	6.4	—	—	6.1
Utah	7,833	—	45.1	71.8	28.2	4.1	46.2	4.2	0.4
Vermont	3,128	33.8	33.8	35.5	64.5	4.1	23.8	2.6	1.9
Virginia	22,213	0.1	31.1	57.4	42.6	3.9	58.8	3.7	2.4
Washington	23,998	8.7	79.9	75.7	24.3	6.1	—	—	5.3
West Virginia	5,092	0.1	52.5	49.9	50.1	2.9	35.6	2.3	6.5
Wisconsin	18,133	0.7	44.0	65.5	34.5	6.5	43.0	5.3	0.5
Wyoming	1,650	16.6	46.2	77.2	22.8	9.8	—	—	27.3
United States	**950,533**	**2.0**	**47.6**	**66.5**	**33.5**	**5.8**	**37.1**	**4.8**	**2.7**

— = Tax not collected by state. **Note:** For fiscal year 2017 (July 1, 2016-June 30, 2017) for all states except AL and MI (ends Sept. 30), NY (Mar. 31), and TX (Aug. 31). (1) Incl. taxes not shown separately. (2) Imposed on sales of particular commodities/services, e.g., alcohol and tobacco, motor fuels, public utilities. (3) Related to the exercise of a privilege, such as owning/operating a motor vehicle. (4) Incl. death and gift taxes and severance taxes (on removal of natural resources).

State Government Personal Income Tax Rates, 2018

Source: Reproduced with permission from *CCH State Tax Guide*, published and copyrighted by CCH Inc., a Wolters Kluwer business **Alaska**, **Florida**, **Nevada**, **South Dakota**, **Texas**, **Washington**, and **Wyoming** did not have state income taxes and are thus not listed. Tax rates apply in stages—for example, a single person in Connecticut making $60,000 in taxable income would pay 3% on the first $10,000 of income, 5% on the next $40,000, and 5.5% on the last $10,000. For further details on some states, see notes at end of table.

Alabama
Single, Head of household, or Married filing separately
$0 to $500 . . . . 2%
$501 to $3,000 . . . . 4%
$3,001 and over 5%
Married filing jointly
$0 to $1,000 . . . . 2%
$1,001 to $6,000 . . . . 4%
$6,001 and over 5%

Arizona[1,2,3]
Single or Married filing separately
$0 to $10,346 . . . . 2.59%
$10,347 to $25,861 . . . . . 2.88%
$25,862 to $51,721 . . . . . 3.36%
$51,722 to $155,159 . . . . 4.24%
$155,160 and over 4.54%
Married filing jointly or Head of household
$0 to $20,690 . . . . 2.59%
$20,691 to $51,721 . . . . . 2.88%
$51,722 to $103,440 . . . . 3.36%
$103,441 to $310,317 . . . 4.24%
$310,318 and over 4.54%

Arkansas[2,3]
For net income less than $21,700:
$0 to $4,399 . . . . 0.9%
$4,400 to $8,699 . . . . 2.4%
$8,700 to $13,099 . . . . . . 3.4%
$13,100 to $21,699 . . . . . 4.4%
For net income from $21,700 to $77,400:
$0 to $4,399 . . . . 0.9%
$4,400 to $8,699 . . . . 2.5%
$8,700 to $13,099 . . . . . . 3.5%
$13,100 to $21,699 . . . . . 4.5%
$21,700 to $36,299 . . . . . . 5%
$36,300 and over 6%
For net income over $77,400:
$0 to $4,399 . . . . 0.9%
$4,400 to $8,699 . . . . 2.5%
$8,700 to $13,099 . . . . . . 3.5%
$13,100 to $21,699 . . . . . 4.5%
$21,700 to $36,299 . . . . . . 6%
$36,300 and over 6.9%

California[1,2,3]
Single or Married/registered domestic partner filing separately
$0 to $8,223 . . . . 1%
$8,224 to $19,495 . . . . 2%
$19,496 to $30,769 . . . . . . 4%
$30,770 to $42,711 . . . . . . 6%
$42,712 to $53,980 . . . . . . 8%
$53,981 to $275,738 . . . . 9.3%
$275,739 to $330,884 . . 10.3%
$330,885 to $551,473 . . 11.3%
$551,474 and over 12.3%
Head of household
$0 to $16,457 . . . . 1%
$16,458 to $38,991 . . . . . . 2%
$38,992 to $50,264 . . . . . . 4%
$50,265 to $62,206 . . . . . . 6%
$62,207 to $73,477 . . . . . . 8%
$73,478 to $375,002 . . . . 9.3%
$375,003 to $450,003 . . 10.3%
$450,004 to $750,003 . . 11.3%
$750,004 and over 12.3%
Married/registered domestic partner filing jointly or Qualifying widow(er)
$0 to $16,446 . . . . 1%
$16,447 to $38,990 . . . . . . 2%
$38,991 to $61,538 . . . . . . 4%
$61,539 to $85,422 . . . . . . 6%
$85,423 to $107,960 . . . . . 8%
$107,961 to $551,476 . . . 9.3%
$551,477 to $661,768 . . 10.3%
$661,769 to $1,102,946 11.3%
$1,102,947 and over . . . 12.3%

Colorado
4.63% of federal taxable income

Connecticut
Single or Married filing separately
$0 to $10,000 . . . . 3%
$10,001 to $50,000 . . . . . . 5%
$50,001 to $100,000 . . . . 5.5%
$100,001 to $200,000 . . . . 6%
$200,001 to $250,000 . . . 6.5%
$250,001 to $500,000 . . . 6.9%
$500,001 and over 6.99%
Head of household
$0 to $16,000 . . . . 3%
$16,001 to $80,000 . . . . . . 5%
$80,001 to $160,000 . . . . 5.5%
$160,001 to $320,000 . . . . 6%
$320,001 to $400,000 . . . 6.5%
$400,001 to $800,000 . . . 6.9%
$800,001 and over 6.99%
Married filing jointly or Qualifying widow(er)
$0 to $20,000 . . . . 3%
$20,001 to $100,000 . . . . . 5%
$100,001 to $200,000 . . . 5.5%
$200,001 to $400,000 . . . . 6%
$400,001 to $500,000 . . . 6.5%
$500,001 to $1,000,000 . . 6.9%
$1,000,001 and over 6.99%

Delaware
$0 to $2,000 . . . . 0%
$2,001 to $5,000 . . . . 2.2%
$5,001 to $10,000 . . . . . . 3.9%
$10,001 to $20,000 . . . . . 4.8%
$20,001 to $25,000 . . . . . 5.2%
$25,001 to $60,000 . . . . 5.55%
$60,001 and over 6.6%

District of Columbia
$0 to $10,000 . . . . 4%
$10,001 to $40,000 . . . . . . 6%
$40,001 to $60,000 . . . . . 6.5%
$60,001 to $350,000 . . . . 8.5%
$350,001 to $1,000,000 8.75%
$1,000,001 and over 8.95%

Georgia
Single
$0 to $750 . . . . 1%
$751 to $2,250 . . . . 2%
$2,251 to $3,750 . . . . 3%
$3,751 to $5,250 . . . . 4%
$5,251 to $7,000 . . . . 5%
$7,001 and over 6%
Head of household, Married filing jointly, or Qualifying widow(er)
$0 to $1,000 . . . . 1%
$1,001 to $3,000 . . . . 2%
$3,001 to $5,000 . . . . 3%
$5,001 to $7,000 . . . . 4%
$7,001 to $10,000 . . . . 5%
$10,001 and over 6%
Married filing separately
$0 to $500 . . . . 1%
$501 to $1,500 . . . . 2%
$1,501 to $2,500 . . . . 3%
$2,501 to $3,500 . . . . 4%
$3,501 to $5,000 . . . . 5%
$5,001 and over 6%

Hawaii
Single or Married filing separately
$0 to $2,400 . . . . 1.4%
$2,401 to $4,800 . . . . 3.2%
$4,801 to $9,600 . . . . 5.5%
$9,601 to $14,400 . . . . . . 6.4%
$14,401 to $19,200 . . . . . 6.8%
$19,201 to $24,000 . . . . . 7.2%
$24,001 to $36,000 . . . . . 7.6%
$36,001 to $48,000 . . . . . 7.9%
$48,001 to $150,000 . . . . 8.25%
$150,001 to $175,000 . . . . .9%
$175,001 to $200,000 . . . .10%
$200,001 and over 11%

Head of household
$0 to $3,600 . . . . 1.4%
$3,601 to $7,200 . . . . 3.2%
$7,201 to $14,400 . . . . . . 5.5%
$14,401 to $21,600 . . . . . 6.4%
$21,601 to $28,800 . . . . . 6.8%
$28,801 to $36,000 . . . . . 7.2%
$36,001 to $54,000 . . . . . 7.6%
$54,001 to $72,000 . . . . . 7.9%
$72,001 to $225,000 . . . . 8.25%
$225,001 to $262,500 . . . . 9%
$262,501 to $300,000 . . . . 10%
$300,001 and over 11%
Married filing jointly or Surviving spouse
$0 to $4,800 . . . . 1.4%
$4,801 to $9,600 . . . . 3.2%
$9,601 to $19,200 . . . . . . 5.5%
$19,201 to $28,800 . . . . . 6.4%
$28,801 to $38,400 . . . . . 6.8%
$38,401 to $48,000 . . . . . 7.2%
$48,001 to $72,000 . . . . . 7.6%
$72,001 to $96,000 . . . . . 7.9%
$96,001 to $300,000 . . . . 8.25%
$300,001 to $350,000 . . . . 9%
$350,001 to $400,000 . . . .10%
$400,001 and over 11%

Idaho[1,2]
Single or Married filing separately
$0 to $1,503 . . . . 1.125%
$1,504 to $3,007 . . . . . 3.125%
$3,008 to $4,510 . . . . . 3.625%
$4,511 to $6,014 . . . . . 4.625%
$6,015 to $7,518 . . . . . 5.625%
$7,519 to $11,278 . . . . 6.625%
$11,279 and over 6.925%
Head of household, Married filing jointly, or Surviving spouse
$0 to $3,007 . . . . 1.125%
$3,008 to $6,015 . . . . . 3.125%
$6,016 to $9,021 . . . . . 3.625%
$9,022 to $12,029 . . . . 4.625%
$12,030 to $15,037 . . . 5.625%
$15,038 to $22,557 . . . 6.625%
$22,558 and over 6.925%

Illinois
4.95% of federal AGI

Indiana
3.23% of AGI

Iowa[2,3]
$0 to $1,573 . . . . 0.36%
$1,574 to $3,146 . . . . . . 0.72%
$3,147 to $6,292 . . . . . . 2.43%
$6,293 to $14,157 . . . . . . 4.5%
$14,158 to $23,595 . . . . 6.12%
$23,596 to $31,460 . . . . 6.48%
$31,461 to $47,190 . . . . . 6.8%
$47,191 to $70,785 . . . . 7.92%
$70,786 and over 8.98%

Kansas
Single, Head of household, or Married filing separately
$0 to $15,000 . . . . 3.1%
$15,001 to $30,000 . . . . . 5.25%
$30,001 and over 5.7%
Married filing jointly
$0 to $30,000 . . . . 3.1%
$30,001 to $60,000 . . . . . 5.25%
$60,001 and over 5.7%

Kentucky
5% of taxable income

Louisiana[1]
Single, Head of household, or Married filing separately
$0 to $12,500 . . . . 2%
$12,501 to $50,000 . . . . . . 4%
$50,001 and over 6%

Maine[2]
Single or Married filing separately
$0 to $21,449 . . . . .5.8%
$21,450 to $50,749 . . . . . .6.75%
$50,750 and over 7.15%
Head of household
$0 to $32,149 . . . . .5.8%
$32,150 to $76,149 . . . . . .6.75%
$76,150 and over 7.15%
Married filing jointly or Qualifying widow(er)
$0 to $42,899 . . . . .5.8%
$42,900 to $101,549 . . . .6.75%
$101,550 and over 7.15%

Maryland
Single, Married filing separately, or Dependent taxpayers
$0 to $1,000 . . . . 2%
$1,001 to $2,000 . . . . 3%
$2,001 to $3,000 . . . . 4%
$3,001 to $100,000 . . . . .4.75%
$100,001 to $125,000 . . . . . 5%
$125,001 to $150,000 . . . 5.25%
$150,001 to $250,000 . . . 5.5%
$250,001 and over 5.75%
Head of household, Married filing jointly, or Qualifying widow(er)
$0 to $1,000 . . . . 2%
$1,001 to $2,000 . . . . 3%
$2,001 to $3,000 . . . . 4%
$3,001 to $150,000 . . . . .4.75%
$150,001 to $175,000 . . . . . 5%
$175,001 to $225,000 . . . 5.25%
$225,001 to $300,000 . . . 5.5%
$300,001 and over 5.75%

Massachusetts
Part A income
  (short-term capital gains) 12%
Part A income
  (interest and dividends) 5.10%
Part B income 5.10%
Part C income 5.10%

Michigan
4.25% of taxable income

Minnesota[2]
Single
$0 to $25,890 . . . . .5.35%
$25,891 to $85,060 . . . .7.05%
$85,061 to $160,020 . . . .7.85%
$160,021 and over 9.85%
Head of household
$0 to $31,880 . . . . .5.35%
$31,881 to $128,090 . . . .7.05%
$128,091 to $213,360 . . .7.85%
$213,361 and over 9.85%
Married filing jointly
$0 to $37,850 . . . . .5.35%
$37,851 to $150,380 . . . .7.05%
$150,381 to $266,700 . . .7.85%
$266,701 and over 9.85%
Married filing separately
$0 to $18,930 . . . . .5.35%
$18,931 to $75,190 . . . .7.05%
$75,191 to $133,350 . . . .7.85%
$133,351 and over 9.85%

Mississippi
$0 to $5,000 . . . . 3%
$5,001 to $10,000 . . . . 4%
$10,001 and over 5%

Missouri[2, 3]

$0 to $100	0%
$101 to $1,008	1.5%
$1,009 to $2,016	2%
$2,017 to $3,024	2.5%
$3,025 to $4,032	3%
$4,033 to $5,040	3.5%
$5,041 to $6,048	4%
$6,049 to $7,056	4.5%
$7,057 to $8,064	5%
$8,065 to $9,072	5.5%
$9,073 and over	6%

Montana[2]

$0 to $3,000	1%
$3,001 to $5,200	2%
$5,201 to $8,000	3%
$8,001 to $10,800	4%
$10,801 to $13,900	5%
$13,901 to $17,900	6%
$17,901 and over	6.9%

Nebraska[2]

Single or Married filing separately

$0 to $3,150	2.46%
$3,151 to $18,880	3.51%
$18,881 to $30,420	5.01%
$30,421 and over	6.84%

Head of household

$0 to $5,870	2.46%
$5,871 to $30,210	3.51%
$30,211 to $45,110	5.01%
$45,111 and over	6.84%

Married filing jointly or
Surviving spouse

$0 to $6,290	2.46%
$6,291 to $37,760	3.51%
$37,761 to $60,840	5.01%
$60,841 and over	6.84%

New Hampshire

5% on interest and dividends only

New Jersey

Single or Married/civil-union
partner filing separately

$0 to $20,000	1.4%
$20,001 to $35,000	1.75%
$35,001 to $40,000	3.5%
$40,001 to $75,000	5.525%
$75,001 to $500,000	6.37%
$500,001 to $5,000,000	8.97%
$5,000,001 and over	10.750%

Head of household, Married/
civil-union couple filing jointly,
or Qualifying widow(er)/Surviving
civil-union partner

$0 to $20,000	1.4%
$20,001 to $50,000	1.75%
$50,001 to $70,000	2.45%
$70,001 to $80,000	3.5%
$80,001 to $150,000	5.525%
$150,001 to $500,000	6.37%
$500,001 to $5,000,000	8.97%
$5,000,001 and over	10.750%

New Mexico[1]

Single

$0 to $5,500	1.7%
$5,501 to $11,000	3.2%
$11,001 to $16,000	4.7%
$16,001 and over	4.9%

Head of household, Married filing
jointly, or Qualifying widow(er)

$0 to $8,000	1.7%
$8,001 to $16,000	3.2%
$16,001 to $24,000	4.7%
$24,001 and over	4.9%

Married filing separately

$0 to $4,000	1.7%
$4,001 to $8,000	3.2%
$8,001 to $12,000	4.7%
$12,001 and over	4.9%

New York[2]

Single or Married filing separately

$0 to $8,500	4%
$8,501 to $11,700	4.5%
$11,701 to $13,900	5.25%
$13,901 to $21,400	5.9%
$21,401 to $80,650	6.33%
$80,651 to $215,400	6.57%
$215,401 to $1,077,550	6.85%
$1,077,551 and over	8.82%

Head of household

$0 to $12,800	4%
$12,801 to $17,650	4.5%
$17,651 to $20,900	5.25%
$20,901 to $32,200	5.9%
$32,201 to $107,650	6.33%
$107,651 to $269,300	6.57%
$269,301 to $1,616,450	6.85%
$1,616,451 and over	8.82%

Married filing jointly or
Qualifying widow(er)

$0 to $17,150	4%
$17,151 to $23,600	4.5%
$23,601 to $27,900	5.25%
$27,901 to $43,000	5.9%
$43,001 to $161,550	6.33%
$161,551 to $323,200	6.57%
$323,201 to $2,155,350	6.85%
$2,155,351 and over	8.82%

North Carolina

5.499% on state taxable income

North Dakota[2]

Single

$0 to $38,700	1.1%
$38,701 to $93,700	2.04%
$93,701 to $195,450	2.27%
$195,451 to $424,950	2.64%
$424,951 and over	2.9%

Head of household

$0 to $51,850	1.1%
$51,851 to $133,850	2.04%
$133,851 to $216,700	2.27%
$216,701 to $424,950	2.64%
$424,951 and over	2.9%

Married filing jointly or
Surviving spouse

$0 to $63,400	1.1%
$63,401 to $156,150	2.04%
$156,151 to $237,950	2.27%
$237,951 to $424,950	2.64%
$424,951 and over	2.9%

Married filing separately

$0 to $32,325	1.1%
$32,326 to $78,075	2.04%
$78,076 to $118,975	2.27%
$118,976 to $212,475	2.64%
$212,476 and over	2.9%

Ohio[3]

$10,651 to $16,000	1.98%
$16,001 to $21,350	2.476%
$21,351 to $42,650	2.969%
$42,651 to $85,300	3.465%
$85,301 to $106,650	3.96%
$106,651 to $213,350	4.597%
$213,351 and over	4.997%

Oklahoma

Single or Married filing separately

$0 to $1,000	0.5%
$1,001 to $2,500	1%
$2,501 to $3,750	2%
$3,751 to $4,900	3%
$4,901 to $7,200	4%
$7,201 and over	5%

Head of household, Married
filing jointly, or Qualifying
widow(er)

$0 to $2,000	0.5%
$2,001 to $5,000	1%
$5,001 to $7,500	2%
$7,501 to $9,800	3%
$9,801 to $12,200	4%
$12,201 and over	5%

Oregon[2]

Single or Married filing
separately

$0 to $3,450	5%
$3,451 to $8,700	7%
$8,701 to $125,000	9%
$125,001 and over	9.9%

Married filing jointly,
Head of household, or
Qualifying widow(er)

$0 to $6,900	5%
$6,901 to $17,400	7%
$17,401 to $250,000	9%
$250,001 and over	9.9%

Pennsylvania

3.07% of taxable compensation,
net profits, net gains from the
sale of property, rent, royalties,
patents or copyrights, income
from estates or trusts, dividends,
interest, and winnings

Rhode Island[2]

$0 to $62,550	3.75%
$62,551 to $142,150	4.75%
$142,151 and over	5.99%

South Carolina[2]

$0 to $2,970	0%
$2,971 to $ 5,940	3%
$5,941 to $8,910	4%
$8,911 to $11,880	5%
$11,881 to $14,860	6%
$14,861 and over	7%

Tennessee

3% on interest and dividends

Utah

4.95% on state taxable income

Vermont

Single

$0 to $38,700	3.35%
$38,701 to $93,700	6.6%
$93,701 to $195,450	7.6%
$195,451 and over	8.75%

Head of household

$0 to $51,850	3.35%
$51,851 to $133,850	6.6%
$133,851 to $216,700	7.6%
$216,701 and over	8.75%

Married or Civil union filing jointly

$0 to $64,600	3.35%
$64,601 to $156,150	6.6%
$156,151 to $237,950	7.6%
$237,951 and over	8.75%

Married or Civil union
filing separately

$0 to $32,300	3.35%
$32,301 to $78,075	6.6%
$78,076 to $118,975	7.6%
$118,976 and over	8.75%

Virginia

$0 to $3,000	2%
$3,001 to $5,000	3%
$5,001 to $17,000	5%
$17,001 and over	5.75%

West Virginia

Single, Head of household,
Married filing jointly, or
Widow(er) with dependent child

$0 to $10,000	3%
$10,001 to $25,000	4%
$25,001 to $40,000	4.5%
$40,001 to $60,000	6%
$60,001 and over	6.5%

Married filing separately

$0 to $5,000	3%
$5,001 to $12,500	4%
$12,501 to $20,000	4.5%
$20,001 to $30,000	6%
$30,001 and over	6.5%

Wisconsin[1,2]

Single or Head of household

$0 to $11,450	4%
$11,451 to $22,900	5.84%
$22,901 to $252,150	6.27%
$252,151 and over	7.65%

Married filing jointly

$0 to $15,270	4%
$15,271 to $30,540	5.84%
$30,541 to $336,200	6.27%
$336,201 and over	7.65%

Married filing separately

$0 to $7,630	4%
$7,631 to $15,270	5.84%
$15,271 to $168,100	6.27%
$168,101 and over	7.65%

AGI = Adjusted gross income; AMT = Alternative minimum tax. (1) Community property state in which, in general, one-half of the community income is taxable to each spouse. (2) Brackets indexed for inflation annually. (3) 2018 adjusted brackets were not available. Bracketed rates listed are for 2017. Other notes, by state: **Arkansas:** For net income from $77,401 to $82,500, deduct bracket adjustment amount as follows: $77,401 to $78,400: deduct $440; $78,401 to $79,400: deduct $340; $79,401 to $80,600: deduct $240; $80,601 to $81,600: deduct $140; $81,601 to $82,600: deduct $40; $82,601 and over: deduct $0. **California:** An additional 1% tax is imposed on taxable income in excess of $1 mil. **Colorado:** Individual taxpayers are subject to an AMT equal to the amount by which 3.47% of their Colorado alternative minimum taxable income exceeds their Colorado normal tax. **Connecticut:** Resident estates and trusts are subject to a 6.99% rate on all income. **Illinois:** Surcharge is imposed on certain types of sales income. **Indiana:** Counties may impose an AGI tax on residents or on nonresidents, or a county option income tax. **Iowa:** An AMT of 6.7% of alternative minimum income is imposed if the minimum tax exceeds the taxpayer's regular income tax liability. **Kansas:** Married filing jointly with taxable income of $5,000 or less, and all other individuals with taxable income of $2,500 or less, have a tax liability of zero. **Massachusetts:** Part A income represents either interest and dividends or short-term capital gains, long-term capital gains from collectibles, and long-term capital gains from pre-1996 installment sales. Part B income represents wages, salaries, tips, pensions, business income, rents, etc. Part C income represents gains from the sale of capital assets held for more than one year. 5.85% optional rate may be elected for Part A interest and dividend income, Part B income after exemptions, and Part C income. **Minnesota:** A 6.75% AMT is imposed. **Montana:** Minimum tax, $1. **Nebraska:** There is an additional tax on taxpayers with federal AGI of more than a certain amount, which is $313,800 for married filing jointly ($261,500 for single filers) in 2017. **New Mexico:** Qualified nonresident taxpayers may pay an alternative tax of 0.75% of gross receipts from sales in New Mexico. **New York:** A supplemental tax is imposed to recapture the tax table benefit. **Vermont:** The tax amount is increased by 24% for certain items.

EDUCATION

U.S. Public Schools: Students, Staff, Spending, 1899-2016
Source: National Center for Education Statistics, U.S. Dept. of Education

	1899-1900	1919-20	1939-40	1959-60	1969-70	1979-80	1989-90	1999-2000	2015-16[1]
Population (thous.)									
Total U.S. population[2]	75,995	104,514	131,028	177,830	201,385	225,055	246,819	279,040	321,419
Population 5-17 years of age	21,573	27,571	30,151	43,881	52,386	48,043	44,947	52,811	53,738
Percentage 5-17 years of age. . . .	28.4%	26.4%	23.0%	24.7%	26.0%	21.3%	18.2%	18.9%	16.7%
Enrollment (thous.)									
Elementary and secondary[3]	15,503	21,578	25,434	36,087	45,550	41,651	40,543	46,857	50,268
Pre-kindergarten and grades 1-8	14,984	19,378	18,833	27,602	32,513	28,034	29,152	33,486	35,298
Grades 9-12	519	2,200	6,601	8,485	13,037	13,616	11,390	13,371	14,970
Percent of pop. ages 5-17 enrolled	71.9%	78.3%	84.4%	82.2%	87.0%	86.7%	90.2%	88.7%	93.5%
High school as percent of all enrolled	3.3%	10.2%	26.0%	23.5%	28.6%	32.7%	28.1%	28.5%	29.8%
High school graduates	62	231	1,143	1,627	2,589	2,748	2,320	2,554	3,192
Instructional staff (thous.)									
Total instructional staff	*	678	912	1,457	2,286	2,406	2,986	3,819	4,250
Teachers, librarians, and other nonsupervisory instructional staff	423	657	875	1,393	2,195	2,300	2,860	3,682	4,068
Revenue and expenditures (mil)									
Total revenue	$220	$970	$2,261	$14,747	$40,267	$96,881	$208,548	$372,944	$648,631
Total expenditures.	215	1,036	2,344	15,613	40,683	95,962	212,770	381,838	652,249
Current expenditures[4]	180	861	1,942	12,329	34,218	86,984	188,229	323,889	575,810
Capital outlay	35	154	258	2,662	4,659	6,506	17,781	43,357	50,613
Interest on school debt	*	18	131	490	1,171	1,874	3,776	9,135	17,413
Others	*	3	13	133	636	598	2,983	5,457	8,413
Salaries and pupil cost									
Avg. annual salary of instruct. staff[5]	$325	$871	$1,441	$4,995	$8,626	$15,970	$31,367	$41,807	$58,064
Expenditure per capita total pop. . . .	3	10	18	88	202	426	862	1,368	2,029
Current expenditure per pupil ADA[4]	17	53	88	375	816	2,272	4,980	7,394	11,930

* = Data not collected. ADA = Average daily attendance. **Note:** Because of rounding, details may not add up to totals. Prior to 1959-60, data do not include Alaska and Hawaii. (1) Revenues and expenditures are fiscal year 2015 (2014-15 school year) provisional data; high school graduates and expenditure per pupil ADA are projected. (2) Data for 1899-1900 are based on total population from the decennial census. From 1919-20 to 1959-60, total population includes armed forces overseas, as of July 1 preceding the school year. Data for later years are for resident population excluding armed forces overseas. (3) Data for 1899-1960 are school year enrollment; data for later years are fall enrollment. (4) Because of changes in the definition of "current expenditures," data for 1959-60 and later years are not entirely comparable with prior years. (5) Data prior to 1959-60 include supervisors, principals, teachers, and nonsupervisory instructional staff.

U.S. Public High School Graduation Rates, 2015-16
Source: National Center for Education Statistics, U.S. Dept. of Education

State	Rate	Rank	State	Rate	Rank	State	Rate	Rank	State	Rate	Rank
Alabama	87.1%	16	Illinois	85.5%	26	Montana	85.6%	24	Rhode Island . . .	82.8%	31
Alaska	76.1	47	Indiana	86.8	19	Nebraska	89.3	4	South Carolina . .	82.6	33
Arizona	79.5	43	Iowa	91.3	1	Nevada	73.6	49	South Dakota . . .	83.9	28
Arkansas	87.0	17	Kansas	85.7	23	New Hampshire. .	88.2	9	Tennessee	88.5	8
California	83.0	30	Kentucky	88.6	7	New Jersey	90.1	2	Texas	89.1	5
Colorado	78.9	45	Louisiana	78.6	46	New Mexico	71.0	50	Utah	85.2	27
Connecticut.	87.4	15	Maine	87.0	18	New York.	80.4	38	Vermont	87.7	11
Delaware	85.5	25	Maryland	87.6	12	North Carolina . .	85.9	22	Virginia	86.7	20
Dist. of Columbia . .	69.2	51	Massachusetts . .	87.5	13	North Dakota . . .	87.5	14	Washington.	79.7	42
Florida	80.7	37	Michigan	79.7	41	Ohio	83.5	29	West Virginia. . . .	89.8	3
Georgia.	79.4	44	Minnesota	82.2	35	Oklahoma	81.6	36	Wisconsin	88.2	10
Hawaii	82.7	32	Mississippi	82.3	34	Oregon	74.8	48	Wyoming	80.0	39
Idaho.	79.7	40	Missouri	89.0	6	Pennsylvania. . . .	86.1	21	**Total U.S.**	84.1	

Note: The 4-year adjusted cohort graduation rate (ACGR) is the number of students who graduate in 4 years with a regular high school diploma divided by the number of students who form the adjusted cohort for the graduating class. From the beginning of 9th grade (or the earliest high school grade), students who are entering that grade for the first time form a cohort that is "adjusted" by adding any students who subsequently transfer into the cohort and subtracting any students who subsequently transfer out, emigrate to another country, or die.

High School Dropouts by Sex, Race, and Ethnicity, 1960-2016
Source: Current Population Survey, U.S. Census Bureau, U.S. Dept. of Commerce
(data for Oct. of year shown unless otherwise noted)

Year[1]	Total dropout rate				Male dropout rate				Female dropout rate			
	All races[2]	White	Black	Hispanic	All races[2]	White	Black	Hispanic	All races[2]	White	Black	Hispanic
1960[3]	27.2%	NA	NA	NA	27.8%	NA	NA	NA	26.7%	NA	NA	NA
1970[4]	15.0	13.2%	27.9%	NA	14.2	12.2%	29.4%	NA	15.7	14.1%	26.6%	NA
1980	14.1	11.4	19.1	35.2%	15.1	12.3	20.8	37.2%	13.1	10.5	17.7	33.2%
1990	12.1	9.0	13.2	32.4	12.3	9.3	11.9	34.3	11.8	8.7	14.4	30.3
2000	10.9	6.9	13.1	27.8	12.0	7.0	15.3	31.8	9.9	6.9	11.1	23.5
2005	9.4	6.0	10.4	22.4	10.8	6.6	12.0	26.4	8.0	5.3	9.0	18.1
2008	8.0	4.8	9.9	18.3	8.5	5.4	8.7	19.9	7.5	4.2	11.1	16.7
2009	8.1	5.2	9.3	17.6	9.1	6.3	10.6	19.0	7.0	4.1	8.1	16.1
2010	7.4	5.1	8.0	15.1	8.5	5.9	9.5	17.3	6.3	4.2	6.7	12.8
2011	7.1	5.0	7.3	13.6	7.7	5.4	8.3	14.6	6.5	4.6	6.4	12.4
2012	6.6	4.3	7.5	12.7	7.3	4.8	8.1	13.9	5.9	3.8	7.0	11.3
2013	6.8	5.1	7.3	11.7	7.2	5.5	8.2	12.6	6.3	4.7	6.6	10.8
2014	6.5	5.2	7.4	10.6	7.1	5.7	7.1	11.8	5.9	4.8	7.7	9.3
2015	5.9	4.6	6.5	9.2	6.3	5.0	6.4	9.9	5.4	4.1	6.5	8.4
2016	6.1	5.2	6.2	8.6	7.1	5.8	8.2	10.1	5.1	4.6	4.3	7.0

NA = Not available. **Note:** Table shows "status" dropouts, defined as 16- to 24-year-olds who are not enrolled in school and who have not completed a high school program, regardless of when they left school. People who have received GED credentials are not shown. Excludes persons in prison or in the military and other persons not living in households. Race categories exclude persons of Hispanic ethnicity unless otherwise noted. (1) Because of changes in data collection procedures, data for years prior to 1992 may not be comparable to later years. For 2005 and after, white and black data exclude persons identifying themselves as being of two or more races. (2) Includes other racial/ethnic categories not separately shown. (3) Based on the Apr. 1960 decennial census. (4) White and black data include persons of Hispanic ethnicity.

Overview of U.S. Public Schools, 2016-17

Source: National Center for Education Statistics, U.S. Dept. of Education; National Education Association (NEA)

State	Local school districts	Elementary schools[1,2]	Secondary schools[2,3]	Classroom teachers	Total enrollment	Pupils per teacher	Teachers' avg. pay	Expend. per pupil
Alabama	137	923	403	46,287	731,607	15.81	$50,391	$9,238
Alaska	54	197	79	8,716	129,753	14.89	68,138	21,261
Arizona	715	1,356	738	45,108	1,060,273	23.51	47,403	7,501
Arkansas	259	701	372	31,401	477,047	15.19	48,304	9,871
California	1,028	7,006	2,550	277,585	6,225,179	22.43	79,128	9,685
Colorado	178	1,311	393	55,298	905,019	16.37	51,808	10,865
Connecticut	196	938	389	41,814	527,169	12.61	73,147	20,861
Delaware	44	163	41	9,278	137,996	14.87	60,214	16,350
Dist. of Columbia	73	176	35	4,958	71,846	14.49	75,692	25,025
Florida	75	2,839	674	143,383	2,817,076	19.65	47,267	9,110
Georgia	207	1,769	449	113,882	1,764,215	15.49	55,532	10,010
Hawaii	1	211	52	10,768	181,357	16.84	56,651	11,964
Idaho	155	448	218	15,985	298,787	18.69	47,504	6,761
Illinois	852	3,046	888	122,997	2,053,720	16.70	64,933	13,875
Indiana	402	1,366	464	59,657	1,020,686	17.11	54,308	7,267
Iowa	333	948	360	36,056	510,932	14.17	55,647	11,017
Kansas	286	928	341	34,406	489,795	14.24	49,422	10,277
Kentucky	173	968	484	40,692	662,097	16.27	52,338	10,508
Louisiana	147	964	276	44,693	723,554	16.19	50,000	11,234
Maine	214	449	146	15,105	180,767	11.97	51,077	8,956
Maryland	24	1,128	243	60,306	886,221	14.70	68,357	14,774
Massachusetts	404	1,421	377	72,090	952,365	13.21	78,100	17,381
Michigan	829	1,769	833	84,505	1,469,287	17.39	62,287	9,968
Minnesota	529	1,339	854	53,415	855,867	16.02	57,346	12,417
Mississippi	165	631	332	32,020	493,429	15.41	42,925	8,361
Missouri	556	1,611	632	74,727	883,879	11.83	48,618	10,826
Montana	406	490	333	10,646	146,375	13.75	51,422	11,129
Nebraska	245	714	309	24,878	318,853	12.82	52,338	11,716
Nevada	17	476	128	17,335	448,220	25.86	57,376	8,165
New Hampshire	165	380	110	14,760	176,314	11.95	57,522	16,495
New Jersey	702	1,959	538	111,497	1,314,857	11.79	69,623	20,556
New Mexico	89	606	238	21,357	334,114	15.64	47,122	10,520
New York	691	3,306	1,131	210,791	2,501,186	11.87	81,902	23,265
North Carolina	115	1,915	536	92,146	1,439,292	15.62	49,970	9,329
North Dakota	176	303	183	8,260	106,863	12.94	52,968	8,176
Ohio	1,026	2,450	1,008	113,335	1,800,329	15.89	58,202	10,669
Oklahoma	512	1,232	564	41,294	693,710	16.80	45,292	8,249
Oregon	196	888	273	29,561	578,947	19.58	61,862	11,595
Pennsylvania	796	2,126	782	118,946	1,716,262	14.43	66,265	15,017
Rhode Island	63	232	75	8,578	139,644	16.28	66,477	15,691
South Carolina	86	919	287	50,440	742,535	14.72	50,000	11,552
South Dakota	150	435	246	9,604	132,520	13.80	46,979	9,000
Tennessee	141	1,373	378	66,064	971,009	14.70	50,099	9,393
Texas	1,203	6,022	2,089	352,809	5,343,893	15.15	52,575	9,387
Utah	141	668	285	28,750	646,888	22.50	47,244	6,906
Vermont	360	231	67	8,030	76,230	9.49	57,349	19,399
Virginia	132	1,490	436	101,699	1,293,538	12.72	51,049	11,141
Washington	307	1,549	640	59,666	1,079,546	18.09	54,433	11,914
West Virginia	55	563	120	19,148	273,170	14.27	45,555	14,274
Wisconsin	422	1,580	559	54,401	875,827	16.10	54,998	11,533
Wyoming	48	245	102	7,461	93,261	12.50	58,187	16,820
Total U.S.	**16,280**	**66,758**	**24,040**	**3,116,588**	**49,753,306**	**15.96**	**59,660**	**11,642**

(1) Includes primary and middle schools (schools with no grade higher than 8th). (2) 2015-16 estimates. (3) Includes schools with no grade lower than 7th.

Students With Disabilities Receiving Educational Services, 1990-2016

Source: Office of Special Education and Rehabilitative Services, U.S. Dept. of Education

Students served by federally funded educational programs for disabled students include children and young adults 3-21 years old. (numbers served in thousands)

Type of disability	1990 -91	2000 -01	2005 -06	2007 -08[1]	2008 -09[1]	2009 -10	2010 -11	2011 -12	2012 -13	2013 -14	2014 -15	2015 -16
Learning disabilities	2,129	2,860	2,740	2,569	2,476	2,431	2,361	2,303	2,277	2,264	2,278	2,298
Speech impairments.	985	1,388	1,468	1,454	1,426	1,416	1,396	1,373	1,356	1,334	1,332	1,337
Intellectual disabilities.	534	624	556	500	478	463	448	435	430	425	423	425
Emotional disturbance	389	480	477	442	420	407	390	373	362	354	349	347
Multiple disabilities	96	131	141	138	130	131	130	132	133	132	132	131
Hearing impairments	58	77	79	79	78	79	78	78	77	77	76	75
Orthopedic impairments. . . .	49	82	71	67	70	65	63	61	59	56	52	47
Other health impairments[2] . .	55	303	570	641	659	689	716	743	779	817	862	909
Visual impairments.	23	29	29	29	29	29	28	28	28	28	28	27
Autism.	—	93	223	296	336	378	417	455	498	538	576	617
Deaf-blindness	1	1	2	2	2	2	2	2	1	1	1	1
Traumatic brain injury	—	16	24	25	26	25	26	26	26	26	26	27
Developmental delay	—	213	339	357	354	368	382	393	402	410	419	434
All disabilities	**4,710**	**6,296**	**6,718**	**6,597**	**6,483**	**6,481**	**6,436**	**6,401**	**6,429**	**6,464**	**6,555**	**6,677**

— = Not available or not reliable data. **Note:** Counts based on reports from states and District of Columbia. Details may not add up to totals because of rounding and/or incomplete enumeration. (1) Vermont not included. (2) Includes limited strength, vitality, or alertness due to chronic or acute health problems such as a heart condition, tuberculosis, rheumatic fever, nephritis, asthma, sickle cell anemia, hemophilia, epilepsy, lead poisoning, leukemia, or diabetes.

Revenues for Public Elementary and Secondary Schools by State, 2014-15

Source: National Center for Education Statistics, U.S. Dept. of Education; amounts in thousands

State/territory	Total	Federal Amount	Federal % of tot. rev.	State Amount	State % of tot. rev.	Local and intermediate Amount	Local and intermediate % of tot. rev.
Alabama	$7,435,758	$835,012	11.2%	$4,129,101	55.5%	$2,471,644	33.2%
Alaska	2,935,538	347,699	11.8	2,037,616	69.4	550,223	18.7
American Samoa	82,212	69,391	84.4	12,573	15.3	248	0.3
Arizona	9,919,670	1,277,021	12.9	4,345,427	43.8	4,297,223	43.3
Arkansas	5,283,244	608,559	11.5	2,720,257	51.5	1,954,428	37.0
California	74,395,627	7,148,875	9.6	42,525,283	57.2	24,721,469	33.2
Colorado	9,764,525	723,032	7.4	4,452,824	45.6	4,588,670	47.0
Connecticut	11,376,740	480,791	4.2	4,661,930	41.0	6,234,018	54.8
Delaware	2,077,887	181,122	8.7	1,199,264	57.7	697,501	33.6
District of Columbia	2,251,430	218,044	9.7	NA	NA	2,033,386	90.3
Florida	26,789,374	3,192,508	11.9	10,661,588	39.8	12,935,279	48.3
Georgia	18,772,155	1,888,388	10.1	8,485,440	45.2	8,398,327	44.7
Guam	316,585	64,901	20.5	NA	NA	251,684	79.5
Hawaii	2,699,827	259,391	9.6	2,381,547	88.2	58,888	2.2
Idaho	2,285,634	246,320	10.8	1,482,298	64.9	557,016	24.4
Illinois	27,304,004	2,264,000	8.3	6,787,531	24.9	18,252,473	66.8
Indiana	12,103,344	988,205	8.2	6,787,225	56.1	4,327,914	35.8
Iowa	6,463,514	475,848	7.4	3,460,804	53.5	2,526,863	39.1
Kansas	6,225,153	556,947	8.9	4,001,451	64.3	1,666,755	26.8
Kentucky	7,453,976	856,715	11.5	4,093,058	54.9	2,504,203	33.6
Louisiana	8,927,289	1,307,850	14.7	3,875,345	43.4	3,744,095	41.9
Maine	2,737,132	192,628	7.0	1,077,156	39.4	1,467,348	53.6
Maryland	14,521,045	821,418	5.7	6,316,683	43.5	7,382,943	50.8
Massachusetts	17,308,265	903,344	5.2	6,836,761	39.5	9,568,160	55.3
Michigan	19,452,849	1,785,600	9.2	11,706,291	60.2	5,960,957	30.6
Minnesota	12,183,690	699,165	5.7	8,131,825	66.7	3,352,701	27.5
Mississippi	4,550,410	672,385	14.8	2,324,855	51.1	1,553,170	34.1
Missouri	10,927,026	979,787	9.0	3,555,885	32.5	6,391,354	58.5
Montana	1,805,295	219,405	12.2	863,889	47.9	722,001	40.0
Nebraska	4,168,349	343,356	8.2	1,350,595	32.4	2,474,399	59.4
Nevada	4,522,125	416,393	9.2	1,621,778	35.9	2,483,954	54.9
New Hampshire	2,992,501	166,235	5.6	1,000,374	33.4	1,825,892	61.0
New Jersey	28,585,120	1,191,041	4.2	11,989,910	41.9	15,404,169	53.9
New Mexico	3,986,781	557,590	14.0	2,771,343	69.5	657,848	16.5
New York	63,213,042	2,831,810	4.5	25,938,520	41.0	34,442,712	54.5
North Carolina	13,681,971	1,662,823	12.2	8,543,954	62.4	3,475,194	25.4
North Dakota	1,578,414	158,647	10.1	926,792	58.7	492,974	31.2
Northern Mariana Islands	65,034	31,420	48.3	33,614	51.7	NA	NA
Ohio	24,516,266	1,850,536	7.5	11,179,287	45.6	11,486,443	46.9
Oklahoma	6,261,170	717,590	11.5	3,090,488	49.4	2,453,092	39.2
Oregon	7,077,486	565,086	8.0	3,678,010	52.0	2,834,391	40.0
Pennsylvania	28,983,071	2,003,649	6.9	10,764,800	37.1	16,214,622	55.9
Puerto Rico	3,098,730	1,065,537	34.4	2,033,132	65.6	61	0.0
Rhode Island	2,444,422	199,039	8.1	990,389	40.5	1,254,995	51.3
South Carolina	8,891,519	855,168	9.6	4,198,817	47.2	3,837,534	43.2
South Dakota	1,420,613	211,164	14.9	431,422	30.4	778,027	54.8
Tennessee	9,428,234	1,126,850	12.0	4,258,683	45.2	4,042,701	42.9
Texas	56,127,791	6,085,723	10.8	22,787,667	40.6	27,254,401	48.6
Utah	5,127,846	450,732	8.8	2,798,042	54.6	1,879,073	36.6
Vermont	1,758,461	105,353	6.0	1,584,246	90.1	68,862	3.9
Virgin Islands (U.S.)	190,235	31,330	16.5	NA	NA	158,905	83.5
Virginia	15,624,013	1,012,211	6.5	6,240,351	39.9	8,371,451	53.6
Washington	13,606,501	1,036,795	7.6	8,301,015	61.0	4,268,691	31.4
West Virginia	3,525,371	362,449	10.3	2,027,143	57.5	1,135,779	32.2
Wisconsin	11,197,990	840,933	7.5	5,139,509	45.9	5,217,548	46.6
Wyoming	1,961,721	120,788	6.2	1,116,909	56.9	724,024	36.9
United States	**648,631,181**	**55,002,019**	**8.5**	**301,631,375**	**46.5**	**291,997,788**	**45.0**

NA = Not applicable.

Enrollment in U.S. Public and Private Schools, 1889-2028

Source: National Center for Education Statistics, U.S. Dept. of Education

Of all students enrolled in private schools in fall 2015, 76% attended religious schools and 24% attended nonsectarian schools.

School year[1]	Public school[2]	Private school[2]	% private[3]	School year[1]	Public school[2]	Private school[2]	% private[3]
1889-90	12,723	1,611	11.2%	1979-80	41,651	5,000[4]	10.7%
1899-1900	15,503	1,352	8.0	1989-90	40,543	5,599	12.1
1909-10	17,814	1,558	8.0	1999-2000	46,857	6,018	11.4
1919-20	21,578	1,699	7.3	2009-10	49,361	5,488	10.0
1929-30	25,678	2,651	9.4	2012-13	49,771	5,333[4]	9.7
1939-40	25,434	2,611	9.3	2013-14	50,045	5,396	9.7
1949-50	25,111	3,380	11.9	2014-15	50,313	5,575[4]	10.0
1959-60	35,182	5,675	13.9	2015-16	50,438	5,751	10.2
1969-70	45,550	5,500[4]	10.8	2027-28[5]	52,059	6,180	10.6

Note: "Private" includes all nonpublic schools. (1) Fall enrollment. (2) In thousands. Data from fall 1980 onward covers an expanded universe of private schools; comparisons with earlier years should be avoided. (3) Percent of U.S. students enrolled in private schools. (4) Estimated. (5) Projected.

Program for International Student Assessment (PISA) Scores, 2000-15

Source: National Center for Education Statistics, U.S. Dept. of Education

Scores are reported on a scale from 0 to 1,000. The PISA test is administered to 15-year-old students.

Education system	Mathematics 2000	Mathematics 2015	Reading 2000	Reading 2015	Science 2000	Science 2015	Education system	Mathematics 2000	Mathematics 2015	Reading 2000	Reading 2015	Science 2000	Science 2015
Albania	—	413	—	405	—	427	Liechtenstein	514	—	483	—	476	—
Algeria	—	360	—	350	—	376	Lithuania	—	478	—	472	—	475
Argentina	—	456	—	475	—	475	Luxembourg*	446	486	441	481	443	483
Australia*	533	494	528	503	528	510	Macau	—	544	—	509	—	529
Austria*	515	497	507	485	519	495	Macedonia	—	371	—	352	—	384
Belgium*	520	507	507	499	496	502	Malta	—	479	—	447	—	465
Brazil	334	377	396	407	375	401	Mexico*	387	408	422	423	422	416
Bulgaria	—	441	—	432	—	446	Moldova	—	420	—	416	—	428
Canada*	533	516	534	527	529	528	Montenegro	—	418	—	427	—	411
Chile*	—	423	—	459	—	447	Netherlands*	—	512	—	503	—	509
China	—	531	—	494	—	518	New Zealand*	537	495	529	509	528	513
Colombia	—	390	—	425	—	416	Norway*	499	502	505	513	500	498
Costa Rica	—	400	—	427	—	420	Peru	—	387	—	398	—	397
Croatia	—	464	—	487	—	475	Poland*	470	504	479	506	483	501
Cyprus	—	437	—	443	—	433	Portugal*	454	492	470	498	459	501
Czech Rep.*	498	492	492	487	511	493	Qatar	—	402	—	402	—	418
Denmark*	514	511	497	500	481	502	Romania	—	444	—	434	—	435
Dominican Republic	—	328	—	358	—	332	Russia	478	494	462	495	460	487
Estonia*	—	520	—	519	—	534	Singapore	—	564	—	535	—	556
Finland*	536	511	546	526	538	531	Slovakia*	—	475	—	453	—	461
France*	517	493	505	499	500	495	Slovenia*	—	510	—	505	—	513
Georgia	—	404	—	401	—	411	Spain*	476	486	493	496	491	493
Germany*	490	506	484	509	487	509	Sweden*	510	494	516	500	512	493
Greece*	447	454	474	467	461	455	Switzerland*	529	521	494	492	496	506
Hong Kong	—	548	—	527	—	523	Taiwan	—	542	—	497	—	532
Hungary*	488	477	480	470	496	477	Thailand	—	415	—	409	—	421
Iceland*	514	488	507	482	496	473	Trinidad and Tobago	—	417	—	427	—	425
Indonesia	—	386	—	397	—	403	Tunisia	—	367	—	361	—	386
Ireland*	503	504	527	521	513	503	Turkey*	—	420	—	428	—	425
Israel*	—	470	—	479	—	467	United Arab Emirates	—	427	—	434	—	437
Italy*	457	490	487	485	478	481	UK*	529	492	523	498	532	509
Japan*	557	532	522	516	550	538	U.S.*	493	470	504	497	499	496
Jordan	—	380	—	408	—	409	Uruguay	—	418	—	437	—	435
Korea, South*	547	524	525	517	552	516	Vietnam	—	495	—	487	—	525
Kosovo	—	362	—	347	—	378	**OECD average[1]**	**500**	**490**	**500**	**493**	**500**	**493**
Latvia*	463	482	458	488	460	490							
Lebanon	—	396	—	347	—	386							

— = Not available. * = Organization for Economic Cooperation and Development (OECD) nation as of 2015. (1) The average of the national averages of the OECD member countries, with each country weighted equally.

Mathematics, Reading, and Science Achievement of U.S. Students, 1998-2017

Source: National Assessment of Educational Progress, National Center for Education Statistics, U.S. Dept. of Education

Percent of public school students in a grade who scored at or above basic levels in national tests. Basic level denotes a partial mastery of prerequisite knowledge and skills fundamental for proficient work at each grade.

State	4th grade Math 2000	4th grade Math 2017	4th grade Reading 1998	4th grade Reading 2017	8th grade Math 2000	8th grade Math 2017	8th grade Reading 1998	8th grade Reading 2017	8th grade Science 2000	8th grade Science 2015	State	4th grade Math 2000	4th grade Math 2017	4th grade Reading 1998	4th grade Reading 2017	8th grade Math 2000	8th grade Math 2017	8th grade Reading 1998	8th grade Reading 2017	8th grade Science 2000	8th grade Science 2015
AL	55	73	56	63	53	55	67	67	53	54	MT	72	83	72	70	79	76	83	79	79	78
AK	NA	71	NA	56	NA	66	NA	70	NA	NA	NE	65	85	NA	72	73	76	NA	79	52	75
AZ	57	73	51	61	60	71	72	75	55	61	NV	60	73	51	61	55	62	70	71	NA	62
AR	55	73	54	63	49	62	68	71	53	62	NH	NA	85	74	75	NA	81	NA	84	NA	81
CA	50	71	48	61	50	62	63	72	38	56	NJ	NA	87	NA	78	NA	76	NA	82	NA	71
CO	NA	80	67	71	NA	74	77	79	NA	NA	NM	50	69	51	54	48	57	71	66	48	55
CT	76	79	76	74	70	72	81	80	64	70	NY	66	76	62	68	63	68	76	73	NA	63
DE	NA	77	53	67	NA	66	64	72	NA	62	NC	73	81	58	69	67	68	74	74	54	64
DC	24	69	27	56	23	51	44	55	NA	NA	ND	73	85	NA	70	76	78	NA	77	72	79
FL	NA	88	53	75	NA	66	67	77	NA	66	OH	73	81	NA	71	73	74	NA	77	72	72
GA	57	77	54	66	54	68	68	76	52	65	OK	67	80	66	63	62	64	80	74	60	66
HI	55	79	45	62	51	66	59	72	40	58	OR	65	73	58	63	71	70	78	76	68	72
ID	68	81	NA	70	70	74	NA	81	71	76	PA	NA	80	NA	71	NA	73	NA	78	NA	NA
IL	63	76	NA	66	67	68	NA	77	59	63	RI	65	79	64	69	59	66	76	75	58	64
IN	77	86	NA	73	74	75	NA	82	66	70	SC	59	75	53	59	53	62	66	71	48	65
IA	75	83	67	69	NA	76	NA	80	NA	75	SD	NA	83	NA	69	NA	76	NA	80	NA	77
KS	76	82	70	70	76	74	81	78	NA	71	TN	59	77	57	64	52	68	71	73	55	71
KY	59	80	62	70	60	65	74	75	60	73	TX	76	82	59	60	67	70	74	71	52	70
LA	57	71	44	56	47	54	63	67	44	NA	UT	69	81	62	72	66	75	77	79	67	82
ME	73	81	72	67	73	72	83	79	72	77	VT	73	81	NA	73	73	76	NA	82	71	79
MD	60	78	58	69	62	66	70	74	57	67	VA	71	87	62	74	65	77	78	77	61	74
MA	77	87	70	80	70	81	79	85	70	75	WA	NA	80	64	68	NA	75	76	80	NA	70
MI	71	75	62	64	68	67	NA	76	68	69	WV	65	78	60	64	58	62	75	70	57	63
MN	76	86	67	71	80	80	78	79	72	76	WI	NA	79	69	66	NA	76	78	79	NA	75
MS	45	77	47	60	42	59	62	66	41	51	WY	71	89	64	74	69	79	76	80	69	79
MO	71	79	61	69	64	70	75	77	66	75	**U.S.**	**64**	**79**	**58**	**67**	**62**	**69**	**71**	**75**	**57**	**67**

NA = Not administered.

Fighting, Bullying, and Safety Concerns of High School Students, 2017

Source: *Youth Risk Behavior Surveillance–United States, 2017*, Centers for Disease Control and Prevention

	In a physical fight on school property[1]			Bullied on school property[2]			Electronically bullied[2,3]			Did not go to school because of safety concerns[4]		
	Female	Male	Total	Female	Male	Total	Female	Male	Total	Female	Male	Total
Race/ethnicity												
White, non-Hispanic ...	3.1%	10.1%	6.5%	24.6%	18.1%	21.5%	23.0%	11.2%	17.3%	5.7%	3.9%	4.9%
Black, non-Hispanic ...	13.7	16.9	15.3	14.5	11.8	13.2	13.3	8.4	10.9	9.5	8.2	9.0
Hispanic, any race.....	7.0	11.6	9.4	21.0	11.8	16.3	17.2	7.6	12.3	9.3	9.4	9.4
Grade												
9	7.7	16.9	12.3	25.2	20.0	22.7	22.3	10.9	16.7	8.7	6.4	7.6
10	5.8	13.5	9.6	23.6	16.8	20.3	19.7	9.7	14.8	8.6	7.2	7.9
11	4.5	7.5	6.0	23.5	12.8	18.3	19.9	8.2	14.2	5.7	4.8	5.4
12	3.6	6.5	5.0	16.3	11.6	14.0	16.4	10.4	13.5	4.7	5.5	5.2
Sexual identity												
Heterosexual (straight)	4.9	11.3	8.3	20.5	14.2	17.1	18.6	8.8	13.3	6.7	5.5	6.1
Gay, lesbian, or bisexual.........	8.9	11.4	9.6	32.2	35.0	33.0	28.5	22.3	27.1	9.1	12.3	10.0
Not sure	7.3	16.4	11.8	25.2	21.5	24.3	23.3	18.2	22.0	8.0	12.6	10.7
Total	**5.6**	**11.6**	**8.5**	**22.3**	**15.6**	**19.0**	**19.7**	**9.9**	**14.9**	**7.1**	**6.1**	**6.7**

(1) One or more times during the 12 months before the survey. (2) During the 12 months before the survey. (3) Including being bullied through texting, Instagram, Facebook, or other social media. (4) On at least one day during the 30 days before the survey.

Characteristics of Public Charter Schools and Students, 1999-2016

Source: National Center for Education Statistics, U.S. Dept. of Education

	1999-2000	2003-04	2005-06	2007-08	2009-10	2011-12	2013-14	2015-16
Number of charter school students	339,678	789,479	1,012,906	1,276,731	1,610,285	2,057,599	2,519,065	2,845,322
			Percentage of charter school students who were—					
Sex								
Male	51.0%	50.3%	49.9%	49.5%	49.5%	49.6%	49.6%	49.6%
Female	49.0	49.7	50.1	50.5	50.5	50.4	50.4	50.4
Race/ethnicity								
White...................	42.5	41.8	40.5	38.8	37.3	35.6	34.9	33.1
Black..................	33.5	31.9	32.1	31.8	30.3	28.7	27.1	26.8
Asian/Pacific Islander	2.8	3.2	3.6	3.8	3.9	4.0	4.1	4.3
Amer. Ind./Alaska Native	1.5	1.5	1.4	1.2	1.0	0.9	0.8	0.7
Two or more races...........	NA	NA	NA	NA	1.4	2.8	3.0	3.4
Hispanic	19.6	21.5	22.4	24.5	26.0	28.0	30.0	31.7
Number of charter schools	1,524	2,977	3,780	4,388	4,952	5,696	6,465	6,855
			Percentage of charter schools that were—					
School level								
Elementary	54.6%	52.0%	52.1%	53.3%	54.1%	54.9%	56.2%	56.2%
Secondary.................	25.9	26.2	28.0	27.8	26.8	24.9	23.5	23.0
Combined	18.6	21.0	18.6	18.3	18.8	19.5	19.6	20.5
Enrollment size								
Under 300.................	77.1	71.1	69.6	65.6	61.5	55.8	51.7	48.7
300-499.................	12.0	15.6	16.5	19.3	20.8	23.1	24.3	24.7
500-999.................	8.6	10.1	10.9	12.0	14.0	17.0	19.0	20.9
1,000 or more	2.4	3.2	3.0	3.1	3.7	4.2	4.9	5.8
Locale								
City	NA	52.7	52.5	54.3	54.8	55.4	56.5	56.5
Suburban	NA	22.0	22.2	22.0	21.1	21.2	26.1	25.9
Town	NA	9.6	9.4	8.5	8.0	7.4	7.0	6.7
Rural	NA	15.8	16.0	15.2	16.1	16.0	10.4	10.9

NA = Not available. **Note:** Race categories exclude persons of Hispanic ethnicity, who may be of any race.

Homeschooled Students, 2015-16

Source: National Center for Education Statistics, U.S. Dept. of Education

A total of 1,689,726 U.S. students in grades K-12 were homeschooled in 2015-16, down from 1,772,987 in 2012 and up from 1,520,140 in 2007 and 850,171 in 1999. In a 2016 U.S. Dept. of Education survey of parents who homeschool their children, the reason they gave as most important in their decision to homeschool was concern over the school environment, with such factors as safety, drugs, or negative peer pressure (34%); dissatisfaction with academic instruction in schools (17%); desire to provide religious instruction (16%); desire to provide a nontraditional approach to education (6%); the child has other special needs (6%); the child has a physical or mental health problem (6%); and desire to provide moral instruction (5%). In all, 80% cited concern over school environment as one of their reasons, 67% cited dissatisfaction with academic instruction, and 51% cited religious instruction.

Characteristic	No. of students (thous.)	% distrib.	Home-schooling rate[1]	Characteristic	No. of students (thous.)	% distrib.	Home-schooling rate[1]
Household locale				**Parents' education**			
City.................	493	29%	3.0%	High school diploma or less	510	30%	3.3%
Suburban	651	39	2.9	Vocational/technical, assoc. degree, or some college........	418	25	3.1
Town...............	177	10	4.3				
Rural...............	368	22	4.4	Bachelor's degree/some graduate school	501	30	3.6
Race/ethnicity[2]							
White	998	59	3.8	Graduate/professional degree.............	260	15	3.0
Black..............	132	8	1.9				
Asian/Pacific Islander ...	44	3	1.4	**Total**	**1,690**	**NA**	**3.3**
Other[3].............	69	4	2.7				
Hispanic	444	26	3.5				

NA = Not applicable. **Note:** Numbers may not add up to totals because of rounding. Homeschooled students are school-age children in a grade equivalent to K-12 who receive instruction at home all or most of the time. Excludes students enrolled in public or private school more than 25 hours per week or homeschooled because of temporary illness only. (1) Percentage of total subgroup (e.g., all "City" students) that is homeschooled. (2) Race categories exclude persons of Hispanic ethnicity, who may be of any race. (3) Includes two or more races and race ethnicity not reported.

Common Core State Standards
Source: Common Core State Standards Initiative

In 2009, members of the Council of Chief State School Officers and the National Governors Association Center for Best Practices met to develop the Common Core State Standards, a set of college- and career-readiness standards for kindergarten through 12th grade in English language arts/literacy and mathematics. The Common Core State Standards were released in June 2010. As of Aug. 2018, 41 states; Washington, DC; American Samoa; Guam; Northern Mariana Islands; and the U.S. Virgin Islands had adopted and were working to implement the standards, which are designed to ensure that students graduating from high school are prepared to take credit-bearing introductory courses in two- or four-year college programs or to enter the workforce.

Assessment took place starting in the 2014-15 school year. Most states used tests developed by the Partnership for Assessment of Readiness for College and Careers (PARCC) or the Smarter Balanced Assessment Consortium.

The Common Core standards have received both support and criticism. Proponents claimed that the Common Core standards would better prepare students for college or work and make them more competitive globally. Critics claimed that teachers and parents did not have enough input in developing the standards, that the federal government would be too involved in education (in spite of the state-level adoption of Common Core), and that implementing the standards would be too costly.

Population With Upper Secondary Education in Selected Countries, 2017
Source: Organization for Economic Cooperation and Development
Ranked by percentage of the population ages 25-64 that have received at least an upper secondary (senior high school) education.

Country	%	Country	%	Country	%	Country	%	Country	%
Japan	100%	Switzerland	88%	Ireland	82%	Luxembourg	77%	Colombia	54%
Russia[1]	94	Slovenia	88	Norway	82	South Africa	73	Brazil[2]	49
Czech Republic	94	South Korea	88	Denmark	81	Greece	73	Portugal	48
Lithuania	93	Latvia	88	Australia	81	Chile[2]	65	Costa Rica	40
Poland	92	Israel	87	New Zealand	79	United Kingdom	65	Turkey	39
Slovakia	91	Germany	87	France	78	Argentina	61	Indonesia	38
Canada	91	Austria	85	Netherlands	78	Italy	61	Mexico	38
United States	91	Hungary	84	Iceland	77	Spain	59	India[4]	29
Estonia	89	Sweden	83	Belgium	77	Saudi Arabia[3]	55	China[5]	24
Finland	88								

(1) 2016. (2) 2015. (3) 2014. (4) 2011. (5) 2010.

Financial Aid to U.S. Undergraduate Students, 2000-16
Source: National Center for Education Statistics, U.S. Dept. of Education

Type of institution/ year	Number enrolled	Number receiving financial aid	Percent receiving aid	Percent of enrolled students in student aid programs				Average award[1]			
				Federal grants	State/ local grants	Institutional grants	Student loans[2]	Federal grants	State/ local grants	Institutional grants	Student loans[2]
All institutions											
2000-01	1,976,600	1,390,527	70.3%	31.6%	31.2%	31.1%	40.1%	$3,446	$2,826	$6,569	$5,217
2015-16	2,456,811	2,032,503	82.7	42.7	32.3	44.4	45.7	4,765	3,436	10,551	7,117
Public											
2000-01	1,333,236	872,109	65.4	30.0	33.5	22.7	30.7	3,337	2,365	3,152	4,227
2015-16	1,745,701	1,400,491	80.2	42.3	37.3	35.6	38.2	4,717	3,297	5,437	6,426
4-year											
2000-01	804,793	573,430	71.3	26.6	36.5	29.6	40.7	3,561	2,866	3,625	4,451
2015-16	1,143,231	948,160	82.9	36.9	36.8	47.3	47.4	4,795	3,980	5,939	6,832
2-year											
2000-01	528,443	298,679	56.5	35.2	28.8	12.1	15.3	3,080	1,399	1,391	3,320
2015-16	602,470	452,331	75.1	52.6	38.1	13.5	20.9	4,612	2,041	2,105	4,681
Private nonprofit											
2000-01	439,369	363,044	82.6	28.4	31.8	68.1	57.7	3,990	4,154	10,211	5,570
2015-16	540,828	484,699	89.6	35.2	23.8	78.7	60.9	5,090	4,087	18,792	8,073
4-year											
2000-01	419,499	347,638	82.9	27.4	32.2	70.1	58.1	4,061	4,160	10,336	5,543
2015-16	505,542	451,270	89.3	31.9	25.0	82.1	59.2	5,022	4,091	19,173	8,151
2-year											
2000-01	19,870	15,406	77.5	49.2	23.9	25.7	49.5	3,145	4,008	3,004	6,249
2015-16	35,286	33,429	94.7	81.8	7.2	30.0	85.8	5,474	3,886	3,839	7,303
Private for-profit											
2000-01	203,995	155,374	76.2	49.3	15.2	6.2	63.5	3,204	3,456	2,134	7,646
2015-16	170,282	147,313	86.5	69.8	8.6	25.3	74.4	4,544	3,915	2,912	8,263
4-year											
2000-01	81,075	51,739	63.8	36.1	11.9	8.3	57.7	3,181	4,003	2,239	7,967
2015-16	59,524	51,839	87.1	65.4	10.9	38.4	73.4	4,733	3,793	4,203	8,617
2-year											
2000-01	122,920	103,635	84.3	58.0	17.3	4.8	67.3	3,214	3,207	2,013	7,465
2015-16	110,758	95,474	86.2	72.2	7.5	18.2	74.9	4,453	4,010	1,451	8,076

Note: Data for full-time, first-time, degree-seeking undergraduate students. (1) Average amounts for students participating in indicated programs, in constant 2016-17 dollars. (2) Includes only loans made directly to students. Does not include Parent Loans for Undergraduate Students (PLUS) and other loans made directly to parents.

Charges at U.S. Institutions of Higher Education, 1969-2017

Source: National Center for Education Statistics, U.S. Dept. of Education

Data are for the entire academic year and are average charges, in current dollars, for full-time students at degree-granting postsecondary institutions. Room and board based on full-time students. For 1989-90 on, board is based on 20 meals per week.

	Tuition and fees			Board rates			Dormitory charges		
Public (in-state)	All institutions	2-yr	4-yr	All institutions	2-yr	4-yr	All institutions	2-yr	4-yr
1969-70	$323	$178	$358	$508	$465	$510	$366	$308	$369
1979-80	583	355	738	867	893	865	715	574	725
1989-90	1,356	756	1,780	1,635	1,581	1,638	1,513	962	1,557
1999-2000	2,504	1,348	3,349	2,364	1,834	2,406	2,440	1,549	2,519
2003-04	3,319	1,702	4,587	2,822	2,221	2,876	3,106	2,089	3,212
2004-05	3,629	1,849	5,027	2,931	2,353	2,981	3,304	2,174	3,418
2005-06	3,874	1,935	5,351	3,035	2,306	3,093	3,545	2,251	3,664
2006-07	4,102	2,018	5,666	3,191	2,390	3,253	3,757	2,407	3,878
2007-08	4,291	2,061	5,943	3,331	2,409	3,404	3,952	2,506	4,082
2008-09	4,512	2,136	6,312	3,554	2,769	3,619	4,190	2,664	4,331
2009-10	4,763	2,283	6,717	3,655	2,571	3,755	4,401	2,854	4,564
2010-11	5,075	2,441	7,132	3,845	2,683	3,956	4,646	2,955	4,832
2011-12	5,563	2,651	7,713	3,946	2,866	4,042	4,849	3,100	5,031
2012-13	5,899	2,792	8,070	4,061	2,888	4,163	5,062	3,247	5,241
2013-14	6,120	2,881	8,312	4,205	2,955	4,308	5,304	3,448	5,479
2014-15	6,370	2,955	8,543	4,313	3,072	4,412	5,504	3,559	5,677
2015-16	6,612	3,038	8,778	4,469	3,118	4,576	5,686	3,759	5,850
2016-17	6,817	3,156	8,804	4,561	3,113	4,666	5,859	3,822	6,017
Private (nonprofit and for-profit)									
1969-70	$1,533	$1,034	$1,562	$560	$546	$561	$434	$413	$436
1979-80	3,130	2,062	3,225	955	923	957	827	766	831
1989-90	8,147	5,196	8,396	1,948	1,811	1,953	1,923	1,663	1,935
1999-2000	14,100	8,225	14,616	2,877	2,753	2,879	3,236	3,067	3,242
2003-04	17,315	11,545	17,763	3,364	4,432	3,354	3,945	3,581	3,952
2004-05	18,154	12,122	18,604	3,485	3,700	3,483	4,178	4,475	4,173
2005-06	18,862	12,450	19,292	3,645	4,781	3,637	4,400	4,173	4,404
2006-07	20,048	12,708	20,517	3,785	3,429	3,788	4,606	4,147	4,613
2007-08	20,972	13,126	21,427	3,992	4,074	3,991	4,804	4,484	4,808
2008-09	21,570	13,562	22,036	4,209	4,627	4,206	5,025	4,537	5,032
2009-10	21,764	14,862	22,269	4,329	4,390	4,329	5,248	5,211	5,248
2010-11	22,042	13,687	22,677	4,430	4,475	4,430	5,403	4,939	5,410
2011-12	22,850	13,961	23,464	4,586	4,475	4,586	5,622	5,169	5,627
2012-13	23,943	14,149	24,523	4,709	3,977	4,712	5,831	5,228	5,837
2013-14	25,110	14,170	25,707	4,864	4,211	4,866	6,021	5,489	6,026
2014-15	26,182	14,261	26,739	5,019	4,560	5,021	6,221	5,506	6,228
2015-16	27,436	14,528	27,942	5,123	4,181	5,128	6,457	5,666	6,464
2016-17	28,947	14,587	29,478	5,268	4,348	5,273	6,710	5,948	6,717

U.S. Student Loan Balances by Age, 2004-17

Source: *2018 Student Loan Update*, Federal Reserve Bank of New York; Equifax

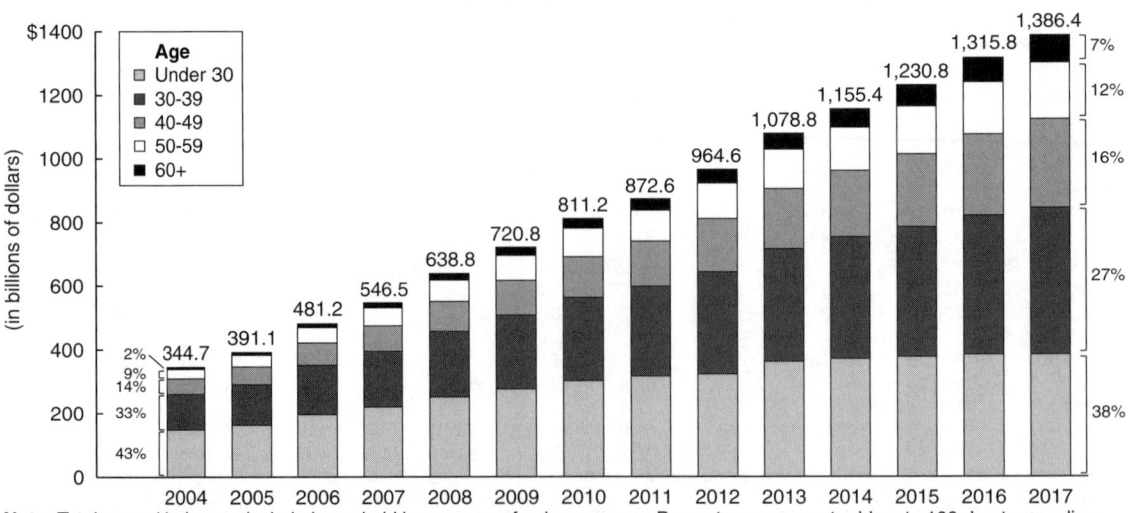

Note: Total annual balances include loans held by persons of unknown ages. Percentages may not add up to 100 due to rounding

Student Loan Debt by State, 2004-16

Source: *Student Debt and the Class of 2016*, Project on Student Debt, Institute for College Access & Success

State[1]	Average debt			% with debt		State[1]	Average debt			% with debt	
	2004	2014	2016	2004	2016		2004	2014	2016	2004	2016
Alabama	$18,042	$29,425	$31,275	57%	50%	Missouri	$15,511	$25,844	$27,532	59%	57%
Alaska	15,648	26,742	26,008	48	49	Montana	18,019	26,946	31,065	68	60
Arizona	18,147	22,609	23,447	48	49	Nebraska	17,384	26,278	26,585	62	61
Arkansas	16,210	25,344	26,859	59	56	Nevada	14,144	20,211	24,128	46	52
California	16,071	21,382	22,744	49	53	New Hampshire	21,441	33,410	36,367	65	74
Colorado	16,352	25,064	26,520	53	53	New Jersey	16,223	28,318	29,878	58	61
Connecticut	18,906	29,750	35,494	57	60	New Mexico	—	18,969	21,373	—	55
Delaware	14,780	33,808	33,838	45	63	New York	18,857	27,822	30,346	62	58
District of						North Carolina	16,863	25,218	25,562	51	58
Columbia	19,357	—	31,054	58	53	North Dakota	22,409	—	—	73	—
Florida	18,857	24,947	24,461	51	52	Ohio	19,182	29,353	30,351	62	64
Georgia	15,354	26,518	27,657	53	60	Oklahoma	16,942	23,430	25,856	55	50
Hawaii	13,509	24,554	26,092	29	50	Oregon	17,267	26,106	27,321	63	58
Idaho	22,273	26,091	27,130	68	66	Pennsylvania	19,556	33,264	35,759	69	68
Illinois	15,650	28,984	29,271	56	61	Rhode Island	19,328	31,841	31,217	68	61
Indiana	19,425	29,222	29,562	54	59	South Carolina	16,775	29,163	30,123	55	60
Iowa	24,204	29,732	29,801	76	65	South Dakota	19,023	26,023	31,362	82	75
Kansas	16,266	25,521	28,776	57	60	Tennessee	16,905	25,510	26,981	41	60
Kentucky	14,250	25,939	28,910	52	63	Texas	17,170	26,250	26,292	51	56
Louisiana	18,993	23,025	27,138	61	50	Utah	12,362	18,921	19,975	43	43
Maine	19,410	30,908	31,295	64	55	Vermont	20,706	29,060	28,662	56	63
Maryland	12,597	27,457	27,455	52	54	Virginia	15,831	26,432	29,296	57	56
Massachusetts	17,021	29,391	31,563	60	60	Washington	17,415	24,804	24,609	56	53
Michigan	18,754	29,450	30,852	58	63	West Virginia	18,246	26,854	27,708	69	77
Minnesota	19,580	31,579	31,915	72	68	Wisconsin	16,560	28,810	30,059	60	67
Mississippi	15,503	26,177	29,384	60	60	Wyoming	15,352	23,708	25,378	44	45
						U.S.	**18,550**	**28,950**	**NA**	**65**	**NA**

— = Usable cases covered less than 30% of bachelor's degree recipients, or underlying data showed a state-level change of 30% or more in average debt from previous year. NA = Not available. (1) Location of surveyed colleges (not necessarily location of degree recipient).

College Enrollment by Selected Characteristics, 1947-2016

Source: National Center for Education Statistics, U.S. Dept. of Education

(numbers in thousands)

Year	Total enrollment[1]	Attendance status			Sex of student		Control of institution			
		Full-time	Part-time	% part-time	Male	Female	Public	Total	Private Nonprofit	For-profit
1947[2]	2,338	NA	NA	NA	1,659	679	1,152	1,186	NA	NA
1950[2]	2,281	NA	NA	NA	1,560	721	1,140	1,142	NA	NA
1955[2]	2,653	NA	NA	NA	1,733	920	1,476	1,177	NA	NA
1965	5,921	4,096	1,825[3]	30.8%	3,630	2,291	3,970	1,951	NA	NA
1970	8,581	5,816	2,765	32.2	5,044	3,537	6,428	2,153	2,134	18
1975	11,185	6,841	4,344	38.8	6,149	5,036	8,835	2,350	2,311	39
1980	12,097	7,098	4,999	41.3	5,874	6,223	9,457	2,640	2,528	112[4]
1985	12,247	7,075	5,172	42.2	5,819	6,429	9,479	2,768	2,572	196
1990	13,819	7,821	5,998	43.4	6,284	7,535	10,845	2,974	2,760	214
1995	14,262	8,129	6,133	43.0	6,343	7,919	11,092	3,169	2,929	240
2000	15,312	9,010	6,303	41.2	6,722	8,591	11,753	3,560	3,109	450
2001	15,928	9,448	6,481	40.7	6,961	8,967	12,233	3,695	3,167	528
2002	16,612	9,946	6,665	40.1	7,202	9,410	12,752	3,860	3,266	594
2003	16,912	10,326	6,585	38.9	7,260	9,651	12,859	4,053	3,341	712
2004	17,272	10,610	6,662	38.6	7,387	9,885	12,980	4,292	3,412	880
2005	17,488	10,797	6,691	38.3	7,456	10,032	13,022	4,466	3,455	1,011
2006	17,759	10,957	6,802	38.3	7,575	10,184	13,180	4,579	3,513	1,066
2007	18,248	11,270	6,978	38.2	7,816	10,432	13,491	4,757	3,571	1,186
2008	19,103	11,748	7,355	38.5	8,189	10,914	13,972	5,131	3,662	1,469
2009	20,314	12,605	7,708	37.9	8,733	11,581	14,811	5,503	3,768	1,735
2010	21,019	13,087	7,932	37.7	9,046	11,974	15,142	5,877	3,855	2,023
2011	21,011	13,003	8,008	38.1	9,034	11,976	15,116	5,894	3,927	1,967
2012	20,644	12,734	7,910	38.3	8,919	11,725	14,885	5,760	3,951	1,808
2013	20,377	12,597	7,780	38.2	8,861	11,515	14,747	5,630	3,971	1,658
2014	20,209	12,454	7,755	38.4	8,798	11,412	14,655	5,554	3,997	1,557
2015	19,988	12,288	7,701	38.5	8,724	11,264	14,573	5,415	4,066	1,349
2016	19,841	12,126	7,715	38.9	8,636	11,205	14,583	5,258	4,078	1,180

NA = Not available. **Note:** Data for 1947-95 are for institutions of higher education, while later data are for degree-granting institutions. Degree-granting institutions grant associate's or higher degrees and participate in Title IV federal financial aid programs. The degree-granting classification is very similar to the earlier higher education classification, but it includes more two-year colleges and excludes a few higher education institutions that do not grant degrees. (1) Fall enrollment. (2) Degree-credit enrollment only. (3) Includes part-time resident students and all extension students (students attending courses at sites separate from the primary reporting campus). In later years, part-time student enrollment was collected as a distinct category. (4) Large increases are due to the addition of schools accredited by the Accrediting Commission of Career Schools and Colleges of Technology.

U.S. Bachelor's Degrees Conferred, 1899-2028

Source: National Center for Education Statistics, U.S. Dept. of Education
(*) figures are projected.

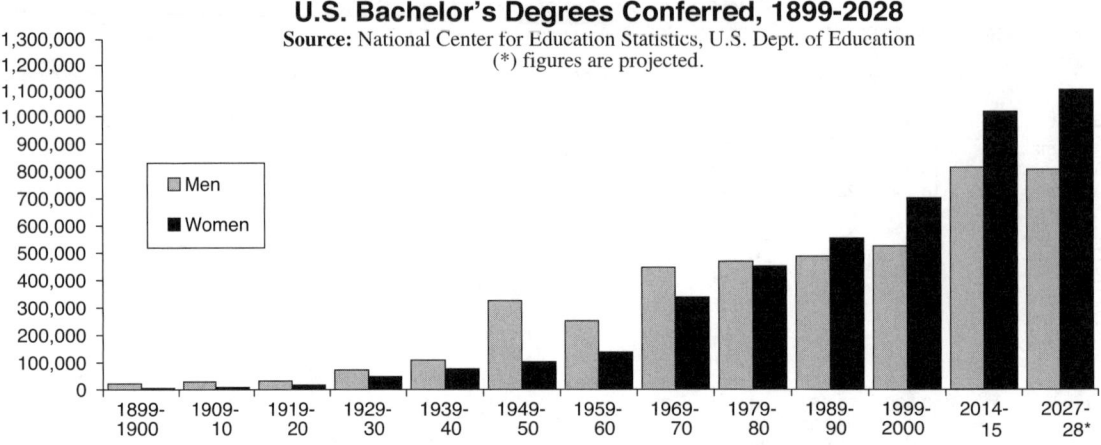

Financial Aid for College and Other Postsecondary Education

Reviewed by National Association of Student Financial Aid Administrators; as of July 2018

The cost of postsecondary education in the U.S. continues to increase, but financial aid—in the form of **grants** (no repayment needed), **loans**, and/or **work-study** programs—is widely available to help families meet these expenses. Most federal aid is limited to families that demonstrate financial need as determined by standard formulas and is designed to help students attend the college of their choice regardless of their ability to pay. Financial aid personnel at each school can provide information about all aid programs (federal, state, institutional, and private) available to students, how to apply, and deadlines.

All applicants for federal aid must file a Free Application for Federal Student Aid (**FAFSA**), generally as soon as possible after Oct. 1 for the academic year starting the following Aug. or Sept. This change from Jan. in prior years allows students to apply for aid earlier. Figures provided should match federal income tax forms filed for the previous year. (The use of tax data that has already been filed ensures timely processing.) Thus, the application for the 2019-20 academic year, available Oct. 1, 2018, should be filed with 2017 tax information. This is made easier by the availability of the IRS Data Retrieval Tool, which allows online applicants to access and transfer IRS tax return information directly into their FAFSA. Many other sources of aid—state governments, employers and unions, civic organizations, and the institutions themselves—also use the FAFSA to determine eligibility for aid. Some federal programs pay for postsecondary education in return for service: AmeriCorps (1-800-942-2677), Reserve Officers' Training Corps (1-800-USA-ROTC [Army], 1-800-USA-NAVY [Navy], and 1-800-522-0033 [Air Force]), the G.I. Bill (1-888-442-4551), and the National Health Service Corps (1-800-221-9393). A student must reapply for aid annually.

Students, parents, and borrowers are required to use an **FSA ID**, made up of a username and password, to access certain U.S. Dept. of Education websites. An FSA ID is used to confirm identity when accessing financial aid information and electronically signing federal student aid documents.

A **federal formula**, based on information provided on the FAFSA, takes into account such factors as family income in the preceding calendar year, parental and student assets (excluding the parents' home, farm, or certain small businesses), and length of time to parents' retirement. Financial aid personnel have the authority to consider unusual expenses, such as very high medical expenses, which are not reported on the FAFSA. Outside scholarships are also taken into account in determining eligibility for federal, institutional, and state financial aid programs.

The formula determines a family's **expected family contribution** (EFC), which is divided among the number of family members—excluding parents—in college. The EFC is subtracted from the total cost of attending college for each person. The difference determines financial need and the maximum federal aid for which the family may be eligible. (Some institutions use a separate formula for need-based institutional aid.) Some schools guarantee they will meet the full financial need of each admitted student. Schools might try to cover a student's financial need using various financial aid but be unable to because of a lack of funds.

The **aid package** offered by each school may include one or more of the following resources: Federal Pell Grants, for those who demonstrate sufficient financial need; Federal Supplemental Educational Opportunity Grants, for those who still have significant need after receiving Federal Pell Grants; grants from the school; Federal Work-Study or other work programs; and federal Direct Subsidized and Unsubsidized Loans (often referred to as Direct Loans). Parents of undergraduates and students in graduate or professional school may apply for a PLUS Loan. Direct Unsubsidized Loans and Direct PLUS Loans are available regardless of financial need, but students and parents must still complete the FAFSA to get these loans.

Loans have varying interest rates and other requirements. Repayment of Direct Subsidized Loans and Direct Unsubsidized Loans generally does not begin until after graduation; deferments, income-based repayment plans, and loan forgiveness are available on federal loans for students who meet certain requirements. For PLUS Loans, parents and graduate-level students must pass a credit check and may need to begin repayment of both principal and interest while the student is still in school.

Terms may vary, but federal student loans must be repaid, even if financial circumstances change, education is incomplete or not as expected, or post-graduation income is less than expected. The loan servicer or lender is required to provide a loan repayment schedule that states the first payment due date, the number and frequency of payments, and the amount due. Some loans have a grace period, a set period of time (in most cases six months) after graduation before repayment begins. Direct loans have a number of repayment plan options—including graduated repayments, extended repayment, income-based repayment—or offer loan consolidation. In most cases, student loan debt cannot be discharged in bankruptcy.

Certain federal income **tax credits and refunds** are available to families who meet requirements.

Rules for financial aid are complex and changeable. Comprehensive resources on financial aid from the U.S. Dept. of Education, including fact sheets, videos, worksheets, and other tools, are available online at studentaid.ed.gov/sa/resources/.

Further information and FAFSA forms are available from schools or from the Federal Student Aid Information Center: 1-800-4-FED-AID, Mon.-Fri., 8 AM-10 PM ET; fafsa.ed.gov.

Endowment Assets of Colleges and Universities, 2017

Source: *2017 NACUBO-Commonfund Study of Endowments*, National Association of College and University Business Officers (NACUBO)

Rank	College/university	Endowment assets[1]	% change, 2016-17	Rank	College/university	Endowment assets[1]	% change, 2016-17
1.	Harvard University	$36,021,516	4.3%	23.	Ohio State University	$4,253,459	18.9%
2.	Yale University	27,176,100	7.0	24.	Vanderbilt University	4,136,465	9.0
3.	University of Texas System	26,535,095	9.6	25.	New York University	3,991,638	14.5
4.	Stanford University	24,784,943	10.7	26.	Pennsylvania State University	3,990,781	10.8
5.	Princeton University	23,812,241	7.5	27.	University of Pittsburgh	3,945,687	11.9
6.	Massachusetts Institute of Technology	14,967,983	11.4	28.	Johns Hopkins University	3,844,918	13.7
7.	University of Pennsylvania	12,213,202	14.0	29.	University of Minnesota and Foundation	3,493,641	6.5
8.	Texas A&M University System	11,556,260	9.6	30.	Brown University	3,245,531	9.5
9.	University of Michigan	10,936,014	12.2	31.	University of North Carolina at Chapel Hill and Foundations	3,027,227	4.8
10.	Northwestern University	10,436,692	8.2	32.	University of Wisconsin Foundation	2,746,470	13.5
11.	Columbia University	9,996,596	10.6	33.	Michigan State University	2,682,869	NA
12.	University of California	9,787,627	17.3	34.	California Institute of Technology	2,606,505	17.5
13.	University of Notre Dame	9,352,376	11.7	35.	University of Illinois and Foundation	2,556,723	12.7
14.	Duke University	7,911,175	15.7	36.	University of Washington	2,529,250	13.0
15.	Washington University in St. Louis	7,860,774	11.4	37.	Williams College	2,508,773	11.2
16.	University of Chicago	7,523,720	7.5	38.	Purdue University	2,424,872	7.6
17.	Emory University	6,905,465	7.9	39.	University of Richmond	2,373,506	8.4
18.	Cornell University	6,757,750	13.2	40.	Boston College	2,317,300	12.3
19.	University of Virginia	6,393,561	9.2				
20.	Rice University	5,814,444	9.2				
21.	University of Southern California	5,128,459	11.3				
22.	Dartmouth College	4,956,494	10.8				

NA = Not available. **Note:** Market value of endowment assets in the fiscal year. (1) In thousands.

Average ACT Scores and Characteristics of College-Bound Students, 1990-2017

Source: ACT, Inc. (formerly American College Testing)

SCORES	Unit	1990	1995	2000	2005	2010	2011	2012	2013	2014	2015	2016	2017
Composite score	Points	**20.6**	**20.8**	**21.0**	**20.9**	**21.0**	**21.1**	**21.1**	**20.9**	**21.0**	**21.0**	**20.8**	**21.0**
Male	Points	21.0	21.0	21.2	21.1	21.2	21.2	21.2	20.9	21.1	21.1	20.9	21.0
Female	Points	20.3	20.7	20.9	20.9	20.9	21.0	21.0	20.9	20.9	21.0	20.9	21.1
English score	Points	**20.5**	**20.2**	**20.5**	**20.4**	**20.5**	**20.6**	**20.5**	**20.2**	**20.3**	**20.4**	**20.1**	**20.3**
Male	Points	20.1	19.8	20.0	20.0	20.1	20.2	20.0	19.8	20.0	20.0	19.8	19.9
Female	Points	20.9	20.6	20.9	20.8	20.8	20.9	20.9	20.6	20.7	20.8	20.6	20.8
Math score	Points	**19.9**	**20.2**	**20.7**	**20.7**	**21.0**	**21.1**	**21.1**	**20.9**	**20.9**	**20.8**	**20.6**	**20.7**
Male	Points	20.7	20.9	21.4	21.3	21.6	21.6	21.7	21.4	21.4	21.3	21.0	21.2
Female	Points	19.3	19.7	20.2	20.2	20.5	20.6	20.6	20.5	20.5	20.4	20.3	20.4
PARTICIPANTS													
Total number	(Thous.)	817	945	1,065	1,186	1,569	1,623	1,666	1,799	1,846	1,924	2,090	2,030
Male	Percent	46%	44%	43%	44%	45%	46%	46%	46%	46%	47%	46%	46%
White	Percent	79	80	72	66	62	60	59	58	56	55	54	52
Black	Percent	9	9	10	12	14	14	13	13	13	13	13	13
Hispanic[1]	Percent	4	5	5	7	10	12	14	14	15	16	16	17
Composite score													
27 or above	Percent	12	13	14	14	16	17	17	13	17	18	17	18
18 or below	Percent	35	34	32	34	35	34	34	36	36	37	39	38

Note: Minimum score, 1; maximum score, 36. Test scores and characteristics of college-bound students are based on the performance of all ACT-tested students who graduated in the spring of a given school year and took the ACT assessment during junior or senior year of high school. (1) Persons of Hispanic origin may be of any race.

Average ACT Composite Scores by State, 2017

Source: ACT, Inc. (formerly American College Testing)

State	Avg. comp. score	% grads taking ACT	State	Avg. comp. score	% grads taking ACT	State	Avg. comp. score	% grads taking ACT
Alabama	19.2	100%	Kentucky	20.0	100%	North Dakota	20.3	98%
Alaska	19.8	65	Louisiana	19.5	100	Ohio	22.0	75
Arizona	19.7	62	Maine	24.3	8	Oklahoma	19.4	100
Arkansas	19.4	100	Maryland	23.6	28	Oregon	21.8	40
California	22.8	31	Massachusetts	25.4	29	Pennsylvania	23.7	23
Colorado	20.8	100	Michigan	24.1	29	Rhode Island	24.0	21
Connecticut	25.2	31	Minnesota	21.5	100	South Carolina	18.7	100
Delaware	24.1	18	Mississippi	18.6	100	South Dakota	21.8	80
District of Columbia	24.2	32	Missouri	20.4	100	Tennessee	19.8	100
Florida	19.8	73	Montana	20.3	100	Texas	20.7	45
Georgia	21.4	55	Nebraska	21.4	84	Utah	20.3	100
Hawaii	19.0	90	Nevada	17.8	100	Vermont	23.6	29
Idaho	22.3	38	New Hampshire	25.5	18	Virginia	23.8	29
Illinois	21.4	93	New Jersey	23.9	34	Washington	21.9	29
Indiana	22.6	35	New Mexico	19.7	66	West Virginia	20.4	69
Iowa	21.9	67	New York	24.2	31	Wisconsin	20.5	100
Kansas	21.7	73	North Carolina	19.1	100	Wyoming	20.2	100

Mean SAT Scores of College-Bound Seniors, 1975-2017
Source: The College Board
(for school year ending in year shown)

	1975	1980	1985	1990	1995	2000	2005	2010	2011	2012	2013	2014	2015	2016[2,3]	2017[3]
Reading and writing[1]	**512**	**502**	**509**	**500**	**504**	**505**	**508**	**500**	**497**	**496**	**496**	**497**	**495**	**494**	**533**
Male	515	506	514	505	505	507	513	502	500	498	499	499	497	495	532
Female	509	498	503	496	502	504	505	498	495	493	494	495	493	493	534
Math score...........	**498**	**492**	**500**	**501**	**506**	**514**	**520**	**515**	**514**	**514**	**514**	**513**	**511**	**508**	**527**
Male	518	515	522	521	525	533	538	533	531	532	531	530	527	524	538
Female	479	473	480	483	490	498	504	499	500	499	499	499	496	494	516
Writing score.........	**NA**	**NA**	**NA**	**NA**	**NA**	**NA**	**NA**	**491**	**489**	**488**	**488**	**487**	**484**	**482**	**NA**
Male	NA	NA	NA	NA	NA	NA	NA	485	482	481	482	481	478	475	NA
Female	NA	NA	NA	NA	NA	NA	NA	497	496	494	493	492	490	487	NA

NA = Not applicable. **Note:** In 1995, the College Board recentered the scoring scale for the SAT. Earlier scores have been adjusted to account for this recentering. (1) Verbal section, 1975-2005; critical reading, 2006-16. (2) Through Jan. 2016. (3) Beginning in Mar. 2016, students took a redesigned SAT. The College Board advised against comparing 2016 and 2017 SAT results with earlier data.

Mean SAT Scores by State, 1990-2017
Source: The College Board; National Center for Education Statistics, U.S. Dept. of Education
(for school year ending in year shown; V = Verbal, M = Math, CR = Critical reading, W = Writing, ERW = Evidence-based reading and writing)

	1990		2000		2010			2015			2017[1]		% grads
State	V	M	V	M	CR	M	W	CR	M	W	ERW	M	taking SAT[2]
Alabama	545	534	559	555	556	550	544	545	538	533	593	572	5%
Alaska	514	501	519	515	518	515	491	509	503	482	547	533	38
Arizona	521	520	521	523	519	525	500	523	527	502	563	553	30
Arkansas	545	532	563	554	566	566	552	568	569	551	614	594	3
California	494	508	497	518	501	516	500	495	506	491	531	524	53
Colorado	533	534	534	537	568	572	555	582	587	567	606	595	11
Connecticut	506	496	508	509	509	514	513	504	506	504	530	512	100
Delaware	510	496	502	496	493	495	481	462	461	445	503	492	100
District of Columbia	483	467	494	486	474	464	466	441	440	432	482	468	90
Florida	495	493	498	500	496	498	479	486	480	468	520	497	83
Georgia	478	473	488	486	488	490	475	490	485	475	535	515	61
Hawaii	480	505	488	519	483	505	470	487	508	477	544	541	55
Idaho	542	524	540	541	543	541	517	467	463	442	513	493	93
Illinois	542	547	568	586	585	600	577	599	616	587	559	556	9
Indiana	486	486	498	501	494	505	477	496	499	478	542	532	63
Iowa	584	588	589	600	603	613	582	589	600	566	641	635	2
Kansas	566	563	574	580	590	595	567	588	592	568	632	628	4
Kentucky	548	541	548	550	575	575	563	588	587	574	631	616	4
Louisiana	551	537	562	558	555	550	547	563	559	553	611	586	4
Maine	501	490	504	500	468	467	454	468	473	451	513	499	95
Maryland	506	502	507	509	501	506	495	491	493	478	536	524	69
Massachusetts	503	498	511	513	512	526	509	516	529	507	555	551	76
Michigan	529	534	557	569	585	605	576	594	609	585	509	495	100
Minnesota	552	558	581	594	594	607	580	595	607	576	644	651	3
Mississippi	552	538	562	549	566	548	552	580	563	570	634	607	2
Missouri	548	541	572	577	593	595	580	596	599	582	640	631	3
Montana	540	542	543	546	538	538	517	561	556	538	605	591	10
Nebraska	559	562	560	571	585	593	568	589	590	576	629	625	3
Nevada	511	511	510	517	496	501	473	494	494	470	563	553	26
New Hampshire	518	510	520	519	520	524	510	525	530	511	532	520	96
New Jersey	495	498	498	513	495	514	497	500	521	499	530	526	70
New Mexico	554	546	549	543	553	549	534	551	544	528	577	561	11
New York	489	496	494	506	484	499	478	489	502	478	528	523	67
North Carolina	478	470	492	496	497	511	477	498	504	476	546	535	49
North Dakota	579	578	588	609	580	594	559	597	608	586	635	621	2
Ohio	526	522	533	539	538	548	522	557	563	537	578	570	12
Oklahoma	553	542	563	560	569	568	547	576	569	548	530	517	7
Oregon	515	509	527	527	523	524	499	523	521	502	560	548	43
Pennsylvania	497	490	498	497	492	501	480	499	504	482	540	531	65
Rhode Island	498	488	505	500	494	495	488	494	494	484	539	524	71
South Carolina	475	467	484	482	484	495	468	488	487	467	543	521	50
South Dakota	580	570	587	588	592	603	571	592	597	564	612	603	3
Tennessee	558	544	563	553	576	571	565	581	574	568	623	604	5
Texas	490	489	493	500	484	505	473	470	486	454	513	507	62
Utah	566	555	570	569	568	559	547	579	575	554	624	614	3
Vermont	507	493	513	508	519	521	506	523	524	507	562	551	60
Virginia	501	496	509	500	512	512	497	518	516	499	561	541	65
Washington	513	511	526	528	524	532	508	502	510	484	541	534	64
West Virginia	520	514	526	511	515	507	500	509	497	495	558	528	14
Wisconsin	552	559	584	597	595	604	579	591	605	575	642	649	3
Wyoming	534	538	545	545	570	567	546	589	586	562	626	604	3
National average	**500**	**501**	**505**	**514**	**501**	**516**	**492**	**495**	**511**	**484**	**533**	**527**	**NA**

NA = Not available. **Note:** In 1995, the College Board recentered the scoring scale for the SAT. In 2005, the Verbal portion became Critical reading, and a writing test was added. In 2016, this portion became Evidence-based reading and writing. (1) Beginning in Mar. 2016, students took a redesigned SAT test. The College Board advised against comparing 2017 SAT results with earlier data. (2) Percentage of students from the class of 2017 who took the SAT during high school.

Four-Year Colleges and Universities

Source: Peterson's College Database © 2018 Peterson's, LLC. All rights reserved.

Note: These listings include only accredited degree-granting institutions in the U.S. and U.S. territories with a total enrollment of 1,200 or more. Only four-year colleges and universities that award a bachelor's degree as their highest undergraduate degree are included. Data reported for institutions that provided updated information on Peterson's Annual Survey of Undergraduate Institutions for the 2017-18 academic year, with some exceptions.

All institutions are coeducational except those where the ZIP code is followed directly by a number in parentheses: (1) = men only; (2) = primarily men; (3) = women only; (4) = primarily women; (5) undergraduate: men only, graduate: coed; (6) undergraduate: women only, graduate: coed.

The **Tuition & fees** column shows the annual tuition and required fees for full-time students or, where indicated, the tuition and standard fees per unit for part-time students. Where tuition varies according to residence, the figure is given for the most local resident and is coded as follows: (A) = area residents, (S) = state residents; all other figures apply to all students regardless of residence. Where annual expenses are expressed as a lump sum (including full-time tuition, mandatory fees, and room and board), the figure is entered under Tuition & fees and coded (C) = comprehensive fee. **Room & board** is the typical cost for one academic year.

Control: 1 = independent (nonprofit), 2 = independent-religious, 3 = proprietary (profit-making), 4 = federal, 5 = state, 6 = commonwealth (Puerto Rico), 7 = territory (U.S. territories), 8 = county, 9 = district, 10 = city, 11 = state and local, 12 = state-related, 13 = private (unspecified), 14 = public (unspecified). **Degree** means the highest degree offered: B = bachelor's, M = master's, D = doctorate.

Enrollment is the total number of matriculated undergraduate and (if applicable) graduate students.

Faculty is the total number of full-time and part-time faculty members teaching courses.

Grad. rate is the percentage of full-time, first-time bachelor's (or equivalent) degree-seeking undergraduate students entering school in 2011 (or most recent available year prior) who obtained their degrees within six years.

NA indicates category is inapplicable, or data is not available from a consistent source.

Name, address	Year founded	Tuition & fees	Room & board	Control, degree	Enrollment	Faculty	Grad. rate
Abilene Christian Univ., Abilene, TX 79699	1906	$33,330	$10,378	2-D	5,149	449	61%
Abraham Baldwin Agr. Coll., Tifton, GA 31793	1933	NA	NA	5-B	3,327	162	NA
Acad. of Art Univ., San Francisco, CA 94105-3410.	1929	$27,810	$16,648	3-M	11,672	1,292	39
Adams State Univ., Alamosa, CO 81101	1921	$9,444 (S)	$7,215	5-D	3,308	254	36
Adelphi Univ., Garden City, NY 11530-0701.	1896	$37,170	$15,500	1-D	7,978	1,062	68
Adrian Coll., Adrian, MI 49221-2575.	1859	$35,740	$10,740	2-M	1,656	195	54
Adventist Univ. of Health Sciences, Orlando, FL 32803	1992	$15,150	$4,200	1-D	1,809	242	NA
Alabama A&M Univ., Huntsville, AL 35811.	1875	$9,857 (S)	$7,302	5-D	5,814	290	100
Alabama State Univ., Montgomery, AL 36101-0271.	1867	$11,068 (S)	$6,050	5-D	4,760	445	28
Albany Coll. of Pharm. & Health Sci., Albany, NY 12208	1881	$31,981	$10,700	1-D	1,559	132	77
Albany State Univ., Albany, GA 31705-2717.	1903	$5,675 (S)	$8,874	5-M	3,041	155	31
Albertus Magnus Coll., New Haven, CT 06511-1189.	1925	$31,490	$14,016	2-M	1,555	134	44
Albion Coll., Albion, MI 49224-1831.	1835	$45,590	$12,380	2-B	1,568	174	57
Albright Coll., Reading, PA 19612-5234	1856	$45,302	$12,070	2-M	2,036	156	53
Alcorn State Univ., Lorman, MS 39096-7500.	1871	$6,888 (S)	$9,731	5-M	3,716	221	33
Alfred Univ., Alfred, NY 14802-1205.	1836	$33,484	$12,516	1-D	2,362	193	54
Allegheny Coll., Meadville, PA 16335	1815	$47,540	$12,140	1-B	1,802	200	76
Alliant Intl. Univ.–San Diego, San Diego, CA 92131	1952	$17,510	NA	1-D	3,046	520	NA
Alma Coll., Alma, MI 48801-1599.	1886	$38,768	$10,642	2-B	1,426	158	68
Alvernia Univ., Reading, PA 19607-1799	1958	$33,640	$11,890	2-D	2,872	319	53
Alverno Coll., Milwaukee, WI 53234-3922 (6).	1887	$28,277	$8,296	2-D	1,942	211	45
Amberton Univ., Garland, TX 75041-5595	1971	$12,000	NA	2-M	1,379	40	NA
Amer. InterContinental Univ. Online, Schaumburg, IL 60173	1970	NA	NA	3-M	22,424	396	NA
Amer. Intl. Coll., Springfield, MA 01109-3189.	1885	$35,680	$14,300	1-D	3,283	320	41
Amer. Public Univ. System, Charles Town, WV 25414	1991	$6,880	NA	3-D	46,420	1,863	NA
Amer. Univ., Washington, DC 20016-8001.	1893	$48,459	$14,880	2-D	13,858	1,466	79
Amer. Univ. of Puerto Rico, Bayamon, PR 00960-2037	1963	NA	NA	1-M	2,468	162	NA
Amherst Coll., Amherst, MA 01002-5000	1821	$54,310	$14,190	1-B	1,836	291	95
Anderson Univ., Anderson, IN 46012-3495	1917	$29,710	$9,740	2-D	1,877	252	67
Anderson Univ., Anderson, SC 29621-4035.	1911	$26,970	$9,680	2-D	3,497	341	57
Andrews Univ., Berrien Springs, MI 49104.	1874	$28,436	$9,078	2-D	3,348	276	55
Angelo State Univ., San Angelo, TX 76909.	1928	$8,215 (S)	$7,666	5-D	10,417	412	37
Anna Maria Coll., Paxton, MA 01612	1946	$37,130	$13,890	2-D	1,468	NA	34
Appalachian State Univ., Boone, NC 28608.	1899	$7,303 (S)	$8,174	5-D	18,811	1,330	74
Aquinas Coll., Grand Rapids, MI 49506	1886	$32,574	$9,332	2-M	1,716	210	59
Arcadia Univ., Glenside, PA 19038-3295	1853	$42,330	$13,660	2-D	3,811	477	66
Arkansas State Univ., State University, AR 72467	1909	$8,478 (S)	$8,762	5-D	13,410	711	39
Arizona State Univ. at the Downtown Phoenix campus, Phoenix, AZ 85004	2006	$10,370 (S)	$13,310	5-D	11,445	635	66
Arizona State Univ. at the Polytechnic campus, Mesa, AZ 85212.	1996	$9,886 (S)	$11,474	5-D	4,809	219	59
Arizona State Univ. at the Tempe campus, Tempe, AZ 85287	1885	$10,522 (S)	NA	5-D	51,164	2,283	63
Arizona State Univ. at the West campus, Glendale, AZ 85306	1984	$9,886 (S)	$10,754	5-D	4,063	292	58
Arkansas Tech. Univ., Russellville, AR 72801.	1909	$8,880 (S)	$7,338	5-D	11,830	623	41
ArtCenter Coll. of Design, Pasadena, CA 91103	1930	$43,416	NA	1-M	2,251	NA	68
Asbury Univ., Wilmore, KY 40390-1198	1890	$29,500	$6,950	2-M	1,973	204	69
Ashford Univ., San Diego, CA 92123	1918	NA	NA	3-M	10,568	748	NA
Ashland Univ., Ashland, OH 44805-3702.	1878	$20,684	$9,746	2-D	6,579	392	62
Ashworth Coll., Norcross, GA 30092	1987	$1,299	NA	3-M	57,650	NA	NA
Aspen Univ., Denver, CO 80246-1930.	1987	NA	NA	1-D	2,000	NA	NA
Assumption Coll., Worcester, MA 01609-1296.	1904	$40,958	$12,684	2-M	2,334	231	71
Athens State Univ., Athens, AL 35611	1822	$6,690 (S)	NA	5-M	3,001	196	NA
Atlantic Univ. Coll., Guaynabo, PR 00970.	1983	NA	NA	1-M	1,236	NA	NA
Auburn Univ., Auburn, AL 36849.	1856	$10,968 (S)	$13,332	5-D	29,776	1,555	77
Auburn Univ. at Montgomery, Montgomery, AL 36124-4023	1967	$8,236 (S)	$6,980	5-D	4,894	363	28
Augsburg Univ., Minneapolis, MN 55454-1351.	1869	$38,800	$10,280	2-D	3,562	369	63
Augusta Univ., Augusta, GA 30912.	1828	$8,282 (S)	$13,200	5-D	7,938	1,482	26
Augustana Coll., Rock Island, IL 61201-2296.	1860	$42,135	$10,572	2-B	2,647	264	75
Augustana Univ., Sioux Falls, SD 57197	1860	$33,018	$8,248	2-M	2,080	176	71
Aurora Univ., Aurora, IL 60506-4892	1893	$24,260	$11,700	1-D	5,833	451	53
Austin Coll., Sherman, TX 75090-4400	1849	$39,010	$12,334	2-M	1,237	125	73
Austin Peay State Univ., Clarksville, TN 37044.	1927	$8,225 (S)	$9,170	5-M	10,463	675	38
Avila Univ., Kansas City, MO 64145-1698	1916	$19,900	$7,200	2-M	1,703	238	45

Name, address	Year founded	Tuition & fees	Room & board	Control, degree	Enroll- ment	Faculty	Grad. rate
Azusa Pacific Univ., Azusa, CA 91702-7000	1899	$37,506	$5,770	2-D	9,926	1,511	70%
Babson Coll., Babson Park, MA 02457-0310	1919	$51,104	$16,312	1-M	3,329	266	92
Baker Coll., Flint, MI 48507	1911	$9,000	$3,000	1-D	24,677	NA	NA
Baker Univ., Baldwin City, KS 66006-0065	1858	$28,880	$8,310	2-D	1,159	100	57
Baldwin Wallace Univ., Berea, OH 44017-2088	1845	$32,586	$9,554	2-M	3,812	474	67
Ball State Univ., Muncie, IN 47306	1918	$9,774 (S)	$10,034	5-D	22,513	1,291	61
Bard Coll., Annandale-on-Hudson, NY 12504	1860	$52,915	$15,066	1-D	2,284	297	74
Barnard Coll., New York, NY 10027-6598 (3)	1889	$52,662	$16,100	1-B	2,604	363	93
Barry Univ., Miami Shores, FL 33161-6695	1940	$29,700	$11,100	2-D	7,358	735	NA
Baruch Coll. of the City Univ. of New York, New York, NY 10010-5585	1919	$7,115 (S)	NA	11-M	18,289	1,129	70
Bastyr Univ., Kenmore, WA 98028-4966	1978	NA	NA	1-D	1,266	299	NA
Bates Coll., Lewiston, ME 04240-6028	1855	$52,042	$14,678	1-B	1,787	195	92
Bay Path Univ., Longmeadow, MA 01106-2292 (6)	1897	$33,557	$12,799	1-D	3,298	478	58
Bayamón Central Univ., Bayamón, PR 00960-1725	1970	$7,518	NA	2-M	2,221	145	29
Baylor Univ., Waco, TX 76798	1845	$45,542	$12,595	2-D	17,059	1,352	77
Becker Coll., Worcester, MA 01609	1784	$39,200	$13,800	1-M	1,892	267	NA
Belhaven Univ., Jackson, MS 39202-1789	1883	$25,300	$8,500	2-D	4,458	456	52
Bellarmine Univ., Louisville, KY 40205	1950	$41,800	$12,250	2-D	3,757	445	65
Bellevue Univ., Bellevue, NE 68005-3098	1965	$9,340	NA	1-D	10,304	411	37
Belmont Abbey Coll., Belmont, NC 28012-1802	1876	$18,500	$10,094	2-B	1,524	NA	NA
Belmont Univ., Nashville, TN 37212	1951	$32,820	$11,680	2-D	8,012	853	70
Beloit Coll., Beloit, WI 53511-5596	1846	$50,040	$8,830	1-B	1,402	141	86
Bemidji State Univ., Bemidji, MN 56601-2699	1919	$8,394 (S)	$7,924	5-M	5,189	241	47
Benedict Coll., Columbia, SC 29204	1870	$19,958	$8,672	2-B	2,641	NA	NA
Benedictine Coll., Atchison, KS 66002-1499	1859	$28,480	$9,900	2-M	2,167	200	64
Benedictine Univ., Lisle, IL 60532	1887	$34,290	$9,480	2-D	5,101	585	50
Bentley Univ., Waltham, MA 02452-4705	1917	$49,880	$16,320	1-D	5,543	450	91
Berea Coll., Berea, KY 40404	1855	$560	$6,534	1-B	1,670	184	66
Berkeley Coll.–New York City campus, New York, NY 10017	1936	$25,300	NA	3-B	3,836	NA	28
Berkeley Coll.–Woodland Park campus, Woodland Park, NJ 07424	1931	$25,300	NA	3-M	3,739	391	31
Berklee Coll. of Music, Boston, MA 02215-3693	1945	$41,398	$18,000	1-M	5,272	692	49
Berry Coll., Mount Berry, GA 30149-0159	1902	$35,176	$12,260	2-M	2,110	230	64
Beth Medrash Govoha, Lakewood, NJ 08701-2797 (1)	1943	NA	NA	2-M	5,788	NA	NA
Bethel Coll., Mishawaka, IN 46545-5591	1947	$28,590	$9,000	2-M	1,513	183	64
Bethel Univ., McKenzie, TN 38201	1842	$16,552	$9,198	2-M	5,553	325	34
Bethel Univ., St. Paul, MN 55112-6999	1871	$37,300	$10,520	2-D	4,591	297	70
Bethune-Cookman Univ., Daytona Beach, FL 32114-3099	1904	$14,410	$8,912	2-M	4,143	278	37
Binghamton Univ., State Univ. of New York, Binghamton, NY 13902-6000	1946	$9,523 (S)	$14,577	5-D	17,322	1,047	82
Biola Univ., La Mirada, CA 90639-0001	1908	$38,448	$10,972	2-D	6,095	536	72
Birmingham-Southern Coll., Birmingham, AL 35254	1856	$17,650	$12,300	2-B	1,231	114	65
Black Hills State Univ., Spearfish, SD 57799	1883	$8,602 (S)	$6,820	5-M	4,178	128	32
Bloomfield Coll., Bloomfield, NJ 07003-9981	1868	$29,300	$11,700	2-M	2,000	230	32
Bloomsburg Univ. of Pennsylvania, Bloomsburg, PA 17815-1301	1839	$10,500 (S)	$9,430	5-D	9,287	519	58
Bluefield State Coll., Bluefield, WV 24701-2198	1895	$6,728 (S)	NA	5-B	1,362	117	26
Bob Jones Univ., Greenville, SC 29614	1927	$18,150	$6,976	2-D	2,936	217	68
Boise State Univ., Boise, ID 83725-0399	1932	$7,326 (S)	$7,750	5-D	24,154	1,526	NA
Boston Coll., Chestnut Hill, MA 02467-3800	1863	$53,346	$14,142	2-D	13,996	1,641	93
Boston Univ., Boston, MA 02215	1839	$52,082	$15,270	1-D	33,355	2,673	87
Bowdoin Coll., Brunswick, ME 04011	1794	$51,848	$14,132	1-B	1,816	228	95
Bowie State Univ., Bowie, MD 20715-9465	1865	$8,063 (S)	$11,340	5-D	5,669	414	39
Bowling Green State Univ., Bowling Green, OH 43403	1910	$11,057 (S)	$8,918	5-D	17,357	1,134	52
Bradley Univ., Peoria, IL 61625-0002	1897	$32,930	$10,310	1-D	5,844	603	72
Brandeis Univ., Waltham, MA 02454-9110	1948	$53,537	$14,906	1-D	5,722	554	90
Brandman Univ., Irvine, CA 92618	1958	$15,360	NA	1-D	7,812	NA	NA
Brenau Univ., Gainesville, GA 30501 (4)	1878	$29,050	$12,418	1-D	2,932	284	42
Brescia Univ., Owensboro, KY 42301-3023	1950	$22,100	$9,350	2-M	1,338	124	39
Briar Cliff Univ., Sioux City, IA 51104-0100	1930	$29,786	$9,086	2-D	1,316	122	44
Bridgewater Coll., Bridgewater, VA 22812-1599	1880	$35,160	$12,720	2-M	1,889	167	61
Bridgewater State Univ., Bridgewater, MA 02325	1840	$10,312 (S)	$13,000	5-M	11,019	771	59
Brigham Young Univ., Provo, UT 84602-1001	1875	$5,620	$7,628	2-D	34,334	1,840	83
Brigham Young Univ.–Hawaii, Laie, HI 96762-1294	1955	NA	NA	2-B	2,555	228	52
Brigham Young Univ.–Idaho, Rexburg, ID 83460	1888	$2,023	$2,296	2-B	32,458	792	44
Brookline Coll., Phoenix, AZ 85021	1979	NA	NA	3-M	1,468	43	NA
Brooklyn Coll. of the City Univ. of New York, Brooklyn, NY 11210-2889	1930	$6,835 (S)	NA	11-M	17,580	1,286	51
Brown Univ., Providence, RI 02912	1764	$53,419	$14,020	1-D	9,781	916	96
Bryan Coll., Dayton, TN 37321	1930	$25,600	$7,300	2-M	1,592	120	47
Bryant & Stratton Coll.–Wauwatosa campus, Wauwatosa, WI 53226	1854	NA	NA	3-B	1,264	NA	NA
Bryant Univ., Smithfield, RI 02917	1863	$43,973	$15,702	1-M	3,751	300	79
Bryn Mawr Coll., Bryn Mawr, PA 19010-2899 (6)	1885	$50,500	$15,910	1-D	1,640	201	83
Bucknell Univ., Lewisburg, PA 17837	1846	$53,986	$13,150	1-M	3,678	434	90
Buffalo State Coll., State Univ. of New York, Buffalo, NY 14222-1095	1867	$7,976 (S)	$12,982	5-M	9,516	816	47
Butler Univ., Indianapolis, IN 46208-3485	1855	$41,120	$14,690	1-D	5,081	568	79
Cabrini Univ., Radnor, PA 19087	1957	$31,350	$12,140	2-D	2,436	231	60
Caldwell Univ., Caldwell, NJ 07006-6195	1939	$34,715	$13,300	2-D	2,200	293	58
California Baptist Univ., Riverside, CA 92504-3206	1950	$33,478	$12,160	2-D	9,941	872	57
California Coll. of the Arts, San Francisco, CA 94107	1907	$49,138	$10,136	1-M	1,983	485	58
California Coll. San Diego, San Diego, CA 92111	1978	NA	NA	3-B	1,299	NA	NA
California Inst. of the Arts, Valencia, CA 91355-2340	1961	$45,030	NA	1-D	1,448	340	56
California Inst. of Integral Studies, San Francisco, CA 94103	1968	$20,222	NA	1-D	1,417	199	NA
California Inst. of Tech., Pasadena, CA 91125-0001	1891	$49,908	$14,796	1-D	2,238	374	89
California Lutheran Univ., Thousand Oaks, CA 91360-2787	1959	$41,363	$13,320	2-D	4,236	445	71
California Polytechnic State Univ., San Luis Obispo, San Luis Obispo, CA 93407	1901	$9,432 (S)	$13,115	5-M	22,188	1,473	82
California State Polytechnic Univ., Pomona, Pomona, CA 91768-2557	1938	$7,297 (S)	$14,514	5-D	25,894	1,244	66
California State Univ. Channel Islands, Camarillo, CA 93012	2002	NA	NA	5-D	3,599	294	NA
California State Univ., Bakersfield, Bakersfield, CA 93311	1970	$8,249 (S)	NA	5-D	9,341	546	42
California State Univ., Chico, Chico, CA 95929-0722	1887	$12,516 (S)	$12,536	5-M	17,557	996	59
California State Univ., Dominguez Hills, Carson, CA 90747-0001	1960	$8,132 (S)	$12,540	5-M	15,179	842	43
California State Univ., East Bay, Hayward, CA 94542-3000	1957	$6,835 (S)	$13,188	5-D	15,435	882	42
California State Univ., Fresno, Fresno, CA 93740-8027	1911	NA	NA	5-D	24,403	1,360	58
California State Univ., Fullerton, Fullerton, CA 92831-3599	1957	$6,850 (S)	$15,642	5-D	70,681	2,284	66
California State Univ., Long Beach, Long Beach, CA 90840	1949	$6,798 (S)	$12,750	5-D	37,065	2,279	72
California State Univ., Los Angeles, Los Angeles, CA 90032-8530	1947	$6,639 (S)	$13,356	5-D	28,253	1,718	47

Name, address	Year founded	Tuition & fees	Room & board	Control, degree	Enroll-ment	Faculty	Grad. rate
California State Univ., Monterey Bay, Seaside, CA 93955-8001	1994	$7,043 (S)	$12,396	5-M	7,574	487	60%
California State Univ., Northridge, Northridge, CA 91330	1958	$6,875 (S)	$10,402	5-D	39,916	2,125	50
California State Univ., Sacramento, Sacramento, CA 95819	1947	$6,934 (S)	$14,396	5-D	30,670	1,648	33
California State Univ., San Bernardino, San Bernardino, CA 92407	1965	$6,656 (S)	$12,711	5-D	20,461	1,017	54
California State Univ., San Marcos, San Marcos, CA 92096-0001	1990	$13,390 (S)	$13,227	5-M	13,887	865	53
California State Univ., Stanislaus, Turlock, CA 95382	1957	$7,038 (S)	$8,670	5-D	10,003	651	62
California Univ. of Pennsylvania, California, PA 15419-1394	1852	$10,641 (S)	$10,186	5-D	7,788	383	55
Calvin Coll., Grand Rapids, MI 49546-4388	1876	$33,100	$9,990	2-M	3,840	350	72
Cambridge Coll., Boston, MA 02129	1971	$14,940	NA	1-D	3,757	453	NA
Cameron Univ., Lawton, OK 73505-6377	1908	$6,180 (S)	$5,452	5-M	4,524	249	23
Campbell Univ., Buies Creek, NC 27506	1887	$31,190	$10,840	2-D	4,743	305	52
Campbellsville Univ., Campbellsville, KY 42718-2799	1906	$25,400	$8,000	2-D	8,056	285	33
Canisius Coll., Buffalo, NY 14208-1098	1870	$28,488	$11,300	2-M	3,464	368	69
Capella Univ., Minneapolis, MN 55402	1993	NA	NA	3-D	36,375	NA	NA
Capital Univ., Columbus, OH 43209-2394	1830	$35,466	$10,842	2-D	3,384	409	59
Cardinal Stritch Univ., Milwaukee, WI 53217-3985	1937	$28,844	$8,118	2-D	2,355	311	42
Caribbean Univ., Bayamón, PR 00960-0493	1969	$5,264	NA	1-D	3,547	361	20
Carleton Coll., Northfield, MN 55057-4001	1866	$52,782	$13,632	1-B	2,078	261	94
Carlow Univ., Pittsburgh, PA 15213-3165 (4)	1929	$28,596	$11,108	2-D	2,140	260	57
Carnegie Mellon Univ., Pittsburgh, PA 15213-3891	1900	$55,465	$14,418	1-D	14,528	1,074	89
Carroll Coll., Helena, MT 59625-0002	1909	$34,480	$9,608	2-B	1,352	163	66
Carroll Univ., Waukesha, WI 53186-5593	1846	$31,918	$9,896	2-D	3,451	401	66
Carson-Newman Univ., Jefferson City, TN 37760	1851	$27,400	$8,630	2-D	2,514	254	45
Carthage Coll., Kenosha, WI 53140	1847	$43,550	$11,990	2-M	2,867	348	60
Case Western Reserve Univ., Cleveland, OH 44106	1826	$47,500	$14,784	1-D	11,824	1,007	83
Castleton Univ., Castleton, VT 05735	1787	NA	NA	5-M	2,184	228	50
Catawba Coll., Salisbury, NC 28144-2488	1851	$30,520	$10,488	2-M	1,331	159	45
The Catholic Univ. of America, Washington, DC 20064	1887	$44,060	$14,316	2-D	6,000	755	74
Cedar Crest Coll., Allentown, PA 18104-6196 (4)	1867	$39,216	$11,544	2-M	1,664	221	50
Cedarville Univ., Cedarville, OH 45314	1887	$30,270	$7,360	2-D	3,886	385	72
Centenary Univ., Hackettstown, NJ 07840-2100	1867	$32,580	$11,110	2-D	2,203	NA	58
Central Coll., Pella, IA 50219	1853	$34,612	$9,980	2-B	1,274	105	67
Central Connecticut State Univ., New Britain, CT 06050-4010	1849	$10,225 (S)	$11,816	5-D	11,880	932	52
Central Michigan Univ., Mount Pleasant, MI 48859	1892	$12,510 (S)	$9,736	5-D	23,335	1,291	58
Central Penn Coll., Summerdale, PA 17093-0309	1881	$18,714	$7,416	3-M	1,224	102	34
Central State Univ., Wilberforce, OH 45384	1887	$6,246 (S)	$9,934	5-B	1,784	213	20
Central Washington Univ., Ellensburg, WA 98926	1891	$7,849 (S)	$10,684	5-M	11,971	724	53
Centre Coll., Danville, KY 40422-1394	1819	$41,700	$10,480	2-B	1,450	137	82
Chadron State Coll., Chadron, NE 69337	1911	NA	NA	5-M	2,649	NA	NA
Chamberlain Coll. of Nursing, Addison, IL 60101	2005	$19,500	NA	3-D	23,964	1,055	NA
Chaminade Univ. of Honolulu, Honolulu, HI 96816-1578	1955	$25,374	$13,630	2-M	1,719	138	53
Champlain Coll., Burlington, VT 05402-0670	1878	$39,818	$14,906	1-M	3,037	467	60
Chapman Univ., Orange, CA 92866	1861	$52,724	$15,828	2-D	9,392	1,089	79
Charleston Southern Univ., Charleston, SC 29423-8087	1964	$24,830	$9,900	2-M	3,493	315	35
Charter Oak State Coll., New Britain, CT 06053-2142	1973	$9,771 (S)	NA	5-M	1,500	186	NA
Chatham Univ., Pittsburgh, PA 15232-2826 (4)	1869	$37,611	$12,090	1-D	2,269	339	63
Chestnut Hill Coll., Philadelphia, PA 19118-2693	1924	$36,180	$11,000	2-D	1,846	297	55
Chicago State Univ., Chicago, IL 60628	1867	$11,902 (S)	$8,724	5-D	5,211	366	NA
Chowan Univ., Murfreesboro, NC 27855	1848	$24,980	$9,400	2-M	1,503	132	23
Christian Brothers Univ., Memphis, TN 38104-5581	1871	$32,820	$7,400	2-M	1,892	193	44
Christopher Newport Univ., Newport News, VA 23606-3072	1960	$13,654 (S)	$11,224	5-M	5,081	459	75
The Citadel, The Military Coll. of South Carolina, Charleston, SC 29409 (2)	1842	$14,368 (S)	$6,600	5-M	3,717	317	73
City Coll. of the City Univ. of New York, New York, NY 10031-9198	1847	$6,740 (S)	NA	11-D	16,112	1,461	50
City Univ. of Seattle, Seattle, WA 98121	1973	NA	NA	1-D	2,065	332	29
Claflin Univ., Orangeburg, SC 29115	1869	$16,391	$9,112	2-M	1,886	NA	44
Claremont McKenna Coll., Claremont, CA 91711	1946	$52,825	$16,220	1-M	1,347	171	NA
Clarion Univ. of Pennsylvania, Clarion, PA 16214	1867	$10,890 (S)	$11,058	5-D	5,225	294	52
Clark Atlanta Univ., Atlanta, GA 30314	1865	$23,082	$10,878	2-D	3,992	281	40
Clark Univ., Worcester, MA 01610-1477	1887	$45,730	$9,170	1-D	3,153	303	82
Clarkson Univ., Potsdam, NY 13699	1896	$49,444	$14,908	1-D	4,233	359	74
Clayton State Univ., Morrow, GA 30260-0285	1969	$6,410 (S)	$10,490	5-M	7,003	346	33
Clemson Univ., Clemson, SC 29634	1889	$14,712 (S)	$9,592	5-D	24,387	1,648	82
Cleveland State Univ., Cleveland, OH 44115	1964	$9,696 (S)	$12,000	5-D	16,607	1,178	41
Coastal Carolina Univ., Conway, SC 29528-6054	1954	$11,200 (S)	$9,140	5-D	10,663	787	42
Coe Coll., Cedar Rapids, IA 52402-5092	1851	$45,000	$9,480	2-B	1,394	177	68
Colby Coll., Waterville, ME 04901-8840	1813	$53,120	$13,660	1-B	1,917	NA	92
Colegio Universitario de San Juan, San Juan, PR 00918	1971	$2,370 (S)	NA	10-B	1,480	145	NA
Colgate Univ., Hamilton, NY 13346-1386	1819	$53,980	$13,520	1-M	2,881	360	91
The Coll. at Brockport, State Univ. of New York, Brockport, NY 14420-2997	1867	$8,154 (S)	$12,904	5-M	8,313	610	66
Coll. for Creative Studies, Detroit, MI 48202-4034	1926	NA	NA	1-M	1,459	289	62
Coll. of Charleston, Charleston, SC 29424-0001	1770	$12,458 (S)	$12,048	5-M	10,863	939	69
Coll. of Coastal Georgia, Brunswick, GA 31520	1961	$3,971 (S)	$9,520	5-B	3,663	214	23
Coll. of Mount St. Vincent, Riverdale, NY 10471-1093	1911	$37,100	$9,500	1-M	1,910	226	54
The Coll. of New Jersey, Ewing, NJ 08628	1855	$16,149 (S)	$13,200	5-M	7,552	858	87
The Coll. of New Rochelle, New Rochelle, NY 10805-2308	1904	$37,760	$14,562	1-M	2,023	291	48
Coll. of St. Benedict, Saint Joseph, MN 56374 (3)	1913	$43,738	$10,742	2-B	1,937	169	82
The Coll. of St. Rose, Albany, NY 12203-1419	1920	$32,574	$12,714	1-M	3,950	327	59
The Coll. of St. Scholastica, Duluth, MN 55811-4199	1912	$37,212	$9,710	2-D	4,325	419	67
Coll. of Staten Island of the City Univ. of New York, Staten Island, NY 10314-6600	1955	$7,089 (S)	$13,900	11-D	13,594	1,124	47
Coll. of the Holy Cross, Worcester, MA 01610-2395	1843	$50,630	$13,690	2-B	3,051	318	92
Coll. of the Ozarks, Point Lookout, MO 65726	1906	$460	$7,400	2-B	1,508	143	72
The Coll. of William & Mary, Williamsburg, VA 23187-8795	1693	$22,044 (S)	$11,799	5-D	8,740	NA	NA
The Coll. of Wooster, Wooster, OH 44691-2363	1866	$48,600	$11,400	2-B	1,980	212	77
Colorado Christian Univ., Lakewood, CO 80226	1914	$30,370	$10,516	2-M	1,343	NA	NA
The Colorado Coll., Colorado Springs, CO 80903-3294	1874	$52,818	$12,076	1-M	2,114	232	87
Colorado Mesa Univ., Grand Junction, CO 81501-3122	1925	$8,972 (S)	$10,735	5-D	9,735	572	33
Colorado Mountain Coll., Glenwood Springs, CO 81601	1965	$62/cr. hr. (A)	NA	9-B	5,847	544	NA
Colorado Mountain Coll., Leadville, CO 80461	1965	NA	NA	9-B	1,209	NA	NA
Colorado Mountain Coll., Steamboat Springs, CO 80487	1965	$62/credit (A)	NA	9-B	2,606	NA	NA
Colorado Sch. of Mines, Golden, CO 80401-1887	1874	$18,386 (S)	$11,897	5-D	5,876	532	75
Colorado State Univ., Fort Collins, CO 80523	1870	$11,488 (S)	$11,514	5-D	33,237	2,164	69
Colorado State Univ.–Pueblo, Pueblo, CO 81001-4901	1933	$12,851 (S)	$10,068	5-M	6,639	382	35
Colorado Tech. Univ. Colorado Springs, Colorado Springs, CO 80907	1965	NA	NA	3-D	2,359	343	NA

Name, address	Year founded	Tuition & fees	Room & board	Control, degree	Enroll-ment	Faculty	Grad. rate
Colorado Tech. Univ. Online, Colorado Springs, CO 80907	NA	NA	NA	3-M	25,797	613	NA
Columbia Central Univ., Caguas, PR 00725	1966	$9,750	NA	3-M	1,410	120	NA
Columbia Coll., Columbia, SC 29203-5998 (4)	1854	$19,500	$7,900	2-M	1,513	109	49%
Columbia Coll. Chicago, Chicago, IL 60605-1996	1890	$27,309	$14,012	1-M	7,312	979	44
Columbia Southern Univ., Orange Beach, AL 36561	1993	$5,400	NA	3-D	20,818	475	NA
Columbia Univ., New York, NY 10027	1754	$57,208	$13,618	1-D	6,231	NA	95
Columbia Univ. Sch. of General Studies, New York, NY 10027-6939	1754	$55,478	$13,950	1-B	2,068	NA	NA
Columbus State Univ., Columbus, GA 31907-5645	1958	$7,200 (S)	$10,550	5-D	8,452	564	33
Concord Univ., Athens, WV 24712-1000	1872	$7,732 (S)	$8,642	5-M	2,194	172	35
Concordia Coll., Moorhead, MN 56562	1891	$38,378	$8,040	2-M	2,132	246	74
Concordia Coll.–New York, Bronxville, NY 10708-1998	1881	$32,900	$12,690	2-M	1,597	148	46
Concordia Univ. Chicago, River Forest, IL 60305-1499	1864	$32,078	$9,748	2-D	5,700	502	48
Concordia Univ. Irvine, Irvine, CA 92612-3299	1972	$35,400	$11,300	2-D	4,249	396	65
Concordia Univ. Texas, Austin, TX 78726	1926	$29,260	$9,836	2-M	2,504	302	35
Concordia Univ. Wisconsin, Mequon, WI 53097-2402	1881	$28,600	$10,530	2-D	7,288	508	54
Concordia Univ., Nebraska, Seward, NE 68434	1894	$32,220	$8,470	2-M	2,520	253	67
Concordia Univ., Portland, OR 97211-6099	1905	NA	NA	2-M	3,111	259	45
Concordia Univ., St. Paul, St. Paul, MN 55104-5494	1893	$22,775	$9,000	2-D	4,792	441	55
Connecticut Coll., New London, CT 06320	1911	$52,850	$14,590	1-B	1,817	248	85
Converse Coll., Spartanburg, SC 29302 (6)	1889	$18,030	$10,610	1-M	1,319	84	55
Coppin State Univ., Baltimore, MD 21216-3698	1900	$7,474 (S)	$9,752	5-M	3,800	312	NA
Cornell Univ., Ithaca, NY 14853	1865	$52,853	$14,380	1-D	23,016	2,157	93
Cornerstone Univ., Grand Rapids, MI 49525-5897	1941	$24,500	$9,300	2-D	2,361	374	53
Creighton Univ., Omaha, NE 68178-0001	1878	$39,916	$11,036	2-D	8,654	890	81
Crown Coll., St. Bonifacius, MN 55375-9001	1916	NA	NA	2-M	1,269	160	50
The Culinary Inst. of America, Hyde Park, NY 12538-1499	1946	$31,616	$10,870	1-B	3,131	183	NA
Cumberland Univ., Lebanon, TN 37087	1842	$21,810	$8,350	1-M	1,481	159	37
Curry Coll., Milton, MA 02186-9984	1879	$39,720	$15,885	1-M	2,799	324	53
Daemen Coll., Amherst, NY 14226-3592	1947	$27,990	$12,696	1-D	2,636	304	55
Dakota State Univ., Madison, SD 57042-1799	1881	$9,147 (S)	$6,720	5-D	3,307	145	37
Dallas Baptist Univ., Dallas, TX 75211-9299	1965	$28,870	$7,992	2-D	5,067	660	58
Dalton State Coll., Dalton, GA 30720	1963	$4,116 (S)	$7,970	5-B	5,188	271	38
Dartmouth Coll., Hanover, NH 03755	1769	$52,950	$15,159	1-D	6,509	781	96
Davenport Univ., Grand Rapids, MI 49512	1866	$17,558	$9,902	1-M	7,232	832	47
Davidson Coll., Davidson, NC 28035	1837	$49,949	$13,954	2-B	1,796	189	93
Dean Coll., Franklin, MA 02038-1994	1865	$39,434	$16,836	1-B	1,301	140	45
Delaware State Univ., Dover, DE 19901-2277	1891	$7,868 (S)	$11,054	5-D	4,353	NA	37
Delaware Valley Univ., Doylestown, PA 18901-2697	1896	$38,000	$13,950	1-D	2,422	266	56
Delta State Univ., Cleveland, MS 38733-0001	1924	$6,859 (S)	$7,584	5-D	3,614	256	35
Denison Univ., Granville, OH 43023	1831	$50,440	$12,330	1-B	2,341	254	84
DePaul Univ., Chicago, IL 60604-2287	1898	$38,410	NA	2-D	22,769	1,855	71
DePauw Univ., Greencastle, IN 46135	1837	$47,838	$12,529	2-B	2,158	264	81
DeSales Univ., Center Valley, PA 18034-9568	1964	$36,100	$12,800	2-D	2,315	346	70
DeVry Coll. of New York–Midtown Manhattan campus, New York, NY 10016	1998	$15,480	NA	3-M	1,495	87	NA
DeVry Univ. Online, Addison, IL 60101	2000	$14,864	NA	3-M	15,551	1,513	NA
Dickinson Coll., Carlisle, PA 17013-2896	1773	$52,930	$13,236	1-B	2,382	283	83
Dickinson State Univ., Dickinson, ND 58601-4896	1918	$6,765 (S)	$6,898	5-M	1,425	169	32
Dixie State Univ., St. George, UT 84770-3876	1911	$5,080 (S)	$6,328	5-B	8,993	582	18
Dominican Coll., Orangeburg, NY 10962-1210	1952	$29,000	$13,150	1-D	1,954	237	43
Dominican Univ., River Forest, IL 60305-1099	1901	$33,434	$10,241	2-D	3,127	418	62
Dominican Univ. of California, San Rafael, CA 94901-2298	1890	$44,690	$14,650	2-M	1,750	328	72
Dordt Coll., Sioux Center, IA 51250-1697	1955	$29,130	$8,730	2-M	1,405	105	62
Drake Univ., Des Moines, IA 50311-4516	1881	$41,396	$10,158	1-D	4,904	478	79
Drew Univ., Madison, NJ 07940-1493	1867	$39,500	$14,108	2-D	2,117	257	62
Drexel Univ., Philadelphia, PA 19104-2875	1891	$52,002	$13,890	1-D	24,190	2,017	71
Drury Univ., Springfield, MO 65802	1873	$28,365	$9,040	1-M	1,659	131	66
Duke Univ., Durham, NC 27708-0586	1838	$53,500	$14,798	2-D	15,928	1,526	95
Duquesne Univ., Pittsburgh, PA 15282-0001	1878	$36,394	$12,114	2-D	9,190	974	79
D'Youville Coll., Buffalo, NY 14201-1084	1908	$25,870	$11,808	1-D	3,021	295	53
East Carolina Univ., Greenville, NC 27858-4353	1907	$7,143 (S)	$9,835	5-D	29,131	1,502	61
East Central Univ., Ada, OK 74820	1909	$6,600 (S)	$6,730	5-M	3,639	223	33
East Stroudsburg Univ. of Pennsylvania, East Stroudsburg, PA 18301-2999	1893	$10,298 (S)	$8,672	5-D	6,742	353	49
East Tennessee State Univ., Johnson City, TN 37614	1911	$9,015 (S)	$8,038	5-D	14,353	1,144	41
East Texas Baptist Univ., Marshall, TX 75670-1498	1912	$25,470	$8,915	2-M	1,533	141	31
Eastern Connecticut State Univ., Willimantic, CT 06226-2295	1889	$10,919 (S)	$13,050	5-M	5,261	499	56
Eastern Illinois Univ., Charleston, IL 61920	1895	$11,678 (S)	$9,736	5-M	7,415	527	57
Eastern Kentucky Univ., Richmond, KY 40475-3102	1906	$8,996 (S)	$9,728	5-D	16,844	1,144	45
Eastern Mennonite Univ., Harrisonburg, VA 22802-2462	1917	$37,100	$11,160	2-M	1,530	190	63
Eastern Michigan Univ., Ypsilanti, MI 48197	1849	$13,649 (S)	$9,672	5-D	20,313	1,319	44
Eastern New Mexico Univ., Portales, NM 88130	1934	$5,508 (S)	$6,760	5-M	6,027	330	33
Eastern Oregon Univ., La Grande, OR 97850-2899	1929	$8,362 (S)	$9,250	5-M	3,016	170	30
Eastern Univ., St. Davids, PA 19087-3696	1952	$32,882	$11,254	2-D	3,291	484	66
Eastern Washington Univ., Cheney, WA 99004-2431	1882	$7,110 (S)	$11,493	5-D	12,607	676	52
Eckerd Coll., St. Petersburg, FL 33711	1958	$43,044	$12,162	2-B	1,957	184	70
ECPI Univ., Virginia Beach, VA 23462	1966	$15,441	NA	3-M	11,739	1,109	39
Edgewood Coll., Madison, WI 53711-1997	1927	$29,500	$11,020	2-D	2,221	284	61
Edinboro Univ. of Pennsylvania, Edinboro, PA 16444	1857	$10,282 (S)	$11,219	5-D	6,837	371	49
EDP Univ. of Puerto Rico, Hato Rey, PR 00918	1968	$6,200	NA	1-M	1,782	198	55
Elizabeth City State Univ., Elizabeth City, NC 27909-7806	1891	$5,140 (S)	$7,948	5-M	1,357	NA	39
Elizabethtown Coll., Elizabethtown, PA 17022-2298	1899	$46,940	$11,370	2-M	1,735	183	75
Elmhurst Coll., Elmhurst, IL 60126-3296	1871	$37,055	$10,366	2-M	3,483	381	64
Elms Coll., Chicopee, MA 01013-2839	1928	$35,788	$13,106	2-D	1,580	187	57
Elon Univ., Elon, NC 27244-2010	1889	$35,318	$12,230	2-D	6,791	599	84
Embry-Riddle Aeron Univ.–Daytona, Daytona Beach, FL 32114-3900	1926	$35,714	$11,438	1-D	6,338	432	59
Embry-Riddle Aeron Univ.–Prescott, Prescott, AZ 86301-3720	1978	$34,662	$10,468	1-D	2,439	164	63
Embry-Riddle Aeron Univ.–Worldwide, Daytona Beach, FL 32114-3900	1970	$9,076	NA	1-D	15,457	1,264	NA
Emerson Coll., Boston, MA 02116-4624	1880	$46,852	$17,690	1-D	4,466	454	81
Emmanuel Coll., Boston, MA 02115	1919	$39,804	$14,994	2-M	2,083	191	66
Emory & Henry Coll., Emory, VA 24327-0947	1836	$35,050	$11,820	2-D	1,226	147	50
Emory Univ., Atlanta, GA 30322-1100	1836	$51,306	$14,456	2-D	14,273	1,222	91
Emporia State Univ., Emporia, KS 66801-5415	1863	$6,345 (S)	$8,684	5-D	5,732	278	45
Endicott Coll., Beverly, MA 01915-2096	1939	$33,050	$15,276	1-D	5,058	526	75
Eugene Lang Coll. of Liberal Arts, New York, NY 10011-8601	1975	$46,340	$16,250	1-B	1,738	158	74
Evangel Univ., Springfield, MO 65802	1955	$23,421	$4,304	2-D	2,112	NA	NA

Name, address	Year founded	Tuition & fees	Room & board	Control, degree	Enroll-ment	Faculty	Grad. rate
Everglades Univ., Boca Raton, FL 33431	1989	$16,648	NA	1-M	1,451	229	51%
The Evergreen State Coll., Olympia, WA 98505	1967	$7,416 (S)	$9,681	5-M	3,907	223	57
Excelsior Coll., Albany, NY 12203-5159	1970	$510/credit	NA	1-M	31,095	1,529	NA
Fairfield Univ., Fairfield, CT 06824	1942	$47,165	$14,280	2-D	5,192	589	81
Fairleigh Dickinson Univ., Florham campus, Madison, NJ 07940-1099	1942	$41,780	$13,130	1-D	3,512	453	55
Fairleigh Dickinson Univ., Metropolitan campus, Teaneck, NJ 07666-1914	1942	$39,446	$13,086	1-D	7,846	682	48
Fairmont State Univ., Fairmont, WV 26554	1865	$9,066 (S)	$9,184	5-M	4,041	325	29
Farmingdale State Coll., Farmingdale, NY 11735	1912	$8,076 (S)	$12,892	5-M	9,574	743	53
Fashion Inst. of Tech., New York, NY 10001-5992 (4)	1944	$7,463 (S)	$13,945	11-M	8,846	1,116	77
Faulkner Univ., Montgomery, AL 36109-3398	1942	$21,690	$7,550	2-D	3,350	280	28
Fayetteville State Univ., Fayetteville, NC 28301-4298	1867	$5,208 (S)	$7,996	5-D	6,226	333	32
Felician Univ., Lodi, NJ 07644-2117	1942	$34,315	$12,885	2-D	1,996	215	47
Ferris State Univ., Big Rapids, MI 49307	1884	$12,180 (S)	$9,894	5-D	13,798	916	50
Ferrum Coll., Ferrum, VA 24088	1913	$33,025	$11,060	2-B	1,451	116	25
FIDM/Fashion Inst. of Design & Merchandising, Los Angeles campus, Los Angeles, CA 90015-1421	1969	$32,945	NA	3-B	2,367	297	73
Fisher Coll., Boston, MA 02116-1500	1903	$31,384	$15,926	1-M	1,923	188	52
Fitchburg State Univ., Fitchburg, MA 01420-2697	1894	$10,155 (S)	$10,676	5-M	7,075	318	60
Flagler Coll., St. Augustine, FL 32085-1027	1968	$18,950	$11,340	1-M	2,689	249	55
Florida A&M Univ., Tallahassee, FL 32307-3200	1887	$5,785 (S)	$10,594	5-D	9,913	675	41
Florida Atlantic Univ., Boca Raton, FL 33431-0991	1961	$6,039 (S)	$10,388	5-D	30,203	1,321	51
Florida Gulf Coast Univ., Fort Myers, FL 33965-6565	1991	$6,118 (S)	$8,620	5-D	14,983	760	43
Florida Inst. of Tech., Melbourne, FL 32901-6975	1958	$41,850	$12,880	1-D	6,402	526	NA
Florida Intl. Univ., Miami, FL 33199	1965	$6,558 (S)	$10,882	5-D	56,851	2,440	56
Florida Memorial Univ., Miami-Dade, FL 33054	1879	NA	NA	2-M	1,750	173	33
Florida Natl. Univ., Hialeah, FL 33012	1982	$13,850	NA	3-M	4,169	150	63
Florida Southern Coll., Lakeland, FL 33801-5698	1885	$34,774	$11,204	2-D	3,073	287	63
Florida State Univ., Tallahassee, FL 32306	1851	$6,507 (S)	$10,458	5-D	41,447	1,774	80
Fontbonne Univ., St. Louis, MO 63105-3098	1917	$25,460	$9,506	2-M	1,713	201	54
Fordham Univ., New York, NY 10458	1841	$50,986	$17,445	2-D	16,037	1,622	80
Fort Hays State Univ., Hays, KS 67601-4099	1902	$4,007 (S)	$7,615	5-M	14,210	544	42
Fort Lewis Coll., Durango, CO 81301-3999	1911	$5,609 (S)	$9,416	5-M	3,331	264	40
Fort Valley State Univ., Fort Valley, GA 31030	1895	NA	NA	5-M	2,594	142	31
Framingham State Univ., Framingham, MA 01701-9101	1839	$9,920 (S)	$11,820	5-M	5,691	330	54
Francis Marion Univ., Florence, SC 29502-0547	1970	$10,742 (S)	$7,948	5-M	3,786	258	37
Franciscan Missionaries of Our Lady Univ., Baton Rouge, LA 70808	1990	$13,287	NA	2-D	1,362	NA	50
Franciscan Univ. of Steubenville, Steubenville, OH 43952-1763	1946	$26,430	$8,400	2-M	2,759	240	76
Franklin & Marshall Coll., Lancaster, PA 17604-3003	1787	$54,380	$13,580	1-B	2,283	273	85
Franklin Pierce Univ., Rindge, NH 03461-0060	1962	$34,995	$13,082	1-D	2,311	327	43
Franklin Univ., Columbus, OH 43215-5399	1902	NA	NA	1-M	5,734	814	NA
Freed-Hardeman Univ., Henderson, TN 38340-2399	1869	$21,950	$7,950	2-D	1,906	157	57
Fresno Pacific Univ., Fresno, CA 93702-4709	1944	$30,448	$8,400	2-M	3,596	479	64
Friends Univ., Wichita, KS 67213	1898	$28,415	$7,972	2-M	1,698	282	35
Frostburg State Univ., Frostburg, MD 21532-1099	1898	$8,914 (S)	$9,210	5-D	5,396	390	49
Full Sail Univ., Winter Park, FL 32792-7437 (2)	1979	NA	NA	3-M	8,921	702	NA
Furman Univ., Greenville, SC 29613	1826	$48,348	$12,158	1-M	2,949	327	81
Gallaudet Univ., Washington, DC 20002-3625	1864	$16,558	$13,530	1-D	1,566	269	43
Gannon Univ., Erie, PA 16541-0001	1925	$30,042	$11,990	2-D	4,149	403	64
Gardner-Webb Univ., Boiling Springs, NC 28017	1905	$30,730	$5,100	2-D	3,884	300	44
Geneva Coll., Beaver Falls, PA 15010-3599	1848	$26,980	$10,170	2-M	1,599	209	69
George Fox Univ., Newberg, OR 97132-2697	1891	$34,866	$10,886	2-D	3,899	604	71
George Mason Univ., Fairfax, VA 22030	1972	$11,724 (S)	$12,028	5-D	35,960	2,692	71
The George Washington Univ., Washington, DC 20052	1821	$53,518	$13,000	1-D	27,973	NA	81
Georgetown Coll., Georgetown, KY 40324-1696	1829	$38,650	$9,780	2-M	1,766	166	54
Georgetown Univ., Washington, DC 20057	1789	$52,300	$16,670	2-D	19,005	2,166	95
Georgia Coll. & State Univ., Milledgeville, GA 31061	1889	$9,346 (S)	$12,538	5-D	6,952	406	66
Georgia Gwinnett Coll., Lawrenceville, GA 30043	2006	$5,634 (S)	$12,874	5-B	12,287	674	15
Georgia Inst. of Tech., Atlanta, GA 30332-0001	1885	$12,418 (S)	$14,126	5-D	29,370	1,285	85
Georgia Southern Univ., Statesboro, GA 30458	1906	$6,890 (S)	$9,650	5-D	20,418	866	50
Georgia Southern Univ.–Armstrong campus, Savannah, GA 31419-1997	1935	$6,430 (S)	$10,856	5-D	7,041	478	32
Georgia Southwestern State Univ., Americus, GA 31709-4693	1906	$6,332 (S)	$7,910	5-M	3,052	166	25
Georgia State Univ., Atlanta, GA 30302-3083	1913	$10,858 (S)	$14,392	5-D	32,848	1,547	54
Georgian Court Univ., Lakewood, NJ 08701-2697	1908	$32,260	$10,808	2-M	2,390	284	48
Gettysburg Coll., Gettysburg, PA 17325-1483	1832	$52,640	$12,570	2-B	2,409	305	85
Glenville State Coll., Glenville, WV 26351-1200	1872	$9,096 (S)	$10,042	5-B	1,732	130	30
Global Univ., Springfield, MO 65804	1948	NA	NA	2-D	4,551	633	NA
Golden Gate Univ., San Francisco, CA 94105-2968	1901	$16,095	NA	1-D	2,685	489	NA
Goldey-Beacom Coll., Wilmington, DE 19808-1999	1886	NA	NA	1-M	1,352	56	49
Gonzaga Univ., Spokane, WA 99258	1887	$41,330	$11,550	2-D	7,506	770	87
Gordon Coll., Wenham, MA 01984-1899	1889	$37,400	$11,070	2-M	1,963	231	70
Goucher Coll., Baltimore, MD 21204-2794	1885	$43,440	$12,670	1-M	2,172	175	68
Governors State Univ., University Park, IL 60484	1969	$11,746 (S)	$10,104	5-D	5,185	470	NA
Grace Coll., Winona Lake, IN 46590-1294	1948	$23,120	$8,404	2-D	2,333	184	60
Graceland Univ., Lamoni, IA 50140	1895	$29,240	$8,760	2-D	2,262	83	49
Grambling State Univ., Grambling, LA 71245	1901	$7,435 (S)	$10,054	5-D	5,188	176	NA
Grand Canyon Univ., Phoenix, AZ 85017-1097	1949	NA	NA	2-D	NA	NA	NA
Grand Valley State Univ., Allendale, MI 49401-9403	1960	$11,994 (S)	$9,000	5-D	25,049	1,768	66
Grand View Univ., Des Moines, IA 50316-1599	1896	$27,518	$9,178	2-M	1,836	222	50
Granite State Coll., Concord, NH 03301	1972	$7,593 (S)	NA	11-M	2,019	272	46
Grantham Univ., Lenexa, KS 66219	1951	NA	NA	3-M	9,463	10	NA
Greenville Univ., Greenville, IL 62246-0159	1892	$27,108	$9,448	2-M	1,235	168	42
Grinnell Coll., Grinnell, IA 50112-1690	1846	$52,392	$12,810	1-B	1,712	209	87
Grove City Coll., Grove City, PA 16127-2104	1876	$17,254	$9,400	2-B	2,373	246	83
Guilford Coll., Greensboro, NC 27410-4173	1837	$34,215	$10,222	2-M	1,680	185	53
Gustavus Adolphus Coll., St. Peter, MN 56082-1498	1862	$45,100	$9,910	2-B	2,201	224	80
Gwynedd Mercy Univ., Gwynedd Valley, PA 19437-0901	1948	$33,520	$11,980	2-D	2,807	303	58
Hamilton Coll., Clinton, NY 13323-1296	1812	$52,770	$13,400	1-B	1,897	226	94
Hamline Univ., St. Paul, MN 55104-1284	1854	$41,298	$10,358	2-D	3,734	297	67
Hampshire Coll., Amherst, MA 01002	1965	$50,030	$13,606	1-B	1,268	162	62
Hampton Univ., Hampton, VA 23668	1868	$25,442	$11,218	1-D	4,619	367	53
Harding Univ., Searcy, AR 72149-0001	1924	$19,190	$6,894	2-D	5,539	415	67

Name, address	Year founded	Tuition & fees	Room & board	Control, degree	Enroll-ment	Faculty	Grad. rate
Hardin-Simmons Univ., Abilene, TX 79698-0001	1891	$28,990	$8,080	2-D	2,252	228	51%
Harrisburg Univ. of Sci. & Tech., Harrisburg, PA 17101	2005	$23,900	$6,800	1-D	4,071	NA	NA
Harrison Coll., Indianapolis, IN 46204	1902	NA	NA	3-B	3,756	290	33
Harris-Stowe State Univ., St. Louis, MO 63103-2136	1857	$5,340 (S)	$6,500	5-B	1,442	170	7
Hartwick Coll., Oneonta, NY 13820-4020	1797	$45,510	$12,460	1-B	1,201	174	61
Harvard Univ., Cambridge, MA 02138	1636	$48,949	$16,660	1-D	11,168	1,170	96
Harvey Mudd Coll., Claremont, CA 91711-5994	1955	$54,636	$17,592	1-B	844	115	96
Hastings Coll., Hastings, NE 68901	1882	NA	NA	2-M	1,212	119	58
Haverford Coll., Haverford, PA 19041-1392	1833	$52,754	$15,958	1-B	1,296	165	93
Hawai'i Pacific Univ., Honolulu, HI 96813	1965	$25,980	$14,800	1-D	4,146	359	44
Heidelberg Univ., Tiffin, OH 44883-2462	1850	$31,000	$10,400	2-M	1,209	124	49
Henderson State Univ., Arkadelphia, AR 71999-0001	1890	$8,311 (S)	$7,320	5-M	3,565	257	34
Hendrix Coll., Conway, AR 72032-3080	1876	$45,790	$12,284	2-M	1,249	136	75
Heritage Univ., Toppenish, WA 98948-9599	1982	$17,824	NA	1-M	1,241	185	NA
High Point Univ., High Point, NC 27268	1924	$35,118	$14,130	2-D	4,951	462	64
Hillsdale Coll., Hillsdale, MI 49242-1298	1844	$26,742	$10,610	1-D	1,556	199	85
Hiram Coll., Hiram, OH 44234	1850	$34,300	$10,290	1-M	1,221	142	56
Hobart & William Smith Colleges, Geneva, NY 14456	1822	$55,255	$14,035	1-M	2,244	244	81
Hodges Univ., Naples, FL 34119	1990	$13,700	NA	1-M	1,724	119	NA
Hofstra Univ., Hempstead, NY 11549	1935	$43,960	$14,930	1-D	11,131	1,236	63
Holy Family Univ., Philadelphia, PA 19114	1954	$30,346	$13,576	2-D	3,081	310	55
Hood Coll., Frederick, MD 21701-8575	1893	$39,492	$12,700	1-D	2,112	248	61
Hope Coll., Holland, MI 49422-9000	1866	$34,010	$10,310	2-B	3,150	348	80
Hope Intl. Univ., Fullerton, CA 92831-3138	1928	$31,800	$9,930	2-M	1,162	234	48
Houston Baptist Univ., Houston, TX 77074-3298	1960	$32,530	$8,814	2-D	3,325	279	48
Howard Univ., Washington, DC 20059-0002	1867	$25,697	$13,504	1-D	10,002	1,520	60
Humboldt State Univ., Arcata, CA 95521-8299	1913	$7,492 (S)	$13,056	5-M	8,347	574	50
Hunter Coll. of the City Univ. of New York, New York, NY 10065-5085	1870	$6,980 (S)	$4,857	11-D	23,005	2,144	53
Huntington Univ., Huntington, IN 46750-1299	1897	$25,540	$8,456	2-D	1,295	112	65
Husson Univ., Bangor, ME 04401-2999	1898	$17,600	$9,830	1-D	3,640	341	54
Idaho State Univ., Pocatello, ID 83209	1901	$7,166 (S)	$7,024	5-D	12,623	771	29
Illinois Inst. of Tech., Chicago, IL 60616	1890	$46,323	$12,818	1-D	7,792	800	73
Illinois State Univ., Normal, IL 61790	1857	$14,061 (S)	$9,850	5-D	20,784	1,290	69
Illinois Wesleyan Univ., Bloomington, IL 61702-2900	1850	$47,636	$10,984	1-B	1,649	193	78
Immaculata Univ., Immaculata, PA 19345	1920	$27,350	$12,620	2-D	2,517	308	62
Indian River State Coll., Fort Pierce, FL 34981-5596	1960	NA	NA	5-B	17,665	859	NA
Indiana State Univ., Terre Haute, IN 47809	1865	$8,916 (S)	$9,883	5-D	13,771	684	38
Indiana Tech., Fort Wayne, IN 46803-1297	1930	$26,370	$9,580	1-D	7,996	530	34
Indiana Univ. Bloomington, Bloomington, IN 47405-7000	1820	$10,680 (S)	NA	5-D	43,710	2,456	77
Indiana Univ. East, Richmond, IN 47374-1289	1971	$7,344 (S)	NA	5-M	3,490	287	36
Indiana Univ. Kokomo, Kokomo, IN 46902-9003	1945	$7,344 (S)	NA	5-M	3,029	241	40
Indiana Univ. Northwest, Gary, IN 46408-1197	1959	$7,344 (S)	NA	5-M	4,055	364	28
Indiana Univ. of Pennsylvania, Indiana, PA 15705	1875	$12,146 (S)	$12,488	5-D	12,316	678	54
Indiana Univ. South Bend, South Bend, IN 46615	1922	$7,344 (S)	NA	5-M	5,385	453	30
Indiana Univ. Southeast, New Albany, IN 47150-6405	1941	$7,344 (S)	NA	5-M	5,238	438	32
Indiana Univ.–Purdue Univ. Fort Wayne, Fort Wayne, IN 46805-1499	1917	$8,330 (S)	$6,844	5-M	13,214	801	25
Indiana Univ.–Purdue Univ. Indianapolis, Indianapolis, IN 46202	1969	$9,465 (S)	$9,730	5-D	29,791	3,528	45
Indiana Wesleyan Univ., Marion, IN 46953-4974	1920	$25,980	$8,312	2-D	3,071	267	65
Inter Amer. Univ. of Puerto Rico, Aguadilla campus, Aguadilla, PR 00605	1957	$5,898	NA	1-M	4,219	263	30
Inter Amer. Univ. of Puerto Rico, Arecibo campus, Arecibo, PR 00614-4050	1957	NA	NA	1-M	4,878	298	NA
Inter Amer. Univ. of Puerto Rico, Barranquitas campus, Barranquitas, PR 00794	1957	$6,262	NA	1-M	1,884	150	43
Inter Amer. Univ. of Puerto Rico, Bayamón campus, Bayamón, PR 00957	1912	$5,178	$6,114	1-M	4,612	272	32
Inter Amer. Univ. of Puerto Rico, Fajardo campus, Fajardo, PR 00738-7003	1965	$5,898	NA	1-M	2,115	137	26
Inter Amer. Univ. of Puerto Rico, Guayama campus, Guayama, PR 00785	1958	$6,425	NA	1-M	1,927	165	72
Inter Amer. Univ. of Puerto Rico, Metropolitan campus, San Juan, PR 00919-1293	1960	NA	NA	1-D	8,483	606	NA
Inter Amer. Univ. of Puerto Rico, Ponce campus, Mercedita, PR 00715-1602	1962	$5,082	NA	1-D	5,288	284	30
Inter Amer. Univ. of Puerto Rico, San Germán campus, San Germán, PR 00683-5008	1912	$6,300	$2,700	1-D	4,759	330	41
Iona Coll., New Rochelle, NY 10801-1890	1940	$37,682	$14,832	2-M	3,792	330	64
Iowa State Univ. of Sci. & Tech., Ames, IA 50011	1858	$8,636 (S)	$8,546	5-D	35,993	1,874	73
Ithaca Coll., Ithaca, NY 14850	1892	$43,978	$15,562	1-D	6,516	785	76
Jackson State Univ., Jackson, MS 39217	1877	$7,946 (S)	$9,552	5-D	8,558	575	NA
Jacksonville State Univ., Jacksonville, AL 36265-1602	1883	$10,020 (S)	$7,898	5-D	8,514	473	35
Jacksonville Univ., Jacksonville, FL 32211	1934	$35,260	$13,950	1-D	4,222	412	43
James Madison Univ., Harrisonburg, VA 22807	1908	$10,830 (S)	$9,822	5-D	21,836	1,541	83
John Brown Univ., Siloam Springs, AR 72761-2121	1919	$26,928	$9,224	2-M	2,613	239	73
John Carroll Univ., University Heights, OH 44118	1886	$39,790	$11,580	2-M	3,523	442	78
John F. Kennedy Univ., Pleasant Hill, CA 94523-4817 (4)	1964	NA	NA	1-D	1,580	237	NA
John Jay Coll. of Criminal Justice of the City Univ. of New York, New York, NY 10019	1964	$7,070 (S)	$20,007	11-M	14,834	NA	47
Johns Hopkins Univ., Baltimore, MD 21218	1876	$52,170	$15,410	1-D	7,868	655	94
Johnson & Wales Univ., Charlotte, NC 28202	2004	NA	NA	1-B	2,255	120	49
Johnson & Wales Univ., Denver, CO 80220	1993	$30,746	$8,268	1-M	1,388	127	53
Johnson & Wales Univ., North Miami, FL 33181	1992	$30,746	$8,268	1-B	1,752	79	41
Johnson & Wales Univ., Providence, RI 02903-3703	1914	$32,441	NA	1-D	9,454	617	55
Johnson C. Smith Univ., Charlotte, NC 28216-5398	1867	$18,236	$7,100	1-M	1,483	173	44
Judson Univ., Elgin, IL 60123-1498	1963	$29,860	$9,988	2-D	1,283	194	55
Juniata Coll., Huntingdon, PA 16652-2119	1876	$45,597	$12,521	2-M	1,495	156	84
Kalamazoo Coll., Kalamazoo, MI 49006-3295	1833	$48,516	$9,756	2-B	1,436	135	86
Kansas State Univ., Manhattan, KS 66506	1863	$10,135 (S)	$9,430	5-D	22,795	1,281	63
Kean Univ., Union, NJ 07083	1855	$12,107 (S)	$13,513	5-D	14,226	1,432	50
Keene State Coll., Keene, NH 03435	1909	$13,868 (S)	$10,736	5-M	3,866	NA	62
Keiser Univ., Fort Lauderdale, FL 33309	1977	$15,498	NA	1-D	17,129	1,440	55
Kendall Coll., Chicago, IL 60642	1934	$19,828	$11,085	3-B	1,200	279	17
Kennesaw State Univ., Kennesaw, GA 30144	1963	$7,432 (S)	$11,467	5-D	35,846	1,994	42

Name, address	Year founded	Tuition & fees	Room & board	Control, degree	Enroll-ment	Faculty	Grad. rate
Kent State Univ., Kent, OH 44242-0001	1910	$10,012 (S)	$10,916	5-D	28,972	1,846	57%
Kent State Univ. at Geauga, Burton, OH 44021-9500	1964	$5,664 (S)	NA	5-M	2,248	132	17
Kent State Univ. at Stark, Canton, OH 44720-7599	1946	$5,664 (S)	NA	5-M	5,030	276	25
Kentucky State Univ., Frankfort, KY 40601	1886	$7,796 (S)	$6,690	12-D	1,925	130	24
Kenyon Coll., Gambier, OH 43022	1824	$55,930	$12,510	1-B	1,677	214	91
Kettering Univ., Flint, MI 48504	1919	$39,790	$7,780	1-M	2,311	146	62
Keuka Coll., Keuka Park, NY 14478	1890	$30,946	$11,452	2-M	2,003	439	60
Keystone Coll., La Plume, PA 18440	1868	$25,920	$10,700	1-M	1,484	249	36
King Univ., Bristol, TN 37620-2699	1867	$29,714	$4,400	2-D	2,162	272	52
King's Coll., Wilkes-Barre, PA 18711-0801	1946	$35,830	$12,410	2-M	2,468	225	67
Knox Coll., Galesburg, IL 61401	1837	$46,554	$9,870	1-B	1,356	140	76
Kutztown Univ. of Pennsylvania, Kutztown, PA 19530-0730	1866	$9,987 (S)	$10,282	5-D	8,329	445	53
La Roche Coll., Pittsburgh, PA 15237-5898	1963	$28,564	$11,556	2-D	1,535	210	51
La Salle Univ., Philadelphia, PA 19141-1199	1863	$29,500	$14,690	2-D	5,197	547	67
La Sierra Univ., Riverside, CA 92505	1922	$32,130	$8,250	2-D	2,418	115	85
Lafayette Coll., Easton, PA 18042	1826	$50,850	$15,040	2-B	2,594	293	90
Lake Erie Coll., Painesville, OH 44077-3389	1856	$30,862	$9,460	1-M	1,201	103	45
Lake Forest Coll., Lake Forest, IL 60045	1857	$45,548	$10,052	1-M	1,578	186	70
Lake Superior State Univ., Sault Sainte Marie, MI 49783	1946	NA	NA	5-M	2,438	178	40
Lakeland Univ., Plymouth, WI 53073	1862	NA	NA	2-M	3,749	71	42
Lamar Univ., Beaumont, TX 77710	1923	$10,111 (S)	$8,740	5-D	14,506	592	30
Lander Univ., Greenwood, SC 29649-2099	1872	$11,700 (S)	$8,900	5-M	3,049	249	40
Lane Coll., Jackson, TN 38301-4598	1882	$10,690	$7,360	2-B	1,427	75	24
Langston Univ., Langston, OK 73050	1897	$5,950 (S)	$10,094	5-D	2,222	221	50
Lasell Coll., Newton, MA 02466-2709	1851	$36,000	$15,400	1-M	2,100	265	54
Lawrence Tech. Univ., Southfield, MI 48075-1058	1932	$32,130	$9,500	1-D	3,069	341	53
Lawrence Univ., Appleton, WI 54911	1847	$46,101	$10,032	1-B	1,473	214	80
Le Moyne Coll., Syracuse, NY 13214	1946	$34,625	$13,780	2-M	3,431	335	74
Lebanon Valley Coll., Annville, PA 17003-1400	1866	$43,650	$11,860	2-D	1,910	285	73
Lee Univ., Cleveland, TN 37320-3450	1918	$17,690	$8,300	2-M	5,370	463	52
Lehigh Univ., Bethlehem, PA 18015	1865	$50,740	$13,120	1-D	7,017	699	86
Lehman Coll. of the City Univ. of New York, Bronx, NY 10468-1589	1931	$7,010 (S)	NA	11-M	13,829	938	46
Lenoir-Rhyne Univ., Hickory, NC 28601	1891	$35,350	$12,150	2-D	2,557	271	43
Lesley Univ., Cambridge, MA 02138-2790 (4)	1909	$27,600	$16,230	1-D	4,732	603	60
LeTourneau Univ., Longview, TX 75607-7001	1946	$30,210	$9,970	2-M	3,003	227	59
Lewis & Clark Coll., Portland, OR 97219-7899	1867	$48,988	$12,096	1-D	3,419	528	79
Lewis Univ., Romeoville, IL 60446	1932	$32,450	$10,578	2-D	6,506	675	67
Lewis-Clark State Coll., Lewiston, ID 83501-2698	1893	$7,224 (S)	$6,570	5-B	3,633	253	21
Liberty Univ., Lynchburg, VA 24515	1971	$23,940	$9,850	2-D	15,549	NA	60
Life Univ., Marietta, GA 30060-2903	1974	$11,715	$14,400	1-D	2,619	183	28
LIM Coll., New York, NY 10022-5268 (4)	1939	$26,350	$20,350	3-M	1,563	176	47
Lincoln Memorial Univ., Harrogate, TN 37752-1901	1897	$22,010	$8,000	1-D	4,770	343	46
Lincoln Univ., Jefferson City, MO 65101	1866	$7,632 (S)	$6,770	5-M	2,619	153	14
Lincoln Univ., Lincoln University, PA 19352	1854	$10,636 (S)	$9,738	12-M	2,266	207	46
Lindenwood Univ., St. Charles, MO 63301-1695	1827	$16,960	$8,800	2-D	10,045	1,330	50
Lindsey Wilson Coll., Columbia, KY 42728	1903	$24,850	$9,385	2-D	2,565	239	33
Linfield Coll., McMinnville, OR 97128-6894	1858	$41,576	$11,770	2-B	1,535	204	78
Lipscomb Univ., Nashville, TN 37204-3951	1891	$32,144	$12,652	2-D	4,642	561	59
Lock Haven Univ. of Pennsylvania, Lock Haven, PA 17745-2390	1870	$10,576 (S)	$9,968	5-M	3,827	232	55
Logan Univ., Chesterfield, MO 63017	1935	$8,400	NA	1-D	1,371	114	NA
Loma Linda Univ., Loma Linda, CA 92350	1905	NA	NA	2-D	4,270	840	NA
Long Island Univ.–LIU Brooklyn, Brooklyn, NY 11201-8423	1926	$36,978	$13,720	1-D	6,982	729	32
Long Island Univ.–LIU Post, Brookville, NY 11548-1300	1954	$36,978	$13,720	1-D	8,499	650	48
Longwood Univ., Farmville, VA 23909	1839	$13,080 (S)	$10,732	5-M	4,883	340	68
Loras Coll., Dubuque, IA 52004-0178	1839	$34,184	$8,275	2-M	1,467	143	68
Los Angeles Film Sch., Hollywood, CA 90028	1999	$79,000/ deg. prog.	NA	3-B	1,358	116	NA
Louisiana State Univ. & A&M Coll., Baton Rouge, LA 70803	1860	$11,374 (S)	$11,750	5-D	30,861	1,489	67
Louisiana State Univ. at Alexandria, Alexandria, LA 71302-9121	1960	$11,085 (S)	$7,770	5-B	3,277	172	33
Louisiana State Univ. Health Sciences Center, New Orleans, LA 70112-2223	1931	$8,308 (S)	$5,598	5-D	2,777	897	NA
Louisiana State Univ. in Shreveport, Shreveport, LA 71115-2399	1965	$7,075 (S)	NA	5-D	4,428	178	37
Louisiana Tech. Univ., Ruston, LA 71272	1894	$9,645 (S)	$6,360	5-D	12,672	432	53
Lourdes Univ., Sylvania, OH 43560-2898	1958	$21,540	$9,700	2-M	1,426	185	28
Loyola Marymount Univ., Los Angeles, CA 90045-2659	1911	$48,172	$15,185	2-D	9,618	1,160	79
Loyola Univ. Chicago, Chicago, IL 60660	1870	$43,808	NA	2-D	16,673	1,566	77
Loyola Univ. Maryland, Baltimore, MD 21210-2699	1852	$47,725	$14,150	2-D	6,084	553	81
Loyola Univ. New Orleans, New Orleans, LA 70118-6195	1912	$39,692	$13,380	2-D	3,759	437	56
Lubbock Christian Univ., Lubbock, TX 79407-2099	1957	$21,794	$7,478	2-M	1,883	187	47
Luther Coll., Decorah, IA 52101	1861	$42,290	$9,460	2-B	2,053	208	80
Lycoming Coll., Williamsport, PA 17701-5192	1812	$40,090	$12,568	2-B	1,223	124	67
Lynn Univ., Boca Raton, FL 33431-5598	1962	$38,210	$12,170	1-D	3,010	183	51
Macalester Coll., St. Paul, MN 55105-1899	1874	$54,344	$12,156	1-B	2,136	238	87
Madonna Univ., Livonia, MI 48150-1173	1947	$20,700	$9,750	2-D	3,088	282	70
Maharishi Univ. of Mgmt., Fairfield, IA 52557	1971	$27,530	$7,400	1-D	1,648	128	64
Malone Univ., Canton, OH 44709	1892	$30,860	$9,500	2-M	1,729	175	49
Manchester Univ., North Manchester, IN 46962-1225	1889	$32,758	$9,580	2-D	1,572	112	57
Manhattan Coll., Riverdale, NY 10471	1853	$42,087	$15,600	2-M	4,242	436	72
Manhattanville Coll., Purchase, NY 10577-2132	1841	$38,820	$14,520	1-D	2,682	384	55
Mansfield Univ. of Pennsylvania, Mansfield, PA 16933	1857	$12,316 (S)	$11,928	5-M	1,897	145	57
Marian Univ., Fond du Lac, WI 54935-4699	1936	$27,370	$7,222	2-D	1,971	233	NA
Marian Univ., Indianapolis, IN 46222-1997	1851	$34,000	$10,640	2-D	3,429	270	52
Marist Coll., Poughkeepsie, NY 12601-1387	1929	$36,680	$15,900	1-M	6,657	608	83
Marquette Univ., Milwaukee, WI 53201-1881	1881	$39,900	$11,890	2-D	11,426	1,164	80
Mars Hill Univ., Mars Hill, NC 28754	1856	$31,804	$9,300	2-M	1,410	147	34
Marshall Univ., Huntington, WV 25755	1837	$7,798 (S)	$10,126	5-D	13,246	688	49
Martin Univ., Indianapolis, IN 46218-3867	1977	NA	NA	1-M	1,236	43	NA
Mary Baldwin Univ., Staunton, VA 24401-3610 (4)	1842	$31,085	$9,410	1-D	1,654	235	45

Name, address	Year founded	Tuition & fees	Room & board	Control, degree	Enroll- ment	Faculty	Grad. rate
Maryland Inst. Coll. of Art, Baltimore, MD 21217	1826	$48,630	$13,280	1-M	2,090	433	72%
Marymount Manhattan Coll., New York, NY 10021-4597	1936	$33,778	$16,832	1-B	2,150	369	49
Marymount Univ., Arlington, VA 22207-4299	1950	$30,425	$12,805	2-D	3,375	363	53
Maryville Univ. of St. Louis, St. Louis, MO 63141-7299	1872	$28,470	$10,088	1-D	7,689	667	72
Marywood Univ., Scranton, PA 18509-1598	1915	$34,910	$13,900	2-D	2,950	394	69
Massachusetts Coll. of Art & Design, Boston, MA 02115-5882	1873	$13,200 (S)	$13,500	5-M	2,065	290	73
Massachusetts Coll. of Lib. Arts, North Adams, MA 01247-4100.	1894	$10,135 (S)	$10,724	5-M	1,588	166	54
Massachusetts Inst. of Tech., Cambridge, MA 02139-4307.	1861	$51,832	$15,510	1-D	11,466	1,576	94
Massachusetts Maritime Acad., Buzzards Bay, MA 02532-1803.	1891	$8,398 (S)	$12,306	5-M	1,780	143	75
The Master's Univ., Santa Clarita, CA 91321-1200	1927	$25,390	$11,200	2-D	1,908	212	50
McDaniel Coll., Westminster, MD 21157-4390.	1867	$41,800	$11,110	1-M	2,845	564	68
McKendree Univ., Lebanon, IL 62254-1299.	1828	$30,520	$9,920	2-D	2,676	278	51
McNeese State Univ., Lake Charles, LA 70609.	1939	$9,001 (S)	$7,314	5-M	7,638	451	NA
MCPHS Univ., Boston, MA 02115-5896.	1823	$32,705	$16,400	1-D	7,208	738	78
Medaille Coll., Buffalo, NY 14214-2695	1875	NA	NA	1-D	2,383	294	50
Medgar Evers Coll. of the City Univ. of New York, Brooklyn, NY 11225-2298.	1969	$6,650 (S)	NA	11-B	6,652	534	NA
Medical Univ. of South Carolina, Charleston, SC 29425	1824	NA	NA	5-D	2,775	223	NA
Mercer Univ., Macon, GA 31207	1833	$36,000	$12,153	2-D	7,130	743	64
Mercy Coll., Dobbs Ferry, NY 10522-1189.	1951	$18,713	$13,900	2-D	9,506	944	42
Mercy Coll. of Ohio, Toledo, OH 43604 (4)	1993	$14,610	$5,460	2-M	1,416	210	NA
Mercyhurst Univ., Erie, PA 16546	1926	$36,320	$12,210	2-M	2,777	NA	67
Meredith Coll., Raleigh, NC 27607-5298 (6)	1891	$35,916	$10,718	1-M	1,981	222	63
Merrimack Coll., North Andover, MA 01845-5800	1947	$40,190	$15,225	1-M	4,171	429	68
Messiah Coll., Mechanicsburg, PA 17055	1909	$35,160	$10,520	2-D	3,331	368	81
Methodist Univ., Fayetteville, NC 28311-1498.	1956	$32,860	$12,295	2-M	2,416	213	44
Metropolitan State Univ. of Denver, Denver, CO 80204	1963	$7,353 (S)	NA	5-M	20,304	1,449	28
Metropolitan State Univ., St. Paul, MN 55106-5000.	1971	$7,859 (S)	NA	5-D	8,354	NA	NA
Miami Univ., Oxford, OH 45056	1809	$14,578 (S)	$12,725	12-D	19,700	1,281	79
Miami Univ. Hamilton, Hamilton, OH 45011-3399	1968	NA	NA	5-M	4,194	224	NA
Miami Univ. Middletown, Middletown, OH 45042-3497	1966	NA	NA	5-B	2,660	209	NA
Michigan State Univ., East Lansing, MI 48824.	1855	$14,460 (S)	$9,976	5-D	50,019	2,946	80
Michigan Tech. Univ., Houghton, MI 49931	1885	$15,074 (S)	$10,477	5-D	7,319	450	67
MidAmerica Nazarene Univ., Olathe, KS 66062-1899	1966	$30,736	$8,708	2-M	1,888	270	51
Middle Georgia State Univ., Macon, GA 31206	2015	$4,608 (S)	$7,614	5-M	7,341	387	24
Middle Tennessee State Univ., Murfreesboro, TN 37132	1911	$8,948 (S)	$6,408	5-D	21,913	1,238	44
Middlebury Coll., Middlebury, VT 05753-6002	1800	$52,496	$14,968	1-D	2,603	343	95
Midland Coll., Midland, TX 79705-6329	1969	$2,670 (A)	$4,900	11-B	5,564	NA	NA
Midway Univ., Midway, KY 40347-1120.	1847	$23,950	$8,180	2-D	1,600	118	38
Midwestern State Univ., Wichita Falls, TX 76308.	1922	NA	NA	5-M	6,043	345	44
Miles Coll., Fairfield, AL 35064.	1905	NA	NA	2-B	1,738	147	NA
Millersville Univ. of Pennsylvania, Millersville, PA 17551-0302	1855	$11,858 (S)	$13,440	5-D	7,720	497	62
Milligan Coll., Milligan College, TN 37682	1866	$33,700	$7,100	2-D	1,171	147	64
Millikin Univ., Decatur, IL 62522-2084	1901	$33,066	$11,082	2-D	2,040	272	61
Mills Coll., Oakland, CA 94613-1000 (6)	1852	$30,257	$13,448	1-D	1,309	174	64
Milwaukee Sch. of Engineering, Milwaukee, WI 53202-3109 (2)	1903	$40,749	$9,408	1-M	2,823	252	67
Minnesota State Univ. Mankato, Mankato, MN 56001	1868	$8,663 (S)	$8,475	5-D	15,407	754	51
Minnesota State Univ. Moorhead, Moorhead, MN 56563.	1885	$8,496 (S)	$9,280	5-D	6,019	348	46
Minot State Univ., Minot, ND 58707-0002	1913	$6,810 (S)	$6,140	5-M	3,216	291	38
Misericordia Univ., Dallas, PA 18612-1098	1924	$33,240	$13,960	2-D	2,764	304	76
Mississippi Coll., Clinton, MS 39058	1826	$17,392	$9,610	2-D	5,036	433	54
Mississippi State Univ., Mississippi State, MS 39762	1878	$8,318 (S)	$9,614	5-D	21,883	1,142	60
Mississippi Univ. for Women, Columbus, MS 39701-9998.	1884	$6,065 (S)	$6,808	5-D	2,673	201	49
Mississippi Valley State Univ., Itta Bena, MS 38941-1400.	1946	$6,442 (S)	$7,764	5-M	2,455	172	31
Missouri Baptist Univ., St. Louis, MO 63141-8660.	1964	$26,020	$10,380	2-D	5,488	286	37
Missouri Southern State Univ., Joplin, MO 64801-1595.	1937	$6,067 (S)	NA	5-M	5,783	350	36
Missouri State Univ., Springfield, MO 65897	1905	$7,306 (S)	$8,537	5-D	23,697	1,123	55
Missouri Univ. of Sci. & Tech., Rolla, MO 65409	1870	$8,460 (S)	$10,094	5-D	8,884	453	64
Missouri Valley Coll., Marshall, MO 65340-3197	1889	$20,600	$9,150	2-M	1,820	147	29
Missouri Western State Univ., St. Joseph, MO 64507-2294	1915	$6,843 (S)	$8,102	5-M	5,533	343	29
Molloy Coll., Rockville Centre, NY 11571-5002	1955	$30,310	$14,712	1-D	4,980	720	72
Monmouth Univ., West Long Branch, NJ 07764-1898.	1933	$36,732	$13,552	1-D	6,371	646	70
Monroe Coll., Bronx, NY 10468	1933	$14,976	$10,130	3-M	6,862	471	68
Montana State Univ., Bozeman, MT 59717	1893	$7,223 (S)	$9,250	5-D	16,440	1,038	53
Montana State Univ. Billings, Billings, MT 59101.	1927	$5,833 (S)	$7,690	5-M	4,401	325	28
Montana State Univ.–Northern, Havre, MT 59501-7751	1929	$5,480 (S)	$7,500	5-M	1,273	96	30
Montana Technological Univ., Butte, MT 59701-8997	1895	$7,411 (S)	$9,828	5-D	2,678	213	44
Montclair State Univ., Montclair, NJ 07043-1624	1908	$12,455 (S)	$13,466	5-D	21,013	1,855	65
Moody Bible Inst., Chicago, IL 60610-3284	1886	NA	NA	2-M	3,349	211	68
Moravian Coll., Bethlehem, PA 18018-6650	1742	$43,636	$13,378	2-D	2,463	294	63
Morehead State Univ., Morehead, KY 40351.	1922	$8,950 (S)	$9,436	5-D	10,584	411	46
Morehouse Coll., Atlanta, GA 30314 (1).	1867	$27,574	$13,438	1-B	2,202	217	55
Morgan State Univ., Baltimore, MD 21251.	1867	$7,767 (S)	$10,650	5-D	7,005	558	100
Morningside Coll., Sioux City, IA 51106.	1894	$30,390	$9,390	2-M	2,788	233	56
Morrisville State Coll., Morrisville, NY 13408	1908	$8,309 (S)	$13,238	5-B	3,003	253	30
Mount Aloysius Coll., Cresson, PA 16630-1999.	1939	$22,430	$10,338	2-M	1,740	160	NA
Mount Holyoke Coll., South Hadley, MA 01075 (3)	1837	$49,998	$14,660	1-M	2,334	264	86
Mount Mary Univ., Milwaukee, WI 53222-4597 (6)	1913	$30,100	$8,600	2-D	1,358	194	39
Mount Mercy Univ., Cedar Rapids, IA 52402-4797.	1928	$31,998	$9,534	2-D	1,848	160	58
Mount St. Joseph Univ., Cincinnati, OH 45233-1670.	1920	$30,100	$9,442	2-D	2,010	206	61
Mount St. Mary Coll., Newburgh, NY 12550-3494	1960	$31,118	$15,108	1-M	2,365	269	54
Mount St. Mary's Univ., Emmitsburg, MD 21727-7799	1808	$40,550	$12,830	2-M	2,323	208	63
Mount St. Mary's Univ., Los Angeles, CA 90049 (4)	1925	$41,170	$12,235	2-D	3,280	453	66
Mount Vernon Nazarene Univ., Mount Vernon, OH 43050-9500.	1968	$29,194	$8,170	2-M	2,222	251	63
Muhlenberg Coll., Allentown, PA 18104-5586.	1848	$50,830	$11,420	2-B	2,408	297	87
Murray State Univ., Murray, KY 42071.	1922	$8,340 (S)	$8,906	5-D	10,495	686	49
Musicians Inst., Hollywood, CA 90028.	1976	NA	NA	3-B	1,337	204	NA
Muskingum Univ., New Concord, OH 43762	1837	$28,516	$11,480	2-M	2,371	154	54
Natl. Louis Univ., Chicago, IL 60603	1886	$12,846	NA	1-D	4,918	290	50

Name, address	Year founded	Tuition & fees	Room & board	Control, degree	Enroll-ment	Faculty	Grad. rate
Natl. Univ., La Jolla, CA 92037-1011	1971	$13,032	NA	1-M	17,097	1,325	43%
Nazareth Coll. of Rochester, Rochester, NY 14618	1924	$33,324	$13,410	1-D	2,900	508	67
Nebraska Wesleyan Univ., Lincoln, NE 68504-2796	1887	$32,894	$9,150	2-M	2,059	NA	70
Neumann Univ., Aston, PA 19014-1298	1965	$30,050	$12,520	2-D	2,715	241	57
Nevada State Coll., Henderson, NV 89002	2002	$4,830 (S)	NA	5-B	3,747	267	15
New England Coll., Henniker, NH 03242-3293	1946	$36,954	$13,874	1-D	2,625	267	31
New England Inst. of Tech., East Greenwich, RI 02818	1940	$29,940	$11,640	1-M	2,793	329	NA
New Jersey City Univ., Jersey City, NJ 07305-1597	1927	$11,431 (S)	$12,446	5-D	8,284	823	31
New Jersey Inst. of Tech., Newark, NJ 07102	1881	$16,898 (S)	$13,300	5-D	11,446	776	64
New Mexico Highlands Univ., Las Vegas, NM 87701	1893	$6,454 (S)	$7,654	5-M	3,471	249	22
New Mexico Inst. of Mining & Tech., Socorro, NM 87801	1889	$7,183 (S)	$8,202	5-D	2,009	188	47
New Mexico State Univ., Las Cruces, NM 88003-8001	1888	$6,461 (S)	$8,686	5-D	14,432	976	46
New Orleans Baptist Theol. Sem., New Orleans, LA 70126-4858 (2)	1917	NA	NA	2-D	2,036	NA	NA
The New School for Public Engagement, New York, NY 10011	1919	$30,860	$16,250	1-D	1,448	356	NA
New York City Coll. of Tech. of the City Univ. of New York, Brooklyn, NY 11201-2983	1946	$6,850 (S)	NA	11-B	17,282	1,427	25
New York Inst. of Tech., Old Westbury, NY 11568-8000	1955	$36,890	$14,290	1-D	7,422	900	50
New York Univ., New York, NY 10012-1019	1831	$50,464	NA	1-D	51,123	6,498	84
Newman Univ., Wichita, KS 67213-2097	1933	$30,564	$8,406	2-M	1,766	202	51
Niagara Univ., Niagara University, NY 14109	1856	$33,500	$13,200	2-D	3,949	442	68
Nicholls State Univ., Thibodaux, LA 70310	1948	$7,886 (S)	$9,790	5-M	6,298	311	37
Nichols Coll., Dudley, MA 01571-5000	1815	$34,000	$13,800	1-M	1,533	108	51
Norfolk State Univ., Norfolk, VA 23504	1935	$9,036 (S)	$9,866	5-D	6,027	NA	34
North Carolina A&T State Univ., Greensboro, NC 27411	1891	$6,526 (S)	$7,260	5-D	11,877	744	44
North Carolina Central Univ., Durham, NC 27707-3129	1910	$6,566 (S)	$8,446	5-D	8,097	564	42
North Carolina State Univ., Raleigh, NC 27695	1887	$9,100 (S)	$11,078	5-D	34,432	2,607	79
North Carolina Wesleyan Coll., Rocky Mount, NC 27804-8677	1956	$30,150	$10,050	2-B	2,093	313	31
North Central Coll., Naperville, IL 60566-7063	1861	$37,749	$10,650	2-M	2,965	283	68
North Dakota State Univ., Fargo, ND 58102	1890	$8,546 (S)	$8,356	5-D	14,358	776	58
North Greenville Univ., Tigerville, SC 29688-1892	1892	$19,150	$10,240	2-D	2,567	218	55
North Park Univ., Chicago, IL 60625-4895	1891	NA	NA	2-D	3,138	305	56
Northcentral Univ., San Diego, CA 92106	1996	$10,680	NA	3-D	10,698	478	NA
Northeastern Illinois Univ., Chicago, IL 60625-4699	1961	$13,420 (S)	$11,424	5-M	9,538	623	24
Northeastern State Univ., Tahlequah, OK 74464-2399	1846	$6,335 (S)	$7,020	5-D	7,906	448	31
Northeastern Univ., Boston, MA 02115-5096	1898	$49,497	$16,240	1-D	26,660	1,743	87
Northern Arizona Univ., Flagstaff, AZ 86011	1899	$11,060 (S)	$9,944	5-D	31,057	1,725	55
Northern Illinois Univ., DeKalb, IL 60115-2854	1895	$12,262 (S)	$10,880	5-D	18,042	1,067	45
Northern Kentucky Univ., Highland Heights, KY 41099	1968	$9,744 (S)	$9,732	5-D	14,474	1,032	40
Northern Michigan Univ., Marquette, MI 49855-5301	1899	$10,490 (S)	$10,328	5-D	7,612	419	53
Northern New Mexico Coll., Española, NM 87532	1909	NA	NA	5-B	2,272	253	NA
Northern State Univ., Aberdeen, SD 57401-7198	1901	$8,280 (S)	$7,844	5-M	3,611	148	50
Northern Vermont Univ.–Johnson, Johnson, VT 05656	2018	$10,224 (S)	$9,696	5-M	1,662	179	35
Northwest Missouri State Univ., Maryville, MO 64468-6001	1905	$9,572 (S)	$9,770	5-M	6,338	302	49
Northwest Nazarene Univ., Nampa, ID 83686-5897	1913	$29,300	$7,400	2-D	2,223	119	60
Northwest Univ., Kirkland, WA 98033	1934	$31,540	$8,630	2-D	2,583	252	59
Northwestern Coll., Orange City, IA 51041-1996	1882	$31,100	$9,200	2-M	1,251	141	68
Northwestern Oklahoma State Univ., Alva, OK 73717-2799	1897	$7,358 (S)	$4,480	5-D	2,102	156	27
Northwestern State Univ. of Louisiana, Natchitoches, LA 71497	1884	$8,588 (S)	$9,086	5-D	10,572	469	37
Northwestern Univ., Evanston, IL 60208	1851	$52,678	$16,047	1-D	21,474	1,731	94
Northwood Univ., Michigan campus, Midland, MI 48640-2398	1959	$26,080	$10,170	1-M	1,927	155	61
Norwich Univ., Northfield, VT 05663	1819	$37,354	$12,920	1-M	3,672	332	57
Notre Dame Coll., South Euclid, OH 44121-4293	1922	$28,300	$9,550	2-M	1,393	118	NA
Notre Dame de Namur Univ., Belmont, CA 94002-1908	1851	$35,350	$14,494	2-D	1,625	230	48
Notre Dame of Maryland Univ., Baltimore, MD 21210-2476 (4)	1873	$35,019	$11,446	2-D	2,764	136	56
Nova Southeastern Univ., Fort Lauderdale, FL 33314-7796	1964	$29,940	$12,550	1-D	20,793	1,602	52
Nyack Coll., Nyack, NY 10960	1882	$25,350	$9,450	2-D	2,455	262	47
Oakland City Univ., Oakland City, IN 47660-1099	1885	$24,000	$9,900	2-D	1,303	187	49
Oakland Univ., Rochester, MI 48309-4401	1957	$12,420 (S)	$9,910	5-D	19,333	NA	46
Oakwood Univ., Huntsville, AL 35896	1896	$16,720	$9,312	2-M	1,824	171	46
Oberlin Coll., Oberlin, OH 44074	1833	$53,460	$14,402	1-M	2,853	381	86
Occidental Coll., Los Angeles, CA 90041-3314	1887	$52,838	$14,968	1-M	2,055	277	84
Oglethorpe Univ., Atlanta, GA 30319-2797	1835	$36,825	$12,960	1-B	1,250	NA	47
Ohio Christian Univ., Circleville, OH 43113	1948	$12,099	$7,498	2-M	4,661	368	NA
Ohio Dominican Univ., Columbus, OH 43219-2099	1911	$31,080	$10,948	2-M	1,714	169	47
Ohio Northern Univ., Ada, OH 45810-1599	1871	$32,260	$11,650	2-D	3,088	286	73
The Ohio State Univ., Columbus, OH 43210	1870	$10,591 (S)	$12,252	5-D	59,837	5,589	83
The Ohio State Univ. at Newark, Newark, OH 43055-1797	1957	$7,553 (S)	$9,132	5-M	2,623	158	37
Ohio Univ., Athens, OH 45701-2979	1804	$11,896 (S)	$11,498	5-D	29,525	1,370	64
Ohio Univ.–Chillicothe, Chillicothe, OH 45601	1946	NA	NA	5-M	2,200	NA	NA
Ohio Univ.–Lancaster, Lancaster, OH 43130-1097	1968	NA	NA	5-M	1,728	NA	NA
Ohio Univ.–Southern campus, Ironton, OH 45638-2214	1956	NA	NA	5-M	1,836	NA	NA
Ohio Univ.–Zanesville, Zanesville, OH 43701-2695	1946	$5,076 (S)	NA	5-B	1,878	130	NA
Ohio Wesleyan Univ., Delaware, OH 43015	1842	$45,740	$12,430	2-B	1,565	208	70
Oklahoma Baptist Univ., Shawnee, OK 74804	1910	$28,258	$7,350	2-M	2,085	175	57
Oklahoma Christian Univ., Oklahoma City, OK 73136-1100	1950	$22,760	$8,190	2-M	2,470	211	52
Oklahoma City Univ., Oklahoma City, OK 73106-1402	1904	$31,026	$8,896	2-D	2,821	268	63
Oklahoma Panhandle State Univ., Goodwell, OK 73939-0430	1909	$7,120 (S)	$5,002	5-B	1,387	91	38
Oklahoma State Univ., Stillwater, OK 74078	1890	$8,738 (S)	$8,558	5-D	25,254	1,321	63
Oklahoma Wesleyan Univ., Bartlesville, OK 74006-6299	1909	$26,090	$8,344	2-M	1,527	111	45
Old Dominion Univ., Norfolk, VA 23529	1930	$10,350 (S)	$11,268	5-D	24,375	1,500	54
Olivet Nazarene Univ., Bourbonnais, IL 60914	1907	$34,940	$7,900	2-D	4,986	453	66
Oral Roberts Univ., Tulsa, OK 74171	1963	$27,728	$9,450	2-D	3,919	296	57
Oregon Health & Sci. Univ., Portland, OR 97239-3098	1974	$19,602 (S)	NA	12-D	2,895	110	NA
Oregon Inst. of Tech., Klamath Falls, OR 97601-8801	1947	$9,982 (S)	$9,206	5-M	5,490	305	44
Oregon State Univ., Corvallis, OR 97331	1868	$10,797 (S)	$12,540	5-D	30,896	1,697	65
Ottawa Univ., Ottawa, KS 66067-3399	1865	$29,690	$6,000	2-M	2,319	36	37
Otterbein Univ., Westerville, OH 43081	1847	$31,874	NA	2-D	2,936	328	64
Ouachita Baptist Univ., Arkadelphia, AR 71998-0001	1886	$26,790	$7,880	2-B	1,545	177	64
Our Lady of the Lake Univ., San Antonio, TX 78207-4689	1895	$28,740	$9,602	2-D	3,212	315	38

Name, address	Year founded	Tuition & fees	Room & board	Control, degree	Enroll- ment	Faculty	Grad. rate
Pace Univ., New York, NY 10038.	1906	$45,280	$19,200	1-D	9,234	840	51%
Pace Univ., Pleasantville campus, Pleasantville, NY 10570	1906	$45,280	$16,600	1-D	3,475	452	60
Pacific Lutheran Univ., Tacoma, WA 98447.	1890	$40,722	$10,520	2-D	3,064	221	68
Pacific Union Coll., Angwin, CA 94508-9707	1882	$29,469	$8,148	2-M	1,555	143	44
Pacific Univ., Forest Grove, OR 97116-1797	1849	$41,054	$11,822	1-D	3,810	NA	71
Palm Beach Atlantic Univ., West Palm Beach, FL 33416-4708	1968	$31,450	$10,130	2-D	3,839	373	54
Palm Beach State Coll., Lake Worth, FL 33461-4796	1933	$3,070 (S)	NA	5-B	30,052	1,170	NA
Palmer Coll. of Chiropractic, Davenport, IA 52803-5287	1897	NA	NA	1-D	2,310	15	NA
Park Univ., Parkville, MO 64152-3795	1875	NA	NA	1-M	9,800	174	42
Parsons Sch. of Design, New York, NY 10011	1896	$47,920	$15,000	1-M	5,278	993	75
Peirce Coll., Philadelphia, PA 19102-4699 (4)	1865	$15,060	NA	1-M	1,478	99	NA
Penn State Abington, Abington, PA 19001	1950	$14,516 (S)	NA	12-B	3,893	320	50
Penn State Altoona, Altoona, PA 16601.	1939	$15,190 (S)	$11,280	12-B	3,482	288	65
Penn State Berks, Reading, PA 19610	1924	$15,190 (S)	$12,400	12-B	2,719	227	57
Penn State Brandywine, Media, PA 19063	1966	$14,460 (S)	$11,860	12-B	1,438	134	42
Penn State Erie, The Behrend Coll., Erie, PA 16563	1948	$15,190 (S)	$11,280	12-M	4,502	339	66
Penn State Harrisburg, Middletown, PA 17057	1966	$15,190 (S)	$12,940	12-D	5,077	372	58
Penn State Univ. Park, University Park, PA 16802	1855	$18,436 (S)	$11,280	12-D	47,119	3,066	85
Pennsylvania Coll. of Health Sciences, Lancaster, PA 17601	1903	$27,084	NA	1-D	1,793	213	64
Pennsylvania Coll. of Tech., Williamsport, PA 17701-5778	1965	$18,840 (S)	$11,340	12-B	5,382	448	57
Pepperdine Univ., Malibu, CA 90263	1937	$53,932	$15,320	2-D	7,710	678	80
Peru State Coll., Peru, NE 68421.	1867	$7,226 (S)	$7,630	5-M	2,358	109	NA
Pfeiffer Univ., Misenheimer, NC 28109-0960	1885	$29,574	$10,958	2-M	1,306	126	59
Piedmont Coll., Demorest, GA 30535	1897	$24,464	$9,870	2-D	2,361	291	50
Pittsburg State Univ., Pittsburg, KS 66762.	1903	$7,100 (S)	$7,700	5-D	6,907	382	NA
Pitzer Coll., Claremont, CA 91711-6101	1963	$52,236	$16,264	1-B	1,112	118	83
Plymouth State Univ., Plymouth, NH 03264-1595	1871	$13,472 (S)	$11,008	5-D	5,050	426	54
Point Loma Nazarene Univ., San Diego, CA 92106-2899	1902	$35,700	$10,450	2-D	4,467	474	74
Point Park Univ., Pittsburgh, PA 15222-1984.	1960	$30,130	$11,960	1-D	4,224	519	55
Point Univ., West Point, GA 31833.	1937	$20,600	$7,900	2-M	1,952	192	27
Polk State Coll., Winter Haven, FL 33881-4299.	1964	$3,367 (S)	NA	5-B	10,659	392	NA
Polytechnic Univ. of Puerto Rico, Hato Rey, PR 00918.	1966	$8,328	$11,858	1-D	4,317	211	16
Pomona Coll., Claremont, CA 91711	1887	$52,780	$16,716	1-B	1,704	240	97
Pontifical Catholic Univ. of Puerto Rico, Ponce, PR 00717-0777.	1948	$5,370	$4,919	2-D	7,682	385	39
Portland State Univ., Portland, OR 97207-0751.	1946	$8,783 (S)	$12,831	5-D	27,305	1,603	48
Post Univ., Waterbury, CT 06723-2540	1890	$29,550	$10,600	1-M	8,540	NA	NA
Prairie View A&M Univ., Prairie View, TX 77446	1878	$10,533 (S)	$8,743	5-D	9,125	481	32
Pratt Inst., Brooklyn, NY 11205-3899.	1887	$51,870	$12,622	1-M	4,829	1,148	70
Presbyterian Coll., Clinton, SC 29325	1880	$37,842	$10,298	2-D	1,282	104	68
Princeton Univ., Princeton, NJ 08544-1019	1746	$49,330	$16,290	1-D	8,273	1,149	97
Providence Coll., Providence, RI 02918.	1917	$48,764	$14,240	2-M	4,874	535	84
Purchase Coll., State Univ. of New York, Purchase, NY 10577-1400	1967	$8,498 (S)	$13,334	5-M	4,224	461	63
Purdue Univ., West Lafayette, IN 47907	1869	$9,992 (S)	$10,030	5-D	41,573	2,642	79
Purdue Univ. Northwest, Hammond, IN 46323-2094	2016	$7,582 (S)	$7,597	5-D	12,071	706	34
Queens Coll. of the City Univ. of New York, Queens, NY 11367-1597	1937	$7,138 (S)	$15,352	11-M	19,866	1,625	54
Queens Univ. of Charlotte, Charlotte, NC 28274-0002	1857	$33,532	$11,844	2-M	2,286	314	53
Quincy Univ., Quincy, IL 62301-2699.	1860	$27,670	$10,500	2-M	1,293	114	52
Quinnipiac Univ., Hamden, CT 06518-1940.	1929	$47,960	$14,990	1-D	10,200	1,084	75
Radford Univ., Radford, VA 24142.	1910	$10,627 (S)	$9,131	5-D	9,418	739	55
Ramapo Coll. of New Jersey, Mahwah, NJ 07430-1680	1969	$14,080 (S)	$12,180	5-M	6,120	491	74
Randolph-Macon Coll., Ashland, VA 23005-5505	1830	$41,300	$11,860	2-B	1,453	171	66
Rasmussen Coll. Lake Elmo/Woodbury, Lake Elmo, MN 55042	1900	$12,750	NA	3-B	2,169	23	NA
Rasmussen Coll. Ocala, Ocala, FL 34474	1984	$12,750	NA	3-B	1,447	44	NA
Rasmussen Coll. Ocala Sch. of Nursing, Ocala, FL 34471	2016	$12,750	NA	3-B	4,326	43	NA
Reed Coll., Portland, OR 97202-8199	1908	$54,200	$13,670	1-M	1,470	156	80
Regent Univ., Virginia Beach, VA 23464-9800.	1977	$17,478	$8,250	2-D	10,187	837	61
Regis Coll., Weston, MA 02493	1927	$39,820	$14,740	2-D	1,954	210	47
Regis Univ., Denver, CO 80221-1099	1877	$36,810	$11,560	2-D	8,131	779	71
Reinhardt Univ., Waleska, GA 30183-2981	1883	$21,544	$7,948	2-M	1,422	172	36
Rensselaer Polytechnic Inst., Troy, NY 12180-3590	1824	$53,880	$15,260	1-D	7,633	517	83
Rhode Island Coll., Providence, RI 02908-1991	1854	$8,776 (S)	$11,335	5-D	8,174	756	46
Rhode Island Sch. of Design, Providence, RI 02903-2784	1877	$48,470	$13,050	1-M	2,440	438	91
Rhodes Coll., Memphis, TN 38112-1690	1848	$46,504	$11,290	1-M	2,010	222	83
Rice Univ., Houston, TX 77251-1892.	1912	$45,608	$13,850	1-D	7,022	870	91
Rider Univ., Lawrenceville, NJ 08648-3001	1865	$41,310	$14,700	1-D	5,073	602	63
Ringling Coll. of Art & Design, Sarasota, FL 34234-5895	1931	$46,420	$14,670	1-B	1,456	173	65
Rivier Univ., Nashua, NH 03060.	1933	NA	NA	2-D	2,157	209	49
Roanoke Coll., Salem, VA 24153-3794	1842	$44,030	$13,690	2-B	2,037	221	67
Robert Morris Univ., Moon Township, PA 15108-1189	1921	$29,420	$11,180	1-D	5,076	438	61
Robert Morris Univ. Illinois, Chicago, IL 60605	1913	$28,530	NA	1-M	2,307	184	76
Roberts Wesleyan Coll., Rochester, NY 14624-1997	1866	$30,936	$10,430	2-D	1,740	249	60
Rochester Inst. of Tech., Rochester, NY 14623-5603	1829	$40,068	$12,666	1-D	16,584	1,459	70
Rockford Univ., Rockford, IL 61108-2393	1847	$30,930	$8,660	1-M	1,261	NA	41
Rockhurst Univ., Kansas City, MO 64110-2561.	1910	$36,590	$9,970	2-D	3,043	239	75
Roger Williams Univ., Bristol, RI 02809	1956	$32,510	$15,564	1-D	5,024	538	65
Rogers State Univ., Claremore, OK 74017-3252	1909	$6,870 (S)	$8,050	5-M	3,723	236	25
Rollins Coll., Winter Park, FL 32789-4499	1885	$49,760	$14,740	1-M	2,650	232	75
Roosevelt Univ., Chicago, IL 60605	1945	$29,832	$13,223	1-D	4,457	622	41
Rose-Hulman Inst. of Tech., Terre Haute, IN 47803-3999 (2)	1874	$45,762	$14,061	1-M	2,245	202	81
Rowan Univ., Glassboro, NJ 08028-1701	1923	$13,108 (S)	$11,688	5-D	18,484	1,593	69
Rush Univ., Chicago, IL 60612-3832	1969	NA	NA	1-D	1,566	796	NA
Rutgers Univ.–Camden, Camden, NJ 08102-1401	1926	$14,501 (S)	$12,094	5-D	6,853	700	58
Rutgers Univ.–New Brunswick, Piscataway, NJ 08854-8097	1766	$14,638 (S)	$12,452	5-D	49,577	4,525	80
Rutgers Univ.–Newark, Newark, NJ 07102	1908	$14,085 (S)	$13,266	5-D	12,768	1,023	68
Sacred Heart Univ., Fairfield, CT 06825.	1963	$39,820	$14,770	2-D	8,543	NA	72
The Sage Colleges, Troy, NY 12180	1916	$30,857	$12,618	1-D	2,525	297	56
Saginaw Valley State Univ., University Center, MI 48710	1963	$9,819 (S)	$9,465	5-D	8,662	742	40
St. Ambrose Univ., Davenport, IA 52803-2898	1882	$30,894	$10,470	2-D	3,118	346	63

Name, address	Year founded	Tuition & fees	Room & board	Control, degree	Enroll- ment	Faculty	Grad. rate
St. Anselm Coll., Manchester, NH 03102-1310	1889	$41,200	$14,500	2-B	1,964	225	80%
St. Augustine Coll., Chicago, IL 60640-3501	1980	$13,200	NA	1-B	1,430	154	NA
St. Bonaventure Univ., St. Bonaventure, NY 14778-2284	1858	$33,331	$11,815	2-M	2,089	239	69
St. Catherine Univ., St. Paul, MN 55105 (6)	1905	$38,349	$9,196	2-D	4,724	536	58
St. Cloud State Univ., St. Cloud, MN 56301-4498	1869	$8,228 (S)	$8,558	5-D	15,092	744	44
St. Edward's Univ., Austin, TX 78704	1885	$43,050	$12,940	2-M	4,601	481	64
St. Francis Coll., Brooklyn Heights, NY 11201-4398	1884	NA	NA	2-M	2,672	300	52
St. Francis Univ., Loretto, PA 15940-0600	1847	$34,956	$11,928	2-D	2,209	237	71
St. John Fisher Coll., Rochester, NY 14618-3597	1948	$33,120	$12,150	2-D	3,782	449	71
St. John's Univ., Collegeville, MN 56321 (5)	1857	$43,356	$10,116	2-M	1,815	157	74
St. John's Univ., Queens, NY 11439	1870	$40,520	$17,020	2-D	21,346	1,460	58
St. Joseph's Coll., Long Island campus, Patchogue, NY 11772-2399	1916	$26,560	NA	1-M	3,966	422	72
St. Joseph's Coll. of Maine, Standish, ME 04084	1912	$34,610	$13,280	2-M	3,355	126	50
St. Joseph's Univ., Philadelphia, PA 19131-1395	1851	$43,880	$14,840	2-D	8,086	704	82
St. Lawrence Univ., Canton, NY 13617	1856	$54,846	$14,134	1-M	2,493	217	85
St. Leo Univ., Saint Leo, FL 33574-6665	1889	$21,970	$10,570	2-D	5,898	211	40
St. Louis Coll. of Pharm., St. Louis, MO 63110-1088	1864	$30,010	$12,285	1-D	1,309	171	71
St. Louis Univ., St. Louis, MO 63103	1818	$42,166	$10,996	2-D	12,098	1,134	77
St. Martin's Univ., Lacey, WA 98503	1895	$37,356	$11,445	2-M	1,565	196	59
St. Mary's Coll., Notre Dame, IN 46556 (3)	1844	$40,800	$12,100	2-D	1,701	210	77
St. Mary's Coll. of California, Moraga, CA 94575	1863	$47,280	$15,370	2-D	3,913	500	76
St. Mary's Coll. of Maryland, St. Mary's City, MD 20686-3001	1840	$14,496 (S)	$12,816	5-M	1,598	199	78
St. Mary's Univ., San Antonio, TX 78228	1852	$30,600	$10,790	2-D	3,649	385	63
St. Mary's Univ. of Minnesota, Winona, MN 55987-1399	1912	$35,140	$9,080	2-D	5,754	471	58
St. Michael's Coll., Colchester, VT 05439	1904	$45,375	$12,220	2-M	2,077	170	78
St. Norbert Coll., De Pere, WI 54115-2099	1898	$38,129	$9,954	2-M	2,165	209	73
St. Olaf Coll., Northfield, MN 55057-1098	1874	$47,840	$5,200	2-B	3,035	320	88
St. Peter's Univ., Jersey City, NJ 07306-5997	1872	NA	NA	2-D	3,524	322	54
St. Petersburg Coll., St. Petersburg, FL 33733-3489	1927	$3,385 (S)	NA	11-B	29,835	1,585	28
St. Thomas Aquinas Coll., Sparkill, NY 10976	1952	$30,750	$12,750	1-M	1,915	157	54
St. Thomas Univ., Miami Gardens, FL 33054-6459	1961	$31,080	$11,700	2-D	4,549	497	44
St. Vincent Coll., Latrobe, PA 15650-2690	1846	$34,830	$11,399	2-D	1,859	227	69
St. Xavier Univ., Chicago, IL 60655-3105	1847	NA	NA	2-M	4,709	431	52
Salem State Univ., Salem, MA 01970-5353	1854	$10,277 (S)	$12,210	5-M	9,301	NA	46
Salisbury Univ., Salisbury, MD 21801-6837	1925	$9,582 (S)	$11,550	5-D	8,714	666	70
Salve Regina Univ., Newport, RI 02840-4192	1934	$38,986	$14,060	2-D	2,823	289	71
Sam Houston State Univ., Huntsville, TX 77341	1879	$9,891 (S)	$9,180	5-D	20,938	955	51
Samford Univ., Birmingham, AL 35229	1841	$31,650	$10,550	2-D	5,509	547	76
Samuel Merritt Univ., Oakland, CA 94609-3108 (4)	1909	NA	NA	1-D	2,141	392	NA
San Diego State Univ., San Diego, CA 92182	1897	$7,460 (S)	$15,966	5-D	34,828	1,794	75
San Francisco State Univ., San Francisco, CA 94132-1722	1899	$7,254 (S)	$13,248	5-D	29,607	1,763	54
San Jose State Univ., San Jose, CA 95192-0001	1857	$7,417 (S)	$14,107	5-M	32,773	1,755	57
Santa Clara Univ., Santa Clara, CA 95053	1851	$49,858	$14,487	2-D	8,629	906	90
Santa Fe Coll., Gainesville, FL 32606	1966	NA	NA	11-B	15,745	829	NA
Sarah Lawrence Coll., Bronxville, NY 10708-5999	1926	$54,010	$14,856	1-M	1,696	311	79
Savannah Coll. of Art & Design, Savannah, GA 31402-3146	1978	$36,630	$14,550	1-M	13,842	694	65
Savannah State Univ., Savannah, GA 31404	1890	$6,734 (S)	$7,592	5-M	4,800	220	27
School of the Art Inst. of Chicago, Chicago, IL 60603-3103	1866	$47,420	$15,490	1-M	3,570	731	65
School of Visual Arts, New York, NY 10010-3994	1947	$39,900	$20,400	3-M	4,395	1,179	NA
Schreiner Univ., Kerrville, TX 78028-5697	1923	$26,900	$10,152	2-M	1,308	125	45
Scripps Coll., Claremont, CA 91711-3948 (3)	1926	$52,966	$16,294	1-B	1,077	125	88
Seattle Pacific Univ., Seattle, WA 98119-1997	1891	$40,902	$11,178	2-D	3,813	395	69
Seattle Univ., Seattle, WA 98122-1090	1891	$42,885	$12,072	2-D	7,278	736	74
Seton Hall Univ., South Orange, NJ 07079-2697	1856	$40,588	$15,174	2-D	9,903	952	64
Seton Hill Univ., Greensburg, PA 15601	1883	$34,660	$11,280	2-M	2,048	199	58
Shaw Univ., Raleigh, NC 27601-2399	1865	$16,480	$8,158	2-M	1,660	139	19
Shawnee State Univ., Portsmouth, OH 45662	1986	$8,556 (S)	$10,864	5-M	3,582	314	28
Shenandoah Univ., Winchester, VA 22601-5195	1875	$32,530	$10,370	2-D	3,844	460	63
Shepherd Univ., Shepherdstown, WV 25443	1871	$7,548 (S)	$10,500	5-D	3,736	347	42
Shippensburg Univ. of Pennsylvania, Shippensburg, PA 17257-2299	1871	$12,086 (S)	$12,010	5-D	6,581	372	52
Siena Coll., Loudonville, NY 12211-1462	1937	$36,975	$15,000	2-M	3,236	332	78
Siena Heights Univ., Adrian, MI 49221-1796	1919	NA	NA	2-M	2,642	268	51
Simmons Coll., Boston, MA 02115 (6)	1899	$40,800	$15,200	1-D	6,402	1,071	73
Simpson Coll., Indianola, IA 50125-1297	1860	$39,144	$8,380	2-M	1,479	194	68
Skidmore Coll., Saratoga Springs, NY 12866	1903	$52,446	$14,004	1-B	2,684	384	87
Slippery Rock Univ. of Pennsylvania, Slippery Rock, PA 16057-1383	1889	$10,205 (S)	$10,312	5-D	8,895	419	66
Smith Coll., Northampton, MA 01063 (6)	1871	$50,044	$16,730	1-D	2,918	NA	NA
Sonoma State Univ., Rohnert Park, CA 94928-3609	1960	$7,724 (S)	$13,554	5-M	9,223	568	58
South Carolina State Univ., Orangeburg, SC 29117-0001	1896	$10,740 (S)	$9,890	5-D	2,905	191	38
South Dakota Sch. of Mines & Tech., Rapid City, SD 57701-3995	1885	$11,170 (S)	$7,300	5-D	2,859	177	47
South Dakota State Univ., Brookings, SD 57007	1881	$8,460 (S)	$7,110	5-D	12,613	696	55
Southeast Missouri State Univ., Cape Girardeau, MO 63701-4799	1873	$7,185 (S)	$8,715	5-M	11,502	578	52
Southeastern Baptist Theol. Sem., Wake Forest, NC 27587	1950	$11,020	$3,265	2-D	2,717	119	31
Southeastern Louisiana Univ., Hammond, LA 70402	1925	$8,153 (S)	$8,340	5-D	14,338	593	40
Southeastern Oklahoma State Univ., Durant, OK 74701-0609	1909	$6,750 (S)	$6,568	5-M	3,724	251	29
Southeastern Univ., Lakeland, FL 33801-6099	1935	$25,360	$9,550	2-D	7,163	467	40
Southern Adventist Univ., Collegedale, TN 37315-0370	1892	$21,950	$6,940	2-D	3,035	169	50
Southern Arkansas Univ.–Magnolia, Magnolia, AR 71753	1909	$8,346 (S)	$6,028	5-M	4,643	282	34
The Southern Baptist Theol. Sem., Louisville, KY 40280-0004	1858	NA	NA	2-D	3,190	NA	NA
Southern Connecticut State Univ., New Haven, CT 06515-1355	1893	$10,538 (S)	$12,432	5-D	10,320	964	51
Southern Illinois Univ. Carbondale, Carbondale, IL 62901-4701	1869	$13,936 (S)	$10,622	5-D	14,554	998	40
Southern Illinois Univ. Edwardsville, Edwardsville, IL 62026	1957	$12,132 (S)	$9,730	5-D	13,796	852	48
Southern Methodist Univ., Dallas, TX 75275	1911	$54,493	$16,845	2-D	11,789	1,156	81
Southern Nazarene Univ., Bethany, OK 73008	1899	NA	NA	2-M	3,906	NA	60
Southern New Hampshire Univ., Manchester, NH 03106-1045	1932	$31,136	$12,278	1-D	4,092	445	56
Southern Oregon Univ., Ashland, OR 97520	1926	$9,286 (S)	$12,831	5-M	5,916	283	40
Southern Tech. Coll., Fort Myers, FL 33907	1940	NA	NA	3-B	1,259	160	20
Southern Univ. & A&M Coll., Baton Rouge, LA 70813	1880	NA	NA	5-D	7,699	546	29

Name, address	Year founded	Tuition & fees	Room & board	Control, degree	Enroll-ment	Faculty	Grad. rate
Southern Univ. at New Orleans, New Orleans, LA 70126-1009 (4)	1959	NA	NA	5-M	3,141	102	NA
Southern Utah Univ., Cedar City, UT 84720-2498	1897	$6,676 (S)	$7,067	5-M	9,468	581	37%
Southern Wesleyan Univ., Central, SC 29630-1020	1906	NA	NA	2-M	1,883	193	39
Southwest Baptist Univ., Bolivar, MO 65613-2597	1878	$24,010	$7,720	2-D	3,592	333	46
Southwest Minnesota State Univ., Marshall, MN 56258	1963	$8,619 (S)	$7,761	5-M	6,896	194	43
Southwestern Assemblies of God Univ., Waxahachie, TX 75165-5735	1927	$20,952	$7,500	2-M	2,162	148	NA
Southwestern Coll., Winfield, KS 67156-2499	1885	$30,150	$7,760	2-D	1,306	167	41
Southwestern Oklahoma State Univ., Weatherford, OK 73096-3098	1901	$7,005 (S)	$5,500	5-D	5,320	280	35
Southwestern Univ., Georgetown, TX 78626	1840	$42,000	$12,000	2-B	1,387	146	74
Spalding Univ., Louisville, KY 40203-2188	1814	$24,000	$7,900	2-D	2,322	170	47
Spelman Coll., Atlanta, GA 30314-4399 (3)	1881	$29,064	$13,865	1-B	2,137	241	75
Spring Arbor Univ., Spring Arbor, MI 49283-9799	1873	$26,730	$9,270	2-M	3,404	138	52
Spring Hill Coll., Mobile, AL 36608-1791	1830	$37,584	$13,070	2-M	1,501	126	53
Springfield Coll., Springfield, MA 01109-3797	1885	NA	NA	1-D	3,254	211	72
Stanford Univ., Stanford, CA 94305-2004	1891	$49,617	$15,112	1-D	16,914	1,637	94
State Coll. of Florida Manatee-Sarasota, Bradenton, FL 34206-7046	1957	$3,074 (S)	NA	5-B	9,073	444	NA
State Univ. of New York at Fredonia, Fredonia, NY 14063-1136	1826	$8,288 (S)	$12,490	5-M	4,631	442	63
State Univ. of New York at New Paltz, New Paltz, NY 12561	1828	$7,975 (S)	$12,642	5-M	7,565	624	72
State Univ. of New York at Oswego, Oswego, NY 13126	1861	$8,191 (S)	$13,740	5-M	8,026	578	66
State Univ. of New York at Plattsburgh, Plattsburgh, NY 12901-2681	1889	$8,164 (S)	$12,988	5-M	5,719	451	63
State Univ. of New York Coll. at Cortland, Cortland, NY 13045	1868	$8,300 (S)	$12,410	5-M	6,913	619	71
State Univ. of New York Coll. at Geneseo, Geneseo, NY 14454-1401	1871	$8,408 (S)	$13,214	5-M	5,591	365	77
State Univ. of New York Coll. at Old Westbury, Old Westbury, NY 11568-0210	1965	$7,883 (S)	$11,020	5-M	4,461	351	43
State Univ. of New York Coll. at Oneonta, Oneonta, NY 13820-4015	1889	$8,136 (S)	$12,658	5-M	6,358	490	72
State Univ. of New York Coll. at Potsdam, Potsdam, NY 13676	1816	$8,221 (S)	$12,830	5-M	3,587	366	52
State Univ. of New York Coll. of Agr. & Tech. at Cobleskill, Cobleskill, NY 12043	1916	$8,139 (S)	$13,182	5-B	2,298	178	61
State Univ. of New York Coll. of Env. Sci. & Forestry, Syracuse, NY 13210-2779	1911	$8,568 (S)	$16,140	5-D	2,219	159	78
State Univ. of New York Coll. of Tech. at Canton, Canton, NY 13617	1906	$8,129 (S)	$12,450	5-B	3,180	238	37
State Univ. of New York Coll. of Tech. at Delhi, Delhi, NY 13753	1913	$8,120 (S)	$11,980	5-M	3,515	250	57
State Univ. of New York Downstate Med. Ctr., Brooklyn, NY 11203-2098	1858	NA	NA	5-D	1,694	981	NA
State Univ. of New York Empire State Coll., Saratoga Springs, NY 12866-4391	1971	$7,205 (S)	NA	5-M	11,024	913	NA
State Univ. of New York Maritime Coll., Throggs Neck, NY 10465-4198	1874	$8,074 (S)	$12,134	5-M	1,794	149	63
State Univ. of New York Polytechnic Inst., Utica, NY 13502	1966	$7,998 (S)	$12,440	5-D	2,933	274	52
State Univ. of New York Upstate Med. Univ., Syracuse, NY 13210	1950	NA	NA	5-D	1,787	54	NA
Stephen F. Austin State Univ., Nacogdoches, TX 75962	1923	$9,537 (S)	$8,868	5-D	12,614	718	44
Stetson Univ., DeLand, FL 32723	1883	$46,030	$13,052	1-D	4,268	430	62
Stevens Inst. of Tech., Hoboken, NJ 07030	1870	$52,202	$15,244	1-D	6,916	415	83
Stevenson Univ., Stevenson, MD 21153	1952	$36,182	$13,130	1-M	3,876	462	54
Stockton Univ., Galloway, NJ 08205-9441	1969	$13,403 (S)	$12,120	5-D	9,216	719	73
Stonehill Coll., Easton, MA 02357	1948	$41,300	$15,760	2-M	2,498	284	80
Stony Brook Univ., State Univ. of New York, Stony Brook, NY 11794	1957	$9,257 (S)	$13,446	5-D	25,989	1,566	72
Suffolk Univ., Boston, MA 02108-2770	1906	$38,566	$15,582	1-D	7,288	685	60
Sul Ross State Univ., Alpine, TX 79832	1920	$8,071 (S)	NA	5-M	1,973	148	NA
Sullivan Univ., Louisville, KY 40205	1962	NA	NA	3-D	3,489	266	NA
Susquehanna Univ., Selinsgrove, PA 17870	1858	$45,470	$12,090	2-B	2,266	260	71
Swarthmore Coll., Swarthmore, PA 19081-1397	1864	$50,822	$14,952	1-B	1,620	220	94
Syracuse Univ., Syracuse, NY 13244	1870	$46,755	$15,558	1-D	22,484	1,691	83
Tarleton State Univ., Stephenville, TX 76402	1899	$9,078 (S)	$9,872	5-D	13,019	766	48
Taylor Univ., Upland, IN 46989-1001	1846	$32,885	$9,245	2-M	2,145	193	79
Temple Univ., Philadelphia, PA 19122-6096	1884	$16,658 (S)	$11,566	12-D	39,948	2,831	71
Tennessee State Univ., Nashville, TN 37209-1561	1912	$7,458 (S)	NA	5-D	8,753	658	NA
Tennessee Tech. Univ., Cookeville, TN 38505	1915	$8,513 (S)	$9,274	5-D	10,504	645	49
Texas A&M Univ., College Station, TX 77843	1876	$10,403 (S)	$12,250	5-D	67,580	3,585	82
Texas A&M Univ.–Central Texas, Killeen, TX 76549	2009	$23,716 (S)	NA	5-M	2,602	190	NA
Texas A&M Univ.–Comm, Commerce, TX 75429	1889	$8,748 (S)	$8,326	5-D	12,490	674	50
Texas A&M Univ.–Corpus Christi, Corpus Christi, TX 78412	1947	$8,969 (S)	$10,410	5-D	12,236	723	35
Texas A&M Univ.–Intl., Laredo, TX 78041	1969	$8,320 (S)	$8,160	5-D	7,640	370	43
Texas A&M Univ.–Kingsville, Kingsville, TX 78363	1925	$8,462 (S)	$8,760	5-D	8,674	NA	NA
Texas A&M Univ.–Texarkana, Texarkana, TX 75503	1971	$7,635 (S)	$7,462	5-D	2,066	NA	30
Texas Christian Univ., Fort Worth, TX 76129-0002	1873	$44,760	$12,360	2-D	10,489	1,020	83
Texas Lutheran Univ., Seguin, TX 78155-5999	1891	$29,960	$10,150	2-M	1,394	127	52
Texas Southern Univ., Houston, TX 77004-4584	1947	NA	NA	5-D	9,233	605	NA
Texas State Univ., San Marcos, TX 78666	1899	$10,621 (S)	$8,100	5-D	38,666	2,013	54
Texas Tech. Univ., Lubbock, TX 79409	1923	$10,772 (S)	$5,956	5-D	36,996	1,790	59
Texas Wesleyan Univ., Fort Worth, TX 76105	1890	$27,800	$9,538	2-D	2,619	234	30
Texas Woman's Univ., Denton, TX 76204 (4)	1901	$9,360 (S)	$8,181	5-D	15,472	937	36
Thomas Coll., Waterville, ME 04901-5097	1894	$25,722	$10,228	1-M	1,367	87	45
Thomas Edison State Univ., Trenton, NJ 08608	1972	$7,300 (S)	NA	5-D	16,233	NA	NA
Thomas Jefferson Univ., Philadelphia, PA 19107	1824	NA	NA	1-D	3,326	215	NA
Thomas More Coll., Crestview Hills, KY 41017-3495	1921	$30,270	$7,592	2-M	1,959	139	50
Thomas Univ., Thomasville, GA 31792-7499	1950	$16,940	$7,040	1-M	1,596	53	NA
Tiffin Univ., Tiffin, OH 44883-2161	1888	$25,000	$11,200	1-M	3,149	361	33
Toccoa Falls Coll., Toccoa Falls, GA 30598	1907	$22,744	$8,330	2-B	1,411	125	53
Touro Coll., New York, NY 10010	1971	$17,900	NA	1-D	12,021	1,335	59
Touro Univ. Worldwide, Los Alamitos, CA 90720	2008	$10,800	NA	1-D	1,304	119	NA
Towson Univ., Towson, MD 21252-0001	1866	$9,694 (S)	$12,544	5-D	22,705	1,711	72
Trevecca Nazarene Univ., Nashville, TN 37210-2877	1901	$25,598	$8,400	2-D	3,620	268	54
Trine Univ., Angola, IN 46703-1764	1884	$31,540	$10,570	1-D	4,302	165	NA
Trinity Coll., Hartford, CT 06106-3100	1823	$52,760	$13,680	1-M	2,397	295	86
Trinity Intl. Univ., Deerfield, IL 60015-1284	1897	NA	NA	2-D	2,671	82	52
Trinity Univ., San Antonio, TX 78212-7200	1869	$42,976	$13,464	2-M	2,604	322	80
Trinity Washington Univ., Washington, DC 20017-1094 (3)	1897	NA	NA	2-M	1,630	NA	NA
Troy Univ., Troy, AL 36082	1887	$12,155 (S)	$7,946	5-D	17,521	1,079	41
Truett McConnell Univ., Cleveland, GA 30528	1946	$19,480	$7,400	2-M	2,187	NA	NA
Truman State Univ., Kirksville, MO 63501-4221	1867	$7,656 (S)	$8,630	5-M	6,272	398	75
Tufts Univ., Medford, MA 02155	1852	$54,318	$14,054	1-D	11,449	1,077	93
Tulane Univ., New Orleans, LA 70118-5669	1834	$52,960	$14,536	1-D	11,248	1,188	83
Tusculum Coll., Greeneville, TN 37743-9997	1794	$24,860	$9,190	2-M	1,767	147	33

Name, address	Year founded	Tuition & fees	Room & board	Control, degree	Enrollment	Faculty	Grad. rate
Tuskegee Univ., Tuskegee, AL 36088	1881	$20,320	$9,320	1-D	2,995	207	46%
Union Coll., Barbourville, KY 40906-1499	1879	$26,080	$7,400	2-M	1,202	81	26
Union Coll., Schenectady, NY 12308-2311	1795	$53,490	$13,119	1-B	2,267	229	85
Union Univ., Jackson, TN 38305-3697	1823	$32,890	$10,200	2-D	2,189	228	69
United States Air Force Acad., USAF Academy, CO 80840-5025	1954	$0 (C)	NA	4-B	4,237	502	83
United States Military Acad., West Point, NY 10996	1802	$0 (C)	NA	4-B	4,491	611	85
United States Naval Acad., Annapolis, MD 21402-5000	1845	$0 (C)	NA	4-B	4,525	592	86
United Talmudical Sem., Brooklyn, NY 11211 (1).	1949	NA	NA	2-M	1,500	NA	NA
Univ. at Albany, State Univ. of New York, Albany, NY 12222-0001	1844	$9,490 (S)	$13,864	5-D	17,743	1,185	65
Univ. at Buffalo, State Univ. of New York, Buffalo, NY 14260	1846	$9,828 (S)	$13,782	5-D	30,648	1,839	75
The Univ. of Akron, Akron, OH 44325	1870	$10,270 (S)	$12,296	5-D	20,169	1,452	43
The Univ. of Alabama at Birmingham, Birmingham, AL 35294	1969	$10,635 (S)	$11,682	5-D	20,902	975	53
The Univ. of Alabama in Huntsville, Huntsville, AL 35899	1950	$10,280 (S)	$9,748	5-D	8,468	542	49
The Univ. of Alabama, Tuscaloosa, AL 35487	1831	$10,780 (S)	$10,102	5-D	38,563	1,898	68
Univ. of Alaska Anchorage, Anchorage, AK 99508	1954	$6,186 (S)	$11,962	5-D	17,321	1,406	NA
Univ. of Alaska Fairbanks, Fairbanks, AK 99775-7520	1917	$8,800 (S)	$8,930	5-D	7,744	831	39
Univ. of Alaska Southeast, Juneau, AK 99801	1972	NA	NA	5-M	3,458	229	31
The Univ. of Arizona, Tucson, AZ 85721	1885	$12,200 (S)	$12,550	5-D	44,831	2,347	64
Univ. of Arkansas, Fayetteville, AR 72701	1871	$9,062 (S)	$10,704	5-D	27,558	1,384	62
Univ. of Arkansas–Fort Smith, Fort Smith, AR 72913-3649	1928	$6,935 (S)	NA	11-M	6,823	412	27
Univ. of Arkansas at Little Rock, Little Rock, AR 72204-1099	1927	$9,430 (S)	$5,900	5-D	11,645	740	24
Univ. of Arkansas at Monticello, Monticello, AR 71656	1909	NA	NA	5-M	3,920	240	24
Univ. of Arkansas at Pine Bluff, Pine Bluff, AR 71601-2799	1873	$7,408 (S)	$7,672	5-D	2,658	199	26
Univ. of Arkansas for Med. Sci., Little Rock, AR 72205-7199	1879	$8,147 (S)	$7,560	5-D	2,869	521	NA
Univ. of Baltimore, Baltimore, MD 21201-5779	1925	NA	NA	5-D	3,526	405	NA
Univ. of Bridgeport, Bridgeport, CT 06604	1927	$32,250	$13,590	1-D	5,434	559	42
Univ. of California, Berkeley, Berkeley, CA 94720-1500	1868	$14,170 (S)	$15,716	5-D	38,204	2,258	91
Univ. of California, Davis, Davis, CA 95616	1908	$14,463 (S)	$15,765	5-D	37,278	NA	85
Univ. of California, Irvine, Irvine, CA 92697	1965	$15,516 (S)	$14,829	5-D	35,242	1,634	85
Univ. of California, Los Angeles, Los Angeles, CA 90095	1919	$13,584 (S)	$15,143	5-D	45,428	2,706	91
Univ. of California, Merced, Merced, CA 95343	2005	$13,598 (S)	$16,790	5-D	6,685	373	66
Univ. of California, Riverside, Riverside, CA 92521-0102	1954	$15,642 (S)	$17,000	5-D	23,278	1,164	75
Univ. of California, San Diego, La Jolla, CA 92093	1959	$14,050 (S)	$13,307	5-D	35,772	1,348	84
Univ. of California, Santa Barbara, Santa Barbara, CA 93106-2014	1909	$14,472 (S)	$15,673	5-D	25,057	1,163	87
Univ. of California, Santa Cruz, Santa Cruz, CA 95064	1965	$14,028 (S)	$16,055	5-D	19,457	NA	77
Univ. of Central Arkansas, Conway, AR 72035-0001	1907	$8,524 (S)	$6,518	5-D	11,350	726	41
Univ. of Central Florida, Orlando, FL 32816	1963	$6,368 (S)	$10,011	5-D	66,183	2,051	70
Univ. of Central Missouri, Warrensburg, MO 64093	1871	$7,520 (S)	$8,536	5-M	12,333	655	48
Univ. of Central Oklahoma, Edmond, OK 73034-5209	1890	$7,100 (S)	$8,050	5-M	15,973	1,030	37
Univ. of Charleston, Charleston, WV 25304-1099	1888	$30,900	$9,180	1-D	2,481	NA	49
Univ. of Chicago, Chicago, IL 60637-1513	1890	$54,825	$15,726	1-D	13,736	1,671	93
Univ. of Cincinnati, Cincinnati, OH 45221	1819	$11,000 (S)	$11,118	5-D	37,204	3,511	69
Univ. of Colorado Boulder, Boulder, CO 80309	1876	$12,086 (S)	$13,998	5-D	35,230	NA	69
Univ. of Colorado Colorado Springs, Colorado Springs, CO 80918	1965	$10,201 (S)	$10,100	5-D	12,932	774	43
Univ. of Colorado Denver, Denver, CO 80217-3364	1912	$11,258 (S)	$12,190	5-D	24,839	4,825	45
Univ. of Connecticut, Storrs, CT 06269	1881	$14,880 (S)	$12,514	5-D	26,541	1,589	81
Univ. of Dallas, Irving, TX 75062-4736	1955	$38,716	$11,960	2-D	2,520	211	68
Univ. of Dayton, Dayton, OH 45469	1850	$21,450	$13,580	2-D	10,882	1,034	79
Univ. of Delaware, Newark, DE 19716	1743	$13,160 (S)	$12,332	12-D	22,168	1,686	83
Univ. of Denver, Denver, CO 80208	1864	$50,556	$13,005	1-D	11,434	1,290	75
Univ. of Detroit Mercy, Detroit, MI 48221	1877	$41,158	$9,452	2-D	4,875	790	68
Univ. of Dubuque, Dubuque, IA 52001-5099	1852	$29,710	$9,450	2-D	2,340	385	43
Univ. of Evansville, Evansville, IN 47722	1854	$36,416	$12,460	2-D	2,516	262	73
The Univ. of Findlay, Findlay, OH 45840-3653	1882	$33,320	$9,720	2-D	4,888	274	61
Univ. of Florida, Gainesville, FL 32611	1853	$6,381 (S)	$9,910	5-D	52,668	NA	87
Univ. of Georgia, Athens, GA 30602	1785	$11,818 (S)	$10,060	5-D	37,606	2,307	85
Univ. of Guam, Mangilao, GU 96923	1952	$5,578 (S)	$3,850	7-M	3,917	NA	35
Univ. of Hartford, West Hartford, CT 06117-1599	1877	$40,694	$12,476	1-D	6,561	875	58
Univ. of Hawaii at Hilo, Hilo, HI 96720-4091	1970	NA	NA	5-D	3,924	338	38
Univ. of Hawaii at Manoa, Honolulu, HI 96822	1907	$11,970 (S)	$13,689	5-D	17,612	1,404	60
Univ. of Hawaii–West Oahu, Kapolei, HI 96707	1976	$7,440 (S)	NA	5-B	2,692	77	29
Univ. of Holy Cross, New Orleans, LA 70131-7399	1916	$13,220	NA	2-M	1,298	NA	NA
Univ. of Houston, Houston, TX 77204	1927	$11,887 (S)	$9,984	5-D	45,364	2,428	54
Univ. of Houston–Clear Lake, Houston, TX 77058-1002	1971	$6,873 (S)	$4,852	5-D	8,542	510	NA
Univ. of Houston–Downtown, Houston, TX 77002	1974	$7,832 (S)	NA	5-M	13,919	748	21
Univ. of Houston–Victoria, Victoria, TX 77901-4450	1973	$7,627 (S)	$7,698	5-M	4,407	239	NA
Univ. of Idaho, Moscow, ID 83844-2282	1889	$7,488 (S)	$8,670	5-D	12,072	798	55
Univ. of Illinois at Chicago, Chicago, IL 60607-7128	1946	$13,614 (S)	$10,960	5-D	30,538	1,613	57
Univ. of Illinois at Springfield, Springfield, IL 62703-5407	1969	$12,445 (S)	$11,660	5-D	4,956	375	50
Univ. of Illinois at Urbana-Champaign, Champaign, IL 61820	1867	$15,868 (S)	$11,308	5-D	44,942	NA	84
Univ. of Indianapolis, Indianapolis, IN 46227-3697	1902	$28,390	$9,988	2-D	5,711	NA	55
The Univ. of Iowa, Iowa City, IA 52242-1316	1847	$7,486 (S)	$10,450	5-D	31,387	1,616	70
The Univ. of Kansas, Lawrence, KS 66045	1866	$10,824 (S)	$10,060	5-D	27,625	1,625	63
Univ. of Kentucky, Lexington, KY 40506-0032	1865	$13,134 (S)	$12,184	5-D	29,465	NA	65
Univ. of La Verne, La Verne, CA 91750-4443	1891	$41,450	$13,140	1-D	4,803	516	67
Univ. of Louisiana at Lafayette, Lafayette, LA 70504	1898	NA	NA	5-D	17,508	793	46
Univ. of Louisiana at Monroe, Monroe, LA 71209-0001	1931	$8,470 (S)	$7,454	5-D	9,181	480	42
Univ. of Louisville, Louisville, KY 40292-0001	1798	$11,264 (S)	$8,700	5-D	21,403	1,336	54
Univ. of Lynchburg, Lynchburg, VA 24501-3199	1903	$37,690	$10,680	2-D	2,808	270	59
Univ. of Maine at Augusta, Augusta, ME 04330-9410	1965	$7,808 (S)	NA	5-B	4,683	260	NA
Univ. of Maine at Farmington, Farmington, ME 04938	1863	$9,458 (S)	$9,334	5-M	2,080	202	51
Univ. of Maine at Fort Kent, Fort Kent, ME 04743-1292	1878	$8,115 (S)	$7,910	5-B	1,760	93	33
Univ. of Maine, Orono, ME 04469	1865	$10,902 (S)	$10,136	5-D	11,240	838	58
Univ. of Maine at Presque Isle, Presque Isle, ME 04769-2888	1903	$8,034 (S)	$8,406	5-B	1,408	102	26
Univ. of Mgmt. & Tech., Arlington, VA 22209-1609	1998	$9,450	NA	3-D	1,293	NA	NA
Univ. of Mary, Bismarck, ND 58504-9652	1959	$18,150	$6,970	2-D	2,872	272	70
Univ. of Mary Hardin-Baylor, Belton, TX 76513	1845	$26,890	$8,446	2-D	3,914	281	48
Univ. of Mary Washington, Fredericksburg, VA 22401-5358	1908	$11,630 (S)	$11,118	5-M	4,808	402	71
Univ. of Maryland Eastern Shore, Princess Anne, MD 21853	1886	NA	NA	5-D	3,492	307	38
Univ. of Maryland Univ. Coll., Adelphi, MD 20783	1947	$7,296 (S)	NA	5-D	59,379	3,691	NA

Name, address	Year founded	Tuition & fees	Room & board	Control, degree	Enroll- ment	Faculty	Grad. rate
Univ. of Maryland, Baltimore Cty, Baltimore, MD 21250	1963	$11,518 (S)	$11,486	5-D	13,662	838	64%
Univ. of Maryland, Coll. Park, College Park, MD 20742.	1856	$10,399 (S)	$12,082	5-D	40,521	2,633	85
Univ. of Massachusetts Amherst, Amherst, MA 01003	1863	$15,411 (S)	$12,258	5-D	30,340	1,495	77
Univ. of Massachusetts Boston, Boston, MA 02125-3393	1964	$13,828 (S)	NA	5-D	16,415	1,146	48
Univ. of Massachusetts Dartmouth, North Dartmouth, MA 02747-2300	1895	$13,571 (S)	$12,936	5-D	8,406	595	49
Univ. of Massachusetts Lowell, Lowell, MA 01854.	1894	$14,800 (S)	$12,496	5-D	18,316	1,119	60
Univ. of Memphis, Memphis, TN 38152	1912	$9,701 (S)	$9,366	5-D	21,521	1,482	44
Univ. of Miami, Coral Gables, FL 33124.	1925	$48,484	$13,666	1-D	17,003	1,614	84
Univ. of Michigan, Ann Arbor, MI 48109.	1817	$14,826 (S)	$11,198	5-D	44,718	3,434	91
Univ. of Michigan–Dearborn, Dearborn, MI 48128.	1959	$12,472 (S)	NA	5-D	9,339	567	58
Univ. of Michigan–Flint, Flint, MI 48502-1950	1956	$11,334 (S)	$8,437	5-D	7,836	573	44
Univ. of Minnesota, Crookston, Crookston, MN 56716-5001	1966	$12,202 (S)	$7,658	5-D	2,823	116	45
Univ. of Minnesota, Duluth, Duluth, MN 55812-2496	1947	$13,344 (S)	$7,608	5-D	11,168	596	59
Univ. of Minnesota, Morris, Morris, MN 56267-2134	1959	$13,072 (S)	$8,150	5-B	1,627	165	59
Univ. of Minnesota, Twin Cities campus, Minneapolis, MN 55455-0213	1851	$14,417 (S)	$9,852	5-D	51,848	3,706	80
Univ. of Mississippi, University, MS 38677.	1844	$8,290 (S)	$10,502	5-D	23,136	1,344	60
Univ. of Mississippi Med. Ctr., Jackson, MS 39216-4505	1955	NA	NA	5-D	2,092	836	NA
Univ. of Missouri, Columbia, MO 65211.	1839	$9,787 (S)	$10,676	5-D	30,870	1,314	68
Univ. of Missouri–Kansas City, Kansas City, MO 64110-2499.	1929	$9,764 (S)	$10,383	5-D	16,944	1,207	53
Univ. of Missouri–St. Louis, St. Louis, MO 63121	1963	$10,275 (S)	$9,363	5-D	16,740	825	56
Univ. of Mobile, Mobile, AL 36613	1961	$22,210	$9,600	2-M	1,604	172	45
Univ. of Montana, Missoula, MT 59812	1893	$7,244 (S)	$9,544	5-D	11,865	728	48
The Univ. of Montana Western, Dillon, MT 59725-3598	1893	$5,502 (S)	$7,744	5-B	1,505	90	52
Univ. of Montevallo, Montevallo, AL 35115	1896	$12,400 (S)	$7,512	5-M	2,717	221	NA
Univ. of Mount Olive, Mount Olive, NC 28365	1951	$19,700	$8,150	2-M	3,855	183	44
Univ. of Mount Union, Alliance, OH 44601-3993	1846	$30,860	$10,200	2-D	2,257	255	62
Univ. of Nebraska, Lincoln, NE 68588	1869	$8,887 (S)	$11,044	5-D	26,079	1,129	68
Univ. of Nebraska at Kearney, Kearney, NE 68849-0001	1903	$7,326 (S)	$9,688	5-M	6,644	457	61
Univ. of Nebraska at Omaha, Omaha, NE 68182	1908	$7,630 (S)	$9,406	5-D	15,227	1,044	42
Univ. of Nebraska Med. Ctr., Omaha, NE 68198	1869	NA	NA	5-D	3,625	1,232	NA
Univ. of Nevada, Las Vegas, Las Vegas, NV 89154	1957	$7,800 (S)	$10,780	5-D	30,471	1,778	42
Univ. of Nevada, Reno, Reno, NV 89557.	1874	$7,764 (S)	$10,868	5-D	21,657	1,274	55
Univ. of New England, Biddeford, ME 04005-9526	1831	$36,530	$13,580	1-D	8,291	599	60
Univ. of New Hampshire, Durham, NH 03824	1866	$18,499 (S)	$11,588	5-D	15,364	1,059	77
Univ. of New Haven, West Haven, CT 06516	1920	$38,170	$15,610	1-D	6,984	647	60
Univ. of New Mexico, Albuquerque, NM 87131-2039.	1889	$7,146 (S)	$9,662	5-D	26,278	1,451	48
Univ. of New Orleans, New Orleans, LA 70148	1958	$8,694 (S)	$10,575	5-D	7,964	387	32
Univ. of North Alabama, Florence, AL 35632-0001	1830	$10,370 (S)	$7,684	5-M	7,457	429	44
Univ. of North Carolina at Asheville, Asheville, NC 28804-3299	1927	$7,145 (S)	$9,106	5-M	3,852	324	62
The Univ. of North Carolina at Chapel Hill, Chapel Hill, NC 27599	1789	$8,986 (S)	$11,190	5-D	29,911	2,313	91
The Univ. of North Carolina at Charlotte, Charlotte, NC 28223-0001	1946	$7,023 (S)	$10,780	5-D	29,317	1,666	54
The Univ. of North Carolina at Greensboro, Greensboro, NC 27412-5001	1891	$7,164 (S)	$8,834	5-D	19,922	1,077	53
The Univ. of North Carolina at Pembroke, Pembroke, NC 28372-1510.	1887	$5,955 (S)	$8,782	5-M	6,252	387	38
The Univ. of North Carolina Wilmington, Wilmington, NC 28403-3297	1947	$7,048 (S)	$9,736	5-D	16,487	1,067	72
Univ. of North Dakota, Grand Forks, ND 58202	1883	$8,447 (S)	$8,226	5-D	14,406	715	54
Univ. of North Florida, Jacksonville, FL 32224	1965	$6,394 (S)	$9,772	5-D	16,309	967	54
Univ. of North Georgia, Dahlonega, GA 30597	1873	$7,395 (S)	$10,800	5-D	18,782	984	54
Univ. of North Texas, Denton, TX 76203	1890	$11,514 (S)	$9,610	5-D	38,081	1,683	52
Univ. of North Texas at Dallas, Dallas, TX 75241	2001	$7,848 (S)	$8,948	5-D	3,509	167	NA
Univ. of Northern Colorado, Greeley, CO 80639	1890	$9,545 (S)	$10,982	5-D	12,968	852	48
Univ. of Northern Iowa, Cedar Falls, IA 50614.	1876	$8,699 (S)	$8,781	5-D	11,907	703	67
Univ. of Northwestern Ohio, Lima, OH 45805-1498.	1920	$10,650	$2,850	1-M	3,848	127	NA
Univ. of Northwestern–St. Paul, St. Paul, MN 55113-1598	1902	NA	NA	2-M	3,427	208	63
Univ. of Notre Dame, Notre Dame, IN 46556.	1842	$53,391	$15,410	2-D	12,467	1,348	95
Univ. of Oklahoma, Norman, OK 73019-0390	1890	$9,063 (S)	$10,588	5-D	28,527	1,454	68
Univ. of Oklahoma Health Sciences Ctr., Oklahoma City, OK 73190	1890	$7,153 (S)	NA	5-D	3,139	408	NA
Univ. of Oregon, Eugene, OR 97403	1876	$11,571 (S)	$12,450	5-D	22,887	1,666	72
Univ. of Pennsylvania, Philadelphia, PA 19104	1740	$55,584	$15,616	1-D	21,907	2,028	96
Univ. of Phoenix–Central Valley campus, Fresno, CA 93720-1552.	2004	NA	NA	3-M	2,235	272	NA
Univ. of Phoenix–Dallas campus, Dallas, TX 75251	2001	NA	NA	3-M	1,371	181	NA
Univ. of Phoenix–Houston campus, Houston, TX 77079-2004	2001	NA	NA	3-M	2,748	325	NA
Univ. of Phoenix–Las Vegas campus, Las Vegas, NV 89135	1994	NA	NA	3-M	3,162	279	NA
Univ. of Phoenix–Online campus, Phoenix, AZ 85034-7209	1989	NA	NA	3-D	292,797	11,477	NA
Univ. of Phoenix–Phoenix campus, Tempe, AZ 85282-2371.	1976	NA	NA	3-M	5,379	985	NA
Univ. of Phoenix–Sacramento Valley campus, Sacramento, CA 95833-4334.	1993	NA	NA	3-M	3,842	518	NA
Univ. of Phoenix–San Diego campus, San Diego, CA 92123	1988	NA	NA	3-M	3,212	399	NA
Univ. of Pikeville, Pikeville, KY 41501	1889	$20,950	$7,800	2-D	2,335	105	31
Univ. of Pittsburgh, Pittsburgh, PA 15260	1787	$19,080 (S)	$10,950	12-D	28,642	2,339	83
Univ. of Pittsburgh at Bradford, Bradford, PA 16701-2812.	1963	$13,900 (S)	$9,058	12-B	1,340	154	47
Univ. of Pittsburgh at Greensburg, Greensburg, PA 15601-5860	1963	$13,870 (S)	$10,270	12-B	1,523	NA	54
Univ. of Pittsburgh at Johnstown, Johnstown, PA 15904-2990	1927	$13,388 (S)	$9,684	12-B	2,769	151	53
Univ. of Portland, Portland, OR 97203-5798	1901	NA	NA	2-D	4,338	363	78
Univ. of Puerto Rico–Aguadilla, Aguadilla, PR 00604	1972	NA	NA	6-B	3,076	NA	NA
Univ. of Puerto Rico–Arecibo, Arecibo, PR 00614.	1967	NA	NA	6-B	4,352	NA	NA
Univ. of Puerto Rico–Bayamón, Bayamón, PR 00959 .	1971	$2,082 (S)	NA	6-B	4,927	254	34
Univ. of Puerto Rico–Carolina, Carolina, PR 00984-4800	1974	NA	NA	6-B	4,321	NA	NA
Univ. of Puerto Rico–Cayey, Cayey, PR 00736.	1967	NA	NA	6-B	3,830	164	42
Univ. of Puerto Rico–Humacao, Humacao, PR 00792	1962	$2,117 (S)	NA	6-B	3,723	254	51
Univ. of Puerto Rico–Mayagüez, Mayagüez, PR 00681-9000	1911	NA	NA	6-D	13,852	NA	NA
Univ. of Puerto Rico–Medical Sci. campus, San Juan, PR 00936-5067 (4).	1950	NA	NA	6-D	2,381	NA	NA
Univ. of Puerto Rico–Ponce, Ponce, PR 00732-7186	1970	$2,082 (S)	NA	6-B	3,229	188	38
Univ. of Puerto Rico–Río Piedras, San Juan, PR 00931-3300	1903	NA	NA	6-D	18,966	1,084	47
Univ. of Puerto Rico–Utuado, Utuado, PR 00641-2500	1979	NA	NA	6-B	1,623	107	NA
Univ. of Puget Sound, Tacoma, WA 98416	1888	$49,776	$12,540	1-D	2,701	288	78
Univ. of Redlands, Redlands, CA 92373-0999.	1907	$46,570	$13,480	1-D	5,215	NA	72
Univ. of Rhode Island, Kingston, RI 02881.	1892	$13,792 (S)	$7,774	5-D	18,098	1,146	66
Univ. of Richmond, University of Richmond, VA 23173	1830	$52,610	$12,250	1-D	3,503	438	88
Univ. of Rio Grande, Rio Grande, OH 45674	1876	NA	NA	1-M	2,161	175	39
Univ. of Rochester, Rochester, NY 14627	1850	$53,825	$15,860	1-D	7,121	NA	NA
Univ. of San Diego, San Diego, CA 92110-2492	1949	$49,358	$12,980	2-D	8,905	909	82
Univ. of San Francisco, San Francisco, CA 94117-1080	1855	$48,066	$14,830	2-D	11,080	1,182	77

Name, address	Year founded	Tuition & fees	Room & board	Control, degree	Enroll-ment	Faculty	Grad. rate
Univ. of Sioux Falls, Sioux Falls, SD 57105-1699	1883	$18,280	$7,350	2-M	1,453	169	49%
Univ. of South Alabama, Mobile, AL 36688-0002.	1963	$9,390 (S)	$7,490	5-D	15,569	1,033	40
Univ. of South Carolina, Columbia, SC 29208	1801	$12,262 (S)	$11,200	5-D	34,731	2,200	75
Univ. of South Carolina Aiken, Aiken, SC 29801	1961	$10,502 (S)	$7,592	5-M	3,506	288	41
Univ. of South Carolina Beaufort, Bluffton, SC 29909	1959	$10,166 (S)	$7,800	5-B	1,980	NA	23
Univ. of South Carolina Upstate, Spartanburg, SC 29303-4999	1967	$11,160 (S)	$8,142	5-M	5,821	451	42
Univ. of South Dakota, Vermillion, SD 57069	1862	$8,772 (S)	$7,672	5-D	10,261	594	57
Univ. of South Florida, St. Petersburg, St. Petersburg, FL 33701	1965	$5,821 (S)	$10,808	5-M	4,980	301	37
Univ. of South Florida, Tampa, FL 33620-9951	1956	$6,410 (S)	$10,325	5-D	42,861	1,737	NA
Univ. of South Florida Sarasota-Manatee, Sarasota, FL 34243	1956	$5,587 (S)	NA	5-M	2,117	151	NA
Univ. of Southern California, Los Angeles, CA 90089	1880	$54,323	$14,885	1-D	45,687	3,523	92
Univ. of Southern Indiana, Evansville, IN 47712-3590	1965	$7,970 (S)	$8,838	5-D	9,014	686	40
Univ. of Southern Maine, Portland, ME 04103	1878	$9,220 (S)	$9,200	5-D	7,855	662	34
Univ. of Southern Mississippi, Hattiesburg, MS 39406-0001	1910	$8,108 (S)	$10,638	5-D	14,478	899	NA
Univ. of St. Francis, Fort Wayne, IN 46808-3994.	1890	$30,430	$9,840	2-D	2,322	299	56
Univ. of St. Francis, Joliet, IL 60435-6169	1920	$32,320	NA	2-D	2,479	266	63
Univ. of St. Joseph, West Hartford, CT 06117-2700 (4).	1932	$39,172	$11,428	2-D	2,405	301	68
Univ. of St. Mary, Leavenworth, KS 66048-5082	1923	$28,690	$8,140	2-D	1,310	183	44
Univ. of St. Thomas, Houston, TX 77006-4696	1947	$33,580	NA	2-D	3,312	350	60
Univ. of St. Thomas, St. Paul, MN 55105-1096	1885	$41,133	$10,054	2-D	9,878	810	77
Univ. of the Cumberlands, Williamsburg, KY 40769-1372	1889	$23,000	$9,000	2-D	7,693	378	37
Univ. of the District of Columbia, Washington, DC 20008-1175.	1976	NA	NA	9-D	4,803	576	NA
Univ. of the Incarnate Word, San Antonio, TX 78209-6397	1881	$29,990	$12,436	2-D	8,603	711	53
Univ. of the Pacific, Stockton, CA 95211-0197.	1851	$46,346	$13,356	1-D	6,255	823	66
Univ. of the Sacred Heart, San Juan, PR 00914-0383.	1935	NA	NA	2-M	5,666	367	35
Univ. of the Sciences, Philadelphia, PA 19104-4495	1821	$39,994	$15,738	1-D	2,664	419	72
The Univ. of Scranton, Scranton, PA 18510.	1888	$43,310	$14,618	2-D	4,993	468	77
The Univ. of Tampa, Tampa, FL 33606-1490	1931	$28,426	$10,502	1-M	8,839	742	59
The Univ. of Tennessee, Knoxville, TN 37996	1794	$12,970 (S)	$10,696	5-D	28,321	1,752	70
The Univ. of Tennessee at Chattanooga, Chattanooga, TN 37403-2598	1886	$8,664 (S)	$8,676	5-D	11,587	717	45
The Univ. of Tennessee at Martin, Martin, TN 38238.	1900	$9,236 (S)	$5,976	5-M	6,800	486	50
The Univ. of Texas at Arlington, Arlington, TX 76019	1895	$9,952 (S)	$8,924	5-D	39,740	NA	42
The Univ. of Texas at Austin, Austin, TX 78712-1111	1883	$10,398 (S)	$10,070	5-D	51,525	3,133	83
The Univ. of Texas at Dallas, Richardson, TX 75080.	1969	$12,528 (S)	$11,112	5-D	27,642	1,319	69
The Univ. of Texas at El Paso, El Paso, TX 79968-0001.	1913	$7,651 (S)	$9,495	5-D	25,078	1,327	41
The Univ. of Texas at San Antonio, San Antonio, TX 78249-0617	1969	$9,380 (S)	$7,190	5-D	30,768	1,276	37
The Univ. of Texas at Tyler, Tyler, TX 75799-0001	1971	NA	NA	5-D	8,785	NA	41
The Univ. of Texas Health Sci. Ctr. at Houston, Houston, TX 77225-0036	1972	NA	NA	5-D	4,811	128	95
The Univ. of Texas Health Sci. Ctr. at San Antonio, San Antonio, TX 78229-3900	1976	NA	NA	5-D	3,093	NA	NA
The Univ. of Texas Med. Branch, Galveston, TX 77555	1891	NA	NA	5-D	2,430	NA	NA
The Univ. of Texas of the Permian Basin, Odessa, TX 79762-0001	1969	$7,124 (S)	$10,944	5-M	7,022	290	43
The Univ. of Texas Rio Grande Valley, Edinburg, TX 78539	1927	$9,055 (S)	$7,986	5-D	27,708	NA	NA
The Univ. of the Arts, Philadelphia, PA 19102-4944	1876	$44,780	$16,322	1-M	1,860	467	63
The Univ. of the South, Sewanee, TN 37383-1000	1857	$45,120	$12,880	2-D	1,778	242	77
The Univ. of Toledo, Toledo, OH 43606-3390	1872	$9,240 (S)	$11,151	5-D	20,579	1,080	42
The Univ. of Tulsa, Tulsa, OK 74104-3189	1894	$41,024	$11,116	1-D	4,433	456	69
Univ. of Utah, Salt Lake City, UT 84112-1107	1850	$8,824 (S)	$9,867	5-D	32,760	2,196	67
The Univ. of Virginia's Coll. at Wise, Wise, VA 24293	1954	$9,825 (S)	$10,314	5-B	2,095	162	41
Univ. of the Virgin Islands, St. Thomas, VI 00802	1962	$5,235 (S)	$9,900	7-D	2,170	216	24
Univ. of Vermont, Burlington, VT 05405.	1791	$17,740 (S)	$12,022	5-D	13,340	826	75
Univ. of Virginia, Charlottesville, VA 22903	1819	$16,146 (S)	$11,220	5-D	24,360	1,575	95
Univ. of Washington, Bothell, Bothell, WA 98011.	1990	$10,690 (S)	$10,833	5-M	5,990	347	64
Univ. of Washington, Seattle, WA 98195	1861	$10,753 (S)	$11,691	5-D	46,166	2,636	84
Univ. of Washington, Tacoma, Tacoma, WA 98402-3100	1990	$10,831 (S)	$10,230	5-D	5,164	345	60
The Univ. of West Alabama, Livingston, AL 35470	1835	$9,204 (S)	$7,080	5-M	4,646	277	32
Univ. of West Florida, Pensacola, FL 32514-5750	1963	$6,359 (S)	$9,942	5-D	12,798	606	47
Univ. of West Georgia, Carrollton, GA 30118.	1933	$7,292 (S)	$10,218	5-D	13,520	705	41
Univ. of Wisconsin–Eau Claire, Eau Claire, WI 54702-4004	1916	$8,816 (S)	$7,538	5-D	10,737	570	67
Univ. of Wisconsin–Green Bay, Green Bay, WI 54311-7001	1968	$7,878 (S)	$7,306	5-M	7,030	308	50
Univ. of Wisconsin–La Crosse, La Crosse, WI 54601-3742.	1909	$8,922 (S)	$6,206	5-D	10,473	632	71
Univ. of Wisconsin–Madison, Madison, WI 53706-1380	1848	$10,534 (S)	$10,842	5-D	43,820	2,858	87
Univ. of Wisconsin–Milwaukee, Milwaukee, WI 53201-0413	1956	$11,010 (S)	$10,728	5-D	25,381	1,519	41
Univ. of Wisconsin–Oshkosh, Oshkosh, WI 54901	1871	$7,544 (S)	$7,466	5-D	14,411	628	54
Univ. of Wisconsin–Parkside, Kenosha, WI 53141-2000.	1968	$7,649 (S)	$7,924	5-M	4,308	261	34
Univ. of Wisconsin–Platteville, Platteville, WI 53818-3099.	1866	$7,543 (S)	$7,526	5-M	8,429	441	51
Univ. of Wisconsin–River Falls, River Falls, WI 54022.	1874	$8,013 (S)	$6,576	5-M	6,110	374	53
Univ. of Wisconsin–Stevens Point, Stevens Point, WI 54481-3897.	1894	$9,734 (S)	$7,290	5-D	8,109	476	65
Univ. of Wisconsin–Stout, Menomonie, WI 54751	1891	$9,456 (S)	$6,744	5-D	9,401	483	NA
Univ. of Wisconsin–Superior, Superior, WI 54880-4500	1893	$8,109 (S)	$6,730	5-M	2,590	224	44
Univ. of Wisconsin–Whitewater, Whitewater, WI 53190-1790.	1868	$7,662 (S)	$6,492	5-D	12,430	636	NA
Univ. of Wyoming, Laramie, WY 82071	1886	$5,217 (S)	$10,320	5-D	12,397	732	55
Universidad Adventista de las Antillas, Mayagüez, PR 00681-0118	1957	$6,470	$5,300	2-M	1,351	107	34
Universidad del Este, Carolina, PR 00984	1949	NA	NA	1-M	13,058	NA	25
Universidad del Turabo, Gurabo, PR 00778-3030.	1972	NA	NA	1-D	17,509	1,171	NA
Universidad Metropolitana, San Juan, PR 00928-1150	1980	NA	NA	1-D	13,919	1,250	26
Upper Iowa Univ., Fayette, IA 52142-1857	1857	$30,450	$8,460	1-M	4,944	518	43
Urbana Univ.–A Branch campus of Franklin Univ., Urbana, OH 43078-2091	1850	$22,452	$9,308	1-M	1,551	120	NA
Ursinus Coll., Collegeville, PA 19426.	1869	$52,050	$12,750	1-B	1,507	171	77
Utah State Univ., Logan, UT 84322	1888	$7,175 (S)	$6,060	5-D	27,679	1,231	49
Utah Valley Univ., Orem, UT 84058-5999	1941	$5,652 (S)	NA	5-M	37,282	1,982	26
Utica Coll., Utica, NY 13502-4892	1946	$20,676	$10,834	1-D	5,258	452	49
Valdosta State Univ., Valdosta, GA 31698.	1906	$6,410 (S)	$7,900	5-D	11,341	559	37
Valencia Coll., Orlando, FL 32802-3028	1967	$2,473 (S)	NA	5-B	44,833	1,956	41
Valley City State Univ., Valley City, ND 58072.	1890	$7,406 (S)	$6,328	5-M	1,522	106	35
Valparaiso Univ., Valparaiso, IN 46383	1859	$40,260	$11,860	2-D	4,053	417	72
Vanderbilt Univ., Nashville, TN 37240-1001	1873	$47,664	$15,584	1-D	12,587	1,225	92
Vanguard Univ. of Southern California, Costa Mesa, CA 92626	1920	$33,700	$10,520	2-M	2,116	247	61
Vassar Coll., Poughkeepsie, NY 12604	1861	$55,210	$12,900	1-M	2,353	336	90
Vaughn Coll. of Aeronautics & Tech., Flushing, NY 11369 (2).	1932	$24,877	$14,185	1-M	1,501	189	52
Vermont Tech. Coll., Randolph Center, VT 05061-0500	1866	$15,510 (S)	$10,598	5-M	1,621	172	44
Villanova Univ., Villanova, PA 19085-1699	1842	$51,284	$13,548	2-D	10,983	1,039	90
Virginia Coll. in Birmingham, Birmingham, AL 35209.	1989	NA	NA	3-M	3,826	NA	NA
Virginia Commonwealth Univ., Richmond, VA 23284-9005	1838	$13,570 (S)	$10,187	5-D	31,036	2,152	63
Virginia Military Inst., Lexington, VA 24450	1839	$18,214 (S)	$9,236	5-B	1,722	207	77

Name, address	Year founded	Tuition & fees	Room & board	Control, degree	Enrollment	Faculty	Grad. rate
Virginia Polytechnic Inst. & State Univ., Blacksburg, VA 24061	1872	$13,230 (S)	$8,690	5-D	34,440	2,032	85%
Virginia State Univ., Petersburg, VA 23806-0001	1882	$8,726 (S)	$10,880	5-D	4,584	480	44
Virginia Union Univ., Richmond, VA 23220-1170	1865	$17,448	$8,512	2-D	1,922	138	32
Virginia Wesleyan Univ., Virginia Beach, VA 23455	1961	$36,660	$9,256	2-M	1,470	128	52
Viterbo Univ., La Crosse, WI 54601-4797	1890	$26,920	$8,760	2-D	2,761	324	46
Wagner Coll., Staten Island, NY 10301-4495	1883	$45,380	$13,650	1-D	2,289	265	70
Wake Forest Univ., Winston-Salem, NC 27109	1834	$53,322	$16,032	1-D	8,116	NA	88
Walden Univ., Minneapolis, MN 55401	1970	NA	NA	3-D	52,799	2,754	NA
Waldorf Univ., Forest City, IA 50436	1903	$22,076	$7,524	2-M	2,487	171	29
Walla Walla Univ., College Place, WA 99324	1892	$27,495	$7,350	2-M	1,894	171	51
Walsh Coll. of Accountancy & Bus. Admin., Troy, MI 48083	1922	$16,935	NA	1-M	2,299	113	NA
Walsh Univ., North Canton, OH 44720-3396	1958	$29,150	$10,530	2-D	2,759	242	61
Wartburg Coll., Waverly, IA 50677-0903	1852	$41,280	$9,995	2-B	1,527	160	66
Washburn Univ., Topeka, KS 66621	1865	$8,300 (S)	$7,527	10-D	6,615	512	36
Washington & Jefferson Coll., Washington, PA 15301	1781	$46,628	$12,318	1-M	1,412	162	70
Washington & Lee Univ., Lexington, VA 24450	1749	$50,170	$11,730	1-D	2,220	234	92
Washington Adventist Univ., Takoma Park, MD 20912	1904	$23,400	$8,930	2-M	1,493	134	26
Washington Coll., Chestertown, MD 21620-1197	1782	$47,006	$12,190	1-B	1,484	175	73
Washington State Univ., Pullman, WA 99164	1890	$11,391 (S)	$11,356	5-D	20,508	1,854	63
Washington State Univ.–Spokane, Spokane, WA 99210-1495	1989	$10,285 (S)	NA	5-D	1,616	NA	91
Washington State Univ.–Tri-Cities, Richland, WA 99354	1989	$10,342 (S)	NA	5-D	1,937	NA	49
Washington State Univ.–Vancouver, Vancouver, WA 98686	1989	$10,129 (S)	NA	5-D	3,546	NA	59
Washington Univ. in St. Louis, St. Louis, MO 63130-4899	1853	$53,399	$16,440	1-D	15,303	1,300	94
Wayland Baptist Univ., Plainview, TX 79072-6998	1908	$19,430	$7,534	2-D	4,827	554	20
Wayne State Coll., Wayne, NE 68787	1910	$6,824 (S)	$7,430	5-M	3,292	204	51
Wayne State Univ., Detroit, MI 48202	1868	$13,776 (S)	$10,106	5-D	27,089	1,740	47
Waynesburg Univ., Waynesburg, PA 15370-1222	1849	$24,010	$9,820	2-D	1,736	211	66
Weber State Univ., Ogden, UT 84408-1001	1889	$5,712 (S)	$8,400	5-M	27,949	1,404	35
Webster Univ., St. Louis, MO 63119-3194	1915	$27,100	$11,050	1-D	4,090	NA	61
Wellesley Coll., Wellesley, MA 02481 (3)	1870	$51,148	$15,836	1-B	2,508	359	90
Wentworth Inst. of Tech., Boston, MA 02115-5998	1904	$34,977	$13,844	1-M	4,454	354	67
Wesley Coll., Dover, DE 19901-3875	1873	$25,646	$11,244	2-M	1,770	170	22
Wesleyan Univ., Middletown, CT 06459	1831	$52,474	$14,466	1-D	3,213	441	90
West Chester Univ. of Pennsylvania, West Chester, PA 19383	1871	$10,111 (S)	$9,060	5-D	17,306	952	73
West Coast Univ., North Hollywood, CA 91606	1909	NA	NA	3-M	1,792	NA	NA
West Liberty Univ., West Liberty, WV 26074	1837	$7,380 (S)	$9,320	5-M	2,340	NA	48
West Texas A&M Univ., Canyon, TX 79015	1909	$7,885 (S)	$7,196	5-D	10,060	444	41
West Virginia State Univ., Institute, WV 25112-1000	1891	$8,167 (S)	$11,892	5-M	3,879	193	26
West Virginia Univ. Inst. of Tech., Beckley, WV 25801	1895	$6,960 (S)	$11,304	5-B	1,623	117	22
West Virginia Univ., Morgantown, WV 26506	1867	$8,376 (S)	$10,576	5-D	28,410	1,486	57
West Virginia Wesleyan Coll., Buckhannon, WV 26201	1890	$31,640	$8,856	2-M	1,449	150	50
Western Carolina Univ., Cullowhee, NC 28723	1889	$7,191 (S)	$9,164	5-D	10,805	688	57
Western Connecticut State Univ., Danbury, CT 06810-6885	1903	$10,458 (S)	$12,416	5-D	5,664	620	44
Western Governors Univ., Salt Lake City, UT 84107	1998	NA	NA	1-M	57,821	1,654	NA
Western Illinois Univ., Macomb, IL 61455-1390	1899	$11,267 (S)	$9,630	5-D	9,441	608	50
Western Kentucky Univ., Bowling Green, KY 42101	1906	$10,202 (S)	$8,350	5-D	20,257	1,192	51
Western Michigan Univ., Kalamazoo, MI 49008	1903	$11,943 (S)	$9,848	5-D	22,894	1,451	51
Western New England Univ., Springfield, MA 01119	1919	$35,740	$13,442	1-D	3,813	367	59
Western New Mexico Univ., Silver City, NM 88062-0680	1893	NA	NA	5-M	2,697	259	NA
Western Oregon Univ., Monmouth, OR 97361	1856	$9,198 (S)	$10,203	5-M	5,285	378	44
Western State Colorado Univ., Gunnison, CO 81231	1901	$9,802 (S)	$9,546	5-M	2,814	169	41
Western Washington Univ., Bellingham, WA 98225-5996	1893	$7,933 (S)	$11,400	5-M	15,915	953	69
Westfield State Univ., Westfield, MA 01086	1839	$9,715 (S)	$10,689	5-M	6,237	524	65
Westminster Coll., New Wilmington, PA 16172-0001	1852	$36,230	$11,020	2-M	1,254	144	70
Westminster Coll., Salt Lake City, UT 84105-3697	1875	$34,040	$10,245	1-M	2,570	382	63
Westmont Coll., Santa Barbara, CA 93108-1099	1937	$44,044	$13,886	2-B	1,303	157	78
Wheaton Coll., Norton, MA 02766	1834	$52,626	$13,424	1-B	1,688	189	78
Wheaton Coll., Wheaton, IL 60187-5593	1860	$36,420	$10,180	2-D	2,900	321	89
Wheeling Jesuit Univ., Wheeling, WV 26003-6295	1954	$28,110	$8,996	2-D	1,289	155	58
Whitman Coll., Walla Walla, WA 99362-2083	1859	$51,746	$13,174	1-B	1,510	222	88
Whittier Coll., Whittier, CA 90608-0634	1887	$46,120	$13,328	1-D	1,904	165	69
Whitworth Univ., Spokane, WA 99251-0001	1890	$43,640	$11,496	2-M	2,627	361	75
Wichita State Univ., Wichita, KS 67260	1895	$8,325 (S)	$6,782	5-D	15,081	771	47
Widener Univ., Chester, PA 19013-5792	1821	$44,166	$14,024	1-D	6,518	622	57
Wilkes Univ., Wilkes-Barre, PA 18766-0002	1933	$34,896	$14,270	1-D	5,545	416	60
Willamette Univ., Salem, OR 97301-3931	1842	$50,074	$12,440	2-D	2,819	250	73
William Carey Univ., Hattiesburg, MS 39401	1906	$12,300	$6,267	2-M	3,248	NA	NA
William Paterson Univ. of New Jersey, Wayne, NJ 07470-8420	1855	$12,804 (S)	$11,218	5-D	10,245	1,042	55
William Penn Univ., Oskaloosa, IA 52577-1799	1873	$25,600	$6,952	2-M	1,372	134	30
William Woods Univ., Fulton, MO 65251-1098	1870	$24,185	$9,700	2-D	2,281	240	59
Williams Coll., Williamstown, MA 01267	1793	$53,550	$14,150	1-M	2,117	364	94
Wilmington Coll., Wilmington, OH 45177	1870	$25,000	$9,600	2-M	1,458	119	52
Wilmington Univ., New Castle, DE 19720-6491	1967	$8,762	NA	1-D	14,118	2,466	28
Wingate Univ., Wingate, NC 28174	1896	$31,120	$10,780	2-D	3,193	307	54
Winona State Univ., Winona, MN 55987	1858	$9,379 (S)	$8,730	5-D	7,953	526	61
Winston-Salem State Univ., Winston-Salem, NC 27110-0003	1892	$8,481 (S)	$9,482	5-M	6,427	336	37
Winthrop Univ., Rock Hill, SC 29733	1886	$15,350 (S)	$8,740	5-M	6,073	561	57
Wittenberg Univ., Springfield, OH 45501-0720	1845	$39,500	$10,356	2-M	1,884	185	67
Wofford Coll., Spartanburg, SC 29303-3663	1854	$43,865	$12,685	2-B	1,592	173	81
Woodbury Univ., Burbank, CA 91504	1884	$39,780	$11,920	1-M	1,160	213	52
Worcester Polytechnic Inst., Worcester, MA 01609-2280	1865	$48,628	$14,218	1-D	6,642	516	89
Worcester State Univ., Worcester, MA 01602-2597	1874	$9,532 (S)	$12,006	5-M	6,434	441	55
Wright State Univ., Dayton, OH 45435	1964	$8,730 (S)	$11,376	5-D	15,957	NA	36
Xavier Univ., Cincinnati, OH 45207	1831	$37,230	$12,150	2-D	6,538	699	71
Xavier Univ. of Louisiana, New Orleans, LA 70125	1925	$23,746	$9,534	2-D	3,044	243	44
Yale Univ., New Haven, CT 06520	1701	$51,400	$15,500	1-D	12,458	1,718	98
Yeshiva Univ., New York, NY 10033-3201	1886	$42,000	$11,950	1-D	6,203	1,028	92
York Coll. of Pennsylvania, York, PA 17403-3651	1787	$20,100	$11,200	1-D	4,415	470	56
York Coll. of the City Univ. of New York, Jamaica, NY 11451	1967	$6,957 (S)	NA	11-M	8,360	NA	30
Youngstown State Univ., Youngstown, OH 44555-0001	1908	$8,899 (S)	NA	5-D	12,642	1,044	36

DIRECTORY

Associations and Organizations

Source: World Almanac research

Selected list, generally by category and first distinctive key word in each title. Listed by acronym when that is the official name. Year established is in parentheses. Entries for religious organizations include addresses and leadership information for 2018.

Academic and Educational

Academies, Natl. (1863): (202) 334-2000; www.nationalacademies.org

African American Life and History, Assn. for the Study of (1915): (202) 238-5910; www.asalh.org

Alpha Delta Kappa (1947): (816) 363-5525; www.alphadeltakappa.org

AMIDEAST (America-Mideast Educational and Training Services, Inc.) (1951): (202) 776-9600; www.amideast.org

Anthropological Assn., American (1902): (703) 528-1902; www.aaanet.org

Archaeological Institute of America (1879): (857)-305-9350; www.archaeological.org

Arts, Americans for the (1960): (202) 371-2830; www.artsusa.org

Arts and Sciences, American Academy of (1780): (617) 576-5000; www.amacad.org

Beta Gamma Sigma Inc. (1913): (314) 432-5650; www.betagammasigma.org

Beta Sigma Phi Intl. (1931): (816) 444-6800; bspinternational.org

Biological Sciences, American Institute of (1947): (703) 674-2500; www.aibs.org

Classical Studies, Society for (fmr. American Philological Assn.) (1869): (215) 898-4975; www.classicalstudies.org

College Board (1900): (212) 713-8000; www.collegeboard.org

Colleges and Universities, Assn. of American (1915): (202) 387-3760; www.aacu.org

Community Colleges, American Assn. of (1920): (202) 728-0200; www.aacc.nche.edu

Consumer Interests, American Council on (1953): (727) 493-2131; www.consumerinterests.org

Delta Kappa Gamma Society Intl. (1929): (512) 478-5748; www.dkg.org

Education, American Council on (1918): (202) 939-9300; www.acenet.edu

Education, Council for Advancement and Support of (1974): (202) 328-2273; www.case.org

Education of Young Children, Natl. Assn. for the (1926): (202) 232-8777; www.naeyc.org

Educators for World Peace, Intl. Assn. of (1973): (256) 534-5501

English-Speaking Union of the U.S. (1920): (212) 818-1200; www.esuus.org

Entomological Society of America (1889): (301) 731-4535; www.entsoc.org

Family Relations, Natl. Council on (1938): (888) 781-9331; www.ncfr.org

Foreign Study, American Institute for (1964): (866) 906-2437; www.aifs.com

Freedom of Information Coalition, Natl. (1958): (573) 882-4856; www.nfoic.org

French Institute/Alliance Française (1971): (212) 355-6100; www.fiaf.org

Genealogical Society, Natl. (1903): (703) 525-0050; www.ngsgenealogy.org

Genetic Assn., American (1914): (541) 264-5612; www.theaga.org

Geological Society of America (1888): (303) 357-1000; www.geosociety.org

Hemispheric Affairs, Council on (1975): (202) 223-4975; www.coha.org

Industrial and Applied Mathematics, Society for (1952): (215) 382-9800; www.siam.org

Intl. Education, Institute of (1919): (212) 883-8200; www.iie.org

Intl. Educational Exchange, Council on (1947): (207) 553-4000; www.ciee.org

Intl. Law, American Society of (1906): (202) 939-6000; www.asil.org

Irish American Cultural Inst. (1962): (973) 605-1991; www.iaci-usa.org

IRTS Foundation (fmr. Intl. Radio and TV Society Foundation) (1939): (212) 867-6650; www.irts.org

Law Libraries, American Assn. of (1906): (312) 939-4764; www.aallnet.org

Learned Societies, American Council of (1919): (212) 697-1505; www.acls.org

Libraries Assn., Special (1909): (703) 647-4900; www.sla.org

Linguistic Society of America (1924): (202) 835-1714; www.linguisticsociety.org

Literacy Assn., Intl. (fmr. Intl. Reading Assn.) (1956): (302) 731-1600; www.literacyworldwide.org

Mathematical Society, American (1888): (401) 455-4000; www.ams.org

Mensa, Ltd., American (1960): (817) 607-0060; www.us.mensa.org

Meteorological Society, American (1919): (617) 227-2425; www.ametsoc.org

Metric Assn., Inc., U.S. (1916): www.us-metric.org

Microbiology, American Society for (1899): (202) 737-3600; www.asm.org

Modern Language Assn. of America (1883): (646) 576-5000; www.mla.org

Museums, American Alliance of (1906): (202) 289-1818; www.aam-us.org

Music Education, Natl. Assn. for (fmr. Music Educators Natl. Conference) (1907): (703) 860-4000; www.nafme.org

Musicological Society, American (1934): (877) 679-7648; www.ams-net.org

Negro College Fund, United (1944): (800) 331-2244; www.uncf.org

Oriental Society, American (1842): (734) 647-4760; www.americanorientalsociety.org

ORT America (1922): (212) 505-7700; www.ortamerica.org

PEN American Center (1922): (212) 334-1660; www.pen.org

Phi Beta Kappa Society (1776): (202) 265-3808; www.pbk.org

Phi Theta Kappa Honor Society (1918): (800) 946-9995; www.ptk.org

Philosophical Assn., American (1900): (302) 831-1112; www.apaonline.org

Physics, American Inst. of (1931): (301) 209-3100; www.aip.org

Physiological Society, American (1887): (301) 634-7164; www.the-aps.org

Poetry Society of America (1910): (212) 254-9628; www.poetrysociety.org

Poets, Academy of American (1934): (212) 274-0343; www.poets.org

Political Science, Academy of (1880): (212) 870-2500; www.psqonline.org

Religion, American Academy of (1909): (404) 727-3049; www.aarweb.org

Science, American Assn. for the Advancement of (1848): (202) 326-6400; www.aaas.org

Science Fiction Society, World (1939): www.wsfs.org

Sciences, Natl. Academy of (1863): (202) 334-2000; www.nasonline.org

Sigma Beta Delta (1994): (314) 516-4723; www.sigmabetadelta.org

Sociological Assn., American (1905): (202) 383-9005; www.asanet.org

Tau Beta Pi Assn. (1885): (865) 546-4578; www.tbp.org

Teach For America (1990): (212) 279-2080; www.teachforamerica.org

Theological Schools in the U.S. and Canada, Assn. of (1918): (412) 788-6505; www.ats.edu

Theosophical Society in America (1875): (630) 668-1571; www.theosophical.org

Universities, Assn. of American (1900): (202) 408-7500; www.aau.edu

World Learning (1932): (802) 257-7751; www.worldlearning.org

Animal Welfare and Environment

Animal Welfare Institute (1951): (202) 337-2332; www.awionline.org

Animals, American Society for the Prevention of Cruelty to (ASPCA) (1866): (212) 876-7700; www.aspca.org

Animals, People for the Ethical Treatment of (PETA) (1980): (757) 622-7382; www.peta.org

Appalachian Trail Conservancy (1925): (304) 535-6331; www.appalachiantrail.org

Audubon Society, Natl. (1905): (212) 979-3000; www.audubon.org

Cat Fanciers' Assn., Inc., The (1906): (330) 680-4070; www.cfa.org

Conservation Intl. (1987): (703) 341-2400; www.conservation.org

Defenders of Wildlife (1947): (800) 385-9712; www.defenders.org

Ducks Unlimited (1937): (901) 758-3825; www.ducks.org

Forest History Society (1946): (919) 682-9319; www.foresthistory.org

Foresters, Society of American (1900): (301) 897-8720; www.safnet.org

Friends of the Earth (1969): (202) 783-7400; www.foe.org

Garden Club of America (1913): (212) 753-8287; www.gcamerica.org

Garden Clubs, Inc., Natl. (1929): (314) 776-7574; www.gardenclub.org

Geographic Society, Natl. (1888): (202) 857-7000; www.nationalgeographic.org

Green Mountain Club (1910): (802) 244-7037; www.greenmountainclub.org

Greenpeace (1971): (202) 462-1177; www.greenpeaceusa.org

Hiking Society, American (1976): (301) 565-6704; www.americanhiking.org

Horse Council, American (1969): (202) 296-4031; www.horsecouncil.org

Humane Society of the U.S., The (1954): (202) 452-1100; www.humanesociety.org

Natural Resources Defense Council (1970): (212) 727-2700; www.nrdc.org

Nature Conservancy, The (1951): (703) 841-5300; www.nature.org

Ocean Conservancy (1972): (202) 429-5609; www.oceanconservancy.org

Ornithological Society, American (fmr. Amer. Ornithologists' Union) (1883): www.americanornithology.org

Recreation and Park Assn., Natl. (1965): (800) 626-6772; www.nrpa.org

Recycling Coalition, Inc., Natl. (1978): (202) 618-2107; www.nrcrecycles.org

Rose Society, American (1892): (318) 938-5402; www.rose.org

Save the Redwoods League (1918): (415) 362-2352; www.savetheredwoods.org

Sierra Club (1892): (415) 977-5500; www.sierraclub.org

Water Environment Federation (1928): (800) 666-0206; www.wef.org

Wildflower Center, Lady Bird Johnson (1982): (512) 232-0100; www.wildflower.org

Wildlife Federation, Natl. (1936): (800) 822-9919; www.nwf.org

World Wildlife Fund (1961): (202) 293-4800; www.worldwildlife.org

Children and Social Services

Big Brothers Big Sisters of America (1904): (813) 720-8778; www.bbbs.org

Boy Scouts of America: see Scouts BSA

Boys & Girls Clubs of America (1906): (404) 487-5700; www.bgca.org

Camp Fire (fmr. Camp Fire Boys & Girls) (1910): (816) 285-2010; www.campfire.org

Child Welfare League of America (1920): (202) 688-4200; www.cwla.org

Children's Book Council, The (1945): (212) 966-1990; www.cbcbooks.org

Feeding America (fmr. America's Second Harvest) (1976): (800) 771-2303; www.feedingamerica.org

4-H Council, Natl. (1914): (301) 961-2800; www.4-h.org

Future Business Leaders of America-Phi Beta Lambda, Inc. (1942): (800) 325-2946; www.fbla-pbl.org

Future Farmers of America Org., Natl. (1928): (317) 802-6060; www.ffa.org

Gifted Children, Natl. Assn. for (1954): (202) 785-4268; www.nagc.org

Girl Scouts of the USA (1912): (212) 852-8000; www.girlscouts.org

Honor Society, Natl. (1921): (703) 860-0200; www.nhs.us

Junior Achievement USA® (1919): (719) 540-8000; www.ja.org

Junior Auxiliaries, Inc., Natl. Assn. of (1941): (662) 332-3000; www.najanet.org

Junior Chamber Intl. USA (1914): (636) 778-3010; www.jciusa.org

Junior Honor Society, Natl. (1929): (703) 860-0200; www.njhs.us

Missing and Exploited Children, Natl. Center for (1984): (703) 224-2150; www.missingkids.com

Pilot Intl. (1921): (478) 477-1208; www.pilotinternational.org

Scouts BSA (fmr. Boy Scouts of America, as of Feb. 2019) (1910), (972) 580-2000; www.scouting.org

Student Council, Natl. (1931): (703) 860-0200; www.natstuco.org

Fraternal

Eagles, Fraternal Order of (1898): (614) 883-2200; www.foe.com

Eastern Star, General Grand Chapter, Order of the (1876): (202) 667-4737; www.easternstar.org

Elks of the USA, Benevolent and Protective Order of (1868): (773) 755-4700; www.elks.org

Freemasonry, Scottish Rite of, Supreme Council, 33° Northern Masonic Jurisdiction (1813): (781) 862-4410; www.scottishritenmj.org

Freemasonry, Scottish Rite of, Supreme Council, 33° Southern Jurisdiction (1802): (202) 232-3579; scottishrite.org

Kiwanis Intl. (1915): (317) 875-8755; www.kiwanis.org

Knights of Columbus (1882): (203) 752-4000; www.kofc.org

Knights of Pythias, Order of (1864): (781) 341-2422; www.pythias.org

Lions Clubs Intl. (1917): (630) 571-5466; www.lionsclubs.org

Moose Intl., Inc. (1888): (630) 859-2000; www.mooseintl.org

Odd Fellows, Independent Order of (1819): (336) 725-5955; www.ioof.org

Rotary Intl. (1905): (847) 866-3000; www.rotary.org

Shriners Intl. (1872): (813) 281-0300; www.shrinersinternational.org

Sons and Daughters of Italy in America, Order (1905): (202) 547-2900; www.osia.org

Sons of Norway (1895): (612) 827-3611; www.sofn.com

Woodmen of America, Modern (1883): (800) 447-9811; www.modernwoodmen.org

Historical

Civil War Trust (1987): (202) 367-1861; www.civilwar.org

Colonial Dames XVII Century, Natl. Soc. (1915): (202) 293-1700; www.colonialdames17c.org

Daughters of the American Revolution (1890): (202) 628-1776; www.dar.org

Daughters of the Confederacy, United (1894): (804) 355-1636; www.hqudc.org

Historic Preservation, Natl. Trust for (1949): (202) 588-6000; www.preservationnation.org

Historical Assn., American (1884): (202) 544-2422; www.historians.org

Lewis and Clark Trail Heritage Foundation (1969): (406) 454-1234; lewisandclark.org

Mayflower Descendants, General Soc. of (1897): (508) 746-3188; www.themayflowersociety.org

Pilgrims, Natl. Soc. Sons and Daughters of (1908): www.nationalssdp.org

Railway Historical Society, Natl. (1935): (215) 557-6606; www.nrhs.com

Sons of the American Revolution (1889): (502) 589-1776; www.sar.org

Sons of Confederate Veterans (1896): (800) 380-1896; www.scv.org

State and Local History, American Assn. for (1940): (615) 320-3203; www.aaslh.org

Supreme Court Historical Society (1974): (202) 543-0400; www.supremecourthistory.org

Theodore Roosevelt Assn. (1920): (516) 921-6319; www.theodoreroosevelt.org

Thoreau Society (1941): (978) 369-5310; www.thoreausociety.org

Titanic Historical Society, Inc. (1963): (413) 543-4770; www.titanichistoricalsociety.org

Victorian Society in America (1966): (215) 636-9872; www.victoriansociety.org

Industrial and Trade

Aerospace Industries Assn. (1919): (703) 358-1000; www.aia-aerospace.org

Better Business Bureaus, Council of (1912): (703) 276-0100; www.bbb.org

Chamber of Commerce, U.S. (1912): (202) 659-6000; www.uschamber.com

Chemistry Council, American (1872): (202) 249-7000; www.americanchemistry.com

Construction Specifications Institute (1948): (800) 689-2900; www.csinet.org

CropLife America (1933): (202) 296-1585; www.croplifeamerica.org

Electrical Manufacturers Assn., Natl. (1926): (703) 841-3200; www.nema.org

Fire Protection Assn., Natl. (NFPA) (1896): (617) 770-3000; www.nfpa.org

Fisheries Soc., American (1870): (301) 897-8616; www.fisheries.org

Foreign Trade Council, Natl. (1914): (202) 887-0278; www.nftc.org

Funeral Consumers Alliance (1963): (802) 865-8300; www.funerals.org

Hotel & Lodging Assn., American (1910): (202) 289-3100; www.ahla.com

Insurance Assn., American (1866): (202) 828-7100; www.aiadc.org

Magazine Media, Assn. of (1919): (212) 872-3700; www.magazine.org

Manufacturers, Natl. Assn. of (1895): (202) 637-3000; www.nam.org

News Media Alliance (fmr. Newspaper Assn. of America) (1992): (571) 366-1000; www.newsmediaalliance.org

Nuclear Society, American (1954): (708) 352-6611; www.ans.org

Orchestras, League of American (1942): (212) 262-5161; www.americanorchestras.org

Petroleum Institute, American (1919): (202) 682-8000; www.api.org

Printing Industries of America, Inc. (1887): (412) 741-6860; www.printing.org

Publishers, Assn. of American (1970): (212) 255-1041; www.publishers.org

Retail Federation, Natl. (1908): (202) 783-7971; www.nrf.com

Safety Council, Natl. (1913): (630) 285-1121; www.nsc.org

Shipbuilders Council of America (1920): (202) 737-3234; www.shipbuilders.org

Small Business Assn., Natl. (1937): (800) 345-6728; www.nsba.biz

Software & Information Industry Assn. (1999): (202) 289-7442; www.siia.net

Tall Buildings and Urban Habitat, Council on (1969): (312) 567-3487; www.ctbuh.org

Toy Industry Assn., Inc. (1916): (212) 675-1141; www.toyassociation.org

Water Works Assn., American (1881): (303) 794-7711; www.awwa.org

Zoos & Aquariums, Assn. of (1924): (301) 562-0777; www.aza.org

Lifestyle and Travel

AAA (American Automobile Assn.) (1902): (407) 444-7000; www.aaa.com

AARP (fmr. American Assn. of Retired Persons) (1958): (888) 687-2277; www.aarp.org

AFS Intercultural Programs USA (1947): (800) 237-4636; www.afsusa.org

Aircraft Owners and Pilots Assn. (1939): (800) 872-2672; www.aopa.org

Appalachian Mountain Club (1876): (617) 523-0636; www.outdoors.org

Boat Owners Assn. of the U.S. (1966): (800) 395-2628; www.boatus.com

Camp Assn., American (1910): (765) 342-8456; www.acacamps.org

Consumer Federation of America (1968): (202) 387-6121; www.consumerfed.org

Consumers Union (1936): (914) 378-2000; www.consumersunion.org

Green America (fmr. Co-op America) (1982): (800) 584-7336; www.greenamerica.org

Hostelling Intl. USA (1934): (240) 650-2100; www.hiusa.org

Jewish Community Centers Assn. of North America (1917): (212) 532-4949; www.jcca.org

Motorcyclist Assn., American (1924): (614) 856-1900; www.americanmotorcyclist.com

Parents Without Partners, Inc. (1957): (800) 637-7974; www.parentswithoutpartners.org

Planetary Society (1980): (626) 793-5100; www.planetary.org

SCRABBLE® Players Assn., N. American (2009): www.scrabbleplayers.org

Sports Car Club of America (1944): (785) 357-7222; www.scca.org

Toastmasters Intl. (1924): (949) 858-8255; www.toastmasters.org

Vertical Flight Society (fmr. American Helicopter Society Intl.) (1943): (703) 684-6777; www.vtol.org

YMCA (Young Men's Christian Assn.) of the USA (1851): (800) 872-9622; www.ymca.net

YWCA (Young Women's Christian Assn.) USA (1858): (202) 467-0801; www.ywca.org

Military and Veterans

Air Force Assn. (1946): (703) 247-5800; www.afa.org

American Legion (1919): (317) 630-1200; www.legion.org

American Legion Auxiliary (1919): (317) 569-4500; www.alaforveterans.org

AMVETS (American Veterans) (1944): (877) 726-8387; www.amvets.org

Army, Assn. of the United States (1950): (703) 841-4300; www.ausa.org

Blinded Veterans Assn. (1958): (800) 669-7079; www.bva.org

Civil Air Patrol (1941): (877) 227-9142; www.gocivilairpatrol.com

Coast Guard Combat Veterans Assn. (1985): (610) 539-1000; www.coastguardcombatvets.org

Disabled American Veterans (1920): (859) 441-7300; www.dav.org

82nd Airborne Division Assn., Inc. (1944): (910) 223-1182; www.82ndairborneassociation.org

Ex-Prisoners of War, American (1942): (817) 649-2979; www.axpow.org

Fleet Reserve Assn. (1924): (703) 683-1400; www.fra.org

Iraq and Afghanistan Veterans of America (2004): (212) 982-9699; www.iava.org

Jewish War Veterans of the U.S.A. (1896): (202) 265-6280; www.jwv.org

Legion of Valor Museum (1991): (559) 498-0510; www.fresnovetsmuseum.com

Marine Corps League (1937): (703) 207-9588; www.mclnational.org

Military Officers Assn. of America (1929): (703) 549-2311; www.moaa.org

Military Order of the World Wars (1919): (703) 683-4911; www.moww.org

National Guard Assn. of the U.S. (1878): (202) 789-0031; www.ngaus.org

Naval Institute, U.S. (1873): (410) 268-6110; www.usni.org

Navy League of the United States (1902): (703) 528-1775; www.navyleague.org

Ninety-Nines, Inc. (Intl. Org. of Women Pilots) (1929): (405) 685-7969; www.ninety-nines.org

Non-Commissioned Officers Assn. (1960): (210) 653-6161; www.ncoausa.org

Paralyzed Veterans of America (1946): (800) 424-8200; www.pva.org

POW/MIA Families, Natl. League of (1970): (703) 465-7432; www.pow-miafamilies.org

Purple Heart, Military Order of the (1932): (703) 642-5360; www.purpleheart.org

Reserve Officers Assn. of the U.S. (1922): (202) 479-2200; www.roa.org

Sons of the American Legion (1932): (317) 630-1200; www.legion.org/sons

Tin Can Sailors (Natl. Assn. of Destroyer Veterans) (1976): (800) 223-5535; www.destroyers.org

Uniformed Services, Natl. Assn. for (1968): (800) 842-3451; www.naus.org

USO, Inc. (United Service Org.) (1941): (888) 484-3876; www.uso.org

USS Missouri Memorial Assn., Inc. (1998): (808) 455-1600; www.ussmissouri.org

Veterans of Foreign Wars (1899): (816) 756-3390; www.vfw.org

Veterans of Foreign Wars Auxiliary (1914): (816) 561-8655; vfwauxiliary.org

Vietnam Veterans of America (1978): (301) 585-4000; www.vva.org

Women's Army Corps Veterans' Assn. (1946): (256) 820-6824; www.armywomen.org

Wounded Warrior Project (2002): (877) 832-6997; www.woundedwarriorproject.org

Political

Abortion Federation, Natl. (1977): (202) 667-5881; www.prochoice.org
Action Network, American (2010): (202) 559-6420; americanactionnetwork.org
Advancement and Support of Education, Council for (1974): (202) 328-2273; www.case.org
American Indians, Natl. Congress of (1944): (202) 466-7767; www.ncai.org
American-Islamic Relations, Council on (1994): (202) 488-8787; www.cair.com
Black Lives Matter (2012): www.blacklivesmatter.com
Brady Campaign to Prevent Gun Violence (1974): (202) 370-8100; www.bradycampaign.org
Center for Responsive Politics (1983): (202) 857-0044; www.opensecrets.org
Cities, Natl. League of (1924): (202) 626-3100; www.nlc.org
Civil Liberties Union, American (ACLU) (1920): (212) 549-2500; www.aclu.org
Coalition to Stop Gun Violence (1974): (202) 408-0061; www.csgv.org
Common Cause (1970): (202) 833-1200; www.commoncause.org
Concerned Women for America (1979): (202) 488-7000; www.cwfa.org
Congress of Racial Equality (CORE) (1942): (212) 598-4000; www.core-online.org
Conservation Voters, League of (1969): (202) 785-8683; www.lcv.org
Constitution Party (1992): (717) 390-1993; www.constitutionparty.com
Counties, Natl. Assn. of (1935): (202) 393-6226; www.naco.org
Crime and Delinquency, Natl. Council on (1907): (800) 306-6223; www.nccdglobal.org
Crossroads GPS (Grassroots Political Strategies) (2010): (202) 706-7051; www.crossroadsgps.org
Democratic Natl. Committee (1848): (202) 863-8000; www.democrats.org
Democratic Socialists of America (1982): (212) 727-8610; www.dsausa.org
Everytown for Gun Safety (2013): (646) 324-8250; www.everytown.org
Feminists for Life of America (1972): (703) 836-3354; www.feministsforlife.org
Future Fund, Amer. (2007): (515) 661-4233; www.americanfuturefund.com
Gay & Lesbian Alliance Against Defamation (GLAAD) (1985): (212) 629-3322; www.glaad.org
Governors Assn., Natl. (1908): (202) 624-5300; www.nga.org
Grange of the Order of Patrons of Husbandry, Natl. (1867): (202) 628-3507; www.nationalgrange.org
Gray Panthers (1970): (202) 737-6637
Green Party of the USA (1984): (202) 319-7191; www.gp.org
Hispanic Leadership Agenda, Natl. (1991): (202) 637-5120; www.nationalhispanic leadership.org
Homeless, Natl. Coalition for the (1984): (202) 462-4822; www.nationalhomeless.org
Human Rights Campaign (1980): (202) 628-4160; www.hrc.org
Immigration Equality (1994): (212) 714-2904; immigrationequality.org
Immigration Reform, Federation for American (FAIR) (1979): (202) 328-7004; www.fairus.org
Japanese American Citizens League (1929): (415) 921-5225; www.jacl.org
Jewish Committee, American (1906): (212) 751-4000; www.ajc.org
John Birch Society (1958): (920) 749-3780; www.jbs.org
LGBTQ Task Force, Natl. (fmr. Natl. Gay and Lesbian Task Force) (1973): (202) 393-5177; www.thetaskforce.org
Libertarian Party (1971): (202) 333-0008; www.lp.org
Mayors, U.S. Conference of (1932): (202) 293-7330; www.usmayors.org
Men, Natl. Coalition for (1977): (888) 223-1280; www.ncfm.org
NAACP (Natl. Assn. for the Advancement of Colored People) (1909): (410) 580-5777; www.naacp.org

NRA (National Rifle Assn.) (1871): (800) 672-3888; www.nra.org
Parliamentarians, Natl. Assn. of (1930): (816) 833-3892; www.parliamentarians.org
Patriot Majority (2005): www.patriot majority.org
Progress, Center for American (2003): (202) 682-1611; www.americanprogress. org
Reform Party Natl. Committee (1995): (972) 275-9297; www.reformparty.org
Republican Natl. Committee (1856): (202) 863-8500; www.gop.com
Southern Christian Leadership Conference (1957): (404) 522-1420; nationalsclc.org
Southern Poverty Law Center (1971): (334) 956-8200; www.splcenter.org
State Governments, Council of (1933): (859) 244-8000; www.csg.org
Tax Foundation (1937): (202) 464-6200; www.taxfoundation.org
Tax Reform, Americans for (1985): (202) 785-0266; www.atr.org
Taxpayers Union, Natl. (1969): (703) 683-5700; www.ntu.org
Tea Party Patriots (2009): www.teapartypatriots.org
Term Limits, U.S. (1992): (202) 261-3532; www.termlimits.org
Urban League, Natl. (1910): (212) 558-5300; www.nul.org
Women, Natl. Organization for (NOW) (1966): (202) 628-8669; www.now.org
Women and Families, Natl. Partnership for (1971): (202) 986-2600; www.nationalpartnership.org
Women Voters, League of (1920): (202) 429-1965; www.lwv.org
Women's Christian Temperance Union (1874): (847) 864-1397; www.wctu.org
Zionist Organization of America (1897): (212) 481-1500; www.zoa.org

Religious

African Methodist Episcopal Church (1787): 500 8th Ave. S., Nashville, TN 37203; (615) 254-0911; www.ame-church. com; Gen. Sec., Dr. Jeffery Cooper
African Methodist Episcopal Zion Church (1796): 3225 Sugar Creek Rd., Charlotte, NC 28269; (704) 599-4630; www.amez.org; Senior Bishop, George E. Battle Jr.
American Baptist Churches USA (1907): P.O. Box 851, Valley Forge, PA 19482; (610) 768-2000; www.abc-usa.org; Gen. Sec., Rev. Dr. Lee B. Spitzer
Antiochian Orthodox Christian Archdiocese of North America (1895): P.O. Box 5238, Englewood, NJ 07631; (201) 871-1355; www.antiochian.org; Primate, Archbishop Metropolitan Joseph
Armenian Apostolic Church of America: *Eastern Prelacy* (1958): 138 E. 39th St., New York, NY 10016; (212) 689-7810; www.armenianprelacy.org; Prelate, Archbishop Oshagan Choloyan; *Western Prelacy* (1973): 6252 Honolulu Ave., La Crescenta, CA 91214; (818) 248-7737; www.westernprelacy.org; Prelate, Archbishop Moushegh Mardirossian
Assemblies of God USA (1914): 1445 N. Boonville Ave., Springfield, MO 65802; (417) 862-2781; www.ag.org; Gen. Supt., Doug Clay
Atheists, American (1963): 225 Cristiani St., Cranford, NJ 07016; (908) 276-7300; www.atheists.org; Board Chair, Neal Cary
Bahá'ís of the U.S., Natl. Spiritual Assembly of the (1909): 1233 Central St., Evanston, IL 60201; (847) 733-3400; www.bahai.us; Sec., Kenneth E. Bowers
Baptist Bible Fellowship Intl. (1950): 720 E. Kearney St., Springfield, MO 65803; (417) 862-5001; www.bbfi.org; Pres., Eddie Lyons
Baptist Convention, Southern (1845): 901 Commerce St., Nashville, TN 37203; (615) 244-2355; www.sbc.net; Pres., J.D. Greear
Baptist Convention, USA, Inc., Natl. (1886): 1700 Baptist World Center Dr., Nashville, TN 37207; (615) 228-6292; www.nationalbaptist.com; Pres., Dr. Jerry Young

Baptist Convention of America Intl., Inc., Natl. (1880): 777 S.R.L. Thornton Fwy., Ste. 210, Dallas, TX 75203; (214) 942-3311; www.nbcainc.com; Pres., Rev. Samuel C. Tolbert Jr.
Baptist Convention of America, Natl. Missionary (1880): 6925 Wofford Dr., Dallas, TX 75227; (877) 886-6222; www.nmbca.com; Pres., Dr. Louis Jones
Bible Society, American (1816): 101 N. Independence Mall East FL8, Philadelphia, PA 19106; (215) 309-0900; www.americanbible.org; Pres., Dr. Roy L. Peterson
Biblical Literature, Society of (1880): 825 Houston Mill Rd., Atlanta, GA 30329; (404) 727-3100; www.sbl-site.org; Exec. Dir., Dr. John F. Kutsko
B'nai B'rith Intl. (1843): 1120 20th St. NW, Ste. 300 N, Washington, DC 20036; (202) 857-6600; www.bnaibrith.org; Pres., Gary P. Saltzman
Brethren in Christ Church (c. 1778): 431 Grantham Rd., Mechanicsburg, PA 17055; (717) 697-2634; www.bicus.org; Natl. Dir., Dr. Alan Robinson
Buddhist Churches of America (1899): 1710 Octavia St., San Francisco, CA 94109; (415) 776-5600; www.buddhist churche sofamerica.org; Pres., Richard A. Stambul
Catholic Bishops, U.S. Conference of (2001): 3211 4th St. NE, Washington, DC 20017; (202) 541-3000; www.usccb.org; Gen. Sec., Msgr. J. Brian Bransfield
Christian Church (Disciples of Christ) (1832): Disciples Center, P.O. Box 1986, Indianapolis, IN 46206; (317) 635-3100; www.disciples.org; Gen. Min. and Pres., Rev. Teresa Hord Owens
Christian Methodist Episcopal Church (1870): 4466 Elvis Presley Blvd., Memphis, TN 38116; (901) 345-0580; www.thecmechurch.org; Senior Bishop, Lawrence L. Reddick III
Church of the Brethren (1708): General Offices, 1451 Dundee Ave., Elgin, IL 60120; (847) 742-5100; www.brethren.org; Gen. Sec., David A. Steele
Church of Christ (1830): P.O. Box 472, Independence, MO 64051; (816) 206-0147; www.churchofchrist-tl.org; Sec., Council of Apostles, Duane L. Ely
Church of God (Anderson, IN) (1881): Box 2420, Anderson, IN 46018; (765) 642-0256; www.jesusisthesubject.org; Gen. Dir., Jim Lyon
Church of God (Cleveland, TN) (1886): 2490 Keith St. NW, Cleveland, TN 37311; (423) 472-3361; www.churchofgod.org; Gen. Overseer, Tim Hill
Church of God in Christ (1897): Mason Temple, 930 Mason St., Memphis, TN 38126; (901) 947-9300; www.cogic.org; Presiding Bishop, Bishop Charles E. Blake Sr.
Church of Jesus Christ (1862): World Operations Ctr., 110 Walton Tea Room Rd., Greensburg, PA 15601; (724) 837-4425; www.thechurchofjesuschrist.org
Church of the Nazarene (1908): Global Ministry Center, 17001 Prairie Star Pkwy., Lenexa, KS 66220; (913) 577-0500; www.nazarene.org; Gen. Sec., David P. Wilson
Community of Christ (reorganized Church of Jesus Christ of Latter-day Saints) (1830): Intl. Headquarters, 1001 W. Walnut, Independence, MO 64050; (816) 833-1000; www.cofchrist.org; Pres., Stephen M. Veazey
Community Churches, International Council of (1950): 21116 Washington Pkwy., Frankfort, IL 60423; (815) 464-5690; www.icccnow.org; Exec. Dir., Rev. Phil Tom
Conservative Judaism, United Synagogue of (1913): 120 Broadway, Ste. 1540, New York, NY 10271; (212) 533-7800; www.uscj.org; Intl. Pres., Margo Gold
Converge Worldwide (fmr. Baptist General Conference) (1852): 2002 S. Arlington Heights Rd., Arlington Heights, IL 60005; (800) 323-4215; www.converge.org; Pres., Scott Ridout

Cumberland Presbyterian Church (1810): 8207 Traditional Pl., Cordova, TN 38016; (901) 276-4572; www.cumberland.org

Episcopal Church (1789): 815 Second Ave., New York, NY 10017; (212) 716-6000; www.episcopalchurch.org; Presiding Bishop and Primate, Most Rev. Michael B. Curry

Evangelical Lutheran Church in America (1988): 8765 W. Higgins Rd., Chicago, IL 60631; (773) 380-2700; www.elca.org; Presiding Bishop, Rev. Elizabeth A. Eaton

First Church of Christ, Scientist, The (1879): 210 Massachusetts Ave., Boston, MA 02115; (617) 450-2000; www.christianscience.com; Pres., Keith Wommack

Free Methodist Church USA (1860): 770 N. High School Rd., Indianapolis, IN 46214; (317) 244-3660; www.fmcusa.org; Chief Operating Officer, Mark Dowley

Freedom From Religion Foundation (1978): P.O. Box 750, Madison, WI 53701; (608) 256-8900; www.ffrf.org; Pres., Annie Laurie Gaylor and Dan Barker

Friends General Conference (1900): 1216 Arch St., #2B, Philadelphia, PA 19107; (215) 561-1700; www.fgcquaker.org; Gen. Sec., Barry Crossno

Gideons Intl., The (1899): P.O. Box 140800, Nashville, TN 37214; (615) 564-5000; www.gideons.org; Exec. Dir., Dan Heighway

Greek Orthodox Archdiocese of America (1922): 8 E. 79th St., New York, NY 10075; (212) 570-3500; www.goarch.org; Primate, Archbishop Demetrios

Hadassah, the Women's Zionist Organization of America, Inc. (1912): 40 Wall St., New York, NY 10005; (800) 664-5646; www.hadassah.org; Exec. Dir. and CEO, Janice Weinman

Interfaith Alliance (1994): 2101 L St. NW, Ste. 400, Washington, DC 20037; (202) 466-0567; www.interfaithalliance.org; Pres., Rabbi Jack Moline

Islamic Society of North America: 6555 S. County Rd. 750 East, Plainfield, IN 46168; (317) 839-8157; www.isna.net; Pres., Azhar Azeez

Jehovah's Witnesses (1931): 900 Red Mills Rd., Wallkill, NY 12589; (845) 744-6000; www.jw.org

Jewish Congress, American (1918): 745 Fifth Ave., 30th Fl., New York, NY 10151; (212) 879-4500; www.ajcongress.org; Pres., Jack Rosen

Jewish Reconstructionist Communities (2012): 1299 Church Rd., Wyncote, PA 19095; (215) 576-0800; www.reconstructingjudaism.org; Pres., Rabbi Deborah Waxman

Jewish Women, Natl. Council of (1893): 475 Riverside Dr., Ste. 1901, New York, NY 10115; (212) 645-4048; www.ncjw.org; Pres., Beatrice Kahn

Latter-day Saints, The Church of Jesus Christ of (Mormons) (1830): 50 W. North Temple St., Salt Lake City, UT 84150; (801) 240-2640; www.lds.org; Pres., Russell M. Nelson

Lutheran Church—Missouri Synod (1847): 1333 S. Kirkwood Rd., St. Louis, MO 63122; (800) 248-1930; www.lcms.org; Pres., Rev. Dr. Matthew C. Harrison

Mennonite Church USA (2001): 718 N. Main St., Newton, KS 67114; (316) 283-5100; www.mennoniteusa.org; Exec. Dir., Glen Guyton

Moravian Church in North America (1735): www.moravian.org; *Northern Prov.*: 1021 Center St., P.O. Box 1245, Bethlehem, PA 18016; (610) 867-7566; Pres., Rev. Dr. Betsy Miller; *Southern Prov.*: 459 S. Church St., Winston-Salem, NC 27101; (336) 725-5811; Pres., Rev. David Guthrie

North American Shia Ithna-asheri Muslim Communities, Org. of (1986): P.O. Box 29691, Minneapolis, MN 55429; (905) 763-7512; www.nasimco.org; Pres., Br. Razak Damani

Orthodox Union (1898): 11 Broadway, New York, NY 10004; (212) 563-4000; www.ou.org; Pres., Mark Bane

Pentecostal Assemblies of the World, Inc. (1906): 3939 N. Meadows Dr., Indianapolis, IN 46205; (317) 547-9541; www.pawinc.org; Presiding Bishop, Charles H. Ellis, III

Presbyterian Church (U.S.A.) (1983): 100 Witherspoon St., Louisville, KY 40202; (800) 728-7228; www.pcusa.org; Pres. and Exec. Dir., Diane Moffett

Progressive Natl. Baptist Convention, Inc. (1961): 601 50th St. NE, Washington, DC 20019; (202) 396-0558; www.pnbc.org; Pres., Dr. James C. Perkins

Rabbis, Central Conference of American (1889): 355 Lexington Ave., New York, NY 10017; (212) 972-3636; www.ccarnet.org; Chief Exec., Rabbi Steven A. Fox

Reform Judaism, Union for (1873): 633 3rd Ave., New York, NY 10017; (212) 650-4000; www.urj.org; Pres., Rabbi Rick Jacobs

Secular Humanism, Council for (1980): P.O. Box 664, Amherst, NY 14226; (716) 636-7571; www.secularhumanism.org; Pres., Robyn A. Blumner

Separation of Church and State, Americans United for (1947): 1310 L St. NW, Ste. 200, Washington, DC 20005; (202) 466-3234; www.au.org; Pres. and CEO, Rachel Laser

Seventh-day Adventist Church (1863): 12501 Old Columbia Pike, Silver Spring, MD 20904; (301) 680-6000; www.adventist.org; Pres., Ted N. C. Wilson

Seventh Day Baptist (1802): P.O. Box 1678, Janesville, WI 53547; (608) 752-5055; www.seventhdaybaptist.org; Gen. Sec., Rev. Andrew Samuels

Unitarian Universalist Assn. of Congregations (1961): 24 Farnsworth St., Boston, MA 02210; (617) 742-2100; www.uua.org; Pres., Rev. Susan Frederick-Gray

United Church of Christ (1957): 700 Prospect Ave., Cleveland, OH 44115; (216) 736-2100; www.ucc.org; Pres., Rev. John C. Dorhauer

United Methodist Church (1968): 100 Maryland Ave. NE, Washington, DC 20002; (202) 488-5600; www.umc.org

United Pentecostal Church Intl. (1945): 36 Research Park Court, Weldon Spring, MO 63304; (636) 229-7900; www.upci.org; Gen. Supt., David K. Bernard

Wesleyan Church, The (1843): 13300 Olio Rd., Fishers, IN 46037; (317) 774-7900; www.wesleyan.org; Gen. Supt., Rev. Dr. Wayne Schmidt

Businesses and Corporations

Source: World Almanac research

Listed below are major corporations offering products and services to U.S. consumers, as of Aug. 2018. Alphabetization is by first key word or founder last name. Listings generally include examples of products offered.

Company name (NYSE/Nasdaq symbol, if traded on those markets): Address; Telephone number; Website; Top executive; Business, products, or services.

Abbott Laboratories (ABT): 100 Abbott Park Rd., Abbott Park, IL 60064; (224) 667-6100; www.abbott.com; Miles D. White; develops, mfr. pharmaceutical, nutritional, diagnostic prods. Acquired medical device company St. Jude Medical, 1/4/2017; acquired diagnostics maker Alere, 10/3/2017.

AbbVie Inc. (ABBV): 1 N. Waukegan Rd., N. Chicago, IL 60064; (847) 932-7900; www.abbvie.com; Richard A. Gonzalez; pharmaceuticals. Acquired Pharmacyclics, 5/26/2015.

ABC: see Walt Disney Co.

Accenture Inc. (ACN): 161 N. Clark St., Chicago, IL 60601; (312) 737-8842; www.accenture.com; Pierre Nanterme; management consulting. Acquired Dutch digital serv. co. MOBGEN, 7/19/2016.

Activision Blizzard Inc. (ATVI): 3100 Ocean Park Blvd., Santa Monica, CA 90405; (310) 255-2000; www.activisionblizzard.com; Bobby Kotick; video game publisher (*World of Warcraft, Call of Duty, Candy Crush Saga*).

adidas Group: Adi-Dassler-Strasse 1, D-91074 Herzogenaurach, Germany; +49 (0) 9132-84-0; www.adidas-group.com; Kasper Rorsted; apparel and accessories mfr. (Reebok, TaylorMade Golf).

Advance Publications, Inc.: 950 W. Fingerboard Rd., Staten Island, NY, 10305; (718) 981-1234; www.advance.net; Steven Newhouse; communications, newspaper and magazine publisher

(Condé Nast subsids.: *New Yorker, Vanity Fair, Vogue*).

Aetna, Inc. (AET): 151 Farmington Ave., Hartford, CT 06156; (860) 273-0123; www.aetna.com; Mark T. Bertolini; health care, employee benefits. Terminated Humana buyout following federal injunction, 2/14/2016. Agreed to $77 bil buyout by CVS Health Corp., 12/3/2017.

Aflac, Inc. (AFL): 1932 Wynnton Rd., Columbus, GA 31999; (706) 596-3272; www.aflac.com; Daniel P. Amos; supplemental health and life insurance.

Airbnb: 888 Brannan St., San Francisco, CA 94103; (415) 800-5959; www.airbnb.com; Brian Chesky; online marketplace for short-term global accommodations.

Alaska Air Group, Inc. (ALK): 19300 International Blvd., Seattle, WA 98188; (206) 433-3200; www.alaskaair.com; Bradley D. Tilden; airline carriers (Alaska Airlines, Horizon Air). Acquired Virgin America airline, 12/14/2016.

Alcoa Inc. (AA): 201 Isabella St., Pittsburgh, PA 15212; (412) 553-4545; www.alcoa.com; Roy Harvey; prod., mfr. of aluminum, aluminum prods. (aerospace, automotive, industrial materials and components). Acquired RTI Intl. Metals, 7/23/2015.

Alibaba Group (BABA): 969 West Wen Yi Road, Yu Hang District, Hangzhou 311121, China; +86 571-8502-2088; www.alibaba.com; Jack Ma; online shopping, logistics, marketing; data mgmt.; financial serv. Record-high U.S.

IPO, 9/19/2014. Acquired Pakistani online retailer Daraz Group, 5/8/2018.

Allstate Corp. (ALL): 2775 Sanders Rd., Northbrook, IL 60062; (847) 402-5000; www.allstate.com; Thomas J. Wilson; personal property and casualty insurance; financial services.

Alphabet Inc. (GOOG): 1600 Amphitheatre Pkwy., Mountain View, CA 94043; (650) 253-0000; www.abc.xyz; Larry Page; Google and other internet-related prods. and services (leading search engine, ad sales; YouTube). Reorganized corp. as Alphabet, 10/2/2015. Acquired game developer Owlchemy Labs, 5/10/2017. Agreed to acquire Israeli cloud migration startup Velostrata, 5/9/2018.

Altice USA (ATUS): 1111 Stewart Ave., Bethpage, NY 11714; (516) 803-2300; www.altice.net; Dexter Goei; telecom, internet, cable provider. Formed 6/21/2016 through Dutch parent co. buyout of Cablevision Systems Corp. and acquisition of Suddenlink, 12/21/2015. IPO, 6/22/2017. Spun off from parent co. Altice, 6/8/2018.

Altria Group, Inc. (MO): 6601 W. Broad St., Richmond, VA 23230; (804) 484-8897; www.altria.com; Howard A. Willard III; tobacco co. (Marlboro, Merit, Parliament, Virginia Slims). (Altria spun off Philip Morris's intl. operations in 2008 but owns Philip Morris brands in U.S.)

Amazon.com, Inc. (AMZN): 440 Terry Ave. N., Seattle, WA 98109; (206) 266-1000;

www.amazon.com; Jeffrey P. Bezos; online retailer of books, music, other consumer and household prods. Acquired video firm Elemental Technologies, 10/19/2015. Acquired grocer Whole Foods, 8/28/2017. Announced plans for second headquarters, 9/7/2017.

American Airlines Group, Inc. (AAL): 4333 Amon Carter Blvd., Ft. Worth, TX 76155; (817) 963-1234; www.aa.com; Doug Parker; airlines (American Airlines, American Eagle).

American Electric Power Co., Inc. (AEP): 1 Riverside Plz., Columbus, OH 43215; (614) 716-1000; www.aep.com; Nicholas K. Akins; public utilities.

American Express Co. (AXP): World Financial Ctr., 200 Vesey St., 50th Fl., NY, NY 10285; (212) 640-2000; www.american express.com; Stephen J. Squeri; charge and credit cards, travel-related services.

American Greetings Corp.: 1 American Blvd., Cleveland, OH 44145; (216) 252-7300; www.americangreetings.com; John W. Beeder; greeting cards, stationery, party goods, gift items.

American Intl. Group, Inc. (AIG): 175 Water St., 15th Fl., NY, NY 10038; (212) 770-7000; www.aigcorporate.com; Brian Duperreault; insurance, financial services. AIG received $182 bil in govt. bailouts, 2008.

AmerisourceBergen (ABC): 1300 Morris Dr., Chesterbrook, PA, 19087; (610) 727-7000; www.amerisourcebergen.com; Steven H. Collis; distrib. of generic and brand-name pharmaceuticals.

Amgen, Inc. (AMGN): 1 Amgen Center Dr., Thousand Oaks, CA 91320; (805) 447-1000; www.amgen.com; Robert A. Bradway; biopharmaceuticals.

Anheuser-Busch InBev (BUD): Brouwerijplein 1, 3000 Leuven, Belgium; +32 (16) 276111; www.ab-inbev.com; Carlos Brito; brewer (Budweiser, Bud Light, Michelob, Corona, Foster's, Stella Artois), soft drinks. Acquired brewing competitor SABMiller for $100 bil+, 10/10/2016.

Anthem, Inc. (ANTM): 120 Monument Cir., Indianapolis, IN 46204; (317) 488-6000; www.anthem.com; Gail K. Boudreaux; health insurance co. Terminated $48-bil bid to acquire Cigna following federal injunction, 5/12/2017.

Apple Inc. (AAPL): 1 Infinite Loop, Cupertino, CA 95014; (408) 996-1010; www.apple.com; Tim Cook; mfr. of computers (Mac), digital media devices (iPod, iPhone, iPad) and distrib. (iTunes store, Apple Music). Acquired Faceshift, 11/2015; A.I. firm Lattice Data, 2017; Agreed to buy music ID app Shazam, 12/11/2017; subscription app Texture, 3/12/2018.

ARAMARK Corp. (ARMK): 2400 Market St., Philadelphia, PA 19103; (215) 238-3000; www.aramark.com; Eric J. Foss; food/support services to institutions and facilities, uniforms and career apparel.

ArcelorMittal USA, Inc.: 1 South Dearborn, Chicago, IL 60603; (312) 899-3440; www.usaarcelormittal.com; John L. Brett; steel; U.S. subsidiary of Arcelor Mittal, based in Luxembourg.

Archer Daniels Midland Co. (ADM): 77 W. Wacker Dr., Ste. 4600, Chicago, IL 60601; (312) 634-8100; www.adm.com; Juan R. Luciano; agricultural commodities and prods. Sold global cocoa business to Olam Intl. Ltd., 10/16/2015. Acquired French mfr. Chamtor, 7/3/2017.

Armstrong World Industries, Inc. (AWI): 2500 Columbia Ave., P.O. Box 3001, Lancaster, PA 17604; (717) 672-9611; www.armstrong.com; Victor D. Grizzle; mfr. of flooring, ceiling prods., cabinets.

AT&T Inc. (T): 208 S. Akard St., Dallas, TX 75202; (210) 821-4105; www.att.com; Randall L. Stephenson; telecommunications, global information management. Acquired DirecTV, 7/24/2015; Quickplay Media, 6/28/2016; CNN and HBO owner Time Warner in $85.4 bil buyout, 6/14/2018.

Automatic Data Processing, Inc. (ADP): 1 ADP Blvd., Roseland, NJ 07068; (973) 974-5000; www.adp.com; Carlos A. Rodriguez; payroll and tax processing serv.

AutoNation, Inc. (AN): 200 SW 1st Ave., Ste. 1600, Ft. Lauderdale, FL 33301; (954) 769-6000; www.autonation.com; Mike Jackson; auto retailer; new and used vehicles; auto parts, maintenance, and repair; auto finance and insurance.

Avon Products, Inc. (AVP): Bldg. 6, Chiswick Park, London, W4 5HR, UK; (203) 682-8200; www.avon.com; Jan Zijderveld; cosmetics, fragrances, skin and personal care items; fashion. Split off N. American business as New Avon, 3/1/2016. Moved HQ to UK, 2017.

Bank of America Corp. (BAC): 100 N. Tryon St., Charlotte, NC 28255; (704) 386-5681; www.bankofamerica.com; Brian T. Moynihan; banking and financial services.

Barnes & Noble, Inc. (BKS): 122 Fifth Ave., NY, NY 10011; (212) 633-3300; www.barnesandnoble.com; Leonard S. Riggio; leading U.S. bookseller (retail and college), publisher (Sterling Pub. Co.). Spun off college bookstores business Barnes & Noble Education, 8/3/2015.

Baxter International Inc. (BAX): 1 Baxter Pkwy., Deerfield, IL 60015; (224) 948-2000; www.baxter.com; José Almeida; mfr. of health care prods. Spun off pharmaceutical business into Baxalta, 7/1/2015.

Bear Stearns Cos. Inc.: see JPMorgan Chase & Co.

Becton, Dickinson & Co. (BDX): 1 Becton Dr., Franklin Lakes, NJ 07417; (201) 847-6800; www.bd.com; Vincent A. Forlenza; medical, laboratory, diagnostic prods. Acquired medical tech co. C.R. Bard Inc., 12/29/2017.

Berkshire Hathaway Inc. (BRK.A): 3555 Farnam St., Ste. 1440, Omaha, NE 68131; (402) 346-1400; www.berkshirehathaway.com; Warren E. Buffett; diversified holdings incl. insurance (GEICO), building materials (Benjamin Moore & Co., Shaw), apparel (Fruit of the Loom), food (Dairy Queen). Acquired Precision Castparts, 1/29/2016; Duracell, 2/29/2016.

Bertelsmann AG: Carl-Bertelsmann-Str. 270, 33311 Gütersloh, Germany; +49 (0) 5241-80-62321; www.bertelsmann.de; Thomas Rabe; intl. media corp., trade book publisher (Penguin Random House: Knopf, Doubleday).

Best Buy Co., Inc. (BBY): 7601 Penn Ave. S., Richfield, MN 55423; (612) 291-1000; www.bestbuy.com; Hubert Joly; retailer of software, appliances, cellular phones, consumer electronics.

Blackstone Group LP, The (BX): 345 Park Ave., NY, NY 10154; (212) 583-5000; www.blackstone.com; Stephen A. Schwarzman; asset mgmt., financial services. Acquired Aon's HR platform, 5/1/2017.

Boeing Co. (BA): 100 N. Riverside, Chicago, IL 60606; (312) 544-2000; boeing.com; Dennis A. Muilenburg; world's leading aerospace co., mfr. of commercial jet and military aircraft; one of the largest U.S. defense contractors.

Booking Holdings Inc. (BKNG) (fmr. The Priceline Group): 800 Connecticut Ave., Norwalk, CT 06854; (203) 299-8000; www.bookingholdings.com; Glenn D. Fogel; online travel/hospitality services (Priceline, booking.com, Kayak, Open Table).

Brink's Co., The (BCO): 1801 Bayberry Ct., P.O. Box 18100, Richmond, VA 23226; (804) 289-9600; www.brinkscompany.com; Doug A. Pertz; security (armored transport, money processing, trans. of valuables).

Bristol-Myers Squibb Co. (BMY): 430 E. 29th St., 14th Fl., NY, NY 10016; (212) 546-4000; www.bms.com; Giovanni Caforio; development, mfr., and sale of pharmaceuticals (Plavix, Eliquis, Atripla). Acquired Cormorant Pharmaceuticals, 7/5/2016.

Brown-Forman Corp. (BF.B): 850 Dixie Hwy., Louisville, KY 40210; (502) 585-1100; www.brown-forman.com; Paul C. Varga; distilled spirits (Jack Daniel's, Finlandia), wine and champagne (Sonoma-Cutrer, Korbel). Sold Southern Comfort and Tuaca brands to Sazerac, 3/1/2016.

Brunswick Corp. (BC): 26125 N. Riverwoods Blvd., Ste. 500, Mettawa, IL 60045; (847) 735-4700; www.brunswick.com;

Mark D. Schwabero; leisure and recreation prods., incl. marine engines and boats; fitness equip.

Burger King: see Restaurant Brands Intl.

Caesars Entertainment Corp. (CZR): One Caesars Palace Dr., Las Vegas, NV 89109; (702) 407-6000; www.caesars.com; Mark Frissora; casinos; gambling services (Caesars, Harrah's, Horseshoe, World Series of Poker).

Campbell Soup Co. (CPB): One Campbell Pl., Camden, NJ 08103; (856) 342-4800; www.campbellsoupcompany.com; Keith R. McLoughlin; soup mfr.; sauces (Pace, Prego), V8 juice, Pepperidge Farm prods.; Garden Fresh Gourmet. Agreed to buy Snyder's-Lance (Pop Secret, Cape Cod/Kettle chips), 12/18/2017.

Capital One Financial Corporation (COF): 1680 Capital One Dr., McLean, VA 22102; (703) 720-1000; www.capitalone.com; Richard D. Fairbank; financial services.

Cardinal Health, Inc. (CAH): 7000 Cardinal Pl., Dublin, OH 43017; (614) 757-5000; www.cardinalhealth.com; George S. Barrett; pharmaceutical and med. equip. dist. co. Acquired Medtronic's medical supplies assets, 7/30/2017.

Carlyle Group, The (CG): 1001 Pennsylvania Ave. NW, Washington, DC 20004; (202) 729-5399; www.carlyle.com; William E. Conway Jr.; private equity group.

Caterpillar Inc. (CAT): 501 SW Jefferson Ave., Peoria, IL 61630; (309) 675-2337; www.caterpillar.com; Jim Umpleby; mfr. of construction and mining equip.

CBRE Group, Inc. (CBRE): 400 S. Hope St., 25th Fl., Los Angeles, CA 90071; (213) 613-3333; www.cbre.com; Bob Sulentic; commercial real estate.

CBS Corp. (CBS): 51 W. 52nd St., NY, NY 10019; (212) 975-4321; www.cbscorporation.com; Leslie Moonves; TV networks (CBS, Showtime), distribution, radio stations; book publishing (Simon & Schuster).

CenturyLink, Inc. (CTL): 100 CenturyLink Dr., Monroe, LA 71203; (318) 388-9000; www.centurylink.com; Jeff Storey; telecommunications provider.

Charter Communications, Inc. (CHTR): 400 Atlantic St., Stamford, CT 06901; (203) 905-7801; www.charter.com; Tom Rutledge; internet, cable TV, telecom provider. Rebranded Time Warner Cable and Bright House Networks, acquired 5/18/2016, as Spectrum.

Chevron Corp. (CVX): 6001 Bollinger Canyon Rd., San Ramon, CA 94583; (925) 842-1000; www.chevron.com; Michael K. Wirth; integrated energy co.

Chiquita Brands Intl., Inc.: 1855 Griffin Rd., Ste. C-436, Ft. Lauderdale, FL, 33004; (980) 636-5000; www.chiquita.com; Brian W. Kocher; fruits and vegetables. Acquired by Cutrale-Safra, 1/6/2015.

CHS, Inc. (CHSCP): 5500 Cenex Dr., Inver Grove Heights, MN 55077; (651) 355-6000; www.chsinc.com; Jay Debertin; grain marketing, oil refining, and pipeline operations.

Chubb Ltd. (CB): 15 Mountain View Rd., Warren, NJ 07059; (908) 903-2000; www.chubb.com; Evan Greenberg; property/casualty insurance. ACE Limited acquired The Chubb Corporation, 1/14/16.

Church & Dwight Co., Inc. (CHD): Princeton South Corporate Center, 500 Charles Ewing Blvd., Ewing, NJ 08628; (609) 806-1200; www.churchdwight.com; Matthew T. Farrell; ARM & HAMMER baking soda; household and personal care prods. (OxiClean, Arrid, Trojan, First Response).

Cigna Corp. (CI): 900 Cottage Grove Rd., Bloomfield, CT 06002; (860) 226-6000; www.cigna.com; David M. Cordani; insurance provider. Acquisition by Anthem terminated following federal injunction, 5/12/2016. Agreed to acquire Express Scripts Holding Co. for $67 bil, 3/8/2018.

Cintas Corp. (CTAS): 6800 Cintas Blvd., Cincinnati, OH 45262; (513) 459-1200;

www.cintas.com; Scott D. Farmer; uniform supplier.

Cisco Systems, Inc. (CSCO): 170 W. Tasman Dr., San Jose, CA 95134; (408) 526-4000; www.cisco.com; Chuck Robbins; networking and communication prods. Bought comm. services co. BroadSoft, 2/2/2018. Agreed to acquire cloud-based authentication provider Duo Security, 8/2/2018.

Citigroup, Inc. (C): 388 Greenwich St., NY, NY 10013; (212) 559-1000; www.citigroup.com; Michael L. Corbat; diversified financial services.

Clorox Co. (CLX): 1221 Broadway, Oakland, CA 94612; (510) 271-7000; www.clorox.com; Benno Dorer; consumer prods. (Clorox, Formula 409, Pine-Sol, S.O.S., Tilex, Scoop Away, Fresh Step, Kingsford, Hidden Valley, Glad, Brita, Burt's Bees). Acquired Renew Life probiotics, 5/3/2016.

Coach, Inc.: see Tapestry.

Coca-Cola Co. (KO): 1 Coca-Cola Plz. NW, Atlanta, GA 30313; (404) 676-2121; www.coca-cola.com; James Quincey; beverages (Coca-Cola, Sprite, Dasani, Fanta, Minute Maid, Vitaminwater).

Colgate-Palmolive Co. (CL): 300 Park Ave., NY, NY 10022; (212) 310-2000; www.colgate.com; Ian M. Cook; soap (Irish Spring), detergent (Palmolive), household cleansers (Ajax), toothpaste (Colgate, Tom's of Maine), pet food (Hill's Science Diet).

Comcast Corp. (CMCSA): 1701 JFK Blvd., Philadelphia, PA 19103; (215) 286-1700; www.comcast.com; Brian L. Roberts; cable provider; broadband media services; programming (E!, NBC, Bravo, USA, Telemundo). Acquired DreamWorks Animation, 8/22/2016.

ConAgra Foods, Inc. (CAG): 222 W. Merchandise Mart Plaza, Ste. 1300, Chicago, IL 60654; (312) 549-5000; www.conagrafoods.com; Sean Connolly; food processor (Chef Boyardee, Healthy Choice frozen dinners, Egg Beaters, Reddi-wip); food service supplier.

ConocoPhillips Co. (COP): 600 N. Dairy Ashford, P.O. Box 2197, Houston, TX 77252; (281) 293-1000; www.conocophillips.com; Ryan M. Lance; oil and gas exploration and prod. co. Spun off refining and marketing segment, 5/1/2012, as Phillips 66.

Consolidated Edison, Inc. (ED): 100 Summit Lake Dr., Ste. 410, Valhalla, NY 10595; (914) 286-7000; www.conedison.com; John McAvoy; electric, natural gas utilities.

Continental Airlines, Inc.: see United Continental Holdings, Inc.

Corning Inc. (GLW): 1 Riverfront Plz., Corning, NY 14831; (607) 974-9000; www.corning.com; Wendell P. Weeks; mfr. of telecommunications, specialty equip., fiber optics. Acquired Samsung's fiber-optics business, 3/31/2015.

Costco Wholesale Corp. (COST): 999 Lake Dr., Issaquah, WA 98027; (425) 313-8100; www.costco.com; W. Craig Jelinek; wholesale warehouse stores.

Countrywide Financial: see Bank of America Corp.

Crown Holdings, Inc. (CCK): 1 Crown Way, Philadelphia, PA 19154; (215) 698-5100; www.crowncork.com; Timothy J. Donahue; leading producer of packaging prods. Acquired Empaque, 2/18/2015.

CSX Corp. (CSX): 500 Water St., 15th Fl., Jacksonville, FL 32202; (904) 359-3200; www.csx.com; James M. Foote; rail freight transport.

CVS Health (CVS): 1 CVS Dr., Woonsocket, RI 02895; (401) 765-1500; www.cvs.com; Larry J. Merlo; retail drugstores. Acquired Target's pharmacy/clinic businesses, 12/16/2015. Announced plans to acquire health insurer Aetna for $77 bil, 12/3/2017.

Dana Holding Corp. (DAN): 3939 Technology Dr., Maumee, OH 43537; (419) 887-3000; www.dana.com; James Kamsickas; truck and auto parts, supplies.

Darden Restaurants, Inc. (DRI): 1000 Darden Center Dr., Orlando, FL 32837; (407) 245-4000; www.darden.com; Eugene Lee Jr.; casual-dining restaurants (Olive Garden, LongHorn Steakhouse). Acquired Cheddar's Scratch Kitchen, 4/24/2017.

Dean Foods Co. (DF): 2711 N. Haskell Ave., Ste. 3400, Dallas, TX 75204; (214) 303-3400; www.deanfoods.com; Ralph P. Scozzafava; milk and specialty dairy prods. (Land O'Lakes). Acquired Friendly's ice cream prods., 6/20/2016.

Deere & Co. (DE): One John Deere Pl., Moline, IL 61265; (309) 765-8000; www.deere.com; Samuel R. Allen; mfr. of farm equip., industrial equip., lawn and garden tractors.

Dell Inc.: 1 Dell Way, Round Rock, TX 78682; (512) 338-4400; www.dell.com; Michael S. Dell; laptop and desktop computers, network accessories, peripherals, tablets, smartphones. Acquired EMC Corp. for $67 bil, 9/7/2016; sold subsidiary Perot Systems to NTT Data, 11/3/2016.

Delta Air Lines, Inc. (DAL): 1030 Delta Blvd., Atlanta, GA (404) 715-2600; www.delta.com; Ed Bastian; air transportation.

Dillard's, Inc. (DDS): 1600 Cantrell Rd., Little Rock, AR 72201; (501) 376-5200; www.dillards.com; William Dillard II; dept. store chain.

Dish Network Corp. (DISH): 9601 S. Meridian Blvd., Englewood, CO 80112; (303) 723-1000; www.dish.com; W. Erik Carlson; satellite media services.

Walt Disney Co., The (DIS): 500 S. Buena Vista St., Burbank, CA 91521; (818) 560-1000; disney.go.com; Robert A. Iger; motion pictures (Lucasfilm, Touchstone, Pixar); TV (ABC, ESPN) and radio; publishing; theme parks (Walt Disney World, Disneyland) and resorts. Announced $52.4-bil buyout plan of 21st Century Fox, 12/14/2017; amended buyout to $71.3 bil, 6/20/2018.

Doctor's Associates Inc.: 325 Sub Way, Milford, CT 06461; (203) 877-4281; www.subway.com; Trevor Haynes; restaurants (Subway).

Dole Food Co., Inc.: One Dole Dr., Westlake Village, CA 91362; (818) 879-6600; www.dole.com; Johan Linden; food prods., fresh fruits, vegetables.

Dollar Tree (DLTR): 500 Volvo Pkwy., Chesapeake, VA 23320; (757) 321-5000; www.dollartree.com; Gary M. Philbin; discount retailer. Acquired Family Dollar, 7/6/2015.

R. R. Donnelley & Sons Co. (RRD): 35 W. Wacker Dr., Chicago, IL 60601; (312) 326-8000; www.rrdonnelley.com; Daniel L. Knotts; commercial printing; photos/graphics, translation; printer of *The World Almanac*. Acquired Courier Corp., 6/8/2015.

DowDuPont (DWDP): 2211 H.H. Dow Way, Midland, MI 48674; (989) 636-1000; www.dow-dupont.com; Edward D. Breen; chemicals, plastics, seed and crop protection. Formed from $130-bil merger between Dow and DuPont, 8/31/2017, with plan to split later into three publicly traded companies.

Dow Jones & Co., Inc.: see News Corp.

Dr Pepper Snapple Group, Inc.: see Keurig Dr Pepper.

Duke Energy Corp. (DUK): 550 S. Tryon St., Charlotte, NC 28202; (980) 373-8649; www.duke-energy.com; Lynn J. Good; utilities, fiber optic networks.

Dun & Bradstreet Corp. (DNB): 103 JFK Pkwy., Short Hills, NJ 07078; (973) 921-5500; www.dnb.com; Thomas J. Manning; business information, research.

Dupont (E. I. du Pont de Nemours & Co.): see DowDuPont.

DXC Technology (DXC): 1775 Tysons Blvd., Tysons, VA 22102; (703) 245-9700; www.dxc.technology; John M. Lawrie; information tech. serv. Formed through merger of Computer Sciences Corp and Hewlett Packard Enterprise's enterprise serv. unit, 4/3/2017.

Eastman Kodak Co. (KODK): 343 State St., Rochester, NY 14650; (585) 724-4000; www.kodak.com; Jeffrey J. Clarke; imaging technology and services.

Eaton Corp. (ETN): 1000 Eaton Blvd., Cleveland, OH 44122; (440) 523-5000; www.eaton.com; Craig Arnold; mfr. vehicle components, controls.

eBay Inc. (EBAY): 2065 Hamilton Ave., San Jose, CA 95125; (408) 376-7400; www.ebay.com; Devin N. Wenig; e-commerce (StubHub). Spun off PayPal, 7/17/2015.

Edison Intl. (EIX): 2244 Walnut Grove Ave., Rosemead, CA 91770; (626) 302-2222; www.edison.com; Pedro Pizarro; electric utilities.

Electronic Arts Inc. (EA): 209 Redwood Shores Pkwy., Redwood City, CA 94065; (650) 628-1500; www.ea.com; Andrew Wilson; video game publisher (*Madden NFL*, *Battlefield*, *The Sims*, *UFC*).

Electronic Data Systems: see Hewlett Packard Enterprise.

Eli Lilly and Co. (LLY): Lilly Corporate Center, Indianapolis, IN 46285; (317) 276-2000; www.lilly.com; David A. Ricks; pharmaceutical research, development, and manufacturing (Prozac, Strattera, Cialis). Acquired Novartis Animal Health, 1/1/2015.

EMC Corp.: see Dell Inc.

Emerson Electric Co. (EMR): 8000 W. Florissant Ave., St. Louis, MO 63136; (314) 553-2000; www.emerson.com; David N. Farr; electrical, electronics prods. and systems.

Energizer Holdings, Inc. (ENR): 533 Maryville Univ. Dr., St. Louis, MO 63141; (314) 985-2000; www.energizer.com; Alan Hoskins; batteries, flashlights, personal care prods.

Enterprise Products Partners L.P. (EPD): 1100 Louisiana St., 10th Fl., Houston, TX 77002; (713) 381-6500; www.enterpriseproducts.com; A.J. Teague; oil processing/transport and waterborne freight.

Estée Lauder Cos. Inc. (EL): 767 Fifth Ave., NY, NY 10153; (212) 572-4200; www.elcompanies.com; Fabrizio Freda; cosmetics (Clinique, Bobbi Brown), fragrance, skin care prods. Acquired GLAMGLOW, 1/16/2015.

Exelon Corp. (EXC): 10 S. Dearborn St., 48th Fl., Chicago, IL 60680; (800) 483-3220; www.exeloncorp.com; Christopher M. Crane; electricity generation/distrib.; natural gas. Acquired Pepco Holdings, 3/23/2016.

Express Scripts Holding Co. (ESRX): 1 Express Way, St. Louis, MO 63121; (314) 996-0900; www.express-scripts.com; Tim Wentworth; U.S. pharmacy benefits mgmt. co. Agreed to $67-bil buyout by Cigna, 3/8/2018.

ExxonMobil Corp. (XOM): 5959 Las Colinas Blvd., Irving, TX 75039; (972) 444-1000; www.exxonmobil.com; Darren W. Woods; integrated energy, oil co. Announced doubling of Permian basin resources in $6.6-bil deal, 1/17/2017.

Facebook, Inc. (FB): 1 Hacker Way, Menlo Park, CA 94025; (650) 308-7300; www.facebook.com; Mark Zuckerberg; social networking/messaging platforms, services (Facebook, WhatsApp).

Federal Home Loan Mortgage Corp. (Freddie Mac): 8200 Jones Branch Dr., McLean, VA 22102; (703) 903-2000; www.freddiemac.com; Donald H. Layton; residential mortgage provider. Under U.S. govt. mgmt. since 9/7/2008.

Federal Natl. Mortgage Assn. (Fannie Mae): 3900 Wisconsin Ave. NW, Washington, DC 20016; (202) 752-7000; www.fanniemae.com; Timothy J. Mayopoulos; provider of residential mortgage funds. Under U.S. govt. mgmt. since 9/7/2008.

FedEx Corp. (FDX): 942 S. Shady Grove Rd., Memphis, TN 38120; (901) 818-7500; www.fedex.com; Frederick W. Smith; delivery services. Acquired TNT Express, 5/25/2016.

First Data Corp. (FDC): 5565 Glenridge Connector NE, Ste. 2000, Atlanta, GA 30342; (404) 890-2000; www.firstdata.com; Frank Bisignano; financial transaction processing. IPO, 10/1/2015.

FirstEnergy Corp. (FE): 76 S. Main St., Akron, OH 44308; (800) 736-3402; www.firstenergycorp.com; Charles E. Jones; public electricity supplier.

Fluor Corp. (FLR): 6700 Las Colinas Blvd., Irving, TX 75039; (469) 398-7000; www.fluor.com; David T. Seaton; international engineering and construction co.

Foot Locker, Inc. (FL): 330 W. 34th St., NY, NY 10001; (212) 720-3700; www.

footlocker-inc.com; Richard A. Johnson; retail athletic stores (Footaction, Foot Locker, Champs Sports).

Ford Motor Co. (F): 1 American Rd., Dearborn, MI 48126; (313) 322-3000; www.ford.com; William C. Ford Jr.; auto mfr.; motor vehicle sales (Ford, Lincoln); auto financing (Ford Motor Credit).

Fox: see News Corp. or 21st Century Fox.

Gannett Co., Inc. (GCI): 7950 Jones Branch Dr., McLean, VA 22107; (703) 854-6000; www.gannett.com; Robert Dickey; newspaper publisher (*USA Today*). Original Gannett Co., spun off network and cable TV and digital media divisions as TEGNA, Inc., 6/29/2015, newspapers as new entity retaining name.

Gap Inc. (GPS): 2 Folsom St., San Francisco, CA 94105; (650) 952-4400; www.gapinc.com; Art Peck; casual apparel retailer (Gap, Banana Republic, Old Navy).

General Dynamics Corp. (GD): 2941 Fairview Park Dr., Ste. 100, Falls Church, VA 22042; (703) 876-3000; www.general dynamics.com; Phebe N. Novakovic; defense contractor: aerospace, combat systems, marine systems, computing devices.

General Electric Co. (GE): 41 Farnsworth St., Boston, MA 02210; (617) 443-3000; www.ge.com; John L. Flannery; electrical, electronic equip., financial services, radio and TV broadcasting, aircraft engines, power generation. Sold appliances business to China's Haier Group, 6/6/2016.

General Mills, Inc. (GIS): One General Mills Blvd., Minneapolis, MN 55426; (763) 764-7600; www.generalmills.com; Jeff Harmening; food mfr. (Annie's Homegrown, Betty Crocker, Bisquick, Cheerios, Chex, Häagen-Dazs, Pillsbury, Progresso, Total, Wheaties, Yoplait). Sold vegetable brands Green Giant and LeSeur to B&G Foods, 11/2/2015. Acquired Blue Buffalo Pet Prods., 4/24/2018.

General Motors Co. (GM): 300 Renaissance Ctr., Detroit, MI 48265; (313) 556-5000; www.gm.com; Mary T. Barra; auto mfr. (Chevrolet, Cadillac, Buick, GMC); auto financing (GM Financial); vehicle security (OnStar). General Motors Corp. filed for Chap. 11 reorganization, 6/1/2009; sold profitable components to a new, smaller co. called General Motors Co., 7/10/2009. Sold European brands to France's Peugeot, 7/31/2018.

Genuine Parts Co. (GPC): 2999 Wildwood Pkwy., Atlanta, GA 30339; (678) 934-5000; www.genpt.com; Paul D. Donahue; distrib. auto (NAPA), industrial replacement parts.

Gilead Sciences, Inc., (GILD): 333 Lakeside Dr., Foster City, CA 94404; (650) 574-3000; www.gilead.com; John F. Milligan, PhD; biopharmaceuticals.

Goldman Sachs Group, Inc. (GS): 200 West St., 29th Fl., NY, NY 10282; (212) 902-1000; www.goldmansachs.com; David Solomon; investment banking, asset mgmt., securities services.

Goodyear Tire & Rubber Co. (GT): 200 Innovation Way, Akron, OH 44316; (330) 796-2121; www.goodyear.com; Richard J. Kramer; tires and other auto prods.

Google, Inc.: see Alphabet Inc.

Graham Holdings Co. (GHC): 1300 N. 17th St. NW, Arlington, VA 22209; (703) 345-6300; www.ghco.com; Timothy O'Shaughnessy; media (newspapers, Slate.com, TV), education (Kaplan), home health care. Fmr. Washington Post Co.; renamed after 2013 sale of newspaper.

Great Atlantic & Pacific Tea Co., Inc.: 2 Paragon Dr., Montvale, NJ 07645; (201) 573-9700; www.aptea.com; Paul Hertz; supermarkets (A&P, Food Basics, Food Emporium, Super Fresh, Waldbaum's, Pathmark).

Halliburton Co. (HAL): 3000 N. Sam Houston Pkwy. E., Houston, TX 77032; (281) 871-4000; www.halliburton.com; Jeff Miller; oil field mgmt., energy services.

Hanesbrands Inc. (HBI): 1000 E. Hanes Mill Rd., Winston-Salem, NC 27105; (336) 519-8080; www.hanesbrands.com; Gerald W. Evans Jr.; apparel mfr. (Hanes, Barely There, Bali, Champion, Gear for Sports, Just My Size, L'eggs, Maidenform,

Playtex, Wonderbra). Acquired Knights Apparel, 4/8/2015; Pacific Brands Ltd., 7/15/2016.

Harley-Davidson, Inc. (HOG): 3700 W. Juneau Ave., Milwaukee, WI 53208; (414) 342-4680; www.harley-davidson.com; Matt Levatich; mfr. motorcycles, parts, accessories.

Hartford Financial Services Group, Inc. (HIG): One Hartford Plz., Hartford, CT 06155; (860) 547-5000; www.thehartford.com; Christopher J. Swift; insurance, financial services.

Hasbro, Inc. (HAS): 1027 Newport Ave., Pawtucket, RI 02862; (401) 431-8697; www.hasbro.com; Brian Goldner; toy and game mfr. (Playskool, G.I. Joe, Nerf, Play-Doh). Acquired Boulder Media, 7/13/2016.

HCA Holdings, Inc. (HCA): 1 Park Plz., Nashville, TN 37203; (615) 344-9551; www.hcahealthcare.com; R. Milton Johnson; owns and operates hospitals; other diagnostic, surgical, health treatment centers.

H. J. Heinz Co.: see Kraft Heinz Co.

Henkel Corp.: 200 Elm St., Stamford, CT 06902; (475) 210-0230; www.henkelna.com; Jerry Perkins; consumer prods. (Dial soap, Purex detergent, Right Guard antiperspirant, Renuzit air fresheners); U.S. subsidiary of Germany's Henkel co.

Hershey Co., The (HSY): 100 Crystal A Dr., Hershey, PA 17033; (717) 534-4200; www.thehersheycompany.com; Michele Buck; chocolate prods. mfr. (Almond Joy, Brookside, Jolly Rancher, Kit Kat, Milk Duds, Reese's, Twizzlers, York). Agreed to acquire Amplify Snack Brands, 12/18/2017.

Hertz Global Holdings, Inc. (HTZ): 225 Brae Blvd., Park Ridge, NJ 07656; (201) 307-2000; www.hertz.com; Kathryn V. Marinello; car rentals.

Hess Corp. (HES): 1185 Ave. of the Americas, 40th Fl., NY, NY 10036; (212) 997-8500; www.hess.com; John B. Hess; integrated oil and gas co.

Hewlett Packard Enterprise (HPE): 3000 Hanover St., Palo Alto, CA 94304; (650) 857-2246; www.hpe.com; Antonio Neri; computer prods. (software, servers, storage), consulting, support. Spun off from Hewlett-Packard Co., now HP Inc., 11/2/2015. Spun off and merged enterprise serv. unit with Computer Sciences Corp. to form DXC Technology, 4/3/2017; sold non-core software unit to UK's Micro Focus Intl., 9/1/2017.

Hillshire Brands Co.: see Tyson Foods, Inc.

Hilton Worldwide (HLT): 7930 Jones Branch Dr., Ste. 1100, McLean, VA 22102; (703) 883-1000; www.hiltonworldwide.com; Christopher J. Nassetta; hotels and resorts (Doubletree, Embassy, Hampton). Sold landmark Waldorf Astoria, 2/11/2015.

Home Depot, Inc. (HD): 2455 Paces Ferry Rd. NW, Atlanta, GA 30339; (770) 433-8211; www.homedepot.com; Craig Menear; home improvement warehouse stores. Acquired Blinds.com, 1/23/2014.

Honeywell Intl. Inc. (HON): 115 Tabor Rd., Morris Plains, NJ 07962; (973) 455-2000; www.honeywell.com; Darius Adamczyk; industrial and home control systems, aerospace guidance systems. Acquired Datamax-O'Neil, 3/2/2015. Announced plans to spinoff homes, ADI global dist., and transport systems businesses into two public cos., 10/10/2017.

Hormel Foods Corp. (HRL): 1 Hormel Pl., Austin, MN 55912; (507) 437-5611; www.hormelfoods.com; Jim Snee; food processor, primarily meat (SPAM, Dinty Moore, Jennie-O, Skippy). Acquired Muscle Milk, 8/12/2014; Applegate Farms, 7/13/2015. Sold Diamond Crystal Brands, 4/26/2016.

Hostess Brands (TWNK): 1 E Armour Blvd., Kansas City, MO 64111; (816) 701-4600; www.hostessbrands.com; Andrew P. Callahan; baked goods wholesaler, distrib. IPO, 11/7/2016.

Houghton Mifflin Harcourt Co. (HMHC): 125 High St., Boston, MA 02110; (617) 351-5000; www.hmhco.com; John J. Lynch Jr.; publisher of textbooks and other educational prods. (Holt McDougal, Clarion), trade and

reference books. Acquired Scholastic's educational tech. business, 5/29/2015.

HP Inc. (HPQ): 1501 Page Mill Rd., Palo Alto, CA 94304; (650) 857-1501; www.hp.com; Dion Weisler; computers, electronic prods. and systems.

H&R Block, Inc. (HRB): 1301 Main St., Kansas City, MO 64105; (816) 854-3000; www.hrblock.com; Jeffrey J. Jones II; tax return preparation; business and consulting services.

Humana Inc. (HUM): 500 W. Main St., Louisville, KY 40202; (502) 580-1000; www.humana.com; Bruce D. Broussard; managed health care service provider, related specialty prods. Merger with Aetna terminated following federal injunction, 2/14/2016.

IAC/InterActiveCorp (IAC): 555 W. 18th St., NY, NY 10011; (212) 314-7300; www.iac.com; Barry Diller; internet conglomerate (Ask.com, Match.com, Citysearch, The Daily Beast, Vimeo).

iHeartMedia, Inc.: 200 E. Basse Rd., Ste. 100, San Antonio, TX 78209; (210) 822-2828; www.iheartmedia.com; Robert Pittman; radio stations; outdoor advertising. Fmr. Clear Channel Communications; renamed 9/16/2014. Filed for Ch. 11 bankruptcy, 3/15/2018.

Illinois Tool Works Inc. (ITW): 155 Harlem Ave., Glenview, IL 60025; (847) 724-7500; www.itw.com; E. Scott Santi; consumer, industrial tools; food equip. (Hobart), packaging (Zip-Pak).

Ingersoll-Rand plc (IR): 170/175 Lakeview Dr., Airside Business Park, Swords, Dublin, Ireland; 353-1-870-7400; company.ingersollrand.com; Michael W. Lamach; low-speed vehicles (Club Car); refrigeration equip. (Thermo King); industrial equip.; air conditioning systems (Trane, American Standard).

Intel Corp. (INTC): 2200 Mission College Blvd., Santa Clara, CA 95054; (408) 765-8080; www.intel.com; Robert Swan; mfr. semiconductors, microprocessors (Core, Centrino). Acquired Altera Corp., 12/28/2015.

International Business Machines Corp. (IBM): One New Orchard Rd., Armonk, NY 10504; (914) 499-1900; www.ibm.com; Virginia M. Rometty; advanced information processing technology equip., services. Sold chip-mfr. unit to GlobalFoundries, 7/1/2015.

International Paper Co. (IP): 6400 Poplar Ave., Memphis, TN 38197; (901) 419-9000; www.internationalpaper.com; Mark Sutton; paper/forest prods. Spun off distr. business xpedx, which merged with Unisource to form Veritiv Corp., 7/1/2014.

INTL FCStone Inc. (INTL): 708 Third Ave., 15th Fl., NY, NY 10017; (212) 485-3500; www.intlfcstone.com; Sean O'Connor; securities and commodities advising.

J.C. Penney Co., Inc. (JCP): 6501 Legacy Dr., Plano, TX 75024; (972) 431-1000; www.jcpenney.com; Ronald W. Tysoe; dept. store retailer, general merchandise catalog sales.

J.Crew Group, Inc.: 770 Broadway, NY, NY 10003; (212) 209-2500; www.jcrew.com; Jim W. Brett; retail and mail order apparel and accessories.

JetBlue Airways Corp. (JBLU): 27-01 Queens Plz. N., Long Island City, NY 11101; (718) 286-7900; www.jetblue.com; Robin Hayes; air transportation.

Jo-Ann Stores, Inc.: 5555 Darrow Rd., Hudson, OH 44236; (330) 656-2600; www.joann.com; Jill Soltau; specialty fabric and craft stores.

Johnson Controls Intl. (JCI): 5757 N. Green Bay Ave., Milwaukee, WI 53209; (414) 524-1200; www.johnsoncontrols.com; George R. Oliver; equip. and controls for heating, ventilating, AC, refrigeration, and building security; auto interiors, batteries. Acquired security/fire co. Tyco, 9/6/2016. Spun off auto interiors unit as separate co. Adient, 10/31/2016.

Johnson & Johnson (JNJ): 1 Johnson & Johnson Plz., New Brunswick, NJ 08933; (732) 524-0400; www.jnj.com; Alex Gorsky; health care prods. (Band-Aid, Neosporin), pharmaceuticals (Tylenol, Motrin,

Sudafed), toiletries (Neutrogena, Aveeno). Sold Ortho-Clinical Diagnostics to The Carlyle Group, 6/30/2014. Acquired hair care co. Vogue Intl., 7/18/2016.

S. C. Johnson & Son, Inc.: 1525 Howe St., Racine, WI 53403; (262) 260-2000; www.scjohnson.com; H. Fisk Johnson; cleaning and other household prods. (Windex, Pledge, Fantastik, Raid, OFF!, Shout, Glade, Scrubbing Bubbles, Ziploc). Acquired HomeBrands A.S., 3/2/2015; UK-based Deb Group, 3/26/2015.

JPMorgan Chase & Co. (JPM): 270 Park Ave., 12th Fl., NY, NY 10017; (212) 270-6000; www.jpmorganchase.com; James Dimon; financial services.

Kate Spade & Co.: see Tapestry, Inc.

KBR, Inc. (KBR): 601 Jefferson St., Ste. 3400, Houston, TX 77002; (713) 753-2000; www.kbr.com; Stuart Bradie; engineering; construction mgmt. services.

Kellogg Co. (K): One Kellogg Sq., Battle Creek, MI 49016; (269) 961-2000; www.kelloggcompany.com; Steven A. Cahillane; mfr. of ready-to-eat cereals, other food prods. (Frosted Flakes, Rice Krispies, Pop-Tarts, Nutri-Grain, Keebler, Eggo, Pringles, Gardenburger).

Kelly Services, Inc. (KELYA): 999 W. Big Beaver Rd., Troy, MI 48084; (248) 362-4444; www.kellyservices.com; George Corona; temporary staffing services.

Keurig Dr Pepper (KDP): 53 South Ave., Burlington, MA 01803; (866) 901-2739; www.keurigdrpepper.com; Robert Gamgort; coffee, tea, and nonalcoholic beverages (Green Mountain Coffee, Caribou Coffee, Straight Up Tea, Dr Pepper, 7UP, Snapple, Mott's).

Kimberly-Clark Corp. (KMB): 351 Phelps Dr., Irving, TX 75038; (972) 281-1200; www.kimberly-clark.com; Thomas J. Falk; personal care prods. (Kleenex, Scott, Cottonelle, Huggies, Kotex).

Kinder Morgan, Inc. (KMI): 1001 Louisiana St., Ste. 1000, Houston, TX 77002; (713) 369-9000; www.kindermorgan.com; Richard D. Kinder; energy trans. and storage. Acquired Kinder Morgan Energy Partners, Kinder Morgan Management, and El Paso Pipeline Partners, 11/26/2014; Hiland Partners, 2/13/2015.

Kmart Corp.: see Sears Holdings Corp.

Koch Industries, Inc.: P.O. Box 2256, Wichita, KS 67201; (316) 828-5500; www.kochind.com; Charles G. Koch; forest prod. mfr.; oil refineries/pipeline; chemicals; pollution-control equip.; ranching.

Kraft Heinz Co. (KHC): 1 PPG Pl., Ste. 3100, Pittsburgh, PA 15222; (412) 456-5700; www.kraftheinzcompany.com; Bernardo Hees; food and beverage mfr. (Ore-Ida, 57 Varieties ketchup, Velveeta, Crystal Light, Maxwell House, Kool-Aid, Lunchables, Jell-O, Oscar Mayer). Formed from merger of Kraft Foods Group with H.J. Heinz Co., 7/2/2015.

Kroger Co. (KR): 1014 Vine St., Cincinnati, OH 45202; (513) 762-4000; www.the krogerco.com; W. Rodney McMullen; grocery, convenience, and mall jewelry stores.

L Brands, Inc. (LB) (fmr. Limited Brands): 3 Limited Pkwy., Columbus, OH 43230; (614) 415-7000; www.lb.com; Leslie H. Wexner; apparel stores (La Senza, Victoria's Secret, PINK, Henri Bendel), home decor, personal care (Bath & Body Works).

Las Vegas Sands Corp. (LVS): 3355 Las Vegas Blvd. S., Las Vegas, NV 89109; (702) 414-1000; www.sands.com; Sheldon G. Adelson; casino-resort operator (Venetian, Palazzo, Sands Macao).

La-Z-Boy Inc. (LZB): 1284 N. Telegraph Rd., Monroe, MI 48162; (734) 242-1444; www.la-z-boy.com; Kurt L. Darrow; reclining chairs, other furniture.

Levi Strauss & Co.: 1155 Battery St., San Francisco, CA 94111; (415) 501-6000; www.levistrauss.com; Charles Bergh; blue jeans, casual sportswear (Dockers).

Liberty Mutual Holding Co. Inc.: 175 Berkeley St., Boston, MA 02116; (617) 357-9500; www.libertymutual.com; David H. Long; insurance prods. and services.

LinkedIn Corp.: 605 W. Maude Ave., Sunnyvale, CA, 94085; (650) 687-3600; www.linkedin.com; Jeff Weiner; social

networking services. Acquired by Microsoft, 12/8/2016.

Liz Claiborne, Inc.: see J.C. Penney Co., Inc.

L.L.Bean, Inc.: 15 Casco St., Freeport, ME 04033; (207) 552-2000; www.llbean.com; Stephen Smith; catalog and retail outdoor apparel, footwear, gear.

Lockheed Martin Corp. (LMT): 6801 Rockledge Dr., Bethesda, MD 20817; (301) 897-6000; www.lockheedmartin.com; Marillyn A. Hewson; leading U.S. defense contractor; aircraft, electronics, missiles, information tech., and communications. Acquired Zeta Associates, 8/18/2014. Bought Sikorsky Aircraft from United Technologies, 11/6/2015.

Loews Corp. (L): 667 Madison Ave., NY, NY 10065; (212) 521-2000; www.loews.com; James S. Tisch; hotels, insurance (CNA Financial), offshore drilling (Diamond).

Lorillard, Inc.: see Reynolds American Inc.

Lowe's Cos., Inc. (LOW): 1000 Lowe's Blvd., Mooresville, NC 28117; (704) 758-1000; www.lowes.com; Marvin R. Ellison; building material and home improvement superstores.

Macy's, Inc. (M): 7 W. 7th St., Cincinnati, OH 45202; (513) 579-7000; www.macysinc.com; Jeff Gennette; dept. stores (Macy's, Bloomingdale's). Acquired cosmetics retailer Bluemercury, Inc., 3/9/2015.

ManpowerGroup (MAN): 100 Manpower Pl., Milwaukee, WI 53212; (414) 961-1000; www.manpowergroup.com; Jonas Prising; employment services.

Marathon Oil Corp. (MRO): 5555 San Felipe St., Houston, TX 77056; (713) 629-6600; www.marathonoil.com; Lee M. Tillman; integrated oil co.

Marriott International, Inc. (MAR): 10400 Fernwood Rd., Bethesda, MD 20817; (301) 380-3000; www.marriott.com; Arne M. Sorenson; hotels (Renaissance, Courtyard, Fairfield Inn, Ritz-Carlton). Acquired Protea Hospitality Group, 4/1/2014; Delta Hotels and Resorts, 4/1/2015. Acquired Starwood Hotels & Resorts to create world's largest hotel co., 9/23/2016.

Mars, Inc.: 6885 Elm St., McLean, VA 22101; (703) 821-4900; www.mars.com; Grant F. Reid; food mfr., including of chocolate (M&M's, Snickers, Dove), food (Uncle Ben's), pet food (Pedigree, Whiskas, Iams, Eukanuba, Sheba). Acquired pet hospital chain VCA Inc., 9/12/2017.

Massachusetts Mutual Life Insurance Co. (MassMutual Financial Group): 1295 State St., Springfield, MA 01111; (413) 744-1000; www.massmutual.com; Roger W. Crandall; financial planning and investment, life insurance.

MasterCard Inc. (MA): 2000 Purchase St., Purchase, NY 10577; (914) 249-2000; www.mastercard.com; Ajay Banga; financial services.

Mattel, Inc. (MAT): 333 Continental Blvd., El Segundo, CA 90245; (310) 252-2000; www.mattel.com; Ynon Kreiz; toymaker (Barbie, Fisher-Price, Hot Wheels, Matchbox, American Girls). Acquired MEGA Brands, 4/30/2014.

McClatchy Co. (MNI): 2100 Q St., Sacramento, CA 95816; (916) 321-1855; www.mcclatchy.com; Craig I. Forman; newspaper publisher.

McDonald's Corp. (MCD): 2111 McDonald's Plz., Oak Brook, IL 60523; (630) 623-3000; www.mcdonalds.com; Steve Easterbrook; fast food.

McGraw-Hill Financial: see S&P Global, Inc.

McKesson Corp. (MCK): 1 Post St., San Francisco, CA 94104; (415) 983-8300; www.mckesson.com; John H. Hammergren; distrib. of drugs and toiletries; provides mgmt. software and services.

Medco Health Solutions, Inc.: see Express Scripts Holding Co.

Merck & Co., Inc. (MRK): 2000 Galloping Hill Rd., Kenilworth, NJ 07033; (908) 740-4000; www.merck.com; Kenneth C. Frazier; pharmaceuticals (Gardasil, Propecia, Singulair, Vytorin, Zocor). Acquired Idenix Pharmaceuticals, 8/5/2014; Cubist Pharmaceuticals, 1/21/2015. Sold consumer care business to Bayer, 10/1/2014.

Meredith Corp. (MDP): 1716 Locust St., Des Moines, IA 50309; (515) 284-3000; www.meredith.com; Tom Harty; magazine publishing (*Better Homes and Gardens*, *Eating Well*, *Parents*, *Family Circle*, *Every Day With Rachael Ray*, *FamilyFun*), book publishing, broadcasting, online media (allrecipes.com). Acquired publisher Time Inc. (*Time*, *People*, *Sports Illustrated*), 1/31/2018.

Merrill Lynch & Co., Inc.: see Bank of America Corp.

MetLife, Inc. (MET): 200 Park Ave., NY, NY 10166; (212) 578-2211; www.metlife.com; Steven A. Kandarian; insurance, financial services. Spun off U.S. retail business as Brighthouse Financial, 8/7/2017.

MGM Resorts Intl. (MGM): 3600 Las Vegas Blvd. S., Las Vegas, NV 89109; (702) 693-7120; www.mgmresorts.com; James J. Murren; hotel-casino operator (Mirage, New York-New York, Luxor, Bellagio, Circus Circus, Monte Carlo). Announced formation of joint venture hotel co. MGM Hakkasan Hospitality, 4/15/2014.

Microsoft Corp. (MSFT): One Microsoft Way, Redmond, WA 98052; (425) 882-8080; www.microsoft.com; Satya Nadella; software (Windows, Word, Excel); video game consoles (Xbox). Acquired Nokia's devices and services businesses, 4/25/2014; *Minecraft* developer Mojang, 11/6/2014; networking site LinkedIn, 12/8/2016. Announced plans to acquire code repository GitHub, 6/4/2018; AI start-up Bonsai, 6/20/2018.

Molson Coors Brewing Co. (TAP): 1801 California St. Ste. 4600, Denver, CO 80202; (303) 927-2337; www.molson coors.com; Mark Hunter; brewer. Acquired SABMiller's global Miller brands and majority stake in joint venture, MillerCoors, following Anheuser-Busch InBev's buyout of SABMiller, 10/11/2016.

Mondelēz International, Inc. (MDLZ): 100 Deforest Ave., East Hanover, NJ 07936; (855) 535-5648; www.mondelez international.com; Dirk Van de Put; global food mfr., including Nabisco (Oreo), Cadbury, Tang, Trident.

Monsanto Co.: 800 N. Lindbergh Blvd., St. Louis, MO 63167; (314) 694-1000; www.monsanto.com; Hugh Grant; agricultural biotechnology. Acquired by Bayer in $63-bil buyout, 6/7/2017.

Morgan Stanley (MS): 1585 Broadway, NY, NY 10036; (212) 761-4000; www.morgan stanley.com; James P. Gorman; diversified financial services.

Motorola Solutions, Inc. (MSI): 500 W Monroe St., Ste. 4400, Chicago, IL 60661; (847) 576-5000; www.motorolasolutions.com; Gregory Q. Brown; electronic equip. and components; communication devices. Sold enterprise business to Zebra Tech. Corp., 10/27/2014.

Nationwide Mutual Insurance Co.: One Nationwide Plz., Columbus, OH 43215; (614) 249-7111; www.nationwide.com; Stephen S. Rasmussen; property/casualty, life insurance; financial services.

Navistar Intl. Corp. (NAV): 2701 Navistar Dr., Lisle, IL 60532; (331) 332-5000; www.navistar.com; Troy Clarke; mfr. heavy-duty trucks, parts, school buses.

NBC Universal: 30 Rockefeller Plz., NY, NY 10112; (212) 664-4444; www.nbcuni.com; Stephen B. Burke; news/entertainment producer; TV and CATV stations (NBC, Bravo, USA, Telemundo); film production. Owned by Comcast and General Electric.

NCR Corp. (NCR): 864 Spring St. NW, Atlanta, GA 30308; (937) 445-1936; www.ncr.com; Michael Hayford; mfr. ATMs, retail technology, hardware and software; computer services and supplies.

Nestlé USA, Inc.: 800 N. Brand Blvd., Glendale, CA 91203; (818) 549-6000; www.nestleusa.com; Steve Presley; candy (Baby Ruth, Raisinets), beverages (Nestea, Ovaltine), food (Buitoni, Coffee-Mate), frozen foods (Stouffer's, Häagen-Dazs, Lean Cuisine), pet foods (Purina, Alpo, Friskies). Subsidiary of Nestlé SA in Switzerland, which announced plans to sell U.S. candy business to Italy's Ferrero, 1/16/2018.

Netflix, Inc. (NFLX): 100 Winchester Cir., Los Gatos, CA 95032; (408) 540-3700; www.netflix.com; Reed Hastings; online DVD rentals; streaming video.

New York Life Insurance Co.: 51 Madison Ave., NY, NY 10010; (212) 576-7000; www.newyorklife.com; Theodore A. Mathas; life insurance, annuities, mutual funds.

New York Times Co. (NYT): 620 8th Ave., NY, NY 10018; (212) 556-1234; www.nytco.com; A. G. Sulzberger; newspapers.

Newell Brands (NWL): 6655 Peachtree Dunwoody Rd., Atlanta, GA 30328; (770) 418-7000; www.newellbrands.com; Michael B. Polk; housewares (Rubbermaid, Calphalon); hair accessories (Goody); writing utensils (Parker, Sharpie, Paper Mate); juvenile prods. (Graco). Sold tools/hardware unit (Irwin, Lenox) to Stanley Black & Decker, 3/10/2017.

News Corp. (NWS): 1211 Ave. of the Americas, NY, NY 10036; (212) 416-3400; www.newscorp.com; K. Rupert Murdoch; publisher (HarperCollins; *Wall Street Journal, Barron's*); digital media (MarketWatch).

NextEra Energy, Inc. (NEE): 700 Universe Blvd., Juno Beach, FL 33408; (561) 694-4000; www.nexteraenergy.com; James L. Robo; electricity generation/distrib.

NIKE, Inc. (NKE): 1 Bowerman Dr., Beaverton, OR 97005; (503) 671-6453; www.nike.com; Mark G. Parker; athletic footwear and apparel mfr.

Nokia (NOK): Karaportti 3, Espoo 02610, Finland; +358 (0) 10 44 88 000; www.nokia.com; Rajeev Suri; telecom. equip., computer software. Acquired Alcatel-Lucent, 1/4/2016.

Nordstrom, Inc. (JWN): 1600 7th Ave., Ste. 2600, Seattle, WA 98101; (206) 628-2111; www.nordstrom.com; Blake W. Nordstrom; upscale dept. store chain.

Norfolk Southern Corp. (NSC): Three Commercial Pl., Norfolk, VA 23510; (855) 667-3655; www.nscorp.com; James A. Squires; railway operator; freight carrier.

Northrop Grumman Corp. (NOC): 2980 Fairview Park Dr., Falls Church, VA 22042; (703) 280-2900; www.northropgrumman.com; Wes Bush; defense contractor: aircraft, electronics, data systems, information systems, missiles.

Northwest Airlines Corp.: see Delta Air Lines, Inc.

Northwestern Mutual Life Insurance Co.: 720 E. Wisconsin Ave., Milwaukee, WI 53202; (414) 271-1444; www.northwesternmutual.com; John E. Schlifske; life insurance, investment prods. and services, annuities. Sold Russell Investments to London Stock Exchange Group, 12/3/2014.

Oath Inc.: 770 Broadway, New York, NY 10003; (212) 652 6400; www.oath.com; Tim Armstrong; digital media, social networking (AOL, Flickr, HuffPost, Mapquest, Yahoo); subsidiary of Verizon. Yahoo announced, 10/3/2017, all 3 bil of its user accounts were hacked in 2013.

Occidental Petroleum Corp. (OXY): Five Greenway Plz., Ste. 110, Houston, TX 77046; (713) 215-7000; www.oxy.com; Vicki A. Hollub; oil, natural gas, chemicals, plastics. Spun off California assets into separate co., 12/1/2014.

Office Depot, Inc. (ODP): 6600 N. Military Trl., Boca Raton, FL 33496; (561) 438-4800; www.officedepot.com; Gerry P. Smith; office supply retail stores. Terminated merger with Staples, Inc. following federal injunction, 5/16/2016.

Omnicom Group Inc. (OMC): 437 Madison Ave., NY, NY 10022; (212) 415-3600; www.omnicomgroup.com; John D. Wren; advertising, marketing, interactive/digital media.

Oracle Corp. (ORCL): 500 Oracle Pkwy., Redwood Shores, CA 94065; (650) 506-7000; www.oracle.com; Lawrence J. Ellison; database and file mgmt. software. Acquired Datalogix, 1/23/2015; CloudMonkey, 8/6/2015. Agreed to acquire DataScience.com, 5/16/2018.

Payless ShoeSource, Inc.: 3231 SE 6th Ave., Topeka, KS 66607; (785) 233-5171; www.collectivebrands.com; Martin R. Wade III; shoe mfr./retailer.

PepsiCo, Inc. (PEP): 700 Anderson Hill Rd., Purchase, NY 10577; (914) 253-2000; www.pepsico.com; Ramon Laguarta; soft drinks and other beverages (Pepsi-Cola, Mountain Dew, Gatorade, Tropicana), snacks and cereals (Fritos, Lay's, Ruffles, Quaker).

Pfizer, Inc. (PFE): 235 E. 42nd St., NY, NY 10017; (212) 733-2323; www.pfizer.com; Ian Read; biopharmaceuticals (Celebrex, Lipitor, Viagra, Zoloft); human and animal health care prods. Acquired Hospira, 9/3/2015. Terminated $160-bil merger with Allergan following new anti-inversion rules, 4/6/2016. Acquired Anacor Pharmaceuticals, 6/24/2016.

PG&E Corp. (PCG): 77 Beale St., 24th Fl., San Francisco, CA 94105; (415) 973-8200; www.pgecorp.com; Geisha J. Williams; operates Pacific Gas and Electric public utility.

Philip Morris Intl. Inc. (PM): 120 Park Ave., 7th Fl., NY, NY 10017; (917) 663-2000; www.pmi.com; André Calantzopoulos; intl. mfr. and distrib. of tobacco. (Altria spun off intl. Philip Morris operations in 2008 but owns Philip Morris brands in U.S.) Acquired Nicocigs, Ltd., 6/26/2014.

Phillips 66 Co. (PSX): P.O. Box 421959, Houston, TX 77242; (281) 293-6600; www.phillips66.com; Greg C. Garland; oil, gas refining and marketing.

Pitney Bowes Inc. (PBI): 3001 Summer St., Stamford, CT 06926; (203) 356-5000; www.pb.com; Marc B. Lautenbach; postage meters and mailing equip.

Post Holdings, Inc. (POST): 2503 S. Hanley Rd., St. Louis, MO 63144; (314) 644-7600; www.postfoods.com; Robert V. Vitale; ready-to-eat cereals. Acquired MOM Brands Co., 5/4/2015; Weetabix, 7/3/2017.

PPG Industries, Inc. (PPG): 1 PPG Pl., Pittsburgh, PA 15272; (412) 434-3131; www.ppg.com; Michael H. McGarry; glass prods., silicas, fiberglass, chemicals, sealants. Acquired Masterwork Paint Co., 7/1/2014; Comex, 11/5/2014.

Priceline Group Inc.: see Booking Holdings.

Procter & Gamble Co. (PG): 1 Procter & Gamble Plz., Cincinnati, OH 45202; (513) 983-1100; www.pg.com; David S. Taylor; soaps and detergents (Ivory, Cheer, Tide, Mr. Clean); toiletries (Crest, Scope, Head & Shoulders, Old Spice); pharmaceuticals (Pepto-Bismol, Vicks cough medicines); paper prods. (Charmin toilet tissues, Bounty towels), Tampax tampons; disposable diapers (Pampers, Luvs); Gillette razors. Sold Duracell to Berkshire Hathaway, 2/29/2016.

Prudential Financial, Inc. (PRU): 751 Broad St., Newark, NJ 07102; (973) 802-6000; www.prudential.com; John R. Strangfeld Jr.; insurance, financial services.

Publix Super Markets Inc.: 3300 Publix Corporate Pkwy., Lakeland, FL 33811; (863) 688-1188; www.publix.com; Todd Jones; supermarket chain.

PVH Corp. (PVH): 200 Madison Ave., NY, NY 10016; (212) 381-3500; www.pvh.com; Emanuel Chirico; apparel mfr., including licensed brands (Calvin Klein, IZOD, Tommy Hilfiger).

Qualcomm Inc. (QCOM): 5775 Morehouse Dr., San Diego, CA 92121; (858) 587-1121; www.qualcomm.com; Steve Mollenkopf; semiconductor, telecommunications equip. design. Merger with Singapore-based Broadcom blocked by White House over natl. security, 3/12/2018.

Quest Diagnostics Inc. (DGX): 500 Plaza Dr., Seacaucus, NJ 07094; (973) 520-2700; www.questdiagnostics.com; Stephen Rusckowski; leading clinical laboratory. Acquired Summit Health, 4/21/2014.

RadioShack Corp.: 300 RadioShack Cir., Fort Worth, TX 76102; (817) 415-3011; www.radioshack.com; Dene Rogers; consumer electronics retailer. Filed for Ch. 11 reorganization, 2/5/2015. General Wireless, Inc. acquired 1,743 remaining Radio Shack stores, 3/31/2015. Filed for second Ch. 11, 3/9/2017.

Ralcorp Holdings, Inc.: see ConAgra Foods, Inc.

Ralph Lauren Corp. (RL): 650 Madison Ave., NY, NY 10022; (212) 318-7000; www.ralphlauren.com; Patrice Louvet; men's and women's apparel, home furnishings, fragrances.

Raytheon Co. (RTN): 870 Winter St., Waltham, MA 02451; (781) 522-3000; www.raytheon.com; Thomas A. Kennedy; defense, communications systems. Acquired cybersecurity co. Websense, 5/29/2015.

Reader's Digest Assn., Inc.: see Trusted Media Brands, Inc.

Republic Services, Inc. (RSG): 18500 N. Allied Way, Phoenix, AZ 85054; (480) 627-2700; www.republicservices.com; Donald W. Slager; waste mgmt. co.

Restaurant Brands Intl. (QSR): 226 Wyecroft Rd., Oakville, ON L6K 3X7, Canada; (905) 845-6511; www.rbi.com; Daniel Schwartz; fast food restaurants (Burger King, Tim Hortons). Co. formed through acquisition of Tim Hortons, Inc. by former co. Burger King Worldwide, 12/12/2014. Acquired Popeyes, 3/27/2017.

Revlon, Inc. (REV): One New York Plaza, NY, NY 10004; (212) 527-4000; www.revlon.com; Debra G. Perelman; cosmetics, skin care. Acquired CBBeauty, 4/30/2015.

Reynolds American Inc.: 401 N. Main St., Winston-Salem, NC 27101; (336) 741-2000; www.reynoldsamerican.com; Ricardo Oberlander; cigarettes (Camel, Pall Mall, Doral, Newport), smokeless tobacco (Grizzly, Kodiak), e-cigarettes (VUSE). Acquired Lorillard, 6/12/2015. Bought out by British American Tobacco for $49.4 bil, which created world's largest tobacco co., 7/25/2017.

Rite Aid Corp. (RAD): 30 Hunter Ln., Camp Hill, PA 17011; (717) 761-2633; www.riteaid.com; John T. Standley; retail drugstores. Bought pharmacy-benefit manager EnvisionRx, 6/24/2015. Sold 1,932 stores and related assets to Walgreens Boots Alliance, 3/27/2018.

Rockwell Automation, Inc. (ROK): 1201 S. 2nd St., Milwaukee, WI 53204; (414) 382-2000; www.rockwellautomation.com; Blake Moret; industrial automation co. Acquired conveying system mfr. MagneMotion, 4/18/2016.

Ryder System, Inc. (R): 11690 NW 105th St., Miami, FL 33178; (305) 500-3726; www.ryder.com; Robert E. Sanchez; truck-leasing service.

SABMiller plc: see Anheuser-Busch InBev.

Safeway Inc.: 5918 Stoneridge Mall Rd., Pleasanton, CA 94588; (925) 467-3000; www.safeway.com; Bob Miller; supermarkets. Acquired by Albertson Holdings LLC, 1/30/2015.

S&P Global, Inc. (SPGI): 55 Water St., NY, NY 10041; (212) 438-1000; www.spglobal.com; Douglas L. Peterson; financial information, services (Standard & Poor's). Formerly McGraw-Hill Financial; renamed 4/27/16. Sold J.D. Power & Associates to XIO Group, 9/7/16.

Schering-Plough Corp.: see Merck & Co., Inc.

Schlumberger Limited Co. (SLB): 300 Schlumberger Dr., Sugar Land, TX 77478; (713) 375-3400; www.slb.com; Paal Kibsgaard; oil equip. and services.

Sears Holdings Corp. (SHLD): 3333 Beverly Rd., Hoffman Estates, IL 60179; (847) 286-2500; www.searsholdings.com; Edward S. Lampert; U.S. retailer. Spun off Land's End, Inc., 4/4/2014.

Shell Oil Co.: 1000 Main St., Ste. 1700, Houston, TX 77002; (713) 767-5300; www.shell.us; Ben van Beurden; integrated oil co.; subsidiary of Royal Dutch Shell.

Sherwin-Williams Co. (SHW): 101 W. Prospect Ave., Cleveland, OH 44115; (216) 566-2000; www.sherwin-williams.com; John G. Morikis; paint and varnish producer (Dutch Boy, Krylon, Minwax). Acquired Valspar Corp., 6/1/2017.

Simon Property Group, Inc. (SPG): 225 W. Washington St., Indianapolis, IN 46204;

(317) 636-1600; www.simon.com; David E. Simon; global real estate.

Sinclair Broadcast Group, Inc. (SBGI): 10706 Beaver Dam Rd., Hunt Valley, MD 21030; (410) 568-1500; www.sbgi.net; Christopher S. Ripley; TV broadcasting (192 stations); local news producer.

Sirius XM Holdings Inc. (SIRI): 1221 Ave. of the Americas, 36th Fl., NY, NY 10020; (212) 584-5100; www.siriusxm.com; James E. Meyer; satellite radio.

Smithfield Foods, Inc.: 200 Commerce St., Smithfield, VA 23430; (757) 365-3000; www.smithfieldfoods.com; Kenneth M. Sullivan; pork producer and processor. Subsidiary of China-based WH Group since 9/26/2013.

J. M. Smucker Co. (SJM): One Strawberry Ln., Orrville, OH 44667; (330) 682-3000; www.smuckers.com; Mark T. Smucker; leading producer of fruit spreads, peanut butter (Jif), oils (Crisco), coffee (Folgers), baking prods. (Pillsbury), pet foods (Milk-Bone, Kibbles 'n Bits).

Snap Inc. (SNAP): 63 Market St., Venice, CA 90291; (310) 399-3339; www.snap.com; Evan Spiegel; social media and tech co. (Bitmoji, Snapchat, Spectacles). Acquired personal emoji creator Bitstrips, 2016. IPO, 3/3/2017.

Sony Corp. of America: 25 Madison Ave., NY, NY 10016; (212) 833-6800; www.sony.com; Kenichiro Yoshida; U.S. subsidiary of Japan-based Sony Corp.; electronics, movies, music.

Southwest Airlines Co. (LUV): 2702 Love Field Dr., Dallas, TX 75235; (214) 792-4000; www.southwest.com; Gary C. Kelly; air transportation.

Sprint Nextel Corp. (S): 6200 Sprint Pkwy., Overland Park, KS 66251; (703) 433-4000; www.sprint.com; Michel Combes; wireless and long-distance telecommunications. Agreed to acquisition by T-Mobile, 4/29/2018.

Stanley Black & Decker, Inc. (SWK): 1000 Stanley Dr., New Britain, CT 06053; (860) 225-5111; www.stanleyblackanddecker.com; James M. Loree; hand and power tools (DeWalt, Bostitch), fastening prods. (Gripco, Masterfix). Acquired tools/hardware unit (Irwin, Lenox) from Newell Brands, 3/10/2017.

Staples, Inc.: 500 Staples Dr., Framingham, MA 01702; (508) 253-5000; www.staples.com; J. Alexander Douglas; office-supply retailer. Acquired PNI Digital Media, 7/11/2014. Terminated Office Depot acquisition following federal injunction, 5/16/2016.

Starbucks Corp. (SBUX): 2401 Utah Ave. S., Seattle, WA 98134; (206) 447-1575; www.starbucks.com; Kevin Johnson; coffee producer; world's leading specialty coffee retailer.

Starwood Hotels & Resorts Worldwide, Inc.: see Marriott International, Inc.

State Farm Mutual Automobile Ins. Co.: 1 State Farm Plz., Bloomington, IL 61710; (309) 766-2311; www.statefarm.com; Michael L. Tipsord; auto/homeowners insurance. Sold Canadian operations to Desjardins Group, 1/1/2015.

Sun Microsystems, Inc.: see Oracle Corp.

SuperValu Inc. (SVU): East View Innovation Ctr., 11840 Valley View Rd., Eden Prairie, MN 55344; (952) 828-4000; www.supervalu.com; Mark Gross; food retailer, wholesale distrib. (Cub Foods, Shoppers). Sold Save-A-Lot stores to Canada's Onex Corp., 12/6/2016.

Sysco Corp. (SYY): 1390 Enclave Pkwy., Houston, TX 77077; (281) 584-1390; www.sysco.com; Tom Bené; food-service distrib. Acquired European food distributor Brakes Group, 7/5/2016.

Tapestry, Inc. (TPR) (fmr. Coach Inc.): 10 Hudson Yards, NY, NY 10001; (212) 594-1850; www.tapestry.com; Victor Luis; luxury fashion brands (Coach, Kate Spade, Stuart Weitzman).

Target Corp. (TGT): 1000 Nicollet Mall, Minneapolis, MN 55403; (612) 304-6073; www.target.com; Brian Cornell; discount retailer.

TEGNA, Inc. (TGNA): 7950 Jones Branch Dr., McLean, VA 22107; (703) 873-6600;

www.tegna.com; Dave Lougee; network and cable TV, digital marketing, websites. Spun off from Gannett Co., 6/29/2015. Spun off cars.com into separate co., 6/1/2017.

Tenneco Inc. (TEN): 500 N. Field Dr., Lake Forest, IL 60045; (847) 482-5000; www.tenneco.com; Brian Kesseler; automotive parts (Monroe, Walker).

Tesla Motors, Inc. (TSLA): 3500 Deer Creek Rd., Palo Alto, CA 94304; (650) 681-5000; www.teslamotors.com; Elon Musk; electric vehicles and batteries. Acquired SolarCity, 11/21/2016.

Texas Instruments Inc. (TXN): 12500 TI Blvd., Dallas, TX 75243; (972) 995-2011; www.ti.com; Richard K. Templeton; processors, semiconductors, software, handheld calculators.

Textron Inc. (TXT): 40 Westminster St., Providence, RI 02903; (401) 421-2800; www.textron.com; Scott C. Donnelly; aircraft (Cessna, Bell, Beechcraft); pilot training; industrial, auto prods.; financial services.

3M Co. (MMM): 3M Center, St. Paul, MN 55144; (651) 733-1110; www.3m.com; Michael F. Roman; abrasives, adhesives, electrical, health care, cleaning (Scotch-Brite, O-Cel-O sponges, Scotchgard), printing, consumer prods. (Scotch Tape, Post-it).

TIAA: 730 Third Ave., NY, NY 10017; (401) 490-9000; www.tiaa.org; Roger W. Ferguson Jr.; financial services provider.

Time Inc.: see Meredith Corp.

TJX Cos., Inc. (TJX): 770 Cochituate Rd., Framingham, MA 01701; (508) 390-1000; www.tjx.com; Ernie Herrman; off-price apparel retailer (T.J. Maxx, Marshalls); home furnishing retailer (HomeGoods).

T-Mobile US, Inc. (TMUS): 12920 SE 38th St., Bellevue, WA 98006; (425) 378-4000; www.t-mobile.com; John J. Legere; wireless telecommunications. Agreed to acquire Sprint, 4/29/2018.

Toro Co. (TTC): 8111 Lyndale Ave. S, Bloomington, MN 55420; (952) 888-8801; www.thetorocompany.com; Richard M. Olson; lawn and turf maintenance prods. (Lawn-Boy), snow removal equip.; irrigation systems.

Toys "R" Us, Inc.: 1 Geoffrey Way, Wayne, NJ 07470; (973) 617-3500; www.toysrus.com; David A. Brandon; children's specialty retailer; filed for Ch.11 bankruptcy on 9/18/2017. Closed all 735 of its U.S. stores 6/29/2018.

The Travelers Companies, Inc. (TRV): 485 Lexington Ave., New York, NY 10017; (917) 778-6000; www.travelers.com; Alan D. Schnitzer; insurance.

Tribune Media Co. (TRCO): 435 N. Michigan Ave., Chicago, IL 60611; (312) 222-9100; www.tribunemedia.com; Peter M. Kern; broadcasting (incl. WGN and 41 other owned/operated television stations, radio), Tribune Studios.

Tronc, Inc. (TRNC): 435 N. Michigan Ave., Chicago, IL 60611; (312) 222-9100; www.tronc.com; Justin Dearborn; newspaper publisher (*Chicago Tribune*). Fmr. Tribune Publishing Co., spun off from Tribune Media, 8/4/2014. Acquired *NY Daily News*, 9/3/2017; sold *L.A. Times*, 6/18/2018.

Trusted Media Brands, Inc.: 750 Third Ave., 3rd Fl., NY, NY 10017; (914) 238-1000; www.tmbi.com; Bonnie Kintzer; publisher (*Taste of Home, Reader's Digest, Birds & Blooms*); marketer of books, music, video prods. Formerly Reader's Digest Assn., Inc., renamed 9/28/2015.

21st Century Fox, Inc. (FOXA): 1211 Ave. of the Americas, New York, NY 10036; (212) 852-7000; www.21cf.com; James Murdoch; TV and film production; broadcast and cable channels (Fox, FX, Fox Sports, National Geographic); media streaming (Hulu). Spun off from News Corp., 6/28/2013. Agreed to $71.3-bil buy-out by Walt Disney Co., 6/20/2018.

Twitter, Inc. (TWTR): 1355 Market St., Ste. 900, San Francisco, CA, 94103; (415) 222-9670; twitter.com; Jack Dorsey; microblogging/social networking services. Acquired video-streaming startup Periscope, 3/9/2015; employee/management feedback startup Peer, 4/7/2016.

Tyco Intl. Ltd.: see Johnson Controls Intl.

Tyson Foods, Inc. (TSN): 2200 W. Don Tyson Pkwy., Springdale, AR 72762; (479) 290-4000; www.tysonfoods.com; Tom Haynes; fresh and processed poultry; beef and pork prods. (Ball Park, Hillshire Farm, Jimmy Dean); Sara Lee prods.

Uber: 1455 Market St., 4th Fl., San Francisco, CA, 94103; (415) 986-2715; www.uber.com; Dara Khosrowshahi; mobile app-based taxi and food delivery services.

UBS Financial Services Inc.: 1285 Ave. of the Americas, NY, NY 10019; (212) 713-2000; www.ubs.com; Sergio P. Ermotti; financial services; subsidiary of Switzerland's UBS AG.

Unilever USA (UN/UL): 800 Sylvan Ave., Englewood Cliffs, NJ 07632; (201) 894-4000; www.unileverusa.com; Paul Polman; food (Hellmann's, Knorr, Lipton, Klondike), hygiene prods. (Dove, Q-tips, Vaseline). Subsidiary of Unilever NV (Neth.) and Unilever plc (UK). Acquired Dermalogica skincare, 8/3/2015; Murad Skincare, 9/1/2015.

Union Pacific Corp. (UNP): 1400 Douglas St., Omaha, NE, 68179; (402) 544-5000; www.up.com; Lance M. Fritz; one of the largest railroad freight cos. in U.S.

Unisys Corp. (UIS): 801 Lakeview Dr., Ste. 100, Blue Bell, PA 19422; (215) 986-4011; www.unisys.com; Peter A. Altabef; designs, manuf. IT systems; IT consulting.

United Continental Holdings, Inc. (UAL): 233 S. Wacker Dr., Chicago IL 60606; (312) 997-8000; www.united.com; Oscar Munoz; air transportation (United Airlines).

United Parcel Service, Inc. (UPS): 55 Glenlake Pkwy. NE, Atlanta, GA 30328; (404) 828-6000; www.ups.com; David Abney; shipping, logistics. Acquired UK-based Polar Speed, 2/11/2014.

United States Steel Corp. (X): 600 Grant St., Pittsburgh, PA 15219; (412) 433-1121; www.ussteel.com; David B. Burritt; steel, tin prods., resource mgmt.

United Technologies Corp. (UTX): 10 Farm Springs Rd., Farmington, CT 06032; (860) 728-7000; www.utc.com; Gregory J. Hayes; aerospace, industrial prods. and services (Carrier, Otis, Pratt & Whitney). Sold Sikorsky Aircraft to Lockheed Martin, 11/6/2015. Agreed to acquire avionics and aircraft interiors co. Rockwell Collins, 9/4/2017.

UnitedHealth Group Inc. (UNH): UHG Center, 9900 Bren Rd. E., Minnetonka, MN 55343; (952) 936-1300; www.unitedhealthgroup.com; David S. Wichmann; health insurance. Acquired benefit mgmt. co. Catamaran Corp., 7/23/2015.

U.S. Bancorp (USB): 800 Nicollet Mall, Minneapolis, MN, 55402; (651) 466-3000; www.usbank.com; Andrew Cecere; financial services.

Valero Energy Corp. (VLO): One Valero Way, San Antonio, TX 78249; (210) 345-2000; www.valero.com; Joe Gorder; fuel mfg. and marketing.

Verizon Communications Inc. (VZ): 1 Verizon Way, Basking Ridge, NJ 07920; (908) 559-5490; www.verizon.com; Hans Vestberg; telecom services; digital media. Sold CA, FL, TX wireline operations to Frontier Communications, 4/1/2016. Subsidiary Oath Inc. formed through acquisition of Yahoo's core internet business, 6/13/2017, merged with AOL (acquired 2015).

VF Corp. (VFC): 105 Corporate Center Blvd., Greensboro, NC 27408; (336) 424-6000; www.vfc.com; Steve Rendle; apparel (Lee, Wrangler, North Face, Timberland).

Viacom Inc. (VIA): 1515 Broadway, NY, NY 10036; (212) 258-6000; www.viacom.com; Robert Bakish; media networks (BET, Comedy Central, MTV, VH1, Nickelodeon); movies (Paramount).

Visa Inc. (V): 900 Metro Center Blvd., Foster City, CA 94404; (650) 432-3200; www.visa.com; Alfred F. Kelly Jr.; financial services. Acquired Visa Europe Ltd., 6/21/2016.

Visteon Corp. (VC): One Village Center Dr., Van Buren Twp., MI 48111; (734) 710-5000; www.visteon.com; Sachin Lawande; automotive parts mfr.

Walgreens Boots Alliance, Inc. (WBA): 108 Wilmot Rd., Deerfield, IL 60015; (847) 315-3700; www.walgreensbootsalliance.com; Stefano Pessina; retail drugstores, pharmaceutical wholesale/distrib. (Alliance Healthcare). Acquired 1,932 RiteAid stores and related assets, 3/27/2018.

Walmart Inc. (WMT): 702 SW 8th St., Bentonville, AR 72716; (479) 273-4000; www.walmartstores.com; Doug McMillon; discount stores, warehouse clubs (Sam's Club). Acquired online retailer Bonobos, 2017. Announced imminent closure of 63 Sam's Club stores, 1/11/2018. Agreed to acquire 77% stake in Indian retail giant Flipkart, 5/9/2018.

Warner Media Inc. (fmr. Time Warner): One Time Warner Ctr., NY, NY 10019; (212) 484-8000; www.warnermediagroup.com; John Stankey; TV and CATV (Cartoon Network, HBO, CNN, TBS, TNT), motion pictures (Warner Bros.), recordings. AOL and Time Warner completed the largest corporate merger in history in 2001; spun off AOL, 12/9/2009. Acquired by AT&T in $85.4-bil buyout, 6/14/2018, renamed WarnerMedia.

Washington Post Co.: see Graham Holdings Co.

Waste Management, Inc. (WM): 1001 Fannin St., Ste. 4000, Houston, TX 77002;

(713) 512-6200; www.wm.com; James C. Fish Jr.; waste, recycling. Acquired Deffenbaugh Disposal, 3/26/2015.

WellPoint, Inc.: see Anthem, Inc.

Wells Fargo & Co. (WFC): 420 Montgomery St., San Francisco, CA 94104; (866) 249-3302; www.wellsfargo.com; Timothy J. Sloan; financial services.

Wendy's Co. (WEN): 1 Dave Thomas Blvd., Dublin, OH 43017; (614) 764-3100; www.aboutwendys.com; Todd A. Penegor; fast food restaurants.

Western Union Co. (WU): 12500 E. Belford Ave., Englewood, CO 80112; (720) 332-1000; www.westernunion.com; Hikmet Ersek; money transfers, payment services.

WestRock Co. (WRK): 1000 Abernathy Rd. NE, Atlanta, GA 30328; (770) 448-2193; www.westrock.com; Steven C. Vorhees; packaging, shipping containers; chemicals. Formed through merger of Rock-Tenn Co. and MeadWestvaco Corp., 7/1/2015.

Weyerhaeuser Co. (WY): 220 Occidental Ave. S., Seattle, WA 98104; (206) 539-3000; www.weyerhaeuser.com; Doyle R. Simons; produces, distributes wood prods.; real estate development. Acquired rival Plumb Creek Timber Co., 2/19/2016.

Whirlpool Corp. (WHR): 2000 N. M-63, Benton Harbor, MI 49022; (269) 923-5000; www.whirlpoolcorp.com; Marc Bitzer; mfr.

of major home appliances (KitchenAid, Amana, Maytag). Acquired American Dryer Corp., 7/3/2015.

Whole Foods Market, Inc.: 550 Bowie St., Austin, TX 78703; (512) 477-4455; www.wholefoodsmarket.com; John P. Mackey; grocery stores specializing in natural/organic foods. Acquired by Amazon, 8/28/2017.

Winnebago Industries, Inc. (WGO): 605 W. Crystal Lake Rd., Forest City, IA 50436; (641) 585-3535; www.winnebagoind.com; Michael J. Happe; mfr. of motor homes, recreational vehicles (RVs).

Wm. Wrigley Jr. Co.: see Mars, Inc.

World Fuel Services Corp. (INT): 9800 NW 41st St., Ste. 400, Miami, FL 33178; (305) 428-8000; www.wfscorp.com; Michael J. Kasbar; marketer and financer of fuel to large-scale aviation and marine-related firms. Acquired Watson Petroleum Ltd., 3/10/2014.

Xerox Corp. (XRX): 201 Merritt 7, Norwalk, CT 06851; (203) 968-3000; www.xerox.com; John Visentin; printers, multifunction devices, document publishing technology and support. Acquired RSA Medical, 9/10/2015.

Yum! Brands, Inc. (YUM): 1441 Gardiner Ln., Louisville, KY 40213; (502) 874-8300; www.yum.com; Greg Creed; fast food restaurants (Pizza Hut, KFC, Taco Bell).

Labor Unions and Professional Organizations

Source: Bureau of Labor Statistics, U.S. Dept. of Labor; AFL-CIO; World Almanac research

= Member of Change to Win Federation, formed in 2005 by unions disaffiliated from AFL-CIO. * = Independent union or one not otherwise affiliated with Change to Win or AFL-CIO. All other unions listed are affiliated with AFL-CIO as of 2018. Year established is in parentheses.

Labor Unions

Air Line Pilots Assn. (ALPA) (1931): 58,129 members, 34 U.S. and Canadian airlines; (703) 689-2270; www.alpa.org

American Federation of Labor and Congress of Industrial Organizations (AFL-CIO) (1955): federation of 55 unions, 12,502,587 members; (202) 637-5000; www.aflcio.org

Automobile, Aerospace & Agricultural Implement Workers of America, International Union, United (UAW) (1935): 430,871 members, 600+ locals; (313) 926-5000; www.uaw.org

Bakery, Confectionery, Tobacco Workers, and Grain Millers International Union (BCTGM) (1886): 66,825 members, 143 locals; (301) 933-8600; www.bctgm.org

Bricklayers and Allied Craftworkers, International Union of (BAC) (1865): 73,411 members, 40+ locals; (202) 783-3788; www.bacweb.org

***Carpenters and Joiners of America, United Brotherhood of (UBC) (1881)**: 424,826 members, 600+ locals; (202) 546-6206; www.carpenters.org

#Change to Win Federation (2005): 3 unions, ex-affiliates of AFL-CIO, 3,289,606 members; (202) 721-0660; www.changetowin.org

Communications Workers of America (CWA) (1938): 646,759 members, 1,200 locals; (202) 434-1100; www.cwa-union.org

***Education Assn., Natl. (NEA) (1857)**: 2,987,077 members, 14,000+ affiliates; (202) 833-4000; www.nea.org

Electrical Workers, International Brotherhood of (IBEW) (1891): 671,076 members, 900 locals; (202) 833-7000; www.ibew.org

Engineers, International Union of Operating (IUOE) (1896): 380,596 members, 123 locals; (202) 429-9100; www.iuoe.org

#Farm Workers of America, United (UFW) (1962): 9,961 members; (661) 823-6151; www.ufw.org

Federal Employees, Natl. Federation of (NFFE; affiliated with IAM) (1917): 110,000 members, about 200 locals; (202) 216-4420; www.nffe.org

Fire Fighters, International Assn. of (IAFF) (1918): 309,343 members, 3,100+ locals; (202) 737-8484; www.iaff.org

Flight Attendants, Assn. of (AFA-CWA) (1945): 37,700 members, 20 airlines; merged with Communications Workers of

America in 2004; (202) 434-1300; www.afanet.org

Food and Commercial Workers International Union, United (UFCW) (1979): 1,255,743 members, 1,000+ locals; (202) 223-3111; www.ufcw.org

Glass, Molders, Pottery, Plastics and Allied Workers Intl. Union (GMP) (1842): 23,857 members, 250+ locals; (610) 565-5051; www.gmpiu.org

Government Employees, American Federation of (AFGE) (1932): 332,274 members, 1,100 locals; (202) 737-8700; www.afge.org

#Graphic Communications Conference (GCC/IBT) (1983): 62,148 members; merged with Teamsters in 2005; (202) 462-1400; www.gciu.org

Iron Workers, Intl. Assn. of Bridge, Structural, Ornamental, and Reinforcing (1896): 127,991 members, 200+ locals; (202) 383-4800; www.ironworkers.org

Laborers' International Union of North America (LiUNA) (1903): 576,475 members, 400 locals; (202) 737-8320; www.liuna.org

Letter Carriers, Natl. Assn. of (NALC) (1889): 293,862 members, 2,000+ locals; (202) 393-4695; www.nalc.org

#Locomotive Engineers and Trainmen, Brotherhood of (BLET) (1863): 56,770 members, 500+ locals; (216) 241-2630; www.ble-t.org

Longshoremen's Assn., Intl. (ILA) (1892): 32,727 members, approx. 200 locals; (212) 425-1200; www.ilaunion.org

Machinists and Aerospace Workers, International Assn. of (IAM) (1888): 564,953 members, affiliated with TCU in 2005; (301) 967-4500; www.goiam.org

#Maintenance of Way Employes, Division of the Intl. Brotherhood of Teamsters; Brotherhood of (BMWED) (1887): 34,962 members, 770 locals; merged with Teamsters in 2004; (248) 662-2660; www.bmwe.org (Note: In honor of tradition, the union maintains the variant spelling of "employes" in its logo.)

Mine Workers of America, United (UMWA) (1890): 63,202 members, 600 locals; (703) 291-2400; www.umwa.org

Musicians of the United States and Canada, American Federation of (AFM) (1896): 73,617 members, 240+ locals; (212) 869-1330; www.afm.org

NewsGuild—Communications Workers of America, The (TNG) (CWA) (1933):

25,000 members, 90 locals; (202) 434-7177; www.newsguild.org

***Nurses Assn., American (ANA) (1911)**: 195,884 members, 54 constituent state and territorial assns.; (301) 628-5000; www.nursingworld.org

Office and Professional Employees Intl. Union (OPEIU) (1945): 103,231 members, 200 locals; (800) 346-7348; www.opeiu.org

Painters and Allied Trades, International Union of (IUPAT) (1887): 110,027 members, 425 locals; (410) 564-5900; www.iupat.org

Plumbing and Pipe Fitting Industry of the U.S. and Canada, United Assn. of Journeymen and Apprentices of the (UA) (1889): 340,000 members, 300+ locals; (410) 269-2000; www.ua.org

***Police, Fraternal Order of (1915)**: 326,257 members, 2,200+ affiliates; (615) 399-0900; www.fop.net

Police Assns., International Union of (IUPA) (1979): 100,000+ members; (941) 487-2560; www.iupa.org

Postal Workers Union, American (APWU) (1971): 241,893 members, 900+ locals; (202) 842-4200; www.apwu.org

Roofers, Waterproofers and Allied Workers, United Union of (1906): 21,726 members; (202) 463-7663; www.unionroofers.com

***Rural Letter Carriers' Assn., Natl. (1903)**: 113,309 members, 50 state orgs.; (703) 684-5545; www.nrlca.org

***Security, Police, Fire Professionals of America, Intl. Union, (SPFPA) (1948)**: 17,555 members, 200 locals; (586) 772-7250; www.spfpa.org

#Service Employees International Union (SEIU) (1921): 1,919,358 members, 150+ locals; (202) 730-7000; www.seiu.org

Sheet Metal, Air, Rail, and Transportation Workers, Int. Assn. of (SMART) (2008, from merger of Sheet Metal Workers' Intl. Assn. and United Transportation Union): 202,402 members, 700 locals; (202) 662-0800; www.smart-union.org

State, County, and Municipal Employees, American Federation of (AFSCME) (1932): 1,299,644 members, 3,400 locals; (202) 429-1000; www.afscme.org

Steel, Paper and Forestry, Rubber, Manufacturing, Energy, Allied Industrial and Service Workers International Union, United (USW) (2005): 559,558 members, 1,800+ locals; formed from merger of United Steelworkers of America (USWA)

(1936) and Paper, Allied-Industrial, Chemical and Energy Workers (PACE) (1999); (412) 562-2400; www.usw.org

Teachers, American Federation of (AFT) (1916): 1,591,911 members, 3,000+ locals; (202) 879-4400; www.aft.org

#Teamsters, International Brotherhood of (IBT) (1903): 1,279,752 members, 475 locals; (202) 624-6800; www.teamster.org

Theatrical Stage Employees, Moving Picture Technicians, Artists and Allied Crafts of the U.S., Its Territories, and Canada, Intl. Alliance of (IATSE) (1893): 133,052 members, 375+ locals; (212) 730-1770; www.iatse.net

Transit Union, Amalgamated (ATU) (1892): 199,968 members, 270 locals; (301) 431-7100; www.atu.org

Transport Workers Union of America (TWU) (1934): 131,844 members, 100 locals; (202) 719-3900; www.twu.org

Transportation Communications Intl. Union (TCU) (1899): affiliated with IAM in 2005; see Machinists and Aerospace Workers.

***Treasury Employees Union, Natl.** (NTEU) (1938): 79,725 members, 200+ chapters; (202) 572-5500; www.nteu.org

UNITE HERE (UNITE, 1900; HERE, 1891; merged 2004): 280,389 members, 132 locals; (212) 265-7000; www.unitehere.org

#Workers United (affiliated with SEIU) (2009): 86,375 members

***Writers Guild of America, West** (1933): 23,245 members; (323) 951-4000; www.wga.org

Professional Organizations and Societies

Accountants, American Institute of Certified Public (1887): 410,000+ members; (888) 777-7077; www.aicpa.org

ACMP—The Chamber Music Network (1947): 2,500+ members; (212) 645-7424; www.acmp.net

Actuaries, Soc. of (1949): nearly 28,000 members; (847) 706-3500; www.soa.org

Administrative Professionals, Intl. Assn. of (1942): 24,000 members; (816) 891-6600; www.iaap-hq.org

Agricultural and Biological Engineers, American Soc. of (1907): 8,000+ members; (269) 429-0300; www.asabe.org

AIGA (fmr. American Institute of Graphic Arts) (1914): 25,000+ members; (212) 807-1990; www.aiga.org

Air & Waste Management Assn. (1907): 5,000+ members; (412) 232-3444; www.awma.org

AMSUS—The Society of the Federal Health Professionals (1891): nearly 8,000 members; (301) 897-8800; www.amsus.org

APICS—The Assn. for Operations Management (1957): 45,000+ members; (773) 867-1777; www.apics.org

Architects, American Institute of (1857): 90,000+ members; (202) 626-7300; www.aia.org

ASIS Intl. (fmr. Amer. Soc. for Industrial Security) (1955): 35,000 members; (703) 519-6200; www.asisonline.org

Astrologers, Inc., American Federation of (1938): 4,000 members; (480) 838-1751; www.astrologers.com

Astronomical Society, American (1899): 7,000 members; (202) 328-2010; www.aas.org

Authors Guild, The (1912): 9,000+ members; (212) 563-5904; www.authorsguild.org

Bankers of America, Independent Community (1930): nearly 5,700 banks; (202) 659-8111; www.icba.org

Bar Assn., American (1878): nearly 400,000 members; (312) 988-5000; www.abanet.org

Bar Assn., Federal (1920): 19,000+ members; (571) 481-9100; www.fedbar.org

Biochemistry and Molecular Biology, American Society for (1906): 12,000+ members; (240) 283-6600; www.asbmb.org

Broadcasters, Natl. Assn. of (1923): 8,300 members; (202) 429-5300; www.nab.org

Business Women's Assn., American (1949): 40,000 members; (800) 228-0007; www.abwa.org

Cartoonists Society, Natl. (1946): 500+ members; (407) 994-6703; www.reuben.org

Ceramic Society, American (1898): 11,000+ members; (240) 646-7054; www.ceramics.org

Chemical Society, American (1876): 150,000+ members; (202) 872-4600; www.chemistry.org

Chiefs of Police, Intl. Assn. of (1893): 20,000+ members; (703) 836-6767; www.theiacp.org

Chiropractic Assn., American (1963): 15,000+ members; (703) 276-8800; www.acatoday.org

Civil Engineers, American Soc. of (1852): 150,000+ members; (703) 295-6300; www.asce.org

College Admission Counseling, Natl. Assn. for (1937): nearly 16,000 members; (703) 836-2222; www.nacacnet.org

Communication Assn., Natl. (1914): 8,000+ members; (202) 464-4622; www.natcom.org

Composers, Authors & Publishers, American Soc. of (ASCAP) (1914): 670,000 members; (212) 621-6000; www.ascap.com

Computing Machinery, Assn. for (1947): 100,000+ members; (212) 626-0500; www.acm.org

Computing Professionals, Institute for the Certification of (1973): nearly 55,000 members; (847) 299-4227; www.iccp.org

Counseling Assn., American (1952): 50,000+ members; (800) 347-6647; www.counseling.org

Country Music Assn. (1958): 7,500+ members; (615) 244-2840; www.cmaworld.com

Dental Assn., American (1859): 161,000+ members; (312) 440-2500; www.ada.org

Directors Guild of America (1936): 16,000+ members; (310) 289-2000; www.dga.org

Electrical and Electronics Engineers, Institute of (1963): 423,000+ members; (732) 562-5501; www.ieee.org

Electronics Technicians, Intl. Soc. of Certified (1980): 50,000+ members; (817) 921-9101; www.iscet.org

Emergency Medical Technicians, Natl. Assn. of (1975): 65,000+ members; (601) 924-7744; www.naemt.org

Energy Engineers, Assn. of (1977): 18,000+ members; (770) 447-5083; www.aeecenter.org

Engineers, Natl. Society of Professional (1934): 31,000+ members; (703) 684-2800; www.nspe.org

Environmental Assessment Assn. (1972): 3,500 members; (877) 743-6806; www.eaa-assoc.org

Environmental Health Assn., Natl. (1937): 5,000 members; (303) 756-9090; www.neha.org

Family Physicians, American Academy of (1947): 131,400 members; (913) 906-6000; www.aafp.org

Farm Bureau Federation, American (1919): 6.2 mil+ members; (202) 406-3600; www.fb.org

Farmers Union, Natl. (1902): 200,000 families; (202) 554-1600; www.nfu.org

Financial Professionals, Assn. for (1979): 16,000+ members; (301) 907-2862; www.afponline.org

Financial Service Professionals, Soc. of (1928): 11,000 members; (610) 526-2500; www.financialpro.org

Fire Chiefs, Intl. Assn. of (1873): nearly 12,000 members; (703) 273-0911; www.iafc.org

Fire Protection Engineers, Soc. of (1950): 4,600+ members; (301) 718-2910; www.sfpe.org

Food Technologists, Institute of (1939): 17,600 members; (312) 782-8424; www.ift.org

Forensic Sciences, American Academy of (1948): 6,600+ members; (719) 636-1100; www.aafs.org

Funeral Directors Assn., Natl. (1882): 20,000+ members; (262) 789-1880; www.nfda.org

General Contractors of America, Associated (1918): 26,000+ cos.; (703) 548-3118; www.agc.org

Geographers, Assn. of American (1904): 10,000 members; (202) 234-1450; www.aag.org

Ground Water Assn., Natl. (1948): 12,000+ members; (614) 898-7791; www.ngwa.org

Heating, Refrigerating and Air-Conditioning Engineers, Inc., American Soc. of (1894): 56,000+ members; (404) 636-8400; www.ashrae.org

Home Builders, Natl. Assn. of (1942): 140,000+ members; (202) 266-8200; www.nahb.org

Human Resource Management, Soc. for (SHRM) (1948): 300,000 members; (703) 548-3440; www.shrm.org

Illustrators, Society of (1901): 1,000 members; (212) 838-2560; www.societyillustrators.org

Industrial Designers Society of America (1965): 3,200+ members; (703) 707-6000; www.idsa.org

Intelligence Officers, Assn. of Former (1975): 24 chap., 5,000+ members; (703) 790-0320; www.afio.com

Interior Designers, American Soc. of (1975): 25,000+ members; (202) 546-3480; www.asid.org

Jail Assn., American (1981): 4,000+ members; (301) 790-3930; www.aja.org

Journalists, Society of Professional (1909): nearly 7,500 members; (317) 927-8000; www.spj.org

Landscape Architects, American Society of (1899): 15,000+ members; (202) 898-2444; www.asla.org

Legal Administrators, Assn. of (1971): nearly 9,000 members; (847) 267-1252; www.alanet.org

Library Assn., American (1876): 59,000+ members; (800) 545-2433; www.ala.org

Lifesaving Assn., U.S. (1964): 12,600+ members; (866) 367-8752; www.usla.org

Logistics, Intl. Society of (SOLE) (1966): 3,000+ members; (301) 459-8446; www.sole.org

Magicians, Intl. Brotherhood of (1922): 10,000 members; (636) 724-2400; www.magician.org

Management Accountants, Inst. of (1919): 100,000+ members; (201) 573-9000; www.imanet.org

Management Assn., American (1923): 4,100 cos., 38,000 ind.; (877) 566-9441; www.amanet.org

Marketing Assn., American (1937): 30,000+ members; (312) 542-9000; www.ama.org

Master Brewers Assn. of the Americas (1887): 4,000+ members; (651) 454-7250; www.mbaa.com

Material and Process Engineering, Soc. for the Advancement of (1944): 5,000+ members; (626) 331-0616; www.sampe.org

Mechanical Engineers, American Soc. of (1880): 130,000+ members; (973) 882-1170; www.asme.org

Medical Assn., American (1847): 250,000 members; (800) 621-8335; www.ama-assn.org

Medical Library Assn. (1898): 4,000+ members; (312) 419-9094; www.mlanet.org

Motion Picture Arts & Sciences, Academy of (1927): 8,000+ members; (310) 247-3000; www.oscars.org

Motion Picture and Television Engineers, Soc. of (1916): 7,000+ members; (914) 761-1100; www.smpte.org

Mystery Writers of America (1945): 3,000+ members; (212) 888-8171; www.mysterywriters.org

NALS…the association for legal professionals (fmr. Natl. Assn. of Legal Secretaries) (1929): 6,000 members; (918) 582-5188; www.nals.org

Notaries, American Society of (1965): approx. 20,000 members; (850) 671-5164; www.notaries.org

Nursing, Natl. League for (1893): 40,000 members, 1,200 institutions; (800) 669-1656; www.nln.org

Operations Management, Assn. for (APICS) (1957): 45,000+ members, 300+ intl. partners; (773) 867-1777; www.apics.org

Optometric Assn., American (1898): 44,000+ members; (800) 365-2219; www.aoa.org

Organists, American Guild of (1896): 14,700 members; (212) 870-2310; www.agohq.org

Pharmacists Assn., American (1852): 62,000+ members; (202) 628-4410; www.pharmacist.com

Physical Therapy Assn., American (1921): 100,000+ members; (703) 684-2782; www.apta.org

Plastics Engineers, Society of (1942): 22,500+ members; (203) 775-0471; www.4spe.org

Police Assn.—United States Section, Intl. (1962): 10,000 members; (855) 241-9998; www.ipa-usa.org

Population Assn. of America (1930): 3,000 members; (301) 565-6710; www.populationassociation.org

Postmasters of the U.S., Natl. Assn. of (1898): 42,000+ members, 95 clubs; (703) 683-9027; www.napus.org

Press Club, Natl. (1908): 3,500+ members; (202) 662-7500; www.press.org

Professional Ball Players of America, Assn. of (1924): 100,900+ members; (714) 528-2012; www.apbpa.org

Professional Beauty Assn. (1904): 7,000+ indiv. members, 1,900+ cos.; (480) 281-0424; www.probeauty.org

Psychiatric Assn., American (1844): 37,800+ members; (703) 907-7300; www.psychiatry.org

Psychological Assn., American (1892): nearly 115,700+ members; (202) 336-5500; www.apa.org

Public Administration, American Soc. for (1939): 8,000 members; (202) 393-7878; www.aspanet.org

Public Health Assn., American (1872): 25,000+ members; (202) 777-2742; www.apha.org

Public Relations Soc. of America (1947): 30,000+ members; (212) 460-1400; www.prsa.org

Range Management, Society for (1948): 4,000+ members; (303) 986-3309; www.rangelands.org

Real Estate Appraisers, Natl. Assn. of (1966): 10,000+ members; (877) 743-6806; www.narea-assoc.org

Rehabilitation Assn., Natl. (1923): 5,600 members; (703) 836-0850; www.nationalrehab.org

Road & Transportation Builders Assn., American (1902): 6,000+ members; (202) 289-4434; www.artba.org

Safety Engineers, American Soc. of (1911): 38,000+ members; (847) 699-2929; www.asse.org

School Administrators, American Assn. of (1865): 13,000+ members; (703) 528-0700; www.aasa.org

Science Teachers Assn., Natl. (1944): 50,000 members; (703) 243-7100; www.nsta.org

Screen Actors Guild—American Federation of Television and Radio Artists (2012): 160,000 members; (855) 724-2387; www.sagaftra.org

Songwriters Guild of America (1931): 5,000+ members; (615) 742-9945; www.songwritersguild.com

Sportscasters Assn., American (1979): 500+ members; (212) 227-8080; www.americansportscastersonline.com

Surgeons, American College of (1913): 80,000+ members; (312) 202-5000; www.facs.org

Tax Administrators, Federation of (1937): (202) 624-5890; www.taxadmin.org

Teachers of English, Natl. Council of (1911): 25,000+ members; (217) 328-3870; www.ncte.org

Teachers of English to Speakers of Other Languages, Inc. (1966): 12,000+ members; (703) 836-0774; www.tesol.org

Teachers of French, American Assn. of (1927): nearly 10,000 members; (815) 310-0490; www.frenchteachers.org

Teachers of German, American Assn. of (1926): nearly 4,000 members; (856) 795-5553; www.aatg.org

Teachers of Mathematics, Natl. Council of (1920): 60,000 members; (703) 620-9840; www.nctm.org

Teachers of Spanish and Portuguese, American Assn. of (1917): 11,000+ members; (248) 960-2180; www.aatsp.org

Television Arts and Sciences, Natl. Academy of (1955): (212) 586-8424; www.emmyonline.org

Theological Library Assn., American (1946): 800+ members; (312) 454-5100; www.atla.com

Transportation Engineers, Inst. of (1930): 15,000+ members; (202) 785-0060; www.ite.org

Travel Agents, American Soc. of (1931): 12,000 members; (703) 739-2782; www.asta.org

Underwriters, Soc. of Chartered Property and Casualty (1944): nearly 20,000 members; (800) 932-2728; www.cpcusociety.org

University Women, American Assn. of (1881): 100,000+ members; (202) 785-7700; www.aauw.org

Veterinary Medical Assn., American (1863): 91,000+ members; (800) 248-2862; www.avma.org

Women in Communications, The Assn. for (1909): 1,100+ members; (417) 886-8606; www.womcom.org

Women Engineers, Society of (1950): 35,000 members; (877) 793-4636; societyofwomenengineers.swe.org

Women in Media, Alliance for (1951): nearly 10,000 members; (202) 750-3664; www.allwomeninmedia.org

Professional Sports Organizations

Source: World Almanac research

Major League Baseball

Office of the Commissioner, 245 Park Ave., 31st Fl., New York, NY 10167; (212) 931-7800; www.mlb.com

American League

Baltimore Orioles (1953): 333 W. Camden St., Baltimore, MD 21201; (410) 685-9800; www.orioles.com

Boston Red Sox (1901): 4 Jersey St., Boston, MA 02215; (617) 267-9440; www.redsox.com

Chicago White Sox (1900, as Chicago White Stockings): 333 W. 35th St., Chicago, IL 60616; (312) 674-1000; www.whitesox.com

Cleveland Indians (1901, as Cleveland Blues): 2401 Ontario St., Cleveland, OH 44115; (216) 420-4200; www.indians.com

Detroit Tigers (1901): 2100 Woodward Ave., Detroit, MI 48201; (313) 471-2000; www.tigers.com

Houston Astros (1962, as Houston Colt 45s): 501 Crawford St., Houston, TX 77002; (713) 259-8000; www.astros.com (National League, 1962-2012; AL West, 2013-present.)

Kansas City Royals (1969): One Royal Way, Kansas City, MO 64129; (816) 921-8000; www.royals.com

Los Angeles Angels of Anaheim (1961): 2000 Gene Autry Way, Anaheim, CA 92806; (714) 940-2000; www.angels.com

Minnesota Twins (1960): 1 Twins Way, Minneapolis, MN 55403; (612) 659-3400; www.twinsbaseball.com

New York Yankees (1903): One E. 161st St., Bronx, NY 10451; (718) 293-4300; www.yankees.com

Oakland Athletics (1901, as Philadelphia Athletics): 7000 Coliseum Way, Oakland, CA 94621; (510) 638-4900; www.athletics.com

Seattle Mariners (1977): P.O. Box 4100, Seattle, WA 98104; (206) 346-4000; www.mariners.com

Tampa Bay Rays (1995, as Tampa Bay Devil Rays): 1 Tropicana Field Dr., St. Petersburg, FL 33705; (727) 825-3137; www.raysbaseball.com

Texas Rangers (1960, as Washington Senators): 1000 Ballpark Way, Arlington, TX 76011; (817) 273-5222; www.texasrangers.com

Toronto Blue Jays (1976): One Blue Jays Way, Ste. 3200, Toronto, ON M5V 1J1, Canada; (416) 341-1000; www.bluejays.com

National League

Arizona Diamondbacks (1998): 401 E. Jefferson St., Phoenix, AZ 85004; (602) 462-6500; www.dbacks.com

Atlanta Braves (1876, as Boston Red Stockings): 755 Battery Ave., Atlanta, GA 30339; (404) 522-7630; www.braves.com

Chicago Cubs (1876, as Chicago White Stockings): 1060 W. Addison, Chicago, IL 60613; (773) 404-2827; www.cubs.com

Cincinnati Reds (1869, as Cincinnati Red Stockings): 100 Main St., Cincinnati, OH 45202; (513) 765-7000; www.reds.com

Colorado Rockies (1991): 2001 Blake St., Denver, CO 80205; (303) 292-0200; www.rockies.com

Los Angeles Dodgers (1890): 1000 Elysian Park Ave., Los Angeles, CA 90012; (323) 224-1500; www.dodgers.com

Miami Marlins (1991, as Florida Marlins): 501 Marlins Way, Miami, FL 33125; (305) 480-1300; www.marlins.com

Milwaukee Brewers (1970): One Brewers Way, Milwaukee, WI 53214; (414) 902-4400; www.brewers.com

New York Mets (1961): Citi Field, 120-01 Roosevelt Ave., Queens, NY 11368; (718) 507-6387; www.mets.com

Philadelphia Phillies (1883): One Citizens Bank Way, Philadelphia, PA 19148; (215) 463-6000; www.phillies.com

Pittsburgh Pirates (1887, as Pittsburgh Alleghenies): 115 Federal St., Pittsburgh, PA 15212; (412) 323-5000; www.pirates.com

St. Louis Cardinals (1892, as St. Louis Browns): 700 Clark St., St. Louis, MO 63102; (314) 345-9600; www.cardinals.com

San Diego Padres (1969): 100 Park Blvd., San Diego, CA 92101; (619) 795-5000; www.padres.com

San Francisco Giants (1883, as New York Gothams): 24 Willie Mays Plz., San Francisco, CA 94107; (415) 972-2000; www.sfgiants.com

Washington Nationals (1969, as Montréal Expos): 1500 South Capitol St., SE, Washington, DC 20003; (202) 675-6287; www.nationals.com

National Basketball Association

League Office, 645 Fifth Ave., New York, NY 10022; (212) 407-8000; www.nba.com

Atlanta Hawks (1949, as Tri-Cities Blackhawks): 101 Marietta St. NW, Ste. 1900, Atlanta, GA 30303; (866) 715-1500; www.nba.com/hawks

Boston Celtics (1946): 226 Causeway St., 4th Fl., Boston, MA 02114; (866) 423-5849; www.nba.com/celtics

Brooklyn Nets (1967, as New Jersey Americans): 15 MetroTech Ctr., 11th Fl., Brooklyn, NY 11201; (718) 933-3000; www.nba.com/nets

Charlotte Hornets (2004, as Charlotte Bobcats): 333 E. Trade St., Charlotte, NC 28202; (704) 688-8600; www.nba.com/hornets

Chicago Bulls (1966): 1901 W. Madison St., Chicago, IL 60612; (312) 455-4000; www.nba.com/bulls

Cleveland Cavaliers (1970): One Center Ct., Cleveland, OH 44115; (216) 420-2000; www.nba.com/cavaliers

Dallas Mavericks (1980): 2909 Taylor St., Dallas, TX 75226; (214) 747-6287; www.nba.com/mavericks

Denver Nuggets (1967, as Denver Rockets): 1000 Chopper Cir., Denver, CO 80204; (303) 405-1100; www.nba.com/nuggets

Detroit Pistons (1957): 66 Sibley St., Detroit, MI 48201; (248) 377-0100; www.nba.com/pistons

Golden State Warriors (1946, as Philadelphia Warriors): 1011 Broadway, Oakland, CA 94607; (510) 986-2200; www.nba.com/warriors

Houston Rockets (1967, as San Diego Rockets): 1510 Polk St., Houston, TX 77002; (713) 627-3865; www.nba.com/rockets

Indiana Pacers (1967): 125 S. Pennsylvania St., Indianapolis, IN 46204; (317) 917-2500; www.nba.com/pacers

Los Angeles Clippers (1970, as Buffalo Braves): 1111 S. Figueroa St., Ste. 1100, Los Angeles, CA 90015; (213) 742-7500; www.nba.com/clippers

Los Angeles Lakers (1947, as Minneapolis Lakers): 555 N. Nash St., El Segundo, CA 90245; (310) 426-6000; www.nba.com/lakers

Memphis Grizzlies (1995, as Vancouver Grizzlies): 191 Beale St., Memphis, TN 38103; (901) 888-4667; www.nba.com/grizzlies

Miami Heat (1988): 601 Biscayne Blvd., Miami, FL 33132; (786) 777-1000; www.nba.com/heat

Milwaukee Bucks (1968): 1111 Vel R. Phillips Ave., Milwaukee, WI 53203; (414) 227-0599; www.nba.com/bucks

Minnesota Timberwolves (1989): 600 Hennepin Ave., Ste. 300, Minneapolis, MN 55403; (612) 673-1600; www.nba.com/timberwolves

New Orleans Pelicans (1988, as Charlotte Hornets): 5800 Airline Dr., Metairie, LA 70003; (504) 593-4700; www.nba.com/pelicans

New York Knickerbockers (1946): Two Pennsylvania Plz., New York, NY 10121; (212) 465-6471; www.nba.com/knicks

Oklahoma City Thunder (1967, as Seattle SuperSonics): 208 Thunder Dr., Oklahoma City, OK 73102; (405) 208-4800; www.nba.com/thunder

Orlando Magic (1989): 8701 Maitland Summit Blvd., Orlando, FL 32810; (407) 916-2400; www.nba.com/magic

Philadelphia 76ers (1937, as Syracuse Nationals): 3601 S. Broad St., Philadelphia, PA 19148; (215) 339-7676; www.nba.com/sixers

Phoenix Suns (1968): 201 E. Jefferson St., Phoenix, AZ 85004; (602) 379-7900; www.nba.com/suns

Portland Trail Blazers (1970): One Center Ct., Ste. 200, Portland, OR 97227; (503) 234-9291; www.nba.com/blazers

Sacramento Kings (1945, as Rochester Royals): 500 David J. Stern Walk, Sacramento, CA 95814; (916) 928-0000; www.nba.com/kings

San Antonio Spurs (1967, as Dallas Chaparrals): One AT&T Center, San Antonio, TX 78219; (210) 444-5000; www.nba.com/spurs

Toronto Raptors (1995): 40 Bay St., Toronto, ON M5J 2X2, Canada; (416) 366-3865; www.nba.com/raptors

Utah Jazz (1974, as New Orleans Jazz): 301 W. South Temple, Salt Lake City, UT 84101; (801) 325-2500; www.nba.com/jazz

Washington Wizards (1961, as Chicago Packers): 601 F St. NW, Washington, DC 20004; (202) 661-5000; www.nba.com/wizards

National Hockey League

NHL Headquarters, 1185 Ave. of the Americas, 15th Fl., New York, NY 10036; (212) 789-2000; www.nhl.com

Anaheim Ducks (1993): 2695 E. Katella Ave., Anaheim, CA 92806; (877) 945-3946; ducks.nhl.com

Arizona Coyotes (1979, as Winnipeg Jets): 9400 W. Maryland Ave., Glendale, AZ 85305; (623) 772-3200; coyotes.nhl.com

Boston Bruins (1924): 100 Legends Way, Boston, MA 02114; (617) 624-1900; bruins.nhl.com

Buffalo Sabres (1970): One Seymour H. Knox III Plz., Buffalo, NY 14203; (716) 855-4100; sabres.nhl.com

Calgary Flames (1980): P.O. Box 1540, Station M, Calgary, AB T2P 3B9, Canada; (403) 777-2177; flames.nhl.com

Carolina Hurricanes (1972, as New England Whalers): 1400 Edwards Mill Rd., Raleigh, NC 27607; (919) 467-7825; hurricanes.nhl.com

Chicago Blackhawks (1926): 1901 W. Madison St., Chicago, IL 60612; (312) 455-7000; blackhawks.nhl.com

Colorado Avalanche (1972, as Quebec Nordiques): 1000 Chopper Cir., Denver, CO 80204; (303) 405-1100; avalanche.nhl.com

Columbus Blue Jackets (2000): 200 W. Nationwide Blvd., Suite Level, Columbus, OH 43215; (614) 246-4625; bluejackets.nhl.com

Dallas Stars (1967, as Minnesota North Stars): 2601 Ave. of the Stars, Frisco, TX 75034; (214) 387-5500; stars.nhl.com

Detroit Red Wings (1926, as Detroit Cougars): 66 Sibley St., Detroit, MI 48201; (313) 471-7444; redwings.nhl.com

Edmonton Oilers (1972, as Alberta Oilers): 300, 10214 104 Ave. NW, Edmonton, AB T5G 0H6, Canada; (780) 414-4000; oilers.nhl.com

Florida Panthers (1993): One Panther Pkwy., Sunrise, FL 33323; (954) 835-7000; panthers.nhl.com

Los Angeles Kings (1967): 1111 S. Figueroa St., Ste. 3100, Los Angeles, CA 90015; (213) 742-7100; kings.nhl.com

Minnesota Wild (2000): 317 Washington St., St. Paul, MN 55102; (651) 602-6000; wild.nhl.com

Montréal Canadiens (1917): 1909, avenue des Canadiens-de-Montréal, Montréal, QC H4B 5G0, Canada; (514) 932-2582; canadiens.nhl.com

Nashville Predators (1998): 501 Broadway, Nashville, TN 37203; (615) 770-2355; predators.nhl.com

New Jersey Devils (1974, as Kansas City Scouts): Prudential Center, 25 Lafayette St., Newark, NJ 07102; (973) 757-6100; devils.nhl.com

New York Islanders (1972): 168 39th St., 7th Fl., Brooklyn, NY 11231; (917) 618-6700; islanders.nhl.com

New York Rangers (1926): Two Pennsylvania Plz., New York, NY 10121; (212) 465-6000; rangers.nhl.com

Ottawa Senators (1992): 1000 Palladium Dr., Ottawa, ON K2V 1A5, Canada; (613) 599-0250; senators.nhl.com

Philadelphia Flyers (1967): 3601 S. Broad St., Philadelphia, PA 19148; (215) 336-3600; flyers.nhl.com

Pittsburgh Penguins (1967): 1001 5th Ave., Pittsburgh, PA 15219; (412) 642-1800; penguins.nhl.com

St. Louis Blues (1967): 1401 Clark Ave. at Brett Hull Way, St. Louis, MO 63103; (314) 622-2500; blues.nhl.com

San Jose Sharks (1991): 525 W. Santa Clara St., San Jose, CA 95113; (408) 287-7070; sharks.nhl.com

Tampa Bay Lightning (1992): 401 Channelside Dr., Tampa, FL 33602; (813) 301-6500; lightning.nhl.com

Toronto Maple Leafs (1919, as Toronto St. Pats): 40 Bay St., Ste. 400, Toronto, ON M5J 2X2, Canada; (416) 815-5700; mapleleafs.nhl.com

Vancouver Canucks (1946, joined NHL in 1970): 800 Griffiths Way, Vancouver, BC V6B 6G1, Canada; (604) 899-7400; canucks.nhl.com

Vegas Golden Knights (2017): 3780 S. Las Vegas Blvd., Las Vegas, NV 89158; (702) 645-4259; goldenknights.nhl.com

Washington Capitals (1974): 627 N. Glebe Rd., Ste. 850, Arlington, VA 22203; (202) 266-2200; capitals.nhl.com

Winnipeg Jets (1999, as Atlanta Thrashers): 345 Graham Ave., Winnipeg, MB R3C 5S6, Canada; (204) 987-7825; jets.nhl.com

National Football League

League Office, 345 Park Ave., New York, NY 10154; (212) 450-2000; www.nfl.com

Arizona Cardinals (1898, as Morgan Athletic Club): P.O. Box 888, Phoenix, AZ 85001; (602) 379-0101; www.azcardinals.com

Atlanta Falcons (1966): 4400 Falcon Pkwy., Flowery Branch, GA 30542; (770) 965-3115; www.atlantafalcons.com

Baltimore Ravens (1996): 1101 Russell St., Baltimore, MD 21230; (410) 261-7283; www.baltimoreravens.com

Buffalo Bills (1960): One Bills Dr., Orchard Park, NY 14127; (716) 648-1800; www.buffalobills.com

Carolina Panthers (1995): 800 S. Mint St., Charlotte, NC 28202; (704) 358-7000; www.panthers.com

Chicago Bears (1920, as Decatur Staleys): 1920 Football Dr., Lake Forest, IL 60045; (847) 615-2327; www.chicagobears.com

Cincinnati Bengals (1968): One Paul Brown Stadium, Cincinnati, OH 45202; (513) 621-3550; www.bengals.com

Cleveland Browns (1946): 76 Lou Groza Blvd., Berea, OH 44017; (440) 824-3434; www.clevelandbrowns.com

Dallas Cowboys (1960): One AT&T Way, Arlington, TX 76011; (817) 892-4000; www.dallascowboys.com

Denver Broncos (1960): 13655 Broncos Pkwy., Englewood, CO 80112; (303) 649-9000; www.denverbroncos.com

Detroit Lions (1930, as Portsmouth Spartans): 222 Republic Dr., Allen Park, MI 48101; (313) 262-2000; www.detroitlions.com

Green Bay Packers (1919): 1265 Lombardi Ave., Green Bay, WI 54304; (920) 569-7500; www.packers.com

Houston Texans (2002): Two NRG Park, Houston, TX 77054; (832) 667-2002; www.houstontexans.com

Indianapolis Colts (1953, as Baltimore Colts): 7001 W. 56th St., Indianapolis, IN 46254; (317) 297-2658; www.colts.com

Jacksonville Jaguars (1995): One EverBank Field Dr., Jacksonville, FL 32202; (904) 633-2000; www.jaguars.com

Kansas City Chiefs (1960, as Dallas Texans): One Arrowhead Dr., Kansas City, MO 64129; (816) 920-9300; www.kcchiefs.com

Los Angeles Chargers (1960): 18400 Avalon Blvd., Carson, CA 92626; (714) 540-7100; www.chargers.com

Los Angeles Rams (1937, as Cleveland Rams): 29899 Agoura Rd., Agoura Hills, CA 91301; (310) 277-4700; www.therams.com

Miami Dolphins (1966): 347 Don Shula Dr., Miami Gardens, FL 33056; (305) 943-8000; www.miamidolphins.com

Minnesota Vikings (1961): 9520 Viking Dr., Eden Prairie, MN 55344; (952) 828-6500; www.vikings.com

New England Patriots (1960): One Patriot Pl., Foxboro, MA 02035; (508) 543-8200; www.patriots.com

New Orleans Saints (1967): 5800 Airline Dr., Metairie, LA 70003; (504) 733-0255; www.neworleanssaints.com

New York Giants (1925): 1925 Giants Dr., E. Rutherford, NJ 07073; (201) 935-8111; www.giants.com

New York Jets (1960, as New York Titans): One Jets Dr., Florham Park, NJ 07932; (800) 469-5387; www.newyorkjets.com

Oakland Raiders (1960): 1220 Harbor Bay Pkwy., Alameda, CA 94502; (510) 864-5000; www.raiders.com

Philadelphia Eagles (1933): One NovaCare Way, Philadelphia, PA 19145; (215) 463-2500; www.philadelphiaeagles.com

Pittsburgh Steelers (1933): 3400 S. Water St., Pittsburgh, PA 15203; (412) 432-7800; www.steelers.com

San Francisco 49ers (1946): 4949 Centennial Blvd., Santa Clara, CA 95054; (408) 562-4949; www.49ers.com

Seattle Seahawks (1976): 12 Seahawks Way, Renton, WA 98056; (888) 635-4295; www.seahawks.com

Tampa Bay Buccaneers (1976): One Buccaneer Pl., Tampa, FL 33607; (813) 870-2700; www.buccaneers.com

Tennessee Titans (1960, as Houston Oilers): 460 Great Circle Rd., Nashville, TN 37228; (615) 565-4000; www.titansonline.com

Washington Redskins (1932, as Boston Braves): 21300 Redskin Park Dr., Ashburn, VA 20147; (703) 726-7000; www.redskins.com

Health Organizations

Source: World Almanac research

Entries are roughly alphabetized by the basic condition addressed or organization name. Year established is in parentheses. Always check with a physician before any new health-related undertaking.

Al-Anon Family Groups (1951): (757) 563-1600; al-anon.org

Alcoholics Anonymous (1935): (212) 870-3400; www.aa.org

Alcoholism and Drug Dependence, Inc., Natl. Council on (1944): (212) 269-7797; www.ncadd.org

Aging, Natl. Institute on (1974): (800) 222-2225; www.nia.nih.gov

Aging's Eldercare Locator, Admin. on (1991): (800) 677-1116; www.eldercare.gov

AIDSinfo: (800) 448-0440; www.aidsinfo. nih.gov

Allergy, Asthma and Immunology, American Academy of (1943): (414) 272-6071; www.aaaai.org

ALS Assn. [Lou Gehrig's disease] (1985): (202) 407-8580; www.alsa.org

Alzheimer's Assn. (1979): (800) 272-3900; www.alz.org

Anorexia Nervosa and Associated Disorders, Natl. Assn. of (1976): (630) 577-1333; www.anad.org

Arc of the United States, The [intellectual/developmental disabilities] (1950): (800) 433-5255; www.thearc.org

Arthritis Foundation (1948): (800) 283-7800; www.arthritis.org

Arthritis and Musculoskeletal and Skin Diseases, Natl. Institute of (1986): (877) 226-4267; www.niams.nih.gov

Asthma and Allergy Foundation of America (1953): (800) 727-8462; www.aafa.org

Autism Society (1965): (800) 328-8476; www.autism-society.org

Blind, American Council of the (1961): (202) 467-5081; (800) 424-8666; www.acb.org

Blind, Natl. Federation of the (1940): (410) 659-9314; www.nfb.org

Blindness, Foundation Fighting (1971): (800) 683-5555; www.blindness.org

Blindness, Prevent (1908): (800) 331-2020; www.preventblindness.org

Brain Tumor Society, Natl. (2008): (617) 924-9997; www.braintumor.org

Breast Cancer Diagnosis, After (ABCD) (1999): (414) 977-1780; (800) 977-4121; www.abcdbreastcancersupport.org

Cancer Institute's Cancer Information Service, Natl. (1975): (800) 422-6237; www.cancer.gov/contact/contact-center

Cancer Society, American (1913): (800) 227-2345; www.cancer.org

Centers for Disease Control and Prevention (CDC) (1946): (800) 232-4636; www.cdc.gov

Cerebral Palsy, United (1949): (202) 776-0406; (800) 872-5827; www.ucp.org

Child Abuse and Family Violence, Natl. Council on (1984): (202) 429-6695; www.nccafv.org

Childhelp Natl. Child Abuse Hotline (1959): (800) 422-4453; www.childhelp.org

Children, Natl. Center for Missing and Exploited (1984): (703) 224-2150; (800) 843-5678; www.missingkids.com

Children's Tumor Foundation (1978): (212) 344-6633; (800) 323-7938; www.ctf.org

Chronic Pain Assn., American (1980): (800) 533-3231; www.theacpa.org

Continence, Natl. Assn. for (1982): (843) 419-5307; (800) 252-3337; www.nafc.org

Cooley's Anemia Foundation (1954): (800) 522-7222; www.thalassemia.org

Crohn's and Colitis Foundation of America (1967): (800) 932-2423; www.ccfa.org

Cystic Fibrosis Foundation (1955): (800) 344-4823 or (301) 951-4422; www.cff.org

Deaf, Natl. Assn. of the (1880): (301) 587-1788, TTY (301) 587-1789; www.nad.org

Depression and Bipolar Support Alliance (1985): (800) 826-3632; www.dbsalliance.org

Diabetes Assn., American (1940): (800) 342-2383; www.diabetes.org

Diabetes and Digestive and Kidney Diseases, Natl. Institute of (1950): (301) 496-3583; www.kidney.niddk.nih.gov

Dial-A-Hearing Screening Test: (800) 222-EARS (222-3277)

Domestic Violence Hotline, Natl. (1996): (800) 799-7233, TTY (800) 787-3224; www.thehotline.org

Down Syndrome Congress, Natl. (1973): (800) 232-6372; www.ndsccenter.org

Down Syndrome Society, Natl. (1979): (800) 221-4602; www.ndss.org

Dyslexia Assn., Intl. (1949): (410) 296-0232; dyslexiaida.org

Easterseals [special needs] (1919): (800) 221-6827; www.easterseals.com

Endometriosis Assn. (1980): (414) 355-2200; www.endometriosisassn.org

Epilepsy Foundation (1967): (800) 332-1000; www.epilepsy.com

Fat Acceptance, Natl. Assn. to Advance (1969): (916) 558-6880; www.naafa.org

First Candle [sudden infant death syndrome] (1987): (800) 221-7437; www.sidsalliance.org

FoodSafety.gov: Food: (888) 723-3366; Meat, poultry, eggs: (888) 674-6854; Illness or food poisoning: (800) 232-4636 (CDC)

Gamblers Anonymous (1957): (626) 960-3500; www.gamblersanonymous.org

Geriatrics Society, American (1942): (212) 308-1414; www.americangeriatrics.org

Headache Foundation, Natl. (1970): (888) 643-5552; www.headaches.org

HealthyWomen (1988): (877) 986-9472; www.healthywomen.org

Hearing Society, Intl. (1951): (734) 522-7200; www.ihsinfo.org

Heart Assn., American (1924): (800) 242-8721; www.heart.org

Hearts, Inc., Mended (1951): (888) 432-7899; www.mendedhearts.org

Hospice Foundation of America (1982): (800) 854-3402; www.hospicefoundation. org

Hospice Intl., Children's (1983): (703) 684-0330; www.chionline.org

Hospital Assn., American (1899): (312) 422-3000; (800) 424-4301; www.aha.org

Huntington's Disease Society of America (1967): (800) 345-4372; www.hdsa.org

JDRF (fmr. Juvenile Diabetes Research Foundation) (1970): (800) 533-2873; www.jdrf.org

Kidney Foundation, Natl. (1950): (800) 622-9010; www.kidney.org

Kidney Fund, American (1971): (866) 300-2900; www.kidneyfund.org

La Leche League Intl. [breastfeeding] (1957): (800) 525-3243; www.llli.org

Leukemia and Lymphoma Society (1949): (800) 955-4572; www.lls.org

Lighthouse Guild [visual impairments] (1914): (800) 284-4422; www.napvi.org

Liver Foundation, American (1976): (800) 465-4837; www.liverfoundation.org

Living Bank [organ donation] (1968): (713) 961-9431; (800) 528-2971; www.livingbank.org

Lung Assn., American (1904): (800) 586-4872; www.lung.org

Lung Line (1983): (800) 222-5864; www.nationaljewish.org/about/contact/lung-line/

Lupus Foundation of America, Inc. (1977): (202) 349-1155; (800) 558-0121; www.lupus.org

March of Dimes [babies' health] (1938): (914) 997-4488; www.marchofdimes.org

Marfan Foundation. (1981): (800) 8-MARFAN (862-7326); www.marfan.org

Mayo Clinic (1889): (507) 284-2511; www.mayoclinic.org

ME/CFS Initiative, Solve [myalgic encephalomyelitis/chronic fatigue syndrome] (1987): (704) 364-0016; solvecfs.org

Mental Health, Natl. Institute of (1946): (866) 615-6464; www.nimh.nih.gov

Mental Health America (1909): (703) 684-7722; (800) 969-6642; www.nmha.org

Mental Illness, Natl. Alliance on (1979): (800) 950-6264; www.nami.org

Multiple Sclerosis Society, Natl. (1946): (800) 344-4867; www.nationalmssociety.org

Muscular Dystrophy Assn. (1950): (800) 572-1717; www.mda.org

Myeloma Foundation, Intl. (1990): (800) 452-2873; www.myeloma.org

Narcotics Anonymous (1953): (818) 773-9999; www.na.org

Natl. Health Council (1920): (202) 785-3910; www.nationalhealthcouncil.org

Natl. Health Information Center (1979): (240) 453-8280; www.health.gov/NHIC/

Natl. Institutes of Health (NIH) (1887): (301) 496-4000; www.nih.gov

Neurological Disorders and Stroke, Natl. Institute of (1950): (301) 496-5751; (800) 352- 9424; www.ninds.nih.gov

Organ Sharing, United Network for (1984): (804) 782-4800; (888) 894-6361; www.unos.org

Osteoporosis Foundation, Natl. (1984): (800) 231-4222; www.nof.org

Overeaters Anonymous (1960): (505) 891-2664; www.oa.org

Parkinson's Foundation (1957): (800) 473-4636; www.parkinson.org

Pediatrics, American Academy of (1930): (800) 433-9016; www.aap.org

Phoenix House [substance abuse] (1967): (888) 671-9392; www.phoenixhouse.org

Planned Parenthood Federation of America, Inc. (1916): (800) 230-7526; www.plannedparenthood.org

Plastic Surgeons, American Society of (1931): (800) 514-5058; www.plastic surgery.org

Post-Polio Health Intl. (1960): (314) 534-0475; www.post-polio.org

Psoriasis Foundation, Natl. (1966): (800) 723-9166; www.psoriasis.org

RAINN (Rape, Abuse, & Incest Natl. Network) (1994): (800) 656-4673; www.rainn. org

Rare Disorders, Natl. Org. for (1983): (203) 744-0100; www.rarediseases.org

Rehabilitation Information Center, Natl. (1977): (800) 346-2742, TTY (301) 459-5984; www.naric.com

Reye's Syndrome Foundation, Natl. (1974): (800) 233-7393; www.reyessyndrome.org

Runaway Safeline, Natl. (1971): (800) 786-2929; www.1800runaway.org

Scleroderma Foundation (1989): (978) 463-5843; (800) 722-4673; www. scleroderma.org

Sexual Health Assn., American (1914): (919) 361-8400; www.ashastd.org

Sickle Cell Disease Assn. of America (1971): (410) 528-1555; (800) 421-8453; www.sicklecelldisease.org

Sjögren's Syndrome Foundation (1983): (800) 475-6473; www.sjogrens.org

Speech-Language-Hearing Assn., American (1925): (800) 638-8255; TTY (301) 296-5650; www.asha.org

Spinal Assn., United (1946): (718) 803-3782; www.spinalcord.org

Stroke Assn., Natl. (1984): (800) 787-6537; www.stroke.org

Stuttering Assn., Natl. (1977): (212) 944-4050; (800) 937-8888; www.nsastutter.org

Stuttering Foundation of America (1947): (800) 992-9392; www.stutteringhelp.org

Substance Abuse and Mental Health Services Admin.: (877) 726-4727; www. samhsa.gov

Sudden Infant Death Syndrome Institute, Amer. (1983): (239) 431-5425; www.sids.org

Suicide Prevention Lifeline, Natl. (2004): (800) 273-TALK (8255); www.suicidepreventionlifeline.org

Therapy Dogs Intl. (1976): (973) 252-9800; www.tdi-dog.org

Tourette Assn. of America (fmr. Tourette Syndrome Assn.) (1972): (718) 224-2999; www.tourette.org

Tuberous Sclerosis Alliance (1974): (301) 562-9890; (800) 225-6872; www.tsalliance.org

Urological Assn., American (1902): (866) 746-4282; www.auanet.org

Women's Health Network, Natl. (1975): (202) 682-2640; www.nwhn.org

UNITED STATES FACTS

Superlative U.S. Statistics

Source: U.S. Geological Survey, U.S. Dept. of the Interior; U.S. Census Bureau, U.S. Dept. of Commerce; World Almanac research

Superlative Statistics for the 50 States

Total area for 50 states and Washington, DC		3,796,742 sq mi
Land area for 50 states and Washington, DC		3,531,905 sq mi
Water area for 50 states and Washington, DC		264,837 sq mi
Largest state	Alaska	665,384 sq mi
Smallest state	Rhode Island	1,545 sq mi
Largest county (excluding Alaska)	San Bernardino County, CA	20,105 sq mi
Smallest county	Arlington County, VA[1]	26 sq mi
Largest incorporated city (by area, pop. 1,000+)	Sitka, AK	4,815 sq mi
Northernmost city	Utqiagvik (formerly Barrow), AK	71°17′ N
Northernmost point	Point Barrow, AK	71°23′ N
Southernmost city	Hilo, HI	19°43′ N
Southernmost settlement	Naalehu, HI	19°03′ N
Southernmost point	Ka Lae (South Cape), island of Hawaii	18°55′ N (155°41′ W)
Easternmost city	Eastport, ME	66°59′24′′ W
Easternmost settlement[2]	Attu Station, AK	173°11′ E
Easternmost point[2]	Pochnoi Point, Semisopochnoi Island, AK	179°52′ E
Westernmost city	Adak (formerly Adak Station), AK	173°11′ W
Westernmost settlement	Adak (formerly Adak Station), AK	173°11′ W
Westernmost point	Amatignak Island, AK	179°09′ W
Highest incorporated city	Leadville, CO	10,158 ft
Lowest settlement	Bombay Beach, CA	−208 ft
Highest point on Atlantic coast	Cadillac Mountain, Mount Desert Island, ME	1,530 ft
Oldest national park	Yellowstone National Park (1872), WY-MT-ID	2,219,791 acres
Largest national park	Wrangell-St. Elias, AK	8,323,146 acres
Longest river system	Mississippi-Missouri-Red Rock	3,710 mi
Highest mountain	Denali (formerly Mt. McKinley), AK	20,310 ft
Lowest point	Death Valley, CA	−282 ft
Deepest lake	Crater Lake, OR	1,949 ft
Rainiest spot	Mount Waialeale, Kauai, HI	annual avg. rainfall 422 in.
Largest gorge	Grand Canyon, Colorado River, AZ	277 mi long, 600 ft to 18 mi wide, 1 mi deep
Deepest gorge	Hells Canyon, Snake River, OR-ID	7,900 ft
Largest dam	New Cornelia Tailings, Ten Mile Wash, AZ[3]	274,026,000 cu yds material used
Tallest building	One World Trade Center, New York, NY	1,782 ft
Largest building	Boeing Everett Production Facility, Everett, WA	472,000,000 cu ft; covers 98 acres
Largest office building	Pentagon, Arlington, VA	77,015,000 cu ft; covers 29 acres
Tallest supported structure	KVLY-TV Tower, Blanchard, ND	2,063 ft
Tallest freestanding tower	Stratosphere Tower, Las Vegas, NV	1,149 ft
Longest bridge span	Verrazano-Narrows Bridge, New York, NY	4,260 ft
Highest bridge	Royal Gorge Bridge, Cañon City, CO	1,053 ft above water
Deepest well (onshore)	Bertha Rogers No. 1 (inactive gas well), Washita County, OK	31,441 ft

Superlative Statistics for the 48 Contiguous States

Total area for 48 states and Washington, DC		3,129,611 sq mi
Land area for 48 states and Washington, DC		2,958,868 sq mi
Water area for 48 states and Washington, DC		170,743 sq mi
Largest state	Texas	268,596 sq mi
Northernmost city	Bellingham, WA	48°46′ N
Northernmost settlement	Angle Inlet, MN	49°20′ N
Northernmost point	Northwest Angle, MN	49°21′ N
Southernmost city	Key West, FL	24°33′ N
Southernmost mainland city	Florida City, FL	25°27′ N
Southernmost point	Ballast Key, FL	24°31′ N
Easternmost settlement	Lubec, ME	66°58′49′′ W
Easternmost point	West Quoddy Head, ME	66°57′ W
Westernmost town	La Push, WA	124°38′ W
Westernmost point	Bodelteh Islands, WA	124°46′ W
Highest mountain	Mount Whitney, CA	14,505 ft

(1) Smallest county by land area is Kalawao County, Hawaii, at 12 sq mi; its total area (including water) is 53 sq mi. Superlative shown is for smallest total area. (2) As measured if the prime meridian and 180° longitude are considered east-west boundaries. (3) Privately owned industrial dam composed of tailings, remnants of a mining process.

Highest and Lowest Elevations in U.S. States and Territories

Source: U.S. Geological Survey, U.S. Dept. of the Interior
(negative sign indicates below sea level)

State/territory	Highest point Name	County	Elev. (ft)	Lowest point Name	County	Elev. (ft)
Alabama	Cheaha Mountain	Cleburne	2,413	Gulf of Mexico		Sea level
Alaska	Denali (fmr. Mt. McKinley)	Denali	20,310	Pacific Ocean		Sea level
American Samoa	Lata Mountain	Tau Island	3,160	Pacific Ocean		Sea level
Arizona	Humphreys Peak	Coconino	12,637	Colorado R.	Yuma	70
Arkansas	Magazine Mountain	Logan	2,753	Ouachita R.	Ashley-Union	55
California	Mount Whitney	Inyo-Tulare	14,505	Death Valley	Inyo	−282
Colorado	Mount Elbert	Lake	14,440	Arikaree R.	Yuma	3,315
Connecticut	S. slope of Mt. Frissell (peak in MA)	Litchfield	2,380	Long Island Sound		Sea level
Delaware	Nr. Ebright Azimuth	New Castle	450	Atlantic Ocean		Sea level
Dist. of Columbia	Fort Reno Park	NW quadrant	409	Potomac R.		1
Florida	Britton Hill	Walton	345	Atlantic Ocean		Sea level
Georgia	Brasstown Bald	Towns-Union	4,840	Atlantic Ocean		Sea level
Guam	Mount Lamlam	Agat District	1,332	Pacific Ocean		Sea level
Hawaii	Pu'u Wekiu, Mauna Kea	Hawaii	13,796	Pacific Ocean		Sea level
Idaho	Borah Peak	Custer	12,668	Snake R.	Nez Perce	710
Illinois	Charles Mound	Jo Daviess	1,235	Mississippi R.	Alexander	279
Indiana	Hoosier Hill	Wayne	1,257	Ohio R.	Posey	320
Iowa	Hawkeye Point	Osceola	1,670	Mississippi R.	Lee	480
Kansas	Mount Sunflower	Wallace	4,039	Verdigris R.	Montgomery	679
Kentucky	Black Mountain	Harlan	4,139	Mississippi R.	Fulton	257
Louisiana	Driskill Mountain	Bienville	535	New Orleans	Orleans	−8
Maine	Mount Katahdin	Piscataquis	5,269	Atlantic Ocean		Sea level
Maryland	Hoye Crest	Garrett	3,360	Bloody Point Hole, Chesapeake Bay	Queen Anne	−174
Massachusetts	Mount Greylock	Berkshire	3,491	Atlantic Ocean		Sea level
Michigan	Mount Arvon	Baraga	1,979	Lake Erie		571
Minnesota	Eagle Mountain	Cook	2,301	Lake Superior		601
Mississippi	Woodall Mountain	Tishomingo	806	Gulf of Mexico		Sea level
Missouri	Taum Sauk Mountain	Iron	1,772	St. Francis R.	Dunklin	230
Montana	Granite Peak	Park	12,807	Kootenai R.	Lincoln	1,800
Nebraska	Panorama Point	Kimball	5,424	Missouri R.	Richardson	840
Nevada	Boundary Peak	Esmeralda	13,146	Colorado R.	Clark	479
New Hampshire	Mount Washington	Coos	6,289	Atlantic Ocean		Sea level
New Jersey	High Point	Sussex	1,803	Atlantic Ocean		Sea level
New Mexico	Wheeler Peak	Taos	13,167	Red Bluff Reservoir	Eddy	2,842
New York	Mount Marcy	Essex	5,343	Atlantic Ocean		Sea level
North Carolina	Mount Mitchell	Yancey	6,683	Atlantic Ocean		Sea level
North Dakota	White Butte	Slope	3,506	Red R. of the North	Pembina	750
Northern Mariana Isls.	Mount Agrihan	Agrihan Island	3,166	Pacific Ocean		Sea level
Ohio	Campbell Hill	Logan	1,550	Ohio R.	Hamilton	455
Oklahoma	Black Mesa	Cimarron	4,973	Little R.	McCurtain	289
Oregon	Mount Hood	Clackamas-Hood R.	11,247	Pacific Ocean		Sea level
Pennsylvania	Mount Davis	Somerset	3,213	Delaware R.	Delaware	Sea level
Puerto Rico	Cerro de Punta	Ponce District	4,390	Atlantic Ocean		Sea level
Rhode Island	Jerimoth Hill	Providence	812	Atlantic Ocean		Sea level
South Carolina	Sassafras Mountain	Pickens	3,560	Atlantic Ocean		Sea level
South Dakota	Harney Peak	Pennington	7,244	Big Stone Lake	Roberts	966
Tennessee	Clingmans Dome	Sevier	6,644	Mississippi R.	Shelby	178
Texas	Guadalupe Peak	Culberson	8,751	Gulf of Mexico		Sea level
Utah	Kings Peak	Duchesne	13,518	Beaver Dam Wash	Washington	2,000
Vermont	Mount Mansfield	Chittenden	4,395	Lake Champlain		95
Virgin Islands	Crown Mountain	St. Thomas Island	1,556	Atlantic Ocean		Sea level
Virginia	Mount Rogers	Grayson-Smyth	5,729	Atlantic Ocean		Sea level
Washington	Mount Rainier	Pierce	14,410	Pacific Ocean		Sea level
West Virginia	Spruce Knob	Pendleton	4,863	Potomac R.	Jefferson	240
Wisconsin	Timms Hill	Price	1,951	Lake Michigan		579
Wyoming	Gannett Peak	Fremont	13,810	Belle Fourche R.	Crook	3,099

U.S. Coastline by State

Source: National Oceanic and Atmospheric Administration, U.S. Dept. of Commerce
(in statute miles; only states with coastline or shoreline are shown)

	Coastline[1]	Shoreline[2]		Coastline[1]	Shoreline[2]
Atlantic Coast	**2,069**	**28,673**	**Gulf Coast**	**1,631**	**17,141**
Connecticut	0	618	Alabama	53	607
Delaware	28	381	Florida	770	5,095
Florida	580	3,331	Louisiana	397	7,721
Georgia	100	2,344	Mississippi	44	359
Maine	228	3,478	Texas	367	3,359
Maryland	31	3,190			
Massachusetts	192	1,519	**Pacific Coast**	**7,623**	**40,298**
New Hampshire	13	131	Alaska	5,580	31,383
New Jersey	130	1,792	California	840	3,427
New York	127	1,850	Hawaii	750	1,052
North Carolina	301	3,375	Oregon	296	1,410
Pennsylvania	0	89	Washington	157	3,026
Rhode Island	40	384	**Arctic Coast**	**1,060**	**2,521**
South Carolina	187	2,876			
Virginia	112	3,315	**United States**	**12,383**	**88,633**

(1) Length of general outline of seacoast. Measurements were made in 1948 with a unit measure of 30 minutes of latitude on charts as near the scale of 1:1,200,000 as possible. Includes coastlines of large sounds and bays. (2) Shoreline of outer coast, offshore islands, sounds, bays, rivers, and creeks to the head of tidewater or to a point where tidal waters narrow to a width of 100 ft. Figures obtained in 1939-40 with a recording instrument on the largest-scale charts and maps then available.

States: Capitals, Key Dates, Geographic Data

Source: *Statistical Abstract of the United States*, U.S. Census Bureau, U.S. Dept. of Commerce

The 13 colonies that declared independence from Great Britain and fought the War of Independence (American Revolution) became the 13 original states. They were, in the order in which they ratified the Constitution: Delaware, Pennsylvania, New Jersey, Georgia, Connecticut, Massachusetts, Maryland, South Carolina, New Hampshire, Virginia, New York, North Carolina, and Rhode Island.

State	Settled[1]	Capital	Entered Union Date	Entered Union Order	Extent (mi) Length (approx. mean)	Extent (mi) Width (approx. mean)	Area (sq mi) Land	Area (sq mi) Water	Area (sq mi) Total	Rank by tot. area
AL	1702	Montgomery	Dec. 14, 1819	22	330	190	50,645	1,775	52,420	30
AK	1784	Juneau	Jan. 3, 1959	49	1,480[2]	810	570,641	94,743	665,384	1
AZ	1776	Phoenix	Feb. 14, 1912	48	400	310	113,594	396	113,990	6
AR	1686	Little Rock	June 15, 1836	25	260	240	52,035	1,143	53,179	29
CA	1769	Sacramento	Sept. 9, 1850	31	770	250	155,779	7,916	163,695	3
CO	1858	Denver	Aug. 1, 1876	38	380	280	103,642	452	104,094	8
CT	1634	Hartford	Jan. 9, 1788	5	110	70	4,842	701	5,543	48
DE	1638	Dover	Dec. 7, 1787	1	96	30	1,949	540	2,489	49
DC	NA	NA	NA	NA	NA	NA	61	7	68	51
FL	1565	Tallahassee	Mar. 3, 1845	27	447	361	53,625	12,133	65,758	22
GA	1733	Atlanta	Jan. 2, 1788	4	300	230	57,513	1,912	59,425	24
HI	1820	Honolulu	Aug. 21, 1959	50	NA	NA	6,423	4,509	10,932	43
ID	1842	Boise	July 3, 1890	43	479	305	82,643	926	83,569	14
IL	1720	Springfield	Dec. 3, 1818	21	390	210	55,519	2,395	57,914	25
IN	1733	Indianapolis	Dec. 11, 1816	19	270	140	35,826	593	36,420	38
IA	1788	Des Moines	Dec. 28, 1846	29	310	200	55,857	416	56,273	26
KS	1727	Topeka	Jan. 29, 1861	34	400	210	81,759	520	82,278	15
KY	1774	Frankfort	June 1, 1792	15	380	140	39,486	921	40,408	37
LA	1699	Baton Rouge	Apr. 30, 1812	18	380	130	43,204	9,174	52,378	31
ME	1624	Augusta	Mar. 15, 1820	23	320	190	30,843	4,537	35,380	39
MD	1634	Annapolis	Apr. 28, 1788	7	250	90	9,707	2,699	12,406	42
MA	1620	Boston	Feb. 6, 1788	6	190	50	7,800	2,754	10,554	44
MI	1668	Lansing	Jan. 26, 1837	26	490	240	56,539	40,175	96,714	11
MN	1805	St. Paul	May 11, 1858	32	400	250	79,627	7,309	86,936	12
MS	1699	Jackson	Dec. 10, 1817	20	340	170	46,923	1,509	48,432	32
MO	1735	Jefferson City	Aug. 10, 1821	24	300	240	68,742	965	69,707	21
MT	1809	Helena	Nov. 8, 1889	41	630	280	145,546	1,494	147,040	4
NE	1823	Lincoln	Mar. 1, 1867	37	430	210	76,824	524	77,348	16
NV	1849	Carson City	Oct. 31, 1864	36	490	320	109,781	791	110,572	7
NH	1623	Concord	June 21, 1788	9	190	70	8,953	397	9,349	46
NJ	1660	Trenton	Dec. 18, 1787	3	150	70	7,354	1,368	8,723	47
NM	1610	Santa Fe	Jan. 6, 1912	47	370	343	121,298	292	121,590	5
NY	1614	Albany	July 26, 1788	11	330	283	47,126	7,429	54,555	27
NC	1660	Raleigh	Nov. 21, 1789	12	500	150	48,618	5,201	53,819	28
ND	1812	Bismarck	Nov. 2, 1889	39	340	211	69,001	1,698	70,698	19
OH	1788	Columbus	Mar. 1, 1803	17	220	220	40,861	3,965	44,826	34
OK	1889	Oklahoma City	Nov. 16, 1907	46	400	220	68,595	1,304	69,899	20
OR	1811	Salem	Feb. 14, 1859	33	360	261	95,988	2,391	98,379	9
PA	1682	Harrisburg	Dec. 12, 1787	2	283	160	44,743	1,312	46,054	33
RI	1636	Providence	May 29, 1790	13	40	30	1,034	511	1,545	50
SC	1670	Columbia	May 23, 1788	8	260	200	30,061	1,960	32,020	40
SD	1859	Pierre	Nov. 2, 1889	40	370	210	75,811	1,305	77,116	17
TN	1769	Nashville	June 1, 1796	16	491	115	41,235	909	42,144	36
TX	1682	Austin	Dec. 29, 1845	28	790	660	261,232	7,365	268,596	2
UT	1847	Salt Lake City	Jan. 4, 1896	45	350	270	82,170	2,727	84,897	13
VT	1724	Montpelier	Mar. 4, 1791	14	160	80	9,217	400	9,616	45
VA	1607	Richmond	June 25, 1788	10	430	200	39,490	3,285	42,775	35
WA	1811	Olympia	Nov. 11, 1889	42	360	240	66,456	4,842	71,298	18
WV	1727	Charleston	June 20, 1863	35	240	130	24,038	192	24,230	41
WI	1766	Madison	May 29, 1848	30	310	260	54,158	11,339	65,496	23
WY	1834	Cheyenne	July 10, 1890	44	360	280	97,093	720	97,813	10

NA = Not applicable. **Note:** Land and water areas may not add up to totals because of rounding. (1) First permanent settlement by Europeans. (2) Does not include Aleutian Islands or Alexander Archipelago.

Continental Divide of the U.S.

The Continental Divide of the U.S., also known as the Great Divide, is located at the watershed created by the mountain ranges, or tablelands, of the Rocky Mountains. This watershed separates the waters that ultimately drain into the Atlantic Ocean and its marginal seas from those waters that drain into the Pacific Ocean. The majority of water flowing E in the U.S. drains into the Gulf of Mexico and then the Atlantic. The majority of water flowing W drains through the Columbia River or Colorado River, which flows into the Gulf of California before reaching the Pacific.

The location and route of the Continental Divide across the U.S. can be described as follows:

Beginning at the U.S.-Mexico border, near longitude 108°45′ W, the Divide, in a northerly direction, crosses New Mexico along the western edge of the Rio Grande drainage basin, entering Colorado near longitude 106°41′ W. From there by an irregular route N across Colorado along the western summits of the Rio Grande and Arkansas, South Platte, and North Platte river basins, and across Rocky Mountain National Park, entering Wyoming near longitude 106°52′ W.

From there in a northwesterly direction, forming the western rims of the North Platte, Big Horn, and Yellowstone river basins, crossing the SW portion of Yellowstone National Park. From there in a westerly and then northerly direction forming the boundary between Idaho and Montana, to a point on the boundary near longitude 114°00′ W. From there northeasterly and northwesterly through Montana and Glacier National Park, entering Canada near longitude 114°04′ W.

Depending on how a "divide" is defined, the U.S. can also be characterized as having a Northern (or Laurentian) Divide, Eastern Divide, and St. Lawrence Seaway Divide. Some of the waters at the Northern Divide drain into Hudson Bay and the Arctic Ocean. The Appalachian Mountains mark the Eastern Divide, with waters joining the Atlantic or Gulf of Mexico. The waters at the St. Lawrence Seaway Divide, near Chicago, flow into the Gulf of St. Lawrence or Gulf of Mexico.

Chronological List of Territories, With State Admissions to Union

Source: U.S. National Archives and Records Administration

Territory	Date of act creating territory	When act took effect	Date of admission as state	Years as terr.
Northwest Territory[1]	July 13, 1787	No fixed date	Mar. 1, 1803[2]	16
Territory South of Ohio River (Southwest Territory)	May 26, 1790	No fixed date	June 1, 1796[3]	6
Mississippi	Apr. 7, 1798	When president acted	Dec. 10, 1817	19
Indiana	May 7, 1800	July 4, 1800	Dec. 11, 1816	16
Orleans	Mar. 26, 1804	Oct. 1, 1804	Apr. 30, 1812[4]	7
Michigan	Jan. 11, 1805	June 30, 1805	Jan. 26, 1837	31
Louisiana-Missouri[5]	Mar. 3, 1805	July 4, 1805	Aug. 10, 1821	16
Illinois	Feb. 3, 1809	Mar. 1, 1809	Dec. 3, 1818	9
Alabama	Mar. 3, 1817	When MS formed state govt.	Dec. 14, 1819	2
Arkansas	Mar. 2, 1819	July 4, 1819	June 15, 1836	17
Florida	Mar. 30, 1822	No fixed date	Mar. 3, 1845	23
Wisconsin	Apr. 20, 1836	July 3, 1836	May 29, 1848	12
Iowa	June 12, 1838	July 3, 1838	Dec. 28, 1846	8
Oregon	Aug. 14, 1848	Date of act	Feb. 14, 1859	10
Minnesota	Mar. 3, 1849	Date of act	May 11, 1858	9
New Mexico	Sept. 9, 1850	On president's proclamation	Jan. 6, 1912	61
Utah	Sept. 9, 1850	Date of act	Jan. 4, 1896	46
Washington	Mar. 2, 1853	Date of act	Nov. 11, 1889	36
Kansas	May 30, 1854	Date of act	Jan. 29, 1861	6
Nebraska	May 30, 1854	Date of act	Mar. 1, 1867	12
Colorado	Feb. 28, 1861	Date of act	Aug. 1, 1876	15
Dakota	Mar. 2, 1861	Date of act	Nov. 2, 1889	28
Nevada	Mar. 2, 1861	Date of act	Oct. 31, 1864	3
Arizona	Feb. 24, 1863	Date of act	Feb. 14, 1912	49
Idaho	Mar. 3, 1863	Date of act	July 3, 1890	27
Montana	May 26, 1864	Date of act	Nov. 8, 1889	25
Wyoming	July 25, 1868	When officers were qualified	July 10, 1890	22
Alaska	May 17, 1884[6]	No fixed date	Jan. 3, 1959	75
Oklahoma	May 2, 1890	Date of act	Nov. 16, 1907	17
Hawaii	Apr. 30, 1900	June 14, 1900	Aug. 21, 1959	59

Note: California was never organized as a territory. It was administered by the military after its acquisition from Mexico (1848) until its admission as a state (1850). (1) Included what is now Ohio, Indiana, Illinois, Michigan, Wisconsin, and E Minnesota. (2) Date of admission for Ohio, the first state created out of territory, based on the date its General Assembly first met. Congress approved Ohio's entry into the Union on Feb. 19, 1803. (3) Admitted as the state of Tennessee. (4) Admitted as the state of Louisiana. (5) The act renaming Louisiana Territory as Missouri Territory (June 4, 1812) became effective Dec. 7, 1812. (6) Act constituted Alaska as a district, though it was often referred to and administered as a territory. The Territory of Alaska was formally organized by an act of Aug. 24, 1912.

U.S. Geographic Centers

Source: U.S. Geological Survey, U.S. Dept. of the Interior

There is no generally accepted definition of a geographic center and no uniform method for determining it. Geographic center is defined here as the center of gravity of the surface of an area, or that point on which an area would balance if it were a plane of uniform thickness.

No government agency has officially established any points marking the geographic center of the U.S., the conterminous U.S. (48 states), or the North American continent. In 1941, private citizens erected a monument in Lebanon, KS, marking it as the geographic center of the then U.S. (conterminous). Residents of Rugby, ND, installed a cairn after the U.S. Geologic Survey, in 1931, determined it to be the center of the North American continent. In 2017, a Univ. at Buffalo geography professor announced that Center, ND, was the continental center according to a mathematical method he developed. The geographic centers in the following list are approximate. They are indicated by county then city unless otherwise noted.

U.S. (50 states): W of Castle Rock, Butte County, South Dakota; 44°58′ N, 103°46′ W
Conterminous U.S. (48 states): nr. Lebanon, Smith County, Kansas; 39°50′ N, 98°35′ W
North American continent: 6 mi W of Balta, Pierce County, North Dakota; 48°10′ N, 100°10′ W
Alabama: Chilton, 12 mi SW of Clanton
Alaska: approx. 60 mi NW of Denali; 63°50′ N, 152° W
Arizona: Yavapai, 55 mi E-SE of Prescott
Arkansas: Pulaski, 12 mi NW of Little Rock
California: Madera, 38 mi E of Madera
Colorado: Park, 30 mi NW of Pikes Peak
Connecticut: Hartford, at East Berlin
Delaware: Kent, 11 mi S of Dover
District of Columbia: near 4th and L Sts. NW
Florida: Hernando, 12 mi N of Brooksville
Georgia: Twiggs, 18 mi SE of Macon
Hawaii: off Maui; 20°15′ N, 156°20′ W
Idaho: Custer, SW of Challis
Illinois: Logan, 28 mi NE of Springfield
Indiana: Boone, 14 mi N-NW of Indianapolis
Iowa: Story, 5 mi NE of Ames
Kansas: Barton, 15 mi NE of Great Bend
Kentucky: Marion, 3 mi N-NW of Lebanon
Louisiana: Avoyelles, 3 mi SE of Marksville
Maine: Piscataquis, 18 mi N of Dover
Maryland: Prince George's, 4.5 mi NW of Davidsonville
Massachusetts: Worcester, N part of city of Worcester
Michigan: Wexford, 5 mi N-NW of Cadillac
Minnesota: Crow Wing, 10 mi SW of Brainerd
Mississippi: Leake, 9 mi W-NW of Carthage
Missouri: Miller, 20 mi SW of Jefferson City
Montana: Fergus, 11 mi W of Lewistown
Nebraska: Custer, 10 mi NW of Broken Bow
Nevada: Lander, 26 mi SE of Austin
New Hampshire: Belknap, 3 mi E of Ashland
New Jersey: Mercer, 5 mi SE of Trenton
New Mexico: Torrance, 12 mi S-SW of Willard
New York: Madison, 12 mi S of Oneida and 26 mi SW of Utica
North Carolina: Chatham, 10 mi NW of Sanford
North Dakota: Sheridan, 5 mi SW of McClusky
Ohio: Delaware, 25 mi N-NE of Columbus
Oklahoma: Oklahoma, 8 mi N of Oklahoma City
Oregon: Crook, 25 mi S-SE of Prineville
Pennsylvania: Centre, 2.5 mi SW of Bellefonte
Rhode Island: Kent, 1 mi S-SW of Crompton
South Carolina: Richland, 13 mi SE of Columbia
South Dakota: Hughes, 8 mi NE of Pierre
Tennessee: Rutherford, 5 mi NE of Murfreesboro
Texas: McCulloch, 15 mi NE of Brady
Utah: Sanpete, 3 mi N of Manti
Vermont: Washington, 3 mi E of Roxbury
Virginia: Buckingham, 5 mi SW of Buckingham
Washington: Chelan, 10 mi W-SW of Wenatchee
West Virginia: Braxton, 4 mi E of Sutton
Wisconsin: Wood, 9 mi SE of Marshfield
Wyoming: Fremont, 58 mi E-NE of Lander

Lengths of U.S. Boundaries

The length of the boundary between the U.S. and Canada is 5,525 mi—3,987 mi between the conterminous U.S. and Canada and 1,538 mi between Alaska and Canada. A 1925 treaty established a permanent International Boundary Commission to maintain the boundary. The U.S.-Mexican border, first established by treaty in 1848, is 1,954-miles long. It largely follows the Rio Grande and Colorado River, from the Gulf of Mexico to the Pacific Ocean. It is overseen by the International Boundary and Water Commission.

Origins of the Names of U.S. States and Territories

Source: State officials; Smithsonian Institution; Topographic Division, U.S. Geological Survey, U.S. Dept. of the Interior

Alabama: Choctaw word for a Chickasaw tribe. First noted in accounts of Hernando de Soto expedition.

Alaska: Russian version of Aleutian (Eskimo) word *alakshak* for "peninsula," "great lands," or "land that is not an island."

American Samoa: Etymology varies.

Arizona: Spanish version of Pima Indian word for "little spring place" or Aztec *arizuma*, meaning "silver-bearing."

Arkansas: Algonquin name for Quapaw Indians, meaning "south wind."

California: Bestowed by Spanish conquistadors (possibly Hernán Cortés). It was the name of an imaginary island in the 1510 Spanish novel *Las Sergas de Esplandián* (The Exploits of Esplandián), by Garci Rodríguez de Montalvo. The Spanish first visited *Baja* (Lower) *California* in 1533. The present-day U.S. state was called *Alta* (Upper) *California*.

Colorado: From Spanish for "red," first applied to Colorado River.

Connecticut: From Mohican and other Algonquin words meaning "long river place."

Delaware: Named for Lord De La Warr, early governor of Virginia; first applied to river, then to Indian tribe (Lenni-Lenape).

District of Columbia: For Christopher Columbus, 1791.

Florida: Named by Juan Ponce de León *Pascua Florida*, "Flowery Easter," on Easter Sunday, 1513.

Georgia: Named by colonial administrator James Oglethorpe for King George II of England in 1732.

Guam: From Chamorro name, *Guahan*, meaning "we have."

Hawaii: Possibly derived from *Hawaiki* or *Owhyhee*, Polynesian word for "homeland."

Idaho: Said to be a coined name with the invented meaning "gem of the mountains"; suggested for the Pikes Peak mining territory (Colorado), then applied to the new mining territory of the Pacific Northwest. Another theory suggests *Idaho* may be Kiowa Apache term for the Comanche.

Illinois: French for *Illini* or "land of *Illini*," Algonquin word meaning "men" or "warriors."

Indiana: Means "land of the Indians."

Iowa: Indian word variously translated as "here I rest" or "beautiful land." Named for the Iowa River, which was named for the Iowa Indians.

Kansas: Sioux word for "south wind people."

Kentucky: Indian word variously translated as "dark and bloody ground," "meadowland," and "land of tomorrow."

Louisiana: Part of territory called Louisiana by René-Robert Cavelier Sieur de La Salle for French King Louis XIV.

Maine: From Maine, historic French province. Also descriptive, referring to the mainland as distinct from coastal islands.

Maryland: For Queen Henrietta Maria, wife of Charles I of England.

Massachusetts: From Indian tribe whose name meant "at or about the Great Hill" in Blue Hills region south of Boston.

Michigan: From Chippewa *mici gama*, meaning "great water," after lake of the same name.

Minnesota: From Dakota Sioux word meaning "cloudy water" or "sky-tinted water" of the Minnesota River.

Mississippi: Probably Chippewa *mici zibi*, meaning "great river" or "gathering-in of all the waters." Also Algonquin word *messipi*.

Missouri: Algonquin Indian term meaning "river of the big canoes."

Montana: Latin or Spanish for "mountainous."

Nebraska: From Omaha or Otos Indian word meaning "broad water" or "flat river," describing the Platte River.

Nevada: Spanish, meaning "snow-clad."

New Hampshire: Named by Capt. John Mason of Plymouth Council, in 1629, for his home county in England.

New Jersey: The Duke of York, in 1664, gave a patent to Lord John Berkeley and Sir George Carteret for *Nova Caesaria*, or New Jersey, after England's Isle of Jersey.

New Mexico: Spaniards in Mexico applied term to land north and west of Rio Grande in the 16th century.

New York: For James, Duke of York and Albany, who received patent for New Netherland from his brother Charles II and sent an expedition to capture it, 1664.

North Carolina: In 1619, Charles I gave patent to Sir Robert Heath for Province of Carolana, from *Carolus*, Latin name for Charles. Charles II granted a new patent to Earl of Clarendon and others. Divided into North and South Carolina, 1710.

North Dakota: Sioux word *Dakota*, meaning "friend" or "ally."

Northern Mariana Isls.: For Mariana of Austria, queen regent of Spain.

Ohio: Iroquois word for "fine or good river."

Oklahoma: Choctaw word meaning "red man," proposed by Rev. Allen Wright, Choctaw-speaking Indian.

Oregon: Origin unknown. One theory is that the name derives from *wauregan*, meaning "beautiful," term used by Indians in New England.

Pennsylvania: William Penn, Quaker who was made full proprietor of area by King Charles II in 1681, suggested "Sylvania," or "woodland," for his tract. The king's government owed 16,000 pounds to Penn's father, Adm. William Penn, and the land was granted as partial settlement. Charles II added "Penn" to "Sylvania," against the modest proprietor's desires, in honor of the admiral.

Puerto Rico: Spanish for "rich port."

Rhode Island: Origin unknown. One theory notes that Giovanni de Verrazzano recorded observing an island about the size of the Greek island of Rhodes in 1524. Another theory is that Dutch explorer Adriaen Block named the state *Roode Eylandt* for its red clay.

South Carolina: See North Carolina.

South Dakota: See North Dakota.

Tennessee: *Tanasi* was the name of Cherokee villages on the Little Tennessee River. From 1784 to 1788, this was the State of Franklin, or Frankland.

Texas: Variant of word used by Caddo and other Indians meaning "friends" or "allies" and applied to them by the Spanish in eastern Texas. Also written *Texias, Tejas, Teysas*.

Utah: From a Navajo word meaning "upper," or "higher up," as applied to Shoshone tribe called Ute. Proposed name *Deseret*, "land of honeybees," from Book of Mormon, was rejected by Congress.

Vermont: From French words *vert* (green) and *mont* (mountain). The Green Mountains were said to have been named by Samuel de Champlain. When the state was formed in 1777, Dr. Thomas Young suggested combining *vert* and *mont*.

Virgin Islands, U.S.: From Spanish name *Las Once Mil Virgenes* (11,000 Virgins), which Christopher Columbus gave to island group.

Virginia: Named by Sir Walter Raleigh, who outfitted an expedition in 1584, in honor of England's Queen Elizabeth, the Virgin Queen.

Washington: Named after George Washington. When the bill creating the Territory of Columbia was introduced in the 32nd Congress, its name was changed to Washington because of the existence of the District of Columbia.

West Virginia: So named when western counties of Virginia refused to secede from the U.S. in 1863.

Wisconsin: Indian name, spelled *Ouisconsin* or *Mesconsing* by early chroniclers, believed to mean "grassy place" in Chippewa. Congress made it *Wisconsin*.

Wyoming: From Algonquin words for "large prairie place," "at the big plains," or "on the great plain."

Territorial Sea of the U.S.

According to a Dec. 27, 1988, proclamation by Pres. Ronald Reagan, "The territorial sea of the United States henceforth extends to 12 nautical miles from the baselines of the United States determined in accordance with international law. In accordance with international law, as reflected in the applicable provisions of the 1982 United Nations Convention on the Law of the Sea, within the territorial sea of the United States, the ships of all countries enjoy the right of innocent passage and the ships and aircraft of all countries enjoy the right of transit passage through international straits."

Major Accessions of Territory by the U.S.

Source: U.S. Dept. of the Interior; U.S. Census Bureau, U.S. Dept. of Commerce

Not including territories such as the Panama Canal Zone and the Philippines, which are no longer under U.S. jurisdiction.

Accession	Date	Area (sq mi)	Accession	Date	Area (sq mi)	Accession	Date	Area (sq mi)
Territory in 1790[1]	NA	888,685	Mexican Cession	1848	529,017	Guam[3]	1899	212
Louisiana Purchase	1803	827,192	Gadsden Purchase	1853	29,640	American Samoa[4]	1900	76
Treaty of Florida	1819	72,003	Alaska	1867	586,412	U.S. Virgin Islands	1917	133
Texas	1845	390,143	Hawaii	1898	6,450	Northern Marianas[5]	1986	179
Oregon Territory	1846	285,680	Puerto Rico[2]	1899	3,435			

NA = Not applicable. (1) Includes that part of a drainage basin of Red River of the North, south of 49th parallel, sometimes considered part of Louisiana Purchase. (2) Ceded by Spain in 1898, ratified in 1899, and became the Commonwealth of Puerto Rico by Act of Congress on July 25, 1952. (3) Acquired in 1898; ratified 1899. (4) Acquired in 1899; ratified 1900. (5) Part of the UN Trust Territory of the Pacific Islands, which U.S. began administering in 1947; became U.S. commonwealth Nov. 3, 1986.

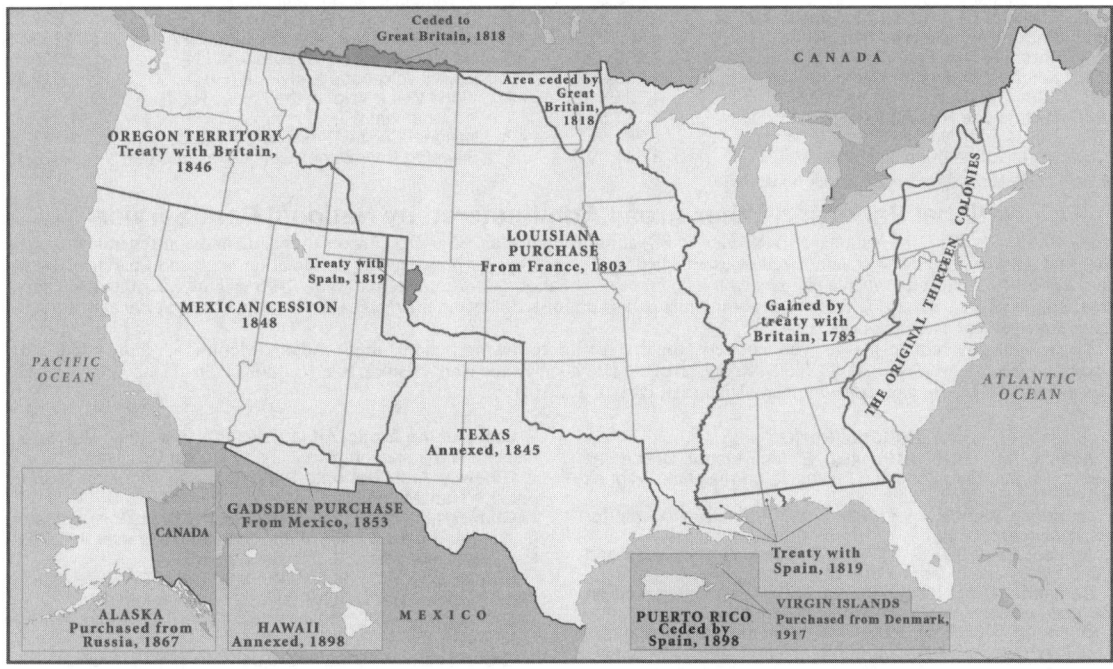

National Park System Recreation Visits, 1904-2017

Source: National Park Service (NPS), U.S. Dept. of the Interior

An NPS site, regardless of its designation (as a park, monument, or preserve, etc.), is generally referred to as a unit. Not all units report public use statistics.

Year	Units reporting visits	Recreation visits	Year	Units reporting visits	Recreation visits
1904	6	120,690	1995	328	269,564,307
1905	6	140,954	2000	344	285,891,275
1910	9	173,416	2001	345	279,873,926
1915	12	314,299	2002	349	277,299,880
1920	26	1,022,091	2003	353	266,230,290
1925	39	1,900,499	2004	356	276,908,337
1930	45	3,038,935	2005	356	273,488,751
1935	85	7,435,659	2006	359	272,623,980
1940	113	16,410,148	2007	360	275,581,547
1945	143	10,855,548	2008	360	274,852,949
1950	139	32,706,172	2009	360	285,579,941
1955	150	48,891,000	2010	363	281,303,769
1960	166	71,586,000	2011	367	278,939,216
1965	182	118,662,500	2012	367	282,765,682
1970	217	168,135,100	2013	370	273,630,895
1975	251	188,085,700	2014	376	292,800,082
1980	275	220,463,211	2015	378	307,247,252
1985	303	263,441,808	2016	382	330,971,689
1990	316	255,581,467	2017	385	330,882,751

Most-Visited Sites in the National Park System, 2017

Source: National Park Service (NPS), U.S. Dept. of the Interior

Attendance at 385 of 417 NPS sites totaled 330,882,751 recreation visits in 2017. (Not all units report public use statistics.)

Rank	Site (location)	Rec. visits	Rank	Site (location)	Rec. visits
1.	Blue Ridge Parkway (NC-VA)	16,093,765	26.	Acadia Natl. Park (ME)	3,509,271
2.	Golden Gate Natl. Recreation Area (CA)	14,981,897	27.	Franklin Delano Roosevelt Memorial (DC)	3,507,402
3.	Great Smoky Mountains Natl. Park (NC-TN)	11,338,893	28.	Boston Natl. Historical Park (MA)	3,425,606
4.	Gateway Natl. Recreation Area (NJ-NY)	9,190,610	29.	Olympic Natl. Park (WA)	3,401,996
5.	Lincoln Memorial (DC)	7,956,117	30.	Delaware Water Gap Natl. Recreation Area (NJ-PA)	3,400,944
6.	Lake Mead Natl. Recreation Area (AZ-NV)	7,882,339	31.	Thomas Jefferson Memorial (DC)	3,366,571
7.	George Washington Memorial Parkway (DC-MD-VA)	7,562,793	32.	Colonial Natl. Historical Park (VA)	3,333,448
8.	Natchez Trace Parkway (MS-AL-TN)	6,326,062	33.	Grand Teton Natl. Park (WY)	3,317,000
9.	Grand Canyon Natl. Park (AZ)	6,254,238	34.	Glacier Natl. Park (MT)	3,305,512
10.	Vietnam Veterans Memorial (DC)	5,072,589	35.	Joshua Tree Natl. Park (CA)	2,853,619
11.	World War II Memorial (DC)	4,876,842	36.	Chattahoochee River Natl. Recreation Area (GA)	2,768,499
12.	Chesapeake & Ohio Canal Natl. Historical Park (DC-MD-WV)	4,859,573	37.	Kennesaw Mountain Natl. Battlefield Park (GA)	2,593,725
13.	Independence Natl. Historical Park (PA)	4,790,758	38.	Bryce Canyon Natl. Park (UT)	2,571,684
14.	Castle Clinton Natl. Monument (NY)	4,737,113	39.	Rock Creek Park (DC)	2,483,788
15.	Glen Canyon Natl. Rec. Area (AZ-UT)	4,574,940	40.	Point Reyes Natl. Seashore (CA)	2,456,669
16.	Zion Natl. Park (UT)	4,504,812	41.	Mount Rushmore Natl. Memorial (SD)	2,437,800
17.	San Francisco Maritime Natl. Historical Park (CA)	4,493,519	42.	Cape Hatteras Natl. Seashore (NC)	2,433,703
18.	Statue of Liberty Natl. Monument (NY)	4,441,988	43.	Assateague Island Natl. Seashore (MD-VA)	2,347,167
19.	Rocky Mountain Natl. Park (CO)	4,437,215	44.	Cuyahoga Valley Natl. Park (OH)	2,226,879
20.	Yosemite Natl. Park (CA)	4,336,890	45.	Valley Forge Natl. Historical Park (PA)	2,159,592
21.	Korean War Veterans Memorial (DC)	4,155,947	46.	Indiana Dunes Natl. Lakeshore (IN)	2,158,471
22.	Cape Cod Natl. Seashore (MA)	4,125,418	47.	Hawaii Volcanoes Natl. Park (HI)	2,016,702
23.	Yellowstone Natl. Park (ID-MT-WY)	4,116,524	48.	World War II Valor in the Pacific Natl. Monument (HI)	1,947,495
24.	Gulf Islands Natl. Seashore (FL-MS)	3,952,941	49.	National Capital Parks Central[1] (DC)	1,932,762
25.	Martin Luther King Jr. Memorial (DC)	3,651,093	50.	Sleeping Bear Dunes Natl. Lakeshore (MI)	1,678,126

(1) Incl. recreation visits to Constitution Gardens.

National Parks and Other Areas Administered by National Park Service

As of Dec. 31, 2017, the National Park Service (NPS) administered about 85,040,323 acres of federal and non-federal land across 417 sites. Date when area was authorized or established by Congress or by presidential proclamation is given in parentheses; any date that follows indicates when a site received its current designation or was transferred to the NPS. Figure after the date is gross area acres as of Dec. 31, 2017. Table does not include parks administered by other agencies, such as the Forest Service or Bureau of Land Management. NA = Not available.

The federal government has not yet acquired property for the following planned units: Adams Mem. (DC, authorized 2001), Dwight D. Eisenhower Mem. (DC, 2002), Ronald Reagan Boyhood Home Natl. Historic Site (IL, 2002), Ste. Genevieve Natl. Historical Park (MO, 2014), or Coltsville Natl. Historical Park (CT, 2014).

National Parks

Acadia, ME (1916/1919): 49,075. Incl. Mount Desert Isl., half of Isle au Haut, Schoodic Peninsula on mainland. Highest elevation on Eastern seaboard.

American Samoa, AS (1988): 8,257. Paleotropical rain forest, coral reef.

Arches, UT (1929/1971): 76,679. Contains giant red sandstone arches and other products of erosion.

Badlands, SD (1939/1978): 242,756. Reformations and native prairie; animal fossils 25-37 mil years old.

Big Bend, TX (1935): 801,163. Rio Grande, Chisos Mtns.

Biscayne, FL (1968/1980): 172,971. Aquatic park encompassing chain of islands south of Miami.

Black Canyon of the Gunnison, CO (1933/1999): 30,781. Has canyon 2,900 ft deep and 40 ft wide at narrowest part.

Bryce Canyon, UT (1923/1928): 35,835. Colorful display of erosion effects.

Canyonlands, UT (1964): 337,598. At junction of Colorado and Green Rivers; extensive evidence of prehistoric peoples.

Capitol Reef, UT (1937/1971): 241,905. 70+-mi-long uplift of sandstone cliffs (Waterpocket Fold) dissected by gorges.

Carlsbad Caverns, NM (1923/1930): 46,766. More than 119 limestone caves, incl. Carlsbad Cavern; Chihuahuan Desert.

Channel Islands, CA (1938/1980): 249,561. Sea lion breeding place, nesting seabirds, unique plants.

Congaree, SC (1976/2003): 26,539. Largest intact tract of old-growth bottomland hardwood forest in U.S.

Crater Lake, OR (1902): 183,224. Deepest U.S. lake, in crater of Mt. Mazama, volcano that erupted about 7,700 years ago.

Cuyahoga Valley, OH (1974/2000): 32,572. Along Ohio and Erie Canal system between Akron and Cleveland.

Death Valley, CA-NV (1933/1994): 3,373,063. Large desert. Incl. lowest point in North America and Scotty's Castle (closed until 2020 due to flood damage).

Denali, AK (1917/1980): 4,740,911. Formerly known as Mt. McKinley; highest mountain in U.S.

Dry Tortugas, FL (1935/1992): 64,701. Ft. Jefferson and seven coral reef and sand islands near Key West.

Everglades, FL (1934): 1,508,934. Largest remaining subtropical wilderness in continental U.S; incl. East Everglades Expansion Area acreage added in 1989.

Gates of the Arctic, AK (1978/1980): 7,523,897. Vast wilderness in north central region. Limited federal facilities.

Gateway Arch National Park, MO: *see* Jefferson Natl. Expansion Natl. Memorial.

Glacier, MT (1910): 1,013,126. Rocky Mt. scenery, numerous glaciers and glacial lakes. Part of Waterton-Glacier Intl. Peace Park established by U.S. and Canada in 1932.

Glacier Bay, AK (1925/1980): 3,223,383. Tidewater glaciers that move down mountainsides and break up into sea.

Grand Canyon, AZ (1919/1919): 1,201,647. Carved by Colorado River.

Grand Teton, WY (1929): 310,044. Incl. highest peaks of Teton Mtns.; summer feeding ground of largest American elk herd.

Great Basin, NV (1922/1986): 77,180. Incl. Wheeler Peak, Lexington Arch, Lehman Caves.

Great Sand Dunes, CO (1932/2004): 107,342. North America's tallest dunes.

Great Smoky Mountains, NC-TN (1926/1934): 522,427. Largest Eastern U.S. mountain range; magnificent forests.

Guadalupe Mountains, TX (1966): 86,367. Extensive Permian limestone fossil reef; tremendous earth fault.

Haleakalā, HI (1916/1960): 33,265. Dormant volcano on island of Maui with large craters.

Hawai'i Volcanoes, HI (1916/1961): 323,431. Contains Kilauea and Mauna Loa, active volcanoes.

Hot Springs, AR (1832/1921): 5,548. Waters from park's 47 hot springs used for bathing and drinking.

Isle Royale, MI (1931): 571,790. Largest island in Lake Superior.

Joshua Tree, CA (1936/1994): 790,636. Desert region incl. Joshua trees, other plant and animal life.

Katmai, AK (1918/1980): 3,674,529. "Valley of Ten Thousand Smokes," scene of 1912 volcanic eruption.

Kenai Fjords, AK (1978/1980): 669,650. Marine mammals, birdlife; over 30 glaciers flow from Harding Icefield.

Kings Canyon, CA (1890/1940): 461,901. Mountain wilderness, dominated by Kings River Canyons and High Sierra; giant sequoias.

Kobuk Valley, AK (1978/1980): 1,750,716. Contains geological and recreational sites. Limited federal facilities.

Lake Clark, AK (1978/1980): 2,619,816. Across Cook Inlet from Anchorage; scenic wilderness, fish and wildlife. Limited federal facilities.

Lassen Volcanic, CA (1907/1916): 106,589. Contains Lassen Peak, recently active volcano; other volcanic phenomena.

Mammoth Cave, KY (1926/1941): 54,012. Longest known cave system in world (more than 405 mi currently surveyed), river 300 ft below surface.

Mesa Verde, CO (1906): 52,485. Most notable and best preserved prehistoric cliff dwellings in U.S.

Mount Rainier, WA (1899): 236,382. Most glaciated peak in contiguous U.S.

North Cascades, WA (1968): 504,781. Mountainous region with many glaciers, lakes.

Olympic, WA (1909/1938): 922,649. Wilderness containing glacier-capped mountains, remnant of temperate rain forest, shoreline, endemic animal species.

Petrified Forest, AZ (1906/1962): 221,390. Extensive petrified wood and Indian artifacts. Contains part of Painted Desert.

Pinnacles, CA (1908/2013): 26,686. A release site for captive-bred California condors; talus caves.

Redwood, CA (1968): 138,999. 40 mi of Pacific coastline, groves of ancient redwoods, the world's tallest trees.

Rocky Mountain, CO (1915): 265,795. On Continental Divide; incl. peaks over 14,000 ft.

Saguaro, AZ (1933/1994): 91,716. Part of Sonoran Desert; incl. giant saguaro cacti, unique to region.

Sequoia, CA (1890): 404,063. Giant sequoia groves; world's largest tree (by volume). Mt. Whitney, highest mountain in conterminous U.S.

Shenandoah, VA (1926): 199,218. Portion of Blue Ridge Mtns. Overlooks Shenandoah Valley; Skyline Drive.

Theodore Roosevelt, ND (1947/1978): 70,447. Contains part of Roosevelt's ranch and scenic badlands.

Virgin Islands, VI (1956): 14,940. Covers more than half of St. John Isl. and nearly all of Hassel Isl.; beaches, Carib Indian petroglyphs, evidence of colonial Danes.

Voyageurs, MN (1971): 218,200. Abundant lakes, forests, wildlife.

Wind Cave, SD (1903): 33,971. Limestone caverns in Black Hills; extensive wildlife incl. bison herd.

Wrangell-St. Elias, AK (1978/1980): 8,323,146. Largest area in park system; most peaks over 16,000 ft.

Yellowstone, ID-MT-WY (1872): 2,219,791. World's first national park. World's greatest concentration of geysers with about 10,000 geysers, hot springs; Yellowstone River falls and canyons; grizzly bear, largest bison herd on U.S. public land.

Yosemite, CA (1890): 761,748. Yosemite Valley, country's highest waterfall, grove of sequoias, mountains.

Zion, UT (1909/1919): 147,237. Unusual shapes, landscapes resulting from erosion, faulting; evidence of past volcanic activity.

National Historical Parks

Abraham Lincoln Birthplace, Hodgenville, KY (1916/2009): 345. Memorial building, sinking spring.

Adams, Quincy, MA (1946/1998): 24. Home of Pres. John Adams, John Quincy Adams, and descendants.

Appomattox Court House, VA (1930/1954): 1,775. Where Confederate Gen. Lee surrendered to Gen. Grant, signaling Civil War's end.

Blackstone River Valley, MA-RI (2014): 1,489. Preserves the valley's industrial heritage.

Boston, MA (1974): 44. Incl. Faneuil Hall, Old North Church, Bunker Hill, Paul Revere House.

Cane River Creole, LA (1994): 206. Preserves Creole culture as it developed along the Cane River.

Cedar Creek and Belle Grove, VA (2002): 3,706. Civil War battle site and an antebellum plantation in Shenandoah Valley.

Chaco Culture, NM (1907/1980): 33,960. Ruins of pueblos built by prehistoric peoples incl. Pueblo, Hopi, and Navajo.

Chesapeake & Ohio Canal, MD-DC-WV (1938/1971): 19,612. 184.5-mi historic canal; DC to Cumberland, MD.

Colonial, VA (1930/1936): 8,677. Incl. most of Jamestown Isl., site of first successful English colony; Yorktown, site of Cornwallis's surrender to George Washington; Colonial Parkway.

Cumberland Gap, KY-TN-VA (1940): 24,547. Mountain pass of Wilderness Road, which carried first great migration of pioneers into America's interior.

Dayton Aviation Heritage, OH (1992): 111. Commemorates area's involvement in aviation.

First State, DE-PA (2013/2014): 1,155. Locations date from colonial past of DE, first state to ratify Constitution.

George Rogers Clark, Vincennes, IN (1966): 26. Commemorates American defeat of British in West during Revolution.

Harpers Ferry, MD-VA-WV (1944/1963): 3,656. At confluence of Shenandoah and Potomac Rivers, the site of John Brown's 1859 raid on the Army arsenal.

Harriet Tubman, NY (2017): 32. Buildings incl. her home, a church, Tubman Home for the Aged.

Harriet Tubman Underground Railroad, MD (2013/2014): 480. Protects landscapes on the Eastern Shore, where Tubman was born and guided other slaves to freedom.

Hopewell Culture, OH (1923/1992): 1,770. Remains of ceremonial mounds built in the Ohio River Valley, 200 BCE-500 CE.

Independence, Philadelphia, PA (1948): 45. Several properties associated with American Revolution and founding of U.S., incl. Independence Hall, Liberty Bell Center.

Jean Lafitte (and Preserve), LA (1907/1978): 22,421. Incl. Chalmette, site of 1815 Battle of New Orleans; French Quarter.

Kalaupapa, HI (1980): 10,779. Former colony on Molokai Isl. for those with Hansen's disease (leprosy).

Kaloko-Honokohau, HI (1978): 1,163. Preserves native culture of Hawaii.

Keweenaw, MI (1992): 1,870. Site of first significant copper mine in U.S.

Klondike Gold Rush, AK-WA (1976): 12,996. Preserves Chilkoot Trail used in 1898 Gold Rush. Museum in Seattle.

Lewis and Clark, OR-WA (1958/2004): 3,410. Lewis and Clark encampment, 1805-06. Incorporates former Fort Clatsop Natl. Mem. Park.

Lowell, MA (1978): 142. Textile mills, canal, 19th-cent. structures; park shows planned city of Industrial Revolution.

Lyndon B. Johnson, TX (1969/1980): 1,572. 36th president's birthplace, boyhood home, ranch.

Manhattan Project, NM-TN-WA (2014): 114. Jointly operated with Dept. of Energy, consists of three sites (Los Alamos, NM; Oak Ridge, TN; Hanford, WA) where U.S. developed world's first atomic weapons.

Marsh-Billings-Rockefeller, VT (1992): 643. Boyhood home of conservationist George Perkins Marsh.

Martin Luther King Jr., GA: see National Historic Sites

Minute Man, MA (1959): 1,028. Where Minute Men battled British, Apr. 19, 1775. Also includes The Wayside, home to authors Louisa May Alcott and Nathaniel Hawthorne.

Morristown, NJ (1933): 1,711. Site of important military encampments during the American Revolution; Washington's headquarters, 1779-80.

Natchez, MS (1988): 108. Mansions, townhouses, and villas related to history of Natchez.

New Bedford Whaling, MA (1996): 34. Preserves structures and relics associated with the city's 19th-cent. whaling industry.

New Orleans Jazz, LA (1994): 5. Preserves, educates, and interprets jazz as it has evolved in New Orleans.

Nez Perce, ID-MT-OR-WA (1965): 4,565. Illustrates history and culture of Nez Perce, or Nimiipuu, homeland (38 separate sites).

Palo Alto Battlefield, TX (1978/2009): 3,442. Scene of first battle of the Mexican War.

Paterson Great Falls, NJ (2011): 51. Falls helped make city one of U.S.'s earliest industrial centers.

Pecos, NM (1965/1990): 6,693. Ruins of ancient Pueblo of Pecos, archaeological sites, and two associated Spanish colonial missions from 17th and 18th centuries.

Pu'uhonua o Hōnaunau, HI (1955/1978): 420. Until 1819, a sanctuary for Hawaiians vanquished in battle and for those guilty of crimes or breaking taboos.

Rosie the Riveter/WWII Home Front, Richmond, CA (2000): 145. Site of shipyard that employed thousands of women during WWII; commemorates women who worked in wartime industries.

Salt River Bay (and Ecological Preserve), St. Croix, VI (1992): 989. Only known site where, in 1493, members of a Columbus party landed on what is now U.S. territory.

San Antonio Missions, TX (1978): 948. Four Spanish missions, 18th-cent. irrigation system.

San Francisco Maritime, CA (1988): 50. Artifacts, photographs, and historic vessels related to development of the Pacific Coast.

San Juan Island, WA (1966): 2,146. Commemorates peaceful relations between U.S., Canada, and Great Britain since the 1872 boundary disputes.

Saratoga, NY (1938): 3,579. Scene of a major 1777 battle that became a turning point in the American Revolution.

Sitka, AK (1910/1972): 116. Scene of Tlingit Indians' last major resistance to Russian colonizers, 1804.

Thomas Edison, West Orange, NJ (1955/2009): 21. Inventor's home and laboratory.

Tumacacori, AZ (1908/1990): 360. Historic Spanish mission building near site first visited by Father Kino in 1691.

Valley Forge, PA (1976): 3,468. Continental Army campsite in 1777-78 winter.

War in the Pacific, GU (1978): 2,031. Seven distinct units illustrating the Pacific theater of WWII.

Women's Rights, NY (1980): 7. Seneca Falls site where Lucretia Mott, Elizabeth Cady Stanton organized movement in 1848.

National Battlefields/Parks/Sites

Antietam, MD (1890/1978): 3,230. Battle here ended first Confederate invasion of North, Sept. 17, 1862.

Big Hole, MT (1910/1963): 976. Site of major battle with Nez Perce Indians, Aug. 9-10, 1877.

Brices Cross Roads, Baldwyn, MS (1929): 1. Site of Confederate victory, June 10, 1864.

Cowpens, SC (1929/1972): 842. American Revolution battlefield, Jan. 17, 1781.

Fort Donelson, TN-KY (1928/1985): 1,319. Site of first major Union victory, Feb. 16, 1862.

Fort Necessity, PA (1931/1961): 903. Site of first battle of French and Indian War, July 3, 1754.

Kennesaw Mountain, GA (1917/1935): 2,894. Site of major battle of Atlanta campaign in Civil War.

Manassas, VA (1940): 5,073. Scene of two Civil War battles.

Monocacy, MD (1934/1976): 1,647. Civil War battle in defense of Washington, DC, fought here, July 9, 1864.

Moores Creek, Currie, NC (1926/1980): 88. Commemorates Feb. 27, 1776, battle between Patriots and Loyalists.

Petersburg, VA (1926/1962): 9,368. Scene of Union campaigns, 1864-65.

Richmond, VA (1936): 8,171. Site of battles defending Confederate capital.

River Raisin, Monroe, MI (2010): 42. Site of major battles of War of 1812.

Stones River, TN (1927/1960): 709. Scene of battle that began federal offensive to trisect Confederacy, Dec. 31, 1862-Jan. 2, 1863.

Tupelo, MS (1929/1961): 1. Site of crucial battle over Union Gen. Sherman's supply line, July 14-15, 1865.

Wilson's Creek, MO (1960/1970): 2,408. Site of second major Civil War battle, Aug. 10, 1861, for control of Missouri.

National Military Parks

Chickamauga and Chattanooga, GA-TN (1890): 9,523. Where Gen. Sherman and Union armies gained control of TN, 1863.

Fredericksburg and Spotsylvania, VA (1927/1933): 8,405. Sites of several major Civil War battles and campaigns.

Gettysburg, PA (1895/1933): 6,033. Site of decisive Confederate defeat in North, July 1863, and of Gettysburg Address.

Guilford Courthouse, NC (1917/1933): 253. American Revolution battle site.

Horseshoe Bend, AL (1956): 2,040. On Tallapoosa River, where Gen. Andrew Jackson broke power of Upper Creek Indian Confederacy on Mar. 27, 1814.

Kings Mountain, SC (1931/1933): 3,945. Site of American Revolution battle, fought on Oct. 7, 1780.

Pea Ridge, AR (1956): 4,300. Civil War battle, Mar. 7-8, 1862.

Shiloh, TN-MS (1894/1933): 7,932. Major Civil War battle site, Apr. 6-7, 1862; incl. Shiloh Indian burial mounds.

Vicksburg, MS-LA (1899/1933): 1,815. Union victory gave North control of Mississippi and split Confederate forces.

National Memorials

Arkansas Post, AR (1960): 758. First permanent French settlement in lower Mississippi River valley.

Arlington House, The Robert E. Lee Memorial, VA (1925/1972): 28. Lee's home overlooking the Potomac River.

Chamizal, El Paso, TX (1966/1974): 55. Commemorates 1963 settlement of 99-year border dispute with Mexico.

Coronado, AZ (1941/1952): 4,830. Commemorates first European exploration of the Southwest.

De Soto, Bradenton, FL (1948): 30. Commemorates 16th-cent. Spanish explorations.

Federal Hall, New York, NY (1939/1955): 0.45. First seat of U.S. government under the Constitution.

Flight 93, Shanksville, PA (2002): 2,319. Commemorates passengers and crew of Flight 93, who died thwarting an attack on Sept. 11, 2001. First features of memorial completed and dedicated in 2011.

Fort Caroline, Jacksonville, FL (1950): 138. On St. Johns River, site of first attempt by France, in 16th cent., at permanent North American settlement.

Franklin Delano Roosevelt Memorial, DC (1982): 8. Statues of Pres. Roosevelt and Eleanor Roosevelt; waterfalls and gardens.

General Grant, New York, NY (1958): 0.76. Tomb of Ulysses Grant and wife; largest mausoleum in U.S.

Hamilton Grange, New York, NY (1962): 1.75. Home of Alexander Hamilton.

Jefferson National Expansion, St. Louis, MO (1935): 193. Commemorates 19th cent. westward expansion; incl. Gateway Arch (authorized 1954). Renamed/redesignated Gateway Arch National Park in 2018.

Johnstown Flood, PA (1964): 178. Commemorates 1889 flood.

Korean War Veterans Memorial, DC (1986/1995): 1.56. Honors those who served in the Korean War.

Lincoln Boyhood, Lincoln City, IN (1962): 200. Site of Abraham Lincoln's boyhood home and grave site of his mother.

Lincoln Memorial, DC (1911/1933): 7. Marble statue of 16th president.

Lyndon Baines Johnson Memorial Grove on the Potomac, DC (1973): 17. Overlooks Potomac River; vista of the Capitol.

Martin Luther King Jr., DC (1996): 2.74. Granite statue of Dr. King close to where he delivered "I Have a Dream" speech.

Mount Rushmore, SD (1925): 1,278. Widely recognized sculpture of presidents Washington, Jefferson, Lincoln, T. Roosevelt.

Perry's Victory and International Peace Memorial, Put-in-Bay, OH (1936/1972): 25. World's most massive Doric column promotes pursuit of peace through arbitration and disarmament.

Port Chicago Naval Magazine, Danville, CA (2009): 5. Where 1944 munitions ship explosion killed 320 men.

Roger Williams, Providence, RI (1965): 4.56. Memorial to founder of Rhode Island.

Thaddeus Kosciuszko, Philadelphia, PA (1972): 0.02. Memorial to Polish hero of American Revolution.

Theodore Roosevelt Island, DC (1932/1933): 89. Statue of Roosevelt in wooded island sanctuary.

Thomas Jefferson Memorial, DC (1934/1943): 18. Statue of Jefferson in an inscribed circular, colonnaded structure.

Vietnam Veterans Memorial, DC (1980): 2.18. Black granite wall with names of those missing or killed in action in Vietnam War.

Washington Monument, DC (1876/1933): 106. Obelisk honoring the first U.S. president. Construction began in 1848 with private funding.

World War I Memorial, DC (1981/2014): 1.39. Formerly Pershing Park, dedicated to Gen. John J. Pershing.

World War II Memorial, DC (1993/2004): 8. Oval plaza with central pool commemorating those who fought and died.

Wright Brothers, Kill Devil Hills, NC (1927/1953): 428. Site of first powered flight, by Orville and Wilbur Wright.

National Historic Sites

Allegheny Portage Railroad, PA (1964): 1,284. Linked Pennsylvania Canal system and the West.

Andersonville, GA (1970): 516. Civil War POW camp.

Andrew Johnson, Greeneville, TN (1935/1963): 17. Two homes, his tailor shop, and cemetery where 17th U.S. president is buried.

Bent's Old Fort, CO (1960): 799. Replica of fort on Sante Fe Trail.

Boston African-American, MA (1980): 0.59. Pre-Civil War black-owned structures.

Brown v. Board of Education, Topeka, KS (1992): 1.85. Commemorates landmark 1954 U.S. Supreme Court decision, which ended legal segregation in schools.

Carl Sandburg Home, Flat Rock, NC (1968): 264. Home of Pulitzer Prize-winning poet and biographer.

Carter G. Woodson Home, DC (1976/2006): 0.15. Home of "Father of Black History."

Charles Pinckney, Mt. Pleasant, SC (1988): 28. Farm of a principal author and signer of the Constitution.

Christiansted, St. Croix, VI (1952/1961): 27. Preserves historic structures from time of Danish colony.

Clara Barton, Glen Echo, MD (1974): 9. Home of American Red Cross founder.

Edgar Allan Poe, Philadelphia, PA (1978/1980): 0.52. Writer's home.

Eisenhower, Gettysburg, PA (1967): 690. Home of 34th president.

Eleanor Roosevelt, Hyde Park, NY (1977): 181. Former first lady's personal retreat.

Eugene O'Neill, Danville, CA (1976): 13. Home where playwright wrote his final plays, incl. *The Iceman Cometh.*

First Ladies, Canton, OH (2000): 0.46. Home of first lady Ida Sexton McKinley. Library now devoted to U.S. first ladies.

Ford's Theatre, DC (1866/1970): 0.3. Incl. theater where Lincoln was assassinated, house where he died, and Lincoln Museum.

Fort Bowie, AZ (1964): 999. Focal point of operations against Geronimo and Apaches.

Fort Davis, TX (1961): 523. Frontier outpost in West Texas; established to guard the San Antonio-El Paso Road.

Fort Laramie, WY (1938/1960): 873. Military post on Oregon Trail.

Fort Larned, KS (1964/1966): 718. Military post on Santa Fe Trail.

Fort Point, CA (1970): 29. West Coast fortification; protected San Francisco during and after Civil War.

Fort Raleigh, NC (1941): 513. First attempted English settlement in North America.

Fort Scott, KS (1965/1978): 17. Commemorates U.S. frontier. Focal point of black troop activity, training during Civil War.

Fort Smith, AR-OK (1961): 75. One of the earliest U.S. posts in Missouri Territory, active 1817-96.

Fort Union Trading Post, MT-ND (1966): 440. Principal fur-trading post on upper Missouri, 1829-67.

Fort Vancouver, WA-OR (1948/1961): 207. Headquarters for Hudson's Bay Company.

Frederick Douglass, DC (1962/1988): 9. Home of black abolitionist, writer, orator.

Frederick Law Olmsted, Brookline, MA (1979): 7. Home of city planner, famous for designing Central Park in NYC.

Friendship Hill, PA (1978): 675. Home of Albert Gallatin, Jefferson's and Madison's secretary of treasury.

Golden Spike, UT (1957): 2,735. Commemorates completion of first transcontinental railroad in 1869.

Grant-Kohrs Ranch, MT (1972): 1,618. Ranch house owned by John Grant, 19th-cent. range-cattle industry pioneer.

Hampton, Towson, MD (1948): 62. 18th-cent. Georgian mansion, which in 1790 was largest house in U.S.

Harry S. Truman, Independence, MO (1982/1983): 13. House of 33rd pres. from 1919 on and farm where he worked as young man.

Herbert Hoover, West Branch, IA (1965): 187. Birthplace and boyhood home of 31st president.

Home of Franklin D. Roosevelt, Hyde Park, NY (1944): 833. FDR's birthplace, home, and "summer White House."

Hopewell Furnace, PA (1938/1985): 848. 19th-cent. iron-making village.

Hubbell Trading Post, AZ (1965): 160. Oldest continuously operating trading post in SW; founded in 1878 on Navajo Nation.

James A. Garfield, Mentor, OH (1980): 8. Home of 20th president; site of his front-porch campaign.

Jimmy Carter, Plains, GA (1987): 72. Birthplace and home of 39th president.

John Fitzgerald Kennedy, Brookline, MA (1967): 0.09. Birthplace and childhood home of 35th president.

John Muir, Martinez, CA (1964): 344. Home of Sierra Club co-founder and "Father of the National Park Service."

Knife River Indian Villages, ND (1974): 1,749. Remnants of villages last occupied by Hidatsa and Mandan Indians.

Lincoln Home, Springfield, IL (1971): 12. Lincoln's residence when he was elected 16th president, 1860.

Little Rock Central High School, AR (1998): 27. Commemorates 1957 desegregation during which federal troops were called in to protect nine black students.

Longfellow House—Washington's Headquarters, Cambridge, MA (1972/2010): 1.98. Poet's home, 1837-82; Washington's headquarters during Boston siege, 1775-76.

Maggie L. Walker, Richmond, VA (1978): 1.29. Home of black leader and first female bank president, daughter of former slave.

Manzanar, Lone Pine, CA (1992): 814. Manzanar War Relocation Ctr., a WWII Japanese-American internment camp.

Martin Luther King Jr., Atlanta, GA (1980): 39. Birthplace, grave, church of the civil rights leader. Redesignated a national historical park in 2018.

Martin Van Buren, Kinderhook, NY (1974): 285. Lindenwald, home of 8th president.

Mary McLeod Bethune Council House, DC (1982/1991): 0.07. Commemorates Bethune's leadership in the black women's movement.

Minidoka, ID (2001/2008): 396. WWII Japanese internment ctr.

Minuteman Missile, SD (1999): 44. Missile launch facilities dating back to Cold War era.

Nicodemus, KS (1996): 18. Only remaining Western town established by African Americans during Reconstruction.

Ninety Six, SC (1976): 1,022. Colonial trading village and site of Gen. Nathanael Greene's siege on Loyalist-held fort in 1781.

Pennsylvania Avenue, DC (1965/1996): 18. Incl. area between Capitol and White House, encompassing U.S. Navy Memorial, Freedom Plaza, Old Post Office Pavilion, other sites.

President William Jefferson Clinton Birthplace Home, Hope, AR (2010): 0.68. Birthplace and early home of 42nd president.

Puʻukoholā Heiau, Kawaihae, HI (1972): 86. Ruins of temple built by King Kamehameha, first king of united Hawaiian islands.

Sagamore Hill, Oyster Bay, NY (1962): 83. Home of Pres. Theodore Roosevelt from 1885 until his death in 1919.

Saint-Gaudens, Cornish, NH (1964): 191. Home, studio, and gardens of American sculptor Augustus Saint-Gaudens.

Saint Paul's Church, New York, NY (1943/1978): 6. Site associated with John Peter Zenger's "freedom of the press" trial.

Salem Maritime, MA (1938): 9. Major fishing and whaling port famous for 1692 witchcraft trials.

San Juan, PR (1949): 75. 16th-cent. Spanish fortifications.

Sand Creek Massacre, CO (2000): 12,583. Site where around 230 Cheyenne and Arapaho Indians—mostly women, children, and elderly—were killed by U.S. soldiers in 1864.

Saugus Iron Works, MA (1974): 9. Reconstructed 17th-cent. colonial ironworks.

Springfield Armory, MA (1974): 55. Small-arms manufacturing center for nearly 200 years.

Steamtown, Scranton, PA (1986): 62. Rail yard, roadhouse, repair shops of former Delaware, Lackawanna & Western Railroad.

Theodore Roosevelt Birthplace, New York, NY (1962): 0.11. Reconstructed brownstone where 26th president was born.

Theodore Roosevelt Inaugural, Buffalo, NY (1966): 1.18. Wilcox House, where 26th president took oath of office, 1901.

Thomas Stone, Port Tobacco, MD (1978): 328. Haberdeventure, home of signer of Declaration of Independence.

Tuskegee Airmen, AL (1998): 90. Airfield where pilots of all-black WWII air corps unit received flight training.

Tuskegee Institute, AL (1974): 58. College founded by Booker T. Washington in 1881 for blacks.

Ulysses S. Grant, St. Louis, MO (1989): 10. Home of Grant during pre-Civil War years.

Vanderbilt Mansion, Hyde Park, NY (1940): 212. Mansion of 19th-cent. financier.

Washita Battlefield, OK (1996): 315. Scene of Nov. 27, 1868, battle between Plains tribes and U.S. army.

Weir Farm, Wilton, CT (1990): 74. Home and studio of American impressionist painter J. Alden Weir.

Whitman Mission, Walla Walla, WA (1936/1963): 139. Site of Protestant missionaries to Cayuse Indians beginning in 1830s.

William Howard Taft, Cincinnati, OH (1969): 3.64. Birthplace and early home of 27th president.

Name	Location	Year[1]	Acreage
National Lakeshores			
Apostle Islands	WI	1970	69,377
Indiana Dunes	IN	1966	15,347
Pictured Rocks	MI	1966	73,236
Sleeping Bear Dunes	MI	1970	71,251
National Monuments			
African Burial Ground	NY	2006	0.35
Agate Fossil Beds	NE	1965	3,058
Alibates Flint Quarries	TX	1965	1,371
Aniakchak[2]	AK	1980	137,176
Aztec Ruins	NM	1923	318
Bandelier	NM	1916	33,677
Belmont-Paul Women's Equality	DC	2016	0.34
Birmingham Civil Rights	AL	2017	0.88
Booker T. Washington	VA	1956	239
Buck Island Reef	VI	1961	19,015
Cabrillo	CA	1913	160
Canyon de Chelly	AZ	1931	83,840
Cape Krusenstern	AK	1978	649,096
Capulin Volcano	NM	1916	793
Casa Grande Ruins	AZ	1918	473
Castillo de San Marcos	FL	1924	19
Castle Clinton	NY	1946	1
Castle Mountains	CA	2016	21,026
Cedar Breaks	UT	1933	6,155
César E. Chávez	CA	2012	117
Charles Young Buffalo Soldiers	OH	2013	60
Chiricahua	AZ	1924	12,025
Colorado	CO	1911	20,536
Craters of the Moon	ID	1924	53,438
Devils Postpile	CA	1911	800
Devils Tower	WY	1906	1,347
Dinosaur	CO-UT	1915	210,282
Effigy Mounds	IA	1949	2,526
El Malpais	NM	1987	114,347
El Morro	NM	1906	1,279
Florissant Fossil Beds	CO	1969	5,998

Name	Location	Year[1]	Acreage
Fort Frederica	GA	1936	284
Fort Matanzas	FL	1924	300
Fort McHenry (and Historic Shrine)	MD	1939	43
Fort Monroe	VA	2011	367
Fort Pulaski	GA	1924	5,623
Fort Stanwix	NY	1935	16
Fort Sumter	SC	1948	235
Fort Union	NM	1954	721
Fossil Butte	WY	1972	8,198
Freedom Riders	AL	2017	6
George Washington Birthplace	VA	1930	653
George Washington Carver	MO	1943	210
Gila Cliff Dwellings	NM	1907	533
Governors Island	NY	2001	23
Grand Portage	MN	1958	710
Hagerman Fossil Beds	ID	1988	4,351
Hohokam Pima[3]	AZ	1972	1,690
Homestead NM of America	NE	1936	211
Honouliuli	HI	2015	154
Hovenweep	CO-UT	1923	785
Jewel Cave	SD	1908	1,274
John Day Fossil Beds	OR	1974	14,062
Katahdin Woods and Waters	ME	2016	87,564
Lava Beds	CA	1925	46,692
Little Bighorn Battlefield	MT	1946	765
Montezuma Castle	AZ	1906	1,016
Muir Woods	CA	1908	554
Natural Bridges	UT	1908	7,636
Navajo	AZ	1909	360
Ocmulgee	GA	1934	704
Oregon Caves (and Preserve)	OR	1909	4,554
Organ Pipe Cactus	AZ	1937	330,689
Petroglyph	NM	1990	7,209
Pipe Spring	AZ	1923	40
Pipestone	MN	1937	282
Poverty Point[2]	LA	1988	911
Pullman	IL	2015	0.40

Name	Location	Year[1]	Acreage
Rainbow Bridge	UT	1910	160
Reconstruction Era	SC	2017	16
Russell Cave	AL	1961	310
Salinas Pueblo Missions	NM	1909	1,071
Scotts Bluff	NE	1919	3,005
Statue of Liberty	NJ-NY	1924	58
Stonewall	NY	2016	8
Sunset Crater Volcano	AZ	1930	3,040
Timpanogos Cave	UT	1922	250
Tonto	AZ	1907	1,120
Tule Springs Fossil Beds	NV	2014	22,650
Tuzigoot	AZ	1939	812
Virgin Islands Coral Reef	VI	2001	12,708
Waco Mammoth	TX	2015	107
Walnut Canyon	AZ	1915	3,529
White Sands	NM	1933	143,704
World War II Valor in the Pacific	HI-CA	2008	59
Wupatki	AZ	1924	35,422
Yucca House[2]	CO	1919	34

National Parkways

Name	Location	Year[1]	Acreage
Blue Ridge	NC-VA	1933	98,860
George Washington Memorial	MD-DC-VA	1930	7,035
John D. Rockefeller Jr. Memorial	WY	1972	23,777
Natchez Trace	MS-TN-AL	1938	52,302

National Preserves

Name	Location	Year[1]	Acreage
Aniakchak[2]	AK	1980	464,118
Bering Land Bridge	AK	1980	2,697,391
Big Cypress[4]	FL	1974	720,564
Big Thicket	TX	1974	113,122
Craters of the Moon	ID	2002	698,940
Denali	AK	1980	1,334,118
Gates of the Arctic	AK	1980	948,608
Glacier Bay	AK	1980	58,406
Great Sand Dunes	CO	2004	41,686
Katmai	AK	1980	418,699
Lake Clark	AK	1980	1,410,294
Little River Canyon	AL	1992	15,289
Mojave	CA	1994	1,545,685
Noatak	AK	1980	6,587,071
Tallgrass Prairie	KS	1996	10,883
Timucuan Ecological and Historic	FL	1988	46,263
Valles Caldera	NM	2014	89,766
Wrangell-St. Elias	AK	1980	4,852,645
Yukon-Charley Rivers	AK	1980	2,526,512

National Recreation Areas

Name	Location	Year[1]	Acreage
Amistad	TX	1990	58,500
Bighorn Canyon	MT-WY	1966	120,296
Boston Harbor Islands	MA	1996	1,482
Chattahoochee River	GA	1978	11,256
Chickasaw	OK	1976	9,899
Curecanti	CO	1965	43,591
Delaware Water Gap	NJ-PA	1965	68,664
Gateway	NJ-NY	1972	26,607
Gauley River	WV	1988	11,566
Glen Canyon	AZ-UT	1972	1,254,117
Golden Gate	CA	1972	82,027
Lake Chelan	WA	1968	61,946
Lake Mead	AZ-NV	1964	1,495,816
Lake Meredith	TX	1990	44,977
Lake Roosevelt (fmr. Coulee Dam)	WA	1946	100,390
Ross Lake	WA	1968	117,575
Santa Monica Mountains	CA	1978	156,618
Whiskeytown-Shasta-Trinity[5]	CA	1972	42,503

National Reserves

Name	Location	Year[1]	Acreage
City of Rocks	ID	1988	14,407
Ebey's Landing Historical	WA	1978	19,334

National Rivers

Name	Location	Year[1]	Acreage
Big South Fork (and Rec. Area)	KY-TN	1991	123,694
Buffalo	AR	1972	94,293
Mississippi (and Rec. Area)	MN	1988	53,775
New River Gorge	WV	1978	72,186
Ozark Scenic Riverways	MO	1972	80,785

National Seashores

Name	Location	Year[1]	Acreage
Assateague Island[6]	MD-VA	1965	41,347
Canaveral	FL	1975	57,662
Cape Cod	MA	1966	43,608
Cape Hatteras	NC	1953	30,351
Cape Lookout	NC	1966	28,243
Cumberland Island	GA	1972	36,347
Fire Island	NY	1964	19,580
Gulf Islands	FL-MS	1971	138,306
Padre Island	TX	1968	130,434
Point Reyes	CA	1972	71,053

International Historic Site

Name	Location	Year[1]	Acreage
Saint Croix Island	ME	1984	7

Other Designations

Name	Location	Year[1]	Acreage
Catoctin Mountain Park	MD	1954	5,891
Constitution Gardens	DC	1974	39
Fort Washington Park	MD	1940	341
Greenbelt Park	MD	1950	1,175
National Capital Parks	DC-MD	1933	8,693
National Mall	DC	1933	156
Piscataway Park	MD	1961	4,626
Prince William Forest Park	VA	1948	16,081
Rock Creek Park	DC	1933	1,755
White House	DC	1933	18
Wolf Trap National Park for the Performing Arts	VA	2002	130

National Wild and Scenic Rivers

Rivers in this system are designated by Congress or the Secretary of the Interior. As of Dec. 2014 (the last designation), the system included 12,734 miles of 208 rivers in 40 states and Puerto Rico. Not all of the rivers that the NPS administers are official units of the park system. Only official NPS units are listed here.

Name	Location	Year[1]	Acreage
Alagnak Wild[2]	AK	1980	30,665
Bluestone Scenic	WV	1988	4,310
Delaware Scenic	NJ-PA	1978	1,973
Great Egg Harbor Scenic and Rec.	NJ	1992	43,311
Missouri Recreational	NE-SD	1991	48,457
Niobrara Scenic	NE	1991	29,101
Obed	TN	1976	5,496
Rio Grande	TX	1978	9,600
Saint Croix Scenic Riverway[7]	MN-WI	1968	92,743
Upper Delaware Scenic and Rec.	NY-PA	1978	75,000

Affiliated Areas

Affiliated areas are administered in connection with the NPS but are not owned by that agency.

Name	Location	Year[1]	Acreage
Aleutian World War II Natl. Historic Area	AK	1996	135
American Memorial Park	MP	1978	133
Benjamin Franklin Natl. Memorial (NMEM)	PA	1972	NA
Chicago Portage Natl. Historic Site (NHS)	IL	1952	91
Chimney Rock NHS	NE	1956	83
Fallen Timbers Battlefield and Fort Miamis NHS	OH	1999	185
Father Marquette NMEM	MI	1975	52
Gloria Dei (Old Swedes') Church NHS	PA	1942	3.71
Green Springs Natl. Historic Landmark District	VA	1974	15,645
Historic Camden Revolutionary War Site	SC	1982	107
Ice Age Natl. Scientific Reserve	WI	1964	32,500
International Peace Garden	ND-MB	1949	2,330
Iñupiat Heritage Center	AK	1999	0
Jamestown NHS	VA	1940	22
Kate Mullany NHS	NY	2004	0.06
Lower East Side Tenement NHS	NY	1998	1.2
New Jersey Coastal Heritage Trail Route	NJ	1988	NA
Oklahoma City NMEM	OK	2004	6
Pinelands Natl. Reserve	NJ	1978	1,164,025
Red Hill Patrick Henry NMEM	VA	1986	NA
Roosevelt Campobello Intl. Park	NB	1964	2,722
Sewall-Belmont House NHS	DC	1974	0.35
Thomas Cole NHS	NY	1999	3.4
Touro Synagogue NHS	RI	1946	0.23
Wing Luke Museum of the Asian Pacific American Experience	WA	2013	NA

NA = Not available. (1) Year established or current designation received. (2) No federal facilities; state services may be available at certain sites. (3) Located on Gila River Indian Reservation; not open to the public. (4) Total incl. acreage added in 1988 expansion. (5) Shasta and Trinity units are administered by the Forest Service. Figure given is NPS acreage only. (6) Figure given includes acreage administered by U.S. Fish and Wildlife Service. (7) Total incl. Lower Saint Croix acreage added in 1972.

National Trails System

Source: National Park Service and Bureau of Land Management, U.S. Dept. of the Interior; U.S. Forest Service, USDA

As of mid-2018, the National Trails System included 11 national scenic trails, 19 national historic trails, almost 1,300 national recreation trails, and 7 connecting and side trails. National scenic trails and national historic trails are established by Congress and administered by the NPS, Forest Service, or BLM. Official NPS units are indicated by an asterisk.

Name	Location	Year[1]	Length (mi)[2]	Name	Location	Year[1]	Length (mi)[2]
National Scenic Trails				El Camino Real de los Tejas....	TX-LA	2004	2,580
*Appalachian	ME to GA	1968	2,180+	El Camino Real de Tierra Adentro	NM-TX	2000	404
Arizona....................	AZ	2009	800	Iditarod	AK	1978	2,350
Continental Divide	MT, ID, WY,			Juan Bautista de Anza	AZ-CA	1990	1,200
	CO, NM	1978	3,100	Lewis and Clark	IL to Pacific	1978	3,700
Florida	FL	1983	1,300	Mormon Pioneer.............	IL to UT	1978	1,300
Ice Age	WI	1980	1,200	Nez Perce (Nee-Me-Poo)	OR to MT	1986	1,170
*Natchez Trace.............	MS-AL-TN	1983	65	Old Spanish	NM to CA	2002	2,700
New England	MA-CT	2009	215	Oregon	MO to OR	1978	2,170
North Country...............	NY to ND	1980	4,600	Overmountain Victory.........	NC, SC,		
Pacific Crest	CA-OR-WA	1968	2,638		TN, VA	1980	330
Pacific Northwest	MT-ID-WA	2009	1,200	Pony Express	MO to CA	1992	2,000
*Potomac Heritage	VA to PA	1983	924	Santa Fe...................	MO, KS, OK,		
National Historic Trails[3]					CO, NM	1987	1,203
Ala Kahakai	HI	2000	175	Selma to Montgomery	AL	1996	54
California	MO, NE to			Star-Spangled Banner	VA-DC-MD	2008	290
	CA, OR	1992	5,600	Trail of Tears	GA, NC, KY		
Capt. John Smith Chesapeake...	VA, DC,				to OK	1987	5,045
	MD, DE	2006	3,000	Washington-Rochambeau			
				Revolutionary Route	MA to VA	2009	680+

(1) Year designation was received. (2) Authorized or currently completed length. (3) Trails may include both overland and water routes.

U.S. Forest Service Special Designated Areas

Source: U.S. Forest Service, U.S. Dept. of Agriculture; as of Sept. 30, 2017

These areas within the National Forest System have been specially designated by presidential proclamation or act of Congress. Size does not include acreage within National Forest boundaries not federally owned or administered by the Forest Service.

NM = Natl. Monument; NRA = Natl. Recreation Area; NS(A) = Natl. Scenic (Area); NVM = Natl. Volcanic Monument; SMA = Special Management Area.

Area	Location	Estab.	Acreage	Area	Location	Estab.	Acreage
Admiralty Island NM	AK	1980	997,226	Jewel Cave NM	SD	1908	2,531
Allegheny NRA...................	PA	1984	23,790	Kelly Butte SMA	WA	1998	5,669
Ancient Bristlecone Pine Forest	CA	2009	31,799	Kings River SMA	CA	1987	50,888
Arapaho NRA....................	CO	1978	31,102	Land Between the Lakes NRA	KY-TN	1998	171,251
Barkshead (Ozark #2) Natl. Game				Livingston (Ozark #1) Natl. Game			
Refuge....................	AR	1926	5,851	Refuge....................	AR	1926	8,755
Bear Creek NSA.................	VA	2009	5,122	Misty Fiords NM	AK	1980	2,293,162
Beech Creek NSA & Botanical Area..				Moccasin (Ozark #3) Natl. Game			
Beech Creek NSA..............	OK	1988	8,042	Refuge....................	AR	1926	4,048
Beech Creek Natl. Botanical Area	OK	1988	538	Mono Basin NSA	CA	1984	51,320
Berryessa Snow Mountain NM......	CA	2015	197,360	Moosalamoo NRA	VT	2006	15,913
Big Levels Game Refuge	VA	1935	12,147	Mount Baker NRA...............	WA	1984	8,789
Black Mountain (Ozark #5)				Mount Hood NRA................	OR	2009	34,465
Natl. Game Refuge...........	AR	1926	18,929	Mount Pleasant NSA	VA	1994	6,864
Bowen Gulch Protection Area	CO	1993	10,768	Mount Rogers NRA	VA	1966	114,223
Bridgeport Winter Recreation Area...	CA	2009	7,250	Mount St. Helens NVM	WA	1989	112,864
Browns Canyon NM	CO	2015	11,819	Newberry NVM..................	OR	1990	56,563
Caney Creek (Ouachita #4)				Noontootly Natl. Game Refuge......	GA	1938	24,670
Natl. Game Refuge...........	AR	1935	8,038	Norbeck Wildlife Preserve	SD	1920	27,630
Cascade Head NS Research Area ...	OR	1974	7,162	North Cascades NSA	WA	1984	88,039
Catahoula Wildlife Mgmt. Preserve ..	LA	1941	37,629	Oak Mountain (Ouachita #2)			
Cherokee Natl. Game Refuge #1....	TN	1924	9,862	Natl. Game Refuge...........	AR	1935	8,551
Chimney Rock NM	CO	2012	4,724	Ocala Natl. Game Refuge	FL	1930	68,241
Columbia River Gorge NSA	OR-WA	1986	83,077	Opal Creek Scenic Recreation Area..	OR	1996	13,666
Burdoin Mountain SMA.........	WA	1986	7,253	Oregon Dunes NRA	OR	1972	30,230
Gates of the Columbia R. Gorge SMA	OR-WA	1986	53,297	Ouachita Natl. Wildlife Preserve.....	AR	1935	137,958
Rowena SMA	OR-WA	1986	3,606	Quinault SMA	WA	1988	5,415
Wind Mountain SMA............	WA	1986	14,803	Piedra SMA	CO	1993	60,498
Coosa Bald NSA................	GA	1991	7,044	Pigeon Creek (Ouachita #1)			
Cradle of Forestry in America				Natl. Game Refuge...........	AR	1935	8,107
Natl. Historic Area..........	NC	1968	7,793	Pine Ridge NRA...............	NE	1986	6,636
Crystal Springs Watershed.........	OR	2009	2,094	Pisgah Natl. Game Preserve	NC	1916	71,893
Cultus Creek....................	OR	2009	278	Rattlesnake NRA	MT	1980	60,081
Ed Jenkins NRA.................	GA	1991	23,541	Red Dirt Natl. Wildlife Mgmt. Pres. ..	LA	1941	40,213
Flaming Gorge NRA..............	UT-WY	1968	187,121	Robert S. Kerr Botanical Area	OK	1988	7,971
Fossil Ridge Rec. Mgmt. Area	CO	1993	43,383	Robert T. Stafford White Rocks NRA	VT	1984	36,563
Francis Marion Natl. Wildlife Pres....	SC	1948	53,188	Roubideau SMA................	CO	1993	18,837
Frank Church-River of No Return				San Gabriel Mountains NM	CA	2014	336,534
Special Mining Mgmt. Zone-Clear				Sand to Snow NM..............	CA	2016	70,942
Creek	ID	1980	40,517	Santa Rosa & San Jacinto Mtns. NM	CA	2000	69,384
Giant Sequoia NM	CA	2000	328,411	Sawtooth NRA	ID	1972	731,774
Grand Canyon Natl. Game Preserve	AZ	1906	622,273	Seng Mountain NSA.............	VA	2009	5,195
Grand Island NRA	MI	1990	13,335	Sheep Mountain Game Refuge	WY	1924	21,526
Grey Towers Natl. Historic Site	PA	2004	95	Smith River NRA	CA	1990	323,137
Haw Creek (Ozark #4) Natl. Game				Spring Mountains NRA...........	NV	1993	316,698
Refuge....................	AR	1926	3,783	Spruce Knob-Seneca Rocks NRA ...	WV	1965	57,511
Hells Canyon NRA	OR-ID	1975	634,579	Tabeguache SMA...............	CO	1993	8,945
Hermosa Creek SMA	CO	2014	69,938	Tahquitz Natl. Game Preserve	CA	1926	18,813
Indian Nations Scenic Wildlife Area ..	OK	1988	44,519	Upper Big Bottom..............	OR	2009	1,581
James Peak Protection Area	CO	2002	17,509	Whiskeytown-Shasta-Trinity NRA ...	CA	1965	173,065
Jemez NRA	NM	1993	48,841	Winding Stair Mountain NRA	OK	1988	26,617

National Heritage Areas

Source: National Park Service (NPS), U.S. Dept. of the Interior; Alliance of National Heritage Areas

National Heritage Areas (NHAs) are designated by Congress for their national importance. NHAs are not units of the National Park system, though the NPS advises and provides limited financial assistance. NHC = Natl. Heritage Corridor.

Name	Location	Year[1]	Size (sq mi)	Name	Location	Year[1]	Size (sq mi)
Abraham Lincoln	IL	2008	25,975	The Last Green Valley NHC	CT-MA	1994	1,105
Arabia Mountain	GA	2006	64	Mississippi Delta	MS	2009	10,976
Atchafalaya	LA	2006	10,400	Mississippi Gulf Coast	MS	2004	4,289
Augusta Canal	GA	1996	3+	Mississippi Hills	MS	2009	NA[4]
Baltimore	MD	2009	18	Mormon Pioneer	UT	2006	16,070
Blue Ridge	NC	2003	10,515	MotorCities	MI	1998	10,000+
Cache La Poudre River[2]	CO	2009	45	Muscle Shoals	AL	2009	3,913
Cane River	LA	1994	181	National Aviation Heritage Area	OH	2004	NA[5]
Champlain Valley Natl. Heritage Partnership	NY-VT	2006	NA[3]	National Coal Heritage Area	WV	1996	5,300
Crossroads of the American Revolution	NJ	2006	2,155	Niagara Falls[2]	NY	2008	13
				Northern Plains	ND	2009	800
Delaware & Lehigh NHC[2]	PA	1988	165	Northern Rio Grande	NM	2006	10,000
Erie Canalway NHC	NY	2000	4,834	Ohio & Erie Canalway[2]	OH	1996	110
Essex	MA	1996	500	Oil Region	PA	2004	708
Freedom's Frontier	KS-MO	2006	31,021	Path of Progress Natl. Heritage Tour Route[2]	PA	1988	500
Freedom's Way	MA-NH	2009	994	Rivers of Steel	PA	1996	5,000+
Great Basin Natl. Heritage Route	NV-UT	2006	15,704	Sangre de Cristo	CO	2009	3,000+
Gullah Geechee Cultural Heritage Corridor	NC, SC, GA, FL	2006	12,818	Schuylkill River Valley	PA	2000	1,750
Hudson River Valley	NY	1996	6,250	Shenandoah Valley Battlefields Natl. Historic District	VA	1996	3,939
Illinois & Michigan Canal NHC	IL	1984	862	Silos & Smokestacks	IA	1996	20,000+
John H. Chafee Blackstone River Valley NHC	MA-RI	1986	720+	South Carolina NHC	SC	1996	NA[6]
Journey Through Hallowed Ground[2]	PA, MD, WV, VA	2008	180	South Park	CO	2009	1,800
				Tennessee Civil War[7]	TN	1996	42,144
Kenai Mountains-Turnagain Arm	AK	2009	650	Upper Housatonic Valley	MA-CT	2006	964
				Wheeling	WV	2000	12
Lackawanna Heritage Valley	PA	2000	350	Yuma Crossing	AZ	2000	21

NA = Not available. (1) Year designation was received. (2) Figure given is length of area. (3) Covers 11 counties in both states. (4) Parts of 30 counties. (5) 8 counties. (6) 17 counties. (7) Spans entire state of Tennessee.

Attractions in and Around Washington, DC

Most attractions are free. Hours are subject to change, especially on holidays, when some attractions may be closed. For a free official visitors guide and map, visit washington.org or call Destination DC at 1-800-422-8644.

Arlington

Arlington National Cemetery, on the former Custis-Lee estate in Arlington, VA, was first used as a burial site during the Civil War. It is the final resting place of Pres. William Howard Taft and Pres. John F. Kennedy and his wife, Jacqueline Bouvier Kennedy Onassis. More than 400,000 U.S. military personnel from every major war are buried at Arlington. The **Tomb of the Unknown Soldier**, dedicated in 1921, is guarded by soldiers 24 hrs. a day.

A number of monuments and memorials are located throughout the 624-acre cemetery. They include the **Women in Military Service for America Memorial** (dedicated 1997), which honors the nearly 3 mil women who have served or currently serve in the U.S. military. Open daily 8 AM-5 PM (8 AM-7 PM, Apr.-Sept.). Arlington, VA; (877) 907-8585. **Website:** www.arlingtoncemetery.mil

The **U.S. Marine Corps War Memorial** stands north of Arlington National Cemetery. A bronze statue depicts the raising of the U.S. flag on Mt. Suribachi, Feb. 23, 1945, during the World War II battle of Iwo Jima. The memorial grounds are open daily 6 AM-midnight; (703) 235-1530. **Website:** www.nps.gov/gwmp/

Bureau of Engraving and Printing

The Bureau of Engraving and Printing of the U.S. Treasury Dept. is the headquarters for the making of U.S. paper money. Free public tours are offered Mon.-Fri., 9 AM-6 PM, Mar.-Aug., with same-day tickets distributed first-come first-served. 14th and C Sts. SW; (866) 874-2330. **Website:** www.moneyfactory.gov

The Capitol

The United States Capitol was originally designed by Dr. William Thornton, an amateur architect, whose submission in 1793 won him $500 and a city lot. Three other architects designed or supervised construction of the Capitol before its completion.

The present cast-iron dome at its greatest exterior height measures 135 ft, 5 in. and is topped by the bronze Statue of Freedom, which stands 19½ ft and weighs 14,985 lbs. On its base are the words *E Pluribus Unum* (out of many, one). Restoration work on the dome was completed before the presidential inauguration in Jan. 2017.

The Capitol Visitor Center is open to the public Mon.-Sat., 8:30 AM-4:30 PM. Free guided tours are available by pass 8:40 AM to 3:20 PM. The Senate and House galleries are not part of the tour. To enter either gallery or to observe Congress in session, those living in the U.S. may obtain tickets from their U.S. representative or senators. Visitors from other countries may inquire at the House and Senate appointment desks. Between Constitution and Independence Aves., bounded by First St.; (202) 226-8000. **Website:** www.visitthecapitol.gov

Federal Bureau of Investigation

The Federal Bureau of Investigation discontinued tours of its headquarters following the Sept. 11, 2001, terrorist attacks. In 2014, the agency opened to the public the FBI Education Center; it was renovated in 2017 so that visitors could take a self-guided tour called the FBI Experience. Visits must be arranged in advance through the office of one's congressional delegate. J. Edgar Hoover Bldg., Pennsylvania Ave., between 9th and 10th Sts. NW; (202) 324-3000. **Website:** www.fbi.gov

Folger Shakespeare Library

The Folger Shakespeare Library, on Capitol Hill, is a research institution with the world's largest collection of Shakespearean materials and other rare books and manuscripts of the Renaissance period. Open to the public Mon.-Sat., 10 AM-5 PM, and Sun., 12 PM-5 PM. Building and garden tours are available. 201 E. Capitol St. SE; (202) 544-4600. **Website:** www.folger.edu

Holocaust Memorial Museum

The U.S. Holocaust Memorial Museum (opened 1993) documents the Holocaust through artifacts and interactive videos and educates the public on other genocides. The permanent exhibition is recommended for visitors age 11 and up.

The museum is open daily, 10 AM-5:20 PM. Entry into the permanent exhibition is timed, Mar. through Aug. Timed passes are available at the door each day on a first-come, first-served basis; advance passes can be ordered online for a fee. 100 Raoul Wallenberg Pl. SW; (202) 488-0400. **Website:** www.ushmm.org

Jefferson Memorial

Dedicated Apr. 13, 1943, the Thomas Jefferson Memorial stands on the south shore of the Tidal Basin in West Potomac Park. The circular stone structure combines architectural elements of the dome of the Pantheon in Rome and the rotunda designed by Jefferson for the Univ. of Virginia.

The memorial is open 24 hrs. a day and staffed 9:30 AM-10 PM. Ohio and E. Basin Drs. SW; (202) 426-6841. **Website:** www.nps.gov/thje/

Kennedy Center

The John F. Kennedy Center for the Performing Arts opened in 1971. Designed by Edward Durell Stone, it includes an opera house, concert hall, theaters, restaurants, and a library. Free tours available Mon.-Fri., 10 AM-5 PM, and Sat.-Sun., 10 AM-1 PM. 2700 F St. NW; (800) 444-1324. **Website:** www.kennedy-center.org

Martin Luther King Jr. Memorial

The MLK Jr. Memorial (dedicated 2011) features a 30-ft figure of Dr. King emerging from a block of granite. The memorial, with a sculpture by artist Lei Yixin, is located on the Tidal Basin between the Lincoln and Jefferson Memorials.

The memorial is open 24 hrs. a day and staffed 9:30 AM-10 PM. Independence Ave. SW and West Basin Dr. SW; (202) 426-6841. **Website:** www.nps.gov/mlkm/

Korean War Veterans Memorial

The Korean War Veterans Memorial, dedicated 1995 at the Mall's west end, features a multiservice formation of 19 combat-ready soldiers in ponchos. A granite wall, with images of service members, juts into the Pool of Remembrance.

The memorial is open 24 hrs. a day and staffed 9:30 AM-10 PM. Independence Ave. SW and French Dr. SW; (202) 426-6841. **Website:** www.nps.gov/kowa/

Library of Congress

Established by and for Congress in 1800, the Library of Congress extends its services to other government agencies and libraries, scholars, and the public. It contains more than 167 mil items in some 470 languages, making it the world's largest library.

The Thomas Jefferson Building (Main Reading Room and exhibition galleries) is open Mon.-Sat., 8:30 AM-4:30 PM. The James Madison Memorial and John Adams Buildings have longer hours. First St. SE between Independence Ave. SE and East Capitol St.; (202) 707-8000. **Website:** www.loc.gov

Lincoln Memorial

Designed by Henry Bacon and dedicated in 1922, the Lincoln Memorial in West Potomac Park is a large marble hall enclosing a statue, designed by Daniel Chester French, of Abraham Lincoln seated in an armchair. The text of the Gettysburg Address is engraved in the south chamber, that of Lincoln's second inaugural speech in the north chamber.

The memorial is open 24 hrs. a day and staffed 9:30 AM-10 PM. Independence Ave. and French Dr. SW; (202) 426-6841. **Website:** www.nps.gov/linc/

Mount Vernon

Mount Vernon, George Washington's estate, is about 15 mi from Washington, DC, in northern Virginia. The house is believed to be an enlargement of one built by Augustine Washington in 1735. His son Lawrence renamed the estate after British Adm. Edward Vernon. George Washington, Lawrence's half brother, inherited it in 1761. The estate has been restored to its 18th-cent. appearance. Washington and his wife, Martha, are buried on the grounds.

Open all year; hours vary seasonally. Mount Vernon, VA; (703) 780-2000. Admission (in-person price; discounted online): adults $20, seniors (62+) $19, youth (6-11) $12, ages 5 and under free. **Website:** www.mountvernon.org

National Archives and Records

Original copies of the Declaration of Independence, the Constitution, and the Bill of Rights are on display at the National Archives Museum. The National Archives also holds other U.S. government records, historic maps, photographs, and manuscripts.

The museum is open daily 10 AM-5:30 PM. Constitution Ave. bet. 7th and 9th Sts. NW; (866) 272-6272. **Website:** www.archives.gov

National Gallery of Art

The National Gallery of Art, established by Congress, opened in 1941. The original West Building was designed by John Russell Pope. The East Building, opened in 1978, was designed by I. M. Pei. Galleries are open Mon.-Sat., 10 AM-5 PM, and Sun., 11 AM-6 PM. The Sculpture Garden has extended hours in summer. Constitution Ave NW between 3rd and 9th Sts.; (202) 737-4215. **Website:** www.nga.gov

The Pentagon

The Pentagon, headquarters of the Dept. of Defense, is the largest low-rise office building in the U.S. It houses some 26,000 employees in offices occupying 3,705,793 sq ft. The building was severely damaged when struck by a plane on Sept. 11, 2001.

Tours are free and available by reservation only, which must be made online 14-90 days in advance. Visitors over 17 years of age must present a current valid photo ID. Arlington, VA; (703) 697-1776. **Website:** pentagontours.osd.mil

Franklin Delano Roosevelt Memorial

Opened in 1997, the FDR Memorial features four spaces with bronze statues and panels depicting FDR through his four terms in office. The 8.14-acre memorial is on the Tidal Basin.

Open daily with staff on grounds 9:30 AM-10 PM. Ohio and W. Basin Drs. SW; (202) 426-6841. **Website:** www.nps.gov/frde/

Smithsonian Institution

The Smithsonian Institution, established in 1846, is the world's largest museum and research complex. It holds some 154.8 mil artifacts and specimens in its trust. Seventeen of its 19 museums and the **National Zoo** are in the DC area. The **Smithsonian Institution Building** (or The Castle) houses the Smithsonian Information Center. Also on the National Mall are the **National Museum of African American History and Culture**, the **National Museum of African Art**, the **National Air and Space Museum**, **National Museum of American History**, the **National Museum of the American Indian**, the **Arts and Industries Building** (a special-events space), the **Freer Gallery of Art**, the **Hirshhorn Museum and Sculpture Garden**, the **National Museum of Natural History**, and the **Arthur M. Sackler Gallery**. Located nearby are the **National Postal Museum**, the **National Museum of American Art**, the **National Portrait Gallery**, and the **Renwick Gallery**. The **Anacostia Community Museum** is in SE DC. The Air and Space Museum's **Udvar-Hazy Center** is near Dulles Airport in Virginia.

Most museums are open daily, 10 AM-5:30 PM (later in summer); (202) 633-1000. **Website:** www.si.edu

Vietnam Veterans Memorial

Originally dedicated in 1982, the Vietnam Veterans Memorial recognizes those who served in the Vietnam War. The names of more than 58,000 Americans who lost their lives or remain missing are inscribed on polished black-granite walls arranged to form a V, designed by Maya Ying Lin.

Two additions have been made to Lin's design, the Frederick Hart sculpture *Three Servicemen* (1984), and the Vietnam Women's Memorial (1993), sculpted by Glenna Goodacre, honoring the more than 11,500 women who served in Vietnam.

The memorial is open 24 hrs. a day and staffed 9:30 AM-10 PM. Constitution Ave. and Bacon Dr. NW; (202) 426-6841. **Website:** www.nps.gov/vive/

Washington Monument

The Washington Monument, dedicated in 1885, is a tapering shaft, or obelisk, of white marble, 554 ft, $7^{11}\!/_{32}$ in. in height and 55 ft, $1\frac{1}{2}$ in. square at the base. Eight small windows, two on each side, are located on the observation deck at the 500-ft level.

In Aug. 2016, the monument was closed so that its elevator could be modernized; a new screening facility will also be constructed. The refurbished Washington Monument is expected to reopen in spring 2019. 15th St. and Constitution Ave. NW; (202) 426-6841. **Website:** www.nps.gov/wamo/

White House

The White House, the president's residence, stands on 18 acres on the south side of Pennsylvania Ave., between the Treasury and the old Executive Office Building. The sandstone walls, quarried at Aquia Creek, VA, were first made white with lime-based whitewash in 1798, though the name did not become official until 1901.

Free self-guided tours of the residence's public areas are available Tues.-Thurs., 7:30-11:30 AM, and Fri. and Sat., 7:30 AM-1:30 PM. Tour requests must be made at least 21 days in advance through one's member of Congress. Foreign visitors may make requests through their embassy. Tours are scheduled on a first-come, first-served basis. 1600 Pennsylvania Ave. NW; (202) 456-7041. **Website:** www.whitehouse.gov

The White House Visitor Center at 1450 Pennsylvania Ave. NW is open daily 7:30 AM-4 PM; (202) 208-1631. **Website:** www. nps.gov/whho/

National World War II Memorial

The National WWII Memorial, opened in 2004, is dedicated to the approx. 16 mil veterans who served and the more than 400,000 who died in the war. The 8.25-acre site is at the east end of the Lincoln Memorial Reflecting Pool.

The 43-ft archways at the north and south entrances represent the Atlantic and Pacific theaters. A wall of 4,048 gold stars, each representing 100 American deaths, stands in an oval plaza surrounded by 56 pillars standing for the states, territories, and the Dist. of Columbia.

The memorial is open 24 hrs. a day and staffed 9:30 AM-10 PM. 17th St. and Independence Ave. SW; (202) 426-6841. **Website:** www.nps.gov/wwii/

1492 Christopher Columbus and crew sighted land Oct. 12 in what is now the Bahamas.

1513 Juan Ponce de León explored Florida coast.

1524 Giovanni da Verrazzano led French expedition along coast from Carolina north to Nova Scotia; entered New York Harbor.

1526 San Miguel de Guadalupe, **first European settlement** in what became U.S. territory, was established in the summer off South Carolina coast; abandoned in Oct.

1539 Hernando de Soto landed in Florida May 28; crossed Mississippi River, 1541.

1540 Francisco Vásquez de Coronado explored Southwest north of Rio Grande. **Hernando de Alarcón** reached Colorado River; **García López de Cárdenas** reached Grand Canyon. Others explored California coast.

1562 First French colony in what became U.S. territory founded on Parris Island off South Carolina coast; abandoned, 1564.

1565 St. Augustine, FL, oldest continuously occupied European settlement in U.S., founded Sept. 8 by Pedro Menéndez de Avilés. Spain ceded settlement to U.S. in 1821.

1579 Sir Francis Drake entered San Francisco Bay and claimed region for Britain.

1585 First English colony in America, sponsored by Sir Walter Raleigh, founded on **Roanoke Island**, off North Carolina coast; colony failed.

1587 Second colony attempted on Roanoke Island. Virginia Dare of colony became **first English infant born** in the New World. Settlers of second colony found to have vanished, 1590.

1607 Capt. **John Smith** and 105 cavaliers in three ships landed on Virginia coast and started Jamestown, **first permanent English settlement** in New World.

1609 Henry Hudson, English explorer of Northwest Passage, employed by Dutch, sailed into New York Harbor in Sept. and up Hudson to Albany. **Samuel de Champlain** explored Lake Champlain, to the north. Spaniards settled **Santa Fe, NM**.

1619 House of Burgesses, **first representative assembly** in New World, elected July 30 at Jamestown, VA. **First black laborers**—indentured servants—in English North American colonies, brought by Dutch to Jamestown in Aug. Chattel slavery legally recognized, 1650.

1620 Pilgrims, Puritan separatists, left Plymouth, England, Sept. 16 on *Mayflower*; reached Cape Cod Nov. 19; 103 passengers landed at Plymouth, Dec. 26. **Mayflower Compact**, signed Nov. 11, was agreement to form a self-government. Half of colony died during harsh winter.

1624 Dutch settled in Albany and along Hudson River, establishing the colony of **New Netherland** in May.

1626 Peter Minuit bought **Manhattan** for Dutch West India Co. from Manahatta Indians during summer for goods valued at $24; named island **New Amsterdam**.

1630 Settlement of **Boston** established by Massachusetts colonists led by John Winthrop; Winthrop began *The History of New England*. **William Bradford**, a governor of Plymouth Colony, began his chronicle *History of Plymouth Plantation (1620-1647)*, first published in entirety in 1856.

1634 Maryland founded as Catholic colony under charter to Lord Baltimore. Act of Toleration passed 1649 provided for religious tolerance.

1626: Dutch colonial governor Peter Minuit acquires the island of Manhattan from Native Americans.

1635 Boston Latin School, **oldest public school** in continuous existence in U.S., founded Apr. 23.

1636 Roger Williams founded **Providence, RI**, in June, as a democratically ruled colony with separation of church and state. Charter granted, 1644. **Harvard College** founded; oldest institution of higher learning in U.S.

1640 First book printed in America, the so-called *Bay Psalm Book*.

1647 Liberal constitution drafted in Rhode Island. First law in America providing for **free compulsory basic education** enacted in Massachusetts.

1660 British Parliament passed first **Navigation Act** Dec. 1, regulating colonial commerce to suit English needs.

1661 Missionary John Eliot's translation of the New Testament into Algonquian became the **first Bible printed** in North America.

1664 British troops Sept. 8 seized New Netherland from Dutch. Charles II granted New Netherland and city of New Amsterdam to brother, Duke of York; both renamed **New York**. Dutch recaptured colony 1673 but ceded it to Britain Nov. 10, 1674.

1670 Charles Town, SC, founded by English colonists in Apr.

1673 Regular mail service on horseback instituted Jan. 1 between New York and Boston. **Jacques Marquette** and **Louis Jolliet** reached the upper Mississippi and traveled down it.

1674 Future **Salem witch trial** judge Samuel Sewall began renowned diary covering events through 1729.

1676 Bloody **Indian war** in New England ended Aug. 12. King Philip, Wampanoag chief, and Narragansett Indians killed. **Nathaniel Bacon** led planters against autocratic British Gov. Sir William Berkeley, burned Jamestown, VA, Sept. 19. Rebellion collapsed when Bacon died; 23 followers executed.

1678 A book of poetry by **Anne Bradstreet** (first published in Britain) revised and expanded for posthumous publication in Massachusetts. Considered first female poet in American colonies.

1679 Fire destroyed 150 houses in Boston. City imported **first fire engines** from England.

1681 John Bunyan's *The Pilgrim's Progress* published in America; became best seller.

1682 René-Robert Cavelier, Sieur de La Salle, claimed lower Mississippi River country for France and called it Louisiana Apr. 9. Had French outposts built in Illinois and Texas, 1684. Killed during mutiny, 1687. Spanish colonists became the **first Europeans to settle Texas**, at site of present-day El Paso.

1683 William Penn signed treaty with Delaware Indians Apr. 23 and made payment for **Pennsylvania** lands. The **first German colonists** in America settled near Philadelphia.

1689 New York's English colonial governor, **Sir Edmund Andros**, resigned after armed uprising in Boston on Apr. 18.

1690 First colonial newspaper, *Publick Occurrences*, published by Benjamin Harris but shut down after one issue for lack of official permission. Harris also published *New England Primer* for use as elementary school textbook. Large-scale **whaling** operations began in Nantucket, MA.

1692 Hysteria over **witchcraft** began in Salem Village (now Danvers), MA; 14 women and 6 men were executed by special court.

1697 *The Essays* of **Sir Francis Bacon**, first published in England in 1597, was published in America; it became a best seller.

1699 Former privateer Capt. **William Kidd** arrested and sent to England; hanged for piracy, 1701. French settlements made in Mississippi, Louisiana.

1702 Legislation enacted making **Church of England** the established church in Maryland.

1704 Indians and French allies attacked **Deerfield**, MA, Feb. 29; killed 40, captured and marched off 100. *Boston News Letter*, **first regular newspaper**, started by postmaster John Campbell.

1710 British-colonial troops captured French fort, Port Royal, Nova Scotia, in **Queen Anne's War**, 1702-13. France yielded Nova Scotia by treaty, 1713.

1712 A group of **black slaves rebelled against white colonists** in New York City Apr. 6 and 9 whites were killed; 40 rebels put on trial and around 20 executed, with 6 committing suicide.

1716 First theater in colonies opened in Williamsburg, VA.

1692: Witch trials begin in Salem Village; of more than 200 people accused of witchcraft, 14 women and 6 men are executed.

1726 **Great Awakening**, general revival of evangelical religion, began in colonies.

1731 America's **first subscription library** (paying members could freely borrow books) cofounded in Philadelphia by Benjamin Franklin.

1732 Benjamin Franklin published the **first** *Poor Richard's Almanack*; published annually until 1757. Georgia, last of 13 colonies, chartered.

1733 **Influenza epidemic** swept through New York City and Philadelphia.

1735 Editor **John Peter Zenger** was acquitted of libel Aug. 5 in New York City after criticizing the British governor's conduct in office.

1739 A series of **slave uprisings** put down in South Carolina.

1741 Famous sermon "Sinners in the Hands of an Angry God," delivered July 8 at Enfield, MA, by Jonathan Edwards, one of the most important preachers in the **Great Awakening** religious revival. Danish navigator **Vitus Bering**, commanding Russian expedition, reached Alaska.

1744 **King George's War** pitted British and colonials versus French. Colonials captured Louisbourg, Cape Breton Isl., Nova Scotia, June 17, 1745. Returned to France 1748 by Treaty of Aix-la-Chapelle.

1752 According to legend, **Benjamin Franklin**, flying kite in thunderstorm, proved lightning is electricity, June 15; invented lightning rod. **Liberty Bell**, cast in England, was delivered to Pennsylvania.

1754 **French and Indian War** began with Ft. Necessity campaign in Pennsylvania. Skirmish May 28, battle at fort July 3-4. British moved Acadian French from Nova Scotia to Louisiana Oct. 8, 1755. British captured Québec Sept. 18, 1759, in battles in which French Gen. Joseph de Montcalm and British Gen. James Wolfe were killed. Peace pact signed Feb. 10, 1763. French lost Canada and Midwest. Delegates from seven colonies to New York for **Albany Congress**, July 19, approved plan of union by Benjamin Franklin; plan rejected by the colonies.

1757 **First streetlights** appeared in Philadelphia.

1764 **Sugar Act**, Apr. 5, placed duties on lumber, foodstuffs in colonies. First law passed by Parliament to specifically raise revenue from colonies, alleviate French and Indian War debts. British enforced this act, unlike with **Molasses Act** of 1733.

1765 **Stamp Act**, enacted by Parliament Mar. 22, required revenue stamps to help fund royal troops. Nine colonies, at Stamp Act Congress in New York Oct. 7-25, adopted Declaration of Rights. Stamp Act repealed Mar. 17, 1766. **Quartering Act**, requiring colonists to house British troops, went into effect Mar. 24.

1767 **Townshend Acts** levied taxes on glass, lead, paper, paint, and tea. In 1770 all duties except on tea were repealed.

1770 British troops fired Mar. 5 into Boston mob, killed five including **Crispus Attucks**, a black man, reportedly leader of group; later called **Boston Massacre**.

1773 East India Co. tea ships turned back at Boston, New York, and Philadelphia in May. Cargo ship burned at Annapolis, Oct. 14; cargo thrown overboard at **Boston Tea Party**, Dec. 16, to protest the tea tax. **First museum** in the colonies was officially established in Charleston, SC; later named the Charleston Museum.

1774 **"Intolerable Acts"** of Parliament curtailed Massachusetts self-rule; barred use of Boston Harbor until dumped tea was paid for. **First Continental Congress** held in Philadelphia Sept. 5-Oct. 26; called for civil disobedience against British. Rhode Island **abolished slavery**.

1775 **Patrick Henry** addressed Virginia convention, Mar. 23, said, "Give me liberty, or give me death!" **Paul Revere, William Dawes**, and Dr. **Samuel Prescott**, Apr. 18, rode to alert patriots that British were on their way to Concord, MA, to destroy arms. At **Lexington**, MA, Apr. 19, Minutemen lost eight. On return from **Concord**, British suffered 273 casualties. Col. Ethan Allen (joined by Col. Benedict Arnold) captured **Ft. Ticonderoga** in New York, May 10, also Crown Point. Colonials headed for **Bunker Hill** and fortified nearby Breed's Hill, Charlestown, MA. Repulsed British under Gen. William Howe twice before retreating, June 17. Continental Congress June 15 named **George Washington** commander in chief; established a postal system, July 26. Benjamin Franklin became the **first postmaster general**.

1776 **Thomas Paine's** *Common Sense*, famous pro-independence pamphlet, published Jan. 10; quickly sold some 100,000 copies. France and Spain agreed May 2 to provide arms to U.S. In Continental Congress June 7, Richard Henry Lee (VA) moved "that these United Colonies are, and of right ought to be, free and independent states." Resolution adopted July 2. **Declaration of Independence** approved July 4, signed Aug. 2. Col. William Moultrie's batteries at **Charleston, SC**, repulsed British sea attack June 28. Washington lost **Battle of Long Island** Aug. 27; evacuated New York. **Nathan Hale** executed as spy by British Sept. 22. Brig. Gen. Arnold's Lake Champlain fleet was defeated in **Battle of Valcour Island** Oct. 11, but British returned to Canada. Howe failed to destroy Washington's army at White Plains, NY, Oct. 28. Hessians captured Ft. Washington, Manhattan, and 3,000 men, Nov. 16; captured Ft. Lee, NJ, Nov. 20. Washington, in Pennsylvania, recrossed **Delaware River** Dec. 25-26, defeated Hessians at **Battle of Trenton**, NJ, Dec. 26.

1777 Washington defeated Lord Charles Cornwallis at **Princeton**, NJ, Jan. 3. Continental Congress, June 14, authorized an **American flag**, the Stars and Stripes. Maj. Gen. John Burgoyne's force of 8,000 from Canada captured **Ft. Ticonderoga**, NY, July 6. Americans beat back Burgoyne at Bemis Heights, Oct. 7, cut off British escape route. Burgoyne surrendered 5,000 men at Saratoga, NY, Oct. 17. **Articles of Confederation** adopted by Continental Congress, Nov. 15; took effect Mar. 1, 1781.

1778 France signed treaty of aid with U.S. Feb. 6; sent fleet. British evacuated Philadelphia, June 18.

1779 **George Rogers Clark** took Ft. Vincennes in what is now Indiana in Feb. **John Paul Jones** on the *Bonhomme Richard* defeated *Serapis* in British North Sea waters, Sept. 23.

1780 Charleston, SC, fell to the British May 12, but Loyalists were defeated in battle of **Kings Mountain**, NC, Oct. 7 in what Thomas Jefferson called "the turn of the tide of success." **Benedict Arnold** found to be a traitor Sept. 23. Arnold escaped, made brigadier general in British army.

1781 Bank of North America, **first commercial bank**, incorporated May 26. Cornwallis retired to **Yorktown, VA**. French fleet under Adm. François-Joseph-Paul, count de Grasse, gained control of harbor; Washington's troops and French force led by Jean Baptiste de Rochambeau arrived near Yorktown, Sept. 28. After long siege, **Cornwallis surrendered** Oct. 19.

1782 New British cabinet agreed in Mar. to **recognize U.S. independence**. Preliminary agreement signed in Paris, Nov. 30. Use of **scarlet letter A**, sewn on clothing or branded on skin of adulterers, discontinued in New England.

1783 Massachusetts Supreme Court decision in final Quock Walker trial **declared slavery illegal**. Newspapers typically published weekly; **first regular daily newspaper**, *Pennsylvania Evening Post*, went on sale in Philadelphia, May 30. Britain, U.S. signed **Paris peace treaty**, Sept. 3, recognizing American independence; Congress ratified it Jan. 14, 1784. Washington ordered army disbanded Nov. 3, bade farewell to his officers at Fraunces Tavern, New York City, Dec. 4.

1784 Thomas Jefferson's proposal to **ban slavery in new territories** after 1802 was narrowly defeated, Mar. 1.

1785 Regular **stagecoach routes** established between Albany, NY; New York City; and Philadelphia.

1786 Delegates from five states at Annapolis, MD, Sept. 11-14 asked Congress to call a **constitutional convention**.

1787 Shays's Rebellion of debt-ridden farmers in Massachusetts failed, Jan. 25. **Constitutional convention** opened in Philadelphia, May 25, with Washington presiding. Constitution accepted by delegates, Sept. 17. Delaware was first state to ratify it, Dec. 7; Pennsylvania and New Jersey followed. **Northwest Ordinance** adopted July 13 by Continental Congress for Northwest Territory, north of Ohio River, west of New York; made rules for statehood and guaranteed freedom of religion, support for schools, no slavery. *Federalist Papers* first appeared in *NY Independent Journal*.

1788 A large fire in **New Orleans**, then a Spanish territory, destroyed much of the city, Mar. 21. **Constitution adopted** June 21 after being ratified by the requisite ninth state (New Hampshire); also ratified by Georgia, Connecticut, Massachusetts, Maryland, South Carolina, Virginia, and New York throughout the year. **First U.S. senators elected** Sept. 30, from Pennsylvania.

1789 George Washington chosen president by all electors voting (73 eligible, 69 voting, 4 absent); **John Adams**, vice president, got 34 votes. **First Congress** met at Federal Hall, New York City, and declared Constitution in effect, Mar. 4; Washington inaugurated there Apr. 30; **first inaugural ball** held May 7. U.S. **State Dept.** established by Congress July 27. (Thomas Jefferson installed as first secretary of state Feb. 1790.) **War Dept.** created Aug. 7, with Henry Knox as secretary; **Treasury Dept.** created Sept. 2, with Alexander Hamilton to be secretary. **Supreme Court** created by Federal Judiciary Act, Sept. 24; **John Jay** confirmed by Congress as first Supreme Court chief justice, Sept. 26.

1790 First Supreme Court session held Feb. 2 in New York City. Congress, Mar. 1, authorized decennial **U.S. census**. Collection of data took 18 months. **Naturalization Act** (two-year residency) passed Mar. 26. John Carroll consecrated as **first American Catholic bishop**, Aug. 15. Congress met in **Philadelphia**, new temporary capital, Dec. 6.

1791 Bill of Rights, submitted to states, Sept. 25, 1789, went into effect Dec. 15. First Bank of the United States, **first bank chartered by federal government**, established in Philadelphia.

1792 Coinage Act established **U.S. Mint** in Philadelphia, Apr. 2. Gen. **"Mad" Anthony Wayne** made commander in Ohio-Indiana area, trained American Legion, established string of forts. Routed Indians at Fallen Timbers on Maumee River, Aug. 20, 1794; checked British at Fort Miami, OH, same year. **White House** cornerstone laid Oct. 13.

1793 Washington inaugurated for second term, Mar. 4, having received 132 electoral votes; **John Adams** again became vice president, having received second highest total, 77. Washington declared **U.S. neutrality**, Apr. 22, in war between Britain and France. Eli Whitney invented **cotton gin** (patented 1794), reviving Southern slavery.

1794 Whiskey Rebellion, western Pennsylvania farmers protesting liquor tax of 1791, suppressed by federal militia in Sept. **Jay's Treaty**, controversial treaty with Britain negotiated by John Jay, signed Nov. 19, ratified June 24, 1795. This treaty intended to settle long-standing differences between U.S. and Britain.

1795 U.S. bought peace from **Algerian pirates** by paying $1 mil ransom for 115 seamen Sept. 5, followed by annual tributes. Gen. Wayne signed **Treaty of Greenville** with Indians, opening Northwest Territory to settlers. Univ. of North Carolina became **first operating state university**.

1796 Washington's farewell address as president delivered Sept. 17. Warned against permanent alliances with foreign powers, big public debt, large military establishment, and devices of "small, artful, enterprising minority."

1797 John Adams inaugurated as second president Mar. 4, having received 71 electoral votes; **Thomas Jefferson** became vice president, having received 68. U.S. frigate *United States* launched at Philadelphia, May 10; *Constellation* at Baltimore, Sept. 7; *Constitution* (Old Ironsides) at Boston, Oct. 21.

1798 Alien and Sedition Acts passed by Federalists June-July; intended to silence political opposition. **War with France threatened** over French raids on U.S. shipping and rejection of U.S. diplomats. Navy (45 ships) and 365 privateers captured 84 French ships. USS *Constellation* took

1787: Fifty-five delegates representing 12 states meet in Philadelphia, PA, beginning May 25, and draft a new U.S. Constitution.

French warship *Insurgente*, 1799. Napoleon stopped French raids after becoming first consul.

1800 Federal government moved to **Washington, DC**.

1801 John Marshall named Supreme Court chief justice, Jan. 20. **Thomas Jefferson**, who had received same number of electoral votes as Aaron Burr in 1800 election, won out over Burr in House vote Feb. 17; Burr named vice president. **Tripoli declared war** June 10 against U.S., which refused added tribute to commerce-raiding Arab corsairs. Land and naval campaigns forced Tripoli to negotiate peace, June 4, 1805. **Oldest U.S. art institution**, Pennsylvania Academy of Fine Arts, founded in Philadelphia.

1802 Congress established U.S. Military Academy at **West Point**, NY.

1803 Supreme Court, in *Marbury v. Madison*, overturned U.S. law for first time, Feb. 24. Napoleon sold all of Louisiana, stretching to Canadian border, to U.S. for $11.25 mil in bonds, plus $3.75 mil indemnities to American citizens with claims against France. U.S. took title Dec. 20. **Louisiana Purchase** doubled U.S. area.

1804 Meriwether Lewis and **William Clark** expedition ordered by Pres. Thomas Jefferson to explore what is now Northwest U.S. Started from St. Louis May 14; ended Sept. 23, 1806, back in St. Louis. Vice Pres. **Aaron Burr** shot Alexander Hamilton in duel July 11 in Weehawken, NJ; Hamilton died next day.

1805 U.S. Marines aided by Arab mercenaries, Apr. 27, captured Tripolitan port of Derna. Major victory in war against **Barbary pirates**; inspiration for "to the shores of Tripoli" in Marines Corps hymn.

1807 Robert Fulton made **first practical steamboat trip**; left New York City Aug. 17 and reached Albany, NY, 150 mi away, in 32 hr. **Embargo Act** banned all trade with foreign countries, forbidding ships to set sail for foreign ports Dec. 22.

1808 Legislation **outlawing slave imports** goes into effect. Some 250,000 people were illegally imported as slaves, 1808-60.

1810 Third U.S. Census found population of 7,239,881. The enslaved population was put at 1,191,364 and the population of all other non-white free persons at 186,446.

1811 Indiana Territory governor William Henry Harrison defeated Indians led by Tenskwatawa, called the Prophet, in **Battle of Tippecanoe**, Nov. 7. Construction began on **Cumberland Road** in Cumberland, MD; road became important route to West. About 400 **slaves revolted** in Louisiana and marched on New Orleans. The insurrection was suppressed; two whites, some 75 slaves killed.

1812 War of 1812 had three main causes: Britain seized U.S. ships trading with France; Britain had seized 4,000 naturalized U.S. sailors by 1810; Britain armed Indians, who raided Western border. U.S. stopped trade with Europe 1807 and 1809. Trade with Britain only was stopped 1810. Unaware that Britain had raised blockade against France two days before, **Congress declared war** June 18. British took **Detroit** Aug. 16.

1813 Oliver H. Perry defeated British fleet at **Battle of Lake Erie**, Sept. 10. U.S. won **Battle of the Thames**, Ontario, Oct. 5, but failed in Canadian invasion attempts. York (Toronto) and Buffalo, NY, were burned.

1814 Troops under Andrew Jackson defeated Creek Indians led by Chief Weatherford at Battle of Horseshoe Bend in

Alabama, Mar. 29, ending **Creek Indian War**, begun a year earlier. British landed in Maryland in Aug., defeated U.S. force Aug. 24, **burned Capitol and White House**. Maryland militia stopped British advance, Sept. 12. British bombardment of Ft. McHenry, Baltimore, for 25 hr., Sept. 13-14, failed, inspiring **Francis Scott Key** to write the words to **"The Star-Spangled Banner."** U.S. won naval **Battle of Lake Champlain** Sept. 11. Peace treaty with Great Britain signed at Ghent, Belgium, Dec. 24.

1815 Some 5,300 British, unaware of peace treaty, attacked U.S. entrenchments near **New Orleans**, Jan. 8. British had more than 2,000 casualties; Americans lost 71. U.S. flotilla finally ended attacks by **pirates** from Ottoman states of Algiers, Tunis, Tripoli.

1816 Second Bank of the U.S. chartered Apr. 10. The **American Colonization Society**, which sought to address slavery issue by transporting freed blacks to Africa, formed in Washington, DC, Dec. 1816-Jan. 1817.

1817 Thomas Hopkins Gallaudet established the **first free public school for the deaf** in Hartford, CT.

1818 Connecticut expanded **suffrage** among white male voters. Massachusetts followed suit in 1820, and New York in 1821, reducing or eliminating property qualifications.

1819 Spain ceded **Florida** to U.S. Feb. 22. American steamship *Savannah* made first part-steam-powered, part-sail-powered **crossing of Atlantic**, traveling from Savannah, GA, to Liverpool, England, in 29 days. **Washington Irving**'s *Sketch Book* became best seller.

1820 First organized immigration of blacks to Africa from U.S. began with 86 free blacks sailing to Sierra Leone in Feb. Henry Clay's **Missouri Compromise** bill passed by Congress, Mar. 3. Slavery was allowed in Missouri but not west of the Mississippi River, north of 36° 30′ (the southern line of Missouri). Compromise repealed 1854.

1821 Emma Willard founded Troy Female Seminary, **first U.S. women's college**. Stephen Austin established **first American community in Texas**, San Felipe de Austin. **James Fenimore Cooper**'s *The Spy*, novel set during American Revolution, published and became a best seller.

1822 Tension between sports and academics surfaced when Yale College Pres. Timothy Dwight banned a **primitive form of football**, setting fines for violators.

1823 Monroe Doctrine, opposing European intervention in the Americas, enunciated by Pres. James Monroe Dec. 2. The **Hudson River School**, painters who focused on the beauties of nature, began to receive public attention.

1824 Pawtucket, RI, **weavers strike** is first organized factory strike in U.S. and one of earliest known involving women workers. **Slavery abolished** in state of Illinois Aug. 2.

1825 After a deadlocked election, **John Quincy Adams** was elected president by the House, Feb. 9. **Erie Canal** opened; first boat left Buffalo, NY, Oct. 26, reached New York City Nov. 4. John Stevens, of Hoboken, NJ, built and operated **first experimental steam locomotive** in U.S.

1826 Thomas Jefferson and **John Adams** both died July 4. **James Fenimore Cooper**'s *The Last of the Mohicans* published.

1827 Massachusetts became first state to pass a law providing for tax-supported **public high schools**.

1828 Baltimore & Ohio, the **first U.S. passenger railroad**, began operations July 4. South Carolina Dec. 19 declared right of **state nullification of federal laws**, opposing the "Tariff of Abominations." **Noah Webster** published his *American Dictionary of the English Language*.

1829 Andrew Jackson inaugurated as president, Mar. 4.

1830 Famous **debate** culminating Jan. 27 between Sen. **Daniel Webster** (MA) and Robert Hayne (SC), on state right to nullify federal law. **Mormon church** organized by Joseph Smith in Fayette, NY, Apr. 6. Pres. Jackson, May 28, signed **Indian Removal Act**, granting president authority to negotiate treaties whereby Indians living east of Mississippi R. give up lands in exchange for lands in West.

1831 William Lloyd Garrison began **abolitionist newspaper** *The Liberator* Jan. 1. **Nat Turner**, black slave in Virginia, led local slave rebellion, starting Aug. 21; 57 whites killed. Troops called in, 100 slaves killed. Turner captured, tried, and hanged Nov. 11.

1832 Black Hawk War in Illinois and Wisconsin Apr.-Sept. pushed Sauk and Fox Indians west across Mississippi.

1833 American Anti-Slavery Society founded in Philadelphia, Dec. 4. **Oberlin College** became first to adopt coeducation in U.S.

1835 According to tradition, the **Liberty Bell** cracked July 8 while tolling death of Chief Justice John Marshall. **Seminole Indians** in Florida under Osceola began attacks Nov. 1, protesting forced removal. The unpopular war ended Aug. 14, 1842; most of the Indians sent to Oklahoma. **Texas** proclaimed right to secede from Mexico; **Sam Houston** put in command of Texas army, Nov. 2-4. **Gold** discovered on Cherokee land in Georgia. Indians forced to cede lands, Dec. 20, and to cross Mississippi.

1836 Texans besieged at **Alamo** in San Antonio by Mexicans under Antonio López de Santa Anna, Feb. 23-Mar. 6; entire garrison killed. Texas independence had been declared, Mar. 2. At San Jacinto Apr. 21, Sam Houston and Texans defeated Mexicans. Ralph Waldo Emerson published his first work, *Nature*, espousing his philosophy of **transcendentalism**. Marcus Whitman, H. H. Spaulding, and wives reached Fort Walla Walla on Columbia River, OR, **first white women to cross the Continental Divide**, in the Rocky Mountains.

1838 Cherokee Indians forced to walk **"Trail of Tears"** from southeast U.S. to area in present-day Oklahoma. At least 4,000—nearly one-fifth of Cherokee population—are estimated to have died.

1841 First emigrant wagon train bound for California, 47 people, left Independence, MO, May 1; reached California Nov. 4. Edgar Allan Poe published one of the **first American detective stories**, *The Murders in the Rue Morgue*.

1842 Webster-Ashburton Treaty signed Aug. 9, fixing U.S.-Canada border in Maine and Minnesota. **First use of anesthetic** (sulfuric ether gas) in an operation performed by Georgia doctor Crawford Long.

1843 More than 1,000 settlers left Independence, MO, for Oregon May 22, arriving in Oct. via **Oregon Trail**.

1844 First message over first telegraph line sent May 24 by inventor Samuel F. B. Morse from Washington to Baltimore: "What hath God wrought?"

1845 Congress **overrode a presidential veto for the first time**, Mar. 3, after Pres. John Tyler vetoed a tariff bill. Congress of **Texas** voted for annexation by U.S., July 4; Texas admitted to Union, Dec. 29. **Edgar Allan Poe**'s poem "The Raven" published.

1846 Mexican War began after Pres. James K. Polk ordered Gen. Zachary Taylor to seize disputed Texan land settled by Mexicans. After border clash, U.S. declared war May 13; Mexico declared war May 23. About 12,000 U.S. troops took Vera Cruz Mar. 27, 1847, and Mexico City Sept. 14, 1847. Treaty signed Feb. 2, 1848, ended war, and Mexico ceded claims to Texas, California, and other territory. Bear flag of **Republic of California** raised by American settlers at Sonoma, June 14. Treaty with Britain June 15 set **Oregon territory** boundary at 49th parallel (extension of existing line). Expansionists had used slogan "54°40′ or fight." The term **"manifest destiny,"** coined by journalist in 1845, also came into play. **Mormons**, after violent clashes with settlers over polygamy, left Nauvoo, IL, for West under Brigham Young. They settled July 1847 at Salt Lake City, UT. Elias Howe invented **sewing machine**.

1838: Cherokee population is marched from their homes in southeast U.S. to present-day Oklahoma on the "Trail of Tears."

1863: President Abraham Lincoln's Emancipation Proclamation frees the enslaved population in seceding states.

1847 First adhesive U.S. postage stamps—Benjamin Franklin 5¢, Washington 10¢—sold July 1. **Henry Wadsworth Longfellow**'s *Evangeline* published.
1848 Gold discovered Jan. 24 in California; 80,000 prospectors emigrated in 1849. Lucretia Mott and Elizabeth Cady Stanton led Seneca Falls, NY, **Women's Rights Convention** July 19-20.
1850 Sen. Henry Clay's **Compromise of 1850** admitted California as 31st state Sept. 9, with slavery forbidden; made Utah and New Mexico territories; made **Fugitive Slave Law** harsher; and ended District of Columbia slave trade. **Nathaniel Hawthorne**'s *The Scarlet Letter* published.
1851 Herman Melville's *Moby-Dick* published.
1852 Harriet Beecher Stowe's *Uncle Tom's Cabin* published.
1853 Japan receives Comm. Matthew C. Perry, July 14. He negotiated treaty to **open Japan** to U.S. ships. New York City hosted **first World's Fair** in the U.S., beginning July 14. **Stephen Foster** published "My Old Kentucky Home."
1854 Republican Party formed at Ripon, WI, Feb. 28. Opposed Kansas-Nebraska Act, which left issue of slavery to vote of settlers. Act became law May 30. Treaty ratified with Mexico Apr. 25, providing for **Gadsden Purchase** of a strip of land. **Henry David Thoreau**'s *Walden* published.
1855 First railroad train crossed Mississippi River on river's first bridge, between Rock Island, IL, and Davenport, IA, Apr. 21. **Walt Whitman**'s *Leaves of Grass* published.
1856 Proslavery group sacked **Lawrence, KS**, May 21; abolitionist John Brown led antislavery contingent against Missourians at Osawatomie, KS, Aug. 30. Antislavery Republican Party's **first presidential nominee**, John C. Frémont, defeated by James Buchanan. Abraham Lincoln made 50 speeches for Frémont. **First U.S. kindergarten** opened in Watertown, WI.
1857 In **Dred Scott** case, which involved determination of constitutionality of already-repealed Missouri Compromise, Supreme Court decided Mar. 6 that enslaved individuals did not become free in a free state, and black persons were not and could not be citizens. **Currier & Ives**, firm of American lithographers, issued their first print.
1858 First Atlantic cable completed by Cyrus W. Field Aug. 5. **Lincoln-Douglas debates** in Illinois, Aug. 21-Oct. 15.
1859 Edwin L. Drake drilled the **first commercially productive oil well** near Titusville, PA, Aug. 27. Abolitionist John Brown, with 21 men, seized U.S. armory at **Harpers Ferry**, WV, Oct. 16. U.S. Marines captured raiders, killing several. Brown was hanged for treason Dec. 2.
1860 Shoeworkers in Lynn, MA, went on strike Feb. 22. Within a week, strike spread to include 20,000 shoeworkers throughout New England in country's **largest strike to date**. **First Pony Express** between Sacramento, CA, and St. Joseph, MO, started Apr. 3. Republican **Abraham Lincoln** elected president Nov. 6 in four-way race.
1861 Seven southern states set up **Confederate States of America** Feb. 8, with **Jefferson Davis** as president. **Civil War** began as Confederates fired on **Ft. Sumter** in Charleston, SC, Apr. 12; they captured it Apr. 14. Pres. Lincoln called for 75,000 volunteers Apr. 15. Lincoln blockaded Southern ports Apr. 19, cutting off vital exports and aid. By May, 11 states had seceded. Confederates repelled Union forces at first **Battle of Bull Run**, July 21. **First transcontinental telegraph line** put in operation.
1862 Union forces were victorious in Western campaigns, took New Orleans May 1. Battles in East were largely inconclusive despite heavy casualties. The **Battle of Antietam**, in western Maryland Sept. 17, was bloodiest one-day battle of war; each side lost more than 2,000 men. **Homestead Act**, which granted free farms to settlers, approved May 20. **Land Grant Act**, which provided for public land sale to benefit agricultural education, approved July 7. It eventually led to establishment of state university systems.
1863 Pres. Lincoln issued **Emancipation Proclamation** Jan. 1, freeing "all slaves in areas still in rebellion." Union forces won major victory at Gettysburg, PA, July 1-3. Confederate forces under siege surrendered **Vicksburg, MS**, to Union forces under Gen. Ulysses S. Grant, July 4; control of Mississippi River in Union hands. About 1,000 were killed or wounded in **draft riots** in New York City; some blacks were hanged by mobs July 13-16. Pres. Lincoln gave his **Gettysburg Address** Nov. 19. Lincoln declared **Thanksgiving** a national holiday.
1864 Gen. **William Tecumseh Sherman** marched through Georgia, taking Atlanta Sept. 1 and Savannah Dec. 22. **Sand Creek massacre** of Cheyenne and Arapaho Indians Nov. 29. Soldiers drove Indians out of village; about 150 killed.
1865 Gen. **Robert E. Lee surrendered** 27,800 Confederate troops to Gen. Grant at Appomattox Court House in VA, Apr. 9. J. E. Johnston surrendered 31,200 to Sherman at Durham Station, NC, Apr. 18. Last rebel troops surrendered May 26. Pres. Lincoln shot Apr. 14 by **John Wilkes Booth** in Ford's Theater, Washington, DC; died the following morning. Vice Pres. **Andrew Johnson** was sworn in as president. Booth was hunted down and fatally wounded, perhaps by his own hand, Apr. 26. Four co-conspirators were hanged July 7. **13th Amendment**, abolishing slavery, ratified Dec. 6.
1866 Congress took control of Southern **Reconstruction**, backed freedmen's rights in legislation vetoed by Pres. Andrew Johnson; veto overridden by Congress, Apr. 9. **Ku Klux Klan** formed secretly in South to terrorize blacks who voted. Disbanded 1869-71.
1867 Alaska sold to U.S. by Russia for $7.2 mil Mar. 30, through efforts of Sec. of State William H. Seward. Fraternal society the **Grange** was organized Dec. 4 to protect farmer interests. **Horatio Alger**'s *Ragged Dick* published.
1868 Pres. Andrew Johnson dismissed Sec. of War Edwin M. Stanton without Senate approval. **Johnson impeached** by the House Feb. 24 for violation of Tenure of Office Act, though charges were actually made in response to his opposition to congressional Reconstruction. He was acquitted by the Senate Mar.-May. **14th Amendment**, providing for citizenship of all persons born or naturalized in U.S. and subject to the jurisdiction thereof, ratified July 9. **Louisa May Alcott**'s *Little Women* published. *The World Almanac*, a publication of the *New York World* newspaper, appeared for first time.
1869 Transcontinental railroad completed; golden spike driven at Promontory Summit, UT, May 10, marking junction of Central Pacific and Union Pacific lines. Attempt to "corner" gold led to financial **"Black Friday"** in New York Sept. 24. **Woman suffrage law** passed in Wyoming Territory Dec. 10. **Knights of Labor** labor union formed in Philadelphia. By 1886, it had 700,000 members nationally.
1870 15th Amendment, making race no bar to voting rights, ratified Feb. 8. **First U.S. boardwalk** completed, in Atlantic City, NJ. **U.S. Weather Bureau** founded.
1871 Great **Chicago fire** destroyed city Oct. 8-11. **National Rifle Association (NRA)** founded.
1872 Amnesty Act May 22 restored civil rights to citizens of the South, except for 500 Confederate leaders. Congress established Yellowstone, **first national park**. James McNeill Whistler painted famous portrait known informally as **"Whistler's Mother."**
1873 First U.S. postal card issued May 1. **Jesse James** and his gang robbed their first passenger train July 21. Banks failed, panic began in Sept. **Depression** lasted five years. **"Boss" William Tweed** of New York City was convicted Nov. 19 of stealing public funds; he died in jail in 1878. New York's Bellevue Hospital started **first nursing school**.
1874 Women's Christian Temperance Union established in Cleveland. **First public zoo** in U.S. established in Philadelphia.

1875 Congress passed **Civil Rights Act** Mar. 1, giving equal rights to blacks in public accommodations and jury duty. Supreme Court invalidated act in 1883. First **Kentucky Derby** held May 17. First **Jim Crow segregation law** enacted, in Tennessee.

1876 **Alexander Graham Bell** patented the telephone Mar. 7. Col. **George A. Custer** and 264 soldiers of the 7th Cavalry were killed June 25 in "last stand," **Battle of the Little Bighorn**, MT, in Sioux Indian War. Democrat **Samuel J. Tilden** received majority of popular votes for president over Republican **Rutherford B. Hayes**, Nov. 7, but 22 electoral votes were in dispute. Congress agreed to certify Hayes as winner in Feb. 1877 after Republicans agreed to end federal Reconstruction of South.

1877 **Molly Maguires**—Irish terrorist society in mining areas of Scranton, PA—was broken up by hanging, June 21, of 11 leaders for murders of mine officials and police. Pres. Hayes sent federal troops to control violent national **railroad strike**, which began in July.

1878 **First commercial telephone exchange** opened, New Haven, CT, Jan. 28. **Thomas A. Edison** founded Edison Electric Light Co. on Oct. 15.

1879 **F. W. Woolworth** opened his first five-and-ten store, in Utica, NY, Feb. 22. French actress **Sarah Bernhardt** made her U.S. debut Nov. 8 at New York City's Booth Theater. Economist and social philosopher **Henry George** published *Progress & Poverty*, advocating single tax on land.

1881 **Clara Barton** founded **American Red Cross** May 21. Pres. **James A. Garfield** shot in Washington, DC, July 2, by mentally disturbed office seeker; died Sept. 19. Famous gun battle between the Earp brothers and outlaw rustlers Oct. 26 near the **OK Corral**, Tombstone, AZ. **Booker T. Washington** founded Tuskegee Institute for black students. **Helen Hunt Jackson**'s *A Century of Dishonor*, about mistreatment of Indians, published.

1882 **Chinese Exclusion Act**, barring immigration of Chinese laborers for 10 years, later made permanent, passed by Congress May 6; first significant law to restrict immigration to U.S.

1883 Civil Service Act, or **Pendleton Act**, passed Jan. 16, created foundations of American civil service system. The **Brooklyn Bridge** opened May 24 as world's longest suspension bridge. Transcontinental **Northern Pacific Railroad** was completed Sept. 8. **Buffalo Bill Cody**'s Wild West Show began its 30-year touring run.

1884 Switchback Railway—**first U.S. roller coaster** built as amusement park ride—opened at Coney Island in New York City. **Mark Twain**'s *The Adventures of Huckleberry Finn* published.

1885 **Washington Monument** dedicated Feb. 21.

1886 **Haymarket riot** and bombing, May 4, followed labor battles for 8-hr. work day in Chicago; seven police and four workers died. Eight anarchists found guilty Aug. 20; four hanged Nov. 11. **Coca-Cola** first sold, May 8, at Jacob's Pharmacy in Atlanta. Apache Indian **Geronimo** surrendered Sept. 4, ending last major Indian war. **Statue of Liberty** dedicated Oct. 28. **American Federation of Labor** (AFL) formed Dec. 8 by 25 craft unions.

1887 **Interstate Commerce Act** enacted Feb. 4, created Interstate Commerce Commission.

1888 **Great blizzard** struck Eastern U.S. Mar. 11-14, causing about 400 deaths. Ernest Thayer's poem **"Casey at the Bat"** recited for first time in public at New York City theater in May.

1889 U.S. opened 2-mil acre **Oklahoma District** to settlement Apr. 22, initiating land run; "sooner" settlers illegally entered the territory before that date to stake favorable claims. More than 2,200 lives lost in **Johnstown flood** (PA) May 31. **Electric lights** installed at White House.

1890 **Sherman Antitrust Act** passed July 2, began federal effort to curb monopolies. Massacre at **Wounded Knee**, SD, Dec. 29, the last major conflict between Indians and U.S. troops; about 200 Lakota Sioux men, women, and children and 29 soldiers were killed. **Jacob Riis**'s *How the Other Half Lives*, about city slums, published, instigating reform legislation in New York City. **Emily Dickinson**'s poems published, four years after her death.

1891 **Forest Reserve Act**, Mar. 3, let president close public forest land to settlement for establishment of national parks. **Carnegie Hall**, in New York City, opened May 5.

1892 **Ellis Island**, in New York Bay, opened Jan. 1 to receive immigrants; closed 1954. **Homestead strike** (PA) at Carnegie steel mills; 7 guards and 11 strikers and spectators shot to death July 6. James J. Corbett defeated John L. Sullivan Sept. 7 to become **first world heavyweight champion** under Marquess of Queensbury rules.

1893 **Columbian Exposition** world's fair held May-Oct. in Chicago. Financial panic led to four-year **depression**. **Mormon Temple** dedicated in Salt Lake City, UT.

1894 Thomas A. Edison's **kinetoscope**, for motion pictures (invented 1887), given first public showing Apr. 14. **Jacob S. Coxey** led army of unemployed from the Midwest, reaching Washington, DC, Apr. 30. Coxey arrested May 1 for trespassing on Capitol grounds; his army disbanded. **Pullman strike** began May 11 at railroad car plant in Chicago. Milton Hershey started **Hershey Chocolate Company**.

1895 **"America, the Beautiful"** appeared for first time, in church publication, July 4. **Stephen Crane**'s *The Red Badge of Courage* published.

1896 Supreme Court, in *Plessy v. Ferguson*, May 18, approved racial segregation under the **"separate but equal"** doctrine. **William Jennings Bryan** delivered "Cross of Gold" speech July 9; won Democratic Party nomination. **John Philip Sousa** composed "Stars and Stripes Forever" on Dec. 25.

1897 **Olney-Pauncefote Treaty** with Britain, Jan. 11, gave wide scope to arbitration in settling disputes; never ratified by U.S. John J. McDermott won **first Boston Marathon** Apr. 19. First Klondike gold arrived in San Francisco July 14, helping set off **Klondike gold rush**. **First subway service** in country opens to public in Boston, Sept. 1.

1898 U.S. battleship *Maine* exploded Feb. 15 in Havana, Cuba; 260 killed. U.S. blockaded Cuba Apr. 22 in aid of independence forces. U.S. declared **war on Spain** Apr. 24; destroyed Spanish fleet in Philippines May 1; took Guam June 20. U.S. took **Puerto Rico** July 25-Aug. 12. Spain agreed Dec. 10 to cede Philippines, Puerto Rico, and Guam, and approved independence for Cuba. Annexation of **Hawaii** signed by Pres. William McKinley, July 7.

1899 Filipino insurgents, unable to get recognition of independence from U.S., started guerrilla war Feb. 4. Their leader, Emilio Aguinaldo, captured May 23, 1901. **Philippine insurrection** ended 1902. Some 200,000 civilians and 20,000 Filipino troops died, mostly from disease and starvation. Pres. McKinley signed treaty officially ending **Spanish-American War**, Feb. 10. U.S. declared **Open Door Policy** Sept. 6, to make China an open international market. Philosopher **John Dewey**'s *School and Society*, advocating progressive education ("learn by doing"), published. Pianist Scott Joplin's "Maple Leaf Rag" published, popularizing **ragtime music**.

1900 **International Ladies' Garment Workers Union** founded in New York City June 3. Fought sweatshop working conditions. **Carry Nation**, Kansas temperance leader, began raiding saloons with a hatchet. U.S. helped suppress **Boxer Rebellion** in Beijing, China. Eastman Kodak Co. introduced the **Brownie camera**, popularizing picture-taking.

1869: The ceremonial golden spike is driven at Promontory Summit, UT, marking the completion of the transcontinental railroad.

1901 Texas had first significant oil strike at **Spindletop** well near Beaumont, Jan. 10. U.S. withdrew troops from **Cuba** May 20, and Cuba became independent. Pres. **McKinley** shot Sept. 6 in Buffalo, NY, by anarchist Leon Czolgosz; died Sept. 14. Vice Pres. **Theodore Roosevelt** sworn in as youngest-ever president, at age 42 years, 11 months. **Booker T. Washington**'s *Up From Slavery* published.

1902 Permanent **Bureau of the Census** established Mar. 6. **Helen Keller** autobiography appeared in serial form.

1903 Treaty between U.S. and Colombia to have U.S. dig **Panama Canal** signed Jan. 22, but rejected by Colombia's Congress. Panama declared independence from Colombia with U.S. support Nov. 3; recognized by Pres. Roosevelt Nov. 6. U.S., Panama signed canal treaty Nov. 18. Wisconsin set first **direct primary voting system**, May 23. **Henry Ford** founded Ford Motor Co., June 16. Boston defeated Pittsburgh, 5 games to 3, Oct. 13 in **first modern World Series. First successful flight** in heavier-than-air mechanically propelled airplane by **Orville Wright** Dec. 17 near Kitty Hawk, NC, 120 ft in 12 sec. Later flight same day by **Wilbur Wright**, 852 ft in 59 sec. Improved plane patented, 1906. **Iroquois Theater fire** in Chicago killed about 600 out of 1,900 in audience, Dec. 30. Pioneering film *Great Train Robbery* produced.

1904 St. Louis hosted **first Olympics in U.S.**, July 1-Nov. 23. First section of **New York City subway** system opened, Oct. 27. **Ida Tarbell** published muckraking *The History of the Standard Oil Company*. **Henry James**'s last major novel, *The Golden Bowl*, published.

1905 Industrial Workers of the World, which advocated Marxian theory of class struggle between workers and capitalists, founded in Chicago, June 27. **Rotary**, oldest service club organization in U.S., founded in Chicago.

1906 San Francisco earthquake and fire, Apr. 18-19, caused more than 3,000 deaths and $400 mil in damages. **Upton Sinclair**'s *The Jungle*, which exposed working conditions in meat-packing industry, published. Helped spur passage of the **Pure Food and Drug Act** and **Meat Inspection Act** June 30.

1907 Financial panic and **depression** started Mar. 13. Pres. Roosevelt sent **"Great White Fleet"** of 16 U.S. battleships around the world in show of power.

1908 Springfield, IL, torn by **anti-black rioting**, Aug. 14-15. Henry Ford introduced **Model T** car, priced at $850, Oct. 1.

1909 Adm. Robert E. Peary claimed to have reached **North Pole** Apr. 6 on sixth attempt, accompanied by black explorer Matthew Henson and four Inuit; may have fallen short. National Conference on the Negro convened May 30, leading to founding of **National Association for the Advancement of Colored People** (NAACP).

1910 Boy Scouts of America founded Feb. 8. Former Pres. Roosevelt called for **"new nationalism"** in famous speech in Kansas, Aug. 10.

1911 Building with New York City's **Triangle Shirtwaist Co.** factory caught fire Mar. 25; 146 died. Supreme Court ruled May 15 that **Standard Oil Co.** must be dissolved because it unreasonably restrained trade. **First transcontinental airplane flight** (with numerous stops) by C. P. Rodgers,

from New York, NY, to Pasadena, CA, Sept. 17-Nov. 5; time in air 82 hr., 4 min.

1912 American Girl Guides founded Mar. 12; name changed in 1913 to **Girl Scouts**. U.S. Marines, Aug. 14, sent to **Nicaragua**, which was in default of loans to U.S. and Europe.

1913 16th Amendment, authorizing federal income tax, ratified Feb. 3. The **Armory Show** in New York City brought modern art to U.S. for first time, Feb. 17. **17th Amendment**, providing for direct popular election of U.S. senators (originally elected by state legislatures), ratified Apr. 8. **Federal Reserve System** authorized Dec. 23, in major reform of U.S. banking and finance.

1914 Ford Motor Co. raised basic wage rates from $2.40 for 9-hr. day to $5 for 8-hr. day, Jan. 5, increasing stability in labor force. When U.S. sailors were arrested in Tampico, Mexico, Apr. 9, Atlantic fleet was sent to **Veracruz**, occupied city. Pres. Woodrow Wilson proclaimed **U.S. neutrality** in the European war, Aug. 4. The **Panama Canal** officially opened Aug. 15. The **Clayton Antitrust Act** passed Oct. 15, strengthening federal antimonopoly powers.

1915 First transcontinental telephone call, New York to San Francisco, completed Jan. 25 by Alexander Graham Bell and Thomas A. Watson. British ship *Lusitania* sunk May 7 by German submarine; 1,198 passengers died, including 128 Americans. (In notice in morning newspapers the day *Lusitania* set sail, Germany had warned Americans against taking passage on British vessels.) As result of U.S. campaign, Germany issued apology and promise of payments, Oct. 5. U.S. troops landed in **Haiti**, July 28. Haiti became virtual U.S. protectorate under Sept. 16 treaty. Pres. Wilson asked for a military fund increase, Dec. 7. D. W. Griffith's film *The Birth of a Nation* released. William J. Simmons partly inspired by film to revive **Ku Klux Klan**, which peaks in 1920s.

1916 Gen. **John J. Pershing** entered Mexico in Mar. to pursue **Francisco (Pancho) Villa**, who had raided U.S. border areas. Forces withdrew Feb. 5, 1917. **Rural Credits Acts** passed July 17, followed by **Warehouse Act** Aug. 11; both provided financial aid to farmers. Bomb exploded during **San Francisco Preparedness Day parade** July 22, killed 10. Thomas J. Mooney, labor organizer, and Warren K. Billings, shoeworker, convicted 1917; both later pardoned. U.S. bought **Virgin Islands** from Denmark Aug. 4. U.S. established military government in the **Dominican Republic** Nov. 29. Jeannette Rankin (R, MT) elected to House of Representatives, **first woman to be a member of Congress**.

1917 Germany, suffering from British blockade, declared almost unrestricted **submarine warfare** Jan. 31. U.S. cut diplomatic ties with Germany Feb. 3 and formally **declared war** Apr. 6. Jones Act, passed Mar. 2, made **Puerto Rico** a U.S. territory, its inhabitants U.S. citizens. **Conscription law** passed May 18. First U.S. troops arrived in **France** June 26.

1918 Pres. Wilson set out his **14 Points** as basis for peace, Jan. 8. More than 1 mil American troops were in Europe by July. Allied counteroffensive launched at Château-Thierry July 18. War ended with signing of **armistice** Nov. 11. **Influenza pandemic** killed an estimated 50-100 mil worldwide, 675,000 in U.S.

1919 18th Amendment, providing for prohibition of manufacture, sale, or transportation of alcoholic beverages, ratified Jan. 16, to take effect on Jan. 16, 1920. **First transatlantic flight**, by U.S. Navy seaplane, left Rockaway, NY, May 8; stopped at Newfoundland, Azores, Lisbon May 27. **Boston police strike** Sept. 9, earliest strike conducted by government employees. About 250 **foreign-born radicals** deported Dec. 21 to Soviet Union.

1920 In national **Red Scare**, some 2,700 Communists, anarchists, and other radicals were arrested Jan.-May. **League of Women Voters** founded Feb. 14. Senate refused Mar. 19 to ratify **League of Nations Covenant**. Nicola Sacco and Bartolomeo Vanzetti accused of killing two men in Massachusetts payroll holdup Apr. 15; found guilty 1921. A seven-year campaign for their release failed; both executed Aug. 23, 1927. Verdict repudiated 1977 by proclamation of Massachusetts Gov. Michael Dukakis. **19th Amendment** ratified Aug. 18, giving women the vote. **First regular licensed radio broadcasting** began Aug. 20. **Wall St. bombing** in New York City killed 30, injured 100, did $2 mil damage, Sept. 16. **Sinclair Lewis**'s *Main Street* published.

1903: Orville and Wilbur Wright achieve the first sustained, controlled flight in a powered airplane near Kitty Hawk, NC.

1918: So-called Spanish flu strikes the U.S., infecting more than 25 million and causing over a half-million American deaths.

1921 Congress sharply curbed immigration, set **national quota system** May 19. **"Black Wall Street"** in Tulsa, OK, looted and burned by white rioters, May 31-June 1. Joint congressional resolution declaring **peace with Germany, Austria, and Hungary** signed July 2 by Pres. Warren G. Harding; treaties were signed in Aug. In so-called **Black Sox scandal**, eight Chicago White Sox players were banned from baseball Aug. 4 for conspiring with gamblers to throw the 1919 World Series. Limitation of Armaments Conference met in Washington, DC, Nov. 12-Feb. 6, 1922. Major powers agreed to curtail naval construction, outlaw poison gas, restrict submarine attacks on merchant vessels, and respect China's integrity.

1922 During nationwide coal strike, union miners killed some 21 strikebreakers at Herrin, IL, June 21-22, in incident referred to as the **Herrin Massacre**. T. S. Eliot's *The Waste Land* published.

1923 **First sound-on-film motion picture**, *Phonofilm*, shown at Rivoli Theater, New York City, beginning in Apr. Pres. Calvin Coolidge addressed Congress, Dec. 6; **first radio broadcast of president's annual speech**.

1924 Law approved by Congress June 15 made all **Native Americans U.S. citizens**. **Immigration law** enacted May 26 established permanent national quotas favoring N and W Europeans. **Nellie Tayloe Ross** elected governor of Wyoming, and **Miriam (Ma) Ferguson** elected governor of Texas Nov. 9. Ross inaugurated as nation's **first female governor** Jan. 5, 1925. Ferguson installed Jan. 20, 1925. **George Gershwin** wrote "Rhapsody in Blue."

1925 In so-called "Monkey Trial," John T. Scopes found guilty of having taught **evolution** in Dayton, TN, high school and fined, July 24. **F. Scott Fitzgerald**'s *The Great Gatsby* published.

1926 Dr. Robert H. Goddard, Mar. 16, demonstrated **first liquid-fuel rocket**. Congress established **Army Air Corps** July 2. **Air Commerce Act** passed Nov. 2, established government agencies for development of airports, radio navigation, and other services. **Ernest Hemingway**'s *The Sun Also Rises* published.

1927 Capt. **Charles A. Lindbergh** left Roosevelt Field, NY, May 20 alone in *Spirit of St. Louis* on first New York-Paris nonstop flight. Reached Le Bourget airfield May 21, 3,610 mi in 33½ hr. *The Jazz Singer*, **first feature-length film** in which **spoken dialogue was part of narrative action**, released Oct. 6. The musical *Show Boat* opened in New York City Dec. 27.

1928 **Amelia Earhart** became first woman to fly across the Atlantic, June 17. **Herbert Hoover** elected president Nov. 6, defeating New York Gov. Alfred E. Smith, a Catholic.

1929 Gangsters killed seven rivals in Chicago **St. Valentine's Day massacre** Feb. 14, which won Al Capone control of Chicago's underworld. Stock market crash Oct. 29 marked end of past prosperity as stock prices plummeted. Stock losses for 1929-31 estimated at $50 bil; beginning of **Great Depression**. Albert B. Fall, former interior sec., was convicted of accepting $10,000 bribe in leasing of the **Elk Hills (Teapot Dome)** naval oil reserve; sentenced Nov. 1 to a year in prison and fined. **William Faulkner**'s *The Sound and the Fury* published.

1930 London **Naval Reduction Treaty** signed by U.S., Britain, Italy, France, and Japan Apr. 22; in effect Jan. 1,

1931; expired Dec. 31, 1936. **Hawley-Smoot Tariff** signed; rate hikes slash world trade. **Sinclair Lewis** became first American to win a Nobel Prize in literature. **Dashiell Hammett**'s *The Maltese Falcon* published.

1931 **Empire State Building** opened in New York City May 1, displacing NYC's Chrysler Building as world's tallest. **Al Capone** convicted of tax evasion Oct. 17. **Charlie Chaplin** film *City Lights* released.

1932 **Reconstruction Finance Corp.** established Jan. 22 to stimulate banking and business. Unemployment at 12 mil. Twenty-month-old **Charles Lindbergh Jr.** kidnapped Mar. 1; found dead May 12. Bruno Hauptmann found guilty Feb. 1935; executed Apr. 3, 1936. Unemployed World War I veterans demanding Congress pay promised bonus early launched **Bonus March** on Washington, DC, May 29. **Franklin D. Roosevelt** elected president for first time in Democratic landslide, Nov. 8. Chicago Bears won **first NFL title game** Dec. 18, defeating the Portsmouth (OH) Spartans, 9-0.

1933 Pres. Roosevelt named **Frances Perkins** U.S. sec. of labor; **first woman in U.S. cabinet**. Pres. Roosevelt ordered **all U.S. banks closed** Mar. 6. In a "100 days" special session, Mar. 9-June 16, Congress passed **New Deal**, including measures to regulate banks, distribute funds to the jobless, create jobs, raise agricultural prices, and set wage and production standards for industry. **Gold standard** dropped by U.S. in favor of "modified gold bullion standard"; announced by Pres. Roosevelt Apr. 19, ratified by Congress June 5. **Tennessee Valley Authority (TVA)** created by act of Congress, May 18. **Prohibition** ended in the U.S. as 36th state ratified **21st Amendment** Dec. 5. Pres. Roosevelt foreswore armed intervention in **Western Hemisphere** nations, Dec. 26.

1934 Pres. Roosevelt signed law creating **Securities and Exchange Commission**, June 6. U.S. troops pulled out of **Haiti**, Aug. 6.

1935 **Works Progress Administration (WPA)** instituted May 6. Rural Electrification Administration created May 11. National Industrial Recovery Act struck down by Supreme Court May 27. **Boulder Dam** (later renamed **Hoover Dam**) completed, May 29. **Social Security Act** passed by Congress Aug. 8-9. Comedian **Will Rogers** and aviator Wiley Post killed Aug. 15 in Alaska plane crash. Sen. **Huey Long**, former Louisiana governor, shot Sept. 8 by a political rival's son-in-law; died Sept. 10. George Gershwin's jazz opera *Porgy and Bess* opened Oct. 10 in New York. **Committee for Industrial Organization** (later Congress of Industrial Organizations) formed to expand industrial unionism Nov. 9.

1936 **Jesse Owens** won four gold medals at the **Berlin Olympics** in Aug. **Baseball Hall of Fame** founded in Cooperstown, NY. **Margaret Mitchell**'s *Gone With the Wind* published.

1937 Airship *Hindenburg* caught fire May 6 as it was landing in Lakehurst, NJ; 36 killed. **Golden Gate Bridge** in San Francisco opened May 27. **Joe Louis** knocked out James J. Braddock to become world heavyweight champ June 22. Aviator **Amelia Earhart** and copilot Fred Noonan disappeared July 2 near Howland Isl., in the Pacific. Pres. Roosevelt proposed judicial reforms that would allow him to appoint additional Supreme Court justices; his **"court-packing" plan** defeated. **Auto, steel labor unions** won first big contracts.

1938 **National minimum wage** enacted June 25. Orson Welles's radio dramatization of H. G. Wells's *War of the Worlds*, Oct. 30, caused Martian invasion scare among some who had missed the introduction. **Seabiscuit** beat War Admiral in match race of the century, at Pimlico track, MD, Nov. 1. The work of folk artist Anna Mary Robertson Moses, **"Grandma Moses,"** discovered. **Thornton Wilder**'s *Our Town* produced on Broadway.

1939 Opera singer **Marian Anderson** performed for integrated crowd of 75,000 at Lincoln Memorial Apr. 9 after Daughters of the American Revolution refused to let Anderson sing in DC's Constitution Hall. **New York World's Fair**—theme: "The World of Tomorrow"—opened Apr. 30, closed Oct. 31. Reopened for second season May 11-Oct. 27, 1940. **Lou Gehrig**, seriously ill with disease that would come to bear his name, said farewell to fans at Yankee Stadium, July 4. Albert Einstein alerted Pres. Roosevelt to **A-bomb possibilities** in Aug. 2 letter. **U.S. declared its neutrality** in European war Sept. 1. Pres. Roosevelt proclaimed limited **national emergency** Sept. 8, unlimited emergency May 27, 1941. Both ended by Pres. Harry Truman, Apr. 28, 1952.

1942: Pres. Franklin D. Roosevelt orders the relocation of 117,000 Japanese-Americans to detention camps for the duration of the war.

Pocket Books, **first paperback publisher** in U.S., established. **John Steinbeck**'s *The Grapes of Wrath* published. *The Wizard of Oz* and *Gone With the Wind* released, the latter to become highest-grossing film of all time (inflation-adjusted).

1940 U.S. OK'd sale of **surplus war material** to Britain June 3; announced transfer of 50 overaged destroyers Sept. 3. **First peacetime military draft** in U.S. history approved, Sept. 14. **Forty-hour work week** went into effect, Oct. 24. Pres. **Roosevelt** elected Nov. 5 to third presidential term. **Richard Wright**'s *Native Son* published.

1941 **Four Freedoms**—freedom of speech and religion, freedom from want and fear—termed essential by Pres. Roosevelt in speech to Congress Jan. 6. **Lend-Lease Act** signed Mar. 11 provided $7 bil in military credits for Britain. Lend-lease for USSR approved in Nov. Pres. Roosevelt signed executive order June 25 barring federal government and war contractors from **racial discrimination**. Order also established Fair Employment Practice Committee. The **Atlantic Charter**, 8-point declaration of principles, issued by Pres. Roosevelt and British Prime Min. Winston Churchill, Aug. 14. Japan attacked **Pearl Harbor**, Hawaii, 7:55 AM Hawaiian time, Dec. 7; 19 ships sunk or damaged, 2,403 dead. Pres. Roosevelt called it "a date which will live in infamy." U.S. declared war on Japan Dec. 8. Germany and Italy declared war on U.S. Dec. 11. U.S. responded with declaration of war later on same day. Japanese invaded **Philippines**, Dec. 22; Wake Island fell, Dec. 23. *Citizen Kane*, directed by Orson Welles, released.

1942 Pres. Roosevelt issued executive order Feb. 19 authorizing relocation of Japanese-Americans. Federal government began forcibly moving 117,000 Japanese-Americans from West Coast to **detention camps**; exclusion lasted three years. Japanese troops took **Bataan** peninsula Apr. 8 and **Corregidor** May 6. **Battle of Midway** June 4-7 was Japan's first major defeat. Marines landed on **Guadalcanal** Aug. 7; last Japanese not expelled until Feb. 9, 1943. U.S., Britain invaded **North Africa** Nov. 8. **First nuclear chain reaction** (fission of uranium isotope U-235) produced at Univ. of Chicago under physicists Arthur Compton, Enrico Fermi, others, Dec. 2. The movie *Casablanca*, starring Humphrey Bogart and Ingrid Bergman, released.

1943 *Oklahoma!* opened Mar. 31 on Broadway. Pres. Roosevelt signed June 10 pay-as-you-go income tax bill. Starting July 1, wage and salary earners were subject to **paycheck withholding tax**. **Detroit race riot** June 21 left 34 dead, 700 injured. Six killed in riot in New York City's **Harlem** section Aug. 2. U.S., Britain invaded **Sicily** July 9, Italian **mainland** Sept. 3. Marines in Nov. recaptured the **Gilbert Islands**, captured by Japan in 1941 and 1942.

1944 U.S., Allied forces invaded Europe at Normandy, France, on **"D-Day,"** June 6, in massive amphibious operation. **GI Bill of Rights**, providing benefits to veterans, signed by Pres. Roosevelt June 22. Representatives of the U.S. and other major powers met at **Dumbarton Oaks**, Washington, DC, Aug. 21-Oct. 7, to work out formation of postwar world organization that would become the **United Nations**. U.S. forces

landed on **Leyte**, Philippines, Oct. 20. Pres. **Roosevelt** elected to fourth term as president Nov. 7. **Battle of the Bulge**, failed Nazi counteroffensive, waged Dec. 16 to Jan. 28, 1945.

1945 **Yalta Conference** met in the Crimea, USSR, Feb. 4-11. Pres. Roosevelt, Prime Min. Churchill, and Soviet leader Joseph Stalin agreed that their countries, plus France, would occupy Germany and that the Soviet Union would enter war against Japan. Marines landed on **Iwo Jima** Feb. 19, declared victory Mar. 26 after heavy casualties. U.S. forces invaded **Okinawa** Apr. 1, captured it June 21. Pres. **Roosevelt** died in Warm Springs, GA, Apr. 12; Vice Pres. **Harry S. Truman** became president. Germany surrendered May 7; May 8 proclaimed **V-E Day**. **First atomic bomb**, produced at Los Alamos, NM, exploded at Alamogordo, NM, July 16. Bomb dropped on **Hiroshima**, Japan, Aug. 6, killing about 75,000; bomb dropped on **Nagasaki**, Japan, Aug. 9, killing about 40,000. Japan agreed to surrender Aug. 14; formally surrendered Sept. 2. At **Potsdam Conference**, July 17-Aug. 2, leaders of U.S., USSR, and Britain agreed on disarmament of Germany, occupation zones, war crimes trials. **Empire State Building** struck accidentally by Army B-25 bomber, July 28, killing 14. U.S. forces entered **Korea** south of 38th parallel to displace Japanese Sept. 8. Gen. **Douglas MacArthur** took over supervision of Japan Sept. 9.

1946 **Steel strike** by 750,000 started Jan. 21, settled in four weeks. Strike by 400,000 **mine workers** began Apr. 1 (settled May 29); other industries (including rail, maritime) followed. Former Prime Min. Winston Churchill employed the phrase **"Iron Curtain"** in Mar. 5 speech at Westminster College in Fulton, MO. Atomic bomb tested off **Bikini Atoll** in Pacific, July 1. In all, U.S. conducted 23 nuclear tests between 1946 and 1958. **Philippines** given independence by U.S. July 4. Mother Frances Xavier Cabrini **first American to be canonized**, July 7. Dr. Benjamin Spock's *Baby and Child Care* published as **baby boom** began.

1947 Pres. Truman asked Congress for financial and military aid for Greece and Turkey to help combat Communist subversion, Mar. 12; **Truman Doctrine** approved May 15. UN Security Council voted Apr. 2 to place under U.S. trusteeship the **Pacific islands** formerly mandated to Japan. **Jackie Robinson** joined Brooklyn Dodgers Apr. 11, breaking color barrier in major league baseball. The **Marshall Plan** for U.S. aid to European countries proposed by Sec. of State George C. Marshall June 5. Congress authorized some $12 bil in next four years. **Taft-Hartley Labor Act** restricting labor union power vetoed by Pres. Truman June 20; Congress overrode veto. Air Force Capt. **Chuck Yeager** broke sound barrier, Oct. 14, in X-1 rocket plane.

1948 **Organization of American States** (OAS) founded Apr. 30 by 21 countries. USSR halted all surface traffic into **West Berlin** June 24; in response, U.S. and British troops launched an **airlift**. Soviet blockade halted May 12, 1949; airlift ended Sept. 30. Pres. **Truman** elected Nov. 2, defeating NY Gov. Thomas E. Dewey in historic upset. Former State Dept. official **Alger Hiss** indicted Dec. 15 for perjury, after denying he had passed government documents to Whittaker Chambers to go to a Communist spy ring; convicted Jan. 21, 1950. **Kinsey Report** on sexuality in the human male published.

1949 North Atlantic Treaty Organization (**NATO**) established Aug. 24 by U.S., Canada, and 10 Western European nations, agreeing that an armed attack against one would be considered an attack against all. Eleven leaders of U.S. **Communist Party** convicted Oct. 14 of advocating violent overthrow of U.S. government; sentenced to prison. Supreme Court upheld convictions, 1951. Pres. Truman, Oct. 26, signed legislation raising **federal minimum wage** from 40¢ an hour to 75¢. **Arthur Miller**'s *Death of a Salesman* opened on Broadway.

1950 Masked bandits robbed **Brink's, Inc.**, Boston express office, Jan. 17, of $2.8 mil. Case solved 1956; eight sentenced to life. Pres. Truman authorized production of **H-bomb** Jan. 31. Special Senate committee to investigate organized crime established May 3, chaired by Sen. **Estes Kefauver** (D, TN).

North Korean forces **invaded South Korea** June 25. UN asked for troops to restore peace. Pres. Truman ordered Air Force and Navy to Korea June 27. Truman approved ground forces, airstrikes against North Korea June 30. U.S. sent

1944: More than 160,000 Allied troops storm a heavily fortified stretch of French coastline on D-Day (June 6).

35 military advisers to **South Vietnam** June 27 and agreed to aid anti-Communist government. U.S. forces landed at **Inchon**, South Korea, Sept. 15. UN forces took Pyongyang Oct. 20, reached China border Nov. 20. China sent troops across border Nov. 26. U.S. banned shipments Dec. 8 to **Communist China** and to Asiatic ports trading with it.

Army **seized all U.S. railroads** Aug. 27 on Truman's order to prevent general strike; returned to owners in 1952. Two members of **Puerto Rican nationalist movement** tried to kill Pres. Truman Nov. 1.

Peanuts comic strip appeared in newspapers. Variety show *Your Show of Shows* debuted on TV. David Riesman's *The Lonely Crowd* published.

1951 **22nd Amendment**, limiting presidential term of office, ratified Feb. 27. **Julius Rosenberg**; his wife, **Ethel Rosenberg**; and **Morton Sobell** found guilty Mar. 29 of conspiracy to commit wartime espionage. Rosenbergs received death penalty. Sobell sentenced to 30 years; released 1969.

Pres. Truman removed Gen. **Douglas MacArthur** from Korea command Apr. 11 for unauthorized policy statements. **Korea cease-fire** talks began in July; lasted two years. Fighting ended July 27, 1953.

Transcontinental TV began Sept. 4 with Pres. Truman's address at Japanese Peace Treaty Conference in San Francisco. **Japanese peace treaty** signed in San Francisco Sept. 8 by U.S., Japan, and 47 other nations. **J. D. Salinger**'s *Catcher in the Rye* published. *I Love Lucy* sitcom premiered on TV.

1952 Pres. Truman ordered seizure of nation's **steel mills** Apr. 8 to avert strike; ruled illegal by Supreme Court June 2. **Peace contract** between West Germany, U.S., Great Britain, and France signed May 26. **Immigration** measure, passed over veto June 26-27, barred those deemed subversive and removed some barriers to Asian immigration, though quotas remained for nationalities and regions. **Puerto Rico** proclaimed commonwealth July 25, after referendum Mar. 3. Richard Nixon, as vice-pres. candidate, gave **"Checkers" speech**, so called because of sentimental reference to his dog Checkers, Sept. 23. **First hydrogen device explosion** Nov. 1 in Pacific. **Ralph Ellison**'s *Invisible Man* published.

1953 Federal jury in New York convicted 13 **Communist** leaders on conspiracy charges, Jan. 20. **Julius and Ethel Rosenberg** executed in electric chair, June 19, for relaying nuclear secrets to Soviet Union. **Korean War armistice** signed July 27. California Gov. **Earl Warren** sworn in Oct. 5 as 14th chief justice of U.S. Supreme Court.

1954 *Nautilus*, **first atomic-powered submarine**, launched at Groton, CT, Jan. 21. Five members of Congress were wounded in the House Mar. 1 by four **Puerto Rican independence supporters** who fired at random from a spectators' gallery.

At televised hearings, Apr. 22-June 17, before a Senate subcommittee, Army officials accused Sen. **Joseph McCarthy** (R, WI) of seeking preferential treatment for a draftee, and McCarthy accused Army of hindering probe of Communist infiltration. McCarthy was cleared in the hearings, but the Senate later voted to condemn him, 67-22, for abuse of the Senate during hearings and debates.

Supreme Court ruled unanimously May 17 that racial segregation in public schools was unconstitutional, in *Brown v.*

Board of Education of Topeka. **Ernest Hemingway** won Nobel Prize in literature for *The Old Man and the Sea*.

1955 U.S. agreed Feb. 12 to help train **South Vietnamese army**. Supreme Court ordered "all deliberate speed" in **integration** of public schools, May 31. A summit meeting of leaders of **Big 4**—U.S., Britain, France, and USSR—took place July 18-23 in Geneva, Switzerland.

Rosa Parks refused Dec. 1 to give her seat to white man on bus in Montgomery, AL. Her arrest, detention, and conviction sparked boycott of bus system, organized by Rev. **Martin Luther King Jr.**, by Montgomery's black community, Dec. 5. Bus segregation ordinance declared unconstitutional by federal court in 1956. Boycott ended Dec. 23 of that year.

America's two largest labor organizations merged Dec. 5, creating **AFL-CIO**. Russian-born U.S. citizen **Vladimir Nabokov**'s *Lolita* published.

1956 Massive resistance to Supreme Court **desegregation rulings** was called for Mar. 12 by 101 Southern congressmen. U.S. Supreme Court, Apr. 23, unanimously ruled against **racial segregation** on intrastate buses.

Federal-Aid Highway Act signed June 29, creating **interstate highway system**. **First transatlantic telephone cable** activated Sept. 25. In Game 5, Oct. 8, Yankee right-hander Don Larsen pitched **only perfect World Series game**. **Eugene O'Neill**'s *Long Day's Journey Into Night* opened Nov. 7 on Broadway.

1957 Congress approved **Civil Rights Act of 1957**, Apr. 29, first such bill since Reconstruction to protect voting rights. Pres. Dwight D. Eisenhower signed act into law Sept. 9; provided for creation of Civil Rights Commission. The U.S. surgeon general July 12 said studies showed "direct link" between cigarette **smoking and lung cancer**.

Arkansas Gov. Orval Faubus (D) called National Guardsmen Sept. 4 to bar nine black students from entering all-white high school in **Little Rock**. Faubus complied Sept. 21 with federal court order to remove Guardsmen, but local authorities ordered black students to withdraw. Pres. Eisenhower sent troops Sept. 24 to enforce court order.

Jack Kerouac's *On the Road* published.

1958 Army launched **first U.S. Earth-orbiting satellite**, *Explorer I*, Jan. 31 from Cape Canaveral, FL; discovered Van Allen radiation belt. U.S. Marines sent to **Lebanon** to protect elected government from threatened overthrow July-Oct. Nuclear sub *Nautilus* made **first undersea crossing of North Pole** Aug. 5. Presidential aide **Sherman Adams** resigned Sept. 22 over scandal involving alleged improper gifts. **First domestic jet airline passenger service** in U.S. opened by National Airlines Dec. 10 between New York and Miami.

1959 **Alaska** admitted as 49th state, Jan. 3; **Hawaii** admitted as 50th, Aug. 21. **St. Lawrence Seaway** linking Atlantic Ocean and Great Lakes opened to traffic, Apr. 25.

Vice Pres. Richard Nixon, on tour of USSR, held **"kitchen debate,"** July 24, with Soviet Prem. Nikita Khrushchev at U.S. exhibit in Moscow. Prem. **Khrushchev** paid unprecedented visit to U.S. Sept. 15-27; made transcontinental tour.

Pres. Eisenhower issued injunction Oct. 12, upheld and made effective by Supreme Court Nov. 7, ending record **116-day steel strike**. In **quiz show scandal**, Columbia Univ. Prof. Charles Van Doren admitted to U.S. House subcommittee Nov. 2 that he had been coached before appearances on NBC-TV's *21* in 1956; he had won $129,000. William Wyler's *Ben-Hur* released; the movie won a record 11 Academy Awards the following year.

1960 **Sit-ins** began Feb. 1 when four black college students in Greensboro, NC, refused to move from a Woolworth lunch counter after being denied service. By Sept. 1961, more than 70,000 students, whites and blacks, had participated in sit-ins. Pres. Eisenhower signed **Civil Rights Act** May 6.

A U.S. **U-2 reconnaissance plane** was shot down in the Soviet Union May 1; pilot Gary Powers captured. The incident led to cancellation of Paris summit conference; Powers traded for Soviet spy, 1962. A **birth control pill** approved as safe for first time by Food and Drug Administration May 9. Vice Pres. **Richard Nixon** and Sen. **John F. Kennedy** faced each other Sept. 26 in first in series of televised debates. Kennedy defeated Nixon to win presidency, Nov. 8. U.S. announced Dec. 15 its backing of rightist group in **Laos**, which took power the next day.

Alfred Hitchcock film *Psycho* released.

1963: The March on Washington for Jobs and Freedom protests racial discrimination; demonstrators demand equality and support civil rights legislation pending in Congress.

1961 U.S. severed diplomatic and consular relations with Cuba Jan. 3, after disputes over nationalizations of U.S. firms, U.S. military presence at Guantánamo base. U.S.-directed invasion of Cuba's **Bay of Pigs** Apr. 17 by Cuban exiles unsuccessfully attempted to overthrow the regime of Prem. Fidel Castro.

Peace Corps created by executive order, Mar. 1. **23rd Amendment**, giving DC citizens the right to vote in presidential elections, ratified Mar. 29. Alan B. Shepard Jr. rocketed from Cape Canaveral, FL, in a Mercury capsule May 5, in **first U.S.-crewed suborbital space flight**.

"Freedom Rides" from Washington, DC, across Deep South were launched May 20 to protest segregation in interstate transportation.

Joseph Heller's *Catch-22* published.

1962 Pres. Kennedy said Feb. 14 that U.S. military advisers in **Vietnam** would fire if fired upon. Lt. Col. John H. Glenn Jr. became **first American in orbit** Feb. 20 when he circled the Earth three times in the Mercury capsule *Friendship 7*.

In *Baker v. Carr*, Mar. 26, U.S. Supreme Court ruled that constitutional challenges to unequal distribution of voters among legislative districts could be resolved by federal courts. **James Meredith** became first black student at Univ. of Mississippi Oct. 1 after 3,000 federal troops put down riots.

A Soviet **offensive missile buildup** in Cuba was revealed Oct. 22 by Pres. Kennedy, who ordered naval and air quarantine on shipment of offensive military equipment to the island. He and Soviet Prem. Khrushchev agreed Oct. 28 on formula to end crisis. Kennedy announced Nov. 2 that missile bases in Cuba were being dismantled. **Rachel Carson**'s *Silent Spring* launched environmentalist movement.

1963 In *Gideon v. Wainwright*, Mar. 18, Supreme Court ruled that all criminal defendants have a right to counsel.

March for civil rights began May 2 in Birmingham, AL; led to desegregation accord, which in turn sparked rioting and violence. Univ. of Alabama **desegregated** after Gov. George Wallace stepped aside when confronted by federally deployed National Guard troops June 11. Civil rights leader **Medgar Evers** assassinated June 12. On Aug. 28, 200,000 joined in **March on Washington** in support of black demands for equal rights led by **Rev. Martin Luther King Jr.**; highlight was King's **"I Have a Dream" speech**.

Supreme Court ruled June 17 that laws requiring **recitation of Lord's Prayer or Bible verses** in public schools were unconstitutional. Pres. Kennedy, on Europe trip, addressed huge crowd in **West Berlin**, June 23. **Limited nuclear test-ban treaty** agreed upon July 25 by the U.S., the Soviet Union, and Britain. Four black girls killed in bombing of **16th St. Baptist Church** in Birmingham, AL, Sept. 15.

South Vietnam Pres. **Ngo Dinh Diem** assassinated Nov. 2; U.S. had earlier withdrawn support. Pres. **Kennedy** shot and fatally wounded Nov. 22 as he rode in motorcade through downtown Dallas, TX. Vice Pres. **Lyndon B. Johnson** sworn in as president. **Lee Harvey Oswald** arrested and charged with murder but was himself shot and fatally wounded Nov. 24. Nightclub owner **Jack Ruby** convicted of Oswald's murder; Ruby died in 1967 while awaiting retrial following reversal of his conviction. **Betty Friedan**'s feminist work *The Feminine Mystique* published.

1964 **Panama** suspended relations with U.S. Jan. 9 after riots. U.S. offered Dec. 18 to negotiate new canal treaty. **The Beatles** appeared Feb. 9 on *The Ed Sullivan Show*. Supreme Court ruled Feb. 17 that **congressional districts** as near as practicable be equal in population. U.S. reported May 27 it was sending military planes to **Laos**.

Three **civil rights workers** reported missing in Mississippi June 22; bodies found Aug. 4. Eighteen white men tried. On Oct. 20, 1967, an all-white federal jury convicted seven of conspiracy in the slayings. Omnibus **civil rights bill** signed by Pres. Johnson July 2, banning discrimination in voting, jobs, public accommodations.

Congress Aug. 7 passed **Tonkin Gulf Resolution**, authorizing presidential action in Vietnam, after North Vietnamese boats reportedly attacked U.S. destroyers Aug. 2. (Resolution repealed, 1971.) Congress approved War on Poverty bill Aug. 11, providing for a domestic Peace Corps (**VISTA**), **Job Corps**, and antipoverty funding. The **Warren Commission** released a report Sept. 27 concluding that Lee Harvey Oswald was solely responsible for the Kennedy assassination. Pres. **Johnson** elected to full term, Nov. 3, defeating Sen. **Barry Goldwater** (R, AZ) in landslide. **Verrazano-Narrows Bridge** opened in New York City, Nov. 21, with world's then-longest suspension span.

1965 In State of the Union address Jan. 4, Pres. Johnson outlined plans for **"Great Society,"** program of civil rights, antipoverty, and health-care legislation. Johnson in Feb. ordered continuous bombing of **North Vietnam** below 20th parallel.

Malcolm X assassinated by Nation of Islam members Feb. 21 at New York City rally. March from **Selma to Montgomery**, AL, Mar. 21-25, by Rev. Martin Luther King Jr. to demand federal protection of blacks' voting rights. Some 14,000 U.S. troops sent to **Dominican Republic** during civil war Apr. 28. All troops withdrawn by next year. Bill establishing **Medicare**, government health insurance program for elderly, signed by Pres. Johnson July 30.

New **Voting Rights Act**, which banned literacy tests and other voter qualification tests, signed Aug. 6. Arrest of black motorist by white police officers precipitated **Watts riot** in predominantly-black Los Angeles neighborhood Aug. 11-16. Riots resulted in 34 deaths and $200 mil in property damage.

Major **immigration law**, signed Oct. 3, replaced national quota system with emphasis on immigrants' skills and family unification. **Electric power failure** blacked out most of northeastern U.S., parts of two Canadian provinces the night of Nov. 9-10.

1966 U.S. forces began firing into **Cambodia** May 1. Bombing of **Hanoi** area of North Vietnam by U.S. planes began June 29. By Dec. 31, 385,300 U.S. troops were stationed in South Vietnam, plus 60,000 offshore and 33,000 in Thailand.

Supreme Court ruled June 13, in *Miranda v. Arizona*, that suspects must be read their rights before police questioning. **Medicare** began July 1. In **Univ. of Texas shooting** rampage, 25-year-old student Charles Whitman killed 15 and wounded 31 from tower observation deck on Austin campus, Aug. 1; shot dead by police.

Dept. of Transportation created, Oct. 15. Edward Brooke (R, MA) elected Nov. 8 as first black U.S. senator in 85 years.

1967: As U.S. deployment in Vietnam reaches nearly a half-million troops, major antiwar demonstrations draw tens of thousands of protesters.

Robert C. Weaver named secretary of newly created Dept. of Housing and Urban Development, becoming **first black cabinet member**.

1967 Green Bay Packers beat Kansas City Chiefs, 35-10, in **first Super Bowl**, Jan. 15, in Los Angeles. Three astronauts died Jan. 27 in *Apollo 1* fire on ground at Cape Canaveral, FL. **25th Amendment**, providing for presidential succession, ratified Feb. 10. Pres. Johnson and Soviet Prem. **Aleksei Kosygin** met June 23 and 25 at Glassboro State College in New Jersey; agreed not to let any crisis push them into war.

Riots erupted among residents of predominantly black **Newark**, NJ, July 12-17; 26 killed, 1,500 injured, more than 1,000 arrested. In **Detroit**, MI, July 23-30, 43 died, 2,000 injured; 5,000 left homeless by rioting, looting, and burning in city's black neighborhoods. **Thurgood Marshall** sworn in Oct. 2 as first black U.S. Supreme Court justice. **Antiwar march** on Washington, DC, Oct. 21-22, drew at least 70,000 participants. Carl B. Stokes (D, Cleveland) and Richard G. Hatcher (D, Gary, IN) elected **first black mayors** of major U.S. cities Nov. 7.

1968 In **"Tet offensive,"** Communist troops attacked several provincial capitals and other major cities, including Saigon, Jan. 30, but suffered heavy casualties. Pres. Johnson **curbed bombing** of North Vietnam Mar. 31. Peace talks began in Paris May 10. All bombing of North halted Oct. 31.

Rev. **Martin Luther King Jr.** assassinated Apr. 4 in Memphis, TN. **James Earl Ray**, an escaped convict, pleaded guilty to slaying, was sentenced to 99 years. Students at **Columbia Univ.**, Apr. 23-24, seized school buildings in protest against school's involvement in military research, among other issues. Sen. **Robert F. Kennedy** (D, NY) shot June 5 in Los Angeles after celebrating presidential primary victories, died June 6. **Sirhan Sirhan** convicted of murder, 1969; death sentence commuted to life in prison, 1972.

Vice Pres. Hubert Humphrey nominated for president at **Democratic National Convention** in Chicago, marked by clash between police and antiwar protesters, Aug. 26-29. Republican nominee **Richard Nixon** won presidency, defeating Humphrey in close race Nov. 5.

Apollo 8 **orbited moon** in five-day mission, Dec. 21-27. North Korea released 82-man crew of the **USS Pueblo** Dec. 22, 11 months after seizing the ship in Sea of Japan; one crew member had been killed in battle.

1969 Expanded four-party **Vietnam peace talks** began Jan. 18. U.S. force peaked at 543,400 in Apr.; withdrawal started July 8. Pres. Nixon set Vietnamization policy of expanding role of South Vietnamese forces Nov. 3. Earl Warren retired upon swearing in **Warren Burger**, June 23, as Supreme Court chief justice. In incident that marked birth of **gay rights** movement, police clashed with patrons of gay bar, the **Stonewall Inn**, in New York City June 28.

U.S. astronaut **Neil Armstrong**, commander of the *Apollo 11* mission, became the **first person to set foot on the moon**, July 20, followed by astronaut **Edwin "Buzz" Aldrin**. Astronaut **Michael Collins** remained aboard command module.

Woodstock rock music festival near Bethel, NY, drew 400,000 people, Aug. 15-18. **Anti-Vietnam War demonstrations** held in cities across the U.S., marking Vietnam Moratorium day, Oct. 15; on Nov. 12, some 250,000 marched in Washington, DC. Massacre of hundreds of civilians by U.S. troops at **My Lai**, South Vietnam, in 1968 reported Nov. 16. **Kurt Vonnegut**'s *Slaughterhouse Five* published. *Sesame Street* launched on public TV.

1970 A federal jury Feb. 18 found the **"Chicago 7"** antiwar activists not guilty of conspiring to incite riots during 1968 Democratic National Convention. However, five were convicted of crossing state lines with intent to incite riots.

Three astronauts safely returned to Earth Apr. 17 after oxygen tank on *Apollo 13* ruptured. Lunar landing had been canceled. Millions of Americans participated in antipollution demonstrations Apr. 22 to mark **first Earth Day**.

U.S. and South Vietnamese forces crossed **Cambodian** borders Apr. 30 to get at enemy bases. Four students killed May 4 at **Kent State Univ.** in Ohio by National Guardsmen during war protest. In protest at **Jackson State Univ.** in Mississippi, two killed when police fired on protesters.

1969: *Apollo 11* **lands on the lunar surface; Neil Armstrong and Edwin "Buzz" Aldrin are first humans to walk on the moon.**

First female U.S. generals appointed June 11. **Postal reform** measure signed Aug. 12 created an independent U.S. Postal Service. Pres. Nixon, Dec. 31, signed **clean air bill** calling for development of cleaner auto engine and national air quality standards for 10 major pollutants. Garry Trudeau's *Doonesbury* comic strip launched in 30 papers.

1971 **Charles Manson** and three of his cult followers found guilty Jan. 25 of first-degree murder in 1969 slaying of actress Sharon Tate and six others. A court-martial jury Mar. 29 convicted Lt. **William Calley** in murder of 22 South Vietnamese at **My Lai** on Mar. 16, 1968. He was sentenced to life in prison Mar. 31, later reduced to 20 years.

Pres. Nixon, Apr. 14, relaxed 20-year **trade embargo with China**. *New York Times* began publishing June 13 classified **Pentagon Papers**, secret Pentagon study on U.S. involvement in Vietnam leaked by Daniel Ellsberg, military analyst consulting for government. Supreme Court June 30 upheld, 6-3, right to publish the documents. **26th Amendment**, lowering the minimum voting age to 18, ratified June 30. Pres. Nixon, Aug. 15, instituted 90-day **wage and price freeze**.

U.S. bombers initiated massive five-day strike Dec. 26 in North Vietnam in retaliation for alleged violations of agreements reached prior to 1968 bombing halt.

1972 Pres. Nixon arrived in **Beijing** Feb. 21 for eight-day visit to China, in "journey for peace." Joint communiqué released Feb. 27 called for increased Sino-U.S. contacts. Senate, Mar. 22, approved **Equal Rights Amendment** banning discrimination on basis of sex; sent measure to states for ratification.

North Vietnamese forces launched biggest attacks in four years across the demilitarized zone Mar. 30. The U.S. responded Apr. 15 with **resumption of bombing** of Hanoi and Haiphong. Pres. Nixon announced May 8 the mining of North Vietnam ports.

Gov. **George C. Wallace** (D, AL), campaigning for president at Laurel, MD, shopping center May 15, shot and seriously wounded. **Arthur Bremer** convicted Aug. 4, sentenced to 63 years for shooting Wallace and three others. In **first visit of U.S. president to Moscow**, Pres. Nixon arrived May 22 for summit talks with Kremlin leaders that culminated in landmark strategic arms pact (**SALT I**). Five men arrested June 17 for breaking into Democratic National Committee offices in **Watergate** office complex in Washington, DC. U.S. Supreme Court in *Furman v. Georgia* June 29 ruled **capital punishment** as practiced was unconstitutional.

Mark Spitz won seven gold medals in world record times at the Munich Olympics in Aug.-Sept.

Last U.S. combat troops left Vietnam Aug. 11. Pres. **Nixon** reelected Nov. 7 in landslide, carrying 49 states to defeat Sen. George McGovern (D, SD). Three astronauts, part of

Apollo 17, made 6th and last lunar landing on Dec. 11. Full-scale **bombing of North Vietnam** resumed after Paris peace negotiations reached impasse Dec. 18.

The Godfather, directed by Francis Ford Coppola, is released.

1973 In *Roe v. Wade*, Supreme Court ruled, 7-2, Jan. 22, fetus not a person with constitutional rights and that right to privacy protected woman's decision to have abortion; states may not ban abortions during first three months of pregnancy but may regulate, not ban, abortions during second trimester.

Four-party **Vietnam peace pacts** signed in Paris Jan. 27. **End of military draft** announced on same day. Last U.S. troops left Vietnam Mar. 29. North Vietnam released some 590 U.S. prisoners by Apr. 1. Pres. Nixon announced, Apr. 30, resignation of top Nixon aides H. R. Haldeman and John Ehrlichman and firing of White House Counsel **John Dean** as a consequence of the widening **Watergate** scandal. Dean told Senate hearings June 25 that Nixon, his aides, and Justice Dept. had conspired to cover up Watergate facts. The U.S. officially ceased bombing in **Cambodia** at midnight Aug. 14 in accord with June congressional action.

Vice Pres. **Spiro Agnew**, Oct. 10, resigned and pleaded no contest to charge of tax evasion while Maryland governor. **Gerald R. Ford**, Oct. 12, became **first appointed vice president** under 25th Amendment; sworn in Dec. 6. The **"Saturday Night Massacre"** occurred Oct. 20, when Pres. Nixon ordered Atty. Gen. Elliot Richardson to fire Watergate special prosecutor **Archibald Cox**, who had sought handover of Nixon's subpoenaed **White House tapes**. Richardson refused to comply and resigned; Dep. Atty. Gen. William Ruckelshaus refused and was fired. Solicitor Gen. Robert Bork, as acting atty. gen., then fired Cox. Nixon administration named **Leon Jaworski**, Nov. 1, to succeed Cox.

Skylab, **first U.S. space station**, launched May 14. **Secretariat** became first Triple Crown winner since **Citation** in 1948 by winning Belmont Stakes June 9 in record time. **Billie Jean King** defeated Bobby Riggs in three straight sets in tennis's nationally televised "Battle of the Sexes," Sept. 20. Total **ban on oil exports** to U.S. imposed by Arab oil-producing nations Oct. 19-21 after outbreak of an Arab-Israeli war; lifted Mar. 1974. Congress overrode Nov. 7 Pres. Nixon's veto of **war powers bill** curbing president's power to commit forces to hostilities abroad without congressional approval.

1974 On Apr. 8, **Hank Aaron** of the Atlanta Braves hit his 715th career home run to break Babe Ruth's record.

House Judiciary Committee opened **impeachment** hearings May 9 against Pres. Nixon. John Ehrlichman and three **White House "plumbers"** found guilty July 12 of conspiring to violate the civil rights of the psychiatrist of **Pentagon Papers** leaker Daniel Ellsberg by breaking into psychiatrist's office. Supreme Court ruled, 8-0, July 24 that Pres. Nixon had to turn over 64 **audio tapes of White House conversations**. House Judiciary Committee, in televised hearings July 24-30, recommended **articles of impeachment** against Pres. Nixon, involving conspiracy to obstruct justice in Watergate cover-up, abuses of power, and defiance of committee subpoenas.

Pres. **Nixon** announced his **resignation**, Aug. 8, and stepped down the next day. His support in Congress had begun to collapse Aug. 5 after release of tapes appearing to implicate him in Watergate cover-up. Vice Pres. **Ford** sworn in Aug. 9 as 38th U.S. president. Pres. Ford, Aug. 20, nominated **Nelson Rockefeller** to be vice president; Rockefeller sworn in Dec. 10. Citing need to move on, Pres. Ford, Sept. 8, issued **pardon to Nixon** for any federal crimes he committed while president.

New York Times published article Dec. 22 on CIA engagement in illegal domestic surveillance. Reports of other apparently illegal CIA activities, recorded in **"family jewels"** file kept by the CIA, leaked out over the years.

1975 Former Atty. Gen. John Mitchell and ex-presidential advisers H. R. Haldeman and John Ehrlichman found guilty Jan. 1 of **Watergate cover-up** charges. Mitchell released 1979, last of 25 jailed over scandal to leave prison.

Bill Gates and Paul Allen founded Microsoft, Apr. 4. U.S. launched **evacuation from Saigon** of Americans and some South Vietnamese Apr. 29 as Communist forces completed takeover of South Vietnam; **South Vietnamese** government officially surrendered Apr. 30. U.S. merchant ship *Mayaguez* and its crew of 39 seized by Cambodian forces in Gulf of Siam May 12. In rescue operation, U.S. Marines attacked Koh Tang Island, recovered ship and crew but inadvertently left three Marines behind. Congress voted $405 mil for **South Vietnam refugees** May 16; 140,000 flown to U.S.

Publishing heiress **Patricia (Patty) Hearst**, kidnapped Feb. 5, 1974, by Symbionese Liberation Army (SLA), captured in San Francisco Sept. 18 with other militants. She was convicted Mar. 20, 1976, of bank robbery.

1976 In **right-to-die** case, New Jersey Supreme Court, Mar. 31, allowed comatose Karen Ann Quinlan to be removed from respirator; she survived until 1985. U.S. Supreme Court reinstated **death penalty**, July 2, subject to conditions.

U.S. celebrated **200th anniversary of independence** July 4 with festivals, parades, and New York City's Operation Sail, gathering of tall ships from around the world. **"Legionnaire's disease"** killed 29 people who attended American Legion convention July 21-24 in Philadelphia.

Viking 1 made successful landing on Mars, July 20. Two U.S. officers on routine mission near DMZ slain by **North Korean soldiers** Aug. 18; North Korea stated "regret."

1977 Convicted murderer Gary Gilmore executed by Utah firing squad Jan. 17; **first use of capital punishment** in U.S. since 1967. Pres. Jimmy Carter Jan. 21 pardoned most Vietnam War **draft evaders**.

Natural gas shortage caused by severe winter weather led Congress Feb. 2 to approve emergency gas bill temporarily authorizing reallocation from surplus areas. Pres. Carter signed act Aug. 4 creating new cabinet-level **Energy Dept.** FBI Dec. 7 released 40,000 pages of previously secret files relating to **Kennedy assassination**.

George Lucas's first *Star Wars* film released.

1978 Senate voted Apr. 18 to turn over **Panama Canal** to Panama on Dec. 31, 1999; Mar. 16 vote had given approval to treaty guaranteeing area's neutrality after the year 2000. Californians, June 6, approved **Proposition 13**, state constitutional amendment slashing property taxes.

Supreme Court, June 28, ruled that while race could be a factor in admission to institutions of higher education, **numerical quotas** could not be used.

Egyptian Pres. **Anwar al-Sadat** and Israeli Prem. **Menachem Begin** reached accord on "framework for peace," Sept. 17, after Pres. Carter-mediated talks at **Camp David**. New York's Chemical Bank Dec. 20 initiated industry-wide move to raise **lending rate** to near-record 11.75%.

1979 Partial meltdown released radioactive material Mar. 28 at nuclear reactor on **Three Mile Island** near Middletown, PA. American Airlines DC-10 **jetliner crashed** May 25 after losing an engine following takeoff from Chicago, killing 275 people.

In speech July 15, Pres. Carter spoke of national "crisis of confidence" and outlined proposed 10-year, $140-bil program to reduce **dependence on foreign oil**. Militant followers of **Ayatollah Khomeini** took hostage some 90 people, including 66 Americans, Nov. 4 at **American embassy in Tehran**, Iran. Khomeini demanded return of ailing former Shah Muhammad Reza Pahlavi to stand trial.

1980 Pres. Carter announced, Jan. 4, economic sanctions against USSR in retaliation for Soviet invasion of Afghanistan. At Carter's request, U.S. Olympic Committee voted, Apr. 12, against U.S. participation in **Moscow Summer Olympics**. At **Winter Olympics** in Lake Placid, NY, U.S. hockey team defeated Russian team Feb. 22 en route to gold medal in "miracle on ice."

Eight Americans were killed, Apr. 24, in ill-fated attempt to rescue hostages held by Iranian militants. **Mt. St. Helens**, in Washington state, erupted May 18. The blast, with others May 25 and June 12, left 57 dead. In sweeping victory, Nov. 4, **Ronald Reagan** (R) was elected 40th president, defeating incumbent Pres. Carter. Republicans gained control of Senate. Former Beatle **John Lennon** was shot and killed by Mark David Chapman, Dec. 8, in New York City.

1981 Minutes after Reagan's inauguration Jan. 20, 52 **American hostages in Iran** were freed after being held for 444 days. Pres. **Reagan** was shot and seriously wounded, Mar. 30, in Washington, DC; also seriously wounded were a Secret Service agent, a police officer, and Press Sec. **James**

1981: Pres. Ronald Reagan nominates Sandra Day O'Connor to be the first woman to serve on the U.S. Supreme Court.

Brady. **John W. Hinckley Jr.** arrested, found not guilty by reason of insanity in 1982, and committed to mental institution (released in 2016).

World's **first reusable spacecraft**, space shuttle *Columbia*, sent into space, Apr. 12. U.S. Centers for Disease Control, June 5, reported first cases of what became known as **AIDS**.

Air controllers went on **strike** Aug. 3; most were fired by Pres. Reagan after defying back-to-work order. Reagan signed into law Aug. 13 **tax-cut legislation**, expected to save taxpayers $750 bil over five years, largest tax cut to date. The Senate confirmed, Sept. 21, appointment of **Sandra Day O'Connor** as **first female Supreme Court justice**.

1982 The 13-year-old Justice Dept. lawsuit against **AT&T** was settled Jan. 8. AT&T agreed to give up 22 Bell System companies and was allowed to expand. **Equal Rights Amendment**, sent to states in 1972, defeated when deadline for ratification passed June 30 with support from only 35 of the 38 states needed. The economy showed signs of recovery from a **recession** that began in mid-1981, as Dow Jones industrial average hit 1,016.93 Oct. 13, its highest level in 18 months.

NFL strike ended Nov. 16 after 57 days when players and team owners settled with $1.6-bil pact. Singer **Michael Jackson**'s album *Thriller*, released Nov. 30, became monumental best-seller. Retired dentist Dr. Barney B. Clark became **first permanent artificial heart recipient**, Dec. 2; he died Mar. 23, 1983. The House, Dec. 16, cited EPA administrator Anne Gorsuch for contempt after she refused to release records relating to enforcement of **Superfund** law.

1983 Pres. Reagan, Jan. 3, declared Times Beach, MO, a federal disaster area because of toxic **dioxin** in soil, prompting evacuations and town's closure. Harold Washington (D) elected Apr. 12 as **first black mayor of Chicago**. On Apr. 20, Pres. Reagan signed compromise bipartisan bill designed to save **Social Security** from bankruptcy.

Sally Ride became **first American woman to travel in space**, June 18, when space shuttle *Challenger* launched from Cape Canaveral, FL. On Sept. 1, **South Korean passenger jet** in Soviet air space was apparently misidentified and shot down; 269 people, including 61 Americans, killed.

On Oct. 23, 241 U.S. Marines and sailors were killed when TNT-laden **suicide truck bomb** blew up Marine barracks at Beirut International Airport in **Lebanon**. U.S. troops, with small force from six Caribbean nations, invaded **Grenada** Oct. 25; deposed Marxist regime.

1984 Seven regional companies took over **local telephone service** from AT&T, Jan. 1. On space shuttle *Challenger*'s fourth trip, launched Feb. 3, two astronauts became **first humans to fly free of a spacecraft**. On May 7, Vietnam War veterans reached settlement with chemical companies in class-action suit over the herbicide **Agent Orange**.

Former Vice Pres. **Walter Mondale** won Democratic presidential nomination, June 6. He chose Rep. **Geraldine Ferraro** (D, NY) as vice presidential candidate, first woman to be nominated for position by major political party. Pres. Reagan signed bill July 17 cutting federal transportation aid to states

that keep their **drinking age** under 21. Pres. **Reagan** reelected Nov. 6 in Republican landslide, carrying 49 states for record 525 electoral votes. **Bernhard Goetz** shot and wounded four allegedly menacing teenage boys on NYC subway train, Dec. 22; acquitted of major charges but successfully sued.

1985 First international **AIDS conference** met in Atlanta, GA, Apr. 15-17. Visiting Germany, Pres. Reagan, May 5, laid wreath at Bergen-Belsen Nazi concentration camp site and at military cemetery at **Bitburg**, where some Nazis were buried. Philadelphia police bombed a rowhouse occupied by **MOVE radical group**, May 13; 11 killed, and fire damaged two blocks of houses. On June 14, **terrorists seized TWA jet** after takeoff from Athens, Greece, with 153 passengers and crew. Thirty-nine Americans held hostage for 17 days; one U.S. service member killed.

Reversing an Apr. 23 decision, the **Coca-Cola Co.** said, July 10, it would resume marketing soda made under its original "Classic" formula. **Live Aid** rock concert broadcast around the world July 13, raised $70 mil for famine relief in Ethiopia.

On Oct. 7, four **Palestinian hijackers** seized Italian cruise ship *Achille Lauro* in the Mediterranean for two days. One American, Leon Klinghoffer, killed. For first time in six years U.S. and Soviet leaders met at **summit in Geneva**, Nov. 19-20. **General Electric** agreed Dec. 11 to buy RCA Corp.

1986 The U.S. officially observed **Martin Luther King Jr. Day** for first time Jan. 20. Space shuttle *Challenger* exploded 73 seconds after liftoff, Jan. 28, killing six astronauts and Teacher in Space Project participant Christa McAuliffe. In four-day extravaganza in July, the U.S. celebrated 100th birthday of the **Statue of Liberty**.

The Senate confirmed, Sept. 17, Reagan's nomination of **William Rehnquist** as chief justice and **Antonin Scalia** as associate justice of U.S. Supreme Court. Congress completed action Oct. 2 overriding a veto to place economic sanctions on **South Africa**. Lebanese newspaper first broke news of **Iran-Contra scandal** Nov. 3, involving secret U.S. sale of arms to Iran and diversion of some of the proceeds to support the Contras, a right-wing, anti-Communist insurgent movement in Nicaragua. Pres. Reagan signed into law, Nov. 7, immigration measure; 2.7 mil **undocumented immigrants** who had applied for amnesty by May 4, 1987, were granted legal status.

Financier **Ivan Boesky** agreed Nov. 14 to pay $100 mil in fines and illicit profits for **insider trading**. Robert Penn Warren named America's **first poet laureate**.

1987 Pres. Reagan produced nation's **first trillion-dollar budget**, Jan. 5. FDA approved, Mar. 20, AZT—first drug shown to be effective in fight against **AIDS**.

Joint public hearings by Senate and House committees investigating **Iran-Contra affair** opened May 5. Lt. Col. **Oliver North**, former National Security Council staff member, said he had believed all his activities were authorized by his superiors. Hearings ended Aug. 3. Pres. Reagan in speech to nation, Aug. 12, denied knowing of diversion of funds to Contras.

An **Iraqi missile** killed 37 sailors on the USS *Stark* in the Persian Gulf, May 17. Iraq called it an accident. The 200th anniversary of **U.S. Constitution** signing was observed, Sept. 17, in Philadelphia and around the U.S. **Stock market crashed**, Oct. 19, with the Dow Jones industrial average plummeting a then-record 508 points to 1,738, ending bull market that began mid-1982. Pres. Reagan and Soviet leader Mikhail Gorbachev Dec. 8, signed **pact to dismantle** all 1,752 U.S. and 859 Soviet intermediate- and shorter-range (300-3,400 mi) missiles.

1988 *Phantom of the Opera* opened Jan. 26; it would go on to be longest-running Broadway show ever. In report issued May 16, Surgeon Gen. C. Everett Koop declared **cigarettes addictive**.

A missile, fired from U.S. Navy warship *Vincennes* in the Persian Gulf, mistakenly struck a commercial **Iranian airliner**, July 3, killing all 290 aboard. **George H. W. Bush** (R) elected 41st U.S. president, Nov. 8, decisively defeating Massachusetts Gov. **Michael Dukakis** (D). **Pan Am Flight 103** exploded and crashed, due to terrorist bomb, into town of Lockerbie, Scotland, Dec. 21, killing all 259 people aboard and 11 on the ground. Investment firm **Drexel Burnham Lambert** agreed, Dec. 21, to plead guilty to insider trading and other violations, and pay penalties of $650 mil. U.S. suffered widespread **drought** conditions, the worst in over 50 years.

1989 Major oil spill occurred when *Exxon Valdez* struck Bligh Reef in Alaska's Prince William Sound, Mar. 24. Oliver North convicted, May 4, on charges related to **Iran-Contra scandal**. Conviction thrown out on appeal in 1991 because of his immunized testimony. TV comedy series *Seinfeld* premiered July 5 on NBC.

A measure to rescue **savings and loan industry** signed into law, Aug. 9, by Pres. Bush, launching largest federal rescue to date. Army Gen. **Colin Powell** became **first black chairman of Joint Chiefs of Staff** after being nominated Aug. 10 by Pres. Bush.

Baseball legend **Pete Rose** banned from game for life Aug. 24 for involvement with gamblers. **Hurricane Hugo** swept through the Carolinas Sept. 22, causing at least 86 deaths and $7 bil damage. An **earthquake** struck the San Francisco Bay area just before a World Series game, Oct. 17, causing 63 deaths.

L. Douglas Wilder (D) declared governor of Virginia Nov. 27, **first elected black governor** in U.S. history. U.S. troops invaded Panama, Dec. 20, overthrowing the government of **Manuel Noriega**. Noriega, wanted by U.S. authorities on drug charges, surrendered Jan. 3, 1990.

1990 Junk bond financier **Michael Milken** pleaded guilty to fraud-related charges, Apr. 14; agreed to pay $500 mil in restitution and sentenced Nov. 21 to 10 years in prison. Pres. Bush signed **Americans With Disabilities Act** barring discrimination against and requiring accommodations for the disabled, July 26.

Operation Desert Shield forces left for Saudi Arabia Aug. 7 to defend that country following invasion of **Kuwait** by Iraq, Aug. 2. David Souter confirmed Sept. 27 to serve on Supreme Court, replacing retiring Justice **William Brennan**. Pres. Bush Nov. 15 signed new **Clean Air Act**, focused on urban pollution, cancer-causing emissions from industrial sources.

1991 The U.S. and its allies defeated Iraq in **Persian Gulf War** and liberated Kuwait, which Iraq had invaded. They launched air attacks, Jan. 16, followed by ground war, starting Feb. 24; Bush declared cease-fire, Feb. 27.

An 8-month **recession** showed signs of having ended in Mar. The **Dow Jones** industrial average closed above 3,000 for first time, Apr. 17. Supreme Court Justice **Thurgood Marshall** announced, June 17, plans to retire. Senate, voting 52-48 on Oct. 15, confirmed nomination of **Clarence Thomas** to replace Marshall, after contentious hearings marked by allegations that Thomas had sexually harassed former aide Anita Hill. House Speaker Tom Foley announced Oct. 3 closure of **House Bank** by end of year after revelations that House members had written numerous bad checks.

1992 Major U.S. carrier Trans World Airlines (**TWA**) filed for bankruptcy, Jan. 31. **Riots** swept South Central Los Angeles Apr. 29 after jury acquitted four white police officers on all but one count in 1991 videotaped beating of black motorist **Rodney King**. Death toll in L.A. violence was put at 53. **27th Amendment**, regarding congressional pay raises, ratified May 7.

Hurricane Andrew ravaged South Florida and Louisiana Aug. 24-26, causing 65 deaths. White supremacist and fugitive Randall Weaver surrendered Aug. 31 after 11-day

1992: As AIDS becomes the leading cause of death for Americans aged 25-44, grassroots groups such as ACT UP raise awareness and demand resources.

FBI siege at his **Ruby Ridge**, ID, cabin, during which his wife, son, and a deputy sheriff were killed.

Bill Clinton (D) elected 42nd president, Nov. 3, defeating Pres. Bush (R) and independent Ross Perot. A UN-sanctioned military force, led by U.S. troops, arrived in **Somalia** Dec. 9. Presidents of U.S., Canada, and Mexico Dec. 17 signed North American Free Trade Agreement (**NAFTA**), which took effect Jan. 1, 1994.

1993 A bomb exploded in a parking garage beneath the **World Trade Center** in New York City, Feb. 26, killing six. Four men found guilty, Mar. 4, 1994. Four federal agents killed, Feb. 28, during unsuccessful raid on **Branch Davidian** compound near **Waco**, TX. A 51-day siege by agents ended Apr. 19 when the compound burned down, leaving more than 70 cult members dead. Eleven cult members acquitted Feb. 26, 1994, of deaths of federal agents.

Janet Reno became **first female attorney general** Mar. 12. Federal jury, Apr. 17, found two Los Angeles police officers guilty and two not guilty of violating civil rights of motorist **Rodney King** in 1991 videotaped beating.

In a May 14 plebiscite, voters in **Puerto Rico** supported continuing commonwealth status with U.S. **"Motor-voter" bill** signed by Pres. Clinton, May 20, easing voting procedures. **"Great Flood of 1993"** inundated parts of nine Midwestern states in summer, leaving about 50 dead and $15 bil in damages.

Pres. Clinton, July 2, approved recommendations that 33 major U.S. military bases be closed. On July 19 he announced **"don't ask, don't tell, don't pursue"** policy for homosexuals in the military. **Ruth Bader Ginsburg** sworn in to U.S. Supreme Court, Aug. 10, replacing retiring Justice **Byron White**. Pres. Clinton, Aug. 10, signed measure designed to **cut federal budget deficits** by $496 bil over five years, through spending cuts and new taxes. **Brady Bill**, a major gun-control measure, signed into law Nov. 30.

1994 A predawn **earthquake** in the Los Angeles area, Jan. 17, claimed 61 lives. Pres. Clinton Feb. 3 lifted 19-year ban on U.S. trade with **Vietnam**. Byron De La Beckwith convicted Feb. 5 of 1963 murder of civil rights leader **Medgar Evers**. Longtime CIA officer **Aldrich Ames** and his wife charged, Feb. 21, with spying for Russians. Under plea bargain, he received life in prison, while she drew 63 months.

U.S. troops, Mar. 25, officially ended peacekeeping and humanitarian aid mission in **Somalia**, begun in 1992. Kenneth Starr named Aug. 5 as independent counsel to probe **Whitewater** affair. Major league baseball players went on strike following Aug. 11 games. World Series canceled; strike ended Apr. 25, 1995. Senate Majority Leader **George Mitchell** (D, ME), Sept. 26, dropped efforts to pass Pres. Clinton's **health-care reform** package.

Republicans gained control of Congress in Nov. 8 elections after many years of Democratic control. House Speaker **Tom Foley** (WA) was among the defeated Democrats.

1995 **Newt Gingrich** (R, GA) elected U.S. House speaker. A bill to end Congress's exemption from federal labor laws, first in series of measures in Republicans' **"Contract With America,"** cleared Congress Jan. 17; signed into law Jan. 23. Pres. Clinton, Jan. 31, authorized $20-bil loan to **Mexico**. Last UN peacekeeping troops withdrew from **Somalia** Feb. 28-Mar. 3, with aid of U.S. Marines. In **Haiti**, peacekeeping responsibilities were transferred from U.S. to UN forces Mar. 31, with U.S. providing 2,400 soldiers.

Truck **bomb exploded outside Oklahoma City federal office building** Apr. 19, killing 168 people; antigovernment extremist Timothy McVeigh arrested, Apr. 21. U.S. space shuttle *Atlantis* made first in series of dockings with Russian space station *Mir*, June 29-July 4. The U.S. announced July 11 it was reestablishing **relations with Vietnam**.

Ten Muslim militants convicted, Oct. 1, in failed plot to blow up **UN Headquarters**, other buildings and assassinate political leaders. Former football star **O.J. Simpson** found not guilty Oct. 3 of June 1994 murders of former wife, Nicole Brown Simpson, and a friend of hers. Hundreds of thousands of black men participated in **Million Man March** and rally in Washington, DC, Oct. 16, organized by Rev. Louis Farrakhan.

Cumulative number of **AIDS** cases reported in the U.S. since 1981 passed 500,000 by Oct. 31, with more than 310,000 deaths. Five Americans among seven killed, Nov. 13, in **bombing** of U.S. military post in **Riyadh, Saudi Arabia**. Budget impasse between Congress and Pres. Clinton led to

1994: The predawn Northridge earthquake causes widespread damage and more than 60 deaths in southern California.

partial **government shutdown** Nov. 14; operations resumed Nov. 20 under continuing resolutions. After talks outside Dayton, OH, warring parties in **Bosnia and Herzegovina** reached agreement Nov. 21 to end their conflict; treaty signed Dec. 14, and U.S. peacekeeping troops arrived. A 1973 federal law imposing **55-mph speed limit** repealed Nov. 28.

1996 Senate, Jan. 26, approved, 87-4, Second Strategic Arms Reduction Treaty (**START II**) with Russia. Congress, Mar. 27-28, approved **line item veto**; struck down by Supreme Court, June 1998.

James and Susan McDougal convicted May 28 of fraud and conspiracy in **Whitewater** case; Arkansas Gov. Jim Guy Tucker (D) convicted on similar charges. The antitax **Freemen** surrendered to federal authorities June 13 after 81-day standoff near Jordan, MT; four were convicted, July 1998, of conspiring to defraud banks.

Bomb exploded at **Khobar Towers** military complex near Dhahran, Saudi Arabia, June 25, killing 19 American service personnel. Homemade pipe bomb exploded July 27 in **Atlanta**, GA, park during **Summer Olympics**; one person killed.

Major **welfare reform bill** signed into law, Aug. 22. Defense of Marriage Act (**DOMA**), passed by wide margins and signed Sept. 21, barred federal recognition of same-sex marriages. U.S. signed **Comprehensive Test Ban Treaty**, Sept. 24, which banned all nuclear weapons tests; Senate failed to ratify treaty. Pres. **Clinton reelected**, Nov. 5.

1997 **Madeleine Albright** sworn in as sec. of state Jan. 23, becoming first female State Dept. head. Former CIA official Harold Nicholson pleaded guilty, Mar. 3, to **spying for Russia**. Thirty-nine members of **Heaven's Gate** religious cult found dead in Rancho Santa Fe, CA, house Mar. 26, in apparent mass suicide.

Timothy McVeigh convicted of conspiracy and murder, June 2, in 1995 **Oklahoma City** bombing; executed June 2001. Co-conspirator Terry Nichols convicted Dec. 23 on related charges; later sentenced to life in prison. Two Islamic militants convicted, Nov. 12, of key roles in 1993 bombing of **World Trade Center**. The film *Titanic*, released Dec. 14, went on to win 11 Oscars.

1998 Media outlets reported Jan. 21 on evidence of sexual relationship between Pres. Clinton and former White House intern **Monica Lewinsky**. Clinton initially denied affair, but in address to the nation, Aug. 17, acknowledged relationship that was "not appropriate." On Sept. 9, independent counsel **Kenneth Starr** sent findings to House; the Judiciary Committee, Oct. 5, voted to recommend full inquiry. House, Dec. 19, approved two articles of **impeachment**.

"Unabomber" **Theodore Kaczynski**, arrested in Montana in 1993, pleaded guilty Jan. 22 to California and New Jersey bombings that killed three people; sentenced in May to four life terms plus 30 years. **Karla Faye Tucker** executed Feb. 3; first woman executed in Texas in 135 years.

Bombs at **U.S. embassies** in Nairobi, Kenya, and Dar es Salaam, Tanzania, killed at least 257, Aug. 7; U.S. launched retaliatory strikes, Aug. 20, against targets in Afghanistan and Sudan. On Sept. 30, Pres. Clinton announced federal **budget surplus** of $70 bil for fiscal 1998, first since 1969.

Pres. Clinton, Nov. 13, settled suit by agreeing to pay $850,000 to **Paula Jones**, who alleged he had made an unwanted sexual advance in 1991. Biggest U.S. **tobacco companies**, in settlement Nov. 23, agreed to pay states and territories $206 bil over 25 years to cover public health costs.

1999 *The Sopranos* TV drama debuted, Jan. 10. Pres. **Clinton** was acquitted, Feb. 12, at end of Senate **impeachment trial**. Perjury article failed with 45 votes; obstruction of justice article drew 50-50 vote, short of the needed two-thirds.

Dr. **Jack Kevorkian** convicted of second-degree murder Mar. 26 in death of terminally ill man. One man pleaded guilty Apr. 5, another convicted Nov. 4, in 1998 kidnapping and beating death of **Matthew Shepard**, an openly gay student at the Univ. of Wyoming.

Eric Harris, 18, and Dylan Klebold, 17, killed 12 fellow students and a teacher Apr. 20 at **Columbine High School** in Littleton, CO, then fatally shot themselves. **John F. Kennedy Jr.** killed in crash of private plane July 16.

2000 Across U.S., midnight celebrations marked changeover to year 2000; feared **Y2K** computer glitch caused few problems. Vermont Gov. Howard Dean (D) on Apr. 26 signed first state law recognizing **same-sex civil unions**. U.S. and British scientists, June 26, announced they had determined structure of the **human genome**. Six-year-old **Elián González** was returned to his father in Cuba June 28, months after rescue from a refugee boat wreck in which his mother drowned. **Tiger Woods** became youngest player, at age 24, to win all four of golf's majors, July 23.

FDA announced, Sept. 28, approval of **RU-486**, a pill that induces abortion. Seventeen U.S. sailors died Oct. 12 in terrorist bombing of **USS *Cole***, in Aden, Yemen.

With Nov. 7 presidential election result still unknown in **Florida**, where Texas Gov. **George W. Bush** (R) was barely ahead of Vice Pres. **Al Gore** (D), Florida Supreme Court, Dec. 8, ordered partial manual recounts. U.S. Supreme Court reversed that decision, Dec. 12, leaving Bush as winner.

2001 **AOL-Time Warner megamerger** completed Jan. 11. FBI agent **Robert Hanssen** arrested Feb. 20, charged with longtime spying for Russians; sentenced in 2002 to life in prison. **U.S. Navy spy plane** collided with Chinese fighter plane over South China Sea Apr. 1, killing fighter pilot; 24 U.S. crew members detained in Hainan until U.S. apology, Apr. 12. Pres. Bush signed, June 7, $1.35-tril tax-cut package. On Aug. 9 he announced he would allow federal funding of limited research on existing **stem-cell** lines from human embryos.

In worst-ever **terrorist attack** on U.S., **Sept. 11**, two hijacked airliners struck **World Trade Center twin towers** in New York City. A third plane destroyed part of the **Pentagon**; a fourth crashed in a field near Shanksville, PA. Some 3,000 people were killed, including about 2,750 at World Trade Center. U.S. and Britain, Oct. 7, launched airstrikes against Afghan-based terrorist organization **al-Qaeda** and Afghanistan's ruling **Taliban** militia. Bush Oct. 26 signed USA **Patriot Act**, with wide-ranging provisions aimed at preventing terrorism. **Taliban** surrendered Kabul, Nov. 13, and fled from Kandahar, their stronghold, Dec. 7. U.S. government, Dec. 11, indicted al-Qaeda operative **Zacarias Moussaoui** as Sept. 11 co-conspirator; he was sentenced in 2006 to life in prison. Five people died and 14 became ill from exposure to **anthrax** through U.S. postal system, Oct. 4-Nov. 21.

2001: The attacks of Sept. 11, 2001, kill more than 2,750 people in New York, including 343 firefighters.

Energy-trading company **Enron** filed for bankruptcy, Dec. 2. Bush announced, Dec. 13, U.S. withdrawal from **1972 Antiballistic Missile Treaty** with Russians.

2002 Taliban and al-Qaeda fighters captured in Afghanistan sent to U.S. naval base at **Guantánamo Bay** in Cuba, starting Jan. 11. In State of the Union address, Jan. 29, Pres. Bush called Iran, Iraq, and North Korea part of **"axis of evil."** By Mar. 6, 1,200 U.S. troops were involved in **Operation Anaconda** against al-Qaeda and Taliban forces in Afghanistan.

Independent prosecutor's report, Mar. 20, found insufficient evidence that Pres. Clinton or Hillary Clinton committed a crime in connection with **Whitewater**. Pres. Bush, Mar. 27, signed McCain-Feingold **campaign-finance reform bill** banning unregulated, unrestricted "soft money" donations (part of bill struck down by Supreme Court, June 2007).

Ceremonial last girder removed May 30 from **World Trade Center** site, signaling end of massive recovery operation. **"Shoe-Bomber"** Richard Reid pleaded guilty Oct. 4 in Dec. 2001 attempted attack aboard an airliner; sentenced 2003 to life in prison. On Oct. 10-11 the House, 296-133, and Senate, 77-23, gave Bush backing to use military force against **Iraq**. Bush administration revealed Oct. 16 that **North Korea** had acknowledged developing nuclear arms in violation of a 1994 agreement. Bush signed measure, Nov. 25, creating cabinet **Dept. of Homeland Security**.

U.S. Catholic bishops, Nov. 13, revised policies for dealing with priests who **sexually abuse** minors. **Trent Lott** (R, MS) bowed out as Senate majority leader Dec. 20 after remarks that appeared to support segregation.

2003 Space shuttle *Columbia* broke apart Feb. 1 during descent; all seven crew members killed. Report issued Aug. 26 cited "broken safety culture" at NASA. Senate, Mar. 6, approved the **Strategic Offensive Reductions Treaty** (SORT) for reducing nuclear stockpiles.

U.S.-led military offensive aimed at **ousting Saddam Hussein** began Mar. 19, as 40 Tomahawk cruise missiles hit targets in Baghdad. U.S. forces Mar. 21 seized oil fields near Basra; by Apr. 9 reported control over much of Baghdad. Pres. Bush, speaking from aircraft carrier May 1, declared **end of major combat operations in Iraq**, though insurgents continued to mount attacks.

Pres. Bush signed bill May 28 providing $330 bil in **tax cuts** over several years. A power failure caused **blackouts** affecting some 50 mil people, mostly in northeastern U.S. and Canada, Aug. 14. The archdiocese of Boston agreed to pay up to $85 mil in **sex abuse settlement** announced Sept. 9. Californians, Oct. 7, voted to recall Gov. Gray Davis (D) and replace him with actor-turned-politician **Arnold Schwarzenegger** (R). Rev. Gene Robinson consecrated Nov. 2 as Episcopal Church's **first openly gay bishop**.

Virginia jury, Nov. 17, found John Muhammad guilty in 2002 Washington, DC, area **sniper attacks** that killed 10; Muhammad sentenced to death. His 17-year-old accomplice, convicted Dec. 18, was sentenced to life.

Pres. Bush signed bill Dec. 8 to overhaul **Medicare**, adding prescription drug benefit and expanding role of private insurers. Former Iraqi leader **Saddam Hussein** captured by U.S. forces Dec. 13, in underground hideout southeast of Tikrit.

2004 *The Lord of the Rings: The Return of the King* won a record-tying 11 Oscars, Feb. 29.

Photos showing abuse of **Abu Ghraib prison** inmates in Iraq by American soldiers emerged Apr. 3; two soldiers later found guilty (2005) and sentenced to prison. U.S.-led coalition transferred power to interim Iraqi government, June 28. **9/11 Commission Report**, released July 22, called for restructuring U.S. intelligence operations.

On May 17, pursuant to a 2003 court decision, Massachusetts became the first state where **same-sex marriage** was legal. **Boston Red Sox** won World Series Oct. 27, for first time since 1918.

Pres. **Bush reelected** Nov. 2, defeating Sen. **John Kerry** (D, MA). Bush signed intelligence reform bill Dec. 17, creating a director of national intelligence.

2005 **Condoleezza Rice** became first black woman sec. of state, Jan. 26. **Terri Schiavo**, in vegetative state since 1990, died Mar. 31, after feeding tube was removed following legal battle.

Hurricane Katrina hit Gulf coast, Aug. 29, causing devastation in Louisiana, Mississippi, and Alabama; relief efforts widely criticized as insufficient. **John G. Roberts Jr.** was confirmed by Senate, Sept. 29, to replace U.S Chief Justice **William H. Rehnquist**, who died Sept. 3.

Tom DeLay (R, TX) resigned as U.S. House majority leader after indictment, Sept. 28, for violating campaign finance law (conviction overturned, 2013). *NY Times*, Dec. 16, reported that Pres. Bush in 2002 had secretly authorized Natl. Security Agency to **eavesdrop without court warrant** on people in U.S. suspected of terrorist activities. Bush, Dec. 30, signed **anti-torture legislation**.

2006 Former top Republican lobbyist **Jack Abramoff** pleaded guilty Jan. 3 to bribery and other charges; sentenced to prison. More than 20 others eventually pleaded or were found guilty on corruption-related charges.

Bush nominee **Samuel Alito Jr.** confirmed, Jan. 31, to replace retiring Supreme Court Justice **Sandra Day O'Connor**. The Court ruled June 29 that system for trying terrorism detainees at **Guantánamo Bay** was unauthorized. Bush, July 19, issued his first veto, on bill to end funding constraints on human embryonic **stem cell research**. On Sept. 6 he confirmed existence of **secret overseas prisons**, run by CIA, for terrorism suspects.

Democrats won control of House and Senate in **midterm elections** Nov. 7. Bush announced Nov. 8 that Defense Sec. **Donald Rumsfeld**, a focus of criticism over Iraq war, had resigned.

2007 Rep. Nancy Pelosi (D, CA) chosen Jan. 4 as **first woman Speaker** of the House. On Jan. 10, Pres. Bush announced troop **"surge"** in Iraq. Reports of substandard conditions at **Walter Reed Army Medical Center** in Washington, DC, led to ousters of military officials, Mar. 1-2. I. Lewis **"Scooter" Libby**, former chief of staff for Vice Pres. Cheney, convicted Mar. 6 of perjury and obstructing justice in investigation into a leak exposing undercover CIA agent; he was fined and disbarred but Bush commuted prison sentence.

A **Virginia Tech** student fatally shot 32 people on campus, Apr. 16, before killing himself. On Apr. 18, Supreme Court upheld, 5-4, a 2003 federal law that banned so-called **partial-birth abortions**.

Congress May 24 approved Iraq and Afghanistan war funding, with benchmarks for withdrawal of troops from Iraq; the same bill raised federal hourly **minimum wage** from $5.15 to $7.25 over two years. Pres. Bush issued an executive order July 20 banning "cruel, inhuman, or degrading" treatment of imprisoned **terror suspects**.

Harry Potter and the Deathly Hallows, final novel in J. K. Rowling's blockbuster series, released July 21. Congress, Aug. 4, cleared bill allowing **NSA** to monitor communications without warrants if believed related to terrorism. Barry Bonds tied Hank Aaron's all-time career **home-run record** at 755 on Aug. 4 and hit No. 756 on Aug. 7.

Atty. Gen. **Alberto Gonzales**, blamed for alleged politically motivated firings of U.S. attorneys, announced resignation Aug. 27.

2005: Hurricane Katrina and subsequent failure of levees cause unprecedented destruction in New Orleans and along the Gulf Coast.

Report by former U.S. Sen. George J. Mitchell, released Dec. 13, presented evidence of **performance-enhancing drug use** by 86 Major League Baseball players. Under law signed Dec. 17, New Jersey became the first state to **repeal the death penalty** since Supreme Court reinstated it in 1976. An energy bill mandating an increase in automobile **fuel-economy standards** signed by Pres. Bush Dec. 19.

2008 The Fed cut key interest rates, Jan. 22 and 30, to aid economy; $168-bil **economic stimulus** package, signed Feb. 13 by Pres. Bush, provided tax rebates. **Oil prices spiked** above $140 per barrel in June; national average price for gallon of regular gas topped $4.

With financial system in crisis, federal government Sept. 7 took control of mortgage finance companies **Fannie Mae** and **Freddie Mac**. A week later, investment titan **Merrill Lynch** agreed to sell itself to **Bank of America**, and **Lehman Brothers** declared bankruptcy. U.S., Sept. 16, took over insurance giant **AIG** in $85-bil bailout. On Sept. 20, a Treasury Dept. plan was introduced to purchase up to $700 bil of **"toxic" mortgage-backed securities**. Revised Troubled Asset Relief Program (**TARP**) cleared Congress Oct. 3; gave Treasury immediate access to half of $700 bil in TARP funds. On Oct. 21 Fed pledged $540 bil as a backup to protect **money market** funds.

After defeating Sen. **Hillary Clinton** (NY) for the Democratic nomination, Sen. **Barack Obama** (IL) was elected, Nov. 4, as **first African-American president** in U.S. history, defeating Republican Sen. **John McCain** (AZ). California voters approved **Proposition 8**, banning same-sex marriages.

U.S. government Nov. 23 announced massive bailout to protect **Citigroup** from mortgage losses. Dow Jones industrial average dropped 7.7% Dec. 1 after report that the economy was in **recession** that began Dec. 2007; it closed the year down 33.8%, its worst since 1931. Obama named Hillary Clinton, Dec. 1, to be sec. of state. **Fed**, Dec. 16, cut **benchmark interest rate** to near zero. Pres. Bush, Dec. 19, announced that $17 bil in **TARP funds** would be used to help keep **General Motors** and **Chrysler** afloat.

2009 Inaugurated Jan. 20, Pres. **Obama** issued executive orders Jan. 22 restricting CIA interrogation practices and calling for U.S. military prison at **Guantánamo Bay**, Cuba, to close (closing blocked by Congress). Illinois Gov. **Rod Blagojevich** (D) was convicted of corruption in state senate trial and **removed from office** Jan. 29.

Treasury Sec. **Timothy Geithner**, Feb. 10, outlined $2-tril program to stabilize banking and ease credit markets with **stress tests** for banks. Pres. Obama signed **stimulus** bill Feb. 17, with $212 bil in tax cuts and $575 bil in new spending; introduced $275-bil program Feb. 18 to aid homeowners. Geithner, Mar. 23, introduced Public-Private Investment Program (PPIP), offering incentives to encourage purchases of **"toxic assets."**

After outbreak of **swine flu**, U.S. officials declared public health emergency Apr. 26. **Chrysler** filed for bankruptcy protection Apr. 30; labor union given stake in reorganized company. Obama, May 19, tightened vehicle **fuel efficiency** standards. **General Motors** filed for bankruptcy June 1, under plan providing new federal funds. On June 9, 10 financial firms received go-ahead from U.S. Treasury to return some $68 bil in **TARP funds**.

George Tiller, Kansas doctor who performed **late-term abortions**, was murdered May 31; anti-abortion extremist convicted Jan. 2010 and sentenced to life in prison.

Speaking June 4 in Egypt, Pres. Obama called for "new beginning" in relations with **Muslim world**. Financier **Bernard Madoff** sentenced June 29 to 150 years in prison after pleading guilty in massive **Ponzi scheme**. U.S. Supreme Court's first Hispanic justice, **Sonia Sotomayor**, confirmed Aug. 6 to fill vacancy left by retirement of **David Souter**.

Government reported Oct. 29 that GDP grew at 3.5% annual rate July-Sept., signaling technical **end of recession**. Obama announced Oct. 30 end to travel and immigration restrictions on people with **AIDS**. On Nov. 5, 13 were killed in shooting at **Ft. Hood**, TX. The shooter, an Army major, was convicted; sentenced to death, 2013.

Obama, Nov. 6, signed measure to extend unemployment benefits and give $8,000 tax credit to first-time homebuyers. A surge of 30,000 troops to **Afghanistan** was announced

Dec. 1. Obama received **Nobel Peace Prize**, Dec. 10, and brokered multination **greenhouse-gas accord**, reached Dec. 18 in Copenhagen.

Detroit-bound air passengers, Dec. 25, thwarted attempt by Nigerian man to ignite **explosives in his underwear**.

2010 In *Citizens United v. FEC*, U.S. Supreme Court Jan. 21 held that corporations and unions could spend unlimited funds on advertising to influence election outcomes.

Obama, Mar. 18, signed $18-bil **job-stimulus** measure. On Mar. 21, the House, with no GOP support, approved **"Obamacare"** health-care reform bill as passed by Senate in Dec. 2009. Pres. Obama and Russian Pres. **Dmitri Medvedev**, Apr. 8, signed New Strategic Arms Reduction Treaty, or **New START** (ratified by Senate Dec. 2010).

On Apr. 20, *Deepwater Horizon* drilling platform exploded in Gulf of Mexico, killing 11 and creating huge oil spill; $20-bil settlement against energy giant **BP** approved in 2016.

Elena Kagan was confirmed Aug. 5 to replace retiring Supreme Court Justice **John Paul Stevens**. Obama signed **financial reform** bill, July 21. More than 75,000 Afghanistan documents, many of them classified, were published July 25 on **WikiLeaks** website and in some news outlets. Last **U.S. combat unit left Iraq** Aug. 19 and Obama, Aug. 31, declared U.S. combat mission in Iraq ended; 50,000 troops remained in noncombat units.

The **Fed** Nov. 3 announced plan to buy $600 bil in Treasury securities to stimulate economy. Bipartisan **Simpson-Bowles** commission, Dec. 1, called for deep cuts in both government spending and entitlements to stabilize national debt. Obama, Dec. 17, signed $858-bil compromise measure that temporarily extended G. W. **Bush-era tax cuts** and unemployment insurance benefits. **"Don't ask, don't tell"** policy for gays in military repealed Dec. 22.

2011 John Boehner (R, OH) elected House Speaker, Jan. 5. Gunman in Tucson, AZ, Jan. 8, killed 6 people and injured 13, including Rep. **Gabrielle Giffords** (D, AZ). A measure to limit collective bargaining by public sector employees, championed by Gov. **Scott Walker** (R), passed Wisconsin state legislature Mar. 9-10.

On May 2, in Abbottabad, Pakistan, a CIA-led squadron of U.S. Navy SEALs killed al-Qaeda leader **Osama bin Laden**. On May 26 Obama signed measure extending key provisions of USA **Patriot Act**.

The **deadliest U.S. tornado** in over a half-century hit Joplin, MO, May 22, claiming about 160 lives. **Budget control act**, passed by bipartisan votes, Aug. 1-2, raised **debt ceiling** and cut some $900 bil in spending, with another $1.5 tril in cuts to be worked out by supercommittee. Standard & Poor's, Aug. 5, downgraded nation's **credit rating**.

NASA's **space shuttle** program ended with landing of *Atlantis*, July 21. A left-wing movement that began Sept. 17 in New York City as **Occupy Wall Street** expanded to demonstrations across the U.S. and abroad.

Anwar al-Awlaki, a Muslim cleric and U.S. citizen linked to terrorist attacks in U.S., was killed Sept. 30 in U.S. drone attack in **Yemen**. U.S. military mission in **Iraq** formally ended Dec. 15; last troop convoy left Dec. 18.

2011: As administration officials monitor the operation from Washington, U.S. forces kill Osama bin Laden, mastermind of the Sept. 11, 2001, terrorist attacks.

2012 Pres. Obama Feb. 10 announced compromise **health insurance** mandate that avoided requiring religiously affiliated employers to directly provide contraceptive coverage. Wisconsin Gov. **Scott Walker** (R) easily survived June 5 recall election.

Obama June 15 announced Deferred Action for Childhood Arrivals (**DACA**) administrative program, shielding from deportation certain undocumented immigrants who entered as minors. Jerry Sandusky, former assistant football coach at **Penn State**, was convicted June 22 in sexual abuse of 10 boys. Twelve people were killed July 20, in **movie-theater shooting** in Aurora, CO; shooter was convicted in July 2015, sentenced to multiple life terms. A gunman opened fire Aug. 5 at a **Sikh temple** in Oak Creek, WI, leaving six dead, before killing himself. NASA rover *Curiosity* landed on **Mars** Aug. 6.

Islamist terrorists attacked U.S. facility in **Benghazi**, Libya, Sept. 11-12, killing ambassador Chris Stevens and three other Americans; report released Dec. 18 blamed State Dept. for "grossly inadequate" security. Inspector general's report, Sept. 19, cited flaws in Justice Dept. gun-buying **Operation Fast and Furious**. **Hurricane Sandy** made landfall in the U.S. Oct. 29, devastating mid-Atlantic coastal areas and leaving over 200 dead.

Pres. Obama reelected Nov. 6, defeating former Massachusetts Gov. **Mitt Romney** (R). Colorado and Washington became first states to vote to decriminalize recreational use of **marijuana**.

David Petraeus resigned as CIA director Nov. 9 after revelations of an extramarital affair and related security breaches; reached plea deal with Justice Dept. in 2015. A gunman fatally shot 20 young children and 6 adults before killing himself, Dec. 14, at **Sandy Hook** Elementary School in Newtown, CT.

2013 Averting **"fiscal cliff,"** Senate passed compromise Jan. 1, making Bush-era tax cuts permanent up to certain ceilings, while deferring automatic spending cuts (sequestration). Sen. **John Kerry** confirmed as sec. of state, Jan. 29. **Sequestration** took effect Mar. 1, triggering $1.2 tril in spending cuts to defense and domestic programs over 10 years.

Bombs at the **Boston Marathon**, Apr. 15, killed three spectators and injured 264; two Chechen-born brothers were implicated. In battle with police, one was shot, run over by vehicle driven by his brother, and died; the other, captured Apr. 19, was convicted and sentenced to death in 2015.

IRS executive Lois Lerner, implicated in alleged IRS focus on groups with conservative-leaning names, invoked Fifth Amendment before House committee, May 22. **Boy Scouts** leadership voted May 23 to let openly gay youths be members.

The *Guardian* newspaper, June 5, disclosed details of classified **NSA electronic surveillance** program; NSA contractor **Edward Snowden** claimed responsibility for leaks after having left the country. Supreme Court, June 25, struck down key provision of the 1965 **Voting Rights Act** and, June 26, struck down part of 1996 Defense of Marriage Act (**DOMA**) that denied federal benefits to same-sex couples.

A jury, July 13, found George Zimmerman not guilty in the 2012 killing of **Trayvon Martin**, an unarmed black teenager, in Sanford, FL. **Detroit** filed for **bankruptcy**, July 18. A military judge Aug. 21 sentenced Army Pfc. **Chelsea Manning** (formerly Bradley Manning) to 30 years for releasing over 700,000 U.S. military and diplomatic documents to **WikiLeaks**. Army Staff Sgt. Robert Bales, who pleaded guilty to having killed 16 Afghan civilians, was sentenced to life Aug. 23. A gunman killed 12 people at the **Navy Yard** in Washington, DC, Sept. 16; he was killed by responding police.

Federal and state health insurance exchanges opened Oct. 1 in **Obamacare** rollout plagued by technical glitches. U.S. **government partially shut down** Oct. 1 over budget impasse; resolved by Congress Oct. 16. **JPMorgan Chase** agreed, Nov. 19, to $13-bil settlement on charges of deceptive practices in sales of troubled mortgages. Dow Jones industrial average closed 2013 up 26.5%, its biggest yearly gain since 1995.

2014 **Janet Yellen** was confirmed Jan. 6 as first woman to chair the Federal Reserve. **General Motors**, Feb. 7, began recall of vehicles with defects ultimately linked to over 120 deaths. **Toyota** agreed Mar. 19 to a $1.2-bil fine on charges it concealed information about defective parts.

Gunman killed 6 people and injured 13 before killing himself, May 23, in Isla Vista, near Univ. of California-Santa Barbara. U.S. Army Sgt. **Bowe Bergdahl**, captured by the Taliban in 2009 after leaving his post in Afghanistan, was freed May 31 in exchange for U.S. release of five Taliban captives; Bergdahl later given dishonorable discharge. Veterans Affairs Sec. **Eric Shinseki** resigned May 30 after revelations that **VA hospitals** had deliberately hidden long waiting times.

The Sunni extremist group Islamic State of Iraq and Syria (**ISIS**) expanded its territory, declaring a **"caliphate"** June 29. Pres. Obama announced June 19 that the U.S. would send up to 300 military advisers to Iraq; he authorized airstrikes there, Aug. 7. ISIS released videos in Aug.-Nov. showing **beheadings** of three Americans.

U.S. Supreme Court ruled June 30 that "closely held corporations" could not be required to offer contraceptive coverage against owners' religious beliefs. A white police officer fatally shot unarmed black 18-year-old **Michael Brown**, Aug. 9, in **Ferguson**, MO, precipitating sometimes violent protests; grand jury declined to indict the officer.

Bank of America agreed Aug. 21 to $16.65-bil settlement on charges it misled investors. U.S. announced Sept. 16 it would send 3,000 military personnel to West Africa in response to **Ebola** epidemic. A man armed with a knife broke into the White House, Sept. 19, sparking congressional inquiry; **Secret Service** Dir. Julia Pierson resigned Oct. 1.

Afghan and U.S. officials signed agreement Sept. 30 providing for 9,800 American and at least 2,000 NATO troops to remain in **Afghanistan** after end of combat mission in Dec. 2014. U.S. jury Oct. 22 convicted four former **Blackwater** (now Academi) security guards in 2007 shootings that killed 17 Iraqi civilians. New York City's **One World Trade Center** welcomed first tenants Nov. 3.

GOP gained control of Senate and strengthened House majority in **midterm elections** Nov. 4. Obama Nov. 7 approved approximate doubling of U.S. noncombat military personnel in Iraq, to about 3,000. Labor Dept. announced Nov. 7 that the Oct. **unemployment rate** had dipped to 5.8%, lowest since July 2008.

Obama and Chinese Pres. **Xi Jinping** announced agreement Nov. 12 to reduce carbon outputs in effort to fight **climate change**. House Intelligence Committee report, released Nov. 21, found no intelligence failure prior to 2012 **Benghazi** attack.

Tamir Rice, a black 12-year-old holding a pellet gun, was fatally shot by a white police officer, Nov. 22, in Cleveland, OH; grand jury declined to indict. A grand jury decided Dec. 3 not to indict a New York City police officer for using a nonregulation chokehold to detain **Eric Garner**, a black man who died July 17 in custody. A black man shot and killed two **New York City police** officers in their patrol car, Dec. 20, then killed himself.

A Senate Intelligence Committee report released Dec. 9 condemned CIA use of so-called **enhanced interrogation techniques**. Hackers accessed Sony Pictures Entertainment data and, Dec. 16, threatened violence against U.S. theaters showing comedy about plot to assassinate North Korean dictator **Kim Jong Un**. U.S.-led NATO mission in **Afghanistan** ended combat operations Dec. 28 after over 13 years.

Centers for Disease Control confirmed 667 **measles** cases for 2014, highest since measles was declared eliminated from the U.S. in 2000. Dow Jones industrial average closed 2014 up 7.5%, in sixth straight year of growth.

2015 **Standard & Poor's** agreed Feb. 3 to pay $1.4 bil to settle suits over alleged inflated ratings for subprime mortgage

2015: Pope Francis, the first leader of the Roman Catholic Church from the Americas, visits the U.S. for the first time.

2015: A Supreme Court decision effectively legalizes same-sex marriage nationwide.

bonds. **Morgan Stanley**, Feb. 15, agreed to pay $2.6 bil to resolve claims of deception over mortgage-backed securities. Justice Dept. Mar. 4 released report exposing widespread mistreatment of African Americans by **Ferguson**, MO, police and court system, mandating policy changes.

A New York court Mar. 5 approved $8.5-bil settlement between **Bank of America** and investors in mortgage securities issued by **Countrywide Financial Corp.** Federal judge, Mar. 20, approved settlement in which **AIG** paid its shareholders $970.5 mil, settling claims they were misled over high-risk mortgage loans.

Facing a fourth year of severe drought, California Gov. **Jerry Brown** (D) issued **mandatory water restrictions** Apr. 1. GOP governors in Indiana and Arkansas, Apr. 2, signed so-called **religious freedom laws** (both later revised).

By July, 17 Republicans announced they would seek the party's 2016 presidential nomination, including real estate mogul **Donald Trump**. Former Sec. of State **Hillary Clinton** launched presidential campaign Apr. 12, followed by main challenger Sen. **Bernie Sanders** (I, VT).

On Apr. 11, Pres. Obama met in Panama with Cuban Pres. **Raúl Castro** in first formal talks between leaders of the two countries in over 50 years. The Apr. 19 death of a black man, **Freddie Gray**, from injury sustained in a **Baltimore** police van spurred riots and led to indictment of six officers; no convictions resulted. Obama June 2 signed a bill to end NSA's bulk collection of phone data, with telecom companies to hold custody of data instead.

American Pharoah, June 6, became first in 37 years to take horse racing's **Triple Crown**.

A white supremacist fatally shot nine African Americans, June 17, at a historic black church in Charleston, SC; shooter sentenced to death, 2017. On June 26, the Supreme Court ruled that **same-sex couples** had constitutional right to marry. Defense Sec. **Ashton Carter** revealed July 7 that a $500-mil program to train some 15,000 Syrian moderate opposition fighters against ISIS had yielded only 60 trainees. The federal Office of Personnel Management July 9 announced hackers had stolen personal information of about 22 mil people.

Iran and six world powers led by the U.S. formally agreed July 14 on a deal to limit **Iranian nuclear capability** in return for lifting economic sanctions; a Senate effort to block the agreement failed, Sept. 10.

NASA's *New Horizons* spacecraft, July 14, carried out the first-ever flyby of **Pluto**.

U.S. and **Cuba** reopened embassies in their respective countries July 20, reestablishing relations. Pres. Obama Aug. 3 unveiled a final EPA **Clean Power Plan** for imposing mandatory limits on carbon dioxide emissions from power plants (enforcement suspended pending litigation). **General Motors** agreed Sept. 17 to pay $900 mil to settle Justice Dept. criminal investigation into its failure to issue recall for a defect that led to at least 124 deaths.

Pope Francis visited the U.S. Sept. 22-27, and addressed joint session of Congress. A student shooter at a community college, Oct. 1, in **Roseburg, OR**, killed nine; he was wounded by police and killed himself. A U.S. airstrike on an Afghanistan hospital operated by **Doctors Without Borders**,

Oct. 3, killed more than 40; Obama apologized and pledged reconstruction funds.

Officials from the U.S. and 11 other nations completed negotiations, Oct. 5, on the **Trans-Pacific Partnership** trade agreement. Rep. **Paul Ryan** (R, WI) was elected Speaker of the House, Oct. 29, replacing **John Boehner** (R, OH). Congress, Oct. 30, cleared a budget bill that increased spending by $80 bil through 2017.

An Oct. 22 joint mission by U.S. and Iraqi forces freed about 70 hostages held by **ISIS** in Iraq; one U.S. soldier was killed. On Oct. 30, Pres. Obama announced he would deploy dozens of special operations forces to fight ISIS in Syria.

After years of delay, Pres. Obama Nov. 6 announced final decision against building the **Keystone XL oil pipeline**. Two civilians and a police officer were killed Nov. 27 at a **Planned Parenthood** clinic in Colorado Springs, CO; alleged shooter was found incompetent to stand trial and hospitalized.

A married couple said by the FBI to be **Muslim extremists** fatally shot 14 people at a Dec. 2 office holiday party in San Bernardino, CA; both died in shootout with police. Defense Sec. Ash Carter Dec. 3 announced that all military combat positions would be opened to women. Pres. Obama Dec. 10 signed into law a revision of the **No Child Left Behind** education law that gave more discretion to states and localities. Officials representing the U.S. and 194 other parties reached agreement in Paris, Dec. 12, on plan to reduce greenhouse gases linked to **climate change**. The Fed, Dec. 16, raised key **interest rates** a fraction of a percent from near-zero levels. Obama signed a $1.8-tril spending and tax relief package Dec. 18.

2016 Oil prices in Jan.-Feb sank to lowest levels in 12 years. Armed protesters, Jan. 2, began 41-day occupation of **Oregon**'s Malheur National Wildlife Refuge, in land dispute; one protester fatally shot, Jan. 26, in confrontation with law enforcement. Obama declared a federal state of emergency in **Flint, MI**, Jan. 16, because of **lead-contaminated** drinking water.

Donald Trump easily won the New Hampshire Republican primary Feb. 9. By month's end the GOP field had narrowed to five. **Hillary Clinton** lost to Sen. **Bernie Sanders** in New Hampshire Democratic primary. The State Dept., Feb. 29, released last batch of the 52,000 emails from Clinton's **private email server**; over 2,000 in all contained information deemed (but not specifically marked as) classified. With victory in the May 3 **Indiana primary**, Trump had enough support to win the GOP presidential nomination; Clinton had enough delegates and superdelegates after winning in **Puerto Rico**, June 5.

Pres. Obama Mar. 16 nominated appellate court judge **Merrick Garland** to Supreme Court seat vacated by the death in Feb. of **Antonin Scalia**; Republican Senate leaders refused to hold confirmation hearings. Obama visited **Cuba**, Mar. 20-22; first sitting U.S. president to do so since 1928.

North Carolina Gov. **Pat McCrory** (R) Mar. 23 signed **"bathroom bill"** providing that persons use state facilities corresponding to birth-certificate gender; boycotts followed. (Measure partly repealed, 2017.) U.S. Depts. of Justice and Education, May 13, issued guidance advising public schools to allow students to use facilities matching their **gender identity** (guidance revoked by Trump administration). The Justice Dept. announced Apr. 11 that **Goldman Sachs** would pay $5.1 bil to settle charges of selling faulty mortgage-backed securities.

U.S. drone strike killed Afghan Taliban leader **Akhtar Muhammad Mansour** May 21. On a trip to East Asia, May 21-28, Obama became first sitting U.S. president to visit **Hiroshima**, Japan, and declared, in Hanoi, that the U.S. would end its arms embargo against **Vietnam**. A gunman who declared allegiance to **ISIS** killed 49 mostly Hispanic people June 12 at a **gay nightclub** in Orlando, FL. The musical *Hamilton* won 11 Tony Awards June 12.

Iraqi troops and Shiite-dominated militias, aided by U.S. airstrikes, gained control of **Fallujah** June 26. A House Select Committee, June 28, released final report on 2012 attack in **Benghazi**, Libya, showing no evidence of wrongdoing by then-Sec. of State Clinton.

In settlement announced June 28, **Volkswagen** agreed to pay some $15 bil for having cheated **emissions tests**. Defense Sec. Ash Carter announced, June 30, that **transgender individuals** would be able to openly serve in the military.

Protests followed the fatal shooting of a black man in each of two unrelated encounters with police in **Baton Rouge**,

LA, July 5, and a **St. Paul**, MN, suburb, July 6. (No charges brought in Baton Rouge incident; a 2017 trial in MN ended in officer's acquittal.) In attacks by two unconnected gunmen, apparently motivated by revenge, five police officers were killed by a sniper, July 7, in **Dallas**, TX, and three officers were killed in an ambush, July 17, in **Baton Rouge**.

After investigating Hillary Clinton's use of a private email server as sec. of state, FBI Dir. **James Comey**, July 5, said she did not show intent to violate the law but had been "extremely careless" in handling of classified information. Meeting July 18-21 in Cleveland, OH, **Republicans nominated Donald Trump** for president and Gov. **Mike Pence** (IN) for vice president. **WikiLeaks** July 22 published Democratic National Committee emails perceived as showing bias by DNC officials against Bernie Sanders; DNC chair **Debbie Wasserman Schultz** resigned in response. Meeting July 25-28 in Philadelphia, **Democrats nominated Hillary Clinton** for president and Sen. **Tim Kaine** (VA) for vice president. Fox News Channel chair and CEO **Roger Ailes** resigned July 21 amid sexual harassment charges.

A Justice Dept. report released Aug. 10 concluded that **Baltimore** police routinely used **excessive force** against black residents. Riots broke out in **Milwaukee**, WI, Aug. 13-15, following police shooting of an armed black man fleeing a traffic stop (the officer, who was black, was tried and acquitted). An unarmed black motorist was fatally shot Sept. 16 in encounter with police in **Tulsa**, OK (officer acquitted of manslaughter). In **Charlotte**, NC, Sept. 20, a police officer fatally shot an allegedly armed black man (no charges brought).

Regulators fined **Wells Fargo** $185 mil Sept. 8 for scheme to generate revenues by applying for credit cards in retail customers' names. Following protests by the **Standing Rock** Sioux Tribe, the Obama administration Sept. 9 temporarily blocked construction on the **Dakota Access oil pipeline** (later resumed; pipeline opened June 2017).

The *Washington Post* Oct. 7 made public 2005 video footage that showed Trump bragging about **groping women**; a number of women subsequently reported Trump had sexually harassed them. Portions of Trump's 1995 **income tax** records, leaked and published Oct. 1, showed he had declared a $916-mil business loss to offset tax liability. **WikiLeaks** Oct. 7 began releasing apparently hacked emails from Clinton campaign chair **John Podesta**. FBI Dir. **Comey** informed Congress Oct. 28 that the agency had found more Hillary Clinton emails but Nov. 6 said that their review found no basis for charges.

AT&T agreed Oct. 22 to acquire Time Warner for about $85 bil. Two **Des Moines**-area police officers were killed in ambushes by gunman, Nov. 2. **Chicago Cubs** won World Series Nov. 2, for first time since 1908.

In Nov. 8 presidential election, **Donald Trump** (R) defeated **Hillary Clinton** (D), ultimately receiving 304 electoral votes out of 538 but losing the popular vote by about 2.9 mil. On Nov. 13, Pres.-elect Trump named Republican National Committee chair **Reince Priebus** as chief of staff and former right-wing media executive **Steve Bannon** as chief strategist and senior counselor. Retired Lt. Gen. **Michael Flynn** signed on, Nov. 18, as national security adviser. Trump named Exxon Mobil CEO **Rex Tillerson**, Dec. 13, as sec.

of state. On Nov. 18, Trump agreed to pay $25 mil to settle fraud suits against the former **Trump University** real estate training program.

The Fed Dec. 14 announced a quarter-point hike to its benchmark rate. Tech pioneer **Yahoo** Dec. 14 revealed an Aug. 2013 hack, ultimately said to have endangered all 3 bil user accounts. Following evidence of **Russian hacking** that might have influenced the Nov. election, Obama Dec. 29 expelled 35 Russian diplomats. The **Dow Jones** industrial average finished 2016 up 13.4%, best gain in three years.

2017 Pres. Obama commuted sentences of document leaker **Chelsea Manning**, Jan. 17, and Jan. 19 of 330 more inmates, the majority of whom were convicted of nonviolent drug offenses. Pres.-elect Trump said, Jan. 11, he would delegate control of his business assets to his two oldest sons and others, while retaining ownership; **Trump inaugurated** Jan. 20. **Women's Marches**, Jan. 21, in Washington, DC, and other cities collectively drew millions of protesters.

On Jan. 23, Trump withdrew the U.S. from the unratified **Trans-Pacific Partnership** trade agreement and reinstated a ban on federal funding for foreign health care organizations providing abortions. He signed an order the next day advancing construction of the **Keystone XL oil pipeline**, and on Jan. 25, an order to build a Mexican **border wall**, hire more immigration personnel, and pull federal funding from so-called **sanctuary cities**.

Citing national security, Pres. Trump Jan. 27 issued a controversial executive order banning admission of travelers from certain **Muslim-majority nations**. Implementation was blocked in part by court challenges. The order was superseded by revised versions, issued Mar. 6 and Sept. 24, that attempted to overcome legal objections.

The Senate Feb. 7 confirmed charter-school advocate **Betsy DeVos** as education secretary. National Security Adviser Michael Flynn resigned Feb. 13 after the Justice Dept. reported Flynn had misled the administration and lied to the FBI about contacts with Russia's U.S. ambassador. The Fed, Mar. 15, raised its **benchmark interest rate** by a quarter point.

A Mar. 17 coalition airstrike in **Mosul**, Iraq, triggered ISIS bombs that killed over 100 noncombatants. After a suspected **chemical attack** that killed over 80 civilians Apr. 4, Pres. Trump authorized a cruise-missile strike against a Syrian government airfield believed linked to the attack. The U.S. military, Apr. 13, dropped its most powerful nonnuclear bomb on a complex of caves and tunnels in **Afghanistan**; 94 ISIS-affiliated militants reportedly killed.

After Senate Republicans used the so-called **nuclear option** to end a Democratic filibuster, the Senate voted, 54-45, to confirm Trump's nomination of **Neil Gorsuch** to the Supreme Court on Apr. 7.

Alabama Gov. **Robert Bentley** (R) resigned Apr. 10 in a scandal over an extramarital affair and cover-up. **Fox News** separated from longtime host **Bill O'Reilly** Apr. 19, following reports of sexual harassment.

With funding for the government set to expire at midnight, Congress Apr. 28 passed a stopgap measure that included money for Obamacare subsidies; an omnibus spending bill, cleared the next day, included an increase in defense and border security funds, but no money for a border wall. With $123 bil in debt and unfunded pension obligations, **Puerto Rico** filed for a form of bankruptcy, May 3.

Pres. Trump fired FBI Dir. **James Comey** May 9, prompting charges the action was an attempt to derail inquiry into any links between the president and **Russian interference** in the 2016 presidential election. The *NY Times* May 16 reported that, according to a Comey memo, Trump had asked him to halt investigation of former national security adviser **Michael Flynn**. On May 17, the Justice Dept. appointed former FBI Dir. **Robert Mueller III** as special counsel to head the investigation into Russian election meddling and any related matters.

Pres. Trump, May 11, established a commission to investigate what he claimed was widespread **voter fraud** in the 2016 election (disbanded Jan. 2018, without reporting evidence of fraud). **New Orleans**, May 19, took down a statue of Gen. Robert E. Lee, the fourth Confederacy-themed monument removed by the city in recent weeks.

After 146 years, financially ailing Ringling Brothers and Barnum & Bailey Circus held its final "**Greatest Show on Earth**" May 21 in Uniondale, NY.

2016: A federal state of emergency is declared in Flint, MI, as 100,000 residents are forced to avoid using the city's lead-contaminated water supply.

2017: Real estate magnate Donald J. Trump, who campaigned as a Washington outsider, is inaugurated as the 45th U.S. president.

Citing fears of job losses, Pres. Trump announced June 1 that he intended to pull the U.S. out of the 2015 **Paris climate change agreement**.

A gunman targeting Republicans June 14 at a practice in Alexandria, VA, for the bipartisan **Congressional Baseball Game** critically injured House majority whip **Steve Scalise** (R, LA) and wounded four others.

Iraqi Prime Min. Haider al-Abadi announced July 9 that Iraqi security forces, supported by the U.S.-backed coalition, had **recaptured Mosul**, ISIS's last urban stronghold.

Embattled White House press secretary **Sean Spicer** resigned July 21, after Trump appointed financier **Anthony Scaramucci** as communications director. In an expletive-laced interview published by the *New Yorker*, Scaramucci blamed White House chief of staff **Reince Priebus** for leaks; Priebus resigned, to be replaced by Homeland Security Sec. **John Kelly**. At Kelly's request, the president fired Scaramucci on July 31.

Pres. Trump Aug. 2 reluctantly signed a bill passed nearly unanimously by Congress that imposed new **economic sanctions against Russia** and limited his authority to lift them. It also extended sanctions on Iran and on **North Korea**, which July 4 had launched what was thought to be its first intercontinental-capable **ballistic missile**. Trump warned North Korea Aug. 8 it could be met with "fire and fury like the world has never seen"; nevertheless, North Korea threatened possible missile strikes against the U.S. territory of **Guam**.

A **white nationalist rally** in **Charlottesville**, VA, Aug. 12, erupted in violent clashes with counterdemonstrators, including **Black Lives Matter** and **"antifa"** (antifascist) activists. One white nationalist drove a car into a crowd, killing a counterprotester and injuring 19 others. After a widely denounced statement that condemned "hatred, bigotry, and violence on many sides," Pres. Trump issued a statement Aug. 14 that branded white supremacist protesters as "thugs." Trump's chief strategist and former Breitbart CEO Steve Bannon left the administration Aug. 18.

On Aug. 21, millions viewed the first coast-to-coast **total solar eclipse** seen in the U.S. since 1918. Pres. Trump Aug. 25 pardoned former Maricopa (AZ) County sheriff **Joe Arpaio**, convicted July 31 of criminal contempt for ignoring judge's order to stop detaining people solely on suspicion of their immigration status. On Aug. 28 several antifa protesters attacked participants in a previously peaceful anti-Marxist rally in **Berkeley**, CA.

Hurricane Harvey hit Texas, Aug. 25, causing 89 deaths; damage was projected at $126.3 bil, costliest storm since Katrina. **North Korea** Sept. 3 conducted its sixth **nuclear weapons test**, claiming it was a hydrogen bomb; the UN and U.S. imposed economic sanctions.

The Trump administration, Sept. 5, announced it would phase out the Deferred Action for Childhood Arrivals (**DACA**) program. **Facebook** told congressional investigators Sept. 6 it had unwittingly sold advertisements to a covert Russian company that sought to influence the 2016 U.S. election. Credit reporting firm **Equifax** revealed Sept. 7 that hackers had gained access to its personal information on some 143 mil Americans.

Pres. Trump Sept. 6 signed a measure to keep the government solvent for three months, with $15 bil in aid to areas affected by Hurricane Harvey. Hurricane **Irma** struck Florida Sept. 10; responsible for heavy damage and about 90 deaths. Hurricane **Maria** hit Puerto Rico, Sept. 20, causing at least 65 deaths and widespread devastation; federal relief efforts were criticized and later estimates of the death toll put the number into the hundreds or thousands.

A former **St. Louis**, MO, police officer was acquitted Sept. 15 in the fatal 2011 shooting of a black motorist after a police chase, sparking sometimes violent demonstrations. NASA retired the unmanned Saturn probe *Cassini*, sending it into Saturn's atmosphere Sept. 15, after an almost 20-year mission. **Toys R Us** retail chain filed for bankruptcy protection, Sept. 18.

In the **deadliest U.S. massacre** yet by a single shooter, a gunman firing from a hotel balcony killed 58 people and injured hundreds attending an outdoor country music concert, Oct. 1 in **Las Vegas**.

Four U.S. service members were killed in **Niger** in an Oct. 4 ambush attributed to an ISIS affiliate.

Attorney Gen. **Jeff Sessions** Oct. 5 reversed an Obama-era policy extending workplace discrimination protections to **transgender employees**. Environmental Protection Agency head Scott Pruitt signed a proposal Oct. 10 to repeal Obama's **Clean Power Plan**.

An Oct. 5 *NY Times* report detailing multiple accusations of sexual assault or harassment against movie producer **Harvey Weinstein** set off a wave of **"Me Too"** allegations by others victimized by sexual misconduct. Among prominent figures implicated by the end of the year, in varying degrees, were actor **Kevin Spacey**, political analyst **Mark Halperin**, broadcast journalists **Matt Lauer** and **Charlie Rose**, conductor **James Levine**, humorist **Garrison Keillor**, comedian **Louis C.K.**, and music producer **Russell Simmons**, as well as U.S. Rep. **John Conyers** (D, MI) and Sen. **Al Franken** (D, MN). Alabama chief justice **Roy Moore** (R), accused of misconduct with a 14-year-old girl, ran in and lost a special election, Dec. 12, for a longtime Republican-held U.S. Senate seat.

Pres. Trump announced Oct. 13 that he would not certify **Iran**'s compliance with the 2015 multinational nuclear weapons deal, while not yet pulling the U.S. out of it. U.S.-backed Syrian militias, Oct. 20, reported they had seized control of **Raqqa**, de facto capital of ISIS's self-proclaimed caliphate.

Trump, Oct. 26, declared the ongoing **opioid addiction epidemic** a public health emergency.

Russia probe special counsel **Robert Mueller** Oct. 30 announced the indictment of former Trump campaign manager **Paul Manafort** and associate **Rick Gates**; charges included laundering some $18 mil obtained by lobbying for a pro-Russia party in Ukraine. Related filings showed that former Trump campaign adviser **George Papadopoulos** had pleaded guilty to lying to the FBI about contacts with Russians. Former Trump adviser **Michael Flynn** pleaded guilty Dec. 1 to lying to the FBI about communications with a Russian official in waning days of the Obama administration.

An Uzbek immigrant, apparently inspired by **ISIS**, drove a truck into a crowd in New York City, Oct. 31, killing 8 people. A white gunman, apparently motivated by a domestic dispute, killed 26 people, Nov. 5, at a Baptist church Nov. 5 in **Sutherland Springs**, TX.

A U.S. Navy report, Nov. 1, blamed multiple personnel errors for **collisions at sea** involving the USS *Fitzgerald* (June 17; 7 sailors killed) and USS *John S. McCain* (Aug. 21; 10 sailors killed).

Fire broke out Dec. 4 in **California**'s Ventura County, burning more than 280,000 acres. Over 8,500 firefighters battled the blaze; one was killed. Claiming federal overreach, Trump, Dec. 4, announced that two **national monuments** in Utah would be slashed in acreage; tribal and environmental groups filed legal challenges.

Pres. Trump, Dec. 6, recognized **Jerusalem** as Israel's capital and announced plans to move the U.S. Embassy there.

Congress avoided a government shutdown by passing another stopgap funding measure, Dec. 21. On Dec. 22, in his first major legislative victory, Pres. Trump signed a **comprehensive tax-reform measure**. The bill, passed with no Democratic votes and projected to cost $1.5 tril over 10 years, permanently reduced the top corporate tax rate and cut personal income tax rates until 2025. It also permitted oil drilling in **Alaska**'s Arctic National Wildlife Refuge and repealed Obamacare's **individual mandate**.

The **Dow Jones** industrial average closed 2017 up 25% over the close of 2016.

U.S. HISTORY: DOCUMENTS, SPEECHES, AND SYMBOLS

Patrick Henry's Speech to the Virginia Convention

The following is an excerpt from Patrick Henry's speech to the Virginia Convention, which met at St. John's Church in Richmond, on Mar. 23, 1775, to react to British oppression.

Gentlemen may cry, peace, peace—but there is no peace. The war is actually begun! The next gale that sweeps from the north will bring to our ears the clash of resounding arms! Our brethren are already in the field! Why stand we here idle? What is it that gentlemen wish? What would they have? Is life so dear, or peace so sweet, as to be purchased at the price of chains and slavery? Forbid it, Almighty God! I know not what course others may take; but as for me, give me liberty, or give me death!

Adoption of the Declaration of Independence

On June 7, 1776, Richard Henry Lee, who had issued the first call for a congress of the colonies, introduced in the Continental Congress at Philadelphia a resolution declaring "that these United Colonies are, and of right ought to be, free and independent states, that they are absolved from all allegiance to the British Crown, and that all political connection between them and the state of Great Britain is, and ought to be, totally dissolved."

The resolution, seconded by John Adams on behalf of the Massachusetts delegation, came up again June 11 when a committee of five chaired by Thomas Jefferson (VA) was appointed to express the purpose of the resolution in a declaration of independence. The other four were John Adams, Benjamin Franklin (PA), Robert R. Livingston (NY), and Roger Sherman (CT).

Drafting the Declaration was assigned to Jefferson, who worked on a portable desk of his own construction in a room at Market and 7th St. The committee reported the result on June 28, 1776. The members of the Congress suggested a number of changes, which Jefferson called "deplorable." They did not approve Jefferson's arraignment of the British people and King George III for encouraging and fostering the slave trade, which Jefferson called "an execrable commerce." They eliminated 630 words and added 146, leaving 1,322 words in the final draft. In its final form, capitalization was erratic. Jefferson had written that men were endowed with "inalienable" rights; in the final copy it came out as "unalienable."

The Lee-Adams resolution of independence was adopted by 12 yeas on July 2—the actual date of the act of independence. The Declaration, which explains the act, was adopted July 4.

After the Declaration was adopted, July 4, 1776, it was turned over to printer John Dunlap to be printed on broadsides. The original copy was lost and one of his broadsides was attached to a page in the journal of the Congress. It was read aloud July 8 in Philadelphia; Easton, PA; and Trenton, NJ. On July 9, it was read by order of Gen. George Washington to the troops assembled on the Common in New York City (now City Hall Park).

The Continental Congress of July 19, 1776, adopted the following resolution:

"Resolved, That the Declaration passed on the 4th, be fairly engrossed on parchment with the title and stile of 'The Unanimous Declaration of the thirteen United States of America' and that the same, when engrossed, be signed by every member of Congress." (Engrossing meant clearly writing out an official document.)

Not all delegates who signed the engrossed Declaration had been present on July 4. Among them were Robert Morris (PA), William Williams (CT), and Samuel Chase (MD), who signed on Aug. 2. Oliver Wolcott (CT), George Wythe (VA), Richard Henry Lee (VA), and Elbridge Gerry (MA) signed in Aug. and Sept.; Matthew Thornton (NH) joined the Congress Nov. 4 and signed later. Thomas McKean (DE) rejoined Washington's army before signing and said later that he signed in 1781.

Charles Carroll of Carrollton was appointed a delegate by Maryland on July 4, 1776, presented his credentials July 18, and signed the engrossed Declaration on Aug. 2. Born Sept. 19, 1737, he was 95 years old and the last surviving signer when he died Nov. 14, 1832.

Two Pennsylvania delegates who did not support the Declaration July 4, 1776, were replaced. The four New York delegates did not have authority from their state to vote on July 4. On July 9, the New York state convention authorized its delegates to approve the Declaration, and the Congress was so notified on July 15, 1776. The four signed the Declaration on Aug. 2.

Declaration of Independence

The Declaration of Independence was adopted by the Continental Congress in Philadelphia on July 4, 1776. John Hancock was president of the Congress, and Charles Thomson was secretary. A copy of the Declaration, engrossed (i.e., written in a clear hand) on parchment, was signed by members of Congress on and after Aug. 2, 1776. On Jan. 18, 1777, Congress ordered that "an authenticated copy, with the names of the members of Congress subscribing the same, be sent to each of the United States, and that they be desired to have the same put on record." Authenticated copies were printed in broadside form in Baltimore, where the Continental Congress was then in session. The following text is that of the original printed by John Dunlap in Philadelphia for the Continental Congress. The original is on display at the National Archives in Washington, DC.

In CONGRESS, July 4, 1776.
A DECLARATION
By the REPRESENTATIVES of the
UNITED STATES OF AMERICA,
In GENERAL CONGRESS assembled.

When in the Course of human Events, it becomes necessary for one People to dissolve the Political Bands which have connected them with another, and to assume among the Powers of the Earth, the separate and equal Station to which the Laws of Nature and of Nature's God entitle them, a decent Respect to the Opinions of Mankind requires that they should declare the causes which impel them to the Separation.

We hold these Truths to be self-evident, that all Men are created equal, that they are endowed by their Creator with certain unalienable Rights, that among these are Life, Liberty, and the Pursuit of Happiness—That to secure these Rights, Governments are instituted among Men, deriving their just Powers from the Consent of the Governed, that whenever any Form of Government becomes destructive of these Ends, it is the Right of the People to alter or to abolish it, and to institute new Government, laying its Foundation on such Principles, and organizing its Powers in such Form, as to them shall seem most likely to effect their Safety and Happiness. Prudence, indeed, will dictate that Governments long established should not be changed for light and transient Causes; and accordingly all Experience hath shewn, that Mankind are more disposed to suffer, while Evils are sufferable, than to right themselves by abolishing the Forms to which they are accustomed. But when a long Train of Abuses and Usurpations, pursuing invariably the same Object, evinces a Design to reduce them under absolute Despotism, it is their Right, it is their Duty, to throw off such Government, and to provide new Guards for their future Security. Such has been the patient Sufferance of these Colonies; and such is now the Necessity which constrains them to alter their former Systems of Government. The History of the present King of Great Britain is a History of repeated Injuries and Usurpations, all having in direct Object the Establishment of an absolute Tyranny over these States. To prove this, let Facts be submitted to a candid World.

He has refused his Assent to Laws, the most wholesome and necessary for the public Good.

He has forbidden his Governors to pass Laws of immediate and pressing Importance, unless suspended in their Operation till his Assent should be obtained; and when so suspended, he has utterly neglected to attend to them.

He has refused to pass other Laws for the Accommodation of large Districts of People, unless those People would relinquish the Right of Representation in the Legislature, a Right inestimable to them, and formidable to Tyrants only.

He has called together Legislative Bodies at Places unusual, uncomfortable, and distant from the Depository of their Public Records, for the sole Purpose of fatiguing them into Compliance with his Measures.

He has dissolved Representative Houses repeatedly, for opposing with manly Firmness his Invasions on the Rights of the People.

He has refused for a long Time, after such Dissolutions, to cause others to be elected; whereby the Legislative Powers, incapable of Annihilation, have returned to the People at large for their exercise; the State remaining in the mean time exposed to all the Dangers of Invasion from without, and Convulsions within.

He has endeavoured to prevent the Population of these States; for that Purpose obstructing the Laws for Naturalization of Foreigners; refusing to pass others to encourage their Migrations hither, and raising the Conditions of new Appropriations of Lands.

He has obstructed the Administration of Justice, by refusing his Assent to Laws for establishing Judiciary Powers.

He has made Judges dependent on his Will alone, for the Tenure of their Offices, and the Amount and payment of their Salaries.

He has erected a Multitude of new Offices, and sent hither Swarms of Officers to harrass our People, and eat out their Substance.

He has kept among us, in Times of Peace, Standing Armies, without the consent of our Legislatures.

He has affected to render the Military independent of, and superior to the Civil Power.

He has combined with others to subject us to a Jurisdiction foreign to our Constitution, and unacknowledged by our Laws; giving his Assent to their Acts of pretended Legislation:

For Quartering large bodies of armed troops among us:

For protecting them, by a mock Trial, from Punishment for any Murders which they should commit on the Inhabitants of these States:

For cutting off our Trade with all Parts of the World:

For imposing Taxes on us without our Consent:

For depriving us, in many Cases, of the Benefits of Trial by Jury:

For transporting us beyond Seas to be tried for pretended Offences:

For abolishing the free System of English Laws in a neighbouring Province, establishing therein an arbitrary Government, and enlarging its Boundaries, so as to render it at once an Example and fit Instrument for introducing the same absolute Rule into these Colonies:

For taking away our Charters, abolishing our most valuable Laws, and altering fundamentally the Forms of our Governments:

For suspending our own Legislatures, and declaring themselves invested with Power to legislate for us in all Cases whatsoever.

He has abdicated Government here, by declaring us out of his Protection and waging War against us.

He has plundered our Seas, ravaged our Coasts, burnt our towns, and destroyed the Lives of our People.

He is, at this Time, transporting large Armies of foreign Mercenaries to complete the works of Death, Desolation, and Tyranny, already begun with circumstances of Cruelty

and Perfidy, scarcely paralleled in the most barbarous Ages, and totally unworthy the Head of a civilized Nation.

He has constrained our fellow Citizens taken Captive on the high Seas to bear Arms against their Country, to become the Executioners of their Friends and Brethren, or to fall themselves by their Hands.

He has excited domestic Insurrections amongst us, and has endeavoured to bring on the Inhabitants of our Frontiers, the merciless Indian Savages, whose known Rule of Warfare, is an undistinguished Destruction, of all Ages, Sexes and Conditions.

In every stage of these Oppressions we have Petitioned for Redress in the most humble Terms: Our repeated Petitions have been answered only by repeated Injury. A Prince, whose Character is thus marked by every act which may define a Tyrant, is unfit to be the Ruler of a free People.

Nor have we been wanting in Attentions to our British Brethren. We have warned them from Time to Time of Attempts by their Legislature to extend an unwarrantable Jurisdiction over us. We have reminded them of the Circumstances of our Emigration and Settlement here. We have appealed to their native Justice and Magnanimity, and we have conjured them by the Ties of our common Kindred to disavow these Usurpations, which, would inevitably interrupt our Connections and Correspondence. They too have been deaf to the Voice of Justice and of Consanguinity. We must, therefore, acquiesce in the Necessity, which denounces our Separation, and hold them, as we hold the rest of Mankind, Enemies in War, in Peace, Friends.

We, therefore, the Representatives of the UNITED STATES OF AMERICA, in General Congress, Assembled, appealing to the Supreme Judge of the World for the Rectitude of our Intentions, do, in the Name, and by Authority of the good People of these Colonies, solemnly Publish and Declare, That these United Colonies are, and of Right ought to be, Free and Independent States; that they are absolved from all Allegiance to the British Crown, and that all political Connection between them and the State of Great Britain, is and ought to be totally dissolved; and that as Free and Independent States, they have full Power to levy War, conclude Peace, contract Alliances, establish Commerce, and to do all other Acts and Things which Independent States may of right do. And for the support of this declaration, with a firm Reliance on the Protection of Divine Providence, we mutually pledge to each other our lives, our Fortunes, and our sacred Honor.

JOHN HANCOCK, President.

Attest.

CHARLES THOMSON, Secretary.

Signers of the Declaration of Independence

Delegate (state)	Occupation	Birthplace	Born	Died
Adams, John (MA)	Lawyer	Braintree (Quincy), MA	Oct. 30, 1735	July 4, 1826
Adams, Samuel (MA)	Merchant, brewer	Boston, MA	Sept. 27, 1722	Oct. 2, 1803
Bartlett, Josiah (NH)	Physician, judge	Amesbury, MA	Nov. 21, 1729	May 19, 1795
Braxton, Carter (VA)	Plantation owner	Newington Plantation, VA	Sept. 10, 1736	Oct. 10, 1797
Carroll, Charles, of Carrollton (MD)	Plantation owner	Annapolis, MD	Sept. 19, 1737	Nov. 14, 1832
Chase, Samuel (MD)	Lawyer, judge	Princess Anne, MD	Apr. 17, 1741	June 19, 1811
Clark, Abraham (NJ)	Surveyor	Elizabethtown, NJ	Feb. 15, 1726	Sept. 15, 1794
Clymer, George (PA)	Merchant	Philadelphia, PA	Mar. 16, 1739	Jan. 23, 1813
Ellery, William (RI)	Lawyer	Newport, RI	Dec. 22, 1727	Feb. 15, 1820
Floyd, William (NY)	Plantation owner, soldier	Brookhaven, NY	Dec. 17, 1734	Aug. 4, 1821
Franklin, Benjamin (PA)	Printer, inventor	Boston, MA	Jan. 17, 1706	Apr. 17, 1790
Gerry, Elbridge (MA)	Merchant	Marblehead, MA	July 17, 1744	Nov. 23, 1814
Gwinnett, Button (GA)	Merchant	Gloucester, England	c. 1735	May 19, 1777
Hall, Lyman (GA)	Physician	Wallingford, CT	Apr. 12, 1724	Oct. 19, 1790
Hancock, John (MA)	Merchant	Braintree (Quincy), MA	Jan. 12, 1737	Oct. 8, 1793
Harrison, Benjamin (VA)	Plantation owner	Charles City County, VA	Apr. 5, 1726	Apr. 24, 1791
Hart, John (NJ)	Plantation owner	Stonington, CT	c. 1713	May 11, 1779
Hewes, Joseph (NC)	Merchant	Kingston, NJ	Jan. 23, 1730	Nov. 10, 1779
Heyward, Thomas, Jr. (SC)	Lawyer, plantation owner	St. Luke's Parish, SC	July 28, 1746	Mar. 6, 1809
Hooper, William (NC)	Lawyer	Boston, MA	June 17, 1742	Oct. 14, 1790
Hopkins, Stephen (RI)	Judge, merchant	Providence, RI	Mar. 7, 1707	July 13, 1785
Hopkinson, Francis (NJ)	Composer, lawyer	Philadelphia, PA	Oct. 2, 1737	May 9, 1791
Huntington, Samuel (CT)	Lawyer, judge	Windham, CT	July 3, 1731	Jan. 5, 1796
Jefferson, Thomas (VA)	Lawyer, plantation owner	Shadwell, VA	Apr. 13, 1743	July 4, 1826
Lee, Francis Lightfoot (VA)	Plantation owner	Westmoreland County, VA	Oct. 14, 1734	Jan. 11, 1797
Lee, Richard Henry (VA)	Plantation owner	Westmoreland County, VA	Jan. 20, 1732	June 19, 1794
Lewis, Francis (NY)	Merchant	Llandaff, Wales	Mar. 21, 1713	Dec. 31, 1802
Livingston, Philip (NY)	Merchant	Albany, NY	Jan. 15, 1716	June 12, 1778
Lynch, Thomas, Jr. (SC)	Plantation owner	Winyah, SC	Aug. 5, 1749	(at sea) 1779
McKean, Thomas (DE)	Lawyer	New London, PA	Mar. 19, 1734	June 24, 1817
Middleton, Arthur (SC)	Plantation owner	Charleston, SC	June 26, 1742	Jan. 1, 1787
Morris, Lewis (NY)	Farmer, judge	Morrisania (Bronx County), NY	Apr. 8, 1726	Jan. 22, 1798
Morris, Robert (PA)	Merchant	Liverpool, England	Jan. 31, 1734	May 8, 1806
Morton, John (PA)	Surveyor	Ridley, PA	c. 1724	Apr. 1777
Nelson, Thomas, Jr. (VA)	Merchant	Yorktown, VA	Dec. 26, 1738	Jan. 4, 1789
Paca, William (MD)	Lawyer, judge	Abingdon, MD	Oct. 31, 1740	Oct. 23, 1799
Paine, Robert Treat (MA)	Lawyer, judge	Boston, MA	Mar. 11, 1731	May 11, 1814
Penn, John (NC)	Lawyer	Caroline County, VA	May 17, 1741	Sept. 14, 1788
Read, George (DE)	Lawyer, judge	Cecil County, MD	Sept. 18, 1733	Sept. 21, 1798
Rodney, Caesar (DE)	Farmer, judge	Dover, DE	Oct. 7, 1728	June 26, 1784
Ross, George (PA)	Lawyer, judge	New Castle, DE	May 10, 1730	July 14, 1779
Rush, Benjamin (PA)	Physician	Byberry Twp. (Philadelphia), PA	Jan. 4, 1746	Apr. 19, 1813
Rutledge, Edward (SC)	Lawyer, plantation owner	Charleston, SC	Nov. 23, 1749	Jan. 23, 1800
Sherman, Roger (CT)	Lawyer, judge	Newton, MA	Apr. 19, 1721	July 23, 1793
Smith, James (PA)	Lawyer	Ireland	c. 1719	July 11, 1806
Stockton, Richard (NJ)	Lawyer	Princeton, NJ	Oct. 1, 1730	Feb. 28, 1781
Stone, Thomas (MD)	Lawyer	Charles County, MD	c. 1743	Oct. 5, 1787
Taylor, George (PA)	Iron mfr., judge	Ireland	c. 1716	Feb. 23, 1781
Thornton, Matthew (NH)	Physician	Ireland	c. 1714	June 24, 1803
Walton, George (GA)	Lawyer, judge	Cumberland County, VA	c. 1749	Feb. 2, 1804
Whipple, William (NH)	Merchant, judge	Kittery, ME	Jan. 14, 1730	Nov. 28, 1785
Williams, William (CT)	Merchant	Lebanon, CT	c. 1731	Aug. 2, 1811
Wilson, James (PA)	Lawyer	Carskerdo, Scotland	Sept. 14, 1742	Aug. 21, 1798
Witherspoon, John (NJ)	Clergyman, educator	Gifford, Scotland	Feb. 5, 1723	Nov. 15, 1794
Wolcott, Oliver (CT)	Lawyer, judge	Windsor, CT	Nov. 20, 1726	Dec. 1, 1797
Wythe, George (VA)	Lawyer	Elizabeth City County, VA	c. 1726	June 8, 1806

Origin of the Constitution

The War of Independence was conducted by delegates from the original 13 states, who composed the Congress of the United States of America, known as the Continental Congress. In 1777 the Congress submitted to the legislatures of the states the Articles of Confederation and Perpetual Union, which were ratified by New Hampshire, Massachusetts, Rhode Island, Connecticut, New York, New Jersey, Pennsylvania, Delaware, Virginia, North Carolina, South Carolina, Georgia, and finally, in 1781, Maryland.

The first article read: "The stile of this confederacy shall be the United States of America." This did not signify a sovereign nation, because the states delegated only those powers they could not handle individually, such as to wage war, make treaties, and contract debts for general expenses (e.g., paying the army). Taxes for payment of such debts were levied by the individual states. The president signed himself "President of the United States in Congress assembled," but here the United States were considered in the plural, a cooperating group.

When the war was over, it became evident that a stronger federal union was needed. The Congress left the initiative to the legislatures. Virginia in Jan. 1786 appointed commissioners to meet with representatives of other states; delegates from Virginia, Delaware, New York, New Jersey, and Pennsylvania met at Annapolis. Alexander Hamilton prepared their call asking delegates from all states to meet in Philadelphia in May 1787 "to render the Constitution of the federal government adequate to the exigencies of the union." Congress endorsed the plan on Feb. 21, 1787. Delegates were appointed by all states except Rhode Island.

The convention was called for May 14, 1787, but a quorum was not present until May 25. George Washington was chosen president (presiding officer). The states certified 65 delegates, but 10 did not attend. The work was done by 55, not all of whom were present at all sessions. Of the 55 attending delegates, 39 signed Sept. 17, 1787, some with reservations, and 16 failed to sign. Some historians have said 74 delegates (nine more than the 65 actually certified) were named, and 19 failed to attend. These additional persons refused the appointment, were never delegates, and were never counted as absentees. Washington sent the Constitution to Congress, and that body, Sept. 28, 1787, ordered it sent to the legislatures, "in order to be submitted to a convention of delegates chosen in each state by the people thereof."

The Constitution was ratified by votes of state conventions as follows: Delaware, Dec. 7, 1787, unanimous; Pennsylvania, Dec. 12, 1787, 46 to 23; New Jersey, Dec. 18, 1787, unanimous; Georgia, Jan. 2, 1788, unanimous; Connecticut, Jan. 9, 1788, 128 to 40; Massachusetts, Feb. 6, 1788, 187 to 168; Maryland, Apr. 28, 1788, 63 to 11; South Carolina, May 23, 1788, 149 to 73; New Hampshire, June 21, 1788, 57 to 46; Virginia, June 25, 1788, 89 to 79; New York, July 26, 1788, 30 to 27. Nine states were needed to establish the operation of the Constitution "between the states so ratifying the same," and New Hampshire was the ninth state. The government did not declare the Constitution in effect until the first Wednesday in Mar. 1789, which was Mar. 4. After that, North Carolina ratified it on Nov. 21, 1789, 194 to 77; and Rhode Island, May 29, 1790, 34 to 32. Vermont in convention ratified it on Jan. 10, 1791, and by act of Congress approved on Feb. 18, 1791, was admitted into the Union as the 14th state, Mar. 4, 1791.

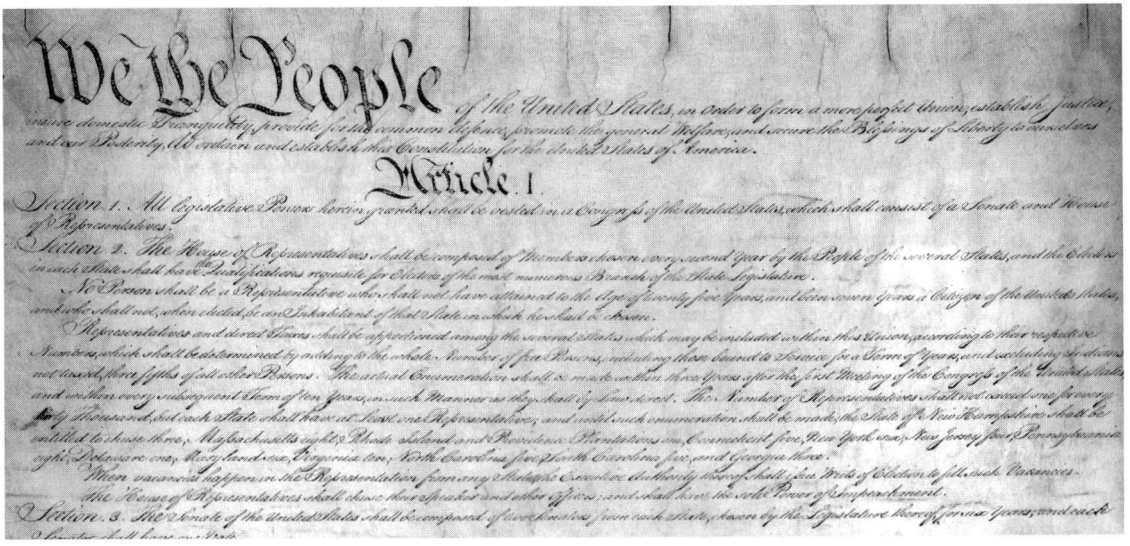

Constitution of the United States

The text of the Constitution given here is from the centennial edition of *The Constitution of the United States of America: Analysis and Interpretation*, prepared by the Library of Congress and issued by the U.S. Government Printing Office. Aug. 26, 2017. Text in brackets indicates that an item has been superseded or amended, or provides background information. **Boldface text** preceding an article, section, or amendment is a brief summary, added by *The World Almanac*.

The Original Seven Articles

PREAMBLE

We the People of the United States, in Order to form a more perfect Union, establish Justice, insure domestic Tranquility, provide for the common defence, promote the general Welfare, and secure the Blessings of Liberty to ourselves and our Posterity, do ordain and establish this Constitution for the United States of America.

ARTICLE I.

Section 1—Legislative powers, in whom vested.

All legislative Powers herein granted shall be vested in a Congress of the United States, which shall consist of a Senate and House of Representatives.

Section 2—House of Representatives, how and by whom chosen. Qualifications of a Representative. Representatives and direct taxes, how apportioned and enumerated. Vacancies to be filled. Choosing of officers and power of impeachment.

The House of Representatives shall be composed of Members chosen every second Year by the People of the several States, and the Electors in each State shall have the Qualifications requisite for Electors of the most numerous Branch of the State Legislature.

No Person shall be a Representative who shall not have attained to the Age of twenty five Years, and been seven Years a Citizen of the United States, and who shall not, when elected, be an Inhabitant of that State in which he shall be chosen.

[Representatives and direct Taxes shall be apportioned among the several States which may be included within this Union, according to their respective Numbers, which shall be determined by adding to the whole Number of free Persons, including those bound to Service for a Term of Years, and excluding Indians not taxed, three fifths of all other Persons.] *[The part of the previous sentence regarding apportionment of representatives among the states was changed by Amendment XIV, section 2, and apportionment of taxes by Amendment XVI.]* The actual Enumeration shall be made within three Years after the first Meeting of the Congress of the United States, and within every subsequent Term of ten Years, in such Manner as they shall by Law direct. The Number of Representatives shall not exceed one for every thirty Thousand, but each State shall have at Least one Representative; and until such enumeration shall be made, the State of New Hampshire shall be entitled to chuse three, Massachusetts eight, Rhode-Island and Providence Plantations one, Connecticut five, New York six, New Jersey four, Pennsylvania eight, Delaware one, Maryland six, Virginia ten, North Carolina five, South Carolina five, and Georgia three.

When vacancies happen in the Representation from any State, the Executive Authority thereof shall issue Writs of Election to fill such Vacancies.

The House of Representatives shall chuse their Speaker and other Officers; and shall have the sole Power of Impeachment.

Section 3—Senators, how and by whom chosen. How assembled. Qualifications of a Senator. President of the Senate. President pro tempore and other officers of the Senate, how chosen. Power to try impeachments. Judgment in cases of impeachment.

The Senate of the United States shall be composed of two Senators from each State, [chosen by the Legislature] *[The preceding words were superseded by Amendment XVII.]* thereof, for six Years; and each Senator shall have one Vote.

Immediately after they shall be assembled in Consequence of the first Election, they shall be divided as equally as may be into three Classes. The Seats of the Senators of the first Class shall be vacated at the Expiration of the second Year, of the second Class at the Expiration of the fourth Year, and of the third Class at the Expiration of the sixth Year, so that one third may be chosen every second Year; [and if Vacancies happen by Resignation, or otherwise, during the Recess of the Legislature of any State, the Executive thereof may make temporary Appointments until the next Meeting of the Legislature, which shall then fill such Vacancies.] *[The words in brackets were superseded by Amendment XVII.]*

No Person shall be a Senator who shall not have attained to the Age of thirty Years, and been nine Years a Citizen of the United States, and who shall not, when elected, be an Inhabitant of that State for which he shall be chosen.

The Vice President of the United States shall be President of the Senate, but shall have no Vote, unless they be equally divided.

The Senate shall chuse their other Officers, and also a President pro tempore, in the Absence of the Vice President, or when he shall exercise the Office of President of the United States.

The Senate shall have the sole Power to try all Impeachments. When sitting for that Purpose, they shall be on Oath or Affirmation. When the President of the United States is tried, the Chief Justice shall preside: And no Person shall be convicted without the Concurrence of two thirds of the Members present.

Judgment in Cases of Impeachment shall not extend further than to removal from Office, and disqualification to hold and enjoy any Office of honor, Trust or Profit under the United States: but the Party convicted shall nevertheless be liable and subject to Indictment, Trial, Judgment and Punishment, according to Law.

Section 4—Times, places, manner of elections. Time of assembly.

The Times, Places and Manner of holding Elections for Senators and Representatives, shall be prescribed in each State by the Legislature thereof; but the Congress may at any time by Law make or alter such Regulations, except as to the Places of chusing Senators.

The Congress shall assemble at least once in every Year, and such Meeting shall be [on the first Monday in December], *[The words in brackets were superseded by Amendment XX, section 2.]* unless they shall by Law appoint a different Day.

Section 5—Membership, quorums, adjournments. Rules of proceedings. Journal of proceedings. Time of adjournments.

Each House shall be the Judge of the Elections, Returns and Qualifications of its own Members, and a Majority of each shall constitute a Quorum to do Business; but a smaller Number may adjourn from day to day, and may be authorized to compel the Attendance of absent Members, in such Manner, and under such Penalties as each House may provide.

Each House may determine the Rules of its Proceedings, punish its Members for disorderly Behaviour, and, with the Concurrence of two thirds, expel a Member.

Each House shall keep a Journal of its Proceedings, and from time to time publish the same, excepting such Parts as may in their Judgment require Secrecy; and the Yeas and Nays of the Members of either House on any question shall, at the Desire of one fifth of those Present, be entered on the Journal.

Neither House, during the Session of Congress, shall, without the Consent of the other, adjourn for more than three days, nor to any other Place than that in which the two Houses shall be sitting.

Section 6—Compensation, privileges. Incompatible offices.

The Senators and Representatives shall receive a Compensation for their Services, to be ascertained by Law, and paid out of the Treasury of the United States. They shall in all Cases, except Treason, Felony and Breach of the Peace, be privileged from Arrest during their Attendance at the Session of their respective Houses, and in going to and returning from the same; and for any Speech or Debate in either House, they shall not be questioned in any other Place.

No Senator or Representative shall, during the Time for which he was elected, be appointed to any civil Office under the Authority of the United States, which shall have been created, or the Emoluments whereof shall have been encreased during such time; and no Person holding any Office under the United States, shall be a Member of either House during his Continuance in Office.

Section 7—House to originate revenue bills. Legislative process; bill presented to the President before becoming law. Passing of bill over objections of President, veto.

All Bills for raising Revenue shall originate in the House of Representatives; but the Senate may propose or concur with Amendments as on other Bills.

Every Bill which shall have passed the House of Representatives and the Senate, shall, before it become a Law, be presented to the President of the United States; If he approve he shall sign it, but if not he shall return it, with his Objections to that House in which it shall have originated, who shall enter the Objections at large on their Journal, and proceed to reconsider it. If after such Reconsideration two thirds of that House shall agree to pass the Bill, it shall be sent, together with the Objections, to the other House, by which it shall likewise be reconsidered, and if approved by two thirds of that House, it shall become a Law. But in all such Cases the Votes of both Houses shall be determined by Yeas and Nays, and the Names of the Persons voting for and against the Bill shall be entered on the Journal of each House respectively. If any Bill shall not be returned by the President within ten Days (Sundays excepted) after it shall have been presented to him, the Same shall be a Law, in like Manner as if he had signed it, unless the Congress by their Adjournment prevent its Return, in which Case it shall not be a Law.

Every Order, Resolution, or Vote to which the Concurrence of the Senate and House of Representatives may be necessary (except on a question of Adjournment) shall be presented to the President of the United States; and before the Same shall take Effect, shall be approved by him, or being disapproved by him, shall be repassed by two thirds of the Senate and House of Representatives, according to the Rules and Limitations prescribed in the Case of a Bill.

Section 8—Powers of Congress.

The Congress shall have Power To lay and collect Taxes, Duties, Imposts and Excises, to pay the Debts and provide for the common Defence and general Welfare of the United States; but all Duties, Imposts and Excises shall be uniform throughout the United States;

To borrow Money on the credit of the United States;

To regulate Commerce with foreign Nations, and among the several States, and with the Indian Tribes;

To establish an uniform Rule of Naturalization, and uniform Laws on the subject of Bankruptcies throughout the United States;

To coin Money, regulate the Value thereof, and of foreign Coin, and fix the Standard of Weights and Measures;

To provide for the Punishment of counterfeiting the Securities and current Coin of the United States;

To establish Post Offices and post Roads;

To promote the Progress of Science and useful Arts, by securing for limited Times to Authors and Inventors the exclusive Right to their respective Writings and Discoveries;

To constitute Tribunals inferior to the supreme Court;

To define and punish Piracies and Felonies committed on the high Seas, and Offences against the Law of Nations;

To declare War, grant Letters of Marque and Reprisal, and make Rules concerning Captures on Land and Water;

To raise and support Armies, but no Appropriation of Money to that Use shall be for a longer Term than two Years;

To provide and maintain a Navy;

To make Rules for the Government and Regulation of the land and naval Forces;

To provide for calling forth the Militia to execute the Laws of the Union, suppress Insurrections and repel Invasions;

To provide for organizing, arming, and disciplining, the Militia, and for governing such Part of them as may be employed in the Service of the United States, reserving to the States respectively, the Appointment of the Officers, and the Authority of training the Militia according to the discipline prescribed by Congress;

To exercise exclusive Legislation in all Cases whatsoever, over such District (not exceeding ten Miles square) as may, by Cession of particular States, and the Acceptance of Congress, become the Seat of the Government of the United States, and to exercise like Authority over all Places purchased by the Consent of the Legislature of the State in which the Same shall be, for the Erection of Forts, Magazines, Arsenals, dock-Yards, and other needful Buildings;—And

To make all Laws which shall be necessary and proper for carrying into Execution the foregoing Powers, and all other Powers vested by this Constitution in the Government of the United States, or in any Department or Officer thereof.

Section 9—Powers denied to Congress: Importation of slaves. Habeas corpus. Bills of attainder. Taxes, how apportioned. Export duty. Preference to ports. Money, how drawn from Treasury. Titles of nobility.

The Migration or Importation of such Persons as any of the States now existing shall think proper to admit, shall not be prohibited by the Congress prior to the Year one thousand eight hundred and eight, but a Tax or duty may be imposed on such Importation, not exceeding ten dollars for each Person.

The Privilege of the Writ of Habeas Corpus shall not be suspended, unless when in Cases of Rebellion or Invasion the public Safety may require it.

No Bill of Attainder or ex post facto Law shall be passed.

No Capitation, or other direct, Tax shall be laid, unless in Proportion to the Census or Enumeration herein before directed to be taken.

No Tax or Duty shall be laid on Articles exported from any State.

No Preference shall be given by any Regulation of Commerce or Revenue to the Ports of one State over those of another: nor shall Vessels bound to, or from, one State, be obliged to enter, clear, or pay Duties in another.

No Money shall be drawn from the Treasury, but in Consequence of Appropriations made by Law; and a regular Statement and Account of the Receipts and Expenditures of all public Money shall be published from time to time.

No Title of Nobility shall be granted by the United States: And no Person holding any Office of Profit or Trust under them, shall, without the Consent of the Congress, accept of any present, Emolument, Office, or Title, of any kind whatever, from any King, Prince, or foreign State.

Section 10—States prohibited from the exercise of certain powers.

No State shall enter into any Treaty, Alliance, or Confederation; grant Letters of Marque and Reprisal; coin Money; emit Bills of Credit; make any Thing but gold and silver Coin a Tender in Payment of Debts; pass any Bill of Attainder, ex post facto Law, or Law impairing the Obligation of Contracts, or grant any Title of Nobility.

No State shall, without the Consent of the Congress, lay any Imposts or Duties on Imports or Exports, except what may be absolutely necessary for executing it's inspection Laws: and the net Produce of all Duties and Imposts, laid by any State on Imports or Exports, shall be for the Use of the Treasury of the United States; and all such Laws shall be subject to the Revision and Controul of the Congress.

No State shall, without the Consent of Congress, lay any Duty of Tonnage, keep Troops, or Ships of War in time of Peace, enter into any Agreement or Compact with another State, or with a foreign Power, or engage in War, unless actually invaded, or in such imminent Danger as will not admit of delay.

ARTICLE II.

Section 1—President, powers and term of office. Electors, number and how appointed. Electors to vote for President. Qualifications of President. On whom duties devolve in case of removal, death, etc., of President. President's compensation. Oath of office.

The executive Power shall be vested in a President of the United States of America. He shall hold his Office during the Term of four Years, and, together with the Vice President, chosen for the same Term, be elected, as follows:

Each State shall appoint, in such Manner as the Legislature thereof may direct, a Number of Electors, equal to the whole Number of Senators and Representatives to which the State may be entitled in the Congress: but no Senator or Representative, or Person holding an Office of Trust or Profit under the United States, shall be appointed an Elector.

[The Electors shall meet in their respective States, and vote by Ballot for two Persons, of whom one at least shall not be an Inhabitant of the same State with themselves. And they shall make a List of all the Persons voted for, and of the Number of Votes for each; which List they shall sign and certify, and transmit sealed to the Seat of the Government of the United States, directed to the President of the Senate. The President of the Senate shall, in the Presence of the Senate and House of Representatives, open all the Certificates, and the Votes shall then be counted. The Person having the greatest Number of Votes shall be the President, if such Number be a Majority of the whole Number of Electors appointed; and if there be more than one who have such Majority, and have an equal Number of Votes, then the House of Representatives shall immediately chuse by Ballot one of them for President; and if no Person have a Majority, then from the five highest on the List the said House shall in like Manner chuse the President. But in chusing the President, the Votes shall be taken by States, the Representation from each State having one Vote; A quorum for this Purpose shall consist of a Member or Members from two thirds of the States, and a Majority of all the States shall be necessary to a Choice. In every Case, after the Choice of the President, the Person having the greatest Number of Votes of the Electors shall be the Vice President. But if there should remain two or more who have equal Votes, the Senate shall chuse from them by Ballot the Vice President.] *[This clause was superseded by Amendment XII.]*

The Congress may determine the Time of chusing the Electors, and the Day on which they shall give their Votes; which Day shall be the same throughout the United States.

No Person except a natural born Citizen, or a Citizen of the United States, at the time of the Adoption of this Constitution, shall be eligible to the Office of President; neither shall any Person be eligible to that Office who shall not have attained to the Age of thirty five Years, and been fourteen Years a Resident within the United States. *[For qualification of the Vice President, see Amendment XII.]*

[In Case of the Removal of the President from Office, or of his Death, Resignation, or Inability to discharge the Powers and Duties of the said Office, the Same shall devolve on the Vice President, and the Congress may by Law provide for the Case of Removal, Death, Resignation or Inability, both of the President and Vice President, declaring what Officer shall then act as President, and such Officer shall act accordingly, until the Disability be removed, or a President shall be elected.] *[This clause was superseded by Amendment XXV.]*

The President shall, at stated Times, receive for his Services, a Compensation, which shall neither be encreased nor diminished during the Period for which he shall have been elected, and he shall not receive within that Period any other Emolument from the United States, or any of them.

Before he enter on the Execution of his Office, he shall take the following Oath or Affirmation:—

"I do solemnly swear (or affirm) that I will faithfully execute the Office of President of the United States, and will to the best of my Ability, preserve, protect and defend the Constitution of the United States."

Section 2—President to be Commander in Chief. Power to make treaties; nominations for, appointments to certain offices. Power to fill vacancies during Senate recess.

The President shall be Commander in Chief of the Army and Navy of the United States, and of the Militia of the several States, when called into the actual Service of the United States; he may require the Opinion, in writing, of the principal Officer in each of the executive Departments, upon any Subject relating to the Duties of their respective Offices, and he shall have Power to Grant Reprieves and Pardons for Offences against the United States, except in Cases of Impeachment.

He shall have Power, by and with the Advice and Consent of the Senate, to make Treaties, provided two thirds of the Senators present concur; and he shall nominate, and by and with the Advice and Consent of the Senate, shall appoint Ambassadors, other public Ministers and Consuls, Judges of the supreme Court, and all other Officers of the United States, whose Appointments are not herein otherwise provided for, and which shall be established by Law: but the Congress may by Law vest the Appointment of such inferior Officers, as they think proper, in the President alone, in the Courts of Law, or in the Heads of Departments.

The President shall have Power to fill up all Vacancies that may happen during the Recess of the Senate, by granting Commissions which shall expire at the End of their next Session.

Section 3—President shall communicate to, may convene and adjourn Congress; shall receive ambassadors, execute laws, and commission officers.

He shall from time to time give to the Congress Information on the State of the Union, and recommend to their Consideration such Measures as he shall judge necessary and expedient; he may, on extraordinary Occasions, convene both Houses, or either of them, and in Case of Disagreement between them, with Respect to the Time of Adjournment, he may adjourn them to such Time as he shall think proper; he shall receive Ambassadors and other public Ministers; he shall take Care that the Laws be faithfully executed, and shall Commission all the Officers of the United States.

Section 4—All civil offices forfeited for certain crimes.

The President, Vice President and all civil Officers of the United States, shall be removed from Office on Impeachment for, and Conviction of, Treason, Bribery, or other high Crimes and Misdemeanors.

ARTICLE III.

Section 1—Judicial powers, tenure, compensation.

The judicial Power of the United States, shall be vested in one supreme Court, and in such inferior Courts as the Congress may from time to time ordain and establish. The Judges, both of the supreme and inferior Courts, shall hold their Offices during good Behaviour, and shall, at stated Times, receive for their Services, a Compensation, which shall not be diminished during their Continuance in Office.

Section 2—Judicial power, cases to which it extends. Jurisdiction of Supreme Court. Trial by jury; where held.

The judicial Power shall extend to all Cases, in Law and Equity, arising under this Constitution, the Laws of the United States, and Treaties made, or which shall be made, under their Authority;—to all Cases affecting Ambassadors, other public Ministers and Consuls;—to all Cases of admiralty and maritime Jurisdiction;—to Controversies to which the United States shall be a Party;—to Controversies between two or more States;—[between a State and Citizens of another State;]—between Citizens of different States;—between Citizens of the same State claiming Lands under Grants of different States, [and between a State, or the Citizens thereof, and foreign States, Citizens or Subjects.] *[This section was modified by Amendment XI.]*

In all Cases affecting Ambassadors, other public Ministers and Consuls, and those in which a State shall be Party, the supreme Court shall have original Jurisdiction. In all the other Cases before mentioned, the supreme Court shall have appellate Jurisdiction, both as to Law and Fact, with such Exceptions, and under such Regulations as the Congress shall make.

The Trial of all Crimes, except in Cases of Impeachment, shall be by Jury; and such Trial shall be held in the State where the said Crimes shall have been committed; but when not committed within any State, the Trial shall be at such Place or Places as the Congress may by Law have directed.

Section 3—Treason defined. Punishment of.

Treason against the United States, shall consist only in levying War against them, or in adhering to their Enemies, giving them Aid and Comfort. No Person shall be convicted of Treason unless on the Testimony of two Witnesses to the same overt Act, or on Confession in open Court.

The Congress shall have Power to declare the Punishment of Treason, but no Attainder of Treason shall work Corruption of Blood, or Forfeiture except during the Life of the Person attainted.

ARTICLE IV.

Section 1—Each State to give credit to the public acts, etc., of every other State.

Full Faith and Credit shall be given in each State to the public Acts, Records, and judicial Proceedings of every other State. And the Congress may by general Laws prescribe the Manner in which such Acts, Records and Proceedings shall be proved, and the Effect thereof.

Section 2—Privileges of citizens of each State. Fugitives from justice to be delivered up. Fugitives from service or labor, to be delivered up.

The Citizens of each State shall be entitled to all Privileges and Immunities of Citizens in the several States.

A Person charged in any State with Treason, Felony, or other Crime, who shall flee from Justice, and be found in another State, shall on Demand of the executive Authority of the State from which he fled, be delivered up, to be removed to the State having Jurisdiction of the Crime.

[No Person held to Service or Labour in one State, under the Laws thereof, escaping into another, shall, in Consequence of any Law or Regulation therein, be discharged from such Service or Labour, but shall be delivered up on Claim of the Party to whom such Service or Labour may be due.] *[This clause was superseded by Amendment XIII.]*

Section 3—Admission of new States. Power of Congress over territory and other property.

New States may be admitted by the Congress into this Union; but no new State shall be formed or erected within the Jurisdiction of any other State; nor any State be formed by the Junction of two or more States, or Parts of States, without the Consent of the Legislatures of the States concerned as well as of the Congress.

The Congress shall have Power to dispose of and make all needful Rules and Regulations respecting the Territory or other Property belonging to the United States; and nothing in this Constitution shall be so construed as to Prejudice any Claims of the United States, or of any particular State.

Section 4—Republican form of government guaranteed; each State to be protected.

The United States shall guarantee to every State in this Union a Republican Form of Government, and shall protect each of them against Invasion; and on Application of the Legislature, or of the Executive (when the Legislature cannot be convened) against domestic Violence.

ARTICLE V.

Constitution, how amended; proviso.

The Congress, whenever two thirds of both Houses shall deem it necessary, shall propose Amendments to this Constitution, or, on the Application of the Legislatures of two thirds of the several States, shall call a Convention for proposing Amendments, which, in either Case, shall be valid to all Intents and Purposes, as Part of this Constitution, when ratified by the Legislatures of three fourths of the several States, or by Conventions in three fourths thereof, as the one or the other Mode of Ratification may be proposed by the Congress; Provided that no Amendment which may be made prior to the Year One thousand eight hundred and eight shall in any Manner affect the first and fourth Clauses in the Ninth Section of the first Article; and that no State, without its Consent, shall be deprived of its equal Suffrage in the Senate.

ARTICLE VI.

Certain debts and engagements shall be valid. Constitution, laws and treaties made, shall be supreme law of the United States. Oath to support Constitution, by whom taken; no religious test shall be required.

All Debts contracted and Engagements entered into, before the Adoption of this Constitution, shall be as valid against the United States under this Constitution, as under the Confederation.

This Constitution, and the Laws of the United States which shall be made in Pursuance thereof; and all Treaties made, or which shall be made, under the Authority of the United States, shall be the supreme Law of the Land; and the Judges in every State shall be bound thereby, any Thing in the Constitution or Laws of any State to the Contrary notwithstanding.

The Senators and Representatives before mentioned, and the Members of the several State Legislatures, and all executive and judicial Officers, both of the United States and of the several States, shall be bound by Oath or Affirmation, to support this Constitution; but no religious Test shall ever be required as a Qualification to any Office or public Trust under the United States.

ARTICLE VII.

Ratification to establish the Constitution.

The Ratification of the Conventions of nine States, shall be sufficient for the Establishment of this Constitution between the States so ratifying the Same.

done in Convention by the Unanimous Consent of the States present the Seventeenth Day of September in the Year of our Lord one thousand seven hundred and Eighty seven and of the Independance of the United States of America the Twelfth. In witness whereof We have hereunto subscribed our Names,

G°. Washington, Presid^t. and deputy from Virginia

New Hampshire—John Langdon, Nicholas Gilman

Massachusetts—Nathaniel Gorham, Rufus King

Connecticut—W^m. Saml. Johnson, Roger Sherman

New York—Alexander Hamilton

New Jersey—Wil: Livingston, David Brearley, W^m. Paterson, Jona: Dayton

Pennsylvania—B Franklin, Thomas Mifflin, Robt. Morris, Geo. Clymer, Thos. FitzSimons, Jared Ingersoll, James Wilson, Gouv Morris

Delaware—Geo: Read, Gunning Bedford jun, John Dickinson, Richard Bassett, Jaco: Broom

Maryland—James McHenry, Dan of St Thos. Jenifer, Danl Carroll

Virginia—John Blair, James Madison Jr.

North Carolina—W^m. Blount, Rich^d. Dobbs Spaight, Hu Williamson

South Carolina—J. Rutledge, Charles Cotesworth Pinckney, Charles Pinckney, Pierce Butler

Georgia—William Few, Abr Baldwin

[George Washington was first to sign the Constitution on Sept. 17, 1787, followed by state delegates in order of geography, from north to south. In total, 38 delegates signed the Constitution, although Delaware delegate George Reed signed for absent delegate John Dickinson, bringing the total signatures to 39. Three delegates abstained from signing in protest of the absent Bill of Rights.]

Origin of the Bill of Rights

Congress, at its first session in New York, NY, submitted to the states 12 amendments Sept. 25, 1789, to clarify certain individual and state rights not named in the Constitution. They are generally called the Bill of Rights.

Influential in framing these amendments was the Declaration of Rights of Virginia, written by George Mason (1725-92) in 1776. Mason, a Virginia delegate to the Constitutional Convention, did not sign the Constitution and opposed its ratification on the ground that it did not sufficiently oppose slavery or safeguard individual rights.

In the preamble to the resolution offering the proposed amendments, Congress said: "The Conventions of a number of the States, having at the time of their adopting the Constitution, expressed a desire, in order to prevent misconstruction or abuse of its powers, that further declaratory and restrictive clauses should be added: And as extending the ground of public confidence in the Government, will best insure the beneficent ends of its institution."

Ten of these amendments, originally three to 12 inclusive, were ratified by the states as follows: New Jersey, Nov. 20, 1789; Maryland, Dec. 19, 1789; North Carolina, Dec. 22, 1789; South Carolina, Jan. 19, 1790; New Hampshire, Jan. 25, 1790; Delaware, Jan. 28, 1790; New York, Feb. 27, 1790; Pennsylvania, Mar. 10, 1790; Rhode Island, June 7, 1790; Vermont, Nov. 3, 1791; Virginia, Dec. 15, 1791; Massachusetts, Mar. 2, 1939; Georgia, Mar. 18, 1939; Connecticut, Apr. 19, 1939. These original 10 ratified amendments follow as Amendments I to X inclusive.

Of the two original proposed amendments that were not ratified promptly by the necessary number of states, the first related to apportionment of Representatives; the second, relating to compensation of members of Congress, was ratified in 1992 and became Amendment XXVII.

The Bill of Rights
In force Dec. 15, 1791

AMENDMENT I.

Religious establishment prohibited. Freedom of speech and of press; right to assemble and to petition.

Congress shall make no law respecting an establishment of religion, or prohibiting the free exercise thereof; or abridging the freedom of speech, or of the press; or the right of the people peaceably to assemble, and to petition the Government for a redress of grievances.

AMENDMENT II.

Right to keep and bear arms.

A well regulated Militia, being necessary to the security of a free State, the right of the people to keep and bear Arms shall not be infringed.

AMENDMENT III.

Conditions for quartering of soldiers.

No Soldier shall, in time of peace be quartered in any house, without the consent of the Owner, nor in time of war, but in a manner to be prescribed by law.

AMENDMENT IV.

Protection from unreasonable search and seizure.

The right of the people to be secure in their persons, houses, papers, and effects, against unreasonable searches and seizures, shall not be violated, and no Warrants shall issue but upon probable cause, supported by Oath or affirmation, and particularly describing the place to be searched, and the persons or things to be seized.

AMENDMENT V.

Provisions concerning prosecution and due process of law. Compensation of private property taken for public use.

No person shall be held to answer for a capital, or otherwise infamous crime, unless on a presentment or indictment of a Grand Jury, except in cases arising in the land or naval forces, or in the Militia, when in actual service in time of War or public danger; nor shall any person be subject for the same offence to be twice put in jeopardy of life or limb; nor shall be compelled in any criminal case to be a witness against himself, nor be deprived of life, liberty, or property, without due process of law; nor shall private property be taken for public use, without just compensation.

AMENDMENT VI.

Rights of accused in criminal prosecutions.

In all criminal prosecutions, the accused shall enjoy the right to a speedy and public trial, by an impartial jury of the State and district wherein the crime shall have been committed, which district shall have been previously ascertained by law, and to be informed of the nature and cause of the accusation; to be confronted with the witnesses against him; to have compulsory process for obtaining witnesses in his favor, and to have the Assistance of Counsel for his defense.

AMENDMENT VII.

Right of trial by jury in civil cases.

In Suits at common law, where the value in controversy shall exceed twenty dollars, the right of trial by jury shall be preserved, and no fact tried by a jury, shall be otherwise reexamined in any Court of the United States, than according to the rules of the common law.

AMENDMENT VIII.

Excessive bail or fines; cruel and unusual punishment.

Excessive bail shall not be required, nor excessive fines imposed, nor cruel and unusual punishments inflicted.

AMENDMENT IX.

Unenumerated rights.

The enumeration in the Constitution, of certain rights, shall not be construed to deny or disparage others retained by the people.

AMENDMENT X.

Rights reserved to States.

The powers not delegated to the United States by the Constitution, nor prohibited by it to the States, are reserved to the States respectively, or to the people.

Amendments Since the Bill of Rights

AMENDMENT XI.

Judicial powers construed.

[Proposed by Congress Mar. 4, 1794. Ratification complete Feb. 7, 1795, though official announcement of ratification not made until Jan. 8, 1798.]

The Judicial power of the United States shall not be construed to extend to any suit in law or equity, commenced or prosecuted against one of the United States by Citizens of another State, or by Citizens or Subjects of any Foreign State.

AMENDMENT XII.

Election of President and Vice-President.

[Proposed by Congress Dec. 9, 1803; ratified June 15, 1804.]
The Electors shall meet in their respective states and vote by ballot for President and Vice-President, one of whom, at least, shall not be an inhabitant of the same state with themselves; they shall name in their ballots the person voted for as President, and in distinct ballots the person voted for as Vice-President, and they shall make distinct lists of all persons voted for as President, and of all persons voted for as Vice-President, and of the number of votes for each, which lists they shall sign and certify, and transmit sealed to the seat of the government of the United States, directed to the President of the Senate;—The President of the Senate shall, in the presence of the Senate and House of Representatives, open all the certificates and the votes shall then be counted;—The person having the greatest number of votes for President, shall be the President, if such number be a majority of the whole number of Electors appointed; and if no person have such majority, then from the persons having the highest numbers not exceeding three on the list of those voted for as President, the House of Representatives shall choose immediately, by ballot, the President. But in choosing the President, the votes shall be taken by states, the representation from each state having one vote; a quorum for this purpose shall consist of a member or members from two-thirds of the states, and a majority of all the states shall be necessary to a choice. [And if the House of Representatives shall not choose a President whenever the right of choice shall devolve upon them, before the fourth day of March next following, then the Vice-President shall act as President, as in the case of the death or other constitutional disability of the President.] *[The words in brackets were superseded by Amendment XX, section 3.]* The person having the greatest number of votes as Vice-President, shall be the Vice-President, if such number be a majority of the whole number of Electors appointed, and if no person have a majority, then from the two highest numbers on the list, the Senate shall choose the Vice-President; a quorum for the purpose shall consist of two-thirds of the whole number of Senators, and a majority of the whole number shall be necessary to a choice. But no person constitutionally ineligible to the office of President shall be eligible to that of Vice-President of the United States.

THE RECONSTRUCTION AMENDMENTS

[Amendments XIII, XIV, and XV are commonly known as the Reconstruction Amendments inasmuch as they followed the Civil War and were drafted by Republicans who wanted to impose their own policy of reconstruction on the South. Southern postbellum legislatures in states including Mississippi, South Carolina, and Georgia had set up laws that effectively perpetuated slavery under other names.]

AMENDMENT XIII.

Slavery abolished.

[Proposed by Congress Jan. 31, 1865; ratified Dec. 6, 1865.]
Section 1. Neither slavery nor involuntary servitude, except as a punishment for crime whereof the party shall have been duly convicted, shall exist within the United States, or any place subject to their jurisdiction.
Section 2. Congress shall have power to enforce this article by appropriate legislation.

AMENDMENT XIV.

Citizenship rights not to be abridged.

[Proposed by Congress June 13, 1866, ratified July 9, 1868, and declared to have been ratified in a proclamation by the Secretary of State, July 28, 1868.]
Section 1. All persons born or naturalized in the United States, and subject to the jurisdiction thereof, are citizens of the United States and of the State wherein they reside. No State shall make or enforce any law which shall abridge the privileges or immunities of citizens of the United States; nor shall any State deprive any person of life, liberty, or property, without due process of law; nor deny to any person within its jurisdiction the equal protection of the laws.
Section 2. Representatives shall be apportioned among the several States according to their respective numbers, counting the whole number of persons in each State, excluding Indians not taxed. But when the right to vote at any election for the choice of electors for President and Vice-President of the United States, Representatives in Congress, the Executive and Judicial officers of a State, or the members of the Legislature thereof, is denied to any of the male inhabitants of such State, being [twenty-one] *[The words in brackets were changed by Amendment XXVI.]* years of age, and citizens of the United States, or in any way abridged, except for participation in rebellion, or other crime, the basis of representation therein shall be reduced in the proportion which the number of such male citizens shall bear to the whole number of male citizens twenty-one years of age in such State.
Section 3. No person shall be a Senator or Representative in Congress, or elector of President and Vice-President, or hold any office, civil or military, under the United States, or under any State, who, having previously taken an oath, as a member of Congress, or as an officer of the United States, or as a member of any State legislature, or as an executive or judicial officer of any State, to support the Constitution of the United States, shall have engaged in insurrection or rebellion against the same, or given aid or comfort to the enemies thereof. But Congress may by a vote of two-thirds of each House, remove such disability.
Section 4. The validity of the public debt of the United States, authorized by law, including debts incurred for payment of pensions and bounties for services in suppressing insurrection or rebellion, shall not be questioned. But neither the United States nor any State shall assume or pay any debt or obligation incurred in aid of insurrection or rebellion against the United States, or any claim for the loss or emancipation of any slave; but all such debts, obligations and claims shall be held illegal and void.
Section 5. The Congress shall have power to enforce, by appropriate legislation, the provisions of this article.

AMENDMENT XV.

Race no bar to voting rights.

[Proposed by Congress Feb. 26, 1869; ratified Feb. 3, 1870.]
Section 1. The right of citizens of the United States to vote shall not be denied or abridged by the United States or by any State on account of race, color, or previous condition of servitude.
Section 2. The Congress shall have power to enforce this article by appropriate legislation.

AMENDMENT XVI.

Taxes on income.

[Proposed by Congress July 12, 1909; ratified Feb. 3, 1913.]
The Congress shall have power to lay and collect taxes on incomes, from whatever source derived, without apportionment among the several States, and without regard to any census or enumeration.

AMENDMENT XVII.

Popular election of Senators.

[Proposed by Congress May 13, 1912; ratified Apr. 8, 1913.]
The Senate of the United States shall be composed of two Senators from each State, elected by the people thereof, for six years; and each Senator shall have one vote. The electors in each State shall have the qualifications requisite for electors of the most numerous branch of the State legislatures.

When vacancies happen in the representation of any State in the Senate, the executive authority of such State shall issue writs of election to fill such vacancies: Provided, That the legislature of any State may empower the executive thereof to make temporary appointments until the people fill the vacancies by election as the legislature may direct.

This amendment shall not be so construed as to affect the election or term of any Senator chosen before it becomes valid as part of the Constitution.

AMENDMENT XVIII.

Liquor prohibition amendment.

[Proposed by Congress Dec. 18, 1917; ratified Jan. 16, 1919. Repealed by Amendment XXI, effective Dec. 5, 1933.]

Section 1. After one year from the ratification of this article the manufacture, sale, or transportation of intoxicating liquors within, the importation thereof into, or the exportation thereof from the United States and all territory subject to the jurisdiction thereof for beverage purposes is hereby prohibited.

Section 2. The Congress and the several States shall have concurrent power to enforce this article by appropriate legislation.

Section 3. This article shall be inoperative unless it shall have been ratified as an amendment to the Constitution by the legislatures of the several States, as provided in the Constitution, within seven years from the date of the submission hereof to the States by the Congress.

AMENDMENT XIX.

Nationwide suffrage to women.

[Proposed by Congress June 4, 1919; ratified Aug. 18, 1920.]

The right of citizens of the United States to vote shall not be denied or abridged by the United States or by any State on account of sex.

Congress shall have power to enforce this article by appropriate legislation.

AMENDMENT XX.

Commencement of terms of office

[Proposed by Congress Mar. 2, 1932; ratified Jan. 23, 1933.]

Section 1. The terms of the President and Vice President shall end at noon on the 20th day of January, and the terms of Senators and Representatives at noon on the 3d day of January, of the years in which such terms would have ended if this article had not been ratified; and the terms of their successors shall then begin.

Section 2. The Congress shall assemble at least once in every year, and such meeting shall begin at noon on the 3d day of January, unless they shall by law appoint a different day.

Section 3. If, at the time fixed for the beginning of the term of the President, the President elect shall have died, the Vice President elect shall become President. If a President shall not have been chosen before the time fixed for the beginning of his term, or if the President elect shall have failed to qualify, then the Vice President elect shall act as President until a President shall have qualified; and the Congress may by law provide for the case wherein neither a President elect nor a Vice President elect shall have qualified, declaring who shall then act as President, or the manner in which one who is to act shall be selected, and such person shall act accordingly until a President or Vice President shall have qualified.

Section 4. The Congress may by law provide for the case of the death of any of the persons from whom the House of Representatives may choose a President whenever the right of choice shall have devolved upon them, and for the case of the death of any of the persons from whom the Senate may choose a Vice President whenever the right of choice shall have devolved upon them.

Section 5. Sections 1 and 2 shall take effect on the 15th day of October following the ratification of this article.

Section 6. This article shall be inoperative unless it shall have been ratified as an amendment to the Constitution by the legislatures of three-fourths of the several States within seven years from the date of its submission.

AMENDMENT XXI.

Repeal of Amendment XVIII.

[Proposed by Congress Feb. 20, 1933; ratified Dec. 5, 1933.]

Section 1. The eighteenth article of amendment to the Constitution of the United States is hereby repealed.

Section 2. The transportation or importation into any State, Territory, or possession of the United States for delivery or use therein of intoxicating liquors, in violation of the laws thereof, is hereby prohibited.

Section 3. This article shall be inoperative unless it shall have been ratified as an amendment to the Constitution by conventions in the several States, as provided in the Constitution, within seven years from the date of the submission hereof to the States by the Congress.

AMENDMENT XXII.

Limit on presidential terms of office.

[Proposed by Congress Mar. 24, 1947; ratified Feb. 27, 1951.]

Section 1. No person shall be elected to the office of the President more than twice, and no person who has held the office of President, or acted as President, for more than two years of a term to which some other person was elected President shall be elected to the office of the President more than once. But this Article shall not apply to any person holding the office of President when this Article was proposed by Congress, and shall not prevent any person who may be holding the office of President, or acting as President, during the term within which this Article becomes operative from holding the office of President or acting as President during the remainder of such term.

Section 2. This Article shall be inoperative unless it shall have been ratified as an amendment to the Constitution by the legislatures of three-fourths of the several States within seven years from the date of its submission to the States by the Congress.

AMENDMENT XXIII.

Presidential vote for District of Columbia.

[Proposed by Congress June 16, 1960; ratified Mar. 29, 1961.]

Section 1. The District constituting the seat of Government of the United States shall appoint in such manner as the Congress may direct:

A number of electors of President and Vice President equal to the whole number of Senators and Representatives in Congress to which the District would be entitled if it were a State, but in no event more than the least populous State; they shall be in addition to those appointed by the States, but they shall be considered, for the purposes of the election of President and Vice President, to be electors appointed by a State; and they shall meet in the District and perform such duties as provided by the twelfth article of amendment.

Section 2. The Congress shall have power to enforce this article by appropriate legislation.

AMENDMENT XXIV.

Poll tax barred in federal elections.

[Proposed by Congress Sept. 14, 1962; ratified Jan. 23, 1964.]

Section 1. The right of citizens of the United States to vote in any primary or other election for President or Vice President, for electors for President or Vice President, or for Senator or Representative in Congress, shall not be denied or abridged by the United States or any State by reason of failure to pay any poll tax or other tax.

Section 2. The Congress shall have power to enforce this article by appropriate legislation.

AFGHANISTAN	ALBANIA	ALGERIA	ANDORRA	ANGOLA
ANTIGUA AND BARBUDA	ARGENTINA	ARMENIA	AUSTRALIA	AUSTRIA
AZERBAIJAN	THE BAHAMAS	BAHRAIN	BANGLADESH	BARBADOS
BELARUS	BELGIUM	BELIZE	BENIN	BHUTAN
BOLIVIA	BOSNIA AND HERZEGOVINA	BOTSWANA	BRAZIL	BRUNEI
BULGARIA	BURKINA FASO	BURUNDI	CABO VERDE	CAMBODIA
CAMEROON	CANADA	CENTRAL AFRICAN REPUBLIC	CHAD	CHILE
CHINA	COLOMBIA	COMOROS	CONGO, DEM. REP. OF THE	CONGO REPUBLIC
COSTA RICA	CÔTE D'IVOIRE	CROATIA	CUBA	CYPRUS
CZECHIA (CZECH REPUBLIC)	DENMARK	DJIBOUTI	DOMINICA	DOMINICAN REPUBLIC
ECUADOR	EGYPT	EL SALVADOR	EQUATORIAL GUINEA	ERITREA

Note: Flag proportions have been standardized to fit page.

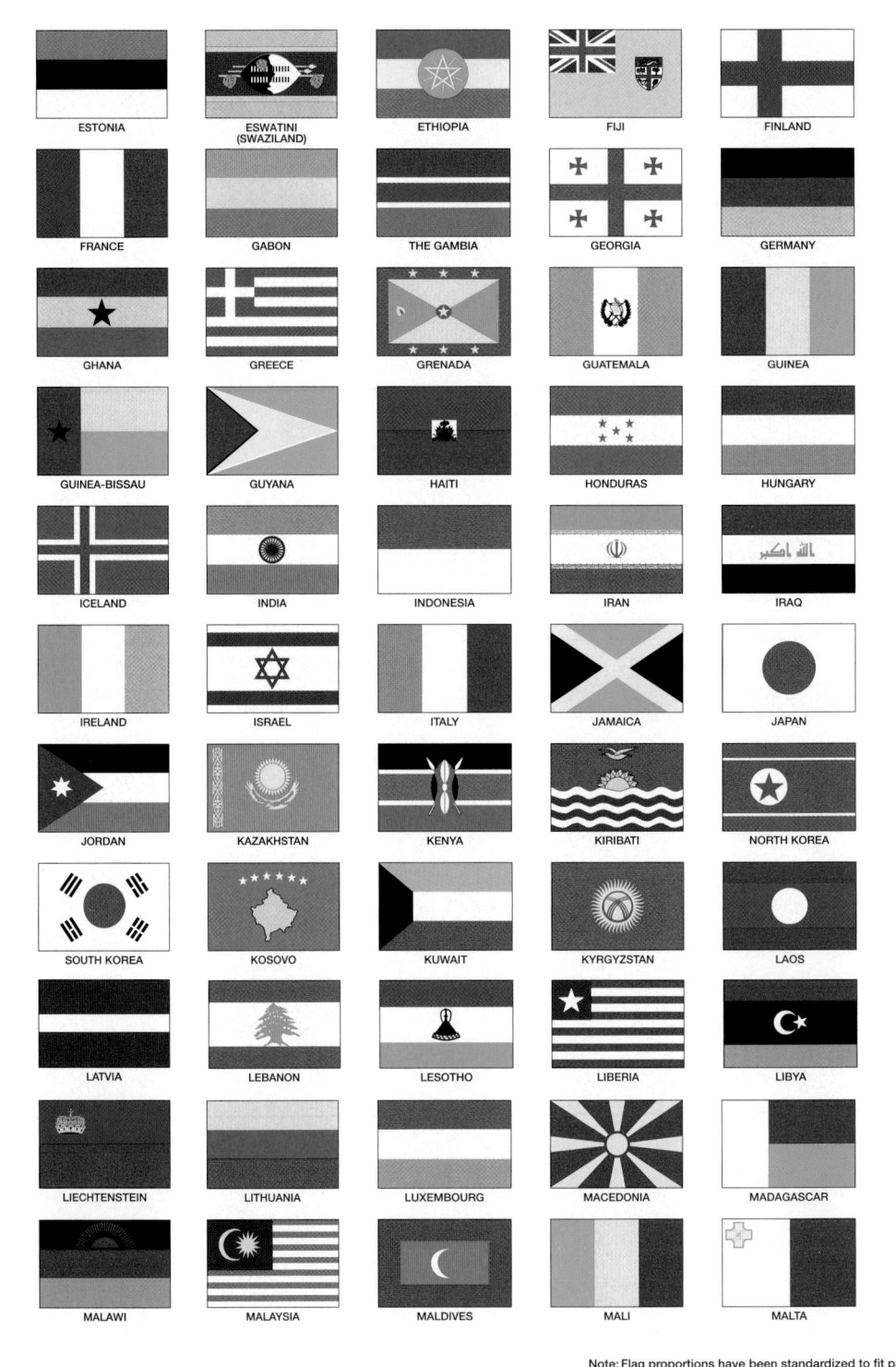

ESTONIA	ESWATINI (SWAZILAND)	ETHIOPIA	FIJI	FINLAND
FRANCE	GABON	THE GAMBIA	GEORGIA	GERMANY
GHANA	GREECE	GRENADA	GUATEMALA	GUINEA
GUINEA-BISSAU	GUYANA	HAITI	HONDURAS	HUNGARY
ICELAND	INDIA	INDONESIA	IRAN	IRAQ
IRELAND	ISRAEL	ITALY	JAMAICA	JAPAN
JORDAN	KAZAKHSTAN	KENYA	KIRIBATI	NORTH KOREA
SOUTH KOREA	KOSOVO	KUWAIT	KYRGYZSTAN	LAOS
LATVIA	LEBANON	LESOTHO	LIBERIA	LIBYA
LIECHTENSTEIN	LITHUANIA	LUXEMBOURG	MACEDONIA	MADAGASCAR
MALAWI	MALAYSIA	MALDIVES	MALI	MALTA

Note: Flag proportions have been standardized to fit page.

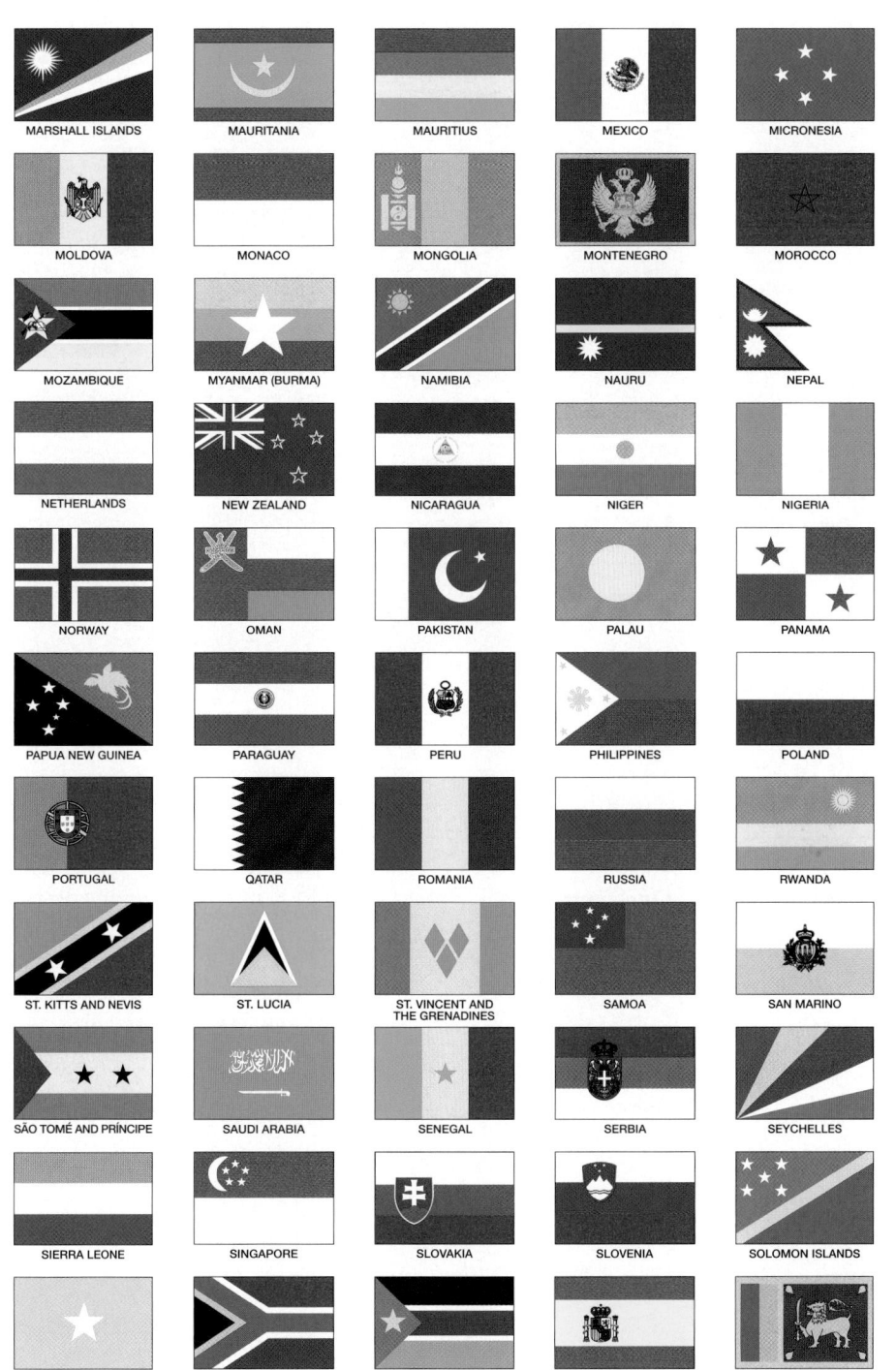

MARSHALL ISLANDS | MAURITANIA | MAURITIUS | MEXICO | MICRONESIA

MOLDOVA | MONACO | MONGOLIA | MONTENEGRO | MOROCCO

MOZAMBIQUE | MYANMAR (BURMA) | NAMIBIA | NAURU | NEPAL

NETHERLANDS | NEW ZEALAND | NICARAGUA | NIGER | NIGERIA

NORWAY | OMAN | PAKISTAN | PALAU | PANAMA

PAPUA NEW GUINEA | PARAGUAY | PERU | PHILIPPINES | POLAND

PORTUGAL | QATAR | ROMANIA | RUSSIA | RWANDA

ST. KITTS AND NEVIS | ST. LUCIA | ST. VINCENT AND THE GRENADINES | SAMOA | SAN MARINO

SÃO TOMÉ AND PRÍNCIPE | SAUDI ARABIA | SENEGAL | SERBIA | SEYCHELLES

SIERRA LEONE | SINGAPORE | SLOVAKIA | SLOVENIA | SOLOMON ISLANDS

SOMALIA | SOUTH AFRICA | SOUTH SUDAN | SPAIN | SRI LANKA

Note: Flag proportions have been standardized to fit page.

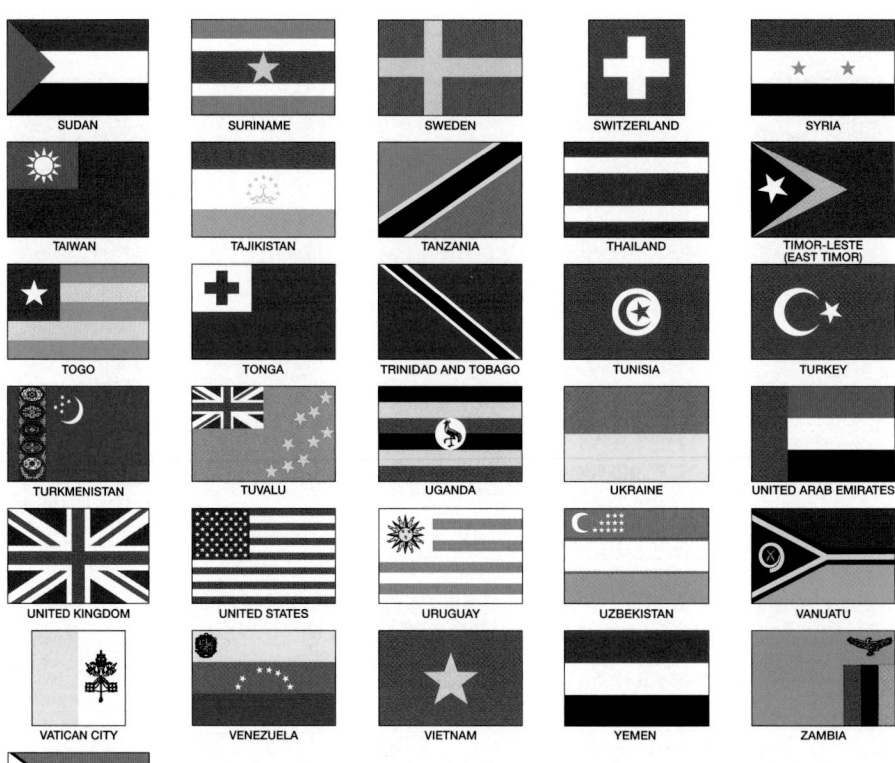

SUDAN | SURINAME | SWEDEN | SWITZERLAND | SYRIA

TAIWAN | TAJIKISTAN | TANZANIA | THAILAND | TIMOR-LESTE (EAST TIMOR)

TOGO | TONGA | TRINIDAD AND TOBAGO | TUNISIA | TURKEY

TURKMENISTAN | TUVALU | UGANDA | UKRAINE | UNITED ARAB EMIRATES

UNITED KINGDOM | UNITED STATES | URUGUAY | UZBEKISTAN | VANUATU

VATICAN CITY | VENEZUELA | VIETNAM | YEMEN | ZAMBIA

ZIMBABWE

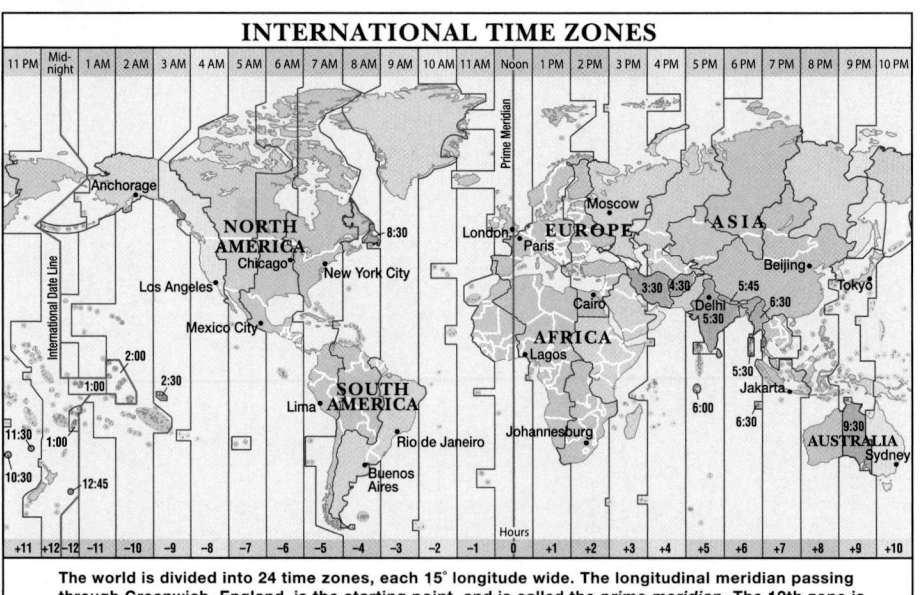

INTERNATIONAL TIME ZONES

The world is divided into 24 time zones, each 15° longitude wide. The longitudinal meridian passing through Greenwich, England, is the starting point, and is called the *prime meridian*. The 12th zone is divided by the 180th meridian (International Date Line). When the line is crossed going west, the date is advanced one day; when crossed going east, the date becomes a day earlier.

Note: Flag proportions have been standardized to fit page.

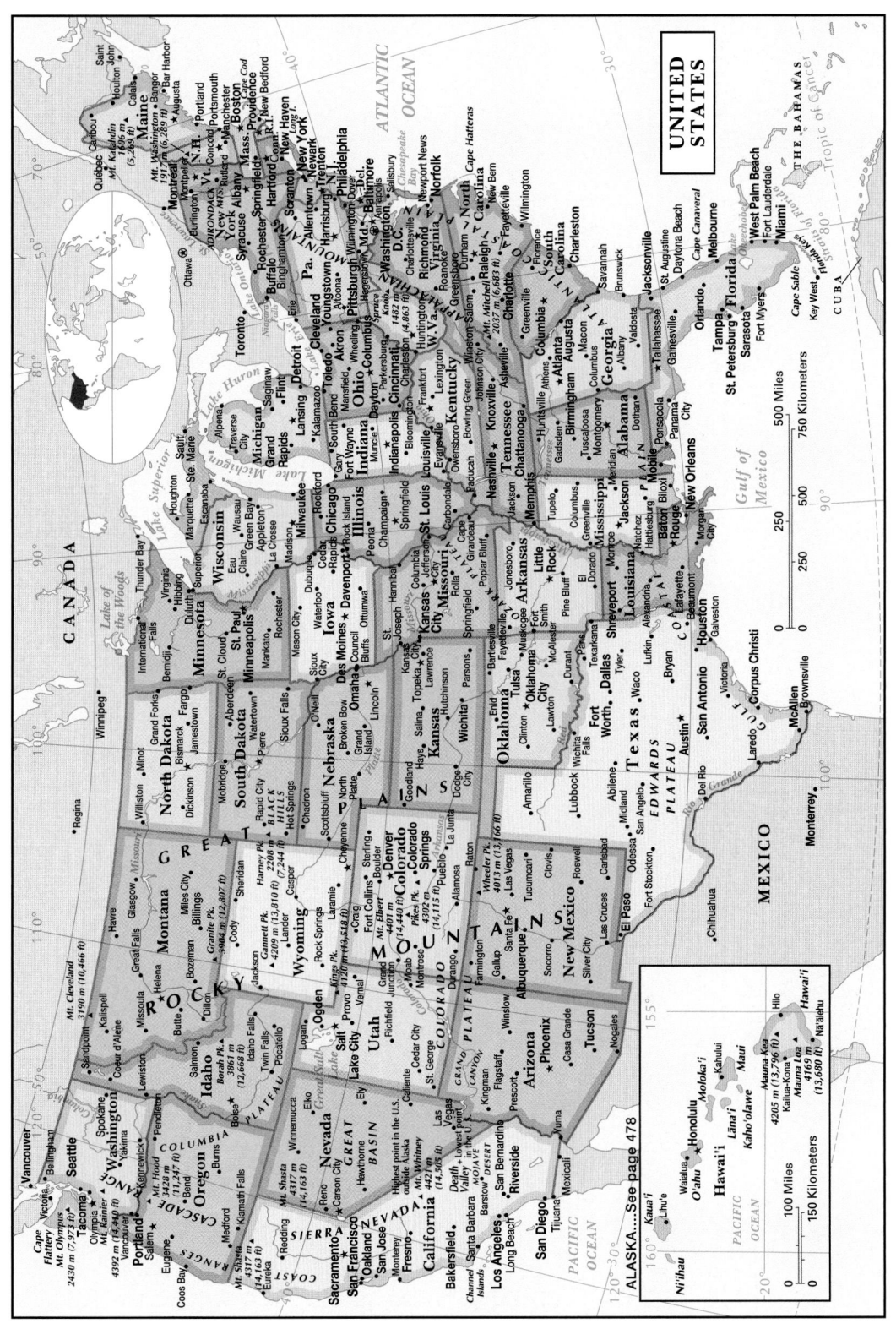

UNITED STATES

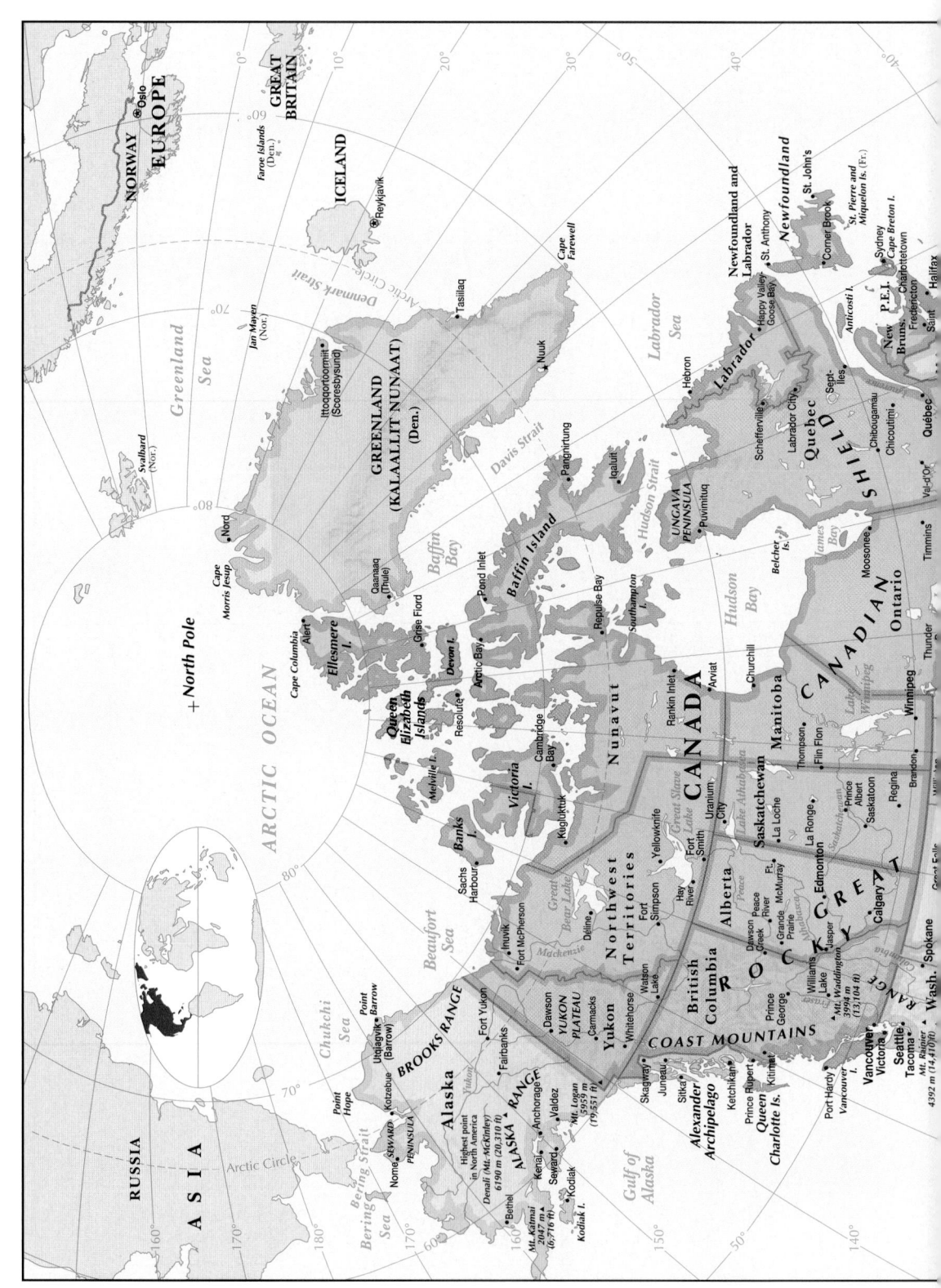

NORWAY
EUROPE
Oslo

GREAT BRITAIN

Faroe Islands (Den.)

ICELAND

Reykjavík

Greenland Sea

Denmark Strait

Arctic Circle

Cape Farewell

Jan Mayen (Nor.)

Tasiilaq

GREENLAND (KALAALLIT NUNAAT) (Den.)

Nuuk

Hebron

Labrador Sea

Labrador

Newfoundland and Labrador

St. Anthony

St. John's

St. Pierre and Miquelon Is. (Fr.)

Corner Brook

Sydney

Cape Breton I.

Newfoundland

Anticosti I.

New P.E.I.

Charlottetown

Fredericton

Saint

Halifax

Svalbard (Nor.)

Ittoqqortoormiit (Scoresbysund)

Nord

Davis Strait

Pangnirtung

Iqaluit

Sept-Îles

Labrador City

Schefferville

Québec

Chibougamau

Chicoutimi

Val-d'Or

Québec

Baffin Bay

Cape Morris Jesup

Qaanaaq (Thule)

Grise Fiord

Pond Inlet

Baffin Island

Hudson Strait

UNGAVA PENINSULA

Puvirnituq

Belcher Is.

James Bay

CANADIAN SHIELD

Timmins

Moosonee

Ontario

Thunder

North Pole

+

Cape Columbia

Ellesmere I.

Alert

Arctic Bay

Repulse Bay

Southampton I.

Hudson Bay

Churchill

Winnipeg

ARCTIC OCEAN

Queen Elizabeth Islands

Devon I.

Resolute

Cambridge Bay

Rankin Inlet

Arviat

CANADA

Manitoba

Lake Winnipeg

Brandon

Melville I.

Victoria I.

Kugluktuk

Nunavut

Thompson

Flin Flon

Regina

Banks I.

Déline

Yellowknife

Uranium City

Fort Smith

Prince Albert

Saskatoon

Saskatchewan

Sachs Harbour

Great Bear Lake

Fort Simpson

Hay River

Lake Athabasca

La Ronge

La Loche

Fort McMurray

Edmonton

Calgary

Beaufort Sea

Inuvik

Fort McPherson

Great Slave Lake

Northwest Territories

Peace River

Grande Prairie

Alberta

Ft. McMurray

Prince Albert

GREAT

Mackenzie

Watson Lake

Dawson Creek

ROCKY

Chukchi Sea

Point Barrow

Utqiagvik (Barrow)

Yukon

YUKON PLATEAU

Carmacks

Whitehorse

British Columbia

Williams Lake

Prince George

Mt. Waddington 3994 m (13,104 ft)

RANGE

BROOKS RANGE

Dawson

Fort Yukon

Spokane

Wash.

Point Hope

Kotzebue

Fairbanks

COAST MOUNTAINS

Skagway

Juneau

Sitka

Prince Rupert

Kitimat

Port Hardy

Vancouver

Victoria

Seattle

Tacoma

Mt. Rainier 4392 m (14,410 ft)

RUSSIA

ASIA

Nome

SEWARD PENINSULA

Bethel

Alaska

ALASKA RANGE

Highest point in North America Denali (Mt. McKinley) 6190 m (20,310 ft)

Anchorage

Valdez

Mt. Logan 5959 m (19,551 ft)

Alexander Archipelago

Ketchikan

Queen Charlotte Is.

Bering Strait

Bering Sea

Kenai Peninsula

Kenai

Seward

Kodiak I.

Mt. Katmai 2047 m (6,716 ft)

Gulf of Alaska

Vancouver I.

Arctic Circle

478

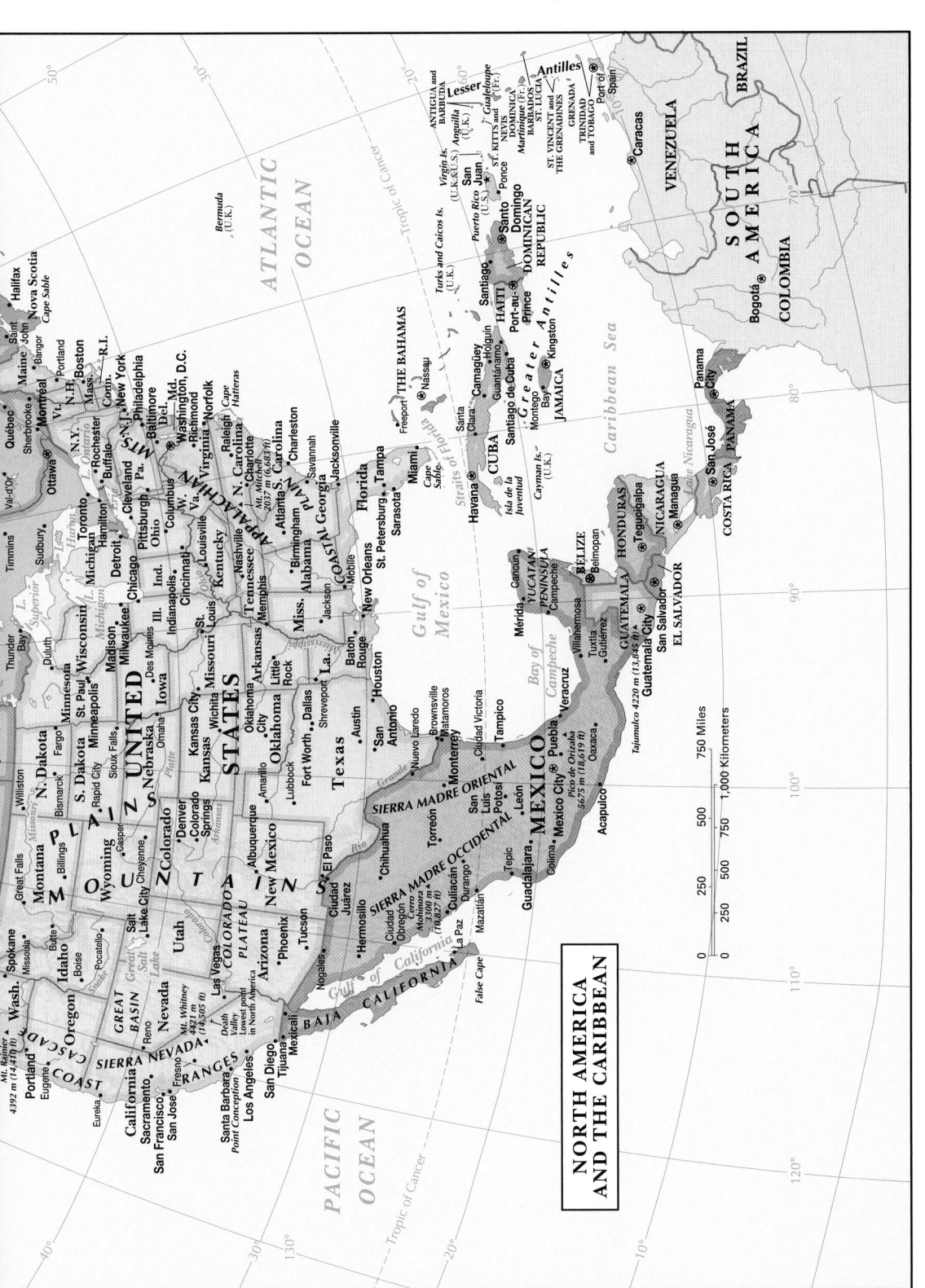

NORTH AMERICA
AND THE CARIBBEAN

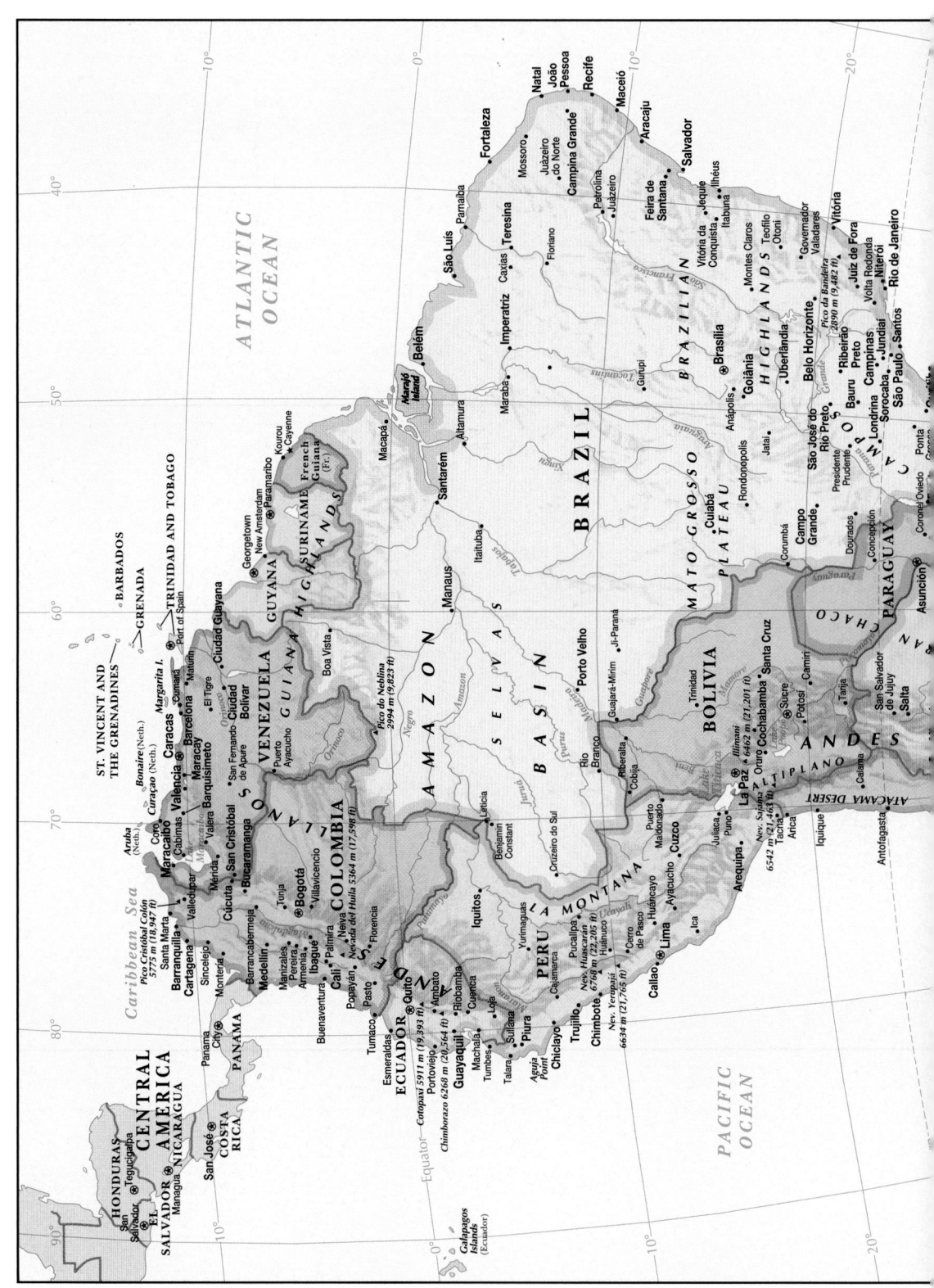

CENTRAL AMERICA

HONDURAS
San Salvador
Tegucigalpa
EL SALVADOR
Managua
NICARAGUA
COSTA RICA
San José
Panama City
PANAMA

ATLANTIC OCEAN

Caribbean Sea

ST. VINCENT AND THE GRENADINES
Bonaire (Neth.)
Curaçao (Neth.)
Aruba (Neth.)
BARBADOS
GRENADA
TRINIDAD AND TOBAGO
Port of Spain

Pico Cristóbal Colón
5775 m (18,947 ft)
Santa Marta
Barranquilla
Cartagena
Maracaibo
Coro
Valencia Caracas
Barcelona
Maracay
Barquisimeto
Valera
Cabimas
Margarita I.
Cumaná
Maturín

VENEZUELA

El Tigre
Ciudad Guayana
Ciudad Bolívar
San Fernando de Apure
Puerto Ayacucho

Georgetown
New Amsterdam
Paramaribo
GUYANA
SURINAME
French Guiana (Fr.)
Kourou
Cayenne

GUIANA HIGHLANDS

Sincelejo
Montería
Barrancabermeja
Valledupar
Cúcuta
Mérida
San Cristóbal
Bucaramanga
Medellín
Manizales
Pereira
Tunja
Villavicencio
Armenia
Bogotá
Ibagué
Cali
Palmira
Nevada del Huila 5364 m (17,598 ft)
Popayán
Florencia
Pasto

COLOMBIA

LLANOS

Boa Vista

Pico do Neblina
2994 m (9,823 ft)

Negro

AMAZON

SELVAS

BASIN

Branco

Manaus

Itaituba

Santarém

Altamira

Belém

Marajó Island

Macapá

São Luís
Parnaíba

Fortaleza

Natal
João Pessoa
Recife
Maceió
Aracaju
Salvador

Mossoró
Juazeiro do Norte
Campina Grande
Petrolina
Juazeiro
Ilhéus
Jequié
Itabuna

Caxias
Teresina
Imperatriz
Marabá
Floriano

BRAZIL

Tocantins

Gurupi

Feira de Santana
Vitória da Conquista
Montes Claros
Teófilo Otoni
Governador Valadares
Belo Horizonte
Pico da Bandeira
2890 m (9,482 ft)
Ouro Preto
Juiz de Fora
Volta Redonda
Niterói
Rio de Janeiro
Vitória

HIGHLANDS

BRAZILIAN

São Francisco

Goiânia
Brasília
Uberlândia
Anápolis

Cuiabá
Rondonópolis
Jataí

MATO GROSSO PLATEAU

São José do Rio Preto
Bauru
Londrina
Campinas
Ribeirão Preto
São Paulo
Sorocaba
Jundiaí
Santos
Presidente Prudente

Paraná

CAMPOS

Ponta

Grande

Xingu

Tapajós

Madeira

Porto Velho
Ji-Paraná

Guajará-Mirim

Riberalta

Cobija

Puerto Maldonado

BOLIVIA
Trinidad
Santa Cruz
Cochabamba
La Paz
Nev. Sajama 6542 m (21,463 ft)
Oruro
Sucre
Potosí
Illimani 6462 m (21,201 ft)
Camiri

ANDES
ALTIPLANO
Lake Titicaca

Corumbá
Campo Grande
Dourados
Concepción
San Salvador de Jujuy
Coronel Oviedo
Asunción
PARAGUAY
CHACO
GRAN

Tarija
Salta

Calama
ATACAMA DESERT
Antofagasta

PERU

LA MONTAÑA

Ucayali

Marañón

Huallaga

Iquitos
Leticia
Benjamin Constant
Orcruzeiro do Sul
Pucallpa

Purus

Juruá

Rio

Nev. Huascarán 6768 m (22,205 ft)
Yurimaguas
Cajamarca
Chiclayo
Trujillo
Chimbote
Nev. Yerupajá 6634 m (21,765 ft)
Cerro de Pasco
Huánuco
Huancayo
Ayacucho
Lima
Callao
Ica
Cuzco
Abancay

Arequipa
Tacna
Arica
Juliaca
Puno
Moquegua
Iquique

ECUADOR
Quito
Ambato
Riobamba
Cotopaxi 5911 m (19,393 ft)
Chimborazo 6268 m (20,564 ft)
Cuenca
Loja
Portoviejo
Guayaquil
Machala
Tumbes
Sullana
Piura
Talara
Aguja Point
Esmeraldas
Tumaco
Buenaventura

Galapagos Islands (Ecuador)

Equator

PACIFIC OCEAN

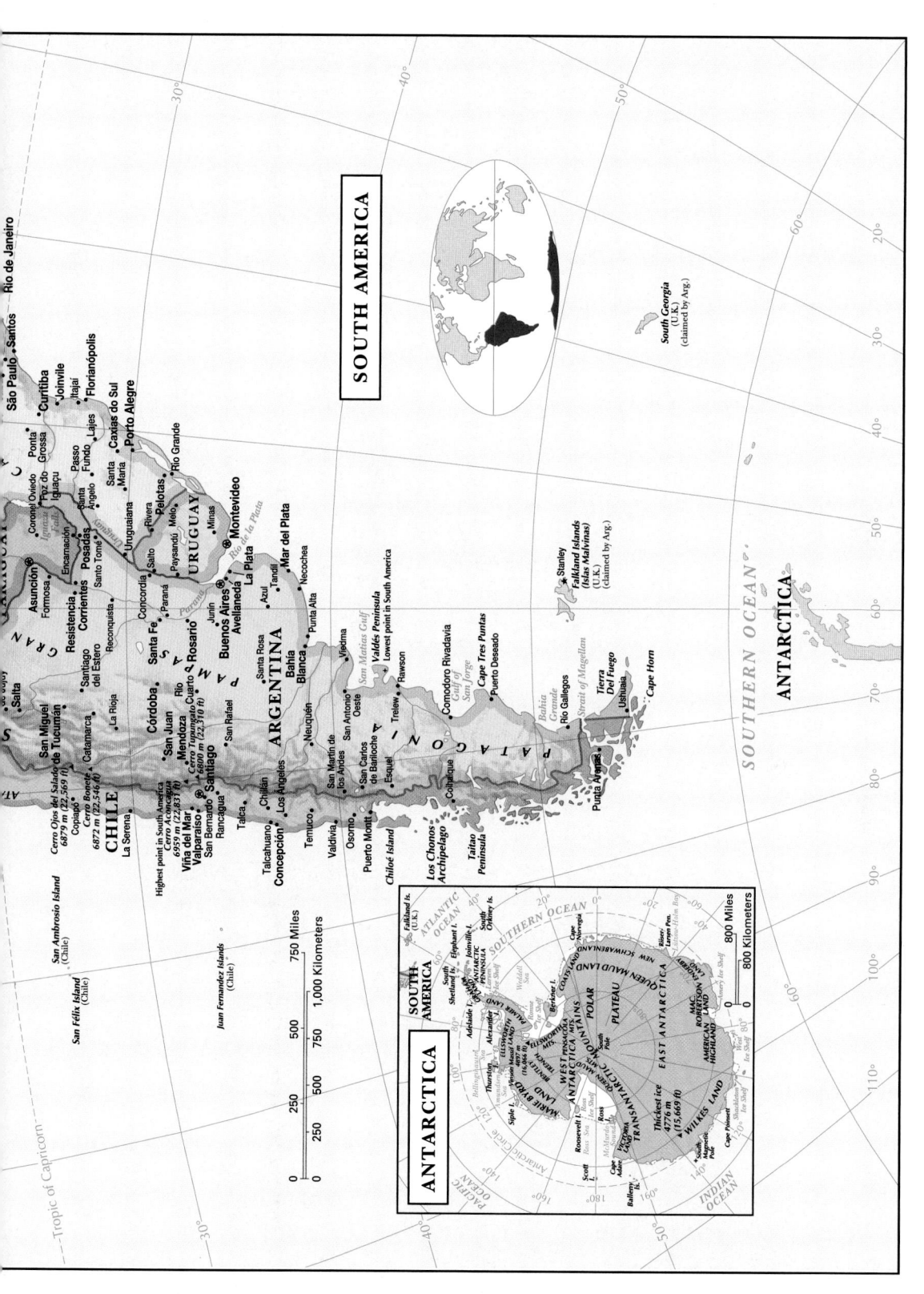

SOUTH AMERICA

South Georgia
(U.K.)
(claimed by Arg.)

Rio de Janeiro
Santos
São Paulo
Curitiba
Joinville
Itajaí
Florianópolis
Lajes
Caxias do Sul
Passo
Fundo
Santa
Maria
Porto Alegre
Ponta
Grossa
Coronel Oviedo
Iguazu
Rio Grande
Santa
Angelo
Pelotas
Uruguaiana
Rivera
Santo Tomé
Paysandú
Melo
ASUNCIÓN
Formosa
Encarnación
Posadas
Salto
URUGUAY
Minas
Resistencia
Corrientes
Concordia
MONTEVIDEO
Santa Fe
Paraná
La Plata
Mar del Plata
Santiago
del Estero
Reconquista
Rosario
Buenos Aires
Avellaneda
Tandil
Necochea
Salta
Córdoba
Junín
Azul
San Miguel
de Tucumán
San Juan
Río
Cuarto
Bahía
Blanca
Punta Alta
Catamarca
Mendoza
Santa Rosa
La Rioja
ARGENTINA
Viedma
San Rafael
Lowest point in South America
Cerro Ojos del Salado
6879 m (22,569 ft)
Copiapó
Cerro Aconcagua
6959 m (22,831 ft)
Cerro Tupungato
6800 m (22,310 ft)
San Antonio
Oeste
Valdés Peninsula
Cerro Bonete
6872 m (22,546 ft)
Highest point in South America
San Martín de
los Andes
Neuquén
Trelew
Comodoro Rivadavia
Valparaíso
Viña del Mar
San Bernardo
Rancagua
SANTIAGO
Los Angeles
San Carlos
de Bariloche
Rawson
Cape Tres Puntas
Esquel
Puerto Deseado
La Serena
CHILE
Talca
Chillán
Concepción
Talcahuano
Coihaique
Río Gallegos
Temuco
PATAGONIA
Valdivia
Osorno
Puerto Montt
Los Chonos
Archipelago
Taitao
Peninsula
Chiloé Island
Tierra
Del Fuego
Ushuaia
Punta Arenas
Cape Horn
Stanley
Falkland Islands
(Islas Malvinas)
(U.K.)
(claimed by Arg.)
Strait of Magellan
Bahía
Grande

San Ambrosio Island
(Chile)

San Félix Island
(Chile)

Juan Fernández Islands
(Chile)

SOUTHERN OCEAN

ANTARCTICA

Tropic of Capricorn

0   250   500   750 Miles
0   250   500   750   1,000 Kilometers

ANTARCTICA

Falkland Is.
(U.K.)
ATLANTIC
OCEAN
South
Orkney
Is.
SOUTHERN OCEAN
SOUTH
AMERICA
South
Shetland
Is.
Elephant I.
Joinville I.
ANTARCTIC
PENINSULA
Weddell
Sea
Cape
Norvegia
NEW SCHWABENLAND
QUEEN MAUD LAND
Berkner I.
Adelaide I.
Alexander
I.
PALMER
LAND
COATS LAND
Ronne
Ice Shelf
Filchner
Ice Shelf
MAC.
ROBERTSON
LAND
AMERICAN
HIGHLAND
Thurston
I.
ELLSWORTH
LAND
WEST
ANTARCTICA
Vinson
Massif
4897 m
(16,066 ft)
TRANSANTARCTIC
MOUNTAINS
EAST ANTARCTICA
POLAR
PLATEAU
South
Pole
Enderby
Land
QUEEN
ELIZABETH
AMERY
ICE SHELF
Prydz
Bay
Lars
Christensen
Coast
Lambert
Glacier
80°
Siple
Station
MARIE BYRD
LAND
Roosevelt I.
Ross
Ice Shelf
Ross
Sea
McMurdo
Sound
Scott
Cape
Adare
Thickest Ice
4776 m
(15,669 ft)
WILKES LAND
South
Magnetic
Pole
Balleny Is.
INDIAN
OCEAN
Antarctic Circle
PACIFIC OCEAN

481

EUROPE

GREENLAND
(KALAALLIT NUNAAT)
(Denmark)

Ísafjördur

Akureyri
Keflavík • ICELAND
Reykjavík

Seydhisfjördhur

Arctic Circle

Narvik

Bodø

Norwegian Sea

Namsos

Faroe
Torshavn *Islands*
(Den.)

Trondheim
Molde
Ålesund

Östersund

Sundsvall

Shetland
Islands
(U.K.)

NORWAY SWEDEN

Bergen

Orkney
Islands
Thurso

Haugesund

Stavanger

Drammen Oslo

Skien Karlstad

Borlänge

Uppsala
Örebro

Inverness

Hebrides

Scotland

Aberdeen

Dundee

Kristiansand

Göteborg

Örebro
Stockholm

Norrköping Linköping

Jönköping

Vänern

Vättern

Londonderry
Northern
Ireland
Belfast

Glasgow

Ayr

Edinburgh

Jutland Århus

Halmstad Växjö

Öland

Go...
(Sw.)

UNITED Newcastle

North

Esbjerg Odense Malmö

Bornholm
(Den.)

KINGDOM

Galway
IRELAND Dublin

Limerick

Waterford

Liverpool

Manchester

Leeds

Kingston upon Hull

Sheffield

Sea

Copenhagen Helsingborg
DENMARK Odense Malmö

Gdańsk

Cork

Birmingham

Wales Swansea

Cardiff

Bristol

Coventry

Norwich

England

NETHERLANDS

London Amsterdam

Kiel

Lübeck Rostock

Groningen
Bremen

Hamburg

NORTHERN

Szczecin

Bydgoszcz

Poznań

POLAND

Plymouth

Land's End

Portsmouth

The Hague
Rotterdam

Dover

Hannover

Bielefeld

Magdeburg

Elbe

Oder

English Channel

Channel Is.
(U.K.)

Le Havre

Brest

Caen Rouen

Rennes

Paris

Le Mans

Nantes

Loire

Brussels

Lille

BELGIUM Liège

Antwerp

Essen

Cologne

Bonn

LUXEMBOURG

Luxembourg

Frankfurt

Wiesbaden

Mannheim

GERMANY

Kassel

Erfurt

Chemnitz

Leipzig

Dresden

Prague

Wrocław

Wałbrzych

Liberec

Plzen

CZECHIA Ostrava
(CZECH REP.)

Brno

Nancy

Strasbourg

Saarbrucken

Nürnberg

Regensburg

Bratislava

Orleans

Seine

Tours

Dijon

Basel

Bern

Stuttgart

Augsburg

Munich

Linz

Vienna

AUSTRIA

Győr

HUNG...

FRANCE

Limoges

Zürich

Innsbruck

Salzburg

Klagenfurt

Graz

Clermont-Ferrand

SWITZERLAND

Lyon

ALPS

LIECHTENSTEIN

Pécs

Bordeaux

Saint-Étienne

Geneva

Mt. Blanc
4810 m (15,781 ft)

Grenoble

Matterhorn
4478 m (14,692 ft)

Bergamo

Udine

Trieste

SLOVENIA

Ljubljana Zagreb

CROATIA

A Coruña

Gijón

Santander

Bilbao

Donostia-
San Sebastián

Vigo

Leon

Vitoria-Gasteiz

Porto Braga

Pamplona

Toulouse

PYRENEES

Avignon

Marseille

Toulon

Milan

Torino

Verona

Venice

Po

Genoa

Parma

Rijeka

Banja
Luka

BOS. &
HERZ.

Sarajevo

Split

DINARIC

Bay
of
Biscay

Montpellier

Nice

MONACO

Pisa

Florence

Perugia

SAN
MARINO

Ancona

Adriatic Sea

Dubrovnik

MO...

Coimbra

Salamanca

Valladolid

Duero

Pico de Aneto
3404 m
(11,168 ft)

ANDORRA

IBERIAN

PORTUGAL

Lisbon

Setubal

Badajoz

Tagus

Toledo

Madrid

SPAIN

Zaragoza

Barcelona

Tarragona

Corsica
(Fr.)

Ajaccio

Elba

Rome

VATICAN CITY

ITALY

Foggia

Bari

APENNINES

Cape
St. Vincent

PENINSULA

Cordoba

Valencia

Castellon de la Plana

Sassari

Naples

Vesuvius
1277 m (4,190 ft)

Salerno

Taranto

Seville

Alicante

Murcia

Palma de
Mallorca

Majorca

Minorca

Balearic
Is.
(Sp.)

Sardinia
(It.)

Ionian
Sea

Co...

Cádiz

Málaga Granada

Cartagena

Cagliari

Tyrrhenian

Sea

Strait of
Gibraltar

GIBRALTAR
(U.K.)

Almería

Mediter

Palermo

Messina
Etna
3369 m (11,053 ft)

Reggio di
Calabria

Rabat

Algiers

Tunis

Sicily
(It.)

Catania

AFRICA

0		250		500 Miles
0	250	500	750 Kilometers	

TUNISIA

MALTA Valletta

Sea

MOROCCO

ALGERIA

ranean

Barents Sea

Novaya Zemlya

North Cape
Hammerfest
Vardø
Tromsø
Murmansk
Ivalo
Apatity KOLA PENINSULA
Kiruna
LAPLAND
Rovaniemi
Nar'yan-Mar
Pechora
Ukhta
ASIA
URAL
RUSSIA
Luleå
Oulu
Skellefteå
Belomorsk
White Sea
Arkhangel'sk
Berezniki
MOUNTAINS
Umeå
FINLAND
Perm'
Syktyvkar
Kotlas
Dvina
Vaasa
Kuopio
Lake Onega
Kirov
Izhevsk
Ufa
Naberezhnye Chelny
Pori
Jyvaskyla
Lahti
Lake Ladoga
Petrozavodsk
Sterlitamak
Tampere
Kama
Turku
Kotka
Helsinki
Cherepovets
Vologda
Yoshkar Ola
Kazan
Åland Is. (Fin.)
St. Petersburg
Rybinsk
Kostroma
Nizhniy Novgorod
Cheboksary
Orsk
Gotland (Swe.)
Tallinn
ESTONIA
Velikiy Novgorod
Yaroslavl'
Ivanovo
Ul'yanovsk
Orenburg
Tartu
Pskov
Tver'
Vladimir
Saransk
Tol'yatti
Riga
Moscow
Ryazan'
Penza
Samara
Liepaja
LATVIA
Kaluga
Tula
Volga
Klaipeda
Daugavpils
Vitsyebsk
Smolensk
Tambov
Saratov
LITHUANIA
Kaunas
Vilnius
PLAIN
Ural
Kaliningrad (RUSSIA)
Minsk
Mahilyow
Lipetsk
Voronezh
KAZAKHSTAN
EUROPEAN
Hrodna
Babruysk
Bryansk
Bialystok
BELARUS
Homyel'
Warsaw
Brest
Pinsk
Chernihiv
Sumy
Kursk
Belgorod
Łódź
Radom
Lublin
Kyiv (Kiev)
Kharkiv
Volgograd
Cherkasy
Poltava
Astrakhan'
Katowice
Zhytomyr
Luhansk
Kraków
UKRAINE
Vinnytsia
Dnipro
Donetsk
Horlivka
Don
CARPATHIAN
Chernivtsi
Kryvyy Rih
Mariupol
Rostov-na-Donu
SLOVAKIA
MOUNTAINS
MOLDOVA
Iasi
Chisinau
Mykolaiv
Caspian
Budapest
Debrecen
Odesa
CRIMEA PENINSULA (disputed territory)
Krasnodar
Stavropol
Groznyy
Makhachkala
Sea
UNGARY
Oradea
Cluj-Napoca
Galati
Sevastopol
Simferopol
Sea of Azov
Mt. Elbrus 5642 m (18,510 ft) Highest point in Europe
Nal'chik
Vladikavkaz
CAUCASUS MTS.
Baku
ROMANIA
Brasov
Ploiesti
GEORGIA
Bucharest
Constanta
Tbilisi
SERBIA
Craiova
Ruse
Varna
Black Sea
ARMENIA
AZERBAIJAN
BULGARIA
Sofia
Stara Zagora
Burgas
Yerevan
AZER.
Skopje
Plovdiv
Istanbul
MACEDONIA
Thessaloniki
Ankara
TURKEY
IRAN
ALBANIA
GREECE
Larisa
Aegean Sea
ASIA
Athens
SYRIA
Baghdad
Rhodes (Gr.)
Nicosia
IRAQ
Crete
CYPRUS
LEBANON
Beirut
Damascus

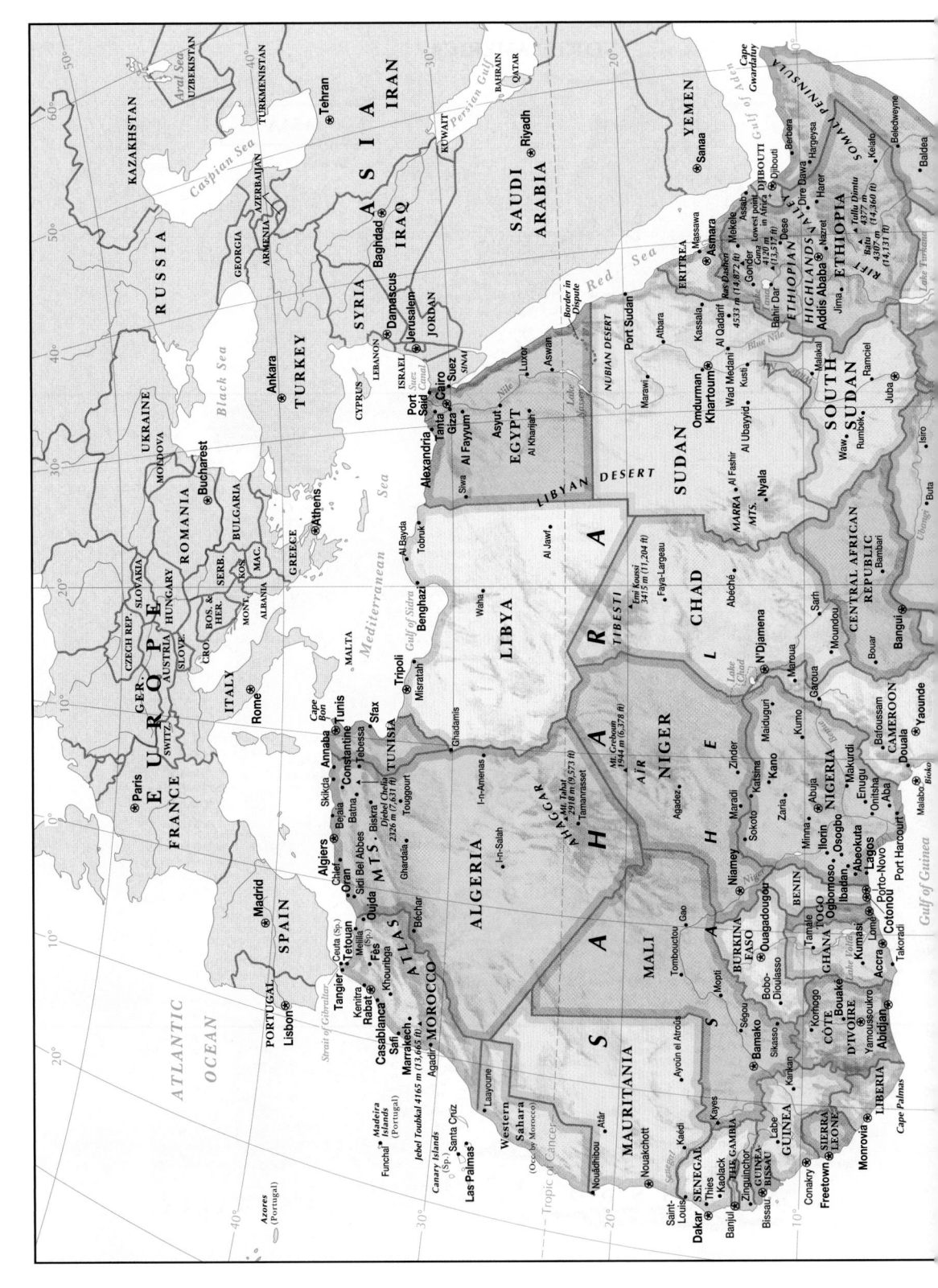

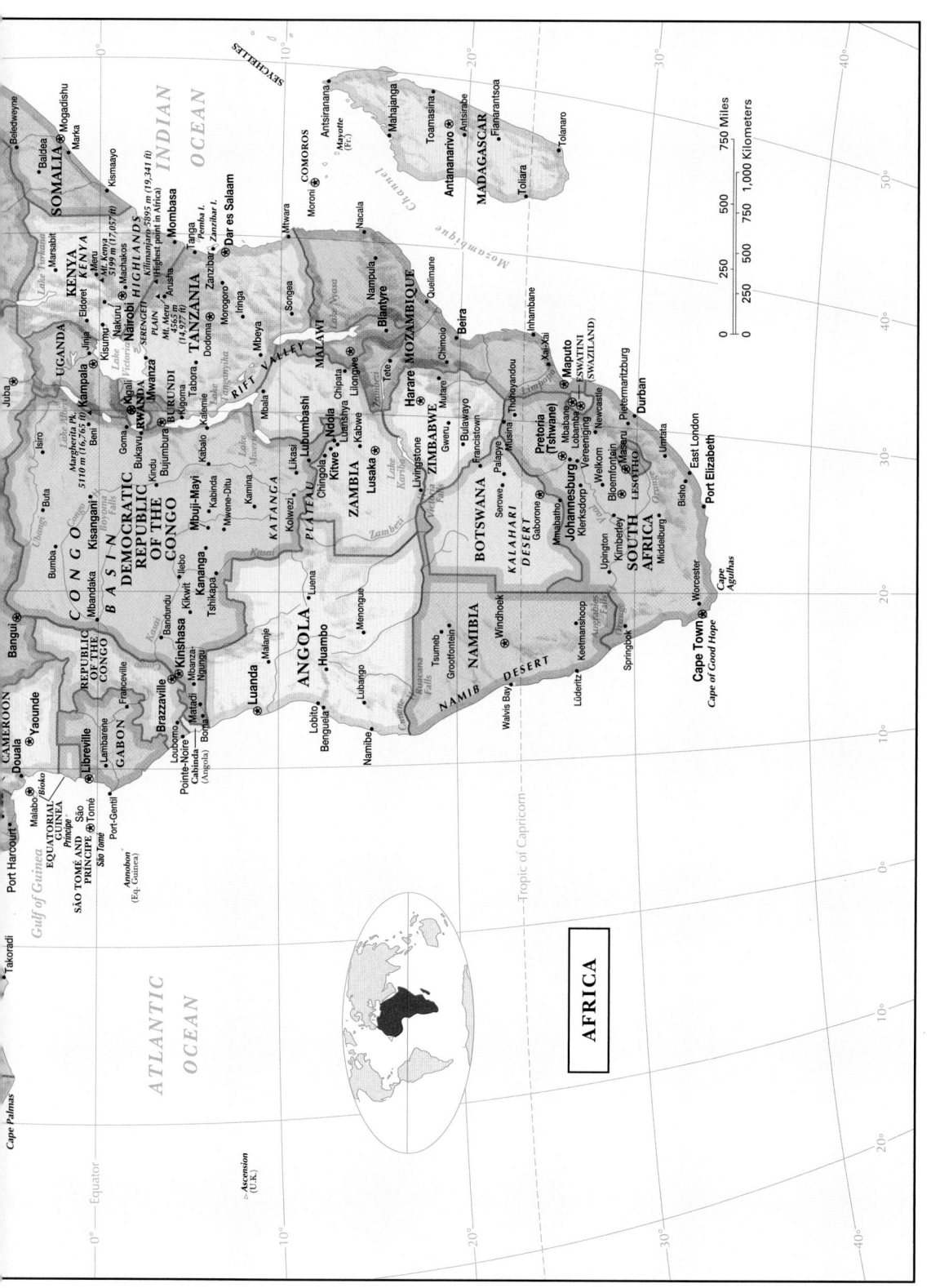

AFRICA

ATLANTIC OCEAN

INDIAN OCEAN

SEYCHELLES

SOMALIA
Mogadishu
Marka
Baidoa
Beledweyne
Kismaayo

KENYA
Nairobi
Mombasa
Machakos
Meru
Marsabit
Eldoret
Nakuru
Lake Turkana

Mt. Kenya 5199 m (17,057 ft)

UGANDA
Kampala
Jinja
Juba
Lake Victoria

RWANDA
Kigali

BURUNDI
Bujumbura

TANZANIA
Dodoma
Dar es Salaam
Zanzibar
Tanga
Arusha
Tabora
Mwanza
Mbeya
Iringa
Songea
Mtwara

Mt. Meru 4565 m (14,977 ft)

SERENGETI PLAIN

Kilimanjaro 5895 m (19,341 ft) (Highest point in Africa)

HIGHLANDS

COMOROS
Moroni
Mayotte (Fr.)

Mozambique Channel

MADAGASCAR
Antananarivo
Mahajanga
Toamasina
Antsiranana
Antsirabe
Fianarantsoa
Toliara
Tolanaro

Pemba I.
Zanzibar I.

Mwara
Nacala
Nampula
Quelimane
Mozambique

MOZAMBIQUE
Blantyre
Beira
Chimoio
Tete
Inhambane
Xai-Xai
Maputo

MALAWI
Lilongwe
Chipata

Lake Nyasa

ZAMBIA
Lusaka
Ndola
Kitwe
Kabwe
Livingstone
Chingola
Luanshya
Mbala
Kalemie

ZIMBABWE
Harare
Bulawayo
Gweru
Mutare
Masvingo
Gwanda

Lake Kariba

KATANGA PLATEAU
Lubumbashi
Likasi
Kolwezi

DEMOCRATIC REPUBLIC OF THE CONGO
Kinshasa
Mbuji-Mayi
Kananga
Kikwit
Kindu
Kabalo
Kalemie
Goma
Bukavu
Beni
Isiro
Butembo
Kabinda
Mwene-Ditu
Kamina
Tshikapa
Mbandaka
Kisangani
Bumba
Buta

Margherita Pk. 5110 m (16,765 ft)

CONGO BASIN

RIFT VALLEY

Lake Tanganyika
Lake Mweru
Lake Edward
Lake Albert
Lake Kivu

Uele
Kasai

ESWATINI (SWAZILAND)
Mbabane
Lobamba

BOTSWANA
Gaborone
Francistown
Serowe
Palapye

KALAHARI DESERT

SOUTH AFRICA
Pretoria (Tshwane)
Johannesburg
Bloemfontein
Kimberley
Cape Town
Durban
East London
Port Elizabeth
Vereeniging
Welkom
Klerksdorp
Newcastle
Pietermaritzburg
Upington
Mmabatho
Springbok
Bisho
Middelburg
Worcester
Umtata

Cape of Good Hope
Cape Agulhas

LESOTHO
Maseru

NAMIBIA
Windhoek
Walvis Bay
Tsumeb
Grootfontein
Keetmanshoop
Lüderitz

NAMIB DESERT

Okavango
Orange
Limpopo

Ruacana Falls

ANGOLA
Luanda
Huambo
Lobito
Benguela
Lubango
Namibe
Malanje
Menongue
Luena
Cabinda (Angola)

REPUBLIC OF THE CONGO
Brazzaville
Pointe-Noire
Loubomo
Franceville
Cabinda

GABON
Libreville
Lambarene
Port-Gentil

CAMEROON
Yaounde
Douala

EQUATORIAL GUINEA
Malabo
São Tomé

SÃO TOMÉ AND PRÍNCIPE
São Tomé
Príncipe
Bioko

Annobon (Eq. Guinea)

Gulf of Guinea

Takoradi
Cape Palmas
Port Harcourt

Bangui
Bumba
Mbandaka

Ubangi
Congo

Ascension (U.K.)

Equator
Tropic of Capricorn

Miles
0   250   500   750   1,000 Kilometers
0   250   500   750 Miles

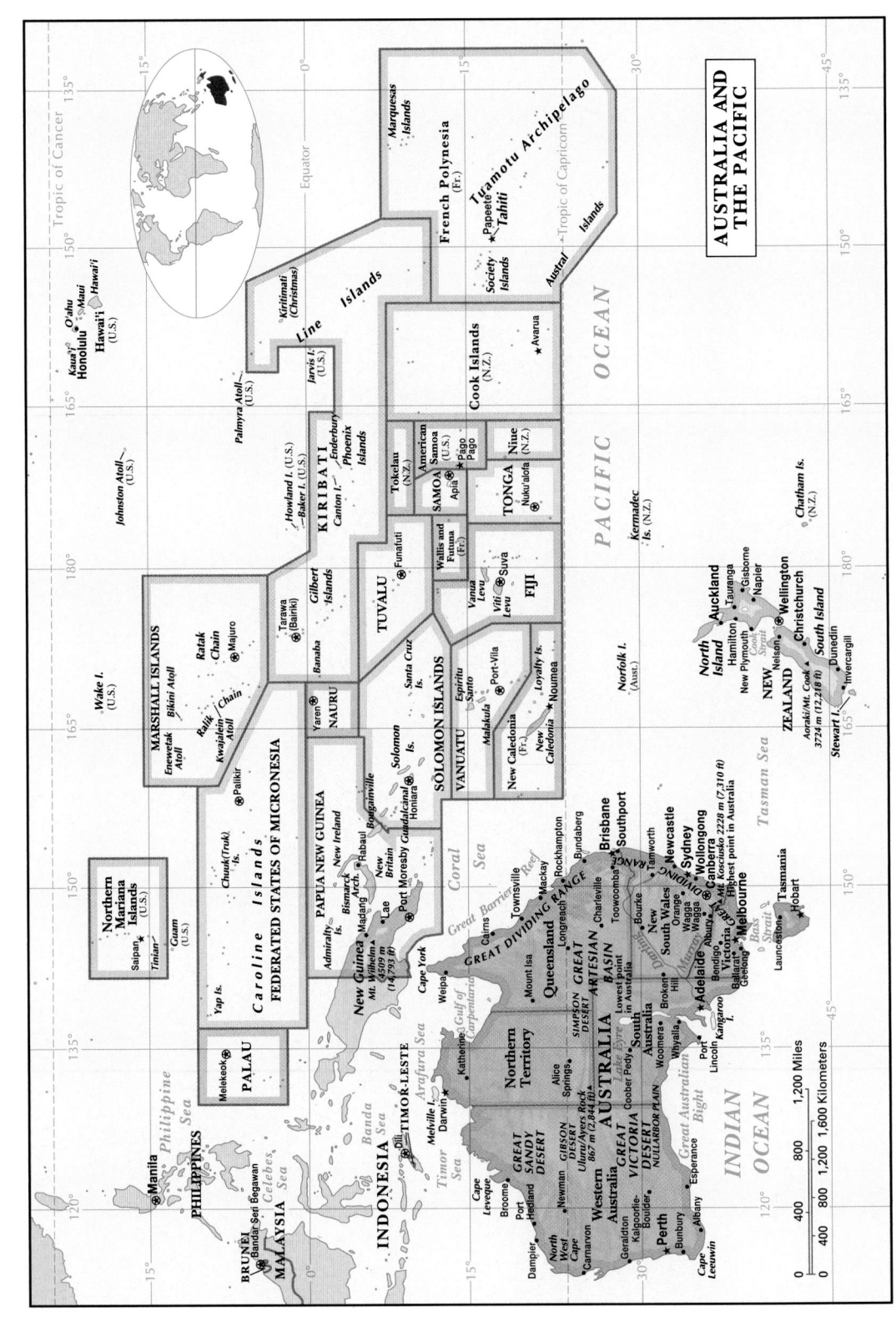

AUSTRALIA AND
THE PACIFIC

AMENDMENT XXV.

Presidential vacancy, inability, and succession.

[Proposed by Congress July 6, 1965; ratified Feb. 10, 1967.]

Section 1. In case of the removal of the President from office or of his death or resignation, the Vice President shall become President.

Section 2. Whenever there is a vacancy in the office of the Vice President, the President shall nominate a Vice President who shall take office upon confirmation by a majority vote of both Houses of Congress.

Section 3. Whenever the President transmits to the President pro tempore of the Senate and the Speaker of the House of Representatives his written declaration that he is unable to discharge the powers and duties of his office, and until he transmits to them a written declaration to the contrary, such powers and duties shall be discharged by the Vice President as Acting President.

Section 4. Whenever the Vice President and a majority of either the principal officers of the executive departments or of such other body as Congress may by law provide, transmit to the President pro tempore of the Senate and the Speaker of the House of Representatives their written declaration that the President is unable to discharge the powers and duties of his office, the Vice President shall immediately assume the powers and duties of the office as Acting President.

Thereafter, when the President transmits to the President pro tempore of the Senate and the Speaker of the House of Representatives his written declaration that no inability exists, he shall resume the powers and duties of his office unless the Vice President and a majority of either the principal officers of the executive department or of such other body as Congress may by law provide, transmit within four days to the President pro tempore of the Senate and the Speaker of the House of Representatives their written declaration that the President is unable to discharge the powers and duties of his office. Thereupon Congress shall decide the issue, assembling within forty-eight hours for that purpose if not in session. If the Congress, within twenty-one days after receipt of the latter written declaration, or, if Congress is not in session, within twenty-one days after Congress is required to assemble, determines by two-thirds vote of both Houses that the President is unable to discharge the powers and duties of his office, the Vice President shall continue to discharge the same as Acting President; otherwise, the President shall resume the powers and duties of his office.

AMENDMENT XXVI.

Voting age lowered to 18 years.

[Proposed by Congress Mar. 23, 1971; ratified July 1, 1971.]

Section 1. The right of citizens of the United States, who are eighteen years of age or older, to vote shall not be denied or abridged by the United States or by any State on account of age.

Section 2. The Congress shall have power to enforce this article by appropriate legislation.

AMENDMENT XXVII.

Congressional pay.

[Proposed by Congress Sept. 25, 1789; ratified May 7, 1992.]

No law, varying the compensation for the services of the Senators and Representatives, shall take effect, until an election of Representatives shall have intervened.

How a Bill Becomes a Law

A senator or representative introduces a bill in Congress by sending it to the clerk of the Senate or the House, who assigns it a number and title. This procedure is termed the first reading. The clerk then refers the bill to the appropriate committee of the Senate or House.

If the committee does not wish to consider the bill, it will table it. Otherwise, the committee holds hearings to gather information, such as by inviting experts and other members of the public to testify. The committee then debates the bill and may offer amendments. A vote is taken, and if favorable, the bill is sent back to the clerk of the Senate or House.

The clerk reads the bill to the house—the second reading. Members may then debate the bill and suggest amendments.

After debate and any amendments, the bill is given a third reading, simply of the title, and put to a voice or roll-call vote.

If the bill passes, it goes to the other house, where it may be defeated or passed, with or without amendments. If defeated, the bill dies. If passed with amendments, a conference committee made up of members of both houses works out the differences between the two bills and arrives at a compromise.

After passage of the final version by both houses, the bill is sent to the president. If the president signs it, the bill becomes a law. The president may instead veto the bill by refusing to sign it and sending it back to the house where it originated, with reasons for the veto.

The president's objections are then read and debated, and a roll-call vote is taken. If the bill receives less than a two-thirds majority, it is defeated. If it receives at least two-thirds, it is sent to the other house. If that house also passes it by at least a two-thirds majority, the president's veto is overridden, and the bill becomes a law.

If the president neither signs nor vetoes the bill within 10 days—not including Sundays—it automatically becomes a law even without the president's signature. However, if Congress adjourns within those 10 days, the bill is automatically killed; this indirect rejection is termed a pocket veto.

Under the Line Item Veto Act, effective Jan. 1, 1997, the president was authorized, under certain circumstances, to veto a bill in part. The legislation was found unconstitutional by the Supreme Court, June 25, 1998.

Presidential Oath of Office

The Constitution (Article II, Section 1) directs that the president-elect shall take the following oath to be inaugurated: "I do solemnly swear [affirm] that I will faithfully execute the office of President of the United States, and will, to the best of my ability, preserve, protect, and defend the Constitution of the United States."

Custom decrees the addition of the words "So help me God" at the end of the oath when taken by the president-elect, with the left hand on the Bible for the duration of the oath, and the right hand slightly raised.

Presidential Succession

If, by reason of death, resignation, removal from office, inability, or failure to qualify, there is neither a president nor vice president to discharge the powers and duties of the office of president, then the speaker of the House of Representatives shall, upon his resignation as speaker and as representative, act as president. The same rule shall apply in the case of the death, resignation, removal from office, or inability of an individual acting as president.

If, at the time when a speaker is to begin the discharge of the powers and duties of the office of president, there is no speaker, or the speaker fails to qualify as acting president, then the president pro tempore of the Senate, upon his resignation as president pro tempore and as senator, shall act as president.

An individual acting as president shall continue to act until the expiration of the then current presidential term, except that (1) if his discharge of the powers and duties of the office is founded in whole or in part in the failure of both the president-elect and the vice president-elect to qualify, then he shall act only until a president or vice president qualifies, and (2) if his discharge of the powers and duties of the office is founded in whole or in part on the inability of the president or vice president, then he shall act only until the removal of the disability of one of such individuals.

If, by reason of death, resignation, removal from office, or failure to qualify, there is no president pro tempore to act as president, then the officer of the United States who is highest on the following list, and who is not under any disability to discharge the powers and duties of president shall act as president: the secretaries of state, treasury, and defense; the attorney general; the secretaries of interior, agriculture, commerce, labor, health and human services, housing and urban development, transportation, energy, education, veterans affairs, and homeland security.

Legislation approved July 18, 1947; amended Sept. 9, 1965, Oct. 15, 1966, Aug. 4, 1977, Sept. 27, 1979, and Mar. 9, 2006. See also Constitutional Amendment XXV.

Confederate States: Secession and Government

The American Civil War (1861-65) grew out of sectional disputes over the continued existence of slavery in the South. Southern legislators contended that the states retained many rights, including the right to own slaves and the right to secede.

The war was not fought by state against state but by one federal regime against another. A Confederate government in Richmond, VA, assumed control over the economic, political, and military life of the seceding states, under protest from Georgia and South Carolina.

South Carolina voted unanimously in convention to secede from the Union, repealing its 1788 ratification of the U.S. Constitution on Dec. 20, 1860, to take effect on Dec. 24. Other states seceded in 1861. Their votes in conventions were Mississippi, Jan. 9, 84-15; Florida, Jan. 10, 62-7; Alabama, Jan. 11, 61-39; Georgia, Jan. 19, 208-89; Louisiana, Jan. 26, 113-17; Texas, Feb. 1, 166-7, ratified by popular vote (34,794 to 11,325) Feb. 23; Virginia, Apr. 17, 88-55, ratified by popular vote (128,884 to 32,134) May 23; Arkansas, May 6, 69-1; Tennessee, May 7, ratified by popular vote (104,019 to 47,238) June 8; and North Carolina, unanimous, May 20.

Missouri Unionists stopped secession in conventions Feb. 28 and Mar. 9, 1861. Under the protection of Confederate troops, secessionist members of the legislature adopted a resolution of secession at Neosho, Oct. 31. The Confederate Congress seated the secessionists' representatives.

Kentucky did not secede, and its government remained Unionist. In a part of the state occupied by Confederate troops, Kentuckians approved secession, and the Confederate Congress admitted their representatives.

The Maryland legislature voted against secession Apr. 27, 1861, 53-13. Delaware did not secede. Pro-Union residents of western Virginia held conventions at Wheeling and, on June 17, 1861, formed the Restored Government of Virginia. It was admitted to the Union as West Virginia on June 20, 1863. Its constitution provided for gradual abolition of slavery.

Forty-two delegates from South Carolina, Georgia, Alabama, Mississippi, Louisiana, and Florida met in convention in Montgomery, AL, on Feb. 4, 1861. They adopted a provisional constitution of the Confederate States of America and elected Jefferson Davis (MS) as provisional president and Alexander H. Stephens (GA) as provisional vice president.

A permanent constitution was adopted Mar. 11. It banned the African slave trade but did not bar interstate commerce in slaves. On July 20 the Congress moved to Richmond. Davis was elected president in Nov. 1861 and was inaugurated Feb. 22, 1862.

The Confederate Congress adopted a flag ("The Stars and Bars") consisting of one white stripe and two red stripes and a blue canton with a circle of white stars. The Confederate battle flag, carried by the Army of Northern Virginia, was more popularly known. It has blue diagonal crossbars with 13 white stars, for the 11 states in the Confederacy plus Kentucky and Missouri, against a red field.

The Gettysburg Address

Delivered by Pres. Abraham Lincoln at the dedication of the Soldiers' National Cemetery in Gettysburg, PA, on Nov. 19, 1863. Five handwritten copies of the Gettysburg Address as made by Lincoln are known to exist. The text differs slightly between copies. The Bliss copy, made for Alexander Bliss, is shown here. The copy is kept on display in the White House.

Four score and seven years ago our fathers brought forth on this continent, a new nation, conceived in Liberty, and dedicated to the proposition that all men are created equal.

Now we are engaged in a great civil war, testing whether that nation, or any nation so conceived and so dedicated, can long endure. We are met on a great battle-field of that war. We have come to dedicate a portion of that field, as a final resting place for those who here gave their lives that that nation might live. It is altogether fitting and proper that we should do this.

But, in a larger sense, we can not dedicate—we can not consecrate—we can not hallow—this ground. The brave men, living and dead, who struggled here, have consecrated it, far above our poor power to add or detract. The world will little note, nor long remember what we say here, but it can never forget what they did here.

It is for us the living, rather, to be dedicated here to the unfinished work which they who fought here have thus far so nobly advanced. It is rather for us to be here dedicated to the great task remaining before us—that from these honored dead we take increased devotion to that cause for which they gave the last full measure of devotion—that we here highly resolve that these dead shall not have died in vain—that this nation, under God, shall have a new birth of freedom—and that government of the people, by the people, for the people, shall not perish from the earth.

Origin of the United States National Motto

In God We Trust, designated as the U.S. National Motto by Congress in 1956, originated during the Civil War as an inscription for U.S. coins. On Nov. 13, 1861, the Rev. M. R. Watkinson, of Ridleyville, PA, wrote to Treasury Sec. Salmon P. Chase requesting "recognition of the Almighty God in some form on our coins." Chase ordered designs prepared with the inscription *In God We Trust* and backed coinage legislation that authorized use of this slogan. The motto first appeared on some U.S. coins in 1864 and sporadically thereafter until 1938, after which all U.S. coins bear the inscription. A joint resolution passed by the 84th Congress and signed by Pres. Dwight D. Eisenhower July 30, 1956, declared *In God We Trust* the national motto of the United States.

Great Seal of the U.S.

On July 4, 1776, the Continental Congress appointed a committee consisting of Benjamin Franklin, John Adams, and Thomas Jefferson "to bring in a device for a seal of the United States of America." The designs submitted by this and a subsequent committee were considered unacceptable. After many delays, a third committee, appointed early in 1782, presented a design prepared by lawyer William Barton. Charles Thomson, the secretary of Congress, suggested certain changes, and Congress finally approved the design on June 20, 1782. The obverse side of the seal shows an American bald eagle. In its mouth is a ribbon bearing the motto *E Pluribus Unum* (out of many, one). In the eagle's talons are 13 arrows of war and an olive branch of peace. The reverse side shows an unfinished pyramid with an eye (Eye of Providence) above it.

The Flag of the U.S.—The Stars and Stripes

The 50-star flag of the United States was raised for the first time officially at 12:01 AM on July 4, 1960, at Ft. McHenry National Monument in Baltimore, MD. The 50th star had been added for Hawaii; just a year earlier, the 49th star was added for Alaska.

There are so many myths and legends surrounding the history of the Stars and Stripes that the facts are difficult, and in some cases impossible, to establish. For example, it is not certain who designed the Stars and Stripes, who made the first such flag, or even whether it ever flew during any battle of the American Revolution.

Historians agree, however, that the Stars and Stripes originated as the result of a resolution offered by the Marine Committee of the Second Continental Congress at Philadelphia and adopted on June 14, 1777. It read:

"Resolved: that the flag of the United States be thirteen stripes, alternate red and white; that the union be thirteen stars, white in a blue field, representing a new constellation."

Congress gave no hint as to the designer of the flag, no instructions as to the arrangement of the stars, and no information on its appropriate uses.

The resolution establishing the flag was not published until Sept. 2, 1777. Despite repeated requests, George Washington did not get the flags until 1783, after the war was over. And there is no certainty that they were the Stars and Stripes.

Early Flags

Many historians consider the first flag of the U.S. to have been the Grand Union (sometimes called Great Union) flag, although the Continental Congress never officially adopted it. This flag was a modification of the British Meteor flag, which had the red cross of St. George and the white cross of St. Andrew combined in the blue canton. For the Grand Union flag, six horizontal stripes were imposed on the red field, dividing it into 13 alternating red and white stripes. On Jan. 1, 1776, when the Continental Army came into formal existence, this flag was unfurled on Prospect Hill, Somerville, MA. Washington wrote that "we hoisted the Union Flag in compliment to the United Colonies."

One of several flags about which controversy has raged is in Easton, PA. Containing the devices of the national flag in reversed order, this flag has been in the public library in Easton for more than 150 years. Some contend that this flag was actually the first Stars and Stripes, first displayed on July 8, 1776. This flag has 13 red and white stripes in the canton and 13 white stars centered in a blue field.

A flag was hastily improvised from garments by the defenders of Ft. Schuyler at Rome, NY, Aug. 3-22, 1777. Historians believe it was the Grand Union Flag.

The Sons of Liberty had a flag of nine red and white stripes, to signify nine colonies, when they met in New York in 1765 to oppose the Stamp Tax. By 1775, the flag had grown to 13 red and white stripes, with a rattlesnake on it.

At Concord, MA, Apr. 19, 1775, the minutemen from Bedford, MA, are said to have carried a flag having a silver arm with sword on a red field. At Cambridge, MA, the Sons of Liberty used a plain red flag with a green pine tree on it.

In June 1775, Washington went from Philadelphia to Boston to take command of the army. He was escorted to New York by the Philadelphia Light Horse Troop, which carried a yellow flag that had an elaborate coat of arms—the shield charged with 13 knots, the motto "For These We Strive"—and a canton of 13 blue and silver stripes.

In Feb. 1776, Col. Christopher Gadsden, a member of the Continental Congress, gave the South Carolina Provincial Congress a flag "such as is to be used by the commander-in-chief of the American Navy." It had a yellow field, with a rattlesnake about to strike and the words "Don't Tread on Me."

At the Battle of Bennington, Aug. 16, 1777, patriots used a flag of seven white and six red stripes with a blue canton extending down nine stripes. Eleven white stars arch over the figure 76 in the canton; a star appears in each of the canton's upper corners. The stars are seven-pointed. This flag is preserved in a museum in Bennington, VT.

At the Battle of Cowpens, Jan. 17, 1781, the 3rd Maryland Regiment is said to have carried a flag of 13 red and white stripes, with a blue canton containing 12 stars in a circle around one star.

Who Designed the Flag? No one knows for certain. Francis Hopkinson, designer of a naval flag, declared he had designed the flag and in 1781 asked Congress to reimburse him for his services. Congress did not do so.

Who Called the Flag "Old Glory"? The flag is said to have been named Old Glory by William Driver, a sea captain of Salem, MA. One legend has it that he did so when he raised the flag on his brig in 1824. But his daughter said he named it at his 21st birthday celebration on Mar. 17, 1824, when his mother presented the homemade flag to him.

The Betsy Ross Legend. The widely publicized legend that Betsy Ross made the first Stars and Stripes in June 1776, at the request of a committee composed of George Washington, Robert Morris, and George Ross, an uncle, was first made public in 1870, by a grandson of Ross. Historians have been unable to find a historical record of such a meeting or committee.

Adding New Stars

On the admission of Vermont and Kentucky to the Union, Congress designated that after May 1, 1795, the flag should have 15 stripes, alternating red and white, and 15 white stars on a blue field.

When more new states were admitted, it became evident that the flag would become burdened with stripes. Congress ordered that after July 4, 1818, the flag should have 13 stripes, symbolizing 13 original states; that the union have 20 stars; and that whenever a new state was admitted a new star should be added on the July 4 following admission.

No law designates the permanent arrangement of the stars. However, since 1912, when a new state has been admitted, the new design has been announced by executive order. No star is specifically identified with any state.

Pledge of Allegiance to the Flag

I pledge allegiance to the flag of the United States of America, and to the republic for which it stands, one nation under God, indivisible, with liberty and justice for all.

This, the current official version of the Pledge of Allegiance, developed from a pledge first published in the Sept. 8, 1892, issue of *Youth's Companion*, a weekly magazine. The original pledge contained the phrase "my flag," which was changed more than 30 years later to "flag of the United States of America." A 1954 act of Congress added the words "under God." (In 2002, the 9th Circuit U.S. Court of Appeals ruled that recitation of the pledge in public schools could not include that phrase. In 2004, however, the U.S. Supreme Court voted to decline to decide the case on a technicality. The lower court's decision was thus overturned.)

The authorship of the pledge was in dispute for many years. *Youth's Companion* stated in 1917 that the original draft was written by James B. Upham, an executive of the magazine who died in 1910. A leaflet circulated by the magazine later named Upham as the originator of the first draft.

Francis Bellamy, a former member of the *Youth's Companion* editorial staff, publicly claimed authorship of the pledge in 1923. In 1939, the United States Flag Association, acting on the advice of a committee named to study the controversy, upheld the claim by Bellamy, who had died eight years earlier. In 1957 the Library of Congress issued a report attributing the authorship to Bellamy.

According to the federal Flag Code, the pledge should be given while standing at attention facing the flag with the right hand over the heart. Those not in military uniform should remove any non-religious head coverings with their right hand and hold it at the left shoulder, the hand being over the heart. Those in uniform should remain silent, face the flag, and render a military salute. Members and veterans of the Armed Forces not in uniform may also render the military salute in the manner provided for persons in uniform.

History of the U.S. National Anthem

"The Star-Spangled Banner" was formally designated the national anthem by Act of Congress, Mar. 3, 1931. The words were written by Francis Scott Key, of Georgetown, MD, marking the bombardment of Ft. McHenry in Baltimore, MD, Sept. 13-14, 1814. Key was a lawyer, a graduate of St. John's College in Annapolis, MD, and a volunteer in a light artillery company. When a friend, Dr. William Beanes, a Maryland physician, was arrested by the British for interfering with British deserters and straggling ground troops, Key and U.S. Col. John Skinner, with permission from Pres. Madison, went to the fleet under a flag of truce to ask for Beanes's release. The British consented, but as the fleet was about to sail up the Patapsco River to bombard Ft. McHenry, Key was detained for the duration of the battle.

The bombardment of Ft. McHenry began at 7 AM, Sept. 13, and lasted 25 hours. The British fired more than 1,500 shells. They were unable to approach closely because the U.S. had sunk 22 vessels to form a barrier. Only four Americans were killed and 24 wounded. A British bomb ship was disabled.

The morning after the shelling, Sept. 14, inspired by the flag still flying above the garrison, Key began to draft the poem. Released from British custody in Baltimore Sept. 16, Key

revised the poem and gave it to his brother-in-law, Joseph Nicholson, who encouraged its printing on handbills. The first versions were titled "The Defence of Fort McHenry" and included a note suggesting use of the tune "Anacreon in Heaven" (attributed to British composer John Stafford Smith). The poem appeared in several newspapers within days and spread quickly.

The garrison flag that Key saw the morning after the bombardment is preserved at the Smithsonian Institution's National Museum of American History in Washington, DC. Major George Armistead, the commander of the militia unit stationed at Fort McHenry, had ordered a flag "so large that the British will have no difficulty seeing it from a distance." A government contract paid Baltimore flagmaker Mary Pickersgill $405.90 in 1813 for the garrison flag and $168.54 for a smaller storm flag (which was flown during the battle itself). The garrison flag originally measured 30 by 42 ft and had 15 alternating red and white stripes and 15 stars, for the original 13 states plus Kentucky and Vermont. The preserved flag measures 30 by 34 ft and is missing one star. Before the flag was placed in a museum, the family holding the flag would give clippings of it away as souvenirs.

The Star-Spangled Banner

I

Oh, say can you see by the dawn's early light
What so proudly we hailed at the twilight's last gleaming?
Whose broad stripes and bright stars through the perilous fight,
O'er the ramparts we watched were so gallantly streaming?
And the rockets' red glare, the bombs bursting in air,
Gave proof through the night that our flag was still there.
Oh, say does that star-spangled banner yet wave
O'er the land of the free and the home of the brave?

II

On the shore, dimly seen through the mists of the deep,
Where the foe's haughty host in dread silence reposes,
What is that which the breeze, o'er the towering steep,
As it fitfully blows, half conceals, half discloses?
Now it catches the gleam of the morning's first beam,
In full glory reflected now shines in the stream:
'Tis the star-spangled banner! Oh long may it wave
O'er the land of the free and the home of the brave!

III

And where is that band who so vauntingly swore
That the havoc of war and the battle's confusion,
A home and a country should leave us no more!
Their blood has washed out their foul footsteps' pollution.
No refuge could save the hireling and slave
From the terror of flight, or the gloom of the grave:
And the star-spangled banner in triumph doth wave
O'er the land of the free and the home of the brave!

IV

Oh! thus be it ever, when freemen shall stand
Between their loved home and the war's desolation!
Blest with victory and peace, may the heav'n rescued land
Praise the Power that hath made and preserved us a nation.
Then conquer we must, when our cause it is just,
And this be our motto: "In God is our trust."
And the star-spangled banner in triumph shall wave
O'er the land of the free and the home of the brave!

Statue of Liberty National Monument

Since 1886, the Statue of Liberty, formally known as "Liberty Enlightening the World," has stood as a symbol of freedom in New York Harbor. As a gift from the people of France to the people of the U.S., it also commemorates French-American friendship. It was designed by French sculptor Frédéric Auguste Bartholdi (1834-1904).

On Washington's Birthday, Feb. 22, 1877, Congress approved the use of a site on Bedloe's Island suggested by Bartholdi. This island of 12 acres had been owned in the 17th cent. by a Walloon colonist named Isaac Bedloe. (On Aug. 3, 1956, Pres. Dwight Eisenhower approved a measure changing the name to Liberty Island.)

The statue was finished on May 21, 1884, and presented to the U.S. minister to France, Levi Parsons Morton, July 4, 1884, by French diplomat Ferdinand de Lesseps.

On Aug. 5, 1884, the cornerstone for the granite pedestal—designed by architect Richard Morris Hunt—was laid on the foundations of Fort Wood, erected by the government in 1811. The American Committee for the Statue of Liberty had raised an inadequate $125,000, and *New York World* newspaper owner Joseph Pulitzer appealed Mar. 16, 1885, for general donations. By Aug. 11, 1885, he had raised $100,000. The statue itself arrived dismantled, in 214 packing cases, from Rouen, France, in June 1885. The last rivet of the statue was driven on Oct. 28, 1886, when Pres. Grover Cleveland dedicated the monument.

The Statue of Liberty National Monument was designated as such in 1924. It is administered by the National Park Service. A $2.5-mil building housing the American Museum of Immigration was opened by Pres. Richard Nixon on Sept. 26, 1972, at the base of the statue. It houses a permanent exhibition tracing the history of American immigration.

Four years of restoration work funded and led by the Statue of Liberty-Ellis Island Foundation were completed before the statue's 1986 centennial. The $87-mil project included the replacement of the 1,600 wrought iron bands that hold the statue's copper skin to its frame, replacement of the torch, and installation of an elevator. A four-day extravaganza of concerts, tall ships, cultural and heritage festivals, and fireworks, July 3-6, 1986, celebrated the 100th anniversary. U.S. Supreme Court Chief Justice Warren E. Burger swore in 5,000 new citizens on Ellis Island, while 20,000 others across the country were sworn in through a satellite telecast. Other ceremonies followed on Oct. 28, 1986, the statue's exact 100th birthday.

After the Sept. 11, 2001, terrorist attacks, Liberty Island was closed to visitors. On Dec. 20, 2001, the secretary of the interior reopened the island after installing airport-type screening facilities at passenger embarkation areas at Battery Park in Manhattan and Liberty State Park in New Jersey.

The federal government increased security throughout the park before reopening the statue. In addition to federally funded security upgrades, significant building safety improvements were made. Public access to the statue was restored on Aug. 3, 2004.

Following the 125th anniversary celebration Oct. 28, 2011, the statue was closed. A $30-mil renovation brought the statue up to contemporary safety standards and allowed for increased visitor access. The statue interior reopened Oct. 28, 2012, but damages caused by Hurricane Sandy the next week forced all of Liberty Island to close again. The island and the statue officially reopened to visitors July 4, 2013.

Advance reservations are recommended for visiting the museum and statue pedestal and are required for the crown. Reservations can be made at www.statuecruises.com or by calling 1-877-LADY-TIX. Fees start at $18.50 for adults ($9 child/$14 senior), with $3 more added for crown visits. Visitors to the statue's interior must follow a number of guidelines including age and height restrictions. Park rangers conduct English-language tours throughout the day. Standard self-guided audio tours are available in nine languages; a children's version of the audio tour is available in five languages.

A 26,000-sq-ft, freestanding Statue of Liberty Museum was expected to open in 2019. There is no additional admission fee for the museum. For more information, visit www.nps.gov/stli and www.libertyellisfoundation.org.

Statue Statistics

The statue weighs 450,000 lbs, or 225 tons. The copper sheeting weighs 200,000 lbs. There are 377 steps from the main lobby to the crown platform. There are 146 steps from the top of the pedestal (the statue's feet) to the crown platform.

	Measurement	
Statue feature	Ft	In.
Height from base to torch tip	151	1
Foundation of pedestal to torch tip	305	1
Heel to top of head	111	1
Hand, length	16	5
Index finger, length	8	0
Fingernail size		13x10
Head from chin to cranium	17	3
Head thickness, ear to ear	10	0
Nose, length	4	6
Right arm, length	42	0
Right arm, max. thickness	12	0
Waist, thickness	35	0
Mouth, width	3	0
Tablet, length	23	7
Tablet, width	13	7

Ellis Island

Ellis Island was the gateway to America for over 12 mil immigrants between 1892 and 1924. In the late 18th cent., Samuel Ellis, a New York City merchant, purchased the island. From Ellis, it passed to New York state before the U.S. government bought it in 1808. On Jan. 1, 1892, the government opened the first federal immigration center in the U.S. there. The 27.5-acre site eventually supported more than 35 buildings, including the Main Building with its Great Hall, which was designed to process 5,000 people a day. In Ellis Island's peak year, 1907, it received 1,004,756 immigrants; on its peak day (Apr. 17, 1907), 11,747 immigrants were processed.

Closed as an immigration station in 1954, Ellis Island was proclaimed part of the Statue of Liberty National Monument in 1965 by Pres. Lyndon B. Johnson. After a six-year, $170-mil restoration project funded by the Statue of Liberty-Ellis Island Foundation, Ellis Island was reopened as a museum in 1990, now called the Ellis Island National Museum of Immigration. Artifacts, historic photographs and documents, oral

histories, and ethnic music depicting 400 years of American immigration are housed in the museum.

In 1998, the U.S. Supreme Court ruled that nearly 90% of the island (the 24.2 acres that are landfill) lies in New Jersey, while the original 3.3 acres, on which the museum is located, are in New York. (The decision settled the issue of jurisdiction over potential development.)

The American Family Immigration History Center opened in Apr. 2001. Visitors there can access immigrant arrival records on more than 51 million individuals who entered the U.S. through the Port of New York and Ellis Island from 1892 to 1957. The searchable digitized archives include ships' images and manifests and passenger information such as age, ethnicity, and port of departure. **Website:** www.libertyellisfoundation.org

Damage caused by storm surges from Hurricane Sandy in late Oct. 2012 forced Ellis Island to close for repairs. New galleries opened May 20, 2015, focusing on post-Ellis Island era immigration.

PRESIDENTS OF THE UNITED STATES

U.S. Presidents

	Name	Politics	Born	Birthplace	Inaug.	Age at inaug.	Died	Age at death
1.	George Washington	Fed.	1732, Feb. 22	VA	1789	57	1799, Dec. 14	67
2.	John Adams	Fed.	1735, Oct. 30	MA	1797	61	1826, July 4	90
3.	Thomas Jefferson	Dem.-Rep.	1743, Apr. 13	VA	1801	57	1826, July 4	83
4.	James Madison	Dem.-Rep.	1751, Mar. 16	VA	1809	57	1836, June 28	85
5.	James Monroe	Dem.-Rep.	1758, Apr. 28	VA	1817	58	1831, July 4	73
6.	John Quincy Adams	Dem.-Rep.	1767, July 11	MA	1825	57	1848, Feb. 23	80
7.	Andrew Jackson	Dem.	1767, Mar. 15	SC	1829	61	1845, June 8	78
8.	Martin Van Buren	Dem.	1782, Dec. 5	NY	1837	54	1862, July 24	79
9.	William Henry Harrison	Whig	1773, Feb. 9	VA	1841	68	1841, Apr. 4	68
10.	John Tyler	Whig	1790, Mar. 29	VA	1841	51	1862, Jan. 18	71
11.	James Knox Polk	Dem.	1795, Nov. 2	NC	1845	49	1849, June 15	53
12.	Zachary Taylor	Whig	1784, Nov. 24	VA	1849	64	1850, July 9	65
13.	Millard Fillmore	Whig	1800, Jan. 7	NY	1850	50	1874, Mar. 8	74
14.	Franklin Pierce	Dem.	1804, Nov. 23	NH	1853	48	1869, Oct. 8	64
15.	James Buchanan	Dem.	1791, Apr. 23	PA	1857	65	1868, June 1	77
16.	Abraham Lincoln	Rep.	1809, Feb. 12	KY	1861	52	1865, Apr. 15	56
17.	Andrew Johnson	Dem.[1]	1808, Dec. 29	NC	1865	56	1875, July 31	66
18.	Ulysses S. Grant	Rep.	1822, Apr. 27	OH	1869	46	1885, July 23	63
19.	Rutherford Birchard Hayes	Rep.	1822, Oct. 4	OH	1877	54	1893, Jan. 17	70
20.	James Abram Garfield	Rep.	1831, Nov. 19	OH	1881	49	1881, Sept. 19	49
21.	Chester Alan Arthur	Rep.	1829, Oct. 5	VT	1881	51	1886, Nov. 18	57
22.	Grover Cleveland	Dem.	1837, Mar. 18	NJ	1885	47	1908, June 24	71
23.	Benjamin Harrison	Rep.	1833, Aug. 20	OH	1889	55	1901, Mar. 13	67
24.	Grover Cleveland	Dem.	1837, Mar. 18	NJ	1893	55	1908, June 24	71
25.	William McKinley	Rep.	1843, Jan. 29	OH	1897	54	1901, Sept. 14	58
26.	Theodore Roosevelt	Rep.	1858, Oct. 27	NY	1901	42	1919, Jan. 6	60
27.	William Howard Taft	Rep.	1857, Sept. 15	OH	1909	51	1930, Mar. 8	72
28.	(Thomas) Woodrow Wilson	Dem.	1856, Dec. 28	VA	1913	56	1924, Feb. 3	67
29.	Warren Gamaliel Harding	Rep.	1865, Nov. 2	OH	1921	55	1923, Aug. 2	57
30.	(John) Calvin Coolidge	Rep.	1872, July 4	VT	1923	51	1933, Jan. 5	60
31.	Herbert Clark Hoover	Rep.	1874, Aug. 10	IA	1929	54	1964, Oct. 20	90
32.	Franklin Delano Roosevelt	Dem.	1882, Jan. 30	NY	1933	51	1945, Apr. 12	63
33.	Harry S. Truman	Dem.	1884, May 8	MO	1945	60	1972, Dec. 26	88
34.	Dwight David Eisenhower	Rep.	1890, Oct. 14	TX	1953	62	1969, Mar. 28	78
35.	John Fitzgerald Kennedy	Dem.	1917, May 29	MA	1961	43	1963, Nov. 22	46
36.	Lyndon Baines Johnson	Dem.	1908, Aug. 27	TX	1963	55	1973, Jan. 22	64
37.	Richard Milhous Nixon[2]	Rep.	1913, Jan. 9	CA	1969	56	1994, Apr. 22	81
38.	Gerald Rudolph Ford	Rep.	1913, July 14	NE	1974	61	2006, Dec. 26	93
39.	James Earl (Jimmy) Carter	Dem.	1924, Oct. 1	GA	1977	52		
40.	Ronald Wilson Reagan	Rep.	1911, Feb. 6	IL	1981	69	2004, June 5	93
41.	George Herbert Walker Bush	Rep.	1924, June 12	MA	1989	64		
42.	Wm. Jefferson (Bill) Clinton	Dem.	1946, Aug. 19	AR	1993	46		
43.	George Walker Bush	Rep.	1946, July 6	CT	2001	54		
44.	Barack Hussein Obama	Dem.	1961, Aug. 4	HI	2009	47		
45.	Donald John Trump	Rep.	1946, June 14	NY	2017	70		

(1) Andrew Johnson, a Democrat, had been nominated vice president by Republicans and elected with Lincoln on National Union ticket. (2) Resigned Aug. 9, 1974.

U.S. Presidents, Vice Presidents, Congresses

President	Service	Vice President	Congresses
1. George Washington	Apr. 30, 1789-Mar. 3, 1797	1. John Adams	1, 2, 3, 4
2. John Adams	Mar. 4, 1797-Mar. 3, 1801	2. Thomas Jefferson	5, 6
3. Thomas Jefferson	Mar. 4, 1801-Mar. 3, 1805	3. Aaron Burr	7, 8
	Mar. 4, 1805-Mar. 3, 1809	4. George Clinton	9, 10
4. James Madison	Mar. 4, 1809-Mar. 3, 1813	George Clinton[1]	11, 12
	Mar. 4, 1813-Mar. 3, 1817	5. Elbridge Gerry[2]	13, 14
5. James Monroe	Mar. 4, 1817-Mar. 3, 1825	6. Daniel D. Tompkins	15, 16, 17, 18
6. John Quincy Adams	Mar. 4, 1825-Mar. 3, 1829	7. John C. Calhoun	19, 20
7. Andrew Jackson	Mar. 4, 1829-Mar. 3, 1833	John C. Calhoun[3]	21, 22
	Mar. 4, 1833-Mar. 3, 1837	8. Martin Van Buren	23, 24
8. Martin Van Buren	Mar. 4, 1837-Mar. 3, 1841	9. Richard M. Johnson	25, 26
9. William Henry Harrison[4]	Mar. 4, 1841-Apr. 4, 1841	10. John Tyler	27
10. John Tyler	Apr. 6, 1841-Mar. 3, 1845	(None)	27, 28
11. James K. Polk	Mar. 4, 1845-Mar. 3, 1849	11. George M. Dallas	29, 30
12. Zachary Taylor[4]	Mar. 5, 1849-July 9, 1850	12. Millard Fillmore	31
13. Millard Fillmore	July 10, 1850-Mar. 3, 1853	(None)	31, 32
14. Franklin Pierce	Mar. 4, 1853-Mar. 3, 1857	13. William R. King[5]	33, 34
15. James Buchanan	Mar. 4, 1857-Mar. 3, 1861	14. John C. Breckinridge	35, 36
16. Abraham Lincoln[4]	Mar. 4, 1861-Mar. 3, 1865	15. Hannibal Hamlin	37, 38
	Mar. 4, 1865-Apr. 15, 1865	16. Andrew Johnson	39
17. Andrew Johnson	Apr. 15, 1865-Mar. 3, 1869	(None)	39, 40
18. Ulysses S. Grant	Mar. 4, 1869-Mar. 3, 1873	17. Schuyler Colfax	41, 42
	Mar. 4, 1873-Mar. 3, 1877	18. Henry Wilson[6]	43, 44
19. Rutherford B. Hayes	Mar. 4, 1877-Mar. 3, 1881	19. William A. Wheeler	45, 46
20. James A. Garfield[4]	Mar. 4, 1881-Sept. 19, 1881	20. Chester A. Arthur	47
21. Chester A. Arthur	Sept. 20, 1881-Mar. 3, 1885	(None)	47, 48
22. Grover Cleveland[7]	Mar. 4, 1885-Mar. 3, 1889	21. Thomas A. Hendricks[8]	49, 50
23. Benjamin Harrison	Mar. 4, 1889-Mar. 3, 1893	22. Levi P. Morton	51, 52
24. Grover Cleveland[7]	Mar. 4, 1893-Mar. 3, 1897	23. Adlai E. Stevenson	53, 54
25. William McKinley[4]	Mar. 4, 1897-Mar. 3, 1901	24. Garret A. Hobart[9]	55, 56
	Mar. 4, 1901-Sept. 14, 1901	25. Theodore Roosevelt	57
26. Theodore Roosevelt	Sept. 14, 1901-Mar. 3, 1905	(None)	57, 58
	Mar. 4, 1905-Mar. 3, 1909	26. Charles W. Fairbanks	59, 60
27. William H. Taft	Mar. 4, 1909-Mar. 3, 1913	27. James S. Sherman[10]	61, 62

President	Service	Vice President	Congresses
28. Woodrow Wilson	Mar. 4, 1913-Mar. 3, 1921	28. Thomas R. Marshall	63, 64, 65, 66
29. Warren G. Harding[4]	Mar. 4, 1921-Aug. 2, 1923	29. Calvin Coolidge	67
30. Calvin Coolidge	Aug. 3, 1923-Mar. 3, 1925	(None)	68
	Mar. 4, 1925-Mar. 3, 1929	30. Charles G. Dawes	69, 70
31. Herbert C. Hoover	Mar. 4, 1929-Mar. 3, 1933	31. Charles Curtis	71, 72
32. Franklin D. Roosevelt[4,11]	Mar. 4, 1933-Jan. 20, 1941	32. John N. Garner	73, 74, 75, 76, 77
	Jan. 20, 1941-Jan. 20, 1945	33. Henry A. Wallace	77, 78, 79
	Jan. 20, 1945-Apr. 12, 1945	34. Harry S. Truman	79
33. Harry S. Truman	Apr. 12, 1945-Jan. 20, 1949	(None)	79, 80, 81
	Jan. 20, 1949-Jan. 20, 1953	35. Alben W. Barkley	81, 82, 83
34. Dwight D. Eisenhower	Jan. 20, 1953-Jan. 20, 1961	36. Richard M. Nixon	83, 84, 85, 86, 87
35. John F. Kennedy[4]	Jan. 20, 1961-Nov. 22, 1963	37. Lyndon B. Johnson	87, 88
36. Lyndon B. Johnson	Nov. 22, 1963-Jan. 20, 1965	(None)	88, 89
	Jan. 20, 1965-Jan. 20, 1969	38. Hubert H. Humphrey	89, 90, 91
37. Richard M. Nixon[13]	Jan. 20, 1969-Jan. 20, 1973	39. Spiro T. Agnew[12]	91, 92, 93
	Jan. 20, 1973-Aug. 9, 1974	40. Gerald R. Ford[14]	93
38. Gerald R. Ford[15]	Aug. 9, 1974-Jan. 20, 1977	41. Nelson A. Rockefeller[16]	93, 94, 95
39. Jimmy Carter	Jan. 20, 1977-Jan. 20, 1981	42. Walter F. Mondale	95, 96, 97
40. Ronald W. Reagan	Jan. 20, 1981-Jan. 20, 1989	43. George H. W. Bush	97, 98, 99, 100, 101
41. George H. W. Bush	Jan. 20, 1989-Jan. 20, 1993	44. Dan Quayle	101, 102, 103
42. Bill Clinton	Jan. 20, 1993-Jan. 20, 2001	45. Al Gore	103, 104, 105, 106, 107
43. George W. Bush	Jan. 20, 2001-Jan. 20, 2009	46. Dick Cheney	107, 108, 109, 110, 111
44. Barack H. Obama	Jan. 20, 2009-Jan. 20, 2017	47. Joe Biden	111, 112, 113, 114, 115
45. Donald J. Trump	Jan. 20, 2017-	48. Mike Pence	115

(1) Died Apr. 20, 1812. (2) Died Nov. 23, 1814. (3) Resigned Dec. 28, 1832, to become U.S. senator. (4) Died in office. (5) Died Apr. 18, 1853. (6) Died Nov. 22, 1875. (7) Terms not consecutive. (8) Died Nov. 25, 1885. (9) Died Nov. 21, 1899. (10) Died Oct. 30, 1912. (11) First president to be inaugurated under 20th Amendment, Jan. 20, 1937. (12) Resigned Oct. 10, 1973, after pleading no contest to a charge of tax evasion. (13) Resigned Aug. 9, 1974. (14) First nonelected vice president, chosen under 25th Amendment procedure. (15) First president never elected president or vice president. (16) Second nonelected vice president, chosen under 25th Amendment. Confirmed Dec. 19, 1974.

Vice Presidents of the U.S.

The numerals given vice presidents do not coincide with those given presidents because some presidents (Tyler, Fillmore, A. Johnson, Arthur) had none, and some had more than one.

Name	Birthplace	Born	Home	Inaug.	Politics/ party	Place of death	Died	Age at death
1. John Adams	Quincy, MA	1735	MA	1789	Fed.	Quincy, MA	1826	90
2. Thomas Jefferson	Shadwell, VA	1743	VA	1797	Dem.-Rep.	Monticello, VA	1826	83
3. Aaron Burr	Newark, NJ	1756	NY	1801	Dem.-Rep.	Staten Island, NY	1836	80
4. George Clinton	Little Britain, NY	1739	NY	1805	Dem.-Rep.	Washington, DC	1812	73
5. Elbridge Gerry	Marblehead, MA	1744	MA	1813	Dem.-Rep.	Washington, DC	1814	70
6. Daniel D. Tompkins	Scarsdale, NY	1774	NY	1817	Dem.-Rep.	Staten Island, NY	1825	51
7. John C. Calhoun[1]	Abbeville, SC	1782	SC	1825	Dem.-Rep.	Washington, DC	1850	68
8. Martin Van Buren	Kinderhook, NY	1782	NY	1833	Dem.	Kinderhook, NY	1862	79
9. Richard M. Johnson[2]	Louisville, KY	1780	KY	1837	Dem.	Frankfort, KY	1850	70
10. John Tyler	Greenway, VA	1790	VA	1841	Whig	Richmond, VA	1862	71
11. George M. Dallas	Philadelphia, PA	1792	PA	1845	Dem.	Philadelphia, PA	1864	72
12. Millard Fillmore	Cayuga Co., NY	1800	NY	1849	Whig	Buffalo, NY	1874	74
13. William R. King	Sampson Co., NC	1786	AL	1853	Dem.	Cahaba, AL	1853	67
14. John C. Breckinridge	Lexington, KY	1821	KY	1857	Dem.	Lexington, KY	1875	54
15. Hannibal Hamlin	Paris, ME	1809	ME	1861	Rep.	Bangor, ME	1891	81
16. Andrew Johnson	Raleigh, NC	1808	TN	1865	Dem.[3]	Carter Co., TN	1875	66
17. Schuyler Colfax	New York, NY	1823	IN	1869	Rep.	Mankato, MN	1885	62
18. Henry Wilson	Farmington, NH	1812	MA	1873	Rep.	Washington, DC	1875	63
19. William A. Wheeler	Malone, NY	1819	NY	1877	Rep.	Malone, NY	1887	68
20. Chester A. Arthur	Fairfield, VT	1829	NY	1881	Rep.	New York, NY	1886	57
21. Thomas A. Hendricks	Zanesville, OH	1819	IN	1885	Dem.	Indianapolis, IN	1885	66
22. Levi P. Morton	Shoreham, VT	1824	NY	1889	Rep.	Rhinebeck, NY	1920	96
23. Adlai E. Stevenson[4]	Christian Co., KY	1835	IL	1893	Dem.	Chicago, IL	1914	78
24. Garret A. Hobart	Long Branch, NJ	1844	NJ	1897	Rep.	Paterson, NJ	1899	55
25. Theodore Roosevelt	New York, NY	1858	NY	1901	Rep.	Oyster Bay, NY	1919	60
26. Charles W. Fairbanks	Unionville Centre, OH	1852	IN	1905	Rep.	Indianapolis, IN	1918	66
27. James S. Sherman	Utica, NY	1855	NY	1909	Rep.	Utica, NY	1912	57
28. Thomas R. Marshall	N. Manchester, IN	1854	IN	1913	Dem.	Washington, DC	1925	71
29. Calvin Coolidge	Plymouth Notch, VT	1872	MA	1921	Rep.	Northampton, MA	1933	60
30. Charles G. Dawes	Marietta, OH	1865	IL	1925	Rep.	Evanston, IL	1951	85
31. Charles Curtis	Topeka, KS	1860	KS	1929	Rep.	Washington, DC	1936	76
32. John Nance Garner	Red River Co., TX	1868	TX	1933	Dem.	Uvalde, TX	1967	98
33. Henry A. Wallace	Adair County, IA	1888	IA	1941	Dem.	Danbury, CT	1965	77
34. Harry S. Truman	Lamar, MO	1884	MO	1945	Dem.	Kansas City, MO	1972	88
35. Alben W. Barkley	Graves Co., KY	1877	KY	1949	Dem.	Lexington, VA	1956	78
36. Richard M. Nixon	Yorba Linda, CA	1913	CA	1953	Rep.	New York, NY	1994	81
37. Lyndon B. Johnson	Stonewall, TX	1908	TX	1961	Dem.	San Antonio, TX	1973	64
38. Hubert H. Humphrey	Wallace, SD	1911	MN	1965	Dem.	Waverly, MN	1978	66
39. Spiro T. Agnew[5]	Baltimore, MD	1918	MD	1969	Rep.	Berlin, MD	1996	77
40. Gerald R. Ford[6]	Omaha, NE	1913	MI	1973	Rep.	Rancho Mirage, CA	2006	93
41. Nelson A. Rockefeller[7]	Bar Harbor, ME	1908	NY	1974	Rep.	New York, NY	1979	70
42. Walter F. Mondale	Ceylon, MN	1928	MN	1977	Dem.			
43. George H. W. Bush	Milton, MA	1924	TX	1981	Rep.			
44. James Danforth (Dan) Quayle Jr.	Indianapolis, IN	1947	IN	1989	Rep.			
45. Albert A. Gore	Washington, DC	1948	TN	1993	Dem.			
46. Richard B. Cheney	Lincoln, NE	1941	WY	2001	Rep.			
47. Joseph R. Biden Jr.	Scranton, PA	1942	DE	2009	Dem.			
48. Michael R. Pence	Columbus, IN	1959	IN	2017	Rep.			

(1) Resigned Dec. 28, 1832, having been elected to the Senate to fill a vacancy. (2) Richard M. Johnson was the only vice president to be chosen by the Senate because of a tied vote in the Electoral College. (3) Democrat Andrew Johnson was nominated vice president by Republicans and elected with Lincoln on the National Union ticket. (4) Grandfather of Democratic candidate for president in 1952 and 1956. (5) Resigned Oct. 10, 1973, after pleading no contest to a charge of tax evasion. (6) First nonelected vice president, chosen under 25th Amendment procedure. (7) Second nonelected vice president, chosen under 25th Amendment.

Biographies of the Presidents

George Washington (1789-97), first president, Federalist, was born on Feb. 22, 1732, in Wakefield on Pope's Creek, Westmoreland Co., VA, the son of Augustine and Mary Ball Washington. He spent his early childhood on a farm near Fredericksburg. His father died when Washington was 11. He studied mathematics and surveying, and at 16, he went to live with his elder half brother, Lawrence, who built and named Mount Vernon in Virginia. Washington surveyed the lands of Thomas Fairfax in the Shenandoah Valley. He accompanied Lawrence to Barbados, West Indies, where he contracted smallpox and was deeply scarred. Lawrence died in 1752, and Washington inherited his property. He valued land, and when he died, he was a slaveholder who owned 70,000 acres in Virginia and 40,000 acres in what is now West Virginia.

Washington's military service began in 1753, when Lt. Gov. Robert Dinwiddie of Virginia sent him on missions deep into Ohio country. He clashed with the French and had to surrender Fort Necessity on July 3, 1754. He was an aide to the British general Edward Braddock and was at his side when the army was ambushed and defeated (July 9, 1755) on a march to Fort Duquesne. He helped take Fort Duquesne from the French in 1758.

After Washington's marriage to Martha Dandridge Custis, a widow, in 1759, he managed his family estate at Mount Vernon. Although not in favor of independence initially, he opposed the repressive measures of the British crown and took charge of the Virginia troops before war broke out. He was made commander of the newly created Continental Army by the Continental Congress on June 15, 1775.

The American victory was due largely to Washington's leadership. He was resourceful, a disciplinarian, and a dependable force for unity. Washington favored a federal government. He became chairman of the Constitutional Convention of 1787 and helped get the Constitution ratified. Unanimously elected president by the Electoral College, he was inaugurated Apr. 30, 1789, on the balcony of New York's Federal Hall. He was reelected in 1792. Washington made an effort to avoid partisan politics as president.

Refusing to consider a third term, Washington retired to Mount Vernon in Mar. 1797. A ride in snow and rain around his estate led to what present-day doctors believe to have been an attack of acute epiglottitis. Doctors were unsuccessful in treating the inflammation in his throat, and Washington died Dec. 14, 1799.

John Adams (1797-1801), second president, Federalist, was born on Oct. 30, 1735, in Braintree (now Quincy), MA, the son of John and Susanna Boylston Adams. He was a great-grandson of Henry Adams, who came from England in 1636. He graduated from Harvard in 1755, then taught school and studied law. He married Abigail Smith in 1764. In 1770, he successfully defended in court the British soldiers who fired on civilians in the Boston Massacre. He was a delegate to the Continental Congress and a signer of the Declaration of Independence. In 1778, Congress sent Adams and John Jay to join Benjamin Franklin as diplomatic representatives in Europe. Because he ran second to Washington in Electoral College balloting in Feb. 1789, Adams became the nation's first vice president, a post he characterized as highly insignificant; he was reelected in 1792.

In 1796 Adams was chosen president by the electors. His administration was marked by growing conflict with fellow Federalist Alexander Hamilton and with those in his cabinet who shared Hamilton's anti-French position. Adams avoided a declared war with France but became unpopular, especially after securing passage of the Alien and Sedition Acts, which restricted speech critical of the government, in 1798. His foreign policy contributed significantly to the election of Thomas Jefferson in 1800.

Adams lived for a quarter century after he left office, during which time he wrote extensively. He died July 4, 1826, on the same day as his rival Thomas Jefferson (the 50th anniversary of the Declaration of Independence).

Thomas Jefferson (1801-09), third president, Democratic-Republican, was born on Apr. 13, 1743, in Shadwell in Goochland (now Albemarle) Co., VA, the son of Peter and Jane Randolph Jefferson. His father died when Jefferson was 14, leaving him 2,750 acres and his slaves. Jefferson attended (1760-62) the College of William and Mary, read Greek and Latin classics, and played the violin. In 1769 he was elected to the Virginia House of Burgesses. In 1770 he began building his home, Monticello, and in 1772 he married Martha Wayles Skelton, a wealthy widow. Jefferson helped establish the Virginia Committee of Correspondence. As a member of the Second Continental Congress he drafted the Declaration of Independence. He also was a member of the Virginia House of Delegates (1776-79) and was elected governor of Virginia in 1779. He resigned in 1781, after British troops invaded Virginia. During his term he wrote the Virginia Statute of Religious Freedom. After his wife's death in 1782, Jefferson again became a delegate to the Congress, and in 1784 he drafted the report that was the basis for the Ordinances of 1784, 1785, and 1787. He was minister to France from 1785 to 1789, when George Washington appointed him secretary of state.

Jefferson's strong faith in the consent of the governed conflicted with the emphasis on executive control, favored by Sec. of the Treasury Alexander Hamilton, and Jefferson resigned as secretary of state on Dec. 31, 1793. In the 1796 election Jefferson was the Democratic-Republican candidate for president; John Adams won the election, and Jefferson became vice president. In 1800, Jefferson and Aaron Burr received equal numbers of Electoral College votes; the House of Representatives elected Jefferson president. Jefferson was a strong advocate of westward expansion; major events of his first term were the Louisiana Purchase (1803) and the Lewis and Clark expedition. His second term saw the passage of the Embargo Act, barring U.S. ships from setting sail to foreign ports and forbidding foreign ships from loading cargo in U.S. ports. Jefferson established the Univ. of Virginia and designed its buildings. He died July 4, 1826, on the same day as John Adams (the 50th anniversary of the Declaration of Independence).

Jefferson called slavery a "moral depravity" and violation of natural rights, but he profited from it as a slaveholder. He advocated gradual emancipation through voting, in conjunction with deportation. Based partly on DNA taken from descendants of Jefferson and of Sally Hemings, an enslaved woman who lived at Monticello from a young age, many historians conclude that Jefferson fathered one or more of her six children.

James Madison (1809-17), fourth president, Democratic-Republican, was born on Mar. 16, 1751, in Port Conway, King George Co., VA, the son of James and Eleanor Rose Conway Madison. Madison graduated from the College of New Jersey in 1771. He served in the Virginia Constitutional Convention (1776), and, in 1780, became a delegate to the Seond Continental Congress. He was chief recorder at the Constitutional Convention in 1787 and supported ratification in the *Federalist Papers*, written with Alexander Hamilton and John Jay. In 1789, Madison was elected to the House of Representatives, where he helped frame the Bill of Rights and fought against passage of the Alien and Sedition Acts. In the 1790s, he helped found the Democratic-Republican Party, which ultimately became the Democratic Party. He became Jefferson's secretary of state in 1801.

Madison was elected president in 1808. His first term was marked by tensions with Great Britain, and his conduct of foreign policy was criticized by the Federalists and by his own party. Nevertheless, he was reelected in 1812, the year war was declared on Great Britain. The war that many considered a second American revolution ended with a treaty that did not settle any of the issues. Madison's most important action after the war was demilitarizing the U.S.-Canadian border.

In 1817, Madison retired to his plantation, Montpelier, which made use of slave labor. He edited his famous papers on the Constitutional Convention and helped found the Univ. of Virginia, of which he became rector in 1826. He died June 28, 1836.

James Monroe (1817-25), fifth president, Democratic-Republican, was born on Apr. 28, 1758, in Westmoreland Co., VA, the son of Spence and Elizabeth Jones Monroe. He entered the College of William and Mary in 1774 but left to serve in the Third Virginia Regiment during the American Revolution. After the war, he studied law with Thomas Jefferson. In 1782 he was elected to the Virginia House of Delegates, and he served (1783-86) as a delegate to the Continental Congress. He opposed ratification of the Constitution because it lacked a bill of rights. Monroe was elected to the U.S. Senate in 1790. In 1794, Pres. Washington appointed Monroe minister to France. He was again minister to France (1803) under Pres. Jefferson as well as minister to Great Britain (1803-07). He served twice as governor of Virginia (1799-1802, 1811).

In 1816 Monroe was elected president; he was reelected in 1820 with all but one Electoral College vote. His administration became known as the Era of Good Feeling. He obtained Florida from Spain, settled boundary disputes with Britain over Canada, and eliminated border forts. Though a slaveholder himself, he supported the antislavery position that led to the Missouri Compromise. His most significant contribution was the Monroe Doctrine, which opposed European intervention in the Western Hemisphere and became a cornerstone of U.S. foreign policy.

Although Monroe retired to Oak Hill, VA, financial problems forced him to sell his property and move to New York City. He died there on July 4, 1831.

John Quincy Adams (1825-29), sixth president, independent Federalist, later Democratic-Republican, was born on July 11, 1767, in Braintree (now Quincy), MA, the son of John and Abigail Adams. His father was the second president. He studied abroad and at Harvard College, from which he graduated in 1787. In 1803, he was elected to the U.S. Senate. President Monroe chose him as his secretary of state in 1817. In this capacity he negotiated the cession of Florida from Spain, supported exclusion of slavery in the Missouri Compromise, and helped formulate the Monroe Doctrine.

After no candidate won an Electoral College majority in 1824, the presidential election was decided by the House of Representatives. Adams won with support from rival Henry Clay, whom he named secretary of state, fueling accusations of a "corrupt bargain." His expansion of executive powers was strongly opposed, and in the 1828 election he lost to Andrew Jackson. In 1831 he entered the House of Representatives and served 17 years. He opposed slavery, the annexation of Texas, and the Mexican War. He helped establish the Smithsonian Institution.

Adams suffered a stroke in the House and died in the Speaker's Room on Feb. 23, 1848.

Andrew Jackson (1829-37), seventh president, Democratic-Republican, later a Democrat, was born on Mar. 15, 1767, in the Waxhaw district, on the border of North and South Carolina, the son of Andrew and Elizabeth Hutchinson Jackson. At the age of 13, he joined the militia to fight in the American Revolution and was captured. Orphaned at age 14, Jackson was raised by an uncle. By age 20, he was practicing law, and he later served as prosecuting attorney in Nashville, TN. In 1796 he helped draft the constitution of Tennessee, and for a year he occupied its one seat in the House of Representatives. The next year he served in the U.S. Senate.

In the War of 1812, Jackson crushed the Creek Indians at Horseshoe Bend, AL (1814), and, with a greatly outnumbered army consisting chiefly of militia members, privateers, Choctaw Indians, and other volunteer fighters, defeated Gen. Edward Pakenham's British troops at the Battle of New Orleans (1815). Nicknamed "Old Hickory" for his toughness, he emerged a national hero.

In 1818 Jackson briefly invaded Spanish Florida to quell Seminoles and outlaws who harassed frontier settlements. He ran for president against John Quincy Adams in 1824, but did not achieve a majority despite winning the most popular and electoral votes. The House of Representatives decided the election and chose Adams. In the 1828 election, however, Jackson, a slaveholder, defeated Adams by carrying the West and the South.

As president, Jackson introduced what became known as the spoils system—rewarding party members with government posts. A self-professed champion of the common man, he also viewed the Second Bank of the U.S. as a bastion of privilege and made it a major issue in the election of 1832, the first where candidates were chosen at national conventions rather than in congressional caucuses. Defeating Henry Clay, Jackson increasingly diverted funds from the national bank into so-called pet banks run by members of his own party. When South Carolina refused to collect imports under a federal tariff, which it declared null and void, Jackson won passage of legislation confirming his right to use military force to obtain compliance; eventually the tariff rate was reduced and the nullifiers backed down. After leaving office in 1837, he retired to the Hermitage, his estate outside Nashville, where he died on June 8, 1845.

Martin Van Buren (1837-41), eighth president, Democrat, was born on Dec. 5, 1782, in Kinderhook, NY, the son of Abraham and Maria Hoes Van Buren. After attending local schools, he studied law and became a lawyer at the age of 20. A consummate politician, Van Buren began his career in the New York state senate and then served as state attorney general (1816-19). He was elected to the U.S. Senate in 1821. He helped swing Eastern support to Andrew Jackson in the 1828 election and served as Jackson's secretary of state from 1829 to 1831. In 1832 he was elected vice president. Known as the "Little Magician," Van Buren was extremely influential in Jackson's administration.

In 1836, Van Buren defeated William Henry Harrison for president and took office as the financial panic of 1837 initiated a nationwide depression. Although he instituted the independent treasury system, his refusal to spend land revenues led to his defeat by William Henry Harrison in 1840. In 1844 he lost the Democratic nomination to James K. Polk. In 1848 he again ran for president on the Free Soil ticket but lost. He died in Kinderhook on July 24, 1862.

William Henry Harrison (1841), ninth president, Whig, who served only 31 days, was born on Feb. 9, 1773, in Berkeley, Charles City Co., VA, the son of Benjamin Harrison—a signer of the Declaration of Independence—and of Elizabeth Bassett Harrison. He attended Hampden-Sydney College. Harrison served as secretary of the Northwest Territory in 1798 and was its delegate to the House of Representatives in 1799. He was the first governor of Indiana Territory and served as superintendent of Indian affairs. Leading some 950 troops, he repelled an attack by Shawnee Indians at Tippecanoe, IN, on Nov. 7, 1811. A generation later, in 1840, he waged a rousing presidential campaign using the slogan "Tippecanoe and Tyler Too." The Tyler of the slogan was his running mate, John Tyler.

Although born to one of the wealthiest, most prestigious, and most influential families in Virginia, Harrison also campaigned with the slogan "Log Cabin and Hard Cider." He died Apr. 4, 1841, after only one month in office, of what doctors now believe was typhoid fever.

John Tyler (1841-45), 10th president, independent Whig, was born on Mar. 29, 1790, in Greenway, Charles City Co., VA, the son of John and Mary Armistead Tyler. His father was governor of Virginia (1808-11). Tyler graduated from the College of William and Mary in 1807 and in 1811 was elected to the Virginia legislature. In 1816 he was chosen for the U.S. House of Representatives. He served in the Virginia legislature again from 1823 to 1825, when he was elected governor of Virginia. After a stint in the U.S. Senate (1827-36), he was elected vice president (1840).

When William Henry Harrison died only a month after taking office, Tyler succeeded him. Because he was the first person to occupy the presidency without having been elected to that office, he was referred to as "His Accidency." He gained passage of the Preemption Act of 1841, which gave squatters on government land the right to buy 160 acres at the minimum auction price. His last act as president was to sign a resolution annexing Texas. Tyler accepted renomination in 1844 from some Democrats but withdrew in favor of the official party candidate, James K. Polk. A slaveholder who consistently supported its expansion, he served briefly in the Confederate House of Representatives before he died in Richmond, VA, on Jan. 18, 1862.

James Knox Polk (1845-49), 11th president, Democrat, was born on Nov. 2, 1795, in Mecklenburg Co., NC, the son of Samuel and Jane Knox Polk. He graduated from the Univ. of North Carolina in 1818 and served in the Tennessee state legislature from 1823 to 1825. He served in the U.S. House of Representatives from 1825 to 1839, the last four years as Speaker. He was governor of Tennessee from 1839 to 1841. In 1844, after the Democratic National Convention became deadlocked, it nominated Polk, who became the first "dark horse" candidate for president. He was nominated primarily because he favored annexation of Texas and tolerated slavery.

As president, Polk reestablished the independent treasury system originated by Van Buren. He was so intent on acquiring California from Mexico that he sent troops to the Mexican border and declared a state of war after Mexicans attacked. The Mexican War ended with the annexation of California and much of the Southwest as part of America's "manifest destiny." Polk compromised on the Oregon boundary ("54-40 or fight!") by accepting the 49th parallel and yielding Vancouver Island to the British. Polk died in Nashville, TN, on June 15, 1849, a few months after leaving office.

Zachary Taylor (1849-50), 12th president, Whig, who served only 16 months, was born on Nov. 24, 1784, in Orange Co., VA, the son of Richard and Sarah Strother Taylor. He grew up on his father's plantation near Louisville, KY, where the work was done by enslaved persons and he was educated by private tutors. In 1808 Taylor joined the regular army and was commissioned first lieutenant. He fought in the War of 1812, the Black Hawk War (1832), and the second Seminole War (beginning in 1837). He was called "Old Rough and Ready" for his military prowess. In 1846 Pres. Polk sent him with an army to the Rio Grande. When the Mexicans attacked him, Polk declared war. Outnumbered four to one, Taylor defeated Antonio López de Santa Anna at Buena Vista (1847).

A national hero, Taylor received the Whig nomination in 1848 and was elected president, even though he had never bothered to vote. He resumed the spoils system and, though a slaveholder, worked to admit California as a free state. He fell ill, likely from a case of acute gastroenteritis, and died in office on July 9, 1850.

Millard Fillmore (1850-53), 13th president, Whig, was born on Jan. 7, 1800, in Cayuga Co., NY, the son of Nathaniel and Phoebe Millard Fillmore. Although he had little schooling, he became a law clerk at the age of 22 and was admitted to the bar a year later. He was elected to the New York state assembly in 1828 and served until 1831. From 1833 until 1835 and again from 1837 to 1843, he represented his district in the U.S. House of Representatives. He opposed the entrance of Texas as a slave state and voted for a protective tariff. In 1844 he was defeated for governor of New York.

In 1848, he was elected vice president; he became president after Taylor's death. Fillmore favored the Compromise of 1850 and signed the Fugitive Slave Law. His policies pleased neither expansionists nor slaveholders, and he was not renominated in 1852. In 1856 he was nominated by the American (Know-Nothing) Party, but despite the support of the Whigs, he was defeated by James Buchanan. He died in Buffalo, NY, on Mar. 8, 1874.

Franklin Pierce (1853-57), 14th president, Democrat, was born on Nov. 23, 1804, in Hillsboro, NH, the son of Benjamin Pierce, Revolutionary War general and governor of New Hampshire, and Anna Kendrick. He graduated from Bowdoin College in 1824 and was admitted to the bar in 1827. He was elected to the New Hampshire state legislature in 1829 and was chosen Speaker in 1831. He went to the U.S. House in 1833 and was elected a U.S. senator in 1837. He enlisted in the Mexican War and became brigadier general under Gen. Winfield Scott.

In 1852 Pierce was nominated as the Democratic presidential candidate on the 49th ballot. He decisively defeated Gen. Scott, his Whig opponent, in the election. Although he was against slavery, Pierce was influenced by proslavery Southerners. He supported the controversial Kansas-Nebraska Act, which left the question of slavery in the new territories of Kansas and Nebraska to popular vote. Pierce signed a reciprocity treaty with Canada and approved the Gadsden Purchase, from Mexico, of a border area on a proposed railroad route. Denied renomination, he spent most of his remaining years in Concord, NH, where he died on Oct. 8, 1869.

James Buchanan (1857-61), 15th president, Federalist, later Democrat, was born on Apr. 23, 1791, near Mercersburg, PA, the son of James and Elizabeth Speer Buchanan. He graduated from Dickinson College in 1809 and was admitted to the bar in 1812. He fought in the War of 1812 as a volunteer. He was twice elected to the Pennsylvania general assembly, and in 1821 he entered the U.S. House of Representatives. After briefly serving (1832-33) as minister to Russia, he was elected U.S. senator from Pennsylvania. As Polk's secretary of state (1845-49), he ended the Oregon dispute with Britain and supported the Mexican War and annexation of Texas. As minister to Great Britain, he signed the Ostend Manifesto (1854), declaring a U.S. right to take Cuba by force should efforts to purchase it fail.

Nominated by Democrats, Buchanan was elected president in 1856. On slavery he favored popular sovereignty and choice by state constitutions but did not consistently uphold this position. He denied the right of states to secede but opposed coercion and attempted to keep peace by not provoking secessionists. Buchanan left office having failed to deal decisively with the situation. He died at Wheatland, his estate, near Lancaster, PA, on June 1, 1868.

Abraham Lincoln (1861-65), 16th president, Whig, then Republican, was born on Feb. 12, 1809, in a log cabin on a farm in Hardin (now Larue) Co., KY, the son of Thomas and Nancy Hanks Lincoln. The Lincolns moved to Spencer Co., IN, near Gentryville, when Lincoln was 7. After Lincoln's mother died, his father married Mrs. Sarah Bush Johnston in 1819. In 1830 the family moved to Macon Co., IL.

Defeated in 1832 in a race for the state legislature, Lincoln was elected on the Whig ticket two years later and served in the lower house from 1834 to 1842. In 1837 Lincoln was admitted to the bar and became partner in a Springfield, IL, law office. In 1846, he was elected to Congress, where he attracted attention during a single term for his opposition to the Mexican War and his position on slavery. In 1856 he campaigned for the newly founded Republican Party, and in 1858 he became its senatorial candidate against Stephen A. Douglas. Although he lost the election, Lincoln gained national recognition from his debates with Douglas.

In 1860, Lincoln was nominated for president by the Republican Party on a platform of restricting slavery. He ran against Douglas, a northern Democrat; John C. Breckinridge, a Southern proslavery Democrat; and John Bell, of the Constitutional Union Party. In response to Lincoln's victory, South Carolina seceded from the Union on Dec. 20, 1860, soon followed by six other Southern states.

The Civil War erupted when South Carolina's Fort Sumter, which Lincoln decided to resupply, was attacked by Confederate forces on Apr. 12, 1861. Lincoln called for recruits from the North, and four more Southern states seceded. Hundreds of thousands of Union and Confederate soldiers were killed or wounded in four years of battle that followed. On Sept. 22, 1862, five days after the Battle of Antietam, Lincoln announced that slaves in territory then in rebellion would be free Jan. 1, 1863, under his Emancipation Proclamation. His speeches, including his Gettysburg and inaugural addresses, are remembered for their eloquence.

Lincoln was reelected, in 1864, over Gen. George B. McClellan, a Democrat. Confederate Gen. Robert E. Lee surrendered on Apr. 9, 1865. On Apr. 14, Lincoln was shot by actor John Wilkes Booth in Ford's Theater, in Washington, DC. He died the next day.

Andrew Johnson (1865-69), 17th president, Democrat, was born on Dec. 29, 1808, in Raleigh, NC, the son of Jacob and Mary McDonough Johnson. He was apprenticed to a tailor as a youth but ran away after two years and eventually settled in Greeneville, TN, where he was elected councilman and later mayor. In 1835 he was sent to the state general assembly. In 1843 he was elected to the U.S. House of Representatives, where he served for 10 years. Johnson was also governor of Tennessee from 1853 to 1857, when he was elected to the U.S. Senate.

Although Johnson had held slaves, he opposed secession and tried to prevent Tennessee from seceding. In Mar. 1862, Lincoln appointed him military governor of occupied Tennessee.

In 1864, in order to balance Lincoln's ticket with a Southern Democrat, the Republicans nominated Johnson for vice president. He was elected vice president with Lincoln and succeeded to the presidency upon Lincoln's death. Soon afterward, in conflict with Congress over the president's power over the South, he proclaimed an amnesty to all Confederates, except certain leaders, if they would ratify the 13th Amendment abolishing slavery. States doing so added anti-Negro provisions that enraged Congress, which restored military control over the South. When Johnson removed Sec. of War Edwin M. Stanton without notifying the Senate, the House impeached him in Feb. 1868 on the charge of violating the Tenure of Office Act. In reality, the House was responding to his opposition to harsh congressional Reconstruction, expressed in repeated vetoes. He was acquitted in the Senate by one-vote margins on each of two counts.

Johnson was denied renomination but remained politically active. He was reelected to the Senate in 1874. Johnson died July 31, 1875, at Carter Station, TN.

Ulysses S. Grant (1869-77), 18th president, Republican, was born on Apr. 27, 1822, in Point Pleasant, OH, the son of Jesse R. and Hannah Simpson Grant. The next year the family moved to Georgetown, OH. Grant was named Hiram Ulysses. Upon entering West Point in 1839, he found his name had been put down as Ulysses S. Grant, with his middle name first and his mother's maiden name as his middle name. He eventually adopted it as his true name but maintained the "S" did not stand for anything. Grant graduated in 1843.

During the Mexican War, Grant served under both Gen. Zachary Taylor and Gen. Winfield Scott. In 1854, he resigned his commission because of loneliness and drinking problems, and in the following years he engaged in generally unsuccessful farming and business ventures. With the start of the Civil War, he was named colonel and then brigadier general of the Illinois Volunteers. He took Forts Henry and Donelson and fought at Shiloh. His brilliant campaign against Vicksburg and his victory at Chattanooga made him so prominent that Lincoln placed him in command of all Union armies. Grant accepted Confederate Gen. Robert E. Lee's surrender at Appomattox Court House on Apr. 9, 1865.

Grant was nominated for president by the Republicans in 1868 and elected over Democrat Horatio Seymour. The 15th Amendment, the amnesty bill, and peaceful settlement of disputes with Great Britain were events of his administration. The Liberal Republicans and Democrats opposed him with Horace Greeley in the 1872 election, but Grant was reelected. His second administration was marked by scandals, including the Crédit Mobilier affair, the Whiskey Ring, in which high-ranked officials conspired to defraud the government of taxes, and the impeachment of his secretary of war. An attempt by the Stalwarts (Old Guard Republicans) to nominate him in 1880 failed. Left penniless by the 1884 collapse of an investment firm in which he was a partner, he wrote his well-regarded memoirs while suffering from cancer to provide income for his family. He died at Mt. McGregor, NY, on July 23, 1885.

Rutherford Birchard Hayes (1877-81), 19th president, Republican, was born on Oct. 4, 1822, in Delaware, OH, the son of Rutherford and Sophia Birchard Hayes. He was reared by his uncle, Sardis Birchard. Hayes graduated from Kenyon College in 1842 and from Harvard Law School in 1845. He practiced law in Lower Sandusky (now Fremont), OH, and was city solicitor of Cincinnati from 1858 to 1861. During the Civil War, he was major of the 23rd Ohio Volunteers. He was wounded several times, and by the end of the war he had risen to the rank of brevet major general. While serving (1865-67) in the U.S. House of Representatives, Hayes supported Reconstruction and Johnson's impeachment. He was twice elected governor of Ohio (1867, 1869). After losing a race for the U.S. House in 1872, he was reelected governor of Ohio in 1875.

In 1876, Hayes was nominated for president. He believed he had lost the election to Democrat Samuel J. Tilden. But a few Southern states submitted two sets of electoral votes, and the result was in dispute. An electoral commission, consisting of 8 Republicans and 7 Democrats, awarded all disputed votes to Hayes, allowing him to become president by one electoral vote. Hayes, keeping a promise to Southerners, withdrew troops from areas still occupied in the South, ending the era of Reconstruction. He proposed civil service reforms, alienating those favoring the spoils system, and advocated repeal of the Tenure of Office Act restricting presidential power to dismiss officials. He supported sound money and specie payments.

Hayes died in Fremont, OH, on Jan. 17, 1893.

James Abram Garfield (1881), 20th president, Republican, was born on Nov. 19, 1831, in Orange, Cuyahoga Co., OH, the son of Abram and Eliza Ballou Garfield. His father died in 1833, and he was reared in poverty by his mother. He worked as a canal bargeman, a farmer, and a carpenter. He attended Western Reserve Eclectic Institute and graduated from Williams College in 1856. He returned to Western Reserve to teach and in 1857, at age 25, he became the school's president. In 1859 he was elected to the Ohio legislature. Antislavery and antisecession, he volunteered for military service in the Civil War, becoming colonel of the 42nd Ohio Infantry and brigadier in 1862. He fought at Shiloh, TN, was chief of staff for Gen. William Starke Rosecrans, and was made major general for gallantry at Chickamauga, GA. He entered Congress as a radical Republican in 1863, calling for execution or exile of Confederate leaders, but he moderated his views after the Civil War. On the electoral commission in 1877 he voted for Hayes against Tilden on strict party lines.

Garfield was a senator-elect in 1880 when he became the Republican nominee for president. He was chosen as a compromise over Gen. Grant, James G. Blaine, and John Sherman, and won election despite some bitterness among Grant's supporters. For much of his brief tenure as president, Garfield was concerned with a fight with New York Sen. Roscoe Conkling, who opposed two major appointments made by Garfield. On July 2, 1881, Garfield was shot and seriously wounded by a mentally disturbed office seeker, Charles J. Guiteau, while entering a railroad station in Washington, DC. He died on Sept. 19, 1881, in Elberon, NJ.

Chester Alan Arthur (1881-85), 21st president, Republican, was born on Oct. 5, 1829, in Fairfield, VT, to William and Malvina Stone Arthur. He graduated from Union College in 1848, taught school in Vermont, then studied law and practiced in New York City. In 1853, he argued in a fugitive slave case that slaves transported through New York State were thereby freed. In 1871, he was appointed collector of the Port of New York. Pres. Hayes, an opponent of the spoils system, forced him to resign in 1878. This made the New York machine enemies of Hayes. Arthur and the Stalwarts (Old Guard Republicans) tried to nominate Grant for a third term as president in 1880. When Garfield was nominated, Arthur was nominated for vice president in the interests of harmony.

Upon Garfield's assassination, Arthur became president. Despite his past connections, he signed major civil service reform legislation. Arthur tried to dissuade Congress from enacting the high protective tariff of 1883. He was defeated for renomination in 1884 by James G. Blaine. He died in New York City on Nov. 18, 1886.

Grover Cleveland (1885-89; 1893-97) *(According to a State Dept. ruling, Grover Cleveland should be counted as both the 22nd and the 24th president because his two terms were not consecutive)*, Democrat, was born Stephen Grover Cleveland on Mar. 18, 1837, in Caldwell, NJ, the son of Richard F. and Ann Neal Cleveland. When he was a small boy, his family moved to New York. Prevented by his father's death from attending college, he studied on his own and was admitted to the bar in Buffalo, NY, in 1859. In succession he became assistant district attorney (1863), sheriff (1871), mayor (1881), and governor of New York (1882). He was an independent, honest administrator who hated corruption. Cleveland was nominated for president over opposition from New York City's Tammany Hall in 1884 and defeated Republican James G. Blaine.

As president, he enlarged the civil service and vetoed many pension raids on the Treasury. In the 1888 election he was defeated by Benjamin Harrison, although his popular vote was larger. Reelected over Harrison in 1892, he faced a money crisis brought about by a lowered gold reserve, circulation of paper, and exorbitant silver purchases under the Sherman Silver Purchase Act. He obtained a repeal of the Sherman Act but was unable to secure effective tariff reform. A severe economic depression and labor troubles racked his administration, but he refused to interfere in business matters and rejected business owner Jacob Coxey's demand for unemployment relief. In 1894, he broke the Pullman strike. Cleveland was not renominated in 1896. He died in Princeton, NJ, on June 24, 1908.

Benjamin Harrison (1889-93), 23rd president, Republican, was born on Aug. 20, 1833, in North Bend, OH, the son of John Scott and Elizabeth Irwin Harrison. His great-grandfather, Benjamin Harrison, was a signer of the Declaration of Independence; his grandfather, William Henry Harrison, was the ninth president; his father was a member of Congress. He attended school on his father's farm and graduated from Miami Univ. in Oxford, OH, in 1852. He was admitted to the bar in 1854 and practiced in Indianapolis, IN. During the Civil War, he rose to the rank of brevet brigadier general and fought at Kennesaw Mountain, Peachtree Creek, Nashville, and in the Atlanta campaign. He lost the 1876 gubernatorial election in Indiana but succeeded in becoming a U.S. senator in 1881.

In 1888 he defeated Cleveland for president despite receiving fewer popular votes. As president, he expanded the pension list and signed the McKinley high tariff bill, the Sherman Antitrust Act, and the Sherman Silver Purchase Act. During his administration, six states were admitted to the Union. He was defeated for reelection in 1892. He died in Indianapolis, IN, on Mar. 13, 1901.

William McKinley (1897-1901), 25th president, Republican, was born on Jan. 29, 1843, in Niles, OH, the son of William and Nancy Allison McKinley. McKinley briefly attended Allegheny College. When the Civil War broke out in 1861, he enlisted and served for the duration. He rose to captain and in 1865 was made brevet major. After studying law in Albany, NY, he opened a law office in Canton, OH (1867). He served twice in the U.S. House (1877-83; 1885-91) and led the fight there for the McKinley Tariff, passed in 1890; he was not reelected to the House as a result. He served two terms (1892-96) as governor of Ohio.

In 1896 he was elected president as a proponent of a protective tariff and sound money (gold standard) over William Jennings Bryan, the Democrat and a proponent of free silver. McKinley was reluctant to intervene in Cuba, but the loss of the battleship *Maine* at Havana crystallized opinion. He demanded Spain's withdrawal from Cuba; Spain made some concessions, but Congress announced a state of war as of Apr. 21, 1898. He was reelected in the 1900 campaign, defeating Bryan's anti-imperialist arguments with the promise of a "full dinner pail." He was known for a conservative stance on business issues. On Sept. 6, 1901, at the Pan-American Exposition, in Buffalo, NY, he was shot by Leon Czolgosz, an anarchist. He died Sept. 14.

Theodore Roosevelt (1901-09), 26th president, Republican, was born on Oct. 27, 1858, in New York City, the son of Theodore and Martha Bulloch Roosevelt. He was a fifth cousin of Franklin D. Roosevelt and an uncle of Eleanor Roosevelt. Roosevelt graduated from Harvard Univ. in 1880. He attended Columbia Law School briefly but abandoned law to enter politics. He was elected to the New York State Assembly in 1881 and served until 1884. He spent the next two years ranching and hunting in the Dakota Territory. In 1886, he ran unsuccessfully for mayor of New York City. He was civil service commissioner in Washington, DC, from 1889 to 1895. From 1895 to 1897, he served as New York City's police commissioner. He was assistant secretary of the Navy under McKinley. The Spanish-American War made him nationally known. He organized the First U.S. Volunteer Cavalry (Rough Riders) and, as lieutenant colonel, led the charge up Kettle Hill in San Juan, Cuba. Elected New York governor in 1898, he fought the spoils system and achieved taxation of corporation franchises.

Nominated for vice president in 1900, Roosevelt became the nation's youngest president at the age of 42 when McKinley was assassinated. He was reelected in 1904. As president he fought corruption of politics by big business, dissolved the Northern Securities Co. and others for violating antitrust laws, intervened in the 1902 coal strike on behalf of the public, obtained the Elkins Law (1903) forbidding rebates to favored corporations, and helped pass the Hepburn Railway Rate Act of 1906 (extending jurisdiction of the Interstate Commerce Commission). He helped obtain passage of the Pure Food and Drug Act (1906) and of employers' liability laws. Roosevelt vigorously organized conservation efforts. He mediated the peace between Japan and Russia in 1905, for which he won the Nobel Peace Prize. He abetted the 1903 revolution in Panama that led to U.S. acquisition of territory for the Panama Canal.

In 1908 Roosevelt obtained the nomination of William H. Taft, who was elected. Feeling that Taft had abandoned his policies, he unsuccessfully sought the nomination in 1912. He then ran on the Progressive "Bull Moose" ticket against Taft and Woodrow Wilson, splitting the Republicans and ensuring Wilson's election. During the campaign he was shot by a mentally deranged man but was not seriously wounded. In 1916, after unsuccessfully seeking the presidential nomination, he supported the Republican candidate, Charles E. Hughes. He strongly promoted U.S. intervention in World War I.

Roosevelt was a voracious reader and wrote some 40 books, including *The Winning of the West*. He died Jan. 6, 1919, at Sagamore Hill, his home in Oyster Bay, NY.

William Howard Taft (1909-13), 27th president, Republican, and 10th chief justice of the U.S., was born on Sept. 15, 1857, in Cincinnati, OH, the son of Alphonso and Louisa Maria Torrey Taft. His father was secretary of war and attorney general in Grant's cabinet and minister to Austria and Russia under Arthur. Taft graduated from Yale in 1878 and from Cincinnati Law School in 1880. After working as a law reporter for Cincinnati newspapers, he served as assistant prosecuting attorney (1881-82), assistant county solicitor (1885), superior court judge (1887), U.S. solicitor-general (1890), and federal circuit judge (1892). In 1900 he became head of the U.S. Philippines Commission and was the first civil governor of the Philippines (1901-04). In 1904 he served as secretary of war, and in 1906 he was sent to Cuba to help avert a threatened revolution.

Taft was groomed for the presidency by Theodore Roosevelt and elected over William Jennings Bryan in 1908. Taft vigorously continued Roosevelt's trust-busting, instituted the Dept. of Labor, and drafted amendments calling for direct election of senators and an income tax. However, his tariff and conservation policies angered progressives. Although renominated in 1912, he was opposed by Roosevelt, who ran on the Progressive Party ticket; the result was Wilson's election.

Taft, with reservations, supported the League of Nations. After leaving office, he was professor of constitutional law at Yale (1913-21) and chief justice of the U.S. (1921-30). Taft was the only person to have been both president and chief justice. He died in Washington, DC, on Mar. 8, 1930.

(Thomas) Woodrow Wilson (1913-21), 28th president, Democrat, was born on Dec. 28, 1856, in Staunton, VA, the son of Joseph Ruggles and Janet (Jessie) Woodrow Wilson. He grew up in Georgia and South Carolina. He attended Davidson College in North Carolina before graduating from Princeton Univ. in 1879. He studied law at the Univ. of Virginia and political science at Johns Hopkins Univ., where he received his PhD in 1886. He taught at Bryn Mawr (1885-88) and at Wesleyan (1888-90) before joining the faculty at Princeton. He was president of Princeton from 1902 until 1910, when he was elected governor of New Jersey. In 1912 he was nominated for president with the aid of William Jennings Bryan, who sought to block James "Champ" Clark and New York City's Tammany Hall. Wilson won because Theodore Roosevelt, running as a "Bull Moose" Progressive, siphoned votes away from Republican candidate Taft.

As president, Wilson protected American interests in revolutionary Mexico and fought for American rights on the high seas. He oversaw the creation of the Federal Reserve system, cut the tariff, and developed a reputation as a reformer. His sharp warnings to Germany led to the resignation of his secretary of state, Bryan, a pacifist. In 1916 he was reelected by a slim margin with the slogan "He kept us out of war," although his attempts to mediate in the war failed. After several American ships were sunk by the Germans, he secured a declaration of war against Germany on Apr. 6, 1917.

Wilson outlined his peace program on Jan. 8, 1918, in the Fourteen Points, a state paper that enunciated a doctrine of self-determination for the settlement of territorial disputes. The Germans accepted his terms and an armistice on Nov. 11, 1918. Wilson went to Paris to help negotiate the peace treaty, the crux of which he considered the League of Nations. The Senate demanded reservations that would not make the U.S. subordinate to the votes of other nations in case of war. Wilson refused and toured the country to get support. After he suffered a severe stroke in Oct. 1919, his wife, Edith Wilson, concealed the extent of his infirmity, controlled access to him, and in effect largely acted in his place.

Wilson was awarded the 1919 Nobel Peace Prize, but the treaty embodying the League of Nations was ultimately rejected by the Senate in 1920. He left the White House in Mar. 1921. He died in Washington, DC, on Feb. 3, 1924.

Warren Gamaliel Harding (1921-23), 29th president, Republican, was born on Nov. 2, 1865, near Corsica (now Blooming Grove), OH, the son of George Tyron and Phoebe Elizabeth Dickerson Harding. He attended Ohio Central College, studied law, and became editor and publisher of a county newspaper. He entered the political arena as state senator (1901-04) and then served as lieutenant governor (1904-06). In 1910 he ran unsuccessfully for governor of Ohio; in 1914 he was elected to the U.S. Senate. In the Senate he voted for antistrike legislation, women's suffrage, and the Volstead Prohibition Enforcement Act over Pres. Wilson's veto. He opposed the League of Nations.

In 1920 he was nominated for president and defeated James M. Cox in the election. The Republicans capitalized on war weariness and fear that Wilson's League of Nations would curtail U.S. sovereignty. Harding stressed a return to "normalcy" and worked for tariff revision and the repeal of excess profits law and high income taxes. In the so-called Teapot Dome scandal, his secretary of the interior, Albert B. Fall, resigned and was later convicted of accepting bribes in the leasing of government-owned oil reserves to private companies.

As rumors began to circulate about the corruption in his administration, Harding fell ill after a trip to Alaska, and he died suddenly of a likely heart attack in San Francisco on Aug. 2,

1923. Harding's letters to a longtime mistress were made public by the Library of Congress in 2014, and DNA evidence in 2015 confirmed another mistress's claim that he had fathered her daughter.

(John) Calvin Coolidge (1923-29), 30th president, Republican, was born on July 4, 1872, in Plymouth Notch, VT, the son of John Calvin and Victoria J. Moor Coolidge. Coolidge graduated from Amherst College in 1895. He entered Republican state politics and served as mayor of Northampton, MA, as state senator, as lieutenant governor, and, in 1919, as governor. In Sept. 1919, Coolidge attained national prominence by calling out the state guard in the Boston police strike. He declared, "There is no right to strike against the public safety by anybody, anywhere, anytime." This brought his name before the Republican convention of 1920, where he was nominated for vice president.

Coolidge succeeded to the presidency on Harding's death. As president, he opposed the League of Nations and the soldiers' bonus bill, which was passed over his veto. In 1924 he was elected to the presidency by a huge majority. He substantially reduced the national debt. He twice vetoed legislation to aid financially hard-pressed farmers.

With Republicans eager to renominate him, Coolidge simply announced on Aug. 2, 1927, "I do not choose to run for president in 1928." He died in Northampton, MA, on Jan. 5, 1933.

Herbert Clark Hoover (1929-33), 31st president, Republican, was born on Aug. 10, 1874, in West Branch, IA, the son of Jesse Clark and Hulda Randall Minthorn Hoover. Hoover grew up in Indian Territory (now Oklahoma) and Oregon and graduated from Stanford Univ. with a degree in geology in 1895. He worked briefly with the U.S. Geological Survey and then managed mines in Australia, Asia, Europe, and Africa. While chief engineer of imperial mines in China, he directed food relief for victims of the Boxer Rebellion. He gained a reputation not only as an engineer but as a humanitarian as he directed the American Relief Committee, London (1914-15) and the U.S. Commission for Relief in Belgium (1915-19). He was U.S. Food Administrator (1917-19), American Relief Administrator (1918-23), and in charge of Russian Relief (1918-23). He served as secretary of commerce under both Harding and Coolidge.

In 1928 Hoover was elected president over Alfred E. Smith. In 1929 the stock market crashed, and the economy collapsed. During the Great Depression, Hoover inaugurated some government assistance programs, but he was opposed to administration of aid through a federal bureaucracy. As the effects of the Depression continued, he was defeated in the 1932 election by Franklin D. Roosevelt. Hoover remained active after leaving office. Pres. Truman named him coordinator of the European Food Program (1946) and chairman of the Commission on Organization of the Executive Branch (1947-49); he was later appointed by Pres. Eisenhower to serve in the same role (1953-55).

Hoover died in New York City on Oct. 20, 1964.

Franklin Delano Roosevelt (1933-45), 32nd president, Democrat, was born on Jan. 30, 1882, in Hyde Park, NY, the son of James and Sara Delano Roosevelt, and a fifth cousin of former Pres. Theodore Roosevelt. He graduated from Harvard Univ. in 1903. He attended Columbia University Law School without taking a degree and was admitted to the New York State bar in 1907. His political career began when he was elected to the New York State senate in 1910. In 1913 Pres. Wilson appointed him assistant secretary of the navy, a post he held during World War I.

In 1920 Roosevelt ran for vice president with James Cox and was defeated. From 1921 to 1928 he worked in his New York law office and was also vice president of a bank. In Aug. 1921, he was stricken with poliomyelitis, which left his legs paralyzed. As a result of therapy, he was able to stand and walk a few steps with the aid of leg braces.

Roosevelt served two terms as governor of New York (1929-33). In 1932, Democratic convention delegate W. G. McAdoo, pledged to nominee John N. Garner, threw his votes to Roosevelt, who was nominated for president. The Depression and the promise to repeal Prohibition ensured his election. He asked for emergency powers, proclaimed the New Deal, and put into effect a vast number of administrative changes. Foremost was the use of public funds for relief and public works, resulting in deficit financing. He greatly expanded the federal government's regulation of business and by an excess profits tax and progressive income taxes produced a redistribution of earnings on an unprecedented scale. He also promoted legislation establishing the Social Security system. He was the last president inaugurated on Mar. 4 (1933) and the first inaugurated on Jan. 20 (1937).

Roosevelt was the first president to use radio for "fireside chats." When the Supreme Court nullified some New Deal laws, he sought power to "pack" the Court with additional justices, but Congress refused to give him the authority. He was the first president to break the no-third-term tradition (1940) and was elected to a fourth term in 1944 despite failing health.

Roosevelt was openly hostile to fascist governments before World War II and launched a lend-lease program on behalf of the Allies. With British Prime Min. Winston Churchill he wrote a declaration of principles to be followed after Nazi defeat (the Atlantic Charter of Aug. 14, 1941) and urged the Four Freedoms (freedom of speech, of worship, from want, from fear) Jan. 6, 1941. After Japan attacked Pearl Harbor on Dec. 7, 1941, the U.S. entered the war. Roosevelt guided the nation through the war and conferred with allied heads of state but did not live to see the end of the war. He died of a cerebral hemorrhage in Warm Springs, GA, on Apr. 12, 1945.

Harry S. Truman (1945-53), 33rd president, Democrat, was born on May 8, 1884, in Lamar, MO, the son of John Anderson and Martha Ellen Young Truman. A family disagreement over whether his middle name should be Shipp or Solomon, after his two grandfathers, resulted in his using only the middle initial S. After graduating from high school (1901) in Independence, MO, he worked in the mailroom of the *Kansas City Star*, as a railroad timekeeper, and as a clerk in Kansas City banks until about 1905. He ran his family's farm from 1906 to 1917, then served in France during World War I. After the war he opened a haberdashery, was a judge on the Jackson Co. Court (1922-24), and attended Kansas City School of Law (1923-25).

Truman was elected to the U.S. Senate in 1934 and reelected in 1940. In 1944, with Roosevelt's backing, he was nominated for vice president and elected. On Roosevelt's death in 1945, Truman became president. In 1948, in a famous upset victory, he defeated Republican Thomas E. Dewey to win a new term.

Truman authorized the first uses of the atomic bomb (Hiroshima and Nagasaki, Aug. 6 and 9, 1945), bringing World War II to a rapid end. He was responsible for what came to be called the Truman Doctrine to aid nations such as Greece and Turkey threatened by Communist takeover, and his strong commitment to NATO and to the Marshall Plan helped bring the two about. In 1948-49, he broke a Soviet blockade of West Berlin with a massive airlift. When Communist North Korea invaded South Korea (June 1950), he won UN approval for a "police action" and, without prior congressional consent, sent in forces under Gen. Douglas MacArthur. When MacArthur opposed his policy of limited objectives, Truman removed him.

He died in Kansas City, MO, on Dec. 26, 1972.

Dwight David Eisenhower (1953-61), 34th president, Republican, was born on Oct. 14, 1890, in Denison, TX, the son of David Jacob and Ida Elizabeth Stover Eisenhower, as David Dwight Eisenhower. He grew up on a small farm in Abilene, KS, and graduated from West Point in 1915. He was on the staff of Gen. Douglas MacArthur in the Philippines from 1935 to 1939. In 1942, he was made commander of Allied forces landing in North Africa; the next year he was made full general. He became supreme Allied commander in Europe that same year and led the Normandy invasion (June 6, 1944). He was subsequently given the rank of general of the Army.

On May 7, 1945, Eisenhower received the surrender of Germany at Rheims, France. He returned to the U.S. to serve as chief of staff (1945-48). His memoir, *Crusade in Europe* (1948), was a best-seller. In 1948 he became president of Columbia Univ.; in 1950 he became commander of NATO forces.

Eisenhower was nominated for president by the Republicans in 1952. He defeated Illinois Gov. Adlai E. Stevenson in the 1952 election and defeated Stevenson in 1956 to win reelection. Eisenhower called himself a moderate, favored the "free market system" versus government price and wage controls, kept government out of labor disputes, reorganized the defense establishment, and promoted missile programs. He continued foreign aid, helped negotiate a cease-fire truce in the Korean War, endorsed Taiwan and SE Asia defense treaties, backed the UN in condemning the Anglo-French raid on Egypt, and advocated the "open skies" policy of mutual inspection with the USSR. He sent U.S. troops into Little Rock, AR, in Sept. 1957, to enforce school integration.

Eisenhower died on Mar. 28, 1969, in Washington, DC.

John Fitzgerald Kennedy (1961-63), 35th president, Democrat, was born on May 29, 1917, in Brookline, MA, the son of Rose Fitzgerald Kennedy and Joseph P. Kennedy, a wealthy businessman. He graduated from Harvard Univ. in 1940. While serving in the Navy (1941-45), he commanded a PT (patrol torpedo) boat in the Solomons and won the Navy and Marine Corps Medal for heroism. In 1956, while recovering from spinal surgery, he wrote *Profiles in Courage*, which won a Pulitzer Prize in 1957. He served in the U.S. House of Representatives from 1947 to 1953 and was elected to the Senate in 1952 and 1958. In 1960, he won the Democratic nomination for president and narrowly defeated Republican Vice Pres. Richard M. Nixon. At 43 years of age, Kennedy was the youngest president ever elected to the office and the first Catholic.

Despite the image of youth and vigor he conveyed to the public, Kennedy suffered from serious medical problems, including Addison's disease and severe chronic back pain that required him to wear a back brace. The public was not aware of the extent of these problems or of his frequent sexual liaisons.

In Apr. 1961, the new Kennedy administration suffered a severe setback when an invasion force of anti-Castro Cubans, trained and directed by the CIA, failed to establish a beachhead at the Bay of Pigs in Cuba. But he weathered a major foreign crisis with his successful demand on Oct. 22, 1962, that the Soviet Union dismantle its missile bases in Cuba. Kennedy also defied Soviet attempts to force the Allies out of Berlin. He established the Peace Corps, spurred space exploration, and won passage of other "New Frontier" legislation. But Congress balked at initiatives such as medical coverage for the elderly and aid to education. After some delay he introduced major civil rights legislation, but died before it could be passed.

On Nov. 22, 1963, Kennedy was assassinated while riding in a motorcade in Dallas, TX. A commission chaired by Chief Justice Earl Warren concluded in Sept. 1964 that the sole assassin had been Lee Harvey Oswald, a former U.S. Marine and an ardent Marxist. Oswald was captured shortly after the assassination and charged but was shot dead by nightclub owner Jack Ruby while being moved to a county jail.

Lyndon Baines Johnson (1963-69), 36th president, Democrat, was born on Aug. 27, 1908, near Stonewall, TX, the son of Rebekah Baines Johnson and Sam Ealy Johnson, a state legislator. He graduated from Southwest Texas State Teachers College in 1930, with formative experience as a student teacher of underprivileged Mexican-American students in a segregated school, and briefly attended Georgetown University Law School. He taught public speaking in Houston (1930-31) and then served as secretary to Rep. R. M. Kleberg (1931-35). In 1935, Johnson became director of the Texas branch of the New Deal National Youth Administration; two years later he won an election to fill the vacancy left by the death of a U.S. representative. A tireless campaigner, he was elected in 1938 to the first of five full terms. During 1941 and 1942 he also served in the Navy. He won a U.S. Senate seat after a close 1948 primary widely regarded as marred by fraud. He rose quickly in the ranks and, after reelection in 1954, served as a skillful Senate majority leader. At the 1960 party convention he was vice president on the ticket led by the successful Democratic nominee, John F. Kennedy.

Johnson became president when Kennedy was assassinated. He was elected to a full term in 1964, defeating Sen. Barry Goldwater (R, AZ) in a landslide. Johnson won passage of landmark civil rights, anti-poverty, education (Head Start), and healthcare (Medicare, Medicaid) legislation—the "Great Society" program. However, in the face of increasing division in the nation and in his own party over his escalation of the Vietnam war, Johnson declined to seek another term.

Johnson died on Jan. 22, 1973, at his ranch in Stonewall, TX.

Richard Milhous Nixon (1969-74), 37th president, Republican, was born on Jan. 9, 1913, in Yorba Linda, CA, the son of Francis Anthony and Hannah Milhous Nixon. He graduated from Whittier College in 1934 and from Duke University Law School in 1937. After practicing law in Whittier, CA, and serving briefly in the Office of Price Administration in 1942, he entered the Navy and served in the South Pacific. Nixon was elected to the U.S. House of Representatives in 1946 and 1948. He achieved prominence as the House Un-American Activities Committee member who forced the showdown leading to the Alger Hiss perjury conviction. In 1950 he was elected to the Senate.

Nixon was elected vice president in the Eisenhower landslides of 1952 and 1956. He won the Republican nomination for president in 1960 but was narrowly defeated by John F. Kennedy. He ran unsuccessfully for governor of California in 1962. In 1968 he again won the GOP presidential nomination, then defeated Vice Pres. Hubert Humphrey for the presidency.

As president, Nixon appointed four Supreme Court justices, including the chief justice, moving the court to the right. As a New Federalist, he sought to shift greater responsibility to state and local governments. At the same time, he championed important federal initiatives, including creation of the Office of Management and Budget and the Environmental Protection Agency. The economy suffered periods of high unemployment and inflation, and he imposed wage and price controls in 1971.

In foreign affairs, Nixon dramatically altered relations with China, which he visited in 1972—the first U.S. president to do so. With adviser Henry Kissinger, he pursued détente with the Soviet Union, signing major arms limitation and other treaties and increasing trade. He began a gradual withdrawal from Vietnam, but U.S. troops remained there through his first term. He ordered an incursion into Cambodia (1970) and the bombing of Hanoi and mining of Haiphong Harbor (1972). Reelected by a large majority in Nov. 1972, he secured a Vietnam cease-fire in Jan. 1973.

Nixon's second term was cut short by scandal, after disclosures relating to a June 1972 burglary of Democratic Party headquarters in the Watergate office complex in DC. The courts and Congress sought tapes of Nixon's office conversations; Nixon claimed executive privilege, but the Supreme Court ruled against him. In July 1974, the House Judiciary Committee recommended adoption of three impeachment articles charging him with obstruction of justice, abuse of power, and contempt of Congress. On Aug. 5, he released transcripts of conversations that linked him to cover-up activities. He resigned on Aug. 9, becoming the first president ever to do so.

In later years, Nixon emerged as an elder statesman. He died Apr. 22, 1994, in New York City.

Gerald Rudolph Ford (1974-77), 38th president, Republican, was born on July 14, 1913, in Omaha, NE, the son of Leslie and Dorothy Gardner King, and was named Leslie Lynch King Jr. When he was two, his parents divorced, and he and his mother moved to Grand Rapids, MI. There she married Gerald R. Ford, who formally adopted him and gave him his name. Ford graduated from the Univ. of Michigan in 1935 and from Yale Law School in 1941. He began practicing law in Grand Rapids, but in 1942, he joined the Navy and served in the Pacific, leaving the service in 1946 as a lieutenant commander. He entered the U.S. House of Representatives in 1949 and spent 25 years in the House, eight of them as Republican leader.

On Oct. 12, 1973, after Vice Pres. Spiro T. Agnew resigned, Pres. Nixon nominated Ford to replace him. It was the first use of the procedures set out in the 25th Amendment. When Nixon resigned, Aug. 9, 1974, because of the Watergate scandal, Ford became president; he was the only president who was never elected either to the presidency or to the vice presidency.

Ford was widely credited with helping rebuild morale after the Nixon presidency, though his pardoning of Nixon for any federal crimes in office was controversial. He vetoed 48 bills in his first 21 months in office, mostly in the interest of fighting high inflation; he was less successful in curbing high unemployment. In foreign policy, he continued to pursue détente.

Ford was narrowly defeated in the 1976 election. He died Dec. 26, 2006, at home in Rancho Mirage, CA.

James Earl (Jimmy) Carter (1977-81), 39th president, Democrat, was the first president from the Deep South since before the Civil War. He was born on Oct. 1, 1924, in Plains, GA, the son of James and Lillian Gordy Carter. Carter graduated from the U.S. Naval Academy in 1946 and in 1952 entered the Navy's nuclear submarine program as an aide to Capt. (later Adm.) Hyman Rickover. He studied nuclear physics at Union College. Carter's father died in 1953, and he left the Navy to take over the family peanut farming businesses. He served in the Georgia state senate (1963-67) and as governor of Georgia (1971-75). In 1976, Carter won the Democratic nomination and defeated Pres. Gerald R. Ford.

On taking office, Carter pardoned all Vietnam draft evaders. He played a major role in the negotiations leading to the 1979 peace treaty between Israel and Egypt, and he won passage of new treaties with Panama providing for U.S. control of the Panama Canal to end in 2000. Carter was widely criticized, however, for the poor state of the economy and was viewed by some as weak in handling foreign policy. In Nov. 1979, Iranian student militants attacked the U.S. embassy in Tehran and held members of the embassy staff hostage. Efforts to obtain release of the hostages were a major preoccupation for the rest of his term. He reacted to the Soviet invasion of Afghanistan by imposing a grain embargo and boycotting the Moscow Olympic Games.

Carter was defeated by Ronald Reagan in the 1980 election. The 52 American hostages in Iran were finally released on inauguration day, 1981, just after Reagan officially became president. After leaving office, Carter played an active role in diplomatic and humanitarian efforts around the world, especially through the Carter Center, which he founded with his wife, Rosalynn, in 1982. He was awarded the Nobel Peace Prize in 2002.

Ronald Wilson Reagan (1981-89), 40th president, Republican, was born on Feb. 6, 1911, in Tampico, IL, the son of John Edward and Nellie Wilson Reagan. Reagan graduated from Eureka College in 1932, after which he worked as a sports announcer. He began a successful career as a movie actor in 1937. During World War II Reagan served in the Army Air Force, making training films. He was president of the Screen Actors Guild in 1947-52 and in 1959-60. Reagan served two terms as California governor (1967-75).

In 1980, Reagan gained the Republican presidential nomination and won a landslide victory over Jimmy Carter. He was easily reelected in 1984. Reagan forged a bipartisan coalition in Congress, which led to enactment of his program of large-scale tax cuts, cutbacks in many government programs, and a major defense buildup. He signed a Social Security reform bill designed to provide for the long-term solvency of the system. In 1986, he signed into law a major tax-reform bill. He was shot and seriously wounded in 1981 by John Hinckley, who was tried and found not guilty by reason of insanity.

In 1982, the U.S. joined France and Italy in maintaining a peacekeeping force in Beirut, Lebanon; the next year Reagan sent a task force to invade Grenada after two Marxist coups on the island. Reagan's opposition to international terrorism led to the U.S. bombing of Libyan military installations in 1986. He strongly supported El Salvador, the Nicaraguan contras, and other anticommunist governments and forces throughout the world. He also held four summit meetings with Soviet leader Mikhail Gorbachev and signed a treaty in 1987 eliminating short- and medium-range missiles from Europe.

In 1986, it was revealed that the U.S. had sold weapons through Israeli brokers to Iran in exchange for the release of U.S. hostages being held in Lebanon and that subsequently some of the money had been illegally diverted to the Nicaraguan contras. The scandal led to the resignation of leading White House aides, but no proof of Reagan's involvement was discovered. As Reagan left office in Jan. 1989, the nation was experiencing its sixth consecutive year of economic prosperity, while also piling up large budget deficits.

In 1994, Reagan revealed that he was suffering from Alzheimer's disease. He died on June 5, 2004, in Los Angeles, CA.

George Herbert Walker Bush (1989-93), 41st president, Republican, was born June 12, 1924, in Milton, MA, the son of U.S. Sen. Prescott Bush (R, CT, 1952-63) and Dorothy Walker Bush. He saw combat as a Navy pilot in World War II and was awarded the Distinguished Flying Cross. After graduating from Yale Univ. in 1948, he settled in Texas, where he helped found an oil company. After losing a bid for a U.S. Senate seat in 1964, he was elected to the House of Representatives in 1966 and 1968. He lost a second Senate race in 1970. Subsequently he served as U.S. ambassador to the United Nations (1971-73), head of the U.S. Liaison Office in Beijing (1974-75), and CIA director (1976-77). Following an unsuccessful bid for the 1980 Republican presidential nomination, Bush became Ronald Reagan's running mate, and served as vice president (1981-89).

In 1988, Bush, as the GOP presidential nominee, defeated Gov. Michael Dukakis (D, MA) to win the presidency. He faced a severe budget deficit annually, struggled with military cutbacks, and vetoed abortion-rights legislation. In 1990 he agreed to a deficit-reduction plan that included tax hikes, despite a campaign promise to the contrary, angering many conservatives. Abroad, Bush supported Soviet reforms, Eastern Europe democratization, and good relations with Beijing. In Dec. 1989, he sent troops to Panama; they overthrew the government and captured military dictator Gen. Manuel Noriega. Bush reacted to Iraq's Aug. 1990 invasion of Kuwait by assembling a U.S.-led, UN-backed military coalition, including NATO and Arab League members. After a month-long air war, in Feb. 1991, Allied forces retook Kuwait in a four-day ground assault, but did not seek to drive Iraqi leader Saddam Hussein from power. The quick victory, with extremely light U.S. casualties, gave Bush one of the highest presidential approval ratings in history. His popularity plummeted by the end of the year, however, as the economy slipped into recession. He was defeated by Bill Clinton in the 1992 election.

Bush saw his son George W. inaugurated as the 43rd president in 2001. In 2005 the elder Bush teamed with former Pres. Clinton to raise money for natural disaster victims.

William Jefferson (Bill) Clinton (1993-2001), 42nd president, Democrat, was born Aug. 19, 1946, in Hope, AR, son of William Blythe and Virginia Cassidy Blythe, and was named William Jefferson Blythe IV. Blythe died in an auto accident before his son was born. His widow married Roger Clinton, whose last name Bill Clinton took. Clinton earned his undergraduate degree from Georgetown Univ. in 1968. While attending Oxford Univ. as a Rhodes scholar, he legally avoided the draft and possible service in Vietnam, according to some critics by misleading his draft board. Clinton worked on George McGovern's 1972 presidential campaign and earned a degree from Yale Law School in 1973. He taught at the Univ. of Arkansas law school until 1976, when he was elected state attorney general. In 1978 he was elected governor, becoming the nation's youngest at the time. Though defeated for reelection in 1980, he was returned to office several times thereafter. He married law school classmate Hillary Rodham in 1975; their daughter Chelsea was born in 1980.

Positioning himself as a centrist "New Democrat" in a crowded field, he won the party's 1992 presidential nomination and was elected president, defeating Pres. George H. W. Bush and independent candidate H. Ross Perot. In 1993, he won passage of a deficit reduction measure and congressional approval of the North American Free Trade Agreement. However, his administration's plan for major health care reform legislation died in Congress. After 1994 midterm elections, Clinton faced Republican majorities in both houses of Congress. He followed a centrist

course at home, sent troops to Bosnia to help implement a peace settlement, and cultivated relations with Russia and China.

Buoyed by a strong economy, Clinton won reelection in 1996, easily defeating Sen. Bob Dole (R, KS), with Reform Party candidate Ross Perot trailing behind. He achieved federal budget surpluses in several years. Clinton was ultimately cleared of involvement in improprieties by associates in the Whitewater land-development venture, but investigation into the matter turned up evidence of a sexual relationship between Clinton and White House intern Monica Lewinsky. In 1998, he was impeached by the House of Representatives, charged with perjury and obstruction of justice in an attempted cover-up of the affair. He was acquitted in a Senate trial, but later in a separate proceeding he agreed to a fine and temporary suspension of his Arkansas law license. In 1999 the United States joined other NATO nations in an aerial bombing campaign that induced Serbia to withdraw troops from Kosovo, where they had been terrorizing ethnic Albanians.

After leaving office, Clinton actively supported the political career of senator (D, NY), secretary of state, and presidential candidate Hillary Clinton. He also founded what became the Bill, Hillary and Chelsea Clinton Foundation. His published works include a 2004 autobiography.

George Walker Bush (2001-09), 43rd president, Republican, was born on July 6, 1946, in New Haven, CT. He was the oldest of six children born to the 41st president, George Herbert Walker Bush, and the former Barbara Pierce. He became the first son of a former president to take office as president since John Quincy Adams in 1825.

Bush grew up in Midland and Houston, TX. He attended Phillips Academy in Andover, MA, and graduated from Yale Univ. in 1968. Eligible for the draft, he fulfilled his military service requirement with the Texas Air National Guard. After earning an MBA from Harvard, he returned to Midland in 1975 and went into the oil business. Two years later he married Laura Welch, a librarian; they had twin daughters, Barbara and Jenna, in 1981. After aiding his father's winning 1988 presidential campaign, he became managing partner of the Texas Rangers baseball team. He was elected governor of Texas in 1994 and reelected in 1998.

In 2000, Bush and running mate Dick Cheney defeated the Democratic ticket led by Vice Pres. Al Gore in one of the closest-ever U.S. presidential elections. The result was not settled until a mid-Dec. ruling by the U.S. Supreme Court left Florida's crucial electoral votes in Bush's column.

Bush called his governing philosophy "compassionate conservatism." During his first term he won a number of policy victories, including two major tax cuts, legislation to renew so-called fast-track trade authority, as well as the No Child Left Behind education bill and a Medicare reform bill addressing prescription drug coverage. He established an office to facilitate social welfare activities by religious groups and signed a measure in 2003 banning so-called partial birth abortions. In 2001 he banned federal funding for research on new human embryonic stem cell lines.

But Bush's first term was dominated by the Sept. 11, 2001, terrorist attacks on the U.S. and the nation's response. In Oct. 2001, he signed the USA Patriot Act, greatly expanding the surveillance powers of the federal government, and created an Office of Homeland Security, which became a cabinet-level department in 2003 after legislation reorganized the U.S. intelligence system.

The U.S. military, aided by allies, had by Dec. 2001 deposed Afghanistan's Taliban regime, which was sheltering al-Qaeda terrorists. However, an operation in the Tora Bora cave complex to capture al-Qaeda leader Osama bin Laden, the architect of the Sept. 11 attacks, failed when he escaped to Pakistan. The U.S., aided mainly by UK forces, also launched an air and ground war against Iraq in 2003 and deposed its autocratic anti-Western leader, Saddam Hussein. However, no evidence was found that his regime had developed weapons of mass destruction, the key rationale for the war. A new Iraqi government was formed in June 2004, but insurgent violence and U.S. troop casualties continued.

Reelected in 2004, Bush pressed unsuccessfully for Social Security and immigration reforms, and his administration drew criticism for its response to Hurricane Katrina (2005). But he won Senate confirmation for John G. Roberts Jr. (2005) as Supreme Court chief justice and Samuel A. Alito Jr. (2006) as associate justice. After Democrats won majorities in House and

Senate midterm elections in 2006, Bush accepted the resignation of Defense Sec. Donald Rumsfeld, a target of widespread criticism over the Iraq war. Two months later, Bush announced a "surge" in U.S. troop strength in Iraq; a sharp drop in casualties ensued, aided by a shift in alliances. In 2008, the administration reached an agreement with Iraq allowing U.S. troops to remain there through 2011. But the Taliban was gaining strength in Afghanistan, and the Bush administration was damaged by revelations of prisoner abuse and extreme interrogation methods.

The U.S. economy fell into recession in Dec. 2007; Bush and congressional leaders responded with a $168-bil stimulus plan. Problems in home finance and credit markets triggered a deep economic crisis by Sept. 2008. The Treasury Dept. bailed out mortgage finance firms Fannie Mae and Freddie Mac, Lehman Bros. filed for bankruptcy, and the Federal Reserve rescued insurance giant AIG with a line of credit reaching $144 bil. An administration-backed plan to buy up to $700 bil in devalued mortgage-related assets cleared Congress in Oct., after a severe stock market plunge bolstered support. The crisis contributed to the GOP's losses in the 2008 election.

In 2010 Bush and former Pres. Clinton established a nonprofit organization to raise funds for earthquake relief in Haiti. Bush published a memoir, *Decision Points* (2010); a biography of his father, *41* (2014); and *Portraits of Courage* (2017), featuring his paintings of U.S. war veterans, along with their stories.

Barack Hussein Obama (2009-17), 44th president, Democrat, was born Aug. 4, 1961, in Honolulu, HI, son of Barack Obama Sr., a black Kenyan, and Stanley Ann Dunham, a white American. They divorced and, after his mother remarried, the family moved to Indonesia. Obama lived with his maternal grandparents in Hawaii while attending high school. He graduated from Columbia Univ. (1983) and, after working as a community organizer in Chicago, earned a law degree from Harvard Univ. (1991), where he was president of the law review. Obama practiced civil rights law in Chicago and taught at the Univ. of Chicago Law School. In 1992, he married attorney Michelle Robinson; they have two daughters, Malia and Natasha (Sasha).

Obama served eight years (1997-2004) in the Illinois state senate. Known for his 1995 memoir *Dreams From My Father*, he gained wider attention with his keynote address at the 2004 Democratic National Convention and was easily elected to the U.S. Senate in Nov. Stressing his opposition to the Iraq war and a message of "hope and change," Obama won the 2008 Democratic presidential nomination, defeating expected front-runner Sen. Hillary Clinton (NY). As a major recession deepened, Obama, with running mate Sen. Joe Biden (DE), defeated the Republican ticket, headed by Sen. John McCain (AZ), and he became the nation's first African-American president.

Pres. Obama was awarded the 2009 Nobel Peace Prize for "efforts to strengthen international diplomacy and cooperation between peoples." He gradually pulled U.S. troops from Iraq, though as sectarian strife heightened they were reintroduced, in what were called noncombat roles. He began force reductions in Afghanistan, but stepped up drone strikes against Islamist militants abroad and authorized a 2011 raid that killed al-Qaeda leader Osama bin Laden. He oversaw U.S. participation in NATO airstrikes leading to the overthrow of Libyan dictator Muammar al-Qaddafi. But rival militias in Libya refused to disarm; the U.S. ambassador and three other Americans were killed in an attack (Sept. 2012) by Islamist radicals on a U.S. consulate in Benghazi.

The administration won passage of a $787-bil economic stimulus package early in 2009, and the U.S. pulled out of recession, though growth was slow. In Mar. 2010, Obama won passage of his signature health care reform bill (dubbed "Obamacare"), aimed at extending coverage to the uninsured. But Democrats lost their House majority in Nov. 2010 elections, limiting Obama's legislative agenda. In 2012, he signed an executive order ending deportations for most young undocumented immigrants who came to the U.S. as children and his administration finalized regulations greatly tightening fuel emission standards for motor vehicles.

After Obama was reelected in 2012, a compromise in Congress averted a year-end "fiscal cliff" by making expiring Bush tax cuts permanent for most people, while postponing a "sequester" (later implemented) involving equal across-the-board cuts. Battles over the federal budget, debt ceiling, and Obamacare funding continued. The administration was also criticized over allegations that the Internal Revenue Service had singled out Tea Party organizations for special scrutiny. Other missteps included the botched rollout of Obamacare and revelations of mismanagement at the Dept. of Veterans Affairs. Leaks of classified information indicating extensive U.S. surveillance by the Natl. Security Agency also drew criticism. Terrorism remained a threat within the U.S. (as in the Boston Marathon bombing, 2013, and Orlando nightclub massacre, 2016).

Abroad, Russian forces annexed the Crimean region of Ukraine (Mar. 2014), and pro-Russian separatists, reportedly bolstered by Russian forces, fought the government in eastern Ukraine; Obama joined Europe in imposing limited economic sanctions. The administration revived Arab-Israeli peace talks, but they broke down. Obama called for an end to the repressive regime of Syria's Bashar al-Assad, pitted against rebel factions in a bloody civil war, but when Assad forces appeared to have launched a chemical weapons attack on civilians in 2013, crossing what Obama had called a "red line," he agreed to a Russian-brokered disarmament pact with the regime. After the Islamic State in Iraq and Syria (ISIS) took over large areas of both countries, proclaiming an Islamic "caliphate" (June 2014) and persecuting religious minorities, Obama sent military advisers into Iraq. Spurred by videos showing executions of abducted Westerners, he also authorized U.S. airstrikes against ISIS in both Iraq and Syria and eventually provided arms to moderate Syrian rebels.

After Nov. 2014 midterm elections, which left Republicans with majorities in both houses of Congress, Obama issued an executive order expanding protection of undocumented immigrants from deportation but it was blocked in court. In 2015, his administration unveiled a Clean Power Plan, aimed especially at cutting carbon emissions from coal-fired power plants, and Obama halted work on the Keystone XL oil pipeline. In 2016 the U.S. signed onto the Paris agreement aimed at global reductions in greenhouse gas emissions linked to climate change.

Under Obama the U.S. in 2015 officially restored relations with Cuba, severed since 1961. Obama also spearheaded a multination accord with Iran (July 2015) intended to curb Iranian nuclear weapons development for 10-15 years in return for ending economic sanctions. The administration participated in trade negotiations for a 12-nation Trans-Pacific Partnership but it was not ratified by Congress.

Responding to the mass shooting of children at Sandy Hook Elementary School in Newtown, CT (Dec. 2012), Obama unsuccessfully called for federal gun control legislation. He also confronted racial violence (as in the June 2015 massacre in a black Charleston, SC, church); racial tensions over the deaths of black people in encounters with police (as in Ferguson, MO, Aug. 2014), and revenge killings of police officers. In Mar. 2016 Obama nominated U.S. Appeals Court Judge Merrick Garland to the Supreme Court, but the Republican-controlled Senate refused to consider the nomination.

Obama left office with an approval rating close to 60%.

Donald John Trump (2017-), 45th president, Republican, was born June 14, 1946, in Queens, NY, the son of Frederick C. Trump, a wealthy real estate developer, and Mary Anne MacLeod Trump, a Scottish immigrant. At age 13 he was sent to a military boarding school. He earned a bachelor's degree from the Wharton School of Finance in 1968.

By then Trump was already working in his father's real estate development enterprise, which he came to control. In 1973 the Justice Dept. sued the Trump Organization for racial discrimination in housing; the suit was settled with a monitoring arrangement and no admission of guilt. Meanwhile, Trump spearheaded a successful expansion from New York City's outer boroughs into Manhattan. He also developed casinos in Atlantic City, NJ, though they eventually failed. While Trump has declined to release income tax returns, leaked portions of his 1995 return showed he declared a $916-mil loss, possibly offsetting tax liabilities over a number of years.

Trump coauthored several business-advice books and hosted his reality TV series *The Apprentice* and *Celebrity Apprentice* (2008-15). He also licensed his name to the now-defunct Trump Univ., a real estate and entrepreneurial training program. (A fraud suit against Trump Univ. was settled in 2018 for $25 mil.) Trump's 2018 net worth was estimated by *Forbes* at $3.1 bil. As president he surrendered control, but not ownership, of the Trump Organization to his elder sons.

After two marriages that ended in divorce, he married Melania Knauss in 2005. Their son Barron was born in 2006. He also has two sons, Donald Jr. (b. 1977) and Eric (b. 1984), and a daughter, Ivanka (b. 1981), from his first marriage, and a daughter, Tiffany (b. 1993), from his second.

Trump had explored running for president as a third-party candidate in 2000. He later became an outspoken "birther," questioning whether Barack Obama was born in the U.S. In June 2015 Trump announced his candidacy for the Republican presidential nomination, blaming illegal immigration for job losses, drugs, and crime, and presenting himself as a skilled negotiator, outsider, and populist. His often provocative rhetoric at rallies and in offhand tweets—which he continued in the White House—energized supporters, and he forged ahead in primaries as a total of 16 more conventional candidates fell away. Nominated in July 2016, he chose Indiana Gov. Mike Pence as his running mate. Details of Trump's crude private remarks about women, notably in a 2005 *Access Hollywood* video released in Oct., and other alleged sexual advances became public but did not derail the campaign. In the Nov. 2016 election he captured key Rust Belt states to prevail with a comfortable electoral majority over Democratic nominee Hillary Clinton.

Inaugurated Jan. 20, 2017, Trump issued a flurry of executive orders. These included orders to minimize any "unwarranted" burdens imposed under Obamacare, deny federal funding to so-called sanctuary cities for undocumented immigrants (blocked in court), plan for a wall along the Mexican border (delayed in funding disputes), and ban immigration from seven Muslim-majority nations (later modified; upheld by the Supreme Court). Trump also announced U.S. withdrawal from the Trans-Pacific Partnership (TPP), Obama's signature trade agreement. Later in 2017 Trump said the U.S. would begin withdrawal from the 2015 Paris Agreement on climate change and launch a process to repeal Obama's Clean Power Plan. In 2018 the administration unveiled proposals to roll back fuel efficiency mandates for vehicles and to challenge the right of states to impose their own strict standards.

Trump's inner-circle advisers included his son-in-law Jared Kushner and daughter Ivanka. A number of other top aides and officials quit or were eased out, including former alt-right media executive Steve Bannon as senior adviser; former GOP chair Reince Priebus, replaced as chief of staff by retired Gen. John Kelly; and former Exxon Mobil CEO Rex Tillerson, replaced as secretary of state by CIA director Mike Pompeo. EPA Administrator Scott Pruitt resigned in July 2018 amidst multiple investigations.

Investigations into Russian interference in the 2016 presidential election led to particular turmoil in the administration. In Feb. 2017, national security adviser Mike Flynn resigned after FBI surveillance found he had lied about a conversation with the Russian ambassador. In May 2017, Trump fired FBI director James Comey, who had been in charge of the FBI's Russia probe. After Attorney Gen. Jeff Sessions recused himself from the Russia investigation, the deputy attorney general appointed former FBI director Robert Mueller as a special counsel, with wide powers to oversee the probe, including any links between the Russian government and the Trump campaign. Trump called for an end to what he termed a "witch hunt" but said in May 2017 he was in part considering "this Russia thing" when firing Comey and in 2018 that his son Donald had met with a Russian attorney in June 2016, hoping to get dirt on Hillary Clinton. Among offshoots of the probe, 12 Russians were indicted in July 2018 on charges of hacking and releasing Democratic organizations' data and emails. In Aug. 2018, former Trump campaign chief Paul Manafort was convicted of various financial crimes, and Trump's longtime personal attorney, Michael Cohen, pleaded guilty to campaign finance violations and other charges. Cohen also implicated Trump in directing hush money payments to two women alleging sexual liaisons.

In Apr. 2017, Trump won confirmation of appellate court judge Neil Gorsuch to the U.S. Supreme Court. In July 2018, Trump nominated another conservative, appellate court judge Brett Kavanaugh, to fill a second Supreme Court vacancy.

Trump was widely denounced when he appeared to equally blame "both sides" for violence at an Aug. 2017 white nationalist rally in Charlottesville, VA, at which one counter-demonstrator was killed. Later events, such as the fatal shootings of students at a Parkland, FL, high school (Feb. 2018) fueled debates over gun control. In Apr. 2018, the administration began separating children from parents detained as part of a "zero-tolerance" policy on illegal immigration; the practice was suspended amid widespread protest. Meanwhile, administration plans to end the Obama-era Deferred Action for Childhood Arrivals (DACA) program, protecting many young undocumented immigrants who arrived in the U.S. as minors, were tied up in court.

In Sept. 2018 a book by reporter Bob Woodward, dismissed by the administration as a fabrication, portrayed Trump as uninformed and irresponsible, and the anonymous author of a *NY Times* opinion essay, described as a "senior official in the Trump administration," said they were working with others to thwart Trump's "more misguided impulses."

Abroad, Trump continued U.S. military engagement in the Middle East, while breaking with past policy to officially recognize Jerusalem as Israel's capital in Dec. 2017. In 2018 he announced U.S. withdrawal from the 2015 multination nuclear deal with Iran and unilaterally imposed heavy U.S. sanctions the deal had removed. While Trump's "America First" stance toward traditional allies strained relationships (G7 summit, June 2018), he cultivated ties with Russian Pres. Vladimir Putin, with whom he met privately in a July 2018 summit in Helsinki, and drew bipartisan criticism for appearing to accept Putin's claim of non-interference in the 2016 U.S. election. After a series of threats and counterthreats between the U.S. and North Korea raised fears that conflict could seriously escalate, Trump met with North Korea's leader Kim Jong Un in June 2018; they agreed on seeking "complete denuclearization of the Korean peninsula," but the effect of the meeting and agreement were unclear.

In Dec. 2017, Trump signed a major GOP tax cut bill, which also in effect repealed the Obamacare health insurance mandate. Stocks, economic output, and employment showed strong gains through summer 2018, although a trade war threatened to develop as Trump imposed new tariffs on certain goods. Opinion of Trump's performance as president was sharply divided, with overall approval in late summer 2018 averaging around 40%, according to RealClearPolitics poll aggregations.

Presidential Rankings, 2017

Source: © 2017 C-SPAN

As assessed by historians and other professional observers of the presidency, 91 of whom participated in the 2017 survey. Participants rated each president on 10 qualities of presidential leadership; rankings here reflect overall score.

Rank	President	2009 rank	2000 rank	Rank	President	2009 rank	2000 rank
1.	Lincoln	1	1	23.	Cleveland	21	17
2.	Washington	2	3	24.	Taft	24	24
3.	F. D. Roosevelt	3	2	25.	Ford	22	23
4.	T. Roosevelt	4	4	26.	Carter	25	22
5.	Eisenhower	8	9	27.	Coolidge	26	27
6.	Truman	5	5	28.	Nixon	27	25
7.	Jefferson	7	7	29.	Garfield	28	29
8.	Kennedy	6	8	30.	B. Harrison	30	31
9.	Reagan	10	11	31.	Taylor	29	28
10.	L. B. Johnson	11	10	32.	Hayes	33	26
11.	Wilson	9	6	33.	G. W. Bush	36	NA
12.	Obama	NA	NA	34.	Van Buren	31	30
13.	Monroe	14	14	35.	Arthur	32	32
14.	Polk	12	12	36.	Hoover	34	34
15.	Clinton	15	21	37.	Fillmore	37	35
16.	McKinley	16	15	38.	W. H. Harrison	39	37
17.	Madison	20	18	39.	Tyler	35	36
18.	Jackson	13	13	40.	Harding	38	38
19.	J. Adams	17	16	41.	Pierce	40	39
20.	G. H. W. Bush	18	20	42.	A. Johnson	41	40
21.	J. Q. Adams	19	19	43.	Buchanan	42	41
22.	Grant	23	33				

NA = Not applicable.

Presidential Facts

Oldest president: Ronald Reagan, who was 77 when he left office

Oldest person elected to first term as president: Donald J. Trump, who was 70 when elected in 2016

Youngest president: Theodore Roosevelt, who was 42 when sworn in after McKinley's death

Youngest person elected president: John F. Kennedy, who was 43 when elected in 1960

Tallest president: Abraham Lincoln, who was 6 feet, 4 inches

Shortest president: James Madison, who was 5 feet, 4 inches

Heaviest president: William Howard Taft, who was 332 pounds in 1911

First president to live in the White House: John Adams, who moved there in 1800

First president whose parents were immigrants: Andrew Jackson; his parents emigrated from Ireland in 1765

First president born a U.S. citizen: Martin Van Buren, in Kinderhook, NY, 1782

First president born outside the original colonies: Abraham Lincoln, in Kentucky, 1809

First president born west of the Mississippi: Herbert Hoover, in West Branch, IA, 1874

Most common presidential home state: Virginia, with 8 presidents

First president born in a hospital: Jimmy Carter, in Plains, GA, 1924

First president to have a telephone in the White House: Rutherford B. Hayes, in 1879

First president to travel outside U.S. while in office: Theodore Roosevelt visited Panama Canal site, 1906

First president to address the nation on radio: Warren G. Harding, in 1922

First president to appear on TV: Franklin D. Roosevelt, at opening ceremonies for the 1939 World's Fair

First president to give a live, televised news conference: John F. Kennedy, in 1961

First president to hold an Internet chat: Bill Clinton, in 1999

Presidents who lost the popular vote while winning election: John Quincy Adams, in 1824 (elected by the House after general election failed to produce a majority); Rutherford B. Hayes, in 1876; Benjamin Harrison, in 1888; George W. Bush, in 2000; Donald J. Trump, in 2016. (Popular vote totals before 1824 are unknown.)

Only presidents chosen by the House of Representatives: Thomas Jefferson (1st term) and John Quincy Adams

Only president never elected either president or vice president: Gerald Ford; named vice president when Spiro Agnew resigned (1973), became president when Nixon resigned (1974)

Only president who never previously held government or military office: Donald J. Trump

Left-handed presidents: James Garfield, Herbert Hoover, Harry Truman, Gerald Ford, Ronald Reagan, George H. W. Bush, Bill Clinton, and Barack Obama

Only Catholic president: John F. Kennedy; the most common religious affiliations have been Episcopalian (11) and Presbyterian (8)

Only bachelor presidents: James Buchanan, who never married, and Grover Cleveland, who married Frances Folsom in the White House in 1886

First divorced president: Ronald Reagan; divorced from Jane Wyman in 1948, married Nancy Davis in 1952

Presidents who died on July 4: John Adams and Thomas Jefferson (both 1826) and James Monroe (1831)

Only president buried in Washington, DC: Woodrow Wilson, interred at Washington National Cathedral

Presidential Libraries

Presidential libraries are coordinated by the National Archives and Records Administration (www.archives.gov/presidential-libraries/). Materials for presidents before Herbert Hoover are held by private institutions. NARA's Barack Obama Presidential Library (www.obamalibrary.gov) will be a fully digital library. The Obama Presidential Center in Chicago, IL, will be a privately operated, non-governmental organization. Under the Presidential Records Act, material is available through Freedom of Information Act requests starting five years after a president has left office.

Herbert Hoover Library and Museum
210 Parkside Dr.
West Branch, IA 52358
Phone: (319) 643-5301
Email: hoover.library@nara.gov
Website: hoover.archives.gov

Franklin D. Roosevelt Library and Museum
4079 Albany Post Rd.
Hyde Park, NY 12538-1990
Phone: (800) FDR-VISIT
Email: roosevelt.library@nara.gov
Website: www.fdrlibrary.marist.edu

Harry S. Truman Library and Museum
500 West U.S. Hwy. 24
Independence, MO 64050-2481
Phone: (800) 833-1225
Email: truman.library@nara.gov
Website: www.trumanlibrary.org

Dwight D. Eisenhower Library
200 SE 4th St.
Abilene, KS 67410-2900
Phone: (877) RING-IKE
Email: eisenhower.library@nara.gov
Website: eisenhower.archives.gov

John F. Kennedy Library and Museum
Columbia Pt.
Boston, MA 02125-3312
Phone: (866) JFK-1960
Email: kennedy.library@nara.gov
Website: www.jfklibrary.org

Lyndon Baines Johnson Library and Museum
2313 Red River St.
Austin, TX 78705-5737
Phone: (512) 721-0200
Email: johnson.library@nara.gov
Website: www.lbjlibrary.org

Richard Nixon Library and Museum
18001 Yorba Linda Blvd.
Yorba Linda, CA 92886-3903
Phone: (714) 983-9120
Email: nixon@nara.gov
Website: www.nixonlibrary.gov

Gerald R. Ford Library and Museum
Library: 1000 Beal Ave.
Ann Arbor, MI 48109-2109
Phone: (734) 205-0555
Museum: 303 Pearl St. NW
Grand Rapids, MI 49504-5353
Phone: (616) 254-0400
Email: ford.library@nara.gov
Website: www.fordlibrarymuseum.gov

Jimmy Carter Library and Museum
441 Freedom Pkwy.
Atlanta, GA 30307-1498
Phone: (404) 865-7100

Email: carter.library@nara.gov
Website: www.jimmycarterlibrary.gov

Ronald Reagan Library and Museum
40 Presidential Dr.
Simi Valley, CA 93065-0600
Phone: (800) 410-8354
Email: reagan.library@nara.gov
Website: reaganlibrary.gov

George H. W. Bush Library and Museum
1000 George Bush Dr. West
College Station, TX 77845
Phone: (979) 691-4000
Email: library.bush@nara.gov
Website: www.bush41.org

William J. Clinton Library and Museum
1200 President Clinton Ave.
Little Rock, AR 72201
Phone: (501) 374-4242
Email: clinton.library@nara.gov
Website: www.clintonlibrary.gov

George W. Bush Library and Museum
2943 SMU Blvd.
Dallas, TX 75205
Phone: (214) 346-1650
Email: gwbush.library@nara.gov
Website: www.georgewbushlibrary.smu.edu

Presidential Impeachment in U.S. History

The U.S. Constitution provides for impeachment and removal from office of federal officials on grounds of "Treason, Bribery, or other high Crimes and Misdemeanors" (Article II, Sect. 4). Impeachment is the bringing of charges by the House of Representatives, whose members can adopt impeachment articles on a simple majority vote. It is followed by a Senate trial; a two-thirds majority vote of Senators present is needed for conviction and removal from office.

In 1868, **Andrew Johnson** became the first president impeached by the House, for his removal of Sec. of War Edwin M. Stanton without first notifying the Senate. He was tried but not convicted. In 1974, impeachment articles against Pres. **Richard Nixon**, in connection with the Watergate scandal, were adopted by the House Judiciary Committee. He resigned Aug. 9, and the House accepted the committee report without taking further action. In 1998, Pres. **Bill Clinton** was impeached by the House in connection with his cover-up of a sexual relationship with former White House intern Monica Lewinsky. He was tried in the Senate in 1999 and acquitted.

Spouses and Children of the Presidents

Name (born-died; married)	Birth-place	Sons/daughters	Name (born-died; married)	Birth-place	Sons/daughters
Martha Dandridge Custis Washington (1731-1802; 1759)	VA	None	Mary Scott Lord Dimmick Harrison (1858-1948; 1896)	PA	0/1
Abigail Smith Adams (1744-1818; 1764)	MA	3/2	Ida Saxton McKinley (1847-1907; 1871)	OH	0/2
Martha Wayles Skelton Jefferson (1748-82; 1772)	VA	1/5	Alice Hathaway Lee Roosevelt (1861-84; 1880)	MA	0/1
Dolley Payne Todd Madison (1768-1849; 1794)	NC	None	Edith Kermit Carow Roosevelt (1861-1948; 1886)	CT	4/1
Elizabeth Kortright Monroe (1768-1830; 1786)	NY	1/2	Helen Herron Taft (1861-1943; 1886)	OH	2/1
Louisa Catherine Johnson Adams (1775-1852; 1797)	Eng.[1]	3/1	Ellen Louise Axson Wilson (1860-1914; 1885)	GA	0/3
Rachel Donelson Robards Jackson (1767-1828; 1791)	VA	1/0[2]	Edith Bolling Galt Wilson (1872-1961; 1915)	VA	None
Hannah Hoes Van Buren (1783-1819; 1807)	NY	4/0	Florence Kling De Wolfe Harding (1860-1924; 1891)	OH	None
Anna Tuthill Symmes Harrison (1775-1864; 1795)	NJ	6/4	Grace Anna Goodhue Coolidge (1879-1957; 1905)	VT	2/0
Letitia Christian Tyler (1790-1842; 1813)	VA	3/5	Lou Henry Hoover (1875-1944; 1899)	IA	2/0
Julia Gardiner Tyler (1820-89; 1844)	NY	5/2	Anna Eleanor Roosevelt (1884-1962; 1905)	NY	5/1
Sarah Childress Polk (1803-91; 1824)	TN	None	Elizabeth Virginia (Bess) Wallace Truman (1885-1982; 1919)	MO	0/1
Margaret (Peggy) Mackall Smith Taylor (1788-1852; 1810)	MD	1/5	Mamie Geneva Doud Eisenhower (1896-1979; 1916)	IA	2/0
Abigail Powers Fillmore (1798-1853; 1826)	NY	1/1	Jacqueline Lee Bouvier Kennedy (1929-94; 1953)	NY	2/1
Caroline Carmichael McIntosh Fillmore (1813-81; 1858)	NJ	None	Claudia (Lady Bird) Alta Taylor Johnson (1912-2007; 1934)	TX	0/2
Jane Means Appleton Pierce (1806-63; 1834)	NH	3/0	Thelma Catherine Patricia Ryan Nixon (1912-93; 1940)	NV	0/2
Mary Todd Lincoln (1818-82; 1842)	KY	4/0	Elizabeth (Betty) Bloomer Warren Ford (1918-2011; 1948)	IL	3/1
Eliza McCardle Johnson (1810-76; 1827)	TN	3/2	Eleanor Rosalynn Smith Carter (1927- ; 1946)	GA	3/1
Julia Boggs Dent Grant (1826-1902; 1848)	MO	3/1	Anne Frances (Nancy) Robbins Davis Reagan (1921-2016; 1952)	NY	1/1[3]
Lucy Ware Webb Hayes (1831-89; 1852)	OH	7/1	Barbara Pierce Bush (1925-2018; 1945)	NY	4/2
Lucretia Rudolph Garfield (1832-1918; 1858)	OH	5/2	Hillary Diane Rodham Clinton (1947- ; 1975)	IL	0/1
Ellen Lewis Herndon Arthur (1837-80; 1859)	VA	2/1	Laura Lane Welch Bush (1946- ; 1977)	TX	0/2
Frances Folsom Cleveland (1864-1947; 1886)	NY	2/3	Michelle LaVaughn Robinson Obama (1964- ; 1992)	IL	0/2
Caroline Lavinia Scott Harrison (1832-92; 1853)	OH	1/1	Melania Knauss Trump (1970- ; 2005)	Slovenia	1/0[4]

Note: Pres. Buchanan was unmarried. Children not born to the marriages shown are not listed unless otherwise noted. (1) Born in London, father a MD citizen. (2) Adopted son. (3) Pres. Reagan's first wife, whom he later divorced, was Jane Wyman (m. 1940-48). They had two daughters, one of whom died in infancy, and an adopted son. (4) Pres. Trump had four children from two previous marriages: two sons (Donald Jr., Eric) and one daughter (Ivanka) with Ivana Marie Zelníčková Trump (m. 1977-92) and one daughter (Tiffany) with Marla Maples (m. 1993-99).

First Lady Melania Trump

Melania Trump was born Melanija Knavs (later Germanized to Melania Knauss) on Apr. 26, 1970, in Novo Mesto, Slovenia (then part of Yugoslavia). She matriculated at Univ. of Ljubljana in Slovenia but moved to New York City in 1996 to further a modeling career. She and Donald Trump were married in Jan. 2005; their son Barron was born in Mar. 2006, the same year Melania Trump became a U.S. citizen. She was the second first lady born outside of the U.S. (The first was English-born Louisa Adams, wife of John Quincy Adams.) She was the first Catholic first lady since Jacqueline Kennedy. In May 2018, Melania Trump launched the "Be Best" initiative directed at youth, focusing especially on avoidance of cyberbullying and drug abuse.

Burial Places of the Presidents

President	Burial place	President	Burial place	President	Burial place
Washington	Mt. Vernon, VA	Pierce	Concord, NH	Wilson	Wash. Natl. Cathedral, DC
J. Adams	Quincy, MA	Buchanan	Lancaster, PA		
Jefferson	Charlottesville, VA	Lincoln	Springfield, IL	Harding	Marion, OH
Madison	Montpelier Station, VA	A. Johnson	Greeneville, TN	Coolidge	Plymouth Notch, VT
Monroe	Richmond, VA	Grant	New York, NY	Hoover	West Branch, IA
J. Q. Adams	Quincy, MA	Hayes	Fremont, OH	F. Roosevelt	Hyde Park, NY
Jackson	Nashville, TN	Garfield	Cleveland, OH	Truman	Independence, MO
Van Buren	Kinderhook, NY	Arthur	Albany, NY	Eisenhower	Abilene, KS
W. H. Harrison	North Bend, OH	Cleveland	Princeton, NJ	Kennedy	Arlington Natl. Cem., VA
Tyler	Richmond, VA	B. Harrison	Indianapolis, IN	L. B. Johnson	Stonewall, TX
Polk	Nashville, TN	McKinley	Canton, OH	Nixon	Yorba Linda, CA
Taylor	Louisville, KY	T. Roosevelt	Oyster Bay, NY	Ford	Grand Rapids, MI
Fillmore	Buffalo, NY	Taft	Arlington Natl. Cem., VA	Reagan	Simi Valley, CA

PRESIDENTIAL ELECTIONS

Electoral and Popular Vote, 2012 and 2016

Source: Federal Election Commission; as of Dec. 2017

	2016					2012					
	Electoral vote		Popular vote			Electoral vote		Popular vote			
State	Clinton	Trump	Clinton	Trump	Johnson	Obama	Romney	Obama	Romney	Johnson	State
AL	0	9	729,547	1,318,255	44,467	0	9	795,696	1,255,925	12,328	AL
AK	0	3	116,454	163,387	18,725	0	3	122,640	164,676	7,392	AK
AZ	0	11	1,161,167	1,252,401	106,327	0	11	1,025,232	1,233,654	32,100	AZ
AR	0	6	380,494	684,872	29,949	0	6	394,409	647,744	16,276	AR
CA	55	0	8,753,792	4,483,814	478,500	55	0	7,854,285	4,839,958	143,221	CA
CO	9	0	1,338,870	1,202,484	144,121	9	0	1,323,102	1,185,243	35,545	CO
CT	7	0	897,572	673,215	48,676	7	0	905,083	634,892	12,580	CT
DE	3	0	235,603	185,127	14,757	3	0	242,584	165,484	3,882	DE
DC	3	0	282,830	12,723	4,906	3	0	267,070	21,381	2,083	DC
FL	0	29	4,504,975	4,617,886	207,043	29	0	4,237,756	4,163,447	44,726	FL
GA	0	16	1,877,963	2,089,104	125,306	0	16	1,773,827	2,078,688	45,324	GA
HI	3	0	266,891	128,847	15,954	4	0	306,658	121,015	3,840	HI
ID	0	4	189,765	409,055	28,331	0	4	212,787	420,911	9,453	ID
IL	20	0	3,090,729	2,146,015	209,596	20	0	3,019,512	2,135,216	56,229	IL
IN	0	11	1,033,126	1,557,286	133,993	0	11	1,152,887	1,420,543	50,111	IN
IA	0	6	653,669	800,983	59,186	6	0	822,544	730,617	12,926	IA
KS	0	6	427,005	671,018	55,406	0	6	440,726	692,634	20,456	KS
KY	0	8	628,854	1,202,971	53,752	0	8	679,370	1,087,190	17,063	KY
LA	0	8	780,154	1,178,638	37,978	0	8	809,141	1,152,262	18,157	LA
ME	3	1	357,735	335,593	38,105	4	0	401,306	292,276	9,352	ME
MD	10	0	1,677,928	943,169	79,605	10	0	1,677,844	971,869	30,195	MD
MA	11	0	1,995,196	1,090,893	138,018	11	0	1,921,290	1,188,314	30,920	MA
MI	0	16	2,268,839	2,279,543	172,136	16	0	2,564,569	2,115,256	7,774	MI
MN	10	0	1,367,716	1,322,951	112,972	10	0	1,546,167	1,320,225	35,098	MN
MS	0	6	485,131	700,714	14,435	0	6	562,949	710,746	6,676	MS
MO	0	10	1,071,068	1,594,511	97,359	0	10	1,223,796	1,482,440	43,151	MO
MT	0	3	177,709	279,240	28,037	0	3	201,839	267,928	14,165	MT
NE	0	5	284,494	495,961	38,946	0	5	302,081	475,064	11,109	NE
NV	6	0	539,260	512,058	37,384	6	0	531,373	463,567	10,968	NV
NH	4	0	348,526	345,790	30,777	4	0	369,561	329,918	8,212	NH
NJ	14	0	2,148,278	1,601,933	72,477	14	0	2,125,101	1,477,568	21,045	NJ
NM	5	0	385,234	319,667	74,541	5	0	415,335	335,788	27,788	NM
NY	29	0	4,556,118	2,819,533	176,598	29	0	4,485,741	2,490,431	47,256	NY
NC	0	15	2,189,316	2,362,631	130,126	0	15	2,178,391	2,270,395	44,515	NC
ND	0	3	93,758	216,794	21,434	0	3	124,827	188,163	5,231	ND
OH	0	18	2,394,164	2,841,005	174,498	18	0	2,827,709	2,661,437	49,493	OH
OK	0	7	420,375	949,136	83,481	0	7	443,547	891,325	—	OK
OR	7	0	1,002,106	782,403	94,231	7	0	970,488	754,175	24,089	OR
PA	0	20	2,926,441	2,970,733	146,715	20	0	2,990,274	2,680,434	49,991	PA
RI	4	0	252,525	180,543	14,746	4	0	279,677	157,204	4,388	RI
SC	0	9	855,373	1,155,389	49,204	0	9	865,941	1,071,645	16,321	SC
SD	0	3	117,458	227,721	20,850	0	3	145,039	210,610	5,795	SD
TN	0	11	870,695	1,522,925	70,397	0	11	960,709	1,462,330	18,623	TN
TX	0	36	3,877,868	4,685,047	283,492	0	38	3,308,124	4,569,843	88,580	TX
UT	0	6	310,676	515,231	39,608	0	6	251,813	740,600	12,572	UT
VT	3	0	178,573	95,369	10,078	3	0	199,239	92,698	3,487	VT
VA	13	0	1,981,473	1,769,443	118,274	13	0	1,971,820	1,822,522	31,216	VA
WA	8	0	1,742,718	1,221,747	160,879	12	0	1,755,396	1,290,670	42,202	WA
WV	0	5	188,794	489,371	23,004	0	5	238,269	417,655	6,302	WV
WI	0	10	1,382,536	1,405,284	106,674	10	0	1,620,985	1,410,966	20,439	WI
WY	0	3	55,973	174,419	13,287	0	3	69,286	170,962	5,326	WY
Total	**227**	**304**	**65,853,514**	**62,984,828**	**4,489,341**	**332**	**206**	**65,915,795**	**60,933,504**	**1,275,971**	**Total**

— = Not listed on state's ballot. **Note:** In 2016, 7 electors (1 from HI, 2 from TX, 4 from WA) voted for candidates to whom they were not pledged; their votes are not included here. Maine and Nebraska are the only two states with laws that allow electoral votes to be split between candidates.

Presidential Popular Vote, 2016

Source: Federal Election Commission; as of Dec. 2017

Candidate (party)	Vote total	Percent of vote
Hillary Clinton (Democrat)	65,853,514	48.18%
Donald J. Trump (Republican)	62,984,828	46.09
Gary Johnson (Libertarian)	4,489,341	3.28
Jill Stein (Green)	1,457,218	1.07
Evan McMullin (Independent/ no party affiliation)	731,991	0.54
Darrell L. Castle (Constitution)	203,090	0.15
Gloria La Riva (Peace and Freedom/ Socialism and Liberation)	74,401	0.05
Rocky De La Fuente (Reform/ American Delta)	33,136	0.02
Richard Duncan (Nonpartisan)	24,307	0.02
Dan R. Vacek (Legal Marijuana Now)	13,537	0.01
Alyson Kennedy (Socialist Workers)	12,467	0.01
Mike Smith (Independent)	9,338	0.01
Chris Keniston (Veterans)	7,211	0.01
Michael A. Maturen (American Solidarity)	6,462	<0.01
Lynn S. Kahn (Independent)	5,733	<0.01
Jim Hedges (Independent/Prohibition)	5,617	<0.01
Tom Hoefling (America's Party)	4,779	<0.01%
Monica Moorehead (Workers World)	4,317	<0.01
Laurence Kotlikoff (Independent)	3,581	<0.01
Peter Skewes (American)	3,250	<0.01
Rocky Giordani (Independent American)	2,752	<0.01
Emidio Soltysik (Natural Law/Socialist)	2,691	<0.01
Scott Copeland (Constitution)	2,356	<0.01
Kyle Kopitke (Independent American)	1,096	<0.01
Joseph Allen Maldonado (Independent)	962	<0.01
Ryan Alan Scott (Unaffiliated)	754	<0.01
Rod Silva (Nutrition)	751	<0.01
Princess Jacob (Independent)	749	<0.01
Jerry White (Socialism Equality Anti-War)	475	<0.01
Bradford Lyttle (Nonviolent Resistance/Pacifist)	382	<0.01
Frank Atwood (Approval Voting)	337	<0.01
Write-in votes (other/miscellaneous)	698,990	0.51
None of these candidates (Nevada)	28,863	0.02
Total	**136,669,276**	

Note: Party designations vary from one state to another; party label listed may not necessarily represent a political party organization. Vote totals for the candidates listed above include any write-in votes.

Electoral Votes for President, 2016

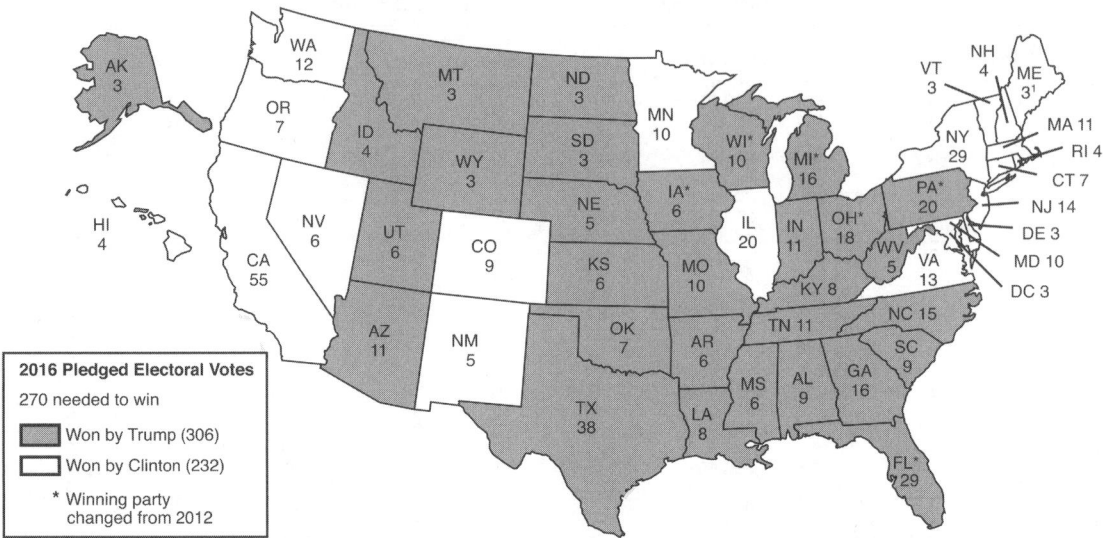

2016 Pledged Electoral Votes

270 needed to win

▨ Won by Trump (306)

☐ Won by Clinton (232)

* Winning party changed from 2012

Note: Electoral votes based on the 2010 Census were in force beginning with the 2012 elections. In 2016, 7 electors (1 from HI, 2 from TX, 4 from WA) defected and voted for candidates to whom they were not pledged. Map shows allotments before defections. (1) Trump was awarded one of Maine's four electoral votes; the other three went to Clinton.

The Electoral College

The president and the vice president are the only elective federal officials not chosen by direct vote of the people. They are elected by the members of the Electoral College, an institution provided for in the U.S. Constitution.

On presidential election day, the first Tuesday after the first Monday in Nov. of every fourth year, each state chooses as many electors as it has senators and representatives in Congress. In 1964, for the first time, as provided by the 23rd Amendment to the Constitution, the District of Columbia voted for three electors. Thus, with 100 senators and 435 representatives, there are 538 members of the Electoral College, with a majority of 270 electoral votes needed to elect the president and vice president.

Political parties were not part of the Founding Fathers' original plan. But today, each political party chooses its electors, by nomination at a state convention or by vote of the party central committee in each state. An elector cannot be a member of Congress or federal office holder. In some states, electors' names may be printed below the names of the presidential and vice presidential candidates on the Nov. ballot. In any case, the electors of the party receiving the highest vote count are elected under a winner-take-all system. Two states, Maine and Nebraska, allow for proportional allocation.

The electors meet on the first Monday after the second Wednesday in Dec. in their respective state capitals or in some other place prescribed by state legislatures. By long-established custom, they vote for their party nominees, although this is not required by federal law. They may be bound to do so by state law or party pledge.

The Constitution requires electors to cast a ballot for at least one person who is not an inhabitant of that elector's home state. This ensures that presidential and vice presidential candidates from the same party will not be from the same state.

Certified and sealed lists of the votes of the electors in each state are sent to the president of the U.S. Senate. He or she then opens them in the presence of members of the Senate and House of Representatives in a joint session held in early Jan. The electoral votes of all the states are then officially counted.

If no candidate for president has a majority, the House of Representatives chooses a president from the top three candidates, with all representatives from each state combining to cast one vote for that state. The House decided the outcomes of the 1800 and 1824 presidential elections. If no candidate for vice president has a majority, the Senate chooses from the top two, with the senators voting as individuals. The Senate chose the vice president following the 1836 election.

Under the electoral college system, a candidate who fails to be the top vote-getter in the popular vote still may win a majority of electoral votes. This happened in the elections of 1876, 1888, 2000, and 2016.

Voter Turnout in Presidential Elections, 1932-2016

Source: U.S. Census Bureau, U.S. Dept. of Commerce; Office of the Clerk, U.S. House of Representatives

Year	Candidates	Voter participation % of voting-age citizen pop.	% of voting-age pop.	Year	Candidates	Voter participation % of voting-age citizen pop.	% of voting-age pop.
1932	F. D. Roosevelt-Hoover . . .	NA	52.6%	1976	Carter-Ford.	NA	59.2%
1936	F. D. Roosevelt-Landon . . .	NA	56.9	1980	Reagan-Carter	64.0%	59.3
1940	F. D. Roosevelt-Willkie	NA	58.8	1984	Reagan-Mondale	64.9	59.9
1944	F. D. Roosevelt-Dewey. . . .	NA	56.1	1988	G. H. W. Bush-Dukakis. . . .	62.2	57.4
1948	Truman-Dewey.	NA	51.1	1992	Clinton-G. H. W. Bush-Perot	67.7	61.3
1952	Eisenhower-Stevenson. . . .	NA	61.6	1996	Clinton-Dole-Perot	58.4	54.2
1956	Eisenhower-Stevenson. . . .	NA	59.3	2000	G. W. Bush-Gore	59.5	54.7
1960	Kennedy-Nixon.	NA	62.8	2004	G. W. Bush-Kerry	63.8	58.3
1964	L. B. Johnson-Goldwater . .	NA	69.3	2008	Obama-McCain	63.6	58.2
1968	Nixon-Humphrey.	NA	67.8	2012	Obama-Romney.	61.8	56.5
1972	Nixon-McGovern.	NA	63.0	2016	Trump-Clinton.	61.4	56.0

NA = Not available. **Note:** Data prior to 1964 is from a legacy source and may not be directly comparable to more recent data. The 1972 presidential election was the first for which eligible voters included 18- to 20-year-olds. The voting-age citizen pop. includes those who are ineligible to vote due to imprisonment or prior felony convictions. The voting-age pop. comprises the former group as well as residents who are ineligible to vote because they are not U.S. citizens.

Popular and Electoral Vote for President, 1789-2016

(D) Democrat; (DR) Democratic Republican; (F) Federalist; (LB) Libertarian; (LR) Liberal Republican; (NR) National Republican; (P) People's/Populist (PR) Progressive; (R) Republican; (W) Whig; * = See notes below table.

Year	President elected	Popular	Elec.	Major losing candidate(s)	Popular	Elec.
1789	George Washington	Unknown	69	No major opposition	—	—
1792	George Washington	Unknown	132	No major opposition	—	—
1796	John Adams (F)	Unknown	71	Thomas Jefferson (DR)	Unknown	68
1800*	Thomas Jefferson (DR)	Unknown	73	Aaron Burr (DR)	Unknown	73
				John Adams (F)	Unknown	65
1804	Thomas Jefferson (DR)	Unknown	162	Charles Pinckney (F)	Unknown	14
1808	James Madison (DR)	Unknown	122	Charles Pinckney (F)	Unknown	47
1812	James Madison (DR)	Unknown	128	DeWitt Clinton (F)	Unknown	89
1816	James Monroe (DR)	Unknown	183	Rufus King (F)	Unknown	34
1820	James Monroe (DR)	Unknown	231	John Quincy Adams (DR)	Unknown	1
1824*	John Quincy Adams (DR)	113,122	84	Andrew Jackson (DR)	151,271	99
				Henry Clay (DR)	46,587	37
				William H. Crawford (DR)	44,282	41
1828	Andrew Jackson (D)	642,553	178	John Quincy Adams (NR)	500,897	83
1832	Andrew Jackson (D)	701,780	219	Henry Clay (NR)	484,205	49
1836	Martin Van Buren (D)	764,176	170	William H. Harrison (W)	550,816	73
1840	William H. Harrison (W)	1,275,390	234	Martin Van Buren (D)	1,128,854	60
1844	James K. Polk (D)	1,339,494	170	Henry Clay (W)	1,300,004	105
1848	Zachary Taylor (W)	1,361,393	163	Lewis Cass (D)	1,223,460	127
				Martin Van Buren (Free Soil)	291,501	—
1852	Franklin Pierce (D)	1,607,510	254	Winfield Scott (W)	1,386,942	42
1856	James Buchanan (D)	1,836,072	174	John C. Frémont (R)	1,342,345	114
				Millard Fillmore (American/Know-Nothing)	873,053	8
1860	Abraham Lincoln (R)	1,865,908	180	Stephen A. Douglas (D)	848,019	12
				John C. Breckinridge (D)	845,763	72
				John Bell (Constitutional Union)	589,581	39
1864	Abraham Lincoln (R)	2,218,388	212	George McClellan (D)	1,812,807	21
1868	Ulysses S. Grant (R)	3,013,650	214	Horatio Seymour (D)	2,708,744	80
1872*	Ulysses S. Grant (R)	3,598,235	286	Horace Greeley (D-LR)	2,834,671	—
1876*	Rutherford B. Hayes (R)	4,034,311	185	Samuel J. Tilden (D)	4,288,546	184
1880	James A. Garfield (R)	4,446,158	214	Winfield S. Hancock (D)	4,444,260	155
1884	Grover Cleveland (D)	4,874,621	219	James G. Blaine (R)	4,848,936	182
1888	Benjamin Harrison (R)	5,443,892	233	Grover Cleveland (D)	5,534,488	168
1892	Grover Cleveland (D)	5,551,883	277	Benjamin Harrison (R)	5,179,244	145
				James Weaver (P)	1,027,329	22
1896	William McKinley (R)	7,108,480	271	William J. Bryan (D-P)	6,511,495	176
1900	William McKinley (R)	7,218,039	292	William J. Bryan (D)	6,358,345	155
1904	Theodore Roosevelt (R)	7,626,593	336	Alton B. Parker (D)	5,082,898	140
1908	William H. Taft (R)	7,676,258	321	William J. Bryan (D)	6,406,801	162
1912	Woodrow Wilson (D)	6,293,152	435	Theodore Roosevelt (PR)	4,119,207	88
				William H. Taft (R)	3,483,922	8
1916	Woodrow Wilson (D)	9,126,300	277	Charles E. Hughes (R)	8,546,789	254
1920	Warren G. Harding (R)	16,153,115	404	James M. Cox (D)	9,133,092	127
1924	Calvin Coolidge (R)	15,719,921	382	John W. Davis (D)	8,386,704	136
				Robert M. La Follette (PR)	4,822,856	13
1928	Herbert Hoover (R)	21,437,277	444	Alfred E. Smith (D)	15,007,698	87
1932	Franklin D. Roosevelt (D)	22,829,501	472	Herbert Hoover (R)	15,760,684	59
1936	Franklin D. Roosevelt (D)	27,757,333	523	Alfred Landon (R)	16,684,231	8
1940	Franklin D. Roosevelt (D)	27,313,041	449	Wendell Willkie (R)	22,348,480	82
1944	Franklin D. Roosevelt (D)	25,612,610	432	Thomas E. Dewey (R)	22,117,617	99
1948	Harry S. Truman (D)	24,179,345	303	Thomas E. Dewey (R)	21,991,291	189
				Strom Thurmond (States' Rights)	1,169,021	39
				Henry A. Wallace (PR)	1,157,172	—
1952	Dwight D. Eisenhower (R)	33,936,234	442	Adlai E. Stevenson (D)	27,314,992	89
1956*	Dwight D. Eisenhower (R)	35,590,472	457	Adlai E. Stevenson (D)	26,022,752	73
1960*	John F. Kennedy (D)	34,226,731	303	Richard M. Nixon (R)	34,108,157	219
1964	Lyndon B. Johnson (D)	43,129,566	486	Barry M. Goldwater (R)	27,178,188	52
1968	Richard M. Nixon (R)	31,785,480	301	Hubert H. Humphrey (D)	31,275,166	191
				George C. Wallace (Amer. Indep.)	9,906,473	46
1972*	Richard M. Nixon (R)	47,169,911	520	George S. McGovern (D)	29,170,383	17
1976*	Jimmy Carter (D)	40,830,763	297	Gerald R. Ford (R)	39,147,793	240
1980	Ronald Reagan (R)	43,904,153	489	Jimmy Carter (D)	35,483,883	49
				John B. Anderson (independent)	5,719,437	—
1984	Ronald Reagan (R)	54,455,075	525	Walter F. Mondale (D)	37,577,185	13
1988*	George H. W. Bush (R)	48,886,097	426	Michael S. Dukakis (D)	41,809,074	111
1992	Bill Clinton (D)	44,909,889	370	George H. W. Bush (R)	39,104,545	168
				H. Ross Perot (independent)	19,742,267	—
1996	Bill Clinton (D)	47,402,357	379	Bob Dole (R)	39,198,755	159
				H. Ross Perot (Reform)	8,085,402	—
2000*	George W. Bush (R)	50,456,002	271	Al Gore (D)	50,999,897	266
				Ralph Nader (Green)	2,882,955	—
2004*	George W. Bush (R)	62,040,610	286	John Kerry (D)	59,028,444	251
2008	Barack H. Obama (D)	69,498,516	365	John McCain (R)	59,948,283	173
2012	Barack H. Obama (D)	65,915,795	332	Mitt Romney (R)	60,933,504	206
2016*	Donald J. Trump (R)	62,984,828	304	Hillary Clinton (D)	65,853,514	227

Note: Not all candidates who received electoral votes are shown. *1800—Elected by House of Representatives because of tied electoral vote. 1824—Elected by House of Representatives because no candidate polled a majority. By 1824, the Democratic Republicans had become a loose coalition of competing political groups. By 1828, Andrew Jackson supporters were known as Democrats and John Q. Adams and Henry Clay supporters as National Republicans. 1872—Greeley died Nov. 29, 1872. His electoral votes were split among four individuals. 1876—FL, LA, OR, and SC election returns were disputed. Congress in joint session (Mar. 2, 1877) declared Hayes and Wheeler elected president and vice president. 1956—Democrats elected 74 electors, but one from AL refused to vote for Stevenson. 1960—Sen. Harry F. Byrd (D, VA) received 15 electoral votes. 1972—John Hospers of CA received a vote from an elector of VA. 1976—Ronald Reagan of CA received a vote from an elector of WA. 1988—Sen. Lloyd Bentsen (D, TX) received a vote from an elector of WV. 2000—One Gore elector from Washington, DC, abstained. Nader was listed as "independent" on the ballot in some states; he was not on the ballot in all states. 2004—One MN elector voted for VP candidate John Edwards for both president and vice president. 2016—Seven electors from three states (HI, TX, WA) did not vote for the candidate to whom they were pledged (two Trump electors defected, as did five pledged to Clinton).

Major-Party Nominees for President and Vice President, 1856-2016

Asterisk (*) denotes winning ticket.

Democratic			Republican		
Year	President	Vice President	Year	President	Vice President
1856	James Buchanan*	John Breckinridge	1856	John Frémont	William Dayton
1860	Stephen A. Douglas[1]	Herschel V. Johnson	1860	Abraham Lincoln*	Hannibal Hamlin
1864	George McClellan	G. H. Pendleton	1864	Abraham Lincoln*	Andrew Johnson
1868	Horatio Seymour	Francis Blair	1868	Ulysses S. Grant*	Schuyler Colfax
1872	Horace Greeley	B. Gratz Brown	1872	Ulysses S. Grant*	Henry Wilson
1876	Samuel J. Tilden	Thomas Hendricks	1876	Rutherford B. Hayes*	William Wheeler
1880	Winfield Hancock	William English	1880	James A. Garfield*	Chester A. Arthur
1884	Grover Cleveland*	Thomas Hendricks	1884	James G. Blaine	John Logan
1888	Grover Cleveland	A. G. Thurman	1888	Benjamin Harrison*	Levi Morton
1892	Grover Cleveland*	Adlai Stevenson	1892	Benjamin Harrison	Whitelaw Reid
1896	William J. Bryan	Arthur Sewall	1896	William McKinley*	Garret Hobart
1900	William J. Bryan	Adlai Stevenson	1900	William McKinley*	Theodore Roosevelt
1904	Alton Parker	Henry Davis	1904	Theodore Roosevelt*	Charles Fairbanks
1908	William J. Bryan	John Kern	1908	William H. Taft*	James Sherman
1912	Woodrow Wilson*	Thomas Marshall	1912	William H. Taft	James Sherman[2]
1916	Woodrow Wilson*	Thomas Marshall	1916	Charles E. Hughes	Charles Fairbanks
1920	James M. Cox	Franklin D. Roosevelt	1920	Warren G. Harding*	Calvin Coolidge
1924	John W. Davis	Charles W. Bryan	1924	Calvin Coolidge*	Charles G. Dawes
1928	Alfred E. Smith	Joseph T. Robinson	1928	Herbert Hoover*	Charles Curtis
1932	Franklin D. Roosevelt*	John N. Garner	1932	Herbert Hoover	Charles Curtis
1936	Franklin D. Roosevelt*	John N. Garner	1936	Alfred M. Landon	Frank Knox
1940	Franklin D. Roosevelt*	Henry A. Wallace	1940	Wendell L. Willkie	Charles McNary
1944	Franklin D. Roosevelt*	Harry S. Truman	1944	Thomas E. Dewey	John W. Bricker
1948	Harry S. Truman*	Alben W. Barkley	1948	Thomas E. Dewey	Earl Warren
1952	Adlai E. Stevenson	John J. Sparkman	1952	Dwight D. Eisenhower*	Richard M. Nixon
1956	Adlai E. Stevenson	Estes Kefauver	1956	Dwight D. Eisenhower*	Richard M. Nixon
1960	John F. Kennedy*	Lyndon B. Johnson	1960	Richard M. Nixon	Henry Cabot Lodge
1964	Lyndon B. Johnson*	Hubert H. Humphrey	1964	Barry M. Goldwater	William E. Miller
1968	Hubert H. Humphrey	Edmund S. Muskie	1968	Richard M. Nixon*	Spiro T. Agnew
1972	George S. McGovern	R. Sargent Shriver Jr.[3]	1972	Richard M. Nixon*	Spiro T. Agnew
1976	Jimmy Carter*	Walter F. Mondale	1976	Gerald R. Ford	Bob Dole
1980	Jimmy Carter	Walter F. Mondale	1980	Ronald Reagan*	George H. W. Bush
1984	Walter F. Mondale	Geraldine Ferraro	1984	Ronald Reagan*	George H. W. Bush
1988	Michael S. Dukakis	Lloyd Bentsen	1988	George H. W. Bush*	Dan Quayle
1992	Bill Clinton*	Al Gore	1992	George H. W. Bush	Dan Quayle
1996	Bill Clinton*	Al Gore	1996	Bob Dole	Jack Kemp
2000	Al Gore	Joseph Lieberman	2000	George W. Bush*	Richard Cheney
2004	John Kerry	John Edwards	2004	George W. Bush*	Richard Cheney
2008	Barack Obama*	Joe Biden	2008	John McCain	Sarah Palin
2012	Barack Obama*	Joe Biden	2012	Mitt Romney	Paul Ryan
2016	Hillary Clinton	Tim Kaine	2016	Donald J. Trump*	Mike Pence

(1) Douglas and Johnson were nominated at the Baltimore convention. An earlier convention in Charleston, SC, failed to reach a consensus and resulted in a split in the party. The Southern faction of the Democrats nominated John Breckinridge for president and Joseph Lane for vice president. (2) Died Oct. 30; replaced on ballot by Nicholas Butler. (3) Chosen by Democratic National Committee after Thomas Eagleton withdrew because of controversy over past treatments for depression.

Third-Party and Independent Presidential Candidates

In most elections since 1860, fewer than one vote in 20 has been cast for a third-party candidate. Still, independent and third-party candidates often bring attention to prominent issues and can affect the outcome between major-party candidates.

Major vote-getters among third-party and independent candidates include James B. Weaver (People's Party), 1892; former Pres. Theodore Roosevelt (Progressive Party), 1912; Robert M. La Follette (Progressive Party), 1924; George C. Wallace (American Independent Party), 1968; and H. Ross Perot, as an independent in 1992 and with the Reform Party in 1996. In these six elections, non-major-party candidates combined polled at least 10% of the vote.

Roosevelt outpolled the Republican candidate, William Howard Taft, in 1912, capturing 28% of the popular vote and 88 electoral votes. In 1948, Strom Thurmond (States' Rights [Dixiecrat]) won 39 electoral votes from five Southern states; however, third-party candidates received only 5.75% of the popular vote. George Wallace's popularity in the same region in 1968 allowed him to get 46 electoral votes and 13.5% of the popular vote.

In 1992, Ross Perot captured 19% of the popular vote but failed to win a single electoral vote. In 1996, Perot won 8% of the popular vote; all third-party candidates combined won just over 10%. In 2000, Ralph Nader (Green, independent) won about 3% of the vote. Gary Johnson (Libertarian) won about 3% in 2016.

Notable Third-Party and Independent Campaigns by Year

Party	Presidential nominee	Year	Issues	Strength in
Anti-Masonic	William Wirt	1832	Against secret societies and oaths	PA, VT
Liberty	James G. Birney	1844	Anti-slavery	North
Free Soil	Martin Van Buren	1848	Anti-slavery	NY, OH
American (Know-Nothing)	Millard Fillmore	1856	Anti-immigrant	Northeast, South
Greenback	Peter Cooper	1876	For "cheap money," labor rights	National
Greenback	James B. Weaver	1880	For "cheap money," labor rights	National
Prohibition	John P. St. John	1884	Anti-liquor	National
People's (Populist)	James B. Weaver	1892	For "cheap money," end of national banks	South, West
Socialist	Eugene V. Debs	1900-12; 1920	For public ownership	National
Progressive (Bull Moose)	Theodore Roosevelt	1912	Against high tariffs	Midwest, West
Progressive	Robert M. La Follette	1924	For farmer and labor rights	Midwest, West
Socialist	Norman Thomas	1928-48	For liberal reforms	National
Union	William Lemke	1936	Anti-New Deal	National
States' Rights (Dixiecrat)	Strom Thurmond	1948	For states' rights	South
Progressive	Henry A. Wallace	1948	Anti-Cold War	NY, CA
American Independent	George C. Wallace	1968	For states' rights	South
American	John G. Schmitz	1972	For "law and order"	West, OH, LA
None (independent)	John B. Anderson	1980	A third choice	National
None (independent)	H. Ross Perot	1992	Federal budget deficit	National
Reform	H. Ross Perot	1996	Deficit, campaign finance	National
Green, independent	Ralph Nader	2000-08	Corporate power, domestic priorities	National
Libertarian	Gary Johnson	2012-16	Public debt, civil liberties	National

Presidential Election Results by State and County, 1960-2016

Source: Federal Election Commission (FEC); local secretaries of state and state elections offices. Some candidates who did not appear on ballots are omitted from historical results.

Alabama

County	2016 Clinton (D)	2016 Trump (R)	2012 Obama (D)	2012 Romney (R)
Autauga	5,936	18,172	6,363	17,379
Baldwin	18,458	72,883	18,424	66,016
Barbour	4,871	5,454	5,912	5,550
Bibb	1,874	6,738	2,202	6,132
Blount	2,156	22,859	2,970	20,757
Bullock	3,530	1,140	4,061	1,251
Butler	3,726	4,901	4,374	5,087
Calhoun	13,242	32,865	15,511	30,278
Chambers	5,784	7,843	6,871	7,626
Cherokee	1,547	8,953	2,132	7,506
Chilton	2,911	15,081	3,397	13,932
Choctaw	3,109	4,106	3,786	4,152
Clarke	5,749	7,140	6,334	7,470
Clay	1,237	5,245	1,777	4,817
Cleburne	684	5,764	971	5,272
Coffee	4,221	15,875	4,925	14,666
Colbert	7,312	16,746	9,166	13,936
Conecuh	3,080	3,420	3,555	3,439
Coosa	1,782	3,381	2,191	3,049
Covington	2,387	13,267	3,158	12,153
Crenshaw	1,664	4,513	2,050	4,331
Cullman	3,798	32,989	5,052	28,999
Dale	4,413	13,808	5,286	13,108
Dallas	12,836	5,789	14,612	6,288
De Kalb	3,622	21,405	5,239	18,331
Elmore	8,443	27,634	8,954	26,253
Escambia	4,605	9,935	5,489	9,287
Etowah	10,442	32,353	12,803	29,130
Fayette	1,362	6,712	1,817	6,054
Franklin	2,197	9,466	3,171	7,567
Geneva	1,525	9,994	2,039	9,175
Greene	4,013	838	4,521	804
Hale	4,775	3,173	5,411	3,210
Henry	2,292	5,632	3,083	5,628
Houston	10,664	30,728	12,367	29,270
Jackson	3,673	16,672	5,822	14,439
Jefferson	156,873	134,768	159,876	141,683
Lamar	1,036	5,823	1,646	5,457
Lauderdale	9,952	27,899	12,511	23,911
Lawrence	3,627	10,833	5,069	8,874
Lee	21,230	34,617	21,381	32,194
Limestone	9,468	29,067	9,829	25,295
Lowndes	4,883	1,751	5,747	1,756
Macon	7,566	1,431	9,045	1,331
Madison	62,822	89,520	62,015	90,884
Marengo	5,615	5,233	6,167	5,336
Marion	1,432	11,274	2,249	9,697
Marshall	4,917	29,233	6,299	25,867
Mobile	72,186	95,116	78,760	94,893
Monroe	4,332	5,795	4,914	5,741
Montgomery	58,916	34,003	63,085	38,332
Morgan	11,254	37,486	13,439	35,391
Perry	3,824	1,407	4,568	1,506
Pickens	3,972	5,456	4,455	5,124
Pike	5,056	7,693	6,035	7,963
Randolph	2,291	7,705	3,078	7,224
Russell	9,579	9,210	10,500	8,278
St. Clair	5,589	31,651	5,801	29,031
Shelby	22,977	73,020	20,051	71,436
Sumter	4,746	1,581	5,421	1,586
Talladega	12,121	20,614	13,905	19,246
Tallapoosa	5,519	13,594	6,319	12,396
Tuscaloosa	31,762	47,723	32,048	45,748
Walker	4,497	24,266	6,557	21,651
Washington	2,374	6,042	2,976	5,761
Wilcox	4,339	1,742	4,868	1,679
Winston	872	9,228	1,286	8,312
Totals	**729,547**	**1,318,255**	**795,696**	**1,255,925**

Alabama Vote Since 1960

2016: Trump, R, 1,318,255; Clinton, D, 729,547; Johnson, Ind., 44,467; Stein, Ind., 9,391.

2012: Romney, R, 1,255,925; Obama, D, 795,696; Johnson, Ind., 12,328; Stein, Ind., 3,397; Goode, Ind., 2,981.

2008: McCain, R, 1,266,546; Obama, D, 813,479; Nader, Ind., 6,788; Barr, Ind., 4,991; Baldwin, Ind., 4,310.

2004: Bush, R, 1,176,394; Kerry, D, 693,933; Nader, Ind., 6,701; Badnarik, Ind., 3,529; Peroutka, Ind., 1,994.

2000: Bush, R, 941,173; Gore, D, 692,611; Nader, Ind., 18,323; Buchanan, Ind., 6,351; Browne, LB, 5,893; Phillips, Ind., 775; Hagelin, Ind., 447.

1996: Dole, R, 769,044; Clinton, D, 662,165; Perot, RF, 92,149; Browne, LB, 5,290; Phillips, Ind., 2,365; Hagelin, Natural Law, 1,697; Harris, Ind., 516.

1992: Bush, R, 804,283; Clinton, D, 690,080; Perot, Ind., 183,109; Marrou, LB, 5,737; Fulani, New Alliance, 2,161.

1988: Bush, R, 815,576; Dukakis, D, 549,506; Paul, LB, 8,460; Fulani, Ind., 3,311.

1984: Reagan, R, 872,849; Mondale, D, 551,899; Bergland, LB, 9,504.

1980: Reagan, R, 654,192; Carter, D, 636,730; Anderson, Ind., 16,481; Rarick, Amer. Ind., 15,010; Clark, LB, 13,318; Bubar, Statesman, 1,743; Hall, Comm., 1,629; DeBerry, Soc. Workers, 1,303; McReynolds, Soc., 1,006; Commoner, Citizens, 517.

1976: Carter, D, 659,170; Ford, R, 504,070; Maddox, Amer. Ind., 9,198; Bubar, Prohib., 6,669; Hall, Comm., 1,954; MacBride, LB, 1,481.

1972: Nixon, R, 728,701; McGovern, D, 219,108 plus Natl. Dem. Party of AL, 37,815; Schmitz, Conservative, 11,918; Munn, Prohib., 8,551.

1968: Wallace, 3rd party, 691,425; Humphrey, D, 196,579; Nixon, R, 146,923; Munn, Prohib., 4,022.

1964: Goldwater, R, 479,085; D (electors unpledged), 209,848; scattered, 105.

1960: Kennedy, D, 324,050; Nixon, R, 237,981; Faubus, States' Rights, 4,367; Decker, Prohib., 2,106; King, Afro-Americans, 1,485; scattered, 236.

Alaska

	2016 Clinton (D)	2016 Trump (R)	2012 Obama (D)	2012 Romney (R)
Totals	116,454	163,387	122,640	164,676

Alaska Vote Since 1960

2016: Trump, R, 163,387; Clinton, D, 116,454; Johnson, LB, 18,725; Stein, Green, 5,735; Castle, Const., 3,866; De La Fuente, unaff., 1,240.

2012: Romney, R, 164,676; Obama, D, 122,640; Johnson, LB, 7,392; Stein, Green, 2,917.

2008: McCain, R, 193,841; Obama, D, 123,594; Nader, Ind., 3,783; Baldwin, AK Ind., 1,660; Barr, LB, 1,589.

2004: Bush, R, 190,889; Kerry, D, 111,025; Nader, Populist, 5,069; Peroutka, AK Ind., 2,092; Badnarik, LB, 1,675; Cobb, Green, 1,058.

2000: Bush, R, 167,398; Gore, D, 79,004; Nader, Green, 28,747; Buchanan, RF, 5,192; Browne, LB, 2,636; Hagelin, Natural Law, 919; Phillips, Const., 596.

1996: Dole, R, 122,746; Clinton, D, 80,380; Perot, RF, 26,333; Nader, Green, 7,597; Browne, LB, 2,276; Phillips, U.S. Taxpayers, 925; Hagelin, Natural Law, 729.

1992: Bush, R, 102,000; Clinton, D, 78,294; Perot, Ind., 73,481; Gritz, Populist/America First, 1,379; Marrou, LB, 1,378.

1988: Bush, R, 119,251; Dukakis, D, 72,584; Paul, LB, 5,484; Fulani, New Alliance, 1,024.

1984: Reagan, R, 138,377; Mondale, D, 62,007; Bergland, LB, 6,378.

1980: Reagan, R, 86,112; Carter, D, 41,842; Clark, LB, 18,479; Anderson, Ind., 11,155; write-in, 857.

1976: Ford, R, 71,555; Carter, D, 44,058; MacBride, LB, 6,785.

1972: Nixon, R, 55,349; McGovern, D, 32,967; Schmitz, Amer., 6,903.

1968: Nixon, R, 37,600; Humphrey, D, 35,411; Wallace, 3rd party, 10,024.

1964: Johnson, D, 44,329; Goldwater, R, 22,930.

1960: Nixon, R, 30,953; Kennedy, D, 29,809.

Arizona

County	2016 Clinton (D)	2016 Trump (R)	2012 Obama (D)	2012 Romney (R)
Apache	17,083	8,240	17,147	8,250
Cochise	17,450	28,092	18,546	29,497
Coconino	32,404	21,108	29,257	21,220
Gila	7,003	14,182	7,697	13,455
Graham	3,301	8,025	3,609	8,076
Greenlee	1,092	1,892	1,310	1,592
La Paz	1,575	4,003	1,880	3,714

County	2016		2012	
	Clinton (D)	Trump (R)	Obama (D)	Romney (R)
Maricopa	702,907	747,361	602,288	749,885
Mohave	17,455	58,282	19,533	49,168
Navajo	16,459	20,577	16,945	19,884
Pima	224,661	167,428	201,251	174,779
Pinal	47,892	72,819	44,306	62,079
Santa Cruz	11,690	3,897	9,486	4,235
Yavapai	35,590	71,330	33,918	64,468
Yuma	24,605	25,165	18,059	23,352
Totals	1,161,167	1,252,401	1,025,232	1,233,654

Arizona Vote Since 1960

2016: Trump, R, 1,252,401; Clinton, D, 1,161,167; Johnson, LB, 106,327; Stein, Green, 34,345; McMullin, Ind., 17,449; Castle, Const., 1,058.

2012: Romney, R, 1,233,654; Obama, D, 1,025,232; Johnson, LB, 32,100; Stein, Green, 7,816.

2008: McCain, R, 1,230,111; Obama, D, 1,034,707; Barr, LB, 12,555; Nader, New Prog., 11,301; McKinney, Green, 3,406.

2004: Bush, R, 1,104,294; Kerry, D, 893,524; Badnarik, LB, 11,856.

2000: Bush, R, 781,652; Gore, D, 685,341; Nader, Green, 45,645; Buchanan, RF, 12,373; Smith, LB, 5,775; Hagelin, Natural Law, 1,120.

1996: Clinton, D, 653,288; Dole, R, 622,073; Perot, RF, 112,072; Browne, LB, 14,358.

1992: Bush, R, 572,086; Clinton, D, 543,050; Perot, Ind., 353,741; Gritz, Populist/America First, 8,141; Marrou, LB, 6,759; Hagelin, Natural Law, 2,267.

1988: Bush, R, 702,541; Dukakis, D, 454,029; Paul, LB, 13,351; Fulani, New Alliance, 1,662.

1984: Reagan, R, 681,416; Mondale, D, 333,854; Bergland, LB, 10,585.

1980: Reagan, R, 529,688; Carter, D, 246,843; Anderson, Ind., 76,952; Clark, LB, 18,784; DeBerry, Soc. Workers, 1,100; Commoner, Citizens, 551; Hall, Comm., 25; Griswold, Workers World, 2.

1976: Ford, R, 418,642; Carter, D, 295,602; McCarthy, Ind., 19,229; MacBride, LB, 7,647; Camejo, Soc. Workers, 928; Anderson, Amer., 564; Maddox, Amer. Ind., 85.

1972: Nixon, R, 402,812; McGovern, D, 198,540; Jenness, Soc. Workers, 30,945; Schmitz, Amer. Ind., 21,208.

1968: Nixon, R, 266,721; Humphrey, D, 170,514; Wallace, 3rd party, 46,573; McCarthy, New Party, 2,751; Cleaver, Peace/ Freedom, 217; Halstead, Soc. Workers, 85; Blomen, Soc. Labor, 75.

1964: Goldwater, R, 242,535; Johnson, D, 237,753; Hass, Soc. Labor, 482.

1960: Nixon, R, 221,241; Kennedy, D, 176,781; Hass, Soc. Labor, 469.

Arkansas

County	2016		2012	
	Clinton (D)	Trump (R)	Obama (D)	Romney (R)
Arkansas	1,939	3,826	2,455	3,897
Ashley	2,408	5,338	2,859	4,867
Baxter	4,169	14,682	5,172	13,688
Benton	28,005	60,871	22,636	54,646
Boone	2,926	12,235	3,772	11,159
Bradley	1,317	2,164	1,449	2,134
Calhoun	639	1,556	660	1,458
Carroll	3,342	6,786	3,696	6,125
Chicot	2,350	1,716	2,649	1,670
Clark	3,620	4,404	3,811	4,343
Clay	1,199	3,781	1,738	3,225
Cleburne	2,101	9,458	2,620	8,693
Cleveland	723	2,462	845	2,313
Columbia	3,140	5,456	3,557	5,790
Conway	2,656	4,849	3,005	4,514
Craighead	10,538	22,892	10,527	20,350
Crawford	4,488	16,686	4,881	15,145
Crittenden	8,410	6,964	9,487	6,998
Cross	1,999	4,584	2,279	4,269
Dallas	1,165	1,509	1,337	1,665
Desha	2,228	1,919	2,443	1,896
Drew	2,365	3,968	2,630	3,887
Faulkner	14,629	29,346	13,621	26,722
Franklin	1,376	5,039	1,726	4,631
Fulton	1,067	3,471	1,452	2,949
Garland	12,311	26,087	13,804	26,014

County	2016		2012	
	Clinton (D)	Trump (R)	Obama (D)	Romney (R)
Grant	1,373	5,725	1,468	4,829
Greene	3,071	10,720	4,000	9,071
Hempstead	2,377	4,401	2,468	4,284
Hot Spring	3,149	8,172	3,830	7,097
Howard	1,351	3,157	1,471	2,892
Independence	2,881	9,936	3,281	8,728
Izard	1,113	4,042	1,524	3,575
Jackson	1,583	3,267	2,095	3,072
Jefferson	15,772	9,250	17,470	9,520
Johnson	2,427	6,091	2,799	5,064
Lafayette	1,032	1,758	1,173	1,713
Lawrence	1,263	4,064	1,788	3,536
Lee	1,735	1,229	2,107	1,280
Lincoln	1,252	2,455	1,425	2,199
Little River	1,397	3,605	1,552	3,385
Logan	1,715	5,746	2,009	5,079
Lonoke	5,664	19,958	5,625	17,880
Madison	1,588	4,928	2,099	4,263
Marion	1,434	5,336	2,037	4,774
Miller	4,273	11,294	4,518	10,622
Mississippi	5,670	7,061	6,467	6,603
Monroe	1,312	1,489	1,583	1,585
Montgomery	748	2,643	920	2,369
Nevada	1,157	2,000	1,314	1,996
Newton	699	2,875	993	2,508
Ouachita	4,321	5,351	4,633	5,521
Perry	1,049	3,008	1,187	2,581
Phillips	4,310	2,446	5,202	2,598
Pike	685	3,150	851	2,847
Poinsett	1,880	5,502	2,390	4,974
Polk	1,212	6,618	1,556	5,955
Pope	5,000	16,256	5,126	14,763
Prairie	814	2,505	880	2,153
Pulaski	89,574	61,257	87,248	68,984
Randolph	1,425	4,509	2,046	3,701
St. Francis	4,031	3,195	4,910	3,368
Saline	13,256	35,863	12,869	32,963
Scott	602	2,731	897	2,631
Searcy	601	2,955	814	2,699
Sebastian	12,300	29,127	13,092	29,169
Sevier	1,075	3,282	1,042	3,136
Sharp	1,472	5,407	2,092	4,921
Stone	1,203	4,113	1,356	3,776
Union	5,855	10,456	6,196	10,699
Van Buren	1,549	5,382	1,832	4,365
Washington	33,366	41,476	28,236	39,688
White	5,170	21,077	5,765	20,011
Woodruff	1,118	1,347	1,340	1,227
Yell	1,480	4,608	1,722	4,042
Totals	380,494	684,872	394,409	647,744

Arkansas Vote Since 1960

2016: Trump, R, 684,872; Clinton, D, 380,494; Johnson, LB, 29,949; McMullin, Better For America, 13,176; Stein, Green, 9,473; Hedges, Ind., 4,709; Castle, Const., 4,613; Kahn, Ind., 3,390.

2012: Romney, R, 647,744; Obama, D, 394,409; Johnson, LB, 16,276; Stein, Green, 9,305; Lindsay, Socialism/Liberation, 1,734.

2008: McCain, R, 638,017; Obama, D, 422,310; Nader, Ind., 12,882; Barr, LB, 4,776; Baldwin, Const., 4,023; McKinney, Green, 3,470; La Riva, Socialism/Liberation, 1,139.

2004: Bush, R, 572,898; Kerry, D, 469,953; Nader, Populist, 6,171; Badnarik, LB, 2,352; Peroutka, Const., 2,083; Cobb, Green, 1,488.

2000: Bush, R, 472,940; Gore, D, 422,768; Nader, Green, 13,421; Buchanan, RF, 7,358; Browne, LB, 2,781; Phillips, Const., 1,415; Hagelin, Natural Law, 1,098.

1996: Clinton, D, 475,171; Dole, R, 325,416; Perot, RF, 69,884; Nader, Ind., 3,649; Browne, Ind., 3,076; Phillips, Ind., 2,065; Forbes, Ind., 932; Collins, Ind., 823; Masters, Ind., 749; Moorehead, Ind., 747; Hagelin, Ind., 729; Hollis, Ind., 538; Dodge, Ind., 483.

1992: Clinton, D, 505,823; Bush, R, 337,324; Perot, Ind., 99,132; Phillips, U.S. Taxpayers, 1,437; Marrou, LB, 1,261; Fulani, New Alliance, 1,022.

1988: Bush, R, 466,578; Dukakis, D, 349,237; Duke, Populist, 5,146; Paul, LB, 3,297.

1984: Reagan, R, 534,774; Mondale, D, 338,646; Bergland, LB, 2,220.

1980: Reagan, R, 403,164; Carter, D, 398,041; Anderson, Ind., 22,468; Clark, LB, 8,970; Commoner, Citizens, 2,345; Bubar, Statesman, 1,350; Hall, Comm., 1,244.

1976: Carter, D, 498,604; Ford, R, 267,903; McCarthy, Ind., 639; Anderson, Amer. Ind., 389.

1972: Nixon, R, 445,751; McGovern, D, 198,899; Schmitz, Amer. Ind., 3,016.

1968: Wallace, 3rd party, 235,627; Nixon, R, 189,062; Humphrey, D, 184,901.

1964: Johnson, D, 314,197; Goldwater, R, 243,264; Kasper, Natl. States' Rights, 2,965.

1960: Kennedy, D, 215,049; Nixon, R, 184,508; Faubus, Natl. States' Rights, 28,952.

California

County	2016		2012	
---	Clinton (D)	Trump (R)	Obama (D)	Romney (R)
Alameda	514,842	95,922	469,684	108,182
Alpine	334	217	389	236
Amador	6,004	10,485	6,830	10,281
Butte	41,567	45,144	42,669	44,479
Calaveras	7,944	13,511	8,670	12,365
Colusa	2,661	3,551	2,314	3,601
Contra Costa	319,287	115,956	290,824	136,517
Del Norte	3,485	5,134	3,791	4,614
El Dorado	36,404	49,247	35,166	50,973
Fresno	141,341	124,049	129,129	124,490
Glenn	3,065	5,788	3,301	5,632
Humboldt	33,200	18,373	34,457	18,825
Imperial	32,667	12,704	25,136	12,777
Inyo	3,155	4,248	3,422	4,340
Kern	98,689	129,584	89,495	126,618
Kings	13,617	18,093	12,979	17,671
Lake	11,496	10,599	13,163	9,200
Lassen	2,224	7,574	3,053	7,296
Los Angeles	2,464,364	769,743	2,216,903	885,333
Madera	17,029	23,357	16,018	22,852
Marin	108,707	21,771	99,896	30,684
Mariposa	3,122	5,185	3,498	5,140
Mendocino	22,079	10,888	23,193	9,658
Merced	37,317	28,725	33,005	27,581
Modoc	877	2,696	1,111	2,777
Mono	2,773	2,111	2,733	2,285
Monterey	89,088	34,895	82,920	37,390
Napa	39,199	17,411	35,870	19,526
Nevada	26,053	23,365	24,663	24,986
Orange	609,961	507,148	512,440	582,332
Placer	73,509	95,138	66,818	99,921
Plumas	3,459	5,420	4,026	5,721
Riverside	373,695	333,243	329,063	318,127
Sacramento	326,023	189,789	300,503	202,514
San Benito	12,521	7,841	11,276	7,343
San Bernardino	340,833	271,240	305,109	262,358
San Diego	735,476	477,766	626,957	536,726
San Francisco	345,084	37,688	301,723	47,076
San Joaquin	121,124	88,936	114,121	86,071
San Luis Obispo	67,107	56,164	61,258	59,967
San Mateo	237,882	57,929	206,085	72,756
Santa Barbara	107,142	56,365	94,129	64,606
Santa Clara	511,684	144,826	450,818	174,843
Santa Cruz	95,249	22,438	90,805	24,047
Shasta	22,301	51,778	25,819	48,067
Sierra	601	1,048	653	1,056
Siskiyou	7,234	11,341	8,046	11,077
Solano	102,360	51,920	96,783	52,092
Sonoma	160,435	51,408	153,942	54,784
Stanislaus	81,647	78,494	77,724	73,459
Sutter	13,076	18,176	12,192	18,122
Tehama	6,809	15,494	7,934	14,235
Trinity	2,214	2,812	2,674	2,716
Tulare	47,585	58,299	41,752	56,956
Tuolumne	9,123	14,551	9,998	13,880
Ventura	194,402	132,323	170,929	147,958
Yolo	54,752	20,739	48,715	23,368
Yuba	7,910	13,170	7,711	11,275
Totals	**8,753,792**	**4,483,814**	**7,854,285**	**4,839,958**

California Vote Since 1960

2016: Clinton, D, 8,753,792; Trump, R, 4,483,814; Johnson, LB, 478,500; Stein, Green, 278,658; Sanders, Ind., 79,341; La Riva, Peace/Freedom, 66,101; McMullin, Ind., 39,596.

2012: Obama, D, 7,854,285; Romney, R, 4,839,958; Johnson, LB, 143,221; Stein, Green, 85,638; Barr, Peace/Freedom, 53,824; Hoefling, Amer. Ind., 38,372.

2008: Obama, D, 8,274,473; McCain, R, 5,011,781; Nader, Peace/Freedom, 108,381; Barr, LB, 67,582; Alan Keyes, Amer. Ind., 40,673; McKinney, Green, 38,774.

2004: Kerry, D, 6,745,485; Bush, R, 5,509,826; Badnarik, LB, 50,165; Cobb, Green, 40,771; Peltier, Peace/Freedom, 27,607; Peroutka, Amer. Ind., 26,645.

2000: Gore, D, 5,861,203; Bush, R, 4,567,429; Nader, Green, 418,707; Browne, LB, 45,520; Buchanan, RF, 44,987; Phillips, Amer. Ind., 17,042; Hagelin, Natural Law, 10,934.

1996: Clinton, D, 5,119,835; Dole, R, 3,828,380; Perot, RF, 697,847; Nader, Green, 237,016; Browne, LB, 73,600; Feinland, Peace/Freedom, 25,332; Phillips, Amer. Ind., 21,202; Hagelin, Natural Law, 15,403.

1992: Clinton, D, 5,121,325; Bush, R, 3,630,575; Perot, Ind., 2,296,006; Marrou, LB, 48,139; Daniels, Ind., 18,597; Phillips, U.S. Taxpayers, 12,711.

1988: Bush, R, 5,054,917; Dukakis, D, 4,702,233; Paul, LB, 70,105; Fulani, Ind., 31,181.

1984: Reagan, R, 5,305,410; Mondale, D, 3,815,947; Bergland, LB, 48,400.

1980: Reagan, R, 4,524,858; Carter, D, 3,083,661; Anderson, Ind., 739,833; Clark, LB, 148,434; Commoner, Ind., 61,063; Smith, Peace/Freedom, 18,116; Rarick, Amer. Ind., 9,856.

1976: Ford, R, 3,882,244; Carter, D, 3,742,284; McCarthy, write-in, 58,412; MacBride, LB, 56,388; Maddox, Amer. Ind., 51,098; Wright, People's, 41,731; Camejo, Soc. Workers, 17,259; Hall, Comm., 12,766; write-in, 4,935.

1972: Nixon, R, 4,602,096; McGovern, D, 3,475,847; Schmitz, Amer. Ind., 232,554; Spock, Peace/Freedom, 55,167; Hospers, LB, 980; Jenness, Soc. Workers, 574; Hall, Comm., 373; Fisher, Soc. Labor, 197; Munn, Prohib., 53; Green, Universal, 21.

1968: Nixon, R, 3,467,664; Humphrey, D, 3,244,318; Wallace, 3rd party, 487,270; Peace/Freedom, 27,707; McCarthy, Alternative, 20,721; Gregory, write-in, 3,230; Blomen, Soc. Labor, 341; Mitchell, Comm., 260; Munn, Prohib., 59; Soeters, Defense, 17.

1964: Johnson, D, 4,171,877; Goldwater, R, 2,879,108; Hass, Soc. Labor, 489; DeBerry, Soc. Workers, 378; Munn, Prohib., 305; Hensley, Universal, 19.

1960: Nixon, R, 3,259,722; Kennedy, D, 3,224,099; Decker, Prohib., 21,706; Hass, Soc. Labor, 1,051.

Colorado

County	2016		2012	
---	Clinton (D)	Trump (R)	Obama (D)	Romney (R)
Adams	96,558	80,082	100,649	70,972
Alamosa	3,189	3,046	3,811	2,705
Arapahoe	159,885	117,053	153,905	125,588
Archuleta	2,500	4,264	2,679	3,872
Baca	283	1,753	467	1,559
Bent	590	1,188	815	1,075
Boulder	132,334	41,396	125,091	49,981
Broomfield	19,731	14,367	16,966	15,008
Chaffee	4,888	5,391	5,086	5,070
Cheyenne	132	925	172	889
Clear Creek	2,729	2,575	3,119	2,430
Conejos	1,771	1,914	2,213	1,835
Costilla	1,125	588	1,340	446
Crowley	339	1,079	535	924
Custer	797	2,061	868	1,788
Delta	4,087	11,655	4,622	10,915
Denver	244,551	62,690	222,018	73,111
Dolores	242	944	334	859
Douglas	68,657	102,573	61,094	104,397
Eagle	14,099	8,990	12,792	9,411
El Paso	108,010	179,228	111,819	170,952
Elbert	3,134	11,705	3,603	10,266
Fremont	5,297	15,122	6,704	13,174
Garfield	11,271	13,132	11,305	12,535
Gilpin	1,634	1,566	1,892	1,346
Grand	3,358	4,494	3,684	4,253
Gunnison	5,128	3,289	5,044	3,341
Hinsdale	197	339	229	353
Huerfano	1,633	1,883	1,953	1,646
Jackson	171	629	216	600
Jefferson	160,776	138,177	159,296	144,197
Kiowa	91	728	118	677
Kit Carson	536	2,967	838	2,785
La Plata	15,525	12,587	15,489	12,794
Lake	1,616	1,270	1,839	1,098
Larimer	93,113	83,430	92,747	82,376
Las Animas	2,650	3,710	3,445	3,263
Lincoln	409	1,892	552	1,687
Logan	1,851	7,282	2,712	6,179
Mesa	21,729	49,779	23,846	47,472
Mineral	237	344	291	344
Moffat	874	5,305	1,330	4,695
Montezuma	3,973	7,853	4,542	7,401
Montrose	5,466	14,382	6,138	13,552
Morgan	3,151	8,145	3,912	6,602
Otero	2,943	4,928	3,647	4,382
Ouray	1,697	1,351	1,646	1,481
Park	3,421	6,135	3,862	5,236

County	2016		2012	
	Clinton (D)	Trump (R)	Obama (D)	Romney (R)
Phillips	436	1,791	588	1,637
Pitkin	7,333	2,550	6,849	3,024
Prowers	1,186	3,531	1,519	3,230
Pueblo	35,875	36,265	42,551	31,894
Rio Blanco	436	2,791	568	2,724
Rio Grande	2,001	3,085	2,478	2,918
Routt	7,600	5,230	7,547	5,469
Saguache	1,417	1,147	1,865	964
San Juan	265	215	266	212
San Miguel	2,975	1,033	2,992	1,154
Sedgwick	267	1,015	419	881
Summit	9,557	5,100	9,347	5,571
Teller	3,603	9,745	4,333	8,702
Washington	296	2,299	468	2,076
Weld	46,519	76,651	49,050	63,775
Yuma	726	3,850	987	3,490
Totals	1,338,870	1,202,484	1,323,102	1,185,243

Colorado Vote Since 1960

2016: Clinton, D, 1,338,870; Trump, R, 1,202,484; Johnson, LB, 144,121; Stein, Green, 38,437; McMullin, unaff., 28,917; Castle, Const., 11,699; Keniston, Veterans, 5,028; Smith, unaff., 1,819; De La Fuente, Amer. Delta, 1,255; Kopitke, Independent Amer., 1,096; Maldonado, Ind., 872; Maturen, Amer. Solidarity, 862; Silva, Nutrition, 751; Scott, unaff., 749; Hoefling, America's Party, 710; La Riva, Socialism/Liberation, 531; Kennedy, Soc. Workers, 452; Kotlikoff, Ind., 392; Lyttle, Nonviolent/Pacifist, 382; Atwood, Approval Voting, 337; Soltysik, Soc. USA, 271; Hedges, Prohib., 185.

2012: Obama, D, 1,323,102; Romney, R, 1,185,243; Johnson, LB, 35,545; Stein, Green, 7,508; Goode, Const., 6,234; Barr, Peace/Freedom, 5,059; Reed, unaff., 2,589; Anderson, Justice, 1,260; Tittle, We the People, 792; Hoefling, Amer. Ind., 679; La Riva, Socialism/Liberation, 317; Alexander, Soc. USA, 308; Miller, A3P, 266; Stevens, Objectivist, 235; Harris, Soc. Workers, 192; White, Soc. Equality, 189.

2008: Obama, D, 1,288,633; McCain, R, 1,073,629; Nader, unaff., 13,352; Barr, LB, 10,898; Baldwin, Const., 6,233; Alan Keyes, Amer. Ind., 3,051; McKinney, Green, 2,822; McEnulty, unaff., 829; Jay, Boston Tea, 598; Allen, HeartQuake '08, 348; Stevens, Objectivist, 336; Moore, Soc. USA, 226; La Riva, Socialism/Liberation, 158; Harris, Soc. Workers, 154; Lyttle, U.S. Pacifist, 110; Amondson, Prohib., 85.

2004: Bush, R, 1,101,255; Kerry, D, 1,001,732; Nader, RF, 12,718; Badnarik, LB, 7,664; Peroutka, Amer. Const., 2,562; Cobb, Green, 1,591; Andress, Ind., 804; Amondson, Concerns of People, 378; Van Auken, Soc. Equal., 329; Harris, Soc. Workers, 241; Brown, Soc., 216; Dodge, Prohib., 140.

2000: Bush, R, 883,748; Gore, D, 738,227; Nader, Green, 91,434; Browne, LB, 12,799; Buchanan, RF, 10,465; Hagelin, RF, 2,240; Phillips, Amer. Const., 1,319; McReynolds, Soc., 712; Harris, Soc. Workers, 216; Dodge, Prohib., 208.

1996: Dole, R, 691,848; Clinton, D, 671,152; Perot, RF, 99,629; Nader, Green, 25,070; Browne, LB, 12,392; Phillips, Amer. Const., 2,813; Collins, Ind., 2,809; Hagelin, Natural Law, 2,547; Hollis, Soc., 669; Moorehead, Workers World, 599; Templin, Amer., 557; Dodge, Prohib., 375; Harris, Soc. Workers, 244.

1992: Clinton, D, 629,681; Bush, R, 562,850; Perot, Ind., 366,010; Marrou, LB, 8,669; Fulani, New Alliance, 1,608.

1988: Bush, R, 728,177; Dukakis, D, 621,453; Paul, LB, 15,482; Dodge, Prohib., 4,604.

1984: Reagan, R, 821,817; Mondale, D, 454,975; Bergland, LB, 11,257.

1980: Reagan, R, 652,264; Carter, D, 367,973; Anderson, Ind., 130,633; Clark, LB, 25,744; Commoner, Citizens, 5,614; Bubar, Statesman, 1,180; Pulley, Soc., 520; Hall, Comm., 487.

1976: Ford, R, 584,367; Carter, D, 460,353; McCarthy, Ind., 26,107; MacBride, LB, 5,330; Bubar, Prohib., 2,882.

1972: Nixon, R, 597,189; McGovern, D, 329,980; Schmitz, Amer., 17,269; Fisher, Soc. Labor, 4,361; Spock, People's, 2,403; Hospers, LB, 1,111; Jenness, Soc. Workers, 555; Munn, Prohib., 467; Hall, Comm., 432.

1968: Nixon, R, 409,345; Humphrey, D, 335,174; Wallace, 3rd party, 60,813; Blomen, Soc. Labor, 3,016; Gregory, New Party, 1,393; Munn, Prohib., 275; Halstead, Soc. Workers, 235.

1964: Johnson, D, 476,024; Goldwater, R, 296,767; DeBerry, Soc. Workers, 2,537; Munn, Prohib., 1,356; Hass, Soc. Labor, 302.

1960: Nixon, R, 402,242; Kennedy, D, 330,629; Hass, Soc. Labor, 2,803; Dobbs, Soc. Workers, 572.

Connecticut

City	2016		2012	
	Clinton (D)	Trump (R)	Obama (D)	Romney (R)
Fairfield	243,852	160,077	217,294	175,168
Hartford	240,403	148,173	244,639	143,238
Litchfield	39,775	53,051	43,856	47,201
Middlesex	45,357	38,867	47,855	34,591
New Haven	205,609	159,048	218,998	138,364
New London	62,278	54,058	67,144	46,119
Tolland	38,506	34,194	39,366	30,450
Windham	21,792	25,747	25,957	19,768
Totals	897,572	673,215	905,083	634,892

Connecticut Vote Since 1960

2016: Clinton, D, 897,572; Trump, R, 673,215; Johnson, LB, 48,676; Stein, Green, 22,841; McMullin, Ind., 2,108.

2012: Obama, D, 905,083; Romney, R, 634,892; Johnson, LB, 12,580; Anderson, Ind., 5,487.

2008: Obama, D, 997,772; McCain, R, 629,428; Nader, Ind., 19,162.

2004: Kerry, D, 857,488; Bush, R, 693,826; Nader, petitioning cand., 12,969; Cobb, Green, 9,564; Badnarik, LB, 3,367; Peroutka, Concerned Citizens, 1,543.

2000: Gore, D, 816,015; Bush, R, 561,094; Nader, Green, 64,452; Phillips, Concerned Citizens, 9,695; Buchanan, RF, 4,731; Browne, LB, 3,484.

1996: Clinton, D, 735,740; Dole, R, 483,109; Perot, RF, 139,523; Nader, Green, 24,321; Browne, LB, 5,788; Phillips, Concerned Citizens, 2,425; Hagelin, Natural Law, 1,703.

1992: Clinton, D, 682,318; Bush, R, 578,313; Perot, Ind., 348,771; Marrou, LB, 5,391; Fulani, New Alliance, 1,363.

1988: Bush, R, 750,241; Dukakis, D, 676,584; Paul, LB, 14,071; Fulani, New Alliance, 2,491.

1984: Reagan, R, 890,877; Mondale, D, 569,597.

1980: Reagan, R, 677,210; Carter, D, 541,732; Anderson, Ind., 171,807; Clark, LB, 8,570; Commoner, Citizens, 6,130; scattered, 836.

1976: Ford, R, 719,261; Carter, D, 647,895; Maddox, George Wallace Party, 7,101; LaRouche, U.S. Labor, 1,789.

1972: Nixon, R, 810,763; McGovern, D, 555,498; Schmitz, Amer., 17,239; scattered, 777.

1968: Humphrey, D, 621,561; Nixon, R, 556,721; Wallace, 3rd party, 76,650; scattered, 1,300.

1964: Johnson, D, 826,269; Goldwater, R, 390,996; scattered, 1,313.

1960: Kennedy, D, 657,055; Nixon, R, 565,813.

Delaware

County	2016		2012	
	Clinton (D)	Trump (R)	Obama (D)	Romney (R)
Kent	33,351	36,991	35,527	32,135
New Castle	162,919	85,525	167,082	81,230
Sussex	39,333	62,611	39,975	52,119
Totals	235,603	185,127	242,584	165,484

Delaware Vote Since 1960

2016: Clinton, D, 235,603; Trump, R, 185,127; Johnson, LB, 14,757; Stein, Green, 6,103; McMullin, Ind., 706.

2012: Obama, D, 242,584; Romney, R, 165,484; Johnson, LB, 3,882; Stein, Green, 1,940.

2008: Obama, D, 255,459; McCain, R, 152,374; Nader, Ind. (DE), 2,401; Barr, LB, 1,109; Baldwin, Const., 626; McKinney, Green, 385; Calero, Soc. Workers, 58.

2004: Kerry, D, 200,152; Bush, R, 171,660; Nader, Ind., 2,153; Badnarik, LB, 586; Peroutka, Const., 289; Cobb, Green, 250; Brown, Natural Law, 100.

2000: Gore, D, 180,068; Bush, R, 137,288; Nader, Green, 8,307; Buchanan, RF, 777; Browne, LB, 774; Phillips, Const., 208; Hagelin, Natural Law, 107.

1996: Clinton, D, 140,355; Dole, R, 99,062; Perot, RF, 28,719; Browne, LB, 2,052; Phillips, U.S. Taxpayers, 348; Hagelin, Natural Law, 274.

1992: Clinton, D, 126,054; Bush, R, 102,313; Perot, Ind., 59,213; Fulani, New Alliance, 1,105.

1988: Bush, R, 139,639; Dukakis, D, 108,647; Paul, LB, 1,162; Fulani, New Alliance, 443.

1984: Reagan, R, 152,190; Mondale, D, 101,656; Bergland, LB, 268.

1980: Reagan, R, 111,252; Carter, D, 105,754; Anderson, Ind., 16,288; Clark, LB, 1,974; Greaves, Amer., 400.

1976: Carter, D, 122,596; Ford, R, 109,831; McCarthy, nonpartisan, 2,437; Anderson, Amer., 645; LaRouche, U.S. Labor, 136; Bubar, Prohib., 103; Levin, Soc. Labor, 86.

1972: Nixon, R, 140,357; McGovern, D, 92,283; Schmitz, Amer., 2,638; Munn, Prohib., 238.

1968: Nixon, R, 96,714; Humphrey, D, 89,194; Wallace, 3rd party, 28,459.

1964: Johnson, D, 122,704; Goldwater, R, 78,078; Munn, Prohib., 425; Hass, Soc. Labor, 113.

1960: Kennedy, D, 99,590; Nixon, R, 96,373; Faubus, States' Rights, 354; Decker, Prohib., 284; Hass, Soc. Labor, 82.

District of Columbia

	2016		2012	
	Clinton (D)	Trump (R)	Obama (D)	Romney (R)
Totals	282,830	12,723	267,070	21,381

District of Columbia Vote Since 1964

2016: Clinton, D, 282,830; Trump, R, 12,723; Johnson, LB, 4,906; Stein, Green, 4,258.

2012: Obama, D, 267,070; Romney, R, 21,381; Stein, DC Statehood Green, 2,458; Johnson, LB, 2,083.

2008: Obama, D, 245,800; McCain, R, 17,367; Nader, Ind., 958; McKinney, Green, 590.

2004: Kerry, D, 202,970; Bush, R, 21,256; Nader, Ind., 1,485; Cobb, DC Statehood Green, 737; Badnarik, LB, 502; Harris, Soc. Workers, 130.

2000: Gore, D, 171,923; Bush, R, 18,073; Nader, Green, 10,576; Browne, LB, 669; Harris, Soc. Workers, 114.

1996: Clinton, D, 158,220; Dole, R, 17,339; Nader, Green, 4,780; Perot, RF, 3,611; Browne, LB, 588; Hagelin, Natural Law, 283; Harris, Soc. Workers, 257.

1992: Clinton, D, 192,619; Bush, R, 20,698; Perot, Ind., 9,681; Fulani, New Alliance, 1,459; Daniels, Ind., 1,186.

1988: Dukakis, D, 159,407; Bush, R, 27,590; Fulani, New Alliance, 2,901; Paul, LB, 554.

1984: Mondale, D, 180,408; Reagan, R, 29,009; Bergland, LB, 279.

1980: Carter, D, 130,231; Reagan, R, 23,313; Anderson, Ind., 16,131; Commoner, Citizens, 1,826; Clark, LB, 1,104; Hall, Comm., 369; DeBerry, Soc. Workers, 173; Griswold, Workers World, 62; write-in, 690.

1976: Carter, D, 137,818; Ford, R, 27,873; Camejo, Soc. Workers, 545; MacBride, LB, 274; Hall, Comm., 219; LaRouche, U.S. Labor, 157.

1972: McGovern, D, 127,627; Nixon, R, 35,226; Reed, Soc. Workers, 316; Hall, Comm., 252.

1968: Humphrey, D, 139, 566; Nixon, R, 31,012.

1964: Johnson, D, 169,796; Goldwater, R, 28,801.

Florida

	2016		2012	
County	Clinton (D)	Trump (R)	Obama (D)	Romney (R)
Alachua	75,820	46,834	69,699	48,797
Baker	2,112	10,294	2,311	8,975
Bay	21,797	62,194	22,051	56,876
Bradford	2,924	8,913	3,325	8,219
Brevard	119,679	181,848	122,993	159,300
Broward	553,320	260,951	508,312	244,101
Calhoun	1,241	4,655	1,664	4,366
Charlotte	33,445	60,218	35,906	47,996
Citrus	22,789	54,456	28,460	44,662
Clay	27,822	74,963	25,759	70,022
Collier	61,085	105,423	51,698	96,520
Columbia	7,601	20,368	8,462	18,429
De Soto	3,781	6,778	4,174	5,587
Dixie	1,270	5,822	1,798	5,052
Duval	205,704	211,672	196,737	211,615
Escambia	57,461	88,808	58,185	88,711
Flagler	22,026	33,850	23,207	26,969
Franklin	1,744	4,125	1,845	3,570
Gadsden	15,020	6,728	15,770	6,630
Gilchrist	1,458	6,740	1,885	5,917
Glades	1,271	2,996	1,603	2,344
Gulf	1,720	5,329	2,014	4,995
Hamilton	1,904	3,443	2,228	3,138
Hardee	2,149	5,242	2,463	4,696
Hendry	4,615	6,195	4,751	5,355
Hernando	31,795	58,970	37,830	44,938
Highlands	14,937	29,565	16,148	25,915
Hillsborough	307,965	266,870	286,467	250,186
Holmes	853	7,483	1,264	6,919
Indian River	29,043	48,620	27,492	43,450
Jackson	6,397	14,257	7,342	13,418
Jefferson	3,541	3,930	3,945	3,808
Lafayette	518	2,809	687	2,668
Lake	62,838	102,188	61,799	87,643

	2016		2012	
County	Clinton (D)	Trump (R)	Obama (D)	Romney (R)
Lee	124,908	191,551	110,157	154,163
Leon	92,068	53,821	90,881	55,805
Levy	5,101	13,775	6,119	12,054
Liberty	651	2,543	942	2,301
Madison	3,526	4,851	4,176	4,474
Manatee	71,224	101,944	66,503	85,627
Marion	62,041	107,833	66,831	93,043
Martin	30,185	53,204	30,107	48,183
Miami-Dade	624,146	333,999	541,440	332,981
Monroe	18,971	21,904	19,404	19,234
Nassau	10,869	34,266	10,251	29,929
Okaloosa	23,780	71,893	23,421	70,168
Okeechobee	3,959	9,356	4,856	7,328
Orange	329,894	195,216	273,665	188,589
Osceola	85,458	50,301	67,239	40,592
Palm Beach	374,673	272,402	349,651	247,398
Pasco	90,142	142,101	98,263	112,427
Pinellas	233,701	239,201	239,104	213,258
Polk	117,433	157,430	114,622	131,577
Putnam	10,094	22,138	11,667	19,326
St. Johns	43,099	88,684	35,190	78,513
St. Lucie	68,881	70,289	65,869	56,202
Santa Rosa	18,464	65,339	17,768	58,186
Sarasota	97,870	124,438	95,119	110,504
Seminole	105,914	109,443	96,445	109,943
Sumter	22,638	52,730	19,524	40,646
Suwannee	3,964	14,287	4,751	12,672
Taylor	2,152	6,930	2,764	6,249
Union	1,014	4,568	1,339	3,980
Volusia	109,091	143,007	114,748	117,490
Wakulla	4,348	10,512	5,175	9,290
Walton	6,876	25,756	6,671	21,490
Washington	2,264	8,637	2,820	8,038
Totals	**4,504,975**	**4,617,886**	**4,237,756**	**4,163,447**

Florida Vote Since 1960

2016: Trump, R, 4,617,886; Clinton, D, 4,504,975; Johnson, LB, 207,043; Stein, Green, 64,399; Castle, Const., 16,475; De La Fuente, RF, 9,108.

2012: Obama, D, 4,237,756; Romney, R, 4,163,447; Johnson, LB, 44,726; Stein, Green, 8,947; Barr, Peace/Freedom, 8,154; Stevens, Objectivist, 3,856; Goode, Const., 2,607; Anderson, Justice, 1,754; Hoefling, Amer. Ind., 946; Barnett, RF, 820; Alexander, Soc., 799; Lindsay, Socialism/Liberation, 322.

2008: Obama, D, 4,282,074; McCain, R, 4,045,624; Nader, Ecology (FL), 28,124; Barr, LB, 17,218; Baldwin, Const., 7,915; McKinney, Green, 2,887; Keyes, Amer. Ind., 2,550; La Riva, Socialism/Liberation, 1,516; Jay, Boston Tea, 795; Harris, Soc. Workers, 533; Stevens, Objectivist, 419; Moore, Soc. USA, 405; Amondson, Prohib., 293.

2004: Bush, R, 3,964,522; Kerry, D, 3,583,544; Nader, RF, 32,971; Badnarik, LB, 11,996; Peroutka, Const., 6,626; Cobb, Green, 3,917; Brown, Soc., 3,502; Harris, Soc. Workers, 2,732.

2000: Bush, R, 2,912,790; Gore, D, 2,912,253; Nader, Green, 97,488; Buchanan, RF, 17,484; Browne, LB, 16,415; Hagelin, Natural Law, 2,281; Moorehead, Workers World, 1,804; Phillips, Const., 1,371; McReynolds, Soc., 622; Harris, Soc. Workers, 562.

1996: Clinton, D, 2,545,968; Dole, R, 2,243,324; Perot, RF, 483,776; Browne, LB, 23,312.

1992: Bush, R, 2,171,781; Clinton, D, 2,071,651; Perot, Ind., 1,052,481; Marrou, LB, 15,068.

1988: Bush, R, 2,616,597; Dukakis, D, 1,655,851; Paul, LB, 19,796; Fulani, New Alliance, 6,655.

1984: Reagan, R, 2,728,775; Mondale, D, 1,448,344.

1980: Reagan, R, 2,046,951; Carter, D, 1,419,475; Anderson, Ind., 189,692; Clark, LB, 30,524; write-in, 285.

1976: Carter, D, 1,636,000; Ford, R, 1,469,531; McCarthy, Ind., 23,643; Anderson, Amer., 21,325.

1972: Nixon, R, 1,857,759; McGovern, D, 718,117; scattered, 7,407.

1968: Nixon, R, 886,804; Humphrey, D, 676,794; Wallace, 3rd party, 624,207.

1964: Johnson, D, 948,540; Goldwater, R, 905,941.

1960: Nixon, R, 795,476; Kennedy, D, 748,700.

Georgia

	2016		2012	
County	Clinton (D)	Trump (R)	Obama (D)	Romney (R)
Appling	1,434	5,494	1,758	5,233
Atkinson	697	1,878	930	1,938
Bacon	608	3,364	791	3,093
Baker	650	775	794	785

County	2016 Clinton (D)	Trump (R)	2012 Obama (D)	Romney (R)	County	2016 Clinton (D)	Trump (R)	2012 Obama (D)	Romney (R)
Baldwin	7,970	7,697	8,483	7,589	Liberty	9,556	6,134	10,457	5,565
Banks	684	6,134	780	5,354	Lincoln	1,273	2,759	1,586	2,807
Barrow	6,580	21,108	6,028	18,725	Long	1,360	2,626	1,442	2,306
Bartow	8,212	29,911	8,396	26,876	Lowndes	15,064	21,635	17,470	21,327
Ben Hill	2,101	3,739	2,512	3,396	Lumpkin	2,220	9,619	2,055	8,647
Berrien	1,047	5,422	1,273	4,843	Macon	2,705	1,540	3,211	1,545
Bibb	36,787	24,043	38,585	25,623	Madison	2,425	9,201	2,494	8,443
Bleckley	1,101	3,719	1,269	3,587	Marion	1,213	1,921	1,412	1,733
Brantley	619	5,567	939	4,964	McDuffie	3,699	5,432	4,044	5,475
Brooks	2,528	3,701	3,138	3,554	McIntosh	2,303	3,487	2,864	3,409
Bryan	4,014	10,529	3,707	9,560	Meriwether	3,804	5,222	4,331	4,856
Bulloch	9,261	15,097	9,593	14,174	Miller	623	1,891	852	1,905
Burke	4,731	4,491	5,405	4,301	Mitchell	3,493	4,279	4,081	4,155
Butts	2,566	6,717	2,968	6,306	Monroe	3,571	8,832	3,785	8,361
Calhoun	1,179	830	1,298	883	Montgomery	847	2,670	1,135	2,662
Camden	5,930	12,310	6,377	11,343	Morgan	2,663	6,559	2,753	6,186
Candler	1,026	2,664	1,157	2,344	Murray	1,800	10,341	2,542	8,443
Carroll	12,464	30,029	12,688	28,280	Muscogee	39,851	26,976	42,573	27,510
Catoosa	4,771	20,876	5,365	17,858	Newton	21,943	20,913	21,851	20,982
Charlton	1,004	2,951	1,197	2,527	Oconee	5,581	13,425	4,421	13,098
Chatham	62,290	45,688	60,246	47,204	Oglethorpe	1,831	4,625	1,914	4,251
Chattahoochee	594	751	729	735	Paulding	18,025	44,662	15,825	40,846
Chattooga	1,613	6,462	2,232	5,452	Peach	5,100	5,413	6,148	5,287
Cherokee	25,231	80,649	19,841	76,514	Pickens	1,979	11,651	1,975	10,547
Clarke	29,603	12,717	25,431	13,815	Pierce	903	6,302	1,124	5,667
Clay	697	566	862	537	Pike	1,240	7,278	1,356	6,668
Clayton	78,220	12,645	81,479	14,164	Polk	2,867	11,014	3,615	9,811
Clinch	686	1,727	852	1,598	Pulaski	1,104	2,437	1,219	2,444
Cobb	160,121	152,912	133,124	171,722	Putnam	2,758	6,544	2,926	6,215
Coffee	4,094	9,588	5,057	9,248	Quitman	461	575	612	510
Colquitt	3,463	9,898	3,973	9,243	Rabun	1,444	6,287	1,559	5,754
Columbia	18,887	43,085	16,451	41,765	Randolph	1,598	1,271	1,770	1,271
Cook	1,753	4,176	2,042	3,935	Richmond	48,814	24,461	52,560	25,845
Coweta	16,583	42,533	15,168	39,653	Rockdale	23,255	13,478	22,023	15,716
Crawford	1,421	3,635	1,706	3,368	Schley	401	1,472	448	1,286
Crisp	2,837	4,549	3,167	4,182	Screven	2,300	3,305	2,774	3,287
Dade	965	5,051	1,411	4,471	Seminole	1,189	2,345	1,478	2,245
Dawson	1,448	9,900	1,241	8,847	Spalding	9,357	15,646	9,898	14,911
Decatur	4,124	6,020	4,591	5,824	Stephens	1,837	7,686	2,131	7,221
DeKalb	251,370	51,468	238,224	64,392	Stewart	1,222	805	1,323	745
Dodge	1,839	5,021	2,442	5,214	Sumter	5,520	5,276	6,375	5,378
Dooly	1,872	1,951	2,285	1,985	Talbot	2,002	1,196	2,265	1,202
Dougherty	23,311	10,232	26,295	11,449	Taliaferro	545	349	636	323
Douglas	31,005	24,817	28,441	26,241	Tattnall	1,681	5,096	1,897	4,706
Early	2,168	2,552	2,765	2,557	Taylor	1,296	2,064	1,572	1,948
Echols	156	1,007	173	917	Telfair	1,313	2,450	1,805	2,480
Effingham	4,853	17,874	4,947	15,596	Terrell	2,267	1,874	2,544	1,834
Elbert	2,539	5,292	3,181	4,859	Thomas	7,142	11,228	7,653	11,156
Emanuel	2,435	5,335	2,927	5,100	Tift	4,347	9,584	4,660	9,185
Evans	1,130	2,404	1,268	2,268	Toombs	2,338	6,615	2,746	6,524
Fannin	1,923	9,632	2,028	7,857	Towns	1,210	5,383	1,273	4,876
Fayette	23,284	35,048	19,736	38,075	Treutlen	862	1,809	1,074	1,652
Floyd	9,159	24,114	9,640	22,733	Troup	9,713	15,750	10,547	15,179
Forsyth	23,462	69,851	14,571	65,908	Turner	1,246	2,095	1,510	2,028
Franklin	1,243	7,054	1,499	6,114	Twiggs	1,971	2,035	2,270	1,907
Fulton	297,051	117,783	255,470	137,124	Union	1,963	9,852	2,139	8,773
Gilmer	1,965	10,477	1,958	8,926	Upson	3,475	7,292	3,959	7,230
Glascock	138	1,235	176	1,135	Walker	4,215	18,950	5,274	16,247
Glynn	11,775	21,512	11,950	20,893	Walton	8,292	31,125	8,148	29,036
Gordon	3,181	15,191	3,440	13,197	Ware	3,440	8,513	3,900	7,941
Grady	3,013	6,053	3,419	5,924	Warren	1,314	991	1,529	990
Greene	3,199	5,490	3,201	5,071	Washington	4,200	4,149	4,714	4,035
Gwinnett	166,153	146,989	132,509	159,855	Wayne	2,041	8,153	2,596	7,557
Habersham	2,483	13,190	2,301	12,166	Webster	473	630	582	601
Hall	16,180	51,733	12,999	47,481	Wheeler	646	1,421	772	1,366
Hancock	2,701	843	3,308	769	White	1,674	9,761	1,671	8,651
Haralson	1,475	9,585	1,789	8,446	Whitfield	7,937	21,537	7,210	19,305
Harris	4,086	11,936	4,145	11,197	Wilcox	852	2,096	1,060	2,053
Hart	2,585	7,286	2,870	6,517	Wilkes	1,848	2,572	2,087	2,635
Heard	743	3,370	948	3,160	Wilkinson	1,894	2,333	2,181	2,246
Henry	50,057	45,724	43,761	46,774	Worth	2,020	6,152	2,487	5,869
Houston	22,553	35,430	22,702	34,662	**Totals**	**1,877,963**	**2,089,104**	**1,773,827**	**2,078,688**
Irwin	891	2,716	1,141	2,538					
Jackson	4,491	21,784	4,238	19,135					
Jasper	1,544	4,360	1,845	4,136					
Jeff Davis	901	4,104	1,275	3,996					
Jefferson	3,821	3,063	4,261	2,999					
Jenkins	1,123	1,895	1,488	1,887					
Johnson	1,136	2,519	1,305	2,440					
Jones	3,961	8,305	4,274	7,744					
Lamar	2,270	5,190	2,602	4,899					
Lanier	806	1,984	1,114	1,820					
Laurens	6,752	12,411	7,513	11,950					
Lee	3,170	10,646	3,196	10,314					

Georgia Vote Since 1960

2016: Trump, R, 2,089,104; Clinton, D, 1,877,963 Johnson, LB, 125,306; McMullin, Ind., 13,017; Stein, Ind., 7,674; Castle, Ind., 1,110.

2012: Romney, R, 2,078,688; Obama, D, 1,773,827; Johnson, LB, 45,324.

2008: McCain, R, 2,048,759; Obama, D, 1,844,123; Barr, LB, 28,731.

2004: Bush, R, 1,914,254; Kerry, D, 1,366,149; Badnarik, LB, 18,387.
2000: Bush, R, 1,419,720; Gore, D, 1,116,230; Browne, LB, 36,332; Buchanan, Ind., 10,926.
1996: Dole, R, 1,080,843; Clinton, D, 1,053,849; Perot, RF, 146,337; Browne, LB, 17,870.
1992: Clinton, D, 1,008,966; Bush, R, 995,252; Perot, Ind., 309,657; Marrou, LB, 7,110.
1988: Bush, R, 1,081,331; Dukakis, D, 714,792; Paul, LB, 8,435; Fulani, New Alliance, 5,099.
1984: Reagan, R, 1,068,722; Mondale, D, 706,628.
1980: Carter, D, 890,955; Reagan, R, 654,168; Anderson, Ind., 36,055; Clark, LB, 15,627.
1976: Carter, D, 979,409; Ford, R, 483,743; write-in, 4,306.
1972: Nixon, R, 881,496; McGovern, D, 289,529; Schmitz, Amer., 812; scattered, 2,935.
1968: Wallace, 3rd party, 535,550; Nixon, R, 380,111; Humphrey, D, 334,440; write-in, 162.
1964: Goldwater, R, 616,600; Johnson, D, 522,557.
1960: Kennedy, D, 458,638; Nixon, R, 274,472; write-in, 239.

Hawaii

County	2016		2012	
	Clinton (D)	Trump (R)	Obama (D)	Romney (R)
Hawaii	41,259	17,501	47,224	14,753
Honolulu	175,696	90,326	204,349	88,461
Kauai	16,456	7,574	18,641	6,121
Maui	33,480	13,446	36,052	11,602
Overseas	NA	NA	392	78
Totals	266,891	128,847	306,658	121,015

Hawaii Vote Since 1960

2016: Clinton, D, 266,891; Trump, R, 128,847; Johnson, LB, 15,594; Stein, Green, 12,737; Castle, Const., 4,508.
2012: Obama, D, 306,658; Romney, R, 121,015; Johnson, LB, 3,840; Stein, Green, 3,184.
2008: Obama, D, 325,871; McCain, R, 120,566; Nader, Ind. (HI), 3,825; Barr, LB, 1,314; Baldwin, Const., 1,013; McKinney, Green, 979.
2004: Kerry, D, 231,708; Bush, R, 194,191; Cobb, Green, 1,737; Badnarik, LB, 1,377.
2000: Gore, D, 205,286; Bush, R, 137,845; Nader, Green, 21,623; Browne, LB, 1,477; Buchanan, RF, 1,071; Phillips, Const., 343; Hagelin, Natural Law, 306.
1996: Clinton, D, 205,012; Dole, R, 113,943; Perot, RF, 27,358; Nader, Green, 10,386; Browne, LB, 2,493; Hagelin, Natural Law, 570; Phillips, Taxpayers, 358.
1992: Clinton, D, 179,310; Bush, R, 136,822; Perot, Ind., 53,003; Gritz, Populist/America First, 1,452; Marrou, LB, 1,119.
1988: Dukakis, D, 192,364; Bush, R, 158,625; Paul, LB, 1,999; Fulani, New Alliance, 1,003.
1984: Reagan, R, 184,934; Mondale, D, 147,098; Bergland, LB, 2,167.
1980: Carter, D, 135,879; Reagan, R, 130,112; Anderson, Ind., 32,021; Clark, LB, 3,269; Commoner, Citizens, 1,548; Hall, Comm., 458.
1976: Carter, D, 147,375; Ford, R, 140,003; MacBride, LB, 3,923.
1972: Nixon, R, 168,865; McGovern, D, 101,409.
1968: Humphrey, D, 141,324; Nixon, R, 91,425; Wallace, 3rd party, 3,469.
1964: Johnson, D, 163,249; Goldwater, R, 44,022.
1960: Kennedy, D, 92,410; Nixon, R, 92,295.

Idaho

County	2016		2012	
	Clinton (D)	Trump (R)	Obama (D)	Romney (R)
Ada	75,677	93,752	77,137	97,554
Adams	415	1,556	577	1,413
Bannock	10,342	17,180	13,214	21,010
Bear Lake	255	2,203	302	2,489
Benewah	770	3,103	1,164	2,596
Bingham	2,924	10,907	3,822	13,440
Blaine	6,416	3,340	5,992	3,939
Boise	777	2,673	1,053	2,284
Bonner	5,819	13,343	6,500	11,367
Bonneville	8,930	26,699	9,903	32,276
Boundary	933	3,789	1,225	3,138
Butte	160	914	258	1,001
Camas	110	410	159	402
Canyon	16,883	47,222	19,866	44,369

County	2016		2012	
	Clinton (D)	Trump (R)	Obama (D)	Romney (R)
Caribou	271	2,275	386	2,608
Cassia	1,036	5,949	1,098	7,154
Clark	44	203	66	235
Clearwater	704	2,852	1,032	2,541
Custer	427	1,777	530	1,744
Elmore	1,814	5,816	2,513	5,227
Franklin	385	3,901	325	5,195
Fremont	651	4,090	810	4,907
Gem	1,229	5,980	1,957	5,311
Gooding	930	3,743	1,287	3,696
Idaho	1,196	6,441	1,708	5,921
Jefferson	976	8,436	1,303	9,895
Jerome	1,329	4,644	1,699	4,804
Kootenai	16,264	44,449	18,851	39,381
Latah	8,093	7,265	8,306	7,589
Lemhi	733	3,011	960	3,029
Lewis	270	1,202	396	1,173
Lincoln	360	1,184	469	1,141
Madison	1,201	8,941	832	13,445
Minidoka	1,167	4,887	1,390	5,442
Nez Perce	4,828	10,699	6,451	9,967
Oneida	184	1,531	217	1,838
Owyhee	591	3,052	833	2,794
Payette	1,507	6,489	2,271	6,004
Power	699	1,666	982	1,870
Shoshone	1,384	3,297	2,277	2,699
Teton	2,159	2,167	1,926	2,458
Twin Falls	6,233	19,828	7,541	19,773
Valley	1,913	2,906	2,095	2,664
Washington	776	3,283	1,104	3,128
Totals	189,765	409,055	212,787	420,911

Idaho Vote Since 1960

2016: Trump, R, 409,055; Clinton, D, 189,765; McMullin, Ind., 46,476; Johnson, LB, 28,331; Stein, Ind., 8,496; Castle, Ind., 4,403; Copeland, Const., 2,356; De La Fuente, Ind., 1,373.
2012: Romney, R, 420,911; Obama, D, 212,787; Johnson, LB, 9,453; Stein, Ind., 4,402; Anderson, Ind., 2,499; Goode, Const., 2,222.
2008: McCain, R, 403,012; Obama, D, 236,440; Nader, Ind., 7,175; Baldwin, Const., 4,747; Barr, LB, 3,658.
2004: Bush, R, 409,235; Kerry, D, 181,098; Badnarik, LB, 3,844; Peroutka, Const., 3,084.
2000: Bush, R, 336,937; Gore, D, 138,637; Buchanan, RF, 7,615; Browne, LB, 3,488; Phillips, Const., 1,469; Hagelin, Natural Law, 1,177.
1996: Dole, R, 256,595; Clinton, D, 165,443; Perot, RF, 62,518; Browne, LB, 3,325; Phillips, U.S. Taxpayers, 2,230; Hagelin, Natural Law, 1,600.
1992: Bush, R, 202,645; Clinton, D, 137,013; Perot, Ind., 130,395; Gritz, Populist/America First, 10,281; Marrou, LB, 1,167.
1988: Bush, R, 253,881; Dukakis, D, 147,272; Paul, LB, 5,313; Fulani, Ind., 2,502.
1984: Reagan, R, 297,523; Mondale, D, 108,510; Bergland, LB, 2,823.
1980: Reagan, R, 290,699; Carter, D, 110,192; Anderson, Ind., 27,058; Clark, LB, 8,425; Rarick, Amer., 1,057.
1976: Ford, R, 204,151; Carter, D, 126,549; Maddox, Amer., 5,935; MacBride, LB, 3,558; LaRouche, U.S. Labor, 739.
1972: Nixon, R, 199,384; McGovern, D, 80,826; Schmitz, Amer., 28,869; Spock, People's, 903.
1968: Nixon, R, 165,369; Humphrey, D, 89,273; Wallace, 3rd party, 36,541.
1964: Johnson, D, 148,920; Goldwater, R, 143,557.
1960: Nixon, R, 161,597; Kennedy, D, 138,853.

Illinois

County	2016		2012	
	Clinton (D)	Trump (R)	Obama (D)	Romney (R)
Adams	7,676	22,790	9,648	20,416
Alexander	1,262	1,496	1,965	1,487
Bond	2,068	4,888	3,020	4,095
Boone	8,986	12,282	9,883	11,096
Brown	476	1,796	787	1,513
Bureau	6,029	9,281	8,134	8,164
Calhoun	739	1,721	1,080	1,440
Carroll	2,447	4434	3,665	3,555
Cass	1,621	3,216	2,053	2,707
Champaign	50,137	33,368	40,831	35,312
Christian	3,992	10,543	5,494	8,885

County	2016 Clinton (D)	Trump (R)	2012 Obama (D)	Romney (R)
Clark	1,877	5,622	2,591	5,144
Clay	1,020	5,021	1,584	4,190
Clinton	3,945	12,412	5,596	10,524
Coles	7,309	13,003	9,262	11,631
Cook	1,611,946	453,287	1,488,537	495,542
Crawford	1,992	6,277	2,858	5,585
Cumberland	1,031	4,206	1,641	3,509
DeKalb	20,466	19,091	21,207	18,934
DeWitt	1,910	5,077	2,601	4,579
Douglas	1,949	5,698	2,430	5,334
DuPage	228,622	166,415	199,460	195,046
Edgar	1,793	5,645	2,565	5,132
Edwards	434	2,778	754	2,405
Effingham	3,083	13,635	3,861	12,501
Fayette	1,819	7,372	2,853	5,951
Ford	1,414	4,480	1,656	4,229
Franklin	4,727	13,116	7,254	10,267
Fulton	6,133	8,492	8,328	6,632
Gallatin	657	1,942	1,029	1,492
Greene	1,205	4,145	2,023	3,451
Grundy	8,065	13,454	9,451	11,343
Hamilton	802	3,206	1,269	2,566
Hancock	2,139	6,430	3,650	5,271
Hardin	420	1,653	742	1,535
Henderson	1,155	2,155	1,978	1,541
Henry	8,871	13,985	12,332	11,583
Iroquois	2,504	9,750	3,413	9,120
Jackson	11,634	10,843	13,319	9,864
Jasper	924	3,975	1,436	3,514
Jefferson	4,425	11,695	6,089	9,811
Jersey	2,679	7,748	3,667	6,039
Jo Daviess	4,462	6,121	5,667	5,534
Johnson	1,142	4,649	1,572	3,963
Kane	103,665	82,734	90,332	88,335
Kankakee	18,971	25,129	21,595	23,136
Kendall	24,884	24,961	22,471	24,047
Knox	10,083	10,737	13,451	9,408
Lake	171,095	109,767	153,757	129,764
LaSalle	19,543	26,689	23,073	23,256
Lawrence	1,290	4,521	2,011	3,857
Lee	5,528	8,612	6,937	8,059
Livingston	4,023	10,208	5,020	9,753
Logan	3,313	8,181	3,978	7,844
Macon	18,343	26,866	22,780	25,309
Macoupin	6,689	14,322	9,464	10,946
Madison	50,587	70,490	58,922	60,608
Marion	4,369	11,859	6,225	9,248
Marshall	1,789	3,785	2,455	3,290
Mason	2,014	4,058	2,867	3,265
Massac	1,558	4,846	2,092	4,278
McDonough	5,288	6,795	5,967	6,147
McHenry	60,803	71,612	59,797	71,598
McLean	36,196	37,237	31,883	39,947
Menard	1,817	4,231	2,100	3,948
Mercer	3,071	4,807	4,507	3,876
Monroe	5,535	12,629	6,215	10,888
Montgomery	3,504	8,630	5,058	6,776
Morgan	4,696	9,076	5,806	7,972
Moultrie	1,481	4,455	2,144	3,784
Ogle	8,050	14,352	9,514	13,422
Peoria	38,060	35,633	40,209	36,774
Perry	2,462	6,855	3,819	5,507
Piatt	2,645	5,634	3,090	5,413
Pike	1,413	5,754	2,278	4,860
Pope	375	1,678	650	1,512
Pulaski	962	1,675	1,389	1,564
Putnam	1,147	1,767	1,559	1,502
Randolph	3,439	10,023	5,759	8,290
Richland	1,584	5,739	2,362	4,756
Rock Island	32,298	26,998	39,157	24,934
St. Clair	60,756	53,857	67,285	50,125
Saline	2,572	8,276	3,701	6,806
Sangamon	40,907	49,944	42,107	50,225
Schuyler	1,075	2,524	1,727	2,069
Scott	535	1,966	910	1,587
Shelby	2,288	8,229	3,342	6,843
Stark	751	1,778	1,095	1,528
Stephenson	7,768	11,083	10,165	10,512
Tazewell	20,685	38,707	24,438	35,335
Union	2,402	5,790	3,137	4,957
Vermilion	10,039	19,087	12,878	16,892
Wabash	1,151	4,047	1,590	3,478
Warren	2,987	4,275	4,044	3,618
Washington	1,448	5,571	2,450	4,792

County	2016 Clinton (D)	Trump (R)	2012 Obama (D)	Romney (R)
Wayne	1,048	6,967	1,514	5,988
White	1,412	5,640	2,188	4,731
Whiteside	11,035	12,615	14,833	10,448
Will	151,927	132,720	144,229	128,969
Williamson	8,581	21,570	10,647	17,909
Winnebago	55,713	55,624	61,732	55,138
Woodford	5,092	13,207	5,572	12,961
Totals	3,090,729	2,146,015	3,019,512	2,135,216

Illinois Vote Since 1960

2016: Clinton, D, 3,090,729; Trump, R, 2,146,015; Johnson, LB, 209,596; Stein, Green, 76,802; McMullin, Ind., 11,655; Castle, Const., 1,138.

2012: Obama, D, 3,019,512; Romney, R, 2,135,216; Johnson, LB, 56,229; Stein, Green, 30,222.

2008: Obama, D, 3,419,348; McCain, R, 2,031,179; Nader, Ind., 30,948; Barr, LB, 19,642; McKinney, Green, 11,838; Baldwin, Const., 8,256; Polachek, New Party, 1,149.

2004: Kerry, D, 2,891,550; Bush, R, 2,345,946; Badnarik, LB, 32,442.

2000: Gore, D, 2,589,026; Bush, R, 2,019,421; Nader, Green, 103,759; Buchanan, Ind., 16,106; Browne, LB, 11,623; Hagelin, RF, 2,127.

1996: Clinton, D, 2,341,744; Dole, R, 1,587,021; Perot, RF, 346,408; Browne, LB, 22,548; Phillips, U.S. Taxpayers, 7,606; Hagelin, Natural Law, 4,606.

1992: Clinton, D, 2,453,350; Bush, R, 1,734,096; Perot, Ind., 840,515; Marrou, LB, 9,218; Fulani, New Alliance, 5,267; Gritz, Populist/America First, 3,577; Hagelin, Natural Law, 2,751; Warren, Soc. Workers, 1,361.

1988: Bush, R, 2,310,939; Dukakis, D, 2,215,940; Paul, LB, 14,944; Fulani, Solidarity, 10,276.

1984: Reagan, R, 2,707,103; Mondale, D, 2,086,499; Bergland, LB, 10,086.

1980: Reagan, R, 2,358,049; Carter, D, 1,981,413; Anderson, Ind., 346,754; Clark, LB, 38,939; Commoner, Citizens, 10,692; Hall, Comm., 9,711; Griswold, Workers World, 2,257; DeBerry, Soc. Workers, 1,302; write-in, 604.

1976: Ford, R, 2,364,269; Carter, D, 2,271,295; McCarthy, Ind., 55,939; Hall, Comm., 9,250; MacBride, LB, 8,057; Camejo, Soc. Workers, 3,615; Levin, Soc. Labor, 2,422; LaRouche, U.S. Labor, 2,018; write-in, 1,968.

1972: Nixon, R. 2,788,179; McGovern, D, 1,913,472; Fisher, Soc. Labor, 12,344; Hall, Comm., 4,541; Schmitz, Amer., 2,471; others, 2,229.

1968: Nixon, R, 2,174,774; Humphrey, D, 2,039,814; Wallace, 3rd party, 390,958; Blomen, Soc. Labor, 13,878; write-in, 325.

1964: Johnson, D, 2,796,833; Goldwater, R, 1,905,946; write-in, 62.

1960: Kennedy, D, 2,377,846; Nixon, R, 2,368,988; Hass, Soc. Labor, 10,560; write-in, 15.

Indiana

County	2016 Clinton (D)	Trump (R)	2012 Obama (D)	Romney (R)
Adams	2,805	9,648	3,806	8,937
Allen	55,382	83,930	60,036	84,613
Bartholomew	9,841	20,640	10,625	18,083
Benton	860	2,579	1,159	2,329
Blackford	1,243	3,350	1,927	2,711
Boone	10,181	19,654	8,328	18,808
Brown	2,518	5,016	3,060	4,332
Carroll	1,892	6,273	2,635	4,999
Cass	3,759	9,701	5,371	8,443
Clark	18,808	30,035	20,807	25,450
Clay	2,306	8,531	3,460	7,096
Clinton	2,819	8,531	3,308	6,338
Crawford	1,323	3,015	2,041	2,421
Daviess	1,800	8,545	2,437	7,638
Dearborn	4,883	18,113	6,528	15,394
Decatur	2,121	8,490	2,941	7,119
DeKalb	3,942	12,054	5,419	10,587
Delaware	18,153	24,263	22,654	21,251
Dubois	5,389	13,365	6,522	11,654
Elkhart	20,740	41,867	24,399	42,378
Fayette	2,252	6,839	3,555	5,045
Floyd	13,945	21,432	14,812	19,878
Fountain	1,476	5,662	2,237	4,664
Franklin	1,969	8,669	2,909	7,424
Fulton	1,960	6,010	2,621	5,317

County	2016 Clinton (D)	Trump (R)	2012 Obama (D)	Romney (R)
Gibson	3,721	11,081	4,928	9,487
Grant	7,010	17,008	9,589	15,151
Greene	2,929	10,277	4,350	8,457
Hamilton	57,263	87,404	43,796	90,747
Hancock	8,904	25,074	9,319	22,796
Harrison	4,783	12,943	6,607	10,640
Hendricks	22,600	48,337	21,112	44,312
Henry	5,124	13,895	7,613	10,838
Howard	11,215	23,675	15,135	20,327
Huntington	3,506	11,649	4,596	10,862
Jackson	3,843	12,859	5,838	10,419
Jasper	3,329	9,382	4,672	7,955
Jay	1,889	5,697	3,063	4,645
Jefferson	4,326	8,546	5,728	7,096
Jennings	2,364	8,224	3,821	6,120
Johnson	17,318	45,456	17,260	39,513
Knox	3,772	11,077	5,228	9,612
Kosciusko	6,313	23,935	6,862	22,558
LaGrange	2,080	7,025	2,898	6,231
Lake	116,935	75,625	130,897	68,431
LaPorte	19,798	22,687	24,107	18,615
Lawrence	4,210	14,035	5,779	11,622
Madison	18,595	32,376	24,407	26,769
Marion	212,899	130,360	216,336	136,509
Marshall	4,798	12,288	6,137	11,260
Martin	881	3,697	1,351	3,262
Miami	2,766	9,975	4,222	8,174
Monroe	34,216	20,592	33,436	22,481
Montgomery	3,362	11,059	4,271	9,824
Morgan	6,040	23,674	7,969	19,591
Newton	1,404	4,077	2,212	3,291
Noble	3,904	12,198	5,229	10,680
Ohio	686	2,118	994	1,759
Orange	2,048	5,803	2,939	4,617
Owen	1,946	6,153	2,823	5,062
Parke	1,441	4,863	2,110	4,234
Perry	3,062	4,556	4,316	3,403
Pike	1,297	4,398	2,125	3,627
Porter	33,676	38,832	37,252	34,406
Posey	3,521	8,404	4,533	7,430
Pulaski	1,327	3,854	1,899	3,366
Putnam	3,356	10,637	4,507	9,005
Randolph	2,446	7,517	3,769	6,218
Ripley	2,471	9,806	3,241	7,484
Rush	1,525	5,292	2,221	4,633
St. Joseph	52,252	52,021	56,460	52,578
Scott	2,642	6,074	3,998	4,539
Shelby	4,247	12,718	5,359	10,978
Spencer	2,861	6,572	4,026	5,515
Starke	2,489	6,367	3,809	4,738
Steuben	3,744	10,133	4,853	8,547
Sullivan	2,113	6,138	3,191	4,902
Switzerland	930	2,558	1,437	1,872
Tippecanoe	27,282	30,768	26,711	28,757
Tipton	1,587	5,589	2,432	4,773
Union	715	2,445	1,018	2,022
Vanderburgh	28,530	40,496	31,725	39,389
Vermillion	2,081	4,513	2,979	3,426
Vigo	15,931	21,937	19,712	19,369
Wabash	3,018	9,821	3,973	8,644
Warren	839	2,898	1,324	2,377
Warrick	9,086	19,113	8,793	15,351
Washington	2,636	8,209	3,909	6,533
Wayne	8,322	16,028	10,591	14,321
Wells	2,586	10,005	3,436	9,256
White	2,590	6,893	3,637	5,970
Whitley	3,379	11,358	4,420	10,258
Totals	**1,033,126**	**1,557,286**	**1,152,887**	**1,420,543**

Indiana Vote Since 1960

2016: Trump, R, 1,557,286; Clinton, D, 1,033,126; Johnson, LB, 133,993; Stein, Green, 7,841; Castle, Const., 1,937.

2012: Romney, R, 1,420,543; Obama, D, 1,152,887; Johnson, LB, 50,111.

2008: Obama, D, 1,374,039; McCain, R, 1,345,648; Barr, LB, 29,257.

2004: Bush, R, 1,479,438; Kerry, D, 969,011; Badnarik, LB, 18,058.

2000: Bush, R, 1,245,836; Gore, D, 901,980; Buchanan, Ind., 16,959; Browne, LB, 15,530.

1996: Dole, R, 1,006,693; Clinton, D, 887,424; Perot, RF, 224,299; Browne, LB, 15,632.

1992: Bush, R, 989,375; Clinton, D, 848,420; Perot, Ind., 455,934; Marrou, LB, 7,936; Fulani, New Alliance, 2,583.

1988: Bush, R, 1,297,763; Dukakis, D, 860,643; Fulani, New Alliance, 10,215.

1984: Reagan, R, 1,377,230; Mondale, D, 841,481; Bergland, LB, 6,741.

1980: Reagan, R, 1,255,656; Carter, D, 844,197; Anderson, Ind., 111,639; Clark, LB, 19,627; Commoner, Citizens, 4,852; Greaves, Amer., 4,750; Hall, Comm., 702; DeBerry, Soc., 610.

1976: Ford, R, 1,185,958; Carter, D, 1,014,714; Anderson, Amer., 14,048; Camejo, Soc. Workers, 5,695; LaRouche, U.S. Labor, 1,947.

1972: Nixon, R, 1,405,154; McGovern, D, 708,568; Reed, Soc. Workers, 5,575; Spock, Peace/Freedom, 4,544; Fisher, Soc. Labor, 1,688.

1968: Nixon, R, 1,067,885; Humphrey, D, 806,659; Wallace, 3rd party, 243,108; Munn, Prohib., 4,616; Halstead, Soc. Workers, 1,293; Gregory, write-in, 36.

1964: Johnson, D, 1,170,848; Goldwater, R, 911,118; Munn, Prohib. 8,266; Hass, Soc. Labor, 1,374.

1960: Nixon, R, 1,175,120; Kennedy, D, 952,358; Decker, Prohib., 6,746; Hass, Soc. Labor, 1,136.

Iowa

County	2016 Clinton (D)	Trump (R)	2012 Obama (D)	Romney (R)
Adair	1,133	2,461	1,790	2,114
Adams	565	1,395	1,028	1,108
Allamakee	2,421	4,093	3,553	3,264
Appanoose	1,814	4,033	2,951	3,161
Audubon	1,080	2,136	1,611	1,802
Benton	4,678	8,232	6,862	6,940
Black Hawk	32,233	27,476	39,821	26,235
Boone	5,541	7,484	7,512	6,556
Bremer	5,356	7,208	6,763	6,405
Buchanan	3,970	5,510	5,911	4,450
Buena Vista	2,856	4,903	3,700	4,554
Butler	2,157	4,921	3,329	4,106
Calhoun	1,398	3,468	2,238	2,891
Carroll	3,309	6,638	4,947	5,601
Cass	1,951	4,761	2,858	4,217
Cedar	3,599	5,295	4,972	4,529
Cerro Gordo	9,862	11,621	13,316	10,128
Cherokee	1,679	4,192	2,634	3,662
Chickasaw	2,266	3,742	3,554	2,836
Clarke	1,465	2,713	2,189	2,124
Clay	2,249	5,877	3,385	4,951
Clayton	3,237	5,317	4,806	4,164
Clinton	10,095	11,276	15,141	9,432
Crawford	1,991	4,617	3,066	3,595
Dallas	15,701	19,339	16,576	20,988
Davis	977	2,723	1,520	2,138
Decatur	1,201	2,296	1,791	1,947
Delaware	2,957	5,694	4,616	4,636
Des Moines	8,212	9,529	11,888	8,136
Dickinson	3,056	6,753	4,095	5,912
Dubuque	22,850	23,460	28,768	21,280
Emmet	1,357	3,124	2,099	2,507
Fayette	3,689	5,620	5,732	4,492
Floyd	3,179	4,375	4,680	3,472
Franklin	1,493	3,163	2,266	2,823
Fremont	963	2,407	1,637	1,972
Greene	1,691	2,820	2,375	2,380
Grundy	1,856	4,527	2,635	4,215
Guthrie	1,732	3,628	2,569	3,171
Hamilton	2,726	4,463	3,782	3,991
Hancock	1,587	3,977	2,521	3,317
Hardin	2,787	5,254	4,075	4,670
Harrison	2,131	4,902	3,136	4,065
Henry	2,904	5,779	4,460	5,035
Howard	1,677	2,611	2,768	1,795
Humboldt	1,252	3,568	1,972	3,099
Ida	792	2,655	1,321	2,286
Iowa	3,084	5,205	4,144	4,569
Jackson	3,837	5,824	5,907	4,177
Jasper	7,109	10,560	10,257	8,877
Jefferson	3,710	3,748	4,798	3,436
Johnson	50,200	21,044	50,666	23,698
Jones	3,787	5,720	5,534	4,721
Keokuk	1,342	3,390	2,303	2,843
Kossuth	2,543	5,653	3,850	4,937
Lee	6,215	8,803	10,714	7,785
Linn	58,935	48,390	68,581	47,622
Louisa	1,648	3,069	2,452	2,420

County	2016		2012	
	Clinton (D)	Trump (R)	Obama (D)	Romney (R)
Lucas	1,239	2,877	1,987	2,254
Lyon	920	5,192	1,423	4,978
Madison	2,678	5,360	3,630	4,638
Mahaska	2,619	7,432	4,213	6,448
Marion	5,482	10,962	7,507	9,828
Marshall	7,652	9,146	10,257	8,472
Mills	2,090	5,067	2,848	4,216
Mitchell	1,888	3,190	2,831	2,643
Monona	1,247	3,120	2,101	2,557
Monroe	1,056	2,638	1,731	2,026
Montgomery	1,314	3,436	1,922	3,001
Muscatine	8,368	9,584	11,323	8,168
O'Brien	1,315	5,752	1,969	5,266
Osceola	552	2,531	912	2,230
Page	1,807	4,893	2,613	4,348
Palo Alto	1,398	3,081	2,139	2,660
Plymouth	2,885	9,680	4,164	8,597
Pocahontas	963	2,702	1,523	2,396
Polk	119,804	93,492	128,465	96,096
Pottawattamie	15,355	24,447	19,644	21,860
Poweshiek	4,304	4,946	5,357	4,424
Ringgold	753	1,824	1,186	1,368
Sac	1,270	3,703	2,122	3,094
Scott	40,440	39,149	50,652	38,251
Shelby	1,662	4,362	2,469	3,911
Sioux	2,300	14,785	2,700	14,407
Story	25,709	19,458	26,192	19,668
Tama	3,196	4,971	4,768	4,098
Taylor	758	2,111	1,262	1,683
Union	1,922	3,525	3,043	2,813
Van Buren	845	2,527	1,402	2,064
Wapello	5,594	8,715	8,663	6,789
Warren	10,411	14,814	12,551	13,052
Washington	3,943	6,173	5,115	5,562
Wayne	719	2,069	1,251	1,583
Webster	6,305	10,056	9,537	8,469
Winnebago	1,931	3,447	2,903	2,906
Winneshiek	5,254	5,344	6,256	4,622
Woodbury	16,210	24,727	22,302	21,841
Worth	1,530	2,453	2,350	1,744
Wright	1,896	3,800	2,836	3,349
Totals	**653,669**	**800,983**	**822,544**	**730,617**

Iowa Vote Since 1960

2016: Trump, R, 800,983; Clinton, D, 653,669; Johnson, LB, 59,186; McMullin, petitioning cand., 12,366; Stein, Green, 11,479; Castle, Const., 5,335; Kahn, New Independent, 2,247; Vacek, Legal Marijuana, 2,246; De La Fuente, petitioning cand., 451; La Riva, Socialism/Liberation, 323.

2012: Obama, D, 822,544; Romney, R, 730,617; Johnson, LB, 12,926; Stein, Green, 3,769; Goode, Const., 3,038; Litzel, Ind., 1,027; Harris, Soc. Workers, 445; La Riva, Socialism/Liberation, 372.

2008: Obama, D, 828,940; McCain, R, 682,379; Nader, Peace/Freedom, 8,014; Barr, LB, 4,590; Baldwin, Const., 4,445; McKinney, Green, 1,423; Harris, Soc. Workers, 292; Moore, Soc. USA, 182; La Riva, Socialism/Liberation, 121.

2004: Bush, R, 751,957; Kerry, D, 741,898; Nader, petitioning cand., 5,973; Badnarik, LB, 2,992; Peroutka, Const., 1,304; Cobb, Green, 1,141; Harris, Soc. Workers, 373; Van Auken, petitioning cand., 176.

2000: Gore, D, 638,517; Bush, R, 634,373; Nader, Green, 29,374; Buchanan, RF, 5,731; Browne, LB, 3,209; Hagelin, Ind., 2,281; Phillips, Const., 613; Harris, Soc. Workers, 190; McReynolds, Soc., 107.

1996: Clinton, D, 620,258; Dole, R, 492,644; Perot, RF, 105,159; Nader, Green, 6,550; Hagelin, Natural Law, 3,349; Browne, LB, 2,315; Phillips, Taxpayers, 2,229; Harris, Soc. Workers, 331.

1992: Clinton, D, 586,353; Bush, R, 504,891; Perot, Ind., 253,468; Hagelin, Natural Law, 3,079; Gritz, Populist/America First, 1,177; Marrou, LB, 1,076.

1988: Dukakis, D, 670,557; Bush, R, 545,355; LaRouche, Ind., 3,526; Paul, LB, 2,494.

1984: Reagan, R, 703,088; Mondale, D, 605,620; Bergland, LB, 1,844.

1980: Reagan, R, 676,026; Carter, D, 508,672; Anderson, Ind., 115,633; Clark, LB, 13,123; Commoner, Citizens, 2,273; McReynolds, Soc., 534; Hall, Comm., 298; DeBerry, Soc. Workers, 244; Greaves, Amer., 189; Bubar, Statesman, 150; scattered, 519.

1976: Ford, R, 632,863; Carter, D, 619,931; McCarthy, Ind., 20,051; Anderson, Amer., 3,040; MacBride, LB, 1,452.

1972: Nixon, R, 706,207; McGovern, D, 496,206; Schmitz, Amer., 22,056; Jenness, Soc. Workers, 488; Hall, Comm., 272; Green, Universal, 199; Fisher, Soc. Labor, 195; scattered, 321.

1968: Nixon, R, 619,106; Humphrey, D, 476,699; Wallace, 3rd party, 66,422; Halstead, Soc. Workers, 3,377; Cleaver, Peace/Freedom, 1,332; Munn, Prohib., 362; Blomen, Soc. Labor, 241.

1964: Johnson, D, 733,030; Goldwater, R, 449,148; Munn, Prohib., 1,902; Hass, Soc. Labor, 182; DeBerry, Soc. Workers, 159.

1960: Nixon, R, 722,381; Kennedy, D, 550,565; Hass, Soc. Labor, 230; write-in, 634.

Kansas

County	2016		2012	
	Clinton (D)	Trump (R)	Obama (D)	Romney (R)
Allen	1,433	3,651	1,869	3,316
Anderson	672	2,435	944	2,276
Atchison	1,989	4,049	2,567	3,917
Barber	286	1,850	482	1,772
Barton	1,839	7,888	2,297	7,874
Bourbon	1,336	4,424	1,996	4,102
Brown	863	2,906	1,076	2,829
Butler	6,573	19,073	7,282	18,157
Chase	316	969	358	875
Chautauqua	197	1,236	280	1,304
Cherokee	2,005	6,182	2,930	5,456
Cheyenne	181	1,173	233	1,159
Clark	120	825	174	805
Clay	677	2,891	834	2,788
Cloud	761	2,919	974	2,954
Coffey	727	3,050	898	2,903
Comanche	102	715	143	767
Cowley	3,551	8,270	4,319	8,081
Crawford	5,199	8,624	6,826	7,708
Decatur	178	1,210	266	1,218
Dickinson	1,609	6,029	2,020	5,832
Doniphan	587	2,606	902	2,414
Douglas	31,195	14,688	29,267	17,401
Edwards	212	1,037	298	1,059
Elk	160	1,048	281	1,049
Ellis	2,742	8,466	3,057	8,399
Ellsworth	521	1,969	702	1,930
Finney	3,195	6,350	2,682	6,219
Ford	2,149	5,114	2,600	5,602
Franklin	2,892	7,185	3,694	6,984
Geary	2,722	4,274	3,332	4,372
Gove	149	1,140	176	1,168
Graham	188	1,025	256	1,056
Grant	441	1,804	456	1,811
Gray	263	1,698	324	1,603
Greeley	83	534	113	543
Greenwood	485	2,160	478	1,590
Hamilton	121	705	163	693
Harper	393	1,996	550	1,759
Harvey	5,068	8,668	5,373	8,588
Haskell	245	1,040	215	1,159
Hodgeman	124	855	179	868
Jackson	1,512	3,939	1,901	3,527
Jefferson	2,518	5,213	2,977	4,827
Jewell	180	1,223	229	1,235
Johnson	129,852	137,490	110,526	158,401
Kearny	174	1,075	268	1,097
Kingman	599	2,530	733	2,397
Kiowa	114	900	163	976
Labette	2,291	5,335	3,117	4,742
Lane	106	718	172	739
Leavenworth	10,209	17,638	11,357	17,059
Lincoln	215	1,179	289	1,165
Linn	736	3,484	1,170	3,177
Logan	149	1,132	197	1,126
Lyon	4,649	6,552	5,111	6,470
Marion	1,204	4,003	1,385	3,889
Marshall	1,072	3,307	1,469	3,195
McPherson	3,226	8,549	3,449	8,545
Meade	210	1,415	258	1,428
Miami	3,991	10,003	4,712	9,858
Mitchell	477	2,308	584	2,327
Montgomery	2,637	8,679	3,501	8,630
Morris	601	1,820	718	1,773
Morton	147	995	189	1,072
Nemaha	725	4,124	1,000	3,930
Neosho	1,501	4,431	2,050	4,272
Ness	162	1,228	218	1,209
Norton	281	1,840	398	1,878

County	2016 Clinton (D)	Trump (R)	2012 Obama (D)	Romney (R)
Osage	1,753	4,826	2,268	4,427
Osborne	233	1,460	324	1,479
Ottawa	424	2,283	558	2,295
Pawnee	579	1,904	718	1,836
Phillips	300	2,233	382	2,135
Pottawatomie	2,225	7,612	2,335	6,804
Pratt	771	2,838	980	2,771
Rawlins	163	1,220	190	1,223
Reno	6,837	15,513	8,085	15,718
Republic	375	2,024	477	2,134
Rice	695	2,837	911	2,676
Riley	9,341	10,107	8,977	11,507
Rooks	275	2,031	361	2,038
Rush	233	1,197	367	1,166
Russell	461	2,574	593	2,553
Saline	6,317	13,828	7,040	13,840
Scott	236	1,865	277	1,728
Sedgwick	69,627	104,353	71,977	106,506
Seward	1,628	3,159	1,490	3,617
Shawnee	33,926	35,934	36,975	37,782
Sheridan	127	1,197	168	1,154
Sherman	347	2,089	577	1,976
Smith	297	1,661	358	1,624
Stafford	304	1,490	404	1,385
Stanton	115	492	143	605
Stevens	220	1,599	252	1,749
Sumner	2,076	6,984	2,658	6,260
Thomas	473	2,908	598	2,788
Trego	198	1,227	291	1,261
Wabaunsee	776	2,372	918	2,256
Wallace	46	721	68	719
Washington	387	2,194	524	2,316
Wichita	140	769	157	821
Wilson	594	2,788	1,636	5,650
Woodson	273	1,082	380	1,035
Wyandotte	30,146	15,806	34,302	15,496
Totals	**427,005**	**671,018**	**440,726**	**692,634**

Kansas Vote Since 1960

2016: Trump, R, 671,018; Clinton, D, 427,005; Johnson, LB, 55,406; Stein, Ind., 23,506; McMullin, Ind., 6,520.

2012: Romney, R, 692,634; Obama, D, 440,726; Johnson, LB, 20,456; Baldwin, RF, 5,017.

2008: McCain, R, 699,655; Obama, D, 514,765; Nader, Ind., 10,527; Barr, LB, 6,706; Baldwin, RF, 4,148.

2004: Bush, R, 736,456; Kerry, D, 434,993; Nader, RF, 9,348; Badnarik, LB, 4,013; Peroutka, Ind., 2,899.

2000: Bush, R, 622,332; Gore, D, 399,276; Nader, Ind., 36,086; Buchanan, RF, 7,370; Browne, LB, 4,525; Hagelin, Ind., 1,373; Phillips, Const., 1,254.

1996: Dole, R, 583,245; Clinton, D, 387,659; Perot, RF, 92,639; Browne, LB, 4,557; Phillips, Ind., 3,519; Hagelin, Ind., 1,655.

1992: Bush, R, 449,951; Clinton, D, 390,434; Perot, Ind., 312,358; Marrou, LB, 4,314.

1988: Bush, R, 554,049; Dukakis, D, 422,636; Paul, Ind., 12,553; Fulani, Ind., 3,806.

1984: Reagan, R, 674,646; Mondale, D, 332,471; Bergland, LB, 3,585.

1980: Reagan, R, 566,812; Carter, D, 326,150; Anderson, Ind., 68,231; Clark, LB, 14,470; Shelton, Amer., 1,555; Hall, Comm., 967; Bubar, Statesman, 821; Rarick, Conservative, 789.

1976: Ford, R, 502,752; Carter, D, 430,421; McCarthy, Ind., 13,185; Anderson, Amer., 4,724; MacBride, LB, 3,242; Maddox, Conservative, 2,118; Bubar, Prohib., 1,403.

1972: Nixon, R, 619,812; McGovern, D, 270,287; Schmitz, Conservative, 21,808; Munn, Prohib., 4,188.

1968: Nixon, R, 478,674; Humphrey, D, 302,996; Wallace, 3rd party, 88,921; Munn, Prohib., 2,192.

1964: Johnson, D, 464,028; Goldwater, R, 386,579; Munn, Prohib., 5,393; Hass, Soc. Labor, 1,901.

1960: Nixon, R, 561,474; Kennedy, D, 363,213; Decker, Prohib., 4,138.

Kentucky

County	2016 Clinton (D)	Trump (R)	2012 Obama (D)	Romney (R)
Adair	1,323	6,637	1,660	5,841
Allen	1,349	6,466	1,808	5,184
Anderson	2,634	8,242	3,315	6,822
Ballard	816	3,161	1,189	2,647
Barren	4,275	13,483	5,400	10,922
Bath	1,361	3,082	1,770	2,275
Bell	1,720	7,764	2,224	7,127
Boone	15,026	39,082	15,629	35,922
Bourbon	2,791	5,569	3,075	4,692
Boyd	6,021	13,591	7,776	10,884
Boyle	4,281	8,040	4,471	7,703
Bracken	705	2,711	1,147	2,029
Breathitt	1,537	3,991	1,562	3,318
Breckinridge	1,960	6,484	2,825	5,025
Bullitt	8,255	26,210	9,971	21,306
Butler	947	4,428	1,293	3,716
Caldwell	1,260	4,507	1,852	3,904
Calloway	4,749	10,367	5,317	9,440
Campbell	14,658	25,050	15,080	24,240
Carlisle	432	2,094	750	1,835
Carroll	1,106	2,588	1,629	1,999
Carter	2,276	7,587	3,383	5,279
Casey	767	5,482	1,086	4,904
Christian	7,188	14,108	8,252	13,475
Clark	4,706	10,710	5,228	9,931
Clay	752	5,861	1,111	6,176
Clinton	547	3,809	752	3,569
Crittenden	617	3,290	960	2,839
Cumberland	459	2,502	599	2,216
Daviess	14,163	28,907	16,208	25,092
Edmonson	979	4,135	1,374	3,232
Elliott	740	2,000	1,186	1,126
Estill	1,108	4,236	1,356	3,749
Fayette	69,778	56,894	62,080	60,795
Fleming	1,348	4,722	1,911	3,780
Floyd	4,015	11,993	4,733	9,784
Franklin	10,717	11,819	11,535	11,345
Fulton	774	1,549	1,022	1,425
Gallatin	749	2,443	1,238	1,758
Garrard	1,453	5,904	1,661	5,310
Grant	1,910	7,268	2,810	5,664
Graves	3,308	12,671	4,547	10,699
Grayson	1,959	8,219	2,744	6,404
Green	832	4,372	1,165	3,634
Greenup	4,146	11,546	6,027	8,855
Hancock	1,244	2,788	1,833	2,212
Hardin	13,944	26,971	15,214	23,357
Harlan	1,372	9,129	1,830	8,652
Harrison	2,031	5,435	2,471	4,556
Hart	1,730	5,320	2,283	4,257
Henderson	6,707	12,159	8,091	10,296
Henry	1,828	4,944	2,530	3,940
Hickman	449	1,657	686	1,431
Hopkins	4,310	15,277	5,789	13,681
Jackson	482	4,889	612	4,365
Jefferson	190,836	143,768	186,181	148,423
Jessamine	6,144	15,474	6,001	14,233
Johnson	1,250	8,043	1,723	7,095
Kenton	24,214	42,958	24,920	41,389
Knott	1,245	4,357	1,420	4,130
Knox	1,761	9,885	2,484	8,467
LaRue	1,278	4,799	1,733	3,911
Laurel	3,440	20,592	3,905	18,151
Lawrence	1,045	4,816	1,520	3,995
Lee	444	2,151	595	1,977
Leslie	400	4,015	433	4,439
Letcher	1,542	7,293	1,702	6,811
Lewis	785	4,363	1,342	3,326
Lincoln	1,865	7,338	2,582	6,416
Livingston	887	3,570	1,346	3,089
Logan	2,755	7,778	3,469	6,899
Lyon	1,045	2,789	1,373	2,412
Madison	11,793	23,431	11,512	21,128
Magoffin	1,172	3,824	1,433	3,391
Marion	2,679	5,122	3,418	3,800
Marshall	3,672	12,322	5,022	10,402
Martin	363	3,503	574	3,180
Mason	1,970	4,944	2,592	4,197
McCracken	9,134	20,774	10,062	19,979
McCreary	664	5,012	1,069	4,564
McLean	988	3,381	1,432	2,705
Meade	3,026	8,660	4,122	6,606
Menifee	700	2,010	1,048	1,484
Mercer	2,395	7,740	2,966	6,820
Metcalfe	976	3,491	1,425	2,676
Monroe	601	4,278	936	3,762
Montgomery	3,158	7,856	3,701	6,398
Morgan	1,006	3,628	1,369	3,021
Muhlenberg	3,272	9,393	4,771	7,762

County	2016		2012	
	Clinton (D)	Trump (R)	Obama (D)	Romney (R)
Nelson	6,434	13,431	7,611	10,673
Nicholas	787	1,957	948	1,583
Ohio	2,080	7,942	2,987	6,470
Oldham	10,268	20,469	9,240	20,179
Owen	1,062	3,745	1,501	2,971
Owsley	256	1,474	283	1,279
Pendleton	1,164	4,604	1,859	3,556
Perry	2,136	8,158	2,047	8,040
Pike	4,280	19,747	5,646	17,590
Powell	1,272	3,513	1,620	2,766
Pulaski	4,208	22,902	4,976	20,714
Robertson	222	759	340	579
Rockcastle	915	5,609	1,097	5,028
Rowan	3,295	5,174	3,438	4,035
Russell	1,093	6,863	1,445	6,346
Scott	7,715	15,052	7,532	12,679
Shelby	6,276	13,196	6,634	11,790
Simpson	2,144	5,077	2,650	4,355
Spencer	1,921	7,196	2,549	5,726
Taylor	2,553	8,320	3,285	7,551
Todd	1,042	3,612	1,403	3,247
Trigg	1,587	4,931	2,115	4,520
Trimble	879	2,771	1,355	2,133
Union	1,331	4,701	1,942	3,955
Warren	16,966	28,673	16,805	26,384
Washington	1,420	4,013	1,669	3,495
Wayne	1,431	6,371	1,855	5,289
Webster	1,240	4,397	1,765	3,607
Whitley	2,067	11,312	2,683	10,232
Wolfe	753	1,804	976	1,542
Woodford	4,958	7,697	4,883	7,219
Totals	**628,854**	**1,202,971**	**679,370**	**1,087,190**

Kentucky Vote Since 1960

2016: Trump, R, 1,202,971; Clinton, D, 628,854; Johnson, LB, 53,752; McMullin, Ind., 22,780; Stein, Green, 13,913; De La Fuente, Amer. Delta, 1,128.

2012: Romney, R, 1,087,190; Obama, D, 679,370; Johnson, LB, 17,063; Terry, Ind., 6,872; Stein, Green, 6,337.

2008: McCain, R, 1,048,462; Obama, D, 751,985; Nader, Ind., 15,378; Barr, LB, 5,989; Baldwin, Const., 4,694.

2004: Bush, R, 1,069,439; Kerry, D, 712,733; Nader, Ind., 8,856; Badnarik, LB, 2,619; Peroutka, Const., 2,213.

2000: Bush, R, 872,520; Gore, D, 638,923; Nader, Green, 23,118; Buchanan, RF, 4,152; Browne, LB, 2,885; Hagelin, Natural Law, 1,513; Phillips, Const., 915.

1996: Clinton, D, 636,614; Dole, R, 623,283; Perot, RF, 120,396; Browne, LB, 4,009; Phillips, U.S. Taxpayers, 2,204; Hagelin, Natural Law, 1,493.

1992: Clinton, D, 665,104; Bush, R, 617,178; Perot, Ind., 203,944; Marrou, LB, 4,513.

1988: Bush, R, 734,281; Dukakis, D, 580,368; Duke, Populist, 4,494; Paul, LB, 2,118.

1984: Reagan, R, 815,345; Mondale, D, 536,756.

1980: Reagan, R, 635,274; Carter, D, 616,417; Anderson, Ind., 31,127; Clark, LB, 5,531; McCormack, Respect for Life, 4,233; Commoner, Citizens, 1,304; Pulley, Soc., 393; Hall, Comm., 348.

1976: Carter, D, 615,717; Ford, R, 531,852; Anderson, Amer., 8,308; McCarthy, Ind., 6,837; Maddox, Amer. Ind., 2,328; MacBride, LB, 814.

1972: Nixon, R, 676,446; McGovern, D, 371,159; Schmitz, Amer., 17,627; Spock, People's, 1,118; Jenness, Soc. Workers, 685; Hall, Comm., 464.

1968: Nixon, R, 462,411; Humphrey, D, 397,547; Wallace, 3rd party, 193,098; Halstead, Soc. Workers, 2,843.

1964: Johnson, D, 669,659; Goldwater, R, 372,977; Kasper, Natl. States' Rights, 3,469.

1960: Nixon, R, 602,607; Kennedy, D, 521,855.

Louisiana

Parish	2016		2012	
	Clinton (D)	Trump (R)	Obama (D)	Romney (R)
Acadia	5,638	21,162	6,560	19,931
Allen	2,106	6,867	2,617	6,495
Ascension	16,476	36,143	16,349	33,856
Assumption	3,931	6,714	4,754	6,083
Avoyelles	5,035	11,165	6,077	10,670
Beauregard	2,393	12,238	2,828	11,112
Bienville	3,129	3,756	3,490	3,641
Bossier	12,641	35,474	12,956	34,988

Parish	2016		2012	
	Clinton (D)	Trump (R)	Obama (D)	Romney (R)
Caddo	53,483	49,006	58,042	52,459
Calcasieu	26,296	54,191	28,359	51,850
Caldwell	788	3,822	1,016	3,640
Cameron	323	3,256	408	3,260
Catahoula	1,322	3,479	1,408	2,744
Claiborne	2,717	3,585	3,014	3,649
Concordia	3,272	5,477	3,833	5,450
DeSoto	5,165	8,068	5,553	7,353
East Baton Rouge	102,828	84,660	102,656	92,292
East Carroll	1,838	1,059	2,478	1,508
East Feliciana	4,235	5,569	4,648	5,397
Evangeline	4,208	10,360	5,330	10,181
Franklin	2,506	6,514	2,921	6,294
Grant	1,181	7,408	1,422	7,082
Iberia	10,698	20,903	12,132	20,892
Iberville	8,324	7,320	9,548	7,271
Jackson	2,139	5,169	2,305	5,132
Jefferson	73,670	100,398	70,384	102,536
Jefferson Davis	3,080	10,775	3,484	10,014
Lafayette	32,726	68,195	31,768	64,992
Lafourche	8,423	31,959	9,623	28,592
LaSalle	605	5,836	764	5,726
Lincoln	7,107	10,761	7,956	10,739
Livingston	6,950	48,824	7,451	45,513
Madison	2,744	1,927	3,154	2,000
Morehouse	5,155	6,502	5,888	6,591
Natchitoches	7,144	8,968	7,942	9,077
Orleans	133,996	24,292	126,722	28,003
Ouachita	24,428	41,734	26,645	40,948
Plaquemines	3,347	6,900	3,599	6,471
Pointe Coupee	4,764	6,789	5,436	6,548
Rapides	18,322	36,816	20,045	37,193
Red River	1,938	2,391	2,253	2,483
Richland	3,157	6,287	3,387	5,846
Sabine	1,703	7,879	2,194	7,738
St. Bernard	4,960	10,237	5,059	8,501
St. Charles	8,559	16,621	8,896	15,937
St. Helena	3,353	2,497	3,780	2,529
St. James	6,418	5,456	7,059	5,209
St. John the Baptist	12,661	7,569	13,179	7,620
St. Landry	17,209	21,971	19,668	21,475
St. Martin	8,266	16,873	9,422	15,653
St. Mary	8,050	14,359	9,450	13,885
St. Tammany	27,717	90,915	25,728	84,723
Tangipahoa	16,878	33,959	17,722	31,590
Tensas	1,332	1,182	1,564	1,230
Terrebonne	10,665	31,902	12,074	29,503
Union	2,691	7,972	3,075	7,561
Vermilion	4,857	20,063	5,720	18,910
Vernon	2,665	13,471	3,173	12,150
Washington	5,692	12,556	6,466	11,798
Webster	6,260	11,542	6,802	11,400
West Baton Rouge	5,383	6,927	5,692	6,922
West Carroll	715	3,970	853	3,628
West Feliciana	2,248	3,390	2,441	3,257
Winn	1,644	4,608	1,919	4,541
Totals	**780,154**	**1,178,638**	**809,141**	**1,152,262**

Louisiana Vote Since 1960

2016: Trump, R, 1,178,638; Clinton, D, 780,154; Johnson, LB, 37,978; Stein, Green, 14,031; McMullin, Courage/Char./Serv., 8,547; Castle, Const., 3,129; Keniston, Veterans, 1,881; Hoefling, Life/Fam./Const., 1,581; Kotlikoff, It's Our Children, 1,048; Jacob, Loyal/Trust., 749; Kennedy, Soc. Workers, 480; La Riva, Socialism/Liberation, 446; White, Soc./Eq./Anti-War, 370.

2012: Romney, R, 1,152,262; Obama, D, 809,141; Johnson, LB, 18,157; Stein, Green, 6,978; Goode, Const., 2,508; Tittle, We the People, 1,767; Anderson, Justice, 1,368; Lindsay, Socialism/Liberation, 622; Fellure, Prohib., 518; Harris, Soc. Workers, 389; White, Soc. Equality, 355.

2008: McCain, R, 1,148,275; Obama, D, 782,989; Paul, LA Taxpayers, 9,368; McKinney, Green, 9,187; Nader, Ind., 6,997; Baldwin, Const., 2,581; Harris, Soc. Workers, 735; La Riva, Socialism/Liberation, 354; Amondson, Prohib., 275.

2004: Bush, R, 1,102,169; Kerry, D, 820,299; Nader, Better Life, 7,032; Peroutka, Const., 5,203; Badnarik, LB, 2,781; Brown, Protect Working Families, 1,795; Amondson, Prohib., 1,566; Cobb, Green, 1,276; Harris, Soc. Workers, 985.

2000: Bush, R, 927,871; Gore, D, 792,344; Nader, Green, 20,473; Buchanan, RF, 14,356; Phillips, Const., 5,483; Browne, LB, 2,951; Harris, Soc. Workers, 1,103; Hagelin, Natural Law, 1,075.

1996: Clinton, D, 927,837; Dole, R, 712,586; Perot, RF, 123,293; Browne, LB, 7,499; Nader, Liberty, Ecology, Community, 4,719; Phillips, U.S. Taxpayers, 3,366; Hagelin, Natural Law, 2,981; Moorehead, Workers World, 1,678.

1992: Clinton, D, 815,971; Bush, R, 733,386; Perot, Ind., 211,478; Gritz, Populist/America First, 18,545; Marrou, LB, 3,155; Daniels, Ind., 1,663; Phillips, U.S. Taxpayers, 1,552; Fulani, New Alliance, 1,434; LaRouche, Ind., 1,136.

1988: Bush, R, 883,702; Dukakis, D, 717,460; Duke, Populist, 18,612; Paul, LB, 4,115.

1984: Reagan, R, 1,037,299; Mondale, D, 651,586; Bergland, LB, 1,876.

1980: Reagan, R, 792,853; Carter, D, 708,453; Anderson, Ind., 26,345; Rarick, Amer. Ind., 10,333; Clark, LB, 8,240; Commoner, Citizens, 1,584; DeBerry, Soc. Workers, 783.

1976: Carter, D, 661,365; Ford, R, 587,446; Maddox, Amer., 10,058; Hall, Comm., 7,417; McCarthy, Ind., 6,588; MacBride, LB, 3,325.

1972: Nixon, R, 686,852; McGovern, D, 298,142; Schmitz, Amer., 52,099; Jenness, Soc. Workers, 14,398.

1968: Wallace, 3rd party, 530,300; Humphrey, D, 309,615; Nixon, R, 257,535.

1964: Goldwater, R, 509,225; Johnson, D, 387,068.

1960: Kennedy, D, 407,339; Nixon, R, 230,890; States' Rights (unpledged), 169,572.

Maine

County	2016		2012	
	Clinton (D)	Trump (R)	Obama (D)	Romney (R)
Androscoggin	23,009	28,227	28,989	22,232
Aroostook	13,386	19,419	17,777	15,196
Cumberland	102,981	57,709	101,950	57,821
Franklin	7,016	7,918	9,367	6,369
Hancock	16,117	13,705	17,569	12,324
Kennebec	29,302	31,675	35,068	26,519
Knox	12,443	9,148	13,223	8,248
Lincoln	10,241	9,727	11,315	8,899
Oxford	12,172	16,210	16,330	11,996
Penobscot	32,838	41,622	38,811	36,547
Piscataquis	3,098	5,406	4,149	4,530
Sagadahoc	10,664	9,304	11,821	8,429
Somerset	9,092	15,001	12,216	11,800
Waldo	10,440	10,378	11,296	9,058
Washington	6,075	9,093	7,803	7,550
York	55,844	50,403	61,551	43,900
Outside U.S.	3,017	648	2,071	858
Totals	357,735	335,593	401,306	292,276

Maine Vote Since 1960

2016: Clinton, D, 357,735; Trump, R, 335,593; Johnson, LB, 38,105; Stein, Green, 14,251; McMullin, Ind., 1,887; Castle, Const., 333.

2012: Obama, D, 401,306; Romney, R, 292,276; Johnson, LB, 9,352; Stein, Green, 8,119.

2008: Obama, D, 421,923; McCain, R, 295,273; Nader, Ind., 10,636; McKinney, Green, 2,900.

2004: Kerry, D, 396,842; Bush, R, 330,201; Nader, Better Life, 8,069; Cobb, Green, 2,936; Badnarik, LB, 1,965; Peroutka, Const., 735.

2000: Gore, D, 319,951; Bush, R, 286,616; Nader, Green, 37,127; Buchanan, RF, 4,443; Browne, LB, 3,074; Phillips, Const., 579.

1996: Clinton, D, 312,788; Dole, R, 186,378; Perot, RF, 85,970; Nader, Green, 15,279; Browne, LB, 2,996; Phillips, Taxpayers, 1,517; Hagelin, Natural Law, 825.

1992: Clinton, D, 263,420; Perot, Ind., 206,820; Bush, R, 206,504; Marrou, LB, 1,681.

1988: Bush, R, 307,131; Dukakis, D, 243,569; Paul, LB, 2,700; Fulani, New Alliance, 1,405.

1984: Reagan, R, 336,500; Mondale, D, 214,515.

1980: Reagan, R, 238,522; Carter, D, 220,974; Anderson, Ind., 53,327; Clark, LB, 5,119; Commoner, Citizens, 4,394; Hall, Comm., 591; write-in, 84.

1976: Ford, R, 236,320; Carter, D, 232,279; McCarthy, Ind., 10,874; Bubar, Prohib., 3,495.

1972: Nixon, R, 256,458; McGovern, D, 160,584; scattered, 229.

1968: Humphrey, D, 217,312; Nixon, R, 169,254; Wallace, 3rd party, 6,370.

1964: Johnson, D, 262,264; Goldwater, R, 118,701.

1960: Nixon, R, 240,608; Kennedy, D, 181,159.

Maryland

County	2016		2012	
	Clinton (D)	Trump (R)	Obama (D)	Romney (R)
Allegany	7,875	21,270	9,805	19,230
Anne Arundel	128,419	122,403	126,635	126,832
Baltimore	218,412	149,477	220,322	154,908
Calvert	18,225	26,176	20,529	23,952
Caroline	4,009	9,368	4,970	8,098
Carroll	26,567	58,215	27,939	56,761
Cecil	13,650	28,868	16,557	24,806
Charles	49,341	25,614	48,774	25,178
Dorchester	6,245	8,413	7,257	7,976
Frederick	56,522	59,522	55,146	58,798
Garrett	2,567	10,776	3,124	9,743
Harford	47,077	77,860	49,729	72,911
Howard	102,597	47,484	91,393	57,758
Kent	4,575	4,876	4,842	4,870
Montgomery	357,837	92,704	323,400	123,353
Prince George's	344,049	32,811	347,938	35,734
Queen Anne's	7,973	16,993	8,556	15,823
St. Mary's	17,534	28,663	19,711	26,797
Somerset	4,196	5,341	5,240	5,042
Talbot	8,653	10,724	8,808	11,339
Washington	21,129	40,998	25,042	36,074
Wicomico	18,050	22,198	19,635	21,764
Worcester	9,753	17,210	11,014	15,951
City				
Baltimore	202,673	25,205	221,478	28,171
Totals	1,677,928	943,169	1,677,844	971,869

Maryland Vote Since 1960

2016: Clinton, D, 1,677,928; Trump, R, 943,169; Johnson, LB, 79,605; Stein, Green, 35,945; McMullin, Ind., 9,630; Castle, Const., 566; Maturen, Ind., 504.

2012: Obama, D, 1,677,844; Romney, R, 971,869; Johnson, LB, 30,195; Stein, Green, 17,110.

2008: Obama, D, 1,629,467; McCain, R, 959,862; Nader, MD Ind., 14,713; Barr, LB, 9,842; McKinney, Green, 4,747; Baldwin, RF, 3,760.

2004: Kerry, D, 1,334,493; Bush, R, 1,024,703; Nader, Populist, 11,854; Badnarik, LB, 6,094; Cobb, Green, 3,632; Peroutka, Const., 3,421.

2000: Gore, D, 1,144,008; Bush, R, 813,827; Nader, Green, 53,768; Browne, LB, 5,310; Buchanan, RF, 4,248; Phillips, Const., 918.

1996: Clinton, D, 966,207; Dole, R, 681,530; Perot, RF, 115,812; Browne, LB, 8,765; Phillips, Taxpayers, 3,402; Hagelin, Natural Law, 2,517.

1992: Clinton, D, 988,571; Bush, R, 707,094; Perot, Ind., 281,414; Marrou, LB, 4,715; Fulani, New Alliance, 2,786.

1988: Bush, R, 876,167; Dukakis, D, 826,304; Paul, LB, 6,748; Fulani, New Alliance, 5,115.

1984: Reagan, R, 879,918; Mondale, D, 787,935; Bergland, LB, 5,721.

1980: Carter, D, 726,161; Reagan, R, 680,606; Anderson, Ind., 119,537; Clark, LB, 14,192.

1976: Carter, D, 759,612; Ford, R, 672,661.

1972: Nixon, R, 829,305; McGovern, D, 505,781; Schmitz, Amer., 18,726.

1968: Humphrey, D, 538,310; Nixon, R, 517,995; Wallace, 3rd party, 178,734.

1964: Johnson, D, 730,912; Goldwater, R, 385,495; write-in, 50.

1960: Kennedy, D, 565,800; Nixon, R, 489,538.

Massachusetts

County	2016		2012	
	Clinton (D)	Trump (R)	Obama (D)	Romney (R)
Barnstable	72,430	54,099	70,822	60,446
Berkshire	43,714	16,839	48,843	14,252
Bristol	129,540	105,443	142,962	93,752
Dukes	8,400	2,477	7,978	2,792
Essex	222,310	136,316	210,302	150,480
Franklin	24,478	10,364	27,072	9,344
Hampden	112,590	78,685	123,619	73,392

County	2016 Clinton (D)	Trump (R)	2012 Obama (D)	Romney (R)
Hampshire	55,367	21,790	57,359	21,480
Middlesex	520,360	219,793	471,804	267,321
Nantucket	4,146	1,892	3,830	2,187
Norfolk	221,819	119,723	202,714	148,393
Plymouth	135,513	115,369	131,845	121,086
Suffolk	245,751	50,421	223,896	59,999
Worcester	198,778	157,682	198,244	163,390
Totals	1,995,196	1,090,893	1,921,290	1,188,314

Massachusetts Vote Since 1960

2016: Clinton, D, 1,995,196; Trump, R, 1,090,893; Johnson, LB, 138,018; Stein, Green, 47,661; McMullin, Ind., 2,719.

2012: Obama, D, 1,921,290; Romney, R, 1,188,314; Johnson, LB, 30,920; Stein, Green, 20,691.

2008: Obama, D, 1,904,097; McCain, R, 1,108,854; Nader, Ind., 28,841; Barr, LB, 13,189; McKinney, Green, 6,550; Baldwin, RF, 4,971.

2004: Kerry, D, 1,803,800; Bush, R, 1,071,109; Badnarik, LB, 15,022; Cobb, Green, 10,623.

2000: Gore, D, 1,616,487; Bush, R, 878,502; Nader, Green, 173,564; Browne, LB, 16,366; Buchanan, RF, 11,149; Hagelin, Natural Law, 2,884.

1996: Clinton, D, 1,571,509; Dole, R, 718,058; Perot, RF, 227,206; Browne, LB, 20,424; Hagelin, Natural Law, 5,183; Moorehead, Workers World, 3,276.

1992: Clinton, D, 1,318,639; Bush, R, 805,039; Perot, Ind., 630,731; Marrou, LB, 9,021; Fulani, New Alliance, 3,172; Phillips, U.S. Taxpayers, 2,218; Hagelin, Natural Law, 1,812; LaRouche, Ind., 1,027.

1988: Dukakis, D, 1,401,415; Bush, R, 1,194,635; Paul, LB, 24,251; Fulani, New Alliance, 9,561.

1984: Reagan, R, 1,310,936; Mondale, D, 1,239,606.

1980: Reagan, R, 1,057,631; Carter, D, 1,053,802; Anderson, Ind., 382,539; Clark, LB, 22,038; DeBerry, Soc. Workers, 3,735; Commoner, Citizens, 2,056; McReynolds, Soc., 62; Bubar, Statesman, 34; Griswold, Workers World, 19; scattered, 2,382.

1976: Carter, D, 1,429,475; Ford, R, 1,030,276; McCarthy, Ind., 65,637; Camejo, Soc. Workers, 8,138; Anderson, Amer., 7,555; LaRouche, U.S. Labor, 4,922; MacBride, LB, 135.

1972: McGovern, D, 1,332,540; Nixon, R, 1,112,078; Jenness, Soc. Workers, 10,600; Schmitz, Amer., 2,877; Fisher, Soc. Labor, 129; Spock, People's, 101; Hall, Comm., 46; Hospers, LB, 43; scattered, 342.

1968: Humphrey, D, 1,469,218; Nixon, R, 766,844; Wallace, 3rd party, 87,088; Blomen, Soc. Labor, 6,180; Munn, Prohib., 2,369; scattered, 53; blank, 25,394.

1964: Johnson, D, 1,786,422; Goldwater, R, 549,727; Hass, Soc. Labor, 4,755; Munn, Prohib., 3,735; scattered, 159; blank, 48,104.

1960: Kennedy, D, 1,487,174; Nixon, R, 976,750; Hass, Soc. Labor, 3,892; Decker, Prohib., 1,633; others, 31; blank and void, 26,024.

Michigan

County	2016 Clinton (D)	Trump (R)	2012 Obama (D)	Romney (R)
Alcona	1,732	4,201	2,472	3,571
Alger	1,663	2,585	2,212	2,330
Allegan	18,050	34,183	20,806	31,123
Alpena	4,877	9,090	6,549	7,298
Antrim	4,448	8,469	5,107	7,917
Arenac	2,384	4,950	3,669	4,057
Baraga	1,156	2,158	1,574	1,866
Barry	9,114	19,202	11,491	16,655
Bay	21,642	28,328	27,877	24,911
Benzie	4,108	5,539	4,685	5,075
Berrien	29,495	38,647	33,465	38,209
Branch	5,061	11,786	6,913	10,035
Calhoun	24,157	31,494	29,267	28,333
Cass	7,270	14,243	9,591	12,659
Charlevoix	5,137	8,674	5,939	8,000
Cheboygan	4,302	8,683	5,831	7,286
Chippewa	5,379	9,122	7,100	8,278
Clare	4,249	8,505	6,338	6,988
Clinton	16,492	21,636	18,191	20,650
Crawford	2,110	4,354	2,994	3,744
Delta	6,436	11,121	8,330	9,534
Dickinson	3,923	8,580	4,952	7,688
Eaton	24,938	27,609	27,913	26,197

County	2016 Clinton (D)	Trump (R)	2012 Obama (D)	Romney (R)
Emmet	6,972	10,616	7,225	10,253
Genesee	102,751	84,175	128,978	71,808
Gladwin	3,794	8,124	5,760	6,661
Gogebic	2,925	4,018	4,058	3,444
Grand Traverse	20,965	27,413	20,875	26,534
Gratiot	5,666	9,880	7,610	8,241
Hillsdale	4,799	14,095	7,106	11,727
Houghton	6,018	8,475	6,801	8,196
Huron	4,579	10,692	6,518	8,806
Ingham	79,110	43,868	80,847	45,306
Ionia	8,352	16,635	11,018	14,315
Iosco	4,345	8,345	6,242	6,909
Iron	2,004	3,675	2,687	3,224
Isabella	11,404	12,338	13,038	10,800
Jackson	25,795	39,793	32,301	36,298
Kalamazoo	67,148	51,034	69,051	52,662
Kalkaska	2,280	6,116	3,272	4,901
Kent	138,683	148,180	133,408	155,925
Keweenaw	527	814	582	774
Lake	1,939	3,159	2,752	2,487
Lapeer	12,734	30,037	18,796	23,734
Leelanau	6,774	7,239	6,576	7,483
Lenawee	16,750	26,430	21,776	22,351
Livingston	34,384	65,680	37,216	60,083
Luce	681	1,756	991	1,580
Mackinac	2,085	3,744	2,652	3,397
Macomb	176,317	224,665	208,016	191,913
Manistee	4,979	6,915	6,473	5,737
Marquette	16,042	14,646	18,115	13,606
Mason	5,281	8,505	6,856	7,580
Mecosta	5,827	10,305	7,515	9,176
Menominee	3,539	6,702	5,242	5,564
Midland	15,635	23,846	17,450	23,919
Missaukee	1,565	5,386	2,274	4,665
Monroe	26,863	43,261	36,310	35,593
Montcalm	7,874	16,907	11,430	13,621
Montmorency	1,287	3,498	2,049	2,928
Muskegon	37,304	36,127	44,436	30,884
Newaygo	6,212	15,173	8,728	12,457
Oakland	343,070	289,203	349,002	296,514
Oceana	3,973	7,228	5,063	6,239
Ogemaw	3,030	6,827	4,791	5,437
Ontonagon	1,176	2,066	1,586	1,906
Osceola	2,705	7,336	3,981	6,141
Oscoda	1,044	2,843	1,657	2,308
Otsego	3,556	8,266	4,681	7,011
Ottawa	44,973	88,467	42,737	88,166
Presque Isle	2,400	4,488	3,192	3,794
Roscommon	4,287	8,141	6,198	6,701
Saginaw	44,396	45,469	54,381	42,720
St. Clair	24,553	49,051	33,983	39,271
St. Joseph	7,526	14,884	10,112	12,978
Sanilac	4,873	13,446	7,212	10,963
Schoolcraft	1,369	2,556	1,865	2,142
Shiawassee	12,546	19,230	17,197	15,962
Tuscola	7,429	17,102	11,425	14,240
Van Buren	13,258	17,890	16,290	16,141
Washtenaw	128,483	50,631	120,890	56,412
Wayne	519,444	228,993	595,846	213,814
Wexford	4,436	10,000	6,184	8,450
Totals	2,268,839	2,279,543	2,564,569	2,115,256

Michigan Vote Since 1960

2016: Trump, R, 2,279,543; Clinton, D, 2,268,839; Johnson, LB, 172,136; Stein, Green, 51,463; Castle, U.S. Taxpayers, 16,139; McMullin, Ind., 8,177; Soltysik, Natural Law, 2,209.

2012: Obama, D, 2,564,569; Romney, R, 2,115,256; Stein, Green, 21,897; Goode, U.S. Taxpayers, 16,119; Johnson, Ind., 7,774; Anderson, Natural Law, 5,147;

2008: Obama, D, 2,872,579; McCain, R, 2,048,639; Nader, Natural Law, 33,085; Barr, LB, 23,716; Baldwin, U.S. Taxpayers, 14,685; McKinney, Green, 8,892.

2004: Kerry, D, 2,479,183; Bush, R, 2,313,746; Nader, Ind., 24,035; Badnarik, LB, 10,552; Cobb, Green, 5,325; Peroutka, U.S. Taxpayers, 4,980; Brown, Natural Law, 1,431.

2000: Gore, D, 2,170,418; Bush, R, 1,953,139; Nader, Green, 84,165; Browne, LB, 16,711; Phillips, U.S. Taxpayers, 3,791; Hagelin, Natural Law, 2,426.

1996: Clinton, D, 1,989,653; Dole, R, 1,481,212; Perot, RF, 336,670; Browne, LB, 27,670; Hagelin, Natural Law, 4,254; Moorehead, Workers World, 3,153; White, Soc. Equality, 1,554.

1992: Clinton, D, 1,871,182; Bush, R, 1,554,940; Perot, Ind., 824,813; Marrou, LB, 10,175; Phillips, U.S. Taxpayers, 8,263; Hagelin, Natural Law, 2,954.

1988: Bush, R, 1,965,486; Dukakis, D, 1,675,783; Paul, LB, 18,336; Fulani, Ind., 2,513.

1984: Reagan, R, 2,251,571; Mondale, D, 1,529,638; Bergland, LB, 10,055.

1980: Reagan, R, 1,915,225; Carter, D, 1,661,532; Anderson, Ind., 275,223; Clark, LB, 41,597; Commoner, Citizens, 11,930; Hall, Comm., 3,262; Griswold, Workers World, 30; Greaves, Amer., 21; Bubar, Statesman, 9.

1976: Ford, R, 1,893,742; Carter, D, 1,696,714; McCarthy, Ind., 47,905; MacBride, LB, 5,406; Wright, People's, 3,504; Camejo, Soc. Workers, 1,804; LaRouche, U.S. Labor, 1,366; Levin, Soc. Labor, 1,148; scattered, 2,160.

1972: Nixon, R, 1,961,721; McGovern, D, 1,459,435; Schmitz, Amer., 63,321; Fisher, Soc. Labor, 2,437; Jenness, Soc. Workers, 1,603; Hall, Comm., 1,210.

1968: Humphrey, D, 1,593,082; Nixon, R, 1,370,665; Wallace, 3rd party, 331,968; Halstead, Soc. Workers, 4,099; Blomen, Soc. Labor, 1,762; Cleaver, New Politics, 4,585; Munn, Prohib., 60; scattered, 29.

1964: Johnson, D, 2,136,615; Goldwater, R, 1,060,152; DeBerry, Soc. Workers, 3,817; Hass, Soc. Labor, 1,704; Prohib. (no candidate listed), 699; scattered, 145.

1960: Kennedy, D, 1,687,269; Nixon, R, 1,620,428; Dobbs, Soc. Workers, 4,347; Decker, Prohib., 2,029; Daly, Tax Cut, 1,767; Hass, Soc. Labor, 1,718; Ind. Amer. (unpledged), 539.

Minnesota

County	2016		2012	
	Clinton (D)	Trump (R)	Obama (D)	Romney (R)
Aitkin	3,134	5,516	4,412	4,533
Anoka	75,500	93,339	88,614	93,430
Becker	5,208	10,880	6,829	9,204
Beltrami	8,688	10,783	11,818	9,637
Benton	5,640	12,872	8,173	10,849
Big Stone	921	1,608	1,345	1,385
Blue Earth	14,428	15,667	18,164	14,916
Brown	3,763	8,708	5,630	7,938
Carlton	8,460	8,160	11,389	6,586
Carver	21,508	29,056	20,745	31,155
Cass	4,949	9,982	6,858	8,957
Chippewa	1,978	3,764	3,083	2,967
Chisago	9,278	18,441	12,524	16,227
Clay	12,971	13,543	15,208	12,920
Clearwater	1,100	2,925	1,753	2,359
Cook	1,912	1,156	1,993	1,221
Cottonwood	1,678	3,679	2,433	3,316
Crow Wing	10,982	22,287	14,760	19,415
Dakota	110,483	99,583	116,255	109,516
Dodge	3,102	6,527	4,487	5,522
Douglas	6,227	13,966	8,653	11,884
Faribault	2,153	4,659	3,407	4,104
Fillmore	3,872	6,271	5,713	4,913
Freeborn	6,041	8,808	9,326	6,969
Goodhue	9,446	14,041	12,212	12,986
Grant	1,105	2,063	1,647	1,748
Hennepin	429,288	191,770	423,982	240,073
Houston	4,145	5,616	5,281	4,951
Hubbard	3,423	7,261	4,676	6,622
Isanti	5,657	13,635	8,024	11,675
Itasca	9,015	12,920	12,852	10,501
Jackson	1,492	3,609	2,268	3,044
Kanabec	2,327	5,230	3,593	4,328
Kandiyohi	7,266	12,785	9,805	11,240
Kittson	823	1,349	1,241	1,095
Koochiching	2,306	3,569	3,451	2,841
Lac Qui Parle	1,305	2,293	1,974	1,938
Lake	3,077	2,932	4,043	2,610
Lake of the Woods	553	1,540	859	1,306
Le Sueur	4,623	9,182	6,753	7,715
Lincoln	860	1,931	1,429	1,595
Lyon	3,825	7,256	5,465	6,594
Mahnomen	930	991	1,276	871
Marshall	1,225	3,208	1,998	2,569
Martin	2,733	7,062	4,054	6,657
McLeod	4,978	12,155	6,968	11,069
Meeker	3,191	8,104	4,969	6,913
Mille Lacs	3,710	8,340	5,829	6,951
Morrison	3,637	12,925	6,153	10,159
Mower	7,437	8,823	11,129	6,938

County	2016		2012	
	Clinton (D)	Trump (R)	Obama (D)	Romney (R)
Murray	1,295	2,974	2,160	2,504
Nicollet	7,886	8,437	9,652	8,214
Nobles	2,733	5,299	3,793	4,581
Norman	1,264	1,699	1,730	1,384
Olmsted	36,268	35,668	39,338	36,832
Otter Tail	9,340	20,939	12,165	18,860
Pennington	2,147	4,000	3,024	3,305
Pine	4,580	8,191	6,750	6,845
Pipestone	1,127	3,338	1,725	2,826
Polk	4,712	8,979	6,773	7,615
Pope	2,106	3,793	2,981	3,142
Ramsey	177,738	70,894	184,938	86,800
Red Lake	540	1,141	928	978
Redwood	1,887	5,137	3,008	4,570
Renville	2,117	4,890	3,394	4,149
Rice	14,437	15,429	17,054	14,384
Rock	1,373	3,091	1,946	2,810
Roseau	1,856	5,451	2,772	4,409
St. Louis	57,771	44,630	73,378	39,131
Scott	28,502	39,948	29,712	40,323
Sherburne	13,293	31,053	17,597	27,848
Sibley	1,954	5,193	2,916	4,693
Stearns	25,576	47,617	33,551	43,015
Steele	6,241	11,198	8,706	9,903
Stevens	2,116	2,799	2,742	2,766
Swift	1,686	2,963	2,751	2,248
Todd	2,783	8,485	4,819	6,719
Traverse	630	1,049	943	861
Wabasha	3,866	6,989	5,415	6,049
Wadena	1,684	4,837	2,492	4,143
Waseca	2,838	5,967	4,370	5,116
Washington	67,086	64,428	70,203	69,137
Watonwan	1,814	2,768	2,494	2,517
Wilkin	893	2,129	1,258	1,884
Winona	11,366	12,122	14,980	11,480
Wright	20,334	43,274	25,741	40,466
Yellow Medicine	1,524	3,382	2,465	2,806
Totals	**1,367,716**	**1,322,951**	**1,546,167**	**1,320,225**

Minnesota Vote Since 1960

2016: Clinton, D, 1,367,716; Trump, R, 1,322,951; Johnson, LB, 112,972; McMullin, Ind., 53,076; Stein, Green, 36,985; Vacek, Legal Marijuana, 11,291; Castle, Const., 9,456; Kennedy, Soc. Workers, 1,672; De La Fuente, Amer. Delta, 1,431.

2012: Obama, D, 1,546,167; Romney, R, 1,320,225; Johnson, LB, 35,098; Stein, Green, 13,023; Goode, Const., 3,722; Carlson, Grassroots, 3,149; Anderson, Justice, 1,996; Morstad, Constitutional, 1,092; Harris, Soc. Workers, 1,051; Lindsay, Socialism/Liberation, 397.

2008: Obama, D, 1,573,354; McCain, R, 1,275,409; Nader, Ind., 30,152; Barr, LB, 9,174; Baldwin, Const., 6,787; McKinney, Green, 5,174; Calero, Soc. Workers, 790.

2004: Kerry, D, 1,445,014; Bush, R, 1,346,695; Nader, Better Life, 18,683; Badnarik, LB, 4,639; Cobb, Green, 4,408; Peroutka, Const., 3,074; Harens, other, 2,387; Van Auken, Soc. Equal., 539; Calero, Soc. Workers, 416.

2000: Gore, D, 1,168,266; Bush, R, 1,109,659; Nader, Green, 126,696; Buchanan, RF MN, 22,166; Browne, LB, 5,282; Phillips, Const., 3,272; Hagelin, RF, 2,294; Harris, Soc. Workers, 1,022.

1996: Clinton, D, 1,120,438; Dole, R, 766,476; Perot, RF, 257,704; Nader, Green, 24,908; Browne, LB, 8,271; Peron, Grass Roots, 4,898; Phillips, U.S. Taxpayers, 3,416; Hagelin, Natural Law, 1,808; Birrenbach, Ind. Grass Roots, 787; Harris, Soc. Workers, 684; White, Soc. Equality, 347.

1992: Clinton, D, 1,020,997; Bush, R, 747,841; Perot, Ind., 562,506; Marrou, LB, 3,373; Gritz, Populist/America First, 3,363; Hagelin, Natural Law, 1,406.

1988: Dukakis, D, 1,109,471; Bush, R, 962,337; McCarthy, MN Prog., 5,403; Paul, LB, 5,109.

1984: Mondale, D, 1,036,364; Reagan, R, 1,032,603; Bergland, LB, 2,996.

1980: Carter, D, 954,173; Reagan, R, 873,268; Anderson, Ind., 174,997; Clark, LB, 31,593; Commoner, Citizens, 8,406; Hall, Comm., 1,117; DeBerry, Soc. Workers, 711; Griswold, Workers World, 698; McReynolds, Soc., 536; write-in, 281.

1976: Carter, D, 1,070,440; Ford, R, 819,395; McCarthy, Ind., 35,490; Anderson, Amer., 13,592; Camejo, Soc. Workers, 4,149; MacBride, LB, 3,529; Hall, Comm., 1,092.

1972: Nixon, R, 898,269; McGovern, D, 802,346; Schmitz, Amer., 31,407; Fisher, Soc. Labor, 4,261; Spock, People's, 2,805; Jenness, Soc. Workers, 940; Hall, Comm., 662; scattered, 962.

1968: Humphrey, D, 857,738; Nixon, R, 658,643; Wallace, 3rd party, 68,931; Cleaver, Peace/Freedom, 935; Halstead, Soc. Workers, 808; McCarthy, write-in, 585; Mitchell, Comm., 415; Blomen, Industrial Govt., 285; scattered, 2,613.

1964: Johnson, D, 991,117; Goldwater, R, 559,624; Hass, Industrial Govt., 2,544; DeBerry, Soc. Workers, 1,177.

1960: Kennedy, D, 779,933; Nixon, R, 757,915; Dobbs, Soc. Workers, 3,077; Hass, Industrial Govt., 962.

Mississippi

County	2016		2012	
	Clinton (D)	Trump (R)	Obama (D)	Romney (R)
Adams	7,757	5,874	9,061	6,293
Alcorn	2,684	11,819	3,511	11,111
Amite	2,697	4,289	3,242	4,414
Attala	3,242	4,897	3,927	5,126
Benton	1,719	2,251	2,051	2,041
Bolivar	9,046	4,590	10,582	4,701
Calhoun	1,910	4,390	2,586	4,412
Carroll	1,680	3,799	2,007	3,960
Chickasaw	3,649	4,127	4,378	3,994
Choctaw	1,218	2,788	1,428	2,812
Claiborne	3,708	540	4,838	625
Clarke	2,585	5,137	3,111	5,049
Clay	5,722	4,150	6,712	4,291
Coahoma	6,378	2,426	7,792	2,712
Copiah	6,741	6,103	7,749	6,282
Covington	3,276	5,435	3,878	5,405
DeSoto	20,591	43,089	21,575	43,559
Forrest	11,716	15,461	13,272	16,574
Franklin	1,502	2,721	1,726	2,735
George	1,027	8,696	1,359	8,376
Greene	974	4,335	1,325	4,531
Grenada	4,424	5,970	5,288	5,986
Hancock	3,344	13,811	3,917	12,964
Harrison	21,169	40,354	23,119	39,470
Hinds	67,594	25,275	76,112	29,664
Holmes	6,689	1,309	7,812	1,435
Humphreys	3,071	1,151	3,903	1,293
Issaquena	395	298	479	302
Itawamba	1,117	8,470	1,706	7,393
Jackson	14,657	33,629	17,299	35,747
Jasper	4,368	4,038	5,097	4,193
Jefferson	3,337	490	3,951	468
Jefferson Davis	3,720	2,466	4,267	2,507
Jones	7,791	20,133	9,211	20,687
Kemper	2,827	1,778	3,239	1,789
Lafayette	7,969	10,872	8,091	11,075
Lamar	5,190	18,751	5,494	19,101
Lauderdale	11,269	17,741	13,814	18,700
Lawrence	2,195	4,091	2,468	4,192
Leake	3,584	4,782	4,079	4,863
Lee	10,029	22,220	12,563	22,415
Leflore	7,787	3,212	9,119	3,587
Lincoln	4,458	10,550	5,471	10,839
Lowndes	11,819	13,271	13,388	13,518
Madison	20,343	28,265	20,722	28,507
Marion	3,677	7,836	4,393	8,237
Marshall	8,023	6,587	9,650	6,473
Monroe	5,524	10,167	7,056	9,723
Montgomery	2,115	2,818	2,675	2,947
Neshoba	2,715	7,679	3,089	7,837
Newton	2,756	6,548	3,319	6,394
Noxubee	4,347	1,200	4,920	1,325
Oktibbeha	8,859	8,576	9,095	8,761
Panola	7,431	7,449	9,079	7,629
Pearl River	3,604	17,782	4,366	17,549
Perry	1,220	4,135	1,527	4,137
Pike	8,043	8,009	9,650	8,181
Pontotoc	2,386	10,336	2,804	9,448
Prentiss	2,067	7,648	2,817	7,075
Quitman	2,312	1,001	2,837	1,116
Rankin	14,110	47,178	14,988	48,444
Scott	4,268	6,122	5,031	6,089
Sharkey	1,479	692	1,782	737
Simpson	3,874	7,393	4,723	7,424
Smith	1,617	5,928	1,979	6,049

County	2016		2012	
	Clinton (D)	Trump (R)	Obama (D)	Romney (R)
Stone	1,573	5,306	2,003	5,420
Sunflower	6,725	2,794	8,199	2,929
Tallahatchie	3,337	2,462	3,959	2,499
Tate	3,926	7,495	4,933	7,332
Tippah	1,842	7,240	2,317	6,717
Tishomingo	999	7,166	1,643	6,133
Tunica	2,667	853	3,475	883
Union	2,012	9,235	2,742	8,498
Walthall	2,790	4,056	3,422	4,051
Warren	9,284	9,767	10,786	10,457
Washington	11,380	5,244	13,981	5,651
Wayne	3,524	5,990	4,148	6,111
Webster	1,019	3,976	1,190	3,992
Wilkinson	2,857	1,318	3,412	1,415
Winston	3,850	4,910	4,607	5,168
Yalobusha	2,582	3,376	3,030	3,276
Yazoo	5,369	4,598	6,603	4,941
Totals	**485,131**	**700,714**	**562,949**	**710,746**

Mississippi Vote Since 1960

2016: Trump, R, 700,714; Clinton, D, 485,131; Johnson, LB, 14,435; Castle, Const., 3,987; Stein, Green, 3,731; Hedges, Prohib., 715; De La Fuente, Amer. Delta, 644.

2012: Romney, R, 710,746; Obama, D, 562,949; Johnson, LB, 6,676; Goode, Const., 2,609; Stein, Green, 1,588; Washer, RF, 1,016.

2008: McCain, R, 724,597; Obama, D, 554,662; Nader, Ind., 4,011; Baldwin, Const., 2,551; Barr, LB, 2,529; McKinney, Green, 1,034; Weill, RF, 481.

2004: Bush, R, 684,981; Kerry, D, 458,094; Nader, RF, 3,177; Badnarik, LB, 1,793; Peroutka, Const., 1,759; Harris, Ind., 1,268; Cobb, Green, 1,073.

2000: Bush, R, 572,844; Gore, D, 404,614; Nader, Ind., 8,122; Phillips, Const., 3,267; Buchanan, RF, 2,265; Browne, LB, 2,009; Harris, Ind., 613; Hagelin, Natural Law, 450.

1996: Dole, R, 439,838; Clinton, D, 394,022; Perot, RF, 52,222; Browne, LB, 2,809; Phillips, U.S. Taxpayers, 2,314; Hagelin, Natural Law, 1,447; Collins, Ind., 1,205.

1992: Bush, R, 487,793; Clinton, D, 400,258; Perot, Ind., 85,626; Fulani, New Alliance, 2,625; Marrou, LB, 2,154; Phillips, U.S. Taxpayers, 1,652; Hagelin, Natural Law, 1,140.

1988: Bush, R, 557,890; Dukakis, D, 363,921; Duke, Ind., 4,232; Paul, LB, 3,329.

1984: Reagan, R, 582,377; Mondale, D, 352,192; Bergland, LB, 2,336.

1980: Reagan, R, 441,089; Carter, D, 429,281; Anderson, Ind., 12,036; Clark, LB, 5,465; Griswold, Workers World, 2,402; Pulley, Soc. Workers, 2,347.

1976: Carter, D, 381,309; Ford, R, 366,846; Anderson, Amer., 6,678; McCarthy, Ind., 4,074; Maddox, Ind., 4,049; Camejo, Soc. Workers, 2,805; MacBride, LB, 2,609.

1972: Nixon, R, 505,125; McGovern, D, 126,782; Schmitz, Amer., 11,598; Jenness, Soc. Workers, 2,458.

1968: Wallace, 3rd party, 415,349; Humphrey, D, 150,644; Nixon, R, 88,516.

1964: Goldwater, R, 356,528; Johnson, D, 52,618.

1960: D. (electors unpledged), 116,248; Kennedy, D, 108,362; Nixon, R, 73,561. Mississippi's victorious slate of 8 unpledged Dem. electors cast their votes for Sen. Harry F. Byrd (D, VA).

Missouri

County	2016		2012	
	Clinton (D)	Trump (R)	Obama (D)	Romney (R)
Adair	3,500	6,030	4,219	5,651
Andrew	2,045	6,665	2,649	5,457
Atchison	541	2,060	756	1,902
Audrain	2,570	6,981	3,539	6,186
Barry	2,710	11,428	3,667	9,832
Barton	795	4,959	1,230	4,418
Bates	1,618	6,001	2,557	5,020
Benton	2,025	7,213	2,925	6,069
Bollinger	705	4,827	1,213	4,095
Boone	41,125	36,200	39,847	37,404
Buchanan	12,013	21,320	15,594	18,660
Butler	3,036	13,650	4,363	12,248
Caldwell	838	3,232	1,312	2,721
Callaway	4,989	13,057	6,071	11,745

County	2016 Clinton (D)	Trump (R)	2012 Obama (D)	Romney (R)
Camden	4,768	16,944	6,458	15,092
Cape Girardeau	8,492	27,017	9,728	25,370
Carroll	745	3,480	1,154	3,072
Carter	436	2,324	754	1,978
Cass	14,846	33,098	17,044	30,912
Cedar	1,011	5,021	1,537	4,376
Chariton	888	2,950	1,339	2,402
Christian	8,508	30,946	9,813	27,473
Clark	724	2,458	1,398	1,730
Clay	45,304	57,476	47,310	56,191
Clinton	2,572	7,067	3,688	5,931
Cole	10,913	24,616	12,005	24,490
Cooper	1,932	5,624	2,474	4,887
Crawford	1,824	7,724	2,951	6,434
Dade	637	3,184	939	2,895
Dallas	1,272	5,895	2,122	4,992
Daviess	730	2,767	1,125	2,290
DeKalb	824	3,540	1,194	3,056
Dent	978	5,600	1,585	4,883
Douglas	984	5,486	1,710	4,649
Dunklin	2,360	8,026	3,636	6,850
Franklin	12,341	35,430	16,347	29,396
Gasconade	1,520	5,670	2,099	4,895
Gentry	605	2,304	937	1,988
Greene	42,728	78,035	46,219	76,900
Grundy	780	3,462	1,212	3,030
Harrison	574	2,965	984	2,624
Henry	2,357	7,075	3,606	6,229
Hickory	1,016	3,542	1,733	2,835
Holt	347	1,926	551	1,725
Howard	1,283	3,277	1,723	3,017
Howell	2,881	13,893	4,395	11,544
Iron	933	3,173	1,669	2,252
Jackson	71,237	91,557	78,283	93,199
Jasper	10,572	35,070	12,809	31,349
Jefferson	31,568	69,036	41,564	53,978
Johnson	5,930	13,719	7,667	12,763
Knox	379	1,416	698	1,205
Laclede	2,553	12,881	4,093	10,934
Lafayette	4,053	10,988	5,655	9,803
Lawrence	2,901	13,089	4,017	11,421
Lewis	934	3,344	1,508	2,677
Lincoln	5,575	18,159	7,734	14,332
Linn	1,240	4,088	2,041	3,344
Livingston	1,265	4,879	1,906	4,006
Macon	1,548	5,798	2,309	4,701
Madison	1,005	4,102	1,588	3,227
Maries	794	3,561	1,299	3,165
Marion	2,994	9,419	4,031	7,923
McDonald	1,329	6,599	1,920	5,694
Mercer	216	1,486	353	1,255
Miller	1,750	9,285	2,651	8,099
Mississippi	1,458	3,600	1,858	2,997
Moniteau	1,237	5,347	1,608	4,704
Monroe	853	3,159	1,398	2,564
Montgomery	1,119	4,127	1,740	3,490
Morgan	1,768	6,760	2,773	5,733
New Madrid	1,933	5,270	2,814	4,284
Newton	4,990	20,553	6,425	18,181
Nodaway	2,529	6,380	3,172	5,593
Oregon	865	3,671	1,419	2,886
Osage	998	5,856	1,473	5,329
Ozark	724	3,639	1,261	3,080
Pemiscot	1,947	3,964	2,671	3,598
Perry	1,520	6,908	2,184	5,669
Pettis	4,324	12,810	5,904	10,842
Phelps	4,766	12,709	5,798	11,895
Pike	1,806	5,274	2,582	4,577
Platte	20,057	25,933	19,175	25,618
Polk	2,631	10,438	3,580	9,252
Pulaski	2,922	9,876	4,199	9,092
Putnam	353	1,936	587	1,673
Ralls	1,138	3,969	1,736	3,231
Randolph	2,283	7,529	3,031	6,667
Ray	3,090	7,104	4,275	5,815
Reynolds	540	2,406	1,157	1,931
Ripley	830	4,522	1,396	3,743
St. Charles	68,626	121,650	71,838	110,784

County	2016 Clinton (D)	Trump (R)	2012 Obama (D)	Romney (R)
St. Clair	936	3,501	1,460	3,019
St. Francois	6,250	17,468	8,829	13,248
St. Louis Co.	286,704	202,434	297,097	224,742
Ste. Genevieve	2,542	5,496	3,813	4,055
Saline	2,789	5,977	3,790	5,104
Schuyler	354	1,505	697	1,174
Scotland	365	1,525	643	1,246
Scott	3,575	13,168	5,122	11,623
Shannon	776	2,966	1,302	2,262
Shelby	606	2,524	966	2,188
Stoddard	1,876	11,079	3,153	9,496
Stone	2,887	13,158	3,923	11,787
Sullivan	526	1,884	908	1,610
Taney	4,373	18,276	5,479	15,746
Texas	1,728	8,875	2,871	7,618
Vernon	1,707	6,533	2,580	5,758
Warren	3,915	11,111	5,219	9,150
Washington	1,926	7,048	3,417	5,071
Wayne	948	4,658	1,813	3,790
Webster	3,177	12,840	4,409	10,708
Worth	195	808	341	664
Wright	1,170	6,707	1,953	5,830
City				
Kansas City	97,735	24,654	105,670	29,509
St. Louis	104,235	20,832	118,780	22,943
Totals	**1,071,068**	**1,594,511**	**1,223,796**	**1,482,440**

Missouri Vote Since 1960

2016: Trump, R, 1,594,511; Clinton, D, 1,071,068; Johnson, LB, 97,359; Stein, Green, 25,419; Castle, Const., 13,092; McMullin, Ind., 7,071.

2012: Romney, R, 1,482,440; Obama, D, 1,223,796; Johnson, LB, 43,151; Goode, Const., 7,936.

2008: McCain, R, 1,445,814; Obama, D, 1,441,911; Nader, Ind., 17,813; Barr, LB, 11,386; Baldwin, Const., 8,201.

2004: Bush, R, 1,455,713; Kerry, D, 1,259,171; Badnarik, LB, 9,831; Peroutka, Const., 5,355.

2000: Bush, R, 1,189,924; Gore, D, 1,111,138; Nader, Green, 38,515; Buchanan, RF, 9,818; Browne, LB, 7,436; Phillips, Const., 1,957; Hagelin, Natural Law, 1,104.

1996: Clinton, D, 1,025,935; Dole, R, 890,016; Perot, RF, 217,188; Phillips, U.S. Taxpayers, 11,521; Browne, LB, 10,522; Hagelin, Natural Law, 2,287.

1992: Clinton, D, 1,053,873; Bush, R, 811,159; Perot, Ind., 518,741; Marrou, LB, 7,497.

1988: Bush, R, 1,084,953; Dukakis, D, 1,001,619; Fulani, New Alliance, 6,656; Paul, write-in, 434.

1984: Reagan, R, 1,274,188; Mondale, D, 848,583.

1980: Reagan, R, 1,074,181; Carter, D, 931,182; Anderson, Ind., 77,920; Clark, LB, 14,422; DeBerry, Soc. Workers, 1,515; Commoner, Citizens, 573; write-in, 31.

1976: Carter, D, 999,163; Ford, R, 928,808; McCarthy, Ind., 24,329.

1972: Nixon, R, 1,154,058; McGovern, D, 698,531.

1968: Nixon, R, 811,932; Humphrey, D, 791,444; Wallace, 3rd party, 206,126.

1964: Johnson, D, 1,164,344; Goldwater, R, 653,535.

1960: Kennedy, D, 972,201; Nixon, R, 962,221.

Montana

County	2016 Clinton (D)	Trump (R)	2012 Obama (D)	Romney (R)
Beaverhead	1,143	3,353	1,371	3,289
Big Horn	2,094	1,853	2,882	1,667
Blaine	1,202	1,268	1,616	1,178
Broadwater	573	2,348	764	2,152
Carbon	1,828	3,748	2,146	3,533
Carter	70	678	96	678
Cascade	12,175	19,632	15,232	18,345
Chouteau	732	1,679	978	1,758
Custer	1,176	3,657	1,833	3,373
Daniels	168	730	237	740
Dawson	787	3,320	1,219	3,029
Deer Lodge	2,058	1,763	2,860	1,448
Fallon	154	1,279	237	1,128
Fergus	1,202	4,269	1,640	4,257
Flathead	13,293	30,240	13,892	28,309

County	2016 Clinton (D)	Trump (R)	2012 Obama (D)	Romney (R)
Gallatin	24,246	23,802	21,961	24,358
Garfield	34	653	66	622
Glacier	3,121	1,620	2,924	1,415
Golden Valley	71	365	110	351
Granite	472	1,192	533	1,107
Hill	2,371	3,478	3,403	3,164
Jefferson	1,998	4,177	2,272	4,055
Judith Basin	235	872	337	854
Lake	4,776	7,530	5,805	7,135
Lewis and Clark	14,478	16,895	15,620	16,803
Liberty	206	698	257	702
Lincoln	2,041	6,729	2,552	6,057
Madison	1,180	3,297	1,289	3,130
McCone	154	862	223	745
Meagher	193	729	269	670
Mineral	519	1,330	700	1,216
Missoula	31,543	22,250	32,824	22,652
Musselshell	332	1,967	492	1,833
Park	3,595	4,980	3,783	4,709
Petroleum	30	278	49	240
Phillips	318	1,723	471	1,688
Pondera	738	1,799	975	1,673
Powder River	127	884	170	833
Powell	551	2,029	888	1,806
Prairie	100	556	167	520
Ravalli	6,223	14,810	7,285	14,307
Richland	671	3,908	1,002	3,510
Roosevelt	1,560	1,797	2,086	1,514
Rosebud	987	2,253	1,422	2,004
Sanders	1,218	4,286	1,720	3,980
Sheridan	477	1,241	665	1,207
Silver Bow	8,619	6,376	10,857	5,430
Stillwater	908	3,661	1,248	3,337
Sweet Grass	402	1,595	475	1,594
Teton	808	2,170	1,082	2,113
Toole	402	1,497	582	1,440
Treasure	59	351	114	319
Valley	886	2,698	1,385	2,337
Wheatland	179	702	272	693
Wibaux	55	463	98	421
Yellowstone	22,171	40,920	26,403	40,500
Totals	177,709	279,240	201,839	267,928

Montana Vote Since 1960

2016: Trump, R, 279,240; Clinton, D, 177,709; Johnson, LB, 28,037; Stein, Green, 7,970; McMullin, Ind., 2,297; De La Fuente, Amer. Delta, 1,570.
2012: Romney, R, 267,928; Obama, D, 201,839; Johnson, LB, 14,165.
2008: McCain, R, 242,763; Obama, D, 231,667; Paul, Const., 10,638; Nader, Ind., 3,686; Barr, LB, 1,355.
2004: Bush, R, 266,063; Kerry, D, 173,710; Nader, Ind., 6,168; Peroutka, Const., 1,764; Badnarik, LB, 1,733; Cobb, Green, 996.
2000: Bush, R, 240,178; Gore, D, 137,126; Nader, Green, 24,437; Buchanan, RF, 5,697; Browne, LB, 1,718; Phillips, Const., 1,155; Hagelin, Natural Law, 675.
1996: Dole, R, 179,652; Clinton, D, 167,922; Perot, RF, 55,229; Browne, LB, 2,526; Hagelin, Natural Law, 1,754.
1992: Clinton, D, 154,507; Bush, R, 144,207; Perot, Ind., 107,225; Gritz, Populist/America First, 3,658.
1988: Bush, R, 190,412; Dukakis, D, 168,936; Paul, LB, 5,047; Fulani, New Alliance, 1,279.
1984: Reagan, R, 232,450; Mondale, D, 146,742; Bergland, LB, 5,185.
1980: Reagan, R, 206,814; Carter, D, 118,032; Anderson, Ind., 29,281; Clark, LB, 9,825.
1976: Ford, R, 173,703; Carter, D, 149,259; Anderson, Amer., 5,772.
1972: Nixon, R, 183,976; McGovern, D, 120,197; Schmitz, Amer., 13,430.
1968: Nixon, R, 138,835; Humphrey, D, 114,117; Wallace, 3rd party, 20,015; Munn, Prohib., 510; Caton, New RF, 470; Halstead, Soc. Workers, 457.
1964: Johnson, D, 164,246; Goldwater, R, 113,032; Kasper, Natl. States' Rights, 519; Munn, Prohib., 499; DeBerry, Soc. Workers, 332.
1960: Nixon, R, 141,841; Kennedy, D, 134,891; Decker, Prohib., 456; Dobbs, Soc. Workers, 391.

Nebraska

County	2016 Clinton (D)	Trump (R)	2012 Obama (D)	Romney (R)
Adams	3,302	9,287	4,062	8,316
Antelope	383	2,732	571	2,596
Arthur	17	244	30	227
Banner	19	357	55	346
Blaine	30	276	29	268
Boone	414	2,299	615	2,138
Box Butte	965	3,617	1,692	2,869
Boyd	128	983	188	873
Brown	153	1,385	224	1,302
Buffalo	4,763	14,569	5,365	13,570
Burt	930	2,367	1,291	2,029
Butler	691	3,079	1,045	2,738
Cass	3,484	8,452	4,367	7,556
Cedar	571	3,532	958	3,278
Chase	171	1,648	254	1,584
Cherry	317	2,623	436	2,557
Cheyenne	711	3,665	1,084	3,449
Clay	477	2,422	667	2,232
Colfax	859	2,171	969	2,051
Cuming	719	3,122	1,031	2,876
Custer	641	4,695	1,083	4,296
Dakota	2,314	3,616	2,922	3,094
Dawes	801	2,632	1,132	2,478
Dawson	2,136	5,984	2,199	5,460
Deuel	120	809	215	763
Dixon	556	2,041	870	1,745
Dodge	4,544	9,933	5,673	8,995
Douglas	113,798	108,077	106,456	113,220
Dundy	89	823	176	792
Fillmore	613	2,130	807	2,007
Franklin	250	1,347	384	1,112
Frontier	161	1,110	271	1,007
Furnas	304	1,921	423	1,782
Gage	2,935	6,380	3,903	5,513
Garden	153	869	242	829
Garfield	121	821	149	769
Gosper	166	794	230	734
Grant	20	367	30	322
Greeley	210	912	340	820
Hall	6,282	14,408	7,161	12,646
Hamilton	878	3,783	1,146	3,600
Harlan	254	1,496	354	1,395
Hayes	30	472	51	476
Hitchcock	161	1,232	274	1,178
Holt	531	4,354	882	3,922
Hooker	40	355	59	330
Howard	544	2,284	914	1,890
Jefferson	837	2,399	1,195	2,166
Johnson	563	1,355	790	1,225
Kearney	550	2,531	773	2,349
Keith	571	3,235	928	3,044
Keya Paha	40	460	80	393
Kimball	230	1,330	395	1,235
Knox	720	3,188	1,059	2,885
Lancaster	61,898	61,588	62,015	62,434
Lincoln	2,913	12,164	4,450	10,728
Logan	32	400	68	356
Loup	48	323	62	290
Madison	2,711	10,628	3,485	10,062
McPherson	14	257	41	237
Merrick	602	2,926	925	2,490
Morrill	284	1,802	455	1,681
Nance	281	1,261	481	1,106
Nemaha	785	2,116	1,128	2,012
Nuckolls	353	1,726	568	1,574
Otoe	2,025	4,860	2,561	4,258
Pawnee	279	974	400	899
Perkins	161	1,217	238	1,135
Phelps	572	3,849	880	3,400
Pierce	382	3,052	637	2,707
Platte	2,646	10,965	3,148	10,061
Polk	413	2,028	528	1,890
Red Willow	645	4,258	952	3,891
Richardson	818	2,769	1,191	2,443
Rock	70	687	103	672
Saline	1,733	3,004	2,289	2,557
Sarpy	28,033	45,143	26,671	43,213
Saunders	2,523	7,555	3,307	6,770

County	2016 Clinton (D)	2016 Trump (R)	2012 Obama (D)	2012 Romney (R)
Scotts Bluff	3,207	10,076	4,327	9,648
Seward	1,875	5,454	2,386	5,003
Sheridan	287	2,211	390	2,021
Sherman	340	1,150	552	927
Sioux	81	616	101	624
Stanton	417	2,187	614	1,949
Thayer	499	2,051	728	1,874
Thomas	30	344	42	360
Thurston	919	1,043	1,247	939
Valley	339	1,780	498	1,657
Washington	2,623	7,424	3,132	6,899
Wayne	835	2,693	1,074	2,493
Webster	306	1,330	442	1,258
Wheeler	62	377	93	345
York	1,186	4,700	1,373	4,874
Totals	**284,494**	**495,961**	**302,081**	**475,064**

Nebraska Vote Since 1960

2016: Trump, R, 495,961; Clinton, D, 284,494; Johnson, LB, 38,946; Stein, petitioning cand., 8,775.

2012: Romney, R, 475,064; Obama, D, 302,081; Johnson, LB, 11,109; Terry, petitioning cand., 2,408.

2008: McCain, R, 452,979; Obama, D, 333,319; Nader, petitioning cand., 5,406; Baldwin, Nebraska, 2,972; Barr, LB, 2,740; McKinney, Green, 1,028.

2004: Bush, R, 512,814; Kerry, D, 254,328; Nader, petitioning cand., 5,698; Badnarik, LB, 2,041; Peroutka, Nebraska, 1,314; Cobb, Green, 978; Calero, petitioning cand., 82.

2000: Bush, R, 433,862; Gore, D, 231,780; Nader, Green, 24,540; Buchanan, Ind., 3,646; Browne, LB, 2,245; Hagelin, Natural Law, 478; Phillips, Ind., 468.

1996: Dole, R, 363,467; Clinton, D, 236,761; Perot, RF, 71,278; Browne, LB, 2,792; Phillips, Ind., 1,928; Hagelin, Natural Law, 1,189.

1992: Bush, R, 343,678; Clinton, D, 216,864; Perot, Ind., 174,104; Marrou, LB, 1,340.

1988: Bush, R, 397,956; Dukakis, D, 259,235; Paul, LB, 2,534; Fulani, New Alliance, 1,740.

1984: Reagan, R, 459,135; Mondale, D, 187,475; Bergland, LB, 2,075.

1980: Reagan, R, 419,214; Carter, D, 166,424; Anderson, Ind., 44,854; Clark, LB, 9,041.

1976: Ford, R, 359,219; Carter, D, 233,287; McCarthy, Ind., 9,383; Maddox, Amer. Ind., 3,378; MacBride, LB, 1,476.

1972: Nixon, R, 406,298; McGovern, D, 169,991; scattered, 817.

1968: Nixon, R, 321,163; Humphrey, D, 170,784; Wallace, 3rd party, 44,904.

1964: Johnson, D, 307,307; Goldwater, R, 276,847.

1960: Nixon, R, 380,553; Kennedy, D, 232,542.

Nevada

County	2016 Clinton (D)	2016 Trump (R)	2012 Obama (D)	2012 Romney (R)
Churchill	2,210	7,830	2,961	7,061
Clark	402,227	320,057	389,936	289,053
Douglas	8,454	17,415	9,297	16,276
Elko	3,401	13,551	3,511	12,014
Esmeralda	65	329	92	317
Eureka	74	723	107	663
Humboldt	1,386	4,521	1,737	3,810
Lander	403	1,828	534	1,580
Lincoln	285	1,671	400	1,691
Lyon	6,146	16,005	7,380	13,520
Mineral	637	1,179	863	1,080
Nye	5,094	13,324	6,320	10,566
Pershing	430	1,403	632	1,167
Storey	752	1,616	920	1,321
Washoe	97,379	94,758	95,409	88,453
White Pine	707	2,723	983	2,601
City				
Carson City	9,610	13,125	10,291	12,394
Totals	**539,260**	**512,058**	**531,373**	**463,567**

Nevada Vote Since 1960

2016: Clinton, D, 539,260; Trump, R, 512,058; Johnson, LB, 37,384; None of These Candidates, 28,863; Castle, Ind. Amer., 5,268; De La Fuente, unaff., 2,552.

2012: Obama, D, 531,373; Romney, R, 463,567; Johnson, LB, 10,968; None of These Candidates, 5,770; Goode, Ind. Amer., 3,240.

2008: Obama, D, 533,736; McCain, R, 412,827; None of These Candidates, 6,267; Nader, Ind., 6,150; Barr, LB, 4,263; Baldwin, Const., 3,194; McKinney, Green, 1,411.

2004: Bush, R, 418,690; Kerry, D, 397,190; Nader, Ind., 4,838; None of These Candidates, 3,688; Badnarik, LB, 3,176; Peroutka, Ind. Amer., 1,152; Cobb, Green, 853.

2000: Bush, R, 301,575; Gore, D, 279,978; Nader, Green, 15,008; Buchanan, Citizens First, 4,747; None of These Candidates, 3,315; Browne, LB, 3,311; Phillips, Ind. Amer., 621; Hagelin, Natural Law, 415.

1996: Clinton, D, 203,974; Dole, R, 199,244; Perot, RF, 43,986; None of These Candidates, 5,608; Nader, Green, 4,730; Browne, LB, 4,460; Phillips, Ind. Amer., 1,732; Hagelin, Natural Law, 545.

1992: Clinton, D, 189,148; Bush, R, 175,828; Perot, Ind., 132,580; Gritz, Populist/America First, 2,892; Marrou, LB, 1,835.

1988: Bush, R, 206,040; Dukakis, D, 132,738; Paul, LB, 3,520; Fulani, New Alliance, 835.

1984: Reagan, R, 188,770; Mondale, D, 91,655; Bergland, LB, 2,292.

1980: Reagan, R, 155,017; Carter, D, 66,666; Anderson, Ind., 17,651; Clark, LB, 4,358.

1976: Ford, R, 101,273; Carter, D, 92,479; MacBride, LB, 1,519; Maddox, Amer. Ind., 1,497; scattered, 5,108.

1972: Nixon, R, 115,750; McGovern, D, 66,016.

1968: Nixon, R, 73,188; Humphrey, D, 60,598; Wallace, 3rd party, 20,432.

1964: Johnson, D, 79,339; Goldwater, R, 56,094.

1960: Kennedy, D, 54,880; Nixon, R, 52,387.

New Hampshire

County	2016 Clinton (D)	2016 Trump (R)	2012 Obama (D)	2012 Romney (R)
Belknap	13,517	19,315	15,890	17,571
Carroll	12,987	14,635	13,977	14,207
Cheshire	22,064	16,876	25,380	15,156
Coos	6,563	7,952	9,095	6,342
Grafton	28,510	19,010	29,826	18,208
Hillsborough	99,589	100,013	102,303	99,991
Merrimack	40,198	37,674	44,756	34,524
Rockingham	79,994	90,447	80,142	87,921
Strafford	34,894	29,072	36,026	26,729
Sullivan	10,210	10,796	12,166	9,269
Totals	**348,526**	**345,790**	**369,561**	**329,918**

New Hampshire Vote Since 1960

2016: Clinton, D, 348,526; Trump, R, 345,790; Johnson, LB, 30,777; Stein, Green, 6,496; De La Fuente, Amer. Delta, 678.

2012: Obama, D, 369,561; Romney, R, 329,918; Johnson, LB, 8,212; Goode, Const., 708.

2008: Obama, D, 384,826; McCain, R, 316,534; Nader, Ind., 3,503; Barr, LB, 2,217; Phillies, LB, 531.

2004: Kerry, D, 340,511; Bush, R, 331,237; Nader, Ind., 4,479.

2000: Bush, R, 273,559; Gore, D, 266,348; Nader, Green, 22,198; Browne, LB, 2,757; Buchanan, Independence, 2,615; Phillips, Const., 328.

1996: Clinton, D, 246,166; Dole, R, 196,486; Perot, RF, 48,387; Browne, LB, 4,214; Phillips, Taxpayers, 1,344.

1992: Clinton, D, 209,040; Bush, R, 202,484; Perot, Ind., 121,337; Marrou, LB, 3,548.

1988: Bush, R, 281,537; Dukakis, D, 163,696; Paul, LB, 4,502; Fulani, New Alliance, 790.

1984: Reagan, R, 267,051; Mondale, D, 120,377; Bergland, LB, 735.

1980: Reagan, R, 221,705; Carter, D, 108,864; Anderson, Ind., 49,693; Clark, LB, 2,067; Commoner, Citizens, 1,325; Hall, Comm., 129; Griswold, Workers World, 76; DeBerry, Soc. Workers, 72; scattered, 68.

1976: Ford, R, 185,935; Carter, D, 147,645; McCarthy, Ind., 4,095; MacBride, LB, 936; Reagan, write-in, 388; LaRouche, U.S. Labor, 186; Camejo, Soc. Workers, 161; Levin, Soc. Labor, 66; scattered, 215.

1972: Nixon, R, 213,724; McGovern, D, 116,435; Schmitz, Amer., 3,386; Jenness, Soc. Workers, 368; scattered, 142.

1968: Nixon, R, 154,903; Humphrey, D, 130,589; Wallace, 3rd party, 11,173; New Party, 421; Halstead, Soc. Workers, 104.

1964: Johnson, D, 182,065; Goldwater, R, 104,029.

1960: Nixon, R, 157,989; Kennedy, D, 137,772.

New Jersey

County	2016 Clinton (D)	2016 Trump (R)	2012 Obama (D)	2012 Romney (R)
Atlantic	60,924	52,690	65,600	46,522
Bergen	231,211	175,529	212,754	169,070
Burlington	121,725	89,272	126,377	87,401
Camden	146,717	72,631	153,682	69,476
Cape May	18,750	28,446	21,657	25,781
Cumberland	27,771	24,453	34,055	20,658
Essex	240,837	63,176	236,618	64,406
Gloucester	66,870	67,544	74,013	59,456
Hudson	163,917	49,043	153,108	42,369
Hunterdon	28,898	38,712	26,876	38,687
Mercer	104,775	46,193	104,377	47,355
Middlesex	193,044	122,953	190,555	107,310
Monmouth	137,181	166,723	133,145	147,513
Morris	115,249	126,071	100,146	124,947
Ocean	87,150	179,079	102,300	146,474
Passaic	116,759	72,902	115,926	64,523
Salem	11,904	16,381	14,719	14,334
Somerset	85,689	65,505	74,592	66,603
Sussex	24,212	46,658	26,104	40,625
Union	147,414	68,114	139,752	68,314
Warren	17,281	29,858	18,745	25,744
Totals	2,148,278	1,601,933	2,125,101	1,477,568

New Jersey Vote Since 1960

2016: Clinton, D, 2,148,278; Trump, R, 1,601,933; Johnson, LB, 72,477; Stein, Green, 37,772; Castle, Const., 6,161; Kennedy, Soc. Workers, 2,156; De La Fuente, Amer. Delta, 1,838; Moorehead, Workers World, 1,749; La Riva, Socialism/Liberation, 1,682.

2012: Obama, D, 2,125,101; Romney, R, 1,477,568; Johnson, LB, 21,045; Stein, Green, 9,888; Goode, Const., 2,064; Anderson, Justice, 1,724; Boss, Ind., 1,007; Harris, Soc. Workers, 710; Miller, A3P, 664; Lindsay, Socialism/Liberation, 521.

2008: Obama, D, 2,215,422; McCain, R, 1,613,207; Nader, Ind., 21,298; Barr, Ind., 8,441; Baldwin, Ind., 3,956; McKinney, Ind., 3,636; Moore, Ind., 699; Boss, Ind., 639; Calero, Ind., 523; La Riva, Ind., 416.

2004: Kerry, D, 1,911,430; Bush, R, 1,670,003; Nader, Ind., 19,418; Badnarik, Ind., 4,514; Peroutka, Ind., 2,750; Cobb, Ind., 1,807; Brown, Ind., 664; Van Auken, Ind., 575; Calero, Ind., 530.

2000: Gore, D, 1,788,850; Bush, R, 1,284,173; Nader, Ind., 94,554; Buchanan, Ind., 6,989; Browne, Ind., 6,312; Hagelin, Ind., 2,215; McReynolds, Ind., 1,880; Phillips, Ind., 1,409; Harris, Ind., 844.

1996: Clinton, D, 1,652,361; Dole, R, 1,103,099; Perot, RF, 262,134; Nader, Green, 32,465; Browne, LB, 14,763; Hagelin, Natural Law, 3,887; Phillips, U.S. Taxpayers, 3,440; Harris, Soc. Workers, 1,837; Moorehead, Workers World, 1,337; White, Soc. Equality, 537.

1992: Clinton, D, 1,436,206; Bush, R, 1,356,865; Perot, Ind., 521,829; Marrou, LB, 6,822; Fulani, New Alliance, 3,513; Phillips, U.S. Taxpayers, 2,670; LaRouche, Ind., 2,095; Warren, Soc. Workers, 2,011; Daniels, Ind., 1,996; Gritz, Populist/America First, 1,867; Hagelin, Natural Law, 1,353.

1988: Bush, R, 1,740,604; Dukakis, D, 1,317,541; Lewin, Peace/Freedom, 9,953; Paul, LB, 8,421.

1984: Reagan, R, 1,933,630; Mondale, D, 1,261,323; Bergland, LB, 6,416.

1980: Reagan, R, 1,546,557; Carter, D, 1,147,364; Anderson, Ind., 234,632; Clark, LB, 20,652; Commoner, Citizens, 8,203; McCormack, Right to Life, 3,927; Lynen, Middle Class, 3,694; Hall, Comm., 2,555; Pulley, Soc. Workers, 2,198; McReynolds, Soc., 1,973; Gahres, Down With Lawyers, 1,718; Griswold, Workers World, 1,288; Wendelken, Ind., 923.

1976: Ford, R, 1,509,688; Carter, D, 1,444,653; McCarthy, Ind., 32,717; MacBride, LB, 9,449; Maddox, Amer., 7,716; Levin, Soc. Labor, 3,686; Hall, Comm., 1,662; LaRouche, U.S. Labor, 1,650; Camejo, Soc. Workers, 1,184; Wright, People's, 1,044; Bubar, Prohib., 554; Zeidler, Soc., 469.

1972: Nixon, R, 1,845,502; McGovern, D, 1,102,211; Schmitz, Amer., 34,378; Spock, People's, 5,355; Fisher, Soc. Labor, 4,544; Jenness, Soc. Workers, 2,233; Mahalchik, America First, 1,743; Hall, Comm., 1,263.

1968: Nixon, R, 1,325,467; Humphrey, D, 1,264,206; Wallace, 3rd party, 262,187; Halstead, Soc. Workers, 8,667; Gregory, Peace/Freedom, 8,084; Blomen, Soc. Labor, 6,784.

1964: Johnson, D, 1,867,671; Goldwater, R, 963,843; DeBerry, Soc. Workers, 8,181; Hass, Soc. Labor, 7,075.

1960: Kennedy, D, 1,385,415; Nixon, R, 1,363,324; Dobbs, Soc. Workers, 11,402; Lee, Conservative, 8,708; Hass, Soc. Labor, 4,262.

New Mexico

County	2016 Clinton (D)	2016 Trump (R)	2012 Obama (D)	2012 Romney (R)
Bernalillo	143,417	94,698	150,739	106,408
Catron	427	1,464	560	1,494
Chaves	5,534	12,872	6,604	13,088
Cibola	3,741	3,195	4,961	2,998
Colfax	2,129	2,585	2,828	2,699
Curry	3,121	9,035	4,022	9,251
De Baca	193	620	287	586
Doña Ana	37,947	25,374	37,139	27,322
Eddy	5,033	13,147	6,142	12,583
Grant	6,276	5,288	7,090	5,358
Guadalupe	970	595	1,488	557
Harding	156	311	260	327
Hidalgo	784	910	995	899
Lea	3,930	12,495	4,080	12,548
Lincoln	2,331	5,896	2,942	5,961
Los Alamos	5,562	3,359	5,191	4,796
Luna	3,195	3,478	3,583	3,670
McKinley	13,576	5,104	15,841	5,546
Mora	1,536	665	1,955	595
Otero	6,124	11,887	6,829	12,451
Quay	1,017	2,212	1,383	2,202
Rio Arriba	9,592	3,599	11,465	3,397
Roosevelt	1,454	3,884	1,727	4,043
San Juan	12,865	27,946	15,855	28,849
San Miguel	7,285	2,313	8,850	2,303
Sandoval	27,707	25,905	27,236	24,387
Santa Fe	50,793	14,332	50,872	15,500
Sierra	1,612	3,010	1,964	2,928
Socorro	3,313	2,616	4,058	2,722
Taos	10,668	2,727	11,978	2,730
Torrance	1,785	3,714	2,428	3,529
Union	320	1,216	472	1,236
Valencia	10,841	13,215	13,511	12,825
Totals	385,234	319,667	415,335	335,788

New Mexico Vote Since 1960

2016: Clinton, D, 385,234; Trump, R, 319,667; Johnson, LB, 74,541; Stein, Green, 9,879; McMullin, Better for Amer., 5,825; Castle, Const., 1,514; La Riva, Socialism/Liberation, 1,184; De La Fuente, Amer. Delta, 475.

2012: Obama, D, 415,335; Romney, R, 335,788; Johnson, LB, 27,788; Stein, Green, 2,691; Anderson, Ind., 1,174; Goode, Const., 982.

2008: Obama, D, 472,422; McCain, R, 346,832; Nader, Ind., 5,327; Barr, LB, 2,428; Baldwin, Const., 1,597; McKinney, Green, 1,552.

2004: Bush, R, 376,930; Kerry, D, 370,942; Nader, Ind., 4,053; Badnarik, LB, 2,382; Cobb, Green, 1,226; Peroutka, Const., 771.

2000: Gore, D, 286,783; Bush, R, 286,417; Nader, Green, 21,251; Browne, LB, 2,058; Buchanan, RF, 1,392; Hagelin, Natural Law, 361; Phillips, Const., 343.

1996: Clinton, D, 273,495; Dole, R, 232,751; Perot, RF, 32,257; Nader, Green, 13,218; Browne, LB, 2,996; Phillips, Taxpayers, 713; Hagelin, Natural Law, 644.

1992: Clinton, D, 261,617; Bush, R, 212,824; Perot, Ind., 91,895; Marrou, LB, 1,615.

1988: Bush, R, 270,341; Dukakis, D, 244,497; Paul, LB, 3,268; Fulani, New Alliance, 2,237.

1984: Reagan, R, 307,101; Mondale, D, 201,769; Bergland, LB, 4,459.

1980: Reagan, R, 250,779; Carter, D, 167,826; Anderson, Ind., 29,459; Clark, LB, 4,365; Commoner, Citizens, 2,202; Bubar, Statesman, 1,281; Pulley, Soc. Workers, 325.

1976: Ford, R, 211,419; Carter, D, 201,148; Camejo, Soc. Workers, 2,462; MacBride, LB, 1,110; Zeidler, Soc., 240; Bubar, Prohib., 211.

1972: Nixon, R, 235,606; McGovern, D, 141,084; Schmitz, Amer., 8,767; Jenness, Soc. Workers, 474.

1968: Nixon, R, 169,692; Humphrey, D, 130,081; Wallace, 3rd party, 25,737; Chavez, 1,519; Halstead, Soc. Workers, 252.

1964: Johnson, D, 194,017; Goldwater, R, 131,838; Hass, Soc. Labor, 1,217; Munn, Prohib., 543.
1960: Kennedy, D, 156,027; Nixon, R, 153,733; Decker, Prohib., 777; Hass, Soc. Labor, 570.

New York

County	2016		2012	
	Clinton (D)	Trump (R)	Obama (D)	Romney (R)
Albany	83,071	47,808	87,556	45,064
Allegany	4,882	12,525	6,139	10,390
Bronx[1]	353,646	37,797	339,211	29,967
Broome	39,212	40,943	41,970	37,641
Cattaraugus	9,497	19,692	12,649	16,569
Cayuga	13,522	17,384	17,007	13,454
Chautauqua	19,091	31,594	23,812	27,971
Chemung	13,757	20,097	16,797	17,612
Chenango	6,775	11,921	9,116	9,713
Clinton	15,059	14,449	18,961	11,115
Columbia	15,284	13,756	16,221	12,225
Cortland	8,771	9,900	10,482	8,695
Delaware	6,627	11,942	8,304	9,938
Dutchess	62,261	61,797	65,312	56,025
Erie	215,456	188,303	237,356	169,675
Essex	7,762	7,958	9,784	6,647
Franklin	7,297	8,221	9,894	5,740
Fulton	6,496	13,462	8,607	10,814
Genesee	7,650	16,915	9,601	14,607
Greene	7,405	13,073	9,030	11,174
Hamilton	949	2,064	1,128	1,932
Herkimer	8,083	16,699	11,273	13,282
Jefferson	13,809	21,763	17,099	18,122
Kings (Brooklyn)[1]	640,553	141,044	604,443	124,551
Lewis	3,146	7,400	4,724	5,651
Livingston	10,697	17,290	11,705	14,448
Madison	11,667	15,936	13,871	13,622
Monroe	188,592	136,582	193,501	133,362
Montgomery	6,595	11,301	8,493	9,334
Nassau	332,154	292,025	302,695	259,308
New York (Manhattan)[1]	579,013	64,930	502,674	89,559
Niagara	35,559	51,961	43,986	43,240
Oneida	33,743	51,437	40,468	44,530
Onondaga	112,337	83,649	122,254	78,831
Ontario	22,233	26,029	23,087	23,820
Orange	68,278	76,645	73,315	65,367
Orleans	4,470	10,936	5,787	8,594
Oswego	17,095	27,688	23,515	19,980
Otsego	10,451	13,308	12,117	11,461
Putnam	19,366	27,024	19,512	24,083
Queens[1]	517,220	149,341	470,732	118,589
Rensselaer	32,717	33,726	37,408	29,113
Richmond (Staten Island)[1]	74,143	101,437	78,181	74,223
Rockland	69,342	60,911	65,657	57,363
St. Lawrence	16,488	19,942	21,353	15,138
Saratoga	50,913	54,575	52,957	50,382
Schenectady	33,747	28,953	36,844	26,568
Schoharie	4,240	8,831	5,427	7,467
Schuyler	3,091	5,050	3,674	4,281
Seneca	5,697	7,236	7,094	5,889
Steuben	12,526	26,831	15,787	21,954
Suffolk	303,951	350,570	304,079	282,131
Sullivan	12,568	15,931	15,268	12,705
Tioga	7,526	13,260	8,930	12,117
Tompkins	28,890	10,371	27,244	11,107
Ulster	44,597	35,239	47,752	29,759
Warren	13,091	15,751	14,806	14,119
Washington	9,098	13,610	11,523	11,085
Wayne	13,473	23,380	16,635	20,060
Westchester	272,926	131,238	240,785	143,122
Wyoming	3,904	12,442	5,661	10,348
Yates	3,659	5,660	4,488	4,798
Totals	**4,556,118**	**2,819,533**	**4,485,741**	**2,490,431**

(1) Borough of New York City.

New York Vote Since 1960

2016: Clinton, D, 4,556,118; Trump, R, 2,819,533; Johnson, LB, 176,598; Stein, Green, 107,935; McMullin, Ind., 10,397.
2012: Obama, D, 4,485,741; Romney, R, 2,490,431; Johnson, LB, 47,256; Stein, Green, 39,982; Goode, Const., 6,274; Lindsay, Socialism/Liberation, 2,050.

2008: Obama, D, 4,804,945; McCain, R, 2,752,771; Nader, Populist, 41,249; Barr, LB, 19,596; McKinney, Green, 12,801; Calero, Soc. Workers, 3,615; La Riva, Socialism/Liberation, 1,639.
2004: Kerry, D, 4,314,280; Bush, R, 2,962,567; Nader, Ind., 99,873; Badnarik, LB, 11,607; Calero, Soc. Workers, 2,405.
2000: Gore, D, 4,112,965; Bush, R, 2,405,570; Nader, Green, 244,360; Buchanan, RF, 31,554; Hagelin, Independence, 24,369; Browne, LB, 7,664; Harris, Soc. Workers, 1,790; Phillips, Const., 1,503.
1996: Clinton, D, 3,756,177; Dole, R, 1,933,492; Perot, RF, 503,458; Nader, Green, 75,956; Phillips, Right to Life, 23,580; Browne, LB, 12,220; Hagelin, Natural Law, 5,011; Moorehead, Workers World, 3,473; Harris, Soc. Workers, 2,762.
1992: Clinton, D, 3,444,450; Bush, R, 2,346,649; Perot, Ind., 1,090,721; Warren, Soc. Workers, 15,472; Marrou, LB, 13,451; Fulani, New Alliance, 11,318; Hagelin, Natural Law, 4,420.
1988: Dukakis, D, 3,347,882; Bush, R, 3,081,871; Marra, Right to Life, 20,497; Fulani, New Alliance, 15,845.
1984: Reagan, R, 3,664,763; Mondale, D, 3,119,609; Bergland, LB, 11,949.
1980: Reagan, R, 2,893,831; Carter, D, 2,728,372; Anderson, Liberal, 467,801; Clark, LB, 52,648; McCormack, Right to Life, 24,159; Commoner, Citizens, 23,186; Hall, Comm., 7,414; DeBerry, Soc. Workers, 2,068; Griswold, Workers World, 1,416; scattered, 1,064.
1976: Carter, D, 3,389,558; Ford, R, 3,100,791; MacBride, LB, 12,197; Hall, Comm., 10,270; Camejo, Soc. Workers, 6,996; LaRouche, U.S. Labor, 5,413; blank, void, and scattered, 143,037.
1972: Nixon, R, 3,824,642; McGovern, D, 2,767,956 and Liberal, 183,128 (total, 2,951,084); Reed, Soc. Workers, 7,797; Fisher, Soc. Labor, 4,530; Hall, Comm., 5,641; blank, void, and scattered, 161,641.
1968: Humphrey, D, 3,378,470; Nixon, R, 3,007,932; Wallace, 3rd party, 358,864; Gregory, Peace/Freedom, 24,517; Halstead, Soc. Workers, 11,851; Blomen, Soc. Labor, 8,432; blank, void, and scattered, 171,624.
1964: Johnson, D, 4,913,156; Goldwater, R, 2,243,559; Hass, Soc. Labor, 6,085; DeBerry, Soc. Workers, 3,215; scattered, 188; blank and void, 151,383.
1960: Kennedy, D, 3,423,909 and Liberal, 406,176 (total, 3,830,085); Nixon, R, 3,446,419; Dobbs, Soc. Workers, 14,319; scattered, 256; blank and void, 88,896.

North Carolina

County	2016		2012	
	Clinton (D)	Trump (R)	Obama (D)	Romney (R)
Alamance	29,833	38,815	28,875	38,170
Alexander	3,767	13,893	4,611	12,253
Alleghany	1,306	3,814	1,583	3,390
Anson	5,859	4,506	7,019	4,166
Ashe	3,500	9,412	4,116	8,242
Avery	1,689	6,298	1,882	5,766
Beaufort	8,764	14,543	9,435	13,977
Bertie	5,778	3,456	6,695	3,387
Bladen	7,058	8,550	8,062	7,748
Brunswick	23,282	42,720	22,038	34,743
Buncombe	75,452	55,716	70,625	54,701
Burke	11,251	26,238	13,701	22,267
Cabarrus	35,521	53,819	32,849	49,557
Caldwell	8,425	26,621	10,898	23,229
Camden	1,274	3,546	1,508	3,109
Carteret	9,939	26,569	10,301	24,775
Caswell	4,792	6,026	5,348	5,594
Catawba	21,216	48,324	24,069	44,538
Chatham	21,065	17,105	18,361	16,665
Cherokee	2,860	10,844	3,378	9,278
Chowan	2,992	4,014	3,556	3,891
Clay	1,367	4,437	1,579	3,973
Cleveland	14,964	28,479	17,062	25,793
Columbus	9,063	14,272	11,050	12,941
Craven	17,630	27,731	18,763	26,928
Cumberland	71,605	51,265	75,792	50,666
Currituck	2,913	9,163	3,562	7,496
Dare	7,222	11,460	7,393	10,248
Davidson	18,109	54,317	20,624	49,383
Davie	5,270	15,602	5,735	14,687
Duplin	8,283	12,217	9,033	11,416
Durham	121,250	28,350	111,224	33,769
Edgecombe	16,224	8,261	18,310	8,546

County	2016 Clinton (D)	Trump (R)	2012 Obama (D)	Romney (R)
Forsyth	94,464	75,975	92,323	79,768
Franklin	12,874	16,368	13,436	14,603
Gaston	31,177	61,798	33,171	56,138
Gates	2,385	2,874	2,786	2,564
Graham	768	3,283	1,119	2,750
Granville	12,909	13,591	13,598	12,405
Greene	3,605	4,374	3,778	4,411
Guilford	149,248	98,062	146,365	104,789
Halifax	15,748	9,031	17,176	8,763
Harnett	16,737	27,614	17,331	25,565
Haywood	10,473	18,929	11,833	15,633
Henderson	19,827	35,809	18,642	32,994
Hertford	6,910	3,099	7,843	3,007
Hoke	9,726	7,760	10,076	6,819
Hyde	965	1,288	1,163	1,193
Iredell	24,734	54,754	26,076	49,299
Jackson	7,713	9,870	8,095	8,254
Johnston	28,362	54,372	27,290	48,427
Jones	2,065	2,974	2,352	2,837
Lee	10,469	13,712	10,801	13,158
Lenoir	12,634	13,613	13,948	13,980
Lincoln	9,897	28,806	11,024	25,267
Macon	4,876	12,127	5,712	10,835
Madison	3,926	6,783	4,484	5,404
Martin	5,846	5,897	6,583	5,995
McDowell	4,667	14,568	6,031	11,775
Mecklenburg	294,562	155,518	272,262	171,668
Mitchell	1,596	6,282	1,838	5,806
Montgomery	4,150	7,130	4,706	6,404
Moore	16,329	30,490	16,505	29,495
Nash	23,235	23,319	24,313	23,842
New Hanover	50,979	55,344	48,668	53,385
Northampton	6,144	3,582	7,232	3,483
Onslow	17,514	37,122	18,490	32,243
Orange	59,923	18,557	53,901	21,539
Pamlico	2,448	4,258	2,647	4,051
Pasquotank	8,615	8,180	10,282	7,633
Pender	9,354	17,639	9,632	14,617
Perquimans	2,319	4,177	2,759	3,822
Person	7,833	11,185	8,418	10,496
Pitt	41,824	35,691	41,843	36,214
Polk	3,735	6,768	4,013	6,236
Randolph	13,194	49,430	14,773	45,160
Richmond	8,501	10,383	9,904	9,332
Robeson	19,016	20,762	24,988	17,510
Rockingham	14,228	26,830	16,351	25,227
Rowan	19,400	42,810	22,650	38,775
Rutherford	7,512	21,871	9,374	18,954
Sampson	10,547	14,838	11,566	14,422
Scotland	7,319	6,256	8,215	5,831
Stanly	7,094	21,964	8,431	19,904
Stokes	4,665	17,116	6,018	15,237
Surry	7,488	23,671	9,112	19,923
Swain	2,196	3,565	2,618	2,976
Transylvania	6,558	10,520	6,826	9,634
Tyrrell	720	975	837	930
Union	34,337	66,707	32,473	61,107
Vance	12,229	7,332	13,323	7,429
Wake	302,736	196,082	267,262	211,596
Warren	6,413	3,214	6,978	3,140
Washington	3,510	2,564	3,833	2,622
Watauga	14,138	13,697	13,002	13,861
Wayne	21,770	27,540	23,314	27,641
Wilkes	6,638	23,752	8,148	20,515
Wilson	19,663	17,531	20,875	17,954
Yadkin	3,160	13,880	3,957	12,578
Yancey	3,196	6,385	3,981	5,278
Totals	2,189,316	2,362,631	2,178,391	2,270,395

North Carolina Vote Since 1960

2016: Trump, R, 2,362,631; Clinton, D, 2,189,316; Johnson, LB, 130,126; Stein, Ind., 12,105.
2012: Romney, R, 2,270,395; Obama, D, 2,178,391; Johnson, LB, 44,515.
2008: Obama, D, 2,142,651; McCain, R, 2,128,474; Barr, LB, 25,722.
2004: Bush, R, 1,961,166; Kerry, D, 1,525,849; Badnarik, LB, 11,731.

2000: Bush, R, 1,631,163; Gore, D, 1,257,692; Browne, LB, 13,891; Buchanan, RF, 8,874.
1996: Dole, R, 1,225,938; Clinton, D, 1,107,849; Perot, RF, 168,059; Browne, LB, 8,740; Hagelin, Natural Law, 2,771.
1992: Bush, R, 1,134,661; Clinton, D, 1,114,042; Perot, Ind., 357,864; Marrou, LB, 5,171.
1988: Bush, R, 1,237,258; Dukakis, D, 890,167; Fulani, New Alliance, 5,682; Paul, write-in, 1,263.
1984: Reagan, R, 1,346,481; Mondale, D, 824,287; Bergland, LB, 3,794.
1980: Reagan, R, 915,018; Carter, D, 875,635; Anderson, Ind., 52,800; Clark, LB, 9,677; Commoner, Citizens, 2,287; DeBerry, Soc. Workers, 416.
1976: Carter, D, 927,365; Ford, R, 741,960; Anderson, Amer., 5,607; MacBride, LB, 2,219; LaRouche, U.S. Labor, 755.
1972: Nixon, R, 1,054,889; McGovern, D, 438,705; Schmitz, Amer., 25,018.
1968: Nixon, R, 627,192; Wallace, 3rd party, 496,188; Humphrey, D, 464,113.
1964: Johnson, D, 800,139; Goldwater, R, 624,844.
1960: Kennedy, D, 713,136; Nixon, R, 655,420.

North Dakota

County	2016 Clinton (D)	Trump (R)	2012 Obama (D)	Romney (R)
Adams	216	909	328	918
Barnes	1,597	3,160	2,394	2,964
Benson	842	929	1,235	868
Billings	59	495	89	472
Bottineau	736	2,494	1,183	2,280
Bowman	227	1,446	414	1,280
Burke	119	895	230	769
Burleigh	10,881	32,532	14,122	27,951
Cass	31,361	39,816	34,712	36,855
Cavalier	476	1,357	818	1,195
Dickey	554	1,667	853	1,610
Divide	245	867	385	733
Dunn	358	1,771	508	1,506
Eddy	355	791	486	634
Emmons	215	1,677	383	1,435
Foster	347	1,241	607	1,030
Golden Valley	99	796	162	742
Grand Forks	10,851	16,340	14,032	15,060
Grant	185	1,108	334	1,025
Griggs	298	847	536	771
Hettinger	168	1,050	313	1,000
Kidder	179	1,111	393	870
LaMoure	502	1,481	740	1,377
Logan	114	888	232	810
McHenry	490	2,050	943	1,678
McIntosh	235	1,100	459	1,035
McKenzie	698	3,670	927	2,458
McLean	1,081	3,860	1,670	3,141
Mercer	621	3,759	1,166	3,152
Morton	3,080	11,336	4,469	8,680
Mountrail	1,220	2,582	1,403	1,962
Nelson	536	1,025	767	865
Oliver	119	830	281	693
Pembina	681	2,208	1,253	1,899
Pierce	431	1,437	660	1,465
Ramsey	1,505	3,217	2,164	2,665
Ransom	838	1,210	1,343	1,009
Renville	201	993	398	851
Richland	2,064	4,767	3,198	4,229
Rolette	2,099	1,217	3,353	1,092
Sargent	694	1,088	1,075	879
Sheridan	95	650	163	642
Sioux	758	260	900	225
Slope	43	362	83	341
Stark	1,753	9,755	2,812	8,521
Steele	361	538	518	498
Stutsman	2,498	6,718	3,585	5,685
Towner	305	733	516	623
Traill	1,241	2,265	1,811	1,996
Walsh	1,167	2,995	1,985	2,656
Ward	5,806	18,636	8,441	16,230
Wells	419	1,796	673	1,654
Williams	1,735	10,069	2,322	7,184
Totals	93,758	216,794	124,827	188,163

North Dakota Vote Since 1960

2016: Trump, R, 216,794; Clinton, D, 93,758; Johnson, LB, 21,434; Stein, Green, 3,780; Castle, Const., 1,833; De La Fuente, Amer. Delta, 364.

2012: Romney, R, 188,163; Obama, D, 124,827; Johnson, LB, 5,231; Stein, Green, 1,361; Goode, Const., 1,185.

2008: McCain, R, 168,601; Obama, D, 141,278; Nader, Ind., 4,189; Barr, LB, 1,354; Baldwin, Const., 1,199.

2004: Bush, R, 196,651; Kerry, D, 111,052; Nader, Ind., 3,756; Badnarik, LB, 851; Peroutka, Const., 514.

2000: Bush, R, 174,852; Gore, D, 95,284; Nader, Ind., 9,486; Buchanan, RF, 7,288; Browne, Ind., 660; Phillips, Const., 373; Hagelin, Ind., 313.

1996: Dole, R, 125,050; Clinton, D, 106,905; Perot, RF, 32,515; Browne, LB, 847; Phillips, Ind., 745; Hagelin, Natural Law, 349.

1992: Bush, R, 136,244; Clinton, D, 99,168; Perot, Ind., 71,084.

1988: Bush, R, 166,559; Dukakis, D, 127,739; Paul, LB, 1,315; LaRouche, Natl. Econ. Recovery, 905.

1984: Reagan, R, 200,336; Mondale, D, 104,429; Bergland, LB, 703.

1980: Reagan, R, 193,695; Carter, D, 79,189; Anderson, Ind., 23,640; Clark, LB, 3,743; Commoner, LB, 429; McLain, Natl. People's League, 296; Greaves, Amer., 235; Hall, Comm., 93; DeBerry, Soc. Workers, 89; McReynolds, Soc., 82; Bubar, Statesman, 54.

1976: Ford, R, 153,470; Carter, D, 136,078; Anderson, Amer., 3,698; McCarthy, Ind., 2,952; Maddox, Amer. Ind., 269; MacBride, LB, 256; scattered, 371.

1972: Nixon, R, 174,109; McGovern, D, 100,384; Schmitz, Amer., 5,646; Jenness, Soc. Workers, 288; Hall, Comm., 87.

1968: Nixon, R, 138,669; Humphrey, D, 94,769; Wallace, 3rd party, 14,244; Halstead, Soc. Workers, 128; Munn, Prohib., 38; Troxell, Ind., 34.

1964: Johnson, D, 149,784; Goldwater, R, 108,207; DeBerry, Soc. Workers, 224; Munn, Prohib., 174.

1960: Nixon, R, 154,310; Kennedy, D, 123,963; Dobbs, Soc. Workers, 158.

Ohio

County	2016		2012	
	Clinton (D)	Trump (R)	Obama (D)	Romney (R)
Adams	2,326	8,659	3,976	6,865
Allen	13,294	30,487	17,914	29,502
Ashland	5,740	17,493	8,281	15,519
Ashtabula	15,577	23,318	23,803	18,298
Athens	16,370	11,354	18,307	8,543
Auglaize	3,980	18,658	5,831	17,169
Belmont	8,785	21,108	14,156	16,758
Brown	4,353	14,573	7,107	11,916
Butler	58,642	106,976	62,388	105,176
Carroll	3,154	9,254	5,543	7,315
Champaign	4,594	12,631	7,044	11,045
Clark	23,328	35,205	31,297	31,820
Clermont	26,715	67,518	30,458	64,208
Clinton	4,066	13,838	5,791	12,009
Columbiana	12,432	31,676	19,821	25,251
Coshocton	4,013	10,785	6,940	8,390
Crawford	4,625	13,611	7,507	11,852
Cuyahoga	398,271	184,211	447,273	190,660
Darke	4,470	20,012	6,826	18,108
Defiance	5,368	11,688	7,732	10,176
Delaware	40,872	57,568	37,292	60,194
Erie	16,057	19,648	21,793	16,952
Fairfield	24,881	44,314	29,890	41,034
Fayette	2,739	7,995	4,249	6,620
Franklin	351,198	199,331	346,373	215,997
Fulton	6,069	13,709	9,073	11,738
Gallia	2,628	9,822	4,557	7,750
Geauga	17,569	30,227	19,659	30,589
Greene	28,943	48,540	32,256	49,819
Guernsey	4,359	11,445	7,450	8,993
Hamilton	215,719	173,665	219,927	193,326
Hancock	9,609	24,183	12,564	22,443
Hardin	2,920	8,717	4,619	7,489
Harrison	1,688	5,098	2,950	4,019
Henry	3,756	9,301	5,658	8,257
Highland	3,773	14,020	6,054	11,413
Hocking	3,775	8,497	6,157	6,285
Holmes	1,788	8,720	2,608	8,702
Huron	7,192	16,226	11,006	13,060
Jackson	3,226	9,949	5,166	7,904
Jefferson	9,675	21,117	15,385	17,034
Knox	8,171	19,131	10,470	17,266
Lake	46,397	64,255	57,680	58,744
Lawrence	6,974	18,689	10,744	14,651
Licking	27,376	51,241	34,201	45,503
Logan	4,647	15,957	7,062	13,633
Lorain	66,949	66,818	81,464	59,405
Lucas	110,833	75,698	136,616	69,940
Madison	4,779	11,631	6,845	10,342
Mahoning	57,381	53,616	77,059	42,641
Marion	7,928	16,961	12,504	14,265
Medina	32,182	54,810	38,785	50,418
Meigs	2,260	7,309	4,027	5,895
Mercer	3,384	17,506	4,745	16,561
Miami	13,120	37,079	16,383	34,606
Monroe	1,662	4,868	3,035	3,548
Montgomery	122,016	123,909	137,139	124,841
Morgan	1,736	4,431	2,814	3,179
Morrow	3,761	11,948	5,933	9,865
Muskingum	11,123	24,056	17,002	19,264
Noble	1,221	4,549	2,131	3,563
Ottawa	8,285	12,653	11,503	10,538
Paulding	2,093	6,500	3,538	5,354
Perry	4,138	10,228	7,033	7,627
Pickaway	6,529	17,076	9,684	14,037
Pike	3,539	7,902	5,684	5,685
Portage	32,397	39,971	39,453	35,242
Preble	4,325	15,446	6,211	13,535
Putnam	2,922	14,961	4,318	13,721
Richland	16,085	36,590	22,687	33,867
Ross	10,356	18,652	14,569	15,008
Sandusky	9,929	16,316	14,541	13,755
Scioto	9,132	20,550	15,077	15,492
Seneca	7,404	14,825	11,353	13,243
Shelby	4,243	18,590	6,343	17,142
Stark	68,146	98,388	89,432	88,581
Summit	134,256	112,026	153,041	111,001
Trumbull	43,014	49,024	61,672	38,279
Tuscarawas	12,188	26,918	18,407	22,242
Union	7,718	18,096	8,805	16,289
Van Wert	2,697	10,469	4,029	9,585
Vinton	1,351	3,883	2,436	2,856
Warren	33,730	77,643	32,909	76,564
Washington	8,026	20,514	11,651	17,284
Wayne	15,031	32,270	19,808	30,251
Williams	4,358	11,939	7,266	10,047
Wood	27,318	32,498	32,802	29,704
Wyandot	2,515	7,468	4,137	6,180
Totals	**2,394,164**	**2,841,005**	**2,827,709**	**2,661,437**

Ohio Vote Since 1960

2016: Trump, R, 2,841,005; Clinton, D, 2,394,164; Johnson, LB, 174,498; Stein, Green, 46,271; Duncan, Ind., 24,235; McMullin, Ind., 12,574; Castle, Const., 1,887.

2012: Obama, D, 2,827,709; Romney, R, 2,661,437; Johnson, LB, 49,493; Stein, Green, 18,573; Duncan, Ind., 12,502; Goode, Const., 8,152; Alexander, Soc., 2,944.

2008: Obama, D, 2,940,044; McCain, R, 2,677,820; Nader, Ind., 42,337; Barr, LB, 19,917; Baldwin, Const., 12,565; McKinney, Green, 8,518; Duncan, Ind., 3,905; Moore, Soc., 2,735.

2004: Bush, R, 2,859,768; Kerry, D, 2,741,167; Badnarik, nonpartisan, 14,676; Peroutka, nonpartisan, 939.

2000: Bush, R, 2,351,209; Gore, D, 2,186,190; Nader, Ind., 117,857; Buchanan, Ind., 26,724; Browne, LB, 13,475; Hagelin, Natural Law, 6,169; Phillips, Ind., 3,823.

1996: Clinton, D, 2,148,222; Dole, R, 1,859,883; Perot, RF, 483,207; Browne, Ind., 12,851; Moorehead, Ind., 10,813; Hagelin, Natural Law, 9,120; Phillips, Ind., 7,361.

1992: Clinton, D, 1,984,942; Bush, R, 1,894,310; Perot, Ind., 1,036,426; Marrou, LB, 7,252; Fulani, New Alliance, 6,413; Gritz, Populist/America First, 4,699; Hagelin, Natural Law, 3,437; LaRouche, Ind., 2,446.

1988: Bush, R, 2,416,549; Dukakis, D, 1,939,629; Fulani, Ind., 12,017; Paul, Ind., 11,926.
1984: Reagan, R, 2,678,559; Mondale, D, 1,825,440; Bergland, LB, 5,886.
1980: Reagan, R, 2,206,545; Carter, D, 1,752,414; Anderson, Ind., 254,472; Clark, LB, 49,033; Commoner, Citizens, 8,564; Hall, Comm., 4,729; Congress, Ind., 4,029; Griswold, Workers World, 3,790; Bubar, Statesman, 27.
1976: Carter, D, 2,011,621; Ford, R, 2,000,505; McCarthy, Ind., 58,258; Maddox, Amer. Ind., 15,529; MacBride, LB, 8,961; Hall, Comm., 7,817; Camejo, Soc. Workers, 4,717; LaRouche, U.S. Labor, 4,335; scattered, 130.
1972: Nixon, R, 2,441,827; McGovern, D, 1,558,889; Schmitz, Amer., 80,067; Fisher, Soc. Labor, 7,107; Hall, Comm., 6,437; Wallace, Ind., 460.
1968: Nixon, R, 1,791,014; Humphrey, D, 1,700,586; Wallace, 3rd party, 467,495; Gregory, 372; Blomen, Soc. Labor, 120; Halstead, Soc. Workers, 69; Mitchell, Comm., 23; Munn, Prohib., 19.
1964: Johnson, D, 2,498,331; Goldwater, R, 1,470,865.
1960: Nixon, R, 2,217,611; Kennedy, D, 1,944,248.

Oklahoma

County	2016 Clinton (D)	Trump (R)	2012 Obama (D)	Romney (R)
Adair	1,382	4,787	2,127	4,381
Alfalfa	216	1,933	322	1,761
Atoka	795	4,084	1,243	3,538
Beaver	176	1,993	244	2,062
Beckham	960	6,308	1,417	5,508
Blaine	711	2,884	992	2,824
Bryan	2,804	10,478	3,681	9,520
Caddo	2,420	6,482	3,164	5,687
Canadian	11,674	39,986	10,537	35,625
Carter	4,002	13,752	4,908	12,214
Cherokee	5,456	9,994	6,144	8,162
Choctaw	1,067	4,206	1,494	3,572
Cimarron	71	963	115	1,082
Cleveland	38,829	62,538	34,771	59,116
Coal	411	1,898	649	1,710
Comanche	11,463	19,183	12,521	17,664
Cotton	424	2,054	657	1,796
Craig	1,252	4,283	1,747	3,559
Creek	5,841	21,575	7,128	18,986
Custer	2,104	7,826	2,359	7,446
Delaware	3,311	11,826	4,196	10,080
Dewey	222	1,965	301	1,792
Ellis	155	1,611	226	1,575
Garfield	4,397	16,009	4,733	15,177
Garvin	1,855	8,253	2,559	6,925
Grady	3,882	17,316	4,786	14,833
Grant	288	1,827	393	1,675
Greer	323	1,482	488	1,344
Harmon	225	715	264	659
Harper	134	1,318	173	1,261
Haskell	882	3,701	1,175	3,069
Hughes	961	3,388	1,370	2,838
Jackson	1,473	5,969	1,954	5,965
Jefferson	365	1,910	605	1,634
Johnston	786	3,093	1,137	2,649
Kay	3,738	12,172	4,627	11,499
Kingfisher	786	5,156	898	4,870
Kiowa	767	2,596	1,106	2,316
Latimer	797	3,100	1,170	2,628
Le Flore	3,250	13,362	4,662	11,177
Lincoln	2,430	10,854	3,273	9,553
Logan	4,248	13,633	4,724	12,314
Love	735	2,922	1,034	2,436
Major	310	2,948	446	2,700
Marshall	1,096	4,206	1,396	3,744
Mayes	3,423	11,555	4,823	9,637
McClain	2,894	13,169	3,194	11,112
McCurtain	1,802	8,656	2,440	7,635
McIntosh	2,123	5,505	2,779	4,509
Murray	1,087	4,175	1,540	3,606
Muskogee	7,977	15,043	9,952	13,404
Noble	901	3,715	1,143	3,488
Nowata	742	3,321	1,244	2,832

County	2016 Clinton (D)	Trump (R)	2012 Obama (D)	Romney (R)
Okfuskee	943	2,800	1,256	2,335
Oklahoma	112,813	141,569	106,982	149,728
Okmulgee	4,385	8,944	5,432	7,731
Osage	5,597	12,577	6,704	11,242
Ottawa	2,584	7,631	3,509	6,466
Pawnee	1,344	4,729	1,813	4,232
Payne	8,788	16,651	9,198	16,481
Pittsburg	3,711	12,753	4,831	10,841
Pontotoc	3,637	10,431	3,947	8,945
Pottawatomie	6,015	17,848	7,188	16,250
Pushmataha	748	3,581	1,043	3,087
Roger Mills	151	1,547	272	1,402
Rogers	7,902	30,913	9,148	27,553
Seminole	2,071	5,613	2,600	4,856
Sequoyah	3,061	10,888	4,193	9,578
Stephens	3,086	14,182	3,939	12,908
Texas	858	4,621	862	4,930
Tillman	657	1,944	906	1,815
Tulsa	87,847	144,258	82,744	145,062
Wagoner	6,723	23,005	7,791	20,900
Washington	5,048	15,825	5,532	15,668
Washita	588	3,854	822	3,494
Woods	522	2,947	671	2,727
Woodward	873	6,347	1,133	5,945
Totals	**420,375**	**949,136**	**443,547**	**891,325**

Oklahoma Vote Since 1960

2016: Trump, R, 949,136; Clinton, D, 420,375; Johnson, LB, 83,481.
2012: Romney, R, 891,325; Obama, D, 443,547.
2008: McCain, R, 960,165; Obama, D, 502,496.
2004: Bush, R, 959,792; Kerry, D, 503,966.
2000: Bush, R, 744,337; Gore, D, 474,276; Buchanan, RF, 9,014; Browne, LB, 6,602.
1996: Dole, R, 582,315; Clinton, D, 488,105; Perot, RF, 130,788; Browne, LB, 5,505.
1992: Bush, R, 592,929; Clinton, D, 473,066; Perot, Ind., 319,878; Marrou, LB, 4,486.
1988: Bush, R, 678,367; Dukakis, D, 483,423; Paul, LB, 6,261; Fulani, New Alliance, 2,985.
1984: Reagan, R, 861,530; Mondale, D, 385,080; Bergland, LB, 9,066.
1980: Reagan, R, 695,570; Carter, D, 402,026; Anderson, Ind., 38,284; Clark, LB, 13,828.
1976: Ford, R, 545,708; Carter, D, 532,442; McCarthy, Ind., 14,101.
1972: Nixon, R, 759,025; McGovern, D, 247,147; Schmitz, Amer., 23,728.
1968: Nixon, R, 449,697; Humphrey, D, 301,658; Wallace, 3rd party, 191,731.
1964: Johnson, D, 519,834; Goldwater, R, 412,665.
1960: Nixon, R, 533,039; Kennedy, D, 370,111.

Oregon

County	2016 Clinton (D)	Trump (R)	2012 Obama (D)	Romney (R)
Baker	1,797	6,218	2,369	5,702
Benton	29,193	13,445	27,776	14,991
Clackamas	102,095	88,392	95,493	88,592
Clatsop	9,252	8,138	9,861	7,249
Columbia	10,167	13,217	12,004	10,772
Coos	10,448	17,865	12,845	14,673
Crook	2,637	8,511	3,104	6,790
Curry	4,300	7,212	4,625	6,598
Deschutes	42,444	45,692	36,961	42,463
Douglas	14,096	34,582	17,145	30,776
Gilliam	239	671	371	639
Grant	739	3,210	853	2,926
Harney	683	2,912	832	2,607
Hood River	6,510	3,272	6,058	3,429
Jackson	44,447	53,870	44,468	49,020
Jefferson	2,980	5,483	3,301	4,642
Josephine	13,453	26,923	14,953	23,673
Klamath	7,210	20,435	8,302	18,898
Lake	639	3,022	770	2,808
Lane	102,753	67,141	102,652	62,509

County	2016 Clinton (D)	Trump (R)	2012 Obama (D)	Romney (R)
Lincoln	12,501	10,039	13,401	8,686
Linn	17,995	33,488	20,378	28,944
Malheur	2,246	7,194	2,759	6,851
Marion	57,788	63,377	56,376	60,190
Morrow	1,017	2,721	1,202	2,532
Multnomah	292,561	67,954	274,887	75,302
Polk	16,420	18,940	16,292	17,819
Sherman	202	732	319	678
Tillamook	5,768	6,538	6,293	5,684
Umatilla	7,673	17,059	8,584	15,499
Union	3,249	8,431	3,973	7,636
Wallowa	1,116	2,848	1,253	2,804
Wasco	4,781	5,833	5,211	5,229
Washington	153,251	83,197	135,291	93,974
Wheeler	155	591	266	545
Yamhill	19,301	23,250	19,260	22,045
Totals	**1,002,106**	**782,403**	**970,488**	**754,175**

Oregon Vote Since 1960

2016: Clinton, D, 1,002,106; Trump, R, 782,403; Johnson, LB, 94,231; Stein, Pacific Green, 50,002.

2012: Obama, D, 970,488; Romney, R, 754,175; Johnson, LB, 24,089; Stein, Pacific Green, 19,427; Christensen, Const., 4,432; Anderson, OR Prog., 3,384.

2008: Obama, D, 1,037,291; McCain, R, 738,475; Nader, Peace Party of OR, 18,614; Baldwin, Const., 7,693; Barr, LB, 7,635; McKinney, Pacific Green, 4,543.

2004: Kerry, D, 943,163; Bush, R, 866,831; Badnarik, LB, 7,260; Cobb, Pacific Green, 5,315; Peroutka, Const., 5,257.

2000: Gore, D, 720,342; Bush, R, 713,577; Nader, Green, 77,357; Browne, LB, 7,447; Buchanan, Ind., 7,063; Hagelin, RF, 2,574; Phillips, Const., 2,189.

1996: Clinton, D, 649,641; Dole, R, 538,152; Perot, RF, 121,221; Nader, Pacific, 49,415; Browne, LB, 8,903; Phillips, Taxpayers, 3,379; Hagelin, Natural Law, 2,798; Hollis, Soc., 1,922.

1992: Clinton, D, 621,314; Bush, R, 475,757; Perot, Ind., 354,091; Marrou, LB, 4,277; Fulani, New Alliance, 3,030.

1988: Dukakis, D, 616,206; Bush, R, 560,126; Paul, LB, 14,811; Fulani, Ind., 6,487.

1984: Reagan, R, 658,700; Mondale, D, 536,479.

1980: Reagan, R, 571,044; Carter, D, 456,890; Anderson, Ind., 112,389; Clark, LB, 25,838; Commoner, Citizens, 13,642; scattered, 1,713.

1976: Ford, R, 492,120; Carter, D, 490,407; McCarthy, Ind., 40,207; write-in, 7,142.

1972: Nixon, R, 486,686; McGovern, D, 392,760; Schmitz, Amer., 46,211; write-in, 2,289.

1968: Nixon, R, 408,433; Humphrey, D, 358,866; Wallace, 3rd party, 49,683; write-ins: McCarthy, 1,496; N. Rockefeller, 69; others, 1,075.

1964: Johnson, D, 501,017; Goldwater, R, 282,779; write-in, 2,509.

1960: Nixon, R, 408,060; Kennedy, D, 367,402.

Pennsylvania

County	2016 Clinton (D)	Trump (R)	2012 Obama (D)	Romney (R)
Adams	14,219	31,423	15,091	26,767
Allegheny	367,617	259,480	352,687	262,039
Armstrong	7,178	23,484	9,045	20,142
Beaver	32,531	48,167	37,055	42,344
Bedford	3,645	19,552	4,788	16,702
Berks	78,437	96,626	83,011	54,702
Blair	13,958	39,135	16,276	33,319
Bradford	6,369	18,141	8,624	14,410
Bucks	167,060	164,361	160,521	156,579
Butler	28,584	64,428	28,550	59,761
Cambria	18,867	42,258	24,249	35,163
Cameron	531	1,589	724	1,359
Carbon	8,936	18,743	11,580	13,504
Centre	37,088	35,274	34,176	34,001
Chester	141,682	116,114	124,311	124,840
Clarion	4,273	12,576	5,056	10,828

County	2016 Clinton (D)	Trump (R)	2012 Obama (D)	Romney (R)
Clearfield	8,200	24,932	11,121	20,347
Clinton	4,744	10,022	5,734	7,303
Columbia	8,934	18,004	10,937	14,236
Crawford	10,971	24,987	13,883	20,901
Cumberland	47,085	69,076	44,367	64,809
Dauphin	64,706	60,863	64,965	57,450
Delaware	177,402	110,667	171,792	110,853
Elk	3,853	10,025	5,463	7,579
Erie	58,112	60,069	68,036	49,025
Fayette	17,946	34,590	21,971	26,018
Forest	626	1,683	896	1,383
Franklin	17,465	49,768	18,995	43,260
Fulton	912	5,694	1,310	4,814
Greene	4,482	10,849	5,852	8,428
Huntingdon	4,539	14,494	5,409	11,979
Indiana	11,528	24,888	14,473	21,257
Jefferson	3,650	15,192	4,787	13,048
Juniata	1,821	8,273	2,547	6,862
Lackawanna	51,983	48,384	61,838	35,085
Lancaster	91,093	137,914	88,481	130,669
Lawrence	14,009	25,428	17,513	21,047
Lebanon	18,953	40,525	19,900	35,872
Lehigh	81,324	73,690	78,283	66,874
Luzerne	52,451	78,688	64,307	58,325
Lycoming	13,020	35,627	15,203	30,658
McKean	4,025	11,635	5,297	9,545
Mercer	18,733	31,544	24,232	25,925
Mifflin	3,877	14,094	4,273	11,939
Monroe	33,918	33,386	35,221	26,867
Montgomery	256,082	162,731	233,356	174,381
Montour	2,857	5,288	3,053	4,652
Northampton	66,272	71,736	67,606	61,446
Northumberland	9,788	25,427	13,072	19,518
Perry	4,632	15,616	5,685	13,120
Philadelphia	584,025	108,748	588,806	96,467
Pike	9,256	16,056	10,210	12,786
Potter	1,302	6,251	1,897	5,231
Schuylkill	16,770	44,001	24,546	32,278
Snyder	4,002	11,725	4,687	10,073
Somerset	7,376	27,379	9,436	23,984
Sullivan	750	2,291	1,034	1,868
Susquehanna	5,123	12,891	6,935	10,800
Tioga	3,901	13,614	5,357	11,342
Union	6,180	10,622	6,109	9,896
Venango	6,309	16,021	7,945	13,815
Warren	5,145	12,477	6,995	10,010
Washington	36,322	61,386	40,345	53,230
Wayne	7,008	16,244	8,396	12,896
Westmoreland	59,669	116,522	63,722	103,932
Wyoming	3,811	8,837	5,061	6,587
York	68,524	128,528	73,191	113,304
Totals	**2,926,441**	**2,970,733**	**2,990,274**	**2,680,434**

Pennsylvania Vote Since 1960

2016: Trump, R, 2,970,733; Clinton, D, 2,926,441; Johnson, LB, 146,715; Stein, Green, 49,941; Castle, Const., 21,572.

2012: Obama, D, 2,990,274; Romney, R, 2,680,434; Johnson, LB, 49,991; Stein, Green, 21,341.

2008: Obama, D, 3,276,363; McCain, R, 2,655,885; Nader, Ind., 42,977; Barr, LB, 19,912.

2004: Kerry, D, 2,938,095; Bush, R, 2,793,847; Badnarik, LB, 21,185; Cobb, Green, 6,319; Peroutka, Const., 6,318.

2000: Gore, D, 2,485,967; Bush, R, 2,281,127; Nader, Green, 103,392; Buchanan, RF, 16,023; Phillips, Const., 14,428; Browne, LB, 11,248.

1996: Clinton, D, 2,215,819; Dole, R, 1,801,169; Perot, RF, 430,984; Browne, LB, 28,000; Phillips, Const., 19,552; Hagelin, Natural Law, 5,783.

1992: Clinton, D, 2,239,164; Bush, R, 1,791,841; Perot, Ind., 902,667; Marrou, LB, 21,477; Fulani, New Alliance, 4,661.

1988: Bush, R, 2,300,087; Dukakis, D, 2,194,944; McCarthy, Consumer, 19,158; Paul, LB, 12,051.

1984: Reagan, R, 2,584,323; Mondale, D, 2,228,131; Bergland, LB, 6,982.

1980: Reagan, R, 2,261,872; Carter, D, 1,937,540; Anderson, Ind., 292,921; Clark, LB, 33,263; DeBerry, Soc. Workers, 20,291; Commoner, Consumer, 10,430; Hall, Comm., 5,184.

1976: Carter, D, 2,328,677; Ford, R, 2,205,604; McCarthy, Ind., 50,584; Maddox, Const., 25,344; Camejo, Soc. Workers, 3,009; LaRouche, U.S. Labor, 2,744; Hall, Comm., 1,891; others, 2,934.

1972: Nixon, R, 2,714,521; McGovern, D, 1,796,951; Schmitz, Amer., 70,593; Jenness, Soc. Workers, 4,639; Hall, Comm., 2,686; others, 2,715.

1968: Humphrey, D, 2,259,405; Nixon, R, 2,090,017; Wallace, 3rd party, 378,582; Gregory, Peace/Freedom, 7,821; Blomen, Soc. Labor, 4,977; Halstead, Soc. Workers, 4,862; others, 2,264.

1964: Johnson, D, 3,130,954; Goldwater, R, 1,673,657; DeBerry, Soc. Workers, 10,456; Hass, Soc. Labor, 5,092; scattered, 2,531.

1960: Kennedy, D, 2,556,282; Nixon, R, 2,439,956; Hass, Soc. Labor, 7,185; Dobbs, Soc. Workers, 2,678; scattered, 440.

Rhode Island

City	2016		2012	
	Clinton (D)	Trump (R)	Obama (D)	Romney (R)
Barrington	6,153	2,898	5,557	3,836
Bristol	5,771	4,080	6,359	3,707
Coventry	7,032	9,199	9,122	6,969
Cranston	18,763	15,934	21,388	13,008
Cumberland	8,655	7,444	9,291	7,106
East Providence	11,904	7,134	14,095	5,752
Johnston	5,652	7,563	7,503	5,417
Lincoln	5,279	5,410	6,028	4,866
Newport	6,287	2,644	6,174	2,959
North Kingstown	7,793	6,147	7,847	6,451
North Providence	7,760	6,936	9,613	5,404
Pawtucket	15,574	6,221	18,155	5,228
Portsmouth	4,945	3,922	5,017	4,165
Providence	45,053	7,682	43,885	7,335
Smithfield	4,402	5,254	5,293	4,681
South Kingstown	8,677	4,627	8,611	4,720
Warwick	20,038	18,338	24,448	15,027
West Warwick	5,540	5,724	6,956	4,332
Westerly	5,291	5,031	6,071	4,382
Woonsocket	6,346	5,442	7,985	4,114
Other	45,610	42,913	50,279	37,745
Totals	**252,525**	**180,543**	**279,677**	**157,204**

Rhode Island Vote Since 1960

2016: Clinton, D, 252,525; Trump, R, 180,543; Johnson, LB, 14,746; Stein, Green, 6,220; De La Fuente, Amer. Delta, 671.

2012: Obama, D, 279,677; Romney, R, 157,204; Johnson, LB, 4,388; Stein, Green, 2,421; Goode, Const., 430; Anderson, Justice, 416; Lindsay, Socialism/Liberation, 132.

2008: Obama, D, 296,571; McCain, R, 165,391; Nader, Ind., 4,829; Barr, LB, 1,382; McKinney, Green, 797; Baldwin, Const., 675; La Riva, Socialism/Liberation, 122.

2004: Kerry, D, 259,765; Bush, R, 169,046; Nader, RF, 4,651; Cobb, Green, 1,333; Badnarik, LB, 907; Peroutka, Const., 339; Parker, Workers World, 253.

2000: Gore, D, 249,508; Bush, R, 130,555; Nader, Ind., 25,052; Buchanan, RF, 2,273; Browne, Ind., 742; Hagelin, Ind., 271; Moorehead, Ind., 199; Phillips, Ind., 97; McReynolds, Ind., 52; Harris, Ind., 34.

1996: Clinton, D, 233,050; Dole, R, 104,683; Perot, RF, 43,723; Nader, Green, 6,040; Browne, LB, 1,109; Phillips, U.S. Taxpayers, 1,021; Hagelin, Natural Law, 435; Moorehead, Workers World, 186.

1992: Clinton, D, 213,299; Bush, R, 131,601; Perot, Ind., 105,045; Fulani, New Alliance, 1,878.

1988: Dukakis, D, 225,123; Bush, R, 177,761; Paul, LB, 825; Fulani, New Alliance, 280.

1984: Reagan, R, 212,080; Mondale, D, 197,106; Bergland, LB, 277.

1980: Carter, D, 198,342; Reagan, R, 154,793; Anderson, Ind., 59,819; Clark, LB, 2,458; Hall, Comm., 218; McReynolds, Soc., 170; DeBerry, Soc. Workers, 90; Griswold, Workers World, 77.

1976: Carter, D, 227,636; Ford, R, 181,249; MacBride, LB, 715; Camejo, Soc. Workers, 462; Hall, Comm., 334; Levin, Soc. Labor, 188.

1972: Nixon, R, 220,383; McGovern, D, 194,645; Jenness, Soc. Workers, 729.

1968: Humphrey, D, 246,518; Nixon, R, 122,359; Wallace, 3rd party, 15,678; Halstead, Soc. Workers, 383.

1964: Johnson, D, 315,463; Goldwater, R, 74,615.

1960: Kennedy, D, 258,032; Nixon, R, 147,502.

South Carolina

County	2016		2012	
	Clinton (D)	Trump (R)	Obama (D)	Romney (R)
Abbeville	3,741	6,763	4,543	5,981
Aiken	25,455	46,025	25,322	44,042
Allendale	2,735	789	3,297	838
Anderson	21,097	56,232	22,405	48,709
Bamberg	3,898	2,204	4,624	2,194
Barnwell	4,400	4,889	5,188	4,659
Beaufort	32,138	42,922	29,848	42,687
Berkeley	30,705	44,587	28,542	38,475
Calhoun	3,573	3,787	4,045	3,707
Charleston	89,299	75,443	81,487	77,629
Cherokee	6,092	15,167	7,231	13,314
Chester	6,579	7,265	7,891	6,367
Chesterfield	6,858	9,312	7,958	8,490
Clarendon	7,732	7,386	9,091	7,071
Colleton	7,627	9,091	8,475	8,443
Darlington	13,888	14,989	15,457	14,434
Dillon	5,834	5,637	7,523	5,427
Dorchester	24,055	34,987	23,445	32,531
Edgefield	4,491	6,842	4,967	6,512
Fairfield	6,945	4,027	7,777	3,999
Florence	26,710	29,573	28,614	28,961
Georgetown	13,310	17,389	14,163	16,526
Greenville	74,483	127,832	68,070	121,685
Greenwood	10,711	16,961	11,972	16,348
Hampton	5,170	3,488	5,834	3,312
Horry	39,410	89,288	38,885	72,127
Jasper	5,956	5,187	5,757	4,169
Kershaw	10,330	17,542	11,259	16,324
Lancaster	13,812	23,719	13,419	19,333
Laurens	8,889	16,816	10,318	14,746
Lee	5,199	2,803	5,977	2,832
Lexington	35,230	80,026	34,148	76,662
Marion	8,569	5,444	9,688	5,164
Marlboro	5,954	4,267	6,100	3,676
McCormick	2,479	2,652	2,653	2,467
Newberry	6,217	10,017	6,913	9,260
Oconee	7,998	24,178	8,550	21,611
Orangeburg	26,318	11,931	30,720	12,022
Pickens	10,354	36,236	11,156	33,474
Richland	108,000	52,469	103,989	53,105
Saluda	2,813	5,526	3,328	5,135
Spartanburg	39,997	76,277	41,461	66,969
Sumter	24,047	18,745	27,589	19,274
Union	4,729	7,061	5,796	6,584
Williamsburg	9,953	4,864	11,335	4,824
York	41,593	66,754	39,131	59,546
Totals	**855,373**	**1,155,389**	**865,941**	**1,071,645**

South Carolina Vote Since 1960

2016: Trump, R, 1,155,389; Clinton, D, 855,373; Johnson, LB, 49,204; McMullin, Ind., 21,016; Stein, Green, 13,034; Castle, Const., 5,765; Skewes, American, 3,246.

2012: Romney, R, 1,071,645; Obama, D, 865,941; Johnson, LB, 16,321; Stein, Green, 5,446; Goode, Const., 4,765.

2008: McCain, R, 1,034,896; Obama, D, 862,449; Barr, LB, 7,283; Baldwin, Const., 6,827; Nader, petitioning cand., 5,053; McKinney, Green, 4,461.

2004: Bush, R, 937,974; Kerry, D, 661,699; Nader, Ind., 5,520; Peroutka, Const., 5,317; Badnarik, LB, 3,608; Brown, United Citizens, 2,124; Cobb, Green, 1,488.

2000: Bush, R, 786,892; Gore, D, 566,039; Nader, United Citizens, 20,279; Browne, LB, 4,898; Buchanan, RF, 3,309; Phillips, Const., 1,682; Hagelin, Natural Law, 943.
1996: Dole, R, 573,458; Clinton, D, 506,283; Perot, RF/Patriot, 64,386; Browne, LB, 4,271; Phillips, U.S. Taxpayers, 2,043; Hagelin, Natural Law, 1,248.
1992: Bush, R, 577,507; Clinton, D, 479,514; Perot, Ind., 138,872; Marrou, LB, 2,719; Phillips, U.S. Taxpayers, 2,680; Fulani, New Alliance, 1,235.
1988: Bush, R, 606,443; Dukakis, D, 370,554; Paul, LB, 4,935; Fulani, United Citizens, 4,077.
1984: Reagan, R, 615,539; Mondale, D, 344,459; Bergland, LB, 4,359.
1980: Reagan, R, 439,277; Carter, D, 428,220; Anderson, Ind., 13,868; Clark, LB, 4,807; Rarick, Amer. Ind., 2,086.
1976: Carter, D, 450,807; Ford, R, 346,149; Anderson, Amer., 2,996; Maddox, Amer. Ind., 1,950; write-in, 681.
1972: Nixon, R, 477,044; McGovern, D, 184,559, and United Citizens, 2,265 (total, 186,824); Schmitz, Amer., 10,075; write-in, 17.
1968: Nixon, R, 254,062; Wallace, 3rd party, 215,430; Humphrey, D, 197,486.
1964: Goldwater, R, 309,048; Johnson, D, 215,700; write-ins: Wallace, 5; Nixon, 1; Powell, 1; Thurmond, 1.
1960: Kennedy, D, 198,129; Nixon, R, 188,558; write-in, 1.

South Dakota

County	2016		2012	
	Clinton (D)	Trump (R)	Obama (D)	Romney (R)
Aurora	340	974	556	804
Beadle	1,912	4,455	2,881	4,230
Bennett	412	666	548	626
Bon Homme	704	2,105	1,167	1,830
Brookings	4,879	6,748	5,827	6,220
Brown	5,452	9,613	7,250	8,321
Brule	571	1,565	824	1,499
Buffalo	296	171	472	166
Butte	696	3,357	1,002	3,073
Campbell	105	704	153	616
Charles Mix	935	2,382	1,483	2,230
Clark	398	1,139	713	1,067
Clay	2,608	2,109	2,955	2,147
Codington	3,174	7,764	4,588	6,696
Corson	535	588	648	515
Custer	1,121	3,293	1,335	3,062
Davison	2,355	5,157	3,042	4,757
Day	974	1,627	1,497	1,320
Deuel	570	1,366	941	1,175
Dewey	888	723	1,207	663
Douglas	214	1,338	332	1,334
Edmunds	380	1,433	622	1,264
Fall River	821	2,511	1,140	2,258
Faulk	204	858	331	765
Grant	971	2,382	1,493	2,034
Gregory	391	1,600	599	1,507
Haakon	77	936	138	940
Hamlin	555	2,051	921	1,803
Hand	334	1,391	575	1,242
Hanson	424	1,497	760	1,627
Harding	38	695	82	638
Hughes	2,450	5,174	2,786	5,219
Hutchinson	692	2,517	923	2,451
Hyde	125	543	189	531
Jackson	323	722	426	661
Jerauld	264	648	452	538
Jones	69	450	108	490
Kingsbury	703	1,680	1,092	1,451
Lake	2,314	4,038	2,724	3,419
Lawrence	3,356	7,411	3,973	7,025
Lincoln	8,076	15,499	7,982	13,611
Lyman	369	977	605	933
Marshall	754	1,056	1,061	889
McCook	623	1,794	905	1,655
McPherson	192	892	272	921
Meade	2,223	8,441	2,928	7,566
Mellette	238	402	375	381

County	2016		2012	
	Clinton (D)	Trump (R)	Obama (D)	Romney (R)
Miner	281	706	479	636
Minnehaha	30,610	42,043	34,674	40,342
Moody	1,043	1,731	1,429	1,535
Oglala Lakota	2,510	241	2,937	188
Pennington	14,074	29,804	15,125	28,232
Perkins	188	1,333	319	1,205
Potter	215	1,071	339	1,029
Roberts	1,540	2,144	2,302	1,883
Sanborn	241	819	389	688
Spink	919	1,854	1,300	1,670
Stanley	329	1,148	435	1,063
Sully	137	679	186	613
Todd	1,505	487	1,976	498
Tripp	462	2,069	737	1,905
Turner	961	2,937	1,411	2,715
Union	2,227	5,290	2,782	4,698
Walworth	457	1,896	671	1,731
Yankton	3,301	5,659	4,226	5,495
Ziebach	353	368	439	314
Totals	**117,458**	**227,721**	**145,039**	**210,610**

South Dakota Vote Since 1960

2016: Trump, R, 227,721; Clinton, D, 117,458; Johnson, LB, 20,850; Castle, Const., 4,064.
2012: Romney, R, 210,610; Obama, D, 145,039; Johnson, LB, 5,795; Goode, Const., 2,371.
2008: McCain, R, 203,054; Obama, D, 170,924; Nader, Ind., 4,267; Baldwin, Const., 1,895; Barr, Ind., 1,835.
2004: Bush, R, 232,584; Kerry, D, 149,244; Nader, Ind., 4,320; Peroutka, Const., 1,103; Badnarik, LB, 964.
2000: Bush, R, 190,700; Gore, D, 118,804; Buchanan, RF, 3,322; Phillips, Ind., 1,781; Browne, LB, 1,662.
1996: Dole, R, 150,543; Clinton, D, 139,333; Perot, RF, 31,250; Browne, LB, 1,472; Phillips, Taxpayers, 912; Hagelin, Natural Law, 316.
1992: Bush, R, 136,718; Clinton, D, 124,888; Perot, Ind., 73,295.
1988: Bush, R, 165,415; Dukakis, D, 145,560; Paul, LB, 1,060; Fulani, New Alliance, 730.
1984: Reagan, R, 200,267; Mondale, D, 116,113.
1980: Reagan, R, 198,343; Carter, D, 103,855; Anderson, Ind., 21,431; Clark, LB, 3,824; Pulley, Soc. Workers, 250.
1976: Ford, R, 151,505; Carter, D, 147,068; MacBride, LB, 1,619; Hall, Comm., 318; Camejo, Soc. Workers, 168.
1972: Nixon, R, 166,476; McGovern, D, 139,945; Jenness, Soc. Workers, 994.
1968: Nixon, R, 149,841; Humphrey, D, 118,023; Wallace, 3rd party, 13,400.
1964: Johnson, D, 163,010; Goldwater, R, 130,108.
1960: Nixon, R, 178,417; Kennedy, D, 128,070.

Tennessee

County	2016		2012	
	Clinton (D)	Trump (R)	Obama (D)	Romney (R)
Anderson	9,013	19,212	10,122	18,968
Bedford	3,395	11,486	4,211	10,034
Benton	1,474	4,716	2,258	3,850
Bledsoe	897	3,622	1,267	3,022
Blount	12,100	37,443	12,934	35,441
Bradley	7,070	29,768	8,037	27,422
Campbell	2,248	9,870	3,328	8,604
Cannon	1,127	4,007	1,564	3,309
Carroll	2,327	7,756	3,475	7,225
Carter	3,453	16,898	4,789	15,503
Cheatham	3,878	11,297	4,659	10,268
Chester	1,243	5,081	1,624	4,684
Claiborne	1,832	8,602	2,433	7,617
Clay	707	2,141	1,037	1,747
Cocke	1,981	9,791	2,804	8,459
Coffee	4,743	14,417	5,870	13,023
Crockett	1,303	3,982	1,669	3,783
Cumberland	5,202	20,413	6,261	18,653
Davidson	148,864	84,550	143,120	97,622
Decatur	894	3,588	1,303	2,874

County	2016 Clinton (D)	Trump (R)	2012 Obama (D)	Romney (R)
DeKalb	1,569	5,171	2,174	4,143
Dickson	4,722	13,233	6,233	11,296
Dyer	2,816	10,180	3,757	9,921
Fayette	5,874	13,055	6,688	12,689
Fentress	1,100	6,038	1,561	5,243
Franklin	4,374	11,532	5,603	10,262
Gibson	5,258	13,786	6,564	12,883
Giles	2,917	7,970	3,760	6,915
Grainger	1,154	6,626	1,668	5,470
Greene	4,216	18,562	6,225	17,245
Grundy	999	3,636	1,643	2,516
Hamblen	4,075	15,857	5,234	14,522
Hamilton	55,316	78,733	58,836	79,933
Hancock	322	1,843	475	1,527
Hardeman	4,185	4,919	5,482	4,865
Hardin	1,622	8,012	2,467	7,886
Hawkins	3,507	16,648	5,088	14,382
Haywood	3,711	3,013	4,569	2,960
Henderson	1,800	8,138	2,517	7,421
Henry	3,063	9,508	4,339	8,193
Hickman	1,824	5,695	2,698	4,758
Houston	866	2,182	1,400	1,579
Humphreys	1,967	4,930	2,905	3,833
Jackson	1,129	3,236	1,739	2,383
Jefferson	3,494	14,776	4,232	13,038
Johnson	988	5,410	1,483	4,611
Knox	62,878	105,767	59,399	109,707
Lake	577	1,357	884	1,163
Lauderdale	3,056	4,884	4,011	4,616
Lawrence	2,821	12,420	4,237	10,770
Lewis	890	3,585	1,447	3,117
Lincoln	2,554	10,398	3,290	9,803
Loudon	4,919	17,610	5,058	16,707
Macon	1,072	6,263	1,552	5,260
Madison	15,448	21,335	18,367	21,993
Marion	2,832	7,696	3,953	6,272
Marshall	2,852	8,184	3,725	6,832
Maury	10,038	23,799	11,825	20,708
McMinn	3,510	14,691	4,609	12,967
McNairy	1,848	7,841	2,645	7,015
Meigs	856	3,342	1,163	2,734
Monroe	3,186	13,374	4,372	11,731
Montgomery	21,699	32,341	24,499	30,245
Moore	496	2,325	705	2,053
Morgan	1,054	5,441	1,725	4,669
Obion	2,426	9,526	3,321	8,814
Overton	1,945	6,059	2,805	4,775
Perry	597	2,167	992	1,578
Pickett	536	2,021	712	1,712
Polk	1,252	5,097	1,856	4,108
Putnam	6,851	19,002	7,802	17,254
Rhea	1,942	8,660	2,628	7,802
Roane	4,837	15,880	6,018	14,724
Robertson	6,637	19,410	8,290	17,643
Rutherford	36,706	64,515	36,414	60,846
Scott	934	6,044	1,452	5,117
Sequatchie	1,053	4,441	1,489	3,541
Sevier	6,297	28,629	7,418	25,984
Shelby	208,992	116,344	232,443	135,649
Smith	1,689	5,494	2,470	4,495
Stewart	1,222	3,864	2,069	2,963
Sullivan	12,578	46,979	15,321	43,562
Sumner	18,161	50,129	18,579	46,003
Tipton	5,785	16,910	7,133	16,672
Trousdale	946	2,103	1,240	1,612
Unicoi	1,262	5,671	1,913	5,032
Union	1,012	5,053	1,478	4,282
Van Buren	539	1,820	875	1,386
Warren	3,535	9,540	4,752	8,010
Washington	13,024	34,252	14,325	32,808
Wayne	717	5,036	1,163	4,253
Weakley	2,772	9,008	3,548	8,605
White	1,845	7,671	2,795	6,197
Williamson	31,013	68,212	25,142	69,850
Wilson	14,385	39,406	14,695	36,109
Totals	**870,695**	**1,522,925**	**960,709**	**1,462,330**

Tennessee Vote Since 1960

2016: Trump, R, 1,522,925; Clinton, D, 870,695; Johnson, Ind., 70,397; Stein, Green, 15,993; McMullin, Ind., 11,991; Smith, Ind., 7,276; De La Fuente, Ind., 4,075; Kennedy, Ind., 2,877; Castle, Ind., 1,584.

2012: Romney, R, 1,462,330; Obama, D, 960,709; Johnson, Ind., 18,623; Stein, Green, 6,515; Goode, Const., 6,022; Anderson, Ind., 2,639, Miller, Ind., 1,739.

2008: McCain, R, 1,479,178; Obama, D, 1,087,437; Nader, Ind., 11,560; Barr, Ind., 8,547; Baldwin, Ind., 8,191; McKinney, Ind., 2,499; Moore, Ind., 1,326; Jay, Ind., 1,011.

2004: Bush, R, 1,384,375; Kerry, D, 1,036,477; Nader, Ind., 8,992; Badnarik, Ind., 4,866; Peroutka, Ind., 2,570.

2000: Bush, R, 1,061,949; Gore, D, 981,720; Nader, Green, 19,781; Browne, LB, 4,284; Buchanan, RF, 4,250; Brown, Ind., 1,606; Phillips, Ind., 1,015; Hagelin, RF, 613; Venson, Ind., 535.

1996: Clinton, D, 909,146; Dole, R, 863,530; Perot, RF, 105,918; Nader, Ind., 6,427; Browne, Ind., 5,020; Phillips, Ind., 1,818; Collins, Ind., 688; Hagelin, Ind., 636; Michael, Ind., 408; Dodge, Ind., 324.

1992: Clinton, D, 933,521; Bush, R, 841,300; Perot, Ind., 199,968; Marrou, LB, 1,847.

1988: Bush, R, 947,233; Dukakis, D, 679,794; Paul, Ind., 2,041; Duke, Ind., 1,807.

1984: Reagan, R, 990,212; Mondale, D, 711,714; Bergland, LB, 3,072.

1980: Reagan, R, 787,761; Carter, D, 783,051; Anderson, Ind., 35,991; Clark, LB, 7,116; Commoner, Citizens, 1,112; Bubar, Statesman, 521; McReynolds, Soc., 519; Hall, Comm., 503; DeBerry, Soc. Workers, 490; Griswold, Workers World, 400; write-in, 152.

1976: Carter, D, 825,879; Ford, R, 633,969; Anderson, Amer., 5,769; McCarthy, Ind., 5,004; Maddox, Amer. Ind., 2,303; MacBride, LB, 1,375; Hall, Comm., 547; LaRouche, U.S. Labor, 512; Bubar, Prohib., 442; Miller, Ind., 316; write-in, 230.

1972: Nixon, R, 813,147; McGovern, D, 357,293; Schmitz, Amer., 30,373; write-in, 369.

1968: Nixon, R, 472,592; Wallace, 3rd party, 424,792; Humphrey, D, 351,233.

1964: Johnson, D, 635,047; Goldwater, R, 508,965; write-in, 34.
1960: Nixon, R, 556,577; Kennedy, D, 481,453; Faubus, States' Rights, 11,304; Decker, Prohib., 2,458.

Texas

County	2016 Clinton (D)	Trump (R)	2012 Obama (D)	Romney (R)
Anderson	3,369	13,201	3,813	12,262
Andrews	836	3,927	795	3,639
Angelina	7,538	21,668	7,834	20,303
Aransas	2,465	7,740	2,704	6,830
Archer	394	3,786	525	3,600
Armstrong	70	924	98	828
Atascosa	4,651	8,618	5,133	7,461
Austin	2,320	9,637	2,252	9,265
Bailey	397	1,344	466	1,339
Bandera	1,726	8,163	1,864	7,426
Bastrop	10,569	16,328	9,864	14,033
Baylor	191	1,267	267	1,297
Bee	3,444	4,744	3,452	4,356
Bell	37,801	51,998	35,512	49,574
Bexar	319,550	240,333	264,856	241,617
Blanco	1,244	4,212	1,220	3,638
Borden	31	330	32	324
Bosque	1,278	6,339	1,367	5,885
Bowie	8,838	24,924	10,196	24,869
Brazoria	43,200	72,791	34,421	70,862
Brazos	23,121	38,738	17,477	37,209
Brewster	1,873	2,077	1,765	1,976
Briscoe	91	625	117	578
Brooks	1,937	613	1,886	507
Brown	1,621	12,017	1,904	11,895
Burleson	1,491	5,316	1,705	4,671
Burnet	3,797	14,638	3,674	12,843
Caldwell	4,795	6,691	4,791	6,021
Calhoun	2,118	4,638	2,410	4,144
Callahan	569	4,865	751	4,378
Cameron	59,402	29,472	49,975	26,099

County	2016 Clinton (D)	Trump (R)	2012 Obama (D)	Romney (R)	County	2016 Clinton (D)	Trump (R)	2012 Obama (D)	Romney (R)
Camp	1,260	3,201	1,428	2,881	Hockley	1,260	5,809	1,486	5,546
Carson	249	2,620	292	2,451	Hood	4,008	21,382	3,843	18,409
Cass	2,391	9,726	2,924	8,763	Hopkins	2,510	10,707	2,777	9,836
Castro	526	1,414	630	1,470	Houston	1,978	6,205	2,265	5,880
Chambers	2,948	13,339	2,790	11,787	Howard	1,770	6,637	2,110	6,453
Cherokee	3,469	12,919	3,875	12,094	Hudspeth	324	503	379	471
Childress	253	1,802	320	1,665	Hunt	6,396	23,910	6,671	21,011
Clay	536	4,377	740	4,266	Hutchinson	854	7,042	1,045	6,804
Cochran	190	679	256	649	Irion	90	660	112	668
Coke	140	1,265	179	1,218	Jack	314	2,973	303	2,580
Coleman	388	3,177	442	3,012	Jackson	904	4,266	1,070	3,906
Collin	140,624	201,014	101,415	196,888	Jasper	2,590	10,609	3,423	9,957
Collingsworth	145	983	177	962	Jeff Davis	422	695	440	719
Colorado	1,987	6,325	2,029	6,026	Jefferson	42,443	42,862	44,668	43,242
Comal	14,238	45,136	11,450	39,318	Jim Hogg	1,635	430	1,301	356
Comanche	789	4,333	890	3,944	Jim Wells	6,694	5,420	6,492	4,598
Concho	148	885	194	793	Johnson	10,988	44,382	10,496	37,661
Cooke	2,352	13,181	2,246	11,951	Jones	936	4,819	1,226	4,262
Coryell	5,064	12,225	5,158	11,220	Karnes	1,145	2,965	1,325	2,825
Cottle	92	506	180	555	Kaufman	10,278	29,587	9,472	24,846
Crane	299	1,049	275	985	Kendall	3,643	15,700	3,043	14,508
Crockett	372	980	480	957	Kenedy	99	84	82	84
Crosby	468	1,181	639	1,132	Kent	59	360	66	335
Culberson	454	280	568	295	Kerr	4,681	17,727	4,338	17,274
Dallam	222	1,261	253	1,248	Kimble	206	1,697	217	1,667
Dallas	461,080	262,945	405,571	295,813	King	5	149	5	139
Dawson	835	2,636	1,019	2,591	Kinney	458	936	522	880
Deaf Smith	1,185	2,911	1,239	3,042	Kleberg	4,716	4,367	4,754	4,058
Delta	400	1,836	454	1,524	Knox	247	1,078	332	1,160
Denton	110,890	170,603	80,978	157,579	La Salle	1,129	872	965	669
DeWitt	1,163	5,519	1,467	5,122	Lamar	3,583	14,561	4,181	12,826
Dickens	128	755	216	793	Lamb	771	3,111	998	3,058
Dimmit	2,173	974	2,141	762	Lampasas	1,483	6,385	1,479	5,621
Donley	191	1,225	226	1,287	Lavaca	1,170	7,347	1,428	6,796
Duval	2,783	1,316	3,331	980	Lee	1,372	4,997	1,632	4,507
Eastland	776	6,011	970	5,444	Leon	909	6,391	1,062	5,814
Ector	10,249	25,020	8,118	24,010	Liberty	4,862	18,892	5,202	17,323
Edwards	303	746	232	642	Limestone	1,778	5,796	2,208	5,288
El Paso	147,843	55,512	112,952	57,150	Lipscomb	135	1,159	119	1,044
Ellis	16,253	44,941	13,881	39,574	Live Oak	742	3,464	919	3,154
Erath	2,160	11,210	1,965	10,329	Llano	1,825	8,299	1,822	7,610
Falls	1,684	3,441	2,033	3,356	Loving	4	58	9	54
Fannin	2,132	9,548	2,486	8,161	Lubbock	28,023	65,651	26,271	63,469
Fayette	2,144	8,743	2,315	8,106	Lynn	403	1,546	506	1,439
Fisher	403	1,265	512	1,094	Madison	881	3,351	967	3,028
Floyd	435	1,474	551	1,523	Marion	1,165	2,983	1,495	2,733
Foard	113	383	140	348	Martin	266	1,455	248	1,368
Fort Bend	134,686	117,291	101,144	116,126	Mason	354	1,656	380	1,565
Franklin	665	3,585	751	3,446	Matagorda	3,500	8,366	3,980	8,040
Freestone	1,471	6,026	1,850	5,646	Maverick	10,397	2,816	8,303	2,171
Frio	2,444	1,856	2,376	1,559	McCulloch	482	2,552	537	2,419
Gaines	597	3,907	535	3,484	McLennan	27,063	48,260	25,694	47,903
Galveston	43,658	73,757	39,511	69,059	McMullen	40	454	67	431
Garza	230	1,225	279	1,263	Medina	4,634	12,085	4,784	11,079
Gillespie	2,288	10,446	2,055	10,306	Menard	154	682	171	665
Glasscock	34	553	44	526	Midland	10,025	36,973	8,286	35,689
Goliad	973	2,620	1,127	2,294	Milam	2,051	6,364	2,636	5,481
Gonzales	1,571	4,587	1,777	4,216	Mills	243	1,951	279	1,882
Gray	701	6,500	886	6,443	Mitchell	354	1,780	538	1,756
Grayson	10,301	35,325	10,670	30,936	Montague	885	7,526	1,116	6,549
Gregg	11,677	28,764	12,398	28,742	Montgomery	45,835	150,314	32,920	137,969
Grimes	2,194	7,065	2,339	6,141	Moore	1,098	3,977	964	3,968
Guadalupe	18,391	36,632	15,744	33,117	Morris	1,425	3,446	1,858	3,232
Hale	2,101	6,366	2,243	6,490	Motley	40	566	55	538
Hall	164	893	265	832	Nacogdoches	6,846	14,771	6,465	13,925
Hamilton	479	3,060	591	2,918	Navarro	4,002	11,994	4,350	10,847
Hansford	171	1,730	159	1,788	Newton	1,156	4,288	1,677	4,112
Hardeman	249	1,207	302	1,176	Nolan	1,029	3,552	1,216	3,282
Hardin	2,780	19,606	3,359	17,746	Nueces	49,198	50,766	45,772	48,966
Harris	707,914	545,955	587,044	586,073	Ochiltree	274	2,628	253	2,719
Harrison	7,151	18,749	8,456	17,512	Oldham	78	850	71	790
Hartley	173	1,730	184	1,708	Orange	5,735	25,513	6,800	23,366
Haskell	314	1,403	553	1,424	Palo Pinto	1,708	8,284	1,811	7,393
Hays	33,224	33,826	25,537	31,661	Panola	1,835	8,445	2,211	7,950
Hemphill	181	1,462	192	1,298	Parker	8,344	46,473	7,853	39,243
Henderson	5,669	23,650	6,106	21,231	Parmer	485	1,915	529	2,011
Hidalgo	118,809	48,642	97,969	39,865	Pecos	1,554	2,468	1,591	2,512
Hill	2,547	10,108	2,752	9,132	Polk	4,187	15,176	4,859	14,071

County	2016 Clinton (D)	Trump (R)	2012 Obama (D)	Romney (R)
Potter	7,657	19,630	7,126	18,918
Presidio	1,458	652	1,282	504
Rains	628	3,968	761	3,279
Randall	8,367	43,462	7,574	41,447
Reagan	167	709	158	676
Real	262	1,382	277	1,236
Red River	1,149	3,926	1,482	3,549
Reeves	1,659	1,417	1,655	1,188
Refugio	1,034	1,830	998	1,663
Roberts	20	524	33	468
Robertson	2,203	4,668	2,798	4,419
Rockwall	9,655	28,451	8,120	27,113
Runnels	453	3,250	519	3,104
Rusk	3,935	14,675	4,451	13,924
Sabine	614	3,998	807	3,727
San Augustine	910	2,622	1,193	2,469
San Jacinto	2,038	8,059	2,410	7,107
San Patricio	7,871	13,030	7,856	12,005
San Saba	293	2,025	323	1,905
Schleicher	208	821	221	787
Scurry	733	4,410	838	4,124
Shackelford	103	1,378	131	1,218
Shelby	1,758	7,179	2,322	6,879
Sherman	96	807	121	908
Smith	22,300	58,930	21,456	57,331
Somervell	541	3,206	613	2,871
Starr	9,289	2,224	10,260	1,547
Stephens	348	3,034	475	2,892
Sterling	70	549	31	459
Stonewall	135	555	160	507
Sutton	313	1,075	369	1,110
Swisher	462	1,671	579	1,655
Tarrant	288,392	345,921	253,071	348,920
Taylor	10,085	33,250	9,750	32,904
Terrell	140	288	184	358
Terry	753	2,459	1,059	2,602
Throckmorton	84	715	109	700
Titus	2,597	6,511	2,648	6,084
Tom Green	9,173	27,494	9,294	26,878
Travis	308,260	127,209	232,788	140,152
Trinity	1,154	4,737	1,614	4,537
Tyler	1,248	6,624	1,668	5,910
Upshur	2,380	13,209	2,971	12,015
Upton	286	1,007	333	953
Uvalde	3,867	4,835	3,825	4,529
Val Verde	6,964	5,890	6,285	5,635
Van Zandt	2,799	18,473	3,084	15,794
Victoria	8,866	21,275	8,802	19,692
Walker	6,091	12,884	6,252	12,140
Waller	5,748	10,531	6,514	9,244
Ward	783	2,547	841	2,366
Washington	3,382	10,945	3,381	10,857
Webb	42,307	12,947	37,597	11,078
Wharton	4,238	10,149	4,235	9,750
Wheeler	194	2,087	232	1,878
Wichita	8,770	27,631	10,525	29,812
Wilbarger	809	3,166	971	2,956
Willacy	3,422	1,547	3,600	1,416
Williamson	84,468	104,175	61,875	97,006
Wilson	4,790	13,998	4,821	12,218
Winkler	420	1,403	398	1,311
Wise	3,412	20,670	3,221	17,207
Wood	2,630	15,700	3,056	14,351
Yoakum	426	1,797	409	1,698
Young	876	6,601	992	6,225
Zapata	2,063	1,029	2,527	997
Zavala	2,636	694	3,042	574
Totals	3,877,868	4,685,047	3,308,124	4,569,843

Texas Vote Since 1960

2016: Trump, R, 4,685,047; Clinton, D, 3,877,868; Johnson, LB, 283,492; Stein, Green, 71,558; McMullin, Ind., 42,366.

2012: Romney, R, 4,569,843; Obama, D, 3,308,124; Johnson, LB, 88,580; Stein, Green, 24,657.

2008: McCain, R, 4,479,328; Obama, D, 3,528,633 Barr, LB, 56,116.

2004: Bush, R, 4,526,917; Kerry, D, 2,832,704; Badnarik, LB, 38,787.

2000: Bush, R, 3,799,639; Gore, D, 2,433,746; Nader, Green, 137,994; Browne, LB, 23,160; Buchanan, Ind., 12,394.

1996: Dole, R, 2,736,167; Clinton, D, 2,459,683; Perot, RF, 378,537; Browne, LB, 20,256; Phillips, U.S. Taxpayers, 7,472; Hagelin, Natural Law, 4,422.

1992: Bush, R, 2,496,071; Clinton, D, 2,281,815; Perot, Ind., 1,354,781; Marrou, LB, 19,699.

1988: Bush, R, 3,036,829; Dukakis, D, 2,352,748; Paul, LB, 30,355; Fulani, New Alliance, 7,208.

1984: Reagan, R, 3,433,428; Mondale, D, 1,949,276.

1980: Reagan, R, 2,510,705; Carter, D, 1,881,147; Anderson, Ind., 111,613; Clark, LB, 37,643; write-in, 528.

1976: Carter, D, 2,082,319; Ford, R, 1,953,300; McCarthy, Ind., 20,118; Anderson, Amer., 11,442; Camejo, Soc. Workers, 1,723; write-in, 2,982.

1972: Nixon, R, 2,298,896; McGovern, D, 1,154,289; Jenness, Soc. Workers, 8,664; Schmitz, Amer., 6,039; others, 3,393.

1968: Humphrey, D, 1,266,804; Nixon, R, 1,227,844; Wallace, 3rd party, 584,269; write-in, 489.

1964: Johnson, D, 1,663,185; Goldwater, R, 958,566; Lightburn, Const., 5,060.

1960: Kennedy, D, 1,167,932; Nixon, R, 1,121,699; Sullivan, Const., 18,169; Decker, Prohib., 3,870; write-in, 15.

Utah

County	2016 Clinton (D)	Trump (R)	2012 Obama (D)	Romney (R)
Beaver	264	1,838	346	2,174
Box Elder	2,282	12,230	1,984	17,101
Cache	8,563	21,139	6,244	35,039
Carbon	1,717	5,275	2,275	5,090
Daggett	77	331	94	406
Davis	28,776	62,219	21,889	96,861
Duchesne	500	5,508	581	5,698
Emery	380	3,425	569	3,777
Garfield	358	1,606	308	1,832
Grand	1,960	1,975	1,727	1,996
Iron	2,450	11,561	2,148	14,200
Juab	442	2,827	451	3,448
Kane	741	2,265	744	2,522
Millard	431	3,860	431	4,478
Morgan	577	3,188	403	4,114
Piute	47	626	74	697
Rich	104	797	83	915
Salt Lake	175,863	138,043	146,147	223,811
San Juan	2,042	2,645	2,139	3,074
Sanpete	1,061	6,673	980	8,406
Sevier	695	6,740	738	7,207
Summit	10,503	7,333	8,072	8,884
Tooele	4,573	11,169	4,524	14,268
Uintah	995	9,810	997	10,421
Utah	28,522	102,182	17,281	156,950
Wasatch	3,063	6,115	2,191	7,220
Washington	10,288	42,650	8,337	44,698
Wayne	271	966	215	1,089
Weber	23,131	40,235	19,841	54,224
Totals	310,676	515,231	251,813	740,600

Utah Vote Since 1960

2016: Trump, R, 515,231; Clinton, D, 310,676; McMullin, unaff., 243,690; Johnson, LB, 39,608; Stein, Green, 9,438; Castle, Const., 8,032; Giordani, Ind. Ameri., 2,752; De La Fuente, unaff., 883; Moorehead, unaff., 544; Kennedy, unaff., 521.

2012: Romney, R, 740,600; Obama, D, 251,813; Johnson, LB, 12,572; Anderson, Justice, 5,335; Stein, Green, 3,817; Goode, Const., 2,871; La Riva, unaff., 393.

2008: McCain, R, 596,030; Obama, D, 327,670; Baldwin, Const., 12,012; Nader, unaff., 8,416; Barr, LB, 6,966; McKinney, unaff., 982; La Riva, unaff., 262.

2004: Bush, R, 663,742; Kerry, D, 241,199; Nader, Ind., 11,305; Peroutka, Const., 6,841; Badnarik, LB, 3,375; Jay, Personal Choice, 946; Harris, Soc. Workers, 393.

2000: Bush, R, 515,096; Gore, D, 203,053; Nader, Green, 35,850; Buchanan, RF, 9,319; Browne, LB, 3,616; Phillips, Ind. American, 2,709; Hagelin, Natural Law, 763; Harris, Soc. Workers, 186; Youngkeit, Ind., 161.

1996: Dole, R, 361,911; Clinton, D, 221,633; Perot, RF, 66,461; Nader, Green, 4,615; Browne, LB, 4,129; Phillips, Taxpayers, 2,601; Templin, Ind. American, 1,290; Crane, Ind., 1,101; Hagelin, Natural Law, 1,085; Moorehead, Workers World, 298; Harris, Soc. Workers, 235; Dodge, Prohib., 111.
1992: Bush, R, 322,632; Perot, Ind., 203,400; Clinton, D, 183,429; Gritz, Populist/America First, 28,602; Marrou, LB, 1,900; Hagelin, Natural Law, 1,319; LaRouche, Ind., 1,089.
1988: Bush, R, 428,442; Dukakis, D, 207,352; Paul, LB, 7,473; Dennis, Amer., 2,158.
1984: Reagan, R, 469,105; Mondale, D, 155,369; Bergland, LB, 2,447.
1980: Reagan, R, 439,687; Carter, D, 124,266; Anderson, Ind., 30,284; Clark, LB, 7,226; Commoner, Citizens, 1,009; Greaves, Amer., 965; Rarick, Amer. Ind., 522; Hall, Comm., 139; DeBerry, Soc. Workers, 124.
1976: Ford, R, 337,908; Carter, D, 182,110; Anderson, Amer., 13,304; McCarthy, Ind., 3,907; MacBride, LB, 2,438; Maddox, Amer. Ind., 1,162; Camejo, Soc. Workers, 268; Hall, Comm., 121.
1972: Nixon, R, 323,643; McGovern, D, 126,284; Schmitz, Amer., 28,549.
1968: Nixon, R, 238,728; Humphrey, D, 156,665; Wallace, 3rd party, 26,906; Peace/Freedom, 180; Halstead, Soc. Workers, 89.
1964: Johnson, D, 219,628; Goldwater, R, 181,785.
1960: Nixon, R, 205,361; Kennedy, D, 169,248; Dobbs, Soc. Workers, 100.

Vermont

County	2016		2012	
	Clinton (D)	Trump (R)	Obama (D)	Romney (R)
Addison	11,219	5,297	12,257	5,203
Bennington	9,539	5,925	11,514	5,687
Caledonia	6,445	5,534	8,192	5,088
Chittenden	54,814	18,601	53,626	21,571
Essex	1,019	1,506	1,539	1,164
Franklin	9,351	8,752	12,057	7,405
Grand Isle	2,094	1,487	2,531	1,471
Lamoille	7,241	3,570	8,371	3,342
Orange	7,541	5,007	9,076	4,588
Orleans	5,185	5,159	7,117	4,306
Rutland	13,635	12,479	17,088	10,835
Washington	18,594	7,993	20,351	8,093
Windham	14,340	5,454	16,026	5,347
Windsor	17,556	8,605	19,494	8,598
Totals	**178,573**	**95,369**	**199,239**	**92,698**

Vermont Vote Since 1960

2016: Clinton, D, 178,573; Trump, R, 95,369; Sanders, write-in, 18,218; Johnson, LB, 10,078; Stein, Green, 6,758; De La Fuente, Ind., 1,063; La Riva, Liberty Union, 327.
2012: Obama, D, 199,239; Romney, R, 92,698; Johnson, LB, 3,487; Anderson, Justice, 1,128; Lindsay, Socialism/Liberation, 695.
2008: Obama, D, 219,262; McCain, R, 98,974; Nader, Ind., 3,339; Barr, LB, 1,067; Baldwin, Const., 500; Calero, Soc. Workers, 150; La Riva, Socialism/Liberation, 149; Moore, Liberty Union, 141.
2004: Kerry, D, 184,067; Bush, R, 121,180; Nader, Ind., 4,494; Badnarik, LB, 1,102; Parker, Liberty Union, 265; Calero, Soc. Workers, 244.
2000: Gore, D, 149,022; Bush, R, 119,775; Nader, Green, 20,374; Buchanan, RF, 2,192; Lane, Grass Roots, 1,044; Browne, LB, 784; Hagelin, Natural Law, 219; McReynolds, Liberty Union, 161; Phillips, Const., 153; Harris, Soc. Workers, 70.
1996: Clinton, D, 137,894; Dole, R, 80,352; Perot, RF, 31,024; Nader, Green, 5,585; Browne, LB, 1,183; Hagelin, Natural Law, 498; Peron, Grass Roots, 480; Phillips, Taxpayers, 382; Hollis, Liberty Union, 292; Harris, Soc. Workers, 199.
1992: Clinton, D, 133,590; Bush, R, 88,122; Perot, Ind., 65,985.
1988: Bush, R, 124,331; Dukakis, D, 115,775; Paul, LB, 1,000; LaRouche, Ind., 275.
1984: Reagan, R, 135,865; Mondale, D, 95,730; Bergland, LB, 1,002.
1980: Reagan, R, 94,598; Carter, D, 81,891; Anderson, Ind., 31,760; Commoner, Citizens, 2,316; Clark, LB, 1,900; McReynolds, Liberty Union, 136; Hall, Comm., 118; DeBerry, Soc. Workers, 75; scattered, 413.
1976: Ford, R, 100,387; Carter, D, 77,798 and Ind. Vermonters, 991 (total, 78,789); McCarthy, Ind., 4,001; Camejo, Soc. Workers, 430; LaRouche, U.S. Labor, 196; scattered, 99.

1972: Nixon, R, 117,149; McGovern, D, 68,174; Spock, Liberty Union, 1,010; Jenness, Soc. Workers, 296; scattered, 318.
1968: Nixon, R, 85,142; Humphrey, D, 70,255; Wallace, 3rd party, 5,104; Gregory, New Party, 579; Halstead, Soc. Workers, 295.
1964: Johnson, D, 107,674; Goldwater, R, 54,868.
1960: Nixon, R, 98,131; Kennedy, D, 69,186.

Virginia

County	2016		2012	
	Clinton (D)	Trump (R)	Obama (D)	Romney (R)
Accomack	6,740	8,583	7,655	8,213
Albemarle	33,345	19,259	29,757	23,297
Alleghany	2,166	4,874	3,403	3,595
Amelia	2,128	4,708	2,490	4,331
Amherst	5,057	9,719	5,900	8,876
Appomattox	2,023	5,715	2,453	5,340
Arlington	92,016	20,186	81,269	34,474
Augusta	8,177	26,163	9,451	23,624
Bath	603	1,548	894	1,274
Bedford	9,768	30,659	10,209	26,679
Bland	453	2,573	735	2,144
Botetourt	4,494	13,375	5,452	12,479
Brunswick	4,481	3,046	4,994	2,968
Buchanan	1,721	7,296	3,094	6,436
Buckingham	3,128	3,950	3,750	3,569
Campbell	6,664	19,551	7,595	17,695
Caroline	6,432	7,147	7,276	6,151
Carroll	2,559	10,663	3,685	8,736
Charles City	2,496	1,476	2,772	1,396
Charlotte	2,155	3,479	2,503	3,311
Chesterfield	81,074	85,045	77,694	90,934
Clarke	3,051	4,661	3,239	4,296
Craig	541	2,140	830	1,757
Culpeper	7,759	13,349	8,285	11,580
Cumberland	2,036	2,697	2,422	2,538
Dickenson	1,335	4,932	2,473	4,274
Dinwiddie	5,765	7,447	6,550	6,875
Essex	2,542	2,657	3,016	2,602
Fairfax	355,133	157,710	315,273	206,773
Fauquier	12,971	22,127	13,965	21,034
Floyd	2,300	5,293	2,732	4,673
Fluvanna	5,760	7,025	5,893	6,678
Franklin	7,257	18,569	9,090	16,718
Frederick	11,932	26,083	12,690	22,858
Giles	1,950	5,910	2,730	4,660
Gloucester	5,404	13,096	6,764	12,137
Goochland	4,889	8,384	4,676	8,448
Grayson	1,407	5,592	2,068	4,801
Greene	2,924	5,945	3,290	5,569
Greensville	2,558	1,737	3,135	1,766
Halifax	6,897	9,704	7,766	8,694
Hanover	19,382	39,630	18,294	39,940
Henrico	93,935	59,857	89,594	70,449
Henry	8,198	15,208	10,317	13,984
Highland	371	958	459	924
Isle of Wight	7,881	12,204	8,761	11,802
James City	19,105	21,306	17,879	22,843
King and Queen	1,468	2,099	1,745	1,865
King George	4,007	7,341	4,477	6,604
King William	2,760	5,975	3,344	5,466
Lancaster	2,869	3,523	3,149	3,753
Lee	1,627	7,543	2,583	6,847
Loudoun	100,795	69,949	82,479	75,292
Louisa	6,212	10,528	6,953	9,215
Lunenburg	2,227	3,204	2,684	2,969
Madison	2,203	4,419	2,639	3,869
Mathews	1,563	3,517	1,807	3,488
Mecklenburg	6,285	8,288	6,921	7,973
Middlesex	2,108	3,670	2,370	3,619
Montgomery	20,021	19,459	19,903	20,006
Nelson	3,689	4,154	4,171	3,947
New Kent	3,546	8,118	3,555	7,246
Northampton	3,255	2,686	3,741	2,676
Northumberland	2,852	4,302	3,191	4,310
Nottoway	2,829	3,712	3,344	3,409
Orange	5,957	10,521	6,870	9,244
Page	2,514	7,831	3,724	6,344
Patrick	1,768	6,454	2,417	5,622
Pittsylvania	9,199	21,554	10,858	19,263
Powhatan	4,060	11,885	4,088	11,200
Prince Edward	4,591	4,101	5,132	3,952
Prince George	6,419	9,157	6,991	8,879
Prince William	113,144	71,721	103,331	74,458

County	2016		2012	
	Clinton (D)	Trump (R)	Obama (D)	Romney (R)
Pulaski	4,172	10,322	5,292	8,920
Rappahan-nock	1,747	2,539	1,980	2,311
Richmond	1,347	2,213	1,574	2,160
Roanoke	17,200	31,408	18,711	31,624
Rockbridge	3,508	6,680	4,088	5,898
Rockingham	9,366	25,990	10,065	24,186
Russell	2,330	9,521	3,718	8,180
Scott	1,581	8,247	2,395	7,439
Shenandoah	5,273	14,094	6,469	12,538
Smyth	2,665	9,750	4,171	8,379
Southampton	3,595	5,035	4,437	4,733
Spotsylvania	24,207	34,623	25,165	31,844
Stafford	27,908	33,868	27,182	32,480
Surry	2,272	1,819	2,576	1,671
Sussex	2,879	2,055	3,358	2,021
Tazewell	2,895	15,168	3,661	13,843
Warren	5,169	11,773	6,452	9,869
Washington	5,553	19,320	7,076	18,141
Westmoreland	3,836	4,448	4,295	3,731
Wise	2,701	12,086	3,760	11,076
Wythe	2,770	10,046	3,783	8,324
York	12,999	18,837	13,183	20,204
City				
Alexandria	57,242	13,285	52,199	20,249
Bristol	1,835	4,892	2,492	4,780
Buena Vista	693	1,430	919	1,564
Charlottesville	17,901	2,960	16,510	4,844
Chesapeake	52,627	54,047	55,052	53,900
Colonial Heights	2,367	5,681	2,544	5,941
Covington	914	1,349	1,319	975
Danville	11,059	7,303	12,218	7,763
Emporia	1,530	789	1,793	886
Fairfax	7,367	3,702	6,651	4,775
Falls Church	5,819	1,324	5,015	2,147
Franklin	2,519	1,421	2,833	1,496
Fredericks-burg	6,707	3,744	7,131	4,060
Galax	681	1,603	900	1,332
Hampton	41,312	17,902	46,966	18,640
Harrisonburg	10,212	6,262	8,654	6,565
Hopewell	4,724	3,885	5,179	3,739
Lexington	1,514	766	1,486	1,146
Lynchburg	14,792	17,982	15,948	19,806
Manassas	8,423	5,953	8,478	6,463
Manassas Park	3,204	1,733	2,879	1,699
Martinsville	3,533	2,149	3,855	2,312
Newport News	45,618	25,468	51,100	27,230
Norfolk	57,023	21,552	62,687	23,147
Norton	383	1,021	566	895
Petersburg	12,021	1,451	14,283	1,527
Poquoson	1,601	5,092	1,679	5,312
Portsmouth	28,497	12,795	32,501	12,858
Radford	2,925	2,638	2,732	2,520
Richmond	81,259	15,581	75,921	20,050
Roanoke	22,286	14,789	24,134	14,991
Salem	4,202	7,226	4,760	7,299
Staunton	5,333	5,133	5,728	5,272
Suffolk	23,280	18,006	24,267	17,820
Virginia Beach	91,032	98,224	94,299	99,291
Waynesboro	3,764	4,801	3,840	4,790
Williamsburg	5,206	1,925	4,903	2,682
Winchester	5,164	4,790	5,094	4,946
Totals	**1,981,473**	**1,769,443**	**1,971,820**	**1,822,522**

Virginia Vote Since 1960

2016: Clinton, D, 1,981,473; Trump, R, 1,769,443; Johnson, LB, 118,274; McMullin, Ind., 54,054; Stein, Green, 27,638.

2012: Obama, D, 1,971,820; Romney, R, 1,822,522; Johnson, LB, 31,216; Goode, Const., 13,058; Stein, Green, 8,627.

2008: Obama, D, 1,959,532; McCain, R, 1,725,005; Nader, Ind., 11,483; Barr, LB, 11,067; Baldwin, Ind. Green, 7,474; McKinney, Green, 2,344.

2004: Bush, R, 1,716,959; Kerry, D, 1,454,742; Badnarik, LB, 11,032; Peroutka, Const., 10,161.

2000: Bush, R, 1,437,490; Gore, D, 1,217,290; Nader, Green, 59,398; Browne, LB, 15,198; Buchanan, RF, 5,455; Phillips, Const., 1,809.

1996: Dole, R, 1,138,350; Clinton, D, 1,091,060; Perot, RF, 159,861; Phillips, Taxpayers, 13,687; Browne, LB, 9,174; Hagelin, Natural Law, 4,510.

1992: Bush, R, 1,150,517; Clinton, D, 1,038,650; Perot, Ind., 348,639; LaRouche, Ind., 11,937; Marrou, LB, 5,730; Fulani, New Alliance, 3,192.

1988: Bush, R, 1,309,162; Dukakis, D, 859,799; Fulani, Ind., 14,312; Paul, LB, 8,336.

1984: Reagan, R, 1,337,078; Mondale, D, 796,250.

1980: Reagan, R, 989,609; Carter, D, 752,174; Anderson, Ind., 95,418; Commoner, Citizens, 14,024; Clark, LB, 12,821; DeBerry, Soc. Workers, 1,986.

1976: Ford, R, 836,554; Carter, D, 813,896; Camejo, Soc. Workers, 17,802; Anderson, Amer., 16,686; LaRouche, U.S. Labor, 7,508; MacBride, LB, 4,648.

1972: Nixon, R, 988,493; McGovern, D, 438,887; Schmitz, Amer., 19,721; Fisher, Soc. Labor, 9,918.

1968: Nixon, R, 590,319; Humphrey, D, 442,387; Wallace, 3rd party, 320,272*; Blomen, Soc. Labor, 4,671; Gregory, Peace/Freedom, 1,680; Munn, Prohib., 601. *10,561 votes for Wallace were omitted in the count.

1964: Johnson, D, 558,038; Goldwater, R, 481,334; Hass, Soc. Labor, 2,895.

1960: Nixon, R, 404,521; Kennedy, D, 362,327; Coiner, Conservative, 4,204; Hass, Soc. Labor, 397.

Washington

County	2016		2012	
	Clinton (D)	Trump (R)	Obama (D)	Romney (R)
Adams	1,299	3,083	1,540	3,171
Asotin	3,134	5,741	4,003	5,654
Benton	26,360	47,194	28,145	49,461
Chelan	13,032	18,114	13,112	18,402
Clallam	17,677	18,794	18,580	18,437
Clark	92,757	92,441	93,382	92,951
Columbia	526	1,497	645	1,568
Cowlitz	17,908	24,185	22,726	20,746
Douglas	4,918	9,603	5,166	9,425
Ferry	1,098	2,202	1,294	1,995
Franklin	8,886	13,206	8,398	13,748
Garfield	279	851	336	913
Grant	7,810	18,518	8,950	17,852
Gray's Harbor	12,020	14,067	15,960	11,914
Island	20,960	18,465	21,478	19,605
Jefferson	12,656	6,037	12,739	6,405
King	718,322	216,339	668,004	275,700
Kitsap	63,156	49,018	67,277	52,846
Kittitas	7,489	10,100	7,949	9,782
Klickitat	4,194	5,789	4,598	5,316
Lewis	9,654	21,992	12,664	20,452
Lincoln	1,244	4,108	1,673	4,063
Mason	11,993	13,677	14,764	12,761
Okanogan	6,298	9,610	7,108	9,221
Pacific	4,620	5,360	5,711	4,499
Pend Oreille	1,934	4,373	2,508	3,952
Pierce	172,538	146,824	186,430	148,467
San Juan	7,172	2,688	7,125	3,111
Skagit	26,690	24,736	28,688	25,071
Skamania	2,232	2,928	2,628	2,687
Snohomish	185,227	128,255	188,516	133,016
Spokane	93,767	113,435	102,295	115,285
Stevens	5,767	15,161	7,762	13,691
Thurston	68,798	48,624	74,037	49,287
Wahkiakum	832	1,344	1,094	1,119
Walla Walla	9,694	13,651	9,768	14,648
Whatcom	60,340	40,599	57,089	42,703
Whitman	8,146	7,403	8,037	8,507
Yakima	31,291	41,735	33,217	42,239
Totals	**1,742,718**	**1,221,747**	**1,755,396**	**1,290,670**

Washington Vote Since 1960

2016: Clinton, D, 1,742,718; Trump, R, 1,221,747; Johnson, LB, 160,879; Stein, Green, 58,417; Castle, Const., 17,623; Kennedy, Soc. Workers, 4,307; La Riva, Socialism/Liberation, 3,523.

2012: Obama, D, 1,755,396; Romney, R, 1,290,670; Johnson, LB, 42,202; Stein, Green, 20,928; Goode, Const., 8,851; Anderson, Justice, 4,946; Lindsay, Socialism/Liberation, 1,318; Harris, Soc. Workers, 1,205.

2008: Obama, D, 1,750,848; McCain, R, 1,229,216; Nader, Ind., 29,489; Barr, LB, 12,728; Baldwin, Const., 9,432; McKinney, Green, 3,819; La Riva, Socialism/Liberation, 705; Harris, Soc. Workers, 641.

2004: Kerry, D, 1,510,201; Bush, R, 1,304,894; Nader, Ind., 23,283; Badnarik, LB, 11,955; Peroutka, Const., 3,922; Cobb,

Green, 2,974; Parker, Workers World, 1,077; Harris, Soc. Workers, 547; Van Auken, Soc. Equality, 231.

2000: Gore, D, 1,247,652; Bush, R, 1,108,864; Nader, Green, 103,002; Browne, LB, 13,135; Buchanan, Freedom, 7,171; Hagelin, Natural Law, 2,927; Phillips, Const., 1,989; Moorehead, Workers World, 1,729; McReynolds, Soc., 660; Harris, Soc. Workers, 304.

1996: Clinton, D, 1,123,323; Dole, R, 840,712; Perot, RF, 201,003; Nader, Ind., 60,322; Browne, LB, 12,522; Hagelin, Natural Law, 6,076; Phillips, U.S. Taxpayers, 4,578; Collins, Ind., 2,374; Moorehead, Workers World, 2,189; Harris, Soc. Workers, 738.

1992: Clinton, D, 993,037; Bush, R, 731,234; Perot, Ind., 541,780; Marrou, LB, 7,533; Gritz, Populist/America First, 4,854; Hagelin, Natural Law, 2,456; Phillips, U.S. Taxpayers, 2,354; Fulani, New Alliance, 1,776; Daniels, Ind., 1,171.

1988: Dukakis, D, 933,516; Bush, R, 903,835; Paul, LB, 17,240; LaRouche, Ind., 4,412.

1984: Reagan, R, 1,051,670; Mondale, D, 798,352; Bergland, LB, 8,844.

1980: Reagan, R, 865,244; Carter, D, 650,193; Anderson, Ind., 185,073; Clark, LB, 29,213; Commoner, Citizens, 9,403; DeBerry, Soc. Workers, 1,137; McReynolds, Soc., 956; Hall, Comm., 834; Griswold, Workers World, 341.

1976: Ford, R, 777,732; Carter, D, 717,323; McCarthy, Ind., 36,986; Maddox, Amer. Ind., 8,585; Anderson, Amer., 5,046; MacBride, LB, 5,042; Wright, People's, 1,124; Camejo, Soc. Workers, 905; LaRouche, U.S. Labor, 903; Hall, Comm., 817; Levin, Soc. Labor, 713; Zeidler, Soc., 358.

1972: Nixon, R, 837,135; McGovern, D, 568,334; Schmitz, Amer., 58,906; Spock, Ind., 2,644; Hospers, LB, 1,537; Fisher, Soc. Labor, 1,102; Jenness, Soc. Workers, 623; Hall, Comm., 566.

1968: Humphrey, D, 616,037; Nixon, R, 588,510; Wallace, 3rd party, 96,990; Cleaver, Peace/Freedom, 1,609; Blomen, Soc. Labor, 488; Mitchell, Free Ballot, 377; Halstead, Soc. Workers, 270.

1964: Johnson, D, 779,699; Goldwater, R, 470,366; Hass, Soc. Labor, 7,772; DeBerry, Freedom Soc., 537.

1960: Nixon, R, 629,273; Kennedy, D, 599,298; Hass, Soc. Labor, 10,895; Curtis, Const., 1,401; Dobbs, Soc. Workers, 705.

West Virginia

County	2016 Clinton (D)	Trump (R)	2012 Obama (D)	Romney (R)
Barbour	1,222	4,527	1,768	3,824
Berkeley	12,321	28,244	14,275	22,156
Boone	1,790	6,504	2,790	5,467
Braxton	1,321	3,537	1,998	2,725
Brooke	2,568	6,625	4,005	5,060
Cabell	11,447	19,850	13,568	17,985
Calhoun	456	2,035	818	1,319
Clay	568	2,300	931	1,971
Doddridge	362	2,358	575	2,130
Fayette	4,290	10,357	5,419	8,350
Gilmer	545	1,896	840	1,595
Grant	512	4,346	718	3,783
Greenbrier	3,765	9,556	4,710	7,930
Hampshire	1,580	6,692	2,299	5,523
Hancock	3,262	8,909	4,627	7,226
Hardy	1,155	4,274	1,482	3,536
Harrison	7,694	18,750	9,732	15,876
Jackson	2,663	9,020	3,854	7,408
Jefferson	9,518	13,204	10,398	11,258
Kanawha	28,263	43,850	32,480	41,364
Lewis	1,347	5,274	1,736	4,375
Lincoln	1,459	5,307	2,227	4,383
Logan	2,092	9,897	3,469	8,222
Marion	6,964	14,668	8,959	12,054
Marshall	2,918	9,666	4,484	8,135
Mason	2,081	7,654	3,778	5,741
McDowell	1,438	4,629	2,109	3,959
Mercer	4,704	17,404	5,432	15,450
Mineral	2,050	9,070	2,885	7,833
Mingo	1,370	7,911	2,428	6,191
Monongalia	14,699	18,432	13,826	16,831
Monroe	1,111	4,443	1,455	3,616
Morgan	1,573	5,732	2,363	4,513
Nicholas	1,840	7,251	2,664	5,898
Ohio	5,493	11,139	6,786	10,768

County	2016 Clinton (D)	Trump (R)	2012 Obama (D)	Romney (R)
Pendleton	729	2,398	1,074	2,095
Pleasants	621	2,358	955	1,825
Pocahontas	928	2,496	1,303	2,182
Preston	2,470	9,538	2,931	7,889
Putnam	5,884	17,788	7,256	16,032
Raleigh	6,443	22,048	7,739	20,614
Randolph	2,735	7,629	3,342	6,160
Ritchie	496	3,405	768	2,921
Roane	1,222	3,781	1,939	2,982
Summers	1,190	3,455	1,621	2,981
Taylor	1,491	4,733	1,941	3,840
Tucker	751	2,565	880	2,176
Tyler	507	2,996	890	2,314
Upshur	1,766	7,005	2,158	5,939
Wayne	3,357	11,152	4,931	8,688
Webster	556	2,302	947	1,710
Wetzel	1,359	4,519	2,217	3,473
Wirt	386	1,911	676	1,427
Wood	8,400	25,434	11,230	22,183
Wyoming	1,062	6,547	1,583	5,769
Totals	**188,794**	**489,371**	**238,269**	**417,655**

West Virginia Vote Since 1960

2016: Trump, R, 489,371; Clinton, D, 188,794; Johnson, LB, 23,004; Stein, Mountain, 8,075; Castle, Const., 3,807.

2012: Romney, R, 417,655; Obama, D, 238,269; Johnson, LB, 6,302; Stein, Mountain, 4,406; Terry, NPA, 3,806.

2008: McCain, R, 397,466; Obama, D, 303,857; Nader, unaff., 7,219; Baldwin, Const., 2,465; McKinney, Mountain, 2,355.

2004: Bush, R, 423,778; Kerry, D, 326,541; Nader, Ind., 4,063; Badnarik, LB, 1,405.

2000: Bush, R, 336,475; Gore, D, 295,497; Nader, Green, 10,680; Buchanan, RF, 3,169; Browne, LB, 1,912; Hagelin, Natural Law, 367.

1996: Clinton, D, 327,812; Dole, R, 233,946; Perot, RF, 71,639; Browne, LB, 3,062.

1992: Clinton, D, 331,001; Bush, R, 241,974; Perot, Ind., 108,829; Marrou, LB, 1,873.

1988: Dukakis, D, 341,016; Bush, R, 310,065; Fulani, New Alliance, 2,230.

1984: Reagan, R, 405,483; Mondale, D, 328,125.

1980: Carter, D, 367,462; Reagan, R, 334,206; Anderson, Ind., 31,691; Clark, LB, 4,356.

1976: Carter, D, 435,864; Ford, R, 314,726.

1972: Nixon, R, 484,964; McGovern, D, 277,435.

1968: Humphrey, D, 374,091; Nixon, R, 307,555; Wallace, 3rd party, 72,560.

1964: Johnson, D, 538,087; Goldwater, R, 253,953.

1960: Kennedy, D, 441,786; Nixon, R, 395,995.

Wisconsin

County	2016 Clinton (D)	Trump (R)	2012 Obama (D)	Romney (R)
Adams	3,745	5,966	5,542	4,644
Ashland	4,226	3,303	5,399	2,820
Barron	7,889	13,614	10,890	11,443
Bayfield	4,953	4,124	6,033	3,603
Brown	53,382	67,210	62,526	64,836
Buffalo	2,525	4,048	3,570	3,364
Burnett	2,949	5,410	3,986	4,550
Calumet	9,642	15,367	11,489	14,539
Chippewa	11,887	17,916	15,237	15,322
Clark	4,221	8,652	6,172	7,412
Columbia	13,528	14,163	17,175	13,026
Crawford	3,419	3,836	4,629	3,067
Dane	217,697	71,275	216,071	83,644
Dodge	13,968	26,635	18,762	25,211
Door	8,014	8,580	9,357	8,121
Douglas	11,357	9,661	14,863	7,705
Dunn	9,034	11,486	11,316	10,224
Eau Claire	27,340	23,331	30,666	23,256
Florence	665	1,898	953	1,645
Fond du Lac	17,387	31,022	22,379	30,355
Forest	1,579	2,787	2,425	2,172
Grant	10,051	12,350	13,594	10,255
Green	9,122	8,693	11,206	7,857
Green Lake	2,693	6,216	3,793	5,782
Iowa	6,669	4,809	8,105	4,287
Iron	1,275	2,081	1,784	1,790

County	2016		2012	
	Clinton (D)	Trump (R)	Obama (D)	Romney (R)
Jackson	3,818	4,906	5,298	3,900
Jefferson	16,569	23,417	20,158	23,517
Juneau	4,073	7,130	6,242	5,411
Kenosha	35,799	36,037	44,867	34,977
Kewaunee	3,627	6,618	5,153	5,747
La Crosse	32,406	26,378	36,693	25,751
Lafayette	3,288	3,977	4,536	3,314
Langlade	3,250	6,478	4,573	5,816
Lincoln	5,371	8,401	7,563	7,455
Manitowoc	14,538	23,244	20,403	21,604
Marathon	26,481	39,014	32,363	36,617
Marinette	6,409	13,122	9,882	10,619
Marquette	2,808	4,709	4,014	3,992
Menominee	1,002	267	1,191	179
Milwaukee	288,822	126,069	332,438	154,924
Monroe	7,052	11,356	9,515	9,675
Oconto	5,940	13,345	8,865	10,741
Oneida	8,109	12,132	10,452	10,917
Outagamie	38,068	49,879	45,659	47,372
Ozaukee	20,170	30,464	19,159	36,077
Pepin	1,344	2,206	1,876	1,794
Pierce	8,399	11,272	10,235	10,397
Polk	7,565	13,810	10,073	12,094
Portage	18,529	17,305	22,075	16,615
Price	2,667	4,559	3,887	3,884
Racine	42,641	46,681	53,008	49,347
Richland	3,569	4,013	4,969	3,573
Rock	39,339	31,493	49,219	30,517
Rusk	2,171	4,564	3,397	3,676
St. Croix	17,482	26,222	19,910	25,503
Sauk	14,690	14,799	18,736	12,838
Sawyer	3,503	5,185	4,486	4,442
Shawano	6,068	12,769	9,000	11,022
Sheboygan	23,000	32,514	27,918	34,072
Taylor	2,393	6,579	3,763	5,601
Trempealeau	5,636	7,366	7,605	5,707
Vernon	6,371	7,004	8,044	5,942
Vilas	4,770	8,166	5,951	7,749
Walworth	18,710	28,863	22,552	29,006
Washburn	3,282	5,436	4,447	4,699
Washington	20,852	51,740	23,166	54,765
Waukesha	79,224	142,543	78,779	162,798
Waupaca	8,451	16,209	11,578	14,002
Waushara	3,791	7,667	5,335	6,562
Winnebago	37,047	43,445	45,449	42,122
Wood	14,225	21,498	18,581	19,704
Totals	**1,382,536**	**1,405,284**	**1,620,985**	**1,407,966**

Wisconsin Vote Since 1960

2016: Trump, R, 1,405,284; Clinton, D, 1,382,536; Johnson, LB, 106,674; Stein, WI Green, 31,072; Castle, Const., 12,162; McMullin, Ind., 11,855; Moorehead, Ind., 1,770; De La Fuente, Ind., 1,502.

2012: Obama, D, 1,620,985; Romney, R, 1,407,966; Johnson, LB, 20,439; Stein, Green, 7,665; White, Soc. Equality, 553; La Riva, Socialism/Liberation, 526.

2008: Obama, D, 1,677,211; McCain, R, 1,262,393; Nader, Ind., 17,605; Barr, LB, 8,858; Baldwin, Ind., 5,072; McKinney, Green, 4,216; Wamboldt, Ind., 764; Moore, Ind., 540; La Riva, Ind., 237.

2004: Kerry, D, 1,489,504; Bush, R, 1,478,120; Nader, Ind., 16,390; Badnarik, LB, 6,464; Cobb, Green, 2,661; Brown, Ind., 471; Harris, Ind., 411.

2000: Gore, D, 1,242,987; Bush, R, 1,237,279; Nader, Green, 94,070; Buchanan, RF, 11,446; Browne, LB, 6,640; Phillips, Const., 2,042; Moorehead, Workers World, 1,063; Hagelin, RF, 878; Harris, Soc. Workers, 306.

1996: Clinton, D, 1,071,971; Dole, R, 845,029; Perot, RF, 227,339; Nader, Green, 28,723; Phillips, U.S. Taxpayers, 8,811; Browne, LB, 7,929; Hagelin, Natural Law, 1,379; Moorehead, Workers World, 1,333; Hollis, Soc., 848; Harris, Soc. Workers, 483.

1992: Clinton, D, 1,041,066; Bush, R, 930,855; Perot, Ind., 544,479; Marrou, LB, 2,877; Gritz, Populist/America First, 2,311; Daniels, Ind., 1,883; Phillips, U.S. Taxpayers, 1,772; Hagelin, Natural Law, 1,070.

1988: Dukakis, D, 1,126,794; Bush, R, 1,047,499; Paul, LB, 5,157; Duke, Populist, 3,056.

1984: Reagan, R, 1,198,584; Mondale, D, 995,740; Bergland, LB, 4,883.

1980: Reagan, R, 1,088,845; Carter, D, 981,584; Anderson, Ind., 160,657; Clark, LB, 29,135; Commoner, Citizens, 7,767; Rarick, Const., 1,519; McReynolds, Soc., 808; Hall, Comm., 772; Griswold, Workers World, 414; DeBerry, Soc. Workers, 383; scattered, 1,337.

1976: Carter, D, 1,040,232; Ford, R, 1,004,987; McCarthy, Ind., 34,943; Maddox, Amer. Ind., 8,552; Zeidler, Soc., 4,298; MacBride, LB, 3,814; Camejo, Soc. Workers, 1,691; Wright, People's, 943; Hall, Comm., 749; LaRouche, U.S. Labor, 738; Levin, Soc. Labor, 389; scattered, 2,839.

1972: Nixon, R, 989,430; McGovern, D, 810,174; Schmitz, Amer., 47,525; Spock, Ind., 2,701; Fisher, Soc. Labor, 998; Hall, Comm., 663; Reed, Ind., 506; scattered, 893.

1968: Nixon, R, 809,997; Humphrey, D, 748,804; Wallace, 3rd party, 127,835; Blomen, Soc. Labor, 1,338; Halstead, Soc. Workers, 1,222; scattered, 2,342.

1964: Johnson, D, 1,050,424; Goldwater, R, 638,495; DeBerry, Soc. Workers, 1,692; Hass, Soc. Labor, 1,204.

1960: Nixon, R, 895,175; Kennedy, D, 830,805; Dobbs, Soc. Workers, 1,792; Hass, Soc. Labor, 1,310.

Wyoming

County	2016		2012	
	Clinton (D)	Trump (R)	Obama (D)	Romney (R)
Albany	6,890	7,602	7,458	7,866
Big Horn	604	4,067	868	4,285
Campbell	1,324	15,778	2,163	14,953
Carbon	1,279	4,409	2,110	4,148
Converse	668	5,520	1,089	5,043
Crook	273	3,348	426	3,109
Fremont	4,200	11,167	5,333	11,075
Goshen	924	4,418	1,458	4,178
Hot Springs	400	1,939	523	1,895
Johnson	638	3,477	749	3,363
Laramie	11,573	24,847	14,295	23,904
Lincoln	1,105	6,779	1,287	7,144
Natrona	6,577	23,552	8,961	22,132
Niobrara	115	1,116	200	1,022
Park	2,535	11,115	2,927	11,234
Platte	719	3,437	1,223	3,136
Sheridan	2,927	10,266	3,618	10,267
Sublette	644	3,409	767	3,472
Sweetwater	3,231	12,154	4,774	11,428
Teton	7,314	3,921	6,213	4,858
Uinta	1,202	6,154	1,628	6,615
Washakie	532	2,911	794	3,014
Weston	299	3,033	422	2,821
Totals	**55,973**	**174,419**	**69,286**	**170,962**

Wyoming Vote Since 1960

2016: Trump, R, 174,419; Clinton, D, 55,973; Johnson, LB, 13,287; Stein, Ind., 2,515; Castle, Const., 2,042; De La Fuente, Ind., 709.

2012: Romney, R, 170,962; Obama, D, 69,286; Johnson, LB, 5,326; Goode, Const., 1,452.

2008: McCain, R, 164,958; Obama, D, 82,868; Nader, Ind., 2,525; Barr, LB, 1,594; Baldwin, Ind., 1,192.

2004: Bush, R, 167,629; Kerry, D, 70,776; Nader, Ind., 2,741; Badnarik, LB, 1,171; Peroutka, Ind., 631.

2000: Bush, R, 147,947; Gore, D, 60,481; Buchanan, RF, 2,724; Browne, LB, 1,443; Phillips, Ind., 720; Hagelin, Natural Law, 411.

1996: Dole, R, 105,388; Clinton, D, 77,934; Perot, RF, 25,928; Browne, LB, 1,739; Hagelin, Natural Law, 582.

1992: Bush, R, 79,347; Clinton, D, 68,160; Perot, Ind., 51,263.

1988: Bush, R, 106,867; Dukakis, D, 67,113; Paul, LB, 2,026; Fulani, New Alliance, 545.

1984: Reagan, R, 133,241; Mondale, D, 53,370; Bergland, LB, 2,357.

1980: Reagan, R, 110,700; Carter, D, 49,427; Anderson, Ind., 12,072; Clark, LB, 4,514.

1976: Ford, R, 92,717; Carter, D, 62,239; McCarthy, Ind., 624; Reagan, Ind., 307; Anderson, Amer., 290; MacBride, LB, 89; Brown, Ind., 47; Maddox, Amer. Ind., 30.

1972: Nixon, R, 100,464; McGovern, D, 44,358; Schmitz, Amer., 748.

1968: Nixon, R, 70,927; Humphrey, D, 45,173; Wallace, 3rd party, 11,105.

1964: Johnson, D, 80,718; Goldwater, R, 61,998.

1960: Nixon, R, 77,451; Kennedy, D, 63,331.

UNITED STATES GOVERNMENT

EXECUTIVE BRANCH	LEGISLATIVE BRANCH	JUDICIAL BRANCH
President	**CONGRESS**	**Supreme Court of the United States**
Vice President	**Senate/House of Representatives**	Courts of Appeals
Executive Office of the President	Architect of the Capitol	District Courts
Council of Economic Advisers	Congressional Budget Office	Territorial Courts
Council on Environmental Quality	Government Accountability Office	Court of International Trade
Executive Residence	Government Publishing Office	Court of Federal Claims
National Security Council	Library of Congress	Bankruptcy Courts
Office of Administration	Medicare Payment Advisory Commission	Tax Court
Office of Management and Budget	Stennis Center for Public Service	Court of Appeals for the Armed Forces
Office of National Drug Control Policy	U.S. Botanic Garden	Court of Appeals for Veterans Claims
Office of Science and Technology Policy		Administrative Office of the Courts
Office of the U.S. Trade Representative		Federal Judicial Center
Office of the Vice President		Sentencing Commission
White House Office*		Judicial Panel on Multidistrict Litigation

*Includes Domestic Policy Council, National Security Advisor, National Economic Council, Office of Cabinet Affairs, Office of the Chief of Staff, Office of Communications, Office of Digital Strategy, Office of the First Lady, Office of Legislative Affairs, Office of Management and Administration, Oval Office Operations, Office of Presidential Personnel, Office of Public Engagement and Intergovernmental Affairs, Office of Scheduling and Advance, Office of the Staff Secretary, and Office of the White House Counsel.

Trump Administration

1600 Pennsylvania Ave. NW, 20500; www.whitehouse.gov
As of Sept. 2018. Mailing addresses are for Washington, DC, except where otherwise noted.
Terms of office of the president and vice president: Jan. 20, 2017, to Jan. 20, 2021.

President: By law, Pres. Donald J. Trump received an annual salary of $400,000 (taxable) and an annual expense allowance of $50,000 (nontaxable) for costs resulting from official duties. This does not include amounts available for expenditures within the Executive Office of the President, including $3,850,000 for necessary expenses for the White House, up to $100,000 a year for travel expenses, and up to $19,000 for official entertainment.

Website: www.whitehouse.gov/people/donald-j-trump/

Vice President: By law, Vice Pres. Michael R. Pence received an annual salary of $243,500 (taxable) and an annual expense allowance of $20,000 for costs resulting from official duties, plus $90,000 for official entertainment expenses (nontaxable).

Website: www.whitehouse.gov/people/mike-pence/

Cabinet Department Heads

(Salary: $210,700 per year)

Secretary of State: Mike Pompeo
Secretary of the Treasury: Steven T. Mnuchin
Secretary of Defense: James Mattis
Attorney General (Dept. of Justice): Jeff Sessions
Secretary of the Interior: Ryan Zinke
Secretary of Agriculture: Sonny Perdue
Secretary of Commerce: Wilbur L. Ross Jr.
Secretary of Labor: R. Alexander Acosta
Secretary of Health and Human Services: Alex Azar
Secretary of Housing and Urban Development: Ben Carson
Secretary of Transportation: Elaine L. Chao
Secretary of Energy: Rick Perry
Secretary of Education: Betsy DeVos
Secretary of Veterans Affairs: Robert Wilkie
Secretary of Homeland Security: Kirstjen M. Nielsen

Executive Offices

Council of Economic Advisers: Kevin Hassett, chair; www.whitehouse.gov/cea/
Council on Environmental Quality: Mary Neumayr, acting chair; www.whitehouse.gov/ceq/
Office of Administration: Marcia Kelly, dir.; www.whitehouse.gov/oa/
Office of Management and Budget: Mick Mulvaney, dir.; www.whitehouse.gov/omb/
Office of Natl. Drug Control Policy: Jim Carroll, acting dir.; www.whitehouse.gov/ondcp/
Office of Science and Technology Policy: vacant; www.whitehouse.gov/ostp/
Office of the U.S. Trade Representative: Robert E. Lighthizer, amb.; www.ustr.gov
Office of the Director of National Intelligence (not formally an executive office): Daniel Coats, dir.; www.dni.gov

White House Staff

Assistants to the President:
  Chief of Staff: John F. Kelly

Deputy Chief of Staff for Communications: Bill Shine
Deputy Chief of Staff for Policy Coordination: Chris Liddell
Deputy Chief of Staff for Operations: Daniel Walsh
Senior Counselor: Kellyanne Conway
Counselor: John DeStefano
Senior Adviser: Jared Kushner
Senior Adviser for Policy: Stephen Miller
Senior Adviser for Strategic Communications: Mercedes Schlapp
Adviser to the President: Ivanka Trump
Counsel to the President: Donald F. McGahn II
Special Counsel to the President: Emmet Flood
White House Press Secretary: Sarah Huckabee Sanders
National Security Adviser: John Bolton
Deputy National Security Adviser: Mira Ricardel
Director of Domestic Policy Council: Andrew Bremberg
Director of National Economic Council: Lawrence Kudlow
Director of Legislative Affairs: Shahira Knight
Director of Management and Administration: Marcia Kelly
Director of Social Media: Dan Scavino
Special Rep. for International Negotiations: Jason Greenblatt
Strategic Initiatives: Brooke Rollins
Trade and Manufacturing Policy: Peter Navarro
White House Staff Secretary: Derek Lyons
Chief of Staff to the First Lady: Lindsay Reynolds

Deputy Assistants to the President:
  Cabinet Secretary: Bill McGinley
  Director of Intergovernmental Affairs: Douglas Hoelscher
  Director of Oval Office Operations: Michael Karem
  Director of the Office of Public Liaison: Justin Clark
  Director of Political Affairs: Bill Stepien
  Director of Presidential Advance: Robert L. Peede Jr.
  Director of Presidential Personnel: Sean E. Doocy
  Principal Deputy Press Secretary: Raj Shah
  White House Social Secretary: Anna Cristina "Rickie" Niceta

The Cabinet

The heads of major executive departments of the federal government constitute the Cabinet. This institution, not provided for in the U.S. Constitution, developed as an advisory body out of the desire of presidents to consult on policy matters. Aside from its advisory role, the Cabinet as a body has no formal function and wields no executive authority. Individual members exercise authority as heads of their departments, reporting to the president. The Cabinet meets at times set by the president. In addition, the Cabinet commonly includes other officials designated by the president as being of Cabinet rank.

The officials so designated by Pres. Donald Trump include Vice Pres. Mike Pence, White House Chief of Staff John F. Kelly, Acting Environmental Protection Agency Administrator Andrew Wheeler, Office of Management and Budget Director Mick Mulvaney, Director of National Intelligence Daniel Coats, U.S. Trade Representative Ambassador Robert Lighthizer, U.S. Ambassador to the United Nations Nikki R. Haley, Central Intelligence Agency Director Gina Haspel, and Small Business Administration Administrator Linda McMahon.

Department of State

2201 C St. NW, 20520; www.state.gov

The Dept. of Foreign Affairs was created by act of Congress on July 27, 1789, and the name changed to Dept. of State on Sept. 15, 1789. Conducts U.S. foreign policy. The Foreign Service protects American citizens and interests through embassies in some 180 countries under eight geographic bureaus. Maintains contact with foreign governments, negotiates agreements and treaties, and supports U.S. foreign trade. Promotes democracy, international security, human rights—including issues related to AIDS, human trafficking, war crimes, and migration—and arms and narcotics control. Represents the nation in international organizations. Issues passports to U.S. citizens and visas to foreigners. **Budget:** $26.5 bil (2015); $29.4 bil (2016); $27.1 bil (2017); $30.1 bil (est. 2018). Budget for other intl. programs: $21.0 bil (2015); $16.2 bil (2016); $18.9 bil (2017); $16.3 bil (est. 2018).

- Bureau of Intl. Information Programs; www.state.gov/r/iip/
- Bureau of Intl. Narcotics and Law Enforcement Affairs; www.state.gov/j/inl/
- Bureau of Intl. Organization Affairs; www.state.gov/p/io/
- Bureau of Population, Refugees, and Migration; www.state.gov/j/prm/
- Intl. Boundary and Water Commission (4171 North Mesa, Ste. C-100, El Paso, TX 79902); www.ibwc.gov
- Office of the U.S. Global AIDS Coordinator and Health Diplomacy (SA-22, Rm. 10300, 20522); www.state.gov/s/gac/

Secretaries of State

President	Secretary	Home	Sworn in
Washington	Thomas Jefferson	VA	1789
	Edmund J. Randolph	VA	1794
	Timothy Pickering	PA	1795
Adams, J.	Timothy Pickering	PA	1797
	John Marshall	VA	1800
Jefferson	James Madison	VA	1801
Madison	Robert Smith	MD	1809
	James Monroe	VA	1811
Monroe	John Quincy Adams	MA	1817
Adams, J. Q.	Henry Clay	KY	1825
Jackson	Martin Van Buren	NY	1829
	Edward Livingston	LA	1831
	Louis McLane	DE	1833
	John Forsyth	GA	1834
Van Buren	John Forsyth	GA	1837
Harrison, W. H.	Daniel Webster	MA	1841
Tyler	Daniel Webster	MA	1841
	Abel P. Upshur	VA	1843
	John C. Calhoun	SC	1844
Polk	John C. Calhoun	SC	1845
	James Buchanan	PA	1845
Taylor	James Buchanan	PA	1849
	John M. Clayton	DE	1849
Fillmore	John M. Clayton	DE	1850
	Daniel Webster	MA	1850
	Edward Everett	MA	1852
Pierce	William L. Marcy	NY	1853
Buchanan	William L. Marcy	NY	1857
	Lewis Cass	MI	1857
	Jeremiah S. Black	PA	1860
Lincoln	Jeremiah S. Black	PA	1861
	William H. Seward	NY	1861
Johnson, A.	William H. Seward	NY	1865
Grant	Elihu B. Washburne	IL	1869
	Hamilton Fish	NY	1869
Hayes	Hamilton Fish	NY	1877
	William M. Evarts	NY	1877
Garfield	William M. Evarts	NY	1881
	James G. Blaine	ME	1881
Arthur	James G. Blaine	ME	1881
	F. T. Frelinghuysen	NJ	1881
Cleveland	F. T. Frelinghuysen	NJ	1885
	Thomas F. Bayard	DE	1885
Harrison, B.	Thomas F. Bayard	DE	1889
	James G. Blaine	ME	1889
	John W. Foster	IN	1892
Cleveland	Walter Q. Gresham	IN	1893
	Richard Olney	MA	1895
McKinley	Richard Olney	MA	1897
	John Sherman	OH	1897
	William R. Day	OH	1898
	John M. Hay	DC	1898

President	Secretary	Home	Sworn in
Roosevelt, T.	John M. Hay	DC	1901
	Elihu Root	NY	1905
	Robert Bacon	NY	1909
Taft	Robert Bacon	NY	1909
	Philander C. Knox	PA	1909
Wilson	Philander C. Knox	PA	1913
	William J. Bryan	NE	1913
	Robert Lansing	NY	1915
	Bainbridge Colby	NY	1920
Harding	Charles E. Hughes	NY	1921
Coolidge	Charles E. Hughes	NY	1923
	Frank B. Kellogg	MN	1925
Hoover	Frank B. Kellogg	MN	1929
	Henry L. Stimson	NY	1929
Roosevelt, F. D.	Cordell Hull	TN	1933
	Edward R. Stettinius Jr.	VA	1944
Truman	Edward R. Stettinius Jr.	VA	1945
	James F. Byrnes	SC	1945
	George C. Marshall	PA	1947
	Dean G. Acheson	CT	1949
Eisenhower	John Foster Dulles	NY	1953
	Christian A. Herter	MA	1959
Kennedy	D. Dean Rusk	GA	1961
Johnson, L. B.	D. Dean Rusk	GA	1963
Nixon	William P. Rogers	NY	1969
	Henry A. Kissinger	DC	1973
Ford	Henry A. Kissinger	DC	1974
Carter	Cyrus R. Vance	NY	1977
	Edmund S. Muskie	ME	1980
Reagan	Alexander M. Haig Jr.	CT	1981
	George P. Shultz	CA	1982
Bush, G. H. W.	James A. Baker III	TX	1989
	Lawrence S. Eagleburger	MI	1992
Clinton	Warren M. Christopher	CA	1993
	Madeleine K. Albright	DC	1997
Bush, G. W.	Colin L. Powell	NY	2001
	Condoleezza Rice	AL	2005
Obama	Hillary Rodham Clinton	NY	2009
	John Kerry	MA	2013
Trump	Rex W. Tillerson	TX	2017
	Mike Pompeo	KS	2018

Department of the Treasury

1500 Pennsylvania Ave. NW, 20220; www.treasury.gov

Organized by act of Congress on Sept. 2, 1789. Responsible for the fiscal affairs of the U.S. Serves as the government's financial agent; collects, borrows, and disburses funds for the federal government. Monitors the nation's financial infrastructure and economic development; recommends domestic and international financial, monetary, economic, trade, and tax policies. Manufactures currency and coins. Carries out monetary and tax law enforcement activities, sanctions, embargoes, and fights illicit finance—counterfeiting, money laundering, narcotics trafficking, terrorist financing. **Budget** (including interest on the public debt): $485.6 bil (2015); $526.1 bil (2016); $546.4 bil (2017); $606.7 bil (est. 2018).

- Alcohol and Tobacco Tax and Trade Bureau (1310 G St. NW, Box 12, 20005); www.ttb.gov
- Bureau of Engraving and Printing (14th and C Sts. SW, 20228); www.moneyfactory.gov
- Bureau of the Fiscal Service (401 14th St. SW, 20227); www.fiscal.treasury.gov
- Financial Crimes Enforcement Network; www.fincen.gov
- Internal Revenue Service (1111 Constitution Ave. NW, 20224); www.irs.gov
- U.S. Mint (801 9th St. NW, 20220); www.usmint.gov

Secretaries of the Treasury

President	Secretary	Home	Sworn in
Washington	Alexander Hamilton	NY	1789
	Oliver Wolcott Jr.	CT	1795
Adams, J.	Oliver Wolcott Jr.	CT	1797
	Samuel Dexter	MA	1801
Jefferson	Samuel Dexter	MA	1801
	Albert Gallatin	PA	1801
Madison	Albert Gallatin	PA	1809
	George W. Campbell	TN	1814
	Alexander J. Dallas	PA	1814
	William H. Crawford	GA	1816
Monroe	William H. Crawford	GA	1817
Adams, J. Q.	Richard Rush	PA	1825

President	Secretary	Home	Sworn in
Jackson	Samuel D. Ingham	PA	1829
	Louis McLane	DE	1831
	William J. Duane	PA	1833
	Roger B. Taney	MD	1833
	Levi Woodbury	NH	1834
Van Buren	Levi Woodbury	NH	1837
Harrison, W. H.	Thomas Ewing	OH	1841
Tyler	Thomas Ewing	OH	1841
	Walter Forward	PA	1841
	John C. Spencer	NY	1843
	George M. Bibb	KY	1844
Polk	Robert J. Walker	MS	1845
Taylor	William M. Meredith	PA	1849
Fillmore	Thomas Corwin	OH	1850
Pierce	James Guthrie	KY	1853
Buchanan	Howell Cobb	GA	1857
	Phillip F. Thomas	MD	1860
	John A. Dix	NY	1861
Lincoln	Salmon P. Chase	OH	1861
	William P. Fessenden	ME	1864
	Hugh McCulloch	IN	1865
Johnson, A.	Hugh McCulloch	IN	1865
Grant	George S. Boutwell	MA	1869
	William A. Richardson	MA	1873
	Benjamin H. Bristow	KY	1874
	Lot M. Morrill	ME	1876
Hayes	John Sherman	OH	1877
Garfield	William Windom	MN	1881
Arthur	Charles J. Folger	NY	1881
	Walter Q. Gresham	IN	1884
	Hugh McCulloch	IN	1884
Cleveland	Daniel Manning	NY	1885
	Charles S. Fairchild	NY	1887
Harrison, B.	William Windom	MN	1889
	Charles Foster	OH	1891
Cleveland	John G. Carlisle	KY	1893
McKinley	Lyman J. Gage	IL	1897
Roosevelt, T.	Lyman J. Gage	IL	1901
	Leslie M. Shaw	IA	1902
	George B. Cortelyou	NY	1907
Taft	Franklin MacVeagh	IL	1909
Wilson	William G. McAdoo	NY	1913
	Carter Glass	VA	1918
	David F. Houston	MO	1920
Harding	Andrew W. Mellon	PA	1921
Coolidge	Andrew W. Mellon	PA	1923
Hoover	Andrew W. Mellon	PA	1929
	Ogden L. Mills	NY	1932
Roosevelt, F. D.	William H. Woodin	NY	1933
	Henry Morgenthau Jr.	NY	1934
Truman	Fred M. Vinson	KY	1945
	John W. Snyder	MO	1946
Eisenhower	George M. Humphrey	OH	1953
	Robert B. Anderson	CT	1957
Kennedy	C. Douglas Dillon	NJ	1961
Johnson, L. B.	C. Douglas Dillon	NJ	1963
	Henry H. Fowler	VA	1965
	Joseph W. Barr	IN	1968
Nixon	David M. Kennedy	IL	1969
	John B. Connally	TX	1971
	George P. Shultz	IL	1972
	William E. Simon	NJ	1974
Ford	William E. Simon	NJ	1974
Carter	W. Michael Blumenthal	MI	1977
	G. William Miller	RI	1979
Reagan	Donald T. Regan	NY	1981
	James A. Baker III	TX	1985
	Nicholas F. Brady	NJ	1988
Bush, G. H. W.	Nicholas F. Brady	NJ	1989
Clinton	Lloyd M. Bentsen	TX	1993
	Robert E. Rubin	NY	1995
	Lawrence H. Summers	CT	1999
Bush, G. W.	Paul H. O'Neill	MO	2001
	John W. Snow	OH	2003
	Henry M. Paulson Jr.	FL	2006
Obama	Timothy F. Geithner	NY	2009
	Jack Lew	NY	2013
Trump	Steven T. Mnuchin	NY	2017

Department of Defense

1400 Defense Pentagon, 20301; www.defense.gov

The Dept. of Defense, originally designated the National Military Establishment, was created on Sept. 18, 1947. Directs and controls the armed forces and assists the president in protecting the nation's security. Military departments of the Army, Navy, and Air Force are each separately organized under its own secretary but all function under the command of the secretary of defense. They conduct military operations as unified commands. The chairman of the Joint Chiefs of Staff is the principal military adviser to the president. Undersecretaries supervise acquisition, technology, and logistics; intelligence; personnel and readiness; and policy. **Budget** for military programs: $562.5 bil (2015); $565.4 bil (2016); $568.9 bil (2017); $612.5 bil (est. 2018). **Budget** for civil programs: $69.7 bil (2015); $70.9 bil (2016); $65.1 bil (2017); $62.74 bil (est. 2018).

- Def. Advanced Research Projects Agency (675 N. Randolph St., Arlington, VA 22203); www.darpa.mil
- Def. Intelligence Agency (200 MacDill Blvd., 20340); www.dia.mil
- Def. Security Cooperation Agency (2800 Defense Pentagon, 20301); www.dsca.mil
- Missile Def. Agency (5700 18th St., Bldg. 245, Fort Belvoir, VA 22060-5573)
- Natl. Geospatial-Intelligence Agency (7500 GEOINT Dr., Springfield, VA 22150); www.nga.mil
- Natl. Security Agency/Central Security Service (9800 Savage Rd., Ste. 6272, Ft. George G. Meade, MD 20755); www.nsa.gov

Secretaries of Defense

President	Secretary	Home	Sworn in
Truman	James V. Forrestal	NY	1947
	Louis A. Johnson	WV	1949
	George C. Marshall	PA	1950
	Robert A. Lovett	NY	1951
Eisenhower	Charles E. Wilson	MI	1953
	Neil H. McElroy	OH	1957
	Thomas S. Gates Jr.	PA	1959
Kennedy	Robert S. McNamara	MI	1961
Johnson, L. B.	Robert S. McNamara	MI	1963
	Clark M. Clifford	MD	1968
Nixon	Melvin R. Laird	WI	1969
	Elliot L. Richardson	MA	1973
	James R. Schlesinger	VA	1973
Ford	James R. Schlesinger	VA	1974
	Donald H. Rumsfeld	IL	1975
Carter	Harold Brown	CA	1977
Reagan	Caspar W. Weinberger	CA	1981
	Frank C. Carlucci	PA	1987
Bush, G. H. W.	Richard B. Cheney	WY	1989
Clinton	Les Aspin	WI	1993
	William J. Perry	CA	1994
	William S. Cohen	ME	1997
Bush, G. W.	Donald H. Rumsfeld	IL	2001
	Robert M. Gates	TX	2006
Obama	Robert M. Gates	TX	2009
	Leon E. Panetta	CA	2011
	Chuck Hagel	NE	2013
	Ashton Carter	PA	2015
Trump	James Mattis	WA	2017

Secretaries of War

The War Dept. (which included jurisdiction over the Navy until 1798) was created by act of Congress on Aug. 7, 1789.

President	Secretary	Home	Sworn in
Washington	Henry Knox	MA	1789
	Timothy Pickering	PA	1795
	James McHenry	MD	1796
Adams, J.	James McHenry	MD	1797
	Samuel Dexter	MA	1800
Jefferson	Henry Dearborn	MA	1801
Madison	William Eustis	MA	1809
	John Armstrong	NY	1813
	James Monroe	VA	1814
	William H. Crawford	GA	1815
Monroe	John C. Calhoun	SC	1817
Adams, J. Q.	James Barbour	VA	1825
	Peter B. Porter	NY	1828
Jackson	John H. Eaton	TN	1829
	Lewis Cass	MI	1831
	Benjamin F. Butler	NY	1837
Van Buren	Joel R. Poinsett	SC	1837
Harrison, W. H.	John Bell	TN	1841
Tyler	John Bell	TN	1841
	John C. Spencer	NY	1841
	James M. Porter	PA	1843
	William Wilkins	PA	1844
Polk	William L. Marcy	NY	1845
Taylor	George W. Crawford	GA	1849
Fillmore	Charles M. Conrad	LA	1850
Pierce	Jefferson Davis	MS	1853

President	Secretary	Home	Sworn in
Buchanan	John B. Floyd	VA	1857
	Joseph Holt	KY	1861
Lincoln	Simon Cameron	PA	1861
	Edwin M. Stanton	PA	1862
Johnson, A.	Edwin M. Stanton	PA	1865
	John M. Schofield	IL	1868
Grant	John A. Rawlins	IL	1869
	William T. Sherman	OH	1869
	William W. Belknap	IA	1869
	Alphonso Taft	OH	1876
	James D. Cameron	PA	1876
Hayes	George W. McCrary	IA	1877
	Alexander Ramsey	MN	1879
Garfield	Robert T. Lincoln	IL	1881
Arthur	Robert T. Lincoln	IL	1881
Cleveland	William C. Endicott	MA	1885
Harrison, B.	Redfield Proctor	VT	1889
	Stephen B. Elkins	WV	1891
Cleveland	Daniel S. Lamont	NY	1893
McKinley	Russell A. Alger	MI	1897
	Elihu Root	NY	1899
Roosevelt, T.	Elihu Root	NY	1901
	William H. Taft	OH	1904
	Luke E. Wright	TN	1908
Taft	Jacob M. Dickinson	TN	1909
	Henry L. Stimson	NY	1911
Wilson	Lindley M. Garrison	NJ	1913
	Newton D. Baker	OH	1916
Harding	John W. Weeks	MA	1921
Coolidge	John W. Weeks	MA	1923
	Dwight F. Davis	MO	1925
Hoover	James W. Good	IL	1929
	Patrick J. Hurley	OK	1929
Roosevelt, F. D.	George H. Dern	UT	1933
	Harry H. Woodring	KS	1937
	Henry L. Stimson	NY	1940
Truman	Robert P. Patterson	NY	1945
	Kenneth C. Royall[1]	NC	1947

(1) Last member of Cabinet with this title. The War Dept. became the Dept. of the Army with the creation of the Defense Dept. in 1947, though the Army secretary maintained Cabinet-level status until 1949.

President	Secretary	Home	Sworn in
Hayes	Richard W. Thompson	IN	1877
	Nathan Goff Jr.	WV	1881
Garfield	William H. Hunt	LA	1881
Arthur	William E. Chandler	NH	1882
Cleveland	William C. Whitney	NY	1885
Harrison, B.	Benjamin F. Tracy	NY	1889
Cleveland	Hilary A. Herbert	AL	1893
McKinley	John D. Long	MA	1897
Roosevelt, T.	John D. Long	MA	1901
	William H. Moody	MA	1902
	Paul Morton	IL	1904
	Charles J. Bonaparte	MD	1905
	Victor H. Metcalf	CA	1906
	Truman H. Newberry	MI	1908
Taft	George von L. Meyer	MA	1909
Wilson	Josephus Daniels	NC	1913
Harding	Edwin Denby	MI	1921
Coolidge	Edwin Denby	MI	1923
	Curtis D. Wilbur	CA	1924
Hoover	Charles Francis Adams	MA	1929
Roosevelt, F. D.	Claude A. Swanson	VA	1933
	Charles Edison	NJ	1940
	Frank Knox	IL	1940
	James V. Forrestal	NY	1944
Truman	James V. Forrestal[1]	NY	1945

(1) Last member of Cabinet with this title. The Navy Dept. became a branch of the Dept. of Defense when the latter was created in 1947, though the Navy secretary maintained Cabinet-level status until 1949.

Department of Justice

950 Pennsylvania Ave. NW, 20530; www.justice.gov

The Office of Attorney General was established by act of Congress on Sept. 24, 1789. It officially reached Cabinet rank in Mar. 1792, when the first attorney general, Edmund Randolph, attended his initial Cabinet meeting. The Dept. of Justice, headed by the attorney general, was created June 22, 1870. Provides for the enforcement of federal laws and investigation of violations; furnishes legal counsel in cases involving the federal government and interprets laws relating to the activities of other federal departments; supervises federal penal institutions. The attorney general and Office of Legal Counsel render legal advice, upon request, to the president and department heads. The solicitor general conducts all suits brought before the U.S. Supreme Court in which the federal government is concerned. The Civil Division represents the U.S. government in many civil or criminal matters. The 93 U.S. attorneys (for 94 federal districts) are the principal litigators in the U.S. and its territories. **Budget:** $26.9 bil (2015); $29.5 bil (2016); $31.0 bil (2017); $38.5 bil (est. 2018).

- Bureau of Alcohol, Tobacco, Firearms and Explosives (99 New York Ave. NE, 20226); www.atf.gov
- Drug Enforcement Admin. (8701 Morrissette Dr., Springfield, VA 22152); www.dea.gov
- Executive Office for Immigration Review (5107 Leesburg Pike, Ste. 1902, Falls Church, VA 22041); www.justice.gov/eoir/
- Federal Bureau of Investigation (935 Pennsylvania Ave. NW, 20535); www.fbi.gov
- Federal Bureau of Prisons (320 First St. NW, 20534); www.bop.gov
- INTERPOL Washington (U.S. Natl. Central Bureau) (20530); www.justice.gov/interpol-washington/
- U.S. Marshals Service (20530-1000); www.usmarshals.gov
- U.S. Parole Commission (90 K St. NE, 3rd Fl., 20530); www.justice.gov/uspc/

Secretaries of the Navy

The Navy Dept. was created by act of Congress on Apr. 30, 1798. The Marine Corps is part of this department.

President	Secretary	Home	Sworn in
Adams, J.	Benjamin Stoddert	MD	1798
Jefferson	Benjamin Stoddert	MD	1801
	Robert Smith	MD	1801
Madison	Paul Hamilton	SC	1809
	William Jones	PA	1813
	Benjamin W. Crowninshield	MA	1814
Monroe	Benjamin W. Crowninshield	MA	1817
	Smith Thompson	NY	1818
	Samuel L. Southard	NJ	1823
Adams, J. Q.	Samuel L. Southard	NJ	1825
Jackson	John Branch	NC	1829
	Levi Woodbury	NH	1831
	Mahlon Dickerson	NJ	1834
Van Buren	Mahlon Dickerson	NJ	1837
	James K. Paulding	NY	1838
Harrison, W. H.	George E. Badger	NC	1841
Tyler	George E. Badger	NC	1841
	Abel P. Upshur	VA	1841
	David Henshaw	MA	1843
	Thomas W. Gilmer	VA	1844
	John Y. Mason	VA	1844
Polk	George Bancroft	MA	1845
	John Y. Mason	VA	1846
Taylor	William B. Preston	VA	1849
Fillmore	William A. Graham	NC	1850
	John P. Kennedy	MD	1852
Pierce	James C. Dobbin	NC	1853
Buchanan	Isaac Toucey	CT	1857
Lincoln	Gideon Welles	CT	1861
Johnson, A.	Gideon Welles	CT	1865
Grant	Adolph E. Borie	PA	1869
	George M. Robeson	NJ	1869

Attorneys General

President	Attorney General	Home	Sworn in
Washington	Edmund J. Randolph	VA	1789
	William Bradford	PA	1794
	Charles Lee	VA	1795
Adams, J.	Charles Lee	VA	1797
Jefferson	Levi Lincoln	MA	1801
	John Breckenridge	KY	1805
	Caesar A. Rodney	DE	1807
Madison	Caesar A. Rodney	DE	1807
	William Pinkney	MD	1811
	Richard Rush	PA	1814
Monroe	Richard Rush	PA	1817
	William Wirt	VA	1817

President	Attorney General	Home	Sworn in
Adams, J. Q.	William Wirt	VA	1825
Jackson	John M. Berrien	GA	1829
	Roger B. Taney	MD	1831
	Benjamin F. Butler	NY	1833
Van Buren	Benjamin F. Butler	NY	1837
	Felix Grundy	TN	1838
	Henry D. Gilpin	PA	1840
Harrison, W. H.	John J. Crittenden	KY	1841
Tyler	John J. Crittenden	KY	1841
	Hugh S. Legaré	SC	1841
	John Nelson	MD	1843
Polk	John Y. Mason	VA	1845
	Nathan Clifford	ME	1846
	Isaac Toucey	CT	1848
Taylor	Reverdy Johnson	MD	1849
Fillmore	John J. Crittenden	KY	1850
Pierce	Caleb Cushing	MA	1853
Buchanan	Jeremiah S. Black	PA	1857
	Edwin M. Stanton	PA	1860
Lincoln	Edward Bates	MO	1861
	James Speed	KY	1864
Johnson, A.	James Speed	KY	1865
	Henry Stanbery	OH	1866
	William M. Evarts	NY	1868
Grant	Ebenezer R. Hoar	MA	1869
	Amos T. Akerman	GA	1870
	George H. Williams	OR	1871
	Edwards Pierrepont	NY	1875
	Alphonso Taft	OH	1876
Hayes	Charles Devens	MA	1877
Garfield	I. Wayne MacVeagh	PA	1881
Arthur	Benjamin H. Brewster	PA	1882
Cleveland	Augustus H. Garland	AR	1885
Harrison, B.	William H. H. Miller	IN	1889
Cleveland	Richard Olney	MA	1893
	Judson Harmon	OH	1895
McKinley	Joseph McKenna	CA	1897
	John W. Griggs	NJ	1898
	Philander C. Knox	PA	1901
Roosevelt, T.	Philander C. Knox	PA	1901
	William H. Moody	MA	1904
	Charles J. Bonaparte	MD	1906
Taft	George W. Wickersham	NY	1909
Wilson	James C. McReynolds	TN	1913
	Thomas W. Gregory	TX	1914
	A. Mitchell Palmer	PA	1919
Harding	Harry M. Daugherty	OH	1921
Coolidge	Harry M. Daugherty	OH	1923
	Harlan F. Stone	NY	1924
	John G. Sargent	VT	1925
Hoover	William D. Mitchell	MN	1929
Roosevelt, F. D.	Homer S. Cummings	CT	1933
	Frank Murphy	MI	1939
	Robert H. Jackson	NY	1940
	Francis Biddle	PA	1941
Truman	Thomas C. Clark	TX	1945
	J. Howard McGrath	RI	1949
	James P. McGranery	PA	1952
Eisenhower	Herbert Brownell Jr.	NY	1953
	William P. Rogers	MD	1957
Kennedy	Robert F. Kennedy	MA	1961
Johnson, L. B.	Robert F. Kennedy	MA	1963
	Nicholas Katzenbach	IL	1964
	W. Ramsey Clark	TX	1967
Nixon	John N. Mitchell	NY	1969
	Richard G. Kleindienst	AZ	1972
	Elliot L. Richardson	MA	1973
	William B. Saxbe	OH	1974
Ford	William B. Saxbe	OH	1974
	Edward H. Levi	IL	1975
Carter	Griffin B. Bell	GA	1977
	Benjamin R. Civiletti	MD	1979
Reagan	William French Smith	CA	1981
	Edwin Meese III	CA	1985
	Richard L. Thornburgh	PA	1988
Bush, G. H. W.	Richard L. Thornburgh	PA	1989
	William P. Barr	NY	1991
Clinton	Janet Reno	FL	1993
Bush, G. W.	John Ashcroft	MO	2001
	Alberto R. Gonzales	TX	2005
	Michael B. Mukasey	NY	2007
Obama	Eric H. Holder Jr.	DC	2009
	Loretta E. Lynch	NY	2015
Trump	Jeff Sessions	AL	2017

Department of the Interior

1849 C St. NW, 20240; www.doi.gov

Created by act of Congress on Mar. 3, 1849. Custodian of natural resources. Has the responsibility of protecting and conserving the country's land, water, minerals, fish, and wildlife; of promoting the wise use of all these natural resources; of maintaining national parks and recreation areas; and of preserving historic places. It also provides for the welfare of American Indian reservation communities and of inhabitants of island territories under U.S. administration. **Budget:** $12.3 bil (2015); $12.6 bil (2016); $12.2 bil (2017); $14.4 bil (est. 2018).

- Bureau of Indian Affairs (1849 C St. NW, MS-4606-MIB, 20240); www.indianaffairs.gov
- Bureau of Land Management (1849 C St. NW, Rm. 5665, 20240); www.blm.gov
- Bureau of Ocean Energy Management (1849 C St. NW, 20240); www.boem.gov
- Bureau of Reclamation (1849 C St. NW, 20240); www.usbr.gov
- Bureau of Safety and Environmental Enforcement (1849 C St. NW, 20240); www.bsee.gov
- National Park Service (1849 C St. NW, 20240); www.nps.gov
- Office of Surface Mining Reclamation and Enforcement (1849 C St. NW, 20240); www.osmre.gov
- U.S. Fish and Wildlife Service (1849 C St. NW, 20240); www.fws.gov
- U.S. Geological Survey (12201 Sunrise Valley Dr., Reston, VA 20192); www.usgs.gov

Secretaries of the Interior

President	Secretary	Home	Sworn in
Taylor	Thomas Ewing	OH	1849
Fillmore	Thomas M. T. McKennan	PA	1850
	Alex H. H. Stuart	VA	1850
Pierce	Robert McClelland	MI	1853
Buchanan	Jacob Thompson	MS	1857
Lincoln	Caleb B. Smith	IN	1861
	John P. Usher	IN	1863
Johnson, A.	John P. Usher	IN	1865
	James Harlan	IA	1865
	Orville H. Browning	IL	1866
Grant	Jacob D. Cox	OH	1869
	Columbus Delano	OH	1870
	Zachariah Chandler	MI	1875
Hayes	Carl Schurz	MO	1877
Garfield	Samuel J. Kirkwood	IA	1881
Arthur	Henry M. Teller	CO	1882
Cleveland	Lucius Q. C. Lamar	MS	1885
	William F. Vilas	WI	1888
Harrison, B.	John W. Noble	MO	1889
Cleveland	M. Hoke Smith	GA	1893
	David R. Francis	MO	1896
McKinley	Cornelius N. Bliss	NY	1897
	Ethan A. Hitchcock	MO	1898
Roosevelt, T.	Ethan A. Hitchcock	MO	1901
	James R. Garfield	OH	1907
Taft	Richard A. Ballinger	WA	1909
	Walter L. Fisher	IL	1911
Wilson	Franklin K. Lane	CA	1913
	John B. Payne	IL	1920
Harding	Albert B. Fall	NM	1921
	Hubert Work	CO	1923
Coolidge	Hubert Work	CO	1923
	Roy O. West	IL	1929
Hoover	Ray Lyman Wilbur	CA	1929
Roosevelt, F. D.	Harold L. Ickes	IL	1933
Truman	Harold L. Ickes	IL	1945
	Julius A. Krug	WI	1946
	Oscar L. Chapman	CO	1949
Eisenhower	Douglas McKay	OR	1953
	Fred A. Seaton	NE	1956
Kennedy	Stewart L. Udall	AZ	1961
Johnson, L. B.	Stewart L. Udall	AZ	1963
Nixon	Walter J. Hickel	AK	1969
	Rogers C. B. Morton	MD	1971
Ford	Rogers C. B. Morton	MD	1971
	Stanley K. Hathaway	WY	1975
	Thomas S. Kleppe	ND	1975
Carter	Cecil D. Andrus	ID	1977
Reagan	James G. Watt	CO	1981
	William P. Clark	CA	1983
	Donald P. Hodel	OR	1985
Bush, G. H. W.	Manuel Lujan	NM	1989
Clinton	Bruce Babbitt	AZ	1993
Bush, G. W.	Gale Norton	CO	2001
	Dirk Kempthorne	ID	2006
Obama	Kenneth L. Salazar	CO	2009
	Sally Jewell	WA	2013
Trump	Ryan Zinke	MT	2017

Department of Agriculture

1400 Independence Ave. SW, 20250; www.usda.gov
Created by act of Congress on May 15, 1862. On Feb. 8, 1889, its commissioner was renamed secretary of agriculture and became a member of the Cabinet. Provides leadership on food, agriculture, and natural resources; supports scientific research and education for agriculture, nutrition, and food safety. Develops nutrition assistance programs, promotes healthy eating, supplies food stamps, grades and inspects the commercial supply of food. Responsible for the health of the land through sustainable management and conservation, manages public lands in national forests and grasslands; safeguards against invasive pests and diseases; ensures the health and care of animals and plants. Oversees assistance and conservation programs for farmers and ranchers and programs to improve the rural economy and quality of life. Facilitates domestic and international marketing of U.S. agricultural products. **Budget:** $139.1 bil (2015); $138.2 bil (2016); $127.6 bil (2017); $145.8 bil (est. 2018).

- Agricultural Research Service (1400 Independence Ave. SW, 20250); www.ars.usda.gov
- Economic Research Service (1400 Independence Ave. SW, Mail Stop 1800, 20250); www.ers.usda.gov
- Food and Nutrition Service (3101 Park Center Dr., Alexandria, VA 22302); www.fns.usda.gov
- Food Safety and Inspection Service (1400 Independence Ave. SW, 20250); www.fsis.usda.gov
- Foreign Agricultural Service (1400 Independence Ave. SW, Mail Stop 1001, 20250); www.fas.usda.gov
- Natl. Agricultural Statistics Service (1400 Independence Ave. SW, 20250); www.nass.usda.gov
- Natural Resources Conservation Service (1400 Independence Ave. SW, 20250); www.nrcs.usda.gov
- U.S. Forest Service (1400 Independence Ave. SW, 20250); www.fs.fed.us

Secretaries of Agriculture

President	Secretary	Home	Sworn in
Cleveland	Norman J. Colman	MO	1889
Harrison, B.	Jeremiah M. Rusk	WI	1889
Cleveland	J. Sterling Morton	NE	1893
McKinley	James Wilson	IA	1897
Roosevelt, T.	James Wilson	IA	1901
Taft	James Wilson	IA	1909
Wilson	David F. Houston	MO	1913
	Edwin T. Meredith	IA	1920
Harding	Henry C. Wallace	IA	1921
Coolidge	Henry C. Wallace	IA	1923
	Howard M. Gore	WV	1924
	William M. Jardine	KS	1925
Hoover	Arthur M. Hyde	MO	1929
Roosevelt, F. D.	Henry A. Wallace	IA	1933
	Claude R. Wickard	IN	1940
Truman	Clinton P. Anderson	NM	1945
	Charles F. Brannan	CO	1948
Eisenhower	Ezra Taft Benson	UT	1953
Kennedy	Orville L. Freeman	MN	1961
Johnson, L. B.	Orville L. Freeman	MN	1963
Nixon	Clifford M. Hardin	IN	1969
	Earl L. Butz	IN	1971
Ford	Earl L. Butz	IN	1974
	John A. Knebel	VA	1976
Carter	Bob Bergland	MN	1977
Reagan	John R. Block	IL	1981
	Richard E. Lyng	CA	1986
Bush, G. H. W.	Clayton K. Yeutter	NE	1989
	Edward Madigan	IL	1991
Clinton	Mike Espy	MS	1993
	Dan Glickman	KS	1995
Bush, G. W.	Ann M. Veneman	CA	2001
	Mike Johanns	NE	2005
	Ed Schafer	ND	2008
Obama	Thomas J. Vilsack	IA	2009
Trump	Sonny Perdue	GA	2017

Department of Commerce

1401 Constitution Ave. NW, 20230; www.commerce.gov
The Dept. of Commerce was formed by Congress Mar. 4, 1913, when it divided the Dept. of Commerce and Labor into two departments. Fosters, serves, and promotes the nation's economic development and technological advancement; supports the comprehension and use of the environment and its oceanic life; assists states, communities, and individuals with economic progress; promotes trade abroad and ensures an effective export control and treaty compliance system. Issues trademarks and patents, maintains measurement standards, and manages the federal telecommunications spectrum. Collects, analyzes, and distributes statistics regarding the nation and the economy through the Bureaus of the Census and of Economic Analysis. NOAA explores, monitors, and conserves oceans and coasts, tracks weather and other environmental data. **Budget:** $9.0 bil (2015); $9.2 bil (2016); $10.3 bil (2017); $9.9 bil (est. 2018).

- Bureau of Economic Analysis (4600 Silver Hill Rd., 20233); www.bea.gov
- Minority Business Development Agency (1401 Constitution Ave. NW, 20230); www.mbda.gov
- Natl. Institute of Standards and Technology (100 Bureau Dr., Gaithersburg, MD 20899); www.nist.gov
- Natl. Oceanic and Atmospheric Admin. (1401 Constitution Ave. NW, Rm. 5128, 20230); www.noaa.gov
- Natl. Technical Information Service (5301 Shawnee Rd., Alexandria, VA 22312); www.ntis.gov
- Natl. Telecommunications and Information Admin. (1401 Constitution Ave. NW, 20230); www.ntia.doc.gov
- U.S. Census Bureau (4600 Silver Hill Rd., 20233); www.census.gov

Secretaries of Commerce

President	Secretary	Home	Sworn in
Wilson	William C. Redfield	NY	1913
	Joshua W. Alexander	MO	1919
Harding	Herbert C. Hoover	CA	1921
Coolidge	Herbert C. Hoover	CA	1923
	William F. Whiting	MA	1928
Hoover	Robert P. Lamont	IL	1929
	Roy D. Chapin	MI	1932
Roosevelt, F. D.	Daniel C. Roper	SC	1933
	Harry L. Hopkins	NY	1939
	Jesse H. Jones	TX	1940
	Henry A. Wallace	IA	1945
Truman	Henry A. Wallace	IA	1945
	W. Averell Harriman	NY	1947
	Charles W. Sawyer	OH	1948
Eisenhower	Sinclair Weeks	MA	1953
	Lewis L. Strauss	NY	1958
	Frederick H. Mueller	MI	1959
Kennedy	Luther H. Hodges	NC	1961
Johnson, L. B.	Luther H. Hodges	NC	1963
	John T. Connor	NJ	1965
	Alex B. Trowbridge	NJ	1967
	Cyrus R. Smith	NY	1968
Nixon	Maurice H. Stans	MN	1969
	Peter G. Peterson	IL	1972
	Frederick B. Dent	SC	1973
Ford	Frederick B. Dent	SC	1974
	Rogers C. B. Morton	MD	1975
	Elliot L. Richardson	MA	1975
Carter	Juanita M. Kreps	NC	1977
	Philip M. Klutznick	IL	1979
Reagan	Malcolm Baldrige	CT	1981
	C. William Verity Jr.	OH	1987
Bush, G. H. W.	Robert A. Mosbacher	TX	1989
	Barbara H. Franklin	PA	1992
Clinton	Ronald H. Brown	DC	1993
	Mickey Kantor	CA	1996
	William M. Daley	IL	1997
	Norman Y. Mineta	CA	2000
Bush, G. W.	Donald L. Evans	TX	2001
	Carlos M. Gutierrez	MI	2005
Obama	Gary F. Locke	WA	2009
	John Bryson	CA	2011
	Penny Pritzker	IL	2013
Trump	Wilbur L. Ross Jr.	NJ	2017

Secretaries of Commerce and Labor

The Dept. of Commerce and Labor was created by Congress on Feb. 14, 1903.

President	Secretary	Home	Sworn in
Roosevelt, T.	George B. Cortelyou	NY	1903
	Victor H. Metcalf	CA	1904
	Oscar S. Straus	NY	1906
Taft	Charles Nagel	MO	1909

Department of Labor

200 Constitution Ave. NW, 20210; www.dol.gov
The Dept. of Labor was formed by Congress Mar. 4, 1913, when it divided the Dept. of Commerce and Labor into two departments. Administers federal labor laws to foster, promote, and develop the welfare of job seekers, wage earners, and retirees of the U.S.; to improve working conditions; and to advance

opportunities for profitable employment. Administers standards for wages and overtime pay, safety and health conditions, workers' compensation. Tracks changes in employment, prices, and other national economic measurements. Regulates pension and welfare benefit plans, the hiring and employment of migrant and seasonal workers, and requirements pertaining to the mining, construction, and transportation industries. Monitors labor unions and their funds. **Budget:** $45.2 bil (2015); $41.4 bil (2016); $40.1 bil (2017); $39.4 bil (est. 2018).

- Bureau of Labor Statistics (2 Massachusetts Ave. NE, 20212); www.bls.gov
- Employment and Training Admin. (200 Constitution Ave. NW, 20210); www.doleta.gov
- Mine Safety and Health Admin. (201 12th St. S, Ste. 401, Arlington, VA 22202); www.msha.gov
- Occupational Safety and Health Admin. (200 Constitution Ave. NW, 20210); www.osha.gov
- Office of Federal Contract Compliance Programs (200 Constitution Ave. NW, 20210); www.dol.gov/ofccp/
- Office of Labor-Management Standards (200 Constitution Ave. NW, 20210); www.dol.gov/olms/
- Office of Workers' Compensation Programs (200 Constitution Ave. NW, 20210); www.dol.gov/owcp/
- Wage and Hour Div. (200 Constitution Ave. NW, 20210); www.dol.gov/whd/

Secretaries of Labor

President	Secretary	Home	Sworn in
Wilson	William B. Wilson	PA	1913
Harding	James J. Davis	PA	1921
Coolidge	James J. Davis	PA	1923
Hoover	James J. Davis	PA	1929
	William N. Doak	VA	1930
Roosevelt, F. D.	Frances Perkins	NY	1933
Truman	L. B. Schwellenbach	WA	1945
	Maurice J. Tobin	MA	1949
Eisenhower	Martin P. Durkin	IL	1953
	James P. Mitchell	NJ	1953
Kennedy	Arthur J. Goldberg	IL	1961
	W. Willard Wirtz	IL	1962
Johnson, L. B.	W. Willard Wirtz	IL	1963
Nixon	George P. Shultz	IL	1969
	James D. Hodgson	CA	1970
	Peter J. Brennan	NY	1973
Ford	Peter J. Brennan	NY	1974
	John T. Dunlop	CA	1975
	W. J. Usery Jr.	GA	1976
Carter	F. Ray Marshall	TX	1977
Reagan	Raymond J. Donovan	NJ	1981
	William E. Brock	TN	1985
	Ann D. McLaughlin	DC	1987
Bush, G. H. W.	Elizabeth H. Dole	NC	1989
	Lynn Martin	IL	1991
Clinton	Robert B. Reich	MA	1993
	Alexis M. Herman	AL	1997
Bush, G. W.	Elaine L. Chao	KY	2001
Obama	Hilda L. Solis	CA	2009
	Thomas E. Perez	MD	2013
Trump	R. Alexander Acosta	FL	2017

Department of Housing and Urban Development

451 7th St. SW, 20410; www.hud.gov

Created by act of Congress on Sept. 9, 1965. Responsible for housing needs and the improvement and development of urban areas. Supports affordable housing, provides grants for community development and redevelopment. Enforces fair and safe housing standards. Provides funds to assist homeless individuals and families with emergency and transitional shelters. The Federal Housing Administration provides mortgage insurance on loans made by approved lenders. **Budget:** $35.5 bil (2015); $26.4 bil (2016); $55.5 bil (2017); $54.9 bil (est. 2018).

- Fannie Mae (Federal Natl. Mortgage Association) (3900 Wisconsin Ave. NW, 20016); www.fanniemae.com
- Federal Housing Admin. (20410); www.hud.gov/federal_housing_administration
- Freddie Mac (Federal Home Loan Mortgage Corporation) (8200 Jones Branch Dr., McLean, VA 22102); www.freddiemac.com
- Ginnie Mae (Government Natl. Mortgage Association) (451 7th St. SW, Rm. B-133, 20410); www.ginniemae.gov

Note: Fannie Mae and Freddie Mac are government-sponsored enterprises (GSEs).

Secretaries of Housing and Urban Development

President	Secretary	Home	Sworn in
Johnson, L. B.	Robert C. Weaver	WA	1966
	Robert C. Wood	MA	1969
Nixon	George W. Romney	MI	1969
	James T. Lynn	OH	1973
Ford	James T. Lynn	OH	1974
	Carla Anderson Hills	CA	1975
Carter	Patricia Roberts Harris	DC	1977
	Moon Landrieu	LA	1979
Reagan	Samuel R. Pierce Jr.	NY	1981
Bush, G. H. W.	Jack F. Kemp	NY	1989
Clinton	Henry G. Cisneros	TX	1993
	Andrew M. Cuomo	NY	1997
Bush, G. W.	Mel Martinez	FL	2001
	Alphonso Jackson	TX	2004
	Steve Preston	VA	2008
Obama	Shaun L. S. Donovan	NY	2009
	Julián Castro	TX	2014
Trump	Ben Carson	MD	2017

Department of Transportation

1200 New Jersey Ave. SE, 20590; www.transportation.gov

Created by act of Congress on Oct. 15, 1966. Promotes and develops rapid, safe, efficient, and convenient transportation in the U.S.; monitors and administers assistance to transportation industries; negotiates and implements international transportation agreements. Manages airspace, commercial space transportation, and the movement of hazardous materials. Resolves railroad rate and service disputes and reviews proposed railroad mergers. Analyzes and shares research and statistics to develop and improve transportation. Develops and enforces regulations on the nation's pipeline transportation system. The Maritime Administration maintains a fleet of cargo ships in reserve for war or national emergencies and commissions officers of the Merchant Marine. Operates the U.S. portion of the St. Lawrence Seaway between Montréal and Lake Erie. **Budget:** $75.4 bil (2015); $78.4 bil (2016); $79.4 bil (2017); $79.7 bil (est. 2018).

- Federal Aviation Admin. (800 Independence Ave. SW, 20591); www.faa.gov
- Federal Highway Admin. (1200 New Jersey Ave. SE, 20590); www.fhwa.dot.gov
- Federal Railroad Admin. (1200 New Jersey Ave. SE, 20590); www.fra.dot.gov
- Federal Transit Admin. (1200 New Jersey Ave. SE, 20590); www.transit.dot.gov
- Maritime Admin. (1200 New Jersey Ave. SE, 20590); www.marad.dot.gov
- Natl. Highway Traffic Safety Admin. (1200 New Jersey Ave. SE, 20590); www.nhtsa.gov
- Office of the Asst. Sec. for Research and Technology (1200 New Jersey Ave. SE, 20590); www.transportation.gov/administrations/research-and-technology

Secretaries of Transportation

President	Secretary	Home	Sworn in
Johnson, L. B.	Alan S. Boyd	FL	1966
Nixon	John A. Volpe	MA	1969
	Claude S. Brinegar	CA	1973
Ford	Claude S. Brinegar	CA	1974
	William T. Coleman Jr.	PA	1975
Carter	Brock Adams	WA	1977
	Neil E. Goldschmidt	OR	1979
Reagan	Andrew L. Lewis Jr.	PA	1981
	Elizabeth H. Dole	NC	1983
	James H. Burnley	NC	1987
Bush, G. H. W.	Samuel K. Skinner	IL	1989
	Andrew H. Card Jr.	MA	1992
Clinton	Federico F. Peña	CO	1993
	Rodney E. Slater	AR	1997
Bush, G. W.	Norman Y. Mineta	CA	2001
	Mary E. Peters	AZ	2006
Obama	Raymond L. LaHood	IL	2009
	Anthony Foxx	NC	2013
Trump	Elaine L. Chao	KY	2017

Department of Energy

1000 Independence Ave. SW, 20585; www.energy.gov

Created by federal law on Aug. 4, 1977. Secures the nation's energy and promotes scientific and technological innovation. Oversees the national energy supply and electric grid. Investigates and promotes clean and reliable energy. Manages and cleans up nuclear and other radioactive material, including nuclear weapons. The Office of Scientific and Technical Information supports much of America's scientific research through program offices, education initiatives, national laboratories, and technology centers. Four power marketing administrations sell power from federal hydroelectric projects across the West and Southeast. **Budget:** $25.4 bil (2015); $25.9 bil (2016); $25.8 bil (2017); $28.3 bil (est. 2018).

- Federal Energy Regulatory Commission (independent regulatory agency) (888 1st St. NE, 20426); www.ferc.gov
- Natl. Nuclear Security Admin. (1000 Independence Ave. SW, 20585); www.energy.gov/nnsa/national-nuclear-security-administration
- Office of Scientific and Technical Information (P.O. Box 62, Oak Ridge, TN 37831); www.osti.gov
- U.S. Energy Information Admin. (1000 Independence Ave. SW, 20585); www.eia.gov

Secretaries of Energy

President	Secretary	Home	Sworn in
Carter	James R. Schlesinger	VA	1977
	Charles W. Duncan Jr.	WY	1979
Reagan	James B. Edwards	SC	1981
	Donald P. Hodel	OR	1982
	John S. Herrington	CA	1985
Bush, G. H. W.	James D. Watkins	CA	1989
Clinton	Hazel R. O'Leary	MN	1993
	Federico F. Peña	CO	1997
	Bill Richardson	NM	1998
Bush, G. W.	Spencer Abraham	MI	2001
	Samuel W. Bodman	MA	2005
Obama	Steven Chu	CA	2009
	Ernest Moniz	MA	2013
Trump	Rick Perry	TX	2017

Department of Health and Human Services

200 Independence Ave. SW, 20201; www.hhs.gov

The Dept. of Health, Education, and Welfare was created by Congress on Apr. 11, 1953. On Sept. 27, 1979, Congress approved creation of a separate Dept. of Education. The existing department was renamed the Dept. of Health and Human Services. Administers a wide range of programs in the fields of health care and social services that affect nearly all Americans. Medicare and Medicaid provide health care insurance for one in four Americans. The HRSA improves health care services for people who are uninsured, isolated, or medically vulnerable; oversees organ, tissue, and blood cell donations. The FDA assures the safety of food, drugs, cosmetics, biological products, and medical devices. The CDC monitors and safeguards against disease outbreaks. The NIH supports research projects nationwide and 27 health institutes and centers. The surgeon general is the nation's chief health educator and leads the U.S. Public Health Service Commissioned Corps. **Budget:** $1.02 tril (2015); $1.10 tril (2016); $1.12 tril (2017); $1.17 tril (est. 2018).

- Agency for Healthcare Research and Quality (5600 Fishers Ln., 7th Fl., Rockville, MD 20857); www.ahrq.gov
- Centers for Disease Control and Prevention (1600 Clifton Rd., Atlanta, GA 30329); www.cdc.gov
- Centers for Medicare and Medicaid Services (7500 Security Blvd., Baltimore, MD 21244); www.cms.gov
- Health Resources and Services Admin. (5600 Fishers Ln., Rockville, MD 20857); www.hrsa.gov
- Natl. Institutes of Health (9000 Rockville Pike, Bethesda, MD 20892); www.nih.gov
- Office of the Surgeon General (200 Independence Ave. SW, 20201); www.surgeongeneral.gov
- U.S. Food and Drug Admin. (10903 New Hampshire Ave., Silver Spring, MD 20993); www.fda.gov

Secretaries of Health and Human Services

President	Secretary	Home	Sworn in
Carter	Patricia Roberts Harris	DC	1979
Reagan	Richard S. Schweiker	PA	1981
	Margaret M. Heckler	MA	1983
Reagan	Otis R. Bowen	IN	1985
Bush, G. H. W.	Louis W. Sullivan	GA	1989
Clinton	Donna E. Shalala	WI	1993
Bush, G. W.	Tommy Thompson	WI	2001
	Michael O. Leavitt	UT	2005
Obama	Kathleen Sebelius	KS	2009
	Sylvia Mathews Burwell	WV	2014
Trump	Thomas E. Price	GA	2017
	Alex Azar	IN	2018

Secretaries of Health, Education, and Welfare

President	Secretary	Home	Sworn in
Eisenhower	Oveta Culp Hobby	TX	1953
	Marion B. Folsom	NY	1955
	Arthur S. Flemming	OH	1958
Kennedy	Abraham A. Ribicoff	CT	1961
	Anthony J. Celebrezze	OH	1962
Johnson, L. B.	Anthony J. Celebrezze	OH	1963
	John W. Gardner	NY	1965
	Wilbur J. Cohen	MI	1968
Nixon	Robert H. Finch	CA	1969
	Elliot L. Richardson	MA	1970
	Caspar W. Weinberger	CA	1973
Ford	Caspar W. Weinberger	CA	1974
	Forrest D. Mathews	AL	1975
Carter	Joseph A. Califano Jr.	DC	1977
	Patricia Roberts Harris	DC	1979

Department of Education

400 Maryland Ave. SW, 20202; www.ed.gov

The Dept. of Health, Education, and Welfare was created by Congress on Apr. 11, 1953. On Sept. 27, 1979, Congress approved creation of a separate Dept. of Education. Works with state agencies and local systems to ensure equal access to all levels of education and seeks to improve the quality of that education through federal support, research programs, and information sharing. Oversees a variety of financial aid distributed through competition, need-based requests, or a set formula. Sets policy goals and initiatives like No Child Left Behind. Conducts research and gathers educational information to disseminate to educators and the general public. **Budget:** $90.0 bil (2015); $77.0 bil (2016); $111.7 bil (2017); $63.9 bil (est. 2018).

Secretaries of Education

President	Secretary	Home	Sworn in
Carter	Shirley Hufstedler	CA	1979
Reagan	Terrel H. Bell	UT	1981
	William J. Bennett	NY	1985
	Lauro F. Cavazos	TX	1988
Bush, G. H. W.	Lauro F. Cavazos	TX	1989
	Lamar Alexander	TN	1991
Clinton	Richard W. Riley	SC	1993
Bush, G. W.	Roderick R. Paige	TX	2001
	Margaret Spellings	TX	2005
Obama	Arne Duncan	IL	2009
	John King	NY	2016
Trump	Betsy DeVos	MI	2017

Department of Veterans Affairs

810 Vermont Ave. NW, 20420; www.va.gov

Pres. Ronald Reagan signed a bill in 1988 granting Cabinet-level status to the Veterans Administration. The agency became the Dept. of Veterans Affairs on Mar. 15, 1989. Supports veterans and their families with nationwide programs for health care, financial assistance, and burial benefits. Compensates for disabilities incurred during wartime. Provides pensions for veterans with low incomes, education assistance, loan guaranty, and life insurance. Manages America's largest medical education and health professions training program, which includes hospitals, clinics, nursing homes, veterans centers, rehabilitation treatment, readjustment counseling, and home-care programs. Also funds medical research pertaining to veterans issues. Manages 135 national cemeteries; provides headstones and markers. **Budget:** $159.2 bil (2015); $174.0 bil (2016); $176.1 bil (2017); $176.8 bil (est. 2018).

Secretaries of Veterans Affairs

President	Secretary	Home	Sworn in
Bush, G. H. W.	Edward J. Derwinski	IL	1989
Clinton	Jesse Brown	IL	1993
	Togo D. West Jr.	NC	1998
Bush, G. W.	Anthony J. Principi	CA	2001
	R. James Nicholson	CO	2005
	James B. Peake	MO	2007
Obama	Eric K. Shinseki	VA	2009
	Robert A. McDonald	OH	2014
Trump	David J. Shulkin	PA	2017
	Robert Wilkie	NC	2018

Department of Homeland Security

20528 (requires no street address); www.dhs.gov

Created by act of Congress on Nov. 25, 2002. Provides a unified core for the national network of organizations and institutions involved in efforts to secure the U.S., its borders, infrastructure, and major events. Provides funding, intelligence, and training for law enforcement and disaster relief. Leads and coordinates response teams to natural and manmade emergencies. Identifies threats, administers the Natl. Terrorism Advisory

System. **Budget:** $42.6 bil (2015); $45.2 bil (2016); $50.5 bil (2017); $84.2 bil (est. 2018).

- Fed. Emergency Management Agency (500 C St. SW, 20472); www.fema.gov
- Transportation Security Admin. (601 S. 12th St., Arlington, VA 20598); www.tsa.gov
- U.S. Citizenship and Immigration Services (111 Massachusetts Ave. NW, MS 2260, 20529); www.uscis.gov
- U.S. Coast Guard (2703 Martin Luther King Jr. Ave. SE, 20593); www.uscg.mil
- U.S. Customs and Border Protection (1300 Pennsylvania Ave. NW, 20229); www.cbp.gov
- U.S. Fire Admin. (16825 S. Seton Ave., Emmitsburg, MD 21727); www.usfa.fema.gov
- U.S. Immigration and Customs Enforcement (500 12th St. SW, 20536); www.ice.gov
- U.S. Secret Service (245 Murray Ln., 20223); www.secretservice.gov

Secretaries of Homeland Security

President	Secretary	Home	Sworn in
Bush, G. W.	Thomas Ridge	PA	2003
	Michael Chertoff	NJ	2005
Obama	Janet A. Napolitano	AZ	2009
	Jeh Johnson	NY	2014
Trump	John F. Kelly	MA	2017
	Kirstjen M. Nielsen	FL	2017

Other Notable U.S. Government Agencies

Source: *The U.S. Government Manual*; National Archives and Records Administration; World Almanac research
All addresses are for Washington, DC, unless otherwise noted; as of Sept. 2018.

Administrative Conference of the U.S.: Matthew L. Wienerk, acting chair (1120 20th St. NW, Ste. 706S, 20036); www.acus.gov

African Development Foundation: C. D. Glin, pres. and CEO (1400 I St. NW, 20005); www.usadf.gov

AMTRAK: Richard H. Anderson, pres. and CEO (60 Massachusetts Ave. NE, 20002); www.amtrak.com

Broadcasting Board of Governors: Kenneth Weinstein, chair (330 Independence Ave. SW, 20237); www.bbg.gov

Central Intelligence Agency: Gina Haspel, dir. (20505); www.cia.gov

Commodity Futures Trading Commission: J. Christopher Giancarlo, chair (3 Lafayette Centre, 1155 21st St. NW, 20581); www.cftc.gov

Consumer Financial Protection Bureau: Mick Mulvaney, acting dir. (P.O. Box 2900, Clinton, IA 52733); www.consumerfinance.gov

Consumer Product Safety Commission: Ann Marie Buerkle, acting chair (4330 East-West Hwy., Bethesda, MD 20814); www.cpsc.gov

Corp. for Natl. and Community Service: Barbara Stewart, CEO (250 E St. SW, 20525); www.nationalservice.gov

Defense Nuclear Facilities Safety Board: Bruce Hamilton, acting chair (625 Indiana Ave. NW, Ste. 700, 20004); www.dnfsb.gov

Election Assistance Commission: Thomas Hicks, chair (1335 East-West Hwy., Ste. 4300, Silver Spring, MD 20910); www.eac.gov

Environmental Protection Agency: Andrew Wheeler, acting admin. (Cabinet rank) (1200 Pennsylvania Ave. NW, 20460); www.epa.gov

Equal Employment Opportunity Commission: Victoria A. Lipnic, acting chair (131 M St. NE, 20507); www.eeoc.gov

Export-Import Bank of the U.S.: Jeffrey Gerrish, pres. and chair (811 Vermont Ave. NW, 20571); www.exim.gov

Farm Credit Admin.: Dallas P. Tonsager, chair and CEO (1501 Farm Credit Dr., McLean, VA 22102); www.fca.gov

Federal Communications Commission: Ajit Pai, chair (445 12th St. SW, 20554); www.fcc.gov

Federal Deposit Insurance Corp.: Jelena McWilliams, chair (550 17th St. NW, 20429); www.fdic.gov

Federal Election Commission: Caroline C. Hunter, chair (999 E St. NW, 20463); www.fec.gov

Federal Housing Finance Agency: Melvin L. Watt, dir. (400 7th St. SW, 20219); www.fhfa.gov

Federal Labor Relations Authority: Colleen Duffy Kiko, chair (1400 K St. NW, 20424); www.flra.gov

Federal Maritime Commission: Michael A. Khouri, acting chair (800 N. Capitol St. NW, 20573); www.fmc.gov

Federal Mediation and Conciliation Service: Richard Giacolone, acting dir. (250 E St. SW, 20427); www.fmcs.gov

Federal Mine Safety and Health Review Commission: Michael G. Young, acting chair (1331 Pennsylvania Ave. NW, Ste. 520N, 20004); www.fmshrc.gov

Federal Reserve System: Jerome H. Powell, chair (20th St. and Constitution Ave. NW, 20551); www.federalreserve.gov

Federal Retirement Thrift Investment Board: Michael Kennedy, chair (77 K St. NE, Ste. 1000, 20002); www.frtib.gov

Federal Trade Commission: Joseph J. Simons, chair (600 Pennsylvania Ave. NW, 20580); www.ftc.gov

General Services Admin.: Emily W. Murphy, admin. (1800 F St. NW, 20405); www.gsa.gov

Institute of Museum and Library Services: Kathryn K. Matthew, dir. (955 L'Enfant Plaza North SW, Ste. 4000, 20024); www.imls.gov

Inter-American Foundation: Paloma Adams-Allen, pres. and CEO (1331 Pennsylvania Ave. NW, Ste. 1200N, 20004); www.iaf.gov

Merit Systems Protection Board: Mark A. Robbins, vice chair (1615 M St. NW, 20419); www.mspb.gov

Natl. Aeronautics and Space Admin.: Jim Bridenstine, admin. (300 E St. SW, Ste. 5R30, 20546); www.nasa.gov

Natl. Archives and Records Admin.: David S. Ferriero, archivist (8601 Adelphi Rd., College Park, MD 20740); www.archives.gov

Natl. Capital Planning Commission: L. Preston Bryant Jr., chair (401 9th St. NW, Ste. 500N, 20004); www.ncpc.gov

Natl. Council on Disability: Neil Romano, chair (1331 F St. NW, Ste. 850, 20004); www.ncd.gov

Natl. Credit Union Admin.: J. Mark McWatters, chair (1775 Duke St., Alexandria, VA 22314); www.ncua.gov

Natl. Endowment for the Arts: Mary Anne Carter, acting chair (400 7th St. SW, 20506); www.arts.gov

Natl. Endowment for the Humanities: Jon Parrish Peede, chair (400 7th St. SW, 20506); www.neh.gov

Natl. Indian Gaming Commission: Jonodev Osceola Chaudhuri, chair (1849 C St. NW, Mail Stop 1621, 20240); www.nigc.gov

Natl. Labor Relations Board: John F. Ring, chair (1015 Half St. SE, 20570); www.nlrb.gov

Natl. Mediation Board: Gerald W. Fauth III, chair (1301 K St. NW, Ste. 250E, 20005); www.nmb.gov

Natl. Science Foundation: France A. Córdova, dir. (2415 Eisenhower Ave., Arlington, VA 22314); www.nsf.gov

Natl. Transportation Safety Board: Robert L. Sumwalt, chair (490 L'Enfant Plaza SW, 20594); www.ntsb.gov

Nuclear Regulatory Commission: Kristine L. Svinicki, chair (20555); www.nrc.gov

Nuclear Waste Technical Review Board: Jean M. Bahr, chair (2300 Clarendon Blvd., Ste. 1300, Arlington, VA 22201); www.nwtrb.gov

Occupational Safety and Health Review Commission: Heather L. MacDougall, chair (1120 20th St. NW, 9th Fl., 20036); www.oshrc.gov

Office of the Dir. of Natl. Intelligence: Daniel Coats, dir. (20511); www.dni.gov

Office of Government Ethics: Emory A. Rounds III, dir. (1201 New York Ave. NW, Ste. 500, 20005); www.oge.gov

Office of Personnel Management: Jeff T.H. Pon, dir. (1900 E St. NW, 20415); www.opm.gov

Office of Special Counsel: Henry Kerner, spec. counsel (1730 M St. NW, Ste. 218, 20036); osc.gov

Overseas Private Investment Corp.: Ray W. Washburne, pres. and CEO (1100 New York Ave. NW, 20527); www.opic.gov

Peace Corps: Josephine Olsen, dir. (1111 20th St. NW, 20526); www.peacecorps.gov

Pension Benefit Guaranty Corp.: W. Thomas Reeder Jr., dir. (1200 K St. NW, 20005); www.pbgc.gov

Postal Regulatory Commission: Robert G. Taub, chair (901 New York Ave. NW, Ste. 200, 20268); www.prc.gov

Railroad Retirement Board: chair vacant (844 N. Rush St., Chicago, IL 60611); www.rrb.gov

Securities and Exchange Commission: Jay Clayton, chair (100 F St. NE, 20549); www.sec.gov

Selective Service System: Donald M. Benton, dir. (Natl. Headquarters, Arlington, VA 22209); www.sss.gov

Small Business Admin.: Linda McMahon, admin. (Cabinet rank) (409 3rd St. SW, 20416); www.sba.gov

Social Security Admin.: Nancy A. Berryhill, acting comm. (1100 West High Rise, 6401 Security Blvd., Baltimore, MD 21235); www.ssa.gov

Tennessee Valley Authority: Bill Johnson, CEO and pres. (400 W. Summit Hill Dr., Knoxville, TN 37902); www.tva.gov

U.S. Agency for Intl. Development: Mark Green, admin. (Ronald Reagan Bldg., 20523); www.usaid.gov

U.S. Commission on Civil Rights: Catherine E. Lhamon, chair (1331 Pennsylvania Ave. NW, Ste. 1150, 20425); www.usccr.gov

U.S. Intl. Trade Commission: David S. Johanson, chair (500 E St. SW, 20436); www.usitc.gov

U.S. Postal Service: Megan J. Brennan, postmaster general and CEO (475 L'Enfant Plaza SW, 20260); www.usps.com

U.S. Trade and Development Agency: dir. vacant (1101 Wilson Blvd., Ste. 1100, Arlington, VA 22209); www.ustda.gov

CONGRESS

Floor Leaders in the U.S. Senate, 1920-2018

MAJORITY LEADERS				MINORITY LEADERS			
Name	Party	State	Tenure	Name	Party	State	Tenure
Charles Curtis[1]	Rep.	KS	1925-1929	Oscar W. Underwood[2]	Dem.	AL	1920-1923
James E. Watson	Rep.	IN	1929-1933	Joseph T. Robinson	Dem.	AR	1923-1933
Joseph T. Robinson	Dem.	AR	1933-1937	Charles L. McNary	Rep.	OR	1933-1944
Alben W. Barkley	Dem.	KY	1937-1947	Wallace H. White	Rep.	ME	1944-1947
Wallace H. White	Rep.	ME	1947-1949	Alben W. Barkley	Dem.	KY	1947-1949
Scott W. Lucas	Dem.	IL	1949-1951	Kenneth S. Wherry	Rep.	NE	1949-1951
Ernest W. McFarland	Dem.	AZ	1951-1953	Henry Styles Bridges	Rep.	NH	1952-1953
Robert A. Taft	Rep.	OH	1953	Lyndon B. Johnson	Dem.	TX	1953-1955
William F. Knowland	Rep.	CA	1953-1955	William F. Knowland	Rep.	CA	1955-1959
Lyndon B. Johnson	Dem.	TX	1955-1961	Everett M. Dirksen	Rep.	IL	1959-1969
Mike Mansfield	Dem.	MT	1961-1977	Hugh D. Scott	Rep.	PA	1969-1977
Robert C. Byrd	Dem.	WV	1977-1981	Howard H. Baker Jr.	Rep.	TN	1977-1981
Howard H. Baker Jr.	Rep.	TN	1981-1985	Robert C. Byrd	Dem.	WV	1981-1987
Robert J. Dole	Rep.	KS	1985-1987	Robert J. Dole	Rep.	KS	1987-1995
Robert C. Byrd	Dem.	WV	1987-1989	Thomas A. Daschle	Dem.	SD	1995-2001[3]
George J. Mitchell	Dem.	ME	1989-1995	Trent Lott	Rep.	MS	2001-2002[3,4]
Robert J. Dole	Rep.	KS	1995-1996	Thomas A. Daschle	Dem.	SD	2003-2005
Trent Lott	Rep.	MS	1996-2001[3]	Harry M. Reid	Dem.	NV	2005-2007
Thomas A. Daschle	Dem.	SD	2001-2003[3]	Mitch McConnell	Rep.	KY	2007-2015
William Frist	Rep.	TN	2003-2007[4]	Harry M. Reid	Dem.	NV	2015-2017
Harry M. Reid	Dem.	NV	2007-2015	Charles E. Schumer	Dem.	NY	2017-
Mitch McConnell	Rep.	KY	2015-				

Note: The offices of party (majority and minority) leaders in the Senate did not evolve until the 20th century. (1) First Republican to be formally designated floor leader. Henry Cabot Lodge (MA) served as unofficial party leader prior to Curtis's election. (2) First Democrat to be designated floor leader. (3) Democrats held the majority Jan. 3, 2001, until Dick Cheney (R) was installed as vice pres., Jan. 20. Republicans subsequently lost the majority when Jim Jeffords (VT) switched his affiliation from Republican to Independent, June 6, 2001. (4) Trent Lott resigned from Republican leadership Dec. 20, 2002. William Frist was elected Republican leader Dec. 23, 2002, and began service Jan. 7, 2003, as majority leader.

Speakers of the U.S. House of Representatives, 1789-2018

Name	Party	State	Tenure	Name	Party	State	Tenure
Frederick A. C. Muhlenberg	Federalist	PA	1789-1791	Michael C. Kerr	Dem.	IN	1875-1876
Jonathan Trumbull	Federalist	CT	1791-1793	Samuel J. Randall	Dem.	PA	1876-1881
Frederick A. C. Muhlenberg	Federalist	PA	1793-1795	J. Warren Keifer	Rep.	OH	1881-1883
Jonathan Dayton	Federalist	NJ	1795-1799	John G. Carlisle	Dem.	KY	1883-1889
Theodore Sedgwick	Federalist	MA	1799-1801	Thomas B. Reed	Rep.	ME	1889-1891
Nathaniel Macon	Dem.-Rep.	NC	1801-1807	Charles F. Crisp	Dem.	GA	1891-1895
Joseph B. Varnum	Dem.-Rep.	MA	1807-1811	Thomas B. Reed	Rep.	ME	1895-1899
Henry Clay	Dem.-Rep.	KY	1811-1814	David B. Henderson	Rep.	IA	1899-1903
Langdon Cheves	Dem.-Rep.	SC	1814-1815	Joseph G. Cannon	Rep.	IL	1903-1911
Henry Clay	Dem.-Rep.	KY	1815-1820	Champ Clark	Dem.	MO	1911-1919
John W. Taylor	Dem.-Rep.	NY	1820-1821	Frederick H. Gillett	Rep.	MA	1919-1925
Philip P. Barbour	Dem.-Rep.	VA	1821-1823	Nicholas Longworth	Rep.	OH	1925-1931
Henry Clay	Dem.-Rep.	KY	1823-1825	John N. Garner	Dem.	TX	1931-1933
John W. Taylor	Dem.	NY	1825-1827	Henry T. Rainey	Dem.	IL	1933-1934
Andrew Stevenson	Dem.	VA	1827-1834	Joseph W. Byrns	Dem.	TN	1935-1936
John Bell	Dem.	TN	1834-1835	William B. Bankhead	Dem.	AL	1936-1940
James K. Polk	Dem.	TN	1835-1839	Sam Rayburn	Dem.	TX	1940-1947
Robert M. T. Hunter	Dem.	VA	1839-1841	Joseph W. Martin Jr.	Rep.	MA	1947-1949
John White	Whig	KY	1841-1843	Sam Rayburn	Dem.	TX	1949-1953
John W. Jones	Dem.	VA	1843-1845	Joseph W. Martin Jr.	Rep.	MA	1953-1955
John W. Davis	Dem.	IN	1845-1847	Sam Rayburn	Dem.	TX	1955-1961
Robert C. Winthrop	Whig	MA	1847-1849	John W. McCormack	Dem.	MA	1962-1971
Howell Cobb	Dem.	GA	1849-1851	Carl B. Albert	Dem.	OK	1971-1977
Linn Boyd	Dem.	KY	1851-1855	Thomas P. O'Neill Jr.	Dem.	MA	1977-1987
Nathaniel P. Banks	American	MA	1856-1857	James C. Wright Jr.	Dem.	TX	1987-1989
James L. Orr	Dem.	SC	1857-1859	Thomas S. Foley	Dem.	WA	1989-1995
William Pennington	Rep.	NJ	1860-1861	Newt Gingrich	Rep.	GA	1995-1999
Galusha A. Grow	Rep.	PA	1861-1863	J. Dennis Hastert	Rep.	IL	1999-2007
Schuyler Colfax	Rep.	IN	1863-1869	Nancy Pelosi	Dem.	CA	2007-2011
Theodore M. Pomeroy	Rep.	NY	1869	John Boehner	Rep.	OH	2011-2015
James G. Blaine	Rep.	ME	1869-1875	Paul Ryan	Rep.	WI	2015-

Political Divisions of Congress, 1901-2018

Source: Office of the Clerk, U.S. House of Representatives; Congressional Research Service, Library of Congress

All figures reflect post-election party breakdown except where noted; **boldface** denotes party in majority immediately after election.

		SENATE					HOUSE OF REPRESENTATIVES				
Congress	Years	Total members	Dem.	Rep.	Other parties	Vacant	Total members	Dem.	Rep.	Other parties	Vacant
57th	1901-1903	90	29	**56**	3	2	357	153	**198**	5	1
58th	1903-1905	90	32	**58**			386	178	**207**		1
59th	1905-1907	90	32	**58**			386	136	**250**		
60th	1907-1909	92	29	**61**		2	386	164	**222**		
61st	1909-1911	92	32	**59**		1	391	172	**219**		
62nd	1911-1913	92	42	**49**		1	391	**228**	162	1	
63rd	1913-1915	96	**51**	44	1		435	**290**	127	18	
64th	1915-1917	96	**56**	39	1		435	**231**	193	8	3
65th	1917-1919	96	**53**	42	1		435	210[1]	216	9	
66th	1919-1921	96	47	**48**	1		435	191	**237**	7	
67th	1921-1923	96	37	**59**			435	132	**300**	1	2
68th	1923-1925	96	43	**51**	2		435	207	**225**	3	

		SENATE					HOUSE OF REPRESENTATIVES				
Congress	Years	Total members	Dem.	Rep.	Other parties	Vacant	Total members	Dem.	Rep.	Other parties	Vacant
69th	1925-1927	96	40	**54**	1	1	435	183	**247**	5	
70th	1927-1929	96	47	**48**	1		435	195	**237**	3	
71st	1929-1931	96	39	**56**	1		435	163	**267**	1	4
72nd	1931-1933	96	47	**48**	1		435	216[2]	**218**	1	
73rd	1933-1935	96	**59**	36	1		435	**313**	117	5	
74th	1935-1937	96	**69**	25	2		435	**322**	103	10	
75th	1937-1939	96	**75**	17	4		435	**333**	89	13	
76th	1939-1941	96	**69**	23	4		435	**262**	169	4	
77th	1941-1943	96	**66**	28	2		435	**267**	162	6	
78th	1943-1945	96	**57**	38	1		435	**222**	209	4	
79th	1945-1947	96	**57**	38	1		435	**243**	190	2	
80th	1947-1949	96	45	**51**			435	188	**246**	1	
81st	1949-1951	96	**54**	42			435	**263**	171	1	
82nd	1951-1953	96	**48**	47	1		435	**234**	199	2	
83rd	1953-1955	96	46	**48**	2		435	213	**221**	1	
84th	1955-1957	96	**48**	47	1		435	**232**	203		
85th	1957-1959	96	**49**	47			435	**234**	201		
86th	1959-1961	98	**64**	34			436[3]	**283**	153		
87th	1961-1963	100	**64**	36			437[3]	**262**	175		
88th	1963-1965	100	**67**	33			435	**258**	176		1
89th	1965-1967	100	**68**	32			435	**295**	140		
90th	1967-1969	100	**64**	36			435	**248**	187		
91st	1969-1971	100	**58**	42			435	**243**	192		
92nd	1971-1973	100	**54**	44	2		435	**255**	180		
93rd	1973-1975	100	**56**	42	2		435	**242**	192	1	
94th	1975-1977	100	**61**	37	2		435	**291**	144		
95th	1977-1979	100	**61**	38	1		435	**292**	143		
96th	1979-1981	100	**58**	41	1		435	**277**	158		
97th	1981-1983	100	46	**53**	1		435	**242**	192	1	
98th	1983-1985	100	46	**54**			435	**269**	166		
99th	1985-1987	100	47	**53**			435	**253**	182		
100th	1987-1989	100	**55**	45			435	**258**	177		
101st	1989-1991	100	**55**	45			435	**260**	175		
102nd	1991-1993	100	**56**	44			435	**267**	167	1	
103rd	1993-1995	100	**57**	43			435	**258**	176	1	
104th	1995-1997	100	48	**52**			435	204	**230**	1	
105th	1997-1999	100	45	**55**			435	207	**226**	2	
106th	1999-2001	100	45	**55**			435	211	**223**	1	
107th	2001-2003	100	50	**50**[4]			435	212	**221**	2	
108th	2003-2005	100	48	**51**	1		435	204	**229**	1	1
109th	2005-2007	100	44	**55**	1		435	202	**232**	1	
110th	2007-2009	100	49	49	2[5]		435	**233**	202		
111th	2009-2011	100	**55**	41	2[5]	2	435	**256**	178		1
112th	2011-2013	100	**51**	47	2[5]		435	193	**242**		
113th	2013-2015	100	**53**	45	2[5]		435	200	**234**		1
114th	2015-2017	100	44	**54**	2[5]		435	188	**247**		
115th	2017-	100	46	**52**	2[5]		435	194	**241**		

(1) Democrats organized the House with help of other parties. (2) Democrats organized the House because of Republican deaths. (3) Number of House seats was increased temporarily when proclamations were issued declaring Alaska (Jan. 3, 1959) and Hawaii (Aug. 21, 1959) new states. (4) While the Senate was split 50-50, control was held by whichever party had an incumbent vice president. Republican Sen. Jim Jeffords (VT) changed his party designation to Independent on June 6, 2001, switching control of the Senate to Democrats. (5) Both Independent senators chose to caucus with the Democrats.

Congressional Bills Vetoed, 1789-2018

Source: Virtual Reference Desk, U.S. Senate; as of Sept. 1, 2018

The president has 10 days (excluding Sundays) to consider a bill or joint resolution passed by Congress. The president can sign it into law or exercise a veto. Only a two-thirds vote in both the Senate and the House can override a regular veto. (A pocket veto cannot be overridden as it takes effect when Congress is adjourned.)

President	Regular vetoes	Pocket vetoes	Total vetoes	Vetoes overridden	President	Regular vetoes	Pocket vetoes	Total vetoes	Vetoes overridden
Washington	2	—	2	—	Cleveland[2]	42	128	170	5
J. Adams	—	—	—	—	McKinley	6	36	42	—
Jefferson	—	—	—	—	T. Roosevelt	42	40	82	1
Madison	5	2	7	—	Taft	30	9	39	1
Monroe	1	—	1	—	Wilson	33	11	44	6
J. Q. Adams	—	—	—	—	Harding	5	1	6	—
Jackson	5	7	12	—	Coolidge	20	30	50	4
Van Buren	—	1	1	—	Hoover	21	16	37	3
W. H. Harrison	—	—	—	—	F. D. Roosevelt	372	263	635	9
Tyler	6	4	10	1	Truman	180	70	250	12
Polk	2	1	3	—	Eisenhower	73	108	181	2
Taylor	—	—	—	—	Kennedy	12	9	21	—
Fillmore	—	—	—	—	L. Johnson	16	14	30	—
Pierce	9	—	9	5	Nixon	26	17	43	7
Buchanan	4	3	7	—	Ford	48	18	66	11
Lincoln	2	5	7	—	Carter	13	18	31	2
A. Johnson	21	8	29	15	Reagan	39	39	78	9
Grant	45	48	93	4	G. H. W. Bush[3]	29	15	44	1
Hayes	12	1	13	1	Clinton[4]	36	1	37	2
Garfield	—	—	—	—	G. W. Bush	12	—	12	4
Arthur	4	8	12	1	Obama	12	—	12	1
Cleveland[1]	304	110	414	2	Trump				
B. Harrison	19	25	44	1	**Total**[3,4]	**1,508**	**1,066**	**2,574**	**111**

— = 0. (1) First term only. (2) Second term only. (3) Excluded from the figures are two bills that Pres. George H. W. Bush claimed were pocket vetoed but which Congress considered to be enacted because the president had failed to return them during a Congressional recess. (4) Does not include line-item vetoes, which were ruled unconstitutional by the U.S. Supreme Court on June 25, 1998.

Congressional Firsts and Milestones

Cities where Congress has convened: New York City (1789-90); Philadelphia (1790-1800); Washington, DC (1800-).

First meeting of Congress in the Capitol Building: Nov. 17, 1800.

First Congressional override of a presidential veto: Pres. John Tyler's veto of an appropriation bill, Mar. 3, 1845.

House of Representatives

First House meeting: Mar. 4, 1789, at Federal Hall in New York, NY. A quorum of 30 representatives was not reached until Apr. 1, 1789.

First House meeting in its current Capitol Building chamber: Dec. 16, 1857.

First former president to serve as representative: John Quincy Adams (MA, 1831-48); president, 1825-29.

First woman representative: Jeannette Rankin (R, MT, 1917-19, 1941-43).

First woman House speaker: Nancy Pelosi (D, CA), on Jan. 4, 2007.

First black representative: Joseph Rainey (R, SC, 1870-79).

First black woman representative: Shirley Chisholm (D, NY, 1969-83).

First elected Hispanic-American representative: Romualdo Pacheco (R, CA, 1877-83); Pacheco was born in California when it was Mexican territory.

First Asian-Pacific American representative: India-born Dalip Saund (D, CA, 1957-63).

First representative to give birth in office: Yvonne Brathwaite Burke (D, CA, 1973-79), on Nov. 23, 1973.

Longest-serving representative: John Dingell Jr. (D, MI, 1955-2015), with more than 59 years of service.

Longest-serving House speaker: Sam Rayburn (D, TX, 1913-61) served as House speaker for 17 years, 2 months, and 2 days (non-consecutive).

Longest consecutive service by a single family: A member of the Dingell family has represented one of Michigan's districts since 1933: John Dingell (D, 1933-55), John Dingell Jr. (D, 1955-2015), and Debbie Dingell (D, 2015-).

Oldest representative: Ralph Hall (D-R, TX, 1981-2015); retired at age 91.

Oldest-known freshman representative: James B. Bowler (D, IL), who won a special election July 7, 1953, aged 78.

Youngest representative: William Charles Cole Claiborne (TN), who was elected at 22 years of age and began service Nov. 23, 1797. The House chose to seat him then and two years later when he was reelected despite the Constitutional requirement that U.S. representatives be at least 25 years of age.

First live-TV broadcast of House proceedings: Mar. 19, 1979, by public television and C-SPAN. Al Gore Jr. (D, TN) was the first representative to give a speech before cameras that day.

First declaration of war made by the House: June 4, 1812, against Great Britain and Ireland.

Senate

First Senate meeting: Mar. 4, 1789, at Federal Hall in New York, NY. A quorum of senators (12) was not reached until Apr. 6, 1789.

First Senate meeting in its current chamber in the Capitol Building: Jan. 4, 1859.

First woman senator: Rebecca Felton (D, GA, 1922). Appointed to a seat left vacant by a death, 87-year-old Felton served only 24 hours after being sworn in Nov. 21. (Felton was also the oldest freshman senator and the last senator to have been a slave owner.)

First elected woman senator: Hattie Caraway (D, AR, 1931-45). Appointed in 1931 to fill the vacancy left by the death of her husband, Thaddeus H. Caraway, she was elected in 1932.

First black senator: Hiram R. Revels (R, MS, 1870-71).

First black woman senator: Carol Moseley-Braun (D, IL, 1993-99).

First American Indian senators: Charles Curtis (Kaw) (R, KS, 1907-13, 1915-29) and Robert Owen (Cherokee) (D, OK, 1907-25).

First Hispanic-American senator: Mexico-born Octaviano Larrazolo (R, NM, 1928-29).

First Asian-American senator: Hiram L. Fong (R, HI, 1959-77).

First Jewish senator: David Levy Yulee (D, FL, 1845-51, 1855-61).

First senator to give birth in office: Tammy Duckworth (D, IL, 2017-), on Apr. 9, 2018.

Longest-serving senator: Robert C. Byrd (D, WV, 1959-2010) died while in office, having served 51 years, 5 months, and 26 days.

Oldest senator: Strom Thurmond (R, SC), who turned 100 years of age on Dec. 5, 2002, one month before he retired from office.

Youngest senator: John H. Eaton (TN), who was 28 years, 5 months old when he was sworn in Nov. 16, 1818, despite the Constitutional requirement that U.S. senators be at least 30 years old.

Longest speech by a senator (since 1900): 24 hours, 18 minutes, by Strom Thurmond (D, SC) in his filibuster against the 1957 Civil Rights Act, Aug. 28-29, 1957.

First Senate impeachment trial of a president: Pres. Andrew Johnson, on Mar. 5, 1868; he was acquitted by a one-vote margin.

Number of Senate impeachment trials: 19, resulting in 7 acquittals, 8 convictions, 3 dismissals, and 1 resignation with no further action.

First regular live-TV broadcast from the Senate chamber: June 2, 1986, by the C-SPAN network.

Number of senators who have received the Nobel Peace Prize: 5 (Elihu Root, Frank Kellogg, Cordell Hull, Al Gore, Barack Obama). Root is the only one of the five to receive the award while serving as senator.

Number of senators who have changed party affiliation during their Senate service (since 1890): 21.

Congressional Activity, 1947-2018

Source: *Congressional Record*, U.S. Govt. Publishing Office; Library of Congress

Congress in recent years has been widely perceived as being less productive than in previous sessions. The data below shows the number of public laws and measures passed in every session of Congress since 1947.

Congress (years)	Public laws passed	Measures passed	Congress (years)	Public laws passed	Measures passed
80th (1947-48)	906	4,132	98th (1983-84)	623	2,670
81st (1949-50)	921	5,764	99th (1985-86)	664	2,698
82nd (1951-52)	594	4,593	100th (1987-88)	713	2,932
83rd (1953-54)	781	5,201	101st (1989-90)	650	2,691
84th (1955-56)	1,028	5,713	102nd (1991-92)	590	2,615
85th (1957-58)	936	5,126	103rd (1993-94)	465	2,054
86th (1959-60)	800	4,165	104th (1995-96)	333	1,834
87th (1961-62)	885	4,769	105th (1997-98)	394	2,077
88th (1963-64)	666	3,425	106th (1999-2000)	580	2,779
89th (1965-66)	810	4,116	107th (2001-02)	377	2,163
90th (1967-68)	640	3,390	108th (2003-04)	498	2,674
91st (1969-70)	695	3,318	109th (2005-06)	482	2,684
92nd (1971-72)	607	2,840	110th (2007-08)	460	3,336
93rd (1973-74)	649	3,088	111th (2009-10)	383	2,939
94th (1975-76)	588	3,176	112th (2011-12)	283	1,744
95th (1977-78)	633	3,211	113th (2013-14)	296	1,788
96th (1979-80)	613	2,960	114th (2015-16)	329	2,110
97th (1981-82)	473	2,267	115th (2017-18)	236*	1,937*

* = As of Aug. 31, 2018. Incomplete congressional session; should not be compared to earlier years. **Note:** Public laws are bills or joint resolutions that have been enacted. Measures passed refers to bills, joint resolutions, concurrent resolutions, or simple resolutions approved by the House or Senate.

U.S. SUPREME COURT

Justices of the U.S. Supreme Court

The Supreme Court comprises the chief justice of the U.S. and eight associate justices, all appointed for life by the president with advice and consent of the U.S. Senate. Names of chief justices are in **boldface**. Terms of service begin with the year each justice took the judicial oath. Service years are the number of complete years served by a justice. 2018 salaries: chief justice, $267,000; associate justice, $255,300. The U.S. Supreme Court Building is at 1 First St. NE, Washington, DC 20543.

Website: www.supremecourt.gov

Name, appointed from	Service Term	Yrs.	Born	Died	Name, appointed from	Service Term	Yrs.	Born	Died
John Jay, NY	1789-1795	5	1745	1829	William H. Moody, MA	1906-1910	3	1853	1917
John Rutledge, SC[1]	1790-1791	1	1739	1800	Horace H. Lurton, TN	1910-1914	4	1844	1914
William Cushing, MA.	1790-1810*	20	1732	1810	Charles E. Hughes, NY[1]	1910-1916	5	1862	1948
James Wilson, PA.	1789-1798	8	1742	1798	Willis Van Devanter, WY	1911-1937	26	1859	1941
John Blair, VA	1790-1795*	5	1732	1800	Joseph R. Lamar, GA	1911-1916	5	1857	1916
James Iredell, NC	1790-1799	9	1751	1799	**Edward D. White**, LA[2]	1910-1921	10	1845	1921
Thomas Johnson, MD	1792-1793	<1	1732	1819	Mahlon Pitney, NJ.	1912-1922	10	1858	1924
William Paterson, NJ.	1793-1806	13	1745	1806	James C. McReynolds, TN	1914-1941	26	1862	1946
John Rutledge, SC[2,3]	1795	<1	1739	1800	Louis D. Brandeis, MA	1916-1939	22	1856	1941
Samuel Chase, MD.	1796-1811	15	1741	1811	John H. Clarke, OH.	1916-1922	5	1857	1945
Oliver Ellsworth, CT	1796-1800	4	1745	1807	**William H. Taft**, CT	1921-1930	8	1857	1930
Bushrod Washington, VA	1799-1829*	30	1762	1829	George Sutherland, UT	1922-1938	15	1862	1942
Alfred Moore, NC	1800-1804	3	1755	1810	Pierce Butler, MN	1923-1939	16	1866	1939
John Marshall, VA.	1801-1835	34	1755	1835	Edward T. Sanford, TN.	1923-1930	7	1865	1930
William Johnson, SC	1804-1834	30	1771	1834	Harlan F. Stone, NY[1]	1925-1941	16	1872	1946
Henry B. Livingston, NY	1807-1823	16	1757	1823	**Charles E. Hughes**, NY[2]	1930-1941	11	1862	1948
Thomas Todd, KY	1807-1826	18	1765	1826	Owen J. Roberts, PA	1930-1945	15	1875	1955
Gabriel Duvall, MD	1811-1835	23	1752	1844	Benjamin N. Cardozo, NY.	1932-1938	6	1870	1938
Joseph Story, MA	1812-1845*	33	1779	1845	Hugo L. Black, AL	1937-1971	34	1886	1971
Smith Thompson, NY	1823-1843	20	1768	1843	Stanley F. Reed, KY.	1938-1957	19	1884	1980
Robert Trimble, KY	1826-1828	2	1777	1828	Felix Frankfurter, MA	1939-1962	23	1882	1965
John McLean, OH.	1830-1861*	31	1785	1861	William O. Douglas, CT.	1939-1975	36[4]	1898	1980
Henry Baldwin, PA	1830-1844	14	1780	1844	Frank Murphy, MI	1940-1949	9	1890	1949
James M. Wayne, GA	1835-1867	32	1790	1867	**Harlan F. Stone**, NY[2]	1941-1946	4	1872	1946
Roger B. Taney, MD	1836-1864	28	1777	1864	James F. Byrnes, SC	1941-1942	1	1879	1972
Philip P. Barbour, VA	1836-1841	4	1783	1841	Robert H. Jackson, NY	1941-1954	13	1892	1954
John Catron, TN	1837-1865	28	1786	1865	Wiley B. Rutledge, IA	1943-1949	6	1894	1949
John McKinley, AL	1838-1852*	14	1780	1852	Harold H. Burton, OH	1945-1958	13	1888	1964
Peter V. Daniel, VA	1842-1860*	18	1784	1860	**Fred M. Vinson**, KY	1946-1953	7	1890	1953
Samuel Nelson, NY	1845-1872	27	1792	1873	Tom C. Clark, TX.	1949-1967	17	1899	1977
Levi Woodbury, NH.	1845-1851	5	1789	1851	Sherman Minton, IN	1949-1956	7	1890	1965
Robert C. Grier, PA.	1846-1870	23	1794	1870	**Earl Warren**, CA.	1953-1969	15	1891	1974
Benjamin R. Curtis, MA	1851-1857	5	1809	1874	John Marshall Harlan, NY.	1955-1971	16	1899	1971
John A. Campbell, AL	1853-1861*	8	1811	1889	William J. Brennan Jr., NJ.	1956-1990	33	1906	1997
Nathan Clifford, ME	1858-1881	23	1803	1881	Charles E. Whittaker, MO	1957-1962	5	1901	1973
Noah H. Swayne, OH	1862-1881	18	1804	1884	Potter Stewart, OH	1958-1981	22	1915	1985
Samuel F. Miller, IA	1862-1890	28	1816	1890	Byron R. White, CO.	1962-1993	31	1917	2002
David Davis, IL	1862-1877	14	1815	1886	Arthur J. Goldberg, IL	1962-1965	2	1908	1990
Stephen J. Field, CA	1863-1897	33	1816	1899	Abe Fortas, TN	1965-1969	3	1910	1982
Salmon P. Chase, OH	1864-1873	8	1808	1873	Thurgood Marshall, NY.	1967-1991	24	1908	1993
William Strong, PA	1870-1880	10	1808	1895	**Warren E. Burger**, VA	1969-1986	17	1907	1995
Joseph P. Bradley, NJ	1870-1892	21	1813	1892	Harry A. Blackmun, MN	1970-1994	24	1908	1999
Ward Hunt, NY	1873-1882	9	1810	1886	Lewis F. Powell Jr., VA	1972-1987	15	1907	1998
Morrison R. Waite, OH	1874-1888	14	1816	1888	William H. Rehnquist, AZ[1]	1972-1986	14	1924	2005
John M. Harlan, KY.	1877-1911	33	1833	1911	John Paul Stevens, IL	1975-2010	34	1920	
William B. Woods, GA.	1881-1887	6	1824	1887	Sandra Day O'Connor, AZ	1981-2006	24	1930	
Stanley Matthews, OH	1881-1889	7	1824	1889	**William H. Rehnquist**, VA[2]	1986-2005	18	1924	2005
Horace Gray, MA	1882-1902	20	1828	1902	Antonin Scalia, VA	1986-2016	29	1936	2016
Samuel Blatchford, NY	1882-1893	11	1820	1893	Anthony M. Kennedy, CA	1988-2018	30	1936	
Lucius Q. C. Lamar, MS	1888-1893	5	1825	1893	David H. Souter, NH	1990-2009	18	1939	
Melville W. Fuller, IL	1888-1910	21	1833	1910	Clarence Thomas, GA	1991-		1948	
David J. Brewer, KS	1890-1910	20	1837	1910	Ruth Bader Ginsburg, NY.	1993-		1933	
Henry B. Brown, MI.	1891-1906	15	1836	1913	Stephen G. Breyer, MA.	1994-		1938	
George Shiras Jr., PA.	1892-1903	10	1832	1924	**John G. Roberts Jr.**, MD.	2005-		1955	
Howell E. Jackson, TN	1893-1895	2	1832	1895	Samuel A. Alito Jr., NJ	2006-		1950	
Edward D. White, LA[1]	1894-1910	16	1845	1921	Sonia Sotomayor, NY	2009-		1954	
Rufus W. Peckham, NY.	1896-1909	13	1838	1909	Elena Kagan, MA	2010-		1960	
Joseph McKenna, CA.	1898-1925	26	1843	1926	Neil M. Gorsuch, CO.	2017-		1967	
Oliver W. Holmes, MA.	1902-1932	29	1841	1935	Brett Kavanaugh, DC	2018-		1965	
William R. Day, OH	1903-1922	19	1849	1923					

* = Because of inadequate government record keeping, date of oath is estimated. (1) Later, chief justice, as listed. (2) Formerly associate justice. (3) Named acting chief justice; confirmation rejected by the Senate. (4) Longest term of service.

Supreme Court History and Notable Firsts

The U.S. Supreme Court first convened Feb. 1, 1790, in New York, NY. Acting on the authority of Congress as outlined in the Judiciary Act of 1789, the court consisted of Chief Justice John Jay and five associate justices who held sessions for a few weeks in Feb. and Aug. The justices also served twice a year in each of the nation's then-13 judicial districts, a requirement known as riding circuit. Since it was established, 113 justices have served on the court for an average of 16 years.

The court's first major legal decision, *Chisholm v. Georgia* (1793), ruled that federal courts held jurisdiction over disputes between individual states and citizens of other states. (The 11th Amendment, which the states ratified in 1795, removed that jurisdiction.) The court over time has expanded its impact on the nation's affairs. Since 1803 it has declared unconstitutional 170 acts of Congress and more than 1,070 state and territorial laws and municipal statutes. The court hears oral arguments in about 70-80 cases per term.

Of 162 nominations to the court (including chief justice nominations), the Senate has voted to reject just 12, most recently Robert Bork in 1987. George W. Bush-nominee Harriet Miers withdrew her nomination before the Senate considered it, in 2005. The Senate did not hold hearings on the Obama-nominated appellate court judge Merrick Garland in 2016.

Justices may be removed from the court by impeachment. In 1804, the House of Representatives, in the control of Jeffersonian Republicans, impeached Samuel Chase, a Federalist; he was acquitted by the Senate in 1805.

First fully vested justice: James Wilson, who took the Constitutional Oath of the Court Oct. 5, 1789
First Jewish justice: Louis D. Brandeis (1916-39)
First and only person to serve as both U.S. president and chief justice: William Howard Taft (president, 1909-13; chief justice, 1921-30)

First justice to take an oath at the White House: Frank Murphy, Jan. 18, 1940
First African-American justice: Thurgood Marshall (1967-91)
First woman justice: Sandra Day O'Connor (1981-2006)
First Hispanic justice: Sonia Sotomayor (2009-)

U.S. Supreme Court Decisions by Issue and Leadership Era, 1946-2018

Source: Supreme Court Database, supremecourtdatabase.org

Decisions through the end of the 2017-18 term. Figures are the number of cases decided in each issue category (number of 5-4 decisions in parentheses). The Court begins its term the first Monday in Oct. and typically recesses in late June.

	Number of decisions under Chief Justice—				
Issue	Vinson (1946-53)	Warren (1953-69)	Burger (1969-86)	Rehnquist (1986-2005)	Roberts (2005-)
Attorneys[1]	2 (0)	12 (1)	37 (5)	31 (7)	19 (3)
Civil rights	74 (7)	316 (27)	555 (78)	326 (69)	171 (32)
Criminal procedure	123 (29)	462 (70)	627 (109)	509 (136)	294 (62)
Due process	47 (6)	40 (5)	144 (18)	86 (23)	28 (6)
Economic activity	224 (37)	493 (48)	452 (52)	346 (39)	207 (21)
Federal taxation	49 (2)	118 (5)	75 (7)	56 (3)	13 (3)
Federalism	33 (1)	94 (3)	107 (6)	125 (27)	44 (8)
First amendment	44 (8)	206 (44)	236 (56)	140 (36)	50 (14)
Interstate relations	12 (2)	14 (0)	40 (0)	23 (1)	10 (2)
Judicial power	135 (18)	299 (20)	366 (33)	286 (28)	134 (25)
Miscellaneous[2]	1 (0)	1 (0)	4 (0)	10 (0)	7 (1)
Privacy	4 (0)	2 (0)	48 (9)	42 (6)	18 (2)
Private action[3]	0 (0)	0 (0)	0 (0)	0 (0)	3 (1)
Unions	41 (4)	131 (8)	109 (24)	55 (11)	23 (7)
Total	**789 (114)**	**2,188 (231)**	**2,800 (397)**	**2,035 (386)**	**1,021 (187)**

Note: Decision types include orally argued judgments, per curiams, and opinions; per curiams without oral arguments; equally divided votes; and decrees. (1) Includes cases on commercial fees, attorneys' fees, admission to state or federal bar, attorney discipline, and disbarment. (2) Includes cases that could not be classified. (3) Includes cases on civil procedures, commercial transactions, contracts, evidence, personal and real property, torts, and wills and trusts.

Selected Landmark Decisions of the U.S. Supreme Court

1803: *Marbury v. Madison.* The Court ruled that Congress exceeded its power in the Judiciary Act of 1789. The Court thus established its power to review acts of Congress and to declare invalid those it found to be in conflict with the Constitution.

1819: *Trustees of Dartmouth College v. Woodward.* The Court ruled that a state could not arbitrarily alter the terms of a college's contract. The Court later used a similar principle to limit the states' ability to interfere with business contracts.

1819: *McCulloch v. Maryland.* The Court ruled that Congress had the authority to charter a national bank, under the Constitution's granting of power to enact all laws "necessary and proper" to responsibilities of government.

1824: *Gibbons v. Ogden.* The Court ruled that New York state had overstepped its authority in granting a monopoly to two steamboat operators. According to the ruling, Congress's power to regulate interstate commerce included transportation.

1857: *Dred Scott v. Sandford.* The Court declared unconstitutional the already-repealed Missouri Compromise of 1820 because it deprived a person of property—a slave—without due process of law. The Court also ruled that slaves were not citizens of any state nor of the U.S. The latter part of the decision was overturned by ratification of the 14th Amendment in 1868.

1880: *Strauder v. West Virginia.* The Court struck down a state law mandating that jurors must be white, ruling it a violation of the right to equal protection under the 14th Amendment.

1896: *Plessy v. Ferguson.* The Court ruled that a state law requiring federal railroad trains to provide separate but equal facilities for black and white passengers neither infringed upon federal authority to regulate interstate commerce nor violated the 13th and 14th Amendments. The "separate but equal" doctrine remained in effect until the 1954 *Brown v. Board of Education* decision.

1904: *Northern Securities Co. v. U.S.* The Court ruled that a holding company formed solely to eliminate competition between two railroad lines was a combination in restraint of trade, violating the 1890 federal Sherman Antitrust Act.

1908: *Muller v. Oregon.* The Court upheld a state law limiting the working hours of women. (Louis D. Brandeis, counsel for the state, cited evidence from social workers, physicians, and factory inspectors that long work hours were harmful to women.)

1911: *Standard Oil Co. of New Jersey v. U.S.* The Court ruled that the Standard Oil Trust must be dissolved because of its unreasonable restraint of trade.

1919: *Schenck v. U.S.* The Court sustained the Espionage Act of 1917, maintaining that freedom of speech and press could be constrained if "the words used ... create a clear and present danger."

1925: *Gitlow v. New York.* The Court ruled that the 1st Amendment prohibition against government abridgment of the freedom of speech applied to the states as well as to the federal government. The decision was the first of a number of rulings holding that the 14th Amendment extended the guarantees of the Bill of Rights to state action.

1935: *Schechter Poultry Corp. v. U.S.* The Court ruled that Congress exceeded its authority to delegate legislative powers and to regulate interstate commerce when it enacted the National Industrial Recovery Act (1933), which afforded the U.S. president too much discretionary power.

1944: *Korematsu v. U.S.* The Court upheld the constitutionality of an order barring all persons of Japanese ancestry, including U.S. citizens, from much of the West Coast, forcing them into internment camps, ruling that the need to prevent espionage outweighed the petitioner's civil rights. The ruling, never officially overturned, followed *Hirabayashi v. U.S.* (1943), in which the Court upheld the imposition of curfews on minority populations perceived to be a potential wartime threat.

1951: *Dennis v. U.S.* The Court upheld convictions under the Smith Act of 1940 for invoking Communist theory advocating the forcible overthrow of the government. In *Yates v. U.S.* (1957), the Court moderated this ruling by allowing such advocacy in the abstract, if not connected to action to achieve the goal.

1952: *Youngstown Sheet & Tube Co. v. Sawyer.* The Court ruled that the president had exceeded his wartime power in ordering the seizure of private steel mills during a nationwide steelworkers' strike. The Court held that neither the Constitution nor his role as commander-in-chief gave the president the authority to interfere in labor issues.

1954: *Brown v. Board of Education of Topeka.* The Court ruled that separate public schools for black and white students were inherently unequal, so state-sanctioned segregation in public schools violated the equal protection guarantee of the 14th Amendment. The Court decided *Bolling v. Sharpe* the same year, ruling that the congressionally mandated segregated public school system in the District of Columbia violated the 5th Amendment's due process guarantee of personal liberty. In *Brown II* (1955), the Court ordered the integration of schools with "all deliberate speed." The Brown rulings also led to abolition of state-sponsored segregation in other public facilities.

1957: *Roth v. U.S.*; *Alberts v. California.* The Court ruled obscene material—defined as appealing primarily to "prurient interest" in the view of "the average person, applying contemporary community standards"—was not protected by 1st Amendment guarantees of freedom of speech and press, being "utterly without redeeming social importance." This definition was modified in later decisions, including *Miller v. California* (1973).

1958: *Cooper v. Aaron.* The Court held that Arkansas could not nullify *Brown v. Board of Education* (1954) through the passage of legislation or constitutional amendments barring integration. The opinion of the Court affirmed its reading of the Constitution as the "supreme law of the land."

1961: *Mapp v. Ohio.* The Court ruled that evidence obtained in violation of the 4th Amendment guarantee against unreasonable search and seizure must be excluded from use in state as well as federal trials.

1962: *Baker v. Carr.* The Court held that constitutional challenges to the unequal distribution of voters among legislative districts could be resolved by federal courts.

1962: *Engel v. Vitale.* The Court held that government bodies could not encourage the recitation of a state-composed prayer in public schools, even if nondenominational, because that would be an unconstitutional attempt to establish religion.

1963: *Gideon v. Wainwright.* The Court ruled that indigent defendants, even in state cases, have a right to legal counsel as guaranteed by the 6th Amendment.

1964: *New York Times Co. v. Sullivan.* The Court ruled that the 1st Amendment protected the press from libel suits for defamatory reports about public officials unless an injured party could prove that a defamatory report was made out of "actual malice," with "reckless disregard" for the truth.

1964: *Heart of Atlanta Motel v. U.S.* The Court upheld the constitutionality of Title II of the 1964 Civil Rights Act banning racial discrimination in motels/hotels engaged in interstate commerce (by accommodating travelers from other states). The Court in *Katzenbach v. McClung* (1964) held that Title II also applied to restaurants and businesses that purchased a substantial percentage of food or goods from other states.

1965: *Griswold v. Connecticut.* The Court ruled that a state unconstitutionally interfered with privacy in a marriage when it prohibited all persons, including married couples, from using contraceptives.

1966: *Miranda v. Arizona.* The Court ruled that, under the guarantee of due process, suspects in custody, before being questioned, must be informed that they have the right to remain silent, that anything they say may be used against them, and that they have the right to counsel.

1967: *Loving v. Virginia.* The Court unanimously struck down all state laws banning interracial marriage.

1968: *Terry v. Ohio.* The Court ruled that a "stop and frisk" performed without a warrant or probable cause was not a violation of 4th Amendment rights, provided that the law enforcement officer had a reasonable suspicion that the subject was armed and dangerous, or had committed or was about to commit a crime.

1969: *Brandenburg v. Ohio.* The Court held that government cannot restrict inflammatory speech unless it is "directed to inciting or producing imminent lawless action AND is likely to incite or produce such action." The so-called Brandenburg test refined the "clear and present danger" outlined in *Schenck v. U.S.* (1927) and overturned the holding in *Whitney v. California* (1927) that speech advocating violence could be prohibited.

1973: *Roe v. Wade*; *Doe v. Bolton.* The Court ruled that the fetus was not a "person" with constitutional rights and that a right to privacy inherent in the 14th Amendment's due process guarantee of personal liberty protected a woman's decision to have an abortion. During the first trimester of pregnancy, the Court maintained, the decision should be left entirely to a woman and her physician. Some regulation of abortion procedures was allowed in the second trimester and some restriction of abortion in the third.

1974: *U.S. v. Nixon.* The Court ruled that neither the separation of powers nor the need to preserve the confidentiality of presidential communications could alone justify an absolute executive privilege of immunity from judicial demands for evidence to be used in a criminal trial.

1976: *Gregg v. Georgia*; *Proffitt v. Florida*; *Jurek v. Texas.* The Court held that death, as a punishment for persons convicted of first-degree murder, was not in and of itself cruel and unusual punishment in violation of the 8th Amendment. But the Court ruled that the sentencing judge and jury must consider the character of the offender and the circumstances of the particular crime.

1978: *Regents of the Univ. of Calif. v. Bakke.* The Court ruled that an admissions program for a state medical school, under which a set number of places were reserved for minorities, violated the 1964 Civil Rights Act, which forbids the exclusion of anyone from a federally funded program based on race. However, the Court ruled that race could be considered as one of a complex of factors.

1985: *New Jersey v. T.L.O.* The Court ruled that officials who carry out searches on school grounds do not violate students' 4th Amendment rights because students' privacy rights may be outweighed by schools' need to maintain learning environments. The ruling put in place less stringent standards of required "reasonableness" for such searches.

1986: *Bowers v. Hardwick.* The Court refused to extend any right of privacy to homosexual activity, upholding a Georgia antisodomy law that in effect made such activity a crime. Georgia's supreme court struck down the law in 1998, and in *Lawrence v. Texas* (2003), the U.S. Supreme Court struck down all state antisodomy laws as violations of liberty prohibited in the 14th Amendment's due process clause. In *Romer v. Evans* (1996), the Court struck down a Colorado constitutional provision that barred homosexuals from recognition as a protected class, ruling that it violated the 14th Amendment's Equal Protection clause.

1989: *Texas v. Johnson.* The Court held the actions of a political activist who burned an American flag outside of the 1984 Republican National Convention were expressive and therefore protected by the 1st Amendment. The ruling invalidated laws in 48 states prohibiting flag desecration.

1990: *Cruzan v. Missouri.* The Court ruled that while a person had the right to refuse life-sustaining medical treatment, a state could require evidence that a comatose patient would not have wanted to live before withholding treatment. In two 1997 rulings, *Washington v. Glucksberg* and *Vacco v. Quill*, the Court ruled that states could ban doctor-assisted suicide.

1995: *U.S. Term Limits, Inc. v. Thornton.* The Court ruled that neither states nor Congress could limit terms of members of Congress because the Constitution reserves to the people the right to choose federal lawmakers.

1995: *Adarand Constructors, Inc. v. Peña.* The Court held that federal programs that classify people by race, unless "narrowly tailored" to further a "compelling governmental interest," may violate the right to equal protection and are thus subject to strict scrutiny.

1997: *Clinton v. Jones.* Rejecting an appeal by Pres. Clinton in a sexual harassment suit, the Court ruled that a sitting president did not have temporary immunity from a lawsuit for actions outside the realm of official duties.

1997: *City of Boerne v. Flores.* The Court overturned the portion of a 1993 law banning enforcement of state laws that "substantially burden" religious practice unless there is a "compelling governmental interest" to do so. The Court held that the act was an unwarranted intrusion by Congress on states' prerogatives and an infringement of the judiciary's role.

1997: *Reno v. ACLU.* Citing the right to free expression, the Court overturned a provision making it a crime to display or distribute "obscene or indecent" or "patently offensive" material on the Internet. The Court ruled, however, in ***NEA v. Finley*** (1998) that "general standards of decency" may be used as a criterion in federal arts funding.

1998: *Clinton v. City of New York.* The Court struck down the Line-Item Veto Act (1996), holding that it unconstitutionally gave the president "the unilateral power to change the text of duly enacted statutes."

1998: *Faragher v. City of Boca Raton*; *Burlington Industries, Inc. v. Ellerth.* The Court issued new guidelines for workplace sexual harassment suits, holding employers responsible for misconduct by supervisory employees. And in ***Oncale v. Sundowner Offshore Services, Inc.*** the same year, the Court ruled that the law against discrimination based on sex applies even if the harasser and harassed are the same sex.

1999: *Dept. of Commerce v. U.S. House of Representatives.* Upholding a challenge to plans for the 2000 census, the Court prohibited statistical sampling, favored by Democrats, in apportioning seats in the U.S. House. The Court maintained that an actual head count was required.

1999: *Alden v. Maine*; *Florida Prepaid v. College Savings Bank*; *College Savings Bank v. Florida Prepaid.* In a series of rulings, the Court applied the principle of sovereign immunity to shield states in large part from being sued under federal law.

2000: *Boy Scouts of America v. Dale.* The Court ruled that the Boy Scouts could dismiss a troop leader after learning he was gay, holding that the right to freedom of association outweighed a New Jersey antidiscrimination statute.

2000: *Bush v. Gore.* The Court ruled that manual recounts in Florida of ballots cast in the 2000 presidential election could not proceed because inconsistent evaluation standards violated the equal protection clause. In effect, the ruling meant the existing official results would stand, making George W. Bush the narrow winner of the election.

2001: *Good News Club v. Milford Central School.* The justices found that a private religious organization could not be denied equal access to a public school facility for after-school meetings because that would be a violation of the group's free speech rights.

2002: *Federal Maritime Commission v. South Carolina State Ports Authority.* The Court ruled that the 11th Amendment gave states immunity from private lawsuits involving federal agencies.

2002: *Atkins v. Virginia.* The Court ruled that the execution of mentally retarded criminals violated the 8th Amendment ban on cruel and unusual punishment. The Court ruled in ***Roper v. Simmons*** (2005) that executions of convicts who committed their crimes before age 18 were also prohibited on the same grounds.

2002: *Zelman v. Simmons-Harris.* The Court ruled that publicly funded tuition vouchers could be used at religious schools without violating the separation of church and state.

2003: *Grutter v. Bollinger*; *Gratz v. Bollinger.* The Court upheld the use of race as a factor in the Univ. of Michigan Law School's admissions policies because of the school's interest in a diverse student body. In a second decision, however, the Court ruled against a strict point system based on racial and ethnic backgrounds as used in the university's undergraduate admissions process.

2004: *Tennessee v. Lane.* The Court ruled that disabled individuals could sue states under the Americans With Disabilities Act (1990) for failing to provide adequate access to state courthouses, despite states' usual immunity from private lawsuits in federal court under the 11th Amendment, which the Court ruled on in ***Federal Maritime Commission v. South Carolina State Ports Authority*** (2002).

2004: *Locke v. Davey.* The justices decided that a scholarship program provided by the state of Washington did not violate the right to free exercise of religion in denying aid to students preparing for the clergy.

2004: *Ashcroft v. ACLU.* The Court struck down federal legislation passed in 1998 to restrict online access to pornography by minors, on the basis that the law violated the 1st Amendment right of free speech.

2005: *Kelo v. City of New London.* The Court ruled that local governments could force property owners to sell their land in order to facilitate private development projects deemed to be economically beneficial to the community.

2006: *Garcetti v. Ceballos.* The Court ruled that the 1st Amendment guarantee of free speech did not protect statements made by public employees in the course of their official duties.

2006: *Hamdan v. Rumsfeld.* The Court ruled that Pres. George W. Bush's system for trying terrorism detainees at the U.S. military base in Guantánamo Bay, Cuba, was unauthorized under federal law and the international Geneva Conventions. The Court furthermore ruled in ***Boumediene v. Bush*** (2008) that detainees had a right to challenge their detention in federal court by applying for a writ of habeas corpus.

2007: *Gonzales v. Carhart*; *Gonzales v. Planned Parenthood Federation of America.* The Court upheld a 2003 federal law prohibiting the abortion procedure known as intact dilation and extraction, or "partial-birth" abortion.

2007: *Parents Involved in Community Schools v. Seattle School District No. 1*; *Meredith v. Jefferson County Board of Education.* The Court ruled that two school districts could not, to encourage diversity, use "racial classifications in making school assignments."

2008: *Crawford v. Marion County Election Board.* The Court upheld the constitutionality of an Indiana law requiring in-person voters to present valid government photo identification.

2008: *District of Columbia v. Heller.* The Court overturned DC's handgun ban, ruling that the 2nd Amendment protected an individual's right to own guns for personal use.

2010: *Citizens United v. Federal Election Commission.* The Court ruled that a federal law barring corporations from using general funds to finance campaign advertisements was unconstitutional. The decision cast doubt on many laws restricting political spending by corporations and unions.

2011: *Snyder v. Phelps.* The justices found that an antigay church whose members protested at the funeral of a Marine could not be held liable for intrusion or the emotional distress of the father of the deceased because the protests were protected by the 1st Amendment.

2012: *U.S. v. Jones.* The Court ruled that attaching a GPS tracking device to a suspect's car and monitoring its movements requires a search warrant, as the 4th Amendment prohibition against unreasonable search and seizure applies.

2012: *Miller v. Alabama.* The Court ruled that mandatory life sentences without the possibility of parole violate juvenile offenders' 8th Amendment right to freedom from cruel and unusual punishment. The decision extended ***Graham v. Florida***, a 2010 case in which the Court held that juveniles may not receive life sentences for nonhomicide crimes.

2012: *Natl. Federation of Independent Business v. Sebelius.* The Court ruled Congress acted within its powers of taxation in enacting the individual-mandate provision of the Patient Protection and Affordable Care Act (ACA), which required Americans without government- or employer-provided health insurance to purchase it or pay a fine. The Court ruled unconstitutional the provision of the act's Medicaid expansion that threatened non-compliant states with loss of funding.

2013: *Shelby County v. Holder.* The justices ruled that a key provision of the 1965 Voting Rights Act, meant to prevent discriminatory voting regulations from being enacted, was unconstitutional because it relied on outdated information to identify jurisdictions for additional scrutiny.

2013: *U.S. v. Windsor.* The Court struck down the central provision of the 1996 federal Defense of Marriage Act (DOMA), which prohibited federal recognition of same-sex marriages. A separate decision the same year, in ***Hollingsworth v. Perry***, had the effect of legalizing same-sex marriage in California.

2014: *Riley v. California*; *U.S. v. Wurie.* The Court unanimously decided that police generally could not search the mobile telephones of arrested individuals without first obtaining a search warrant.

2014: *Burwell v. Hobby Lobby Stores*; *Conestoga Wood Specialties Corp. v. Burwell.* The justices ruled that some closely held corporations could claim an exemption—based on their owners' religious beliefs and the 1993 Religious Freedom Restoration Act—from a 2010 ACA mandate requiring many businesses to provide health insurance that covers contraception.

2015: *Obergefell v. Hodges.* The court ruled that state bans on same-sex marriage violated same-sex couples' rights under the due process and equal protection clauses of the 14th Amendment.

2016: *Whole Woman's Health v. Hellerstedt.* The justices ruled that a Texas law that included stringent regulations on abortion providers did not pass the "undue burden" standard the Court established in 1992's ***Planned Parenthood v. Casey***.

See also Year in Review: Notable Supreme Court Decisions.

Sources: Population: Decennial Censuses and Population Estimates Program, U.S. Census Bureau, U.S. Dept. of Commerce; population as of July 1, 2017, unless otherwise noted. **Pop. density** is for land area only. **Racial distribution** categories are abbreviated; their full forms are white, black or African American, Asian, American Indian and Alaska Native, Native Hawaiian and other Pacific Islander, two or more races. Categories may not add up to 100% due to rounding. **Hispanic** or Latino persons may be of any race. **Area:** Geography Division, U.S. Census Bureau, U.S. Dept. of Commerce. **Acres forested:** U.S. Forest Service, U.S. Dept. of Agriculture; source year may vary. **Chief airports:** Federal Aviation Admin., U.S. Dept. of Transportation. Chief airports had 500,000+ boardings in 2017; not all states had airports meeting this threshold. All **Economy** data as of 2017 unless otherwise noted. **Chief manuf. goods:** Manufacturing and Construction Division, U.S. Census Bureau, U.S. Dept. of Commerce. **Chief crops:** Natl. Agricultural Statistics Service, U.S. Dept. of Agriculture. **Farm income:** Economic Research Service, U.S. Dept. of Agriculture; 2016 cash receipts. **Nonfuel minerals:** Office of Mineral Information, U.S. Dept. of Interior; estimated 2017 data. Some states exclude small amounts to avoid disclosing proprietary data. **Commercial fishing:** Natl. Marine Fisheries Service, U.S. Dept. of Commerce; 2016 value. **Gross state product** and **Per cap. pers. income:** Bureau of Economic Analysis, U.S. Dept. of Commerce; as of Dec. 2017. **Sales tax:** Federation of Tax Administrators; as of Jan. 1, 2018. **Gasoline tax:** American Petroleum Institute; as of July 2, 2018; incl. state excise tax, federal excise tax (18.4 cents per gallon), and other state fees. **Employment distrib.** and **Unemployment:** Bureau of Labor Statistics, U.S. Dept. of Labor; distribution is for non-farm jobs as of May 2018; annual unemployment rate for 2017. **Min. wage/hr.:** U.S. Dept. of Labor; as of July 1, 2018. If a state has no minimum wage, or the state minimum wage is lower than the federal minimum wage, the federal rate of $7.25 applies. Small businesses may have lower minimum wages. Some municipalities may have different minimum wages. **New private housing:** Manufacturing and Construction Division, U.S. Census Bureau, U.S. Dept. of Commerce. Figures are building permits issued and est. value of the construction. **Broadband internet:** Industry Analysis and Tech. Division, Fed. Communications Commission; Natl. Telecommunications and Information Administration, U.S. Dept. of Commerce. Broadband connections have minimum speeds of at least 3 megabits per second (Mbps) downstream and 200 kilobits per second (kbps) upstream as of Dec. 2016; figure given is broadband as a percentage of total internet connections. **Commercial banks** and **Savings institutions:** Federal Deposit Insurance Corp., as of June 30, 2017; FDIC-insured institutions only. **Lottery:** North American Assn. of State and Provincial Lotteries, FY 2017. Data may be unaudited and in some cases were gathered by third party; profit is amount of total funds transferred to public beneficiaries, after prizes to players/retailers and administrative costs. **Fed. civ. employees:** Office of Personnel Mgmt., U.S. Dept. of Labor; as of Mar. 2018. **Education:** Natl. Ctr. for Education Statistics; high school graduation rates as of 2015-16 school year; number of colleges/univ. as of 2016-17. Data for **4-yr. private** institutions does not include for-profit colleges/universities. **Energy:** Energy Information Admin., U.S. Dept. of Energy; average per capita monthly electricity consumption and cost for residential customers in 2016. **Tourism:** U.S. Travel Assn.; **tourist spending** in 2016. Other information from sources in individual states. NA = Not available; AFB = air force base; JRB = joint reserve base; NAS = naval air station.

Famous persons lists may include non-natives associated with the state as well as persons born there. **Websites** are subject to change and are not endorsed by *The World Almanac*.

Alabama (AL)
Heart of Dixie, Camellia State

People. Population: 4,874,747; rank: 24. **Pop. change** (2010-17): 2.0%. **Pop. density:** 96.3 per sq mi. **Racial distribution:** 69.2% white; 26.8% black; 1.5% Asian; 0.7% Amer. Ind.; 0.1% Pac. Isl.; 2+ races, 1.7%. **Hispanic pop.:** 4.3%.

Geography. Total area: 52,420 sq mi; rank: 24. **Land area:** 50,645 sq mi; rank: 28. **Acres forested:** 23.1 mil. **Location:** East South Central state extending N-S from Tennessee to the Gulf of Mexico; E of the Mississippi R. **Climate:** long, hot summers; mild winters; generally abundant rain. **Topography:** coastal plains, including Prairie Black Belt, give way to hills, broken terrain; highest elevation 2,413 ft. **Capital:** Montgomery. **Chief airports:** Birmingham, Huntsville.

Economy. Chief industries: chemicals, electronics, apparel, primary metals, lumber and wood products, food processing, fabricated metals, automotive tires, oil and gas exploration. **Chief manuf. goods:** poultry processing, paper and paperboard, iron and steel, petroleum, automotive tires, aerospace, aluminum, auto body and parts. **Chief crops:** cotton, greenhouse and nursery, hay, peanuts, corn, soybeans. **Farm income:** crops, $1.07 bil; livestock, $3.88 bil. **Nonfuel minerals:** $1.3 bil; stone (crushed), cement (portland), lime, sand and gravel (construction), cement (masonry). **Commercial fishing:** $65.6 mil. **Chief port:** Mobile. **Gross state product:** $211.0 bil. **Sales tax:** 4.0%. **Gasoline tax:** 39.31 cents/gal. **Employment distrib.:** 19.0% govt.; 18.5% trade/trans./util.; 13.1% mfg.; 11.9% ed./health; 11.9% prof./bus. serv.; 10.4% leisure/hosp.; 4.7% finance; 4.8% constr./mining/log.; 1.0% info.; 4.6% other serv. **Unemployment:** 4.4%. **Min. wage/hr.:** none ($7.25). **Per cap. pers. income:** $39,976. **New private housing:** 14,799 units/$2.8 bil. **Broadband internet:** 93.3%. **Commercial banks:** 154; deposits: $99.8 bil. **Savings institutions:** 7; deposits: $635.0 mil.

Federal govt. Fed. civ. employees: 37,687; **avg. salary:** $84,510. **Notable fed. facilities:** Redstone Arsenal; Ft. Rucker; Marshall Space Flight Ctr., Huntsville; Anniston Army Depot; Maxwell AFB and Gunter Annex; Army Corps of Engineers, Mobile District.

Education. High school grad. rate: 87.1%. **4-yr. public coll./univ.:** 14; **2-yr. public:** 25; **4-yr. private:** 20.

Energy. Electricity use/cost: 1,214 kWh; $145.55.

State data. Motto: Audemus Jura Nostra Defendere (We dare defend our rights). **Flower:** Camellia. **Bird:** Northern flicker (yellowhammer is local nickname). **Tree:** Southern longleaf pine. **Song:** "Alabama." **Entered union:** Dec. 14, 1819; rank: 22nd.

Tourism. Tourist spending: $9.3 bil. **Attractions:** First White House of the Confederacy, Civil Rights Memorial, Alabama Shakespeare Festival, Legacy Museum, National Memorial for Peace and Justice, in Montgomery; Ivy Green (Helen Keller birthplace), Tuscumbia; Barber Vintage Motorsports Museum, Civil Rights Institute, Vulcan Park and Museum (world's largest cast iron statue), in Birmingham; G. W. Carver Interpretive Museum, Tuskegee; W. C. Handy Home, Museum, and Library, Frank Lloyd Wright's Rosenbaum House, in Florence; U.S. Space & Rocket Ctr., Huntsville; Moundville Archaeological Park; USS *Alabama* Memorial Park, Mobile; Gulf State Park, Gulf Shores. **Information:** Alabama Tourism Dept., 401 Adams Ave., Ste. 126, P.O. Box 4927, Montgomery, AL 36103; 1-800-ALABAMA, (334) 242-4169; alabama.travel

History. Alabama was inhabited by the Creek, Cherokee, Chickasaw, Alabama, and Choctaw peoples when Spanish explorers arrived in the early 1500s. The French made the first permanent settlement at Ft. Louis, 1702, and founded Mobile, 1711. France later gave up the entire region to England under the Treaty of Paris, 1763. Spanish forces took control of the Mobile Bay area, 1780, and it remained under Spanish control until seized by U.S. troops, 1813. Most of present-day Alabama was held by the Creeks until Gen. Andrew Jackson broke their power, 1814. When Alabama became a state, 1819, enslaved black people made up about one-third of the population. The Indian Removal Act of 1830 forced most remaining Creeks west. The state seceded, 1861, and the Confederate states were organized Feb. 4, at Montgomery, the first capital. The state was readmitted, 1868. Birmingham, founded 1871, became a center for iron- and steelmaking. The Montgomery bus boycott, 1955, sparked by Rosa Parks, helped launch the civil rights movement. Other confrontations occurred at Birmingham, 1963, and Selma, 1965. The leading political figure from the 1960s through the '80s, four-term gov. George Wallace, started as a segregationist but later won with black support. Growth in the auto industry boosted the economy as the 21st cent. began. A string of tornadoes in 2011 killed at least 248. Jefferson County, which includes Birmingham, filed the then-most expensive municipal bankruptcy in 2011. Gov. Robert Bentley pleaded guilty to misdemeanor charges connected with a sex scandal and resigned, 2017. Roy Moore, a former state chief justice, was upset by Doug Jones (D) in a special election for the U.S. Senate in Dec. 2017 after several women alleged a history of sexual misconduct.

Famous Alabamians. Hank Aaron, Tallulah Bankhead, Charles Barkley, Hugo L. Black, Paul "Bear" Bryant, George Washington Carver, Nat King Cole, Courteney Cox, William Christopher "W. C." Handy, Polly Holliday, Bo Jackson, Helen Keller, Coretta Scott King, Harper Lee, Joe Louis, Willie Mays, Jim Nabors, Jesse Owens, Terrell Owens, Rosa Parks, Condoleezza Rice, Lionel Richie, Robin Roberts, Octavia Spencer, Channing Tatum, George C. Wallace, Booker T. Washington, Hank Williams.

Website. www.alabama.gov

Alaska (AK)
The Last Frontier (unofficial)

People. Population: 739,795; rank: 48. **Pop. change** (2010-17): 4.2%. **Pop. density:** 1.3 per sq mi. **Racial distri-**

bution: 65.8% white; 3.7% black; 6.5% Asian; 15.3% Amer. Ind.; 1.4% Pac. Isl.; 2+ races, 7.4%. **Hispanic pop.:** 7.1%.

Geography. Total area: 665,384 sq mi; rank: 1. **Land area:** 570,641 sq mi; rank: 1. **Acres forested:** 12.0 mil. **Location:** NW corner of North America, bordered on E by Canada. **Climate:** SE, SW, and central regions, moist and mild; far N extremely dry. Extended summer days, winter nights throughout. **Topography:** includes Pacific and Arctic mountain systems, central plateau, and Arctic slope. Denali, formerly Mt. McKinley, 20,310 ft, is the highest point in N. America. **Capital:** Juneau. **Chief airports:** Anchorage, Fairbanks.

Economy. Chief industries: petroleum, tourism, fishing, mining, forestry, transportation, aerospace. **Chief manuf. goods:** petroleum, seafood. **Chief crops:** greenhouse products, barley, oats, hay, potatoes, carrots. **Farm income:** crops, $28.84 mil; livestock, $6.03 mil. **Nonfuel minerals:** $3.5 bil; zinc, gold, lead, silver, sand and gravel (construction). **Commercial fishing:** $1.6 bil. **Chief ports:** Anchorage, Dutch Harbor, Kodiak, Juneau, Sitka, Valdez. **Gross state product:** $52.8 bil. **Sales tax:** none. **Gasoline tax:** 33.05 cents/gal. **Employment distrib.:** 24.9% govt.; 19.8% trade/trans./util.; 3.2% mfg.; 15.1% ed./health; 8.5% prof./bus. serv.; 11.1% leisure/hosp.; 3.5% finance; 8.8% constr./mining/log.; 1.8% info.; 3.3% other serv. **Unemployment:** 7.2%. **Min. wage/hr.:** $9.84. **Per cap. pers. income:** $56,042. **New private housing:** 1,539 units/$395.7 mil. **Broadband internet:** 87.0%. **Commercial banks:** 6; deposits $11.9 bil. **Savings institutions:** 1; deposits $307.0 mil.

Federal govt. Fed. civ. employees: 10,718; **avg. salary:** $82,929. **Notable fed. facilities:** Joint Base Elmendorf-Richardson; Ft. Wainwright; Eielson AFB; Ft. Greely.

Education. High school grad. rate: 76.1%. **4-yr. public coll./univ.:** 3; **2-yr. public:** 1; **4-yr. private:** 2.

Energy. Electricity use/cost: 590 kWh, $119.84.

State data. Motto: North to the future. **Flower:** Forget-me-not. **Bird:** Willow ptarmigan. **Tree:** Sitka spruce. **Song:** "Alaska's Flag." **Entered union:** Jan. 3, 1959; rank: 49th.

Tourism. Tourist spending: $2.7 bil. **Attractions:** Portage Glacier, in Chugach Natl. Forest; Mendenhall Glacier, in Tongass Natl. Forest; Totem Heritage Ctr., Ketchikan; Glacier Bay Natl. Park and Preserve; Denali (formerly Mt. McKinley, N. America's highest peak), in Denali Natl. Park and Preserve; Mt. Roberts Tramway, Juneau; Alaska Maritime Natl. Wildlife Refuge; St. Michael's Cathedral, Alaska Raptor Ctr., in Sitka; White Pass & Yukon Route railroad, Skagway; Katmai Natl. Park and Preserve; Univ. of Alaska Museum of the North, Fairbanks. **Information:** Alaska Travel Industry Association, 2600 Cordova St., Ste. 201, Anchorage, AK 99503; 1-800-327-9372; www.travelalaska.com

History. Early inhabitants included the Tlingit-Haida and Athabascan peoples. Ancestors of the Aleut and Inuit (Eskimo) probably arrived from Siberia between 10,000 and 6,000 years ago. Vitus Bering, a Dane sailing for Russia, was the first European to land in Alaska, 1741. Russians, pursuing the fur trade, established a permanent settlement on Kodiak Island, 1784. Sec. of State William H. Seward bought Alaska from Russia for $7.2 mil in 1867, a deal some called "Seward's Folly." Discovery of gold in the Klondike region of Canada's Yukon Territory, 1896, triggered an Alaskan gold rush. Alaska became a territory, 1912, and a state, 1959. A huge oil find at Prudhoe Bay, 1968, led to construction of the Trans-Alaska Pipeline, 1974-77. The *Exxon Valdez* supertanker ran aground, 1989, spilling about 11 mil gallons of crude oil; the cleanup cost more than $2.2 bil. Congress included a measure permitting oil and gas drilling in the Arctic National Wildlife Refuge in the tax bill passed in Dec. 2017, ending a four-decade battle.

Famous Alaskans. Tom Bodett, Susan Butcher, Ernest Gruening, Jewel (Kilcher), Tony Knowles, Sydney Laurence, Sarah Palin, Libby Riddles, Curt Schilling, Jefferson "Soapy" Smith.

Website. www.alaska.gov

Arizona (AZ)
Grand Canyon State

People. Population: 7,016,270; rank: 14. **Pop. change** (2010-17): 9.8%. **Pop. density:** 61.8 per sq mi. **Racial distribution:** 83.1% white; 5.0% black; 3.5% Asian; 5.3% Amer. Ind.; 0.3% Pac. Isl.; 2+ races, 2.8%. **Hispanic pop.:** 31.4%.

Geography. Total area: 113,990 sq mi; rank: 6. **Land area:** 113,594 sq mi; rank: 6. **Acres forested:** 18.4 mil. **Location:** southwestern U.S. **Climate:** clear and dry in southern regions and northern plateau; high central areas have heavy winter snows. **Topography:** Colorado Plateau in the N, containing the Grand Canyon; Mexican Highlands run NW to SE;

Sonoran Desert in the SW. **Capital:** Phoenix. **Chief airports:** Mesa, Phoenix, Tucson.

Economy. Chief industries: manufacturing, construction, tourism, mining, agriculture. **Chief manuf. goods:** aerospace, semiconductors, navigational instruments, cement, plastics, structural metals, dairy, printing, furniture. **Chief crops:** cotton, grapes, apples, lettuce, hay, potatoes, sorghum, barley, corn, wheat. **Farm income:** crops, $2.64 bil; livestock, $1.52 bil. **Nonfuel minerals:** $6.6 bil; copper, sand and gravel (construction), molybdenum concentrates, cement (portland), stone (crushed). **Gross state product:** $319.9 bil. **Sales tax:** 5.6%. **Gasoline tax:** 37.40 cents/gal. **Employment distrib.:** 14.7% govt.; 18.6% trade/trans./util.; 6.0% mfg.; 15.5% ed./health; 15.0% prof./bus. serv.; 11.7% leisure/hosp.; 7.7% finance; 5.9% constr./mining/log.; 1.6% info.; 3.2% other serv. **Unemployment:** 4.9%. **Min. wage/hr.:** $10.50. **Per cap. pers. income:** $41,633. **New private housing:** 39,472 units/$8.7 bil. **Broadband internet:** 96.5% **Commercial banks:** 60; deposits $120.9 bil. **Savings institutions:** 7; deposits: $3.8 bil. **Lottery:** total sales: $852.0 mil; profit: $198.2 mil.

Federal govt. Fed. civ. employees: 31,659; **avg. salary:** $71,309. **Notable fed. facilities:** Luke AFB; Davis-Monthan AFB; Ft. Huachuca; Yuma Proving Ground.

Education. High school grad. rate: 79.5%. **4-yr. public coll./univ.:** 10; **2-yr. public:** 20; **4-yr. private:** 12.

Energy. Electricity use/cost: 1,030 kWh, $125.19.

State data. Motto: Ditat Deus (God enriches). **Flower:** Blossom of the saguaro cactus. **Bird:** Cactus wren. **Tree:** Paloverde. **Song:** "Arizona." **Entered union:** Feb. 14, 1912; rank: 48th.

Tourism. Tourist spending: $19.3 bil. **Attractions:** Grand Canyon; Painted Desert, in Grand Canyon and Petrified Forest Natl. Parks; Glen Canyon Natl. Recreation Area; Canyon de Chelly Natl. Monument; Meteor Crater, near Winslow; London Bridge, Lake Havasu City; Biosphere 2, Oracle; Navajo Natl. Monument; Tombstone historic mining town; Tempe Town Lake. **Information:** Arizona Office of Tourism, 1110 W. Washington St., Ste. 155, Phoenix, AZ 85007; 1-866-275-5816; www.visitarizona.com

History. Paleo-Indians hunted large game in the area at least 12,000 years ago. Anasazi, Mogollon, and Hohokam civilizations lived there c. 300 BCE-1300 CE; Navajo and Apache came c. 15th cent. Marcos de Niza, a Spanish Franciscan, and Estevanico, a black former slave, explored, 1539; explorer Francisco Vásquez de Coronado visited, 1540. Eusebio Francisco Kino, a Jesuit missionary, taught Indians, 1692-1711, and left missions. Tubac, a Spanish fort, became the first European settlement, 1752. Spain ceded Arizona to Mexico, 1821. The U.S. took over, 1848, after the Mexican War. The area below the Gila R. came from Mexico in the Gadsden Purchase, 1853. Arizona became a territory, 1863. Apache wars ended with Geronimo's surrender, 1886. Arizona became a state, 1912, and grew rapidly after 1960 with a fourfold rise in population over the next four decades. Barry Goldwater was a leading conservative voice in the U.S. Senate (1953-65, 1969-87). The border with Mexico is a major gateway for illegal immigration to the U.S. In 2012, the U.S. Supreme Court struck down most provisions of a 2010 state immigration law that allowed police to make warrantless arrests of those reasonably suspected of having immigrated illegally. A statewide teacher walkout in Apr. 2018 demanded increased pay and school funding.

Famous Arizonans. Bruce Babbitt, Cochise, Alice Cooper, Geronimo, Gabrielle Giffords, Barry Goldwater, Zane Grey, Carl Hayden, George W. P. Hunt, Helen Hull Jacobs, Bil Keane, Percival Lowell, John McCain, John J. Rhodes, Linda Ronstadt, Emma Stone, Morris K. Udall, Stewart L. Udall, Frank Lloyd Wright.

Website. www.az.gov

Arkansas (AR)
Natural State, Razorback State

People. Population: 3,004,279; rank: 32. **Pop. change** (2010-17): 3.0%. **Pop. density:** 57.7 per sq mi. **Racial distribution:** 79.3% white; 15.7% black; 1.6% Asian; 1.0% Amer. Ind.; 0.3% Pac. Isl.; 2+ races, 2.1%. **Hispanic pop.:** 7.6%.

Geography. Total area: 53,179 sq mi; rank: 29. **Land area:** 52,035 sq mi; rank: 27. **Acres forested:** 19.0 mil. **Location:** West South Central state. **Climate:** long, hot summers, mild winters; generally abundant rainfall. **Topography:** eastern delta and prairie, southern lowland forests, and the northwestern highlands, which include the Ozark Plateaus. **Capital:** Little Rock. **Chief airports:** Bentonville, Little Rock.

Economy. Chief industries: manufacturing, agriculture, tourism, forestry. **Chief manuf. goods:** poultry processing, motor vehicles and parts, iron and steel, paper and paperboard, plastics, preserved fruits and vegetables, aerospace, rubber. **Chief crops:** rice, soybeans, cotton, hay, wheat, corn, sorghum, tomatoes, peaches, watermelons, pecans, blueberries, grapes. **Farm income:** crops, $3.50 bil; livestock, $4.71 bil. **Nonfuel minerals:** $771 mil; stone (crushed), bromine, cement (portland), sand and gravel (construction), sand and gravel (industrial). **Chief port:** Helena. **Gross state product:** $124.9 bil. **Sales tax:** 6.5%. **Gasoline tax:** 40.20 cents/gal. **Employment distrib.:** 17.1% govt.; 20.0% trade/trans./util.; 12.8% mfg.; 15.1% ed./health; 11.8% prof./bus. serv.; 9.5% leisure/hosp.; 4.3% finance; 4.5% constr./mining/log.; 1.0% info.; 3.9% other serv. **Unemployment:** 3.7%. **Min. wage/hr.:** $8.50. **Per cap. pers. income:** $40,791. **New private housing:** 10,795 units/$1.8 bil. **Broadband internet:** 92.7%. **Commercial banks:** 121; deposits: $64.2 bil. **Savings institutions:** 1; deposits: $42.0 mil. **Lottery:** total sales: $499.1 mil; profit: $85.2 mil.

Federal govt. Fed. civ. employees: 12,923; **avg. salary:** $68,583. **Notable fed. facilities:** Little Rock AFB; Pine Bluff Arsenal; Natl. Ctr. for Toxicological Research, Jefferson.

Education. High school grad. rate: 87.0%. **4-yr. public coll./univ.:** 11; **2-yr. public:** 22; **4-yr. private:** 12.

Energy. Electricity use/cost: 1,083 kWh, $107.44.

State data. Motto: Regnat Populus (The people rule). **Flower:** Apple blossom. **Bird:** Northern mockingbird. **Tree:** Pine. **Song:** "Arkansas." **Entered union:** June 15, 1836; rank: 25th.

Tourism. Tourist spending: $7.0 bil. **Attractions:** Eureka Springs; Ozark Folk Ctr. State Park, Mountain View; Blanchard Springs Caverns, in Ozark Natl. Forest; Crater of Diamonds State Park, Murfreesboro; Toltec Mounds Archeological State Park, Scott; Buffalo Natl. River; Hot Springs Natl. Park; Pea Ridge Natl. Military Park; William J. Clinton Presidential Library and Museum, Little Rock Central High School Natl. Historic Site, in Little Rock; Crystal Bridges Museum of American Art, Bentonville. **Information:** Arkansas Dept. of Parks & Tourism, 1 Capitol Mall, Little Rock, AR 72201; 1-800-NATURAL; www.arkansas.com

History. Quapaw, Caddo, Osage, Cherokee, and Choctaw peoples lived in the area at the time of European contact. The first European explorers were Hernando de Soto, 1541; Jacques Marquette and Louis Jolliet, 1673; and René-Robert Cavelier, sieur de La Salle, 1682. French fur trader Henri de Tonty founded the first settlement, 1686, at Arkansas Post. In 1762, the area was ceded by France to Spain, then given back, 1800, and was part of the Louisiana Purchase, 1803. It was made a territory, 1819, and entered the Union as a slave state, 1836. Arkansas seceded in 1861, after the Civil War began; it was readmitted, 1868. Pres. Eisenhower sent federal troops, 1957, to keep Gov. Orval Faubus from blocking racial integration at Central High School in Little Rock. Walmart, now the world's leading retailer, opened its first store in Rogers, 1962. Elected five times as governor, Bill Clinton later served two terms as president (1993-2001). His presidential library opened, 2004, in Little Rock. After 12 years without an execution, the state put to death four inmates in eight days in 2017.

Famous Arkansans. Daisy Bates, Dee Brown, Paul "Bear" Bryant, Glen Campbell, Hattie Wyatt Caraway, Johnny Cash, Wesley Clark, Bill Clinton, Jay Hanna "Dizzy" Dean, Orval Faubus, James William Fulbright, Al Green, John Grisham, Levon Helm, John H. Johnson, Douglas MacArthur, John Little McClellan, James S. McDonnell, Scottie Pippen, Dick Powell, Brooks Robinson, Winthrop Rockefeller, Mary Steenburgen, Edward Durell Stone, Billy Bob Thornton, Sam Walton, Archibald Yell.

Website. www.arkansas.gov

California (CA)
Golden State

People. Population: 39,536,653; rank: 1. **Pop. change** (2010-17): 6.1%. **Pop. density:** 253.8 per sq mi. **Racial distribution:** 72.4% white; 6.5% black; 15.2% Asian; 1.6% Amer. Ind.; 0.5% Pac. Isl.; 2+ races, 3.9%. **Hispanic pop.:** 39.1%.

Geography. Total area: 163,695 sq mi; rank: 3. **Land area:** 155,779 sq mi; rank: 3. **Acres forested:** 31.8 mil. **Location:** western coast of U.S. **Climate:** moderate temperatures and rainfall along the coast; extremes in the interior. **Topography:** long mountainous coastline; central valley; Sierra Nevada on the E; desert basins in southern interior; rugged mountains in N. **Capital:** Sacramento. **Chief airports:** Burbank, Fresno, Long Beach, Los Angeles, Oakland, Ontario, Palm Springs, Sacramento, San Diego, San Francisco, San Jose, Santa Ana.

Economy. Chief industries: agriculture, tourism, apparel, electronics, telecommunications, entertainment. **Chief manuf. goods:** petroleum, aerospace, precision instruments, semiconductors, telecom and broadcasting equip., pharmaceutical, wineries, plastics, medical equip., preserved fruits and vegetables, printing, dairy, cut and sew apparel, motor vehicles. **Chief crops:** grapes, nursery products, almonds, lettuce, hay, strawberries, floriculture, tomatoes, cotton, oranges, pistachios, walnuts, broccoli, carrots, rice, peaches, lemons. **Farm income:** crops, $35.59 bil; livestock, $10.45 bil. **Nonfuel minerals:** $3.5 bil; sand and gravel (construction), cement (portland), boron minerals, stone (crushed), gold. **Commercial fishing:** $216.1 mil. **Chief ports:** Long Beach, Los Angeles, San Diego, Port Hueneme, Richmond, Oakland, San Francisco, Stockton. **Gross state product:** $2.7 tril. **Sales tax:** 7.25%. **Gasoline tax:** 73.62 cents/gal. **Employment distrib.:** 15.3% govt.; 17.7% trade/trans./util.; 7.7% mfg.; 15.8% ed./health; 15.2% prof./bus. serv.; 11.7% leisure/hosp.; 4.9% finance; 5.1% constr./mining/log.; 3.1% info.; 3.3% other serv. **Unemployment:** 4.8%. **Min. wage/hr.:** $11.00. **Per cap. pers. income:** $58,272. **New private housing:** 114,780 units/$27.8 bil. **Broadband internet:** 97.2%. **Commercial banks:** 202; deposits: $1.3 tril. **Savings institutions:** 14; deposits: $15.8 bil. **Lottery:** total sales: $6.2 bil; profit: $1.5 bil.

Federal govt. Fed. civ. employees: 139,979; **avg. salary:** $85,981. **Notable fed. facilities:** USMC Camp Pendleton; Naval Base Coronado; Marine Corps Air Ground Combat Ctr., 29 Palms; Marine Corps Air Station Miramar; Travis AFB; Naval Research Lab, Monterey; Lawrence Livermore Natl. Lab; Lawrence Berkeley Natl. Lab; NASA Jet Propulsion Lab, Pasadena; Edwards AFB (NASA Dryden Flight Research Ctr., AF Test Ctr.); San Francisco Mint.

Education. High school grad. rate: 83.0%. **4-yr. public coll./univ.:** 46; **2-yr. public:** 105; **4-yr. private:** 142.

Energy. Electricity use/cost: 547 kWh, $95.20.

State data. Motto: Eureka (I have found it). **Flower:** Golden poppy. **Bird:** California valley quail. **Tree:** California redwood. **Song:** "I Love You, California." **Entered union:** Sept. 9, 1850; rank: 31st.

Tourism. Tourist spending: $133.5 bil. **Attractions:** Queen Mary, Aquarium of the Pacific, in Long Beach; Palomar Observatory, Palomar Mountain; Disneyland Resort, Anaheim; Getty Center, Universal Studios Hollywood, Griffith Observatory, in Los Angeles; Tournament of Roses and Rose Bowl, Pasadena; The California Museum, California State Railroad Museum, in Sacramento; San Diego Zoo, USS Midway Museum, in San Diego; Yosemite Valley; Lassen Volcanic, Sequoia, and Kings Canyon Natl. Parks; Mojave and Sonoran Deserts; Death Valley; Golden Gate Park, Alcatraz Island, in San Francisco; Napa Valley wine region; Monterey Bay Aquarium, Monterey Peninsula; Ancient Bristlecone Pine Forest (oldest known living trees on Earth), in Inyo Natl. Forest; Redwood Natl. and State Parks; Muir Woods Natl. Monument, Mill Valley. **Information:** California Tourism, P.O. Box 1499, Sacramento, CA 95812-1499; 1-877-225-4367; www.visitcalifornia.com

History. Early inhabitants included more than 100 different Native American tribes with multiple dialects. The first European explorers were Juan Rodríguez Cabrillo, 1542, and Sir Francis Drake, 1579. The first settlement was the Spanish Alta California mission at San Diego, 1769, first in a string founded by Franciscan Father Junípero Serra. California became a province of independent Mexico, 1821. U.S. traders and settlers arrived in the 19th cent. and staged the Bear Flag revolt, 1846, in protest against Mexican rule; later that year U.S. forces occupied California. At the end of the Mexican War, Mexico ceded the territory to the U.S., 1848; that same year gold was discovered, and the famed gold rush began. California became a state, 1850. An economic downturn in the 1870s spurred riots against Chinese immigrants, who had come as laborers in the boom years. An earthquake and related fires devastated San Francisco, 1906. During World War II, Japanese Americans, many of them U.S. citizens, were held in detention camps, 1942-45. Ronald Reagan, a former movie actor, became state governor (1967-75) and U.S. president (1981-89). A budget crisis, 2003, resulted in the recall of Gov. Gray Davis and the election of another actor, Arnold Schwarzenegger. Led by Hollywood in entertainment and Silicon Valley in technology, the state's economy dwarfs that of most nations. In 2015, Gov. Jerry Brown ordered a mandatory statewide reduction in water use; the 6-year-old drought mostly ended in 2017. Wildfires caused 54 deaths in Oct.-Dec. 2017 and destroyed thousands of homes and other structures. Mudslides in fire-affected Montecito killed 21 people in early 2018, and major summer wildfires again proved deadly.

Famous Californians. Tom Brady, Edmund G. (Pat) Brown, Jerry Brown, Luther Burbank, Julia Child, Ted Danson, Cameron Diaz, Leonardo DiCaprio, Joe DiMaggio, Landon Donovan, Clint Eastwood, Dianne Feinstein, John C. Fremont, Tom Hanks, William Randolph Hearst, Helen Hunt, Steve Jobs, Jimmie Johnson, Angelina Jolie, Jack Kemp, Jason Kidd, Brie Larson, Lisa Leslie, Monica Lewinsky, Jack London, George Lucas, Phil Mickelson, Marilyn Monroe, John Muir, Richard M. Nixon, Gwyneth Paltrow, George S. Patton Jr., Gregory Peck, Nancy Pelosi, Ronald Reagan, Sally K. Ride, William Saroyan, Arnold Schwarzenegger, Junípero Serra, O. J. Simpson, Kevin Spacey, Leland Stanford, Gwen Stefani, John Steinbeck, Shirley Temple, Earl Warren, Serena Williams, Ted Williams, Venus Williams, Tiger Woods.

Website. www.ca.gov

Colorado (CO)
Centennial State

People. Population: 5,607,154; rank: 21. **Pop. change** (2010-17): 11.5%. **Pop. density:** 54.1 per sq mi. **Racial distribution:** 87.3% white; 4.5% black; 3.4% Asian; 1.6% Amer. Ind.; 0.2% Pac. Isl.; 2+ races, 3.0%. **Hispanic pop.:** 21.5%.

Geography. Total area: 104,094 sq mi; rank: 8. **Land area:** 103,642 sq mi; rank: 8. **Acres forested:** 22.9 mil. **Location:** W central U.S. **Climate:** low relative humidity, abundant sun, wide daily/seasonal temperature ranges; alpine conditions in the high mountains. **Topography:** eastern dry high plains; hilly to mountainous central plateau; western Rocky Mts. of high ranges with broad valleys, deep, narrow canyons. **Capital:** Denver. **Chief airports:** Colorado Springs, Denver.

Economy. Chief industries: manufacturing, construction, government, tourism, agriculture, aerospace, electronics equip. **Chief manuf. goods:** animal slaughtering, beer, petroleum, pharmaceuticals, aerospace, medical equip., precision instruments, printing, semiconductors. **Chief crops:** hay, corn, potatoes, wheat, onions, dry edible beans, sunflowers, sugar beets, barley, proso millet, cabbage, peaches, lettuce, apples, cantaloupes. **Farm income:** crops, $2.01 bil.; livestock, $4.16 bil. **Nonfuel minerals:** $1.7 bil; gold, cement (portland), sand and gravel (construction), molybdenum concentrates, stone (crushed). **Gross state product:** $342.7 bil. **Sales tax:** 2.9%. **Gasoline tax:** 40.40 cents/gal. **Employment distrib.:** 16.7% govt.; 17.2% trade/trans./util.; 5.4% mfg.; 12.4% ed./health; 15.8% prof./bus. serv.; 12.4% leisure/hosp.; 6.1% finance; 7.3% constr./mining/log.; 2.7% info.; 4.0% other serv. **Unemployment:** 2.8%. **Min. wage/hr.:** $10.20. **Per cap. pers. income:** $53,504. **New private housing:** 40,673 units/$9.5 bil. **Broadband internet:** 95.1%. **Commercial banks:** 125; deposits: $129.3 bil. **Savings institutions:** 15; deposits: $3.3 bil. **Lottery:** total sales: $555.3 mil.; profit: $133.5 mil.

Federal govt. Fed. civ. employees: 35,922; **avg. salary:** $85,783. **Notable fed. facilities:** U.S. Air Force Academy; Peterson AFB; Denver Mint; Ft. Carson; Natl. Renewable Energy Lab, Golden; Transportation Tech. Ctr., Pueblo; NORAD and USNORTHCOM Alt. Command Ctr., Cheyenne Mtn. Complex; Denver Fed. Ctr.; Natl. Ctr. for Atmospheric Research, Natl. Inst. of Standards & Technology, NOAA Earth System Environmental Lab, Boulder; Natl. Wildlife Research Ctr., Fort Collins.

Education. High school grad. rate: 78.9%. **4-yr. public coll./univ.:** 16; **2-yr. public:** 12; **4-yr. private:** 14.

Energy. Electricity use/cost: 694 kWh, $83.85.

State data. Motto: Nil Sine Numine (Nothing without Providence). **Flower:** Rocky Mountain columbine. **Bird:** Lark bunting. **Tree:** Colorado blue spruce. **Songs:** "Where the Columbines Grow"; "Rocky Mountain High." **Entered union:** Aug. 1, 1876; rank: 38th.

Tourism. Tourist spending: $18.9 bil. **Attractions:** Denver Museum of Nature & Science, Denver Botanic Gardens, Denver Zoo; Red Rocks Park and Amphitheatre, Morrison; Natl. Ctr. for Atmospheric Research, Boulder; Rocky Mountain, Black Canyon of the Gunnison, and Mesa Verde (Anasazi cliff dwellings) Natl. Parks; Aspen, Breckenridge, Steamboat, and Vail ski resorts; Garden of the Gods, Colorado Springs; Great Sand Dunes Natl. Park and Preserve; Dinosaur and Colorado Natl. Monuments; Pikes Peak and Mount Evans; Grand Mesa Natl. Forest; historic mining towns of Central City, Silverton, Cripple Creek; Bent's Old Fort Natl. Historic Site, near La Junta; Georgetown Loop Historic Mining and Railroad Park; Durango & Silverton Narrow Gauge Railroad Museum, Durango; Cumbres & Toltec Scenic Railroad, Antonito; gambling in Black Hawk, Central City, Cripple Creek and on tribal land in Ignacio and Towaoc. **Information:** Colorado Tourism Office, 1625 Broadway, Ste. 1700, Denver, CO 80202; 1-800-265-6723; www.colorado.com

History. Paleo-Indians hunted big game in the area at least 11,000 years ago. Anasazi cliff dwellers flourished around Mesa Verde until about 1300 CE; other Native Americans were the Ute, Pueblo, Cheyenne, and Arapaho. The region was claimed by Spain but passed to France, 1800. The U.S. acquired eastern Colorado in the Louisiana Purchase, 1803. Lt. Zebulon M. Pike explored the area, 1806, sighting the peak that bears his name. After the Mexican War, 1846-48, U.S. immigrants settled in the east, former Mexicans in the south. Gold was discovered in 1858, causing a population boom. Congress created Colorado Territory, 1861. Conflict between newcomers and displaced Native Americans led to the Sand Creek Massacre, 1864, in which U.S. soldiers and settlers killed some 150 Cheyenne and Arapaho. U.S. Army troops forced the removal to reservations (mostly in present-day Oklahoma) of most Native Americans in the state, 1867. The 1870s brought statehood, 1876, and rich silver finds that turned Leadville into a boomtown. Federal military and civilian employment in Colorado surged in the 1940s and '50s; since then, tourism and technology have fueled the economy. The state's Hispanic population grew from 5.8% in 1980 to 20.7% in 2010. Colorado became the first state in the U.S. to legalize selling recreational marijuana in 2014. The state raised $223 mil in fees and tax revenue from combined medical and recreational marijuana sales in FY2016-17.

Famous Coloradans. Tim Allen, Chauncey Billups, Frederick Bonfils, Molly Brown, William N. Byers, M. Scott Carpenter, Lon Chaney, Jack Dempsey, Mamie Eisenhower, Douglas Fairbanks, Barney Ford, Neil Gorsuch, Roy Halladay, Ouray, Trey Parker, "Baby Doe" Tabor, Lowell Thomas, Byron R. White, Paul Whiteman.

Website. www.colorado.gov

Connecticut (CT)
Constitution State, Nutmeg State

People. Population: 3,588,184; rank: 29. **Pop. change** (2010-17): 0.4%. **Pop. density:** 741.1 per sq mi. **Racial distribution:** 80.3% white; 11.9% black; 4.8% Asian; 0.5% Amer. Ind.; 0.1% Pac. Isl.; 2+ races, 2.4%. **Hispanic pop.:** 16.1%.

Geography. Total area: 5,543 sq mi; rank: 48. **Land area:** 4,842 sq mi; rank: 48. **Acres forested:** 1.8 mil. **Location:** New England state in NE corner of U.S. **Climate:** moderate; winters avg. slightly below freezing; warm, humid summers. **Topography:** western upland, the Berkshires, in the NW, highest elevations; narrow central lowland N-S; hilly eastern upland drained by rivers. **Capital:** Hartford. **Chief airport:** Windsor Locks.

Economy. Chief industries: manufacturing, retail trade, government, services, finances, insurance, real estate. **Chief manuf. goods:** aerospace, chemicals, fabricated metals, precision instruments, toiletries, medical equip., printing, plastics. **Chief crops:** nursery stock, Christmas trees, mushrooms, sweet corn, apples, tobacco, hay. **Farm income:** crops, $346.89 mil.; livestock, $167.37 mil. **Nonfuel minerals:** $183 mil; stone (crushed), sand and gravel (construction), stone (dimension), clays (common), gemstones (natural). **Commercial fishing:** $15.0 mil. **Chief ports:** New Haven, Bridgeport, New London. **Gross state product:** $260.8 bil. **Sales tax:** 6.35%. **Gasoline tax:** 62.20 cents/gal. **Employment distrib.:** 13.8% govt.; 17.6% trade/trans./util.; 9.6% mfg.; 19.9% ed./health; 13.1% prof./bus. serv.; 9.3% leisure/hosp.; 7.5% finance; 3.7% constr./mining/log.; 1.8% info.; 3.8% other serv. **Unemployment:** 4.7%. **Min. wage/hr.:** $10.10. **Per cap. pers. income:** $70,121. **New private housing:** 4,547 units/$1.2 bil. **Broadband internet:** 98.9%. **Commercial banks:** 33; deposits: $109.9 bil. **Savings institutions:** 29; deposits: $23.4 bil. **Lottery:** total sales: $1.2 bil; profit: $332.3 mil.

Federal govt. Fed. civ. employees: 8,028; **avg. salary:** $83,374. **Notable fed. facilities:** U.S. Coast Guard Academy; Naval Sub Base New London.

Education. High school grad. rate: 87.4%. **4-yr. public coll./univ.:** 9; **2-yr. public:** 12; **4-yr. private:** 18.

Energy. Electricity use/cost: 711 kWh, $142.19.

State data. Motto: Qui Transtulit Sustinet (He who transplanted still sustains). **Flower:** Mountain laurel. **Bird:** American robin. **Tree:** White oak. **Song:** "Yankee Doodle."

Fifth of the 13 original states to ratify the Constitution, Jan. 9, 1788.

Tourism. Tourist spending: $11.2 bil. **Attractions:** Mark Twain House and Museum, Hartford; Yale Univ. Art Gallery, Peabody Museum of Natural History, in New Haven; Mystic Seaport, Mystic Aquarium; Barnum Museum, Bridgeport; Gillette Castle State Park, East Haddam; USS *Nautilus* (1st nuclear-powered submarine) at Submarine Force Library and Museum, Groton; Mashantucket Pequot Museum and Research Ctr.; Foxwoods Resort Casino, Ledyard; Mohegan Sun, Uncasville; Lake Compounce (est. 1846; oldest continuously operating amusement park in U.S.), Bristol; Philip Johnson Glass House, New Canaan. **Information:** Connecticut Office of Tourism, 450 Columbus Blvd., Ste. 5, Hartford, CT 06103; 1-888-CTVISIT, (860) 256-2800; www.ctvisit.com

History. At the time of European contact, inhabitants of the area were Algonquian peoples, including the Mohegan and Pequot. Dutch explorer Adriaen Block was the first European visitor, 1614. By 1634, English settlers from Plymouth had started colonies along the Connecticut R.; in 1637 they defeated the Pequots. The Colony of Connecticut was chartered by England, 1662; New Haven colony was added, 1665. A Patriot stronghold in the American Revolution, the state actively supported the antislavery movement and the Union cause in the Civil War. The state economy prospered in the 20th cent. from insurance- and defense-related industries. *Nautilus*, the first nuclear-powered submarine, was launched at Groton, 1954. Connecticut Sen. Joseph Lieberman was the Democratic nominee for vice president in 2000. American Indian casinos, starting with Foxwoods in 1992, were an economic boon to the state, but tourism revenues declined sharply with the recession that began in late 2007. Twenty children and six staff members were killed in a mass shooting at Sandy Hook Elementary School in Newtown, Dec. 14, 2012.

Famous "Nutmeggers." Ethan Allen, P. T. Barnum, Michael Bolton, Glenn Close, Samuel Colt, Ann Coulter, Jonathan Edwards, Nathan Hale, Katharine Hepburn, Isaac Hull, Norman Lear, Seth MacFarlane, John Mayer, Robert Mitchum, J. P. Morgan, Ralph Nader, Israel Putnam, Wallace Stevens, Harriet Beecher Stowe, Mark Twain, Noah Webster, Eli Whitney.

Website. www.ct.gov

Delaware (DE)
First State, Diamond State

People. Population: 961,939; rank: 45. **Pop. change** (2010-17): 7.1%. **Pop. density:** 493.6 per sq mi. **Racial distribution:** 69.7% white; 22.8% black; 4.1% Asian; 0.6% Amer. Ind.; 0.1% Pac. Isl.; 2+ races, 2.6%. **Hispanic pop.:** 9.3%.

Geography. Total area: 2,489 sq mi; rank: 49. **Land area:** 1,949 sq mi; rank: 49. **Acres forested:** 0.4 mil. **Location:** Delmarva Peninsula on the Atlantic coastal plain. **Climate:** moderate. **Topography:** Piedmont Plateau to the N, sloping to a near sea-level plain. **Capital:** Dover.

Economy. Chief industries: chemicals, agriculture, finance, poultry, shellfish, tourism, auto assembly, food processing, transportation equip. **Chief manuf. goods:** pharmaceuticals, poultry processing, soap and cleaning compounds, precision instruments, basic chemicals, plastics. **Chief crops:** soybeans, corn, greenhouse and nursery, wheat, potatoes, barley, hay, watermelons, lima beans, green peas, pumpkins, mushrooms, cabbage. **Farm income:** crops, $280.85 mil; livestock, $929.06 mil. **Nonfuel minerals:** $25 mil; sand and gravel (construction), magnesium compounds, stone (crushed), gemstones (natural). **Commercial fishing:** $11.5 mil. **Chief port:** Wilmington. **Gross state product:** $73.5 bil. **Sales tax:** none. **Gasoline tax:** 41.40 cents/gal. **Employment distrib.:** 14.6% govt.; 17.7% trade/trans./util.; 5.6% mfg.; 16.9% ed./health; 13.9% prof./bus. serv.; 11.0% leisure/hosp.; 10.3% finance; 4.9% constr./mining/log.; 0.9% info.; 4.1% other serv. **Unemployment:** 4.6%. **Min. wage/hr.:** $8.25. **Per cap. pers. income:** $49,125. **New private housing:** 6,601 units/$806.5 mil. **Broadband internet:** 98.3%. **Commercial banks:** 37; deposits: $354.2 bil. **Savings institutions:** 5; deposits: $4.4 bil. **Lottery:** total sales: $624.5 mil; profit: $205.7 mil.

Federal govt. Fed. civ. employees: 3,097; **avg. salary:** $73,847. **Notable fed. facilities:** Dover AFB; Bombay Hook Natl. Wildlife Refuge.

Education. High school grad. rate: 85.5%. **4-yr. public coll./univ.:** 3; **2-yr. public:** 0; **4-yr. private:** 3.

Energy. Electricity use/cost: 947 kWh, $127.03.

State data. Motto: Liberty and independence. **Flower:** Peach blossom. **Bird:** Blue hen chicken. **Tree:** American holly.

Song: "Our Delaware." **First** of original 13 states to ratify the Constitution, Dec. 7, 1787.

Tourism. Tourist spending: $2.1 bil. **Attractions:** Fort Christina (site of founding of colony of New Sweden), Holy Trinity (Old Swedes) Church (erected 1698, oldest church in U.S. still standing as built and in use), Hagley Museum and Library, Nemours Mansion and Gardens, in Wilmington; Winterthur Museum, Garden, and Library, near Wilmington; New Castle Historic District; John Dickinson "Penman of the Revolution" Plantation, First State Heritage Park, Dover Intl. Speedway, in Dover; Rehoboth Beach. **Information:** Delaware Tourism Office, 99 Kings Hwy., Dover, DE 19901; 1-866-2VISITDE; www.visitdelaware.com

History. The Lenni Lenape (Delaware) people lived in the region at the time of European contact. Henry Hudson located the Delaware R., 1609. In 1610, English explorer Samuel Argall entered Delaware Bay and named the area after Virginia's governor, Lord De La Warr. Dutch, Swedish, and Finnish settlers were followed by the British, who took control in 1664. After 1682, Delaware became part of Pennsylvania, and in 1704 it was granted its own assembly. It adopted a constitution as the state of Delaware, 1776, and was the first state to ratify the federal Constitution, 1787. Although it remained in the Union during the Civil War, Delaware retained slavery until the 13th Amendment abolished it in 1865. The DuPont company, founded as a gunpowder mill in 1802, became an industrial giant in the 20th cent. making nylon, Teflon, and other synthetics. Pro-business laws drew many out-of-state firms to incorporate in Delaware. In 2000, Ruth Ann Minner was elected Delaware's first woman governor. Joe Biden, the state's former U.S. senator, served as U.S. vice president, 2009-17.

Famous Delawareans. Thomas F. Bayard, Joe Biden, Henry Seidel Canby, E. I. du Pont, John P. Marquand, Aubrey Plaza, Howard Pyle, Caesar Rodney, Susan Stroman.

Website. www.delaware.gov

Florida (FL)
Sunshine State

People. Population: 20,984,400; rank: 3. **Pop. change** (2010-17): 11.6%. **Pop. density:** 391.3 per sq mi. **Racial distribution:** 77.4% white; 16.9% black; 2.9% Asian; 0.5% Amer. Ind.; 0.1% Pac. Isl.; 2+ races, 2.1%. **Hispanic pop.:** 25.6%.

Geography. Total area: 65,758 sq mi; rank: 22. **Land area:** 53,625 sq mi; rank: 26. **Acres forested:** 17.1 mil. **Location:** peninsula jutting southward 500 mi between the Atlantic and Gulf of Mexico. **Climate:** subtropical N of Bradenton-Lake Okeechobee-Vero Beach line; tropical S of line. **Topography:** land is flat or rolling; highest point is 345 ft in the NW. **Capital:** Tallahassee. **Chief airports:** Clearwater, Fort Lauderdale, Fort Myers, Jacksonville, Miami, Orlando, Pensacola, Punta Gorda, Sanford, Sarasota, Tampa, Valparaiso, West Palm Beach.

Economy. Chief industries: tourism, agriculture, manufacturing, construction, services, international trade. **Chief manuf. goods:** navigational instruments, medical equip., cement, broadcasting equip., beverages, phosphatic fertilizer, preserved fruits and vegetables, structural metal, printing. **Chief crops:** greenhouse and nursery, oranges, sugarcane, tomatoes, green peppers, grapefruit, strawberries, snap beans, sweet corn, potatoes, cucumbers, tangerines. **Farm income:** crops, $6.08 bil; livestock, $1.66 bil. **Nonfuel minerals:** $3.2 bil; phosphate rock, stone (crushed), cement (portland), sand and gravel (construction), cement (masonry). **Commercial fishing:** $236.6 mil. **Chief ports:** Pensacola, Tampa, Port Manatee, Miami, Port Everglades, Jacksonville, Canaveral. **Gross state product:** $967.3 bil. **Sales tax:** 6.0%. **Gasoline tax:** 59.76 cents/gal. **Employment distrib.:** 12.7% govt.; 20.0% trade/trans./util.; 4.3% mfg.; 14.8% ed./health; 15.4% prof./bus. serv.; 14.4% leisure/hosp.; 6.6% finance; 6.2% constr./mining/log.; 1.6% info.; 4.0% other serv. **Unemployment:** 4.2%. **Min. wage/hr.:** $8.25. **Per cap. pers. income:** $46,858. **New private housing:** 122,719 units/$28.1 bil. **Broadband internet:** 97.3%. **Commercial banks:** 206; deposits: $533.8 bil. **Savings institutions:** 21; deposits: $30.2 bil. **Lottery:** total sales: $6.2 bil; profit: $1.7 bil.

Federal govt. Fed. civ. employees: 79,045; **avg. salary:** $77,600. **Notable fed. facilities:** John F. Kennedy Space Ctr.; Eglin AFB; MacDill AFB; Hurlburt Field; Pensacola NAS; Jacksonville NAS; Mayport Naval Sta.

Education. High school grad. rate: 80.7%. **4-yr. public coll./univ.:** 39; **2-yr. public:** 3; **4-yr. private:** 66.

Energy. Electricity use/cost: 1,123 kWh, $123.37.

State data. Motto: In God we trust. **Flower:** Orange blossom. **Bird:** Northern mockingbird. **Tree:** Sabal palmetto palm.

Song: "Old Folks at Home." **Entered union:** Mar. 3, 1845; rank: 27th.

Tourism. Tourist spending: $94.0 bil. **Attractions:** Miami Beach; Castillo de San Marcos Natl. Monument, St. Augustine Lighthouse & Museum, Lightner Museum, in St. Augustine (oldest permanent European settlement in U.S.); Walt Disney World Resort, SeaWorld Orlando, Universal Studios, Discovery Cove, in Orlando; Kennedy Space Ctr., U.S. Astronaut Hall of Fame; Everglades Natl. Park; Ringling Museum of Art, Ringling Circus Museum, in Sarasota; Cypress Gardens at Legoland Florida, Winter Haven; Busch Gardens, Big Cat Rescue, in Tampa; Florida Caverns State Park, Marianna; Key West. **Information:** Visit Florida, 2540 W. Executive Center Cir., Ste. 200, Tallahassee, FL 32301; 1-888-7FLA-USA; www.visitflorida.com

History. Florida has been inhabited for at least 12,000 years. Timucua, Apalachee, and Calusa peoples were living in the region when the earliest Europeans came; later the Seminole migrated from Georgia to Florida, becoming dominant there in the early 18th cent. The first European to see Florida was Spain's Ponce de León, 1513. France established a colony, Ft. Caroline, on the St. Johns R., 1564. Spain settled St. Augustine, 1565, and Spanish troops massacred most of the French. Britain's Sir Francis Drake burned St. Augustine, 1586. In 1763, Spain ceded Florida to Great Britain, which held the area 20 years before returning it to Spain. Florida was ceded to the U.S. in the Adams-Onís Treaty, 1819. The Seminole War, 1835-42, resulted in the removal of most Native Americans to Indian Territory. Florida joined the Union in 1845, seceded in 1861, and was readmitted in 1868. In the late 19th cent., hotel and railroad builder Henry M. Flagler laid the foundations of the tourism industry. The state experienced phenomenal population growth in the 20th cent., especially after 1950. The first U.S. astronaut was launched into space from Cape Canaveral, 1961. Walt Disney World opened near Orlando, 1971. Hurricane Andrew slammed Florida, 1992, causing at least $25 bil in property damage. A dispute over Florida's presidential vote in 2000 was decided by the U.S. Supreme Court and resulted in George W. Bush's Electoral College victory. Four hurricanes hit the state in 2004, causing more than $40 bil in damages. In June 2016, a gunman carried out the then-deadliest mass shooting in modern U.S. history when he killed 49 people at a gay nightclub in Orlando. After 49 days, the CDC in Sept. 2016 lifted its first-ever travel warning for a part of the continental U.S. when a Miami neighborhood was declared free of Zika virus. The Palm Beach private club Mar-a-Lago in 2017-18 frequently hosted its owner, Pres. Donald Trump. A Feb. 2018 mass shooting at a Parkland high school killed 17 and galvanized a wave of youth-led activism against gun violence.

Famous Floridians. Edna Buchanan, Jeb Bush, Marjory Stoneman Douglas, Henry Morrison Flagler, Carl Hiaasen, Perez Hilton, Zora Neale Hurston, James Weldon Johnson, Deacon Jones, MacKinlay Kantor, Osceola, Claude Pepper, Tom Petty, Henry B. Plant, A. Philip Randolph, Marjorie Kinnan Rawlings, Janet Reno, Marco Rubio, Deion Sanders, Emmitt Smith, Joseph W. Stilwell, Amar'e Stoudemire, Charles P. Summerall.

Website. www.myflorida.com

Georgia (GA)
Empire State of the South, Peach State

People. Population: 10,429,379; rank: 8. **Pop. change** (2010-17): 7.6%. **Pop. density:** 181.3 per sq mi. **Racial distribution:** 60.8% white; 32.2% black; 4.2% Asian; 0.5% Amer. Ind.; 0.1% Pac. Isl.; 2+ races, 2.1%. **Hispanic pop.:** 9.6%.

Geography. Total area: 59,425 sq mi; rank: 24. **Land area:** 57,513 sq mi; rank: 21. **Acres forested:** 24.6 mil. **Location:** South Atlantic state. **Climate:** maritime tropical air masses dominate in summer; polar air masses in winter; E central area drier. **Topography:** most southerly of the Blue Ridge Mts. cover NE and N central; central Piedmont extends to the fall line of rivers; coastal plain levels to the coast flatlands. **Capital:** Atlanta. **Chief airports:** Atlanta, Savannah.

Economy. Chief industries: services, manufacturing, retail trade. **Chief manuf. goods:** carpet and rugs, animal slaughtering and processing, motor vehicles and parts, plastics, aircrafts, paper, chemicals, food. **Chief crops:** cotton, greenhouse and nursery, peanuts, pecans, corn, tomatoes, cucumbers, onions, watermelons, tobacco, squash, blueberries, hay, cabbage, soybeans, peaches, snap beans, wheat. **Farm income:** crops, $3.14 bil; livestock, $5.29 bil. **Nonfuel minerals:** $1.8 bil; clays (kaolin), stone (crushed), sand and gravel (construction), cement (portland), clays (montmorillonite).

Commercial fishing: $13.5 mil. **Chief ports:** Savannah, Brunswick. **Gross state product:** $554.3 bil. **Sales tax:** 4.0%. **Gasoline tax:** 49.99 cents/gal. **Employment distrib.:** 15.2% govt.; 21.1% trade/trans./util.; 8.8% mfg.; 12.9% ed./health; 14.7% prof./bus. serv.; 11.1% leisure/hosp.; 5.3% finance; 4.6% constr./mining/log.; 2.5% info.; 3.6% other serv. **Unemployment:** 4.7%. **Min. wage/hr.:** $5.15 ($7.25). **Per cap. pers. income:** $43,270. **New private housing:** 51,240 units/$9.9 bil. **Broadband internet:** 95.5%. **Commercial banks:** 213; deposits: $238.0 bil. **Savings institutions:** 14; deposits: $2.8 bil. **Lottery:** total sales: $4.5 bil; profit: $1.1 bil.

Federal govt. Fed. civ. employees: 71,511; **avg. salary:** $79,186. **Notable fed. facilities:** Ft. Benning; Ft. Stewart; Fed. Law Enforcement Training Ctr., Brunswick; Robins AFB; Ft. Gordon; Naval Sub Base Kings Bay; Moody AFB; Centers for Disease Control, Atlanta; Marine Corps Logistics Base Albany.

Education. High school grad. rate: 79.4%. **4-yr. public coll./univ.:** 30; **2-yr. public:** 23; **4-yr. private:** 33.

Energy. Electricity use/cost: 1,138 kWh, $130.87.

State data. Motto: Wisdom, justice, and moderation. **Flower:** Cherokee rose. **Bird:** Brown thrasher. **Tree:** Southern live oak. **Song:** "Georgia on My Mind." **Fourth** of the 13 original states to ratify the Constitution, Jan. 2, 1788.

Tourism. Tourist spending: $28.5 bil. **Attractions:** Georgia State Capitol, Stone Mountain, Centennial Olympic Park, Six Flags Over Georgia, Martin Luther King Jr. Natl. Historic Site, Jimmy Carter Library and Museum, Atlanta Botanical Garden, Georgia Aquarium (largest in Western Hemisphere), in Atlanta; Kennesaw Mountain Natl. Battlefield Park; Chickamauga and Chattanooga Natl. Military Park; Chattahoochee-Oconee Natl. Forest; Dahlonega, site of earliest U.S. gold rush; Brasstown Bald (highest mtn. in state); Franklin D. Roosevelt's Little White House Historic Site, Warm Springs; Callaway Gardens, Pine Mountain; Andersonville Natl. Historic Site (Confederate military prison); Okefenokee Natl. Wildlife Refuge; Jekyll, St. Simons, and Cumberland barrier islands; Savannah Historic District. **Information:** Dept. of Economic Development, 75 Fifth St., NW, Ste. 1200, Atlanta, GA 30308; 1-800-VISITGA; www.exploregeorgia.org

History. Creek and Cherokee peoples were living in the region when Spaniards founded Santa Catalina mission, 1566, on Saint Catherines Island. Gen. James Oglethorpe established a colony at Savannah, 1733, for the poor and religiously persecuted. Oglethorpe defeated a Spanish army from Florida at Bloody Marsh, 1742. Georgia was a battleground in the American Revolution, with the British finally evacuating Savannah in 1782. When Georgia entered the Union, 1788, its plantation economy relied on slaves for rice and cotton growing. The Cherokee were removed to Indian Territory, 1838-39, and thousands died on the long march, known as the Trail of Tears. By 1860 the number of slaves exceeded 462,000 (nearly 44% of the total population). Georgia seceded from the Union, 1861, and was invaded by Union forces, 1864, under Gen. William T. Sherman, who took Atlanta, Sept. 2, and proceeded on his famous "march to the sea," ending in Savannah in Dec. Georgia was readmitted, 1870. Born 1929 in Atlanta, Martin Luther King Jr. made the city his base during the civil rights struggles of the 1960s. Atlanta became the leading city of the "New South," world headquarters of Coca-Cola and CNN, and host of the 1996 Summer Olympic Games. More than 70 tornadoes struck the South in late Jan. 2017, killing 16 people in southern Georgia. With the state offering significant tax breaks and other economic incentives, film and TV production was a $2.7-bil industry in 2018.

Famous Georgians. Kim Basinger, Griffin Bell, James Brown, Erskine Caldwell, Jimmy Carter, Ray Charles, Ty Cobb, James Dickey, Walt Frazier, John C. Fremont, Newt Gingrich, Nancy Grace, Joel Chandler Harris, "Doc" Holliday, Larry Holmes, Holly Hunter, Alan Jackson, Martin Luther King Jr., Gladys Knight, Sidney Lanier, Little Richard, Juliette Gordon Low, Margaret Mitchell, Jessye Norman, Sam Nunn, Flannery O'Connor, Otis Redding, Burt Reynolds, Julia Roberts, Jackie Robinson, Ryan Seacrest, Clarence Thomas, Travis Tritt, Ted Turner, Carl Vinson, Alice Walker, Herschel Walker, Joanne Woodward, Trisha Yearwood, Andrew Young.

Website. www.georgia.gov

Hawai'i (HI)
Aloha State

People. Population: 1,427,538; rank: 40. **Pop. change** (2010-17): 4.9%. **Pop. density:** 222.3 per sq mi. **Racial distribution:** 25.7% white; 2.2% black; 37.8% Asian; 0.4% Amer. Ind.; 10.2% Pac. Isl.; 2+ races, 23.8%. **Hispanic pop.:** 10.5%.

Geography. Total area: 10,932 sq mi; rank: 43. **Land area:** 6,423 sq mi; rank: 47. **Acres forested:** 1.5 mil. **Location:** Pacific archipelago of about 132 islands 2,100 mi SW of U.S. mainland. **Climate:** subtropical, with wide variations in rainfall; Mt. Waialeale, on Kaua'i, wettest spot in U.S. (annual avg. rainfall 422 in., 1912-2015). **Topography:** islands are tops of a chain of submerged volcanic mountains; Mauna Loa, Kilauea are active volcanoes. **Capital:** Honolulu. **Chief airports:** Hilo, Honolulu, Kahului, Kailua Kona, Lihue.

Economy. Chief industries: tourism, defense, sugar, pineapples. **Chief manuf. goods:** concrete, printing, baked goods, sugar, preserved fruits and vegetables, apparel. **Chief crops:** flowers and nursery, pineapples, seed crops, sugarcane, macadamia nuts, coffee, algae, papayas, tomatoes, bananas, basil, ginger. **Farm income:** crops, $496.23 mil; livestock, $152.33 mil. **Nonfuel minerals:** $105 mil; stone (crushed), sand and gravel (construction), gemstones (natural). **Commercial fishing:** $118.1 mil. **Chief ports:** Honolulu, Hilo, Barbers Point, Kahului. **Gross state product:** $88.1 bil. **Sales tax:** 4.0%. **Gasoline tax:** 66.28 cents/gal. **Employment distrib.:** 19.4% govt.; 18.3% trade/trans./util.; 2.1% mfg.; 13.0% ed./health; 12.6% prof./bus. serv.; 19.2% leisure/hosp.; 4.4% finance; 5.5% constr./mining/log.; 1.4% info.; 4.2% other serv. **Unemployment:** 2.4%. **Min. wage/hr.:** $10.10. **Per cap. pers. income:** $51,939. **New private housing:** 4,035 units/$1.1 bil. **Broadband internet:** 99.0%. **Commercial banks:** 9; deposits: $36.9 bil. **Savings institutions:** 3; deposits: $7.3 bil.

Federal govt. Fed. civ. employees: 22,319; **avg. salary:** $78,583. **Notable fed. facilities:** Joint Base Pearl Harbor-Hickam; Schofield Barracks; Marine Corps Base Hawaii, Kaneohe Bay; Tripler Army Med. Ctr.; Ft. Shafter; Wheeler Army Airfield; Prince Kuhio Federal Bldg., Honolulu.

Education. High school grad. rate: 82.7%. **4-yr. public coll./univ.:** 4; **2-yr. public:** 6; **4-yr. private:** 6.

Energy. Electricity use/cost: 505 kWh, $138.73.

State data. Motto: Ua mau ke ea o ka aina i ka pono (The life of the land is perpetuated in righteousness). **Flower:** Yellow hibiscus. **Bird:** Hawaiian goose. **Tree:** Kukui (candlenut). **Song:** "Hawai'i Pono'i" (Hawai'i's Own). **Entered union:** Aug. 21, 1959; rank: 50th.

Tourism. Tourist spending: $24.6 bil. **Attractions:** Oahu Isl.: Natl. Memorial Cemetery of the Pacific, Waikiki Beach, Diamond Head, in Honolulu; USS *Arizona* Memorial, Pearl Harbor; Polynesian Cultural Ctr., Laie; Hanauma Bay; Nu'uanu Pali. Kaua'i Isl.: Waimea Canyon. Maui Isl.: Haleakala Natl. Park. Hawai'i Isl.: Hawaii Volcanoes Natl. Park, Wailoa and Wailuku River State Parks. **Information:** Hawaii Visitors and Conventions Bureau, 2270 Kalakaua Ave., Ste. 801, Honolulu, HI 96815; 1-800-GOHAWAII; www.gohawaii.com

History. Polynesians from islands 2,000 mi to the S settled the Hawaiian Islands, probably 300-600 CE. The first European visitor was British captain James Cook, 1778. King Kamehameha I united the islands by 1810. Christian missionaries arrived, 1819, bringing Western culture. Under the reign, 1825-54, of King Kamehameha III, a constitution, legislature, and public school system were instituted. Sugar production began, 1835, and it became the dominant industry. Queen Liliuokalani was deposed, 1893, and a republic was established, 1894, headed by Sanford B. Dole, born in Hawaii to American missionaries. Annexation by the U.S. came in 1898. The Japanese attack on Pearl Harbor, Dec. 7, 1941, brought the U.S. into World War II. Hawai'i attained statehood, 1959. Hurricane Iniki pounded Kaua'i, 1992, causing about $1 bil in damage. In 2006, Pres. George W. Bush designated the Northwestern Hawaiian Islands Natl. Monument, a marine area of 140,000 sq mi. A false alert in Jan. 2018 warned Hawaiian residents of an inbound ballistic missile threat via mobile devices, radio, and TV. The Kilauea volcano on Hawaii's Big Island started to erupt, May 2018, forcing a series of evacuations.

Famous Islanders. Bernice Pauahi Bishop, Tia Carrere, Alexander Cartwright, St. Damien de Veuster, Don Ho, Daniel K. Inouye, Duke Kahanamoku, King Kamehameha, Nicole Kidman, Brook Mahealani Lee, Jason Scott Lee, Queen Liliuokalani, Bruno Mars, Bette Midler, Barack Obama, Ellison S. Onizuka, Michelle Wie.

Website. portal.ehawaii.gov

Idaho (ID)
Gem State

People. Population: 1,716,943; rank: 39. **Pop. change** (2010-17): 9.5%. **Pop. density:** 20.8 per sq mi. **Racial distribution:** 93.2% white; 0.9% black; 1.5% Asian; 1.7% Amer. Ind.; 0.2% Pac. Isl.; 2+ races, 2.4%. **Hispanic pop.:** 12.5%.

Geography. Total area: 83,569 sq mi; rank: 14. **Land area:** 82,643 sq mi; rank: 11. **Acres forested:** 21.7 mil. **Location:** northwestern Mountain state bordering British Columbia, Canada. **Climate:** tempered by Pacific westerly winds; drier, colder, continental climate in SE; altitude an important factor. **Topography:** Snake R. plains in the S; central region of mountains, canyons, gorges (Hells Canyon, 7,900 ft, deepest in N. America); subalpine northern region. **Capital:** Boise. **Chief airport:** Boise.

Economy. Chief industries: manufacturing, agriculture, tourism, lumber, mining, electronics. **Chief manuf. goods:** computers and electronics, preserved fruits and vegetables, cheese, lumber. **Chief crops:** potatoes, wheat, hay, sugar beets, barley, greenhouse and nursery, onions, dry beans, corn, mint, apples, hops, peaches, lentils, peas, cherries, plums and prunes, oats. **Farm income:** crops, $2.83 bil; livestock, $4.30 bil. **Nonfuel minerals:** $191 mil; phosphate rock, sand and gravel (construction), stone (crushed), lead, silver. **Chief port:** Lewiston. **Gross state product:** $71.9 bil. **Sales tax:** 6.0%. **Gasoline tax:** 51.40 cents/gal. **Employment distrib.:** 17.4% govt.; 19.0% trade/trans./util.; 9.4% mfg.; 14.3% ed./health; 12.7% prof./bus. serv.; 10.5% leisure/hosp.; 5.0% finance; 6.9% constr./mining/log.; 1.2% info.; 3.5% other serv. **Unemployment:** 3.2%. **Min. wage/hr.:** $7.25. **Per cap. pers. income:** $40,507. **New private housing:** 14,183 units/$2.8 bil. **Broadband internet:** 93.6%. **Commercial banks:** 31; deposits: $24.5 bil. **Savings institutions:** 1; deposits: $527.0 mil. **Lottery:** total sales: $239.9 mil; profit: $48.5 mil.

Federal govt. Fed. civ. employees: 8,419; **avg. salary:** $70,217. **Notable fed. facilities:** Idaho Natl. Lab, Idaho Falls; Mountain Home AFB.

Education. High school grad. rate: 79.7%. **4-yr. public coll./univ.:** 4; **2-yr. public:** 4; **4-yr. private:** 6.

Energy. Electricity use/cost: 953 kWh, $94.90.

State data. Motto: Esto Perpetua (It is perpetual). **Flower:** Syringa. **Bird:** Mountain bluebird. **Tree:** White pine. **Song:** "Here We Have Idaho." **Entered union:** July 3, 1890; rank: 43rd.

Tourism. Tourist spending: $4.5 bil. **Attractions:** Hells Canyon (deepest river gorge in N. America); World Ctr. for Birds of Prey, Boise Art Museum, in Boise; Craters of the Moon Natl. Monument and Preserve; Sun Valley; Shoshone Falls, near Twin Falls; Lava Hot Springs; Lake Coeur d'Alene; Sawtooth Natl. Recreation Area; Frank Church-River of No Return Wilderness Area; Nez Perce Natl. Historical Park. **Information:** Idaho Division of Tourism Development, 700 W. State St., P.O. Box 83720, Boise, ID 83720; 1-800-VISITID; www.visitidaho.org

History. Paleo-Indian hunters roamed the land over 13,000 years ago; later inhabitants included Shoshone, Northern Paiute, Bannock, and Nez Percé peoples. The Meriwether Lewis and William Clark Expedition took place 1804-06. Next came fur traders, 1809-34, and missionaries, 1830s-50s. Mormons made their first permanent settlement at Franklin, 1860. Idaho's gold rush began the same year and brought thousands of permanent settlers. A series of Indian wars followed, including a campaign by Chief Joseph and the Nez Percé that ended with his surrender in Montana, 1877. Idaho became a territory, 1863, and a state, 1890. In the 20th cent., it emerged as a leader in potato, lumber, and silver output. The Sun Valley ski resort opened in 1936, boosting tourism. Startup of Lewiston's river port, 1975, opened Idaho to oceangoing trade. Fueled by technology job growth, the state's population jumped 21.2% in 2000-10.

Famous Idahoans. William Borah, Frank Church, Lou Dobbs, Fred Dubois, W. Mark Felt, Chief Joseph, Harmon Killebrew, Ezra Pound, Marilynne Robinson, Sacagawea, Picabo Street, Lana Turner.

Website. www.idaho.gov

Illinois (IL)
Prairie State

People. Population: 12,802,023; rank: 6. **Pop. change** (2010-17): −0.2%. **Pop. density:** 230.6 per sq mi. **Racial distribution:** 77.1% white; 14.6% black; 5.7% Asian; 0.6% Amer. Ind.; 0.1% Pac. Isl.; 2+ races, 2.0%. **Hispanic pop.:** 17.3%.

Geography. Total area: 57,914 sq mi; rank: 25. **Land area:** 55,519 sq mi; rank: 24. **Acres forested:** 5.0 mil. **Location:** East North Central state; western, southern, and eastern boundaries formed by Mississippi, Ohio, and Wabash Rivers, respectively. **Climate:** temperate; typically cold, snowy winters, hot summers. **Topography:** prairie and fertile plains throughout; open hills in the southern region. **Capital:** Springfield. **Chief airports:** Chicago (2).

Economy. Chief industries: services, manufacturing, travel, wholesale and retail trade, finance, insurance, real estate, construction, health care, agriculture. **Chief manuf. goods:** food, petroleum, plastics, chemicals, agricultural machinery, pharmaceuticals, motor vehicles, printing. **Chief crops:** corn, soybeans, hay, wheat, greenhouse and nursery, apples, peaches, sorghum. **Farm income:** crops, $13.97 bil; livestock, $2.29 bil. **Nonfuel minerals:** $1.4 bil; sand and gravel (industrial), stone (crushed), cement (portland), sand and gravel (construction), tripoli. **Chief port:** Chicago. **Gross state product:** $820.4 bil. **Sales tax:** 6.25%. **Gasoline tax:** 55.72 cents/gal. **Employment distrib.:** 13.8% govt.; 19.8% trade/trans./util.; 9.6% mfg.; 15.2% ed./health; 15.3% prof./bus. serv.; 10.2% leisure/hosp.; 6.5% finance; 3.9% constr./mining/log.; 1.5% info.; 4.1% other serv. **Unemployment:** 5.0%. **Min. wage/hr.:** $8.25. **Per cap. pers. income:** $52,808. **New private housing:** 24,992 units/$4.6 bil. **Broadband internet:** 97.2%. **Commercial banks:** 456; deposits: $457.5 bil. **Savings institutions:** 61; deposits: $20.9 bil. **Lottery:** total sales: $2.8 bil; profit: $723.2 mil.

Federal govt. Fed. civ. employees: 40,658; **avg. salary:** $84,541. **Notable fed. facilities:** Great Lakes Naval Station; Fermi Natl. Accelerator Lab, Batavia; Argonne Natl. Lab, Lemont; Scott AFB; Rock Island Arsenal.

Education. High school grad. rate: 85.5%. **4-yr. public coll./univ.:** 12; **2-yr. public:** 48; **4-yr. private:** 82.

Energy. Electricity use/cost: 733 kWh, $91.83.

State data. Motto: State sovereignty, national union. **Flower:** Native violet. **Bird:** Northern cardinal. **Tree:** White oak. **Song:** "Illinois." **Entered union:** Dec. 3, 1818; rank: 21st.

Tourism. Tourist spending: $38.4 bil. **Attractions:** Art Institute of Chicago, Field Museum of Natural History, Shedd Aquarium, Millennium Park, Navy Pier, in Chicago; Illinois State Museum, Abraham Lincoln Presidential Library and Museum, in Springfield; Cahokia Mounds State Historic Site, Collinsville; Starved Rock State Park; Crab Orchard Natl. Wildlife Refuge; Forts Kaskaskia, de Chartres, Massac; Shawnee Natl. Forest; Dickson Mounds Museum, Lewistown. **Information:** Illinois Bureau of Tourism, 100 W. Randolph St., Ste. 3-400, Chicago, IL 60601; 1-800-226-6632; www.enjoyillinois.com

History. The region has been inhabited for at least 10,000 years; seminomadic Algonquian peoples, including the Peoria, Illinois, Kaskaskia, and Tamaroa, lived there at the time of European contact. Fur traders were the first Europeans in Illinois, followed shortly by Louis Jolliet and Jacques Marquette, 1673, and René-Robert Cavelier, sieur de La Salle, 1680, who built a fort near present-day Peoria. French priests established the first permanent settlements at Cahokia, near present-day St. Louis, 1699, and Kaskaskia, 1703. France ceded the area to Britain, 1763, and in 1778, American Gen. George Rogers Clark took Kaskaskia from the British without a shot. Illinois became a separate territory, 1809, and a state, 1818. Defeat of Native American tribes in the Black Hawk War, 1832, and canal, rail, and road construction brought rapid change. Mormon settlers at Nauvoo, 1839, met with hostility, and a Carthage mob killed Mormon leader Joseph Smith and his brother, 1844. The Great Chicago Fire, 1871, destroyed the city's downtown. Illinois became a center for the labor movement, leading to bitter conflicts such as the Haymarket riot, 1886, and Pullman strike, 1894. Social reformer Jane Addams founded Hull House, 1889, to aid immigrants and the poor. The expansion of manufacturing, 1900-70, drew African Americans from the South in the Great Migration. Chicago police violently suppressed antiwar protests at the 1968 Democratic National Convention. Barack Obama, elected in 2004, was only the fifth African American to serve in the U.S. Senate; he became the 44th U.S. president in 2009. Political corruption and criminality have plagued the state; since 1960, five former governors have been charged with criminal offenses. Dennis Hastert, the longest serving Republican Speaker of the House, 1999-2007, was sentenced to 15 months in prison in 2016 on charges related to payments he made to conceal his sexual abuse of teen boys in the 1960s-70s. A U.S. Justice Dept. investigation of the Chicago Police Dept., launched after a video of a white officer fatally shooting a black teen sparked protests, found in Jan. 2017 that officers used excessive force too often and without repercussions.

Famous Illinoisans. Jane Addams, Saul Bellow, John Belushi, Jack Benny, Ray Bradbury, Gwendolyn Brooks, St. Frances Xavier Cabrini, Al Capone, Hillary Rodham Clinton, Clarence Darrow, John Deere, Stephen A. Douglas, Katherine Dunham, Wyatt Earp, Roger Ebert, James T. Farrell, Marshall Field, Harrison Ford, Betty Friedan, Benny Goodman, Ulysses S. Grant, Dennis Hastert, Hugh Hefner, Ernest Hemingway, Charlton Heston, Jennifer Hudson, Henry J. Hyde, Abraham Lincoln, Vachel Lindsay, David Mamet, Edgar Lee Masters, Oscar Mayer, Cyrus McCormick, Eliot Ness, Bob Newhart, Michelle Obama, Ronald Reagan, Shonda Rhimes, Donald Rumsfeld, Carl Sandburg, Shel Silverstein, Adlai E. Stevenson, James Watson, Frank Lloyd Wright, Philip K. Wrigley.

Website. www.illinois.gov

Indiana (IN)
Hoosier State

People. Population: 6,666,818; rank: 17. **Pop. change** (2010-17): 2.8%. **Pop. density:** 186.1 per sq mi. **Racial distribution:** 85.4% white; 9.7% black; 2.4% Asian; 0.4% Amer. Ind.; 0.1% Pac. Isl.; 2+ races, 2.1%. **Hispanic pop.:** 7.0%.

Geography. Total area: 36,420 sq mi; rank: 38. **Land area:** 35,826 sq mi; rank: 38. **Acres forested:** 4.9 mil. **Location:** East North Central state; Lake Michigan on N border. **Climate:** four distinct seasons with temperate climate. **Topography:** hilly southern region; fertile rolling plains of central region; flat, heavily glaciated N; dunes along Lake Michigan shore. **Capital:** Indianapolis. **Chief airport:** Indianapolis.

Economy. Chief industries: manufacturing, services, agriculture, government, wholesale and retail trade, transportation, public utilities. **Chief manuf. goods:** motor vehicles and parts, iron and steel mills, pharmaceuticals, petroleum, plastics, medical equip., printing. **Chief crops:** corn, soybeans, greenhouse and nursery, wheat, hay, tomatoes, watermelons, apples. **Farm income:** crops, $6.67 bil; livestock, $3.38 bil. **Nonfuel minerals:** $1.0 bil; stone (crushed), cement (portland), sand and gravel (construction), lime, stone (dimension). **Chief ports:** Burns Harbor-Portage, Mt. Vernon, Jeffersonville. **Gross state product:** $359.1 bil. **Sales tax:** 7.0%. **Gasoline tax:** 61.30 cents/gal. **Employment distrib.:** 13.6% govt.; 19.2% trade/trans./util.; 17.0% mfg.; 15.1% ed./health; 10.9% prof./bus. serv.; 9.9% leisure/hosp.; 4.4% finance; 4.8% constr./mining/log.; 0.9% info.; 4.1% other serv. **Unemployment:** 3.5%. **Min. wage/hr.:** $7.25. **Per cap. pers. income:** $44,165. **New private housing:** 21,664 units/$4.6 bil. **Broadband internet:** 96.4%. **Commercial banks:** 123; deposits: $119.7 bil. **Savings institutions:** 27; deposits: $4.7 bil. **Lottery:** total sales: $1.2 bil; profit: $288.0 mil.

Federal govt. Fed. civ. employees: 23,233; **avg. salary:** $73,432. **Notable fed. facilities:** Naval Surface Warfare Ctr., Crane Div.; Grissom Air Reserve Base.

Education. High school grad. rate: 86.8%. **4-yr. public coll./univ.:** 15; **2-yr. public:** 1; **4-yr. private:** 40.

Energy. Electricity use/cost: 975 kWh, $114.96.

State data. Motto: Crossroads of America. **Flower:** Peony. **Bird:** Northern cardinal. **Tree:** Tulip poplar. **Song:** "On the Banks of the Wabash, Far Away." **Entered union:** Dec. 11, 1816; rank: 19th.

Tourism. Tourist spending: $11.3 bil. **Attractions:** Lincoln Boyhood Natl. Memorial, Lincoln City; George Rogers Clark Natl. Historical Park, Vincennes; Tippecanoe Battlefield Museum and Park, Battle Ground; Benjamin Harrison Presidential Site, Indianapolis Motor Speedway and Hall of Fame Museum, Indianapolis Museum of Art, in Indianapolis; Indiana Dunes Natl. Lakeshore, Chesterton; College Football Hall of Fame, Studebaker Natl. Museum, in South Bend; Hoosier Natl. Forest. **Information:** Indiana Office of Tourism Development, 1 North Capital, Ste. 600, Indianapolis, IN 46204; 1-800-677-9800; www.visitindiana.com

History. When the Europeans arrived, Miami, Potawatomi, Kickapoo, Piankashaw, Wea, and Shawnee peoples inhabited the region. René-Robert Cavelier, sieur de La Salle, visited the present South Bend area, 1679 and 1681. The first French fort was built near present-day Lafayette, 1717. A French trading post was established, 1731-32, at Vincennes. France ceded the area to Britain, 1763. During the American Revolution, American Gen. George Rogers Clark captured Vincennes, 1778, and defeated British forces, 1779. Indiana became a territory, 1800, and a state, 1816. The Miami were beaten, 1794, at Fallen Timbers, and Gen. William H. Harrison defeated Tecumseh's Indian confederation, 1811, at Tippecanoe. Manufacturing grew rapidly after the Civil War. U.S. Steel founded Gary, 1906. An automotive test track was the site of the first Indianapolis 500 race, 1911. The auto industry remains key to the state economy; in 2008, Honda opened a $550-mil plant near Greensburg. Heavy rain in June 2008 flooded southwest and central Indiana. Some rights groups and businesses criticized the state's Religious Freedom Restoration Act as discriminatory to LGBT individuals. Mike Pence, the state's governor, 2013-17, was sworn in as U.S. vice president in Jan. 2017.

Famous "Hoosiers." Larry Bird, Ambrose Burnside, Meg Cabot, Hoagy Carmichael, Jim Davis, James Dean, Eugene V. Debs, John Dillinger, Theodore Dreiser, Paul Dresser, Jeff Gordon, Benjamin Harrison, Gil Hodges, Michael Jackson, David Letterman, Carole Lombard, Marjorie Main, John Mellencamp, Jane Pauley, Cole Porter, Gene Stratton Porter, Ernie Pyle, Dan Quayle, James Whitcomb Riley, Oscar Robertson, Red Skelton, Tony Stewart, Booth Tarkington, Kurt Vonnegut, Lew Wallace, Ryan White, Wendell L. Willkie, Wilbur Wright.

Website. www.in.gov

Iowa (IA)
Hawkeye State

People. Population: 3,145,711; rank: 30. **Pop. change** (2010-17): 3.2%. **Pop. density:** 56.3 per sq mi. **Racial distribution:** 91.1% white; 3.8% black; 2.6% Asian; 0.5% Amer. Ind.; 0.1% Pac. Isl.; 2+ races, 1.9%. **Hispanic pop.:** 6.0%.

Geography. Total area: 56,273 sq mi; rank: 26. **Land area:** 55,857 sq mi; rank: 23. **Acres forested:** 2.9 mil. **Location:** West North Central state bordered by Mississippi R. on the E, Missouri R. on the W. **Climate:** humid, continental. **Topography:** watershed from NW to SE; soil especially rich and land level in the N central counties. **Capital:** Des Moines. **Chief airports:** Cedar Rapids, Des Moines.

Economy. Chief industries: agriculture, communications, construction, finance, insurance, trade, services, manufacturing. **Chief manuf. goods:** machinery, vegetable oils, animal slaughtering and processing, laundry equip., plastics, motor vehicles and parts. **Chief crops:** corn, soybeans, hay, greenhouse and nursery, oats. **Farm income:** crops, $14.74 bil; livestock, $12.10 bil. **Nonfuel minerals:** $583 mil; stone (crushed), cement (portland), sand and gravel (construction), sand and gravel (industrial), lime. **Gross state product:** $190.2 bil. **Sales tax:** 6.0%. **Gasoline tax:** 48.90 cents/gal. **Employment distrib.:** 16.5% govt.; 19.7% trade/trans./util.; 14.0% mfg.; 14.6% ed./health; 8.9% prof./bus. serv.; 9.3% leisure/hosp.; 6.9% finance; 5.2% constr./mining/log.; 1.4% info.; 3.5% other serv. **Unemployment:** 3.1%. **Min. wage/hr.:** $7.25. **Per cap. pers. income:** $45,996. **New private housing:** 13,948 units/$2.5 bil. **Broadband internet:** 92.6%. **Commercial banks:** 318; deposits: $80.8 bil. **Savings institutions:** 9; deposits: $3.2 bil. **Lottery:** total sales: $352.2 mil; profit: $80.8 mil.

Federal govt. Fed. civ. employees: 8,655; **avg. salary:** $69,544. **Notable fed. facilities:** Ames Lab; Natl. Animal Disease Ctr.

Education. High school grad. rate: 91.3%. **4-yr. public coll./univ.:** 3; **2-yr. public:** 16; **4-yr. private:** 33.

Energy. Electricity use/cost: 864 kWh, $103.17.

State data. Motto: Our liberties we prize, and our rights we will maintain. **Flower:** Wild rose. **Bird:** Eastern goldfinch. **Tree:** Oak. **Song:** "The Song of Iowa." **Entered union:** Dec. 28, 1846; rank: 29th.

Tourism. Tourist spending: $8.4 bil. **Attractions:** Des Moines Art Ctr., Iowa State Fairgrounds, Iowa State Capitol, in Des Moines; Natl. Czech & Slovak Museum & Library, Cedar Rapids; Herbert Hoover Natl. Historic Site, Presidential Library and Museum, in West Branch; Effigy Mounds Natl. Monument, Marquette; Amana Colonies (former communal society); Figge Art Museum, Davenport; Living History Farms, Urbandale; Adventureland, Altoona; Boone & Scenic Valley Railroad and Museum; riverboat cruises and casino gambling, Mississippi and Missouri Rivers; Iowa Great Lakes, Okoboji; American Gothic House, Eldon; *Field of Dreams* movie site, Dyersville; Natl. Mississippi River Museum & Aquarium, Dubuque. **Information:** Iowa Tourism Office, Iowa Dept. of Economic Development, 200 E. Grand Ave., Des Moines, IA 50309; 1-800-345-IOWA; www.traveliowa.com

History. Early inhabitants were Mound Builders who dwelt on Iowa's fertile plains. Later, Iowa and Yankton Sioux lived in the area. The first Europeans, Jacques Marquette and Louis Jolliet, gave France its claim to the area, 1673. In 1762, France ceded the region to Spain, but Napoleon took it back, 1800. It became part of the U.S. through the Louisiana Purchase, 1803. Native American Sauk and Fox tribes moved into the area but relinquished their land in defeat after the 1832 uprising led by Sauk chieftain Black Hawk. Iowa became a territory in 1838 and a free state in 1846, strongly supporting the Union. Fertile land lured farmers from eastern states, 1850-1900, and the population rose rapidly. Growth slowed in the

20th cent., as farming became mechanized. Severe flooding in eastern Iowa in June 2008 caused billions of dollars in damages and forced the evacuation of thousands of residents. The Iowa caucuses have been the first statewide electoral event in the presidential nomination process since 1972.

Famous Iowans. Tom Arnold, Johnny Carson, William F. "Buffalo Bill" Cody, Mamie Dowd Eisenhower, Michael Emerson, Bob Feller, George Gallup, Susan Glaspell, James Norman Hall, Herbert Hoover, Shawn Johnson, Ashton Kutcher, Ann Landers, Cloris Leachman, Glenn Miller, Lillian Russell, Billy Sunday, James A. Van Allen, Abigail Van Buren, Carl Van Vechten, Henry Wallace, Kurt Warner, John Wayne, Meredith Willson, Elijah Wood, Grant Wood.

Website. www.iowa.gov

Kansas (KS)
Sunflower State

People. Population: 2,913,123; rank: 35. **Pop. change** (2010-17): 2.1%. **Pop. density:** 35.6 per sq mi. **Racial distribution:** 86.5% white; 6.2% black; 3.1% Asian; 1.2% Amer. Ind.; 0.1% Pac. Isl.; 2+ races, 3.0%. **Hispanic pop.:** 11.9%.

Geography. Total area: 82,278 sq mi; rank: 15. **Land area:** 81,759 sq mi; rank: 13. **Acres forested:** 2.5 mil. **Location:** West North Central state with Missouri R. on E. **Climate:** temperate but continental, with great extremes between summer and winter. **Topography:** hilly Osage Plains in the E; central region level prairie and hills; high plains in the W. **Capital:** Topeka. **Chief airport:** Wichita.

Economy. Chief industries: manufacturing, finance, insurance, real estate, services. **Chief manuf. goods:** animal slaughtering and processing, aerospace, petroleum, plastics, machinery, navigational instruments, printing. **Chief crops:** wheat, corn, soybeans, hay, sorghum, sunflowers, cotton, potatoes. **Farm income:** crops, $6.49 bil; livestock, $8.98 bil. **Nonfuel minerals:** $598 mil; helium (Grade-A), cement (portland), salt, stone (crushed), helium (crude). **Chief port:** Kansas City. **Gross state product:** $157.8 bil. **Sales tax:** 6.5%. **Gasoline tax:** 42.43 cents/gal. **Employment distrib.:** 18.5% govt.; 18.9% trade/trans./util.; 11.6% mfg.; 13.9% ed./health; 12.8% prof./bus. serv.; 9.3% leisure/hosp.; 5.5% finance; 4.7% constr./mining/log.; 1.3% info.; 3.5% other serv. **Unemployment:** 3.6%. **Min. wage/hr.:** $7.25. **Per cap. pers. income:** $47,603. **New private housing:** 8,984 units/$1.8 bil. **Broadband internet:** 95.4%. **Commercial banks:** 287; deposits: $65.7 bil. **Savings institutions:** 14; deposits: $7.6 bil. **Lottery:** total sales: $258.0 mil; profit: $75.3 mil.

Federal govt. Fed. civ. employees: 15,946; **avg. salary:** $71,573. **Notable fed. facilities:** Ft. Riley; Leavenworth Fed. Penitentiary, Dwight D. Eisenhower VA Medical Ctr., Leavenworth; McConnell AFB; Colmery-O'Neil VA Medical Ctr., Topeka.

Education. High school grad. rate: 85.7%. **4-yr. public coll./univ.:** 8; **2-yr. public:** 25; **4-yr. private:** 24.

Energy. Electricity use/cost: 899 kWh, $117.34.

State data. Motto: Ad Astra per Aspera (To the stars through difficulties). **Flower:** Native sunflower. **Bird:** Western meadowlark. **Tree:** Cottonwood. **Song:** "Home on the Range." **Entered union:** Jan. 29, 1861; rank: 34th.

Tourism. Tourist spending: $7.4 bil. **Attractions:** Eisenhower Presidential Library and Museum, Abilene; Natl. Agricultural Ctr. and Hall of Fame, Bonner Springs; Boot Hill Museum, Dodge City; Old Cowtown Museum, Wichita; Ft. Scott and Ft. Larned Natl. Historic Sites; Kansas Cosmosphere and Space Ctr., Hutchinson; U.S. Cavalry Museum, Ft. Riley; Tallgrass Prairie Natl. Preserve, Strong City; Kansas Speedway, Kansas City. **Information:** Kansas Dept. of Commerce, Travel and Tourism Div., 1000 SW Jackson St., Ste. 100, Topeka, KS 66612; (785) 296-2009; www.travelks.com

History. Wichita, Pawnee, Kansa, and Osage peoples lived in the area when Spain's Francisco de Coronado explored it in 1541. These Native Americans—hunters who also farmed—were joined on the Plains by the nomadic Cheyenne, Arapaho, Comanche, and Kiowa about 1800. France claimed the region, 1682, ceded its claim to Spain, 1762, then regained control, 1800, before selling it to the U.S. in the Louisiana Purchase, 1803. After 1830, thousands of Native Americans were removed from more eastern states to Kansas. Organized as a territory, 1854, the area witnessed violent clashes between pro- and antislavery settlers and became known as "Bleeding Kansas." It entered the Union as a free state, 1861. After the Civil War, rail construction and huge cattle drives from Texas turned Abilene and Dodge City into cowboy capitals. Russian Mennonite immigrants brought a new strain of winter wheat, 1874, transforming Kansas agriculture. Carry

Nation launched her anti-saloon crusade in the 1890s. Part of the Dust Bowl, the state experienced drought and depression in the 1930s. Topeka was the focus of the famous *Brown v. Board of Education* decision, 1954, that led to desegregation of U.S. public schools. Bob Dole represented Kansas in the U.S. Senate (1969-96) but failed in several efforts to win higher office.

Famous Kansans. Kirstie Alley, Roscoe "Fatty" Arbuckle, Ed Asner, John Brown, Walter P. Chrysler, Glenn Cunningham, John Steuart Curry, Robert Joseph "Bob" Dole, Amelia Earhart, Dwight D. Eisenhower, Melissa Etheridge, Ron Evans, Georgia Neese Clark Gray, Maurice Greene, James Butler "Wild Bill" Hickok, Cyrus K. Holliday, Dennis Hopper, William Inge, Don Johnson, Walter Johnson, Nancy Landon Kassebaum, Buster Keaton, Emmett Kelly, Alfred M. "Alf" Landon, Hattie McDaniel, Oscar Micheaux, Carry Nation, Charlie Parker, Gordon Parks, Jim Ryun, Barry Sanders, Vivian Vance, William Allen White, Jess Willard.

Website. www.kansas.gov

Kentucky (KY)
Bluegrass State

People. Population: 4,454,189; rank: 26. **Pop. change** (2010-17): 2.6%. **Pop. density:** 112.8 per sq mi. **Racial distribution:** 87.8% white; 8.4% black; 1.6% Asian; 0.3% Amer. Ind.; 0.1% Pac. Isl.; 2+ races, 1.9%. **Hispanic pop.:** 3.7%.

Geography. Total area: 40,408 sq mi; rank: 37. **Land area:** 39,486 sq mi; rank: 37. **Acres forested:** 12.4 mil. **Location:** East South Central state bordered on N by Illinois, Indiana, Ohio; on E by West Virginia and Virginia; on S by Tennessee; on W by Missouri. **Climate:** moderate, with plentiful rainfall. **Topography:** mountainous in E; rounded hills of the Knobs region in the N; Bluegrass region in heart of state; wooded rocky hillsides of the Pennyroyal Plateau; Western Coal Field; the fertile Jackson Purchase region in the SW. **Capital:** Frankfort. **Chief airports:** Cincinnati, Lexington, Louisville.

Economy. Chief industries: manufacturing, services, finance, insurance and real estate, retail trade, public utilities. **Chief manuf. goods:** motor vehicles and parts, aluminum, basic chemicals, plastics, iron and steel, rubber, printing. **Chief crops:** hay, corn, soybeans, tobacco, wheat. **Farm income:** crops, $2.49 bil.; livestock, $2.95 bil. **Nonfuel minerals:** $592 mil; stone (crushed), lime, cement (portland), sand and gravel (construction), sand and gravel (industrial). **Chief ports:** Louisville, Hickman-Fulton County. **Gross state product:** $202.5 bil. **Sales tax:** 6.0%. **Gasoline tax:** 44.40 cents/gal. **Employment distrib.:** 16.5% govt.; 21.3% trade/trans./util.; 12.7% mfg.; 14.1% ed./health; 11.0% prof./bus. serv.; 10.5% leisure/hosp.; 4.8% finance; 4.5% constr./mining/log.; 1.1% info.; 3.4% other serv. **Unemployment:** 4.9%. **Min. wage/hr.:** $7.25. **Per cap. pers. income:** $39,393. **New private housing:** 12,630 units/$2.0 bil. **Broadband internet:** 94.2%. **Commercial banks:** 165; deposits $77.5 bil. **Savings institutions:** 15; deposits $1.8 bil. **Lottery:** total sales: $1.0 bil; profit: $248.6 mil.

Federal govt. Fed. civ. employees: 22,455; **avg. salary:** $66,783. **Notable fed. facilities:** U.S. Bullion Depository, Ft. Knox; Ft. Campbell; Fed. Medical Ctr., Lexington; Army Corps of Engineers, Louisville District.

Education. High school grad. rate: 88.6%. **4-yr. public coll./univ.:** 8; **2-yr. public:** 16; **4-yr. private:** 25.

Energy. Electricity use/cost: 1,121 kWh, $117.65.

State data. Motto: United we stand, divided we fall. **Flower:** Goldenrod. **Bird:** Northern cardinal. **Tree:** Tulip poplar. **Song:** "My Old Kentucky Home." **Entered union:** June 1, 1792; rank: 15th.

Tourism. Tourist spending: $9.2 bil. **Attractions:** Churchill Downs (Kentucky Derby), Louisville Slugger Museum and Factory, in Louisville; Land Between the Lakes Natl. Recreation Area (Kentucky and Barkley Lakes); Mammoth Cave Natl. Park (world's longest known cave system); Abraham Lincoln Birthplace Natl. Historical Park, Hodgenville; My Old Kentucky Home State Park, Bardstown; Cumberland Gap Natl. Historical Park, Middlesboro; Creation Museum, Petersburg; Kentucky Horse Park, Lexington; Shaker Village of Pleasant Hill, Harrodsburg; Natl. Corvette Museum, Bowling Green. **Information:** Kentucky Dept. of Tourism, 100 Airport Road, 2nd Fl., Frankfort, KY 40601; 1-800-225-8747; www.kentuckytourism.com

History. Paleo-Indians first arrived about 14,000 years ago. Much later, Shawnee, Wyandot, Delaware, and Cherokee peoples used the area mostly for hunting. Explored by Thomas Walker and Christopher Gist, 1750-51, Kentucky was the first area W of the Alleghenies settled by American pioneers. The first permanent settlement was Harrodsburg, 1774. Daniel Boone blazed the Wilderness Trail through the Cumberland Gap and founded Ft. Boonesborough, 1775. Clashes with Native Americans were frequent, 1774-94. Virginia dropped its claims to the region, and Kentucky became a state, 1792. Tobacco growing, horse breeding, coal mining, and bourbon whiskey making were major industries in the 19th cent. A slave state, Kentucky tried to stay neutral in the Civil War, but then opted for the Union; many Kentuckians sided with the Confederacy. The U.S. gold depository at Ft. Knox opened, 1937. Prior to the 2008 economic downturn, auto manufacturing had grown in recent decades. A Rowan County clerk attracted national attention after being jailed in 2015 for refusing to issue marriage licenses to same-sex couples. A statewide teacher walkout in Mar.-Apr. 2018 demanded increased pay and school funding.

Famous Kentuckians. Muhammad Ali, Alben W. Barkley, Ned Beatty, Louis D. Brandeis, John C. Breckinridge, Kit Carson, Albert B. "Happy" Chandler, Henry Clay, George Clooney, Rosemary Clooney, Jefferson Davis, D. W. Griffith, "Casey" Jones, Jennifer Lawrence, Abraham Lincoln, Mary Todd Lincoln, Thomas Hunt Morgan, Carry Nation, Colonel Harland Sanders, Diane Sawyer, Chris Stapleton, Jesse Stuart, Zachary Taylor, Hunter S. Thompson, Robert Penn Warren, Whitney M. Young Jr.

Website. www.kentucky.gov

Louisiana (LA)
Pelican State

People. Population: 4,684,333; rank: 25. **Pop. change** (2010-17): 3.3%. **Pop. density:** 108.4 per sq mi. **Racial distribution:** 63.0% white; 32.6% black; 1.9% Asian; 0.8% Amer. Ind.; 0.1% Pac. Isl.; 2+ races, 1.7%. **Hispanic pop.:** 5.2%.

Geography. Total area: 52,378 sq mi; rank: 31. **Land area:** 43,204 sq mi; rank: 33. **Acres forested:** 15.1 mil. **Location:** West South Central state on the Gulf Coast. **Climate:** subtropical, affected by continental weather patterns. **Topography:** lowlands of marshes and Mississippi R. floodplain; Red R. Valley lowlands; upland hills in the Florida Parishes; avg. elevation, 100 ft. **Capital:** Baton Rouge. **Chief airport:** Metairie.

Economy. Chief industries: wholesale and retail trade, tourism, manufacturing, construction, transportation, communication, public utilities, finance, insurance, real estate, mining. **Chief manuf. goods:** petroleum, chemicals, plastics material and resin, pesticides and fertilizers, cleaning prods., paper and paperboard, ships, structural metals. **Chief crops:** sugarcane, cotton, rice, soybeans, corn, sweet potatoes. **Farm income:** crops, $1.79 bil; livestock, $1.03 bil. **Nonfuel minerals:** $477 mil; salt, sand and gravel (construction), stone (crushed), sand and gravel (industrial), clays (common). **Commercial fishing:** $427.5 mil. **Chief ports:** New Orleans, Baton Rouge, Lake Charles, Port of S. Louisiana (La Place), Shreveport, Plaquemine, St. Bernard, Alexandria. **Gross state product:** $246.3 bil. **Sales tax:** 5.0%. **Gasoline tax:** 38.41 cents/gal. **Employment distrib.:** 16.4% govt.; 19.1% trade/trans./util.; 6.9% mfg.; 15.9% ed./health; 10.8% prof./bus. serv.; 12.1% leisure/hosp.; 4.6% finance; 9.2% constr./mining/log.; 1.2% info.; 3.8% other serv. **Unemployment:** 5.1%. **Min. wage/hr.:** none ($7.25). **Per cap. pers. income:** $43,491. **New private housing:** 15,224 units/$3.0 bil. **Broadband internet:** 94.3%. **Commercial banks:** 121; deposits $101.2 bil. **Savings institutions:** 19; deposits $3.5 bil. **Lottery:** total sales: $455.0 mil; profit: $159.2 mil.

Federal govt. Fed. civ. employees: 18,555; **avg. salary:** $72,639. **Notable federal facilities:** Ft. Polk (Joint Readiness Training Ctr.); Barksdale AFB; Strategic Petroleum Reserve, Michoud Assembly Facility, USDA Southern Regional Research Ctr., New Orleans NAS JRB.

Education. High school grad. rate: 78.6%. **4-yr. public coll./univ.:** 17; **2-yr. public:** 16; **4-yr. private:** 12.

Energy. Electricity use/cost: 1,240 kWh, $115.79.

State data. Motto: Union, justice, and confidence. **Flower:** Magnolia blossom. **Bird:** Eastern brown pelican. **Tree:** Bald cypress. **Song:** "Give Me Louisiana." **Entered union:** Apr. 30, 1812; rank: 18th.

Tourism. Tourist spending: $12.3 bil. **Attractions:** Mardi Gras, French Quarter, Bourbon Street, in New Orleans; Jean Lafitte Natl. Historical Park and Preserve; Longfellow-Evangeline State Historic Site, St. Martinville; Kent Plantation House, Alexandria; Oak Alley Plantation, Vacherie; Whitney Plantation, Wallace; Hodges Gardens State Park, Florien; USS *Kidd* Veterans Memorial, Baton Rouge. **Information:** Louisiana Office of Tourism, P.O. Box 94291, Baton Rouge, LA 70804-9291; 1-800-677-4082; www.louisianatravel.com

History. Caddo, Tunica, Choctaw, Chitimacha, and Cha-wash peoples lived in the region at the time of European contact. Spanish explorers in the early 16th cent. reached the mouth of the Mississippi. René-Robert Cavelier, sieur de La Salle, 1682, claimed the region for France. Early French and Spanish settlers were the ancestors of Louisiana Creoles. Cajuns descended from the Acadians, French settlers expelled by the British from Nova Scotia, Canada, in 1755. France ceded the Louisiana region to Spain, 1762, took it back, 1800, and sold it to the U.S., 1803, in the Louisiana Purchase. Admitted as a state in 1812, Louisiana witnessed the Battle of New Orleans, 1815. Cotton and sugar plantations relied on black slaves, who made up close to 47% of the population in 1860, on the eve of the Civil War. Louisiana seceded, 1861, and was readmitted, 1868. Jazz was born in New Orleans in the early 20th cent. As governor (1928-32), Huey Long pushed populist programs. Many tropical storms and floods have battered Louisiana, including Hurricane Katrina and subsequent flooding, 2005, which devastated New Orleans. The offshore oil and gas industry developed after World War II. An oil rig explosion off the state's Gulf coast spilled millions of barrels of oil, damaging coastal wetlands and many of the state's marine-dependent industries in 2010. Rain caused severe flooding in and around Baton Rouge and Lafayette in 2016. In May 2017, New Orleans removed several monuments honoring the Confederacy and a racially motivated Reconstruction-era attack.

Famous Louisianans. Louis Armstrong, Pierre Beauregard, Judah P. Benjamin, Braxton Bragg, Kate Chopin, Harry Connick Jr., Ellen DeGeneres, Fats Domino, George "Buddy" Guy, Lillian Hellman, Grace King, Jerry Lee Lewis, Bob Livingston, Huey Long, Eli Manning, Peyton Manning, Wynton Marsalis, Tim McGraw, Leonidas K. Polk, Anne Rice, Bill Russell, Henry Miller Shreve, Britney Spears, Madam C. J. Walker (Sarah Breedlove), Edward Douglass White Jr.

Website. www.louisiana.gov

Maine (ME)
Pine Tree State

People. Population: 1,335,907; rank: 42. **Pop. change** (2010-17): 0.6%. **Pop. density:** 43.3 per sq mi. **Racial distribution:** 94.7% white; 1.6% black; 1.2% Asian; 0.7% Amer. Ind.; <0.05% Pac. Isl.; 2+ races, 1.8%. **Hispanic pop.:** 1.6%.

Geography. Total area: 35,380 sq mi; rank: 39. **Land area:** 30,843 sq mi; rank: 39. **Acres forested:** 17.6 mil. **Location:** New England state at northeastern tip of U.S. **Climate:** southern interior and coast influenced by air masses from the S and W; northern clime harsher, avg. over 100 in. snow in winter. **Topography:** Appalachian Mts. extend through state; western borders have rugged terrain; long sand beaches on southern coast; northern coast mainly rocky promontories, peninsulas, fjords. **Capital:** Augusta. **Chief airport:** Portland.

Economy. Chief industries: manufacturing, agriculture, fishing, services, trade, government, finance, insurance, real estate, construction. **Chief manuf. goods:** paper, ships and boats, cardboard, frozen/canned fruits and vegetables, plastics, baked goods. **Chief crops:** potatoes, greenhouse and nursery, wild blueberries, apples, hay, maple syrup. **Farm income:** crops, $382.61 mil; livestock, $297.07 mil. **Nonfuel minerals:** $104 mil; sand and gravel (construction), cement (portland), stone (crushed), stone (dimension), peat. **Commercial fishing:** $635.8 mil. **Chief ports:** Searsport, Portland, Eastport. **Gross state product:** $61.4 bil. **Sales tax:** 5.5%. **Gasoline tax:** 48.41 cents/gal. **Employment distrib.:** 16.2% govt.; 19.0% trade/trans./util.; 8.2% mfg.; 20.5% ed./health; 10.7% prof./bus. serv.; 10.7% leisure/hosp.; 5.0% finance; 5.1% constr./mining/log.; 1.2% info.; 3.4% other serv. **Unemployment:** 3.3%. **Min. wage/hr.:** $10.00. **Per cap. pers. income:** $45,072. **New private housing:** 4,358 units/$827.7 mil. **Broadband internet:** 94.8%. **Commercial banks:** 11; deposits: $16.6 bil. **Savings institutions:** 20; deposits: $11.4 bil. **Lottery:** total sales: $265.9 mil; profit: $58.7 mil.

Federal govt. Fed. civ. employees: 10,413; **avg. salary:** $70,326. **Notable fed. facilities:** Portsmouth Naval Shipyard.

Education. High school grad. rate: 87.0%. **4-yr. public coll./univ.:** 8; **2-yr. public:** 7; **4-yr. private:** 11.

Energy. Electricity use/cost: 546 kWh, $86.48.

State data. Motto: Dirigo (I direct). **Flower:** White pine cone and tassel. **Bird:** Black-capped chickadee. **Tree:** Eastern white pine. **Song:** "State of Maine Song." **Entered union:** Mar. 15, 1820; rank: 23rd.

Tourism. Tourist spending: $4.0 bil. **Attractions:** Acadia Natl. Park, Bar Harbor, on Mt. Desert Island; Old Orchard Beach; Old Port historic waterfront, Victoria Mansion, Port-

land; Portland Head Light, Cape Elizabeth; Maine Maritime Museum, Bath; Baxter State Park; L.L. Bean flagship store and outlet shopping, Freeport. **Information:** Maine Office of Tourism, 59 State House Station, Augusta, ME 04330; 1-888-624-6345; www.visitmaine.com

History. Paleo-Indians arrived about 11,500 years ago. Maine was inhabited by Algonquian peoples including the Abnaki, Penobscot, and Passamaquoddy at the time of European contact. French settled, 1604, at the St. Croix R., the English, c. 1607, on the Kennebec; both settlements failed. A royal charter, 1691, made Maine part of Massachusetts. Maine broke off, 1819, and became a separate state, 1820. Drawing on vast forest resources, the pulp and paper industry developed after the Civil War. Bath Iron Works began building U.S. Navy vessels and other ships in the 1890s. Mail-order and retail giant L.L. Bean was founded, 1912. Women have fared well in state politics: Margaret Chase Smith became the first woman to serve in both houses of Congress (House, 1940-49; Senate, 1949-73), and Olympia Snowe and Susan Collins represented Maine in the Senate since the mid-1990s (Snowe retired in Jan. 2013).

Famous "Down Easters." Leon Leonwood (L. L.) Bean, James G. Blaine, Patrick Dempsey, Hannibal Hamlin, Sarah Orne Jewett, Stephen King, Henry Wadsworth Longfellow, Sir Hiram and Hudson Maxim, Edna St. Vincent Millay, George J. Mitchell, Edmund Muskie, Judd Nelson, Edwin Arlington Robinson, Joan Benoit Samuelson, Liv Tyler, Kate Douglas Wiggin, Ben Ames Williams.

Website. www.maine.gov

Maryland (MD)
Old Line State, Free State

People. Population: 6,052,177; rank: 19. **Pop. change** (2010-17): 4.8%. **Pop. density:** 623.5 per sq mi. **Racial distribution:** 59.0% white; 30.8% black; 6.7% Asian; 0.6% Amer. Ind.; 0.1% Pac. Isl.; 2+ races, 2.8%. **Hispanic pop.:** 10.1%.

Geography. Total area: 12,406 sq mi; rank: 42. **Land area:** 9,707 sq mi; rank: 42. **Acres forested:** 2.5 mil. **Location:** South Atlantic state stretching from the ocean to the Allegheny Mts. **Climate:** continental in the W; humid subtropical in the E. **Topography:** coastal plain on Eastern Shore separated by Chesapeake Bay from coastal plain, Piedmont Plateau, and the Blue Ridge. **Capital:** Annapolis. **Chief airport:** Glen Burnie.

Economy. Chief industries: manufacturing, biotechnology and information technology, services, tourism. **Chief manuf. goods:** navigational instruments, pharmaceutical and medicine, broadcasting equip., plastics, printing, milk and ice cream. **Chief crops:** greenhouse and nursery, corn, soybeans, wheat, hay, tomatoes, watermelons, barley, potatoes, apples. **Farm income:** crops, $876.93 mil; livestock, $1.23 bil. **Nonfuel minerals:** $379 mil; cement (portland), stone (crushed), sand and gravel (construction), cement (masonry), stone (dimension). **Commercial fishing:** $90.4 mil. **Chief port:** Baltimore. **Gross state product:** $393.6 bil. **Sales tax:** 6.0%. **Gasoline tax:** 53.70 cents/gal. **Employment distrib.:** 18.6% govt.; 17.1% trade/trans./util.; 3.9% mfg.; 17.1% ed./health; 16.3% prof./bus. serv.; 10.4% leisure/hosp.; 5.1% finance; 6.0% constr./mining/log.; 1.3% info.; 4.2% other serv. **Unemployment:** 4.1%. **Min. wage/hr.:** $10.10. **Per cap. pers. income:** $59,524. **New private housing:** 16,224 units/$3.3 bil. **Broadband internet:** 98.0%. **Commercial banks:** 75; deposits: $138.5 bil. **Savings institutions:** 20; deposits: $4.4 bil. **Lottery:** total sales: $3.4 bil; profit: $1.0 bil.

Federal govt. Fed. civ. employees: 128,653; **avg. salary:** $108,498. **Notable fed. facilities:** U.S. Naval Academy; Beltsville Agriculture Res. Ctr.; Ft. Meade; Aberdeen Proving Ground; Joint Base Andrews; Naval Air Sys. Command; Goddard Space Flight Ctr.; Natl. Inst. of Standards & Technology, Gaithersburg; Food & Drug Admin., Natl. Marine Fisheries Serv., Natl. Oceanic and Atmospheric Admin., Silver Spring; Bureau of the Census, Suitland; Natl. Inst. of Health, Walter Reed Natl. Military Med. Ctr., Bethesda.

Education. High school grad. rate: 87.6%. **4-yr. public coll./univ.:** 13; **2-yr. public:** 16; **4-yr. private:** 19.

Energy. Electricity use/cost: 995 kWh, $141.53.

State data. Motto: Fatti Maschii, Parole Femine (Manly deeds, womanly words). **Flower:** Black-eyed Susan. **Bird:** Baltimore oriole. **Tree:** White oak. **Song:** "Maryland, My Maryland." **Seventh** of original 13 states to ratify the Constitution, Apr. 28, 1788.

Tourism. Tourist spending: $17.0 bil. **Attractions:** Ocean City; Ft. McHenry—the defense of which inspired Francis

Scott Key to write "The Star-Spangled Banner," Pimlico Race Course (Preakness Stakes), Edgar Allan Poe House and Museum, Oriole Park at Camden Yards, Natl. Aquarium, Inner Harbor, in Baltimore; Antietam Natl. Battlefield, Sharpsburg; South Mountain State Battlefield, Middletown; U.S. Naval Academy, Maryland State House (oldest in continuous legislative use in U.S.), in Annapolis; Natl. Cryptologic Museum, Ft. Meade. **Information:** Maryland Office of Tourism Development, 401 E. Pratt St., 14th Fl., Baltimore, MD 21202; 1-866-639-3526; www.visitmaryland.org

History. Europeans encountered Algonquian-speaking Nanticoke and Piscataway and Iroquois-speaking Susquehannock when they first visited the area. Italian navigator Giovanni da Verrazzano reached the Chesapeake region in the early 16th cent. English Capt. John Smith explored and mapped the area, 1608. William Claiborne set up a trading post on Kent Island in Chesapeake Bay, 1631. King Charles I granted land to Cecilius Calvert, Lord Baltimore, 1632; Calvert's brother Leonard, with about 200 settlers, founded St. Mary's, 1634. During the Revolutionary War, Baltimore (1776-77) and Annapolis (1783-84) served as temporary capitals of the U.S. When a British fleet tried to take Ft. McHenry in the War of 1812, Marylander Francis Scott Key wrote "The Star-Spangled Banner," 1814. Born into slavery at Tuckahoe in 1818, Frederick Douglass became a leading abolitionist. Although a slaveholding state, Maryland stayed in the Union during the Civil War and was the site of the battle of Antietam, 1862. Gov. Spiro Agnew, elected U.S. vice pres., 1968 and 1972, pleaded no contest to tax evasion and resigned, 1973. Israeli and Egyptian leaders reached a historic peace accord at the Camp David presidential retreat, 1978. A major effort is under way to clean up pollution in the Chesapeake Bay watershed. The death of a young black man in police custody touched off sometimes violent protests in Baltimore in 2015. Six law enforcement officers were charged in his death; after three were acquitted, charges against the others were dropped. According to a 2016 Justice Dept. report, Baltimore's police dept. regularly violated the constitutional rights of black residents. A gunman in June 2018 fatally shot five employees at the office of Annapolis's *Capital Gazette*.

Famous Marylanders. John Astin, Benjamin Banneker, Tom Clancy, Frederick Douglass, Matthew Henson, Francis Scott Key, Thurgood Marshall, H. L. Mencken, Kweisi Mfume, Ogden Nash, Charles Willson Peale, Michael Phelps, William Pinkney, Edgar Allan Poe, Cal Ripken Jr., Babe Ruth, Upton Sinclair, Roger B. Taney, Harriet Tubman, John Waters, Montel Williams.

Website. www.maryland.gov

Massachusetts (MA)
Bay State, Old Colony

People. Population: 6,859,819; rank: 15. **Pop. change** (2010-17): 4.8%. **Pop. density:** 879.5 per sq mi. **Racial distribution:** 81.3% white; 8.8% black; 6.9% Asian; 0.5% Amer. Ind.; 0.1% Pac. Isl.; 2+ races, 2.4%. **Hispanic pop.:** 11.9%.

Geography. Total area: 10,554 sq mi; rank: 44. **Land area:** 7,800 sq mi; rank: 45. **Acres forested:** 3.0 mil. **Location:** New England state on Atlantic seaboard. **Climate:** temperate, with colder, drier clime in western region. **Topography:** jagged indented coast from Rhode Island around Cape Cod; flat land yields to stony upland pastures near central region and gentle hilly country in W; except in W, land is rocky, sandy, and not fertile. **Capital:** Boston. **Chief airport:** Boston.

Economy. Chief industries: services, trade, manufacturing. **Chief manuf. goods:** electronics and instruments, pharmaceuticals, telecom and broadcasting equip., plastics, medical equip., printing. **Chief crops:** greenhouse and nursery, cranberries, tomatoes, sweet corn, apples, hay, tobacco. **Farm income:** crops, $270.97 mil; livestock, $115.91 mil. **Nonfuel minerals:** $296 mil; stone (crushed), sand and gravel (construction), stone (dimension), lime, clays (common). **Commercial fishing:** $551.1 mil. **Chief ports:** Boston, Fall River. **Gross state product:** $527.5 bil. **Sales tax:** 6.25%. **Gasoline tax:** 44.94 cents/gal. **Employment distrib.:** 12.6% govt.; 15.8% trade/trans./util.; 6.7% mfg.; 21.8% ed./health; 16.0% prof./bus. serv.; 10.3% leisure/hosp.; 6.0% finance; 4.4% constr./mining/log.; 2.5% info.; 3.8% other serv. **Unemployment:** 3.7%. **Min. wage/hr.:** $11.00. **Per cap. pers. income:** $65,890. **New private housing:** 17,728 units/$4.1 bil. **Broadband internet:** 98.1%. **Commercial banks:** 43; deposits: $272.2 bil. **Savings institutions:** 115; deposits: $77.9 bil. **Lottery:** total sales: $5.1 bil; profit: $1.0 bil.

Federal govt. Fed. civ. employees: 24,384; **avg. salary:** $87,230. **Notable fed. facilities:** Thomas P. O'Neill Jr. Fed.

Bldg., J.W. McCormack Bldg., JFK Fed. Bldg., Boston; Hanscom AFB; Army Natick Soldier Systems Ctr.

Education. High school grad. rate: 87.5%. **4-yr. public coll./univ.:** 15; **2-yr. public:** 16; **4-yr. private:** 79.

Energy. Electricity use/cost: 599 kWh, $113.77.

State data. Motto: Ense Petit Placidam Sub Libertate Quietem (By the sword we seek peace, but peace only under liberty). **Flower:** Mayflower. **Bird:** Black-capped chickadee. **Tree:** American elm. **Song:** "All Hail to Massachusetts." **Sixth** of original 13 states to ratify the Constitution, Feb. 6, 1788.

Tourism. Tourist spending: $21.8 bil. **Attractions:** Provincetown art colony; Cape Cod; Plymouth Rock, Plimoth Plantation, Mayflower II, in Plymouth; Freedom Trail, Museum of Fine Arts, New England Aquarium, Faneuil Hall, Boston Harbor Isls. Natl. Recreation Area, Boston Public Garden, in Boston; Tanglewood, Hancock Shaker Village, Berkshire Scenic Railway Museum, Norman Rockwell Museum, in the Berkshires region; Peabody Essex Museum, House of the Seven Gables, in Salem; Old Sturbridge Village; Historic Deerfield; Walden Pond, Louisa May Alcott's Orchard House, in Concord; Naismith Memorial Basketball Hall of Fame, Springfield. **Information:** Massachusetts Office of Travel & Tourism, 136 Blackstone St., 5th Fl., Boston, MA 02109; 1-800-227-MASS; www.massvacation.com

History. Early inhabitants were Algonquian peoples: Nauset, Wampanoag, Massachuset, Pennacook, Nipmuc, and Pocumtuc. Pilgrims settled in Plymouth, 1620, giving thanks for their survival with a Thanksgiving feast alongside Wampanoag living there, 1621. About 20,000 new settlers arrived, 1630-40. Colonist-Native American relations deteriorated, leading to King Philip's War, 1675-76, which the colonists won. Witch trials at Salem, 1692, led to the execution of 20 people. Demonstrations against British restrictions set off the Boston Massacre, 1770, and the Boston Tea Party, 1773. The first bloodshed of American Revolution was at Lexington, 1775. After statehood, Massachusetts prospered from shipbuilding, seafaring, and the making of textiles, shoes, and metal goods, while artists, writers, and social reformers flourished. The controversial Sacco-Vanzetti case, 1920-27, ended with the execution of two Italian immigrants on murder and robbery charges. After World War II, old industries declined, knowledge-intensive enterprises thrived, and the Kennedys became a dominant political family. The state's highest court ruled, 2003, that same-sex couples could legally marry. Two bombs exploded Apr. 15, 2013, near the finish line of the Boston Marathon, killing three and injuring more than 250. The surviving of two brothers believed to have planted the bombs was convicted on multiple charges in Apr. 2015 and sentenced to death.

Famous "Bay Staters." John Adams, John Quincy Adams, Samuel Adams, Louisa May Alcott, Horatio Alger, Susan B. Anthony, Crispus Attucks, Clara Barton, Michael Bloomberg, George H. W. Bush, Steve Carell, John Cheever, E. E. Cummings, Bette Davis, Emily Dickinson, Charles Eliot, Ralph Waldo Emerson, William Lloyd Garrison, Edward Everett Hale, John Hancock, Nathaniel Hawthorne, Oliver Wendell Holmes Jr., Winslow Homer, Elias Howe, John F. Kennedy, Jack Kerouac, John Kerry, Emeril Lagasse, Jack Lemmon, James Russell Lowell, Cotton Mather, Maria Mitchell, Samuel F. B. Morse, Conan O'Brien, Paul Revere, Norman Rockwell, Dr. Seuss (Theodor Seuss Geisel), Henry David Thoreau, Barbara Walters, James Abbott McNeil Whistler, John Greenleaf Whittier.

Website. www.mass.gov

Michigan (MI)
Great Lakes State, Wolverine State

People. Population: 9,962,311; rank: 10. **Pop. change** (2010-17): 0.8%. **Pop. density:** 176.2 per sq mi. **Racial distribution:** 79.4% white; 14.1% black; 3.2% Asian; 0.7% Amer. Ind.; <0.05% Pac. Isl.; 2+ races, 2.4%. **Hispanic pop.:** 5.1%.

Geography. Total area: 96,714 sq mi; rank: 11. **Land area:** 56,539 sq mi; rank: 22. **Acres forested:** 20.3 mil. **Location:** East North Central state bordering four of the Great Lakes, divided into an Upper and Lower Peninsula by the Straits of Mackinac, which link Lakes Michigan and Huron. **Climate:** well-defined seasons tempered by the Great Lakes. **Topography:** low rolling hills give way to northern tableland of hilly belts in Lower Peninsula; Upper Peninsula is level in the E with swampy areas; western region is higher and more rugged. **Capital:** Lansing. **Chief airports:** Detroit, Grand Rapids.

Economy. Chief industries: manufacturing, services, tourism, agriculture, forestry/lumber. **Chief manuf. goods:** motor vehicles and parts, plastics, metalworking machinery, non-wood office furniture, fabricated metals. **Chief crops:** greenhouse and nursery, soybeans, corn, wheat, sugar beets, apples, blueberries, potatoes, dry beans, cherries, hay, cucumbers, tomatoes, grapes. **Farm income:** crops, $4.49 bil; livestock, $2.91 bil. **Nonfuel minerals:** $2.5 bil; iron ore, cement (portland), sand and gravel (construction), nickel concentrates, stone (crushed). **Commercial fishing:** $9.8 mil. **Chief ports:** Detroit, Escanaba, Calcite, Port Inland, Muskegon, Port Huron. **Gross state product:** $505.0 bil. **Sales tax:** 6.0%. **Gasoline tax:** 62.53 cents/gal. **Employment distrib.:** 13.6% govt.; 17.8% trade/trans./util.; 13.9% mfg.; 15.2% ed./health; 14.9% prof./bus. serv.; 10.2% leisure/hosp.; 5.0% finance; 4.2% constr./mining/log.; 1.2% info.; 3.9% other serv. **Unemployment:** 4.6%. **Min. wage/hr.:** $9.25. **Per cap. pers. income:** $45,255. **New private housing:** 23,623 units/$4.9 bil. **Broadband internet:** 96.9%. **Commercial banks:** 115; deposits: $199.5 bil. **Savings institutions:** 11; deposits: $11.1 bil. **Lottery:** total sales: $3.3 bil; profit: $924.7 mil.

Federal govt. Fed. civ. employees: 25,470; **avg. salary:** $83,020. **Notable fed. facilities:** Army TACOM Life Cycle Mgmt., Detroit Arsenal; DLA Logistics Info. Service; Selfridge Air Natl. Guard Base; Hart-Dole-Inouye Fed. Ctr., Battle Creek.

Education. High school grad. rate: 79.7%. **4-yr. public coll./univ.:** 21; **2-yr. public:** 25; **4-yr. private:** 39.

Energy. Electricity use/cost: 668 kWh, $101.64.

State data. Motto: Si Quaeris Peninsulam Amoenam, Circumspice (If you seek a pleasant peninsula, look about you). **Flower:** Apple blossom. **Bird:** American robin. **Tree:** White pine. **Song:** "Michigan, My Michigan." **Entered union:** Jan. 26, 1837; rank: 26th.

Tourism. Tourist spending: $23.7 bil. **Attractions:** Henry Ford Museum and Greenfield Village, Dearborn; Frederik Meijer Gardens and Sculpture Park, Grand Rapids; Tahquamenon Falls (of Longfellow's poem *Song of Hiawatha*); De Zwaan windmill, Tulip Time Festival, in Holland; Soo Locks (bet. Lakes Superior and Huron), Sault Ste. Marie; Air Zoo, Portage; Mackinac Island; Belle Isle Park, Detroit Institute of Arts, Charles H. Wright Museum of African-American History, Motown Historical Museum, in Detroit. **Information:** Michigan Economic Development Corp., 300 N. Washington Sq., Lansing, MI 48913; 1-888-784-7328; www.michigan.org

History. Hunting and fishing peoples lived in the region as early as 11,000 years ago. Ojibwa, Ottawa, Miami, Potawatomi, and Huron inhabited the area at the time of European contact. French fur traders and missionaries arrived in the 17th cent. and established a settlement at Sault Ste. Marie, 1668. British took over, 1763, and crushed a Native American uprising led by Ottawa chieftain Pontiac. The area was ceded to the U.S. by the Treaty of Paris, 1783, but the British remained until 1796. Michigan was organized as a territory, 1805. The British seized Ft. Mackinac and Detroit, 1812, but the U.S. regained control, 1814. The opening of the Erie Canal, 1825, and new land laws and Native American cessions led the way for a flood of settlers. Strongly antislavery, Michigan became a state, 1837, and supplied 90,000 soldiers to the Union army in the Civil War. In the 20th cent., automobile manufacturing was the backbone of the economy. Henry Ford launched the Model T car, 1908; the United Auto Workers union was founded, 1935. Motown music flourished in Detroit in the 1960s, but riots in 1967 dealt the city a heavy blow. As the auto industry faltered, Michigan lost more than 20% of its automotive-related jobs in 2002-07. In 2009, the federal government loaned billions of dollars to GM and Chrysler to keep them solvent. Detroit formally emerged from a 17-month bankruptcy process—the largest in U.S. municipal history—in Dec. 2014, having shed nearly $7 bil in debts. The state closed its last four bottled water distribution centers in Flint in Apr. 2018; 11 state and local officials were still facing criminal charges over their alleged roles in the lead-contamination crisis that began in 2014 in Flint's municipal water supply system. Michigan State Univ. in May 2018 agreed to pay $500 mil to settle sexual abuse lawsuits related to claims against former MSU doctor Larry Nassar.

Famous Michiganders. Ralph Bunche, Paul de Kruif, Thomas Edison, Eminem (Marshall Mathers), Edna Ferber, Gerald R. Ford, Henry Ford, Aretha Franklin, Edgar Guest, Lee Iacocca, Magic Johnson, Casey Kasem, Will Kellogg, Ring Lardner, Elmore Leonard, Charles Lindbergh, Joe Louis, Madonna, Malcolm X, Terry McMillan, Michael Moore, Larry Page, Pontiac, Gilda Radner, Mitt Romney, Diana Ross, Tom Selleck, Sinbad (David Adkins), John Smoltz, Lily Tomlin, Serena Williams.

Website. www.michigan.gov

Minnesota (MN)
North Star State, Gopher State

People. Population: 5,576,606; rank: 22. **Pop. change** (2010-17): 5.1%. **Pop. density:** 70.0 per sq mi. **Racial distribution:** 84.4% white; 6.5% black; 5.1% Asian; 1.4% Amer. Ind.; 0.1% Pac. Isl.; 2+ races, 2.5%. **Hispanic pop.:** 5.1%.

Geography. Total area: 86,936 sq mi; rank: 12. **Land area:** 79,627 sq mi; rank: 14. **Acres forested:** 17.7 mil. **Location:** West North Central state bounded on the E by Wisconsin and Lake Superior, on the N by Canada, on the W by the Dakotas, and on the S by Iowa. **Climate:** northern part of state lies in the moist Great Lakes storm belt; the western border lies at the edge of the semiarid Great Plains. **Topography:** central hill and lake region covers approx. half the state; to the NE, rocky ridges and deep lakes; to the NW, flat plain; to the S, rolling plains and deep river valleys. **Capital:** St. Paul. **Chief airport:** Minneapolis.

Economy. Chief industries: agribusiness, forest products, mining, manufacturing, tourism. **Chief manuf. goods:** petroleum and asphalt, computers and electronics, milk and cheese, printing, animal slaughtering, paper and prod., medical equip. **Chief crops:** corn, soybeans, hay, sugar beets, wheat, potatoes, greenhouse and nursery, dry edible beans, green peas, sunflowers. **Farm income:** crops, $9.97 bil; livestock, $7.09 bil. **Nonfuel minerals:** $3.2 bil; iron ore, sand and gravel (construction), sand and gravel (industrial), stone (crushed), stone (dimension). **Commercial fishing:** $0.2 mil. **Chief ports:** Two Harbors, Silver Bay, Duluth, St. Paul. **Gross state product:** $351.1 bil. **Sales tax:** 6.875%. **Gasoline tax:** 47.00 cents/gal. **Employment distrib.:** 14.6% govt.; 18.2% trade/trans./util.; 10.9% mfg.; 18.1% ed./health; 12.6% prof./bus. serv.; 9.5% leisure/hosp.; 6.1% finance; 4.4% constr./mining/log.; 1.7% info.; 3.9% other serv. **Unemployment:** 3.5%. **Min. wage/hr.:** $9.65. **Per cap. pers. income:** $53,043. **New private housing:** 21,953 units/$4.8 bil. **Broadband internet:** 94.9%. **Commercial banks:** 346; deposits: $230.2 bil. **Savings institutions:** 17; deposits: $4.0 bil. **Lottery:** total sales: $563.5 mil; profit: $139.2 mil.

Federal govt. Fed. civ. employees: 16,538; **avg. salary:** $77,548. **Notable fed. facilities:** Bishop Henry Whipple Fed. Bldg.; Minneapolis-St. Paul Air Reserve Station.

Education. High school grad. rate: 82.2%. **4-yr. public coll./univ.:** 12; **2-yr. public:** 31; **4-yr. private:** 34.

Energy. Electricity use/cost: 764 kWh, $96.79.

State data. Motto: L'Etoile du Nord (The star of the north). **Flower:** Pink and white lady's-slipper. **Bird:** Common loon. **Tree:** Red pine. **Song:** "Hail! Minnesota." **Entered union:** May 11, 1858; rank: 32nd.

Tourism. Tourist spending: $14.1 bil. **Attractions:** Minneapolis Institute of Arts, Walker Art Center, Minneapolis Sculpture Garden, Minnehaha Falls (in Longfellow's poem *Song of Hiawatha*), Guthrie Theater, in Minneapolis; Mall of America, Bloomington; Ordway Ctr. for the Performing Arts, Science Museum of Minnesota, in St. Paul; Voyageurs Natl. Park; Mayo Clinic, Rochester; North Shore (Lake Superior); Lake Minnetonka; Boundary Waters Canoe Area Wilderness; Superior Natl. Forest; Aerial Lift Bridge, Duluth. **Information:** Explore Minnesota Tourism, Metro Square, 121 7th Pl. E., Ste. 360, St. Paul, MN 55101; 1-888-VISITMN; www.explore minnesota.com

History. Inhabited for at least 10,000 years, the region was home to Dakota Sioux when Europeans arrived. French fur traders Pierre Esprit Radisson and Médard Chouart, sieur des Groseilliers, explored in the mid-17th cent. In 1679, Daniel Greysolon, sieur Duluth, claimed the entire region for France. Ojibwa arrived in the 18th cent. and warred with the Sioux for over 100 years. Britain took the area east of the Mississippi, 1763. The U.S. took over that portion after the American Revolution and gained the western area, 1803, in the Louisiana Purchase. The U.S. built Ft. St. Anthony (now Ft. Snelling), 1819, and bought Native American lands, 1837, spurring an influx of settlers from the east. Minnesota became a territory, 1849, and a state, 1858. The Sioux staged a bloody uprising, the Battle of Wood Lake, 1862, and were driven from the state. Railroad construction after the Civil War spurred the growth of the grain, timber, and iron mining industries. The opening of the St. Lawrence Seaway, 1959, aided the port of Duluth. Elected as a reformer, former pro wrestler Jesse Ventura served as governor, 1999-2003. Sen. Paul Wellstone (D) died when his campaign plane crashed, 2002. The I-35W Mississippi River Bridge in Minneapolis collapsed in 2007, killing 13. Former comedian and two-term Sen. Al Franken (D) resigned in Jan. 2018 amid allegations of sexual misconduct.

Famous Minnesotans. Andrews Sisters, Warren E. Burger, Ethan and Joel Coen, Bob Dylan, F. Scott Fitzgerald, Al Franken, Judy Garland, Cass Gilbert, Hubert H. Humphrey, Garrison Keillor, Sister Elizabeth Kenny, Jessica Lange, Sinclair Lewis, Paul Manship, E. G. Marshall, William J. and Charles H. Mayo, Eugene McCarthy, Walter F. Mondale, Prince (Prince Rogers Nelson), Charles M. Schulz, Ann Sothern, Harold Stassen, Thorstein Veblen, Jesse Ventura, Lindsey Vonn, Paul Wellstone.

Website. www.minnesota.gov

Mississippi (MS)
Magnolia State

People. Population: 2,984,100; rank: 34. **Pop. change** (2010-17): 0.5%. **Pop. density:** 63.6 per sq mi. **Racial distribution:** 59.2% white; 37.8% black; 1.1% Asian; 0.6% Amer. Ind.; 0.1% Pac. Isl.; 2+ races, 1.3%. **Hispanic pop.:** 3.2%.

Geography. Total area: 48,432 sq mi; rank: 32. **Land area:** 46,923 sq mi; rank: 31. **Acres forested:** 19.3 mil. **Location:** East South Central state bordered on the W by the Mississippi R., on the S by the Gulf of Mexico. **Climate:** semitropical, with abundant rainfall and long growing season. **Topography:** low, fertile delta between the Yazoo and Mississippi Rivers; loess bluffs stretch around delta border; sandy gulf coastal terraces followed by piney woods and prairie; rugged, high sandy hills in extreme NE followed by Prairie Black Belt, Pontotoc Ridge, and flatwoods into the N central highlands. **Capital:** Jackson.

Economy. Chief industries: warehousing and distribution, services, manufacturing, government, wholesale and retail trade. **Chief manuf. goods:** petroleum, upholstered furniture, poultry processing, motor vehicle parts, plastics, ships and boats, chemicals. **Chief crops:** cotton, soybeans, rice, hay, corn, sweet potatoes. **Farm income:** crops, $2.19 bil; livestock, $3.02 bil. **Nonfuel minerals:** $216 mil; sand and gravel (construction), stone (crushed), clays (montmorillonite), sand and gravel (industrial), clays (ball). **Commercial fishing:** $29.4 mil. **Chief ports:** Pascagoula, Vicksburg, Gulfport, Biloxi, Greenville. **Gross state product:** $111.7 bil. **Sales tax:** 7.0%. **Gasoline tax:** 37.19 cents/gal. **Employment distrib.:** 20.9% govt.; 19.9% trade/trans./util.; 12.4% mfg.; 12.6% ed./health; 9.7% prof./bus. serv.; 11.8% leisure/hosp.; 3.8% finance; 4.4% constr./mining/log.; 0.9% info.; 3.5% other serv. **Unemployment:** 5.1%. **Min. wage/hr.:** none ($7.25). **Per cap. pers. income:** $36,346. **New private housing:** 7,481 units/$1.3 bil. **Broadband internet:** 91.8%. **Commercial banks:** 95; deposits: $52.7 bil. **Savings institutions:** 4; deposits: $358.0 mil.

Federal govt. Fed. civ. employees: 17,408; **avg. salary:** $70,805. **Notable fed. facilities:** Keesler AFB; Meridian NAS; Columbus AFB; NASA Stennis Space Ctr.; Army Corps of Eng. Waterways Experiment Sta., Vicksburg; Naval Constr. Battalion Ctr., Gulfport.

Education. High school grad. rate: 82.3%. **4-yr. public coll./univ.:** 8; **2-yr. public:** 15; **4-yr. private:** 9.

Energy. Electricity use/cost: 1,203 kWh, $125.91.

State data. Motto: Virtute et Armis (By valor and arms). **Flower:** Magnolia. **Bird:** Northern mockingbird. **Tree:** Magnolia. **Song:** "Go, Mississippi!" **Entered union:** Dec. 10, 1817; rank: 20th.

Tourism. Tourist spending: $6.4 bil. **Attractions:** Vicksburg Natl. Military Park and Cemetery; Natchez Trace Parkway; antebellum home tours in Natchez and other cities; Tupelo Natl. Battlefield, Elvis Presley Birthplace, in Tupelo; Smith Robertson Museum and Cultural Ctr., Mynelle Gardens, Eudora Welty House, in Jackson; Mardi Gras parades on Gulf Coast; Beauvoir (Jefferson Davis Home and Presidential Library), Biloxi; Gulf Islands Natl. Seashore; Delta Blues Museum, Clarksdale. **Information:** Mississippi Division of Tourism, P.O. Box 849, Jackson, MS 39205; 1-866-SEE-MISS; www.visitmississippi.org

History. Choctaw, Chickasaw, and Natchez peoples were living in the region at the time of European contact. The Spaniard Hernando de Soto explored the area, 1540-41. René-Robert Cavelier, sieur de La Salle, traced the Mississippi R. from Illinois to its mouth and claimed the entire Mississippi Valley for France, 1682. The first settlement was the French Ft. Maurepas, 1699, on Biloxi Bay. The region was ceded to Britain, 1763, and claimed by Spain, 1779-98, then became a U.S. territory, 1798, and a state, 1817. Slavery spread along with cotton plantations; slaves made up 55% of the population, 1860. Mississippi seceded, 1861. In the Civil War, Union forces captured Vicksburg, 1863, and caused extensive damage elsewhere. Mississippi reentered the Union, 1870. For the next 100 years, resistance to desegregation and violence

against blacks made the state a battleground for the civil rights movement. Hurricanes Camille, 1969, and Katrina, 2005, caused substantial damage to the Gulf Coast. Since the early 1990s, casino gambling has boosted the economy, but the state's poverty rate remained the highest in the nation in 2010.

Famous Mississippians. Margaret Walker Alexander, Dana Andrews, Jimmy Buffett, Bo Diddley, Medgar Evers, William Faulkner, Brett Favre, Shelby Foote, Morgan Freeman, John Grisham, Fannie Lou Hamer, Jim Henson, Faith Hill, John Lee Hooker, Robert Johnson, James Earl Jones, B. B. King, L. Q. C. Lamar, Trent Lott, Gerald McRaney, Willie Morris, Walter Payton, Elvis Presley, Leontyne Price, Charley Pride, LeAnn Rimes, Robin Roberts, Muddy Waters, Eudora Welty, Tennessee Williams, Oprah Winfrey, Johnny Winter, Richard Wright, Tammy Wynette.

Website. www.ms.gov

Missouri (MO)
Show Me State

People. Population: 6,113,532; rank: 18. **Pop. change** (2010-17): 2.1%. **Pop. density:** 88.9 per sq mi. **Racial distribution:** 83.1% white; 11.8% black; 2.1% Asian; 0.6% Amer. Ind.; 0.1% Pac. Isl.; 2+ races, 2.3%. **Hispanic pop.:** 4.2%.

Geography. Total area: 69,707 sq mi; rank: 21. **Land area:** 68,742 sq mi; rank: 18. **Acres forested:** 15.3 mil. **Location:** West North Central state near the geographic center of the conterminous U.S.; bordered on the E by Mississippi R., on the NW by Missouri R. **Climate:** continental, susceptible to cold Canadian air; moist, warm Gulf air; and drier SW air. **Topography:** rolling hills, open, fertile plains, and well-watered prairie N of the Missouri R.; S of the river, land is rough and hilly with deep, narrow valleys; alluvial plain in the SE; low elevation in the W. **Capital:** Jefferson City. **Chief airports:** Kansas City, St. Louis.

Economy. Chief industries: agriculture, manufacturing, aerospace, tourism. **Chief manuf. goods:** motor vehicles and parts, aerospace, pharmaceuticals, plastics, soap, animal slaughtering and processing, printing. **Chief crops:** soybeans, corn, hay, cotton and cottonseed, wheat, rice, sorghum. **Farm income:** crops, $4.76 bil; livestock, $4.16 bil. **Nonfuel minerals:** $2.5 bil; cement (portland), stone (crushed), lime, lead, sand and gravel (industrial). **Gross state product:** $304.9 bil. **Sales tax:** 4.225%. **Gasoline tax:** 35.75 cents/gal. **Employment distrib.:** 15.3% govt.; 18.9% trade/trans./util.; 9.2% mfg.; 16.1% ed./health; 13.6% prof./bus. serv.; 10.8% leisure/hosp.; 6.0% finance; 4.3% constr./mining/log.; 1.8% info.; 4.0% other serv. **Unemployment:** 3.8%. **Min. wage/hr.:** $7.85. **Per cap. pers. income:** $43,661. **New private housing:** 18,811 units/$3.5 bil. **Broadband internet:** 94.0%. **Commercial banks:** 308; deposits: $155.9 bil. **Savings institutions:** 16; deposits: $21.7 bil. **Lottery:** total sales: $1.3 bil; profit: $291.6 mil.

Federal govt. Fed. civ. employees: 35,719; **avg. salary:** $68,523. **Notable fed. facilities:** Federal Reserve banks; Ft. Leonard Wood; Jefferson Barracks Natl. Cemetery; Natl. Personnel Records Ctr., St. Louis; Whiteman AFB.

Education. High school grad. rate: 89.0%. **4-yr. public coll./univ.:** 13; **2-yr. public:** 14; **4-yr. private:** 52.

Energy. Electricity use/cost: 1,041 kWh, $116.63.

State data. Motto: Salus Populi Suprema Lex Esto (Let the welfare of the people be the supreme law). **Flower:** Hawthorn. **Bird:** Eastern bluebird. **Tree:** Flowering dogwood. **Song:** "Missouri Waltz." **Entered union:** Aug. 10, 1821; rank: 24th.

Tourism. Tourist spending: $14.3 bil. **Attractions:** Silver Dollar City, Branson; Mark Twain Boyhood Home and Museum, Hannibal; Pony Express Natl. Museum, St. Joseph; Harry S. Truman Library and Museum, Independence; Gateway Arch (part of Jefferson Natl. Expansion Memorial), Ulysses S. Grant Natl. Historic Site, St. Louis Zoo, in St. Louis; Worlds of Fun amusement park, Kansas City; Lake of the Ozarks; Ozark Natl. Scenic Riverways; Natl. Churchill Museum, Fulton; State Capitol, Jefferson City; Wilson's Creek Natl. Battlefield; George Washington Carver Natl. Monument, Diamond; Bass Pro Shops Outdoor World, Springfield. **Information:** Missouri Division of Tourism, P.O. Box 1055, Jefferson City, MO 65102; 1-800-519-2100; www.visitmo.com

History. In the 17th cent., when French explorers arrived, Algonquian-speaking Sauk, Fox, and Illinois as well as Siouan-speaking Osage, Iowa, and Kansa peoples were living in the region; few remained by the 1830s. French hunters and lead miners made the first settlement, c. 1735, at Ste. Genevieve. The territory was ceded to Spain by the French,

1762, then returned to France, 1800, and acquired by the U.S. in the Louisiana Purchase, 1803. Powerful earthquakes rocked New Madrid, 1811-12. Missouri became a territory, 1812, and entered the Union as a slave state, 1821. St. Louis became the gateway for pioneers heading west. Though Missouri stayed with the Union, pro- and antislavery forces battled there during the Civil War. In the late 19th cent. railroad building and the cattle trade made Kansas City a boomtown. The most notable Missourian of the 20th cent., Harry S. Truman, was U.S. president, 1945-53. The state, a political bellwether, voted for the winner in every presidential election from 1960 to 2004. In May 2011, a tornado in Joplin killed about 162. The police-shooting death of Michael Brown in Ferguson in Aug. 2014 touched off major protests that spread nationwide and revived debate over the relationship between law enforcement officers and the communities they serve. With the state legislature considering impeachment, Gov. Eric Greitens resigned his office effective June 1, 2018, four months after he was indicted on felony charges related to an extramarital affair. In July, an amphibious duckboat sank in Table Rock Lake in Branson, killing 17 people.

Famous Missourians. Maya Angelou, Robert Altman, John Ashcroft, Burt Bacharach, Josephine Baker, Scott Bakula, Thomas Hart Benton, Yogi Berra, Chuck Berry, George Caleb Bingham, Daniel Boone, Omar Bradley, William S. Burroughs, Kate Capshaw, Dale Carnegie, George Washington Carver, Bob Costas, Walter Cronkite, Sheryl Crow, Walt Disney, T. S. Eliot, Richard "Dick" Gephardt, John Goodman, Betty Grable, Jon Hamm, Edwin Hubble, Jesse James, Rush Limbaugh, Marianne Moore, Reinhold Niebuhr, J. C. Penney, John J. Pershing, Brad Pitt, Joseph Pulitzer, Ginger Rogers, Bess Truman, Harry S. Truman, Kathleen Turner, Tina Turner, Mark Twain, Dick Van Dyke, Tennessee Williams, Lanford Wilson, Shelley Winters, Jane Wyman.

Website. www.mo.gov

Montana (MT)
Treasure State

People. Population: 1,050,493; rank: 44. **Pop. change** (2010-17): 6.2%. **Pop. density:** 7.2 per sq mi. **Racial distribution:** 89.1% white; 0.6% black; 0.8% Asian; 6.7% Amer. Ind.; 0.1% Pac. Isl.; 2+ races, 2.8%. **Hispanic pop.:** 3.8%.

Geography. Total area: 147,040 sq mi; rank: 4. **Land area:** 145,546 sq mi; rank: 4. **Acres forested:** 25.8 mil. **Location:** Mountain state bounded on the E by the Dakotas, on the S by Wyoming, on the SSW by Idaho, on the N by Canada. **Climate:** colder, continental climate with low humidity. **Topography:** Rocky Mts. in western third of state; eastern two-thirds gently rolling northern Great Plains. **Capital:** Helena. **Chief airport:** Bozeman.

Economy. Chief industries: agriculture, timber, mining, tourism, oil and gas. **Chief manuf. goods:** sawmills, softwood veneer and plywood, petroleum. **Chief crops:** wheat, barley, hay, sugar beets, potatoes, dry beans, flaxseed, cherries, corn, oats. **Farm income:** crops, $2.04 bil; livestock, $1.63 bil. **Nonfuel minerals:** $1.1 bil; palladium metal, copper, platinum metal, sand and gravel (construction), molybdenum concentrates. **Gross state product:** $48.1 bil. **Sales tax:** none. **Gasoline tax:** 50.65 cents/gal. **Employment distrib.:** 19.6% govt.; 19.6% trade/trans./util.; 4.2% mfg.; 16.0% ed./health; 8.9% prof./bus. serv.; 13.8% leisure/hosp.; 5.1% finance; 7.7% constr./mining/log.; 1.3% info.; 4.0% other serv. **Unemployment:** 4.0%. **Min. wage/hr.:** $8.30. **Per cap. pers. income:** $43,907. **New private housing:** 4,932 units/$847.4 mil. **Broadband internet:** 90.7%. **Commercial banks:** 57; deposits: $22.9 bil. **Savings institutions:** 2; deposits: $82.0 mil. **Lottery:** total sales: $52.7 mil; profit: $9.2 mil.

Federal govt. Fed. civ. employees: 9,102; **avg. salary:** $68,620. **Notable fed. facilities:** Malmstrom AFB and missile silos; Ft. Peck, Hungry Horse, Libby, Yellowtail, and other dams.

Education. High school grad. rate: 85.6%. **4-yr. public coll./univ.:** 6; **2-yr. public:** 11; **4-yr. private:** 4.

Energy. Electricity use/cost: 813 kWh, $88.95.

State data. Motto: Oro y Plata (Gold and silver). **Flower:** Bitterroot. **Bird:** Western meadowlark. **Tree:** Ponderosa pine. **Song:** "Montana." **Entered union:** Nov. 8, 1889; rank: 41st.

Tourism. Tourist spending: $4.4 bil. **Attractions:** Glacier and Yellowstone Natl. Parks; Museum of the Rockies, Bozeman; Museum of the Plains Indian, Blackfeet Reservation, in Browning; Custer Natl. Cemetery at Little Bighorn Battlefield Natl. Monument; Lewis and Clark Caverns State Park, Whitehall; Lewis and Clark Natl. Historic Trail Interpretive Ctr., Great

Falls. **Information:** Travel Montana, Dept. of Commerce, 301 S. Park Ave., P.O. Box 200533, Helena, MT 59601; 1-800-VIS-ITMT; www.visitmt.com

History. Paleo-Indian hunters reached the area over 12,000 years ago. Cheyenne, Blackfoot, Crow, Assiniboin, Salish (Flatheads), Kootenai, and Kalispel peoples lived in the region before Europeans arrived. French explorers visited the region, 1742. The U.S. acquired the area partly through the Louisiana Purchase, 1803, partly through the Lewis and Clark Expedition, 1804-06. Fur traders and missionaries established posts in the early 19th cent. Gold was discovered on Grasshopper Creek, 1862, and Montana Territory was established, 1864. Indian uprisings reached their peak with the defeat of Gen. George Custer at the Battle of Little Bighorn, 1876. Chief Joseph and the Nez Percé tribe surrendered in Montana, 1877, after being driven from their lands in Oregon. Mining activity and the coming of the Northern Pacific Railway, 1883, brought population growth. Montana became a state, 1889. Copper wealth from the Butte pits resulted in the turn of the century "War of Copper Kings" as feuding factions contended for "the richest hill on earth." During the first half of the 20th cent., the Anaconda Copper firm wielded enormous political influence. Jeannette Rankin, a suffragist and pacifist, was the first woman elected to Congress, 1916. Mike Mansfield served 34 years in Congress and was Senate Democratic leader, 1961-77. An 18-year hunt for notorious "Unabomber" Theodore Kaczynski ended with his arrest, 1996, at his cabin near Lincoln. Ryan Zinke became the first Montanan in the president's cabinet since statehood when he was sworn in as interior secretary in Mar. 2017.

Famous Montanans. Dana Carvey, Gary Cooper, Marcus Daly, Chet Huntley, Phil Jackson, Will James, Myrna Loy, David Lynch, Mike Mansfield, Brent Musburger, Jeannette Rankin, Charles M. Russell, Lester Thurow.

Website. www.mt.gov

Nebraska (NE)
Cornhusker State

People. Population: 1,920,076; rank: 37. **Pop. change** (2010-17): 5.1%. **Pop. density:** 25.0 per sq mi. **Racial distribution:** 88.6% white; 5.1% black; 2.6% Asian; 1.5% Amer. Ind.; 0.1% Pac. Isl.; 2+ races, 2.2%. **Hispanic pop.:** 11.0%.

Geography. Total area: 77,348 sq mi; rank: 16. **Land area:** 76,824 sq mi; rank: 15. **Acres forested:** 1.5 mil. **Location:** West North Central state with the Missouri R. for a border on NE and E. **Climate:** continental semiarid. **Topography:** till plains of the central lowland in the eastern third rises to the Great Plains and hill country of the N central and NW. **Capital:** Lincoln. **Chief airport:** Omaha.

Economy. Chief industries: agriculture, manufacturing. **Chief manuf. goods:** animal slaughtering, grain and oilseed, farm machinery, medical equip., motor vehicle parts, printing, structural metals. **Chief crops:** corn, sorghum, soybeans, hay, wheat, dry beans, oats, potatoes, sugar beets. **Farm income:** crops, $9.41 bil; livestock, $12.15 bil. **Nonfuel minerals:** $192 mil; cement (portland), stone (crushed), sand and gravel (construction), sand and gravel (industrial), lime. **Gross state product:** $121.8 bil. **Sales tax:** 5.5%. **Gasoline tax:** 47.30 cents/gal. **Employment distrib.:** 17.0% govt.; 19.7% trade/trans./util.; 9.8% mfg.; 14.9% ed./health; 11.5% prof./bus. serv.; 9.4% leisure/hosp.; 7.3% finance; 5.2% constr./mining/log.; 1.6% info.; 3.6% other serv. **Unemployment:** 2.9%. **Min. wage/hr.:** $9.00. **Per cap. pers. income:** $50,395. **New private housing:** 8,863 units/$1.4 bil. **Broadband internet:** 95.7%. **Commercial banks:** 186; deposits: $58.6 bil. **Savings institutions:** 8; deposits: $5.8 bil. **Lottery:** total sales: $173.8 mil; profit: $41.3 mil.

Federal govt. Fed. civ. employees: 9,692; **avg. salary:** $73,169. **Notable fed. facilities:** Offutt AFB.

Education. High school grad. rate: 89.3%. **4-yr. public coll./univ.:** 7; **2-yr. public:** 8; **4-yr. private:** 17.

Energy. Electricity use/cost: 973 kWh, $105.47.

State data. Motto: Equality before the law. **Flower:** Giant goldenrod. **Bird:** Western meadowlark. **Tree:** Cottonwood. **Song:** "Beautiful Nebraska." **Entered union:** Mar. 1, 1867; rank: 37th.

Tourism. Tourist spending: $4.9 bil. **Attractions:** Univ. of Nebraska State Museum at Morrill Hall, Nebraska State Capitol, in Lincoln; Stuhr Museum of the Prairie Pioneer, Grand Island; Boys Town; Omaha's Henry Doorly Zoo and Aquarium, Joslyn Art Museum, The Durham Museum, in Omaha; Ashfall Fossil Beds State Hist. Park, near Royal; Strategic Air and Space Museum, Ashland; Arbor Lodge State Historical Park, Nebraska City; Buffalo Bill Ranch State Historical Park, North

Platte; Pioneer Village, Minden; Oregon Trail landmarks, incl. at Scotts Bluff Natl. Monument and Chimney Rock Natl. Historic Site; Great Platte River Road Archway, Museum of Nebraska Art, in Kearney. **Information:** Nebraska Tourism Commission, 301 Centennial Mall S., Lincoln, NE 68508; 1-888-444-1867; www.visitnebraska.com

History. When Europeans arrived, Pawnee, Ponca, Omaha, and Oto peoples lived in the region. Spanish and French explorers and fur traders visited the area prior to its acquisition in the Louisiana Purchase, 1803. Meriwether Lewis and William Clark passed through, 1804-06. The first permanent settlement was Bellevue, near Omaha, 1823. The 1834 Indian Intercourse Act declared Nebraska Indian country and excluded white settlement, but conflicts with settlers eventually forced Native Americans to move to reservations. Nebraska became a territory, 1854, and a state, 1867. Many Civil War veterans settled under free land terms of the 1862 Homestead Act; as agriculture grew, struggles followed between homesteaders and ranchers. Since the mid-1930s, Nebraska has been the only state with a unicameral legislature. A leader in agribusiness, Nebraska has also become a major telemarketing center. The "Oracle of Omaha," investor Warren Buffett, one of the world's wealthiest men, said in 2006 he would give most of his then-$44-bil fortune to charity.

Famous Nebraskans. Grover Cleveland Alexander, Fred Astaire, Marlon Brando, Charles W. Bryan, William Jennings Bryan, Warren Buffett, Johnny Carson, Willa Cather, Dick Cavett, Dick Cheney, Loren Eiseley, Father Edward J. Flanagan, Henry Fonda, Bob Gibson, Rollin Kirby, Harold Lloyd, Malcolm X, J. Sterling Morton, John G. Neihardt, Nick Nolte, George W. Norris, Tom Osborne, Roscoe Pound, Red Cloud, Mari Sandoz, Robert Taylor, Darryl F. Zanuck.

Website. www.nebraska.gov

Nevada (NV)
Sagebrush State, Battle Born State, Silver State

People. Population: 2,998,039; rank: 33. **Pop. change** (2010-17): 11.0%. **Pop. density:** 27.3 per sq mi. **Racial distribution:** 74.6% white; 9.8% black; 8.8% Asian; 1.7% Amer. Ind.; 0.8% Pac. Isl.; 2+ races, 4.3%. **Hispanic pop.:** 28.8%.

Geography. Total area: 110,572 sq mi; rank: 7. **Land area:** 109,781 sq mi; rank: 7. **Acres forested:** 10.5 mil. **Location:** Mountain state bordered on N by Oregon and Idaho, on E by Utah, on SE by Arizona, and on SW and W by California. **Climate:** semiarid and arid. **Topography:** rugged N-S mountain ranges; highest elevation, Boundary Peak, 13,146 ft; southern area is within the Mojave Desert; lowest elevation, Colorado R., at southern tip of state, 479 ft. **Capital:** Carson City. **Chief airports:** Las Vegas, Reno.

Economy. Chief industries: gaming, tourism, mining, manufacturing, government, retailing, warehousing, trucking. **Chief manuf. goods:** gaming machines, cement and concrete, plastics, printing, architectural and structural metals, electricity instruments. **Chief crops:** hay, onions, potatoes, alfalfa, wheat, garlic, mint, barley. **Farm income:** crops, $151.38 mil; livestock, $444.87 mil. **Nonfuel minerals:** $8.7 bil; gold, copper, stone (crushed), sand and gravel (construction), silver. **Gross state product:** $156.3 bil. **Sales tax:** 6.85%. **Gasoline tax:** 52.18 cents/gal. **Employment distrib.:** 12.2% govt.; 18.3% trade/trans./util.; 3.9% mfg.; 10.0% ed./health; 13.4% prof./bus. serv.; 25.8% leisure/hosp.; 4.8% finance; 7.5% constr./mining/log.; 1.1% info.; 3.1% other serv. **Unemployment:** 5.0%. **Min. wage/hr.:** $8.25. **Per cap. pers. income:** $44,626. **New private housing:** 19,544 units/$2.8 bil. **Broadband internet:** 97.8%. **Commercial banks:** 37; deposits: $67.3 bil. **Savings institutions:** 10; deposits: $163.9 bil.

Federal govt. Fed. civ. employees: 10,981; **avg. salary:** $73,316. **Notable fed. facilities:** Nevada Natl. Security Site; Hawthorne Army Depot; Creech AFB; Nellis AFB; Fallon NAS; Natl. Wild Horse & Burro Ctr. at Palomino Valley.

Education. High school grad. rate: 73.6%. **4-yr. public coll./univ.:** 6; **2-yr. public:** 1; **4-yr. private:** 4.

Energy. Electricity use/cost: 925 kWh, $105.48.

State data. Motto: All for our country. **Flower:** Sagebrush. **Bird:** Mountain bluebird. **Trees:** Single-leaf piñon and bristlecone pine. **Song:** "Home Means Nevada." **Entered union:** Oct. 31, 1864; rank: 36th.

Tourism. Tourist spending: $39.8 bil. **Attractions:** Legalized gambling, incl. at Lake Tahoe, Reno, Las Vegas, Laughlin, and Elko; Hoover Dam, Lake Mead Natl. Recreation Area, near Boulder City; Great Basin Natl. Park; Valley of Fire State Park; Red Rock Canyon Natl. Conservation Area; Las Vegas Strip, Fremont St., Natl. Atomic Testing Museum, Pinball Hall of Fame, Las Vegas Motor Speedway, in Las Vegas;

Natl. Automobile Museum, Reno. **Information:** Commission on Tourism, 401 N. Carson St., Carson City, NV 89701; 1-800-NEVADA-8; www.travelnevada.com

History. Shoshone, Paiute, Bannock, and Washoe peoples lived in the area at the time of European contact. Nevada was first explored by Spaniards, 1776. In the 1820s, fur traders Peter Skene Ogden, a Canadian, and Jedediah Smith separately explored the area. It was acquired by the U.S., 1848, at the end of the Mexican War. A trading post at Mormon Station, now Genoa, was established, 1850. Discovery of the Comstock Lode, rich in gold and silver, 1859, spurred a population boom. Nevada became a territory, 1861, and a state, 1864. Hoover Dam was built, 1931-36. With gambling legal since 1931, a surge in resort casino construction after World War II turned Las Vegas into one of the nation's most popular tourist destinations. An influx of both native and foreign-born Hispanics and Asians, attracted by the thriving service and construction industries, helped make Nevada the fastest-growing state in the U.S. in 1990-2005. The 2007-09 recession had an equally powerful effect, with high unemployment and foreclosures. In the deadliest mass shooting in modern U.S. history, a gunman killed 58 when he fired indiscriminately from his 32nd floor Las Vegas hotel suite on an outdoor country music festival in Oct. 2017.

Famous Nevadans. Andre Agassi, Kurt Busch, Kyle Busch, Walter Van Tilburg Clark, George W. G. Ferris, Sarah Winnemucca Hopkins, Paul Laxalt, Dat So La Lee, John William Mackay, Anne Henrietta Martin, Pat McCarran, Key Pittman, William Morris Stewart.

Website. www.nv.gov

New Hampshire (NH)
Granite State

People. Population: 1,342,795; rank: 41. **Pop. change** (2010-17): 2.0%. **Pop. density:** 150.0 per sq mi. **Racial distribution:** 93.6% white; 1.6% black; 2.8% Asian; 0.3% Amer. Ind.; <0.05% Pac. Isl.; 2+ races, 1.7%. **Hispanic pop.:** 3.7%.

Geography. Total area: 9,349 sq mi; rank: 46. **Land area:** 8,953 sq mi; rank: 44. **Acres forested:** 4.7 mil. **Location:** New England state bounded on S by Massachusetts, on W by Vermont, on N by Canada, on E by Maine and the Atlantic Ocean. **Climate:** highly varied, due to its nearness to high mountains and ocean. **Topography:** low, rolling coast followed by countless hills and mountains rising out of a central plateau. **Capital:** Concord. **Chief airport:** Manchester.

Economy. Chief industries: tourism, manufacturing, agriculture, trade, mining. **Chief manuf. goods:** navigational instruments, circuit boards, electrical equip., fabricated metal, machinery, medical equip., plastics. **Chief crops:** greenhouse and nursery, apples, sweet corn, hay, Christmas trees, berries, maple syrup. **Farm income:** crops, $95.96 mil; livestock, $113.98 mil. **Nonfuel minerals:** $78 mil; stone (crushed), sand and gravel (construction), stone (dimension), gemstones (natural). **Commercial fishing:** $33.2 mil. **Chief port:** Portsmouth. **Gross state product:** $80.5 bil. **Sales tax:** none. **Gasoline tax:** 42.23 cents/gal. **Employment distrib.:** 13.5% govt.; 20.7% trade/trans./util.; 10.2% mfg.; 18.5% ed./health; 12.0% prof./bus. serv.; 10.6% leisure/hosp.; 5.1% finance; 4.2% constr./mining/log.; 1.8% info.; 3.6% other serv. **Unemployment:** 2.7%. **Min. wage/hr.:** $7.25. **Per cap. pers. income:** $57,574. **New private housing:** 3,625 units/$758.3 mil. **Broadband internet:** 95.9%. **Commercial banks:** 18; deposits: $26.5 bil. **Savings institutions:** 24; deposits: $6.6 bil. **Lottery:** total sales: $299.2 mil; profit: $76.1 mil.

Federal govt. Fed. civ. employees: 4,315; **avg. salary:** $87,594. **Notable fed. facilities:** Army Cold Regions Res. and Engineering Lab, Hanover.

Education. High school grad. rate: 88.2%. **4-yr. public coll./univ.:** 6; **2-yr. public:** 7; **4-yr. private:** 11.

Energy. Electricity use/cost: 604 kWh, $110.95.

State data. Motto: Live free or die. **Flower:** Purple lilac. **Bird:** Purple finch. **Tree:** White birch. **Song:** "Old New Hampshire." **Ninth** of original 13 states to ratify the Constitution, June 21, 1788.

Tourism. Tourist spending: $4.1 bil. **Attractions:** Mt. Washington Cog Railway, Mt. Washington (highest peak in Northeast); Lake Winnipesaukee; Crawford, Franconia, Pinkham Notches (mountain passes), Flume Gorge, Cannon Mountain Aerial Tramway, in White Mountains region; Strawbery Banke Museum, Portsmouth; Canterbury Shaker Village; Saint-Gaudens Natl. Historic Site, Cornish; Mt. Monadnock; Santa's Village, Jefferson. **Information:** Division of Travel & Tourism Development, 172 Pembroke Rd., P.O. Box 1856; Concord, NH 03302; 1-800-FUN-IN-NH; www.visitnh.gov

History. The area has been inhabited for about 10,000 years. Algonquian-speaking peoples, including the Pennacook, lived in the region when the Europeans arrived. The first explorers to visit the area were England's Martin Pring, 1603, and France's Samuel de Champlain, 1605. The first settlement was Odiorne's Point (now port of Rye), 1623. Before the American Revolution, New Hampshire residents raided a British fort at Portsmouth, 1774, and drove the royal governor out, 1775. New Hampshire became the first colony to adopt its own constitution, 1776. After statehood, 1788, New Hampshire became a textile manufacturing center. The mill towns declined in the first half of the 20th cent., but tourism and technology industries, lured by low taxes, have revived the economy since the 1960s. A state law requires it to hold the first primary of the presidential campaign season.

Famous New Hampshirites. Dan Brown, Salmon P. Chase, Ralph Adams Cram, Mary Baker Eddy, Daniel Chester French, Robert Frost, Horace Greeley, Sarah Josepha Buell Hale, John Irving, Seth Meyers, Bode Miller, Franklin Pierce, Augustus Saint-Gaudens, Adam Sandler, Alan B. Shepard Jr., Sarah Silverman, David H. Souter, Daniel Webster.

Website. www.nh.gov

New Jersey (NJ)
Garden State

People. Population: 9,005,644; rank: 11. **Pop. change** (2010-17): 2.4%. **Pop. density:** 1,224.6 per sq mi. **Racial distribution:** 72.1% white; 15.0% black; 10.1% Asian; 0.6% Amer. Ind.; 0.1% Pac. Isl.; 2+ races, 2.2%. **Hispanic pop.:** 20.4%.

Geography. Total area: 8,723 sq mi; rank: 47. **Land area:** 7,354 sq mi; rank: 46. **Acres forested:** 2.0 mil. **Location:** Middle Atlantic state bounded on N and E by New York and Atlantic Ocean, on S and W by Delaware and Pennsylvania. **Climate:** moderate, with marked difference between NW and SE extremities. **Topography:** Appalachian Valley in NW also has highest elevation, High Pt., 1,803 ft; Appalachian Highlands, flat-topped NE-SW mountain ranges; Piedmont Plateau, low plains broken by high ridges (Palisades) rising 400-500 ft; Coastal Plain, covering three-fifths of state in SE, rises from sea level to gentle slopes. **Capital:** Trenton. **Chief airports:** Atlantic City, Newark.

Economy. Chief industries: pharmaceuticals, telecommunications, biotechnology, printing and publishing. **Chief manuf. goods:** petroleum, pharmaceuticals, toiletries, chemicals, plastics, printing, navigational instruments, medical equip., paper prod. **Chief crops:** greenhouse and nursery, blueberries, peaches, corn, hay, tomatoes, bell peppers, cranberries, soybeans, apples. **Farm income:** crops, $907.47 mil; livestock, $118.41 mil. **Nonfuel minerals:** $265 mil; stone (crushed), sand and gravel (construction), sand and gravel (industrial), peat, gemstones. **Commercial fishing:** $191.1 mil. **Chief ports:** Newark-Elizabeth, Camden. **Gross state product:** $591.7 bil. **Sales tax:** 6.625%. **Gasoline tax:** 55.50 cents/gal. **Employment distrib.:** 14.9% govt.; 21.4% trade/trans./util.; 6.0% mfg.; 17.0% ed./health; 16.3% prof./bus. serv.; 9.1% leisure/hosp.; 5.9% finance; 3.6% constr./mining/log.; 1.7% info.; 4.2% other serv. **Unemployment:** 4.6%. **Min. wage/hr.:** $8.60. **Per cap. pers. income:** $62,554. **New private housing:** 28,501 units/$4.1 bil. **Broadband internet:** 98.3%. **Commercial banks:** 87; deposits: $272.7 bil. **Savings institutions:** 50; deposits: $58.6 bil. **Lottery:** total sales: $3.2 bil; profit: $994.0 mil.

Federal govt. Fed. civ. employees: 20,315; **avg. salary:** $95,059. **Notable fed. facilities:** Joint Base McGuire-Dix-Lakehurst; Picatinny Arsenal; FAA William J. Hughes Technical Ctr.

Education. High school grad. rate: 90.1%. **4-yr. public coll./univ.:** 13; **2-yr. public:** 19; **4-yr. private:** 29.

Energy. Electricity use/cost: 691 kWh, $108.58.

State data. Motto: Liberty and prosperity. **Flower:** Purple violet. **Bird:** Eastern goldfinch. **Tree:** Red oak. **Third** of the original 13 states to ratify the Constitution, Dec. 18, 1787.

Tourism. Tourist spending: $21.8 bil. **Attractions:** 130 mi of beaches, boardwalks on the Jersey Shore at Atlantic City (with gambling), Seaside Heights, Ocean City, Wildwood; Grover Cleveland Birthplace, Caldwell; Cape May Historic District; Thomas Edison Natl. Historical Park, West Orange; Six Flags Great Adventure, Jackson; Liberty State Park, Liberty Science Ctr., in Jersey City; Pine Barrens wilderness; Princeton Univ., Princeton Battlefield State Park, in Princeton; Morristown Natl. Historical Park; Adventure Aquarium, Battleship *New Jersey*, Walt Whitman House, in Camden. **Information:** Dept. of State, Division of Travel and Tourism, P.O. Box 460, Trenton, NJ 08625; 1-800-VISITNJ; www.visitnj.org

History. The Lenni Lenape (Delaware) peoples lived in the region and had mostly peaceful relations with European colonists, who arrived after the explorers Giovanni da Verrazzano,

1524, and Henry Hudson, 1609. The first permanent European settlement was Dutch, at Bergen (now Jersey City), 1660. When the British took New Netherland, 1664, the area between the Delaware and Hudson Rivers was given to Lord John Berkeley and Sir George Carteret. During the American Revolution, New Jersey was the scene of many major battles, including Trenton, 1776; Princeton, 1777; and Monmouth, 1778. New Jersey was the third state to ratify the Constitution, 1787, and the first to approve the Bill of Rights, 1789. In a duel at Weehawken, 1804, Vice Pres. Aaron Burr fatally shot former Treasury Sec. Alexander Hamilton. Canal and railroad building stimulated the growth of cities and industries in the 19th cent. The 20th-cent. arrival of large numbers of African Americans, Italians, Irish, European Jews, Puerto Ricans, South Asians, and other groups made New Jersey one of the most diverse states in the U.S. Construction of resort casinos in Atlantic City from the late 1970s revitalized tourism. Gov. James McGreevey resigned, 2004, after acknowledging an extramarital affair with a man identified as his former homeland security adviser. An estimated 37 people in New Jersey were killed when Hurricane Sandy (by then downgraded to a tropical storm) made landfall in 2012. Two members of Gov. Chris Christie's administration were convicted in 2016 on federal charges related to allegations that officials had created traffic jams to punish a political opponent.

Famous New Jerseyans. Buzz Aldrin, Jason Alexander, Samuel Alito, Count Basie, Judy Blume, Jon Bon Jovi, Bill Bradley, Aaron Burr, Grover Cleveland, Stephen Crane, Danny DeVito, Thomas Edison, Albert Einstein, James Gandolfini, Allen Ginsberg, Alexander Hamilton, Ed Harris, Whitney Houston, Joyce Kilmer, Jack Nicholson, Shaquille O'Neal, Thomas Paine, Bill Parcells, Dorothy Parker, Joe Pesci, Molly Pitcher, Paul Robeson, Philip Roth, Antonin Scalia, Wally Schirra, H. Norman Schwarzkopf, Frank Sinatra, Bruce Springsteen, Martha Stewart, Meryl Streep, Dave Thomas, John Travolta, Walt Whitman, William Carlos Williams, Woodrow Wilson.

Website. www.nj.gov

New Mexico (NM)
Land of Enchantment

People. Population: 2,088,070; rank: 36. **Pop. change** (2010-17): 1.4%. **Pop. density:** 17.2 per sq mi. **Racial distribution:** 82.2% white; 2.5% black; 1.7% Asian; 10.9% Amer. Ind.; 0.2% Pac. Isl.; 2+ races, 2.5%. **Hispanic pop.:** 48.8%.

Geography. Total area: 121,590 sq mi; rank: 5. **Land area:** 121,298 sq mi; rank: 5. **Acres forested:** 24.6 mil. **Location:** southwestern state bounded by Colorado on the N; Oklahoma, Texas, and Mexico on the E and S; Arizona on the W. **Climate:** dry, with temperatures rising or falling 5°F with every 1,000 ft elevation. **Topography:** eastern third, Great Plains; central third, Rocky Mts. (85% of the state is over 4,000-ft elevation); western third, high plateau. **Capital:** Santa Fe. **Chief airport:** Albuquerque.

Economy. Chief industries: government, services, trade. **Chief manuf. goods:** semiconductors, medical equip., navigational/measuring/medical/control instruments, aircraft, chemicals, jewelry. **Chief crops:** hay, pecans, corn, greenhouse and nursery, chiles, onions, cotton, wheat, peanuts. **Farm income:** crops, $711.09 mil; livestock, $2.15 bil. **Nonfuel minerals:** $1.3 bil; copper, potash, sand and gravel (construction), stone (crushed), cement (portland). **Gross state product:** $97.1 bil. **Sales tax:** 5.125%. **Gasoline tax:** 37.28 cents/gal. **Employment distrib.:** 22.2% govt.; 16.4% trade/trans./util.; 3.2% mfg.; 16.5% ed./health; 12.7% prof./bus. serv.; 11.9% leisure/hosp.; 4.2% finance; 8.2% constr./mining/log.; 1.4% info.; 3.4% other serv. **Unemployment:** 6.2%. **Min. wage/hr.:** $7.50. **Per cap. pers. income:** $39,023. **New private housing:** 4,741 units/$941.8 mil. **Broadband internet:** 91.9%. **Commercial banks:** 53; deposits: $29.7 bil. **Savings institutions:** 5; deposits: $830.0 mil. **Lottery:** total sales: $126.0 mil; profit: $37.8 mil.

Federal govt. Fed. civ. employees: 21,192; **avg. salary:** $74,260. **Notable fed. facilities:** Kirtland, Cannon, Holloman AF Bases; Los Alamos Natl. Lab; White Sands Missile Range; Natl. Solar Observatory, Sunspot; Natl. Radio Astronomy Observatory (Very Large Array), Socorro; Sandia Natl. Labs, Albuquerque.

Education. High school grad. rate: 71.0%. **4-yr. public coll./univ.:** 9; **2-yr. public:** 19; **4-yr. private:** 3.

Energy. Electricity use/cost: 631 kWh, $75.96.

State data. Motto: Crescit Eundo (It grows as it goes). **Flower:** Yucca. **Bird:** Roadrunner. **Tree:** Piñon. **Songs:** "O, Fair New Mexico"; "Asi Es Nuevo Mexico." **Entered union:** Jan. 6, 1912; rank: 47th.

Tourism. Tourist spending: $6.9 bil. **Attractions:** Carlsbad Caverns Natl. Park (with Lechuguilla Cave, among world's longest caves); Petroglyph Natl. Monument, Sandia Peak Tramway, in Albuquerque; New Mexico History Museum, Museum of Intl. Folk Art, in Santa Fe (oldest U.S. capital); White Sands Natl. Monument (world's largest gypsum dune field); Chaco Culture Natl. Historical Park; Acoma Pueblo, or Sky City, built atop a 367-ft mesa; Taos Art Colony, Taos Ski Valley; Elephant Butte Lake State Park; Shiprock volcanic remnant; Intl. UFO Museum and Research Ctr., Roswell. **Information:** New Mexico Dept. of Tourism, 491 Old Santa Fe Trl., Santa Fe, NM 87501; 1-800-733-6396; www.newmexico.org

History. Inhabited for more than 10,000 years, the region was home to Sandia, Clovis, Folsom, Mogollon, and Anasazi cultures, followed by the Pueblo people, Anasazi descendants; later, nomadic Navajo and Apache came. Spanish Franciscan Marcos de Niza and a former black slave, Estevanico, explored the area, 1539, seeking gold; Coronado followed, 1540. First settlements were near San Juan Pueblo, 1598, and at Santa Fe, 1610. Settlers alternately traded and fought with the Apache, Comanche, and Navajo. Trade on the Santa Fe Trail to Missouri started, 1821. After the Mexican War began, 1846, Gen. Stephen Kearny took Santa Fe without firing a shot, and declared New Mexico part of the U.S. All Hispanic New Mexicans and Pueblo became U.S. citizens by terms of the 1848 treaty ending the war. New Mexico became a territory, 1850, but did not attain statehood until 1912. Mexican revolutionary leader Pancho Villa raided Columbus, 1916, and U.S. troops were sent to the area. The world's first atomic bomb was exploded at a test site near Alamogordo, 1945. An underground nuclear waste depository opened near Carlsbad, 1999. Spaceport America, a state-owned commercial spaceport, hosted its first test launch in 2006.

Famous New Mexicans. Ben Abruzzo, Maxie Anderson, Jeff Bezos, William Bonney (Billy the Kid), Kit Carson, Bob Foster, Neil Patrick Harris, Tony Hillerman, Peter Hurd, Jean Baptiste Lamy, Nancy Lopez, Bill Mauldin, Georgia O'Keeffe, Bill Richardson, Kim Stanley, Al Unser, Bobby Unser.

Website. www.newmexico.org

New York (NY)
Empire State

People. Population: 19,849,399; rank: 4. **Pop. change** (2010-17): 2.4%. **Pop. density:** 421.2 per sq mi. **Racial distribution:** 69.6% white; 17.7% black; 9.1% Asian; 1.0% Amer. Ind.; 0.1% Pac. Isl.; 2+ races, 2.5%. **Hispanic pop.:** 19.2%.

Geography. Total area: 54,555 sq mi; rank: 27. **Land area:** 47,126 sq mi; rank: 30. **Acres forested:** 18.8 mil. **Location:** Middle Atlantic state bordered by the New England states, Atlantic Ocean on E; New Jersey and Pennsylvania on S; Lakes Ontario and Erie on W; Canada on N. **Climate:** variable; the SE region moderated by the ocean. **Topography:** highest and most rugged mountains in the NE Adirondack upland; St. Lawrence-Champlain lowlands extend from Lake Ontario NE along the Canadian border; Hudson-Mohawk lowland follows rivers N and W, 10-30 mi wide; Atlantic coastal plain in the SE; Appalachian Highlands, covering half the state westward from the Hudson Valley, include the Catskill Mts., Finger Lakes; plateau of Erie-Ontario lowlands. **Capital:** Albany. **Chief airports:** Albany, Buffalo, Islip, New York (2), Rochester, Syracuse, White Plains.

Economy. Chief industries: manufacturing, finance, communications, tourism, transportation, services. **Chief manuf. goods:** pharmaceuticals, photographic chemicals, electronics, automotive parts, toiletries, printing, plastics, apparel. **Chief crops:** greenhouse and nursery, apples, corn, hay, cabbage, onions, soybeans, potatoes, snap beans, grapes, squash, pumpkins, tomatoes, wheat, cucumbers, green peas. **Farm income:** crops, $1.97 bil; livestock, $3.09 bil. **Nonfuel minerals:** $1.3 bil; salt, stone (crushed), sand and gravel (construction), cement (portland), clays (common). **Commercial fishing:** $52.4 mil. **Chief ports:** New York, Buffalo, Albany. **Gross state product:** $1.5 tril. **Sales tax:** 4.0%. **Gasoline tax:** 64.16 cents/gal. **Employment distrib.:** 15.1% govt.; 16.3% trade/trans./util.; 4.6% mfg.; 21.3% ed./health; 13.9% prof./bus. serv.; 10.1% leisure/hosp.; 7.4% finance; 4.2% constr./mining/log.; 2.7% info.; 4.4% other serv. **Unemployment:** 4.7%. **Min. wage/hr.:** $10.40. **Per cap. pers. income:** $60,991. **New private housing:** 39,350 units/$7.0 bil. **Broadband internet:** 98.3%. **Commercial banks:** 153; deposits: $1.6 tril. **Savings institutions:** 51; deposits: $72.9 bil. **Lottery:** total sales: $9.7 bil; profit: $3.3 bil.

Federal govt. Fed. civ. employees: 51,472; **avg. salary:** $82,002. **Notable fed. facilities:** Ft. Drum; West Point Military Academy; Merchant Marine Academy, Kings Point; NY

Fed. Reserve; U.S. Army Watervliet Arsenal; Brookhaven Natl. Lab; U.S. Mission to the United Nations.

Education. High school grad. rate: 80.4%. **4-yr. public coll./univ.:** 43; **2-yr. public:** 36; **4-yr. private:** 170.

Energy. Electricity use/cost: 595 kWh, $104.58.

State data. Motto: Excelsior (Ever upward). **Flower:** Rose. **Bird:** Eastern bluebird. **Tree:** Sugar maple. **Song:** "I Love New York." **Eleventh** of original 13 states to ratify the Constitution, July 26, 1788.

Tourism. Tourist spending: $76.4 bil. **Attractions:** New York City; Adirondack and Catskill Mountains; Watkins Glen State Park; Thousand Islands region; Niagara Falls; Saratoga Race Course, Saratoga Springs; Philipsburg Manor, Old Dutch Church of Sleepy Hollow, in Sleepy Hollow; Washington Irving's Sunnyside, Tarrytown; Corning Museum of Glass; Fenimore Art Museum, Natl. Baseball Hall of Fame and Museum, in Cooperstown; Ft. Ticonderoga; New York State Capitol, Albany; Home of Franklin D. Roosevelt Natl. Historic Site, Hyde Park; Long Island beaches; Sagamore Hill (Theodore Roosevelt's "Summer White House"), Oyster Bay. **Information:** Empire State Development, Travel Information Center, 30 South Pearl St., Albany, NY 12245; 1-800-CALLNYS; www.iloveny.com

History. When Europeans arrived, Algonquians including the Mahican, Wappinger, and Lenni Lenape inhabited the region, as did the Iroquoian Mohawk, Oneida, Onondaga, Cayuga, and Seneca tribes, who established the League of the Five Nations. Italian Giovanni da Verrazzano entered New York harbor, 1524. In 1609, England's Henry Hudson visited the river later named for him, and France's Samuel de Champlain explored the lake that now bears his name. The first permanent settlement was Dutch, near present-day Albany, 1624. New Amsterdam was settled, 1626, at the southern tip of Manhattan island. A British fleet seized New Netherland, 1664. Key battles of the American Revolution included Saratoga, 1777. In the 19th cent., New York City emerged as one of the world's great metropolitan areas, a center for trade, finance, and arts, and a haven for millions of immigrants. Completion of the Erie Canal, 1825, established the state as a gateway to the West. The first women's rights convention was held in Seneca Falls, 1848. Although the state backed the Union in the Civil War, an 1863 military draft triggered three days of riots in New York City. Industry declined in the 20th cent., and California and Texas passed New York in population. Attica was the scene of a bloody prison revolt, 1971. Two jet aircraft hijacked by terrorists on Sept. 11, 2001, destroyed the World Trade Center in lower Manhattan and killed thousands. An estimated 65 people in New York state were killed when Hurricane Sandy (by then downgraded to a tropical storm) made landfall in Oct. 2012. Citing concerns over health risks, Gov. Andrew Cuomo in Dec. 2014 announced a statewide ban on hydraulic fracturing (or "fracking") as a method to access the state's natural gas resources.

Famous New Yorkers. Woody Allen, Susan B. Anthony, James Baldwin, Lucille Ball, Ann Bancroft, L. Frank Baum, Milton Berle, Humphrey Bogart, Barbara Boxer, Mel Brooks, Benjamin Cardozo, De Witt Clinton, James Fenimore Cooper, Peter Cooper, Aaron Copland, Francis Ford Coppola, Tom Cruise, Robert De Niro, George Eastman, Jimmy Fallon, Millard Fillmore, Lou Gehrig, George and Ira Gershwin, Ruth Bader Ginsburg, Rudolph Giuliani, Jackie Gleason, Stephen Jay Gould, Julia Ward Howe, Charles Evans Hughes, Washington Irving, Henry and William James, John Jay, Edward Koch, Fiorello LaGuardia, Herman Melville, Arthur Miller, Lin-Manuel Miranda, J. Pierpont Morgan Jr., Eddie Murphy, Joyce Carol Oates, Carroll O'Connor, Rosie O'Donnell, Eugene O'Neill, Jerry Orbach, George Pataki, Colin Powell, Nancy Reagan, John Roberts, John D. Rockefeller, Nelson Rockefeller, Richard Rodgers, Ray Romano, Eleanor Roosevelt, Franklin D. Roosevelt, Theodore Roosevelt, J. D. Salinger, Caroline Kennedy Schlossberg, Jerry Seinfeld, Al Sharpton, Paul Simon, Alfred E. Smith, Elizabeth Cady Stanton, Barbra Streisand, Donald Trump, William (Boss) Tweed, Martin Van Buren, Luther Vandross, Gore Vidal, Denzel Washington, Edith Wharton, Walt Whitman, Mark Zuckerberg.

Website. www.ny.gov

North Carolina (NC)
Tar Heel State, Old North State

People. Population: 10,273,419; rank: 9. **Pop. change** (2010-17): 7.7%. **Pop. density:** 211.3 per sq mi. **Racial distribution:** 70.8% white; 22.2% black; 3.1% Asian; 1.6% Amer. Ind.; 0.1% Pac. Isl.; 2+ races, 2.2%. **Hispanic pop.:** 9.5%.

Geography. Total area: 53,819 sq mi; rank: 28. **Land area:** 48,618 sq mi; rank: 29. **Acres forested:** 18.8 mil. **Location:**

South Atlantic state bounded on N by Virginia, on S by South Carolina, on SW by Georgia, on W by Tennessee, and on E by Atlantic. **Climate:** subtropical in SE, medium-continental in mountain region; tempered by the Gulf Stream and mountains in W. **Topography:** coastal plain and tidewater in two-fifths of state, extending to the fall line of the rivers; Piedmont Plateau in another two-fifths has gentle to rugged hills; southern Appalachian Mts. contain the Blue Ridge and Great Smoky Mts. **Capital:** Raleigh. **Chief airports:** Charlotte, Greensboro, Raleigh.

Economy. Chief industries: manufacturing, agriculture, tourism. **Chief manuf. goods:** transportation, tobacco, pharmaceuticals, toiletries, plastics, animal slaughtering and processing, household furniture, fabric and apparel. **Chief crops:** greenhouse and nursery, tobacco, cotton, soybeans, corn, Christmas trees, sweet potatoes, wheat, peanuts, blueberries, cucumbers, tomatoes, hay, potatoes. **Farm income:** crops, $3.36 bil; livestock, $7.21 bil. **Nonfuel minerals:** $1.1 bil; stone (crushed), phosphate rock, sand and gravel (construction), sand and gravel (industrial), clays (common). **Commercial fishing:** $94.0 mil. **Chief ports:** Morehead City, Wilmington. **Gross state product:** $538.3 bil. **Sales tax:** 4.75%. **Gasoline tax:** 53.75 cents/gal. **Employment distrib.:** 16.6% govt.; 18.6% trade/trans./util.; 10.5% mfg.; 13.4% ed./health; 14.2% prof./bus. serv.; 11.3% leisure/hosp.; 5.2% finance; 5.0% constr./mining/log.; 1.8% info.; 3.4% other serv. **Unemployment:** 4.6%. **Min. wage/hr.:** $7.25. **Per cap. pers. income:** $43,303. **New private housing:** 67,047 units/$12.7 bil. **Broadband internet:** 95.9%. **Commercial banks:** 71; deposits $360.0 bil. **Savings institutions:** 21; deposits $3.4 bil. **Lottery:** total sales: $2.4 bil; profit: $624.5 mil.

Federal govt. Fed. civ. employees: 43,603; **avg. salary:** $74,196. **Notable fed. facilities:** Ft. Bragg; Camp Lejeune Marine Base, Marine Corps Air Station Cherry Point; NOAA Natl. Centers for Environmental Information, Asheville; Natl. Inst. of Environmental Health Sciences, EPA Research and Dev. Labs, all in Research Triangle Park.

Education. High school grad. rate: 85.9%. **4-yr. public coll./univ.:** 16; **2-yr. public:** 59; **4-yr. private:** 49.

Energy. Electricity use/cost: 1,101 kWh, $121.44.

State data. Motto: Esse Quam Videri (To be rather than to seem). **Flower:** Dogwood. **Bird:** Cardinal. **Tree:** Pine. **Song:** "The Old North State." **Twelfth** of the original 13 states to ratify the Constitution, Nov. 21, 1789.

Tourism. Tourist spending: $23.9 bil. **Attractions:** Cape Hatteras and Cape Lookout Natl. Seashores; Great Smoky Mountains Natl. Park; Guilford Courthouse Natl. Military Park; Moore's Creek Natl. Battlefield (1776 victory ended British rule in colony); Bennett Place (site of largest troop surrender of Civil War), Durham; Ft. Raleigh Natl. Historic Site, North Carolina Aquarium, on Roanoke Island; Wright Brothers Natl. Mem., Kill Devil Hills; USS *North Carolina*, Wilmington; North Carolina Zoo, Asheboro; North Carolina Symphony, Marbles Kids Museum, North Carolina Museum of Art, North Carolina Museum of Natural Sciences, in Raleigh; Carl Sandburg Home, Flat Rock; Biltmore House and Gardens, North Carolina Arboretum, in Asheville; U.S. Natl. Whitewater Ctr., Discovery Place, in Charlotte; Fort Macon State Park, Atlantic Beach. **Information:** North Carolina Dept. of Commerce, Tourism Div., 15000 Weston Pkwy., Cary, NC 27513; 1-800-VISIT-NC, (919) 733-8372; www.visitnc.com

History. Algonquian, Siouan, and Iroquoian peoples lived in the region at the time of European contact. Sir Walter Raleigh tried to found a colony, 1584-87; the "Lost Colony" on Roanoke Island, 1587, seemingly disappeared. Permanent settlers came from Virginia in the mid-17th cent. The province's congress was the first to vote for independence, 1776. In the Revolutionary War, Gen. Charles Cornwallis's forces were defeated at Kings Mountain, 1780, and forced out after Guilford Courthouse, 1781. The state ratified the Constitution, 1789, only after Congress passed the Bill of Rights. North Carolina, where one-third of the population was slaves, seceded from the Union, 1861, and provided more troops to the Confederacy than any other state; it was readmitted, 1868. The Wright brothers made the first powered airplane flight at Kitty Hawk, 1903. Sit-ins at segregated Greensboro lunch counters, 1960, drew national attention to the civil rights movement. Long reliant on tobacco, textiles, and wood products, North Carolina has prospered since the 1960s from advanced technologies in the Raleigh-Durham-Chapel Hill area and banking in Charlotte. The hurricane-prone state was hit hard by Hazel, 1954, Fran, 1996, and Floyd, 1999. The state drew immediate backlash in 2016 after passing a "bathroom bill" requiring people to use public facilities that correspond with the sex assigned on their birth certificate; a revised bill was passed in 2017.

Famous North Carolinians. David Brinkley, Shirley Caesar, John Coltrane, Rick Dees, Elizabeth Hanford Dole, Dale Earnhardt Sr., John Edwards, Ava Gardner, Richard Jordan Gatling, Billy Graham, Andy Griffith, O. Henry, Andrew Jackson, Andrew Johnson, Michael Jordan, William Rufus King, Charles Kuralt, Meadowlark Lemon, Dolley Madison, Thelonious Monk, Edward R. Murrow, Richard Petty, James K. Polk, Charlie Rose, Carl Sandburg, Enos Slaughter, Dean Smith, James Taylor, Thomas Wolfe.

Website. www.nc.gov

North Dakota (ND)
Peace Garden State

People. Population: 755,393; rank: 47. **Pop. change** (2010-17): 12.3%. **Pop. density:** 10.9 per sq mi. **Racial distribution:** 87.5% white; 3.1% black; 1.6% Asian; 5.5% Amer. Ind.; 0.1% Pac. Isl.; 2+ races, 2.2%. **Hispanic pop.:** 3.7%.

Geography. Total area: 70,698 sq mi; rank: 19. **Land area:** 69,001 sq mi; rank: 17. **Acres forested:** 0.8 mil. **Location:** West North Central state situated exactly in the middle of North America, bounded on the N by Canada, on the E by Minnesota, on the S by South Dakota, on the W by Montana. **Climate:** continental, with a wide range of temperatures and moderate rainfall. **Topography:** Central Lowland in the E comprises the flat Red R. Valley and the Rolling Drift Prairie; Missouri Plateau of the Great Plains on the W. **Capital:** Bismarck.

Economy. Chief industries: agriculture, mining, tourism, manufacturing, telecommunications, energy, food processing. **Chief manuf. goods:** machinery, wood prods., motor vehicles and parts, furniture, processed foods. **Chief crops:** wheat, soybeans, corn, sugar beets, barley, dry beans, sunflowers, canola, potatoes, flaxseed, hay, dry peas, lentils, oats. **Farm income:** crops, $7.07 bil; livestock, $1.11 bil. **Nonfuel minerals:** $72 mil; sand and gravel (construction), lime, stone (crushed), clays (common), sand and gravel (industrial). **Gross state product:** $55.5 bil. **Sales tax:** 5.0%. **Gasoline tax:** 41.40 cents/gal. **Employment distrib.:** 19.1% govt.; 21.6% trade/trans./util.; 5.7% mfg.; 14.7% ed./health; 8.0% prof./bus. serv.; 9.0% leisure/hosp.; 5.7% finance; 10.8% constr./mining/log.; 1.4% info.; 3.8% other serv. **Unemployment:** 2.6%. **Min. wage/hr.:** $7.25. **Per cap. pers. income:** $54,643. **New private housing:** 3,411 units/$606.7 mil. **Broadband internet:** 96.6%. **Commercial banks:** 84; deposits $25.5 bil. **Savings institutions:** 2; deposits $1.8 bil. **Lottery:** total sales: $27.6 mil; profit: $6.9 mil.

Federal govt. Fed. civ. employees: 5,489; **avg. salary:** $68,492. **Notable fed. facilities:** Minot AFB; Grand Forks AFB; Northern Prairie Wildlife Res. Ctr., Jamestown; Garrison Dam Natl. Fish Hatchery; Grand Forks Human Nutrition Res. Ctr.

Education. High school grad. rate: 87.5%. **4-yr. public coll./univ.:** 9; **2-yr. public:** 5; **4-yr. private:** 5.

Energy. Electricity use/cost: 1,046 kWh, $106.28.

State data. Motto: Liberty and union, now and forever, one and inseparable. **Flower:** Wild prairie rose. **Bird:** Western meadowlark. **Tree:** American elm. **Song:** "North Dakota Hymn." **Entered union:** Nov. 2, 1889; rank: 39th.

Tourism. Tourist spending: $2.9 bil. **Attractions:** North Dakota Heritage Ctr., North Dakota State Capitol, in Bismarck; Bonanzaville, West Fargo; Ft. Union Trading Post Natl. Historic Site; Intl. Peace Garden, Dunseith; Elkhorn Ranch site, in Theodore Roosevelt Natl. Park; Ft. Abraham Lincoln State Park and Museum, Mandan; Dakota Dinosaur Museum, Dickinson; Knife River Indian Villages Natl. Historic Site; Scandinavian Heritage Park, Minden. **Information:** North Dakota Tourism Division, Century Center, 1600 E. Century Ave., Ste. 2, P.O. Box 2057, Bismarck, ND 58502; 1-800-435-5663; www.ndtourism.com

History. Paleo-Indian peoples hunted in the area at least 11,000 years ago. At the time of European contact, the Ojibwa, Yanktonai and Teton Sioux, Mandan, Arikara, and Hidatsa peoples lived in the region. Pierre de Varennes, sieur de La Vérendrye, was the first French fur trader in the area, 1738, followed by the English at the end of the 18th cent. Lewis and Clark built Ft. Mandan, near present-day Washburn, 1804-05, and wintered there. The first permanent settlement was at Pembina, 1812. Missouri River steamboats reached the area, 1832. Dakota Territory was organized, 1861. The first railroad arrived, 1872. The "bonanza farm" craze of the 1870s-80s led to statehood, 1889. The Nonpartisan League, a farmers' group favoring state ownership of industries, helped elect Lynn Frazier as governor, 1916, but he and others were ousted in a recall vote, 1921. The predominantly agricultural state has one of the nation's lowest unemployment rates, mostly due to increased oil production since late 2008 in the state's Bakken Formation. Construction of the Dakota Access Pipeline drew international attention and vigorous protests in 2016-17, in particular from the Standing Rock Sioux tribe.

Famous North Dakotans. Maxwell Anderson, Angie Dickinson, Josh Duhamel, John Bernard Flannagan, Phil Jackson, Louis L'Amour, Peggy Lee, Roger Maris, Eric Sevareid, Vilhjalmur Stefansson, Lawrence Welk.

Website. www.nd.gov

Ohio (OH)
Buckeye State

People. Population: 11,658,609; rank: 7. **Pop. change** (2010-17): 1.1%. **Pop. density:** 285.3 per sq mi. **Racial distribution:** 82.2% white; 12.9% black; 2.3% Asian; 0.3% Amer. Ind.; 0.1% Pac. Isl.; 2+ races, 2.3%. **Hispanic pop.:** 3.8%.

Geography. Total area: 44,826 sq mi; rank: 34. **Land area:** 40,861 sq mi; rank: 35. **Acres forested:** 8.0 mil. **Location:** East North Central state bounded on the N by Michigan and Lake Erie; on the E and S by Pennsylvania, West Virginia, and Kentucky; on the W by Indiana. **Climate:** temperate but variable; weather subject to much precipitation. **Topography:** generally rolling plain; Allegheny Plateau in E; Lake Erie Plains extend southward; central plains in the W. **Capital:** Columbus. **Chief airports:** Akron, Cleveland, Columbus, Dayton.

Economy. Chief industries: manufacturing, trade, services. **Chief manuf. goods:** motor vehicles and parts, petroleum, plastics and rubber, iron and steel, aircraft, machinery, fabricated metal, printing. **Chief crops:** corn, soybeans, hay, wheat, grapes, potatoes, tomatoes, apples, strawberries, tobacco. **Farm income:** crops, $5.32 bil; livestock, $3.03 bil. **Nonfuel minerals:** $1.1 bil; stone (crushed), salt, sand and gravel (construction), lime, cement (portland). **Commercial fishing:** $5.0 mil. **Chief ports:** Cincinnati, Toledo, Conneaut, Cleveland, Ashtabula. **Gross state product:** $649.1 bil. **Sales tax:** 5.75%. **Gasoline tax:** 46.41 cents/gal. **Employment distrib.:** 14.1% govt.; 18.5% trade/trans./util.; 12.3% mfg.; 16.7% ed./health; 12.9% prof./bus. serv.; 10.4% leisure/hosp.; 5.6% finance; 4.3% constr./mining/log.; 1.3% info.; 4.0% other serv. **Unemployment:** 5.0%. **Min. wage/hr.:** $8.30. **Per cap. pers. income:** $45,615. **New private housing:** 23,917 units/$5.0 bil. **Broadband internet:** 97.0%. **Commercial banks:** 145; deposits: $307.1 bil. **Savings institutions:** 78; deposits: $29.5 bil. **Lottery:** total sales: $3.9 bil; profit: $1.0 bil.

Federal govt. Fed. civ. employees: 49,457; **avg. salary:** $81,842. **Notable fed. facilities:** Wright-Patterson AFB; Defense Supply Ctr., Columbus; NASA Glenn Research Ctr., Cleveland; Joint Systems Manufacturing Ctr., Lima.

Education. High school grad. rate: 83.5%. **4-yr. public coll./univ.:** 35; **2-yr. public:** 25; **4-yr. private:** 67.

Energy. Electricity use/cost: 891 kWh, $111.15.

State data. Motto: With God, all things are possible. **Flower:** Scarlet carnation. **Bird:** Northern cardinal. **Tree:** Ohio buckeye. **Song:** "Beautiful Ohio." **Entered union:** Mar. 1, 1803; rank: 17th.

Tourism. Tourist spending: $19.3 bil. **Attractions:** Hopewell Culture Natl. Historical Park, Chillicothe; Cuyahoga Valley Natl. Park; Armstrong Air and Space Museum, Wapakoneta; Natl. Museum of the U.S. Air Force, near Dayton; Pro Football Hall of Fame, First Ladies Natl. Historic Site, in Canton; Kings Island amusement park, Mason; Lake Erie Islands; Cedar Point amusement park, in Sandusky; birthplaces, homes of, and memorials to presidents W. H. Harrison, Grant, Hayes, Garfield, B. Harrison, McKinley, Taft, and Harding; Amish Country, particularly in Holmes County; German Village historic neighborhood, Franklin Park Conservatory and Botanical Gardens, in Columbus; Rock and Roll Hall of Fame and Museum, West Side Market, Cleveland Metroparks Zoo, in Cleveland; Cincinnati Museum Center at Union Terminal; Toledo Zoo. **Information:** TourismOhio, P.O. Box 1001, Columbus, OH 43216; 1-800-BUCKEYE; www.ohio.org

History. Paleo-Indians hunted in the area about 11,000 years ago; the Adena and Hopewell cultures followed. Wyandot, Delaware, Miami, and Shawnee peoples sparsely occupied the area when the first Europeans arrived. René-Robert Cavelier, sieur de La Salle, visited the region, 1669. France claimed it, 1682, but ceded it to Britain, 1763. After the American Revolution, Ohio became part of the Northwest Territory, 1787. The first permanent settlement was at Marietta, 1788. Cincinnati was also founded, 1788; Cleveland, 1796. Indian warfare abated with the Treaty of Greenville, 1795. Ohio became a state, 1803. In the War of 1812, Oliver Hazard Perry's victory on Lake Erie and William Henry Harrison's

invasion of Canada, 1813, ended British incursions. Columbus, founded 1812, became the state capital, 1816. Before the Civil War, Ohioans aided the Underground Railroad, helping runaway slaves. Agricultural for much of the 19th cent., the state became an industrial powerhouse in the 20th cent. but struggled to replace well-paying manufacturing jobs that began disappearing even before the 2007-09 recession. Cleveland hosted the Republican Natl. Convention in July 2016; no Republican has ever won the presidency without winning Ohio's electoral votes.

Famous Ohioans. Berenice Abbott, Sherwood Anderson, Neil Armstrong, George Bellows, Halle Berry, Ambrose Bierce, Erma Bombeck, Drew Carey, Hart Crane, George Custer, Clarence Darrow, Paul Laurence Dunbar, Thomas Edison, Clark Gable, John Glenn, Zane Grey, Bob Hope, William Dean Howells, LeBron James, Maya Lin, Toni Morrison, Paul Newman, Jack Nicklaus, Annie Oakley, Jesse Owens, Jack Paar, Pontiac, Eddie Rickenbacker, John D. Rockefeller Sr. and Jr., Roy Rogers, Pete Rose, Arthur Schlesinger Jr., Gen. William Sherman, Steven Spielberg, Gloria Steinem, Harriet Beecher Stowe, Robert A. Taft, William H. Taft, Tecumseh, James Thurber, Orville and Wilbur Wright.

Website. www.ohio.gov

Oklahoma (OK)
Sooner State

People. Population: 3,930,864; rank: 28. **Pop. change** (2010-17): 4.8%. **Pop. density:** 57.3 per sq mi. **Racial distribution:** 74.3% white; 7.8% black; 2.3% Asian; 9.2% Amer. Ind.; 0.2% Pac. Isl.; 2+ races, 6.1%. **Hispanic pop.:** 10.6%.

Geography. Total area: 69,899 sq mi; rank: 20. **Land area:** 68,595 sq mi; rank: 19. **Acres forested:** 12.2 mil. **Location:** West South Central state bounded on the N by Colorado and Kansas, on the E by Missouri and Arkansas, on the S and W by Texas and New Mexico. **Climate:** temperate; southern humid belt merging with colder northern continental; humid eastern and dry western zones. **Topography:** high plains predominate in the W, hills and small mountains in the E; the E central region is dominated by the Arkansas R. Basin, and the S by the Red R. Plains. **Capital:** Oklahoma City. **Chief airports:** Oklahoma City, Tulsa.

Economy. Chief industries: manufacturing, mineral and energy exploration and production, agriculture, services. **Chief manuf. goods:** animal slaughtering and processing, petroleum, plastics and rubber, fabricated metals, machinery, motor vehicles and parts. **Chief crops:** wheat, greenhouse and nursery, hay, cotton, corn, soybeans, pecans, sorghum, peanuts. **Farm income:** crops, $1.35 bil; livestock, $4.84 bil. **Nonfuel minerals:** $700 mil; stone (crushed), cement (portland), sand and gravel (construction), sand and gravel (industrial), gypsum (crude). **Chief port:** Catoosa. **Gross state product:** $189.2 bil. **Sales tax:** 4.5%. **Gasoline tax:** 38.40 cents/gal. **Employment distrib.:** 21.1% govt.; 18.1% trade/trans./util.; 7.7% mfg.; 14.0% ed./health; 11.2% prof./bus. serv.; 10.4% leisure/hosp.; 4.7% finance; 7.7% constr./mining/log.; 1.1% info.; 4.1% other serv. **Unemployment:** 4.3%. **Min. wage/hr.:** $7.25. **Per cap. pers. income:** $43,449. **New private housing:** 11,092 units/$2.2 bil. **Broadband internet:** 96.0%. **Commercial banks:** 223; deposits: $80.9 bil. **Savings institutions:** 4; deposits: $5.4 bil. **Lottery:** total sales: $151.5 mil; profit: $53.8 mil.

Federal govt. Fed. civ. employees: 38,337; **avg. salary:** $69,632. **Notable fed. facilities:** Tinker AFB; FAA Mike Monroney Aeronautical Ctr., Oklahoma City; Ft. Sill; Altus AFB; McAlester Army Ammunition Plant; Vance AFB; Natl. Severe Storms Lab, Norman.

Education. High school grad. rate: 81.6%. **4-yr. public coll./univ.:** 17; **2-yr. public:** 14; **4-yr. private:** 14.

Energy. Electricity use/cost: 1,093 kWh, $111.49.

State data. Motto: Labor Omnia Vincit (Labor conquers all things). **Flower:** Oklahoma rose. **Bird:** Scissor-tailed flycatcher. **Tree:** Redbud. **Song:** "Oklahoma!" **Entered union:** Nov. 16, 1907; rank: 46th.

Tourism. Tourist spending: $7.6 bil. **Attractions:** Cherokee Heritage Ctr., Tahlequah; Oklahoma City Natl. Memorial and Museum, Natl. Cowboy and Western Heritage Museum, White Water Bay and Frontier City amusement parks, Museum of Osteology, Bricktown neighborhood, in Oklahoma City; Will Rogers Memorial Museum and Birthplace Ranch, Claremore and Oologah; Gathering Place, Philbrook Museum of Art, Gilcrease Museum, in Tulsa; Wichita Mountains Wildlife Refuge; Woolaroc Museum and Wildlife Preserve, Price Tower Arts Center, in Bartlesville; Sequoyah's Cabin, Sallisaw; Sam Noble Museum of Natural History, Norman. **Information:** Oklahoma Tourism Dept., Travel Promotion Division, 900

N. Stiles Ave., Oklahoma City, OK 73104-3234; 1-800-652-6552; www.travelok.com

History. Few Native Americans inhabited the region when Spanish explorer Coronado arrived, 1541; in the 16th and 17th cent., French traders visited. Part of the Louisiana Purchase, 1803, Oklahoma was known as Indian Country and, from 1834, Indian Territory. It became home to the "Five Civilized Tribes"—Cherokee, Choctaw, Chickasaw, Creek, and Seminole—after the forced removal of Indians from the eastern U.S., 1828-46. The land was also used by Comanche, Osage, and other Plains Indians. As white settlers pressed west, land was opened for homesteading by "runs" and lottery. The first run was in 1889; the most famous run, 1893, was to the Cherokee Outlet. Oklahoma became a state, 1907. In the early 20th cent., oil finds brought wealth to the Tulsa area; Tulsa's Greenwood section, then known as the "Negro Wall Street," was looted and destroyed by a white mob, 1921. Depression and drought drove many "Okies" from the Dust Bowl to California in the 1930s. A truck bomb in Oklahoma City, 1995, destroyed a federal office building, killing 168 people; an anti-government extremist was executed for the crime, 2001. A tornado in Moore killed 23 people May 20, 2013; the widest tornado on record touched down in El Reno May 31, 2013, killing 10 people. Since 2010, Oklahoma has experienced thousands of earthquakes (more than 1,400 greater than 3 magnitude in 2015-16 alone) believed to be connected with the use of disposal wells for wastewater from oil and gas operations. A teacher walkout in Apr. 2018 demanded increased pay and school funding.

Famous Oklahomans. Troy Aikman, Carl Albert, Gene Autry, Johnny Bench, William Boyd (Hopalong Cassidy), Garth Brooks, Lon Chaney, Gordon Cooper, Ralph Ellison, John Hope Franklin, James Garner, Vince Gill, Woody Guthrie, Paul Harvey, Ron Howard, Patrick J. Hurley, Ben Johnson, Jeane Kirkpatrick, Louis L'Amour, Shannon Lucid, Wilma Mankiller, Mickey Mantle, Reba McEntire, Wiley Post, Tony Randall, Oral Roberts, Will Rogers, Barry Switzer, Maria Tallchief, Jim Thorpe, Carrie Underwood, J. C. Watts Jr.

Website. www.ok.gov

Oregon (OR)
Beaver State

People. Population: 4,142,776; rank: 27. **Pop. change** (2010-17): 8.1%. **Pop. density:** 43.2 per sq mi. **Racial distribution:** 87.1% white; 2.2% black; 4.7% Asian; 1.8% Amer. Ind.; 0.4% Pac. Isl.; 2+ races, 3.8%. **Hispanic pop.:** 13.1%.

Geography. Total area: 98,379 sq mi; rank: 9. **Land area:** 95,988 sq mi; rank: 10. **Acres forested:** 29.7 mil. **Location:** Pacific state bounded on N by Washington, on E by Idaho, on S by Nevada and California, on W by the Pacific. **Climate:** mild and humid on coast; continental dryness and extreme temperatures in the interior. **Topography:** Coast Range of rugged mountains; fertile Willamette R. Valley to E and S; Cascade Mt. Range of volcanic peaks E of the valley; plateau E of Cascades, remaining two-thirds of state. **Capital:** Salem. **Chief airports:** Eugene, Portland.

Economy. Chief industries: manufacturing, services, trade, finance, insurance, real estate, government, construction. **Chief manuf. goods:** wood prods., frozen produce, printing, computers and electronics, transportation equip., industrial machinery. **Chief crops:** greenhouse and nursery, grass seed, hay, wheat, potatoes, Christmas trees, onions, pears, hazelnuts, corn, grapes, cherries, blackberries, blueberries, peppermint, snap beans, apples, hops. **Farm income:** crops, $3.12 bil; livestock, $1.48 bil. **Nonfuel minerals:** $474 mil; stone (crushed), sand and gravel (construction), cement (portland), diatomite, perlite (crude). **Commercial fishing:** $151.7 mil. **Chief ports:** Portland, Coos Bay. **Gross state product:** $236.2 bil. **Sales tax:** none. **Gasoline tax:** 55.17 cents/gal. **Employment distrib.:** 15.8% govt.; 18.4% trade/trans./util.; 10.0% mfg.; 15.4% ed./health; 12.8% prof./bus. serv.; 11.3% leisure/hosp.; 5.3% finance; 5.8% constr./mining/log.; 1.8% info.; 3.4% other serv. **Unemployment:** 4.1%. **Min. wage/hr.:** $10.75. **Per cap. pers. income:** $46,361. **New private housing:** 20,053 units/$4.2 bil. **Broadband internet:** 95.6%. **Commercial banks:** 44; deposits: $74.9 bil. **Savings institutions:** 5; deposits: $983.0 mil. **Lottery:** total sales: $1.2 bil; profit: $662.4 mil.

Federal govt. Fed. civ. employees: 18,413; **avg. salary:** $77,016. **Notable fed. facilities:** Bonneville Power Admin.

Education. High school grad. rate: 74.8%. **4-yr. public coll./univ.:** 9; **2-yr. public:** 17; **4-yr. private:** 24.

Energy. Electricity use/cost: 907 kWh, $96.71.

State data. Motto: She flies with her own wings. **Flower:** Oregon grape. **Bird:** Western meadowlark. **Tree:** Douglas fir.

Song: "Oregon, My Oregon." **Entered union:** Feb. 14, 1859; rank: 33rd.

Tourism. Tourist spending: $11.7 bil. **Attractions:** John Day Fossil Beds Natl. Monument; Multnomah Falls, Columbia River Gorge; Timberline Lodge, Mount Hood Natl. Forest; Crater Lake Natl. Park; Oregon Dunes Natl. Recreation Area; Ft. Clatsop (Lewis and Clark Natl. Historical Park), Astoria Column, in Astoria; Oregon Caves Natl. Monument; Intl. Rose Test Garden, Lan Su Chinese Garden, Pittock Mansion, Oregon Museum of Science and Industry, in Portland; Oregon Shakespeare Festival, Ashland; High Desert Museum, Bend; "Spruce Goose" (largest aircraft ever built), Evergreen Aviation and Space Museum, McMinnville; Yaquina Head Outstanding Natural Area, Oregon Coast Aquarium, in Newport. **Information:** Travel Oregon, 530 Center St. NE, Ste. 200, Salem, OR 97301; 1-800-547-7842; www.traveloregon.com

History. More than 100 Native American tribes inhabited the area at the time of European contact, including the Chinook, Yakima, Cayuse, Modoc, and Nez Percé. Capt. Robert Gray sighted and sailed into the Columbia R., 1792. Lewis and Clark, traveling overland, wintered at its mouth, 1805-06. Fur traders sent by John Jacob Astor established the Astoria trading post in the Columbia River region, 1811. Settlers arrived in the Willamette Valley, 1834. In 1843, the first large wave of settlers arrived via the Oregon Trail. Oregon became a territory, 1848, and a state, 1859. Early in the 20th cent., the "Oregon System"—political reforms that included initiative, referendum, recall, direct primary, and woman suffrage—was adopted. Originally dominated by forest products, the economy diversified after World War II, with technology firms clustering in the "Silicon Forest" area around Portland. Oregonians were the first in the U.S. to pass measures allowing physician-assisted suicide for terminally ill patients, 1994, and establishing an all-mail voting system, 1998. Gov. John Kitzhaber resigned a month into his unprecedented fourth term in 2015, amidst an ethics scandal. A 41-day armed occupation of Malheur Natl. Wildlife Refuge ended in Feb. 2016.

Famous Oregonians. Ernest Bloch, Bill Bowerman, Ty Burrell, Beverly Cleary, Matt Groening, Ernest Haycox, Chief Joseph, Ken Kesey, Phil Knight, Ursula K. Le Guin, Edwin Markham, Tom McCall, John McLoughlin, Joaquin Miller, Bob Packwood, Linus Pauling, Steve Prefontaine, John "Jack" Reed, Alberto Salazar, Mary Decker Slaney, William Simon U'Ren.

Website. www.oregon.gov

Pennsylvania (PA)
Keystone State

People. Population: 12,805,537; rank: 5. **Pop. change** (2010-17): 0.8%. **Pop. density:** 286.2 per sq mi. **Racial distribution:** 82.1% white; 11.9% black; 3.6% Asian; 0.4% Amer. Ind.; 0.1% Pac. Isl.; 2+ races, 2.0%. **Hispanic pop.:** 7.3%.

Geography. Total area: 46,054 sq mi; rank: 33. **Land area:** 44,743 sq mi; rank: 32. **Acres forested:** 16.8 mil. **Location:** Middle Atlantic state bordered on the E by the Delaware R., on the S by the Mason-Dixon Line, on the W by West Virginia and Ohio, on the N/NE by Lake Erie and New York. **Climate:** continental with wide fluctuations in seasonal temperatures. **Topography:** Allegheny Mts. run SW-NE, with Piedmont and Coast Plain in the SE triangle; Allegheny Front a diagonal spine across the state's center; N and W rugged plateau falls to Lake Erie Lowland. **Capital:** Harrisburg. **Chief airports:** Harrisburg, Philadelphia, Pittsburgh.

Economy. Chief industries: agribusiness, advanced manufacturing, health care, travel and tourism, depository institutions, biotechnology, printing and publishing, research and consulting, trucking and warehousing, transportation by air, engineering and management, legal services. **Chief manuf. goods:** petroleum, pharmaceuticals, plastics, iron and steel, printing, paper and paperboard, confectionery and snacks, animal slaughtering and processing. **Chief crops:** greenhouse and nursery, mushrooms, corn, hay, soybeans, apples, tomatoes, wheat, grapes, peaches, potatoes, strawberries, tobacco. **Farm income:** crops, $2.49 bil; livestock, $3.91 bil. **Nonfuel minerals:** $1.9 bil; stone (crushed), cement (portland), lime, sand and gravel (construction), sand and gravel (industrial). **Commercial fishing:** $0.1 mil. **Chief ports:** Philadelphia, Pittsburgh. **Gross state product:** $752.1 bil. **Sales tax:** 6.0%. **Gasoline tax:** 77.10 cents/gal. **Employment distrib.:** 11.8% govt.; 18.7% trade/trans./util.; 9.4% mfg.; 21.1% ed./health; 13.6% prof./bus. serv.; 9.8% leisure/hosp.; 5.4% finance; 4.8% constr./mining/log.; 1.3% info.; 4.4% other serv. **Unemployment:** 4.9%. **Min. wage/hr.:** $7.25. **Per cap. pers. income:** $52,096. **New private housing:** 22,584 units/$4.4 bil. **Broadband internet:** 96.3%. **Commercial banks:** 136; deposits: $329.7 bil. **Savings institutions:** 60; deposits: $59.9 bil. **Lottery:** total sales: $4.0 bil; profit: $1.0 bil.

Federal govt. Fed. civ. employees: 59,639; **avg. salary:** $76,413. **Notable fed. facilities:** Army War College, Carlisle Barracks; Naval Supply Systems Command (NAVSUP), Mechanicsburg; Philadelphia Mint, Defense Supply Ctr., Naval Surface Warfare Ctr., in Phila.; DLA Distribution Ctr. Susquehanna, New Cumberland, Mechanicsburg; Tobyhanna Army Depot; Letterkenny Army Depot.

Education. High school grad. rate: 86.1%. **4-yr. public coll./univ.:** 45; **2-yr. public:** 17; **4-yr. private:** 104.

Energy. Electricity use/cost: 841 kWh, $116.67.

State data. Motto: Virtue, liberty, and independence. **Flower:** Mountain laurel. **Bird:** Ruffed grouse. **Tree:** Eastern hemlock. **Song:** "Pennsylvania." **Second** of the original 13 states to ratify the Constitution, Dec. 12, 1787.

Tourism. Tourist spending: $25.1 bil. **Attractions:** Liberty Bell Ctr. at Independence Natl. Historical Park, Franklin Institute, Philadelphia Museum of Art, in Philadelphia; Valley Forge Natl. Historical Park, King of Prussia; Gettysburg Natl. Military Park; Pennsylvania Dutch Country, Lancaster County; Hersheypark, Hershey; Duquesne Incline, Carnegie Museums of Pittsburgh, Heinz Hall for the Performing Arts, in Pittsburgh; Pocono Mountains; Pine Creek Gorge (Pennsylvania Grand Canyon), Allegheny Natl. Forest; Fallingwater (house designed by Frank Lloyd Wright), Mill Run; Johnstown Flood Natl. Memorial; Steamtown Natl. Historic Site, Scranton; U.S. Brig *Niagara*, Erie Maritime Museum, Presque Isle State Park, in Erie; Oil Region Natl. Heritage Area; Longwood Gardens, Kennett Square. **Information:** Pennsylvania Tourism Office, Dept. of Community and Economic Development, Commonwealth Keystone Building, 4th Fl., 400 North St., Harrisburg, PA 17120-0225; 1-800-VISITPA; www.visitpa.com

History. When Europeans came, Algonquian-speaking Lenni Lenape (Delaware) and Shawnee and the Iroquoian Susquehannocks, Erie, and Seneca occupied the region. Swedish explorers made the first permanent settlement, 1643, on Tinicum Island. The Dutch seized the settlement, 1655, but lost it to the British, 1664. The region was given by Charles II to William Penn, 1681. Philadelphia ("brotherly love") was the capital of the colonies during most of the American Revolution and of the U.S., 1790-1800; the Declaration of Independence, 1776, and Constitution, 1787, were signed here. Philadelphia was taken by the British, 1777. George Washington's troops encamped at Valley Forge in the bitter winter of 1777-78. Slavery was abolished, 1780. Union victory at the Battle of Gettysburg, July 1-3, 1863, marked a turning point in the Civil War. A dam collapse at Johnstown, 1889, killed at least 2,200 people. From the late 19th to the mid-20th cent., Pittsburgh prospered from coal and steel; later, heavy industry declined, but the city revived as a hub of finance, health care, and research. The Three Mile Island nuclear plant near Harrisburg had a near-meltdown, 1979. One of four hijacked planes on Sept. 11, 2001, crashed near Shanksville; the Flight 93 national memorial was officially dedicated on the site in 2011. In June 2018, East Pittsburgh police fatally shot unarmed black teen Antwon Rose Jr. in the back, sparking protests; the officer was charged with criminal homicide.

Famous Pennsylvanians. Marian Anderson, Maxwell Anderson, George Blanda, Kobe Bryant, James Buchanan, Andrew Carnegie, Rachel Carson, Wilt Chamberlain, Noam Chomsky, Perry Como, Bill Cosby, Cyrus H. K. Curtis, Thomas Eakins, Tina Fey, Stephen Foster, Benjamin Franklin, Robert Fulton, Martha Graham, Milton Hershey, Gene Kelly, Grace Kelly (Princess Grace of Monaco), Dan Marino, George C. Marshall, Chris Matthews, John J. McCloy, Margaret Mead, Andrew W. Mellon, Joe Montana, Stan Musial, Joe Namath, John O'Hara, Arnold Palmer, Robert E. Peary, Mike Piazza, Pink (Alecia Beth Moore), Mary Roberts Rinehart, Fred Rogers, Betsy Ross, Will Smith, Jimmy Stewart, Taylor Swift, Jim Thorpe, Johnny Unitas, John Updike, Honus Wagner, Andy Warhol, Benjamin West.

Website. www.pa.gov

Rhode Island (RI)
Little Rhody, Ocean State

People. Population: 1,059,639; rank: 43. **Pop. change** (2010-17): 0.6%. **Pop. density:** 1,024.8 per sq mi. **Racial distribution:** 84.1% white; 8.2% black; 3.7% Asian; 1.0% Amer. Ind.; 0.2% Pac. Isl.; 2+ races, 2.8%. **Hispanic pop.:** 15.5%.

Geography. Total area: 1,545 sq mi; rank: 50. **Land area:** 1,034 sq mi; rank: 50. **Acres forested:** 0.4 mil. **Location:**

New England state. **Climate:** invigorating and changeable. **Topography:** eastern lowlands of Narragansett Basin; western uplands of flat and rolling hills. **Capital:** Providence. **Chief airport:** Warwick.

Economy. Chief industries: services, manufacturing. **Chief manuf. goods:** plastics, fabricated metals, electrical equip., jewelry. **Chief crops:** greenhouse and nursery, sweet corn, berries, potatoes, apples, hay. **Farm income:** crops, $48.54 mil; livestock, $23.54 mil. **Nonfuel minerals:** $63 mil; stone (crushed), sand and gravel (construction), sand and gravel (industrial), gemstones (natural). **Commercial fishing:** $94.0 mil. **Chief ports:** Providence, Davisville, Newport. **Gross state product:** $59.5 bil. **Sales tax:** 7.0%. **Gasoline tax:** 52.40 cents/gal. **Employment distrib.:** 12.3% govt.; 15.3% trade/trans./util.; 8.2% mfg.; 21.5% ed./health; 13.8% prof./bus. serv.; 11.9% leisure/hosp.; 7.3% finance; 3.9% constr./mining/log.; 1.2% info.; 4.8% other serv. **Unemployment:** 4.5%. **Min. wage/hr.:** $10.10. **Per cap. pers. income:** $51,503. **New private housing:** 1,153 units/$246.9 mil. **Broadband internet:** 98.6%. **Commercial banks:** 11; deposits: $26.9 bil. **Savings institutions:** 11; deposits: $3.3 bil. **Lottery:** total sales: $872.4 mil; profit: $362.7 mil.

Federal govt. Fed. civ. employees: 7,319; **avg. salary:** $90,719. **Notable fed. facilities:** Naval War College, Naval Undersea Warfare Ctr., Newport; EPA Atlantic Ecology Div. Lab, Narragansett.

Education. High school grad. rate: 82.8%. **4-yr. public coll./univ.:** 2; **2-yr. public:** 1; **4-yr. private:** 10.

Energy. Electricity use/cost: 586 kWh, $109.02.

State data. Motto: Hope. **Flower:** Common blue violet. **Bird:** Rhode Island red chicken. **Tree:** Red maple. **Song:** "Rhode Island." **Thirteenth** of original 13 states to ratify the Constitution, May 29, 1790.

Tourism. Tourist spending: $2.1 bil. **Attractions:** Block Island; mansions (The Breakers, The Elms, others), Cliff Walk, Intl. Tennis Hall of Fame and Museum, Touro Synagogue (completed 1763, oldest in U.S.), in Newport; First Baptist Church in America, Rhode Island School of Design Museum of Art, WaterFire art installation, in Providence; Slater Mill Historic Site, Pawtucket; Gilbert Stuart Birthplace and Museum, Saunderstown. **Information:** Rhode Island Tourism Division, 315 Iron Horse Way, Ste. 101, Providence, RI 02908; 1-800-556-2484; www.visitrhodeisland.com

History. When Europeans arrived, Narragansett, Niantic, Nipmuc, and Wampanoag peoples lived in the region. Italian Giovanni da Verrazzano visited the area, 1524. The first permanent settlement was founded at Providence, 1636, by Roger Williams, who was exiled from the Massachusetts Bay Colony. Anne Hutchinson, also exiled, settled Portsmouth, 1638. Quaker and Jewish immigrants seeking freedom of worship began arriving, 1650s-60s. The colonists broke the power of the Narragansett in the Great Swamp Fight, 1675, the decisive battle in King Philip's War. The colony was the first to formally renounce all allegiance to King George III, May 4, 1776. Initially opposed to joining the Union, Rhode Island was the last of the 13 colonies to ratify the Constitution, 1790. Trade, textiles, and metal goods dominated the economy in the 19th cent., and Newport became a fashionable resort after the Civil War. The U.S. Navy was the state's largest civilian employer, 1945-73, until the destroyer force was relocated from Newport. A nightclub fire in West Warwick killed 100 people in 2003.

Famous Rhode Islanders. Ambrose Burnside, George M. Cohan, Viola Davis, Nelson Eddy, Jabez Gorham, Nathanael Greene, Elisabeth Hasselbeck, Christopher and Oliver La Farge, Cormac McCarthy, John McLaughlin, Matthew C. and Oliver Hazard Perry, Gilbert Stuart, Meredith Vieira.

Website. www.ri.gov

South Carolina (SC)
Palmetto State

People. Population: 5,024,369; rank: 23. **Pop. change** (2010-17): 8.6%. **Pop. density:** 167.1 per sq mi. **Racial distribution:** 68.5% white; 27.3% black; 1.7% Asian; 0.5% Amer. Ind.; 0.1% Pac. Isl.; 2+ races, 1.9%. **Hispanic pop.:** 5.7%.

Geography. Total area: 32,020 sq mi; rank: 40. **Land area:** 30,061 sq mi; rank: 40. **Acres forested:** 12.9 mil. **Location:** South Atlantic state bordered by North Carolina on the N; Georgia on the SW and W; the Atlantic Ocean on the E, SE, and S. **Climate:** humid subtropical. **Topography:** Blue Ridge province in NW has highest peaks; piedmont lies between the mountains and the fall line; coastal plain covers two-thirds of state. **Capital:** Columbia. **Chief airports:** Charleston, Columbia, Greer, Myrtle Beach.

Economy. Chief industries: tourism, agriculture, manufacturing. **Chief manuf. goods:** chemicals and synthetics, motor vehicles and parts, plastics, paper and paper prods., turbines, rubber, textiles. **Chief crops:** greenhouse and nursery, tobacco, soybeans, cotton, corn, peaches, wheat, tomatoes, peanuts. **Farm income:** crops, $851.38 mil; livestock, $1.27 bil. **Nonfuel minerals:** $784 mil; stone (crushed), cement (portland), gold, sand and gravel (construction), clays (kaolin). **Commercial fishing:** $20.8 mil. **Chief ports:** Charleston, Georgetown. **Gross state product:** $219.1 bil. **Sales tax:** 6.0%. **Gasoline tax:** 39.15 cents/gal. **Employment distrib.:** 17.4% govt.; 19.0% trade/trans./util.; 11.4% mfg.; 11.8% ed./health; 13.2% prof./bus. serv.; 12.6% leisure/hosp.; 4.7% finance; 4.9% constr./mining/log.; 1.3% info.; 3.7% other serv. **Unemployment:** 4.3%. **Min. wage/hr.:** none ($7.25). **Per cap. pers. income:** $40,421. **New private housing:** 35,521 units/$8.0 bil. **Broadband internet:** 95.7%. **Commercial banks:** 72; deposits: $83.4 bil. **Savings institutions:** 12; deposits: $1.1 bil. **Lottery:** total sales: $1.6 bil; profit: $410.5 mil.

Federal govt. Fed. civ. employees: 20,968; **avg. salary:** $73,173. **Notable fed. facilities:** Ft. Jackson; Joint Base Charleston; Marine Corps Recruit Depot Parris Island; Shaw AFB; USMC Air Station Beaufort; Savannah River Site.

Education. High school grad. rate: 82.6%. **4-yr. public coll./univ.:** 13; **2-yr. public:** 20; **4-yr. private:** 21.

Energy. Electricity use/cost: 1,155 kWh, $146.09.

State data. Motto: Dum Spiro Spero (While I breathe, I hope). **Flower:** Yellow jessamine. **Bird:** Carolina wren. **Tree:** Palmetto. **Song:** "Carolina." **Eighth** of the original 13 states to ratify the Constitution, May 23, 1788.

Tourism. Tourist spending: $13.9 bil. **Attractions:** Historic Charleston, Waterfront Park, Charleston Museum (est. 1773, oldest in U.S.), Middleton Place, Magnolia Plantation and Gardens, Drayton Hall, in Charleston; Ft. Sumter Natl. Monument (where first shots of Civil War were fired), in Charleston Harbor; Cypress Gardens, Moncks Corner; Boone Hall Plantation and Gardens, Mt. Pleasant; Brookgreen Gardens, Murrells Inlet; Myrtle Beach; Hilton Head Island; Andrew Jackson State Park, Lancaster; South Carolina State Museum, Riverbanks Zoo, in Columbia. **Information:** SC Dept. of Parks, Recreation, and Tourism, 1205 Pendleton St., Columbia, SC 29201; 1-866-224-9339, (803) 734-1700; discoversouthcarolina.com

History. When Europeans arrived, Cherokee, Catawba, and Muskogean peoples lived in the area. Spanish and French came in the 16th cent. The first English colonists settled near the Ashley R., 1670, and moved to the site of present-day Charleston, 1680. The colonists seized the government, 1775, and the royal governor fled. The British took Charleston, 1780, but were defeated at Kings Mountain that same year and at Cowpens, 1781. In the 1830s, South Carolinians, angered by federal protective tariffs, adopted the Nullification Doctrine, holding that a state can void an act of Congress. Plantation agriculture relied on slave labor to cultivate rice and cotton; slaves made up 57% of the population in 1860, when South Carolina was the first state to secede from the Union. Confederate troops fired on and forced the surrender of U.S. troops at Ft. Sumter, in Charleston Harbor, 1861, launching the Civil War. The state was readmitted to the Union, 1868. Strom Thurmond, who ran for president as a segregationist in 1948, later served 48 years in the U.S. Senate (1955-2003). Formerly dependent on textiles, the state has attracted new industries by courting foreign investment. The state removed the Confederate flag from its capitol grounds in July 2015 after an alleged white supremacist shot and killed nine black parishioners at a Charleston church the previous month; the shooter was sentenced to death in 2017.

Famous South Carolinians. Aziz Ansari, Charles F. Bolden Jr., Chadwick Boseman, James F. Byrnes, John C. Calhoun, Stephen Colbert, Marian Wright Edelman, Joe Frazier, DuBose Heyward, Ernest F. Hollings, Andrew Jackson, Jesse Jackson, "Shoeless" Joe Jackson, Jasper Johns, Andie MacDowell, Francis Marion, Ronald E. McNair, Charles Pinckney, John Rutledge, Thomas Sumter, Strom Thurmond, John B. Watson.

Website. www.sc.gov

South Dakota (SD)
Coyote State, Mount Rushmore State

People. Population: 869,666; rank: 46. **Pop. change** (2010-17): 6.8%. **Pop. density:** 11.5 per sq mi. **Racial distribution:** 84.9% white; 2.1% black; 1.5% Asian; 9.0% Amer. Ind.; 0.1% Pac. Isl.; 2+ races, 2.4%. **Hispanic pop.:** 3.8%.

Geography. Total area: 77,116 sq mi; rank: 17. **Land area:** 75,811 sq mi; rank: 16. **Acres forested:** 2.0 mil. **Location:** West North Central state bounded on the N by North Dakota, on the E by Minnesota and Iowa, on the S by Nebraska, on the W by Wyoming and Montana. **Climate:** characterized by extremes of temperature, persistent winds, low precipitation and humidity. **Topography:** Prairie Plains in the E; rolling hills of the Great Plains in the W; the Black Hills, rising 3,500 ft, in the SW corner. **Capital:** Pierre. **Chief airport:** Sioux Falls.

Economy. Chief industries: agriculture, services, manufacturing. **Chief manuf. goods:** animal slaughtering, machinery, semiconductors, surgical appliances. **Chief crops:** corn, soybeans, wheat, hay, sunflowers, sorghum, oats, barley. **Farm income:** crops, $5.71 bil; livestock, $3.63 bil. **Nonfuel minerals:** $372 mil; gold, cement (portland), sand and gravel (construction), stone (crushed), lime. **Gross state product:** $49.9 bil. **Sales tax:** 4.5%. **Gasoline tax:** 48.40 cents/gal. **Employment distrib.:** 18.5% govt.; 19.6% trade/trans./util.; 10.0% mfg.; 16.5% ed./health; 7.3% prof./bus. serv.; 10.6% leisure/hosp.; 6.7% finance; 5.6% constr./mining/log.; 1.3% info.; 3.9% other serv. **Unemployment:** 3.3%. **Min. wage/hr.:** $8.85. **Per cap. pers. income:** $48,281. **New private housing:** 5,407 units/$894.3 mil. **Broadband internet:** 96.6%. **Commercial banks:** 79; deposits: $533.3 bil. **Savings institutions:** 4; deposits: $3.3 bil. **Lottery:** total sales: $261.7 mil; profit: $118.1 mil.

Federal govt. Fed. civ. employees: 8,262; **avg. salary:** $65,006. **Notable fed. facilities:** Ellsworth AFB.

Education. High school grad. rate: 83.9%. **4-yr. public coll./univ.:** 7; **2-yr. public:** 5; **4-yr. private:** 7.

Energy. Electricity use/cost: 981 kWh, $112.53.

State data. Motto: Under God, the people rule. **Flower:** Pasqueflower. **Bird:** Chinese ring-necked pheasant. **Tree:** Black Hills spruce. **Song:** "Hail, South Dakota." **Entered union:** Nov. 2, 1889; rank: 40th.

Tourism. Tourist spending: $2.8 bil. **Attractions:** Mt. Rushmore Natl. Memorial, Keystone; Harney Peak (tallest E of Rockies); Custer State Park; Crazy Horse Memorial (mtn. carving in progress); Wind Cave Natl. Park, near Hot Springs; Black Hills Natl. Forest; Needles Hwy., part of Peter Norbeck Natl. Scenic Byway; Minuteman Missile Natl. Historic Site; Deadwood (1876 gold rush town); Jewel Cave Natl. Monument, near Custer; Badlands Natl. Park; Great Lakes of South Dakota; Great Plains Zoo and Delbridge Museum of Natural History, Sioux Falls; Corn Palace, Mitchell; Reptile Gardens, Chapel in the Hills, Bear Country USA, in Rapid City. **Information:** Dept. of Tourism, Dolly Reed Plaza, 711 E. Wells Ave., c/o 500 E. Capitol Ave., Pierre, SD 57501; 1-800-SDAKOTA; www.travelsd.com

History. Paleo-Indians hunted in the region at least 11,500 years ago. At the time of first European contact, Mandan, Hidatsa, Arikara, and Sioux lived in the area. The French Vérendrye brothers explored the region, 1742-43. The U.S. acquired the territory in the Louisiana Purchase, 1803, and Meriwether Lewis and William Clark passed through, 1804-06. In 1817 a trading post opened at what would become Ft. Pierre. Dakota Territory was established, 1861. Gold was discovered, 1874, in the Black Hills on Lakota Sioux land; the "Great Dakota Boom" began in 1879. South Dakota became a state, 1889. The massacre of more than 200 Native American men, women, and children at Wounded Knee, 1890, ended Sioux resistance. Armed supporters of the American Indian Movement, a Native American rights group, occupied the area, leading to a 70-day standoff, 1973. Major economic activities include agribusiness and, since the 1980s, credit card services. Republicans scored a key election victory, 2004, with the defeat of three-term U.S. Sen. Tom Daschle, a national Democratic leader.

Famous South Dakotans. Sparky Anderson, Bob Barker, Black Elk, Tom Brokaw, Crazy Horse, Tom Daschle, Myron Floren, Mary Hart, Cheryl Ladd, Ernest O. Lawrence, George McGovern, Russell Means, Billy Mills, Allen H. Neuharth, Pat O'Brien, Sitting Bull.

Website. www.sd.gov

Tennessee (TN)
Volunteer State

People. Population: 6,715,984; rank: 16. **Pop. change** (2010-17): 5.8%. **Pop. density:** 162.9 per sq mi. **Racial distribution:** 78.6% white; 17.1% black; 1.9% Asian; 0.5% Amer. Ind.; 0.1% Pac. Isl.; 2+ races, 1.9%. **Hispanic pop.:** 5.5%.

Geography. Total area: 42,144 sq mi; rank: 36. **Land area:** 41,235 sq mi; rank: 34. **Acres forested:** 13.9 mil. **Location:** East South Central state bounded on the N by Kentucky and

Virginia; on the E by North Carolina; on the S by Georgia, Alabama, and Mississippi; on the W by Arkansas and Missouri. **Climate:** humid continental to the N; humid subtropical to the S. **Topography:** rugged country in the E; the Great Smoky Mts. of the Unakas; low ridges of the Appalachian Valley; flat Cumberland Plateau; slightly rolling terrain and knobs of the Interior Low Plateau, the largest region; Eastern Gulf Coastal Plain to the W, laced with streams; Mississippi Alluvial Plain, a narrow strip of swamp and floodplain in the extreme W. **Capital:** Nashville. **Chief airports:** Alcoa, Memphis, Nashville.

Economy. Chief industries: manufacturing, trade, services, tourism, finance, insurance, real estate. **Chief manuf. goods:** motor vehicles and parts, computers and electronics, food, chemicals, plastics, printing, appliances, aluminum. **Chief crops:** greenhouse and nursery, soybeans, cotton, corn, tobacco, hay, tomatoes, wheat. **Farm income:** crops, $1.98 bil; livestock, $1.32 bil. **Nonfuel minerals:** $1.1 bil; stone (crushed), zinc, cement (portland), sand and gravel (construction), sand and gravel (industrial). **Chief ports:** Memphis, Nashville, Chattanooga. **Gross state product:** $345.2 bil. **Sales tax:** 7.0%. **Gasoline tax:** 44.80 cents/gal. **Employment distrib.:** 14.3% govt.; 20.5% trade/trans./util.; 11.4% mfg.; 14.3% ed./health; 13.5% prof./bus. serv.; 11.4% leisure/hosp.; 5.3% finance; 4.1% constr./mining/log.; 1.5% info.; 3.8% other serv. **Unemployment:** 3.7%. **Min. wage/hr.:** none ($7.25). **Per cap. pers. income:** $44,266. **New private housing:** 37,912 units/$7.0 bil. **Broadband internet:** 96.0%. **Commercial banks:** 189; deposits: $144.6 bil. **Savings institutions:** 10; deposits: $3.0 bil. **Lottery:** total sales: $1.6 bil; profit: $386.7 mil.

Federal govt. Fed. civ. employees: 25,945; **avg. salary:** $70,620. **Notable fed. facilities:** Tennessee Valley Authority, Knoxville; Oak Ridge Natl. Lab; Arnold Engineering Development Ctr.; Ft. Campbell; NSA Mid-South, Millington.

Education. High school grad. rate: 88.5%. **4-yr. public coll./univ.:** 10; **2-yr. public:** 13; **4-yr. private:** 45.

Energy. Electricity use/cost: 1,238 kWh, $128.89.

State data. Motto: Agriculture and commerce. **Flower:** (cultivated) iris; (wildflower) passion flower, Tennessee coneflower. **Bird:** Northern mockingbird. **Tree:** Tulip poplar. **Songs:** "My Homeland, Tennessee"; "When It's Iris Time in Tennessee"; "My Tennessee"; "Tennessee Waltz"; "Rocky Top"; "Smoky Mountain Rain." **Entered union:** June 1, 1796; rank: 16th.

Tourism. Tourist spending: $19.5 bil. **Attractions:** Lookout Mountain, Tennessee Aquarium, Ruby Falls, in Chattanooga; Great Smoky Mountains Natl. Park; Lost Sea (largest underground lake in U.S.), Sweetwater; Cherokee Natl. Forest; Cumberland Gap Natl. Historical Park; James K. Polk Ancestral Home, Columbia; American Museum of Science and Energy, Oak Ridge; The Hermitage (home of Pres. Andrew Jackson), Country Music Hall of Fame and Museum, Ryman Auditorium, Belle Meade Plantation, Parthenon replica, Grand Ole Opry, in Nashville; Dollywood theme park, Pigeon Forge; Graceland (home of Elvis Presley), Sun Studio, in Memphis; Alex Haley Museum and Interpretive Ctr., Henning; Casey Jones Village, Jackson; Bristol Motor Speedway. **Information:** Dept. of Tourist Development, Wm. Snodgrass/Tennessee Tower, 312 Rosa L. Parks Ave., 13th Fl., Nashville, TN 37243; 1-800-462-8366; www.tnvacation.com

History. Inhabited for at least 20,000 years, the region was home to Creek and Yuchi peoples when the first Europeans arrived; the Cherokee moved into the region in the early 18th cent. Spanish explorers visited the area, 1540. English traders crossed the Great Smoky Mtns. from the east, while France's Jacques Marquette and Louis Jolliet sailed down the Mississippi on the west, 1673. The first permanent settlement was of Virginians on the Watauga R., 1769. After the American Revolution, in which Tennesseans fought in eastern campaigns, the region became a territory, 1790, and a state, 1796. Slavery was widespread in western Tennessee, where cotton was the main crop, but much less common in the east. The state seceded, 1861, and saw many Civil War engagements; some 187,000 Tennesseans fought for the Confederacy and 51,000 for the Union. Tennessee was readmitted in 1866, the only former Confederate state not to have a postwar military government. The famous Scopes trial, 1925, questioned the teaching of evolution in public schools. In the 1930s, the Tennessee Valley Authority, a federal program, brought electric power to rural areas. Nashville became the capital of country music while Memphis fostered the blues and, with Elvis Presley in the 1950s, rock 'n' roll. Martin Luther King Jr. was assassinated in Memphis, 1968. Since the 1970s, auto plants have become major employers, as has Federal Express. Al Gore Jr., U.S. vice pres. (1993-2001), lost his 2000 presidential bid partly because he failed to carry his home state of Tennessee. Record amounts of rainfall flooded Nashville in 2010. Wildfires killed 14 in East Tennessee in Nov. 2016.

Famous Tennesseans. Roy Acuff, Kenny Chesney, Davy Crockett, David Farragut, Ernie Ford, Aretha Franklin, Bill Frist, Al Gore Jr., Alex Haley, William C. Handy, Sam Houston, Cordell Hull, Andrew Jackson, Andrew Johnson, Casey Jones, Estes Kefauver, Grace Moore, Dolly Parton, Minnie Pearl, James Polk, Elvis Presley, Wilma Rudolph, Dinah Shore, Bessie Smith, Fred Thompson, Justin Timberlake, Tina Turner, Hank Williams Jr., Alvin York.

Website. www.tn.gov

Texas (TX)
Lone Star State

People. Population: 28,304,596; rank: 2. **Pop. change** (2010-17): 12.6%. **Pop. density:** 108.4 per sq mi. **Racial distribution:** 79.2% white; 12.7% black; 5.0% Asian; 1.0% Amer. Ind.; 0.1% Pac. Isl.; 2+ races, 2.0%. **Hispanic pop.:** 39.4%.

Geography. Total area: 268,596 sq mi; rank: 2. **Land area:** 261,232 sq mi; rank: 2. **Acres forested:** 62.2 mil. **Location:** southwestern state bounded on the SE by the Gulf of Mexico; on the SW by Mexico, separated by the Rio Grande; surrounding states are Louisiana, Arkansas, Oklahoma, New Mexico. **Climate:** extremely varied; driest region is the Trans-Pecos; wettest is the NE. **Topography:** Gulf Coast Plain in the S and SE; North Central Plains slope upward with some hills; the Great Plains extend over the Panhandle, are broken by low mountains; the Trans-Pecos is the southern extension of the Rockies. **Capital:** Austin. **Chief airports:** Austin, Dallas, El Paso, Fort Worth, Houston (2), Midland, San Antonio.

Economy. Chief industries: manufacturing, trade, oil and gas extraction, services. **Chief manuf. goods:** petroleum, chemicals and resins, computers and electronics, animal slaughtering and processing, plastics, aerospace. **Chief crops:** cotton, greenhouse and nursery, corn, wheat, sorghum, hay, peanuts, onions, rice, pecans, grapefruit. **Farm income:** crops, $7.72 bil; livestock, $13.15 bil. **Nonfuel minerals:** $5.2 bil; stone (crushed), cement (portland), sand and gravel (construction), sand and gravel (industrial), lime. **Commercial fishing:** $196.9 mil. **Chief ports:** Houston, Galveston, Brownsville, Beaumont, Port Arthur, Corpus Christi, Texas City, Freeport. **Gross state product:** $1.7 tril. **Sales tax:** 6.25%. **Gasoline tax:** 38.40 cents/gal. **Employment distrib.:** 15.7% govt.; 19.9% trade/trans./util.; 6.9% mfg.; 13.5% ed./health; 13.8% prof./bus. serv.; 11.0% leisure/hosp.; 6.1% finance; 8.0% constr./mining/log.; 1.6% info.; 3.5% other serv. **Unemployment:** 4.3%. **Min. wage/hr.:** $7.25. **Per cap. pers. income:** $46,942. **New private housing:** 175,112 units/$32.5 bil. **Broadband internet:** 97.0%. **Commercial banks:** 491; deposits: $727.8 bil. **Savings institutions:** 39; deposits: $90.3 bil. **Lottery:** total sales: $5.1 bil; profit: $1.3 bil.

Federal govt. Fed. civ. employees: 117,154; **avg. salary:** $75,822. **Notable fed. facilities:** Ft. Hood; Ft. Bliss; Sheppard, Dyess, Goodfellow AF Bases; Joint Base San Antonio; NASA Johnson Space Ctr., Houston; Naval Air Training School, Corpus Christi NAS; Red River Army Depot; Western Currency Facility, Ft. Worth.

Education. High school grad. rate: 89.1%. **4-yr. public coll./univ.:** 47; **2-yr. public:** 60; **4-yr. private:** 64.

Energy. Electricity use/cost: 1,156 kWh, $127.10.

State data. Motto: Friendship. **Flower:** Bluebonnet. **Bird:** Northern mockingbird. **Tree:** Pecan. **Song:** "Texas, Our Texas." **Entered union:** Dec. 29, 1845; rank: 28th.

Tourism. Tourist spending: $68.5 bil. **Attractions:** Big Bend and Guadalupe Mountains Natl. Parks; Fort Davis Natl. Historic Site; Six Flags Over Texas, Arlington; SeaWorld San Antonio, Six Flags Fiesta Texas, The Alamo, San Antonio Missions Natl. Historical Park, San Antonio River Walk, in San Antonio; Natl. Cowgirl Museum and Hall of Fame, Kimbell Art Museum, Ft. Worth Zoo, Bureau of Engraving and Printing, in Ft. Worth; Lyndon B. Johnson Natl. Historical Park, Johnson City; LBJ Presidential Library and Museum, Bullock Texas State History Museum, Austin; George Bush Presidential Library and Museum, College Station; Dallas Arboretum and Botanical Garden, Sixth Floor Museum at Dealey Plaza, George W. Bush Presidential Library and Museum, in Dallas; USS Lexington, Texas State Aquarium, Padre Island Natl. Seashore, in Corpus Christi. **Information:** Texas Tourism, P.O. Box 141009, Austin, TX 78714; 1-800-452-9292, (512) 486-5876; www.traveltexas.com

History. Humans have lived in the region for at least 12,000 years. Coahuiltecan, Karankawa, Caddo, Jumano, and Tonkawa peoples were in the area when the first Europeans came; later, Apache, Comanche, Cherokee, and Wichita arrived. Early Spanish explorers included Alonso Alvarez de Pineda, who sailed along the Texas coast, 1519; Cabeza de Vaca, shipwrecked near Galveston along with the former slave Estevanico, 1528; and Coronado, who crossed the Panhandle, 1541. Spaniards made the first settlement at Ysleta, near El Paso, 1682. Americans moved into the land early in the 19th cent. Mexico, of which Texas was a part, won independence from Spain, 1821. Texans rebelled, 1836, losing to Mexican Gen. Santa Anna at the Alamo but winning decisively under Sam Houston at San Jacinto. With Houston as president, 1836-38 and 1841-44, the Republic of Texas functioned as a nation until admitted to the Union. With a slave population of 30%, Texas seceded, 1861; mostly unscathed by the Civil War, it was readmitted, 1870. In 1900 a powerful hurricane lashed Galveston, killing at least 8,000. Cotton and cattle were dominant until 1901, when the Spindletop gusher, near Beaumont, launched the petroleum and petrochemical industries. With wealth and population came political power, notably in the presidencies of Lyndon B. Johnson (1963-69), George H. W. Bush (1989-93), and George W. Bush (2001-09). Amid backlash over police killings of black men, a black military veteran in 2016 fatally shot five police officers in Dallas. Hurricane Harvey brought historic rainfall and flooding to Houston and surrounding areas in Aug. 2017, displacing thousands from homes and businesses. A shooter killed 26 at a Baptist church in Sutherland Springs in Nov. 2017. A string of bombings, Mar. 2018, unleashed terror in Austin and killed two. A shooter at a Santa Fe High School killed 10 in May 2018.

Famous Texans. Lance Armstrong, Stephen F. Austin, Lloyd Bentsen, James Bowie, Drew Brees, Carol Burnett, George H. W. Bush, George W. Bush, Earl Campbell, Joan Crawford, Dwight T. Eisenhower, Morgan Fairchild, Farrah Fawcett, George Foreman, Sam Houston, Howard Hughes, Molly Ivins, Lyndon B. Johnson, Tommy Lee Jones, Janis Joplin, Barbara Jordan, Beyoncé Knowles, Mary Martin, Matthew McConaughey, Chester Nimitz, Sandra Day O'Connor, H. Ross Perot, Katherine Anne Porter, Dan Rather, Sam Rayburn, Ann Richards, Michael Strahan, George Strait, Babe Didrikson Zaharias.

Website. www.texas.gov

Utah (UT)
Beehive State

People. Population: 3,101,833; rank: 31. **Pop. change (2010-17):** 12.2%. **Pop. density:** 37.7 per sq mi. **Racial distribution:** 90.9% white; 1.4% black; 2.6% Asian; 1.5% Amer. Ind.; 1.0% Pac. Isl.; 2+ races, 2.5%. **Hispanic pop.:** 14.0%.

Geography. Total area: 84,897 sq mi; rank: 13. **Land area:** 69,891 sq mi; rank: 12. **Acres forested:** 18.1 mil. **Location:** middle Rocky Mountain state; its SE corner touches Colorado, New Mexico, and Arizona and is the only spot in the U.S. where four states join. **Climate:** arid; ranges from warm desert in SW to alpine in NE. **Topography:** high Colorado Plateau is cut by brilliantly colored canyons of the SE; broad, flat, desertlike Great Basin of the W; the Great Salt Lake and Bonneville Salt Flats to the NW; Middle Rockies in the NE run E-W; valleys and plateaus of the Wasatch Front. **Capital:** Salt Lake City. **Chief airport:** Salt Lake City.

Economy. Chief industries: services, trade, manufacturing, government, transportation, utilities. **Chief manuf. goods:** food, petroleum, nonferrous metal, motor vehicles and parts, aerospace, sporting goods, fabricated metal, computers and electronics. **Chief crops:** hay, greenhouse and nursery, wheat, cherries, onions, apples, barley, peaches, corn. **Farm income:** crops, $412.97 mil; livestock, $1.24 bil. **Nonfuel minerals:** $2.6 bil; copper, magnesium metal, gold, potash, sand and gravel (construction). **Gross state product:** $165.5 bil. **Sales tax:** 5.95%. **Gasoline tax:** 47.81 cents/gal. **Employment distrib.:** 16.8% govt.; 19.0% trade/trans./util.; 8.8% mfg.; 13.3% ed./health; 14.2% prof./bus. serv.; 9.6% leisure/hosp.; 5.7% finance; 7.4% constr./mining/log.; 2.5% info.; 2.7% other serv. **Unemployment:** 3.2%. **Min. wage/hr.:** $7.25. **Per cap. pers. income:** $42,043. **New private housing:** 24,679 units/$5.2 bil. **Broadband internet:** 96.4%. **Commercial banks:** 52; deposits: $371.3 bil. **Savings institutions:** 3; deposits: $95.8 bil.

Federal govt. Fed. civ. employees: 28,221; **avg. salary:** $69,891. **Notable fed. facilities:** Hill AFB; Tooele Army Depot; Army Dugway Proving Ground; NSA Utah Data Ctr.

Education. High school grad. rate: 85.2%. **4-yr. public coll./univ.:** 7; **2-yr. public:** 1; **4-yr. private:** 10.

Energy. Electricity use/cost: 750 kWh, $82.57.

State data. Motto: Industry. **Flower:** Sego lily. **Bird:** (California) sea gull. **Tree:** Blue spruce. **Song:** "Utah, This Is the Place." **Entered union:** Jan. 4, 1896; rank: 45th.

Tourism. Tourist spending: $8.5 bil. **Attractions:** Temple Square (site of Mormon Church headquarters), Salt Lake City; Great Salt Lake; Zion, Canyonlands, Bryce Canyon, Arches, and Capitol Reef Natl. Parks; Dinosaur, Rainbow Bridge, Timpanogos Cave, and Natural Bridges Natl. Monuments; Lake Powell; Flaming Gorge Natl. Recreation Area; Utah Olympic Park, Sundance Film Festival, in Park City. **Information:** Utah Office of Tourism, Council Hall/Capitol Hill, 300 N. State St., Salt Lake City, UT 84114; 1-800-200-1160; visit www.visitutah.com

History. Ute, Gosiute, Southern Paiute, and Navajo peoples lived in the region at the time of European contact. Spanish Franciscans visited the area, 1776; American fur traders followed. Permanent settlement began with the arrival of the Latter-day Saints, or Mormons, 1847, who created a prosperous economy. Organized in 1849, the State of Deseret asked admission to the Union; instead, Congress established Utah Territory, 1850, and appointed Brigham Young governor. The Union Pacific and Central Pacific railroads met near Promontory Point, May 10, 1869, creating the first transcontinental railroad. Statehood was not achieved until 1896, after a long controversy over the Mormon practices of economic isolationism and polygamy (the church renounced the latter in 1890). The 20th cent. brought expansion in mining, defense-related industries, and, more recently, information technologies. More than two-thirds of Utahans are Mormons; the church has its world headquarters in Salt Lake City. Utah experienced 60% population growth, 1990-2010. Environmentalists and tribal groups said they would challenge a Trump administration decision in Dec. 2017 to drastically cut the land area covered by Bears Ears and Grand Staircase-Escalante National Monuments.

Famous Utahans. Maude Adams, Roseanne Barr, Ezra Taft Benson, John Moses Browning, Butch Cassidy, Marriner S. Eccles, Philo T. Farnsworth, David M. Kennedy, J. Willard Marriott, Merlin Olsen, the Osmonds, Ivy Baker Priest, George W. Romney, Wallace Stegner, Brigham Young, Loretta Young.

Website. www.utah.gov

Vermont (VT)
Green Mountain State

People. Population: 623,657; rank: 50. **Pop. change (2010-17):** −0.3%. **Pop. density:** 67.7 per sq mi. **Racial distribution:** 94.5% white; 1.4% black; 1.8% Asian; 0.4% Amer. Ind.; <0.05% Pac. Isl.; 2+ races, 1.9%. **Hispanic pop.:** 1.9%.

Geography. Total area: 9,616 sq mi; rank: 45. **Land area:** 9,217 sq mi; rank: 43. **Acres forested:** 4.5 mil. **Location:** northern New England state. **Climate:** temperate, with considerable temperature extremes; heavy snowfall in mountains. **Topography:** Green Mts. N-S backbone 20-36 mi wide; avg. altitude 1,000 ft. **Capital:** Montpelier. **Chief airport:** Burlington.

Economy. Chief industries: manufacturing, tourism, agriculture, trade, finance, insurance, real estate, government. **Chief manuf. goods:** dairy, plastics, printing, wood furniture, sporting goods, metalworking machinery. **Chief crops:** greenhouse and nursery, hay, maple syrup, apples, berries, sweet corn. **Farm income:** crops, $202.10 mil; livestock, $583.84 mil. **Nonfuel minerals:** $149 mil; stone (crushed), sand and gravel (construction), stone (dimension), talc (crude), gemstones (natural). **Gross state product:** $32.2 bil. **Sales tax:** 6.0%. **Gasoline tax:** 49.62 cents/gal. **Employment distrib.:** 18.1% govt.; 17.6% trade/trans./util.; 9.3% mfg.; 21.3% ed./health; 9.2% prof./bus. serv.; 10.7% leisure/hosp.; 4.0% finance; 5.3% constr./mining/log.; 1.4% info.; 3.2% other serv. **Unemployment:** 3.0%. **Min. wage/hr.:** $10.50. **Per cap. pers. income:** $51,114. **New private housing:** 1,749 units/$326.5 mil. **Broadband internet:** 84.8%. **Commercial banks:** 15; deposits: $11.1 bil. **Savings institutions:** 8; deposits: $2.0 bil. **Lottery:** total sales: $122.4 mil; profit: $25.7 mil.

Federal govt. Fed. civ. employees: 3,329; **avg. salary:** $74,802. **Notable fed. facilities:** Law Enforcement Support Ctr., Williston.

Education. High school grad. rate: 87.7%. **4-yr. public coll./univ.:** 5; **2-yr. public:** 1; **4-yr. private:** 16.

Energy. Electricity use/cost: 549 kWh, $95.31.

State data. Motto: Freedom and unity. **Flower:** Red clover. **Bird:** Hermit thrush. **Tree:** Sugar maple. **Song:** "These Green Mountains." **Entered union:** Mar. 4, 1791; rank: 14th.

Tourism. Tourist spending: $2.5 bil. **Attractions:** Shelburne Museum; Shelburne Farms; Vermont Marble Museum, Proctor; Bennington Battle Monument; Pres. Calvin Coolidge Homestead, Plymouth; Ben & Jerry's Factory, Waterbury; Stowe, Killington, and Burke ski resorts: Hildene (Robert Todd Lincoln home), Manchester; Marsh-Billings-Rockefeller Natl. Historical Park, Woodstock. **Information:** Vermont Dept. of Tourism and Marketing, Natl. Life Building, 6th Fl., Montpelier, VT 05620; 1-800-VERMONT, (802) 828-3237; www.vermontvacation.com

History. Inhabited for 10,000 years or more, the region attracted Abenaki and Mahican peoples before Europeans arrived. France's Champlain explored the lake that now bears his name, 1609. The first European settlement was on Isle la Motte in Lake Champlain, 1666. During the American Revolution, Ethan Allen and the Green Mountain Boys captured Ft. Ticonderoga (NY), 1775. Under a constitution that provided for public schools and abolished slavery, settlers declared a republic, 1777. Vermont joined the Union, 1791. Agriculture dominated in the 19th cent. Still mainly rural, the state expanded tourism and manufacturing after World War II, and IBM became the largest private employer. Vermont was the first state to recognize same-sex civil unions (2000) and to enact equal same-sex marriage rights via legislation (2009). Legislation to legalize recreational marijuana went into effect in July 2018.

Famous Vermonters. Ethan Allen, Chester A. Arthur, Calvin Coolidge, Howard Dean, John Deere, George Dewey, John Dewey, Stephen A. Douglas, Dorothy Canfield Fisher, James Fisk, James "Jim" Jeffords, Bernie Sanders, Jody Williams.

Website. www.vermont.gov

Virginia (VA)
Old Dominion

People. Population: 8,470,020; rank: 12. **Pop. change** (2010-17): 5.9%. **Pop. density:** 214.5 per sq mi. **Racial distribution:** 69.7% white; 19.8% black; 6.8% Asian; 0.5% Amer. Ind.; 0.1% Pac. Isl.; 2+ races, 3.0%. **Hispanic pop.:** 9.4%.

Geography. Total area: 42,775 sq mi; rank: 35. **Land area:** 39,490 sq mi; rank: 36. **Acres forested:** 16.1 mil. **Location:** South Atlantic state bounded by the Atlantic Ocean on the E and surrounded by North Carolina, Tennessee, Kentucky, West Virginia, and Maryland. **Climate:** mild and equable. **Topography:** mountain and valley region in the W, including the Blue Ridge Mts.; rolling Piedmont Plateau; tidewater, or coastal plain, including the Eastern Shore. **Capital:** Richmond. **Chief airports:** Arlington, Dulles, Highland Springs, Norfolk.

Economy. Chief industries: services, trade, government, manufacturing, tourism, agriculture. **Chief manuf. goods:** beverages and tobacco, transportation equip., animal slaughtering and processing, plastics, textiles, paper and paper prods., printing, pharmaceuticals, furniture, chemicals. **Chief crops:** greenhouse and nursery, soybeans, tomatoes, corn, tobacco, hay, cotton, apples, wheat, peanuts, potatoes. **Farm income:** crops, $1.14 bil; livestock, $2.20 bil. **Nonfuel minerals:** $1.3 bil; stone (crushed), cement (portland), sand and gravel (construction), lime, kyanite. **Commercial fishing:** $209.0 mil. **Chief ports:** Norfolk Harbor, Newport News, Richmond, Hopewell. **Gross state product:** $508.7 bil. **Sales tax:** 5.3%. **Gasoline tax:** 40.80 cents/gal. **Employment distrib.:** 17.9% govt.; 16.7% trade/trans./util.; 5.9% mfg.; 13.3% ed./health; 18.5% prof./bus. serv.; 10.4% leisure/hosp.; 5.2% finance; 5.3% constr./mining/log.; 1.7% info.; 5.2% other serv. **Unemployment:** 3.8%. **Min. wage/hr.:** $7.25. **Per cap. pers. income:** $54,244. **New private housing:** 33,760 units/$5.7 bil. **Broadband internet:** 96.7%. **Commercial banks:** 119; deposits: $265.3 bil. **Savings institutions:** 7; deposits: $42.3 bil. **Lottery:** total sales: $2.0 bil; profit: $558.3 mil.

Federal govt. Fed. civ. employees: 134,043; **avg. salary:** $95,695. **Notable fed. facilities:** Pentagon; Norfolk Naval Sta., Shipyard, and other Hampton Roads military bases; Ft. Belvoir; Joint Base Langley-Eustis; NASA Langley Res. Ctr.; CIA George Bush Ctr. for Intelligence, Langley; FBI Academy, Quantico USMC Base; Dahlgren Nav. Surface Warfare Ctr. and Lab; USDA Food and Nutrition Serv., Alexandria; U.S. Geological Survey Natl. Ctr., Reston.

Education. High school grad. rate: 86.7%. **4-yr. public coll./univ.:** 16; **2-yr. public:** 24; **4-yr. private:** 40.

Energy. Electricity use/cost: 1,120 kWh, $127.14.

State data. Motto: Sic Semper Tyrannis (Thus always to tyrants). **Flower:** American dogwood. **Bird:** Northern cardinal.

Tree: American dogwood. **Song emeritus:** "Carry Me Back to Old Virginia." **Tenth** of original 13 states to ratify the Constitution, June 25, 1788.

Tourism. Tourist spending: $24.6 bil. **Attractions:** Colonial Williamsburg, Busch Gardens Williamsburg, Jamestown Settlement, in Williamsburg; Yorktown Victory Ctr.; Wolf Trap Natl. Park for the Performing Arts, near Vienna; Arlington Natl. Cemetery; George Washington's Mount Vernon; Thomas Jefferson's Monticello, Charlottesville; Stratford Hall (Robert E. Lee birthplace); Appomattox Court House Natl. Historical Park; Shenandoah Natl. Park; Blue Ridge Natl. Parkway; Virginia Beach; Kings Dominion amusement park, Doswell. **Information:** Virginia Tourism Corp., 901 E. Cary St., Ste. 900, Richmond, VA 23219; 1-800-VISITVA; www.virginia.org

History. Cherokee and Susquehanna peoples and the Algonquians of the Powhatan Confederacy were in the region when Europeans arrived. English settlers founded Jamestown, 1607. Four of the first five U.S. presidents—Washington, Jefferson, Madison, and Monroe—came from Virginia. The conclusive battle of the American Revolution took place at Yorktown, 1781. The state profited from tobacco, cotton, and the slave trade; in 1860, slaves made up nearly one-third of the population. Virginia seceded from the Union, 1861, and Richmond became the capital of the Confederacy. Western counties, loyal to the Union, split off to become West Virginia, 1863. The war ended with Robert E. Lee's surrender to Ulysses S. Grant at Appomattox, 1865; Virginia was readmitted to the Union, 1870. In the 20th cent., expansion of federal civilian jobs and military facilities transformed the economy. State officials pledged "massive resistance" to racial integration in the mid-1950s but eventually accommodated it. In 1989, L. Douglas Wilder became the first elected black governor in U.S. history. On Sept. 11, 2001, terrorist hijackers crashed a jet into U.S. defense headquarters at the Pentagon, in Arlington. Seven-term Rep. Eric Cantor became the first House majority leader ever to lose a primary race in 2014.

Famous Virginians. Arthur Ashe, Sandra Bullock, Richard E. Byrd, James B. Cabell, Henry Clay, Katie Couric, Gabby Douglas, Jubal Early, Jerry Falwell, William Henry Harrison, Patrick Henry, A. P. Hill, Thomas Jefferson, Joseph E. Johnston, Robert E. Lee, Meriwether Lewis and William Clark, James Madison, John Marshall, George Mason, James Monroe, Sean Parker, George Pickett, Pocahontas, Edgar Allan Poe, John Randolph, Walter Reed, Rev. Pat Robertson, John Smith, J. E. B. Stuart, William Styron, Zachary Taylor, John Tyler, Maggie Walker, Booker T. Washington, George Washington, L. Douglas Wilder, Woodrow Wilson.

Website. www.virginia.gov

Washington (WA)
Evergreen State

People. Population: 7,405,743; rank: 13. **Pop. change** (2010-17): 10.1%. **Pop. density:** 111.4 per sq mi. **Racial distribution:** 79.5% white; 4.2% black; 8.9% Asian; 1.9% Amer. Ind.; 0.8% Pac. Isl.; 2+ races, 4.7%. **Hispanic pop.:** 12.7%.

Geography. Total area: 71,298 sq mi; rank: 18. **Land area:** 66,456 sq mi; rank: 20. **Acres forested:** 22.1 mil. **Location:** Pacific state bordered by Canada on the N, Idaho on the E, Oregon on the S, the Pacific Ocean on the W. **Climate:** mild, dominated by the Pacific Ocean and protected by the Cascades. **Topography:** Olympic Mts. on NW peninsula; open land along coast to Columbia R.; flat terrain of Puget Sound Lowland; high peaks of Cascade Mts. to the E; Columbia Basin in central portion; highlands to the NE; mountains to the SE. **Capital:** Olympia. **Chief airports:** Seattle, Spokane.

Economy. Chief industries: advanced technology, aerospace, biotechnology, intl. trade, forestry, tourism, recycling, agriculture and food processing. **Chief manuf. goods:** aerospace, petroleum, food, paper, milled lumber, plastics, structural metals, computers and electronics. **Chief crops:** apples, potatoes, wheat, hay, cherries, greenhouse and nursery, forest products, pears, grapes, onions, hops, sweet corn, Christmas trees, mint, raspberries. **Farm income:** crops, $7.44 bil; livestock, $2.48 bil. **Nonfuel minerals:** $901 mil; sand and gravel (construction), stone (crushed), gold, zinc, cement (portland). **Commercial fishing:** $287.5 mil. **Chief ports:** Seattle, Tacoma, Vancouver, Kelso-Longview, Anacortes. **Gross state product:** $506.4 bil. **Sales tax:** 6.5%. **Gasoline tax:** 67.80 cents/gal. **Employment distrib.:** 17.7% govt.; 18.8% trade/trans./util.; 8.4% mfg.; 14.3% ed./health; 12.6% prof./bus. serv.; 9.9% leisure/hosp.; 4.6% finance; 6.3% constr./mining/log.; 3.8% info.; 3.5% other serv. **Unemployment:** 4.8%. **Min. wage/hr.:** $11.50. **Per cap. pers. income:** $56,283. **New private housing:** 45,794 units/$9.9 bil. **Broad-**

band internet: 96.0%. **Commercial banks:** 72; deposits: $148.0 bil. **Savings institutions:** 11; deposits: $5.9 bil. **Lottery:** total sales: $673.3 mil; profit: $161.9 mil.

Federal govt. Fed. civ. employees: 53,317; **avg. salary:** $78,866. **Notable fed. facilities:** Bonneville Power Admin.; Lewis-McChord Joint Base; Fairchild AFB; Hanford Site (fmr. nuclear weapons production facility); Naval Base Kitsap (Bremerton and Bangor); Whidbey Island NAS; Pacific Northwest Natl. Lab, Richland.

Education. High school grad. rate: 79.7%. **4-yr. public coll./univ.:** 31; **2-yr. public:** 12; **4-yr. private:** 21.

Energy. Electricity use/cost: 955 kWh, $90.56.

State data. Motto: Alki (By and by). **Flower:** Western rhododendron. **Bird:** Willow goldfinch. **Tree:** Western hemlock. **Song:** "Washington, My Home." **Entered union:** Nov. 11, 1889; rank: 42nd.

Tourism. Tourist spending: $18.0 bil. **Attractions:** Seattle Center, Space Needle, EMP Museum, Museum of Flight, Pike Place Market, Underground Tour, in Seattle; Mount Rainier, Olympic, and North Cascades Natl. Parks; Mount St. Helens Natl. Volcanic Monument; Puget Sound; San Juan Islands; Grand Coulee Dam; Columbia R. Gorge Natl. Scenic Area; Riverfront Park, Spokane; Snoqualmie Falls. **Information:** Washington Tourism Alliance, 506 2nd Ave., 30th Fl., P.O. Box 953, Seattle, WA 98104; 1-800-544-1800; www.experience wa.com

History. People of the Clovis culture lived in the region 11,000 years ago. At the time of European contact, Native Americans in the area included Nez Percé, Spokane, Yakima, Cayuse, Okanogan, Walla Walla, and Colville peoples in the interior, and Nooksak, Chinook, Nisqually, Clallam, Makah, Quinault, and Puyallup peoples along the coast. Spain's Bruno de Heceta sailed the coast, 1775. In 1792, British naval officer George Vancouver mapped the Puget Sound area, and American Capt. Robert Gray sailed up the Columbia R. Fur traders and missionaries arrived in the first half of the 19th cent. Final agreement on the border of Washington and Canada was made with Britain, 1846. Completion in 1883 of a transcontinental rail link between Puget Sound and the eastern U.S. aided immigration, and Washington became a state in 1889. In the 20th cent., cheap hydroelectric power spurred growth in the aluminum and aircraft industries. Founded in 1975, Microsoft became a computer software giant. Mount St. Helens erupted, 1980. With Starbucks coffee and Amazon.com, Seattle became a national trendsetter in the 1990s. Violent street protests disrupted a World Trade Organization meeting there in 1999. Gary Locke, in office 1997-2005, was the first U.S. governor of Chinese ancestry. A mudslide in Mar. 2014 killed 43 people in a rural area north of Seattle.

Famous Washingtonians. Paul Allen, Glenn Beck, Raymond Carver, Kurt Cobain, Bing Crosby, William O. Douglas, Bill Gates, Jimi Hendrix, Henry M. Jackson, Gary Larson, Mary McCarthy, Robert Motherwell, Edward R. Murrow, Apolo Ohno, Chris Pratt, Theodore Roethke, Ann Rule, Hope Solo, Hilary Swank, Julia Sweeney, Adam West, Marcus Whitman, Minoru Yamasaki.

Website. access.wa.gov

West Virginia (WV)
Mountain State

People. Population: 1,815,857; rank: 38. **Pop. change** (2010-17): –2.0%. **Pop. density:** 75.5 per sq mi. **Racial distribution:** 93.6% white; 3.6% black; 0.8% Asian; 0.2% Amer. Ind.; <0.05% Pac. Isl.; 2+ races, 1.7%. **Hispanic pop.:** 1.6%.

Geography. Total area: 24,230 sq mi; rank: 41. **Land area:** 24,038 sq mi; rank: 41. **Acres forested:** 12.1 mil. **Location:** South Atlantic state bounded on the N by Pennsylvania, Maryland; on the S, W, and NW by Virginia, Kentucky, Ohio; on the E by Maryland and Virginia. **Climate:** humid continental climate except for marine modification in the lower panhandle. **Topography:** hilly to mountainous; Allegheny Plateau in the W covers two-thirds of state; mountains here are the highest in the state, over 4,000 ft. **Capital:** Charleston.

Economy. Chief industries: manufacturing, services, mining, tourism. **Chief manuf. goods:** chemicals, aluminum, motor vehicle parts, lumber and plywood, primary and fabricated metals. **Chief crops:** hay, apples, corn, peaches, soybeans, tobacco, wheat. **Farm income:** crops, $142.02 mil; livestock, $548.59 mil. **Nonfuel minerals:** $245 mil; stone (crushed), cement (portland), sand and gravel (industrial), lime, sand and gravel (construction). **Chief port:** Huntington. **Gross state product:** $76.8 bil. **Sales tax:** 6.0%. **Gasoline tax:** 54.10 cents/gal. **Employment distrib.:** 21.7% govt.; 17.4% trade/trans./util.; 6.2% mfg.; 17.2% ed./health; 8.6%

prof./bus. serv.; 10.0% leisure/hosp.; 3.5% finance; 7.5% constr./mining/log.; 1.1% info.; 6.9% other serv. **Unemployment:** 5.2%. **Min. wage/hr.:** $8.75. **Per cap. pers. income:** $37,924. **New private housing:** 2,719 units/$463.1 mil. **Broadband internet:** 97.2%. **Commercial banks:** 70; deposits: $32.1 bil. **Savings institutions:** 4; deposits: $803.0 mil. **Lottery:** total sales: $1.1 bil; profit: $480.4 mil.

Federal govt. Fed. civ. employees: 14,996; **avg. salary:** $76,011. **Notable fed. facilities:** Natl. Radio Astronomy Observatory, Green Bank; Bureau of the Fiscal Service Bldg.; Alderson Fed. Prison Camp; FBI Criminal Justice Information Services.

Education. High school grad. rate: 89.8%. **4-yr. public coll./univ.:** 13; **2-yr. public:** 9; **4-yr. private:** 10.

Energy. Electricity use/cost: 1,102 kWh, $126.10.

State data. Motto: Montani Semper Liberi (Mountaineers are always free). **Flower:** Big rhododendron. **Bird:** Cardinal. **Tree:** Sugar maple. **Songs:** "The West Virginia Hills"; "This Is My West Virginia"; "West Virginia, My Home, Sweet Home." **Entered union:** June 20, 1863; rank: 35th.

Tourism. Tourist spending: $3.9 bil. **Attractions:** Harpers Ferry Natl. Historical Park, Appalachian Trail Conservancy and Visitor Ctr., in Harpers Ferry; Clay Center for the Arts and Sciences and Avampato Discovery Museum, Charleston; The Greenbrier resort, White Sulphur Springs; Berkeley Springs State Park; Seneca Rocks State Park; New River Gorge Natl. River; Beckley Exhibition Coal Mine; Monongahela Natl. Forest; Fenton Art Glass Company, Williamstown; Mountain State Forest Festival, Elkins; Mountain State Art & Craft Fair, Ripley; Green Bank Telescope (world's largest fully steerable radio telescope); Cass Scenic Railroad State Park. **Information:** West Virginia Tourism Office, Bldg. 3, Ste. 100, State Capitol Complex, 1900 Kanawha Blvd. East, Charleston, WV 25305; 1-800-CALLWVA; wvtourism.com

History. Sparsely inhabited at the time of European contact, the area was primarily Native American hunting grounds. British explorers Thomas Batts and Robert Fallam reached the New R., 1671. Coal, discovered in 1742, was mined extensively by the mid-19th cent. White settlement led to conflicts with Native Americans, including a major battle in which settlers defeated an Indian confederacy at Point Pleasant, 1774. The region joined the Union as part of Virginia, 1788. Longstanding tensions between the E and W parts of the state came to a head in 1861, when Virginia seceded. Delegates of western counties, meeting at Wheeling, repudiated the act and created a new state, Kanawha, later renamed West Virginia, which was admitted to the Union in 1863. Poverty has been a problem for much of the state's subsequent history. It continued to rank low in per capita personal income, despite billions of dollars in federal contracts brought to the state by nine-term U.S. Sen. Robert Byrd, who passed away in 2010. Coal mining, though dangerous and challenged by environmental concerns, continues to be a major industry; nearly 30 miners were killed in a mine explosion in 2010. Flash flooding across the state killed at least 23 people in late June 2016. A statewide teacher walkout in Apr. 2018 demanded increased pay and school funding.

Famous West Virginians. George Brett, Pearl S. Buck, Robert C. Byrd, Henry Louis Gates Jr., Stonewall Jackson, Don Knotts, Michael Joseph Owens, Brad Paisley, Mary Lou Retton, Walter Reuther, Cyrus Vance, Jerry West, Charles "Chuck" Yeager.

Website. www.wv.gov

Wisconsin (WI)
Badger State

People. Population: 5,795,483; rank: 20. **Pop. change** (2010-17): 1.9%. **Pop. density:** 107.0 per sq mi. **Racial distribution:** 87.3% white; 6.7% black; 2.9% Asian; 1.2% Amer. Ind.; 0.1% Pac. Isl.; 2+ races, 1.9%. **Hispanic pop.:** 6.9%.

Geography. Total area: 65,496 sq mi; rank: 23. **Land area:** 54,158 sq mi; rank: 25. **Acres forested:** 17.0 mil. **Location:** East North Central state bounded on the N by Lake Superior and Upper Michigan, on the E by Lake Michigan, on the S by Illinois, on the W by the St. Croix and Mississippi Rivers. **Climate:** long, cold winters and short, warm summers tempered by the Great Lakes. **Topography:** narrow Lake Superior Lowland plain met by Northern Highland, which slopes gently to the sandy crescent Central Plain; Western Upland in the SW; three broad parallel limestone ridges running N-S are separated by wide and shallow lowlands in the SE. **Capital:** Madison. **Chief airports:** Madison, Milwaukee.

Economy. Chief industries: services, manufacturing, trade, government, agriculture, tourism. **Chief manuf. goods:** transportation, dairy, animal slaughtering and processing, paper, printing, plastics, computers and electronics. **Chief crops:** corn, greenhouse and nursery, soybeans, potatoes, cranberries, hay, wheat, snap beans, apples, peas. **Farm income:** crops, $3.46 bil; livestock, $7.31 bil. **Nonfuel minerals:** $1.5 bil; sand and gravel (industrial), stone (crushed), sand and gravel (construction), lime, stone (dimension). **Commercial fishing:** $3.8 mil. **Chief ports:** Superior, Milwaukee, Green Bay. **Gross state product:** $324.1 bil. **Sales tax:** 5.0%. **Gasoline tax:** 51.30 cents/gal. **Employment distrib.:** 14.0% govt.; 18.1% trade/trans./util.; 16.1% mfg.; 15.2% ed./health; 11.0% prof./bus. serv.; 9.7% leisure/hosp.; 5.0% finance; 4.3% constr./mining/log.; 1.6% info.; 5.1% other serv. **Unemployment:** 3.3%. **Min. wage/hr.:** $7.25. **Per cap. pers. income:** $47,850. **New private housing:** 19,545 units/$3.9 bil. **Broadband internet:** 95.1%. **Commercial banks:** 214; deposits: $145.2 bil. **Savings institutions:** 27; deposits: $9.9 bil. **Lottery:** total sales: $602.8 mil; profit: $183.8 mil.

Federal govt. Fed. civ. employees: 15,378; **avg. salary:** $70,568. **Notable fed. facilities:** Ft. McCoy; USDA Forest Products Lab, Madison.

Education. High school grad. rate: 88.2%. **4-yr. public coll./univ.:** 15; **2-yr. public:** 16; **4-yr. private:** 30.

Energy. Electricity use/cost: 683 kWh, $96.08.

State data. Motto: Forward. **Flower:** Wood violet. **Bird:** American robin. **Tree:** Sugar maple. **Song:** "On, Wisconsin!" **Entered union:** May 29, 1848; rank: 30th.

Tourism. Tourist spending: $11.1 bil. **Attractions:** Wade House, Greenbush; Villa Louis, Prairie du Chien; Circus World Museum, Baraboo; Wisconsin Dells; Old World Wisconsin, Eagle; shoreline and state parks of Door County; Chequamegon-Nicolet Natl. Forest; House on the Rock, Taliesin, in Spring Green; Monona Terrace Community and Convention Ctr., Madison; Milwaukee Art Museum, Pabst Mansion, in Milwaukee. **Information:** Wisconsin Dept. of Tourism, 201 W. Washington Ave., P.O. Box 8690, Madison, WI 53703; 1-800-432-TRIP; www.travelwisconsin.com

History. At the time of European contact, Ojibwa, Menominee, Winnebago, Kickapoo, Sauk, Fox, and Potawatomi peoples inhabited the area. French explorer Jean Nicolet reached Green Bay, 1634; French missionaries and fur traders followed. The British took over, 1763. The U.S. won the land after the American Revolution but did not wield control until forts were established at Green Bay and Prairie du Chien, 1816. Native Americans rebelled against the seizure of tribal lands in the Black Hawk War, 1832, but were defeated and relocated to reservations. Wisconsin became a territory, 1836, and a state, 1848. Some 96,000 soldiers served the Union cause during the Civil War. Many immigrants arrived from Germany, Poland, and Scandinavia. Wisconsin agriculture focused on dairy; Milwaukee became a manufacturing center. As governor, 1901-06, Robert La Follette pushed Progressive reforms such as direct primary voting and consumer protection laws. The era of McCarthyism ended when anti-Communist crusader U.S. Sen. Joseph McCarthy of Wisconsin was censured by the Senate, 1954. The state legislature passed controversial measures in 2011 to restrict collective bargaining by some 170,000 public-sector employees and in 2014 became the 25th state to pass a "right-to-work" law allowing private-sector workers to choose not to join unions and pay dues even if they benefit from union contracts.

Famous Wisconsinites. Don Ameche, Carrie Chapman Catt, Willem Dafoe, Edna Ferber, Hamlin Garland, King Camp Gillette, Harry Houdini, Robert La Follette, (Vladzio Valentino) Liberace, Alfred Lunt, Pat O'Brien, Georgia O'Keeffe, Danica Patrick, Les Paul, William H. Rehnquist, John Ringling, Donald K. "Deke" Slayton, Spencer Tracy, Orson Welles, Laura Ingalls Wilder, Thornton Wilder, Frank Lloyd Wright.

Website. www.wisconsin.gov

Wyoming (WY)

Equality State, Cowboy State

People. Population: 579,315; rank: 51. **Pop. change** (2010-17): 2.8%. **Pop. density:** 6.0 per sq mi. **Racial distribution:** 92.8% white; 1.3% black; 1.0% Asian; 2.7% Amer. Ind.; 0.1% Pac. Isl.; 2+ races, 2.1%. **Hispanic pop.:** 10.0%.

Geography. Total area: 97,813 sq mi; rank: 10. **Land area:** 97,093 sq mi; rank: 9. **Acres forested:** 10.4 mil. **Location:** Mountain state in the high western plateaus of the Great Plains. **Climate:** semidesert conditions throughout; true desert in the Bighorn and Great Divide Basins. **Topography:** eastern Great Plains rise to the foothills of the Rocky Mts.;

the Continental Divide crosses the state from the NW to the SE. **Capital:** Cheyenne.

Economy. Chief industries: mineral extraction, oil, natural gas, tourism and recreation, agriculture. **Chief manuf. goods:** petroleum, chemicals, fabricated metal, beet sugar, lumber. **Chief crops:** hay, sugar beets, barley, dry beans, wheat, corn, greenhouse and nursery, oats. **Farm income:** crops, $341.32 mil; livestock, $1.05 bil. **Nonfuel minerals:** $2.4 bil; soda ash, helium (Grade-A), clays (bentonite), sand and gravel (construction), cement (portland). **Gross state product:** $40.3 bil. **Sales tax:** 4.0%. **Gasoline tax:** 42.40 cents/gal. **Employment distrib.:** 24.7% govt.; 18.3% trade/trans./util.; 3.3% mfg.; 9.8% ed./health; 6.7% prof./bus. serv.; 12.7% leisure/hosp.; 4.0% finance; 14.4% constr./mining/log.; 1.3% info.; 5.0% other serv. **Unemployment:** 4.2%. **Min. wage/hr.:** $5.15 ($7.25). **Per cap. pers. income:** $56,724. **New private housing:** 1,926 units/$526.3 mil. **Broadband internet:** 91.8%. **Commercial banks:** 44; deposits: $14.9 bil. **Savings institutions:** 2; deposits: $429.0 mil. **Lottery:** total sales: $25.3 mil; profit: $2.7 mil.

Federal govt. Fed. civ. employees: 5,487; **avg. salary:** $66,640. **Notable fed. facilities:** Warren AFB.

Education. High school grad. rate: 80.0%. **4-yr. public coll./univ.:** 1; **2-yr. public:** 7; **4-yr. private:** 1.

Energy. Electricity use/cost: 850 kWh, $94.66.

State data. Motto: Equal rights. **Flower:** Indian paintbrush. **Bird:** Western meadowlark. **Tree:** Plains cottonwood. **Song:** "Wyoming." **Entered union:** July 10, 1890; rank: 44th.

Tourism. Tourist spending: $3.2 bil. **Attractions:** Yellowstone Natl. Park (est. 1872, first U.S. national park); Grand Teton Natl. Park; Natl. Elk Refuge, Jackson; Devils Tower Natl. Monument; Ft. Laramie Natl. Historic Site; Oregon Trail ruts, Guernsey; Buffalo Bill Historical Ctr., Cody; Cheyenne Frontier Days. **Information:** Wyoming Office of Tourism, 5611 High Plains Rd., Cheyenne, WY 82007; 1-800-225-5996; www.travelwyoming.com

History. Inhabited for at least 12,000 years, the region supported Shoshone, Crow, Cheyenne, Oglala Sioux, and Arapaho peoples when Europeans arrived. France's Vérendrye brothers were the first Europeans to see the region, 1742-43. John Colter, an American, traversed the Yellowstone area, 1807-08. Trappers and fur traders followed in the 1820s. Forts Laramie and Bridger became important stops on trails to the West Coast. Population grew after the Union Pacific railroad crossed the state, 1867-68. Wyoming became a territory, 1868, and the first to extend full voting rights to women, 1869. Statehood was attained, 1890. Disputes between large landowners and small ranchers culminated in the Johnson County Cattle War, 1892; federal troops were called in to restore order. Nellie Tayloe Ross was the first woman governor to take office in the U.S., 1925. Wyoming, the least populous state, has relied on the energy, tourism, and ranching industries in recent decades. Dick Cheney, Wyoming's representative in the U.S. House, 1979-89, served as U.S. vice pres. (2001-09).

Famous Wyomingites. James Bridger, Dick Cheney, William F. "Buffalo Bill" Cody, Curt Gowdy, Esther Hobart Morris, Nellie Tayloe Ross.

Website. www.wyoming.gov

District of Columbia (DC)

People. Population: 693,972; rank: 49. **Pop. change** (2010-17): 15.3%. **Pop. density:** 11,376.6 per sq mi. **Racial distribution:** 45.1% white; 47.1% black; 4.3% Asian; 0.6% Amer. Ind.; 0.1% Pac. Isl.; 2+ races, 2.7%. **Hispanic pop.:** 11.0%.

Geography. Total area: 68 sq mi; rank: 51. **Land area:** 61 sq mi; rank: 51. **Acres forested:** NA. **Location:** at the confluence of the Potomac and Anacostia Rivers, flanked by Maryland on the N, E, and SE and by Virginia on the SW. **Climate:** hot humid summers, mild winters. **Topography:** low hills rise toward the N away from the Potomac R. and slope to the S; highest elevation, 409 ft; lowest on Potomac R., 1 ft.

Economy. Chief industries: government, legal, publishing, medical, service, tourism. **Gross state product:** $131.0 bil. **Sales tax:** 5.75%. **Gasoline tax:** 41.90 cents/gal. **Employment distrib.:** 29.8% govt.; 4.3% trade/trans./util.; 0.2% mfg.; 16.9% ed./health; 21.1% prof./bus. serv.; 10.1% leisure/hosp.; 3.9% finance; 2.0% constr./mining/log.; 2.3% info.; 9.5% other serv. **Unemployment:** 6.1%. **Min. wage/hr.:** $13.25. **Per cap. pers. income:** $76,986. **New private housing:** 6,037 units/$689.5 mil. **Broadband internet:** 97.1%. **Commercial banks:** 29; deposits: $47.1 bil. **Savings institutions:** 1; deposits: $42.0 mil. **Lottery:** total sales: $218.7 mil; profit: $45.6 mil.

Federal govt. Fed. civ. employees: 141,941; **avg. salary:** $119,805.

Education. High school grad. rate: 69.2%. **4-yr. public coll./univ.:** 2; **2-yr. public:** 0; **4-yr. private:** 12.

Energy. Electricity use/cost: 804 kWh, $98.79.

District data. Motto: Justitia omnibus (Justice for all). **Flower:** American beauty rose. **Bird:** Wood thrush. **Tree:** Scarlet oak.

Tourism. Tourist spending: $12.7 bil. **Attractions:** See Attractions in and Around Washington, DC, pp. 438-39. **Information:** Destination DC, 901 7th St. NW, 4th Fl., Washington, DC, 20001-3719; 1-800-422-8644; www.washington.org

History. The District of Columbia, coextensive with the city of Washington, is the seat of the U.S. federal government. It lies on the west central edge of Maryland on the Potomac R., opposite Virginia. The Piscataway, an Algonquian-speaking people, were living in the region when Europeans arrived in the 17th cent. Proposals for a "federal town" for the deliberations of the Continental Congress were made in 1783. Authorized by Congress, 1790, Pres. George Washington chose the Potomac site and persuaded landowners to sell their holdings to the government. Its area was originally 100 sq mi taken from the sovereignty of Maryland and Virginia. Virginia's portion south of the Potomac was given back to that state in 1846.

Pres. Washington chose Pierre Charles L'Enfant, a Frenchman, to plan the capital. Surveyor Andrew Ellicott finished the official map and design of the city, assisted by Benjamin Banneker, a black architect and astronomer. Washington laid the cornerstone of the north wing of the Capitol building, 1793, and Pres. John Adams moved to the new national capital, 1800. The City of Washington was incorporated, 1802. British troops invaded, 1814, setting fire to the Capitol, the President's House (as the White House was then called), and other buildings. Pres. Abraham Lincoln ended slavery in the district, 1862. Many African Americans arrived after the Civil War, but racial segregation remained legal until the mid-20th cent. After federal government expansion spurred population growth, 1930-50, an exodus to the suburbs shrank the city's population, 1950-2005.

The 23rd Amendment (1961) granted residents the right to vote for president and vice president. Congress, which has legislative authority over the District under the Constitution, approved legislation in 1970 giving the District one delegate to the House of Representatives, who could vote in committee but not on the floor. Voters approved, 1974, a congressionally drafted charter giving them the right to elect their own mayor and city council. The district won the right to levy taxes, but Congress retained power to veto council actions and approve the city budget. Security measures were dramatically increased after terrorists attacked the U.S. on Sept. 11, 2001. After a 34-year absence, major league baseball returned to the city in 2005.

Famous Washingtonians. Edward Albee, Michael Chabon, Frederick Douglass, John Foster Dulles, Kevin Durant, Edward Kennedy, "Duke" Ellington, Marvin Gaye, Katharine Graham, Goldie Hawn, Taraji P. Henson, J. Edgar Hoover, Bill Nye, Pete Sampras, John Philip Sousa.

Website. www.dc.gov

OUTLYING U.S. AREAS

American Samoa (AS)

People. Population: 51,504. **Pop. change** (2010-17): –7.2%. **Pop. density:** 677.7 per sq mi. **Racial distribution** (2010): 92.6% Hawaiian/Pacific Islander; 3.6% Asian; 1.2% other; 2+ races, 2.7%. **Languages:** Samoan, English, Tongan.

Geography. Total area: 581 sq mi. **Land area:** 76 sq mi. **Acres forested:** 39,155. **Location:** most southerly of all lands under U.S. sovereignty, about 2,300 mi SW of Honolulu. It is an unincorporated territory consisting of seven islands: Samoan group: **Tutuila** (52.59 sq mi), **Aunu'u** (0.59 sq mi); Manu'a group: **Ta'u** (17.57 sq mi), **Olosega** (2.03 sq mi), **Ofu** (2.83 sq mi); and the atolls **Rose** (0.03 sq mi) and **Swains** (1.38 sq mi). **Climate:** marine tropical, avg. temp 82°F with little seasonal variation; avg. annual rainfall about 36 in. **Topography:** volcanic islands, rugged peaks, and limited coastal plains. About 70% of the land is bush and mountains. **Capital:** Pago Pago, on Tutuila. **Airport:** Pago Pago.

Economy. Chief industries: tuna fishing and processing, trade, services, tourism. **Chief crops:** giant taro, taro, yams, coconuts, breadfruits, bananas, papayas. **Livestock** (2008): 35,709 chickens, 16,904 hogs/pigs. **Nonfuel minerals:** crushed stone, trap rock. **Commercial fishing** (2008): $9.7 mil. **Unemployment** (2007): 29.8%. **Min. wage/hr.:** $4.58-$5.99. **Gross domestic product** (2016): $658 mil. **Broadband internet** (Dec. 2013): 96.8%. **Commercial banks:** 2; deposits: $177.0 mil.

Fed. govt. Fed. civ. employees: 99; **avg. salary:** $61,719.

Education. 4-yr. public coll./univ.: 1; **2-yr. public:** 0; **4-yr. private:** 0.

Energy. Total electricity production (2015 est.): 161 mil kWh.

Misc. data. Motto: Samoa Muamua le Atua (In Samoa, God is first). **Flower:** Paogo (Ula-fala). **Plant:** Ava. **Song:** "Amerika Samoa."

Tourism. Attractions: Natl. Park of American Samoa; Natl. Marine Sanctuary of American Samoa; Jean P. Haydon Museum. **Information:** American Samoa Visitors Bureau, Ground Fl., Fagatogo Sq., Route 001, Fagatogo, AS 96799; (684) 633-9805; www.americansamoa.travel

History. A tripartite agreement between Great Britain, Germany, and the U.S. in 1899 gave the U.S. sovereignty over the eastern islands of the Samoan group; these islands became American Samoa. Local chiefs ceded Tutuila and Aunu'u to the U.S. in 1900 and the Manu'a group and Rose Island in 1904; Swains Island was annexed in 1925. Samoa (Western), comprising the larger islands of the Samoan group, was a New Zealand mandate and UN Trusteeship until it became independent Jan. 1, 1962 (now called Samoa).

From 1900 to 1951, American Samoa was under the jurisdiction of the U.S. Navy. Since 1951, it has been under the Interior Dept. On Jan. 3, 1978, the first popularly elected Samoan governor and lieutenant governor were inaugurated. Previously, the governor was appointed by the Sec. of the Interior. American Samoa has a bicameral legislature and elects a delegate to the U.S. House of Representatives who has a voice but no vote, except in committees.

Five of the seven islands are volcanoes. Scientists discovered a rapidly growing volcano, Vailulu'u, between Ta'u and Rose in 1975.

The tuna canning industry has been the backbone of the economy since the 1950s, but one of two canneries closed in 2009, and a third cannery closed in 2016 after opening the year before. An 8.1 magnitude earthquake in Sept. 2009 triggered a tsunami that severely damaged Tutuila.

American Samoans are of Polynesian origin. They are nationals of the U.S. As of 2010, 109,637 lived in the U.S., including 18,287 in Hawaii and 40,100 in California.

Website. www.americansamoa.gov

Guam (GU)

People. Population: 167,358. **Pop change** (2010-17): 5.0%. **Pop. density:** 796.9 per sq mi. **Racial/ethnic distribution** (2010 est.): 37.3% Chamorro; 26.3% Filipino; 12.0% other Pac. Isl.; 7.1% white. **Languages:** English, Chamorro, Philippine/other Pacific Island languages.

Geography. Total area: 571 sq mi. **Land area:** 210 sq mi. **Acres forested:** 69,851. **Location:** largest and southernmost of the Mariana Islands in the West Pacific, 3,700 mi W of Hawaii. **Climate:** tropical, with temperatures from 70° to 90°F; rainy July to Nov., avg. annual rainfall about 80-100 in. **Topography:** coralline limestone plateau in the N; southern chain of low volcanic mountains slope gently to the W, more steeply to coastal cliffs on the E; general elevation, 500 ft; highest point, Mt. Lamlam, 1,332 ft. **Capital:** Hagåtña. **Chief airport:** Tamuning.

Economy. Chief industries: U.S. military, tourism, construction, shipping, concrete products, printing and publishing. **Chief manuf. goods:** textiles, foods. **Chief crops:** watermelons, cucumbers, eggplant, long beans, bananas, corn. **Livestock** (2007): 533 chickens, 112 cattle, 635 hogs/pigs, 124 goats. **Nonfuel minerals** (2008): $3.8 mil; crushed stone. **Commercial fishing** (2008): $499,095. **Chief port:** Apra Harbor. **Gross domestic product** (2016 est.): $5.8 bil. **Employment distrib.** (Dec. 2017): 28.8% serv.; 24.6% govt.; 23.4% trade; 9.3% constr.; 7.0% trans.; 4.2% insur./real estate/finance; 2.4% mfg.; 0.4% agric. **Unemployment** (Mar. 2018): 4.4%. **Min. wage/hr.:** $8.25. **Per capita income** (2014): $31,809. **Broadband internet** (Dec. 2013): 99.2%. **Commercial banks:** 4; deposits: $2.7 bil. **Savings institutions:** 1; deposits: $87.0 mil.

Federal govt. Fed. civ. employees: 2,389; **avg. salary:** $67,210. **Notable fed. facilities:** Andersen AFB.

Education. 4-yr. public coll./univ.: 1; **2-yr. public:** 1; **4-yr. private:** 1.

Energy. Total electricity production (2015 est.): 1.6 bil kWh.

Misc. data. Motto: Where America's day begins. **Flower:** Puti Tai Nobio (Bougainvillea). **Bird:** Ko'ko (Guam rail). **Tree:** Ifit (Intsia bijuga). **Song:** "Stand Ye Guamanians."

Tourism. Attractions: Ritidian Point, Guam Natl. Wildlife Refuge; War in the Pacific Natl. Historical Park; Chamorro Village; Two Lovers Point. **Information:** Guam Visitors Bureau, 401 Pale San Vitores Rd., Tumon, Guam 96913; (671) 646-5278; www.visitguam.com

History. Guam was probably settled by voyagers from the Indonesian-Philippine archipelago by 3rd cent. BCE. Pottery, rice cultivation, and megalithic technology show strong East Asian cultural influence. Centralized, village clan-based communities engaged in agriculture and offshore fishing. The estimated population by the early 16th cent. was 50,000-75,000. Portuguese explorer Ferdinand Magellan, sailing for Spain, arrived in the Marianas Mar. 6, 1521. They were colonized in 1668 by Spanish missionaries, who named them the Mariana Islands in honor of Maria Anna, queen of Spain. When Spain ceded Guam to the U.S., it sold the other Marianas to Germany. Japan obtained a League of Nations mandate over the German islands in 1919; in Dec. 1941 it seized Guam, which was retaken by the U.S. in July-Aug. 1944.

Guam is a self-governing organized unincorporated U.S. territory. The Organic Act of 1950 provided for a governor, elected to a four-year term, and a 21-member unicameral legislature, elected biennially by the residents, who are American citizens. In 1970, the first governor was elected. In 1972, a U.S. law gave Guam one U.S. House delegate, who has a voice but no vote except in committees.

Guam's quest to change its status to a U.S. commonwealth began in the late 1970s. The Guam Commission on Self-Determination, created in 1984, developed a draft Commonwealth Act. In 1993, legislation proposing a change of status was submitted to the U.S. Congress. In 1994, the U.S. Congress passed legislation transferring 3,200 acres of land on Guam from federal to local control. The Navy approved in 2015 a plan to move 5,000 Marines stationed in Okinawa, Japan, to Guam by 2021. North Korea in Aug. 2017 threatened to target Guam in the wake of new UN sanctions and increasingly heated rhetoric from Pres. Trump.

Website. www.guam.gov

Commonwealth of the Northern Mariana Islands (MP)

People. Population: 52,263. **Pop. change** (2010-17): –3.0%. **Pop. density:** 287.2 per sq mi. **Racial/ethnic distribution** (2010 est.): 50.0% Asian; 34.9% Hawaiian/Pacific Islander; 2.5% other; 2+ races/ethnicities, 12.7%. **Languages:** Philippine languages, Chinese, Chamorro (official), English (official), other Pacific Island languages.

Geography. Total area: 1,976 sq mi. **Land area:** 182 sq mi. **Acres forested:** 60,206. **Location:** between Guam and the Tropic of Cancer, the 14 islands of the Northern Marianas form a 300-mi-long archipelago. The indigenous population is concentrated on the three largest of the six inhabited islands: **Saipan,** the seat of government and commerce, **Rota,** and **Tinian.** **Climate:** tropical, with avg. temperature around 82°F, moderated by NE trade winds; avg. annual rainfall 80-100 in. **Topography:** limestone southern islands with even terraces, coral reefs; volcanic northern isles. **Capital:** Saipan. **Airport:** Saipan.

Economy. Chief industries: banking, construction, fishing, mining, tourism, apparel manufacturing, retail. **Chief manuf. goods:** apparel, stone, clay and glass prods. **Chief crops:** bananas, cucumbers, sweet potatoes, taro, watermelons. **Livestock** (2007): 9,700 chickens, 1,395 cattle, 1,483 hogs/pigs. **Commercial fishing** (2010 est.): $608,971. **Chief port:** Saipan. **Gross domestic product** (2016): $1.2 bil. **Employment distrib.:** 1.9% agriculture; 10.0% industry; 88.1% serv. **Unemployment** (2010): 11.2%. **Min. wage/hr.:** $7.25. **Broadband internet** (Dec. 2013): 80.9%. **Commercial banks:** 3; deposits: $901.0 mil. **Savings institutions:** 1; deposits: $8.0 mil.

Federal govt. Fed. civ. employees: 60; **avg. salary:** $68,965.

Education. 4-yr. public coll./univ.: 1; **2-yr. public:** 0; **4-yr. private:** 0.

Energy. Total electricity production (2009): 60,600 kWh.

Misc. data. Flower: Plumeria. **Bird:** Mariana fruit-dove. **Tree:** Flame tree. **Song:** "Gi Talo Gi Halom Tasi" (In the Middle of the Sea).

Tourism. Attractions: House of Taga; American Memorial Park; Banzai Cliff. **Information:** Marianas Visitors Authority, P.O. Box 500861, Saipan, MP 96950; (670) 664-3200; www.mymarianas.com

History. The people of the Northern Marianas are predominantly of Chamorro cultural extraction, although Carolinians

and immigrants from other areas of E. Asia and Micronesia have also settled in the islands. English is among the several languages commonly spoken.

The German-controlled Northern Marianas were placed under Japanese control by a League of Nations mandate after World War I. The U.S. captured the islands during World War II. From July 18, 1947, the U.S. administered the Northern Marianas under a trusteeship agreement with the UN Security Council. In 1975, the residents voted to become a U.S. commonwealth.

The Northern Mariana Islands has been self-governing since 1978, when a constitution drafted and adopted by the people became effective and a popularly elected bicameral legislature (two-year term), with offices of governor (four-year term) and lieut. governor, was inaugurated. Pres. Ronald Reagan proclaimed the Northern Marianas a commonwealth, 1986, and the UN formally ended its trusteeship, 1990. In 2008, U.S. law gave the islands one delegate to the U.S. House of Representatives who has a voice but no vote, except in committees.

Under the 1976 Commonwealth Covenant with the U.S., the islands are exempt from federal immigration and import laws, and minimum wage is lower than on the mainland. The garment-making industry, which has since boomed, has drawn accusations of sweatshop conditions from some critics. As mandated by legislation passed in 2007, the minimum wage finally reached the federal rate in Sept. 2018.

Website. gov.mp

Commonwealth of Puerto Rico (PR)
Estado Libre Asociado de Puerto Rico

People. Population: 3,337,177 (about 5 mil additional Puerto Ricans reside in mainland U.S.). **Pop. change** (2010-17): –10.4%. **Pop. density:** 974.6 per sq mi. **Racial distribution** (2010): 75.8% white; 12.4% black; 0.2% Asian; 0.5% Amer. Ind.; <0.05% Pac. Isl.; 2+ races, 3.3%. **Hispanic pop.:** 99.0%. **Languages:** Spanish and English are joint official languages.

Geography. Total area: 5,325 sq mi. **Land area:** 3,424 sq mi. **Acres forested:** 1.2 mil. **Location:** island between the Atlantic to the N and the Caribbean to the S; it is easternmost of the West Indies group called the Greater Antilles, of which Cuba, Hispaniola, and Jamaica are the larger islands. **Climate:** mild, with a mean temperature of 77°F. **Topography:** mountainous throughout three-fourths of its rectangular area, surrounded by a broken coastal plain; highest peak, Cerro de Punto, 4,390 ft. **Capital:** San Juan. **Chief airport:** San Juan.

Economy. Chief industries: manufacturing, service, tourism. **Chief manuf. goods:** pharmaceuticals, medical equip., electronics, apparel, food products. **Chief crops:** pumpkins, coffee, watermelons, plantains, yams, oranges, pineapples, sugarcane, bananas. **Livestock** (2012): 10.9 mil chickens, 257,285 cattle, 12,539 sheep, 48,262 hogs/pigs. **Nonfuel minerals** (2013): $66.3 mil; crushed stone, lime, salt, cement (portland), clays (common), cement (masonry). **Commercial fishing** (2008): $3.8 mil. **Chief ports:** San Juan, Ponce, Mayagüez. **Gross domestic product** (2017 est.): $98.8 bil. **Employment distrib.:** 24.5% govt.; 19.5% trade/trans./util.; 8.2% mfg.; 14.0% ed./health; 13.1% prof./bus. serv.; 9.3% leisure/hosp.; 4.9% finance; 2.4% constr./mining/log.; 2.0% info.; 2.0% other serv. **Unemployment** (June 2018): 9.3%. **Min. wage/hr.:** $7.25. **Per capita income** (2015): $18,347. **Broadband internet:** 80.0%. **Commercial banks:** 7; deposits: $74.1 bil. **Lottery** (2009): total sales: $421.2 mil; profit: $146.9 mil.

Federal govt. Fed. civ. employees: 11,306; **avg. salary:** $60,699. **Notable fed. facilities:** PR Natl. Guard Training Area at Camp Santiago; Ft. Buchanan; Intl. Inst. of Tropical Forestry, San Juan; Vieques Natl. Wildlife Refuge; USGS Caribbean Water Science Ctr., Guaynabo.

Education. 4-yr. public coll./univ.: 14; **2-yr. public:** 4; **4-yr. private:** 45.

Energy. Total electricity production (2015 est.): 20.3 bil kWh.

Misc. data. Motto: Joannes Est Nomen Eius (John is his name). **Flower:** Maga. **Bird:** Reinita. **Tree:** Ceiba. **Anthem:** "La Borinqueña."

Tourism. Attractions: Museo de Arte de Ponce; San Felipe del Morro and San Cristóbal forts, San Juan Natl. Historic Site, Walled City of Old San Juan, Casa Blanca in San Juan; Arecibo Observatory; Cordillera Central mtn. range; El Yunque Natl. Forest (only tropical rain forest in Natl. Forest system); Cathedral of San Juan Bautista; Porta Coeli (Doorway to Heaven) Church and Religious Art Museum, San Germán; Río Camuy Cave Park, Camuy; Mosquito Bay. **Information:** The Puerto Rico Tourism Company, La Princesa

Bldg. #2, Paseo La Princesa, Old San Juan, PR 00902; (800) 981-7575; www.prtourism.com

History. Puerto Rico (or Borinquen, after the original Arawak Indian name, Boriquen) was visited by Christopher Columbus on his second voyage, Nov. 19, 1493. In 1508, the Spanish arrived.

Sugarcane was introduced, 1515, and slaves were imported three years later. Gold mining petered out, 1570. Spaniards fought off a series of British and Dutch attacks; slavery was abolished, 1873. Under the Treaty of Paris, Puerto Rico was ceded to the U.S. after the Spanish-American War, 1898. In 1952 the people voted in favor of commonwealth status.

The Commonwealth of Puerto Rico is a self-governing part of the U.S. with a primarily Hispanic culture. The island's citizens have virtually the same control over their internal affairs as do the 50 states of the U.S. However, they do not vote in national general elections, only in national primaries.

Puerto Rico is represented in the U.S. House of Representatives by a Resident Commissioner who has a voice but no vote, except in committees.

No federal income tax is collected from residents on income earned from local sources in Puerto Rico. Nevertheless, as part of the U.S. legal system, Puerto Rico is subject to the provisions of the U.S. Constitution; most federal laws apply as they do in the 50 states.

Puerto Rico's famous "Operation Bootstrap," begun in the late 1940s, succeeded in changing the island from the "Poorhouse of the Caribbean" to an area with the highest per capita income in Latin America. This program encouraged manufacturing and development of the tourist trade by selective tax exemptions, low-interest loans, and other incentives. Despite the marked success of Puerto Rico's development efforts over an extended period of time, per capita income in Puerto Rico is low in comparison to that of the 50 states.

In plebiscites held in 1967, 1993, and 1998, voters chose to retain commonwealth status. In 2012, a half-million ballots were left blank, with 61.1% of those casting votes favoring statehood over free association (33.3%) or independence (5.6%). In a June 2017 referendum, 97% favored statehood, but only 23% of eligible voters participated, rendering the result indecisive. Protests mounted in the late 1990s over the U.S. Navy's use of Vieques Island for live ammunition training; official military exercises there were terminated, 2003. Puerto Rico went into default for the first time in its history Aug. 2015 after it missed a bond payment. Pres. Barack Obama signed contentious debt-relief legislation in 2016. The island in May 2017 officially filed to restructure its debt load of more than $70 bil. Hurricane Maria in Sept. 2017 caused some $90 bil in damages, including widespread devastation of infrastructure. A Harvard study published May 2018 in the *New England Journal of Medicine* estimated at least 4,645 deaths were linked with the hurricane and its aftermath, far greater than the government estimate of 64. A separate analysis, commissioned and accepted by the government, raised the official death toll to 2,975 in Aug. 2018.

Cultural facilities and events. Festival Casals classical music concerts, mid-June; Puerto Rico Symphony Orchestra at Music Conservatory; Botanical Garden and Museum of Anthropology, Art, and History at the Univ. of Puerto Rico; Institute of Puerto Rican Culture, at the Dominican Convent.

Famous Puerto Ricans. Julia de Burgos, Marta Casals Istomin, Pablo Casals, José Celso Barbosa, Orlando Cepeda, Roberto Clemente, José de Diego, José Feliciano, Doña Felisa Rincón de Gautier, Luis A. Ferré, José Ferrer, Commodore Diégo E. Hernández, Miguel Hernández Agosto, Rafael Hernández (El Jibarito), Rafael Hernández Colón, Raúl Juliá, René Marqués, Ricky Martin, Concha Meléndez, Rita Moreno, Luis Muñoz Marín, Luis Palés Matos, Joaquin Phoenix, Adm. Horacio Rivero.

Website. www.pr.gov (in Spanish)

Virgin Islands (VI)

St. John, St. Croix, St. Thomas

People. Population: 107,268. **Pop. change** (2010-17): 0.8%. **Pop. density:** 800.5 per sq mi. **Racial distribution** (2010): 76.0% black; 15.6% white; 6.2% other race; 2+ races, 2.1%. **Languages:** English (official), Spanish, Creole.

Geography. Total area: 733 sq mi. **Land area:** 134 sq mi. **Acres forested:** 46,967. **Location:** 3 larger and 50 smaller islands and cays in the S and W of the V.I. group (British V.I. colony to the N and E), which is situated 70 mi E of Puerto Rico; W of Anegada Passage, a major channel connecting the Atlantic Ocean and Caribbean Sea. **Climate:** subtropical; sun tempered by gentle trade winds; humidity is low; avg. temperature 78°F. **Topography:** St. Thomas is mainly a ridge of hills running E-W and has little tillable land; St. Croix rises

abruptly in the N, slopes to flatlands and lagoons in the S; St. John has steep, lofty hills and valleys with little level tillable land. **Capital:** Charlotte Amalie, on St. Thomas. **Chief airport:** Charlotte Amalie.

Economy. Chief industries: retail, petroleum, tourism, prof. consulting. **Chief manuf. goods:** rum, stone, glass and clay products, electronics, textiles. **Chief crops:** cucumbers, coconuts, mangoes, tomatoes, bananas. **Livestock** (2007): 699 chickens, 776 cattle, 2,981 sheep, 1,125 hogs/pigs, 2,331 goats. **Nonfuel minerals:** crushed stone, limestone, trap rock. **Commercial fishing** (2011): $7.1 mil. **Chief port:** Charlotte Amalie. **Gross domestic product** (2016): $3.9 bil. **Employment distrib.:** 29.0% govt.; 20.3% trade/trans./util.; 1.7% mfg.; 7.0% ed./health; 9.2% prof./bus. serv.; 17.0% leisure/hosp.; 5.8% finance; 5.8% constr./mining/log.; 1.7% info.; 2.5% other serv. **Unemployment** (2017 est.): 10.4%. **Min. wage/hr.:** $10.50. **Per capita income** (2012): $19,982. **Broadband internet:** 85.1%. **Commercial banks:** 3; deposits: $1.8 bil. **Savings institutions:** 1; deposits: $140.0 mil.

Federal govt. Fed. civ. employees: 424; **avg. salary:** $62,405.

Education. 4-yr. public coll./univ.: 1; **2-yr. public:** 0; **4-yr. private:** 0.

Energy. Total electricity production (2016 est.): 636.2 mil kWh.

Misc. data. Motto: United in pride and hope. **Flower:** Yellow cedar. **Bird:** Bananaquit (yellow breast). **Song:** "Virgin Islands March."

Tourism. Attractions: St. Croix Isl.: Salt River Bay Natl. Historic Park and Ecological Preserve, Christiansted Natl. Historic Site. St. John and Hassel Isls.: Virgin Islands Natl. Park. St. Thomas Isl.: Blackbeard's Castle, Coral World Ocean Park, Magens Bay, 99 Steps. **Information:** USVI Division of Tourism, P.O. Box 6400, St. Thomas, USVI 00804; 1-800-372-USVI; www.visitusvi.com

History. The islands were visited by Columbus in 1493. Spanish forces, 1555, defeated the Caribes and claimed the territory; by 1596 the native population was annihilated. The first permanent settlement in the U.S. territory, 1672, was by the Danes; U.S. purchased the islands, 1917, for defense purposes.

The Virgin Islands has a republican form of government, headed by a governor and lieut. governor elected, since 1970, by popular vote for four-year terms. There is a 15-member unicameral legislature, elected by popular vote for a two-year term. Residents of the V.I. have been U.S. citizens since 1927. Since 1973 they have elected a U.S. House delegate, who has a voice but no vote except in committees. Hurricanes Maria and Irma in Sept. 2017 caused some $5.5 bil in damages, according to Gov. Kenneth Mapp.

Website. www.vi.gov

Other Islands

Navassa lies between Haiti and Jamaica, 100 mi S of Guantánamo Bay, Cuba, in the Caribbean. It covers 1,147 acres and is uninhabited. Claimed 1857, a Coast Guard lighthouse was built 1917, now inoperative. Natl. Wildlife Refuge since 1999. Administered by the Dept. of Interior.

The three coral islands of **Wake Atoll—Wake, Wilkes**, and **Peale**—lie in the Pacific Ocean on a direct route from Hawaii to Hong Kong, about 2,300 mi W of Honolulu and 1,500 mi NE of Guam. The group is 4.5 mi long, 1.5 mi wide. Land area totals 2.5 sq mi. The U.S. annexed Wake Atoll Jan. 17, 1899. Japan occupied Wake 1941-45. Designated a National Historic Landmark in 1985. Wake is owned by the U.S. Air Force, administered by the Dept. of Interior, and used by the Army as a missile launch facility. The population consists of military personnel and contractors. Most infrastructure was damaged by super typhoon Ioke in 2006.

The following mostly uninhabited islands are part of the **Pacific/Remote Islands National Wildlife Refuge Complex**, which along with Wake Atoll are administered by the Dept. of Interior: **Midway Atoll**, acquired in 1867, has three main islands—Sand, Spit, and Eastern—1,250 mi WNW of Honolulu, with an area of about 1,500 acres. Naval activity ended in 1997. Has the world's largest albatross colony (Laysan and black-footed). **Johnston Atoll**, 800 mi WSW of Honolulu, is two natural and two artificial islands across 107 sq mi administered by the Navy. Johnston was a nuclear test site in 1958, 1962; the Army disposed of chemical weapons 1990-2000. Cleanup ended in 2005. **Kingman Reef** is a barren coral atoll 932 mi S of Hawaii, annexed 1922. **Palmyra Atoll** is about 54 islets over 753 sq mi, 1,052 mi S of Hawaii; annexed with Hawaii in 1898. Part privately owned by the Nature Conservancy. **Jarvis Island** covers 1,086 acres, 1,300 mi S of Honolulu near the equator. West of Jarvis are **Howland and Baker Islands**, 36 mi apart and about 1,600 mi SW of Honolulu.

100 MOST POPULOUS U.S. CITIES

Sources: Population: Decennial Census and Population Estimates Program, U.S. Census Bureau, U.S. Dept. of Commerce. Population is as of July 1, 2017; population rank is indicated within parentheses. **Pop. density** specifies the number of persons per square mile (sq mi) of land area. Unless otherwise noted, **all other figures** are estimates for 2012-16 by American Community Survey, U.S. Census Bureau. **Racial distribution** categories are abbreviated; their full forms are white, black or African American, Asian, American Indian and Alaska Native, Native Hawaiian and Other Pacific Islander, some other race, two or more races. **Hispanic** or Latino persons may be of any race. **Language** is what is spoken at home. **Employment:** Bureau of Labor Statistics, U.S. Dept. of Labor for 2017. **Per capita income:** Bureau of Economic Analysis, U.S. Dept. of Commerce; figures apply to MSAs for 2016. **Educational attainment** is the percentage of persons age 25 and up who have graduated high school (HS) and who have a bachelor's degree or higher. **Avg. commute** is the time it takes for workers 16 years and over to travel from home to work. "Drive" includes only those who drive to work alone. Forms of transport used by less than 10% are omitted. **Avg. home:** National Association of Realtors®. Figures represent median 2017 sales price of existing single-family homes in the metropolitan area; data not available for all cities. **Avg. rent** is the median gross rent (rent asked plus est. avg. cost of utilities) per month. **Crime rates:** *Crime in the United States, 2016*, Federal Bureau of Investigation, U.S. Dept. of Justice. Rates are per 100,000 in population. Violent crimes include murder, nonnegligent manslaughter, rape, robbery, aggravated assault; property crimes include burglary, larceny-theft, motor vehicle theft. **Mayor** (or other city leader) and **website:** World Almanac research as of mid-2018; subject to change. A nonpartisan mayor is one whose party affiliation was not indicated on the ballot.

Included here are the 100 most populous U.S. cities, according to U.S. Census Bureau estimates released in May 2018. Most data are for the city proper; some, where noted, apply to the Metropolitan Statistical Area (MSA). Inc. = incorporated; est. = established.

Albuquerque, New Mexico

Population: 558,545 (32). **Pop. density:** 2,984. **Pop. change (2010-17):** 2.3%. **Area:** 187.2 sq mi. **Racial distribution:** 72.1% white; 3.3% black; 2.6% Asian; 4.4% Amer. Ind.; 0.1% Pac. Isl.; 13.1% other; 2+ races 4.4%. **Hispanic pop.:** 47.9%. **Foreign born:** 10.4%. **U.S. citizens:** 93.6%. **Language:** 70.6% English only; 23.7% Spanish.
Employment: 259,948 employed; 5.5% unemployment. **Per capita income:** $39,665; change (2015-16): 2.6%. **Below poverty:** 18.9%; 14.7% of families. **Educational attainment:** 89.1% HS; 33.8% bachelor's. **Avg. commute:** 21.1 min. 79.7% drive. **Housing units:** 242,070; 91.4% occupied. **Home ownership:** 59.3%. **Avg. home:** $240,200; change (2015-17): 32.9%. **Avg. rent:** $816. **Crime rates:** violent: 1,112; property: 6,861.
Mayor: Tim Keller, nonpartisan
History: Founded 1706 by the Spanish; inc. 1891.
Website: www.cabq.gov

Anaheim, California

Population: 352,497 (55). **Pop. density:** 7,061. **Pop. change (2010-17):** 4.8%. **Area:** 49.9 sq mi. **Racial distribution:** 69.9% white; 2.2% black; 16.0% Asian; 0.4% Amer. Ind.; 0.5% Pac. Isl.; 7.9% other; 2+ races 3.1%. **Hispanic pop.:** 53.6%. **Foreign born:** 36.9%. **U.S. citizens:** 79.3%. **Language:** 38.2% English only; 44.9% Spanish.
Employment: 165,378 employed; 3.7% unemployment. **Per capita income:** $57,160; change (2015-16): 2.8%. **Below poverty:** 16.2%; 13.2% of families. **Educational attainment:** 76.0% HS; 24.8% bachelor's. **Avg. commute:** 28.4 min. 76.6% drive, 12.8% carpool. **Housing units:** 104,763; 95.5% occupied. **Home ownership:** 45.3%. **Avg. home:** $780,000; change (2015-17): 11.4%. **Avg. rent:** $1,402. **Crime rates:** violent: 342; property: 2,720.
Mayor: Tom Tait, nonpartisan
History: Founded 1857; inc. 1876. Home of Disneyland, the Anaheim Ducks, and the Los Angeles Angels.
Website: www.anaheim.net

Anchorage, Alaska

Population: 294,356 (67). **Pop. density:** 173. **Pop. change (2010-17):** 0.9%. **Area:** 1,706.4 sq mi. **Racial distribution:** 64.3% white; 5.7% black; 8.9% Asian; 7.0% Amer. Ind.; 2.3% Pac. Isl.; 2.1% other; 2+ races 9.8%. **Hispanic pop.:** 8.7%. **Foreign born:** 10.3%. **U.S. citizens:** 95.9%. **Language:** 82.5% English only; 5.0% Spanish.
Employment: 146,175 employed; 6.0% unemployment. **Per capita income:** $57,796; change (2015-16): -2.5%. **Below poverty:** 8.1%; 5.6% of families. **Educational attainment:** 93.3% HS; 34.3% bachelor's. **Avg. commute:** 19.1 min. 75.3% drive, 11.9% carpool. **Housing units:** 114,443; 91.7% occupied. **Home ownership:** 60.3%. **Avg. rent:** $1,231. **Crime rates:** violent: 1,144; property: 4,898.
Mayor: Ethan Berkowitz, nonpartisan
History: Founded 1914 as a railroad construction port; HQ of Alaska Defense Command, WWII. Severely damaged in earthquake, 1964.
Website: www.muni.org

Arlington, Texas

Population: 396,394 (48). **Pop. density:** 4,138. **Pop. change (2010-17):** 8.5%. **Area:** 95.8 sq mi. **Racial distribution:** 65.0% white; 20.8% black; 6.9% Asian; 0.4% Amer. Ind.; 0.1% Pac. Isl.; 4.0% other; 2+ races 2.8%. **Hispanic pop.:** 28.7%. **Foreign born:** 20.3%. **U.S. citizens:** 87.4%. **Language:** 67.2% English only; 22.3% Spanish.
Employment: 200,582 employed; 3.7% unemployment. **Per capita income:** $51,099; change (2015-16): 0.1%. **Below poverty:** 16.6%; 13.0% of families. **Educational attainment:** 84.6% HS; 29.3% bachelor's. **Avg. commute:** 26.8 min. 81.4% drive, 11.1% carpool. **Housing units:** 147,231; 91.6% occupied. **Home ownership:** 55.5%. **Avg. home:** $247,400; change (2015-17): 19.4%. **Avg. rent:** $896. **Crime rates:** violent: 557; property: 3,154.
Mayor: Jeff Williams, nonpartisan

History: Anglo-Americans began to settle in 1840s; inc. 1884.
Website: www.arlington-tx.gov

Atlanta, Georgia

Population: 486,290 (38). **Pop. density:** 3,644. **Pop. change (2010-17):** 15.8%. **Area:** 133.4 sq mi. **Racial distribution:** 40.1% white; 52.4% black; 4.0% Asian; 0.3% Amer. Ind.; <0.05% Pac. Isl.; 1.1% other; 2+ races 2.2%. **Hispanic pop.:** 4.8%. **Foreign born:** 7.0%. **U.S. citizens:** 95.4%. **Language:** 90.2% English only; 4.4% Spanish.
Employment: 237,761 employed; 5.2% unemployment. **Per capita income:** $47,348; change (2015-16): 3.1%. **Below poverty:** 24.0%; 18.8% of families. **Educational attainment:** 89.5% HS; 48.3% bachelor's. **Avg. commute:** 25.8 min. 68.6% drive, 10.0% public trans. **Housing units:** 231,432; 81.8% occupied. **Home ownership:** 43.0%. **Avg. home:** $198,500; change (2015-17): 14.3%. **Avg. rent:** $998. **Crime rates:** violent: 1,084; property: 5,249.
Mayor: Keisha Lance Bottoms, nonpartisan
History: Founded as Terminus, 1837; renamed Atlanta, 1845; inc. 1847. Played major role in Civil War; became state capital, 1868. Birthplace of civil rights movement; host to 1996 Olympic Games.
Website: www.atlantaga.gov

Aurora, Colorado

Population: 366,623 (54). **Pop. density:** 2,388. **Pop. change (2010-17):** 12.8%. **Area:** 153.5 sq mi. **Racial distribution:** 61.8% white; 15.9% black; 5.5% Asian; 0.8% Amer. Ind.; 0.3% Pac. Isl.; 10.2% other; 2+ races 5.6%. **Hispanic pop.:** 28.5%. **Foreign born:** 19.5%. **U.S. citizens:** 87.3%. **Language:** 67.9% English only; 21.0% Spanish.
Employment: 183,534 employed; 3.1% unemployment. **Per capita income:** $56,892; change (2015-16): -0.3%. **Below poverty:** 14.7%; 10.8% of families. **Educational attainment:** 87.0% HS; 27.9% bachelor's. **Avg. commute:** 28.8 min. 76.2% drive, 11.3% carpool. **Housing units:** 131,511; 95.3% occupied. **Home ownership:** 57.1%. **Avg. home:** $414,700; change (2015-17): 17.3%. **Avg. rent:** $1,092. **Crime rates:** violent: 529; property: 3,060.
Mayor: Bob LeGare, nonpartisan
History: Founded as Fletcher, 1891; renamed Aurora, 1907; inc. 1928. Early growth stimulated by military bases; fast-growing trade, technology, and med. science center.
Website: www.auroragov.org

Austin, Texas

Population: 950,715 (11). **Pop. density:** 2,964. **Pop. change (2010-17):** 20.3%. **Area:** 320.8 sq mi. **Racial distribution:** 75.9% white; 7.6% black; 6.8% Asian; 0.4% Amer. Ind.; 0.1% Pac. Isl.; 6.1% other; 2+ races 3.2%. **Hispanic pop.:** 34.5%. **Foreign born:** 18.2%. **U.S. citizens:** 87.5%. **Language:** 67.6% English only; 24.3% Spanish.
Employment: 555,738 employed; 2.9% unemployment. **Per capita income:** $51,566; change (2015-16): 0.9%. **Below poverty:** 16.7%; 11.1% of families. **Educational attainment:** 88.0% HS; 47.7% bachelor's. **Avg. commute:** 23.8 min. 73.7% drive. **Housing units:** 388,316; 92.3% occupied. **Home ownership:** 45.3%. **Avg. home:** $295,800; change (2015-17): 12.3%. **Avg. rent:** $1,106. **Crime rates:** violent: 408; property: 3,506.
Mayor: Steve Adler, nonpartisan
History: First permanent Anglo-American settlement, 1830s; capital of Rep. of Texas, 1839; named after Stephen Austin.
Website: www.austintexas.gov

Bakersfield, California

Population: 380,874 (53). **Pop. density:** 2,544. **Pop. change (2010-17):** 9.6%. **Area:** 149.7 sq mi. **Racial distribution:** 67.5% white; 7.8% black; 7.2% Asian; 1.3% Amer. Ind.; 0.2% Pac. Isl.; 12.4% other; 2+ races 3.6%. **Hispanic pop.:** 48.3%. **Foreign born:** 19.0%. **U.S. citizens:** 89.0%. **Language:** 59.0% English only; 33.7% Spanish.

Employment: 163,309 employed; 6.5% unemployment. **Per capita income:** $37,714; change (2015-16): –0.3%. **Below poverty:** 19.7%; 16.1% of families. **Educational attainment:** 79.6% HS; 21.3% bachelor's. **Avg. commute:** 22.6 min. 80.9% drive, 11.8% carpool. **Housing units:** 121,291; 93.7% occupied. **Home ownership:** 56.8%. **Avg. rent:** $1,005. **Crime rates:** violent: 481; property: 4,524.

Mayor: Karen Goh, nonpartisan
History: Named after Col. Thomas Baker, an early settler; inc. 1898.
Website: www.bakersfieldcity.us

Baltimore, Maryland

Population: 611,648 (30). **Pop. density:** 7,556. **Pop. change (2010-17):** –1.5%. **Area:** 80.9 sq mi. **Racial distribution:** 30.3% white; 63.0% black; 2.5% Asian; 0.3% Amer. Ind.; 0.1% Pac. Isl.; 1.6% other; 2+ races 2.3%. **Hispanic pop.:** 4.8%. **Foreign born:** 7.8%. **U.S. citizens:** 95.2%. **Language:** 90.7% English only; 4.0% Spanish.
Employment: 276,206 employed; 6.1% unemployment. **Per capita income:** $57,189; change (2015-16): 3.1%. **Below poverty:** 23.1%; 18.3% of families. **Educational attainment:** 83.5% HS; 29.7% bachelor's. **Avg. commute:** 30.5 min. 59.8% drive, 18.4% public trans. **Housing units:** 296,923; 81.6% occupied. **Home ownership:** 46.6%. **Avg. home:** $262,900; change (2015-17): 8.3%. **Avg. rent:** $974. **Crime rates:** violent: 1,780; property: 4,778.

Mayor: Catherine E. Pugh, Democrat
History: Founded by Maryland legislature, 1729; inc. 1797. British artillery barrage of Ft. McHenry (1814) inspired "Star-Spangled Banner." Birthplace of America's railroads, 1828; rebuilt after fire, 1904. Site of National Aquarium.
Website: www.baltimorecity.gov

Baton Rouge, Louisiana

Population: 225,374 (99). **Pop. density:** 2,623. **Pop. change (2010-17):** –1.8%. **Area:** 85.9 sq mi. **Racial distribution:** 38.6% white; 55.2% black; 3.6% Asian; 0.2% Amer. Ind.; <0.05% Pac. Isl.; 1.0% other; 2+ races 1.4%. **Hispanic pop.:** 3.1%. **Foreign born:** 5.3%. **U.S. citizens:** 96.8%. **Language:** 91.8% English only; 2.8% Spanish.
Employment: 109,157 employed; 4.8% unemployment. **Per capita income:** $43,197; change (2015-16): 0.0%. **Below poverty:** 26.1%; 17.5% of families. **Educational attainment:** 87.6% HS; 32.3% bachelor's. **Avg. commute:** 21.5 min. 79.2% drive, 10.4% carpool. **Housing units:** 101,838; 86.2% occupied. **Home ownership:** 49.5%. **Avg. home:** $198,600; change (2015-17): 9.4%. **Avg. rent:** $797. **Crime rates:** violent: 938; property: 4,350.

Mayor-President: Sharon Weston Broome, Democrat
History: Claimed by Spain at time of Louisiana Purchase, 1803; est. independence by rebellion, 1810; inc. as town, 1817. Became state capital, 1849; Union-held most of Civil War.
Website: www.brla.gov

Boise, Idaho

Population: 226,570 (98). **Pop. density:** 2,764. **Pop. change (2010-17):** 10.2%. **Area:** 82.0 sq mi. **Racial distribution:** 89.0% white; 1.8% black; 3.4% Asian; 0.8% Amer. Ind.; 0.1% Pac. Isl.; 1.5% other; 2+ races 3.4%. **Hispanic pop.:** 8.5%. **Foreign born:** 7.5%. **U.S. citizens:** 95.7%. **Language:** 89.6% English only; 4.6% Spanish.
Employment: 121,801 employed; 2.7% unemployment. **Per capita income:** $40,943; change (2015-16): 1.6%. **Below poverty:** 14.1%; 8.4% of families. **Educational attainment:** 94.4% HS; 40.6% bachelor's. **Avg. commute:** 18.1 min. 79.7% drive. **Housing units:** 93,172; 94.7% occupied. **Home ownership:** 59.9%. **Avg. home:** $226,700; change (2015-17): 20.1%. **Avg. rent:** $834. **Crime rates:** violent: 298; property: 2,326.

Mayor: David H. Bieter, nonpartisan
History: Gold discovered in area, 1862; proclaimed capital of Idaho Terr., 1864; inc. 1866; on Oregon Trail.
Website: www.cityofboise.org

Boston, Massachusetts

Population: 685,094 (21). **Pop. density:** 14,171. **Pop. change (2010-17):** 10.9%. **Area:** 48.3 sq mi. **Racial distribution:** 53.0% white; 25.4% black; 9.3% Asian; 0.4% Amer. Ind.; <0.05% Pac. Isl.; 6.9% other; 2+ races 4.9%. **Hispanic pop.:** 19.0%. **Foreign born:** 27.6%. **U.S. citizens:** 85.5%. **Language:** 62.9% English only; 16.6% Spanish.
Employment: 361,592 employed; 3.4% unemployment. **Per capita income:** $70,157; change (2015-16): 2.1%. **Below poverty:** 21.1%; 16.7% of families. **Educational attainment:** 85.7% HS; 46.4% bachelor's. **Avg. commute:** 30.3 min. 38.9% drive, 33.6% public trans., 14.8% walk. **Housing units:** 281,417; 92.1% occupied. **Home ownership:** 34.7%. **Avg. home:** $452,900; change (2015-17): 12.1%. **Avg. rent:** $1,369. **Crime rates:** violent: 707; property: 2,150.

Mayor: Martin J. Walsh, nonpartisan
History: Settled 1630 by John Winthrop; capital of Mass. Bay Colony; figured strongly in American Revolution; inc. 1822.
Website: www.boston.gov

Buffalo, New York

Population: 258,612 (81). **Pop. density:** 6,404. **Pop. change (2010-17):** –1.0%. **Area:** 40.4 sq mi. **Racial distribution:** 48.1% white; 37.3% black; 4.9% Asian; 0.4% Amer. Ind.; <0.05% Pac. Isl.; 5.7% other; 2+ races 3.6%. **Hispanic pop.:** 10.9%. **Foreign born:** 8.9%. **U.S. citizens:** 94.6%. **Language:** 83.2% English only; 7.8% Spanish.
Employment: 103,127 employed; 6.7% unemployment. **Per capita income:** $46,511; change (2015-16): 2.0%. **Below poverty:** 31.2%; 25.9% of families. **Educational attainment:** 83.3% HS; 25.3% bachelor's. **Avg. commute:** 20.9 min. 67.1% drive, 10.9% carpool, 11.6% public trans. **Housing units:** 130,977; 83.7% occupied. **Home ownership:** 41.4%. **Avg. home:** $142,700; change (2015-17): 9.9%. **Avg. rent:** $710. **Crime rates:** violent: 1,110; property: 4,117.

Mayor: Byron W. Brown, Democrat
History: Settled 1780 by Seneca Indians; raided by British in War of 1812; inc. 1832. Served as western terminus for Erie Canal and a center for trade and manufacturing.
Website: www.buffalony.gov

Chandler, Arizona

Population: 253,458 (84). **Pop. density:** 3,901. **Pop. change (2010-17):** 7.3%. **Area:** 65.0 sq mi. **Racial distribution:** 77.0% white; 4.8% black; 9.3% Asian; 1.7% Amer. Ind.; 0.1% Pac. Isl.; 2.8% other; 2+ races 4.3%. **Hispanic pop.:** 22.2%. **Foreign born:** 14.5%. **U.S. citizens:** 92.7%. **Language:** 76.9% English only; 12.8% Spanish.
Employment: 136,672 employed; 3.8% unemployment. **Per capita income:** $42,218; change (2015-16): 1.9%. **Below poverty:** 9.3%; 6.9% of families. **Educational attainment:** 92.0% HS; 41.2% bachelor's. **Avg. commute:** 23.7 min. 78.5% drive, 11.0% carpool. **Housing units:** 92,375; 92.9% occupied. **Home ownership:** 61.2%. **Avg. home:** $246,700; change (2015-17): 14.0%. **Avg. rent:** $1,162. **Crime rates (MSA):** violent: 427; property: 2,870.

Mayor: Jay Tibshraeny, nonpartisan
History: Formed 1912; population doubled in 1990s when marketed as "the high-tech oasis of the Silicon Desert."
Website: www.chandleraz.gov

Charlotte, North Carolina

Population: 859,035 (17). **Pop. density:** 2,806. **Pop. change (2010-17):** 17.4%. **Area:** 306.2 sq mi. **Racial distribution:** 50.7% white; 35.3% black; 6.0% Asian; 0.3% Amer. Ind.; 0.1% Pac. Isl.; 4.9% other; 2+ races 2.8%. **Hispanic pop.:** 13.7%. **Foreign born:** 16.0%. **U.S. citizens:** 89.5%. **Language:** 79.2% English only; 11.8% Spanish.
Employment: 458,575 employed; 4.4% unemployment. **Per capita income:** $46,679; change (2015-16): 2.3%. **Below poverty:** 15.8%; 12.2% of families. **Educational attainment:** 88.4% HS; 42.0% bachelor's. **Avg. commute:** 25.1 min. 76.5% drive, 10.4% carpool. **Housing units:** 337,375; 91.9% occupied. **Home ownership:** 53.3%. **Avg. home:** $226,900; change (2015-17): 17.0%. **Avg. rent:** $966. **Crime rates:** violent: NA; property: NA.

Mayor: Vi Alexander Lyles, Democrat
History: Scotch-Irish immigrants arrived, c. 1750; inc. 1768 and named after Queen Charlotte, George III's wife. Site of first major U.S. gold discovery, 1799.
Website: charlottenc.gov

Chesapeake, Virginia

Population: 240,397 (92). **Pop. density:** 710. **Pop. change (2010-17):** 8.2%. **Area:** 338.5 sq mi. **Racial distribution:** 62.2% white; 29.7% black; 3.2% Asian; 0.2% Amer. Ind.; 0.1% Pac. Isl.; 1.3% other; 2+ races 3.2%. **Hispanic pop.:** 5.3%. **Foreign born:** 5.0%. **U.S. citizens:** 98.0%. **Language:** 92.8% English only; 3.4% Spanish.
Employment: 114,953 employed; 3.9% unemployment. **Per capita income:** $47,019; change (2015-16): 1.1%. **Below poverty:** 9.5%; 7.8% of families. **Educational attainment:** 91.4% HS; 30.4% bachelor's. **Avg. commute:** 25.7 min. 86.1% drive. **Housing units:** 87,807; 94.0% occupied. **Home ownership:** 70.1%. **Avg. home:** $225,000; change (2015-17): 7.7%. **Avg. rent:** $1,180. **Crime rates (MSA):** violent: 352; property: 2,811.

Mayor: Rick West, Republican
History: First English colonies on banks of Elizabeth River, 1620s; home to Dismal Swamp Canal, first envisioned by George Washington in 1763. Battle of Great Bridge fought here Dec. 1775; inc. 1963.
Website: www.cityofchesapeake.net

Chicago, Illinois

Population: 2,716,450 (3). **Pop. density:** 11,949. **Pop. change (2010-17):** 0.8%. **Area:** 227.3 sq mi. **Racial distribution:** 48.7% white; 30.9% black; 6.1% Asian; 0.3% Amer. Ind.; <0.05% Pac. Isl.; 11.4% other; 2+ races 2.5%. **Hispanic pop.:** 29.1%. **Foreign born:** 20.9%. **U.S. citizens:** 88.1%. **Language:** 63.8% English only; 24.6% Spanish.
Employment: 1,289,325 employed; 5.5% unemployment. **Per capita income:** $55,621; change (2015-16): 2.0%. **Below**

poverty: 21.7%; 17.6% of families. **Educational attainment:** 83.1% HS; 36.5% bachelor's. **Avg. commute:** 34.4 min. 49.5% drive, 27.8% public trans. **Housing units:** 1,194,098; 87.3% occupied. **Home ownership:** 44.1%. **Avg. home:** $248,500; change (2015-17): 13.5%. **Avg. rent:** $987. **Crime rates:** violent: 1,105; property: 3,191.

Mayor: Rahm Emanuel, nonpartisan

History: First nonnative residence established by Point Du Sable, 1780s; Fort Dearborn built, 1803; significant white settlement began with completion of Erie Canal, 1825; inc. 1837. Boomed with arrival of railroads and canal to Mississippi R.; one-third of city destroyed by fire, 1871. Major Great Migration destination, 1910-30.

Website: www.cityofchicago.org

Chula Vista, California

Population: 270,471 (76). **Pop. density:** 5,450. **Pop. change (2010-17):** 10.9%. **Area:** 49.6 sq mi. **Racial distribution:** 67.2% white; 4.7% black; 15.2% Asian; 0.3% Amer. Ind.; 0.5% Pac. Isl.; 6.7% other; 2+ races 5.3%. **Hispanic pop.:** 58.6%. **Foreign born:** 31.0%. **U.S. citizens:** 84.8%. **Language:** 41.7% English only; 46.6% Spanish.

Employment: 116,818 employed; 4.4% unemployment. **Per capita income:** $55,168; change (2015-16): 2.2%. **Below poverty:** 12.2%; 10.5% of families. **Educational attainment:** 80.8% HS; 27.9% bachelor's. **Avg. commute:** 28.0 min. 78.7% drive, 10.6% carpool. **Housing units:** 84,401; 92.2% occupied. **Home ownership:** 58.1%. **Avg. home:** $599,000; change (2015-17): 13.1%. **Avg. rent:** $1,351. **Crime rates** (MSA): violent: 234; property: 1,309.

Mayor: Mary Casillas Salas, nonpartisan

History: Visited by Spanish, 1542; became part of Spanish land grant, 1795; claimed by U.S. in Mexican-American War, 1847; inc. 1911. WWII brought aircraft industry and growth.

Website: www.chulavistaca.gov

Cincinnati, Ohio

Population: 301,301 (66). **Pop. density:** 3,867. **Pop. change (2010-17):** 1.5%. **Area:** 77.9 sq mi. **Racial distribution:** 50.7% white; 43.1% black; 1.8% Asian; 0.2% Amer. Ind.; <0.05% Pac. Isl.; 1.1% other; 2+ races 3.1%. **Hispanic pop.:** 3.2%. **Foreign born:** 5.1%. **U.S. citizens:** 96.8%. **Language:** 92.4% English only; 2.9% Spanish.

Employment: 138,154 employed; 4.8% unemployment. **Per capita income:** $48,668; change (2015-16): 1.8%. **Below poverty:** 29.9%; 24.0% of families. **Educational attainment:** 86.2% HS; 33.8% bachelor's. **Avg. commute:** 22.6 min. 72.0% drive. **Housing units:** 161,162; 83.5% occupied. **Home ownership:** 37.7%. **Avg. home:** $162,000; change (2015-17): 11.4%. **Avg. rent:** $662. **Crime rates:** violent: 910; property: 5,147.

Mayor: John Cranley, nonpartisan

History: Founded 1788; named after Society of the Cincinnati, an organization of Revolutionary War officers; chartered as town, 1802; inc. 1819.

Website: www.cincinnati-oh.gov

Cleveland, Ohio

Population: 385,525 (51). **Pop. density:** 4,962. **Pop. change (2010-17):** −2.8%. **Area:** 77.7 sq mi. **Racial distribution:** 40.3% white; 50.8% black; 2.0% Asian; 0.5% Amer. Ind.; <0.05% Pac. Isl.; 2.8% other; 2+ races 3.5%. **Hispanic pop.:** 10.8%. **Foreign born:** 4.9%. **U.S. citizens:** 97.2%. **Language:** 87.4% English only; 8.0% Spanish.

Employment: 147,580 employed; 7.4% unemployment. **Per capita income:** $48,968; change (2015-16): 2.0%. **Below poverty:** 36.0%; 31.4% of families. **Educational attainment:** 78.4% HS; 16.1% bachelor's. **Avg. commute:** 24.3 min. 69.5% drive, 10.0% carpool, 10.6% public trans. **Housing units:** 211,387; 79.0% occupied. **Home ownership:** 41.9%. **Avg. home:** $140,400; change (2015-17): 12.2%. **Avg. rent:** $660. **Crime rates:** violent: 1,631; property: 5,316.

Mayor: Frank G. Jackson, nonpartisan

History: Surveyed in 1796; inc. as village, 1814; inc. as city, 1836; annexed Ohio City 1854. Major Great Lakes port and early hub for steel, oil industries.

Website: www.city.cleveland.oh.us

Colorado Springs, Colorado

Population: 464,474 (42). **Pop. density:** 2,384. **Pop. change (2010-17):** 11.5%. **Area:** 194.8 sq mi. **Racial distribution:** 78.8% white; 6.4% black; 3.0% Asian; 0.5% Amer. Ind.; 0.3% Pac. Isl.; 5.6% other; 2+ races 5.4%. **Hispanic pop.:** 17.4%. **Foreign born:** 7.8%. **U.S. citizens:** 95.9%. **Language:** 86.7% English only; 8.5% Spanish.

Employment: 223,958 employed; 3.2% unemployment. **Per capita income:** $44,458; change (2015-16): 1.1%. **Below poverty:** 12.8%; 9.0% of families. **Educational attainment:** 93.4% HS; 37.8% bachelor's. **Avg. commute:** 21.4 min. 79.1% drive, 10.9% carpool. **Housing units:** 189,017; 94.1% occupied. **Home ownership:** 58.0%. **Avg. home:** $281,600; change (2015-17): 18.0%. **Avg. rent:** $958. **Crime rates:** violent: 496; property: 3,561.

Mayor: John Suthers, nonpartisan

History: Founded 1871 at the foot of Pikes Peak; inc. 1886.

Website: coloradosprings.gov

Columbus, Ohio

Population: 879,170 (14). **Pop. density:** 4,022. **Pop. change (2010-17):** 11.7%. **Area:** 218.6 sq mi. **Racial distribution:** 61.1% white; 28.0% black; 4.9% Asian; 0.2% Amer. Ind.; <0.05% Pac. Isl.; 1.7% other; 2+ races 4.1%. **Hispanic pop.:** 5.8%. **Foreign born:** 11.6%. **U.S. citizens:** 93.0%. **Language:** 85.3% English only; 4.2% Spanish.

Employment: 444,418 employed; 4.1% unemployment. **Per capita income:** $47,725; change (2015-16): 1.8%. **Below poverty:** 21.2%; 16.3% of families. **Educational attainment:** 88.8% HS; 34.8% bachelor's. **Avg. commute:** 21.5 min. 80.1% drive. **Housing units:** 383,071; 88.8% occupied. **Home ownership:** 45.0%. **Avg. home:** $189,900; change (2015-17): 15.3%. **Avg. rent:** $856. **Crime rates:** violent: 522; property: 4,070.

Mayor: Andrew J. Ginther, nonpartisan

History: Laid out as state capital, 1812; inc. 1834.

Website: www.columbus.gov

Corpus Christi, Texas

Population: 325,605 (59). **Pop. density:** 1,865. **Pop. change (2010-17):** 6.7%. **Area:** 174.6 sq mi. **Racial distribution:** 86.6% white; 4.3% black; 2.0% Asian; 0.5% Amer. Ind.; 0.1% Pac. Isl.; 4.8% other; 2+ races 1.8%. **Hispanic pop.:** 61.9%. **Foreign born:** 8.6%. **U.S. citizens:** 94.9%. **Language:** 61.9% English only; 35.4% Spanish.

Employment: 144,086 employed; 5.3% unemployment. **Per capita income:** $41,052; change (2015-16): −0.9%. **Below poverty:** 16.6%; 12.5% of families. **Educational attainment:** 81.8% HS; 21.1% bachelor's. **Avg. commute:** 19.5 min. 82.4% drive, 10.6% carpool. **Housing units:** 129,357; 89.7% occupied. **Home ownership:** 56.0%. **Avg. home:** $186,300; change (2015-17): 2.6%. **Avg. rent:** $920. **Crime rates:** violent: 710; property: 3,719.

Mayor: Joe McComb, nonpartisan

History: Anglo-Americans settled, 1838-39; inc. 1852. One of the largest U.S. ports.

Website: www.cctexas.com

Dallas, Texas

Population: 1,341,075 (9). **Pop. density:** 3,945. **Pop. change (2010-17):** 12.0%. **Area:** 340.0 sq mi. **Racial distribution:** 61.0% white; 24.6% black; 3.3% Asian; 0.3% Amer. Ind.; <0.05% Pac. Isl.; 8.4% other; 2+ races 2.5%. **Hispanic pop.:** 41.5%. **Foreign born:** 24.3%. **U.S. citizens:** 81.6%. **Language:** 57.0% English only; 37.7% Spanish.

Employment: 653,102 employed; 3.8% unemployment. **Per capita income:** $51,099; change (2015-16): 0.1%. **Below poverty:** 22.9%; 19.4% of families. **Educational attainment:** 75.3% HS; 31.0% bachelor's. **Avg. commute:** 26.3 min. 76.3% drive, 11.2% carpool. **Housing units:** 543,275; 89.8% occupied. **Home ownership:** 41.9%. **Avg. home:** $247,400; change (2015-17): 19.4%. **Avg. rent:** $888. **Crime rates:** violent: 762; property: 3,400.

Mayor: Mike Rawlings, nonpartisan

History: First nonnatives settled, 1841; inc. 1871. Developed as financial and commercial hub; center of TX oil boom from 1930s.

Website: dallascityhall.com

Denver, Colorado

Population: 704,621 (19). **Pop. density:** 4,596. **Pop. change (2010-17):** 17.4%. **Area:** 153.3 sq mi. **Racial distribution:** 77.0% white; 9.8% black; 3.5% Asian; 0.9% Amer. Ind.; 0.1% Pac. Isl.; 5.4% other; 2+ races 3.4%. **Hispanic pop.:** 30.8%. **Foreign born:** 15.9%. **U.S. citizens:** 89.5%. **Language:** 72.9% English only; 20.6% Spanish.

Employment: 386,225 employed; 2.8% unemployment. **Per capita income:** $56,892; change (2015-16): −0.3%. **Below poverty:** 16.4%; 12.2% of families. **Educational attainment:** 86.4% HS; 45.7% bachelor's. **Avg. commute:** 25.1 min. 70.2% drive. **Housing units:** 299,338; 93.9% occupied. **Home ownership:** 49.4%. **Avg. home:** $414,700; change (2015-17): 17.3%. **Avg. rent:** $1,035. **Crime rates:** violent: 657; property: 3,590.

Mayor: Michael B. Hancock, nonpartisan

History: Miners arrived, 1858; inc. 1861; became territorial capital, 1867. Growth spurred by gold and silver boom; became financial, industrial, cultural center of Rocky Mtn. region.

Website: www.denvergov.org

Des Moines, Iowa

Population: 217,521 (100). **Pop. density:** 2,460. **Pop. change (2010-17):** 6.9%. **Area:** 88.4 sq mi. **Racial distribution:** 77.1% white; 11.0% black; 5.5% Asian; 0.5% Amer. Ind.; 0.1% Pac. Isl.; 2.4% other; 2+ races 3.4%. **Hispanic pop.:** 12.6%. **Foreign born:** 11.9%. **U.S. citizens:** 92.6%. **Language:** 82.7% English only; 9.1% Spanish.

Employment: 108,134 employed; 3.7% unemployment. **Per capita income:** $50,677; change (2015-16): 1.8%. **Below poverty:** 19.0%; 14.4% of families. **Educational attainment:** 87.2% HS; 25.2% bachelor's. **Avg. commute:** 18.8 min. 80.3% drive,

10.4% carpool. **Housing units:** 90,437; 91.9% occupied. **Home ownership:** 60.2%. **Avg. home:** $194,000; change (2015-17): 7.0%. **Avg. rent:** $775. **Crime rates:** violent: 708; property: 4,199.
Mayor: Frank Cownie, nonpartisan
History: Fort founded, 1843; inc. as city and became capital, 1857.
Website: www.dmgov.org

Detroit, Michigan

Population: 673,104 (23). **Pop. density:** 4,852. **Pop. change (2010-17):** −5.7%. **Area:** 138.7 sq mi. **Racial distribution:** 13.6% white; 79.7% black; 1.4% Asian; 0.4% Amer. Ind.; <0.05% Pac. Isl.; 2.9% other; 2+ races 2.0%. **Hispanic pop.:** 7.5%. **Foreign born:** 5.5%. **U.S. citizens:** 96.5%. **Language:** 89.5% English only; 6.5% Spanish.
Employment: 224,958 employed; 9.3% unemployment. **Per capita income:** $48,692; change (2015-16): 2.9%. **Below poverty:** 39.4%; 34.7% of families. **Educational attainment:** 79.0% HS; 13.8% bachelor's. **Avg. commute:** 26.6 min. 68.8% drive, 13.3% carpool. **Housing units:** 365,859; 70.2% occupied. **Home ownership:** 48.2%. **Avg. rent:** $754. **Crime rates:** violent: 2,047; property: 4,723.
Mayor: Mike Duggan, nonpartisan
History: Founded by French, 1701; controlled by British, 1760; acquired by U.S., 1796; inc. 1815; capital of state 1837-47. First automobile factory opened, 1899. Major Great Migration destination, 1910-30.
Website: www.detroitmi.gov

Durham, North Carolina

Population: 267,743 (77). **Pop. density:** 2,427. **Pop. change (2010-17):** 17.3%. **Area:** 110.3 sq mi. **Racial distribution:** 47.9% white; 40.0% black; 5.1% Asian; 0.4% Amer. Ind.; <0.05% Pac. Isl.; 3.6% other; 2+ races 3.0%. **Hispanic pop.:** 13.9%. **Foreign born:** 14.5%. **U.S. citizens:** 89.7%. **Language:** 79.9% English only; 12.8% Spanish.
Employment: 137,889 employed; 4.1% unemployment. **Per capita income:** $49,315; change (2015-16): 1.9%. **Below poverty:** 18.5%; 13.6% of families. **Educational attainment:** 87.0% HS; 48.3% bachelor's. **Avg. commute:** 22.5 min. 74.6% drive, 11.2% carpool. **Housing units:** 111,470; 92.5% occupied. **Home ownership:** 48.7%. **Avg. home:** $254,700; change (2015-17): 14.3%. **Avg. rent:** $913. **Crime rates:** violent: NA; property: NA.
Mayor: Steve Schewel, nonpartisan
History: Inc. 1869. Trinity College moved to Durham, 1892, renamed Duke Univ.,1924.
Website: durhamnc.gov

El Paso, Texas

Population: 683,577 (22). **Pop. density:** 2,656. **Pop. change (2010-17):** 5.3%. **Area:** 257.4 sq mi. **Racial distribution:** 83.6% white; 3.8% black; 1.3% Asian; 0.6% Amer. Ind.; 0.2% Pac. Isl.; 8.3% other; 2+ races 2.2%. **Hispanic pop.:** 80.2%. **Foreign born:** 24.4%. **U.S. citizens:** 86.5%. **Language:** 29.7% English only; 68.0% Spanish.
Employment: 283,061 employed; 4.4% unemployment. **Per capita income:** $32,952; change (2015-16): 1.9%. **Below poverty:** 21.0%; 17.8% of families. **Educational attainment:** 78.6% HS; 23.6% bachelor's. **Avg. commute:** 22.6 min. 80.4% drive, 11.3% carpool. **Housing units:** 242,682; 91.3% occupied. **Home ownership:** 59.2%. **Avg. home:** $151,500; change (2015-17): 6.6%. **Avg. rent:** $769. **Crime rates:** violent: 390; property: 1,798.
Mayor: Dee Margo, nonpartisan
History: First nonnatives settled, 1598; inc. 1873; arrival of railroad, 1881, boosted population and industries.
Website: www.elpasotexas.gov

Fort Wayne, Indiana

Population: 265,904 (78). **Pop. density:** 2,404. **Pop. change (2010-17):** 4.8%. **Area:** 110.6 sq mi. **Racial distribution:** 74.3% white; 15.2% black; 4.0% Asian; 0.2% Amer. Ind.; 0.1% Pac. Isl.; 2.3% other; 2+ races 3.9%. **Hispanic pop.:** 8.5%. **Foreign born:** 7.8%. **U.S. citizens:** 95.4%. **Language:** 88.2% English only; 6.1% Spanish.
Employment: 121,394 employed; 3.5% unemployment. **Per capita income:** $42,267; change (2015-16): 2.5%. **Below poverty:** 18.3%; 14.1% of families. **Educational attainment:** 88.2% HS; 26.8% bachelor's. **Avg. commute:** 20.5 min. 83.6% drive. **Housing units:** 114,888; 90.5% occupied. **Home ownership:** 62.2%. **Avg. home:** $132,900; change (2015-17): 14.7%. **Avg. rent:** $681. **Crime rates:** violent: 397; property: 3,411.
Mayor: Tom Henry, Democrat
History: U.S. fort founded, 1794; inc. 1840 prior to Wabash-Erie Canal completion, 1843.
Website: www.cityoffortwayne.org

Fort Worth, Texas

Population: 874,168 (15). **Pop. density:** 2,535. **Pop. change (2010-17):** 17.9%. **Area:** 344.8 sq mi. **Racial distribution:** 65.2% white; 19.2% black; 3.8% Asian; 0.4% Amer. Ind.; 0.1% Pac. Isl.; 8.0% other; 2+ races 3.3%. **Hispanic pop.:** 34.1%. **Foreign born:** 17.2%. **U.S. citizens:** 88.2%. **Language:** 67.0% English only; 27.0% Spanish.
Employment: 398,298 employed; 3.8% unemployment. **Per capita income:** $51,099; change (2015-16): 0.1%. **Below poverty:** 18.0%; 14.1% of families. **Educational attainment:** 81.2% HS; 27.6% bachelor's. **Avg. commute:** 26.8 min. 81.7% drive, 11.1% carpool. **Housing units:** 306,326; 91.2% occupied. **Home ownership:** 56.7%. **Avg. home:** $247,400; change (2015-17): 19.4%. **Avg. rent:** $931. **Crime rates:** violent: 526; property: 3,302.
Mayor: Betsy Price, nonpartisan
History: Established as military post, 1849; inc. 1873; oil discovered, 1917.
Website: fortworthtexas.gov

Fremont, California

Population: 234,962 (96). **Pop. density:** 3,033. **Pop. change (2010-17):** 9.7%. **Area:** 77.5 sq mi. **Racial distribution:** 26.4% white; 3.2% black; 55.9% Asian; 0.5% Amer. Ind.; 0.9% Pac. Isl.; 7.3% other; 2+ races 5.8%. **Hispanic pop.:** 13.3%. **Foreign born:** 46.4%. **U.S. citizens:** 79.4%. **Language:** 40.8% English only; 8.2% Spanish.
Employment: 116,367 employed; 3.3% unemployment. **Per capita income:** $84,675; change (2015-16): 4.2%. **Below poverty:** 5.3%; 3.3% of families. **Educational attainment:** 93.0% HS; 54.0% bachelor's. **Avg. commute:** 32.8 min. 72.3% drive, 10.2% carpool. **Housing units:** 75,875; 96.2% occupied. **Home ownership:** 61.6%. **Avg. home:** $900,000; change (2015-17): 15.2%. **Avg. rent:** $1,868. **Crime rates (MSA):** violent: 478; property: 3,348.
Mayor: Lily Mei, nonpartisan
History: Spanish mission founded, 1797; inc. 1956 as consolidation of five communities.
Website: fremont.gov

Fresno, California

Population: 527,438 (34). **Pop. density:** 4,644. **Pop. change (2010-17):** 6.6%. **Area:** 113.6 sq mi. **Racial distribution:** 54.2% white; 8.1% black; 13.4% Asian; 1.1% Amer. Ind.; 0.2% Pac. Isl.; 18.6% other; 2+ races 4.4%. **Hispanic pop.:** 48.6%. **Foreign born:** 20.7%. **U.S. citizens:** 87.9%. **Language:** 57.2% English only; 29.3% Spanish.
Employment: 217,612 employed; 6.7% unemployment. **Per capita income:** $40,101; change (2015-16): 2.5%. **Below poverty:** 30.0%; 24.8% of families. **Educational attainment:** 75.3% HS; 20.5% bachelor's. **Avg. commute:** 21.6 min. 76.4% drive, 13.0% carpool. **Housing units:** 175,978; 93.2% occupied. **Home ownership:** 46.5%. **Avg. rent:** $901. **Crime rates:** violent: 611; property: 3,911.
Mayor: Lee Brand, nonpartisan
History: Founded by railroad company, 1872; inc. 1885.
Website: www.fresno.gov

Garland, Texas

Population: 238,002 (95). **Pop. density:** 4,173. **Pop. change (2010-17):** 4.9%. **Area:** 57.0 sq mi. **Racial distribution:** 55.7% white; 13.7% black; 10.6% Asian; 0.5% Amer. Ind.; <0.05% Pac. Isl.; 14.8% other; 2+ races 4.7%. **Hispanic pop.:** 41.5%. **Foreign born:** 28.1%. **U.S. citizens:** 82.5%. **Language:** 62.9% English only; 35.5% Spanish.
Employment: 118,794 employed; 3.6% unemployment. **Per capita income:** $51,099; change (2015-16): 0.1%. **Below poverty:** 15.9%; 13.6% of families. **Educational attainment:** 76.2% HS; 22.5% bachelor's. **Avg. commute:** 28.4 min. 78.8% drive, 13.1% carpool. **Housing units:** 79,948; 94.3% occupied. **Home ownership:** 61.9%. **Avg. home:** $247,400; change (2015-17): 19.4%. **Avg. rent:** $973. **Crime rates (MSA):** violent: 360; property: 2,476.
Mayor: Lori Barnett Dodson, nonpartisan
History: Settled 1850s; inc. 1891.
Website: www.garlandtx.gov

Gilbert, Arizona

Population: 242,354 (91). **Pop. density:** 3,563. **Pop. change (2010-17):** 16.3%. **Area:** 68.0 sq mi. **Racial distribution:** 83.7% white; 3.0% black; 6.2% Asian; 0.9% Amer. Ind.; 0.2% Pac. Isl.; 2.2% other; 2+ races 3.8%. **Hispanic pop.:** 16.0%. **Foreign born:** 9.4%. **U.S. citizens:** 96.6%. **Language:** 86.2% English only; 6.4% Spanish.
Employment: 126,888 employed; 3.5% unemployment. **Per capita income:** $42,218; change (2015-16): 1.9%. **Below poverty:** 6.2%; 4.7% of families. **Educational attainment:** 95.7% HS; 42.4% bachelor's. **Avg. commute:** 27.4 min. 79.2% drive. **Housing units:** 77,444; 92.8% occupied. **Home ownership:** 71.6%. **Avg. home:** $246,700; change (2015-17): 14.0%. **Avg. rent:** $1,315. **Crime rates (MSA):** violent: 427; property: 2,870.
Mayor: Jenn Daniels, nonpartisan
History: Est. 1902; inc. 1920.
Website: www.gilbertaz.gov

Glendale, Arizona

Population: 246,709 (87). **Pop. density:** 4,147. **Pop. change (2010-17):** 8.8%. **Area:** 59.5 sq mi. **Racial distribution:** 78.6% white; 6.2% black; 4.0% Asian; 1.6% Amer. Ind.; 0.1% Pac. Isl.;

5.4% other; 2+ races 4.0%. **Hispanic pop.:** 37.0%. **Foreign born:** 17.3%. **U.S. citizens:** 89.1%. **Language:** 68.4% English only; 24.2% Spanish.

Employment: 115,782 employed; 4.5% unemployment. **Per capita income:** $42,218; change (2015-16): 1.9%. **Below poverty:** 21.5%; 16.9% of families. **Educational attainment:** 83.4% HS; 21.3% bachelor's. **Avg. commute:** 27.2 min. 74.9% drive, 13.9% carpool. **Housing units:** 90,977; 89.5% occupied. **Home ownership:** 54.0%. **Avg. home:** $246,700; change (2015-17): 14.0%. **Avg. rent:** $880. **Crime rates:** violent: 112; property: 1,700.

Mayor: Jerry Weiers, nonpartisan

History: Est. 1892; inc. 1910.

Website: www.glendaleaz.com

Greensboro, North Carolina

Population: 290,222 (68). **Pop. density:** 2,258. **Pop. change (2010-17):** 7.6%. **Area:** 128.5 sq mi. **Racial distribution:** 48.1% white; 41.8% black; 4.3% Asian; 0.4% Amer. Ind.; 0.1% Pac. Isl.; 2.9% other; 2+ races 2.3%. **Hispanic pop.:** 7.4%. **Foreign born:** 10.6%. **U.S. citizens:** 93.0%. **Language:** 86.9% English only; 5.8% Spanish.

Employment: 137,278 employed; 4.9% unemployment. **Per capita income:** $40,663; change (2015-16): 1.6%. **Below poverty:** 19.9%; 15.3% of families. **Educational attainment:** 89.2% HS; 36.8% bachelor's. **Avg. commute:** 20.4 min. 81.7% drive. **Housing units:** 128,570; 88.9% occupied. **Home ownership:** 50.1%. **Avg. home:** $157,200; change (2015-17): 3.8%. **Avg. rent:** $787. **Crime rates:** violent: NA; property: NA.

Mayor: Nancy Vaughan, nonpartisan

History: Est. c. 1740; site of Revolutionary War conflict, 1781, between namesake Gen. Nathanael Greene and Gen. Cornwallis; inc. 1807. Origin of civil rights sit-in movement.

Website: www.greensboro-nc.gov

Henderson, Nevada

Population: 302,539 (64). **Pop. density:** 2,889. **Pop. change (2010-17):** 17.4%. **Area:** 104.7 sq mi. **Racial distribution:** 78.0% white; 5.6% black; 7.2% Asian; 0.5% Amer. Ind.; 0.4% Pac. Isl.; 3.9% other; 2+ races 4.4%. **Hispanic pop.:** 15.8%. **Foreign born:** 12.5%. **U.S. citizens:** 95.6%. **Language:** 82.2% English only; 9.5% Spanish.

Employment: 143,779 employed; 4.8% unemployment. **Per capita income:** $42,284; change (2015-16): 0.9%. **Below poverty:** 9.2%; 6.5% of families. **Educational attainment:** 92.7% HS; 31.1% bachelor's. **Avg. commute:** 23.3 min. 82.7% drive. **Housing units:** 120,516; 89.1% occupied. **Home ownership:** 61.6%. **Avg. home:** $256,500; change (2015-17): 18.3%. **Avg. rent:** $1,151. **Crime rates:** violent: 212; property: 1,881.

Mayor: Debra March, nonpartisan

History: Early growth spurred by WWII magnesium mining; inc. 1953.

Website: www.cityofhenderson.com

Hialeah, Florida

Population: 239,673 (94). **Pop. density:** 11,160. **Pop. change (2010-17):** 6.7%. **Area:** 21.5 sq mi. **Racial distribution:** 93.6% white; 2.7% black; 0.3% Asian; <0.05% Amer. Ind.; <0.05% Pac. Isl.; 2.7% other; 2+ races 0.6%. **Hispanic pop.:** 96.3%. **Foreign born:** 74.0%. **U.S. citizens:** 64.3%. **Language:** 6.4% English only; 93.1% Spanish.

Employment: 109,298 employed; 5.1% unemployment. **Per capita income:** $52,210; change (2015-16): 1.5%. **Below poverty:** 26.2%; 23.5% of families. **Educational attainment:** 70.5% HS; 13.3% bachelor's. **Avg. commute:** 24.8 min. 78.6% drive. **Housing units:** 73,452; 95.9% occupied. **Home ownership:** 45.7%. **Avg. home:** $330,000; change (2015-17): 17.9%. **Avg. rent:** $1,035. **Crime rates** (MSA): violent: 486; property: 3,215.

Mayor: Carlos Hernandez, nonpartisan

History: Inc. 1925. Industrial and residential city NW of Miami; site of major race track.

Website: www.hialeahfl.gov

Honolulu, Hawaii

Population: 350,395 (56). **Pop. density:** 5,787. **Pop. change (2010-17):** 3.9%. **Area:** 60.5 sq mi. **Racial distribution:** 18.0% white; 1.7% black; 53.8% Asian; 0.1% Amer. Ind.; 8.5% Pac. Isl.; 0.8% other; 2+ races 17.0%. **Hispanic pop.:** 6.9%. **Foreign born:** 27.2%. **U.S. citizens:** 87.2%. **Language:** 63.0% English only; 1.3% Spanish.

Employment: 460,776 employed; 2.2% unemployment. **Per capita income:** $54,229; change (2015-16): 2.9%. **Below poverty:** 12.1%; 7.8% of families. **Educational attainment:** 88.3% HS; 36.0% bachelor's. **Avg. commute:** 23.2 min. 56.0% drive, 13.5% carpool, 12.6% public trans. **Housing units:** 147,569; 86.5% occupied. **Home ownership:** 43.1%. **Avg. home:** $757,300; change (2015-17): 7.0%. **Avg. rent:** $1,357. **Crime rates** (MSA): violent: 335; property: 3,073.

Mayor: Kirk Caldwell, nonpartisan

History: Europeans entered harbor, 1794; declared capital of the Hawaii Kingdom by King Kamehameha III, 1850. Pearl Harbor naval base attacked by Japanese, Dec. 7, 1941.

Website: www.honolulu.gov

Houston, Texas

Population: 2,312,717 (4). **Pop. density:** 3,633. **Pop. change (2010-17):** 10.2%. **Area:** 636.5 sq mi. **Racial distribution:** 58.3% white; 22.8% black; 6.7% Asian; 0.4% Amer. Ind.; 0.1% Pac. Isl.; 9.8% other; 2+ races 2.0%. **Hispanic pop.:** 44.3%. **Foreign born:** 29.0%. **U.S. citizens:** 79.3%. **Language:** 52.0% English only; 38.4% Spanish.

Employment: 1,093,835 employed; 4.8% unemployment. **Per capita income:** $51,913; change (2015-16): −3.6%. **Below poverty:** 21.9%; 18.8% of families. **Educational attainment:** 77.4% HS; 31.2% bachelor's. **Avg. commute:** 26.8 min. 76.3% drive, 11.7% carpool. **Housing units:** 937,245; 88.7% occupied. **Home ownership:** 43.2%. **Avg. home:** $231,100; change (2015-17): 8.3%. **Avg. rent:** $898. **Crime rates:** violent: 1,026; property: 4,321.

Mayor: Sylvester Turner, Democrat

History: Founded 1836; inc. 1837; capital of Rep. of Texas, 1837-39; developed rapidly after completion of channel to Gulf of Mexico, 1914. World center of oil, natural gas technology.

Website: www.houstontx.gov

Indianapolis, Indiana

Population: 863,002 (16). **Pop. density:** 2,388. **Pop. change (2010-17):** 5.2%. **Area:** 361.4 sq mi. **Racial distribution:** 61.6% white; 28.0% black; 2.8% Asian; 0.3% Amer. Ind.; <0.05% Pac. Isl.; 4.4% other; 2+ races 2.9%. **Hispanic pop.:** 9.9%. **Foreign born:** 8.8%. **U.S. citizens:** 93.6%. **Language:** 87.0% English only; 8.6% Spanish.

Employment: 421,536 employed; 3.6% unemployment. **Per capita income:** $49,681; change (2015-16): 3.1%. **Below poverty:** 20.9%; 16.1% of families. **Educational attainment:** 85.5% HS; 29.0% bachelor's. **Avg. commute:** 23.0 min. 81.9% drive. **Housing units:** 382,055; 86.8% occupied. **Home ownership:** 53.0%. **Avg. home:** $171,500; change (2015-17): 11.9%. **Avg. rent:** $811. **Crime rates:** violent: 1,374; property: 4,795.

Mayor: Joe Hogsett, Democrat

History: Founded 1821; became planned state capital, 1825.

Website: www.indy.gov

Irvine, California

Population: 277,453 (73). **Pop. density:** 4,231. **Pop. change (2010-17):** 30.6%. **Area:** 65.6 sq mi. **Racial distribution:** 48.8% white; 2.1% black; 41.2% Asian; 0.1% Amer. Ind.; 0.2% Pac. Isl.; 2.7% other; 2+ races 4.9%. **Hispanic pop.:** 9.7%. **Foreign born:** 39.0%. **U.S. citizens:** 82.5%. **Language:** 51.7% English only; 5.9% Spanish.

Employment: 135,218 employed; 3.4% unemployment. **Per capita income:** $57,160; change (2015-16): 2.8%. **Below poverty:** 12.7%; 7.0% of families. **Educational attainment:** 96.6% HS; 68.0% bachelor's. **Avg. commute:** 24.9 min. 77.9% drive. **Housing units:** 95,209; 94.5% occupied. **Home ownership:** 47.8%. **Avg. home:** $780,000; change (2015-17): 11.4%. **Avg. rent:** $1,997. **Crime rates:** violent: 57; property: 1,401.

Mayor: Donald P. Wagner, nonpartisan

History: Univ. of CA–Irvine campus announced, 1959; planned city developed around campus; inc. 1971.

Website: www.cityofirvine.org

Irving, Texas

Population: 240,373 (93). **Pop. density:** 3,585. **Pop. change (2010-17):** 11.1%. **Area:** 67.1 sq mi. **Racial distribution:** 53.4% white; 13.0% black; 17.3% Asian; 0.5% Amer. Ind.; 0.2% Pac. Isl.; 12.7% other; 2+ races 3.0%. **Hispanic pop.:** 41.3%. **Foreign born:** 35.3%. **U.S. citizens:** 74.0%. **Language:** 44.4% English only; 36.6% Spanish.

Employment: 126,934 employed; 3.5% unemployment. **Per capita income:** $51,099; change (2015-16): 0.1%. **Below poverty:** 15.0%; 12.6% of families. **Educational attainment:** 79.8% HS; 35.0% bachelor's. **Avg. commute:** 24.0 min. 78.3% drive, 11.8% carpool. **Housing units:** 90,805; 93.0% occupied. **Home ownership:** 37.2%. **Avg. home:** $247,400; change (2015-17): 19.4%. **Avg. rent:** $953. **Crime rates:** violent: 216; property: 2,696.

Mayor: Richard H. Stopfer, nonpartisan

History: Founded 1903; inc. 1914; remained small until 1950s.

Website: www.cityofirving.org

Jacksonville, Florida

Population: 892,062 (12). **Pop. density:** 1,193. **Pop. change (2010-17):** 8.6%. **Area:** 747.6 sq mi. **Racial distribution:** 59.7% white; 30.7% black; 4.5% Asian; 0.2% Amer. Ind.; 0.1% Pac. Isl.; 1.2% other; 2+ races 3.5%. **Hispanic pop.:** 8.8%. **Foreign born:** 9.9%. **U.S. citizens:** 95.4%. **Language:** 86.2% English only; 6.3% Spanish.

Employment: 437,370 employed; 4.2% unemployment. **Per capita income:** $45,468; change (2015-16): 1.4%. **Below poverty:** 17.0%; 13.1% of families. **Educational attainment:** 88.5% HS; 27.0% bachelor's. **Avg. commute:** 24.2 min. 80.3% drive. **Housing units:** 372,432; 86.5% occupied. **Home ownership:** 57.9%. **Avg. home:** $228,900; change (2015-17): 17.4%. **Avg. rent:** $955. **Crime rates:** violent: 625; property: 3,582.

Mayor: Lenny Curry, Republican

History: Settled as Cow Ford; renamed after Andrew Jackson, 1822; inc. 1832; scene of Civil War conflict, 1864.
Website: www.coj.net

Jersey City, New Jersey

Population: 270,753 (75). **Pop. density:** 18,300. **Pop. change (2010-17):** 9.4%. **Area:** 14.8 sq mi. **Racial distribution:** 35.3% white; 24.8% black; 25.0% Asian; 0.3% Amer. Ind.; <0.05% Pac. Isl.; 11.4% other; 2+ races 3.1%. **Hispanic pop.:** 28.1%. **Foreign born:** 41.1%. **U.S. citizens:** 77.3%. **Language:** 47.4% English only; 22.6% Spanish.
Employment: 133,752 employed; 4.7% unemployment. **Per capita income:** $65,846; change (2015-16): 1.8%. **Below poverty:** 19.4%; 16.4% of families. **Educational attainment:** 85.9% HS; 44.1% bachelor's. **Avg. commute:** 36.6 min. 32.4% drive, 47.3% public trans. **Housing units:** 111,331; 89.5% occupied. **Home ownership:** 27.9%. **Avg. home:** $382,500; change (2015-17): –4.0%. **Avg. rent:** $1,233. **Crime rates:** violent: 479; property: 1,684.
Mayor: Steven M. Fulop, nonpartisan
History: Chartered as town by British 1668; scene of Revolutionary War conflict, 1779. Important station on Underground Railroad.
Website: www.cityofjerseycity.com

Kansas City, Missouri

Population: 488,943 (37). **Pop. density:** 1,553. **Pop. change (2010-17):** 6.3%. **Area:** 314.9 sq mi. **Racial distribution:** 60.1% white; 29.1% black; 2.6% Asian; 0.4% Amer. Ind.; 0.1% Pac. Isl.; 4.4% other; 2+ races 3.3%. **Hispanic pop.:** 10.0%. **Foreign born:** 7.3%. **U.S. citizens:** 95.8%. **Language:** 88.5% English only; 6.5% Spanish.
Employment: 247,621 employed; 4.3% unemployment. **Per capita income:** $48,514; change (2015-16): 0.2%. **Below poverty:** 18.3%; 14.0% of families. **Educational attainment:** 89.1% HS; 33.0% bachelor's. **Avg. commute:** 21.6 min. 80.1% drive. **Housing units:** 227,768; 86.2% occupied. **Home ownership:** 53.7%. **Avg. home:** $194,800; change (2015-17): 14.3%. **Avg. rent:** $826. **Crime rates:** violent: NA; property: NA.
Mayor: Sly James, nonpartisan
History: Est. by 1838 at confluence of Missouri and Kansas Rivers; inc. 1850.
Website: www.kcmo.org

Laredo, Texas

Population: 260,654 (80). **Pop. density:** 2,504. **Pop. change (2010-17):** 10.4%. **Area:** 104.1 sq mi. **Racial distribution:** 94.7% white; 0.4% black; 0.6% Asian; 0.2% Amer. Ind.; <0.05% Pac. Isl.; 3.4% other; 2+ races 0.6%. **Hispanic pop.:** 95.4%. **Foreign born:** 26.4%. **U.S. citizens:** 81.3%. **Language:** 9.9% English only; 89.5% Spanish.
Employment: 105,318 employed; 4.1% unemployment. **Per capita income:** $29,426; change (2015-16): 0.2%. **Below poverty:** 31.3%; 27.5% of families. **Educational attainment:** 66.8% HS; 17.9% bachelor's. **Avg. commute:** 21.1 min. 81.2% drive, 12.6% carpool. **Housing units:** 73,196; 92.4% occupied. **Home ownership:** 62.7%. **Avg. rent:** $764. **Crime rates:** violent: 362; property: 3,043.
Mayor: Pete Saenz, nonpartisan
History: Founded by Spanish colonists, 1755; part of U.S. from 1848. Fast growth fueled by immigration; principal port of entry into Mexico.
Website: www.cityoflaredo.com

Las Vegas, Nevada

Population: 641,676 (28). **Pop. density:** 4,762. **Pop. change (2010-17):** 9.9%. **Area:** 134.7 sq mi. **Racial distribution:** 64.0% white; 11.8% black; 6.5% Asian; 0.6% Amer. Ind.; 0.6% Pac. Isl.; 11.8% other; 2+ races 4.7%. **Hispanic pop.:** 32.2%. **Foreign born:** 21.0%. **U.S. citizens:** 87.9%. **Language:** 66.5% English only; 25.4% Spanish.
Employment: 287,331 employed; 5.4% unemployment. **Per capita income:** $42,284; change (2015-16): 0.9%. **Below poverty:** 16.8%; 12.6% of families. **Educational attainment:** 83.5% HS; 22.4% bachelor's. **Avg. commute:** 25.4 min. 77.5% drive, 10.8% carpool. **Housing units:** 251,862; 87.0% occupied. **Home ownership:** 52.1%. **Avg. home:** $256,500; change (2015-17): 18.3%. **Avg. rent:** $985. **Crime rates:** violent: 849; property: 2,889.
Mayor: Carolyn G. Goodman, nonpartisan
History: Occupied by Mormons 1855-57; bought by railroad 1903; city of Las Vegas inc. 1911; gambling legalized 1931.
Website: www.lasvegasnevada.gov

Lexington, Kentucky

Population: 321,959 (60). **Pop. density:** 1,135. **Pop. change (2010-17):** 8.8%. **Area:** 283.6 sq mi. **Racial distribution:** 75.8% white; 14.5% black; 3.5% Asian; 0.3% Amer. Ind.; <0.05% Pac. Isl.; 2.7% other; 2+ races 3.0%. **Hispanic pop.:** 6.8%. **Foreign born:** 8.9%. **U.S. citizens:** 93.5%. **Language:** 87.9% English only; 6.1% Spanish.
Employment: 167,944 employed; 3.6% unemployment. **Per capita income:** $42,894; change (2015-16): 0.1%. **Below poverty:** 18.9%; 12.3% of families. **Educational attainment:** 89.9% HS;

41.4% bachelor's. **Avg. commute:** 20.6 min. 79.0% drive. **Housing units:** 138,858; 91.1% occupied. **Home ownership:** 53.6%. **Avg. home:** $162,700; change (2015-17): 9.9%. **Avg. rent:** $793. **Crime rates:** violent: 339; property: 4,108.
Mayor: Jim Gray, nonpartisan
History: Site founded and named in 1775 after site of the Revolutionary War's opening battle at Lexington, MA; chartered 1782. Merged with Fayette County, 1974.
Website: www.lexingtonky.gov

Lincoln, Nebraska

Population: 284,736 (71). **Pop. density:** 3,065. **Pop. change (2010-17):** 10.2%. **Area:** 92.9 sq mi. **Racial distribution:** 85.8% white; 4.3% black; 4.4% Asian; 0.7% Amer. Ind.; 0.1% Pac. Isl.; 1.6% other; 2+ races 3.1%. **Hispanic pop.:** 7.1%. **Foreign born:** 8.1%. **U.S. citizens:** 95.4%. **Language:** 88.0% English only; 4.5% Spanish.
Employment: 148,355 employed; 2.7% unemployment. **Per capita income:** $45,511; change (2015-16): 1.5%. **Below poverty:** 15.5%; 9.9% of families. **Educational attainment:** 92.9% HS; 37.1% bachelor's. **Avg. commute:** 18.0 min. 81.1% drive. **Housing units:** 114,631; 95.3% occupied. **Home ownership:** 56.5%. **Avg. home:** $175,400; change (2015-17): 11.9%. **Avg. rent:** $750. **Crime rates:** violent: 358; property: 3,105.
Mayor: Chris Beutler, nonpartisan
History: Originally called Lancaster; chosen state capital, 1867, renamed after Abraham Lincoln; inc. 1871.
Website: lincoln.ne.gov

Long Beach, California

Population: 469,450 (39). **Pop. density:** 9,332. **Pop. change (2010-17):** 1.6%. **Area:** 50.3 sq mi. **Racial distribution:** 53.1% white; 13.0% black; 13.0% Asian; 1.2% Amer. Ind.; 0.9% Pac. Isl.; 13.2% other; 2+ races 5.5%. **Hispanic pop.:** 42.4%. **Foreign born:** 26.0%. **U.S. citizens:** 86.5%. **Language:** 54.1% English only; 33.7% Spanish.
Employment: 228,998 employed; 4.8% unemployment. **Per capita income:** $57,160; change (2015-16): 2.8%. **Below poverty:** 20.3%; 15.7% of families. **Educational attainment:** 79.5% HS; 29.5% bachelor's. **Avg. commute:** 29.9 min. 73.9% drive. **Housing units:** 173,040; 94.7% occupied. **Home ownership:** 39.8%. **Avg. home:** $550,800; change (2015-17): 14.7%. **Avg. rent:** $1,150. **Crime rates:** violent: 597; property: 2,985.
Mayor: Robert Garcia, nonpartisan
History: Settled c. 1784 by Spanish; by 1884, developed as harbor; inc. 1888; oil discovered 1921.
Website: www.longbeach.gov

Los Angeles, California

Population: 3,999,759 (2). **Pop. density:** 8,534. **Pop. change (2010-17):** 5.5%. **Area:** 468.7 sq mi. **Racial distribution:** 52.4% white; 9.0% black; 11.6% Asian; 0.7% Amer. Ind.; 0.2% Pac. Isl.; 22.6% other; 2+ races 3.6%. **Hispanic pop.:** 48.6%. **Foreign born:** 37.8%. **U.S. citizens:** 79.2%. **Language:** 40.2% English only; 42.7% Spanish.
Employment: 1,970,782 employed; 4.7% unemployment. **Per capita income:** $57,160; change (2015-16): 2.8%. **Below poverty:** 21.5%; 17.2% of families. **Educational attainment:** 75.9% HS; 32.5% bachelor's. **Avg. commute:** 30.5 min. 68.5% drive, 10.1% public trans. **Housing units:** 1,447,026; 93.7% occupied. **Home ownership:** 36.6%. **Avg. home:** $550,800; change (2015-17): 14.7%. **Avg. rent:** $1,241. **Crime rates:** violent: 719; property: 2,474.
Mayor: Eric Garcetti, nonpartisan
History: Est. by Mexicans near Spanish mission, 1781; ceded to U.S., 1848; inc. 1850; grew rapidly after coming of railroads, 1876 and 1885. Film and defense industries drove 20th-century growth.
Website: www.lacity.org

Louisville, Kentucky

Population: 621,349 (29). **Pop. density:** 2,356. **Pop. change (2010-17):** 4.0%. **Area:** 263.7 sq mi. **Racial distribution:** 70.9% white; 22.9% black; 2.4% Asian; 0.1% Amer. Ind.; 0.1% Pac. Isl.; 0.6% other; 2+ races 3.1%. **Hispanic pop.:** 4.9%. **Foreign born:** 6.9%. **U.S. citizens:** 95.9%. **Language:** 91.3% English only; 3.9% Spanish.
Employment: 376,784 employed; 4.4% unemployment. **Per capita income:** $45,525; change (2015-16): 2.1%. **Below poverty:** 17.7%; 12.6% of families. **Educational attainment:** 88.0% HS; 28.3% bachelor's. **Avg. commute:** 22.4 min. 81.0% drive. **Housing units:** 274,374; 90.1% occupied. **Home ownership:** 59.6%. **Avg. home:** $171,600; change (2015-17): 11.1%. **Avg. rent:** $748. **Crime rates:** violent: 676; property: 4,424.
Mayor: Greg Fischer, Democrat
History: Est. 1778; named for Louis XVI of France; inc. 1828; base for Union forces in Civil War.
Website: www.louisvilleky.gov

Lubbock, Texas

Population: 253,888 (83). **Pop. density:** 1,988. **Pop. change (2010-17):** 10.6%. **Area:** 127.7 sq mi. **Racial distribution:** 78.7%

white; 7.9% black; 2.4% Asian; 0.9% Amer. Ind.; 0.1% Pac. Isl.; 7.0% other; 2+ races 3.0%. **Hispanic pop.:** 34.5%. **Foreign born:** 5.8%. **U.S. citizens:** 96.6%. **Language:** 77.1% English only; 19.6% Spanish.

Employment: 127,130 employed; 3.2% unemployment. **Per capita income:** $38,658; change (2015-16): 0.6%. **Below poverty:** 20.9%; 13.0% of families. **Educational attainment:** 85.5% HS; 28.7% bachelor's. **Avg. commute:** 16.2 min. 80.7% drive, 12.4% carpool. **Housing units:** 101,486; 90.3% occupied. **Home ownership:** 52.2%. **Avg. rent:** $854. **Crime rates:** violent: 1,084; property: 5,006.

Mayor: Dan Pope, nonpartisan
History: Became county seat, 1891; inc. 1909.
Website: ci.lubbock.tx.us

Madison, Wisconsin

Population: 255,214 (82). **Pop. density:** 3,314. **Pop. change (2010-17):** 9.4%. **Area:** 77.0 sq mi. **Racial distribution:** 78.7% white; 7.0% black; 8.6% Asian; 0.4% Amer. Ind.; <0.05% Pac. Isl.; 1.8% other; 2+ races 3.4%. **Hispanic pop.:** 6.5%. **Foreign born:** 11.0%. **U.S. citizens:** 93.0%. **Language:** 84.4% English only; 5.3% Spanish.

Employment: 153,434 employed; 2.3% unemployment. **Per capita income:** $53,595; change (2015-16): 2.0%. **Below poverty:** 18.6%; 8.2% of families. **Educational attainment:** 95.2% HS; 56.3% bachelor's. **Avg. commute:** 19.2 min. 63.4% drive. **Housing units:** 110,540; 95.7% occupied. **Home ownership:** 47.6%. **Avg. home:** $267,900; change (2015-17): 12.6%. **Avg. rent:** $959. **Crime rates:** violent: 330; property: 2,749.

Mayor: Paul R. Soglin, nonpartisan
History: Selected as site for state capital, named for James Madison, 1836; chartered 1856.
Website: www.cityofmadison.com

Memphis, Tennessee

Population: 652,236 (25). **Pop. density:** 2,055. **Pop. change (2010-17):** 0.8%. **Area:** 317.4 sq mi. **Racial distribution:** 29.6% white; 63.6% black; 1.5% Asian; 0.2% Amer. Ind.; <0.05% Pac. Isl.; 3.3% other; 2+ races 1.7%. **Hispanic pop.:** 6.8%. **Foreign born:** 6.1%. **U.S. citizens:** 95.6%. **Language:** 90.6% English only; 6.1% Spanish.

Employment: 278,956 employed; 4.8% unemployment. **Per capita income:** $43,498; change (2015-16): 2.9%. **Below poverty:** 27.6%; 22.7% of families. **Educational attainment:** 84.0% HS; 25.1% bachelor's. **Avg. commute:** 21.7 min. 80.1% drive, 11.6% carpool. **Housing units:** 299,160; 84.1% occupied. **Home ownership:** 47.9%. **Avg. home:** $166,700; change (2015-17): 13.4%. **Avg. rent:** $842. **Crime rates:** violent: 1,820; property: 5,635.

Mayor: Jim Strickland, nonpartisan
History: French, Spanish, and U.S. forts by 1797; settled by 1819; inc. 1826; surrendered charter to state 1879 after yellow fever epidemics; rechartered as city 1893.
Website: memphistn.gov

Mesa, Arizona

Population: 496,401 (36). **Pop. density:** 3,597. **Pop. change (2010-17):** 13.1%. **Area:** 138.0 sq mi. **Racial distribution:** 84.7% white; 3.5% black; 2.0% Asian; 2.2% Amer. Ind.; 0.3% Pac. Isl.; 4.3% other; 2+ races 2.9%. **Hispanic pop.:** 27.1%. **Foreign born:** 12.0%. **U.S. citizens:** 92.1%. **Language:** 78.8% English only; 17.4% Spanish.

Employment: 229,728 employed; 4.2% unemployment. **Per capita income:** $42,218; change (2015-16): 1.9%. **Below poverty:** 16.2%; 12.2% of families. **Educational attainment:** 87.8% HS; 25.6% bachelor's. **Avg. commute:** 24.9 min. 76.9% drive, 11.3% carpool. **Housing units:** 204,833; 84.3% occupied. **Home ownership:** 60.1%. **Avg. home:** $246,700; change (2015-17): 14.0%. **Avg. rent:** $907. **Crime rates:** violent: 429; property: 2,345.

Mayor: John Giles, nonpartisan
History: Founded by Mormons from Utah and Idaho, 1878; inc. 1883.
Website: www.mesaaz.gov

Miami, Florida

Population: 463,347 (43). **Pop. density:** 12,875. **Pop. change (2010-17):** 16.0%. **Area:** 36.0 sq mi. **Racial distribution:** 75.6% white; 18.8% black; 0.9% Asian; 0.2% Amer. Ind.; <0.05% Pac. Isl.; 3.0% other; 2+ races 1.4%. **Hispanic pop.:** 71.2%. **Foreign born:** 57.6%. **U.S. citizens:** 69.3%. **Language:** 23.2% English only; 69.7% Spanish.

Employment: 218,121 employed; 4.7% unemployment. **Per capita income:** $52,210; change (2015-16): 1.5%. **Below poverty:** 27.6%; 22.9% of families. **Educational attainment:** 74.2% HS; 25.0% bachelor's. **Avg. commute:** 27.7 min. 70.2% drive, 11.3% public trans. **Housing units:** 194,277; 83.2% occupied. **Home ownership:** 30.5%. **Avg. home:** $330,000; change (2015-17): 17.9%. **Avg. rent:** $995. **Crime rates:** violent: 887; property: 4,221.

Mayor: Francis Suarez, nonpartisan

History: Site of fort, 1836; inc. 1896. Modern city developed into financial and tourism center. Land speculation in 1920s added to city's growth.
Website: www.miamigov.com

Milwaukee, Wisconsin

Population: 595,351 (31). **Pop. density:** 6,191. **Pop. change (2010-17):** 0.1%. **Area:** 96.2 sq mi. **Racial distribution:** 46.0% white; 39.2% black; 3.8% Asian; 0.6% Amer. Ind.; <0.05% Pac. Isl.; 6.7% other; 2+ races 3.7%. **Hispanic pop.:** 18.2%. **Foreign born:** 9.7%. **U.S. citizens:** 93.6%. **Language:** 80.6% English only; 13.8% Spanish.

Employment: 268,452 employed; 4.6% unemployment. **Per capita income:** $51,444; change (2015-16): 1.6%. **Below poverty:** 28.4%; 24.1% of families. **Educational attainment:** 82.5% HS; 23.5% bachelor's. **Avg. commute:** 22.4 min. 71.4% drive, 10.3% carpool. **Housing units:** 256,971; 89.8% occupied. **Home ownership:** 41.7%. **Avg. home:** $239,600; change (2015-17): 8.7%. **Avg. rent:** $798. **Crime rates:** violent: 1,533; property: 4,064.

Mayor: Tom Barrett, Democrat
History: Indian trading post by 1674; inc. 1846. Famous beer industry.
Website: city.milwaukee.gov

Minneapolis, Minnesota

Population: 422,331 (46). **Pop. density:** 7,821. **Pop. change (2010-17):** 10.4%. **Area:** 54.0 sq mi. **Racial distribution:** 64.8% white; 18.8% black; 5.9% Asian; 1.2% Amer. Ind.; <0.05% Pac. Isl.; 4.4% other; 2+ races 4.9%. **Hispanic pop.:** 9.6%. **Foreign born:** 15.3%. **U.S. citizens:** 91.3%. **Language:** 79.1% English only; 8.0% Spanish.

Employment: 231,184 employed; 3.1% unemployment. **Per capita income:** $56,723; change (2015-16): 2.0%. **Below poverty:** 21.3%; 14.6% of families. **Educational attainment:** 89.0% HS; 47.7% bachelor's. **Avg. commute:** 22.7 min. 61.3% drive, 13.1% public trans. **Housing units:** 181,348; 93.6% occupied. **Home ownership:** 47.4%. **Avg. home:** $252,100; change (2015-17): 12.7%. **Avg. rent:** $898. **Crime rates:** violent: 1,109; property: 4,222.

Mayor: Jacob Frey, Democrat (DFL)
History: Visited by French missionary Louis Hennepin, 1680; included in area of military reservations, 1819; inc. 1867.
Website: minneapolismn.gov

Nashville, Tennessee

Population: 667,560 (24). **Pop. density:** 1,403. **Pop. change (2010-17):** 11.0%. **Area:** 475.9 sq mi. **Racial distribution:** 62.3% white; 28.0% black; 3.5% Asian; 0.3% Amer. Ind.; 0.1% Pac. Isl.; 3.4% other; 2+ races 2.4%. **Hispanic pop.:** 10.3%. **Foreign born:** 12.5%. **U.S. citizens:** 91.5%. **Language:** 83.1% English only; 9.0% Spanish.

Employment: 377,454 employed; 2.7% unemployment. **Per capita income:** $52,450; change (2015-16): 3.4%. **Below poverty:** 18.0%; 13.3% of families. **Educational attainment:** 87.2% HS; 37.6% bachelor's. **Avg. commute:** 24.3 min. 79.4% drive, 10.1% carpool. **Housing units:** 284,276; 91.3% occupied. **Home ownership:** 53.5%. **Avg. home:** $241,700; change (2015-17): 18.4%. **Avg. rent:** $902. **Crime rates:** violent: 1,102; property: 3,697.

Mayor: David Briley, nonpartisan
History: Est. 1779; first chartered, 1806; became permanent state capital 1843. Home of Grand Ole Opry.
Website: www.nashville.gov

New Orleans, Louisiana

Population: 393,292 (49). **Pop. density:** 2,321. **Pop. change (2010-17):** 14.4%. **Area:** 169.4 sq mi. **Racial distribution:** 34.0% white; 59.8% black; 2.9% Asian; 0.2% Amer. Ind.; <0.05% Pac. Isl.; 1.3% other; 2+ races 1.6%. **Hispanic pop.:** 5.5%. **Foreign born:** 5.9%. **U.S. citizens:** 96.7%. **Language:** 91.1% English only; 4.2% Spanish.

Employment: 170,264 employed; 5.1% unemployment. **Per capita income:** $47,205; change (2015-16): −1.4%. **Below poverty:** 26.2%; 20.6% of families. **Educational attainment:** 85.7% HS; 36.2% bachelor's. **Avg. commute:** 23.7 min. 69.5% drive. **Housing units:** 192,358; 80.5% occupied. **Home ownership:** 46.4%. **Avg. home:** $198,400; change (2015-17): 16.9%. **Avg. rent:** $929. **Crime rates:** violent: 1,070; property: 3,920.

Mayor: LaToya Cantrell, Democrat
History: Founded by French colonists, 1718; became major seaport on Mississippi R.; acquired by U.S. in Louisiana Purchase, 1803; inc. 1805. Hurricane Katrina, 2005, inflicted major damage and killed 1,450+.
Website: www.nola.gov

New York, New York

Population: 8,622,698 (1). **Pop. density:** 28,708. **Pop. change (2010-17):** 5.5%. **Area:** 300.4 sq mi. **Racial distribution:** 43.1% white; 24.4% black; 13.7% Asian; 0.4% Amer. Ind.; <0.05% Pac. Isl.; 15.1% other; 2+ races 3.3%. **Hispanic pop.:** 29.0%. **Foreign born:** 37.2%. **U.S. citizens:** 83.0%. **Language:** 51.0% English only; 24.5% Spanish.

Employment: 4,032,497 employed; 4.5% unemployment. **Per capita income:** $65,846; change (2015-16): 1.8%. **Below poverty:** 20.3%; 17.0% of families. **Educational attainment:** 80.8% HS; 36.2% bachelor's. **Avg. commute:** 40.3 min. 22.0% drive, 56.6% public trans., 10.0% walk. **Housing units:** 3,436,084; 91.0% occupied. **Home ownership:** 32.0%. **Avg. home:** $382,500; change (2015-17): –4.0%. **Avg. rent:** $1,294. **Crime rates:** violent: 573; property: 1,462.
Mayor: Bill de Blasio, Democrat
History: Trading post est., 1624; British took control from Dutch, 1664, named city New York; U.S. capital, 1785-90. Under new charter, 1898, city expanded to include five boroughs: Bronx, Brooklyn, Queens, and Staten Island, as well as Manhattan. Sept. 11, 2001, terrorist attacks destroyed World Trade Center, killed more than 2,750.
Website: www.nyc.gov

Newark, New Jersey

Population: 285,154 (70). **Pop. density:** 11,811. **Pop. change (2010-17):** 2.9%. **Area:** 24.1 sq mi. **Racial distribution:** 24.4% white; 50.2% black; 1.8% Asian; 0.5% Amer. Ind.; 0.1% Pac. Isl.; 20.2% other; 2+ races 2.9%. **Hispanic pop.:** 36.0%. **Foreign born:** 28.3%. **U.S. citizens:** 82.8%. **Language:** 53.7% English only; 32.4% Spanish.
Employment: 108,048 employed; 7.5% unemployment. **Per capita income:** $65,846; change (2015-16): 1.8%. **Below poverty:** 29.1%; 25.7% of families. **Educational attainment:** 73.3% HS; 13.7% bachelor's. **Avg. commute:** 34.7 min. 49.9% drive, 12.3% carpool, 26.5% public trans. **Housing units:** 110,847; 84.9% occupied. **Home ownership:** 21.8%. **Avg. home:** $379,300; change (2015-17): –1.2%. **Avg. rent:** $981. **Crime rates:** violent: 937; property: 2,241.
Mayor: Ras J. Baraka, nonpartisan
History: Est. by Puritans, 1666; inc. as city, 1836. Major industry and shipping hub from mid-19th century.
Website: www.newarknj.gov

Norfolk, Virginia

Population: 244,703 (88). **Pop. density:** 4,593. **Pop. change (2010-17):** 0.8%. **Area:** 53.3 sq mi. **Racial distribution:** 47.7% white; 42.2% black; 3.4% Asian; 0.5% Amer. Ind.; 0.1% Pac. Isl.; 2.5% other; 2+ races 3.7%. **Hispanic pop.:** 7.4%. **Foreign born:** 7.1%. **U.S. citizens:** 96.5%. **Language:** 89.6% English only; 5.0% Spanish.
Employment: 106,502 employed; 4.7% unemployment. **Per capita income:** $47,019; change (2015-16): 1.1%. **Below poverty:** 21.0%; 16.4% of families. **Educational attainment:** 87.5% HS; 26.6% bachelor's. **Avg. commute:** 21.8 min. 74.3% drive. **Housing units:** 96,631; 90.4% occupied. **Home ownership:** 42.8%. **Avg. home:** $225,000; change (2015-17): 7.7%. **Avg. rent:** $980. **Crime rates:** violent: 658; property: 3,914.
Mayor: Kenneth Cooper Alexander, nonpartisan
History: Founded 1682; burned by colonists to prevent capture by British during Revolutionary War. Inc. as city, 1845. Site of world's largest naval base; major commercial port.
Website: www.norfolk.gov

North Las Vegas, Nevada

Population: 242,975 (90). **Pop. density:** 2,479. **Pop. change (2010-17):** 12.0%. **Area:** 98.0 sq mi. **Racial distribution:** 53.0% white; 20.0% black; 6.0% Asian; 0.6% Amer. Ind.; 0.9% Pac. Isl.; 14.5% other; 2+ races 5.1%. **Hispanic pop.:** 40.4%. **Foreign born:** 21.3%. **U.S. citizens:** 87.5%. **Language:** 60.2% English only; 33.4% Spanish.
Employment: 103,477 employed; 5.8% unemployment. **Per capita income:** $42,284; change (2015-16): 0.9%. **Below poverty:** 15.8%; 12.9% of families. **Educational attainment:** 79.2% HS; 16.3% bachelor's. **Avg. commute:** 26.1 min. 81.3% drive, 11.2% carpool. **Housing units:** 77,525; 89.1% occupied. **Home ownership:** 54.6%. **Avg. home:** $256,500; change (2015-17): 18.3%. **Avg. rent:** $1,118. **Crime rates (MSA):** violent: 771; property: 2,728.
Mayor: John J. Lee, nonpartisan
History: Inc. 1946.
Website: www.cityofnorthlasvegas.com

Oakland, California

Population: 425,195 (45). **Pop. density:** 7,607. **Pop. change (2010-17):** 8.8%. **Area:** 55.9 sq mi. **Racial distribution:** 38.2% white; 24.7% black; 16.0% Asian; 0.8% Amer. Ind.; 0.6% Pac. Isl.; 13.1% other; 2+ races 6.6%. **Hispanic pop.:** 26.7%. **Foreign born:** 27.3%. **U.S. citizens:** 85.2%. **Language:** 59.7% English only; 22.0% Spanish.
Employment: 205,152 employed; 4.2% unemployment. **Per capita income:** $84,675; change (2015-16): 4.2%. **Below poverty:** 20.0%; 16.1% of families. **Educational attainment:** 80.5% HS; 39.7% bachelor's. **Avg. commute:** 31.0 min. 52.1% drive, 11.6% carpool, 20.8% public trans. **Housing units:** 169,654; 93.7% occupied. **Home ownership:** 39.6%. **Avg. home:** $900,000; change (2015-17): 15.2%. **Avg. rent:** $1,189. **Crime rates:** violent: 1,426; property: 5,636.
Mayor: Libby Schaaf, nonpartisan

History: Area settled by Spanish, 1820; inc. 1854.
Website: www.oaklandnet.com

Oklahoma City, Oklahoma

Population: 643,648 (27). **Pop. density:** 1,062. **Pop. change (2010-17):** 11.0%. **Area:** 606.3 sq mi. **Racial distribution:** 67.7% white; 14.3% black; 4.4% Asian; 3.0% Amer. Ind.; <0.05% Pac. Isl.; 3.8% other; 2+ races 6.7%. **Hispanic pop.:** 18.5%. **Foreign born:** 12.2%. **U.S. citizens:** 91.6%. **Language:** 79.9% English only; 14.7% Spanish.
Employment: 301,742 employed; 3.9% unemployment. **Per capita income:** $44,646; change (2015-16): –1.0%. **Below poverty:** 17.8%; 13.5% of families. **Educational attainment:** 85.3% HS; 29.3% bachelor's. **Avg. commute:** 21.1 min. 82.2% drive, 11.4% carpool. **Housing units:** 265,168; 88.8% occupied. **Home ownership:** 58.6%. **Avg. home:** $154,300; change (2015-17): 3.1%. **Avg. rent:** $793. **Crime rates:** violent: 783; property: 3,901.
Mayor: David Holt, nonpartisan
History: Settled during land rush, 1889; inc. 1890; became capital, 1910; oil discovered, 1928. Bomb in 1995 destroyed federal office bldg., killed 168 people.
Website: www.okc.gov

Omaha, Nebraska

Population: 466,893 (40). **Pop. density:** 3,388. **Pop. change (2010-17):** 14.2%. **Area:** 137.8 sq mi. **Racial distribution:** 77.3% white; 12.7% black; 3.3% Asian; 0.6% Amer. Ind.; <0.05% Pac. Isl.; 3.2% other; 2+ races 3.0%. **Hispanic pop.:** 13.8%. **Foreign born:** 10.2%. **U.S. citizens:** 92.8%. **Language:** 83.9% English only; 10.7% Spanish.
Employment: 221,660 employed; 3.2% unemployment. **Per capita income:** $53,613; change (2015-16): 1.7%. **Below poverty:** 16.3%; 11.9% of families. **Educational attainment:** 87.8% HS; 34.7% bachelor's. **Avg. commute:** 18.6 min. 82.0% drive. **Housing units:** 189,070; 92.5% occupied. **Home ownership:** 57.5%. **Avg. home:** $175,900; change (2015-17): 10.6%. **Avg. rent:** $819. **Crime rates:** violent: 567; property: 3,767.
Mayor: Jean Stothert, nonpartisan
History: Founded 1854; inc. 1857. Large food-processing, telecommunications, information-processing center.
Website: www.cityofomaha.org

Orlando, Florida

Population: 280,257 (72). **Pop. density:** 2,664. **Pop. change (2010-17):** 17.6%. **Area:** 105.2 sq mi. **Racial distribution:** 61.0% white; 26.4% black; 3.8% Asian; 0.3% Amer. Ind.; <0.05% Pac. Isl.; 5.7% other; 2+ races 2.7%. **Hispanic pop.:** 29.2%. **Foreign born:** 18.4%. **U.S. citizens:** 89.8%. **Language:** 66.6% English only; 23.9% Spanish.
Employment: 159,456 employed; 3.5% unemployment. **Per capita income:** $40,169; change (2015-16): 2.1%. **Below poverty:** 19.9%; 16.3% of families. **Educational attainment:** 89.5% HS; 35.0% bachelor's. **Avg. commute:** 25.1 min. 79.1% drive. **Housing units:** 126,537; 85.8% occupied. **Home ownership:** 35.5%. **Avg. home:** $244,900; change (2015-17): 23.1%. **Avg. rent:** $1,040. **Crime rates:** violent: 838; property: 5,220.
Mayor: Buddy Dyer, Democrat
History: Ft. Gatlin built just south of present-day Orlando, 1838; name changed from Jernigan, 1856; inc. 1875. Walt Disney World opened, 1971.
Website: www.cityoforlando.net

Philadelphia, Pennsylvania

Population: 1,580,863 (6). **Pop. density:** 11,782. **Pop. change (2010-17):** 3.6%. **Area:** 134.2 sq mi. **Racial distribution:** 41.3% white; 42.9% black; 6.9% Asian; 0.4% Amer. Ind.; 0.1% Pac. Isl.; 5.7% other; 2+ races 2.8%. **Hispanic pop.:** 13.8%. **Foreign born:** 13.1%. **U.S. citizens:** 93.4%. **Language:** 77.6% English only; 10.3% Spanish.
Employment: 660,073 employed; 6.2% unemployment. **Per capita income:** $58,589; change (2015-16): 2.2%. **Below poverty:** 25.9%; 20.4% of families. **Educational attainment:** 82.6% HS; 26.3% bachelor's. **Avg. commute:** 32.7 min. 50.8% drive, 25.7% public trans. **Housing units:** 671,125; 86.8% occupied. **Home ownership:** 52.4%. **Avg. home:** $230,000; change (2015-17): 2.8%. **Avg. rent:** $943. **Crime rates:** violent: 989; property: 3,141.
Mayor: Jim F. Kenney, Democrat
History: Named Philadelphia, 1682; chartered 1701. Continental Congresses convened 1774, 1775; Declaration of Independence signed, 1776; U.S. capital, 1790-1800.
Website: www.phila.gov

Phoenix, Arizona

Population: 1,626,078 (5). **Pop. density:** 3,141. **Pop. change (2010-17):** 12.5%. **Area:** 517.7 sq mi. **Racial distribution:** 72.6% white; 6.8% black; 3.5% Asian; 2.0% Amer. Ind.; 0.2% Pac. Isl.; 11.5% other; 2+ races 3.4%. **Hispanic pop.:** 41.8%. **Foreign born:** 19.8%. **U.S. citizens:** 86.4%. **Language:** 62.9% English only; 30.8% Spanish.

Employment: 776,624 employed; 4.3% unemployment. **Per capita income:** $42,218; change (2015-16): 1.9%. **Below poverty:** 22.3%; 17.7% of families. **Educational attainment:** 80.9% HS; 27.4% bachelor's. **Avg. commute:** 25.1 min. 74.9% drive, 12.1% carpool. **Housing units:** 605,756; 89.0% occupied. **Home ownership:** 52.7%. **Avg. home:** $246,700; change (2015-17): 14.0%. **Avg. rent:** $914. **Crime rates:** violent: 674; property: 3,690.

Mayor (acting): Thelda Williams, nonpartisan

History: Founded 1867; inc. 1881; became territorial capital, 1889.

Website: www.phoenix.gov

Pittsburgh, Pennsylvania

Population: 302,407 (65). **Pop. density:** 5,461. **Pop. change (2010-17):** −1.1%. **Area:** 55.4 sq mi. **Racial distribution:** 66.3% white; 24.3% black; 5.5% Asian; 0.2% Amer. Ind.; <0.05% Pac. Isl.; 0.5% other; 2+ races 3.2%. **Hispanic pop.:** 2.8%. **Foreign born:** 8.5%. **U.S. citizens:** 94.4%. **Language:** 89.2% English only; 2.2% Spanish.

Employment: 149,318 employed; 4.9% unemployment. **Per capita income:** $51,187; change (2015-16): 1.1%. **Below poverty:** 22.3%; 15.6% of families. **Educational attainment:** 92.0% HS; 40.7% bachelor's. **Avg. commute:** 23.5 min. 56.0% drive, 17.1% public trans., 11.1% walk. **Housing units:** 153,785; 86.4% occupied. **Home ownership:** 47.7%. **Avg. rent:** $844. **Crime rates:** violent: 782; property: 3,263.

Mayor: William "Bill" Peduto, Democrat

History: Settled around Ft. Pitt, 1758; inc. 1816; became an inland port; a center for iron production by Civil War.

Website: pittsburghpa.gov

Plano, Texas

Population: 286,143 (69). **Pop. density:** 3,993. **Pop. change (2010-17):** 10.1%. **Area:** 71.7 sq mi. **Racial distribution:** 67.8% white; 8.0% black; 19.1% Asian; 0.4% Amer. Ind.; 0.1% Pac. Isl.; 1.7% other; 2+ races 2.9%. **Hispanic pop.:** 14.8%. **Foreign born:** 24.7%. **U.S. citizens:** 87.0%. **Language:** 67.6% English only; 11.6% Spanish.

Employment: 157,479 employed; 3.4% unemployment. **Per capita income:** $51,099; change (2015-16): 0.1%. **Below poverty:** 7.5%; 5.4% of families. **Educational attainment:** 93.6% HS; 55.6% bachelor's. **Avg. commute:** 26.3 min. 81.8% drive. **Housing units:** 109,915; 95.7% occupied. **Home ownership:** 61.8%. **Avg. home:** $247,400; change (2015-17): 19.4%. **Avg. rent:** $1,196. **Crime rates:** violent: 138; property: 1,901.

Mayor: Harry LaRosiliere, nonpartisan

History: Settled 1846; inc. 1873.

Website: www.plano.gov

Portland, Oregon

Population: 647,805 (26). **Pop. density:** 4,854. **Pop. change (2010-17):** 11.0%. **Area:** 133.5 sq mi. **Racial distribution:** 77.7% white; 5.7% black; 7.6% Asian; 0.7% Amer. Ind.; 0.6% Pac. Isl.; 2.4% other; 2+ races 5.2%. **Hispanic pop.:** 9.7%. **Foreign born:** 13.7%. **U.S. citizens:** 92.7%. **Language:** 81.0% English only; 6.8% Spanish.

Employment: 362,123 employed; 3.6% unemployment. **Per capita income:** $50,489; change (2015-16): 2.6%. **Below poverty:** 16.9%; 10.5% of families. **Educational attainment:** 91.6% HS; 47.0% bachelor's. **Avg. commute:** 25.6 min. 57.8% drive, 12.1% public trans. **Housing units:** 272,551; 94.1% occupied. **Home ownership:** 53.1%. **Avg. home:** $381,800; change (2015-17): 22.3%. **Avg. rent:** $1,025. **Crime rates:** violent: 493; property: 5,153.

Mayor: Ted Wheeler, nonpartisan

History: Est. 1843; developed as trading center, aided by California Gold Rush, 1849; city chartered, 1851.

Website: www.portlandoregon.gov

Raleigh, North Carolina

Population: 464,758 (41). **Pop. density:** 3,204. **Pop. change (2010-17):** 15.1%. **Area:** 145.1 sq mi. **Racial distribution:** 59.6% white; 28.9% black; 4.6% Asian; 0.3% Amer. Ind.; 0.1% Pac. Isl.; 3.9% other; 2+ races 2.5%. **Hispanic pop.:** 10.8%. **Foreign born:** 13.1%. **U.S. citizens:** 91.6%. **Language:** 83.1% English only; 9.6% Spanish.

Employment: 243,250 employed; 4.2% unemployment. **Per capita income:** $50,444; change (2015-16): 1.5%. **Below poverty:** 14.9%; 10.4% of families. **Educational attainment:** 91.3% HS; 49.2% bachelor's. **Avg. commute:** 22.7 min. 78.6% drive. **Housing units:** 190,286; 91.4% occupied. **Home ownership:** 51.1%. **Avg. home:** $266,800; change (2015-17): 12.0%. **Avg. rent:** $966. **Crime rates:** violent: NA; property: NA.

Mayor: Nancy McFarlane, nonpartisan

History: Named after Sir Walter Raleigh; chosen state capital, 1788; inc. 1795; occupied by Union Gen. Sherman, 1865.

Website: www.raleighnc.gov

Reno, Nevada

Population: 248,853 (86). **Pop. density:** 2,290. **Pop. change (2010-17):** 10.5%. **Area:** 108.7 sq mi. **Racial distribution:** 78.5% white; 2.6% black; 6.5% Asian; 1.1% Amer. Ind.; 0.8% Pac. Isl.; 6.2% other; 2+ races 4.4%. **Hispanic pop.:** 25.1%. **Foreign born:** 16.5%. **U.S. citizens:** 90.5%. **Language:** 74.3% English only; 17.8% Spanish.

Employment: 123,971 employed; 4.2% unemployment. **Per capita income:** $49,653; change (2015-16): 1.5%. **Below poverty:** 18.4%; 12.1% of families. **Educational attainment:** 86.2% HS; 30.7% bachelor's. **Avg. commute:** 19.4 min. 76.4% drive, 11.2% carpool. **Housing units:** 103,210; 90.9% occupied. **Home ownership:** 46.4%. **Avg. home:** $345,100; change (2015-17): 21.7%. **Avg. rent:** $872. **Crime rates:** violent: 702; property: 3,244.

Mayor: Hillary Schieve, nonpartisan

History: Originally named Lake's Crossing; name changed to Reno, after a Union Civil War general, 1868, with arrival of transcontinental railroad.

Website: www.reno.gov

Richmond, Virginia

Population: 227,032 (97). **Pop. density:** 3,789. **Pop. change (2010-17):** 11.2%. **Area:** 59.9 sq mi. **Racial distribution:** 44.2% white; 48.6% black; 2.1% Asian; 0.5% Amer. Ind.; <0.05% Pac. Isl.; 1.1% other; 2+ races 3.5%. **Hispanic pop.:** 6.3%. **Foreign born:** 6.5%. **U.S. citizens:** 95.7%. **Language:** 90.6% English only; 5.3% Spanish.

Employment: 111,499 employed; 4.4% unemployment. **Per capita income:** $51,685; change (2015-16): 1.4%. **Below poverty:** 25.4%; 19.4% of families. **Educational attainment:** 84.0% HS; 36.7% bachelor's. **Avg. commute:** 21.9 min. 71.0% drive, 10.7% carpool. **Housing units:** 99,883; 89.1% occupied. **Home ownership:** 41.4%. **Avg. home:** $250,500; change (2015-17): 10.2%. **Avg. rent:** $916. **Crime rates:** violent: NA; property: NA.

Mayor: Levar Stoney, nonpartisan

History: First explored, 1607; became capital of Virginia, 1779; attacked by British, 1781; inc. as city, 1782; capital of Confederate States of America, 1861-65.

Website: www.richmondgov.com

Riverside, California

Population: 327,728 (58). **Pop. density:** 4,033. **Pop. change (2010-17):** 7.9%. **Area:** 81.3 sq mi. **Racial distribution:** 64.8% white; 6.0% black; 6.9% Asian; 0.8% Amer. Ind.; 0.3% Pac. Isl.; 16.2% other; 2+ races 5.0%. **Hispanic pop.:** 52.0%. **Foreign born:** 22.4%. **U.S. citizens:** 87.1%. **Language:** 58.4% English only; 34.3% Spanish.

Employment: 145,075 employed; 4.6% unemployment. **Per capita income:** $36,807; change (2015-16): 2.9%. **Below poverty:** 17.8%; 12.8% of families. **Educational attainment:** 79.0% HS; 22.6% bachelor's. **Avg. commute:** 29.9 min. 74.4% drive, 14.4% carpool. **Housing units:** 98,109; 93.7% occupied. **Home ownership:** 54.5%. **Avg. home:** $336,000; change (2015-17): 15.6%. **Avg. rent:** $1,194. **Crime rates:** violent: 529; property: 3,457.

Mayor: William "Rusty" Bailey, nonpartisan

History: Founded 1870; inc. 1883. Known for citrus industry; home of the parent navel orange tree.

Website: riversideca.gov

Sacramento, California

Population: 501,901 (35). **Pop. density:** 5,141. **Pop. change (2010-17):** 7.6%. **Area:** 97.6 sq mi. **Racial distribution:** 49.7% white; 13.7% black; 18.4% Asian; 0.7% Amer. Ind.; 1.5% Pac. Isl.; 9.4% other; 2+ races 6.6%. **Hispanic pop.:** 28.1%. **Foreign born:** 22.4%. **U.S. citizens:** 89.8%. **Language:** 62.5% English only; 17.9% Spanish.

Employment: 220,686 employed; 4.7% unemployment. **Per capita income:** $51,370; change (2015-16): 2.7%. **Below poverty:** 21.4%; 17.1% of families. **Educational attainment:** 87.7% HS; 30.7% bachelor's. **Avg. commute:** 24.9 min. 73.8% drive, 11.3% carpool. **Housing units:** 194,034; 92.7% occupied. **Home ownership:** 46.8%. **Avg. home:** $340,000; change (2015-17): 16.8%. **Avg. rent:** $1,057. **Crime rates:** violent: 716; property: 3,085.

Mayor: Darrell Steinberg, nonpartisan

History: Est. 1839; important trading center during Gold Rush; became state capital, 1854.

Website: www.cityofsacramento.org

St. Louis, Missouri

Population: 308,626 (62). **Pop. density:** 4,981. **Pop. change (2010-17):** −3.3%. **Area:** 62.0 sq mi. **Racial distribution:** 45.6% white; 47.9% black; 3.1% Asian; 0.2% Amer. Ind.; 0.1% Pac. Isl.; 0.9% other; 2+ races 2.2%. **Hispanic pop.:** 3.9%. **Foreign born:** 6.3%. **U.S. citizens:** 96.3%. **Language:** 91.1% English only; 3.1% Spanish.

Employment: 148,881 employed; 4.4% unemployment. **Per capita income:** $49,519; change (2015-16): 1.3%. **Below poverty:** 26.7%; 21.3% of families. **Educational attainment:** 84.5% HS; 33.0% bachelor's. **Avg. commute:** 24.1 min. 71.6% drive. **Housing units:** 175,538; 79.8% occupied. **Home ownership:** 43.3%. **Avg. home:** $169,400; change (2015-17): 7.2%. **Avg. rent:** $759. **Crime rates:** violent: 1,913; property: 5,931.

Mayor: Lyda Krewson, Democrat

History: Founded 1764 as French fur trading post on Mississippi R., near confluence with Missouri R.; acquired by U.S., 1803; chartered as city, 1823.
Website: www.stlouis-mo.gov

St. Paul, Minnesota

Population: 306,621 (63). **Pop. density:** 5,900. **Pop. change (2010-17):** 7.6%. **Area:** 52.0 sq mi. **Racial distribution:** 58.6% white; 15.7% black; 17.3% Asian; 0.8% Amer. Ind.; <0.05% Pac. Isl.; 2.7% other; 2+ races 4.8%. **Hispanic pop.:** 9.4%. **Foreign born:** 18.8%. **U.S. citizens:** 90.4%. **Language:** 71.7% English only; 6.8% Spanish.
Employment: 152,489 employed; 3.3% unemployment. **Per capita income:** $56,723; change (2015-16): 2.0%. **Below poverty:** 21.6%; 16.3% of families. **Educational attainment:** 86.7% HS; 40.0% bachelor's. **Avg. commute:** 23.4 min. 69.1% drive, 10.1% carpool. **Housing units:** 119,625; 94.1% occupied. **Home ownership:** 49.5%. **Avg. home:** $252,100; change (2015-17): 12.7%. **Avg. rent:** $865. **Crime rates:** violent: 648; property: 3,228.
Mayor: Melvin Carter, nonpartisan
History: Est. c. 1840 as Pig's Eye Landing; became capital of Minnesota territory, 1849; chartered as St. Paul, 1854.
Website: www.stpaul.gov

St. Petersburg, Florida

Population: 263,255 (79). **Pop. density:** 4,262. **Pop. change (2010-17):** 7.6%. **Area:** 61.8 sq mi. **Racial distribution:** 69.0% white; 23.5% black; 3.3% Asian; 0.2% Amer. Ind.; <0.05% Pac. Isl.; 1.1% other; 2+ races 2.8%. **Hispanic pop.:** 7.7%. **Foreign born:** 10.4%. **U.S. citizens:** 95.9%. **Language:** 88.1% English only; 5.3% Spanish.
Employment: 135,455 employed; 3.7% unemployment. **Per capita income:** $43,807; change (2015-16): 1.0%. **Below poverty:** 16.4%; 11.2% of families. **Educational attainment:** 89.9% HS; 32.2% bachelor's. **Avg. commute:** 23.3 min. 79.5% drive. **Housing units:** 129,336; 82.4% occupied. **Home ownership:** 57.7%. **Avg. home:** $220,000; change (2015-17): 26.5%. **Avg. rent:** $959. **Crime rates:** violent: 665; property: 4,934.
Mayor: Rick Kriseman, nonpartisan
History: Founded 1888; inc. 1903. Site of Salvador Dali Museum.
Website: www.stpete.org

San Antonio, Texas

Population: 1,511,946 (7). **Pop. density:** 3,280. **Pop. change (2010-17):** 13.9%. **Area:** 461.0 sq mi. **Racial distribution:** 78.8% white; 7.1% black; 2.7% Asian; 0.7% Amer. Ind.; 0.1% Pac. Isl.; 8.0% other; 2+ races 2.6%. **Hispanic pop.:** 63.6%. **Foreign born:** 14.2%. **U.S. citizens:** 91.1%. **Language:** 56.0% English only; 40.1% Spanish.
Employment: 690,631 employed; 3.5% unemployment. **Per capita income:** $44,284; change (2015-16): 0.4%. **Below poverty:** 19.5%; 15.7% of families. **Educational attainment:** 81.6% HS; 25.2% bachelor's. **Avg. commute:** 23.9 min. 79.0% drive, 11.2% carpool. **Housing units:** 537,596; 91.5% occupied. **Home ownership:** 54.1%. **Avg. home:** $217,200; change (2015-17): 11.4%. **Avg. rent:** $882. **Crime rates:** violent: 718; property: 5,190.
Mayor: Ron Nirenberg, nonpartisan
History: First Spanish mission est., 1718; Battle of the Alamo, 1836; city subsequently captured by Texans; inc. 1837.
Website: www.sanantonio.gov

San Diego, California

Population: 1,419,516 (8). **Pop. density:** 4,371. **Pop. change (2010-17):** 8.6%. **Area:** 324.8 sq mi. **Racial distribution:** 64.6% white; 6.4% black; 16.8% Asian; 0.5% Amer. Ind.; 0.4% Pac. Isl.; 6.3% other; 2+ races 4.9%. **Hispanic pop.:** 30.2%. **Foreign born:** 26.5%. **U.S. citizens:** 87.3%. **Language:** 59.2% English only; 23.1% Spanish.
Employment: 686,466 employed; 3.9% unemployment. **Per capita income:** $55,168; change (2015-16): 2.2%. **Below poverty:** 15.0%; 10.3% of families. **Educational attainment:** 87.5% HS; 43.6% bachelor's. **Avg. commute:** 23.5 min. 74.8% drive. **Housing units:** 527,049; 93.0% occupied. **Home ownership:** 46.5%. **Avg. home:** $599,000; change (2015-17): 13.1%. **Avg. rent:** $1,427. **Crime rates:** violent: 377; property: 2,025.
Mayor: Kevin L. Faulconer, nonpartisan
History: Claimed by Spanish, 1542; first mission est., 1769; scene of conflict during Mexican-American War, 1846; inc. 1850.
Website: www.sandiego.gov

San Francisco, California

Population: 884,363 (13). **Pop. density:** 18,854. **Pop. change (2010-17):** 9.8%. **Area:** 46.9 sq mi. **Racial distribution:** 48.1% white; 5.4% black; 33.9% Asian; 0.3% Amer. Ind.; 0.4% Pac. Isl.; 7.0% other; 2+ races 4.9%. **Hispanic pop.:** 15.3%. **Foreign born:** 34.9%. **U.S. citizens:** 86.6%. **Language:** 56.0% English only; 11.1% Spanish.
Employment: 552,223 employed; 2.9% unemployment. **Per capita income:** $84,675; change (2015-16): 4.2%. **Below pov-erty:** 12.5%; 7.0% of families. **Educational attainment:** 87.4% HS; 54.8% bachelor's. **Avg. commute:** 32.4 min. 35.0% drive, 33.6% public trans., 10.6% walk. **Housing units:** 386,755; 92.3% occupied. **Home ownership:** 36.8%. **Avg. home:** $900,000; change (2015-17): 15.2%. **Avg. rent:** $1,632. **Crime rates:** violent: 711; property: 5,441.
Mayor: London N. Breed, nonpartisan
History: Est. by 1776; claimed by U.S., 1846; became major city during Gold Rush, 1849; inc. 1850. Devastated by earthquake, 1906.
Website: sfgov.org

San Jose, California

Population: 1,035,317 (10). **Pop. density:** 5,832. **Pop. change (2010-17):** 9.4%. **Area:** 177.5 sq mi. **Racial distribution:** 42.2% white; 3.1% black; 34.1% Asian; 0.5% Amer. Ind.; 0.4% Pac. Isl.; 14.7% other; 2+ races 5.0%. **Hispanic pop.:** 32.6%. **Foreign born:** 38.9%. **U.S. citizens:** 82.7%. **Language:** 43.5% English only; 23.3% Spanish.
Employment: 532,763 employed; 3.3% unemployment. **Per capita income:** $87,643; change (2015-16): 4.2%. **Below poverty:** 10.9%; 7.6% of families. **Educational attainment:** 82.9% HS; 40.2% bachelor's. **Avg. commute:** 28.5 min. 76.3% drive, 11.6% carpool. **Housing units:** 328,185; 96.7% occupied. **Home ownership:** 57.1%. **Avg. home:** $1,180,000; change (2015-17): 25.5%. **Avg. rent:** $1,689. **Crime rates:** violent: 373; property: 2,376.
Mayor: Sam Liccardo, nonpartisan
History: Founded by Spanish, 1777, between San Francisco and Monterey; state capital, 1849-51; inc. 1850.
Website: www.sanjoseca.gov

Santa Ana, California

Population: 334,136 (57). **Pop. density:** 12,309. **Pop. change (2010-17):** 3.0%. **Area:** 27.1 sq mi. **Racial distribution:** 47.9% white; 1.0% black; 11.0% Asian; 0.6% Amer. Ind.; 0.2% Pac. Isl.; 37.5% other; 2+ races 1.7%. **Hispanic pop.:** 77.9%. **Foreign born:** 46.1%. **U.S. citizens:** 69.4%. **Language:** 17.9% English only; 71.0% Spanish.
Employment: 153,592 employed; 3.6% unemployment. **Per capita income:** $57,160; change (2015-16): 2.8%. **Below poverty:** 21.2%; 18.7% of families. **Educational attainment:** 55.5% HS; 12.4% bachelor's. **Avg. commute:** 24.8 min. 73.1% drive, 14.0% carpool. **Housing units:** 77,106; 97.4% occupied. **Home ownership:** 44.2%. **Avg. home:** $780,000; change (2015-17): 11.4%. **Avg. rent:** $1,354. **Crime rates:** violent: 478; property: 2,069.
Mayor: Miguel Pulido, nonpartisan
History: Founded by Spanish, 1769; inc. 1886.
Website: www.santa-ana.org

Scottsdale, Arizona

Population: 249,950 (85). **Pop. density:** 1,359. **Pop. change (2010-17):** 15.0%. **Area:** 183.9 sq mi. **Racial distribution:** 88.4% white; 1.7% black; 4.1% Asian; 1.2% Amer. Ind.; 0.1% Pac. Isl.; 2.5% other; 2+ races 2.0%. **Hispanic pop.:** 10.2%. **Foreign born:** 11.1%. **U.S. citizens:** 95.2%. **Language:** 86.8% English only; 6.5% Spanish.
Employment: 134,968 employed; 3.5% unemployment. **Per capita income:** $42,218; change (2015-16): 1.9%. **Below poverty:** 9.2%; 5.9% of families. **Educational attainment:** 96.2% HS; 55.6% bachelor's. **Avg. commute:** 22.2 min. 79.1% drive, 10.7% work at home. **Housing units:** 130,007; 80.9% occupied. **Home ownership:** 65.8%. **Avg. home:** $246,700; change (2015-17): 14.0%. **Avg. rent:** $1,184. **Crime rates:** violent: 153; property: 2,365.
Mayor: W. J. "Jim" Lane, nonpartisan
History: Founded 1888 by namesake Army Chaplain Winfield Scott; inc. 1951.
Website: www.scottsdaleaz.gov

Seattle, Washington

Population: 724,745 (18). **Pop. density:** 8,645. **Pop. change (2010-17):** 19.1%. **Area:** 83.8 sq mi. **Racial distribution:** 69.2% white; 7.1% black; 14.1% Asian; 0.6% Amer. Ind.; 0.4% Pac. Isl.; 2.1% other; 2+ races 6.5%. **Hispanic pop.:** 6.6%. **Foreign born:** 18.0%. **U.S. citizens:** 91.1%. **Language:** 78.3% English only; 4.2% Spanish.
Employment: 430,608 employed; 3.4% unemployment. **Per capita income:** $64,553; change (2015-16): 2.7%. **Below poverty:** 13.0%; 6.9% of families. **Educational attainment:** 93.9% HS; 60.4% bachelor's. **Avg. commute:** 26.9 min. 49.2% drive, 20.8% public trans., 10.1% walk. **Housing units:** 322,795; 94.2% occupied. **Home ownership:** 46.2%. **Avg. home:** $465,800; change (2015-17): 22.7%. **Avg. rent:** $1,266. **Crime rates:** violent: 613; property: 5,488.
Mayor: Jenny A. Durkan, nonpartisan
History: Settled 1851; inc. 1869. Suffered severe fire, 1889; played prominent role in Alaska Gold Rush, 1897; growth followed opening of Panama Canal 1914. Center of aircraft industry during WWII.
Website: www.seattle.gov

Stockton, California

Population: 310,496 (61). **Pop. density:** 5,033. **Pop. change (2010-17):** 6.4%. **Area:** 61.7 sq mi. **Racial distribution:** 43.5% white; 11.5% black; 21.8% Asian; 0.7% Amer. Ind.; 0.8% Pac. Isl.; 12.7% other; 2+ races 8.9%. **Hispanic pop.:** 41.7%. **Foreign born:** 26.0%. **U.S. citizens:** 86.3%. **Language:** 53.9% English only; 27.1% Spanish.
Employment: 120,937 employed; 8.0% unemployment. **Per capita income:** $40,458; change (2015-16): 3.5%. **Below poverty:** 23.7%; 19.7% of families. **Educational attainment:** 74.8% HS; 17.4% bachelor's. **Avg. commute:** 28.4 min. 76.9% drive, 15.3% carpool. **Housing units:** 101,494; 92.1% occupied. **Home ownership:** 47.9%. **Avg. rent:** $967. **Crime rates:** violent: 1,421; property: 3,773.
Mayor: Michael Tubbs, nonpartisan
History: Est. 1849 to serve gold miners; inc. 1850.
Website: www.stocktongov.com

Tampa, Florida

Population: 385,430 (52). **Pop. density:** 3,398. **Pop. change (2010-17):** 14.8%. **Area:** 113.4 sq mi. **Racial distribution:** 65.4% white; 24.3% black; 4.0% Asian; 0.3% Amer. Ind.; 0.1% Pac. Isl.; 2.8% other; 2+ races 3.1%. **Hispanic pop.:** 24.3%. **Foreign born:** 15.6%. **U.S. citizens:** 91.8%. **Language:** 73.8% English only; 19.0% Spanish.
Employment: 189,317 employed; 4.0% unemployment. **Per capita income:** $43,807; change (2015-16): 1.0%. **Below poverty:** 21.2%; 16.0% of families. **Educational attainment:** 87.0% HS; 35.5% bachelor's. **Avg. commute:** 23.6 min. 78.4% drive. **Housing units:** 162,903; 88.8% occupied. **Home ownership:** 48.4%. **Avg. home:** $220,000; change (2015-17): 26.5%. **Avg. rent:** $983. **Crime rates:** violent: 507; property: 2,075.
Mayor: Bob Buckhorn, nonpartisan
History: U.S. army fort on site, 1824; inc. 1855.
Website: www.tampagov.net

Toledo, Ohio

Population: 276,491 (74). **Pop. density:** 3,426. **Pop. change (2010-17):** –3.7%. **Area:** 80.7 sq mi. **Racial distribution:** 63.5% white; 27.2% black; 1.4% Asian; 0.3% Amer. Ind.; <0.05% Pac. Isl.; 2.7% other; 2+ races 4.9%. **Hispanic pop.:** 8.2%. **Foreign born:** 3.4%. **U.S. citizens:** 98.2%. **Language:** 93.1% English only; 3.4% Spanish.
Employment: 121,558 employed; 6.6% unemployment. **Per capita income:** $43,458; change (2015-16): 2.7%. **Below poverty:** 27.5%; 22.7% of families. **Educational attainment:** 85.7% HS; 18.0% bachelor's. **Avg. commute:** 19.6 min. 83.2% drive. **Housing units:** 138,573; 85.5% occupied. **Home ownership:** 52.3%. **Avg. home:** $118,200; change (2015-17): 10.2%. **Avg. rent:** $651. **Crime rates:** violent: 1,192; property: 4,020.
Mayor: Wade Kapszukiewicz, nonpartisan
History: Site of Ft. Industry, 1800; figured in Toledo War between OH and MI over borders, 1835-36; inc. 1837.
Website: toledo.oh.gov

Tucson, Arizona

Population: 535,677 (33). **Pop. density:** 2,260. **Pop. change (2010-17):** 3.0%. **Area:** 237.0 sq mi. **Racial distribution:** 73.5% white; 5.0% black; 3.0% Asian; 2.9% Amer. Ind.; 0.2% Pac. Isl.; 11.0% other; 2+ races 4.5%. **Hispanic pop.:** 42.6%. **Foreign born:** 15.2%. **U.S. citizens:** 91.0%. **Language:** 65.9% English only; 28.8% Spanish.
Employment: 242,237 employed; 4.7% unemployment. **Per capita income:** $39,541; change (2015-16): 1.6%. **Below poverty:** 25.1%; 18.4% of families. **Educational attainment:** 84.4% HS; 25.8% bachelor's. **Avg. commute:** 22.2 min. 73.8% drive, 10.7% carpool. **Housing units:** 234,323; 88.6% occupied. **Home ownership:** 48.7%. **Avg. home:** $210,300; change (2015-17): 15.0%. **Avg. rent:** $772. **Crime rates:** violent: 795; property: 5,859.
Mayor: Jonathan Rothschild, Democrat
History: Est. 1775 by Spanish as a presidio; acquired by U.S. in Gadsden Purchase, 1854; inc. 1877.
Website: www.tucsonaz.gov

Tulsa, Oklahoma

Population: 401,800 (47). **Pop. density:** 2,034. **Pop. change (2010-17):** 2.5%. **Area:** 197.5 sq mi. **Racial distribution:** 64.5% white; 15.0% black; 3.0% Asian; 4.3% Amer. Ind.; 0.1% Pac. Isl.; 5.2% other; 2+ races 7.9%. **Hispanic pop.:** 15.4%. **Foreign born:** 10.6%. **U.S. citizens:** 92.2%. **Language:** 83.0% English only; 12.6% Spanish.
Employment: 188,441 employed; 4.5% unemployment. **Per capita income:** $50,117; change (2015-16): –7.0%. **Below poverty:** 20.3%; 16.3% of families. **Educational attainment:** 87.0% HS; 30.7% bachelor's. **Avg. commute:** 18.3 min. 80.4% drive, 11.0% carpool. **Housing units:** 187,553; 88.0% occupied. **Home ownership:** 51.1%. **Avg. home:** $160,200; change (2015-17): 6.7%. **Avg. rent:** $757. **Crime rates:** violent: 1,095; property: 5,904.
Mayor: G.T. Bynum, nonpartisan

History: Settled in 1836 by Creek Indians; modern town founded 1882; inc. 1898; oil discovered early 20th century.
Website: www.cityoftulsa.org

Virginia Beach, Virginia

Population: 450,435 (44). **Pop. density:** 1,841. **Pop. change (2010-17):** 2.8%. **Area:** 244.7 sq mi. **Racial distribution:** 67.6% white; 19.1% black; 6.5% Asian; 0.3% Amer. Ind.; 0.1% Pac. Isl.; 1.5% other; 2+ races 4.9%. **Hispanic pop.:** 7.6%. **Foreign born:** 9.1%. **U.S. citizens:** 96.5%. **Language:** 87.9% English only; 4.4% Spanish.
Employment: 224,148 employed; 3.6% unemployment. **Per capita income:** $47,019; change (2015-16): 1.1%. **Below poverty:** 8.2%; 6.4% of families. **Educational attainment:** 93.2% HS; 34.2% bachelor's. **Avg. commute:** 23.4 min. 81.9% drive. **Housing units:** 182,016; 92.0% occupied. **Home ownership:** 63.2%. **Avg. home:** $225,000; change (2015-17): 7.7%. **Avg. rent:** $1,258. **Crime rates:** violent: 155; property: 2,176.
Mayor: Louis R. Jones, nonpartisan
History: Settlement by Capt. John Smith, 1607; formed by merger with Princess Anne Co., 1963.
Website: www.vbgov.com

Washington, District of Columbia

Population: 693,972 (20). **Pop. density:** 11,351. **Pop. change (2010-17):** 15.3%. **Area:** 61.1 sq mi. **Racial distribution:** 40.4% white; 48.3% black; 3.6% Asian; 0.3% Amer. Ind.; <0.05% Pac. Isl.; 4.5% other; 2+ races 2.8%. **Hispanic pop.:** 10.5%. **Foreign born:** 14.0%. **U.S. citizens:** 91.8%. **Language:** 82.6% English only; 8.8% Spanish.
Employment: 376,633 employed; 6.1% unemployment. **Per capita income:** $66,733; change (2015-16): 2.4%. **Below poverty:** 17.9%; 14.1% of families. **Educational attainment:** 90.0% HS; 55.4% bachelor's. **Avg. commute:** 29.9 min. 33.7% drive, 36.8% public trans., 13.3% walk. **Housing units:** 306,711; 90.2% occupied. **Home ownership:** 40.7%. **Avg. home:** $406,700; change (2015-17): 6.1%. **Avg. rent:** $1,362. **Crime rates:** violent: 1,132; property: 4,648.
Mayor: Muriel Bowser, Democrat
History: U.S. capital; planned site on Potomac R. chosen by George Washington, 1790, on land ceded from VA and MD (portion S of Potomac returned to VA, 1846). Congress first met there, 1800; inc. 1802; sacked by British, War of 1812.
Website: dc.gov

Wichita, Kansas

Population: 390,591 (50). **Pop. density:** 2,432. **Pop. change (2010-17):** 2.2%. **Area:** 160.6 sq mi. **Racial distribution:** 76.2% white; 11.2% black; 5.0% Asian; 1.0% Amer. Ind.; <0.05% Pac. Isl.; 2.5% other; 2+ races 4.0%. **Hispanic pop.:** 16.4%. **Foreign born:** 10.3%. **U.S. citizens:** 94.1%. **Language:** 83.1% English only; 11.3% Spanish.
Employment: 177,439 employed; 4.4% unemployment. **Per capita income:** $47,395; change (2015-16): 0.1%. **Below poverty:** 17.1%; 12.6% of families. **Educational attainment:** 87.4% HS; 28.9% bachelor's. **Avg. commute:** 18.2 min. 84.5% drive. **Housing units:** 168,793; 89.7% occupied. **Home ownership:** 59.7%. **Avg. home:** $132,900; change (2015-17): 0.0%. **Avg. rent:** $736. **Crime rates:** violent: 1,057; property: 5,382.
Mayor: Jeff Longwell, nonpartisan
History: Founded 1864; inc. 1871.
Website: www.wichita.gov

Winston-Salem, North Carolina

Population: 244,605 (89). **Pop. density:** 1,846. **Pop. change (2010-17):** 6.5%. **Area:** 132.5 sq mi. **Racial distribution:** 56.7% white; 34.9% black; 2.0% Asian; 0.1% Amer. Ind.; 0.1% Pac. Isl.; 3.8% other; 2+ races 2.4%. **Hispanic pop.:** 14.9%. **Foreign born:** 9.7%. **U.S. citizens:** 93.3%. **Language:** 83.4% English only; 13.4% Spanish.
Employment: 111,461 employed; 4.7% unemployment. **Per capita income:** $40,910; change (2015-16): 0.8%. **Below poverty:** 24.3%; 18.1% of families. **Educational attainment:** 86.1% HS; 34.2% bachelor's. **Avg. commute:** 20.2 min. 82.5% drive. **Housing units:** 105,723; 89.3% occupied. **Home ownership:** 54.1%. **Avg. home:** $155,000; change (2015-17): 7.9%. **Avg. rent:** $734. **Crime rates:** violent: NA; property: NA.
Mayor: Allen Joines, Democrat
History: Salem founded, 1766; Winston founded, 1849; became Winston-Salem, 1913. Reynolds Building, completed 1929, used as model for Empire State Building (designed by same architects).
Website: www.cityofws.org

UNITED STATES POPULATION

Census Origins and Methods

A census is conducted in the U.S. every 10 years. The primary purpose is to apportion seats in the House of Representatives. Census data is also used to determine the boundaries of state legislative districts and the distribution of federal funds to local, state, and tribal governments.

The first U.S. census, mandated by the Constitution, was conducted in 1790, a little more than a year after George Washington became president. It counted the numbers of free white males ages 16 and over (as a measure of available workers and military personnel), free white males under 16, free white females, all other free persons, and slaves. The data was collected over 18 months, at a cost of about $44,000, or $1.2 million in current dollars. (The 2020 census, as of Oct. 2017, was expected to cost an est. $15.6 billion in total.) The 1790 census counted a total of 3.9 million people, resulting in an increase from 65 to 105 seats in the U.S. House of Representatives.

As the nation grew, so did the scope of the census. The first inquiries on manufacturing were made in 1810. Questions on "the pursuits, industry, education, and resources of the country" were added to the 1840 census. It took a full 10 years to publish the results of the 1880 and 1890 censuses due to the number of questions asked. Because of those delays, Congress limited the 1900 census to questions on population, mortality, agriculture, and manufacturing.

Today, the secretary of commerce and the Census Bureau are directed by law to collect data on population, housing, employment, agriculture, manufacturing, trade, construction, transportation, and governments, among other things, at stated intervals. They also conduct smaller-scale surveys on behalf of other federal agencies. At the Dept. of Justice's request, the Commerce Dept. announced it would add a question on citizenship status to the 2020 census.

U.S. marshals administered the earliest decennial censuses by visiting each household and reporting to the president (1790), to the secretary of state (1800-40), or to the secretary of the interior (1850-70). Trained census-takers were hired for the 1880 census and thereafter. In 1902, Congress authorized a permanent Census Office within the Interior Department. In 1903, the agency was transferred to the new Department of Commerce and Labor and remained with the Commerce Department when a separate labor department was created in 1913.

The 1790 through 1820 decennial censuses were officially enumerated the first Monday in Aug. The 1830-1900 censuses were as of June 1, though the 1890 census was not started until June 2 (June 1 was a Sunday). The 1910 census was as of Apr. 15, the 1920 census as of Jan. 1, and every census since 1930 has been for Apr. 1.

The Census Bureau began using statistical sampling techniques in the 1940s, the first modern computer in the 1950s, and enumeration by mail in the 1960s. These innovations allowed the Bureau to publish data more quickly, at a lower cost and with less burden on the public. Any personally identifiable information gathered is withheld from the public for 72 years, after which records are made available through the National Archives. The 1940 census records, the most recent set to be released, can be accessed at 1940census.archives.gov.

Prior to 2010, about five in six households responded to the short-form census while one in six households answered a long-form questionnaire, which asked about details such as ancestry, marital status, and occupation. The 2005 implementation of the American Community Survey (ACS) made the long-form questionnaire no longer necessary. Conducted yearly on a random sample of the population, the ACS gathers demographic, economic, and housing information on communities across the country.

U.S. Population by State and Region, 2000, 2017

Source: Population Estimates Program and Decennial Census, U.S. Census Bureau, U.S. Dept. of Commerce
(ranked by 2017 resident population)

Rank	State	2017[1]	2000[2]	% change, 2000-17	Rank	State	2017[1]	2000[2]	% change, 2000-17
1.	California	39,536,653	33,871,653	16.7%	29.	Connecticut	3,588,184	3,405,602	5.4%
2.	Texas	28,304,596	20,851,790	35.7	30.	Iowa	3,145,711	2,926,382	7.5
3.	Florida	20,984,400	15,982,824	31.3	31.	Utah	3,101,833	2,233,198	38.9
4.	New York	19,849,399	18,976,821	4.6	32.	Arkansas	3,004,279	2,673,400	12.4
5.	Pennsylvania	12,805,537	12,281,054	4.3	33.	Nevada	2,998,039	1,998,257	50.0
6.	Illinois	12,802,023	12,419,647	3.1	34.	Mississippi	2,984,100	2,844,656	4.9
7.	Ohio	11,658,609	11,353,145	2.7	35.	Kansas	2,913,123	2,688,824	8.3
8.	Georgia	10,429,379	8,186,816	27.4	36.	New Mexico	2,088,070	1,819,046	14.8
9.	North Carolina	10,273,419	8,046,485	27.7	37.	Nebraska	1,920,076	1,711,265	12.2
10.	Michigan	9,962,311	9,938,480	0.2	38.	West Virginia	1,815,857	1,808,350	0.4
11.	New Jersey	9,005,644	8,414,347	7.0	39.	Idaho	1,716,943	1,293,956	32.7
12.	Virginia	8,470,020	7,079,030	19.6	40.	Hawaii	1,427,538	1,211,537	17.8
13.	Washington	7,405,743	5,894,141	25.6	41.	New Hampshire	1,342,795	1,235,786	8.7
14.	Arizona	7,016,270	5,130,632	36.8	42.	Maine	1,335,907	1,274,923	4.8
15.	Massachusetts	6,859,819	6,349,105	8.0	43.	Rhode Island	1,059,639	1,048,319	1.1
16.	Tennessee	6,715,984	5,689,267	18.0	44.	Montana	1,050,493	902,195	16.4
17.	Indiana	6,666,818	6,080,517	9.6	45.	Delaware	961,939	783,600	22.8
18.	Missouri	6,113,532	5,596,683	9.2	46.	South Dakota	869,666	754,844	15.2
19.	Maryland	6,052,177	5,296,507	14.3	47.	North Dakota	755,393	642,200	17.6
20.	Wisconsin	5,795,483	5,363,715	8.0	48.	Alaska	739,795	626,931	18.0
21.	Colorado	5,607,154	4,302,015	30.3	49.	Dist. of Columbia	693,972	572,059	21.3
22.	Minnesota	5,576,606	4,919,492	13.4	50.	Vermont	623,657	608,827	2.4
23.	South Carolina	5,024,369	4,011,816	25.2	51.	Wyoming	579,315	493,782	17.3
24.	Alabama	4,874,747	4,447,351	9.6		**United States**	**325,719,178**	**281,424,603**	**15.7**
25.	Louisiana	4,684,333	4,468,958	4.8		Northeast[3]	56,470,581	53,594,784	5.4
26.	Kentucky	4,454,189	4,042,285	10.2		Midwest[4]	68,179,351	64,395,194	5.9
27.	Oregon	4,142,776	3,421,436	21.1		South[5]	123,658,624	100,235,846	23.4
28.	Oklahoma	3,930,864	3,450,652	13.9		West[6]	77,410,622	63,198,779	22.5

Note: The U.S. resident population consists of individuals whose usual residence, or where they live and sleep most of the time, is in one of the 50 states or DC. It excludes overseas U.S. military personnel and civilian U.S. citizens living abroad. (1) Estimates are as of July 1. (2) Figures are for Apr. 1 of decennial census year. Population figures may reflect revisions/corrections to initial tabulated census counts. (3) Incl. the states of the New England (Connecticut, Maine, Massachusetts, New Hampshire, Rhode Island, Vermont) and Middle Atlantic (New Jersey, New York, Pennsylvania) divisions. (4) Incl. the states of the East North Central (Illinois, Indiana, Michigan, Ohio, Wisconsin) and West North Central (Iowa, Kansas, Minnesota, Missouri, Nebraska, North Dakota, South Dakota) divisions. (5) Incl. the states of the South Atlantic (Delaware, DC, Florida, Georgia, Maryland, North Carolina, South Carolina, Virginia, West Virginia), East South Central (Alabama, Kentucky, Mississippi, Tennessee), and West South Central (Arkansas, Louisiana, Oklahoma, Texas) divisions. (6) Incl. the states of the Mountain (Arizona, Colorado, Idaho, Montana, Nevada, New Mexico, Utah, Wyoming) and Pacific (Alaska, California, Hawaii, Oregon, Washington) divisions.

Density of U.S. Population by State, 1930-2010

Source: Decennial Censuses, U.S. Census Bureau, U.S. Dept. of Commerce

(per square mile of land area, as measured for the 2010 census)

State	1930	1950	1970	1990	2010	State	1930	1950	1970	1990	2010
AL......	52.3	60.5	68.0	79.8	94.4	MT	3.7	4.1	4.8	5.5	6.8
AK......	0.1	0.2	0.5	1.0	1.2	NE......	17.9	17.3	19.3	20.5	23.8
AZ......	3.8	6.6	15.6	32.3	56.3	NV......	0.8	1.5	4.5	10.9	24.6
AR......	35.6	36.7	37.0	45.2	56.0	NH	52.0	59.6	82.4	123.9	147.0
CA......	36.4	68.0	128.1	191.0	239.1	NJ......	549.5	657.5	974.7	1,051.1	1,195.5
CO	10.0	12.8	21.3	31.8	48.5	NM	3.5	5.6	8.4	12.5	17.0
CT......	331.8	414.5	626.1	678.8	738.1	NY......	267.1	314.7	387.0	381.7	411.2
DE......	122.3	163.2	281.3	341.9	460.8	NC	65.2	83.5	104.5	136.3	196.1
DC	7,975.1	13,140.0	12,392.0	9,941.3	9,856.5	ND	9.9	9.0	9.0	9.3	9.7
FL......	27.4	51.7	126.6	241.3	350.6	OH	162.7	194.5	260.7	265.5	282.3
GA	50.6	59.9	79.8	112.6	168.4	OK	34.9	32.6	37.3	45.9	54.7
HI	57.3	77.8	119.7	172.6	211.8	OR	9.9	15.8	21.8	29.6	39.9
ID	5.4	7.1	8.6	12.2	19.0	PA......	215.3	234.6	263.6	265.6	283.9
IL......	137.4	156.9	200.2	205.9	231.1	RI	665.0	766.0	915.8	970.6	1,018.1
IN	90.4	109.8	145.0	154.8	181.0	SC......	57.8	70.4	86.2	116.0	153.9
IA	44.2	46.9	50.6	49.7	54.5	SD......	9.1	8.6	8.8	9.2	10.7
KS......	23.0	23.3	27.5	30.3	34.9	TN......	63.5	79.8	95.2	118.3	153.9
KY......	66.2	74.6	81.5	93.3	109.9	TX......	22.3	29.5	42.9	65.0	96.3
LA......	48.6	62.1	84.3	97.7	104.9	UT......	6.2	8.4	12.9	21.0	33.6
ME	25.9	29.6	32.2	39.8	43.1	VT......	39.0	41.0	48.2	61.1	67.9
MD	168.1	241.4	404.1	492.6	594.8	VA	61.3	84.0	117.7	156.7	202.6
MA	544.8	601.3	729.4	771.3	839.4	WA	23.5	35.8	51.3	73.2	101.2
MI......	85.6	112.7	157.0	164.4	174.8	WV	71.9	83.4	72.6	74.6	77.1
MN	32.2	37.5	47.8	54.9	66.6	WI......	54.3	63.4	81.6	90.3	105.0
MS	42.8	46.4	47.2	54.8	63.2	WY	2.3	3.0	3.4	4.7	5.8
MO	52.8	57.5	68.0	74.4	87.1	**U.S.**	**34.7**	**42.6**	**57.5**	**70.4**	**87.4**

Note: For the sake of comparison, the densities of Alaska and Hawaii in 1930 and 1950 are included though they were not yet states.

U.S. Area and Population, 1790-2010

Source: Decennial Censuses, U.S. Census Bureau, U.S. Dept. of Commerce

Census date	AREA (square miles)			RESIDENT POPULATION			
	Total area[1]	Land area	Water area[1]	Number	Per sq mi of land	Increase over preceding census Number	%
1790 (Aug. 2)	891,364	864,746	24,065	3,929,214	4.5	—	—
1800 (Aug. 4)	891,364	864,746	24,065	5,308,483	6.1	1,379,269	35.1%
1810 (Aug. 6)	1,722,685	1,681,828	34,175	7,239,881	4.3	1,931,398	36.4
1820 (Aug. 7)	1,792,552	1,749,462	38,544	9,638,453	5.5	2,398,572	33.1
1830 (June 1)	1,792,552	1,749,462	38,544	12,860,702	7.4	3,222,249	33.4
1840 (June 1)	1,792,552	1,749,462	38,544	17,063,453	9.8	4,203,751	32.7
1850 (June 1)	2,991,655	2,940,042	52,705	23,191,876	7.9	6,128,423	35.9
1860 (June 1)	3,021,295	2,969,640	52,747	31,443,321	10.6	8,251,445	35.6
1870 (June 1)	3,612,299	3,540,705	68,082	38,558,371	10.9	7,115,050	22.6
1880 (June 1)	3,612,299	3,540,705	68,082	50,189,209	14.2	11,630,838	30.2
1890 (June 1)	3,612,299	3,540,705	68,082	62,979,766	17.8	12,790,557	25.5
1900 (June 1)	3,618,770	3,547,314	67,901	76,212,168	21.5	13,232,402	21.0
1910 (Apr. 15)	3,618,770	3,547,045	68,170	92,228,496	26.0	16,016,328	21.0
1920 (Jan. 1)	3,618,770	3,546,931	68,284	106,021,537	29.9	13,793,041	15.0
1930 (Apr. 1)	3,618,770	3,554,608	60,607	123,202,624	34.7	17,181,087	16.2
1940 (Apr. 1)	3,618,770	3,554,608	60,607	132,164,569	37.2	8,961,945	7.3
1950 (Apr. 1)	3,618,770	3,552,206	63,005	151,325,798	42.6	19,161,229	14.5
1960 (Apr. 1)	3,618,770	3,540,911	74,212	179,323,175	50.6	27,997,377	18.5
1970 (Apr. 1)	3,618,770	3,536,855	78,444	203,302,031	57.5	23,978,856	13.4
1980 (Apr. 1)	3,618,770	3,539,289	79,481	226,542,199	64.0	23,240,168	11.4
1990 (Apr. 1)	3,717,796	3,536,278	181,518	248,718,302	70.3	22,176,103	9.8
2000 (Apr. 1)	3,794,083	3,537,438	256,645	281,424,603	79.6	32,706,301	13.1
2010 (Apr. 1)	3,796,742	3,531,905	264,837	308,746,065	87.4	27,321,462	9.7

Note: Area and population density figures represent the area within the boundaries of the U.S. under its jurisdiction on the date in question including, in some cases, considerable areas not organized or settled and not covered by the census. Beginning in 1870, area data include Alaska; from 1900 on, data include Hawaii. Population figures may reflect revisions/corrections to initial tabulated census counts. (1) Figures for 1790-1980 cover inland water only. Figures for 1990 include inland, coastal, and Great Lakes water. Figures for 2000-10 include additional territorial water.

U.S. Congressional Apportionment by Census Year, 1850-2010

Source: Decennial Censuses, U.S. Census Bureau, U.S. Dept. of Commerce

The U.S. Constitution, in Article 1, Section 2, mandates that the population be counted every 10 years so that the number of U.S. representatives can be apportioned among the states. Every state is entitled to at least one House seat. The size of a state's resident population, both citizens and noncitizens, determines if it may send additional representatives to Congress. A congressional apportionment has been made after every decennial census except for that of 1920. Prior to 1870, slaves were counted as being only three-fifths of a person in the apportionment population. Since the 1970 census (excluding 1980), overseas military personnel and federal civilian employees as well as their dependents have been allocated to a home state for apportionment purposes. Residents of the District of Columbia, Puerto Rico, and U.S. island areas are not included in the apportionment population as they lack voting seats in the U.S. House.

Under a law approved in 1941, House seats are allocated using the Huntington-Hill, or equal proportions, method. It allows for the least possible variation in the average number of people each House member represents.

The first House of Representatives, in 1789, had 65 members as provided by the Constitution. Virginia (10), Massachusetts (8), and Pennsylvania (8) had the most representatives. As the nation's population grew, the number of representatives was increased. A 1911 act fixed the total House membership at 435. (Alaska and Hawaii each gained one House seat when they became states, temporarily raising the total to 437 representatives until after the 1960 census was conducted.)

State	2010	2000	1990	1970	1950	1900	1850
AL	7	7	7	7	9	9	7
AK	1	1	1	1	1	NA	NA
AZ	9	8	6	4	2	NA	NA
AR	4	4	4	4	6	7	2
CA	53	53	52	43	30	8	2
CO	7	7	6	5	4	3	NA
CT	5	5	6	6	6	5	4
DE	1	1	1	1	1	1	1
FL	27	25	23	15	8	3	1
GA	14	13	11	10	10	11	8
HI	2	2	2	2	1	NA	NA
ID	2	2	2	2	2	1	NA
IL	18	19	20	24	25	25	9
IN	9	9	10	11	11	13	11
IA	4	5	5	6	8	11	2
KS	4	4	4	5	6	8	NA
KY	6	6	6	7	8	11	10
LA	6	7	7	8	8	7	4
ME	2	2	2	2	3	4	6
MD	8	8	8	8	7	6	6
MA	9	10	10	12	14	14	11
MI	14	15	16	19	18	12	4
MN	8	8	8	8	9	9	2
MS	4	4	5	5	6	8	5
MO	8	9	9	10	11	16	7
MT	1	1	1	2	2	1	NA
NE	3	3	3	3	4	6	NA
NV	4	3	2	1	1	1	NA
NH	2	2	2	2	2	2	3
NJ	12	13	13	15	14	10	5
NM	3	3	3	2	2	NA	NA
NY	27	29	31	39	43	37	33
NC	13	13	12	11	12	10	8
ND	1	1	1	1	2	2	NA
OH	16	18	19	23	23	21	21
OK	5	5	6	6	6	5	NA
OR	5	5	5	4	4	2	1
PA	18	19	21	25	30	32	25
RI	2	2	2	2	2	2	2
SC	7	6	6	6	6	7	6
SD	1	1	1	2	2	2	NA
TN	9	9	9	8	9	10	10
TX	36	32	30	24	22	16	2
UT	4	3	3	2	2	1	NA
VT	1	1	1	1	1	2	3
VA	11	11	11	10	10	10	13
WA	10	9	9	7	7	3	NA
WV	3	3	3	4	6	5	NA
WI	8	8	9	9	10	11	3
WY	1	1	1	1	1	1	NA
Total	**435**	**435**	**435**	**435**	**437**	**391**	**237**

NA = Not applicable.

U.S. Enslaved and "Free Colored" Population, 1790, 1820, 1860

Source: Decennial Censuses, U.S. Census Bureau, U.S. Dept. of Commerce

	1790			1820			1860		
	Enslaved	% enslaved[1]	Free colored	Enslaved	% enslaved[1]	Free colored	Enslaved	% enslaved[1]	Free colored
Northern states[2]	**40,354**	**2.1%**	**27,070**	**19,108**	**0.4%**	**99,307**	**18**	**0.0%**	**225,224**
Connecticut	2,764	1.2	2,808	97	0.0	7,870	0	0.0	8,627
New Jersey	11,423	6.2	2,762	7,557	2.7	12,460	18	0.0	25,318
New York	21,324	6.3	4,654	10,088	0.7	29,279	0	0.0	49,005
Pennsylvania	3,737	0.9	6,537	211	0.0	30,202	0	0.0	56,949
Border/disputed states	**124,353**	**27.5**	**12,056**	**248,860**	**22.4**	**55,794**	**429,403**	**13.2**	**118,652**
Delaware	8,887	15.0	3,899	4,509	6.2	12,958	1,798	1.6	19,829
Kansas	—	—	—	—	—	—	2	0.0	625
Kentucky	12,430	16.9	114	126,732	22.5	2,759	225,483	19.5	10,684
Maryland	103,036	32.2	8,043	107,397	26.4	39,730	87,189	12.7	83,942
Missouri	—	—	—	10,222	15.4	347	114,931	9.7	3,572
Southern states	**532,974**	**35.3**	**20,401**	**1,265,534**	**37.8**	**75,775**	**3,521,110**	**38.7**	**132,760**
Alabama	—	—	—	41,879	32.7	571	435,080	45.1	2,690
Arkansas	—	—	—	1,617	11.3	59	111,115	25.5	144
Florida	—	—	—	—	—	—	61,745	44.0	932
Georgia	29,264	35.5	398	149,656	43.9	1,763	462,198	43.7	3,500
Louisiana	—	—	—	69,064	45.0	10,476	331,726	46.9	18,647
Mississippi	—	—	—	32,814	43.5	458	436,631	55.2	773
North Carolina	100,572	25.5	4,975	204,917	32.1	14,712	331,059	33.4	30,463
South Carolina	107,094	43.0	1,801	258,475	51.4	6,826	402,406	57.2	9,914
Tennessee	3,417	9.6	361	80,107	18.9	2,737	275,719	24.8	7,300
Texas	—	—	—	—	—	—	182,566	30.2	355
Virginia	292,627	39.1	12,866	427,005	39.7	38,173	490,865	30.7	58,042
Total territories[3]	**—**	**—**	**—**	**4,520**	**19.4**	**2,758**	**3,229**	**1.1**	**11,434**
Total states and territories	**697,681**	**17.8**	**59,527**	**1,538,022**	**16.0**	**233,634**	**3,953,760**	**12.6**	**488,070**

Note: "Free colored" was an official Census Bureau designation in these decades. States are grouped roughly by allegiance in the Civil War. (1) Percentage of total pop., all races. (2) The following states are not listed separately but are included in totals for Northern states (relevant census years in parentheses): CA (1860), IL (1820, 1860), IN (1820, 1860), IA (1860), ME (1790, 1820, 1860), MA (1790, 1820, 1860), MI (1820, 1860), MN (1860), NH (1790, 1820, 1860), OH (1820, 1860), OR (1860), RI (1790, 1820, 1860), VT (1790, 1820, 1860), WI (1820, 1860). (3) Incl. AZ (1860), CO (1860), Dakota (1860), DC (1820, 1860), NE (1860), NV (1860), NM (1860), UT (1860), WA (1860).

U.S. Population by Official

Source: Decennial Censuses, U.S. Census Bureau,
(population figures for 1790-1860

State	1790	1800	1810	1820	1830	1840	1850	1860	1870	1880	1890	1900	1910	1920
AL	—	1	9	128	310	591	772	964	996,992	1,262,505	1,513,401	1,828,697	2,138,093	2,348,174
AK	—	—	—	—	—	—	—	—	—	33,426	32,052	63,592	64,356	55,036
AZ	—	—	—	—	—	—	—	—	9,658	40,440	88,243	122,931	204,354	334,162
AR	—	—	1	14	30	98	210	435	484,471	802,525	1,128,211	1,311,564	1,574,449	1,752,204
CA	—	—	—	—	—	—	93	380	560,247	864,694	1,213,398	1,485,053	2,377,549	3,426,861
CO	—	—	—	—	—	—	—	34	39,864	194,327	413,249	539,700	799,024	939,629
CT	238	251	262	275	298	310	371	460	537,454	622,700	746,258	908,420	1,114,756	1,380,631
DE	59	64	73	73	77	78	92	112	125,015	146,608	168,493	184,735	202,322	223,003
DC[1]	—	8	15	23	30	34	52	75	131,700	177,624	230,392	278,718	331,069	437,571
FL	—	—	—	—	35	54	87	140	187,748	269,493	391,422	528,542	752,619	968,470
GA	83	163	251	341	517	691	906	1,057	1,184,109	1,542,180	1,837,353	2,216,331	2,609,121	2,895,832
HI	—	—	—	—	—	—	—	—	—	—	—	154,001	191,874	255,881
ID	—	—	—	—	—	—	—	—	14,999	32,610	88,548	161,772	325,594	431,866
IL	—	—	12	55	157	476	851	1,712	2,539,891	3,077,871	3,826,352	4,821,550	5,638,591	6,485,280
IN	—	6	25	147	343	686	988	1,350	1,680,637	1,978,301	2,192,404	2,516,462	2,700,876	2,930,390
IA	—	—	—	—	—	43	192	675	1,194,020	1,624,615	1,912,297	2,231,853	2,224,771	2,404,021
KS	—	—	—	—	—	—	—	107	364,399	996,096	1,428,108	1,470,495	1,690,949	1,769,257
KY[1]	74	221	407	564	688	780	982	1,156	1,321,011	1,648,690	1,858,635	2,147,174	2,289,905	2,416,630
LA	—	—	77	153	216	352	518	708	726,915	939,946	1,118,588	1,381,625	1,656,388	1,798,509
ME[2]	97	152	229	298	399	502	583	628	626,915	648,936	661,086	694,466	742,371	768,014
MD	320	342	381	407	447	470	583	687	780,894	934,943	1,042,390	1,188,044	1,295,346	1,449,661
MA[2]	379	423	472	523	610	738	995	1,231	1,457,351	1,783,085	2,238,947	2,805,346	3,366,416	3,852,356
MI	—	—	5	7	28	212	398	749	1,184,059	1,636,937	2,093,890	2,420,982	2,810,173	3,668,412
MN	—	—	—	—	—	—	6	172	439,706	780,773	1,310,283	1,751,394	2,075,708	2,387,125
MS	—	8	31	75	137	376	607	791	827,922	1,131,597	1,289,600	1,551,270	1,797,114	1,790,618
MO	—	—	20	67	140	384	682	1,182	1,721,295	2,168,380	2,679,185	3,106,665	3,293,335	3,404,055
MT	—	—	—	—	—	—	—	—	20,595	39,159	142,924	243,329	376,053	548,889
NE	—	—	—	—	—	—	—	29	122,993	452,402	1,062,656	1,066,300	1,192,214	1,296,372
NV	—	—	—	—	—	—	—	7	42,491	62,266	47,355	42,335	81,875	77,407
NH	142	184	214	244	269	285	318	326	318,300	346,991	376,530	411,588	430,572	443,083
NJ	184	211	246	278	321	373	490	672	906,096	1,131,116	1,444,933	1,883,669	2,537,167	3,155,900
NM	—	—	—	—	—	—	62	94	91,874	119,565	160,282	195,310	327,301	360,350
NY	340	589	959	1,373	1,919	2,429	3,097	3,881	4,382,759	5,082,871	6,003,174	7,268,894	9,113,614	10,385,227
NC	394	478	557	639	738	753	869	993	1,071,361	1,399,750	1,617,949	1,893,810	2,206,287	2,559,123
ND[3]	—	—	—	—	—	—	—	—	2,405	36,909	190,983	319,146	577,056	646,872
OH	—	42	231	581	938	1,519	1,980	2,340	2,665,260	3,198,062	3,672,329	4,157,545	4,767,121	5,759,394
OK[4]	—	—	—	—	—	—	—	—	—	—	258,657	790,391	1,657,155	2,028,283
OR	—	—	—	—	—	—	12	52	90,923	174,768	317,704	413,536	672,765	783,389
PA	434	602	810	1,049	1,348	1,724	2,312	2,906	3,521,951	4,282,891	5,258,113	6,302,115	7,665,111	8,720,017
RI	69	69	77	83	97	109	148	175	217,353	276,531	345,506	428,556	542,610	604,397
SC	249	346	415	503	581	594	669	704	705,606	995,577	1,151,149	1,340,316	1,515,400	1,683,724
SD[3]	—	—	—	—	—	—	—	5	11,776	98,268	348,600	401,570	583,888	636,547
TN	36	106	262	423	682	829	1,003	1,110	1,258,520	1,542,359	1,767,518	2,020,616	2,184,789	2,337,885
TX	—	—	—	—	—	—	213	604	818,579	1,591,749	2,235,527	3,048,710	3,896,542	4,663,228
UT	—	—	—	—	—	—	11	40	86,336	143,963	210,779	276,749	373,351	449,396
VT	85	154	218	236	281	292	314	315	330,551	332,286	332,422	343,641	355,956	352,428
VA[1]	692	808	878	938	1,044	1,025	1,119	1,220	1,225,163	1,512,565	1,655,980	1,854,184	2,061,612	2,309,187
WA	—	—	—	—	—	—	1	12	23,955	75,116	357,232	518,103	1,141,990	1,356,621
WV[1]	56	79	105	137	177	225	302	377	442,014	618,457	762,794	958,800	1,221,119	1,463,701
WI	—	—	—	—	—	31	305	776	1,054,670	1,315,497	1,693,330	2,069,042	2,333,860	2,632,067
WY	—	—	—	—	—	—	—	—	9,118	20,789	62,555	92,531	145,965	194,402
U.S.[5]	**3,929**	**5,308**	**7,240**	**9,638**	**12,861**	**17,063**	**23,192**	**31,443**	**38,558,371**	**50,189,209**	**62,979,766**	**76,212,168**	**92,228,496**	**106,021,537**

Note: With some exceptions, pop. shown is number of residents in a state (or territory of the same name) at the time of each decennial census. Figures may differ from originally published census data because of revisions. Excl. overseas U.S. military personnel and civilian U.S. citizens living abroad. (1) 1790-1860 VA figures are for present-day boundaries. That is, they incl. pop. in areas then part of DC (1800-40) and excl. pop. of areas that went to KY (1790) and WV (1790-1860). (2) 1790-1810 figures for MA do not incl. district taken to form state of ME in 1820. (3) 1860 SD figure is for area reported as "unorganized Dakota"; 1870-80 figures are for present-day ND and SD. (4) 1860-1900 figures incl. pop. for Indian Terr. (5) 1830-40 totals excl. persons (5,318 in 1830; 6,100 in 1840) on public ships in service of the U.S. not credited to any state. 1890 total incl. Indian Terr. and Indian Reservations pop. (325,464) specially enumerated.

Estimated Population of American Colonies, 1630-1780

Source: U.S. Census Bureau, U.S. Dept. of Commerce
(numbers in thousands)

Colony	1630	1650	1670	1690	1700	1720	1740	1750	1760	1770	1780
Total	4.6	50.4	111.9	210.4	250.9	466.2	905.6	1,170.8	1,593.6	2,148.1	2,780.4
Connecticut	—	4.1	12.6	21.6	26.0	58.8	89.6	111.3	142.5	183.9	206.7
Delaware	—	0.2	0.7	1.5	2.5	5.4	19.9	28.7	33.3	35.5	45.4
Georgia	—	—	—	—	—	—	2.0	5.2	9.6	23.4	56.1
Kentucky[1]	—	—	—	—	—	—	—	—	—	15.7	45.0
Maine (counties)[2]	0.4	1.0	—	—	—	—	—	—	20.0	31.3	49.1
Maryland	—	4.5	13.2	24.0	29.6	66.1	116.1	141.1	162.3	202.6	245.5
Massachusetts and Plymouth[2,3]	0.9	15.6	35.3	56.9	55.9	91.0	151.6	188.0	202.6	235.3	268.6
New Hampshire	0.5	1.3	1.8	4.2	5.0	9.4	23.3	27.5	39.1	62.4	87.8
New Jersey	—	—	1.0	8.0	14.0	29.8	51.4	71.4	93.8	117.4	139.6
New York	0.4	4.1	5.8	13.9	19.1	36.9	63.7	76.7	117.1	162.9	210.5
North Carolina	—	—	3.9	7.6	10.7	21.3	51.8	73.0	110.4	197.2	270.1
Pennsylvania	—	—	—	11.4	18.0	31.0	85.6	119.7	183.7	240.1	327.3
Rhode Island	—	0.8	2.2	4.2	5.9	11.7	25.3	33.2	45.5	58.2	52.9
South Carolina	—	—	0.2	3.9	5.7	17.0	45.0	64.0	94.1	124.2	180.0
Tennessee[4]	—	—	—	—	—	—	—	—	—	1.0	10.0
Vermont[5]	—	—	—	—	—	—	—	—	—	10.0	47.6
Virginia	2.5	18.7	35.3	53.0	58.6	87.8	180.4	231.0	339.7	447.0	538.0

Note: With the exception of KY, ME, Plymouth, TN, and VT, colonies shown are the original 13 states (ratified the Constitution 1787-90). (1) Admitted as state 1792. (2) For 1660-1750, the pop. of ME counties are included with MA. ME was annexed by MA in the 1650s but became a separate state in 1820. (3) Plymouth became part of Prov. of Massachusetts in 1691. (4) Admitted as state 1796. (5) Admitted as state 1791.

Census, 1790-2010
U.S. Dept. of Commerce
only are in thousands)

1930	1940	1950	1960	1970	1980	1990	2000	2010	State
2,646,248	2,832,961	3,061,743	3,266,740	3,444,354	3,894,025	4,040,389	4,447,351	4,779,753	AL
59,278	72,524	128,643	226,167	302,583	401,851	550,043	626,931	710,235	AK
435,573	499,261	749,587	1,302,161	1,775,399	2,716,546	3,665,339	5,130,632	6,392,017	AZ
1,854,482	1,949,387	1,909,511	1,786,272	1,923,322	2,286,357	2,350,624	2,673,400	2,915,919	AR
5,677,251	6,907,387	10,586,223	15,717,204	19,971,069	23,667,764	29,758,213	33,871,653	37,253,956	CA
1,035,791	1,123,296	1,325,089	1,753,947	2,209,596	2,889,735	3,294,473	4,302,015	5,029,196	CO
1,606,903	1,709,242	2,007,280	2,535,234	3,032,217	3,107,564	3,287,116	3,405,602	3,574,097	CT
238,380	266,505	318,085	446,292	548,104	594,338	666,168	783,600	897,934	DE
486,869	663,091	802,178	763,956	756,668	638,432	606,900	572,059	601,767	DC
1,468,211	1,897,414	2,771,305	4,951,560	6,791,418	9,746,961	12,938,071	15,982,824	18,801,332	FL
2,908,506	3,123,723	3,444,578	3,943,116	4,587,930	5,462,982	6,478,149	8,186,816	9,687,850	GA
368,300	422,770	499,794	632,772	769,913	964,691	1,108,229	1,211,537	1,360,301	HI
445,032	524,873	588,637	667,191	713,015	944,127	1,006,734	1,293,956	1,567,652	ID
7,630,654	7,897,241	8,712,176	10,081,158	11,110,285	11,427,409	11,430,602	12,419,647	12,830,632	IL
3,238,503	3,427,796	3,934,224	4,662,498	5,195,392	5,490,210	5,544,156	6,080,517	6,483,802	IN
2,470,939	2,538,268	2,621,073	2,757,537	2,825,368	2,913,808	2,776,831	2,926,382	3,046,355	IA
1,880,999	1,801,028	1,905,299	2,178,611	2,249,071	2,364,236	2,477,588	2,688,824	2,853,118	KS
2,614,589	2,845,627	2,944,806	3,038,156	3,220,711	3,660,324	3,686,892	4,042,285	4,339,367	KY
2,101,593	2,363,880	2,683,516	3,257,022	3,644,637	4,206,116	4,220,164	4,468,958	4,533,372	LA
797,423	847,226	913,774	969,265	993,722	1,125,043	1,227,928	1,274,923	1,328,361	ME
1,631,526	1,821,244	2,343,001	3,100,689	3,923,897	4,216,933	4,780,753	5,296,507	5,773,626	MD
4,249,614	4,316,721	4,690,514	5,148,578	5,689,170	5,737,093	6,016,425	6,349,105	6,547,629	MA
4,842,325	5,256,106	6,371,766	7,823,194	8,881,826	9,262,044	9,295,287	9,938,480	9,883,706	MI
2,563,953	2,792,300	2,982,483	3,413,864	3,806,103	4,075,970	4,375,665	4,919,492	5,303,925	MN
2,009,821	2,183,796	2,178,914	2,178,141	2,216,994	2,520,770	2,575,475	2,844,656	2,967,297	MS
3,629,367	3,784,664	3,954,653	4,319,813	4,677,623	4,916,766	5,116,901	5,596,683	5,988,927	MO
537,606	559,456	591,024	674,767	694,409	786,690	799,065	902,195	989,415	MT
1,377,963	1,315,834	1,325,510	1,411,330	1,485,333	1,569,825	1,578,417	1,711,265	1,826,341	NE
91,058	110,247	160,083	285,278	488,738	800,508	1,201,675	1,998,257	2,700,551	NV
465,293	491,524	533,242	606,921	737,681	920,610	1,109,252	1,235,786	1,316,470	NH
4,041,334	4,160,165	4,835,329	6,066,782	7,171,112	7,365,011	7,730,188	8,414,347	8,791,909	NJ
423,317	531,818	681,187	951,023	1,017,055	1,303,302	1,515,069	1,819,046	2,059,181	NM
12,588,066	13,479,142	14,830,192	16,782,304	18,241,391	17,558,165	17,990,778	18,976,821	19,378,102	NY
3,170,276	3,571,623	4,061,929	4,556,155	5,084,411	5,880,095	6,632,448	8,046,485	9,535,483	NC
680,845	641,935	619,636	632,446	617,792	652,717	638,800	642,200	672,591	ND
6,646,697	6,907,612	7,946,627	9,706,397	10,657,423	10,797,603	10,847,115	11,353,145	11,536,504	OH
2,396,040	2,336,434	2,233,351	2,328,284	2,559,463	3,025,487	3,145,576	3,450,652	3,751,351	OK
953,786	1,089,684	1,521,341	1,768,687	2,091,533	2,633,156	2,842,337	3,421,436	3,831,074	OR
9,631,350	9,900,180	10,498,012	11,319,366	11,800,766	11,864,720	11,882,842	12,281,054	12,702,379	PA
687,497	713,346	791,896	859,488	949,723	947,154	1,003,464	1,048,319	1,052,567	RI
1,738,765	1,899,804	2,117,027	2,382,594	2,590,713	3,120,729	3,486,310	4,011,816	4,625,364	SC
692,849	642,961	652,740	680,514	666,257	690,768	696,004	754,844	814,191	SD
2,616,556	2,915,841	3,291,718	3,567,089	3,926,018	4,591,023	4,877,203	5,689,267	6,346,105	TN
5,824,715	6,414,824	7,711,194	9,579,677	11,198,655	14,225,513	16,986,335	20,851,790	25,145,565	TX
507,847	550,310	688,862	890,627	1,059,273	1,461,037	1,722,850	2,233,198	2,763,885	UT
359,611	359,231	377,747	389,881	444,732	511,456	562,758	608,827	625,741	VT
2,421,851	2,677,773	3,318,680	3,966,949	4,651,448	5,346,797	6,189,197	7,079,030	8,001,024	VA
1,563,396	1,736,191	2,378,963	2,853,214	3,413,244	4,132,353	4,866,669	5,894,141	6,724,540	WA
1,729,205	1,901,974	2,005,552	1,860,421	1,744,237	1,950,186	1,793,477	1,808,350	1,852,994	WV
2,939,006	3,137,587	3,434,575	3,951,777	4,417,821	4,705,642	4,891,769	5,363,715	5,686,986	WI
225,565	250,742	290,529	330,066	332,416	469,557	453,589	493,782	563,626	WY
123,202,624	132,164,569	151,325,798	179,323,175	203,302,031	226,542,199	248,718,302	281,424,603	308,746,065	U.S.

U.S. Center of Population, 1790-2010

Source: Decennial Censuses, Geography Division, U.S. Census Bureau, U.S. Dept. of Commerce

The country's **(mean) center of population** is the center of population gravity. In other words, it is the point upon which the U.S. would balance if the country were a rigid, weightless plane and its population was distributed thereon, with each individual assuming an equal weight.

Census year	N Latitude °	′	″	W Longitude °	′	″	Approximate location
1790	39	16	30	76	11	12	Kent Co., MD, 23 miles east of Baltimore
1800	39	16	6	76	56	30	Howard Co., MD, 18 miles west of Baltimore
1810	39	11	30	77	37	12	Loudoun Co., VA, 40 miles northwest by west of Washington, DC
1820	39	5	42	78	33	0	Hardy Co., WV[1], 16 miles east of Moorefield
1830	38	57	54	79	16	54	Grant Co., WV[1], 19 miles west-southwest of Moorefield
1840	39	2	0	80	18	0	Upshur Co., WV[1], 16 miles south of Clarksburg
1850	38	59	0	81	19	0	Wirt Co., WV[1], 23 miles southeast of Parkersburg
1860	39	0	24	82	48	48	Pike Co., OH, 20 miles south by east of Chillicothe
1870	39	12	0	83	35	42	Highland Co., OH, 48 miles east by north of Cincinnati
1880	39	4	8	84	39	40	Boone Co., KY, 8 miles west by south of Cincinnati, OH
1890	39	11	56	85	32	53	Decatur Co., IN, 20 miles east of Columbus
1900	39	9	36	85	48	54	Bartholomew Co., IN, 6 miles southeast of Columbus
1910	39	10	12	86	32	20	Monroe Co., IN, in the city of Bloomington
1920	39	10	21	86	43	15	Owen Co., IN, 8 miles south-southeast of Spencer
1930	39	3	45	87	8	6	Greene Co., IN, 3 miles northeast of Linton
1940	38	56	54	87	22	35	Sullivan Co., IN, 2 miles southeast by east of Carlisle
1950	38	50	21	88	9	33	Richland Co., IL, 8 miles north-northwest of Olney
1950[2]	38	48	15	88	22	8	Clay Co., IL, 3 miles northeast of Louisville
1960[2]	38	35	58	89	12	35	Clinton Co., IL, 6.5 miles northwest of Centralia
1970[2]	38	27	47	89	42	22	St. Clair Co., IL, 5 miles east-southeast of Mascoutah
1980[2]	38	8	13	90	34	26	Jefferson Co., MO, 0.25 mile west of DeSoto
1990[2]	37	52	20	91	12	55	Crawford Co., MO, 9.7 miles southeast of Steelville
2000[2]	37	41	49	91	48	34	Phelps Co., MO, 2.8 miles east of Edgar Springs
2010[2]	37	31	3	92	10	23	Texas Co., MO, 2.7 miles northeast of Plato

(1) Pres. Lincoln signed a bill Dec. 31, 1862, approving statehood for West Virginia (made up of former Virginia counties). It was admitted to the Union June 20, 1863. (2) Incl. Alaska and Hawaii.

U.S. Population by Sex, Race, Residence, and Median Age, 1790-2010

Source: Decennial Censuses, U.S. Census Bureau, U.S. Dept. of Commerce

(numbers in thousands, unless otherwise noted)

Census date	SEX Male	SEX Female	RACE[2] White	RACE[2] Black Number	RACE[2] Black % tot. pop.	RACE[2] Other	RESIDENCE Urban[3]	RESIDENCE Rural	MEDIAN AGE (years) All races	MEDIAN AGE (years) White[2]	MEDIAN AGE (years) Black[2]
Conterminous U.S.[1]											
1790 (Aug. 2)	NA	NA	3,172	757	19.3%	NA	202	3,728	NA	NA	NA
1800 (Aug. 4)	NA	NA	4,306	1,002	18.9	NA	322	4,986	NA	NA	NA
1810 (Aug. 6)	NA	NA	5,862	1,378	19.0	NA	525	6,714	NA	16.0	NA
1820 (Aug. 7)	4,897	4,742	7,867	1,772	18.4	NA	693	8,945	16.7	16.6	17.2
1830 (June 1)	6,532	6,334	10,537	2,329	18.1	NA	1,127	11,733	17.2	17.3	17.2
1840 (June 1)	8,689	8,381	14,196	2,874	16.8	NA	1,845	15,218	17.8	17.9	17.6
1850 (June 1)	11,838	11,354	19,553	3,639	15.7	NA	3,574	19,617	18.9	19.2	17.4
1860 (June 1)	16,085	15,358	26,923	4,442	14.1	79	6,217	25,227	19.4	19.7	17.5
1870 (June 1)	19,494	19,065	33,589	4,880	12.7	89	9,902	28,656	20.2	20.4	18.5
1880 (June 1)	25,519	24,637	43,403	6,581	13.1	172	14,130	36,059	20.9	21.4	18.0
1890 (June 1)	32,237	30,711	55,101	7,489	11.9	358	22,106	40,874	22.0	22.5	17.8
1900 (June 1)	38,816	37,178	66,809	8,834	11.6	351	30,215	45,997	22.9	23.4	19.4
1910 (Apr. 15).......	47,332	44,640	81,732	9,828	10.7	413	42,064	50,164	24.1	24.5	20.8
1920 (Jan. 1)	53,900	51,810	94,821	10,463	9.9	427	54,253	51,768	25.3	25.5	22.3
1930 (Apr. 1).......	62,137	60,638	110,287	11,891	9.7	597	69,161	54,042	26.5	26.9	23.5
1940 (Apr. 1).......	66,062	65,608	118,215	12,866	9.8	589	74,705	57,459	29.0	29.5	25.3
United States											
1950 (Apr. 1).......	74,833	75,864	135,150	15,045	10.0	713	96,847	54,479	30.2	30.8	26.1
1960 (Apr. 1).......	88,331	90,992	158,832	18,872	10.5	1,620	125,269	54,054	29.5	30.3	23.5
1970 (Apr. 1).......	98,926	104,309	178,098	22,581	11.1	2,557	149,647	53,565	28.1	28.9	22.4
1980 (Apr. 1).......	110,053	116,493	194,713	26,683	11.8	5,150	167,051	59,495	30.0	30.9	24.9
1990 (Apr. 1).......	121,284	127,507	208,741	30,517	12.3	9,533	187,053	61,656	32.8	33.7	27.9
2000 (Apr. 1).......	138,054	143,368	194,553	34,658	12.3	13,118	222,361	59,061	35.3	38.6	30.2
2010 (Apr. 1).......	151,781	156,964	196,818	38,929	12.6	18,147	249,253	59,492	37.2	42.0	32.4

NA = Not available. **Note:** Population figures may reflect revisions/corrections to initial tabulated census counts. (1) Excludes Alaska and Hawaii. (2) New race categories were introduced in the 2000 census. Race data for 2000 and on are for people who reported being of one race alone. "White" does not include people who reported being of Hispanic or Latino origin. "Other" comprises Asians, Native Hawaiians and other Pacific Islanders, American Indians and Alaska Natives. Because of these changes, race data from 2000 on are not comparable to figures from previous years. (3) The Census Bureau's definition of "urban" has changed over time. Figures for 2000 and 2010 include residents of urbanized areas (50,000 or more inhabitants) and urban clusters (at least 2,500 but fewer than 50,000 inhabitants).

U.S. Population by Race and Hispanic Origin, 2000-10

Source: Decennial Censuses, U.S. Census Bureau, U.S. Dept. of Commerce

	2010 One race alone	2010 One or more races[1]	2000 One race alone	2000 One or more races[1]	% change, 2000-10[2] One race alone	% change, 2000-10[2] One or more races
Total population	299,736,465	308,746,065	274,595,678	281,421,906	9.2%	9.7%
Race						
White.........................	223,553,265	231,040,398	211,460,626	216,930,975	5.7	6.5
Black or African American...........	38,929,319	42,020,743	34,658,190	36,419,434	12.3	15.4
Asian.........................	14,674,252	17,320,856	10,242,998	11,898,828	43.3	45.6
American Indian and Alaska Native ...	2,932,248	5,220,579	2,475,956	4,119,301	18.4	26.7
Native Hawaiian and other Pac. Isl. ...	540,013	1,225,195	398,835	874,414	35.4	40.1
Some other race	19,107,368	21,748,084	15,359,073	18,521,486	24.4	17.4
Hispanic origin and race						
Hispanic or Latino, any race	47,435,002	50,477,594	33,081,736	35,305,818	43.4	43.0
Not Hispanic or Latino..............	252,301,463	258,267,944	241,513,942	246,116,088	4.5	4.9
White	196,817,552	201,856,108	194,552,774	198,177,900	1.2	1.9
Black or African American	37,685,848	40,123,525	33,947,837	35,383,751	11.0	13.4
Asian	14,465,124	16,722,710	10,123,169	11,579,494	42.9	44.4
American Indian and Alaska Native..	2,247,098	4,029,675	2,068,883	3,444,700	8.6	17.0
Native Hawaiian and other Pac. Isl.	481,576	1,014,888	353,509	748,149	36.2	35.7
Some other race	604,265	1,033,866	467,770	1,770,645	29.2	−41.6

Note: Population figures may reflect revisions/corrections to initial tabulated census counts. (1) Alone or in combination with one or more of the other races listed. Numbers do not add up to totals because of individuals reporting more than one race. (2) An error in data processing resulted in the overstatement in the 2000 census of the number of people reporting more than one race, in particular race combinations involving some other race. Percent change in multiple-race populations between 2000 and 2010 should ideally be calculated with specific race combinations (e.g., White and Black or White and Asian).

U.S. Population Growth by Race and Hispanic Origin, 1970-2030

Source: Decennial Censuses and Population Projections Program, U.S. Census Bureau, U.S. Dept. of Commerce
(numbers in millions)

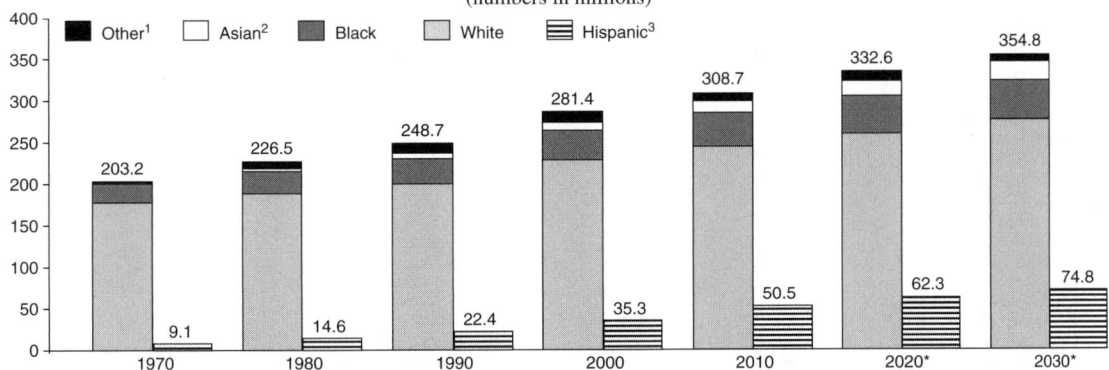

*Projected. **Note:** Because of changes in census questions and methods, data on race and Hispanic origin are not wholly comparable over time. Population figures may reflect revisions/corrections to initial tabulated census counts. (1) Includes American Indians and Alaska Natives as well as other races not shown. For 2000 and on, this category also includes Native Hawaiians and other Pacific Islanders along with persons reporting two or more races. (2) Figures for 1970-90 include Pacific Islanders. (3) May be of any race. 1970 figure is based on sample of households.

State Population by Race and Hispanic Origin, 2010

Source: Decennial Census, U.S. Census Bureau, U.S. Dept. of Commerce
(percentage of state or country's total population)

State	One race alone[1]						Two or more races[1]	Hispanic or Latino, any race
	White	Black or African American	Asian	American Indian and Alaska Native	Native Hawaiian and other Pacific Islander	Some other race		
Alabama	67.0%	26.0%	1.1%	0.5%	0.04%	0.08%	1.3%	3.9%
Alaska	64.1	3.1	5.3	14.4	1.02	0.16	6.4	5.5
Arizona	57.8	3.7	2.7	4.0	0.17	0.13	1.8	29.6
Arkansas	74.5	15.3	1.2	0.7	0.19	0.07	1.6	6.4
California	40.1	5.8	12.8	0.4	0.35	0.23	2.6	37.6
Colorado	70.0	3.8	2.7	0.6	0.11	0.15	2.0	20.7
Connecticut	71.2	9.4	3.8	0.2	0.03	0.34	1.7	13.4
Delaware	65.3	20.8	3.2	0.3	0.03	0.17	2.0	8.2
District of Columbia	34.8	50.0	3.5	0.2	0.04	0.24	2.1	9.1
Florida	57.9	15.2	2.4	0.3	0.05	0.26	1.5	22.5
Georgia	55.9	30.0	3.2	0.2	0.05	0.20	1.6	8.8
Hawaii	22.7	1.5	37.7	0.2	9.43	0.14	19.4	8.9
Idaho	84.0	0.6	1.2	1.1	0.14	0.10	1.7	11.2
Illinois	63.7	14.3	4.5	0.1	0.02	0.12	1.4	15.8
Indiana	81.5	9.0	1.6	0.2	0.03	0.13	1.5	6.0
Iowa	88.7	2.9	1.7	0.3	0.06	0.07	1.4	5.0
Kansas	78.2	5.7	2.3	0.8	0.07	0.10	2.3	10.5
Kentucky	86.3	7.7	1.1	0.2	0.05	0.11	1.5	3.1
Louisiana	60.3	31.8	1.5	0.6	0.03	0.15	1.3	4.2
Maine	94.4	1.1	1.0	0.6	0.02	0.08	1.4	1.3
Maryland	54.7	29.0	5.5	0.2	0.04	0.21	2.2	8.2
Massachusetts	76.1	6.0	5.3	0.2	0.02	0.94	1.9	9.6
Michigan	76.6	14.0	2.4	0.6	0.02	0.10	1.9	4.4
Minnesota	83.1	5.1	4.0	1.0	0.04	0.11	1.9	4.7
Mississippi	58.0	36.9	0.9	0.5	0.03	0.06	0.9	2.7
Missouri	81.0	11.5	1.6	0.4	0.10	0.09	1.8	3.5
Montana	87.8	0.4	0.6	6.1	0.06	0.05	2.2	2.9
Nebraska	82.1	4.4	1.7	0.8	0.05	0.12	1.6	9.2
Nevada	54.1	7.7	7.1	0.9	0.57	0.18	2.9	26.5
New Hampshire	92.3	1.0	2.1	0.2	0.02	0.14	1.4	2.8
New Jersey	59.3	12.8	8.2	0.1	0.02	0.31	1.5	17.7
New Mexico	40.5	1.7	1.3	8.5	0.06	0.18	1.4	46.3
New York	58.3	14.4	7.3	0.3	0.03	0.42	1.7	17.6
North Carolina	65.3	21.2	2.2	1.1	0.06	0.16	1.6	8.4
North Dakota	88.9	1.1	1.0	5.3	0.04	0.05	1.5	2.0
Ohio	81.1	12.0	1.7	0.2	0.03	0.13	1.8	3.1
Oklahoma	68.7	7.3	1.7	8.2	0.11	0.08	5.1	8.9
Oregon	78.5	1.7	3.6	1.1	0.33	0.14	2.9	11.7
Pennsylvania	79.5	10.4	2.7	0.1	0.02	0.13	1.4	5.7
Rhode Island	76.4	4.9	2.8	0.4	0.03	0.84	2.2	12.4
South Carolina	64.1	27.7	1.3	0.4	0.05	0.12	1.4	5.1
South Dakota	84.7	1.2	0.9	8.5	0.04	0.06	1.8	2.7
Tennessee	75.6	16.5	1.4	0.3	0.04	0.10	1.4	4.6
Texas	45.3	11.5	3.8	0.3	0.07	0.14	1.3	37.6
Utah	80.4	0.9	2.0	1.0	0.87	0.13	1.8	13.0
Vermont	94.3	0.9	1.3	0.3	0.02	0.09	1.6	1.5
Virginia	64.8	19.0	5.5	0.3	0.06	0.19	2.3	7.9
Washington	72.5	3.4	7.1	1.3	0.58	0.18	3.7	11.2
West Virginia	93.2	3.4	0.7	0.2	0.02	0.06	1.3	1.2
Wisconsin	83.3	6.2	2.3	0.9	0.03	0.07	1.4	5.9
Wyoming	85.9	0.8	0.8	2.1	0.06	0.08	1.5	8.9
United States	**63.7**	**12.2**	**4.7**	**0.7**	**0.16**	**0.20**	**1.9**	**16.3**

Note: Population figures may reflect revisions/corrections to initial tabulated census counts. (1) Not Hispanic or Latino.

American Indian and Alaska Native Population by State, 2010

Source: Decennial Census, U.S. Census Bureau, U.S. Dept. of Commerce
(ranked by one race alone)

Rank	State	One race alone[1]	More than one race[2]	Rank	State	One race alone[1]	More than one race[2]
1.	California	362,801	360,424	27.	Kansas	28,150	30,980
2.	Oklahoma	321,687	161,073	28.	Missouri	27,376	45,000
3.	Arizona	296,529	56,857	29.	Pennsylvania	26,843	54,249
4.	New Mexico	193,222	26,290	30.	Ohio	25,292	64,832
5.	Texas	170,972	144,292	31.	Arkansas	22,248	25,340
6.	North Carolina	122,110	61,972	32.	Idaho	21,441	14,944
7.	New York	106,906	114,152	33.	Maryland	20,420	38,237
8.	Alaska	104,871	33,441	34.	Tennessee	19,994	34,880
9.	Washington	103,869	95,129	35.	South Carolina	19,524	22,647
10.	South Dakota	71,817	10,256	36.	Massachusetts	18,850	31,855
11.	Florida	71,458	91,104	37.	Indiana	18,462	31,276
12.	Montana	62,555	16,046	38.	Nebraska	18,427	11,389
13.	Michigan	62,007	77,088	39.	Mississippi	15,030	10,880
14.	Minnesota	60,916	40,984	40.	Wyoming	13,336	5,260
15.	Colorado	56,010	51,822	41.	Connecticut	11,256	19,884
16.	Wisconsin	54,526	31,702	42.	Iowa	11,084	13,427
17.	Oregon	53,203	56,020	43.	Kentucky	10,120	21,235
18.	Illinois	43,963	57,488	44.	Maine	8,568	9,914
19.	North Dakota	36,591	6,405	45.	Rhode Island	6,058	8,336
20.	Utah	32,927	17,137	46.	Delaware	4,181	5,718
21.	Georgia	32,151	51,873	47.	Hawaii	4,164	29,306
22.	Nevada	32,062	23,883	48.	West Virginia	3,787	9,527
23.	Louisiana	30,579	24,500	49.	New Hampshire	3,150	7,374
24.	Virginia	29,225	51,699	50.	Vermont	2,207	5,172
25.	New Jersey	29,026	41,690	51.	District of Columbia	2,079	4,442
26.	Alabama	28,218	28,900		**United States**	**2,932,248**	**2,288,331**

(1) Respondents who self-identified as American Indian and Alaska Native (AIAN) alone. (2) Respondents who self-identified as AIAN in combination with one or more other races.

American Indian and Alaska Native Population by Selected Tribal Groupings, 2010

Source: Decennial Census, U.S. Census Bureau, U.S. Dept. of Commerce
(ranked by American Indian and Alaska Native [AIAN] alone, one tribal grouping alone)

Tribal grouping	AIAN alone — One tribal grouping alone[1]	AIAN alone — One or more tribal groupings[2]	AIAN alone or in combination — One or more tribal groupings[3]	Tribal grouping	AIAN alone — One tribal grouping alone[1]	AIAN alone — One or more tribal groupings[2]	AIAN alone or in combination — One or more tribal groupings[3]
Total	2,879,638	2,932,248	5,220,579	Crow	10,332	10,860	15,203
AIAN tribes, not specified	693,709	693,709	1,545,963	Kiowa	9,437	10,355	13,787
Amer. Ind. tribes, specified	1,935,363	2,032,133	3,397,251	Paiute	9,340	10,205	13,767
Navajo	286,731	295,016	332,129	Osage	8,938	10,063	18,576
Cherokee	284,247	300,463	819,105	Yakama	8,786	9,096	11,527
Mexican Amer. Ind.	121,221	123,550	175,494	Menominee	8,374	8,627	11,133
Chippewa	112,757	115,402	170,742	Houma	8,169	8,240	10,768
Sioux	112,176	116,477	170,110	Colville	8,114	8,314	10,549
Choctaw	103,910	110,308	195,764	Arapaho	8,014	8,402	10,861
Apache	63,193	69,694	111,810	Shoshone	7,852	8,462	13,002
Lumbee	62,306	62,957	73,691	Delaware	7,843	8,215	18,264
Pueblo	49,695	52,026	62,540	Yuman	7,727	8,278	10,089
Creek	48,352	52,948	88,332	Ute	7,435	8,220	11,491
Iroquois	40,570	42,461	81,002	Ottawa	7,272	8,048	13,033
Chickasaw	27,973	30,206	52,278	Canadian/French Amer. Ind.	6,433	7,051	14,822
Blackfeet	27,279	31,798	105,304	Cree	2,211	2,950	7,983
Pima	22,040	23,205	26,655	All other Amer. Ind. tribes	270,141	282,747	429,629
Yaqui	21,679	23,195	32,595	Amer. Ind. tribes, not specified	131,943	132,060	234,320
S. Amer. Ind.	20,901	21,380	47,233	AK Native tribes, specified	98,892	103,086	138,850
Potawatomi	20,412	20,874	33,771	Yup'ik	28,927	29,618	33,889
Tohono O'Odham	19,522	20,247	23,478	Inupiat[4]	24,859	25,736	33,360
Central Amer. Ind.	15,882	16,454	27,844	Alaskan Athabascan	15,623	16,427	22,484
Puget Sound Salish	14,320	14,535	20,260	Tlingit-Haida	15,256	16,115	26,080
Seminole	14,080	16,448	31,971	Aleut	11,920	12,643	19,282
Spanish Amer. Ind.	13,460	13,758	19,951	Tsimshian	2,307	2,547	3,755
Hopi	12,580	14,634	18,327	AK Native tribes, not specified	19,731	19,904	29,933
Comanche	12,284	13,471	23,330				
Cheyenne	11,375	12,493	19,051				

Note: This table measures the number of responses, not respondents. Respondents who self-identified with multiple tribal groupings are counted more than once. A tribal grouping refers to combined individual tribes (e.g., Fort Sill Apache and San Carlos Apache as Apache or King Salmon Tribe and Native Village of Kanatak as Aleut). (1) For example, Navajo or Alaskan Athabascan. (2) As in footnote 1 or in combination with other tribal groupings (e.g., Yakama and Aleut). (3) As in footnotes 1 or 2 or in combination with another race (e.g., Apache, Navajo, and white; or Inupiat, white, and black). (4) Eskimo in previous censuses.

Largest U.S. Cities by Population, 1850-2017

Source: Population Estimates Program and Decennial Censuses, U.S. Census Bureau, U.S. Dept. of Commerce
(ranked by 2017 population)

Rank	City	2017	2000	1990	1980	1970	1950	1900	1850
1.	New York, NY	8,622,698	8,008,654	7,322,564	7,071,639	7,895,563	7,891,957	3,437,202	515,547
2.	Los Angeles, CA	3,999,759	3,694,742	3,485,557	2,968,528	2,811,801	1,970,358	102,479	1,610
3.	Chicago, IL	2,716,450	2,896,016	2,783,726	3,005,072	3,369,537	3,620,962	1,698,575	29,963
4.	Houston, TX	2,312,717	1,953,631	1,630,864	1,595,138	1,233,535	596,163	44,633	2,396
5.	Phoenix, AZ	1,626,078	1,321,045	983,392	789,704	584,303	106,818	5,544	—
6.	Philadelphia, PA	1,580,863	1,517,550	1,585,577	1,688,210	1,949,996	2,071,605	1,293,697	121,376
7.	San Antonio, TX	1,511,946	1,144,646	935,393	785,940	654,153	408,442	53,321	3,488
8.	San Diego, CA	1,419,516	1,223,400	1,110,623	875,538	697,471	334,387	17,700	—
9.	Dallas, TX	1,341,075	1,188,580	1,007,618	904,599	844,401	434,462	42,638	—
10.	San Jose, CA	1,035,317	894,943	782,224	629,400	459,913	95,280	21,500	—
11.	Austin, TX	950,715	656,562	465,648	345,890	253,539	132,459	22,258	629
12.	Jacksonville, FL[1]	892,062	735,617	635,230	540,920	504,265	204,517	28,429	1,045
13.	San Francisco, CA[2]	884,363	776,733	723,959	678,974	715,674	775,357	342,782	34,776
14.	Columbus, OH	879,170	711,470	632,945	565,021	540,025	375,901	125,560	17,882
15.	Fort Worth, TX	874,168	534,694	447,619	385,164	393,455	278,778	26,688	—
16.	Indianapolis, IN[1]	863,002	791,926	741,915	710,868	746,992	427,173	169,164	8,091
17.	Charlotte, NC	859,035	540,167	395,934	315,474	241,420	134,042	18,091	1,065
18.	Seattle, WA	724,745	563,376	516,259	493,846	530,831	467,591	80,671	—
19.	Denver, CO	704,621	553,693	467,610	492,686	514,678	415,786	133,859	—
20.	Washington, DC	693,972	572,059	606,900	638,432	756,668	802,178	278,718	40,001
21.	Boston, MA	685,094	589,141	574,283	562,994	641,071	801,444	560,892	136,881
22.	El Paso, TX	683,577	563,662	515,342	425,259	322,261	130,485	15,906	—
23.	Detroit, MI	673,104	951,270	1,027,974	1,203,368	1,514,063	1,849,568	285,704	21,019
24.	Nashville-Davidson, TN[1]	667,560	569,892	510,786	477,811	447,877	174,307	80,865	10,165
25.	Memphis, TN	652,236	650,100	610,337	646,174	623,988	396,000	102,320	8,841
26.	Portland, OR	647,805	529,121	438,802	368,148	379,967	373,628	90,426	—
27.	Oklahoma City, OK	643,648	506,132	444,724	404,014	368,164	243,504	10,037	—
28.	Las Vegas, NV	641,676	479,137	258,204	164,674	125,787	24,624	—	—
29.	Louisville/Jefferson Co., KY[1]	621,349	256,231	269,555	298,694	361,706	369,129	204,731	43,194
30.	Baltimore, MD	611,648	651,154	736,014	786,741	905,787	949,708	508,957	169,054
31.	Milwaukee, WI	595,351	596,974	628,088	636,297	717,372	637,392	285,315	20,061
32.	Albuquerque, NM	558,545	448,607	384,619	332,619	244,920	96,815	6,238	—
33.	Tucson, AZ	535,677	486,699	405,371	330,537	262,933	45,454	7,531	—
34.	Fresno, CA	527,438	427,652	354,091	217,491	165,655	91,669	12,470	—
35.	Sacramento, CA	501,901	407,018	369,365	275,741	257,105	137,572	29,282	6,820
36.	Mesa, AZ	496,401	396,375	288,104	152,404	63,049	16,790	722	—
37.	Kansas City, MO	488,943	441,545	434,829	448,028	507,330	456,622	163,752	—
38.	Atlanta, GA	486,290	416,267	393,929	425,022	495,039	331,314	89,872	2,572
39.	Long Beach, CA	469,450	461,522	429,321	361,498	358,879	250,767	2,252	—
40.	Omaha, NE	466,893	390,007	335,719	313,939	346,929	251,117	102,555	—
41.	Raleigh, NC	464,758	276,094	212,092	150,255	122,830	65,679	13,643	4,518
42.	Colorado Springs, CO	464,474	360,890	280,430	215,105	135,517	45,472	21,085	—
43.	Miami, FL	463,347	362,470	358,648	346,681	334,859	249,276	1,681	—
44.	Virginia Beach, VA	450,435	425,257	393,089	262,199	172,106	5,390	—	—
45.	Oakland, CA	425,195	399,484	372,242	339,337	361,561	384,575	66,960	—
46.	Minneapolis, MN	422,331	382,747	368,383	370,951	434,400	521,718	202,718	—
47.	Tulsa, OK	401,800	393,049	367,302	360,919	330,350	182,740	1,390	—
48.	Arlington, TX	396,394	332,969	261,717	160,113	90,229	7,692	1,079	—
49.	New Orleans, LA	393,292	484,674	496,938	557,927	593,471	570,445	287,104	116,375
50.	Wichita, KS	390,591	346,753	304,017	279,838	276,554	168,279	24,671	—
51.	Cleveland, OH	385,525	477,459	505,616	573,822	750,879	914,808	381,768	17,034
52.	Tampa, FL	385,430	303,447	280,015	271,577	277,714	124,681	15,839	—
53.	Bakersfield, CA	380,874	246,889	174,978	105,611	69,515	34,784	4,836	—
54.	Aurora, CO	366,623	275,921	222,103	158,588	74,974	11,421	202	—
55.	Anaheim, CA	352,497	328,014	266,406	219,494	166,408	14,556	1,456	—
56.	Urban Honolulu, HI[3]	350,395	371,657	365,272	365,048	324,871	248,034	39,306	—
57.	Santa Ana, CA	334,136	337,977	293,827	204,023	155,710	45,533	4,933	—
58.	Riverside, CA	327,728	255,166	226,546	170,591	140,089	46,764	7,973	—
59.	Corpus Christi, TX	325,605	277,454	257,453	232,134	204,525	108,287	4,703	—
60.	Lexington-Fayette Urban Co., KY[1]	321,959	260,512	225,366	204,165	108,137	55,534	26,369	8,159
61.	Stockton, CA	310,496	243,771	210,943	148,283	109,963	70,853	17,506	—
62.	St. Louis, MO	308,626	348,189	396,685	452,801	622,236	856,796	575,238	77,860
63.	St. Paul, MN	306,621	286,840	272,235	270,230	309,866	311,349	163,065	1,112
64.	Henderson, NV	302,539	175,381	64,948	24,363	16,395		—	—
65.	Pittsburgh, PA	302,407	334,563	369,879	423,959	520,089	676,806	321,616	46,601
66.	Cincinnati, OH	301,301	331,285	364,040	385,409	453,514	503,998	325,902	115,435
67.	Anchorage, AK	294,356	260,283	226,338	174,431	48,081	11,254	—	—
68.	Greensboro, NC	290,222	223,891	183,894	155,642	144,076	74,389	10,035	—
69.	Plano, TX	286,143	222,030	127,885	72,331	17,872	2,126	1,304	—
70.	Newark, NJ	285,154	272,537	275,221	329,248	381,930	438,776	246,070	38,894
71.	Lincoln, NE	284,736	225,581	191,972	171,932	149,518	98,884	40,169	—
72.	Orlando, FL	280,257	185,951	164,674	128,291	99,006	52,367	2,481	—
73.	Irvine, CA	277,453	143,072	110,330	62,134	—	—	—	—
74.	Toledo, OH	276,491	313,782	332,943	354,635	383,062	303,616	131,822	3,829
75.	Jersey City, NJ	270,753	240,055	228,517	223,532	260,350	299,017	206,433	6,856
76.	Chula Vista, CA	270,471	173,556	135,160	83,927	67,901	15,927	—	—
77.	Durham, NC	267,743	187,035	136,612	101,149	95,438	71,311	6,679	—
78.	Fort Wayne, IN	265,904	205,727	172,971	172,391	178,269	133,607	45,115	4,282
79.	St. Petersburg, FL	263,255	248,232	240,318	238,647	216,159	96,738	1,575	—
80.	Laredo, TX	260,654	176,576	122,899	91,449	69,024	51,910	13,429	—

Rank City	2017	2000	1990	1980	1970	1950	1900	1850
81. Buffalo, NY	258,612	292,648	328,175	357,870	462,768	580,132	352,387	42,261
82. Madison, WI	255,214	208,054	190,766	170,616	171,809	96,056	19,164	1,525
83. Lubbock, TX	253,888	199,564	186,206	174,361	149,101	71,747	—	—
84. Chandler, AZ	253,458	176,581	89,862	29,673	13,763	3,799	—	—
85. Scottsdale, AZ	249,950	202,705	130,069	88,412	67,823	2,032	—	—
86. Reno, NV	248,853	180,480	133,850	100,756	72,863	32,497	4,500	—
87. Glendale, AZ	246,709	218,812	147,864	97,172	36,228	8,179	—	—
88. Norfolk, VA	244,703	234,403	261,250	266,979	307,951	213,513	46,624	14,326
89. Winston-Salem, NC	244,605	185,776	143,485	131,885	133,683	87,811	13,650	—
90. North Las Vegas, NV	242,975	115,488	47,849	42,739	46,067	—	—	—
91. Gilbert, AZ	242,354	109,697	29,122	5,717	1,971	1,114	—	—
92. Chesapeake, VA	240,397	199,184	151,982	114,486	89,580	—	—	—
93. Irving, TX	240,373	191,615	155,037	109,943	97,260	2,621	—	—
94. Hialeah, FL	239,673	226,419	188,008	145,254	102,452	19,676	—	—
95. Garland, TX	238,002	215,768	180,635	138,857	81,437	10,571	819	—
96. Fremont, CA	234,962	203,413	173,339	131,945	100,869	—	—	—
97. Richmond, VA	227,032	197,790	202,798	219,214	249,332	230,310	85,050	27,570
98. Boise City, ID	226,570	185,787	125,551	102,249	74,990	34,393	5,957	—
99. Baton Rouge, LA	225,374	227,818	219,531	220,394	165,291	125,629	11,269	3,905
100. Des Moines, IA	217,521	198,682	193,189	191,003	210,404	177,965	62,139	—

— = Not available. **Note:** 2017 population estimates are as of July 1. Decennial census figures for 1950-2000 are for Apr. 1; 1850 and 1900 are for June 1. Figures may reflect revisions/corrections to initial tabulated census counts. Cities are incorporated places unless otherwise noted. (1) Consolidated city-county government. For years predating consolidation, city population figures are shown. (2) 1850 figure is for 1852, from state census. 1850 census results were destroyed by fire. (3) Census designated place (CDP). Figures for years prior to 2017 are for Honolulu CDP and are not directly comparable.

Population Change in Largest U.S. Cities, 2010-17

Source: Population Estimates Program and Decennial Census, U.S. Census Bureau, U.S. Dept. of Commerce

(ranked by % change, 2010-17; 2017 estimates are as of July 1; 2010 decennial census figures are for Apr. 1)

Cities With Most Growth

Rank City	Population 2017	2010	% change, 2010-17
1. Irvine, CA	277,453	212,375	30.6%
2. Austin, TX	950,715	790,390	20.3
3. Seattle, WA	724,745	608,660	19.1
4. Fort Worth, TX	874,168	741,206	17.9
5. Orlando, FL	280,257	238,300	17.6
6. Charlotte, NC	859,035	731,424	17.4
7. Denver, CO	704,621	600,158	17.4
8. Henderson, NV	302,539	257,729	17.4
9. Durham, NC	267,743	228,330	17.3
10. Gilbert, AZ	242,354	208,453	16.3
11. Miami, FL	463,347	399,457	16.0
12. Atlanta, GA	486,290	420,003	15.8
13. Washington, DC	693,972	601,723	15.3
14. Raleigh, NC	464,758	403,892	15.1
15. Scottsdale, AZ	249,950	217,385	15.0
16. Tampa, FL	385,430	335,709	14.8
17. New Orleans, LA	393,292	343,829	14.4
18. Omaha, NE	466,893	408,958	14.2
19. San Antonio, TX	1,511,946	1,327,407	13.9
20. Mesa, AZ	496,401	439,041	13.1

Cities With Least Growth

Rank City	Population 2017	2010	% change, 2010-17
1. Detroit, MI	673,104	713,777	−5.7%
2. Toledo, OH	276,491	287,208	−3.7
3. St. Louis, MO	308,626	319,294	−3.3
4. Cleveland, OH	385,525	396,815	−2.8
5. Baton Rouge, LA	225,374	229,493	−1.8
6. Baltimore, MD	611,648	620,961	−1.5
7. Pittsburgh, PA	302,407	305,704	−1.1
8. Buffalo, NY	258,612	261,310	−1.0
9. Milwaukee, WI	595,351	594,833	0.1
10. Chicago, IL	2,716,450	2,695,598	0.8
11. Norfolk, VA	244,703	242,803	0.8
12. Memphis, TN	652,236	646,889	0.8
13. Anchorage, AK	294,356	291,826	0.9
14. Cincinnati, OH	301,301	296,943	1.5
15. Long Beach, CA	469,450	462,257	1.6
16. Wichita, KS	390,591	382,368	2.2
17. Albuquerque, NM	558,545	545,852	2.3
18. Tulsa, OK	401,800	391,906	2.5
19. Virginia Beach, VA	450,435	437,994	2.8
20. Newark, NJ	285,154	277,140	2.9

Note: This table shows which of the 100 largest U.S. cities by 2017 population size experienced the most and least population growth since 2010. Figures may reflect revisions/corrections to initial tabulated census counts. Cities are typically incorporated places.

Largest U.S. Counties by Population, 2000, 2017

Source: Population Estimates Program and Decennial Census, U.S. Census Bureau, U.S. Dept. of Commerce

(ranked by 2017 population, estimated as of July 1; 2000 decennial census figures are for Apr. 1)

Rank County	2017	2000	% change, 2000-17	Rank County	2017	2000	% change, 2000-17
1. Los Angeles Co., CA	10,163,507	9,519,338	6.8%	16. Bexar Co., TX	1,958,578	1,392,931	40.6%
2. Cook Co., IL	5,211,263	5,376,815	−3.1	17. Santa Clara Co., CA	1,938,153	1,682,585	15.2
3. Harris Co., TX	4,652,980	3,400,578	36.8	18. Broward Co., FL	1,935,878	1,623,018	19.3
4. Maricopa Co., AZ	4,307,033	3,072,149	40.2	19. Wayne Co., MI	1,753,616	2,061,162	−14.9
5. San Diego Co., CA	3,337,685	2,813,833	18.6	20. New York Co., NY	1,664,727	1,537,372	8.3
6. Orange Co., CA	3,190,400	2,846,289	12.1	21. Alameda Co., CA	1,663,190	1,443,741	15.2
7. Miami-Dade Co., FL	2,751,796	2,253,779	22.1	22. Middlesex Co., MA	1,602,947	1,466,394	9.3
8. Kings Co., NY	2,648,771	2,465,525	7.4	23. Philadelphia Co., PA	1,580,863	1,517,550	4.2
9. Dallas Co., TX	2,618,148	2,218,774	18.0	24. Sacramento Co., CA	1,530,615	1,223,499	25.1
10. Riverside Co., CA	2,423,266	1,545,387	56.8	25. Suffolk Co., NY	1,492,953	1,419,369	5.2
11. Queens Co., NY	2,358,582	2,229,379	5.8	26. Bronx Co., NY	1,471,160	1,332,650	10.4
12. Clark Co., NV	2,204,079	1,375,765	60.2	27. Palm Beach Co., FL	1,471,150	1,131,191	30.1
13. King Co., WA	2,188,649	1,737,044	26.0	28. Hillsborough Co., FL	1,408,566	998,948	41.0
14. San Bernardino Co., CA	2,157,404	1,709,434	26.2	29. Nassau Co., NY	1,369,514	1,334,544	2.6
15. Tarrant Co., TX	2,054,475	1,446,219	42.1	30. Orange Co., FL	1,348,975	896,344	50.5

Note: Decennial pop. figures may reflect revisions/corrections to initial tabulated census counts. The 10 smallest counties or county equivalents by estimated 2017 population: (1) Kalawao Co., HI (pop. 88); (2) Loving Co., TX (134); (3) King Co., TX (296); (4) Kenedy Co., TX (417); (5) Arthur Co., NE (457); (6) Blaine Co., NE (482); (7) McPherson Co., NE (499); (8) Petroleum Co., MT (523); (9) Yakutat City and Borough, AK (605); and (10) Loup Co., NE (609).

Largest U.S. Metropolitan Areas by Population, 2000-17

Source: Population Estimates Program and Decennial Censuses, U.S. Census Bureau, U.S. Dept. of Commerce

Metropolitan Statistical Areas (MSAs) are defined, or delineated geographically, for federal statistical use by the Office of Management and Budget (OMB) with technical assistance from the Census Bureau. An MSA consists of at least one urbanized area of 50,000 or more inhabitants, plus adjacent territory closely integrated socially and economically with the core as measured by commuting ties. The Census Bureau's 2017 population estimates are for delineations issued by the OMB in Aug. 2017, which designated 383 MSAs in the U.S. About 85.7% of the resident population lived in an MSA in 2017.

(ranked by 2017 population, estimated as of July 1; 2000 and 2010 decennial census figures are for Apr. 1)

Rank	Metropolitan Statistical Area	Population 2017	Population 2010	Population 2000	Percent change 2010-17	Percent change 2000-17
1.	New York-Newark-Jersey City, NY-NJ-PA	20,320,876	19,567,410	18,944,519	3.9%	7.3%
2.	Los Angeles-Long Beach-Anaheim, CA	13,353,907	12,828,837	12,365,627	4.1	8.0
3.	Chicago-Naperville-Elgin, IL-IN-WI	9,533,040	9,461,105	9,098,316	0.8	4.8
4.	Dallas-Fort Worth-Arlington, TX	7,399,662	6,426,214	5,204,126	15.1	42.2
5.	Houston-The Woodlands-Sugar Land, TX	6,892,427	5,920,416	4,693,161	16.4	46.9
6.	Washington-Arlington-Alexandria, DC-VA-MD-WV	6,216,589	5,636,232	4,837,428	10.3	28.5
7.	Miami-Fort Lauderdale-West Palm Beach, FL	6,158,824	5,564,635	5,007,564	10.7	23.0
8.	Philadelphia-Camden-Wilmington, PA-NJ-DE-MD	6,096,120	5,965,343	5,687,147	2.2	7.2
9.	Atlanta-Sandy Springs-Roswell, GA	5,884,736	5,286,728	4,263,438	11.3	38.0
10.	Boston-Cambridge-Newton, MA-NH	4,836,531	4,552,402	4,391,344	6.2	10.1
11.	Phoenix-Mesa-Scottsdale, AZ	4,737,270	4,192,887	3,251,876	13.0	45.7
12.	San Francisco-Oakland-Hayward, CA	4,727,357	4,335,391	4,123,740	9.0	14.6
13.	Riverside-San Bernardino-Ontario, CA	4,580,670	4,224,851	3,254,821	8.4	40.7
14.	Detroit-Warren-Dearborn, MI	4,313,002	4,296,250	4,452,557	0.4	-3.1
15.	Seattle-Tacoma-Bellevue, WA	3,867,046	3,439,809	3,043,878	12.4	27.0
16.	Minneapolis-St. Paul-Bloomington, MN-WI	3,600,618	3,348,859	3,031,918	7.5	18.8
17.	San Diego-Carlsbad, CA	3,337,685	3,095,313	2,813,833	7.8	18.6
18.	Tampa-St. Petersburg-Clearwater, FL	3,091,399	2,783,243	2,395,997	11.1	29.0
19.	Denver-Aurora-Lakewood, CO	2,888,227	2,543,482	2,179,240	13.6	32.5
20.	Baltimore-Columbia-Towson, MD	2,808,175	2,710,489	2,552,994	3.6	10.0
21.	St. Louis, MO-IL	2,807,338	2,787,701	2,675,343	0.7	4.9
22.	Charlotte-Concord-Gastonia, NC-SC	2,525,305	2,217,012	1,717,372	13.9	47.0
23.	Orlando-Kissimmee-Sanford, FL	2,509,831	2,134,411	1,644,561	17.6	52.6
24.	San Antonio-New Braunfels, TX	2,473,974	2,142,508	1,711,703	15.5	44.5
25.	Portland-Vancouver-Hillsboro, OR-WA	2,453,168	2,226,009	1,927,881	10.2	27.2
26.	Pittsburgh, PA	2,333,367	2,356,285	2,431,087	-1.0	-4.0
27.	Sacramento—Roseville—Arden-Arcade, CA	2,324,884	2,149,127	1,796,857	8.2	29.4
28.	Las Vegas-Henderson-Paradise, NV	2,204,079	1,951,269	1,375,765	13.0	60.2
29.	Cincinnati, OH-KY-IN	2,179,082	2,114,580	1,994,830	3.1	9.2
30.	Kansas City, MO-KS	2,128,912	2,009,342	1,811,254	6.0	17.5
31.	Austin-Round Rock, TX	2,115,827	1,716,289	1,249,763	23.3	69.3
32.	Columbus, OH	2,078,725	1,901,974	1,675,013	9.3	24.1
33.	Cleveland-Elyria, OH	2,058,844	2,077,240	2,148,143	-0.9	-4.2
34.	Indianapolis-Carmel-Anderson, IN	2,028,614	1,887,877	1,658,462	7.5	22.3
35.	San Jose-Sunnyvale-Santa Clara, CA	1,998,463	1,836,911	1,735,819	8.8	15.1
36.	Nashville-Davidson—Murfreesboro—Franklin, TN	1,903,045	1,670,890	1,381,287	13.9	37.8
37.	Virginia Beach-Norfolk-Newport News, VA-NC	1,725,246	1,676,822	1,580,057	2.9	9.2
38.	Providence-Warwick, RI-MA	1,621,122	1,600,852	1,582,997	1.3	2.4
39.	Milwaukee-Waukesha-West Allis, WI	1,576,236	1,555,908	1,500,741	1.3	5.0
40.	Jacksonville, FL	1,504,980	1,345,596	1,122,750	11.8	34.0
41.	Oklahoma City, OK	1,383,737	1,252,987	1,095,421	10.4	26.3
42.	Memphis, TN-MS-AR	1,348,260	1,324,829	1,213,230	1.8	11.1
43.	Raleigh, NC	1,335,079	1,130,490	797,071	18.1	67.5
44.	Richmond, VA	1,294,204	1,208,101	1,055,683	7.1	22.6
45.	Louisville/Jefferson County, KY-IN	1,293,953	1,235,708	1,121,109	4.7	15.4
46.	New Orleans-Metairie, LA	1,275,762	1,189,866	1,337,726	7.2	-4.6
47.	Hartford-West Hartford-East Hartford, CT	1,210,259	1,212,381	1,148,618	-0.2	5.4
48.	Salt Lake City, UT	1,203,105	1,087,873	939,122	10.6	28.1
49.	Birmingham-Hoover, AL	1,149,807	1,128,047	1,052,238	1.9	9.3
50.	Buffalo-Cheektowaga-Niagara Falls, NY	1,136,856	1,135,509	1,170,111	0.1	-2.8
51.	Rochester, NY	1,077,948	1,079,671	1,062,452	-0.2	1.5
52.	Grand Rapids-Wyoming, MI	1,059,113	988,938	930,670	7.1	13.8
53.	Tucson, AZ	1,022,769	980,263	843,746	4.3	21.2

Population by Urban and Rural Residency, 1790-2010

Source: Decennial Censuses, U.S. Census Bureau, U.S. Dept. of Commerce

The Census Bureau currently defines an area as urban if it has at least 2,500 people (at least 1,500 of whom do not reside in institutional group quarters, such as a correctional facility). All other areas are rural. Prior to 1950, the definition of urban was limited to incorporated places and other areas meeting certain criteria.

Year	Total pop.	No. of places of 2,500 or more	% of total pop. Urban	% of total pop. Rural
Pre-1950 urban definition				
1790	3,929,214	24	5.1%	94.9%
1800	5,308,483	33	6.1	93.9
1810	7,239,881	46	7.3	92.7
1820	9,638,453	61	7.2	92.8
1830	12,860,702	90	8.8	91.2
1840	17,063,353	131	10.8	89.2
1850	23,191,876	237	15.4	84.6
1860	31,443,321	392	19.8	80.2
1870	38,558,371	663	25.7	74.3
1880	50,189,209	939	28.2	71.8
1890	62,979,766	1,348	35.1	64.9
1900	76,212,168	1,740	39.6	60.4
1910	92,228,496	2,266	45.6	54.4
1920	106,021,537	2,725	51.2	48.8

Year	Total pop.	No. of places of 2,500 or more	% of total pop. Urban	% of total pop. Rural
1930	123,202,624	3,183	56.1%	43.9%
1940	132,164,569	3,485	56.5	43.5
1950	151,325,798	4,077	59.6	40.4
1960	179,323,175	5,023	63.1	36.9
1950-90 urban definition				
1950	151,325,798	4,307	64.0	36.0
1960	179,323,175	5,445	69.9	30.1
1970	203,302,031	6,433	73.6	26.3
1980	226,542,199	7,749	73.7	26.3
1990	248,718,302	8,510	75.2	24.8
Current urban definition				
1990	248,718,302	8,510	78.0	22.0
2000	281,424,603	9,063	79.0	21.0
2010	308,746,065	9,644	80.7	19.3

Note: Figures may not add up to 100 due to rounding.

Mobility of U.S. Population by Selected Characteristics, 2016-17

Source: Annual Social and Economic Supplement, Current Population Survey (CPS), U.S. Census Bureau, U.S. Dept. of Commerce
(numbers in thousands)

	Total movers	Location of new residence					Total movers	Location of new residence			
		Same county	Diff. county, same state	Diff. state	Abroad			Same county	Diff. county, same state	Diff. state	Abroad
Age						**Marital status[1]**					
1 to 14 years.........	7,094	4,504	1,313	1,068	208	Married, spouse present	9,747	5,747	1,765	1,800	435
15 years and older	27,808	17,110	5,355	4,297	1,047	Married, spouse absent	590	276	109	128	77
25 years and older	20,780	12,634	3,980	3,343	821	Widowed............	831	521	163	120	27
65 years and older	1,818	1,042	378	319	78	Divorced	2,961	1,865	644	415	37
85 years and older	246	138	49	48	11	Separated...........	851	526	183	116	25
Income[1]						Never married........	12,828	8,173	2,490	1,717	446
Without income.......	3,533	2,082	610	490	351	**Educational attainment[2]**					
Under $5,000 or loss ..	2,265	1,238	463	377	187	Not a HS graduate	1,976	1,320	391	184	82
$5,000-$9,999	1,944	1,212	400	292	41	High school graduate ..	5,568	3,673	1,020	697	178
$10,000-$19,999	4,160	2,639	783	626	111	Some college or					
$20,000-$29,999	3,694	2,366	735	501	90	associate's degree ..	5,890	3,556	1,229	951	154
$30,000-$39,999	3,297	2,091	662	496	48	Bachelor's degree.....	4,512	2,577	841	867	227
$40,000-$59,999	3,977	2,612	706	572	88	Prof. or grad. degree ...	2,831	1,508	498	649	178
$60,000-$74,999	1,677	972	356	315	35	**Tenure**					
$75,000-$99,999	1,380	815	294	246	24	In owner-occupied unit	11,502	6,910	2,477	1,821	294
$100,000 and over	1,883	1,084	347	381	71	In renter-occupied unit[3]	23,400	14,704	4,191	3,545	961
						Total movers	**34,903**	**21,614**	**6,668**	**5,365**	**1,255**

Note: Total movers consists of persons ages 1 and older who moved to a new residence in the 12 months preceding the survey. Figures may not add up to totals due to rounding. (1) Ages 15 and older. (2) Ages 25 and older. (3) Includes units occupied without payment of cash rent.

Mobility of U.S. Population, 1948-2017

Source: Annual Social and Economic Supplement, Current Population Survey (CPS), U.S. Census Bureau, U.S. Dept. of Commerce
(numbers in thousands unless otherwise noted)

Mobility period	Total movers		Location of new residence							
			Same county		Diff. county, same state		Diff. state		Abroad	
	No.	% of pop.	No.	% distrib.	No.	% distrib.	No.	% distrib.	No.	% distrib.
1947-48	28,672	20.2%	19,202	67.0%	4,638	16.2%	4,370	15.2%	462	1.6%
1950-51	31,464	21.2	20,694	65.8	5,276	16.8	5,188	16.5	306	1.0
1955-56	34,040	21.1	22,186	65.2	5,859	17.2	5,053	14.8	942	2.8
1960-61	36,533	20.6	24,289	66.5	5,493	15.0	5,753	15.7	998	2.7
1965-66	37,586	19.8	24,165	64.3	6,275	16.7	6,263	16.7	883	2.3
1970-71	37,705	18.7	23,018	61.0	6,197	16.4	6,946	18.4	1,544	4.1
1975-76	36,793	17.7	22,399	60.9	7,106	19.3	6,140	16.7	1,148	3.1
1980-81	38,200	17.2	23,097	60.5	7,614	19.9	6,175	16.2	1,313	3.4
1985-86	43,237	18.6	26,401	61.1	8,665	20.0	6,971	16.1	1,200	2.8
1990-91	41,539	17.0	25,151	60.5	7,881	19.0	7,122	17.1	1,385	3.3
1995-96	42,537	16.3	26,696	62.8	8,009	18.8	6,471	15.2	1,361	3.2
2000-01	39,007	14.2	21,918	56.2	7,550	19.4	7,783	20.0	1,756	4.5
2005-06	39,837	13.7	24,851	62.4	8,010	20.1	5,679	14.3	1,296	3.3
2010-11	35,038	11.6	23,330	66.6	5,868	16.7	4,756	13.6	1,084	3.1
2015-16	35,138	11.2	21,588	61.4	7,501	21.3	4,768	13.6	1,281	3.6
2016-17	34,902	11.0	21,614	61.9	6,668	19.1	5,366	15.4	1,255	3.6

Note: Total movers consists of persons ages 1 and older who moved to a new residence in the 12 months preceding the survey. Figures may not add up to totals due to rounding. Because of changes in survey processing, numbers may not be comparable over time.

U.S. Households by Size, 1900-2010

Source: Decennial Censuses, U.S. Census Bureau, U.S. Dept. of Commerce

The household population does not include those living in group quarters (either institutionalized like a correctional facility or noninstitutionalized like a college dormitory). Data not available for 1930; 1950 figures are based on a sample of the population. Average household size is shown above each bar.

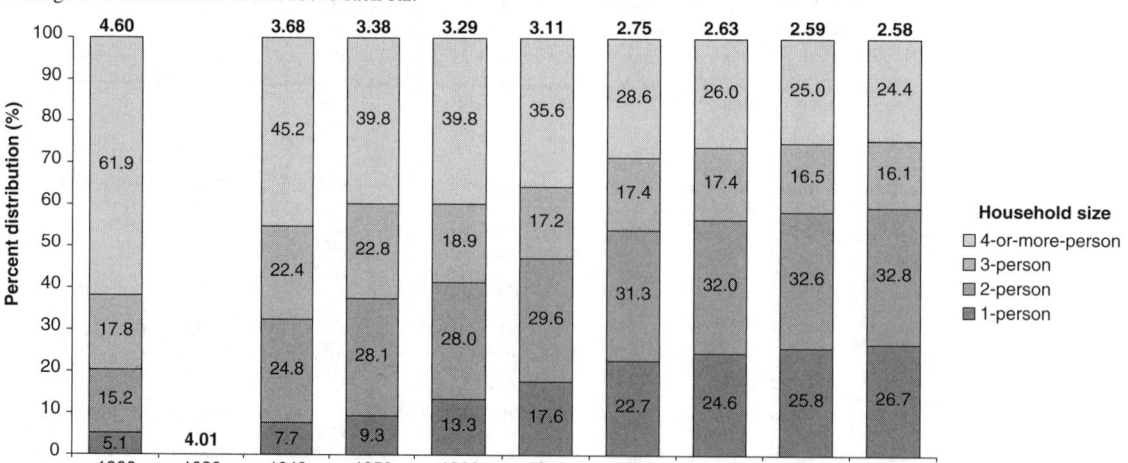

U.S. Population by Age, Sex, and Household, 2017

Source: American Community Survey (ACS), U.S. Census Bureau, U.S. Dept. of Commerce

	Number	% of tot.		Number	% of tot.
Total population[1]	325,719,178	100.0%	Sex		
Age			Male	160,402,504	49.2%
Under 5 years.	19,795,159	6.1	Female	165,316,674	50.8
5 to 14 years.	41,226,715	12.7	Total households[2]	120,062,818	100.0%
15 to 17 years.	12,626,809	3.9	Family households	78,631,163	65.5
18 years and over.	252,070,495	77.4	2-person household	34,546,577	28.8
Male	122,729,360	37.7	3-person household	17,611,556	14.7
Female	129,341,135	39.7	4-person household	14,927,463	12.4
18 to 24 years	30,820,412	9.5	5-or-more-person household	11,545,567	9.6
25 to 34 years	44,965,735	13.8	Married-couple family household . . .	57,847,574	48.2
35 to 44 years	41,117,905	12.6	Male HH, no wife present	5,886,661	4.9
45 to 54 years	42,330,955	13.0	Female HH, no husband present	14,896,928	12.4
55 to 64 years	42,019,776	12.9	Nonfamily households	41,431,655	34.5
65 years and over	50,815,712	15.6	1-person household, or HH living alone	33,513,155	27.9
75 years and over	21,083,836	6.5	HH 65 years and over	12,942,049	10.8
85 years and over	6,259,473	1.9	2-person household	6,447,116	5.4
Median age (years).	38.1	NA	3-or-more-person household	1,471,384	1.2
			Average household size	2.65	NA

NA = Not applicable. HH = Householder, or person in whose name a home is owned or rented. **Note:** Data based on sample and subject to sampling variability. (1) Includes population living in group quarters (institutional and noninstitutional, e.g., correctional facilities, university housing). (2) Number of occupied housing units, not household members. Group quarters are not considered households.

Elderly U.S. Population, 1900-2060

Source: Decennial Censuses and Population Projections Program, U.S. Census Bureau, U.S. Dept. of Commerce
(numbers of resident population in thousands)

	65 and over		85 and over			65 and over		85 and over	
Year	Number	% tot. pop.	Number	% tot. pop.	Year	Number	% tot. pop.	Number	% tot. pop.
1900[1]	3,080	4.1%	122	0.2%	2010	40,268	13.0%	5,493	1.8%
1920[1]	4,933	4.7	210	0.2	2020	56,052	16.9	6,701	2.0
1940[1]	9,019	6.8	365	0.3	2030	73,138	20.6	9,074	2.6
1960	16,560	9.2	929	0.5	2040	80,827	21.7	14,430	3.9
1980	25,549	11.3	2,240	1.0	2050	85,675	22.1	18,561	4.8
2000	34,992	12.4	4,240	1.5	2060	94,676	23.5	19,019	4.7

Note: 1900 figures are for June 1; 1920 figures are for Jan. 1; and 1940-2010 figures are for Apr. 1. 2020-60 projections are as of July 1. (1) Excludes Alaska and Hawaii.

U.S. Population Projections by Age, 2020-60

Source: Population Projections Program, U.S. Census Bureau, U.S. Dept. of Commerce
(numbers of resident population in thousands)

	2020		2030		2040		2050		2060	
Age	No.	% distrib.	No.	% distrib.	No.	% distrib.	No.	% distrib.	No.	% distrib.
Total	332,555	100.0%	354,840	100.0%	373,121	100.0%	388,335	100.0%	403,697	100.0%
Under 5 years	20,354	6.1	20,895	5.9	21,033	5.6	21,514	5.5	22,047	5.5
5 to 13 years.	36,780	11.1	37,873	10.7	38,431	10.3	38,905	10.0	39,909	9.9
14 to 17 years.	16,748	5.0	16,623	4.7	17,385	4.7	17,510	4.5	17,832	4.4
18 to 24 years.	30,380	9.1	30,612	8.6	31,244	8.4	32,015	8.2	32,362	8.0
25 to 44 years.	88,843	26.7	94,370	26.6	95,067	25.5	97,280	25.1	99,898	24.7
45 to 64 years.	83,398	25.1	81,329	22.9	89,135	23.9	95,437	24.6	96,973	24.0
65 years and over. . .	56,052	16.9	73,138	20.6	80,827	21.7	85,675	22.1	94,676	23.5
85 years and over. . .	6,701	2.0	9,074	2.6	14,430	3.9	18,561	4.8	19,019	4.7
100 years and over. .	92	0.03	140	0.04	196	0.05	386	0.10	589	0.15

Note: Projections are as of July 1 of given year. They are based on assumptions about future births, deaths, and net international migration.

Disability Status of U.S. Population by Age, 2017

Source: American Community Survey (ACS), U.S. Census Bureau, U.S. Dept. of Commerce
(numbers in thousands, by difficulty type)

Characteristic	Number	% of pop.	Characteristic	Number	% of pop.
Total population (all ages)	320,775	100.00%	Total population (5 years and over) . . .	300,982	100.00%
With a disability[1]	40,679	12.68	With a cognitive difficulty[2]	15,382	5.11
Under 5 years.	146	0.05	5 to 17 years.	2,268	0.75
Under 18 years.	3,094	0.96	18 to 64 years.	8,836	2.94
18 to 64 years.	20,444	6.37	65 years and over.	4,278	1.42
65 years and over.	17,141	5.34	With an ambulatory difficulty[3]	20,903	6.94
With a hearing difficulty	11,515	3.59	5 to 17 years.	324	0.11
Under 5 years.	98	0.03	18 to 64 years.	9,715	3.23
Under 18 years.	409	0.13	65 years and over.	10,864	3.61
18 to 64 years.	3,956	1.23	With a self-care difficulty[4]	7,951	2.64
65 years and over.	7,150	2.23	5 to 17 years.	526	0.17
With a vision difficulty	7,556	2.36	18 to 64 years.	3,543	1.18
Under 5 years.	85	0.03	65 years and over.	3,883	1.29
Under 18 years.	568	0.18			
18 to 64 years.	3,869	1.21	Total population (18 years and over) . .	247,266	100.00%
65 years and over.	3,118	0.97	With an independent living difficulty[5]	14,300	5.78
			18 to 64 years.	7,279	2.94
			65 years and over.	7,021	2.84

Note: Data based on sample and subject to sampling variability. Does not include military personnel and civilian institutionalized population (i.e., those under formal supervision or custody in a facility). (1) Identified by the ACS as persons "who exhibit difficulty with specific functions and may, in the absence of accommodation, have a disability." (2) Concentrating, remembering, or making decisions. (3) Walking or climbing stairs. (4) Dressing or bathing. (5) Doing errands alone, such as visiting a doctor's office or shopping.

Marital Status of the U.S. Population, 1960-2017

Source: Annual Social and Economic Supplements, Current Population Surveys (CPS), U.S. Census Bureau, U.S. Dept. of Commerce
(numbers in millions)

Marital status	Both sexes 2017	2000	1980	1960	Male 2017	2000	1980	1960	Female 2017	2000	1980	1960
Total.................	259.1	213.8	171.9	124.9	125.7	103.1	81.9	60.3	133.4	110.7	89.9	64.6
Married[1].............	135.8	120.2	104.8	84.4	67.7	59.7	51.8	41.8	68.1	60.5	53.0	42.6
Never married	82.9	60.0	44.5	27.5	43.8	32.3	24.2	15.3	39.1	27.8	20.2	12.3
Divorced	25.5	19.9	9.9	2.8	10.9	8.6	3.9	1.1	14.6	11.3	6.0	1.7
Widowed	14.9	13.7	12.7	10.2	3.3	2.6	2.0	2.1	11.6	11.1	10.8	8.1
% of total or subset pops.												
Married[1].............	52.4%	56.2%	61.0%	67.6%	53.8%	57.9%	63.2%	69.3%	51.0%	54.7%	58.9%	65.9%
Never married	32.0	28.1	25.9	22.0	34.9	31.3	29.6	25.3	29.3	25.1	22.5	19.0
Divorced	9.8	9.3	5.8	2.3	8.7	8.3	4.8	1.8	10.9	10.2	6.6	2.6
Widowed	5.8	6.4	7.4	8.1	2.6	2.5	2.4	3.5	8.7	10.0	12.0	12.5

Note: Total population for 1980, 2000, and 2017 is persons ages 15 and older and for 1960, persons ages 14 and older. Data is based on sample of occupied households in the civilian noninstitutional population. Figures may not add up to totals due to rounding. (1) Comprises subcategories Married, spouse present; Married, spouse absent; and Separated.

Household Characteristics of Couples in the U.S., 2016

Source: American Community Survey (ACS), U.S. Census Bureau, U.S. Dept. of Commerce
(as percent of all households with same couple relationship type, unless otherwise noted)

Household characteristics	Opposite-sex couples Married	Unmarried	Same-sex couples Married Total same-sex married couples	Male couple	Female couple	Same-sex couples Unmarried Total same-sex unmarried couples	Male couple	Female couple
Total number of households (thous.)	56,480.8	6,821.1	487.0	235.2	251.8	400.5	200.7	199.8
Age of householder								
15-24 years....................	1.2%	11.6%	1.5%	0.9%	2.1%	7.1%	6.3%	7.9%
25-34 years....................	13.0	34.8	13.8	10.8	16.6	25.5	23.8	27.1
35-44 years....................	19.7	21.1	18.6	17.9	19.4	19.4	20.5	18.3
45-54 years....................	21.7	15.7	24.0	26.1	22.1	21.9	23.1	20.7
55-64 years....................	21.4	10.4	21.0	22.1	20.0	16.7	17.8	15.6
65 years and over	23.0	6.4	21.0	22.2	19.9	9.3	8.4	10.2
Average age of householder (years) ...	52.2	39.4	51.6	52.9	50.5	44.1	44.4	43.8
Household income								
Less than $35,000	13.5	23.2	12.1	9.8	14.2	15.5	11.6	19.3
$35,000-$49,999.................	10.7	15.1	9.1	7.7	10.4	10.5	9.2	11.8
$50,000-$74,999.................	18.5	22.5	15.8	14.4	17.1	18.3	16.2	20.5
$75,000-$99,999.................	16.1	15.0	14.4	13.3	15.4	16.0	15.4	16.7
$100,000 or more	41.3	24.2	48.6	54.8	42.9	39.7	47.6	31.7
Median household income (dollars)	$85,581	$61,909	$97,252	$108,614	$88,514	$83,578	$95,283	$72,714
Households with children[1]	39.2%	39.1%	19.4%	12.8%	25.5%	13.0%	5.6%	20.4%

Note: Data based on sample and subject to sampling variability. Householder is person in whose name a home is owned or rented. Categories are for one race alone, not in combination with any other race, unless otherwise noted. (1) Includes own children and nonrelatives of the householder under 18 years.

Same-Sex Couple Households in the U.S., 2008-16

Source: American Community Survey (ACS), U.S. Census Bureau, U.S. Dept. of Commerce
(in thousands)

Year	Total same-sex couples Total	Male couple	Female couple	Same-sex married couples Total	Male couple	Female couple	Same-sex unmarried partner couples Total	Male couple	Female couple
2008	539.2	281.3	257.9	142.5	62.2	80.3	396.7	195.8	201.0
2009	581.3	280.4	300.9	152.1	66.3	85.8	429.2	214.1	215.0
2010	593.3	287.7	305.6	152.3	68.5	83.8	441.0	219.2	221.8
2011	605.5	284.3	321.2	168.1	69.5	98.6	437.4	214.8	222.6
2012	639.4	305.8	333.6	181.9	80.7	101.2	457.5	225.1	232.5
2013	726.6	352.6	374.0	251.7	117.5	134.2	474.9	235.1	239.8
2014	783.1	377.9	405.2	334.8	163.2	171.6	448.3	214.7	233.6
2015	858.9	412.0	446.9	425.4	201.8	223.6	433.5	210.2	223.3
2016	887.5	435.9	451.6	487.0	235.2	251.8	400.5	200.7	199.8

Note: Data based on sample and subject to sampling variability.

Children in the U.S. by Selected Characteristics, 2017

Source: Annual Social and Economic Supplement, Current Population Survey (CPS), U.S. Census Bureau, U.S. Dept. of Commerce
(numbers in thousands)

Characteristic	Number	% of tot.	Characteristic	Number	% of tot.
All children	**73,781**	**100.0%**	Presence of siblings in living arrangement		
Age of child			None.............................	15,520	21.0%
Under 1 year......................	3,822	5.2	One sibling	28,629	38.8
1-2 years.........................	8,185	11.1	Two siblings	17,904	24.3
3-5 years.........................	11,889	16.1	Three siblings.....................	7,467	10.1
6-8 years.........................	12,255	16.6	Four siblings	2,773	3.8
9-11 years........................	12,468	16.9	Five or more siblings................	1,488	2.0
12-14 years.......................	12,343	16.7	Presence of grandparents in living		
15-17 years.......................	12,818	17.4	arrangement		
Race of child			Grandparent is householder		
White alone, not Hispanic............	37,613	51.0	Grandmother and grandfather	2,491	3.4
Black alone.......................	11,151	15.1	Grandmother only	2,051	2.8
Asian alone.......................	3,872	5.2	Grandfather only	349	0.5
Hispanic (any race).................	18,415	25.0	No grandparents present	66,114	89.6

Note: Children are defined as all persons under 18 years of age excluding those who are a family reference person or spouse. Data based on sample of occupied households in the civilian noninstitutional population.

Persons Granted Lawful Permanent Resident Status by State, 2016

Source: Office of Immigration Statistics, U.S. Dept. of Homeland Security

(ranked by fiscal year 2016 number)

State/territory	Number	State/territory	Number	State/territory	Number	State/territory	Number
Total	**1,183,505**	North Carolina	20,811	Hawaii	6,285	New Hampshire	2,332
California	223,141	Arizona	20,694	Oklahoma	5,960	Delaware	2,204
New York	159,878	Ohio	17,251	Louisiana	5,784	Mississippi	2,149
Florida	136,337	Minnesota	15,603	Kansas	5,709	Maine	1,748
Texas	110,651	Colorado	14,225	Nebraska	5,654	Alaska	1,726
New Jersey	56,187	Connecticut	12,669	Iowa	5,299	North Dakota	1,595
Illinois	43,207	Nevada	11,555	South Carolina	5,104	South Dakota	1,229
Massachusetts	35,706	Oregon	10,033	Alabama	4,736	Guam	1,147
Georgia	29,572	Tennessee	10,032	Rhode Island	4,194	West Virginia	928
Virginia	29,242	Indiana	9,946	New Mexico	4,104	Vermont	886
Washington	27,304	Utah	7,271	Puerto Rico	3,581	Montana	566
Pennsylvania	27,217	Wisconsin	7,111	Arkansas	3,158	Wyoming	462
Maryland	26,077	Kentucky	7,098	Dist. of Columbia	3,114	Other[1]	1,225
Michigan	22,569	Missouri	6,868	Idaho	2,562	Unknown	1,809

Note: Applicants for lawful permanent resident (LPR) status, or "green cards," may already live in the U.S. They include refugees and asylees, temp. workers, foreign students, family members of U.S. citizens, and unauthorized immigrants. Applicants from outside the U.S. are granted LPR status upon entry with a visa. (1) Incl. Amer. Samoa, Northern Mariana Isls., U.S. Virgin Isls., and armed forces posts.

Persons Granted Lawful Permanent Resident Status by Top Areas of Residence, 2016

Source: Office of Immigration Statistics, U.S. Dept. of Homeland Security

(ranked by fiscal year 2016 number)

Area of residence[1]	Number	% of total	Area of residence[1]	Number	% of total
Total	**1,183,505**	**100.0%**	Detroit-Warren-Dearborn, MI	15,864	1.3%
New York-Newark-Jersey City, NY-NJ-PA	195,593	16.5	Phoenix-Mesa-Scottsdale, AZ	14,485	1.2
Los Angeles-Long Beach-Anaheim, CA	88,743	7.5	Orlando-Kissimmee-Sanford, FL	13,273	1.1
Miami-Fort Lauderdale-West Palm Beach, FL	88,651	7.5	Minneapolis-Saint Paul-Bloomington, MN-WI	12,233	1.0
Washington-Arlington-Alexandria, DC-VA-MD-WV	40,642	3.4	Tampa-Saint Petersburg-Clearwater, FL	11,792	1.0
Chicago-Naperville-Elgin, IL-IN-WI	39,749	3.4	Sacramento–Roseville–Arden-Arcade, CA	11,306	1.0
Houston-The Woodlands-Sugar Land, TX	37,777	3.2	Las Vegas-Henderson-Paradise, NV	9,832	0.8
San Francisco-Oakland-Hayward, CA	36,476	3.1	Denver-Aurora-Lakewood, CO	9,738	0.8
Dallas-Fort Worth-Arlington, TX	33,605	2.8	Baltimore-Columbia-Towson, MD	8,599	0.7
Boston-Cambridge-Newton, MA-NH	28,677	2.4	Portland-Vancouver-Hillsboro, OR-WA	8,443	0.7
Atlanta-Sandy Springs-Roswell, GA	23,620	2.0	Austin-Round Rock, TX	8,336	0.7
Seattle-Tacoma-Bellevue, WA	20,582	1.7	Charlotte-Concord-Gastonia, NC-SC	6,693	0.6
San Jose-Sunnyvale-Santa Clara, CA	19,790	1.7	San Antonio-New Braunfels, TX	6,462	0.5
Philadelphia-Camden-Wilmington, PA-NJ-DE-MD	19,318	1.6	Columbus, OH	6,443	0.5
San Diego-Carlsbad, CA	18,690	1.6	Providence-Warwick, RI-MA	5,363	0.5
Riverside-San Bernardino-Ontario, CA	16,559	1.4	Other CBSAs	309,512	26.2
			Non-CBSA or unknown	16,659	1.4

Note: Applicants for lawful permanent resident (LPR) status, or "green cards," may already live in the U.S. They include refugees and asylees, temporary workers, foreign students, family members of U.S. citizens, and unauthorized immigrants. Applicants from outside the U.S. are granted LPR status upon entry with a visa. (1) Residence by "Core Based Statistical Areas," or CBSAs, which refer collectively to metropolitan and micropolitan statistical areas. These areas are defined for federal statistical use by the Office of Management and Budget with Census Bureau assistance.

Unauthorized Immigrant Population in the U.S., 2000, 2014

Source: Pew Research Center

About 10% of the unauthorized immigrant population in 2014 were covered by the Deferred Action for Childhood Arrivals (DACA) program or the federal government's Temporary Protected Status program for people from countries where war, natural disaster, or disease make return dangerous.

(ranked by 2014 est. population; numbers in thousands)

Country of Birth

Country	Est. population 2014	Est. population 2000	% change, 2000-14
All countries	**11,100**	**8,600**	**29.1%**
Mexico	5,850	4,450	31.5
El Salvador	700	500	40.0
Guatemala	525	200	162.5
India	500	240	108.3
Honduras	350	140	150.0
China[1]	325	325	0.0
Philippines	180	120	50.0
Dominican Republic	170	180	−5.6
Korea[2]	160	110	45.5
Ecuador	130	90	44.4
Colombia	130	150	−13.3
Peru	100	100	0.0
Haiti	100	130	−23.1
Brazil	100	90	11.1
Canada	100	55	81.8

State of Residence

State	Est. population 2014	Est. population 2000	% change, 2000-14
All states	**11,100**	**8,600**	**29.1%**
California	2,350	2,250	4.4
Texas	1,650	1,050	57.1
Florida	850	900	−5.6
New York	775	750	3.3
New Jersey	500	325	53.8
Illinois	450	375	20.0
Georgia	375	170	120.6
North Carolina	350	220	59.1
Arizona	325	350	−7.1
Virginia	300	200	50.0
Washington	250	150	66.7
Maryland	250	160	56.3
Massachusetts	210	170	23.5
Nevada	210	170	23.5
Colorado	200	130	53.8

Note: Unauthorized immigrant population estimates are made using the residual method. The estimated number of immigrants residing legally in the country is subtracted from the total foreign-born pop. Numbers are rounded independently and may not add up to totals. (1) Incl. Hong Kong and Taiwan. (2) Incl. North and South Korea.

Active U.S. DACA Population by Birth Country, 2018

Source: U.S. Citizenship and Immigration Services, U.S. Dept. of Homeland Security

The Deferred Action for Childhood Arrivals (DACA) program conveys (1) temporary protection from deportation and (2) permission to legally work to undocumented individuals living in the U.S. who were brought to the country as children.

(number of valid DACA recipients as of Mar. 31, 2018, ranked by country of birth)

Country of birth	Number	Country of birth	Number	Country of birth	Number
Total	693,850	Colombia	4,910	Trinidad and Tobago	1,850
Mexico	553,200	Argentina	3,880	Bolivia	1,660
El Salvador	26,160	Philippines	3,800	Costa Rica	1,570
Guatemala	17,920	India	2,570	Chile	1,390
Honduras	16,420	Jamaica	2,530	Poland	1,380
Peru	7,220	Venezuela	2,420	Nicaragua	1,370
South Korea	7,150	Dominican Republic	2,310	Pakistan	1,310
Brazil	5,730	Uruguay	1,930	Nigeria	1,010
Ecuador	5,360				

Note: Numbers are approximate and rounded and may not add up to total. Countries with fewer than 1,000 valid DACA recipients are not shown here. Does not include individuals who have obtained lawful permanent resident status or U.S. citizenship.

Refugee Arrivals in the U.S. by Region and Nationality, 2007-16

Source: Office of Immigration Statistics, U.S. Dept. of Homeland Security; Bureau of Population, Refugees, and Migration, U.S. Dept. of State

Under the Refugee Act of 1980, the president in consultation with Congress establishes a refugee admissions ceiling and regional allocations before each fiscal year (Oct. 1-Sept. 30). Applicants for refugee status are outside of the U.S. whereas applicants seeking asylum are in the U.S. or at a U.S. port of entry.

(countries ranked by nationality of most refugee arrivals in fiscal year 2016)

Region/country of nationality	2007	2008	2009	2010	2011	2012	2013	2014	2015	2016
Total ceiling	70,000	80,000	80,000	80,000	80,000	76,000	70,000	70,000	70,000	85,000
Total refugee arrivals	48,218	60,107	74,602	73,293	56,384	58,179	69,909	69,975	69,920	84,989
COUNTRY										
Congo, Dem. Rep. of	848	727	1,135	3,174	977	1,863	2,563	4,540	7,876	16,370
Syria	17	24	25	29	29	31	36	105	1,682	12,587
Myanmar (Burma)	13,896	18,139	18,202	16,693	16,972	14,160	16,299	14,598	18,386	12,347
Iraq	1,608	13,822	18,838	18,016	9,388	12,163	19,487	19,769	12,676	9,880
Somalia	6,969	2,523	4,189	4,884	3,161	4,911	7,608	9,000	8,858	9,020
Bhutan	0	5,320	13,452	12,363	14,999	15,070	9,134	8,434	5,775	5,817
Iran	5,482	5,270	5,381	3,543	2,032	1,758	2,579	2,846	3,109	3,750
Afghanistan	441	576	349	515	428	481	661	753	910	2,737
Ukraine	1,605	1,022	601	449	428	372	227	490	1,451	2,543
Eritrea	963	251	1,571	2,570	2,032	1,346	1,824	1,488	1,596	1,949
Sudan	705	375	683	558	334	1,077	2,160	1,315	1,578	1,458
Ethiopia	1,028	299	321	668	560	620	765	728	626	1,131
Burundi	4,545	2,889	762	530	110	186	193	68	1,186	694
Pakistan	30	104	67	59	54	274	158	240	159	545
Colombia	54	94	57	123	46	126	230	252	521	529
Moldova	565	487	445	356	331	255	119	142	333	465
Russia	1,773	426	495	326	165	197	125	139	281	462
Central African Republic	15	56	59	45	182	136	318	25	270	401
El Salvador	0	0	0	0	0	0	0	0	0	364
Cuba	2,922	4,177	4,800	4,818	2,920	1,948	4,205	4,062	1,527	354
All other countries[1]	4,749	3,519	3,167	3,573	1,230	1,199	1,211	976	1,115	1,582
REGION										
Africa	17,486	8,943	9,678	13,325	7,693	10,629	15,984	17,501	22,492	31,648
Asia	23,564	44,819	58,309	52,695	44,583	44,416	48,840	47,197	43,115	48,287
Europe	4,192	2,059	1,693	1,238	996	908	482	818	2,164	3,664
North America	2,922	4,177	4,800	4,856	2,930	1,948	4,206	4,066	1,528	811
Oceania	0	0	0	0	0	0	0	0	0	0
South America	54	100	57	126	46	130	233	252	522	529
Unknown	0	9	65	1,053	136	148	164	141	99	50

Note: Excludes Amerasian immigrants (children born in Cambodia, Korea, Laos, Thailand, or Vietnam in 1950-82 and fathered by a U.S. citizen). (1) Includes admissions from Palestinian Territory and unknown.

Persons Granted Asylum and Refugee Arrivals in the U.S., 1980-2017

Source: U.S. Dept. of Homeland Security (DHS), U.S. Dept. of Justice (DOJ), U.S. Dept. of State

Individuals apply for asylum from within the U.S. or at a U.S. port of entry. Applicants for refugee status are outside of the U.S.

Year	Number granted asylum	Number of refugee arrivals	Year	Number granted asylum	Number of refugee arrivals	Year	Number granted asylum	Number of refugee arrivals
1980	—	207,116	1993	9,543	114,181	2006	26,352	41,094
1981	—	159,252	1994	13,828	111,680	2007	25,318	48,218
1982	—	98,096	1995	20,703	98,973	2008	23,026	60,107
1983	—	61,218	1996	23,532	75,421	2009	22,288	74,602
1984	—	70,393	1997	22,939	69,653	2010	19,755	73,293
1985	—	67,704	1998	20,507	76,712	2011	23,570	56,384
1986	—	62,146	1999	26,571	85,285	2012	28,010	58,179
1987	—	64,528	2000	32,514	72,165	2013	24,997	69,909
1988	—	76,483	2001	39,148	68,920	2014	23,296	69,975
1989	—	107,070	2002	36,937	26,785	2015	25,971	69,920
1990	8,472	122,066	2003	28,743	28,286	2016	20,455	84,989
1991	5,035	113,389	2004	27,376	52,840	2017	—	53,716
1992	6,307	115,548	2005	25,304	53,738			

— = Not available. **Note:** Fiscal year (Oct. 1-Sept. 30) data. Excludes Amerasians (children born in Cambodia, Korea, Laos, Thailand, or Vietnam after Dec. 31, 1950, and before Oct. 22, 1982, and fathered by a U.S. citizen) except in fiscal years 1989-91.

U.S. Foreign-Born Population

Source: Annual Social and Economic Supplements, Current Population Surveys (CPS), U.S. Census Bureau, U.S. Dept. of Commerce

Foreign-Born as a Percentage of U.S. Population, 1900-2017

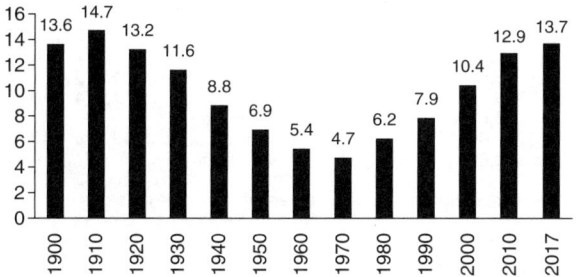

Foreign-Born Population by Region of Birth, 1995-2016

(numbers in thousands)

Region	2016[1] No.	2016[1] %	2000	1995
Asia	12,832	29.8%	7,916	6,121
Under 18	819	30.8	696	767
Europe	4,523	10.5	4,382	3,937
Under 18	254	9.5	247	232
Latin America	22,449	52.1	15,323	11,777
Under 18	1,201	45.2	1,786	1,451
Other[2]	3,266	7.6	2,364	2,658
Under 18	386	14.5	249	275
All regions	**43,070**	**100.0**	**29,985**	**24,493**
Under 18	**2,660**	**100.0**	**2,977**	**2,726**

(1) Figures are percentage of total foreign-born population or of all foreign-born under 18 years of age. (2) Including those born at sea.

U.S. Foreign-Born Population: Top Countries of Origin, 1880-2017

Source: American Community Survey (ACS), Decennial Censuses, U.S. Census Bureau, U.S. Dept. of Commerce

(numbers in thousands; percentage is of all foreign-born excluding population born at sea)

1880 Country	No.	%	1920 Country	No.	%	1960 Country	No.	%	2000 Country	No.	%	2017[4] Country	No.	%
Germany	1,967	29.4	Germany	1,686	12.1	Italy	1,257	12.9	Mexico	9,177	29.5	Mexico	11,270	25.3
Ireland	1,855	27.8	Italy	1,610	11.6	Germany	990	10.2	China[2]	1,519	4.9	India	2,611	5.9
UK	918	13.7	USSR	1,400	10.1	Canada	953	9.8	Philippines	1,369	4.4	China[2]	2,217	5.0
Canada	717	10.7	Poland	1,140	8.2	UK	765	7.9	India	1,023	3.3	Philippines	2,008	4.5
Sweden	194	2.9	Canada	1,138	8.2	Poland	748	7.7	Vietnam	988	3.2	El Salvador	1,402	3.1
Norway	182	2.7	UK	1,135	8.2	USSR	691	7.1	Cuba	873	2.8	Vietnam	1,343	3.0
France	107	1.6	Ireland	1,037	7.5	Mexico	576	5.9	Korea[3]	864	2.8	Cuba	1,312	2.9
China[1]	104	1.6	Sweden	626	4.5	Ireland	339	3.5	Canada	821	2.6	Dominican Republic	1,163	2.6
Switzerland	89	1.3	Austria	576	4.1	Austria	305	3.1	El Salvador	817	2.6	Korea[3]	1,063	2.4
Czech.	85	1.3	Mexico	486	3.5	Hungary	245	2.5	Germany	707	2.3	Guatemala	959	2.2
Total	**6,680**	**100.0**	**Total**	**13,921**	**100.0**	**Total**	**9,738**	**100.0**	**Total**	**31,108**	**100.0**	**Total**	**44,525**	**100.0**

(1) Incl. Taiwan. (2) Incl. Hong Kong and Taiwan. (3) North and South Korea. (4) Data based on sample and subject to sampling variability. The Census Bureau collects data from residents regardless of immigration status, so the foreign-born population implicitly includes unauthorized migrants.

Language Spoken at Home by the U.S. Population, 2017

Source: American Community Survey (ACS), U.S. Census Bureau, U.S. Dept. of Commerce

(number of speakers 5 years of age and over by language or language group most often used)

Language	Number (thous.)	% of tot. pop.	% English inability[1]
Total population	305,924.0	100.00%	8.5%
Speak only English	239,331.7	78.23	NA
Speak another language	66,592.3	21.77	39.0
Spanish			
Spanish	41,017.6	13.41	40.1
Other Indo-European languages			
Armenian	248.2	0.08	43.2
Bengali	350.9	0.11	40.2
French (incl. Cajun)	1,202.1	0.39	20.9
German	917.8	0.30	14.6
Greek	267.8	0.09	24.5
Gujarati	434.3	0.14	34.0
Haitian	886.8	0.29	38.9
Hindi	863.1	0.28	19.1
Italian	567.3	0.19	25.7
Malayalam, Kannada, other Dravidian	245.5	0.08	21.5
Nepali, Marathi, other Indic	433.4	0.14	35.3
Persian (incl. Farsi, Dari)	420.1	0.14	38.1
Polish	520.3	0.17	37.1
Portuguese	794.8	0.26	36.3
Punjabi	310.7	0.10	41.0
Russian	936.3	0.31	42.8
Serbo-Croatian	250.1	0.08	31.7
Tamil	286.7	0.09	15.9
Telugu	415.4	0.14	19.4
Ukrainian or other Slavic	331.4	0.11	35.5
Urdu	507.3	0.17	27.9

Language	Number (thous.)	% of tot. pop.	% English inability[1]
Yiddish, Penn. Dutch, other West Germanic	505.8	0.17%	28.0%
Other Indo-European languages	573.0	0.19	29.3
Asian and Pacific Island languages			
Chinese (incl. Mandarin, Cantonese)	3,462.1	1.13	54.6
Hmong	234.0	0.08	39.3
Ilocano, Samoan, Hawaiian, other Austronesian	459.0	0.15	36.9
Japanese	467.0	0.15	39.9
Khmer	207.5	0.07	52.5
Korean	1,095.2	0.36	51.8
Tagalog (incl. Filipino)	1,746.3	0.57	30.7
Thai, Lao, other Tai-Kadai	315.4	0.10	49.2
Vietnamese	1,498.9	0.49	58.3
Other Asian languages	406.4	0.13	54.5
All other languages			
Amharic, Somali, other Afro-Asiatic	526.2	0.17	43.7
Arabic	1,227.8	0.40	37.2
Hebrew	226.2	0.07	14.0
Navajo	169.1	0.06	18.7
Swahili or other Central/ Eastern/Southern Africa	267.8	0.09	34.2
Yoruba, Twi, Igbo, other Western Africa	541.0	0.18	22.1
Other Native North American	181.9	0.06	11.9
Other and unspecified	273.9	0.09	28.0

NA = Not applicable. **Note:** Data based on sample and subject to sampling variability. (1) Percent of respondents who speak the language at left who indicated that they spoke English less than "very well." For example, 43.2% of respondents who use Armenian at home do not speak English very well.

U.S. Population by Ancestry Reported, 2017

Source: American Community Survey (ACS), U.S. Census Bureau, U.S. Dept. of Commerce
(numbers in thousands; ranked by number)

Ancestry	Number	% of total	Ancestry	Number	% of total	Ancestry	Number	% of total
Total population	325,719	100.0%	European	5,322	1.6%	French Canadian	2,110	0.6%
German	43,094	13.2	Norwegian	4,296	1.3	Arab[3]	2,005	0.6
Irish	31,479	9.7	Dutch	3,906	1.2	British	1,891	0.6
English	23,075	7.1	Sub-Saharan African[1]	3,894	1.2	Welsh	1,801	0.6
American	20,025	6.1	Swedish	3,683	1.1	Czech	1,379	0.4
Italian	16,651	5.1	West Indian (excl. Hispanic groups)[2]	3,023	0.9	Hungarian	1,374	0.4
Polish	9,012	2.8	Scotch-Irish	3,008	0.9	Other ancestry not shown here	142,223	43.7
French (excl. Basque)	7,674	2.4	Russian	2,608	0.8	Unclassified or not reported	60,142	18.5
Scottish	5,399	1.7						

Note: Data based on sample and subject to sampling variability. Because respondents could self-identify with more than one ancestry, numbers do not add up to total. (1) Incl. Cabo Verdean, Ethiopian, Ghanian, Kenyan, Liberian, Nigerian, Senegalese, Sierra Leonean, Somali, South African, Sudanese, Ugandan, Zimbabwean, African, and other sub-Saharan African. (2) Incl. Bahamian, Barbadian, Belizean, Bermudan, British or Dutch West Indian, Haitian, Jamaican, Trinidadian and Tobagonian, U.S. Virgin Islander, West Indian, and other West Indian. (3) Incl. Egyptian, Iraqi, Jordanian, Lebanese, Moroccan, Palestinian, Syrian, Arab, and other Arab.

U.S. Population by Race, Hispanic Origin, and Age, 2017

Source: American Community Survey (ACS), U.S. Census Bureau, U.S. Dept. of Commerce

Race and origin/age	Number	% of group	Race and origin/age	Number	% of group
White (not Hispanic or Latino)	**197,285,202**	**100.0%**	**Native Hawaiian and other Pacific Islander**	**608,219**	**100.0%**
Under 5 years	9,786,584	5.0	Under 5 years	41,061	6.8
Under 18 years	37,159,867	18.8	Under 18 years	154,549	25.4
18 to 64 years	121,071,003	61.4	18 to 64 years	400,043	65.8
65 years and over	39,054,332	19.8	65 years and over	53,627	8.8
85 years and over	5,053,979	2.6	85 years and over	5,105	0.8
Black or African American	**41,393,491**	**100.0**	**Some other race**	**16,552,940**	**100.0**
Under 5 years	2,749,795	6.6	Under 5 years	1,284,584	7.8
Under 18 years	10,332,978	25.0	Under 18 years	4,897,799	29.6
18 to 64 years	26,404,108	63.8	18 to 64 years	10,688,748	64.6
65 years and over	4,656,405	11.2	65 years and over	966,393	5.8
85 years and over	469,574	1.1	85 years and over	85,946	0.5
Asian	**18,215,328**	**100.0**	**Two or more races**	**10,715,465**	**100.0**
Under 5 years	948,630	5.2	Under 5 years	1,524,469	14.2
Under 18 years	3,594,578	19.7	Under 18 years	4,885,308	45.6
18 to 64 years	12,370,375	67.9	18 to 64 years	5,286,195	49.3
65 years and over	2,250,375	12.4	65 years and over	543,962	5.1
85 years and over	238,423	1.3	85 years and over	47,632	0.4
American Indian and Alaska Native	**2,726,278**	**100.0**	**Hispanic or Latino (any race)**	**58,846,134**	**100.0**
Under 5 years	191,296	7.0	Under 5 years	5,124,300	8.7
Under 18 years	731,274	26.8	Under 18 years	18,550,211	31.5
18 to 64 years	1,711,953	62.8	18 to 64 years	36,113,635	61.4
65 years and over	283,051	10.4	65 years and over	4,182,288	7.1
85 years and over	24,516	0.9	85 years and over	444,248	0.8

Note: Data based on sample and subject to sampling variability. Categories are for one race alone, not in combination with any other race, unless otherwise noted.

Educational Attainment of the U.S. Population, 2017

Source: American Community Survey (ACS), U.S. Census Bureau, U.S. Dept. of Commerce
(numbers in thousands; population 25 years of age and over)

Race and origin/highest ed. completed	Number	% of group	Race and origin/highest ed. completed	Number	% of group
White alone (not Hispanic or Latino)	**143,648**	**100.0%**	**Native Hawaiian and other Pacific Islander**	**382**	**100.0%**
Less than HS diploma	10,221	7.1	Less than HS diploma	47	12.4
HS diploma or equiv. credential	39,085	27.2	HS diploma or equiv. credential	135	35.5
Some college or associate's degree	42,945	29.9	Some college or associate's degree	132	34.5
Bachelor's degree or higher	51,397	35.8	Bachelor's degree or higher	68	17.7
Black or African American	**26,473**	**100.0**	**Some other race**	**9,679**	**100.0**
Less than HS diploma	3,742	14.1	Less than HS diploma	3,609	37.3
HS diploma or equiv. credential	8,387	31.7	HS diploma or equiv. credential	2,827	29.2
Some college or associate's degree	8,687	32.8	Some college or associate's degree	2,109	21.8
Bachelor's degree or higher	5,657	21.4	Bachelor's degree or higher	1,135	11.7
Asian	**12,886**	**100.0**	**Two or more races**	**4,502**	**100.0**
Less than HS diploma	1,682	13.1	Less than HS diploma	504	11.2
HS diploma or equiv. credential	1,932	15.0	HS diploma or equiv. credential	1,026	22.8
Some college or associate's degree	2,334	18.1	Some college or associate's degree	1,547	34.4
Bachelor's degree or higher	6,939	53.8	Bachelor's degree or higher	1,425	31.7
American Indian and Alaska Native	**1,702**	**100.0**	**Hispanic or Latino (any race)**	**33,474**	**100.0**
Less than HS diploma	337	19.8	Less than HS diploma	10,478	31.3
HS diploma or equiv. credential	528	31.0	HS diploma or equiv. credential	9,412	28.1
Some college or associate's degree	587	34.5	Some college or associate's degree	8,224	24.6
Bachelor's degree or higher	250	14.7	Bachelor's degree or higher	5,361	16.0

HS = High school. **Note:** Data based on sample and subject to sampling variability. Categories are for one race alone, not in combination with any other race, unless otherwise noted.

Populations, ZIP, and Area Codes for U.S. Places of 10,000 or More

Source: Decennial Census and Population Estimates Program, U.S. Census Bureau, U.S. Dept. of Commerce; NeuStar Inc.; www.usps.com

The following is a list of places of 10,000 or more residents according to the U.S. Census Bureau's population estimates for 2017 and the results of the 2010 census.

This list includes **places incorporated** under state law as cities, towns, villages, or boroughs, and **Census designated places (CDPs)**, marked with a (c). This list also includes, in italics, **minor civil divisions (MCDs)** in Connecticut, Maine, Massachusetts, New Hampshire, Rhode Island, and Vermont. **Townships are not included.** Neither CDPs nor MCDs are incorporated areas. The Census Bureau delineates CDPs as statistical counterparts to incorporated places but does not typically include CDPs in its estimates program. MCDs are often the primary political or administrative divisions of a county. (Balance) indicates that the population given is for a consolidated area minus the residents of any separately incorporated places within its boundaries.

An asterisk (*) denotes that the **ZIP code** given is for general delivery; mail routes and/or P.O. boxes within the place may use a different one. Telephone **area codes** are given in parentheses. New phone numbers may be assigned a different area code from that of existing phone numbers in an area. These areas of overlay are noted. When two or more area codes are listed for one place, consult local operators for assistance. Area codes based on latest information as of mid-2018. — = Not available.

Alabama
Area code 938 overlays area code 256.

ZIP	Place	Area code	2010 population	2017 estimate
*35007	Alabaster	(205)	30,352	33,202
*35950	Albertville	(256)	21,160	21,392
*35010	Alexander City	(256)	14,875	14,595
*36201	Anniston	(256)	23,106	21,770
*35611	Athens	(256)	21,897	25,616
*36830	Auburn	(334)	53,380	63,973
*35020	Bessemer	(205)	27,456	26,386
*35203	Birmingham	(205)	212,237	210,710
35040	Calera	(205)	11,620	13,979
*35215	Center Point	(205)	16,921	16,313
35043	Chelsea	(205)	10,183	13,011
*35055	Cullman	(256)	14,775	15,385
*36526	Daphne	(251)	21,570	25,960
*35601	Decatur	(256)	55,683	54,405
*36301	Dothan	(334)	65,496	68,202
*36330	Enterprise	(334)	26,562	28,247
*36027	Eufaula	(334)	13,137	12,044
35064	Fairfield	(205)	11,117	10,683
*36532	Fairhope	(251)	15,326	20,935
*35630	Florence	(256)	39,319	39,852
*36535	Foley	(251)	14,618	18,288
35214	Forestdale (c)	(205)	10,162	—
*35967	Fort Payne	(256)	14,012	14,071
*35901	Gadsden	(256)	36,856	35,409
35071	Gardendale	(205)	13,893	13,906
36542	Gulf Shores	(251)	9,741	11,809
35640	Hartselle	(256)	14,255	14,373
*35080	Helena	(205)	16,793	19,072
*35209	Homewood	(205)	25,167	25,476
*35216	Hoover	(205)	81,619	84,920
*35023	Hueytown	(205)	16,105	15,460
*35801	Huntsville	(256)	180,105	194,585
35210	Irondale	(205)	12,349	12,468
36265	Jacksonville	(256)	12,548	12,612
*35501	Jasper	(205)	14,352	13,618
35094	Leeds	(205)	11,773	12,031
*35758	Madison	(256)	42,938	48,861
36054	Millbrook	(334)	14,640	15,318
*36602	Mobile	(251)	195,111	190,265
*36104	Montgomery	(334)	205,764	199,518
35004	Moody	(205)	11,726	12,956
*35223	Mountain Brook	(205)	20,413	20,381
*35661	Muscle Shoals	(256)	13,146	14,022
*35476	Northport	(205)	23,330	25,094
*36801	Opelika	(334)	26,477	30,240
36203	Oxford	(256)	21,348	21,180
*36360	Ozark	(334)	14,907	14,428
35124	Pelham	(205)	21,352	23,493
*35125	Pell City	(205)	12,695	13,676
*36867	Phenix City	(334)	32,822	36,219
35127	Pleasant Grove	(205)	10,110	10,104
*36066	Prattville	(334)	33,960	35,498
*36610	Prichard	(251)	22,659	21,732
36206	Saks (c)	(256)	10,744	—
36571	Saraland	(251)	13,405	14,576
*35768	Scottsboro	(256)	14,770	14,484
*36701	Selma	(334)	20,756	18,370
*35150	Sylacauga	(256)	12,749	12,264
*35160	Talladega	(256)	15,676	15,426
36619	Tillman's Corner (c)	(251)	17,398	—
*36081	Troy	(334)	18,033	19,037
35173	Trussville	(205)	19,933	21,827
*35401	Tuscaloosa	(205)	90,468	100,287
*35216	Vestavia Hills	(205)	34,033	34,291

Alaska
Area code 907 applies to the entire state.

ZIP	Place	2010 population	2017 estimate
*99501	Anchorage	291,826	294,356
99711	Badger (c)	19,482	—
*99708	College (c)	12,964	—
*99701	Fairbanks	31,535	31,644
*99801	Juneau	31,275	32,094
99654	Knik-Fairview (c)	14,923	—
*99623	Wasilla	7,831	10,151

Arizona

ZIP	Place	Area code	2010 population	2017 estimate
85086	Anthem (c)	(623)	21,700	—
*85119	Apache Junction	(480)	35,840	40,538
*85123	Arizona City (c)	(520)	10,475	—
*85323	Avondale	(623)	76,238	84,025
*85326	Buckeye	(623)	50,876	68,453
*86442	Bullhead City	(928)	39,540	40,252
86322	Camp Verde	(928)	10,873	11,201
*85122	Casa Grande	(520)	48,571	55,477
85740	Casas Adobes (c)	(520)	66,795	—
85718	Catalina Foothills (c)	(520)	50,796	—
*85225	Chandler	(480)	236,123	253,458
86323	Chino Valley	(928)	10,817	11,705
85128	Coolidge	(520)	11,825	12,698
86326	Cottonwood	(928)	11,265	12,023
*85607	Douglas	(520)	17,378	16,165
*85746	Drexel Heights (c)	(520)	27,749	—
85335	El Mirage	(623)	31,797	35,216
85131	Eloy	(520)	16,631	19,168
*86001	Flagstaff	(928)	65,870	71,975
85132	Florence	(520)	25,536	26,074
85705	Flowing Wells (c)	(520)	16,419	—
*86427	Fort Mohave (c)	(928)	14,364	—
*85367	Fortuna Foothills (c)	(928)	26,265	—
*85268	Fountain Hills	(480)	22,489	24,583
*85234	Gilbert	(480)	208,453	242,354
*85301	Glendale	(623)	226,721	246,709
85118	Gold Canyon (c)	(480)	10,159	—
*85338	Goodyear	(623)	65,275	79,858
*85622	Green Valley (c)	(520)	21,391	—
*86401	Kingman	(928)	28,068	29,472
*86403	Lake Havasu City	(928)	52,527	54,411
*85653	Marana	(520)	34,961	44,792
*85138	Maricopa	(520)	43,482	48,007
*85201	Mesa	(480)	439,041	496,401
86401	New Kingman-Butler (c)	(928)	12,134	—
*85087	New River (c)	(623)	14,952	—
*85621	Nogales	(520)	20,837	20,076
*85737	Oro Valley	(520)	41,011	44,350
85253	Paradise Valley	(480)	12,820	14,293
*85541	Payson	(928)	15,301	15,520
*85345	Peoria	(623)	154,065	168,181
*85003	Phoenix	(480)/(602)/(623)	1,445,632	1,626,078
*86301	Prescott	(928)	39,843	42,731
*86314	Prescott Valley	(928)	38,822	44,466
*85142	Queen Creek	(480)	26,361	39,184
85648	Rio Rico (c)	(520)	18,962	—
85629	Sahuarita	(520)	25,259	29,318
85349	San Luis	(928)	25,505	32,446
*85142	San Tan Valley (c)	(480)	81,321	—
*85251	Scottsdale	(480)	217,385	249,950
*86336	Sedona	(928)	10,031	10,336
*85901	Show Low	(928)	10,660	11,098
*85635	Sierra Vista	(520)	43,888	42,912
85650	Sierra Vista Southeast (c)	(520)	14,797	—
85350	Somerton	(928)	14,287	16,120
*85351	Sun City (c)	(623)	37,499	—
*85375	Sun City West (c)	(623)	24,535	—
85248	Sun Lakes (c)	(480)	13,975	—
*85374	Surprise	(623)	117,517	134,085
85749	Tanque Verde (c)	(520)	16,901	—
*85281	Tempe	(480)	161,719	185,038
*85701	Tucson	(520)	520,116	535,677
85735	Tucson Estates (c)	(520)	12,192	—
85641	Vail (c)	(520)	10,208	—
86326	Verde Village (c)	(928)	11,605	—
*85364	Yuma	(928)	93,064	95,502

Arkansas

ZIP	Place	Area code	2010 population	2017 estimate
*71923	Arkadelphia	(870)	10,714	10,650
*72501	Batesville	(870)	10,248	10,727
*72714	Bella Vista	(479)	26,461	28,511
*72015	Benton	(501)	30,681	35,789
*72712	Bentonville	(479)	35,301	49,298
*72315	Blytheville	(870)	15,620	14,051

ZIP	Place	Area code	2010 population	2017 estimate
*72022	Bryant	(501)	16,688	20,194
72023	Cabot	(501)	23,776	26,141
*71701	Camden	(870)	12,183	11,030
72719	Centerton	(479)	9,515	14,001
*72032	Conway	(501)	58,908	65,782
*71730	El Dorado	(870)	18,884	18,030
*72701	Fayetteville	(479)	73,580	85,257
*72335	Forrest City	(870)	15,371	14,291
*72901	Fort Smith	(479)	86,209	88,037
*72601	Harrison	(870)	12,943	13,079
72342	Helena-West Helena	(870)	12,282	10,701
*71901	Hot Springs	(501)	35,193	36,915
*71909	Hot Springs Village (c)	(501)	12,807	—
*72076	Jacksonville	(501)	28,364	28,513
*72401	Jonesboro	(870)	67,263	75,866
*72201	Little Rock	(501)	193,524	198,606
*71753	Magnolia	(870)	11,577	11,467
72104	Malvern	(501)	10,318	10,839
72364	Marion	(870)	12,345	12,440
72113	Maumelle	(501)	17,163	18,214
*72653	Mountain Home	(870)	12,448	12,332
*72114	North Little Rock	(501)	62,304	65,911
*72450	Paragould	(870)	26,113	28,488
*71601	Pine Bluff	(870)	49,083	42,984
*72756	Rogers	(479)	55,964	66,430
*72801	Russellville	(479)	27,920	29,318
*72143	Searcy	(501)	22,858	23,916
*72120	Sherwood	(501)	29,523	31,081
72761	Siloam Springs	(479)	15,039	16,842
*72764	Springdale	(479)	69,797	79,599
71854	Texarkana	(870)	29,919	30,259
*72956	Van Buren	(479)	22,791	23,509
*72301	West Memphis	(870)	26,245	24,860

California

Area code 279 overlays area code 916. Area code 323 overlays 213. Area code 424 overlays 310. Area code 442 overlays 760. Area code 628 overlays 415. Area code 657 overlays 714. Area code 669 overlays 408. Area code 747 overlays 818. Area code 820 overlays 805.

ZIP	Place	Area code	2010 population	2017 estimate
92301	Adelanto	(760)	31,765	34,066
*91301	Agoura Hills	(818)	20,330	20,692
*94501	Alameda	(510)	73,812	79,177
94507	Alamo (c)	(925)	14,570	—
*94706	Albany	(510)	18,539	20,143
*91801	Alhambra	(626)	83,089	85,396
*92656	Aliso Viejo	(949)	47,823	51,671
*91901	Alpine (c)	(619)	14,236	—
*91001	Altadena (c)	(626)	42,777	—
95127	Alum Rock (c)	(408)	15,536	—
*94503	American Canyon	(707)	19,454	20,247
96007	Anderson	(530)	9,932	10,370
95843	Antelope (c)	(916)	45,770	—
*94509	Antioch	(925)	102,372	111,674
*92307	Apple Valley	(760)	69,135	73,077
*91006	Arcadia	(626)	56,364	58,799
*95521	Arcata	(707)	17,231	18,000
*95825	Arden-Arcade (c)	(916)	92,186	—
*93420	Arroyo Grande	(805)	17,252	18,123
*90701	Artesia	(562)	16,522	16,904
93203	Arvin	(661)	19,304	21,270
94577	Ashland (c)	(510)	21,925	—
*93422	Atascadero	(805)	28,310	30,418
95301	Atwater	(209)	28,168	29,397
*95603	Auburn	(530)	13,330	13,997
93204	Avenal	(559)	15,505	12,440
91746	Avocado Heights (c)	(626)	15,411	—
91702	Azusa	(626)	46,361	49,864
*93301	Bakersfield	(661)	347,483	380,874
91706	Baldwin Park	(626)	75,390	76,402
92220	Banning	(951)	29,603	31,230
*92310	Barstow	(760)	22,639	23,916
94565	Bay Point (c)	(925)	21,349	—
92223	Beaumont	(951)	36,877	46,967
*90201	Bell	(323)	35,477	35,811
*90201	Bell Gardens	(213)/(562)	42,072	42,747
*90706	Bellflower	(562)	76,616	77,772
94002	Belmont	(650)	25,835	27,140
94510	Benicia	(707)	26,997	28,343
*94704	Berkeley	(510)	112,580	122,324
*90210	Beverly Hills	(310)	34,109	34,484
*92314	Big Bear City (c)	(909)	12,304	—
92316	Bloomington (c)	(951)	23,851	—
*92225	Blythe	(760)	20,817	19,630
*91902	Bonita (c)	(619)	12,538	—
92021	Bostonia (c)	(619)	15,379	—
92227	Brawley	(760)	24,953	26,390
*92821	Brea	(714)	39,282	42,777
94513	Brentwood	(925)	51,481	62,433
*90620	Buena Park	(714)	80,530	83,015
*91502	Burbank	(818)	103,340	104,834

ZIP	Place	Area code	2010 population	2017 estimate
*94010	Burlingame	(650)	28,806	30,686
*91301	Calabasas	(747)	23,058	24,202
*92231	Calexico	(760)	38,572	40,351
*93505	California City	(760)	14,120	13,972
*93010	Camarillo	(805)	65,201	67,845
95682	Cameron Park (c)	(530)	18,228	—
92058	Camp Pendleton South (c)	(760)	10,616	—
*95008	Campbell	(408)	39,349	41,544
92587	Canyon Lake	(951)	10,561	11,223
95010	Capitola	(831)	9,918	10,180
*92008	Carlsbad	(760)	105,328	115,330
*95608	Carmichael (c)	(916)	61,762	—
*93013	Carpinteria	(805)	13,040	13,622
*90745	Carson	(310)	91,714	92,735
*91941	Casa de Oro-Mt. Helix (c)	(619)	18,762	—
*91384	Castaic (c)	(661)	19,015	—
*94546	Castro Valley (c)	(510)	61,388	—
*92234	Cathedral City	(760)	51,200	54,596
95307	Ceres	(209)	45,417	48,697
90703	Cerritos	(562)	49,041	51,020
*94541	Cherryland (c)	(510)	14,728	—
*95926	Chico	(530)	86,187	93,293
*91708	Chino	(909)	77,983	89,797
91709	Chino Hills	(909)	74,799	80,374
93610	Chowchilla	(559)	18,720	18,558
*91910	Chula Vista	(619)	243,916	270,471
91702	Citrus (c)	(626)	10,866	—
*95610	Citrus Heights	(916)	83,301	87,931
91711	Claremont	(909)	34,926	36,015
94517	Clayton	(925)	10,897	12,150
95422	Clearlake	(707)	15,250	15,066
*93612	Clovis	(559)	95,631	109,691
92236	Coachella	(760)	40,704	45,443
93210	Coalinga	(559)	13,380	16,766
92324	Colton	(909)	52,154	54,828
*90040	Commerce	(323)	12,823	12,947
*90220	Compton	(310)	96,455	97,612
*94520	Concord	(925)	122,067	129,783
*93212	Corcoran	(559)	24,813	21,835
*92882	Corona	(951)	152,374	167,836
*92118	Coronado	(619)	18,912	24,417
*92626	Costa Mesa	(714)/(949)	109,960	113,825
92679	Coto de Caza (c)	(949)	14,866	—
*91722	Covina	(626)	47,796	48,462
92325	Crestline (c)	(909)	10,770	—
90201	Cudahy	(213)	23,805	24,076
*90230	Culver City	(310)	38,883	39,283
*95014	Cupertino	(408)	58,302	60,777
*90630	Cypress	(714)	47,802	49,064
*94015	Daly City	(415)/(650)	101,123	107,074
*92629	Dana Point	(949)	33,351	33,934
*94526	Danville	(925)	42,039	44,786
*95616	Davis	(530)	65,622	68,986
90250	Del Aire (c)	(310)/(323)	10,001	—
*93215	Delano	(661)	53,041	53,138
95315	Delhi (c)	(209)	10,755	—
*92240	Desert Hot Springs	(760)	25,938	28,757
*91765	Diamond Bar	(909)	55,544	56,665
95619	Diamond Springs (c)	(530)	11,037	—
93618	Dinuba	(559)	21,453	24,034
*94514	Discovery Bay (c)	(925)	13,352	—
95620	Dixon	(707)	18,351	20,202
*90240	Downey	(562)	111,772	113,092
*91008	Duarte	(626)	21,321	21,757
94568	Dublin	(925)	46,036	60,939
92544	East Hemet (c)	(951)	17,418	—
90022	East Los Angeles (c)	(213)	126,496	—
94303	East Palo Alto	(650)	28,155	29,765
90221	East Rancho Dominguez (c)	(310)/(323)	15,135	—
91775	East San Gabriel (c)	(626)	14,874	—
*91752	Eastvale[1]	(909)/(951)	53,668	63,211
*92020	El Cajon	(619)	99,478	103,894
*92243	El Centro	(760)	42,598	44,364
94530	El Cerrito	(510)	23,549	25,515
95762	El Dorado Hills (c)	(916)	42,108	—
*91731	El Monte	(626)	113,475	116,109
*93446	El Paso de Robles (Paso Robles)	(805)	29,793	31,918
90245	El Segundo	(310)	16,654	16,853
*94803	El Sobrante (c) (Contra Costa Co.)	(510)	12,669	—
92503	El Sobrante (c) (Riverside Co.)	(714)/(909)	12,723	—
*95624	Elk Grove	(916)	153,015	171,844
*94608	Emeryville	(510)	10,080	11,758
*92024	Encinitas	(760)	59,518	63,184
*92025	Escondido	(760)	143,911	151,969
*95501	Eureka	(707)	27,191	27,177
93221	Exeter	(559)	10,334	10,553
95628	Fair Oaks (c)	(916)	30,912	—
*94533	Fairfield	(707)	105,321	116,266
94541	Fairview (c)	(510)	10,003	—
*92028	Fallbrook (c)	(760)	30,534	—

ZIP	Place	Area code	2010 population	2017 estimate
93223	Farmersville	(559)	10,588	10,778
*93015	Fillmore	(805)	15,002	15,812
90001	Florence-Graham (c)	(213)	63,387	—
95828	Florin (c)	(916)	47,513	—
*95630	Folsom	(916)	72,203	78,038
*92335	Fontana	(909)	196,069	211,815
95841	Foothill Farms (c)	(916)	33,121	—
95540	Fortuna	(707)	11,926	12,191
94404	Foster City	(650)	30,567	34,412
*92704	Fountain Valley	(714)	55,313	56,313
*94538	Fremont	(510)	214,089	234,962
92596	French Valley (c)	(951)	23,067	—
*93721	Fresno	(559)	494,665	527,438
*92831	Fullerton	(714)	135,161	140,392
95632	Galt	(209)	23,647	26,172
95215	Garden Acres (c)	(209)	10,648	—
*92840	Garden Grove	(714)	170,883	174,226
*90247	Gardena	(310)	58,829	60,224
*95020	Gilroy	(408)	48,821	57,664
92509	Glen Avon (c)	(951)	20,199	—
*91201	Glendale	(818)	191,719	203,054
*91741	Glendora	(626)	50,073	52,445
*93117	Goleta	(805)	29,888	31,116
*92313	Grand Terrace	(951)	12,040	12,595
95746	Granite Bay (c)	(916)	20,402	—
*95945	Grass Valley	(530)	12,860	12,997
93927	Greenfield	(831)	16,330	17,517
*93433	Grover Beach	(805)	13,156	13,628
91745	Hacienda Heights (c)	(626)	54,038	—
94019	Half Moon Bay	(650)	11,324	12,870
*93230	Hanford	(559)	53,967	56,499
90716	Hawaiian Gardens	(562)	14,254	14,450
*90250	Hawthorne	(310)	84,293	87,854
*94541	Hayward	(510)	144,186	160,500
95448	Healdsburg	(707)	11,254	11,840
*92543	Hemet	(951)	78,657	85,160
94547	Hercules	(510)	24,060	25,545
90254	Hermosa Beach	(310)	19,506	19,708
*92344	Hesperia	(760)	90,173	94,859
92346	Highland	(909)	53,104	55,342
94010	Hillsborough	(650)	10,825	11,486
*95023	Hollister	(831)	34,928	38,404
92879	Home Gardens (c)	(909)	11,570	—
*92647	Huntington Beach	(714)	189,992	201,874
90255	Huntington Park	(323)	58,114	58,822
92251	Imperial	(760)	14,758	17,550
*91932	Imperial Beach	(619)	26,324	27,418
*92201	Indio	(760)	76,036	89,793
*90301	Inglewood	(310)	109,673	110,598
*92602	Irvine	(949)	212,375	277,453
93117	Isla Vista (c)	(805)	23,096	—
*91752	Jurupa Valley[2]	(951)	95,005	106,028
93630	Kerman	(559)	13,544	14,932
93930	King City	(831)	12,874	14,055
93631	Kingsburg	(559)	11,382	12,002
*91011	La Cañada Flintridge	(818)	20,246	20,413
*91214	La Crescenta-Montrose (c)	(818)	19,653	—
*90631	La Habra	(562)	60,239	62,466
*91941	La Mesa	(619)	57,065	60,021
*90638	La Mirada	(562)/(714)	48,527	49,095
90623	La Palma	(714)	15,568	15,722
91977	La Presa (c)	(619)	34,169	—
*91744	La Puente	(626)	39,816	40,322
*92253	La Quinta	(760)	37,467	41,304
95401	La Riviera (c)	(916)	10,802	—
91750	La Verne	(909)	31,063	32,461
92694	Ladera Ranch (c)	(949)	22,980	—
94549	Lafayette	(925)	23,893	26,440
*92651	Laguna Beach	(949)	22,723	23,147
*92653	Laguna Hills	(949)	30,344	31,318
*92677	Laguna Niguel	(949)	62,979	66,334
*92637	Laguna Woods	(949)	16,192	16,200
92352	Lake Arrowhead (c)	(909)	12,424	—
*92530	Lake Elsinore	(951)	51,821	66,411
*92630	Lake Forest	(949)	77,264	84,293
*93535	Lake Los Angeles (c)	(661)	12,328	—
92530	Lakeland Village (c)	(909)/(951)	11,541	—
92040	Lakeside (c)	(619)	20,648	—
*90712	Lakewood	(562)	80,048	80,967
93241	Lamont (c)	(661)	15,120	—
*93534	Lancaster	(661)	156,633	160,316
*94939	Larkspur	(415)	11,926	12,396
95330	Lathrop	(209)	18,023	22,781
*90260	Lawndale	(310)	32,769	33,078
*91945	Lemon Grove	(619)	25,320	27,108
95824	Lemon Hill (c)	(916)	13,729	—
*93245	Lemoore	(559)	24,531	26,355
90304	Lennox (c)	(310)	22,753	—
95648	Lincoln	(916)	42,819	47,674
95901	Linda (c)	(530)	17,773	—
93247	Lindsay	(559)	11,768	13,303
95953	Live Oak (c)	(530)	17,158	—
*94550	Livermore	(925)	80,968	90,295
95334	Livingston	(209)	13,058	14,140
*95240	Lodi	(209)	62,134	65,884
*92354	Loma Linda	(909)	23,261	24,196
90717	Lomita	(310)	20,256	20,707
*93436	Lompoc	(805)	42,434	43,542
*90802	Long Beach	(562)	462,257	469,450
*90720	Los Alamitos	(562)	11,449	11,603
*94022	Los Altos	(650)	28,976	30,743
*90012	Los Angeles	(213)	3,792,621	3,999,759
93635	Los Banos	(209)	35,972	39,183
*95030	Los Gatos	(408)	29,413	30,724
*93402	Los Osos (c)	(805)	14,276	—
90262	Lynwood	(310)	69,772	71,099
*93638	Madera	(559)	61,416	65,508
95954	Magalia (c)	(530)	11,310	—
*90265	Malibu	(310)	12,645	12,877
*90266	Manhattan Beach	(310)	35,135	35,924
*95336	Manteca	(209)	67,096	79,268
93933	Marina	(831)	19,718	22,145
94553	Martinez	(925)	35,824	38,373
95901	Marysville	(530)	12,072	12,413
90270	Maywood	(323)	27,395	27,586
93250	McFarland	(661)	12,707	15,093
*95521	McKinleyville (c)	(707)	15,177	—
92570	Mead Valley (c)	(951)	18,510	—
93640	Mendota	(559)	11,014	11,438
*92586	Menifee	(951)	77,519	90,595
*94025	Menlo Park	(650)	32,026	34,357
*95340	Merced	(209)	78,958	83,081
*94941	Mill Valley	(415)	13,903	14,335
94030	Millbrae	(650)	21,532	22,718
*95035	Milpitas	(408)	66,790	78,106
91752	Mira Loma (c)	(951)	21,930	—
*92691	Mission Viejo	(949)	93,305	96,016
*95350	Modesto	(209)	201,165	214,221
*91016	Monrovia	(626)	36,590	37,061
*91763	Montclair	(909)	36,664	39,276
90640	Montebello	(323)	62,500	63,192
*93940	Monterey	(831)	27,810	28,639
*91754	Monterey Park	(323)/(626)	60,269	61,044
*93021	Moorpark	(805)	34,421	36,802
*94556	Moraga	(925)	16,016	17,630
*92551	Moreno Valley	(951)	193,365	207,226
*95037	Morgan Hill	(408)	37,882	45,037
*93442	Morro Bay	(805)	10,234	10,635
*94041	Mountain View	(650)	74,066	81,438
*92562	Murrieta	(951)	103,466	113,326
92407	Muscoy (c)	(909)	10,644	—
*94558	Napa	(707)	76,915	79,774
*91950	National City	(619)	58,582	61,363
94560	Newark	(510)	42,573	47,531
95360	Newman	(209)	10,224	11,361
*92657	Newport Beach	(949)	85,186	86,160
93444	Nipomo (c)	(805)	16,714	—
92860	Norco	(951)	27,063	26,761
95603	North Auburn (c)	(530)	13,022	—
94025	North Fair Oaks (c)	(650)	14,687	—
95660	North Highlands (c)	(916)	42,694	—
92705	North Tustin (c)	(714)	24,917	—
*90650	Norwalk	(562)	105,549	106,084
*94947	Novato	(415)	51,904	55,980
*91377	Oak Park (c)	(805)/(818)	13,811	—
95361	Oakdale	(209)	20,675	23,150
*94601	Oakland	(510)	390,724	425,195
94561	Oakley	(925)	35,432	41,714
*92054	Oceanside	(760)	167,086	176,193
93308	Oildale (c)	(661)	32,684	—
95961	Olivehurst (c)	(530)	13,656	—
*91761	Ontario	(909)	163,924	175,841
*92866	Orange	(714)	136,416	140,560
95662	Orangevale (c)	(916)	33,960	—
*93455	Orcutt (c)	(805)	28,905	—
94563	Orinda	(925)	17,643	19,730
*95965	Oroville	(530)	15,546	19,121
*93030	Oxnard	(805)	197,899	210,037
93950	Pacific Grove	(831)	15,041	15,698
94044	Pacifica	(650)	37,234	39,087
*92260	Palm Desert	(760)	48,445	52,932
*92262	Palm Springs	(760)	44,552	48,142
*93550	Palmdale	(661)	152,750	157,519
*94303	Palo Alto	(650)	64,403	67,178
*90274	Palos Verdes Estates	(310)	13,438	13,544
*95969	Paradise	(530)	26,218	26,682
90723	Paramount	(562)	54,098	54,909
95823	Parkway (c)	(916)	14,670	—
93648	Parlier	(559)	14,494	15,250
*91101	Pasadena	(323)/(626)/(818)	137,122	142,647
	Paso Robles. *See* El Paso de Robles			
95363	Patterson	(209)	20,413	22,124
92509	Pedley (c)	(951)	12,672	—
*92570	Perris	(951)	68,386	77,879
*94952	Petaluma	(707)	57,941	60,870
*92371	Phelan (c)	(760)	14,304	—
*90660	Pico Rivera	(562)	62,942	63,522
*94611	Piedmont	(510)	10,667	11,378

ZIP	Place	Area code	2010 population	2017 estimate
94564	Pinole	(510)	18,390	19,364
94565	Pittsburg	(925)	63,264	72,141
*92870	Placentia	(714)	50,533	52,157
95667	Placerville	(530)	10,389	10,936
94523	Pleasant Hill	(925)	33,152	34,987
*94566	Pleasanton	(925)	70,285	83,007
*91765	Pomona	(909)	149,058	152,939
*93041	Port Hueneme	(805)	21,723	22,327
*93257	Porterville	(559)	54,165	59,145
*92064	Poway	(858)	47,811	50,041
93907	Prunedale (c)	(831)	17,560	—
*93536	Quartz Hill (c)	(661)	10,912	—
92065	Ramona (c)	(760)	20,292	—
*95670	Rancho Cordova	(916)	64,776	73,563
*91730	Rancho Cucamonga	(909)	165,269	177,452
92270	Rancho Mirage	(760)	17,218	18,306
90275	Rancho Palos Verdes	(310)	41,643	42,364
*92019	Rancho San Diego (c)	(619)	21,208	—
92688	Rancho Santa Margarita	(949)	47,853	48,793
96080	Red Bluff	(530)	14,076	14,287
*96001	Redding	(530)	89,861	91,794
*92373	Redlands	(909)	68,747	71,554
*90277	Redondo Beach	(310)	66,748	67,908
*94063	Redwood City	(650)	76,815	86,685
93654	Reedley	(559)	24,194	25,620
*92376	Rialto	(909)	99,171	103,562
*94801	Richmond	(510)	103,701	110,040
*93555	Ridgecrest	(760)	27,616	28,880
95673	Rio Linda (c)	(916)	15,106	—
95366	Ripon	(209)	14,297	15,677
95367	Riverbank	(209)	22,678	24,740
*92501	Riverside	(951)	303,871	327,728
*95677	Rocklin	(916)	56,974	64,838
*94928	Rohnert Park	(707)	40,971	42,838
93560	Rosamond (c)	(661)	18,150	—
93314	Rosedale (c)	(661)	14,058	—
*91770	Rosemead	(626)	53,764	54,554
95826	Rosemont (c)	(916)	22,681	—
*95678	Roseville	(916)	118,788	135,329
90720	Rossmoor (c)	(714)	10,244	—
91748	Rowland Heights (c)	(626)	48,993	—
92509	Rubidoux (c)	(951)	34,280	—
*95814	Sacramento	(916)	466,488	501,901
95368	Salida (c)	(209)	13,722	—
*93901	Salinas	(831)	150,441	157,596
*94960	San Anselmo	(415)	12,336	12,580
*92401	San Bernardino	(909)	209,924	216,995
94066	San Bruno	(650)	41,114	43,299
*93001	San Buenaventura (Ventura)	(805)	106,433	110,790
94070	San Carlos	(650)	28,406	30,499
*92672	San Clemente	(949)	63,522	65,267
*92101	San Diego	(619)/(858)	1,307,402	1,419,516
92065	San Diego Country Estates (c)	(760)	10,109	—
91773	San Dimas	(909)	33,371	34,326
*91340	San Fernando	(818)	23,645	24,714
*94102	San Francisco	(415)	805,235	884,363
*91775	San Gabriel	(626)	39,718	40,514
*92582	San Jacinto	(951)	44,199	48,254
*95113	San Jose	(408)	945,942	1,035,317
*92675	San Juan Capistrano	(949)	34,593	36,064
*94577	San Leandro	(510)	84,950	90,553
94580	San Lorenzo (c)	(510)	23,452	—
*93401	San Luis Obispo	(805)	45,119	47,541
*92069	San Marcos	(760)	83,781	96,198
*91108	San Marino	(626)	13,147	13,327
*94403	San Mateo	(650)	97,207	104,748
*94806	San Pablo	(510)	29,139	31,156
*94901	San Rafael	(415)	57,713	59,070
*94583	San Ramon	(925)	72,148	75,931
93657	Sanger	(559)	24,270	25,161
*92701	Santa Ana	(714)/(949)	324,528	334,136
*93101	Santa Barbara	(805)	88,410	92,101
*95050	Santa Clara	(408)	116,468	127,134
*91355	Santa Clarita	(661)	176,320	210,888
*95060	Santa Cruz	(831)	59,946	65,021
90670	Santa Fe Springs	(562)	16,223	17,980
*93454	Santa Maria	(805)	99,553	107,014
*90401	Santa Monica	(310)	89,736	92,306
*93060	Santa Paula	(805)	29,321	30,313
*95401	Santa Rosa	(707)	167,815	175,269
*92071	Santee	(619)	53,413	58,113
*95070	Saratoga	(408)	29,926	30,905
*95066	Scotts Valley	(831)	11,580	11,945
90740	Seal Beach	(562)	24,168	24,326
93955	Seaside	(831)	33,025	34,150
93662	Selma	(559)	23,219	24,782
93263	Shafter	(661)	16,988	19,608
*96019	Shasta Lake	(916)	10,164	10,190
*91024	Sierra Madre	(626)	10,917	11,038
*90755	Signal Hill	(562)	11,016	11,622
*93065	Simi Valley	(805)	124,237	126,878
92075	Solana Beach	(858)	12,867	13,444

ZIP	Place	Area code	2010 population	2017 estimate
93960	Soledad	(831)	25,738	26,273
95476	Sonoma	(707)	10,648	11,108
91733	South El Monte	(626)	20,116	20,987
90280	South Gate	(323)	94,396	95,430
*96150	South Lake Tahoe	(530)	21,403	21,978
*91030	South Pasadena	(323)/(626)	25,619	25,888
*94080	South San Francisco	(650)	63,632	67,429
91744	South San Jose Hills (c)	(626)	20,551	—
90605	South Whittier (c)	(562)	57,156	—
*91977	Spring Valley (c) (San Diego Co.)	(619)	28,205	—
*94305	Stanford (c)	(650)	13,809	—
90680	Stanton	(714)	38,186	38,528
91381	Stevenson Ranch (c)	(661)	17,557	—
*95202	Stockton	(209)	291,707	310,496
*94585	Suisun City	(707)	28,111	29,639
93543	Sun Village (c)	(661)	11,565	—
*94086	Sunnyvale	(408)	140,081	153,656
*96130	Susanville	(530)	17,947	15,326
94941	Tamalpais-Homestead Valley (c)	(415)	10,735	—
*93561	Tehachapi	(661)	14,414	12,630
*92590	Temecula	(951)	100,097	114,327
92883	Temescal Valley (c)	(951)	22,535	—
91780	Temple City	(626)	35,558	36,367
*91360	Thousand Oaks	(805)	126,683	128,995
*90503	Torrance	(310)	145,438	146,758
*95376	Tracy	(209)	82,922	90,889
*96161	Truckee	(916)	16,180	16,553
*93274	Tulare	(559)	59,278	63,855
*95380	Turlock	(209)	68,549	73,556
*92780	Tustin	(714)/(949)	75,540	80,498
*92277	Twentynine Palms	(760)	25,048	26,542
*95482	Ukiah	(707)	16,075	16,036
94587	Union City	(510)	69,516	75,343
*91784	Upland	(909)	73,732	76,999
*95687	Vacaville	(707)	92,428	100,032
91744	Valinda (c)	(626)	22,822	—
92343	Valle Vista (c)	(951)	14,578	—
*94590	Vallejo	(707)	115,942	122,105
	Ventura. See San Buenaventura			
*92392	Victorville	(760)	115,903	122,441
90043	View Park-Windsor Hills (c)	(310)	11,075	—
91722	Vincent (c)	(925)	15,922	—
95829	Vineyard (c)	(916)	24,836	—
*93277	Visalia	(559)	124,442	133,010
*92084	Vista	(760)	93,834	101,568
*91789	Walnut	(909)	29,172	30,199
*94596	Walnut Creek	(925)	64,173	69,773
90255	Walnut Park (c)	(213)	15,966	—
93280	Wasco	(661)	25,545	26,994
*95076	Watsonville	(831)	51,199	54,098
90502	West Carson (c)	(310)	21,699	—
*91790	West Covina	(626)	106,098	107,598
*90069	West Hollywood	(310)/(323)	34,399	37,080
91746	West Puente Valley (c)	(626)	22,636	—
*95691	West Sacramento	(916)	48,744	53,512
*90606	West Whittier-Los Nietos (c)	(562)	25,540	—
*92683	Westminster	(714)	89,701	91,564
*90047	Westmont (c)	(213)	31,853	—
*90602	Whittier	(562)	85,331	86,838
92595	Wildomar	(951)	32,176	36,932
*90222	Willowbrook (c)	(323)	35,983	—
95492	Windsor	(707)	26,801	27,548
92040	Winter Gardens (c)	(619)	20,631	—
95388	Winton (c)	(209)	10,613	—
92504	Woodcrest (c)	(909)/(951)	14,347	—
*95695	Woodland	(530)	55,468	60,012
*92886	Yorba Linda	(714)	64,234	68,229
*95991	Yuba City	(530)	64,925	66,860
92399	Yucaipa	(909)	51,367	53,683
*92284	Yucca Valley	(760)	20,700	21,748

(1) Incorporated after the 2010 Census was conducted. Data in 2010 column is for Eastvale CDP. (2) Incorporated after the 2010 Census was conducted. Data in 2010 column is Census Bureau estimate.

Colorado

Area code 720 overlays area code 303.

ZIP	Place	Area code	2010 population	2017 estimate
*80004	Arvada	(303)	106,433	118,807
*80010	Aurora	(303)	325,078	366,623
80221	Berkley (c)	(970)	11,207	—
*80908	Black Forest (c)	(719)	13,116	—
*80302	Boulder	(303)	97,385	107,125
*80601	Brighton	(303)	33,352	40,562
*80020	Broomfield	(303)	55,889	68,341
*81212	Cañon City	(719)	16,400	16,539
80108	Castle Pines[1]	(303)	10,360	10,523
*80104	Castle Rock	(303)	48,231	62,276
*80015	Centennial	(303)	100,377	110,250

ZIP	Place	Area code	2010 population	2017 estimate
80111	Cherry Creek (c)	(303)	11,120	—
81222	Cimarron Hills (c)	(719)	16,161	—
81520	Clifton (c)	(970)	19,889	—
*80903	Colorado Springs	(719)	416,427	464,474
*80128	Columbine (c)	(303)	24,280	—
*80022	Commerce City	(303)	45,913	55,923
80304	Dakota Ridge (c)	(303)	32,005	—
*80202	Denver	(303)	600,158	704,621
*81301	Durango	(970)	16,887	18,465
81632	Edwards (c)	(970)	10,266	—
*80110	Englewood	(303)	30,255	34,407
*80516	Erie	(303)	18,135	24,234
*80620	Evans	(970)	18,537	20,470
80221	Federal Heights	(303)	11,467	12,744
*80520	Firestone	(303)	10,147	13,825
80913	Fort Carson (c)	(719)	13,813	—
*80521	Fort Collins	(970)	143,986	165,080
*80701	Fort Morgan	(970)	11,315	11,281
80817	Fountain	(719)	25,846	29,804
*80530	Frederick	(303)	8,679	12,687
81521	Fruita	(970)	12,646	13,294
*80401	Golden	(303)	18,867	20,571
*81501	Grand Junction	(970)	58,566	62,475
*80631	Greeley	(970)	92,889	105,448
*80111	Greenwood Village	(303)	13,925	15,721
*80126	Highlands Ranch (c)	(303)	96,713	—
80534	Johnstown	(970)	9,887	15,478
*80127	Ken Caryl (c)	(303)	32,438	—
80026	Lafayette	(303)	24,453	28,328
*80226	Lakewood	(303)	142,980	154,958
*80120	Littleton	(303)	41,737	47,734
*80124	Lone Tree	(303)	10,218	13,566
*80501	Longmont	(303)	86,270	94,341
80027	Louisville	(303)	18,376	21,128
*80537	Loveland	(970)	66,859	76,701
*81401	Montrose	(970)	19,132	19,305
*80233	Northglenn	(303)	35,789	38,928
*80134	Parker	(303)	45,297	54,202
*81003	Pueblo	(719)	106,595	111,127
81007	Pueblo West (c)	(719)	29,637	—
80911	Security-Widefield (c)	(719)	32,882	—
80221	Sherrelwood (c)	(303)	18,287	—
*80487	Steamboat Springs	(970)	12,088	12,965
*80751	Sterling	(970)	14,777	13,961
80027	Superior	(303)	12,483	12,951
80134	The Pinery (c)	(303)	10,517	—
*80229	Thornton	(303)	118,772	136,978
80229	Welby (c)	(303)	14,846	—
*80031	Westminster	(303)	106,114	112,812
*80033	Wheat Ridge	(303)	30,166	31,294
*80550	Windsor	(970)	18,644	25,330

(1) Place was incorporated after the 2010 Census was conducted. Data in 2010 column is Census Bureau estimate.

Connecticut

Area code 475 overlays area code 203. Area code 959 overlays 860. See introductory note.

ZIP	Place	Area code	2010 population	2017 estimate
06401	Ansonia	(203)	19,249	18,813
06001	Avon	(860)	18,098	18,352
06037	Berlin	(860)	19,866	20,505
06801	Bethel	(203)	18,584	19,802
06002	Bloomfield	(860)	20,486	21,406
06405	Branford	(203)	28,026	28,111
*06604	Bridgeport	(203)	144,229	146,579
*06010	Bristol	(860)	60,477	60,223
06804	Brookfield	(203)	16,452	17,133
06019	Canton	(860)	10,292	10,298
*06410	Cheshire	(203)	29,261	29,330
06413	Clinton	(860)	13,260	12,957
*06415	Colchester	(860)	16,068	16,029
06238	Coventry	(860)	12,435	12,439
06416	Cromwell	(860)	14,005	13,956
*06810	Danbury	(203)	80,893	85,246
*06820	Darien	(203)	20,732	21,887
06418	Derby	(203)	12,902	12,581
*06424	East Hampton	(860)	12,959	12,901
*06108	East Hartford	(860)	51,252	50,319
*06512	East Haven	(203)	29,257	28,857
06333	East Lyme	(860)	19,159	18,789
06088	East Windsor	(860)	11,162	11,395
06029	Ellington	(860)	15,602	16,195
*06082	Enfield	(860)	44,654	44,585
*06824	Fairfield	(203)	59,404	62,105
*06032	Farmington	(860)	25,340	25,572
06033	Glastonbury	(860)	34,427	34,575
06035	Granby	(860)	11,282	11,357
*06830	Greenwich	(203)	61,171	62,855
*06830	Greenwich (c)	(203)	12,942	—
06351	Griswold	(860)	11,951	11,687
*06340	Groton	(860)	40,115	39,075
06437	Guilford	(203)	22,375	22,283
*06514	Hamden	(203)	60,960	61,284
*06103	Hartford	(860)	124,775	123,400
*06239	Killingly	(860)	17,370	17,172
06339	Ledyard	(860)	15,051	14,837
06443	Madison	(203)	18,269	18,196
*06040	Manchester	(860)	58,241	57,932
*06040	Manchester (c)	(860)	30,577	—
*06250	Mansfield	(860)	26,543	25,912
*06450	Meriden	(203)	60,868	59,927
*06457	Middletown	(860)	47,648	46,478
*06460	Milford (balance)	(203)	51,271	52,970
*06460	Milford	(203)	52,759	54,508
06468	Monroe	(203)	19,479	19,635
*06353	Montville	(860)	19,571	19,149
06770	Naugatuck	(203)	31,862	31,461
*06051	New Britain	(860)	73,206	72,710
06840	New Canaan	(203)	19,738	20,376
06812	New Fairfield	(203)	13,881	14,017
*06511	New Haven	(203)	129,779	131,014
06320	New London	(860)	27,620	27,072
06776	New Milford	(860)	28,142	27,099
*06111	Newington	(860)	30,562	30,404
06470	Newtown	(203)	27,560	27,965
06471	North Branford	(203)	14,407	14,208
06473	North Haven	(203)	24,093	23,751
*06850	Norwalk	(203)	85,603	89,005
*06360	Norwich	(860)	40,493	39,470
06475	Old Saybrook	(860)	10,242	10,132
06477	Orange	(203)	13,956	13,997
06478	Oxford	(203)	12,683	13,035
06374	Plainfield	(860)	15,405	15,093
06062	Plainville	(860)	17,716	17,705
06782	Plymouth	(860)	12,243	11,718
*06877	Ridgefield	(203)	24,638	25,187
06067	Rocky Hill	(860)	19,709	20,105
*06483	Seymour	(203)	16,540	16,583
06484	Shelton	(203)	39,559	41,397
06070	Simsbury	(860)	23,511	24,952
06071	Somers	(860)	11,444	11,106
06074	South Windsor	(860)	25,709	25,937
06488	Southbury	(203)	19,904	19,571
06489	Southington	(860)	43,069	43,863
*06075	Stafford	(860)	12,087	11,944
*06614	Stamford	(203)	122,643	130,824
06378	Stonington	(860)	18,545	18,593
*06268	Storrs (c)	(860)	15,344	—
*06614	Stratford	(203)	51,384	52,345
*06078	Suffield	(860)	15,735	15,698
06084	Tolland	(860)	15,052	14,722
*06790	Torrington	(860)	36,383	34,538
06611	Trumbull	(203)	36,018	36,154
06066	Vernon	(860)	29,179	29,289
*06492	Wallingford	(203)	45,135	44,741
06492	Wallingford Center (c)	(203)	18,209	—
*06702	Waterbury	(203)	110,366	108,629
06385	Waterford	(860)	19,517	19,007
*06795	Watertown	(860)	22,514	21,740
*06105	West Hartford	(860)	63,268	63,133
06516	West Haven	(203)	55,564	54,843
06883	Weston	(203)	10,179	10,331
*06880	Westport	(203)	26,391	28,042
*06109	Wethersfield	(860)	26,668	26,195
06226	Willimantic (c)	(860)	17,737	—
06897	Wilton	(203)	18,062	18,581
*06098	Winchester	(860)	11,242	10,739
06280	Windham	(860)	25,268	24,686
*06095	Windsor	(860)	29,044	28,898
*06096	Windsor Locks	(860)	12,498	12,554
*06716	Wolcott	(203)	16,680	16,672

Delaware

Area code 302 applies to the entire state.

ZIP	Place	2010 population	2017 estimate
19701	Bear (c)	19,371	—
19713	Brookside (c)	14,353	—
*19901	Dover	36,047	37,538
19702	Glasgow (c)	14,303	—
19707	Hockessin (c)	13,527	—
19709	Middletown	18,871	21,897
19963	Milford	9,559	11,075
*19711	Newark	31,454	33,858
19808	Pike Creek Valley (c)	11,217	—
19977	Smyrna	10,023	11,584
*19801	Wilmington	70,851	71,106

District of Columbia

Area code 202 applies to the entire district.

ZIP	Place	2010 population	2017 estimate
*20001	Washington	601,723	693,972

Florida

Part of area code 321 overlays area code 407. Area code 754 overlays 954. Area code 786 overlays 305.

ZIP	Place	Area code	2010 population	2017 estimate
*32828	Alafaya (c)	(407)	78,113	—
*32701	Altamonte Springs	(407)	41,496	44,277
33572	Apollo Beach (c)	(813)	14,055	—
*32712	Apopka	(407)	41,542	51,564
32233	Atlantic Beach	(904)	12,655	13,608
*33823	Auburndale	(863)	13,507	15,973
*33160	Aventura	(305)	35,762	38,202
*33825	Avon Park	(863)	8,836	10,408
32807	Azalea Park (c)	(407)	12,556	—
*33830	Bartow	(863)	17,298	19,597
34667	Bayonet Point (c)	(727)	23,467	—
*33507	Bayshore Gardens (c)	(941)	16,323	—
*33756	Bellair-Meadowbrook Terrace (c)	(904)	13,343	—
33430	Belle Glade	(561)	17,467	19,666
*34420	Belleview (c)	(352)	23,355	—
*33509	Bloomingdale (c)	(813)	22,711	—
*33431	Boca Raton	(561)	84,392	98,150
*34135	Bonita Springs	(239)	43,914	56,088
*33436	Boynton Beach	(561)	68,217	77,702
*34201	Bradenton	(941)	49,546	56,508
*33510	Brandon (c)	(813)	103,483	—
32503	Brent (c)	(850)	21,804	—
33142	Brownsville (c)	(305)	15,313	—
34743	Buenaventura Lakes (c)	(407)	26,079	—
32404	Callaway	(850)	14,405	15,144
32920	Cape Canaveral	(321)	9,912	10,413
*33990	Cape Coral	(239)	154,305	183,365
*33618	Carrollwood (c)	(813)	33,365	—
*32707	Casselberry	(407)	26,241	28,395
33558	Cheval (c)	(813)	10,702	—
33625	Citrus Park (c)	(813)	24,252	—
*33755	Clearwater	(727)	107,685	115,513
*34711	Clermont	(352)	28,742	35,211
*32922	Cocoa	(321)	17,140	18,532
*32931	Cocoa Beach	(321)	11,231	11,733
*33063	Coconut Creek	(954)	52,909	61,010
32809	Conway (c)	(407)	13,467	—
*33328	Cooper City	(954)	28,547	35,732
*33134	Coral Gables	(305)	46,780	51,095
*33065	Coral Springs	(954)	121,096	133,037
33157	Coral Terrace (c)	(305)	24,376	—
33015	Country Club (c)	(305)	47,105	—
33196	Country Walk (c)	(305)	15,997	—
*32536	Crestview	(850)	20,978	23,856
*33189	Cutler Bay	(305)	40,286	45,101
33919	Cypress Lake (c)	(239)	11,846	—
*33004	Dania Beach	(954)	29,639	32,030
*33314	Davie	(954)	91,992	105,149
*32114	Daytona Beach	(386)	61,005	68,055
*32713	DeBary	(386)	19,320	20,784
*33441	Deerfield Beach	(954)	75,018	80,571
*32720	DeLand	(386)	27,031	32,506
*33444	Delray Beach	(561)	60,522	68,749
*32738	Deltona	(386)	85,182	90,746
*32541	Destin	(850)	12,305	13,765
*32819	Doctor Phillips (c)	(407)	10,981	—
*33166	Doral	(305)	45,704	61,130
*34698	Dunedin	(727)	35,321	36,545
*34685	East Lake (c)	(727)	30,962	—
33619	East Lake-Orient Park (c)	(813)	22,753	—
32583	East Milton (c)	(850)	11,074	—
*32132	Edgewater	(386)	20,750	22,399
33614	Egypt Lake-Leto (c)	(813)	35,282	—
34680	Elfers (c)	(727)	13,986	—
*34223	Englewood (c)	(941)	14,863	—
32534	Ensley (c)	(850)	20,602	—
*33928	Estero[1]	(239)	22,612	33,048
*32726	Eustis	(352)	18,558	20,827
32804	Fairview Shores (c)	(305)	10,239	—
*32034	Fernandina Beach	(904)	11,487	12,292
32514	Ferry Pass (c)	(850)	28,921	—
33547	Fish Hawk (c)	(813)	14,087	—
*32003	Fleming Island (c)	(904)	27,126	—
*33034	Florida City	(305)	11,245	12,155
32960	Florida Ridge (c)	(772)	18,164	—
32714	Forest City (c)	(407)	13,854	—
*33301	Fort Lauderdale	(954)	165,521	180,072
*33901	Fort Myers	(239)	62,298	79,943
*34950	Fort Pierce	(772)	41,590	45,581
*32548	Fort Walton Beach	(850)	19,507	21,895
33172	Fountainebleau (c)	(305)	59,764	—
34747	Four Corners (c)	(863)	26,116	—
32259	Fruit Cove (c)	(904)	29,362	—
34232	Fruitville (c)	(941)	13,224	—
*32601	Gainesville	(352)	124,354	132,249
33534	Gibsonton (c)	(813)	14,234	—
33138	Gladeview (c)	(954)	11,535	—
33143	Glenvar Heights (c)	(305)	16,898	—
34116	Golden Gate (c)	(239)	23,961	—
33055	Golden Glades (c)	(305)	33,145	—
32733	Goldenrod (c)	(407)	12,039	—
32560	Gonzalez (c)	(850)	13,273	—
33170	Goulds (c)	(305)	10,103	—
*33463	Greenacres	(561)	37,573	40,719
*34736	Groveland	(352)	8,729	13,474
33581	Gulf Gate Estates (c)	(941)	10,911	—
*33707	Gulfport	(727)	12,029	12,371
*33844	Haines City	(863)	20,535	24,304
*33009	Hallandale Beach	(954)	37,113	39,831
*33010	Hialeah	(305)	224,669	239,673
*33016	Hialeah Gardens	(305)	21,744	24,156
33846	Highland City (c)	(863)	10,834	—
*33455	Hobe Sound (c)	(772)	11,521	—
*34690	Holiday (c)	(727)	22,403	—
*33019	Holly Hill	(386)	11,659	12,218
*33019	Hollywood	(954)	140,768	153,627
*33030	Homestead	(305)	60,512	69,907
34447	Homosassa Springs (c)	(352)	13,791	—
34787	Horizon West (c)	(352)	14,000	—
*34667	Hudson (c)	(727)	12,158	—
32837	Hunters Creek (c)	(407)	14,321	—
*34142	Immokalee (c)	(239)	24,154	—
33908	Iona (c)	(239)	15,369	—
33162	Ives Estates (c)	(305)	19,525	—
*32202	Jacksonville	(904)	821,784	892,062
*32250	Jacksonville Beach	(904)	21,362	23,518
33568	Jasmine Estates (c)	(727)	18,989	—
*34957	Jensen Beach (c)	(772)	11,707	—
*33458	Jupiter	(561)	55,156	64,976
33478	Jupiter Farms (c)	(561)	11,994	—
33183	Kendale Lakes (c)	(305)	56,148	—
*33156	Kendall (c)	(305)	75,371	—
33193	Kendall West (c)	(305)	36,154	—
33149	Key Biscayne	(305)	12,344	13,182
33037	Key Largo (c)	(305)	10,433	—
*33040	Key West	(305)	24,649	25,208
33556	Keystone (c)	(813)	24,039	—
*34741	Kissimmee	(407)	59,682	71,104
*32159	Lady Lake	(352)	13,926	15,317
32054	Lake Butler (c)	(386)	15,400	—
*32055	Lake City	(386)	12,046	12,163
33612	Lake Magdalene (c)	(813)	28,509	—
*32746	Lake Mary	(407)	13,822	16,474
*33853	Lake Wales	(863)	14,225	16,066
*33460	Lake Worth	(561)	34,910	38,107
*33801	Lakeland	(863)	97,422	108,054
33801	Lakeland Highlands (c)	(863)	11,056	—
32073	Lakeside (c)	(904)	30,943	—
34951	Lakewood Park (c)	(772)	11,323	—
*34639	Land O' Lakes (c)	(813)	31,996	—
*33462	Lantana	(561)	10,423	11,824
*33770	Largo	(727)	77,648	84,754
*33319	Lauderdale Lakes	(954)	32,593	36,069
*33313	Lauderhill	(954)	66,887	71,970
33714	Lealman (c)	(727)	19,879	—
*34748	Leesburg	(352)	20,117	22,689
*33936	Lehigh Acres (c)	(239)	86,784	—
*33033	Leisure City (c)	(305)	22,655	—
*33064	Lighthouse Point	(954)	10,344	11,242
32810	Lockhart (c)	(407)	13,060	—
*32750	Longwood	(407)	13,657	15,061
*33549	Lutz (c)	(813)	19,344	—
32444	Lynn Haven	(850)	18,493	20,922
*32751	Maitland	(407)	15,751	17,554
33550	Mango (c)	(813)	11,313	—
*34145	Marco Island	(239)	16,413	17,904
*33063	Margate	(954)	53,284	58,430
32824	Meadow Woods (c)	(407)	25,558	—
*32901	Melbourne	(321)	76,068	82,011
*32953	Merritt Island (c)	(321)	34,743	—
33125	Miami	(305)	399,457	463,347
*33140	Miami Beach	(305)	87,779	92,307
*33014	Miami Gardens	(305)	107,167	113,750
*33014	Miami Lakes	(305)	29,361	31,087
33138	Miami Shores	(305)	10,493	10,649
*33166	Miami Springs	(305)	13,809	14,424
*32068	Middleburg (c)	(904)	13,008	—
32563	Midway (c) (Santa Rosa Co.)	(850)	16,115	—
34715	Minneola	(352)	9,403	11,529
*33023	Miramar	(305)	122,041	140,328
*32757	Mount Dora	(352)	12,370	13,916
32526	Myrtle Grove (c)	(850)	15,870	—
*34102	Naples	(239)	19,537	21,948
32566	Navarre (c)	(850)	31,378	—
*34653	New Port Richey	(727)	14,911	16,256
34653	New Port Richey East (c)	(727)	10,036	—
*32168	New Smyrna Beach	(386)	22,464	26,470
*32578	Niceville	(850)	12,749	15,249
*33917	North Fort Myers (c)	(239)	39,407	—
*33068	North Lauderdale	(954)	41,023	44,198
*33161	North Miami	(305)	58,786	62,225
*33160	North Miami Beach	(305)	41,523	44,124
*33408	North Palm Beach	(561)	12,015	13,057
*34286	North Port	(941)	57,357	66,300

ZIP	Place	Area code	2010 population	2017 estimate
*33624	Northdale (c).	(813)	22,079	—
33860	Oak Ridge (c)	(407)	22,685	—
*33334	Oakland Park	(954)	41,363	45,035
32065	Oakleaf Plantation (c)	(904)	20,315	—
*34470	Ocala	(352)	56,315	59,110
34761	Ocoee	(407)	35,579	46,402
*33163	Ojus (c)	(305)	18,036	—
34677	Oldsmar	(813)	13,591	14,617
*33265	Olympia Heights (c)	(305)	13,488	—
*33054	Opa-locka	(305)	15,219	16,479
*32763	Orange City	(386)	10,599	11,697
*32801	Orlando	(407)	238,300	280,257
*32174	Ormond Beach	(386)	38,137	42,816
*32765	Oviedo	(407)	33,342	40,785
32571	Pace (c)	(850)	20,039	—
*32177	Palatka	(386)	10,558	10,389
*32905	Palm Bay	(321)	103,190	111,657
*33410	Palm Beach Gardens	(561)	48,452	55,036
*34990	Palm City (c)	(772)	23,120	—
*32137	Palm Coast	(386)	75,180	86,516
*34683	Palm Harbor (c)	(727)	57,439	—
*33601	Palm River-Clair Mel (c)	(813)	21,024	—
*33406	Palm Springs	(561)	18,928	24,892
32082	Palm Valley (c)	(904)	20,019	—
*34221	Palmetto	(941)	12,606	13,661
*33157	Palmetto Bay	(305)	23,410	24,710
33157	Palmetto Estates (c)	(305)	13,535	—
*32401	Panama City	(850)	36,484	36,986
*32413	Panama City Beach	(850)	12,018	12,757
*33067	Parkland	(954)	23,962	32,202
*33026	Pembroke Pines	(954)	154,750	170,712
*32502	Pensacola	(850)	51,923	52,590
*32809	Pine Castle (c)	(407)	10,805	—
*32808	Pine Hills (c)	(407)	60,076	—
*33156	Pinecrest	(305)	18,223	19,651
*33781	Pinellas Park	(727)	49,079	52,854
33168	Pinewood (c)	(305)	16,520	—
*33566	Plant City	(813)	34,721	38,714
*33311	Plantation	(954)	84,955	93,909
*34758	Poinciana (c)	(407)	53,193	—
*33060	Pompano Beach	(954)	99,845	110,473
*33952	Port Charlotte (c)	(941)	54,392	—
*32129	Port Orange	(386)	56,048	63,203
32927	Port St. John (c)	(321)	12,267	—
*34953	Port St. Lucie	(772)	164,603	189,344
34992	Port Salerno (c)	(772)	10,091	—
*33032	Princeton (c)	(305)	22,038	—
*33950	Punta Gorda	(941)	16,641	19,761
*33177	Richmond West (c)	(305)	31,973	—
*33569	Riverview (c)	(813)	71,050	—
*33404	Riviera Beach	(561)	32,488	34,674
*32955	Rockledge	(321)	24,926	27,476
*33411	Royal Palm Beach	(561)	34,140	38,592
*33570	Ruskin (c)	(813)	17,208	—
34695	Safety Harbor	(727)	16,884	17,844
*32084	Saint Augustine	(904)	12,975	14,243
*34769	Saint Cloud	(407)	35,183	51,282
*33701	Saint Petersburg	(727)	244,769	263,255
33912	San Carlos Park (c)	(239)	16,824	—
*32771	Sanford	(407)	53,570	59,317
*34231	Sarasota	(941)	51,917	56,994
33577	Sarasota Springs (c)	(941)	14,395	—
32937	Satellite Beach	(321)	10,109	11,056
*32958	Sebastian	(772)	21,929	25,174
*33870	Sebring	(863)	10,491	10,696
*33772	Seminole	(727)	17,233	18,576
34610	Shady Hills (c)	(727)	11,523	—
33505	South Bradenton (c)	(941)	22,178	—
*32119	South Daytona	(386)	12,252	12,936
*33143	South Miami	(305)	11,657	12,281
33157	South Miami Heights (c)	(305)	35,696	—
33595	South Venice (c)	(941)	13,949	—
32824	Southchase (c)	(407)	15,921	—
*34604	Spring Hill (c)	(352)	98,621	—
*34994	Stuart	(772)	15,593	16,543
*33573	Sun City Center (c)	(813)	19,258	—
33160	Sunny Isles Beach	(305)	20,832	22,348
*33325	Sunrise	(954)	84,439	94,323
*33283	Sunset (c)	(305)	16,389	—
*33144	Sweetwater	(305)	13,499	21,028
*32301	Tallahassee	(850)	181,376	191,049
*33321	Tamarac	(954)	60,427	65,669
*33184	Tamiami (c)	(305)	55,271	—
*33602	Tampa	(813)	335,709	385,430
*34689	Tarpon Springs	(727)	23,484	25,331
32778	Tavares	(352)	13,951	16,865
*33617	Temple Terrace	(813)	24,541	26,489
33412	The Acreage (c)	(561)	38,704	—
33186	The Crossings (c)	(305)	22,758	—
33196	The Hammocks (c)	(305)	51,003	—
*32162	The Villages (c)	(352)	51,442	—
33592	Thonotosassa (c)	(813)	13,014	—
33186	Three Lakes (c)	(305)	15,047	—
*32780	Titusville	(321)	43,761	46,263
33615	Town 'n' Country (c)	(813)	78,442	—

ZIP	Place	Area code	2010 population	2017 estimate
34655	Trinity (c)	(813)	10,907	—
33613	University (c) (Hillsborough Co.)	(813)	41,163	—
32826	University (c) (Orange Co.)	(407)	31,084	—
33165	University Park (c)	(305)	26,995	—
32401	Upper Grand Lagoon (c)	(850)	13,963	—
*33594	Valrico (c)	(813)	35,545	—
*34285	Venice	(941)	20,748	23,020
*32960	Vero Beach	(772)	15,220	16,919
*32960	Vero Beach South (c)	(772)	23,092	—
32955	Viera East (c)	(321)	10,757	—
33901	Villas (c)	(239)	11,569	—
32507	Warrington (c)	(850)	14,531	—
32779	Wekiwa Springs (c)	(407)	21,998	—
*33414	Wellington	(561)	56,508	64,848
*33544	Wesley Chapel (c)	(813)	44,092	—
33714	West Lealman (c)	(727)	15,651	—
33147	West Little River (c)	(305)	34,699	—
*32904	West Melbourne	(321)	18,355	22,089
*33401	West Palm Beach	(561)	99,919	110,222
33023	West Park	(954)	14,156	15,153
32505	West Pensacola (c)	(850)	21,339	—
33626	Westchase (c)	(813)	21,747	—
33165	Westchester (c)	(305)	29,862	—
*33326	Weston	(954)	65,333	70,944
33165	Westwood Lakes (c)	(305)	11,838	—
*33305	Wilton Manors	(954)	11,632	12,773
*34787	Winter Garden	(407)	34,568	43,536
*33880	Winter Haven	(863)	33,874	41,280
*32789	Winter Park	(407)	27,852	30,879
*32708	Winter Springs	(407)	33,282	36,635
32092	World Golf Village (c)	(904)	12,310	—
32547	Wright (c)	(850)	23,127	—
*32097	Yulee (c)	(904)	11,491	—
*33540	Zephyrhills	(813)	13,288	15,247

(1) Place was incorporated after the 2010 Census was conducted. Data in 2010 column is for Estero CDP.

Georgia

Area codes 470/678/770 overlay area code 404. Area code 762 overlays 706.

ZIP	Place	Area code	2010 population	2017 estimate
*30101	Acworth	(770)	20,425	22,698
*31701	Albany	(229)	77,434	73,179
*30004	Alpharetta	(770)	57,551	65,799
*31709	Americus	(229)	17,041	15,400
*30601	Athens-Clarke Co. (balance)	(706)	115,452	125,691
*30303	Atlanta	(404)	420,003	486,290
*30901	Augusta-Richmond Co. (balance)	(706)	195,844	197,166
*39817	Bainbridge	(229)	12,697	12,111
30032	Belvedere Park (c)	(404)	15,152	—
30517	Braselton	(706)	7,511	10,947
*30319	Brookhaven[1]	(404)	49,312	53,518
*31520	Brunswick	(912)	15,383	16,287
*30518	Buford	(404)	12,225	14,868
*30701	Calhoun	(706)	15,650	16,414
30032	Candler-McAfee (c)	(404)	23,025	—
*30114	Canton	(770)	22,958	27,936
*30117	Carrollton	(770)	24,388	26,815
*30120	Cartersville	(770)	19,731	20,978
*30341	Chamblee	(770)	9,892	29,428
30021	Clarkston	(404)	7,554	12,848
*30337	College Park	(404)	13,942	14,959
*31901	Columbus	(706)	189,885	194,058
*30013	Conyers	(404)	15,195	16,015
*31015	Cordele	(229)	11,147	10,726
*30014	Covington	(770)	13,118	14,044
31805	Cusseta-Chattahoochee Co.	(706)	11,267	10,343
*30132	Dallas	(770)	11,544	13,237
*30720	Dalton	(706)	33,128	33,748
*30030	Decatur	(404)	19,335	23,832
*30340	Doraville	(770)	8,330	10,540
*31533	Douglas	(912)	11,589	11,430
*30134	Douglasville	(770)	30,961	33,675
30333	Druid Hills (c)	(404)	14,568	—
*31021	Dublin	(478)	16,201	15,811
*30096	Duluth	(770)	26,600	29,463
*30338	Dunwoody	(770)	46,267	49,609
*30344	East Point	(404)	33,712	35,282
30809	Evans (c)	(706)	29,011	—
30213	Fairburn	(770)	12,950	15,520
*30214	Fayetteville	(770)	15,945	17,802
*30297	Forest Park	(404)	18,468	19,823
*30501	Gainesville	(770)	33,804	40,359
39854	Georgetown (c)	(912)	11,823	—
*30223	Griffin	(770)	23,643	22,770
30813	Grovetown	(706)	11,216	14,109
*31313	Hinesville	(912)	33,437	33,140
*30114	Holly Springs	(770)	9,189	11,935

ZIP	Place	Area code	2010 population	2017 estimate
30549	Jefferson	(706)	9,432	11,136
*30097	Johns Creek	(404)	76,728	84,350
*30144	Kennesaw	(770)	29,783	34,344
31548	Kingsland	(912)	15,946	17,077
*30240	LaGrange	(706)	29,588	30,472
*30045	Lawrenceville	(770)	28,546	29,873
*30047	Lilburn	(404)	11,596	12,700
30122	Lithia Springs (c)	(770)	15,491	—
30052	Loganville	(770)	10,458	12,062
30126	Mableton (c)	(770)	37,115	—
*31201	Macon-Bibb Co.[1]	(478)	155,303	152,663
*30060	Marietta	(404)	56,579	61,048
30907	Martinez (c)	(706)	35,795	—
*30253	McDonough	(770)	22,084	24,755
*31061	Milledgeville	(478)	17,715	18,575
*30004	Milton	(770)	32,661	38,924
*30655	Monroe	(770)	13,234	13,484
*31768	Moultrie	(229)	14,268	14,160
30075	Mountain Park (c)	(770)	11,554	—
*30263	Newnan	(770)	33,039	38,909
*30071	Norcross	(770)	9,116	16,845
30319	North Atlanta (c)	(770)	40,456	—
30033	North Decatur (c)	(404)	16,698	—
30033	North Druid Hills (c)	(404)	18,947	—
*30269	Peachtree City	(770)	34,364	35,262
*30092	Peachtree Corners[1]	(678)	38,006	43,268
31069	Perry	(478)	13,839	16,684
31322	Pooler	(912)	19,140	23,816
30127	Powder Springs	(404)	13,940	15,052
30074	Redan (c)	(770)	33,015	—
31324	Richmond Hill	(912)	9,281	12,632
*30274	Riverdale	(404)	15,134	16,439
*30161	Rome	(706)	36,303	36,375
*30075	Roswell	(404)	88,346	94,786
31558	Saint Marys	(912)	17,121	18,019
31522	Saint Simons (c)	(912)	12,743	—
*30350	Sandy Springs	(404)	93,853	106,739
*31401	Savannah	(912)	136,286	146,444
30079	Scottdale (c)	(404)	10,631	—
*30080	Smyrna	(770)	51,271	56,685
*30078	Snellville	(404)	18,242	19,738
*30458	Statesboro	(912)	28,422	31,379
30281	Stockbridge	(770)	25,636	29,114
*30038	Stonecrest[1]	(404)	50,200	54,471
30518	Sugar Hill	(770)	18,522	23,180
30024	Suwanee	(770)	15,355	19,549
*31792	Thomasville	(229)	18,413	18,515
*31794	Tifton	(229)	16,350	16,733
*30084	Tucker[2]	(404)	27,581	36,130
30291	Union City	(404)	19,456	21,370
*31601	Valdosta	(229)	54,518	56,085
*30474	Vidalia	(912)	10,473	10,485
30180	Villa Rica	(770)	13,956	15,345
*31088	Warner Robins	(478)	66,588	74,854
*31501	Waycross	(912)	14,649	13,876
31410	Wilmington Island (c)	(912)	15,138	—
30680	Winder	(770)	14,099	16,244
*30188	Woodstock	(770)	23,896	31,564

(1) Incorporated after the 2010 Census was conducted. Data in 2010 column is Census Bureau estimate. (2) Incorporated after the 2010 Census. Data in 2010 column is for Tucker CDP.

Hawaii
Area code 808 applies to the entire state.

ZIP	Place	2000 population	2010 population
96821	East Honolulu (c)	—	49,914
96706	Ewa Beach (c)	14,650	14,955
96706	Ewa Gentry (c)	4,939	22,690
96701	Halawa (c)	13,891	14,014
96749	Hawaiian Paradise Park (c)	7,051	11,404
*96720	Hilo (c)	40,759	43,263
*96813	Honolulu, urban (c)	371,657	337,256[1]
*96732	Kahului (c)	20,146	26,337
96740	Kailua (c) (Hawaii Co.)	9,870	11,975
96734	Kailua (c) (Honolulu Co.)	36,513	38,635
96744	Kaneohe (c)	34,970	34,597
96746	Kapaa (c)	9,472	10,699
*96707	Kapolei (c)	—	15,186
96753	Kihei (c)	16,749	20,881
*96761	Lahaina (c)	9,118	11,704
96707	Makakilo (c)	13,156	18,248
96789	Mililani Mauka (c)	—	21,039
96789	Mililani Town (c)	28,608	27,629
96792	Nanakuli (c)	10,814	12,666
96782	Pearl City (c)	30,976	47,698
96797	Royal Kunia (c)	—	14,525
96857	Schofield Barracks (c)	14,428	16,370
96786	Wahiawa (c)	16,151	17,821
96792	Waianae (c)	10,506	13,177
96793	Wailuku (c)	12,296	15,313
96701	Waimalu (c)	29,371	13,730
96797	Waipahu (c)	33,108	38,216
96797	Waipio (c)	11,672	11,674

(1) 2017 est. pop. was 350,395.

Idaho
Area code 986 overlays area code 208, which applies to the entire state.

ZIP	Place	2010 population	2017 estimate
*83401	Ammon	13,816	15,540
83221	Blackfoot	11,899	11,922
*83702	Boise	205,671	226,570
83318	Burley	10,345	10,474
*83605	Caldwell	46,237	54,660
83202	Chubbuck	13,922	14,869
*83814	Coeur d'Alene	44,137	50,665
83616	Eagle	19,908	26,089
*83714	Garden City	10,972	11,890
83835	Hayden	13,294	14,693
*83402	Idaho Falls	56,813	61,076
83338	Jerome	10,890	11,636
83634	Kuna	15,210	19,200
83501	Lewiston	31,894	32,800
*83642	Meridian	75,092	99,926
*83843	Moscow	23,800	25,146
83647	Mountain Home	14,206	14,224
*83651	Nampa	81,557	93,590
*83201	Pocatello	54,255	55,193
*83854	Post Falls	27,574	33,290
*83440	Rexburg	25,484	28,337
*83301	Twin Falls	44,125	49,202

Illinois
Area code 224 overlays area code 847. Area code 331 overlays 630. Area code 779 overlays 815. Area code 872 overlays 312/773.

ZIP	Place	Area code	2010 population	2017 estimate
60101	Addison	(630)	36,942	36,820
*60102	Algonquin	(847)	30,046	31,017
60803	Alsip	(708)	19,277	19,059
62002	Alton	(618)	27,865	26,725
60002	Antioch	(847)	14,430	14,235
*60005	Arlington Heights	(847)	75,101	75,634
*60505	Aurora	(630)	197,899	200,965
*60010	Barrington	(847)	10,327	10,297
*60103	Bartlett	(630)	41,208	41,149
*60510	Batavia	(630)	26,045	26,563
*60083	Beach Park	(847)	13,638	13,995
*62220	Belleville	(618)	44,478	41,649
60104	Bellwood	(708)	19,071	19,019
61008	Belvidere	(815)	25,585	25,181
*60106	Bensenville	(630)	18,352	18,330
60402	Berwyn	(708)	56,657	55,550
*60108	Bloomingdale	(630)	22,018	22,016
*61701	Bloomington	(309)	76,610	77,934
60406	Blue Island	(708)	23,706	23,361
*60440	Bolingbrook	(630)	73,366	75,201
60914	Bourbonnais	(815)	18,631	18,420
60915	Bradley	(815)	15,895	15,344
60455	Bridgeview	(708)	16,446	16,335
60513	Brookfield	(708)	18,978	18,694
60089	Buffalo Grove	(847)	41,496	41,226
60459	Burbank	(708)	28,925	28,793
60527	Burr Ridge	(630)	10,559	10,818
62206	Cahokia	(618)	15,241	14,151
60409	Calumet City	(708)	37,042	36,633
*60119	Campton Hills	(630)/(847)	11,131	11,282
61520	Canton	(309)	14,704	13,865
*62901	Carbondale	(618)	25,902	25,899
*60188	Carol Stream	(630)	39,711	39,989
60110	Carpentersville	(847)	37,691	38,162
60013	Cary	(847)	18,271	17,885
62801	Centralia	(618)	13,032	12,452
*61820	Champaign	(217)	81,055	87,432
60410	Channahon	(815)	12,560	12,805
61920	Charleston	(217)	21,838	20,996
62629	Chatham	(217)	11,500	12,624
*60602	Chicago	(312)/(773)	2,695,598	2,716,450
*60411	Chicago Heights	(708)	30,276	29,901
60415	Chicago Ridge	(708)	14,305	14,186
60804	Cicero	(708)	83,891	82,552
62234	Collinsville	(618)	25,579	24,703
62236	Columbia	(618)	9,707	10,274
60478	Country Club Hills	(708)	16,541	16,564
*60403	Crest Hill	(815)	20,837	21,175
60445	Crestwood	(708)	10,950	10,846
*60014	Crystal Lake	(815)	40,743	40,421
*61832	Danville	(217)	33,027	31,424
60561	Darien	(630)	22,086	22,061
*62521	Decatur	(217)	76,122	72,174
60015	Deerfield	(847)	18,225	18,946
60115	DeKalb	(815)	43,862	43,193
*60018	Des Plaines	(847)	58,364	58,193
61021	Dixon	(815)	15,733	15,202
60419	Dolton	(708)	23,153	22,793
*60515	Downers Grove	(630)	47,833	49,540
61244	East Moline	(309)	21,302	21,109
*61611	East Peoria	(309)	23,402	22,739

ZIP	Place	Area code	2010 population	2017 estimate
*62201	East St. Louis	(618)	27,006	26,662
*62025	Edwardsville	(618)	24,293	24,967
62401	Effingham	(217)	12,328	12,589
*60120	Elgin	(847)	108,188	112,456
*60007	Elk Grove Village	(847)	33,127	32,776
60126	Elmhurst	(630)	44,121	46,662
60707	Elmwood Park	(708)	24,883	24,537
*60201	Evanston	(847)	74,486	74,756
60805	Evergreen Park	(708)	19,852	19,542
*62208	Fairview Heights	(618)	17,078	16,588
*60130	Forest Park	(708)	14,167	13,951
60020	Fox Lake	(847)	10,579	10,554
60423	Frankfort	(815)	17,782	19,009
*60131	Franklin Park	(847)	18,333	18,012
61032	Freeport	(815)	25,638	24,091
60030	Gages Lake (c)	(847)	10,198	—
*61401	Galesburg	(309)	32,195	30,769
60134	Geneva	(630)	21,495	22,010
62034	Glen Carbon	(618)	12,934	12,985
*60137	Glen Ellyn	(630)	27,450	28,045
*60139	Glendale Heights	(630)	34,208	34,058
*60025	Glenview	(847)	44,692	47,659
62035	Godfrey	(618)	17,982	17,650
62040	Granite City	(618)	29,849	28,746
60030	Grayslake	(847)	20,957	20,957
60031	Gurnee	(847)	31,295	30,767
60133	Hanover Park	(630)	37,973	37,982
*60426	Harvey	(708)	25,282	24,908
60429	Hazel Crest	(708)	14,100	13,837
62948	Herrin	(618)	12,501	12,880
*60457	Hickory Hills	(708)	14,049	13,950
*60035	Highland Park	(847)	29,763	29,767
*60521	Hinsdale	(630)	16,816	17,705
*60195	Hoffman Estates	(847)	51,895	51,567
*60491	Homer Glen	(708)	24,220	24,591
*60430	Homewood	(708)	19,323	19,089
60142	Huntley	(847)	24,291	27,207
*62650	Jacksonville	(217)	19,446	18,454
*60436	Joliet	(815)	147,433	148,462
60458	Justice	(708)	12,926	12,836
60901	Kankakee	(815)	27,537	26,216
61443	Kewanee	(309)	12,916	12,473
60525	La Grange	(708)	15,550	15,581
60526	La Grange Park	(708)	13,579	13,433
60045	Lake Forest	(847)	19,375	19,612
*60102	Lake in the Hills	(847)	28,965	28,936
*60047	Lake Zurich	(847)	19,631	19,903
60438	Lansing	(708)	28,331	27,962
*60439	Lemont	(630)	16,000	17,075
60048	Libertyville	(847)	20,315	20,490
62656	Lincoln	(217)	14,504	13,816
*60645	Lincolnwood	(847)	12,590	12,483
60046	Lindenhurst	(847)	14,462	14,467
60532	Lisle	(630)	22,390	22,912
*60441	Lockport	(815)	24,839	25,434
60148	Lombard	(630)	43,165	43,745
*61111	Loves Park	(815)	23,996	23,387
60534	Lyons	(708)	10,729	10,585
*61115	Machesney Park	(815)	23,499	22,733
61455	Macomb	(309)	19,288	18,267
62959	Marion	(618)	17,193	17,762
*60426	Markham	(708)	12,508	12,538
60443	Matteson	(708)	19,009	19,418
*61938	Mattoon	(217)	18,555	17,886
*60153	Maywood	(708)	24,090	23,640
*60050	McHenry	(815)	26,992	26,911
*60160	Melrose Park	(708)	25,411	25,197
60445	Midlothian	(708)	14,819	14,634
60447	Minooka	(815)	10,924	11,307
60448	Mokena	(708)	18,740	20,293
*61265	Moline	(309)	43,483	42,231
60538	Montgomery	(630)	18,438	19,701
60450	Morris	(815)	13,636	14,651
61550	Morton	(309)	16,267	16,301
60053	Morton Grove	(847)	23,270	23,142
60056	Mount Prospect	(847)	54,167	53,930
62864	Mount Vernon	(618)	15,277	14,956
60060	Mundelein	(847)	31,064	31,385
*60540	Naperville	(630)	141,853	147,682
60451	New Lenox	(815)	24,394	26,575
60714	Niles	(847)	29,803	29,482
*61761	Normal	(309)	52,497	54,284
*60634	Norridge	(708)	14,572	14,437
60542	North Aurora	(630)	16,760	18,245
*60064	North Chicago	(847)	32,574	29,842
*60062	Northbrook	(847)	33,170	33,400
60164	Northlake	(708)	12,323	12,364
60452	Oak Forest	(708)	27,962	27,685
*60453	Oak Lawn	(708)	56,690	56,087
*60301	Oak Park	(708)	51,878	52,261
62269	O'Fallon	(618)	28,281	29,272
*60462	Orland Park	(708)	56,767	58,765
60543	Oswego	(630)	30,355	34,833
61350	Ottawa	(815)	18,768	18,180
*60067	Palatine	(847)	68,557	68,644
60463	Palos Heights	(708)	12,515	12,403
60465	Palos Hills	(708)	17,484	17,358
*60466	Park Forest	(708)	21,975	21,682
60068	Park Ridge	(847)	37,480	37,494
*61554	Pekin	(309)	34,094	32,731
*61602	Peoria	(309)	115,007	112,883
*60544	Plainfield	(815)	39,581	43,926
60545	Plano	(630)	10,856	11,588
61764	Pontiac	(815)	11,931	11,809
60070	Prospect Heights	(847)	16,256	16,180
*62301	Quincy	(217)	40,633	40,303
61866	Rantoul	(217)	12,941	12,769
60471	Richton Park	(708)	13,646	13,505
60305	River Forest	(708)	11,172	11,132
60171	River Grove	(708)	10,227	10,093
60827	Riverdale	(708)	13,549	13,352
*61201	Rock Island	(309)	39,018	38,110
*61101	Rockford	(815)	152,871	147,051
60008	Rolling Meadows	(847)	24,099	23,988
60446	Romeoville	(815)	39,680	39,632
61073	Roscoe	(815)	10,785	10,505
60172	Roselle	(630)	22,763	22,794
60073	Round Lake	(847)	18,289	18,444
60073	Round Lake Beach	(847)	28,115	27,607
*60174	Saint Charles	(630)	32,974	32,714
60411	Sauk Village	(708)	10,506	10,452
*60193	Schaumburg	(847)	74,227	74,184
*60176	Schiller Park	(847)	11,793	11,640
*62269	Shiloh	(618)	12,651	13,090
*60436	Shorewood	(815)	15,615	17,249
*60077	Skokie	(847)	64,784	63,978
60177	South Elgin	(847)	21,985	22,549
60473	South Holland	(708)	22,030	21,732
*62701	Springfield	(217)	116,250	114,868
61081	Sterling	(815)	15,370	14,766
60107	Streamwood	(630)	39,858	39,978
61364	Streator	(815)	13,710	13,135
60501	Summit	(708)	11,054	11,278
*62221	Swansea	(618)	13,430	13,518
60178	Sycamore	(815)	17,519	18,022
62568	Taylorville	(217)	11,246	10,650
*60477	Tinley Park	(708)	56,703	56,668
62294	Troy	(618)	9,888	10,176
*61801	Urbana	(217)	41,250	41,989
60061	Vernon Hills	(847)	25,113	26,253
60181	Villa Park	(630)	21,904	21,836
60555	Warrenville	(630)	13,140	13,269
61571	Washington	(309)	15,134	16,811
62298	Waterloo	(618)	9,811	10,355
60084	Wauconda	(847)	13,603	13,737
*60085	Waukegan	(847)	89,078	87,729
*60185	West Chicago	(630)	27,086	27,182
60154	Westchester	(708)	16,718	16,461
60558	Western Springs	(708)	12,975	13,479
60559	Westmont	(630)	24,685	24,756
*60187	Wheaton	(630)	52,894	53,373
60090	Wheeling	(847)	37,648	38,562
60091	Wilmette	(847)	27,087	27,418
60093	Winnetka	(847)	12,187	12,480
*60191	Wood Dale	(630)	13,770	13,798
62095	Wood River	(618)	10,657	10,263
60517	Woodridge	(630)	32,971	33,598
60098	Woodstock	(815)	24,770	25,286
60482	Worth	(708)	10,789	10,661
60560	Yorkville	(630)	16,921	19,388
60099	Zion	(847)	24,413	23,952

Indiana

Area code 463 overlays area code 317. Area code 930 overlays 812.

ZIP	Place	Area code	2010 population	2017 estimate
*46011	Anderson	(765)	56,129	55,076
46706	Auburn	(260)	12,731	13,169
46123	Avon	(317)	12,446	17,568
47421	Bedford	(812)	13,413	13,296
46107	Beech Grove	(317)	14,192	14,795
*47408	Bloomington	(812)	80,405	85,071
46714	Bluffton	(260)	9,897	10,030
46112	Brownsburg	(317)	21,285	25,911
*46032	Carmel	(317)	79,191	92,198
46303	Cedar Lake	(219)	11,560	12,470
46304	Chesterton	(219)	13,068	13,503
*47129	Clarksville	(812)	21,724	21,694
*47201	Columbus	(812)	44,061	47,143
47331	Connersville	(765)	13,481	12,866
47933	Crawfordsville	(765)	15,915	16,174
*46307	Crown Point	(219)	27,317	29,625
*46311	Dyer	(219)	16,390	15,941
*46312	East Chicago	(219)	29,698	28,215
*46514	Elkhart	(574)	50,949	52,558
*47708	Evansville	(812)	117,429	118,930
*46038	Fishers	(317)	76,794	91,832
*46802	Fort Wayne	(260)	253,691	265,904

ZIP	Place	Area code	2010 population	2017 estimate
*46041	Frankfort	(765)	16,422	15,827
46131	Franklin	(317)	23,712	25,089
*46402	Gary	(219)	80,294	76,008
*46526	Goshen	(574)	31,719	33,220
46530	Granger (c)	(574)	30,465	—
46135	Greencastle	(765)	10,326	10,529
46140	Greenfield	(317)	20,602	22,094
47240	Greensburg	(812)	11,492	11,902
*46142	Greenwood	(317)	49,791	57,375
46319	Griffith	(219)	16,893	16,152
*46320	Hammond	(219)	80,830	76,618
*46322	Highland	(219)	23,727	22,585
46342	Hobart	(219)	29,059	28,255
46750	Huntington	(260)	17,391	17,084
*46201	Indianapolis (balance)	(317)	820,445	863,002
*47546	Jasper	(812)	15,038	15,519
*47130	Jeffersonville	(812)	44,953	47,383
*46902	Kokomo	(765)	45,468	57,836
*46350	La Porte	(219)	22,053	21,681
*47901	Lafayette	(765)	67,140	72,390
46405	Lake Station	(219)	12,572	11,965
46226	Lawrence	(317)	46,001	48,704
46052	Lebanon	(765)	15,792	15,959
46947	Logansport	(574)	18,396	17,755
47250	Madison	(812)	11,967	11,777
*46952	Marion	(765)	29,948	28,327
46151	Martinsville	(765)	11,828	11,603
*46410	Merrillville	(219)	35,246	34,871
*46360	Michigan City	(219)	31,479	31,056
*46544	Mishawaka	(574)	48,252	49,177
*47302	Muncie	(765)	70,085	68,625
46321	Munster	(219)	23,603	22,717
*47150	New Albany	(812)	36,372	36,461
47362	New Castle	(765)	18,114	17,351
46774	New Haven	(260)	14,794	15,560
*46060	Noblesville	(317)	51,969	61,882
*46970	Peru	(765)	11,417	11,024
*46168	Plainfield	(317)	27,631	32,865
46368	Portage	(219)	36,828	36,672
47907	Purdue University (c)	(765)	12,183	—
*47374	Richmond	(765)	36,812	35,455
46373	Saint John	(219)	14,850	17,259
46375	Schererville	(219)	29,243	28,633
47274	Seymour	(812)	17,503	19,480
46176	Shelbyville	(765)	19,191	19,070
*46601	South Bend	(574)	101,168	102,245
46224	Speedway	(317)	11,812	12,140
*47802	Terre Haute	(812)	60,785	60,774
*46383	Valparaiso	(219)	31,730	33,376
47591	Vincennes	(812)	18,423	17,729
46992	Wabash	(260)	10,666	10,112
*46580	Warsaw	(574)	13,559	14,748
47501	Washington	(812)	11,509	12,114
*47906	West Lafayette	(765)	29,596	46,269
*46074	Westfield	(317)	30,068	39,493
47396	Yorktown	(765)	9,405	11,199
46077	Zionsville	(317)	14,160	26,710

Iowa

ZIP	Place	Area code	2010 population	2017 estimate
50009	Altoona	(515)	14,541	18,699
*50010	Ames	(515)	58,965	66,498
*50021	Ankeny	(515)	45,582	62,416
52722	Bettendorf	(563)	33,217	35,813
*50036	Boone	(515)	12,661	12,510
52601	Burlington	(319)	25,663	25,022
*50613	Cedar Falls	(319)	39,260	41,570
*52401	Cedar Rapids	(319)	126,326	132,228
*52732	Clinton	(563)	26,885	25,480
50325	Clive	(515)	15,447	17,172
52241	Coralville	(319)	18,907	20,881
*51501	Council Bluffs	(712)	62,230	62,316
*52801	Davenport	(563)	99,685	102,320
*50309	Des Moines	(515)	203,433	217,521
*52001	Dubuque	(563)	57,637	58,276
*52556	Fairfield	(641)	9,464	10,420
50501	Fort Dodge	(515)	25,206	24,305
52627	Fort Madison	(319)	11,051	10,520
50111	Grimes	(515)	8,246	12,742
50125	Indianola	(515)	14,782	15,990
*52240	Iowa City	(319)	67,862	75,798
50131	Johnston	(515)	17,278	21,562
52632	Keokuk	(319)	10,780	10,343
52302	Marion	(319)	34,768	39,400
50158	Marshalltown	(641)	27,552	27,280
*50401	Mason City	(641)	28,079	27,399
52761	Muscatine	(563)	22,886	23,782
50208	Newton	(641)	15,254	15,109
52317	North Liberty	(319)	13,374	18,813
50211	Norwalk	(515)	8,945	10,896
52577	Oskaloosa	(641)	11,463	11,546
52501	Ottumwa	(641)	25,023	24,454
50219	Pella	(641)	10,352	10,225

ZIP	Place	Area code	2010 population	2017 estimate
*51101	Sioux City	(712)	82,684	82,514
51301	Spencer	(712)	11,233	11,045
50588	Storm Lake	(712)	10,600	10,611
*50322	Urbandale	(515)	39,463	43,592
*50701	Waterloo	(319)	68,406	67,587
50263	Waukee	(515)	13,790	20,649
50677	Waverly	(319)	9,874	10,126
*50265	West Des Moines	(515)	56,609	65,608

Kansas

ZIP	Place	Area code	2010 population	2017 estimate
67002	Andover	(316)	11,791	13,111
67005	Arkansas City	(620)	12,415	11,866
66002	Atchison	(913)	11,021	10,636
67037	Derby	(316)	22,158	23,673
*67801	Dodge City	(620)	27,340	27,720
67042	El Dorado	(316)	13,021	12,993
66801	Emporia	(620)	24,916	24,724
*67846	Garden City	(620)	26,658	26,895
*66030	Gardner	(913)	19,123	21,583
67530	Great Bend	(620)	15,995	15,344
*67601	Hays	(785)	20,510	20,845
67060	Haysville	(316)	10,826	11,278
*67501	Hutchinson	(620)	42,080	40,772
*66441	Junction City	(785)	23,353	22,988
*66101	Kansas City	(913)	145,786	152,938
66043	Lansing	(913)	11,265	11,947
*66044	Lawrence	(785)	87,643	96,892
*66048	Leavenworth	(913)	35,251	36,210
*66211	Leawood	(913)	31,867	34,659
*66215	Lenexa	(913)	48,190	53,553
*67901	Liberal	(620)	20,525	19,826
*66502	Manhattan	(785)	52,281	54,832
67460	McPherson	(620)	13,155	13,201
*66202	Merriam	(913)	11,003	11,212
*67114	Newton	(316)	19,132	18,869
*66061	Olathe	(913)	125,872	137,472
66067	Ottawa	(785)	12,649	12,342
*66212	Overland Park	(913)	173,372	191,278
*66762	Pittsburg	(620)	20,233	20,216
*66208	Prairie Village	(913)	21,447	22,368
*67401	Salina	(785)	47,707	46,994
*66203	Shawnee	(913)	62,209	65,513
*66603	Topeka	(785)	127,473	126,587
*67202	Wichita	(316)	382,368	390,591
67156	Winfield	(620)	12,301	12,104

Kentucky

Area code 364 overlays area code 270.

ZIP	Place	Area code	2010 population	2017 estimate
*41101	Ashland	(606)	21,684	20,669
40004	Bardstown	(502)	11,700	13,165
*40403	Berea	(859)	13,561	15,597
*42101	Bowling Green	(270)	58,067	67,067
41005	Burlington (c)	(859)	15,926	—
*42718	Campbellsville	(270)	9,108	11,415
*41011	Covington	(859)	40,640	40,455
*40422	Danville	(859)	16,218	16,735
*42701	Elizabethtown	(270)	28,531	30,023
*41018	Erlanger	(859)	18,082	18,840
*41042	Florence	(859)	29,951	32,305
42223	Fort Campbell North (c)	(270)	13,685	—
40121	Fort Knox (c)	(270)	10,124	—
41075	Fort Thomas	(859)	16,325	16,263
*40601	Frankfort	(502)	25,527	27,621
40324	Georgetown	(502)	29,098	33,660
*42141	Glasgow	(270)	14,028	14,362
*42420	Henderson	(270)	28,757	28,657
*42240	Hopkinsville	(270)	31,577	30,789
41051	Independence	(859)	24,757	27,634
*40269	Jeffersontown	(502)	26,595	27,395
40342	Lawrenceburg	(502)	10,505	11,318
*40507	Lexington-Fayette	(859)	295,803	321,959
*40202	Louisville-Jefferson Co. (balance)	(502)	597,337	621,349
*40222	Lyndon	(502)	11,002	11,485
42431	Madisonville	(270)	19,591	19,067
40047	Mount Washington	(502)	9,117	14,554
42071	Murray	(270)	17,741	19,200
*41071	Newport	(859)	15,273	15,033
*40356	Nicholasville	(859)	28,015	30,553
*42301	Owensboro	(270)	57,265	59,404
*42003	Paducah	(270)	25,024	24,941
*40160	Radcliff	(270)	21,688	22,576
*40475	Richmond	(859)	31,364	35,397
*40207	Saint Matthews	(502)	17,472	18,139
*40066	Shelbyville	(502)	14,045	15,872
40165	Shepherdsville	(502)	11,222	12,260
*40216	Shively	(502)	15,264	15,800
*42501	Somerset	(606)	11,196	11,423
*40391	Winchester	(859)	18,368	18,486

Louisiana

ZIP	Place	Area code	2010 population	2017 estimate
*70510	Abbeville	(337)	12,257	12,272
*71301	Alexandria	(318)	47,723	47,334
70714	Baker	(225)	13,895	13,537
71220	Bastrop	(318)	11,365	10,395
*70801	Baton Rouge	(225)	229,493	225,374
70360	Bayou Blue (c)	(985)	12,352	—
*70364	Bayou Cane (c)	(985)	19,355	—
*70037	Belle Chasse (c)	(504)	12,679	—
*70427	Bogalusa	(985)	12,232	11,789
*71111	Bossier City	(318)	61,315	68,554
70518	Broussard	(337)	8,197	12,042
70837	Central	(225)	26,864	28,984
*70043	Chalmette (c)	(504)	16,751	—
70433	Claiborne (c)	(985)	11,507	—
*70433	Covington	(985)	8,765	10,416
*70526	Crowley	(337)	13,265	12,839
70634	DeRidder	(337)	10,578	10,797
70047	Destrehan (c)	(985)	11,535	—
70072	Estelle (c)	(504)	16,377	—
70535	Eunice	(337)	10,398	10,113
*70810	Gardere (c)	(225)	10,580	—
*70737	Gonzales	(225)	9,781	10,771
*70053	Gretna	(504)	17,736	17,935
*70401	Hammond	(985)	20,019	20,480
*70058	Harvey (c)	(504)	20,348	—
*70360	Houma	(985)	33,727	33,278
70121	Jefferson (c)	(504)	11,193	—
70546	Jennings	(337)	10,383	10,002
*70062	Kenner	(504)	66,702	67,451
*70501	Lafayette	(337)	120,623	126,848
*70601	Lake Charles	(337)	71,993	77,117
*70068	LaPlace (c)	(985)	29,872	—
70070	Luling (c)	(985)	12,119	—
*70471	Mandeville	(985)	11,560	12,318
*70072	Marrero (c)	(504)	33,141	—
*70001	Metairie (c)	(504)	138,481	—
*71055	Minden	(318)	13,082	12,319
*71201	Monroe	(318)	48,815	48,371
*70380	Morgan City	(985)	12,404	11,221
70611	Moss Bluff (c)	(337)	11,557	—
*71457	Natchitoches	(318)	18,323	18,048
*70560	New Iberia	(337)	30,617	29,620
*70112	New Orleans	(504)	343,829	393,292
*70570	Opelousas	(337)	16,634	16,323
*71360	Pineville	(318)	14,555	14,429
70769	Prairieville (c)	(225)	26,895	—
70394	Raceland (c)	(985)	10,193	—
70123	River Ridge (c)	(504)	13,494	—
*71270	Ruston	(318)	21,859	22,234
70817	Shenandoah (c)	(318)	18,399	—
*71101	Shreveport	(318)	199,311	192,036
*70458	Slidell	(985)	27,068	27,883
*70663	Sulphur	(337)	20,410	20,278
70056	Terrytown (c)	(504)	23,319	—
*70301	Thibodaux	(985)	14,566	14,713
70056	Timberlane (c)	(504)	10,243	—
70094	Waggaman (c)	(504)	10,015	—
*71291	West Monroe	(318)	13,065	12,657
70058	Woodmere (c)	(504)	12,080	—
70592	Youngsville	(337)	8,105	13,424
70791	Zachary	(225)	14,960	17,538

Maine

Area code 207 applies to the entire state. See introductory note.

ZIP	Place	2010 population	2017 estimate
*04210	Auburn	23,055	23,033
*04330	Augusta	19,136	18,594
*04401	Bangor	33,039	31,903
*04005	Biddeford	21,277	21,488
04011	Brunswick	20,278	20,619
04011	Brunswick (c)	15,175	—
04105	Falmouth	11,185	12,162
04038	Gorham	16,381	17,450
04043	Kennebunk	10,798	11,380
*04240	Lewiston	36,592	36,221
*04473	Orono	10,362	11,305
*04101	Portland	66,194	66,882
04072	Saco	18,482	19,485
04073	Sanford[1]	20,796	21,028
*04074	Scarborough	18,919	19,922
*04106	South Portland	25,002	25,483
04084	Standish	9,874	10,166
*04901	Waterville	15,722	16,600
04090	Wells	9,589	10,305
*04092	Westbrook	17,494	18,730
*04062	Windham	17,001	18,071
03909	York	12,529	13,088

(1) Place was incorporated after the 2010 Census was conducted. Data in 2010 column is Census Bureau estimate.

Maryland

Area code 240 overlays area code 301. Area codes 443/667 overlay 410.

ZIP	Place	Area code	2010 population	2017 estimate
21001	Aberdeen	(410)	14,959	16,049
20607	Accokeek (c)	(301)	10,573	—
*20783	Adelphi (c)	(301)	15,086	—
*21401	Annapolis	(410)	38,394	39,321
21403	Annapolis Neck (c)	(410)	10,950	—
21227	Arbutus (c)	(410)	20,483	—
21012	Arnold (c)	(410)	23,106	—
*20906	Aspen Hill (c)	(301)	48,759	—
21220	Ballenger Creek (c)	(410)	18,274	—
*21201	Baltimore	(410)	620,961	611,648
*21014	Bel Air	(410)	10,120	10,037
21050	Bel Air North (c)	(410)	30,568	—
*21015	Bel Air South (c)	(410)	47,709	—
*20705	Beltsville (c)	(301)	16,772	—
20603	Bensville (c)	(301)	11,923	—
*20814	Bethesda (c)	(301)	60,858	—
*20715	Bowie	(301)	54,727	58,859
21225	Brooklyn Park (c)	(410)	14,373	—
20619	California (c)	(301)	11,857	—
20705	Calverton (c)	(301)	17,724	—
21613	Cambridge	(410)	12,326	12,376
*20748	Camp Springs (c)	(301)	19,096	—
21234	Carney (c)	(410)	29,941	—
21228	Catonsville (c)	(410)	41,567	—
20657	Chesapeake Ranch Estates (c)	(301)	10,519	—
20782	Chillum (c)	(301)	33,513	—
20871	Clarksburg (c)	(301)	13,766	—
20735	Clinton (c)	(301)	35,970	—
20904	Cloverly (c)	(301)	15,126	—
21030	Cockeysville (c)	(410)	20,776	—
*20904	Colesville (c)	(301)	14,647	—
*20740	College Park	(301)	30,413	32,303
*21044	Columbia (c)	(410)	99,615	—
21114	Crofton (c)	(410)	27,348	—
*21502	Cumberland	(301)	20,859	19,707
20872	Damascus (c)	(301)	15,257	—
21222	Dundalk (c)	(410)	63,597	—
20737	East Riverdale (c)	(301)	15,509	—
*21601	Easton	(410)	15,945	16,514
21040	Edgewood (c)	(410)	25,562	—
21784	Eldersburg (c)	(410)	30,531	—
21075	Elkridge (c)	(410)	15,593	—
*21921	Elkton	(410)	15,443	15,652
*21043	Ellicott City (c)	(410)	65,834	—
21221	Essex (c)	(410)	39,262	—
20904	Fairland (c)	(301)	23,681	—
21061	Ferndale (c)	(410)	16,746	—
*20747	Forestville (c)	(301)	12,353	—
*20744	Fort Washington (c)	(301)	23,717	—
*21701	Frederick	(301)	65,239	71,408
*20877	Gaithersburg	(301)	59,933	68,710
*20874	Germantown (c)	(301)	86,395	—
20745	Glassmanor (c)	(301)	17,295	—
*21061	Glen Burnie (c)	(410)	67,639	—
20906	Glenmont (c)	(301)	13,529	—
20769	Glenn Dale (c)	(301)	13,466	—
*20770	Greenbelt	(301)	23,068	23,489
*21740	Hagerstown	(301)	39,662	40,306
21740	Halfway (c)	(301)	10,701	—
21078	Havre de Grace	(410)	12,952	13,576
20748	Hillcrest Heights (c)	(301)	16,469	—
*20781	Hyattsville	(301)	17,557	18,333
21043	Ilchester (c)	(410)	23,476	—
21085	Joppatowne (c)	(410)	12,616	—
20902	Kemp Mill (c)	(301)	12,564	—
*20774	Kettering (c)	(301)	12,790	—
*21122	Lake Shore (c)	(410)	19,477	—
20785	Landover (c)	(301)	23,078	—
*20787	Langley Park (c)	(301)	18,755	—
*20706	Lanham (c)	(301)	10,157	—
*20774	Largo (c)	(301)	10,709	—
*20707	Laurel	(301)	25,115	25,906
20653	Lexington Park (c)	(410)	11,626	—
21090	Linthicum (c)	(410)	10,324	—
21207	Lochearn (c)	(410)	25,333	—
20724	Maryland City (c)	(301)	16,093	—
21093	Mays Chapel (c)	(410)	11,420	—
21220	Middle River (c)	(410)	25,191	—
*21244	Milford Mill (c)	(410)	29,042	—
*20716	Mitchellville (c)	(301)	10,967	—
*20886	Montgomery Village (c)	(301)	32,032	—
20784	New Carrollton	(301)	12,135	13,023
*20852	North Bethesda (c)	(301)	43,828	—
20878	North Potomac (c)	(301)	24,410	—
21811	Ocean Pines (c)	(410)	11,710	—
21113	Odenton (c)	(410)	37,132	—
*20832	Olney (c)	(301)	33,844	—
21236	Overlea (c)	(410)	12,275	—

ZIP	Place	Area code	2010 population	2017 estimate
21117	Owings Mills (c)	(410)	30,622	—
*20745	Oxon Hill (c)	(301)	17,722	—
21234	Parkville (c)	(410)	30,734	—
21401	Parole (c)	(410)	15,922	—
*21122	Pasadena (c)	(410)	24,287	—
21128	Perry Hall (c)	(410)	28,474	—
*21207	Pikesville (c)	(410)	30,764	—
*20850	Potomac (c)	(301)	44,965	—
21133	Randallstown (c)	(410)	32,430	—
20855	Redland (c)	(301)	17,242	—
*21136	Reisterstown (c)	(410)	25,968	—
*21122	Riviera Beach (c)	(410)	12,677	—
*20850	Rockville	(301)	61,209	68,401
20772	Rosaryville (c)	(301)	10,697	—
21237	Rosedale (c)	(410)	19,257	—
21221	Rossville (c)	(410)	15,147	—
*21801	Salisbury	(410)	30,343	32,807
20723	Scaggsville (c)	(301)	24,333	—
*20706	Seabrook (c)	(301)	17,287	—
21144	Severn (c)	(410)	44,231	—
21146	Severna Park (c)	(410)	37,634	—
*20901	Silver Spring (c)	(301)	71,452	—
20707	South Laurel (c)	(301)	26,112	—
*20746	Suitland (c)	(301)	25,825	—
21842	Summerfield (c)	(410)	10,898	—
*20912	Takoma Park	(301)	16,715	17,885
*21204	Towson (c)	(410)	55,197	—
20854	Travilah (c)	(301)	12,159	—
*20602	Waldorf (c)	(301)	67,752	—
20743	Walker Mill (c)	(301)	11,302	—
*21157	Westminster	(410)	18,590	18,593
*20902	Wheaton (c)	(301)	48,284	—
20904	White Oak (c)	(301)	17,403	—
21207	Woodlawn (c) (Baltimore Co.)	(410)	37,879	—

Massachusetts

Area code 339 overlays area code 781. Area code 351 overlays 978. Area code 774 overlays 508. Area code 857 overlays 617. See introductory note.

ZIP	Place	Area code	2010 population	2017 estimate
02351	Abington	(781)	15,985	16,396
*01720	Acton	(978)	21,924	23,777
*02743	Acushnet	(508)	10,303	10,544
01001	Agawam	(413)	28,438	28,849
01913	Amesbury	(978)	16,283	17,457
*01002	Amherst	(413)	37,819	40,046
*01002	Amherst Center (c)	(413)	19,065	—
*01810	Andover	(978)	33,201	35,937
*02476	Arlington	(781)	42,844	45,510
01721	Ashland	(508)	16,593	17,706
*01331	Athol	(978)	11,584	11,711
02703	Attleboro	(508)	43,593	44,590
01501	Auburn	(508)	16,188	16,702
02630	Barnstable	(508)	45,193	44,163
*01730	Bedford	(781)	13,320	14,197
01007	Belchertown	(413)	14,649	15,100
02019	Bellingham	(508)	16,332	17,093
02478	Belmont	(617)	24,729	26,458
01915	Beverly	(978)	39,502	41,816
*01821	Billerica	(978)	40,243	43,962
*02108	Boston	(617)	617,594	685,094
*02532	Bourne	(508)	19,754	19,879
*02184	Braintree	(781)	35,744	37,156
*02324	Bridgewater	(508)	26,563	27,478
*02301	Brockton	(508)	93,810	95,672
*02446	Brookline	(617)	58,732	59,157
*01803	Burlington	(781)	24,498	27,176
*02139	Cambridge	(617)	105,162	113,630
02021	Canton	(781)	21,561	23,444
*02330	Carver	(508)	11,509	11,715
01507	Charlton	(508)	12,981	13,571
01824	Chelmsford	(978)	33,802	35,099
02150	Chelsea	(617)	35,177	40,227
*01020	Chicopee	(413)	55,298	55,515
01510	Clinton	(978)	13,606	13,963
01742	Concord	(978)	17,668	19,237
01923	Danvers	(978)	26,493	27,558
*02747	Dartmouth	(508)	34,032	34,336
*02026	Dedham	(781)	24,729	25,364
02638	Dennis	(508)	14,207	13,917
01826	Dracut	(978)	29,457	31,619
01571	Dudley	(508)	11,390	11,768
*02332	Duxbury	(781)	15,059	15,928
02333	East Bridgewater	(508)	13,794	14,465
*01028	East Longmeadow	(413)	15,720	16,291
01027	Easthampton	(413)	16,053	16,050
*02356	Easton	(508)	23,112	24,984
02149	Everett	(617)	41,667	46,324
02719	Fairhaven	(508)	15,873	16,055
*02720	Fall River	(508)	88,857	89,420
*02540	Falmouth	(508)	31,531	31,101
01420	Fitchburg	(978)	40,318	40,793

ZIP	Place	Area code	2010 population	2017 estimate
02035	Foxborough	(508)	16,865	17,574
*01701	Framingham	(508)	68,318	72,032
02038	Franklin	(508)	31,635	32,996
*01440	Gardner	(978)	20,228	20,640
*01930	Gloucester	(978)	28,789	30,172
01519	Grafton	(508)	17,765	18,761
*01301	Greenfield	(413)	17,456	17,442
*01450	Groton	(978)	10,646	11,364
*02339	Hanover	(781)	13,879	14,444
*02341	Hanson	(781)	10,209	10,777
02645	Harwich	(508)	12,243	12,145
*01830	Haverhill	(978)	60,879	63,639
*02043	Hingham	(781)	22,157	23,415
02343	Holbrook	(781)	10,791	11,026
01520	Holden	(508)	17,346	18,943
01746	Holliston	(508)	13,547	14,753
*01040	Holyoke	(413)	39,880	40,341
01748	Hopkinton	(508)	14,925	18,035
01749	Hudson	(978)	19,063	19,944
01749	Hudson (c)	(978)	14,907	—
02045	Hull	(781)	10,293	10,449
01938	Ipswich	(978)	13,175	13,995
02364	Kingston	(781)	12,629	13,565
02347	Lakeville	(508)	10,602	11,424
*01840	Lawrence	(978)	76,377	80,162
01524	Leicester	(508)	10,970	11,373
01453	Leominster	(978)	40,759	41,615
*02420	Lexington	(781)	31,394	33,727
*01460	Littleton	(978)	8,924	10,115
*01028	Longmeadow	(413)	15,784	15,864
*01850	Lowell	(978)	106,519	111,346
01056	Ludlow	(413)	21,103	21,502
*01462	Lunenburg	(978)	10,086	11,312
*01901	Lynn	(781)	90,329	94,063
01940	Lynnfield	(781)	11,596	12,942
02148	Malden	(781)	59,450	61,246
*02048	Mansfield	(508)	23,184	23,946
01945	Marblehead	(781)	19,808	20,554
01752	Marlborough	(508)	38,499	39,873
*02050	Marshfield	(781)	25,132	25,836
02649	Mashpee	(508)	14,006	14,191
01754	Maynard	(978)	10,106	10,665
02052	Medfield	(508)	12,024	12,845
*02155	Medford	(781)	56,173	57,797
02053	Medway	(508)	12,752	13,329
02176	Melrose	(781)	26,983	28,367
01844	Methuen	(978)	47,255	50,259
*02346	Middleborough	(508)	23,116	24,873
01757	Milford	(508)	27,999	28,933
01757	Milford (c)	(508)	25,055	—
*01527	Millbury	(508)	13,261	13,733
02186	Milton	(617)	27,003	27,575
*02584	Nantucket	(508)	10,172	11,229
01760	Natick	(508)	33,006	36,246
*02494	Needham	(781)	28,886	30,999
*02740	New Bedford	(508)	95,072	95,120
01950	Newburyport	(978)	17,416	18,060
*02456	Newton	(617)	85,146	88,994
02056	Norfolk	(508)	11,227	11,793
01247	North Adams	(413)	13,708	12,970
01845	North Andover	(978)	28,352	31,013
*02760	North Attleborough	(508)	28,712	29,153
*01864	North Reading	(978)	14,892	15,735
*01060	Northampton	(413)	28,549	28,593
01532	Northborough	(508)	14,155	15,033
01534	Northbridge	(508)	15,707	16,630
*02766	Norton	(508)	19,031	19,882
02061	Norwell	(781)	10,506	11,067
02062	Norwood	(781)	28,602	29,195
01540	Oxford	(508)	13,709	13,980
01069	Palmer	(413)	12,140	12,279
*01960	Peabody	(978)	51,251	52,987
*02359	Pembroke	(781)	17,837	18,377
01463	Pepperell	(978)	11,497	12,146
*01201	Pittsfield	(413)	44,737	42,591
*02360	Plymouth	(508)	56,468	59,885
*02169	Quincy	(617)	92,271	94,166
02368	Randolph	(781)	32,112	34,272
*02767	Raynham	(508)	13,383	14,203
01867	Reading	(781)	24,747	26,106
02769	Rehoboth	(508)	11,608	12,188
02151	Revere	(781)	51,755	53,993
02370	Rockland	(781)	17,489	17,957
*01970	Salem	(978)	41,340	43,453
*02563	Sandwich	(508)	20,675	20,303
01906	Saugus	(781)	26,628	28,251
*02066	Scituate	(781)	18,133	18,688
02771	Seekonk	(508)	13,722	15,548
02067	Sharon	(781)	17,612	18,227
*01545	Shrewsbury	(508)	35,608	37,387
*02725	Somerset	(508)	18,165	18,176
*02143	Somerville	(617)	75,754	81,360
01075	South Hadley	(413)	17,514	17,791

ZIP	Place	Area code	2010 population	2017 estimate
02664	South Yarmouth (c)	(508)	11,092	—
*01745	Southborough	(508)	9,767	10,136
01550	Southbridge	(508)	16,719	16,911
01562	Spencer	(508)	11,688	11,954
*01103	Springfield	(413)	153,060	154,758
02180	Stoneham	(781)	21,437	22,036
02072	Stoughton	(781)	26,962	28,528
01776	Sudbury	(978)	17,659	18,867
01907	Swampscott	(781)	13,787	15,177
02777	Swansea	(508)	15,865	16,528
*02780	Taunton	(508)	55,874	57,139
01876	Tewksbury	(978)	28,961	31,247
01879	Tyngsborough	(978)	11,292	12,357
01569	Uxbridge	(508)	13,457	13,997
01880	Wakefield	(781)	24,932	27,157
02081	Walpole	(508)	24,070	25,073
*02451	Waltham	(781)	60,632	62,442
02571	Wareham	(508)	21,822	22,640
*02742	Watertown	(617)	31,915	35,756
01778	Wayland	(508)	12,994	13,954
01570	Webster	(508)	16,767	17,020
01570	Webster (c)	(508)	11,412	—
*02457	Wellesley	(781)	27,982	29,479
*01089	West Springfield	(413)	28,391	28,704
*01581	Westborough	(508)	18,272	19,109
*01085	Westfield	(413)	41,094	41,700
01886	Westford	(978)	21,951	24,310
02493	Weston	(781)	11,261	12,150
02790	Westport	(508)	15,532	15,910
02090	Westwood	(781)	14,618	16,056
*02188	Weymouth	(781)	53,743	56,664
02382	Whitman	(781)	14,489	15,022
01095	Wilbraham	(413)	14,219	14,671
01887	Wilmington	(978)	22,325	23,803
01475	Winchendon	(978)	10,300	10,862
01890	Winchester	(781)	21,374	22,838
02152	Winthrop	(617)	17,497	18,625
*01801	Woburn	(781)	38,120	39,701
*01602	Worcester	(508)	181,045	185,677
*02093	Wrentham	(508)	10,955	11,838
*02664	Yarmouth	(508)	23,793	23,339

Michigan

Area code 947 overlays area code 248.

ZIP	Place	Area code	2010 population	2017 estimate
49221	Adrian	(517)	21,133	20,689
48101	Allen Park	(313)	28,210	27,156
49401	Allendale (c)	(616)	17,579	—
*48103	Ann Arbor	(734)	113,934	121,477
*48326	Auburn Hills	(248)	21,412	23,296
*49014	Battle Creek	(269)	52,347	51,286
*48708	Bay City	(989)	34,932	33,188
48505	Beecher (c)	(810)	10,232	—
48072	Berkley	(248)	14,970	15,331
48025	Beverly Hills	(248)	10,267	10,425
49307	Big Rapids	(231)	10,601	10,378
*48009	Birmingham	(248)	20,103	21,142
*48509	Burton	(810)	29,999	28,643
49601	Cadillac	(231)	10,355	10,445
*48017	Clawson	(248)	11,825	11,946
49036	Coldwater	(517)	10,945	10,764
49321	Comstock Park (c)	(616)	10,088	—
49508	Cutlerville (c)	(616)	14,370	—
*48120	Dearborn	(313)	98,153	94,491
*48127	Dearborn Heights	(313)	57,774	55,758
*48201	Detroit	(313)	713,777	673,104
*49506	East Grand Rapids	(616)	10,694	11,731
*48823	East Lansing	(517)	48,579	48,844
48021	Eastpointe	(586)	32,442	32,511
49829	Escanaba	(906)	12,616	12,223
*48333	Farmington	(248)	10,372	10,578
*48331	Farmington Hills	(248)	79,740	81,050
48430	Fenton	(810)	11,756	11,286
48220	Ferndale	(248)	19,900	20,070
*48502	Flint	(810)	102,434	96,448
49506	Forest Hills (c)	(616)	25,867	—
48026	Fraser	(586)	14,480	14,608
*48135	Garden City	(734)	27,692	26,650
49417	Grand Haven	(616)	10,412	10,905
*49503	Grand Rapids	(616)	188,040	198,829
*49418	Grandville	(616)	15,378	15,970
48230	Grosse Pointe Park	(313)	11,555	11,125
48230	Grosse Pointe Woods	(313)	16,135	15,560
*48212	Hamtramck	(313)	22,423	21,752
48225	Harper Woods	(313)	14,236	13,743
48840	Haslett (c)	(517)	19,220	—
48030	Hazel Park	(248)	16,422	16,489
48203	Highland Park	(313)	11,776	10,900
*49423	Holland	(616)	33,051	33,366
48842	Holt (c)	(517)	23,973	—
48141	Inkster	(313)/(734)	25,369	24,453
48846	Ionia	(616)	11,394	11,188

ZIP	Place	Area code	2010 population	2017 estimate
*49201	Jackson	(517)	33,534	32,704
*49428	Jenison (c)	(616)	16,538	—
*49001	Kalamazoo	(269)	74,262	75,807
*49508	Kentwood	(616)	48,707	51,747
*48915	Lansing	(517)	114,297	116,986
48146	Lincoln Park	(313)	38,144	36,655
*48150	Livonia	(734)	96,942	94,105
48071	Madison Heights	(248)	29,694	30,050
49855	Marquette	(906)	21,355	20,629
48122	Melvindale	(313)	10,715	10,341
*48640	Midland	(989)	41,863	41,950
*48161	Monroe	(734)	20,733	19,875
*48046	Mount Clemens	(586)	16,314	16,312
*48858	Mount Pleasant	(989)	26,016	25,847
*49440	Muskegon	(231)	38,401	38,131
49444	Muskegon Heights	(231)	10,856	10,735
*48047	New Baltimore	(586)	12,084	12,380
*49120	Niles	(269)	11,600	11,208
49505	Northview (c)	(616)	14,541	—
*49441	Norton Shores	(231)	23,994	24,501
*48374	Novi	(248)	55,224	59,715
48237	Oak Park	(248)	29,319	29,654
*48864	Okemos (c)	(517)	21,369	—
*48867	Owosso	(906)	15,194	14,539
*48340	Pontiac	(248)	59,515	59,792
*48060	Port Huron	(810)	30,184	29,051
*49024	Portage	(269)	46,292	48,816
*48192	Riverview	(734)	12,486	12,107
*48308	Rochester	(248)	12,711	13,029
*48306	Rochester Hills	(248)	70,995	74,205
48174	Romulus	(313)/(734)	23,989	23,457
48066	Roseville	(586)	47,299	47,501
*48067	Royal Oak	(248)	57,236	59,112
*48601	Saginaw	(989)	51,508	48,677
*48080	Saint Clair Shores	(586)	59,715	59,635
*49783	Sault Ste. Marie	(906)	14,144	13,631
48178	South Lyon	(248)	11,327	11,741
*48033	Southfield	(248)	71,739	73,208
48195	Southgate	(734)	30,047	29,084
*48310	Sterling Heights	(586)	129,699	132,631
49091	Sturgis	(269)	10,994	10,824
48180	Taylor	(313)/(734)	63,131	61,276
*49684	Traverse City	(231)	14,674	15,515
48183	Trenton	(734)	18,853	18,255
*48083	Troy	(248)	80,980	83,813
*49534	Walker	(616)	23,537	24,822
*48088	Warren	(586)	134,056	135,022
48917	Waverly (c)	(517)	23,925	—
48184	Wayne	(734)	17,593	16,947
*48185	Westland	(734)	84,094	81,747
48393	Wixom	(248)	13,498	13,831
48183	Woodhaven	(734)	12,875	12,486
*48192	Wyandotte	(734)	25,883	24,977
*49509	Wyoming	(616)	72,125	75,938
*48197	Ypsilanti	(734)	19,435	21,076

Minnesota

ZIP	Place	Area code	2010 population	2017 estimate
56007	Albert Lea	(507)	18,016	17,703
56308	Alexandria	(320)	11,070	13,592
*55304	Andover	(763)	30,598	32,902
*55303	Anoka	(612)	17,142	17,522
55124	Apple Valley	(952)	49,084	52,435
*55112	Arden Hills	(651)	9,552	10,362
55912	Austin	(507)	24,718	24,933
*56601	Bemidji	(218)	13,431	15,366
55309	Big Lake	(763)	10,060	10,915
*55014	Blaine	(763)	57,186	64,557
*55420	Bloomington	(952)	82,893	85,866
*56401	Brainerd	(218)	13,590	13,428
*55430	Brooklyn Center	(763)	30,104	31,006
*55443	Brooklyn Park	(763)	75,781	80,581
55313	Buffalo	(763)	15,453	16,201
*55337	Burnsville	(952)	60,306	61,439
55316	Champlin	(763)	23,089	25,022
55317	Chanhassen	(952)	22,952	25,558
55318	Chaska	(952)	23,770	26,561
55720	Cloquet	(218)	12,124	11,938
55421	Columbia Heights	(612)	19,496	20,254
*55433	Coon Rapids	(763)	61,476	62,656
55016	Cottage Grove	(651)	34,589	36,793
*55422	Crystal	(763)	22,151	23,165
*55802	Duluth	(218)	86,265	86,066
*55121	Eagan	(651)	64,206	66,627
*55005	East Bethel	(763)	11,626	11,928
*55344	Eden Prairie	(952)	60,797	64,400
*55424	Edina	(952)	47,941	51,958
55330	Elk River	(763)	22,974	24,506
56031	Fairmont	(507)	10,666	10,126
55021	Faribault	(507)	23,352	23,750
*55024	Farmington	(651)	21,086	23,067
*56537	Fergus Falls	(218)	13,138	13,783

ZIP	Place	Area code	2010 population	2017 estimate
55025	Forest Lake	(651)	18,375	19,879
*55432	Fridley	(763)	27,208	27,853
*55427	Golden Valley	(763)	20,371	21,520
*55744	Grand Rapids	(218)	10,869	11,242
*55304	Ham Lake	(763)	15,296	16,528
55033	Hastings	(651)	22,172	22,722
*55746	Hibbing	(218)	16,361	16,041
*55343	Hopkins	(952)	17,591	18,678
55038	Hugo	(651)	13,332	14,828
55350	Hutchinson	(320)	14,178	13,895
*55076	Inver Grove Heights	(651)	33,880	35,392
55044	Lakeville	(952)	55,954	63,748
*55014	Lino Lakes	(651)	20,216	21,407
*55109	Little Canada	(651)	9,773	10,477
*56001	Mankato	(507)	39,309	42,264
*55311	Maple Grove	(763)	61,567	71,066
*55109	Maplewood	(651)	38,018	40,918
56258	Marshall	(507)	13,680	13,710
*55118	Mendota Heights	(651)	11,071	11,343
*55401	Minneapolis	(612)	382,578	422,331
*55345	Minnetonka	(952)	49,734	53,085
*55362	Monticello	(763)	12,759	13,599
*56560	Moorhead	(218)	38,065	43,122
55112	Mounds View	(763)	12,155	13,098
55112	New Brighton	(651)	21,456	22,787
*54427	New Hope	(763)	20,339	21,063
56073	New Ulm	(507)	13,522	13,238
55056	North Branch	(651)	10,125	10,462
*56002	North Mankato	(507)	13,394	13,746
55109	North St. Paul	(651)	11,460	12,444
55057	Northfield	(507)	20,007	20,474
*55128	Oakdale	(651)	27,378	28,083
*55330	Otsego	(763)	13,571	16,755
55060	Owatonna	(507)	25,599	25,794
*55446	Plymouth	(763)	70,576	78,395
*55372	Prior Lake	(952)	22,796	26,401
*55303	Ramsey	(763)	23,668	26,587
55066	Red Wing	(651)	16,459	16,412
55423	Richfield	(612)	35,228	36,151
55422	Robbinsdale	(763)	13,953	14,544
*55901	Rochester	(507)	106,769	115,733
55374	Rogers	(763)	8,597	12,984
55068	Rosemount	(651)	21,874	24,344
*55113	Roseville	(651)	33,660	36,314
*56301	Saint Cloud	(320)	65,842	67,984
*55416	Saint Louis Park	(952)	45,250	49,029
55376	Saint Michael	(763)	16,399	17,565
*55101	Saint Paul	(651)	285,068	306,621
56082	Saint Peter	(507)	11,196	11,906
56377	Sartell	(320)	15,876	17,752
56379	Sauk Rapids	(320)	12,773	13,722
55378	Savage	(952)	26,911	31,352
*55379	Shakopee	(952)	37,076	40,893
55126	Shoreview	(651)	25,043	26,794
*55075	South St. Paul	(651)	20,160	20,242
*55082	Stillwater	(651)	18,225	19,388
*55127	Vadnais Heights	(651)	12,302	13,561
*55387	Waconia	(952)	10,697	12,232
*55118	West St. Paul	(651)	19,540	19,767
*55110	White Bear Lake	(651)	23,797	25,888
56201	Willmar	(320)	19,610	19,628
55987	Winona	(507)	27,592	26,928
*55125	Woodbury	(651)	61,961	69,756
56187	Worthington	(507)	12,764	13,247

Mississippi

Area code 769 overlays area code 601.

ZIP	Place	Area code	2010 population	2017 estimate
39520	Bay St. Louis	(228)	9,260	13,043
*39530	Biloxi	(228)	44,054	45,908
*39042	Brandon	(601)	21,705	23,999
*39601	Brookhaven	(601)	12,513	12,173
39272	Byram	(601)	11,489	11,671
39046	Canton	(601)	13,189	12,725
*38614	Clarksdale	(662)	17,962	15,732
*38732	Cleveland	(662)	12,334	11,729
*39056	Clinton	(601)	25,216	25,154
*39701	Columbus	(662)	23,640	24,041
*38834	Corinth	(662)	14,573	14,643
39540	D'Iberville	(228)	9,486	11,610
39553	Gautier	(228)	18,572	18,512
*38701	Greenville	(662)	34,400	30,686
*38930	Greenwood	(662)	15,205	13,996
*38901	Grenada	(662)	13,092	12,511
*39501	Gulfport	(228)	67,793	71,822
*39401	Hattiesburg	(601)	45,989	46,377
38632	Hernando	(662)	14,090	15,981
38637	Horn Lake	(662)	26,066	27,095
*39201	Jackson	(601)	173,514	166,965
*39440	Laurel	(601)	18,540	18,493
39560	Long Beach	(228)	14,792	15,642
*39110	Madison	(601)	24,149	25,627

ZIP	Place	Area code	2010 population	2017 estimate
*39648	McComb	(601)	12,790	12,799
*39301	Meridian	(601)	41,148	37,940
*39563	Moss Point	(228)	13,704	13,398
*39120	Natchez	(601)	15,792	14,886
*39564	Ocean Springs	(228)	17,442	17,682
38654	Olive Branch	(662)	33,484	37,435
*38655	Oxford	(662)	18,916	23,639
*39567	Pascagoula	(228)	22,392	21,733
*39208	Pearl	(601)	25,092	26,534
39465	Petal	(601)	10,454	10,633
39466	Picayune	(601)	10,878	10,382
*39157	Ridgeland	(601)	24,047	24,266
*38671	Southaven	(662)	48,982	54,031
*39759	Starkville	(662)	23,888	25,352
*38801	Tupelo	(662)	34,546	38,114
*39180	Vicksburg	(601)	23,856	22,489
39773	West Point	(662)	11,307	10,675
39194	Yazoo City	(662)	11,403	10,987

Missouri

ZIP	Place	Area code	2010 population	2017 estimate
63123	Affton (c)	(314)	20,307	—
63010	Arnold	(636)	20,808	21,113
*63011	Ballwin	(636)	30,404	30,181
63137	Bellefontaine Neighbors	(314)	10,860	10,628
64012	Belton	(816)	23,116	23,480
*64015	Blue Springs	(816)	52,575	54,945
*65613	Bolivar	(417)	10,325	10,885
*65616	Branson	(417)	10,520	11,467
63044	Bridgeton	(314)	11,550	11,648
*63701	Cape Girardeau	(573)	37,941	39,151
*64836	Carthage	(417)	14,378	14,350
*63017	Chesterfield	(636)	47,484	47,588
*63105	Clayton	(314)	15,939	16,805
*65201	Columbia	(573)	108,500	121,717
*63128	Concord (c)	(314)	16,421	—
63126	Crestwood	(314)	11,912	11,870
63141	Creve Coeur	(314)	17,833	18,702
*63366	Dardenne Prairie	(636)	11,494	13,310
63025	Eureka	(636)	10,189	10,574
64024	Excelsior Springs	(816)	11,084	11,560
63640	Farmington	(573)	16,240	18,425
63135	Ferguson	(314)	21,203	20,728
63028	Festus	(636)	11,602	12,034
*63031	Florissant	(314)	52,158	51,443
65473	Fort Leonard Wood (c)	(573)	15,061	—
65251	Fulton	(573)	12,790	12,844
*64118	Gladstone	(816)	25,410	27,140
64029	Grain Valley	(816)	12,854	13,996
64030	Grandview	(816)	24,475	25,159
63401	Hannibal	(573)	17,916	17,590
64701	Harrisonville	(816)	10,019	10,103
*63042	Hazelwood	(314)	25,703	25,290
*64050	Independence	(816)	116,830	117,306
63755	Jackson	(573)	13,758	14,932
*65101	Jefferson City	(573)	43,079	42,895
63136	Jennings	(314)	14,712	14,674
*64801	Joplin	(417)	50,150	52,288
*64106	Kansas City	(816)	459,787	488,943
64060	Kearney	(816)	8,381	10,049
63857	Kennett	(573)	10,932	10,399
63501	Kirksville	(660)	17,505	17,536
63122	Kirkwood	(314)	27,540	27,653
63367	Lake St. Louis	(636)	14,545	15,936
65536	Lebanon	(417)	14,474	14,611
*64063	Lee's Summit	(816)	91,364	97,290
63125	Lemay (c)	(314)	16,645	—
*64068	Liberty	(816)	29,149	31,507
*63011	Manchester	(636)	18,094	18,112
65340	Marshall	(660)	13,065	12,708
63043	Maryland Heights	(314)	27,472	26,996
64468	Maryville	(660)	11,972	11,757
63129	Mehlville (c)	(314)	28,380	—
65265	Mexico	(573)	11,543	11,506
65270	Moberly	(660)	13,974	13,783
*64850	Neosho	(417)	11,835	12,031
65714	Nixa	(417)	19,022	21,321
63129	Oakville (c)	(314)	36,143	—
*63366	O'Fallon	(636)	79,329	87,597
63034	Old Jamestown (c)	(314)	19,184	—
63114	Overland	(314)	16,062	15,708
65721	Ozark	(417)	17,820	19,905
*63901	Poplar Bluff	(573)	17,023	17,070
64083	Raymore	(816)	19,206	21,167
*64133	Raytown	(816)	29,526	29,211
65738	Republic	(417)	14,751	16,294
*65401	Rolla	(573)	19,559	20,293
63074	Saint Ann	(314)	13,020	12,737
*63301	Saint Charles	(636)	65,794	70,329
*64501	Saint Joseph	(816)	76,780	76,442
*63101	Saint Louis	(314)	319,294	308,626
*63376	Saint Peters	(636)	52,575	57,178
*65301	Sedalia	(660)	21,387	21,568

ZIP	Place	Area code	2010 population	2017 estimate
63801	Sikeston	(573)	16,318	16,155
63138	Spanish Lake (c)	(314)	19,650	—
*65802	Springfield	(417)	159,498	167,376
63017	Town and Country	(314)	10,815	11,115
63379	Troy	(314)	10,540	12,015
63084	Union	(636)	10,204	11,524
63130	University City	(314)	35,371	34,549
64093	Warrensburg	(660)	18,838	20,168
63090	Washington	(636)	13,982	13,966
64870	Webb City	(417)	10,996	11,334
63119	Webster Groves	(314)	22,995	22,886
63385	Wentzville	(636)	29,070	39,414
65775	West Plains	(417)	11,986	12,248
*63040	Wildwood	(636)	35,517	35,501

Montana
Area code 406 applies to the entire state.

ZIP	Place	2010 population	2017 estimate
*59101	Billings	104,170	109,642
*59715	Bozeman	37,280	46,596
*59701	Butte-Silver Bow (balance)	33,525	33,901
*59401	Great Falls	58,505	58,876
*59601	Helena	28,190	31,429
*59901	Kalispell	19,927	23,212
*59801	Missoula	66,788	73,340

Nebraska
Area code 531 overlays area code 402.

ZIP	Place	Area code	2010 population	2017 estimate
68310	Beatrice	(402)	12,459	12,295
*68005	Bellevue	(402)	50,137	53,424
68138	Chalco (c)	(402)	10,994	—
*68601	Columbus	(402)	22,111	23,128
*68025	Fremont	(402)	26,397	26,457
*68801	Grand Island	(308)	48,520	51,390
*68901	Hastings	(402)	24,907	24,989
*68847	Kearney	(308)	30,787	33,835
*68128	La Vista	(402)	15,758	17,116
68850	Lexington	(308)	10,230	10,024
*68502	Lincoln	(402)	258,379	284,736
*68701	Norfolk	(402)	24,210	24,434
*69101	North Platte	(308)	24,733	23,888
*68104	Omaha	(402)	408,958	466,893
*68046	Papillion	(402)	18,894	19,539
*69361	Scottsbluff	(308)	15,039	14,874
68776	South Sioux City	(402)	13,353	12,911

Nevada
Area code 725 overlays area code 702.

ZIP	Place	Area code	2010 population	2017 estimate
*89005	Boulder City	(702)	15,023	15,971
*89701	Carson City	(775)	55,274	54,745
*89801	Elko	(775)	18,297	20,451
89124	Enterprise (c)	(702)	108,481	—
89408	Fernley	(775)	19,368	19,863
*89410	Gardnerville Ranchos (c)	(775)	11,312	—
*89015	Henderson	(702)	257,729	302,539
*89101	Las Vegas	(702)	583,756	641,676
*89027	Mesquite	(702)	15,276	18,541
*89030	North Las Vegas	(702)	216,961	242,975
*89048	Pahrump (c)	(775)	36,441	—
*89121	Paradise (c)	(702)	223,167	—
*89501	Reno	(775)	225,221	248,853
*89441	Spanish Springs (c)	(775)	15,064	—
*89431	Sparks	(775)	90,264	100,888
89815	Spring Creek (c)	(702)	12,361	—
89147	Spring Valley (c)	(702)	178,395	—
89135	Summerlin South (c)	(702)	24,085	—
89433	Sun Valley (c)	(775)	19,299	—
*89110	Sunrise Manor (c)	(702)	189,372	—
89122	Whitney (c)	(702)	38,585	—
*89121	Winchester (c)	(702)	27,978	—

New Hampshire
Area code 603 applies to the entire state. See introductory note.

ZIP	Place	2010 population	2017 estimate
03031	Amherst	11,201	11,229
03110	Bedford	21,203	22,458
03570	Berlin	10,051	10,225
03743	Claremont	13,355	12,982
*03301	Concord	42,695	43,019
03818	Conway	10,115	10,147
03038	Derry	33,109	33,440
03038	Derry (c)	22,015	—
*03820	Dover	29,987	31,398
03824	Durham	14,638	16,523
03824	Durham (c)	10,345	—

ZIP	Place	2010 population	2017 estimate
03833	Exeter	14,306	15,082
03045	Goffstown	17,651	17,937
*03842	Hampton	15,430	15,491
03755	Hanover	11,260	11,485
03106	Hooksett	13,451	14,175
03051	Hudson	24,467	25,139
*03431	Keene	23,409	22,949
*03246	Laconia	15,951	16,464
*03766	Lebanon	13,151	13,522
*03053	Londonderry	24,129	26,126
*03053	Londonderry (c)	11,037	—
*03101	Manchester	109,565	111,196
03054	Merrimack	25,494	25,660
03055	Milford	15,115	15,449
*03060	Nashua	86,494	88,341
03076	Pelham	12,897	13,681
*03801	Portsmouth	20,779	21,796
03077	Raymond	10,138	10,376
*03867	Rochester	29,752	30,797
03079	Salem	28,776	29,046
03878	Somersworth	11,766	11,900
03087	Windham	13,592	14,562

New Jersey
Area code 551 overlays area code 201. Area code 640 overlays 609. Area code 848 overlays 732. Area code 862 overlays 973.

ZIP	Place	Area code	2010 population	2017 estimate
07712	Asbury Park	(732)	16,116	15,767
*08401	Atlantic City	(609)	39,558	38,429
07001	Avenel (c)	(732)	17,011	—
07002	Bayonne	(201)	63,024	67,186
08722	Beachwood	(732)	11,045	11,248
*08031	Bellmawr	(856)	11,583	11,489
07621	Bergenfield	(201)	26,764	27,927
08805	Bound Brook	(732)	10,402	10,468
08807	Bradley Gardens (c)	(908)	14,206	—
08302	Bridgeton	(856)	25,349	24,505
08015	Browns Mills (c)	(609)	11,223	—
*08102	Camden	(856)	77,344	74,532
07008	Carteret	(732)	22,844	24,084
08002	Cherry Hill Mall (c)	(856)	14,171	—
07010	Cliffside Park	(201)	23,594	25,142
*07013	Clifton	(973)	84,136	86,607
*08108	Collingswood	(856)	13,926	14,027
07067	Colonia (c)	(732)	17,795	—
*07801	Dover	(973)	18,157	18,232
07628	Dumont	(201)	17,479	17,998
*07018	East Orange	(973)	64,270	65,378
*07724	Eatontown	(732)	12,709	12,376
08043	Echelon (c)	(856)	10,743	—
07020	Edgewater	(201)	11,513	12,368
*07201	Elizabeth	(908)	124,969	130,215
07407	Elmwood Park	(201)	19,403	20,429
*07631	Englewood	(201)	27,147	29,112
07410	Fair Lawn	(201)	32,457	33,710
07022	Fairview	(201)	13,835	14,537
07932	Florham Park	(973)	11,696	11,765
08863	Fords	(732)	15,187	—
07024	Fort Lee	(201)	35,345	37,907
07417	Franklin Lakes	(201)	10,590	11,255
08823	Franklin Park (c)	(732)	13,295	—
07728	Freehold	(732)	12,052	11,894
07026	Garfield	(973)	30,487	32,393
08028	Glassboro	(856)	18,579	20,011
07452	Glen Rock	(201)	11,601	12,045
08030	Gloucester City	(856)	11,456	11,342
*08053	Greentree (c)	(856)	11,367	—
07093	Guttenberg	(201)	11,176	11,695
*07601	Hackensack	(201)	43,010	45,248
08033	Haddonfield	(856)	11,593	11,435
08690	Hamilton Square (c)	(609)	12,784	—
08037	Hammonton	(609)	14,791	14,369
07029	Harrison	(973)	13,620	17,643
07604	Hasbrouck Heights	(201)	11,842	12,277
*07506	Hawthorne	(973)	18,791	19,101
08904	Highland Park	(732)	13,982	14,164
07642	Hillsdale	(201)	10,219	10,581
07030	Hoboken	(201)	50,005	55,131
*08753	Holiday City-Berkeley (c)	(732)	12,831	—
07843	Hopatcong	(973)	15,147	14,298
08830	Iselin (c)	(732)	18,695	—
*07302	Jersey City	(201)	247,597	270,753
*07302	Kearny	(201)/(973)	40,684	42,670
07405	Kinnelon	(973)	10,248	10,213
08701	Lakewood (c)	(732)	53,805	—
07035	Lincoln Park	(973)	10,521	10,468
07036	Linden	(732)/(908)	40,499	43,056
08021	Lindenwold	(856)	17,613	17,471
07643	Little Ferry	(201)	10,626	11,000
07644	Lodi	(973)	24,136	24,961
07740	Long Branch	(732)	30,719	30,762
07940	Madison	(973)	15,845	16,033

ZIP	Place	Area code	2010 population	2017 estimate
08835	Manville	(908)	10,344	10,414
08053	Marlton (c)	(856)	10,133	—
08836	Martinsville (c)	(908)	11,980	—
08619	Mercerville (c)	(609)	13,230	—
08840	Metuchen	(732)	13,574	14,349
08846	Middlesex	(732)	13,635	13,867
08332	Millville	(856)	28,400	27,918
08057	Moorestown-Lenola (c)	(856)	14,217	—
*07960	Morristown	(973)	18,411	19,037
*08901	New Brunswick	(732)	55,181	57,073
07646	New Milford	(201)	16,341	16,868
07974	New Providence	(908)	12,171	13,308
*07102	Newark	(973)	277,140	285,154
07031	North Arlington	(201)	15,392	16,009
*07060	North Plainfield	(908)	21,936	22,060
07436	Oakland	(201)	12,754	13,224
*08050	Ocean Acres (c)	(609)	16,142	—
08226	Ocean City	(609)	11,701	11,206
08857	Old Bridge (c)	(732)	23,753	—
07650	Palisades Park	(201)	19,622	20,988
*07652	Paramus	(201)	26,342	27,032
07055	Passaic	(973)	69,781	71,247
*07505	Paterson	(973)	146,199	148,678
08070	Pennsville (c)	(856)	11,888	—
*08861	Perth Amboy	(732)	50,814	52,823
08865	Phillipsburg	(908)	14,950	14,459
08021	Pine Hill	(856)	10,233	10,536
*07060	Plainfield	(908)	49,808	51,327
08232	Pleasantville	(609)	20,249	20,732
08742	Point Pleasant	(732)	18,392	18,651
07442	Pompton Lakes	(973)	11,097	11,206
*08540	Princeton	(609)	12,307	31,822
08536	Princeton Meadows (c)	(609)	13,834	—
07065	Rahway	(732)	27,346	30,131
07446	Ramsey	(201)	14,473	15,242
*07701	Red Bank	(732)	12,206	12,150
07657	Ridgefield	(201)	11,032	11,435
07660	Ridgefield Park	(201)	12,729	13,154
*07450	Ridgewood	(201)	24,958	25,692
07456	Ringwood	(973)	12,228	12,454
07661	River Edge	(201)	11,340	11,724
07751	Robertsville (c)	(732)	11,297	—
07203	Roselle	(908)	21,085	21,976
07204	Roselle Park	(908)	13,297	13,821
07070	Rutherford	(201)	18,061	18,782
*08872	Sayreville	(732)	42,704	45,325
*07094	Secaucus	(201)	16,264	20,215
07078	Short Hills (c)	(973)	13,165	—
08244	Somers Point	(609)	10,795	10,480
*08873	Somerset (c)	(732)	22,083	—
08876	Somerville	(908)	12,098	12,418
07080	South Plainfield	(732)/(908)	23,385	24,435
*08882	South River	(732)	16,008	16,349
08003	Springdale (c)	(856)	14,518	—
*07901	Summit	(908)	21,457	22,323
07670	Tenafly	(201)	14,488	14,900
*07724	Tinton Falls	(732)	17,892	17,789
*08753	Toms River (c)	(732)	88,791	—
*07512	Totowa	(973)	10,804	10,817
*08608	Trenton	(609)	84,913	84,964
07087	Union City	(201)	66,455	70,387
07043	Upper Montclair (c)	(973)	11,565	—
08406	Ventnor City	(609)	10,650	10,239
*08360	Vineland	(856)	60,724	60,392
07463	Waldwick	(201)	9,625	10,092
07057	Wallington	(201)/(973)	11,335	11,781
07465	Wanaque	(201)/(973)	11,116	11,994
07728	West Freehold (c)	(908)	13,613	—
07093	West New York	(201)	49,708	54,227
*07090	Westfield	(908)	30,316	30,433
*07675	Westwood	(201)	10,908	11,326
08094	Williamstown (c)	(609)/(856)	15,567	—
07095	Woodbridge (c)	(732)	19,265	—
07424	Woodland Park	(973)	11,819	12,834

New Mexico

ZIP	Place	Area code	2010 population	2017 estimate
*88310	Alamogordo	(575)	30,403	31,248
*87101	Albuquerque	(505)	545,852	558,545
*88210	Artesia	(575)	11,301	11,921
*88220	Carlsbad	(575)	26,138	28,774
*88021	Chaparral (c)	(575)	14,631	—
*88101	Clovis	(575)	37,775	38,962
*88030	Deming	(575)	14,855	14,183
*87532	Española	(505)	10,224	10,029
*87401	Farmington	(505)	45,877	45,450
*87301	Gallup	(505)	21,678	21,960
*88240	Hobbs	(575)	34,122	37,764
*88001	Las Cruces	(575)	97,618	101,712
*87701	Las Vegas	(505)	13,753	13,201
*87544	Los Alamos (c)	(505)	12,019	—
87031	Los Lunas	(505)	14,835	15,501

ZIP	Place	Area code	2010 population	2017 estimate
88260	Lovington	(575)	11,009	11,152
87107	North Valley (c)	(505)	11,333	—
*88130	Portales	(575)	12,280	11,850
*87124	Rio Rancho	(505)	87,521	96,159
*88201	Roswell	(575)	48,366	47,775
*87501	Santa Fe	(505)	67,947	83,776
87105	South Valley (c)	(505)	40,976	—
*88063	Sunland Park	(575)	14,106	17,061

New York

Area codes 347/929 overlay area code 718. Area codes 332/646/917 overlay 212. Area code 680 overlays 315. Area code 838 overlays 518. Area code 934 overlays 631.

ZIP	Place	Area code	2010 population	2017 estimate
*12202	Albany	(518)	97,856	98,251
12010	Amsterdam	(518)	18,620	17,844
*13021	Auburn	(315)	27,687	26,704
*11702	Babylon	(631)	12,166	12,145
11510	Baldwin (c)	(516)	24,033	—
*14020	Batavia	(585)	15,465	14,661
11706	Bay Shore (c)	(631)	26,337	—
12508	Beacon	(845)	15,541	14,289
11710	Bellmore (c)	(516)	16,218	—
11714	Bethpage (c)	(516)	16,429	—
*13901	Binghamton	(607)	47,376	45,179
11716	Bohemia (c)	(631)	10,180	—
11717	Brentwood (c)	(631)	60,664	—
*14610	Brighton (c)	(585)	36,609	—
*14201	Buffalo	(716)	261,310	258,612
*14424	Canandaigua	(585)	10,545	10,289
11720	Centereach (c)	(631)	31,578	—
*11722	Central Islip (c)	(631)	34,450	—
*14227	Cheektowaga (c)	(716)	75,178	—
12047	Cohoes	(518)	16,168	16,875
11725	Commack (c)	(631)	36,124	—
11726	Copiague (c)	(631)	22,993	—
11727	Coram (c)	(631)	39,113	—
*14830	Corning	(607)	11,183	10,709
13045	Cortland	(607)	19,204	18,698
11729	Deer Park (c)	(631)	27,745	—
14043	Depew	(716)	15,303	15,193
*11746	Dix Hills (c)	(631)	26,892	—
10522	Dobbs Ferry	(914)	10,875	11,147
*14048	Dunkirk	(716)	12,563	11,848
11730	East Islip (c)	(631)	14,475	—
11758	East Massapequa (c)	(516)	19,069	—
11554	East Meadow (c)	(516)	38,132	—
11731	East Northport (c)	(631)	20,217	—
11772	East Patchogue (c)	(631)	22,469	—
10709	Eastchester (c)	(914)	19,554	—
14226	Eggertsville (c)	(716)	15,019	—
*14901	Elmira	(607)	29,200	27,773
11003	Elmont (c)	(516)	33,198	—
11731	Elwood (c)	(631)	11,177	—
*13760	Endicott	(607)	13,392	12,828
13762	Endwell (c)	(607)	11,446	—
13219	Fairmount (c)	(315)	10,224	—
11738	Farmingville (c)	(631)	15,481	—
*11001	Floral Park	(516)	15,863	16,103
*13602	Fort Drum (c)	(315)	12,955	—
11768	Fort Salonga (c)	(631)	10,008	—
11010	Franklin Square (c)	(516)	29,320	—
14063	Fredonia	(716)	11,230	10,567
11520	Freeport	(516)	42,860	43,508
13069	Fulton	(315)	11,896	11,324
*11530	Garden City	(516)	22,371	22,698
14456	Geneva	(315)	13,261	12,886
11542	Glen Cove	(516)	26,964	27,500
12801	Glens Falls	(518)	14,700	14,439
12078	Gloversville	(518)	15,665	14,951
*11023	Great Neck	(516)	9,989	10,303
14616	Greece (c)	(585)	14,519	—
11740	Greenlawn (c)	(631)	13,742	—
11946	Hampton Bays (c)	(631)	13,603	—
10528	Harrison	(914)	27,472	28,587
*11788	Hauppauge (c)	(631)	20,882	—
10927	Haverstraw	(845)	11,910	12,216
*11550	Hempstead	(516)	53,891	55,806
*11801	Hicksville (c)	(516)	41,547	—
11741	Holbrook (c)	(631)	27,195	—
11742	Holtsville (c)	(631)	19,714	—
11743	Huntington (c)	(631)	18,046	—
*11746	Huntington Station (c)	(631)	33,029	—
*14617	Irondequoit (c)	(585)	51,692	—
11751	Islip (c)	(631)	18,689	—
*14850	Ithaca	(607)	30,014	31,006
*14701	Jamestown	(716)	31,146	29,591
*10535	Jefferson Valley-Yorktown (c)	(914)	14,142	—
11753	Jericho (c)	(516)	13,567	—
13790	Johnson City	(607)	15,174	14,508
*14217	Kenmore	(716)	15,423	15,217
11754	Kings Park (c)	(631)	17,282	—

ZIP	Place	Area code	2010 population	2017 estimate
*12401	Kingston	(845)	23,893	23,169
10950	Kiryas Joel	(845)	20,175	24,155
14218	Lackawanna	(716)	18,141	17,934
11755	Lake Grove	(631)	11,163	11,155
11779	Lake Ronkonkoma (c)	(631)	20,155	—
*14086	Lancaster	(716)	10,352	10,179
11756	Levittown (c)	(516)	51,881	—
11757	Lindenhurst	(631)	27,253	27,153
*14094	Lockport	(716)	21,165	20,569
11561	Long Beach	(516)	33,275	33,750
11563	Lynbrook	(516)	19,427	19,716
10543	Mamaroneck	(914)	18,929	19,423
11949	Manorville (c)	(631)	14,314	—
11758	Massapequa (c)	(516)	21,685	—
11762	Massapequa Park	(516)	17,008	17,266
13662	Massena	(315)	10,936	10,368
11950	Mastic (c)	(631)	15,481	—
11951	Mastic Beach[1]	(631)	12,930	14,762
11763	Medford (c)	(631)	24,142	—
11747	Melville (c)	(631)	18,985	—
11566	Merrick (c)	(516)	22,097	—
11953	Middle Island (c)	(631)	10,483	—
*10940	Middletown	(845)	28,086	27,891
11764	Miller Place (c)	(631)	12,339	—
11501	Mineola	(516)	18,799	19,387
10952	Monsey (c)	(845)	18,412	—
10549	Mount Kisco	(914)	10,877	10,998
11766	Mount Sinai (c)	(631)	12,118	—
*10550	Mount Vernon	(914)	67,292	68,703
10954	Nanuet (c)	(845)	17,882	—
11767	Nesconset (c)	(631)	13,387	—
11590	New Cassel (c)	(516)	14,059	—
10956	New City (c)	(845)	33,559	—
*10801	New Rochelle	(914)	77,062	79,946
*10001	New York	(212)/(718)	8,175,133	8,622,698
*12550	Newburgh	(845)	28,866	28,363
*14301	Niagara Falls	(716)	50,193	48,460
11701	North Amityville (c)	(631)	17,862	—
11703	North Babylon (c)	(631)	17,509	—
11706	North Bay Shore (c)	(631)	18,944	—
11710	North Bellmore (c)	(516)	19,941	—
11713	North Bellport (c)	(631)	11,545	—
11757	North Lindenhurst (c)	(631)	11,652	—
11758	North Massapequa (c)	(516)	17,886	—
11566	North Merrick (c)	(516)	12,272	—
11040	North New Hyde Park (c)	(516)	14,899	—
14120	North Tonawanda	(716)	31,568	30,475
11580	North Valley Stream (c)	(516)	16,628	—
11793	North Wantagh (c)	(516)	11,960	—
11572	Oceanside (c)	(516)	32,109	—
13669	Ogdensburg	(315)	11,128	10,687
14760	Olean	(585)/(716)	14,452	13,711
13421	Oneida	(315)	11,393	10,997
13820	Oneonta	(607)	13,901	14,057
10562	Ossining	(914)	25,060	25,403
13126	Oswego	(315)	18,142	17,465
11772	Patchogue	(631)	11,798	12,489
10965	Pearl River (c)	(845)	15,876	—
10566	Peekskill	(914)	23,583	24,272
11803	Plainview (c)	(516)	26,217	—
*12901	Plattsburgh	(518)	19,989	19,696
*10573	Port Chester	(914)	28,967	29,711
*11050	Port Washington (c)	(516)	15,846	—
12601	Poughkeepsie	(845)	32,736	30,614
11961	Ridge (c)	(631)	13,336	—
11901	Riverhead (c)	(631)	13,299	—
*14604	Rochester	(585)	210,565	208,046
*11570	Rockville Centre	(516)	24,023	24,848
11778	Rocky Point (c)	(631)	14,014	—
*13440	Rome	(315)	33,725	32,473
*11779	Ronkonkoma (c)	(631)	19,082	—
11575	Roosevelt (c)	(516)	16,258	—
12306	Rotterdam (c)	(518)	20,652	—
10580	Rye	(914)	15,720	16,009
11780	Saint James (c)	(631)	13,338	—
13454	Salisbury (c)	(315)	12,093	—
12866	Saratoga Springs	(518)	26,586	28,027
11782	Sayville (c)	(631)	16,853	—
*10583	Scarsdale	(914)	17,166	18,079
*12305	Schenectady	(518)	66,135	65,625
11783	Seaford (c)	(516)	15,294	—
11784	Selden (c)	(631)	19,851	—
11733	Setauket-East Setauket (c)	(631)	15,477	—
11967	Shirley (c)	(631)	27,854	—
10591	Sleepy Hollow	(914)	9,870	10,218
*11787	Smithtown (c)	(631)	26,470	—
11735	South Farmingdale (c)	(516)	14,486	—
10977	Spring Valley	(845)	31,347	32,724
*11790	Stony Brook (c)	(631)	13,740	—
10980	Stony Point (c)	(845)	12,147	—
10901	Suffern	(845)	10,723	10,995
*11791	Syosset (c)	(516)	18,829	—
*13202	Syracuse	(315)	145,170	143,396
10591	Tarrytown	(914)	11,277	11,572
11776	Terryville (c)	(631)	11,849	—

ZIP	Place	Area code	2010 population	2017 estimate
*14150	Tonawanda	(716)	15,130	14,904
*14150	Tonawanda (c)	(716)	58,144	—
*12180	Troy	(518)	50,129	49,565
*11553	Uniondale (c)	(516)	24,759	—
*13501	Utica	(315)	62,235	60,635
*11580	Valley Stream	(516)	37,511	37,935
11793	Wantagh (c)	(516)	18,871	—
*13601	Watertown	(315)	27,023	25,687
12189	Watervliet	(518)	10,254	10,131
*11704	West Babylon (c)	(631)	43,213	—
10993	West Haverstraw	(845)	10,165	10,388
11552	West Hempstead (c)	(516)	18,862	—
11795	West Islip (c)	(631)	28,335	—
*14224	West Seneca (c)	(716)	44,711	—
*11590	Westbury	(516)	15,146	15,493
*10601	White Plains	(914)	56,853	59,047
11797	Woodbury	(845)	10,686	11,075
11598	Woodmere (c)	(516)	17,121	—
11798	Wyandanch (c)	(631)	11,647	—
*10701	Yonkers	(914)	195,976	202,019

(1) Place was incorporated after the 2010 Census was conducted. Data in 2010 column is for Mastic Beach CDP.

North Carolina

Area code 743 overlays area code 336. Area code 980 overlays 704. Area code 984 overlays 919.

ZIP	Place	Area code	2010 population	2017 estimate
*28001	Albemarle	(704)	15,903	15,977
*27502	Apex	(919)	37,476	50,451
27263	Archdale	(336)	11,415	11,518
*27203	Asheboro	(336)	25,012	25,863
*28801	Asheville	(828)	83,393	91,902
28012	Belmont	(704)	10,076	12,046
*28607	Boone	(828)	17,122	19,205
*27215	Burlington	(336)	49,963	53,077
27510	Carrboro	(919)	19,582	21,544
*27511	Cary	(919)	135,234	165,904
*27514	Chapel Hill	(919)	57,233	59,862
*28202	Charlotte	(704)	731,424	859,035
*27520	Clayton	(919)	16,116	21,405
27012	Clemmons	(336)	18,627	20,420
*28025	Concord	(704)	79,066	92,067
28031	Cornelius	(704)	24,866	29,191
*28036	Davidson	(704)	10,944	12,684
*27701	Durham	(919)	228,330	267,743
*27288	Eden	(336)	15,527	15,041
*27909	Elizabeth City	(252)	18,683	17,756
27244	Elon	(336)	9,419	10,227
*28301	Fayetteville	(910)	200,564	209,889
27526	Fuquay-Varina	(919)	17,937	27,906
27529	Garner	(919)	25,745	28,858
*28052	Gastonia	(704)	71,741	76,593
*27530	Goldsboro	(919)	36,437	35,197
27253	Graham	(336)	14,153	14,814
*27401	Greensboro	(336)	269,666	290,222
*27834	Greenville	(252)	84,554	92,156
28075	Harrisburg	(704)	11,526	15,728
*28532	Havelock	(252)	20,735	20,008
*27536	Henderson	(252)	15,368	14,852
*28739	Hendersonville	(828)	13,137	13,954
*28601	Hickory	(828)	40,010	40,611
*27260	High Point	(336)	104,371	111,513
27540	Holly Springs	(919)	24,661	35,223
28348	Hope Mills	(910)	15,176	16,135
*28078	Huntersville	(704)	46,773	56,212
28079	Indian Trail	(704)	33,518	38,980
*28540	Jacksonville	(910)	70,145	72,447
*28081	Kannapolis	(704)	42,625	48,806
*27284	Kernersville	(336)	23,123	24,386
28086	Kings Mountain	(704)	10,296	10,791
*28501	Kinston	(252)	21,677	20,509
*27545	Knightdale	(919)	11,401	15,849
*28352	Laurinburg	(910)	15,962	15,156
28451	Leland	(910)	13,527	19,976
*28645	Lenoir	(828)	18,228	17,943
27023	Lewisville	(336)	12,639	13,913
*27292	Lexington	(336)	18,931	18,775
*28092	Lincolnton	(704)	10,486	10,776
*28358	Lumberton	(910)	21,542	21,040
*28105	Matthews	(704)	27,198	32,117
27302	Mebane	(919)	11,393	14,973
28227	Mint Hill	(704)	22,722	26,748
*28110	Monroe	(704)	32,797	35,065
*28115	Mooresville	(704)	32,711	37,820
28655	Morganton	(828)	16,918	16,519
27560	Morrisville	(919)	18,576	26,461
*27030	Mount Airy	(336)	10,388	10,232
28120	Mount Holly	(704)	13,656	15,635
28411	Murraysville (c)	(910)	14,215	—
*28560	New Bern	(252)	29,524	29,590
28658	Newton	(828)	12,968	13,098
*28374	Pinehurst	(910)	13,124	16,028

ZIP	Place	Area code	2010 population	2017 estimate
28399	Piney Green (c)	(910)	13,293	—
*27601	Raleigh	(919)	403,892	464,758
*27320	Reidsville	(336)	14,520	13,857
27870	Roanoke Rapids	(252)	15,754	14,787
*27801	Rocky Mount	(252)	57,477	54,523
*28144	Salisbury	(704)	33,662	33,849
*27330	Sanford	(919)	28,094	29,313
*28150	Shelby	(704)	20,323	20,018
27577	Smithfield	(919)	10,966	12,309
*28387	Southern Pines	(910)	12,334	14,029
*28390	Spring Lake	(910)	11,964	12,580
28104	Stallings	(704)	13,831	15,647
*28677	Statesville	(704)	24,532	26,657
27358	Summerfield	(336)	10,232	11,198
27886	Tarboro	(252)	11,415	10,856
*27360	Thomasville	(336)	26,757	26,615
*27587	Wake Forest	(919)	30,117	42,269
28173	Waxhaw	(704)	9,859	15,147
28104	Weddington	(704)	9,459	10,773
*28401	Wilmington	(910)	106,476	119,045
*27893	Wilson	(252)	49,167	49,348
*27101	Winston-Salem	(336)	229,617	244,605

North Dakota

Area code 701 applies to the entire state.

ZIP	Place	2010 population	2017 estimate
*58501	Bismarck	61,272	72,865
*58601	Dickinson	17,787	22,186
*58102	Fargo	105,549	122,359
*58201	Grand Forks	52,838	57,056
*58401	Jamestown	15,427	15,387
58554	Mandan	18,331	22,228
*58701	Minot	40,888	47,822
58078	West Fargo	25,830	35,708
*58801	Williston	14,716	25,586

Ohio

Area code 220 overlays area code 740. Area code 234 overlays 330. Area code 380 overlays 614. Area code 567 overlays 419.

ZIP	Place	Area code	2010 population	2017 estimate
*44301	Akron	(330)	199,110	197,846
44601	Alliance	(330)	22,322	21,791
44001	Amherst	(440)	12,021	12,088
44805	Ashland	(419)	20,362	20,455
*44004	Ashtabula	(440)	19,124	18,144
45701	Athens	(740)	23,832	25,214
44202	Aurora	(330)	15,548	15,982
*44515	Austintown (c)	(330)	29,677	—
44011	Avon	(440)	21,193	23,054
44012	Avon Lake	(440)	22,581	24,184
44203	Barberton	(330)	26,550	26,120
44140	Bay Village	(440)	15,651	15,344
44122	Beachwood	(216)	11,953	11,696
*45432	Beavercreek	(937)	45,193	46,948
44146	Bedford	(216)/(440)	13,074	12,627
*44146	Bedford Heights	(216)/(440)	10,751	10,580
43311	Bellefontaine	(937)	13,370	13,161
44141	Brecksville	(440)	13,656	13,632
45211	Bridgetown (c)	(513)	14,407	—
44147	Broadview Heights	(440)	19,400	19,227
44142	Brook Park	(216)/(440)	19,212	18,626
44144	Brooklyn	(216)	11,169	10,792
44212	Brunswick	(330)	34,255	34,867
44820	Bucyrus	(419)	12,362	11,817
*43725	Cambridge	(740)	10,635	10,411
*44702	Canton	(330)	73,007	70,909
*45822	Celina	(419)	10,400	10,290
*45458	Centerville	(937)	23,999	23,787
45601	Chillicothe	(740)	21,901	21,499
*45202	Cincinnati	(513)	296,943	301,301
43113	Circleville	(740)	13,314	13,930
45315	Clayton	(937)	13,209	13,215
*44102	Cleveland	(216)	396,815	385,525
*44118	Cleveland Heights	(216)	46,121	44,562
*43201	Columbus	(614)	787,033	879,170
44030	Conneaut	(440)	12,841	12,642
43812	Coshocton	(740)	11,216	11,044
*44221	Cuyahoga Falls	(330)	49,652	49,247
*45402	Dayton	(937)	141,527	140,371
43512	Defiance	(419)	16,494	16,687
43015	Delaware	(740)	34,753	39,267
*45247	Dent (c)	(513)	10,497	—
44622	Dover	(330)	12,826	12,766
*43016	Dublin	(614)	41,751	47,619
*44112	East Cleveland	(216)	17,843	17,187
43920	East Liverpool	(330)	11,195	10,691
*44095	Eastlake	(440)	18,577	18,172
*44035	Elyria	(440)	54,533	53,883
45322	Englewood	(937)	13,465	13,470
*44117	Euclid	(216)	48,920	47,201
45324	Fairborn	(937)	32,352	33,541
*45011	Fairfield	(513)	42,510	42,566
44126	Fairview Park	(440)	16,826	16,292
*45840	Findlay	(419)	41,202	41,321
*45224	Finneytown (c)	(513)	12,741	—
45240	Forest Park	(513)	18,720	18,690
45230	Forestville (c)	(513)	10,532	—
44830	Fostoria	(419)	13,441	13,256
45005	Franklin	(513)	11,771	11,735
43420	Fremont	(419)	16,734	16,193
43230	Gahanna	(614)	33,248	35,297
44833	Galion	(419)	10,512	10,032
*44125	Garfield Heights	(216)	28,849	27,835
44232	Green	(330)	25,699	25,747
45331	Greenville	(937)	13,227	12,771
43123	Grove City	(614)	35,575	41,022
*45011	Hamilton	(513)	62,477	62,092
45030	Harrison	(513)	9,897	11,300
43056	Heath	(740)	10,310	10,713
43026	Hilliard	(614)	28,435	35,939
45424	Huber Heights	(937)	38,101	37,986
*44236	Hudson	(330)	22,262	22,245
45638	Ironton	(740)	11,129	10,722
*44240	Kent	(330)	28,904	29,915
*45429	Kettering	(937)	56,163	55,175
44107	Lakewood	(216)	52,131	50,249
43130	Lancaster	(740)	38,780	40,280
45036	Lebanon	(513)	20,033	20,622
*45801	Lima	(419)	38,771	37,149
43140	London	(740)	9,904	10,138
*44052	Lorain	(440)	64,097	63,841
*45140	Loveland	(513)	12,081	12,770
44124	Lyndhurst	(216)/(440)	14,001	13,557
*44056	Macedonia	(330)	11,188	11,940
*45248	Mack (c)	(513)	11,585	—
*44902	Mansfield	(419)	47,821	46,160
44137	Maple Heights	(216)	23,138	22,400
45750	Marietta	(740)	14,085	13,673
*43302	Marion	(740)	36,837	35,997
*43040	Marysville	(937)	22,094	23,912
*45036	Mason	(513)	30,712	33,235
*44646	Massillon	(330)	32,149	32,342
43537	Maumee	(419)	14,286	13,787
44124	Mayfield Heights	(440)	19,155	18,682
*44256	Medina	(330)	26,678	26,190
*44060	Mentor	(440)	47,159	47,121
*45343	Miamisburg	(937)	20,181	19,985
44130	Middleburg Heights	(216)/(440)	15,946	15,587
*45042	Middletown	(513)	48,694	48,823
*45247	Monfort Heights (c)	(513)	11,948	—
*45050	Monroe	(513)	12,442	13,683
45242	Montgomery	(513)	10,251	10,746
43050	Mount Vernon	(740)	16,990	16,659
43054	New Albany	(614)	7,724	10,718
*44216	New Franklin	(330)	14,227	14,165
44663	New Philadelphia	(330)	17,288	17,424
*43055	Newark	(740)	47,573	49,423
44446	Niles	(330)	19,266	18,473
*44720	North Canton	(330)	17,488	17,290
44070	North Olmsted	(440)	32,718	31,734
*44039	North Ridgeville	(440)	29,465	33,436
44133	North Royalton	(440)	30,444	30,294
*45251	Northbrook (c)	(513)	10,668	—
44203	Norton	(330)	12,085	12,013
44857	Norwalk	(419)	17,012	16,824
45212	Norwood	(513)	19,207	19,870
*43616	Oregon	(419)	20,291	19,973
45056	Oxford	(513)	21,371	22,859
44077	Painesville	(440)	19,563	19,813
*44129	Parma	(216)/(440)	81,601	79,167
44130	Parma Heights	(440)	20,718	20,053
43062	Pataskala	(740)	14,962	15,566
*43551	Perrysburg	(419)	20,623	21,482
43147	Pickerington	(614)/(740)	18,291	20,402
45356	Piqua	(937)	20,522	20,987
*45662	Portsmouth	(740)	20,226	20,443
43065	Powell	(614)	11,500	13,204
44266	Ravenna	(330)	11,724	11,461
*45215	Reading	(513)	10,385	10,260
*43068	Reynoldsburg	(614)	35,893	37,847
44143	Richmond Heights	(216)/(440)	10,546	10,417
45431	Riverside	(937)	25,201	25,094
44116	Rocky River	(216)/(440)	20,213	20,216
44460	Salem	(330)	12,303	11,782
*44870	Sandusky	(419)	25,793	24,845
*44131	Seven Hills	(216)/(440)	11,804	11,663
*44120	Shaker Heights	(216)	28,448	27,440

ZIP	Place	Area code	2010 population	2017 estimate
45241	Sharonville	(513)	13,560	13,797
*45365	Sidney	(937)	21,229	20,614
44139	Solon	(440)	23,348	22,962
*44121	South Euclid	(216)/(440)	22,295	21,598
45066	Springboro	(513)	17,409	18,610
45246	Springdale	(513)	11,223	11,213
*45502	Springfield	(937)	60,608	59,208
*43952	Steubenville	(740)	18,659	18,003
44224	Stow	(330)	34,837	34,769
44241	Streetsboro	(330)	16,028	16,365
*44136	Strongsville	(440)	44,750	44,744
44471	Struthers	(330)	10,713	10,254
43560	Sylvania	(419)	18,965	18,941
44278	Tallmadge	(330)	17,537	17,552
44883	Tiffin	(419)	17,963	17,546
*43604	Toledo	(419)	287,208	276,491
45067	Trenton	(513)	11,869	12,912
*45426	Trotwood	(937)	24,431	24,386
*45373	Troy	(937)	25,058	25,865
44087	Twinsburg	(330)	18,795	18,959
*44122	University Heights	(216)	13,539	13,028
*43221	Upper Arlington	(614)	33,771	35,337
43078	Urbana	(937)	11,793	11,405
45891	Van Wert	(419)	10,846	10,654
45377	Vandalia	(937)	15,246	15,053
*44089	Vermilion	(440)	10,594	10,453
*44281	Wadsworth	(330)	21,567	23,476
*44481	Warren	(330)	41,557	39,562
*44122	Warrensville Heights	(216)	13,542	13,251
43160	Washington Court House	(740)	14,192	14,215
*45449	West Carrollton	(937)	13,143	12,924
*43081	Westerville	(614)	36,120	39,737
44145	Westlake	(440)	32,729	32,297
*45239	White Oak (c)	(513)	19,167	—
43213	Whitehall	(614)	18,062	18,913
44092	Wickliffe	(440)	12,750	12,736
*44094	Willoughby	(440)	22,268	22,860
44095	Willowick	(440)	14,171	14,148
45177	Wilmington	(937)	12,520	12,398
44691	Wooster	(330)	26,119	26,618
43085	Worthington	(614)	13,575	14,646
45385	Xenia	(937)	25,719	26,562
*44503	Youngstown	(330)	66,982	64,604
*43701	Zanesville	(740)	25,487	25,388

Oklahoma

Area code 539 overlays area code 918.

ZIP	Place	Area code	2010 population	2017 estimate
*74820	Ada	(580)	16,810	17,280
*73521	Altus	(580)	19,813	18,849
*73401	Ardmore	(580)	24,283	24,779
*74003	Bartlesville	(918)	35,750	36,389
73008	Bethany	(405)	19,051	19,402
74008	Bixby	(918)	20,884	26,724
*74012	Broken Arrow	(918)	98,850	108,303
*73018	Chickasha	(405)	16,036	16,276
73020	Choctaw	(405)	11,146	12,524
*74017	Claremore	(918)	18,581	18,729
*73115	Del City	(405)	21,332	21,798
*73533	Duncan	(580)	23,431	22,484
*74701	Durant	(580)	15,856	17,764
*73034	Edmond	(405)	81,405	91,950
73036	El Reno	(405)	16,749	18,948
*73644	Elk City	(580)	11,693	11,555
*73701	Enid	(580)	49,379	50,122
*74033	Glenpool	(918)	10,808	13,814
73044	Guthrie	(405)	10,191	11,350
73942	Guymon	(580)	11,442	11,545
74037	Jenks	(918)	16,924	22,578
*73501	Lawton	(580)	96,867	93,714
*74501	McAlester	(918)	18,383	18,044
*74354	Miami	(918)	13,570	13,212
*73110	Midwest City	(405)	54,371	57,308
*73160	Moore	(405)	55,081	61,523
*74401	Muskogee	(918)	39,223	37,858
73064	Mustang	(405)	17,395	21,222
*73069	Norman	(405)	110,925	122,843
*73102	Oklahoma City	(405)	579,999	643,648
74447	Okmulgee	(918)	12,321	11,998
74055	Owasso	(918)	28,915	36,215
*74601	Ponca City	(580)	25,387	24,220
74063	Sand Springs	(918)	18,906	19,909
*74066	Sapulpa	(918)	20,544	20,843
*74801	Shawnee	(405)	29,857	31,232
*74074	Stillwater	(405)	45,688	49,829
*74464	Tahlequah	(918)	15,753	16,736
*74103	Tulsa	(918)	391,906	401,800
*73112	Warr Acres	(405)	10,043	10,333
73096	Weatherford	(580)	10,833	11,832
*73801	Woodward	(580)	12,051	12,268
*73099	Yukon	(405)	22,709	26,830

Oregon

Area code 458 overlays area code 541. Area code 971 overlays 503.

ZIP	Place	Area code	2010 population	2017 estimate
*97321	Albany	(541)	50,158	53,503
*97006	Aloha (c)	(503)	49,425	—
97603	Altamont (c)	(541)	19,257	—
97520	Ashland	(541)	20,078	21,117
*97005	Beaverton	(503)	89,803	97,514
*97701	Bend	(541)	76,639	94,520
97229	Bethany (c)	(503)	20,646	—
97013	Canby	(503)	15,829	17,759
97291	Cedar Mill (c)	(503)	14,546	—
97502	Central Point	(541)	17,169	18,234
97420	Coos Bay	(541)	15,967	16,295
97113	Cornelius	(503)	11,869	12,493
*97330	Corvallis	(541)	54,462	57,961
97424	Cottage Grove	(541)	9,686	10,169
97338	Dallas	(503)	14,583	16,301
*97009	Damascus	(503)	10,539	11,155
*97401	Eugene	(541)	156,185	168,916
97116	Forest Grove	(503)	21,083	24,141
97301	Four Corners (c)	(503)	15,947	—
97027	Gladstone	(503)	11,497	12,207
*97526	Grants Pass	(541)	34,533	37,579
*97030	Gresham	(503)	105,594	111,053
*97015	Happy Valley	(503)	13,903	21,196
97303	Hayesville (c)	(503)	19,936	—
97838	Hermiston	(541)	16,745	17,428
*97123	Hillsboro	(503)	91,611	106,894
97351	Independence	(503)	8,590	10,053
*97303	Keizer	(503)	36,478	39,315
*97601	Klamath Falls	(541)	20,840	21,359
97850	La Grande	(541)	13,082	13,173
*97034	Lake Oswego	(503)	36,619	39,196
97355	Lebanon	(541)	15,518	16,878
97128	McMinnville	(503)	32,187	34,347
*97501	Medford	(541)	74,907	81,780
*97222	Milwaukie	(503)	20,291	20,801
97361	Monmouth	(503)	9,534	10,338
97132	Newberg	(503)	22,068	23,609
*97365	Newport	(541)	9,989	10,592
97268	Oak Grove (c)	(503)	16,629	—
97006	Oak Hills (c)	(503)	11,333	—
97267	Oatfield (c)	(503)	13,415	—
97914	Ontario	(541)	11,366	11,009
97045	Oregon City	(503)	31,859	36,360
97801	Pendleton	(541)	16,612	16,677
*97201	Portland	(503)	583,776	647,805
97754	Prineville	(541)	9,253	10,055
97756	Redmond	(541)	26,215	30,011
*97470	Roseburg	(541)	21,181	22,321
97051	Saint Helens	(503)	12,883	13,701
*97301	Salem	(503)	154,637	169,798
97055	Sandy	(503)	9,570	11,149
97140	Sherwood	(503)	18,194	19,467
97381	Silverton	(503)	9,222	10,313
*97477	Springfield	(541)	59,403	62,353
97058	The Dalles	(541)	13,620	15,646
*97223	Tigard	(503)	48,035	53,148
97060	Troutdale	(503)	15,962	16,554
97062	Tualatin	(503)	26,054	27,478
97068	West Linn	(503)	25,109	26,703
97070	Wilsonville	(503)	19,509	24,058
97071	Woodburn	(503)	24,080	25,780

Pennsylvania

Area code 223 overlays area code 717. Area codes 267/445 overlay 215. Area code 272 overlays 570. Area code 484 overlays 610. Area code 878 overlays 412/724.

ZIP	Place	Area code	2010 population	2017 estimate
*18101	Allentown	(610)	118,032	121,283
15101	Allison Park (c)	(412)/(724)	21,552	—
*16601	Altoona	(814)	46,320	44,098
19003	Ardmore (c)	(610)	12,455	—
15234	Baldwin	(412)	19,767	19,610
18603	Berwick	(570)	10,477	10,086
15102	Bethel Park	(412)	32,313	32,404
*18016	Bethlehem	(610)	74,982	75,707
17815	Bloomsburg	(570)	14,855	14,231
19008	Broomall (c)	(610)	10,789	—
*16001	Butler	(724)	13,757	13,107
*17013	Carlisle	(717)	18,682	19,259
15108	Carnot-Moon (c)	(412)	11,372	—
*17201	Chambersburg	(717)	20,268	20,878
*19013	Chester	(610)	33,972	34,077
19320	Coatesville	(610)	13,100	13,123
17109	Colonial Park (c)	(717)	13,229	—
17512	Columbia	(717)	10,400	10,432
19023	Darby	(610)	10,687	10,700
19026	Drexel Hill (c)	(610)	28,043	—
*18512	Dunmore	(570)	14,057	13,069
*18301	East Stroudsburg	(570)	9,840	10,287

ZIP	Place	Area code	2010 population	2017 estimate
*18042	Easton	(610)	26,800	27,109
17022	Elizabethtown	(717)	11,545	11,586
*18049	Emmaus	(610)	11,211	11,454
17522	Ephrata	(717)	13,394	13,885
*16501	Erie..................	(814)	101,786	97,369
16063	Fernway (c)	(724)	12,414	—
15237	Franklin Park........	(412)	13,470	14,552
18052	Fullerton (c)	(610)	14,925	—
*15601	Greensburg..........	(724)	14,892	14,299
*17331	Hanover	(717)	15,289	15,607
*17101	Harrisburg..........	(717)	49,528	49,192
*18201	Hazleton	(570)	25,340	24,723
16148	Hermitage..........	(724)	16,220	15,635
17033	Hershey (c)..........	(717)	14,257	—
19044	Horsham (c)	(215)	14,842	—
*15701	Indiana	(724)	13,975	13,149
15025	Jefferson Hills	(412)	10,619	11,226
*15901	Johnstown..........	(814)	20,978	19,643
*19406	King of Prussia (c) ...	(610)	19,936	—
18704	Kingston	(570)	13,182	12,878
*17601	Lancaster	(717)	59,322	59,708
19446	Lansdale...........	(215)	16,269	16,588
19050	Lansdowne	(610)	10,620	10,646
*17042	Lebanon	(717)	25,477	25,770
*19055	Levittown (c)	(215)	52,983	—
15068	Lower Burrell......	(724)	11,761	11,228
*15132	McKeesport........	(412)	19,731	19,245
*16335	Meadville	(814)	13,388	12,973
*15146	Monroeville .... (412)/(724)		28,386	27,716
18936	Montgomeryville (c)	(215)	12,624	—
18707	Mountain Top (c)......	(570)	10,982	—
15120	Munhall............	(412)	11,406	11,158
*15668	Murrysville ...... (412)/(724)		20,079	19,800
18634	Nanticoke	(570)	10,465	10,279
*16101	New Castle..........	(724)	23,273	22,069
*15068	New Kensington	(724)	13,116	12,466
*19401	Norristown	(610)	34,324	34,510
*19107	Philadelphia	(215)	1,526,006	1,580,863
*19460	Phoenixville	(610)	16,440	16,943
*15201	Pittsburgh	(412)	305,704	302,407
15239	Plum..............	(412)	27,126	27,258
*19464	Pottstown	(610)	22,377	22,741
17901	Pottsville	(570)	14,324	13,625
*19601	Reading	(610)	88,082	88,423
15857	Saint Marys........	(814)	13,070	12,370
*18503	Scranton	(570)	76,089	77,605
*16146	Sharon	(724)	14,038	13,259
17404	Shiloh (c)	(717)	11,218	—
*16801	State College	(814)	42,034	42,430
15241	Upper St. Clair (c).......	(412)	19,229	—
15301	Washington	(724)	13,663	13,566
*17268	Waynesboro	(717)	10,568	10,877
17315	Weigelstown (c)	(717)	12,875	—
*19380	West Chester	(610)	18,461	20,060
*15122	West Mifflin	(412)	20,313	19,839
18052	Whitehall	(412)	13,944	13,733
*18701	Wilkes-Barre	(570)	41,498	40,806
15221	Wilkinsburg........	(412)	15,930	15,554
*17701	Williamsport	(570)	29,381	28,462
19090	Willow Grove (c)	(215)	15,726	—
19610	Wyomissing	(610)	10,461	10,454
19050	Yeadon	(610)	11,443	11,505
*17401	York..................	(717)	43,718	44,132

Rhode Island

Area code 401 applies to the entire state. See introductory note.

ZIP	Place	2010 population	2017 estimate
02806	Barrington..................	16,310	16,176
02809	Bristol....................	22,954	22,290
*02830	Burrillville	15,955	16,727
02863	Central Falls	19,376	19,359
*02816	Coventry....................	35,014	34,933
*02905	Cranston..................	80,387	81,202
02864	Cumberland	33,506	34,927
02818	East Greenwich	13,146	13,099
02914	East Providence	47,037	47,600
*02814	Glocester	9,746	10,135
02919	Johnston..................	28,769	29,332
*02865	Lincoln	21,105	21,863
02842	Middletown	16,150	16,081
*02882	Narragansett..............	15,868	15,504
02840	Newport	24,672	24,942
02842	Newport East (c)...........	11,769	—
02852	North Kingstown..........	26,486	26,160
*02908	North Providence	32,078	32,511
02896	North Smithfield	11,967	12,438
*02860	Pawtucket................	71,148	72,001
02871	Portsmouth	17,389	17,510
*02903	Providence	178,042	180,393
*02857	Scituate	10,329	10,611
*02917	Smithfield	21,430	21,767
*02879	South Kingstown	30,639	30,788
02878	Tiverton..................	15,780	15,874
02864	Valley Falls (c)	11,547	—

ZIP	Place	2010 population	2017 estimate
02885	Warren	10,611	10,446
*02886	Warwick..................	82,672	80,871
02893	West Warwick..............	29,191	28,626
02891	Westerly..................	22,787	22,567
02891	Westerly (c)	17,936	—
02895	Woonsocket	41,186	41,759

South Carolina

Area code 854 overlays area code 843.

ZIP	Place	Area code	2010 population	2017 estimate
*29801	Aiken.................	(803)	29,524	30,721
*29621	Anderson	(864)	26,686	27,293
*29902	Beaufort	(843)	12,361	13,729
29611	Berea (c)............	(864)	14,295	—
*29910	Bluffton	(843)	12,530	21,085
*29033	Cayce	(803)	12,528	14,086
*29401	Charleston	(843)	120,083	134,875
*29631	Clemson	(864)	13,905	16,649
*29201	Columbia	(803)	129,272	133,114
*29526	Conway	(843)	17,103	23,714
29204	Dentsville (c)........	(803)	14,062	—
*29640	Easley................	(864)	19,993	21,053
29681	Five Forks (c)	(864)	14,140	—
*29501	Florence	(843)	37,056	37,778
29206	Forest Acres	(803)	10,361	10,380
*29715	Fort Mill............	(803)	10,811	17,557
*29341	Gaffney	(864)	12,414	12,782
29605	Gantt (c)	(864)	14,229	—
29445	Goose Creek	(843)	35,938	42,619
*29601	Greenville	(864)	58,409	68,219
*29646	Greenwood	(864)	23,222	23,262
29650	Greer	(864)	25,515	30,899
29410	Hanahan............	(843)	17,997	24,885
*29928	Hilton Head Island	(843)	37,099	40,055
29063	Irmo	(803)	11,097	12,250
29412	James Island[1]	(843)	11,216	12,083
29456	Ladson (c)..........	(843)	13,790	—
*29072	Lexington	(803)	17,870	21,265
29662	Mauldin	(864)	22,889	25,130
29461	Moncks Corner	(843)	7,885	10,933
*29464	Mount Pleasant.......	(843)	67,843	86,668
*29572	Myrtle Beach	(843)	27,109	32,795
29108	Newberry	(803)	10,277	10,302
*29841	North Augusta	(803)	21,348	22,930
*29410	North Charleston	(843)	97,471	110,861
*29582	North Myrtle Beach	(843)	13,752	16,310
29073	Oak Grove (c)........	(803)	10,291	—
*29115	Orangeburg..........	(803)	13,964	12,954
29611	Parker (c)	(864)	11,431	—
29935	Port Royal	(843)	10,678	12,886
29020	Red Hill (c)	(843)	13,223	—
*29730	Rock Hill	(803)	66,154	73,068
29407	Saint Andrews (c)	(803)	20,493	—
29210	Seven Oaks (c)........	(803)	15,144	—
*29681	Simpsonville	(864)	18,238	22,072
29577	Socastee (c)	(843)	19,952	—
*29306	Spartanburg	(864)	37,013	37,498
*29483	Summerville	(843)	43,392	50,388
*29150	Sumter	(803)	40,524	39,982
29687	Taylors (c)..........	(864)	21,617	—
*29708	Tega Cay	(803)	7,620	10,339
*29607	Wade Hampton (c)	(864)	20,622	—
*29169	West Columbia	(803)	14,988	17,265

(1) Place was incorporated after the 2010 Census was conducted. Data in 2010 column is Census Bureau estimate.

South Dakota

Area code 605 applies to the entire state.

ZIP	Place	2010 population	2017 estimate
*57401	Aberdeen	26,091	28,388
*57006	Brookings	22,056	23,938
*57350	Huron	12,592	13,118
57301	Mitchell	15,254	15,603
57501	Pierre	13,646	14,004
*57701	Rapid City	67,956	74,421
*57103	Sioux Falls	153,888	176,888
*57783	Spearfish	10,494	11,609
57069	Vermillion	10,571	10,772
57201	Watertown..................	21,482	22,222
57078	Yankton....................	14,454	14,516

Tennessee

Area code 629 overlays area code 615.

ZIP	Place	Area code	2010 population	2017 estimate
37701	Alcoa.................	(865)	8,449	10,228
38002	Arlington	(901)	11,517	11,696
*37303	Athens	(423)	13,458	13,615
*38133	Bartlett	(901)	54,613	59,102
*37027	Brentwood	(615)	37,060	42,667
*37620	Bristol	(423)	26,702	26,842
*37402	Chattanooga	(423)	167,674	179,139

ZIP	Place	Area code	2010 population	2017 estimate
*37040	Clarksville	(931)	132,929	153,205
*37311	Cleveland	(423)	41,285	44,483
*37716	Clinton	(865)	9,841	10,103
37315	Collegedale	(423)	8,282	11,659
*38017	Collierville	(901)	43,965	50,286
*38401	Columbia	(931)	34,681	38,266
*38501	Cookeville	(931)	30,435	33,452
*38555	Crossville	(931)	10,795	11,449
*37055	Dickson	(615)	14,538	15,509
*38024	Dyersburg	(731)	17,145	16,473
37412	East Ridge	(423)	20,979	21,118
*37643	Elizabethton	(423)	14,176	13,743
*37922	Farragut	(865)	20,676	22,729
*37064	Franklin	(615)	62,487	78,321
37066	Gallatin	(615)	30,278	37,351
*38138	Germantown	(901)	38,844	39,141
*37072	Goodlettsville	(615)	15,921	16,867
*37743	Greeneville	(423)	15,062	14,888
37074	Hartsville/Trousdale Co.	(615)	7,870	10,083
*37075	Hendersonville	(615)	51,372	57,517
*38301	Jackson	(731)	65,211	66,847
*37601	Johnson City	(423)	63,152	66,391
*37660	Kingsport	(423)	48,205	53,374
*37902	Knoxville	(865)	178,874	187,347
*37086	La Vergne	(615)	32,588	35,717
38002	Lakeland	(901)	12,430	12,618
38464	Lawrenceburg	(931)	10,428	10,772
*37087	Lebanon	(615)	26,190	32,226
37091	Lewisburg	(931)	11,100	11,857
*37355	Manchester	(931)	10,102	10,642
38237	Martin	(731)	11,473	10,543
*37801	Maryville	(865)	27,465	28,765
*37110	McMinnville	(931)	13,605	13,662
*38103	Memphis	(901)	646,889	652,236
37343	Middle Valley (c)	(423)	12,684	—
*38053	Millington	(901)	10,176	11,033
*37813	Morristown	(423)	29,137	29,771
*37122	Mount Juliet	(615)	23,671	34,726
*37130	Murfreesboro	(615)	108,755	136,372
*37201	Nashville-Davidson (balance)	(615)	601,222	667,560
*37830	Oak Ridge	(865)	29,330	29,096
38242	Paris	(731)	10,156	10,094
37148	Portland	(615)	11,480	12,697
37415	Red Bank	(423)	11,651	11,754
*37862	Sevierville	(865)	14,807	16,716
37865	Seymour (c)	(865)	10,919	—
*37160	Shelbyville	(931)	20,335	21,532
37167	Smyrna	(615)	39,974	49,969
*37379	Soddy-Daisy	(423)	12,714	13,693
37174	Spring Hill	(931)	29,036	39,602
37172	Springfield	(615)	16,440	16,838
*37388	Tullahoma	(931)	18,655	19,229
*38261	Union City	(731)	10,895	10,420
37188	White House	(615)	10,255	11,608

Texas

Area code 346 overlays area codes 281/713/832. Area code 430 overlays 903. Area codes 469/972 overlay 214. Area code 682 overlays 817. Area code 726 overlays 210. Area code 737 overlays 512.

ZIP	Place	Area code	2010 population	2017 estimate
*79601	Abilene	(325)	117,063	121,885
75001	Addison	(214)	13,056	15,458
78516	Alamo	(956)	18,353	19,679
77039	Aldine (c)	(281)	15,869	—
*78332	Alice	(361)	19,104	18,949
*75002	Allen	(214)	84,246	100,685
78573	Alton	(956)	12,341	17,278
*77511	Alvin	(281)	24,236	26,474
*79101	Amarillo	(806)	190,695	199,826
79714	Andrews	(432)	11,088	13,472
*77515	Angleton	(979)	18,862	19,544
75409	Anna	(972)	8,249	12,753
*76001	Arlington	(817)	365,438	396,394
77346	Atascocita (c)	(281)	65,844	—
*75751	Athens	(903)	12,710	12,704
*78701	Austin	(512)	790,390	950,715
76020	Azle	(817)	10,947	12,495
*75180	Balch Springs	(214)	23,728	25,357
*77414	Bay City	(979)	17,614	17,528
*77520	Baytown	(281)/(832)	71,802	76,804
*77701	Beaumont	(409)	118,296	119,114
*76021	Bedford	(817)	46,979	49,486
*78102	Beeville	(361)	12,863	12,937
*77401	Bellaire	(713)	16,855	18,797
*76704	Bellmead	(254)	9,901	10,503
76513	Belton	(254)	18,216	21,734
*76126	Benbrook	(817)	21,234	23,590
*79720	Big Spring	(432)	27,282	27,905
*78006	Boerne	(830)	10,471	16,056
75418	Bonham	(903)	10,127	10,193
*79007	Borger	(806)	13,251	12,754
*77833	Brenham	(979)	15,716	16,951
*78520	Brownsville	(956)	175,023	183,299
*76801	Brownwood	(325)	19,288	18,831

ZIP	Place	Area code	2010 population	2017 estimate
78717	Brushy Creek (c)	(512)	21,764	—
*77801	Bryan	(979)	76,201	84,021
*78610	Buda	(512)	7,295	16,163
76354	Burkburnett	(940)	10,811	11,170
*76028	Burleson	(817)	36,690	46,145
*79015	Canyon	(806)	13,303	15,306
*78130	Canyon Lake (c)	(830)	21,262	—
*75006	Carrollton	(214)	119,097	135,710
*75104	Cedar Hill	(214)	45,028	48,710
*78613	Cedar Park	(512)	48,937	75,704
77530	Channelview (c)	(281)	38,289	—
78108	Cibolo	(210)	15,349	29,249
77450	Cinco Ranch (c)	(281)	18,274	—
*76031	Cleburne	(817)	29,337	30,230
77015	Cloverleaf (c)	(713)	22,942	—
77531	Clute	(979)	11,211	11,634
*77840	College Station	(979)	93,857	113,564
76034	Colleyville	(817)	22,807	26,674
*77301	Conroe	(936)	56,207	84,378
78109	Converse	(210)	18,198	23,375
*75019	Coppell	(214)	38,659	41,941
76522	Copperas Cove	(254)	32,032	32,706
*76208	Corinth	(940)	19,935	21,152
*78401	Corpus Christi	(361)	305,215	325,605
*75110	Corsicana	(903)	23,770	23,683
76036	Crowley	(817)	12,838	15,389
*75201	Dallas	(214)	1,197,816	1,341,075
77536	Deer Park	(281)	32,010	33,891
*78840	Del Rio	(830)	35,591	36,006
*75020	Denison	(903)	22,682	24,380
*76201	Denton	(940)	113,383	136,268
*75115	DeSoto	(214)	49,047	53,568
77539	Dickinson	(281)	18,680	20,359
78537	Donna	(956)	15,798	16,638
79029	Dumas	(806)	14,691	14,785
*75116	Duncanville	(214)	38,524	39,487
*78852	Eagle Pass	(830)	26,248	28,945
*78539	Edinburg	(956)	77,100	90,280
*77437	El Campo	(979)	11,602	11,751
*79901	El Paso	(915)	649,121	683,577
*75119	Ennis	(214)	18,513	19,261
*76039	Euless	(817)	51,277	55,174
*75234	Farmers Branch	(214)	28,616	37,088
*75087	Fate	(214)	6,357	12,090
*75022	Flower Mound	(214)	64,669	76,681
*76119	Forest Hill	(817)	12,355	12,953
75126	Forney	(214)	14,661	20,336
76544	Fort Hood (c)	(254)	29,589	—
*76102	Fort Worth	(817)	741,206	874,168
77498	Four Corners (c)	(281)	12,382	—
78624	Fredericksburg	(830)	10,530	11,369
*77541	Freeport	(979)	12,049	12,169
77545	Fresno (c)	(281)	19,069	—
*77546	Friendswood	(281)	35,805	39,839
*75034	Frisco	(214)	116,989	177,286
*77441	Fulshear	(281)/(713)	1,134	10,044
*76240	Gainesville	(940)	16,002	16,419
77547	Galena Park	(713)	10,887	10,989
*77550	Galveston	(409)	47,743	50,497
*75040	Garland	(214)	226,876	238,002
*76528	Gatesville	(254)	15,751	12,387
*78626	Georgetown	(512)	47,400	70,685
75154	Glenn Heights	(214)	11,278	13,084
*75051	Grand Prairie	(214)	175,396	193,837
*76051	Grapevine	(817)	46,334	53,982
77479	Greatwood (c)	(281)	11,538	—
*75401	Greenville	(903)	25,557	27,443
77619	Groves	(409)	16,144	15,769
*76117	Haltom City	(817)	42,409	44,417
76548	Harker Heights	(254)	26,700	31,075
*78550	Harlingen	(956)	64,849	65,467
*75652	Henderson	(903)	13,712	13,300
79045	Hereford	(806)	15,370	14,888
76643	Hewitt	(254)	13,549	14,435
78557	Hidalgo	(956)	11,198	13,931
75077	Highland Village	(214)	15,056	16,587
*79927	Horizon City	(915)	16,735	19,562
*77002	Houston	(281)/(713)/(832)	2,099,451	2,312,717
*77338	Humble	(281)	15,133	15,997
*77340	Huntsville	(936)	38,548	41,277
*77053	Hurst	(817)	37,337	39,051
78634	Hutto	(512)	14,698	25,367
78362	Ingleside	(361)	9,387	10,302
*75060	Irving	(214)	216,290	240,373
77029	Jacinto City	(281)	10,553	10,661
75766	Jacksonville	(903)	14,544	14,910
78729	Jollyville (c)	(512)	16,151	—
*77449	Katy	(281)/(713)	14,102	18,282
*76248	Keller	(817)	39,627	47,266
*78028	Kerrville	(830)	22,347	23,386
*75662	Kilgore	(903)	12,975	14,782
*76541	Killeen	(254)	127,921	145,482
*78363	Kingsville	(361)	26,213	25,482
78640	Kyle	(512)	28,016	43,480
78572	La Homa (c)	(956)	11,985	—
77568	La Marque	(409)	14,509	16,766
*77571	La Porte	(281)/(832)	33,800	35,371

ZIP	Place	Area code	2010 population	2017 estimate
77566	Lake Jackson	(979)	26,849	27,473
*78734	Lakeway	(512)	11,391	15,154
*75146	Lancaster	(214)	36,361	39,386
*78040	Laredo	(956)	236,091	260,654
*77573	League City	(281)	83,560	104,903
*78641	Leander	(512)	26,521	49,234
*78238	Leon Valley	(210)	10,151	11,426
*79336	Levelland	(806)	13,542	13,628
*75057	Lewisville	(214)	95,290	106,021
75068	Little Elm	(214)	25,898	46,548
*78233	Live Oak	(210)	13,131	15,820
78644	Lockhart	(512)	12,698	13,788
*75601	Longview	(903)	80,455	81,522
*79401	Lubbock	(806)	229,573	253,888
*75901	Lufkin	(936)	35,067	35,837
77657	Lumberton	(409)	11,943	12,829
76063	Mansfield	(817)	56,368	68,928
77578	Manvel	(281)	5,179	10,115
*75670	Marshall	(903)	23,523	23,195
*78501	McAllen	(956)	129,877	142,696
*75070	McKinney	(214)	131,117	181,330
78570	Mercedes	(956)	15,570	16,734
*75149	Mesquite	(214)	139,824	143,949
*79701	Midland	(432)	111,147	136,089
76065	Midlothian	(214)	18,037	25,254
*76067	Mineral Wells	(940)	16,788	14,962
*78572	Mission	(956)	77,058	84,424
*77083	Mission Bend (c)	(281)	36,501	—
*77489	Missouri City	(281)	67,358	74,497
*75455	Mount Pleasant	(903)	15,564	16,257
*75094	Murphy	(214)	17,708	20,673
*75961	Nacogdoches	(936)	32,996	33,614
77627	Nederland	(409)	17,547	17,491
*78130	New Braunfels	(830)	57,740	79,152
77479	New Territory (c)	(281)	15,186	—
*76117	North Richland Hills	(817)	63,343	70,441
*79761	Odessa	(432)	99,940	116,861
*77630	Orange	(409)	18,595	19,072
*75801	Palestine	(903)	18,712	18,306
*79065	Pampa	(806)	17,994	17,475
*75460	Paris	(903)	25,171	24,800
*77502	Pasadena....(281)/(713)/	(832)	149,043	153,520
*77581	Pearland......(281)/(713)/	(832)	91,252	119,940
78061	Pearsall	(830)	9,146	10,345
78721	Pecan Grove (c)	(254)	15,963	—
*78660	Pflugerville	(512)	46,936	63,359
78577	Pharr	(956)	70,400	79,487
*79072	Plainview	(806)	22,194	20,767
*75074	Plano	(214)	259,841	286,143
78064	Pleasanton	(830)	8,934	10,490
*77640	Port Arthur	(409)	53,818	55,498
77979	Port Lavaca	(361)	12,248	12,212
77651	Port Neches	(409)	13,040	12,898
78374	Portland	(361)	15,099	17,287
75407	Princeton	(214)	6,807	10,159
75078	Prosper	(214)	9,423	20,312
*78580	Raymondville	(956)	11,284	11,003
75154	Red Oak	(214)	10,769	12,780
76140	Rendon (c)	(817)	12,552	—
*75080	Richardson	(214)	99,223	116,783
*77469	Richmond.....(281)/(713)/	(832)	11,679	12,064
78582	Rio Grande City	(956)	13,834	14,518
76701	Robinson	(254)	10,509	11,617
78380	Robstown	(361)	11,487	11,385
*78382	Rockport	(361)	8,766	10,555
*75087	Rockwall	(214)	37,490	44,208
78584	Roma	(956)	9,765	11,425
*77471	Rosenberg	(832)	30,618	37,661
*78681	Round Rock	(512)	99,887	123,678
*75088	Rowlett	(214)	56,199	62,868
75189	Royse City	(214)	9,349	12,567
75048	Sachse	(214)	20,329	25,937
*76179	Saginaw	(817)	19,806	23,014
*76901	San Angelo	(325)	93,200	100,119
*78201	San Antonio	(210)	1,327,407	1,511,946
78586	San Benito	(956)	24,250	24,528
79849	San Elizario (c)	(915)	13,603	—
78589	San Juan	(956)	33,856	36,981
*78666	San Marcos	(512)	44,894	63,071
*77510	Santa Fe	(409)	12,222	13,442
*78154	Schertz	(210)	31,465	40,092
77586	Seabrook	(281)	11,952	13,693
75159	Seagoville	(214)	14,835	16,715
*78155	Seguin	(830)	25,175	28,983
78154	Selma	(214)	5,540	10,712
*75090	Sherman	(903)	38,521	41,917
77459	Sienna Plantation (c)	(281)	13,721	—
*79549	Snyder	(325)	11,202	11,320
*79927	Socorro	(915)	32,013	34,048
77587	South Houston	(713)	16,983	17,543
76092	Southlake	(817)	26,575	31,824
*77373	Spring (c).....(281)/(713)/	(832)	54,298	—
*77477	Stafford	(281)	17,693	18,315
*76401	Stephenville	(254)	17,123	20,797
*77478	Sugar Land....(281)/(713)/	(832)	78,817	88,485
*75482	Sulphur Springs	(903)	15,449	16,029
79556	Sweetwater	(325)	10,906	10,579
76574	Taylor	(512)	15,191	16,982

ZIP	Place	Area code	2010 population	2017 estimate
*76501	Temple	(254)	66,102	74,503
*75160	Terrell	(214)	15,816	17,842
*75501	Texarkana	(903)	36,411	37,333
*77590	Texas City	(409)	45,099	48,558
75056	The Colony	(214)	36,328	42,721
*77381	The Woodlands (c)	(281)	93,847	—
78260	Timberwood Park (c)	(830)	13,447	—
*77375	Tomball	(281)	10,753	11,707
76262	Trophy Club	(817)	8,024	12,340
*75702	Tyler	(903)	96,900	104,991
*78148	Universal City	(210)	18,530	20,532
75205	University Park	(214)	23,068	25,201
*78801	Uvalde	(830)	15,751	16,298
*76384	Vernon	(940)	11,002	10,346
*77901	Victoria	(361)	62,592	67,106
*77662	Vidor	(409)	10,579	10,854
*76701	Waco	(254)	124,805	136,436
*76148	Watauga	(817)	23,497	24,602
*75165	Waxahachie	(214)	29,621	35,340
*76086	Weatherford	(817)	25,250	30,654
77598	Webster	(281)	10,400	11,123
78728	Wells Branch (c)	(512)	12,120	—
*78596	Weslaco	(956)	35,670	40,358
79764	West Odessa (c)	(432)	22,707	—
77005	West University Place	(713)	14,787	15,608
76108	White Settlement	(817)	16,116	17,828
*76301	Wichita Falls	(940)	104,553	104,747
75098	Wylie	(214)	41,427	49,826

Utah

Area code 385 overlays area code 801.

ZIP	Place	Area code	2010 population	2017 estimate
84004	Alpine	(801)	9,555	10,371
84003	American Fork	(801)	26,263	29,527
84065	Bluffdale	(801)	7,598	13,484
*84010	Bountiful	(801)	42,552	44,107
84302	Brigham City	(435)	17,899	19,182
*84720	Cedar City	(435)	28,857	31,806
84062	Cedar Hills	(801)	9,796	10,334
84014	Centerville	(801)	15,335	17,657
*84015	Clearfield	(801)	30,112	31,363
84015	Clinton	(801)	20,426	21,971
*84047	Cottonwood Heights	(801)	33,433	33,996
84020	Draper	(801)	42,274	47,710
*84005	Eagle Mountain	(801)	21,415	32,204
84025	Farmington	(801)	18,275	24,066
*84029	Grantsville	(435)	8,893	11,000
*84032	Heber City	(435)	11,362	15,792
*84096	Herriman	(801)	21,785	39,224
84003	Highland	(801)	15,523	18,957
*84117	Holladay	(801)	26,472	30,709
84737	Hurricane	(435)	13,748	17,135
84037	Kaysville	(801)	27,300	31,776
84118	Kearns (c)	(801)	35,731	—
*84041	Layton	(801)	67,311	76,691
*84043	Lehi	(801)	47,407	62,712
84042	Lindon	(801)	10,070	10,968
*84321	Logan	(435)	48,174	51,115
84044	Magna (c)	(801)	26,505	—
*84047	Midvale	(801)	27,964	33,208
*84106	Millcreek[1]	(801)	62,139	60,192
*84107	Murray	(801)	46,746	49,295
84341	North Logan	(435)	8,269	10,646
*84404	North Ogden	(801)	17,357	19,465
84054	North Salt Lake	(801)	16,322	20,507
*84401	Ogden	(801)	82,825	87,031
*84057	Orem	(801)	88,328	97,839
84651	Payson	(801)	18,294	19,892
*84062	Pleasant Grove	(801)	33,509	38,845
*84414	Pleasant View	(801)	7,979	10,287
*84601	Provo	(801)	112,488	117,335
*84065	Riverton	(801)	38,753	43,344
*84067	Roy	(801)	36,884	38,595
*84770	Saint George	(435)	72,897	84,405
*84101	Salt Lake City	(801)	186,440	200,544
*84070	Sandy	(801)	87,461	96,145
84655	Santaquin	(801)	9,128	11,652
*84043	Saratoga Springs	(801)	17,781	29,608
84335	Smithfield	(435)	9,495	11,374
*84095	South Jordan	(801)	50,418	70,954
*84403	South Ogden	(801)	16,532	17,101
*84115	South Salt Lake	(801)	23,617	24,956
84660	Spanish Fork	(801)	34,691	39,443
*84663	Springville	(801)	29,466	33,294
84075	Syracuse	(801)	24,331	29,507
*84118	Taylorsville	(801)	58,652	59,992
84074	Tooele	(435)	31,605	34,628
*84078	Vernal	(435)	9,089	10,291
*84780	Washington	(435)	18,761	26,405
84401	West Haven	(801)	10,272	13,532
*84084	West Jordan	(801)	103,712	113,905
84015	West Point	(801)	9,511	10,603
*84119	West Valley City	(801)	129,480	136,170
*84087	Woods Cross	(801)	9,761	11,362

(1) Place was incorporated after the 2010 Census was conducted.
Data in 2010 column is for Millcreek CDP.

Vermont

Area code 802 applies to the entire state. See introductory note.

ZIP	Place	2010 population	2017 estimate
05201	Bennington...............	15,764	15,003
*05301	Brattleboro.................	12,046	11,487
*05401	Burlington................	42,417	42,239
*05446	Colchester................	17,067	17,287
*05452	Essex......................	19,587	21,519
*05452	Essex Junction............	9,271	10,691
05468	Milton...................	10,352	10,940
*05701	Rutland..................	16,495	15,440
*05403	South Burlington.............	17,904	19,141

Virginia

Area code 571 overlays area code 703.

ZIP	Place	Area code	2010 population	2017 estimate
*22314	Alexandria.............	(703)	139,966	160,035
22003	Annandale (c)..........	(703)	41,008	—
*22201	Arlington (c)	(703)	207,627	—
*20147	Ashburn (c)...........	(703)	43,511	—
22041	Bailey's Crossroads (c)...	(703)	23,643	—
*24060	Blacksburg..........	(540)	42,620	44,563
23235	Bon Air (c)............	(804)	16,366	—
23112	Brandermill (c)	(804)	13,173	—
*24201	Bristol	(276)	17,835	16,790
20148	Broadlands (c)	(703)	12,313	—
20111	Buckhall (c)...........	(703)	16,293	—
20109	Bull Run (c)...........	(703)	14,983	—
*22015	Burke (c)	(703)	41,055	—
22015	Burke Centre (c)........	(703)	17,326	—
*20165	Cascades (c)	(434)	11,912	—
24018	Cave Spring (c)........	(540)	24,922	—
*20120	Centreville (c)	(703)	71,135	—
*20151	Chantilly (c)...........	(703)	23,039	—
*22901	Charlottesville	(434)	43,475	48,019
22026	Cherry Hill (c)	(703)	16,000	—
*23320	Chesapeake	(757)	222,209	240,397
*23831	Chester (c)	(804)	20,987	—
*24073	Christiansburg	(540)	21,041	22,259
23834	Colonial Heights	(804)	17,411	17,830
20165	Countryside (c)	(703)	10,072	—
22701	Culpeper..............	(540)	16,379	18,413
22193	Dale City (c)	(703)	65,969	—
*24541	Danville..............	(434)	43,055	41,130
20170	Dranesville (c).........	(703)	11,921	—
23222	East Highland Park (c) ...	(804)	14,796	—
22033	Fair Oaks (c)...........	(703)	30,223	—
*22030	Fairfax...............	(703)	22,565	24,097
22039	Fairfax Station (c)	(703)	12,030	—
*22046	Falls Church	(703)	12,332	14,583
22308	Fort Hunt (c)	(703)	16,045	—
*22310	Franconia (c)..........	(703)	18,245	—
20171	Franklin Farm (c)	(703)	19,288	—
*22401	Fredericksburg	(540)	24,286	28,360
22630	Front Royal	(540)	14,440	15,239
*20155	Gainesville (c)	(703)	11,481	—
*23060	Glen Allen (c)	(804)	14,774	—
22066	Great Falls (c)..........	(703)	15,427	—
22306	Groveton (c)	(703)	14,598	—
*23669	Hampton..............	(757)	137,436	134,669
*22801	Harrisonburg	(540)	48,914	54,215
*20170	Herndon..............	(703)	23,292	24,532
23075	Highland Springs (c).....	(804)	15,711	—
24019	Hollins (c)	(540)	14,673	—
23860	Hopewell..............	(804)	22,591	22,621
22303	Huntington (c)..........	(703)	11,267	—
22306	Hybla Valley (c)........	(703)	15,801	—
22043	Idylwood (c)...........	(703)	17,288	—
22038	Kings Park West (c)	(703)	13,390	—
22315	Kingstowne (c)	(703)	15,556	—
22192	Lake Ridge (c)	(703)	41,058	—
23228	Lakeside (c)	(804)	11,849	—
20176	Lansdowne (c)	(703)	11,253	—
23060	Laurel (c)	(804)	16,713	—
*20175	Leesburg.............	(703)	42,616	54,215
22312	Lincolnia (c)..........	(703)	22,855	—
20136	Linton Hall (c)	(703)	35,725	—
*22079	Lorton (c)	(703)	18,610	—
20165	Lowes Island (c)	(703)	10,756	—
*24501	Lynchburg.............	(434)	75,568	80,995
24572	Madison Heights (c)	(434)	11,285	—
*20110	Manassas.............	(703)	37,821	41,501
*20111	Manassas Park.........	(703)	14,273	16,591
23235	Manchester (c).........	(804)	10,804	—
*24112	Martinsville...........	(276)	13,821	13,142
22191	Marumsco (c).........	(703)	35,036	—
*22101	McLean (c)...........	(703)	48,115	—
20171	McNair (c)............	(703)	17,513	—
23234	Meadowbrook (c).......	(804)	18,312	—
*23111	Mechanicsville (c).......	(804)	36,348	—
*22081	Merrifield (c)	(703)	15,212	—
22025	Montclair (c)...........	(703)	19,570	—
22121	Mount Vernon (c)	(703)	12,416	—
22191	Neabsco (c)	(703)	12,068	—

ZIP	Place	Area code	2010 population	2017 estimate
22122	Newington (c)	(703)	12,943	—
22153	Newington Forest (c)	(703)	12,442	—
*23607	Newport News	(757)	180,719	179,388
*23502	Norfolk...............	(757)	242,803	244,703
*22124	Oakton (c)..............	(703)	34,166	—
*23704	Petersburg	(804)	32,420	31,750
23662	Poquoson	(757)	12,150	12,053
*23704	Portsmouth	(757)	95,535	94,707
*24141	Radford..............	(540)	16,408	17,658
*20190	Reston (c)	(703)	58,404	—
*23219	Richmond .... (276)/(804)		204,214	227,032
*24011	Roanoke	(540)	97,032	99,837
24281	Rose Hill (c) (Fairfax Co.)	(276)	20,226	—
24153	Salem................	(540)	24,802	25,862
23233	Short Pump (c)	(804)	24,729	—
20152	South Riding (c)	(703)	24,256	—
*22150	Springfield (c)	(703)	30,484	—
*24401	Staunton	(540)	23,746	24,528
*20164	Sterling (c)	(703)	27,822	—
20109	Sudley (c)	(703)	16,203	—
*23434	Suffolk...............	(757)	84,585	90,237
20164	Sugarland Run (c)	(703)	11,799	—
24502	Timberlake (c).........	(434)	12,183	—
23229	Tuckahoe (c)..........	(804)	44,990	—
*22102	Tysons Corner (c)	(703)	19,627	—
*22180	Vienna	(703)	15,687	16,544
*23451	Virginia Beach	(757)	437,994	450,435
23888	Wakefield (c)..........	(757)	11,275	—
22980	Waynesboro	(540)	21,006	22,327
*22042	West Falls Church (c)	(703)	29,207	—
22152	West Springfield (c)	(703)	22,460	—
*23185	Williamsburg	(757)	14,068	15,031
*22601	Winchester	(540)	26,203	27,932
*22182	Wolf Trap (c)	(703)	16,131	—
24381	Woodlawn (c) (Fairfax Co.)	(276)	20,804	—

Washington

Area code 564 overlays area code 360.

ZIP	Place	Area code	2010 population	2017 estimate
98520	Aberdeen	(360)	16,896	16,462
*98221	Anacortes.............	(360)	15,778	16,953
98223	Arlington..............	(360)	17,926	19,212
98335	Artondale (c)..........	(253)	12,653	—
*98001	Auburn	(253)	70,180	80,776
98110	Bainbridge Island	(206)	23,025	24,522
98604	Battle Ground	(360)	17,571	20,576
*98004	Bellevue	(425)	122,363	144,444
*98225	Bellingham	(360)	80,885	89,045
98391	Bonney Lake...........	(253)	17,374	20,675
*98011	Bothell...............	(425)	33,505	45,533
98036	Bothell West (c)	(425)	16,607	—
*98337	Bremerton.............	(360)	37,729	41,041
98178	Bryn Mawr-Skyway (c) ...	(206)	15,645	—
*98166	Burien...............	(206)	33,313	51,671
98607	Camas	(360)	19,355	23,331
98531	Centralia	(360)	16,336	17,216
99004	Cheney	(509)	10,590	12,446
98072	Cottage Lake (c)	(425)	22,494	—
98042	Covington	(253)	17,575	20,916
*98198	Des Moines...........	(206)	29,673	31,238
*98031	East Hill-Meridian (c)	(253)	29,878	—
98056	East Renton Highlands (c)	(425)	11,140	—
98802	East Wenatchee	(509)	13,190	13,983
98204	Eastmont (c)...........	(425)	20,101	—
*98372	Edgewood	(253)	9,387	11,213
*98020	Edmonds	(425)	39,709	42,209
98387	Elk Plain (c)	(253)	14,205	—
*98926	Ellensburg	(509)	18,174	20,326
98022	Enumclaw	(360)	10,669	11,784
*98201	Everett	(425)	103,019	110,079
98058	Fairwood (c) (King Co.)....	(425)	19,102	—
*98001	Federal Way	(253)	89,306	96,690
98248	Ferndale	(360)	11,415	14,026
98424	Fife	(253)	9,173	10,154
98597	Five Corners (c)	(360)	18,159	—
98433	Fort Lewis (c)	(253)	11,046	—
98375	Frederickson (c)	(253)	18,719	—
98338	Graham (c)	(253)	23,491	—
98930	Grandview	(509)	10,862	11,129
98665	Hazel Dell (c)	(360)	19,435	—
*98011	Inglewood-Finn Hill (c) ...	(425)	22,707	—
*98027	Issaquah..............	(425)	30,434	37,487
98626	Kelso................	(360)	11,925	12,110
98028	Kenmore	(425)	20,460	22,867
*99336	Kennewick	(509)	73,917	81,607
*98031	Kent .... (253)/(425)		92,411	128,458
98033	Kingsgate (c)	(425)	13,065	—
*98033	Kirkland	(425)	48,787	88,630
98029	Klahanie (c)	(425)	10,674	—
*98503	Lacey	(360)	42,393	49,748
98155	Lake Forest Park	(206)	12,598	13,392
98042	Lake Morton-Berrydale (c) ..... (253)/(425)		10,160	—
98258	Lake Stevens	(425)	28,069	32,785

ZIP	Place	Area code	2010 population	2017 estimate
98391	Lake Tapps (c)	(253)	11,859	—
98002	Lakeland North (c)	(253)	12,942	—
98002	Lakeland South (c)	(253)	11,574	—
*98498	Lakewood	(253)	58,163	60,296
98632	Longview	(360)	36,648	37,602
98264	Lynden	(360)	11,951	14,259
*98036	Lynnwood	(425)	35,836	38,273
*98290	Maltby (c)	(360)/(425)	10,830	—
98038	Maple Valley	(425)	22,684	25,758
98012	Martha Lake (c)	(425)	15,473	—
*98270	Marysville	(360)	60,020	68,864
98040	Mercer Island	(206)	22,699	25,261
*98012	Mill Creek	(425)	18,244	20,832
*98012	Mill Creek East (c)	(425)	15,709	—
98272	Monroe	(360)	17,304	18,789
98837	Moses Lake	(509)	20,366	23,328
*98273	Mount Vernon	(360)	31,743	35,051
98043	Mountlake Terrace	(425)	19,909	21,337
98275	Mukilteo	(425)	20,254	21,469
*98056	Newcastle	(425)	10,380	11,681
*98037	North Lynnwood (c)	(425)	16,574	—
*98277	Oak Harbor	(360)	22,075	23,187
*98501	Olympia	(360)	46,478	51,609
98662	Orchards (c)	(360)	19,556	—
*98444	Parkland (c)	(253)	35,803	—
*99301	Pasco	(509)	59,781	73,013
*98362	Port Angeles	(360)	19,038	19,872
*98366	Port Orchard	(360)	11,144	13,997
98370	Poulsbo	(360)	9,200	10,670
*98390	Prairie Ridge (c)	(360)	11,464	—
*99163	Pullman	(509)	29,799	33,354
*98371	Puyallup	(253)	37,022	41,001
*98052	Redmond	(425)	54,144	64,291
*98057	Renton	(425)	90,927	101,379
*99352	Richland	(509)	48,058	56,243
*98685	Salmon Creek (c)	(360)	19,686	—
*98074	Sammamish	(425)	45,780	64,548
*98148	SeaTac	(206)	26,909	29,140
*98101	Seattle	(206)/(425)	608,660	724,745
98284	Sedro-Woolley	(360)	10,540	11,838
98584	Shelton	(360)	9,834	10,146
*98133	Shoreline	(206)	53,007	56,189
98208	Silver Firs (c)	(206)/(425)	20,891	—
*98315	Silverdale (c)	(360)	19,204	—
*98290	Snohomish	(360)	9,098	10,089
98065	Snoqualmie	(425)	10,670	13,500
*98373	South Hill (c)	(253)	52,431	—
98387	Spanaway (c)	(253)	27,227	—
*99201	Spokane	(509)	208,916	217,108
*99206	Spokane Valley	(509)	89,755	97,847
*98390	Sumner	(253)	9,451	10,093
98944	Sunnyside	(509)	15,858	16,407
*98402	Tacoma	(253)	198,397	213,418
*98188	Tukwila	(206)	19,107	20,144
*98501	Tumwater	(360)	17,371	22,973
98053	Union Hill-Novelty Hill (c)	(425)	18,805	—
*98466	University Place	(253)	31,144	33,401
*98660	Vancouver	(360)	161,791	175,673
*98070	Vashon (c)	(206)	10,624	—
99362	Walla Walla	(509)	31,731	32,854
98671	Washougal	(360)	14,095	15,711
*98801	Wenatchee	(509)	31,925	33,962
*99353	West Richland	(509)	11,811	14,596
98166	White Center (c)	(206)	13,495	—
*98072	Woodinville	(425)	10,938	11,997
*98901	Yakima	(509)	91,067	93,667

West Virginia

Area code 681 overlays area code 304; both apply to the entire state.

ZIP	Place	2010 population	2017 estimate
*25801	Beckley	17,614	16,404
*25301	Charleston	51,400	47,929
*26301	Clarksburg	16,578	15,621
*26554	Fairmont	18,704	18,467
*25701	Huntington	49,138	47,079
*25401	Martinsburg	17,227	17,404
*26505	Morgantown	29,660	30,547
*26101	Parkersburg	31,492	30,096
25177	Saint Albans	11,044	10,265
*25303	South Charleston	13,450	12,493
*25526	Teays Valley (c)	13,175	—
*26105	Vienna	10,749	10,370
26062	Weirton	19,746	18,685
26003	Wheeling	28,486	27,066

Wisconsin

Area code 534 overlays area code 715.

ZIP	Place	Area code	2010 population	2017 estimate
54301	Allouez	(920)	13,975	13,886
*54911	Appleton	(920)	72,623	74,653
*54304	Ashwaubenon	(920)	16,963	17,271
53913	Baraboo	(608)	12,048	12,164
53916	Beaver Dam	(920)	16,214	16,369
54311	Bellevue	(920)	14,570	15,687
*53511	Beloit	(608)	36,966	36,773

ZIP	Place	Area code	2010 population	2017 estimate
*53045	Brookfield	(262)	37,920	38,045
*53209	Brown Deer	(414)	11,999	11,964
53105	Burlington	(262)	10,464	10,978
53108	Caledonia	(262)	24,705	25,002
53012	Cedarburg	(262)	11,412	11,465
*54729	Chippewa Falls	(715)	13,661	14,035
53110	Cudahy	(414)	18,267	18,282
54115	De Pere	(920)	23,800	25,034
53532	DeForest	(608)	8,936	10,340
*54701	Eau Claire	(715)	65,883	68,587
*53711	Fitchburg	(608)	25,260	29,485
*54935	Fond du Lac	(920)	43,021	42,809
53538	Fort Atkinson	(920)	12,368	12,482
*54956	Fox Crossing[1]	(920)	10,588	10,980
53132	Franklin	(414)	35,451	36,143
53022	Germantown	(262)	19,749	19,982
*53209	Glendale	(414)	12,872	12,728
53024	Grafton	(262)	11,459	11,643
*54301	Green Bay	(920)	104,057	105,116
53129	Greendale	(414)	14,046	14,159
*53220	Greenfield	(414)	36,720	36,827
53027	Hartford	(262)	14,223	15,064
*54303	Howard	(920)	17,399	19,634
*54016	Hudson	(715)	12,719	13,706
*53545	Janesville	(608)	63,575	64,359
*54130	Kaukauna	(920)	15,462	16,086
*53140	Kenosha	(262)	99,218	99,877
*54601	La Crosse	(608)	51,320	51,834
54140	Little Chute	(920)	10,449	11,403
*53703	Madison	(608)	233,209	255,214
*54220	Manitowoc	(920)	33,736	32,697
54143	Marinette	(715)	10,968	10,607
*54449	Marshfield	(715)	19,118	18,405
54952	Menasha	(920)	17,353	17,748
*53051	Menomonee Falls	(262)	35,626	37,443
54751	Menomonie	(715)	16,264	16,429
*53092	Mequon	(262)	23,132	24,159
*53562	Middleton	(608)	17,442	19,660
*53202	Milwaukee	(414)	594,833	595,351
53566	Monroe	(608)	10,827	10,604
*53406	Mount Pleasant	(262)	26,197	26,525
53150	Muskego	(262)	24,135	24,996
*54956	Neenah	(920)	25,501	25,951
*53151	New Berlin	(262)	39,584	39,740
53154	Oak Creek	(414)	34,451	36,354
53066	Oconomowoc	(262)	15,759	16,717
54650	Onalaska	(608)	17,736	18,712
53575	Oregon	(608)	9,231	10,390
*54901	Oshkosh	(920)	66,083	66,665
53072	Pewaukee	(262)	13,195	14,476
53818	Platteville	(608)	11,224	12,457
53158	Pleasant Prairie	(262)	19,719	20,762
54467	Plover	(715)	12,123	12,772
53074	Port Washington	(262)	11,250	11,762
53901	Portage	(608)	10,324	10,473
*53402	Racine	(262)	78,860	77,542
*53076	Richfield	(262)	11,300	11,696
54022	River Falls	(715)	15,000	15,510
*53081	Sheboygan	(920)	49,288	48,329
53211	Shorewood	(414)	13,162	13,338
53172	South Milwaukee	(414)	21,156	20,988
*54481	Stevens Point	(715)	26,717	26,293
53589	Stoughton	(608)	12,611	13,088
*54173	Suamico	(920)	11,346	12,816
*53590	Sun Prairie	(608)	29,364	32,894
54880	Superior	(715)	27,244	26,194
53089	Sussex	(262)	10,518	10,819
*54241	Two Rivers	(920)	11,712	11,153
53593	Verona	(608)	10,619	13,107
*53094	Watertown	(920)	23,861	23,655
*53186	Waukesha	(262)	70,718	72,489
53597	Waunakee	(608)	12,097	13,755
53963	Waupun	(920)	11,340	11,269
*54403	Wausau	(715)	39,106	38,739
*53213	Wauwatosa	(414)	46,396	48,277
*53214	West Allis	(414)	60,411	59,934
*53095	West Bend	(262)	31,078	31,596
*54476	Weston	(715)	14,868	15,167
*53217	Whitefish Bay	(414)	14,110	13,950
53190	Whitewater	(262)	14,390	14,540
*54494	Wisconsin Rapids	(715)	18,367	17,806

(1) Place was incorporated after the 2010 Census was conducted. Data in 2010 column is Census Bureau estimate.

Wyoming

Area code 307 applies to the entire state.

ZIP	Place	2010 population	2017 estimate
*82601	Casper	55,316	57,814
*82001	Cheyenne	59,466	63,624
*82930	Evanston	12,359	11,866
*82716	Gillette	29,087	30,560
*82935	Green River	12,515	12,070
*83001	Jackson	9,577	10,532
*82070	Laramie	30,816	32,306
82501	Riverton	10,615	11,058
*82901	Rock Springs	23,036	23,350
82801	Sheridan	17,444	17,860

Chronology of World History

Note: In this section, the notation BCE (before the common era) is applied to years dating to the traditional BC (before Christ) era, and CE (common era) is applied to AD (anno domini) dates. This notation is now preferred in many scientific and academic publications. The traditional Gregorian calendar system and its dates and years are unaltered except by these labels.

Other abbreviations used in this chapter include the following: KYA = thousand years ago, MYA = million years ago, c. = circa, fl. = flourished, r. = ruled, b. = born, d. = died.

Prehistory: Our Ancestors Emerge

Reviewed by Marc Kissel, Ph.D., Univ. of Notre Dame, 2016; later updates per World Almanac research.

Evidence of the origins of *Homo sapiens*, the genus and species to which all living humans belong, comes from an ever increasing number of fossils and DNA studies, and from the archaeological record. Put together, the latest evidence suggests that humans evolved from an ape-like ancestor that lived in eastern and central Africa 8 to 5 million years ago.

Current theories trace the first hominin[1] (primates more closely related to humans than to any other living primate) to Africa, where several distinct genera appear in the fossil record 6-4 MYA. Skeletally, hominins are defined by signs of bipedalism (walking on two legs). They lived in a variety of environments, including swampy forest margins, woodlands, and open savannas (usually near lakes or springs).

Claims of the earliest hominin are inherently controversial. The earliest currently proposed species are *Sahelanthropus tchadensis* (c. 7 MYA, Chad) and *Orrorin tugenensis* (c. 6 MYA, Kenya). The recently described species *Ardipithecus ramidus* (4.4 MYA, Ethiopia) had a chimp-sized brain and a fairly primitive body plan but was bipedal.

Although all humans living today are members of a single species, the fossil record confirms that our ancestors coexisted with a number of similar species throughout our evolutionary history. Starting around 4 MYA one of these earliest hominins gave rise to the australopithecines, a genus of early hominins referred to as "bipedal apes." Scientists divided these into two groups, "gracile" and "robust," each containing a number of species.

The robust australopithecines were characterized by larger molar and premolar teeth; they probably went extinct around 1 MYA. Members of this species adapted a new dietary niche of eating hard foods such as nuts and tubers and have been found in both E and S Africa.

The gracile lineage most likely led to modern humans. *Australopithecus sediba* (2 MYA, South Africa) shows a mosaic of both Australopithecus and early *Homo* traits, leading some to suggest that this is the predecessor to our genus; the morphology of its hand is very suggestive of tool-use. However, while originally believed to arise solely within the genus *Homo*, recent work at the sites of Dikika (3.3 MYA, Ethopia) and Lomekwi (3.3 MYA, Kenya) suggest that earlier hominins were making stone tools.

Our genus, *Homo*, arose 3-2 MYA, with fossils showing early members of our genus being fully bipedal, having larger brains, and hands well-adapted to tool use. The Oldowan tools first appear 2.6 MYA and were used to cut and scrape meat. It is not known whether these early hominins had the ability to speak, but they were social primates, had campsites, and subsisted by gathering plants and small animals and by scavenging other kills, as well as perhaps hunting.

Homo ergaster appeared in E Africa around 1.9 MYA and was the first to leave the continent, spreading throughout Eurasia by c. 1.8 MYA. *H. ergaster* is sometimes grouped with *H. erectus*, a species first identified on the Indonesian island of Java. It was capable of hunting large and medium-sized animals, such as antelopes and horses, learned to make and control fire, and produced bifacially-flaked tools (sharpened on both sides).

The ability to control fire enormously expanded the human food niche as well as creating new opportunities in the social world. Fire-making possibly began as early as 1 MYA in Africa and is clearly documented throughout Eurasia after c. 500 KYA. Hearths were found in northern Israel by c. 750 KYA, and by 465 KYA in southwestern France.

After about 800 KYA, Europe provides a particularly rich set of fossil evidence usually assigned to *H. erectus*, *H. antecessor*, or *H. heidelbergensis*. This population gave rise to the Neanderthals, who appeared c. 350 KYA. While originally portrayed as savage and unhuman-like, recent research suggests they could probably speak, were proficient hunters of large game, had sophisticated tools and weapons, had ornamentation and other forms of symbolic expression, and a well-developed social organization. On the island of Flores, Indonesia, remains of a species known as *Homo floresiensis*, a 1.1-m (3.5-ft) tall hominin, date from c. 100-60 KYA. Its small stature may be due to limited food and few predators on the small island.

The remains of *Homo naledi*, dating to c. 335-236 KYA, raised questions about a possible overlap in existence and behaviors with early humans. It has a human-like foot and lower limbs, but other aspects of the skeleton, such as the pelvis and shoulder, are more primitive looking. They seem to have been deliberately deposited into a cave system, suggesting an early form of burial.

Improved dating techniques call into question the age of modern humans. The oldest modern human fossils (*Homo sapiens*) were dated to c. 300 KYA and were found at the Jebel Irhoud site in Morocco. Until that 2017 analysis, the oldest, found in Omo Kibish, Ethiopia, were believed to date to c. 195 KYA. Fossils considered some of the oldest modern humans were also found at the Herto site in Ethiopia's Middle Awash Valley. The species spread out of Africa, reaching Israel by c. 100 KYA, and Romania by c. 35 KYA. Migration from Asia to Australia took place as early as 60 KYA. What happened when they met other hominins is a subject of intense research. Genetic evidence in the form of ancient DNA suggests that Neanderthals interbred with modern humans. Genetic data also tells us about the Denisovans, a population of early humans dated to c. 50 KYA. Some modern populations retain Denisovan DNA, suggesting a complex web of interactions between these populations.

First confirmation for the crossing from Asia to the Americas by the Bering land bridge dates to the end of the last Ice Age, at 14 KYA. Their arrival was rapidly followed by the extinction of the indigenous Pleistocene megafauna (e.g., mammoths, mastodons) due either to overexploitation by humans, climate change, or a combination of both.

Wooden throwing spears about 3 m (10 ft) long were fashioned by big-game hunters 300 KYA at Schöningen, Germany. Scraping tools, dated after 750 KYA in Europe, N Africa, the Middle East, and Central Asia, suggest the preparation of hides for clothing. Some of the oldest evidence of personal adornment date to around 300 KYA in the form of ochre, while various sites around 100 KYA from South Africa, Morocco, and Israel show the use of perforated shell beads, suggestive of symbolic expression. Although they were probably invented much earlier, impressions in burnt clay from the Czech Republic document the ability to weave cloth baskets and nets by 28 KYA.

Some of the earliest well-dated cave paintings come from the island of Sulawesi, Indonesia, where they date to around the same time as the earliest cave paintings in Europe. The painted caves of Cosquer and Chauvet in southern France have (contested) radiocarbon dates of c. 32 KYA. Painting, engraving, and bodily decoration flourished in Europe 15 KYA, along with stone and ivory sculpture. More than 200 western European caves show remarkable examples of naturalistic wall painting. A few musical instruments—bone flutes with precisely bored holes—have been found in sites dated after 40 KYA.

Skeletal data suggests that after 60-30 KYA the number of people who survived to become grandparents increased. With more adults available to provide child care, humans began to develop more complex, multigenerational social systems. In general, as human cognitive capacities slowly expanded over the Pleistocene, a variety of behavioral modes—in toolmaking,

Cave paintings in Lascaux, France, discovered in 1940, have been carbon-dated to 11,000 to 30,000 years before the present.

diet, shelter, social arrangements, and spiritual expression—arose as humans adapted to different geographic and climatic zones. By about 13,000 years ago, sites from all over the world show seasonal migration patterns and efficient exploitation of a wide range of plant and animal foods, some of which were eventually domesticated.

Shortly after 12 KYA, among widely separated foraging communities in both hemispheres, a series of dramatic technological and social changes occurred, marking the Neolithic, or New Stone Age. As the world climate became drier and warmer, population/resource imbalances ensued, creating the conditions that allowed for increased human interference in the life cycles of certain plants and animals. This interference ultimately resulted in the appearance of domestication, initially in the northern Middle East.

Domesticated plants and animals encouraged population growth and the appearance of permanent settlements. Agricultural economies increasingly replaced or assimilated hunting and gathering. Reliance upon domesticated plants and animals, coupled with technological advances like pottery-making, precipitated a dramatic increase in world population and social complexity. Genetic research suggests that mutations related to traits currently found in some human populations, such as Europeans' ability to process lactose, arose after this time.

Sites in the Americas, SE Europe, and the Middle East show roughly contemporaneous (12-6 KYA) evidence of Neolithic domestication economies; similar evidence of E and S Asian, W European, and sub-Saharan African Neolithic adaptations dates to 10-7 KYA. From W Asian sources, farming and the herding of sheep and goats spread rapidly throughout the Mediterranean Basin, perhaps in as short a time interval as 100-200 years. The variety of crops—wheat, barley, rice, maize, squash, beans, and tubers—and a mix of other characteristics suggest that this adaptation occurred independently in as many as 12 or 13 places in both hemispheres.

Evidence for fermented beverages likewise coincides with the early Neolithic settled farming lifestyle. Northern Chinese farmers concocted a wine-like drink from rice, honey, and fruit between 9 and 8 KYA. In highland W Asia, in what is today Iran, vintners were fermenting grapes and making wine by c. 7.4 KYA. The plants and animals associated with the Neolithic Revolution provided the basis for all subsequent social and cultural evolution worldwide.

---

(1) Although "hominid" was standard usage several decades ago, "hominin" is now more commonly used in reference to human ancestors because of developments in the interpretation of primate evolution.

Earliest Civilizations: 4000-1000 BCE

Mesopotamia. Recorded history began with writing in Mesopotamia in the Tigris-Euphrates river valley. The Sumerians used clay tablets with pictographs to keep records after 4000 BCE. A **cuneiform** (wedge-shaped) script, evolved by 3000 BCE as a full syllabic alphabet. Neighboring peoples adapted the script for their own use.

Sumerian life centered, from 4000 BCE, on large cities (Eridu, Ur, Uruk, Nippur, Kish, and Lagash) organized around temples and priestly bureaucracies, with surrounding plains watered by vast irrigation works and worked with traction plows. Sailboats, wheeled vehicles, potter's wheels, and kilns were used. Copper was smelted and tempered from c. 4000 BCE; bronze was produced not long after. Ores, as well as precious stones and metals, were obtained through long-distance ship and caravan trade. Iron was used from c. 2000 BCE. Improved ironworking, developed partly by the Hittites, became widespread by 1200 BCE.

Sumerian political primacy passed among cities and their kingly dynasties. Semitic-speaking peoples, with cultures derived from the Sumerian, founded a succession of dynasties that ruled in Mesopotamia and neighboring areas for most of 1,800 years. Among them were the **Akkadians** (first under Sargon I, c. 2350 BCE), the Amorites (whose laws, codified by **Hammurabi**, c. 1792-1750 BCE, have biblical parallels), and the Assyrians, with interludes of rule by the Hittites, Kassites, and Mitanni.

Mesopotamian learning, preserved in vast libraries, was practically oriented. Scribes maintained lists of astronomical phenomena, plants, animals, and stones. Medical texts listed ailments and herbal cures. The Sumerians worshipped anthropomorphic gods representing natural forces. Sacrifices were made at **ziggurats**, or huge stepped temples.

The Syria-Palestine area, site of some of the earliest urban remains (Jericho, 7000 BCE) and of the **Ebla** civilization (fl. 2500 BCE), experienced Egyptian cultural and political influence along with Mesopotamian. The **Phoenician** coast was an active commercial center. A phonetic alphabet was invented here before 1600 BCE. It became the ancestor of many other alphabets.

Egypt. Agricultural villages along the Nile R. were united by around 3300 BCE into two kingdoms, Upper and Lower Egypt. They were unified (c. 3100 BCE) under the pharaoh Menes, as detailed on the Narmer Palate. A bureaucracy supervised construction of canals and monuments (**pyramids** starting 2700 BCE). Control over Nubia to the S was asserted from 2600 BCE.

Brilliant **Old Kingdom** period achievements in architecture, sculpture, and painting reached their height during the 3rd and 4th dynasties. **Hieroglyphic writing** appeared by 3200 BCE, recording a sophisticated literature that included religious writings, philosophy, history, and science. An ordered hierarchy of gods, including totemistic animal elements, was served by a powerful priesthood in Memphis. The pharaoh was identified with the falcon god Horus. Other trends included belief in an afterlife and short-lived quasi-monotheistic reforms introduced by the pharaoh **Akhenaton** (c. 1379-1362 BCE), who was married to Nefertiti.

After a period of dominance by Semitic Hyksos from Asia (c. 1700-1550 BCE), the **New Kingdom** established an empire in Syria. Egypt became increasingly embroiled in Asiatic wars and

diplomacy. Conquered by Persia in 525 BCE, it eventually faded away as an independent culture.

South Asia. The Bronze Age Indus Civilization spanned more than a million square kilometers in Pakistan and Northwestern India with many sites that expanded beyond the fertile core area of the Indus river system. The civilization independently grew out of local traditions developing complex trade networks and technologies during the Regionalization Era (5500-2600 BCE). The fully urban Harappan 2600-1900 BCE phase featured a standardized system of weights, uniform bricks, stamp seals featuring animals and unicorns, well laid out streets, and water management systems. Long distance trade with Mesopotamia and complex technologies were important. The writing system is one of the last to not be fully deciphered.

The major urban centers such as Dholavira, Harappa, and **Mohenjo-daro** were independent states. The civilization gradually changed due to environmental and cultural changes during the Localization Era (1900-1300 BCE). Post-Indus cultural complexes include the Gandara Grave culture (Swat, c. 1500-500 BCE) and the Painted Grey Ware (1200-800 BCE) culture, which some have associated with Vedic chiefdoms of the **Rig Veda**.

Europe. On Crete, the Bronze Age **Minoan civilization** emerged c. 2500 BCE. A prosperous economy and richly decorative art was supported by seaborne commerce. Mycenae and other cities in mainland Greece and Asia Minor (e.g., **Troy**) preserved elements of the culture until c. 1200 BCE. Cretan Linear A script (c. 2000-1700 BCE) remains undeciphered; Linear B script (c. 1300-1200 BCE) records an early Greek dialect. The possible connection between Mycenaean monumental stonework and the megalithic monuments of Western Europe, Iberia, and Malta (c. 4000-1500 BCE) is unclear.

China. Proto-Chinese Neolithic cultures had long covered N and SE China when the first large political state was organized

The Pyramids of Giza, including the Great Pyramid, were built during Egypt's 4th dynasty (c. 2575-2465 BCE).

in the N by the **Shang dynasty** (c. 1523 BCE). Shang kings called themselves Sons of Heaven, and they presided over a cult of human and animal sacrifice to ancestors and nature gods. The Zhou dynasty, starting c. 1027 BCE, expanded the area of the Sons of Heaven's dominion, but feudal states exercised most temporal power.

A writing system with 2,000 characters was already in use under the Shang, with **pictographs** later supplemented by phonetic characters. Many of its principles and symbols, despite changes in spoken Chinese, were preserved in later writing systems. Technical advances allowed urban specialists to create fine ceramic and jade products, and bronze casting after 1500 BCE was the most advanced in the world. Bronze artifacts discovered in northern Thailand date from 3600 BCE, hundreds of years before similar Middle Eastern finds.

Americas. Olmecs settled (1500 BCE) on the Gulf coast of Mexico and developed the first known civilization in the Western Hemisphere. Temple cities and huge stone sculptures date from 1200 BCE. A rudimentary calendar and writing system existed. Olmec religion—centered on a jaguar god—and art forms influenced later Mesoamerican cultures.

Formation of Classical Societies: 1000-400 BCE

Greece. After a period of decline during the Dorian Greek invasions (1200-1000 BCE), the Aegean area developed a unique civilization. Drawing on Mycenaean traditions, Mesopotamian learning (weights and measures, lunisolar calendar, astronomy, musical scales), the Phoenician alphabet (modified for Greek), and Egyptian art, **Greek city-states** saw a rich elaboration of intellectual life. The two great epic poems attributed to **Homer**, the *Iliad* and the *Odyssey*, were probably composed around the 8th cent. BCE. Long-range commerce was aided by metal coinage (introduced by the Lydians in Asia Minor before 700 BCE). Colonies were founded around the Mediterranean (Cumae in Italy in 760 BCE; Massalia in France c. 600 BCE) and Black Sea shores.

Philosophy, starting with Ionian speculation on the nature of matter (Thales, c. 634-546 BCE), continued by other "Pre-Socratics" (e.g., Heraclitus, c. 540-480 BCE; Parmenides, b. c. 515 BCE), reached a high point in Athens in the rationalist idealism of **Plato** (c. 428-347 BCE), a disciple of **Socrates** (c. 469-399 BCE; executed for alleged impiety), and in **Aristotle** (384-322 BCE), a pioneer in many fields, from natural sciences to logic, ethics, and metaphysics. The arts were highly valued. Architecture culminated in the Parthenon (438 BCE) by Phidias (fl. 490-430 BCE). Poetry (Sappho, c. 610-580 BCE; Pindar, c. 518-438 BCE) and drama (Aeschylus, 525-456 BCE; Sophocles, c. 496-406 BCE; Euripides, c. 484-406 BCE) thrived. Male beauty and strength, a chief artistic theme, were celebrated at the national games at Olympia.

Ruled by local tyrants or **oligarchies**, the Greeks were not politically united but managed to resist inclusion in the Persian Empire. Persian king Darius was defeated at Marathon (490 BCE), his son Xerxes at Salamis (480 BCE), and the Persian army at Plataea (479 BCE). Democracy sprouted in Athens as statesman Pericles (495-429 BCE) sought participation in government from all citizens. Local warfare was common; the **Peloponnesian Wars** (431-404 BCE) ended in Sparta's victory over Athens. Greek political power subsequently waned, but Greek cultural forms spread far and wide.

Hebrews. Nomadic Hebrew tribes entered Canaan before 1200 BCE, settling among other Semitic peoples speaking the same language. They brought from the desert a **monotheistic** faith said to have been revealed to Abraham in Canaan c. 1800 BCE and Moses at Mt. Sinai c. 1250 BCE, after the Hebrews' escape from bondage in Egypt. David (r. 1000-961 BCE) and Solomon (r. 961-922 BCE) united them in a kingdom that briefly dominated the area. **Phoenicians** to the N founded Mediterranean colonies (Carthage, c. 814 BCE) and sailed into the Atlantic.

A temple in Jerusalem became the national religious center, with sacrifices performed by a hereditary priesthood. Polytheistic influences, especially of the fertility cult of Baal, were opposed by **prophets** (Elijah, Amos, Isaiah).

Divided into **two kingdoms** after Solomon, the Hebrews were unable to resist the revived Assyrian empire, which conquered **Israel**, the northern kingdom, in 722 BCE. **Judah**, the southern kingdom, was conquered in 586 BCE by the Babylonians under Nebuchadnezzar II. With the fixing of most of the biblical canon by the mid-4th cent. BCE and the emergence of rabbis, Judaism successfully survived the loss of Hebrew autonomy. A Jewish kingdom was revived under the Hasmoneans (168-42 BCE).

China. During the **Eastern Zhou** dynasty (770-256 BCE), Chinese culture spread E to the sea and S to the Yangtze R. Large feudal states on the periphery of the empire contended for preeminence but continued to recognize the Son of Heaven (king), who retained a purely ritual role enriched with courtly music and dance. In the Age of Warring States (403-221 BCE), when the first sections of the **Great Wall** were built, the Qin state in the W gained supremacy and finally united all of China.

Iron tools entered China c. 500 BCE. Casting techniques were advanced, aiding agriculture. Peasants owned their land and owed civil and military service to nobles. China's cities grew in number and size; barter remained the chief trade medium.

Intellectual ferment among noble scribes and officials produced a classical age of Chinese literature and philosophy. **Confucius** (551-479 BCE) urged a restoration of a supposedly harmonious social order of the past through proper conduct in accordance with one's station and through filial and ceremonial piety. The *Analects* attributed to him are revered throughout E Asia.

Among other thinkers, **Mencius** (d. 289 BCE) added the view that the Mandate of Heaven can be removed from an unjust dynasty. The Legalists sought to curb the supposed natural wickedness of people through new institutions and harsh laws. The Naturalists emphasized the balance of opposites—yin, yang—in the world. **Daoists** sought mystical knowledge through meditation and disengagement.

India. The political and cultural center of India shifted from the Indus to the Ganges River Valley. Buddhism, Jainism, and mystical revisions of orthodox Vedism all developed c. 500-300 BCE. The *Upanishads*, last part of the *Veda*, urged escape from the cycle of rebirth into the physical world. Vedism remained the preserve of the Brahman caste.

In contrast, **Buddhism**, founded by Siddhartha Gautama (c. 563-c. 483 BCE)—Buddha ("Enlightened One")—appealed to merchants in the urban centers and took hold at first (and most lastingly) on the geographic fringes of Indian civilization. The classic Indian epics were composed in this era: the *Ramayana* perhaps c. 300 BCE, the *Mahabharata* over a period starting around 400 BCE.

Northern India was divided into a large number of monarchies and aristocratic republics, probably derived from tribal groupings, when the Magadha kingdom was formed in Bihar c. 542 BCE. It soon became the dominant power. The **Maurya** dynasty, founded by Chandragupta c. 321 BCE, expanded the kingdom, uniting most of Northern India in a centralized bureaucratic empire. The third Mauryan king, **Asoka** (r. c. 274-236 BCE), conquered most of the subcontinent. He converted to Buddhism, inscribed its tenets on pillars throughout India, and downplayed the caste system.

Before its final decline in India, Buddhism developed into a popular worship of heavenly Bodhisattvas ("enlightened beings"), and it produced a refined architecture (the Great Stupa [shrine] at Sanchi, 100 CE) and sculpture (Gandhara reliefs, 1-400 CE).

Persia. Aryan peoples (Persians, Medes) dominated the area of present Iran by the beginning of the 1st millennium BCE. The prophet **Zoroaster** (b. c. 628 BCE) introduced a dualistic religion in which the forces of good (Ahura Mazda, "Lord of Wisdom") and evil (Ahriman) battle for dominance; individuals are judged by their actions and earn damnation or salvation. Zoroaster's hymns (*Gathas*) are included in the *Avesta*, the Zoroastrian scriptures. A version of this faith became the established religion of the Persian Empire.

Africa. Nubia, periodically occupied by Egypt since about 2600 BCE, ruled Egypt c. 750-661 BCE and survived as an independent Egyptianized kingdom (**Kush**; capital Meroe) for 1,000 years. The Iron Age Nok culture flourished c. 500 BCE-200 CE on the Benue Plateau of **Nigeria**.

Americas. The Chavin culture controlled Northern Peru c. 900 BCE to 200 BCE. Its ceremonial centers, featuring the jaguar god, survived long after. Its architecture, ceramics, and textiles had influenced other Peruvian cultures. **Mayan civilization** began to develop in Central America as early as 1500 BCE.

Great Empires Unite the Classical World: 400 BCE-400 CE

Persia and the Mediterranean. Cyrus, ruler of a small kingdom in Persia from 559 BCE, united the Persians and Medes within 10 years and conquered Asia Minor and Babylonia in another 10. His son Cambyses, followed by **Darius** (r. 522-486 BCE), added vast lands to the E and N as far as the Indus Valley and Central Asia, as well as Egypt and Thrace. The whole empire was ruled by an international bureaucracy and army, with Persians holding the chief positions. The resources and styles of all the subject civilizations were exploited to create a rich syncretic art.

The kingdom of Macedon, which under Philip II dominated the Greek world and Egypt, was passed on to Philip's son **Alexander** in 336 BCE. Within 13 years, Alexander had conquered all the Persian dominions. Imbued by his tutor Aristotle with Greek ideals, Alexander encouraged colonization, and Greek-style cities were founded. After his death in 323 BCE, wars of succession divided the empire into three significant dynasties—the **Antigonids** in Asia Minor and Macedon, the **Ptolemies** in Egypt, and the **Seleucids** in Mesopotamia. In the ensuing 300 years (the **Hellenistic Era**), a cosmopolitan Greek-oriented culture permeated the ancient world from Western Europe to the borders of India, absorbing native elites everywhere.

Hellenistic philosophy stressed the private individual's search for happiness. The Cynics followed Diogenes (c. 400-c. 325 BCE), who stressed self-sufficiency and restriction of desires and expressed contempt for luxury and social convention. Zeno (c. 335-c. 263 BCE) and the **Stoics** exalted reason, identified it with virtue, and counseled an ascetic disregard for misfortune. The **Epicureans** tried to build lives of moderate pleasure without political or emotional involvement. Hellenistic arts imitated life realistically, especially in sculpture and literature (comedies of Menander, 342-292 BCE).

The sciences thrived, especially at Alexandria, where the Ptolemies financed a great library and museum. Fields of study included mathematics (**Euclid**'s geometry, c. 300 BCE); astronomy (heliocentric theory of Aristarchus, 310-230 BCE; Julian calendar, 45 BCE; **Ptolemy**'s *Almagest*, c. 150 CE); geography (world map of Eratosthenes, 276-194 BCE); hydraulics (**Archimedes**, 287-212 BCE); medicine (Galen, 130-200 CE); and chemistry. Inventors refined uses for siphons, valves, gears, springs, screws, levers, cams, and pulleys.

A restored Persian empire under the **Parthians** (northern Iranian tribespeople) controlled the eastern Hellenistic world from 250 BCE to 229 CE. The Parthians and the succeeding **Sassanian dynasty** (c. 224-651 CE) fought with Rome periodically. The Sassanians revived Zoroastrianism as a state religion and patronized a nationalistic artistic and scholarly renaissance.

Rome. The city of Rome was founded, according to legend, by Romulus in 753 BCE. Through military expansion and colonization, and by granting citizenship to leading members of conquered tribes, the city annexed all of Italy S of the Po R. in the 100-year period before 268 BCE. The Latin and other Italic tribes were annexed first, followed by the **Etruscans** (founders of a great civilization N of Rome) and Greek colonies in the S. With a large standing army and reserve forces of several hundred thousand, Rome was able to defeat **Carthage** in the three

Punic Wars (264-241 BCE, 218-201 BCE, 149-146 BCE), despite the invasion of Italy by **Hannibal** (218 BCE), thus gaining Sicily and territory in Spain and N Africa.

Rome exploited local disputes to conquer Greece and Asia Minor in the 2nd cent. BCE and Egypt in the 1st (after the defeat and suicide of **Antony and Cleopatra**, 30 BCE). The Mediterranean civilized world, up to the disputed Parthian border, was now Roman and remained so for 500 years. Less civilized regions were added to the Empire: Gaul (conquered by **Julius Caesar**, 58-51 BCE), Britain (43 CE), and Dacia NE of the Danube (107 CE).

The original aristocratic republican government, with democratic features added in the 5th and 4th cent. BCE, deteriorated under the pressures of empire and class conflict (**Gracchus** brothers, social reformers, murdered in 133 and 121 BCE; slave revolts in 135 BCE and 73 BCE). After a series of civil wars (Marius vs. Sulla, 88-82 BCE; Caesar vs. **Pompey**, 49-45 BCE; triumvirate vs. Caesar's assassins, 44-43 BCE; Antony vs. Octavian, 32-30 BCE), the empire came under the rule of a deified monarch (first emperor, **Augustus**, 27 BCE-14 CE).

Provincials (nearly all granted citizenship by Caracalla, 212 CE) came to dominate the army and civil service. Traditional **Roman law**, systematized and interpreted by independent jurists, and local self-rule in provincial cities were supplanted by a vast tax-collecting bureaucracy in the 3rd and 4th cent. The legal rights of women, children, and slaves were strengthened.

Roman innovations in **civil engineering** included water mills, windmills, and rotary mills and the use of cement that hardened under water. Monumental architecture (baths, theaters, temples) relied on the arch and the dome. A network of roads (some still standing) stretched 53,000 mi, passing through mountain tunnels as long as 3.5 mi. Aqueducts brought water to cities; underground sewers removed waste.

Roman art and literature were derivative of Greek models. Innovations were made in sculpture (naturalistic busts, equestrian statues), decorative wall painting (as at Pompeii), satire (**Juvenal**, 60-127 CE), history (**Tacitus**, 56-120 CE), and prose romance (**Petronius**, d. 66 CE). Gladiatorial contests dominated public amusements, which were supported by the state.

India. The **Gupta** monarchs reunited Northern India c. 320 CE. Their peaceful and prosperous reign saw a revival of Hindu religious thought and Brahman power. The old Vedic traditions were combined with devotion to many indigenous deities (who were seen as manifestations of Vedic gods). Caste lines were reinforced, and Buddhist practices gradually disappeared or were integrated with **Hindu** traditions. The art (often erotic), architecture, and literature of the period, patronized by the Gupta court, are considered among India's finest achievements (Kalidasa, poet and dramatist, fl. c. 400 CE). Mathematical innovations included the use of zero and decimal numbers. Invasions by White Huns from the NW led to the empire's destruction c. 550 CE. Rich cultures also developed in Southern India during this period. Emotional Tamil religious poetry contributed to the Hindu revival. The Pallava kingdom controlled much of Southern India c. 350-880 CE and helped to spread Indian civilization to SE Asia.

China. The Qin ruler Shi Huang (r. 221-210 BCE), known as the First Emperor, centralized political authority; standardized the written language, laws, weights, measures, and coinage; and conducted a census. But he tried to destroy most philosophical texts. The **Han** dynasty (202 BCE-220 CE) instituted the Mandarin bureaucracy, which lasted 2,000 years. Local officials were selected by examination in Confucian classics and trained at the imperial university and provincial schools.

The invention of **paper** facilitated this bureaucratic system. Agriculture was promoted, but peasants bore most of the tax burden. Irrigation was improved, water clocks and sundials were used, astronomy and mathematics thrived, and landscape painting was perfected.

With the expansion S and W (to nearly the present borders of today's China), trade was opened with India, SE Asia, and the Middle East over sea and caravan routes. Indian missionaries brought Mahayana Buddhism to China by the 1st cent. CE and spawned a variety of sects. Daoism was revived and merged with popular superstitions. **Daoist and Buddhist monasteries** and convents multiplied in the turbulent centuries after the collapse of the Han dynasty in 220 CE.

China's Great Wall, first built during the Age of Warring States (403-221 BCE), was rebuilt, extended, and modified over thousands of years to protect China from invaders.

Monotheism Spreads: 1-750 CE

Roman Empire. Polytheism was practiced in the Roman Empire, and religions indigenous to particular Middle Eastern nations became international. Roman citizens worshiped **Isis** of Egypt, **Mithras** of Persia, **Demeter** of Greece, and the great mother **Cybele** of Phrygia. Their cults centered on mysteries (secret ceremonies) and the promise of an afterlife, symbolized by the death and rebirth of the god. The Jews of the empire preserved their monotheistic religion, Judaism, the world's oldest (c. 1300 BCE) continuous religion. Its teachings are contained in the Bible (the Old Testament). 1st-cent. CE Judaism embraced several sects, including the **Sadducees**, mostly drawn from the Temple priesthood, who were culturally Hellenized; the **Pharisees**, who upheld the full range of traditional customs and practices as of equal weight to literal scriptural law and elaborated synagogue worship; and the **Essenes**, an ascetic, millenarian sect. Messianic fervor led to repeated, unsuccessful rebellions against Rome (66-70, 135 CE). As a result, the Temple in Jerusalem was destroyed and the population decimated; this event marked the beginning of the Diaspora (living in exile). To preserve the faith, codification of law was begun at the academy of Yavneh. The work continued for some 500 years in Palestine and in Babylonia, ending in the final redaction (c. 600) of the **Talmud**, a huge collection of legal and moral debates, rulings, liturgy, biblical exegesis, and legendary materials.

Christianity. Emerging as a distinct sect by the second half of the 1st cent. CE, Christianity is based on the teachings of **Jesus**, whom believers considered the Savior (Messiah or Christ) and son of God. Missionary activities of the Apostles and such early leaders as **Paul of Tarsus** spread the faith. Intermittent persecution, as in Rome under Nero in 64 CE, on grounds of suspected disloyalty, failed to disrupt Christian communities. Each congregation, generally urban and of plebeian character, was tightly organized under a leader (bishop), elders (presbyters or priests), and assistants (deacons). The four **Gospels** (accounts of the life and teachings of Jesus) and the Acts of the Apostles were written down in the late 1st and early 2nd cent. and circulated along with letters of Paul and other Christian leaders. An authoritative canon of these writings was not fixed until the 4th cent.

A school for priests was established at Alexandria in the 2nd cent. Its teachers (**Origen**, c. 182-251) helped define doctrine and promote the faith in Greek-style philosophical works. Neoplatonism underwent Christian coloration in the writings of Church Fathers such as **Augustine** (354-430). Christian hermits began to associate in monasteries, first in Egypt (St. Pachomius, c. 290-345), then in other eastern lands, then in the W (**St. Benedict's rule**, 529). Devotion to saints, especially Mary, mother of Jesus, spread. Under **Constantine** (r. 306-37), Christianity became in effect the established religion of the Empire. Pagan temples were expropriated, state funds were used to build churches and support the hierarchy, and laws were adjusted in accordance with Christian ideas. Pagan worship was banned by the end of the 4th cent., and severe restrictions were placed on Judaism.

The newly established church was rocked by doctrinal disputes, often exacerbated by regional rivalries. Chief heresies (as defined by church councils, backed by imperial authority) were **Arianism**, which denied the divinity of Jesus; **Monophysitism**, denying the human nature of Christ; **Donatism**, which regarded as invalid any sacraments administered by sinful clergy; and **Pelagianism**, which denied the necessity of unmerited divine aid (grace) for salvation.

Islam. The earliest Arab civilization emerged by the end of the 2nd millennium BCE in the watered highlands of Yemen. Seaborne and caravan trade in frankincense and myrrh connected the area with the Nile and Fertile Crescent. The Minaean, Sabean (Sheba), and Himyarite states successively held sway. By Muhammad's time (7th cent. CE), the region was a province of Sassanian Persia. In the N, the Nabataean kingdom at Petra and the kingdom of Palmyra were Aramaicized, Romanized, and finally absorbed, as neighboring Judea had been, into the Roman Empire. Nomads shared the central region with a few trading towns and oases. Wars between tribes and raids on communities were common and were celebrated in a poetic tradition that by the 6th cent. helped establish a classic literary Arabic.

About 610, **Muhammad**, a 40-year-old Arab man of Mecca, emerged as a prophet. He proclaimed a revelation from the one true God, calling on contemporaries to abandon idolatry and restore the faith of Abraham. He introduced his religion as **Islam**, meaning "submission" to the one God, Allah, as a continuation of the biblical faith of Abraham, Moses, and Jesus, all respected as prophets in this system. His teachings, recorded in the Quran, in many ways were inclusive of Abrahamic monotheistic ideas known to the Jews and Christians in Arabia. A key aspect of the Abrahamic connection was insistence on justice in society, which led to severe opposition among the aristocrats in Mecca. As conditions worsened for Muhammad and his followers, he decided in 622 to make a **hegira** (flight) to Medina, 200 mi to the N. This event marks the beginning of the Muslim lunar calendar. Hostilities between Mecca and Medina increased, and in 629 Muhammad conquered Mecca. By the time he died in 632, nearly all the Arabian peninsula accepted his political and religious leadership.

After his death the majority of Muslims (later known as **Sunni** Muslims) recognized the leadership of the **caliph** (successor) Abu Bakr (632-34), followed by Umar (634-44), Uthman (644-56), and Ali (656-60). A minority, the **Shiites**, insisted instead on the leadership of Ali, Muhammad's cousin and son-in-law. By 644, **Muslim rule** over Arabia was confirmed. Muslim armies had threatened the Byzantine and Persian empires, which were weakened by wars and disaffection among subject peoples (including Coptic and Syriac Christians opposed to the Byzantine Orthodox establishment). Syria, Palestine, Egypt, Iraq, and Persia fell to Muslim armies. The new administration assimilated existing systems in the region; hence the conquered peoples participated in running the empire. The Quran recognized the so-called Peoples of the Book, i.e., Christians, Jews, and Zoroastrians, as tolerated monotheists, and Muslim policy was relatively tolerant to minorities living as "protected" peoples. An expanded tax system, based on conquests of the Persian and Byzantine empires, provided revenue to organize campaigns against neighboring non-Muslim regions.

Under the **Umayyads** (661-750) and **Abbasids** (750-1256), territorial expansion led Muslim armies across N Africa and into Spain (711). Muslim armies in the W were stopped at Tours, France, in 732 by the Frankish ruler **Charles Martel**. Asia Minor, the Indus Valley, and Transoxiana were conquered in the E. The conversion of conquered peoples to Islam was gradual. In many places the official Arabic language supplanted the local tongues. But in the eastern regions the Arab rulers and their armies adopted Persian cultures and language as part of their Muslim identity.

Disputes over succession and pious opposition to injustices in society led to a number of oppositional movements, which led to the factionalization of Muslim community. The **Shiites** supported leadership candidates descended from Muhammad, believing them to be carriers of some kind of divine authority. The **Kharijites** supported an egalitarian system derived from the Quran, opposing and even engaging in battle against those who did not agree with them.

The now-typical use of a minaret as the location for the Muslim call to prayer began at the Mosque of Uqba, or Great Mosque of Kairouan, built from 670 CE in present-day Tunisia.

New Peoples Enter World History: 400-900 CE

Barbarian invasions and fall of Rome. Germanic tribes infiltrated S and E from their Baltic homeland during the 1st millennium BCE, reaching southern Germany by 100 BCE and the Black Sea by 214 CE. Organized into large federated tribes under elected kings, most resisted Roman domination and raided the empire in times of civil war (Goths took Dacia in 214, raided Thrace in 251-69). Germanic troops and commanders dominated the Roman armies by the end of the 4th cent. **Huns,** invaders from Asia, entered Europe in 372, driving more Germans into the empire. Emperor Valens allowed Visigoths to cross the Danube in 376. Huns under Attila (d. 453) raided Gaul, Italy, and the Balkans.

The western empire, weakened by overtaxation and social stagnation, was overrun in the 5th cent. Gaul was effectively lost in 406-07, Spain in 409, Britain in 410, and Africa in 429-39. Rome was sacked in 410 by Visigoths under Alaric and in 455 by Vandals. The **last western emperor**, Romulus Augustulus, was deposed in 476 by the Germanic chief Odoacer.

Celts. Celtic cultures, which in pre-Roman times covered most of W Europe, were confined almost entirely to the British Isles after the Germanic invasions. **St. Patrick** completed (c. 457-92) the conversion of Ireland and a strong monastic tradition took hold. Irish monastic missionaries in Scotland, England, and on the continent (Columba, c. 521-97; Columbanus, c. 543-615) helped restore Christianity after the Germanic invasions. **Monasteries** became centers of classic and Christian learning and presided over the recording of a Christianized Celtic mythology, elaborated by secular writers and bards. An intricate decorative art style developed, especially in book illumination (Lindisfarne Gospels, c. 700; Book of Kells, 8th cent.).

Successor states. The Visigothic kingdom in Spain (from 419) and much of France (to 507) saw continuation of Roman administration, language, and law (Breviary of Alaric, 506) until its destruction by Muslim forces from North Africa (711). The Vandal kingdom in Africa (from 429) was conquered by the Byzantines in 533. Italy was ruled successively by an Ostrogothic kingdom under Byzantine suzerainty (489-554), direct Byzantine government, and German Lombards (568-774). The Lombards divided the peninsula with the Byzantines and papacy under the dynamic reformer **Pope Gregory the Great** (590-604) and successors.

King Clovis (r. 481-511) united the Franks on both sides of the Rhine and, after his conversion to Christianity, defeated the Arian heretics, Burgundians (after 500), and Visigoths (507) with the support of native clergy and the papacy. Under the **Merovingian** kings, a feudal system emerged: power was fragmented among hierarchies of military landowners. Social stratification, which in late Roman times had acquired legal, hereditary sanction, was reinforced.

The Carolingians (747-987) expanded the kingdom and restored central power. **Charlemagne** (r. 768-814) conquered nearly all the Germanic lands, including Lombard Italy. He was crowned emperor by Pope Leo III in Rome in 800. A centuries-long decline in commerce and arts was reversed under Charlemagne's patronage. He welcomed Jews to his kingdom, which became a center of Jewish learning (Rashi, 1040-1105). He sponsored the Carolingian Renaissance of learning under the Anglo-Latin scholar Alcuin (c. 732-804), who reformed church liturgy.

The pyramid of Kukulkan (El Castillo) at Chichen Itza is one of the existing examples of Mayan architecture in present-day Mexico.

Byzantine Empire. Under **Diocletian** (r. 284-305) the Roman empire had been divided into two parts to facilitate administration and defense. **Constantine** founded (330) **Constantinople** (at old Byzantium) as a fully Christian city. Commerce and taxation financed a sumptuous, orientalized court, a class of hereditary bureaucratic families, and magnificent urban construction (Hagia Sophia, 532-37). The city's fortifications and naval innovations repelled assaults by Goths, Huns, Slavs, Bulgars, Avars, Arabs, and Scandinavians. Greek replaced Latin as the official language by c. 700. **Byzantine art,** a solemn, sacral, and stylized variation of late classical styles (mosaics at the Church of San Vitale, Ravenna, Italy, 526-48), was a starting point for medieval art in Eastern and Western Europe.

Justinian (r. 527-65) briefly reconquered parts of Spain, N Africa, and Italy, codified **Roman law** (Codex Justinianus [529] was medieval Europe's chief legal text), closed the Platonic Academy at Athens, and ordered all pagans to convert. Lombards in Italy and Arabs in Africa retook most of his conquests. The Isaurian dynasty from Anatolia (from 717) and the Macedonian dynasty (867-1054) restored military and commercial power. The Iconoclast controversy (726-843) over the permissibility of images helped alienate the Eastern Church from the papacy.

Abbasid Empire. Baghdad (established 762) became seat of the **Abbasid dynasty** (established 750), while Umayyads continued to rule in Spain. A brilliant cosmopolitan civilization emerged, inaugurating a Muslim-Arab golden age. Arabic was the lingua franca of the empire; intellectual sources from Persian, Sanskrit, Greek, and Syriac were rendered into Arabic. Christians and Jews equally participated in this translation movement, which also involved interaction between Jewish legal thought and Islamic law, as much as between Christian theology and Muslim scholasticism. Persian-style court life, with art and music, flourished at the court of **Harun al-Rashid** (786-809), celebrated in the masterpiece known to English readers as *The Arabian Nights*. The sciences, medicine, and mathematics were pursued at Baghdad, Cordova, and Cairo (c. 969). The culmination of this intellectual synthesis in Islamic civilization came with the scientific and philosophical works of **Avicenna** (Ibn Sina, 980-1037), **Averroes** (Ibn Rushd, 1126-98), and **Maimonides** (1135-1204), a Jew who wrote in Arabic. This intellectual tradition was translated into Latin and opened a new period in Christian thought.

The decentralization of the Abbasid empire, from 874, led to the establishment of various Muslim dynasties under different ethnic groups. Persians, Berbers, and Turks ruled different regions, retaining connection with the Abbasid caliph at the religious level. The Abbasid period also saw various religious movements against the orthodox position held by governing authorities. This situation in Islam led to the establishment of different legal, theological, and mystical schools of thought. The most influential mass movement was **Sufism,** which aimed at the reaching out of the average individual in quest of a spiritual path. Al-Ghazali (1058-1111) is credited with reconciling personal Sufism with orthodox Sunni tradition.

Africa. Immigrants from Saba in S Arabia helped set up the **Axum** kingdom in Ethiopia in the 1st cent. (their language, Ge'ez, is preserved by the Ethiopian Church). In the 3rd cent., when the kingdom became Christianized, it defeated Kushite Meroe and expanded its influence into Yemen. Axum was the center of a vast ivory trade and controlled the Red Sea coast until c. 1100. Arab conquest in Egypt cut Axum's political and economic ties with Byzantium.

The Iron Age entered W Africa by the end of the 1st millennium BCE. **Ghana,** the first known sub-Saharan state, ruled in the upper Senegal-Niger region c. 400-1240, controlling the trade of gold from mines in the S to trans-Sahara caravan routes to the N. The **Bantu** peoples, probably of W African origin, began to spread E and S perhaps 2,000 years ago, displacing the Pygmies and Bushmen of central and southern Africa during a 1,500-year period.

Japan. The advanced Neolithic Yayoi period, when irrigation, rice farming, and iron and bronze casting techniques were introduced from China or Korea, persisted to c. 400 CE. The myriad Japanese states were then united by the **Yamato** clan, under an emperor who acted as chief priest of the animistic Shinto cult. Japanese political and military intervention by the 6th cent. in Korea, then under strong Chinese influence, quickened a Chinese cultural invasion of Japan, bringing Buddhism, the Chinese language (which long remained a literary and governmental medium), Chinese ideographs, and Buddhist styles in painting, sculpture, literature, and architecture (7th cent., Horyuji temple at Nara). The Taika Reforms (646) tried unsuccessfully to centralize Japan according to Chinese bureaucratic and Buddhist philosophical values.

A nativist reaction against the Buddhist **Nara** period (710-94) ushered in the **Heian** period (794-1185) centered at the new capital, Kyoto. Japanese elegance and simplicity modified Chinese styles in architecture, scroll painting, and literature; the writing system was also simplified. The courtly novel *Tale of Genji* (1010-20) testifies to the enhanced role of women in medieval Japanese literature and culture.

Southeast Asia. The historic peoples of SE Asia began arriving some 2,500 years ago from China and Tibet, displacing scattered aborigines. Their agriculture relied on rice and yams. Indian cultural influences were strongest; literacy and Hindu and Buddhist ideas followed the S India-China trade route. From the southern tip of Indochina, the kingdom of **Funan** (1st-7th cent.) traded as far W as Persia. It was absorbed by Chenla, itself conquered by the **Khmer** empire (800-1300). The Khmers, under Hindu god-kings (Suryavarman II, 1113-c. 1150), built the monumental Angkor Wat temple center for the royal phallic cult. The **Nam-Viet** kingdom in Annam, dominated by China and Chinese culture for 1,000 years, emerged in the 10th cent., growing at the expense of the Khmers, who also lost ground in the NW to the new, highly organized **Thai** kingdom. On Sumatra, the **Srivijaya** empire controlled vital sea lanes (7th-10th cent.). A Buddhist dynasty, the Sailendras, ruled central **Java**

(8th-9th cent.), building at Borobudur one of the largest stupas (dome-shaped Buddhist shrines) in the world.

China. The Sui dynasty (581-618) ushered in a period of commercial, artistic, and scientific achievement in China, which continued under the **Tang** dynasty (618-906). Inventions like the magnetic compass, gunpowder, the abacus, and printing were introduced or perfected. Medical innovations included cataract surgery. The state, from its cosmopolitan capital, Chang-an, supervised foreign trade, which exchanged Chinese silks, porcelains, and art for spices and ivory over Central Asian caravan routes and sea routes reaching Africa. A golden age of poetry bequeathed valuable works to later generations (Tu Fu, 712-70; Li Po, 701-62). Landscape painting flourished.

Commercial and industrial expansion continued under the **Northern Song** (960-1126), facilitated by paper money and credit notes. But commerce never achieved full respectability; government monopolies expropriated successful merchants. The population, long stable at 50 million, doubled in 200 years with the introduction of early-ripening rice and the double harvest. In art, native Chinese styles were revived.

Americas. From 300 to 600, a Native American empire stretched from the Valley of Mexico to Guatemala, centering on the huge city **Teotihuacán** (founded 100 BCE). To the S, in Guatemala, a high **Mayan** civilization developed (150-900) around hundreds of rural ceremonial centers. The Mayans improved on Olmec writing and the calendar and pursued astronomy and mathematics. In South America, a widespread pre-Inca culture grew from **Tiahuanacu**, Bolivia, near Lake Titicaca (Gateway of the Sun doorway, c. 700).

Christian Europe Regroups and Expands: 900-1300

Scandinavia. Pagan Danish and Norse (Viking) adventurers, traders, and pirates raided the coasts of the British Isles (Dublin, c. 831), France, and even the Mediterranean for over 200 years beginning in the late 8th cent. Inland settlement in the W was limited to Great Britain (King Canute, 994-1035) and Normandy, settled (911) under Rollo, as a fief of France. Vikings also reached Iceland (874), Greenland (c. 986), and North America (**Leif Ericson** and others, c. 1000). Norse traders (**Varangians**) developed Russian river commerce from the 8th to the 11th cent. and helped set up a state at Kiev in the late 9th cent. Conversion to Christianity occurred in the 10th cent., reaching Sweden 100 years later. In the 11th cent. Norman bands conquered Southern Italy and Sicily, and Duke **William of Normandy** conquered (1066) England, bringing feudal government and the French language, essential elements in later English civilization.

Central and East Europe. Slavs began to expand from about 150 CE in all directions in Europe. By the 7th cent. they reached as far S as the Adriatic and Aegean seas. In the Balkan Peninsula they dislocated Romanized local populations or assimilated newcomers (Bulgarians, a Turkic people). The first **Slavic states** were Moravia (628) in Central Europe and the Bulgarian state (680) in the Balkans. Byzantine missions of St. Methodius and Cyril (whose Greek-based cyrillic alphabet is still used by some Southern and Eastern Slavs) converted (863) Moravia.

The Eastern Slavs, part-civilized under the overlordship of the Turkish-Jewish **Khazar** trading empire (7th-10th cent.), gravitated toward Constantinople by the 9th cent. The **Kievan** state adopted (989) Eastern Christianity under Prince Vladimir. King Boleslav I (992-1025) began **Poland**'s long history of conquest. The Magyars (**Hungarians**), in present-day Hungary since 896, accepted (1001) Latin Christianity.

Germany. The German kingdom that emerged after the breakup of Charlemagne's Western Empire remained a confederation of largely autonomous states. Otto I, a Saxon who was king from 936, established the **Holy Roman Empire**—a union of Germany and Northern Italy—in alliance with Pope John XII, who crowned (962) him emperor; he defeated (955) the Magyars. Imperial power was greatest under the **Hohenstaufens** (1138-1254), despite the growing opposition of the papacy, which ruled central Italy, and the Lombard League cities. Frederick II (1194-1250) improved administration and patronized the arts. After his death, German influence was removed from Italy.

Christian Spain. From its northern mountain redoubts, Christian rule slowly migrated S through the 11th cent., when Muslim unity collapsed. After the capture (1085) of **Toledo**, the

kingdoms of Portugal, Castile, and Aragon undertook repeated crusades of reconquest, finally completed in 1492. Elements of Islamic civilization persisted in recaptured areas, influencing all Western Europe.

Crusades. **Pope Urban II** called for a crusade (1095) to restore Asia Minor to Byzantium and the Holy Land to Christendom. This first crusade captured Jerusalem and led to the foundation of four Frankish states in the Levant. The defeat inflicted upon crusaders at the Battle of Hattin (1187) by **Saladin** (c. 1137-93), the Kurdish ruler of Egypt and Syria, effectively negated territorial gains. Many crusades followed until 1291. The 4th crusade sacked Constantinople (1204). Other crusades were launched against Christian heretics (Albigensian Crusade, 1229), pagans, and enemies of the papacy.

Economy. The agricultural base of European life benefited from improvements in **plow design** (c. 1000) and by the draining of lowlands and clearing of forests, leading to a rural population increase. Towns grew in Northern Italy, Flanders, and Northern Germany (Hanseatic League). Improvements in **loom design** permitted factory textile production. **Guilds** dominated urban trades from the 12th cent. Banking (centered in Italy, 12th-15th cent.) facilitated long-distance trade.

Christianity. The split between the Eastern and Western churches was formalized in 1054. Western and Central Europe was divided into 500 bishoprics under one united hierarchy, but conflicts between secular and church authorities were frequent (German **Investiture Controversy**, 1075-1122). Clerical power was first strengthened through the international monastic

The Magna Carta, granted by England's King John to his rebellious barons in 1215, is considered a foundational document for constitutional liberties.

reform begun at Cluny in 910. Popular religious enthusiasm often expressed itself in heretical movements (Waldensians from 1173), but was channeled by the **Dominican** (1215) and **Franciscan** (1223) friars into the religious mainstream.

Arts. **Romanesque** architecture (9th to mid-12th cent.) expanded on late Roman models, using the rounded arch and massed stone to support enlarged basilicas. Painting and sculpture followed Byzantine models. The literature of **chivalry** was exemplified by the epic (*Chanson de Roland*, c. 1100) and by courtly love poems of the troubadours of Provence and minnesingers of Germany. **Gothic** architecture emerged in France (choir of St. Denis, c. 1140) and spread along with French cultural influence. Rib vaulting and pointed arches were used to combine soaring heights with delicacy, and they freed walls for display of stained glass. Exteriors were covered with painted relief sculpture and embellished with elaborate architectural detail.

Learning. Law, medicine, and philosophy were advanced at independent **universities** (Bologna, Paris, 12th cent.), originally corporations of students and masters. Twelfth-cent. translations of Greek classics, especially by Aristotle, encouraged an analytic approach. Scholastic philosophy, from Anselm (1033-1109) to **Aquinas** (1225-74), attempted to understand revelation through reason.

Apogee of Central Asian Power and the Spread of Islam: 1250-1500

Turks. Turkic peoples, of Central Asian ancestry, were a military threat to the Byzantine and Persian Empires from the 6th cent. After several waves of invasions, during which most of the Turks adopted Islam, the **Seljuk Turks** took (1055) Baghdad. They ruled Persia, Iraq, and, after 1071, Asia Minor, where massive numbers of Turks settled. The empire was divided in the 12th cent. into smaller states ruled by Seljuks, Kurds, and Mamluks (a military caste of former Turk, Kurd, and Circassian slaves), which governed Egypt and the Middle East until the Ottoman era (c. 1290-1922).

Osman I (r. c. 1290-1326) and succeeding sultans united Anatolian Turkish warriors in a militaristic state that waged holy war against Byzantism and Balkan Christians. Most of the Balkans had been subdued and Anatolia united when Constantinople fell (1453). By the mid-16th cent., Hungary, the Middle East, and N Africa had been conquered. The Turkish advance was stopped at Vienna (1529) and at the naval battle of Lepanto (1571) by Spain, Venice, and the papacy.

The **Ottoman state** was governed in accordance with orthodox Muslim law. Greek, Armenian, and Jewish communities were segregated and were ruled by religious leaders responsible for taxation; they dominated trade. Many state offices and most army ranks were filled by slaves, in part through a system of child conscription among Christians.

India. Mahmud of Ghazni (971-1030) led repeated Turkish raids into N India. Turkish power was consolidated in 1206 with the start of the **Sultanate at Delhi**. Centralization of state power under the early Delhi sultans went far beyond traditional Indian practice. Muslim rule of much of the subcontinent lasted until the British conquest 600 years later, though Hinduism remained the majority religion.

Mongols. **Genghis Khan** (c. 1167-1227) first united the feuding Mongol tribes and built their armies into an effective offensive force around a core of highly mobile cavalry. He and his immediate successors created the largest land empire in history; by 1279 it stretched from the E coast of Asia to the Danube and from the Siberian steppes to the Arabian Sea. East-West trade and contacts were facilitated (Marco Polo, c. 1254-1324). The western Mongols were Islamized by 1295; successor states soon lost their Mongol character by assimilation. They were briefly reunited under the Turk Tamerlane (1336-1405).

Kublai Khan ruled China from his new capital Beijing (established c. 1264). Naval campaigns against Japan (1274, 1281) and Java (1293) were defeated, the latter by the Hindu-Buddhist maritime kingdom of Majapahit. The **Yuan** dynasty used Mongols and other foreigners (including Europeans) in official posts and tolerated the return of Nestorian Christianity (suppressed 841-45) and the spread of Islam in the S and W. A native reaction expelled the Mongols in 1367-68.

Russia. The Kievan state in Russia, weakened by the decline of Byzantium and the rise of the Catholic Polish-Lithuanian state, was overrun (1238-40) by the Mongols. Only the northern trading republic of Novgorod remained independent. The grand dukes of Moscow emerged as leaders of a coalition of princes that eventually (by 1481) defeated the Mongols. After the fall of Constantinople in 1453, the **Tsars** (Caesars) at Moscow (from Ivan III, r. 1462-1505) set up an independent Russian Orthodox Church. Commerce failed to revive. The isolated Russian state remained agrarian with the peasant class falling into serfdom.

Persia. A revival of Persian literature, making use of the Arab alphabet and literary forms, began in the 10th cent. (epic of Firdausi, 935-1020). An art revival, influenced by Chinese styles introduced after the Mongols came to power in Iran, began in the 13th cent. Persian cultural and political forms, and often the Persian language, were used for centuries by Turkish and Mongol elites from the Balkans to India. Persian mystics from Rumi (1207-73) to Jami (1414-92) promoted **Sufism** in their poetry.

Africa. Two militant Islamic Berber dynasties emerged from the Sahara to carve out empires from the Sahel to central Spain—the **Almoravids** (c. 1050-1140) and the fanatical **Almohads** (c. 1125-1269). The Ghanaian empire was replaced in the upper Niger by Mali (c. 1230-1340), whose Muslim rulers imported Egyptians to help make **Timbuktu** a center of commerce (in gold, leather, and slaves) and learning. The Songhay empire (to 1590) replaced Mali. To the S, forest kingdoms produced refined artworks (Ife terra cotta, **Benin** bronzes).

Other **Muslim states** in Nigeria (Hausas) and Chad originated in the 11th cent. and continued in some form until the 19th-cent. European conquest. Less-developed Bantu kingdoms existed across central Africa.

Some 40 Muslim Arab-Persian trading colonies and city-states were established all along the E African coast from the 10th cent. (Kilwa, Mogadishu). The interchange with Bantu peoples produced the **Swahili** language and culture. Gold, palm oil, and slaves were brought from the interior, stimulating the growth of the Monamatapa kingdom of the Zambezi (15th cent.). The Christian Ethiopian empire (from 13th cent.) continued the traditions of Axum.

Southeast Asia. Islam was introduced into Malaya and the Indonesian islands by Arab, Persian, and Indian traders. Coastal Muslim cities and states (starting before 1300) soon dominated the interior. Chief among these was the **Malacca** state (c. 1400-1511), on the Malay peninsula.

Arts and Statecraft Thrive in Europe; New Asian Empires Rise: 1350-1600

Italy. Distinctive Italian achievements in literature and fine arts during the late Middle Ages (**Dante**, 1265-1321; Giotto, 1276-1337) led to the vigorous new styles of the Renaissance (14th-16th cent.). Patronized by the rulers of the quarreling petty states of Italy (**Medicis** in Florence and the papacy, c. 1400-1737), the plastic arts perfected realistic techniques, including **perspective** (Masaccio, 1401-28; Leonardo **da Vinci**, 1452-1519). Classical motifs were used in architecture, and increased talent and expense were put into secular buildings. The Florentine dialect was refined as a national literary language (**Petrarch**, 1304-74). Greek refugees from the E strengthened the respect of humanist scholars for the classic sources. Soon an international movement aided by the spread of **printing** (Gutenberg, c. 1397-1468), **humanism** was optimistic about the power of human reason (Erasmus of Rotterdam, 1466-1536, **More**'s *Utopia*, 1516) and valued individual effort in the arts and in politics (**Machiavelli**, 1469-1527).

France. The French monarchy, strengthened in its repeated struggles with powerful nobles (Burgundy, Flanders, Aquitaine) by alliances with the growing commercial towns, consolidated bureaucratic control under Philip IV (r. 1285-1314) and extended French influence into Germany and Italy (popes at Avignon, France, 1309-1417). The **Hundred Years War** (1337-1453) ended English dynastic claims in France (battles of Crécy, 1346, and Poitiers, 1356; Joan of Arc executed, 1431). A

French Renaissance, dating from royal invasions (1494, 1499) of Italy, was encouraged at the court of Francis I (r. 1515-47), who centralized taxation and law. French vernacular literature consciously asserted its independence (La Pléiade, 1549).

England. The evolution of England's political institutions began with the **Magna Carta** (1215), by which King John guaranteed the privileges of nobles and church against the monarchy and assured jury trial. After the **Wars of the Roses** (1455-85), the **Tudor** dynasty reasserted royal prerogatives (Henry VIII, r. 1509-47), but the trend toward independent departments and ministerial government also continued. English trade (wool exports from c. 1340) was protected by the nation's growing maritime power (**Spanish Armada** destroyed, 1588).

English replaced French and Latin in the late 14th cent. in law and literature (**Chaucer**, c. 1340-1400), and English translation of the Bible began (Wycliffe, 1380s). **Elizabeth I** (r. 1558-1603) presided over the development of poetry (Spenser, 1552-99), drama (**Shakespeare**, 1564-1616), and music.

German Empire. From among a welter of minor feudal states, church lands, and independent cities, the **Habsburgs** assembled a far-flung territorial domain, based in Austria from 1276. Family members held the title of Holy Roman Emperor from 1438 to the Empire's dissolution in 1806 but failed to centralize its domains, leaving Germany disunited for centuries. Resistance to Turkish expansion brought Hungary under Austrian control from the 16th cent. The Netherlands, Luxembourg, and Burgundy were added in 1477, curbing French expansion.

The Flemish painting tradition of naturalism, technical proficiency, and bourgeois subject matter began in the 15th cent. (Jan van Eyck, c. 1390-1441), the earliest northern manifestation of the Renaissance. Albrecht **Dürer** (1471-1528) typified the merging of late Gothic and Italian trends in 16th-cent. German art. Imposing civic architecture flourished in the prosperous commercial cities.

Black Death. The bubonic plague reached Europe from the E in 1348, killing up to half the population by 1350 (and recurring periodically in most areas until the early 18th cent.). Labor scarcity forced wages to rise and brought greater freedom to the peasantry, making possible **peasant uprisings** (Jacquerie in France, 1358; Wat Tyler's rebellion in England, 1381).

Spain. Despite the unification of Castile and Aragon in 1479, the two countries retained separate governments, and the nobility, especially in Aragon and Catalonia, retained many privileges. Spanish lands in Italy (Naples, Sicily) and the Netherlands entangled the country in European wars through the mid-17th cent., while explorers, traders, and conquerors built up a Spanish empire in the Americas and the Philippines.

From the late 15th cent., a **golden age** of literature and art produced works of social satire (plays of Lope de Vega, 1562-1635; **Cervantes**, 1547-1616), as well as spiritual intensity (**El Greco**, 1541-1614; **Velázquez**, 1599-1660).

Explorations. Organized European maritime exploration began, seeking to evade the Venice-Ottoman monopoly of eastern trade and to promote Christianity. A key goal was to satisfy a growing taste for Asian goods. Beginning in 1418, expeditions from Portugal explored the W coast of Africa, until Vasco da Gama rounded the Cape of Good Hope in 1497 and reached India. A Portuguese trading empire was consolidated by the seizure of Goa (1510) and Malacca (1551). Japan was reached in 1542. The voyages of Christopher **Columbus** (1492-1504) uncovered a world new to Europeans, which Spain hastened to subdue. Navigation schools in Spain and Portugal, the development of large sailing ships (carracks) mounted with cannons, and the invention (c. 1475) of the rifle aided European penetration.

Mughals and Safavids. E of the Ottoman Empire, two Muslim dynasties ruled unchallenged in the 16th and 17th cent. The Mughal dynasty of India, founded by Persianized Turkish invaders from the NW under Babur, dates from their 1526 conquest of the Delhi Sultanate. The dynasty ruled most of India for more than 200 years, surviving nominally until 1857. **Akbar** (r. 1556-1605) consolidated administration at his glorious court, where the Urdu language (Persian-influenced Hindi) developed. Trade relations with Europe increased. Under Shah Jahan (1629-58), a secularized art fusing Hindu and Muslim elements flourished in miniature painting and in architecture (**Taj Mahal**). **Sikhism** (founded late 15th cent.) combined elements of both faiths. Suppression of Hindus and Shiite Muslims in S India in the late 17th cent. weakened the empire.

Intense devotion to the Shiite sect characterized the Safavids (1502-1736) of Persia and led to hostilities with the Sunni Ottomans for more than a century. The prosperity and the strength of the empire are evidenced by the mosques at its capital city, **Isfahan**. The Safavids enhanced Iranian national consciousness.

China. The **Ming** emperors (1368-1644), the last native dynasty in China, wielded strong personal power. European trade (Portuguese monopoly through **Macau** from 1557) was strictly controlled. Jesuit scholars and scientists (Matteo Ricci, 1552-1610) introduced some Western science; their writings familiarized the West with China. The arts thrived, especially in the areas of painting and ceramics. Chinese manufacturing boomed, bringing in new profits from world trade.

Japan. After the decline of the first hereditary *shogunate* (chief generalship) at **Kamakura** (1185-1333), fragmentation of power accelerated, as did the consequent social mobility. Under Kamakura and the Ashikaga shogunate (1338-1573), the *daimyos* (lords) and *samurai* (warriors) grew more powerful and promoted a martial ideology. Japanese pirates and traders plied the China coast. Popular Buddhist movements included the nationalist Nichiren sect (from c. 1250) and **Zen** (brought from China, 1191), which stressed meditation and a disciplined aesthetic (tea ceremony, gardening, martial arts, *No* drama).

Change and Development in Europe: 1500-1700

Reformation. Theological debate and protests against real and perceived clerical corruption existed in the medieval Christian world, expressed by such dissenters as John **Wycliffe** (c. 1320-84) and his followers (the Lollards) in England, and **Huss** (burned as a heretic, 1415) in Bohemia.

Martin **Luther** (1483-1546) preached that faith alone, without the mediation of clergy or good works, leads to salvation. He attacked the authority of the pope, rejected priestly celibacy, and recommended individual study of the Bible (which he translated into German c. 1525). His 95 Theses (1517) led to his excommunication (1521). John **Calvin** (1509-64) said that God's elect were predestined for salvation and all others for damnation; good conduct and success were signs of election. Calvin in Geneva and John **Knox** (1505-72) in Scotland established theocratic states.

Henry VIII asserted English national authority and secular power by breaking away (1534) from the Catholic Church, creating what would become the Anglican Church. Monastic property was confiscated, and some Protestant doctrines given official sanction.

Religious wars. A century and a half of religious wars began with a southern German peasant uprising (1524), repressed with Luther's support. Radical sects—democratic, pacifist, millenarian—arose (Anabaptists ruled Münster, 1534-35) and were suppressed violently. Civil war in France

from 1562 between **Huguenots** (Protestant nobles and merchants) and Catholics ended with the 1598 **Edict of Nantes**, tolerating Protestants (revoked 1685). Habsburg attempts to restore Catholicism in Germany were resisted in 25 years of fighting. The 1555 Peace of Augsburg guarantee of religious independence to local princes and cities was confirmed only after the **Thirty Years' War** (1618-48), when much of Germany was devastated by local and foreign armies (Sweden, France).

A Catholic Reformation, or **Counter-Reformation**, met the Protestant challenge, defining an official theology at the Council of Trent (1545-63). The **Jesuit** order (Society of Jesus), founded in 1534 by Ignatius Loyola (1491-1556), helped reconvert large areas of Poland, Hungary, and S Germany and sent missionaries to the New World, India, and China. The **Inquisition** suppressed heresy in Catholic countries. A revival of religious fervor appeared in devotional literature (Teresa of Avila, 1515-82) and in grandiose **Baroque** art (Bernini, 1598-1680).

Scientific Revolution. The late nominalist thinkers (Ockham, c. 1300-49) of Paris and Oxford challenged Aristotelian orthodoxy, allowing for a freer scientific approach. At the same time, metaphysical values, such as the Neoplatonic faith in an orderly, mathematical cosmos, still motivated and directed inquiry. Nicolaus **Copernicus** (1473-1543) promoted the heliocentric theory, which was confirmed when Johannes

Kepler (1571-1630) discovered the mathematical laws describing the elliptical orbits of the planets. The traditional Christian-Aristotelian belief that the heavens and the Earth were fundamentally different collapsed when **Galileo Galilei** (1564-1642) discovered moving sunspots, irregular moon topography, and moons around Jupiter, but he faced religious opposition (Galileo's retraction, 1633). He and Sir Isaac **Newton** (1642-1727) developed a mechanics that unified cosmic and earthly phenomena. Newton and Gottfried von **Leibniz** (1646-1716) invented calculus. René **Descartes** (1596-1650), best known for his influential philosophy, also invented analytic geometry.

An explosion of **observational science** included the discovery of blood circulation (Harvey, 1578-1657) and microscopic life (Leeuwenhoek, 1632-1723) and advances in anatomy (Vesalius, 1514-64, dissected corpses) and chemistry (Boyle, 1627-91). Scientific research institutes were founded in Florence (1657), London (**Royal Society**, 1660), and Paris (1666). Inventions proliferated (Savery's steam engine, 1698).

Arts. Mannerist trends of the High Renaissance (**Michelangelo**, 1475-1564) exploited virtuosity, grace, novelty, and exotic subjects and poses. The notion of artistic genius was promoted. Private connoisseurs entered the art market. These trends were elaborated in the 17th cent. **Baroque** era on a grander scale. Dynamic movement in painting and sculpture was emphasized by sharp lighting effects, rich materials (colored marble, gilt), and realistic details. Curved facades, broken lines, rich detail, and ceiling decoration characterized Baroque architecture. Monarchs, princes, and prelates, usually Catholic, used Baroque art to enhance and embellish their authority, as in royal portraits (Velázquez, 1599-1660; Van Dyck, 1599-1641).

National styles emerged. In France, a taste for rectilinear order and serenity (Poussin, 1594-1665), linked to the new rational philosophy, was expressed in classical forms. The influence of **classical values** in French literature (tragedies of **Racine**, 1639-99) gave rise to the "battle of the Ancients and Moderns." New forms included the essay (**Montaigne**, 1533-92) and novel (*Princesse de Clèves*, La Fayette, 1678).

Dutch painting of the 17th cent. was unique in its wide social distribution. The Flemish tradition of undemonstrative realism reached its peak in **Rembrandt** (1606-69) and Jan Vermeer (1632-75).

Economy. European economic expansion, known as the **commercial revolution**, was stimulated by new trade with the East, by New World gold and silver, and by a doubling of population (50 million in 1450, 100 million in 1600). **New business and financial techniques** were developed and refined, such as joint-stock companies, insurance, and letters of credit and exchange. The Bank of Amsterdam (1609) and the Bank of England (1694) broke the old monopoly of private banking families. The rise of a business mentality was typified by the spread of clock towers in cities in the 14th cent. By the mid-15th cent., portable clocks were available; the first watch was invented in 1502.

By 1650, most governments had adopted the **mercantile system**, in which they sought to amass metallic wealth by protecting merchants' foreign and colonial trade monopolies. The rise in prices and the new coin-based economy undermined craft guild and feudal manorial systems. Expanding industries (clothweaving, mining) benefited from technical advances. Coal began to replace wood as the chief fuel; it was used to fuel new 16th-cent. blast furnaces making cast iron.

New World. The **Aztecs** united much of the Mesoamerican area in a militarist empire by 1519 from their capital, Tenochtitlán (pop. 300,000), which was the center of a cult requiring ritual human sacrifice. Most of the civilized areas of South America were ruled by the centralized Inca Empire (1476-1534), stretching 2,000 mi from Ecuador to NW Argentina. Lavish and sophisticated traditions in pottery, weaving, sculpture, and architecture were maintained in both regions.

These empires, beset by revolts, fell in two short campaigns to gold-seeking Spanish forces based in the Antilles and Panama. Hernán **Cortés** took Mexico (1519-21); Francisco **Pizarro**, Peru (1532-35). From these centers, land and sea expeditions claimed most of North and South America for Spain. The indigenous high cultures did not survive the impact of **Christian missionaries** and the new upper class of whites. Although the Spanish administration intermittently concerned itself with their

The exact purpose of the Incan city of Machu Picchu, built in the 15th century and abandoned less than 150 years later, is unknown; one theory is that it served as a royal retreat.

welfare, the population was devastated by European diseases and remained impoverished at most levels. New World silver and such native products as potatoes, tobacco, corn, peanuts, chocolate, and rubber exercised a major economic influence on Europe.

Brazil, which the Portuguese reached in 1500 and settled after 1530, and the Caribbean colonies of several European nations developed a plantation economy where sugarcane, tobacco, cotton, coffee, rice, indigo, and lumber were grown by slaves. From the early 16th to late 19th cent., 10 million Africans were transported to **slavery** in the Americas and Caribbean islands.

Netherlands. The urban, Calvinist northern provinces of the Netherlands rebelled (1568) against Habsburg Spain and founded an oligarchic mercantile republic. Their control of the Baltic grain market enabled them to exploit Mediterranean food shortages. Religious refugees—French and Belgian Protestants, Iberian Jews—added to the commercial talent pool. After Spain absorbed Portugal (1580), the Dutch seized Portuguese possessions and created a vast commercial empire ultimately centered in parts of the Caribbean and in Indonesia. The Dutch also challenged or supplanted Portuguese traders in China and Japan. Revolution in 1640 restored Portuguese independence.

England. Anglicanism became firmly established under **Elizabeth I** after a brief Catholic interlude under "Bloody" Mary I (1553-58). But religious and political conflicts led to a rebellion (1642) by Parliament. Forces of the Roundheads (Puritans) defeated the Cavaliers (Royalists); Charles I was beheaded (1649). The new Commonwealth was ruled as a military dictatorship by Oliver **Cromwell**, who also brutally crushed (1649-51) an Irish rebellion. Conflicts within the Puritan camp (democratic Levelers defeated, 1649) aided the Stuart restoration (1660), but Parliament was strengthened and the peaceful **"Glorious Revolution"** (1688) advanced political and religious liberties (writings of **Locke**, 1632-1704). British privateers (Drake, 1540-96) challenged Spanish control of the New World and penetrated Asian trade routes (Madras taken, 1639). North American colonies (Jamestown, 1607; Plymouth, 1620) provided an outlet for private enterprise and religious dissenters from Europe. The British East India Co. gained growing sway in 18th-cent. India, as Mughal power declined.

France. Emerging from the religious civil wars in 1628, France regained military and commercial great power status (under the ministries of **Richelieu**, Mazarin, and Colbert). Under **Louis XIV** (r. 1643-1715), royal absolutism triumphed over nobles and local *parlements* (defeat of Fronde, 1648-53). Durable colonies were founded in Canada (1608), the Caribbean (1626), and India (1674).

Sweden. Sweden seceded from the Scandinavian Union in 1523. The thinly populated agrarian state (with copper, iron, and timber exports) was united by the Vasa kings, whose conquests by the mid-17th cent. made Sweden the dominant Baltic power. The empire collapsed in the Great Northern War (1700-21).

Poland. After the union with Lithuania in 1447, Poland ruled vast territories from the Baltic to the Black Sea, resisting

German and Turkish incursions. Catholic nobles failed to gain the loyalty of their Orthodox Christian subjects in the E; commerce and trades were practiced by German and Jewish immigrants. The bloody 1648-49 Cossack uprising began the kingdom's dismemberment.

Russia. Growing authority of the tsars continued with advancing serfdom. Around 1700, **Peter the Great** imported new Western styles and technologies. Steady territorial expansion created a vast territory touching China, the Ottoman Empire, and east-central Europe.

China. A new dynasty, the **Manchus**, invaded from the NE, seized power in 1644, and expanded Chinese control to its greatest extent in Central and SE Asia. Trade and diplomatic contact with Europe grew, carefully controlled by China. New crops (sweet potato, maize, peanut) allowed economic and population growth (pop. 300 million, in 1800). Traditional arts and literature were pursued with increased sophistication (*Dream of the Red Chamber*, novel, mid-18th cent.).

Japan. Tokugawa Ieyasu, shogun from 1603, finally unified and pacified feudal Japan. Hereditary nobles (daimyos and samurai) monopolized government office and the professions. An urban merchant class grew, literacy spread, and a cultural renaissance occurred (**haiku**, a verse innovation of the poet Basho, 1644-94). Fear of European domination led to persecution of Christian converts from 1597 and to substantial isolation from outside contact from 1640.

Philosophy, Industry, and Revolution: 1700-1800

Science and reason. Greater faith in reason and empirical observation, instead of tradition and religious beliefs, espoused since the Renaissance (Francis Bacon, 1561-1626), was bolstered by scientific discoveries. René **Descartes** (1596-1650) used a rationalistic approach modeled on geometry and introspection to discover "self-evident" truths as a foundation of knowledge. Sir Isaac **Newton** emphasized induction from experimental observation. Baruch de **Spinoza** (1632-77), who called for political and intellectual freedom, developed a systematic rationalistic philosophy in his classic work *Ethics*.

French philosophers assumed leadership of the **Enlightenment** in the 18th cent. Montesquieu (1689-1755) used British history to support his notions of limited government. **Voltaire**'s (1694-1778) diaries and novels of exotic travel illustrated the intellectual trends toward secular ethics and relativism. Jean-Jacques **Rousseau**'s (1712-78) radical concepts of the **social contract** and of the inherent goodness of the common man gave impetus to antimonarchical republicanism. The *Encyclopedia* (1751-72, edited by Diderot and d'Alembert), designed as a monument to reason, was largely devoted to practical technology.

In England, ideals of liberty were connected with empiricist philosophy and science in the followers of John **Locke**. But British empiricism, especially as developed by the skeptical David **Hume** (1711-76), radically reduced the role of reason in philosophy, as did the evolutionary approach to law and politics of Edmund Burke (1729-97) and the utilitarian ethics of Jeremy Bentham (1748-1832). Adam Smith (1723-90) and other economists called for a rationalization of economic activity by removing artificial barriers to a supposedly natural free exchange of goods known as **laissez-faire**.

German writers participated in the new philosophical trends popularized by Christian von Wolff (1679-1754). Immanuel **Kant**'s (1724-1804) transcendental idealism, unifying an empirical epistemology with a priori moral and logical concepts, directed German thought away from skepticism. Italian contributions included work on electricity (Galvani, 1737-98; Volta, 1745-1827), the pioneer historiography of Vico (1668-1744), and writings on penal reform (Beccaria, 1738-94). Benjamin Franklin (1706-90) was celebrated in Europe for his varied achievements.

The growth of the **press** (*Spectator*, 1711-12) and the wide distribution of sentimental **novels** attested to the increase of a large bourgeois public.

Arts. Rococo art, characterized by extravagant decorative effects, asymmetries copied from organic models, and artificial pastoral subjects, was favored by the continental aristocracy for most of the century (Watteau, 1684-1721) and had musical analogies in the ornamentalized polyphony of late Baroque. The **Neoclassical** art after 1750, associated with the new scientific archaeology, was more streamlined and was infused with the supposed moral and geometric rectitude of the Roman Republic (David, 1748-1825). In England, **town planning** on a grand scale began.

Industrial Revolution in England. Agricultural improvements, such as the sowing drill (1701) and livestock breeding, were implemented on the large fields provided by enclosure of common lands by private owners. Profits from agriculture and from colonial and foreign trade (1800 volume, £54 million) were channeled through hundreds of banks and the **Stock Exchange** (est. 1773) into new industrial processes.

The Newcomen steam pump (1712) aided coal mining. Coal fueled the new efficient steam engines patented by James Watt in 1769, and coke-smelting produced cheap, sturdy iron for machinery by the 1730s. The **flying shuttle** (1733) and **spinning jenny** (c. 1764) were used in the large new cotton textile factories, where women and children were much of the workforce. Goods were transported cheaply over **canals** (2,000 mi; built 1760-1800). By the early 19th cent., industrialization spread in Western Europe and North America.

American Revolution. The British colonies in North America attracted a mass immigration of religious dissenters and poor people throughout the 17th and 18th cent., coming from the British Isles, Germany, the Netherlands, and other countries including imported African slaves. The population reached 3 million non-natives by the 1770s. The indigenous population was greatly reduced by European diseases and by wars with the various colonies. British attempts to control colonial trade and to tax the colonists to pay for the costs of colonial administration and defense clashed with local self-government and eventually provoked the colonies to a successful rebellion.

Central and East Europe. The monarchs of the three states that dominated E Europe—Austria, Prussia, and Russia—expanded royal power and centralized institutions in their kingdoms, which were enlarged by the division (1772-95) of Poland.

Under **Frederick II** (the Great) (r. 1740-86), Prussia, with its efficient modern army, doubled in size. State monopolies and tariff protection fostered industry, and some legal reforms were introduced. Austria's heterogeneous realms were unified under **Maria Theresa** (r. 1740-80) and **Joseph II** (r. 1765-90). Reforms in education, law, and religion were enacted, and the Austrian serfs were freed (1781). With its defeat in the Seven Years' War in 1763, Austria failed to regain Silesia, which had been seized by Prussia, but it was compensated by expansion to the E and S (Hungary, Slavonia, 1699; Galicia, 1772).

Russia, whose borders continued to expand, adopted some Western bureaucratic and economic policies under **Peter I** (r. 1682-1725) and **Catherine II** (r. 1762-96). Trade and

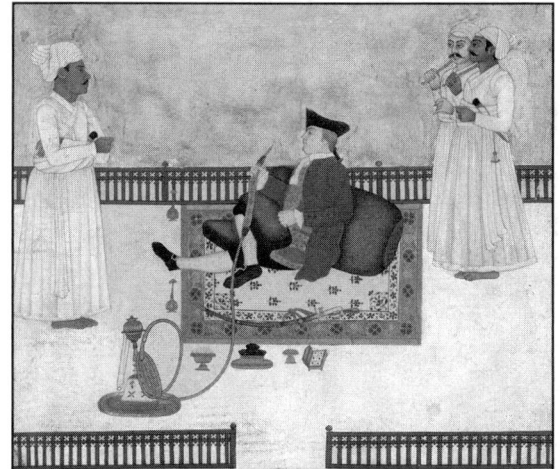

Indian artists created works to document the British East India Company and other colonizers as they expanded their presence in India in the 18th century; these are collectively called "Company paintings."

cultural contacts with the West multiplied from the new Baltic Sea capital, **St. Petersburg** (est. 1703).

French Revolution. The growing French middle class lacked political power and resented aristocratic tax privileges, especially in light of the successful American Revolution. Peasants lacked adequate land and were burdened with feudal obligations to nobles. War with Britain led to the loss of French Canada and drained the treasury, finally forcing the king to call the **Estates-General** in 1789 for the first time since 1614, in an atmosphere of food riots (poor crop in 1788).

Aristocratic resistance to absolutism was soon overshadowed by the reformist Third Estate (middle class), which proclaimed itself the **National Constituent Assembly** June 17 and took the "Tennis Court Oath" on June 20 to secure a constitution. The storming of the **Bastille** fortress/prison on July 14, 1789, by Parisian artisans was followed by looting and the seizure of aristocratic property throughout France. Assembly reforms included abolition of class and regional privileges, a Declaration of Rights, suffrage by taxpayers (75% of male population), and the **Civil Constitution of the Clergy** providing for election and loyalty oaths for priests. A republic was declared Sept. 22, 1792, in spite of royalist pressure from Austria and Prussia, which had declared war in Apr. (joined by Britain the next year). Louis XVI was beheaded Jan. 21, 1793, and Queen Marie Antoinette was beheaded Oct. 16, 1793.

Royalist uprisings in La Vendée and military reverses led to institution of a **reign of terror** in which tens of thousands of opponents of the Revolution and criminals were executed. Radical reforms in the **Convention** period (Sept. 1793-Oct. 1795) included the abolition of colonial slavery, economic measures to aid the poor, support of public education, and a short-lived de-Christianization.

Division among radicals (execution of Hebert, Danton, and Robespierre, 1794) aided the ascendancy of a moderate **Directory**, which consolidated military victories. **Napoleon Bonaparte** (1769-1821), a popular young general, exploited political divisions and participated in a coup Nov. 9, 1799, making himself first consul (dictator).

India. Sikh and Hindu rebels (Rajputs, Marathas) and Afghans destroyed the power of the Mughals during the 18th cent. After France's defeat (1763) in the Seven Years' War, Britain was the primary European trade power in India. Its control of inland **Bengal** and **Bihar** was recognized (1765) by the Mughal shah, who granted the **British East India Co.** (under Clive, 1725-74) the right to collect land revenue there. Despite objections from Parliament (1784 India Act), the company's involvement in local wars and politics led to repeated acquisitions of new territory. The company exported Indian textiles, sugar, and indigo, but industry was discouraged to promote British imports.

Nationalism Gathers Momentum: 1800-40

French ideals and empire spread. Inspired by the ideals of the French Revolution, and supported by the expanding French armies, new republican regimes arose near France: the **Batavian** Republic in the Netherlands (1795-1806), the **Helvetic** Republic in Switzerland (1798-1803), the **Cisalpine** Republic in Northern Italy (1797-1805), the **Ligurian** Republic in Genoa (1797-1805), and the **Parthenopean** Republic in Southern Italy (1799). A Roman Republic existed briefly in 1798 after Pope Pius VI was arrested by French troops. In Italy and Germany, new nationalist sentiments were stimulated both in imitation of and in reaction to developments in France (anti-French and anti-Jacobin peasant uprisings in Italy, 1796-99).

From 1804, when Napoleon declared himself emperor, to 1812, a succession of military victories (Austerlitz, 1805; Jena, 1806) extended his control over most of Europe through puppet states (**Confederation of the Rhine** united W German states for the first time and **Grand Duchy of Warsaw** revived Polish national hopes), expansion of the empire, and alliances.

Among the lasting reforms initiated under Napoleon's absolutist reign were establishment of the Bank of France, centralization of tax collection, codification of law along Roman models (Code Napoléon), and reform and extension of secondary and university education. In an 1801 concordat, the papacy recognized the effective autonomy of the French Catholic Church.

Napoleon's continental successes were offset by a British victory under Adm. Horatio Nelson in the **Battle of Trafalgar** (1805). Some 400,000 French soldiers were killed in the Napoleonic Wars, along with about 600,000 foreign troops.

Last gasp of old regimes. The disastrous 1812 invasion of Russia exposed Napoleon's overextension. After Napoleon's 1814 exile to Elba, his armies were defeated (1815) at **Waterloo** by British and Prussian troops.

At the **Congress of Vienna**, the monarchs and princes of Europe redrew their boundaries, to the advantage of Prussia (in Saxony and the Ruhr), Austria (in Illyria and Venetia), and Russia (in Poland and Finland). British conquest of Dutch and French colonies (S Africa, Ceylon, Mauritius) was recognized. France, under the restored Bourbons, retained its expanded 1792 borders. The settlement brought 50 years of international peace to Europe.

But the Congress was unable to check the advance of liberal ideals and of nationalism among the smaller European nations. The 1825 **Decembrist uprising** by liberal officers in Russia was easily suppressed. But an independence movement in **Greece**, stirred by commercial prosperity and a cultural revival, succeeded in expelling Ottoman rule by 1831, with the aid of Britain, France, and Russia.

A constitutional monarchy was secured in France by the **1830 Revolution**; Louis Philippe became king. The revolutionary contagion spread to **Belgium**, which gained its independence (1830) from the Dutch monarchy, to **Poland**, whose rebellion was defeated (1830-31) by Russia, and to Germany.

Romanticism. A new style in intellectual and artistic life replaced Neoclassicism and Rococo after the mid-18th cent. By the early 19th cent., Romanticism prevailed in Europe.

Rousseau had begun the reaction against rationalism; in education (*Émile*, 1762) he stressed subjective spontaneity over regularized instruction. German writers (Lessing, 1729-81; Herder, 1744-1803) favorably compared the German folk song to classical forms and began a cult of Shakespeare, whose passion and "natural" wisdom was a model for the romantic *Sturm und Drang* (Storm and Stress) movement. **Goethe**'s *Sorrows of Young Werther* (1774) set the model for the tragic, passionate genius.

A new interest in **Gothic architecture** in England after 1760 (Walpole, 1717-97) spread through Europe, associated with an aesthetic Christian and mystic revival (**Blake**, 1757-1827). Celtic, Norse, and German mythology and folk tales were revived or imitated (Grimm's Fairy Tales, 1812-22). The

Haiti's Toussaint L'Ouverture was a leader of the revolution that led to Haiti's establishment as a free, self-governing state in 1804.

medieval revival (Scott's *Ivanhoe*, 1819) led to a new interest in history, stressing national differences and organic growth (**Carlyle**, 1795-1881; Michelet, 1798-1874), corresponding to theories of natural evolution (Lamarck's *Philosophie Zoologique*, 1809; Lyell's *Geology*, 1830-33). A reaction against classicism characterized the English **romantic poets** (beginning with **Wordsworth**, 1770-1850). Revolution and war fed an emphasis on freedom and conflict, expressed by both poets (**Byron**, 1788-1824; **Hugo**, 1802-85) and philosophers (**Hegel**, 1770-1831).

Wild gardens replaced the formal French variety, and painters favored rural, stormy, and mountainous landscapes (**Turner**, 1775-1851; **Constable**, 1776-1837). Clothing became freer, with wigs, hoops, and ruffles discarded. Originality and genius were expected in the life and work of inspired artists (Murger's *Scenes From Bohemian Life*, 1847-49). Exotic locales and themes (as in Gothic horror stories) were used in art and literature (Delacroix, 1798-1863; **Poe**, 1809-49). Music exhibited the new dramatic style and a breakdown of classical forms (**Beethoven**, 1770-1827). The use of folk melodies and modes aided the growth of distinct national traditions (Glinka in Russia, 1804-57).

Latin America. François **Toussaint L'Ouverture** led a successful slave revolt in Haiti, which subsequently became the first Caribbean state to achieve independence (1804). The mainland Spanish colonies won their independence (1810-24) under such leaders as Simón **Bolívar** (1783-1830). Brazil became an independent empire (1822) under the Portuguese prince regent. A new class of military officers divided power with large landholders and the church.

United States. Territory under U.S. control nearly doubled in size with the **Louisiana Purchase** (1803). Heavy immigration and exploitation of ample natural resources fueled rapid economic growth. The spread of the franchise, public education, and antislavery sentiment were signs of a widespread democratic ethic.

China. Failure to keep pace with Western arms technology exposed China to greater European influence and hampered efforts to bar imports of opium, which had damaged Chinese society and drained wealth overseas. In the **Opium War** (1839-42), Britain forced China to expand trade opportunities and to cede Hong Kong.

New Complexities: Reforms and Imperialism: 1840-80

Idea of progress. As a result of the cumulative scientific, economic, and political changes of the preceding eras, the idea took hold among literate people in the West that continuing growth and improvement constituted the usual state of human and natural life.

Charles **Darwin**'s statement of the **theory of evolution** and survival of the fittest (*On the Origin of Species*, 1859), defended by intellectuals and scientists against theological objections, was taken as confirmation that progress was the natural direction of life. The controversy helped define popular ideas of the dedicated scientist and of science's increasing control over the world (Foucault's demonstration of Earth's rotation, 1851; **Pasteur**'s germ theory, 1861).

Liberals following Ricardo (1772-1823) in their faith that unrestrained competition would bring continuous economic expansion sought to adjust political life to new social realities and believed that unregulated competition of ideas would yield truth (**Mill**, 1806-73). In England, successive reform bills (1832, 1867, 1884) gave representation to the new industrial towns and extended the franchise to the middle and lower classes and to Catholics, Dissenters, and Jews. On both sides of the Atlantic, reformists tried to improve conditions for the mentally ill (**Dix**, 1802-87), women (Anthony, 1820-1906), and prisoners. Slavery was barred in the British Empire (1833), the U.S. (1865), and Brazil (1888).

Socialist theories based on ideas of human perfectibility or progress were widely disseminated. Utopian socialists such as Saint-Simon (1760-1825) envisaged an orderly, just society directed by a technocratic elite. A model factory town, New Lanark, Scotland, was set up by utopian Robert Owen (1771-1858), and communal experiments were tried in the U.S. (Brook Farm, MA, 1841-47). Bakunin's (1814-76) anarchism represented the opposite extreme of total freedom. Karl **Marx** (1818-83) posited the inevitable triumph of socialism in industrial countries through a dialectical process of class conflict. Effective development of oceanic steamship lines (Cunard Lines, 1840s) and the opening of the **Suez Canal** accelerated shipping and commerce. Telegraph lines (Australia-Europe,

1871) sped communication. International organizations included the General (later Universal) Postal Union (1874) and conferences to limit epidemics like cholera. The initial **Geneva Convention** (1864) regulated treatment of prisoners of war.

Spread of industry. The technical processes and managerial innovations of the English industrial revolution spread to Europe (especially Germany) and the U.S., causing an explosion of industrial production, demand for raw materials, and competition for markets. Inventors, both trained and self-taught, provided means for larger-scale production (Bessemer steel, 1856; sewing machine, 1846). Many inventions were shown at the universal prosperity-themed 1851 London Great Exhibition at the **Crystal Palace**.

Local specialization and long-distance trade were aided by a revolution in transportation and communication. Railroads were first introduced in the 1820s in England and the U.S. Over 150,000 mi of track had been laid worldwide by 1880, with another 100,000 mi laid in the next decade. Steamships were improved (*Savannah* crossed Atlantic, 1819). The **telegraph**, perfected by 1844 (Morse), connected the Old and New Worlds by cable in 1866 and quickened the pace of international commerce and politics. The first commercial **telephone** exchange went into operation in the U.S. in 1878.

The new class of industrial workers, uprooted from their rural homes, lacked job security and suffered from dangerous overcrowding at work and at home. Many responded by organizing **trade unions** (legalized in England, 1824; France, 1884). The U.S. Knights of Labor had 700,000 members by 1886. The First International (1864-76) tried to unite workers worldwide around a Marxist program. The quasi-Socialist Paris Commune uprising (1871) was violently suppressed. Acts to reduce child labor and regulate conditions were passed (1833-50 in England). Social security measures were introduced by the Bismarck regime (1883-89) in Germany.

Revolutions of 1848. Among the causes of the continent-wide revolutions were an international collapse of credit and resulting unemployment, bad harvests in 1845-47, and a cholera epidemic. The new urban proletariat and expanding bourgeoisie demanded greater political roles. Republics were proclaimed in France, Rome, and Venice. Nationalist feelings reached fever pitch in the Habsburg empire, as Hungary declared independence under Kossuth, a Slav Congress demanded equality, and Piedmont tried to drive Austria from Lombardy. A national liberal assembly at Frankfurt called for German unification.

But riots fueled bourgeois fear of socialism (**Marx** and **Engels**, *Communist Manifesto*, 1848), and peasants remained conservative. The old establishment—the Papacy, the Habsburgs with the help of the Tsarist Russian army—was able to rout the revolutionaries by 1849. The French Republic succumbed to a renewed monarchy by 1852 (Emperor Napoleon III).

Great nations unified. Using the "blood and iron" tactics of Bismarck from 1862, Prussia controlled N Germany by 1867 (war with Denmark, 1864; Austria, 1866). After defeating France in 1870 (annexation of Alsace-Lorraine), it won the allegiance of S German states. A new **German Empire** was proclaimed (1871). **Italy**, inspired by Giuseppe Mazzini (1805-72) and Giuseppe Garibaldi (1807-82), was unified by the reformed Piedmont kingdom through uprisings, plebiscites, and war.

The opening of the Suez Canal, which connected the Mediterranean and Red Seas in 1869, provided a more direct sea route for international trade between the Atlantic and Indian Oceans.

The **United States** expanded its area after the 1846-48 Mexican War and defeated (1861-65) a secession attempt by Southern states in the **Civil War**. Canadian provinces were united in an autonomous **Dominion of Canada** (1867). Control in **India** was removed from the East India Co. and centralized under British administration after the 1857-58 Sepoy rebellion, laying the groundwork for the modern Indian state. Queen Victoria was named Empress of India (1876).

Europe dominates Asia. The Ottoman Empire began to weaken in the face of Balkan nationalisms and European imperial incursions in N Africa (**Suez Canal**, 1869). The Ottomans had lost control of most of both regions by 1882. Russia completed its expansion S by 1884 (despite the temporary setback of the **Crimean War** with Turkey, Britain, and France, 1853-56), taking Turkestan, all the Caucasus, and Chinese areas in the E and sponsoring Balkan Slavs against the Turks. A succession of reformist and reactionary regimes presided over a slow modernization (serfs freed, 1861). Persian independence suffered as Russia and British India competed for influence.

China was forced to sign a series of unequal treaties with European powers and Japan. Overpopulation and an inefficient dynasty brought misery and caused rebellions (Taiping, Muslims) leaving tens of millions dead. **Japan** was forced by the U.S. (Commodore Perry's visits, 1853-54) and Europe to end its isolation. The Meiji restoration (1868) gave power to a Westernizing oligarchy, abolishing feudalism and expanding education. Intensified empire-building gave Burma to Britain (1824-85) and Indochina to France (1862-95). Christian missionary activity followed imperial and trade expansion in Asia.

Arts. The official **Beaux Arts** school in Paris set an international style of imposing public buildings (Paris Opera, 1861-74; Vienna Opera, 1861-69) and uplifting statues (Bartholdi's Statue of Liberty, 1884). Realist painting, influenced by photography (Daguerre, 1837), appealed to a new mass audience with social or historical narrative (Wilkie, 1785-1841; Poynter, 1836-1919) or with serious religious, moral, or social messages (pre-Raphaelites, Millet's *Angelus*, 1858), often drawn from ordinary life. The **Impressionists** (Monet, 1840-1926; Pissarro, 1830-1903; Renoir, 1841-1919) rejected the formalism, sentimentality, and precise techniques of academic art in favor of a spontaneous, undetailed rendering of the world through careful representation of the effect of natural light on objects. They were strongly influenced by Asian and African styles.

Realistic **novelists** presented the full panorama of social classes and personalities but retained sentimentality and moral judgment (**Dickens**, 1812-70; **Eliot**, 1819-80; **Tolstoy**, 1828-1910; **Balzac**, 1799-1850).

Veneer of Stability: 1880-1900

Imperialism triumphant. The vast **African** interior, visited by European explorers (Barth, 1821-65; Livingstone, 1813-73), was conquered by the European powers in rapid, competitive thrusts from their coastal bases after 1880, mostly for domestic political and international strategic reasons. W African Muslim kingdoms (Fulani), Arab slave traders (Zanzibar), and Bantu military confederations (Zulu) were alike subdued. Only Christian Ethiopia (defeat of Italy, 1896) and Liberia resisted successfully. France (W Africa) and Britain ("Cape to Cairo," **Boer War**, 1899-1902) were the major beneficiaries. The ideology of "the white man's burden" (Kipling, *Barrack Room Ballads*, 1892) justified the conquests, which in fact reflected Europe's weapons superiority.

W European foreign capital investment soared to nearly $40 billion by 1914, but most was in E Europe (France, Germany), the Americas (Britain), and Europe's colonies. The foundation of the modern interdependent world economy was laid, with cartels dominating raw material trade. Global developments included a new agreement on international patents (1883), the modern Olympics (1896), and the worldwide spread of department stores.

An industrious world. Industrial and technological proficiency characterized the two new great powers—Germany and the U.S. Coal and iron deposits enabled Germany to reach second- or third-place status in iron, steel, and shipbuilding by the 1900s. German electrical and chemical industries were world leaders. The U.S. post-Civil War boom (interrupted by financial panics—1873, 1884, and 1893) was shaped by massive immigration from S and E Europe from 1880, government subsidy of railroads, and huge private monopolies (Standard Oil, 1870; U.S. Steel, 1901). The **Spanish-American War**, 1898 (Philippine Insurrection, 1899-1902), and the **Open Door policy** in China (1899) made the U.S. a world power.

England led in **urbanization**, with London the world capital of finance, insurance, and shipping. Sewer systems (Paris, 1850s), electric subways (London, 1890), parks, and bargain department stores helped improve living standards for most of the urban population of the industrial world. Birthrates declined in the West while infant mortality rates plunged (demographic transition, 1880-1920).

Upheavals in Asia. Asian reaction to European economic, military, and religious incursions took the form of imitation of Western techniques and adoption of Western ideas of progress and freedom. The Chinese "self-strengthening" movement of the 1860s and 1870s included rail, port, and arsenal improvements and metal and textile mills. Reformers such as **K'ang** Yu-wei (1858-1927) won liberalizing reforms

in 1898, right after the European and Japanese "scramble for concessions."

A universal education system in Japan and importation of foreign industrial, scientific, and military experts aided Japan's rapid modernization after 1868 under the authoritarian Meiji regime. Japan's victory in the **Sino-Japanese War** (1894-95) put Formosa and Korea in its power. Industrialization began in earnest by 1890.

In India, the British alliance with the remaining princely states masked reform sentiment among the Westernized urban elite; higher education had been conducted largely in English for 50 years. The **Indian National Congress**, founded in 1885, demanded a larger government role for Indians.

Fin-de-siècle **sophistication.** **Naturalist** writers pushed realism to its extreme limits, adopting a quasi-scientific attitude and writing about formerly taboo subjects such as sex, crime, extreme poverty, and corruption (Flaubert, 1821-80; Zola, 1840-1902; Hardy, 1840-1928). Unseen or repressed psychological motivations were explored in the clinical and theoretical works of Sigmund **Freud** (1856-1939) and in works of fiction (**Dostoyevsky**, 1821-81; Henry James, 1843-1916; Schnitzler, 1862-1931).

A contempt for bourgeois life or a desire to shock a complacent audience was shared by the French **symbolist** poets (Verlaine, 1844-96; Rimbaud, 1854-91), by neopagan English writers (Swinburne, 1837-1909), by continental dramatists (**Ibsen**, 1828-1906), and by satirists (**Wilde**, 1854-1900). The German philosopher Friedrich **Nietzsche** (1844-1900) was influential in his elitism and pessimism.

Postimpressionist art neglected long-cherished conventions of representation (**Cézanne**, 1839-1906) and showed a willingness to learn from primitive and non-European art (**Gauguin**, 1848-1903; Japanese prints).

Racism. Gobineau (1816-82) gave a pseudobiological foundation to modern racist theories, which spread in Europe in the latter 19th cent., along with **Social Darwinism**, the belief that societies are and should be organized as a struggle for survival of the fittest. The medieval period was interpreted as an era of natural Germanic rule (Chamberlain, 1855-1927), and notions of racial superiority were associated with German national aspirations (Treitschke, 1834-96). **Anti-Semitism**, with a new racist rationale, became a significant political force in Germany (Anti-Semitic Petition, 1880), Austria (Lueger, 1844-1910), and France (**Dreyfus affair**, 1894-1906).

Imperialism's High Point: 1900-09

Alliances. While the peace of Europe (and its dependencies) continued to hold (1907 **Hague Conference** extended the rules of war and international arbitration procedures), imperial rivalries, protectionist trade practices (in Germany and France), and the escalating arms race (British *Dreadnought* battleship launched; Germany widens Kiel canal, 1906) exacerbated minor disputes (German-French Moroccan "crises," 1905, 1911).

Security was sought through balance-of-power alliances: **Triple Alliance** (Germany, Austria-Hungary, Italy; renewed in 1902 and 1907); Anglo-Japanese Alliance (1902), Franco-Russian Alliance (1899), **Entente Cordiale** (Britain, France, 1904), Anglo-Russian Treaty (1907), German-Ottoman friendship. Global developments included the establishment of an international court in The Hague, the first transatlantic radio transmission (1901), and the creation of the first international association for European football (1904).

Ottomans decline. The Ottoman government was unable to resist further loss of territory, and earlier reform efforts gave way to greater authoritarianism. Nearly all European lands were lost in 1912 to Serbia, Greece, Montenegro, and Bulgaria. Italy took Libya and the Dodecanese islands the same year. Britain took Kuwait (1899) and the Sinai (1906). The **Young Turk** revolution in 1908 forced the sultan to restore a constitution, and it introduced some social reform and secularization.

British Empire. British trade and cultural influence remained dominant in the empire, but constitutional reforms presaged its eventual dissolution. The colonies of **Australia** were united in 1901 under a self-governing commonwealth. **New Zealand** acquired dominion status in 1907. The old Boer republics joined Cape Colony and Natal in the self-governing Union of **South Africa** in 1910.

The 1909 Indian Councils Act enhanced the role of elected province legislatures in **India**. The Muslim League (founded 1906) sought separate communal representation.

East Asia. Japan exploited its growing industrial power to expand its empire. Victory in the 1904-05 war against Russia (naval battle of Tsushima, 1905) assured Japan's domination of **Korea** (annexed 1910) and Manchuria (Port Arthur taken, 1905).

In China, central authority began to crumble (empress died, 1908). Reforms (Confucian exam system ended 1905, modernization of the army, building of railroads) were inadequate, and secret societies of reformers and nationalists, inspired by the Westernized **Sun** Yat-sen (1866-1925), fomented periodic uprisings in the S.

Siam, whose independence had been guaranteed by Britain and France in 1896, was split into spheres of influence by those countries in 1907.

Russia. The population of the Russian Empire approached 150 million in 1900. Reforms in education, in law, and in local institutions (*zemstvos*) and an industrial boom starting in the 1880s (oil, railroads) created the beginnings of a modern society, despite the autocratic tsarist regime. Liberals (1903 Union of Liberation), Socialists (Social Democrats founded 1898, Bolsheviks split off 1903), and populists (Social Revolutionaries founded 1901) were periodically repressed, and national minorities were persecuted (anti-Jewish pogroms, 1903, 1905-06).

An industrial crisis after 1900 and harvest failures aggravated poverty among urban workers, and the 1904-05 defeat by Japan (which checked Russia's Asian expansion) sparked the **Revolution of 1905-06**. A **Duma** (parliament) was created under Tsar Nicholas II. Agricultural reform (under Stolypin, prime minister, 1906-11) created a large class of land-owning peasants (*kulaks*).

The world shrinks. Developments in transportation and communication and mass population movements helped create an awareness of an interdependent world. Early **automobiles** (Daimler, Benz, 1885) were experimental or were designed as luxuries. Assembly-line mass production (Ford Motor Co., 1903) made the invention practical, and by 1910 nearly 500,000 motor vehicles were registered in the U.S. alone. **Heavier-than-air flights** began in 1903 in the U.S. (Wright brothers' *Flyer*), preceded by glider, balloon, and model plane advances in several countries. Trade was advanced by improvements in **ship design** (gyrocompass, 1910), speed (*Lusitania* crossed Atlantic in five days, 1907), and reach (Panama Canal begun, 1904).

The first transatlantic **radio** telegraphic transmission occurred in 1901, six years after Marconi discovered radio. Radio transmission of human speech had been made in 1900. Telegraphic transmission of photos was achieved in 1904, lending immediacy to news reports. **Phonographs**, popularized by Caruso's recordings (starting 1902), made for quick international spread of musical styles (ragtime). **Motion pictures**, perfected in the 1890s (Dickson, Lumière brothers), became a popular and artistic medium after 1900; newsreels appeared in 1909.

Emigration from densely populated European countries to the Americas soared in the early 20th century; many landed on Ellis Island, in New York Harbor, en route to U.S. cities.

Emigration from crowded European centers soared in the decade: 9 million migrated to the U.S., and millions more went to Siberia, Canada, Argentina, Australia, South Africa, and Algeria. Some 70 million Europeans emigrated in the century before 1914. Several million Chinese, Indians, and Japanese migrated to SE Asia, where their urban skills often enabled them to take a predominant economic role.

Social reform. The social and economic problems of the poor were kept in the public eye by realist fiction writers (Dreiser's *Sister Carrie*, 1900; Gorky's *Lower Depths*, 1902; Sinclair's *The Jungle*, 1906), journalists (U.S. **muckrakers**—Steffens, Tarbell), and artists (Ashcan school). Frequent labor strikes and occasional assassinations by anarchists or radicals (Empress Elizabeth of Austria, 1898; King Umberto I of Italy, 1900; U.S. Pres. McKinley, 1901; Russian Interior Min. Plehve, 1904; Portugal's King Carlos, 1908) added to social tension and fear of revolution. Feminist agitators for the vote surfaced in several countries.

But democratic reformism responded in part. In Germany, Bernstein's (1850-1932) **revisionist Marxism**, downgrading revolution, was accepted by the powerful Social Democrats and trade unions. The British Fabian Society (the Webbs, Shaw) and the Labour Party (founded 1906) worked for reforms such as social security and union rights (1906), while woman suffragists grew more militant. U.S. **progressives** fought big business (Pure Food and Drug Act, 1906). In France, the 10-hour workday (1904) and separation of church and state (1905) were reform victories, as was universal suffrage in Austria (1907).

Arts. An unprecedented period of experimentation, centered in France, produced several new **painting styles**: Fauvism exploited bold color areas (Matisse, *Woman With Hat*, 1905); expressionism reflected powerful inner emotions (Brücke group, 1905); Cubism combined several views of an object on one flat surface (Picasso, *Demoiselles*, 1906-07); futurism tried to depict speed and motion (Italian Futurist Manifesto, 1910). **Architects** explored new uses of steel structures, with facades either neoclassical (Adler and Sullivan in U.S.), curvilinear Art Nouveau (Gaudi's Casa Mila, 1905-10), or functionally streamlined (Wright's Robie House, 1909).

Music and dance shared the experimental spirit. Ruth St. Denis (1877-1968) and Isadora Duncan (1878-1927) pioneered modern dance, while Sergei Diaghilev in Paris revitalized classic ballet from 1909. Composers explored atonal music (Debussy, 1862-1918) and dissonance (Schoenberg, 1874-1951) or revolutionized classical forms (Stravinsky, 1882-1971), often showing jazz or folk music influences.

War and Revolution: 1910-19

War threatens. Germany under Wilhelm II sought a political and imperial role consonant with its industrial strength, challenging Britain's world supremacy and threatening France, which was still resenting the loss (1871) of Alsace-Lorraine. Austria wanted to curb an expanded Serbia (after 1912) and the threat it posed to its own Slav lands. Russia feared Austrian and German political and economic aims in the Balkans and Turkey.

An accelerated arms race resulted from these circumstances. The German standing army rose to more than 2 million men

by 1914. Russia and France had more than a million each, and Austria and the British Empire nearly a million each. Dozens of enormous battleships were built by the powers after 1906.

The **assassination of Austrian Archduke Franz Ferdinand** by a Serbian nationalist, June 28, 1914, was the trigger for war. The system of alliances made the conflict Europe-wide; Germany's invasion of Belgium to outflank France forced Britain to enter the war. Patriotic fervor was nearly unanimous among all classes in most countries.

Both sides in World War I developed elaborate networks of dug-in trenches from which to fight.

World War I. German forces were stopped in France in one month. The rival armies dug **trench networks**. Artillery and improved machine guns prevented either side from any lasting advance despite repeated assaults (600,000 dead at **Verdun**, Feb.-July 1916). German deployment of poisonous chlorine gas (Ypres, 1915) was first major use of lethal **chemical weapons**. The entrance of more than 1 million U.S. troops tipped the balance after mid-1917, forcing Germany to sue for peace the next year. The formal armistice was signed on Nov. 11, 1918, and the German emperor abdicated.

In the E, the Russian armies were thrown back (battle of **Tannenberg**, Aug. 20, 1914), and the war grew unpopular in Russia. An allied attempt to relieve Russia through Turkey failed (**Gallipoli**, 1915). The **Russian Revolution** (1917) abolished the monarchy. The new Bolshevik regime signed the capitulatory Brest-Litovsk peace in Mar. 1918. Italy entered the war on the allied side in May 1915 but was pushed back by Oct. 1917. A renewed offensive with Allied aid in Oct.-Nov. 1918 forced Austria to surrender.

The British Navy successfully blockaded Germany, which responded with submarine U-boat attacks; **unrestricted submarine warfare** against neutrals after Jan. 1917 helped bring the U.S. into the war. Other battlefields included Palestine and Mesopotamia, both of which Britain wrested from the Turks in 1917, and the African and Pacific colonies of Germany, most of which fell to Britain, France, Australia, Japan, and South Africa.

Settlement. At the **Paris Peace Conference** (Jan.-June 1919), concluded by the **Treaty of Versailles**, and in subsequent negotiations and local wars (Russian-Polish War, 1920), the **map of Europe** was redrawn with a nod to U.S. Pres. Woodrow Wilson's principle of self-determination. Austria and Hungary were separated, and much of their land was given to Yugoslavia (formerly Serbia), Romania, Italy, and the newly independent Poland and Czechoslovakia. Germany lost territory in the W, N, and E, while Finland and the Baltic states were detached from Russia. The Ottoman Empire ended (1922) and most of its Arab lands went to British-sponsored Arab states or to direct French and British rule. Belgium's sovereignty was recognized.

From 1916, the civilian populations and economies of both sides were mobilized to an unprecedented degree. Hardships intensified among fighting nations in 1917 (French mutiny crushed in May). More than 10 million soldiers died in the war.

A huge **reparations** burden and partial demilitarization were imposed on Germany. Pres. Wilson proposed a League of Nations, but the U.S. Senate voted against U.S. involvement.

Russian revolution. Military defeats and high casualties caused a contagious lack of confidence in Tsar Nicholas, who was forced to abdicate Mar. 1917. A liberal provisional government failed to end the war, and massive desertions, riots, and fighting between factions followed. A moderate socialist government under Aleksandr Kerensky was overthrown (Nov. 1917) in a violent coup by the **Bolsheviks** in Petrograd under **Lenin**, who later disbanded the elected Constituent Assembly.

The Bolsheviks brutally suppressed all opposition and ended the war with Germany in Mar. 1918. **Civil war** broke out in the summer between the Red Army (the Bolsheviks and their supporters), and monarchists, anarchists, minority nationalities (Ukrainians, Georgians, Poles), and others. Small U.S., British, French, and Japanese units also opposed the Bolsheviks (1918-19; Japan in Vladivostok to 1922). The civil war, anarchy, and pogroms devastated the country until the 1920 Red Army victory. The **Communist Party** leadership retained absolute power.

Other European revolutions. An unpopular monarchy in **Portugal** was overthrown in 1910. The new republic took severe anticlerical measures in 1911.

After a century of Home Rule agitation, during which **Ireland** was devastated by famine (1 million dead, 1846-47) and emigration, republican militants staged an unsuccessful uprising in Dublin during **Easter 1916**. The execution of the leaders and mass arrests by the British won popular support for the rebels. The **Irish Free State**, comprising all but the six northern counties, achieved dominion status in 1922.

In the aftermath of the world war, radical revolutions were attempted in Germany (**Spartacist** uprising, Jan. 1919), **Hungary** (Kun regime, 1919), and elsewhere. All were suppressed or failed for lack of support.

Chinese revolution. The Qinq, or Manchu, Dynasty was overthrown and a republic proclaimed, 1911-12. Revolutionary leader Sun Yat-sen, who organized the nationalist **Kuomintang** party and led a provisional republican government in Nanjing, resigned in a unification compromise with former imperial viceroy Yuan Shikai. Yuan became president upon the abdication of the emperor in Feb. 1912.

Students launched protests on May 4, 1919, against League of Nations concessions in China to Japan. Nationalist, liberal, and socialist ideas and political groups spread. The **Chinese Communist Party** was founded in 1921. A Communist regime took power in Mongolia with Soviet support in 1921.

India restive. Indian objections to British rule erupted in nationalist riots as well as in the nonviolent tactics of Mahatma **Gandhi** (1869-1948). Nearly 400 unarmed demonstrators were shot at **Amritsar** in Apr. 1919. Britain approved limited self-rule that year.

Mexican revolution. Under the long Díaz dictatorship (1877-1911) the economy advanced, but Indian and mestizo lands were confiscated, and concessions to foreigners (mostly U.S.) damaged the middle class. A revolution in 1910 led to civil wars and U.S. intervention (1914, 1916-17). Land reform and a more democratic constitution (1917) were achieved.

Sciences. Scientific specialization prevailed by the 20th cent. Advances in knowledge and technological aptitude increased with the geometric rise in the number of practitioners. Physicists challenged common-sense views of causality, observation, and a mechanistic universe, putting science further beyond popular grasp (**Einstein**'s general theory of relativity, 1915-16; Bohr's quantum mechanics, 1913; Heisenberg's uncertainty principle, 1927).

Aftermath of War: 1920-29

U.S. Easy credit, technological ingenuity, and war-related industrial decline in Europe caused a long economic boom, in which ownership of new products—**autos**, **phones**, **radios**—became more democratized. **Prosperity**, an increase in women workers, women's suffrage (19th Amendment ratified, 1920), and drastic change in fashion (**flappers**, mannish bob for women, clean-shaven men) created a wide perception of social change despite prohibition of alcoholic beverages (1919-33). Union membership and strikes increased. Fear of

radicals led to Palmer raids (1919-20) and the Sacco-Vanzetti case (1921-27).

Europe sorts itself out. Germany's liberal **Weimar constitution** (1919) could not guarantee a stable government in the face of rightist violence (Foreign Min. Rathenau assassinated, 1922) and Communist refusal to cooperate with Socialists. Reparations and Allied occupation of the Rhineland caused staggering inflation that destroyed middle-class savings, but economic expansion resumed after mid-decade, aided by U.S. loans. A sophisticated, **innovative culture** developed in architecture and design (Bauhaus, 1919-28), film (Lang, *M*, 1931), painting (Grosz), music (Weill, *Threepenny Opera*, 1928), theater (Brecht, *A Man's a Man*, 1926), criticism (Benjamin), philosophy (Jung), and fashion. This culture was considered decadent and socially disruptive by rightists.

England elected its first Labour governments (Jan. 1924, June 1929). A 10-day general strike in support of coal miners failed in May 1926. In **Italy**, strikes, political chaos, and violence by small Fascist bands culminated in the Oct. 1922 Fascist March on Rome, which established **Mussolini**'s dictatorship. Strikes were outlawed (1926), and Italian influence was pressed in the Balkans (Albania made a protectorate, 1926). A conservative dictatorship was also established in **Portugal** in a 1926 military coup.

Czechoslovakia, the only stable democracy to emerge from the war in Central or E Europe, faced opposition from Germans (in the Sudetenland), Ruthenians, and some Slovaks. As the industrial heartland of the old Habsburg empire, it remained fairly prosperous. With French backing, it formed the Little Entente with Yugoslavia (1920) and **Romania** (1921) to block Austrian or Hungarian irredentism. Croats and Slovenes in **Yugoslavia** demanded a federal state until King Alexander I proclaimed (1929) a royal dictatorship. Poland faced internal nationality problems as well (Germans, Ukrainians, Jews); Pilsudski ruled as dictator from 1926. The Baltic states were threatened by traditionally dominant ethnic Germans and by Soviet-supported Communists.

An economic collapse and famine in **Russia** (1921-22) claimed 5 million lives. The New Economic Policy (1921) allowed land ownership by peasants and some private commerce and industry. **Stalin** was absolute ruler within four years of Lenin's death (1924). He inaugurated a brutal collectivization program (1929-32) and used foreign Communist parties for Soviet state advantage. Industrialization advanced rapidly.

Internationalism. Revulsion against World War I led to pacifist agitation, to the Kellogg-Briand Pact renouncing aggressive war (1928), and to **naval disarmament** pacts (Washington, 1922; London, 1930). But the League of Nations was able to arbitrate only minor disputes (Greece-Bulgaria, 1925). A number of countries pulled back from global contacts, as with American isolationism and Russia's separation from international capitalism.

Middle East. Mustafa Kemal (**Ataturk**) led **Turkish** nationalists in resisting Italian, French, and Greek military advances (1919-23). The sultanate was abolished (1922), and elaborate reforms were passed, including secularization of law and adoption of the Latin alphabet. Ethnic conflict led to persecution of **Armenians** (more than 1 million dead in 1915, 1 million expelled), Greeks (forced Greek-Turk population exchange, 1923), and Kurds (1925 uprising).

With evacuation of the Turks from **Arab** lands, the puritanical Wahabi dynasty of E Arabia conquered (1919-25) what is now Saudi Arabia. British, French, and Arab dynastic and nationalist maneuvering resulted in the creation of two more Arab monarchies in 1921—Iraq and Transjordan (both under British control)—and two French mandates—Syria and Lebanon. Jewish immigration into British-mandated **Palestine**, inspired by the Zionist movement, was resisted by Arabs, at times violently (1921, 1929 riots).

Reza Khan ruled **Persia** after his 1921 coup (shah from 1925), centralized control, and created the trappings of a modern secular state.

In 1922, English archaeologist Howard Carter discovered the tomb of the boy pharaoh **Tutankhamun** in the Valley of the Kings in Egypt.

China. The Kuomintang under **Chiang Kai-shek** (1887-1975) subdued the warlords by 1928. The Communists were brutally suppressed after their alliance with the Kuomintang was broken in 1927. Relative peace thereafter allowed for industrial and financial improvements, with some Russian, British, and U.S. cooperation.

Arts. Nearly all bounds of subject matter, style, and attitude were broken in the arts of the period. **Abstract** art first took inspiration from natural forms or narrative themes (Kandinsky from 1911) and then worked free of any representational aims (Malevich's suprematism, 1915-19; Mondrian's geometric style from 1917). The **Dada** movement (from 1916) mocked artistic pretension with absurd collages and constructions. Paradox, illusion, and psychological taboos were exploited by **surrealists** by the late 1920s (Dali, Magritte). Architectural schools celebrated industrial values, whether vigorous abstract constructivism (Tatlin, *Monument to the Third International*, 1919) or the machined, streamlined **Bauhaus** style, which was extended to many design fields (Helvetica typeface).

Prose writers explored revolutionary narrative modes related to dreams (Kafka's *Trial*, 1925), internal monologue (Joyce's *Ulysses*, 1922), and word play (Stein's *Making of Americans*, 1925). Poets and novelists wrote of modern alienation (Eliot's *Waste Land*, 1922) and aimlessness ("The Lost Generation").

Rise of Totalitarians: 1930-39

Depression. A worldwide financial panic and economic depression began with the Oct. 1929 U.S. stock market crash and the May 1931 failure of the Austrian Credit-Anstalt. A credit crunch caused international bankruptcies and **unemployment**: 12 million jobless by 1932 in the U.S., 5.6 million in Germany, 2.7 million in England. Governments responded with **tariff restrictions** (Smoot-Hawley Act, 1930; Ottawa Imperial Conference, 1932), which dried up world trade. Government public works programs were vitiated by deflationary budget balancing.

Germany. As **Nazi Party** leader, **Adolf Hitler** built up a mass movement (feeding on economic hardship, ideas of racial superiority, fear of leftist influence). With a plurality in the Reichstag, he pursuaded Pres. **Hindenburg** to name him chancellor (Jan. 1933); Hindenburg further granted him emergency powers after the Reichstag fire in Feb. Other parties and most forms of opposition, including strikes, were banned, and the media and most aspects of life fell under Nazi control. Severe persecution of Jews began (**Nuremberg Laws**, Sept. 1935). Many Jews, political opponents, and others were sent to concentration camps (Dachau, 1933), where thousands died or were killed. Public works, renewed conscription (1935), arms production, and a four-year plan (1936) all but ended unemployment.

Hitler's expansionism started with reincorporation of the Saar (1935), occupation of the **Rhineland** (Mar. 1936), and annexation of Austria (Mar. 1938). At **Munich** (Sept. 1938) Britain and France attempted to appease Hitler and avoid war by successfully encouraging Czechoslovakia's surrender of the Sudetenland territory.

Russia. Rapid industrialization was achieved through successive **five-year plans** starting in 1928, using severe labor discipline and mass forced labor. Industry was financed by exploitation of agriculture, which was almost totally collectivized by the early 1930s. Millions perished in a series of manufactured disasters: extermination (1929-34) of kulaks (peasant landowners), severe famine (1932-33), party purges and show trials (Great Purge, 1936-38), suppression of nationalities, and poor conditions in labor camps. Purges also increased Stalin's power in the Communist party.

Spain. An industrial revolution during World War I created an urban proletariat, which was attracted to socialism and anarchism; Catalan nationalists challenged central authority. The five years after King Alfonso left Spain in Apr. 1931 were dominated by tension between intermittent leftist and anticlerical governments and clericals, monarchists, and other rightists. Anarchist and Communist rebellions were crushed, but a July 1936 extreme right rebellion led by Gen. Francisco **Franco** and aided by Nazi Germany and Fascist Italy succeeded after a three-year **civil war** (more than 1 million dead in battles and atrocities). The war polarized international public opinion.

Italy. Despite propaganda for the ideal of the Corporate State, few domestic reforms were attempted. An entente with Hungary and Austria (Mar. 1934), a pact with Germany and Japan (Nov. 1937), and intervention by 50,000-75,000 troops in Spain (1936-39) sealed Italy's identification with the fascist bloc (anti-Semitic laws after Mar. 1938). Ethiopia was conquered (1935-36) and Albania annexed (Jan. 1939) in conscious imitation of ancient Rome.

Eastern Europe. Repressive regimes fought for power against an active opposition (liberals, socialists, Communists, peasants, Nazis). Minority groups and Jews were restricted within national boundaries that did not coincide with ethnic population patterns. In the destruction of **Czechoslovakia**, Hungary occupied S Slovakia (Nov. 1938) and Ruthenia (Mar. 1939), and a pro-Nazi regime took power in the rest of Slovakia. Other boundary disputes (e.g., Poland-Lithuania, Yugoslavia-Bulgaria, and Romania-Hungary) doomed attempts to build joint fronts against Germany or Russia. Economic depression was severe.

East Asia. After a period of liberalism in **Japan**, nativist militarists dominated the government with peasant support. Manchuria was seized (Sept. 1931-Feb. 1932), and a puppet state was set up (Manchukuo). Adjacent Jehol (Inner Mongolia) was occupied in 1933. **China** proper was invaded in July 1937; large areas were conquered by Oct. 1938. Hundreds of thousands of rapes, murders, and other atrocities were attributed to the Japanese.

Communist forces left Kuomintang-besieged strongholds in the S of China in a Long March (1934-35) to the N. The Kuomintang-Communist civil war was suspended in Jan. 1937 in the face of threatening Japan.

Democracies. The Franklin Roosevelt administration, in office Mar. 1933, embarked on an extensive program of **New Deal** social reform and economic stimulation, including protection for labor unions (heavy industries organized), Social Security, public works, wage-and-hour laws, and assistance to farmers. Isolationist sentiment (1937 Neutrality Act) prevented U.S. intervention in Europe, but military expenditures were increased in 1939.

French political instability and polarization prevented resolution of economic and international security questions. The Popular Front government under Léon Blum (June 1936-Apr. 1938) passed social reforms (40-hour work week) and raised arms spending. National coalition governments, which ruled Britain from Aug. 1931, brought economic recovery but failed to define a consistent international policy until Chamberlain's government (from May 1937), which practiced **appeasement** of Germany and Italy.

India. Twenty years of agitation for autonomy and then for independence (Gandhi's **salt march**, 1930) achieved some constitutional reform (extended provincial powers, 1935) despite Muslim-Hindu strife. Social issues assumed prominence with peasant uprisings (1921), strikes (1928), Gandhi's efforts for untouchables (1932 "fast unto death"), and social and agrarian reform by the provinces after 1937.

Arts. The streamlined, geometric design motifs of Art Deco (from 1925) prevailed through the 1930s. **Abstract art** flourished (Moore sculptures from 1931) alongside a new **realism** related to social and political concerns (Socialist Realism, the official Soviet style from 1934; Mexican muralist Rivera, 1886-1957; Orozco, 1883-1949), which were also expressed in fiction and poetry (Steinbeck's *Grapes of Wrath*, 1939; Sandburg's *The People, Yes*, 1936). Modern architecture (International Style, 1932) was unchallenged in its use of artificial materials (concrete, glass), lack of decoration, and monumentality (Rockefeller Center, 1929-40). Larger-than-life U.S.-made films captured a worldwide audience (*Gone With the Wind, The Wizard of Oz*, both 1939).

War, Hot and Cold: 1940-49

War in Asia-Pacific. Japan occupied Indochina in Sept. 1940, dominated Thailand in Dec. 1941, and attacked Hawaii (**Pearl Harbor**), the Philippines, Hong Kong, and Malaya on Dec. 7, 1941 (precipitating U.S. entrance into the war). Indonesia was attacked in Jan. 1942, and Burma was conquered in Mar. 1942. The Battle of **Midway** (June 1942) turned back the Japanese advance. "Island-hopping" battles (**Guadalcanal**, Aug. 1942-Jan. 1943; **Leyte Gulf**, Oct. 1944; **Iwo Jima**, Feb.-Mar. 1945; **Okinawa**, Apr. 1945) and massive bombing raids on Japan from June 1944 wore out Japanese defenses. U.S. atom bombs, dropped Aug. 6 and 9 on **Hiroshima** and **Nagasaki**, forced Japan to agree, on Aug. 14, to surrender; formal surrender was on Sept. 2, 1945.

War in Europe. The **Nazi-Soviet nonaggression** pact (Aug. 1939) freed Germany to attack Poland (Sept. 1939). Britain and France, which had guaranteed Polish independence, declared war on Germany. Russia seized E Poland (Sept. 1939),

The U.S. bombing of Hiroshima and Nagasaki, Japan, in 1945 demonstrated the deadly, destructive power of atomic weapons.

attacked Finland (Nov. 1939), and took the Baltic states (July 1940). Mobile German forces staged *blitzkrieg* attacks during Apr.-June 1940, conquering neutral Belgium, Denmark, Luxembourg, Netherlands, and Norway and defeating France; 350,000 British and French troops were evacuated at **Dunkirk**, France (May). The **Battle of Britain** (June-Dec. 1940) denied Germany air superiority. German-Italian campaigns won the Balkans by Apr. 1941. Three million Axis troops **invaded Russia** in June 1941, marching through Ukraine to the Caucasus, and through White Russia and the Baltic republics to Moscow and Leningrad.

Russian winter counterthrusts (1941-42 and 1942-43) stopped the German advance (**Stalingrad**, Sept. 1942-Feb. 1943). Sustaining great casualties, the Russians drove the Axis from all E Europe and the Balkans in the next two years. Invasions of N Africa (Nov. 1942), Italy (Sept. 1943), and **Normandy** (launched on D-Day, June 6, 1944) brought U.S., British, Free French, and allied troops to Germany by spring 1945. In Feb. 1945, the three Allied leaders, Winston **Churchill** (Britain), Joseph **Stalin** (USSR), and Franklin D. **Roosevelt** (U.S.), met in **Yalta** to discuss strategy and resolve political issues, including the postwar Allied occupation of Germany. Germany surrendered May 7, 1945.

Atrocities. The war brought 20th-cent. cruelty to its peak. The Nazi regime systematically killed an estimated 5-6 million Jews, including some 3 million who died in death camps (e.g., **Auschwitz**). The Nazis also killed Roma (also known as Gypsies), political opponents, people with mental or physical disabilities, homosexuals, others deemed undesirable, and vast numbers of Slavs.

German bombs killed 70,000 British civilians. More than 100,000 Chinese civilians were killed by Japanese forces in the capture and occupation of Nanking. Severe retaliation by the Soviet army, E European partisans, Free French, and others took a heavy toll. U.S. and British bombing of Germany killed hundreds of thousands, as did U.S. bombing of Japan (80,000-200,000 at Hiroshima alone). Some 45 million people died in the war.

Settlement. The **United Nations** charter was signed in San Francisco on June 26, 1945, by 50 nations. The International Tribunal at **Nuremberg** convicted 22 German leaders for war crimes in Sept. 1946; 23 Japanese leaders were convicted in Nov. 1948. Postwar border changes included large gains in territory for the USSR, losses for Germany, a shift to the W in Polish borders, and minor losses for Italy. Communist regimes, supported by Soviet troops, took power in most of Eastern Europe, including Soviet-occupied Germany (GDR, a.k.a. East Germany, proclaimed Oct. 1949). Japan lost all overseas lands. Global developments involved establishing new economic coordinating bodies like the International Monetary Fund (1944) and the Universal Declaration of Human Rights (1948).

Recovery. Basic political and social changes were imposed on Japan and W Germany by the Western allies (Japan constitution adopted, Nov. 1946; W German basic law, May 1949). U.S. **Marshall Plan** aid ($12 billion, 1947-51) spurred W European economic recovery after a period of severe inflation and strikes in Europe and the U.S. The British Labour Party introduced a national health service and nationalized basic industries in 1946.

Cold War. Western fears of further Soviet advances (Cominform formed in Oct. 1947; Czechoslovakia coup, Feb. 1948; Berlin blockade, Apr. 1948-Sept. 1949) led to the formation of **NATO**. Civil war in Greece and Soviet pressure on Turkey led to U.S. aid under the **Truman Doctrine** (Mar. 1947). Other anti-Communist security pacts were the Organization of American States (Apr. 1948) and the SE Asia Treaty Organization (Sept. 1954). A new wave of **Soviet purges** and repression intensified in the last years of Stalin's rule, extending to E Europe (Slansky trial in Czechoslovakia, 1951). Only Yugoslavia resisted Soviet control (expelled by Cominform, June 1948; U.S. aid, June 1949).

China, Korea. Communist forces emerged from World War II strengthened by the Soviet takeover of industrial Manchuria. In four years of fighting, the Kuomintang was driven from the mainland; the People's Republic of China was proclaimed Oct. 1, 1949. Korea was divided by USSR and U.S. occupation forces. Separate republics were proclaimed in the two zones in Aug.-Sept. 1948.

India. India and Pakistan became independent dominions on Aug. 15, 1947. Millions of Hindu and Muslim refugees were created by the partition. Riots (1946-47) took hundreds of thousands of lives. Mahatma **Gandhi** was assassinated in Jan. 1948. Burma became completely independent in Jan. 1948; Ceylon (later Sri Lanka) took dominion status in Feb.

Middle East. The UN approved partition of Palestine into Jewish and Arab states. **Israel** was proclaimed a state, May 14, 1948. Arabs rejected partition, but failed to defeat Israel in war (May 1948-July 1949). Immigration from Europe and the Middle East swelled Israel's Jewish population. British and French forces left Lebanon and Syria in 1946. Transjordan occupied most of Arab Palestine.

Southeast Asia. Communists and others fought against restoration of French rule in **Indochina** from 1946; a non-Communist government was recognized by France in Mar. 1949, but fighting continued. Both Indonesia and the Philippines became independent; the former in 1949 after four years of war with the Netherlands, the latter in 1946. Philippine economic and military ties with the U.S. remained strong; a Communist-led peasant rising was checked in 1948.

Arts. New York City became the center of the world art market; **abstract expressionism** was the chief mode (Pollock from 1943, de Kooning from 1947). Literature and philosophy explored **existentialism** (Camus's *The Stranger*, 1942; Sartre's *Being and Nothingness*, 1943). Non-Western attempts to revive or create regional styles (Senghor's Négritude, Mishima's novels) were responses to global cultural influences. Radio and phonograph records spread American popular music (swing, bebop) around the world.

The Cold War Decade: 1950-59

Decolonization. The relatively peaceful decline of European political and military power in Asia and Africa accelerated in the 1950s. Nearly all of **N Africa** was freed by 1956, but France fought bitterly to retain Algeria, with its large European minority, until 1962. **Ghana**, independent in 1957, led a parade of new black African nations (more than two dozen by 1962), which altered the political character of the UN. Ethnic disputes often exploded in the new nations after decolonization (UN troops in Cyprus, 1964; **Nigerian civil war**, 1967-70). Leaders of the new states, mostly sharing socialist ideologies, tried to create an Afro-Asian bloc (Bandung Conference, 1955), but Western economic influence and U.S. political ties remained strong (Baghdad Pact, 1955).

Trade. World trade volume soared, in an atmosphere of monetary stability assured by international accords (**Bretton Woods**, 1944). In Europe, economic integration advanced (**European Economic Community**, 1957; European Free Trade Association, 1960). Comecon (1949) coordinated the economies of Soviet-bloc countries. Global developments included transcontinental jet travel (first South Africa to Britain flight, 1952; introduction of term "jet lag," 1965) and the increasing spread of English in global business, sports, and transportation.

U.S. Economic growth produced an abundance of consumer goods (9.3 million motor vehicles sold, 1955). Suburban housing changed life patterns for middle and working classes (Levittown, NY, 1947-51). Pres. Dwight **Eisenhower**'s landslide election victories (1952, 1956) reflected consensus politics. A system of alliances and military bases bolstered U.S. influence on all continents. Trade and payments surpluses were balanced by overseas investments and foreign aid ($50 billion, 1950-59).

USSR. In the "thaw" after Stalin's death in 1953, relations with the West improved (evacuation of Vienna, Geneva summit conference, both 1955). Repression of scientific and cultural life eased, and many prisoners were freed culminating in **de-Stalinization** (1956). Nikita **Khrushchev**'s leadership aimed at consumer sector growth, but farm production lagged, despite the virgin lands program (from 1954). Soviet crushing of the 1956 Hungarian revolution, the 1960 U-2 spy plane episode, and other incidents renewed E-W tension and domestic curbs.

Eastern Europe. Resentment of Russian domination and Stalinist repression combined with nationalist, economic, and religious factors to produce periodic violence. E Berlin workers rioted (1953), Polish workers rioted in Poznan (June 1956), and a broad-based **revolution** broke out in **Hungary** (Oct. 1956). All were suppressed by Soviet force or threats (at least 7,000 dead in Hungary), but Poland was allowed to restore private ownership of farms, and a degree of personal and economic freedom returned to Hungary. Yugoslavia experimented with worker self-management and a market economy.

Korea. The 1945 division of Korea along the 38th parallel left industry in the N, which was organized into a militant regime and armed by the USSR. The S was politically disunited. More

Cuban revolutionary leader Fidel Castro established diplomatic relations with the USSR and Soviet Premier Nikita Khrushchev in 1959; the two nations quickly developed close economic ties.

than 60,000 N Korean troops invaded the S on June 25, 1950. The U.S., backed by the UN Security Council, sent troops. **UN troops** reached the Chinese border in Nov. Some 200,000 Chinese troops crossed the Yalu R. and drove back UN forces. By spring 1951, battle lines had become stabilized near the original 38th parallel border, but heavy fighting continued. Finally, an armistice was signed on July 27, 1953. U.S. troops remained in the S, and U.S. economic and military aid continued. The war stimulated rapid economic recovery in Japan.

China. Starting in 1952, industry, agriculture, and social institutions were forcibly collectivized. In a massive purge, as many as several million people were executed as Kuomintang supporters or as class and political enemies. The **Great Leap Forward** (1958-60) unsuccessfully tried to force the pace of development by substituting labor for investment.

Southeast Asia. Ho Chi Minh's forces, aided by the USSR and the new Chinese Communist government, fought French and pro-French Vietnamese forces to a standstill and captured the strategic **Dien Bien Phu** camp in May 1954. The Geneva Agreements divided Vietnam in half pending elections (never held) and recognized Laos and Cambodia as independent. The U.S. aided the anti-Communist Republic of Vietnam in the S.

Middle East. Arab revolutions placed leftist, militantly nationalist regimes in power in Egypt (1952) and Iraq (1958). But Arab unity attempts failed (United Arab Republic joined Egypt, Syria, Yemen, 1958-61). Arab refusal to recognize Israel (Arab League economic blockade began Sept. 1951) led to a permanent **state of war**, with repeated incidents (Gaza, 1955). Israel occupied Sinai, and Britain and France took

(Oct. 1956) the Suez Canal, but were replaced by the UN Emergency Force. The Mossadegh government in Iran nationalized (May 1951) the British-owned oil industry in May, but was overthrown (Aug. 1953) in a U.S.-aided coup.

Latin America. Argentinian dictator Juan **Perón**, in office 1946, crushed opposition and enforced land reform, some nationalization, welfare state measures, and curbs on the Roman Catholic Church. A Sept. 1955 coup deposed Perón. The 1952 revolution in Bolivia brought land reform, nationalization of tin mines, and improvement in the status of the indigenous population, who nevertheless remained poor. The Batista regime in Cuba was overthrown (Jan. 1959) by Fidel **Castro**, who imposed a Communist dictatorship, aligned Cuba with the USSR, and improved education and health care. A U.S.-backed anti-Castro invasion (**Bay of Pigs**, Apr. 1961) was crushed. Self-government advanced in the British Caribbean.

Technology. Large outlays on research and development in the U.S. and the USSR focused on military applications (H-bomb in U.S., 1952; USSR, 1953; Britain, 1957; intercontinental missiles, late 1950s). Soviet launching of the **Sputnik** satellite (Oct. 4, 1957) spurred increases in U.S. science education funds (National Defense Education Act).

Literature and film. Alienation from social and literary conventions reached an extreme in the theater of the absurd (Beckett's *Waiting for Godot*, 1952), the "new novel" (Robbe-Grillet's *Voyeur*, 1955), and avant-garde film (Antonioni's *L'Avventura*, 1960). U.S. beatniks (Kerouac's *On the Road*, 1957) and others rejected the supposed conformism of Americans (Riesman's *The Lonely Crowd*, 1950).

Rising Expectations and New Protests: 1960-69

Global economy. The longest sustained economic boom on record spanned almost the entire decade in the capitalist world; the closely watched GNP figure doubled (1960-70) in the U.S., fueled by **Vietnam War**-related budget deficits. The **General Agreement on Tariffs and Trade** (1967) stimulated Western European prosperity, which spread to peripheral areas (Spain, Italy, E Germany). Japan became a top economic power. Foreign investment aided the industrialization of Brazil. There were limited Soviet economic reform attempts. Outside the Soviet zone the global economy was marked by the growing role of multinational corporations (3,000 in 1914; 6,000 by 1970). International nongovernmental organizations (NGOs) also multiplied rapidly (Amnesty International, 1961).

Reform and radicalization. Pres. John F. **Kennedy**, inaugurated 1961, emphasized youthful idealism and vigor; his assassination Nov. 22, 1963, was a national trauma. Political and social reform movements took root in U.S. and other countries. Blacks demonstrated nonviolently and with partial success against segregation and poverty (1963 March on Washington; 1964 **Civil Rights Act**), but some urban areas erupted in riots (Watts, 1965; Detroit, 1967; more than 100 cities following **Martin Luther King Jr.** assassination, Apr. 4, 1968). New concern for the poor (Harrington's *Other America*, 1963) helped lead to Pres. Lyndon Johnson's **"Great Society"** programs (Medicare, Water Quality Act, Higher Education Act, all 1965). Concern for the **environment** surged (Carson's *Silent Spring*, 1962).

Feminism revived as a cultural and political movement (Friedan's *Feminine Mystique*, 1963; National Organization for Women founded, 1966), and a movement for homosexual rights emerged (Stonewall riot in NYC, 1969). Pope John XXIII called the **Second Vatican Council** (1962-65), which liberalized Roman Catholic liturgy and some other aspects of Catholicism.

Opposition to U.S. involvement in Vietnam, especially among university students (**Moratorium** protest, Nov. 1969), turned violent (Weatherman Chicago riots, Oct. 1969). **New Left** and Marxist theories became popular, and membership in radical groups (Students for a Democratic Society, Black Panthers) increased. Maoist groups, especially in Europe, called for total transformation of society. In France, students sparked a nationwide strike affecting 10 million workers in May-June 1968.

China. China's revolutionary militancy under **Mao** Zedong led to border disputes and other conflict with the USSR under "revisionist" Khrushchev, starting in 1960. The **"Great Proletarian Cultural Revolution"** tried to impose a utopian egalitarian program in China and spread revolution abroad; political struggle, often violent, convulsed China in 1965-68.

Southeast Asia. Communist-led guerrillas aided by N Vietnam fought from 1960 against the S Vietnam government of Ngo Dinh Diem (killed 1963). The U.S. military role increased after the 1964 **Tonkin Gulf** incident. Laotian and Cambodian neutrality were threatened by Communist insurgencies, with N Vietnamese aid, and U.S. intrigues.

Developing world. A bloc of authoritarian leftist regimes among the newly independent nations came to dominate the conference of nonaligned nations (Belgrade, 1961; Cairo, 1964; Lusaka, 1970). Soviet political ties and military bases were established in Cuba, Egypt, Algeria, Guinea, and other countries. Some leaders were ousted in coups by pro-Western groups— Dem. Rep. of the Congo's Patrice Lumumba (killed 1961), Ghana's Kwame Nkrumah (exiled 1966), and Indonesia's Sukarno (effectively ousted in 1965 after a Communist coup failed).

Middle East. Arab-Israeli tension erupted into a brief war June 1967. Israel emerged from the war as a major regional power. Military shipments before and after the war increased Soviet influence in much of the Arab world. Most Arab states broke U.S. diplomatic ties, while Communist countries cut their ties to Israel. Intra-Arab disputes continued: Egypt and Saudi Arabia supported rival factions in a bloody Yemen civil war 1962-70; Lebanese troops fought Palestinian commandos 1969.

Eastern Europe. To stop the large-scale exodus of citizens, E German authorities built (Aug. 1961) a fortified

In spite of its short duration, the Arab-Israeli Six-Day War in June 1967 had a wide-ranging impact.

wall across Berlin that enclosed West Berlin. Soviet sway in the Balkans was weakened by Albania's realignment with China (USSR broke ties with Albania in Dec. 1961) and Romania's assertion (1964) of limited autonomy. Liberalization (spring 1968) in **Czechoslovakia** was crushed with massive force by troops of five Warsaw Pact countries. W German treaties (1970) with the USSR and Poland facilitated transfer of German technology and confirmed postwar boundaries.

Arts and styles. The boundary between fine and popular arts was blurred to some extent by Pop Art (Warhol) and rock musicals (*Hair*, 1968). Informality and exaggeration prevailed

in fashion (beards, miniskirts). A nonpolitical "counterculture" developed, rejecting traditional bourgeois life goals and personal habits, and use of marijuana and hallucinogens spread (**Woodstock** festival, Aug. 1969). **The Beatles** brought unprecedented sophistication to rock music.

Science. Achievements in space (**humans on the moon**, July 1969) and electronics (lasers, integrated circuits) encouraged a faith in scientific solutions to problems in agriculture ("green revolution"), medicine (heart transplants, 1967), and other areas. Harmful technology, it was believed, could be controlled (1963 Limited Test Ban Treaty, 1968 Nuclear Nonproliferation Treaty).

New Global Balances and Religious Revivals: 1970-79

U.S.: Caution and neoconservatism. A sluggish economy, energy shortages, and environmental problems contributed to a **"limits of growth"** philosophy. Suspicion of science and technology killed or delayed some projects (supersonic transport dropped, 1971). The Three Mile Island nuclear reactor accident (Mar. 1979) reinforced fears of nuclear energy.

There was some backlash against social change. School busing and racial quotas were challenged (Bakke decision, June 1978); Equal Rights Amendment for women languished; legislation aimed at protecting LGBT individuals from discrimination was opposed.

Completion of Communist forces' takeover of **South Vietnam** (evacuation of U.S. civilians, Apr. 1975), revelations of Central Intelligence Agency misdeeds (Rockefeller Commission report, June 1975), and **Watergate** scandals (Nixon resigned in Aug. 1974) reduced faith in U.S. moral and material capacity to influence world affairs. Revelations of Soviet crimes (Solzhenitsyn's *Gulag Archipelago*, 1974) and Soviet intervention in Africa helped foster a revival of anti-Communist sentiment.

Economy sluggish. The 1960s boom faltered in the 1970s; a severe recession in the U.S. and Europe (1974-75) followed a huge oil price hike (Dec. 1973). Monetary instability (U.S. cut ties to gold in Aug. 1971), the decline of the dollar, and protectionist moves by industrial countries (1977-78) threatened trade. Business investment declined. Severe inflation plagued many countries (25% in Britain, 1975; 18% in U.S., 1979).

China readjusts. After the 1976 deaths of Mao Zedong and Zhou Enlai, pragmatists won the struggle for leadership. A nationwide purge of orthodox Maoists ensued, and the **Gang of Four**, led by Mao's widow, Chiang Ching, was arrested. The new leaders freed more than 100,000 political prisoners and reduced public adulation of Mao. Political and trade ties expanded in Japan, Europe, and the U.S. in the late 1970s, as relations worsened with the USSR, Cuba, and Vietnam (four-week invasion by China, 1979). Ideological guidelines were reversed (bonuses to workers, Dec. 1977; exams for college entrance, Oct. 1977). Some restrictions on cultural expression were eased.

Europe. European unity moves (EEC-EFTA trade accord, 1972) faltered as economic problems appeared (Britain floated pound, 1972; France floated franc, 1974). Germany and Switzerland curbed guest workers from S Europe. Greece and Turkey quarreled over Cyprus and Aegean oil rights.

All non-Communist Europe was under democratic rule after free elections (June 1976) in **Spain** seven months after the death of Franco. The conservative, colonialist regime in **Portugal** was overthrown in Apr. 1974. In **Greece** the seven-year military dictatorship yielded power in 1974. The **British** Labour government imposed (1975) wage curbs and suspended nationalization schemes. Terrorism in **Germany** (1972 Munich Olympics killings) led to laws curbing some civil liberties. **French** "new philosophers" rejected leftist ideologies, and the Socialist-Communist coalition lost a 1978 election bid.

Religion and politics. The improvement in **Muslim** countries' political fortunes by the 1950s (with the exception of Central Asia under Soviet and Chinese rule) and the growth of Arab oil wealth were followed by a resurgence of traditional religious fervor. Libyan dictator Muammar al-**Qaddafi** mixed Islamic laws with socialism. The illegal Muslim Brotherhood in **Egypt** was accused of violence, while extreme groups bombed (1977) theaters to protest Western and secular values.

In **Turkey**, the National Salvation Party was the first Islamic group to share (1974) power since secularization in the 1920s. In **Iran**, Ayatollah Ruhollah **Khomeini** led a revolution that deposed the secular shah (Jan. 1979) and created an Islamic republic. Religiously motivated Muslims took part in

an insurrection in **Saudi Arabia** that briefly seized (1979) the Grand Mosque in Mecca. Muslim puritan opposition to **Pakistan** Pres. Zulfikar al-Bhutto helped lead to his overthrow in July 1977. Muslim solidarity, however, could not prevent Pakistan's eastern province (**Bangladesh**) from declaring (Dec. 1971) independence after a bloody civil war.

Muslim and Hindu resentment of coerced sterilization in **India** helped defeat the Indira Gandhi government, and a coalition including religious Hindu parties replaced it (Mar. 1977). Muslims in the S **Philippines**, aided by Libya, rebelled against central rule from 1973. The Buddhist Soka Gakkai movement launched (1964) the Komeito party in **Japan**, which became a major opposition party in 1972 and 1976 elections.

Evangelical Protestant groups grew in the U.S. A revival of interest in Orthodox Christianity occurred among **Russian** intellectuals (Solzhenitsyn). The secularist **Israeli** Labor party, after decades of rule, was ousted in 1977 by conservatives led by Menachem Begin; religious militants founded settlements on the disputed West Bank, part of biblically promised Israel. Reform Judaism in U.S. revived many traditional practices.

Religious wars raged in **Northern Ireland** (Catholic vs. Protestant, 1969-97) and **Lebanon** (Christian vs. Muslim, 1975-90), while religious militancy complicated the Israel-Arab dispute (1973 Israel-Arab war). The Camp David Accords in 1978, negotiated by Egyptian Pres. Anwar al-Sadat, Israeli Prime Min. Menachem Begin, and U.S. Pres. Jimmy Carter, facilitated the landmark 1979 **Egypt-Israel peace treaty**, but increased militancy on the West Bank impeded further progress.

Latin America. Repressive conservative regimes strengthened their hold, with a violent coup against the elected (Sept. 1973) **Allende** government in **Chile**, military coup in **Argentina** (1976), and coups against reformist regimes in **Bolivia** (1971, 1979) and **Peru** (1976). In Central America, increasing liberal and leftist militancy led to the ouster (1979) of the **Somoza** regime in **Nicaragua** and to civil conflict in **El Salvador**.

Southeast Asia. Communist victories in Vietnam, Cambodia, and Laos by May 1975 led to new turmoil. **Pol Pot**'s Khmer Rouge regime in **Cambodia** ordered millions to resettle in rural areas, in a program of forced labor and terrorism that cost more than 1 million lives (1975-79) and caused hundreds of thousands to flee. The Vietnamese invasion of Cambodia (1979)

The Vietnam War, in which an estimated 2 million Vietnamese and 58,000 Americans died, also engulfed Laos and Cambodia in deadly violence.

swelled the refugee population and contributed to widespread starvation.

Russian expansion. Soviet influence, checked in some countries (troops ousted by Egypt, 1972), was projected farther afield, often with the use of Cuban troops (Angola, 1975-89; Ethiopia, 1977-88). **Détente** with the West—1972 Berlin pact, 1972 strategic arms pact (**SALT**)—gave way to a more antagonistic relationship in the late 1970s, exacerbated by the Soviet invasion (1979) of **Afghanistan**.

Africa. The last remaining European colonies were granted independence (**Spanish Sahara**, 1976; **Djibouti**, 1977), and, after 10 years of civil war, a black government took over (1979) in **Zimbabwe** (Rhodesia); white domination remained in **South Africa**. European involvement in local wars (Russia in **Angola**, **Ethiopia**; France in **Chad**, **Zaire**, **Mauritania**) and the use of tens of thousands of Cuban troops were denounced by some African leaders. Ethnic or tribal clashes made Africa a locus of sustained warfare during the late 1970s.

End of the Cold War and Demand for Democracy: 1980-89

Global developments. International contacts accelerated thanks to new openness in China (1978) and USSR (1985); global consumerism was symbolized by the rapid spread of McDonald's restaurants (Japan, 1971; Russia, 1990).

USSR, Eastern Europe. The late 1980s saw the remaking of the Soviet state and the beginning of the disintegration of the Soviet empire. After the deaths of Gen. Sec. Leonid **Brezhnev** (1982) and two successors, the harsh treatment of dissent and restriction of emigration, and the Soviet invasion (Dec. 1979) of Afghanistan, Gen. Sec. Mikhail **Gorbachev** (in office 1985-91) promoted *glasnost* and *perestroika*—economic, political, and social reform. Supported by the Communist Party, he signed (Dec. 1987) the intermediate-range nuclear forces disarmament treaty. Military withdrawal from Afghanistan was completed in Feb. 1989, and the Soviet people chose (Mar. 1989) part of the new Congress of People's Deputies from competing candidates. By decade's end the **Cold War** appeared to be fading away.

In **Poland**, Solidarity, the labor union founded (1980) by Lech **Walesa**, was outlawed in 1982 but legalized in 1988, after years of unrest. Poland's first free election since the Communist takeover brought **Solidarity** victory (June 1989); Tadeusz Mazowiecki, a Walesa adviser, became prime minister in a government with the Communists. In fall 1989 the failure of Marxist economies in **Hungary**, **East Germany**, **Czechoslovakia**, **Bulgaria**, and **Romania** brought the collapse of the Communist monopoly and a demand for democracy. In a historic step, the **Berlin Wall** was opened in Nov. 1989.

U.S. The **"Reagan Years"** (1981-88) featured new economic policies via budget and tax cuts, deregulation, "junk bond" financing, leveraged buyouts, and mergers. However, there was a stock market crash (Oct. 1987), and federal budget deficits and the trade deficit increased. Foreign policy showed a **strong anti-Communist stance**, via increased defense spending, aid to anti-Communists in Central America, invasion of Cuba-threatened **Grenada**, and championing of the **"Star Wars"** missile defense program. Four Reagan-Gorbachev summits (1985-88) climaxed in the INF treaty (1987). The **Iran-Contra affair** (Oliver North testimony, July 1987) was a major political scandal.

Middle East. The Middle East remained militarily unstable, with sharp divisions along economic, political, racial, and religious lines. In **Iran**, the Islamic revolution of 1979 created a strong anti-U.S. stance (hostage crisis, Nov. 1979-Jan. 1981). In Sept. 1980, **Iraq** repudiated its border agreement with Iran and began major hostilities that led to an eight-year war in which hundreds of thousands were killed.

Libya's support for international terrorism induced the U.S. to close (May 1981) its diplomatic mission there and embargo (Mar. 1982) Libyan oil. Following an attack on a West Berlin disco frequented by U.S. military, U.S. bombed targets in Libya (Apr. 1986).

Israel affirmed (July 1980) all Jerusalem as its capital, destroyed (June 1981) an Iraqi atomic reactor, and invaded **Lebanon**, citing terrorism from the Palestine Liberation Organization; PLO withdrew from Lebanon after cease-fire. A **Palestinian uprising** began (Dec. 1987) in Israeli-occupied Gaza and spread to the West Bank; troops responded with force, killing 300 by the end of 1988, with 6,000 more in detention camps. Israeli withdrawal from Lebanon began in Feb. 1985 and ended in June 1985, as Lebanon continued to be torn by military and political conflict. Artillery duels (Mar.-Apr. 1989) between Christian East Beirut and Muslim West Beirut left 200 dead.

Latin America. In **Nicaragua**, the leftist **Sandinista** National Liberation Front, in power after the 1979 civil war, faced problems as a result of Nicaragua's military aid to leftist guerrillas in El Salvador and U.S. backing of antigovernment contras. The CIA admitted (1984) having directed the mining of Nicaraguan ports, and the U.S. sent humanitarian (1985) and military (1986) aid. Profits from U.S. **secret arms sales** to Iran were found (1987) diverted to contras. Cease-fire talks between the Sandinista government and contras came in 1988, and elections were held in Nicaragua in Feb. 1990.

In **El Salvador**, a military coup (Oct. 1979) failed to halt extremist terrorism. Archbishop Oscar Romero, advocate for poor, was assassinated in Mar. 1980; from Jan. to June some 4,000 civilians were killed in the civil unrest. In 1984, newly elected Pres. José Napoleon Duarte worked to stem human rights abuses, but violence continued. In **Chile**, Gen. Augusto **Pinochet** yielded the presidency after elections (Dec. 1989) but remained as head of the army. He had ruled since 1973, imposing harsh measures against leftists and dissidents.

Africa. The 1980s saw continuing economic decline in virtually all African countries, a result of accelerating desertification, the world economic recession, heavy indebtedness to overseas creditors, rapid population growth, and political instability. Some 60 million Africans faced prolonged hunger in 1981. Much of Africa had one of the worst **droughts** ever in 1983, and by year's end, one-third of the population, or about 150 million, were near **famine**. Live Aid, a marathon rock concert, was presented in July 1985, and the U.S. and Western nations sent aid in Sept. 1985. Wars in **Ethiopia** and **Sudan** and military strife in several other nations continued. **HIV/AIDS** took a heavy toll.

Anti-apartheid sentiment gathered force in **South Africa**, with demonstrations meeting violent police response. White voters approved (Nov. 1983) the first constitution to give people of mixed-race backgrounds and Asians a voice, while still excluding the black majority. Twelve nations imposed economic sanctions in Aug.-Sept. 1985. Pres. P. W. **Botha** was succeeded (Sept. 1989) by F. W. **de Klerk**, who promised negotiation with the black population.

Asia and the Pacific. Benazir **Bhutto** became the first woman to lead a majority-Muslim nation as prime minister of **Pakistan** (Dec. 1988). The "people power" revolt in the **Philippines** ousted Ferdinand **Marcos** (Feb. 1986) after two decades as president; he was replaced by Corazon **Aquino**.

During the 1980s **China**'s Communist government and paramount leader **Deng** Xiaoping expanded commercial and technical ties to the West and the role of market forces. In Apr. 1989 student demonstrators camped out in **Tiananmen Square**, Beijing, in a peaceful call for political reform. Some 100,000 students and workers marched; at least 20 other cities saw protests. In response, martial law was imposed. Army

The Chinese government responded to 1989 pro-democracy demonstrations in Tiananmen Square with force.

troops crushed the demonstration in and around Tiananmen Square on June 3-4, with death toll estimates of 500-7,000, up to 10,000 dissidents arrested, and 31 people tried and executed. The conciliatory Communist Party chief was ousted; the Politburo adopted (July 1989) reforms against official corruption.

Japan's relations with other nations were dominated by **trade imbalances** favoring Japan. Western Europe and the U.S. accused Japan of unfair trade policies.

Europe. With the addition of Greece, Portugal, and Spain, the European Community became a common market of more than 300 million people. Margaret **Thatcher** became the first British prime minister in the 20th cent. to win a third consecutive term (1987). **France** elected (1981) its first socialist president, François **Mitterrand**, who was reelected in 1988. Elections in 1983 brought **Italy** its first socialist premier, Bettino **Craxi**.

International terrorism. With the 1979 **overthrow of the shah** of Iran and with instablity in the Middle East, terrorism became a prominent tactic. In 1979-81, Iranian militants held 52 **U.S. hostages in Iran** for 444 days. In 1983 a truck bomb exploded at U.S. Marine headquarters in Beirut, Lebanon, killing 241 Americans; almost simultaneously a few miles away, a truck bomb blew up a French paratrooper barracks, killing 58. The *Achille Lauro* cruise ship was hijacked in Oct. 1985, and an American passenger killed. Incidents rose to 700 in 1985 and to 1,000 in 1988. **Assassinated leaders** included Egypt's Pres. Anwar al-**Sadat** (1981), India's Prime Min. Indira **Gandhi** (1984), and Lebanese Prem. Rashid **Karami** (1987).

New Regional Tensions in a Post-Cold War World: 1990-99

Soviet Empire collapse. Breakup of the Soviet Union into 15 independent states began with declarations of independence by **Lithuania**, **Latvia**, and **Estonia** during abortive coup against Mikhail **Gorbachev** (Aug. 1991). Other republics followed. In Dec. 1991, **Russia**, **Ukraine**, and **Belarus** declared the Soviet Union dead; Gorbachev resigned. The **Warsaw Pact** and Council for Mutual Economic Assistance (**Comecon**) disbanded. Most former Soviet republics joined in loose confederation (**Commonwealth of Independent States**). Hardship ensued as Russia, under Pres. Boris **Yeltsin**, moved to reboot the economy under a free-market system.

When the Muslim-majority Russian republic of **Chechnya** declared independence, Russian forces invaded (Dec. 1994), withdrawing after 1996 cease-fire. In 1999, Russia forcibly suppressed Muslim insurgents in Russian republic of Dagestan and entered Chechnya, again fighting separatists. Yeltsin resigned presidency, Dec. 1999, with Prime Min. Vladimir **Putin** becoming acting president.

Europe. Yugoslavia broke apart, and hostilities ensued along ethnic and religious lines. **Croatia**, **Slovenia**, and **Macedonia** declared independence (1991), followed by **Bosnia-Herzegovina** (1992). **Serbia** and **Montenegro** remained as the republic of Yugoslavia. Bitter fighting followed, especially in Bosnia, where Serbs engaged in **ethnic cleansing** of the Muslim population; peace plan (**Dayton accord**, 1995) was brokered by the U.S., with **NATO** policing its implementation. In spring 1999, NATO conducted a bombing campaign aimed at stopping Yugoslavia from driving ethnic Albanians from the **Kosovo** region; a June accord brought in NATO peacekeeping troops.

The **two Germanys were reunited** after 45 years (Oct. 1990). Czechoslovakia broke apart (Jan. 1993) into the **Czech Republic** and **Slovakia**. Labor leader Lech **Walesa** was elected president of **Poland** (Dec. 1991). In Jan. 1994, NATO approved the **Partnership for Peace**, coordinating defense of E and Central European countries; Russia later joined. NATO signed a cooperation pact with **Russia** (May 1997) allowing for NATO expansion into former Soviet-bloc countries. Czech Republic, **Hungary**, and **Poland** joined NATO in Jan. 1999. Efforts toward European unity continued with adoption of a single market (Jan. 1993) and conversion of the European Community to the **European Union** as the **Maastricht Treaty** took effect (Nov. 1993). The **euro** was launched as common currency for non-cash uses, Jan. 1999, and as cash, Jan. 2002, in the then-12 Eurozone countries.

An intraparty revolt forced Margaret **Thatcher** out as UK prime minister, to be succeeded by John **Major** (Nov. 1990); Labour took power under Tony **Blair** (May 1997). Prince **Charles** and **Diana** divorced (Aug. 1996); Diana died in a car crash a year later. Talks on **Northern Ireland** led to peace plan, approved in all-Ireland vote (May 1998). In Dec. 1999, Northern Ireland was granted home rule. Voters in **Scotland** (overwhelmingly) and **Wales** (narrowly) approved creation of regional legislatures (1997).

Middle East. In Aug. 1990, **Iraq**'s Saddam Hussein ordered troops to invade **Kuwait**. A UN-approved international force, led by U.S., bombed Iraq (Jan. 1991) and launched a land attack, crushing the invasion; cease-fire agreed to, Apr. 1991. The UN extended sanctions on Iraq for failure to abide by cease-fire terms. Iraq's reported failure to cooperate with UN inspectors seeking to eliminate **weapons of mass destruction** led to airstrikes by U.S. and Britain (1998).

Israel and the **PLO** signed peace accord (Sept. 1993) providing for Palestinian self-government in the **West Bank** and **Gaza** Strip; Prime Min. Yitzhak **Rabin** and Foreign Min. Shimon **Peres** of Israel and Yasir **Arafat** of the PLO shared 1994 Nobel Peace Prize. Six Arab nations relaxed boycott against Israel (1994), and Israel and **Jordan** signed peace treaty (Oct. 1994). Rabin was assassinated (Nov. 1995) by an Israeli extremist; Benjamin **Netanyahu** became prime minister (May 1996). Arafat was elected president of the Palestinian Authority (Jan. 1996).

Asia and the Pacific. Longtime **North Korean** dictator Kim Il Sung died (July 1994), to be succeeded by son **Kim Jong Il**. In Oct. 1994 North Korea signed agreement with U.S. setting timetable for ending **nuclear weapons** program (deal collapsed in 2002). North Korea suffered severe drought and famine. **Palau** achieved independence, Oct. 1994. **Hong Kong** was returned to **China** (July 1997), after 156 years as a British colony, and **Macau** reverted to China (Dec. 1999) after over 400 years of Portuguese rule. **Jiang** Zemin, general secretary of the Chinese Communist Party, also became China's president (Mar. 1993). China released several well-known dissidents but continued to jail and execute many. U.S. and China signed trade pact (Nov. 1999). In **Japan** members of a religious cult released the nerve gas sarin on **Tokyo subway**, killing 12 and injuring more than 5,500 (Mar. 1995).

After years of growing prosperity, **Thailand**, **Indonesia**, and **South Korea** in 1997 began to suffer economic reverses, with worldwide ripple effect, and received IMF **bailout** packages. In South Korea, former dissident **Kim** Dae-jung was elected president (Dec. 1997). In Indonesia, protests over mismanagement led to the resignation of Pres. **Suharto** (May 1998) after 32 years of rule. In a referendum (Aug. 1999), **East Timorese** voted for independence; pro-Indonesian militias rampaged, but a multinational peacekeeping force helped restore order (Sept. 1999).

In **Afghanistan** the radical Islamist **Taliban** gained control of Kabul (Sept. 1996) and, eventually, most of the country. **Indian** forces repeatedly clashed with pro-independence demonstrators in the disputed majority-Muslim region of **Kashmir**, exacerbating relations with **Pakistan**. India and Pakistan both conducted **nuclear tests** in 1998. Conflict between government and the military led to a **bloodless coup** in Pakistan (Oct. 1999).

South Africa abandoned apartheid and transitioned to a nonracial democratic government, with Nelson Mandela (pictured, with U.S. Pres. Bill Clinton) elected president in 1994.

Africa. South Africa's Pres. F. W. **de Klerk** released dissident black leader Nelson **Mandela** from prison (Feb. 1990) after 27 years, and the white minority government repealed **apartheid** laws (1990, 1991); the government also voluntarily dismantled its nuclear weapons program. The African National Congress won in multiracial elections (Apr. 1994), making Mandela president, and a new constitution became law (Dec. 1996). **Namibia** became independent in Mar. 1990, after almost 20 years under UN trusteeship. **Eritrea** achieved independence from **Ethiopia**, July 1993, after over 30 years of war. **Mobutu** Sese Seko, longtime ruler of **Zaire**, was deposed (May 1997) by rebel forces under Laurent **Kabila**, who changed country's name back to **Democratic Republic of the Congo**. In **Nigeria**, former Gen. Olusegun **Obasanjo** was elected (Feb. 1999) as the nation's first civilian leader in 15 years.

Civil war broke out in **Liberia** (Dec. 1989) and lasted, with interruptions, through the 1990s and beyond, leaving hundreds of thousands dead. Factional fighting erupted in **Somalia** (Jan. 1991); a U.S.-led UN peacekeeping force failed to restore order and left (Mar. 1995). In **Algeria**, the army canceled parliamentary elections (Jan. 1992) after the Islamic party won a first round. Ensuing civil war left more than 150,000 dead; a peace and amnesty plan was approved in a Sept. 1999 referendum. Assassination of **Burundi**'s president (June 1993) renewed ethnic violence between **Hutus** and **Tutsis** there. A suspicious plane crash that killed the presidents of Burundi and Rwanda (Apr. 1994) led to genocide in **Rwanda**; some 800,000 died, mostly Tutsis massacred by Hutu militias.

The World Health Organization reported (1995) that Africa accounted for 70% of **AIDS** cases worldwide.

North America. U.S. Pres. Bill **Clinton** (D) (elected 1992, 1996) presided over growing economy, promoted free trade, intervened in Bosnia. Impeached by House (Dec. 1998) on charges stemming from affair with intern, he was acquitted by the Senate. In **Canada**, Liberal Jean **Chrétien** became prime minister (Nov. 1993; reelected 1997). The Canadian territory of **Nunavut** was created (Apr. 1999), carved from Northwest Territories. In **Mexico**, Ernesto **Zedillo** of the ruling PRI party was elected president (July 1994) after PRI's first candidate was assassinated. The country weathered a **monetary crisis** with the help of a 1995 U.S. bailout. The North American Free Trade Agreement (**NAFTA**), liberalizing trade between U.S., Canada, and Mexico, took effect Jan. 1994. Globalization trends drew protests from activists (**World Trade Org.** meeting, Nov.-Dec. 1999).

Central America and the Caribbean. In Haiti, Jean-Bertrand **Aristide** was elected president (Dec. 1990); ousted in a Sept. 1991 military coup, he was restored to office (Oct. 1994) through U.S.-led negotiations. In **Nicaragua**, Violeta **Chamorro** defeated **Sandinista** Pres. Daniel **Ortega** in Feb. 1990 election. In **Panama**, U.S. troops overthrew dictator Manuel **Noriega** (Dec. 1989); convicted on drug and human rights charges, he served time in the U.S., France, and Panama. On Dec. 31, 1999, Panama assumed full control of the **Panama Canal**, in accord with 1977 treaty with U.S.

South America. Alberto **Fujimori** was elected president of **Peru** in June 1990; condemned for human rights abuses but popular for reducing terrorism, he was reelected in 1995. Leftist guerrillas took hostages in Lima (Dec. 1996); one hostage killed during rescue operation (Apr. 1997). Peronist Pres. Carlos Saúl **Menem** was **Argentina**'s president for much of the decade, imposing economic austerity. Former **Chilean** Pres. Augusto **Pinochet** was arrested in London (Oct. 1998) and charged with human-rights violations but judged unfit for trial. In **Brazil**, Fernando Henrique **Cardoso** was elected president (Oct. 1994) and reelected in 1998 despite economic slump; the IMF announced a $42-bil aid package (Nov. 1998). In **Venezuela** two coups were thwarted (1992), but leftist coup leader Hugo **Chávez** was elected president, Dec. 1998.

Terrorism. A bomb exploded in garage beneath New York City's **World Trade Center**, killing six (Feb. 1993); six Islamic fundamentalists were convicted. Bombs outside U.S. embassies in **Kenya** and **Tanzania** killed over 220 (Aug. 1998); U.S. retaliated with airstrikes in Afghanistan and Sudan. Anti-government U.S. radicals bombed a federal building in **Oklahoma City**, OK (Apr. 1995), killing 168.

Science, technology, and environment. The powerful **Hubble Space Telescope** was launched in Apr. 1990. U.S. space shuttle *Atlantis* docked with the orbiting Russian space station *Mir* (June 1995) in first of several joint missions. In Nov. 1998 the first component for a new **International Space Station** was launched into space from **Kazakhstan**. Scottish scientists announced (Feb. 1997) **cloning** of a sheep—first mammal successfully cloned from a cell from an adult animal. Tim **Berners-Lee** launched first **World Wide Web** server (1990); user-friendly graphical browsers (Mosaic, 1993; Netscape, 1994) and internet service providers followed, beginning a transformation of global communications and information access. Efforts to limit **global climate change** intensified with tentative agreements adopted in **Kyoto**, Japan (Dec. 1997).

Globalization and Global Realignments: 2000-09

Terrorism. In Oct. 2000, 17 were killed aboard the USS *Cole* in Aden, **Yemen**, in a suicide bombing tied to **al-Qaeda** terrorist network, based in Afghanistan. Hijackers on Sept. 11, 2001, crashed two jetliners into the twin towers of the **World Trade Center** in New York City and another into the **Pentagon** outside Washington, DC, with a fourth crashing in a Pennsylvania field. The attacks, linked to al-Qaeda and its leader, **Osama bin Laden**, killed nearly 3,000 and destroyed both towers.

A U.S.-led coalition ousted the Taliban regime from Afghanistan in late 2001, but insurgent violence grew and the U.S. sent a surge of 30,000 troops at the end of the decade.

Among other incidents tied to Islamic radicals, a car bomb on the Indonesian island of **Bali** (Oct. 2002) killed over 200. **Commuter trains** were bombed in **Madrid**, Spain, killing about 200 (Mar. 2004). Subway trains and a bus were bombed in **London** (July 2005); 56 died. Explosions killed more than 180 on commuter trains in **Mumbai**, India (July 2006); also in Mumbai (Nov. 2008), terrorists launched coordinated attacks on sites frequented by foreigners, killing more than 160. **Chechen** separatist guerrillas were implicated in an attack on a **Moscow** movie theater (Oct. 2002; over 100 hostages died), bombings in Moscow's subways (Feb. 2004; about 40 killed), suicide bombings on two planes (Aug. 2004; 90 died), and takeover of a school in Beslan (Sept. 2004; over 330 killed). Coordinated bombing attacks on **Yazidi** towns in **Iraq** (Aug. 2007) killed at least 500.

Global economic crisis. Rapid economic growth in **China** and other developing countries contrasted with sluggish rates in traditional economic powers. A global **recession**, beginning in late 2007, led to **financial meltdown** (Sept. 2008). **Iceland**'s banking system collapsed (Oct. 2008); rescued by loans and austerity. **Dubai**'s state-controlled investment company was bailed out (Dec. 2009) by neighboring emirate Abu Dhabi. Soaring food and fuel prices led to an attempted general strike in **Egypt** and riots in **Haiti** (Apr. 2008). **Austerity** measures spurred protests in several European countries.

War in Iraq and Afghanistan. The U.S., with the UK, invaded **Iraq** (Mar. 2003) to oust the regime of Saddam **Hussein**. U.S. Pres. George W. **Bush** declared major combat ended by May, but insurgents caused continuing casualties. Cited as grounds for the invasion, no **weapons of mass destruction** were found. Hussein was captured by U.S. troops (Dec. 2003); convicted and executed by Iraq for crimes against humanity (Dec. 2006). Iraqis voted in **elections** for a transitional assembly (Jan. 2005), democratic constitution (Oct. 2005), and parliament (Dec. 2005); negotiations produced a **Shiite coalition government** under Prime Min. Nouri al-**Maliki** (May 2006). With violence intensifying, Bush announced (Jan. 2007) a **"surge"** of additional U.S. troops; casualties fell sharply, aided by changing sectarian trends.

In **Afghanistan**, a U.S.-led military coalition ousted the **Taliban** regime from power. A transitional government was installed (Dec. 2001), and NATO assumed control of multinational forces (Aug. 2003). Afghans elected Hamid **Karzai** president (Nov. 2004). From 2007, Taliban and other Islamist militants stepped up attacks, often operating from safe havens inside **Pakistan**. U.S. increased its troop strength in Afghanistan (2009) and expanded use of **drones**.

Middle East. **Palestinian suicide bombings** continued, and **Israel** mounted a major offensive (Mar. 2002), reoccupying much of the **West Bank**. The U.S., Russia, UN, and EU introduced (Apr. 2003) **"road map"** for peace negotiations; little progress made. After Palestinian leader Yasir **Arafat** died (Nov. 2004), Mahmoud **Abbas** was elected in his place. In Jan. 2006 the militant Palestinian party **Hamas** won a parliamentary majority, defeating the long-ruling **Fatah** party. Israel launched attacks on **Lebanon** (July 2006) after a raid into N Israel by Lebanon-based **Hezbollah** guerrillas; a cease-fire was declared a month later. In reaction to **Hamas** attacks, Israel launched an offensive in the **Gaza Strip** (Dec. 2008), which killed an estimated 1,300 Palestinians. Prime Min. Ehud **Olmert**, in office since 2006, resigned amid corruption inquiries; Feb. 2009 elections led to a coalition government headed by conservative former Prime Min. Benjamin **Netanyahu**.

In **Yemen**, U.S. used drones to kill suspected **al-Qaeda** terrorists (Nov. 2002), and the government of Pres. Ali Abdullah **Saleh**, from 2004 onward, battled a growing insurgency from **Shiite Houthi** rebels, believed aided by Iran.

Asia. Gen. Pervez **Musharraf**, brought to power in a 1999 coup, assumed **Pakistan**'s presidency (June 2001). Following the Sept. 11, 2001, terrorist attacks in U.S., Pakistan agreed to help in fighting Taliban and al-Qaeda militants. Pakistani former Prime Min. Benazir **Bhutto** was assassinated, Dec. 2007; her party won parliamentary elections, Feb. 2008, and her widower was later elected president. In May 2009, the government launched an offensive against Taliban insurgents in the Swat Valley. **Riots** in the mostly Hindu **Indian** state of Gujarat (Feb.-Apr. 2002) left more than 1,200 dead, mostly Muslims. Pakistan and **India** restored ties (May 2003) and declared cease-fire in disputed territory (Nov. 2003); relations remained tense.

East Timor achieved independence (May 2002). Leaders of **North** and **South Korea** met (June 2000) in first-ever postwar summit. North agreed, Feb. 2007, to end **nuclear weapons** development in exchange for aid but reneged in early 2009. In **China**, **Hu** Jintao was named to succeed retiring **Jiang** Zemin as party chief (Nov. 2002) and president (Mar. 2003). The UN Intl. Atomic Energy Agency (IAEA) censured **Iran** (Dec. 2003) for covering up aspects of its nuclear program; Iran continued enriching uranium in defiance of IAEA deadlines. Pres. Mahmoud **Ahmadinejad** was declared landslide winner in June 2009 Iranian elections widely perceived as rigged; massive protests were crushed.

In **Kyrgyzstan**, protests (Mar. 2005) against election fraud brought down Pres. Askar Akayev in a **"tulip revolution."** **Myanmar**'s military junta cracked down on hundreds of thousands of protesters (Sept. 2007). **Tamil** guerrillas in **Sri Lanka** ended their rebellion (May 2009), which in 26 years had claimed at least 80,000 lives.

A **tsunami** (Dec. 2004) swept ashore, affecting Indian Ocean nations and leaving some 228,000 dead. **Earthquakes** struck Kashmir and other parts of Pakistan and India (Oct. 2005; nearly 80,000 died) and China's Sichuan province (May 2008; nearly 70,000 died). Over 80,000 people were killed in a **cyclone** in Myanmar (May 2008).

Europe. The **European Union** admitted 10 E European nations, May 2004; two more joined in Jan. 2007. Voters in

One of the deadliest natural disasters in recorded history, a 2004 tsunami killed more than 200,000 people in African and Asian countries.

France and the Netherlands rejected a treaty to establish a new EU constitution (May-June 2005); modified plan (**Treaty of Lisbon**) came into force (Dec. 2009) after Irish voters approved it (Oct. 2009).

In Oct. 2000, **Yugoslav** strongman Slobodan **Milosevic** yielded power after a disputed election; tried for **war crimes** by an international tribunal, he died (Mar. 2006) before a verdict was rendered. **Serbia** and **Montenegro** separated into two independent nations, May-June 2006. **Kosovo** unilaterally declared independence, Feb. 2008.

British Prime Min. Tony **Blair** won reelection twice (2001, 2005) and stepped down in June 2007, succeeded by fellow Labourite Gordon Brown. **Germany** elected its first East German and first woman chancellor (Nov. 2005) in Angela **Merkel**, a Christian Democrat. Riots broke out in **France**'s immigrant communities (Nov. 2005). French voters elected conservative Nicolas **Sarkozy** president (May 2007), and France rejoined **NATO** military command (Apr. 2009) after more than 40 years. **Russians** captured capital of **Chechnya** (Feb. 2000) and established direct rule, but the insurgency continued, along with terrorist attacks in Moscow and elsewhere. Russian Pres. Vladimir **Putin** (elected Mar. 2000, 2004), was constitutionally barred from new term in 2008; his protégé, Dmitri **Medvedev**, was elected, Mar. 2008, and Medvedev named Putin prime minister. In **Ukraine**, a tainted presidential runoff election (Nov. 2004) led to the country's "orange revolution"; recount gave power to nationalist Viktor **Yushchenko**.

Africa. **Ethiopia** and **Eritrea** signed a peace treaty (Dec. 2000), ending two-year border war. Liberian Pres. Charles **Taylor** went into exile (Aug. 2003) as part of a deal to end 14-year civil war; Ellen Johnson **Sirleaf** elected pres, Oct. 2005. Other accords were reached aimed at ending civil wars in **Angola** (Apr. 2002) and **Côte d'Ivoire** (Jan. 2003).

Laurent Kabila, president of **Dem. Rep. of the Congo** (DRC), was assassinated, Jan. 2001. A peace agreement in DRC (Apr. 2003) did not end violence there; the nation agreed to work with **Rwanda** to disarm Hutu rebels (Nov. 2007). In **Sudan** the Muslim-led government and rebels from the Christian south signed power-sharing agreement, Jan. 2005. Rebellion in the **Darfur** area of western Sudan led to large-scale violence. Arab militias (**janjaweed**), reportedly backed by the government, were accused of displacing over 2 million people in acts bordering on **genocide**; over 300,000 had been killed by the end of 2009. The Intl. Criminal Court issued an arrest warrant for Sudanese Pres. Omar al-**Bashir** for war crimes (Mar. 2009); he remained in power. Disputed elections sparked violence in **Kenya** (Jan. 2008) and **Zimbabwe** (Apr. 2008). Under Pres. Robert **Mugabe**, Zimbabwe sustained soaring unemployment and hyperinflation. **Guinea-Bissau**'s defense chief and president were assassinated (Mar. 2009).

Americas and the Caribbean. George W. **Bush** (R) served as U.S. president, 2001-09, after close election. He pursued wars in Afghanistan and Iraq following Sept. 2001 terror attack on the U.S. Barack **Obama** (D), first-ever black U.S. president, elected in 2008. The long-supreme Institutional Revolutionary Party (**PRI**) lost power in **Mexico** with election of presidents from a center-right party, Vicente **Fox** (2000) and

Felipe **Calderón** (2006). Calderón launched crackdown on drug trafficking (Dec. 2006); by 2010, over 30,000 people had been killed in drug violence. After 12 years in power, **Canada**'s Liberal Party was defeated in Jan. 2006 elections; Conservative Stephen **Harper** became prime minister, heading minority government.

Leftists held power in several Latin American countries. **Chile** was ruled by Socialist governments under Ricardo **Lagos** Escobar (from 2000) and Michelle **Bachelet** (from 2006). In **Brazil**, Luiz Inácio **Lula** da Silva won a runoff (Oct. 2002) to become president; reelected Oct. 2006. In **Venezuela**, populist Pres. Hugo **Chávez** regained power after a 48-hour coup (Dec. 2002); a subsequent referendum (Feb. 2009) eliminated presidential term limits. Peronist **Nestor Kirchner** was elected president of **Argentina** (Apr. 2003); his wife, **Cristina Kirchner**, was elected (Oct. 2007) to succeed him. In **Bolivia**, Evo **Morales**, another leftist populist, won election as president (Dec. 2005) and passage of a new constitution (Jan. 2009). In **Honduras**, leftist leader Manuel **Zelaya** was elected president (Nov. 2005) but was ousted by the military (June 2009); conservative Porfirio **Lobo** won election (Nov. 2009) to succeed him. In **Nicaragua**, leftist Sandinista leader Daniel **Ortega** won back the presidency, Nov. 2006, and strengthened ties with Cuba and Iran.

In **Peru**, right-wing Pres. Alberto **Fujimori** was reelected (May 2000) but fled the country; he was extradited (2007) and convicted on human rights and corruption charges. **Haiti** was wracked by antigovernment protests, leading to resignation of Jean-Bertrand **Aristide** in Feb. 2004; a UN peacekeeping mission was brought in. Ailing Pres. **Fidel Castro**, **Cuba**'s leader since 1959, ceded powers (July 2006) to his brother, **Raúl**, who instituted limited economic reforms.

Religion. Pope **John Paul II** died, Apr. 2005, after 26 years in the papacy; German Cardinal Joseph Ratzinger was elected as his successor, taking the name **Benedict XVI**. During the decade, reports of **sexual abuse** by Catholic priests and evidence of inaction by church officials emerged and multiplied.

Science and technology. The U.S. **space shuttle** *Columbia* broke up on reentering Earth's atmosphere (Feb. 2003), killing seven crewmembers. NASA landed two rovers, *Spirit* and *Opportunity*, on **Mars** (Jan. 2004); observations verified presence of water. The international Cassini-Huygens mission entered orbit around **Saturn**, June 2004. **China** launched its first manned space flight, Oct. 2003. **Internet** penetration and access to technology expanded exponentially; online commerce, use of **social media** (Facebook, 2004; Twitter, 2006), mobile computing (iPhone, 2007), and file-sharing services became common.

Environment and health. Under the **Kyoto Protocol** (effective Feb. 2005), most industrialized nations agreed to specific reductions in emissions of **greenhouse gases** linked to global warming. Worldwide **AIDS** estimates showed (Nov. 2007) new infections had peaked in the late 1990s. An epidemic of **swine flu**, or influenza A (H1N1), broke out in **Mexico** (Apr. 2009) and spread, killing more than 18,000.

Searching for Resolutions: 2010-mid 2018

Middle East. UN General Assembly granted observer-state status to **Palestine** (Nov. 2012). Arab-Israeli **peace talks** resumed, July 2013, but foundered as **Fatah** and militant **Hamas** factions agreed (Apr. 2014) to aim for unification. **Israel** launched airstrikes on **Gaza** (July-Aug. 2014) after rocket attacks by Hamas-affiliated groups; at least 2,000 Palestinians and 60 Israeli soldiers killed. **Hamas** remained in effective control of Gaza, conducted sporadic terrorist attacks. U.S. recognized **Jerusalem** as Israel's capital, Dec. 2017, and relocated embassy there, May 2018. Demonstrations in Gaza over Israel's economic blockade expanded into mass protest at border fence beginning Mar. 2018, with some violence. Israeli forces responded with tear gas and gunfire; over 150 mostly unarmed protesters killed.

Poverty, religious and ethnic conflict, and government corruption and repression fueled revolts against entrenched regimes. In **Tunisia**, protests forced the ouster of Pres. Zine al-Abidine **Ben Ali** (Jan. 2011); elections followed and a new constitution (Jan. 2014) recognized civil liberties. But the so-called **Arab Spring** also backfired. In **Egypt**, after mass demonstrations led to overthrow of longtime Pres. Hosni **Mubarak** (Feb. 2011), the new **Muslim Brotherhood**-dominated government (elected June 2012) fell in a military coup (July 2013); raids (over 600 killed) and mass arrests followed. Coup leader Abdel Fattah **al-Sisi** was elected president, May 2014. In **Libya**, insurgents with NATO military backing overthrew dictator Muammar al-**Qaddafi**, who was killed (Oct. 2011). A battleground for rival Islamist factions, Libya became increasingly lawless (U.S. consulate attacked in **Benghazi**, Sept. 2012; rebels took over **Tripoli**, Oct. 2014) and served as hub for tens of thousands of migrants heading for Europe. In **Yemen**, Pres. Ali Abdullah **Saleh** yielded power to new leader, Feb. 2012, after protests. **Houthi** rebels, backed by Iran, took over Sanaa, Sept. 2014. A Saudi-led coalition of Arab states (Mar. 2015) launched bombings against Houthi. Civil war continued through 2018, involving multiple militant groups, U.S. airstrikes, massive casualties.

In **Iraq**, the last U.S. combat unit withdrew, Aug. 2010; U.S. military left in Dec. 2011. Death toll, 2003-11: about 4,500 U.S. service members, 300 from allied countries, and Iraqi civilian deaths estimated at over 100,000. But sectarian violence accelerated, with government forces and Shia militia fighting insurgent groups. After taking **Fallujah** and **Mosul**, Sunni extremist rebels of the Islamic State in Iraq and Syria (**ISIS**) declared a caliphate (June 2014); seized **Ramadi**, May 2015. ISIS imposed strict Islamic law, murdered minorities and resisters, and recorded beheadings. Separatist **Kurds** controlled part of Iraq and fought ISIS on the ground. U.S. and allies conducted airstrikes and sent in advisers, and ISIS lost nearly all its territory (including Ramadi, Dec. 2015; Fallujah, June 2016; Mosul, July 2017). Over 300 killed in ISIS bombings in **Baghdad** (July 2016). Iraqi troops seized Kurdish-held **Kirkuk**, Oct. 2017; government asserted liberation from ISIS, Dec. 2017. Nouri al-**Maliki** lost Iraqi premiership to Haider **al-Abadi**, Sept 2014; coalition led by anti-American Shia cleric Muqtada al-**Sadr** won a plurality in May 2018 elections.

In **Afghanistan**, U.S. and NATO-led troops reached about 140,000 by mid-2011, when drawdown began. Combat operations officially ended in Dec. 2014, but thousands of troops remained in support roles under agreement with new unity government headed by Ashraf **Ghani**. Coalition death toll, 2001-14: close to 3,500. Fighting continued, with Taliban gaining ground (45% of country in **Taliban** hands or contested as of Jan. 2018). Taliban bombed civilian areas (150 killed in truck bomb, May 2017, and over 100 killed from explosives in an ambulance, Jan. 2018, both in **Kabul**). UN estimated 28,300 non-combatants died in Afghanistan violence, 2009-17.

In **Syria**, Pres. Bashar al-**Assad**, Mar. 2011, launched offensive against protesters, giving rise to **civil war**. After about 1,400 people were killed in **chemical attacks**, mostly attributed to the regime, the government, Sept. 2013, agreed to a Russian-backed plan for surrender of chemical weapons. Despite sporadic cease-fires, fighting continued (death toll unknown, but estimated at 511,000 in Mar. 2018). In Dec. 2016, after years-long siege and bombings, Syrian government forces, supported by Russia and Iran, gained control of **Aleppo**. In Oct. 2017, U.S.-backed rebels took over **Raqqa**, hitherto the ISIS de facto capital. The Assad regime was suspected in further chemical attacks, as in Apr. 2018, in conjunction with capture of rebel-held eastern Ghouta.

In **Iran**, where moderate cleric Hassan **Rouhani** was elected president (June 2013), the government, July 2015, reached multinational agreement to cut back nuclear weapon capability in return for lifting of sanctions and release of over $100 billion in frozen assets. In Jan. 2016, **Saudi Arabia** broke ties with Iran after Iranians burned Saudi embassy following Saudi execution of an activist Shia cleric. Protests over poor economy spread through Iran, starting Dec. 2017, with thousands arrested. Anti-American protests followed after U.S. withdrew from Iran nuclear agreement, May 2018. In **Jordan**, anti-austerity protests brought down the government, June 2018.

Crime and terrorism. According to U.S. State Dept., terrorist attacks, in 2016 alone, caused over 25,600 deaths globally; 75% were in Iraq, Afghanistan, Syria, Nigeria, or Pakistan. After **al-Qaeda** leader Osama **bin Laden** was killed in U.S. raid in Pakistan (May 2011), al-Qaeda remained entrenched in its base along Afghan-Pakistan border, while **ISIS** and al-Qaeda affiliates were both active on a wide scale.

Among major incidents, **al-Shabab** militants linked to al-Qaeda were behind July 2010 bombings in Kampala, **Uganda** (over 70 killed), Sept. 2013 shootings at a Nairobi, **Kenya**, shopping mall (close to 70 died), and Apr. 2015 massacre at a college in Garissa, Kenya (nearly 150 killed). In **Yemen**, al-Qaeda in the Arabian Peninsula (**AQAP**) attacked military parade rehearsal (May 2012; over 100 killed). **Boko Haram** jihadists, active in Africa, abducted over 200 schoolgirls in **Nigeria** (Apr. 2014). **Taliban** gunmen in **Pakistan** killed some 150 at a Peshawar school (Dec. 2014). Radicalized brothers originally from Chechnya set off bombs at the **Boston Marathon** (Apr. 2013); in **Ottawa**, Canada, a Muslim gunman killed a sentry and attacked Parliament (Oct. 2014). Attackers possibly linked to AQAP killed 17 in and around **Paris**, France, Jan. 2015, most at offices of satirical magazine ***Charlie Hebdo***. Jihadists linked to ISIS murdered 130 in or near Paris, Nov. 2015, and 36 in and around **Brussels**, Mar. 2016.

Jihadists launched attacks in **Tunisia** (Mar., June 2015; about 60 killed) and in **Turkey**, at peace rally (Oct. 2015; over 100 killed) and airport (June 2016; over 40 died). **Russian airliner** exploded over **Egypt** (Oct. 2015, killing 224); bombing in **St. Petersburg** subways killed 16 (Apr. 2017). Couple with Jihadist sympathies killed 14 at a **San Bernardino**, CA, workplace (Dec. 2015); ISIS-inspired shooter killed 49 (June 2016) at gay nightclub in **Orlando**, FL. ISIS claimed responsibility for truck attack in **Nice**, France (July 2016, 86 killed), and bombings at **Istanbul** nightclub (Jan. 2017; 39 killed), plus major attacks in Iraq and Afghanistan. Suicide bombing at pop music concert in **Manchester**, England (May 2017), killed 22. In Egypt, ISIS-affiliated terrorists attacked Coptic Christian churches (Apr.-May 2017; about 75 killed) and a non-Sunni mosque (Nov. 2017; over 300 died). Three radicalized families launched suicide attacks in Surabaya, **Indonesia** (May 2018; 25 died in all). Al-Shabab militants were linked to bombing in Mogadishu, **Somalia** (Oct. 2017; over 350 killed). Jihadist targets also included a church in **Normandy** (July 2016, priest killed), Christmas market in **Berlin** (Dec. 2016; 12 killed), and sites in **London** (Mar., June 2017; 12 killed) and Barcelona (Aug. 2017; 15 killed).

An anti-Muslim extremist killed 77 people in **Norway**, July 2011; another killed six in a **Québec City** mosque, June 2017. In Apr. 2018 a van driver plowed into pedestrians in **Toronto**, killing 10, mostly women. A shooter killed 58 at a **Las Vegas** music festival, Oct. 2017.

Europe. The EU, with IMF help, provided loans to bail out **Greece** (beginning May 2010); a leftist Greek government, elected Jan. 2015, accepted a rescue plan, despite its rejection in a referendum. Also receiving **bailouts** were **Ireland** (2010), **Portugal** (2011), **Spain** (2013), and **Cyprus** (2013). **Croatia** became 28th EU member, July 2013; **Lithuania** became 19th nation to adopt the **euro**, Jan. 2015.

Millions of **migrants**, mostly from Middle East and Africa, sought asylum in Europe 2014-18; thousands drowned crossing the Mediterranean. EU, Sept. 2015, approved plan aimed at redistributing some 120,000 migrants from heavily impacted **Greece** and **Italy**; **Turkey** (Mar. 2016) agreed to limit outflow and accept more migrants in exchange for aid and other concessions. Opposition to migrant influx helped spur growth of populist parties.

Conservatives returned to power in **UK** under David **Cameron** (May 2010) and were reelected in June 2015 but split internally over **Brexit**. UK voted, June 2016, to leave the EU; EU supporter Cameron resigned and new Conservative leader Theresa **May** became prime minister. After June 2017 elections she formed a minority government. In **France**, socialist François **Hollande** defeated conservative Nicolas **Sarkozy** to become president (May 2012). He was succeeded by pro-EU centrist Emmanuel **Macron**, who defeated far-right nationalist Marine **LePen** in May 2017 runoff. Conservative Recep Tayyip **Erdogan**, prime minister of **Turkey** since 2003, was elected president of **Turkey** in Aug. 2014. Erdogan launched crackdown on opponents and journalists following a July 2016 **coup** attempt (160,000 jailed) and an offensive against Kurds in Syria (Jan. 2018). Elections in June 2018 granted Erdogan sweeping new powers. In **Italy**, center-left Prime Min. Matteo **Renzi** resigned, Dec. 2017, leading to elections and formation,

June 2018, of a populist coalition government. In **Spain**, the government imposed direct rule over **Catalonia** in Oct. 2017, after lawmakers there declared independence following a referendum. In May 2018, **ETA**, the Basque separatist group responsible for over 800 deaths in Spain during some 40 years of violence announced its dissolution. Spain's socialists took power in June 2018, after the conservative government fell in a corruption scandal. In **Hungary**, anti-immigration populist Prime Min. Viktor **Orbán** won third term in Apr. 2018 elections.

After interregnum as prime minister, Vladimir **Putin** was elected again as **Russia**'s president (Mar. 2012, 2018). Claiming danger to ethnic Russians, he sent troops to annex Ukrainian territory of **Crimea** in Mar. 2014, resulting in international sanctions. Putin also intervened in Syria (beginning Sept. 2015), providing military support to the Assad regime, and allegedly meddled in 2016 U.S. elections. Hundreds in Russia were arrested in anti-corruption protests, June 2017. After Mar. 2018 **poisoning** in London of a Russian former spy and his daughter appeared to originate in Russia, UK, U.S., and other Western countries expelled Russian diplomats (Russia reciprocated).

Pro-Russian Viktor **Yanukovich**, elected president of **Ukraine** in Feb. 2010, faced mass protests after he rebuffed EU integration; he fled (Feb. 2014). With pro-Russian separatists fighting for control of E Ukraine, pro-European moderate Petro **Poroshenko** was elected Ukraine's president (May 2014) and signed EU trade agreement, June 2014. Multinational talks led to fragile cease-fire, Feb. 2015. UN estimated in 2017 that close to 10,000 had died since Apr. 2014, with many more fleeing or displaced. In **Moldova**, stung by the 2014 disappearance of $1 billion from banks, the election of Pavel **Filip** as prime minister (Jan. 2016) stirred anticorruption protests. Over 20 years after the **Srebrenica massacre** in **Bosnia**, former Bosnian Serb leader Radovan Karadzic (Mar. 2016) and commander Ratko Mladic (Nov. 2017) were convicted of war crimes.

In May 2015 traditionally Catholic **Ireland** became first country to legalize **same-sex marriage** by popular vote; three years later the country voted to repeal constitutional ban on **abortion**. So-called **Panama Papers**, leaked Apr. 2016, showed how politicians concealed assets abroad; implicated were leaders in **Russia**, **Ukraine**, **UK**, and **Iceland**. In royal milestone, May 2018, Britain's **Prince Harry** married U.S.-born Meghan **Markle**, a divorced, biracial actress.

Asia and the Pacific. An **earthquake** and **tsunami** (Mar. 2011) struck **Japan**, killing more than 16,000 and leading to meltdowns at nuclear reactors. Over 8,500 were killed in two earthquakes in **Nepal** (Apr.-May 2015). A **Malaysian airliner** en route to Beijing with 239 aboard veered off course and vanished (Mar. 2014).

Kyrgyzstan's president was ousted (Apr. 2010) after clashes with protesters left at least 85 dead; up to 2,000 killed in ethnic violence, June 2010; in Dec. 2016 voters approve constitutional changes strengthening executive power. **North Korean** dictator **Kim Jong Il** died, Dec. 2011; succeeded by son **Kim Jong Un**,

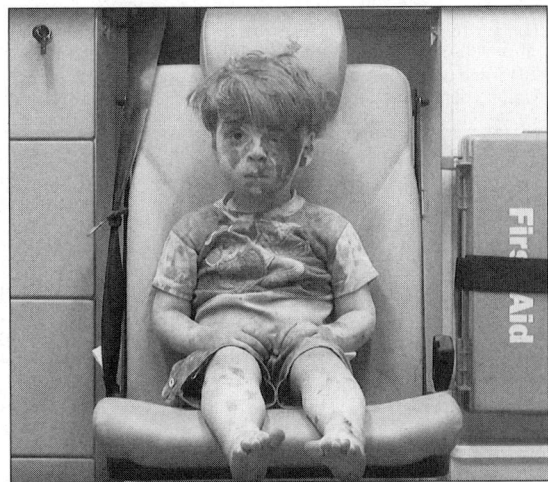

Since the civil war broke out in Syria in 2011, some 12 million Syrians have become refugees or were displaced within Syria.

who resumed nuclear and ballistic missile tests, leading to heavy international sanctions. In **South Korea**, Pres. **Park** Geun-hye was removed from office, Mar. 2017 (convicted of corruption, Apr. 2018) and replaced by center-left **Moon** Jae-in. Moon and Kim Jong Un met in summits, the first between the two nations in more than a decade, Apr.-May 2018. Kim and U.S. Pres. Trump met in Singapore, June 2018, resulting in accord calling for "denuclearization of the Korean peninsula." **Myanmar**'s military-backed party lost Nov. 2015 election to party of dissident leader Aung San **Suu Kyi**. Sectarian and government violence against Myanmar's long-persecuted **Rohingya** Muslim minority surged in 2016-17, in part in response to insurgent attacks. Thousands of Rohingya were killed; hundreds of thousands fled, many to refugee camps in **Bangladesh**.

In **China**, **Xi** Jinping succeeded retiring **Hu** Jintao as Communist party chief, Nov. 2012, and president, Mar. 2013. In Mar. 2018, party reelected Xi and supported constitutional changes eliminating term limits. The party retained firm control (**Hong Kong** pro-democracy protests, Sept.-Dec. 2014). Signs of slowdown in China's economic growth rattled investors globally. Hindu nationalists won majority in May 2014 elections in **India**; Narendra **Modi** became prime minister. Anti-crime hardliner Rodrigo **Duterte** was elected **Philippines** president, May 2016; thousands of alleged drug dealers and users were killed and over a million surrendered in subsequent anti-drug campaign. In Oct. 2017 the Philippine government declared victory over Islamist rebels in the city of Marawi. **Thailand**'s King **Bhumibol** Adulyadej died, Oct. 2016, ending 70-year reign; new king, **Vajiralongkorn**, signed army-drafted constitution, Apr. 2017. In **Malaysian** elections, May 2018, the ruling coalition since independence fell to opposition; 92-year-old former leader **Mahathir** Mohamad became prime minister.

Trans-Pacific Partnership (TPP), trade pact covering 12 Pacific nations, was signed Feb. 2016 but not in force. After new U.S. administration repudiated TPP, remaining nations signed a replacement, Mar. 2018.

Africa. Coups ousted **Niger**'s president (Feb. 2010) and ended elections in **Guinea-Bissau** (Apr. 2012); in both cases, civilian rule returned following new elections. In a referendum, southern Sudanese (mostly Christian or indigenous religion) voted overwhelmingly for separation from the north (mostly Arab Muslim), and **South Sudan** was granted independence as of July 2011. An ethnic-based leadership struggle in 2013 led to **civil war** in South Sudan. Thousands of civilians killed, millions displaced or fled; UN (Feb. 2017) declared **famine** conditions. Former Liberian Pres. Charles **Taylor** convicted of war crimes, Apr. 2012. Low-level soldiers staged coup in **Mali** (Mar. 2012); junta ceded power to civilians, but Islamic rebels seized control in the north. French and West African forces intervened; a peace deal was reached (June 2013) but proved fragile. In **Burkina Faso**, longtime Pres. Blaise **Campaoré** fled amid protests (Oct. 2014); elections in Dec. 2015 brought in new government. In **Nigeria**, former dictator Muhammadu **Buhari** was elected president, Mar. 2015; Muslim herders clashed with Christian farmers (over 80 killed, Jan. 2018) and **Boko Haram** remained active (responsible for thousands of deaths since 2009). Ethnic and political violence plagued **Burundi** in 2015; hundreds killed, at least 250,000 displaced. An African Union court, June 2016, convicted Hissène **Habré** of crimes

against humanity while ruler of **Chad** in the 1980s. In **Gambia** longtime Pres. Yahya **Jammeh** reluctantly yielded power, Jan. 2017, after election defeat. In **Zimbabwe** longtime Pres. Robert **Mugabe** resigned, Nov. 2017, after house arrest by military and impeachment threat; in **South Africa**, Jacob **Zuma**, president since 2009, resigned Feb. 2018, amid intra-party opposition; subsequently charged with corruption.

An **Ebola** epidemic in W Africa (2014-15) caused over 11,000 deaths, mostly in Guinea, Liberia, and Sierra Leone.

Americas and the Caribbean. Poverty and violence related to drug cartels and other organized crime continued to spur migration to the U.S. from **Mexico**, **El Salvador**, **Honduras**, and **Guatemala**. In **Haiti** an **earthquake** (Jan. 2010) killed over 200,000; lingering **cholera** epidemic left thousands more dead. **Canada**'s Conservatives, under Prime Min. Stephen **Harper**, won majority in May 2011 elections, but Liberals came back to win in Oct. 2015 under charismatic party leader Justin **Trudeau**. **Mexico**'s long-dominant Institutional Revolutionary Party lost power with the landslide election (July 2018) of leftist candidate Andrés Manuel **López Obrador**, following a campaign in which over 100 politicians were murdered. U.S., under Pres. Obama, officially restored relations with **Cuba**, July 2015; Miguel **Díaz-Canel** succeeded Raúl Castro as Cuba's president, Apr. 2018. After Nov. 2016 election of real estate magnate Donald **Trump**, "America First" policy prevailed and traditional allies' influence diminished (G7 summit, June 2018).

Several leftist regimes suffered reverses. In **Brazil**, Pres. **Lula** da Silva's chosen successor, Dilma **Rousseff**, won the presidency, Oct. 2010, but a corruption scandal and devastated economy led to mass protests. She was removed (Aug. 2016) after Senate trial. Lula himself was convicted in corruption case, July 2017. In **Nicaragua** leftist Pres. Daniel **Ortega** twice won reelections challenged as flawed (Nov. 2011, 2016); protests were violently suppressed (over 200 killed, Apr.-June 2018). In **Venezuela**, leftist Pres. Hugo **Chávez** died, Mar. 2013. His ally and elected successor Nicolás **Maduro** Moros declared state of emergency (May 2016) as economy collapsed; large-scale protests saw heavy casualties; powers of legislature curbed. Maduro was reelected, May 2018, aided by boycott and irregularities. In **Chile**, billionaire conservative Sebastián **Piñera** replaced leftist Pres. Michelle **Bachelet** following Jan. 2010 election; after she returned for second term, **Piñera** defeated (Dec. 2017) her choice for a successor.

Argentine voters ended 12 years of Peronist rule, choosing center-right candidate Mauricio **Macri** as president (Nov. 2015); debt repayment deal approved, Mar. 2016. **Peru**'s voters elected a conservative, Pedro Pablo **Kuczynski**, as president (June 2016), but he resigned, Mar. 2018, in corruption scandal. After over 50 years of fighting, the **Colombian** government signed revised peace accord (Nov. 2016) with Revolutionary Army of Colombia (**FARC**) guerrillas.

Uruguay (Dec. 2013) and **Canada** (June 2018) became the first countries to fully legalize **marijuana**.

Religion. Pope Benedict XVI resigned after eight years (Feb. 2013); Argentinean Cardinal Jorge Mario Bergoglio was elected to succeed him; took the name **Francis**. U.S. State Dept., Dec. 2017, cited 10 countries as of "particular concern" for violations of **religious freedom**: China, Eritrea, Iran, North Korea, Myanmar, Saudi Arabia, Sudan, Tajikistan, Turkmenistan, and Uzbekistan, with Pakistan put on "watch list."

Science, technology, environment. After 30 years, NASA's **space shuttle** program ended with return of *Atlantis* to Earth (July 2011). NASA's rover *Curiosity* landed on **Mars**, Aug. 2012; China landed unmanned *Yulu* rover on the **Moon**, Dec. 2013. NASA's *New Horizons* space probe made flyby of **Pluto**, July 2015. Scientists, Feb. 2016, reported first-ever direct observation of **gravitational waves**, confirming Einstein prediction. NASA's *Kepler/K2* missions, first launched Mar. 2009, found more than 2,000 confirmed exoplanets by mid-2018.

Ransomware emerged as increasing global threat with launch of CryptoLocker (Sept. 2013) and other cyberattacks. Representatives of 195 nations, meeting in Paris (Dec. 2015), committed to individual plans for reducing greenhouse gas emissions linked to **climate change**; Pres. Trump announced intention to withdraw U.S. from agreement, June 2015. Average global temperatures reached record high in 2016; 2015 and 2017 ranked 2nd- and 3rd-highest.·

Leaders of North Korea and South Korea, two nations still technically at war, held summits in Apr., May, and Sept. 2018.

HISTORICAL FIGURES

Note: Information accurate as of Sept. 2018.

Ancient Greeks and Romans

Greeks

Aeschines, orator, 389-314 BCE
Aeschylus, dramatist, 525-456 BCE
Aesop, fableist, c. 620-c. 560 BCE
Alcibiades, politician, 450-404 BCE
Anacreon, poet, c. 582-c. 485 BCE
Anaxagoras, philosopher, c. 500-428 BCE
Anaximander, philosopher, 611-546 BCE
Anaximenes, philosopher, c. 570-500 BCE
Antiphon, speechwriter, c. 480-411 BCE
Apollonius, mathematician, c. 265-170 BCE
Archimedes, mathematician, 287-212 BCE
Aristophanes, dramatist, c. 448-380 BCE
Aristotle, philosopher, 384-322 BCE
Athenaeus, scholar, fl. c. 200
Callicrates, architect, fl. 5th cent. BCE
Callimachus, poet, c. 305-240 BCE
Cratinus, comic dramatist, 520-421 BCE
Democritus, philosopher, c. 460-370 BCE
Demosthenes, orator, 384-322 BCE
Diodorus, historian, fl. 20 BCE
Diogenes, philosopher, c. 400-c. 325 BCE
Dionysius, historian, d. c. 7 BCE
Empedocles, philosopher, c. 490-430 BCE
Epicharmus, dramatist, c. 530-440 BCE
Epictetus, philosopher, c. 55-c. 135
Epicurus, philosopher, 341-270 BCE
Eratosthenes, scientist, 276-194 BCE
Euclid, mathematician, fl. c. 300 BCE
Euripides, dramatist, c. 484-406 BCE
Galen, physician, 129-200
Heraclitus, philosopher, c. 540-c. 480 BCE
Herodotus, historian, c. 484-420 BCE

Hesiod, poet, 8th cent. BCE
Hippocrates, physician, c. 460-377 BCE
Homer, poet, fl. c. 8th cent. BCE
Isocrates, orator, 436-338 BCE
Menander, dramatist, 342-292 BCE
Parmenides, philosopher, c. 515-440 BCE
Pericles, statesman, c. 495-429 BCE
Phidias, sculptor, fl. 490-430 BCE
Pindar, poet, c. 518-c. 438 BCE
Plato, philosopher, c. 428-347 BCE
Plutarch, biographer, c. 46-120
Polybius, historian, c. 200-c. 118 BCE
Praxiteles, sculptor, 400-330 BCE
Pythagoras, phil., math., c. 580-c. 500 BCE
Sappho, poet, c. 610-c. 580 BCE
Simonides, poet, 556-c. 468 BCE
Socrates, philosopher, 469-399 BCE
Solon, statesman, 640-560 BCE
Sophocles, dramatist, c. 496-406 BCE
Strabo, geographer, c. 63 BCE-24 CE
Thales, philosopher, c. 634-546 BCE
Themistocles, politician, c. 524-c. 460 BCE
Theocritus, poet, c. 310-250 BCE
Theophrastus, phil., c. 372-c. 287 BCE
Thucydides, historian, fl. 5th cent. BCE
Timon, philosopher, c. 320-c. 230 BCE
Xenophon, historian, c. 434-c. 355 BCE
Zeno, philosopher, c. 335-c. 263 BCE

Romans

Ammianus, historian, c. 330-395
Apuleius, satirist, c. 124-c. 170
Boethius, scholar, c. 480-524
Caesar, Julius, leader, 100-44 BCE

Catiline, politician, c. 108-62 BCE
Cato (Elder), statesman, 234-149 BCE
Catullus, poet, c. 84-54 BCE
Cicero, orator, 106-43 BCE
Claudian, poet, c. 370-c. 404
Ennius, poet, 239-170 BCE
Gellius, author, c. 130-c. 165
Horace, poet, 65-8 BCE
Juvenal, satirist, 60-127
Livy, historian, 59 BCE-17 CE
Lucan, poet, 39-65
Lucilius, poet, c. 180-c.102 BCE
Lucretius, poet, c. 99-c. 55 BCE
Martial, epigrammatist, c. 38-c. 103
Nepos, historian, c. 100-c. 25 BCE
Ovid, poet, 43 BCE-17 CE
Persius, satirist, 34-62
Plautus, dramatist, c. 254-c. 184 BCE
Pliny the Elder, scholar, 23-79
Pliny the Younger, author, 62-113
Quintilian, rhetorician, c. 35-c. 97
Sallust, historian, 86-34 BCE
Seneca, philosopher, 4 BCE-65 CE
Silius, poet, c. 25-101
Statius, poet, c. 45-c. 96
Suetonius, biographer, c. 69-c. 122
Tacitus, historian, 56-120
Terence, dramatist, 195/185-c. 159 BCE
Tibullus, poet, c. 55-c. 19 BCE
Vergil, poet, 70-19 BCE
Vitruvius, architect, fl. late 1st cent. BCE

Roman Rulers

From Romulus to the end of the Empire in the West (Rome). Rulers in the East sat in Constantinople and, for a brief period, in Nicaea, until the capture of Constantinople by the Turks in 1453, when Byzantium was succeeded by the Ottoman Empire.

The Kingdom

BCE
753 Romulus (Quirinus)
715 Numa Pompilius
673 Tullus Hostilius
641 Ancus Marcius
616 L. Tarquinius Priscus
579 Servius Tullius
534 L. Tarquinius Superbus

The Republic

509 Consulate established;
Quaestorship instituted
498 Dictatorship introduced
494 Plebeian Tribunate created;
Plebeian Aedileship created
444 Consular Tribunate organized
435 Censorship instituted
366 Praetorship established;
Curule Aedileship created
362 Military Tribunate elected
326 Proconsulate introduced
311 Naval Duumvirate elected
217 Dictatorship of Fabius Maximus
133 Tribunate of Tiberius Gracchus
123 Tribunate of Gaius Gracchus
82 Dictatorship of Sulla
60 First Triumvirate formed
(Caesar, Pompeius, Crassus)
47 Dictatorship of Caesar
43 Second Triumvirate formed
(Octavianus, Antonius, Lepidus)

The Empire

27 Augustus (or Octavian)
CE
14 Tiberius
37 Caligula
41 Claudius
54 Nero
68 Galba
69 Otho; Vitellius; Vespasian,
established Flavian Dynasty
79 Titus
81 Domitian, end of Flavian Dynasty

96 Nerva
98 Trajan
117 Hadrian
138 Antoninus Pius
161 Marcus Aurelius and Lucius Verus
169 Marcus Aurelius (alone)
177 Marcus Aurelius and Commodus
180 Commodus
193 Pertinax
193 Didius Julianus
193 Septimius Severus, founded
Severan Dynasty
211 Caracalla and Geta
212 Caracalla (alone)
217 Macrinus
218 Elagabalus (or Heliogabalus)
222 Alexander Severus, end of dynasty
235 Maximinus (the Thracian)
238 Gordian I and Gordian II
238 Pupienus and Balbinus
238 Gordian III
244 Philip (the Arabian)
249 Decius
251 Gallus and Volusianus
253 Aemilian
253 Valerian and Gallienus
258 Gallienus (alone)
268 Claudius II (or Claudius Gothicus)
270 Quintillus
270 Aurelian
275 Tacitus
276 Florian
276 Probus
282 Carus
283 Carinus and Numerian
284 Diocletian
286 Diocletian and Maximian
305 Galerius and Constantius I
306 Galerius, Maximinus (or
Maximinus Daia), Severus
307 Galerius, Maximinus (Daia),
Constantine I, Licinius, Maxentius
311 Maximinus (Daia), Constantine I,
Licinius, Maxentius

314 Constantine I, Licinius
324 Constantine I (the Great), first
Christian emperor
337 Constantine I, Constans I,
Constantius II
340 Constantius II and Constans I
353 Constantius II (alone)
361 Julian (the Apostate)
363 Jovian

West (Rome) and East (Constantinople)

364 Valentinian I (West),
Valens (East)
367 Valentinian I with Gratian (W),
Valens (E)
375 Gratian with Valentinian II (W),
Valens (E)
379 Gratian with Valentinian II (W),
Theodosius I (E)
383 Magnus Maximus and
Valentinian II (W),
Theodosius I (E)
388 Valentinian II (W), Theodosius I (E)
392 Eugenius (W), Theodosius I (E)
394 Theodosius I (the Great)
395 Honorius (W), Arcadius (E)
408 Honorius (W), Theodosius II (E)
423 Valentinian III (W),
Theodosius II (E)
450 Valentinian III (W), Marcian (E)
455 Petronius Maximus (W),
Marcian (E)
455 Avitus (W), Marcian (E)
457 Majorian (W), Leo I (E)
461 Libius Severus (W), Leo I (E)
467 Anthemius (W), Leo I (E)
472 Olybrius (W), Leo I (E)
473 Glycerius (W), Leo I (E)
474 Julius Nepos (W), Leo II (E)
475 Romulus Augustulus (W), Zeno (E)
476 End of Empire in W when Romulus
Augustulus deposed by Germanic
chief Odoacer, who was later
murdered by King Theodoric of
Ostrogoths, 493

Rulers of England and the United Kingdom

Reign began	England: Saxons and Danes	Age at death[1]
829	Egbert, king of Wessex, won allegiance of all English	NA
839	Ethelwulf, son, king of Wessex, Sussex, Kent, Essex	NA
858	Ethelbald, eldest son, displaced father in Wessex	NA
860	Ethelbert, 2nd son of Ethelwulf, united Kent and Wessex	NA
866	Ethelred I, 3rd son of Ethelwulf, king of Wessex, fought Danes	NA
871	Alfred (the Great), 4th son of Ethelwulf, defeated Danes, fortified London	52
899	Edward (the Elder), son, united English, claimed Scotland	55
924	Athelstan (the Glorious), eldest son, king of Mercia, Wessex	45
940	Edmund, 3rd son of Edward, king of Wessex, Mercia	25
946	Edred, 4th son of Edward	32
955	Edwy (the Fair), eldest son of Edmund, king of Wessex	18
959	Edgar (the Peaceful), 2nd son of Edmund, ruled all English	32
975	Edward (the Martyr), eldest son, murdered by stepmother	17
978; 1014[2]	Ethelred II (the Unready), 2nd son of Edgar, married Emma of Normandy	48
1016	Edmund II (Ironside), son, king of London	27
1016	Canute (the Dane), son of Sweyn, who conquered English territory; gave Wessex to Edmund II; married Emma, Ethelred II's widow	40
1035	Harold I (Harefoot), illegitimate son	NA
1040	Hardecanute, son of Canute by Emma, also king of Denmark	24
1042	Edward (the Confessor), son of Ethelred II, canonized 1161	62
1066	Harold II, brother-in-law, last Saxon king	44
	England: House of Normandy	
1066	William I (the Conqueror), son of Duke Robert I of Normandy, defeated Harold II at Hastings	60
1087	William II (Rufus), 3rd son, killed by arrow while hunting in possible assassination	43
1100	Henry I (Beauclerc), youngest son of William I	67
	England: House of Blois	
1135	Stephen, son of Adela, daughter of William I, and Count of Blois	50
	England: House of Plantagenet	
1154	Henry II, son of Geoffrey Plantagenet (Angevin) by Matilda, daughter of Henry I	56
1189	Richard I (Coeur de Lion), son, crusader	42
1199	John (Lackland), son of Henry II, approved Magna Carta, 1215	50
1216	Henry III, son, acceded at 9, under regency until 1227	65
1272	Edward I (Longshanks), son	68
1307	Edward II, son, deposed by Parliament	43
1327	Edward III (of Windsor), son	65
1377	Richard II, grandson of Edward III, deposed	33
	England: House of Lancaster	
1399	Henry IV (of Bolingbroke), son of John of Gaunt, duke of Lancaster, son of Edward III	47
1413	Henry V, son, victor over French at Agincourt	34
1422; 1470	Henry VI, son, overthrown by Edward IV in 1461 but was returned to throne in 1470. Deposed, died in Tower of London, 1471	49
	England: House of York	
1461; 1471	Edward IV, great-great-grandson of Edward III, son of duke of York. Acclaimed king by Parliament, 1461. Driven into exile in 1470 but regained throne, 1471	40
1483	Edward V, son, murdered in Tower of London	13
1483	Richard III, brother of Edward IV, fell in battle at Bosworth Field against Henry Tudor	32

Reign began	England: House of Tudor	Age at death[1]
1485	Henry VII, son of Edmund Tudor, earl of Richmond, whose father had married Henry V's widow. Descended from Edward III through mother, Margaret Beaufort, via John of Gaunt. Married Elizabeth of York, eldest daughter of Edward IV, to unite Lancaster and York.	53
1509	Henry VIII, 2nd son, by Elizabeth	56
1547	Edward VI, son, by Jane Seymour, his 3rd queen. Was persuaded by John Dudley to name Lady Jane Grey, his cousin and Dudley's daughter-in-law, his successor. Council of State proclaimed her queen, July 10, 1553, but she ruled only nine days before Mary Tudor overthrew her	16
1553	Mary I, daughter of Henry VIII, by his 1st wife, Catherine of Aragon	43
1558	Elizabeth I, daughter of Henry VIII, by his 2nd wife, Anne Boleyn	69
	Great Britain: House of Stuart	
1603	James I (James VI of Scotland), son of Mary, Queen of Scots. First to call self king of Great Britain; this became official with Acts of Union, 1707	59
1625	Charles I, only surviving son of James I	48
	Great Britain: Commonwealth	
1649	Declared upon execution of Charles I	—
	Great Britain: Protectorate	
1653	Oliver Cromwell, served on Council of State, executive body of Commonwealth, following overthrow of monarchy. Named Lord Protector upon creation of Protectorate by 1653 Instrument of Government	59
1658	Richard Cromwell, 3rd son, resigned as Lord Protector amid civil war, 1659	86
	Great Britain: House of Stuart (restored)	
1660	Charles II, eldest son of Charles I, acceded to throne by Restoration, died without issue	55
1685	James II, 2nd son of Charles I, deposed 1688	68
1689	William III, son of William, Prince of Orange, by Mary, daughter of Charles I. Offered joint rule of throne with wife by Parliament	51
1689	Mary II, eldest daughter of James II and wife of William III, died 1694	33
1702	Anne, 2nd daughter of James II, sister-in-law of William III, assumed throne on William's death	49
	United Kingdom of Great Britain[3]: House of Hanover	
1714	George I, son of Elector of Hanover by Sophia, granddaughter of James I	67
1727	George II, only son, married Caroline of Brandenburg	77
1760	George III, grandson, married Charlotte of Mecklenburg	81
1820	George IV, eldest son, prince regent from Feb. 1811	67
1830	William IV, 3rd son of George III, married Adelaide of Saxe-Meiningen	71
1837	Victoria, daughter of Edward, 4th son of George III; married Prince Albert of Saxe-Coburg and Gotha, 1840	81
	United Kingdom of Great Britain[3]: House of Saxe-Coburg-Gotha	
1901	Edward VII, eldest son, married Alexandra, Princess of Denmark	68
	United Kingdom of Great Britain[3]: House of Windsor[4]	
1910	George V, 2nd son, married Princess Mary of Teck	70
1936	Edward VIII, eldest son, acceded Jan. 20, abdicated Dec. 11	77
1936	George VI, 2nd son of George V, married Lady Elizabeth Bowes-Lyon	56
1952	Elizabeth II, elder daughter, acceded Feb. 6	NA

NA = Age/birthdate not certain or not applicable. (1) Except where noted, year of death is the same year the next ruler's reign began. (2) King Sweyn I of Denmark invaded England in 1013 and declared himself king. Ethelred II reclaimed the throne upon Sweyn's death in 1014. (3) Officially the United Kingdom of Great Britain and Ireland after Act of Union 1801 and the United Kingdom of Great Britain and Northern Ireland after Anglo-Irish Treaty of 1921 (name formalized 1927). (4) Name adopted by proclamation of George V, July 17, 1917, because of anti-German feeling during World War I.

Rulers of Scotland

Reign began	Name
846	Kenneth I, first Scot to rule both Scots and Picts
1005	Malcolm II, son of Kenneth II
1034	Duncan I, grandson, first general ruler
1040	Macbeth, seized kingdom, slain by Malcolm Canmore
1057	Malcolm III (Canmore), eldest son of Duncan I
1093	Donald III (the Fair), younger brother
1094	Duncan II, eldest son of Malcolm III by first wife
1095	Donald III (restored)
1097	Edgar, 4th son of Malcolm III and Queen Margaret
1107	Alexander I, brother
1124	David I, brother
1153	Malcolm IV (the Maiden), grandson
1165	William (the Lion), brother
1214	Alexander II, son
1249	Alexander III, son
1286	Margaret (Maid of Norway), granddaughter; died 1290 at age 8. (Interregnum, 1290-92)
1292	John Balliol, proclaimed king of Scotland by Edward I of England. (Interregnum, 1296-1306[1])
1306	Robert I (the Bruce), victor at Bannockburn, 1314. Treaty with England and secured throne, 1328
1329	David II, only surviving son
1371	Robert II (the Steward), son of Robert I's daughter Marjorie and Walter, steward of Scotland. First of Stewart line
1390	Robert III, son
1406	James I, son, assassinated
1437	James II, son
1460	James III, eldest son, possibly assassinated
1488	James IV, eldest son
1513	James V, eldest son, died at Battle of Flodden
1542	Mary (Queen of Scots), daughter, became queen before she was 1 week old. Married Francis II (d. 1560), son of King Henry II of France, 1558. Married her cousin, Henry Stewart, Lord Darnley (d. 1567), 1565. Married James Hepburn, Earl of Bothwell, 1567. Imprisoned by her cousin Elizabeth I of England, 1568; beheaded, 1587
1567	James VI, son of Mary and Lord Darnley, became James I, king of England, on Elizabeth's death, 1603. (Legislative union of Scotland and England as United Kingdom of Great Britain not official until Acts of Union, 1707)

Note: Not all rulers before 1005 are shown. (1) Edward I decreed annexation of Scotland to England, 1296, after defeating Balliol in battle. William Wallace led resistance, 1297-1305.

Prime Ministers of the United Kingdom

Titles are given on first mention only. C = Conservative; La. = Labour; Li. = Liberal; P = Peelite; T = Tory; W = Whig.

Entered office	Name (party)
1721	Sir Robert Walpole (W)[1]
1742	Spencer Compton, 1st Earl of Wilmington (W)
1743	Henry Pelham (W)
1754	Thomas Pelham-Holles, 1st Duke of Newcastle (W)
1756	William Cavendish, 4th Duke of Devonshire (W)
1757	Thomas Pelham-Holles (W)
1762	John Stuart, 3rd Earl of Bute (T)
1763	George Grenville (W)
1765	Charles Watson-Wentworth, 2nd Marquess of Rockingham (W)
1766	William Pitt the Elder, 1st Earl of Chatham (W)
1768	Augustus Henry Fitzroy, 3rd Duke of Grafton (W)
1770	Lord Frederick North (T)
1782	Charles Watson-Wentworth (W)
1782	William Petty, 2nd Earl of Shelburne (W)
1783	William Cavendish-Bentinck, 3rd Duke of Portland (W[2])
1783	William Pitt the Younger (T)
1801	Henry Addington (T)
1804	William Pitt the Younger (T)
1806	William Wyndham Grenville, 1st Baron Grenville (W)
1807	William Cavendish-Bentinck (T)
1809	Spencer Perceval (T)
1812	Robert Banks Jenkinson, 2nd Earl of Liverpool (T)
1827	George Canning (T)
1827	Frederick John Robinson, Viscount Goderich (T)
1828	Arthur Wellesley, 1st Duke of Wellington (T)
1830	Charles Grey, 2nd Earl Grey (W)
1834	William Lamb, 2nd Viscount Melbourne (W)
1834	Arthur Wellesley (T)
1834	Sir Robert Peel, 2nd Baronet (C)
1835	William Lamb (W)
1841	Sir Robert Peel (C)
1846	John Russell, 1st Earl Russell (W)
1852	Edward Stanley, 14th Earl of Derby (C)
1852	George Hamilton Gordon, 4th Earl of Aberdeen (P[2])
1855	Henry John Temple, 3rd Viscount Palmerston (W-Li.)
1858	Edward Stanley (C)
1859	Henry John Temple (W-Li.)
1865	John Russell (Li.)
1866	Edward Stanley (C)
1868	Benjamin Disraeli (C)
1868	William E. Gladstone (Li.)
1874	Benjamin Disraeli (C)
1880	William E. Gladstone (Li.)
1885	Robert Gascoyne-Cecil, 3rd Marquess of Salisbury (C)
1886	William E. Gladstone (Li.)
1886	Robert Gascoyne-Cecil (C)
1892	William E. Gladstone (Li.)
1894	Archibald Primrose, 5th Earl of Rosebery (Li.)
1895	Robert Gascoyne-Cecil (C)
1902	Arthur James Balfour (C)
1905	Sir Henry Campbell-Bannerman (Li.)
1908	Herbert Henry Asquith (Li.[2])
1916	David Lloyd George (Li.[2])
1922	Andrew Bonar Law (C)
1923	Stanley Baldwin (C)
1924	Ramsay MacDonald (La.)
1924	Stanley Baldwin (C)
1929	Ramsay MacDonald (La.[2])
1935	Stanley Baldwin (C[2])
1937	Neville Chamberlain (C[2])
1940	Winston Churchill (C[2])
1945	Clement Attlee (La.)
1951	Winston Churchill (C)
1955	Anthony Eden (C)
1957	Harold Macmillan (C)
1963	Alec Douglas-Home (C)
1964	Harold Wilson (La.)
1970	Edward Heath (C)
1974	Harold Wilson (La.)
1976	James Callaghan (La.)
1979	Margaret Thatcher (C)
1990	John Major (C)
1997	Tony Blair (La.)
2007	Gordon Brown (La.)
2010	David Cameron (C[2])
2016	Theresa May (C)

Note: Prime ministers prior to 1801 are for Great Britain. The Conservative Party was formed in 1834, an outgrowth of the Tory party. (1) Walpole is traditionally regarded as the first prime minister of Britain though the title was not commonly used then and did not become official until 1905. (2) Led a coalition government for all or part of time in office.

Prime Ministers of Canada

C = Conservative; Lib. = Liberal; PC = Progressive Conservative; U = Unionist

Entered office	Name (party)
1867	John A. Macdonald (C)
1873	Alexander Mackenzie (Lib.)
1878	John A. Macdonald (C)
1891	John Abbott (C)
1892	John Thompson (C)
1894	Mackenzie Bowell (C)
1896[1]	Charles Tupper (C)
1896	Wilfrid Laurier (Lib.)
1911	Robert Borden (C/U)[2]
1920	Arthur Meighen (U)
1921	W. L. Mackenzie King (Lib.)
1926[3]	Arthur Meighen (C)
1926	W. L. Mackenzie King (Lib.)
1930	Richard Bedford Bennett (C)
1935	W. L. Mackenzie King (Lib.)
1948	Louis St. Laurent (Lib.)
1957	John G. Diefenbaker (PC)
1963	Lester B. Pearson (Lib.)
1968	Pierre Trudeau (Lib.)
1979	Joe Clark (PC)
1980	Pierre Trudeau (Lib.)
1984[3]	John Turner (Lib.)
1984	Brian Mulroney (PC)
1993[4]	Kim Campbell (PC)
1993	Jean Chrétien (Lib.)
2003	Paul Martin (Lib.)
2006	Stephen Harper (C)
2015	Justin Trudeau (Lib.)

(1) May-July. (2) Conservative 1911-17, Unionist 1917-20. (3) June-Sept. (4) June-Nov.

Rulers of France

Caesar to Charlemagne

Julius Caesar subdued the Gauls, native tribes of Gaul (France), 58 to 51 BCE. The Romans ruled 500 years. The Franks, a Teutonic tribe, reached the Somme from the east c. 250 CE. By the 5th cent., the Merovingian Franks ousted the Romans. In 451, with the help of Visigoths, Burgundians, and others, they defeated Attila and the Huns at Châlons-sur-Marne.

Childeric I became leader of the Merovingians, 458. After son Clovis I (crowned 481) defeated the Alemanni (Germans), 496, he was baptized a Christian and made Paris his capital. Line ended when Childeric III was deposed, 751.

The West Merovingians were called Neustrians, the eastern Austrasians. Pepin of Herstal (687-714), major domus (head of the palace) of Austrasia, took over Neustria as dux (leader) of the Franks. Pepin's son, Charles, called Martel (the Hammer), defeated the Saracens at Tours-Poitiers, 732; was succeeded in 741 by his sons, Pepin the Short and Carloman (abdicated 747). Pepin deposed Childeric III and ruled as king until 768.

His son, Charlemagne, or Charles the Great (742-814), became king of the Franks, 768, with his brother Carloman (751-71). Charlemagne ruled France, Germany, parts of Italy, Spain, and Austria, and enforced Christianity. Crowned Emperor of the Romans by Pope Leo III in Rome, 800. Succeeded by son, Louis I (the Pious), 814. At death, 840, Louis left empire to sons Lothair (Roman emperor), Pepin I (king of Aquitaine), Louis II (the German), and Charles II (the Bald, of France). They quarreled and, by the Treaty of Verdun, 843, divided the empire.

The date preceding each entry is year of accession.

Carolingian Dynasty

843 Charles II (the Bald), Roman emperor, 875
877 Louis II (the Stammerer), son
879 Louis III (d. 882), son, and brother Carloman
885 Charles III (the Fat), son of Louis the German, Roman emperor, 881
888 Eudes (Odo), son of Robert the Strong, elected by nobles
898 Charles III (the Simple), son of Louis II the Stammerer, deposed
922 Robert I, brother of Eudes, defeated forces of Charles III but died in battle
923 Rudolph (Raoul), Robert I's son-in-law, duke of Burgundy
936 Louis IV, son of Charles III (the Simple); struggled with Hugh the Great, son of Robert I
954 Lothair, son, dominated by Hugh the Great
986 Louis V (the Sluggard), left no heirs

House of Capet

987 Hugh Capet, son of Hugh the Great
996 Robert II (the Pious), son
1031 Henry I, son
1060 Philip I (the Fair), son
1108 Louis VI (the Fat), son
1137 Louis VII (the Younger), son
1180 Philip II Augustus, son, crowned at Reims
1223 Louis VIII (the Lion), son
1226 Louis IX, son, arbitrated disputes with English King Henry III; led crusades, 1248 (captured in Egypt, 1250) and 1270, when he died of plague in Tunis. Canonized as St. Louis, 1297
1270 Philip III (the Bold), son
1285 Philip IV (the Fair), son, king at 17
1314 Louis X (the Headstrong), son. His posthumous son, John I, lived and reigned only five days.
1316 Philip V (the Tall), brother of Louis X
1322 Charles IV (the Fair), brother of Louis X

House of Valois

1328 Philip VI (of Valois), grandson of Philip III
1350 John II (the Good), son, retired to England
1364 Charles V (the Wise), son
1380 Charles VI (the Beloved), son
1422 Charles VII (the Victorious), son. In 1429, Joan of Arc defeated English at Orleans and Patay and had Charles crowned at Reims. Joan was captured, 1430, and executed, 1431, at Rouen for heresy.
1461 Louis XI (the Cruel), son, civil reformer
1483 Charles VIII (the Affable), son
1498 Louis XII, great-grandson of Charles V
1515 Francis I, of Angouleme, nephew, son-in-law. Fought four major wars, was patron of the arts
1547 Henry II, son, killed at joust. Husband of Catherine (daughter of Lorenzo) de Médicis and lover of Diane de Poitiers. By marriage to Henry II, Catherine became the mother of Francis II, Charles IX, Henry III, and Queen Margaret (Reine Margot), wife of Henry IV (of Navarre).
1559 Francis II, son. Betrothed in 1548 at age 4 to Mary, Queen of Scots, aged 6; they were married 1558. Francis died 1560, aged 16. Mary returned to rule Scotland, 1561.

1560 Charles IX, brother
1574 Henry III, brother, assassinated

House of Bourbon

1589 Henry IV (of Navarre), grandson of Queen Margaret of Navarre. Made enemies when he gave tolerance to Protestants by Edict of Nantes, 1598. Married Margaret of Valois, daughter of Henry II and Catherine de Médicis; was divorced. Married Marie de Médicis, 1600. She became regent upon Henry's assassination, 1610-17, for her son, Louis XIII; she was exiled by Richelieu, 1631.
1610 Louis XIII (the Just), son, married Anne of Austria. His chief minister (1622-42), Cardinal Richelieu, determined his policies.
1643 Louis XIV (the Sun King), son; was king 72 years. Until 1661, Anne of Austria was regent with Cardinal Mazarin as chief minister; Louis then ruled absolutely. Known for lavish court and arts patronage, he exhausted the economy with wars for territory.
1715 Louis XV (the Beloved), great-grandson. Married a Polish princess, lost Canada to England. Favorite mistresses Mme. de Pompadour and Mme. Du Barry influenced policies. Pompadour's saying "Après moi, le déluge" ("After me, the deluge) is often incorrectly attributed to Louis XV.
1774 Louis XVI, grandson, married Marie Antoinette, daughter of Empress Maria Therese of Austria. Couple beheaded in Revolution, 1793. Louis XVII, son, never ruled and died in prison.

First Republic

1792 National Convention of the French Revolution
1795 Directory, under Viscount of Barras and others
1799 Consulate, Napoleon Bonaparte, first consul. Elected consul for life, 1802

First Empire

1804 Napoleon I (Napoleon Bonaparte), emperor. Josephine (de Beauharnais), empress, 1804-09; Marie Louise, empress, 1810-14. Son, Napoleon II (1811-32), titular king of Rome, later duke of Reichstadt, never ruled. Napoleon I abdicated 1814; died in exile, 1821.

House of Bourbon (restored)

1814 Louis XVIII, brother of Louis XVI, king
1824 Charles X, brother, reactionary, deposed by the July Revolution, 1830

House of Orleans

1830 Louis-Philippe (the Citizen King)

Second Republic

1848 Louis Napoleon Bonaparte, nephew of Napoleon I, president

Second Empire

1852 Napoleon III (Louis Napoleon Bonaparte), emperor; Eugenie (de Montijo), empress. Lost Franco-Prussian war, deposed 1870. Son, Prince Imperial (1856-79), died in Zulu War. Eugenie died 1920.

Third Republic

1871 Adolphe Thiers (1797-1877), president
1873 Patrice de Mac-Mahon (1808-93)
1879 Jules Grévy (1807-91)
1887 Sadi Carnot (1837-94), assassinated
1894 Jean Casimir-Périer (1847-1907)
1895 Félix Faure (1841-99)
1899 Émile Loubet (1838-1929)
1906 Armand Fallières (1841-1931)
1913 Raymond Poincaré (1860-1934)
1920 Paul Deschanel (1855-1922)
1920 Alexandre Millerand (1859-1943)
1924 Gaston Doumergue (1863-1937)
1931 Paul Doumer (1857-1932), assassinated
1932 Albert Lebrun (1871-1950), resigned 1940

Vichy Regime

1940 Philippe Pétain (1856-1951), chief of state, 1940-44, under German armistice

Provisional Government

1944 Charles de Gaulle (1890-1970)
1946 Félix Gouin (1884-1977)
1946 Georges Bidault (1899-1983)

Fourth Republic

1947 Vincent Auriol (1884-1966), president
1954 René Coty (1882-1962)

Fifth Republic

1959 Charles de Gaulle (1890-1970), president; resigned 1969. Alain Poher (1909-96), interim pres., Apr.-June 1969.
1969 Georges Pompidou (1911-74); Poher, interim pres., Apr.-May 1974.
1974 Valéry Giscard d'Estaing (1926-)
1981 François Mitterrand (1916-96)
1995 Jacques Chirac (1932-)
2007 Nicolas Sarkozy (1955-)
2012 François Hollande (1954-)
2017 Emmanuel Macron (1977-)

Rulers of Middle Europe and Germany

Carolingian Dynasty

Charles I (the Great), or Charlemagne, made Roman emperor by pope in Rome, 800. Ruled France, Italy, and Middle Europe; established Ostmark (later Austria). Died 814.

Louis I (Ludwig) (the Pious), son, crowned co-emperor by Charlemagne, 813. Divided empire among sons. Died 840; sons fought for control.

Louis II (the German), son, succeeded to East Francia (Germany), 843-76, with Treaty of Verdun.

Charles III (the Fat), son, inherited Swabia, 876. With brothers' deaths, acquired East Francia and West Francia (France), reuniting empire. Crowned emperor by pope, 881; deposed 887.

Arnulf, nephew, 887-99, took over East Francia; partition of empire.

Louis IV (the Child), son, 900-11, last direct descendant of Charlemagne.

Conrad I, duke of Franconia, first elected German king, 911-18.

Saxon Dynasty; First Reich

Henry I (the Fowler), duke of Saxony, elected king 919-36.

Otto I (the Great), son, 936-73, crowned Holy Roman Emperor by pope, 962.

Otto II, son, 961-83, ruled with Otto I as king, then emperor, 967.

Otto III, son, 983-1002, crowned Holy Roman Emperor, 996.

Henry II (the Saint), great-grandson of Otto the Great, duke of Bavaria, 1002-24. Crowned emperor, 1014.

Salian Dynasty

Conrad II, 1024-39, elected king of Germany.

Henry III (the Black), son, 1039-56, deposed three popes; annexed Burgundy.

Henry IV, son, 1056-1106, with mother, Agnes of Poitou, as regent in early years. He and Pope Gregory VII tried to depose each other. Civil war lasted about 20 years.

Henry V, son, 1106-25, last of Salian Dynasty.

Lothair, duke of Saxony, elected king 1125-37. Crowned emperor in Rome, 1133.

Hohenstaufen Dynasty

Conrad III, duke of Franconia, 1138-52, in Second Crusade.

Frederick I (Barbarossa, Italian for "Redbeard"), nephew, 1152-90.

Henry VI, son, 1190-97, gained kingdom of Sicily through marriage.

Philip of Swabia, brother, 1197-1208. Otto IV, nephew of King Richard I of England, 1198-1215, was elected rival king. Philip's murder, in 1208, led to Otto's win in new election same year. Civil war followed before Otto was deposed, 1215.

Frederick II, son of Henry VI, elected 1212-50. Had earlier succeeded father as king of Sicily; crowned himself king of Jerusalem, 1229, in Sixth Crusade.

Conrad IV, son, 1250-54. Conquered Naples.

(Interregnum, 1254-73. Conradin, son of Conrad IV and last legitimate Hohenstaufen, defeated by Charles of Anjou—brother of King Louis IX of France—and executed, 1268. Rise of electors of German monarch.)

Transition

Rudolf I, of Habsburg, 1273-91, defeated King Ottocar II of Bohemia, 1278. Bequeathed duchies of Austria and Styria to sons.

Adolf of Nassau, 1292-98, killed in war with Albert I.

Albert I, elder son of Rudolf I, 1298-1308, assassinated.

Henry VII, of Luxemburg, 1308-13. Gained Bohemia, 1310; crowned Holy Roman Emperor, 1312.

Louis IV, of Wittelsbach, 1314-46. Also elected was a son of Albert I, Frederick of Austria, whom Louis defeated in 1322. Rejected need for papal confirmation of elected German king.

Charles IV, of Luxemburg, grandson of Henry VII, 1346-78. Took Brandenburg.

Wenceslaus, son, 1378-1400; deposed.

Rupert, of Wittelsbach, elector palatine, 1400-10.

Sigismund, brother of Wenceslaus, 1410-37.

Habsburg Dynasty

Albert II, duke of Austria, son-in-law of Sigismund, elected German king, 1438-39; king of Hungary and Holy Roman Emperor.

Frederick III, cousin, 1440-93, fought Turks.

Maximilian I, son, 1493-1519, archduke of Austria.

Charles V, grandson, 1519-58. King of Spain; assumed title of Holy Roman Emperor. Martin Luther, who had been excommunicated by pope, appeared at Diet of Worms, 1521. Charles attempted church reform and conciliation between Catholicism and Protestantism; abdicated.

Ferdinand I, brother, 1558-64; king of Hungary and Bohemia, 1526 (successive leaders through Maria Theresa will rule these lands as well).

Maximilian II, son, 1564-76.

Rudolf II, son, 1576-1612.

Matthias, brother, 1612-19.

Ferdinand II, grandson of Ferdinand I, 1619-37. Bohemian Protestants, unhappy with Ferdinand's support of Catholic Counter-Reformation, crowned Frederick V, elector palatine. Frederick became known as "Winter King" with defeat in battle, 1620; start of Thirty Years' War.

Ferdinand III, son, 1637-57. Treaties signed, 1648, in Peace of Westphalia ended war.

Leopold I, son, 1658-1705.

Joseph I, son, 1705-11.

Charles VI, brother, 1711-40; died without male heir.

Maria Theresa, daughter, 1740-80. Appointed husband, Francis Stephen of Lorraine, co-regent. Dispute over her inheritance led to War of the Austrian Succession. Charles VII, also known as Charles Albert, elected in opposition to Francis, 1742-45. After Charles's death, Maria Theresa obtained election of her husband as Holy Roman Emperor Francis I, 1745-65. Fought Seven Years' War with Frederick II of Prussia.

Habsburg-Lorraine Dynasty

Joseph II, son, 1765-90, reformer. Ruled jointly with Maria Theresa until her death. Participated in first partition of Poland, with Prussia and Russia.

Leopold II, brother, 1790-92; king of Hungary and Bohemia.

Francis II, son, 1792-1806; king of Hungary and Bohemia. Proclaimed first emperor of Austria, 1804-35. Unsuccessfully fought against Napoleon; forced to abdicate, 1806, as Holy Roman Emperor, last use of title.

Ferdinand, son, 1835-48, emperor of Austria; king of Hungary and Bohemia. Abdicated in favor of nephew after revolution broke out in Vienna.

Austro-Hungarian Monarchy

Francis Joseph I, nephew, 1848-1916, emperor of Austria and king of Hungary. Defeated in Austro-Prussian War, 1866. Formed dual monarchy of Austria-Hungary, 1867. After Serbian nationalist assassinated Francis Joseph's nephew and heir, Archduke Francis Ferdinand, June 28, 1914, Austrian diplomacy precipitated World War I.

Charles I, grandnephew, 1916-18, last emperor of Austria and king of Hungary. Abdicated Nov. 1918; died in exile, 1922.

Second and Third Reichs

William I, brother of Frederick William IV, 1861-88, king of Prussia. Appointed Otto von Bismarck chancellor, 1862. Franco-Prussian War, also known as Franco-German War, 1870-71, unified German states. William proclaimed German emperor, 1871; beginning of Second Reich.

Frederick III, son, 1888.

William II, son, 1888-1918, led Germany into World War I. Abdicated Nov. 1918; died in exile in the Netherlands, 1941.

Germany adopted constitution at Weimar, July 1, 1919, setting up Weimar Republic. Presidents included Friedrich Ebert, 1919-25, and Paul von Hindenburg, 1925-34, field marshal in World War I. Hindenburg appointed Adolf Hitler chancellor, 1933, at beginning of Third Reich. Following Hindenburg's death, Hitler succeeded as Führer and chancellor, 1934-45, with dictatorial powers. Annexed Austria, 1938. Precipitated World War II, 1939-45. Hitler committed suicide, 1945.

Germany After 1945

After World War II, Germany was split between democratic West and Soviet-dominated East. West German chancellors: Konrad Adenauer, 1949-63; Ludwig Erhard, 1963-66; Kurt Georg Kiesinger, 1966-69; Willy Brandt, 1969-74; Helmut Schmidt, 1974-82; Helmut Kohl, 1982-90. East German Communist party leaders: Walter Ulbricht, 1950-71; Erich Honecker, 1971-89; Egon Krenz, 1989. (Berlin Wall fell, Nov. 1989.)

Germany reunited Oct. 3, 1990. Post-reunification chancellors: Helmut Kohl, 1990-98; Gerhard Schröder, 1998-2005; Angela Merkel, 2005- .

Rulers of Hungary

The first king of Hungary was Stephen I, of the Arpad Dynasty, 1000-38. Feuds followed his death.

Charles I, also known as Charles Robert, became king, 1308-42.

Louis I (the Great), son, 1342-82. Succeeded uncle Casimir III as ruler of Poland, 1370.

Mary, elder daughter, 1382-95, ruled with husband, Sigismund of Luxemburg, 1387-1437, who also became king of Bohemia, Germany and Holy Roman Emperor. Hedwig (Jadwiga), younger daughter of Louis I, became queen of Poland. (See **Rulers of Poland**.)

Albert II, duke of Austria, son-in-law of Sigismund, 1438-39. Also king of Germany and Holy Roman Emperor.

Vladislaus I, 1440-44, king of Poland.

Ladislaus V, posthumous son of Albert II, 1444-57, not crowned until 1453. Janos Hunyadi acted as governor under young king, 1446-52; fought Turks.

Matthias I (Corvinus), son of Janos Hunyadi, 1458-90. Shared title of king of Bohemia. Captured Vienna, 1485; annexed Styria, Carinthia.

Vladislaus II, 1490-1516, king of Bohemia.

Louis II, son, 1516-26. Died in Battle of Mohács against Suleiman (the Magnificent), head of Ottoman Empire.

Ferdinand I, of Austria, brother-in-law, and John I, also known as John Zapolya of Transylvania, elected rival kings. Suleiman claimed part of Hungary for Ottoman Empire. Hungary partitioned. (Refer to **Habsburg Dynasty** for continuation.)

Rulers of Prussia

Nucleus of Prussia was the margravate of Brandenburg, an electorate of the Holy Roman Empire. Frederick VI, burgrave of Nuremberg, was made elector of Brandenburg, 1415. Rise of Hohenzollern Dynasty in territory that included Brandenburg and duchy of Prussia.

Frederick William (the Great Elector), 1640-88, elector of Brandenburg.

Frederick III, son, 1688-1713, elector of Brandenburg. Crowned Frederick I, king in Prussia, 1701.

Frederick William I, son, 1713-40.

Frederick II (the Great), son, 1740-86; military strategist who expanded Prussia's holdings.

Frederick William II, nephew, 1786-97.

Frederick William III, son, 1797-1840; Napoleonic Wars.

Frederick William IV, son, 1840-61. Revolution of 1848; constitution adopted, 1850. (Refer to **Second and Third Reichs** for continuation.)

Rulers of Poland

House of Piast

Mieszko I, c. 963-92, duke of Poland; Poland Christianized, 966. Expansion under three with name Boleslaus (reigns not consecutive): Boleslaus I (the Brave), son, 992-1025, crowned first king of Poland, 1025; Boleslaus II (the Bold), great-grandson, 1058-79, exiled after killing bishop of Krakow, Stanislaus (who became a patron saint of Poland); Boleslaus III (the Wry-Mouthed), nephew, 1102-38, divided Poland among four sons with oldest also in control of crown. Period of feudal division followed.

A Polish duke, Conrad of Masovia, asked the Teutonic Knights—a German military religious order—to crusade against Prussia, 1226. Teutonic Knights conquered lands; thereafter warred with Poland. Mongols/Tatars invaded Poland, 1241.

Vladislaus I, 1306-33, reunited most Polish territories; crowned king, 1320. Casimir III (the Great), son, 1333-70, developed economy, cultural life, foreign policy. No male heir. Succeeded by Louis I, nephew, 1370-82, who was also Louis I (the Great) of Hungary.

Jadwiga, daughter, 1384-99.

House of Jagiello

Vladislaus Jagiello, grand duke of Lithuania, married Jadwiga, 1386, and ruled jointly as Vladislaus II, 1386-1434. Poland and Lithuania united; Lithuania converted to Christianity. Defeated Teutonic Knights at Grunwald (Tannenberg), 1410.

Vladislaus III, son, 1434-44, also king of Hungary. Fought Turks; killed in Battle of Varna, 1444.

Casimir IV, brother, 1447-92, put son Vladislaus on throne of Bohemia and Hungary. Victorious over Teutonic Knights; signed treaty, 1466, after 13-year war.

John I, son, 1492-1501.

Alexander I, brother, 1501-05.

Sigismund I, brother, 1506-48, patronized sciences and arts; his and son's reign were golden age. Grand Master of Teutonic Order, Albert Hohenzollern, converted to Protestantism; secularized his state and made first duke of Prussia by Sigismund, 1525.

Sigismund II, son, 1548-72; Union of Lublin, 1569, established dual state of Poland and Lithuania. No male heir.

Elective Kings

Henry of Valois, 1573-74, first king elected by nobility. Left Poland to assume crown of France after brother's death. Interregnum.

Stephen Bathory, 1576-86, prince of Transylvania, married Anna, sister of Sigismund II. Fought Russians.

Sigismund III Vasa, nephew of Sigismund II and son of king of Sweden, 1587-1632. Fought to reclaim Swedish crown, which he'd lost because of his Catholicism; battled Russians and Turks.

Vladislaus IV Vasa, son, 1632-48.

John II Casimir Vasa, brother, 1648-68. Fought Cossacks, Swedish, Russians, Turks, Tatars; period of invasions known as "the Deluge."

Michael Korybut Wisniowiecki, 1669-73.

John III Sobieski, 1674-96, freed Vienna from besieging Turks, 1683.

Augustus II (the Strong), 1697-1733, elector of Saxony.

Augustus III, son, 1733-63, elector of Saxony.

Stanislaus II, 1764-95, last king. Encouraged reforms; first modern constitution in Europe, 1791. Poland lost territory to Russia, Austria, and Prussia in three partitions (1772, 1793, 1795). Thaddeus Kosciusko, American-Polish general, attempted unsuccessful insurrection, 1794.

Poland Under Foreign Rule

Grand duchy of Warsaw created by Napoleon I out of Prussian (formerly Polish) territory. Frederick Augustus I, king of Saxony, ruled grand duchy, 1807-15. Defeat of Napoleon led to Congress of Vienna, 1814-15; part of Poland claimed as kingdom by Russia. Polish uprisings against Russia (1830, 1863) and Austria (1846) repressed. Poland regained independence following World War I.

Second Republic

Jozef Pilsudski, 1918-22, head of state. Presidents: Gabriel Narutowicz, 1922, assassinated by extremist; Stanislaus Wojciechowski, 1922-26, resigned after coup d'état by Pilsudski; Ignacy Moscicki, 1926-39, ruled with Pilsudski (d. 1935) and Pilsudski's military colleagues as virtual dictator during what came to be known as Sanacja (meaning "cleansing" or "healing") regime.

Poland Under Foreign Occupation, Influence

After Hitler and Stalin signed nonaggression pact, Germany invaded Poland Sept. 1, 1939; Russia invaded Sept. 17. Polish government-in-exile was in France, then England. Vladislaus Raczkiewicz, 1939-47, president; Gen. Vladislaus Sikorski, 1939-43, and Stanislaus Mikolajczyk, 1943-44, prime ministers. Polish residents were sent to German concentration camps and Soviet labor camps; about 3 million Jewish Poles were killed in the Holocaust. Thousands of Polish prisoners of war, mostly military officers, massacred in Katyn Forest by Soviet secret police, 1940. Soviet-sponsored Polish Committee of National Liberation took formative role in new government, 1945, renamed Polish People's Republic in 1952. Communist Polish United Workers' Party ruled the country. Brief period of liberalization followed Stalin's death in 1953. Vladislaus Gomulka, 1956-70, and Edward Gierek, 1970-80, led country as first secretary of Polish United Workers' Party.

Election of Cardinal Karol Wojtyla, archbishop of Krakow, as pope (John Paul II) inspired Poles, 1978. Strikes in 1980 prompted creation of Solidarity, an independent trade union headed by Lech Walesa. Solidarity gained control of government in partly free elections, 1985.

Third Republic

Presidents: Lech Walesa, 1990-95; Aleksander Kwasniewski, 1995-2005; Lech Kaczynski, 2005-10, died in plane crash; Bronislaus Komorowski and Grzegorz Schetyna, acting, 2010; Komorowski, 2010-15; Andrzej Duda, 2015- .

Rulers of Denmark, Sweden, Norway

Denmark

Canute (the Great) ruled area that included England, Denmark, and Norway, 1016-35. Valdemar IV Atterdag reunited Denmark, 1361. Margaret I, daughter, married to Haakon VI, king of Norway, 1363. After Valdemar's death, Olaf, Margaret's infant son, made king of Denmark, 1375. He was also crowned king of Norway after death of Haakon, 1380. Following Olaf's death, 1387, Margaret served as regent of Denmark, Norway, and Sweden. She effected the Union of Kalmar of the three kingdoms, 1397. She had her grandnephew, Eric of Pomerania, crowned (she held actual power until her death, 1412).

Succeeding rulers were unable to enforce their claims on Sweden until Christian II, 1512-23, conquered the country, 1520. He was soon deposed; accession of Gustavus I as king of Sweden, 1523, ended Kalmar Union. Denmark continued to dominate Norway until the Napoleonic Wars when Frederick VI, 1808-39, allied with Napoleon I after Danish fleet was attacked by Britain, 1807. By 1814 treaty, Denmark was forced to cede Norway to Sweden.

Succession: House of Oldenborg (began with Christian I, 1448): Christian VIII, 1839-48; Frederick VII, son, 1848-63. House of Glücksborg: Christian IX, 1863-1906; Frederick VIII, son, 1906-12; Christian X, son, 1912-47; Frederick IX, son, 1947-72; Margrethe II, daughter, 1972- .

Sweden

Under King Magnus Ladulas, hereditary nobility established around 1280. Swedish nobles opposed to Albert of Mecklenburg accepted Margaret I, regent of Denmark, as ruler, 1389. Sweden joined Kalmar Union, 1397. After internal unrest, Sweden was conquered anew by Denmark's Christian II, 1520. Execution of Christian's opponents in "Stockholm Bloodbath" led to uprising under Gustavus Vasa, who was elected Swedish king, 1523-60. Gustavus established an independent kingdom with centralized power, state church, and hereditary throne.

Gustavus II Adolphus (Lion of the North), 1611-32, fought Russia, Poland, Germany; died in battle.

Later rulers: Christina, daughter, 1632-54, abdicated; Charles X Gustavus, cousin, 1654-60; Charles XI, son, 1660-97; Charles XII, son, 1697-1718; Ulrika Eleonora, sister, 1718-20, abdicated; Frederick I, of Hesse, husband, 1720-51; Adolphus Frederick, 1751-71; Gustavus III, son, 1771-92; Gustavus IV Adolphus, son, 1792-1809, deposed; Charles XIII, uncle, 1809-18. Charles XIV John (born Jean Baptiste Bernadotte, a general under Napoleon I), 1818-44, founded House of Bernadotte.

Succession: Oscar I, son, 1844-59; Charles XV, son, 1859-72; Oscar II, brother, 1872-1907; Gustavus V, son, 1907-50; Gustavus VI Adolf, son, 1950-73; Carl XVI Gustavus, grandson, 1973- .

Norway

Harald I (Fairhair) overcame rivals to become first king of Norway, c. 885-c. 933. Olaf II Haraldsson, 1015-28, Christianized country; became patron saint of Norway. Haakon V Magnusson, 1299-1319, died without male heir. His daughter Ingeborg was married to Erik, a son of the Norwegian king; their son Magnus VII Eriksson became ruler of Norway, 1319-55, and Sweden, 1319-63. Haakon VI Magnusson, son, 1355-80, married Margaret of Denmark. Olaf IV, son, became king of Norway, 1380-87, and Denmark, 1375-87, with mother as regent. Margaret took over rule upon his death, 1387. Union of Kalmar, 1397, united Norway, Denmark, and Sweden.

After Napoleonic Wars, Denmark ceded Norway to Sweden, 1814. A strong nationalist movement forced Sweden to recognize Norway as an independent kingdom under the Swedish kings. Norwegian constitution, adopted 1814, allowed for creation of the Storting (Norwegian parliament), which governed country domestically. In 1905, the union was dissolved. Prince Charles of Denmark elected king of Norway as Haakon VII, 1905-57; founded House of Glücksburg. Succession: Olav V, son, 1957-91; Harald V, son, 1991- .

Rulers of the Netherlands and Belgium

The Netherlands

William I, son of Prince William V of Orange, came to power after French rule ended in the Netherlands, 1813; crowned king with approval of Congress of Vienna, 1815. Started House of Orange-Nassau. Northern Netherlands was known as Holland. Belgians, in southern Netherlands, rebelled against the Dutch and seceded, Oct. 4, 1830. Dutch formally recognized Belgian independence, Apr. 19, 1839. William I abdicated, 1840.

Succession: William II, son, 1840-49; William III, son, 1849-90; Wilhelmina, daughter, 1890-1948; Juliana, daughter, 1948-80; Beatrix, daughter, 1980-2013; Willem-Alexander, son, 2013- .

Belgium

A national congress elected Prince Leopold of Saxe-Coburg as king. He took the throne July 21, 1831, as Leopold I.

Succession: Leopold II, son, 1865-1909; Albert I, nephew, 1909-34; Leopold III, son, 1934-51, in exile after Germany invaded Belgium, later abdicated; Prince Charles, brother, acted as regent 1944-50; Baudouin I, son of Leopold III, 1951-93; Albert II, brother, 1993-2013; Philippe, son, 2013- .

Rulers of Modern Italy

After the fall of Napoleon, the Congress of Vienna, 1814-15, restored Italy as a political patchwork, comprising the Kingdom of the Two Sicilies (Naples and Sicily), the Papal States, and smaller units. King Victor Emmanuel I of Savoy ruled Sardinia, Piedmont, and Genoa.

Victor Emmanuel I abdicated 1821. Charles Felix, brother, 1821-31, died without issue. Succeeded by Charles Albert, 1831-49; he abdicated upon defeat by the Austrians. Succeeded by Victor Emmanuel II, son, 1849-61. United Italy emerged under Camillo Benso di Cavour, prime minister of the Kingdom of Sardinia, 1852-61. Giuseppe Mazzini and Giuseppe Garibaldi were also figures in Risorgimento ("resurgence") period before Italy's unification.

In 1859, France forced Austria to cede Lombardy to Sardinia. In 1860, Garibaldi led more than 1,000 volunteers in a campaign against King Francis II of the Two Sicilies, taking Sicily and Naples. The House of Savoy subsequently annexed the Two Sicilies, Tuscany, Parma, Modena, Romagna, the Marches, and Umbria. Victor Emmanuel II assumed leadership of a united Kingdom of Italy, Mar. 17, 1861.

In 1866, Victor Emmanuel II allied with Prussia in the Austro-Prussian War and, with Prussia's victory, received Venetia. On Sept. 20, 1870, Italian troops entered Rome, ending the temporal power of the Roman Catholic Church. (The 1929 Lateran Treaty established papal sovereignty in Vatican City.)

Succession: Umberto I, son, 1878-1900, assassinated; Victor Emmanuel III, son, 1900-46; Umberto II, son, 1946, ruled only one month before voters in a referendum chose to establish a republic. In 1919, Benito Mussolini helped found the nationalist Fasci di Combattimento (Fighting Leagues), or Fascists. After Mussolini organized March on Rome, 1922, Victor Emmanuel III agreed to a coalition government. Mussolini eventually became dictator (Il Duce). He entered World War II as an ally of Hitler, 1940. He was dismissed by the king, 1943; executed, 1945.

At a plebiscite, 1946, voters approved a republic. Prime minister Alcide de Gasperi was chief of state, 1945-53; Enrico de Nicola was provisional president. Successive presidents: Luigi Einaudi, 1948-55; Giovanni Gronchi, 1955-62; Antonio Segni, 1962-64; Giuseppe Saragat, 1964-71; Giovanni Leone, 1971-78; Alessandro Pertini, 1978-85; Francesco Cossiga, 1985-92; Oscar Luigi Scalfaro, 1992-99; Carlo Azeglio Ciampi, 1999-2006; Giorgio Napolitano, 2006-15; Sergio Mattarella, 2015- .

Rulers of Spain

From 8th to 11th centuries, Spain was dominated by the Moors (Muslims from North Africa of Arab and Berber origin). A number of small kingdoms—Aragon, Asturias, Castile, Catalonia, Leon, Navarre, and Valencia—undertook a Christian reconquest. In 1474, Isabella I became Queen of Castile and Leon. By the Catholic Monarchs' request, Pope Sixtus IV authorized the Inquisition, 1478. Isabella's husband, Ferdinand V, acceded to the throne of Aragon, 1479. Last Moorish kingdom, Granada, seized 1492. Spain sponsored Christopher Columbus, who led European exploration of New World, 1492. Isabella was succeeded by daughter, Joanna (the Mad), but Ferdinand acted as regent until his death, 1516.

Charles I, son of Joanna and grandson of Habsburg Emperor Maximilian I, became Holy Roman Emperor as Charles V, 1520;

abdicated 1556. Philip II, son, 1556-98, inherited only part of empire. He conquered Portugal, fought against Ottoman Empire, sent Armada in unsuccessful invasion of England. Succession: Philip III, son, 1598-1621; Philip IV, son, 1621-65; Charles II, son, 1665-1700, no issue, left Spain to Philip of Anjou, grandson of Louis XIV of France. As Philip V, he was first of Bourbon dynasty in Spain, 1700-46 (his son Louis ruled briefly in 1724); Ferdinand VI, son, 1746-59; Charles III, brother, 1759-88; Charles IV, son, 1788-1808, abdicated.

Joseph Bonaparte made king of Spain, 1808-13, by his brother Napoleon. Ferdinand VII, son of Charles IV, 1808, 1814-33, lost American colonies except Cuba, Puerto Rico. Maria Christina of the Two Sicilies, wife, was regent until 1843 for Isabella II, daughter, who was driven into exile by revolution, 1868. Amadeo of Savoy elected king by the Cortes (parliament), 1870-73. First Republic, 1873-74. Alfonso XII, son of Isabella II, 1875-85; Alfonso XIII, posthumous son, 1901-31, with mother Maria Christina as regent before he assumed throne. Spain ceded territory after loss in Spanish-American War, 1898. Primo de Rivera ruled as dictator, 1923-30, after military coup but was forced to resign after losing support. Alfonso agreed to exile without formal abdication. Monarchy abolished; Second Republic established with socialist backing. Presidents: Niceto Alcala Zamora, 1931-36; Manuel Azaña, 1936-39.

Revolt by military started Spanish Civil War, 1936-39. Gen. Francisco Franco ruled as head of Nationalist regime, 1939-73. Monarchy restored after 1947 referendum. Juan Carlos, grandson of Alfonso XIII, acceded to throne after Franco's death in 1975; abdicated, 2014. Felipe VI, son, 2014- .

Leaders in the South American Wars of Liberation

Francisco de Miranda, José de San Martín, and Simón Bolívar led early 19th-cent. struggles of South American nations to free themselves from Spain.

Miranda (1750-1816), a Venezuelan, served as an officer in the Spanish army. After a dispute with the army, he fled to the U.S., 1783, where he met leaders of the American Revolution. He traveled seeking support for South American independence from other world leaders. Miranda unsuccessfully attempted a revolt in Venezuela, 1806. Napoleon's invasion of Spain, 1808, prompted the start of a revolution in Venezuela. Miranda returned, 1810, and headed the revolution with dictatorial powers. Venezuela declared independence, 1811. Overcome by royalist forces, 1812, Miranda surrendered and was arrested; he died in a Spanish prison.

San Martín (1778-1850) was born in present-day Argentina. He served in Spanish campaigns in Europe until 1811. He returned to Argentina and joined the independence movement, 1812. In 1817, he invaded Chile through the Andean mountain passes. He and Bernardo O'Higgins defeated the Spanish at Chacabuco, 1817. Chile gained independence, 1819; O'Higgins became first director of Chile, 1817-23. In 1821, San Martín entered Lima and took the port of Callao; he became protector of an independent Peru.

Bolívar (1783-1830) was born into an aristocratic family in Venezuela. He served under Miranda until Miranda's surrender in 1812. Bolívar continued to fight; he captured Caracas and was named Liberator, 1813. But he was forced to flee by royalist forces, 1814. In 1817, Bolívar again fought for control of Venezuela. With Francisco de Paula Santander and José Antonio Páez, he defeated the Spanish at the Battle of Boyacá, 1819, freeing New Granada (present-day Colombia). New Granada, Venezuela, and the area that is now Panama and Ecuador were joined as the Republic of Colombia, or Gran Colombia, with Bolívar as president later that same year, though parts of the republic remained under Spanish control. He decisively defeated the Spanish in the Battle of Carabobo in Venezuela, 1821.

Antonio José de Sucre, Bolívar's chief lieutenant, overcame Spanish forces at the Battle of Pichincha in Ecuador, 1822. Bolívar convinced San Martín to resign as protector of Peru. Peru was declared independent after Bolívar and Sucre won the Battle of Junin, Aug. 1824, and Sucre triumphed at the Battle of Ayacucho, Dec. 1824.

Sucre organized Upper Peru as Republica Bolívar (now Bolivia), 1825, and acted as president in place of Bolívar, who wrote its constitution.

Civil strife caused the Colombian federation to break apart. Bolívar gave up the presidency, 1830.

Rulers of Russia; Leaders of the USSR and Russian Federation

The Varangian (Viking) prince Rurik is considered to be the first leader of the Russians; he established himself at Novgorod, c. 862 CE. His successor, Oleg, and those who followed Oleg ruled as princes of Kiev. Vladimir I, or Saint Vladimir, married sister of Byzantine emperor and converted to Christianity, 988. Yaroslav I (the Wise), brother, 1019-54, was important organizer and lawgiver; his daughters married kings of Norway, Hungary, and France. In 1169, Andrew Bogolyubsky conquered Kiev and began the line of Vladimir.

Daniel, a son of grand prince of Vladimir, Alexander Nevsky, was first to be called prince of Muscovy (Moscow), 1263-1303. Dmitri Ivanovich (Donskoi), prince of Moscow, defeated the Tatars at the Battle of Kulikovo, 1380. His successors were grand princes of Moscow. Ivan III (the Great), 1462-1505, achieved considerable territorial expansion.

Ivan III married Sofia Palaeologus, niece of the last Byzantine emperor. Succession: Vasily III, son. Ivan IV (the Terrible), son, crowned 1547 as Tsar of Russia. Fyodor I, son, reigned 1584-98, but his brother-in-law Boris Godunov had real control before becoming tsar himself, 1598-1605. After years of internal strife ("Time of Troubles"), the Russians united under 16-year-old Michael Romanov, distantly related to Ivan IV's first wife. He ruled 1613-45, establishing the Romanov line.

Tsars, or emperors, of Russia (Romanovs): Peter I (the Great), 1682-1725, with Ivan V, brother, as co-ruler, 1682-96. Catherine I, his widow, 1725-27. Peter II, grandson of Peter I, 1727-30. Anna, daughter of Ivan V and niece of Peter I, 1730-40. Ivan VI, nephew, 1740-41; deposed by Elizabeth, daughter of Peter I, 1741-62. Peter III, nephew, 1762; deposed by his wife, Catherine II (the Great), former princess of Anhalt Zerbst (Germany), 1762-96. Paul I, son, 1796-1801, assassinated. Alexander I, son, 1801-25, defeated Napoleon. Nicholas I, brother, 1825-55. Alexander II, son, 1855-81, assassinated. Alexander III, son, 1881-94. Nicholas II, son, 1894-1917, last tsar of Russia, was forced to abdicate by revolutionaries following losses to Germany in WWI. The tsar, empress, tsarevich (crown prince), and tsar's four daughters were murdered by the Bolsheviks, July 1918.

Premiers of provisional government: Prince Georgi Lvov, followed by Alexander Kerensky, 1917.

Union of Soviet Socialist Republics

Bolshevik Revolution, Nov. 7, 1917, (also known as the October Revolution, based on Russia's then use of the Julian calendar) removed Kerensky from power. Council of People's Commissars formed with Lenin (Vladimir Ilyich Ulyanov) as chair (or premier), 1917-24. Aleksei Rykov (executed 1938) and Vyacheslav M. Molotov held the office, but effective ruler was Joseph Stalin (Joseph Vissarionovich Dzhugashvili), general secretary of the Communist Party. Stalin was chair of the Council of People's Commissars from 1941 until his death in 1953. Succeeded by Georgi M. Malenkov, who also briefly served as general secretary of the Communist Party before being ousted from the position by Nikita S. Khrushchev. Malenkov was forced to resign as premier, 1955, and was expelled from the Communist Party, 1961. Nikolai A. Bulganin was premier, 1955-58, until his replacement by Khrushchev, 1958-64.

Leonid I. Brezhnev ousted Khrushchev as general secretary of the party, a post he held until his death in 1982. Aleksei N. Kosygin was premier, 1964-80. The Central Committee elected former KGB (state security) head Yuri V. Andropov general secretary, 1982-84. After Andropov's death, Konstantin U. Chernenko was chosen for the position, 1984-85. Upon Chernenko's death, he was succeeded by Mikhail Gorbachev. Gorbachev assumed the newly created position of president of the Soviet Union, 1990. Boris Yeltsin was sworn in July 1991 as the Russian Republic's first elected president. Under Yeltsin, Russia became a founding member of the Commonwealth of Independent States. Gorbachev resigned the presidency, Dec. 25, 1991, and the Soviet Union officially disbanded Dec. 31. Each of the 15 former Soviet constituent republics became independent.

Post-Soviet Russia

Presidents of the Russian Federation: Boris Yeltsin, 1991-99; Vladimir Putin, 2000-08; Dmitry Medvedev, 2008-12; Putin, 2012- .

Rulers of China

Where dynastic dates overlap, the rulers or events referred to appeared in different areas of China.

Years in power	Dynasty/ruler(s)
c. 1994-c. 1766 BCE	Xia dynasty, first hereditary Chinese dynasty
c. 1766-c. 1045 BCE	Shang dynasty, first Chinese dynasty with historical records
c. 1045-771 BCE	Western Zhou dynasty, capital near present-day Xi'an
770-256 BCE	Eastern Zhou dynasty, new capital established at Luoyang. During Chunqiu (Spring and Autumn) period (722-481 BCE), Zhou began to lose authority. Period of the Warring States (403-221 BCE) involved major powers of Qi, Chu, Yan, Han, Zhao, Wei, and Qin
221-207 BCE	Qin dynasty, quasi-feudal states unified for first time under self-proclaimed Shi Huang Di, or First Emperor. Prefectures and counties organized under central government with uniform laws and procedures; written language, weights standardized
206 BCE-9 CE	Earlier, or Western Han dynasty, founded by rebel leader Liu Bang. Expansion under Emperor Wudi (born Liu Che), 140-87 BCE; civil service system established
9-23	Xin dynasty, established by Wang Mang, who deposed infant emperor for whom he was regent
25-220	Later, or Eastern Han dynasty
220-265[1]	Wei dynasty, established by son of Han general Cao Cao
221-263[1]	Shu Han dynasty in SW China
222-280[1]	Wu dynasty in SE China
265-317	Western Jin dynasty, established by Sima Yan, Wei dynasty general
317-420	Eastern Jin dynasty, established by prince of Sima family
420-589	Southern dynasties, four short-lived dynasties with capital at Jiankang (present-day Nanjing)
581-618	Sui dynasty, reunified China; established by Emperor Wendi (born Yang Jian), military appointee who usurped throne of non-Chinese Northern Zhou, 581
618-906	Tang dynasty, founded by Li Yuan (known as Emperor Gaozu of Tang), who led rebellion against the Sui. Notable rulers include former imperial concubine Empress Wu, 683-705; Xuanzong, 712-56
907-960	Five Dynasties. Period of disunion with short-lived dynasties in N; Ten Kingdoms (states) in S and W
907-1125	Liao dynasty, of Khitan Mongols, capital at Yanjing (present-day Beijing)
960-1126	Northern Song dynasty, established by military leader Zhao Kuangyin (Emperor Taizu), capital at Kaifeng
1122-1234	Jin dynasty, of Juchen people of Manchuria; drove Song out of N China
1127-1279	Southern Song dynasty, capital at Lin'an (present-day Hangzhou)
1279-1368	Yuan, or Mongol dynasty; Kublai Khan, grandson of Genghis Khan, high point of Mongol power
1368-1644	Ming dynasty, founded by Buddhist monk turned rebel general Zhu Yuanzhang. Country again under Chinese rule; capital in present-day Nanjing, then Beijing after Mongolian tribes' defeat
1644-1912	Qing, or Manchu dynasty, under rule of Manchu people. Height of power of Chinese empire to date. Last imperial dynasty; Emperor Xuantong, or Puyi, last emperor. Sun Yat-sen organized the Kuomintang (Nationalist party) and led provisional republican government in Nanjing, 1911-12. Sun resigned in unification compromise with former imperial viceroy Yuan Shikai, who became president upon emperor's abdication in Feb. 1912
1912-1949	Rep. of China, power passed to provincial warlords upon Yuan's death, 1916. Gen. Chiang Kai-shek sought to reunify China under Kuomintang with new government at Nanjing, 1928. War with Japan, then civil war, led to Nationalist authority collapse, Communist declaration of People's Rep. of China, 1949

(1) Also known as the period of the Three Kingdoms because of warfare between the Wei, Shu Han, and Wu dynasties.

Leaders of People's Republic of China

Name	Title/position, years in power
Mao Zedong	People's Rep. of China (PRC) Chairman, 1949-59; Chinese Communist Party (CCP) Chairman, 1949-76
Zhou Enlai	Premier, 1949-76
Liu Shaoqi	PRC Chairman, 1959-68; one-time Mao successor removed from power during Cultural Revolution (1966-76)
Lin Biao	Red Army commander designated Mao's successor, 1966; government reported his death in plane crash, 1971, after failed coup attempt
Hua Guofeng	Premier, 1976-80; CCP Chairman, 1976-81
Deng Xiaoping	"Paramount leader," 1977-97
Hu Yaobang	CCP General Secretary, 1980-87; CCP Chairman, 1981-82[1]
Zhao Ziyang	Premier, 1980-87; CCP General Secretary, 1987-89
Li Xiannian	President, 1983-88
Yang Shangkun	President, 1988-93
Li Peng	Premier, 1988-98
Jiang Zemin	CCP General Secretary, 1989-2002; President, 1993-2003
Zhu Rongji	Premier, 1998-2003
Hu Jintao	CCP General Secretary, 2002-12; President, 2003-13
Wen Jiabao	Premier, 2003-13
Xi Jinping	CCP General Secretary, 2012- ; President, 2013-
Li Keqiang	Premier, 2013-

(1) Position of CCP chairman was abolished in 1982, making the CCP general secretary the party's highest-ranking official.

Historical Periods of Japan

Years in power	Period	Founding event
c. 300-592	Yamato	Conquest of Yamato plain. Also called Tumulus, or Tomb, period for large mounds built during this time
592-710	Asuka	Accession of Empress Suiko; capital in Asuka region
710-794	Nara	Heijo (Nara) completed; capital moved to Nagaoka, 784
794-1185	Heian	Capital moved to Heian (present-day Kyoto) by Emperor Kammu
858-1160	Fujiwara	Fujiwara no Yoshifusa became regent for his grandson
1160-1185	Taira	Taira no Kiyomoro assumed control; Minamoto no Yoritomo defeated Taira, 1185
1192-1333	Kamakura	Yoritomo became shogun
1334-1392	Namboku	Emperor Godaigo returned to power in Kemmu Restoration; 1336 revolt drove him from Kyoto to establish Southern Court at Yoshino
1392-1573	Muromachi	Unification of Southern and Northern Courts
1467-1600	Sengoku	Onin War began; also known as Warring States period
1573-1603	Momoyama	Oda Nobunaga entered Kyoto, 1568, deposed last Ashikaga shogun, 1573. Tokugawa Ieyasu victor at Battle of Sekigahara, 1600
1603-1867	Edo	Ieyasu established Tokugawa shogunate, became shogun
1868-1912	Meiji	Meiji Restoration of imperial power, with Meiji (reign name of Mutsuhito) ascending throne; Charter Oath, 1868, led to Westernization
1912-1926	Taisho	Accession of Emperor Taisho (reign name of Yoshihito)
1926-1989	Showa	Accession of Emperor Hirohito (posthumous name Showa)
1989-	Heisei	Accession of Emperor Akihito[1]

(1) A 2017 law allowed Akihito to abdicate—the first Japanese emperor to do so in about 200 years—in favor of his eldest son, Crown Prince Naruhito. Akihito was expected to abdicate on Apr. 30, 2019, followed by Naruhito's accession the next day.

WORLD EXPLORATION AND GEOGRAPHY

Early Explorers of the Western Hemisphere

Genetic evidence suggests that beginning around 15,000 years before the present (BP), humans reached the Americas by sailing along the Pacific coast or by crossing the Bering Land Bridge between Siberia and Alaska. Extant remains known as the Anzick child (c. 12,600 BP) of the Clovis people; Xach'itee'aaneh T'eede Gaay (Sunrise Girl-Child) (c. 11,500 BP) of the Ancient Beringians; Luzia Woman (11,500 BP); and Kennewick Man (9,600-9,200 BP) were some of these early arrivals. Modern Native Americans appear to be descended from peoples indigenous to N and Central Asia who arrived in subsequent waves.

Long before Europeans arrived, the Americas were populated mostly by hunter-gatherers and small-scale horticulturalists. Complex chiefdoms and state-level societies appeared in a few areas (SE U.S., Mesoamerica, coastal Chile). The earliest known state in the Americas spanned 700 sq mi across river valleys in coastal Peru between 3,500 and 500 BP.

The Norse, led by Leif Ericson, are usually credited as being the first Europeans to reach America, with at least five voyages occurring about 1000 CE to areas they called Helluland, Markland, and Vinland—possibly present-day Baffin Island, Labrador, and either Newfoundland or somewhere in New England. L'Anse aux Meadows, Newfoundland, is the only documented settlement, with evidence of a small village dating to c. 1000 CE.

Sustained contact between the hemispheres began with Christopher Columbus (born Cristoforo Colombo, c. 1451, near Genoa, Italy), who made four voyages to the Americas with funding from the Spanish monarchs and private investors. He left Spain, Aug. 3, 1492, with 88 men and a fleet of three vessels— the Niña, Pinta, and Santa María—and landed on the island of San Salvador in present-day Bahamas on Oct. 12, 1492. He also visited Cuba, Hispaniola, and many smaller Caribbean islands, then populated by the Taíno. A second expedition in 1493, with 17 ships and 1,200 men, reached the island of Dominica in the Lesser Antilles; a third, in 1498, took Columbus to Trinidad and the adjacent S American coast. A fourth voyage reached Mexico, Honduras, Panama, and what he christened Santiago (the present-day island of Jamaica) in 1502.

In 1497 and 1499, Amerigo Vespucci (for whom the Americas are named), an Italian sailing for Spain, passed along the N and E coasts of S America. He was the first to claim these lands were previously unknown and not part of Asia. Some early explorations are listed below.

Year	Explorer	Nationality (sponsor, if different)	Area reached or explored
1497	John Cabot	Italian (English)	Newfoundland, possibly Nova Scotia
1497-98	Vasco da Gama	Portuguese	Cape of Good Hope (Africa), India
1499	Alonso de Ojeda	Spanish	Northern S Amer. coast, Venezuela
1500	Vicente Yañez Pinzón	Spanish	S American coast, Amazon R.
1500	Pedro Álvarez Cabral	Portuguese	Brazil
1501	Rodrigo de Bastidas	Spanish	Central America
1513	Vasco Núñez de Balboa	Spanish	Panama, Pacific Ocean
1513	Juan Ponce de León	Spanish	Florida, Yucatán Peninsula
1515	Juan de Solis	Spanish	Río de la Plata
1519	Alonso de Pineda	Spanish	Mouth of Mississippi R.
1519	Hernán Cortés	Spanish	Mexico
1519-20	Ferdinand Magellan	Portuguese (Spanish)	Straits of Magellan, Tierra del Fuego
1524	Giovanni da Verrazano	Italian (French)	Atlantic coast, incl. New York Harbor
1528	Álvar Núñez Cabeza de Vaca	Spanish	Texas coast and interior
1532	Francisco Pizarro	Spanish	Peru
1534	Jacques Cartier	French	Canada, Gulf of St. Lawrence
1536	Pedro de Mendoza	Spanish	Up Río de la Plata, Buenos Aires
1539	Francisco de Ulloa	Spanish	California coast
1539	Marcos de Niza	Italian (Spanish)	SW United States
1539-41	Hernando de Soto	Spanish	Mississippi R., near Memphis, TN
1540	Francisco de Coronado	Spanish	SW United States
1540	Hernando de Alarcón	Spanish	Colorado R.
1540	Garcia Lopez de Cárdenas	Spanish	Colorado, Grand Canyon
1541	Francisco de Orellana	Spanish	Amazon R.
1542	Juan Rodriguez Cabrillo	Portuguese (Spanish)	Western Mexico, San Diego Harbor
1565	Pedro Menéndez de Avilés	Spanish	St. Augustine, FL
1576	Sir Martin Frobisher	English	Frobisher Bay, Canada
1577-80	Sir Francis Drake	English	CA coast, on voyage around world
1582	Antonio de Espejo	Spanish	SW U.S. (New Mexico)
1584	Philip Amadas and Arthur Barlowe (for Raleigh)	English	Virginia, Roanoke Isl.
1585-87	Sir Walter Raleigh's men	English	Roanoke Isl., NC
1595	Sir Walter Raleigh	English	Orinoco R., Venezuela
1603-09	Samuel de Champlain	French	Canadian interior, Lake Champlain
1607	John Smith	English	Atlantic coast
1609-10	Henry Hudson	English (Dutch)	Hudson R., Hudson Bay
1634	Jean Nicolet	French	Lake Michigan, Wisconsin
1673	Jacques Marquette and Louis Jolliet	French	Mississippi R., south to Arkansas
1682	René-Robert Cavelier, sieur de La Salle	French	Mississippi R., south to Gulf of Mexico
1727-29	Vitus Bering	Danish (Russian)	Bering Strait, Alaska
1789	Sir Alexander Mackenzie	Canadian	NW Canada
1804-06	Meriwether Lewis and William Clark	American	Missouri R., Rocky Mts., Columbia R.

Arctic Exploration

1596-97: Willem Barents (Dutch) touched Spitsbergen, 79°49′N, and rounded Novaya Zemlya, where he and crew were forced to winter ashore, first W Europeans to successfully do so in the Arctic.

1610: Henry Hudson (Eng.) explored Hudson Strait, Hudson Bay on search for Northwest Passage. After winter ashore, crew mutinied, 1611, and set him, his son, and some others adrift on small boat.

1733-43: Great Northern Expedition (Russ.), led by Vitus Bering (Dan./Russ.), surveyed Siberian Arctic coast. Bering had sailed through what would become known as Bering Strait,

1728, but this second expedition proved that Asia and North America were separate.

1827: William Edward Parry (Eng.), attempting to reach North Pole, made it to 82°45′N via sledge, setting record for farthest north.

1831: James Clark Ross (Eng.) was first to north magnetic pole.

1878-79: Baron Adolf Erik Nordenskiöld (Swed.) was first to navigate Northeast Passage—ocean route connecting Europe's North Sea to Pacific O.

1881-84: Adolphus Greely led 25-person U.S. expedition to Ellesmere Isl. as part of first Intl. Polar Year (1882-83). Only he and five others survived scurvy and starvation after relief ships failed to reach them.

1893-96: Fridtjof Nansen (Nor.) deliberately allowed *Fram* to become icebound and drift from New Siberian Isls. Leaving others in charge of ship, he tried polar dash in 1895 but only reached 86°14′N.

1903-06: Roald Amundsen (Nor.) was first to sail length of Northwest Passage—route linking Atlantic and Pacific via Canada's marine waterways.

1909: Robert E. Peary (U.S.) began dash for North Pole, Mar. 1, from Ellesmere Isl. Reportedly reached the pole, 90°N, Apr. 6, with Matthew Henson and four Inuit. Research suggests he may have fallen short of goal by c. 30-60 mi. (Dr. Frederick Cook [U.S.] claimed to have reached the North Pole in 1908.)

1926: Richard E. Byrd and Floyd Bennett (both U.S.) reputedly flew over North Pole, May 9. Amundsen, Lincoln Ellsworth (U.S.), and Umberto Nobile (Ital.) flew over North Pole May 12 in dirigible *Norge*.

1958: Nuclear-powered submarine USS *Nautilus* crossed the North Pole beneath the ice.

1968: Ralph Plaisted (U.S.) and three amateur explorers on snowmobiles became first independently confirmed surface expedition to reach North Pole.

1978: Naomi Uemura (Jpn.) became first person to reach the North Pole alone, traveling by dog sled in 54-day, 600-mi trek.

1982: Ranulph Fiennes (Eng.) and Charles Burton (S. Afr.-UK) reached the North Pole and became first to circle the Earth from pole to pole. They had reached the South Pole 16 months earlier. The 52,000-mi trek took three years at an est. cost of $18 mil.

1995: Richard Weber (Can.) and Mikhail Malakhov (Russ.) became first to North Pole and back without any mechanical assistance. The 940-mi trip on skis took 121 days.

Antarctic Exploration

Explorers have approached Antarctica since 1773-75, when Capt. James Cook (Eng.) reached 71°10′S. Fabian von Bellingshausen (Russ.) mapped the region on an expedition sponsored by Tsar Alexander I, 1819-21. In 1823, James Weddell (Brit.) reached 74°15′S and found the Weddell Sea.

First to announce existence of the continent of Antarctica was Charles Wilkes (U.S.), who followed the coast for 1,500 mi, 1840. Ross Ice Shelf was found by James Clark Ross (Brit.), 1841-42.

1895: Leonard Kristensen (Nor.) landed a party on Victoria Land, first ashore on main continental mass. C. E. Borchgrevink, a member of that party, returned in 1899 with a Brit. expedition, first to winter on Antarctica.

1901-04: Robert Falcon Scott (Eng.), commander of Brit. Natl. Antarctic Expedition, crossed Ross Ice Shelf to 82°17′S, farthest south then reached.

1911: Roald Amundsen (Nor.) with four men and dog teams were first to South Pole, Dec. 14. Scott and four companions reached South Pole on Jan. 17, 1912; they died on return trip.

1929: Richard E. Byrd (U.S.) crossed South Pole, Nov. 29, with three others on 1,600-mi airplane flight.

1934-35: Byrd led second expedition to Little America base camp, explored 450,000 sq mi, wintered alone at 80°08′S.

1935: Lincoln Ellsworth (U.S.) made first transcontinental crossing by air, flying south along E coast of Palmer Peninsula then across to Little America.

1946-48: Ronne Antarctic Research Expedition Cmdr. Finn Ronne determined Antarctic to be one continent with no strait between Weddell and Ross Seas.

1955-57: Supporting U.S. scientific efforts for Intl. Geophysical Year (IGY), the U.S. Navy's Operation Deep Freeze, led by Byrd, established five coastal stations and three interior stations; explored more than 1 mil sq mi in Wilkes Land.

1957-58: During the IGY, scientists from 12 countries conducted research within network of some 60 stations on Antarctica. Vivian E. Fuchs (Eng.) led 12-person Trans-Antarctic Expedition on first land crossing of Antarctica; completed in Mar. 1958 after traveling 2,158 mi in 99 days.

1959: Argentina, Australia, Belgium, Chile, France, Japan, New Zealand, Norway, South Africa, USSR, UK, and U.S. signed a treaty (in force 1961) affirming the use of Antarctica (specifically the area south of 60°S) "for peaceful purposes only." Territorial claims suspended.

1961-62: Scientists discovered Bentley Trench, running from Ross Ice Shelf into Marie Byrd Land, near the end of the Ellsworth Mts., toward Weddell Sea.

1985: Ocean Drilling Project finds that the ice sheets of E Antarctica are 37 mil years old, main W Antarctic ice sheet about 8 mil years old.

1991: Protocol to the Antarctic Treaty on Environmental Protection, or Madrid Protocol, adopted (in force 1998); it banned activities—except for scientific research—related to mineral resources.

1995: After a 1994 solo expedition to North Pole, Borge Ousland (Nor.) reached South Pole on skis, becoming first to reach both N and S Poles alone. He later became the first to traverse both Antarctica (1996-97) and the Arctic (2001) solo.

Volcanoes

Source: *Volcanoes of the World*, Geoscience Press; Global Volcanism Program, Smithsonian Institution, www.volcano.si.edu

Eruptions have been documented in some 568 volcanoes. More than half to three-quarters of historically active volcanoes can be found on the so-called **Ring of Fire**, which runs along the W coast of the Americas from the southern tip of Chile to Alaska, down the E coast of Asia from Kamchatka to Indonesia, and continues from New Guinea to New Zealand. The Ring of Fire marks boundaries between tectonic plates underlying the Pacific Ocean and the surrounding continents. Volcanic activity also occurs along rift zones like Iceland, where plates pull apart, or over hot spots such as Hawaii, where molten material rises from the mantle to Earth's crust. The majority of Earth's volcanism takes place at submarine rift zones, on the seafloor.

Notable Volcanic Eruptions

In approximately 5,700 BC, Mount Mazama, in southern Oregon, erupted violently, ejecting large amounts of ash and pumice and sending out pyroclastic flows (mixture of volcanic debris and gases). The top of the mountain collapsed, leaving a caldera about 6 mi across and 1 mi deep. This depression filled with water from rain and snow to form Crater Lake.

Date	Volcano	Est. deaths	Date	Volcano	Est. deaths
Aug. 24, 79 CE	Vesuvius, Italy	16,000[1]	Jan. 30, 1911	Taal, Philippines	1,400
1586	Kelut, Java, Indon.	10,000	June 6-8, 1912	Novarupta, AK, U.S.[5]	1
Dec. 15, 1631	Vesuvius, Italy	4,000	May 19, 1919	Kelut, Java, Indon.	5,000
Aug. 12, 1772	Papandayan, Java, Indon.	3,000	Jan. 17-21, 1951	Lamington, Papua New Guinea	3,000
June 8, 1783	Laki, Iceland	9,350	May 18, 1980	St. Helens, WA, U.S.	57
May 21, 1792	Unzen, Japan	14,500	Mar. 28, 1982	El Chichón, Mexico	1,880
Apr. 10-12, 1815	Tambora, Sumbawa, Indon.	92,000[2]	Nov. 13, 1985	Nevado del Ruiz, Colombia	23,000
Aug. 26-27, 1883	Krakatau, Indon.	36,000[3]	Aug. 21, 1986	Lake Nyos, Cameroon	1,700[6]
Apr. 24, 1902	Santa María, Guatemala	1,000[4]	June 15, 1991	Pinatubo, Luzon, Philippines	800[7]
May 8, 1902	Pelée, Martinique	28,000			

(1) Heated mud and ash engulfed Pompeii, Herculaneum, and Stabiae with debris more than 60 ft deep. About 10% of the three towns' pop. were killed. (2) Of these, about 10,000 were directly related to the eruption. Released gases and particles altered the global climate, leading to additional deaths from starvation and disease when crops failed. (3) At least 2,000 died in pyroclastic flows, Aug. 26. Collapse of volcano, Aug. 27, sank most of island, killing over 3,000. Resulting tsunamis were responsible for the majority of deaths, in Java and Sumatra. (4) An additional 3,000 deaths due to a malaria outbreak are sometimes attributed to the eruption. (5) Biggest eruption of 20th cent. by volume. (6) Caused by release of massive amount of carbon dioxide from crater lake. (7) Of these, about 500 were associated with post-eruption lahars (volcanic mudflows).

Notable Active Volcanoes

Source: Global Volcanism Program, Smithsonian Inst.; Volcano Hazards Program, U.S. Geological Survey, U.S. Dept. of the Interior

Active volcanoes display a wide range of activity, including the production of ash plumes and seismic swarms. An eruption may involve the explosive ejection of fragmental material and escape of liquid lava. Year of a volcano's last known or confirmed eruption, as of May 24, 2018, is given. Volcanoes are listed by elevation, which does not reflect eruptive magnitude. Submarine volcanoes are not included.

Volcano (last eruption)	Location	Elev. (ft)
Africa		
Cameroon (2000)	Cameroon	13,435
Nyiragongo (2018)	Dem. Rep. of the Congo	11,385
Nyamuragira (2017)	Dem. Rep. of the Congo	10,033
Ol Doinyo Lengai (2014)	Tanzania	9,718
Fogo (2015)	Cape Verde Isls.	9,281
Piton de la Fournaise (2018)	Réunion Isl. (Fr.), Indian O.	8,635
Karthala (2007)	Comoros	7,746
Nabro (2012)	Eritrea	7,277
Antarctica		
Erebus (2018)	Ross Isl.	12,448
Melbourne (1892)	Victoria Land	8,963
Asia and Oceania		
Ararat (1840)	Turkey	16,946
Klyuchevskoy (2018)	Kamchatka, Russia	15,597
Kerinci (2016)	Sumatra, Indon.	12,467
Fuji (1708)	Honshu, Japan	12,388
Rinjani (2016)	Lombok, Indon.	12,224
Semeru (2018)	Java, Indon.	11,998
Tolbachik (2013)	Kamchatka, Russia	11,847
Koryaksky (2009)	Kamchatka, Russia	11,253
Slamet (2014)	Java, Indon.	11,247
Shiveluch (2018)	Kamchatka, Russia	10,771
Raung (2015)	Java, Indon.	10,696
Dempo (2017)	Sumatra, Indon.	10,308
Ontake (2014)	Honshu, Japan	10,062
Agung (2018)	Bali, Indon.	9,833
Merapi (2018)	Java, Indon.	9,738
Zhupanovsky (2016)	Kamchatka, Russia	9,511
Marapi (2018)	Sumatra, Indon.	9,465
Bezymianny (2018)	Kamchatka, Russia	9,455
Ruapehu (2007)	North Isl., New Zealand	9,177
Heard (2017)	Heard Isl., Australia	9,006
Changbaishan (1903)	China-North Korea	9,003
Avachinsky (2001)	Kamchatka, Russia	8,914
Papandayan (2002)	Java, Indon.	8,743
Talang (2007)	Sumatra, Indon.	8,520
Asama (2015)	Honshu, Japan	8,425
Dieng Volcanic Complex (2018)	Java, Indon.	8,415
Mayon (2018)	Luzon, Philippines	8,077
Sinabung (2018)	Sumatra, Indon.	8,071
Kanlaon (2017)	Negros, Philippines	7,989
Niigata-Yakeyama (1998)	Honshu, Japan	7,874
Kizimen (2013)	Kamchatka, Russia	7,657
Ulawun (2017)	Papua New Guinea	7,657
Tengger Caldera (2016)	Java, Indon.	7,641
Alaid (2016)	Kuril Isls., Russia	7,497
Chokai (1974)	Honshu, Japan	7,336
Galunggung (1984)	Java, Indon.	7,113
Kusatsu-Shirane (2018)	Honshu, Japan	7,103
Sorikmarapi (1986)	Sumatra Isl., Indon.	7,037
Kambalny (2017)	Kamchatka, Russia	6,942
Tangkubanparahu (2013)	Java, Indon.	6,837
Tongariro (2012)	North Isl., New Zealand	6,490
Azuma (1977)	Honshu, Japan	6,394
Sangeang Api (2017)	Lesser Sunda Isls., Indon.	6,394
Kaba (2000)	Sumatra Isl., Indon.	6,365
Nasu (1963)	Honshu, Japan	6,283
Bagana (2018)	Papua New Guinea	6,086
Karkar (2014)	Papua New Guinea	6,033
Chachadake (Tiatia) (1981)	Kunashir Isl., Japan-admin. by Russia	5,978
Bandai (1888)	Honshu, Japan	5,958
Manam (2018)	Papua New Guinea	5,928
Gorely (2010)	Kamchatka, Russia	5,902
Karangetang (Api Siau) (2018)	Siau Isl., Indon.	5,896
Kuju (1996)	Kyushu, Japan	5,876
Soputan (2016)	Sulawesi, Indon.	5,856
Chikurachki (2016)	Kuril Isls., Russia	5,843
Kelut (2014)	Java, Indon.	5,679
Adatara (1996)	Honshu, Japan	5,669
Batur (2000)	Bali, Indon.	5,633
Gamalama (2016)	Ternate, Indon.	5,627
Lewotobi (2003)	Flores Isl., Indon.	5,587
Kirishima (2018)	Kyushu, Japan	5,577
Egon (2008)	Flores, Indon.	5,449
Gamkonora (2007)	Halmahera, Indon.	5,364
Aso (2016)	Kyushu, Japan	5,223
Lokon-Empung (2015)	Sulawesi, Indon.	5,184
Bulusan (2017)	Luzon, Philippines	5,036
Karymsky (2018)	Kamchatka, Russia	4,964
Akan (2008)	Hokkaido, Japan	4,918
Pinatubo (1993)	Luzon, Philippines	4,875

Volcano (last eruption)	Location	Elev. (ft)
Central America and West Indies		
Tacaná (1986)	Mexico-Guatemala	13,333
Acatenango (1972)	Guatemala	13,045
Fuego (2018)	Guatemala	12,346
Santa María (2018)	Guatemala	12,287
Irazú (1994)	Costa Rica	11,260
Turrialba (2018)	Costa Rica	10,958
Poás (2017)	Costa Rica	8,885
Pacaya (2018)	Guatemala	8,428
Santa Ana (2005)	El Salvador	7,812
San Miguel (2018)	El Salvador	6,988
Rincón de la Vieja (2018)	Costa Rica	6,286
San Cristóbal (2018)	Nicaragua	5,725
Concepción (2011)	Nicaragua	5,577
Arenal (2010)	Costa Rica	5,479
Soufrière Guadeloupe (1977)	Guadeloupe (France)	4,813
Pelée (1932)	Martinique (France)	4,573
Momotombo (2016)	Nicaragua	4,255
North America		
Pico de Orizaba (1846)	Mexico	18,255
Popocatépetl (2018)	Mexico	17,694
Rainier (1450)	Washington	14,409
Shasta (1786)	California	14,163
Wrangell (1912)	Alaska	14,035
Colima (2017)	Mexico	12,631
Hood (1866)	Oregon	11,240
Spurr (1992)	Alaska	11,070
Lassen Peak (1917)	California	10,456
Redoubt (2009)	Alaska	10,197
Iliamna (1876)	Alaska	10,016
Shishaldin (2015)	Unimak Isl., Aleutians, AK	9,373
St. Helens (2008)	Washington	8,363
Veniaminof (2013)	Alaska	8,225
Pavlof (2016)	Alaska	8,179
Fourpeaked (2006)	Alaska	6,906
Katmai (1912)	Alaska	6,716
Makushin (1995)	Unalaska Isl., Aleutians, AK	5,906
Great Sitkin (1974)	Great Sitkin Isl., Aleutians, AK	5,709
Cleveland (2018)	Chuginadak Isl., Aleutians, AK	5,676
South America		
Llullaillaco (1877)	Chile-Argentina	22,110
San Pedro-San Pablo (1960)	Chile	20,151
Guallatiri (1960)	Chile	19,918
San José (1960)	Chile-Argentina	19,915
Sabancaya (2018)	Peru	19,554
Cotopaxi (2016)	Ecuador	19,393
El Misti (1985)	Peru	19,101
Ubinas (2017)	Peru	18,609
Tupungatito (1987)	Chile-Argentina	18,570
Láscar (2017)	Chile	18,346
Nevado del Huila (2012)	Colombia	17,598
Sangay (2018)	Ecuador	17,343
Nevado del Ruiz (2017)	Colombia	17,320
Irruputuncu (1995)	Chile-Bolivia	16,993
Tungurahua (2016)	Ecuador	16,480
Guagua Pichincha (2002)	Ecuador	15,696
Puracé (1977)	Colombia	15,256
Galeras (2014)	Colombia	14,029
Planchón-Peteroa (2011)	Chile	13,048
Lautaro (1979)	Chile	11,834
Reventador (2018)	Ecuador	11,686
Nevados de Chillán (2018)	Chile	10,433
Llaima (2009)	Chile	10,253
Europe		
Etna (2018)	Italy	10,810
Vesuvius (1944)	Italy	4,203
Stromboli (2018)	Italy	3,031
Mid-Atlantic		
La Palma (1971)	Canary Isls. (Spain)	7,959
Beerenberg (1985)	Jan Mayen (Norway)	6,841
Bardarbunga (2015)	Iceland	6,562
Grímsvötn (2011)	Iceland	5,640
Eyjafjallajökull (2010)	Iceland	5,417
Hekla (2000)	Iceland	4,888
Mid-Pacific		
Mauna Loa (1984)	Hawaii, HI	13,681
Haleakala (1750)	Maui, HI	10,023
Kilauea (2018)	Hawaii, HI	4,009

Mountains
North America

Source: U.S. Geological Survey, U.S. Dept. of the Interior; National Geodetic Survey, NOAA, U.S. Dept. of Commerce; Natural Resources Canada. Survey dates and elevation sources may differ.

Peak, state/prov., country	Height (ft)	Peak, state/prov., country	Height (ft)	Peak, state/prov., country	Height (ft)
Denali (fmr. McKinley), AK	20,310	La Malinche (Matlalcuéyetl), Mexico	14,636	Wilson, CO	14,246
Logan, Yukon, Canada	19,551	Hunter, AK	14,573	Cameron, CO	14,238
Pico de Orizaba, Mexico	18,619	Browne Tower, AK	14,530	Shavano, CO	14,231
St. Elias, AK-YT, U.S.-Can.	18,009	Whitney, CA	14,505	Princeton, CO	14,204
Popocatépetl, Mexico	17,802	Alverstone, AK-YT, U.S.-Can.	14,500	Belford, CO	14,203
Foraker, AK	17,400	University Peak, AK	14,470	Yale, CO	14,200
Iztaccíhuatl, Mexico	17,159	Elbert, CO	14,440	Crestone Needle, CO	14,197
Lucania, YT, Canada	17,146	Massive, CO	14,421	Bross, CO	14,172
King Peak, YT, Canada	16,972	Harvard, CO	14,421	Kit Carson, CO	14,165
Steele, YT, Canada	16,624	Rainier, WA	14,410	Point Success, WA	14,164
Bona, AK	16,500	Williamson, CA	14,376	Shasta, CA	14,163
Blackburn, AK	16,390	Blanca Peak, CO	14,345	Wrangell, AK	14,163
Sanford, AK	16,237	La Plata Peak, CO	14,336	Maroon Peak, CO	14,163
South Buttress, AK	15,885	Uncompahgre Peak, CO	14,321	Tabeguache, CO	14,162
Wood, YT, Canada	15,873	Crestone Peak, CO	14,294	Oxford, CO	14,160
Vancouver, AK-YT, U.S.-Can.	15,699	Lincoln, CO	14,293	El Diente Peak, CO	14,159
Churchill, AK	15,638	Castle Peak, CO	14,279	Sill, CA	14,159
Nevado de Toluca (Xinantécatl), Mexico	15,354	Grays Peak, CO	14,278	Democrat, CO	14,155
Fairweather, AK-BC, U.S.-Can.	15,299	Antero, CO	14,276	Sneffels, CO	14,150
Macaulay, YT, Canada	15,299	Torreys Peak, CO	14,275	Capitol Peak, CO	14,130
Slaggard, YT, Canada	15,299	Quandary Peak, CO	14,271	Liberty Cap, WA	14,118
Hubbard, AK-YT, U.S.-Can.	15,016	Evans, CO	14,265	Pikes Peak, CO	14,115
Bear, AK	14,831	Longs Peak, CO	14,259	Snowmass, CO	14,099
Walsh, YT, Canada	14,780	McArthur, YT, Canada	14,253	Russell, CA	14,094
East Buttress, AK	14,730	White Mountain Peak, CA	14,252	Eolus, CO	14,083
		North Palisade, CA	14,248	Windom, CO	14,082
				Challenger Point, CO	14,081

Note: The highest point in the West Indies is Pico Duarte (10,417 ft), in the Dominican Republic.

Other Notable U.S. Mountains

Peak, state	Height (ft)	Peak, state	Height (ft)	Peak, state	Height (ft)
Gannett, WY	13,810	Adams, WA	12,281	Mitchell, NC	6,683
Grand Teton, WY	13,775	San Gorgonio, CA	11,503	Clingmans Dome, NC-TN	6,644
Kings, UT	13,518	Hood, OR	11,247	Washington, NH	6,289
Cloud, WY	13,171	Cleveland, MT	10,466	Rogers, VA	5,729
Wheeler, NM	13,167	Lassen, CA	10,461	Marcy, NY	5,343
Boundary, NV	13,146	Granite, CA	10,325	Katahdin, ME	5,269
Granite, MT	12,807	Guadalupe, TX	8,751	Spruce Knob, WV	4,863
Borah, ID	12,668	Olympus, WA	7,973	Mansfield, VT	4,395
Humphreys, AZ	12,637	Harney, SD	7,244	Black Mountain, KY	4,139

South America

Peak, country	Height (ft)	Peak, country	Height (ft)	Peak, country	Height (ft)
Aconcagua, Argentina	22,831	Coropuna, Peru	21,083	Solo, Argentina	20,492
Ojos del Salado, Arg.-Chile	22,569	Laudo, Argentina	20,997	Polleras, Argentina	20,456
Bonete, Argentina	22,546	Ancohuma, Bolivia	20,958	Pular, Chile	20,423
Tupungato, Argentina-Chile	22,310	Ausangate, Peru	20,945	Chani, Argentina	20,341
Pissis, Argentina	22,241	Toro, Argentina-Chile	20,932	Aucanquilcha, Chile	20,295
Mercedario, Argentina	22,211	Illampu, Bolivia	20,873	Juncal, Argentina-Chile	20,276
Huascarán, Peru	22,205	Tres Cruces, Argentina-Chile	20,853	Negro, Argentina	20,184
Llullaillaco, Argentina-Chile	22,109	Huandoy, Peru	20,852	Quela, Argentina	20,128
El Libertador, Argentina	22,047	Parinacota, Bolivia-Chile	20,768	Condoriri, Bolivia	20,095
Cachi, Argentina	22,047	Tortolas, Argentina-Chile	20,745	Palermo, Argentina	20,079
Yerupajá, Peru	21,765	Ampato, Peru	20,702	Solimana, Peru	20,068
Incahuasi, Argentina-Chile	21,720	El Condor, Argentina	20,669	San Juan, Argentina-Chile	20,049
Galan, Argentina	21,654	Salcantay, Peru	20,574	Sierra Nevada, Argentina-Chile	20,023
Nevado Sajama, Bolivia	21,463	Chimborazo, Ecuador	20,561	Antofalla, Argentina	20,013
El Muerto, Argentina-Chile	21,457	Huancarhuas, Peru	20,531	Marmolejo, Argentina-Chile	20,013
Nacimiento, Argentina	21,302	Famatina, Argentina	20,505	Chachani, Peru	19,931
Illimani, Bolivia	21,201	Pumasillo, Peru	20,492		

Africa

Peak, country	Height (ft)	Peak, country	Height (ft)	Peak, country	Height (ft)
Kilimanjaro, Tanzania	19,341	Karisimbi, Congo-Rwanda	14,787	Guna, Ethiopia	13,881
Kenya, Kenya	17,057	Tullu Dimtu, Ethiopia	14,360	Gughe, Ethiopia	13,780
Margherita Pk., Uganda-Congo	16,765	Elgon, Kenya-Uganda	14,178	Jebel Toubkal, Morocco	13,665
Meru, Tanzania	14,977	Batu, Ethiopia	14,131	Cameroon, Cameroon	13,435
Ras Dashen, Ethiopia	14,872				

Australia, New Zealand, SE Asian Islands

Peak, country	Height (ft)	Peak, country	Height (ft)	Peak, country	Height (ft)
Jaya, New Guinea, Indon.	16,024	Wilhelm, Papua New Guinea	14,793	Aoraki/Cook, New Zealand	12,218
Trikora, New Guinea, Indon.	15,585	Kinabalu, Malaysia	13,436	Semeru, Java, Indon.	12,060
Mandala, New Guinea, Indon.	15,420	Kerinci, Sumatra, Indon.	12,467	Kosciusko, Australia	7,310

Height of Mount Everest

Mt. Everest, the world's highest mountain, was considered 29,002 ft when Edmund Hillary and Tenzing Norgay became the first to scale it, in 1953. In 1954, the Surveyor General of the Republic of India set the height at 29,028 ft, plus or minus 10 ft because of snow. In 1999, a team of climbers sponsored by Boston's Museum of Science and the National Geographic Society measured the height at the summit using satellite-based technology. The new measurement, of 29,035 ft, was accepted by other authorities, including the U.S. National Imagery and Mapping Agency, but not by Nepal. In 2018, Nepal's government began a survey to determine a new official height for Everest.

Climbers typically ascend Everest on its north (Tibet) or south face (Nepal). By the end of the 2017 climbing season, which runs from April through May, a total of about 4,833 climbers had made successful ascents while around 288 climbers had died in the attempt. Among the dead were 16 Sherpas killed in an avalanche triggered by falling ice Apr. 18, 2014. Concerns about additional avalanches, the increasing number of tourists on Everest, and fair worker compensation contributed to the decision by most tour operators to cancel the rest of the 2014 season on the south face. A 7.8-magnitude earthquake hit Nepal Apr. 25, 2015, triggering avalanches that swept through Everest Base Camp on the south side, killing 19. The 2015 season was canceled, making it the first year since 1974 that no one reached the top of Everest.

Europe

Peak, country	Height (ft)	Peak, country	Height (ft)	Peak, country	Height (ft)
Alps		Dent D'Herens, Switzerland	13,686	Schalihorn, Switzerland	13,040
		Breithorn, It.-Switzerland	13,665	Scerscen, Switzerland	13,028
Mont Blanc, France-Italy	15,781	Bishorn, Switzerland	13,645	Eiger, Switzerland	13,025
Dufourspitze (highest of Monte		Jungfrau, Switzerland	13,642	Jagerhorn, Switzerland	13,024
Rosa group), Switzerland	15,203	Ecrins, France	13,461	Rottalhorn, Switzerland	13,022
Dom, Switzerland	14,911	Monch, Switzerland	13,448	**Pyrenees**	
Liskamm, It.-Switzerland	14,852	Pollux, Switzerland	13,422		
Weisshorn, Switzerland	14,780	Schreckhorn, Switzerland	13,379	Aneto, Spain	11,168
Taschhorn, Switzerland	14,733	Ober Gabelhorn, Switzerland	13,330	Posets, Spain	11,073
Matterhorn, It.-Switzerland	14,692	Gran Paradiso, Italy	13,323	Perdido, Spain	11,007
Dent Blanche, Switzerland	14,293	Bernina, It.-Switzerland	13,284	Vignemale, France-Spain	10,820
Nadelhorn, Switzerland	14,196	Fiescherhorn, Switzerland	13,283	Long, Spain	10,479
Grand Combin, Switzerland	14,154	Grunhorn, Switzerland	13,266	Estats, Spain	10,304
Lenzpitze, Switzerland	14,088	Lauteraarhorn, Switzerland	13,261	Montcalm, Spain	10,105
Finsteraarhorn, Switzerland	14,022	Durrenhorn, Switzerland	13,238	**Caucasus (Europe-Asia)**	
Castor, Switzerland	13,865	Allalinhorn, Switzerland	13,213		
Zinalrothorn, Switzerland	13,849	Weissmies, Switzerland	13,199	Elbrus, Russia	18,510
Hohberghorn, Switzerland	13,842	Lagginhorn, Switzerland	13,156	Shkhara, Georgia	17,064
Alphubel, Switzerland	13,799	Zupo, Switzerland	13,120	Dykh Tau, Russia	17,054
Rimpfischhorn, Switzerland	13,776	Fletschhorn, Switzerland	13,110	Kashtan Tau, Russia	16,877
Aletschorn, Switzerland	13,763	Adlerhorn, Switzerland	13,081	Janqi, Georgia	16,565
Strahlhorn, Switzerland	13,747	Gletscherhorn, Switzerland	13,068	Kazbek, Georgia	16,558

Asia (Mainland)

Peak, country/region	Height (ft)	Peak, country/region	Height (ft)	Peak, country/region	Height (ft)
Everest, Nepal-Tibet	29,035	Tirich Mir, Pakistan	25,230	Badrinath, India	23,420
K2 (Godwin Austen), Kashmir	28,251	Makalu II, Nepal-Tibet	25,120	Nunkun, Kashmir	23,410
Kanchenjunga, India-Nepal	28,169	Minya Konka, China	24,900	Lenin Peak, Tajikistan	23,406
Lhotse I (Everest), Nepal-Tibet	27,923	Annapurna III, Nepal	24,786	Pyramid, India-Nepal	23,400
Makalu I, Nepal-Tibet	27,824	Kula Gangri, Bhutan-Tibet	24,784	Api, Nepal	23,399
Lhotse II (Everest), Nepal-Tibet	27,560	Changtse (Everest), Nepal-Tibet	24,780	Pauhunri, India-Tibet	23,385
Dhaulagiri, Nepal	26,795	Muztagh Ata, Xinjiang, China	24,757	Trisul, India	23,360
Manaslu I, Nepal	26,781	Skyang Kangri, Kashmir	24,750	Kangto, India-Tibet	23,260
Cho Oyu, Nepal-Tibet	26,750	Annapurna IV, Nepal	24,688	Nyenchen Thanglha, Tibet	23,255
Nanga Parbat, Kashmir	26,660	Ismail Samani Peak, Tajikistan	24,590	Trisuli, India	23,210
Annapurna I, Nepal	26,545	Jongsong Peak,		Pumori, Nepal-Tibet	23,190
Annapurna II, Nepal	26,545	India-Nepal-China	24,472	Dunagiri, India	23,184
Gasherbrum, Kashmir	26,470	Jengish Chokusu, Xinjiang,		Lombo Kangra, Tibet	23,165
Broad, Kashmir	26,400	China-Kyrgyzstan	24,406	Saipal, Nepal	23,100
Gosainthan, Nepal-Tibet	26,287	Sia Kangri, Kashmir	24,350	Macha Pucchare, Nepal	22,958
Gyachung Kang, Nepal-Tibet	25,910	Haramosh Peak, Pakistan	24,270	Khan Tengri, Kazakhstan-	
Disteghil Sar, Kashmir	25,868	Istoro Nal, Pakistan	24,240	Kyrgyzstan-Xinjiang, China	22,949
Himalchuli, Nepal	25,801	Kirat Chuli, India-Nepal	24,165	Numbar, Nepal	22,817
Nuptse (Everest), Nepal-Tibet	25,726	Chomo Lhari, Bhutan-Tibet	24,040	Kanjiroba, Nepal	22,580
Masherbrum, Kashmir	25,660	Chamlang, Nepal	24,012	Ama Dablam, Nepal	22,350
Nanda Devi, India	25,645	Kabru, India-Nepal	24,002	Cho Polu, Nepal	22,093
Rakaposhi, Kashmir	25,550	Alung Gangri, Tibet	24,000	Lingtren, Nepal-Tibet	21,972
Kamet, India-Tibet	25,447	Baltoro Kangri, Kashmir	23,990	Khumbutse, Nepal-Tibet	21,785
Namcha Barwa, Tibet	25,445	Mana, India	23,860	Hlako Gangri, Tibet	21,266
Gurla Mandhata, Tibet	25,355	Baruntse, Nepal	23,688	Grosvenor, China	21,190
Ulugh Muztagh, Xinjiang,		Nepal Peak, India-Nepal	23,500	Thagchhab Gangri, Tibet	20,970
China-Tibet	25,340	Amne Machin, China	23,490	Damavand, Iran	18,406
Kungur, Xinjiang, China	25,325	Gauri Sankar, Nepal-Tibet	23,440	Ararat, Turkey	16,854

Antarctica

Peak	Height (ft)	Peak	Height (ft)	Peak	Height (ft)
Vinson Massif	16,066	Sidley	13,720	Donaldson	12,894
Tyree	15,919	Ostenso	13,710	Ray	12,808
Shinn	15,750	Minto	13,668	Sellery	12,779
Gardner	15,375	Miller	13,650	Waterman	12,730
Epperly	15,100	Long Gables	13,620	Anne	12,703
Kirkpatrick	14,855	Dickerson	13,517	Press	12,566
Elizabeth	14,698	Giovinetto	13,412	Falla	12,549
Markham	14,290	Wade	13,400	Rucker	12,520
Bell	14,117	Fisher	13,386	Goldthwait	12,510
Mackellar	14,098	Fridtjof Nansen	13,350	Morris	12,500
Anderson	13,957	Wexler	13,202	Erebus	12,450
Bentley	13,934	Lister	13,200	Campbell	12,434
Kaplan	13,878	Shear	13,100	Don Pedro Christophersen	12,355
Andrew Jackson	13,750	Odishaw	13,008	Lysaght	12,326

Notable Islands and Their Areas

Figures are for total area in square miles. Boldface figures in parentheses show rank among the world's 10 largest individual islands. Only the largest islands in an island group are shown. Table does not include islands smaller than 10 sq mi in area. Canada's Manitoulin Island (1,068 sq mi), in Lake Huron, is the world's largest island in a freshwater lake.

Antarctica

Adelaide	1,400
Alexander	16,700
Berkner	18,500
Roosevelt	2,900

Arctic Ocean

Amund Ringnes, NU, Can.	2,029
Axel Heiberg, NU, Can.	16,671
Baffin, NU, Can. (5)	195,928
Banks, NT, Can.	27,038
Bathurst, NU, Can.	6,194
Bolshoy Lyakhovsky, Russia	1,776
Borden, NT-NU, Can.	1,079
Bylot, NU, Can.	4,273
Coats, NU, Can.	2,123
Cornwallis, NU, Can.	2,701
Devon, NU, Can.	21,331
Disko, Greenland, Denmark	3,312
Ellef Ringnes, NU, Can.	4,361
Ellesmere, NU, Can. (10)	75,767
Faddayevskiy, Russia	1,930
Franz Josef Land, Russia	8,000
Iturup (Etorofu), Russia	2,596
King William, NU, Can.	5,062
Kotelny, Russia	4,504
Mackenzie King, NT, Can.	1,949
Melville, NT-NU, Can.	16,274
Milne Land, Greenland, Den.	1,400
New Siberian Isls., Russia	14,500
Novaya Zemlya, Russia (2 isls.)	31,730
Prince Charles, NT, Can.	3,676
Prince Patrick, NT, Can.	6,119
Prince of Wales, NU, Can.	12,872
Severnaya Zemlya, Russia (tot. group)	14,175
Bol'shevik	4,368
Komsomolets	3,477
Oktyabr'skoy Revolyutsii	5,471
Somerset, NU, Can.	9,570
Southampton, NU, Can.	15,913
Svalbard, Norway (tot. group)	23,561
Nordaustlandet	5,576
Spitsbergen	14,546
Traill, Greenland, Denmark	1,300
Victoria, NT-NU, Can. (8)	83,897
Wrangel, Russia	2,937

Atlantic Ocean

Anticosti, QC, Can.	3,066
Ascension, UK	35
Azores, Portugal (tot. group)	868
Faial	67
San Miguel	291
Bahama Isls. (tot. group)	5,382
Andros	2,300
Bermuda Isls., UK (tot. group)	21
Bioko Isl., Equatorial Guinea	785
Block Island, RI, U.S.	21
Cabo Verde	1,557
Canary Isls., Spain (tot. group)	2,807
Fuerteventura	688
Gran Canaria	592
Tenerife	795
Cape Breton, NS, Can.	3,981
Caviana, Pará, Brazil	1,918
Channel Isls., UK (tot. group)	75
Guernsey	24
Jersey	45
Falkland Isls., UK (tot. group)	4,700
East Falkland	2,550
West Falkland	1,750
Faroe Isls., Denmark	538
Great Britain, UK (9)	80,823
Greenland, Denmark (1)	836,330
Gurupá, Pará, Brazil	1,878
Hebrides, Scotland, UK	2,744
Iceland	39,958
Ireland, Ireland-UK	32,589
Isle of Man, UK	221
Isle of Wight, England, UK	147
Long Island, NY, U.S.	1,320
Madeira Isls., Portugal	306
Marajo, Brazil	15,444
Martha's Vineyard, MA, U.S.	89

Atlantic Ocean

Mount Desert, ME, U.S.	104
Nantucket, MA, U.S.	45
Newfoundland, Canada	42,031
Orkney Isls., Scotland, UK	383
Prince Edward Isl. (main), Can.	2,170
St. Helena, UK	47
Shetland Isls., Scotland, UK	555
Skye, Scotland, UK	647
South Georgia, UK	1,450
Tierra del Fuego, Chile-Arg.	18,800
Tristan da Cunha, UK	38

Baltic Sea

Aland Isls., Finland	610
Bornholm, Denmark	227
Funen, Denmark	1,154
Gotland, Sweden	1,159
Zealand, Denmark	2,722

Caribbean Sea

Antigua	108
Aruba, Netherlands	69
Barbados	166
Cayman Isls., UK (tot. group)	102
Cuba	40,285
Isle of Youth	934
Curaçao, Netherlands	171
Dominica	290
Guadeloupe, France	687
Hispaniola (Haiti and Dominican Rep.)	29,389
Jamaica	4,244
Martinique, France	436
Montserrat, UK	39
Nevis	36
Puerto Rico, U.S.	3,425
St. Kitts	65
St. Lucia	238
St. Vincent	133
Tobago	116
Trinidad	1,864
Virgin Isls., UK	59
Virgin Isls., U.S.	134

East Indies

Bali, Indonesia	2,171
Bangka, Indonesia	4,375
Borneo, Indonesia-Malaysia-Brunei (3)	290,321
Bougainville, Papua New Guinea	3,880
Buru, Indonesia	3,670
Celebes, Indonesia	69,000
Flores, Indonesia	5,500
Halmahera, Indonesia	6,865
Java (Jawa), Indonesia	48,900
Madura, Indonesia	2,113
Moluccas, Indonesia	32,307
New Britain, PNG	14,093
New Guinea, Indon.-PNG (2)	303,381
New Ireland, PNG	3,707
Seram, Indonesia	6,621
Sumatra, Indonesia (6)	182,543
Sumba, Indonesia	4,306
Sumbawa, Indonesia	5,965
Timor, Indon.–Timor-Leste	13,094
Yos Sudarsa, Indonesia	4,500

Indian Ocean

Andaman Isls., India	2,500
Kerguelen, France	2,247
Madagascar (4)	226,917
Mauritius	720
Pemba, Tanzania	380
Réunion, France	970
Seychelles	176
Sri Lanka	25,332
Zanzibar, Tanzania	640

Mediterranean Sea

Balearic Isls., Spain	1,927
Corfu, Greece	229
Corsica, France	3,369
Crete, Greece	3,189
Cyprus	3,572
Elba, Italy	86
Euboea, Greece	1,411

Mediterranean Sea

Malta	95
Rhodes, Greece	540
Sardinia, Italy	9,301
Sicily, Italy	9,926

Pacific Ocean

Admiralty, AK, U.S.	1,709
Aleutian Isls., AK, U.S. (tot. group)	6,912
Adak	275
Attu	350
Tanaga	195
Umnak	686
Unalaska	1,051
Unimak	1,571
Baranof, AK, U.S.	1,636
Chichagof, AK, U.S.	2,062
Chiloe, Chile	3,241
Easter Isl. (Rapa Nui), Chile	63
Fiji (tot. group)	7,056
Vanua Levu	2,242
Viti Levu	4,109
Galapagos Isls., Ecuador	3,043
Graham Isl., BC, Can.	2,456
Guadalcanal, Solomon Isls.	2,180
Guam, U.S.	210
Hainan, China	13,000
Hawaiian Isls., HI, U.S. (tot. group)	6,428
Hawaii	4,028
Oahu	597
Hong Kong, China	31
Hoste, Chile	1,590
Japan (tot. group)	145,936
Hokkaido	32,210
Honshu (7)	89,239
Kyushu	16,306
Okinawa	881
Shikoku	7,254
Kangaroo, South Australia	1,705
Kiritimati (Christmas), Kiribati	150
Kodiak, AK, U.S.	3,485
Kupreanof, AK, U.S.	1,084
Marquesas Isls., France	492
Marshall Islands	70
Melville, Northern Terr., Australia	2,234
Micronesia	271
New Caledonia, France	6,530
New Zealand (tot. group)	103,362
Chatham Isls.	372
North	44,075
South	58,076
Stewart	649
Northern Mariana Isls., U.S.	179
Nunivak, AK, U.S.	1,600
Palau	188
Philippines (tot. group)	115,831
Leyte	2,787
Luzon	40,680
Mindanao	36,775
Mindoro	3,690
Negros	4,907
Palawan	4,554
Panay	4,446
Samar	5,050
Prince of Wales, AK, U.S.	2,770
Revillagigedo, AK, U.S.	1,134
Riesco, Chile	1,973
St. Lawrence, AK, U.S.	1,780
Sakhalin, Russia	29,500
Samoa Isls. (tot. group)	1,177
American Samoa, U.S.	77
Savaii, Samoa	659
Tutuila, U.S.	55
Upolu, Samoa	432
Santa Catalina, CA, U.S.	75
Santa Ines, Chile	1,407
Tahiti, France	402
Taiwan (tot. group)	13,892
Jinmen Dao (Quemoy)	56
Tasmania, Australia	26,178
Tonga	288
Vancouver Isl., BC, Can.	12,079
Vanuatu	4,707
Wellington, Chile	2,549

Persian Gulf

Bahrain	295

Notable Deserts of the World

Deserts are defined as regions of the Earth receiving less than 10 in. of precipitation annually, usually in combination with an evaporation rate exceeding precipitation.

In addition to areas listed below, the continent of Antarctica, with an area of about 5.4 mil sq mi (of which 108,109 sq mi are ice free), is generally considered a desert. Annual precipitation averages 8 in. along the coast and far less in the deep interior; however, there is little evaporation.

Arabian (Eastern), 86,000 sq mi in Egypt between the Nile R. and Red Sea, extending south into Sudan
Atacama, 600-mi-long area rich in nitrate and copper deposits in northern Chile
Chihuahuan, 140,000 sq mi in TX, NM, AZ, and Mexico
Dasht-e Kavir, approx. 500 mi long by 200 mi wide in north-central Iran
Dasht-e Lut, approx. 300 mi long by 200 mi wide in south-central Iran
Death Valley, 3,300 sq mi in CA and NV
Gibson, 60,232 sq mi in the interior of western Australia
Gobi, 500,000 sq mi in Mongolia and China
Great Sandy, 103,186 sq mi in western Australia
Great Victoria, 134,653 sq mi in southwestern Australia
Kalahari, 275,000 sq mi in southern Africa
Kara Kum, 115,000 sq mi in Turkmenistan
Kyzyl Kum, 115,000 sq mi in Kazakhstan and Uzbekistan
Libyan, 425,000 sq mi in the Sahara, extending from Libya through southwestern Egypt into Sudan

Mojave, 15,000 sq mi in southern CA
Namib, long narrow area (varies 30-100 mi wide) extending 800 mi along SW coast of Africa
Nubian, 157,000 sq mi in the Sahara in northeastern Sudan
Painted Desert, section of high plateau in northern AZ extending 200 mi southeast from Grand Canyon
Patagonia, 300,000 sq mi in southern Argentina
Rub al-Khali (Empty Quarter), 225,000 sq mi in the S Arabian Peninsula
Sahara, 3,500,000 sq mi in N Africa, extending west to the Atlantic. Largest desert in the world
Sonoran, 70,000 sq mi in southwestern AZ and southeastern CA extending into NW Mexico
Syrian, 100,000 sq mi over much of northern Saudi Arabia, eastern Jordan, southern Syria, and western Iraq
Taklamakan, 140,000 sq mi in Xinjiang Prov., China
Tanami, 71,236 sq mi in northern Australia
Thar (Great Indian), 100,000-sq-mi area extending 400 mi along India-Pakistan border

Areas and Average Depths of Oceans, Seas, and Gulfs

Geographers and mapmakers recognize at least four major bodies of water: the Pacific, Atlantic, Indian, and Arctic Oceans. The Atlantic and Pacific Oceans are considered divided at the equator into N and S. The Arctic Ocean is the name for waters north of the continental landmasses in the region of the Arctic Circle. The International Hydrographic Organization delimited a fifth world ocean in 2000. The Southern Ocean extends from the coast of Antarctica north to 60°S latitude, encompassing portions of the Atlantic, Indian, and Pacific Oceans. A Woods Hole Oceanographic Institution study published in 2010 calculated a mean depth of 12,081 ft for the world's oceans.

Body of water	Area (sq mi)	Avg. depth (ft)	Body of water	Area (sq mi)	Avg. depth (ft)
Pacific Ocean	60,060,893	14,040	Sea of Japan	391,100	5,468
Atlantic Ocean	29,637,974	11,810	Hudson Bay	281,900	305
Indian Ocean	26,469,620	12,800	East China Sea	256,600	620
Southern Ocean	7,848,299	14,450	Andaman Sea	218,100	3,667
Arctic Ocean	5,427,052	4,300	Black Sea	196,100	3,906
South China Sea	2,688,429	4,802	Red Sea	174,900	1,764
Caribbean Sea	971,400	8,448	North Sea	164,900	308
Mediterranean Sea	969,100	4,926	Baltic Sea	147,500	180
Bering Sea	873,000	4,893	Yellow Sea	113,500	121
Gulf of Mexico	582,100	5,297	Persian Gulf	88,800	328
Sea of Okhotsk	537,500	3,192	Gulf of California	59,100	2,375

Principal Ocean Depths

Source: Intl. Hydrographic Org. (IHO); Intergovernmental Oceanographic Commission (IOC) of UNESCO; National Geospatial-Intelligence Agency, U.S. Dept. of Defense

Body of water	Location (lat.)	(long.)	Depth (meters)	(fathoms)	(feet)
Pacific Ocean					
Mariana Trench	11°22′ N	142°36′ E	10,994	6,012	36,069
Tonga Trench	23°16′ S	174°44′ W	10,800	5,906	35,433
Philippine Trench	10°38′ N	126°36′ E	10,057	5,499	32,995
Kermadec Trench	31°53′ S	177°21′ W	10,047	5,494	32,963
Bonin Trench	24°30′ N	143°24′ E	9,994	5,464	32,788
Kuril Trench	44°15′ N	150°34′ E	9,750	5,331	31,988
Izu Trench	31°05′ N	142°10′ E	9,695	5,301	31,808
New Britain Trench	06°19′ S	153°45′ E	8,940	4,888	29,331
Yap Trench	08°33′ N	138°02′ E	8,527	4,663	27,976
Japan Trench	36°08′ N	142°43′ E	8,412	4,600	27,599
Peru-Chile Trench	23°18′ S	71°14′ W	8,064	4,409	26,457
Palau Trench	07°52′ N	134°56′ E	8,054	4,404	26,424
Aleutian Trench	50°51′ N	177°11′ E	7,679	4,199	25,194
New Hebrides Trench	20°36′ S	168°37′ E	7,570	4,139	24,836
North Ryukyu Trench	24°00′ N	126°48′ E	7,181	3,927	23,560
Middle America Trench	14°02′ N	93°39′ W	6,662	3,643	21,857
Atlantic Ocean					
Puerto Rico Trench	19°55′ N	65°27′ W	8,605	4,705	28,232
South Sandwich Trench	55°42′ S	25°56′ W	8,325	4,552	27,313
Romanche Gap	0°13′ S	18°26′ W	7,728	4,226	25,354
Cayman Trench	19°12′ N	80°00′ W	7,535	4,120	24,721
Brazil Basin	09°10′ S	23°02′ W	6,119	3,346	20,076
Indian Ocean					
Java Trench	10°19′ S	109°58′ E	7,125	3,896	23,376
Ob' Trench	09°45′ S	67°18′ E	6,874	3,759	22,553
Diamantina Trench	35°50′ S	105°14′ E	6,602	3,610	21,660
Vema Trench	09°08′ S	67°15′ E	6,402	3,501	21,004
Agulhas Basin	45°20′ S	26°50′ E	6,195	3,387	20,325
Arctic Ocean					
Eurasia Basin	82°23′ N	19°31′ E	5,450	2,980	17,881
Mediterranean Sea					
Ionian Basin	36°32′ N	21°06′ E	5,150	2,816	16,896

Note: Greater depths have been reported in some areas but have not been officially confirmed by research vessels.

Major World Rivers

North American rivers are listed in a separate table.

River	Source or upper limit of length	Outflow	Length (mi)
Africa			
Chari	Bamingui-Bangoran region, Central African Republic	Lake Chad	650
Congo	Junction of Lualaba and Luvua Rivers, Dem. Rep. of Congo	Atlantic Ocean	2,720
Cubango (fmr. Okavango)	Central Angola	Okavango Delta	1,000
Gambia	Fouta Djallon Highlands, Guinea	Atlantic Ocean	700
Kasai	Central Angola	Congo River	1,100
Limpopo	Junction of Marico and Ngotwane Rivers, South Africa	Indian Ocean	1,100
Lualaba	Southeastern Dem. Rep. of Congo	Congo River	1,100
Niger	Fouta Djallon Highlands, Guinea	Gulf of Guinea	2,600
Nile	Luvironza River, Burundi	Mediterranean Sea	4,160
Orange	Maluti Mountains, northern Lesotho	Atlantic Ocean	1,300
Sénégal	Junction of Bafing and Bakoy Rivers, Mali	Atlantic Ocean	1,000
Ubangi	Junction of Uele and Bomu Rivers, Dem. Rep. of Congo	Congo River	700
Zambezi	Northwestern Zambia	Indian Ocean	1,700
Asia			
Amu Darya	Junction of Vakhsh and Panj Rivers, Afghanistan-Tajikistan	Aral Sea	1,660
Amur	Junction of Shilka and Argun Rivers, China-Russia	Tartar Strait	1,780
Angara	Lake Baikal, Russia	Yenisei River	1,150
Ayeyarwady (fmr. Irrawaddy)	Junction of Mali and Nmai Rivers, Myanmar	Andaman Sea	1,000
Brahmaputra	Kailas Range, Himalayas, southwestern Tibet	Bay of Bengal	1,800
Chang-Jiang	Tibetan Plateau, southwestern Qinghai, China	East China Sea	3,450
Euphrates	Junction of Kara (Sarasu) and Murat Rivers, Turkey	Shatt al-Arab	1,700
Ganges	Gangotri glacier, Himalayas, India	Bay of Bengal	1,560
Godavari	Western Ghats, Maharashtra, India	Bay of Bengal	900
Hsi (see Xi He)			
Huang-He	Kunlun Mountains, Qinghai, China	Yellow Sea	3,000
Indus	Kailas Range, Himalayas, Tibet	Arabian Sea	1,900
Irtysh	Kazakhstan-Russia	Ob River	2,650
Jordan	Junction of Dan, Banias, and Hazbani streams, Israel	Dead Sea	200
Kolyma	Kolyma and Cherskogo Ranges, Russia	Arctic Ocean	1,500
Krishna	Western Ghats, Maharashtra, India	Bay of Bengal	800
Kura	Northeastern Turkey	Caspian Sea	950
Lena	Western Baikal Range, Russia	Laptev Sea	2,648
Mekong	Eastern Tibetan Plateau, China	South China Sea	2,700
Narmada	Madhya Pradesh, India	Arabian Sea	775
Ob	Junction of Biya and Katun Rivers, Russia	Gulf of Ob	2,300
Salween	Eastern Tibet, China	Gulf of Martaban	1,750
Songhua Jiang	Changbai Mountains, Jilin, China	Amur River	1,150
Sungari (see Songhua Jiang)			
Sutlej	Kailas Range, Himalayas, Tibet	Indus River	900
Syr	Junction of Naryn and Kara Darya Rivers, Uzbekistan	Aral Sea	1,380
Tarim	Junction of Kashi and Yarkant Rivers, China	Lop Nor	1,300
Tigris	Taurus Mountains, Turkey	Shatt al-Arab	1,150
Xi He	Eastern Yunnan, China	South China Sea	1,250
Yamuna	Yamnotri glacier, Uttarakhand, India	Ganges River	850
Yangtze (see Chang-Jiang)			
Yellow (see Huang-He)			
Yenisei	Kyzyl, Tuva Republic, Russia	Kara Sea	2,500
Australia			
Darling	Eastern Highlands, NE New South Wales/SE Queensland	Murray River	1,703
Murray	Australian Alps, SE New South Wales	Southern Ocean	1,558
Murrumbidgee	Australian Alps, SE New South Wales	Murray River	923
Europe			
Buh, Southern	Podolian Upland, Ukraine	Black Sea	532
Buh, Western	Western Ukraine	Vistula River	500
Danube	Brege and Brigach Rivers, Black Forest, southwestern Germany	Black Sea	1,770
Dnieper	Valdai Hills, western Russia	Black Sea	1,420
Dniester	Carpathian Mountains, Ukraine	Black Sea	850
Don	SE of Tula, Russia	Sea of Azov	1,200
Drava	Carnic Alps, northern Italy	Danube River	450
Dvina, North	Near Veliki Ustyug, Vologda, Russia	White Sea	465
Dvina, West	Valdai Hills, Russia	Gulf of Riga	635
Ebro	Cantabrian Mountains, northern Spain	Mediterranean Sea	575
Elbe	Giant Mountains, northwestern Czech Republic	North Sea	725
Garonne	Central Pyrenees, Spain	Bay of Biscay	402
Kama	Ural Mountains, N of Kuliga, Russia	Volga River	1,260
Loire	Mt. Gerbier-de-Jonc, Vivrais Mountains, France	Atlantic Ocean	630
Marne	Langres Plateau, northeastern France	Seine River	325
Meuse	Langres Plateau, northeastern France	North Sea	560
Oder	Sudetes Mountains, northeastern Czech Republic	Baltic Sea	562
Oka	S of Orël, Russia	Volga River	925
Pechora	Northern Ural Mountains, Russia	Barents Sea	1,120
Po	Cottian Alps, Piedmont, northwestern Italy	Adriatic Sea	405
Rhine	Swiss Alps	North Sea	766

River	Source or upper limit of length	Outflow	Length (mi)
Rhône	Rhône glacier, northeastern Valais, Switzerland	Mediterranean Sea	505
Seine	Langres Plateau, northern Burgundy, France	English Channel	480
Shannon	Near Cuilcagh Mountain, northwestern Cavan County, Ireland	Atlantic Ocean	240
Tagus	E of Madrid, Spain	Atlantic Ocean	585
Thames	4 headstreams in the Cotswold Hills, Gloucestershire, England, UK	North Sea	215
Tiber	Etruscan Apennines, Italy	Tyrrhenian Sea	251
Tisza	N of Rakhiv, western Ukraine	Danube River	700
Ural	Southern Ural Mountains, northeastern Bashkortostan, Russia	Caspian Sea	1,580
Vistula (Wisla)	W Beskid range, Carpathian Mountains, southwestern Poland	Gulf of Gdansk	665
Volga	Valdai Hills, Smolensk, Russia	Caspian Sea	2,290
Weser	Junction of Fulda and Werra Rivers, Germany	North Sea	273

South America

River	Source or upper limit of length	Outflow	Length (mi)
Amazon	Junction of Ucayali and Marañón Rivers, Andes Mountains, Peru	Atlantic Ocean	3,900
Araguaía	Serra das Araras, Goiás-Mato Grosso, Brazil	Tocantins River	1,100
Beni	Cordillera Real, La Paz, Bolivia	Madeira River	1,000
Caquetá-Japura	Andes Mountains, southwestern Colombia	Amazon River	1,750
Juruá	Cerros de Canchuyaya, eastern Peru	Amazon River	1,500
Madeira	Junction of Beni and Mamoré Rivers, Bolivia	Amazon River	2,100
Magdalena	Cordillera Central, southwestern Colombia	Caribbean Sea	1,000
Negro	Southeastern Colombia	Amazon River	1,400
Orinoco	Near Mt. Delgado Chalbaud, Guiana Highlands, S Venezuela	Atlantic Ocean	1,600
Paraguay	Central Mato Grosso highlands, Brazil	Paraná River	1,584
Paraná	Junction of Paranaíba and Rio Grande Rivers, SE Brazil	Río de la Plata	2,485
Pilcomayo	E of Lake Poopó, Bolivia	Paraguay River	1,000
Purus	Andes Mountains, eastern Peru	Amazon River	2,100
Putumayo	Andes Mountains, southern Colombia	Amazon River	1,000
Río de la Plata	Estuary of Paraná and Uruguay Rivers, Argentina-Uruguay	Atlantic Ocean	170
São Francisco	Serra de Canastra, southwestern Minas Gerais, Brazil	Atlantic Ocean	1,800
Tocantins	South-central Goiás, Brazil	Para River	1,640
Ucayali	Junction of Apurímac and Urubamba Rivers, eastern Peru	Marañón River	1,000
Uruguay	Southern Brazil	Río de la Plata	1,000
Xingu	Central Mato Grosso, Brazil	Amazon River	1,230

Major Rivers in North America

River	Source or upper limit of length	Outflow	Length (mi)
Alabama	Gilmer County, GA	Mobile River	729
Albany	Lake St. Joseph, ON, Can.	James Bay	610
Allegheny	Potter County, PA	Ohio River	325
Altamaha-Ocmulgee	Junction of Yellow and South Rivers, Newton Co., GA	Atlantic Ocean	392
Apalachicola-Chattahoochee	Towns County, GA	Gulf of Mexico	524
Arkansas	Lake County, CO	Mississippi River	1,459
Assiniboine	Eastern Saskatchewan, Can.	Red River	450
Athabasca	Columbia Icefield, AB, Can.	Lake Athabasca	765
Attawapiskat	Attawapiskat, ON, Can.	James Bay	465
Back (NT)	Contwoyto Lake, NT, Can.	Chantrey Inlet, Arctic Ocean	605
Big Black	Webster County, MS	Mississippi River	330
Brazos	Junction of Salt and Double Mountain Forks, Stonewall Co., TX	Gulf of Mexico	1,280
Canadian	Las Animas County, CO	Arkansas River	906
Cedar (IA)	Dodge County, MN	Iowa River	329
Cheyenne	Junction of Antelope Creek and Dry Fork, Converse Co., WY	Missouri River	290
Churchill, Labrador	Lake Ashuanipi, NL, Can.	Atlantic Ocean	532
Churchill, Manitoba	Methy Lake, SK, Can.	Hudson Bay	1,000
Cimarron	Colfax County, NM	Arkansas River	600
Colorado (AZ)	Rocky Mountain Natl. Park, CO	Gulf of California	1,450
Colorado (TX)	Dawson County, TX	Matagorda Bay	862
Columbia	Columbia Lake, BC, Can.	Pacific Ocean, Astoria, OR	1,243
Columbia, Upper	Columbia Lake, BC, Can.	Mouth of Snake River	890
Connecticut	Third Connecticut Lake, NH	Long Island Sound, CT	407
Coppermine	Lac de Gras, NT, Can.	Coronation Gulf, Arctic Ocean	525
Cumberland	Letcher County, KY	Ohio River	720
Delaware	Schoharie County, NY	Liston Point, Delaware Bay	390
Fraser	Near Mount Robson (on Continental Divide)	Strait of Georgia	851
Gila	Catron County, NM	Colorado River	649
Green (UT-WY)	Junction of Wells and Trail Creeks, Sublette County, WY	Colorado River	730
Hudson	Henderson Lake, Essex County, NY	Upper New York Bay	306
Illinois	St. Joseph County, IN	Mississippi River	420
James (ND-SD)	Wells County, ND	Missouri River	710
James (VA)	Junction of Jackson and Cowpasture Rivers, Botetourt Co., VA	Hampton Roads	340
Kanawha-New	Junction of North and South Forks of New River, NC	Ohio River	352
Kentucky	Junction of North and Middle Forks, Lee County, KY	Ohio River	259
Klamath	Lake Ewauna, Klamath Falls, OR	Pacific O., Klamath, CA	250

River	Source or upper limit of length	Outflow	Length (mi)
Kootenay (Kootenai)	Rocky Mountains, BC, Can.	Columbia River	485
Koyukuk	Endicott Mountains, AK	Yukon River	470
Kuskokwim	Alaska Range	Kuskokwim Bay	724
Liard	Southern Yukon, AK	Mackenzie River	693
Little Missouri	Crook County, WY	Missouri River	560
Mackenzie	Great Slave Lake, NT, Can.	Arctic Ocean	2,635
Milk	Junction of North and South Forks, AB, Can.	Missouri River	624
Minnesota	Big Stone Lake, MN	Mississippi River	332
Mississippi	Lake Itasca, Clearwater County, MN	Gulf of Mexico	2,340
Mississippi-Missouri-Red Rock	Source of Red Rock, Beaverhead County, MT	Gulf of Mexico	3,710
Missouri	Junction of Jefferson, Madison, and Gallatin Rivers, Gallatin County, MT	Mississippi River	2,315
Missouri-Red Rock	Source of Red Rock, Beaverhead County, MT	Mississippi River	2,540
Mobile-Alabama-Coosa	Gilmer County, GA	Mobile Bay	774
Nelson	Lake Winnipeg, MB, Can.	Hudson Bay	400
Neosho	Morris County, KS	Arkansas River, OK	460
Niobrara	Niobrara County, WY	Missouri River, NE	431
North Canadian	Union County, NM	Canadian River, OK	800
North Platte	Junction of Grizzly and Little Grizzly Creeks, Jackson Co., CO	Platte River, NE	618
Ohio	Junction of Allegheny and Monongahela Rivers, Pittsburgh, PA	Mississippi River	981
Ohio-Allegheny	Potter County, PA	Mississippi River	1,310
Osage	East-central Kansas	Missouri River	500
Ottawa	Lake Capimitchigama, QC, Can.	St. Lawrence River	790
Ouachita	Polk County, AR	Black River	605
Peace	Junction of Finlay and Parsnip Rivers, BC, Can.	Slave River	1,195
Pearl	Neshoba County, MS	Gulf of Mexico	411
Pecos	Mora County, NM	Rio Grande	926
Pee Dee-Yadkin	Watauga County, NC	Winyah Bay	435
Pend Oreille-Clark Fork	Near Butte, MT	Columbia River	531
Platte	Junction of North Platte and South Platte Rivers, NE	Missouri River	990
Porcupine	Ogilvie Mountains, AK	Yukon River, AK	569
Potomac	Garrett County, MD	Chesapeake Bay	383
Powder	Junction of South and Middle Forks, WY	Yellowstone River	375
Red (River of the South)	Curry County, NM	Atchafalaya River, LA	1,290
Red River of the North	Junction of Otter Tail and Bois de Sioux Rivers, Wilkin Co., MN	Lake Winnipeg	545
Republican	Junction of North Fork and Arikaree Rivers, NE	Kansas River	445
Rio Grande (Rio Bravo)	San Juan County, CO	Gulf of Mexico	1,900
Roanoke	Junction of North and South Forks, Montgomery Co., VA	Albemarle Sound	380
Rock (IL-WI)	Dodge County, WI	Mississippi River	300
Sabine	Junction of South and Caddo Forks, Hunt Co., TX	Sabine Lake	380
Sacramento	Siskiyou County, CA	Suisun Bay	377
Saguenay	Lake St. John, QC, Can.	St. Lawrence River	434
St. Francis	Iron County, MO	Mississippi River	425
St. John	Northwestern Maine	Bay of Fundy	418
St. Lawrence	Lake Ontario, NY-ON, Can.	Gulf of St. Lawrence, Atlantic Ocean	800
Salmon (ID)	Custer County, ID	Snake River	420
San Joaquin	Junction of South and Middle Forks, Madera Co., CA	Suisun Bay	350
San Juan	Silver Lake, Archuleta County, CO	Colorado River	360
Santee-Wateree-Catawba	McDowell County, NC	Atlantic Ocean	538
Saskatchewan, North	Rocky Mountains, AB, Can.	Saskatchewan R.	800
Saskatchewan, South	Rocky Mountains, AB, Can.	Saskatchewan R.	865
Savannah	Junction of Seneca and Tugaloo Rivers, Anderson Co., SC	Atlantic Ocean, GA-SC	314
Severn (ON)	Sandy Lake, ON, Can.	Hudson Bay	610
Smoky Hill	Cheyenne County, CO	Kansas River, KS	540
Snake	Teton County, WY	Columbia River, WA	1,038
South Platte	Junction of South and Middle Forks, Park County, CO	Platte River	424
Susitna	Alaska Range	Cook Inlet	313
Susquehanna	Otsego Lake, Otsego County, NY	Chesapeake Bay	447
Tallahatchie	Tippah County, MS	Yazoo River	301
Tanana	Wrangell Mountains, AK	Yukon River	659
Tennessee	Junction of French Broad and Holston Rivers, TN	Ohio River	652
Tennessee-French Broad	Courthouse Creek, Transylvania County, NC	Ohio River	886
Tombigbee	Prentiss County, MS	Mobile River	525
Trinity	N of Dallas, TX	Galveston Bay	360
Usumacinta	Junction of Pasión and Chixoy Rivers, Guatemala	Bay of Campeche, Mex.	600
Wabash	Darke County, OH	Ohio River	512
Washita	Hemphill County, TX	Red River, OK	500
White (AR-MO)	Madison County, AR	Mississippi River	722
Willamette	Douglas County, OR	Columbia River	309
Wind-Bighorn	Junction of Wind and Little Wind Rivers, Fremont Co., WY (source of Wind R. is Togwotee Pass, Teton Co., WY)	Yellowstone River	338
Wisconsin	Lac Vieux Desert, Vilas County, WI	Mississippi River	430
Yellowstone	Park County, WY	Missouri River	682
Yukon	McNeil River, YT, Can.	Bering Sea	1,979

Major Natural Lakes of the World

Source: U.S. Geological Survey, U.S. Dept. of the Interior; Natural Resources Canada

A lake is generally defined as a body of water surrounded by land. By this definition some bodies of water that are called seas, such as the Caspian Sea and the Aral Sea, are really lakes. In the following table, the word "lake" is omitted when it is part of the name.

Name	Continent	Area (sq mi)	Length (mi)	Maximum depth (ft)	Elevation (ft)
Caspian Sea[1]	Asia-Europe	143,244	760	3,363	−92
Superior	North America	31,700	350	1,333	601
Victoria	Africa	26,828	209	270	3,720
Huron	North America	23,000	206	750	578
Michigan	North America	22,300	307	923	578
Tanganyika	Africa	12,700	420	4,823	2,534
Baikal	Asia	12,162	395	5,315	1,493
Great Bear	North America	12,096	192	1,463	512
Nyasa (Malawi)	Africa	11,150	360	2,280	1,550
Great Slave	North America	11,030	298	2,014	512
Erie	North America	9,910	241	210	569
Winnipeg	North America	9,416	266	200	712
Ontario	North America	7,340	193	802	243
Balkhash[1]	Asia	7,115	376	85	1,115
Ladoga	Europe	6,835	124	738	13
Maracaibo	South America	5,217	133	115	sea level
Aral Sea[1,2]	Asia	4,040	260	180	175
Onega	Europe	3,710	145	328	108
Eyre[1]	Australia	3,600[3]	90	4	−49
Titicaca	South America	3,200	122	922	12,500
Nicaragua	North America	3,100	102	230	102
Athabasca	North America	3,064	208	407	699
Reindeer	North America	2,568	143	720	1,106
Tonle Sap	Asia	2,500[3]	70	45	NA
Turkana (Rudolf)	Africa	2,473	154	240	1,230
Issyk Kul[1]	Asia	2,355	115	2,303	5,279
Torrens[1]	Australia	2,230[3]	130	NA[3]	92
Vänern	Europe	2,181	91	328	144
Nettilling	North America	2,140	67	(3)	98
Winnipegosis	North America	2,075	141	38	833
Albert	Africa	2,075	100	168	2,030
Nipigon	North America	1,872	72	540	853
Gairdner[1]	Australia	1,840[3]	90	NA[3]	112
Manitoba	North America	1,799	140	21	813
Urmia[1]	Asia	888	90	49	4,177
Chad	Africa	521[4]	175	24	787

NA = Not available. (1) Salt lake. (2) The diversion of its two feeder rivers since the 1960s has devastated the Aral—once the world's fourth-largest lake (26,000 sq mi) with length, max. depth, and elevation shown. By 2000, the Aral had effectively become three lakes, with the total area shown. (3) Subject to great seasonal variation. (4) Once fourth-largest lake in Africa (about 10,000 sq mi in the 1960s), Chad had shrunk to around 5% of its original size by 2006 as a result of irrigation and long-term drought.

The Great Lakes

Source: National Ocean Service, National Oceanic and Atmospheric Administration, U.S. Dept. of Commerce

The Great Lakes form the world's **largest freshwater body** (in surface area) and with their connecting waterways are the largest inland water transportation unit. Draining the north-central basin of the U.S., they enable shipping to get to the Atlantic via their outlet, the St. Lawrence R.; the Gulf of Mexico can be reached via the Illinois Waterway, between Lake Michigan and the Mississippi R. A third outlet connects with the Hudson R. and then the Atlantic via the New York State Barge Canal System. Illinois Waterway and NYS Barge Canal System traffic is limited to recreational boating and small shipping vessels.

Only Lake Michigan is wholly in the U.S.; the other lakes are shared with Canada. Ships move from the shores of Lake Superior to Whitefish Bay in the east, then through the Soo Locks in Sault Ste. Marie, MI, onto St. Mary's R. and into Lake Huron. To reach the Port of Indiana-Burns Harbor and South Chicago, IL, ships travel west from Lake Huron to Lake Michigan through the Straits of Mackinac. Low water datum is based on the International Great Lakes Datum (1985), with Rimouski, Quebec, as the reference zero point. The distance between Duluth, MN, and Lake Ontario's east end is 1,156 mi.

	Superior	Michigan	Huron	Erie	Ontario
Length (mi)	350	307	206	241	193
Breadth (mi)	160	118	183	57	53
Deepest soundings (ft)	1,333	923	750	210	802
Volume of water (cu mi)	2,935	1,180	850	116	393
Area (sq mi) water surface—U.S.	20,600	22,300	9,100	4,980	3,460
Canada	11,100	NA	13,900	4,930	3,880
Area (sq mi) entire drainage basin—U.S.	16,900	45,600	16,200	18,000	15,200
Canada	32,400	NA	35,500	4,720	12,100
Total area (sq mi), U.S. and Canada	**81,000**	**67,900**	**74,700**	**32,630**	**34,850**
Low water datum above mean water level at Rimouski, QC, avg. level (ft)	601.10	577.50	577.50	569.20	243.30
Latitude, N	46°25′	41°37′	43°00′	41°23′	43°11′
	49°00′	46°06′	46°17′	42°52′	44°15′
Longitude, W	84°22′	84°45′	79°43′	78°51′	76°03′
	92°06′	88°02′	84°45′	83°29′	79°53′
National boundary line (mi)	282.8	NA	260.8	251.5	174.6
U.S. shoreline (mainland only) (mi)	863	1,400	580	431	300

NA = Not applicable.

Notable Waterfalls

The magnitude of a waterfall is determined not only by height but also by volume and steadiness of flow, crest width, the angle of a drop, and the number of leaps it may make. A series of low falls over a considerable distance is known as a cascade. Waterfalls are highly variable and few authoritative figures exist. For more information and some alternative measurements, see the World Waterfall Database at www.worldwaterfalldatabase.com.

Estimated mean annual flow (ft³/sec): Niagara, 212,200; Paulo Afonso, 100,000; Iguazú, 61,000; Victoria, 35,400.

Height is total drop in feet in one or more leaps. If river name is not shown, it is the same as the waterfall. # = more than one leap; * = diminishes greatly seasonally; ** = reduces to a trickle or is dry for part of each year; R. = river; (C) = cascade.

Name, location	Height (ft)	Name, location	Height (ft)	Name, location	Height (ft)
Africa		**Switzerland**		Maryland	
Angola-Namibia		Giessbach (C)	984	Great, Potomac R. (C)*	76
Ruacana, Cunene R.	352	Reichenbach#	394	Minnesota	
Lesotho		Staubbach	974	Minnehaha**	53
Maletsunyane*	630	Trümmelbach#	950	New Jersey	
South Africa		**United Kingdom**		Great, Passaic R.	70
Augrabies, Orange R.*	480	Glomach, Scotland	370	New York	
Tugela#.	2,800	Pistyll Rhaeadr, Wales	240	Kaaterskill, Lake Creek*	231
Tanzania-Zambia		**North America**		Niagara (American)	120
Kalambo*	704	**Canada**		Taughannock*	215
Zimbabwe-Zambia		Alberta		Oregon	
Victoria, Zambezi R.*	343	Panther, Nigel Creek	600	Multnomah#	620
Asia and Oceania		British Columbia		Tennessee	
Australia		Della#	1,444	Fall Creek	256
New South Wales		Takakkaw, Daly Glacier#	992	Washington	
Wentworth	614	Ontario		Colonial Creek	2,568
Wollomombi	722	Niagara (Horseshoe)	167	Sluiskin, Paradise R.	300
Queensland		Québec		Snoqualmie**	268
Tully**	984	Montmorency	276	Wisconsin	
Wallaman, Stony Creek	879	**United States**		Big Manitou, Black R. (C)*	165
India		Alabama		Wyoming	
Jog, Sharavati R.*	829	Noccalula Falls	90	Tower	132
Sivasamudram	320	California		Yellowstone (lower)*	308
Japan		Feather*	640	Yellowstone (upper)*	109
Kegon, Lake Chuzenji*	350	Yosemite National Park		**South America**	
New Zealand		Bridalveil*	620	**Argentina-Brazil**	
Helena	722	Illilouette*	370	Iguazú	269
Sutherland, Arthur R.#	1,904	Nevada, Merced R.*	594	**Brazil**	
Europe		Ribbon**	1,612	Cachoeira da Fumaça*	1,312
Austria		Silver Strand,		Paulo Afonso, São Francisco R.	275
Gastein#	487	Meadow Brook**	574	**Colombia**	
Krimml#	1,246	Vernal, Merced R.*	317	Tequendama, Bogota R.*	482
France		Yosemite#**	2,425	**Ecuador**	
Gavarnie*	1,385	Colorado		Agoyan, Pastaza R.*	200
Italy		Seven Falls,		**Guyana**	
Toce (C)	470	S. Cheyenne Creek#	300	Kaieteur, Potaro R.	741
Norway		Hawaii		King George VI, Kamarang R.	1,600
Mardalsfossen#**	2,154	Akaka, Kolekole Stream	420	Marina, Ipobe R.#	500
Skykje**	984	Idaho		**Venezuela**	
Vetti, Morka-Koldedola R.	900	Shoshone, Snake R.**	212	Angel (Kerepakupai Merú),	
Sweden		Kentucky		Churún#*	3,212
Handol#	345	Cumberland	68	Cuquenan	2,000

Latitude and Longitude of World Cities
Source: National Geospatial-Intelligence Agency, U.S. Dept. of Defense

City, country	Lat. ° ′	Long. ° ′	City, country	Lat. ° ′	Long. ° ′
Athens, Greece	37 59 N	23 44 E	Manila, Philippines	14 35 N	121 0 E
Bangkok, Thailand	13 45 N	100 31 E	Mexico City, Mexico	19 26 N	99 8 W
Beijing, China	39 55 N	116 23 E	Moscow, Russia	55 45 N	37 36 E
Berlin, Germany	52 31 N	13 24 E	Mumbai (Bombay), India	18 59 N	72 50 E
Bogotá, Colombia	4 38 N	74 3 W	New Delhi, India	28 36 N	77 12 E
Buenos Aires, Argentina	34 35 S	58 40 W	Paris, France	48 52 N	2 20 E
Cairo, Egypt	30 4 N	31 17 E	Rio de Janeiro, Brazil	22 52 S	43 16 W
Jakarta, Indonesia	6 10 S	106 49 E	Rome, Italy	41 54 N	12 29 E
Jerusalem, Israel	31 45 N	35 0 E	Santiago, Chile	33 27 S	70 40 W
Johannesburg, South Africa	26 12 S	28 2 E	Seoul, South Korea	37 35 N	127 0 E
Kiev, Ukraine	50 26 N	30 31 E	Sydney, Australia	33 51 S	151 12 E
Lagos, Nigeria	6 35 N	3 45 E	Tehran, Iran	35 40 N	51 25 E
London, UK (Greenwich)	51 28 N	0 0	Tokyo, Japan	35 41 N	139 45 E

Highest and Lowest Continental Elevations

Continent	Highest point	Elev. (ft)	Continent	Lowest point	Ft below sea level
Asia	Everest, Nepal-Tibet	29,035	Antarctica	Bentley Subglacial Trench	8,383[1]
South America	Aconcagua, Argentina	22,831	Asia	Dead Sea, Israel-Jordan	1,339
North America	Denali (fmr. McKinley), Alaska, U.S.	20,310	Africa	Lake Assal, Djibouti	509
Africa	Kilimanjaro, Tanzania	19,341	South America	Laguna del Carbón, Argentina	344
Europe	Elbrus, Russia	18,510	North America	Death Valley, California, U.S.	282
Antarctica	Vinson Massif	16,066	Europe	Caspian Sea, Azer.-Kazakh.-Russ.	92
Australia	Kosciusko, New South Wales	7,310	Australia	Lake Eyre, South Australia	49

(1) Estimated level of the continental floor. Lower points that have yet to be discovered may exist beneath the ice.

Latitude, Longitude, and Elevation of U.S. and Canadian Cities

Source: U.S. geographic positions and altitudes provided by U.S. Geological Survey, U.S. Dept. of the Interior. Canadian geographic positions and altitudes provided by Natural Resources Canada.

City, state/province	Lat. N °	′	″	Long. W °	′	″	Elev. (ft)
Albany, NY	42	39	9	73	45	22	149
Albuquerque, NM	35	5	4	106	39	4	4,956
Anchorage, AK	61	13	5	149	54	1	104
Annapolis, MD	38	58	42	76	29	32	43
Atlanta, GA	33	44	56	84	23	17	1,050
Augusta, GA	33	28	15	81	58	29	141
Augusta, ME	44	18	38	69	46	46	123
Austin, TX	30	16	2	97	44	35	489
Baltimore, MD	39	17	25	76	36	44	36
Baton Rouge, LA	30	27	3	91	9	16	46
Billings, MT	45	47	0	108	30	2	3,124
Birmingham, AL	33	31	14	86	48	9	610
Bismarck, ND	46	48	30	100	47	1	1,695
Boise, ID	43	36	49	116	12	12	2,699
Boston, MA	42	21	30	71	3	35	45
Buffalo, NY	42	53	11	78	52	42	600
Burlington, VT	44	28	33	73	12	43	196
Calgary, AB	51	2	45	114	3	27	3,557
Carson City, NV	39	9	50	119	46	3	4,681
Casper, WY	42	52	0	106	18	47	5,105
Cedar Rapids, IA	42	0	30	91	38	39	808
Charleston, SC	32	46	36	79	55	51	11
Charleston, WV	38	20	59	81	37	57	596
Charlotte, NC	35	13	18	80	50	35	762
Charlottetown, PE	46	14	25	63	8	5	160
Cheyenne, WY	41	8	24	104	49	13	6,087
Chicago, IL	41	51	0	87	39	0	586
Churchill, MB	58	46	51	94	11	13	94
Cleveland, OH	41	29	58	81	41	43	653
Colorado Springs, CO	38	50	2	104	49	17	6,010
Columbia, SC	34	0	3	81	2	5	300
Columbus, OH	39	57	40	82	59	56	780
Concord, NH	43	12	29	71	32	15	273
Corpus Christi, TX	27	48	2	97	23	47	7
Dallas, TX	32	46	59	96	48	24	421
Denver, CO	39	44	21	104	59	5	5,277
Des Moines, IA	41	36	2	93	36	33	873
Detroit, MI	42	19	53	83	2	45	598
Dover, DE	39	9	29	75	31	27	28
Durham, NC	35	59	39	78	53	55	400
Edmonton, AB	53	32	4	113	29	25	2,200
El Paso, TX	31	45	31	106	29	13	3,717
Eugene, OR	44	3	7	123	5	12	430
Evansville, IN	37	58	29	87	33	21	388
Fairbanks, AK	64	50	16	147	42	59	445
Fargo, ND	46	52	38	96	47	23	902
Ft. Smith, AR	35	23	9	94	23	55	440
Ft. Wayne, IN	41	7	50	85	7	44	810
Ft. Worth, TX	32	43	31	97	19	15	653
Frankfort, KY	38	12	3	84	52	24	507
Fredericton, NB	45	56	43	66	40	0	67
Greensboro, NC	36	4	21	79	47	31	827
Greenville, SC	34	51	9	82	23	38	984
Gulfport, MS	30	22	3	89	5	34	21
Halifax, NS	44	52	0	63	42	58	477
Hamilton, ON	43	14	34	79	59	22	780
Harrisburg, PA	40	16	25	76	53	4	332
Hartford, CT	41	45	49	72	41	6	29
Helena, MT	46	35	34	112	2	10	4,047
Hilo, HI	19	43	47	155	5	24	59
Honolulu, HI	21	18	25	157	51	30	17
Houston, TX	29	45	48	95	21	48	37
Idaho Falls, ID	43	28	0	112	2	3	4,705
Indianapolis, IN	39	46	6	86	9	29	720
Iqaluit, NU	63	45	0	68	31	0	112
Jackson, MS	32	17	56	90	11	5	280
Jacksonville, FL	30	19	56	81	39	20	15
Jefferson City, MO	38	34	36	92	10	25	630
Jersey City, NJ	40	43	41	74	4	40	34
Juneau, AK	58	18	7	134	25	11	33
Kansas City, MO	39	5	59	94	34	43	898
Knoxville, TN	35	57	38	83	55	15	904
Lansing, MI	42	43	57	84	33	20	853
Laredo, TX	27	30	23	99	30	27	415
Las Vegas, NV	36	10	30	115	8	14	2,001
Lexington, KY	37	59	19	84	28	40	968
Lincoln, NE	40	48	0	96	40	0	1,200
Little Rock, AR	34	44	47	92	17	23	333
Los Angeles, CA	34	3	8	118	14	37	291
Louisville, KY	38	15	15	85	45	34	466
Madison, WI	43	4	23	89	24	4	873
Manchester, NH	42	59	44	71	27	17	258
Memphis, TN	35	8	58	90	2	56	260
Miami, FL	25	46	27	80	11	37	8
Milwaukee, WI	43	2	20	87	54	23	615
Minneapolis, MN	44	58	48	93	15	50	830
Mobile, AL	30	41	40	88	2	35	10
Montgomery, AL	32	22	0	86	18	0	238
Montpelier, VT	44	15	36	72	34	31	526
Montréal, QC	45	31	0	73	39	0	221
Nashville, TN	36	9	57	86	47	4	567
New Orleans, LA	29	57	17	90	4	30	1
New York, NY	40	42	51	74	0	22	35
Newark, NJ	40	44	8	74	10	21	32
Nome, AK	64	30	4	165	24	23	37
Oklahoma City, OK	35	28	3	97	30	59	1,198
Olympia, WA	47	2	16	122	54	3	93
Omaha, NE	41	15	31	95	56	16	1,059
Ottawa, ON	45	20	0	75	35	3	382
Overland Park, KS	38	58	56	94	40	15	1,084
Philadelphia, PA	39	57	8	75	9	50	45
Phoenix, AZ	33	26	54	112	4	27	1,085
Pierre, SD	44	22	6	100	21	3	1,479
Pittsburgh, PA	40	26	26	79	59	45	766
Portland, OR	45	31	24	122	40	34	33
Providence, RI	41	49	26	71	24	46	9
Provo, UT	40	14	2	111	39	31	4,551
Québec, QC	46	49	0	71	13	0	244
Raleigh, NC	35	46	20	78	38	19	315
Rapid City, SD	44	4	50	103	13	52	3,243
Regina, SK	50	27	17	104	36	24	1,894
Reno, NV	39	31	47	119	48	50	4,505
Richmond, VA	37	33	14	77	27	37	213
Rochester, NY	43	9	17	77	36	56	504
Sacramento, CA	38	34	54	121	29	40	27
St. John's, NL	47	28	56	52	47	49	461
St. Louis, MO	38	37	38	90	11	52	464
St. Paul, MN	44	56	34	93	5	36	789
Salem, OR	44	56	35	123	2	6	157
Salt Lake City, UT	40	45	39	111	53	28	4,265
San Antonio, TX	29	25	27	98	29	37	649
San Diego, CA	32	42	55	117	9	26	63
San Francisco, CA	37	46	30	122	25	10	54
San Jose, CA	37	20	22	121	53	42	82
San Juan, PR	18	27	59	66	6	21	26
Santa Fe, NM	35	41	13	105	56	16	6,995
Saskatoon, SK	52	8	23	106	41	10	1,653
Savannah, GA	32	5	1	81	5	59	20
Seattle, WA	47	36	22	122	19	55	177
Shreveport, LA	32	31	31	93	45	1	151
Sioux City, IA	42	30	0	96	24	1	1,201
Sioux Falls, SD	43	33	0	96	42	1	1,473
Spokane, WA	47	39	35	117	25	45	1,732
Springfield, IL	39	48	6	89	38	37	600
Tacoma, WA	47	15	10	122	26	39	250
Tampa, FL	27	56	51	82	27	30	15
Topeka, KS	39	2	54	95	40	41	948
Toronto, ON	43	44	30	79	22	24	251
Trenton, NJ	40	13	1	74	44	35	61
Tucson, AZ	32	13	18	110	55	35	2,490
Tulsa, OK	36	9	14	95	59	34	721
Vancouver, BC	49	15	40	123	6	50	14
Victoria, BC	48	25	42	123	21	53	63
Virginia Beach, VA	36	51	11	75	58	41	11
Washington, DC	38	53	42	77	2	11	24
Whitehorse, YT	60	41	46	135	4	51	2,305
Wichita, KS	37	41	32	97	20	15	1,302
Wilmington, DE	39	44	45	75	32	48	91
Wilmington, NC	34	13	33	77	56	41	36
Winnipeg, MB	49	53	4	97	8	47	783
Yakima, WA	46	36	7	120	30	21	1,068
Yellowknife, NT	62	27	13	114	22	12	675

RELIGION

Religious Affiliation in the U.S., 2015

Source: Todd M. Johnson and Gina A. Zurlo, eds. *World Christian Database* (Leiden/Boston: Brill, Aug. 2018)

Affliation	2015 pop.	Percent	Affliation	2015 pop.	Percent	Affliation	2015 pop.	Percent
Agnostics	48,167,301	15.1%	Christians	249,241,703	77.9%	Muslims	4,359,781	1.4%
Atheists	2,796,769	0.9	Daoists	12,797	—	New religionists	1,669,550	0.5
Baha'is	538,943	0.2	Ethnoreligionists	1,117,792	0.4	Shintoists	64,616	—
Buddhists	4,089,182	1.3	Hindus	1,445,951	0.5	Sikhs	358,321	0.1
Chinese folk religionists	111,975	—	Jains	87,981	—	Spiritists	233,139	0.1
			Jews	5,615,982	1.8	Zoroastrians	18,178	—

— = Less than 0.05%.

Religious Group Membership in the U.S.

Source: Todd M. Johnson and Gina A. Zurlo, eds. *World Christian Database* (Leiden/Boston: Brill, Aug. 2018)

Figures generally are based on collected reports made by each denomination as of 2015 and include only persons affiliated with a congregation of the denomination. Reporting practices vary from one denomination to another but generally include all members, not only full communicants. Denominations with fewer than 50,000 members not generally shown. Broad religious groups are indicated in **boldface**.

Group (congregations)	Members	Group (congregations)	Members
African Methodist Episcopal Church (9,296)	2,779,000	Faith Christian Fellowship Intl. (348)	239,000
African Methodist Episcopal Zion Church (3,414)	1,757,000	Free Methodist Church of North America (1,070)	76,800
Agnosticism (NA)	**48,167,301**	Full Gospel Baptist Church Fellowship (645)	188,000
American Baptist Assn. (1,500)	100,000	Full Gospel Fellowship of Churches and	
American Baptist Churches in the USA (5,708)	1,614,000	Ministers (1,517)	495,000
American Evangelistic Assn. (587)	297,000	General Assn. of General Baptists (838)	96,300
Antiochian Orthodox Christian, N. Amer. (259)	499,000	General Assn. of Regular Baptist Churches (1,284)	140,000
Apostolic Assemblies of Christ Intl. (346)	51,600	Grace Intl. (109)	130,000
Apostolic Assembly of the Faith in Christ Jesus (790)	94,700	Greater Emmanuel Intl. Fellowship of Churches and Ministries (49)	50,400
Armenian Apostolic Church of America (37)	358,000	Greek Orthodox Archdiocese of America (534)	1,488,000
Armenian Church of North America (109)	367,000	**Hinduism (NA)**	**1,445,951**
Assemblies of God Fellowship Intl. (910)	865,000	Independent Assemblies Fellowship (522)	103,000
Assemblies of God USA (12,740)	3,376,000	Independent Assemblies of God Intl. (305)	122,000
Associate Reformed Presbyterian Church (286)	52,300	Independent Churches of the Latter Rain Revival (831)	82,100
Assn. of Faith Churches and Ministries (1,234)	225,000	Independent Fundamental Churches of America (620)	57,300
Assn. of Intl. Gospel Assemblies (260)	270,000	Indian Pentecostal Church of America (383)	229,000
Assyrian Church of the East (23)	115,000	Interdenominational Ministries Intl. (190)	51,600
Atheism (NA)	**2,796,769**	Intl. Church of the Foursquare Gospel (2,067)	555,000
Baha'i Faith (NA)	**538,943**	Intl. Convention of Faith Ministries (428)	105,000
Baptist Bible Fellowship Intl. (4,500)	1,729,000	Intl. Council of Community Churches (127)	64,800
Baptist General Conference (1,315)	181,000	Intl. Evangelical Church (112)	55,500
Baptist Missionary Assn. of America (1,210)	226,000	Intl. Evangelism Crusades (71)	70,100
Bible Way Churches of Our Lord Jesus Christ World-Wide (1,512)	359,000	Intl. Fellowship of Faith Ministries (2,856)	282,000
Brethren in Christ Church (234)	50,700	Intl. Gospel Assemblies (715)	478,000
Buddhism (NA)	**4,089,182**	Intl. Ministers Forum (526)	180,000
Calvary Chapels Intl. (1,171)	523,000	Intl. Pentecostal Holiness Church (2,062)	356,000
Chinese Folk Religions[1] (NA)	**111,975**	**Islam[2] (NA)**	**4,359,781**
Christian and Missionary Alliance (2,044)	484,000	**Jainism (NA)**	**87,981**
Christian Brethren (Open) (1,253)	112,000	Jehovah's Witnesses (13,784)	2,921,000
Christian Church (Disciples of Christ) (3,638)	593,000	**Judaism[3] (NA)**	**5,615,982**
Christian Churches and Churches of Christ (4,821)	1,129,000	Korean American Presbyterian Church (670)	72,000
Christian Congregation (1,608)	129,000	Korean Full Gospel Churches of America (1,044)	328,000
Christian Methodist Episcopal Church (3,886)	987,000	Korean Presbyterian Church of America (1,869)	585,000
Christian Reformed Church in N. America (1,104)	263,000	Latin American Council of Christian Churches (269)	136,000
Christianity (all) (NA)	**249,241,703**	Lighthouse Gospel Fellowship (475)	56,300
Church of Christ, Scientist (2,172)	826,000	Living Faith Christian Centers (310)	62,500
Church of God (Anderson, IN) (2,310)	268,000	Lutheran Church-Missouri Synod (6,200)	2,200,000
Church of God (Cleveland, OH) (6,601)	1,432,000	Malankara Orthodox Syrian Church of the East (102)	50,600
Church of God (Huntsville, AL) (1,592)	82,100	Mennonite Church USA (885)	134,000
Church of God in Christ (24,010)	8,511,000	Ministers Fellowship Intl. (768)	70,600
Church of God of Prophecy (1,849)	95,100	Missionary Church (383)	56,400
Church of Jesus Christ (715)	160,000	Missionary Gospel Church Intl. (853)	50,600
Church of Jesus Christ of Latter-day Saints (14,752)	6,621,000	Natl. Assn. of Free Will Baptists (2,425)	230,000
Church of Our Lord Jesus Christ of Apostolic Faith (553)	671,000	Natl. Baptist Convention of America (12,265)	4,270,000
Church of the Brethren (1,041)	147,000	Natl. Baptist Convention, USA (40,000)	9,195,000
Church of the Nazarene (5,160)	778,000	Natl. Baptist Evangelical Life and Soul Saving Assembly (294)	87,100
Churches of Christ (Non-Instrumental) (12,196)	1,191,000	Natl. David Spiritual Temple of Christ (74)	68,300
Churches on the Rock Intl. (221)	248,000	Natl. Missionary Baptist Conv. of America (271)	417,000
Congregational Christian Churches (405)	62,800	Natl. Primitive Baptist Convention (1,565)	595,000
Conservative Baptist Assn. of America (1,377)	229,000	Native American Church of North America (381)	198,000
Coptic Orthodox Church (250)	500,000	Network of Kingdom Churches (1,331)	311,000
Covenant Ministries Intl. (39)	113,000	New Apostolic Church USA (325)	50,600
Cumberland Presbyterian Church (721)	71,400	**New Religion[1] (NA)**	**1,669,550**
Czechoslovak Hussite Church (41)	59,400	North American Baptist Conference (435)	93,300
Episcopal Church in the USA (4,821)	1,744,000	North American Old Roman Catholic Church (139)	65,300
Ethiopian Orthodox Church in the USA (84)	85,200	Old Order Amish Mennonite Church (977)	121,000
Ethnoreligious[1] (NA)	**1,117,992**	Orthodox Church in America (528)	2,968,000
Evangelical Covenant Church of America (924)	157,000	Palestinian/Jordanian Orthodox Christian Communities in the USA (7)	175,000
Evangelical Fellowship Intl. (306)	91,700	Pentecostal Assemblies of the Apostolic Faith (91)	70,100
Evangelical Free Church of America (1,422)	437,000	Pentecostal Assemblies of the World (1,602)	1,201,000
Evangelical Lutheran Church in America (10,447)	4,339,000	Pentecostal Church of God (1,087)	99,600
Evangelical Presbyterian Church (342)	149,000		
Evangelistic Messengers Assn. (618)	142,000		

Group (congregations)	Members
Pentecostal Churches of the Apostolic Faith (288) ..	75,800
Presbyterian Church (USA) (10,536)	2,422,000
Presbyterian Church in America (1,447).........	415,000
Primitive Baptists (2,997)	133,000
Progressive Natl. Baptist Convention (1,200)	2,163,000
Reformed Church in America (894)	236,000
Reorganized Church of Jesus Christ of Latter Day Saints (905)	171,000
Rhema Bible Churches (593)	180,000
Roman Catholic Church[4] (18,034)	**72,797,730**
Romanian Orthodox Episcopate of America (37) ...	110,000
Russian Orthodox Church Outside Russia (232) ...	94,900
Salvation Army (1,100).......................	400,000
Serbian Orthodox Church in N. and S. Amer. (193)..	68,000
Seventh-day Adventist Church (5,148)	1,341,000
Shintoism (NA)	**64,616**
Sikhism (NA)	**358,321**
Southern Baptist Convention (45,500)	20,000,000
Spanish Christian Churches (363)	89,900
Spiritism (NA)	**232,139**
Taoism (or Daoism) (NA)	**12,797**
Trinity Church Network (22)	142,000
Unitarian Universalist Assn. (1,057)	223,000
United Baptist Churches (400)	52,500

Group (congregations)	Members
United Church of Christ (4,900)	950,000
United Church of Jesus Christ (Apostolic) (130). ...	142,000
United Evangelical Churches (332)	88,100
United Free Will Baptist Church (692)...........	101,000
United House of Prayer for All People (173)	1,746,000
United Methodist Church (33,096)	7,094,000
United Pentecostal Church Intl. (5,173)	839,000
Unity School of Christianity (683)...............	119,000
Victory Fellowship of Ministries (171)............	63,600
Vineyard Churches (USA) (569)...............	210,000
Way of the Cross Church of Christ (74)	77,000
Wesleyan Church (1,835).....................	140,000
Willow Creek Assn. of Churches (2,236)	444,000
Wisconsin Evangelical Lutheran Synod (1,274)....	359,000
Word of Faith Fellowship/Ministries (31)..........	51,600
World Council of Independent Christian Churches (382)	61,900
World Harvest Ministerial Alliance (190)..........	67,800
World Ministry Fellowship (326)	55,500
World Salt (96)	56,300
Worldwide Missionary Evangelism (297)	51,600
Worldwide/Last Churches (211)	142,000
Zoroastrianism (NA).......................	**18,178**

NA = Not available. (1) See definition in World Adherents table on p. 698. (2) Other sources vary. In 2017, the Council on American-Islamic Relations estimated a total of 2,000 mosques and 6-7 mil Muslims in the U.S., and a Pew Research Center report in Jan. 2018 estimated the U.S. Muslim pop. at 3.45 mil. (3) Includes Jewish Reconstructionist Communities (about 90), Union of Orthodox Jewish Congregations of America (500), Other Orthodox congregations (1,200), Chabad (over 2,000), Union for Reform Judaism (850), and United Synagogue of Conservative Judaism (580). Among Jewish adherents in the U.S., about 35% classify themselves as Reform, 18% as Conservative, 10% as Orthodox, 2% as Reconstructionist, the rest as "just Jewish." Source: Ira M. Sheskin and Arnold Dashefsky, "United States Jewish Population, 2018," in *The American Jewish Year Book* (Dordrecht: Springer, 2018). (This source estimates the total American Jewish population at 6.93 mil.) (4) According to another estimate, by the U.S. Center for Research in the Apostolate, there were 74.3 mil self-identified Roman Catholics in the U.S. in 2017.

World Adherents of Religions by Continental Area, 2016

Source: *2017 Encyclopædia Britannica Book of the Year.* All adherents figures are midyear estimates, in thous.

Religion (no. of countries)	Africa	Asia	Europe	Latin America	Northern America	Oceania	World	% of world pop.
Baha'is (224)	2,477	3,680	142	978	610	123	8,010	0.1%
Buddhists (152)	284	512,967	1,883	819	4,776	763	521,492	7.0
Chinese folk religionists (120)	151	439,259	568	204	834	129	441,145	5.9
Christians (234)	591,405	384,404	575,674	591,547	276,225	28,733	2,447,988	32.9
Roman Catholics (234)	212,659	149,877	273,849	508,306	88,450	9,320	1,242,461	16.7
Protestants (231).....	222,513	97,186	92,868	66,015	61,019	12,998	552,599	7.4
Independents (231)...	126,564	154,454	15,530	56,743	73,172	2,128	428,591	5.8
Orthodox (138)	50,968	18,624	204,158	1,307	7,996	1,064	284,117	3.8
Confucianists (17)......	22	8,399	16	500	—	61	8,498	0.1
Ethnoreligionists (145) ..	103,070	157,416	1,212	3,849	1,272	407	267,226	3.6
Hindus (144)..........	3,279	1,011,584	1,173	789	1,959	637	1,019,421	13.7
Jains (20)	110	5,772	21	2	107	6	6,016	0.1
Jews (146)	129	6,607	1,436	438	6,041	127	14,778	0.2
Muslims (215)..........	506,577	1,191,467	45,949	1,733	5,597	722	1,752,045	23.6
Sunnis (212)	499,111	983,652	43,757	1,267	3,881	582	1,532,250	20.6
Shiites (148)	2,849	198,033	2,158	453	1,111	136	204,740	2.8
New religionists (121)...	219	60,975	651	1,988	2,485	133	66,451	0.9
Shintoists (9).........	—	2,742	—	8	65	—	2,816	—
Sikhs (64)	85	24,025	632	8	869	122	25,741	0.3
Spiritists (59).........	3	2	149	14,130	257	9	14,550	0.2
Taoists (7)...........	—	8,671	—	—	13	7	8,691	0.1
Zoroastrians (28)	1	164	6	—	22	4	196	—
All religious adherents (234)	**1,207,812**	**3,818,132**	**629,512**	**616,493**	**301,132**	**31,982**	**6,605,063**	**88.9**
Nonreligious (233)	8,318	618,092	109,337	24,536	59,397	7,919	827,599	11.1
Agnostics (233)......	7,642	504,553	94,753	21,405	55,599	7,337	691,289	9.3
Atheists (223)	676	113,539	14,584	3,131	3,798	582	136,310	1.8

— = Less than 500 adherents or 0.05%. **Note:** Figures may not add up to totals due to rounding. "Religious adherents," or those who indicate attachment to religion, may or may not consider themselves as belonging to a particular religious denomination. Figures shown for adherents to specific religious groups are estimates generally based on self-definition as reported in censuses, surveys, and other data; these people may not all be actually affiliated with a particular congregation as members. Some individuals report attachment to more than one religious group, and subdivisions shown in this table are not necessarily exhaustive. Continental areas are as per UN demographic terminology; "Asia" is defined to include the former Soviet Central Asian states, while "Europe" includes all of Russia, extending to the Pacific coast. Figures in parentheses indicate the number of countries where the religion or type of belief has a significant following. **Buddhists** include Mahayana (72%), Theravada or Hinayana (25%), and Tantrayana (incl. Lamaists, Tibetans) (3%). **Chinese folk religionists** are followers of traditional Chinese religion; it may involve worship of local deities, ancestor veneration, Confucian ethics, divination, and Buddhist or Taoist elements, among other beliefs and practices. **Christians** are usually baptized members of a church belonging to one of the major Christian traditions shown here. Those characterized as Independents belong to sects or groups that consider themselves independent of historical mainstream institutionalized Christianity; these include groups such as Unitarians, Mormons, and Jehovah's Witnesses. **Confucianists** are followers of Confucius, mostly living in China or elsewhere in East/Southeast Asia. **Ethnoreligionists** are followers of local, tribal, animistic, or shamanistic religions, generally belonging to a single ethnic group. **Hindus** include Vaishnavites (38%); Shaivites (36%); and Shaktas, neo-Hindi, and reformed Hindi (26%). **New religionists** include followers of Asian new religions, neoreligious movements, radical new crisis religions, and syncretistic mass religions.

Episcopal Church Liturgical Colors and Calendar, 2018-22

The most common liturgical colors in the Episcopal Church are as follows: **White**—Christmas Day through first Sunday after Epiphany; Maundy Thursday (as an alternative to crimson at the Eucharist); from the Vigil of Easter to the Day of Pentecost (Whitsunday); Trinity Sunday; Feasts of the Lord (except Holy Cross Day); the Confession of St. Peter; the Conversion of St. Paul; St. Joseph; St. Mary Magdalene; St. Mary the Virgin; St. Michael and All Angels; All Saints' Day; St. John the Evangelist; memorials of other saints who were not martyred; Independence Day and Thanksgiving Day; weddings and funerals. **Red**—the Day of Pentecost; Holy Cross Day; feasts of apostles and evangelists (except those previously mentioned); feasts and memorials of martyrs (including Holy Innocents' Day). **Violet**—Advent and Lent. **Crimson** or oxblood (dark red)—Holy Week. **Green**—the seasons after Epiphany and after Pentecost. **Black**—optional alternative for funerals and Good Friday.

The days of fasting are Ash Wednesday and Good Friday. Other days of special devotion (penitence) include the 40 days of Lent. Ember days are days of prayer for the church's ministry. They fall on the Wednesday, Friday, and Saturday after the first Sunday in Lent, the Day of Pentecost, Holy Cross Day, and Dec. 13. Rogation Days, the three days before Ascension Day, are days of prayer for God's blessing on the crops, on commerce and industry, and for conservation of the Earth's resources.

Holy days and other variables	2018	2019	2020	2021	2022
Golden Number	5	6	7	8	9
Sunday Letter	G	F	E/D	C	B
Sundays after Epiphany	6	8	7	6	8
Ash Wednesday	Feb. 14	Mar. 6	Feb. 26	Feb. 17	Mar. 2
First Sunday in Lent	Feb. 18	Mar. 10	Mar. 1	Feb. 21	Mar. 6
Passion/Palm Sunday	Mar. 25	Apr. 14	Apr. 5	Mar. 28	Apr. 10
Good Friday	Mar. 30	Apr. 19	Apr. 10	Apr. 2	Apr. 15
Easter Day	Apr. 1	Apr. 21	Apr. 12	Apr. 4	Apr. 17
Ascension Day	May 10	May 30	May 21	May 13	May 26
Day of Pentecost	May 20	June 9	May 31	May 23	June 5
Trinity Sunday	May 27	June 16	June 7	May 30	June 12
Numbered Proper of 2 Pentecost	#4	#7	#6	#5	#7
First Sunday of Advent	Dec. 2	Dec. 1	Nov. 29	Nov. 28	Nov. 27

Greek Orthodox Movable Ecclesiastical Dates, 2018-22

Feast days and fasting days are determined annually on the basis of the date of Holy Pascha (Easter). Western Easter also included for reference. This ecclesiastical cycle begins with the first day of the Triodion and ends with the Sunday of All Saints, a total of 18 weeks.

Holy days and observances	2018	2019	2020	2021	2022
Triodion begins	Jan. 28	Feb. 17	Feb. 9	Feb. 21	Feb. 13
1st Saturday of Souls	Feb. 10	Mar. 2	Feb. 22	Mar. 6	Feb. 26
Meat-Fare Sunday	Feb. 11	Mar. 3	Feb. 23	Mar. 7	Feb. 27
2nd Saturday of Souls	Feb. 17	Mar. 9	Feb. 29	Mar. 13	Mar. 5
Lent begins	Feb. 19	Mar. 11	Mar. 2	Mar. 15	Mar. 7
St. Theodore—3rd Saturday of Souls	Feb. 24	Mar. 16	Mar. 7	Mar. 20	Mar. 12
Sunday of Orthodoxy	Feb. 25	Mar. 17	Mar. 8	Mar. 21	Mar. 13
Saturday of Lazarus	Mar. 31	Apr. 20	Apr. 11	Apr. 24	Apr. 16
Palm Sunday	Apr. 1	Apr. 21	Apr. 12	Apr. 25	Apr. 17
Holy (Good) Friday	Apr. 6	Apr. 26	Apr. 17	Apr. 30	Apr. 22
Western Easter	Apr. 1	Apr. 21	Apr. 12	Apr. 4	Apr. 17
Orthodox Pascha (Easter)	Apr. 8	Apr. 28	Apr. 19	May 2	Apr. 24
Ascension	May 17	June 6	May 28	June 10	June 2
Saturday of Souls	May 26	June 15	June 6	June 19	June 11
Pentecost	May 27	June 16	June 7	June 20	June 12
All Saints	June 3	June 23	June 14	June 27	June 19
Fast of Holy Apostles (first day)	June 4	June 24	June 15	June 28	June 20
Fast of Holy Apostles lasts—	25 days	5 days	14 days	1 day	9 days

Jewish Holy Days, 5778-5782 (2017-2022)

The Jewish calendar consists of 12 lunar months, alternating between 29 and 30 days. It is lunisolar and adjusts for the solar cycle by adding an extra month (Adar II) in the 3rd, 6th, 8th, 11th, 14th, 17th, and 19th years of a 19-year cycle. The calendar starts on the day of Creation, reckoned in the 2nd-3rd cent. BCE as Tishrei 1, 3,761 years before the common era.

The religious calendar begins with the month Nisan, from which all other months are counted, and the civil calendar with Tishrei. The months are 1) Nisan, 2) Iyar, 3) Sivan, 4) Tammuz, 5) Av (also Abh), 6) Elul, 7) Tishrei, 8) Cheshvan (also Marcheshvan), 9) Kislev, 10) Tevet (also Tebeth), 11) Shevat (also Shebhat), 12) Adar, and 12a) Adar Sheni (II), added in leap years.

All holidays listed below begin at sunset of the previous day and end at nightfall on the last day shown.

Holiday	Date on Jewish cal.	5778 (2017-18)		5779 (2018-19)		5780 (2019-20)		5781 (2020-21)		5782 (2021-22)	
Rosh Hashanah (New Year)	Tishrei 1	Sept. 21	Thu.	Sept. 10	Mon.	Sept. 30	Mon.	Sept. 19	Sat.	Sept. 7	Tue.
	Tishrei 2	Sept. 22	Fri.	Sept. 11	Tue.	Oct. 1	Tue.	Sept. 20	Sun.	Sept. 8	Wed.
Yom Kippur (Day of Atonement)	Tishrei 10	Sept. 30	Sat.	Sept. 19	Wed.	Oct. 9	Wed	Sept. 28	Mon.	Sept. 16	Thu.
Sukkot	Tishrei 15	Oct. 5	Thu.	Sept. 24	Mon.	Oct. 14	Mon.	Oct. 3	Sat.	Sept. 21	Tue.
	Tishrei 21	Oct. 11	Wed.	Sept. 30	Sun.	Oct. 20	Sun.	Oct. 9	Fri.	Sept. 27	Mon.
Shemini Atzeret	Tishrei 22	Oct. 12	Thu.	Oct. 1	Mon.	Oct. 21	Mon.	Oct. 10	Sat.	Sept. 28	Tue.
Simchat Torah	Tishrei 23	Oct. 13	Fri.	Oct. 2	Tue.	Oct. 22	Tue.	Oct. 11	Sun.	Sept. 29	Wed.
Hanukkah	Kislev 25	Dec. 13	Wed.	Dec. 3	Mon.	Dec. 23	Mon.	Dec. 11	Fri.	Nov. 29	Mon.
	Tevet 2 or 3	Dec. 20	Wed.	Dec. 10	Mon.	Dec. 30	Mon.	Dec. 18	Fri.	Dec. 6	Mon.
Purim	Adar 14	Mar. 1	Thu.	Mar. 21	Thu.	Mar. 10	Tue.	Feb. 26	Fri.	Mar. 17	Thu.
Pesach (Passover)	Nisan 15	Mar. 31	Sat.	Apr. 20	Sat.	Apr. 9	Thu.	Mar. 28	Sun.	Apr. 16	Sat.
	Nisan 22	Apr. 7	Sat.	Apr. 27	Sat.	Apr. 16	Thu.	Apr. 4	Sun.	Apr. 23	Sat.
Shavuot (Pentecost)	Sivan 6	May 20	Sun.	June 9	Sun.	May 29	Fri.	May 17	Mon.	June 5	Sun.
	Sivan 7	May 21	Mon.	June 10	Mon.	May 30	Sat.	May 18	Tue.	June 6	Mon.
Fast of the 9th of Av	Av 9	July 22	Sun.*	Aug. 11	Sun.*	July 30	Thu.	July 18	Sun.	Aug. 7	Sun.

* = Date changed to avoid Sabbath.

Hindu Festivals, 2018-22

There are various traditional lunisolar Hindu calendars. Most have similar names for the 12 lunar months, with days beginning at dawn or sunrise, but they differ in various ways, including the numbering of years and the starting point of months. The Indian civil (Saka) calendar, adopted in 1957, is solar-based, and begins Mar. 22 (Mar. 21 in leap years). The year 1941 on the Saka calendar begins Mar. 21, 2019. There are many Hindu holidays and festivals; some are observed only in certain regions. Below are three of the most widely observed.

Festival	2018	2019	2020	2021	2022
Maha Shivaratri (Night of Shiva)[1]	Feb. 14	Mar. 5	Feb. 22	Mar. 12	Mar. 1
Holi (Festival of Color)	Mar. 2	Mar. 21	Mar. 10	Mar. 29	Mar. 18
Diwali (Festival of Lights)	Nov. 7	Oct. 27	Nov. 14	Nov. 4	Oct. 24

(1) Begins the night of the previous day.

Islamic Holy Days, 1439-43 AH (late 2017-22)

The Islamic calendar is a strict lunar calendar reckoned from the year of the Hijra (anno Hegirae, or AH)—Muhammad's flight from Mecca to Medina, in 622 CE. Each year consists of 12 lunar months of 29 or 30 days beginning and ending with each new moon's visible crescent. Common years have 354 days; leap years have 355 days. Some Muslim countries employ a conventionalized calendar with the leap day added to the last month, Dhu'l-Hijja, but for religious purposes the leap date is taken into account by tracking each new moon sighting.

Holy days begin at sunset of the day previous to the day cited. The actual dates may vary slightly from what is shown below, depending on the locality and the times of actual moon sightings as determined by different authorities.

Holy day (date)	1439 (2017-18)	1440 (2018-19)	1441 (2019-20)	1442 (2020-21)	1443 (2021-22)
New Year's Day (Muharram 1)	Sept. 21, 2017	Sept. 11, 2018	Aug. 31, 2019	Aug. 20, 2020	Aug. 10, 2021
Ashura (Muharram 10)	Sept. 30, 2017	Sept. 20, 2018	Sept. 9, 2019	Aug. 29, 2020	Aug. 18, 2021
Mawlid (Rabi' I 12)	Nov. 30, 2017	Nov. 20, 2018	Nov. 10, 2019	Oct. 29, 2020	Oct. 18, 2021
Ramadan begins (Ramadan 1)	May 16, 2018	May 6, 2019	Apr. 24, 2020	Apr. 13, 2021	Apr. 3, 2022
Eid al-Fitr (Shawwal 1)	June 15, 2018	June 4, 2019	May 24, 2020	May 13, 2021	May 3, 2022
Eid al-Adha (Dhu'l-Hijja 10)	Aug. 21, 2018	Aug. 11, 2019	July 31, 2020	July 20, 2021	July 10, 2022

Ash Wednesday and Easter Sunday (Western Churches), 2001-2100

Year	Ash Wed.	Easter Sunday	Year	Ash Wed.	Easter Sunday	Year	Ash Wed.	Easter Sunday	Year	Ash Wed.	Easter Sunday	Year	Ash Wed.	Easter Sunday
2001	Feb. 28	Apr. 15	2021	Feb. 17	Apr. 4	2041	Mar. 6	Apr. 21	2061	Feb. 23	Apr. 10	2081	Feb. 12	Mar. 30
2002	Feb. 13	Mar. 31	2022	Mar. 2	Apr. 17	2042	Feb. 19	Apr. 6	2062	Feb. 8	Mar. 26	2082	Mar. 4	Apr. 19
2003	Mar. 5	Apr. 20	2023	Feb. 22	Apr. 9	2043	Feb. 11	Mar. 29	2063	Feb. 28	Apr. 15	2083	Feb. 17	Apr. 4
2004	Feb. 25	Apr. 11	2024	Feb. 14	Mar. 31	2044	Mar. 2	Apr. 17	2064	Feb. 20	Apr. 6	2084	Feb. 9	Mar. 26
2005	Feb. 9	Mar. 27	2025	Mar. 5	Apr. 20	2045	Feb. 22	Apr. 9	2065	Feb. 11	Mar. 29	2085	Feb. 28	Apr. 15
2006	Mar. 1	Apr. 16	2026	Feb. 18	Apr. 5	2046	Feb. 7	Mar. 25	2066	Feb. 24	Apr. 11	2086	Feb. 13	Mar. 31
2007	Feb. 21	Apr. 8	2027	Feb. 10	Mar. 28	2047	Feb. 27	Apr. 14	2067	Feb. 16	Apr. 3	2087	Mar. 5	Apr. 20
2008	Feb. 6	Mar. 23	2028	Mar. 1	Apr. 16	2048	Feb. 19	Apr. 5	2068	Mar. 7	Apr. 22	2088	Feb. 25	Apr. 11
2009	Feb. 25	Apr. 12	2029	Feb. 14	Apr. 1	2049	Mar. 3	Apr. 18	2069	Feb. 27	Apr. 14	2089	Feb. 16	Apr. 3
2010	Feb. 17	Apr. 4	2030	Mar. 6	Apr. 21	2050	Feb. 23	Apr. 10	2070	Feb. 12	Mar. 30	2090	Mar. 1	Apr. 16
2011	Mar. 9	Apr. 24	2031	Feb. 26	Apr. 13	2051	Feb. 15	Apr. 2	2071	Mar. 4	Apr. 19	2091	Feb. 21	Apr. 8
2012	Feb. 22	Apr. 8	2032	Feb. 11	Mar. 28	2052	Mar. 6	Apr. 21	2072	Feb. 24	Apr. 10	2092	Feb. 13	Mar. 30
2013	Feb. 13	Mar. 31	2033	Mar. 2	Apr. 17	2053	Feb. 19	Apr. 6	2073	Feb. 8	Mar. 26	2093	Feb. 25	Apr. 12
2014	Mar. 5	Apr. 20	2034	Feb. 22	Apr. 9	2054	Feb. 11	Mar. 29	2074	Feb. 28	Apr. 15	2094	Feb. 17	Apr. 4
2015	Feb. 18	Apr. 5	2035	Feb. 7	Mar. 25	2055	Mar. 3	Apr. 18	2075	Feb. 20	Apr. 7	2095	Mar. 9	Apr. 24
2016	Feb. 10	Mar. 27	2036	Feb. 27	Apr. 13	2056	Feb. 16	Apr. 2	2076	Mar. 4	Apr. 19	2096	Feb. 29	Apr. 15
2017	Mar. 1	Apr. 16	2037	Feb. 18	Apr. 5	2057	Mar. 7	Apr. 22	2077	Feb. 24	Apr. 11	2097	Feb. 13	Mar. 31
2018	Feb. 14	Apr. 1	2038	Mar. 10	Apr. 25	2058	Feb. 27	Apr. 14	2078	Feb. 16	Apr. 3	2098	Mar. 5	Apr. 20
2019	Mar. 6	Apr. 21	2039	Feb. 23	Apr. 10	2059	Feb. 12	Mar. 30	2079	Mar. 8	Apr. 23	2099	Feb. 25	Apr. 12
2020	Feb. 26	Apr. 12	2040	Feb. 15	Apr. 1	2060	Mar. 3	Apr. 18	2080	Feb. 21	Apr. 7	2100	Feb. 10	Mar. 28

Roman Catholic Church Hierarchy

The Roman Catholic Church is headed by the pope, or bishop of Rome. He is assisted and advised by members of the College of Cardinals. The church is governed through a central administrative body, the Roman Curia. Dioceses around the world are headed by bishops appointed by the pope; collectively they also play a part in leadership of the church as a whole.

The Papacy

Roman Catholics consider Peter the Apostle to have been the first bishop of Rome and first in a line of popes extending to the present. He is said to have arrived in Rome c. 42 CE and to have been martyred there c. 67; he was later canonized as a saint. Popes through history have had both religious and secular roles. The pope today is the head of state of Vatican City as well as leader of the church.

German-born Pope **Benedict XVI**, formerly Cardinal Joseph Ratzinger, who was elected in Apr. 2005, resigned effective Feb. 28, 2013, citing his age (85) and declining health. Assuming the title of supreme pontiff emeritus, he took up residence in a restored convent near the Vatican.

At a papal conclave in Mar. 2013, 115 cardinals from 48 countries chose Argentinean Cardinal Jorge Mario Bergoglio as pope. He took the name **Francis**, after St. Francis of Assisi (1182-1226), known for his life of poverty and devotion to the poor. Pope Francis was the first member of the Society of Jesus (Jesuits), a Roman Catholic order, to become pope, and the first born outside Europe since Syrian-born Gregory III, who died in 741.

Chronological List of Popes

Source: *Annuario Pontificio*

Table lists year of accession of each pope. * = antipope, an illegitimate claimant to the papal throne.

Year	Pope	Year	Pope	Year	Pope	Year	Pope	Year	Pope
NA	St. Peter	530	Boniface II	884	St. Adrian III	1102	Albert*	1431	Eugene IV
67	St. Linus	530	Dioscorus*	885	Stephen V (VI)	1105	Sylvester IV*	1439	Felix V*
76	St. Anacletus,	533	John II	891	Formosus	1118	Gelasius II	1447	Nicholas V
	or Cletus	535	St. Agapitus I	896	Boniface VI	1118	Gregory VIII*	1455	Callistus III
88	St. Clement I	536	St. Silverius, Martyr	896	Stephen VI (VII)	1119	Callistus II	1458	Pius II
97	St. Evaristus	537	Vigilius	897	Romanus	1124	Honorius II	1464	Paul II
105	St. Alexander I	556	Pelagius I	897	Theodore II	1124	Celestine II*	1471	Sixtus IV
115	St. Sixtus I	561	John III	898	John IX	1130	Innocent II	1484	Innocent VIII
125	St. Telesphorus	575	Benedict I	900	Benedict IV	1130	Anacletus II*	1492	Alexander VI
136	St. Hyginus	579	Pelagius II	903	Leo V	1138	Victor IV*	1503	Pius III
140	St. Pius I	590	St. Gregory I	903	Christopher*	1143	Celestine II	1503	Julius II
155	St. Anicetus	604	Sabinian	904	Sergius III	1144	Lucius II	1513	Leo X
166	St. Soter	607	Boniface III	911	Anastasius III	1145	Bl. Eugene III	1522	Adrian VI
175	St. Eleutherius	608	St. Boniface IV	913	Landus	1153	Anastasius IV	1523	Clement VII
189	St. Victor I	615	St. Deusdedit,	914	John X	1154	Adrian IV	1534	Paul III
199	St. Zephyrinus		or Adeodatus	928	Leo VI	1159	Alexander III	1550	Julius III
217	St. Callistus I	619	Boniface V	928	Stephen VII (VIII)	1159	Victor IV*	1555	Marcellus II
217	St. Hippolytus*	625	Honorius I	931	John XI	1164	Paschal III*	1555	Paul IV
222	St. Urban I	640	Severinus	936	Leo VII	1168	Callistus III*	1559	Pius IV
230	St. Pontian	640	John IV	939	Stephen VIII (IX)	1179	Innocent III*	1566	St. Pius V
235	St. Anterus	642	Theodore I	942	Marinus II	1181	Lucius III	1572	Gregory XIII
236	St. Fabian	649	St. Martin I, Martyr	946	Agapitus II	1185	Urban III	1585	Sixtus V
251	St. Cornelius	654	St. Eugene I	955	John XII	1187	Clement III	1590	Urban VII
251	Novatian*	657	St. Vitalian	963	Leo VIII	1187	Gregory VIII	1590	Gregory XIV
253	St. Lucius I	672	Adeodatus II	964	Benedict V	1191	Celestine III	1591	Innocent IX
254	St. Stephen I	676	Donus	965	John XIII	1198	Innocent III	1592	Clement VIII
257	St. Sixtus II	678	St. Agatho	973	Benedict VI	1216	Honorius III	1605	Leo XI
259	St. Dionysius	682	St. Leo II	974	Boniface VII*	1227	Gregory IX	1605	Paul V
269	St. Felix I	684	St. Benedict II	974	Benedict VII	1241	Celestine IV	1621	Gregory XV
275	St. Eutychian	685	John V	983	John XIV	1243	Innocent IV	1623	Urban VIII
283	St. Caius	686	Conon	984	Boniface VII*	1254	Alexander IV	1644	Innocent X
296	St. Marcellinus	687	Theodore*	985	John XV	1261	Urban IV	1655	Alexander VII
308	St. Marcellus I	687	Paschal*	996	Gregory V	1265	Clement IV	1667	Clement IX
309	St. Eusebius	687	St. Sergius I	997	John XVI*	1271	Bl. Gregory X	1670	Clement X
311	St. Melchiades	701	John VI	999	Sylvester II	1276	Bl. Innocent V	1676	Bl. Innocent XI
314	St. Sylvester I	705	John VII	1003	John XVII	1276	Adrian V	1689	Alexander VIII
336	St. Marcus	708	Sisinnius	1004	John XVIII	1276	John XXI	1691	Innocent XII
337	St. Julius I	708	Constantine	1009	Sergius IV	1277	Nicholas III	1700	Clement XI
352	Liberius	715	St. Gregory II	1012	Benedict VIII	1281	Martin IV	1721	Innocent XIII
355	Felix II*	731	St. Gregory III	1012	Gregory*	1285	Honorius IV	1724	Benedict XIII
366	St. Damasus I	741	St. Zachary	1024	John XIX	1288	Nicholas IV	1730	Clement XII
366	Ursinus*	752	Stephen II (III)[1]	1032	Benedict IX	1294	St. Celestine V	1740	Benedict XIV
384	St. Siricius	757	St. Paul I	1045	Sylvester III	1294	Boniface VIII	1758	Clement XIII
399	St. Anastasius I	767	Constantine*	1045	Benedict IX	1303	Bl. Benedict XI	1769	Clement XIV
401	St. Innocent I	768	Philip*	1045	Gregory VI	1305	Clement V	1775	Pius VI
417	St. Zosimus	768	Stephen III (IV)	1046	Clement II	1316	John XXII	1800	Pius VII
418	St. Boniface I	772	Adrian I	1047	Benedict IX	1328	Nicholas V*	1823	Leo XII
418	Eulalius*	795	St. Leo III	1048	Damasus II	1334	Benedict XII	1829	Pius VIII
422	St. Celestine I	816	Stephen IV (V)	1049	St. Leo IX	1342	Clement VI	1831	Gregory XVI
432	St. Sixtus III	817	St. Paschal I	1055	Victor II	1352	Innocent VI	1846	Pius IX
440	St. Leo I	824	Eugene II	1057	Stephen IX (X)	1362	Bl. Urban V	1878	Leo XIII
461	St. Hilary	827	Valentine	1058	Benedict X*	1370	Gregory XI	1903	St. Pius X
468	St. Simplicius	827	Gregory IV	1059	Nicholas II	1378	Urban VI	1914	Benedict XV
483	St. Felix III (II)	844	John*	1061	Alexander II	1378	Clement VII*	1922	Pius XI
492	St. Gelasius I	844	Sergius II	1061	Honorius II*	1389	Boniface IX	1939	Pius XII
496	Anastasius II	847	St. Leo IV	1073	St. Gregory VII	1394	Benedict XIII*	1958	St. John XXIII
498	St. Symmachus	855	Benedict III	1080	Clement III*	1404	Innocent VII	1963	Paul VI
498	Lawrence* (also in	855	Anastasius*	1086	Bl. Victor III	1406	Gregory XII	1978	John Paul I
	501-505)	858	St. Nicholas I	1088	Bl. Urban II	1409	Alexander V*	1978	St. John Paul II
514	St. Hormisdas	867	Adrian II	1099	Paschal II	1410	John XXIII*	2005	Benedict XVI
523	St. John I, Martyr	872	John VIII	1100	Theodoric*	1417	Martin V	2013	Francis
526	St. Felix IV (III)	882	Marinus I						

NA = Not available. Bl. = Blessed. (1) After St. Zachary, a Roman priest named Stephen was elected who died before assuming the papacy. Another Stephen was then elected to succeed Zachary as Stephen II. He is sometimes listed as Stephen III.

Pope Francis

Pope Francis was born Jorge Mario Bergoglio in Buenos Aires, Argentina, Dec. 17, 1936; his parents were Italian immigrants. He joined the Jesuits in 1958 and was ordained a priest in 1969. Bergoglio served as a parish priest, theology professor, and college administrator. Ordained a bishop in 1992, he was named archbishop of Buenos Aires in 1998 and made a cardinal in 2001.

Soon after his election in 2013, Francis approved measures for reform of the scandal-ridden Vatican Bank and established a commission on clerical sex abuse. In 2015, Francis released an encyclical focusing on consumerism and the environment, and the next year addressed family life, divorce, and inclusion. A 2018 publication offered guidance on holy behavior, including the need to care for poor, sick, and migrant populations. Francis condemned the "atrocities" of clerical sex abuse and the church's response "with shame and repentance," after a Pennsylvania grand jury report showed the church had concealed decades of child sex abuse by 300 priests.

College of Cardinals

Members of the Sacred College of Cardinals are chosen by the pope to be his chief assistants and advisers in the administration of the church. Among their duties is the election of the pope.

In its present form, the College of Cardinals dates from the 12th century. The first cardinals, from about the 6th century, were deacons and priests of the leading churches of Rome and were bishops of neighboring dioceses. The title of cardinal was limited to members of the college in 1567. The number of cardinals was set at 70 in 1586. Pope John XXIII began to increase the number in 1959; however, the number eligible to participate in papal elections was limited to 120. Previous limitations were set aside by Pope John Paul II when he created new cardinals. In 1918, the Code of Canon Law specified that all cardinals must be priests. Pope John XXIII in 1962 ruled that cardinals must ordinarily be bishops. In 1971, Pope Paul VI decreed that at age 80, cardinals must retire from curial departments and offices and cannot be summoned to participate in papal elections.

As of Sept. 2018, there were 224 cardinals from 88 countries, of whom 124 from 65 countries remained eligible to vote.

North American Cardinals

Name	Office	Born	Named cardinal
Carlos Aguiar Retes	Archbishop of Mexico City	1950	2016
Raymond L. Burke	Archbishop emeritus of St. Louis	1948	2010
Thomas C. Collins[1]	Archbishop of Toronto, Canada	1947	2012
Blase J. Cupich	Archbishop of Chicago	1949	2016
Daniel N. DiNardo[2]	Pres., U.S. Conference of Catholic Bishops; archbishop of Galveston-Houston	1949	2007
Timothy M. Dolan	Archbishop of New York	1950	2012
Kevin J. Farrell	Prefect, Dicastery for Laity, Family, and Life; bishop emer. of Dallas	1947	2016
James M. Harvey	Archpriest of St. Paul Outside-the-Walls	1949	2012
Gérald Cyprien Lacroix	Archbishop of Québec, Canada	1957	2014
William Levada[3]	Archbishop emeritus of San Francisco	1936	2006
Javier Lozano Barragán[3]	Bishop emeritus of Zacatecas, Mexico	1933	2003
Roger Mahony[3]	Archbishop emeritus of Los Angeles	1936	1991
Adam Joseph Maida[3]	Archbishop emeritus of Detroit	1930	1994
Sergio Obeso Rivera[3]	Archbishop emeritus of Jalapa, Mexico	1931	2018
Edwin F. O'Brien	Grand Master of Equestrian Order of the Holy Sepulcher of Jerusalem; archbishop emeritus of Baltimore	1939	2012
Sean O'Malley[4]	Archbishop of Boston	1944	2006
Marc Ouellet	Prefect, Congregation for Bishops; pres., Pontifical Commission for Latin America; archbishop emeritus of Québec, Canada	1944	2003
Justin F. Rigali[3]	Archbishop emeritus of Philadelphia	1935	2003
Norberto Rivera Carrera[2]	Archbishop of Mexico City, Mexico	1942	1998
José Francisco Robles Ortega	Archbishop of Guadalajara, Mexico	1949	2007
Juan Sandoval Íñiguez[3]	Archbishop emeritus of Guadalajara, Mexico	1933	1994
James F. Stafford[3]	Archbishop emeritus of Denver	1932	1998
Alberto Suárez Inda	Archbishop emeritus of Morelia, Mexico	1939	2015
Joseph W. Tobin	Archbishop of Newark	1952	2016
Donald W. Wuerl	Archbishop of Washington, DC	1940	2010

Note: Theodore McCarrick, archbishop emeritus of Washington, DC, and named cardinal in 2001, resigned in July 2018 after allegations of sexual abuse. (1) Member, Commission of Cardinals Overseeing the Institute for Works of Religion (Vatican Bank). (2) Member, Council for the Economy. (3) Ineligible to vote in a papal conclave because of age. (4) Member, Council of Cardinals and Pres., Pontifical Commission for the Protection of Minors.

The Ten Commandments

In the Hebrew Bible (Old Testament) the Ten Commandments (also called the Decalogue, from the Greek meaning "ten words") were revealed by God to Moses on Mt. Sinai. They form the covenant between God and the Israelites and the moral code that is the basis for the Jewish and Christian religions. The Ten Commandments appear in two places in the Old Testament—Exodus 20:1-17 and Deuteronomy 5:6-21.

Most Protestant, Anglican, and Orthodox Christians follow Jewish tradition, as shown here, which considers the introduction ("I am the Lord ...") the first commandment and makes the prohibition against idolatry the second. Roman Catholic and Lutheran traditions combine I and II and split the last commandment into two that separately prohibit coveting of a neighbor's wife and of a neighbor's goods. This arrangement alters the numbering of the other commandments by one.

Following is the text as it appears in Exodus 20:1-17 in the King James version of the Bible [Roman numerals added]:

And God spake all these words, saying,

I. I *am* the LORD thy God, which have brought thee out of the land of Egypt, out of the house of bondage. Thou shalt have no other gods before me.

II. Thou shalt not make unto thee any graven image, or any likeness of *any thing* that *is* in heaven above, or that *is* in the earth beneath, or that *is* in the water under the earth. Thou shalt not bow down thyself to them, nor serve them: for I the LORD thy God *am* a jealous God, visiting the iniquity of the fathers upon the children unto the third and fourth *generation* of them that hate me; and shewing mercy unto thousands of them that love me, and keep my commandments.

III. Thou shalt not take the name of the LORD thy God in vain: for the LORD will not hold him guiltless that taketh his name in vain.

IV. Remember the sabbath day, to keep it holy. Six days shalt thou labour, and do all thy work: but the seventh day *is* the sabbath of the LORD thy God: *in it* thou shalt not do any work, thou, nor thy son, nor thy daughter, thy manservant, nor thy maidservant, nor thy cattle, nor thy stranger that *is* within thy gates: for *in* six days the LORD made heaven and earth, the sea, and all that in them *is*, and rested the seventh day: wherefore the LORD blessed the sabbath day, and hallowed it.

V. Honour thy father and thy mother: that thy days may be long upon the land which the LORD thy God giveth thee.

VI. Thou shalt not kill.

VII. Thou shalt not commit adultery.

VIII. Thou shalt not steal.

IX. Thou shalt not bear false witness against thy neighbour.

X. Thou shalt not covet thy neighbour's house, thou shalt not covet thy neighbour's wife, nor his manservant, nor his maidservant, nor his ox, nor his ass, nor any thing that *is* thy neighbour's.

Books of the Bible

Old Testament—Standard Protestant List

Genesis	I Kings	Ecclesiastes	Obadiah
Exodus	II Kings	Song of Solomon	Jonah
Leviticus	I Chronicles	Isaiah	Micah
Numbers	II Chronicles	Jeremiah	Nahum
Deuteronomy	Ezra	Lamentations	Habakkuk
Joshua	Nehemiah	Ezekiel	Zephaniah
Judges	Esther	Daniel	Haggai
Ruth	Job	Hosea	Zechariah
I Samuel	Psalms	Joel	Malachi
II Samuel	Proverbs	Amos	

New Testament List

Matthew	Ephesians	Hebrews
Mark	Philippians	James
Luke	Colossians	I Peter
John	I Thessalonians	II Peter
Acts	II Thessalonians	I John
Romans	I Timothy	II John
I Corinthians	II Timothy	III John
II Corinthians	Titus	Jude
Galatians	Philemon	Revelation

The standard Protestant Old Testament consists of the same 39 books as in the Bible of Judaism, but the latter is organized differently. The Old Testament used by Roman Catholics has 7 additional deuterocanonical books, plus some additional parts of books. The 7 are **Tobit**, **Judith**, **Wisdom**, **Sirach (Ecclesiasticus)**, **Baruch**, **I Maccabees**, and **II Maccabees**. Both Catholic and Protestant versions of the New Testament have 27 books with the same names.

Figures in the Hebrew Bible (Old Testament)

Aaron: First of Hebrew high priests; brother of Moses and Miriam.

Abel: Second son of Adam and Eve; slain by Cain.

Abraham: Founder of monotheism; patriarch; also called Abram.

Adam: First human according to Genesis.

Amos: Herdsman; prophesized against social injustice and oppression of the poor.

Bathsheba: Seduced by King David; mother of King Solomon.

Cain: First son of Adam and Eve; killed his brother Abel.

Cyrus: Persian ruler; sent Jews home from exile.

Daniel: Cast into lion's den for violating decree of King Darius; saved.

David: Israel's greatest king; shepherd, warrior, musician, psalmist.

Deborah: Prophet and judge; ruled over Israel.

Elijah: Great prophet; was victorious over the priests of the Phoenician god Baal.

Elisha: Prophet; successor to Elijah.

Esther: Jewish wife of the king of Persia; saved Jews from annihilation.

Eve: First woman according to Genesis.

Ezekiel: Visionary; prophesized hope to exiled Jews in Babylon.

Ezra: Great Jewish leader; rededicated worship and Torah law after exile.

Goliath: Giant Philistine warrior; slain by David.

Hannah: Childless; promised child to God; mother to the prophet Samuel.

Hosea: Enacted prophecy; asked God's forgiveness for Israel's unfaithfulness.

Isaac: Son of Abraham and Sarah; saved from sacrificial altar.

Isaiah: Highly educated prophet; avoided war with Assyria; Israel destroyed; Jerusalem survived.

Jacob: Son of Isaac; father of the Twelve Tribes; renamed "Israel" by angel.

Jeremiah: Confronted leaders and urged surrender to Babylon.

Jezebel: Phoenician queen of King Ahab; had Israelite prophets killed.

Job: "Blameless" man; allowed by God to lose family, health, and possessions in a test of his faith.

Jonah: Swallowed by a great fish; prophesied destruction of the city of Nineveh, averted when the people repented.

Jonathan: Son of King Saul; friend of David.

Joseph: Favorite of Jacob; interpreted Pharaoh's dreams; brought Hebrews to Egypt.

Joshua: Successor of Moses; led Hebrews into Canaan.

Josiah: Reformist king; repaired Solomon's Temple; restored worship; reintroduced Passover.

Leah: Matriarch; older sister of Rachel; Jacob's wife.

Micah: Prophet; predicted the end of war and beginning of peace.

Miriam: Prophet and great leader of the Hebrews; sister to Moses and Aaron.

Moses: Most important Hebrew prophet; leader of the Israelites; received the Torah.

Nathan: Prophet; confronted King David over his seduction of Bathsheba.

Nebuchadnezzar: Babylonian king; destroyed Jerusalem.

Nehemiah: Led Jews back to Jerusalem from Babylonian exile.

Noah: Man of great faith who, according to Genesis, saved his family and two of every living thing on Earth from a great flood.

Rachel: Matriarch; younger sister of Leah; Jacob's wife; Joseph's mother.

Rebecca: Matriarch; wife of Isaac; mother of Jacob.

Ruth: Moabite convert; ancestor of David.

Samson: Judge and military leader of Israel; possessed super-human strength.

Samuel: Prophet; anointed Saul king of Israel and later anointed David to succeed him.

Sarah: First matriarch of Israel; wife of Abraham; mother of Isaac.

Saul: First king of Israel; father of Jonathan.

Solomon: King of Israel at its zenith; known for great wisdom.

Zechariah: Prophet; encouraged rebuilding of Solomon's Temple destroyed by Babylonians.

Figures in the New Testament

Andrew: One of the Twelve Apostles; brother of Peter and former fisherman; one of the earlier disciples.

Barabbas: Imprisoned with Jesus; set free by Pilate on Passover.

Barnabas: Disciple of Jesus; closely connected with Paul.

Bartholomew: A lesser-known member of the Twelve Apostles; cheerful and prayed often.

Cornelius: Roman convert; defended by Peter, allowing Gentiles to become Christians.

Elizabeth: Mother of John the Baptist; relation of the Virgin Mary.

Gabriel: Archangel; appeared to the Virgin Mary to announce that she was to give birth to the Messiah.

Herod: May refer to Herod the Great, who ordered the death of children after Jesus's birth, or to his son, Herod, who had John the Baptist beheaded.

James: May refer to either of two apostles: James, son of Zebedee, brother of John the Apostle, or the lesser-known James, son of Alphaeus.

Jesus: Central figure of the Gospels; believed to be the Messiah and son of God; crucified by the Romans.

John (Apostle): Beloved disciple of Jesus; one of the Twelve Apostles; possible author of fourth Gospel; brother of James.

John (Baptist): Known as John the Baptist; important prophet and forerunner to Jesus; relation of the Virgin Mary.

Joseph: Husband of the Virgin Mary; descendant of King David.

Judas Iscariot: Betrayer of Jesus; prominent member of the Apostles; committed suicide.

Judas Thaddeus: One of the Twelve Apostles; also called Jude to distinguish him from Judas Iscariot.

Lazarus: Brother of the disciples Martha and Mary of Bethany; raised from the dead by Jesus at their request; possibly the same Lazarus who appears in Jesus's parable of the rich man.

Luke: Traditional author of the Gospel of Luke; possibly a follower of Paul.

Mark: Traditional author of the Gospel of Mark; possibly a disciple of Peter.

Mary, the mother of Jesus: Traditionally believed to be a virgin who conceived without sin; wife of Joseph.

Mary Magdalene: Important female disciple of Jesus; witness to his death and resurrection.

Matthew: One of the Twelve Apostles; possible author of the Gospel of Matthew; former tax collector.

Matthias: Often included on lists of the Twelve Apostles as the apostle who replaced Judas Iscariot after his betrayal.

Paul (Saul): Writer of nearly a quarter of the New Testament; a former persecutor of Christians, converted after a vision; played a significant role in spreading Christianity.

Peter: Considered the foremost of the Twelve Apostles; traditionally the first pope and "rock" of the Christian church; author of epistles; also called Simon and Simon Peter.

Philip: One of the Twelve; considered pragmatic and sensible.

Pilate, Pontius: A Roman prefect; played large role in the trial and crucifixion of Jesus.

Simon: One of the Twelve Apostles; known as "the Zealot" to distinguish him from Simon Peter.

Stephen: Fervently preached that Jesus was the Messiah; stoned to death by angry mob, including Saul (Paul); important figure in Saul's conversion.

Thomas: One of the Twelve Apostles; known as "Doubting Thomas" because he did not believe Jesus was risen until he could touch him.

Timothy: A disciple closely connected with Paul; recipient of epistles.

Zacharias: Father of John the Baptist; husband of Elizabeth; struck dumb when he doubted his barren wife could become pregnant.

Major Christian Denominations:
Brackets indicate some features that tend to

Denom-ination	Origins	Organization	Authority	Special rites
Baptists	In radical Reformation, objections to infant baptism, demands for church and state separation; John Smyth, English Separatist, in 1609; Roger Williams, 1638, Providence, RI.	Congregational; each local church is autonomous.	Scripture; some Baptists, particularly in the South, interpret the Bible literally.	[Baptism, usually early teen years and after, by total immersion]; Lord's Supper.
Church of Christ (Disciples)	Among evangelical Presbyterians in KY (1804) and PA (1809), in distress over Protestant factional-ism and decline of fervor; organized in 1832.	Congregational.	["Where the Scriptures speak, we speak; where the Scriptures are silent, we are silent."]	Adult baptism; Lord's Supper (weekly).
Episco-palians	Henry VIII separated English Catholic Church from Rome, 1534, for political reasons; Protestant Episcopal Church in U.S. founded in 1789.	[Diocesan bishops, in apos-tolic succession, are elected by parish representatives; the national Church is headed by General Conven-tion and Presiding Bishop; part of the Anglican Com-munion.]	Scripture as interpreted by tradition, especially 39 Articles (1563); tri-annual convention of bishops, priests, and lay people.	Infant baptism, Eucharist, and other sacraments; sacrament taken to be symbolic, but as having real spiritual effect.
Jehovah's Witnesses	Founded in 1870 in PA by Charles Taze Russell; incorporated as Watch Tower Bible and Tract Society of PA, 1884; name Jehovah's Witnesses adopted in 1931.	A governing body located in NY coordinates worldwide activities; each congregation cared for by a body of elders; each Witness considered a minister.	The Bible.	Baptism by immersion; annual Lord's Meal ceremony.
Latter-day Saints (Mormons)	In a vision of the Father and the Son reported by Joseph Smith (1820s) in NY; Smith also reported receiving new scripture on golden tablets: the Book of Mormon.	Theocratic; 1st Presidency (church president, two counselors), 12 Apostles preside over international church; local congregations headed by lay priesthood leaders.	Revelation to living prophet (church president). The Bible, Book of Mormon, and other revelations to Smith and his successors.	Baptism at age 8; laying on of hands (which confers the gift of the Holy Ghost); Lord's Supper; temple rites: baptism for the dead, marriage for eternity, others.
Lutherans	Begun by Martin Luther in Wittenberg, Germany, in 1517; objection to Catholic doctrine of salvation and sale of indulgences; break complete, 1519.	Varies from congregational to episcopal; in U.S., a combination of regional synods and congregational polities is most common.	Scripture alone; the *Book of Concord* (1580), which includes the three Ecumenical Creeds, is subscribed to as a correct exposition of Scripture.	Infant baptism; Lord's Supper; Christ's true body and blood present "in, with, and under the bread and wine."
Methodists	Rev. John Wesley began movement in 1738, within Church of England; first U.S. denomination in Baltimore (1784).	Conference and superintendent system; [in United Methodist Church, general superintendents are bishops—not a priestly order, only an office—who are elected for life].	Scripture as interpreted by tradition, reason, and experience.	Baptism of infants or adults; Lord's Supper commanded; other rites: marriage, ordination, solemnization of personal commitments.
Orthodox	Developed in original Christian proselytizing; broke with Rome in 1054 after centuries of doctrinal disputes and diverging traditions.	Synods of bishops in autonomous, usually national, churches elect a patriarch, archbishop, or metropolitan; these men, as a group, are the heads of the church.	Scripture, tradition, and the first seven church councils up to Nicaea II in 787; bishops in council have authority in doctrine and policy.	Seven sacraments: infant baptism and anointing, Eucharist, ordination, penance, marriage, and anointing of the sick.
Pentecostal	In Topeka, KS (1901) and Los Angeles (1906), in reaction to perceived loss of evangelical fervor among Methodists and others.	Originally a movement, not a formal organization, Pentecostalism now has a variety of organized forms and continues also as a movement.	Scripture; individual charismatic leaders, the teachings of the Holy Spirit.	[Spirit baptism, especially as shown in "speaking in tongues"; faith healing; sometimes exorcism]; adult baptism; Lord's Supper.
Presby-terians	In 16th-cent. Calvinist reformation; differed with Lutherans over sacraments, church government; John Knox founded Scotch Presbyterian church about 1560.	[Highly structured representational system of ministers and lay persons (presbyters) in local, regional, and national bodies (synods).]	Scripture.	Infant baptism; Lord's Supper; bread and wine symbolize Christ's spiritual presence.
Roman Catholics	Traditionally, founded by Jesus who named St. Peter the first vicar; developed in early Christian proselytizing, especially after the conversion of imperial Rome in the 4th cent.	[Hierarchy with supreme power vested in pope elected by cardinals]; councils of bishops advise on matters of doctrine and policy.	[The pope, when speak-ing for the whole church in matters of faith and morals, and tradition (which is expressed in church councils and in part contained in Scripture).]	Mass; seven sacraments: baptism, reconciliation, Eucharist, confirmation, marriage, ordination, and anointing of the sick (unction).
United Church of Christ	[By ecumenical union, in 1957, of Congregationalists and Evangelical and Reformed, representing both Calvinist and Lutheran traditions.]	Congregational; a General Synod, representative of all congregations, sets general policy.	Scripture.	Infant baptism; Lord's Supper.

How Do They Differ?

distinguish a denomination sharply from others.

Practice	Ethics	Doctrine	Other	Denomination
Worship style varies from staid to evangelistic; extensive missionary activity.	Usually opposed to alcohol and tobacco; some tendency toward a perfectionist ethical standard.	[No creed; true church is of believers only, who are all equal.]	Believing no authority can stand between the believer and God, the Baptists are strong supporters of church and state separation.	**Baptists**
Tries to avoid any rite not considered part of the 1st-cent. church; some congregations may reject instrumental music.	Some tendency toward perfectionism; increasing interest in social action programs.	Simple New Testament faith; avoids any elaboration not firmly based on Scripture.	Highly tolerant in doctrinal and religious matters; strongly supportive of scholarly education.	**Church of Christ (Disciples)**
Formal, based on *Book of Common Prayer*, updated 1979; services range from austerely simple to highly liturgical.	Tolerant, sometimes permissive; some social action programs.	Scripture; the "historic creeds," which include the Apostles, Nicene, and Athanasian, and the *Book of Common Prayer*; ranges from Anglo-Catholic to low church, with Calvinist influences.	Strongly ecumenical, holding talks with many branches of Christendom.	**Episcopalians**
Meetings are held in Kingdom Halls and members' homes for study and worship; [extensive door-to-door visitations].	High moral code; stress on marital fidelity and family values; avoidance of tobacco and blood transfusions.	[God, by his first creation, Christ, will soon destroy all wickedness; 144,000 faithful ones will rule in heaven with Christ over others on a paradise earth.]	Total allegiance proclaimed only to God's kingdom or heavenly government by Christ; main periodical, *The Watchtower*, is available in over 250 languages.	**Jehovah's Witnesses**
Simple service with prayers, hymns, sermon; private temple ceremonies may be more elaborate.	Temperance; strict moral code; [tithing]; a strong work ethic with communal self-reliance; [strong missionary activity]; family emphasis.	Jesus Christ is the Son of God, the Eternal Father. Jesus's atonement saves all humans; those who are obedient to God's laws may become joint-heirs with Christ in God's kingdom.	Mormons believe theirs is the true church of Jesus Christ, restored by God through Joseph Smith. Official name: The Church of Jesus Christ of Latter-day Saints.	**Latter-day Saints (Mormons)**
Relatively simple, formal liturgy with emphasis on the sermon.	Generally conservative in personal and social ethics; doctrine of "two kingdoms" (worldly and holy) supports conservatism in secular affairs.	Salvation by grace alone through faith; Lutheranism has made major contributions to Protestant theology.	Though still somewhat divided along ethnic lines (German, Swedish, etc.), main divisions are between fundamentalists and liberals.	**Lutherans**
Worship style varies widely by denomination, local church, geography.	Originally pietist and perfectionist; always strong social activist elements.	No distinctive theological development; 25 articles abridged from Church of England's 39, not binding.	In 1968, The United Methodist Church was formed by the union of The Methodist Church and The Evangelical United Brethren Church.	**Methodists**
Elaborate liturgy, usually in the vernacular, though extremely traditional; the liturgy is the essence of Orthodoxy; veneration of icons.	Tolerant; little stress on social action; divorce, remarriage permitted in some cases; bishops are celibate; priests need not be.	Emphasis on Christ's resurrection, rather than crucifixion; the Holy Spirit proceeds from God the Father only.	Orthodox Church in America originally under Patriarch of Moscow, was granted autonomy in 1970; Greek Orthodox do not recognize this autonomy.	**Orthodox**
Loosely structured service with rousing hymns and sermons, culminating in spirit baptism.	Usually, emphasis on perfectionism, with varying degrees of tolerance.	Simple traditional beliefs, usually Protestant, with emphasis on the immediate presence of God in the Holy Spirit.	Once appealed mostly to lower classes; formation of charismatic fellowships in mainline churches expanded reach.	**Pentecostal**
A simple, sober service in which the sermon is central.	Traditionally, a tendency toward strictness, with firm church- and self-discipline; otherwise tolerant.	Emphasizes the sovereignty and justice of God; no longer dogmatic.	Although traces of belief in predestination (that God has foreordained salvation for the "elect") remain, this idea is no longer a central element in Presbyterianism.	**Presbyterians**
Relatively elaborate ritual centered on the Mass; also rosary recitation, novenas.	Traditionally strict but increasingly tolerant in practice; divorce and remarriage not accepted, but annulments sometimes granted; celibate clergy, except in Eastern rite.	Highly elaborated; salvation by merit gained through grace; dogmatic; special veneration of Mary, the mother of Jesus.	Relatively rapid changes followed Vatican Council II (1962-65). Mass held in vernacular instead of Latin; more stress on social action, tolerance, ecumenism.	**Roman Catholics**
Usually simple service with emphasis on the sermon.	Tolerant; some social action emphasis.	Standard Protestant; Statement of Faith (1959) is not binding.	Two main churches in the 1957 union represented earlier unions with small groups of almost every Protestant denomination.	**United Church of Christ**

Major Religions

Islam

Founded: Muhammad received his first revelation in 610 CE.

Founder: Muhammad (c. 570-632 CE), the Prophet.

Sacred texts: Two texts constitute the Muslim sacred canon, the *Quran* (Koran) and the *Hadith*. The Quran provides the foundation for Islamic religion and culture. It is regarded as the final, perfect, and complete word of God as revealed to Muhammad over the course of his life. Received by Muhammad in the Arabic language, it is memorized in Arabic by adherents regardless of their native language. It is divided into 114 chapters of unequal length, the shortest containing only 3 verses, and the longest containing 286 verses. The Quran is the ultimate source of everything Islamic, from metaphysics to theology to sacred history, to ethics and law, to art. The Hadith, which describes Muhammad's actions, attitudes, and teachings, complements the Quran. Due to its long history of oral transmission, the Hadith's lessons are seen as somewhat vulnerable to human error. It is not said to contain God's unadulterated voice as is the Quran but functions as a powerful spiritual and behavioral code nonetheless.

Organization: Muhammad was both the last prophet and a statesman. Muslim leaders have often assumed both civil and moral functions within Islamic states. Within the larger community, there are cultural and national groups, held together by a common religious law, the *Sharia*. Muslims believe that God is the ultimate lawgiver and that human beings cannot devise laws that oppose divine laws. Still, the Sharia is approached differently in different parts of the Islamic world. Over the centuries, Sunnis have developed four major schools of law: the Hanafi, the Shafi'i, the Hanbali, and the Maliki. The Ja'fari is the most important and well-known Shiite school. Before the 20th century, religious scholars known as the *ulama* held much legal power. Judges (*qadis*) and law-interpreters (*muftis*) are people learned in religious law who lead congregational prayers in mosques and perform other religious duties.

Practice: Five duties (of both men and women), known as the Pillars of Islam, are regarded as cardinal in Islam and as central to the life of the Islamic community. In accordance with Islam's absolute commitment to monotheism, the first duty is the profession of faith (the *Shahadah*): "There is no God but Allah and Muhammad is His Prophet." A Muslim must profess this belief publicly at least once in his or her lifetime; it defines the membership of an individual in the Islamic community. The second duty is that of five daily prayers organized in intervals throughout the day: sunrise, early afternoon, late afternoon, immediately after sunset, and before midnight. During prayer, Muslims face the Kaaba, a small, cube-shaped structure in the courtyard of al-Haram (the "inviolate place"), at the Grand Mosque of Mecca in Saudi Arabia. All five prayers in Islam are congregational and are to be offered in a mosque, but they may be offered individually if one cannot be present with a congregation. Congregational prayer is required only at the early afternoon prayer on Friday for men. The third cardinal duty of a Muslim is to pay alms, or *zakat*, which should be 2.5% of one's total wealth. This was originally the tax levied by Muhammad on the wealthy members of the community, primarily to help the poor. Only when zakat has been paid is the rest of a Muslim's property considered purified and legitimate. The fourth duty is the fast of the lunar month of Ramadan. During the fasting month, one must abstain from eating, drinking, smoking, impure thoughts, and sexual intercourse from dawn until sunset, and feed at least one poor person, if able. The fifth duty is the pilgrimage to the Kaaba, known as the hajj, which a Muslim must undertake, with exceptions for poverty and ill health, at least once during his or her lifetime.

Divisions: There are two major groups: the majority **Sunni** (85%-90% of the worldwide Muslim population) and the minority Shiites. Sects first appeared in Islam at the time of Muhammad's death. The group that came to be known as Sunni accepted Abu Bakr, an early convert, as his successor (caliph), while a smaller number, which became the Shia, believed that Ali ibn Abi Talib, the son-in-law and first cousin of the prophet, should have become his successor (Imam). Imams are believed to interpret the Quran infallibly. **Shiites** fall into three major branches: Fivers, Seveners, and Twelvers, reflecting the number of Imams they recognize. Twelvers believe that the 12th Imam has lived an invisible existence since 874, and will return as the Mahdi (a messiah figure) who will usher in a 1,000-year reign of peace and justice. **Sufism** (mystical dimension of Islam) emphasizes personal relation to God and obedience informed by love of God; it is prevalent among both Sunni and Shiites.

Location: W Africa to Philippines, across a band including E Africa, Central Asia and western China, India, Malaysia, Indonesia. Islam has several million adherents in North America and about 30 mil in Europe.

Beliefs: Strictly monotheistic. God is creator of the universe, omnipotent, omniscient, just, forgiving, and merciful. God revealed the Quran to Muhammad to guide humanity to truth and justice. Those who sincerely "submit" (literal meaning of "Islam") to God attain salvation.

World's Largest Muslim Populations, 2015

Source: Todd M. Johnson and Gina A. Zurlo, eds. World Christian Database (Leiden/Boston: Brill, Aug. 2018)

Rank	Country	Muslim population	% of country's pop.
1.	Indonesia	204,671,044	79.3%
2.	India	188,272,157	14.4
3.	Pakistan	182,418,084	96.3
4.	Bangladesh	143,167,192	88.8
5.	Egypt	85,277,278	90.9
6.	Nigeria	83,073,733	45.9
7.	Iran	78,184,167	98.5
8.	Turkey	76,991,982	98.4
9.	Algeria	39,224,098	98.4
10.	Iraq	35,451,542	98.2
11.	Sudan	35,230,531	91.2
12.	Morocco	34,683,762	99.7
13.	Ethiopia	34,336,387	34.4
14.	Afghanistan	33,682,089	99.8
15.	Uzbekistan	29,199,012	94.3
16.	Saudi Arabia	29,053,564	92.1
17.	Yemen	26,696,957	99.2
18.	China	23,048,543	1.6
19.	Niger	18,988,341	95.4
20.	Malaysia	17,361,112	56.5

Baha'i

Founded: Mid-19th century.

Founder: Mirza Husayn-Ali Nuri (1817-92), later known as Baha'u'llah (Arabic for "Glory of God").

Sacred texts: The writings of Baha'u'llah and of his herald the Bab (Siyyid Ali-Muhammad, 1819-50). The primary text is *Kitab-i-Aqdas* (Most Holy Book).

Organization: The Baha'i administrative system consists of elected nine-member councils at the local, national, and international levels. There are also more than 180 National Spiritual Assemblies and an elected, international governing body known as the Universal House of Justice.

Practice: Prayer, meditation, and fasting are key components of the Baha'i Faith. Work performed in a spirit of service to humanity is considered an important form of worship. The Baha'i Faith has no clergy and minimal ritual and congregational worship.

Divisions: In a religion in which unity is perhaps the central spiritual value, the Baha'i Faith has avoided separating into sects with differentiated theologies and practices.

Location: Worldwide.

Beliefs: God has progressively revealed His will and purpose through a series of Divine manifestations including Jesus, Buddha, Muhammad, Zoroaster, and Baha'u'llah. Baha'u'llah's teachings include the oneness of humanity, the equality of men and women, the harmony of science and religion, and the need to abandon all forms of prejudice and eliminate extremes of poverty and wealth.

Buddhism

Founded: About 525 BCE, reportedly near Benares, India.

Founder: Gautama Siddhartha (c. 563-483 BCE), the Buddha, who achieved enlightenment through intense meditation.

Sacred texts: The *Tripitaka*, a collection of the Buddha's teachings, rules of monastic life, and philosophical commentaries on the teachings; also a vast body of Buddhist teachings and commentaries, many of which are called *sutras*.

Organization: The basic institution is the *sangha*, or monastic order, through which traditions are passed down. Monastic life tends to be democratic and antiauthoritarian.

Practice: Varies widely according to the sect and ranges from austere meditation to magical chanting and elaborate temple rites. Many practices, such as exorcism of devils, reflect pre-Buddhist beliefs.

Divisions: A variety of sects grouped into three primary branches: Theravada, which emphasizes the importance of pure thought and deed; Mahayana (includes Zen and Sokagakkai), which ranges from philosophical schools to belief in the saving grace of higher beings or ritual practices and to practical meditative disciplines; and Vajrayana, or Tantrism, a combination of belief in ritual magic and sophisticated philosophy.

Location: Mainly in Asia, from Sri Lanka to Japan.

Beliefs: Life is suffering, and there is no ultimate reality behind it. The cycle of birth and rebirth continues because of desire and attachment to the unreal "self." Meditation and deeds will end the cycle and achieve Nirvana (nothingness, enlightenment).

Hinduism

Founded: About 1500 BCE to 300 CE as a religion and *dharma* (way of life); a diverse synthesis of primarily Indian traditions, practices, and beliefs.

Sacred texts: The *Vedas* (Rig, Sama, Yajur, Atharva); the *Upanishads*, a collection of rituals and commentaries; a vast number of epic stories about gods, heroes, and saints, including the *Puranas*, *Ramayana*, and *Mahabharata*; the *Bhagavad Gita*; and the *Agamas*.

Organization: None, strictly speaking. No single founder, establishment date, authoritative scripture, or central religious organization exist.

Practice: *Sanskara*, or rites of passage (e.g., initiation, marriage, death), and devotionals (*bhakti*). Bhakti may be practiced privately, as at a household shrine, or in a group.

Divisions: There is no concept of orthodoxy in Hinduism, which presents a variety of sects. Three major traditions are those devoted to the gods Vishnu and Shiva and to the goddess Shakti, but others believe in *brahman* (the All) as a more impersonal but infinite spiritual core. Numerous beliefs and practices, often in amalgamation, exist side by side with various philosophical schools.

Location: Mainly India, Nepal, Malaysia, Mauritius, Guyana, Suriname, and Sri Lanka.

Beliefs: Two general beliefs for Hindus include that in the unity of existence as well as in the process of transmigration and rebirth (*samsara*) with no clear beginning or end. Life

in all its forms is an aspect or manifestation of the divine or of divine qualities.

Judaism

Founded: About 2000 BCE.

Founder: Abraham is regarded as the founding patriarch.

Sacred texts: The five books of Moses (the Torah), the basic source of teachings.

Organization: Originally theocratic, Judaism has evolved into a congregational polity. The basic institution is the local synagogue or temple, operated by the congregation and led by a rabbi of their choice. Chief rabbis in France and Great Britain have authority only over those who accept it; in Israel, the two chief rabbis have civil authority in family law.

Practice: Among traditional practitioners, almost all areas of life are governed by strict discipline. Sabbath and holidays are marked by observances, and attendance at public worship is considered especially important. Chief annual observances are Passover, celebrating liberation of the Israelites from Egypt and marked by the Seder meal in homes, and the 10 days from Rosh Hashanah (New Year) to Yom Kippur (Day of Atonement), a period of penitence.

Divisions: Judaism is an unbroken spectrum from ultraconservative to ultraliberal, largely reflecting different points of view regarding the binding character of the prohibitions and duties—particularly the dietary and Sabbath observations—traditionally prescribed for the daily life of the Jew.

Location: Mainly in Israel and the U.S.

Beliefs: Strictly monotheistic. God is the creator and ruler of the universe. God established a particular relationship with the Hebrew people: by obeying a divine law God gave them, they would be a special witness to God's mercy and justice. Judaism stresses ethical behavior (and, among the traditional, careful ritual obedience) as true worship of God.

Sikhism

Founded: Late 15th century in South Asia.

Founder: Guru Nanak Dev ji, Sikhism's first Guru.

Sacred texts: The *Guru Granth Sahib* was compiled by the Sikh Gurus and contains their experiences of the Divine. It also contains writings by other saintly figures of different faiths.

Organization: Each Sikh must make her or his own spiritual journey and not depend on clergy. Congregational prayer led by both men and women takes place in local *Gurdwaras* ("doorway to the Guru"). Harmandir Sahib in Amritsar, Punjab (northern India), is the central place of worship.

Practice: Prayers are required in the morning, evening, and before sleeping. The most important mode of congregational prayer is the singing of hymns from the Guru Granth Sahib. The "Five Ks" are five articles of faith required of all Sikhs: *Kes* (uncut hair), *Kangha* (comb), *Kara* (steel bracelet), *Kirpan* (sword), and *Kaccha* (short pants).

Divisions: The last living Guru, Guru Gobind Singh (1666-1708), crystallized the practices and beliefs of the faith and determined that no future living Guru was needed. Today the religion is guided by joint sovereignty of Guru Granth and Guru Panth. Guru Granth is the Sikh scripture, as the spiritual manifestation of the Guru, while the Guru Panth is the collectivity of all initiated Sikhs worldwide, as the physical manifestation of the Guru.

Location: Many Sikhs have Punjabi backgrounds. The Punjab region was divided between India and Pakistan with the end of British rule.

Beliefs: Sikhism preaches a message of devotion, remembrance of God at all times, truthful living, equality between all human beings, and social justice, while denouncing what is considered superstition and blind ritualism. Sikhism is a monotheistic religion based on revelation.

LANGUAGE

New Words in English

The following new words and definitions were provided by Merriam-Webster Inc., publishers of *Merriam-Webster's Collegiate Dictionary, Eleventh Edition*, and other language references. The words are among those added in 2018 by Merriam-Webster's editors to the digital version of the dictionary, available as the *Merriam-Webster Dictionary* app and at www.merriam-webster.com.

antifa: a person or group actively opposing fascism; or an anti-fascist movement

anti-vaxxer: a person who opposes vaccination or laws that mandate vaccination

aquafaba: the liquid that results when beans are cooked in water *Note:* Aquafaba is used especially in vegan cooking as an egg white substitute.

Arnold Palmer: a cold beverage of iced tea mixed with lemonade

burner phone: a prepaid cell phone that is not bound to a contract with a carrier and is usually intended to be disposed of after use

colony collapse disorder: a disorder of honeybees (*Apis mellifera*) that is of unknown cause and that is characterized by sudden colony death due to the disappearance of all adult worker bees in a hive while immature bees, the queen bee, and the honey remain

cryptocurrency: any form of currency that only exists digitally, that usually has no central issuing or regulating authority but instead uses a decentralized system to record transactions and manage the issuance of new units, and that relies on cryptography to prevent counterfeiting and fraudulent transactions

dashcam: a video camera mounted on the dashboard of a vehicle and used to continuously record activity through the vehicle's windshield

demonym: a word (such as *Nevadan* or *Sooner*) used to denote a person who inhabits or is native to a particular place

dumpster fire: an utterly calamitous or mismanaged situation or occurrence: a disaster

evergreen: universally and continually relevant: not limited in applicability to a particular event or date

fingerling *or* **fingerling potato:** a small, narrow, elongated potato typically ranging in length from two to 5 inches (5 to 13 centimeters) when mature

foodborne: caused by food contaminated with pathogenic microorganisms or toxic substances

glamping: outdoor camping with amenities and comforts (such as beds, electricity, and access to indoor plumbing) not usually used when camping

harissa: a spicy North African paste made from dried chilies, salt, oil, and other seasonings

hate-watch: to watch and take pleasure in laughing at or criticizing (a disliked television show, movie, etc.)

health span: the length of time in one's life during which an individual is in reasonably good health

kabocha: a winter squash (*Curcubita maxima*) of Japanese origin that is round with somewhat flattened top and bottom, typically dark green skin usually streaked or mottled with pale green, and yellowish-orange sweet flesh

life hack: a usually simple and clever tip or technique for accomplishing some familiar task more easily and efficiently

mansplain *of a man*: to explain something to a woman in a condescending way that assumes she has no knowledge about the topic

neoadjuvant: of, relating to, or being treatment (such as chemotherapy or hormone therapy) administered before primary cancer treatment (such as surgery) to enhance the outcome of primary treatment

piloerection: erection or bristling of hairs due to the involuntary contraction of small muscles at the base of hair follicles that occurs as a reflexive response of the sympathetic nervous system especially to cold, shock, or fright

poke: a Hawaiian salad made typically from cubed pieces of raw seafood (such as tuna) marinated with soy sauce and sesame oil and mixed with onions or other ingredients

reconciliation *US government*: a legislative process that enables expedited passage of a bill relating to certain matters in the federal budget by a simple majority of votes

regenerative medicine: a branch of medicine concerned with developing therapies that regenerate or replace injured, diseased, or defective cells, tissues, or organs to restore or establish function and structure

schnoodle: a dog that is a cross between a schnauzer and a poodle

silver alert: a widely publicized bulletin that alerts the public when an elderly person or a person with a cognitive disability goes missing

sizeism: discrimination or prejudice directed against people because of their size and especially because of their weight

subtweet: a usually mocking or critical tweet that alludes to another Twitter user without including a link to the user's account and often without directly mentioning the user's name

wordie: a lover of words: a logophile

Words About Words

alliteration: repetition of same, initial consonant sounds of two or more words in sequence or in short intervals. Ex.: "I have **s**tood **s**till and **s**topped the **s**ound of feet." —Robert Frost, "Acquainted With the Night"

anagram: word or word sequence that is a rearrangement, typically clever, of letters in another word or word sequence. Ex.: The Leaning Tower of Pisa = I spot one giant flaw here.

assonance: repetition of same or similar vowel sounds in words located near each other. Ex.: "Gr**ee**n as a dr**ea**m, and d**ee**p as d**ea**th." —Rupert Brooke, "The Old Vicarage, Grantchester"

cliché: a saying or expression that has been used so often it has lost its effect. Ex.: work like a dog

euphemism: a mild, indirect expression used instead of a plainer one that might be harsh, unpleasant, or offensive. Ex.: restroom instead of toilet; pass away, or pass, instead of die

hyperbole: exaggeration for emphasis or effect. Ex.: "And fired the shot heard round the world." —Ralph Waldo Emerson, "Concord Hymn"

irony: use of an expression in which the literal or surface meaning conceals a hidden intended, often opposite meaning that can be inferred. Ex.: "Yet Brutus says he was ambitious; / And Brutus is an honorable man." —William Shakespeare, *Julius Caesar*

litotes: intentional understatement made by negating the opposite of what is meant. Ex.: This was no small matter.

metaphor: a stated equivalence between two dissimilar things or a reference to one thing rather than another, so as to imply a comparison. Ex.: "Life is a tale told by an idiot, full of sound and fury, signifying nothing." —William Shakespeare, *Macbeth*

metonymy: substitution of one word for another that it suggests. Ex.: The pen is mightier than the sword.

onomatopoeia: words that imitate the sounds they describe. Ex.: buzz, murmur

oxymoron: expression containing seemingly contradictory words. Ex.: deafening silence

palindrome: word or phrase that reads the same backward and forward. Ex: radar, Hannah, "Madam, I'm Adam"

paradox: a statement that is phrased to seem contradictory, odd, or opposed to common sense or expectation, while being presented as true. Ex.: "What a pity that youth must be wasted on the young." —George Bernard Shaw

personification: treatment of objects or abstractions as if they were persons. Ex.: "Because I could not stop for Death— / He kindly stopped for me." —Emily Dickinson, "Because I Could Not Stop for Death"

simile: a comparison between two dissimilar things using the words "like" or "as." Ex.: "My love is like a red, red rose" —Robert Burns, "A Red, Red Rose"

spoonerism: play on words in which the initial sounds of two or more words are transposed, often with comic result. Ex.: blushing crow instead of crushing blow

synecdoche: a form of metonymy; the use of a part for the whole, or the whole for the part. Ex.: All hands on deck!

tautology: useless, often unwitting repetition of the same idea in different wording. Ex.: close proximity. In logic, a proposition that would be self-contradictory to deny. Ex.: All bachelors are male.

National Spelling Bee

The annual Scripps National Spelling Bee, conducted by The E.W. Scripps Company and other newspapers since 1941, was instituted by *The Courier-Journal* of Louisville, KY, in 1925. Students under 16 who are not beyond 8th grade are eligible to compete locally for a chance to advance to the national competition in Washington, DC. Starting in 2017, a runoff round was introduced to avoid a first-place tie. The winner in 2018 was Karthik Nemmani, 14, of McKinney, TX. Naysa Modi, 12, of Frisco, TX, took second place.

Here are the last words given and spelled correctly at the National Spelling Bee in recent years.

1982	psoriasis	1990	fibranne	1998	chiaroscurist	2006	Ursprache	2014	feuilleton
1983	purim	1991	antipyretic	1999	logorrhea	2007	serrefine		stichomythia
1984	luge	1992	lyceum	2000	demarche	2008	guerdon	2015	scherenschnitte
1985	milieu	1993	kamikaze	2001	succedaneum	2009	Laodicean		nunatak
1986	odontalgia	1994	antediluvian	2002	prospicience	2010	stromuhr	2016	Feldenkrais
1987	staphylococci	1995	xanthosis	2003	pococurante	2011	cymotrichous		gesellschaft
1988	elegiacal	1996	vivisepulture	2004	autochthonous	2012	guetapens	2017	marocain
1989	spoliator	1997	euonym	2005	appoggiatura	2013	knaidel	2018	koinonia

Foreign Words and Phrases

A = Arabic; F = French; Ger = German; Gr = Greek; I = Italian; J = Japanese; L = Latin; R = Russian; S = Spanish; Y = Yiddish

ad hoc (L; ad-HOK): for the end or purpose at hand; impromptu

ad hominem (L; ad-HOH-mee-nem): argument that criticizes an opponent, often unfairly, rather than addressing an issue directly

al fresco (I; ahl-FRAYS-koh): outdoors

anime (J; A-nuh-may): Japanese-style animation

antebellum (L; AHN-teh-BEL-lum): pre-war

au courant (F; oh-koo-RAHN): up-to-date, fashionable

belles lettres (F; bel-LET-truh): writing aspiring to artistic merit

bête noire (F; bet-NWAHR): literally, black beast; a thing or person viewed with particular dislike or fear

bildungsroman (Ger; BIL-doongs-roh-mahn): novel embodying coming-of-age story

bodega (S; boh-DAY-gah): grocery store

bon vivant (F; bon-vee-VAHN): a person with refined tastes, esp. for food and drink

bonhomie (F; boh-noh-MEE): friendliness

bourgeois (F; boo-ZHWAH): middle-class; materialistic

carte blanche (F; kahrt-BLANSH): full discretionary power

cause célèbre (F; kawz-suh-LEB): a notorious incident

chutzpah (Y, HUHTS-pah): audacity, nerve

comme il faut (F; cum-eel-FOH): proper; as it should be

contretemps (F; kon-truh-TAHN): awkward situation

coup de grâce (F; kooh-duh-GRAHS): the decisive final blow

cum laude/magna cum laude/summa cum laude (L; kuhm-LOU-day; MAG-na ... ; SOO-ma ...): with praise or honor/with great praise or honor/with the highest praise or honor

de facto (L; day-FAK-toh): in fact, if not by law

de jure (L; dee-JOOR-ee, day-YOOR-ay): by right or by law

de rigueur (F; duh-ree-GUR): required by convention or etiquette

détente (F; day-TAHNT): an easing of strained relations

deus ex machina (L; DAY-uhs-eks-MAH-keh-nah): person/event that provides a solution unexpectedly or suddenly, esp. (in literature) a contrived solution to a plot

doppelgänger (Ger; DAH-pul-gang-ur): a double or ghostly counterpart of a person

double entendre (F; DOO-blahn-TAHN-druh): expression with a double meaning, one meaning of which is often risqué

e pluribus unum (L; eh-PLOO-ree-boos-OO-noom): out of many, one (U.S. motto)

éminence grise (F; ay-meh-nahns-GREEZ): one who wields power behind the scenes

ennui (F; ah-NOOEE): boredom; world-weariness; annoyance

ersatz (Ger; EHR-zats): artificial; being a (usually inferior) substitute

ex post facto (L; eks-pohst-FAK-toh): retroactive(ly)

fait accompli (F; fayt-uh-kom-PLEE): an accomplished fact

fatwa (A; FAHT-wah): in Islam, a legal or religious decree

faux pas (F; foh-PAH): false step; breach of etiquette

habeas corpus (L; HAY-bee-ahs-KOR-pus): an order for a prisoner to be brought to court to challenge his or her detention

hoi polloi (Gr; hoy-puh-LOY): the masses

impresario (I; im-prah-SAH-ri-oh): manager, promoter, or sponsor of a musical or theatrical program or company

imprimatur (L; im-prah-MAH-toor): approval or official permission to print, esp. by the Roman Catholic church

in loco parentis (L; in-LOH-koh-puh-REN-tis): in place of a parent

in medias res (L; in-MAY-dee-oos-rays): into the middle of things

intelligentsia (R; in-te-luh-JEN-see-uh): elite social class made up of intellectuals and educated people

ipso facto (L; ip-soh-FAK-toh): by that fact itself

je ne sais quoi (F; zhuh-nuh-say-KWAH): literally, "I don't know what"; the little something that eludes description

jihad (A; jih-HAHD): Islamic holy war; struggle in devotion to Islam

joie de vivre (F; zhwah-duh-VEEV-ruh): zest for life

kvetch (Y; Kuh-VETCH): complain, gripe

leitmotif (Ger; lyt-moh-TEEF): the central theme or idea, particularly in art and literature

mano a mano (S; MAH-noh-ah-MAH-noh): hand to hand; in direct combat

mea culpa (L; MAY-uh-CUL-puh): through my fault

mensch (Y; MENTSCH): an upright, noble, admirable person

modus operandi (L; MOH-duhs-op-uh-RAN-dee): method of operation

mujahedeen (A; moo-jah-ha-DEEN): Islamic holy warrior

noblesse oblige (F; noh-BLES-oh-BLEEZH): the obligation of nobility to help the less fortunate

nolo contendere (L; NOH-loh-kohn-TEN-duh-ree): a plea of no contest to charges, without admitting guilt

non compos mentis (L; non-KOM-puhs-MEN-tis): not of sound mind

non sequitur (L; non-SEH-kwi-tour): a conclusion that does not logically follow from what preceded it

nouveau riche (F; noo-voh-REESH): a newly rich person, esp. one who spends money conspicuously

ombudsman (Swedish; AHM-budz-muhn): person who receives, investigates, and settles complaints

par excellence (F; par-ek-seh-LANS): best of all; incomparable

persona non grata (L; per-SOH-nah-non-GRAH-tah): unwelcome person

pièce de résistance (F; pee-es-duh-ray-ZEES-tonz): the outstanding item in a series or group

prima facie (L; pry-muh-FAY-shee-ee; pry-muh-FAY-shuh): true at first glance; presumptively valid

pro bono (L; proh-BOH-noh): (work) donated for the public good

quid pro quo (L; kwid-proh-KWOH): something given or received for something else

raison d'être (F; RAY-zohnn-DET-ruh): reason for being

savoir faire (F; sav-wahr-FAIR): dexterity in social affairs

schadenfreude (Ger; SHAH-duhn-froy-deh): joy at another's misfortune

semper fidelis (L; SEM-puhr-fee-DAY-lis): always faithful

sobriquet (F; SOH-bri-kay): nickname or informal descriptive name for someone

sotto voce (I; sah-toh-VOH-chee); in a low voice

sui generis (L; soo-ee-JEN-er-is); unique; one of a kind

terra firma (L; TER-uh-FUR-muh): solid ground

verboten (Ger; ver-BOH-ten): forbidden

vis-à-vis (F; vee-zuh-VEE): compared with; with regard to

voir dire (F; vwar-DEER): examination by lawyers or judge to determine the suitability of a witness or a prospective juror

zeitgeist (Ger; ZITE-gyste): the general intellectual, moral, and cultural climate of an era

Names for Animal Young

calf: cattle, elephant, hippo, camel, others

cheeper: grouse, partridge, quail

chick: chicken, penguin, other birds

cockerel: rooster

codling, sprag: codfish

colt: horse, zebra (male)

cria: llama, alpaca

cub: lion, bear, shark, fox, others

cygnet: swan

duckling: duck

elver: eel

ephyra: jellyfish

eyas: hawk, other birds

fawn: deer, antelope

filly: horse, zebra (female)

fingerling, fry: fish generally

fledgling, nestling: birds generally

foal: horse, zebra, others

gosling: goose

heifer: cow

hoglet: hedgehog

joey: kangaroo, opossum, wombat

kid: goat

kit: beaver, rabbit, ferret, others

kitten: cat, other small mammals

lamb: sheep

larva: frog, sea urchin, insects generally

parr, smolt, grilse: salmon

piglet, shoat, farrow, suckling: pig

polliwog, tadpole: frog

poult: turkey

pullet: hen

pup: dog, fox, seal, rat, others

spat: oyster, other bivalves

spiderling: spider

spike, blinker, tinker: mackerel

squab: pigeon

whelp: dog, tiger, other carnivores

yearling: cattle, sheep, horse, others

Names for Animal Collectives

alligators: congregation

ants: army, colony, swarm

apes: shrewdness, troop

bears: sleuth, sloth

bees: colony, swarm, hive

birds: flight, volery

buffalo: gang, obstinacy

butterflies: flutter

buzzards: wake

camels: caravan, flock, train

cats: clowder, cluster, pounce

cattle: drove

cheetahs: coalition

cockroaches: intrusion

cranes: sedge, siege

crocodiles: bask, nest, float

crows: murder, horde

dolphins: pod

doves: dule, pitying

ducks: brace, team

eagles: convocation, aerie

ferrets: business

finches: charm

fish: school, shoal

flamingos: stand, flamboyance

foxes: skulk

geese: flock, gaggle, skein

giraffes: corps, herd, tower

goats: tribe, trip

gorillas: band, troop, whoop

grasshoppers: cloud

hawks: cast, kettle

hedgehogs: array, prickle

hippopotamuses: bloat

horses: pair, team

hounds: cry, mute, pack

hyenas: cackle

iguanas: mess

jellyfish: smack

kangaroos: mob, troop

larks: exaltation

leopards: leap

lions: pride

locusts: plague, swarm

mice, rats: mischief

moles: labor

monkeys: troop

mules: barren, span

nightingales: watch

otters: romp

owls: parliament

oxen: yoke

peacocks: muster

pheasants: nest, nide, bouquet

ponies: string

raccoons: gaze

ravens: unkindness

rhinoceroses: crash

seals: pod

sheep: flock, drove, hurtle

snakes: nest

squirrels: dray, scurry

starlings: flock, murmuration

swans: bevy

tigers: streak

toads: knot

trout: hover

turkeys: rafter

turtles: bale

vultures: committee

whales: gam, herd, pod

woodchucks: fall

woodpeckers: descent

zebras: herd, zeal

Some Eponyms
(words named for people)

boycott: to avoid trade or dealings with, as a protest; after Charles C. Boycott, an English land agent in County Mayo, Ireland, ostracized in 1880 for refusing to reduce rents

Casanova: an unscrupulous and promiscuous romancer and lover; after Italian adventurer Giovanni Casanova (1725-98)

gerrymander: to draw an irregular election district so as to favor a particular political party; after Elbridge Gerry, who (1812) approved creation of a salamander-shaped district as governor of Massachusetts

guillotine: a machine for beheading; after Joseph Guillotin, French physician who proposed its use in 1789 as more humane than hanging

Luddite: one who opposes new technology; from Ned Ludd, leader of textile workers in England who destroyed machinery in the early 1800s

maudlin: excessively sentimental; from scriptural figure Mary Magdalene, often depicted as weeping

salmonella: bacteria that can cause infections when contaminated food or water is consumed; named after Daniel Elmer Salmon, American veterinarian and public health official

sandwich: slices of bread with a filling in-between; after John Montagu, 4th Earl of Sandwich (1718-92), who supposedly ate these at the gaming table

shrapnel: pieces of shell casings; originally, a projectile designed to produce maximum damage; from Henry Shrapnel (1761-1842), British artillery officer who designed it

silhouette: an outline image; from Étienne de Silhouette (1709-67), a stingy French finance minister

Some Common Abbreviations

(See also Abbreviations in the General Index.) Abbreviations include acronyms, pronounceable words formed from first letters, or syllables, of other words, e.g., AIDS. Some acronyms are words coined as abbreviations and written in lowercase (e.g., sonar). Italicized words below are Latin unless otherwise noted.

A: ampere
AA: Alcoholics Anonymous
ABA: American Bar Association
AC: alternating current; air-conditioning
ACA: Affordable Care Act
ACLU: American Civil Liberties Union
AD: *anno Domini* (in the year of the Lord)
AD(H)D: attention deficit (hyperactivity) disorder
AFL-CIO: American Federation of Labor-Congress of Industrial Organizations
AFSCME: American Federation of State, County, and Municipal Employees
AFT: American Federation of Teachers
AI: artificial intelligence
AIDS: acquired immune deficiency syndrome
ALA: American Library Association
a.m. or **AM:** *ante meridiem* (before noon)
AP: Associated Press
APO: army post office
APR: annual percentage rate
AQAP: al-Qaeda in the Arabian Peninsula
ARM: adjustable rate mortgage
ASAP: as soon as possible
ASCAP: American Society of Composers, Authors, and Publishers
ASCII: American Standard Code for Information Interchange
ATM: automated teller machine
Ave.: Avenue
AWOL: absent without leave
BA: Bachelor of Arts
bbl: barrel(s)
BC: before Christ
BCE: before Common, or Christian, Era
Benelux: Belgium, Netherlands, Luxembourg
bpd or **b/d:** barrels per day
BRB: be right back
Brexit: British exit (from the EU)
BS: Bachelor of Science
Btu: British thermal unit(s)
BTW: by the way
B2B: business-to-business (company)
bu: bushel(s)
BYOB: bring your own bottle
C: Celsius, centigrade
c.: *circa* (about); copyright
C(A)T: computerized (axial) tomography
CD: compact disc
CDC: Centers for Disease Control and Prevention; Community Development Corporation
CE: Common Era; Christian Era
CEO: chief executive officer
cf.: *confer* (compare)
CFO: chief financial officer
CIA: Central Intelligence Agency
COBRA: Consolidated Omnibus Budget Reconciliation Act (health insurance continuation)
COD: cash (or collect) on delivery
COL or **Col.:** Colonel
COLA: cost of living adjustment

COO: chief operating officer
CPA: certified public accountant
CPI: consumer price index
CPL or **Cpl.:** Corporal
CPR: cardiopulmonary resuscitation
CPU: central processing unit
CST: central standard time
CV: curriculum vitae
DA: district attorney
DACA: Deferred Action for Childhood Arrivals
DC: direct current
DD: Doctor of Divinity
DDS: Doctor of Dental Surgery
DEA: Drug Enforcement Administration
DHS: Department of Homeland Security
DJ or **deejay:** disc jockey
DM: direct message
DMD: Doctor of Dental Medicine
DMZ: demilitarized zone
DNA: deoxyribonucleic acid
DNC: Democratic National Committee
DNR: do not resuscitate
DOA: dead on arrival
DOB: date of birth
DoD: Department of Defense
dpi: dots per inch
DPT: diphtheria, pertussis, tetanus
DUI: driving under the influence
DVD: digital video disc
DVM: Doctor of Veterinary Medicine
DWI: driving while intoxicated
ECB: European Central Bank
ed.: edited; edition; editor
EEG: electroencephalogram
e.g.: *exempli gratia* (for example)
EKG or **ECG:** electrocardiogram
EMT: emergency medical technician
EOE: equal opportunity employer
EP: extended play
EPA: Environmental Protection Agency
ERA: Equal Rights Amendment; earned run average
ESL: English as a second language
ESP: extrasensory perception
Esq.: Esquire
EST: eastern standard time
et al.: *et alii* (and others)
etc.: *et cetera* (and so forth)
EU: European Union
F: Fahrenheit
Fannie Mae: Federal National Mortgage Association
FAQ: frequently asked questions
FBI: Federal Bureau of Investigation
FDA: Food and Drug Administration
FDIC: Federal Deposit Insurance Corporation
FEC: Federal Election Commission
FEMA: Federal Emergency Management Agency
ff.: and those following
FICA: Federal Insurance Contributions Act (Social Security)

FIFA: Fédération Internationale de Football Association
fl.: *floruit* (flourished), used for historical figures when life dates uncertain
FLOTUS: First Lady of the United States
Freddie Mac: Federal Home Loan Mortgage Corporation
FTP: file transfer protocol
FWIW: for what it's worth
FY: fiscal year
FYI: for your information
GB: gigabyte(s)
GDP: gross domestic product
GED: general equivalency diploma
GMO: genetically modified organism
GMT: Greenwich mean time
GOP: Grand Old Party (Republican Party)
GPS: Global Positioning System
GTG: got to go
GUI: graphical user interface
ha: hectare
hazmat: HAZardous MATerial
HDTV: high-definition television
HIV: human immunodeficiency virus
HMO: health maintenance organization
HMS: His/Her Majesty's Ship (UK)
Hon.: the Honorable
HOV: high-occupancy vehicle
HRH: Her (His) Royal Highness (UK)
HTML: hypertext markup language
HTTP: hypertext transfer protocol
HUD: Department of Housing and Urban Development
HVAC: heating, ventilating, and air-conditioning
Hz: hertz
ibid.: *ibidem* (in the same place)
ICE: Immigration and Customs Enforcement (agency)
ICU: intensive care unit
i.e.: *id est* (that is)
IM: instant messaging
IMF: International Monetary Fund
IM(H)O: in my (humble) opinion
INS: Immigration and Naturalization Service
IPO: initial public offering
IQ: intelligence quotient
IRA: individual retirement account; Irish Republican Army
IRS: Internal Revenue Service
ISBN: International Standard Book Number
ISIL or **ISIS:** Islamic State of Iraq in the Levant, or of Iraq and Syria
ISP: Internet service provider
IVF: in vitro fertilization
JD: *Juris Doctor* (Doctor of Law)
k: karat; **K:** Kelvin
kWh: kilowatt-hour(s)
laser: Light Amplification by Stimulated Emission of Radiation
lb: pound
LGBT(QIA): lesbian, gay, bisexual, transgender (queer/questioning, intersex, asexual)
LLP: limited liability partnership

loc. cit.: *loco citato* (in the place cited)
LOL: laughing out loud
LSAT: Law School Admission Test
LT or **Lt.:** Lieutenant
MA: Master of Arts
MB: megabyte(s)
MBA: Master of Business Administration
MCAT: Medical College Admission Test
MD: *Medicinae Doctor* (Doctor of Medicine)
MIA: missing in action
modem: MOdulator-DEModulator
MP: member of Parliament (UK)
mph: miles per hour
MRI: magnetic resonance imaging
ms, mss: manuscript(s)
MS: Master of Science; multiple sclerosis
MSG: monosodium glutamate
MST: mountain standard time
MVP: most valuable player
MYOB: mind your own business
NA: not applicable; not available
NAACP: National Association for the Advancement of Colored People
NAFTA: North American Free Trade Agreement
NASA: National Aeronautics and Space Administration
NATO: North Atlantic Treaty Organization
NB or **n.b.:** *nota bene* (note carefully)
NCAA: National Collegiate Athletic Association
NEA: National Education Association; National Endowment for the Arts
NIH: National Institutes of Health
NIMBY: not in my backyard
NOW: National Organization for Women
NPR: National Public Radio
NRA: National Rifle Association
NSA: National Security Agency
NSC: National Security Council
obs.: obsolete
OECD: Organization for Economic Cooperation and Development
OED: Oxford English Dictionary
OMB: Office of Management and Budget
OMG: Oh my goodness/gosh/God!
op., opp.: *opus* (work[s])
OPEC: Organization of Petroleum Exporting Countries
OTC: over-the-counter
oz: ounce
p., pp.: page(s)

PA: public address
PAC: political action committee
PC: personal computer; politically correct
PDA: personal digital assistant
PET: positron emission tomography
PETA: People for the Ethical Treatment of Animals
PhD: *Philosophiae Doctor* (Doctor of Philosophy)
PIN: personal identification number
p.m. or **PM:** post meridiem (after noon)
PM: private message; prime minister
POTUS: President of the United States
PPO: preferred provider organization, a type of health-care provider network
PS: *post scriptum* (postscript)
PST: Pacific standard time
pt: part(s); pint(s); point(s)
PT: physical therapy/training
PTSD: post-traumatic stress disorder
PVT or **Pvt.:** Private
QC: Queen's Council (UK)
QED: *quod erat demonstrandum* (which was to be demonstrated)
radar: RAdio Detecting And Ranging
RAM: random access memory
RC: Roman Catholic
RCMP: Royal Canadian Mounted Police
REM: rapid eye movement
Rev.: Reverend
rev.: revised; reviewed
RIP: *requiescat in pace* (may he/she rest in peace)
RN: registered nurse
RNA: ribonucleic acid
RNC: Republican National Committee
ROFL: rolling on the floor laughing
ROM: read only memory
ROTC: Reserve Officers' Training Corps
rpm: revolutions per minute
RSVP: *répondez s'il vous plaît* (Fr.) (please reply)
SARS: severe acute respiratory syndrome
SASE: self-addressed stamped envelope
SCOTUS: Supreme Court of the United States
SEC: Securities and Exchange Commission
SEO: search engine optimization
SETI: Search for Extraterrestrial Intelligence
SGT or **Sgt.:** Sergeant

SIDS: sudden infant death syndrome
SJ: Society of Jesus (Jesuits)
sonar: SOund NAvigation and Ranging
SOTU: State of the Union
SPCA: Society for the Prevention of Cruelty to Animals
SSI: Supplementary Security Income
St.: Saint; Street
STEM: science, technology, engineering, math
TB: tuberculosis; terabyte(s)
TBA/TBD: to be announced/determined
tbsp: tablespoon
TBT: Throwback Thursday
TEFL: teaching English as a foreign language
TGIF: thank God it's Friday
TIA: transient ischemic attack
TMI: too much information
TPP: Trans-Pacific Partnership (trade agreement)
TSA: Transportation Security Administration
tsp: teaspoon
UFO: unidentified flying object
UPC: Universal Product Code
URL: Universal Resource Locator
USDA: United States Department of Agriculture
USS: United States ship
UTC: coordinated universal time
VA: Department of Veterans Affairs
var.: variant
VAT: value-added tax
VCR: videocassette recorder
VISTA: Volunteers in Service to America
viz: *videlicet* (namely)
VP: vice president
W: watt(s)
WHO: World Health Organization
WMD: weapon of mass destruction
WPM: words per minute
WTF: what the f--- [expletive]
WTO: World Trade Organization
WWW: World Wide Web
YMCA/YWCA: Young Men's/Women's Christian Association
YTD: year to date
yuppie: young urban professional
ZIP: zone improvement plan (U.S. Postal Service)

Most Popular U.S. First Names by Decade or Year of Birth

Source: U.S. Social Security Administration

All names are from Social Security card applications for births that occurred in the United States after 1879. Rankings are based on one spelling of the name; variant spellings and similar sounding names are considered separate names.

BOYS

1880-1889	John, William, James, George, Charles, Frank, Joseph, Henry, Robert, Thomas
1890-1899	John, William, James, George, Charles, Joseph, Frank, Robert, Edward, Henry
1900-1909	John, William, James, George, Charles, Robert, Joseph, Frank, Edward, Thomas
1910-1919	John, William, James, Robert, Joseph, George, Charles, Edward, Frank, Thomas
1920-1929	Robert, John, James, William, Charles, George, Joseph, Richard, Edward, Donald
1930-1939	Robert, James, John, William, Richard, Charles, Donald, George, Thomas, Joseph
1940-1949	James, Robert, John, William, Richard, David, Charles, Thomas, Michael, Ronald
1950-1959	Michael, David, James, John, Robert, Mark, William, Richard, Thomas, Jeffrey
1960-1969	Michael, David, John, James, Robert, Mark, William, Richard, Thomas, Jeffrey
1970-1979	Michael, Christopher, Jason, David, James, John, Robert, Brian, William, Matthew
1980-1989	Michael, Christopher, Matthew, Joshua, David, James, Daniel, Robert, John, Joseph
1990-1999	Michael, Christopher, Matthew, Joshua, Jacob, Nicholas, Andrew, Daniel, Tyler, Joseph
2000-2009	Jacob, Michael, Joshua, Matthew, Daniel, Christopher, Andrew, Ethan, Joseph, William
2017	Liam, Noah, William, James, Logan, Benjamin, Mason, Elijah, Oliver, Jacob

GIRLS

1880-1889	Mary, Anna, Emma, Elizabeth, Margaret, Minnie, Ida, Bertha, Clara, Alice
1890-1899	Mary, Anna, Margaret, Helen, Elizabeth, Ruth, Florence, Ethel, Emma, Marie
1900-1909	Mary, Helen, Margaret, Anna, Ruth, Elizabeth, Dorothy, Marie, Florence, Mildred
1910-1919	Mary, Helen, Dorothy, Margaret, Ruth, Mildred, Anna, Elizabeth, Frances, Virginia
1920-1929	Mary, Dorothy, Helen, Betty, Margaret, Ruth, Virginia, Doris, Mildred, Frances
1930-1939	Mary, Betty, Barbara, Shirley, Patricia, Dorothy, Joan, Margaret, Nancy, Helen
1940-1949	Mary, Linda, Barbara, Patricia, Carol, Sandra, Nancy, Sharon, Judith, Susan
1950-1959	Mary, Linda, Patricia, Susan, Deborah, Barbara, Debra, Karen, Nancy, Donna
1960-1969	Lisa, Mary, Susan, Karen, Kimberly, Patricia, Linda, Donna, Michelle, Cynthia
1970-1979	Jennifer, Amy, Melissa, Michelle, Kimberly, Lisa, Angela, Heather, Stephanie, Nicole
1980-1989	Jessica, Jennifer, Amanda, Ashley, Sarah, Stephanie, Melissa, Nicole, Elizabeth, Heather
1990-1999	Jessica, Ashley, Emily, Sarah, Samantha, Amanda, Brittany, Elizabeth, Taylor, Megan
2000-2009	Emily, Madison, Emma, Olivia, Hannah, Abigail, Isabella, Samantha, Elizabeth, Ashley
2017	Emma, Olivia, Ava, Isabella, Sophia, Mia, Charlotte, Amelia, Evelyn, Abigail

Origins of Popular American Given Names

Source: World Almanac research

Some names listed here are commonly used for either sex and/or have variant spellings that are not shown.

Boys

Aiden: Gaelic *Aodhan*, "little fire," from name of Celtic sun god

Alexander: Gr. *Alexandros*, "defender of man"

Andrew: Gr. *andreios*, "manly"

Anthony: Roman *Antonius*, possibly from Gr. *anthos*, "flower"

Benjamin: Heb. *Binyamin*, "son of the right hand"

Brandon: Eng. place name, "gorse-covered hill"

Brian: Irish, perhaps Celtic *Brigonos*, "high" or "noble"

Charles: Ger. *ceorl*, "free man"

Christopher: Gr. *Christophoros*, "bearing Christ"

Daniel: Heb. "God is my judge"

David: Heb. *Dodavehu*, perhaps "darling"

Edward: Old Eng. *Eadweard*, "wealth-guard"

Elijah: Heb. "the Lord is my God"

Ethan: Heb. "solid, firm"

Francis, Frank: Late Lat. *Franciscus*, "Frenchman"

George: Gr. *georgos*, "soil tiller," "farmer"

Henry: Ger. *Haimric*, "home-power"

Jack: nickname for or variant of John

Jacob: Heb. *Yaakov*, "God protects" or "supplanter"

James: Late Lat. *Iacomus*, form of Jacob

Jason: Gr. *Iason*, "healer"

Jayden: prob. from Jay (short form for many *J* names) and Hayden (Old Eng. "little hollow")

Jeffrey: Norman Fr., from Ger. *Gaufrid*, "land-peace," or *Gisfrid*, "pledge-peace"

John: Heb. *Yohanan*, "God is gracious"

Jonathan: Heb. "God has given"

José: Heb. and Aramaic *Yose*, variant of Joseph

Joseph: Heb. *Yosef*, "[God] shall add"

Joshua: Heb. *Yoshua*, "God saves"

Liam: Gaelic form of William

Logan: Scot. "little hollow"

Mark: Lat. *Marcus*, perhaps from Mars, Roman god of war

Mason: Fr. "stone worker," related to Old Eng. "work"

Matthew: Heb. *Mattathia*, "gift of God"

Michael: Heb. "who could ever be like God?"

Nathan: Heb. "God has given"; modern short form of Nathaniel or Jonathan

Nicholas: Gr. *Nikolaos*, "victory-people"

Noah: Heb. "rest"

Patrick: Lat. *Patricius*, "of noble origin"

Richard: Ger. "power-hardy"

Robert: Ger. *Hrodberht*, "fame-bright"

Ryan: prob. from Irish surname, Gaelic "king"

Samuel: Heb. *Shemuel*, "God heard"

Sean: Gaelic form of John

Steven: Gr. *stephanos*, "crown" or "garland"

Thomas: Aramaic "twin"

Tyler: Old Eng. *tigeler*, "tile layer"

William: Ger. *Wilhelm*, "will-helmet"

Girls

Abigail: Heb. "my father is joy"

Alexis: Gr. "helper" or "defender"

Alyssa: variant of Alicia (Eng., Sp.) or Alice (Eng., Fr.); may mean "noble"

Amanda: 17th-cent. invention from Lat. "lovable"

Amelia: Ger. "hard-working," or from Lat. *aemulus*, "striving"

Amy: Old Fr. *Amee*, "beloved"

Andrea: fem. form of Andrew

Angela: Gr. *angelos*, "messenger [of God]"

Anna: Lat., Gr. form of Hannah; variants include Ann (Eng.), Ana (Sp.), Anne (Eng., Fr., Ger.)

Ashley: Eng. place name, "ash grove"

Ava: prob. modern form of Eva, Lat. form of Heb. *Eve*

Barbara: Gr. *barbarus*, "foreign"

Carol, Charlotte: fem. forms of Charles

Chloe: Gr. "young shoot," "blooming"

Claire, Clara: Lat. *clarus*, "famous"

Deborah: Heb. "bee"

Dorothy: Gr. *Dorothea*, "gift of God"

Elizabeth: Heb. *Elisheba*, "God is my oath" or "God is good fortune"

Ella: prob. variant or nickname for Ellen, variant of Helen, or Eleanor

Emily: prob. derived from Amelia

Emma: Ger. *ermen*, "whole" or "entire"

Eve, Evelyn: Heb. "life-giving"

Grace: Lat. *gratia*, "grace," "blessing"

Hailey: Eng. place name, "hay clearing"

Hannah: Heb. "He [God] has favored me"

Harper: Old Eng. "harp player"

Heather: Middle Eng. *hathir*, "heather"

Isabella, Isabel: Lat., Sp. variant of Elizabeth

Jennifer: Cornish form of Welsh *Gwenhwyfar*, "fair-smooth"

Jessica: Shakesp. invention, prob. fem. form of *Jesse*, Heb. "God exists"

Judith: Heb. "Jewish woman"

Julia: fem. form of Julius, Roman family name, or Lat. "youthful"

Kaitlyn: American spelling of Caitlin, the Irish form of Katherine

Karen: Danish form of Katherine

Katherine: Egyptian *Aikaterine*, later modified to resemble Gr. *katharos*, "pure"

Kelly: Irish Gaelic *Ceallagh*, perhaps "churchgoer" or "bright-headed"

Kimberly: Eng. place name, "Cyneburgh's clearing"

Laura: Lat. *laurus*, "laurel"

Lily: for the flower, symbol of purity

Linda: Sp. "pretty" or Ger. "tender"

Lisa: nickname for Elizabeth

Madison: Middle Eng. surname, "son of Madeline or Maud"

Margaret: Gr. *margaron*, "pearl"

Maria, Marie, Mary: Lat., Fr., Eng. forms for Heb. *Maryam*, perhaps "seeress" or "wished-for child"

Megan: Welsh form of Margaret

Melissa: Gr. "bee"

Mia: Nordic or Ital., short for Maria, etc.

Michelle: Fr. fem. form of Michael

Nancy: medieval Eng. nickname for Agnes (Gr. *hagnos*, "holy"), later also for Ann

Natalie: Fr., from Lat. *natalia*, "birthday [of Christ]"

Nicole: Fr. fem. form of Nicholas

Olivia: Lat. *oliva*, "olive tree"

Patricia: Lat. fem. form of Patrick

Rachel: Heb. "ewe"

Rose, Rosa: for the flower, suggesting beauty

Ruth: Heb., perhaps "companion"

Samantha: colonial American invention, prob. combining Sam from Samuel with *-antha* from Gr. *anthos*, "flower"

Sarah: Heb. "princess"

Sharon: Biblical place name, Heb. "plain"

Sofia, Sophia: Gr. "wisdom"

Stephanie: Fr. fem. form of Steven

Susan: Eng. form of Heb. *Shoshana*, "lily"

Teresa: Sp., perhaps "woman from Therasia"

Victoria: Lat. *victoria*, "victory"

Words and Expressions in Common Languages

English	Arabic	Chinese[1]	French	German	Hebrew	Russian	Spanish
Hello/hi	Salam	Ni hao	Bonjour	Hallo	Shalom	Privet (informal)	Hola
Good morning	Sabah el kheer	Zao shang hao	Bonjour	Guten Morgen	Boker tov	Dobraye utra	Buenos días
Good night	Tosbeho 'ala khair	Wan an	Bonne nuit	Gute Nacht	Layla tov	Spakoynay noci	Buenas noches
Goodbye	Ma'a salama	Zai jian	Au revoir	Auf wiedersehen	Lehitraot	Da svidan'ya	Adiós
Please	Men fadlek	Qing	S'il vous plaît	Bitte	Bevakasha	Pazhalusta	Por favor
Thank you very much	Shokran jazeelan	Xie xie	Merci beaucoup	Danke schön	Toda raba	Spasiba	Muchas gracias
You're welcome	Al' afw	Huan ying	De rien/pas de quoi	Bitte schön	Bevakasha	Pazhalusta	De nada
How are you?	Kaifa haloka?	Ni hao?	Comment allez-vous?	Wie geht's dir/Ihnen?	Ma shelomkha?	Kak dela?	Cómo estás?
I'm fine	Ana bekhair	Hen hao	Je vais bien	Mir geht's gut	Tov	Harasho	Estoy bien
I'm sorry	Aasef	Bao qian	Je suis désolé	Entschuldigung	Ani mamash mitstaer	Prastite	Lo siento
Excuse me	Alma'derah	Bao qian	Pardon	Darf ich mal vorbei?	Selikha	Izvinite	Perdone
yes	na'am	shi [it is so]	oui	ja	ken	da	si
no	laa	bu [not]	non	nein	lo	nyet	no
one	wahed	yi	un	eins	ekhad	adin	uno
two	ithnaan	er	deux	zwei	shenayim	dva	dos
three	thalatha	san	trois	drei	shelosha	tri	tres
four	arba'a	si	quatre	vier	arbaa	chityri	cuatro
five	khamsa	wu	cinq	fünf	khamisha	p'at	cinco

Note: Actual form or usage of some words and expressions may vary depending on dialect, grammar, or circumstances. Transliterations for languages not in Latin alphabet vary. (1) Mandarin.

Principal Languages of the World

Source: Used by permission. © 2018 SIL International, from *Ethnologue: Languages of the World, 20th Edition*

Languages shown in italics are macrolanguages, or language groups that are equivalent in some ways to individual languages. Each language group consists of a number of variants, which may be mutually unintelligible; these variants, when they have 2.5 mil speakers or more, will also appear in the larger table below, and occasionally have the same name as the macrolanguage. Numbers are estimates and count only speakers for whom the language is a first language, or mother tongue.

Languages Spoken by the Most People

Language	Speakers (mil)	Language	Speakers (mil)	Language	Speakers (mil)
Chinese[1]	1,298.6	Japanese	128.2	Marathi	71.8
Spanish	442.4	*Lahnda*[2]	118.9	Vietnamese	68.0
English	378.3	Javanese	84.4	Tamil	66.7
Arabic	315.3	Turkish	78.5	Urdu	69.2
Hindi	260.0	Korean	77.2	Italian	64.8
Bengali	242.7	French	76.8	*Persian*	61.5
Portuguese	222.7	German, Standard	76.0	*Malay*	60.7
Russian	153.9	Telugu	74.8		

(1) Mandarin (908.8 mil speakers), Wu (80.7 mil), and Yue (73.4 mil) are included here under Chinese; not listed separately. (2) Includes Punjabi (Western), which by itself has 92.7 mil speakers.

Languages With at Least 2.5 Million Speakers

Primary country is country of origin, not necessarily the country where the most speakers reside (e.g., Portugal is the primary country for Portuguese, but more Portuguese speakers live in Brazil). Number of speakers is worldwide total for each language.

Primary country	Language	Countries	Population (mil)	Primary country	Language	Countries	Population (mil)
Afghanistan	Pashto, Southern	4	10.9	Ethiopia	Amharic	2	21.9
	Dari	3	9.0		*Oromo*	3	17.5
	Uzbek, Southern	2	4.2		Oromo, West Central	1	8.9
Albania	*Albanian*	19	4.1		Tigrigna	3	7.5
Algeria	Arabic, Algerian Spoken	2	29.4		Oromo, Eastern	1	4.5
	Kabyle	1	5.6		Oromo, Borana-Arsi-Guji	3	3.9
Angola	Umbundu	1	6.0		Sidamo	1	3.0
Armenia	Armenian	5	3.8	Finland	Finnish	4	5.5
Austria	Bavarian	4	14.4	France	French	53	76.8
Azerbaijan	Azerbaijani, North	4	9.2	Georgia	Georgian	3	3.7
Bangladesh	Bengali	4	242.7	Germany	German, Standard	28	76.0
	Rangpuri	2	15.0	Ghana	Akan	1	8.2
	Chittagonian	1	13.0		Ghanaian Pidgin English	1	5.0
	Sylheti	2	10.3		Éwé	2	4.2
Belarus	Belarusian	4	2.6	Greece	Greek	9	13.1
Bosnia and				Guinea	*Mandingo*	7	7.4
Herzegovina	Bosnian	5	2.6		Pular	5	3.8
Botswana	Setswana	4	5.8		Maninkakan, Eastern	3	3.6
Brazil	Hunsrik	1	3.0	Haiti	Haitian Creole	2	7.6
Bulgaria	Bulgarian	8	8.0	Hungary	Hungarian	9	12.6
Burkina Faso	Mòoré	3	6.5	India	Hindi	4	260.0
Burundi	Rundi	1	10.8		Telugu	2	74.8
Cambodia	Khmer	2	16.4		Marathi	1	71.8
China	*Chinese*	38	1,298.6		Tamil	7	66.7
	Chinese, Mandarin	13	908.8		Gujarati	7	46.9
	Chinese, Wu	1	80.7		Bhojpuri	3	39.4
	Chinese, Yue	13	73.4		Kannada	1	37.8
	Chinese, Min Nan	11	49.8		Malayalam	2	35.2
	Chinese, Hakka	13	48.2		Maithili	2	33.9
	Chinese, Jinyu	1	46.5		*Oriya*	5	32.7
	Chinese, Xiang	1	36.9		Odia	1	32.1
	Chinese, Gan	1	21.9		Punjabi, Eastern	3	29.5
	Zhuang	2	14.9		*Marwari*	3	19.7
	Chinese, Min Bei	2	10.9		Magahi	1	14.0
	Uyghur	4	10.4		Chhattisgarhi	1	13.3
	Chinese, Min Dong	6	9.1		*Rajasthani*	3	12.9
	Chinese, Huizhou	1	4.6		Assamese	1	12.8
	Mongolian, Peripheral	2	3.4		Deccan	1	12.8
	Chinese, Min Zhong	1	3.1		Kanauji	1	9.5
	Bouyei	3	2.7		Haryanvi	1	8.0
	Chinese, Pu-Xian	3	2.6		Varhadi-Nagpuri	1	7.0
Congo, Dem. Rep.					Santhali	3	6.2
of the	Luba-Kasai	2	6.4		*Konkani*	3	6.1
	Kongo	3	5.7		Marwari	2	5.6
	Koongo	3	5.0		Malvi	1	5.6
	Kituba	1	4.2		Kashmiri	2	5.5
Côte d'Ivoire	Baoulé	1	3.5		Mewari	1	5.1
Croatia	Croatian	8	5.4		Lambadi	1	4.2
Czechia	Czech	7	10.7		Indian Sign Language	2	4.1
Denmark	Danish	5	5.6		Merwari	1	3.9
Egypt	Arabic, Egyptian Spoken	1	64.4		Mina	1	3.8
	Arabic, Sa'idi Spoken	1	22.4		Konkani, Goan	2	3.6

Primary country	Language	Countries	Population (mil)
India (cont.)	Bhili	1	3.3
	Sadri	2	3.3
	Bundeli	1	3.1
	Awadhi	2	3.0
	Shekhawati	1	3.0
	Godwari	1	3.0
	Garhwali	1	2.9
	Bagheli	1	2.9
	Wagdi	1	2.5
	Haroti	1	2.5
Indonesia	Javanese	3	84.4
	Sunda	1	34.0
	Indonesian	1	23.1
	Madura	2	6.8
	Minangkabau	1	5.5
	Bugis	2	5.0
	Betawi	1	5.0
	Banjar	2	3.5
	Aceh	1	3.5
	Bali	1	3.3
	Musi	1	3.1
Iran	*Persian*	29	61.5
	Persian, Iranian	7	52.5
	Azerbaijani	17	23.1
	Azerbaijani, South	5	13.8
	Kurdish, Southern	2	3.0
Iraq	*Kurdish*	28	25.0
	Arabic, Mesopotamian Spoken	4	15.6
	Arabic, North Mesopotamian Spoken	4	8.7
	Kurdish, Central	2	7.3
Israel	Hebrew	1	5.3
Italy	Italian	14	64.8
	Venetian	5	7.9
	Napoletano-Calabrese	1	5.7
	Sicilian	1	4.7
	Lombard	2	3.9
Jamaica	Jamaican Creole English	3	3.0
Japan	Japanese	2	128.2
Jordan	Arabic, South Levantine Spoken	4	11.5
Kazakhstan	Kazakh	6	12.8
Kenya	Gikuyu	1	6.6
	Oluluyia	3	5.3
	Kalenjin	3	4.9
	Dholuo	2	4.2
	Kamba	2	3.9
Korea, South	Korean	6	77.2
Kuwait	Arabic, Gulf Spoken	10	8.8
Kyrgyzstan	Kyrgyz	5	4.9
Laos	Lao	3	3.6
Lesotho	Sotho, Southern	2	6.0
Libya	Arabic, Libyan Spoken	3	4.8
Lithuania	Lithuanian	2	3.0
Madagascar	*Malagasy*	5	18.1
	Malagasy, Plateau	2	7.5
Malawi	Chichewa	5	9.7
	Yao	4	2.6
Malaysia	*Malay*	18	60.7
	Malay	3	16.1
	Malay, Kedah	2	2.6
Mali	Bamanankan	2	4.1
Mauritania	Hassaniyya	7	8.8
Mongolia	*Mongolian*	8	6.0
	Mongolian, Halh	2	2.6
Morocco	Arabic, Moroccan Spoken	3	27.5
	Tachelhit	2	7.1
	Tamazight, Central Atlas	1	4.7
	Tarifit	2	4.4
Mozambique	Makhuwa	1	3.6
Myanmar (Burma)	Burmese	1	32.9
	Shan	3	3.3
	Rohingya	2	2.5
Nepal	*Nepali*	9	16.2
	Nepali	3	15.5
Netherlands	Dutch	7	23.0
Niger	Zarma	4	3.7
Nigeria	Hausa	9	43.7
	Yoruba	2	37.7
	Igbo	1	27.0

Primary country	Language	Countries	Population (mil)
Nigeria (cont.)	Fulfulde, Nigerian	3	14.5
	Kanuri	6	7.9
	Kanuri, Central	5	7.3
	Ibibio	1	5.5
	Tiv	2	4.0
	Anaang	1	2.6
Norway	Norwegian	1	5.2
Pakistan	*Lahnda*	6	118.9
	Punjabi, Western	2	92.7
	Urdu	7	69.2
	Pushto	10	38.1
	Sindhi	3	24.5
	Pashto, Northern	3	20.8
	Saraiki	2	20.1
	Baluchi	9	8.7
	Pashto, Central	1	6.5
	Balochi, Southern	4	3.6
	Pahari-Potwari	2	3.5
	Balochi, Eastern	2	3.1
Peru	*Quechua*	6	7.7
Philippines	Tagalog	3	23.4
	Cebuano	1	15.9
	Ilocano	1	6.5
	Hiligaynon	1	6.2
	Waray-Waray	1	2.6
Poland	Polish	10	39.6
Portugal	Portuguese	15	222.7
Romania	Romanian	6	23.4
Russia	Russian	18	153.9
	Tatar	4	5.0
Rwanda	Kinyarwanda	3	12.1
Saudi Arabia	*Arabic*	58	315.3
	Arabic, Hijazi Spoken	3	14.5
	Arabic, Najdi Spoken	4	4.0
Senegal	*Fulah*	20	27.8
	Wolof	2	5.3
	Pulaar	6	4.5
Serbia	*Serbo-Croatian*	25	16.7
	Serbian	10	8.6
Slovakia	Slovak	8	5.2
Somalia	Somali	4	16.1
South Africa	Zulu	5	11.8
	Xhosa	2	8.2
	Afrikaans	6	7.2
	Tsonga	4	5.5
	Sotho, Northern	1	4.6
Spain	Spanish	31	442.4
	Catalan	4	4.1
Sri Lanka	Sinhala	2	15.2
Sudan	Arabic, Sudanese Spoken	3	31.9
	Bedawiyet	3	3.4
Sweden	Swedish	3	9.6
Switzerland	German, Swiss	5	5.7
Syria	Arabic, North Levantine Spoken	5	24.2
Tajikistan	Tajik	4	7.9
Tanzania	*Swahili*	17	16.0
	Swahili	8	16.0
	Sukuma	1	8.1
Thailand	Thai	2	20.6
	Thai, Northeastern	1	15.0
	Thai, Northern	2	6.0
	Thai, Southern	1	4.5
Tunisia	Arabic, Tunisian Spoken	1	11.6
Turkey	Turkish	8	78.5
	Kurdish, Northern	9	14.8
Turkmenistan	Turkmen	7	6.7
Uganda	Ganda	1	5.6
	Nyankore	1	3.4
	Soga	1	3.0
	Teso	2	2.7
Ukraine	Ukrainian	10	27.1
United Kingdom	English	118	378.3
	Uzbek	14	29.3
	Uzbek, Northern	6	25.2
Vietnam	Vietnamese	3	68.0
Yemen	Arabic, Sanaani Spoken	1	11.4
	Arabic, Ta'izzi-Adeni Spoken	2	10.5
	Arabic, Hadrami Spoken	1	4.6
Zambia	Bemba	2	4.1
Zimbabwe	Shona	3	7.2

BUILDINGS, BRIDGES, AND TUNNELS

100 Tallest Buildings in the World

Source: Phorio, phorio.com; Council on Tall Buildings and Urban Habitat (CTBUH), www.ctbuh.org

Only buildings that are completed or under construction and topped out as of Oct. 2018, are shown here. Structures under construction and topped out architecturally are denoted by an asterisk (*). Year in parentheses is date of completion or projected completion. Height is generally measured from the lowest significant open-air pedestrian entrance to the architectural top, including spires and other decorative features that are an integral part of the design, but not including flagpoles and antennae. Stories generally counted from street level. NA = Not available.

Building	Ht. (ft)	Stories
Burj Khalifa, Dubai, United Arab Emirates (2010)	2,717	163
Shanghai Tower, Shanghai, China (2015)	2,074	128
Makkah Royal Clock Tower Hotel, Mecca, Saudi Arabia (2013)	1,972	120
Ping An Finance Center, Shenzhen, China (2016)	1,965	115
*Goldin Finance 117, Tianjin, China (NA)	1,957	128
Lotte World Tower, Seoul, South Korea (2017)	1,819	123
One World Trade Center, New York, NY, U.S. (2014)	1,782	94
CTF Finance Centre, Guangzhou, China (2016)	1,739	111
*Chow Tai Fook Binhai Center, Tianjin, China (2020)	1,739	97
*Citic Tower, Beijing, China (2018)	1,732	108
Taipei 101, Taipei, Taiwan (2004)	1,667	101
Shanghai World Financial Center, Shanghai, China (2008)	1,614	101
International Commerce Centre, Hong Kong, China (2010)	1,588	108
*Lakhta Center, St. Petersburg, Russia (2019)	1,517	86
Vincom Landmark 81, Ho Chi Minh City, Vietnam (2018)	1,513	81
Changsha IFS Tower T1, Changsha, China (2018)	1,483	94
Petronas Tower I, Kuala Lumpur, Malaysia (1998)	1,483	88
Petronas Tower II, Kuala Lumpur, Malaysia (1998)	1,483	88
*Suzhou IFS, Suzhou, China (2019)	1,476	98
Zifeng Tower, Nanjing, China (2010)	1,476	66
*The Exchange 106, Kuala Lumpur, Malaysia (2019)	1,461	96
Willis (formerly Sears) Twr., Chicago, IL, U.S. (1974)	1,451	108
KK100, Shenzhen, China (2011)	1,449	100
Guangzhou International Finance Center, Guangzhou, China (2010)	1,439	103
Wuhan Center, Wuhan, China (2018)	1,437	88
432 Park Avenue, New York, NY, U.S. (2015)	1,397	85
Marina 101, Dubai, UAE (2017)	1,394	101
Trump Intl. Hotel & Tower, Chicago, IL, U.S. (2009)	1,389	98
Jin Mao Tower, Shanghai, China (1999)	1,380	88
Princess Tower, Dubai, UAE (2012)	1,356	101
Al Hamra Tower, Kuwait City, Kuwait (2011)	1,354	80
Two International Finance Centre, Hong Kong, China (2003)	1,352	88
*LCT Landmark Tower, Busan, South Korea (2020)	1,350	101
*China Resources Tower, Nanning, China (2019)	1,321	85
China Resources Headquarters, Shenzhen, China (2018)	1,288	66
23 Marina, Dubai, UAE (2012)	1,287	88
CITIC Plaza, Guangzhou, China (1997)	1,280	80
*Sum Yip Upperhills Twr. 1, Shenzhen, China (2019)	1,273	80
*30 Hudson Yards, New York, NY (2019)	1,268	73
*Capital Market Authority Headquarters, Riyadh, Saudi Arabia (2019)	1,260	76
Shun Hing Square, Shenzhen, China (1996)	1,260	69
Eton Place Dalian Tower 1, Dalian, China (2016)	1,257	80
*Logan Century Center 1, Nanning, China (2018)	1,251	82
Burj Mohammed Bin Rashid Tower, Abu Dhabi, UAE (2014)	1,251	88
Empire State Building, New York, NY, U.S. (1931)	1,250	102
Elite Residence, Dubai, UAE (2012)	1,248	87
Central Plaza, Hong Kong, China (1992)	1,227	78
Vostok, Moscow, Russia (2017)	1,226	93
*Dalian Intl. Trade Center, Dalian, China (2019)	1,214	86
*Golden Eagle Tiandi Tower A, Nanjing, China (2019)	1,207	76
Address Boulevard, Dubai, UAE (2017)	1,207	72
Bank of China Tower, Hong Kong, China (1989)	1,205	72
Bank of America Tower, New York, NY, U.S. (2009)	1,200	55
Almas Tower, Dubai, UAE (2008)	1,181	68

Building	Ht. (ft)	Stories
GevoraTower, Dubai, UAE (2017)	1,169	76
JW Marriott Marquis Hotel Dubai Tower 2, Dubai, UAE (2013)	1,166	82
JW Marriott Marquis Hotel Dubai Tower 1, Dubai, UAE (2012)	1,166	82
*Chongqing Raffles City T4N, Chongqing, China (2019)	1,163	81
*Chongqing Raffles City T3N, Chongqing, China (2019)	1,163	81
Emirates Office Tower, Dubai, UAE (2000)	1,163	54
OKO South Tower, Moscow, Russia (2015)	1,160	90
The Torch, Dubai, UAE (2011)	1,155	86
Forum 66 Tower 1, Shenyang, China (2015)	1,150	67
The Pinnacle, Guangzhou, China (2012)	1,149	60
*IFC, Xi'an, China (2019)	1,148	75
Hanking Center, Shenzhen, China (2018)	1,148	65
Tuntex Sky Tower, Kaohsiung, Taiwan (1998)	1,140	85
*Shimao Hunan Center, Changsha, China (2019)	1,138	76
Aon Center, Chicago, IL, U.S. (1973)	1,136	83
The Center, Hong Kong, China (1998)	1,135	73
*Neva Towers 2, Moscow, Russia (2020)	1,132	79
*Xiamen Cross-Strait Financial Centre, Xiamen, China (2018)	1,128	68
875 N. Michigan Ave. (fmr. John Hancock Center), Chicago, IL, U.S. (1969)	1,128	100
Four Seasons Place, Kuala Lumpur, Malay. (2018)	1,124	65
ADNOC Headquarters, Abu Dhabi, UAE (2015)	1,122	65
Comcast Technology Ctr., Phila., PA, U.S. (2018)	1,121	59
*Suning Plaza Tower 1, Zhenjiang, China (2018)	1,120	77
One Shenzhen Bay Tower 7, Shenzhen, China (2018)	1,120	71
*LCT Residential Twr. A, Busan, South Korea (2020)	1,113	85
Chongqing World Financial Center, Chongqing, China (2015)	1,112	72
Mercury City Tower, Moscow, Russia (2013)	1,112	75
Wuxi Intl. Finance Square, Wuxi, China (2014)	1,112	68
Tianjin Modern City Office Tower, Tianjin, China (2016)	1,109	65
Tianjin World Financial Center, Tianjin, China (2011)	1,105	75
*Hengqin IFC, Zhuhai, China (2020)	1,105	69
DAMAC Heights, Dubai, UAE (2018)	1,100	88
Wilshire Grand Center, L.A., CA, U.S. (2017)	1,100	62
*Twin Towers Guiyang East Tower, Guiyang, China (2018)	1,099	74
*Twin Towers Guiyang West Tower, Guiyang, China (2018)	1,099	74
*Shengjing Finance Plaza T2, Shenyang, China (2019)	1,097	68
Shanghai Shimao International Plaza, Shanghai, China (2006)	1,094	60
*LCT Residential Tower B, Busan, South Korea (2020)	1,093	85
Rose Rayhaan by Rotana, Dubai, UAE (2007)	1,093	71
*The Address Residence Fountain Views III, Dubai, UAE (2019)	1,087	77
Minsheng Bank Building, Wuhan, China (2008)	1,087	68
*Ryugyong Hotel, Pyongyang, North Korea (NA)	1,083	105
China World Tower, Beijing, China (2009)	1,083	74
Yuexiu Fortune Center Twr. 1, Wuhan, China (2017)	1,083	69
*Hon Kwok City Centre, Shenzhen, China (2017)	1,081	80
Hanoi Landmark Tower, Hanoi, Vietnam (2012)	1,079	72
Three World Trade Center, New York, NY, U.S. (2018)	1,079	69
Zhuhai St. Regis Hotel & Office Tower, Zhuhai, China (2017)	1,079	66

Tallest Free-Standing Towers in the World

Source: Phorio, phorio.com; Council on Tall Buildings and Urban Habitat (CTBUH), www.ctbuh.org
Year is date of completion or projected completion. As of Oct. 2018.

Tower	Ht. (ft)	Year
Tokyo Sky Tree, Tokyo, Japan	2,080	2012
Canton Tower, Guangzhou, China	1,969	2010
CN Tower, Toronto, ON, Canada	1,815	1976
Ostankino Tower, Moscow, Russia	1,772	1967
Oriental Pearl Television Tower, Shanghai, China	1,535	1995
Milad Tower, Tehran, Iran	1,427	2008
Manara Kuala Lumpur, Kuala Lumpur, Malaysia	1,379	1996
Tianjin Radio & TV Tower, Tianjin, China	1,362	1991
Central Radio & TV Tower, Beijing, China	1,347	1992
Henan Province Radio & Television Emission Tower, Zhengzhou, China	1,273	2010

Tower	Ht. (ft)	Year
Kiev TV Tower, Kiev, Ukraine	1,263	1974
Tashkent Tower, Tashkent, Uzbekistan	1,230	1985
Liberation Tower, Kuwait City, Kuwait	1,220	1996
Alma-Ata Tower, Almaty, Kazakhstan	1,217	1982
TV Tower, Riga, Latvia	1,208	1987
Berliner Fernsehturm, Berlin, Germany	1,207	1969
Camlica TV Tower, Istanbul, Turkey	1,199	2019
Stratosphere Tower, Las Vegas, NV, U.S.	1,149	1996
Lotus Tower, Colombo, Sri Lanka	1,148	2018
West Pearl Tower, Chengdu, China	1,112	2004
Macau Tower, Macau, China	1,109	2001

Tall Buildings in Selected North American Cities

Source: Phorio, phorio.com; Council on Tall Buildings and Urban Habitat (CTBUH), www.ctbuh.org

List includes freestanding towers and other structures that do not have stories and are not technically considered buildings. Structures still under construction as of Oct. 2018, are denoted by an asterisk (*). Year in parentheses is date of completion or projected completion. Height is generally measured from the lowest significant open-air pedestrian entrance to the architectural top, including penthouses, spires, and other decorative features that are an integral part of the design, but not including flagpoles and antennae. Stories generally counted from street level. NA = Not applicable/available.

Building/structure	Ht. (ft)	Stories
Atlanta, GA		
Bank of America Plaza (incl. spire), 600 Peachtree St. NE (1992)	1,023	55
SunTrust Plaza, 303 Peachtree St. NE (1993)[1]	867	60
One Atlantic Center, 1201 W. Peachtree St. (1987)	820	50
191 Peachtree Tower (1991)	770	50
Westin Peachtree Plaza, 210 Peachtree St. NW (1976)[2]	723	73
Georgia Pacific Tower, 133 Peachtree St. NE (1981)	697	51
Promenade II (incl. spire), 1230 Peachtree St. NE (1989)	691	40
AT&T Building, 675 W. Peachtree St. (1980)	677	47
Sovereign, 3344 Peachtree (2008)	665	48
1180 Peachtree (2006)	657	41
GLG Grand/Four Seasons Hotel, 75 14th St. NE (1992)	609	53
The Mansion on Peachtree, 3376 Peachtree Rd. NE (2008)	580	42
Atlantic, 270 17th St. NW (2009)	577	46
State of Georgia Building, 2 Peachtree St. NW (1967)[3]	556	44
Marriott Marquis, 265 Peachtree Center Ave. NE (1985)	554	52
Icon Midtown, 22 14th St. NW (2018)	515	39
Viewpoint, 855 Peachtree St. NE (2008)	501	36
(1) 902 ft incl. antenna. (2) 883 ft incl. antenna. (3) 599 ft incl. antenna.		
Austin, TX		
*The Independent, 301 West Ave. (2019)	688	58
Austonian, 200 Congress Ave. (2010)	683	56
Fairmont Austin (incl. spire), 101 Red River St. (2018)	595	36
360 Condominiums (incl. spire), 360 Nueces St. (2008)	581	45
Frost Bank Tower, 401 N. Congress Ave. (2004)	516	33
Baltimore, MD		
Transamerica Tower, 100 Light St. (1973)	529	40
Bank of America, 10 Light St. (1924)	509	37
414 Light St. (2018)	500	44
Boston, MA		
200 Clarendon (1976)	790	62
Prudential Tower, 800 Boylston St. (1964)[1]	750	52
*Four Seasons Hotel and Private Residences, One Dalton St. (2019)	746	61
Millennium Tower, 426 Washington St. (2016)	681	54
Federal Reserve Bldg., 600 Atlantic Ave. (1978)	604	32
BNY Mellon Center at One Boston Place, 201 Washington St. (1970)	602	41
One International Place, 100 Oliver St. (1987)	600	46
100 Federal St. (1971)	591	37
One Financial Center, 10 Dewey Sq. (1984)	590	46
111 Huntington Ave. (2002)	564	36
Two International Place (1993)	538	35
One Post Office Square (1981)	525	40
1 Federal St. (1975)	520	38
*One Congress Street Tower 1 (2020)	519	45
Exchange Place, 53 State St. (1984)	510	39
Sixty State St. (1977)	509	38
1 Beacon St. (1972)	507	36
State Street Financial Center (incl. spire), 1 Lincoln St. (2003)	503	36
28 State St. (1970)	500	40
(1) 920 ft incl. antenna.		
Burnaby, BC, Canada		
Solo District-Altus (2017)	616	49
*Brentwood Two (2019)	611	53
*Brentwood One (2018)	611	53
*Brentwood Three (2020)	597	55
*6000 McKay (2021)	564	52
*4670 Assembly Way (2018)	535	57
Sovereign, 4509 Kingsway (2014)	511	45
Calgary, AB, Canada		
Brookfield Place Tower One, 225 6th Ave. (2017)	810	56
The Bow, 510 Centre St. (2012)	779	57
*Telus Sky (2019)	729	59
Petro Canada Centre West Tower, 150 6th Ave. SW (1984)	705	53
Eighth Avenue Place East Tower, 8th Ave. and 5th St. SW (2011)	696	49
Bankers Hall West Tower, 888 3rd St. SW (2000)	645	50
Bankers Hall East Tower, 855 2nd St. SW (1989)	645	50
Calgary Tower, 101 9th Ave. SW (1967)	626	NA
Centennial Place 1 (incl. spire), 520 3rd Ave. SW (2010)	599	40
TransCanada Tower, 450 1st St. SW (2001)	581	38

Building/structure	Ht. (ft)	Stories
Canterra Tower, 400 3rd Ave. SW (1988)	580	46
Eighth Avenue Place West Tower, 8th Ave. and 5th St. SW (2014)	580	40
Jamieson Place (incl. spires), 302 4th Ave. SW (2009)	568	38
First Canadian Centre, 350 7th Ave. SW (1982)	547	41
Western Canadian Place-North Tower, 707 6th St. SW (1983)	538	41
Canada Trust, Calgary Eatons Centre, 421 7th Ave. SW (1991)	530	40
CF Calgary City Centre I, 339 2nd Ave. SW (2016)	524	37
Scotia Centre, 700 2nd St. SW (1976)	509	42
Nexen Building, 801 7th Ave. SW (1982)	500	37
Charlotte, NC		
Bank of America Corporate Center, 100 N. Tryon St. (1992)	871	60
Duke Energy Center, 534 S. Tryon St. (2010)	786	48
Hearst Tower, 214 N. Tryon St. (2002)	659	47
*Legacy Union, 620 S. Tryon St. (2019)	632	33
One Wells Fargo Center, 301 S. College St. (1988)	588	42
The Vue, 400 W. 5th St. (2010)	574	50
Bank of America Plaza, 101 S. Tryon St. (1974)	503	40
Chicago, IL		
Willis (fmr. Sears) Tower, 233 S. Wacker Dr. (1974)[1]	1,451	108
Trump International Hotel & Tower (incl. spire), 401 N. Wabash Ave. (2009)	1,389	98
*Vista Tower, 381 E. Wacker Dr. (2020)	1,191	98
Aon Center, 200 E. Randolph St. (1973)	1,136	83
875 N. Michigan Ave. (fmr. John Hancock Center) (1969)[2]	1,128	100
Franklin Center-North Tower (incl. spires), 227 W. Monroe St. (1989)	1,007	60
Two Prudential Plaza (incl. spire), 180 N. Stetson Ave. (1990)	995	64
311 S. Wacker Dr. (1990)	961	65
*NEMA Chicago, 1200 S. Indiana Ave. (2019)	887	76
900 N. Michigan Ave. (1989)	871	66
Chase Tower, 21 S. Clark St. (1969)	868	60
Aqua at Lakeshore East, 225 N. Columbus Dr. (2009)	859	86
Water Tower Place, 845 N. Michigan Ave. (1976)	859	74
Park Tower, 800 N. Michigan Ave. (2000)	844	68
*One Bennett Park, 451 E. Grand Ave. (2018)	843	67
The Legacy at Millennium Park, 21-39 S. Wabash (2010)	818	73
*110 N. Wacker (2020)	800	52
300 N. LaSalle (2009)	785	60
3 First National Plaza, 70 W. Madison St. (1981)	767	57
Grant Thornton Tower, 161 N. Clark St. (1992)	756	50
Blue Cross HQ, 300 E. Randolph St. (2010)	744	54
River Point, 444 W. Lake St. (2017)	732	52
Olympia Centre, 737 N. Michigan Ave. (1986)	731	63
One Museum Park, 1215 S. Prairie Ave. (2009)	726	62
150 North Riverside (2017)	725	53
AMA Plaza, 330 N. Wabash Ave. (1973)	695	52
Waldorf Astoria Chicago, 940 N. Rush St. (2009)	686	60
111 S. Wacker Dr. (2005)	681	51
181 W. Madison St. (1990)	680	50
71 S. Wacker Dr. (2005)	679	48
One Magnificent Mile, 980 N. Michigan Ave. (1983)	673	57
340 on the Park, 340 E. Randolph St. (2007)	672	64
*Wolf Point East Tower (2020)	668	60
United Bldg., 77 W. Wacker Dr. (1992)	668	49
UBS Tower, 1 N. Wacker Dr. (2001)	652	50
Daley Center, 55 W. Washington St. (1965)	648	31
55 E. Erie St. (2004)	647	56
Lake Point Tower, 505 N. Lake Shore Dr. (1968)	645	70
River East Center, 350 E. Illinois St. (2001)	644	58
Grand Plaza I (incl. spire), 540 N. State St. (2003)	641	57
155 N. Wacker Dr. (2009)	638	45
Leo Burnett Bldg., 35 W. Wacker Dr. (1989)	635	46
The Heritage at Millennium Park, 125 N. Wabash Ave. (2005)	631	57
NBC Tower (incl. spire), 455 N. Cityfront Plaza Dr. (1989)	627	37
353 N. Clark (2009)	623	44
*Essex on the Park, 812 S. Michigan Ave. (2019)	620	57
OneEleven, 111 W. Wacker Dr. (2014)	616	58
Millennium Centre, 33 W. Ontario St. (2003)	610	58
Board of Trade (incl. statue), 141 W. Jackson Blvd. (1930)	609	44
Chicago Place, 700 N. Michigan Ave. (1991)	608	49
CNA Plaza, 325 S. Wabash St. (1972)	601	44
One Prudential Plaza, 130 E. Randolph St. (1955)[3]	601	41
Heller International Tower, 500 W. Monroe St. (1992)	600	45
One Madison Plaza, 200 W. Madison St. (1982)	599	44
The Grant, 201 E. Roosevelt Rd. (2010)	595	54

Building/structure	Ht. (ft)	Stories
1000 Lake Shore Plaza (1964)	590	55
The Clare at Water Tower, 55 E. Pearson St. (2008)	589	52
Marina City I, 300 N. State St. (1964)	588	61
Marina City II, 301 N. Dearborn St. (1964)	588	61
Citigroup Center, 500 W. Madison St. (1987)	588	42
Optima Signature, 220 E. Illinois St. (2017)	587	57
The Park Monroe, 65 E. Monroe St. (1972)	583	49
Crain Communications Bldg., 150 N. Michigan Ave. (1983)	582	41
North Pier Apts., 474 N. Lake Shore Dr. (1990)	581	61
Citadel Center, 131 S. Dearborn St. (2003)	580	39
The Fordham, 25 E. Superior St. (2003)	574	52
190 S. LaSalle St. (1987)	573	40
One South Dearborn (2005)	571	39
Onterie Center, 446 E. Ontario St. (1986)	570	58
Loews Chicago Hotel, 455 North Park Dr. (2015)	569	52
CNA Center, 151 N. Franklin St. (2018)	568	36
Chicago Temple, 77 W. Washington St. (1924)	568	23
Palmolive Building (incl. beacon), 919 N. Michigan Ave. (1929)	565	37
Kluczynski Federal Bldg., 230 S. Dearborn St. (1975)	562	42
Huron Plaza Apts., 30 E. Huron St. (1983)	560	56
Boeing International Headquarters, 100 N. Riverside Plz. (1990)	560	36
The Parkshore, 195 N. Harbor Dr. (1991)	556	56
North Harbor Tower, 175 N. Harbor Dr. (1988)	556	55
Civic Opera Bldg., 20 N. Wacker Dr. (1929)	555	45
Streeter Place, 351 E. Ohio St. (2009)	554	55
Harbor Point, 155 N. Harbor Dr. (1975)	554	54
Newberry Plaza, 1000 N. State St. (1974)	553	53
Michigan Plaza South, 205 N. Michigan Ave. (1985)	553	46
30 N. LaSalle St. (1975)	553	44
Pittsfield Building, 55 E. Washington St. (1927)	551	38
One S. Wacker Dr. (1982)	550	40
Park Millennium, 222 N. Columbus Dr. (2002)	544	57
AMLI River North, 401 N. Clark St. (2013)	543	49
Franklin Center-South Tower, 125 S. Franklin St. (1992)	538	35
The Pinnacle, 21 E. Huron St. (2004)	535	48
*465 North Park Drive (2018)	535	47
LaSalle National Bank, 135 S. LaSalle St. (1934)	535	45
Park Place Tower, 655 W. Irving Park Rd. (1971)	531	56
One N. LaSalle St. (1930)	530	48
The Elysees, 111 E. Chestnut St. (1973)	529	56

(1) 1,729 ft incl. antenna. (2) 1,499 ft incl. antenna. (3) 912 ft incl. antenna.

Cleveland, OH

Building/structure	Ht. (ft)	Stories
Key Tower (incl. spire), 127 Public Sq. (1991)	947	57
Terminal Tower, 50 Public Sq. (1928)[1]	708	52
200 Public Sq. (1985)	658	46
Tower at Erieview, 1301 E. 9th St. (1964)	529	40

(1) 771 ft incl. flagpole.

Columbus, OH

Building/structure	Ht. (ft)	Stories
James A. Rhodes State Office Tower, 30 E. Broad St. (1973)	624	41
Leveque-Lincoln Tower, 50 W. Broad St. (1927)	555	47
William Green Building, 30 W. Spring St. (1990)	530	33
Huntington Center, 41 S. High St. (1983)	512	37
Vern Riffe State Office Tower, 77 S. High St. (1988)	503	33

Dallas, TX

Building/structure	Ht. (ft)	Stories
Bank of America Plaza, 901 Main St. (1985)	921	72
Renaissance Tower (incl. spire), 1201 Elm St. (1974)	886	56
Comerica Bank Tower, 1717 Main St. (1987)	787	60
JPMorgan Chase Tower, 2200 Ross Ave. (1987)	738	55
Fountain Place, 1445 Ross Ave. (1986)	720	58
Trammel Crow Center, 2001 Ross Ave. (1984)	686	50
1700 Pacific Ave. (1983)	655	50
Thanksgiving Tower, 1600 Pacific Ave. (1982)	645	50
Energy Plaza, 1601 Bryan St. (1983)	629	49
Elm Place, 1401 Elm St. (1965)	628	52
Gables Republic Tower (incl. spire), 300 N. Ervay (1954)	602	36
Republic Center Tower II, 325 N. St. Paul (1964)	598	50
One AT&T Plaza, 208 S. Akard St. (1984)	580	37
Ross Tower, 500 N. Akard St. (1984)	579	45
Museum Tower, 2112 Flora St. (2013)	560	42
Cityplace Center East, 2711 N. Haskell Ave. (1989)	560	42
Reunion Tower, 300 Reunion Blvd. (1976)	560	NA
Sheraton Dallas Hotel Center Tower, 400 Olive St. (1959)	550	42
Mercantile Bldg. (incl. spire), 1700 Main St. (1943)	523	31
Bryan Tower, 2001 Bryan St. (1973)	512	40

Denver, CO

Building/structure	Ht. (ft)	Stories
Republic Plaza, 330 17th St. (1984)	714	56
1801 California St. (1982)	709	52
Wells Fargo Center, 1700 Lincoln Ave. (1983)	698	50
Four Seasons Hotel and Private Residences, 1111 14th St. (2010)	639	45
1144 Fifteenth (2018)	617	40
1999 Broadway (1985)	544	43
707 17th St. (1981)	522	42
555 17th St. (1978)	507	40

Detroit, MI

Building/structure	Ht. (ft)	Stories
*Hudson's Tower, 1246 Woodward Ave. (2022)	800	58
Marriott Hotel, Renaissance Center I (1977)[1]	727	70
One Detroit Center, 500 Woodward Ave. (1991)	619	43
Penobscot Building, 633 Griswold Ave. (1928)[2]	565	47
Renaissance Center 100 Tower (1976)	508	39
Renaissance Center 200 Tower (1976)	508	39
Renaissance Center 300 Tower (1976)	508	39
Renaissance Center 400 Tower (1976)	508	39

(1) 755 ft incl. antenna. (2) 665 ft incl. antenna.

Fort Worth, TX

Building/structure	Ht. (ft)	Stories
Burnett Plaza, 801 Cherry St. (1983)	567	40
D.R. Horton Tower, 301 Commerce St. (1984)	547	38
Carter Burgess Plaza, 777 Main St. (1982)	525	40

Hartford, CT

Building/structure	Ht. (ft)	Stories
City Place I, 185 Asylum St. (1980)	535	38
Travelers Tower, 26 Grove St. (1919)	527	24
Goodwin Square, 225 Asylum St. (1990)	522	30

Houston, TX

Building/structure	Ht. (ft)	Stories
JPMorganChase Tower, 600 Travis St. (1982)	1,002	75
Wells Fargo Plaza, 1000 Louisiana St. (1983)	992	71
Williams Tower, 2800 Post Oak Blvd. (1982)	901	64
Bank of America Center, 700 Louisiana St. (1983)	780	56
Texaco Heritage Plaza, 1111 Bagby St. (1987)	762	53
Enterprise Plaza, 1100 Louisiana St. (1980)[1]	756	55
609 Main at Texas (2017)	755	48
Centerpoint Energy Plaza, 1111 Louisiana St. (1996)	741	53
1600 Smith St. (1984)	732	55
Fulbright Tower, 1301 McKinney St. (1982)	725	52
One Shell Plaza, 900 Louisiana St. (1970)[2]	714	50
1400 Smith St. (1983)	691	50
3 Allen Center, 333 Clay St. (1980)	685	50
LyondellBassell Tower, 1221 McKinney St. (1978)	678	47
First City Tower, 1001 Fannin St. (1984)	662	47
BG Group Place, 811 Main St. (2011)	632	46
San Felipe Plaza, 5847 San Felipe Blvd. (1984)	625	45
ExxonMobil Building, 800 Bell Ave. (1962)	606	44
1500 Louisiana St. (2002)	600	40
America General Center, 2929 Allen Pkwy. (1983)	590	42
Two Houston Center, 909 Fannin St. (1974)	579	40
*Capitol Tower, 800 Capitol St. (2018)	579	34
San Jacinto Monument, La Porte (1939)	570	NA
Marathon Oil Tower, 5555 San Felipe Blvd. (1983)	562	41
1415 Louisiana (1983)	550	44
KBR Tower, 601 Jefferson St. (1973)	550	40
Memorial Hermann Tower (incl. spires), 929 Gessner Rd. (2009)	542	35
2929 Weslayan (2015)	533	40
Pennzoil Place I, 700 Milam St. (1976)	523	36
Pennzoil Place II, 700 Louisiana St. (1976)	523	36
Devon Energy Center, 1200 Smith St. (1978)	521	36
RRI Energy Plaza, 1000 Main St. (2003)	518	36
Total Plaza, 1201 Louisiana St. (1971)	518	35
Methodist Outpatient Care Center (incl. spires), 6448 Fannin St. (2010)	512	26
The Huntington, 2121 Kirby Dr. (1982)	503	34
Market Square Tower, 777 Preston St. (2017)	502	40
El Paso Energy Building, 1010 Milam St. (1962)	502	33
One Park Place, 1500 McKinney St. (2009)	501	37

(1) 782 ft incl. antenna. (2) 999 ft incl. antenna.

Indianapolis, IN

Building/structure	Ht. (ft)	Stories
Salesforce Tower, 111 Monument Cir. (1990)[1]	701	49
One America Tower, 200 N. Illinois St. (1982)	533	38
One Indiana Square, 200 N. Delaware St. (1970)	504	36

(1) 811 ft incl. antenna.

Jersey City, NJ

Building/structure	Ht. (ft)	Stories
*99 Hudson St. (2019)	889	76
30 Hudson St. (2004)	781	42
URL Harborside Tower 1 (2016)	700	70
J3 (2016)	574	53
101 Hudson St. (1992)	548	42
Trump Plaza I, 88 Morgan St. (2008)	532	55
Newport Tower, 525 Washington Blvd. (1990)	531	37
*90 Columbus (2018)	529	50
70 Columbus (2015)	529	50
Exchange Place Center (incl. spire), 10 Exchange Pl. (1990)	516	32
Hudson Green East Tower, 77 Hudson St. (2009)	509	48
Hudson Green West Tower, 77 Hudson St. (2010)	501	48

Las Vegas, NV

Building/structure	Ht. (ft)	Stories
Stratosphere Tower, 2000 Las Vegas Blvd. S. (1996)	1,149	NA
*The Drew Las Vegas, 2755 Las Vegas Blvd. S. (2020)	735	63
*Resorts World Las Vegas Tower I (2020)	674	57
The Palazzo, 3339 Las Vegas Blvd. S. (2007)	642	53
Encore at Wynn Las Vegas, 3145 Las Vegas Blvd. S. (2008)	631	52
Trump International Hotel and Tower 1, 3128 Las Vegas Blvd. S. (2008)	622	64
Wynn Las Vegas, 3145 Las Vegas Blvd. S. (2005)	613	45

Building/structure	Ht. (ft)	Stories
Cosmopolitan Casino Spa Tower, Las Vegas Blvd. and Harmon Ave. (2010).	603	52
Cosmopolitan Beach Resort Tower, Las Vegas Blvd. and Harmon Ave. (2010).	603	50
Aria Resort and Casino (2009).	600	60
Planet Hollywood Towers, 3667 Las Vegas Blvd. S. (2009).	597	50
VDARA, 2551 W. Harmon Ave. (2009).	556	55
Eiffel Tower, Paris Hotel and Casino, 3645 Las Vegas Blvd. S. (1998).	540	NA
Mandarin Oriental Hotel Las Vegas, 3750 Las Vegas Blvd. S. (2009).	539	47
New York, New York Hotel and Casino, 3790 Las Vegas Blvd. S. (1997).	529	48
Palms Place, 4321 W. Flamingo Rd. (2008).	518	50
Bellagio Hotel and Casino, 3600 Las Vegas Blvd. S. (1998).	508	36
Sky Las Vegas, 2780 Las Vegas Blvd. S. (2007).	500	45

Los Angeles, CA

Building/structure	Ht. (ft)	Stories
Wilshire Grand Center (2017).	1,100	62
US Bank Tower, 633 W. 5th St. (1990).	1,018	73
Aon Center, 707 Wilshire Blvd. (1974).	858	62
Two California Plaza, 350 S. Grand Ave. (1992).	750	52
Gas Company Tower, 555 W. 5th St. (1991).	749	52
Bank of America Plaza, 333 S. Hope St. (1975).	735	55
777 Tower, 777 S. Figueroa St. (1991).	725	53
Wells Fargo Tower, 333 S. Grand Ave. (1983).	723	54
Figueroa at Wilshire, 601 S. Figueroa St. (1989).	717	52
City National Tower, 555 S. Flower St. (1971).	699	52
Paul Hastings Tower, 515 S. Flower St. (1971).	699	52
*Oceanside Plaza Tower I (2019).	677	49
Ritz Carlton/Marriott Marquis Los Angeles, 900 W. Olympic Blvd. (2010).	667	54
*Metropolis Tower D (2019).	647	58
*825 South Hill (2019).	637	49
Citigroup Center, 444 S. Flower St. (1979).	625	48
611 Place, 611 W. 6th St. (1968).	620	42
KPMG Tower, 355 S. Grand Ave. (1984).	606	45
One California Plaza, 300 S. Grand Ave. (1985).	578	42
Century Plaza Tower 1, 2029 Century Park E. (1973)	571	44
Century Plaza Tower 2, 2049 Century Park E. (1973)	571	44
Ernst & Young, LLP Plaza, 725 S. Figueroa St. (1986)	534	41
AIG-SunAmerica Ctr., 1999 Ave. of the Stars (1989)	533	39
*Oceanwide Plaza Tower II (2019).	530	40
*Oceanwide Plaza Tower III (2019).	530	40
*Hope+Flower Tower 1 (2019).	529	40
TCW Tower, 865 S. Figueroa St. (1990).	517	37
Union Bank Plaza, 445 S. Figueroa St. (1967).	516	40
10 Universal City Plaza (1984).	506	36

Mexico City, Mexico

Building/structure	Ht. (ft)	Stories
*Torre Mitikah Residencial, Rio Churubusco 601 (2021).	876	70
Torre Reforma, Paseo de la Reforma 483 (2016).	807	57
*Chapultepec Uno, Reforma 509 (2019).	791	59
Torre BBVA Bancomer, Paseo de la Reforma 506 (2015).	771	50
*Torre Paradox, Av. Santa Fe 562 (2018).	768	62
Torre Mayor, Paseo de la Reforma 505 (2003).	738	55
Torre Ejecutiva Pemex, Marina Nacional 329 Col. Huasteca (1984).	693	51
*Downtown & Be Grand Reforma, La Fragura 7 (2022)	678	49
Torre Altus, Paseo de los Laureles 416 (1999).	640	44
Torre Reforma Latino, Paseo de la Reforma 296 (2016).	607	46
Torre Latino Americana (incl. spire), Eje Central Lazaro Cardenas 2 (1956).	597	45
Torre Cuarzo, Paseo de la Reforma 26 (2017).	591	40
Miyana Tower 1 (2017).	577	43
*Torre M, Rio Churubusco 601 (2019).	577	35
*Peninsula Santa Fe T 300, Santa Fe 578 (2019).	571	53
*Sofitel Hotel Mexico City, Paseo de la Reforma 297 (2019).	561	41
World Trade Center, Montecito 38 Col. Napoles (1972)	565	50
Siroco Elite Residences, Av. Santa Fe 482 (2015).	561	43
Peninsula Tower, Av. Santa Fe 1240 (2014).	539	50
Torre Punta Reforma, Paseo de la Reforma 180 (2015).	537	37
Arcos Torre II, Paseo de los Tamarindos 400 (2008).	529	35
Arcos Torre I, Paseo de los Tamarindos 400 (1997).	529	35
Torre Diana, Rio Lerma 232 (2016).	519	33

Miami, FL

Building/structure	Ht. (ft)	Stories
*One River Point 1 (2021).	928	60
*One River Point 2 (2021).	928	60
Panorama Tower, 1101 Brickell Ave. (2018).	828	81
*Aston Martin Residences, 300 Biscayne Blvd. Way (2021).	817	66
Four Seasons Hotel & Tower, 1441 Brickell Ave. (2003).	789	64
Wachovia Financial Ctr., 200 S. Biscayne Blvd. (1983)	764	55
*Brickell Flatiron, 1001 S. Miami Ave. (2019).	734	64
Marquis, 1100 Biscayne Blvd. (2009).	702	63
*One Thousand Museum, 1000 Biscayne Blvd. (2018).	699	61

Building/structure	Ht. (ft)	Stories
Met 2 Office Tower, 200 SE 3rd St. (2010).	655	47
900 Biscayne Bay, 900 Biscayne Blvd. (2008).	650	63
*Elysee, 700 NE 23rd St. (2019).	649	57
*Missoni Baia, 700 NE 26th Terr. (2021).	646	57
*Paramount Miami Worldcenter (2019).	641	60
Echo Brickell, 1451 Brickell Ave. (2017).	637	57
Mint at Riverfront, 90 SW 3rd St. (2009).	631	55
Infinity at Brickell, 60 W. 13th St. (2008).	630	52
Miami Tower, 100 SE 2nd St. (1987).	625	47
Marinablue, 888 Biscayne Blvd. (2007).	615	57
Plaza on Brickell Tower I, 901 Brickell Ave. (2007).	610	56
Epic Residences & Hotel, 300 Biscayne Blvd. Way (2009).	601	54
*One Paraiso, 620 NE 31st St. (2018).	601	53
SLS Brickell, 1300 S. Miami Ave. (2016).	599	52
SLS Lux Brickell, 801 S. Miami Ave. (2018).	595	57
Icon Brickell North Tower, 495 Brickell Ave. (2008).	586	58
Icon Brickell South Tower, 495 Brickell Ave. (2008).	586	58
Solitair Brickell, 80 SW 8th St. (2018).	555	48
Paramount at Edgewater Square, 2066 N. Bayshore Dr. (2009).	555	47
50 Biscayne Blvd. (2007).	554	55
Quantum on the Bay South Tower, 1900 N. Bayshore Dr. (2008).	554	51
Biscayne Beach, 701 NE 29th St. (2017).	550	51
Brickell Heights North Tower, 850 S. Miami Ave. (2017)	549	52
*GranParaiso, 600 NE 31st St. (2018).	548	55
ParaisoBay, 600 NE 31st St. (2017).	548	55
1010 Brickell (2017).	548	50
Opera Tower, 1750 N. Bayshore Dr. (2007).	543	56
Viceroy, 495 Brickell Ave. (2009).	542	50
Vizcayne North Tower, 244 Biscayne Blvd. (2008).	538	49
Vizcayne South Tower, 244 Biscayne Blvd. (2008).	538	49
Avant at Met Square, 340 SE 3rd St. (2018).	538	46
Quantum on the Bay North Tower, 1900 N. Bayshore Dr. (2008).	536	44
Aria on the Bay, 1770 N. Bayshore Dr. (2018).	535	53
Ten Museum Park, 1040 Biscayne Blvd. (2007).	530	50
Brickell Heights So. Tower, 850 S. Miami Ave. (2017)	529	52
Jade at Brickell Bay, 1331 Brickell Bay Dr. (2004).	528	49
Plaza on Brickell Tower II, 901 Brickell Ave. (2007).	525	48

Minneapolis, MN

Building/structure	Ht. (ft)	Stories
IDS Center, 80 S. 8th St. (1973)[1].	792	55
Capella Tower, 225 S. 6th St. (1992).	776	56
Wells Fargo Center, 90 S. 7th St. (1988).	775	56
33 South Sixth St. (1983).	668	52
Campbell Mithun Tower, 222 S. 9th St. (1985).	582	42
US Bank Plaza I, 200 S. 6th St. (1981).	561	40
RBC Plaza, 60 S. 6th St. (1992).	539	40
Fifth Street Towers II, 150 S. 5th St. (1988).	504	36
(1) 910 ft incl. antenna.		

Monterrey, Mexico

Building/structure	Ht. (ft)	Stories
*T.Op Torre 1 (2019).	984	62
Torre Koi, San Pedro Garza Garcia (2017).	916	67
*Metropolitan Center Torre III (incl. spire), San Pedro Garza Garcia (2019).	755	56
Pabellon M (2015).	674	45
Torre Avalanz, San Pedro Garza Garcia (2000).	597	43
*Santa Maria Business Campus Torre 6 (2019).	591	38
*Metropolitan Center Torre II, San Pedro Garza Garcia (2017).	594	52
Centro de Gobierno Plaza Civica (2010).	591	36
LIU East, San Pedro Garza Garcia (2013).	564	39
*Lola! (2021).	558	40
Torre Sofia, Av. Sofia 440, San Pedro Garza Garcia (2014).	520	40
Torre Helicon, San Pedro Garza Garcia (2012).	512	33

Montréal, QC, Canada

Building/structure	Ht. (ft)	Stories
1250 Boulevard Rene Levesque (incl. spire) (1992).	743	47
1000 Rue de la Gauchetiere (1992).	673	51
Tour de la Bourse, 800 Place Victoria (1964).	624	47
1 Place Villa Marie (1962).	616	43
L'Avenue, 1175 Avenue des Canadiens (2017).	605	51
La Tour CIBC, 1155 Rene Levesque Blvd. (1962)[1].	604	45
Montreal Tower (1987).	574	NA
*Tour des Canadiens 2, 1150 Rue Saint-Antoine Ouest (2019).	551	53
Tour des Canadiens, 1288 Avenue des Canadiens (2016).	548	50
Tour McGill College, 1501 McGill College (1992).	519	38
(1) 740 ft incl. antenna.		

New Orleans, LA

Building/structure	Ht. (ft)	Stories
One Shell Square, 701 Poydras St. (1972).	697	51
CapitalOne Center, 201 St. Charles Ave. (1985).	645	53
Plaza Tower, 1001 Howard Ave. (1969).	531	45
Energy Centre, 1100 Poydras St. (1984).	530	39

New York, NY

Building/structure	Ht. (ft)	Stories
One World Trade Center (incl. spire) (2014).	1,782	94
*Central Park Tower, 217 West 57th St. (2019).	1,550	95
*111 W. 57th St. (2019).	1,428	82
*One Vanderbilt Place, 51 E. 42nd St. (2021).	1,401	58

Building/structure	Ht. (ft)	Stories
432 Park Avenue (2015)	1,397	85
*30 Hudson Yards (2019)	1,268	73
Empire State Building, 350 5th Ave. (1931)[1]	1,250	102
*45 Broad St. (2021)	1,200	68
Bank of America Tower (incl. spire), One Bryant Park (2009)	1,200	55
Three World Trade Center, 175 Greenwich St. (2018)	1,079	69
*9 DeKalb, Brooklyn (2021)	1,066	73
*53 West 53rd St. (2019)	1,050	77
Chrysler Bldg. (incl. spire), 405 Lexington Ave. (1930)	1,046	77
New York Times Tower (incl. spire), 620 8th Ave. (2007)	1,046	52
*50 Hudson Yards, 504 W. 34th St. (2022)	1,011	58
*35 Hudson Yards (2019)	1,009	72
One57, 157 W. 57th St. (2014)	1,005	75
*The Spiral, 435 10th Ave. (2021)	1,005	65
*One Manhattan West, 401 9th Ave. (2019)	995	67
4 World Trade Center, 150 Greenwich St. (2014)	977	65
*220 Central Park South (2018)	952	70
70 Pine (incl. spire) (1932)	952	67
*3 Hudson Boulevard, 555 W. 34th St. (2021)	940	53
*Two Manhattan West (2022)	935	56
The Trump Bldg., 40 Wall St. (1930)	927	71
30 Park Place, 99 Church St. (2016)	926	67
Citigroup Center, 153 E. 53rd St. (1977)	915	63
*15 Hudson Yards (2018)	914	70
*125 Greenwich Street (2020)	912	72
10 Hudson Yards (2016)	878	50
New York by Gehry at Eight Spruce Street (2011)	870	76
Trump World Tower, 845 UN Plaza (2001)	861	72
*425 Park Avenue (2019)	860	44
Comcast Building, 30 Rockefeller Center (1933)	850	70
*One Manhattan Square, 250 South St. (2019)	847	72
56 Leonard Street (2016)	821	57
Cityspire Center, 150 W. 56th St. (1987)	814	75
28 Liberty (1961)	813	60
4 Times Square (1999)[2]	809	48
MetLife Building, 200 Park Ave. (1963)	808	59
Bloomberg Tower, 731 Lexington Ave. (2005)[3]	806	54
*126 Madison Avenue (2021)	805	56
*138 E. 50th St. (2019)	803	64
111 Murray Street (2018)	792	58
Woolworth Building, 233 Broadway (1913)	792	57
520 Park Avenue (2018)	781	52
50 West, 50 West St. (2017)	778	64
Madison Square Park Tower, 41 E. 22nd St. (2017)	778	61
*55 Hudson Yards (2018)	778	51
1 Worldwide Plaza, 935 8th Ave. (1989)	778	47
*50 W. 66th St. (2021)	775	52
*Court Square City View Tower, 23-15 44th Dr., Queens (2021)	762	68
*19 Dutch Street (2019)	758	63
Carnegie Hall Tower, 152 W. 57th St. (1991)	757	60
*The Wall Street Tower, 130 William St. (2020)	755	61
383 Madison Avenue (2001)	755	47
1717 Broadway (2013)	753	67
AXA Center, 787 7th Ave. (1985)	752	51
One Penn Plaza, 250 W. 34th St. (1972)	750	57
1251 Avenue of the Americas (1971)	750	54
Time Warner Center North Tower, 10 Columbus Cir. (2004)	749	55
Time Warner Center South Tower, 10 Columbus Cir. (2004)	749	55
Goldman Sachs HQ, 200 Murray St. (2010)	749	44
60 Wall Street (1989)	745	55
One Astor Plaza, 1515 Broadway (1972)	745	54
One Liberty Plaza, 165 Broadway (1972)	743	54
7 World Trade Center, 250 Greenwich St. (2006)	743	49
Twenty Exchange, 20 Exchange Pl. (1931)	741	57
Three World Financial Center, 200 Vesey St. (1986)	739	51
*ARO, 242 W. 53rd St. (2018)	737	62
1540 Broadway (incl. spire) (1990)	732	42
Times Square Tower, 1459 Broadway (2004)	726	47
Metropolitan Tower, 142 W. 57th St. (1985)	716	68
252 E. 57th Street (2016)	715	59
100 E. 53rd Street (2018)	711	61
JPMorganChase World HQ, 270 Park Ave. (1960)	707	52
General Motors Building, 767 5th Ave. (1968)	705	50
The Eugene, 401 W. 31st St. (2017)	702	64
*23 Park Row (2019)	702	54
Metropolitan Life Tower, 1 Madison Ave. (1909)	700	50
500 5th Avenue (1931)	697	59
*Brooklyn Point, 138 Willoughby St., Brooklyn (2021)	696	57
Americas Tower, 1177 Ave. of the Americas (1992)	692	48
Solow Building, 9 W. 57th St. (1974)	689	49
Marine Midland Building, 140 Broadway (1967)	688	52
55 Water Street (1972)	687	53
277 Park Avenue (1963)	687	50
The Beekman Hotel & Residences, 5 Beekman St. (2017)	687	47
1585 Broadway (1989)	685	42
Random House/Park Imperial, 1739 Broadway (2003)	684	52
Four Seasons Hotel, 57 E. 57th St. (1993)	682	52
Sky, 605 W. 42nd St. (2015)	676	61
McGraw-Hill Bldg., 1221 Ave. of the Americas (1972)	674	51

Building/structure	Ht. (ft)	Stories
Barclay Tower, 10 Barclay St. (2007)	673	56
One Grand Central Place, 60 E. 42nd St. (1930)	673	53
1 Court Square, Queens (1990)	673	50
*One Seaport, 161 Maiden Ln. (2019)	670	60
Paramount Plaza, 1633 Broadway (1970)	670	48
*200 Amsterdam Ave. (2020)	668	55
*45 Park Place (2019)	667	43
*281 5th Avenue (2018)	663	52
Trump Tower, 725 5th Ave. (1982)	664	58
Bank of New York Building, 1 Wall St. (1932)	654	50
Silver Towers East, 600 W. 42nd St. (2009)	653	58
Silver Towers West, 600 W. 42nd St. (2009)	653	58
599 Lexington Avenue (1986)	653	51
712 5th Avenue (1990)	650	53
Chanin Building, 122 E. 42nd St. (1929)	649	56
245 Park Avenue (1967)	648	47
Tower 28, 42-12 28th St., Queens (2017)	647	58
550 Madison Avenue (1983)	647	37
Two World Financial Center, 225 Liberty St. (1986)	645	44
1095 Avenue of the Americas (1974)	645	43
570 Lexington Avenue (1931)	642	50
1 New York Plaza, 1 Water St. (1969)	640	50
1 MiMA Tower, 440 W. 42nd St. (2011)	638	63
1 Dag Hammarskjold Plaza, 885 2nd Ave. (1972)	637	48
345 Park Avenue (1968)	634	44
Langham Place, 400 5th Ave. (2010)	632	58
Mercantile Bldg., 10 E. 40th St. (1929)	632	48
W New York Downtown Hotel & Residences, 123 Washington St. (2010)	631	57
Grace Plaza, 1114 Ave. of the Americas (1972)	630	50
Home Insurance Plaza, 59 Maiden Ln. (1966)	630	44
101 Park Avenue (1982)	629	49
Central Park Place, 301 W. 57th St. (1988)	628	56
888 7th Avenue (1971)	628	45
*11 Hoyt St., Brooklyn (2020)	626	51
Burlington House, 1345 Ave. of the Americas (1969)	625	50
Waldorf Astoria New York, 301 Park Ave. (1931)	625	47
Avalon Willoughby West, 100 Willoughby St., Brooklyn (2015)	624	57
Trump Palace, 200 E. 69th St. (1991)	623	54
One Madison Park, 20 E. 23rd St. (2010)	621	51
Olympic Tower, 645 5th Ave. (1976)	620	51
425 Fifth Avenue (2003)	618	55
The Epic, 125 W. 31st St. (2007)	615	58
919 3rd Avenue (1970)	615	47
Tower 49, 12 E. 49th St. (1985)	615	44
750 7th Avenue (incl. spire) (1989)	615	35
New York Life, 51 Madison Ave. (1928)	615	33
Eventi, 851 6th Ave. (2010)	614	46
551 10th Avenue (2016)	612	52
Credit Lyonnais Building, 1301 Ave. of the Americas (1964)	609	46
Baccarat Hotel & Residences, 20 W. 53rd St. (2014)	605	47
The Orion, 350 W. 42nd St. (2006)	604	58
590 Madison Avenue (1983)	603	41
The Hub, 333 Schermerhorn St., Brooklyn (2017)	602	54
250 W. 55th Street (2013)	602	40
Eleven Times Square, 644 8th Ave. (2011)	601	40
1166 Avenue of the Americas (1974)	600	44
*Eagle Lofts, 43-22 Queens St., Queens (2018)	598	55
Hawthorn Park, 160 W. 62nd St. (2014)	598	54
Hearst Magazine Tower, 959 8th Ave. (2006)	597	46
3 Lincoln Center, 160 W. 66th St. (1993)	595	60
Celanese Building, 1211 Ave. of the Americas (1973)	592	45
The London NYC, 151 W. 54th St. (1990)	590	54
388 Bridge Street, Brooklyn (2014)	590	51
Thurgood Marshall U.S. Courthouse, 505 Pearl St. (1936)	590	37
Museum Tower Apts., 21 W. 53rd St. (1985)	589	52
The Millenium Hilton Hotel, 55 Church St. (1992)	588	58
Sky House, 11 E. 29th St. (2008)	588	55
Time-Life Bldg., 1271 Ave. of the Americas (1959)	587	48
Jacob K. Javits Federal Bldg., 26 Federal Plz. (1967)	587	41
W Times Square, 1567 Broadway (2000)	584	53
Trump International Hotel & Tower, 15 Columbus Cir. (1970)	583	44
*3 Jackson Park, 28-30 Jackson Ave., Queens (2018)	581	54
Stevens Tower, 1185 Ave. of the Americas (1971)	580	42
Municipal Building, 1 Centre St. (1914)	580	34
520 Madison Avenue (1981)	577	43
One World Financial Center, 200 Liberty St. (1985)	577	37
Merchandise Mart, 41 Madison Ave. (1973)	576	42
Park Avenue Plaza, 55 E. 52nd St. (1981)	575	44
300 Madison Avenue (2003)	575	38
Lehman Building, 745 7th Ave. (2001)	575	38
32 Old Slip (1987)	575	37
Marriott Marquis Times Square, 1531 Broadway (1985)	574	50
299 Park Avenue (1967)	574	42
5 Times Square, 590 7th Ave. (2002)	574	40
Socony Mobil Building, 150 E. 42nd St. (1956)	572	42
1290 Avenue of the Americas (1963)	571	43
780 3rd Avenue (1983)	570	49
600 3rd Avenue (1971)	570	42

Building/structure	Ht. (ft)	Stories
The Ashland, 590 Fulton St., Brooklyn (2016)	568	51
450 Lexington Avenue (1991)	568	38
Paramount Tower, 240 E. 39th St. (1998)	567	51
230 Park Avenue (1928)	565	35
New York Palace Hotel, 455 Madison Ave. (1980)	563	51
Continental Bank Building, 30 Broad St. (1932)	562	48
Park Avenue Tower, 65 E. 55th St. (1986)	561	36
Nelson Tower, 450 7th Ave. (1931)	560	46
Sherry-Netherland, 781 5th Ave. (1927)	560	40
623 5th Avenue (1990)	560	36
South Park Tower, 124 W. 60th St. (1986)	558	51
100 UN Plaza, 327 E. 48th St. (1986)	557	52
Continental Can, 633 3rd Ave. (1962)	557	39
222 E. 44th Street (2018)	556	42
3 Park Avenue (1975)	556	42
Continental Center, 180 Maiden Ln. (1983)	555	41
330 Madison Ave. (1964)	555	41
Equitable Building, 120 Broadway (1915)	555	38
Reuters Building, 3 Times Sq. (2001)[4]	555	30
Tower 111, 885 6th Ave. (2011)	554	48
The Belvedere, 10 E. 29th St. (1999)	554	48
Inmont Bldg., 1133 Ave. of the Americas (1970)	552	45
Downtown by Philippe Starck, 15 Broad St. (1927)	551	42
Hyatt Times Square, 135 W. 45th St. (2013)	550	53
Biltmore Tower, 267 W. 47th St. (2003)	550	51
Unisys Building, 605 3rd Ave. (1963)	550	44
2 Grand Central Tower, 140 E. 45th St. (1982)	550	43
The Tower at 15 Central Park West (2008)	550	35
AT&T Long Lines Building, 33 Thomas St. (1974)	550	29
50 UN Plaza, 345 E. 46th St. (2015)	548	44
Bankers Trust, 33 E. 48th St. (1971)	547	41
The Corinthian, 330 E. 38th St. (1988)	546	55
Transportation Building, 225 Broadway (1928)	546	44
MillenniumTower, 101 W. 67th St. (1995)	545	54
The Galleria, 117 E. 57th St. (1975)	544	56
2 Gold Street (2005)	543	51
220 Riverside Blvd. at Trump Place (2003)	542	49
17 State Street (1988)	542	41
Grand Central Plaza, 622 3rd Ave. (1973)	542	38
American Copper Buildings West Tower, 626 1st Ave. (2017)	540	47
New York Telephone, 375 Pearl St. (1976)	540	42
1285 Avenue of the Americas (1960)	540	42
Ritz Tower, 109 E. 57th St. (1925)	540	41
14 Wall (1912)	540	29
Tribeca Tower, 105 Duane St. (1990)	537	53
Lefcourt Colonial Building, 295 Madison Ave. (1929)	537	45
The Encore, 175 W. 60th St. (2016)	533	48
1700 Broadway (1969)	533	41
Westin Hotel New York, 43rd St. and 8th Ave. (2002)	532	45
515 Park Avenue (1999)	532	43
DuMont Building, 515 Madison Ave. (1931)	532	42
The Brooklyner, 111 Lawrence St., Brooklyn (2010)	531	52
One East River Place, 525 E. 72nd St. (1989)	530	49
21 West End Avenue (2016)	529	45
The Metropolis, 150 E. 44th St. (2001)	528	50
William Beaver House, 15 William St. (2010)	528	47
North American Plywood, 800 3rd Ave. (1972)	526	41
City Point Tower II, 336 Flatbush Ave. Ext., Brooklyn (2016)	525	46
The Pierre, 2 E. 61st St. (1930)	525	44
767 3rd Avenue (1980)	525	39

(1) 1,455 ft incl. antenna. (2) 1,118 ft incl. antenna. (3) 941 ft incl. antenna. (4) 659 ft incl. antenna.

Philadelphia, PA

Building/structure	Ht. (ft)	Stories
Comcast Technology Center, 1800 Arch St. (2018)	1,121	59
Comcast Center, 1701 JFK Blvd. (2008)	974	57
One Liberty Place (incl. spire), 1650 Market St. (1987)	945	61
Two Liberty Place (incl. spire), 1601 Chestnut St. (1989)	848	58
BNY Mellon Bank Center, 1735 Market St. (1990)	792	54
Three Logan, 1717 Arch St. (1991)	739	55
FMC Tower at Cira Centre South (2017)	730	49
G. Fred DiBona Jr. Building, 1901 Market St. (1990)	625	45
*The W Philadelphia and Element, 1441 Chestnut St. (2019)	617	51
Commerce Square #2, 2001 Market St. (1992)	572	40
Commerce Square #1, 2005 Market St. (1990)	572	40
City Hall (incl. statue) (1901)	548	7
Residences at Ritz-Carlton, 1416 S. Penn Sq. (2009)	518	46
1818 Market St. (1974)	500	40

Pittsburgh, PA

Building/structure	Ht. (ft)	Stories
US Steel Tower, 600 Grant St. (1970)	841	64
BNY Mellon Center, 500 Grant St. (1983)	725	54
One PPG Place (1984)	635	40
Fifth Avenue Place, 120 5th Ave. (1987)	616	32
One Oxford Centre, 301 Grant St. (1982)	615	46
Gulf Tower, 707 Grant St. (1932)	582	44
The Tower at PNC Plaza (2015)	545	33
University of Pittsburgh Cathedral of Learning, 4200 5th Ave. (1936)	535	42

Building/structure	Ht. (ft)	Stories
3 Mellon Bank Center, 525 Wm. Penn Way (1951)	520	41
K&L Gates Center, 210 6th Ave. (1968)	511	39

Portland, OR

Building/structure	Ht. (ft)	Stories
Wells Fargo Center, 1300 SW 5th Ave. (1973)	546	40
Park Avenue West (incl. spire), 728 SW 9th Ave. (2016)	537	30
U.S. Bancorp Tower, 111 SW 5th Ave. (1983)	536	42
Koin Center, 222 SW Columbia St. (1984)	509	31

Puebla, Mexico

Building/structure	Ht. (ft)	Stories
*Oak 58 High Living (2022)	761	58
*Torre JV Angelopolis (2020)	722	46
*Torre NVBOLA (2018)	574	43

St. Louis, MO

Building/structure	Ht. (ft)	Stories
Gateway Arch, 11 N. 4th St. (1965)	630	NA
Metropolitan Square Tower, 211 N. Broadway (1988)	593	42
AT&T Center, 900 Pine St. (1984)	588	44
Thomas F. Eagleton Federal Courthouse, 111 S. 10th St. (2000)	557	29

San Francisco, CA

Building/structure	Ht. (ft)	Stories
Salesforce Tower, 415 Mission St. (2018)	1,070	61
Sutro Tower (1972)	977	NA
*Oceanwide Center Tower 1 (2021)	910	61
Transamerica Pyramid, 600 Montgomery St. (1972)	853	48
181 Fremont (2018)	802	54
555 California St. (1969)	779	52
345 California Center (1986)	695	48
Millennium Tower, 301 Mission St. (2009)	645	58
*Oceanwide Center Tower 2 (2021)	625	54
One Rincon Hill South Tower, 425 First St. (2008)	605	54
*Park Tower at Transbay (2018)	605	43
101 California Street (1982)	600	48
50 Fremont Center (1985)	600	43
*400 Folsom (2019)	575	55
575 Market St. (1975)	573	40
Four Embarcadero Center, 55 Clay St. (1984)	570	45
One Embarcadero Center, 355 Clay St. (1970)	569	45
44 Montgomery Street (1967)	565	43
Spear Tower, 1 Market St. (1976)	565	42
One Sansome Street (1984)	550	43
One Rincon Hill North Tower, 425 First St. (2014)	541	45
Shaklee Terrace Building, 444 Market St. (1982)	537	38
First Market Tower, 525 Market St. (1972)	529	38
McKesson Plaza, 1 Post St. (1969)	529	38
425 Market St. (1973)	524	38
*706 Mission (2019)	510	43
Telsis Tower, 1 Montgomery St. (1982)	500	38

Seattle, WA

Building/structure	Ht. (ft)	Stories
Columbia Center, 701 5th Ave. (1985)	933	76
*Rainier Square Tower (2020)	850	58
1201 Third Avenue Tower, 1201 3rd Ave. (1988)	772	55
Two Union Square, 601 Union St. (1989)	740	56
Seattle Municipal Tower, 700 5th Ave. (1990)	722	57
F5 Tower, 811 5th Ave. (2017)	660	43
Safeco Plaza, 1001 4th Ave. (1969)	630	50
City Centre, 1420 5th Ave. (1989)	606	44
Space Needle, 203 6th Ave. (1962)	605	NA
Russell Investments Center, 1301 2nd Ave. (2006)	598	42
Wells Fargo Center, 999 3rd Ave. (1983)	574	47
Madison Centre, 505 Madison St. (2017)	560	36
Bank of America Fifth Ave. Plz., 800 5th Ave. (1981)	543	42
901 5th Avenue (1973)	536	41
Amazon Tower I, 2021 7th Ave. (2016)	524	37
Amazon Tower II, 2021 7th Ave. (2017)	521	37
Hyatt Regency Seattle, 808 Howell St. (2018)	520	45
*Amazon Tower III, 2021 7th Ave. (2019)	520	37
Rainier Tower, 1301 5th Ave. (1977)	514	31
Fourth & Madison Building, 915 4th Ave. (2003)	512	40
1918 8th Avenue (2009)	500	37
*2+U, 1201 2nd Ave. (2019)	500	37

Sunny Isles Beach, FL

Building/structure	Ht. (ft)	Stories
*Armani Residences, 18975 Collins Ave. (2018)	649	60
*Turnberry Ocean Club, 18501 Collins Ave. (2019)	649	52
*Muse, 17141 Collins Ave. (2018)	649	47
Porsche Design Tower, 18555 Collins Ave. (2016)	644	58
Mansions at Acqualina, 17749 Collins Ave. (2015)	643	46
*The Ritz-Carlton Residences (2019)	642	52
Jade Signature, 16901 Collins Ave. (2017)	636	57
Jade on the Beach Condominiums, 17001 Collins Ave. (2008)	574	51
Trump Royale, 18201 Collins Ave. (2008)	551	43
Trump Palace, 18101 Collins Ave. (2005)	551	43
Acqualina Ocean Residences, 17875 Collins Ave. (2004)	550	51
Jade Ocean, 17121 Collins Ave. (2009)	543	51

Tampa, FL

Building/structure	Ht. (ft)	Stories
Regions Building, 100 N. Tampa St. (1992)	579	42
Bank of America Plaza, 101 E. Kennedy Blvd. (1986)	577	42

Building/structure	Ht. (ft)	Stories
One Tampa City Center, 201 N. Franklin St. (1981)	537	39
SunTrust Financial Center, 401 E. Jackson St. (1992)	525	36

Toronto, ON, Canada

Building/structure	Ht. (ft)	Stories
CN Tower, 310 Front St. West (1976)	1,815	NA
*The One, 1 Bloor St. West (2022)	1,005	83
First Canadian Place, 100 King St. West (1975)[1]	978	72
The St. Regis Toronto (incl. spire), 325 Bay St. (2012)	908	63
Scotia Tower, 40 King St. West (1989)	902	68
Aura at College Park, 388 Yonge St. (2014)	892	78
Brookfield Place (incl. spire), 161 Bay St. (1990)	856	53
Number One Bloor, 1 Bloor St. East (2017)	844	75
Commerce Court West, 199 Bay St. (1973)[2]	784	57
*CIBC Square I, 81 Bay St. (2020)	780	49
Ice Condos at York Centre 2, 16 York St. (2015)	768	67
Harbour Plaza Residences East, 90 Harbour St. (2017)	764	66
*Sugar Wharf Tower D, 95 Lakeshore East (2022)	755	70
*Eau de Soleil Sky Tower, 2183 Lake Shore Blvd. West, Etobicoke (2019)	749	66
*Ten York (2018)	735	65
Harbour Plaza Residences West, 90 Harbour St. (2017)	735	62
TD Centre-Toronto Dominion Bank Tower, 66 Wellington St. West (1967)	730	56
*Sugar Wharf Tower E, 95 Lakeshore East (2022)	717	65
Bay-Adelaide Center West Tower, 335 Bay St. (2010)	704	52
*The Prestige at Pinnacle One Yonge (2022)	709	65
Living Shangri-La Toronto, 180 University Ave. (2012)	702	65
Ritz-Carlton Hotel and Residences, 185 Wellington St. West (2011)	687	54
*Massey Tower, 199 Yonge St. (2018)	683	60
*The Residences of 488 University Avenue (2019)	679	55
BCE Place, Bay-Wellington Tower, 181 Bay St. (1991)	679	49
L Tower, 1 Front St. (2014)	673	58
88 Scott Street (2017)	669	58
Four Seasons Private Residences West, 48 Yorkville Ave. (2012)	669	55
*YC Condos, 460 Yonge St. (2018)	664	60
Ice Condos at York Centre 1, 16 York St. (2014)	663	57
Bay-Adelaide Center East Tower, 40 Adelaide St. (2016)	643	44
*E Condos South, 8 Eglinton Ave. (2018)	642	58
*Wellesley on the Park, 11 Wellesley St. West (2019)	637	60
*22|21 Yonge, 2221 Yonge St. (2019)	632	58
EY Tower, 100 Adelaide St. West (2017)	617	40
*19 Duncan St. (2022)	612	58
RBC Centre, 155 Wellington St. West (2009)	607	42
CASA II, 42 Charles St. East (2016)	605	57
U Condominiums East Tower, 50 St. Joseph St. (2016)	604	55
*One Yorkville (2019)	601	58
TD North Tower, 77 King St. West (1969)	600	46
Maple Leaf Square North Tower, 65 Bremner Blvd. (2010)	595	54
*Eau de Soleil Water Tower, 2183 Lake Shore Blvd. West, Etobicoke (2019)	593	49
*CASA III, 50 Charles St. East (2018)	589	55
*Rosedale on Bloor, 403 Bloor St. East (2021)	587	52
INDX Condominiums, 70 Temperance St. (2016)	587	54
1 King West (2005)	578	51
*The Well Office Tower, 410 Front St. West (2020)	571	36
Success Tower 2, 33 Bay St. (2010)	569	55
One York Street (2016)	569	35
Royal Bank Plaza-South Tower, 200 Bay St. (1976)	567	41
Maple Leaf Square South Tower, 55 Bremner Blvd. (2010)	562	50
*The Selby Condominiums, 592 Shelbourne St. (2019)	560	49
*Teahouse Condominiums South, 501 Yonge St. (2019)	558	52
Hullmark Centre I, 4789 Yonge St. (2015)	557	45
Lago at the Waterfront, 2151 Lake Shore Blvd. West, Etobicoke (2016)	550	49
44 Charles Street West (1974)	545	51
Karma, 9 Grenville St. (2016)	544	50
Quantum 2, 2195 Yonge St. (2008)	541	51
Theatre Park, 224 King St. West (2015)	541	47
Residences @ College Park I, 763 Bay St. (2006)	535	51
Burano, 832 Bay St. (2012)	535	50
Success Tower 1, 18 Harbour St. (2011)	531	52
X2, 580 Jarvis St. (2015)	529	44
FIVE, 606 Yonge St. (2016)	528	48

(1) 1,116 ft incl. antenna. (2) 942 ft incl. antenna.

Tulsa, OK

Building/structure	Ht. (ft)	Stories
BOK Tower, 1 E. 2nd St. (1975)	667	52
Cityplex Central Tower, 2448 E. 81st St. (1979)	648	60
First Place Tower, 15 E. 5th St. (1973)	516	40
Mid-Continent Tower, 401 S. Boston St. (1984)	513	36

Vancouver, BC, Canada

Building/structure	Ht. (ft)	Stories
Shangri-La Vancouver, 1120 W. Georgia St. (2009)	659	59
Trump International Hotel & Tower, 1153 W. Georgia (2016)	616	58
*One Burrard Place (2020)	551	54
Telus Garden Residential Tower, 777 Richards St. (2016)	550	53
Hotel Georgia, 667 Howe St. (2012)	520	50

Other Tall Buildings in North America

Building/structure	City	Ht. (ft)	Stories
Devon Energy Center (2012)	Oklahoma City, OK	844	52
*Stantec Tower (2019)	Edmonton, AB, Can.	816	66
RSA Battle House Tower (incl. spire) (2007)	Mobile, AL	745	35
Revel Hotel (2012)	Atlantic City, NJ	718	53
Hotel Riu Plaza Guadalajara (2011)	Guadalajara, Mex.	705	44
Great American Tower at Queen City Square (2011)	Cincinnati, OH	665	40
The Tower at First National Center (2002)	Omaha, NE	634	45
801 Grand (1991)	Des Moines, IA	630	44
*JW Marriott-Legends Private Residences (2018)	Edmonton, AB, Can.	627	56
One Kansas City Place (incl. spire) (1988)	Kansas City, MO	623	42
Tower of the Americas (1968)	San Antonio, TX	622	NA
Bank of America Tower (1990)	Jacksonville, FL.	617	42
AT&T Building (1994)	Nashville TN	617	33
U.S. Bank Center (1973)	Milwaukee, WI.	601	42
Town Pavilion (1986)	Kansas City, MO	591	38
Erastus Corning II Twr. (1973)	Albany, NY	589	44
Niagara Falls Hilton Phase 2 (2009)	Niagara Falls, ON, Can.	581	58
Absolute World 56 (2012)	Mississauga, ON, Can.	576	56
*Transit City Condos 1 (2021)	Vaughan, ON, Can.	575	55
*Transit City Condos 2 (2021)	Vaughan, ON, Can.	575	55
Carew Tower (1931)[1]	Cincinnati, OH	574	49
Concourse Corporate Ctr. V (incl. spire) (1988)	Sandy Springs, GA	570	34
Hyatt Regency Andares (2016)	Zapopan, Mex.	568	41
Torre Aura Altitude (2008)	Zapopan, Mex.	563	44
Blue Diamond Tower (2000)	Miami Beach, FL.	559	44
Green Diamond Tower (2000)	Miami Beach, FL.	559	44
Washington Monument (1884)	Washington, DC	555	NA
Concourse Corporate Ctr. VI (incl. spire) (1991)	Sandy Springs, GA	553	34
Northwestern Mutual Tower (2017)	Milwaukee, WI.	550	33
400 West Market (1992)	Louisville, KY	549	35
Simmons Tower (1986)	Little Rock, AR.	546	40
Marriott Rivercenter (incl. spire) (1988)	San Antonio, TX	546	38
RBC Plaza (incl. spire) (2008)	Raleigh, NC	538	32
Modis Tower (1975)	Jacksonville, FL.	535	37
One Seneca Tower (1970)	Buffalo, NY	529	38
Vehicle Assembly Bldg. (1965)	Cape Canaveral, FL	526	40
Harrah's Waterfront Twr. (2008)	Atlantic City, NJ.	525	44
505 (2018)	Nashville, TN.	524	45
Skylon (1965)	Niagara Falls, ON, Can.	520	NA
Absolute World 50 (2012)	Mississauga, ON, Can.	518	50
*3 Civic Plaza (2018)	Surrey, BC, Can.	516	50
The Westin Virginia Beach Town Center and Residences (2007)	Virginia Beach, VA.	508	38
The Beach Club Tower 2 (2006)	Hallandale Beach, FL	505	50
*Corporativo Bansi (2018)	Guadalajara, Mexico	505	32
Chase Tower (1971)	Oklahoma City, OK	500	36
One American Plaza (1991)	San Diego, CA	500	34

(1) 623 ft incl. antenna.

Selected Bridge Styles

Bridges support weight through tension (pulling), compression (pushing), or a combination of both. **Suspension** and **cable-stayed** bridges are characterized by cables under tension. While the deck of a suspension bridge hangs from suspenders, that of a cable-stayed bridge ties directly to a bridge tower. The elements of a **truss** form triangles, which distribute the forces of tension and compression. Truss bridges can thus carry more weight than beam bridges. Steel plates can be welded or bolted together to make a **plate girder**, a kind of beam. A common form is the **box girder**.

A bridge can have a **simple** configuration, whereby its load is supported at both ends. If a bridge is **continuous**, its load extends across multiple supports. In a **cantilever** configuration, structural elements (e.g., trusses or girders) supported at one end project out, or cantilever, to carry a span.

Notable North American Bridges

Source: World Almanac research; Office of Bridge Technology, Federal Highway Administration, U.S. Dept. of Transportation
Asterisk (*) designates a bridge that carries railroads only. All other bridges carry roads or roads and rail unless otherwise noted.
Year is date of completion or projected completion. Span of bridge is the distance between its main supports. As of mid-2018.

Year	Bridge	Location	Main span (ft)
	Suspension		
1964	Verrazano-Narrows	New York, NY	4,260
1937	Golden Gate	San Francisco Bay, CA	4,200
1957	Mackinac	Straits of Mackinac, MI	3,800
1931	George Washington	New York, NY-Fort Lee, NJ	3,500
1950/			
2007	Tacoma Narrows (twin)	Tacoma, WA	2,800
2003	Al Zampa Mem. (New		
	Carquinez) (westbound)	Carquinez Strait, CA	2,388
1936	San Francisco-Oakland Bay	San Francisco-	
	(West Span)[1]	Yerba Buena Isl., CA	2,310
1939	Bronx-Whitestone	East R., New York, NY	2,300
1970	Pierre Laporte	Quebec City, QC, Can.	2,190
1951/	Delaware Mem. (twin)	Pennsville, NJ-	
68		New Castle, DE	2,150
1957	Walt Whitman	Philadelphia, PA-NJ	2,000
1929	Ambassador	Detroit, MI-Windsor, ON,	
		Can.	1,850
1961	Throgs Neck	New York, NY	1,801
1926	Benjamin Franklin	Phila., PA-Camden, NJ	1,750
1924	Bear Mountain	Hudson R., Peekskill, NY	1,632
1969	Claiborne Pell/Newport	Narragansett Bay, RI	1,600
1952/	William Preston Lane Jr.		
73	Memorial (twin)	Sandy Point, MD.	1,600
1903	Williamsburg	East R., New York, NY	1,600
1883	Brooklyn	East R., New York, NY	1,596
1938	Lions Gate	Vancouver, BC, Can.	1,549
1963	Vincent Thomas	L.A. Harbor, CA	1,500
1930	Mid-Hudson	Poughkeepsie, NY	1,495
1909	Manhattan	East R., New York, NY	1,470
1955	Angus L. Macdonald	Halifax, NS, Can.	1,447
1970	A. Murray MacKay	Halifax, NS, Can.	1,400
1936	Triborough (Harlem R.		
	Lift/Bronx Crossing/		
	East R. Suspension)	East R., New York, NY	1,380
2013	San Francisco-Oakland Bay		
	(SAS)[2]	San Francisco Bay, CA	1,263
	Cantilever		
1917	Quebec	Quebec City, QC, Can.	1,800
1974	Commodore Barry	Chester, PA-	
		Bridgeport, NJ	1,644
1958/	Crescent City Connection	Mississippi R.,	
88	(twin)	New Orleans, LA	1,575
1995	Veterans Memorial	Gramercy, LA	1,460
1968	Baton Rouge	Mississippi R., LA	1,235
1955	Tappan Zee (I-287)	Hudson R., Tarrytown, NY	1,212
1930	Lewis and Clark	Longview, WA-Rainier, OR	1,200
1909	Queensboro	East R., New York, NY	1,182
1958	Carquinez (eastbound)	San Francisco Bay, CA.	1,100
1930	Jacques Cartier	Montreal, QC, Can.	1,097
1968	Isaiah D. Hart	Jacksonville, FL	1,088
1956	Richmond-San Rafael (twin)	San Francisco Bay, CA.	1,070
1963/			
80	Newburgh-Beacon (twin)	Hudson R., NY	1,000
	Truss		
1966	Astoria-Megler (U.S. 101)	Columbia R., OR-WA	1,232
1976	Francis Scott Key	Baltimore, MD	1,200
1981	Ravenswood	Ohio R., Ravenswood, WV	902
1995	Taylor-Southgate, Ohio R.	Cincinnati, OH-Newport, KY	850
1943	Julien Dubuque (U.S. 20)	Mississippi R., IA-IL	845
1966	Charles Braga	Fall River, MA	840
1956	Shawneetown (KY 56) (twin)	Ohio R., IL-KY	825
1953	John E. Mathews	Jacksonville, FL	810
1992	Cooper R.	Charleston, SC	800
1957	Kingston-Rhinecliff	Hudson R., NY	800
1950	Maurice J. Tobin	Boston, MA	800
1940	Gov. Nice Mem.	Newburg, MD-	
		Dahlgren, VA	800
1986	Rochester-Monaca	Rochester-Monaca, PA.	780
1973/	Atchafalaya R. (U.S. 190)		
88	(twin)	Krotz Springs, LA	780
1988	Phil G. McDonald		
	(Glade Creek)	Beckley, WV	784
1917	*Sciotoville RR (twin)	Sciotoville, OH-KY	775
1981	Sewickley	Sewickley, PA	750
1977	Jennings Randolph	Chester, WV-	
		E. Liverpool, OH	750
1974	Carroll C. Cropper (I-275)	Ohio R., IN-KY	750

Year	Bridge	Location	Main span (ft)
1940	Glover Cary	Ohio R., Owensboro, KY-IN	750
1984	13th Street	Ohio R., Ashland, KY-OH	740
1959	Monaca-E. Rochester	Monaca-E. Rochester, PA	730
1976	Betsy Ross	Phila., PA-Pennsauken, NJ	729
2013	Milton-Madison (U.S. 421)	Ohio R., KY-IN	727
1967	Matthew E. Welsh	Ohio R., Mauckport, IN-KY	725
1994	Robert C. Byrd	Huntington, WV.	720
1971	Atchafalaya R. (LA 1)	Simmesport, LA	720
1962	U.S. 41 Twin	Ohio R., Evansville, IN-	
		Henderson, KY	720
1929	Irvin S. Cobb (U.S. 45)	Ohio R., Brookport, IL-	
		Paducah, KY	716
1970	Vanport	Vanport, PA.	715
1962	Champlain	Montreal, QC, Can.	707
1973	Girard Point	Philadelphia, PA	700
1963	John F. Kennedy (I-65)	Ohio R., Louisville, KY-	
		Jeffersonville, IN	700
1923	*Mears Mem., Tanana R.	Nenana, AK	700
	Plate and Box Girder		
1997	Confederation[3]	Prince Edward Isl.-NB, Can.	820
2010	Kanawha R. (I-64)	S. Charleston-Dunbar, WV	760
1982	Jesse H. Jones Memorial	Houston, TX	750
1977	LA 27, Intracoastal Canal.	Gibbstown, LA	750
1976	LA 82, Intracoastal Canal.	Forked Isl., LA	750
1967	San Mateo-Hayward	San Francisco Bay, CA	750
1992	Jamestown-Verrazano	Narragansett Bay, RI	674
2002	Vietnam Veterans Mem.	James R., Richmond, VA.	672
1986	Umatilla	Columbia R., OR-WA	660
1969	San Diego-Coronado (twin)	San Diego Bay, CA	660
2007	Benicia-Martinez (new)	Carquinez Strait, CA	659
	Cable-Stayed		
2012	Baluarte Bicentennial	Sinaloa-Durango, Mex.	1,706
2020	New Harbor Bridge	Corpus Christi Ship	
	(U.S. 181)	Channel, TX	1,661
2011	John James Audubon	St. Francisville, LA	1,583
2005	Arthur Ravenel Jr.	Charleston, SC	1,546
2012	Port Mann	Vancouver, BC, Can.	1,542
1986	Alex Fraser	Vancouver, BC, Can.	1,526
2014	Stan Musial Veterans		
	Memorial (I-70)	Miss. R., St. Louis, MO-IL	1,500
2010	U.S. 82, Mississippi R.	Greenville, MS-	
		Lake Village, AR.	1,378
1994	Clark	Alton, IL-MO	1,360
1989	Dames Point	Jacksonville, FL	1,300
2003	Sidney Lanier	Brunswick, GA	1,250
1995	Fred Hartman	Houston Ship Channel,	
		Baytown, TX	1,250
2007	Veterans' Glass City		
	Skyway	Maumee R., Toledo, OH	1,225
1983	Hale Boggs Memorial	Luling, LA	1,222
2017/	New/Mario M. Cuomo		
18	(I-287) (twin)	Hudson R., Tarrytown, NY	1,200
2002	William Natcher, Ohio R.	Owensboro, KY-IN	1,200
1987	Sunshine Skyway (I-275)	Tampa Bay, FL.	1,200
2012	Margaret Hunt Hill	Trinity R., Dallas, TX	1,197
1988	Tampico	Panuco R., Mex.	1,181
2006	Penobscot Narrows	Bucksport, ME	1,161
2003	Bill Emerson Memorial	Cape Girardeau, MO-IL	1,150
1988	Skybridge[4]	Vancouver, BC, Can.	1,115
1991	Talmadge Memorial	Savannah, GA	1,100
2000	Maysville (Wm. H. Harsha)	Savannah, GA	1,050
	Steel Arch		
1977	New River Gorge	Fayetteville, WV	1,700
1931	Bayonne (Kill Van Kull)	Bayonne, NJ-	
		New York, NY	1,675
1973	Fremont	Portland, OR	1,255
1964	Port Mann	Vancouver, BC, Can.	1,200
1967	Laviolette	Trois-Rivières, QC, Can.	1,100
1990	Roosevelt Lake	Roosevelt Lake, AZ	1,080
1959	Glen Canyon	Page, AZ	1,028
1962	Lewiston-Queenston	NY-ON, Can.	1,001
1976	Perrine	Twin Falls, ID	993
1916	*Hell Gate	East R., New York, NY	978
1941	Rainbow	Niagara Falls, NY-ON, Can.	950
1997	Second Blue Water	Port Huron, MI-ON, Can.	922
1977	Moundsville	Ohio R., WV	912
1983/	Jefferson Barracks (I-255)		
92	(twin)	Mississippi R., IL-MO	910

Year	Bridge	Location	Main span (ft)
1973	Hernando DeSoto (I-40) (two spans)	Mississippi R., AR-TN	900
2008	Blennerhassett (U.S. 50)	Parkersburg, WV-OH	878
1936	Henry Hudson	Harlem R., New York, NY	840
1966	Bob Cummings Lincoln Trail	Ohio R., IN-KY	825
1978	I-57, Mississippi R.	Cairo, IL	821
1980	I-65, Mobile R.	Mobile, AL	800
1961	Sherman Minton (I-64)	IN-Louisville, KY	800
1978	I-470, Ohio R.	Wheeling, WV	780
1932	West End	Pittsburgh, PA	780
1971	Piscataqua R. (I-95 High Level)	Portsmouth, NH- Kittery, ME	756
1959	Fort Pitt	Pittsburgh, PA	750

Movable Bridges
Vertical Lift

Year	Bridge	Location	Main span (ft)
1959	*Arthur Kill	New York, NY-Elizabeth, NJ	558
1935	*Cape Cod Canal	Buzzards Bay, MA	544
1896	*Delair	Pennsauken, NJ-Phila., PA	542
1937	Marine Pkwy. Hodges Mem.	Jamaica Bay, New York, NY	540
1931	Burlington-Bristol	Delaware R., NJ-PA	540

Year	Bridge	Location	Main span (ft)
1908	*Burlington Northern RR[5]	Portland, OR	516
1968	*Second Narrows Railway	Vancouver, BC, Can.	499
1911	*Armour-Swift-Burlington	Missouri R., Kansas City, MO	428

Bascule

Year	Bridge	Location	Main span (ft)
1940	Charles Berry Memorial	Lorain, OH	333
1917	Market St./Ch. John Ross.	Chattanooga, TN	310
2003	SW 2nd Avenue	Miami, FL	302

Swing

Year	Bridge	Location	Main span (ft)
1927	Fort Madison (Santa Fe)	Mississippi R., IA	525
1952	George P. Coleman Mem.	Yorktown, VA	500
1991	SW Spokane St.	Seattle, WA	480
1899	*Illinois Central RR	Chicago, IL	479
1914	*Coos Bay RR	Coos Bay, OR	458
1913	East Haddam (Rt. 82)	Connecticut R., CT	456

Floating Pontoon[6]

Year	Bridge	Location	Main span (ft)
2016	New SR 520	Seattle, WA	7,709
1993	Lacey V. Murrow (I-90)	Seattle, WA	6,620
1961	Hood Canal (SR 104)	Kitsap-Jefferson Cos., WA	6,521
1989	Homer M. Hadley (I-90)	Seattle, WA	5,811

Other Notable North American Bridges

Year	Bridge	Type	Location	Tot. length (ft)
1956/69	Lake Pontchartrain Causeway[7]	Twin concrete trestle	Metairie-Mandeville, LA	126,055
1979	Manchac Swamp	Twin concrete trestle	Manchac, LA	120,384
1973	Atchafalaya Basin (I-10)	Twin concrete trestle	Baton Rouge, LA	95,040
1982	Seven Mile (Overseas Hwy., U.S. 1)	Segmental concrete	Florida Keys	35,867
2009/11	I-10 Twin Spans	Twin concrete trestle	Slidell-New Orleans, LA	29,040
2002	Croatan Sound	Continuous post-tensioned girder	Manteo, NC	27,000
1993	Choctawhatchee Mid-Bay	Segmental concrete	Destin-Niceville, FL	19,265
1962	International	Arch truss	Sault Ste. Marie, MI-ON, Can.	9,278
2009	Walkway Over the Hudson[8]	Pedestrian	Poughkeepsie-Highland, NY	6,768
1874	Eads, Mississippi R.[9]	Steel arch	St. Louis, MO-IL	6,442
2013	San Francisco-Oakland Bay (Skyway)	Segmental concrete box girder	San Francisco Bay, CA	6,336
1987	Powder Point	Tropical hardwood	Duxbury, MA	2,200
1969	Silver Memorial, Ohio R.[10]	Cantilever	Pt. Pleasant, WV-OH	1,964
2010	O'Callaghan-Tillman Mem. (U.S. 93)[11]	Concrete arch	Colorado R., AZ-NV	1,900
1994	Natchez Trace Parkway	Concrete arch	Franklin, TN	1,572
1901	Hartland[12]	Covered	St. John R., Hartland, NB, Can.	1,282

(1) Two complete bridges each 2,310-ft long, which share an anchor point. (2) Self-Anchored Suspension Span (SAS); the world's longest single-tower, self-anchored suspension bridge. (3) World's longest bridge crossing ice-covered water, with total length of 8 mi. (4) World's longest cable-stayed bridge carrying mass transit only. (5) Vertical lift replaced swing span in 1989. (6) Length listed is of bridge's floating section. (7) World's longest continuous spans over water. (8) Originally opened in 1889 as a railroad bridge. (9) World's first major structure made of alloy steel. (10) Replaced Silver Bridge, the collapse of which in 1967 led to the creation of National Bridge Inspection Standards in the U.S. (11) Longest single-span concrete arch in Western Hemisphere. (12) World's longest covered bridge.

Oldest U.S. Bridges in Continuous Use

Built in 1697, the stone-arch Frankford Ave. Bridge (U.S. 13) crosses Pennypack Creek in Philadelphia, PA. It is 73-ft long and consists of three spans. The bridge was constructed as part of the King's Road, which connected Philadelphia to New York.

The oldest covered bridge, completed in 1829, is the double-span, 256-ft-long Bath-Haverhill Bridge, which spans the Ammonoosuc River between the towns of Bath and Haverhill, NH. The bridge was bypassed in 1999. It has since reopened to pedestrian traffic only.

Notable World Bridges

Source: World Almanac research

Year is date of completion or projected completion. Span of bridge is the distance between its main supports. As of mid-2018. NA = Not available.

Year	Bridge	Location	Main span (ft)
	Suspension		
1998	Akashi Kaikyo	Japan	6,532
2009	Xihoumen	China	5,413
1998	Storebælt (Great Belt, East Bridge)	Denmark	5,328
2016	Osman Gazi (Izmit Bay)	Turkey	5,085
2012	Yi Sun-sin (Gwangyang)	South Korea	5,069
2005	Runyang Yangtze R. (south)	China	4,888
2012	Nanjing Fourth Yangtze R.	China	4,652
1981	Humber	England	4,625
2016	Yavuz Sultan Selim (Third Bosphorus)	Turkey	4,619
1999	Jiangyin Yangtze R.	China	4,544
1997	Tsing Ma	China	4,518
2013	Hardanger	Norway	4,298
2007	Yangluo Yangtze R.	China	4,199
1997	Höga Kusten	Sweden	3,970
2016	Longjian	China	3,924
2012	Aizhai	China	3,858
2015	Ulsan Grand	South Korea	3,773
2018	Halogaland	Norway	3,756
2008	Huangpu	China	3,635
1988	Minami Bisan-Seto	Japan	3,609
1988	Fatih Sultan Mehmet (Bosphorus II)	Turkey	3,576
2009	Baling R.	China	3,570
2012	Taizhou Yangtze R.[1]	China	3,543
1973	Bosphorus	Turkey	3,524
1999	Kurushima III	Japan	3,379
1999	Kurushima II	Japan	3,346
1966	Ponte 25 de Abril, Tagus R.	Portugal	3,323
1964	Forth Road	Scotland	3,300

Note: Turkey's Çanakkale 1915 bridge across the Dardanelles Strait will have world's longest suspension span (6,637 ft) upon expected completion in 2021. (1) Two consecutive spans of equal length.

Year	Bridge	Location	Main span (ft)
	Steel Arch		
2009	Chaotianmen Yangtze R.	China	1,811
2003	Lupu	China	1,804
2012	Bosideng	China	1,739
1932	Sydney Harbour	Australia	1,650
2005	Wushan Yangtze R.	China	1,614
2019	Chenab (rail)[1]	India	1,532
2013	Xijiang (rail)	China	1,476
2007	Xinguang	China	1,404
2007	Caiyuanba	China	1,378
2010	Daning R.	China	1,312
2007	Lianxiang	China	1,312
2010	Hiroshima Airport	Japan	1,247
1959	Sloboda	Croatia	1,224
2007	Maocao Street	China	1,207
2005	Wanzhou Yangtze R. Railway	China	1,181
2000	Yajisha	China	1,181
1962	Bridge of the Americas	Panama	1,128

(1) Will be world's highest rail bridge (1,178 ft) upon completion.

Year	Bridge	Location	Main span (ft)
Concrete Arch			
2016	Beipanjiang	China	2,362
1997	Wanxian Yangtze R.	China	1,378
2015	Nanpanjiang (rail)	China	1,365
1980	Krk I	Croatia	1,280
2016	Almonte Viaduct	Spain	1,260
Cantilever			
1890	Forth Rail[1]	Scotland	1,710
1974	Minato	Japan	1,673
1943	Rabindra Setu (Howrah)	India	1,500

(1) Two spans of equal length.

Year	Bridge	Location	Main span (ft)
Plate and Box Girder			
2006	Shibanpo	China	1,083
1998	Stolmasundet	Norway	988
1974	Pres. Costa e Silva (Rio-Niterói)	Brazil	984
1998	Raftsund	Norway	978
Cable-Stayed			
2012	Russky Island	Russia	3,622
2008	Sutong Yangtze R.	China	3,570
2009	Stonecutters	China	3,340
2009	Edong	China	3,038
1999	Tatara	Japan	2,920
1995	Normandy	France	2,808
2013	Jiujiang Yangtze R. Expressway	China	2,684
2010	Jingyue Yangtze R.	China	2,677
2009	Incheon	South Korea	2,625
2012	Zolotoy Rog	Russia	2,418
2009	Shanghai Yangtze R.	China	2,395
2009	Minpu	China	2,323
2017	Queensferry	Scotland	2,132
2005	Third Nanjing Yangtze R.	China	2,126
2001	Second Nanjing Yangtze R.	China	2,060
2000	Third Wuhan Yangtze R. (Baishazhou)	China	2,028
2002	Qingzhou Minjiang R.	China	1,985
1993	Yangpu	China	1,975

Year	Bridge	Location	Main span (ft)
1998	Meiko Chuo	Japan	1,936
1997	Xupu	China	1,936
2004	Rion-Antirion	Greece	1,837
2015	La Pepa	Spain	1,772
2014	Bukhang	South Korea	1,772
1991	Skarnsund	Norway	1,739
1999	Shantou Queshi	China	1,699
1995	Tsurumi Tsubasa	Japan	1,673
2008	Tianxingzhou Yangtze R.	China	1,654
2012	Mokpo	South Korea	1,640
2007	Kanchanaphisek	Thailand	1,640
2002	Jingsha	China	1,640
2000	Øresund	Denmark-Sweden	1,608
1991	Ikuchi	Japan	1,608
1994	Higashi Kobe	Japan	1,591
2011	Geo Geum	South Korea	1,575
1998	Zhanjiang	China	1,575
Other Notable World Bridges[1]			
2011	Danyang-Kunshan Grand (rail)[2]	China	538,000
2000	Bang Na Expressway[3]	Thailand	180,446
2011	Qingdao-Haiwan (Jiaozhou Bay)[4]	China	136,417
2007	Hangzhou Bay	China	118,110
2018	Hong Kong-Zhuhai Macau Main[5]	China	75,131
2013	Jiashao	China	33,136
2004	Millau Viaduct[6]	France	8,071
1978	Demerara Harbour (floating)	Guyana	6,074
1994	Nordhordland (floating)	Norway	4,088
1992	Bergsøysund (floating)	Norway	2,772
1991	Ikitsuki[7]	Japan	1,312

(1) Length listed is total length of bridge unless otherwise noted. (2) World's longest bridge. (3) World's longest road bridge. (4) World's longest oversea bridge in aggregate. (5) Part of HZMB link, which consists of multiple bridges, an underwater tunnel, and artificial islands. (6) World's tallest bridge, with max. height of 1,125 ft from top of pylon to valley floor. (7) Length listed is of main span, world's longest continuous truss span.

World's Longest Railway Tunnels

Source: World Almanac research

Year is date of opening or projected opening unless otherwise noted. As of mid-2018.

Year	Tunnel	Location	Operating railway	Length (mi)
2026	Brenner Base (twin)	Austria-Italy	Austrian Federal Railways (ÖBB) and Ferrovie dello Stato (FS)	39.8
2016	Gotthard Base (twin)	Switzerland-Italy	Swiss Federal Railways (SBB)	35.4/35.5
1988	Seikan	Japan	Japan Railways Group	33.5
2016	Yulhyeon	South Korea	SR/Korea Railroad Corporation (Korail)	31.3
1994	English Channel (Chunnel) (twin)	UK-France	Eurotunnel	31.1
2007	Lötschberg Base (twin)	Switzerland	BLS Lötschbergbahn AG	21.0
2014	New Guanjiao	China	Qinghai-Tibet Railway Company	20.3
2007	Guadarrama (twin)	Spain	Renfe	17.6
2009	Taihang (twin)	China	China's Ministry of Railways	17.3
2005	Hakkoda	Japan	Japan Railways Group	16.4
2018	Guangzhou-Shenzhen-Hong Kong Express Rail Link (XRL), Hong Kong section	China	MTR Corporation	16.2
2002	Iwate-Ichinohe	Japan	Japan Railways Group	16.0
NA[1]	Pajares (twin)	Spain	Renfe	15.3
2015	Iiyama	Japan	Japan Railways Group	13.8
1982	Daishimizu	Japan	Japan Railways Group	13.8
2018	Crossrail (twin)	UK	Transport for London	13.0
2008-09	Geumjeong	South Korea	Korea Railroad Corporation (Korail)	12.6
2006	Wushaoling (twin)	China	China's Ministry of Railways	12.5
1906/22	Simplon No. 1 and 2	Switzerland-Italy	BLS Lötschbergbahn AG	12.3
1999	Vereina	Switzerland	Rhätische Bahn (RhB)	11.8
2007	High Speed 1 (Channel Tunnel Rail Link, or CTRL) (twin)	UK-France	London & Continental Railways (LCR)	11.8
1975	Shin-Kanmon (twin)	Japan	Japan Railways Group	11.6
1934	Apennine	Italy	Ferrovie dello Stato (FS)	11.5
2002	Qinling (twin)	China	China's Ministry of Railways	11.5
2028	Fehmarn Belt[2]	Denmark-Germany	Rail Net Denmark (Banedanmark)	11.2
2006	Vaglia	Italy	Ferrovie dello Stato (FS)	10.4
2014	West Qinling (twin)	China	China's Ministry of Railways	10.3

NA = Not available. (1) Tunnels have been dug but are not yet in operation. (2) Would be world's longest immersed tunnel for rail and auto.

Underwater Vehicular Tunnels in North America

Source: World Almanac research

(more than 5,000 ft in length; year is date of opening)

Year	Name	Location	Waterway	Length (ft)
1950	Brooklyn Battery (twin)	New York, NY	East River	9,117
1927	Holland (twin)	New York, NY-Jersey City, NJ	Hudson River	8,558/8,371
1937/45/57	Lincoln (center/north/south tubes)	New York, NY-Weehawken, NJ	Hudson River	8,216/7,482/8,006
1985	Fort McHenry	Baltimore, MD	Patapsco River	7,920
1957/76	Hampton Roads (twin)	Hampton, VA	Hampton Roads	7,479
1957	Baltimore Harbor (twin)	Baltimore, MD	Baltimore Harbor	7,392
1940	Queens Midtown (twin)	New York, NY	East River	6,414
1934	Sumner	Boston, MA	Boston Harbor	5,653
1964	Thimble Shoal	Northampton Co., VA	Chesapeake Bay	5,552
1964	Chesapeake Channel	Northampton Co., VA	Chesapeake Bay	5,237
1930	Detroit-Windsor	Detroit, MI-Windsor, ON, Canada	Detroit River	5,160
1961	Callahan	Boston, MA	Boston Harbor	5,070

Land Vehicular Tunnels in the U.S.

Source: World Almanac research; Federal Highway Administration, U.S. Dept. of Transportation
(3,400 ft or more in length)

Name	Location	Length (ft)	Name	Location	Length (ft)
Anton Anderson Memorial[1]	Whittier, AK	13,300	Lehigh (twin)	PA Turnpike,	4,461/
SR99[2]	Seattle, WA	9,270		NE Extension	4,380
Edwin C. Johnson Memorial (eastbound)	I-70, Clear Creek Co.-Summit Co., CO	8,960	Blue Mountain (twin)	PA Turnpike	4,339
			Wawona	Yosemite Natl. Pk., CA	4,233
Eisenhower Memorial (westbound)	I-70, Clear Creek Co.-Summit Co., CO	8,939	Big Walker Mountain (twin)	Bland Co., VA	4,229
			Squirrel Hill	Pittsburgh, PA	4,225
Ted Williams[3]	MA Turnpike, Boston, MA	8,448	Tom Lantos/Devil's Slide (twin)	San Mateo Co., CA	4,200
Thomas P. O'Neill Jr.	I-93, Boston, MA	7,920	Hanging Lake (twin)	Glenwood Canyon, CO	4,000
Allegheny (twin)	PA Turnpike	6,070	Caldecott (4 tubes)	Oakland, CA	3,771/3,610/
Liberty (twin)	Pittsburgh, PA	5,920			3,610/3,389
Zion-Mount Carmel	Zion Natl. Park, UT	5,808	Fort Pitt (twin)	Pittsburgh, PA	3,614
East River Mountain (twin)	I-77, Rocky Gap, VA-Bluefield, WV	5,412	Mount Baker	I-90, Bellevue-Seattle, WA	3,456
Tuscarora Mountain (twin)	PA Turnpike	5,326	Dingess	Mingo Co., WV	3,400
Tetsuo Harano (twin)	H-3 Freeway, HI	5,165	Mall	Washington, DC	3,400
Kittatinny Mountain (twin)	PA Turnpike	4,727			
Cumberland Gap (twin)	U.S. 25E, KY-TN	4,600			

(1) Vehicles and trains take turns using the tunnel's one lane. (2) Under construction, with expected opening as early as fall 2018. (3) Total length of tunnel is 8,448 ft, 3,960 ft of which is underwater.

Major U.S. Dams and Reservoirs

Source: 2016 National Inventory of Dams, U.S. Army Corps of Engineers

Highest U.S. Dams

Rank	Dam	River	State	Type	Height Feet	Height Meters	Year completed
1.	Oroville	Feather	California	E	770	235	1968
2.	Hoover	Colorado	Nevada	A-G	730	221	1935
3.	Dworshak	N. Fork Clearwater	Idaho	G	717	219	1973
4.	Glen Canyon	Colorado	Arizona	A	710	216	1963
5.	New Bullards Bar	North Yuba	California	A	645	197	1970
6.	Mossyrock	Cowlitz	Washington	A	606	185	1968
7.	Shasta	Sacramento	California	G	602	183	1945
8.	Don Pedro	Tuolumne	California	E	585	178	1971
9.	New Melones	Stanislaus	California	E-R	578	176	1979
10.	Hungry Horse	S. Fork Flathead	Montana	A	564	172	1952

A = Arch; E = Embankment, earthfill; G = Gravity; R = Embankment, rockfill. **Note:** The height of a dam is the vertical distance between the original streambed or excavated foundation and the dam's crest, parapet wall, or maximum design water level. Tailings and other mining dams (i.e., dams built from the waste generated by mining operations) are not included in this list.

Largest U.S. Embankment Dams

Rank	Dam	River	State	Volume Cubic yards (thousands)	Volume Cubic meters (thousands)	Year completed
1.	Fort Peck	Missouri	Montana	125,628	96,049	1957
2.	Oahe	Missouri	South Dakota	92,000	70,339	1966
3.	Oroville	Feather	California	80,000	61,164	1968
4.	B. F. Sisk	San Luis Creek	California	77,670	59,383	1967
5.	Garrison	Missouri	North Dakota	66,500	50,843	1953
6.	Scotts Flat	Deer Creek	California	66,300	50,690	1948
7.	Cochiti	Rio Grande	New Mexico	65,000	49,696	1975
8.	Herbert Hoover	North New River Canal	Florida	54,700	41,821	1965
9.	Fort Randall	Missouri	South Dakota	50,200	38,381	1954
10.	Castaic	Castaic Creek	California	44,000	33,640	1973

Note: An embankment dam is any dam constructed with excavated material, including earth, rocks, and mining or other industrial waste. (In contrast, gravity, arch, and buttress dams are generally made out of concrete or masonry.) The majority of the world's dams are embankment dams. All dams in this list are earthfill, or formed primarily out of layers of compacted earth.

Largest-Capacity U.S. Reservoirs

Rank	Dam	Reservoir	State	Max. reservoir capacity Acre feet (thousands)	Max. reservoir capacity Cubic meters (thousands)	Year completed
1.	Hoover	Lake Mead	Nevada	30,237	37,296,790	1935
2.	Glen Canyon	Lake Powell	Arizona	29,875	36,850,270	1963
3.	Garrison	Lake Sakakawea	North Dakota	24,500	30,220,305	1953
4.	Oahe	Lake Oahe	South Dakota	23,600	29,110,172	1966
5.	Fort Peck	Fort Peck Lake	Montana	19,100	23,559,503	1957
6.	Grand Coulee	Lake Roosevelt	Washington	9,562	11,794,553	1941
7.	Herbert Hoover	Lake Okeechobee	Florida	8,519	10,508,032	1965
8.	Kentucky	Kentucky Lake	Kentucky	7,535	9,294,779	1944
9.	Sam Rayburn	Sam Rayburn Lake	Texas	6,520	8,042,302	1965
10.	Wright Patman	Wright Patman Lake	Texas	6,505	8,023,799	1954

Note: A reservoir is a body of water created by a dam for storage. This water may serve a single or multiple purposes, such as irrigation, flood reduction, and electricity generation.

Major Dams and Reservoirs of the World

Source: World Register of Dams, Intl. Commission on Large Dams (ICOLD)
Asterisk (*) designates structure is planned or under construction as of mid-2018.

World's Highest Dams

Rank	Dam	Country	Meters	Feet
1.	*Rogun	Tajikistan	335	1,099
2.	*Bakhtiari	Iran	315	1,033
3.	Jinping I	China	305	1,001
4.	Nurek	Tajikistan	300	984
5.	*Lianghekou	China	295	968
6.	Xiaowan (Yunnan Gorge)	China	294	965
7.	Xiluodu	China	286	938
8.	Grande Dixence	Switzerland	285	935
9.	*Baihetan	China	277	909
10.	*Diamer-Bhasha	Pakistan	272	892
11.	Inguri	Georgia	272	892
12.	*Yusufeli	Turkey	270	886
13.	Nuozhadu	China	262	860
14.	Chicoasén	Mexico	262	860
15.	Tehri	India	260	853

Height above lowest formation

World's Largest Embankment Dams

Rank	Dam	Country	Volume cubic meters (thousands)
1.	Tarbela	Pakistan	121,000
2.	Fort Peck	U.S.	96,049
3.	Ataturk	Turkey	84,500
4.	Guri	Venezuela	77,971
5.	*Rogun	Tajikistan	74,000
6.	Oahe	U.S.	70,339
7.	Parambikulam	India	69,165
8.	High Island West	China	67,000
9.	Gardiner	Canada	65,440
10.	Yacyretà	Argentina/Paraguay	65,436
11.	Mangla	Pakistan	64,991
12.	Afsluitdijk	Netherlands	63,400
13.	Oroville	U.S.	61,164
14.	B. F. Sisk	U.S.	59,383
15.	Nurek	Tajikistan	56,000

World's Largest-Capacity Reservoirs

Rank	Dam	Country	Max. capacity cubic meters (millions)
1.	Kariba	Zimbabwe/Zambia	180,600
2.	Bratsk	Russia	169,000
3.	High Aswan	Egypt	169,000
4.	Akosombo (Lake Volta)	Ghana	150,000
5.	Daniel-Johnson	Canada	141,851
6.	Guri	Venezuela	135,000
7.	W. A. C. Bennett	Canada	74,300
8.	*Hidase	Ethiopia	74,000
9.	Krasnoyarsk	Russia	73,300
10.	Zeya	Russia	68,400
11.	Robert-Bourassa (La Grande 2)	Canada	61,715
12.	La Grande 3	Canada	60,020
13.	Ust-Ilim	Russia	59,300
14.	Boguchany	Russia	58,200
15.	Kuibyshev	Russia	58,000

World's Largest-Capacity Hydro Plants

Rank	Dam	Country	Installed capacity (MW)
1.	Sanxia (Three Gorges Dam)	China	22,500
2.	Itaipu	Brazil/Paraguay	14,000
3.	Xiluodu	China	13,860
4.	*Baihetan	China	13,050
5.	*Belo Monte	Brazil	11,234
6.	Guri	Venezuela	10,200
7.	Tucuruí	Brazil	8,370
8.	Robert-Bourassa	Canada	7,772
9.	*Ta Sang	Myanmar (Burma)	7,100
10.	Grand Coulee	U.S.	6,809
11.	Xiangjiaba	China	6,400
12.	Sayano-Shushenskaya	Russia	6,400
13.	Longtan	China	6,300
14.	*Hidase	Ethiopia	6,000
15.	*Myitsone	Myanmar (Burma)	6,000
16.	Krasnoyarsk	Russia	6,000

Timeline of Selected Architectural Styles and Structures

Asterisk (*) denotes part of a UNESCO World Heritage site.

Style and period	Location; characteristics; significant examples
Mesopotamian c. 3500-539 BCE	City-states of Sumer, Akkad, Babylon, Assyria (modern-day Iraq). Mud-brick rectangular temples on oval platforms with simple corbel vaults, later ziggurats. Painted terra-cotta mosaics and murals; carved reliefs on columns and walls. **Ziggurat of Nanna**, Ur (Muqayyar, Iraq), ordered by Ur-Nammu, c. 2100 BCE **Anu Ziggurat and White Temple**, Uruk (Warka, Iraq), c. 3000 BCE
Egyptian c. 3000-30 BCE	Along Nile R. Mud-brick and limestone tombs and massive, geometric pyramids, post-and-lintel construction. Highly decorative with colorful hieroglyphics, carvings, columns, obelisks, paintings, and sculpture. ***Stepped Pyramid of Pharaoh Djoser** (Saqqara, Egypt), by Imhotep, c. 2737-2717 BCE ***Great Pyramid of Khufu** (Giza, Egypt), c. 2250 BCE ***Great Temple of Amon-Ra** (Karnak, Egypt), c. 1530-300 BCE ***Mortuary Temple of Queen Hatshepsut**, Deir el-Bahari (Thebes, Egypt), by Senenmut, c. 1479-1458 BCE
Three Dynasties c. 2100-221 BCE	China. Single-level mud-brick or mud-smeared timber structures on earthen platforms with thatched roofs. Later, bracketed wooden-framed structures with brick-tiled floors, roofs with overhanging eaves. **City of Erlitou** (Yanshi, China), c. 1900-1500 BCE
Minoan c. 1800-1450 BCE	Crete. Palaces, tombs in monumental style adapted from Mesopotamia and Egypt. Multilevel stone palaces with large central court, no fortifications. Walls made of doors (*polythyron*); stone porticoes and lintels; wooden ceilings and columns; beehive-shaped tombs (*tholi*). **Palace at Knossos** (Heraklion, Crete, Greece), c. 1700 BCE
Mycenaean c. 1600-1100 BCE	Greece. Adapted Minoan style, with large stone masonry, huge walls, and fortified citadels with complex palaces (*megaron*). ***Treasury of Atreus** (Mycenae, Greece), c. 1250 BCE
Olmec c. 1200-400 BCE	Mexico Gulf Coast. Many religious structures, including stone temple-pyramids centered in cities; also large stone sculptures and mosaic pavement with natural and animistic themes. **Great Pyramid** (La Venta, Mexico), c. 800-400 BCE
Mayan c. 900 BCE-900 CE	Central America. Religious structures with plaster-surfaced stone temple-pyramids with stairs containing tombs. Decorative animistic and geometric relief sculptures, lintels, and stone monuments with hieroglyphics. ***Pyramid of the Magician** (Uxmal, Mexico), c. 700-910 CE ***North Acropolis** (Tikal, Guatemala), c. 200 BCE

Style and period	Location; characteristics; significant examples

Greek
c. 750-323 BCE
	Greek peninsula, Asia Minor, North Africa, western Mediterranean. Religious, civic buildings in monumental style, inspired by Egypt, based on strict rules of form and human proportion; many ornamental details. Marble and limestone structures (including rectangular temples) with pediment, colonnaded porticoes in diverse regional styles, defined by orders of architecture like Ionic, Doric, Corinthian. Most early buildings with timber supports; solid stone in later temples.
	  ***Parthenon, Acropolis** (Athens, Greece), by Ictinus and Callicrates, 447-436 BCE
	  ***Temple of Zeus** (Olympia, Greece), by Libon of Elis, mid-5th cent. BCE
	  Mausoleum of Halicarnassus (Bodrum, Turkey), by Pythis, c. 353 BCE (destroyed)
	  ***Temple of Apollo Epicurius** (Bassae, Greece), by Ictinus, c. 420 BCE

Achaemenid
c. 550-334 BCE
	Persian Empire (Eastern Mediterranean to Indus R.). Palatial complexes influenced by cultures absorbed by the empire; limestone and mud-brick complexes on raised stone terraces with ornamental stairways, rectangular pillared audience halls with porticoes and corner towers; pleasure gardens (*bâgh*) as focal point of architecture.
	  ***Pasargadae** (Iran), founded by Cyrus II, after 547 BCE
	  ***Persepolis** (Iran), founded by Darius I, around 518 BCE

Roman
c. 500 BCE-400 CE
	Roman Empire. Civic and religious structures with grandiose limestone brick and concrete construction in systematic, practical layout. Adapted Greek orders in many structures, including circular temples and large covered halls (basilica), but emphasized movement with rounded arches and domes, geometric vaults.
	  ***Pantheon** (Rome, Italy), ordered by Emperor Hadrian, 118-128 CE
	  ***Colosseum** (Rome, Italy), ordered by Emperor Vespasian, 70-82 CE
	  ***Roman Forum** (Rome, Italy), 500s BCE-608 CE

Qin and Han
c. 221 BCE-220 CE
	China. Massive public works, palaces, tombs, and planned cities; systematic layout and design determined by divination techniques (geomancy). Multistoried timber palace complexes with gardens, courtyards laid along a long hall with a south-north axis for weather; decorative roof with overhanging eaves.
	  ***The Great Wall** (China), ordered by Qin Shi Huang, 220 BCE-c. 1600 CE
	  ***Mausoleum of the First Qin Emperor** (Xianyang [Xi'an], China), c. 210 BCE

Sassanian
226-651
	Iran. Mud-brick, mortared rubble, and stone palaces on platforms. Tall, vaulted entry chambers with one open side (*iwans*). Three-aisled hall chambers covered with rudimentary barrel vaults. Parabolic domes abandoned for square courtyards in later Sassanian period.
	  Palace of Ardashir I (Firuzabad, Iran), c. 224
	  Taq-i Kisra [Arch of Khosrau] (Ctesiphon, Iraq), c. 260 or c. 550

Byzantine
330-1453
	Byzantine Empire, Italy, Russia. Religious structures with masonry construction based on Roman architecture, many salvaged pieces. Centralized cross-in-square layout, with large central dome supported by vaults. Highly decorative, with iconographic frescoes, glass mosaics.
	  ***Hagia Sophia** (Istanbul, Turkey), by Anthemius and Isidorus, 532-37
	  ***St. Mark's Basilica** (Venice, Italy), ordered by Domenico Contarini, 1063-94

Sui and Tang
581-906
	China. Includes influences from other cultures; geomancy used to enhance harmony and social status. Rectangular, multistory modular timber structures with interlinking corridors; single-eaved roofs with exposed beams.
	  Daming Palace (Xi'an, China), 634 (destroyed)
	  ***Hall of the Great Buddha**, Foguang Temple (Mount Wutai, China), ordered rebuilt by Xuan Zhong, 857

Early Islamic (Umayyad)
692-c. 1000
	Syria, Middle East, North Africa, southern Spain. Mosques in adapted Sassanian style. Austere exteriors; simple columned halls with minarets and mihrabs (prayer niches), walled courtyards and gardens, onion domes. Highly decorative interiors with patterned marble, mosaics.
	  ***Dome of the Rock** [Qubbat al-Sakhra] (Jerusalem), ordered by Abd al-Malik, 692
	  ***Great Mosque of Córdoba** (Spain), ordered by Abd al-Rahman I, 784-86

Khmer c. 880-1200s	Indochina. Hindu or Buddhist temple complexes, including brick, later sandstone beehive-shaped shrines with arches atop terraced temple "mountains" symbolizing Mount Meru, Hindu and Buddhist center of the universe, where the gods dwell. Concentric layout of structures mimics the cosmos, relating religious narrative in carved reliefs. ***Angkor Wat** (Cambodia), ordered by Suryavarman II, 12th cent.

Romanesque (Norman)
c. 900s-1100s
	Western Europe. Churches and monasteries in localized Roman style; many reused material from Roman structures. Austere, heavy, simple masonry construction with thick walls, concealed buttresses, small windows, barrel arches, and vaults. Churches like Roman basilica with arched central nave, lower side aisles, apse, transept formed Latin cross. Monumental art and ornaments with Christian narrative throughout, especially on façade and portals.
	  ***Durham Cathedral** (England, UK), ordered by Bishop William de Saint-Calais, 1093-1133
	  ***Cathedral, Baptistery, and "Leaning" Tower** (Pisa, Italy), by various architects, begun in 1063, tower not completed until 1372

Gothic
c. 1100s-1500s
	France, Europe. Cathedrals meant to inspire spirituality with design like Roman basilica: pointed arches and spires that reach toward heavens, skeletal masonry, revealed structure like flying buttresses, ribbed vaults to allow better lighting, large stained-glass windows.
	  Abbey Church of Saint-Denis (France), ordered by Abbot Suger, 1135-44
	  ***Cathedral of Notre-Dame** (Paris, France), ordered by Bishop Maurice de Sully, 1163-1351
	  ***Cologne Cathedral** (Cologne, Germany), ordered by Archbishop Konrad von Hochstaden, 1248-1880
	  ***St. Vitus Cathedral** (Prague, Czech Republic), by Matthias of Arras, later Peter Parler, 1344-1929

Yuan and Ming 1279-1644	China. Mongol-influenced timber and some brick structures influenced by geomancy. Emphasized monumental mass in low-lying, sprawling structures with simple rectangular pavilions, great halls, elaborate wooden latticework, carved and painted details. ***Forbidden City** (Beijing, China), ordered by Emperor Yongle, 1406-20

Renaissance
1420s-1520s
	Italy. The rebirth or rediscovery of ancient Roman design, grounded in a scholarly approach to architecture. Followed rules of proportion in perspective and symmetry, classical orders, and simple but perfected geometric forms; emphasis on human scale.
	  ***Pazzi Chapel** (Florence, Italy), by Filippo Brunelleschi, 1429-61
	  ***Palazzo Medici-Riccardi** (Florence, Italy), by Michelozzo di Bartolomeo, 1444-60
	  ***Tempietto San Pietro** (Rome, Italy), by Donato Bramante, 1502-10
	  ***Villa Almerico Capra, or La Rotonda** (near Vicenza, Italy), by Andrea Palladio, later Vincenzo Scamozzi, 1566-1610

Style and period	Location; characteristics; significant examples

Mughal
1526-1858
	India. Monumental palaces and mosques blending Hindu and Islamic architecture. Sandstone with marble inlay; highly decorative, with semiprecious stones, vegetal and Koranic motifs. Formulaic four-part pleasure gardens (*charbâgh*), exemplified by grounds of Taj Mahal.
	   *Humayun's Tomb (Delhi, India), by Sayyid Muhammad, 1562-72
	   *Taj Mahal (Agra, India), ordered by Emperor Shah Jahan, 1631-48

Baroque
1630s-1700s
	Italy, later Western Europe. Elaborate and theatrical religious and civic structures, focused on dramatic overall effect. Complex geometric shapes and elaborate sculptures meant to be viewed from many angles.
	   St. Carlo alle Quattro Fontane (Rome, Italy), by Francesco Borromini, 1638-41
	   *Palace of Versailles (Versailles, France), royal hunting lodge (built 1631-34) expanded under Louis XIV, 1661-1710
	   Church of San Lorenzo (Turin, Italy), by Guarino Guarini, 1666-79
	   Church of St. John of Nepomuk, or Asamkirche (Munich, Germany), by Cosmas Damian and Egid Quirin Asam, 1733-46

Rococo 1690s-1700s	Europe. Mostly interior, simplified but still fanciful Baroque designs; ornate with natural motifs, gold trim, light and creamy colors, asymmetrical designs, and unusual materials. ***Sanssouci Palace** (Potsdam, Germany), by Georg Wenzeslaus von Knobelsdorff, 1745-47

Neoclassicism
1750-1830
	Europe, Americas. Civic, commercial, and religious structures; chaste, non-decorative designs in reaction to Baroque excess. Grounded in Enlightenment-era principles and simple, strict adherence to classic (Greek, Roman, Renaissance) forms and details. Palladian style in England, Federal style in U.S.
	   Chiswick House (Chiswick, England, UK), by Richard Boyle, 1725-29
	   *Monticello (Charlottesville, VA), by Thomas Jefferson, 1768-1809

Neo-Gothic
1837-1900s
	Britain, U.S. Civic, commercial, and religious structures utilizing Gothic forms in new commercial enterprises like railway stations and hotels. Traditional masonry façade disguised modern structural material like iron and glass.
	   *Westminster Palace (London, England, UK), by Charles Barry and A.W.N. Pugin, 1840-47
	   Hotel fronting St. Pancras Railway Station (London, England, UK), by George Gilbert Scott, 1865-71

Arts and Crafts
1850s-1930s
	England, U.S. Residential structures made of brick and other indigenous materials with pastoral and traditional elements like gabled roofs. Conceived as a reaction against homogenization of style following the Industrial Revolution.
	   Red House (Bexley Heath, England, UK), by Philip Webb, 1859
	   Tigbourne Court (Surrey, England, UK), by Edwin Lutyens, 1898

Beaux-Arts
1870s-1930s
	France, U.S. Grandiose, highly decorative style, using a mix of classical forms taught at the École des Beaux-Arts (School of Fine Arts) in Paris: columns, wall projections, elaborate rooftops, high-relief decoration.
	   Boston Public Library (Boston, MA), by McKim, Mead, and White, 1888-95
	   Grand Central Terminal (New York, NY), Reed & Stem and Warren & Wetmore, 1903-13

Art Nouveau
1884-1905
	Europe (esp. Brussels, Belgium; France). Civic and residential structures using industrial products like metal and glass to mimic natural forms; airy, fluid, and ornate.
	   *Hôtel Tassel (Brussels, Belgium), by Victor Horta, 1892-93
	   Entrances to Métro (subway) (Paris, France), by Hector Guimard, 1900

Prairie
1893-1917
	U.S. Mostly residences, some civic buildings in adapted Arts and Crafts style. Inspired by American Midwest and small-town values. Frank Lloyd Wright most notable architect of the style. Buildings centered on chimney, with overhanging eaves and horizontal emphasis, long bands of windows.
	   Robie House (Chicago, IL), by Frank Lloyd Wright, 1908-10
	   National Farmer's Bank (Owatonna, MN), by Louis Sullivan, 1906-08

Futurism 1913-14	Italy. Purely theoretical style that produced no actual structures. Emphasized concrete, glass, and steel construction; pure geometric forms and straight lines; and exposed structure and utilities. **La Città Nuova (The New City)** (sketches), by Antonio Sant'Elia, 1913
Constructivism 1914-20s	Russia, Europe. Public buildings based on socialist philosophies. Purely utilitarian industrial design, modern materials. **Rusakov Club** (Moscow, Russia), by Konstantin Melnikov, 1927-28
De Stijl 1917-31	Netherlands. Building and fixtures designed as a complete, sculpture-like piece of art; emphasis on primary colors, simple but asymmetrical geometry. Name is Dutch for "The Style." ***Schröder House** (Utrecht, Netherlands), by Gerrit Thomas Rietveld, 1924
Bauhaus 1919-33	Weimar Republic Germany. Art and design school founded by Walter Gropius with philosophy that the machine is the modern medium. Concrete, glass, and steel construction that united industrial crafts and fine arts with simple geometric forms and colors. ***Bauhaus** (Dessau, Germany), by Walter Gropius, 1925-26

International Style
1920s-70s
	Asia, Europe, North America. Reinforced concrete and steel structures, mostly commercial buildings with some residences and civic structures. Post-and-slab construction meant walls no longer supported weight so façades could be continuous strip (ribbon) glass "curtain-walls" with modular interiors. Emphasis on simple forms; glass, marble, and stainless steel; minimal decoration.
	   Philadelphia Savings Fund Society Building (Philadelphia, PA), by George Howe and William Lescaze, 1926-32
	   Villa Savoye (Poissy, France), by Le Corbusier, 1928-31
	   Seagram Building (New York, NY), by Ludwig Mies Van Der Rohe with Philip Johnson, 1954-58

Art Deco
1925-30s
	Europe, U.S. Traditional, symmetric, elegant construction like Beaux-Arts whimsically mixed with modern styles like geometric forms and steel or chrome features.
	   Chrysler Building (New York, NY), by William van Alen, 1928-30
	   Empire State Building (New York, NY), by Shreve, Lamb & Harmon, 1930-31

Postmodernism
1970s-present
	Asia, Europe, North America. Playful reaction against generic, mainstream "orthodox modern architecture," according to Robert Venturi. Token references to traditional architectural elements like pediments or gables on houses; aim to present, Venturi wrote, "old clichés in new settings."
	   Vanna Venturi House (Philadelphia, PA), by Robert Venturi, 1962
	   Public Service Building (Portland, OR), by Michael Graves, 1980-82

World Population Growth

The global population in ancient times can only be very roughly estimated, but there were perhaps 50 mil people in the world in 1000 BCE. The United Nations (UN) Population Division estimates a figure of 300 mil for 1 CE. This diagram shows estimated population growth since then.

Although different sources may provide varying estimates, they agree that the world's population began growing more rapidly in the 18th and 19th centuries and increased at an even greater rate in the 20th century. According to the UN, the total population reached 1 bil in 1804; rose to 2 bil 123 years later, in 1927; to 3 bil 33 years after that, in 1960; to 4 bil in 1974; to 5 bil in 1987; and to 6 bil in 1999.

The UN put the world population in mid-2018 at 7.6 bil. It projects that the population will reach 8 bil by 2023. The UN expects that between 2017 and 2050, nine countries will account for half the increase in the world population: India, Nigeria, Dem. Rep. of the Congo, Pakistan, Ethiopia, Tanzania, U.S., Uganda, and Indonesia (in descending order).

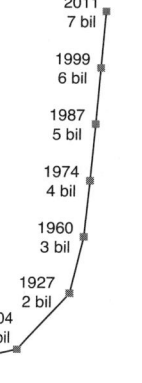

```
2011
7 bil

1999
6 bil

1987
5 bil

1974
4 bil

1960
3 bil

1927
2 bil

1804
1 bil
```

```
1 CE                         1250          1500
300 mil                      400 mil       500 mil
```

Area and Population of the World by Continent/Region

Source: International Data Base, International Programs Center, U.S. Census Bureau, U.S. Dept. of Commerce; *The World Factbook*, Central Intelligence Agency (CIA)

Continent/ region	Land area (sq mi)	Land area (sq km)	% of Earth's land	Population (midyear) 1950	1975	2000	2018	% of world total, 2018	2025[1]
Asia.	11,921,263	30,875,930	21.2	1,437,565,483	2,412,701,231	3,686,050,249	4,450,997,043	59.3	4,692,549,820
Africa	11,494,808	29,771,416	20.4	229,058,740	416,958,705	805,888,233	1,264,314,235	16.8	1,487,078,163
Europe[2].	8,559,255	22,168,368	15.2	547,140,324	678,635,710	730,502,554	748,074,050	10.0	749,663,317
N. America	7,879,783	20,408,544	14.0	165,945,185	238,783,486	313,388,332	365,272,462	4.9	385,028,748
Latin America[3]. .	7,723,205	20,003,009	13.7	165,442,794	320,616,913	518,453,673	636,745,569	8.5	674,582,932
Oceania	3,277,072	8,487,577	5.8	12,476,128	21,114,852	30,420,838	38,424,821	0.5	41,240,203
Antarctica[4] . . .	5,405,430	14,000,000	9.6	NA	NA	NA	NA	NA	NA
World	56,260,816	145,714,844	100.0	2,557,628,654	4,088,810,897	6,084,703,879	7,503,828,180	100.0	8,030,143,183

NA = Not applicable. **Note:** Composition of geographical (continental) regions are as defined by the United Nations. Figures may not add up to totals due to rounding. (1) Projected. (2) Includes all of Russia. (3) Includes the Caribbean. (4) Antarctica has no indigenous inhabitants, though people are present at permanent and seasonal research stations. Only an est. 108,109 sq mi are ice free.

Population of the World's Largest Urban Areas

Source: *World Urbanization Prospects: The 2018 Revision*, Dept. of Economic and Social Affairs, UN Population Division

Population figures are midyear estimates or projections for urban agglomerations, i.e., whole metropolitan areas comprising an urban center and surrounding settlements of lower density. In 2018, 55% of the world's population lived in an urban area. That proportion is expected to increase as the population grows. Data may differ from figures elsewhere in *The World Almanac*. MMA = Major Metropolitan Area.

(ranked by mid-2018 population)

Rank	Urban area, country	Population (thous.) 1975	2000	2018	2035	Rate of change (%) 1975-2000	2000-18	2018-35	Pop. of urban area as % of country's 2018 pop.
1.	Tokyo, Japan.	26,615	34,450	37,468	36,014	29.4%	8.8%	−3.9%	29.5%
2.	Delhi, India	4,436	15,692	28,514	43,345	253.7	81.7	52.0	2.1
3.	Shanghai, China.	5,658	14,247	25,582	34,341	151.8	79.6	34.2	1.8
4.	São Paulo, Brazil	9,614	17,014	21,650	24,490	77.0	27.2	13.1	10.3
5.	Mexico City, Mexico	10,734	18,457	21,581	25,415	72.0	16.9	17.8	16.5
6.	Cairo, Egypt	6,450	13,626	20,076	28,504	111.3	47.3	42.0	20.2
7.	Mumbai (Bombay), India	7,685	16,147	19,980	27,343	110.1	23.7	36.9	1.5
8.	Beijing, China	4,828	10,285	19,618	25,366	113.0	90.7	29.3	1.4
9.	Dhaka, Bangladesh	2,221	10,285	19,578	31,234	363.1	90.4	59.5	11.8
10.	Kinki MMA (Osaka), Japan. . .	16,298	18,660	19,281	18,346	14.5	3.3	−4.9	15.2
11.	New York-Newark, NY-NJ, U.S.	15,880	17,813	18,819	20,817	12.2	5.6	10.6	5.8
12.	Karachi, Pakistan	3,989	9,825	15,400	23,128	146.3	56.7	50.2	7.7
13.	Buenos Aires, Argentina	9,143	12,504	14,967	17,128	36.8	19.7	14.4	33.5
14.	Chongqing, China.	2,545	7,863	14,838	20,531	209.0	88.7	38.4	1.0
15.	Istanbul, Turkey.	3,600	8,744	14,751	17,986	142.9	68.7	21.9	18.0
16.	Kolkata (Calcutta), India	8,166	13,097	14,681	19,564	60.4	12.1	33.3	1.1
17.	Manila, Philippines	4,999	9,958	13,482	18,649	99.2	35.4	38.3	12.7
18.	Lagos, Nigeria	1,890	7,281	13,463	24,419	285.3	84.9	81.4	6.9
19.	Rio de Janeiro, Brazil	7,733	11,307	13,293	14,810	46.2	17.6	11.4	6.3
20.	Tianjin, China.	3,527	6,989	13,215	16,446	98.1	89.1	24.5	0.9
21.	Kinshasa, Dem. Rep. of Congo.	1,482	6,140	13,171	26,682	314.4	114.5	102.6	15.7
22.	Guangzhou, Guangdong, China	1,698	7,812	12,638	16,741	360.0	61.8	32.5	0.9
23.	Los Angeles-Long Beach-Santa Ana, CA, U.S.	8,926	11,798	12,458	13,778	32.2	5.6	10.6	3.8
24.	Moscow, Russia	7,623	10,005	12,410	12,823	31.2	24.0	3.3	8.6
25.	Shenzhen, China	36	6,550	11,908	15,185	18,327.5	81.8	27.5	0.8
26.	Lahore, Pakistan.	2,399	5,576	11,738	19,117	132.5	110.5	62.9	5.8
27.	Bangalore, India	2,111	5,581	11,440	18,066	164.4	105.0	57.9	0.8
28.	Paris, France	8,558	9,737	10,901	12,065	13.8	12.0	10.7	16.7
29.	Bogotá, Colombia.	3,040	6,329	10,574	12,753	108.2	67.1	20.6	21.4
30.	Jakarta, Indonesia	4,813	8,390	10,517	13,688	74.3	25.4	30.2	3.9

National Rankings by Population, Area, Population Density, 2018

Source: International Data Base, International Programs Center, U.S. Census Bureau, U.S. Dept. of Commerce; *The World Factbook*, Central Intelligence Agency (CIA)

Population figures are for midyear. In mid-2018, the world had an estimated population of nearly 7.5 bil, of which China represented nearly one-fifth. Population density is calculated using land area, which does not include inland water.

Largest Populations

Rank	Country	Population
1.	China[1]	1,384,688,986
2.	India	1,296,834,042
3.	United States	329,256,465
4.	Indonesia	262,787,403
5.	Brazil	208,846,892
6.	Pakistan	207,862,518
7.	Nigeria	203,452,505
8.	Bangladesh	159,453,001
9.	Russia	142,122,776
10.	Japan	126,168,156

Smallest Populations

Rank	Country	Population
1.	Vatican City[2]	1,000
2.	Nauru	9,692
3.	Tuvalu	11,147
4.	Palau	21,516
5.	Monaco	30,727
6.	San Marino	33,779
7.	Liechtenstein	38,547
8.	Saint Kitts and Nevis	53,094
9.	Dominica	74,027
10.	Marshall Islands	75,684

Largest Land Areas

Rank	Country	Area (sq mi)	Area (sq km)
1.	Russia	6,323,482	16,377,742
2.	China	3,600,947	9,326,410
3.	United States	3,532,315	9,148,655
4.	Canada	3,511,023	9,093,507
5.	Brazil	3,227,096	8,358,140
6.	Australia	2,966,153	7,682,300
7.	India	1,147,956	2,973,193
8.	Argentina	1,056,642	2,736,690
9.	Kazakhstan	1,042,360	2,699,700
10.	Algeria	919,595	2,381,741

Smallest Land Areas

Rank	Country	Area (sq mi)	Area (sq km)
1.	Vatican City	0.17	0.44
2.	Monaco	0.77	2
3.	Nauru	8	21
4.	Tuvalu	10	26
5.	San Marino	24	61
6.	Liechtenstein	62	160
7.	Marshall Islands	70	181
8.	Saint Kitts and Nevis	101	261
9.	Maldives	115	298
10.	Malta	122	316

Most Densely Populated

Rank	Country	Persons per sq mi	Persons per sq km
1.	Monaco	39,791.3	15,363.5
2.	Singapore	21,903.5	8,454.6
3.	Vatican City[2]	5,886.3	2,272.7
4.	Bahrain	4,916.4	1,898.2
5.	Malta	3,680.4	1,421.0
6.	Maldives	3,411.1	1,317.0
7.	Bangladesh	3,172.6	1,225.0
8.	Taiwan	1,890.4	729.9
9.	Barbados	1,765.6	681.7
10.	Mauritius	1,740.6	672.1

Least Densely Populated

Rank	Country	Persons per sq mi	Persons per sq km
1.	Mongolia	5.2	2.0
2.	Australia	7.9	3.1
3.	Namibia	8.0	3.1
4.	Iceland	8.9	3.4
5.	Mauritania	9.7	3.7
6.	Guyana	9.7	3.8
7.	Libya	9.9	3.8
8.	Suriname	9.9	3.8
9.	Canada	10.2	3.9
10.	Botswana	10.3	4.0

(1) Does not include mid-2018 population of Hong Kong (7,213,338) and Macau (606,340). (2) Population is for mid-2017.

Current Population and Projections for Countries and Other Areas

Source: International Data Base, International Programs Center, U.S. Census Bureau, U.S. Dept. of Commerce; *The World Factbook*, Central Intelligence Agency (CIA)

(midyear figures)

Country/area	2018	2025	2050
Afghanistan	34,940,837	41,117,073	63,795,418
Albania	3,057,220	3,104,932	2,824,012
Algeria	41,657,488	45,841,317	55,444,735
American Samoa	50,826	45,973	29,167
Andorra	85,708	85,112	74,765
Angola	30,355,880	38,467,070	82,179,028
Anguilla	17,422	19,749	26,980
Antigua and Barbuda	95,882	103,830	122,930
Argentina	44,694,198	47,333,842	54,115,246
Armenia	3,038,217	2,961,175	2,468,311
Aruba	116,576	126,130	150,730
Australia	23,470,145	25,053,669	29,012,740
Austria	8,793,370	8,987,330	9,107,912
Azerbaijan	10,046,516	10,533,598	11,209,644
Bahamas, The	332,634	349,116	371,219
Bahrain	1,442,659	1,579,899	1,847,072
Bangladesh	159,453,001	170,280,989	193,092,763
Barbados	293,131	297,015	282,041
Belarus	9,527,543	9,325,020	8,339,664
Belgium	11,570,762	12,037,746	12,772,233
Belize	385,854	433,389	590,608
Benin	11,340,504	13,564,964	22,118,545
Bermuda	71,176	72,851	69,874
Bhutan	766,397	820,143	951,873
Bolivia	11,306,341	12,463,434	16,003,638
Bosnia and Herzegovina	3,849,891	3,787,402	3,216,039
Botswana	2,249,104	2,483,999	3,201,058
Brazil	208,846,892	218,259,140	232,304,177
Brunei	450,565	498,756	638,157
Bulgaria	7,057,504	6,728,056	5,531,820
Burkina Faso	19,742,715	23,599,713	37,009,374
Burundi	11,844,520	14,791,662	30,391,856
Cabo Verde	568,373	619,168	741,842
Cambodia	16,449,519	18,037,946	22,338,891
Cameroon	25,640,965	30,508,842	51,912,309
Canada	35,881,659	37,558,781	41,135,648
Cayman Islands	59,613	67,661	91,118
Central African Republic	5,745,062	6,637,613	10,338,863
Chad	15,833,116	19,676,074	37,468,757
Chile	17,925,262	18,764,737	19,688,474
China	1,384,688,986	1,407,006,788	1,301,627,048
Colombia	48,168,996	51,194,904	56,227,630
Comoros	821,164	905,545	1,169,893
Congo, Dem. Rep. of	85,281,024	99,162,003	144,805,434
Congo Republic	5,062,021	5,947,999	10,201,971
Cook Islands	9,038	7,621	5,460
Costa Rica	4,987,142	5,353,218	6,065,989
Côte d'Ivoire	26,260,582	30,639,091	47,023,289
Croatia	4,270,480	4,125,465	3,538,821
Cuba	11,116,396	10,938,159	9,829,024
Curaçao	150,241	153,501	150,128
Cyprus	1,237,088	1,329,908	1,392,078
Czechia	10,686,269	10,696,842	10,209,638
Denmark	5,809,502	5,994,785	6,266,278
Djibouti	884,017	1,016,919	1,395,810
Dominica	74,027	74,374	64,772
Dominican Republic	10,298,756	10,978,295	12,542,490
Ecuador	16,498,502	17,867,616	21,102,550
Egypt	99,413,317	115,502,146	168,937,974
El Salvador	6,187,271	6,288,430	6,181,181
Equatorial Guinea	797,457	935,553	1,428,139
Eritrea	5,970,646	6,411,164	8,935,060

Country/area	2018	2025	2050
Estonia	1,244,288	1,182,920	923,335
Eswatini (Swaziland)	1,087,200	1,142,871	1,268,089
Ethiopia	108,386,391	131,260,566	228,066,276
Faroe Islands	51,018	53,200	57,112
Fiji	926,276	956,003	1,013,636
Finland	5,537,364	5,630,882	5,475,753
France	67,364,357	68,860,292	69,484,481
French Polynesia	290,373	305,484	324,712
Gabon	2,119,036	2,515,181	4,088,698
Gambia, The	2,092,731	2,369,298	3,210,223
Gaza Strip	1,836,713	2,120,751	3,053,554
Georgia	4,926,087	4,929,789	4,714,548
Germany	80,457,737	79,226,209	71,541,906
Ghana	28,102,471	32,610,058	52,415,526
Gibraltar	29,461	29,753	28,423
Greece	10,761,523	10,670,697	10,035,935
Greenland	57,691	57,174	49,356
Grenada	112,207	114,741	114,205
Guam	167,772	169,588	157,176
Guatemala	16,581,273	18,550,664	24,400,094
Guernsey	66,697	67,710	66,521
Guinea	11,855,411	14,375,261	27,531,955
Guinea-Bissau	1,833,247	2,187,466	4,038,893
Guyana	740,685	781,231	878,028
Haiti	10,788,440	11,749,583	14,542,914
Honduras	9,182,766	10,143,828	12,948,839
Hong Kong	7,213,338	7,296,877	6,623,263
Hungary	9,825,704	9,615,020	8,489,811
Iceland	343,518	366,578	406,766
India	1,296,834,042	1,396,046,308	1,656,553,632
Indonesia	262,787,403	276,746,433	300,183,166
Iran	83,024,745	88,968,954	98,601,804
Iraq	40,194,216	47,656,612	76,519,418
Ireland	5,068,050	5,417,947	6,333,836
Isle of Man	89,407	92,606	92,840
Israel	8,424,904	9,305,235	12,364,874
Italy	62,246,674	62,591,055	61,415,852
Jamaica	2,812,090	2,790,919	2,319,218
Japan	126,168,156	123,385,521	107,209,536
Jersey	99,602	104,140	107,581
Jordan	10,458,413	11,310,890	15,600,166
Kazakhstan	18,744,548	19,809,426	22,237,156
Kenya	48,397,527	53,196,255	70,755,460
Kiribati	109,367	117,779	139,738
Korea, North	25,381,085	26,242,210	26,969,396
Korea, South	51,418,097	52,565,679	47,731,321
Kosovo	1,907,592	1,999,461	2,222,619
Kuwait	2,916,467	3,169,497	3,863,453
Kyrgyzstan	5,849,296	6,218,713	7,063,351
Laos	7,234,171	7,971,675	10,068,995
Latvia	1,923,559	1,772,796	1,249,812
Lebanon	6,100,075	5,396,843	5,621,049
Lesotho	1,962,461	1,970,540	1,920,225
Liberia	4,809,768	5,811,539	10,569,823
Libya	6,754,507	7,374,566	8,970,664
Liechtenstein	38,547	40,505	43,610
Lithuania	2,793,284	2,573,431	1,801,002
Luxembourg	605,764	680,527	864,238
Macau	606,340	630,434	620,184
Macedonia	2,118,945	2,137,317	2,033,994
Madagascar	25,683,610	30,182,920	45,807,534
Malawi	19,842,560	24,957,849	51,780,996
Malaysia	31,809,660	34,683,300	42,928,546
Maldives	392,473	388,681	444,429
Mali	18,429,893	22,636,934	41,656,105
Malta	449,043	471,365	475,293
Marshall Islands	75,684	83,203	103,092
Mauritania	3,840,429	4,425,089	6,536,272
Mauritius	1,364,283	1,412,384	1,441,100
Mexico	125,959,205	134,828,700	150,567,503
Micronesia	103,643	98,948	74,483
Moldova	3,437,720	3,176,863	2,261,208
Monaco	30,727	31,706	29,810
Mongolia	3,103,428	3,301,176	3,669,264
Montenegro	614,249	596,968	484,207
Montserrat	5,315	5,529	5,707
Morocco	34,314,130	36,484,418	42,026,448
Mozambique	27,233,789	32,306,018	58,998,457
Myanmar (Burma)	55,622,506	58,786,637	64,503,165
Namibia	2,533,224	2,879,366	4,156,634
Nauru	9,692	10,008	11,995
Nepal	29,717,587	31,565,692	33,265,760
Netherlands	17,151,228	17,572,113	17,906,594
New Caledonia	282,754	307,452	370,511
New Zealand	4,545,627	4,775,930	5,198,992
Nicaragua	6,085,213	6,493,913	7,233,620
Niger	19,866,231	24,618,828	44,221,854
Nigeria	203,452,505	242,556,503	416,996,080
Northern Mariana Islands	51,994	49,909	38,616
Norway	5,372,191	5,682,068	6,364,008
Oman	3,494,116	3,981,057	5,401,957
Pakistan	207,862,518	228,385,138	290,847,790
Palau	21,516	22,102	22,894
Panama	3,800,644	4,117,882	4,859,334
Papua New Guinea	7,027,332	7,823,210	10,110,027
Paraguay	7,025,763	7,602,853	8,840,105
Peru	31,331,228	33,283,408	36,943,693
Philippines	105,893,381	117,445,897	155,380,252
Poland	38,420,687	37,753,766	32,738,308
Portugal	10,355,493	10,201,334	9,463,025
Puerto Rico	3,294,626	2,980,352	2,089,492
Qatar	2,363,569	2,562,764	2,558,854
Romania	21,457,116	20,872,127	18,060,354
Russia	142,122,776	140,139,049	129,908,086
Rwanda	12,187,400	13,851,378	19,169,209
Saint Barthelemy	7,160	7,056	6,527
Saint Helena, Ascension, and Tristan da Cunha	7,841	7,888	7,296
Saint Kitts and Nevis	53,094	55,405	56,362
Saint Lucia	165,510	168,519	162,356
Saint Martin	32,284	33,048	34,601
Saint Pierre and Miquelon	5,471	5,030	3,516
Saint Vincent and the Grenadines	101,844	100,409	93,507
Samoa	201,316	210,369	245,010
San Marino	33,779	35,203	35,178
São Tomé and Príncipe	204,454	227,395	309,457
Saudi Arabia	33,091,113	37,038,252	46,923,312
Senegal	15,020,945	17,580,816	27,244,158
Serbia	7,078,110	6,845,638	5,869,146
Seychelles	94,633	98,843	100,391
Sierra Leone	6,312,212	7,500,140	13,593,862
Singapore	5,995,991	6,732,999	8,609,518
Sint Maarten	42,677	46,560	53,001
Slovakia	5,445,040	5,405,646	4,850,540
Slovenia	2,102,126	2,093,610	1,922,216
Solomon Islands	660,121	747,001	1,015,731
Somalia	11,259,029	13,274,251	22,626,120
South Africa	55,380,210	59,108,375	68,528,850
South Sudan	10,204,581	13,301,507	23,624,573
Spain	49,331,076	51,415,437	52,490,640
Sri Lanka	22,576,592	23,563,343	25,166,733
Sudan	43,120,843	51,818,208	89,327,551
Suriname	597,927	636,782	717,936
Sweden	10,040,995	10,587,441	12,011,256
Switzerland	8,292,809	8,665,531	9,539,097
Syria	19,454,263	24,537,876	31,225,740
Taiwan	23,545,963	23,642,264	20,834,040
Tajikistan	8,604,882	9,510,130	12,132,365
Tanzania	55,451,343	66,904,889	118,586,412
Thailand	68,615,858	69,588,429	66,063,997
Timor-Leste	1,321,929	1,539,173	2,191,749
Togo	8,176,449	9,741,450	16,583,950
Tonga	106,398	104,648	78,995
Trinidad and Tobago	1,215,527	1,183,838	1,023,741
Tunisia	11,516,189	12,114,586	12,679,219
Turkey	81,257,239	84,544,177	89,290,126
Turkmenistan	5,411,012	5,800,391	6,607,083
Turks and Caicos Islands	53,701	61,293	84,240
Tuvalu	11,147	11,819	13,423
Uganda	40,853,749	50,692,201	93,476,229
Ukraine	43,952,299	42,887,993	37,148,031
United Arab Emirates	6,215,216	7,063,346	8,018,904
United Kingdom	65,105,246	67,243,723	71,153,797
United States	329,256,465	347,334,912	398,328,349
Uruguay	3,369,299	3,431,610	3,495,238
Uzbekistan	30,023,709	31,823,964	35,116,374
Vanuatu	288,037	323,464	432,658
Vatican City[1]	1,000	NA	NA
Venezuela	31,689,176	34,203,406	39,757,122
Vietnam	97,040,334	102,458,828	111,173,583
Virgin Islands, British	35,802	41,324	59,618
Virgin Islands, U.S.	106,977	103,539	79,884
Wallis and Futuna	15,763	16,023	15,598
West Bank	2,798,494	3,153,234	4,213,540
Western Sahara	619,551	735,697	1,173,350
Yemen	28,667,230	32,822,216	46,080,625
Zambia	16,445,079	20,104,997	38,992,619
Zimbabwe	14,030,368	16,030,790	25,552,730
World[2]	7,503,828,180	8,030,143,183	9,488,153,401

NA = Not available. **Note:** Figures for countries do not include the population of any dependencies listed separately in this table. For example, China's population estimate and projections do not include Hong Kong or Macau. (1) Current pop. is as of 2017. (2) Total projected populations do not include countries for which projections were not available.

Countries Ranked by Gross Domestic Product and Per Capita GDP, 2017

Source: *The World Factbook*, Central Intelligence Agency (CIA)

Estimates of gross domestic product (GDP)—the value of all final goods and services that a country produced in a year—were made based on purchasing power parity exchange rates. Per capita GDP is calculated using the estimated population size as of July 1 in a given year. Data may differ from estimates made by the U.S. Bureau of Economic Analysis. GDP figures are 2017 ests. unless otherwise noted.

GDP (in mil)				Per capita GDP			
Highest		**Lowest**		**Highest**		**Lowest**	
1. China[1]	$23,160,000	1. Tuvalu	$42	1. Liechtenstein[2]	$139,100	1. Burundi	$700
2. U.S.	19,390,000	2. Nauru	159	2. Qatar	124,500	Central African Republic	700
3. India	9,459,000	3. Marshall Islands	189	3. Monaco[3]	115,700	3. Congo, Dem. Rep. of	800
4. Japan	5,429,000	4. Kiribati	226	4. Luxembourg	106,300	4. Mozambique	1,200
5. Germany	4,171,000	5. Palau	291	5. Singapore	93,900	Niger	1,200
6. Russia	4,008,000	6. Micronesia	347	6. Brunei	78,200	Malawi	1,200
7. Indonesia	3,243,000	7. Tonga	587	7. Ireland	75,500	7. Yemen	1,300
8. Brazil	3,240,000	8. São Tomé and Príncipe	676	8. Norway	71,800	8. Liberia	1,400
9. UK	2,914,000	9. Vanuatu	770	9. UAE	67,700	9. South Sudan	1,500
10. France	2,836,000	10. Dominica	785	10. Kuwait	66,200	10. Eritrea	1,600
11. Mexico	2,458,000	11. Samoa	1,134	11. Switzerland	61,400	Madagascar	1,600
12. Italy	2,311,000	12. St. Vincent and the Grenadines	1,266	12. U.S.	59,500	Sierra Leone	1,600
						Comoros	1,600
13. Turkey	2,173,000	13. Comoros	1,313	13. San Marino	58,600		
14. South Korea	2,029,000	14. Solomon Islands	1,324	14. Saudi Arabia	54,800	14. North Korea[3]	1,700
15. Spain	1,774,000	15. St. Kitts and Nevis	1,528	15. Netherlands	53,600	Togo	1,700
Saudi Arabia	1,774,000	16. Grenada	1,606	16. Iceland	51,800	The Gambia	1,700
17. Canada	1,769,000	17. San Marino	2,052	17. Sweden	51,500	17. Haiti	1,800
18. Iran	1,645,000	18. Antigua and Barbuda	2,393	18. Germany	50,400	Guinea-Bissau	1,800
19. Australia	1,246,000	19. St. Lucia	2,536	19. Taiwan	50,300	19. Burkina Faso	1,900
20. Thailand	1,234,000	20. Seychelles	2,718	Australia	50,300	20. Guinea	2,000
						Kiribati	2,000
						Afghanistan	2,000

(1) Does not include Hong Kong ($454.9 bil GDP) or Macau ($71.8 bil GDP). (2) 2009 est. (3) 2015 est.

Budget Deficits as Percent of GDP in Selected Countries, 1998-2018

Source: *OECD Economic Outlook*, Organisation for Economic Co-operation and Development (OECD)

Country	1998	2000	2005	2010	2012	2014	2015	2016	2017	2018
Australia	2.3%	1.0%	2.3%	−4.1%	−3.0%	−1.8%	−1.1%	−1.5%	−0.5%	−0.2%
Austria	−2.7	−2.4	−2.5	−4.4	−2.2	−2.7	−1.0	−1.6	−0.7	−0.5
Belgium	−0.9	−0.1	−2.8	−4.0	−4.2	−3.1	−2.5	−2.5	−1.0	−1.3
Brazil*	NA	−3.3	−3.5	−2.4	−2.3	−6.0	−10.2	−9.0	−7.8	−7.6
Canada	0.1	2.6	1.6	−4.7	−2.5	0.2	−0.1	−1.1	−1.0	−1.0
China*	−1.4	−2.7	−0.7	−0.4	0.5	−0.3	−1.3	−3.0	−3.0	−3.0
Colombia*	NA	−5.3	−3.4	−2.2	−0.6	−3.1	−3.2	−4.9	−4.5	−3.9
Czechia	−4.2	−3.6	−3.0	−4.2	−3.9	−2.1	−0.6	0.7	1.6	1.6
Denmark	−0.4	1.9	5.0	−2.7	−3.5	1.1	−1.5	−0.4	1.0	−0.5
Estonia	−0.8	−0.1	1.1	0.2	−0.3	0.7	0.1	−0.3	−0.3	0.4
Finland	1.6	6.9	2.6	−2.6	−2.2	−3.2	−2.8	−1.8	−0.6	−0.8
France	−2.4	−1.3	−3.3	−6.9	−5.0	−3.9	−3.6	−3.4	−2.6	−2.3
Germany	−2.5	0.9	−3.4	−4.2	0.0	0.5	0.8	1.0	1.3	1.5
Greece	−6.3	−4.1	−6.2	−11.2	−8.9	−3.6	−5.7	0.6	0.8	0.5
Hungary	−7.4	−3.0	−7.8	−4.5	−2.4	−2.6	−1.9	−1.7	−2.0	−2.6
Iceland	−0.6	1.2	4.5	−9.7	−3.7	−0.1	−0.8	12.6	1.5	1.4
India*	−9.0	−9.5	−6.7	−7.1	−6.9	−6.7	−6.3	−6.3	−6.5	−6.3
Indonesia*	−1.4	−1.6	0.2	−0.3	−1.3	−1.9	−2.8	−2.4	−2.5	−2.3
Ireland	2.0	4.9	1.6	−32.1	−8.0	−3.6	−1.9	−0.5	−0.3	−0.3
Israel	−6.8	−3.2	−4.1	−3.7	−4.8	−3.3	−2.1	−2.1	−2.1	−2.8
Italy	−3.0	−2.4	−4.1	−4.2	−2.9	−3.0	−2.6	−2.5	−2.3	−1.8
Japan	−10.2	−7.4	−4.4	−9.1	−8.3	−5.4	−3.6	−3.4	−3.5	−3.0
Korea, South	0.6	4.4	1.6	1.0	1.0	1.3	1.3	2.4	2.8	2.1
Latvia	0.0	−2.7	−0.4	−8.7	−1.2	−1.5	−1.4	0.1	−0.5	−0.9
Luxembourg	3.2	5.9	0.1	−0.7	0.3	1.3	1.4	1.6	1.5	0.5
Netherlands	−0.9	1.9	−0.3	−5.0	−3.9	−2.3	−2.1	0.4	1.1	0.7
New Zealand	0.0	1.7	4.6	−7.3	−2.3	0.2	0.2	1.2	0.9	0.2
Norway	3.3	15.1	14.8	11.0	13.8	8.7	6.1	4.0	4.4	4.9
Poland	−4.2	−3.0	−4.0	−7.3	−3.7	−3.6	−2.6	−2.3	−1.7	−1.5
Portugal	−4.4	−3.2	−6.2	−11.2	−5.7	−7.2	−4.4	−2.0	−3.0	−0.7
Russia*	NA	NA	5.0	−1.0	2.0	−2.3	−1.5	−3.6	−1.5	0.3
Slovakia	−5.2	−12.0	−2.9	−7.5	−4.3	−2.7	−2.7	−2.2	−1.0	−0.8
Slovenia	−2.3	−3.6	−1.3	−5.6	−4.0	−5.5	−2.9	−1.9	0.0	0.4
South Africa*	−5.3	−4.1	−2.4	−3.3	−3.6	−3.8	−3.8	−3.5	−4.0	−3.7
Spain	−2.9	−1.1	1.2	−9.4	−10.5	−6.0	−5.3	−4.5	−3.1	−2.4
Sweden	0.8	3.2	1.8	0.0	−1.0	−1.6	0.2	1.2	1.3	1.0
Switzerland	−1.3	0.4	−0.7	0.4	0.4	−0.2	0.6	0.3	1.1	0.7
United Kingdom	−0.3	1.0	−3.4	−9.5	−8.2	−5.7	−4.3	−3.3	−1.8	−1.4
United States	−0.4	0.8	−4.2	−12.2	−9.0	−5.0	−4.3	−5.0	−3.6	−5.5
OECD countries	**−2.3**	**−0.5**	**−2.8**	**−8.1**	**−6.0**	**−3.6**	**−3.0**	**−2.9**	**−2.0**	**−2.6**

* = Not an OECD member nation; excluded from OECD country total. NA = Not available.

Gold Reserves of Selected Central Banks and Governments, 1975-2017

Source: *International Financial Statistics*, International Monetary Fund (IMF)

(in mil fine troy ounces)

Year end	All countries	China[1]	France	Germany[2]	India	Italy	Japan	Nether-lands	Russia	Switzer-land	Turkey	UK	U.S.
1975	1,174.4	NA	100.9	117.6	7.0	82.5	21.1	54.3	NA	83.2	3.6	21.0	274.7
1980	1,149.1	12.8	81.9	95.2	8.6	66.7	24.2	43.9	NA	83.3	3.8	18.8	264.3
1985	1,143.7	12.7	81.9	95.2	9.4	66.7	24.2	43.9	NA	83.3	3.9	19.0	262.7
1990	1,144.2	12.7	81.9	95.2	10.7	66.7	24.2	43.9	NA	83.3	4.1	18.9	261.9
1995	1,114.7	12.7	81.9	95.2	12.8	66.7	24.2	34.8	9.4	83.3	3.7	18.4	261.7
2000	1,066.4	12.7	97.2	111.5	11.5	78.8	24.5	29.3	12.4	77.8	3.7	15.7	261.6
2005	991.6	19.3	90.9	110.2	11.5	78.8	24.6	22.3	12.4	41.5	3.7	10.0	261.6
2006	979.8	19.3	87.4	110.0	11.5	78.8	24.6	20.6	12.9	41.5	3.7	10.0	261.5
2007	963.6	19.3	83.7	109.9	11.5	78.8	24.6	20.0	14.5	36.8	3.7	10.0	261.5
2008	963.2	19.3	80.1	109.7	11.5	78.8	24.6	19.7	16.7	33.4	3.7	10.0	261.5
2009	980.1	33.9	78.3	109.5	17.9	78.8	24.6	19.7	20.9	33.4	3.7	10.0	261.5
2010	990.4	33.9	78.3	109.3	17.9	78.8	24.6	19.7	25.4	33.4	3.7	10.0	261.5
2011	1,002.2	33.9	78.3	109.2	17.9	78.8	24.6	19.7	28.4	33.4	6.3	10.0	261.5
2012	1,017.5	33.9	78.3	109.0	17.9	78.8	24.6	19.7	30.8	33.4	11.6	10.0	261.5
2013	1,023.0	33.9	78.3	108.9	17.9	78.8	24.6	19.7	33.3	33.4	16.7	10.0	261.5
2014	1,028.7	33.9	78.3	108.8	17.9	78.8	24.6	19.7	38.8	33.4	17.0	10.0	261.5
2015	1,051.5	56.7	78.3	108.7	17.9	78.8	24.6	19.7	45.5	33.4	16.6	10.0	261.5
2016	1,069.3	59.2	78.3	108.6	17.9	78.8	24.6	19.7	51.9	33.4	12.1	10.0	261.5
2017	1,082.0	59.2	78.3	108.5	17.9	78.8	24.6	19.7	51.9	33.4	18.2	10.0	261.5

NA = Not available. (1) Figures are for mainland China only and do not include Hong Kong (0.07 mil oz t in 2017) or Macau. (2) West Germany prior to 1991.

Unemployment Rates in Selected Countries, 1970-2017

Source: *OECD Economic Outlook*, Organisation for Economic Co-operation and Development (OECD)

Year	Australia	Canada	France	Germany	Italy	Japan	Sweden	Turkey	UK	U.S.
1970	1.6%	5.7%	2.1%	NA	3.8%	1.2%	2.0%	5.7%	3.5%	5.0%
1975	4.9	6.9	3.4	NA	4.1	1.9	2.1	6.9	4.5	8.5
1980	6.1	7.5	5.3	NA	5.4	2.0	2.6	7.5	6.8	7.2
1985	8.3	10.6	8.9	NA	8.3	2.6	3.6	6.6	11.4	7.2
1990	6.9	8.2	7.9	NA	8.8	2.1	2.1	7.5	7.1	5.6
1995	8.5	9.5	10.0	8.2%	11.2	3.1	10.5	7.1	8.6	5.6
1997	8.4	9.1	10.7	9.6	11.3	3.4	11.7	6.3	7.0	4.9
2000	6.3	6.8	8.5	7.9	10.0	4.7	6.7	6.0	5.5	4.0
2002	6.4	7.7	7.8	8.6	8.5	5.4	6.0	9.8	5.2	5.8
2004	5.4	7.2	8.8	10.3	8.0	4.7	7.4	9.7	4.8	5.5
2005	5.0	6.8	8.8	11.0	7.7	4.4	7.7	9.5	4.8	5.1
2006	4.8	6.3	8.8	10.0	6.8	4.1	7.1	9.0	5.4	4.6
2007	4.4	6.0	8.0	8.6	6.1	3.8	6.1	9.2	5.3	4.6
2008	4.2	6.1	7.3	7.4	6.7	4.0	6.2	10.0	5.7	5.8
2009	5.6	8.3	9.1	7.6	7.7	5.0	8.3	13.0	7.6	9.3
2010	5.2	8.0	9.2	7.0	8.3	5.0	8.6	11.1	7.9	9.6
2011	5.1	7.5	9.1	5.9	8.4	4.6	7.8	9.1	8.1	8.9
2012	5.2	7.3	9.7	5.4	10.7	4.3	8.0	8.4	8.0	8.1
2013	5.7	7.1	10.3	5.2	12.1	4.0	8.0	9.0	7.6	7.4
2014	6.1	6.9	10.3	5.0	12.6	3.6	7.9	9.9	6.2	6.2
2015	6.1	6.9	10.4	4.6	11.9	3.4	7.4	10.3	5.4	5.3
2016	5.7	7.0	10.0	4.2	11.7	3.1	6.9	10.9	4.9	4.9
2017	5.6	6.3	9.4	3.8	11.2	2.8	6.7	10.9	4.4	4.3

NA = Not available. **Note:** Labor market data are subject to differences in definitions across countries. Because of changes in methodology, some data may not be fully comparable over time.

Personal Tax Rates in Selected Countries, 2017

Source: *Taxing Wages*, Organisation for Economic Co-operation and Development (OECD)

Rates are averages for a single person without children at the income level of the average full-time worker.

(as % of total gross earnings before taxes in U.S. dollars with equal purchasing power; ranked by total payment rate)

Country	Total payment rate[1]	Income tax	Employee soc. sec. contribs.	Gross earnings	Country	Total payment rate[1]	Income tax	Employee soc. sec. contribs.	Gross earnings
Belgium.	40.5%	26.5%	14.0%	$58,545	Poland.	25.1%	7.2%	17.8%	$27,816
Germany.	39.9	19.1	20.8	63,551	Sweden.	25.0	18.0	7.0	47,658
Denmark.	36.1	36.1	0.0	56,211	Australia	24.4	24.4	0.0	55,099
Slovenia	33.7	11.6	22.1	31,417	Czechia	24.1	13.1	11.0	27,536
Hungary	33.5	15.0	18.5	26,012	Slovakia	23.5	10.1	13.4	23,484
Austria	32.4	14.4	18.0	57,581	United Kingdom	23.4	14.0	9.4	54,319
Italy.	31.2	21.7	9.5	43,304	Canada	22.8	15.4	7.4	40,983
Netherlands	30.4	17.3	13.1	62,981	Japan	22.3	7.9	14.4	52,946
Finland	30.2	20.9	9.3	49,013	Spain	21.1	14.7	6.4	40,451
Latvia	29.4	18.9	10.5	21,755	Ireland	19.4	15.4	4.0	45,093
France.	29.2	14.8	14.4	48,339	Estonia	18.4	16.8	1.6	26,796
Luxembourg	29.1	16.7	12.3	65,716	New Zealand . . .	18.1	18.1	0.0	39,826
Iceland	28.7	28.3	0.3	63,661	Israel	17.7	9.7	8.0	39,215
Turkey	27.9	12.9	15.0	29,263	Switzerland	16.9	10.7	6.2	70,835
Norway	27.6	19.4	8.2	56,401	South Korea	14.5	6.1	8.4	52,505
Portugal	27.5	16.5	11.0	30,888	Mexico	11.2	9.8	1.4	12,730
United States . . .	26.0	18.4	7.7	52,988	Chile	7.0	0.0	7.0	22,616
Greece	26.0	10.0	16.0	35,165	**OECD[2] . . . .**	**25.5**	**15.7**	**9.8**	**43,791**

(1) Figures may not add up to totals due to rounding. (2) The 35 countries shown here.

Consumer Price Changes in Selected Countries, 1975-2017

Source: *International Financial Statistics*, International Monetary Fund (IMF)
(annual average % change)

Country	1975-80	1980-85	1985-90	1990-95	1995-2000	2000-05	2005-10	2010-11	2011-12	2012-13	2013-14	2014-15	2015-16	2016-17
Canada	8.8%	7.5%	4.5%	2.3%	1.7%	2.3%	1.7%	2.9%	1.5%	0.9%	1.9%	1.1%	1.4%	1.6%
China[1]	NA	NA	9.5	13.1	1.9	1.3	3.0	5.6	2.6	2.6	1.9	1.4	2.0	1.6
France	10.5	9.7	3.0	2.2	1.2	1.9	1.5	2.1	2.0	0.9	0.5	0.04	0.2	1.0
Germany	4.0	3.9	1.4	3.6	1.3	1.5	1.6	2.1	2.0	1.5	0.9	0.2	0.5	1.7
Italy	16.3	13.8	5.7	5.1	2.4	2.4	1.9	2.8	3.0	1.2	0.2	0.04	-0.1	1.2
Japan	6.6	2.8	1.4	1.4	0.3	-0.4	-0.1	-0.3	-0.1	0.3	2.8	0.8	-0.1	0.5
Spain	18.6	12.2	6.5	5.2	2.6	3.2	2.4	3.2	2.4	1.4	-0.2	-0.5	-0.2	2.0
Sweden	10.5	9.0	6.2	4.2	0.5	1.5	1.5	3.0	0.9	-0.04	-0.2	-0.05	1.0	1.8
Switzerland	2.3	4.3	2.5	3.2	0.7	0.8	0.9	0.2	-0.7	-0.2	-0.01	-1.1	-0.4	0.5
United Kingdom	14.4	7.2	4.7	3.8	1.6	1.4	2.6	3.9	2.6	2.3	1.5	0.4	1.0	2.6
United States	8.9	5.5	4.0	3.1	2.5	2.6	2.2	3.2	2.1	1.5	1.6	0.1	1.3	2.1
All countries	NA	NA	NA	NA	NA	NA	0.8	5.1	4.2	4.4	3.8	3.6	3.4	3.9

NA = Not available. (1) Figures for mainland China only and do not include Hong Kong (1.5% in 2016-17) or Macau (1.2% in 2016-17).

Number of Days Off Work Per Year in Selected Countries

Source: OECD Family Database, Organisation for Economic Co-operation and Development (OECD)

Entitlements are generally for full-time, full-year private-sector employees working a five-day week. The U.S. is the only OECD country without a national statute that entitles workers to a minimum number of days off per year.

Country	Paid days off[1]	Public holidays[2]	Total minimum days off	Country	Paid days off[1]	Public holidays[2]	Total minimum days off	Country	Paid days off[1]	Public holidays[2]	Total minimum days off
Australia	20	8	28	Germany....	20	9-13	29-33	Netherlands..	20	9	29
Austria	25	13	38	Greece....	20	11	31	New Zealand	20	11	31
Belgium.....	20	10	30	Hungary	20	10	30	Norway	21	10	31
Bulgaria	20	12	32	Iceland	24	12	36	Poland......	20	12	32
Canada.....	10	9	19	Ireland......	20	9	29	Portugal	22	12	34
Chile	15	15	30	Israel.......	11	10	21	Romania....	20	10	30
Costa Rica ..	10	11	21	Italy........	20	10	30	Slovakia	20	15	35
Croatia	20	13	33	Japan	10	15	25	Slovenia	20	12	32
Cyprus	20	NA	20	Korea, South	15	15	30	Spain	22	14	36
Czech Rep. .	20	13	33	Latvia	20	12	32	Sweden.....	25	11	36
Denmark....	25	9	34	Lithuania....	20	11	31	Switzerland..	20	9	29
Estonia	20	10	30	Luxembourg	25	10	35	Turkey......	12	NA	12
Finland	25	11	36	Malta.......	24	14	38	UK.........	28	9	37
France	25	11	36	Mexico......	6	7	13	U.S.........	0	NA[3]	0

NA = Not applicable. (1) Statutory minimum. (2) Generally set at the national or federal level. May vary at the state level. In some countries, including the U.S., public holidays do not have to be given as paid leave. (3) The government designates 10 federal holidays per year, though private-sector employers decide how much paid leave to offer.

International Migrants by Destination and Origin, 2000, 2017

Source: *Trends in International Migrant Stock: The 2017 Revision*, Dept. of Economic and Social Affairs, UN Population Division
(numbers in thousands)

	Places hosting the most international migrants 2017		2000		Places of origin with the largest diaspora populations 2017		2000	
	Country/terr.	Migrants	Country/terr.	Migrants	Country/terr.	Population	Country/terr.	Population
1.	U.S.	49,777.0	U.S.	34,814.1	India	16,587.7	Russia........	10,735.0
2.	Saudi Arabia ...	12,185.3	Russia........	11,900.3	Mexico	12,964.9	Mexico	9,562.3
3.	Germany......	12,165.1	Germany......	8,992.6	Russia.......	10,636.0	India	7,978.4
4.	Russia........	11,651.5	India	6,411.3	China[1].......	9,962.1	China[1].......	5,787.0
5.	UK............	8,841.7	France........	6,278.7	Bangladesh....	7,499.9	Ukraine........	5,596.5
6.	UAE	8,312.5	Ukraine.......	5,527.1	Syria	6,864.4	Bangladesh....	5,435.4
7.	France........	7,902.8	Canada.......	5,511.9	Pakistan	5,978.6	Afghanistan.....	4,541.2
8.	Canada.......	7,861.2	Saudi Arabia	5,263.4	Ukraine	5,941.7	UK..........	3,866.9
9.	Australia	7,035.6	UK...........	4,730.2	Philippines	5,680.7	Kazakhstan.....	3,554.5
10.	Spain	5,947.1	Australia	4,386.3	UK..........	4,921.3	Pakistan	3,398.4
11.	Italy..........	5,907.5	Pakistan	4,181.9	Afghanistan....	4,826.5	Germany.......	3,350.8
12.	India	5,188.6	Kazakhstan....	2,871.3	Poland.......	4,701.5	Italy..........	3,115.5
13.	Ukraine.......	4,964.3	Iran	2,803.8	Indonesia	4,234.0	Philippines	3,065.9
14.	Turkey........	4,882.0	Hong Kong	2,669.1	Germany.....	4,208.1	Turkey........	2,814.0
15.	South Africa ...	4,036.7	UAE	2,446.7	Kazakhstan....	4,074.4	Palestine......	2,756.0
16.	Kazakhstan....	3,635.2	Italy.........	2,121.7	Palestine.....	3,803.9	Indonesia	2,336.5
17.	Thailand	3,588.9	Côte d'Ivoire	1,994.1	Romania.....	3,578.5	Poland........	2,068.4
18.	Pakistan	3,398.2	Jordan........	1,927.8	Turkey.......	3,418.9	Portugal	2,004.0
19.	Jordan........	3,233.6	Israel.........	1,851.3	Egypt	3,413.0	U.S.	1,988.3
20.	Kuwait........	3,123.4	Japan	1,686.6	Italy.........	3,029.2	South Korea	1,951.8
21.	Hong Kong	2,883.1	Spain	1,657.3	U.S.........	3,016.7	Morocco	1,948.4
22.	Malaysia	2,703.6	Switzerland.....	1,570.8	Morocco	2,898.7	Vietnam	1,874.5
23.	Iran	2,699.2	Netherlands....	1,556.3	Myanmar.....	2,894.7	Egypt........	1,707.4
24.	Singapore	2,623.4	Argentina	1,540.2	Colombia	2,736.2	Belarus	1,688.5
25.	Switzerland....	2,506.4	Uzbekistan	1,405.3	Vietnam	2,727.4	Azerbaijan......	1,629.3
26.	Japan	2,321.5	Singapore	1,351.7	South Korea ...	2,477.6	Puerto Rico....	1,601.4
27.	Côte d'Ivoire ...	2,197.2	Turkey........	1,281.0	Portugal	2,266.7	Uzbekistan	1,599.6
28.	Argentina	2,164.5	Malaysia	1,277.2	France........	2,207.2	France........	1,527.3
29.	Oman	2,073.3	Thailand	1,257.8	Uzbekistan	1,991.9	Bosnia and Herzegovina ..	1,468.8
30.	Netherlands ...	2,056.5	Kuwait........	1,127.6	Somalia.......	1,988.5	Colombia	1,434.9
	World	**257,715.4**	**World**	**172,604.3**	**World**	**257,715.4**	**World**	**172,604.3**

(1) Not incl. Hong Kong or Macau.

Refugees and Other Populations of Concern, 2007-17

Source: *UNHCR Global Trends*, United Nations High Commissioner for Refugees (UNHCR)

Refugees are persons recognized under the 1951 UN Refugee Convention/1967 Protocol or the 1969 OAU (Org. of African Unity) Refugee Convention, those recognized in accordance with the UNHCR Statute, and persons granted or receiving protection. The UNHCR also extends assistance to internally displaced persons (IDPs), although they legally remain under their home country's protection. Stateless persons are not considered nationals under any state under the operation of its laws. Others of concern comprises persons who do not necessarily belong in any one category. Population as of year-end.

Category	2007	2009	2011	2013	2015	2016	2017	% change 2016-17
Refugees	11,391,000	10,396,500	10,404,800	11,699,300	16,111,300	17,187,500	19,941,300	16.0%
Asylum-seekers (pending cases) . . .	740,100	983,900	895,300	1,164,400	3,225,000	2,826,500	3,090,900	9.4
Returned refugees[1] . .	730,600	251,500	531,900	414,600	201,400	552,200	667,400	20.9
IDPs	13,740,200	15,628,100	15,473,400	23,925,500	37,494,200	36,627,100	39,118,500	6.8
Returned IDPs[1]	2,070,100	2,229,500	3,245,800	1,356,200	2,317,300	6,511,100	4,229,000	−35.0
Stateless persons	2,937,300	6,559,600	3,477,100	3,469,200	3,687,800	3,242,200	2,796,200	−13.8
Others of concern	68,700	411,700	1,411,800	836,100	870,700	803,100	1,596,200	98.8
Total	**31,678,000**	**36,460,800**	**35,440,100**	**42,865,300**	**63,907,700**	**67,749,800**	**71,439,500**	**5.4**

(1) Persons who have returned to their place of origin in that year.

Refugees and People in a Refugee-Like Situation, 2017

Source: *UNHCR Global Trends*, United Nations High Commissioner for Refugees (UNHCR)

Refugees are persons recognized under the 1951 UN Refugee Convention/1967 Protocol or the 1969 OAU (Org. of African Unity) Refugee Convention, those recognized in accordance with the UNHCR Statute, and persons granted or receiving protection. Persons outside of their country or territory of origin who face protection risks—but whose refugee status has not been ascertained—are described as being in a refugee-like situation. Only countries hosting 50,000 or more refugees and people in a refugee-like situation are shown; of those countries, only places originating 5,000 or more refugees and people in a refugee-like situation are given, in decreasing order. As of year-end.

Place of asylum	Origin of most refugees (excl. asylum-seekers with pending cases)	Number
Africa		**6,687,326**
Algeria	Western Sahara	94,258
Burundi	Dem. Rep. of the Congo	62,361
Cameroon	Central African Republic, Nigeria	337,388
Chad	Sudan, Central African Republic, Nigeria	411,482
Dem. Rep. of the Congo	Rwanda, Central African Republic, South Sudan, Burundi	537,087
Egypt	Syria, Palestinian[1], Sudan, South Sudan	232,648
Ethiopia	South Sudan, Somalia, Eritrea, Sudan	889,412
Kenya	Somalia, South Sudan, Ethiopia, Dem. Rep. of the Congo	431,901
Mauritania	Mali, Western Sahara	77,427
Niger	Nigeria, Mali	165,732
Rwanda	Burundi, Dem. Rep. of the Congo	170,990
South Africa	Somalia, Dem. Rep. of the Congo, Ethiopia, Congo Republic	88,694
South Sudan	Sudan, Dem. Rep. of the Congo	283,409
Sudan	South Sudan, Eritrea, Syria, Chad	906,599
Tanzania	Burundi, Dem. Rep. of the Congo	308,528
Uganda	South Sudan, Dem. Rep. of the Congo, Burundi, Somalia, Rwanda	1,350,504
Asia		**9,945,930**
Afghanistan	Pakistan	75,928
Bangladesh	Myanmar (Burma)	932,216
China	Vietnam	321,718
India	China, Sri Lanka, Myanmar (Burma), Afghanistan	197,146
Iran	Afghanistan, Iraq	979,435
Iraq	Syria, Turkey, Palestinian[1], Iran	277,672
Jordan	Syria, Iraq	691,023
Lebanon	Syria, Iraq	998,890
Malaysia	Myanmar (Burma)	103,839
Pakistan	Afghanistan	1,393,143
Thailand	Myanmar (Burma)	104,615
Turkey	Syria, Iraq, Iran, Afghanistan	3,480,348
Yemen	Somalia, Ethiopia	270,919
Europe		**2,602,942**
Austria	Syria, Afghanistan, Russia, Iraq, Somalia	115,263
France	Sri Lanka, Dem. Rep. of the Congo, Russia, Afghanistan, Serbia-Kosovo, Syria, Cambodia, Sudan, Turkey, Vietnam, Guinea, Iraq, Laos, Mauritania, Bangladesh	337,177
Germany	Syria, Iraq, Afghanistan, Eritrea, Iran, Turkey, Somalia, Serbia-Kosovo, stateless[2], Russia, Pakistan	970,365
Italy	Nigeria, Afghanistan, Pakistan, Somalia, Mali, The Gambia, Eritrea, Côte d'Ivoire, Senegal, Bangladesh, Iraq	167,335
Netherlands	Syria, Somalia, Eritrea, Iraq, Afghanistan, stateless[2]	103,860
Norway	Eritrea, Syria, Somalia, Afghanistan	59,236
Russia	Ukraine	126,035
Sweden	Syria, Eritrea, Afghanistan, stateless[2], Somalia, Iraq, Iran	240,962
Switzerland	Eritrea, Syria, Afghanistan, Sri Lanka	93,056
United Kingdom	Iran, Eritrea, Afghanistan, Syria, Zimbabwe, Sudan, Pakistan, Sri Lanka	121,837
Latin America and the Caribbean		**252,288**
Ecuador	Colombia	92,416
Venezuela	Colombia	122,810
Northern America		**391,907**
Canada	Colombia, China, Haiti	104,778
United States	China, El Salvador, Haiti, Guatemala, Egypt, Honduras, Ethiopia, Mexico, Syria, Nepal, Iraq, Iran, Russia, Venezuela, Eritrea	287,129
Oceania		**60,954**
Total		**19,941,347**

(1) Number includes Palestinians under the UNHCR mandate only. (2) Persons not considered nationals under any state under the operation of its laws.

Internally Displaced Persons, 2017

Source: Internal Displacement Monitoring Centre, Norwegian Refugee Council

Internally displaced persons (IDPs) are people who have been forced to move due to conflict or disasters (e.g., earthquakes) but who have not crossed into another country. As such, they are not protected by international refugee law and legally remain under the protection of their home country. Estimates shown are of those displaced by conflict and violence only as of year-end 2017; they may comprise only registered IDPs or those displaced from a certain area of a country.

Country	Number	Country	Number	Country	Number
Afghanistan	1,286,000	Guatemala	242,000	Pakistan	249,000
Azerbaijan	393,000	Honduras	190,000	Palestine[2]	231,000
Bangladesh	432,000	India	806,000	Papua New Guinea	12,000
Bosnia and Herzegovina	99,000	Indonesia	13,000	Peru	59,000
Burkina Faso	4,900	Iraq	2,648,000	Philippines	445,000
Burundi	57,000	Kenya	159,000	Russia	19,000
Cameroon	239,000	Kosovo	16,000	Senegal	22,000
Central African Republic	689,000	Lebanon	11,000	Somalia	825,000
Chad	158,000	Libya	197,000	South Sudan[3]	1,899,000
Colombia[1]	6,509,000	Macedonia	140	Sri Lanka	42,000
Congo, Dem. Rep. of	4,480,000	Mali	38,000	Sudan[3]	2,072,000
Congo Republic	108,000	Mexico	345,000	Syria	6,784,000
Côte d'Ivoire	16,000	Mozambique	10,000	Thailand	41,000
Cyprus	217,000	Myanmar (Burma)	635,000	Turkey	1,113,000
Egypt	82,000	Nepal	2	Uganda	24,000
Ethiopia	1,078,000	Niger	144,000	Ukraine	800,000
Georgia	289,000	Nigeria	1,707,000	Yemen	2,014,000
				Total	**40.0 mil**

(1) Cumulative since 1985. (2) Populations in the West Bank, East Jerusalem, and Gaza. (3) Number does not incl. an est. 31,000 IDPs from Abyei Area, disputed territory between Sudan and South Sudan.

Countries With Highest Mortality Rates by Selected Causes of Death

Source: *World Health Statistics 2018*, World Health Organization (WHO)

(per 100,000 live births or 100,000 population)

Rank	Country	Maternal mortality ratio, 2015	Rank	Country	Suicide mortality rate, 2016	Rank	Country	Mortality rate due to homicide, 2016
1.	Sierra Leone	1,360	1.	Lithuania	31.9	1.	Honduras	55.5
2.	Central African Republic	882	2.	Russia	31.0	2.	Venezuela	49.2
3.	Chad	856	3.	Guyana	29.2	3.	El Salvador	46.0
4.	Nigeria	814	4.	Korea, South	26.9	4.	Colombia	43.1
5.	South Sudan	789	5.	Belarus	26.2	5.	Trinidad and Tobago	42.2
6.	Somalia	732	6.	Suriname	22.8	6.	Jamaica	39.1
7.	Liberia	725	7.	Kazakhstan	22.5	7.	Lesotho	35.0
8.	Burundi	712	8.	Ukraine	22.4	8.	South Africa	33.1
9.	The Gambia	706	9.	Lesotho	21.2	9.	Brazil	31.3
10.	Congo, Dem. Rep. of	693		Latvia	21.2	10.	The Bahamas	29.7
11.	Guinea	679	11.	Belgium	20.7	11.	Belize	29.4
12.	Côte d'Ivoire	645	12.	Hungary	19.1	12.	Haiti	28.0
13.	Malawi	634	13.	Slovenia	18.6	13.	Guatemala	25.8
14.	Mauritania	602	14.	Japan	18.5	14.	Panama	20.5
15.	Cameroon	596	15.	Uruguay	18.4	15.	Swaziland	20.0
16.	Mali	587	16.	Estonia	17.8	16.	Guyana	18.8
17.	Niger	553	17.	France	17.7	17.	Namibia	18.3
18.	Guinea-Bissau	549	18.	Switzerland	17.2	18.	Mexico	16.9
19.	Kenya	510	19.	Croatia	16.5	19.	Dominican Republic	16.8
20.	Eritrea	501	20.	Equatorial Guinea	16.4	20.	St. Lucia	15.6
	Global	**216**		**Global**	**10.6**		**Global**	**6.4**

Note: 2016 rankings did not include countries with a population of less than 90,000.

Global HIV/AIDS Status, 2017

Source: HIV Justice Network, Joint United Nations Programme on HIV/AIDS (UNAIDS)

Between 2004—when the number of AIDS-related deaths reached a peak of 1.9 million—and 2017, there was an approximate 50.5% drop in annual deaths due to AIDS. That reduction was particularly notable among children, as pregnant women were increasingly able to access antiretroviral therapy. As of 2017, an estimated 59% of people living with HIV worldwide had access to antiretroviral therapy. While access to treatment has expanded, the risk of HIV infection remained high for certain groups, including sex workers, injecting drug users, transgender persons (particularly transgender women), prisoners, and men who have sex with men. Tuberculosis was still the leading cause of death for those with HIV. Laws allowing specifically for HIV criminalization existed in 72 countries as of mid-2016 and 29 U.S. states as of mid-2018.

An estimated $187 billion was spent on the HIV/AIDS epidemic in 2000-14. At year-end 2017, some $21.3 billion was available to low- and middle-income countries in responding to AIDS.

Current and New HIV/AIDS Cases and Deaths by Region, 2017

Source: Joint United Nations Programme on HIV/AIDS (UNAIDS)

Region	Number living with HIV/AIDS	Percent of world total[1]	New HIV infections	AIDS-related deaths
East and Southern Africa	19,600,000	53.1%	800,000	380,000
West and Central Africa	6,100,000	16.5	370,000	280,000
Asia and the Pacific	5,200,000	14.1	280,000	170,000
Western and Central Europe and North America . .	2,200,000	6.0	70,000	13,000
Latin America	1,800,000	4.9	100,000	37,000
Eastern Europe and Central Asia	1,400,000	3.8	130,000	34,000
Caribbean	310,000	0.8	15,000	10,000
Middle East and North Africa	220,000	0.6	18,000	9,800
World[2]	**36,900,000**	**100.0**	**1,800,000**	**940,000**

(1) Population within a region living with HIV/AIDS as a percentage of population worldwide living with HIV/AIDS. (2) Figures may not add up to totals because of rounding.

Drinking Water and Sanitation, 2015

Source: World Health Organization (WHO) and United Nations Children's Fund (UNICEF)

In 2015, the most recent year for which data was available, an estimated 91% of the world's population had access to improved drinking-water sources, although service and water quality were inconsistent. As of the same year, only 68% of people worldwide used improved sanitation facilities. One in eight people still practiced open defecation. Those without access to improved sanitation are at increased risk of contracting a variety of infectious and parasitic diseases such as diarrhea, malaria, and hepatitis A.

The G7 countries have near-universal (99% or greater) access to improved water and sanitation. In comparison, while 97% of Russia's population had access to improved drinking-water sources, only 72% had access to improved sanitation in 2015. In China, the figures were 95% and 76%, respectively.

Lowest Access to Improved Drinking-Water Sources, 2015

Source: World Health Organization (WHO) and United Nations Children's Fund (UNICEF)

Improved drinking-water sources protect from outside contamination and include household connections, public taps or standpipes, dug wells, and rainwater collection.

(ranked by % of total pop. with access)

Rank	Country/area	Total	Urban	Rural	Rank	Country/area	Total	Urban	Rural
1.	Papua New Guinea	40.0%	88.0%	32.8%	17.	Sierra Leone	62.6%	84.9%	47.8%
2.	Equatorial Guinea	47.9	72.5	31.5	18.	Togo	63.1	91.4	44.2
3.	Angola	49.0	75.4	28.2	19.	Kenya	63.2	81.6	56.8
4.	Chad	50.8	71.8	44.8	20.	Mongolia	64.4	66.4	59.2
5.	Mozambique	51.1	80.6	37.0		Caucasus and Central Asia	88.6	97.8	81.4
6.	Madagascar	51.5	81.6	35.3		Eastern Asia	95.6	97.6	93.0
7.	Congo, Dem. Rep. of	52.4	81.1	31.2		Latin America and the Caribbean	94.6	97.4	83.9
8.	Afghanistan	55.3	78.2	47.0		Northern Africa	92.8	94.9	90.2
9.	Tanzania	55.6	77.2	45.5		Oceania	55.7	94.2	44.1
10.	Ethiopia	57.3	93.1	48.6		Southeastern Asia	90.3	95.5	85.6
11.	Haiti	57.7	64.9	47.6		Southern Asia	92.5	95.5	91.0
12.	Eritrea	57.8	73.2	53.3		Sub-Saharan Africa	67.7	86.8	56.1
13.	Mauritania	57.9	58.4	57.1		Western Asia	94.6	96.5	90.1
14.	Niger	58.2	100.0	48.6		Developed countries	99.2	99.5	97.9
15.	Palestine	58.4	50.7	81.5		**World**	**90.9**	**96.4**	**84.5**
16.	South Sudan	58.7	66.7	56.9					

Lowest Access to Improved Sanitation Facilities, 2015

Source: World Health Organization (WHO) and United Nations Children's Fund (UNICEF)

Sanitation facilities are considered improved if they are private and not shared with other households, including sewer or septic system connections, ventilated improved pit latrines, and composting toilets.

(ranked by % of total pop. with access)

Rank	Country/area	Total	Urban	Rural	Rank	Country/area	Total	Urban	Rural
1.	South Sudan	6.7%	16.4%	4.5%	17.	Mozambique	20.5%	42.4%	10.1%
2.	Niger	10.9	37.9	4.6	18.	Guinea-Bissau	20.8	33.5	8.5
3.	Togo	11.6	24.7	2.9	19.	Central African Republic	21.8	43.6	7.2
4.	Madagascar	12.0	18.0	8.7	20.	Côte d'Ivoire	22.5	32.8	10.3
5.	Chad	12.1	31.4	6.5		Caucasus and Central Asia	95.9	96.3	95.7
6.	Sierra Leone	13.3	22.8	6.9		Eastern Asia	77.4	87.3	64.3
7.	Ghana	14.9	20.2	8.6		Latin America and the Caribbean	83.1	87.9	64.1
8.	Congo Republic	15.0	20.0	5.6		Northern Africa	89.5	92.2	86.1
9.	Tanzania	15.6	31.3	8.3		Oceania	35.5	75.9	23.2
10.	Eritrea	15.7	44.5	7.3		Southeastern Asia	72.2	80.8	64.3
11.	Liberia	16.9	28.0	5.9		Southern Asia	46.9	67.2	36.0
12.	Papua New Guinea	18.9	56.4	13.3		Sub-Saharan Africa	29.7	40.3	23.3
13.	Uganda	19.1	28.5	17.3		Western Asia	93.8	95.8	89.2
14.	Benin	19.7	35.6	7.3		Developed countries	95.6	96.8	91.4
15.	Burkina Faso	19.7	50.4	6.7		**World**	**67.6**	**82.2**	**50.5**
16.	Guinea	20.1	34.1	11.8					

Foreign Development Aid Donors, 2016-17

Source: Development Assistance Committee (DAC), Organisation for Economic Co-operation and Development (OECD)
Listed below is the amount of official development assistance (ODA)—in the form of grants or loans—each DAC member country disbursed in a given year to developing countries. The numbers are net flows, or amounts disbursed less repayments on earlier loans. Both bilateral ODA (made directly to an aid recipient) and multilateral ODA (made to an agency like the World Bank) are included.

(ranked by size of ODA as % of 2017 gross national income [GNI]; 2017 figures are prelim.)

Rank	Donor	ODA as % of GNI 2016	2017	ODA in mil of current U.S. dollars 2016	2017	Rank	Donor	ODA as % of GNI 2016	2017	ODA in mil of current U.S. dollars 2016	2017
1.	Sweden......	0.94%	1.01%	$4,893.74	$5,511.50	18.	Japan	0.20%	0.23%	$10,416.80	$11,475.30
2.	Luxembourg ...	1.00	1.00	391.04	424.48	19.	Australia	0.27	0.23	3,277.52	2,957.14
3.	Norway	1.12	0.99	4,380.08	4,123.10	20.	Spain	0.34	0.19	4,223.67	2,414.54
4.	Denmark......	0.75	0.72	2,369.19	2,401.34	21.	United States ..	0.19	0.18	34,420.98	35,260.98
5.	United Kingdom	0.70	0.70	18,052.80	17,940.43	22.	Portugal	0.17	0.18	343.07	378.32
6.	Germany......	0.70	0.66	24,735.70	24,681.25	23.	Slovenia	0.19	0.16	81.30	76.36
7.	Netherlands ...	0.65	0.60	4,966.26	4,954.87	24.	Greece	0.19	0.16	368.53	316.74
8.	Switzerland....	0.53	0.46	3,582.49	3,096.59	25.	South Korea ...	0.16	0.14	2,246.16	2,204.92
9.	Belgium.......	0.50	0.45	2,300.16	2,203.93	26.	Czech Republic	0.14	0.13	260.24	272.45
10.	France.......	0.38	0.43	9,621.67	11,363.03	27.	Poland........	0.15	0.13	662.95	673.79
11.	Finland	0.44	0.41	1,059.61	1,053.67	28.	Slovakia	0.12	0.12	106.01	112.93
12.	Austria	0.42	0.30	1,635.48	1,229.58	29.	Hungary	0.17	0.11	199.12	148.66
13.	Ireland.......	0.32	0.30	802.59	807.75	**Total DAC**...		**0.32**	**0.31**	**144,920.56**	**146,600.18**
14.	Italy..........	0.27	0.29	5,087.39	5,733.84	**G7 countries[1]**		**0.30**	**0.30**	**106,265.78**	**110,732.26**
15.	Iceland	0.28	0.29	58.72	69.25	**EU institutions**		**NA**	**NA**	**17,106.40**	**16,449.56**
16.	Canada.......	0.26	0.26	3,930.44	4,277.43	**All donors[2]**		**NA**	**NA**	**176,537.39**	**177,595.02**
17.	New Zealand...	0.25	0.23	446.85	436.01						

NA = Not applicable/available. (1) Canada, France, Germany, Italy, Japan, the UK, and the U.S. (2) Incl. countries not shown here.

Recipients of U.S. Official Development Assistance, 2015-16

Source: Development Assistance Committee (DAC), Organisation for Economic Co-operation and Development (OECD)
(net flows of official development assistance, or amounts disbursed less repayments on earlier loans, in mil of current U.S. dollars; ranked by 2016 numbers)

Rank	Country	2015	2016	Rank	Country	2015	2016
1.	Afghanistan................	$1,631.47	$1,375.76	12.	South Africa	$336.05	$489.87
2.	Ethiopia..................	746.43	874.89	13.	Haiti	398.96	424.70
3.	Jordan....................	809.69	873.98	14.	Iraq	346.03	415.11
4.	Kenya....................	711.73	805.72	15.	Liberia...................	514.06	399.56
5.	West Bank and Gaza Strip....	256.71	650.37	16.	Mozambique...............	301.56	389.41
6.	Syria	710.85	637.28	17.	Burundi..................	41.97	388.55
7.	Pakistan	746.10	605.31	18.	Malawi	248.63	370.22
8.	South Sudan..............	595.10	543.54	19.	Zambia	266.80	367.97
9.	Uganda...................	409.87	538.71	20.	Congo, Dem. Rep. of the......	769.23	337.18
10.	Nigeria	490.64	529.58	**All developing countries**		**26,654.11**	**28,544.15**
11.	Tanzania..................	452.58	500.01				

Nuclear Powers of the World

As of Sept. 2018, eight countries were acknowledged nuclear weapons states: the **U.S.**, **UK**, **France**, **China**, **India**, **Pakistan**, **Russia**, and **North Korea**. **Israel** was presumed to have an arsenal. **South Africa** announced in 1993 that it had dismantled its handful of weapons.

All of the more than 40 nations with the knowledge or technology to produce nuclear weapons have signed the Nuclear Non-Proliferation Treaty (NPT) with the exception of Israel, India, and Pakistan. After expelling Intl. Atomic Energy Agency (IAEA) inspectors in Dec. 2002, North Korea announced on Jan. 10, 2003, its withdrawal from the NPT effective the following day.

Iran had argued for the right to pursue the peaceful application of nuclear technology as an NPT signatory, but the IAEA maintained the country had violated the NPT by withholding information. In July 2015, the so-called P5+1 (the five permanent members of the UN Security Council plus Germany) signed a Joint Comprehensive Plan of Action (JCPOA) with Iran, which agreed to curb its ability to enrich uranium as well as reduce its current stockpile of the material. Nuclear-related sanctions on Iran were lifted on Jan. 16, 2016 ("Implementation Day") after the IAEA certified the country had implemented key measures from the JCPOA. The U.S., under Pres. Donald Trump, pulled out of the JCPOA on May 8, 2018, and announced it would reimpose sanctions. The other JCPOA states maintained their commitment to the deal

North Korea conducted six nuclear tests between 2006 and Sept. 2017, as well as two intercontinental ballistic missile tests in July 2017 that appeared to indicate North Korean missiles were capable of reaching the U.S. In response, the UN Security Council unanimously approved new sanctions on North Korea. Trump and North Korean leader Kim Jong Un met in Singapore June 12, 2018, to discuss denuclearization, but any long-term effect of the two nations' summit remained to be seen. There also were three inter-Korean summits in 2018.

Estimated Numbers of Nuclear Weapons by Country, 1945-2018

Source: *Bulletin of the Atomic Scientists*; Carnegie Endowment for International Peace; Federation of American Scientists (FAS); Natural Resources Defense Council (NRDC); Nuclear Threat Initiative (NTI); Stockholm International Peace Research Institute (SIPRI)

Year	United States	USSR/Russia	United Kingdom	France	China	Israel[1]	India	Pakistan	Total[2]
1945	6	—	—	—	—	—	—	—	**6**
1950	369	5	—	—	—	—	—	—	**374**
1960	20,434	1,605	30	—	—	—	—	—	**22,069**
1970	26,662	11,643	280	36	75	8	—	—	**38,696**
1980	24,304	30,062	350	250	280	31	—	—	**55,246**
1990	21,004	37,000	300	505	430	53	—	—	**59,239**
2000	10,577	21,000	185	470	400	72	—	—	**32,632**
2010	9,400	12,300	225	300	240	60-80	60-80	70-90	**22,400**
2018[3]	6,450	6,850	215	300	280	80	130-140	140-150	**14,485**

(1) Israel is widely presumed to have a nuclear stockpile although it has never confirmed nor denied its nuclear status. (2) Numbers may not add up to totals due to rounding and include deployed warheads, those in reserve or in a military stockpile, and retired warheads awaiting dismantlement. (3) As of midyear. North Korea was estimated to have 10-20 warheads, though operational status was difficult to assess.

Nuclear Arms Treaties and Negotiations: A Historical Overview

Aug. 5, 1963: Partial (Limited) Test Ban Treaty signed by the UK, U.S., and USSR, went into effect Oct. 10, 1963. Prohibits parties from testing or participating in the testing of nuclear weapons in the atmosphere, in outer space, and under water.

July 1, 1968: Nuclear Non-Proliferation Treaty (NPT) opened to signatures, went into effect Mar. 5, 1970. With the UK, U.S., and USSR as major signers, the parties agree not to help non-nuclear nations get or make nuclear weapons, though such nations can pursue the peaceful application of nuclear energy.

On May 11, 1995, parties to the treaty voted to extend it indefinitely. As of Sept. 2018, 191 states were party to the treaty, not including North Korea, which withdrew in 2003. Israel, India, and Pakistan were not signatories.

May 26, 1972: The **Strategic Arms Limitation Talks (SALT I)** led to the signing of two agreements by the U.S. and USSR: the **Treaty on the Limitation of Anti-Ballistic Missile Systems** (or **ABM Treaty**) and an interim agreement. These agreements cap the numbers of intercontinental ballistic missile (ICBM) launchers and submarine-launched ballistic missile (SLBM) launchers.

July 3, 1974: Treaty on the Limitation of Underground Nuclear Weapon Tests (or **Threshold Test Ban Treaty**) signed by the U.S. and USSR. Limits underground testing of nuclear weapons to yields of 150 kilotons or less. On May 28, 1976, U.S. and Russia signed the **Peaceful Nuclear Explosions Treaty**, governing explosions outside weapons test sites. Both treaties entered into force Dec. 11, 1990.

June 18, 1979: Strategic Offensive Arms Limitation Treaty (or **SALT II**) signed by the U.S. and USSR. Limited each side to 2,400 missile launchers and heavy bombers; ceiling to apply until Jan. 1, 1985. Never ratified; superseded by START I.

Dec. 8, 1987: Intermediate-Range Nuclear Forces (INF) Treaty signed by the U.S. and USSR. Eliminates all U.S. and Soviet intermediate- and shorter-range nuclear missiles. For the first time, a treaty eliminated an entire category of nuclear weapons and established a comprehensive verification system. Entered into force June 1, 1988.

July 31, 1991: Strategic Arms Reduction Treaty (START I) signed by the USSR and U.S. to reduce long-range nuclear forces no later than seven years after the treaty entered into force. This was the first treaty to mandate reductions in so-called strategic nuclear weapons by the superpowers.

With the Soviet Union breakup in Dec. 1991, four former republics became independent nations with strategic nuclear arms: Russia, Ukraine, Kazakhstan, and Belarus. Under the **Lisbon Protocol** of May 1992, Ukraine, Kazakhstan, and Belarus agreed to accede to the NPT as non-nuclear-weapon states, to destroy or transfer their nuclear weapons to Russia, and to ratify START I. START I expired on Dec. 5, 2009.

Jan. 3, 1993: START II signed by the U.S. and Russia, ratified by the two on Jan. 26, 1996, and Apr. 14, 2000, respectively. Called for further reductions in their long-range nuclear arsenals. Both sides withdrew from the treaty before it went into force.

Sept. 24, 1996: Comprehensive Nuclear-Test-Ban Treaty (CTBT) signed by 71 countries, including the five nuclear-weapons states (China, France, Russia, UK, U.S.). The CTBT bans all nuclear explosions. It is intended to prevent the nuclear powers from developing more advanced weapons while limiting the ability of other states to acquire such devices. As of Aug. 2018, the CTBT had been signed by 183 nations and ratified by 166 of them. It will enter into force only after all Annex 2 states—the 44 states with nuclear capabilities at the time of the treaty's final negotiations—have signed and ratified it. Only 36 have done so to date. Of the remaining Annex 2 countries, five have yet to ratify the CTBT (China, Egypt, Iran, Israel, the U.S.), and three have yet to sign it (India, North Korea, Pakistan).

Dec. 13, 2001: The U.S. announced its intention to withdraw from the **ABM Treaty** in 180 days, arguing that it hindered the government in protecting itself from "future terrorist or rogue state missile attacks." Russia responded by withdrawing from **START II**, stating that U.S. withdrawal from the ABM Treaty effectively invalidated START II.

May 24, 2002: Strategic Offensive Reductions Treaty (SORT or **Moscow Treaty)** signed by the U.S. and Russia, entered into force June 1, 2003. Committed both countries to cutting nuclear arsenals to 1,700-2,200 warheads each by Dec. 31, 2012. SORT lapsed upon entry into force of the New START Treaty.

Apr. 8, 2010: New START Treaty signed by the U.S. and Russia, entered into force Feb. 5, 2011. It limits each country's arsenal of deployed strategic nuclear warheads to 1,550.

Major International Organizations

African Union (AU), inaugurated July 9, 2002, in Durban, South Africa, following disbanding of the Organization of African Unity (OAU). Africa's 55 countries make up its members. (Morocco withdrew in 1984 after the OAU admitted Western Sahara [Sahrawi Arab Dem. Rep.], a territory it claimed, but Morocco rejoined in 2017.) The AU is focused on achieving greater socioeconomic integration and unity among its member states. Its founding document authorized the organization to intervene to stop genocide, war crimes, or human rights abuses within individual member nations. **Headquarters:** Addis Ababa, Ethiopia. **Website:** www.au.int

Asia-Pacific Economic Cooperation (APEC), founded Nov. 1989 as a forum to further cooperation on trade and investment between nations of the region and the rest of the world. Its 21 members are Australia, Brunei, Canada, Chile, China, Hong Kong, Indonesia, Japan, Malaysia, Mexico, New Zealand, Papua New Guinea, Peru, Philippines, Russia, Singapore, South Korea, Taiwan, Thailand, the U.S., and Vietnam. **Secretariat:** Singapore. **Website:** www.apec.org

Association of Southeast Asian Nations (ASEAN), formed Aug. 8, 1967, to promote economic, social, and cultural collaboration and development among the states of Southeast Asia. Its 10 members are Brunei, Cambodia, Indonesia, Laos, Malaysia, Myanmar, Philippines, Singapore, Thailand, and Vietnam. **Secretariat:** Jakarta, Indonesia. **Website:** www.asean.org

Caribbean Community (CARICOM), established Aug. 1, 1973, to coordinate economic integration, foreign policy, social development, and security. Its 15 members are Antigua and Barbuda, The Bahamas, Barbados, Belize, Dominica, Grenada, Guyana, Haiti, Jamaica, Montserrat, St. Kitts and Nevis, St. Lucia, St. Vincent and the Grenadines, Suriname, and Trinidad and Tobago. Anguilla, Bermuda, British Virgin Islands, Cayman Islands, and Turks and Caicos Islands are associate members. **Secretariat:** Georgetown, Guyana. **Website:** www.caricom.org

The Commonwealth, originally called the British Commonwealth of Nations, then the Commonwealth of Nations, in 1949, is an association of nations and dependencies, most part of the former British Empire. Queen Elizabeth II, the current British monarch, is the symbolic head of the Commonwealth. (The secretary-general is chosen by Commonwealth leaders.)

There are 53 independent, sovereign nations in the Commonwealth as of Aug. 2018. Among them are the UK and 15 other nations recognizing the British monarch, represented by a governor-general, as their head of state. **Secretariat:** London, UK. **Website:** www.thecommonwealth.org

Commonwealth of Independent States (CIS), established in Dec. 1991 as an alliance of former Soviet constituent republics. Its members are Armenia, Azerbaijan, Belarus, Kazakhstan, Kyrgyzstan, Moldova, Russia, Tajikistan, and Uzbekistan; Turkmenistan is an associate member. Georgia and Ukraine withdrew from the organization following fighting with Russia over disputed territory. Policy is set through coordinating bodies such as the Council of the Heads of States and Council of the Heads of Governments. **Headquarters:** Minsk, Belarus. **Website:** www.cis.minsk.by or www.cisstat.com/eng/

European Free Trade Association (EFTA), created May 3, 1960, to promote free trade and economic integration. The European Economic Area (EEA) agreement, in force since 1994, set up a single market, with free flow of goods, services, capital, and labor, among EU nations and Iceland, Liechtenstein, and Norway, the EFTA members party to the EEA. Switzerland, the fourth EFTA member, has bilateral agreements with the EU. **Headquarters:** Geneva, Switzerland. **Website:** www.efta.int

European Union (EU), known as the European Community (EC) until 1993, aims to integrate economies, coordinate social developments, and foster political partnerships between member states. As of Jan. 1, 1993, there has been a single market, with no restrictions on the movement of people, goods, services, and money, within the EU.

The EU has its origins in such organizations as the European Coal and Steel Community (ECSC), established by the 1951 Treaty of Paris, and the European Economic Community (EEC, or Common Market) and European Atomic Energy Community (Euratom), created by the 1957 Treaties of Rome. A merger of the three communities' executives went into effect in 1967. As of Aug. 2018, there were 28 EU members: the 12 original members (Belgium, Denmark, France, Germany, Greece, Ireland, Italy, Luxembourg, Netherlands, Portugal, Spain, and UK); 3 that entered in 1995 (Austria, Finland, Sweden); 10 that joined in 2004 (Cyprus, Czech Republic, Estonia, Hungary, Latvia, Lithuania, Malta, Poland, Slovakia, Slovenia); 2 that joined in 2007 (Bulgaria, Romania); and 1 that joined in 2013 (Croatia). Albania, Macedonia, Montenegro, Serbia, and Turkey were candidate countries. UK citizens voted in June 2016 to leave the EU; the country invoked Article 50 of the Lisbon Treaty in Mar. 2017, whereupon the EU and UK had two years to agree on separation terms. All 79 member-states of the Africa, Caribbean, and Pacific (ACP) group of states with the exception of Cuba are affiliated with the EU under the Cotonou Agreement (for the 20-year period ending in 2020). **De facto capital:** Brussels, Belgium. **Website:** europa.eu

Leaders of the then-12 member nations signed the Treaty on European Union, also known as the Maastricht Treaty, on Feb. 7, 1992. It went into effect in 1993, committing the organization to launching a common currency, to establishing common foreign policies, and to taking a lead on social policy among other issues. The European Central Bank was established in 1998. In 1999, 11 of the then-15 EU countries began using the euro. By 2002, national currencies in those 11 countries and Greece were removed from circulation, leaving the euro as the only currency of legal tender. EU peacekeeping forces replaced NATO troops in Macedonia, 2003, the first such mission for the organization. A Treaty Establishing a Constitution for Europe was signed in 2004 by EU members but was never ratified.

Group of Seven (G7), forum of major industrialized countries. France, Germany, Italy, Japan, the UK, and the U.S. first met in 1975 as the Group of Six. Canada joined in 1976; Russia in 1998. The EU is represented at summits. In Mar. 2014, group members condemned Russia for its annexation of Crimea, a region of Ukraine. They boycotted a planned G8 summit in Russia and have met as the Group of Seven since June 2014.

International Criminal Police Organization (INTERPOL), created 1923 as the International Criminal Police Commission before changing its name in 1956, is the world's largest international police organization. There were 192 member nations as of Aug. 2018. **General Secretariat:** Lyon, France. **Website:** www.interpol.int

League of Arab States (Arab League), created Mar. 22, 1945. The League promotes economic, social, political, and military cooperation, mediates disputes, and represents Arab states in certain international negotiations. Its members are Algeria, Bahrain, Comoros, Djibouti, Egypt, Iraq, Jordan, Kuwait, Lebanon, Libya, Mauritania, Morocco, Oman, Palestine (considered an independent state by the League), Qatar, Saudi Arabia, Somalia, Sudan, Syria (membership suspended since 2011), Tunisia, United Arab Emirates, and Yemen. **Headquarters:** Cairo, Egypt. **Website:** www.lasportal.org

North Atlantic Treaty Organization (NATO), created with the signing of what is popularly known as the Washington Treaty Apr. 4, 1949 (in effect Aug. 24, 1949). Its 29 members as of Aug. 2018 are Albania, Belgium, Bulgaria, Canada, Croatia, Czech Republic, Denmark, Estonia, France, Germany, Greece, Hungary, Iceland, Italy, Latvia, Lithuania, Luxembourg, Montenegro, Netherlands, Norway, Poland, Portugal, Romania, Slovakia, Slovenia, Spain, Turkey, UK, and U.S.

Members agree to settle disputes by peaceful means, to develop their capacity to resist armed attack, to regard an attack on one as an attack on all, and to take necessary action to repel an attack under Article 51 of the UN Charter. **Headquarters:** Brussels, Belgium. **Website:** www.nato.int

NATO's military representatives include the Military Committee; International Military Staff, the committee's executive body; and the military command structure (Allied Command Operations and Allied Command Transformation). The North Atlantic Council is NATO's main political decision-making body.

With the end of the Cold War in the early 1990s, members put greater stress on political action and on creating a force that could rapidly deploy to local crises. By the mid-1990s, Russia and other former Soviet republics, among other countries, had joined with NATO in the so-called Partnership for Peace program, which provides for limited joint military exercises and peacekeeping missions. (NATO suspended cooperation with Russia, Apr. 2014, in response to Russia's conflict with Ukraine.) NATO also engages with countries through its Mediterranean Dialogue and Istanbul Cooperation Initiative.

A NATO-led multinational force was deployed to help keep the peace in Bosnia and Herzegovina in 1995. In 1999, a force was deployed in Kosovo. Following the Sept. 2001 terrorist attacks on the U.S., the NATO Council agreed to invoke for the first time Article 5 of the treaty, which stipulates mutual defense of alliance members. NATO assumed control of the International Security Assistance Force in Afghanistan (ISAF), Aug. 2003, marking the first time NATO led a mission outside Europe.

Organization of American States (OAS), which describes itself as the world's oldest regional organization, was officially formed by the signing of a charter on Apr. 30, 1948. Its four main pillars are democracy, human rights, security, and development.

The OAS's 35 members are Antigua and Barbuda, Argentina, The Bahamas, Barbados, Belize, Bolivia, Brazil, Canada, Chile, Colombia, Costa Rica, Cuba, Dominica, Dominican Republic, Ecuador, El Salvador, Grenada, Guatemala, Guyana, Haiti, Honduras, Jamaica, Mexico, Nicaragua, Panama, Paraguay, Peru, St. Kitts and Nevis, St. Lucia, St. Vincent and the Grenadines, Suriname, Trinidad and Tobago, U.S., Uruguay, and Venezuela. **Headquarters:** Washington, DC. **Website:** www.oas.org

Organization for Economic Cooperation and Development (OECD), established Dec. 14, 1960, to promote the economic and social welfare of member countries and to stimulate efforts for developing nations. Its 36 members, as of Aug. 2018, are Australia, Austria, Belgium, Canada, Chile, Czech Republic, Denmark, Estonia, Finland, France, Germany, Greece, Hungary, Iceland, Ireland, Israel, Italy, Japan, Latvia, Lithuania, Luxembourg, Mexico, Netherlands, New Zealand, Norway, Poland, Portugal, Slovakia, Slovenia, South Korea, Spain, Sweden, Switzerland, Turkey, UK, and the U.S. **Headquarters:** Paris, France. **Website:** www.oecd.org

Organization of Petroleum Exporting Countries (OPEC), created Sept. 14, 1960, by Iran, Iraq, Kuwait, Saudi Arabia, and Venezuela. This group made up of most but not all of the major petroleum exporting nations seeks to stabilize the oil market and set world oil prices by controlling production. In addition to the founding countries, members as of Aug. 2018 include Algeria, Angola, Congo Republic, Ecuador, Equatorial Guinea, Gabon, Libya, Nigeria, Qatar, and United Arab Emirates. Indonesia suspended its membership as of Nov. 2016. **Secretariat/headquarters:** Vienna, Austria. **Website:** www.opec.org

Organization for Security and Cooperation in Europe (OSCE), established in 1972 as the Conference on Security and Cooperation in Europe; current name adopted 1995. The group, formed by NATO and Warsaw Pact members, seeks improved East-West relations through a commitment to nonaggression and human rights, and cooperation in economics, science and technology, cultural exchange, and environmental protection. There were 57 member states as of Aug. 2018, making it the world's largest regional security organization. **Secretariat:** Vienna, Austria. **Website:** www.osce.org

United Nations

The 73rd regular session of the United Nations General Assembly opened Sept. 18, 2018, attended by world leaders and other delegates from 193 nations. The UN headquarters is located on 18 acres, considered international territory, in New York, NY.

Proposals to establish an organization for maintenance of world peace led to the convening of the United Nations Conference on International Organization in San Francisco, Apr. 25-June 26, 1945, where the UN charter was drawn. It was signed June 26 by 50 nations and on Oct. 15 by Poland. It went into effect Oct. 24, 1945, upon ratification by the permanent members of the Security Council and a majority of the other signatories.

Purposes. To maintain international peace and security; to promote sustained economic growth and sustainable development; to achieve international cooperation in solving economic, social, cultural, and humanitarian problems; to protect human rights; and to advance justice and international law.

Visitors to the UN. The UN headquarters is open every day except New Year's Day, Good Friday, Memorial Day, Eid al-Fitr, Independence Day, Eid al-Adha, Labor Day, Thanksgiving, and Christmas. It is closed to the public during the UN general debate and may also close on short notice at other times for meetings of heads of state and government. All visitors must obtain a security pass from the check-in office to enter UN headquarters. Visitors age 18 and older must present a government-issued photo ID.

Guided tours lasting 45-60 min., as well as a new tour aimed at 5- to 10-year-olds, are conducted on weekdays only. Tickets can be purchased online. A limited number of tickets for same-day tours may be sold on-site. Groups of 40 or more can reserve directly on the UN website. Children under 5 years of age are not admitted on tours. The UN Visitor Center, in the basement of the General Assembly Building, is the only area open to the public on weekends (Mar.-Dec. only). It includes a post office, book and gift shops, and a cafe. Guided tours are also available at the UN's other headquarters, in Geneva, Switzerland; Vienna, Austria; and Nairobi, Kenya. **Website:** visit.un.org

Six Main Organs of the United Nations

General Assembly. The General Assembly comprises representatives from all member nations. Each nation is entitled to one vote. The General Assembly meets in Sept. for an annual session; the Security Council or a majority of UN members can convoke a special session. Decisions on important issues, such as security, require a two-thirds majority of the General Assembly; a simple majority can decide other issues.

The General Assembly must approve the UN budget and apportion expenses among members. A member in arrears can lose its vote if the amount of arrears equals or exceeds the amount of the contributions due for the preceding two full years. **Website:** www.un.org/en/ga/

Security Council. The Security Council, which has primary responsibility within the UN for maintaining peace and security, consists of 15 members. Five members—China, France, Russia, United Kingdom, and the United States—have permanent seats. The remaining 10 are elected for two-year terms by the General Assembly. Nonpermanent members with terms expiring Dec. 31, 2018, are Bolivia, Ethiopia, Kazakhstan, Netherlands (which had split a two-year term with Italy), and Sweden; those with terms expiring Dec. 31, 2019, are Côte d'Ivoire, Equatorial Guinea, Kuwait, Peru, and Poland. Belgium, Dominican Republic, Germany, Indonesia, and South Africa have been elected to two-year terms starting on Jan. 1, 2019.

Any UN member may participate in Council discussions at its invitation. Decisions on procedural questions are made by an affirmative vote of nine members. On all other matters the affirmative vote of nine members must include the concurring votes of all permanent members (giving them veto power). The Security Council directs the various peacekeeping forces deployed throughout the world. **Website:** www.un.org/en/sc/

Secretariat. The Secretariat is responsible for the UN's day-to-day operations. It is headed by the secretary-general, who is appointed by the General Assembly, on the recommendation of the Security Council, for a five-year, renewable term. The secretary-general reports to the General Assembly and may bring to the attention of the Security Council any matter that threatens international peace. The Secretariat maintained an international staff of 38,105 as of Dec. 31, 2017. **Website:** www.un.org/en/sections/about-un/secretariat/

United Nations Secretaries General

Took office	Secretary, nation
1946	Trygve Lie, Norway
1953	Dag Hammarskjöld, Sweden
1961	U Thant, Burma (Myanmar)
1972	Kurt Waldheim, Austria
1982	Javier Pérez de Cuéllar, Peru
1992	Boutros Boutros-Ghali, Egypt
1997	Kofi Annan, Ghana
2007	Ban Ki-moon, South Korea
2017	António Guterres, Portugal

Economic and Social Council. The Economic and Social Council consists of 54 members elected by the General Assembly to overlapping three-year terms. The council is responsible for economic, social, and environmental issues in relation to sustainable development. It meets with academics, non-governmental organizations, and private-sector representatives throughout the year. A four-week substantive session each July is alternately held in New York and Geneva, Switzerland. **Website:** www.un.org/ecosoc/

International Court of Justice (World Court). The International Court of Justice is the principal judicial organ of the UN. The Court has jurisdiction over cases that UN members or parties to the court's statute submit to it. In addition to rendering judgments, the Court issues advisory opinions.

The court's 15 judges are elected to nine-year terms by the General Assembly and the Security Council. No two judges may come from the same nation, and they should represent the world's principal legal systems. Once elected, the judges no longer act as representatives of a government. The Court remains permanently in session, except during vacations. All questions are decided by a majority. The International Court of Justice sits in The Hague, Netherlands. **Website:** www.icj-cij.org

Trusteeship Council. The Trusteeship Council, made up of the five permanent Security Council members, supervised the administration of UN trust territories. All 11 trust territories have since attained their right to self-determination. The Council formally suspended its work on Nov. 1, 1994, with Palau's independence.

The text of the **UN Charter** is online at www.un.org/en/charter-united-nations/.

Selected UN Programs and Funds, Specialized Agencies, and Related Organizations

UN programs and funds operate with voluntary funding. UN specialized agencies and related organizations are autonomous groups that have a functional relationship or working agreement with the UN. Their financing comes from voluntary and assessed contributions. The location in parentheses is the primary office or headquarters.

Food and Agriculture Org. (FAO) works to achieve food security, eliminate malnutrition, and increase the productivity and sustainability of farms, forests, and fisheries. (Rome, Italy) **Website:** www.fao.org

International Atomic Energy Agency (IAEA) promotes safe, peaceful uses of atomic energy. (Vienna, Austria) **Website:** www.iaea.org

International Civil Aviation Org. (ICAO) sets international civil aviation standards and regulations. (Montréal, Quebec, Canada) **Website:** www.icao.int

International Fund for Agricultural Development (IFAD) seeks to alleviate poverty in rural areas of developing countries. (Rome, Italy) **Website:** www.ifad.org

International Labor Org. (ILO) promotes decent and productive employment standards, the improvement of labor conditions and worker protections, and vocational training. (Geneva, Switzerland) **Website:** www.ilo.org

International Maritime Org. (IMO) seeks cooperation on technical matters affecting international shipping. (London, England, UK) **Website:** www.imo.org

International Monetary Fund (IMF) promotes international monetary cooperation, currency stabilization, and the expansion of international trade. (Washington, DC) **Website:** www.imf.org

International Telecommunication Union (ITU) regulates all aspects of global communication, including setting standards for radio and phone, and allocating the radio-frequency spectrum and satellite orbits. (Geneva, Switzerland) **Website:** www.itu.int

Office of the United Nations High Commissioner for Refugees (UNHCR) safeguards the rights of and provides essential assistance to refugees. (Geneva, Switzerland) **Website:** www.unhcr.org

United Nations Children's Fund (UNICEF) provides financial aid and development assistance to programs for children and mothers in developing countries. (New York, NY) **Website:** www.unicef.org

United Nations Educational, Scientific, and Cultural Org. (UNESCO) works to improve education around the world and to preserve historical and cultural sites. (Paris, France) **Website:** www.unesco.org

United Nations Industrial Development Org. (UNIDO) helps developing and transitional nations pursue sustainable industrial development while promoting international industrial cooperation. (Vienna, Austria) **Website:** www.unido.org

Universal Postal Union (UPU) facilitates international collaboration among postal service providers. (Berne, Switzerland) **Website:** www.upu.int

World Bank Group is focused on ending extreme poverty and promoting the sharing of prosperity worldwide. It encompasses five institutions. The **International Bank for Reconstruction and Development (IBRD)** provides loans and technical assistance for projects in developing member countries. The **International Development Assn. (IDA)** provides funds for development projects on concessionary terms to the poorest countries. The IBRD and IDA make up the World Bank. The **International Finance Corp. (IFC)** promotes private-sector growth in developing countries; encourages the development of local capital markets; and stimulates the international flow of private capital. The **Multilateral Investment Guarantee Agency (MIGA)** promotes foreign direct investment in developing countries by guaranteeing investments from noncommercial political risks. The **International Center for Settlement of Investment Disputes (ICSID)** provides conciliation and arbitration services for disputes between foreign investors and host governments that arise out of an investment. (Washington, DC) **Website:** www.worldbank.org, www.ifc.org, www.miga.org

World Health Org. (WHO) responds to public-health emergencies and works to eradicate life-threatening diseases. (Geneva, Switzerland) **Website:** www.who.int

World Intellectual Property Org. (WIPO) protects literary, industrial, scientific, and artistic works through international cooperation. (Geneva, Switzerland) **Website:** www.wipo.int

World Meteorological Org. (WMO) coordinates the free exchange of world meteorological data. (Geneva, Switzerland) **Website:** www.wmo.int

World Tourism Org. (UNWTO) advocates for responsible, sustainable, and universally accessible tourism. (Madrid, Spain) **Website:** www.unwto.org

World Trade Org. (WTO) administers trade agreements and treaties between nations, attempts to settle disputes, and keeps track of trade measures and statistics. (Geneva, Switzerland) **Website:** www.wto.org

Ongoing UN Peacekeeping Missions, 2018

Source: Dept. of Peacekeeping Operations (DPKO), Dept. of Field Support, Dept. of Management; United Nations Secretariat

Unless otherwise noted, numbers are for peacekeeping operations only (not including political and peacebuilding missions), as of Aug. 31, 2018, unless otherwise noted. Year given in graphic is the year each mission started.

Uniformed personnel (troops, police, military observers, and staff officers)	89,133	Total personnel serving in 14 current peacekeeping operations	103,303
Countries contributing uniformed personnel	124	Approved budget for July 1, 2018-June 30, 2019	$6.7 bil
Civilian personnel (as of May 31, 2018):		Peacekeeping operations since 1948	71
International	4,539	Total fatalities in all peace operations since 1948	3,767
Local	8,393	Est. total cost of operations, 1948 to June 30, 2010	$69 bil

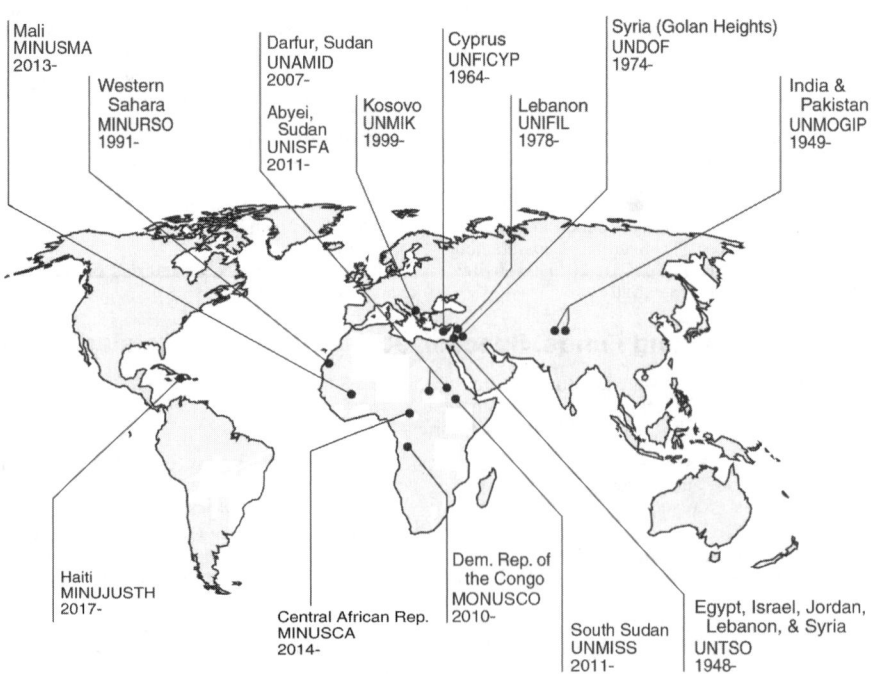

Mali MINUSMA 2013-
Western Sahara MINURSO 1991-
Darfur, Sudan UNAMID 2007-
Abyei, Sudan UNISFA 2011-
Kosovo UNMIK 1999-
Cyprus UNFICYP 1964-
Lebanon UNIFIL 1978-
Syria (Golan Heights) UNDOF 1974-
India & Pakistan UNMOGIP 1949-
Haiti MINUJUSTH 2017-
Central African Rep. MINUSCA 2014-
Dem. Rep. of the Congo MONUSCO 2010-
South Sudan UNMISS 2011-
Egypt, Israel, Jordan, Lebanon, & Syria UNTSO 1948-

Roster of the United Nations

Listed below are the 193 members of the United Nations, with the years in which they were admitted (as of Sept. 2018). Vatican City (Holy See), Kosovo, and China (Taiwan)[1] are not members. Taiwan's repeated bids for UN membership have so far been unsuccessful. Palestine and Vatican City are non-member states of the UN with permanent observer status.

Member	Year	Member	Year	Member	Year	Member	Year
Afghanistan	1946	Dominica	1978	Libya	1955	Saint Vincent and the	
Albania	1955	Dominican Republic	1945	Liechtenstein	1990	Grenadines	1980
Algeria	1962	Ecuador	1945	Lithuania	1991	Samoa	1976
Andorra	1993	Egypt[4]	1945	Luxembourg	1945	San Marino	1992
Angola	1976	El Salvador	1945	Macedonia[2,7]	1993	São Tomé and Príncipe	1975
Antigua and Barbuda	1981	Equatorial Guinea	1968	Madagascar	1960	Saudi Arabia	1945
Argentina	1945	Eritrea	1993	Malawi	1964	Senegal	1960
Armenia	1992	Estonia	1991	Malaysia[8]	1957	Serbia[2,9]	2000
Australia	1945	Ethiopia	1945	Maldives	1965	Seychelles	1976
Austria	1955	Fiji	1970	Mali	1960	Sierra Leone	1961
Azerbaijan	1992	Finland	1955	Malta	1964	Singapore[8]	1965
Bahamas, The	1973	France	1945	Marshall Islands	1991	Slovakia[3]	1993
Bahrain	1971	Gabon	1960	Mauritania	1961	Slovenia[2]	1992
Bangladesh	1974	Gambia, The	1965	Mauritius	1968	Solomon Islands	1978
Barbados	1966	Georgia	1992	Mexico	1945	Somalia	1960
Belarus	1945	Germany[5]	1973	Micronesia	1991	South Africa[11]	1945
Belgium	1945	Ghana	1957	Moldova	1992	South Sudan[12]	2011
Belize	1981	Greece	1945	Monaco	1993	Spain	1955
Benin	1960	Grenada	1974	Mongolia	1961	Sri Lanka	1955
Bhutan	1971	Guatemala	1945	Montenegro[2,9]	2006	Sudan[12]	1956
Bolivia	1945	Guinea	1958	Morocco	1956	Suriname	1975
Bosnia and		Guinea-Bissau	1974	Mozambique	1975	Swaziland	1968
Herzegovina[2]	1992	Guyana	1966	Myanmar (Burma)	1948	Sweden	1946
Botswana	1966	Haiti	1945	Namibia	1990	Switzerland	2002
Brazil	1945	Honduras	1945	Nauru	1999	Syria[3]	1945
Brunei	1984	Hungary	1955	Nepal	1955	Tajikistan	1992
Bulgaria	1955	Iceland	1946	Netherlands	1945	Tanzania[13]	1961
Burkina Faso	1960	India	1945	New Zealand	1945	Thailand	1946
Burundi	1962	Indonesia[6]	1950	Nicaragua	1945	Timor-Leste	2002
Cabo Verde	1975	Iran	1945	Niger	1960	Togo	1960
Cambodia	1955	Iraq	1945	Nigeria	1960	Tonga	1999
Cameroon	1960	Ireland	1955	Norway	1945	Trinidad and Tobago	1962
Canada	1945	Israel	1949	Oman	1971	Tunisia	1956
Central African Rep.	1960	Italy	1955	Pakistan	1947	Turkey	1945
Chad	1960	Jamaica	1962	Palau	1994	Turkmenistan	1992
Chile	1945	Japan	1956	Panama	1945	Tuvalu	2000
China[1]	1945	Jordan	1955	Papua New Guinea	1975	Uganda	1962
Colombia	1945	Kazakhstan	1992	Paraguay	1945	Ukraine	1945
Comoros	1975	Kenya	1963	Peru	1945	United Arab Emirates	1971
Congo, Dem. Rep. of	1960	Kiribati	1999	Philippines	1945	United Kingdom	1945
Congo Republic	1960	Korea, North	1991	Poland	1945	United States	1945
Costa Rica	1945	Korea, South	1991	Portugal	1955	Uruguay	1945
Côte d'Ivoire	1960	Kuwait	1963	Qatar	1971	Uzbekistan	1992
Croatia[2]	1992	Kyrgyzstan	1992	Romania	1955	Vanuatu	1981
Cuba	1945	Laos	1955	Russia[10]	1945	Venezuela	1945
Cyprus	1960	Latvia	1991	Rwanda	1962	Vietnam	1977
Czech Republic[3]	1993	Lebanon	1945	Saint Kitts and Nevis	1983	Yemen[14]	1947
Denmark	1945	Lesotho	1966	Saint Lucia	1979	Zambia	1964
Djibouti	1977	Liberia	1945			Zimbabwe	1980

(1) The General Assembly (GA) voted in 1971 to expel the Chinese government in Taiwan and admit the government in Beijing. (2) The Socialist Federal Republic of Yugoslavia was an original UN member. After four of its six republics (Bosnia and Herzegovina, Croatia, Macedonia, and Slovenia) declared independence in 1991-92, the two remaining republics, Montenegro and Serbia, reconstituted as the Federal Republic of Yugoslavia. They sought to take over the former Yugoslavia's UN seat in 1992 but were expelled a few months later by GA vote. The Federal Republic of Yugoslavia was granted membership in 2000. In 2003, the country changed its name to Serbia and Montenegro. (3) Czechoslovakia, an original UN member from 1945 to 1992, was succeeded by both the Czech Republic and Slovakia in 1993. (4) Egypt and Syria were original UN members. In 1958, Egypt and Syria established the United Arab Republic and continued under a single UN membership. In 1961, Syria resumed separate membership following independence. (5) The Federal Republic of Germany and the German Democratic Republic became UN members in 1973. In 1990, the two formed one sovereign state. (6) Withdrew from the UN in 1965; rejoined within 1966. (7) Provisionally referred to as the former Yugoslav Republic of Macedonia pending settlement of Greece's objection to its constitutional name. (8) The Federation of Malaya joined the UN in 1957. In 1963, it changed its name to Malaysia following the accession of Singapore, Sabah, and Sarawak. Singapore became an independent UN member in 1965. (9) After Montenegro declared independence in 2006, the Republic of Serbia continued Serbia and Montenegro's UN membership. Montenegro was admitted to the UN as the Republic of Montenegro the same month. (10) The USSR was an original UN member. After the USSR's dissolution in 1991, Russia informed the UN it would continue the Soviet Union's membership in the Security Council and all other UN organs with the support of the Commonwealth of Independent States (comprising most of the former Soviet republics). (11) Readmitted in 1994. Its delegation had been suspended from participation in 1974 because of apartheid. (12) The Republic of South Sudan seceded from the Republic of the Sudan in 2011 and was admitted to the UN the same year. (13) Tanganyika was a UN member from 1961 and Zanzibar from 1963. The two countries united in 1964 to form the United Republic of Tanganyika and Zanzibar, which continued a single UN membership. It later changed its name to the United Republic of Tanzania. (14) The Yemen Arab Republic was admitted in 1947; the People's Democratic Republic of Yemen in 1967. In 1990, the two nations formed the Republic of Yemen.

U.S. Representatives to the United Nations, 1946-2018

The U.S. Permanent Representative to the United Nations is head of the U.S. Mission to the UN in New York. He or she is appointed by the president and confirmed by the Senate. Year given is the year each took office.

Year	Representative	Year	Representative	Year	Representative	Year	Representative
1946	Edward R. Stettinius Jr.	1969	Charles W. Yost	1989	Thomas R. Pickering	2004	John C. Danforth
1946	Herschel V. Johnson (act.)	1971	George H. W. Bush	1992	Edward J. Perkins	2005	Anne W. Patterson (act.)
1947	Warren R. Austin	1973	John A. Scali	1993	Madeleine K. Albright		
1953	Henry Cabot Lodge Jr.	1975	Daniel P. Moynihan	1997	Bill Richardson	2005	John R. Bolton
1960	James J. Wadsworth	1976	William W. Scranton	1998	A. Peter Burleigh (act.)	2006	Alejandro D. Wolff (act.)
1961	Adlai E. Stevenson	1977	Andrew Young	1999	Richard C. Holbrooke	2007	Zalmay M. Khalilzad
1965	Arthur J. Goldberg	1979	Donald McHenry	2001	James B. Cunningham (act.)	2009	Susan E. Rice
1968	George W. Ball	1981	Jeane J. Kirkpatrick			2013	Samantha Power
1968	James Russell Wiggins	1985	Vernon A. Walters	2001	John D. Negroponte	2017	Nikki R. Haley

International Criminal Court

The International Criminal Court (ICC) was created when 120 nations signed the Rome Statute on July 17, 1998. Its mission is to try individuals accused of genocide, war crimes, and crimes against humanity, which was undertaken in the past by temporary tribunals. The statute came into force on July 1, 2002. As of Aug. 2018, 123 nations were state parties to the Rome Statute of the ICC. China, Russia, and the U.S. are among those countries that have not yet signed or ratified the treaty.

The ICC, unlike the International Court of Justice (or World Court), is not part of the UN. It is an independent international agency with its own administration and budget, which is made up of funds from member states and voluntary contributions by other institutions, international groups, individuals, and corporations. It consists of 18 judges elected by state parties to nine-year, non-renewable terms. An absolute majority of these 18 judges elect three from among themselves to serve as president and first and second vice presidents. A Registry handles the non-judicial aspects of administration. The Office of the Prosecutor reviews, investigates, and prosecutes cases referred to it by a state or by the UN Security Council.

As of mid-2018, 26 cases had been brought before the ICC. The Office of the Prosecutor was investigating situations in Burundi, Central African Republic, Côte d'Ivoire, Dem. Rep. of the Congo, Georgia, Kenya, Libya, Mali, Sudan (Darfur), and Uganda. It was conducting preliminary examinations in Afghanistan, Colombia, Gabon, Guinea, Iraq (involving UK nationals), Nigeria, Palestine, the Philippines, Ukraine, and Venezuela. The court issued its first-ever conviction in Mar. 2012, when it found the warlord Thomas Lubanga Dyilo guilty of war crimes for his use of child soldiers in the Dem. Rep. of the Congo.

Though jurisdiction is limited to member nations, the ICC is a court of last resort. It may also initiate cases involving non-member nations if it deems the country's authorities have not taken steps to investigate or prosecute a case. The ICC is headquartered in The Hague, Netherlands, though it may sit elsewhere.
Website: www.icc-cpi.int

Geneva Conventions

The Geneva Conventions are four international treaties governing the protection of civilians in times of war, the treatment of prisoners of war, and the care of the wounded and sick in the armed forces. The first convention, covering the sick and wounded in war, was concluded in Geneva, Switzerland, in 1864, at a conference convened by the Swiss government at the urging of the International Committee of the Red Cross. The convention was amended and expanded in 1906. In 1929, two more conventions covering the wounded and prisoners of war were signed. Outrage at the treatment of prisoners and civilians during WWII by some belligerents, notably Germany and Japan, prompted the conclusion, on Aug. 12, 1949, of four new conventions. Three of these restated and strengthened the previous conventions. The fourth codified general principles of international law governing the treatment of civilians in wartime.

The 1949 convention for civilians provided for special safeguards for wounded persons, children under 15 years of age, pregnant women, and the elderly. Discrimination on racial, religious, national, or political grounds was forbidden. Torture, collective punishment, reprisals, unwarranted destruction of property, and forced use of civilians for an occupier's armed forces were also prohibited. Also included was a pledge for the humane treatment, adequate feeding, and delivery of supplies to prisoners. They were not to be forced to disclose more than minimal information. Two additional protocols were adopted in June 1977 dealing with the protection of victims, especially civilians, in international and non-international armed conflicts. (A third protocol, adopted in 2005, created the Red Crystal emblem for use along with the Red Cross and Red Crescent.)

Most countries have formally accepted all or most of the humanitarian conventions as binding. However, there is no permanent international machinery in place to enforce these treaties.

Genocide

Source: Convention on the Prevention and Punishment of the Crime of Genocide, United Nations Treaty Series 277; Rome Statute of the International Criminal Court (ICC)

The term "genocide" (which combines Greek and Latin roots to mean "murder of a race") was coined by Polish-Jewish lawyer Raphael Lemkin in 1944 to describe the intentional or attempted destruction of a national, ethnic, racial, or religious group. Genocide is defined as killing members of a group, causing serious bodily harm to members of a group, or otherwise attempting to bring about a group's destruction, including efforts to prevent births or transfer children away from a group. Although the legal definition of genocide does not extend to political groups, the term is often used colloquially to refer to large-scale political violence.

The prohibition against genocide is part of customary international law and is codified in the Convention on the Prevention and Punishment of the Crime of Genocide, which entered into force on Jan. 12, 1951. As of Sept. 2018, 149 nations, including the U.S., were parties to it. Genocide is also prohibited by the domestic laws of many nations.

The first modern trials for genocide were conducted by the Allies after WWII. Although the charter of the Nuremberg Tribunal—the international court set up to try Nazi war criminals—did not use the term genocide, its definition of "crimes against humanity" included persecution on racial or religious grounds. More recently, the UN Security Council created ad hoc tribunals to try those responsible for genocide and other serious crimes in former Yugoslavia and in Rwanda. The ICC also has jurisdiction to try perpetrators. Sudanese Pres. Omar Hassan al-Bashir is the first person the ICC has charged with the crime of genocide, for the violence in Darfur against the Fur, Masalit, and Zaghawa people. Bashir remained at large and in office as of Sept. 2018.

UN investigators recommended, Aug. 2018, that Myanmar's top military leaders be tried on multiple charges including genocide of the country's Rohingya population. At least 6,700 Rohingya are estimated to have been killed by armed government forces in Aug.-Sept. 2017.

Examples of Genocides Since 1900

Year	Event	Location	Est. deaths
1915	Extermination of Armenians by the nationalist Young Turks	Turkey/Ottoman Empire	1,000,000+
1930s	Intentional infliction of famine on Ukraine	Soviet Union (Ukraine)	6,000,000-7,000,000
1933-45	Attempted destruction of European Jewry (Holocaust)	Europe	6,000,000
1975-79	Khmer Rouge campaign of extermination under Pol Pot[1]	Cambodia	1,500,000-2,000,000
1981-83	Army and paramilitary killings of indigenous Mayan during civil war	Guatemala	200,000+
1988	Anfal Campaign (named by the Iraqi government) against Iraqi Kurds	Iraq	100,000-200,000
1992-95	Ethnic killings during the breakup of Yugoslavia, chiefly Serbs against Bosnian Muslims (known as Bosniaks)	Bosnia-Herzegovina, Serbia, Croatia	200,000
1994	Hutu massacre of Tutsis	Rwanda	800,000
2003-present	Govt. forces and govt.-backed Arab militia (Janjaweed) attacks on non-Arab southern tribes, mainly Fur, Masalit, Zaghawa[2]	Darfur region, Sudan	300,000-600,000
2014-present	Self-proclaimed Islamic State (ISIS) against Yazidi, Christian, and Shia Muslim population	Iraq, Syria	3,100+

Note: Estimates based on historical evidence. The legal definition of "genocide" does not include politically motivated mass killings. Therefore, instances of mass violence against political or class enemies, such as Josef Stalin's purges of some 20 mil Soviets in the 1930s, and Mao Zedong's Cultural Revolution, which killed several million Chinese, are not included. (1) The mass killings during Cambodia's Khmer Rouge regime are often spoken of as genocide, though many of the murders were politically or class motivated. (2) In 2005, a UN commission concluded that although the "international offenses ... that have been committed in Darfur may be no less serious and heinous than genocide," it did not term the situation there a genocide.

NATIONS OF THE WORLD

As of mid-2018, there were **196 nations** in the world. This number includes three nations that are not United Nations (UN) members—Kosovo, Taiwan, and Vatican City (Holy See). Certain regions and territories can be found under the entry for their governing nation. **Sources:** FAOSTAT and AQUASTAT, Food and Agric. Org. of the UN (FAO); Global Health Observatory, World Health Organization (WHO); Intl. Data Base, U.S. Census Bureau; International Energy Statistics, Energy Information Admin., U.S. Dept. of Energy; *International Financial Statistics*, Intl. Monetary Fund (IMF); Joint UN Programme on HIV/AIDS (UNAIDS); *Key Indicators of the Labour Market*, International Labour Organization; *The Military Balance*, Intl. Inst. for Strategic Studies; *Oil & Gas Journal*, PennWell Corp.; *Trends in International Migrant Stock* and *World Urbanization Prospects*, Population Div., UN Dept. of Economic and Social Affairs; UN Educational, Scientific, and Cultural Org. (UNESCO); *UNWTO World Tourism Barometer* © World Tourism Org.; U.S. Dept. of State; Wards Intelligence, a div. of Informa; The World Bank; *The World Factbook*, Central Intelligence Agency (CIA); World Telecommunication/ICT Indicators Database, Intl. Telecommunication Union.

Note: Because of rounding or incomplete enumeration, percentages may not add up to 100%. FY = Fiscal year. NA = Not available/applicable. Figures are for years noted below unless otherwise indicated within a country's profile. **Population, age distrib.**, and **pop. density** are mid-2018 ests. **Growth** gives the avg. annual percent change in the pop. resulting from **births** and **deaths** at midyear 2018 as well as the flow of migrants into and out of a country. International **migrants**, including foreign-born citizens and refugees, as a percent of the total pop. is for mid-2017. Percent of total pop. living in **urban** areas, as defined by each country, are projections for mid-2018. **Languages** are ranked with those most widely spoken listed first. **Arable land** is given as percentage of country's land area. Pop. of **capitals** and **cities** are projected ests. for urban agglomerations as of mid-2018. **Defense budget** is for 2017, **active troops** for 2018. Selected **industries** are ranked by descending value of annual output. Selected **chief agric.** products are listed in descending order of importance. Total renewable **water** resources per inhabitant is for 2014. **Crude oil reserves** are as of Jan. 1, 2018; countries without this entry lack reserves. **Electricity prod.** indicates net, not gross, generated in 2015. **Labor force** percentages are latest available; **unemployment** (percentage of total labor force age 15 and older currently available for and seeking work) are 2017 ests. **Monetary unit** exchange rate is as of Sept. 2018. **GDP** data, 2017 ests. made in Aug. 2018, are based on purchasing power parity exchange rates; **per capita GDP** is calculated using a country's est. pop. size as of July 1 of given year. **GDP growth** is year-over-year. Value of **imports** and **exports**, calculated on an exchange rate basis, are from 2017; trade partners are listed in descending order of importance by percentage of total dollar value. **Tourism** is 2016 or 2017 provisional receipts from intl. visitors; data not available for all countries. **Budget** calculated on an exchange rate basis, not purchasing power parity terms, is 2017 expenditures. **Inflation** is measured by the percent change in the consumer price index (or avg. consumer cost for certain goods and services) between 2016 and 2017. Total length of a country's **railway** network is the latest available. **Motor vehicle** statistics, for cars and comm. vehicles in operation based on registrations, are for 2017. The number of **airports** with paved, usable runways are latest available. Number of fixed-**telephone** subscriptions and mobile-cellular telephone subscriptions offering voice communications are for 2017. Percentage of pop. accessing the **internet**, regardless of device used, and active mobile-**broadband** subscriptions are for 2016. Current health **expend.** (both government and private) is given as a percentage of GDP in 2015. **Life expect.** is in avg. number of years at birth for persons born in 2018. **Infant mortality** measures the probability of a child dying between birth and exact age 1 in 2018. **Undernourished**, or the prevalence of undernourishment, is the probability in 2014-16 that a randomly selected person from the pop. does not consume enough calories for an active, healthy life. **HIV** prevalence is the percentage of a country's pop. of 15- to 49-year-olds living with HIV in 2017. **Education** and **literacy** rate ests. are latest available. Literacy measures the percent of the pop. age 15 and older able to read and write simple statements; some countries define as literate those who have completed certain schooling. **Embassy** addresses are for Wash., DC, area code (202). Current events as of Oct. 1, 2018.

See pages 473-88 for full-color maps and flags of all nations.

Afghanistan
Islamic Republic of Afghanistan

People: Population: 34,940,837 (39). **Age distrib.:** <15: 40.9%; 65+: 2.6%. **Growth:** 2.4%. **Migrants:** 0.4%. **Pop. density:** 138.7 per sq mi, 53.6 per sq km. **Urban:** 25.5%. **Ethnic groups:** Pashtun, Tajik, Hazara, Uzbek, smaller numbers of 10 other constitutionally recognized ethnic groups, Kyrghyz. **Languages:** Afghan Persian or Dari, Pashto (both official); Uzbek, English, Turkmen, Urdu. **Religions:** Sunni Muslim 84.7%-89.7%, Shia Muslim 10%-15%.

Geography: Total area: 251,827 sq mi, 652,230 sq km (40); **Land area:** 251,827 sq mi, 652,230 sq km. **Location:** SW Asia, NW of Indian subcontinent. Pakistan on E, S; Iran on W; Turkmenistan, Uzbekistan, Tajikistan on N. NE tip touches China. **Topography:** Landlocked and mountainous, much of it over 4,000 ft above sea level. The Hindu Kush Mts. tower 16,000 ft above Kabul and reach a height of 25,000 ft to the E. Dry climate with extreme temperatures; large desert regions. **Arable land:** 11.9%. **Capital:** Kabul, 4,011,770.

Government: Type: Presidential Islamic republic. **Head of state and govt.:** Pres. Ashraf Ghani Ahmadzai; b. 1949; in office: Sept. 29, 2014; and Chief Exec. Abdullah Abdullah; b. 1960; in office: Sept. 29, 2014. **Local divisions:** 34 provinces. **Defense budget:** $2.2 bil. **Active troops:** 174,300.

Economy: Industries: small-scale prod. of bricks, textiles, soap, furniture, shoes, fertilizer, apparel, food prods. **Chief agric.:** opium, wheat, fruits, nuts; wool, mutton. **Natural resources:** nat. gas, petroleum, coal, copper, chromite, talc, barites, sulfur, lead, zinc, iron ore, salt, prec./semiprec. stones. **Water:** 2,008 cu m per capita. **Electricity prod.:** 1 bil kWh. **Labor force:** agric. 62.2%, industry 6.7%, services 31.1%. **Unemployment:** 8.8%.

Finance: Monetary unit: Afghani (AFN) (73.82 = $1 U.S.). **GDP:** $69.6 bil; **per capita GDP:** $2,000; **GDP growth:** 2.5%. **Imports:** $7.6 bil; China 21%, Iran 20.5%, Pakistan 11.8%, Kazakhstan 11%, Uzbekistan 6.8%, Malaysia 5.3%. **Exports:** $784 mil (not incl. illicit trade); India 56.5%, Pakistan 29.6%. **Tourism:** $49 mil. **Budget:** $5.3 bil. **Inflation:** 5%.

Transport: Motor vehicles: 63.5 per 1,000 pop. **Airports:** 25. **Communications: Telephone:** 0.3 per 100 pop. **Mobile:** 67.4 per 100 pop. **Broadband:** 14.3 per 100 pop. **Internet:** 10.6%.

Health: Expend.: 10.3%. **Life expect.:** 50.6 male; 53.6 female. **Births:** 37.5 per 1,000 pop. **Deaths:** 13.2 per 1,000 pop. **Infant mortality:** 108.5 per 1,000 live births. **Undernourished:** 30.3%. **HIV:** <0.1%.

Education: Compulsory: ages 7-15. **Literacy:** 38.2%.

Embassy: 2341 Wyoming Ave. NW 20008; 483-6410.

Website: president.gov.af/en/

Afghanistan, occupying a favored invasion route since antiquity, has been variously known as Ariana or Bactria (in ancient times) and Khorasan (in the Middle Ages). Foreign empires alternated rule with local emirs and kings until the 18th cent., when a unified kingdom was established. In 1973, a military coup ushered in a republic.

Pro-Soviet leftists took power in a bloody 1978 coup. In Dec. 1979 the USSR began a massive airlift into Kabul and backed a new coup, leading to the installation of a more pro-Soviet leader. Soviet forces fanned out over Afghanistan and waged a protracted guerrilla war with Muslim rebels, in which some 15,000 Soviet troops reportedly died.

A UN-mediated agreement was signed Apr. 14, 1988, providing for withdrawal of Soviet troops, a neutral Afghan state, and repatriation of refugees. Afghan rebels rejected the pact. The Soviets completed their troop withdrawal Feb. 15, 1989; fighting between Afghan rebels and government forces ensued. Communist Pres. Najibullah resigned Apr. 16, 1992, as competing guerrilla forces advanced on Kabul. The rebels achieved power Apr. 28, ending 14 years of Soviet-backed regimes. More than 2 mil Afghans had been killed, and 6 mil had left the country since 1979.

Clashes between moderates and Islamic fundamentalist forces followed the rebel victory. The Taliban, an insurgent radical-Islamist faction, captured Kabul in Sept. 1996 and empowered Islamic religious police to enforce strict Islamic codes of dress and behavior.

Victories in the northern cities of Mazar-e Sharif, Aug. 8, 1998, and Taloqan, Aug. 8-11, essentially gave the Taliban control over the entire country. On Aug. 20, U.S. cruise missiles struck SE of Kabul, hitting facilities the U.S. said were terrorist training camps run by Osama bin Laden. The UN imposed sanctions Nov. 14, 1999, when Afghanistan refused to turn over bin Laden to the U.S. for prosecution.

After the Sept. 11, 2001, attacks on the World Trade Center and Pentagon, the U.S., blaming bin Laden, demanded that the Taliban surrender him and shut down his al-Qaeda terrorist network. When the Taliban refused, the U.S., with British assistance, began bombing Afghanistan Oct. 7, as part of Operation Enduring Freedom (OEF).

Supported by the U.S., the opposition Northern Alliance recaptured Mazar-e Sharif Nov. 9 and took Kabul 4 days later; Taliban forces abandoned Kandahar, their last stronghold, to southern tribal fighters Dec. 7. A power-sharing agreement signed by four anti-Taliban factions, including the Northern Alliance, provided for an interim government headed by Hamid Karzai, a Pashtun tribal leader. The UN authorized a multinational security force Dec. 20, 2001.

Meeting June 13, 2002, in Kabul, a traditional council (*loya jirga*) chose Karzai to head a new transitional government. Although the U.S. announced the end of major combat operations in Afghanistan, May 1, 2003, resistance continued. NATO officially assumed control of peacekeeping forces—the Intl. Security Assistance Force (ISAF)—Aug. 11, 2003.

The most intense fighting in more than 4 years erupted Mar. 2006 with a new wave of attacks and other strikes by Taliban insurgents. Operating from sanctuaries in Pakistan, Islamist suicide bombers and Taliban insurgents stepped up their activities,

2007-11. Violence escalated in the run-up to the first-round presidential election Aug. 20, 2009. After a Nov. runoff election was canceled when Karzai's lone opponent dropped out, Karzai was sworn in for a second term Nov. 19.

Ending a decade-long manhunt, U.S. commandos killed bin Laden shortly after midnight May 2, 2011, in Abbottabad, Pakistan. Insurgents retaliated Aug. 6 by shooting down a helicopter, killing 30 Americans and 8 Afghans. Other violence included attacks Sept. 13, 2011, on the U.S. embassy and NATO headquarters in Kabul.

Between Jan. 2009 and June 2011, the number of U.S. troops in Afghanistan rose from about 36,000 to 101,000, while the number of allied foreign forces under ISAF increased from nearly 32,000 to more than 42,000. The U.S., June 22, 2011, outlined a timetable for drawing down troops and ending their combat role, with a residual force focusing on combating Islamic extremists and training and advising Afghan troops. OEF and ISAF officially ended Dec. 28, 2014; since Oct. 2001, 2,215 U.S. and 1,270 allied troops had been killed. The NATO-led Resolute Support Mission (RSM) to aid Afghan forces began Jan. 1, 2015. As of mid-2018, there were more than 16,200 RSM troops in Afghanistan, of which almost 8,500 were from the U.S.; including other counterterrorism forces, total U.S. troop strength was about 14,000-15,000. U.S. and other RSM troop strength had increased by more than 4,000 from mid-2017 to mid-2018.

The first round of elections for a new president was held Apr. 5, 2014. A June 14 runoff between the two top vote-getters—former Foreign Min. Abdullah Abdullah and former Finance Min. Ashraf Ghani Ahmadzai—was marred by allegations of electoral fraud. After an internationally supervised audit of all 8 mil runoff ballots, Ghani was declared the winner Sept. 21. Under a U.S.-brokered power-sharing agreement, he appointed Abdullah chief executive of the government. Fighting between government and Taliban forces continued in 2015-18, as did Taliban terrorist attacks in Kabul and other cities. A Taliban bombing in Kabul, Jan. 27, 2018, killed more than 100. Well over 1,000 government troops died in a number of Taliban attacks, Aug.-Sept. 2018. Taliban forces briefly controlled the cities of Farah in May and Ghazni in Aug.

The government announced, July 29, 2015, that longtime Taliban leader Mohammad Omar had died in 2013. A U.S. drone strike in Pakistan, May 21, 2016, killed Omar's successor, Akhtar Muhammad Mansour; Haibatullah Akhundzada replaced Mansour. Beginning in 2014, an affiliate of the Sunni extremist group ISIS gained control of areas in eastern Afghanistan and staged suicide bombings and other attacks in Kabul and elsewhere. The U.S. special inspector general for Afghanistan reconstruction estimated that, in mid-2018, the government effectively controlled about 56% of the country; insurgent groups controlled about 14% and contested 30%. The U.S. increased airstrikes against Taliban and ISIS targets beginning in 2017, including use of a 21,600-lb bomb, Apr. 13, 2017, against an ISIS cave complex—the most powerful non-nuclear bomb ever used by the U.S. Taliban attacks reduced ISIS-controlled territory in 2018.

Combat and terrorist attacks caused high civilian casualties. The UN reported 14,182 conflict-related civilian deaths, 2014-17, and a further 1,692, Jan.-June 2018. Conflict in 2018 had internally displaced more than 225,000 people by Sept. 15. About 2.5 mil refugees from decades of Afghanistan violence were in Pakistan as of 2016. Hundreds of thousands returned in 2016-17, amid accusations that many were forced to return by Pakistan; almost 1.4 mil remained as of Aug. 31, 2018.

Albania
Republic of Albania

People: Population: 3,057,220 (134). **Age distrib.:** <15: 17.8%; 65+: 12.2%. **Growth:** 0.3%. **Migrants:** 1.8%. **Pop. density:** 289 per sq mi, 111.6 per sq km. **Urban:** 60.3%. **Ethnic groups:** Albanian 82.6%. **Languages:** Albanian (official). **Religions:** Muslim 56.7%, Roman Catholic 10%, Orthodox 6.8%, atheist 2.5%.

Geography: Total area: 11,100 sq mi, 28,748 sq km (141); **Land area:** 10,578 sq mi, 27,398 sq km. **Location:** SE Europe, on SE coast of Adriatic Sea. Greece on S; Montenegro, Kosovo on N; Macedonia on E. **Topography:** Narrow coastal plain; hills and mountains covered with scrub forest, cut by small E-W rivers. **Arable land:** 22.4%. **Capital:** Tirana, 475,577.

Government: Type: Parliamentary republic. **Head of state:** Pres. Ilir Meta; b. 1969; in office: July 24, 2017. **Head of govt.:** Prime Min. Edi Rama; b. 1964; in office: Sept. 15, 2013. **Local divisions:** 12 counties. **Defense budget:** $109 mil. **Active troops:** 8,000.

Economy: Industries: food, footwear, apparel, clothing, lumber. **Chief agric.:** wheat, corn, potatoes, vegetables, fruits, olives and olive oil, grapes; meat, dairy prods. **Natural resources:** petroleum, nat. gas, coal, bauxite, chromite, copper, iron ore, nickel, salt, timber, hydropower. **Water:** 10,425 cu m per capita. **Crude oil reserves:** 168.3 mil bbls. **Electricity prod.:** 5.9 bil kWh. **Labor force:** agric. 40.3%, industry 18.6%, services 41.1%. **Unemployment:** 13.9%.

Finance: Monetary unit: Lek (ALL) (109.16 = $1 U.S.). **GDP:** $36 bil (unreported output may be as large as 50% of official GDP);

per capita GDP: $12,500; **GDP growth:** 3.9%. **Imports:** $4.1 bil; Italy 28.5%, Turkey 8.1%, Germany 8%, Greece 8%, China 7.9%. **Exports:** $960.9 mil; Italy 53.4%, Kosovo 7.7%, Spain 5.6%. **Tourism:** $1.9 bil. **Budget:** $3.8 bil. **Inflation:** 2%.

Transport: Railways: 421 mi. **Airports:** 4.

Communications: Telephone: 8.4 per 100 pop. **Mobile:** 119.4 per 100 pop. **Broadband:** 52.6 per 100 pop. **Internet:** 66.4%.

Health: Expend.: 6.8%. **Life expect.:** 76.0 male; 81.6 female. **Births:** 13.2 per 1,000 pop. **Deaths:** 6.9 per 1,000 pop. **Infant mortality:** 11.6 per 1,000 live births. **Undernourished:** 5.5%. **HIV:** <0.1%.

Education: Compulsory: ages 6-15. **Literacy:** 97.6%.

Embassy: 2100 S St. NW 20008; 223-4942.

Website: www.kryeministria.al

Ancient Illyria was conquered by Romans, Slavs, and Turks (15th cent.); the Turks Islamized the population. Independent Albania was proclaimed in 1912; a republic was formed in 1920. King Zog I ruled 1925-39 until Italy invaded.

Communist partisans took over in 1944 and allied Albania with the USSR but broke with the USSR in 1960 over de-Stalinization. Billions of dollars in Chinese financial assistance was cut off in 1978 when Albania attacked China's policies. Large-scale purges of officials occurred during the 1970s.

Enver Hoxha, the nation's ruler for four decades, died Apr. 11, 1985. The new regime introduced some liberalization, including measures in 1990 providing for freedom to travel abroad.

Albania's former Communists were routed in elections Mar. 1992, amid economic collapse and social unrest. Sali Berisha was elected as the first non-Communist president since WWII. Berisha's party claimed a landslide victory in disputed parliamentary elections, May 26 and June 2, 1996. Public protests over the collapse of fraudulent investment schemes in Jan. 1997 led to armed rebellion. The UN Security Council, Mar. 28, authorized a 7,000-member force to restore order. Socialists and their allies won parliamentary elections, June 29 and July 6, and international peacekeepers pulled out by Aug. 11, 1997.

During NATO's air war against Yugoslavia, Mar.-June 1999, Albania hosted some 465,000 Kosovar refugees. A pro-Berisha coalition victory in July 3, 2005, elections ended eight years of Socialist rule. Albania became a full member of NATO Apr. 1, 2009. Socialists won June 23, 2013, parliamentary elections, and Edi Rama became the new prime min. The EU granted Albania official candidate status June 27, 2014. The Socialists won June 25, 2017, elections, after a campaign in which Rama pledged reforms to reduce organized crime and political corruption, key issues for EU-membership negotiations.

Algeria
People's Democratic Republic of Algeria

People: Population: 41,657,488 (34). **Age distrib.:** <15: 29.5%; 65+: 5.8%. **Growth:** 1.6%. **Migrants:** 0.6%. **Pop. density:** 45.3 per sq mi, 17.5 per sq km. **Urban:** 72.6%. **Ethnic groups:** Arab-Berber 99%. **Languages:** Arabic (official), French (lingua franca), Berber or Tamazight (official), Berber dialects. **Religions:** Muslim (official; predom. Sunni) 99%.

Geography: Total area: 919,595 sq mi, 2,381,741 sq km (10). **Land area:** 919,595 sq mi, 2,381,741 sq km. **Location:** NW Africa, from Medit. Sea into Sahara. Morocco, Western Sahara on W; Mauritania, Mali, Niger on S; Libya, Tunisia on E. **Topography:** The Tell, on the coast, comprises fertile plains 50-100 mi wide with a moderate climate and adequate rain. Two major chains of Atlas Mts., running roughly E-W and reaching 7,000 ft, enclose a dry plateau region. The Sahara lies below. **Arable land:** 3.1%. **Capital:** Algiers, 2,693,542. **Cities:** Oran, 881,119.

Government: Type: Presidential republic. **Head of state:** Pres. Abdelaziz Bouteflika; b. 1937; in office: Apr. 28, 1999. **Head of govt.:** Prime Min. Ahmed Ouyahia; b. 1952; in office: Aug. 16, 2017. **Local divisions:** 48 provinces. **Defense budget:** $10 bil. **Active troops:** 130,000.

Economy: Industries: petroleum, nat. gas, light industries, mining, electrical, petrochemical, food proc. **Chief agric.:** wheat, barley, oats, grapes, olives, citrus, fruits; sheep, cattle. **Natural resources:** petroleum, nat. gas, iron ore, phosphates, uranium, lead, zinc. **Water:** 294 cu m per capita. **Crude oil reserves:** 12.2 bil bbls. **Electricity prod.:** 64.7 bil kWh. **Labor force:** agric. 12.8%, industry 47%, services 40.2%. **Unemployment:** 10.1%.

Finance: Monetary unit: Dinar (DZD) (118.70 = $1 U.S.). **GDP:** $632.9 bil; **per capita GDP:** $15,200; **GDP growth:** 2%. **Imports:** $50 bil; China 18.2%, France 9.1%, Italy 8%, Germany 7%, Spain 6.9%. **Exports:** $33.2 bil; Italy 17.4%, Spain 13%, France 11.9%, U.S. 9.4%, Brazil 6.2%, Netherlands 5.5%. **Tourism:** $209 mil. **Budget:** $70.7 bil. **Inflation:** 5.6%.

Transport: Railways: 2,469 mi. **Motor vehicles:** 137.7 per 1,000 pop. **Airports:** 64.

Communications: Telephone: 7.6 per 100 pop. **Mobile:** 120.7 per 100 pop. **Broadband:** 46.8 per 100 pop. **Internet:** 42.9%.

Health: Expend.: 7.1%. **Life expect.:** 75.8 male; 78.7 female. **Births:** 21.5 per 1,000 pop. **Deaths:** 4.3 per 1,000 pop. **Infant mortality:** 18.9 per 1,000 live births. **Undernourished:** 4.7%. **HIV:** <0.1%.

Education: Compulsory: ages 6-15. **Literacy:** 80.2%.
Embassy: 2118 Kalorama Rd. NW 20008; 265-2800.
Website: www.algerianembassy.org or www.premier-ministre.gov.dz

Earliest known inhabitants were ancestors of Berbers, followed by Phoenicians, Romans, Vandals, and Arabs. Turkey ruled 1518-1830, when France took control. Large-scale European immigration followed. Arab nationalists launched a guerrilla war, 1954, that more than 400,000 French troops were unable to suppress. After French Pres. Charles de Gaulle came to power, 1958, colonial rule ended, nearly all Europeans left, and Algeria declared independence July 5, 1962. Ahmed Ben Bella ruled until 1965, when an army coup installed Col. Houari Boumedienne, a former guerrilla leader who held power until his death in 1978.

Hundreds died in anti-government riots protesting economic hardship, Oct. 1988. The government canceled the Jan. 1992 elections and banned all nonreligious activities at Algeria's 10,000 mosques. Pres. Mohammed Boudiaf was assassinated June 29, 1992. Over the next seven years, Muslim fundamentalists attacked high-ranking officials, security forces, and foreigners; pro-government death squads were active.

Liamine Zeroual won the Nov. 16, 1995, presidential election. A new constitution banning Islamic political parties and increasing the president's powers passed in a Nov. 1996 referendum. Abdelaziz Bouteflika, who became president after a flawed Apr. 15, 1999, election, reconciled with rebels and won approval for an amnesty plan in a referendum, Sept. 16. Some 100 people died and thousands were injured in violent protests Apr.-June 2001, chiefly by Algeria's Berber minority. Bouteflika was reelected Apr. 8, 2004, though opponents charged fraud.

Under a reconciliation plan approved by referendum Sept. 2005, the government in Mar. 2006 began freeing Islamists jailed for their role in the 1990s civil war, which left up to 200,000 people dead and 8,000 "disappeared."

Radical Islamists bombed police stations in Oct. 2006 and Feb. 2007. A group known as al-Qaeda in the Islamic Maghreb (AQIM) carried out several suicide bombings throughout 2007, killing more than 100 people. A surge in AQIM violence in Aug. 2008 left another 100+ people dead.

Parliament, Nov. 12, 2008, amended the constitution to abolish presidential term limits, enabling Bouteflika to run for a third term. He claimed more than 90% of the vote in a 2009 election denounced as fraudulent by opposition parties. During Arab Spring uprisings in early 2011, Bouteflika's government suppressed street protests in Algiers, Feb. 12, and used oil revenues to raise salaries of discontented civil servants. The country's governing party, the Natl. Liberation Front (FLN), strengthened its hold on power in May 10, 2012, parliamentary elections that opposition groups called fraudulent. The 77-year-old Bouteflika won a fourth term as president with 81.5% of the vote in the Apr. 17, 2014, election. A Feb. 2016 constitutional amendment restored presidential term limits (two terms). The FLN won May 4, 2017, parliamentary elections.

AQIM members protesting France's involvement in Mali seized the In Amenas gas facility Jan. 16, 2013, holding about 40 foreign workers hostage for 4 days and demanding the release of about 100 Islamist prisoners being held in Algeria. In the end, 38 hostages died, including 3 Americans, as well as some 29 militants at the hands of Algerian special forces attempting to liberate the facility. Algerian officials reported that security forces, May 19, 2015, had killed 21 Islamist extremists planning a terrorist attack on Algiers.

In Algeria's worst air disaster, 257 people died, Apr. 11, 2018, when a military transport plane crashed near Algiers.

Andorra
Principality of Andorra

People: Population: 85,708 (186). **Age distrib.:** <15: 14.1%; 65+: 16.2%. **Growth:** −0.01%. **Migrants:** 53.3%. **Pop. density:** 474.3 per sq mi, 183.1 per sq km. **Urban:** 88.1%. **Ethnic groups:** Andorran 45.5%, Spanish 26.6%, Portuguese 12.9%, French 5.2%. **Languages:** Catalan (official), French, Castilian, Portuguese. **Religions:** Roman Catholic (predom.).

Geography: Total area: 181 sq mi, 468 sq km (180); **Land area:** 181 sq mi, 468 sq km. **Location:** SW Europe, in Pyrenees Mts. Spain on S, France on N. **Topography:** High mountains and narrow valleys across country. **Arable land:** 1.7%. **Capital:** Andorra la Vella, 22,614.

Government: Type: Parliamentary democracy. **Heads of state:** President of France and Bishop of Urgell (Spain), as co-princes. **Head of govt.:** Antoni Martí Petit; b. 1963; in office: May 12, 2011. **Local divisions:** 7 parishes. **Defense budget/active troops:** NA.

Economy: Industries: tourism (skiing), banking, timber, furniture. **Chief agric.:** rye, wheat, barley, oats, vegetables, tobacco; sheep, cattle. **Natural resources:** hydropower, mineral water, timber, iron ore, lead. **Water:** 4,479 cu m per capita. **Labor force:** agric. 0.5%, industry 4.4%, services 95.1%. **Unemployment:** NA. **Finance: Monetary unit:** Euro (EUR) (0.86 = $1 U.S.). **GDP** (2015): $3.3 bil; **per capita GDP** (2015): $49,900; **GDP**

growth (2015): −1.1%. **Imports** (2015): $1.3 bil; Spain 63.6%, France 15.8%. **Exports** (2015): $78.7 mil; Spain 52.6%, France 18.7%. **Budget** (2016): $2.1 bil. **Inflation** (2014-15): −0.9%.

Transport: NA.
Communications: Telephone: 49.9 per 100 pop. **Mobile:** 104.4 per 100 pop. **Broadband:** 47.8 per 100 pop. **Internet:** 97.9%.

Health: Expend.: 12%. **Life expect.:** 80.7 male; 85.3 female. **Births:** 7.3 per 1,000 pop. **Deaths:** 7.4 per 1,000 pop. **Infant mortality:** 3.6 per 1,000 live births. **Undernourished:** NA. **HIV:** NA.

Education: Compulsory: ages 6-15. **Literacy:** 100%.
Embassy: 2 UN Plz., 27th Fl., New York, NY 10017; (212) 750-8064.

Website: www.govern.ad

France and the bishop of Urgell held joint sovereignty over Andorra from 1278 to 1993. Voters chose to adopt a parliamentary system Mar. 14, 1993, although co-princes remain heads of state. Tourism, especially skiing, and banking are economic mainstays. For years, Andorra served as a tax haven, but it began reforms in 2008 and was removed by the OECD from its list of uncooperative tax havens, May 27, 2009. In Mar. 2015, the government seized control of Banca Privada d'Andorra (BPA) and arrested its chief executive after the U.S. Treasury Dept. accused BPA of facilitating money laundering on behalf of global criminal groups. The parliament approved, Nov. 30, 2016, a measure to end, in stages, banking secrecy for foreigners with accounts in Andorra.

Angola
Republic of Angola

People: Population: 30,355,880 (45). **Age distrib.:** <15: 48.1%; 65+: 2.3%. **Growth:** 3.5%. **Migrants:** 2.1%. **Pop. density:** 63.1 per sq mi, 24.3 per sq km. **Urban:** 65.5%. **Ethnic groups:** Ovimbundu 37%, Kimbundu 25%, Bakongo 13%, mestico (mixed European/native African) 2%. **Languages:** Portuguese (official), Umbundu, Kikongo, Kimbundu, Chokwe. **Religions:** Roman Catholic 41.1%, Protestant 38.1%, none 12.3%.

Geography: Total area: 481,354 sq mi, 1,246,700 sq km (22); **Land area:** 481,354 sq mi, 1,246,700 sq km. **Location:** SW Africa on Atlantic coast. Namibia on S, Zambia on E, Dem. Rep. of the Congo on N; Cabinda, an exclave separated from rest of country by short Atlantic coast of Dem. Rep. of the Congo, borders Congo Rep. **Topography:** Mostly plateau 3,000-5,000 ft above sea level, rising from a narrow coastal strip. Temperate highland area in the W-central region, a desert in S, and a tropical rain forest in Cabinda. **Arable land:** 3.9%. **Capital:** Luanda, 7,774,200.

Government: Type: Presidential republic. **Head of state and govt.:** João Lourenço; b. 1954; in office: Sept. 26, 2017. **Local divisions:** 18 provinces. **Defense budget:** $3.2 bil. **Active troops:** 107,000.

Economy: Industries: petroleum, diamonds, cement, metal prods., fish/food proc. **Chief agric.:** bananas, sugarcane, coffee, sisal, corn, cotton, cassava, tobacco; livestock; fish. **Natural resources:** petroleum, diamonds, iron ore, phosphates, copper, feldspar, gold, bauxite, uranium. **Water:** 5,931 cu m per capita. **Crude oil reserves:** 9.5 bil bbls. **Electricity prod.:** 9.4 bil kWh. **Labor force:** agric. 50.6%, industry 8.6%, services 40.8%. Portugal 14%, South Korea 11.2%, U.S. 7%. **Unemployment:** 8.2%.

Finance: Monetary unit: Kwanza (AOA) (280.48 = $1 U.S.). **GDP:** $190.3 bil; **per capita GDP:** $6,800; **GDP growth:** 0.7%. **Imports:** $23 bil; Portugal 17.8%, China 13.5%, U.S. 7.4%, South Africa 6.2%, Brazil 6.1%. **Exports:** $33.8 bil; China 61.2%, India 13%. **Tourism:** $623 mil. **Budget:** $44.6 bil. **Inflation:** 31.7%.

Transport: Railways: 1,772 mi. **Motor vehicles:** 5.3 per 1,000 pop. **Airports:** 31.

Communications: Telephone: 0.5 per 100 pop. **Mobile:** 44.7 per 100 pop. **Broadband:** 17.1 per 100 pop. **Internet:** 13%.

Health: Expend.: 2.9%. **Life expect.:** 58.5 male; 62.7 female. **Births:** 43.7 per 1,000 pop. **Deaths:** 9 per 1,000 pop. **Infant mortality:** 65.8 per 1,000 live births. **Undernourished:** 23.9%. **HIV:** 1.9%.

Education: Compulsory: ages 6-11. **Literacy:** 71.1%.
Embassy: 2100-2108 16th St. NW 20009; 785-1156.
Website: www.governo.gov.ao

From the early centuries CE to 1500, Bantu tribes penetrated most of the region. Portuguese came in 1583, allied with the Bakongo kingdom in the north, and developed the slave trade. Large-scale colonization began in the 20th cent., when 400,000 Portuguese immigrated.

A guerrilla war, 1961-75, ended when Portugal granted Angola independence. Fighting then erupted among rival rebel groups, including the Soviet-backed Popular Movement for the Liberation of Angola (MPLA) and the National Union for the Total Independence of Angola (UNITA), aided by the U.S. and South Africa. Cuban troops and Soviet aid helped the MPLA win control of most of the country by 1976, although fighting continued. The MPLA government and UNITA signed a peace accord May 1, 1991. Elections were held, Sept. 1992, but fighting again broke out when UNITA rejected the results. UNITA signed a new peace treaty with the government, Nov. 20, 1994, but the rebels were slow to demobilize. The UN ended its mission in Angola, Mar. 1999, as the civil war continued. The UN estimated that the war with UNITA had claimed some 1 mil lives and left another 2.5 mil people homeless by mid-2001. Government troops killed rebel leader Jonas Savimbi Feb. 22, 2002. UNITA agreed to a truce Apr. 4, 2002. Separatist rebels in oil-rich Cabinda agreed to a cease-fire July 2006.

With proven petroleum reserves estimated at more than 8 bil barrels, Angola is among Africa's leading oil producers. Wealth is extremely unevenly distributed and corruption has been widespread. The ruling MPLA claimed victory in voting Sept. 2008, in Angola's first parliamentary elections in 16 years. Parliament approved Jan. 21, 2010, a new constitution augmenting the power of MPLA leader José Eduardo dos Santos, Angola's president since 1979. The MPLA won flawed elections, Aug 31, 2012, giving dos Santos another 5-year term. Dos Santos did not seek a new term in 2017, and he campaigned for João Lourenço. The MPLA won disputed Aug. 23 elections and Lourenço took office Sept. 26, 2017. Lourenço dismissed, Nov. 15, dos Santos's daughter as head of the state oil company. On Jan. 11, 2018, he removed as head of the country's sovereign wealth fund dos Santos's son José Filomeno dos Santos, who was later accused of attempting to siphon up to $1.5 bil from the fund.

Antigua and Barbuda

People: Population: 95,882 (184). **Age distrib.:** <15: 22.9%; 65+: 8.3%. **Growth:** 1.2%. **Migrants:** 28.1%. **Pop. density:** 560.6 per sq mi, 216.4 per sq km. **Urban:** 24.6%. **Ethnic groups:** black 87.3%, mixed 4.7%, Hispanic 2.7%. **Languages:** English (official), Antiguan creole. **Religions:** Protestant 68.3% (incl. Anglican 17.6%, Seventh-day Adventist 12.4%, Pentecostal 12.2%, Moravian 8.3%), Roman Catholic 8.2%, none 5.9%.

Geography: Total area: 171 sq mi, 443 sq km (Antigua, 108 sq mi, 280 sq km; Barbuda, 62 sq mi, 161 sq km) (183); **Land area:** 171 sq mi, 443 sq km. **Location:** E Caribbean. St. Kitts and Nevis to W, Guadeloupe (Fr.) to S. **Topography:** Mostly low-lying and limestone coral islands. Antigua is mostly hilly with an indented coast; Barbuda is a flat island with a large lagoon on W. **Arable land:** 9.1%. **Capital:** St. John's, 20,764.

Government: Type: Parliamentary democracy under constitutional monarchy. **Head of state:** Queen Elizabeth II, rep. by Gov.-Gen. Rodney Williams; b. 1947; in office: Aug. 14, 2014. **Head of govt.:** Prime Min. Gaston Browne; b. 1967; in office: June 13, 2014. **Local divisions:** 6 parishes, 2 dependencies. **Defense budget:** $27 mil. **Active troops:** 180.

Economy: Industries: tourism, constr., light mfg. **Chief agric.:** cotton, fruits, vegetables, bananas, coconuts; livestock. **Natural resources:** negligible. **Water:** 566 cu m per capita. **Electricity prod.:** 330 mil kWh. **Labor force:** agric. 7%, industry 11%, services 82%. **Unemployment:** NA.

Finance: Monetary unit: East Caribbean Dollar (XCD) (2.70 = $1 U.S.). **GDP:** $2.4 bil; **per capita GDP:** $26,300; **GDP growth:** 2.8%. **Imports:** $420.7 mil; U.S. 48%. **Exports:** $61.3 mil; Poland 62.2%, Cameroon 9.5%, U.S. 5.1%. **Tourism:** $332 mil. **Budget:** $322.9 mil. **Inflation:** 2.4%.

Transport: Airports: 2.
Communications: Telephone (2016): 22.3 per 100 pop. **Mobile** (2016): 178.3 per 100 pop. **Broadband:** 44.2 per 100 pop. **Internet:** 73%.
Health: Expend.: 4.8%. **Life expect.:** 74.8 male; 79.2 female. **Births:** 15.6 per 1,000 pop. **Deaths:** 5.8 per 1,000 pop. **Infant mortality:** 11.7 per 1,000 live births. **Undernourished:** NA. **HIV:** NA.
Education: Compulsory: ages 5-15. **Literacy:** 99%.
Embassy: 3216 New Mexico Ave. NW 20016; 362-5122.
Website: ab.gov.ag

Christopher Columbus landed on Antigua in 1493. The British colonized it in 1632. The British-associated state of Antigua achieved independence as Antigua and Barbuda on Nov. 1, 1981. Tourism accounts for almost 60% of GDP. The worldwide recession caused the economy to shrink in 2009-11. With the economy still weak, the opposition Antigua and Barbuda Labour Party (ABLP) won June 12, 2014, parliamentary elections, and ABLP leader Gaston Browne became prime minister. The ABLP retained power in Mar. 21, 2018, elections.

Hurricane Irma caused massive damage on Barbuda, Sept. 5-6, 2017. Browne estimated that 95% of buildings were destroyed or extensively damaged. At least one person died.

Argentina
Argentine Republic

People: Population: 44,694,198 (31). **Age distrib.:** <15: 24.4%; 65+: 11.8%. **Growth:** 0.9%. **Migrants:** 4.9%. **Pop. density:** 42.3 per sq mi, 16.3 per sq km. **Urban:** 91.9%. **Ethnic groups:** European (mostly Spanish and Italian) and mestizo (mixed European/Amerindian) 97.2%, Amerindian 2.4%. **Languages:** Spanish (official), Italian, English, German, French, indigenous (Mapudungun, Quechua). **Religions:** nominally Roman Catholic 92%, Protestant 2%, Jewish 2%.

Geography: Total area: 1,073,518 sq mi, 2,780,400 sq km (8); **Land area:** 1,056,642 sq mi, 2,736,690 sq km. **Location:** Occupies most of southern S America. Chile on W; Bolivia, Paraguay on N; Brazil, Uruguay on NE. **Topography:** Andean, Central, Misiones, and Southern mountain ranges in W. Aconcagua (22,831 ft) is highest peak in Western Hemisphere. Heavily wooded plains called the Gran Chaco are E of Andes in the N; fertile, treeless Pampas in the central region. Patagonia, in S, is bleak and arid. Rio de la Plata, an estuary in NE, 170 by 140 mi, is mostly freshwater, from 2,485-mi Parana and 1,000-mi Uruguay Rivers. **Arable land:** 14.3%. **Capital:** Buenos Aires, 14,966,530. **Cities:** Córdoba, 1,548,176; Rosario, 1,488,162; Mendoza, 1,133,373.

Government: Type: Presidential republic. **Head of state and govt.:** Pres. Mauricio Macri; b. 1959; in office: Dec. 10, 2015. **Local divisions:** 23 provinces, 1 autonomous city. **Defense budget:** $6.1 bil. **Active troops:** 74,200.

Economy: Industries: food proc., motor vehicles, consumer durables, textiles, chemicals and petrochemicals. **Chief agric.:** sunflower seeds, lemons, soybeans, grapes, corn, tobacco; livestock. **Natural resources:** lead, zinc, tin, copper, iron ore, manganese, petroleum, uranium. **Water:** 20,181 cu m per capita. **Crude oil reserves:** 2.2 bil bbls. **Electricity prod.:** 133.8 bil kWh. **Labor force:** agric. 0.5%, industry 23.3%, services 76.1%. **Unemployment:** 8.5%.

Finance: Monetary unit: Peso (ARS) (38.97 = $1 U.S.). **GDP:** $920.2 bil; **per capita GDP:** $20,900; **GDP growth:** 2.9%. **Imports:** $60.8 bil; Brazil 26.9%, China 18.5%, U.S. 11.3%. **Exports:** $59.7 bil; Brazil 16.1%, U.S. 7.9%, China 7.5%. **Tourism:** $5.1 bil. **Budget:** $161.1 bil. **Inflation:** 25.7%.

Transport: Railways: 22,939 mi. **Motor vehicles:** 318.5 per 1,000 pop. **Airports:** 161.
Communications: Telephone: 21.5 per 100 pop. **Mobile:** 139.8 per 100 pop. **Broadband:** 80.5 per 100 pop. **Internet:** 71%.
Health: Expend.: 6.8%. **Life expect.:** 74.4 male; 80.8 female. **Births:** 16.5 per 1,000 pop. **Deaths:** 7.5 per 1,000 pop. **Infant mortality:** 9.5 per 1,000 live births. **Undernourished:** 3.8%. **HIV:** 0.4%.
Education: Compulsory: ages 4-17. **Literacy:** 98.1%.
Embassy: 1600 New Hampshire Ave. NW 20009; 238-6400.
Website: www.argentina.gob.ar

Nomadic Indians roamed the Pampas when Spaniards arrived, 1515-16, led by Juan Díaz de Solís. Nearly all the Indians were killed by the late 19th cent. The colonists won independence, 1816. A long period of disorder ended in a strong centralized government.

Large-scale Italian, German, and Spanish immigration in the decades after 1880 spurred modernization. Social reforms were enacted in the 1920s, but military coups prevailed, 1930-46, until Gen. Juan Perón was elected president.

Perón, with his wife, Eva Duarte (d. 1952), introduced labor reforms but suppressed speech and press freedoms, closed religious schools, and ran the country into debt. A 1955 coup exiled Perón. A series of military and civilian regimes followed. Perón returned in 1973 and was again elected president. He died 10 months later. His wife and vice president, Isabel, succeeded him.

A military junta ousted Isabel Perón in 1976 amid charges of corruption. Under a continuing state of siege, the army conducted a "dirty war" against guerrillas and leftists. An estimated 30,000 people "disappeared."

Argentine troops seized control of the British-held Falkland Islands (Islas Malvinas) on Apr. 2, 1982. The British imposed an air and sea blockade around the Falklands. Fighting began May 1. British troops landed on East Falkland May 21. Argentine troops surrendered, June 14.

Democratic rule returned in 1983. On Dec. 9, 1985, five former junta members were found guilty of murder and human rights abuses during the "dirty war" period. Buenos Aires Mayor Fernando de la Rúa won the presidential election Oct. 24, 1999, but resigned in 2001 after a prolonged recession resulted in debt of more than $130 bil. Congress, Jan. 1, 2002, chose a Peronist, Eduardo Alberto Duhalde, to finish de la Rúa's term. Further economic decline and renewed protests led Duhalde, July 2, to schedule an early presidential election for Mar. 2003; another Peronist, Néstor Kirchner, took office May 25, 2003. A new IMF aid deal, approved Sept. 10, 2003, rescued Argentina from default.

The Supreme Court, June 14, 2005, overturned amnesty laws that had barred prosecution for "dirty war" crimes committed while the military ruled Argentina. In July 2010, Argentina became the first Latin American country to extend full marriage rights to same-sex couples.

Cristina Fernández de Kirchner ran as the Peronist candidate after her husband and was elected president Oct. 28, 2007. She was reelected Oct. 23, 2011. In Nov. 2012, leaders of the nation's Jewish population charged the government with anti-Semitism for attempting to ease relations with Iran. In 2013, Argentine special prosecutor Alberto Nisman accused Cristina Kirchner of interfering with his investigation of Iranian involvement in a 1994 Jewish community center bombing in Buenos Aires that killed 85 people.

Nisman was found dead in his home from a gunshot to the head Jan. 18, 2015. Contradicting earlier police reports, a border police investigation concluded, Nov. 2017, that Nisman had been murdered. On Mar. 5, 2018, Cristina Kirchner was ordered to stand trial on charges of covering up Iranian involvement in the Jewish center bombing. She had been indicted, May 13, 2016, for allegedly manipulating the value of the Argentine peso while president, and she was indicted again Dec. 27, 2016, and Apr. 4, 2017, on financial corruption charges. An Aug. 24, 2018, judicial report implicated her in a long-running bribery scheme involving business and government officials; she was indicted on bribery charges Sept. 17.

Former Pres. Carlos Saúl Menem was convicted, Mar. 8, 2013, of weapons smuggling during his 1989-99 term; the conviction was overturned on technical grounds, Oct. 4, 2018. He went on trial, Aug. 6, 2015, on charges of interfering with the 1994 bombing investigation. Menem was convicted, Dec. 1, 2015, of embezzlement of public funds. Defeating Peronist candidate Daniel Scioli in a runoff, Mauricio Macri of the center-right Republican Proposal Party was elected president Nov. 22, 2015.

Pres. Macri, Sept. 3, 2018, announced austerity measures to stem a budget deficit and sharp drop in the value of the peso.

Buenos Aires Archbishop Jorge Mario Bergoglio was elected pope Mar. 13, 2013; he was the first pope from the Americas. He took the name Francis.

Armenia
Republic of Armenia

People: Population: 3,038,217 (135). **Age distrib.:** <15: 18.9%; 65+: 11.7%. **Growth:** −0.3%. **Migrants:** 6.5%. **Pop. density:** 279 per sq mi, 107.7 per sq km. **Urban:** 63.1%. **Ethnic groups:** Armenian 98.1%, Yezidi (Kurd) 1.1%. **Languages:** Armenian (official), Kurdish. **Religions:** Armenian Apostolic 92.6%.

Geography: Total area: 11,484 sq mi, 29,743 sq km (139); **Land area:** 10,889 sq mi, 28,203 sq km. **Location:** SW Asia. Georgia on N, Azerbaijan on E, Iran on S, Turkey on W. **Topography:** Mountainous with many peaks above 10,000 ft. **Arable land:** 15.7%. **Capital:** Yerevan, 1,080,324.

Government: Type: Parliamentary democracy. **Head of state:** Pres. Armen Sarkissian; b. 1953; in office: Apr. 9, 2018. **Head of govt.:** Prime Min. Nikol Pashinyan; b. 1975; in office: May 8, 2018. **Local divisions:** 11 provinces. **Defense budget:** $429 mil. **Active troops:** 44,800.

Economy: Industries: brandy, mining, diamond proc., metal-cutting machine tools, forging/pressing machines, elec. motors, knitted wear. **Chief agric.:** fruit (espec. grapes, apricots), vegetables; livestock. **Natural resources:** gold, copper, molybdenum, zinc, bauxite. **Water:** 2,574 cu m per capita. **Electricity prod.:** 7.4 bil kWh. **Labor force:** agric. 34.4%, industry 16%, services 49.7%. **Unemployment:** 18.2%.

Finance: Monetary unit: Dram (AMD) (483.39 = $1 U.S.). **GDP:** $28.3 bil; **per capita GDP:** $9,500; **GDP growth:** 7.5%. **Imports:** $3.4 bil; Russia 28%, China 11.5%, Turkey 5.5%. **Exports:** $2.2 bil; Russia 24.2%, Bulgaria 12.8%, Switzerland 12%, Georgia 6.9%, Germany 5.9%, China 5.5%, Iraq 5.4%. **Tourism:** $1.1 bil. **Budget:** $2.9 bil. **Inflation:** 1%.

Transport: Railways: 485 mi (only partly operational). **Airports:** 10.

Communications: Telephone: 17.2 per 100 pop. **Mobile:** 119 per 100 pop. **Broadband:** 53.9 per 100 pop. **Internet:** 64.3%.

Health: Expend.: 10.1%. **Life expect.:** 71.8 male; 78.7 female. **Births:** 12.6 per 1,000 pop. **Deaths:** 9.5 per 1,000 pop. **Infant mortality:** 12.3 per 1,000 live births. **Undernourished:** 4.3%. **HIV:** 0.2%.

Education: Compulsory: ages 6-17. **Literacy:** 99.7%.
Embassy: 2225 R St. NW 20008; 319-1976.
Website: www.gov.am

Ancient Armenia extended into parts of what are now Turkey and Iran. Present-day Armenia was set up as a Soviet republic Apr. 2, 1921. It joined Georgian and Azerbaijan SSRs Mar. 12, 1922, to form the Transcaucasian SFSR, which became part of the USSR Dec. 30, 1922. Armenia became a constituent republic of the USSR Dec. 5, 1936. An earthquake struck Armenia Dec. 7, 1988; approximately 25,000 were killed.

Armenia declared independence Sept. 23, 1991, and became an independent state when the USSR disbanded Dec. 26, 1991. Nagorno-Karabakh, an enclave in Azerbaijan with an ethnic Armenian majority, seceded from Azerbaijan in 1988. A 1992-94 war that cost 30,000 lives ended in a cease-fire with Armenian forces in control. Voters in the breakaway region approved a pro-independence constitution Dec. 10, 2006, that was rejected by the EU and OSCE. Deadly clashes between Armenian and Azerbaijani forces occurred in 2015-16 in and near Nagorno-Karabakh; a cease-fire was announced Apr. 5, 2016.

Voters approved, July 5, 1995, a new constitution increasing presidential powers. Pres. Levon Ter-Petrosian won reelection Sept. 22, 1996, amid claims of fraud. He resigned Feb. 3, 1998, and Robert Kocharian, a nationalist born in Nagorno-Karabak,

won the presidency Mar. 30, 1998. Gunmen stormed Parliament Oct. 27, 1999, killing Prime Min. Vazgen Sarkissian and 7 others. Kocharian won a second term Mar. 5, 2003, in a runoff vote that observers viewed as flawed.

Prime Min. Serzh Sargsyan defeated Ter-Petrosian in a Feb. 19, 2008, presidential election and won reelection Feb. 18, 2013. Constitutional revisions approved in a Dec. 6, 2015, referendum transitioned the country's government to a parliamentary system as of 2018, with presidential powers reduced. Sargsyan's party won Apr. 2, 2017, parliamentary elections. Sargsyan became prime min., Apr. 17, 2018, 8 days after his presidential term expired, but large-scale protests led to his resignation Apr. 23. Opposition leader Nikol Pashinyan was elected prime min. by parliament May 8.

Armenia did not ratify an Oct. 2009 treaty it had approved with Turkey over the 1915-18 killing of more than 1 mil Armenians by Ottoman Turks, due to renewed friction between the countries in 2010. On Jan. 2, 2015, Armenia joined the new Russian-led Eurasian Economic Union.

Australia
Commonwealth of Australia

People: Population: 23,470,145 (56). **Age distrib.:** <15: 17.7%; 65+: 16.4%. **Growth:** 1%. **Migrants:** 28.8%. **Pop. density:** 7.9 per sq mi, 3.1 per sq km. **Urban:** 86%. **Ethnic groups:** English 25.9%, Australian 25.4%, Irish 7.5%, Scottish 6.4%, Italian 3.3%, German 3.2%, Chinese 3.1%. **Languages:** English, Chinese, Arabic, Vietnamese, Italian. **Religions:** Protestant 23.1% (incl. Anglican 13.3%), Roman Catholic 22.6%, Muslim 2.6%, Buddhist 2.4%, none 30.1%.

Geography: Total area: 2,988,902 sq mi, 7,741,220 sq km (6); **Land area:** 2,966,153 sq mi, 7,682,300 sq km. **Location:** SE of Asia. Surrounded by Indian O. on W and S, Pacific O. (Coral, Tasman Seas) in E. Tasmania lies 150 mi S of Victoria state, across Bass Strait. Nearest are Indonesia, Papua New Guinea on N; Solomons, Fiji, and New Zealand on E. **Topography:** An island continent. The Great Dividing Range along the E coast has Mt. Kosciusko (7,310 ft). The Western Plateau rises to 2,000 ft, with arid areas in the Great Sandy and Great Victoria Deserts. The NW part of Western Australia and Northern Terr. are arid and hot. The NE has heavy rainfall. Jungles in Cape York Peninsula. **Arable land:** 6%. **Capital:** Canberra, 447,692. **Cities:** Sydney, 4,792,281; Melbourne, 4,770,894; Brisbane, 2,338,120; Perth, 1,990,745; Adelaide, 1,320,323.

Government: Type: Parliamentary democracy under constitutional monarchy. **Head of state:** Queen Elizabeth II, rep. by Gov.-Gen. Peter Cosgrove; b. 1947; in office: Mar. 28, 2014. **Head of govt.:** Prime Min. Scott Morrison; b. 1968; in office: Aug. 24, 2018. **Local divisions:** 6 states, 2 territories. **Defense budget:** $25 bil. **Active troops:** 57,800.

Economy: Industries: mining, industrial and transp. equip., food proc., chemicals, steel. **Chief agric.:** wheat, barley, sugarcane, fruits; cattle, sheep, poultry. **Natural resources:** bauxite, coal, iron ore, copper, tin, gold, silver, uranium, nickel, tungsten, rare earth elements, mineral sands, lead, zinc, diamonds, nat. gas, petroleum. **Water:** 20,527 cu m per capita. **Crude oil reserves:** 1.8 bil bbls. **Electricity prod.:** 239.1 bil kWh. **Labor force:** agric. 2.6%, industry 19.1%, services 78.3%. **Unemployment:** 5.6%.

Finance: Monetary unit: Dollar (AUD) (1.39 = $1 U.S.). **GDP:** $1.2 tril; **per capita GDP:** $50,300; **GDP growth:** 2.3%. **Imports:** $215.4 bil; China 22.9%, U.S. 10.8%, Japan 7.5%, Thailand 5.1%. **Exports:** $224.5 bil; China 33.5%, Japan 14.6%, South Korea 6.6%, India 5%. **Tourism:** $41.7 bil. **Budget:** $484.9 bil. **Inflation:** 1.9%.

Transport: Railways: 20,718 mi. **Motor vehicles:** 788.3 per 1,000 pop. **Airports:** 349.

Communications: Telephone: 34.6 per 100 pop. **Mobile:** 112.7 per 100 pop. **Broadband:** 130.2 per 100 pop. **Internet** (2017): 86.5%.

Health: Expend.: 9.4%. **Life expect.:** 79.9 male; 85.0 female. **Births:** 12 per 1,000 pop. **Deaths:** 7.3 per 1,000 pop. **Infant mortality:** 4.2 per 1,000 live births. **Undernourished:** <2.5%. **HIV:** 0.1%.

Education: Compulsory: ages 6-15. **Literacy:** 99%.
Embassy: 1601 Massachusetts Ave. NW 20036; 797-3000.
Website: www.australia.gov.au

Australia harbors many plant and animal species not found elsewhere, including kangaroos, koalas, platypuses, dingoes (wild dogs), Tasmanian devils, wombats, and barking and frilled lizards.

Capt. James Cook explored the eastern coast in 1770, when the continent and offshore islands were inhabited by Aborigines and other indigenous peoples. The first European settlers, beginning in 1788, were mostly convicts, soldiers, and government officials. By 1830, Britain had claimed the entire continent, and the immigration of free settlers accelerated. The Commonwealth was proclaimed Jan. 1, 1901. Northern Terr. was granted limited self-rule July 1, 1978.

State/territory, capital	Tot. area (sq mi)	Population (2017 est.)
New South Wales, Sydney	309,130	7,915,069
Victoria, Melbourne	87,806	6,385,849
Queensland, Brisbane	668,207	4,965,033
Western Australia, Perth	976,790	2,584,768
South Australia, Adelaide	379,725	1,728,053
Tasmania, Hobart	26,410	524,677
Australian Capital Terr., Canberra	910	415,916
Northern Terr., Darwin	520,902	246,726

Note: Preliminary pop. est. as of Dec. 31. (Source: Australian Bureau of Statistics.)

In a 1967 referendum, Australians voted to change parts of the country's constitution that discriminated against Aborigines. Racially discriminatory immigration policies ended in 1973, after 3 mil Europeans (half British) had entered since 1945.

Australia is among the top exporters of beef, lamb, wool, and wheat. Major mineral deposits have been developed, largely for export. Slumping commodity prices and sluggish exports to China impacted the economy in 2016-18.

Australia led an international peacekeeping force into Timor in Sept. 1999. In a referendum Nov. 6, voters rejected a proposal that would have made Australia a republic.

Australian troops fought in U.S.-led military operations in Afghanistan (since 2001) and Iraq (beginning 2003); about 300 Australian troops were in Afghanistan in mid-2018. Some 2,000 Australian peacekeepers began arriving in the Solomon Isls., July 24, 2003; nearly all were withdrawn by mid-2005. In race riots in Sydney suburbs, Dec. 11-12, 2005, thousands of youths assaulted people of Middle Eastern ancestry, who then retaliated. Australian troops were dispatched, 2006, to suppress disorder in the Solomon Isls. in Apr. and Timor in May. The last Australian troops in Timor returned home on Mar. 27, 2013. Australian warplanes, Oct. 1, 2014, joined the U.S.-led air campaign in Iraq against the Sunni extremist group ISIS. Beginning in late 2014, Australia sent military advisers to train and assist Iraqi armed forces. In Sept. 2015, Australia joined the U.S.-led air campaign against ISIS in Syria. With ISIS-controlled territory sharply reduced, Australia ended air combat missions in Iraq and Syria in Jan. 2018.

Kevin Rudd led the Labor Party to victory in parliamentary elections Nov. 24, 2007. Rudd was forced out June 24, 2010, by his deputy, Julia Gillard, who became Australia's first female prime minister. Downpours from Cyclone Tasha and other storms flooded Queensland in late Dec. 2010 and early Jan. 2011, with three-fourths of the state declared a disaster zone.

Prime Min. Gillard, Mar. 20, 2013, officially apologized for Australia's forced adoption policy (in effect late 1950s-70s), in which the state took the babies of single, teenage, or "unfit" mothers, often under duress, and gave them to childless married couples. Gillard resigned June 26 after being voted out as party leader, and former Prime Min. Rudd returned as premier.

The conservatives returned to power after Sept. 7, 2013, elections. Prime Min. Tony Abbott announced, Sept. 9, 2015, that Australia would accept, in a special program, 12,000 refugees from the conflicts in Syria and Iraq; a total of about 23,000 Syrian and Iraqi refugees arrived in Australia 2015-17. Malcolm Turnbull replaced Abbott as prime min., Sept. 15, 2015, after defeating him in a vote for Liberal Party leader. Turnbull's Liberal/National Party coalition won a narrow victory in July 2, 2016, elections. Scott Morrison replaced Turnbull as prime min., Aug. 24, 2018, after winning a Liberal Party leadership vote.

Australian External Territories

Norfolk Isl., area 14 sq mi, pop. (2016 est.) 1,748, was taken over, 1914. The soil is very fertile, suitable for citrus, bananas, and coffee. Many of the inhabitants are descended from Pitcairn Islanders who moved to Norfolk in 1856 after the British abandoned an attempted penal colony. Australia offered the island limited home rule in 1979 but revoked its autonomy in 2015. The island's legislative assembly was replaced by an elected regional council in 2016. **Website:** www.norfolkisland.com.nf

The only inhabitants of **Coral Sea Isls.**, area <1.2 sq mi, are meteorological staff on Willis Isl.

Ashmore and Cartier Isls., area 1.9 sq mi, in the Indian O., came under Australian authority in 1934. **Heard Isl. and McDonald Isls.**, area 159 sq mi, are administered by the Australian Antarctic Division.

Cocos (Keeling) Isls. are 27 coral islands in the Indian O. about 1,833 mi NW of Australia. Area 5.4 sq mi; pop. (2014 est.) 596. The residents voted to become part of Australia, Apr. 1984. **Website:** www.shire.cc

Christmas Isl., area 52 sq mi, pop. (2016 est.) 2,205; 230 mi S of Java, was transferred by Britain in 1958. Phosphate mining is the main economic activity, though high-grade phosphate deposits are nearly depleted. **Website:** www.shire.gov.cx

Australian Antarctic Territory was claimed by the UK and then transferred to Australian sovereignty in 1933. It comprises some 2.2 mil sq mi of territory S of 60th parallel S lat. between 45°E and 160°E (not incl. France's Adelie Coast) and between 136°E and 142°E.

Austria
Republic of Austria

People: Population: 8,793,370 (96). **Age distrib.:** <15: 14%; 65+: 19.4%. **Growth:** 0.4%. **Migrants:** 19%. **Pop. density:** 276.2 per sq mi, 106.7 per sq km. **Urban:** 58.3%. **Ethnic groups:** Austrian 84.2%, German (incl. Croat, Slovene, Serb, Bosniak) 2.1%. **Languages:** German (official), Turkish, Serbian, Croatian (official in one state). **Religions:** Catholic 73.8%, Protestant 4.9%, Muslim 4.2%, none 12%.

Geography: Total area: 32,383 sq mi, 83,871 sq km (112); **Land area:** 31,832 sq mi, 82,445 sq km. **Location:** S Central Europe. Switzerland, Liechtenstein on W; Germany, Czech Rep. on N; Slovakia, Hungary on E; Slovenia, Italy on S. **Topography:** Primarily mountainous, with the Alps and foothills covering the western and southern provinces. The eastern provinces and Vienna are located in the Danube River Basin. **Arable land:** 16.3%. **Capital:** Vienna, 1,900,547.

Government: Type: Federal parliamentary republic. **Head of state:** Pres. Alexander Van der Bellen; b. 1944; in office: Jan. 26, 2017. **Head of govt.:** Chancellor Sebastian Kurz; b. 1986; in office: Dec. 18, 2017. **Local divisions:** 9 states. **Defense budget:** $3 bil. **Active troops:** 22,400.

Economy: Industries: constr., machinery, vehicles and parts, food, metals, chemicals, lumber and paper, electronics, tourism. **Chief agric.:** grains, potatoes, wine, fruit; dairy prods., cattle, pigs. **Natural resources:** oil, coal, lignite, timber, iron ore, copper, zinc, antimony, magnesite, tungsten, graphite, salt, hydropower. **Water:** 9,093 cu m per capita. **Crude oil reserves:** 41.2 mil bbls. **Electricity prod.:** 56.9 bil kWh. **Labor force:** agric. 4.3%, industry 25.6%, services 70.1%. **Unemployment:** 5.5%.

Finance: Monetary unit: Euro (EUR) (0.86 = $1 U.S.). **GDP:** $439.6 bil; **per capita GDP:** $49,900; **GDP growth:** 2.9%. **Imports:** $168.3 bil; Germany 41.8%, Italy 5.8%, Switzerland 5.5%. **Exports:** $161.8 bil; Germany 29.4%, U.S. 6.3%, Italy 6.2%, Switzerland 5.1%. **Tourism:** $20.4 bil. **Budget:** $199.6 bil. **Inflation:** 2.1%.

Transport: Railways: 3,604 mi. **Motor vehicles:** 614.9 per 1,000 pop. **Airports:** 24.

Communications: Telephone: 43.1 per 100 pop. **Mobile:** 170.8 per 100 pop. **Broadband:** 88.3 per 100 pop. **Internet** (2017): 87.9%.

Health: Expend.: 10.3%. **Life expect.:** 79.0 male; 84.5 female. **Births:** 9.5 per 1,000 pop. **Deaths:** 9.7 per 1,000 pop. **Infant mortality:** 3.4 per 1,000 live births. **Undernourished:** <2.5%. **HIV:** 0.1%.

Education: Compulsory: ages 5-17. **Literacy:** 98%.

Embassy: 3524 International Ct. NW 20008; 895-6700.

Website: www.federal-chancellery.gv.at

Rome conquered Austrian lands from Celtic tribes around 15 BCE. In 788 the territory was incorporated into Charlemagne's empire. By 1300, the House of Habsburg had gained control; it added vast territories in all parts of Europe to the realm in the next few hundred years.

Austrian dominance of Germany was undermined in the 18th cent. and ended by Prussia by 1866. But the Congress of Vienna, 1815, confirmed Austrian control of a large empire in SE Europe consisting of Germans, Hungarians, Slavs, Italians, and others. The dual Austro-Hungarian monarchy was established in 1867, giving autonomy to Hungary and almost 50 years of peace.

World War I, which started after the June 28, 1914, assassination of Archduke Franz Ferdinand, the Habsburg heir, by a Serbian nationalist, destroyed the empire. By 1918 Austria was reduced to a small republic, with the borders it has today.

Nazi Germany, ruled by the Austrian-born Adolf Hitler, annexed Austria Mar. 13, 1938. The republic was reestablished in 1945, under Allied occupation. Full independence and neutrality were restored in 1955. Austria joined the EU Jan. 1, 1995.

The right-wing, anti-immigrant Austrian Freedom Party (FPO) challenged the dominance of the Social Democratic Party (SPO) beginning in the late 1990s. However, the SPO won parliamentary elections in Oct. 2006, Sept. 2008, and Sept. 2013. Former Green Party leader Alexander Van der Bellen defeated FPO candidate Norbert Hofer in a Dec. 4, 2016, presidential runoff election, 53.8% to 46.2%. The conservative Austrian People's Party (OVP) won the most votes in Oct. 15, 2017, parliamentary elections; after forming a coalition with the FPO, OVP leader Sebastian Kurz became chancellor Dec. 18.

Hundreds of thousands of migrants fleeing war and hardship in Syria and elsewhere entered Austria in 2015, many en route to Germany or elsewhere in N Europe. About 90,000 migrants applied for asylum in Austria in 2015, and nearly 40,000 in 2016. The government, Feb. 16, 2016, announced sharp limits on the number of migrants per day allowed to transit or apply for asylum. A law passed Apr. 27, 2016, made it easier to deny asylum claims.

Azerbaijan
Republic of Azerbaijan

People: Population: 10,046,516 (90). **Age distrib.:** <15: 23%; 65+: 6.8%. **Growth:** 0.8%. **Migrants:** 2.6%. **Pop. density:**

314.9 per sq mi, 121.6 per sq km. **Urban:** 55.7%. **Ethnic groups:** Azerbaijani 91.6%, Lezghin 2%. **Languages:** Azerbaijani (Azeri) (official), Russian, Armenian. **Religions:** Muslim (predom. Shia) 96.9%, Christian 3%.

Geography: Total area: 33,436 sq mi, 86,600 sq km (111); **Land area:** 31,903 sq mi, 82,629 sq km. **Location:** SW Asia. Russia, Georgia on N; Iran on S; Armenia on W; Caspian Sea on E. **Topography:** The Great Caucasus Mts. in N, Karabakh Upland in W border the Kur-Araz lowland. Arid climate except in subtropical SE. **Arable land:** 23.4%. **Capital:** Baku, 2,285,729.

Government: Type: Presidential republic. **Head of state:** Pres. Ilham Aliyev; b. 1961; in office: Oct. 31, 2003. **Head of govt.:** Prime Min. Novruz Mammadov; b. 1947; in office: Apr. 21, 2018. **Local divisions:** 66 rayons, 11 cities. **Defense budget:** $1.6 bil. **Active troops:** 66,950.

Economy: Industries: petroleum/petroleum prods., nat. gas, oil field equip.; steel, iron ore; cement. **Chief agric.:** fruit, vegetables, grain, rice; cattle, pigs, sheep, goats. **Natural resources:** petroleum, nat. gas, iron ore, nonferrous metals, bauxite. **Water:** 3,555 cu m per capita. **Crude oil reserves:** 7 bil bbls. **Electricity prod.:** 23.3 bil kWh. **Labor force:** agric. 37.4%, industry 14.1%, services 48.5%. **Unemployment:** 5%.

Finance: Monetary unit: Manat (AZN) (1.70 = $1 U.S.). **GDP:** $171.8 bil; **per capita GDP:** $17,500; **GDP growth:** 0.1%. **Imports:** $8.7 bil; Russia 17.7%, Turkey 14.8%, China 9.9%, U.S. 8.3%, Ukraine 5.3%, Germany 5.1%. **Exports:** $15.7 bil; Italy 23.2%, Turkey 13.6%, Israel 6.1%, Russia 5.4%, Germany 5%. **Tourism:** $3 bil. **Budget:** $10.4 bil. **Inflation:** 12.9%.

Transport: Railways: 1,830 mi. **Motor vehicles:** 163.5 per 1,000 pop. **Airports:** 30.

Communications: Telephone: 17.2 per 100 pop. **Mobile:** 103 per 100 pop. **Broadband:** 57.4 per 100 pop. **Internet** (2017): 79%.

Health: Expend.: 6.7%. **Life expect.:** 70.0 male; 76.4 female. **Births:** 15.3 per 1,000 pop. **Deaths:** 7 per 1,000 pop. **Infant mortality:** 23 per 1,000 live births. **Undernourished:** <2.5%. **HIV:** 0.1%.

Education: Compulsory: ages 5-14. **Literacy:** 99.8%.
Embassy: 2741 34th St. NW 20008; 337-3500.
Website: www.president.az

Azerbaijan was home to Scythian tribes and part of the Roman Empire. Overrun by Turks in the 11th cent. and conquered by Russia in 1806 and 1813, it joined the USSR Dec. 30, 1922, and became a constituent republic in 1936. Azerbaijan gained independence when the Soviet Union disbanded Dec. 26, 1991.

Nagorno-Karabakh, an enclave with a majority population of ethnic Armenians, seceded from Azerbaijan in 1988, triggering a war between mostly Muslim Azerbaijan and mostly Christian Armenia, 1992-94, in which 30,000 lives were lost.

Voters approved a new constitution expanding presidential powers, Nov. 12, 1995. Pres. Haydar Aliyev, a pro-Russian former Communist, was reelected Oct. 11, 1998, but international monitors called the vote seriously flawed. The dying Pres. Aliyev named his son Ilham prime min. Aug. 4, 2003. The younger Aliyev won a flawed Oct. 15, 2003, presidential election. He responded to violent protests Oct. 16 by arresting hundreds of opposition leaders and their supporters. The opening May 25, 2005, of the Baku-Tbilisi-Ceyhan pipeline, providing an outlet for Azerbaijan's vast Caspian oil reserves, transformed the nation's economy. Construction began in 2014 on new pipelines to carry natural gas from Caspian Sea deposits in Azerbaijan to Georgia, Turkey, and Europe.

Pres. Ilham Aliyev won a second term Oct. 15, 2008. A constitutional amendment abolishing presidential term limits was approved by referendum Mar. 18, 2009. In OSCE-criticized elections, Aliyev won a third term Oct. 9, 2013, and a fourth term Apr. 11, 2018.

The first European Games, organized by the European Olympic Committee, were held in Baku June 12-28, 2015—amid international criticism because of Azerbaijan's poor human rights record. The European Parliament voted, Sept. 2017, to investigate a so-called Azerbaijani Laundromat scheme, in which almost $3 bil was reportedly sent out of Azerbaijan, including money allegedly paid to European officials to influence policy toward Azerbaijan.

The Bahamas
Commonwealth of The Bahamas

People: Population: 332,634 (173). **Age distrib.:** <15: 22.4%; 65+: 8%. **Growth:** 0.8%. **Migrants:** 15.6%. **Pop. density:** 86.1 per sq mi, 33.2 per sq km. **Urban:** 83%. **Ethnic groups:** black 90.6%, white 4.7%, black and white 2.1%. **Languages:** English (official), Creole (among Haitian immigrants). **Religions:** Protestant 69.9% (incl. Baptist 34.9%, Anglican 13.7%, Pentecostal 8.9%), Roman Catholic 12%, other Christian 13%.

Geography: Total area: 5,359 sq mi, 13,880 sq km (156); **Land area:** 3,865 sq mi, 10,010 sq km. **Location:** In Atlantic O., SE of Florida. U.S. is on W, Cuba to SW. **Topography:** Nearly 700 islands (30 inhabited) and over 2,000 cays in the W Atlantic O. extend 760 mi NW to SE. **Arable land:** 0.8%. **Capital:** Nassau, 279,668.

Government: Type: Parliamentary democracy under constitutional monarchy. **Head of state:** Queen Elizabeth II, rep. by Gov.-Gen. Marguerite Pindling; b. 1932; in office: July 8, 2014. **Head of govt.:** Prime Min. Hubert Minnis; b. 1954; in office: May 11, 2017. **Local divisions:** 31 districts. **Defense budget:** $99 mil. **Active troops:** 1,300.

Economy: Industries: tourism, banking, oil bunkering, maritime, transshipment, salt, aragonite, pharmaceuticals. **Chief agric.:** citrus, vegetables; poultry; seafood. **Natural resources:** salt, aragonite, timber. **Water:** 1,804 cu m per capita. **Electricity prod.:** 1.8 bil kWh. **Labor force:** agric. 4%, industry 11.7%, other services 84.3%. **Unemployment:** 12.6%.

Finance: Monetary unit: Dollar (BSD) (1.00 = $1 U.S.). **GDP:** $11.6 bil; **per capita GDP:** $31,200; **GDP growth:** 1.3%. **Imports:** $3.1 bil; U.S. 83.2%. **Exports:** $934.7 mil; U.S. 63.9%, Namibia 19.3%. **Tourism:** $2.6 bil. **Budget:** $2.6 bil. **Inflation:** 1.5%.

Transport: Motor vehicles: 422.7 per 1,000 pop. **Airports:** 24.

Communications: Telephone: 28.8 per 100 pop. **Mobile:** 89.4 per 100 pop. **Broadband:** 51.2 per 100 pop. **Internet:** 80%.

Health: Expend.: 7.4%. **Life expect.:** 70.4 male; 75.4 female. **Births:** 15.1 per 1,000 pop. **Deaths:** 7.3 per 1,000 pop. **Infant mortality:** 11.1 per 1,000 live births. **Undernourished:** NA. **HIV:** 1.9%.

Education: Compulsory: ages 5-16. **Literacy:** 95%+.
Embassy: 2220 Massachusetts Ave. NW 20008; 319-2660.
Website: www.bahamas.gov.bs

Christopher Columbus first set foot in the New World on San Salvador (Watling Isl.) in 1492, when Arawak Indians inhabited the islands. British settlement began in 1647; the islands became a British colony in 1783. Internal self-government was granted in 1964; full independence within the Commonwealth was attained July 10, 1973. International banking and investment management have become major industries alongside tourism. The Free Natl. Movement won May 10, 2017, elections, and Hubert Minnis became prime min.

Bahrain
Kingdom of Bahrain

People: Population: 1,442,659 (150). (Immigrants made up about 48% of pop. in 2017.) **Age distrib.:** <15: 18.9%; 65+: 3.1%. **Growth:** 2.2%. **Migrants:** 48.4%. **Pop. density:** 4,916.4 per sq mi, 1,898.2 per sq km. **Urban:** 89.3%. **Ethnic groups:** Bahraini 46%, Asian 45.5%, other Arab 4.7%. **Languages:** Arabic (official), English, Farsi, Urdu. **Religions:** Muslim 70.3%, Christian 14.5%, Hindu 9.8%, Buddhist 2.5%.

Geography: Total area: 293 sq mi, 760 sq km (174); **Land area:** 293 sq mi, 760 sq km. **Location:** SW Asia, in Persian Gulf. Saudi Arabia on W, Qatar on E. **Topography:** Bahrain Island and several adjacent, smaller islands, are flat, hot, and humid with little rain. **Arable land:** 2.1%. **Capital:** Manama, 564,631.

Government: Type: Constitutional monarchy. **Head of state:** King Hamad bin Isa al-Khalifa; b. 1950; in office: as emir Mar. 6, 1999; as king Feb. 14, 2002. **Head of govt.:** Prime Min. Khalifa bin Salman al-Khalifa; b. 1936; in office: 1971. **Local divisions:** 4 governorates. **Defense budget:** $1.5 bil. **Active troops:** 8,200.

Economy: Industries: petroleum proc. and refining, aluminum smelting, iron pelletization, fertilizers, Islamic and offshore banking, insurance. **Chief agric.:** fruit, vegetables; poultry; shrimp, fish. **Natural resources:** oil, nat. gas, fish, pearls. **Water:** 84 cu m per capita. **Crude oil reserves:** 124.6 mil bbls. **Electricity prod.:** 26.8 bil kWh. **Labor force:** agric. 1%, industry 35.1%, services 63.9%. **Unemployment:** 1.2%.

Finance: Monetary unit: Dinar (BHD) (0.38 = $1 U.S.). **GDP:** $70.4 bil; **per capita GDP:** $48,500; **GDP growth:** 3.2%. **Imports:** $14 bil; China 8.8%, UAE 7.2%, U.S. 7.1%, Australia 5.3%. **Exports:** $14.3 bil; UAE 19.6%, Saudi Arabia 11.7%, U.S. 10.8%, Oman 8.1%, China 6.5%, Qatar 5.7%. **Tourism:** $3.8 bil. **Budget** (2018): $9.8 bil. **Inflation:** 1.4%.

Transport: Motor vehicles: 530.1 per 1,000 pop. **Airports:** 4.
Communications: Telephone: 19.1 per 100 pop. **Mobile:** 158.4 per 100 pop. **Broadband:** 162.1 per 100 pop. **Internet** (2017): 95.9%.

Health: Expend.: 5.2%. **Life expect.:** 76.9 male; 81.5 female. **Births:** 13.1 per 1,000 pop. **Deaths:** 2.8 per 1,000 pop. **Infant mortality:** 8.8 per 1,000 live births. **Undernourished:** NA. **HIV:** <0.1%.

Education: Compulsory: ages 6-14. **Literacy:** 95.7%.
Embassy: 3502 International Dr. NW 20008; 342-0741.
Website: www.bahrain.bh

Long ruled by the Khalifa family, Bahrain was a British protectorate from 1861 to Aug. 15, 1971, when it regained independence. Oil was discovered in 1932. Natural gas output has more than doubled since 1990. Low oil prices hurt the economy beginning in 2015. A major offshore oil and gas field discovery was announced in Apr. 2018.

Emir Hamad bin Isa al-Khalifa proclaimed himself king Feb. 14, 2002. Local elections in May 2002 marked the first time Bahraini women were allowed to vote and run for office. The monarchy suppressed Arab Spring demonstrations Feb.-Mar. 2011, aided by a Gulf Cooperation Council force of 1,600 led by Saudi Arabia.

Protests, however, continued, largely by members of the country's Shiite majority against the mostly Sunni ruling elite. The government arrested opposition leaders and other critics. Court rulings July 17, 2016, and May 31, 2017, ordered the dissolution of leading Shiite and secular opposition groups. A Nov. 2015 Human Rights Watch report accused the government of torturing detained dissidents. Forced labor and sexual exploitation of Asian and African immigrants also gained international attention. Beginning Sept. 23, 2014, Bahrain took part in U.S.-led airstrikes against Sunni extremists in Syria. A U.S. ban on military aid to Bahrain, imposed after suppression of Arab Spring protests, was lifted June 29, 2015. Bahrain was one of a Saudi-led group of nations that June 5, 2017, broke diplomatic relations with Qatar, alleging Qatari support for terrorist and sectarian groups.

Bangladesh
People's Republic of Bangladesh

People: Population: 159,453,001 (8). **Age distrib.:** <15: 27.3%; 65+: 6.4%. **Growth:** 1%. **Migrants:** 0.9%. **Pop. density:** 3,172.6 per sq mi, 1,225 per sq km. **Urban:** 36.6%. **Ethnic groups:** Bengali 98%+. **Languages:** Bangla or Bengali (official). **Religions:** Muslim 89.1%, Hindu 10%.

Geography: Total area: 57,321 sq mi, 148,460 sq km (92); **Land area:** 50,259 sq mi, 130,170 sq km. **Location:** S Asia, on N bend of Bay of Bengal. India nearly surrounds country on W, N, E; Myanmar on SE. **Topography:** Mostly a low plain cut by the Ganges and Brahmaputra R. and their delta. Alluvial and marshy along the coast. Hilly only in the extreme SE and NE. Its tropical monsoon climate makes country among the rainiest in the world. **Arable land:** 59.6%. **Capital:** Dhaka, 19,578,421. **Cities:** Dhaka, 19,578,421; Chittagong, 4,815,545.

Government: Type: Parliamentary republic. **Head of state:** Pres. Abdul Hamid; b. 1944; in office: Apr. 24, 2013. **Head of govt.:** Prime Min. Sheikh Hasina; b. 1947; in office: Jan. 6, 2009. **Local divisions:** 8 divisions. **Defense budget:** $2.8 bil. **Active troops:** 157,050.

Economy: Industries: jute, cotton, garments, paper, leather, fertilizer, iron and steel, cement, petroleum prods., tobacco, pharmaceuticals. **Chief agric.:** rice, jute, tea, wheat, sugarcane, potatoes, tobacco, pulses, oilseeds, spices; beef, milk, poultry. **Natural resources:** nat. gas, timber, coal. **Water:** 7,621 cu m per capita. **Crude oil reserves:** 28 mil bbls. **Electricity prod.:** 55.5 bil kWh. **Labor force:** agric. 39.1%, industry 21.1%, services 39.9%. **Unemployment:** 4.4%.

Finance: Monetary unit: Taka (BDT) (83.70 = $1 U.S.). **GDP:** $687.1 bil; **per capita GDP:** $4,200; **GDP growth:** 7.1%. **Imports:** $42.4 bil; China 21.9%, India 15.3%, Singapore 5.7%. **Exports:** $35.9 bil; Germany 12.9%, U.S. 12.2%, UK 8.7%, Spain 5.3%, France 5.1%. **Tourism:** $337 mil. **Budget:** $39.3 bil. **Inflation:** 5.8%.

Transport: Railways: 1,529 mi. **Motor vehicles:** 2.7 per 1,000 pop. **Airports:** 16.

Communications: Telephone: 0.4 per 100 pop. **Mobile:** 88.1 per 100 pop. **Broadband:** 17.8 per 100 pop. **Internet:** 18.2%.

Health: Expend.: 2.6%. **Life expect.:** 71.5 male; 75.9 female. **Births:** 18.6 per 1,000 pop. **Deaths:** 5.4 per 1,000 pop. **Infant mortality:** 30.5 per 1,000 live births. **Undernourished:** 15.2%. **HIV:** <0.1%.

Education: Compulsory: ages 6-10. **Literacy:** 72.8%.

Embassy: 3510 International Dr. NW 20008; 244-0183.

Website: bangladesh.gov.bd

Muslim invaders conquered the formerly Hindu area in the 12th cent. British rule lasted from the 18th cent. to 1947, when East Bengal became part of Pakistan.

Opposing domination by West Pakistan, the Awami League, based in the East, won control of the National Assembly in 1971. Assembly sessions were postponed; riots broke out. Pakistani troops attacked, Mar. 25; Bangladesh independence was proclaimed the next day. In the ensuing civil war, 1 mil died and 10 mil fled to India. War between India and Pakistan broke out Dec. 3, 1971. Pakistan surrendered in the East on Dec. 16. Mujibur Rahman, known as Sheikh Mujib, became prime min.; he was killed in a coup Aug. 15, 1975.

Army rivals killed Pres. Ziaur Rahman in an unsuccessful coup attempt, May 1981. Vice Pres. Abdus Sattar assumed the presidency but was ousted in a coup led by army chief of staff Gen. H. M. Ershad, Mar. 1982. A parliamentary system of government was adopted in 1991. A cyclone, Apr. 1991, killed over 131,000 people.

Political turmoil led to the resignation, Mar. 1996, of Prime Min. Khaleda Zia, Ziaur Rahman's widow. Sheikh Mujib's daughter, known as Sheikh Hasina, led the country after the June 1996 election. Khaleda Zia returned to power following parliamentary elections, Oct. 1, 2001. Militant Islamists set off more than 400 small bombs in more than 50 cities and towns, Aug. 17, 2005, killing 3. Another wave of jihadist bombings killed 22, Nov. 29-Dec. 8, 2005. Bangladeshi economist Muhammad Yunus won the 2006 Nobel Peace Prize for using very small loans (microcredit) to help alleviate the nation's severe poverty.

Amid escalating political violence, Pres. Iajuddin Ahmed declared a state of emergency, Jan. 11, 2007, and a military-backed caretaker government took office. Cyclone Sidr struck Nov. 15, 2007, damaging more than 1.5 mil homes and leaving about 3,400 dead.

The Awami League triumphed in parliamentary elections Dec. 2008, and Sheikh Hasina returned as prime min. Jan. 6, 2009, ending two years of emergency rule. She remained in office when her party won Jan. 5, 2014, elections. Her political rival, Khaleda Zia, was convicted, Feb. 8, 2018, on embezzlement charges Zia claimed were politically motivated.

A garment factory fire Nov. 24, 2012, near Dhaka killed 112 workers. Rana Plaza, a building near Dhaka that housed garment factories, collapsed Apr. 24, 2013, killing more than 1,100 workers in the deadliest garment-industry disaster in world history. The owner of Rana Plaza, Sohel Rana, was among 38 people formally charged, July 18, 2016, with murder in connection with the disaster. With the murder case still pending, Sohel Rana was convicted, Aug. 29, 2017, and sentenced to 3 years in prison on corruption charges.

Security forces in Dhaka, July 1-2, 2015, arrested 12 people said to be affiliated with al-Qaeda, including a man who had claimed responsibility for the Feb. killing of a Bangladeshi-American blogger who had criticized Islamist extremists. Three other so-called secular bloggers had been killed by Aug. 2015. Assassinations of non-Muslims attributed to al-Qaeda or ISIS escalated in 2016. In an attack in Dhaka, July 1-2, 2016, for which ISIS claimed responsibility, 20 people, mostly foreigners, held hostage inside a restaurant were killed, as well as 2 police officers and 5 terrorist gunmen. The suspected plotter of the attack was killed by police in a shootout, Aug. 27.

Beginning in late 2016, recurrent military and vigilante attacks in neighboring Myanmar caused much of the Rohingya population to seek refuge in Bangladesh. Anti-Rohingya violence in Myanmar peaked in Aug.-Sept. 2017, leading hundreds of thousands to flee. As of Sept. 15, 2018, almost 900,000 Rohingya refugees were in Bangladesh.

Barbados

People: Population: 293,131 (174). **Age distrib.:** <15: 17.8%; 65+: 12.4%. **Growth:** 0.3%. **Migrants:** 12.1%. **Pop. density:** 1,765.6 per sq mi, 681.7 per sq km. **Urban:** 31.1%. **Ethnic groups:** black 92.4%, mixed 3.1%, white 2.7%. **Languages:** English (official), Bajan (English-based Creole). **Religions:** Protestant 66.4% (incl. Anglican 23.9%, other Pentecostal 19.5%), Roman Catholic 3.8%, none 20.6%.

Geography: Total area: 166 sq mi, 430 sq km (184); **Land area:** 166 sq mi, 430 sq km. **Location:** In Atlantic O., farthest E of West Indies. Nearest neighbors are St. Lucia and St. Vincent and the Grenadines to the W. **Topography:** Almost completely surrounded by coral reefs. Highest point is Mt. Hillaby (1,102 ft). **Arable land:** 25.6%. **Capital:** Bridgetown, 89,201.

Government: Type: Parliamentary democracy under constitutional monarchy. **Head of state:** Queen Elizabeth II, rep. by Gov.-Gen. Sandra Mason; b. 1965; in office: Jan. 8, 2018. **Head of govt.:** Prime Min. Mia Mottley; b. 1965; in office: May 25, 2018. **Local divisions:** 11 parishes, 1 city. **Defense budget:** $38 mil. **Active troops:** 610.

Economy: Industries: tourism, sugar, light mfg., component assembly for export. **Chief agric.:** sugarcane, vegetables, cotton. **Natural resources:** petroleum, fish, nat. gas. **Water:** 282 cu m per capita. **Crude oil reserves:** 2.5 mil bbls. **Electricity prod.:** 915 mil kWh. **Labor force:** agric. 2.9%, industry 19.2%, services 77.9%. **Unemployment:** 9.7%.

Finance: Monetary unit: Dollar (BBD) (2.00 = $1 U.S.). **GDP:** $5.2 bil; **per capita GDP:** $18,700; **GDP growth:** 0.9%. **Imports:** $1.5 bil; U.S. 38.5%, Trinidad and Tobago 14.6%, China 7.1%. **Exports:** $482.5 mil; U.S. 38%, Trinidad and Tobago 10.2%, Guyana 5.5%, Jamaica 5%. **Tourism:** $1.1 bil. **Budget:** $1.6 bil. **Inflation:** 4.7%.

Transport: Motor vehicles: 394.8 per 1,000 pop. **Airports:** 1.

Communications: Telephone: 48.9 per 100 pop. **Mobile:** 118.2 per 100 pop. **Broadband:** 59.3 per 100 pop. **Internet:** 79.5%.

Health: Expend.: 7.5%. **Life expect.:** 73.3 male; 78.1 female. **Births:** 11.6 per 1,000 pop. **Deaths:** 8.6 per 1,000 pop. **Infant mortality:** 10 per 1,000 live births. **Undernourished:** 3.7%. **HIV:** 1.6%.

Education: Compulsory: ages 5-15. **Literacy:** 99.7%.

Embassy: 2144 Wyoming Ave. NW 20008; 939-9200.

Website: www.gov.bb

Barbados was probably named by Portuguese sailors in reference to bearded fig trees. An English ship visited in 1605, and British settled on the uninhabited island in 1627. Slaves worked the sugarcane plantations until slavery was abolished in 1834. Barbados became independent Nov. 30, 1966. Tourism, banking, and manufacturing have surpassed sugarcane in economic importance since the 1990s. Barbados's slow recovery from the 2008-09 global recession hurt the ruling Democratic Labor Party in the May 24, 2018, elections. The opposition Barbados Labour Party won all 30 House of Assembly seats, making Mia Mottley the country's first female prime min.

A Zika virus outbreak in the Americas affected Barbados from late 2015 to early 2017, with more than 850 confirmed or suspected cases reported.

Belarus
Republic of Belarus

People: Population: 9,527,543 (94). **Age distrib.:** <15: 15.9%; 65+: 15.2%. **Growth:** –0.2%. **Migrants:** 11.4%. **Pop. density:**

121.6 per sq mi, 47 per sq km. **Urban:** 78.6%. **Ethnic groups:** Belarusian 83.7%, Russian 8.3%, Polish 3.1%. **Languages:** Russian, Belarusian (both official). **Religions:** Orthodox 48.3%, Catholic 7.1%, non-believers 41.1%.

Geography: Total area: 80,155 sq mi, 207,600 sq km (84); **Land area:** 78,340 sq mi, 202,900 sq km. **Location:** Eastern Europe. Poland on W; Latvia, Lithuania on N; Russia on E; Ukraine on S. **Topography:** Landlocked country consisting mostly of hilly lowland with significant marsh areas in S. **Arable land:** 28%. **Capital:** Minsk, 2,004,672.

Government: Type: Presidential republic in name. **Head of state:** Pres. Aleksandr Lukashenko; b. 1954; in office: July 20, 1994. **Head of govt.:** Prime Min. Sergei Rumas; b. 1969; in office: Aug. 18, 2018. **Local divisions:** 6 provinces, 1 municipality. **Defense budget:** $528 mil. **Active troops:** 45,350.

Economy: Industries: metal-cutting machine tools, tractors, trucks, earthmovers. **Chief agric.:** grain, potatoes, vegetables, sugar beets, flax; beef, milk. **Natural resources:** timber, peat, oil, nat. gas, granite, dolomitic limestone, marl, chalk, sand, gravel, clay. **Water:** 6,097 cu m per capita. **Crude oil reserves:** 198 mil bbls. **Electricity prod.:** 32.1 bil kWh. **Labor force:** agric. 9.9%, industry 31.2%, services 59%. **Unemployment:** 0.5%.

Finance: Monetary unit: Ruble (BYN) (2.11 = $1 U.S.). **GDP:** $178.9 bil; **per capita GDP:** $18,900; **GDP growth:** 2.4%. **Imports:** $26.2 bil; Russia 57.2%, China 8%, Germany 5.1%. **Exports:** $24.2 bil; Russia 43.9%, Ukraine 11.5%, UK 8.2%. **Tourism:** $790 mil. **Budget:** $22.5 bil. **Inflation:** 6%.

Transport: Railways: 3,435 mi. **Motor vehicles:** 371.1 per 1,000 pop. **Airports:** 33.

Communications: Telephone: 47.5 per 100 pop. **Mobile:** 120.6 per 100 pop. **Broadband:** 69.5 per 100 pop. **Internet** (2017): 74.4%.

Health: Expend.: 6.1%. **Life expect.:** 67.8 male; 79.0 female. **Births:** 10 per 1,000 pop. **Deaths:** 13.2 per 1,000 pop. **Infant mortality:** 3.6 per 1,000 live births. **Undernourished:** <2.5%. **HIV:** 0.4%.

Education: Compulsory: ages 6-14. **Literacy:** 99.7%. **Embassy:** 1619 New Hampshire Ave. NW 20009; 986-1604. **Website:** www.belarus.by

Belarus became a constituent republic of the USSR in 1922. Overrun by German armies in 1941, Belarus was recaptured by Soviet troops in 1944. Following WWII, Belarus increased in area through Soviet annexation of part of NE Poland. Belarus declared independence Aug. 25, 1991, and became independent when the Soviet Union disbanded Dec. 26, 1991.

After a new constitution was adopted, Mar. 15, 1994, Aleksandr Lukashenko was elected president. Russia and Belarus signed a pact, Apr. 2, 1996, linking their political and economic systems. An authoritarian constitution enacted in Nov. gave Lukashenko vast new powers. He retained office in 2001, 2006, 2010, and 2015 elections criticized as seriously flawed by Western observers. Lukashenko crushed protests that followed the Dec. 19, 2010, presidential election. Belarus, Russia, and Kazakhstan signed an agreement, May 29, 2014, to create a Eurasian Economic Union (EEU). The EEU came into existence Jan. 1, 2015, and Armenia and Kyrgyzstan joined in Jan. and May 2015, respectively. Hurt in part by low world commodity prices and an outdated industrial base, Belarus's GDP shrank 3.8% in 2015 and 2.5% in 2016. In early-2017, protests against economic conditions and a new tax on the unemployed were suppressed. GDP growth resumed in 2017 (2.4%).

Belgium
Kingdom of Belgium

People: Population: 11,570,762 (77). **Age distrib.:** <15: 17.2%; 65+: 18.8%. **Growth:** 0.7%. **Migrants:** 11.1%. **Pop. density:** 989.8 per sq mi, 382.2 per sq km. **Urban:** 98%. **Ethnic groups:** Belgian 75%, Italian 4.1%, Moroccan 3.7%, French 2.4%, Turkish 2%, Dutch 2%. **Languages:** Dutch, French, German (all official). **Religions:** Roman Catholic 50%, Muslim 5%, Protestant and other Christian 2.5%, atheist 9.2%, none 32.6%.

Geography: Total area: 11,787 sq mi, 30,528 sq km (137); **Land area:** 11,690 sq mi, 30,278 sq km. **Location:** Western Europe, on North Sea. France on W and S, Luxembourg on SE, Germany on E, Netherlands on N. **Topography:** Mostly flat; trisected by the Scheldt and Meuse, major commercial rivers. The land becomes hilly and forested in the Ardennes region to the SE. **Arable land:** 27.4%. **Capital:** Bruxelles-Brussel, 2,049,510. **Cities:** Antwerpen, 1,032,209.

Government: Type: Federal parliamentary democracy under constitutional monarchy. **Head of state:** King Philippe; b. 1960; in office: July 21, 2013. **Head of govt.:** Prime Min. Charles Michel; b. 1975; in office: Oct. 11, 2014. **Local divisions:** 3 regions. **Defense budget:** $4.3 bil. **Active troops:** 28,800.

Economy: Industries: engineering and metal prods., motor vehicle assembly, transp. equip., scientific instruments, processed food and beverages. **Chief agric.:** sugar beets, vegetables, fruits, grain, tobacco; beef, veal. **Natural resources:** constr. materials, silica sand, carbonates. **Water:** 1,620 cu m per capita. **Electricity**

prod.: 65.7 bil kWh. **Labor force:** agric. 1.3%, industry 21.3%, services 77.4%. **Unemployment:** 7.1%.

Finance: Monetary unit: Euro (EUR) (0.86 = $1 U.S.). **GDP:** $528.5 bil; **per capita GDP:** $46,600; **GDP growth:** 1.7%. **Imports:** $306.1 bil; Netherlands 17.3%, Germany 13.8%, France 9.5%, U.S. 7.1%. **Exports:** $309.1 bil; Germany 16.6%, France 14.9%, Netherlands 12%, UK 8.4%. **Tourism:** $12.2 bil. **Budget:** $257 bil. **Inflation:** 2.1%.

Transport: Railways: 2,232 mi. **Motor vehicles:** 573.3 per 1,000 pop. **Airports:** 26.

Communications: Telephone: 37.2 per 100 pop. **Mobile:** 104.7 per 100 pop. **Broadband:** 66.7 per 100 pop. **Internet** (2017): 87.7%.

Health: Expend.: 10.5%. **Life expect.:** 78.6 male; 83.9 female. **Births:** 11.3 per 1,000 pop. **Deaths:** 9.7 per 1,000 pop. **Infant mortality:** 3.4 per 1,000 live births. **Undernourished:** <2.5%. **HIV:** NA.

Education: Compulsory: ages 6-17. **Literacy:** 99%. **Embassy:** 3330 Garfield St. NW 20008; 333-6900. **Website:** www.belgium.be

Belgium derives its name from the Belgae, the first recorded inhabitants, probably Celts. The land was ruled for 1,800 years by conquerors, including Rome, the Franks, Burgundy, Spain, Austria, and France. After 1815, Belgium was made a part of the Netherlands but became an independent constitutional monarchy in 1830.

King Leopold III surrendered to Germany, May 28, 1940. After WWII, he was forced to abdicate in favor of his son, King Baudouin. Baudouin was succeeded by his brother, Albert II, Aug. 9, 1993. Albert's son Philippe became king July 21, 2013.

The Flemings of northern Belgium speak Dutch, while the Walloons in the south speak French. The language difference is a source of controversy between the two groups. Parliament has passed measures transferring power from the central government to three regions—Wallonia, Flanders, and Brussels. Constitutional changes in 1993 made Belgium a federal state. After elections June 2007, rivalries between Flemings and Walloons created a 9-month political stalemate. June 2010 elections led to a political deadlock that ended when Elio Di Rupo became prime min. Dec. 2011. After May 25, 2014, elections in which Flemish nationalists made gains, Charles Michel was sworn in as prime min. Oct. 11, heading a center-right coalition government.

An Oct. 2014 government report stated that 350 Belgians had traveled to Syria to fight with Islamist extremists. Two suspects were killed Jan. 15, 2015, in a series of police raids in Belgium on alleged Islamist extremists. After evidence emerged that people living in Belgium planned and took part in terrorist attacks in France, Nov. 13, that killed 130, Belgian authorities, fearing similar attacks, closed the Brussels subway system for several days beginning Nov. 21, canceled public events, and urged Brussels residents to stay at home. In Mar. 22, 2016, attacks for which the Sunni extremist group ISIS claimed responsibility, 3 suicide bombers killed 32 others in a Brussels subway station and at the city's airport. In separate incidents May 28-29, 2018, a prisoner on short-term release killed two police officers and two civilians before being fatally shot by police.

Belize

People: Population: 385,854 (171). **Age distrib.:** <15: 33.6%; 65+: 3%. **Growth:** 1.8%. **Migrants:** 16%. **Pop. density:** 43.8 per sq mi, 16.9 per sq km. **Urban:** 45.7%. **Ethnic groups:** mestizo 52.9%, Creole 25.9%, Maya 11.3%, Garifuna 6.1%, East Indian 3.9%, Mennonite 3.6%. **Languages:** English (official), Spanish, Creole, Maya, German, Garifuna. **Religions:** Roman Catholic 40.1%, Protestant 31.5% (incl. Pentecostal 8.4%, Seventh-day Adventist 5.4%), other (incl. Baha'i, Buddhist, Hindu, Mormon, Muslim, Rastafarian) 10.5%, none 15.5%.

Geography: Total area: 8,867 sq mi, 22,966 sq km (148); **Land area:** 8,805 sq mi, 22,806 sq km. **Location:** Eastern coast of Central America. Mexico on N, Guatemala on W and S. **Topography:** Swampy lowlands in N, Maya Mts. in S, coral reefs and cays near coast. Tropical climate. **Arable land:** 3.4%. **Capital:** Belmopan, 22,964.

Government: Type: Parliamentary democracy under constitutional monarchy. **Head of state:** Queen Elizabeth II, rep. by Gov.-Gen. Colville Young; b. 1932; in office: Nov. 17, 1993. **Head of govt.:** Prime Min. Dean Barrow; b. 1951; in office: Feb. 8, 2008. **Local divisions:** 6 districts. **Defense budget:** $23 mil. **Active troops:** 1,500.

Economy: Industries: garment prod., food proc., tourism, constr. **Chief agric.:** bananas, cacao, citrus, sugar; fish, cultured shrimp. **Natural resources:** timber, fish, hydropower. **Water:** 60,479 cu m per capita. **Crude oil reserves:** 6.7 mil bbls. **Electricity prod.:** 248 mil kWh. **Labor force:** agric. 15.4%, industry 15.1%, services 69.5%. **Unemployment:** 9.3%.

Finance: Monetary unit: Dollar (BZD) (2.01 = $1 U.S.). **GDP:** $3.2 bil; **per capita GDP:** $8,300; **GDP growth:** 0.8%. **Imports:** $944.4 mil; U.S. 35.6%, China 11.2%, Mexico 11.2%, Guatemala 6.9%. **Exports:** $483.4 mil; UK 33.9%, U.S. 22%, Jamaica 6.7%, Italy 6.4%, Barbados 5.9%, Ireland 5.5%. **Tourism:** $426 mil. **Budget:** $550 mil. **Inflation:** 1.2%.

Transport: Motor vehicles: 115.2 per 1,000 pop. **Airports:** 6. **Communications: Telephone** (2016): 6.3 per 100 pop. **Mobile** (2016): 61.9 per 100 pop. **Broadband:** 13.8 per 100 pop. **Internet:** 44.6%.

Health: Expend.: 6.2%. **Life expect.:** 73.1 male; 76.3 female. **Births:** 22.9 per 1,000 pop. **Deaths:** 4.2 per 1,000 pop. **Infant mortality:** 12 per 1,000 live births. **Undernourished:** 6.5%. **HIV:** 1.9%.

Education: Compulsory: ages 5-12. **Literacy:** 79.7%.

Embassy: 2535 Massachusetts Ave. NW 20008; 332-9636.

Website: www.belize.gov.bz

Belize (formerly British Honduras) gained independence from Great Britain Sept. 21, 1981. Guatemala claims the southern half of Belize and its islands as its own territory. Belize has become a center for drug trafficking between Colombia and the U.S. Beginning in 2016, thousands of people fleeing violence in El Salvador, Honduras, and Guatemala sought refuge in Belize.

Benin
Republic of Benin

People: Population: 11,340,504 (79). **Age distrib.:** <15: 42.3%; 65+: 2.9%. **Growth:** 2.7%. **Migrants:** 2.3%. **Pop. density:** 265.5 per sq mi, 102.5 per sq km. **Urban:** 47.3%. **Ethnic groups:** Fon and related 38.4%, Adja/related 15.1%, Yoruba/related 12%, Bariba/related 9.6%, Fulani/related 8.6%, Ottamari/related 6.1%, Yoa-Lokpa/related 4.3%, Dendi/related 2.9%. **Languages:** French (official), Fon, Yoruba, tribal langs. **Religions:** Muslim 27.7%, Catholic 25.5%, Protestant 13.5%, Vodoun 11.6%, none 5.8%.

Geography: Total area: 43,484 sq mi, 112,622 sq km (100); **Land area:** 42,711 sq mi, 110,622 sq km. **Location:** W Africa on Gulf of Guinea. Togo on W; Burkina Faso, Niger on N; Nigeria on E. **Topography:** Mostly flat and covered with dense vegetation. The coast is hot, humid, and rainy. **Arable land:** 23.9%. **Capital:** Cotonou (seat), 685,458; Porto-Novo (constitutional), 285,328.

Government: Type: Presidential republic. **Head of state and govt.:** Pres. Patrice Talon; b. 1958; in office: Apr. 6, 2016. **Local divisions:** 12 departments. **Defense budget:** $117 mil. **Active troops:** 7,250.

Economy: Industries: textiles, food proc., constr. materials, cement. **Chief agric.:** cotton, corn, cassava, yams, beans, palm oil. **Natural resources:** offshore oil, limestone, marble, timber. **Water:** 2,426 cu m per capita. **Crude oil reserves:** 8 mil bbls. **Electricity prod.:** 311.6 mil kWh. **Labor force:** agric. 43.2%, industry 18.5%, services 38.3%. **Unemployment:** 2.5%.

Finance: Monetary unit: CFA Franc (XOF) (566.17 = $1 U.S.). **GDP:** $25.3 bil; **per capita GDP:** $2,300; **GDP growth:** 5.6%. **Imports:** $2.4 bil; Thailand 18.1%, India 15.9%, France 8.5%, China 7.5%, Togo 5.9%. **Exports:** $1.8 bil; Bangladesh 18.1%, India 10.7%, Ukraine 9%, Niger 8.1%, China 7.7%, Nigeria 7.2%. **Tourism:** $123 mil. **Budget:** $2.3 bil. **Inflation:** 0.1%.

Transport: Railways: 272 mi. **Motor vehicles:** 3.6 per 1,000 pop. **Airports:** 1.

Communications: Telephone: 0.5 per 100 pop. **Mobile:** 78.5 per 100 pop. **Broadband:** 5.6 per 100 pop. **Internet:** 12%.

Health: Expend.: 4%. **Life expect.:** 61.2 male; 64.2 female. **Births:** 34.5 per 1,000 pop. **Deaths:** 7.7 per 1,000 pop. **Infant mortality:** 51.5 per 1,000 live births. **Undernourished:** 10.4%. **HIV:** 1%.

Education: Compulsory: ages 6-11. **Literacy:** 38.4%.

Embassy: 2124 Kalorama Rd. NW 20008; 232-6656.

Website: www.gouv.bj

The Kingdom of Abomey, rising to power in wars with neighboring kingdoms in the 17th cent., came under French domination in the late 19th cent., and was incorporated into French West Africa by 1904. Under the name Dahomey, the country gained independence Aug. 1, 1960; it became Benin in 1975. In the fifth coup since independence Col. Ahmed Kerekou took power in 1972; two years later he declared a socialist state with a Marxist-Leninist philosophy. In Dec. 1989, Kerekou announced Marxism-Leninism would no longer be the state ideology.

Thomas Boni Yayi, an economist, was elected president, Mar. 19, 2006, and Mar. 13, 2011. Independent Patrice Talon won a presidential runoff election Mar. 20, 2016.

In June 2015, Benin agreed to join Nigeria, Chad, Cameroon, and Niger in contributing troops to a multinational force to fight the Islamist extremist group Boko Haram. The first 150 Benin troops were deployed in Nov. 2017.

Bhutan
Kingdom of Bhutan

People: Population: 766,397 (161). **Age distrib.:** <15: 25.4%; 65+: 6.4%. **Growth:** 1.1%. **Migrants:** 6.5%. **Pop. density:** 51.7 per sq mi, 20 per sq km. **Urban:** 40.9%. **Ethnic groups:** Ngalop or Bhote 50%, ethnic Nepalese (incl. Lhotsampa) 35%, indigenous or migrant tribes 15%. **Languages:** Sharchhopka, Dzongkha (official), Lhotshamkha. **Religions:** Lamaistic Buddhist 75.3%, Indian- and Nepalese-influenced Hinduism 22.1%.

Geography: Total area: 14,824 sq mi, 38,394 sq km (133); **Land area:** 14,824 sq mi, 38,394 sq km. **Location:** S Asia, in eastern Himalayan Mts. India (Sikkim state) on W and S, China on N. **Topography:** Very high mountains in the N, fertile valleys in the center, and thick forests in the Duar Plain in the S. **Arable land:** 2.6%. **Capital:** Thimphu, 203,297.

Government: Type: Constitutional monarchy. **Head of state:** King Jigme Khesar Namgyel Wangchuk; b. 1980; in office: Dec. 14, 2006. **Head of govt.:** Prime Min. Tshering Tobgay; b. 1965; in office: July 27, 2013. **Local divisions:** 20 districts. **Defense budget/active troops:** NA.

Economy: Industries: cement, wood prods., processed fruits, alcoholic beverages, calcium carbide, tourism. **Chief agric.:** rice, corn, root crops, citrus; dairy prods. **Natural resources:** timber, hydropower, gypsum, calcium carbonate. **Water:** 100,671 cu m per capita. **Electricity prod.:** 7.7 bil kWh. **Labor force:** agric. 56.8%, industry 9.8%, services 33.5%. **Unemployment:** 2.4%.

Finance: Monetary unit: Ngultrum (BTN) (71.56 = $1 U.S.). **GDP:** $7.03 bil; **per capita GDP:** $8,700; **GDP growth:** 6%. **Imports:** $1.1 bil; India 89.5%. **Exports:** $580 mil; India 95.3%. **Tourism:** $103 mil. **Budget:** $818.8 mil (nearly one-quarter financed by India's govt.). **Inflation:** 3.9%.

Transport: Airports: 2.

Communications: Telephone: 2.6 per 100 pop. **Mobile:** 90.5 per 100 pop. **Broadband:** 47.9 per 100 pop. **Internet:** 41.8%.

Health: Expend.: 3.5%. **Life expect.:** 70.1 male; 72.2 female. **Births:** 17 per 1,000 pop. **Deaths:** 6.4 per 1,000 pop. **Infant mortality:** 30.3 per 1,000 live births. **Undernourished:** NA. **HIV:** NA.

Education: Compulsory: NA. **Literacy:** 64.9%.

Permanent UN mission: 343 E. 43rd St., New York, NY 10017; (212) 682-2268.

Website: www.bhutan.gov.bt

The region came under Tibetan rule in the 16th cent. British influence grew in the 19th cent. A Buddhist monarchy was set up in 1907. After a 1910 treaty, Britain guided Bhutan's external affairs, while the country remained internally self-governing. Upon independence the treaty was revised, 1949, to allow India to assume Britain's role.

Isolated for much of its history, Bhutan has taken steps toward modernization. King Jigme Singye Wangchuk, in power since 1972, stepped down Dec. 14, 2006, in favor of his son, Jigme Khesar Namgyel Wangchuk. Multiparty parliamentary elections took place Mar. 24, 2008, and a new constitution was ratified July 18, making Bhutan a democratic constitutional monarchy. Tashi Chhozom became the first woman appointed to the country's Supreme Court, Aug. 3, 2012. The ruling party was defeated in July 13, 2013, parliamentary elections, with the opposition People's Democratic Party (PDP) winning 32 out of 47 seats.

Bolivia
Plurinational State of Bolivia

People: Population: 11,306,341 (80). **Age distrib.:** <15: 31.3%; 65+: 5.4%. **Growth:** 1.5%. **Migrants:** 1.3%. **Pop. density:** 27 per sq mi, 10.4 per sq km. **Urban:** 69.4%. **Ethnic groups:** mestizo (mixed white/Amerindian) 68%, indigenous 20%, white 5%, cholo/chola 2%. **Languages:** Spanish, Quechua, Aymara, Guarani (all official). **Religions:** Roman Catholic 76.8%, Evangelical and Pentecostal 8.1%, Protestant 7.9%, none 5.5%.

Geography: Total area: 424,164 sq mi, 1,098,581 sq km (27); **Land area:** 418,265 sq mi, 1,083,301 sq km. **Location:** W central South America, in the Andes Mts. One of two landlocked countries in S America. Peru, Chile on W; Argentina, Paraguay on S; Brazil on E and N. **Topography:** The great central plateau, more than 500 mi long at an elevation of 12,000 ft, lies between two cordilleras having three of the highest peaks in S America. Lake Titicaca, on Peruvian border, is world's highest lake (12,500 ft) navigable by large boats. The E central region has semitropical forests; the llanos, or Amazon-Chaco lowlands, are in E. **Arable land:** 4.1%. **Capital:** La Paz (seat), 1,814,087; Sucre (constitutional/legis. and judic.), 277,910. **Cities:** Santa Cruz, 1,641,421; Cochabamba, 1,237,383.

Government: Type: Presidential republic. **Head of state and govt.:** Pres. Juan Evo Morales Ayma; b. 1959; in office: Jan. 22, 2006. **Local divisions:** 9 departments. **Defense budget:** $543 mil. **Active troops:** 34,100.

Economy: Industries: mining, smelting, electricity, petroleum, food/beverages, handicrafts, clothing, jewelry. **Chief agric.:** soybeans, quinoa, Brazil nuts, sugarcane, coffee, corn, rice, potatoes. **Natural resources:** tin, nat. gas, petroleum, zinc, tungsten, antimony, silver, iron, lead, gold, timber, hydropower. **Water:** 53,520 cu m per capita. **Crude oil reserves:** 211.5 mil bbls. **Electricity prod.:** 8.2 bil kWh. **Labor force:** agric. 27%, industry 22.4%, services 50.6%. **Unemployment:** 3.2%.

Finance: Monetary unit: Boliviano (BOB) (6.89 = $1 U.S.). **GDP:** $83.6 bil; **per capita GDP:** $7,500; **GDP growth:** 4.2%. **Imports:** $9.3 bil; China 21.7%, Brazil 16.8%, Argentina 12.6%, U.S. 8.4%, Peru 6.5%. **Exports:** $8 bil; Brazil 17.9%, Argentina 16%, U.S. 7.8%, Japan 7.3%, India 6.6%, South Korea 6.3%, Colombia 5.8%, China 5.1%. **Tourism:** $784 mil. **Budget:** $17.4 bil. **Inflation:** 2.8%.

Transport: Railways: 2,177 mi. **Motor vehicles:** 76.2 per 1,000 pop. **Airports:** 21.

Communications: Telephone: 7.7 per 100 pop. **Mobile:** 99.2 per 100 pop. **Broadband:** 57.6 per 100 pop. **Internet:** 39.7%.

Health: Expend.: 6.4%. **Life expect.:** 67.0 male; 72.8 female. **Births:** 21.6 per 1,000 pop. **Deaths:** 6.3 per 1,000 pop. **Infant mortality:** 34.2 per 1,000 live births. **Undernourished:** 19.8%. **HIV:** 0.3%.

Education: Compulsory: ages 4-17. **Literacy:** 92.5%.

Embassy: 3014 Massachusetts Ave. NW 20008; 483-4410.

Website: www.bolivia.gob.bo

The Incas conquered the region's earlier Indian inhabitants in the 13th cent. Spanish colonial rule began in the 1530s and lasted until Aug. 6, 1825. The country is named after independence fighter Simón Bolívar. In a series of wars, Bolivia lost its Pacific coast to Chile, the oil-bearing Chaco to Paraguay, and rubber-growing areas to Brazil, 1879-1935.

Economic unrest, especially among militant mine workers, led to continuing political instability. A reformist government under Victor Paz Estenssoro, 1951-64, nationalized tin mines and attempted to improve conditions for the Indian majority but was overthrown by a military junta. A series of coups and countercoups continued until constitutional government was restored in 1982.

U.S. pressure on the government to reduce production of coca, the raw material for cocaine, led to clashes between police and growers and increased anti-U.S. feeling in Bolivia, where chewing coca leaves is fairly common. Gen. Hugo Banzer Suárez, who ruled as a dictator, 1971-78, later governed as president, 1997-2001.

After an inconclusive presidential election June 2002, Congress chose Gonzalo Sánchez de Lozada, a U.S.-educated mining executive, as head of state. He quit Oct. 17, 2003, after indigenous Bolivians staged a month of anti-government protests in which over 70 people died.

Leftist Juan Evo Morales Ayma won the presidential election, Dec. 2005. Bolivia's first indigenous president, he nationalized the hydrocarbon sector and launched a land-redistribution program to benefit poor farmers. He faced resistance and demands for autonomy from leaders of Bolivia's relatively prosperous lowland provinces. Voters, Jan. 25, 2009, approved a new constitution strengthening the rights of Bolivia's indigenous majority and increasing federal control over the country's natural resources. Morales won a second term Dec. 6, 2009. His government nationalized major utility companies in 2012. Morales won reelection Oct. 12, 2014. Miners protesting government regulation killed Bolivia's deputy interior minister, Aug. 25, 2016. A Nov. 28, 2017, Supreme Court ruling abolished term limits, paving the way for Morales to seek a fourth term in 2019.

Bosnia and Herzegovina

People: Population: 3,849,891 (127). **Age distrib.:** <15: 13.2%; 65+: 15%. **Growth:** -0.2%. **Migrants:** 1.1%. **Pop. density:** 194.8 per sq mi, 75.2 per sq km. **Urban:** 48.2%. **Ethnic groups:** Bosniak 50.1%, Serb 30.8%, Croat 15.4%. **Languages:** Bosnian, Serbian, Croatian (all official). **Religions:** Muslim 50.7%, Orthodox 30.7%, Roman Catholic 15.2%.

Geography: Total area: 19,767 sq mi, 51,197 sq km (125); **Land area:** 19,763 sq mi, 51,187 sq km. **Location:** Balkan Peninsula in SE Europe. Serbia, Montenegro on E and SE; Croatia on N and W. **Topography:** Hilly with some mountains. **Arable land:** 20.1%. **Capital:** Sarajevo, 342,577.

Government: Type: Parliamentary republic. **Heads of state:** Collective presidency with rotating leadership every 8 months. **Head of govt.:** Chairman of the Council of Ministers Denis Zvizdic; b. 1964; in office: Feb. 11, 2015. **Local divisions:** 3 first-order admin. divisions. **Defense budget:** $162 mil. **Active troops:** 10,500.

Economy: Industries: steel, coal, iron ore, lead, zinc, manganese, bauxite, aluminum, motor vehicle assembly, textiles, tobacco prods. **Chief agric.:** wheat, corn, fruits, vegetables; livestock. **Natural resources:** coal, iron ore, bauxite, copper, lead, zinc, chromite, cobalt, manganese, nickel, clay, gypsum, salt, sand, timber, hydropower. **Water:** 9,843 cu m per capita. **Electricity prod.:** 15 bil kWh. **Labor force:** agric. 19.1%, industry 32.2%, services 48.7%. **Unemployment:** 25.6%.

Finance: Monetary unit: Convertible Marka (BAM) (1.69 = $1 U.S.). **GDP:** $44.6 bil; **per capita GDP:** $12,700; **GDP growth:** 2.7%. **Imports:** $9.1 bil; Germany 11.6%, Italy 11.3%, Serbia 11.1%, Croatia 10.1%, China 6.5%, Slovenia 5%. **Exports:** $4.8 bil; Germany 14.7%, Croatia 11.8%, Italy 11.1%, Serbia 10%, Slovenia 9%, Austria 8.3%. **Tourism:** $826 mil. **Budget:** $8 bil. **Inflation:** 1.2%.

Transport: Railways: 600 mi. **Airports:** 7.

Communications: Telephone: 21.7 per 100 pop. **Mobile:** 98.1 per 100 pop. **Broadband:** 37.4 per 100 pop. **Internet** (2017): 69.5%.

Health: Expend.: 9.4%. **Life expect.:** 74.1 male; 80.3 female. **Births:** 8.7 per 1,000 pop. **Deaths:** 10.1 per 1,000 pop. **Infant mortality:** 5.4 per 1,000 live births. **Undernourished:** <2.5%. **HIV:** NA.

Education: Compulsory: ages 6-14. **Literacy:** 98.5%.

Embassy: 2109 E St. NW 20037; 337-1500.

Website: www.fbihvlada.gov.ba

Bosnia was ruled by Croatian kings c. 958 CE, and by Hungary 1000-1200. It became organized c. 1200 and later took control of Herzegovina. The kingdom disintegrated after 1391, with the southern part becoming the independent duchy of Herzegovina. It was conquered by Turks in 1463 and made a Turkish province. The area was placed under control of Austria-Hungary in 1878 and made part of the province of Bosnia and Herzegovina, which was formally annexed to Austria-Hungary, 1908. Bosnia became a province of Yugoslavia in 1918. It was reunited with Herzegovina as a federated republic under the 1946 Yugoslav constitution.

Bosnia and Herzegovina declared sovereignty Oct. 15, 1991. A referendum for independence was passed Feb. 29, 1992. Ethnic Serbs' opposition to the referendum spurred violent clashes and bombings. The U.S. and EU recognized the republic Apr. 7. Fierce three-way fighting continued between Bosnia's Serbs, Muslims, and Croats. Serb forces engaged in ethnic cleansing, killing thousands of Bosnian Muslims (Bosniaks) and expelling Muslims and other non-Serbs from areas under Bosnian Serb control. The capital, Sarajevo, was surrounded and besieged by Bosnian Serb forces. Muslims and Croats in Bosnia began a cease-fire Feb. 23, 1994, and signed an accord, Mar. 18, to create a Muslim-Croat confederation in Bosnia. However, by mid-1994, Bosnian Serbs controlled over 70% of the country.

As fighting continued in 1995, the balance of power shifted toward the Muslim-Croat alliance. Massive NATO airstrikes at Bosnian Serb targets beginning Aug. 30 triggered a new round of peace talks, and the siege of Sarajevo was lifted Sept. 15. The new talks produced an agreement to create autonomous regions within Bosnia, with the Serb region (Republika Srpska) constituting 49% of the country.

A 1995 peace agreement was signed in Paris, Dec. 14, 1995, by leaders of Bosnia, Croatia, and Serbia. Some 60,000 NATO troops (about 20,000 from the U.S.) moved in to police the accord. Meanwhile, a UN tribunal—the International Criminal Tribunal for the Former Yugoslavia (ICTY), established in 1993 at The Hague, Netherlands—began bringing charges against suspected war criminals. Elections were held Sept. 14, 1996, for a 3-person collective presidency, for seats in a federal parliament, and for regional offices. In Dec. a revamped NATO Stabilization Force (SFOR) of over 30,000 members (more than 8,000 from the U.S.) received an 18-month mandate, which was later extended.

The ICTY found Radislav Krstic, a Bosnian Serb general, guilty in 2001, in connection with the genocide of thousands of Muslims at Srebrenica in 1995. An EU peacekeeping force (EUFOR), initially with 7,000 members, assumed responsibility from SFOR, Dec. 2, 2004. Accused of complicity in the Sarajevo and Srebrenica atrocities, former Bosnian Serb leader Radovan Karadzic was convicted, Mar. 24, 2016, by the ICTY of genocide, war crimes, and crimes against humanity and sentenced to 40 years in prison. Gen. Ratko Mladic, the former Bosnian Serb military commander accused of directing the Srebrenica massacre, was convicted by the ICTY, Nov. 22, 2017, of genocide, war crimes, and crimes against humanity and sentenced to life in prison. Mladic's close associate Zdravko Tolimir had already been convicted of genocide on Dec. 12, 2012, and sentenced to life in prison, where he died in 2016. The ICTY concluded its work in Dec. 2017. EUFOR strength in Bosnia was about 600 troops in 2018.

Botswana
Republic of Botswana

People: Population: 2,249,104 (141). **Age distrib.:** <15: 31.5%; 65+: 5.3%. **Growth:** 1.5%. **Migrants:** 7.3%. **Pop. density:** 10.3 per sq mi, 4 per sq km. **Urban:** 69.4%. **Ethnic groups:** Tswana or Setswana 79%, Kalanga 11%, Basarwa 3%, other (incl. Kgalagadi, white) 7%. **Languages:** Setswana, Sekalanga, Shekgalagadi, English (official). **Religions:** Christian 79.1%, Badimo 4.1%, none 15.2%.

Geography: Total area: 224,607 sq mi, 581,730 sq km (47); **Land area:** 218,816 sq mi, 566,730 sq km. **Location:** Southern Africa. Namibia on N and W, Zambia on N, Zimbabwe on NE, South Africa on S. **Topography:** The Kalahari Desert, supporting nomadic peoples and wildlife, spreads over SW. Swamplands and farming areas in N; rolling plains in E where livestock are grazed. **Arable land:** 0.7%. **Capital:** Gaborone, 269,338.

Government: Type: Parliamentary republic. **Head of state and govt.:** Pres. Mokgweetsi Masisi; b. 1962; in office: Apr. 1, 2018. **Local divisions:** 10 districts, 6 town councils. **Defense budget:** $492 mil. **Active troops:** 9,000.

Economy: Industries: diamonds, copper, nickel, salt, soda ash, potash, coal, iron ore, silver. **Chief agric.:** livestock; sorghum, maize, millet, beans, sunflowers, groundnuts. **Natural resources:** diamonds, copper, nickel, salt, soda ash, potash, coal, iron ore, silver. **Water:** 5,411 cu m per capita. **Electricity prod.:** 2.8 bil kWh. **Labor force:** agric. 26.2%, industry 13.5%, services 60.3%. **Unemployment:** 17.4%.

Finance: Monetary unit: Pula (BWP) (10.92 = $1 U.S.). **GDP:** $38.9 bil; **per capita GDP:** $17,800; **GDP growth:** 2.2%. **Imports:** $6 bil; South Africa 66.1%, Canada 8.3%, Israel 5.3%. **Exports:**

$7.6 bil; Belgium 20.3%, India 12.6%, UAE 12.4%, South Africa 11.9%, Singapore 8.7%, Israel 7%. **Tourism:** $1.1 bil. **Budget:** $6.1 bil. **Inflation:** 3.3%.

Transport: Railways: 552 mi. **Motor vehicles:** 212.5 per 1,000 pop. **Airports:** 10.

Communications: Telephone: 6.2 per 100 pop. **Mobile:** 141.4 per 100 pop. **Broadband:** 67.9 per 100 pop. **Internet:** 39.4%.

Health: Expend.: 6%. **Life expect.:** 61.8 male; 66.0 female. **Births:** 21.7 per 1,000 pop. **Deaths:** 9.5 per 1,000 pop. **Infant mortality:** 28.6 per 1,000 live births. **Undernourished:** 28.5%. **HIV:** 22.8%.

Education: Free primary and junior secondary; not compulsory. **Literacy:** 88.5%.

Embassy: 1531-1533 New Hampshire Ave. NW 20036; 244-4990.

Website: www.gov.bw

First inhabited by San people, then Bantus, the region became the British protectorate of Bechuanaland in 1886. The country became fully independent Sept. 30, 1966. Cattle raising and mining (diamonds, copper, nickel) have contributed to economic growth. Pres. Festus Mogae transferred power Apr. 1, 2008, to Seretse Khama Ian Khama, son of Botswana's independence leader and first president (1966-80), Sir Seretse Khama. In power since independence, the Botswana Democratic Party won elections in 2014 for the National Assembly, which chooses the president. When Ian Khama stepped down after serving two 5-year terms, Mokgweetsi Eric Masisi became president, Apr. 1, 2018. The government outlawed commercial hunting in 2014, but poaching of big-game animals remained a problem.

Brazil
Federative Republic of Brazil

People: Population: 208,846,892 (5). **Age distrib.:** <15: 21.9%; 65+: 8.6%. **Growth:** 0.7%. **Migrants:** 0.4%. **Pop. density:** 64.7 per sq mi, 25 per sq km. **Urban:** 86.6%. **Ethnic groups:** white 47.7%, mulatto (mixed white/black) 43.1%, black 7.6%. **Languages:** Portuguese (official). **Religions:** Roman Catholic 64.6%, Protestant 22.2% (incl. Adventist 6.5%), none 8%.

Geography: Total area: 3,287,957 sq mi, 8,515,770 sq km (5); **Land area:** 3,227,096 sq mi, 8,358,140 sq km. **Location:** Occupies E half of South America. French Guiana, Suriname, Guyana, Venezuela on N; Colombia, Peru, Bolivia, Paraguay, on W; Argentina, Uruguay on S. **Topography:** Atlantic coastline stretches 4,603 mi. Heavily wooded Amazon basin covers N half of country. Vast network of navigable rivers. The Amazon itself flows 2,093 mi in Brazil. The NE region is semiarid scrubland, heavily settled and poor. Almost half of pop. resides in S central region. Most major cities are in the narrow coastal belt. Almost the entire country has a tropical or semitropical climate. **Arable land:** 9.6%. **Capital:** Brasília, 4,469,585. **Cities:** São Paulo, 21,650,181; Rio de Janeiro, 13,293,172; Belo Horizonte, 5,972,135.

Government: Type: Federal presidential republic. **Head of state and govt.:** Pres. Michel Temer; b. 1940; in office: May 12, 2016. **Local divisions:** 26 states, 1 federal district. **Defense budget:** $29.4 bil. **Active troops:** 334,500.

Economy: Industries: textiles, shoes, chemicals, cement, lumber, iron ore, tin, steel, aircraft, motor vehicles and parts. **Chief agric.:** coffee, soybeans, wheat, rice, corn, sugarcane, cocoa, citrus; beef. **Natural resources:** bauxite, gold, iron ore, manganese, nickel, phosphates, platinum, tin, rare earth elements, uranium, petroleum, hydropower, timber. **Water:** 41,603 cu m per capita. **Crude oil reserves:** 12.6 bil bbls. **Electricity prod.:** 568.7 bil kWh. **Labor force:** agric. 10.3%, industry 20.9%, services 68.8%. **Unemployment:** 13.3%.

Finance: Monetary unit: Real (BRL) (4.16 = $1 U.S.). **GDP:** $3.2 tril; **per capita GDP:** $15,600; **GDP growth:** 1%. **Imports:** $153.2 bil; China 18.1%, U.S. 16.7%, Argentina 6.3%, Germany 6.1%. **Exports:** $217.2 bil; China 21.8%, U.S. 12.5%, Argentina 8.1%. **Tourism:** $5.8 bil. **Budget:** $845.7 bil. **Inflation:** 3.4%.

Transport: Railways: 18,548 mi. **Motor vehicles:** 210.3 per 1,000 pop. **Airports:** 698.

Communications: Telephone: 19.5 per 100 pop. **Mobile:** 113 per 100 pop. **Broadband:** 89.5 per 100 pop. **Internet:** 60.9%.

Health: Expend.: 8.9%. **Life expect.:** 70.7 male; 78.0 female. **Births:** 13.9 per 1,000 pop. **Deaths:** 6.7 per 1,000 pop. **Infant mortality:** 16.9 per 1,000 live births. **Undernourished:** <2.5%. **HIV:** 0.6%.

Education: Compulsory: ages 4-17. **Literacy:** 92.6%.

Embassy: 3006 Massachusetts Ave. NW 20008; 238-2700.

Website: www.brasil.gov.br

Pedro Álvares Cabral, a Portuguese navigator, is generally credited as the first European to reach Brazil, in 1500. The country was thinly settled by various indigenous groups. Only a few survive today, mostly in the Amazon Basin.

In the next centuries, Portuguese colonists gradually pushed inland, bringing along large numbers of African slaves. (Slavery was not abolished until 1888.) The king of Portugal, fleeing Napoleon's army, moved the seat of government to Brazil in 1808. Brazil thereupon became a kingdom under Dom Joao VI. After Joao

VI returned to Portugal, his son Pedro proclaimed Brazil's independence, Sept. 7, 1822, and was crowned emperor. The second emperor, Dom Pedro II, was deposed in 1889, and a republic proclaimed.

A military junta took control in 1930; Getulio Vargas assumed dictatorial power. The military forced him out in 1945. A democratic regime prevailed 1945-64, during which time the capital was moved from Rio de Janeiro to Brasília. Military-backed governments ruled Brazil for the next 20 years. Censorship was imposed, and the opposition was suppressed.

By the 1990s, Brazil had one of the world's largest economies (8th-largest in 2017). Income is unevenly distributed, however, and almost one-fourth of Brazilians live in poverty. Despite protective environmental legislation, development has destroyed much of the Amazon ecosystem.

Democratic presidential elections held in 1985 brought back civilian rule. Fernando Collor de Mello was elected president, Dec. 1989. In Sept. 1992, Collor was charged with corruption. He resigned, Dec. 29.

A new civil code guaranteeing legal equality for women was enacted Aug. 15, 2001. Luiz Inácio Lula da Silva, a union leader and reformer, won a presidential runoff, Oct. 2002. Brazil's space program launched its first rocket into space Oct. 23, 2004.

Despite political corruption scandals, Lula won a second presidential term, Oct. 2006. The nation reported huge offshore oil finds in 2007-08. Lula's former chief of staff, Dilma Rousseff, won a runoff election Oct. 31, 2010, to become Brazil's first woman president. She narrowly won reelection in an Oct. 26, 2014, runoff.

Brazil hosted the men's World Cup soccer tournament, June 12-July 13, 2014. Rio de Janeiro hosted the 2016 Summer Olympics, Aug. 5-21.

A $3-bil bribery and corruption scandal involving Petrobras (the national oil company), Pres. Rousseff's Workers' Party, and high-level government officials led to the resignations of Petrobras's top executives in Feb. 2015 and to arrests, in Nov. 2014 and June 2015, of business executives at Petrobras subcontractors. The Workers' Party's former treasurer was convicted of bribery and sentenced, Sept. 21, 2015, to more than 15 years in prison, while José Dirceu, Lula's former chief of staff, was sentenced, May 18, 2016, to 23 years in prison for money laundering and other Petrobras-related offenses. A similar scandal involved Electrobras, the government's electric utility company. Former Pres. Lula was convicted, July 12, 2017, of bribery and money laundering in connection with the Petrobras scandal. With appeals and other charges still pending, he surrendered to police Apr. 7, 2018, to begin serving his sentence.

With Brazil suffering an economic downturn (real GDP declined 3.6% in 2015 and 3.5% in 2016 before growing 1.0% in 2017), the lower house of Congress, Apr. 17, 2016, charged Pres. Rousseff with illegally manipulating the federal budget to conceal the size of the deficit. The Senate suspended her from office, May 12; her Senate impeachment trial, Aug. 25-31, ended with her conviction and removal from office. Former Vice Pres. Michel Temer (a centrist and political rival who had been acting president since May 12) succeeded Rousseff. Former lower house speaker Eduardo Cunha was sentenced, Mar. 30, 2017, to more than 15 years in prison following his conviction on Petrobras-related corruption and bribery charges. Pres. Temer was twice charged with corruption in 2017, but the lower house of Congress voted not to send him to trial both times. Brazil's prosecutor general brought new corruption charges against Rousseff and other Workers' Party officials, Sept. 5, 2017.

Responding to a Zika virus outbreak and related cases of microcephaly, Brazil declared a public health emergency, Nov. 11, 2015. The emergency was ended May 11, 2017, although some additional cases occurred. Through the end of 2017, health officials confirmed 2,952 microcephaly cases; 369,013 confirmed or suspected Zika infections had occurred.

Brunei
Brunei Darussalam

People: Population: 450,565 (168). **Age distrib.:** <15: 22.8%; 65+: 5.2%. **Growth:** 1.6%. **Migrants:** 25.3%. **Pop. density:** 221.6 per sq mi, 85.6 per sq km. **Urban:** 77.6%. **Ethnic groups:** Malay 65.7%, Chinese 10.3%. **Languages:** Malay (Bahasa Melayu) (official), English, Chinese dialects. **Religions:** Muslim (official) 78.8%, Christian 8.7%, Buddhist 7.8%, other (incl. indigenous beliefs) 4.7%.

Geography: Total area: 2,226 sq mi, 5,765 sq km (165); **Land area:** 2,033 sq mi, 5,265 sq km. **Location:** SE Asia, on the N coast of the island of Borneo. It is surrounded on its landward side by the Malaysian state of Sarawak. **Topography:** Narrow coastal plain with mountains in E, hilly lowlands in W. Swamps in W and NE. Tropical climate. **Arable land:** 0.9%. **Capital:** Bandar Seri Begawan, 40,781.

Government: Type: Absolute monarchy or sultanate. **Head of state and govt.:** Sultan and Prime Min. Sir Hassanal Bolkiah Mu'izzaddin Waddaulah; b. 1946; in office: Jan. 1, 1984 (sultan since Oct. 5, 1967). **Local divisions:** 4 districts. **Defense budget:** $324 mil. **Active troops:** 7,200.

Economy: Industries: petroleum, petroleum refining, liquefied nat. gas, constr. **Chief agric.:** rice, vegetables, fruits; chickens, water buffalo. **Natural resources:** petroleum, nat. gas, timber. **Water:** 20,085 cu m per capita. **Crude oil reserves:** 1.1 bil bbls. **Electricity prod.:** 3.9 bil kWh. **Labor force:** agric. 0.5%, industry 17.7%, services 81.8%. **Unemployment:** 7.1%.

Finance: Monetary unit: Dollar (BND) (1.38 = $1 U.S.). **GDP:** $33.5 bil; **per capita GDP:** $78,200; **GDP growth:** 0.5%. **Imports:** $3.3 bil; China 19.6%, Singapore 19%, Malaysia 18.8%, U.S. 9.2%, Germany 5.9%. **Exports:** $5.8 bil; Japan 27.8%, South Korea 12.4%, Thailand 11.5%, Malaysia 11.3%, India 9.3%, Singapore 7.7%, Switzerland 5%. **Tourism:** $144 mil. **Budget:** $4 bil. **Inflation:** -0.2%.

Transport: Motor vehicles: 893.4 per 1,000 pop. **Airports:** 1. **Communications: Telephone** (2016): 17.5 per 100 pop. **Mobile:** 127.1 per 100 pop. **Broadband:** 116.6 per 100 pop. **Internet:** 90%.

Health: Expend.: 2.6%. **Life expect.:** 75.2 male; 80.0 female. **Births:** 16.9 per 1,000 pop. **Deaths:** 3.7 per 1,000 pop. **Infant mortality:** 9.3 per 1,000 live births. **Undernourished:** 2.6%. **HIV:** NA.

Education: Compulsory: ages 6-14. **Literacy:** 96.7%.

Embassy: 3520 International Ct. NW 20008; 237-1838.

Website: www.gov.bn

The Sultanate of Brunei was a powerful state in the early 16th cent., with authority over all of the island of Borneo as well as parts of the Sulu Islands and the Philippines. In 1888, a treaty placed the state under the protection of Great Britain.

Brunei became a fully sovereign and independent state on Jan. 1, 1984. The country fielded female athletes for the first time at the 2012 Summer Olympics. Brunei began enacting, May 1, 2014, a new penal code based on Islamic law. If fully implemented, the code could make theft punishable by whipping or limb amputation, and adultery and gay sex would become capital crimes. Brunei outlawed public Christmas celebrations and displays in 2015.

Oil and natural gas account for 65% of GDP and 95% of exports. Brunei's GDP per capita is among the world's highest.

Bulgaria
Republic of Bulgaria

People: Population: 7,057,504 (103). **Age distrib.:** <15: 14.6%; 65+: 19.5%. **Growth:** -0.6%. **Migrants:** 2.2%. **Pop. density:** 168.5 per sq mi, 65.1 per sq km. **Urban:** 75%. **Ethnic groups:** Bulgarian 76.9%, Turkish 8%, Romani 4.4%. **Languages:** Bulgarian (official), Turkish, Romani. **Religions:** Eastern Orthodox 59.4%, Muslim 7.8%, none 3.7%.

Geography: Total area: 42,811 sq mi, 110,879 sq km (103); **Land area:** 41,888 sq mi, 108,489 sq km. **Location:** SE Europe, in E Balkan Peninsula on Black Sea. Romania on N; Serbia, Macedonia on W; Greece, Turkey on S. **Topography:** The Stara Planina (Balkan) Mts. stretch E-W across the center of country, with the Danubian plain on N, the Rhodope Mts. on SW, and Thracian Plain on SE. **Arable land:** 32.3%. **Capital:** Sofia, 1,272,418.

Government: Type: Parliamentary republic. **Head of state:** Pres. Rumen Radev; b. 1963; in office: Jan. 22, 2017. **Head of govt.:** Prime Min. Boyko Borisov; b. 1959; in office: May 4, 2017. **Local divisions:** 28 provinces. **Defense budget:** $676 mil. **Active troops:** 31,300.

Economy: Industries: electricity, gas, water; food, beverages, tobacco; machinery and equip. **Chief agric.:** vegetables, fruits, tobacco, wine, wheat, barley, sunflowers, sugar beets; livestock. **Natural resources:** bauxite, copper, lead, zinc, coal, timber. **Water:** 2,979 cu m per capita. **Crude oil reserves:** 15 mil bbls. **Electricity prod.:** 46.3 bil kWh. **Labor force:** agric. 6.3%, industry 29.3%, services 44.5%. **Unemployment:** 6.2%.

Finance: Monetary unit: Lev (BGN) (1.69 = $1 U.S.). **GDP:** $153.1 bil; **per capita GDP:** $21,700; **GDP growth:** 3.6%. **Imports:** $36.3 bil; Germany 12.3%, Russia 10.3%, Italy 7.3%, Romania 7.1%, Turkey 6.2%, Spain 5.3%. **Exports:** $32.1 bil; Germany 13.5%, Italy 8.3%, Romania 8.2%, Turkey 7.7%, Greece 6.5%. **Tourism:** $4 bil. **Budget:** $21.2 bil. **Inflation:** 2.1%.

Transport: Railways: 3,178 mi. **Motor vehicles:** 452.6 per 1,000 pop. **Airports:** 57.

Communications: Telephone: 18.4 per 100 pop. **Mobile:** 120.4 per 100 pop. **Broadband:** 88.4 per 100 pop. **Internet** (2017): 63.4%.

Health: Expend.: 8.2%. **Life expect.:** 71.5 male; 78.3 female. **Births:** 8.5 per 1,000 pop. **Deaths:** 14.5 per 1,000 pop. **Infant mortality:** 8.3 per 1,000 live births. **Undernourished:** 3%. **HIV:** <0.1%.

Education: Compulsory: ages 5-15. **Literacy:** 98.4%.

Embassy: 1621 22nd St. NW 20008; 387-0174.

Website: www.gob.bg

Bulgaria was settled by Slavs in the 6th cent. Turkic Bulgars arrived in the 7th cent., merged with the Slavs, became Christians by the 9th cent., and set up powerful empires in the 10th and 12th cents. Ottomans took over in 1396 and ruled for nearly 500 years.

An 1876 revolt led to an independent kingdom in 1908. Bulgaria expanded after the first Balkan War but lost its Aegean coastline in WWI, when it sided with Germany. Bulgaria joined the Axis in WWII but withdrew in 1944. Communists took power with Soviet aid; the monarchy was abolished Sept. 8, 1946.

On Nov. 10, 1989, Communist Party leader and head of state Todor Zhivkov resigned after 35 years. In Jan. 1990, Parliament voted to revoke the constitutionally guaranteed dominant role of the Communist Party. A new constitution took effect July 13, 1991.

Bulgaria became a full member of NATO, Apr. 2, 2004, and entered the EU, Jan. 1, 2007. Restrictions on Bulgarians' right to work in nine other EU nations ended Jan. 1, 2014.

A terrorist blew up a bus carrying Israeli tourists, July 18, 2012, leaving 5 Israelis, the Bulgarian bus driver, and the bomber dead. An investigation ending Feb. 5, 2013, blamed the attack on the Muslim militant group Hezbollah, which denied involvement. The identity of the bomber, a Lebanese-French citizen, was determined by DNA evidence in July 2014.

Worsening economic conditions in 2012-13 inspired protests that led center-right, pro-EU Prime Min. Boyko Borisov to submit his government's resignation Feb. 20, 2013. No clear winner emerged from May 12 elections. Parliament elected Plamen Oresharski, with no party affiliation, prime min. May 29. Amid a banking crisis, Oresharski resigned July 23, 2014. After Oct. 5 elections, Borisov again became prime min., Nov. 7, 2014. Construction began in 2015 on the second phase of a security fence along the Turkish border, intended to stop Middle Eastern, SW Asian, and African migrants from entering Bulgaria; about 30,000 entered in 2015. Socialist-backed, pro-Moscow candidate Rumen Radev won Bulgaria's presidential runoff election Nov. 13, 2016. Borisov resigned but returned as prime min. after his party won Mar. 26, 2017, parliamentary elections.

Burkina Faso

People: Population: 19,742,715 (61). **Age distrib.:** <15: 44.3%; 65+: 3.2%. **Growth:** 2.8%. **Migrants:** 3.7%. **Pop. density:** 186.8 per sq mi, 72.1 per sq km. **Urban:** 29.4%. **Ethnic groups:** Mossi 52%, Fulani 8.4%, Gurma 7%, Bobo 4.9%, Gurunsi 4.6%, Senufo 4.5%, Bissa 3.7%, Lobi 2.4%, Dagara 2.4%. **Languages:** French (official), native African Sudanic-family langs. **Religions:** Muslim 61.5%, Roman Catholic 23.3%, traditional/animist 7.8%, Protestant 6.5%.

Geography: Total area: 105,869 sq mi, 274,200 sq km (74); **Land area:** 105,715 sq mi, 273,800 sq km. **Location:** W Africa, S of the Sahara. Mali on NW; Niger on NE; Benin, Togo, Ghana, Côte d'Ivoire on S. **Topography:** Landlocked in the savanna region of W Africa. The N is arid, hot, and thinly populated. **Arable land:** 21.9%. **Capital:** Ouagadougou, 2,531,381.

Government: Type: Presidential republic. **Head of state:** Pres. Roch Marc Christian Kaboré; b. 1957; in office: Dec. 29, 2015. **Head of govt.:** Prime Min. Paul Kaba Thieba; b. 1960; in office: Jan. 6, 2016. **Local divisions:** 13 regions. **Defense budget:** $189 mil. **Active troops:** 11,200.

Economy: Industries: cotton lint, beverages, agric. proc., soap, cigarettes, textiles. **Chief agric.:** cotton, peanuts, shea nuts, sesame, sorghum, millet, corn, rice. **Natural resources:** manganese, limestone, marble, gold, phosphates, pumice, salt. **Water:** 746 cu m per capita. **Electricity prod.:** 944 mil kWh. **Labor force:** agric. 28.3%, industry 32%, services 39.8%. France 11.1%, Togo 7.6%. **Unemployment:** 6.3%.

Finance: Monetary unit: CFA Franc (XOF) (566.17 = $1 U.S.). **GDP:** $35.8 bil; **per capita GDP:** $1,900; **GDP growth:** 6.4%. **Imports:** $2.9 bil; China 13.2%, Côte d'Ivoire 9.5%, U.S. 8.2%, Thailand 8.1%, France 6.5%. **Exports:** $2.8 bil; Switzerland 44.9%, India 15.6%, South Africa 11.3%. **Tourism:** $122 mil. **Budget:** $3.3 bil. **Inflation:** 0.4%.

Transport: Railways: 386 mi. **Motor vehicles:** 16 per 1,000 pop. **Airports:** 2.

Communications: Telephone: 0.4 per 100 pop. **Mobile:** 93.5 per 100 pop. **Broadband:** 19.9 per 100 pop. **Internet:** 14%.

Health: Expend.: 5.4%. **Life expect.:** 60.1 male; 63.6 female. **Births:** 36.9 per 1,000 pop. **Deaths:** 8.7 per 1,000 pop. **Infant mortality:** 54.7 per 1,000 live births. **Undernourished:** 21.3%. **HIV:** 0.8%.

Education: Compulsory: ages 6-15. **Literacy:** 36%.

Embassy: 2340 Massachusetts Ave. NW 20008; 332-5577.

Website: www.gouvernement.gov.bf or burkina-usa.org

The Mossi people entered Burkina Faso in the 11th-13th cents. Their kingdoms ruled until they were defeated by the Mali and Songhai empires. French control came by 1896, but Upper Volta (renamed Burkina Faso on Aug. 4, 1984) was not established as a separate territory until 1947. Independence came Aug. 5, 1960; a pro-French government was elected. The military seized power in 1980. A 1987 coup brought to power military officers including Blaise Compaoré, who became sole ruler by 1989. Pres. Compaoré most recently won reelection Nov. 21, 2010. Violent protests in 2014 against economic hardship and attempts to amend the constitution to allow Compaoré to run again led to his resignation Oct. 31. Civilian Michel Kafando became interim president Nov. 18, 2014. Forces loyal to Compaoré ousted Kafando, Sept. 16, 2015. An ECOWAS-negotiated agreement restored Kafando, Sept. 23, and provided for Nov. 29, 2015, elections; former center-left Prime Min. Roch Marc Christian Kaboré was elected president.

Islamist extremist attacks have increased since 2015. An attack on a café and hotel in Ouagadougou the night of Jan. 15-16, 2016, left 30 victims dead. Terrorist gunmen killed at least 19 at an Ouagadougou restaurant, Aug. 13-14, 2017. Separate attacks, Mar. 2, 2018, on army headquarters and the French embassy in Ouagadougou left 8 security personnel and 8 attackers dead.

Burma
See Myanmar.

Burundi
Republic of Burundi

People: Population: 11,844,520 (76). **Age distrib.:** <15: 45.5%; 65+: 2.7%. **Growth:** 3.2%. **Migrants:** 2.8%. **Pop. density:** 1,194.6 per sq mi, 461.2 per sq km. **Urban:** 13%. **Ethnic groups:** Hutu 85%, Tutsi 14%. **Languages:** Kirundi, French (both official). **Religions:** Catholic 62.1%, Protestant 23.9%, Muslim 2.5%.

Geography: Total area: 10,745 sq mi, 27,830 sq km (143); **Land area:** 9,915 sq mi, 25,680 sq km. **Location:** Central Africa. Rwanda on N, Dem. Rep. of the Congo on W, Tanzania on E and S. **Topography:** Mostly grassy highland, with mountains reaching 8,900 ft. The southernmost source of the White Nile is located in Burundi. Lake Tanganyika is the world's second deepest lake (max. depth 4,823 ft). **Arable land:** 46.7%. **Capital:** Bujumbura, 898,968.

Government: Type: Presidential republic. **Head of state and govt.:** Pres. Pierre Nkurunziza; b. 1963; in office: Aug. 26, 2005. **Local divisions:** 18 provinces. **Defense budget:** $63 mil. **Active troops:** 30,050.

Economy: Industries: light consumer goods, assembly of imported components, public works constr., food proc. (fruits). **Chief agric.:** coffee, cotton, tea, corn, beans, sorghum, sweet potatoes, bananas, cassava; beef. **Natural resources:** nickel, uranium, rare earth oxides, peat, cobalt, copper, platinum, vanadium, hydropower, niobium, tantalum, gold, tin, tungsten, kaolin, limestone. **Water:** 1,122 cu m per capita. **Electricity prod.:** 230 mil kWh. **Labor force:** agric. 91.5%, industry 2.5%, services 6.1%. **Unemployment:** 1.6%.

Finance: Monetary unit: Franc (BIF) (1,771.07 = $1 U.S.). **GDP:** $8 bil; **per capita GDP:** $700; **GDP growth:** 0%. **Imports:** $442.1 mil; India 18.5%, China 13%, Kenya 7.9%, UAE 6.8%, Saudi Arabia 6.8%, Uganda 6%, Tanzania 5.4%. **Exports:** $100.3 mil; Dem. Rep. of the Congo 25.5%, Switzerland 18.4%, UAE 14.9%, Belgium 6%. **Tourism:** $2 mil. **Budget:** $748.9 mil. **Inflation:** 16.1%.

Transport: Motor vehicles: 6.5 per 1,000 pop. **Airports:** 1. **Communications: Telephone:** 0.2 per 100 pop. **Mobile:** 54.5 per 100 pop. **Broadband:** 8.3 per 100 pop. **Internet:** 5.2%.

Health: Expend.: 8.2%. **Life expect.:** 59.6 male; 63.2 female. **Births:** 40.9 per 1,000 pop. **Deaths:** 8.6 per 1,000 pop. **Infant mortality:** 57.4 per 1,000 live births. **Undernourished:** NA. **HIV:** 1.1%.

Education: Compulsory: NA. **Literacy:** 85.6%.

Embassy: 2233 Wisconsin Ave. NW, Ste. 408, 20007; 342-2574.

Website: presidence.gov.bi or www.burundiembassydc-usa.org

The pygmy Twa were the first inhabitants, followed by Bantu Hutus, who were conquered in the 16th cent. by the Tutsi (Watusi), probably from Ethiopia. Germany gained control in 1899. Belgium took over in 1916, successively exercising a League of Nations mandate and UN trusteeship over Ruanda-Urundi (now the two countries of Rwanda and Burundi). Burundi became independent July 1, 1962.

An unsuccessful Hutu rebellion in 1972-73 left 10,000 Tutsi and 150,000 Hutu dead. Over 100,000 Hutu fled to Tanzania and Zaire (now Dem. Rep. of the Congo). In the 1980s, Burundi's Tutsi-dominated regime pledged itself to ethnic reconciliation and democratic reform. In the nation's first democratic presidential election, June 1993, a Hutu, Melchior Ndadaye, was elected. He was killed in an attempted coup, Oct. 21, 1993. At least 150,000 Burundians died in ethnic conflicts over the next three years. Pres. Cyprien Ntaryamira, elected Jan. 1994, and the president of Rwanda were killed when missiles shot down their plane, Apr. 6. The incident sparked massive carnage in Rwanda; violence in Burundi, initially far more limited, intensified in 1995. Ethnic strife continued after a military coup, July 25, 1996. Most warring groups signed a draft peace treaty, Aug. 2000. A power-sharing government headed by Pierre Buyoya was sworn in Nov. 1, 2001, but clashes with rebels continued.

Domitien Ndayizeye, a Hutu, became president Apr. 2003. The UN Security Council authorized, May 2004, a peacekeeping force (ONUB) for Burundi. Approval of a power-sharing constitution by referendum, Feb. 28, 2005, paved the way for local and parliamentary elections. Chosen by parliament, Pierre Nkurunziza, former leader of a Hutu rebel group, became president Aug. 2005. ONUB was succeeded by the UN Integrated Office in Burundi (BINUB), 2007-10, and by the UN Office in Burundi (BNUB), 2011-14, both intended to assist with political transition. Under a reconciliation accord reached Dec. 4, 2008, remaining

Hutu rebels began to demobilize. Candidates opposing Nkurunziza dropped out of the June 2010 presidential election, claiming the vote was rigged. The government was accused of ordering extrajudicial killings, 2010-11.

Violent protests began after Nkurunziza's Apr. 2015 decision to seek a constitutionally dubious third term, which he won, July 21, despite a coup attempt. Political violence and government repression continued in Nkurunziza's third term, claiming an est. 1,700 lives between 2015 and May 2018. Nkurunziza signed legislation, Oct. 18, 2016, to withdraw Burundi from the Intl. Criminal Court. Constitutional changes approved in a May 17, 2018, referendum could facilitate Nkurunziza's staying in power beyond the 2020 expiration of his term; amid widespread criticism, Nkurunziza stated, June 7, that he would not seek reelection in 2020. As of Aug. 31, 2018, an est. 418,000 Burundians were refugees in other African countries.

Cabo Verde
Republic of Cabo Verde

People: Population: 568,373 (167). **Age distrib.:** <15: 28.7%; 65+: 5.2%. **Growth:** 1.3%. **Migrants:** 2.8%. **Pop. density:** 365 per sq mi, 140.9 per sq km. **Urban:** 65.7%. **Ethnic groups:** Creole (mulatto) 71%, African 28%. **Languages:** Portuguese (official), Crioulo (Portuguese/West African blend). **Religions:** Roman Catholic 77.3%, Protestant 4.6%, none 10.8%.

Geography: Total area: 1,557 sq mi, 4,033 sq km (167); **Land area:** 1,557 sq mi, 4,033 sq km. **Location:** In Atlantic O., off W tip of Africa. Nearest neighbors are Mauritania, Senegal to E. **Topography:** 15 Cabo Verde islands, volcanic in origin (active crater on Fogo). Landscape is eroded and stark, with vegetation mostly in interior valleys. **Arable land:** 12.4%. **Capital:** Praia, 167,504.

Government: Type: Parliamentary republic. **Head of state:** Pres. Jorge Carlos Fonseca; b. 1950; in office: Sept. 9, 2011. **Head of govt.:** Prime Min. José Ulisses Correia e Silva; b. 1962; in office: Apr. 22, 2016. **Local divisions:** 22 municipalities. **Defense budget:** $10 mil. **Active troops:** 1,200.

Economy: Industries: food and beverages, fish proc., shoes and garments, salt mining, ship repair. **Chief agric.:** bananas, corn, beans, sweet potatoes, sugarcane, coffee, peanuts; fish. **Natural resources:** salt, basalt rock, limestone, kaolin, fish, clay, gypsum. **Water:** 576 cu m per capita. **Electricity prod.:** 462 mil kWh. **Labor force:** agric. 67.7%, industry 6.9%, services 25.4%. **Unemployment:** 10.3%.

Finance: Monetary unit: Escudo (CVE) (95.18 = $1 U.S.). **GDP:** $3.7 bil; **per capita GDP:** $6,900; **GDP growth:** 4%. **Imports:** $724.8 mil; Portugal 43.9%, Spain 11.6%, Netherlands 6.1%, China 6.1%. **Exports:** $158.6 mil; Spain 45.3%, Portugal 40.3%, Netherlands 8.1%. **Tourism:** $436 mil. **Budget:** $463.7 mil. **Inflation:** 0.8%.

Transport: Airports: 9.

Communications: Telephone: 11.9 per 100 pop. **Mobile:** 112.1 per 100 pop. **Broadband:** 70 per 100 pop. **Internet** (2017): 57.2%.

Health: Expend.: 4.8%. **Life expect.:** 70.3 male; 75.1 female. **Births:** 19.7 per 1,000 pop. **Deaths:** 6 per 1,000 pop. **Infant mortality:** 21.1 per 1,000 live births. **Undernourished:** 12.3%. **HIV:** 0.6%.

Education: Compulsory: ages 6-15. **Literacy:** 86.8%.

Embassy: 3415 Massachusetts Ave. NW 20007; 965-6820.

Website: www.governo.cv

The first Portuguese colonists landed in 1462; African slaves were brought soon after, and most Cabo Verdeans descend from both groups. Independence for Cabo Verde (known as Cape Verde until Oct. 2013) came July 5, 1975. Antonio Mascarenhas Monteiro won the nation's first free presidential election Feb. 17, 1991; he was reelected without opposition five years later. Pres. Pedro Pires served two 5-year terms, 2001-11. Jorge Carlos Fonseca won a presidential runoff election Aug. 21, 2011; he easily won reelection, Oct. 2, 2016. Remittances from Cabo Verdean emigrants are a major source of income.

Cambodia
Kingdom of Cambodia

People: Population: 16,449,519 (69). **Age distrib.:** <15: 30.8%; 65+: 4.4%. **Growth:** 1.5%. **Migrants:** 0.5%. **Pop. density:** 241.4 per sq mi, 93.2 per sq km. **Urban:** 23.4%. **Ethnic groups:** Khmer 97.6%. **Languages:** Khmer (official). **Religions:** Buddhist (official) 96.9%, Muslim 1.9%.

Geography: Total area: 69,898 sq mi, 181,035 sq km (88); **Land area:** 68,153 sq mi, 176,515 sq km. **Location:** SE Asia, on Indochina Peninsula. Thailand on W and N, Laos on NE, Vietnam on E. **Topography:** The central area, formed by the Mekong R. basin and Tonle Sap Lake, is level. Hills and mountains in SE; long escarpment in NW separates the country from Thailand. **Arable land:** 21.5%. **Capital:** Phnom Penh, 1,952,329.

Government: Type: Parliamentary constitutional monarchy. **Head of state:** King Norodom Sihamoni; b. 1953; in office: Oct. 29, 2004. **Head of govt.:** Prime Min. Hun Sen; b. 1952; in office: Jan. 14, 1985. **Local divisions:** 24 provinces, 1 municipality. **Defense budget:** $788 mil. **Active troops:** 124,300.

Economy: Industries: tourism, garments, constr., rice milling, fishing, wood and wood prods., rubber, cement, gem mining, textiles. **Chief agric.:** rice, rubber, corn, vegetables, cashews, cassava, silk. **Natural resources:** oil and gas, timber, gemstones, iron ore, manganese, phosphates. **Water:** 30,562 cu m per capita. **Electricity prod.:** 4.2 bil kWh. **Labor force:** agric. 26.7%, industry 27%, services 46.3%. **Unemployment:** 0.2%.

Finance: Monetary unit: Riel (KHR) (4,084.63 = $1 U.S.). **GDP:** $64.3 bil; **per capita GDP:** $4,000; **GDP growth:** 6.9%. **Imports:** $14.3 bil; China 34.1%, Singapore 12.8%, Thailand 12.4%, Vietnam 10.1%. **Exports:** $10.5 bil; U.S. 21.5%, UK 9%, Germany 8.6%, Japan 7.6%, China 6.9%, Canada 6.7%. **Tourism:** $3.2 bil. **Budget:** $4.7 bil. **Inflation:** 2.9%.

Transport: Railways: 399 mi (under restoration). **Airports:** 6. **Communications: Telephone:** 0.8 per 100 pop. **Mobile:** 116 per 100 pop. **Broadband:** 50.2 per 100 pop. **Internet** (2017): 34%. **Health: Expend.:** 6%. **Life expect.:** 62.7 male; 67.9 female. **Births:** 22.5 per 1,000 pop. **Deaths:** 7.4 per 1,000 pop. **Infant mortality:** 46.1 per 1,000 live births. **Undernourished:** 18.5%. **HIV:** 0.5%.

Education: Compulsory: NA. **Literacy:** 77.2%.
Embassy: 4530 16th St. NW 20011; 726-7742.
Website: cnv.org.kh

Early kingdoms dating from that of Funan in the 1st cent. CE culminated in the great Khmer empire that flourished from the 9th cent. to the 13th, encompassing present-day Thailand, Cambodia, Laos, and southern Vietnam. The peripheral areas were lost to invading Siamese and Vietnamese. France established a protectorate in 1863. Independence came in 1953.

Prince Norodom Sihanouk, king (1941-55) and head of state from 1960, tried to maintain neutrality during the Vietnam War. The U.S. bombed Cambodia, 1969-73, targeting suspected border sanctuaries of Vietnamese insurgents.

In 1970, pro-U.S. Prem. Lon Nol seized power, demanded removal of 40,000 North Vietnamese troops, and abolished the monarchy. Open war began between Lon Nol's government and Communist Khmer Rouge guerrillas, led by Pol Pot and supported by Vietnam and China. The U.S. provided Lon Nol with military and economic aid.

Khmer Rouge forces captured Phnom Penh Apr. 17, 1975. Cities were depopulated with the stated goal of making Cambodia a classless agrarian society; Cambodians were executed or forced to work on cooperative farms. An estimated 1.7 mil people died in "killing fields" or from other hardships under Khmer Rouge rule, 1975-79.

Severe border fighting broke out with Vietnam in 1978 and developed into a full-fledged Vietnamese invasion. Formation of a Vietnamese-backed government was announced, Jan. 8, 1979, one day after Phnom Penh was seized. Thousands of refugees fled to Thailand; widespread starvation was reported. Vietnamese troops remained in Cambodia until Sept. 1989 to combat resistance from Khmer Rouge guerrillas.

Following 1993 UN-sponsored elections in Cambodia, two leading parties agreed to share power in an interim government. On Sept. 21, the National Assembly adopted a constitution reestablishing a monarchy with Sihanouk as king. The Khmer Rouge insurgency weakened and splintered by 1996.

Co-Prime Min. Hun Sen staged a coup July 5, 1997, ousting his rival, Prince Norodom Ranariddh. Pol Pot was denounced by his former comrades at a show trial, July 25, 1997, and sentenced to house arrest; he died Apr. 15, 1998. Sihanouk abdicated because of poor health and was succeeded, Oct. 2004, by his son Norodom Sihamoni. A UN-backed war crimes tribunal convicted a former prison warden known as Duch July 2010 for overseeing the killing and torture of more than 14,000 inmates under the Khmer Rouge. Two other Khmer Rouge leaders were convicted of murder, crimes against humanity, and other charges, Aug. 7, 2014, and sentenced to life in prison.

Hun Sen's party retained power through a series of flawed elections, most recently on July 29, 2018, and repressive policies. Opposition leader Kem Sokha was arrested Sept. 3, 2017; in poor health, he was released on bail Sept. 9, 2018. His party was dissolved in Nov. 2017, and several media outlets were shut down by the government. In recent years, Chinese investment, military and other aid, and tourism have increased sharply.

Cameroon
Republic of Cameroon

People: Population: 25,640,965 (53). **Age distrib.:** <15: 42.1%; 65+: 3.2%. **Growth:** 2.5%. **Migrants:** 2.2%. **Pop. density:** 140.5 per sq mi, 54.2 per sq km. **Urban:** 56.4%. **Ethnic groups:** Cameroon Highlander 31%, Equatorial Bantu 19%, Kirdi 11%, Fulani 10%, Northwestern Bantu 8%, Eastern Nigritic 7%. **Languages:** English, French (both official); 24 major African lang. groups. **Religions:** Catholic 38.4%, Protestant 26.3%, Muslim 20.9%, animist 5.6%.

Geography: Total area: 183,568 sq mi, 475,440 sq km (53); **Land area:** 182,514 sq mi, 472,710 sq km. **Location:** Between W and central Africa. Nigeria on NW; Chad, Central African Republic on E; Congo Rep., Gabon, Equatorial Guinea on S. **Topography:** Low coastal plain with rain forests in S; plateaus in center lead to forested mountains in W, including Mt. Cameroon (13,435 ft). Grasslands in N, marshes around Lake Chad. **Arable land:** 13.1%. **Capital:** Yaoundé, 3,655,656. **Cities:** Douala, 3,412,103.

Government: Type: Presidential republic. **Head of state:** Pres. Paul Biya; b. 1933; in office: Nov. 6, 1982. **Head of govt.:** Prime Min. Philemon Yang; b. 1947; in office: June 30, 2009. **Local divisions:** 10 regions. **Defense budget:** $404 mil. **Active troops:** 14,400.

Economy: Industries: petroleum prod./refining, aluminum prod., food proc., light consumer goods, textiles, lumber, ship repair. **Chief agric.:** coffee, cocoa, cotton, rubber, bananas, oilseed, grains, cassava; livestock. **Natural resources:** petroleum, bauxite, iron ore, timber, hydropower. **Water:** 12,127 cu m per capita. **Crude oil reserves:** 200 mil bbls. **Electricity prod.:** 6.6 bil kWh. **Labor force:** agric. 62%, industry 9.3%, services 28.7%. **Unemployment:** 4.2%.

Finance: Monetary unit: Central African CFA Franc (XAF) (566.17 = $1 U.S.). **GDP:** $88.9 bil; **per capita GDP:** $3,700; **GDP growth:** 3.2%. **Imports:** $5.3 bil; China 19%, France 10.3%, Thailand 7.9%. **Exports:** $5.2 bil; Netherlands 15.6%, France 12.6%, China 11.7%, Belgium 6.8%, Italy 6.3%. **Tourism:** $505 mil. **Budget:** $7 bil. **Inflation:** 0.6%.

Transport: Railways: 613 mi. **Motor vehicles:** 16.3 per 1,000 pop. **Airports:** 11. **Communications: Telephone:** 2.9 per 100 pop. **Mobile:** 81.9 per 100 pop. **Broadband:** 9.6 per 100 pop. **Internet** (2017): 23.2%. **Health: Expend.:** 5.1%. **Life expect.:** 58.0 male; 60.9 female. **Births:** 35 per 1,000 pop. **Deaths:** 9.4 per 1,000 pop. **Infant mortality:** 49.8 per 1,000 live births. **Undernourished:** 7.3%. **HIV:** 3.7%. **Education:** Compulsory: ages 6-11. **Literacy:** 75%.
Embassy: 3400 International Dr. NW 20008; 265-8790.
Website: www.spm.gov.cm

Portuguese sailors were the first Europeans to reach Cameroon, in the 15th cent. The European and American slave trade was very active in the area. German control lasted from 1884 to 1916, when France and Britain divided the territory. French Cameroon became independent Jan. 1, 1960; one part of British Cameroon joined Nigeria in 1961 while the other part joined Cameroon. Pres. Paul Biya has retained power since 1982 in a series of elections that were boycotted by opposition parties or disputed as fraudulent.

More than a dozen French citizens were kidnapped during 2013, allegedly in retaliation for France's intervention in Mali, and taken to Nigeria by the Nigerian-based jihadist group Boko Haram. Kidnappings and attacks by Boko Haram in Cameroon continued in 2014-18. Beginning in 2015, Cameroon troops fought in Nigeria against Boko Haram forces, and, U.S. troops were in Cameroon to train and assist them. A July 2017 Amnesty Intl. report accused the Cameroon military of torturing detainees suspected of supporting or having information about Boko Haram.

Since late 2016, government forces have violently suppressed protesters and fought separatists in Anglophone areas of western Cameroon; about 180,000 people were internally displaced or had become refugees by mid-2018.

Canada

People: Population: 35,881,659 (38). **Age distrib.:** <15: 15.4%; 65+: 19.1%. **Growth:** 0.7%. **Migrants:** 21.5%. **Pop. density:** 10.2 per sq mi, 3.9 per sq km. **Urban:** 81.4%. **Ethnic groups:** Canadian 32.2%, English 19.8%, French 15.5%, Scottish 14.4%, Irish 13.8%, German 9.8%, Italian 4.5%, Chinese 4.5%, N. Amer. Indian 4.2%. **Languages:** English, French (both official). **Religions:** Catholic 39%, Protestant 20.3%, Muslim 3.2%, none 23.9%.

Geography: Total area: 3,855,103 sq mi, 9,984,670 sq km (2); **Land area:** 3,511,023 sq mi, 9,093,507 sq km. **Location:** Extends 3,426 mi E-W and S from the North Pole to the U.S. **Topography:** Seacoast includes 36,356 mi of mainland and 115,133 mi of islands, including the Arctic islands almost from Greenland to near the Alaskan border. Generally temperate, though varies from freezing winter cold to blistering summer heat. **Arable land:** 4.8%. **Capital:** Ottawa-Gatineau, 1,363,159. **Cities:** Toronto, 6,082,425; Montréal, 4,171,717; Vancouver, 2,530,746; Calgary, 1,476,598; Edmonton, 1,397,424; Québec City, 815,604; Winnipeg, 800,249; Halifax, 409,124; Victoria, 378,170.

Government: Type: Federal parliamentary democracy under constitutional monarchy. **Head of state:** Queen Elizabeth II, rep. by Gov.-Gen. Julie Payette; b. 1963; in office: Oct. 2, 2017. **Head of govt.:** Prime Min. Justin Trudeau; b. 1971; in office: Nov. 4, 2015. **Local divisions:** 10 provinces, 3 territories. **Defense budget:** $17 bil. **Active troops:** 63,000.

Economy: Industries: transp. equip., chemicals, minerals, food prods., wood and paper prods., fish prods. **Chief agric.:** wheat, barley, oilseed, tobacco, fruits, vegetables; dairy prods.; fish. **Natural resources:** iron ore, nickel, zinc, copper, gold, lead, rare earth elements, molybdenum, potash, diamonds, silver, fish, timber, wildlife, coal, petroleum, nat. gas, hydropower. **Water:** 80,746 cu m per capita. **Crude oil reserves:** 170.5 bil bbls. **Electricity**

Canada's Provinces and Territories

Province/territory	Joined confed.	Tot. area (sq mi)	Population (2017 est.)	Capital	Premier	Party	In office
Alberta	1905	255,541	4,286,134	Edmonton	Rachel Notley	New Democratic	2015
British Columbia	1871	364,764	4,817,160	Victoria	John Horgan	New Democratic	2017
Manitoba.	1870	250,116	1,338,109	Winnipeg	Brian Pallister	Prog. Cons.	2016
New Brunswick.	1867	28,150	759,655	Fredericton	Brian Gallant	Liberal	2014
Newfoundland and Labrador	1949	156,453	528,817	St. John's	Dwight Ball	Liberal	2015
Nova Scotia	1867	21,345	953,869	Halifax	Stephen McNeil	Liberal	2013
Ontario	1867	415,598	14,193,384	Toronto	Doug Ford	Prog. Cons.	2018
Prince Edward Island	1873	2,185	152,021	Charlottetown	Wade MacLauchlan	Liberal	2015
Québec.	1867	595,391	8,394,034	Québec	Philippe Couillard	Liberal	2014
Saskatchewan	1905	251,366	1,163,925	Regina	Scott Moe	Saskatchewan	2018
Northwest Territories[1].	1871	519,734	44,520	Yellowknife	Bob McLeod	Nonpartisan	2011
Nunavut[1,2].	1999	808,185	37,996	Iqaluit	Joe Savikataaq	Nonpartisan	2018
Yukon[1]	1898	186,272	38,459	Whitehorse	Sandy Silver	Liberal	2016

Note: Pop. est. as of July 1. (Source: Statistics Canada.) (1) Territories also have federally appointed commissioners to represent federal interests. (2) Territory created in 1999 from eastern portion of Northwest Territories.

prod.: 647 bil kWh. **Labor force:** agric. 2%, industry 19.6%, services 78.4%. **Unemployment:** 6.3%.

Finance: Monetary unit: Dollar (CAD) (1.32 = $1 U.S.). **GDP:** $1.8 tril; **per capita GDP:** $48,300; **GDP growth:** 3%. **Imports:** $443.7 bil; U.S. 51.5%, China 12.6%, Mexico 6.3%. **Exports:** $433 bil; U.S. 76.4%. **Tourism:** $20.3 bil. **Budget:** $657.3 bil. **Inflation:** 1.6%.

Transport: Railways: 48,425 mi. **Motor vehicles:** 669.4 per 1,000 pop. **Airports:** 523.

Communications: Telephone: 40.1 per 100 pop. **Mobile:** 85.9 per 100 pop. **Broadband:** 66.1 per 100 pop. **Internet:** 91.2%.

Health: Expend.: 10.4%. **Life expect.:** 79.4 male; 84.8 female. **Births:** 10.2 per 1,000 pop. **Deaths:** 8.8 per 1,000 pop. **Infant mortality:** 4.5 per 1,000 live births. **Undernourished:** <2.5%. **HIV:** NA.

Education: Compulsory: ages 6-15. **Literacy:** 99%.

Embassy: 501 Pennsylvania Ave. NW 20001; 682-1740.

Website: www.canada.ca

Indigenous people have lived in Canada for at least 12,000 years. Vikings reached and briefly settled in part of Newfoundland in the 10th cent. Italian seaman Giovanni Caboto (a.k.a. John Cabot) claimed parts of the Atlantic coast for England in 1497 and 1498. After French explorer Jacques Cartier reached the Gulf of St. Lawrence in 1534, France pioneered Canadian settlement by Western Europeans, establishing Québec City (1608) and Montréal (1642) and declaring New France a colony in 1663.

Britain acquired Acadia (later Nova Scotia) in 1717 and defeated French forces in Canada to gain control of all of New France by 1763. The French, through the Quebec Act of 1774, retained rights to their language, religion, and civil law. During the American Revolution, many colonials, calling themselves United Empire Loyalists, moved north to Canada. Fur traders and explorers led Canadians westward across the continent. Sir Alexander Mackenzie reached the Pacific in 1793 and scrawled on a rock, "From Canada by land."

In Upper and Lower Canada (later called Ontario and Quebec) and in the Maritimes, legislative assemblies were formed in the 18th cent. Upper Canada was involved in the War of 1812 between Great Britain and the U.S.

In 1837 political agitation for a more democratic government culminated in rebellions in Upper and Lower Canada and the union of the two into the colony of Canada in 1839. The union lasted until the 1867 British North America Act (now known as the Constitution Act, 1867) launched the Dominion of Canada, consisting of Ontario, Quebec, and the former colonies of Nova Scotia and New Brunswick.

The British North America Act, which was the basis for the country's written constitution, established a federal system of government modeled on the British parliament and cabinet structure under the crown. Canada was proclaimed a self-governing dominion within the British Empire in 1931. The Constitution Act, 1982, gave Canada the right to amend its constitution, thereby severing its last legislative link with Britain.

Failure in 1990 of the so-called Meech Lake Accord, which would have assured constitutional protection for Quebec's efforts to preserve its French language and culture, sparked a separatist revival in Quebec. The Charlottetown agreement, calling for constitutional changes, such as recognition of Quebec as a "distinct society" within the Canadian confederation, was defeated by a national referendum in Oct. 1992. A Quebec referendum on secession, Oct. 1995, also failed.

On Jan. 7, 1998, the government apologized to indigenous peoples for 150 years of mistreatment. Nunavut ("Our Land"), carved from the Northwest Territories as a homeland for the Inuit, was established Apr. 1, 1999.

Victory by the Liberals in national elections Nov. 27, 2000, made Jean Chrétien the first Canadian prime min. in over 50 years to head a third successive majority government. Canada sent troops and warships to aid the U.S.-led coalition in Afghanistan beginning Oct. 2001; 157 Canadian troops had been killed in Afghanistan by the time Canada's combat mission ended July 7, 2011.

Same-sex marriage (already permitted in 8 provinces) became legal throughout the country July 2005.

Twelve years of Liberal Party rule ended when the Conservatives won parliamentary elections, Jan. 23, 2006. Elections Oct. 19, 2015, returned Liberals to power, and Justin Trudeau, son of former Prime Min. Pierre Trudeau, became prime min.

Improved technology has facilitated extracting oil from Alberta's tar sands. The Canadian government approved, Nov. 29, 2016, a major expansion of the Trans Mountain oil pipeline (owned by Kinder Morgan Canada Ltd.) from Alberta to British Columbia; with the project delayed by court challenges, the government purchased the pipeline, Aug. 2018. Pres. Barack Obama's 2015 decision not to approve building the Keystone XL pipeline, to carry Alberta oil through the central U.S. to the Gulf of Mexico, was reversed by Pres. Donald Trump, Mar. 24, 2017. On Oct. 22, 2014, a terrorist gunman in Ottawa, apparently inspired by the Islamist extremist group ISIS, killed a soldier at the Canadian War Memorial and opened fire in the Parliament building before being shot to death. Two days earlier in Montréal, a terrorist with apparently similar motivation ran down two soldiers with his car, killing one, before being fatally shot. Canada joined the U.S.-led campaign of airstrikes against ISIS forces in Iraq (Nov. 2, 2014) and Syria (Apr. 8, 2015). The Trudeau government ended airstrikes Feb. 15, 2016, but continued other military assistance to the anti-ISIS campaign. Canada began a resettlement program for Syrian refugees in Nov. 2015; a total of 57,815 arrived in Canada Nov. 4, 2015-July 31, 2018.

A man drove a van into pedestrians in Toronto, Apr. 23, 2018, killing 10 and injuring 16 before being arrested. A gunman killed 2 and injured 13 in a crowded Toronto neighborhood, July 22. In Fredericton, NB, Aug. 10, a gunman killed 4, including 2 police officers.

The North American Free Trade Agreement among Canada, Mexico, and the U.S. went into effect Jan. 1, 1994. Negotiations, called for by the U.S., on revising the agreement began Aug. 16, 2017. With negotiations ongoing, the Trump administration imposed tariffs, June 1, 2018, on Canadian steel and aluminum exports; Canada imposed tariffs, July 1, 2018, on various U.S. steel products and food items. A draft revised agreement—renamed the U.S.-Mexico-Canada Agreement—was completed Sept. 30, 2018, including auto industry changes and increased U.S. access to the Canadian dairy market; a final signed agreement required Canadian cabinet, U.S. Congress, and Mexican Senate approval. A Canada-EU trade agreement eliminating almost all tariffs was signed Oct. 30, 2016. Canada signed, Mar. 8, 2018, the 11-nation Comprehensive and Progressive Agreement for Trans-Pacific Partnership; the trade-liberalization agreement replaced the proposed 12-nation Trans-Pacific Partnership pact that the U.S. withdrew from in 2017.

Central African Republic

People: Population: 5,745,062 (115). **Age distrib.:** <15: 39.9%; 65+: 3.4%. **Growth:** 2.1%. **Migrants:** 1.9%. **Pop. density:** 23.9 per sq mi, 9.2 per sq km. **Urban:** 41.4%. **Ethnic groups:** Baya 33%, Banda 27%, Mandjia 13%, Sara 10%, Mboum 7%, M'Baka 4%, Yakoma 4%. **Languages:** French (official), Sangho (lingua franca and national lang.), tribal langs. **Religions:** indigenous beliefs 35%, Protestant 25%, Roman Catholic 25%, Muslim 15%.

Geography: Total area: 240,535 sq mi, 622,984 sq km (44); **Land area:** 240,535 sq mi, 622,984 sq km. **Location:** Central Africa. Chad on N, Cameroon on W, Congo Republic and Dem. Rep. of the Congo on S, South Sudan and Sudan on E. **Topography:** Mostly rolling plateau, avg. elevation 2,000 ft, with rivers draining S to the Congo and N to Lake Chad. Open, well-watered savanna covers most of area, with an arid area in NE and tropical rain forest in SW. **Arable land:** 2.9%. **Capital:** Bangui, 850,946.

Government: Type: Presidential republic. **Head of state:** Pres. Faustin-Archange Touadéra; b. 1957; in office: Mar. 30, 2016. **Head of govt.:** Prime Min. Simplice Sarandji; b. 1955; in office: Apr. 2, 2016. **Local divisions:** 14 prefectures, 2 economic prefectures, 1 commune. **Defense budget:** $31 mil. **Active troops:** 7,150.

Economy: Industries: gold, diamond mining; logging; brewing; sugar refining. **Chief agric.:** cotton, coffee, tobacco, cassava, yams, millet, corn, bananas. **Natural resources:** diamonds, uranium, timber, gold, oil, hydropower. **Water:** 28,776 cu m per capita. **Electricity prod.:** 174 mil kWh. **Labor force:** agric. 85.6%, industry 8%, services 6.4%. **Unemployment:** 6%.

Finance: Monetary unit: Central African CFA Franc (XAF) (566.17 = $1 U.S.). **GDP:** $3.4 bil; **per capita GDP:** $700; **GDP growth:** 4%. **Imports:** $380.5 mil; France 17.1%, U.S. 12.3%, India 11.5%, China 8.2%, South Africa 7.4%, Japan 5.8%, Italy 5.1%. **Exports:** $118.5 mil; France 31.2%, Burundi 16.2%, China 12.5%, Cameroon 9.6%, Austria 7.8%. **Tourism** (2010) $11 mil. **Budget:** $271.1 mil. **Inflation** (2014-15): 37.1%.

Transport: Motor vehicles: 1 per 1,000 pop. **Airports:** 2. **Communications: Telephone** (2016): 0.04 per 100 pop. **Mobile** (2016): 27.2 per 100 pop. **Broadband:** 3.3 per 100 pop. **Internet:** 4%.

Health: Expend.: 4.8%. **Life expect.:** 51.9 male; 54.7 female. **Births:** 34 per 1,000 pop. **Deaths:** 12.9 per 1,000 pop. **Infant mortality:** 84.3 per 1,000 live births. **Undernourished:** 61.8%. **HIV:** 4%.

Education: Compulsory: ages 6-15. **Literacy:** 36.8%.

Embassy: 2704 Ontario Rd. NW 20009; 483-7800.

Website: rcawashington.org or www.state.gov/p/af/ci/car/

Various Bantu peoples migrated through the region for centuries before French control was asserted in the late 19th cent., when the region was named Ubangi-Shari. Independence was attained Aug. 13, 1960.

Pres. Jean-Bedel Bokassa, who seized power in a 1965 military coup, proclaimed himself constitutional emperor of the renamed Central African Empire Dec. 1976. Bokassa's rule was characterized by ruthless authoritarianism and human rights violations. He was ousted in a bloodless coup aided by the French government, Sept. 20, 1979. In 1981, Gen. André Kolingba became head of state in another bloodless coup. Elections in Aug. and Sept. 1993 led to civilian rule under Pres. Ange-Félix Patassé.

Patassé was ousted Mar. 15, 2003, by rebels under former army chief François Bozizé. Bozizé won a presidential runoff election May 8, 2005, but insurgent activity by Patassé loyalists and others continued in the north. A national peace conference, Dec. 8-20, 2008, enabled the installation of a unity government Jan. 19, 2009. Pres. Bozizé won reelection Jan. 23, 2011, but was ousted when the largely Muslim rebel group Seleka, led by Michel Djotodia, seized the capital Mar. 24, 2013. Djotodia declared himself president. Bozizé supporters and Christian militias clashed with pro-Djotodia and Muslim fighters, resulting in thousands of deaths. A National Transitional Council elected Catherine Samba-Panza interim pres. Jan. 20, 2014, and other African nations, France, and the EU sent peacekeeping troops. A UN peacekeeping force (MINUSCA) was authorized Apr. 10, 2014. UNICEF reported, Mar. 2016, over 100 mostly underage women alleged sexual abuse by peacekeepers, 2013-15. France ended its peacekeeping mission Oct. 31, 2016. Faustin-Archange Touadéra, a Christian, won a UN-supervised presidential runoff election, Feb. 14, 2016. Violence between Muslims and Christians, as well as between rival militias and ethnic groups, continued in 2017-18. More than 13,000 MINUSCA uniformed personnel were in the country as of Aug. 31, 2018. The UNHCR estimated that, as of Aug. 31, 2018, almost 1.2 mil people had become refugees or were internally displaced.

Chad
Republic of Chad

People: Population: 15,833,116 (71). **Age distrib.:** <15: 48.1%; 65+: 2.4%. **Growth:** 3.2%. **Migrants:** 3.3%. **Pop. density:** 32.6 per sq km, 12.6 per sq km. **Urban:** 23.1%. **Ethnic groups:** Sara (Ngambaye/Sara/Madjingaye/Mbaye) 30.5%, Kanembu/Bornu/Buduma 9.8%, Arab 9.7%, Wadai/Maba/Masalit/Mimi 7%, Gorane 5.8%, Masa/Musseye/Musgum 4.9%, Bulala/Medogo/Kuka 3.7%, Marba/Lele/Mesme 3.5%, Mundang 2.7%, Bidiyo/Migaama/Kenga/Dangleat 2.5%, Dadjo/Kibet/Muro 2.4%, Tupuri/Kera 2%, Gabri/Kabalaye/Nanchere/Somrai 2%. **Languages:** French, Arabic (both official); Sara; 120+ langs. and dialects. **Religions:** Muslim 52.1%, Protestant 23.9%, Roman Catholic 20%.

Geography: Total area: 495,755 sq mi, 1,284,000 sq km (20); **Land area:** 486,180 sq mi, 1,259,200 sq km. **Location:** Central N Africa. Libya on N; Niger, Nigeria, Cameroon on W; Central African Republic on S; Sudan on E. **Topography:** Wooded savanna, steppe, and desert in the S; part of the Sahara in the N. Southern rivers flow N to Lake Chad, surrounded by marshland. **Arable land:** 3.9%. **Capital:** N'Djaména, 1,322,679.

Government: Type: Presidential republic. **Head of state and govt.:** Pres. Idriss Déby Itno; b. 1952; in office: Dec. 4, 1990. (Prime minister position eliminated under 2018 constitution.) **Local divisions:** 23 regions. **Defense budget:** $165 mil. **Active troops:** 30,350.

Economy: Industries: oil, cotton textiles, brewing, natron (sodium carbonate), soap, cigarettes, constr. materials. **Chief agric.:** cotton, sorghum, millet, peanuts, sesame, corn, rice, potatoes, onions, cassava; cattle, sheep, goats, camels. **Natural resources:** petroleum, uranium, natron, kaolin, fish, gold, limestone, sand and gravel, salt. **Water:** 3,256 cu m per capita. **Crude oil reserves:** 1.5 bil bbls. **Electricity prod.:** 215 mil kWh. **Labor force:** agric. 87.2%, industry 4.9%, services 7.9%. China 14.2%, Cameroon 11%, U.S. 6.4%, India 6%, Belgium 5.7%. **Unemployment:** 5.9%.

Finance: Monetary unit: Central African CFA Franc (XAF) (566.17 = $1 U.S.). **GDP:** $28.6 bil; **per capita GDP:** $2,300; **GDP growth:** -3.1%. **Imports:** $2.1 bil; China 19.9%, Cameroon 17.2%, France 17%, U.S. 5.4%. **Exports:** $2.4 bil; U.S. 38.7%, China 16.6%, Netherlands 15.7%, UAE 12.2%, India 6.3%. **Budget:** $1.5 bil. **Inflation** (2014-15) 3.7%.

Transport: Airports: 9.

Communications: Telephone (2016): 0.09 per 100 pop. **Mobile** (2016): 38.6 per 100 pop. **Broadband:** 9.5 per 100 pop. **Internet:** 5%.

Health: Expend.: 4.6%. **Life expect.:** 55.7 male; 59.3 female. **Births:** 43 per 1,000 pop. **Deaths:** 10.5 per 1,000 pop. **Infant mortality:** 71.7 per 1,000 live births. **Undernourished:** 39.7%. **HIV:** 1.3%.

Education: Compulsory: ages 6-15. **Literacy:** 22.3%.

Embassy: 2401 Massachusetts Ave. NW 20008; 652-1312.

Website: www.gouvernement.td

Chad was the site of Paleolithic and Neolithic cultures before the Sahara Desert formed. A succession of kingdoms and Arab slave traders dominated Chad until France took control around 1900. Independence came Aug. 11, 1960. Northern Muslim rebels fought animist and Christian southern government and French troops from 1966.

Rebel forces led by Hissène Habré captured the capital and forced Pres. Goukouni Oueddei to flee the country in June 1982. In Dec. 1990, a Libyan-supported insurgent group, the Patriotic Salvation Movement, overthrew Habré, who went into exile in Senegal. After approval of a new constitution Mar. 1996, Chad's first multiparty presidential election was held in June and July.

Violence along the Sudan border escalated in 2006, as Sudanese janjaweed militias and Chadian rebels attacked civilians, and Darfur rebels preyed on refugee camps. Between 140 and 700 civilians died in N'Djaména, Feb. 2-5, 2008, as more than 2,000 Chadian rebels stormed the capital and clashed with government troops in a failed coup attempt.

On Jan. 15, 2010, Chad and Sudan signed an accord aimed at normalizing relations and suppressing cross-border activities by rebel groups. Established in 2007, a UN peacekeeping force (MINURCAT) completed its mandate Dec. 31, 2010. Almost 335,000 Sudanese refugees were living in Chad as of Aug. 31, 2018, as well as about 100,000 people fleeing violence in the Central African Republic.

Pres. Idriss Déby won reelection for a fifth term, Apr. 10, 2016.

After Islamist groups took over northern Mali and imposed a repressive regime in late 2012, Chad contributed roughly 2,000 soldiers to aid French, Malian, and other African forces in a military intervention. On Apr. 15, 2013, the Chadian government announced it would begin pulling its troops out of Mali. Chadian troops in 2015-18 fought Boko Haram Islamist extremists in Nigeria. Boko Haram fighters and suicide bombers staged attacks in Chad.

Former Pres. Habré, accused of killing and torturing thousands of opponents in the 1980s, was arrested in Senegal June 30, 2013. The Extraordinary African Chambers (created within Senegal's court system) convicted Habré of crimes against humanity, torture, and rape, May 30, 2016, and sentenced him to life in prison. The sentence and most counts of the conviction (except rape) were upheld on appeal, Apr. 27, 2017.

Chile
Republic of Chile

People: Population: 17,925,262 (65). **Age distrib.:** <15: 20%; 65+: 11.1%. **Growth:** 0.8%. **Migrants:** 2.7%. **Pop. density:** 62.4 per sq mi, 24.1 per sq km. **Urban:** 87.6%. **Ethnic groups:** white and non-indigenous 88.9%, Mapuche 9.1%. **Languages:** Spanish (official), English, indigenous. **Religions:** Roman Catholic 66.7%, Evangelical or Protestant 16.4%, none 11.5%.

Geography: Total area: 291,933 sq mi, 756,102 sq km (37); **Land area:** 287,187 sq mi, 743,812 sq km. **Location:** W coast of southern S America. Peru on N, Bolivia on NE, Argentina on E. **Topography:** Andes Mts., with some of world's highest peaks, on E border; on W is 2,650-mi Pacific coast. Width varies 100-250 mi. Atacama Desert in N. **Arable land:** 1.8%. **Capital:** Santiago, 6,680,371; Valparaíso (seat of natl. legislature), 966,531.

Government: Type: Presidential republic. **Head of state and govt.:** Pres. Sebastián Piñera Echenique; b. 1949; in office: Mar. 11, 2018. **Local divisions:** 16 regions. **Defense budget:** $3.9 bil. **Active troops:** 77,200.

Economy: Industries: copper, lithium, other minerals; foodstuffs, fish proc.; iron and steel; wood and wood prods.; transp. equip.; cement; textiles. **Chief agric.:** grapes, apples, pears, onions, wheat, corn, oats, peaches, garlic, asparagus, beans; beef, poultry, wool; fish. **Natural resources:** copper, timber, iron ore, nitrates, prec. metals, molybdenum, hydropower. **Water:** 51,432 cu m per capita. **Crude oil reserves:** 150 mil bbls. **Electricity prod.:** 72.3 bil kWh. **Labor force:** agric. 9.6%, industry 22.8%, services 67.6%. **Unemployment:** 7%.

Finance: Monetary unit: Peso (CLP) (692.53 = $1 U.S.). **GDP:** $451.1 bil; **per capita GDP:** $24,500; **GDP growth:** 1.5%. **Imports:** $59.9 bil; China 23.9%, U.S. 18.1%, Brazil 8.6%. **Exports:** $64.5 bil; China 27.5%, U.S. 14.5%, Japan 9.3%, South Korea 6.2%, Brazil 5%. **Tourism:** $3.6 bil. **Budget:** $64.9 bil. **Inflation:** 2.2%.

Transport: Railways: 4,525 mi. **Motor vehicles:** 265.3 per 1,000 pop. **Airports:** 90.

Communications: Telephone: 17.7 per 100 pop. **Mobile:** 127.5 per 100 pop. **Broadband:** 69 per 100 pop. **Internet** (2017): 82.3%.

Health: Expend.: 8.1%. **Life expect.:** 76.0 male; 82.2 female. **Births:** 13.4 per 1,000 pop. **Deaths:** 6.3 per 1,000 pop. **Infant mortality:** 6.4 per 1,000 live births. **Undernourished:** 3.3%. **HIV:** 0.6%.

Education: Compulsory: ages 5-17. **Literacy:** 97.5%.

Embassy: 1732-1736 Massachusetts Ave. NW 20036; 785-1746. **Website:** www.gob.cl

Northern Chile was under Inca rule before the Spanish conquest, 1536-40. The southern Araucanian Indians resisted until the late 19th cent. Independence was gained 1810-18 under José de San Martin and Bernardo O'Higgins; the latter, as supreme director 1817-23, sought social and economic reforms until deposed. Chile defeated Peru and Bolivia in 1836-39 and 1879-84, gaining mineral-rich northern land. Chile is the world's largest producer of copper, responsible for more than 25% of the world total; copper exports are a mainstay of the economy.

In 1970, Salvador Allende Gossens, a Marxist, became president. His government improved conditions for the poor, but property seizures by left-wing extremists, poorly planned socialist economic programs, and a destabilization campaign backed by the U.S. led to political and financial chaos. A U.S.-backed military junta seized power Sept. 11, 1973. With the presidential palace under attack, Allende refused to surrender; a 2011 autopsy confirmed police reports that he killed himself. The junta, headed by Gen. Augusto Pinochet Ugarte, implemented plans to privatize the economy and "exterminate Marxism." Repression continued into the 1980s.

In Dec. 1989 voters elected a civilian president, although Pinochet continued to head the army until Mar. 10, 1998. In Mar. 1994, a Chilean human rights group estimated that more than 3,100 people were killed or "disappeared" during Pinochet's rule. Efforts to prosecute him failed when courts in Britain and Chile declared him mentally unfit to stand trial.

Ricardo Lagos Escobar, Chile's first Socialist president since the 1973 coup, took office Mar. 11, 2000. Chile and the U.S. signed a free trade accord June 6, 2003. Michelle Bachelet Jeria, also a Socialist, won a runoff election Jan. 2006 and took office in Mar. as Chile's first woman president. Pinochet died Dec. 10, 2006.

Billionaire businessman Sebastián Piñera Echenique, a conservative, won a presidential runoff election Jan. 2010. An earthquake and tsunami, Feb. 27, 2010, killed at least 521 people and caused up to $30 bil in property damage. Despite economic growth, lagging wages sparked labor protests against the Piñera government that continued into 2012 and spread to the student population. Bachelet returned to the presidency after winning a runoff election Dec. 15, 2013. During her second administration, Chile legalized civil unions between same-sex couples, Oct. 22, 2015, and abortion in very limited circumstances, Aug. 2, 2017.

With the Socialists' popularity hurt by a sluggish economy resulting from low copper prices, Piñera returned as president after winning a Dec. 17, 2017, runoff. After a Vatican investigation, Pope Francis, Apr. 11, 2018, apologized for "grave errors" in the handling by Catholic Church officials in Chile of numerous allegations of child sex abuse by clergy.

Tierra del Fuego is the largest (18,800 sq mi) island in the archipelago of the same name at the southern tip of S America. It was visited 1520 by Magellan and named Land of Fire because of its many Indian bonfires. Part of the island is in Chile, part in Argentina. Punta Arenas, on a mainland peninsula, is a center of sheep raising and the world's southernmost city; Puerto Williams is the southernmost settlement.

China
People's Republic of China

(Statistical data do not include Hong Kong or Macau.)

People: Population: 1,384,688,986 (1). **Age distrib.:** <15: 17.2%; 65+: 11.3%. **Growth:** 0.4%. **Migrants:** 0.1%. **Pop. density:** 384.5 per sq mi, 148.5 per sq km. **Urban:** 59.2%. **Ethnic groups:** Han Chinese 91.6%, other (incl. Hui, Manchu, Uighur, Miao, Yi, Tujia, Tibetan, Mongol, Dong, Buyei, Yao, Bai, Korean, Hani, Li, Kazakh, Dai) 7.1%. **Languages:** Standard Chinese or Mandarin (official; Putonghua, based on Beijing dialect), Yue (Cantonese), Wu (Shanghainese), Minbei (Fuzhou), Minnan (Hokkien-Taiwanese), Xiang, Gan. **Religions:** officially atheist; folk religion 21.9%, Buddhist 18.2%, Christian 5.1%, unaffiliated 52.2%.

Geography: Total area: 3,705,407 sq mi, 9,596,960 sq km (4); **Land area:** 3,600,947 sq mi, 9,326,410 sq km. **Location:** Occupies most of the habitable mainland of E Asia. Mongolia on N; Russia on NE and NW; Kazakhstan, Kyrgyzstan, Tajikistan, Afghanistan, Pakistan on W; India, Nepal, Bhutan, Myanmar, Laos, Vietnam on S; North Korea on NE. **Topography:** Two-thirds of territory is mountainous or desert. The Da Xing'an Ling Mts. in N separate Manchuria and Mongolia. Other ranges incl. the Tien Shan in Xinjiang and the Himalayan and Kunlun Mts. in the SW and in Tibet. Three great river systems—the Chang (Yangtze), Huang (Yellow), and Xi—cross the eastern half of China. **Arable land:** 12.7%. **Capital:** Beijing, 19,617,963. **Cities:** Shanghai, 25,582,138; Chongqing, 14,837,823; Tianjin, 13,214,790; Guangzhou, Guangdong, 12,638,305; Shenzhen, 11,907,836; Chengdu, 8,813,478; Nanjing, Jiangsu, 8,244,627; Wuhan, 8,175,602; Xi'an, Shaanxi, 7,444,233; Dongguan, 7,360,496; Hangzhou, 7,235,803; Foshan, 7,195,585.

Government: Type: Communist party-led state. **Head of state:** Pres. Xi Jinping; b. 1953; in office: Mar. 14, 2013 (gen. sec. of Communist Party since Nov. 15, 2012). **Head of govt.:** Prem. Li Keqiang; b. 1955; in office: Mar. 15, 2013. **Local divisions:** 22 provinces (not incl. Taiwan), 5 autonomous regions, 4 municipalities, special admin. regions of Hong Kong (as of July 1, 1997) and Macau (as of Dec. 20, 1999). **Defense budget:** $150.5 bil. **Active troops:** 2,035,000.

Economy: Industries: mining and ore proc., iron, steel, aluminum, other metals, coal; machine building; armaments; textiles and apparel; petroleum; cement; chemicals; fertilizers; consumer prods.; food proc.; transp. equip.; telecom equip.; comm. space launch vehicles, satellites. **Chief agric.:** rice, wheat, potatoes, corn, tobacco, peanuts, tea, apples, cotton; pork, mutton; fish, shrimp. **Natural resources:** coal, iron ore, petroleum, nat. gas, mercury, tin, tungsten, antimony, manganese, molybdenum, vanadium, magnetite, aluminum, lead, zinc, rare earth elements, uranium. **Water:** 2,018 cu m per capita. **Crude oil reserves:** 25.6 bil bbls. **Electricity prod.:** 5.6 tril kWh. **Labor force:** agric. 17.5%, industry 26.6%, services 55.9%. **Unemployment:** 4.7%.

Finance: Monetary unit: Yuan Renminbi (CNY) (6.84 = $1 U.S.). **GDP:** $23.2 tril; **per capita GDP:** $16,700; **GDP growth:** 6.9%. **Imports:** $1.7 tril; South Korea 9.7%, Japan 9.1%, U.S. 8.5%, Germany 5.3%, Australia 5.1%. **Exports:** $2.2 tril; U.S. 19%, Hong Kong 12.4%, Japan 6%. **Tourism:** $32.6 bil. **Budget:** $3.1 tril. **Inflation:** 1.6%.

Transport: Railways: 77,050 mi. **Motor vehicles:** 156.3 per 1,000 pop. **Airports:** 463.

Communications: Telephone: 13.7 per 100 pop. **Mobile:** 104.6 per 100 pop. **Broadband:** 66.8 per 100 pop. **Internet** (2017): 54.3%.

Health: Expend.: 5.3%. **Life expect.:** 73.7 male; 78.1 female. **Births:** 12.1 per 1,000 pop. **Deaths:** 8 per 1,000 pop. **Infant mortality:** 11.8 per 1,000 live births. **Undernourished:** 8.8%. **HIV:** NA.

Education: Compulsory: ages 6-14. **Literacy:** 96.4%.

Embassy: 3505 International Pl. NW 20008; 495-2000. **Website:** www.gov.cn

Remains of various humanlike creatures who lived as early as several hundred thousand years ago have been found in many parts of China. Neolithic agricultural settlements dotted the Huang (Yellow) R. basin from about 5000 BCE. Their language, religion, and art were the sources of later Chinese civilization.

Bronze metallurgy reached a peak and Chinese pictographic writing, similar to today's, was in use in the more developed culture of the Shang Dynasty (c. 1766 BCE-c. 1045 BCE), which ruled much of North China.

A succession of dynasties and interdynastic warring kingdoms ruled China for the next 3,000 years. They expanded Chinese political and cultural domination to the south and west, and developed a technologically and culturally advanced society that was unaffected by foreign rule (Mongols in the Yuan Dynasty, 1279-1368, and Manchus in the Qing Dynasty, 1644-1912).

Rebellions in the 19th cent. left tens of millions dead. Russia, Japan, Britain, and other powers exercised political and economic control in large parts of the country. China became a republic in 1912, when the Qing emperor Puyi abdicated following the Wuchang Uprising inspired by Dr. Sun Yat-sen, founder of the Kuomintang (Nationalist) party. By 1928, the Kuomintang, led by Chiang Kai-shek, succeeded in nominal reunification of China. About the same time, a bloody purge of Communists from the ranks of the Kuomintang fomented hostilities.

For over 50 years, 1894-1945, China was involved in conflicts with Japan. In 1895, China ceded Korea, Taiwan, and other areas. On Sept. 18, 1931, Japan seized the Northeastern Provinces (Manchuria) and set up a puppet state called Manchukuo. Taking advantage of Chinese dissension, Japan invaded China proper July 7, 1937. On Nov. 20 the retreating Nationalist government moved its capital to Chongqing (Chungking) from Nanjing (Nanking), which Japanese troops then ravaged Dec. 13.

From 1939 the Sino-Japanese War (1937-45) became part of the broader world conflict. After its defeat in World War II, Japan relinquished China. Within China, conflicts involving the Kuomintang, Communists, and other factions resumed. China came under the domination of Communist armies, 1949-50. The Kuomintang government fled to Taiwan, Dec. 8, 1949.

The People's Republic of China was proclaimed in Beijing (Peking) Oct. 1, 1949, under Mao Zedong. China and the USSR signed a 30-year treaty of "friendship, alliance, and mutual assistance," Feb. 15, 1950. The U.S. refused to recognize the new regime. On Nov. 26, 1950, the People's Republic sent armies into Korea against U.S. troops and forced a stalemate in the Korean War.

Frequent drastic changes in policy and violent factionalism 1949-52 interfered with economic development. In 1957, Mao admitted an estimated 800,000 people had been executed 1949-54; opponents claimed much higher figures. The Great Leap Forward, 1958-60, tried to accelerate economic development through intensive labor on huge new rural communes and emphasis on ideological purity. Many resisted, and the program was largely abandoned.

By the 1960s, relations with the USSR deteriorated over disagreements on borders, ideology, and leadership of world Communism. The USSR canceled aid accords. The Great Proletarian Cultural Revolution, 1965, an attempt to instruct a new generation in revolutionary principles, resulted in massive purges. Millions of urban teenagers were relocated to rural areas. By 1968 the movement had run its course; many purged officials returned to office in subsequent years, and several ideological reforms were gradually weakened.

On Oct. 25, 1971, the UN General Assembly ousted the Taiwan government from the UN and seated the People's Republic in its place.

U.S. Pres. Richard Nixon visited China Feb. 21-28, 1972, on invitation from Prem. Zhou Enlai, ending years of antipathy between the two nations. China and the U.S. opened liaison offices in each other's capitals, May-June 1973. The U.S., Dec. 15, 1978, formally recognized the People's Republic of China as the sole legal government of China; diplomatic relations between the two were established, Jan. 1, 1979.

Mao died Sept. 9, 1976. By 1978, Vice Prem. Deng Xiaoping had consolidated power, succeeding Mao as "paramount leader" of China. The new ruling group modified Maoist policies in education, culture, and industry, and sought better ties with non-Communist countries. By the mid-1980s, China had enacted far-reaching economic reforms, deemphasizing centralized planning and incorporating market-oriented incentives.

Some 100,000 students and workers marched in Beijing to demand political reforms, May 4, 1989. As the unrest spread, martial law was imposed, May 20. Troops entered Beijing, June 3-4, and crushed the pro-democracy protests, as tanks and armored personnel carriers rolled through Tiananmen Square. It is estimated that hundreds died and thousands were injured, and hundreds of students and workers were arrested.

Deng Xiaoping died Feb. 19, 1997, leaving Jiang Zemin in control as president. Hong Kong reverted to Chinese sovereignty July 1, 1997. Portugal returned Macau to China Dec. 20, 1999.

Hu Jintao was named Communist Party general secretary at the 16th party congress, Nov. 2002, and elected president by the 10th National People's Congress, Mar. 2003. With the successful launch and recovery, Oct. 15-16, 2003, of the *Shenzhou 5* spacecraft, China became the third nation (after the U.S. and USSR) to send a person into space. In Dec. 2013, China became the third nation to reach the Moon with a spacecraft that made a soft landing.

China's industries, exports, and oil demand have increased rapidly since the 1980s. China became the world's largest producer and consumer of coal. In part to diversify energy production, China completed construction in 2006 of the world's largest hydroelectric dam, the Three Gorges Dam on the Yangtze R. However, the burning of fossil fuels has caused severe air pollution. After negotiations with the U.S., China pledged, Nov. 11, 2014, that its CO_2 emissions would peak and then begin to decline no later than 2030 and that 20% of its energy would come from non-fossil fuel sources by that year. China announced, Sept. 3, 2016, that it had ratified the agreement to limit climate change negotiated in Paris in Dec. 2015.

An earthquake in Sichuan prov. May 12, 2008, left 69,226 dead and 17,923 missing. The Nobel Peace Prize was awarded Oct. 8, 2010, to Liu Xiaobo, an incarcerated human rights activist; Liu died of cancer in government custody, July 13, 2017. Xi Jinping was chosen Communist Party general secretary, Nov. 15, 2012. In March 2013, the National People's Congress (NPC) elected Xi as president of China and Li Keqiang as premier. They were reelected Mar. 2018 by the NPC, which also amended the constitution to eliminate presidential term limits, allowing Xi to remain in power indefinitely.

Western computer security experts Jan.-Feb. 2010 blamed hackers in China for cyberattacks on Google and at least 30 other firms. Hackers in China were suspected in two attacks on U.S. government computer systems in 2015; personal data on tens of millions of people was stolen.

China's rapid economic growth has slowed in recent years. GDP growth was under 8% annually 2012-14 and under 7% yearly 2015-17, compared to double-digit gains for many years since the 1980s. However, by 2014, China's GDP (measured by purchasing power parity) was the largest in the world. After a run-up in prices, shares on China's major stock exchanges fell sharply, 2015-16. To boost the economy, China devalued its currency, lowered interest rates, and increased infrastructure spending.

Since 2010, China has been the world's largest exporter. Since 2013, under the $1-tril Belt and Road Initiative, China has been financing and building infrastructure projects in Asia, Africa, and Eastern Europe.

The U.S. trade in goods deficit with China was $375.6 bil in 2017. The U.S. accused China in 2017 of unfair trade practices. Jan. 2018 U.S. tariffs on imported solar panels affected China, which accounts for more than 60% of global production. The U.S. implemented tariffs on Chinese steel and aluminum Mar. 23, 2018. It imposed tariffs on a total of about $250 bil worth of Chinese products July 6, Aug. 23, and Sept. 24; in each case, China retaliated the same day with tariffs on U.S. goods.

China has occupied the Paracel Isls., in the South China Sea, since 1974. Taiwan and Vietnam also claim the resource-rich islands. The Spratly Isls. are similarly in dispute with Taiwan, Vietnam, Malaysia, and the Philippines. The international Permanent Court of Arbitration in The Hague, July 12, 2016, rejected China's claim to most of the South China Sea as territorial waters and ruled that China's building of artificial islands—in some cases militarized—in disputed areas violated international law. After a two-decade shipbuilding program, China had the world's largest navy by 2017.

Autonomous Regions

Guangxi Zhuang is in SE China, bounded on the N by Guizhou and Hunan provinces, E and S by Guangdong, on the SW by Vietnam, and on the W by Yunnan. It produces rice in the river valleys and has valuable forest products. Pop. (2010): 46,026,629. Capital: Nanning.

Inner Mongolia was organized by the People's Republic in 1947. Its boundaries have undergone frequent changes, reaching its greatest extent in 1956 (and restored in 1979), with an area of 454,600 sq mi, allegedly in order to dilute the minority Mongol population. Chinese settlers outnumber the Mongols more than 10 to 1. Pop. (2010) 24,706,321. Capital: Hohhot.

Ningxia Hui, in N central China, is about 60,000 sq mi. Pop. (2010) 6,301,350. Capital: Yinchuan. The climate is mostly semi-arid, with desert areas in the N. The Huang (Yellow) R. flows across the N, furnishing water for irrigation. Coal is mined in the E. The majority of the population is Han; the Hui (Chinese Muslims) constitute about one-third of the population.

Xinjiang Uighur, in Central Asia, is 635,900 sq mi, pop. (2010) 21,813,334 (75% Uighurs, a Turkic Muslim group, with a heavy Han Chinese increase in recent years). Capital: Urumqi. It is China's richest region in strategic minerals. China has moved to suppress Uighur cultural and religious practices and to crack down on Uighur separatists. A protest march July 5, 2009, by Uighurs in Urumqi led to violent clashes with Han Chinese; at least 197 people (mostly Han) were killed. Unrest and domestic terrorist attacks continued, including truck bombings in Urumqi May 22, 2014, that killed more than 40 people. The government's crackdown included the June 16 execution of 13 people convicted of terrorism-related crimes. Violence in Yarkand July 28 left almost 100 people dead. An apparent separatist attack at a coal mine, Sept. 18, 2015, left about 50 dead. Legislation effective Apr. 1, 2017, placed new restrictions on women wearing face veils in public and prohibited baby names with Muslim religious significance. In Aug. 2018, the UN cited "credible reports" that up to 1 mil Uighurs had been detained in "re-education" camps, which the government legalized in Oct. as "vocational" centers.

Tibet, 471,700 sq mi, is a thinly populated region of high plateaus and massive mountains, the Himalayas on the S, the Kunluns on the N. High passes connect with India and Nepal; roads lead into China proper. Capital: Lhasa. Avg. elevation is 15,000 ft. Jiachan, 15,870 ft, is believed to be the highest inhabited town on Earth. Agriculture is primitive. Pop. (2010) 3,002,166 (of whom about 500,000 are Chinese). Another 4 mil Tibetans form the majority of the population of vast adjacent areas that have long been incorporated into China.

China ruled all of Tibet from the 18th cent. Independence came in 1911, but China reasserted control in 1951, and a Communist government was installed in 1953. Serfdom was abolished, but all land remained collectivized. A Tibetan uprising within China in 1956 spread to Lhasa in 1959. The rebellion was crushed by Chinese troops, and Buddhism was almost totally suppressed. The Dalai Lama and 100,000 Tibetans fled to India. Efforts by Chinese authorities to halt peaceful demonstrations by Tibetan monks led to anti-Chinese riots in Lhasa, Mar. 14, 2008; the Chinese government sent troops into Tibet to crush dissent, sparking international criticism. Protests (including more than 150 self-immolations from 2009 to mid-2018) and government repression of dissent continued in subsequent years.

Hong Kong

Hong Kong (Xianggang), located at the mouth of the Zhu Jiang (Pearl R.) in SE China, 90 mi S of Guangzhou, was a British dependency from 1842 until July 1, 1997, when it became a

Special Administrative Region of China. Its nucleus is Hong Kong Isl., 31 sq mi, occupied by the British in 1841 and formally ceded to them in 1842, on which is located the seat of government. Opposite is Kowloon Peninsula, 3 sq mi, and Stonecutters Isl., added to the territory in 1860. An additional 355 sq mi known as the New Territories, a mainland area and islands, were leased from China, 1898, for 99 years. Area 428 sq mi (total); 414 sq mi (land); pop. (2018 est.) 7,213,338. **Website:** www.gov.hk

Hong Kong is a major trade and banking center. Per capita GDP, $61,400 (2017 est.), is among the highest in the world. Principal industries are textiles and apparel, tourism, banking, shipping, and electronics. A majority of tourists are from mainland China. International tourism receipts in 2017 were $33.2 bil. Outside of the public sector, the labor force is engaged in the following sectors: wholesale and retail trade, restaurants, and hotels 54.5%; community and social services 17.1%; financing, insurance, and real estate 12.5%; transport and communications 10.1%; manufacturing 3.8%; and construction 2.0%.

Hong Kong harbor was long an important British naval station and one of the world's great transshipment ports. The colony often provided refuge for exiles from mainland China. It was occupied by Japan during WWII.

From 1949 to 1962, Hong Kong absorbed more than 1 mil refugees fleeing Communist China. Starting in the 1950s, cheap labor led to a boom in light manufacturing, while liberal tax policies attracted foreign investment. Hong Kong became one of the wealthiest, most productive areas in the Far East. In recent years, manufacturing has been shifting from Hong Kong to mainland China.

With the end of the 99-year lease on the New Territories drawing near, Britain and China signed an agreement, Dec. 19, 1984, under which all of Hong Kong was to be returned to China in 1997; under this agreement Hong Kong was to be allowed to keep its capitalist system for 50 years. Following the transfer of government, Hong Kong retained its currency, the Hong Kong dollar, but without the British monarch's picture; in recent years, a growing portion of financial transactions use the Chinese renminbi. Cantonese, English, and Mandarin are official languages.

A mass march by Hong Kong residents, July 1, 2004, protested Beijing's refusal to allow greater freedom. Leung Chun-ying, with close ties to China, was elected chief executive Mar. 2012 by a committee of about 1,200 members. Large pro-democracy protests took place July-Dec. 2014, opposing Chinese plans to restrict candidate selection for a proposed direct election of the chief executive in 2017; Hong Kong's Legislative Council, June 18, 2015, rejected China's direct-election plan. Six activists from the 2014 protests won seats on the Legislative Council in Sept. 4, 2016, elections; they were subsequently barred from serving. Pro-Beijing candidate Carrie Lam was chosen chief executive by the election committee, Mar. 26, 2017. China's foreign ministry stated, June 30, 2017, that the 1984 agreement with Britain no longer had binding force. By mid-2018, at least 16 pro-democracy activists had received prison sentences in connection with 2016 pre-election protests. A pro-independence political party was banned, Sept. 24, 2018.

Macau

Macau, area of 11 sq mi, is a peninsula and two small islands at the mouth of the Xi (Pearl) R. in China. It was established as a Portuguese trading colony in 1557. In 1849, Portugal claimed sovereignty over the territory; this claim was accepted by China in an 1887 treaty. Portugal granted broad autonomy in 1976. Under a 1987 agreement, Macau reverted to China Dec. 20, 1999. As in the case of Hong Kong, the Chinese government guaranteed Macau it would not interfere in its way of life and capitalist system for a period of 50 years. The tourism industry, including casino gambling, is a mainstay of the economy; two-thirds of tourists are from mainland China. International tourism receipts in 2017 were $35.6 bil. A Chinese government campaign against corruption in the gaming industry caused GDP to decline by almost 25% in 2015-16, before rebounding in 2017. Per capita GDP was $111,600 in 2017. A majority of the labor force is occupied in the following areas: gambling 25.9%, restaurants and hotels 15%, wholesale and retail trade 12.4%. Pop. (2018 est.) 606,340. **Website:** www.gov.mo

Colombia
Republic of Colombia

People: Population: 48,168,996 (30). **Age distrib.:** <15: 23.9%; 65+: 7.7%. **Growth:** 1%. **Migrants:** 0.3%. **Pop. density:** 120.1 per sq mi, 46.4 per sq km. **Urban:** 80.8%. **Ethnic groups:** mestizo and white 84.2%, Afro-Colombian (incl. mulatto, Raizal, Palenquero) 10.4%, Amerindian 3.4%. **Languages:** Spanish (official). **Religions:** Roman Catholic 79%, Protestant 14%.

Geography: Total area: 439,736 sq mi, 1,138,910 sq km (25); **Land area:** 401,044 sq mi, 1,038,700 sq km. **Location:** NW corner of S America. Panama on NW, Ecuador and Peru on S, Brazil and Venezuela on E. **Topography:** Three Andes ranges—Western, Central, and Eastern Cordilleras—run N-S. The eastern range consists mostly of high tablelands. The Magdalena R. rises in the

Andes, flows N to Caribbean through a rich alluvial plain. Sparsely settled plains in E are drained by Orinoco and Amazon systems. **Arable land:** 1.5%. **Capital:** Bogotá, 10,574,409. **Cities:** Medellín, 3,933,652; Cali, 2,725,931; Barranquilla, 2,218,443.

Government: Type: Presidential republic. **Head of state and govt.:** Pres. Iván Duque Marquez; b. 1976; in office: Aug. 7, 2018. **Local divisions:** 32 departments, 1 capital district. **Defense budget:** $10 bil. **Active troops:** 293,200.

Economy: Industries: textiles, food proc., oil, clothing and footwear, beverages, chemicals, cement. **Chief agric.:** coffee, cut flowers, bananas, rice, tobacco, corn, sugarcane, cocoa beans, oilseed, vegetables; shrimp. **Natural resources:** petroleum, nat. gas, coal, iron ore, nickel, gold, copper, emeralds, hydropower. **Water:** 48,933 cu m per capita. **Crude oil reserves:** 1.7 bil bbls. **Electricity prod.:** 67.3 bil kWh. **Labor force:** agric. 16.1%, industry 19.4%, services 64.5%. **Unemployment:** 8.9%.

Finance: Monetary unit: Peso (COP) (3,091.78 = $1 U.S.). **GDP:** $714 bil; **per capita GDP:** $14,500; **GDP growth:** 1.8%. **Imports:** $46.9 bil; U.S. 26.3%, China 19.3%, Mexico 7.5%, Brazil 5%. **Exports:** $34.3 bil; U.S. 28.5%, Panama 8.6%, China 5.1%. **Tourism:** $4.8 bil. **Budget:** $96.3 bil. **Inflation:** 4.3%.

Transport: Railways: 1,330 mi. **Motor vehicles:** 123.7 per 1,000 pop. **Airports:** 121.

Communications: Telephone: 14.2 per 100 pop. **Mobile:** 126.8 per 100 pop. **Broadband:** 45.5 per 100 pop. **Internet** (2017): 62.3%.

Health: Expend.: 6.2%. **Life expect.:** 73.0 male; 79.5 female. **Births:** 15.8 per 1,000 pop. **Deaths:** 5.5 per 1,000 pop. **Infant mortality:** 13.2 per 1,000 live births. **Undernourished:** 6.5%. **HIV:** 0.5%.

Education: Compulsory: ages 5-14. **Literacy:** 94.2%.
Embassy: 1724 Massachusetts Ave. NW 20036; 387-8338.
Website: id.presidencia.gov.co

Spain subdued the local Indian kingdoms (Funza, Tunja) by the 1530s and ruled Colombia and neighboring areas as New Granada for 300 years. Independence was won by 1819. Venezuela and Ecuador broke away in 1829-30, and Panama withdrew in 1903.

In the 20th and early 21st cents., Colombia was plagued by rural and urban violence. "La Violencia" of 1948-58 claimed 200,000 lives. Guerrilla warfare and terrorist attacks by leftist rebels, including the Revolutionary Armed Forces of Colombia (FARC), began in the 1960s. Violence by right-wing paramilitary groups became widespread by the 1980s. Government activity against drug cartels sparked retaliation killings of politicians and judges. The FARC engaged in drug trafficking and kidnappings for ransom to finance its operations. The violence led to an internally displaced population estimated by the UNHCR at 7.7 mil at year-end 2017. Since 1999, the U.S. has paid billions of dollars to reduce farming of coca (used to make cocaine) and combat the drug trade.

Álvaro Uribe Vélez, a hardliner, won a presidential election, May 2002, and launched a new government offensive against the FARC. Uribe easily won reelection, May 2006. Key political figures were arrested in 2007 on charges of colluding with paramilitary death squads. Former Defense Min. Juan Manuel Santos Calderón won a presidential runoff election June 2010; he was reelected June 15, 2014. Peace talks with the FARC began in Oct. 2012. The government signed a peace accord with the FARC, Sept. 26, 2016, providing for FARC disarmament and reintegration into civilian life. In an Oct. 2, 2016, referendum, Colombian voters narrowly rejected the accord, believing it treated FARC members too leniently. A revised agreement, still deemed too lenient by many critics, went into effect Dec. 1, 2016, one day after gaining final congressional approval. On Oct. 7, 2016, Santos won the 2016 Nobel Peace Prize. On June 27, 2017, about 7,000 FARC rebels finished surrendering weapons, but violence by criminal gangs, former FARC members, and other rebels continued. Uribe's Conservative protégé Iván Duque, who pledged to revise the FARC agreement, won a June 17, 2018, presidential runoff election.

From 2015 to Aug. 2018, well over 1 mil Venezuelans, fleeing extreme economic hardship and political repression, entered Colombia; by Aug. 2018, more than 880,000 Venezuelans had been granted temporary legal resident status.

Comoros
Union of the Comoros

People: Population: 821,164 (159). **Age distrib.:** <15: 38.5%; 65+: 4%. **Growth:** 1.6%. **Migrants:** 1.5%. **Pop. density:** 951.6 per sq mi, 367.4 per sq km. **Urban:** 29%. **Ethnic groups:** Antalote, Cafre, Makoa, Oimatsaha, Sakalava. **Languages:** Arabic, French, Shikomoro (Swahili/Arabic blend) (all official). **Religions:** Sunni Muslim 98% (Islam official), other (incl. Shia Muslim) 2%.

Geography: Total area: 863 sq mi, 2,235 sq km (170); **Land area:** 863 sq mi, 2,235 sq km. **Location:** 3 islands—Grande Comore (Njazidja), Anjouan (Nzwani), and Moheli (Mwali)—in the Mozambique Channel between NW Madagascar and SE Africa. Nearest neighbor is Mozambique on W. **Topography:** Of volcanic origin; an active volcano on Grande Comore. **Arable land:** 34.9%. **Capital:** Moroni, 62,351.

Government: Type: Federal presidential republic. **Head of state and govt.:** Pres. Azali Assoumani; b. 1959; in office: May 26, 2016. **Local divisions:** 3 islands, 4 municipalities. **Defense budget/active troops:** NA.

Economy: Industries: fishing, tourism, perfume distillation. **Chief agric.:** vanilla, cloves, ylang-ylang, coconuts, bananas, cassava. **Natural resources:** fish. **Water:** 1,522 cu m per capita. **Electricity prod.:** 54 mil kWh. **Labor force:** agric. 54.9%, industry 15.4%, services 29.8%, Pakistan 16%, France 14.6%, UAE 11.2%, India 6.3%. **Unemployment:** 4.3%.

Finance: Monetary unit: Franc (KMF) (424.62 = $1 U.S.). **GDP:** $1.3 bil; **per capita GDP:** $1,600; **GDP growth:** 2.5%. **Imports:** $194.8 mil; UAE 32.8%, France 17.3%, China 13.2%, Madagascar 6.1%. **Exports:** $18.4 mil; France 36.5%, India 12.2%, Germany 8.2%, Pakistan 6.3%, Switzerland 5.8%. **Tourism** (2015) $40 mil. **Budget:** $183.1 mil. **Inflation** (2012-13): –4.3%.

Transport: Airports: 4.

Communications: Telephone: 2.1 per 100 pop. **Mobile:** 54.9 per 100 pop. **Broadband:** NA. **Internet:** 7.9%.

Health: Expend.: 8%. **Life expect.:** 62.6 male; 67.4 female. **Births:** 25.3 per 1,000 pop. **Deaths:** 7.1 per 1,000 pop. **Infant mortality:** 58.3 per 1,000 live births. **Undernourished:** NA. **HIV:** <0.1%. **Education:** Compulsory: ages 6-11. **Literacy:** 77.8%.

Permanent UN Mission: 866 UN Plz., Ste. 418, New York, NY 10017; (212) 750-1637.

Website: www.gouvernement.km or www.state.gov/p/af/ci/cn/

France acquired the islands from Muslim sultans, 1841-1909. The islands became a French overseas territory in 1947 and were granted internal autonomy in 1961. In a 1974 referendum, all islands favored independence except Mayotte. The French National Assembly decided to allow each island to decide its own fate. The Comorian government declared independence July 6, 1975, with Ahmed Abdallah as its president. In a 1976 referendum, Mayotte voted to remain French.

A leftist regime that seized power from Abdallah in 1975 was deposed in a pro-French 1978 coup in which he regained the presidency. In Nov. 1989, Pres. Abdallah was assassinated; soon after, a multiparty system was instituted. A Sept. 1995 military coup, assisted by French mercenaries, ousted Pres. Said Mohamed Djohar. French troops invaded, Oct. 4, and forced coup leaders to surrender.

Anjouan and Moheli seceded from the Comoros in 1997. Unrest on Grande Comore culminated in a military coup, Apr. 1999. Anjouan endorsed secession in a disputed vote Jan. 2000. A constitution adopted in a referendum Dec. 2001 that went into effect the following year reunited Anjouan and Moheli with Grande Comore, granting each a semi-autonomous status and its own president.

Irregularities marred the Apr. 2002 runoff election for national president, won by Azali Assoumani, who led the 1999 coup. Ahmed Abdallah Mohamed Sambi won a presidential runoff vote, May 2006. Sambi's Vice Pres. Ikililou Dhoinine won a runoff election for national president Dec. 2010. Assoumani was again elected president in an Apr. 10, 2016, runoff.

Congo
Democratic Republic of the Congo

(The Democratic Republic of the Congo [formerly Zaire], now commonly called Congo or DRC, is also known as Congo-Kinshasa. The Republic of the Congo, commonly called Congo Republic, is also known as Congo-Brazzaville.)

People: Population: 85,281,024 (16). **Age distrib.:** <15: 41.3%; 65+: 2.7%. **Growth:** 2.3%. **Migrants:** 1.1%. **Pop. density:** 97.4 per sq mi, 37.6 per sq km. **Urban:** 44.5%. **Ethnic groups:** 200+ groups, majority Bantu. Four largest tribes (Mongo, Luba, Kongo [all Bantu], and Mangbetu-Azande [Hamitic]) 45%. **Languages:** French (official), Lingala (lingua franca trade lang.), Kingwana (Kiswahili or Swahili dialect), Kikongo, Tshiluba. **Religions:** Roman Catholic 50%, Protestant 20%, Kimbanguist 10%, Muslim 10%, other (incl. syncretic sects, indigenous beliefs) 10%.

Geography: Total area: 905,355 sq mi, 2,344,858 sq km (11); **Land area:** 875,312 sq mi, 2,267,048 sq km. **Location:** Central Africa. Congo Republic on W; Central African Republic, South Sudan on N; Uganda, Rwanda, Burundi, Tanzania on E; Zambia, Angola on S. **Topography:** Includes the bulk of the Congo R. basin. Central region is a low-lying plateau covered by rain forest. Mountainous terraces in the W, savannas in the S and SE, grasslands toward the N, and Ruwenzori Mts. on the E. A short strip of territory borders the Atlantic O. **Arable land:** 3.1%. **Capital:** Kinshasa, 13,171,256. **Cities:** Mbuji-Mayi, 2,304,603; Lubumbashi, 2,281,421.

Government: Type: Semi-presidential republic. **Head of state:** Pres. Joseph Kabila; b. 1971; in office: Jan. 26, 2001. **Head of govt.:** Prime Min. Bruno Tshibala; in office: Apr. 7, 2017. **Local divisions:** 26 provinces. **Defense budget:** $586 mil. **Active troops:** 134,250.

Economy: Industries: mining, mineral proc., consumer prods., metal prods., processed foods and beverages, timber, cement. **Chief agric.:** coffee, sugar, palm oil, rubber, tea, cotton, cocoa, quinine, cassava, bananas, plantains, peanuts, root crops, corn, fruits. **Natural resources:** cobalt, copper, niobium, tantalum,

petroleum, diamonds, gold, silver, zinc, manganese, tin, uranium, coal, hydropower, timber. **Water:** 16,605 cu m per capita. **Crude oil reserves:** 180 mil bbls. **Electricity prod.:** 8.9 bil kWh. **Labor force:** agric. 81.9%, industry 11.1%, services 7%. **Unemployment:** 3.7%.

Finance: Monetary unit: Franc (CDF) (1,618.47 = $1 U.S.). **GDP:** $68.5 bil; **per capita GDP:** $800; **GDP growth:** 3.4%. **Imports:** $8.8 bil; China 19.9%, South Africa 18%, Zambia 10.4%, Belgium 9.1%. **Exports:** $8.6 bil; China 41.4%, Zambia 22.7%, South Korea 7.2%, Finland 6.2%. **Tourism:** $4.3 mil. **Budget:** $3.4 bil. **Inflation** (2015-16): 2.9%.

Transport: Railways: 2,490 mi. **Motor vehicles:** 25.4 per 1,000 pop. **Airports:** 26.

Communications: Telephone: 0 per 100 pop. **Mobile:** 43.4 per 100 pop. **Broadband:** 14.2 per 100 pop. **Internet:** 6.2%.

Health: Expend.: 4.3%. **Life expect.:** 56.5 male; 59.7 female. **Births:** 32.8 per 1,000 pop. **Deaths:** 9.4 per 1,000 pop. **Infant mortality:** 66.7 per 1,000 live births. **Undernourished:** NA. **HIV:** 0.7%. **Education:** Compulsory: ages 6-11. **Literacy:** 77%.

Embassy: 1100 Connecticut Ave. NW, Ste. 725, 20036; 234-7690.

Website: www.presidentrdc.cd

The earliest inhabitants of Congo may have been the pygmies, followed by Bantus from the east and Nilotic people from the north. The large Bantu Bakongo kingdom ruled much of Congo and Angola when Portuguese explorers visited in the 15th cent.

Leopold II, king of the Belgians, formed an international group to exploit the Congo region in 1876. In 1877, British explorer Henry M. Stanley traveled the Congo R, and in 1878 he returned to organize the region and win over the indigenous leaders. The Conference of Berlin, 1884-85, established the Congo Free State with Leopold as king and chief owner. The colony became known as the Belgian Congo in 1908 when Leopold sold it to the Belgian government. Millions of Congolese rubber plantation workers were exploited and died under brutal European rule between 1880 and 1920.

Belgian and Congolese leaders agreed Jan. 27, 1960, that Congo would become independent in June. In the first general elections, May 31, Patrice Lumumba's party won a plurality in the National Assembly. The Republic of the Congo was proclaimed June 30. Europeans and others fled widespread violence. The UN Security Council, Aug. 9, called on Belgium to withdraw its troops and sent a UN contingent. Lumumba was dismissed as premier in Sept. and murdered Jan. 17, 1961. The last UN troops left the Congo June 30, 1964.

In late 1965, Gen. Joseph D. Mobutu was named president. He later changed his name to Mobutu Sese Seko and ruled as a dictator. The country became the Democratic Republic of the Congo (1966) and the Republic of Zaire (1971). Under Mobutu, economic decline and government corruption plagued the country.

During 1994, Zaire was inundated with refugees from the massive ethnic bloodshed in Rwanda. Ethnic violence spread to eastern Zaire in 1996. In Oct., militant Hutus, who dominated in the refugee camps, fought rebels (mostly Tutsis) in Zaire, precipitating intervention by government troops. As a result of the fighting, Rwandan refugees abandoned the camps; hundreds of thousands returned to Rwanda, while hundreds of thousands more were dispersed throughout eastern Zaire. The rebels, led by Gen. Laurent Kabila, moved west across Zaire. On May 17, 1997, Kabila's troops entered Kinshasa, and Mobutu went into exile. The country again became the Dem. Rep. of the Congo. Mobutu died Sept. 7 in Morocco.

Kabila, who ruled by decree, alienated UN officials, international aid donors, and former allies. Rebels assisted by Rwanda and Uganda threatened Kinshasa in Aug. 1998 but were turned back with help from Angola, Namibia, and Zimbabwe. Rebel groups agreed to a cease-fire, Aug. 31, 1999, but the truce was widely violated. Kabila was assassinated Jan. 16, 2001, and was succeeded by his son Joseph.

The estimated death toll from the civil war and related causes was 3.3 mil through Nov. 2002. By then, Rwanda and Uganda had agreed to pull out their remaining troops. A power-sharing accord signed Apr. 2, 2003, led to the installation of a new Congolese government in July. Under a new constitution in effect as of Feb. 18, 2006, a UN peacekeeping force (MONUC), established in 1999, oversaw July 2006 elections. Kabila defeated former rebel leader Jean-Pierre Bemba in a presidential runoff election, Oct. 2006.

Hundreds reportedly died in Kinshasa, Mar. 22-23, 2007, in clashes between security forces and a militia loyal to Bemba, who fled to Europe. Held responsible for atrocities committed by his forces in the Central African Rep. in 2002-03, Bemba was convicted of war crimes and crimes against humanity, Mar. 21, 2016, by the Intl. Criminal Court (ICC) at The Hague; the conviction was overturned on appeal, June 8, 2018. The ICC fined Bemba, Sept. 17, 2018, for a separate witness tampering conviction. A peace deal with militia groups in eastern Congo, including one led by Tutsi rebel Gen. Laurent Nkunda, was signed Jan. 23, 2008, but Nkunda launched a new offensive Aug. 28; Rwandan authorities arrested him Jan. 2009.

Kabila was reelected, Nov. 28, 2011. A June 2011 study estimated that more than 1,000 women were raped in Congo every day. The ICC convicted Congolese warlord Thomas Lubanga Dyilo Mar. 2012 of war crimes for conscripting child soldiers during the country's civil war. The ICC, May 23, 2014, sentenced rebel leader Germain Katanga to 12 years in prison in connection with a 2003 massacre of more than 200 villagers.

The MONUC peacekeeping mission, reconstituted and renamed MONUSCO as of July 1, 2010, included almost 16,000 uniformed personnel as of Aug. 31, 2018. Eleven African nations signed a peace plan Feb. 24, 2013, designed to end the vio-lence in Congo. Rebel leader Bosco Ntaganda surrendered in Rwanda Mar. 18, 2013, to face charges of war crimes and crimes against human-ity; his trial at the ICC began Sept. 2, 2015. A peace agreement with the M23 militia group was reached in Dec. 2013. About 8,000 rebels laid down their arms, but other fighters remained active. With Kabila legally required to leave office in Dec. 2016, violent protests erupted in Kinshasa in late 2016 over government delays in scheduling the next presidential election. As protests continued, the government announced, Nov. 5, 2017, that the election would be held Dec. 23, 2018. Kabila said, Aug. 8, 2018, that he would not run. Political and ethnic violence in the Kasai region of central Congo and in eastern Congo continued in 2017-18. About 4.5 mil Congolese were internally displaced as of June 30, 2018, and mil-lions of Congolese faced severe food shortages.

Congo Republic
Republic of the Congo

(Congo Republic, officially Republic of the Congo, is also known as Congo-Brazzaville. The Democratic Republic of the Congo [formerly Zaire], now commonly called Congo or DRC, is also known as Congo-Kinshasa.)

People: Population: 5,062,021 (121). **Age distrib.:** <15: 41.8%; 65+: 3.1%. **Growth:** 2.2%. **Migrants:** 7.6%. **Pop. density:** 38.4 per sq mi, 14.8 per sq km. **Urban:** 66.9%. **Ethnic groups:** Kongo 48%; Sangha 20%; M'Bochi 12%; Teke 17%; European, other 3%. **Languages:** French (official); Lingala, Monokutuba (lingua franca trade langs.); many local langs., dialects (Kikongo most widespread). **Religions:** Roman Catholic 33.1%, Awakening Churches/Christian Revival 22.3%, Protestant 19.9%, none 11.3%.

Geography: Total area: 132,047 sq mi, 342,000 sq km (63); **Land area:** 131,854 sq mi, 341,500 sq km. **Location:** W central Africa. Gabon and Cameroon on W, Central African Republic on N, Dem. Rep. of the Congo on E, Angola on SW. **Topography:** Thick forests across much of country. A coastal plain leads to the fertile Niari Valley. The Congo R. basin consists of flood plains in the lower portion and savanna in the upper. **Arable land:** 1.6%. **Capital:** Brazzaville, 2,229,693. **Cities:** Pointe-Noire, 1,137,609.

Government: Type: Presidential republic. **Head of state:** Pres. Denis Sassou-Nguesso; b. 1943; in office: Oct. 25, 1997. **Head of govt.:** Prime Min. Clement Mouamba; in office: Apr. 23, 2016. **Local divisions:** 12 departments. **Defense budget:** $481 mil. **Active troops:** 10,000.

Economy: Industries: petroleum extraction, cement, lumber, brewing, sugar, palm oil, soap. **Chief agric.:** cassava, sugar, rice, corn, peanuts, vegetables, coffee, cocoa. **Natural resources:** petroleum, timber, potash, lead, zinc, uranium, copper, phos-phates, gold, magnesium, nat. gas, hydropower. **Water:** 180,087 cu m per capita. **Crude oil reserves:** 1.6 bil bbls. **Electricity prod.:** 1.7 bil kWh. **Labor force:** agric. 37.2%, industry 25.9%, services 36.9%. **Unemployment:** 11%.

Finance: Monetary unit: Central African CFA Franc (XAF) (566.17 = $1 U.S.). **GDP:** $28.9 bil; **per capita GDP:** $6,600; **GDP growth:** −4.6%. **Imports:** $3.5 bil; France 15%, China 14%, Belgium 12.2%, Norway 8.1%. **Exports:** $5.2 bil; China 53.8%, Angola 6.2%, Gabon 5.7%, Italy 5.4%, Spain 5.4%. **Tourism** (2015): $46 mil. **Budget:** $3.3 bil. **Inflation** (2014-15): 4.5%.

Transport: Railways: 317 mi. **Motor vehicles:** 17.8 per 1,000 pop. **Airports:** 8.

Communications: Telephone (2016): 0.3 per 100 pop. **Mobile:** 96.1 per 100 pop. **Broadband:** NA. **Internet:** 8.1%.

Health: Expend.: 3.4%. **Life expect.:** 59.0 male; 61.6 female. **Births:** 33.7 per 1,000 pop. **Deaths:** 9.2 per 1,000 pop. **Infant mor-tality:** 53.5 per 1,000 live births. **Undernourished:** 37.5%. **HIV:** 3.1%.

Education: Compulsory: ages 6-15. **Literacy:** 79.3%.

Embassy: 1720 16th St. NW 20009; 726-5500.

Website: www.presidence.cg/president/ or www.ambacongo-us.org

The Loango kingdom flourished in the 15th cent., as did the Anzico kingdom of the Batekes; by the late 17th cent. they had weakened. By 1885, France controlled the region. The Republic of the Congo gained independence Aug. 15, 1960.

After a 1963 coup, the country adopted a Marxist-Leninist stance. However, France remained a dominant trade partner and source of technical assistance, and French-owned private enter-prise retained a major economic role. In 1970, the country was renamed People's Republic of the Congo. Since the 1980s, oil has dominated the economy; hurt by low world oil prices, GDP fell in 2016 and 2017. In June 2018, the country joined OPEC.

In 1990, Marxism was renounced and opposition parties were legalized. In 1991 the country's name was changed back to Rep. of the Congo. A democratically elected government came into office in 1992. Factional fighting broke out in Brazzaville, June 1997. Troops loyal to former Marxist dictator Denis Sassou-Nguesso took con-trol of the city Oct. 15, 1997; he claimed lopsided victories in 2002 and 2009 presidential elections. After 2015 constitutional changes allowed him to run again, Sassou-Nguesso was reelected Mar. 20, 2016; the U.S. and EU criticized the fairness of the election. Vio-lence between government forces and opposition militias erupted in the weeks after voting, and opposition leaders were arrested.

Costa Rica
Republic of Costa Rica

People: Population: 4,987,142 (122). **Age distrib.:** <15: 22.4%; 65+: 8.1%. **Growth:** 1.1%. **Migrants:** 8.4%. **Pop. density:** 253 per sq mi, 97.7 per sq km. **Urban:** 79.3%. **Ethnic groups:** white or mestizo 83.6%, mulato 6.7%, indigenous 2.4%. **Lan-guages:** Spanish (official), English. **Religions:** Roman Catholic 76.3%, Evangelical 13.7%, none 3.2%.

Geography: Total area: 19,730 sq mi, 51,100 sq km (126). **Land area:** 19,714 sq mi, 51,060 sq km. **Location:** Central America. Nicaragua on N, Panama on S. **Topography:** Tropical lowlands by the Caribbean. The interior plateau, at an elevation of about 4,000 ft, is temperate. **Arable land:** 4.5%. **Capital:** San José, 1,357,745.

Government: Type: Presidential republic. **Head of state and govt.:** Pres. Carlos Alvarado Quesada; b. 1980; in office: May 8, 2018. **Local divisions:** 7 provinces. **Defense budget:** $389 mil (paramilitary budget). **Active troops:** No armed forces. 9,800 paramilitary-style police only.

Economy: Industries: medical equip., food proc., textiles and clothing, constr. materials, fertilizer, plastic prods. **Chief agric.:** bananas, pineapples, coffee, melons, ornamental plants, sugar, corn, rice, beans, potatoes; beef, poultry, dairy. **Natural resources:** hydropower. **Water:** 23,502 cu m per capita. **Electric-ity prod.:** 10.7 bil kWh. **Labor force:** agric. 12%, industry 18.6%, services 69.5%. **Unemployment:** 8.1%.

Finance: Monetary unit: Colon (CRC) (566.87 = $1 U.S.). **GDP:** $83.9 bil; **per capita GDP:** $16,900; **GDP growth:** 3.2%. **Imports:** $15.6 bil; U.S. 38.1%, China 13.1%, Mexico 7.3%. **Exports:** $10.6 bil; U.S. 40.9%, Belgium 6.3%, Panama 5.6%, Netherlands 5.6%, Nicaragua 5.1%, Guatemala 5%. **Tourism:** $3.9 bil. **Budget:** $11.3 bil. **Inflation:** 1.6%.

Transport: Railways: 173 mi (some sections rehabilitated after entire network fell into disrepair). **Motor vehicles:** 228.8 per 1,000 pop. **Airports:** 47.

Communications: Telephone: 17.2 per 100 pop. **Mobile:** 180.2 per 100 pop. **Broadband:** 109.5 per 100 pop. **Internet** (2017): 71.6%.

Health: Expend.: 8.1%. **Life expect.:** 76.2 male; 81.7 female. **Births:** 15.3 per 1,000 pop. **Deaths:** 4.8 per 1,000 pop. **Infant mor-tality:** 7.8 per 1,000 live births. **Undernourished:** 4.4%. **HIV:** 0.4%.

Education: Compulsory: ages 4-16. **Literacy:** 97.8%.

Embassy: 2114 S St. NW 20008; 499-2991.

Website: presidencia.go.cr

Guaymi Indians inhabited the area when Spaniards arrived, 1502. Independence came in 1821. Costa Rica seceded from the Central American Federation in 1838. Since the civil war of 1948-49, free political institutions have been preserved.

Costa Rica has achieved a relatively high standard of living. Tourism and agricultural exports are important sources of revenue. Nobel Peace Prize-winner Óscar Arias Sánchez, president 1986-90, won a second term in 2006. A 2010 election victory made ruling party candidate Laura Chinchilla Miranda the nation's first female president. The opposition Citizen Action Party (PAC) won the 2014 presidential election. The PAC's Carlos Alvarado Quesada won an Apr. 1, 2018, runoff. Fleeing political violence and repression, tens of thousands of Nicaraguans entered Costa Rica in 2018.

Côte d'Ivoire
Republic of Côte d'Ivoire

People: Population: 26,260,582 (51). **Age distrib.:** <15: 39.6%; 65+: 2.8%. **Growth:** 2.3%. **Migrants:** 9%. **Pop. density:** 213.9 per sq mi, 82.6 per sq km. **Urban:** 50.8%. **Ethnic groups:** Akan 28.8%, Voltaique or Gur 16.1%, Northern Mande 14.5%, Kru 8.5%, Southern Mande 6.9%, non-Ivoirian 42.3%. **Languages:** French (official), 60 native dialects (Dioula most widely spoken). **Religions:** Muslim 42.9%, Catholic 17.2%, Evangelical 11.8%, animist 3.6%, none 19.1%.

Geography: Total area: 124,504 sq mi, 322,463 sq km (68); **Land area:** 122,782 sq mi, 318,003 sq km. **Location:** S coast of W Africa. Liberia, Guinea on W; Mali, Burkina Faso on N; Ghana on E. **Topography:** Forests cover W half of country. A sparse inland plain leads to low mountains in NW. **Arable land:** 9.1%. **Capital:** Yamoussoukro (official), 231,072; Abidjan (de facto), 4,920,776.

Government: Type: Presidential republic. **Head of state:** Pres. Alassane Ouattara; b. 1942; in office: Apr. 11, 2011 (sworn in Dec. 4, 2010). **Head of govt.:** Prime Min. Amadou Gon Coulibaly; b. 1959; in office: Jan. 11, 2017. **Local divisions:** 12 districts, 2 autonomous districts. **Defense budget:** $829 mil. **Active troops:** 25,400.

Economy: Industries: foodstuffs, beverages, wood prods., oil refining, gold mining, truck and bus assembly, textiles, fertilizer. **Chief agric.:** coffee, cocoa beans, bananas, palm kernels, corn, rice, cassava, sweet potatoes, sugar, cotton, rubber. **Natural resources:** petroleum, nat. gas, diamonds, manganese, iron ore, cobalt, bauxite, copper, gold, nickel, tantalum, silica sand, clay, cocoa beans, coffee, palm oil, hydropower. **Water:** 3,706 cu m per capita. **Crude oil reserves:** 100 mil bbls. **Electricity prod.:** 8.3 bil kWh. **Labor force:** agric. 48.3%, industry 6.4%, services 45.3%., China 14.3%, France 11.3%, The Bahamas 5%. **Unemployment:** 2.6%.

Finance: Monetary unit: CFA Franc (XOF) (566.17 = $1 U.S.). **GDP:** $96.9 bil; **per capita GDP:** $3,900; **GDP growth:** 7.8%. **Imports:** $8.8 bil; Nigeria 15%, France 13.4%, China 11.3%. **Exports:** $11.1 bil; Netherlands 11.8%, U.S. 7.9%, France 6.4%, Belgium 6.4%, Germany 5.8%. **Tourism** (2015): $158 mil. **Budget:** $8.9 bil. **Inflation:** 0.7%.

Transport: Railways: 410 mi. **Motor vehicles:** 26.8 per 1,000 pop. **Airports:** 7.

Communications: Telephone: 1.3 per 100 pop. **Mobile:** 130.7 per 100 pop. **Broadband:** 47.5 per 100 pop. **Internet** (2017): 43.8%.

Health: Expend.: 5.4%. **Life expect.:** 58.0 male; 62.4 female. **Births:** 30.1 per 1,000 pop. **Deaths:** 8.4 per 1,000 pop. **Infant mortality:** 62.6 per 1,000 live births. **Undernourished:** 20.7%. **HIV:** 2.8%.

Education: Compulsory: ages 6-15. **Literacy:** 43.9%.

Embassy: 2424 Massachusetts Ave. NW 20008; 797-0300.

Website: www.gouv.ci

A French protectorate from 1842, Côte d'Ivoire became independent in 1960. The name was officially changed from Ivory Coast, Oct. 1985.

Students and workers protested, Feb. 1990, demanding the ouster of longtime Pres. Félix Houphouët-Boigny. Côte d'Ivoire held its first multiparty presidential election Oct. 1990, which Houphouët-Boigny won. He died Dec. 7, 1993. The National Assembly named as successor Henri Konan Bédié. He was reelected Oct. 1995 but was ousted in a military coup Dec. 24, 1999. The coup leader, Robert Guéi, lost a presidential vote Oct. 2000 but claimed victory anyway. After mass protests, he fled, and Laurent Gbagbo became president. Guéi was killed in Abidjan Sept. 19, 2002.

Agreement on power sharing was reached in Mar. 2003, and Gbagbo and former rebel leaders declared an end to their war July 5. The country remained divided, however. Rebels held the north and government forces controlled the south. Under a new accord reached Mar. 2007, rebel leader Guillaume Soro became prime min.

After apparently losing a presidential runoff election, Nov. 28, 2010, to former Prime Min. Alassane Ouattara, Gbagbo clung to power. A violent power struggle followed, claiming several thousand lives and displacing at least 1 mil people. Ouattara loyalists captured Gbagbo in Abidjan, Apr. 2011. Human Rights Watch reported June 2 that after taking power, Ouattara's troops killed at least 149 suspected Gbagbo supporters. In 2013 and 2014 reports, Amnesty Intl. accused the army and its allies of killing and torturing Gbagbo loyalists. Ouattara won reelection Oct. 25, 2015. Legislative elections were held and a new constitution approved in 2016. A UN peacekeeping mission (UNOCI), authorized in 2004, ended in June 2017.

The ICC, June 12, 2014, ordered Gbagbo to stand trial for crimes against humanity; his trial began Jan. 28, 2016. His wife, Simone Gbagbo, was sentenced, Mar. 10, 2015, by a Côte d'Ivoire court to 20 years in prison for her role in the violence that followed the 2010 election. (She was amnestied and released in Aug. 2018.) In attacks, Mar. 13, 2016, for which al-Qaeda in the Islamic Maghreb claimed responsibility, gunmen killed 19 people and wounded more than 30 at 3 resort hotels in Grand-Bassam.

Croatia
Republic of Croatia

People: Population: 4,270,480 (126). **Age distrib.:** <15: 14.2%; 65+: 19.9%. **Growth:** –0.5%. **Migrants:** 13.4%. **Pop. density:** 197.6 per sq mi, 76.3 per sq km. **Urban:** 56.9%. **Ethnic groups:** Croat 90.4%, Serb 4.4%, other (incl. Bosniak, Hungarian, Slovene, Czech, Romani) 4.4%. **Languages:** Croatian (official), Serbian. **Religions:** Roman Catholic 86.3%, Orthodox 4.4%, not religious or atheist 3.8%.

Geography: Total area: 21,851 sq mi, 56,594 sq km (124); **Land area:** 21,612 sq mi, 55,974 sq km. **Location:** SE Europe, on the Balkan Peninsula. Slovenia, Hungary on N; Bosnia and Herzegovina, Serbia, Montenegro on E. **Topography:** Flat plains in NE; highlands, low mts. along Adriatic. **Arable land:** 15.1%. **Capital:** Zagreb, 685,587.

Government: Type: Parliamentary republic. **Head of state:** Pres. Kolinda Grabar-Kitarovic; b. 1968; in office: Feb. 19, 2015. **Head of govt.:** Prime Min. Andrej Plenkovic; b. 1970; in office: Oct. 19, 2016. **Local divisions:** 20 counties, 1 city with special county status. **Defense budget:** $657 mil. **Active troops:** 15,650.

Economy: Industries: chemicals and plastics, machine tools, fabricated metal, electronics. **Chief agric.:** arable crops (incl. wheat, corn, barley, sugar beets); vegetables, fruits, grapes for wine; cattle, pigs. **Natural resources:** oil, coal, bauxite, iron ore, calcium, gypsum, nat. asphalt, silica, mica, clays, salt, hydropower. **Water:** 24,882 cu m per capita. **Crude oil reserves:** 71 mil bbls. **Electricity prod.:** 10.9 bil kWh. **Labor force:** agric. 7.5%, industry 27%, services 65.4%. **Unemployment:** 11.2%.

Finance: Monetary unit: Kuna (HRK) (6.42 = $1 U.S.). **GDP:** $101.3 bil; **per capita GDP:** $24,400; **GDP growth:** 2.8%. **Imports:** $24.6 bil; Germany 15.7%, Italy 12.9%, Slovenia 10.7%, Hungary 7.5%, Austria 7.5%. **Exports:** $15.8 bil; Italy 13.4%, Germany 12.2%, Slovenia 10.6%, Bosnia and Herzegovina 9.8%, Austria 6.2%. **Tourism:** $10.9 bil. **Budget:** $18.7 bil. **Inflation:** 1.1%.

Transport: Railways: 1,691 mi. **Motor vehicles:** 409.7 per 1,000 pop. **Airports:** 24.

Communications: Telephone: 33.5 per 100 pop. **Mobile:** 103 per 100 pop. **Broadband:** 79.7 per 100 pop. **Internet** (2017): 67.1%.

Health: Expend.: 7.4%. **Life expect.:** 73.2 male; 79.6 female. **Births:** 8.8 per 1,000 pop. **Deaths:** 12.4 per 1,000 pop. **Infant mortality:** 9.1 per 1,000 live births. **Undernourished:** <2.5%. **HIV:** NA.

Education: Compulsory: ages 7-14. **Literacy:** 99.3%.

Embassy: 2343 Massachusetts Ave. NW 20008; 588-5899.

Website: vlada.gov.hr

From the 7th cent. the area was inhabited by Croats, a south Slavic people. It was formed into a kingdom under Tomislav in 924, and joined with Hungary in 1102. The Croats became westernized and separated from Slavs under Austro-Hungarian influence. Croatia united with other Yugoslav areas to proclaim the Kingdom of Serbs, Croats, and Slovenes in 1918. A nominally independent state between 1941 and 1945, it became a constituent republic of Yugoslavia in the 1946 constitution.

On June 25, 1991, Croatia declared independence from Yugoslavia. Fighting began between ethnic Serbs and Croats. The Serbs gained control of some Croatian territory, but Croatian troops recaptured most of it Aug. 1995. A peace accord was signed in Dec. The last Serb-held enclave, E Slavonia, was returned to Croatia in 1998. Croatia became a full NATO member Apr. 1, 2009, and joined the EU July 1, 2013.

A UN tribunal convicted six Croat officers May 29, 2013, for ethnic cleansing of Bosnians during the 1990s; one defendant died after drinking poison in court when his 20-year prison sentence was upheld, Nov. 29, 2017. Kolinda Grabar-Kitarovic of the conservative Croatian Democratic Union (HDZ) party narrowly won a runoff election, Jan. 11, 2015, to become Croatia's first woman president. The HDZ won the most seats in Sept. 11, 2016, parliamentary elections, and party leader Andrej Plenkovic formed a coalition government, Oct. 19, 2016.

Beginning Sept. 2015, tens of thousands of Middle Eastern, Asian, and African refugees and other migrants—most trying to reach N Europe—entered Croatia from Serbia. Croatia announced that as of Mar. 9, 2016, it would block virtually all migrants from transiting through the country.

Cuba
Republic of Cuba

People: Population: 11,116,396 (82). **Age distrib.:** <15: 16.4%; 65+: 15.2%. **Growth:** –0.3%. **Migrants:** 0.1%. **Pop. density:** 262.2 per sq mi, 101.2 per sq km. **Urban:** 77%. **Ethnic groups:** white 64.1%, mulatto or mixed 26.6%, black 9.3%. **Languages:** Spanish (official). **Religions:** Roman Catholic (nominally, prior to 1959 revolution) 85%.

Geography: Total area: 42,803 sq mi, 110,860 sq km (104); **Land area:** 42,402 sq mi, 109,820 sq km. **Location:** In Caribbean, westernmost of West Indies. The Bahamas, U.S. to N; Mexico to W; Jamaica to S; Haiti to E. **Topography:** Coastline is about 2,500 mi. The N coast is steep and rocky, the S coast low and marshy. Low hills and fertile valleys cover more than half the country. Three mountain ranges. **Arable land:** 29%. **Capital:** Havana, 2,136,468.

Government: Type: Communist state. **Head of state and govt.:** Pres. Miguel Díaz-Canel Bermúdez; b. 1960; in office: Apr. 19, 2018. **Local divisions:** 15 provinces, 1 special municipality. **Defense budget:** NA. **Active troops:** 49,000.

Economy: Industries: petroleum, nickel, cobalt, pharmaceuticals, tobacco, constr., steel, cement, agric. machinery, sugar. **Chief agric.:** sugar, tobacco, citrus, coffee, rice, potatoes, beans. **Natural resources:** cobalt, nickel, iron ore, chromium, copper, salt, timber, silica, petroleum. **Water:** 3,347 cu m per capita. **Crude**

oil reserves: 124 mil bbls. **Electricity prod.:** 19.1 bil kWh. **Labor force:** agric. 18.6%, industry 16.5%, services 64.9%. **Unemployment:** 2.5%.

Finance: Monetary unit: Peso (CUP) (26.50 = $1 U.S.). **GDP:** $137 bil; **per capita GDP** (2016): $12,300; **GDP growth:** 1.6%. **Imports:** $10.8 bil; China 22%, Spain 14%, Russia 5%, Brazil 5%, Mexico 4.9%, Italy 4.8%, U.S. 4.5%. **Exports:** $2.9 bil; Venezuela 17.8%, Spain 12.2%, Russia 7.9%, Lebanon 6.1%. **Tourism:** $2.9 bil. **Budget:** $62.1 bil. **Inflation:** 4.8%.

Transport: Railways: 5,199 mi. **Motor vehicles:** 45.9 per 1,000 pop. **Airports:** 64.

Communications: Telephone: 11.7 per 100 pop. **Mobile:** 40.2 per 100 pop. **Broadband:** NA. **Internet:** 43%.

Health: Expend.: 10.9%. **Life expect.:** 76.6 male; 81.4 female. **Births:** 10.6 per 1,000 pop. **Deaths:** 8.9 per 1,000 pop. **Infant mortality:** 4.4 per 1,000 live births. **Undernourished:** <2.5%. **HIV:** 0.4%.

Education: Compulsory: ages 6-14. **Literacy:** 99.8%.

Embassy: 2630 16th St. NW 20009; 797-8518.

Website: www.cubagob.cu

Some 50,000 indigenous people lived in Cuba when Christopher Columbus reached it in 1492. Except for British occupation of Havana, 1762-63, Cuba remained Spanish until 1898. A slave-based sugar plantation economy developed from the 18th cent. Sugar remains a leading agricultural product. Spain failed to deliver on rights guaranteed in 1878, prompting a fullscale liberation movement under Jose Martí in 1895.

The Spanish-American War began Apr. 1898 with the sinking of the USS *Maine* in Havana harbor. Spain lost the war and gave up all claims to Cuba. U.S. troops withdrew in 1902, but under 1903 and 1934 agreements, the U.S. continued to lease a site at Guantánamo Bay in the SE as a naval base. U.S. and other foreign investors dominated the economy. In 1952, former Pres. Fulgencio Batista established a dictatorship, which grew increasingly harsh and corrupt. Fidel Castro began a rebellion in 1956. Batista fled Jan. 1, 1959, and Castro took power, becoming premier Feb. 16.

Government-instituted economic and social changes failed to restore promised liberties. Opponents were imprisoned or executed. Some 700,000 Cubans emigrated in the first years after Castro's takeover, mostly to the U.S. By 1960, all banks and industrial companies had been nationalized, including over $1-bil worth of U.S.-owned properties, mostly without compensation. U.S. economic sanctions became a complete trade embargo under legislation passed by Congress in 1961. The U.S. broke diplomatic relations with Cuba in Jan. 1961.

In Apr. 1961, some 1,400 Cubans, trained and backed by the U.S. Central Intelligence Agency, unsuccessfully tried to overthrow the regime. On Oct. 22, 1962, U.S. Pres. John F. Kennedy ordered a naval blockade around Cuba and demanded that Soviet-installed nuclear missiles be withdrawn. The crisis ended Oct. 28 when Soviet Prem. Nikita S. Khrushchev agreed to withdraw the missiles; the U.S. ended the blockade, pledged not to invade Cuba, and removed its own missiles from Turkey.

In 1978 and 1980, the U.S. agreed to accept political prisoners released by Cuba, some of whom were criminals and mental patients. A 1987 agreement provided for 20,000 Cubans to emigrate to the U.S. each year; Cuba agreed to take back some 2,500 jailed in the U.S. since 1980. Cuba's support for left-wing regimes and liberation movements in Central America, Africa, and the Caribbean contributed to poor relations with the U.S.

Cuba's economy, hobbled by U.S. sanctions and dependent on aid from other Communist countries, was shaken by the collapse of the Communist bloc in the late 1980s. Anti-government demonstrations in Aug. 1994 prompted Castro to loosen emigration restrictions. A new U.S.-Cuba accord in Sept. ended the exodus of "boat people" after more than 30,000 had left Cuba. The U.S. also announced May 1995 it would admit 20,000 Cuban refugees held at Guantánamo but would return additional refugees to Cuba.

On July 31, 2006, the ailing Fidel Castro yielded power to his 75-year-old brother Raúl, who served as acting president until formally succeeding Feb. 24, 2008. (Fidel Castro, age 90, died Nov. 25, 2016.) The U.S. in 2009 eased restrictions on remittances and family travel to Cuba. The Cuban government announced, Sept. 2010, economic restructuring plans involving cutting more than 500,000 public jobs. A Communist Party conference, Apr. 2011, approved an expansion of private property rights and private ownership of some small businesses. Legislation to encourage foreign investment was adopted in Mar. 2014.

The U.S., Jan. 11, 2002, began using its naval base at Guantánamo Bay to detain prisoners captured in Afghanistan. The indefinite detention and aggressive interrogation of prisoners were criticized by human rights groups. U.S. Pres. Barack Obama signed, Jan. 22, 2009, an executive order calling for the closure of the Guantánamo detention center, but 41 detainees were still held there at the end of Obama's presidency, Jan. 20, 2017. Pres. Donald Trump said he opposed closing the detention center, which held 40 following a prisoner transfer to Saudi Arabia, announced May 2, 2018.

Pres. Obama announced, Dec. 17, 2014, that the U.S. would restore full diplomatic relations with Cuba. Following the announcement, some travel and economic restrictions were eased. Relations were formally resumed July 20, 2015. Scheduled U.S. commercial flights to Cuba, suspended since the early 1960s, resumed Aug. 31, 2016. On Jan. 12, 2017, the Obama administration ended the "wet foot, dry foot" policy, which since 1995 had allowed any Cuban migrant reaching U.S. soil to remain in the country legally. In a policy directive signed June 16, 2017, Pres. Trump tightened some travel and economic regulations. The U.S. announced, Sept. 29, the withdrawal of nonessential personnel from its Havana embassy, after about two dozen diplomats and family members developed various medical problems (possibly a result of microwave attacks); on Oct. 3, the U.S. expelled 15 Cuban diplomats.

Hurricane Irma, Sept. 8-9, 2017, caused widespread damage, flooding, and at least 10 deaths.

Elected by the National Assembly, Miguel Díaz-Canel Bermúdez became president Apr. 19, 2018, succeeding Raúl Castro, who remained head of the Communist Party.

Cyprus
Republic of Cyprus

People: Population: 1,237,088 (154). **Age distrib.:** <15: 15.6%; 65+: 12.4%. **Growth:** 1.3%. **Migrants:** 16%. **Pop. density:** 346.7 per sq mi, 133.9 per sq km. **Urban:** 66.8%. **Ethnic groups:** Greek 98.8% (govt.-controlled area only). **Languages:** Greek, Turkish (both official); English; Romanian; Russian; Bulgarian. **Religions:** Orthodox Christian 89.1%, Roman Catholic 2.9%.

Geography: Total area: 3,572 sq mi, 9,251 sq km (164); **Land area:** 3,568 sq mi, 9,241 sq km. **Location:** Eastern Mediterranean Sea, off Turkish coast. Nearest neighbors are Turkey to N, Syria and Lebanon to E. **Topography:** Two mountain ranges run E-W, separated by a wide, fertile plain. **Arable land:** 10.7%. **Capital:** Nicosia (Lefkosia), 269,469.

Government: Type: Presidential democracy. **Head of state and govt.:** Pres. Nicos Anastasiades; b. 1946; in office: Feb. 28, 2013. **Local divisions:** 6 districts. **Defense budget:** $397 mil. **Active troops:** 15,000.

Economy: Industries: tourism, food and beverage proc., cement and gypsum, ship repair and refurb., textiles, light chemicals, metal prods. **Chief agric.:** citrus, vegetables, barley, grapes, olives, vegetables; poultry, pork, lamb. **Natural resources:** copper, pyrites, asbestos, gypsum, timber, salt, marble, clay earth pigment. **Water:** 670 cu m per capita. **Electricity prod.:** 4.3 bil kWh. **Labor force:** agric. 3.5%, industry 17%, services 79.4%. **Unemployment:** 11%.

Finance: Monetary unit: Euro (EUR) (0.86 = $1 U.S.). **GDP:** $31.6 bil; **per capita GDP:** $37,000; **GDP growth:** 3.9%. **Imports:** $7.9 bil; Greece 19%, Italy 7.5%, China 7.4%, South Korea 7.3%, Germany 7%, Netherlands 5.1%, UK 5%. **Exports:** $2.9 bil; Libya 9.4%, Greece 7.7%, Norway 6.7%, UK 5.3%. **Tourism:** $3.1 bil. **Budget:** $7.9 bil. **Inflation:** 0.5%.

Transport: Motor vehicles: 655.7 per 1,000 pop. **Airports:** 13.

Communications: Telephone: 37.3 per 100 pop. **Mobile:** 138.5 per 100 pop. **Broadband:** 97.5 per 100 pop. **Internet** (2017): 80.7%.

Health: Expend.: 6.8%. **Life expect.:** 76.2 male; 81.9 female. **Births:** 11.2 per 1,000 pop. **Deaths:** 6.8 per 1,000 pop. **Infant mortality:** 7.7 per 1,000 live births. **Undernourished:** 4.6%. **HIV:** 0.1%.

Education: Compulsory: ages 5-14. **Literacy:** 99.1%.

Embassy: 2211 R St. NW 20008; 462-5772.

Website: www.cyprus.gov.cy

The Ottoman Empire held Cyprus, 1571-1878, until it yielded control to Britain. Agitation for *enosis* (union) with Greece, which the Turkish minority opposed, increased after WWII and led to violence in 1955-56. In 1959, Britain, Greece, Turkey, and Cypriot leaders approved a plan for an independent republic, with constitutional guarantees for the Turkish minority and permanent division of offices on an ethnic basis.

Archbishop Makarios III was elected president, and full independence became final Aug. 16, 1960. Strife between Greek Cypriot and Turkish Cypriot communities prompted the UN to send a peacekeeping force (UNFICYP) in 1964; about 850 UNFICYP uniformed personnel were in Cyprus as of Aug. 31, 2018.

The Cypriot National Guard, led by officers from the Greek army, seized the government July 15, 1974. On July 20, Turkey invaded the island, and by Aug. 16, Turkish forces had occupied the northeastern 40%. Turkish troops remained in northern Cyprus as of mid-2018.

Turkish Cyprus opened its border with Greek Cyprus Apr. 23, 2003, for the first time since partition. In separate referendums Apr. 2004, 65% of Turkish Cypriot voters accepted a UN-sponsored reunification plan, but 76% of Greek Cypriots rejected it. Still divided, Cyprus became a full member of the EU on May 1, 2004. Greek Cyprus began using the euro as its currency in 2008. In a runoff election Feb. 24, 2013, the conservative candidate and head of the Democratic Rally party, Nicos Anastasiades, was elected president; he was reelected in a runoff, Feb. 4, 2018.

In part because Cypriot banks held large amounts of Greek bonds, Cyprus suffered a banking crisis in 2013. The outline of a Cyprus bailout package was agreed upon Mar. 5, 2013, by the Intl. Monetary Fund, the European Central Bank, and eurozone countries. In exchange for $13 bil in IMF and EU assistance, Cyprus agreed to stringent banking reforms and economic austerity measures. Those with deposits of more than 100,000 euros in Cypriot banks lost some or all the money above that amount to help finance the restructuring of the banking system. Cyprus's GDP shrank 2012-14. GDP growth resumed beginning in 2015.

Turkish Republic of Northern Cyprus

A declaration of independence was announced by Turkish-Cypriot leader Rauf Denktash, Nov. 15, 1983. The state, a semi-presidential democracy, is not internationally recognized but has trade relations with some countries. Political moderate Mustafa Akinci won an Apr. 26, 2015, presidential runoff election. Akinci and Anastasiades met in May, and new UN-sponsored reunification talks began in June 2015. After several rounds of negotiations, the UN announced, July 7, 2017, that talks had failed. Area 1,295 sq mi; pop. (2011 census) 286,257, nearly all Turkish. Capital: Nicosia (Lefkosia). Local divisions: 5 districts. Active troops: 3,500. **Website:** www.kktcb.org

Czechia
Czech Republic

(As of May 17, 2016, the country's official short form name in English was Czechia.)

People: Population: 10,686,269 (85). **Age distrib.:** <15: 15.2%; 65+: 19.4%. **Growth:** 0.1%. **Migrants:** 4.1%. **Pop. density:** 358.3 per sq mi, 138.3 per sq km. **Urban:** 73.8%. **Ethnic groups:** Czech 64.3%, Moravian 5%. **Languages:** Czech (official), Slovak. **Religions:** Roman Catholic 10.4%, none 34.5%.

Geography: Total area: 30,451 sq mi, 78,867 sq km (114); **Land area:** 29,825 sq mi, 77,247 sq km. **Location:** E central Europe. Poland on N, Germany on N and W, Austria on S, Slovakia on E and SE. **Topography:** Bohemia, in W, is a plateau surrounded by mountains; Moravia is hilly. **Arable land:** 40.6%. **Capital:** Prague, 1,291,552.

Government: Type: Parliamentary republic. **Head of state:** Pres. Milos Zeman; b. 1944; in office: Mar. 8, 2013. **Head of govt.:** Prime Min. Andrej Babis; b. 1954; in office: Dec. 13, 2017. **Local divisions:** 13 regions, 1 capital city. **Defense budget:** $2.2 bil. **Active troops:** 23,200.

Economy: Industries: motor vehicles, metallurgy, machinery and equip., glass, armaments. **Chief agric.:** wheat, potatoes, sugar beets, hops, fruit; pigs, poultry. **Natural resources:** coal, kaolin, clay, graphite, timber. **Water:** 1,247 cu m per capita. **Crude oil reserves:** 15 mil bbls. **Electricity prod.:** 77.8 bil kWh. **Labor force:** agric. 2.9%, industry 37.9%, services 59.3%. **Unemployment:** 2.9%.

Finance: Monetary unit: Koruna (CZK) (22.22 = $1 U.S.). **GDP:** $375.7 bil; **per capita GDP:** $35,500; **GDP growth:** 4.3%. **Imports:** $147.4 bil; Germany 29.8%, Poland 9.1%, China 7.4%, Slovakia 5.8%, Netherlands 5.3%. **Exports:** $157.4 bil; Germany 32.8%, Slovakia 7.8%, Poland 6.1%, France 5.1%. **Tourism:** $6.9 bil. **Budget:** $82.8 bil. **Inflation:** 2.5%.

Transport: Railways: 5,979 mi. **Motor vehicles:** 596.7 per 1,000 pop. **Airports:** 41.

Communications: Telephone: 15.2 per 100 pop. **Mobile:** 119 per 100 pop. **Broadband:** 76 per 100 pop. **Internet** (2017): 78.7%.

Health: Expend.: 7.3%. **Life expect.:** 76.0 male; 82.1 female. **Births:** 9.2 per 1,000 pop. **Deaths:** 10.5 per 1,000 pop. **Infant mortality:** 2.6 per 1,000 live births. **Undernourished:** <2.5%. **HIV:** <0.1%. **Education:** Compulsory: ages 6-14. **Literacy:** 99%. **Embassy:** 3900 Spring of Freedom St. NW 20008; 274-9100. **Website:** www.czech.cz

Bohemia and Moravia were part of the Great Moravian Empire in the 9th cent. and later became part of the Holy Roman Empire. Under the kings of Bohemia, Prague in the 14th cent. was the cultural center of Central Europe. Bohemia and Hungary became part of Austria-Hungary.

In 1914-18, Thomas G. Masaryk and Eduard Benes formed a provisional government with the support of Slovak leaders, including Milan Stefanik. They proclaimed the Republic of Czechoslovakia Oct. 28, 1918.

By 1938, Nazi Germany had generated disaffection among German-speaking citizens in Sudetenland and demanded its cession. British Prime Min. Neville Chamberlain signed with Adolf Hitler at Munich, Sept. 30, 1938, an agreement to the cession, with a guarantee of peace by Hitler and Italian dictator Benito Mussolini. Germany occupied Sudetenland Oct. 1-2. Hitler on Mar. 15, 1939, dissolved Czechoslovakia, made protectorates of Bohemia and Moravia, and supported the autonomy of Slovakia, proclaimed independent Mar. 14, 1939.

Soviet troops with some Czechoslovak contingents entered eastern Czechoslovakia in 1944 and reached Prague in May 1945; Benes returned as president. In May 1946 elections, the Communist Party won 38% of the votes. In Feb. 1948, the Communists seized power in advance of scheduled elections. The country was renamed the Czechoslovak Socialist Republic. A harsh Stalinist period followed; all opposition was suppressed.

In Jan. 1968 a liberalization movement spread through Czechoslovakia. Long-time Stalinist ruler Antonin Novotny was deposed; the democrat Slovak Alexander Dubcek succeeded him. In July, the USSR and 4 Warsaw Pact nations demanded an end to liberalization. On Aug. 20, the Soviet, Polish, East German, Hungarian, and Bulgarian armies invaded Czechoslovakia. Despite demonstrations and riots by students and workers, press censorship was imposed and liberal leaders were ousted. On Apr. 17, 1969, Dubcek resigned as Communist Party leader and was succeeded by Gustav Husak. Censorship was tightened, and the Communist Party expelled a third of its members.

More than 700 leading Czechoslovak intellectuals and former party leaders signed a human rights manifesto in 1977, called Charter 77, prompting a renewed crackdown by the regime.

The police crushed a massive protest in Prague, Nov. 17, 1989. As protesters demanded free elections, the Communist Party leadership resigned Nov. 24; millions went on strike Nov. 27.

On Dec. 10, 1989, the first cabinet in 41 years without a Communist majority took power; Vaclav Havel, playwright and human rights campaigner, was chosen president, Dec. 29. In Mar. 1990 the country was officially renamed the Czech and Slovak Federal Republic. A Slovak-led coalition blocked Havel's bid to win reelection July 1992.

Slovakia declared sovereignty, July 17, 1992. Czech and Slovak leaders agreed, July 23, on a plan for a peaceful division of Czechoslovakia. It split into two separate states—the Czech Republic and Slovakia—Jan. 1, 1993. Havel was elected president of the Czech Republic on Jan. 26. The country became a full member of NATO in 1999.

Vaclav Klaus replaced the retiring Havel, 2003. The nation became a full EU member May 1, 2004. Inconclusive parliamentary elections, June 2006, led to a political deadlock, after which a minority center-right government took office Sept. 2006. Center-right parties made a strong showing in May 2010 parliamentary elections. Conservative Milos Zeman, a former Social Democrat prime min., was elected president, Jan. 26, 2013; running on an anti-immigration, anti-EU platform, Zeman narrowly won reelection, Jan. 2018.

Billionaire Andrej Babis became prime minister, Dec. 13, 2017, after his new, anti-immigration party ANO won the most seats in Oct. elections. Amid a corruption scandal, Babis lost a no-confidence vote, Jan. 16, 2018, but was reappointed prime minister by Zeman, June 6, after forming a coalition with the Social Democrats. Babis then reached a controversial agreement with Communist legislators, and his new government survived a confidence vote, July 12.

Denmark
Kingdom of Denmark

People: Population: 5,809,502 (114). **Age distrib.:** <15: 16.6%; 65+: 19.4%. **Growth:** 0.6%. **Migrants:** 11.5%. **Pop. density:** 354.6 per sq mi, 136.9 per sq km. **Urban:** 87.9%. **Ethnic groups:** Danish (incl. Greenlandic [predom. Inuit] and Faroese) 86.7%, Turkish 1.1%, other (incl. Polish, Syrian, German, Iraqi, Romanian) 12.2%. **Languages:** Danish, Faroese, Greenlandic, English (predominant second lang.). **Religions:** Evangelical Lutheran (official) 76%, Muslim 4%.

Geography: Total area: 16,639 sq mi, 43,094 sq km (130); **Land area:** 16,384 sq mi, 42,434 sq km. **Location:** Northern Europe, separating North and Baltic Seas. Germany on S, Norway on NW, Sweden on NE. **Topography:** Consists of the Jutland Peninsula and 392 islands; flat and gently rolling plains. **Arable land:** 56%. **Capital:** Copenhagen, 1,320,826.

Government: Type: Parliamentary constitutional monarchy. **Head of state:** Queen Margrethe II; b. 1940; in office: Jan. 14, 1972. **Head of govt.:** Prime Min. Lars Loekke Rasmussen; b. 1964; in office: June 28, 2015. **Local divisions:** 5 regions. **Defense budget:** $3.8 bil. **Active troops:** 16,100.

Economy: Industries: wind turbines, pharmaceuticals, medical equip., shipbuilding and refurbishment, iron, steel, nonferrous metals, chemicals, food proc., machinery and transp. equip., textiles and clothing, electronics, constr., furniture and other wood prods. **Chief agric.:** barley, wheat, potatoes, sugar beets; pork, dairy prods.; fish. **Natural resources:** petroleum, nat. gas, fish, salt, limestone, chalk, stone, gravel and sand. **Water:** 1,058 cu m per capita. **Crude oil reserves:** 439 mil bbls. **Electricity prod.:** 28.4 bil kWh. **Labor force:** agric. 2.6%, industry 18.8%, services 78.6%. **Unemployment:** 5.7%.

Finance: Monetary unit: Krone (DKK) (6.43 = $1 U.S.). **GDP:** $286.8 bil; **per capita GDP:** $49,900; **GDP growth:** 2.1%. **Imports:** $94.6 bil; Germany 21.3%, Sweden 11.9%, Netherlands 7.8%, China 7.1%, Norway 6.3%. **Exports:** $113.2 bil; Germany 15.5%, Sweden 11.6%, UK 8.2%, U.S. 7.5%, Norway 6%. **Tourism:** $7.4 bil. **Budget:** $175.5 bil. **Inflation:** 1.1%.

Transport: Railways: 2,160 mi. **Motor vehicles:** 531.8 per 1,000 pop. **Airports:** 28.

Communications: Telephone: 25.1 per 100 pop. **Mobile:** 121.7 per 100 pop. **Broadband:** 124.2 per 100 pop. **Internet** (2017): 97.1%.

Health: Expend.: 10.3%. **Life expect.:** 79.1 male; 83.1 female. **Births:** 10.9 per 1,000 pop. **Deaths:** 9.3 per 1,000 pop. **Infant mortality:** 3.2 per 1,000 live births. **Undernourished:** <2.5%. **HIV:** 0.1%.

Education: Compulsory: ages 6-15. **Literacy:** 99%.
Embassy: 3200 Whitehaven St. NW 20008; 234-4300.
Website: denmark.dk

Most of the Viking raiders in the early Middle Ages were Danes. The Danish kingdom was a major power until the 17th cent., when it lost its land in southern Sweden. Norway was separated in 1815, and Schleswig-Holstein in 1864. Northern Schleswig was returned in 1920. Nazi Germany occupied Denmark, Apr. 1940-May 1945, but Danes helped more than 7,200 Jews escape to safety in Sweden, Sept. 1943. Voters ratified the Maastricht Treaty, enabling Denmark to join the EU, in May 1993.

The Danish newspaper *Jyllands-Posten* published, Sept. 30, 2005, cartoon images of the prophet Muhammad, offensive to Muslims; the caricatures, republished elsewhere, triggered violent protests and a boycott of Danish products in Islamic countries.

A left-wing coalition won Sept. 2011 parliamentary elections, and Helle Thorning-Schmidt, a Social Democrat, became Denmark's first female prime min. Oct. 3. A bill granting marriage rights to same-sex couples was voted into law, June 7, 2012. In 2014-15, in part as a result of the Syrian refugee crisis, the number of migrants seeking asylum in Denmark rose sharply—nearly 15,000 in 2014 and more than 21,000 in 2015. A center-right coalition returned to power in June 2015 elections in which the anti-immigration Danish People's Party won 21% of the vote. A 2016 law allowed the government to seize the assets of arriving asylum seekers. Asylum applications fell to 12,700 in 2016 and 3,500 in 2017. May 2018 legislation banned wearing a face-covering garment, such as a burqa or niqab, in public. Other 2018 legislation would essentially require preschool education in "Danish values," beginning at age 1, for children living in largely immigrant "ghetto" areas.

The **Faroe Islands** in the N Atlantic, about 300 mi NW of the Shetlands, and 850 mi from Denmark proper, 18 inhabited, have an area of 538 sq mi and pop. (2018 est.) of 51,018. They are an administrative division of Denmark, self-governing in most matters. Capital: Tórshavn; pop. (2018 est.) 20,817. Fish is a primary export. **Website:** www.government.fo

Kalaallit Nunaat (Greenland)

Greenland, an island between the North Atlantic and the Arctic Oceans, is separated from the North American continent by Davis Strait and Baffin Bay. Total area is 836,330 sq mi, about 81% of which is ice-capped. Most of the island is a lofty plateau 9,000-10,000 ft in elevation. The average thickness of the cap is 1,000 ft. Scientists point to accelerated melting of Greenland's ice sheet in recent years as evidence of global warming. The pop. (2018 est.) was 57,691. About 88% of the pop. in 2010 were Inuit. Under the 1953 Danish constitution the colony became an integral part of the realm with representatives in the Folketing (Danish legislature). The Danish parliament, 1978, approved home rule for Greenland, effective May 1, 1979. With home rule, Greenlandic place names came into official use. The technically correct name for Greenland is Kalaallit Nunaat. The official name for its capital is Nuuk (2018 est. pop., 18,406), rather than Godthab. Voters approved the Self-Government Act in Nov. 2008, replacing the home rule government. Per capita GDP was $41,800 (2015 est.). The labor force is distributed as follows: agric. 15.9%, industry 10.1%, services 73.9%. Fish and fish products account for over 90% of exports. Other natural resources include coal, iron ore, lead, zinc, molybdenum, diamonds, gold, platinum, uranium, and hydropower. **Website:** naalakkersuisut.gl

Djibouti
Republic of Djibouti

People: Population: 884,017 (158). **Age distrib.:** <15: 30.7%; 65+: 3.8%. **Growth:** 2.1%. **Migrants:** 12.1%. **Pop. density:** 98.8 per sq mi, 38.1 per sq km. **Urban:** 77.8%. **Ethnic groups:** Somali 60%, Afar 35%, other (incl. French, Arab, Ethiopian, Italian) 5%. **Languages:** French, Arabic (both official); Somali; Afar. **Religions:** Muslim 94%, Christian 6%.

Geography: Total area: 8,958 sq mi, 23,200 sq km (147); **Land area:** 8,950 sq mi, 23,180 sq km. **Location:** E coast of Africa, separated from Arabian Peninsula by strategically vital strait of Bab el-Mandeb. Eritrea on NW, Ethiopia on W and SW, Somalia on SE. **Topography:** Low coastal plain with mountains behind and an interior plateau. Arid, sandy, and desolate. Hot and dry climate. **Arable land:** 0.1%. **Capital:** Djibouti, 561,564.

Government: Type: Semi-presidential republic. **Head of state:** Pres. Ismail Omar Guelleh; b. 1947; in office: May 8, 1999. **Head of govt.:** Prime Min. Abdoulkader Kamil Mohamed; b. 1951; in office:

Apr. 1, 2013. **Local divisions:** 6 districts. **Defense budget:** NA. **Active troops:** 10,450.

Economy: Industries: constr., agric. proc., shipping. **Chief agric.:** fruits, vegetables; goats, sheep, camels. **Natural resources:** potential geothermal power, gold, clay, granite, limestone, marble, salt, diatomite, gypsum, pumice, petroleum. **Water:** 338 cu m per capita. **Electricity prod.:** 405 mil kWh. **Labor force:** agric. 29.8%, industry 29.7%, services 40.5%. **Unemployment:** 5.8%.

Finance: Monetary unit: Franc (DJF) (177.73 = $1 U.S.). **GDP:** $3.6 bil; **per capita GDP:** $3,600; **GDP growth:** 6.7%. **Imports:** $1.2 bil; UAE 25%, France 15.2%, Saudi Arabia 11%, China 9.6%, Ethiopia 6.8%. **Exports:** $155.5 mil; Ethiopia 38.8%, Somalia 17.1%, Qatar 9.1%, Brazil 8.9%. **Tourism:** $33 mil. **Budget:** $865.4 mil. **Inflation:** 0.6%.

Transport: Railways: 60 mi (Djibouti segment of railway jointly controlled with Ethiopia). **Airports:** 3.

Communications: Telephone: 3.8 per 100 pop. **Mobile:** 39 per 100 pop. **Broadband:** 11.6 per 100 pop. **Internet** (2017): 55.7%.

Health: Expend.: 4.4%. **Life expect.:** 61.4 male; 66.6 female. **Births:** 23.3 per 1,000 pop. **Deaths:** 7.5 per 1,000 pop. **Infant mortality:** 44.3 per 1,000 live births. **Undernourished:** 19.7%. **HIV:** 1.3%.

Education: Compulsory: ages 6-15. **Literacy:** NA.
Embassy: 1156 15th St. NW, Ste. 515, 20005; 331-0270.
Website: www.presidence.dj

France gained control of the territory in stages between 1862 and 1900. As French Somaliland, it became an overseas French territory in 1945; in 1967 it was renamed the French Territory of the Afars and the Issas. Ethiopia and Somalia renounced their claims to the area, but each accused the other of trying to gain control. There were clashes between Afars (ethnically related to Ethiopians) and Issas (related to Somalis) in 1976. Immigrants from both countries continued to enter Djibouti until independence on June 27, 1977.

Post-independence economic support has come from France, Arab countries, the U.S., and China. A peace accord Dec. 1994 ended a 3-year Afar rebel uprising. Protests associated with the Arab Spring broke out in late Jan. 2011 demanding the resignation of Pres. Ismail Omar Guelleh. Authorities suppressed the protests, and Guelleh won a third term in an Apr. 2011 election boycotted by the main opposition. The U.S. announced, May 5, 2014, the signing of a new 20-year lease for its military base in Djibouti, used for anti-terrorism and other military operations in the Middle East and Africa. Guelleh won a fourth term in disputed Apr. 8, 2016, elections. A 460-mi Chinese-built railroad linking Addis Ababa, Ethiopia, with Djibouti City began service Oct. 5, 2016. China opened a naval base in Djibouti, Aug. 1, 2017.

Dominica
Commonwealth of Dominica

People: Population: 74,027 (188). **Age distrib.:** <15: 21.6%; 65+: 11.4%. **Growth:** 0.2%. **Migrants:** 9.2%. **Pop. density:** 255.3 per sq mi, 98.6 per sq km. **Urban:** 70.5%. **Ethnic groups:** black 86.6%, mixed 9.1%, indigenous 2.9%. **Languages:** English (official), French patois. **Religions:** Roman Catholic 61.4%, Protestant 28.6% (incl. Evangelical 6.7%, Seventh-day Adventist 6.1%), none 6.1%.

Geography: Total area: 290 sq mi, 751 sq km (175); **Land area:** 290 sq mi, 751 sq km. **Location:** E Caribbean, most northerly Windward Isl. Guadeloupe to N, Martinique to S (both French terr.). **Topography:** Central ridge runs N-S, terminating in cliffs. Volcanic in origin, with numerous thermal springs. **Arable land:** 8%. **Capital:** Roseau, 14,942.

Government: Type: Parliamentary republic. **Head of state:** Pres. Charles A. Savarin; b. 1943; in office: Oct. 2, 2013. **Head of govt.:** Prime Min. Roosevelt Skerrit; b. 1972; in office: Jan. 8, 2004. **Local divisions:** 10 parishes. **Defense budget/active troops:** NA.

Economy: Industries: soap, coconut oil, tourism, copra, furniture, cement blocks, shoes. **Chief agric.:** bananas, citrus, mangoes, root crops, coconuts, cocoa. **Natural resources:** timber, hydropower. **Water:** 2,752 cu m per capita. **Electricity prod.:** 94 mil kWh. **Labor force:** agric. 40%, industry 32%, services 28%. **Unemployment:** NA.

Finance: Monetary unit: East Caribbean Dollar (XCD) (2.70 = $1 U.S.). **GDP:** $785 mil; **per capita GDP:** $11,100; **GDP growth:** –4.2%. **Imports:** $198 mil; U.S. 61.3%, Trinidad and Tobago 9.8%. **Exports:** $47.4 mil; Saudi Arabia 42.6%, Trinidad and Tobago 9.3%, Jamaica 8.1%, St. Kitts and Nevis 7.1%, Guyana 6.7%. **Tourism:** $132 mil. **Budget:** $148.1 mil. **Inflation:** 0.4%.

Transport: Airports: 2.

Communications: Telephone (2016): 18.1 per 100 pop. **Mobile** (2016): 106.7 per 100 pop. **Broadband:** 41 per 100 pop. **Internet:** 67%.

Health: Expend.: 5.4%. **Life expect.:** 74.4 male; 80.5 female. **Births:** 15 per 1,000 pop. **Deaths:** 7.9 per 1,000 pop. **Infant mortality:** 10.3 per 1,000 live births. **Undernourished:** 5.2%. **HIV:** NA.

Education: Compulsory: ages 5-16. **Literacy:** NA.
Embassy: 3216 New Mexico Ave. NW 20016; 364-6781.
Website: www.dominica.gov.dm

A British colony since 1805, Dominica was granted self-government in 1967. Independence was achieved Nov. 3, 1978.

Hurricane David struck, Aug. 30, 1979, devastating the island and destroying the banana plantations, Dominica's economic mainstay. Coups were attempted in 1980 and 1981. Prime Min. Pierre Charles died Jan. 6, 2004, and was succeeded by Roosevelt Skerrit. Tropical storm Erika, Aug. 27, 2015, killed 30 and caused widespread damage. Hurricane Maria, Sept. 18, 2017, left more than 30 dead and damaged or destroyed over 90% of buildings.

Dominican Republic

People: Population: 10,298,756 (88). **Age distrib.:** <15: 27.6%; 65+: 5.9%. **Growth:** 1%. **Migrants:** 3.9%. **Pop. density:** 552 per sq mi, 213.1 per sq km. **Urban:** 81.1%. **Ethnic groups:** mixed 70.4% (mestizo/indio 58%, mulatto 12.4%), black 15.8%, white 13.5%. **Languages:** Spanish (official). **Religions:** Roman Catholic 95%.

Geography: Total area: 18,792 sq mi, 48,670 sq km (128); **Land area:** 18,656 sq mi, 48,320 sq km. **Location:** W Indies, sharing isl. of Hispaniola with Haiti on W, Puerto Rico (U.S.) to E. **Topography:** The Cordillera Central range crosses center, rising to over 10,000 ft, highest in the Caribbean. Cibao Valley to N. **Arable land:** 16.6%. **Capital:** Santo Domingo, 3,172,152.

Government: Type: Presidential republic. **Head of state and govt.:** Pres. Danilo Medina Sánchez; b. 1951; in office: Aug. 16, 2012. **Local divisions:** 10 regions. **Defense budget:** $496 mil. **Active troops:** 56,050.

Economy: Industries: tourism, sugar proc., gold mining, textiles, cement, tobacco. **Chief agric.:** cocoa, tobacco, sugarcane, coffee, cotton, rice, beans, potatoes, corn, bananas; cattle, pigs. **Natural resources:** nickel, bauxite, gold, silver. **Water:** 2,232 cu m per capita. **Electricity prod.:** 15.6 bil kWh. **Labor force:** agric. 12.4%, industry 17.4%, services 70.2%. **Unemployment:** 5.5%.

Finance: Monetary unit: Peso (DOP) (49.90 = $1 U.S.). **GDP:** $172.4 bil; **per capita GDP:** $16,900; **GDP growth:** 4.6%. **Imports:** $19 bil; U.S. 41.4%, China 13.9%. **Exports:** $10.3 bil; U.S. 50.3%, Haiti 9.1%, Canada 8.2%, India 5.6%. **Tourism:** $7.2 bil. **Budget:** $12.8 bil. **Inflation:** 3.3%.

Transport: Railways: 308 mi. **Motor vehicles:** 169.7 per 1,000 pop. **Airports:** 16.

Communications: Telephone: 12.4 per 100 pop. **Mobile:** 81.4 per 100 pop. **Broadband:** 49.2 per 100 pop. **Internet:** 63.9%.

Health: Expend.: 6.2%. **Life expect.:** 69.7 male; 73.1 female. **Births:** 18.9 per 1,000 pop. **Deaths:** 6.4 per 1,000 pop. **Infant mortality:** 22.7 per 1,000 live births. **Undernourished:** 10.4%. **HIV:** 0.9%.

Education: Compulsory: ages 3-17. **Literacy:** 92%.

Embassy: 1715 22nd St. NW 20008; 332-6280.

Website: www.dominicana.gob.do

Carib and Arawak Indians inhabited the island of Hispaniola when Christopher Columbus landed in 1492. The city of Santo Domingo, founded 1496, is the oldest European settlement in the Western Hemisphere.

France took over the western third of the island (now Haiti) in 1697 and Santo Domingo in 1795. Spain returned intermittently 1803-21, as several native republics came and went. Haiti ruled again, 1822-44; Spanish occupation occurred 1861-63. U.S. Marines occupied the country 1916-24.

In 1930, Gen. Rafael Leonidas Trujillo Molina was elected president. The brutal Trujillo era ended with his assassination in 1961. Pres. Joaquín Balaguer, appointed by Trujillo in 1960, resigned under pressure in 1962.

Juan Bosch, elected president in the first free elections in 38 years, was overthrown in 1963. On Apr. 24, 1965, Bosch's followers and others, including a few Communists, launched a revolt. Four days later U.S. Marines intervened against pro-Bosch forces. A provisional government supervised a June 1966 election in which Balaguer defeated Bosch. Balaguer remained in office for most of the next 28 years, but his May 1994 reelection was widely denounced as fraudulent. He called for new elections but did not run, and Leonel Fernández Reyna was elected June 1996. The leftist candidate, Hipólito Mejía, won a presidential vote in 2000. After a banking scandal and soaring inflation, Fernández defeated Mejía in 2004, and he was reelected in 2008. Danilo Medina Sánchez, Fernández's ally, was elected in 2012 and reelected in 2016.

The Constitutional Court ruled, Sept. 23, 2013, that people born in the Dominican Rep. after 1929 to undocumented immigrant parents were not entitled to Dominican citizenship. The decision affected perhaps 200,000 people or more, most of Haitian descent. May 2014 legislation provided a path to citizenship for such people if they completed an application process by June 17, 2015; most did not. In 2015, the government also required undocumented immigrants—estimated at more than 500,000, most of them Haitian—to register by June 17 or face deportation; about half had not registered by the deadline. By the end of 2017, more than 250,000 Haitians had left the country voluntarily or been deported; there were reports of anti-Haitian vigilante violence. A 2015-16 Zika virus outbreak resulted in about 5,250 confirmed or suspected cases.

Ecuador
Republic of Ecuador

People: Population: 16,498,502 (68). **Age distrib.:** <15: 26.6%; 65+: 7.7%. **Growth:** 1.3%. **Migrants:** 2.4%. **Pop. density:** 154.4 per sq mi, 59.6 per sq km. **Urban:** 63.8%. **Ethnic groups:** mestizo (mixed Amerindian/white) 71.9%, Montubio 7.4%, Amerindian 7%, white 6.1%, Afroecuadorian 4.3%. **Languages:** Spanish (Castilian) (official), Quechua. **Religions:** Roman Catholic 74%, Evangelical 10.4%, atheist 7.9%.

Geography: Total area: 109,484 sq mi, 283,561 sq km (73); **Land area:** 106,889 sq mi, 276,841 sq km. **Location:** NW S America, on Pacific coast, astride the equator. Colombia on N, Peru on E and S. **Topography:** Two Andes ranges run N-S, splitting country into 3 zones: hot, humid lowlands on coast; temperate highlands between ranges; and rainy, tropical lowlands to E. **Arable land:** 4.3%. **Capital:** Quito, 1,822,397. **Cities:** Guayaquil, 2,898,796.

Government: Type: Presidential republic. **Head of state and govt.:** Pres. Lenin Moreno; b. 1953; in office: May 24, 2017. **Local divisions:** 24 provinces. **Defense budget:** $1.6 bil. **Active troops:** 40,250.

Economy: Industries: petroleum, food proc., textiles, wood prods., chemicals. **Chief agric.:** bananas, coffee, cocoa, rice, potatoes, cassava, plantains, sugarcane; cattle, sheep, pigs; fish, shrimp. **Natural resources:** petroleum, fish, timber, hydropower. **Water:** 27,403 cu m per capita. **Crude oil reserves:** 8.3 bil bbls. **Electricity prod.:** 25 bil kWh. **Labor force:** agric. 26.9%, industry 18.5%, services 54.5%. **Unemployment:** 3.8%.

Finance: Monetary unit: U.S. Dollar (USD) (1.00 = $1 U.S.). **GDP:** $192.6 bil; **per capita GDP:** $11,500; **GDP growth:** 2.7%. **Imports:** $19 bil; U.S. 22.8%, China 15.4%, Colombia 8.7%, Panama 6.4%. **Exports:** $19.1 bil; U.S. 31.5%, Vietnam 7.6%, Peru 6.7%, Chile 6.5%. **Tourism:** $1.7 bil. **Budget:** $37.7 bil. **Inflation:** 0.4%.

Transport: Railways: 600 mi. **Motor vehicles:** 111.5 per 1,000 pop. **Airports:** 104.

Communications: Telephone: 14.5 per 100 pop. **Mobile:** 83.5 per 100 pop. **Broadband:** 47.2 per 100 pop. **Internet** (2017): 57.3%.

Health: Expend.: 8.5%. **Life expect.:** 74.2 male; 80.3 female. **Births:** 17.6 per 1,000 pop. **Deaths:** 5.1 per 1,000 pop. **Infant mortality:** 15.9 per 1,000 live births. **Undernourished:** 7.8%. **HIV:** 0.3%.

Education: Compulsory: ages 3-17. **Literacy:** 94.4%.

Embassy: 2535 15th St. NW 20009; 234-7200.

Website: www.presidencia.gob.ec

The region, which was the northern Inca empire, was conquered by Spain in 1533. Liberation forces defeated the Spanish May 24, 1822, near Quito. Ecuador became part of the Great Colombia Republic but seceded, May 13, 1830.

Ecuadoran indigenous peoples, demanding greater rights, staged protests in the 1990s. A border war with Peru flared Jan. 26-Mar. 1, 1995. Elected president, July 1996, Abdalá Bucaram—a populist known as El Loco, or "The Crazy One"—imposed stiff price increases and other austerity measures. His rising unpopularity and erratic behavior led the National Congress, Feb. 1997, to dismiss him for "mental incapacity."

Jamil Mahuad Witt won a presidential runoff election July 1998. In Sept. 1998 and Mar. 1999 he imposed emergency measures to cope with a continuing economic crisis. Opposed by Indian groups and military leaders, he was ousted Jan. 2000, and succeeded by Vice Pres. Gustavo Noboa Bejarano. Noboa enacted a plan introduced by Mahuad to replace the sucre with the U.S. dollar as Ecuador's currency. Lucio Gutiérrez Borbúa, a leader in the 2000 coup, won a presidential runoff Nov. 2002.

Gutiérrez imposed economic austerity measures, purged opponents from the Supreme Court, Dec. 2004, and then dissolved it, Apr. 2005. With street protests, Congress ousted Gutiérrez Apr. 20, and Vice Pres. Alfredo Palacio González became president. In May 2006, Ecuador took over oil assets belonging to U.S.-based Occidental Petroleum.

Rafael Correa, a left-wing economist, won a presidential runoff vote Nov. 2006. A revised constitution was approved in a national referendum Sept. 2008. Early in his term, when oil revenues were high, Correa boosted development spending and aid to poor families; later, as oil prices dropped, he restricted imports to prevent an outflow of dollars and, Dec. 2008, allowed Ecuador to default on part of its $10-bil foreign debt.

Correa, reelected Apr. 2009, pressured foreign oil companies in 2010 to renegotiate contracts to increase the government's share of mineral revenues. A confrontation Sept. 30, 2010, between Correa and rebellious police officers led to a shootout between government troops and police; 5 people were killed and at least 38 wounded. Ecuador granted asylum, Aug. 16, 2012, to Julian Assange, the founder of WikiLeaks. Assange had been in Ecuador's UK embassy in London since June 19, avoiding extradition to Sweden for sexual assault charges. Sweden discontinued, May 19, 2017, its investigation of the last remaining charge against Assange. Still facing arrest for failing to surrender to

British authorities, he remained in the embassy as of Sept. 2018. Ecuador announced, Jan. 11, 2018, that it had granted Assange citizenship.

Correa was reelected Feb. 17, 2013. A 2013 communications law limited press freedom. Beginning in 2013, the government encouraged new exploration for oil and other mineral resources in the Amazon. Lenin Moreno Garces won an Apr. 2, 2017, presidential runoff election. In 2018, hundreds of thousands of Venezuelans fleeing economic hardship and repression entered Ecuador; many continued on to Peru or other nations.

The **Galápagos Islands**, pop. (2008 est.) 30,000, about 600 mi to the W, are the home of giant tortoises and other distinctive animals. The oil tanker *Jessica* ran aground Jan. 16, 2001, off San Cristóbal Isl., spilling some 185,000 gallons of fuel.

Egypt
Arab Republic of Egypt

People: Population: 99,413,317 (14). **Age distrib.:** <15: 33.4%; 65+: 4.3%. **Growth:** 2.4%. **Migrants:** 0.5%. **Pop. density:** 258.7 per sq mi, 99.9 per sq km. **Urban:** 42.7%. **Ethnic groups:** Egyptian 99.6%. **Languages:** Arabic (official), English and French widely understood by educated classes. **Religions:** Muslim (predom. Sunni) 90%, Christian (most Coptic Orthodox) 10%.
Geography: Total area: 386,662 sq mi, 1,001,450 sq km (29); **Land area:** 384,345 sq mi, 995,450 sq km. **Location:** NE corner of Africa. Libya on W; Sudan on S; Israel, Gaza Strip on E. **Topography:** Almost entirely desolate and barren with hills and mountains in E and along Nile. Most people live in 550-mi-long Nile Valley. **Arable land:** 2.9%. **Capital:** Cairo, 20,076,002. **Cities:** Alexandria, 5,086,240.
Government: Type: Presidential republic. **Head of state:** Pres. Abdel Fattah al-Sisi; b. 1954; in office: June 8, 2014. **Head of govt.:** Prime Min. Mostafa Madbouly; in office: June 7, 2018. **Local divisions:** 27 governorates. **Defense budget:** $2.7 bil. **Active troops:** 438,500.
Economy: Industries: textiles, food proc., tourism, chemicals, pharmaceuticals, hydrocarbons, constr., cement, metals, light manufactures. **Chief agric.:** cotton, rice, corn, wheat, beans, fruits, vegetables; cattle, water buffalo, sheep, goats. **Natural resources:** petroleum, nat. gas, iron ore, phosphates, manganese, limestone, gypsum, talc, asbestos, lead, rare earth elements, zinc. **Water:** 637 cu m per capita. **Crude oil reserves:** 4.4 bil bbls. **Electricity prod.:** 171.8 bil kWh. **Labor force:** agric. 24.8%, industry 25.5%, services 49.6%. **Unemployment:** 12.1%.
Finance: Monetary unit: Pound (EGP) (17.91 = $1 U.S.). **GDP:** $1.2 tril; **per capita GDP:** $12,700; **GDP growth:** 4.2%. **Imports:** $53 bil; China 7.9%, UAE 5.2%. **Exports:** $23.5 bil; UAE 10.9%, Italy 10%, U.S. 7.4%, UK 5.7%. **Tourism:** $7.8 bil. **Budget:** $58.6 bil. **Inflation:** 29.5%.
Transport: Railways: 3,160 mi. **Motor vehicles:** 60.1 per 1,000 pop. **Airports:** 72.
Communications: Telephone: 6.8 per 100 pop. **Mobile:** 105.5 per 100 pop. **Broadband:** 52.6 per 100 pop. **Internet** (2017): 45%.
Health: Expend.: 4.2%. **Life expect.:** 71.8 male; 74.7 female. **Births:** 28.8 per 1,000 pop. **Deaths:** 4.5 per 1,000 pop. **Infant mortality:** 18.3 per 1,000 live births. **Undernourished:** 4.8%. **HIV:** <0.1%.
Education: Compulsory: ages 6-17. **Literacy:** 75.8%.
Embassy: 3521 International Ct. NW 20008; 895-5400.
Website: www.egypt.gov.eg

Archaeological records of ancient Egyptian civilization date back to 4000 BCE. A unified kingdom arose around 3200 BCE and extended south into Nubia and as far north as Syria. A high culture of rulers and priests was built on an economic base of serfdom, fertile soil, and annual flooding of the Nile.

Imperial decline facilitated conquest by Asian invaders (Hyksos, Assyrians). The last native dynasty fell in 341 BCE to the Persians, who were in turn replaced by Greeks (Alexander and the Ptolemies), Romans, Byzantines, and Arabs, who introduced Islam and the Arabic language. The ancient Egyptian language is preserved only in Coptic Christian liturgy.

Egypt was ruled as part of larger Islamic empires for many centuries. Britain intervened in Egypt in 1882 and ruled the country as a protectorate, 1914-22. A 1936 treaty strengthened Egyptian autonomy, but Britain retained bases in Egypt and a condominium (joint rule with Egypt) over Sudan. When the state of Israel was proclaimed in 1948, Egypt joined other Arab nations invading Israel and was defeated. In 1951 Egypt abrogated the 1936 treaty; Sudan became independent in 1956.

A July 1952 uprising overthrew King Farouk and established a republic. Lt. Col. Gamal Abdel Nasser rose to power, becoming premier in 1954 and president in 1956. Nasser pushed construction of Egypt's Aswan High Dam, completed in 1970.

After guerrilla raids across its border, Israel invaded Egypt's Sinai Peninsula, Oct. 29, 1956. Egypt rejected a cease-fire demand by Britain and France; on Oct. 31 the two nations dropped bombs and on Nov. 5-6 landed forces. Egypt and Israel accepted a UN cease-fire; fighting ended Nov. 7. Subsequently, a UN Emergency Force guarded the border. Full-scale war with Israel broke out again, June 5, 1967; before it ended under a UN cease-fire June 10, Israel had captured Gaza and the Sinai Peninsula and taken control of the E bank of the Suez Canal.

Nasser died Sept. 28, 1970, and was replaced by Vice Pres. Anwar Sadat. In a surprise attack Oct. 6, 1973, Egyptian forces crossed the Suez Canal into the Sinai. (At the same time, Syrian forces attacked Israelis on the Golan Heights.) Israel counterattacked, crossed the canal, and surrounded Suez City. A UN cease-fire took effect Oct. 24. Under an agreement signed Jan. 1974, Israeli forces withdrew from the canal's W bank; limited numbers of Egyptian forces occupied a strip along the E bank. A second accord was signed in 1975, with Israel yielding Sinai oil fields.

Pres. Sadat's surprise visit to Jerusalem, Nov. 1977, opened the prospect of peace with Israel. On Mar. 26, 1979, Egypt and Israel signed a formal peace treaty, ending 30 years of war and establishing diplomatic relations. On Oct. 6, 1981, Muslim extremists within the army assassinated Pres. Sadat, who was succeeded by Hosni Mubarak. Israel returned control of the Sinai to Egypt in Apr. 1982.

Egyptian security forces battled Islamist violence in the 1990s and early 2000s. On Nov. 17, 1997, near Luxor, Muslim extremists killed 58 foreign tourists and 4 Egyptians. Bombs Oct. 7, 2004, in and near Taba, a Sinai tourist site popular with Israelis, killed at least 35 people. Another 88 people were killed in bombings July 23, 2005, at Sharm el Sheikh, a Red Sea resort city. Suicide bombings at the Sinai resort town of Dahab, Apr. 24, 2006, killed at least 18 people; security forces May 9 killed Nasser Khamis al-Mallahi, leader of the group blamed for the Taba, Sharm el Sheikh, and Dahab attacks.

Following 18 days of mass protests in which at least 846 people died in clashes between Arab Spring dissidents and Mubarak loyalists, Mubarak surrendered power Feb. 11, 2011. A transitional military regime prepared for elections and charged Mubarak and associates with corruption and abuse of power. Mubarak was convicted June 2, 2012, in connection with the 2011 deaths of protesters and sentenced to life in prison. The verdict was overturned on appeal Jan. 13, 2013, and the charges were dismissed Nov. 29, 2014. A judge ordered, June 4, 2015, that Mubarak stand trial again, and he was acquitted, Mar. 2, 2017. Mubarak had been convicted of separate corruption charges, May 21, 2014; after that conviction was overturned, Mubarak was re-tried, convicted May 9, 2015, and sentenced to three years in prison. He was released, Mar. 24, 2017, from the military hospital where he had been held.

Islamist candidate Mohammed Morsi of the Muslim Brotherhood was declared winner of the presidential election, June 2012. Morsi overhauled the military leadership Aug. 12. On Oct. 8, 2012, he pardoned select political prisoners detained during the Arab Spring uprising. At least 110 people were injured in violent clashes between Morsi supporters and opponents Oct. 12, and more conflicts erupted Nov. 23 after Morsi announced an edict interpreted as a power-grab. The proposal of a new Islamist constitution prompted demonstrations throughout Dec.; it passed Dec. 23, 2012.

The military forced Morsi out of office July 3, 2013, and cracked down violently, Aug. 14, on pro-Morsi protesters. More than 600 protesters and at least 40 police officers died in confrontations. The military outlawed the Muslim Brotherhood as a terrorist organization Dec. 25, 2013. Under a new constitution approved in a Jan. 2014 referendum, former Gen. Abdel Fattah al-Sisi, one of the leaders in ousting Morsi, won a May presidential election. Violence between Morsi supporters and security forces continued, causing hundreds of deaths on both sides. Muslim Brotherhood leader Mohamed Badie was sentenced to death June 21, 2014, in connection with July 2013 violence; the sentence was reduced to life in prison Aug. 30, 2014. Morsi was sentenced to 20 years in prison, Apr. 21, 2015, in a trial related to Dec. 2012 street violence. The Sisi government carried out a series of arrests of dissidents and journalists and continually suppressed protests. Sisi won a new term as president in a March 2018 election from which opposition candidates were essentially barred.

Beginning in 2013, Islamist militants battled security forces and seized territory in the northern Sinai. Terrorist attacks occurred at major tourist sites in Luxor and Giza in June 2015. A Russian airliner crashed in the Sinai, Oct. 31, 2015, apparently after a bomb onboard exploded, killing all 224 on board; Sinai Province, an ISIS-affiliated Islamist group, claimed responsibility. Egypt announced, Aug. 4, 2016, that it had killed Sinai Province's leader in an airstrike. A suicide bombing, for which ISIS claimed responsibility, killed about 30 people at a Coptic Christian chapel in Cairo, Dec. 11, 2016. About 75 people were killed in three attacks on Coptic Christians, Apr.-May 2017. More than 40 Egyptian soldiers and police were killed in July 7 and Sept. 11, 2017, attacks by Islamist militants in the Sinai; over 50 police officers died in a gun battle with militants SW of Cairo, Oct. 20. An attack on a Sufi mosque in the northern Sinai, Nov. 24, 2017, killed more than 300 dead. The Egyptian military launched a new offensive, Feb. 2018, against Islamist militants in the Sinai and other areas.

The Suez Canal, 103 mi long, links the Mediterranean and Red Seas. It was built by a French corporation 1859-69, but Britain obtained controlling interest in 1875. On July 26, 1956, Egypt nationalized the canal.

El Salvador
Republic of El Salvador

People: Population: 6,187,271 (108). **Age distrib.:** <15: 25.3%; 65+: 7.7%. **Growth:** 0.3%. **Migrants:** 0.7%. **Pop. density:** 773.4 per sq mi, 298.6 per sq km. **Urban:** 72%. **Ethnic groups:** mestizo 86.3%, white 12.7%. **Languages:** Spanish (official), Nawat. **Religions:** Roman Catholic 50%, Protestant 36%, none 12%.

Geography: Total area: 8,124 sq mi, 21,041 sq km (149); **Land area:** 8,000 sq mi, 20,721 sq km. **Location:** Central America. Guatemala on W, Honduras on N. **Topography:** A hot Pacific coastal plain in S rises to a cooler plateau and valley region, densely populated. The N is mountainous with many volcanoes. **Arable land:** 36.2%. **Capital:** San Salvador, 1,106,698.

Government: Type: Presidential republic. **Head of state and govt.:** Pres. Salvador Sánchez Cerén; b. 1944; in office: June 1, 2014. **Local divisions:** 14 departments. **Defense budget:** $146 mil. **Active troops:** 24,500.

Economy: Industries: food proc., beverages, petroleum, chemicals, fertilizer, textiles, furniture, light metals. **Chief agric.:** coffee, sugar, corn, rice, beans, oilseed, cotton, sorghum; beef, dairy prods. **Natural resources:** hydropower, geothermal power, petroleum. **Water:** 4,288 cu m per capita. **Electricity prod.:** 5.9 bil kWh. **Labor force:** agric. 18.8%, industry 21.2%, services 60%. **Unemployment:** 4.5%.

Finance: Monetary unit: Colon (SVC) (8.75 = $1 U.S.). **GDP:** $57 bil; **per capita GDP:** $8,900; **GDP growth:** 2.4%. **Imports:** $10.6 bil; U.S. 36.7%, Guatemala 10.5%, China 8.7%, Mexico 7.4%, Honduras 6.7%. **Exports:** $5.8 bil; U.S. 45.7%, Honduras 13.9%, Guatemala 13.5%, Nicaragua 6.7%. **Tourism:** $873 mil. **Budget:** $6.8 bil. **Inflation:** 1%.

Transport: Railways: 8 mi. **Motor vehicles:** 46.9 per 1,000 pop. **Airports:** 5.

Communications: Telephone: 10.6 per 100 pop. **Mobile:** 156.5 per 100 pop. **Broadband:** 28.5 per 100 pop. **Internet:** 29%.

Health: Expend.: 6.9%. **Life expect.:** 71.8 male; 78.6 female. **Births:** 16.1 per 1,000 pop. **Deaths:** 5.8 per 1,000 pop. **Infant mortality:** 16.3 per 1,000 live births. **Undernourished:** 10.3%. **HIV:** 0.6%.

Education: Compulsory: ages 4-15. **Literacy:** 88%.

Embassy: 1400 16th St. NW, Ste. 100, 20036; 265-9671.

Website: www.presidencia.gob.sv

El Salvador became independent of Spain in 1821, and of the Central American Federation in 1839.

A military coup overthrew Pres. Carlos Humberto Romero in 1979, but a new military-civilian junta failed to quell a rebellion by leftist insurgents, armed by Cuba and Nicaragua. Right-wing death squads organized to eliminate suspected leftists killed thousands in the 1980s. The Reagan administration supported the government with military aid. After taking the lives of some 75,000 people (with thousands more "disappeared"), the 12-year civil war ended Jan. 16, 1992, as the government and leftist rebels signed a formal peace treaty.

Members of the right-wing ARENA party held the presidency from 1989 to 2009. Mauricio Funes, a leftist, won the 2009 presidential election. His vice pres., Salvador Sánchez Cerén, a former rebel commander, narrowly won the 2014 election.

Beginning in late 2013, thousands of undocumented immigrants from El Salvador were caught trying to enter the U.S. from Mexico; many were families or unaccompanied children fleeing widespread gang violence. On Jan. 8, 2018, the Trump administration announced the end, effective Sept. 2019, of temporary residence status for about 263,000 Salvadorans allowed to live in the U.S. following 2001 earthquakes; a U.S. court order, Oct. 3, 2018, temporarily blocked implementation.

A Zika virus outbreak that began in 2015 caused more than 11,800 confirmed or suspected cases through the end of 2017. Mar. 2017 legislation intended to protect scarce water resources banned all metal mining in El Salvador.

Equatorial Guinea
Republic of Equatorial Guinea

People: Population: 797,457 (160). **Age distrib.:** <15: 39.5%; 65+: 3.9%. **Growth:** 2.4%. **Migrants:** 17.5%. **Pop. density:** 73.6 per sq mi, 28.4 per sq km. **Urban:** 72.1%. **Ethnic groups:** Fang 85.7%, Bubi 6.5%, Mdowe 3.6%. **Languages:** Spanish, French (both official); Fang; Bubi. **Religions:** nominally Christian and predom. Roman Catholic, pagan practices.

Geography: Total area: 10,831 sq mi, 28,051 sq km (142); **Land area:** 10,831 sq mi, 28,051 sq km. **Location:** Bioko Isl. off W Africa coast in Gulf of Guinea. Rio Muni, mainland enclave, has Gabon on S, Cameroon on E and N. **Topography:** Bioko Isl. consists of 2 volcanic mountains and connecting valley. Rio Muni, with over 90% of area, has coastal plain and low hills. **Arable land:** 4.3%. **Capital:** Malabo, 296,770. New administrative capital of Oyala has been in development. **Cities:** Bata, 375,896.

Government: Type: Presidential republic. **Head of state:** Pres. Teodoro Obiang Nguema Mbasogo; b. 1942; in office: Aug. 3, 1979. **Head of govt.:** Prime Min. Francisco Pascual Eyegue Obama

Asue; in office: June 23, 2016. **Local divisions:** 7 provinces. **Defense budget:** NA. **Active troops:** 1,450.

Economy: Industries: petroleum, nat. gas, sawmilling. **Chief agric.:** coffee, cocoa, rice, yams, cassava, bananas, palm oil nuts. **Natural resources:** petroleum, nat. gas, timber, gold, bauxite, diamonds, tantalum, sand and gravel, clay. **Water:** 30,766 cu m per capita. **Crude oil reserves:** 1.1 bil bbls. **Electricity prod.:** 425 mil kWh. **Labor force:** agric. 59.5%, industry 6.4%, services 34.1%. **Unemployment:** 6.9%.

Finance: Monetary unit: Central African CFA Franc (XAF) (566.17 = $1 U.S.). **GDP:** $30.4 bil; **per capita GDP:** $36,000; **GDP growth:** –4.4%. **Imports:** $2.6 bil; Spain 20.5%, China 19.4%, U.S. 13%, Côte d'Ivoire 6.2%. **Exports:** $5.4 bil; China 28%, India 11.8%, South Korea 10.3%, Portugal 8.7%, U.S. 6.9%. **Budget:** $3.4 bil. **Inflation:** 0.7%.

Transport: Airports: 6.

Communications: Telephone (2016): 0.9 per 100 pop. **Mobile** (2016): 47.1 per 100 pop. **Broadband:** 0.1 per 100 pop. **Internet:** 23.8%.

Health: Expend.: 2.7%. **Life expect.:** 63.8 male; 66.2 female. **Births:** 31.7 per 1,000 pop. **Deaths:** 7.6 per 1,000 pop. **Infant mortality:** 63.3 per 1,000 live births. **Undernourished:** NA. **HIV:** 6.5%.

Education: Compulsory: ages 7-12. **Literacy:** 95.3%.

Embassy: 2020 16th St. NW 20009; 518-5700.

Website: www.guineaecuatorialpress.com or www.state.gov/p/af/ci/ek/

Fernando Po (now Bioko) Island was reached by Portugal in the late 15th cent. and ceded to Spain in 1778. Independence came Oct. 12, 1968. Anti-Spanish riots erupted in 1969 in Rio Muni province on the mainland.

Masie Nguema Biyogo, a mainlander, became president for life in 1972. His reign, among the most brutal in Africa, left the nation bankrupt; most of the nation's 7,000 Europeans emigrated. He was ousted in a military coup, Aug. 1979. Teodoro Obiang Nguema Mbasogo, leader of the coup, became president. Presidential elections in 1996, 2002, 2009, and 2016 were seriously flawed.

The economy is heavily dependent on oil exports. There have been allegations of government misuse of oil revenue, and poverty remains widespread. Teodorin Obiang, the president's son, was convicted in absentia in France, Oct. 2017, of embezzling oil revenue.

Human Rights Watch reported in 2012 that the Obiang regime "regularly tortures and arbitrarily detains" suspected dissidents. The seat of government moved, Feb. 2017, from Malabo (on Bioko) to a new capital, Oyala, still under construction on the mainland.

Eritrea
State of Eritrea

People: Population: 5,970,646 (112). **Age distrib.:** <15: 39.5%; 65+: 3.9%. **Growth:** 0.9%. **Migrants:** 0.3%. **Pop. density:** 153.1 per sq mi, 59.1 per sq km. **Urban:** 40.1%. **Ethnic groups:** Tigrinya 55%, Tigre 30%, Saho 4%, Kunama 2%, Rashaida 2%, Bilen 2%, other (Afar, Beni Amir, Nera) 5%. **Languages:** Tigrinya, Arabic, English (all official); Tigre; Kunama; Afar. **Religions:** Muslim, Coptic Christian, Roman Catholic, Protestant.

Geography: Total area: 45,406 sq mi, 117,600 sq km (99); **Land area:** 38,996 sq mi, 101,000 sq km. **Location:** E Africa, on SW coast of Red Sea. Sudan on W, Ethiopia on S, Djibouti on SE. **Topography:** Includes many islands of the Dahlak Archipelago. Low coastal plains in S, mountain range with peaks to 9,000 ft in N. **Arable land:** 6.8%. **Capital:** Asmara, 895,863.

Government: Type: Presidential republic. **Head of state and govt.:** Pres. Isaias Afworki; b. 1946; in office: June 8, 1993. **Local divisions:** 6 regions. **Defense budget:** NA. **Active troops:** 201,750.

Economy: Industries: food proc., beverages, clothing and textiles, light mfg., salt, cement. **Chief agric.:** sorghum, lentils, vegetables, corn, cotton, tobacco, sisal; goats; fish. **Natural resources:** gold, potash, zinc, copper, salt, fish. **Water:** 1,399 cu m per capita. **Electricity prod.:** 383.8 mil kWh. **Labor force:** agric. 83.9%, industry 7.1% and services 9.1%. **Unemployment:** 6.4%.

Finance: Monetary unit: Nakfa (ERN) (15.00 = $1 U.S.). **GDP:** $9.4 bil; **per capita GDP:** $1,600; **GDP growth:** 5%. **Imports:** $1.1 bil; UAE 14.5%, China 13.2%, Saudi Arabia 13.2%, Italy 12.9%, Turkey 5.6%. **Exports:** $635.7 mil; China 62%, South Korea 28.3%. **Tourism:** $48 mil. **Budget:** $2.6 bil. **Inflation:** 9%.

Transport: Railways: 190 mi. **Airports:** 4.

Communications: Telephone (2016): 1.3 per 100 pop. **Mobile** (2016): 10.2 per 100 pop. **Broadband:** NA. **Internet:** 1.2%.

Health: Expend.: 3.3%. **Life expect.:** 63.0 male; 68.2 female. **Births:** 29.1 per 1,000 pop. **Deaths:** 7.1 per 1,000 pop. **Infant mortality:** 44.4 per 1,000 live births. **Undernourished:** NA. **HIV:** 0.6%.

Education: Compulsory: ages 6-13. **Literacy:** 73.8%.

Embassy: 1708 New Hampshire Ave. NW 20009; 319-1991.

Website: www.shabait.com or www.state.gov/p/af/ci/er/

Eritrea was part of the Ethiopian kingdom of Aksum. It was an Italian colony from 1890 to 1941, when it was captured by the British. Following a period of British and UN supervision, Eritrea was awarded to Ethiopia as part of a federation in 1952. Ethiopia annexed Eritrea as a province in 1962. After a 31-year struggle, Eritrea formally declared its independence May 24, 1993. A constitution was ratified in 1997 but not implemented.

A border war with Ethiopia erupted in June 1998. Although a peace treaty was signed Dec. 12, 2000, border disputes and tensions continued. Agreements signed July 9, 2018, ended the "state of war between Ethiopia and Eritrea" and restored diplomatic relations as well as communications, transportation, and commercial links.

Many thousands have fled repressive conditions in Eritrea, including defections by the national soccer team in Kenya, 2009, and Uganda, 2012. Four Eritrean athletes sought asylum in the UK during the 2012 Summer Olympics. A coup attempt against Pres. Isaias Afworki failed, Jan. 21, 2013. A UN report, issued June 8, 2016, concluded that the government was committing widespread human rights violations. Tens of thousands of Eritreans were among migrants reaching or trying to reach Europe, 2014-18. Asmara, known for its early-20th-cent. Italian architecture, was named a UNESCO World Heritage Site, July 8, 2017.

Estonia
Republic of Estonia

People: Population: 1,244,288 (153). **Age distrib.:** <15: 16.3%; 65+: 20.2%. **Growth:** –0.6%. **Migrants:** 14.7%. **Pop. density:** 76 per sq mi, 29.4 per sq km. **Urban:** 68.9%. **Ethnic groups:** Estonian 68.7%, Russian 24.8%. **Languages:** Estonian (official), Russian. **Religions:** Orthodox 16.2%, Lutheran 9.9%, none 54.1%.

Geography: Total area: 17,463 sq mi, 45,228 sq km (129); **Land area:** 16,366 sq mi, 42,388 sq km. **Location:** Eastern Europe, bordering Baltic Sea and Gulf of Finland. Russia on E, Latvia on S. **Topography:** Marshy lowland with numerous lakes and swamps. Elongated hills show evidence of former glaciation. More than 800 islands on Baltic coast. **Arable land:** 15.8%. **Capital:** Tallinn, 437,027.

Government: Type: Parliamentary republic. **Head of state:** Pres. Kersti Kaljulaid; b. 1969; in office: Oct. 10, 2016. **Head of govt.:** Prime Min. Juri Ratas; b. 1978; in office: Nov. 23, 2016. **Local divisions:** 15 counties. **Defense budget:** $543 mil. **Active troops:** 6,600.

Economy: Industries: food, engineering, electronics, wood/wood prods., textiles, information tech., telecom. **Chief agric.:** grain, potatoes, vegetables; livestock, dairy prods.; fish. **Natural resources:** oil shale, peat, rare earth elements, phosphorite, clay, limestone, sand, dolomite, sea mud. **Water:** 9,756 cu m per capita. **Electricity prod.:** 9.9 bil kWh. **Labor force:** agric. 3.9%, industry 29.9%, services 66.2%. **Unemployment:** 5.8%.

Finance: Monetary unit: Euro (EUR) (0.86 = $1 U.S.). **GDP:** $41.6 bil; **per capita GDP:** $31,800; **GDP growth:** 4.9%. **Imports:** $15.3 bil; Finland 14%, Germany 10.7%, Lithuania 8.9%, Sweden 8.5%, Latvia 8.2%, Poland 7.2%, Russia 6.7%, Netherlands 5.9%. **Exports:** $14 bil; Finland 16.2%, Sweden 13.5%, Latvia 9.2%, Russia 7.3%, Germany 6.9%, Lithuania 5.9%. **Tourism:** $1.6 bil. **Budget:** $9.8 bil. **Inflation:** 3.4%.

Transport: Railways: 1,333 mi. **Airports:** 13. **Communications: Telephone:** 27.7 per 100 pop. **Mobile:** 145.4 per 100 pop. **Broadband:** 125 per 100 pop. **Internet** (2017): 88.1%.

Health: Expend.: 6.5%. **Life expect.:** 72.3 male; 82.0 female. **Births:** 9.9 per 1,000 pop. **Deaths:** 12.7 per 1,000 pop. **Infant mortality:** 3.8 per 1,000 live births. **Undernourished:** 2.8%. **HIV:** 0.7%.

Education: Compulsory: ages 7-15. **Literacy:** 99.8%.
Embassy: 2131 Massachusetts Ave. NW 20008; 588-0101.
Website: www.eesti.ee

Estonia, a province of imperial Russia before World War I, was independent between World Wars I and II. The USSR conquered it in 1940 and incorporated it as the Estonian SSR. Estonia, Aug. 20, 1991, declared independence, which the Soviet Union recognized Sept. 1991. The first free elections in over 50 years were held Sept. 20, 1992. The last occupying Russian troops departed Aug. 31, 1994.

Estonia became a full member of the EU and NATO, 2004, and adopted the euro, 2011. The government accused Russia of orchestrating a cyberattack in Apr.-May 2007. After his Reform Party won the most votes in Mar. 1, 2015, elections, Taavi Rõivas formed a coalition government. He lost a no-confidence vote in parliament, Nov. 9, 2016, and was replaced as prime min., Nov. 23, by the Center Party's Juri Ratas. NATO leaders, July 2016, agreed to station troops in Estonia to deter Russian aggression. Parliament elected Kersti Kaljulaid, Oct. 3, 2016, to be Estonia's first woman president.

Eswatini
Kingdom of eSwatini

(King Mswati III announced, Apr. 19, 2018, that he was changing the country's name from Swaziland to "eSwatini" to celebrate the 50th anniversary of its independence.)

People: Population: 1,087,200 (156). **Age distrib.:** <15: 34.4%; 65+: 3.8%. **Growth:** 0.8%. **Migrants:** 2.4%. **Pop. density:** 163.7 per sq mi, 63.2 per sq km. **Urban:** 23.8%. **Ethnic groups:** African 97%, European 3%. **Languages:** English (used in govt.), siSwati (both official). **Religions:** Christian 90% (incl. Zionist—

blend of Christianity/indigenous ancestral worship 40%, Roman Catholic 20%), Muslim 2%.

Geography: Total area: 6,704 sq mi, 17,364 sq km (154); **Land area:** 6,643 sq mi, 17,204 sq km. **Location:** Southern Africa, near Indian O. coast. South Africa on N, W, S; Mozambique on E. **Topography:** Descends W-E in broad belts, becoming more arid in low veld region, then rising to plateau in E. **Arable land:** 10.2%. **Capital:** Mbabane (admin.), 68,010; Lobamba (legis./royal).

Government: Type: Constitutional monarchy. **Head of state:** King Mswati III; b. 1968; in office: Apr. 25, 1986. **Head of govt.:** Prime Min. Barnabas Sibusiso Dlamini; b. 1942; in office: Oct. 23, 2008. **Local divisions:** 4 regions. **Defense budget/active troops:** NA.

Economy: Industries: soft drink concentrates, coal, forestry, sugar proc., textiles, apparel. **Chief agric.:** sugarcane, corn, cotton, citrus, pineapples, cattle, goats. **Natural resources:** asbestos, coal, clay, cassiterite, hydropower, forests, small gold and diamond deposits, quarry stone, talc. **Water:** 3,504 cu m per capita. **Electricity prod.:** 431 mil kWh. **Labor force:** agric. 69.1%, industry 12.4%, services 18.5%. **Unemployment:** 26.4%.

Finance: Monetary unit: Lilangeni (SZL) (15.34 = $1 U.S.). **GDP:** $11.3 bil; **per capita GDP:** $9,900; **GDP growth:** 0.2%. **Imports:** $1.5 bil; South Africa 81.6%, China 5.2%. **Exports:** $1.6 bil; South Africa 94%. **Tourism:** $13 mil. **Budget** $1.5 bil. **Inflation:** 6.2%.

Transport: Railways: 187 mi. **Airports:** 2.
Communications: Telephone (2016): 3.1 per 100 pop. **Mobile** (2016): 74.1 per 100 pop. **Broadband:** NA. **Internet:** 28.6%.

Health: Expend.: 7%. **Life expect.:** 55.1 male; 59.3 female. **Births:** 25.8 per 1,000 pop. **Deaths:** 10.7 per 1,000 pop. **Infant mortality:** 46.6 per 1,000 live births. **Undernourished:** 20.7%. **HIV:** 27.4%.

Education: Compulsory: ages 6-12. **Literacy:** 87.5%.
Embassy: 1712 New Hampshire Ave. NW 20009; 234-5002.
Website: www.gov.sz

The royal house of Eswatini traces back 400 years. The Zulus drove the Swazis, a Bantu people, from lands to the N, 1820. Britain and Transvaal (later part of South Africa) later guaranteed their autonomy, and Britain assumed control after 1903. Independence came Sept. 6, 1968. In 1973, the king repealed the constitution and assumed full powers.

A new constitution banning political parties took effect Oct. 13, 1978. Under a revised constitution effective Feb. 8, 2006, nonpartisan parliamentary elections were permitted. An attempt failed in 2012 to unite pro-democracy groups under the People's United Democratic Movement (PUDEMO), which had been outlawed as a terrorist group in 2008. PUDEMO leader Mario Masuku, arrested on terrorism charges May 1, 2014, was released on bail July 14, 2015.

In recent decades, Eswatini has suffered from an AIDS epidemic. AIDS-related deaths fell sharply due to antiretroviral therapy, but as of 2016, about 27% of people ages 15-49 were HIV positive, still the highest rate in the world.

Ethiopia
Federal Democratic Republic of Ethiopia

People: Population: 108,386,391 (12). **Age distrib.:** <15: 43.2%; 65+: 3%. **Growth:** 2.8%. **Migrants:** 1.2%. **Pop. density:** 280.7 per sq mi, 108.4 per sq km. **Urban:** 20.8%. **Ethnic groups:** Oromo 34.4%, Amhara 27%, Somali 6.2%, Tigray 6.1%, Sidama 4%, Gurage 2.5%, Welaita 2.3%. **Languages:** Oromo (official in one state); Amharic (official nationally); Somali, Tigrigna (both official in one state each); Sidamo; Wolaytta; Gurage. **Religions:** Ethiopian Orthodox 43.5%, Muslim 33.9%, Protestant 18.5%, traditional 2.7%.

Geography: Total area: 426,373 sq mi, 1,104,300 sq km (26); **Land area:** 386,102 sq mi, 1,000,000 sq km. **Location:** E Africa. Sudan, South Sudan on W; Kenya on S; Somalia, Djibouti on E; Eritrea on N. **Topography:** A central plateau, 6,000-10,000 ft high, rises to mountains near the Great Rift Valley, cutting in from SW. Blue Nile and other rivers cross the plateau, which descends to plains on W and SE. **Arable land:** 15.1%. **Capital:** Addis Ababa, 4,399,674.

Government: Type: Federal parliamentary republic. **Head of state:** Pres. Mulatu Teshome Wirtu; in office: Oct. 7, 2013. **Head of govt.:** Prime Min. Abiy Ahmed; b. 1976; in office: Apr. 2, 2018. **Local divisions:** 9 states (ethnically based), 2 self-governing administrations. **Defense budget:** $492 mil. **Active troops:** 138,000.

Economy: Industries: food proc., beverages, textiles, leather, garments, chemicals, metals proc., cement. **Chief agric.:** cereals, coffee, oilseed, cotton, sugarcane, vegetables, khat, cut flowers; hides, cattle, sheep, goats; fish. **Natural resources:** gold, platinum, copper, potash, nat. gas, hydropower. **Water:** 1,227 cu m per capita. **Crude oil reserves:** 428 bbls. **Electricity prod.:** 10.3 bil kWh. **Labor force:** agric. 68.2%, industry 9.4%, services 22.4%. **Unemployment:** 5.2%.

Finance: Monetary unit: Birr (ETB) (27.65 = $1 U.S.). **GDP:** $200.2 bil; **per capita GDP:** $2,200; **GDP growth:** 10.9%. **Imports:** $16.8 bil; China 24.1%, Saudi Arabia 10.1%, India 6.4%, Kuwait 5.3%, France 5.2%. **Exports:** $3.1 bil; Sudan 23.3%, Switzerland 10.2%, China 8.1%, Somalia 6.6%, Netherlands 6.2%. **Tourism:** $434 mil. **Budget:** $14.6 bil. **Inflation:** 9.8%.

Transport: Railways: 409 mi (Ethiopian segment of Addis Ababa-Djibouti railroad). **Motor vehicles:** 1.7 per 1,000 pop. **Airports:** 17.

Communications: Telephone: 1.1 per 100 pop. **Mobile:** 59.7 per 100 pop. **Broadband:** 5.3 per 100 pop. **Internet:** 15.4%.

Health: Expend.: 4%. **Life expect.:** 60.5 male; 65.5 female. **Births:** 36 per 1,000 pop. **Deaths:** 7.5 per 1,000 pop. **Infant mortality:** 48.3 per 1,000 live births. **Undernourished:** 21.4%. **HIV:** 0.9%.

Education: Compulsory: ages 7-14. **Literacy:** 49.1%.

Embassy: 3506 International Dr. NW 20008; 364-1200.

Website: www.ethiopia.gov.et

Ethiopian culture was influenced by Egypt and Greece. Italy invaded the region in 1880, but Ethiopia maintained its independence until the Italian invasion of 1936. British forces freed the country in 1941.

A series of droughts in the 1970s killed hundreds of thousands. An army mutiny, strikes, and student demonstrations led to the 1974 dethronement of Ethiopia's Emperor, Haile Selassie I, ending his 58-year reign; he died a prisoner of the ruling junta, known as the Dergue, 1975. The junta dissolved parliament, abolished the monarchy, established a socialist state, redistributed land, curbed the influence of the Coptic Church, and violently suppressed opposition.

The regime, torn by bloody coups, faced uprisings by tribal and political groups aided in part by Sudan and Somalia. In 1978, Soviet advisers and Cuban troops helped defeat Somali forces. Ethiopia and Somalia signed a peace agreement in 1988. A worldwide relief effort began in 1984, as an extended drought precipitated famine; up to 1 mil people died.

The Ethiopian People's Revolutionary Democratic Front (EPRDF), an umbrella organization of rebel groups, launched a major push against government forces in 1991, prompting Pres. Mengistu Haile Mariam's resignation. The EPRDF set up a transitional government.

Eritrea, a province on the Red Sea, declared its independence May 24, 1993. Fighting along the border with Eritrea, which erupted in 1998, intensified in May 2000, as Ethiopian forces entered Eritrean territory; the war displaced 350,000 Ethiopians. Although a peace treaty was signed Dec. 12, 2000, tensions and border conflicts persisted until a July 9, 2018, accord.

The ruling EPRDF won parliamentary elections May 2005. Tried in absentia, former Pres. Mengistu was convicted of genocide Dec. 12, 2006. Drought and other food supply disruptions occurred 2008-09. The EPRDF dominated 2010 parliamentary elections. When Prime Min. Meles Zenawi died Aug. 2012, the EPRDF's Hailemariam Desalegn became prime min. Ethiopian troops joined an African Union peacekeeping force in Somalia in Jan. 2014. As of Aug. 31, 2018, Ethiopia housed more than 900,000 refugees, the largest numbers being from South Sudan, Somalia, and Eritrea.

The EPRDF won every seat in May 24, 2015, parliamentary elections. Following violent protests by members of the Oromo ethnic group that claimed hundreds of lives, Hailemariam declared a 6-month state of emergency, Oct. 9, 2016, limiting speech, assembly, and due process; Human Rights Watch accused the government of torturing detainees. Successive droughts caused severe food shortages in highland regions, 2015-16, and lowland areas, 2016-17, affecting about 18 mil people. Amid continuing ethnic violence in eastern Ethiopia, more than 1 mil people were internally displaced nationwide at the end of 2017. With anti-government protests continuing, Hailemariam resigned, Feb. 15, 2018. New Prime Min. Abiy Ahmed, the country's first leader from the Oromo ethnic group, pledged economic reforms, reduced censorship, freed political prisoners, and allowed political exiles to return. Continuing ethnic violence in 2018 left scores dead and greatly increased the number of IDPs.

Ethiopia began construction, Apr. 2, 2011, of Africa's largest dam, the Grand Renaissance Dam across the Blue Nile. The dam raised concerns in Egypt and Sudan over loss of water resources.

Fiji
Republic of Fiji

People: Population: 926,276 (157). **Age distrib.:** <15: 27.5%; 65+: 6.8%. **Growth:** 0.6%. **Migrants:** 1.5%. **Pop. density:** 131.3 per sq mi, 50.7 per sq km. **Urban:** 56.2%. **Ethnic groups:** iTaukei (predom. Melanesian with Polynesian admixture; name for original, native settlers of Fiji) 56.8%, Indian 37.5%, other (European, part European, other Pac. Islanders, Chinese) 4.5%. **Languages:** English, Fijian (both official); Hindustani. **Religions:** Protestant 45% (incl. Methodist 34.6%), Hindu 27.9%, Roman Catholic 9.1%, Muslim 6.3%.

Geography: Total area: 7,056 sq mi, 18,274 sq km (152); **Land area:** 7,056 sq mi, 18,274 sq km. Viti Levu, largest island of group, has over half the total land area. **Location:** Western S Pacific O. Nearest neighbors are Vanuatu to W, Tonga to E. **Topography:** 322 isls. (about 110 inhabited), many mountainous, with tropical forests and large fertile areas. **Arable land:** 9%. **Capital:** Suva, 178,339.

Government: Type: Parliamentary republic. **Head of state:** Pres. George Konrote; b. 1947; in office: Nov. 12, 2015. **Head of govt.:** Prime Min. Voreqe "Frank" Bainimarama; b. 1954; in office: Sept. 22, 2014 (acting from Jan. 5, 2007). **Local divisions:** 14 provinces, 1 dependency. **Defense budget:** $51 mil. **Active troops:** 3,500.

Economy: Industries: tourism, sugar proc., clothing, copra. **Chief agric.:** sugarcane, coconuts, cassava, rice, sweet potatoes, bananas; cattle, pigs, horses; fish. **Natural resources:** timber, fish, gold, copper, hydropower. **Water:** 32,003 cu m per capita. **Electricity prod.:** 892 mil kWh. **Labor force:** agric. 39.5%, industry 13.3%, services 47.2%, South Korea 15.7%, New Zealand 14.2%, Australia 13.4%, Singapore 8.7%, France 7%. **Unemployment:** 6.3%.

Finance: Monetary unit: Dollar (FJD) (2.13 = $1 U.S.) **GDP:** $8.7 bil; **per capita GDP:** $9,800; **GDP growth:** 3.8%. **Imports:** $1.9 bil; Australia 19.2%, New Zealand 17.2%, Singapore 17%, China 13.8%. **Exports:** $758.6 mil; U.S. 20.8%, Australia 14.9%, New Zealand 7.7%, Tonga 5%. **Tourism:** $885 mil. **Budget:** $1.7 bil. **Inflation:** 3.4%.

Transport: Railways: 371 mi. **Motor vehicles:** 204.6 per 1,000 pop. **Airports:** 4.

Communications: Telephone: 8.4 per 100 pop. **Mobile:** 114.2 per 100 pop. **Broadband:** 54.3 per 100 pop. **Internet:** 46.5%.

Health: Expend.: 3.6%. **Life expect.:** 70.5 male; 76.0 female. **Births:** 18.2 per 1,000 pop. **Deaths:** 6.2 per 1,000 pop. **Infant mortality:** 9.3 per 1,000 live births. **Undernourished:** 4.4%. **HIV:** NA.

Education: Compulsory: NA. **Literacy:** NA.

Embassy: 1707 L St. NW, Ste. 200, 20036; 466-8320.

Website: www.fiji.gov.fj

A British colony since 1874, Fiji became independent Oct. 10, 1970. Cultural differences between the Indian community (mostly descendants of contract laborers brought to the islands in the 19th cent.) and indigenous Fijians have led to political tensions. More than 100,000 Indians left Fiji after a 1987 coup deposed an Indian-majority government.

Fiji's first Indian prime minister, Mahendra Chaudhry, and other government officials were taken captive May 19, 2000, by indigenous Fijian gunmen led by George Speight, culminating in a military takeover, May 29, led by Frank Bainimarama. Release of the last remaining hostages in July 2000 coincided with the installation of an interim military-backed government. Speight was convicted of treason and sentenced to life in prison in 2002. Prime Min. Laisenia Qarase headed an elected civilian government, 2001-06, but was ousted in a military coup Dec. 5, 2006. Bainimarama took office as interim prime min. After a court ruled in 2009 that the 2006 coup was illegal, Pres. Ratu Josefa Iloilo abrogated the constitution, dissolved the judiciary, and reappointed Interim Prime Min. Bainimarama. In July, Bainimarama promised a new constitution and legislative elections. He accepted a draft constitution released Mar. 22, 2013, and he retained office in democratic elections Sept. 17, 2014. The Commonwealth, Sept. 26, 2014, reinstated Fiji's membership, which had been suspended since the 2006 coup; U.S. sanctions were lifted Oct. 2014. A Dec. 2016 Amnesty Intl. report said physical and sexual abuse of detainees by Fiji's police and military was widespread.

Finland
Republic of Finland

People: Population: 5,537,364 (116). **Age distrib.:** <15: 16.4%; 65+: 21.5%. **Growth:** 0.3%. **Migrants:** 6.2%. **Pop. density:** 47.2 per sq mi, 18.2 per sq km. **Urban:** 85.4%. **Ethnic groups:** Finn 93.4%, Swede 5.6%. **Languages:** Finnish, Swedish (both official). **Religions:** Lutheran 70.9%.

Geography: Total area: 130,559 sq mi, 338,145 sq km (64); **Land area:** 117,304 sq mi, 303,815 sq km. **Location:** Northern Europe. Norway on N, Sweden on W, Russia on E. **Topography:** Flat with low hills and many lakes in S and center. The N has mountainous areas 3,000-4,000 ft above sea level. **Arable land:** 7.4%. **Capital:** Helsinki, 1,279,096.

Government: Type: Parliamentary republic. **Head of state:** Pres. Sauli Niinistö; b. 1948; in office: Mar. 1, 2012. **Head of govt.:** Prime Min. Juha Sipilä; b. 1961; in office: May 29, 2015. **Local divisions:** 19 regions. **Defense budget:** $3.2 bil. **Active troops:** 21,500.

Economy: Industries: metals and metal prods., electronics, machinery and scientific instruments, shipbuilding, pulp and paper, foodstuffs, chemicals, textiles, clothing. **Chief agric.:** barley, wheat, sugar beets, potatoes; dairy cattle; fish. **Natural resources:** timber, iron ore, copper, lead, zinc, chromite, nickel, gold, silver, limestone. **Water:** 19,989 cu m per capita. **Electricity prod.:** 66.4 bil kWh. **Labor force:** agric. 3.9%, industry 22.3%, services 73.8%. **Unemployment:** 8.6%.

Finance: Monetary unit: Euro (EUR) (0.86 = $1 U.S.). **GDP:** $244 bil; **per capita GDP:** $44,300; **GDP growth:** 3%. **Imports:** $62.1 bil; Germany 17.7%, Sweden 15.8%, Russia 13.1%, Netherlands 8.7%. **Exports:** $59.6 bil; Germany 14.2%, Sweden 10.1%, U.S. 7%, Netherlands 6.8%, China 5.7%, Russia 5.7%. **Tourism:** $3 bil. **Budget:** $63.2 bil (central govt.). **Inflation:** 0.8%.

Transport: Railways: 3,682 mi. **Motor vehicles:** 619.1 per 1,000 pop. **Airports:** 74.

Communications: Telephone: 6.8 per 100 pop. **Mobile:** 132.3 per 100 pop. **Broadband:** 153 per 100 pop. **Internet** (2017): 87.5%.

Health: Expend.: 9.4%. **Life expect.:** 78.1 male; 84.2 female. **Births:** 10.7 per 1,000 pop. **Deaths:** 10.1 per 1,000 pop. **Infant mortality:** 2.5 per 1,000 live births. **Undernourished:** <2.5%. **HIV:** NA.

Education: Compulsory: ages 6-15. **Literacy:** 100%.

Embassy: 3301 Massachusetts Ave. NW 20008; 298-5800.

Website: valtioneuvosto.fi

Early Finns may have migrated from the Ural region and other areas about 6,000 years ago. Swedish settlers brought the country into Sweden, 1154 to 1809, when Finland became an autonomous grand duchy of the Russian Empire. On Dec. 6, 1917, Finland declared its independence, and in 1919 it became a republic. On Nov. 30, 1939, the Soviet Union invaded, and Finland was forced to cede 16,173 sq mi of territory. After World War II, further cessions were exacted. In 1948, Finland signed a treaty of mutual assistance with the USSR that was renegotiated as a cooperation agreement with Russia, effective July 11, 1992.

Finland entered the EU Jan. 1, 1995. Juha Sipilä's Center Party won the most seats in Apr. 19, 2015, parliamentary elections; he formed a center-right government. More than 32,000 refugees and other migrants applied for asylum in Finland in 2015, and over 5,600 in 2016. The government announced, Jan. 28, 2016, it would deport rejected asylum applicants, and Finland concluded border security agreements with Russia, Mar. 2016, to reduce migrant crossings. During 2016, 7,745 asylum applications were approved and 14,282 rejected. A rejected asylum applicant from Morocco, who claimed to be inspired by ISIS, fatally stabbed two and wounded eight in Turku, Aug. 18, 2017. In June 2018, he was convicted of murder and attempted murder with terrorist intent and sentenced to life in prison.

Aland, or Ahvenanmaa, an autonomous, Swedish-speaking province, is a group of small islands, 590 sq mi, in the Gulf of Bothnia, 25 mi from Sweden, 15 mi from Finland. Mariehamn is the chief port and seat of government. **Website:** www.aland.ax

France
French Republic

People: Population: 67,364,357 (incl. pop. of overseas departments) (21). **Age distrib.:** <15: 18.5%; 65+: 19.8%. **Growth:** 0.4%. **Migrants:** 12.2%. **Pop. density:** 272.4 per sq mi, 105.2 per sq km. **Urban:** 80.4%. **Ethnic groups:** Celtic and Latin with Teutonic, Slavic, North African, Indochinese, Basque minorities. **Languages:** French (official), declining regional dialects and langs. (Provençal, Breton, Alsatian, Corsican, Catalan, Basque, Flemish). **Religions:** Christian (overwhelmingly Roman Catholic) 63%-66%, Muslim 7%-9%, none 23%-28%. France maintains a tradition of secularism.

Geography: Total area: 248,573 sq mi, 643,801 sq km (incl. overseas departments) (42); **Land area:** 247,270 sq mi, 640,427 sq km (incl. overseas departments). **Location:** Western Europe, between Atlantic O. and Medit. Sea. Spain, Andorra, Monaco on S; Italy, Switzerland, Germany on E; Luxembourg, Belgium on N. **Topography:** A wide plain covers more than half of the country, in N and W, drained to W by Seine, Loire, Garonne Rivers. The Alps (Mt. Blanc is tallest in W Europe at 15,781 ft), the lower Jura range, and forested Vosges are in E. The Rhone flows from Lake Geneva to Mediterranean. Pyrenees are on SW border. **Arable land:** 33.7%. **Capital:** Paris, 10,900,952. **Cities:** Lyon, 1,690,105; Marseille-Aix-en-Provence, 1,599,198; Lille, 1,054,088.

Government: Type: Semi-presidential republic. **Head of state:** Pres. Emmanuel Macron; b. 1977; in office: May 14, 2017. **Head of govt.:** Prime Min. Edouard Philippe; b. 1970; in office: May 15, 2017. **Local divisions:** 13 metropolitan regions, 5 overseas regions. **Defense budget:** $48.6 bil. **Active troops:** 202,700.

Economy: Industries: machinery, chemicals, automobiles, metallurgy, aircraft, electronics, textiles, food proc., tourism. **Chief agric.:** wheat, cereals, sugar beets, potatoes, wine grapes; beef, dairy prods.; fish. **Natural resources:** coal, iron ore, bauxite, zinc, uranium, antimony, arsenic, potash, feldspar, fluorspar, gypsum, timber, fish. **Water:** 3,277 cu m per capita. **Crude oil reserves:** 66 mil bbls. **Electricity prod.:** 540.1 bil kWh. **Labor force:** agric. 2.9%, industry 20.4%, services 76.8%. **Unemployment:** 9.4%.

Finance: Monetary unit: Euro (EUR) (0.86 = $1 U.S.). **GDP:** $2.8 tril; **per capita GDP:** $43,800; **GDP growth:** 1.8%. **Imports:** $624.9 bil; Germany 18.5%, Belgium 10.2%, Netherlands 8.3%, Italy 7.9%, Spain 7.1%, UK 5.3%, U.S. 5.2%, China 5.1%. **Exports:** $551.8 bil; Germany 14.8%, Spain 7.7%, Italy 7.5%, U.S. 7.2%, Belgium 7%, UK 6.7%. **Tourism:** $60.7 bil. **Budget:** $1.5 tril. **Inflation:** 1%.

Transport: Railways: 18,417 mi. **Motor vehicles:** 586.9 per 1,000 pop. **Airports:** 294.

Communications: Telephone: 59.5 per 100 pop. **Mobile:** 106.2 per 100 pop. **Broadband:** 81.7 per 100 pop. **Internet** (2017): 80.5%.

Health: Expend.: 11.1%. **Life expect.:** 78.9 male; 85.3 female. **Births:** 12.1 per 1,000 pop. **Deaths:** 9.4 per 1,000 pop. **Infant mortality:** 3.2 per 1,000 live births. **Undernourished:** <2.5%. **HIV:** 0.5%.

Education: Compulsory: ages 6-15. **Literacy:** 99%.

Embassy: 4101 Reservoir Rd. NW 20007; 944-6000.

Website: www.gouvernement.fr

Julius Caesar conquered Celtic Gaul 58-51 BCE; Romans ruled for 500 years. Under Charlemagne, Frankish rule extended over much of Europe. After his death, France emerged as one of the successor kingdoms.

The monarchy was overthrown in the French Revolution (1789-93) and succeeded by the First Republic, followed by the First Empire under Napoleon I (1804-15), a monarchy (1814-48), the Second Republic (1848-52), the Second Empire (1852-70), the Third Republic (1871-1946), the Fourth Republic (1946-58), and the Fifth Republic (1958-present).

France suffered severe losses in people and wealth in WWI (1914-18) when it was invaded by Germany. By the Treaty of Versailles, 1919, France exacted return of Alsace and Lorraine, provinces seized by Germany in 1871 after it defeated France in the Franco-Prussian War. During WWII (1939-45), Germany invaded France in May 1940 and signed an armistice with a government based in Vichy. After the Allies liberated France in 1944, Gen. Charles de Gaulle became head of the provisional government, serving until 1946. De Gaulle again became premier in 1958, during a crisis over Algeria, and obtained voter approval for a new constitution, ushering in the Fifth Republic. He then became president.

France withdrew from Indochina in 1954 and from Morocco and Tunisia in 1956. Most of its remaining African territories, including Algeria, were freed 1958-62.

In May 1968, students in Paris and other centers rioted, battled police, and were joined by workers who launched nationwide strikes. De Gaulle resigned from office in Apr. 1969, after losing a nationwide referendum on constitutional reform. Georges Pompidou was elected to succeed him. After Pompidou's death, in 1974, Valery Giscard d'Estaing was elected president; he continued his predecessors' conservative policies.

In 1981, France elected Socialist François Mitterrand president. Under Mitterrand the government nationalized five major industries and most private banks. After 1986, however, when rightists won a narrow victory in the National Assembly, Mitterrand chose conservative Jacques Chirac as premier. During a two-year period of "cohabitation," France pursued a privatization program, selling many state-owned companies. Mitterrand won a second 7-year term in 1988.

Chirac won the 1995 presidency in a runoff election. He cut government spending to meet budgetary goals for the introduction of the euro. With unemployment at nearly 13%, leftist parties won a decisive victory in 1997 legislative elections, resulting in a new period of cohabitation. Chirac easily won the 2002 presidential election in a runoff, and his center-right allies won parliamentary elections. Parliament gave final approval in 2004 to a law barring the wearing of Islamic head scarves and other religious symbols in public schools.

Displeased with sluggish economic growth, high unemployment, and budget cuts, voters rejected, 2005, a proposed EU constitution supported by the Chirac government. A state of emergency was declared Nov. 8 after 12 days of riots that began in Paris and spread to some 300 French cities and towns; rioters were mainly young immigrants from N and W Africa.

The conservative Nicolas Sarkozy won the 2007 presidential runoff election. Sarkozy responded to the global recession, Dec. 2008, with a $33-bil economic stimulus plan; measures announced Feb. 2009, following labor protests, added $3.3 bil in aid for lower-income people. With France's economy still struggling, the Socialist François Hollande won a presidential runoff over Sarkozy in 2012, and the Socialist Party won parliamentary elections. Hollande, May 18, 2013, signed a bill that legalized same-sex marriage and allowed gay couples to adopt children. After forming a new party, La République en Marche (Onward!), in 2016, centrist Emmanuel Macron was elected president, May 7, 2017, defeating Marine Le Pen of the far-right National Front (renamed National Rally in 2018) in a runoff, 66.1% to 33.9%. Macron pledged reforms to improve GDP growth and reduce unemployment. His party won June 2017 parliamentary elections. On Sept. 22, Macron signed decrees (ratified by the National Assemby, Nov. 28) making it easier for many companies to hire, fire, and negotiate terms with workers. June 2018 legislation reduced government railroad workers' benefits for new hires.

France participated in military operations that ousted Libyan leader Muammar al-Qaddafi, Aug. 23, 2011. Beginning in 2014, France took part in the U.S.-led campaign of airstrikes in Iraq against the Sunni extremist group ISIS. In Sept. 2015, France began airstrikes against ISIS targets in Syria. French troops entered the conflict between government forces in Mali and Islamist militants Jan. 11, 2013; they pushed the militants out of most seized territory. France maintained a counterterrorism force in the region, consisting of about 4,000 troops in 2018.

On Jan. 7, 2015, two French gunmen of Algerian descent attacked the Paris offices of the magazine Charlie Hebdo, which had published satirical images of Muhammad. The gunmen, who claimed affiliation with al-Qaeda in the Arabian Peninsula, killed 12 people. They were killed in a shootout with police, Jan. 9. A third gunman, who claimed loyalty to ISIS, fatally shot a police officer Jan. 8 and killed 4 people and took hostages at a kosher supermarket Jan. 9, before being killed by police. On the night of

Nov. 13, 2015, in coordinated attacks in and near Paris for which ISIS claimed responsibility, terrorist gunmen and suicide bombers killed 130, many in Paris's Bataclan concert hall. In a July 14, 2016, attack ISIS claimed to have inspired, a Tunisian-born French resident drove a truck through a Bastille Day fireworks crowd in Nice, killing 86 before he was fatally shot by police.

France ratified, June 15, 2016, a global agreement to reduce greenhouse gas emissions negotiated at a UN climate conference in Paris, Dec. 2015. The International Olympic Committee announced, Sept. 13, 2017, that Paris would host the 2024 Summer Games. With a 4-2 victory over Croatia, July 15, France won the 2018 men's soccer World Cup.

The island of **Corsica**, in the Mediterranean W of Italy and N of Sardinia, is a territorial collectivity and region of France comprising two departments. It elects 2 senators and 3 deputies to the French Parliament. Area 3,369 sq mi; pop. (2014 est.) 323,092. The capital is Ajaccio, birthplace of Napoleon I. Violence by Corsican separatist groups, especially in the 1980s and 1990s, hurt tourism, a leading industry. Corsicans rejected, 51%-49%, a limited autonomy plan in a referendum July 6, 2003. **Website:** www.isula.corsica

French Overseas Departments

French Guiana is on the NE coast of South America with Suriname on the W and Brazil on the E and S. Its area is 35,135 sq mi (total), 34,421 sq mi (land); pop. (2016 est.) 262,527. Guiana sends 1 senator and 2 deputies to the French Parliament. Guiana is administered by a prefect and has a Council General of 16 elected members; capital is Cayenne, pop. (2018 est.) 57,506.

The famous penal colony, Devil's Island, was phased out between 1938 and 1951. The European Space Agency helps to maintain a satellite-launching center, established by France in 1964, in the city of Kourou.

Immense forests of rich timber cover much of the land. Fishing (especially shrimp), forestry, and gold mining are the most important industries. Natural resources include petroleum, kaolin, niobium, tantalum, and clay.

Guadeloupe, in the West Indies' Leeward Isls., consists of two large islands, Basse-Terre and Grande-Terre, separated by the Salt R., plus Marie Galante and the Saintes group to the S and Desirade to the N. A French possession since 1635, the department is represented in the French Parliament; administration consists of a prefect (governor) as well as an elected general and regional councils.

Area of the islands is 525 sq mi; pop. (2016 est.) 395,725, mainly descendants of slaves; capital is Basse-Terre (2018 est. pop. 58,397) on Basse-Terre Island. The land is fertile; sugar, rum, and bananas are important industry. International tourism receipts in 2015 were $614 mil.

Martinique, the northernmost of the Windward Islands, in the West Indies, has been a possession since 1635, and a department since Mar. 1946. It is represented in the French Parliament by 2 senators and 4 deputies. The island was the birthplace of Napoleon's first wife, Empress Josephine.

It has an area of 425 sq mi (total), 409 sq mi (land); pop. (2016 est.) 376,847, mostly descendants of slaves. The capital is Fort-de-France; pop. (2018 est.) 79,361. It is a popular tourist stop; 2017 international tourism receipts were $490 mil. The chief exports are rum, bananas, and petroleum products. **Website:** www.collectivitedemartinique.mq

Mayotte, claimed by Comoros and administered by France, voted in 1976 to become a territorial collectivity of France. An island NW of Madagascar, area is 144 sq mi, pop. (2012 est.) 235,132. The capital is Mamoudzou; pop. (2018 est.) 6,180. In a Mar. 29, 2009, referendum, 95% of voters endorsed a plan under which Mayotte became an overseas department of France as of Mar. 31, 2011.

Réunion is a volcanic island in the Indian O. about 420 mi E of Madagascar, and has belonged to France since 1665. Area, 972 sq mi (total), 968 sq mi (land); pop. (2016 est.) 850,996, 30% of French extraction. Capital: Saint-Denis; pop. (2018 est.) 147,209. The chief export is sugar. International tourism receipts in 2017 were $401 mil. It elects 5 deputies, 3 senators to the French Parliament. **Website:** www.regionreunion.com

French Overseas Territorial Collectivities

French Polynesia, comprises 130 islands widely scattered among 5 archipelagos in the S Pacific; administered by a Council of Ministers (headed by a president). Territorial Assembly and the Council have headquarters at Papeete, on Tahiti, one of the Society Islands (which include the Windward Isls. and Leeward Isls.). Two deputies and a senator are elected to the French Parliament.

Other groups are the Marquesas Isls.; the Tuamotu Archipelago; the Gambier Isls.; and the Austral, or Tubuai, Isls.

Total area of the islands administered from Tahiti is 1,609 sq mi (total), 1,478 sq mi (land); pop. (2018 est.) 290,373. Tahiti is mountainous with a productive coastline bearing coconuts, citrus, pineapples, and vanilla. Tourism is the largest industry.

Tahiti was visited by Capt. James Cook in 1769 and by Capt. Bligh in the *Bounty*, 1788-89. Its beauty impressed Herman Melville, Paul Gauguin, and Charles Darwin. A coalition favoring independence for French Polynesia within 20 years gained control of

the territorial assembly after elections May 23, 2004. A UN General Assembly resolution May 17, 2013, called on France to grant French Polynesia independence, but anti-independence parties won general elections May 5, 2013, and May 6, 2018. A 2013-14 Zika virus outbreak affected about 28,000 people.

St. Pierre and Miquelon became a territorial collectivity in 1985. It consists of two groups of rocky islands near the SW coast of Newfoundland, inhabited by fishermen. Fish products are the chief export. The St. Pierre group has an area of 10 sq mi; Miquelon, 83 sq mi. Total pop. (2018 est.) 5,471. Capital: Saint-Pierre. Both Mayotte and St. Pierre and Miquelon elect a deputy and a senator to the French Parliament.

St. Barthélemy and **St. Martin**, both formerly part of Guadeloupe, voted for secession in 2003 and became overseas territorial collectivities in 2007. Both suffered severe damage from Hurricane Irma, Sept. 6, 2017, which caused at least 11 deaths. Total area 10 sq mi and 21 sq mi; total pop. (2018 est.) 7,160 and 32,284 respectively.

The territorial collectivity of **Wallis and Futuna** comprises two island groups in the SW Pacific S of Tuvalu, N of Fiji, and W of Samoa. It became an overseas territory July 29, 1961. The islands have a total area of 55 sq mi and pop. (2018 est.) 15,763. Alofi, attached to Futuna, is uninhabited. Capital: Mata-Utu; pop. (2018 est.) 1,025. Chief exports are copra, chemicals, and construction materials. A senator and a deputy are elected to the French Parliament.

Overseas Territory and Special Collectivity

The territory of the **French Southern and Antarctic Lands** comprises island groups in the Indian O. Area: 2,991 sq mi (total), 2,960 sq mi (land).

The U.S. does not recognize French claim to Adelie Land, an area of about 193,051 sq mi on Antarctica. Adelie, reached 1840, has a 185-mi coastline and tapers 1,240 mi inland to the S Pole. It has a research station. The area includes the Ninnis and Mertz glaciers.

The Indian O. groups are as follows: Kerguelen Archipelago, visited 1772, consists of one large and 300 small islands. The chief is 87 mi long, 74 mi wide, and has Mt. Ross (6,429 ft). Principal research station is Port-aux-Français. There are seals, blue whales, coal, peat, semiprecious stones. Crozet Archipelago, reached 1772, covers 136 sq mi. Eastern Island rises to 6,560 ft. Volcanic Saint Paul, in southern Indian O., has warm springs. Amsterdam Island is nearby; both produce cod and rock lobster. Military garrisons and meteorological stations are located on the Scattered Isls.

The special collectivity of **New Caledonia** and Dependencies is a group of islands in the Pacific O. about 1,115 mi E of Australia and approx. the same distance NW of New Zealand. Dependencies are the Loyalty Isls., Isle of Pines, Belep Archipelago, and Huon Isls.

The largest island, New Caledonia, is 6,530 sq mi. Total area of the territory is 7,172 sq mi (total), 7,056 sq mi (land); pop. (2018 est.) 282,754. The group was acquired by France in 1853.

The territory is administered by a High Commissioner. There is a popularly elected Territorial Congress. Two deputies and two senators are elected to the French Parliament. Capital: Nouméa; pop. (2018 est.) 197,787.

Mining is a key industry. New Caledonia is one of the world's largest nickel producers. Chrome, iron, cobalt, manganese, silver, gold, lead, and copper are also found. Tourism is an important industry.

In 1987, New Caledonian voters chose by referendum to remain within France. French and Melanesians (Kanaks) clashed in 1988. An agreement (the Nouméa Accord) signed May 5, 1998, between France and rival New Caledonian factions specified a 20-year period of shared sovereignty and a referendum on independence; the vote was later scheduled for Nov. 4, 2018. Parties favoring remaining part of France won a majority in May 11, 2014, Territorial Congress elections. **Website:** www.gouv.nc

Gabon
Gabonese Republic

People: Population: 2,119,036 (142). **Age distrib.:** <15: 37.4%; 65+: 3.9%. **Growth:** 2.7%. **Migrants:** 13.8%. **Pop. density:** 21.3 per sq mi, 8.2 per sq km. **Urban:** 89.4%. **Ethnic groups:** Bantu tribes, incl. four major groupings (Fang, Bapounou, Nzebi, Obamba). **Languages:** French (official), Fang, Myene, Nzebi, Bapounou/Eschira, Bandjabi. **Religions:** Roman Catholic 42.3%, Protestant 12.3%, other Christian 27.4%, Muslim 9.8%.

Geography: Total area: 103,347 sq mi, 267,667 sq km (76); **Land area:** 99,486 sq mi, 257,667 sq km. **Location:** Atlantic coast of W central Africa. Equatorial Guinea, Cameroon on N; Congo Republic on E and S. **Topography:** Heavily forested, consisting of coastal lowlands; plateaus in N, E, and S; mountains in N, SE, and center. The Ogooue R. system covers most of Gabon. **Arable land:** 1.3%. **Capital:** Libreville, 813,489.

Government: Type: Presidential republic. **Head of state:** Pres. Ali Bongo Ondimba; b. 1959; in office: Oct. 16, 2009. **Head of govt.:** Prime Min. Emmanuel Issoze-Ngondet; b. 1961; in office:

Sept. 29, 2016. **Local divisions:** 9 provinces. **Defense budget:** $302 mil. **Active troops:** 4,700.

Economy: Industries: petroleum extraction and refining; manganese, gold; chemicals, ship repair, food and beverages, textiles. **Chief agric.:** cocoa, coffee, sugar, palm oil, rubber; cattle; fish. **Natural resources:** petroleum, nat. gas, diamonds, niobium, manganese, uranium, gold, timber, iron ore, hydropower. **Water:** 96,232 cu m per capita. **Crude oil reserves:** 2 bil bbls. **Electricity prod.:** 2 bil kWh. **Labor force:** agric. 41.9%, industry 12.6%, services 45.6%. **Unemployment:** 19.7%.

Finance: Monetary unit: Central African CFA Franc (XAF) (566.17 = $1 U.S.). **GDP:** $36.7 bil; **per capita GDP:** $19,200; **GDP growth:** 0.8%. **Imports:** $3.2 bil; France 23.6%, Belgium 19.6%, China 15.2%. **Exports:** $5.1 bil; China 36.4%, U.S. 10%, Ireland 8.5%, Netherlands 6.3%, South Korea 5.1%, Australia 5%. **Budget:** $4 bil. **Inflation** (2015-16): 2.1%.

Transport: Railways: 403 mi. **Airports:** 14.

Communications: Telephone: 1 per 100 pop. **Mobile:** 131.5 per 100 pop. **Broadband:** 66.1 per 100 pop. **Internet:** 48.1%.

Health: Expend.: 2.7%. **Life expect.:** 66.3 male; 69.6 female. **Births:** 26.5 per 1,000 pop. **Deaths:** 6.2 per 1,000 pop. **Infant mortality:** 32.9 per 1,000 live births. **Undernourished:** 9.4%. **HIV:** 4.2%.

Education: Compulsory: ages 6-15. **Literacy:** 83.2%.

Embassy: 2034 20th St. NW 20009; 797-1000.

Website: www.gouvernement.ga or www.state.gov/p/af/ci/gb/

France established control over the region in the second half of the 19th cent. Gabon became independent Aug. 17, 1960. Backed by France, Pres. Albert-Bernard Bongo (later Omar Bongo Ondimba) ruled the country 1967-2009, greatly enriching himself and his family. A multiparty political system was introduced in 1990. Bongo's reelection victories in 1993, 1998, and 2003 were faulted by international observers. After he died June 8, 2009, his son Ali Bongo Ondimba claimed victory in the disputed 2009 presidential election. Bongo was declared the winner of a close Aug. 27, 2016, presidential election. Violent protests followed, and the opposition called the result fraudulent. Constitutional amendments enacted in 2018 strengthened the powers of the president.

Gabon has abundant natural resources (including oil) and is one of the most prosperous African countries, although there is extreme income inequality.

The Gambia
Republic of The Gambia

People: Population: 2,092,731 (143). **Age distrib.:** <15: 37%; 65+: 3.6%. **Growth:** 2%. **Migrants:** 9.8%. **Pop. density:** 535.6 per sq mi, 206.8 per sq km. **Urban:** 61.3%. **Ethnic groups:** Mandinka/Jahanka 34%, Fulani/Tukulur/Lorobo 22.4%, Wolof 12.6%, Jola/Karoninka 10.7%, Serahuleh 6.6%, Serer 3.2%, Manjago 2.1%. **Languages:** English (official), Mandinka, Wolof, Fula, other indigenous vernaculars. **Religions:** Muslim 95.7%, Christian 4.2%.

Geography: Total area: 4,363 sq mi, 11,300 sq km (160); **Land area:** 3,907 sq mi, 10,120 sq km. **Location:** Atlantic coast near W tip of Africa. Surrounded on 3 sides by Senegal. **Topography:** Narrow strip of land on each side of lower Gambia R. **Arable land:** 43.5%. **Capital:** Banjul, 437,161.

Government: Type: Presidential republic. **Head of state and govt.:** Pres. Adama Barrow; b. 1965; in office: Jan. 19, 2017. **Local divisions:** 5 regions, 1 city, 1 municipality. **Defense budget:** NA. **Active troops:** 800.

Economy: Industries: peanuts, fish, hides, tourism, beverages, agric. machinery assembly. **Chief agric.:** rice, millet, sorghum, peanuts, corn, sesame, cassava, palm kernels; cattle, sheep, goats. **Natural resources:** fish, clay, silica sand, titanium, tin, zircon. **Water:** 4,018 cu m per capita. **Electricity prod.:** 240 mil kWh. **Labor force:** agric. 27.1%, industry 15.3%, services 57.6%. **Unemployment:** 9.5%.

Finance: Monetary unit: Dalasi (GMD) (48.03 = $1 U.S.). **GDP:** $3.6 bil; **per capita GDP:** $1,700; **GDP growth:** 3.5%. **Imports:** $316.1 mil; Côte d'Ivoire 11.5%, Brazil 10.6%, Spain 10.2%, China 7.8%, Russia 6.4%, Netherlands 5.3%, India 5%. **Exports:** $109.7 mil; Guinea-Bissau 51.9%, Vietnam 14.6%, Senegal 8.8%, Mali 7.2%. **Tourism:** $116 mil. **Budget:** $369.9 mil. **Inflation** (2015-16): 7.2%.

Transport: Airports: 1.

Communications: Telephone (2016): 1.9 per 100 pop. **Mobile** (2016): 139.2 per 100 pop. **Broadband:** 21.3 per 100 pop. **Internet:** 18.5%.

Health: Expend.: 6.7%. **Life expect.:** 63.0 male; 67.8 female. **Births:** 28.6 per 1,000 pop. **Deaths:** 6.9 per 1,000 pop. **Infant mortality:** 58.4 per 1,000 live births. **Undernourished:** 9.6%. **HIV:** 1.6%.

Education: Compulsory: ages 7-15. **Literacy:** 55.6%.

Embassy: 5630 16th St. NW 20011; 785-1379.

Website: www.state.gov/p/af/ci/ga/

The peoples of The Gambia were at one time associated with the West African empires of Ghana, Mali, and Songhai. The area became Britain's first African possession in 1588.

Independence came Feb. 18, 1965; republic status within the Commonwealth was achieved in 1970. The country suffered from severe famine in the 1970s. Senegambia, a confederation with Senegal, lasted from 1982 to 1989.

On July 22, 1994, after 24 years in power, Pres. Dawda K. Jawara was deposed in a bloodless coup by a military officer, Yahya Jammeh. Jammeh barred political activity, detained potential opponents, and governed by decree. Despite a nominal return to constitutional government in 1996, Jammeh retained a tight grip on power. He won a fourth 5-year term in 2011. Businessman Adama Barrow defeated Jammeh in the Dec. 1, 2016, presidential election. Reversing an earlier statement, Jammeh announced Dec. 9 that he rejected the election result. Barrow was sworn in, Jan. 19, 2017, in Senegal. Under pressure from ECOWAS and the UN, Jammeh left the country Jan. 21.

Georgia

People: Population: 4,926,087 (123). **Age distrib.:** <15: 18.2%; 65+: 16.3%. **Growth:** 0.01%. **Migrants:** 2%. **Pop. density:** 183 per sq mi, 70.7 per sq km. **Urban:** 58.6%. **Ethnic groups:** Georgian 86.8%, Azeri 6.3%, Armenian 4.5%. **Languages:** Georgian (official), Azeri, Armenian, Abkhaz (official in Abkhazia). **Religions:** Orthodox (official) 83.4%, Muslim 10.7%, Armenian Apostolic 2.9%.

Geography: Total area: 26,911 sq mi, 69,700 sq km (119). (About 18% is occupied by Russia.) **Land area:** 26,911 sq mi, 69,700 sq km. **Location:** SW Asia, on E coast of Black Sea. Russia on N and NE, Turkey and Armenia on S, Azerbaijan on SE. **Topography:** Main range of Caucasus Mts. in NE separates country from Russia. **Arable land:** 6.4%. **Capital:** Tbilisi, 1,077,333.

Government: Type: Semi-presidential republic. **Head of state:** Pres. Giorgi Margvelashvili; b. 1969; in office: Nov. 17, 2013. **Head of govt.:** Prime Min. Mamuka Bakhtadze; b. 1982; in office: June 20, 2018. **Local divisions:** 9 regions, 1 city, 2 autonomous republics. **Defense budget:** $303 mil. **Active troops:** 20,650.

Economy: Industries: steel, machine tools, elec. appliances, mining, chemicals, wood prods., wine. **Chief agric.:** citrus, grapes, tea, hazelnuts, vegetables. **Natural resources:** timber, hydropower, manganese, iron ore, copper, minor coal and oil deposits. **Water:** 15,832 cu m per capita. **Crude oil reserves:** 35 mil bbls. **Electricity prod.:** 10.6 bil kWh. **Labor force:** agric. 40.9%, industry 12.5%, services 46.6%. **Unemployment:** 11.6%.

Finance: Monetary unit: Lari (GEL) (2.59 = $1 U.S.). **GDP:** $39.7 bil; **per capita GDP:** $10,700; **GDP growth:** 4.8%. **Imports:** $7.8 bil; Turkey 17.2%, Russia 9.9%, China 9.2%, Azerbaijan 7.6%, Ukraine 5.6%, Germany 5.4%. **Exports:** $3.5 bil; Russia 14.5%, Azerbaijan 10%, Turkey 7.9%, Armenia 7.7%, China 7.6%, Bulgaria 6.6%. **Tourism:** $2.8 bil. **Budget:** $4.9 bil. **Inflation** (2014-15): 4%.

Transport: Railways: 847 mi. **Airports:** 18.

Communications: Telephone: 18.2 per 100 pop. **Mobile:** 146.5 per 100 pop. **Broadband:** 57.7 per 100 pop. **Internet** (2017): 60.5%.

Health: Expend.: 7.9%. **Life expect.:** 72.5 male; 80.9 female. **Births:** 12.1 per 1,000 pop. **Deaths:** 10.9 per 1,000 pop. **Infant mortality:** 14.7 per 1,000 live births. **Undernourished:** 7.4%. **HIV:** 0.4%.

Education: Compulsory: ages 6-14. **Literacy:** 99.8%.

Embassy: 1824-1826 R St. NW 20009; 387-2390.

Website: www.gov.ge

The region, which contained the ancient kingdoms of Colchis and Iberia, was Christianized in the 4th cent. and conquered by Arabs in the 8th cent. Annexed by Russia in 1801, Georgia was forcibly incorporated into the USSR in 1922.

Georgia declared independence Apr. 9, 1991, and became an independent country when the Soviet Union disbanded Dec. 26. After a power struggle, former Soviet Foreign Min. Eduard A. Shevardnadze became president. He survived several coup attempts and won reelection in 1995 and 2000. Parliamentary elections Nov. 2, 2003, denounced as fraudulent sparked massive anti-government protests, causing Shevardnadze to resign Nov. 23. Opposition leader Mikhail Saakashvili won the 2004 presidential election. He survived an apparent assassination attempt along with U.S. Pres. George W. Bush in Tbilisi May 10, 2005. He suppressed an alleged coup plot, Sept. 6, 2006, and cracked down violently on anti-government protests, Nov. 2007. He called early elections, Jan. 2008, which he won. Barred by term limits from seeking reelection in 2013, he left the country. In Jan. and June 2018, he was sentenced to prison terms after convictions in absentia for abuse of power.

Giorgi Margvelashvili of the recently formed Georgian Dream coalition, which won 2012 parliamentary elections, was elected president Oct. 27, 2013. Irakli Garibashvili of Georgian Dream became prime min., Nov. 20, 2013, a post with greatly increased powers under constitutional revisions. Giorgi Kvirikashvili became prime min., Dec. 30, 2015. Georgian Dream won Oct. 2016 parliamentary elections. Kvirikashvili resigned, June 13, 2018, following public protests and was replaced, June 20, by Mamuka Bakhtadze.

Georgia has close economic ties with the EU under a 2014 cooperation agreement.

After independence, secessionist movements in the enclaves of South Ossetia and Abkhazia, supported by Russia, rejected the Tbilisi government. Open warfare between Georgia and Russia erupted when Saakashvili sent troops, Aug. 7, 2008, to suppress insurgent activity in Tskhinvali, the South Ossetian capital. Russia,

Aug. 8-9, dispatched forces to South Ossetia and Abkhazia and attacked key Georgian cities. After a cease-fire signed Aug. 15-16, thousands of Russian troops remained in the breakaway regions. Russia, Aug. 2008, formally recognized South Ossetia and Abkhazia's independence; almost all other nations have not. South Ossetia Pres. Leonid Tibilov signed a military cooperation treaty with Russia, Mar. 18, 2015. Anatoly Bibilov defeated Tibilov in South Ossetia's Apr. 9, 2017, presidential election; voters also approved adding State of Alania to the area's name. Raul Khajimba won an Aug. 2014 presidential election in Abkhazia; he signed a new cooperation agreement with Russia, Nov. 24, 2014.

Germany
Federal Republic of Germany

People: Population: 80,457,737 (19). **Age distrib.:** <15: 12.8%; 65+: 22.4%. **Growth:** –0.2%. **Migrants:** 14.8%. **Pop. density:** 597.7 per sq mi, 230.8 per sq km. **Urban:** 77.3%. **Ethnic groups:** German 91.5%, Turkish 2.4%, other (largely Polish, Italian, Romanian, Syrian, Greek) 6.1%. **Languages:** German (official); Danish, Frisian, Sorbian, Romany (all official minority langs.). **Religions:** Roman Catholic 29%, Protestant 27%, Muslim 4.4%.

Geography: Total area: 137,847 sq mi, 357,022 sq km (62); **Land area:** 134,623 sq mi, 348,672 sq km. **Location:** Central Europe. Denmark on N; Netherlands, Belgium, Luxembourg, France on W; Switzerland, Austria on S; Czech Rep., Poland on E. **Topography:** Flat in N, hilly in center and W, and mountainous in Bavaria in the S. Chief rivers are Elbe, Weser, Ems, Rhine, and Main, all flowing toward North Sea, and Danube, flowing toward Black Sea. **Arable land:** 34%. **Capital:** Berlin, 3,552,123. **Cities:** Hamburg, 1,792,904; Munich, 1,503,708; Cologne, 1,096,152.

Government: Type: Federal parliamentary republic. **Head of state:** Pres. Frank-Walter Steinmeier; b. 1956; in office: Mar. 22, 2017. **Head of govt.:** Chancellor Angela Merkel; b. 1954; in office: Nov. 22, 2005. **Local divisions:** 16 states. **Defense budget:** $41.7 bil. **Active troops:** 178,600.

Economy: Industries: iron, steel, coal, cement, chemicals, machinery, vehicles, machine tools, electronics, automobiles, food and beverages. **Chief agric.:** potatoes, wheat, barley, sugar beets, fruit, cabbages; milk prods.; cattle, pigs, poultry. **Natural resources:** coal, lignite, nat. gas, iron ore, copper, nickel, uranium, potash, salt, constr. materials, timber. **Water:** 1,909 cu m per capita. **Crude oil reserves:** 129.6 mil bbls. **Electricity prod.:** 610.2 bil kWh. **Labor force:** agric. 1.3%, industry 27.3%, services 71.5%. **Unemployment:** 3.8%.

Finance: Monetary unit: Euro (EUR) (0.86 = $1 U.S.). **GDP:** $4.2 tril; **per capita GDP:** $50,400; **GDP growth:** 2.5%. **Imports:** $1.1 tril; Netherlands 13.8%, China 7%, France 6.6%, Belgium 5.9%, Italy 5.4%, Poland 5.4%. **Exports:** $1.4 tril; U.S. 8.8%, France 8.2%, China 6.8%, Netherlands 6.7%, UK 6.6%, Italy 5.1%. **Tourism:** $39.8 bil. **Budget:** $1.6 tril. **Inflation:** 1.7%.

Transport: Railways: 20,872 mi. **Motor vehicles:** 621.5 per 1,000 pop. **Airports:** 318.

Communications: Telephone: 54.1 per 100 pop. **Mobile:** 129.1 per 100 pop. **Broadband:** 80.2 per 100 pop. **Internet** (2017): 84.4%.

Health: Expend.: 11.2%. **Life expect.:** 78.6 male; 83.4 female. **Births:** 8.6 per 1,000 pop. **Deaths:** 11.8 per 1,000 pop. **Infant mortality:** 3.4 per 1,000 live births. **Maternal:** <2.5%. **HIV:** 0.2%.

Education: Compulsory: ages 6-17. **Literacy:** 99%.

Embassy: 4645 Reservoir Rd. NW, 20007; 298-4000.

Website: www.deutschland.de

Julius Caesar defeated Germanic tribes, 55 and 53 BCE, but Roman expansion north of the Rhine was stopped in 9 CE. Charlemagne, ruler of the Franks, consolidated Saxon, Bavarian, Rhenish, Frankish, and other lands; after him the eastern part became the German Empire. The Thirty Years' War, 1618-48, split Germany into small principalities and kingdoms.

Otto von Bismarck, Prussian chancellor, formed the North German Confederation, 1867. In 1870 Bismarck maneuvered Napoleon III into declaring war. After the quick defeat of France, Bismarck formed the German Empire and on Jan. 18, 1871, in Versailles, proclaimed King Wilhelm I of Prussia the German emperor (Deutscher kaiser).

The German Empire reached its peak before WWI in 1914, with 208,780 sq mi, plus overseas colonies. After losing the war in 1918, Germany ceded Alsace-Lorraine to France, West Prussia and Posen (Poznan) province to Poland, and part of Schleswig to Denmark. It lost all colonies and the ports of Memel and Danzig.

Republic of Germany, 1919-33, adopted the Weimar constitution; met reparation payments and elected Friedrich Ebert and Gen. Paul von Hindenburg presidents.

Third Reich, 1933-45: Adolf Hitler led the National Socialist German Workers' (Nazi) party after WWI. Pres. von Hindenburg named Hitler chancellor in 1933; on Aug. 3, 1934, the day after Hindenburg's death, the cabinet joined the offices of president and chancellor and made Hitler *führer* (leader). Hitler abolished freedom of speech and assembly, and began a long series of persecutions culminating in the murder of millions of Jews and others.

He repudiated the Versailles treaty and reparations agreements, remilitarized the Rhineland (1936), and annexed Austria (Anschluss, 1938). At Munich he made an agreement with British Prime Min. Neville Chamberlain, which permitted Germany to annex part of Czechoslovakia. He declared war on Poland Sept. 1, 1939, precipitating WWII. With total defeat near, Hitler committed suicide in Berlin Apr. 1945. The victorious Allies voided all acts and annexations of Hitler's Reich.

Germany was sectioned into four zones of occupation, administered by the Allied Powers (U.S., USSR, UK, and France). The USSR took control of many E German states. The territory E of the so-called Oder-Neisse line was assigned to, and later annexed by, Poland. The USSR annexed Northern East Prussia (now Kaliningrad). Greater Berlin, within but not part of the Soviet zone, was administered by the four occupying powers under the Allied Command. In 1948 the USSR withdrew, established its single command in East Berlin, and cut off supplies. The Western Allies utilized a gigantic airlift to bring food to West Berlin, 1948-49.

In 1949, two separate German states were established. The zones administered by the Western Allies became West Germany; the Soviet sector became East Germany. West Berlin was considered a West German enclave, a status the Soviet bloc disputed.

East Germany. The German Democratic Republic (East Germany) was proclaimed in the Soviet sector of Berlin Oct. 7, 1949. It was declared fully sovereign in 1954, but Soviet troops remained.

Coincident with the entrance of West Germany into the European defense community in 1952, the East German government decreed a prohibited zone 3 mi deep along its 600-mi border with West Germany and cut Berlin's telephone system in two. East Germany also erected a fortified wall dividing Berlin in 1961, after over 3 mil East Germans had fled to the West. The oppressive Communist regime maintained control through the state security police, known as the Stasi.

By the early 1970s, the economy of East Germany was highly industrialized, and the nation was credited with the highest standard of living among Warsaw Pact countries. Growth slowed in the late 1970s because of shortages of natural resources and labor and huge debt. Comparison with the lifestyle in the West caused many young people to emigrate.

In the late 1980s the government firmly resisted following the USSR's policy of openness (*glasnost*) but was faced with nationwide demonstrations demanding reform. Pres. Erich Honecker, in office since 1976, was forced to resign Oct. 18, 1989. On Nov. 9, the East German government announced its decision to open the border with the West, signaling the end of the Berlin Wall. On Aug. 23, 1990, the East German parliament agreed to reunite with West Germany.

West Germany. The Federal Republic of Germany (West Germany) was proclaimed May 23, 1949, in Bonn. The occupying powers—the U.S., Britain, and France—restored civil status, Sept. 21. The Western Allies ended the state of war with Germany in 1951, while the USSR did so in 1955. The powers lifted controls, and the republic became fully independent May 5, 1955.

Dr. Konrad Adenauer, a Christian Democrat, was made chancellor 1949 and was reelected 1953, 1957, 1961. Willy Brandt, heading a coalition of Social Democrats and Free Democrats, became chancellor 1969 and pursued a policy of *Ostpolitik*, or rapprochement with East Germany and the USSR. Brandt resigned May 1974 after a spy scandal. Terrorist acts on German soil in the 1970s included activities of the Baader-Meinhof gang, also known as the Red Army Faction, and the murder of Israeli athletes by Palestinian commandos at the Olympic Games in Munich, Sept. 5, 1972.

Helmut Kohl became chancellor in 1982 and led the Christian Democratic Union (CDU) and its Bavarian sister party Christian Social Union (CSU) to victory in 1983 and 1987.

Unified Germany. In May 1990, NATO ministers voted to make the united Germany a full member of NATO and barred the new Germany from having its own nuclear, chemical, or biological weapons. The merger of the two Germanys took place Oct. 3, and the first all-German elections since 1932 were held Dec. 2, with West German Chancellor Helmut Kohl confirmed as leader of the unified nation. Eastern Germany received over $1 tril in public and private funds from western Germany, 1990-95. In 1991, Berlin again became Germany's official capital; the Bundestag (parliament) relocated from Bonn to Berlin in 1999. The Christian Democrats lost parliamentary elections, Sept. 27, 1998, and Gerhard Schröder, of the Social Democratic Party (SPD), became chancellor. The Christian Democrats, led by Angela Merkel, won a razor-thin plurality in 2005 parliamentary elections, and she became chancellor Nov. 22, heading a "grand coalition" that included the SPD.

Responding to the global recession, the government passed a 50-bil euro economic stimulus plan in early 2009. Merkel led a center-right coalition to victory in 2009 national elections. Merkel led the response to the European debt crisis beginning in late 2009; debtor nations were required to adopt stern austerity measures (sometimes leading to new or deepened recessions) in return for aid.

A report released Jan 19, 2013, contained information from more than 1,100 people describing themselves as victims of child sexual abuse perpetrated by German Catholic priests. A Church-commissioned study, released Sept. 2018, found evidence that more than 3,600 children had been sexually abused, 1946-2014, by over 1,600 members of the clergy.

Merkel's Christian Democrats won Sept. 22, 2013, parliamentary elections but fell short of a majority. She formed a new coalition, including the SPD, in Dec.

Germany was the destination in 2015-16 for many migrants reaching Europe after fleeing war or hardship in the Middle East, SW Asia, or Africa; it also received, in 2015, large numbers of migrants from the Balkans. Almost 900,000 migrants arrived in 2015, according to government statistics, and 280,000 in 2016. About 477,000 people applied for asylum in 2015 and 745,500 in 2016. Germany provided temporary care, set up expedited procedures for asylum applicants, and began repatriating migrants judged not to be refugees. It implemented a series of measures tightening requirements for asylum. About 62% of asylum applications decided in 2016 were approved. Germany played a key role in negotiating a Mar. 2016 EU-Turkey agreement to stem the flow of migrants to Europe. In an attack for which ISIS claimed responsibility, a Tunisian migrant killed 12 when he stole a truck and drove it into a crowded Berlin outdoor market, Dec. 19, 2016.

Legislation legalizing same-sex marriage was signed into law by Germany's president, July 21, 2017.

Merkel's CDU/CSU won a plurality in Sept. 24, 2017, elections. However, its share of the vote dropped sharply, and the far-right, anti-EU, and anti-immigration Alternative for Germany party won 12.6% of the vote. Merkel reached agreement, Feb. 2018, on a new coalition with the SPD. To prevent a CSU defection from the coalition, Merkel agreed, July 2, to institute controls at the Austrian border and set up border camps to screen potential asylum seekers. Agreements with Spain and Greece in Aug. allowed Germany to return to those countries migrants who originally applied for asylum there. Far-right protests and rioting in Chemnitz in Aug. included attacks on apparent immigrants.

Helgoland, an island of 0.66 sq mi in the North Sea, was taken from Denmark by a British naval force in 1807 and ceded to Germany in 1890. The island was surrendered to the UK, May 23, 1945, and returned to then-West Germany, Mar. 1, 1952.

Ghana
Republic of Ghana

People: Population: 28,102,471 (49). **Age distrib.:** <15: 37.8%; 65+: 4.3%. **Growth:** 2.2%. **Migrants:** 1.4%. **Pop. density:** 319.9 per sq mi, 123.5 per sq km. **Urban:** 56.1%. **Ethnic groups:** Akan 45.7%, Mole-Dagbon 16.6%, Ewe 13.9%, Ga-Dangme 7.4%, Gurma 5.7%, Guan 3.7%, Grusi 2.5%. **Languages:** Asante, Ewe, Fante, Boron, Dagomba, Dangme, Dagarte, Kokomba, Akyem, Ga, English (official). **Religions:** Christian 71.2% (incl. Pentecostal/Charismatic 28.3%, Protestant 18.4%, Catholic 13.1%), Muslim 17.6%, traditional 5.2%, none 5.2%.

Geography: Total area: 92,098 sq mi, 238,533 sq km (80). **Land area:** 87,851 sq mi, 227,533 sq km. **Location:** S coast of W Africa. Côte d'Ivoire on W, Burkina Faso on N, Togo on E. **Topography:** Mostly low fertile plains and scrubland, cut by rivers and by the artificial Lake Volta. **Arable land:** 20.7%. **Capital:** Accra, 2,439,389. **Cities:** Kumasi, 3,064,718.

Government: Type: Presidential republic. **Head of state and govt.:** Pres. Nana Addo Dankwa Akufo-Addo; b. 1944; in office: Jan. 7, 2017. **Local divisions:** 10 regions. **Defense budget:** $185 mil. **Active troops:** 15,500.

Economy: Industries: mining, lumbering, light mfg., aluminum smelting, food proc., cement, small comm. shipbuilding. **Chief agric.:** cocoa, rice, cassava, peanuts, corn, shea nuts, bananas. **Natural resources:** gold, timber, industrial diamonds, bauxite, manganese, fish, rubber, hydropower, petroleum, silver, salt, limestone. **Water:** 2,050 cu m per capita. **Crude oil reserves:** 660 mil bbls. **Electricity prod.:** 11.1 bil kWh. **Labor force:** agric. 40.7%, industry 14.1%, services 45.2%. **Unemployment:** 2.4%.

Finance: Monetary unit: Cedi (GHS) (4.78 = $1 U.S.). **GDP:** $133.7 bil; **per capita GDP:** $4,700; **GDP growth:** 8.4%. **Imports:** $12.7 bil; China 16.8%, U.S. 8%, UK 6.2%, Belgium 5.9%. **Exports:** $13.8 bil; India 23.8%, UAE 13.4%, China 10.8%, Switzerland 10.1%, Vietnam 5.2%. **Tourism:** $846 mil. **Budget:** $12.4 bil. **Inflation:** 12.4%.

Transport: Railways: 588 mi. **Motor vehicles:** 6.7 per 1,000 pop. **Airports:** 7.

Communications: Telephone: 1 per 100 pop. **Mobile:** 127.5 per 100 pop. **Broadband:** 71.3 per 100 pop. **Internet:** 34.7%.

Health: Expend.: 5.9%. **Life expect.:** 64.9 male; 70.0 female. **Births:** 30.2 per 1,000 pop. **Deaths:** 6.8 per 1,000 pop. **Infant mortality:** 34.1 per 1,000 live births. **Undernourished:** 6.1%. **HIV:** 1.7%.

Education: Compulsory: ages 4-14. **Literacy:** 76.6%.
Embassy: 3512 International Dr. NW 20008; 686-4520.
Website: www.ghana.gov.gh

Named for an African empire along the Niger R., 400-1240 CE, Ghana was ruled by Britain for 113 years as the Gold Coast. The UN in 1956 approved merger with the British Togoland trust territory. Independence came Mar. 6, 1957, and republic status within the Commonwealth in 1960.

Pres. Kwame Nkrumah built hospitals and schools and promoted development projects but ran the country into debt, jailed opponents, and was accused of corruption. A 1964 referendum gave Nkrumah dictatorial powers and set up a one-party socialist state. A police-army coup overthrew Nkrumah in 1966. Elections were held in 1969, but four further coups occurred in 1972, 1978, 1979, and 1981. A new constitution, allowing multiparty politics, was approved in Apr. 1992. Former coup leader Jerry Rawlings won the 1996 presidential election. Kofi Annan, a career UN diplomat from Ghana, served as UN sec.-gen., 1997-2006.

Opposition leader John Agyekum Kufuor won a 2000 runoff vote and was sworn in Jan. 7, 2001, marking Ghana's first peaceful transfer of power from one elected president to another. He was reelected in 2004. John Atta Mills won a 2008 runoff election. A major offshore oil and gas find was announced June 2007; production began Dec. 2010. When Mills died in 2012, Vice Pres. John Dramani Mahama replaced him. Mahama won a full term in Dec. 2012 elections, but with unemployment high, he was defeated by Nana Addo Dankwa Akufo-Addo in the Dec. 7, 2016, presidential election.

Greece
Hellenic Republic

People: Population: 10,761,523 (84). **Age distrib.:** <15: 13.7%; 65+: 21.1%. **Growth:** −0.07%. **Migrants:** 10.9%. **Pop. density:** 213.3 per sq mi, 82.4 per sq km. **Urban:** 79.1%. **Ethnic groups:** Greek 93%, foreign citizen 7%. (Greece does not collect ethnicity data.) **Languages:** Greek (official). **Religions:** Greek Orthodox (official) 81%-90%, Muslim 2%, none 4%-15%.

Geography: Total area: 50,949 sq mi, 131,957 sq km (95). **Land area:** 50,443 sq mi, 130,647 sq km. **Location:** S end of Balkan Peninsula in SE Europe. Albania, Macedonia, Bulgaria on N; Turkey on E. **Topography:** About three-quarters is non-arable, with mountains in all areas incl. N-S Pindus Mts. Heavily indented coastline is 9,385 mi long. About 2,000 islands, only 169 inhabited, among them Crete, Rhodes, Milos, Kerkira (Corfu), Chios, Lesbos, Samos, Euboea, Delos, Mykonos. **Arable land:** 17.3%. **Capital:** Athens, 3,155,600. **Cities:** Thessaloniki, 810,791.

Government: Type: Parliamentary republic. **Head of state:** Pres. Prokopis Pavlopoulos; b. 1950; in office: Mar. 13, 2015. **Head of govt.:** Prime Min. Alexis Tsipras; b. 1974; in office: Sept. 21, 2015. **Local divisions:** 13 regions, 1 autonomous monastic state. **Defense budget:** $4.7 bil. **Active troops:** 141,350.

Economy: Industries: tourism, food and tobacco proc., textiles, chemicals, metal prods. **Chief agric.:** wheat, corn, barley, sugar beets, olives, tomatoes, wine, tobacco, potatoes; beef. **Natural resources:** lignite, petroleum, iron ore, bauxite, lead, zinc, nickel, magnesite, marble, salt. **Water:** 6,244 cu m per capita. **Crude oil reserves:** 10 mil bbls. **Electricity prod.:** 49.3 bil kWh. **Labor force:** agric. 12.1%, industry 15.3%, services 72.6%. **Unemployment:** 21.5%.

Finance: Monetary unit: Euro (EUR) (0.86 = $1 U.S.). **GDP:** $298.7 bil; **per capita GDP:** $27,700; **GDP growth:** 1.4%. **Imports:** $50.2 bil; Germany 10.4%, Italy 8.2%, Russia 6.8%, Iraq 6.3%, South Korea 6.1%, China 5.4%, Netherlands 5.3%. **Exports:** $29.2 bil; Italy 10.6%, Germany 7.1%, Turkey 6.8%, Cyprus 6.5%. **Tourism:** $16.5 bil. **Budget:** $98.1 bil. **Inflation:** 1.1%.

Transport: Railways: 1,583 mi. **Motor vehicles:** 613.5 per 1,000 pop. **Airports:** 68.

Communications: Telephone: 46.4 per 100 pop. **Mobile:** 115.9 per 100 pop. **Broadband:** 51.3 per 100 pop. **Internet:** 69.1%.

Health: Expend.: 8.4%. **Life expect.:** 78.2 male; 83.6 female. **Births:** 8.3 per 1,000 pop. **Deaths:** 11.4 per 1,000 pop. **Infant mortality:** 4.5 per 1,000 live births. **Undernourished:** <2.5%. **HIV:** 0.2%.

Education: Compulsory: ages 6-14. **Literacy:** 97.7%.
Embassy: 2217 Massachusetts Ave. NW 20008; 939-1300.
Website: primeminister.gr

The achievements of ancient Greece in art, architecture, science, mathematics, philosophy, drama, literature, and democracy became legacies for succeeding ages. Greece reached the height of its power, particularly in the Athenian city-state, in the 5th cent. BCE. Greece fell under Roman rule in the 2nd and 1st cents. BCE. In the 4th cent. CE, it became part of the Byzantine Empire and, after the fall of Constantinople to the Turks in 1453, part of the Ottoman Empire.

Greece won its war of independence from Turkey, 1821-29, and became a kingdom. A republic was established 1924; the monarchy was restored, 1935. In Oct. 1940, Greece rejected an ultimatum from Italy, but the country was defeated and occupied by German, Italian, and Bulgarian forces. By the end of 1944 the invaders withdrew. Communist resistance forces were overcome by Royalist and British troops. A plebiscite restored the monarchy.

Communists waged guerrilla war 1947-49 against the government but were defeated with the aid of the U.S. A period of reconstruction and rapid development followed, mainly with conservative governments under Prem. Constantine Karamanlis. The Center Union, led by Georgios Papandreou, won elections in 1963 and 1964, but King Constantine forced Papandreou to resign. A period of political maneuvers ended with Col. George Papadopoulos's military takeover Apr. 1967. King Constantine tried to reverse the consolidation of the harsh dictatorship Dec. 1967, but failed and fled to Italy. Papadopoulos was ousted Nov. 1973.

Greek army officers serving in the Cyprus National Guard staged a coup on the island July 15, 1974. Turkey invaded Cyprus a week later, precipitating the collapse of the Greek junta. Democratic government returned, and in 1975 the monarchy was abolished.

The 1981 electoral victory of the Panhellenic Socialist Movement (Pasok) of Andreas Papandreou (Georgios's son) substantially changed Greece's internal and external policies. A scandal contributed to the 1989 defeat of the Socialists at the polls. Papandreou, who was acquitted Jan. 1992 of corruption charges, led the Socialists to a comeback victory in 1993 general elections. The Socialists retained power in 1996 and 2000 elections.

The conservative New Democracy (ND) party won 2004 parliamentary elections, and Konstantinos (Costas) Karamanlis became prime min. Beset by scandals and an ailing economy, Karamanlis called early elections for Oct. 4, 2009, won by Pasok under the leadership of the U.S.-born George A. Papandreou (Andreas's son). The IMF and eurozone countries agreed in 2010 on a 110-bil euro loan package to prevent Greece from defaulting on its debt; in return, Greek leaders implemented an austerity plan. As the debt crisis continued, parliament passed, amid violent anti-austerity protests, new austerity measures, Feb. 2012, to obtain a second, 130-bil euro bailout in Mar. The conservative, pro-bailout Antonis Samaras of ND became prime min., June 2012. The government agreed on a plan for 13.5 bil euros in budget cuts and austerity measures Sept. 27, touching off renewed violent protests. Recession and austerity measures, 2007-13, caused Greece's GDP to shrink by 26%. In 2014, 36% of people lived below the poverty line. Campaigning against austerity, the leftist Syriza party won Jan. 25, 2015, elections. Syriza's Alexis Tsipras became prime min. and negotiated with the Intl. Monetary Fund, European Central Bank, and eurozone members (known as the troika) on a third bailout needed by mid-2015 to avert default. In a July 5 referendum, Greek voters decisively rejected further austerity. However, negotiations with the troika after the referendum produced an 86-bil euro bailout agreement (final approval came Aug. 19) with tough austerity terms—including further tax increases and pension cuts, sales of government assets, deregulation of the economy, and banking system reform. Tsipras resigned Aug. 20 and called elections for Sept. 20; Syriza won, and Tsipras again became prime min., Sept. 21. As austerity measures were implemented, unemployment was 24% in 2016 and 22% in 2017. After negotiating extended repayment terms for more than 200 bil euros of eurozone debt, Greece officially exited the bailout program, Aug. 20, 2018, but was still subject to international supervision of government finances.

In 2015, Greece was the most common entry point for undocumented migrants from the Middle East, SW Asia, and Africa trying to reach the EU. More than 850,000 migrants arrived in Greece in 2015. About 174,000 arrived in 2016, 30,000 in 2017, and 23,000 Jan.-Sept. 2018. The leading country of origin was Syria. An EU-Turkey agreement, effective Mar. 20, 2016, reduced the number of undocumented migrants arriving in Greece by boat from Turkey. Most migrants reaching Greece tried to continue to N Europe. However, several countries closed their borders to migrants traveling north, and EU resettlement programs progressed slowly. As of Aug. 31, 2018, about 62,500 migrants were in Greece, some living in harsh conditions in refugee camps.

Amid heat and drought, wildfires near Athens in July 2018 killed almost 100.

Grenada

People: Population: 112,207 (179). **Age distrib.:** <15: 23.8%; 65+: 10.3%. **Growth:** 0.4%. **Migrants:** 6.6%. **Pop. density:** 844.8 per sq mi, 326.2 per sq km. **Urban:** 36.3%. **Ethnic groups:** African descent 82.4%, mixed 13.3%, East Indian 2.2%. **Languages:** English (official), French patois. **Religions:** Protestant 49.2% (incl. Pentecostal 17.2%, Seventh-day Adventist 13.2%), Roman Catholic 36%, none 5.7%.

Geography: Total area: 133 sq mi, 344 sq km (186); **Land area:** 133 sq mi, 344 sq km. **Location:** In Caribbean, 90 mi N of Venezuela. Trinidad and Tobago to S, St. Vincent and the Grenadines to N. **Topography:** Main island is mountainous. Country also comprised of Carriacou and Petite Martinique Isls. **Arable land:** 8.8%. **Capital:** St.George's, 39,297.

Government: Type: Parliamentary democracy. **Head of state:** Queen Elizabeth II, rep. by Gov.-Gen. Cecile La Grenade; b. 1952; in office: May 7, 2013. **Head of govt.:** Prime Min. Keith Mitchell; b. 1946; in office: Feb. 20, 2013. **Local divisions:** 6 parishes, 1 dependency. **Defense budget/active troops:** NA.

Economy: Industries: food and beverages, textiles, light assembly operations, tourism, constr., education, call-center operations. **Chief agric.:** bananas, cocoa, nutmeg, mace, soursop, citrus, avocados, root crops, corn, vegetables; fish. **Natural resources:** timber, tropical fruit. **Water:** 1,873 cu m per capita. **Electricity prod.:** 200 mil kWh. **Labor force:** agric. 11%, industry 20%, services 69%. **Unemployment:** NA.

Finance: Monetary unit: East Caribbean Dollar (XCD) (2.70 = $1 U.S.). **GDP:** $1.6 bil; **per capita GDP:** $14,900; **GDP growth:** 3.5%. **Imports:** $310.2 mil; U.S. 31.7%, Trinidad and Tobago 24.9%, China 6.7%. **Exports:** $43.4 mil; U.S. 25.3%, Japan 10.1%, Guyana 8.7%, Dominica 6.6%, St. Lucia 6.4%. **Tourism:** $149 mil. **Budget** $284.6 mil. **Inflation:** 0.9%.

Transport: Airports: 3.

Communications: Telephone: 30.1 per 100 pop. **Mobile:** 105 per 100 pop. **Broadband:** 32.9 per 100 pop. **Internet:** 55.9%.

Health: Expend.: 5%. **Life expect.:** 72.1 male; 77.6 female. **Births:** 15.2 per 1,000 pop. **Deaths:** 8.2 per 1,000 pop. **Infant mortality:** 9.4 per 1,000 live births. **Undernourished:** NA. **HIV:** NA.

Education: Compulsory: ages 5-16. **Literacy:** NA.

Embassy: 1701 New Hampshire Ave. NW 20009; 265-2561.

Website: www.gov.gd

Christopher Columbus sighted Grenada in 1498. The first European settlers were French, 1650. The island was held alternately by France and England until final British occupation, 1784. Grenada became fully independent Feb. 7, 1974, during a general strike.

On Oct. 14, 1983, a military coup ousted Prime Min. Maurice Bishop, who was put under house arrest, later freed by supporters, rearrested, and executed Oct. 19. U.S. forces, with a token force from six area nations, invaded Grenada, Oct. 25. Resistance from the Grenadian army and Cuban advisors was quickly overcome, and U.S. troops left Grenada in June 1985.

Hurricane Ivan slammed into Grenada, Sept. 7, 2004, killing 39 people and damaging an estimated 90% of the buildings on the island. The New National Party (NNP) won all 15 seats in 2013 and 2018 legislative elections; the NNP's Keith Mitchell became prime min., Feb. 20, 2013.

Guatemala
Republic of Guatemala

People: Population: 16,581,273 (67). **Age distrib.:** <15: 34.6%; 65+: 4.5%. **Growth:** 1.7%. **Migrants:** 0.5%. **Pop. density:** 400.8 per sq mi, 154.7 per sq km. **Urban:** 51.1%. **Ethnic groups:** mestizo or Ladino (mixed Amerindian/Spanish) and European 60.1%, Maya 39.3% (K'iche 11.3%, Q'eqchi 7.6%, Kaqchikel 7.4%, Mam 5.5%). **Languages:** Spanish (official), Maya langs. (incl. K'iche, Q'eqchi, Mam, Kaqchikel). **Religions:** Roman Catholic, Protestant, indigenous Mayan beliefs.

Geography: Total area: 42,042 sq mi, 108,889 sq km (105); **Land area:** 41,374 sq mi, 107,159 sq km. **Location:** Central America. Mexico on N and W, El Salvador on S, Honduras and Belize on E. **Topography:** Central highland and mountain areas bordered by a narrow Pacific coast and lowlands and fertile river valleys on the Caribbean. Numerous volcanoes in S, more than half a dozen over 11,000 ft. **Arable land:** 8.7%. **Capital:** Guatemala City, 2,851,104.

Government: Type: Presidential republic. **Head of state and govt.:** Pres. Jimmy Ernesto Morales; b. 1969; in office: Jan. 14, 2016. **Local divisions:** 22 departments. **Defense budget:** $242 mil. **Active troops:** 18,050.

Economy: Industries: sugar, textiles/clothing, furniture, chemicals, petroleum, metals, rubber, tourism. **Chief agric.:** sugarcane, corn, bananas, coffee, beans, cardamom; cattle, sheep. **Natural resources:** petroleum, nickel, rare woods, fish, chicle, hydropower. **Water:** 7,826 cu m per capita. **Crude oil reserves:** 83.1 mil bbls. **Electricity prod.:** 10.8 bil kWh. **Labor force:** agric. 29.4%, industry 21.1%, services 49.6%. **Unemployment:** 2.7%.

Finance: Monetary unit: Quetzal (GTQ) (7.57 = $1 U.S.). **GDP:** $137.8 bil; **per capita GDP:** $8,100; **GDP growth:** 2.8%. **Imports:** $17.5 bil; U.S. 39.8%, China 10.7%, Mexico 10.7%, El Salvador 5.3%. **Exports:** $10.5 bil; U.S. 33.8%, El Salvador 11.1%, Honduras 8.8%, Nicaragua 5.1%. **Tourism:** $1.6 bil. **Budget:** $10.6 bil. **Inflation:** 4.4%.

Transport: Railways: 497 mi. **Motor vehicles:** 132.2 per 1,000 pop. **Airports:** 16.

Communications: Telephone: 14.6 per 100 pop. **Mobile:** 118.2 per 100 pop. **Broadband:** 13.9 per 100 pop. **Internet:** 34.5%.

Health: Expend.: 5.7%. **Life expect.:** 69.8 male; 73.9 female. **Births:** 24.6 per 1,000 pop. **Deaths:** 5.0 per 1,000 pop. **Infant mortality:** 23.3 per 1,000 live births. **Undernourished:** 15.8%. **HIV:** 0.4%.

Education: Compulsory: ages 6-15. **Literacy:** 81.5%.

Embassy: 2220 R St. NW 20008; 745-4953.

Website: www.presidencia.gob.gt

A Mayan Indian empire flourished in present-day Guatemala for over 1,000 years before Spaniards came. Guatemala was a Spanish colony 1524-1821. A republic was established in 1839.

In 1954, the U.S. Central Intelligence Agency engineered the overthrow of elected Pres. Jacobo Arbenz Guzmán, a left-wing reformer. Since then, the country has experienced a variety of military and civilian governments and periods of insurgency, repression, paramilitary violence, and civil war. After military coups in 1982 and 1983, the nation returned to civilian rule in 1986.

The Guatemalan government and leftist rebels signed a peace accord Dec. 29, 1996. During more than 35 years of armed conflict, some 200,000 people were killed or "disappeared"; most casualties were attributed to the government and its paramilitary allies. Gen. Efraín Ríos Montt, dictator in 1982-83, was found guilty of genocide May 10, 2013, but the Constitutional Court overturned his conviction May 20 and ruled that part of his trial had to be repeated. Ríos Montt died, Apr. 1, 2018, during the retrial. Four former high-level military officers were convicted, May 23, 2018, of crimes against humanity and other charges.

Former Pres. Alfonso Portillo was extradited to the U.S. May 24, 2013, to be tried for money laundering; he pleaded guilty Mar. 18, 2014. Drug trafficking, arms smuggling, police corruption, and one of the world's highest homicide rates posed threats to national stability. Guatemalans made up a sizable portion of the tens of thousands of asylum seekers and other migrants detained trying to enter the U.S. from Mexico 2013-18.

Pres. Otto Pérez Molina's vice president, Roxana Baldetti, resigned, May 2015, following bribery and corruption scandals; Baldetti was arrested Aug. 21, 2015. While her Guatemala cases were pending, she was indicted in the U.S., Feb. 22, 2017, on drug trafficking charges. Following large-scale protests, Pérez Molina resigned Sept. 2, 2015; jailed Sept. 3, he was ordered to stand trial on bribery, corruption, and conspiracy charges Sept. 8. Former comedian Jimmy Ernesto Morales Cabrera won a runoff election for president Oct. 25, 2015. Under investigation by a UN-sponsored anti-corruption panel, Morales announced, Aug. 31, 2018, he would halt the panel's work in 2019.

Guinea
Republic of Guinea

People: Population: 11,855,411 (75). **Age distrib.:** <15: 41.4%; 65+: 3.9%. **Growth:** 2.8%. **Migrants:** 1%. **Pop. density:** 125 per sq mi, 48.2 per sq km. **Urban:** 36.1%. **Ethnic groups:** Fulani (Peul) 32.1%, Malinke 29.8%, Susu 19.8%, Guerze 6.2%, Kissi 4.7%, Toma 2.8%. **Languages:** French (official), ethnic group-specific langs. **Religions:** Muslim 86.2%, Christian 9.7%.

Geography: Total area: 94,926 sq mi, 245,857 sq km (77). **Land area:** 94,872 sq mi, 245,717 sq km. **Location:** Atlantic coast of W Africa. Guinea-Bissau, Senegal, Mali on N; Côte d'Ivoire on E; Liberia, Sierra Leone on S. **Topography:** Narrow coastal belt leads to mountainous middle region, source of the Gambia, Senegal, and Niger Rivers. Upper Guinea, farther inland, is cooler upland. The SE is forested. **Arable land:** 12.6%. **Capital:** Conakry, 1,843,121.

Government: Type: Presidential republic. **Head of state:** Pres. Alpha Condé; b. 1938; in office: Dec. 21, 2010. **Head of govt.:** Prime Min. Ibrahima Kassory Fofana; in office: May 22, 2018. **Local divisions:** 7 regions, 1 governorate. **Defense budget:** $164 mil. **Active troops:** 9,700.

Economy: Industries: bauxite, gold, diamonds, iron ore; light mfg.; agric. proc. **Chief agric.:** rice, coffee, pineapples, mangoes, palm kernels, cocoa, cassava, bananas, potatoes; cattle, sheep, goats. **Natural resources:** bauxite, iron ore, diamonds, gold, uranium, hydropower, fish, salt. **Water:** 17,924 cu m per capita. **Electricity prod.:** 1 bil kWh. **Labor force:** agric. 68.2%, industry 5.9%, services 25.9%. **Unemployment:** 4.5%.

Finance: Monetary unit: Franc (GNF) (9,047.42 = $1 U.S.). **GDP:** $26.5 bil; **per capita GDP:** $2,000; **GDP growth:** 6.7%. **Imports:** $2.5 bil; Netherlands 17.2%, China 13.2%, India 11.8%, Belgium 10%, France 6.9%. **Exports:** $2.1 bil; China 35.8%, Ghana 20.1%, UAE 11.6%. **Tourism:** $16 mil. **Budget:** $1.9 bil. **Inflation:** 8.9%.

Transport: Railways: 675 mi. **Airports:** 4.

Communications: Telephone: 0 per 100 pop. **Mobile** (2016): 87.1 per 100 pop. **Broadband:** 15 per 100 pop. **Internet:** 9.8%.

Health: Expend.: 4.5%. **Life expect.:** 60.4 male; 64.0 female. **Births:** 36.4 per 1,000 pop. **Deaths:** 8.9 per 1,000 pop. **Infant mortality:** 55.3 per 1,000 live births. **Undernourished:** 19.7%. **HIV:** 1.5%.

Education: Compulsory: ages 7-12. **Literacy:** 32%.

Embassy: 2112 Leroy Pl. NW 20008; 986-4300.

Website: www.presidence.gov.gn or www.state.gov/p/af/ci/gv/

Guinea, a French colony, attained independence Oct. 2, 1958. Sékou Touré, Guinea's first president (1958-84), turned to Communist nations for support and set up a one-party state. Thousands of opponents were jailed and tortured, and many were killed in the 1970s after an unsuccessful Portuguese invasion.

The military took control in a bloodless coup after the Mar. 1984 death of Touré. A new constitution was approved in 1991, but movement toward democracy was slow. Gen. Lansana Conté, the incumbent, won a long-awaited presidential election in Dec. 1993, which outside monitors called flawed. Conté suppressed an army mutiny in Conakry, Feb. 2-3, 1996, and won reelection in 1998. Fighting in early 2001 along the border with Liberia and Sierra Leone created a refugee crisis in Guinea; voluntary repatriation of more than 51,000 Liberian refugees was largely completed in 2007.

Major opposition parties boycotted the 2003 presidential election, in which the ailing Conté won 95.6% of the vote. More than 120 died in Jan.-Feb. 2007 strikes and protests that pressured Conté to name a new prime min. from a union-leader approved list; protests followed Prime Min. Lansana Kouyate's ouster by Conté in May 2008. After Conté's death Dec. 22, a military junta took power. More than 150 people were reportedly killed Sept. 28, 2009, when Guinean troops fired into a crowd of about 50,000 anti-government protesters in Conakry. After an assassination attempt Dec. 3, 2009, by a former aide left Pres. Moussa Dadis Camara seriously wounded, Vice Pres. Sékouba Konaté became interim head of state. Presidential elections June-Nov. 2010 brought a civilian government headed by Alpha Condé to power Dec. 21. Condé won reelection, Oct. 11, 2015. In Feb.-Mar. 2018, violent protests related to a teachers' strike and disputed local elections, and a harsh security-forces response, left at least 11 dead.

The largest known outbreak of Ebola virus disease (EVD) began in Guinea in Dec. 2013, spread rapidly to Liberia and Sierra Leone, and caused thousands of deaths. WHO lifted its public health emergency in West Africa, Mar. 29, 2016. By June 10, 2016, WHO had recorded 28,616 EVD cases in the 3 countries (including 3,814 in Guinea) and 11,310 deaths (2,544 in Guinea). Guinea declared an end to the epidemic there, June 1.

Guinea-Bissau
Republic of Guinea-Bissau

People: Population: 1,833,247 (149). **Age distrib.:** <15: 43.5%; 65+: 3%. **Growth:** 2.5%. **Migrants:** 1.3%. **Pop. density:** 168.9 per sq mi, 65.2 per sq km. **Urban:** 43.4%. **Ethnic groups:** Fulani 28.5%, Balanta 22.5%, Mandinga 14.7%, Papel 9.1%, Manjaco 8.3%, Beafada 3.5%, Mancanha 3.1%, Bijago 2.1%. **Languages:** Crioulo (lingua franca), Portuguese (official), Pular, Mandingo. **Religions:** Muslim 45.1%, Christian 22.1%, animist 14.9%.

Geography: Total area: 13,948 sq mi, 36,125 sq km (134). **Land area:** 10,857 sq mi, 28,120 sq km. **Location:** Atlantic coast of W Africa. Senegal on N, Guinea on E and S. **Topography:** A swampy coastal plain covers most of country. Low savanna region to E. **Arable land:** 10.7%. **Capital:** Bissau, 558,399.

Government: Type: Semi-presidential republic. **Head of state:** Pres. José Mário Vaz; b. 1957; in office: June 23, 2014. **Head of govt.:** Prime Min. Aristides Gomes; in office: Apr. 16, 2018. **Local divisions:** 9 regions. **Defense budget:** NA. **Active troops:** 4,450.

Economy: Industries: agric. prods. proc., beer, soft drinks. **Chief agric.:** rice, corn, beans, cassava, cashew nuts, peanuts, palm kernels, cotton; fish. **Natural resources:** fish, timber, phosphates, bauxite, clay, granite, limestone, unexploited petroleum deposits. **Water:** 17,028 cu m per capita. **Electricity prod.:** 34 mil kWh. **Labor force:** agric. 83.5%, industry 7%, services 9.6%. **Unemployment:** 6.1%.

Finance: Monetary unit: CFA Franc (XOF) (566.17 = $1 U.S.). **GDP:** $3.1 bil; **per capita GDP:** $1,800; **GDP growth:** 5.5%. **Imports:** $241.2 mil; Portugal 47.8%, Senegal 12.1%, China 10.4%, Netherlands 8.1%, Pakistan 5.4%. **Exports:** $281.2 mil; India 67.1%, Vietnam 21.1%. **Tourism:** $19 mil. **Budget:** $267 mil. **Inflation:** 1.4%.

Transport: Airports: 2.

Communications: Telephone: 0 per 100 pop. **Mobile:** 77.1 per 100 pop. **Broadband:** 6.9 per 100 pop. **Internet:** 3.8%.

Health: Expend.: 6.9%. **Life expect.:** 59.2 male; 63.6 female. **Births:** 37.3 per 1,000 pop. **Deaths:** 8.5 per 1,000 pop. **Infant mortality:** 54.8 per 1,000 live births. **Undernourished:** 26%. **HIV:** 3.4%.

Education: Compulsory: ages 6-14. **Literacy:** 59.9%.

Permanent UN mission: 336 E. 45th St., 13th Fl., New York, NY 10017; (212) 896-8311.

Website: www.state.gov/p/af/ci/pu/

Portuguese mariners explored the area in the mid-15th cent.; the slave trade flourished in the 17th and 18th cents., and colonization began in the 19th. Independence came Sept. 10, 1974, ending 13 years of guerrilla warfare against the Portuguese rule.

A Nov. 1980 coup gave army chief João Bernardo Vieira absolute power. Vieira eventually initiated political liberalization; multiparty elections were held in 1994. A 1998 army uprising triggered a civil war, with Senegal and Guinea aiding the Vieira regime. After a peace accord signed Nov. 2 broke down, rebel troops ousted Vieira on May 7, 1999.

Civilian rule returned with 1999-2000 elections, but top military officers staged a coup Sept. 14, 2003. Vieira won a presidential runoff election, July 24, 2005. A group of soldiers murdered Vieira, Mar. 2, 2009. Political violence continued as the 2009 presidential election approached; the ruling party candidate, Malam Bacai Sanhá, won a runoff vote July 26. He died Jan. 9, 2012. A military coup Apr. 12 derailed a runoff election scheduled for Apr. 29. The military appointed Manuel Serifo Nhamadjo to lead a transitional government. Drug trafficking increased substantially, with the support of the military. The U.S. arrested and indicted former navy chief Rear Adm. José Américo Bubo Na Tchuto on drug charges Apr. 2013; then-armed forces head Gen. Antonio Injai was indicted in absentia. Na Tchuto pleaded guilty, May 13, 2014. Former Finance Min. José Mário Vaz won a May 18, 2014, presidential runoff.

Guyana
Cooperative Republic of Guyana

People: Population: 740,685 (162). **Age distrib.:** <15: 25.4%; 65+: 6.4%. **Growth:** 0.5%. **Migrants:** 2%. **Pop. density:** 9.7 per sq mi, 3.8 per sq km. **Urban:** 26.6%. **Ethnic groups:** East Indian 39.8%, black (African) 29.3%, mixed 19.9%, Amerindian 10.5%. **Languages:** English (official), Guyanese Creole, Amerindian langs., Indian langs., Chinese. **Religions:** Protestant 34.8% (incl. Pentecostal 22.8%), Hindu 24.8%, Roman Catholic 7.1%, Muslim 6.8%.

Geography: Total area: 83,000 sq mi, 214,969 sq km (83); **Land area:** 76,004 sq mi, 196,849 sq km. **Location:** N coast of S America. Venezuela on W, Brazil on S, Suriname on E. **Topography:** Dense tropical forests cover much of land. A grassy savanna divides it from flat coastal area, where 90% of the pop. lives, with its rich alluvial soil. **Arable land:** 2.1%. **Capital:** Georgetown, 109,934.

Government: Type: Parliamentary republic. **Head of state and govt.:** Pres. David Arthur Granger; b. 1945; in office: May 16, 2015. **Local divisions:** 10 regions. **Defense budget:** $56 mil. **Active troops:** 3,400.

Economy: Industries: bauxite, sugar, rice milling, timber, textiles, gold mining. **Chief agric.:** sugarcane, rice, edible oils; beef, pork, poultry; shrimp, fish. **Natural resources:** bauxite, gold, diamonds, timber, shrimp, fish. **Water:** 353,279 cu m per capita. **Electricity prod.:** 1 bil kWh. **Labor force:** agric. 13.4%, industry 26.5%, services 60.1%. **Unemployment:** 12%.

Finance: Monetary unit: Dollar (GYD) (209.63 = $1 U.S.). **GDP:** $6.3 bil; **per capita GDP:** $8,200; **GDP growth:** 2.1%. **Imports:** $1.8 bil; Trinidad and Tobago 27.5%, U.S. 26.5%, China 8.9%, Suriname 6.1%. **Exports:** $1.5 bil; Canada 24.9%, U.S. 16.5%, Panama 9.6%, UK 7.7%, Jamaica 5.1%, Trinidad and Tobago 5%. **Tourism:** $104 mil. **Budget:** $1.2 bil. **Inflation** (2015-16): 0.8%.

Transport: Motor vehicles: 93.9 per 1,000 pop. **Airports:** 11. **Communications: Telephone:** 17.5 per 100 pop. **Mobile:** 82.7 per 100 pop. **Broadband:** 0.2 per 100 pop. **Internet:** 35.7%.

Health: Expend.: 4.5%. **Life expect.:** 65.9 male; 72.1 female. **Births:** 15.4 per 1,000 pop. **Deaths:** 7.4 per 1,000 pop. **Infant mortality:** 29.5 per 1,000 live births. **Undernourished:** 7.5%. **HIV:** 1.7%.

Education: Compulsory: ages 6-11. **Literacy:** 88.5%. **Embassy:** 2490 Tracy Pl. NW 20008; 265-6900. **Website:** parliament.gov.gy

Guyana became a Dutch possession in the 17th cent., but sovereignty passed to Britain in 1815. Indentured servants from India soon outnumbered freed African slaves. Guyana became independent May 26, 1966.

The Port Kaituma ambush of U.S. Rep. Leo J. Ryan and others investigating mistreatment of American followers of the Rev. Jim Jones's Peoples Temple cult triggered a mass suicide-execution of more than 900 at their commune in Jonestown, Nov. 18, 1978.

The People's National Congress, the party in power since Guyana became independent, was voted out of office with the election of Cheddi Jagan in Oct. 1992. When Pres. Jagan died Mar. 6, 1997, Prime Min. Samuel Hinds succeeded him. Jagan's widow, Janet, became prime min. Mar. 17. She won the presidency in a disputed election Dec. 15. She resigned because of ill health Aug. 1999 and was succeeded by Bharrat Jagdeo. He won reelection in 2001 and 2006. Donald Ramotar, the candidate of Jagdeo's party, was elected president in 2011. An opposition coalition won a 1-seat majority over Ramotar's party in May 11, 2015, elections, and coalition leader David Granger became president, May 16. Offshore oil discoveries were announced in 2015 and 2017.

Haiti
Republic of Haiti

People: Population: 10,788,440 (86). **Age distrib.:** <15: 32.3%; 65+: 4.2%. **Growth:** 1.3%. **Migrants:** 0.4%. **Pop. density:** 1,013.9 per sq mi, 391.5 per sq km. **Urban:** 55.3%. **Ethnic groups:** black 95%, mixed and white 5%. **Languages:** French, Creole (both official). **Religions:** Roman Catholic 54.7%, Protestant 28.5% (incl. Baptist 15.4%), vodou 2.1%, none 10.2%.

Geography: Total area: 10,714 sq mi, 27,750 sq km (144); **Land area:** 10,641 sq mi, 27,560 sq km. **Location:** In Caribbean; occupies western third of isl. of Hispaniola. Dominican Republic on E, Cuba to W. **Topography:** About two-thirds is mountainous. Much of rest is semiarid. Coastal areas are warm and moist. **Arable land:** 38.8%. **Capital:** Port-au-Prince, 2,636,763.

Government: Type: Semi-presidential republic. **Head of state:** Pres. Jovenel Moise; b. 1968; in office: Feb. 7, 2017. **Head of govt.:** Prime Min. Jean-Henry Céant; b. 1956; in office: Aug. 7, 2018. **Local divisions:** 10 departments. **Defense budget:** $7 mil. **Active troops:** 150. UN mission MINUJUSTH, in Oct. 2017, began assisting Haiti in developing a national police.

Economy: Industries: textiles, sugar refining, flour milling, cement, light assembly using imported parts. **Chief agric.:** coffee, mangoes, cocoa, sugarcane, rice, corn, sorghum. **Natural resources:** bauxite, copper, calcium carbonate, gold, marble, hydropower. **Water:** 1,310 cu m per capita. **Electricity prod.:** 979.7 mil kWh. **Labor force:** agric. 41.3%, industry 12.3%, services 46.5%. **Unemployment:** 14%.

Finance: Monetary unit: Gourde (HTG) (68.77 = $1 U.S.). **GDP:** $19.9 bil; **per capita GDP:** $1,800; **GDP growth:** 1.2%. **Imports:** $3.6 bil; U.S. 20.7%, China 18.8%, Netherlands Antilles 15.7%, Indonesia 8.5%. **Exports:** $960.1 mil; U.S. 80.6%. **Tourism:** $504 mil. **Budget:** $2.3 bil. **Inflation:** 14.7%.

Transport: Motor vehicles: 8.8 per 1,000 pop. **Airports:** 4. **Communications: Telephone:** 0.05 per 100 pop. **Mobile:** 59.1 per 100 pop. **Broadband:** 10.3 per 100 pop. **Internet:** 12.2%.

Health: Expend.: 6.9%. **Life expect.:** 61.9 male; 67.2 female. **Births:** 22.6 per 1,000 pop. **Deaths:** 7.5 per 1,000 pop. **Infant mortality:** 45.4 per 1,000 live births. **Undernourished:** 45.8%. **HIV:** 1.9%.

Education: Compulsory: ages 6-11. **Literacy:** 60.7%. **Embassy:** 2311 Massachusetts Ave. NW 20008; 332-4090. **Website:** primature.gouv.ht or www.haiti.org

Haiti, visited by Christopher Columbus in 1492 and a French colony from 1697, attained its independence, 1804, following a rebellion led by former slave Toussaint L'Ouverture. After a period of political violence, the U.S. occupied the country 1915-34.

François Duvalier, known as Papa Doc, was elected president in 1957; in 1964 he was named president for life. Upon his death in 1971, he was succeeded by his son, Jean Claude Duvalier, known as Baby Doc. Following weeks of unrest, Jean Claude fled Haiti aboard a U.S. Air Force jet Feb. 7, 1986. His departure ended the Duvalier family's brutal 28-year dictatorship, but political violence, corruption, poverty, AIDS, and other health problems have continued to plague Haiti.

Jean-Bertrand Aristide was elected president in 1990, but the military arrested and expelled him from the country in Sept. 1991. The U.S. Coast Guard intercepted some 35,000 Haitian refugees as they tried to enter the U.S., 1991-92. Most were returned to Haiti. There was a new upsurge of refugees starting in late 1993.

The UN authorized in 1994 an invasion of Haiti by a U.S.-led multinational force. A full-scale invasion was averted, Sept. 18, when military leaders agreed to step down. Aristide was restored to office Oct. 15. A UN peacekeeping force exercised responsi-bility in Haiti from 1995 to 1997. Aristide transferred power to his elected successor, René Préval, in 1996.

Aristide won the 2000 presidency in an election boycotted by opposition groups. An armed uprising in early 2004 and pressure from France and the U.S. toppled Aristide, who went into exile Feb. 29. A U.S.-led contingent, sent in after the upheaval, yielded authority June 1, 2004, to a UN stabilization force (MINUSTAH). MINUSTAH's mission ended Oct. 15, 2017, and the force was replaced by MINUJUSTH, intended to strengthen the rule of law and develop the national police.

Préval was again elected president in 2006. Skyrocketing prices for food imports sparked riots and mass protests in Apr. 2008. A succession of hurricanes and tropical storms, Aug.-Sept. 2008, left more than 550 Haitians dead and up to 1 mil homeless.

An earthquake Jan. 12, 2010, near Port-au-Prince caused cataclysmic damage. More than 220,000 people were killed, at least 300,000 were injured, and more than 1.5 mil were left homeless. With the central government paralyzed, a massive international relief effort was launched, but rebuilding and recovery proceeded slowly. In 2018, about 37,500 Haitians were still living in displacement camps. In Nov. 2017, the Trump administration announced it would end temporary residency status for almost 59,000 Haitians who had come to the U.S. after the 2010 earthquake, requiring them to return home by July 2019; an Oct. 3, 2018, injunction by a U.S. court temporarily barred implementation.

A severe cholera epidemic began soon after the 2010 earthquake. By 2018 the number of new cases had dropped sharply, but through July, more than 812,000 total cases had been reported and more than 9,600 people had died. The UN publicly acknowledged responsibility for the epidemic Dec. 1, 2016.

After the first round of presidential balloting Nov. 28, 2010, Michel Martelly, an entertainer, was declared ineligible for the second round. Violent protests, allegations of electoral fraud, and diplomatic pressure gained him a place in the runoff Mar. 20, 2011, which he won. After allegations of widespread fraud in the Oct. 25, 2015, first-round election for a new president, an electoral commission ruled that the balloting should be held again Oct. 9, 2016. Postponed, Oct. 5, 2016, after Hurricane Matthew caused widespread damage and about 1,000 deaths, the Nov. 20, 2016, re-vote was won by businessman Jovenel Moise. Government-announced fuel price increases led to violent protests, July 2018, leaving several dead; the increases were suspended, and the prime minister replaced.

Honduras
Republic of Honduras

People: Population: 9,182,766 (95). **Age distrib.:** <15: 32.4%; 65+: 4.4%. **Growth:** 1.6%. **Migrants:** 0.4%. **Pop. density:** 212.6 per sq mi, 82.1 per sq km. **Urban:** 57.1%. **Ethnic groups:** mestizo (mixed Amerindian/European) 90%, Amerindian 7%, black 2%. **Languages:** Spanish (official), Amerindian dialects. **Religions:** Roman Catholic 46%, Protestant 41%, none 9%.

Geography: Total area: 43,278 sq mi, 112,090 sq km (101); **Land area:** 43,201 sq mi, 111,890 sq km. **Location:** Central America. Guatemala on W; El Salvador, Nicaragua on S. **Topography:** Caribbean coast is 500 mi long. Pacific coast, on Gulf of Fonseca, is 40 mi long. Mountainous, with wide fertile valleys and rich forests. **Arable land:** 9.1%. **Capital:** Tegucigalpa, 1,363,041.

Government: Type: Presidential republic. **Head of state and govt.:** Pres. Juan Orlando Hernandez Alvarado; b. 1968; in office: Jan. 27, 2014. **Local divisions:** 18 departments. **Defense budget:** $263 mil. **Active troops:** 14,950.

Economy: Industries: sugar proc., coffee, woven and knit apparel, wood prods., cigars. **Chief agric.:** bananas, coffee, citrus, corn, African palm; beef; shrimp, tilapia, lobster. **Natural resources:** timber, gold, silver, copper, lead, zinc, iron ore, antimony, coal, fish, hydropower. **Water:** 11,413 cu m per capita. **Electricity prod.:** 8.6 bil kWh. **Labor force:** agric. 28.5%, industry 21.2%, services 50.3%. **Unemployment:** 4.5%.

Finance: Monetary unit: Lempira (HNL) (24.02 = $1 U.S.). **GDP:** $46.2 bil; **per capita GDP:** $5,600; **GDP growth:** 4.8%. **Imports:** $10.9 bil; U.S. 40.3%, Guatemala 10.5%, China 8.5%, Mexico 6.2%, El Salvador 5.7%. **Exports:** $8.2 bil; U.S. 34.5%, Germany 8.9%, Belgium 7.7%, El Salvador 7.3%, Netherlands 7.2%, Guatemala 5.2%. **Tourism:** $715 mil. **Budget:** $5.1 bil. **Inflation:** 3.9%.

Transport: Railways: 434 mi. **Motor vehicles:** 19.9 per 1,000 pop. **Airports:** 13.

Communications: Telephone: 5.3 per 100 pop. **Mobile:** 88.9 per 100 pop. **Broadband:** 22.5 per 100 pop. **Internet:** 30%.

Health: Expend.: 7.6%. **Life expect.:** 69.6 male; 73.0 female. **Births:** 22.0 per 1,000. **Deaths:** 5.3 per 1,000. **Infant mortality:** 16.7 per 1,000 live births. **Undernourished:** 15.3%. **HIV:** 0.3%.

Education: Compulsory: ages 5-16. **Literacy:** 89%.

Embassy: 3007 Tilden St. NW, Ste. 4-M, 20008; 966-7702.

Website: www.presidencia.gob.hn

Mayan civilization flourished in Honduras in the 1st millennium CE. Columbus arrived in 1502. Honduras became independent after freeing itself from Spain, 1821, and from the Fed. of Central America, 1838.

In 1975, the army ousted Gen. Oswaldo Lopez Arellano, president for most of the time since 1963, over charges of pervasive bribery by United Brands Co. of the U.S. An elected civilian government took power in 1982.

Honduras was devastated in late Oct. 1998 by Hurricane Mitch, which killed at least 5,600 people and caused more than $850 mil in damage to crops and livestock. On May 4, 2018, the Trump administration announced the termination of temporary residency status for about 86,000 Hondurans who came to the U.S. after Mitch; they would have to leave by Jan. 2020.

Juan Orlando Hernández of the conservative National Party won the Nov. 2013 presidential election. After the Supreme Court, 2015, struck down presidential term limits, Hernández sought reelection, Nov. 26, 2017. On Dec. 17, despite voting irregularities, Honduras's electoral commission, headed by a National Party member, declared Hernández the winner by a narrow margin.

Honduras has become a transshipment point for illegal drugs being smuggled from South America to the U.S. Drug-gang violence and other crime apparently contributed to an increase in Honduran migrants trying to enter the U.S. along the Mexican border, 2013-18. Environmental and indigenous rights activist Berta Cáceres was shot to death in her home, Mar. 3, 2016; two associates were killed later in 2016. The NGO Global Witness estimated in mid-2017 that more than 120 environmental activists or opponents of land seizures for development had been killed since 2009.

Hungary

People: Population: 9,825,704 (92). **Age distrib.:** <15: 14.7%; 65+: 19.5%. **Growth:** –0.3%. **Migrants:** 5.2%. **Pop. density:** 284 per sq mi, 109.7 per sq km. **Urban:** 71.4%. **Ethnic groups:** Hungarian 85.6%, Romani 3.2%. **Languages:** Hungarian (official), English, German. **Religions:** Roman Catholic 37.2%, Calvinist 11.6%, none 18.2%.

Geography: Total area: 35,918 sq mi, 93,028 sq km (108); **Land area:** 34,598 sq mi, 89,608 sq km. **Location:** E central Europe. Ukraine, Slovakia on N; Austria on W; Slovenia, Croatia, Serbia on S; Romania on E. **Topography:** Danube R. forms Slovak border in NW, then swings S to bisect country. Eastern half of Hungary is mainly a great fertile plain, the Alfold. Hilly in W and N. **Arable land:** 48.7%. **Capital:** Budapest, 1,759,497.

Government: Type: Parliamentary republic. **Head of state:** Pres. János Áder; b. 1959; in office: May 10, 2012. **Head of govt.:** Prime Min. Viktor Orbán; b. 1963; in office: May 29, 2010. **Local divisions:** 19 counties, 23 cities with county rights, 1 capital city. **Defense budget:** $1.3 bil. **Active troops:** 27,800.

Economy: Industries: mining, metallurgy, constr. materials, processed foods, textiles, chemicals (espec. pharmaceuticals), motor vehicles. **Chief agric.:** wheat, corn, sunflower seeds, potatoes, sugar beets; pigs, cattle. **Natural resources:** bauxite, coal, nat. gas. **Water:** 10,553 cu m per capita. **Crude oil reserves:** 24 mil bbls. **Electricity prod.:** 28.7 bil kWh. **Labor force:** agric. 5%, industry 30.2%, services 64.8%. **Unemployment:** 4.2%.

Finance: Monetary unit: Forint (HUF) (283.03 = $1 U.S.). **GDP:** $289 bil; **per capita GDP:** $29,500; **GDP growth:** 4%. **Imports:** $93.3 bil; Germany 26.2%, Austria 6.3%, China 5.9%, Poland 5.5%, Slovakia 5.3%, Netherlands 5%. **Exports:** $98.7 bil; Germany 27.7%, Romania 5.4%, Italy 5.1%, Austria 5%. **Tourism:** $6.2 bil. **Budget:** $66.4 bil. **Inflation:** 2.3%.

Transport: Railways: 5,001 mi. **Motor vehicles:** 401.3 per 1,000 pop. **Airports:** 20.

Communications: Telephone: 32.2 per 100 pop. **Mobile:** 123.8 per 100 pop. **Broadband:** 44.5 per 100 pop. **Internet** (2017): 76.8%.

Health: Expend.: 7.2%. **Life expect.:** 72.6 male; 80.2 female. **Births:** 8.9 per 1,000 pop. **Deaths:** 12.8 per 1,000 pop. **Infant mortality:** 4.8 per 1,000 live births. **Undernourished:** <2.5%. **HIV:** <0.1%.

Education: Compulsory: ages 4-16. **Literacy:** 99.4%.

Embassy: 3910 Shoemaker St. NW 20008; 362-6730.

Website: www.kormany.hu

Earliest settlers, chiefly Slav and Germanic, were overrun by Magyars from the east. Stephen I (997-1038) was made king by Pope Sylvester II in 1000 CE. The country suffered repeated Turkish invasions in the 15th-17th cents. After the Turks were defeated, 1686-97, Austria dominated, but Hungary obtained concessions, and regained internal independence in 1867 under a dual monarchy with the emperor of Austria. Defeated with the Central Powers at the end of WWI in 1918, Hungary lost Transylvania to Romania, Croatia and Bacska to Yugoslavia, and Slovakia and Carpatho-Ruthenia to Czechoslovakia. All had large Hungarian minorities. A republic under Michael Karolyi and a Bolshevist revolt under Bela Kun were followed by a vote for a monarchy in 1920 with Adm. Nicholas Horthy as regent.

Hungary allied with Germany before WWII and was allowed to annex, 1938-41, most of its lost territories. Russian troops captured the country, 1944-45. By terms of an armistice with the Allied powers, Hungary agreed to return to its borders of 1937.

A republic was declared Feb. 1, 1946. In 1947 a hard-line Communist, pro-Soviet government was installed. Demonstrations against Communist rule developed into open revolt in 1956. Soviet forces launched a massive attack Nov. 4 against Budapest. About 200,000 persons fled the country. Thousands were arrested and executed.

Major economic reforms were launched early in 1968, switching from a central planning system to one based on market forces and profit. In 1989 Parliament legalized freedom of assembly and association as Hungary shifted away from Communism. In Oct. the Communist Party was formally dissolved. The last Soviet troops left June 19, 1991. Hungary became a full member of NATO in 1999 and of the EU in 2004.

The IMF, EU, and World Bank agreed Oct. 2008 to extend $25.1 bil to rescue Hungary's economy, battered by a global financial crisis. The center-right Fidesz party ousted the Socialists in 2010 parliamentary elections, and former prime min. (1998-2002) Viktor Orbán became prime min. Parliament approved Apr. 2011 a fiscally and socially conservative constitution that went into force Jan. 1, 2012. Fidesz won Apr. 6, 2014, elections and, after an anti-immigration campaign, increased its majority in Apr. 8, 2018, voting.

Hungary was a major transit route in 2015 for migrants from the Balkans, SW Asia, the Middle East, and Africa trying to reach N Europe. More than 411,000 migrants entered or tried to enter Hungary in 2015, almost all before the end of Oct., by which time Hungary had built more than 300 mi of security fencing along its southern borders with Serbia and Croatia. Legislation signed Mar. 15, 2017, authorized incarcerating asylum seekers in border detention camps; June 2018 legislation essentially prohibited NGOs from assisting migrants with asylum claims. The government refused to participate in a 2015 EU refugee resettlement program; a June 2018 constitutional amendment barred such resettlement.

Iceland
Republic of Iceland

People: Population: 343,518 (172). **Age distrib.:** <15: 20.4%; 65+: 14.8%. **Growth:** 1.1%. **Migrants:** 12.5%. **Pop. density:** 8.9 per sq mi, 3.4 per sq km. **Urban:** 93.8%. **Ethnic groups:** homogeneous mix of Norse-Celt descendants 94%, foreign origin 6%. **Languages:** Icelandic, English, Nordic langs., German. **Religions:** Evangelical Lutheran Church of Iceland (official) 69.9%, Roman Catholic 3.8%, none 6.1%.

Geography: Total area: 39,769 sq mi, 103,000 sq km (106); **Land area:** 38,707 sq mi, 100,250 sq km. **Location:** Isl. at N end of Atlantic O. Nearest neighbor is Greenland (Den.) to W. **Topography:** Recent volcanic origin. Three-quarters of surface is wasteland: glaciers, lakes, a lava desert, geysers, and hot springs. The climate is moderated by the Gulf Stream. **Arable land:** 1.2%. **Capital:** Reykjavík, 216,364.

Government: Type: Parliamentary republic. **Head of state:** Pres. Gudni Thorlacius Johannesson; b. 1968; in office: Aug. 1, 2016. **Head of govt.:** Prime Min. Katrin Jakobsdottir; b. 1976; in office: Nov. 30, 2017. **Local divisions:** 74 municipalities. **Defense budget:** $37 mil (Coast Guard budget). **Active troops:** No armed forces; 250 Coast Guard. Relies on NATO allies for air policing and defense.

Economy: Industries: tourism, fish proc., aluminum smelting, geothermal power, hydropower, medical/pharmaceutical prods. **Chief agric.:** potatoes, carrots, green vegetables; mutton, chicken; fish. **Natural resources:** fish, hydropower, geothermal power, diatomite. **Water:** 516,090 cu m per capita. **Electricity prod.:** 18.6 bil kWh. **Labor force:** agric. 3.6%, industry 16.6%, services 79.8%. **Unemployment:** 2.8%.

Finance: Monetary unit: Krona (ISK) (109.45 = $1 U.S.). **GDP:** $17.6 bil; **per capita GDP:** $51,800; **GDP growth:** 3.6%. **Imports:** $5.7 bil; (2015) Norway 10.1%, Germany 8.6%, U.S. 7.9%, China 7.9%, Denmark 7.1%, Netherlands 5.9%, Brazil 5.8%, UK 5%. **Exports:** $4.6 bil; (2015) Netherlands 26.1%, UK 11.6%, Spain 11.5%, Germany 7.4%, France 5.7%, U.S. 5.7%. **Tourism:** $3 bil. **Budget:** $9.7 bil. **Inflation:** 1.8%.

Transport: Motor vehicles: 848.3 per 1,000 pop. **Airports:** 7. **Communications: Telephone:** 43.6 per 100 pop. **Mobile:** 122.6 per 100 pop. **Broadband:** 104 per 100 pop. **Internet:** 98.2%. **Health: Expend.:** 8.6%. **Life expect.:** 80.9 male; 85.5 female. **Births:** 13.6 per 1,000 pop. **Deaths:** 6.5 per 1,000 pop. **Infant mortality:** 2.1 per 1,000 live births. **Undernourished:** <2.5%. **HIV:** NA.

Education: Compulsory: ages 6-15. **Literacy:** 99%. **Embassy:** 2900 K St. NW, Ste. 509, 20007; 265-6653. **Website:** www.iceland.is

Iceland was an independent republic from 930 to 1262, when it joined with Norway. Its language has maintained its purity for 1,000 years. The Althing, or assembly, established in 930, is the world's oldest surviving parliament. Danish rule lasted 1380-1918; the last ties with the Danish crown were severed in 1944.

Iceland's banking system and currency collapsed amid the global financial crisis in Oct. 2008. More than $10 bil in loans from the IMF and European governments restored financial stability; austerity measures were imposed, and the nation entered a deep recession. Political unrest sparked by soaring inflation and unemployment led to the Feb. 2009 installation of a center-left government. An Apr. 2010 eruption of the Eyjafjallajökull volcano disrupted European air traffic. The governing coalition lost Apr. 28, 2013, parliamentary elections, in which center-right parties came to power. Prime Min. Sigmundur David Gunnlaugsson resigned, Apr. 5, 2016, after conflict-of-interest allegations. Following inconclusive Oct. 2016 elections, a new center-right government was formed, Jan. 11, 2017, but collapsed in Sept. After new elections, Oct. 28, 2017, Katrin Jakobsdottir of the Left-Green Movement became prime min. when she formed a coalition with center-right parties.

India
Republic of India

People: Population: 1,296,834,042 (2). **Age distrib.:** <15: 27%; 65+: 6.4%. **Growth:** 1.1%. **Migrants:** 0.4%. **Pop. density:** 1,129.7 per sq mi, 436.2 per sq km. **Urban:** 34%. **Ethnic groups:** Indo-Aryan 72%, Dravidian 25%, Mongoloid and other 3%. **Languages:** Hindi (most widely spoken); 14 other official langs. (incl. Bengali, Telugu, Marathi, Tamil, Urdu, Gujarati); English (subsidiary official lang.; crucial for natl., political, commercial communication); Hindustani (variant of Hindi/Urdu widely spoken throughout N). **Religions:** Hindu 79.8%, Muslim 14.2%.

Geography: Total area: 1,269,219 sq mi, 3,287,263 sq km (7); **Land area:** 1,147,956 sq mi, 2,973,193 sq km. **Location:** Occupies most of Indian subcontinent in S Asia. Pakistan on W; China, Nepal, Bhutan on N; Myanmar, Bangladesh on E. **Topography:** The Himalayan Mts., highest in world, stretch across northern borders. The Ganges Plain below is among the world's most densely populated regions. The climate varies from tropical heat in S to near-Arctic cold in N. Rajasthan Desert is NW. NE Assam Hills get 400 in. of rain a year. **Arable land:** 52.6%. **Capital:** Delhi, 28,513,682. **Cities:** Mumbai (Bombay), 19,979,955; Kolkata (Calcutta), 14,680,613; Bangalore, 11,440,030; Chennai (Madras), 10,455,606; Hyderabad, 9,481,623; Ahmadabad, 7,680,935; Srinagar, 1,514,504; Jammu, 692,531.

Government: Type: Federal parliamentary republic. **Head of state:** Pres. Ram Nath Kovind; b. 1945; in office: July 25, 2017. **Head of govt.:** Prime Min. Narendra Modi; b. 1950; in office: May 26, 2014. **Local divisions:** 29 states, 7 union territories. **Defense budget:** $52.5 bil. **Active troops:** 1,395,100.

Economy: Industries: textiles, chemicals, food proc., steel, transp. equip., cement, mining, petroleum, machinery, software, pharmaceuticals. **Chief agric.:** rice, wheat, oilseed, cotton, jute, tea, sugarcane, lentils, onions, potatoes; dairy prods., sheep, goats; fish. **Natural resources:** coal, iron ore, manganese, mica, bauxite, rare earth elements, titanium ore, chromite, nat. gas, diamonds, petroleum, limestone. **Water:** 1,458 cu m per capita. **Crude oil reserves:** 4.5 bil bbls. **Electricity prod.:** 1.3 tril kWh. **Labor force:** agric. 42.7%, industry 23.8%, services 33.5%. **Unemployment:** 3.5%.

Finance: Monetary unit: Rupee (INR) (71.56 = $1 U.S.). **GDP:** $9.5 tril; **per capita GDP:** $7,200; **GDP growth:** 6.7%. **Imports:** $426.8 bil; China 16.3%, U.S. 5.5%, UAE 5.2%. **Exports:** $299.3 bil; U.S. 15.6%, UAE 10.2%. **Tourism:** $27.4 bil. **Budget:** $330.3 bil. **Inflation:** 3.3%.

Transport: Railways: 42,579 mi. **Motor vehicles:** 36.3 per 1,000 pop. **Airports:** 253. **Communications: Telephone:** 1.7 per 100 pop. **Mobile:** 87.3 per 100 pop. **Broadband:** 16.8 per 100 pop. **Internet:** 29.5%. **Health: Expend.:** 3.9%. **Life expect.:** 67.8 male; 70.5 female. **Births:** 18.7 per 1,000 pop. **Deaths:** 7.3 per 1,000 pop. **Infant mortality:** 37.8 per 1,000 live births. **Undernourished:** 14.8%. **HIV:** 0.2%.

Education: Compulsory: ages 6-13. **Literacy:** 71.2%. **Embassy:** 2107 Massachusetts Ave. NW 20008; 939-7000. **Website:** www.india.gov.in

India has one of the oldest civilizations in the world. Excavations trace the Indus Valley civilization back for at least 5,000 years. Paintings in the mountain caves of Ajanta, richly carved temples, the Taj Mahal in Agra, and the Kutab Minar in Delhi are among treasured relics of the past.

Aryan tribes, speaking Sanskrit, invaded from the NW around 1500 BCE. Asoka ruled most of the Indian subcontinent in the 3rd cent. BCE and established Buddhism. But Hinduism revived and eventually predominated. Under the Guptas, 4th-6th cent. CE, science, literature, and the arts enjoyed a golden age. Arab invaders established a Muslim foothold in the west in the 8th cent., and Turkish Muslims gained control of North India by 1200. The Mughal emperors ruled 1526-1857.

Vasco da Gama established Portuguese trading posts 1498-1503. The Dutch followed. The British East India Co. sent Capt. William Hawkins, 1609, to get concessions from the Mughal emperor for spices and textiles. Operating as the East India Co., the British gained control of most of India. The British parliament assumed political direction; under Lord Bentinck, 1828-35, rule by rajahs (princes) was curbed. After the Sepoy troops mutinied, 1857-58, the British supported the native rulers.

Nationalism grew after WWI. The Indian National Congress and the Muslim League demanded constitutional reform. A leader emerged in Mohandas K. Gandhi (called Mahatma, or Great Soul) (b. Oct. 2, 1869), who advocated self-rule, nonviolence, and an end to caste discrimination against "untouchables." In 1930 he launched a program of civil disobedience, boycotting British goods and rejecting taxes without representation. He was assassinated Jan. 30, 1948.

In 1935, Britain gave India a constitution providing a bicameral federal congress. Muhammad Ali Jinnah, head of the Muslim League, sought creation of a Muslim nation, Pakistan.

The British government partitioned British India into the dominions of India and Pakistan. India became a member of the UN in 1945, a self-governing member of the Commonwealth in 1947, and a democratic republic, Jan. 26, 1950. More than 12 mil Hindu and Muslim refugees crossed the India-Pakistan borders in 1947; about 200,000 were killed in communal fighting.

After Pakistan troops began attacks on Bengali separatists in East Pakistan, Mar. 25, 1971, some 10 mil refugees fled to India. India and Pakistan went to war Dec. 3, 1971, on both the east and west fronts. Pakistan troops, Dec. 16, surrendered in the east, which became Bangladesh; Pakistan agreed to a cease-fire in the west Dec. 17.

Indira Gandhi, India's prime minister since Jan. 1966, invoked emergency powers in June 1975. Thousands of opponents were arrested and press censorship imposed. These and other actions, including population control through forced vasectomies, were widely resented. Opposition parties, united in the Janata coalition, won the 1977 elections.

Gandhi became prime minister for the second time in 1980. She was assassinated by two of her Sikh bodyguards Oct. 31, 1984, in response to the government suppression in June 1984 of a Sikh uprising in Punjab, which included an assault on the Golden Temple at Amritsar, the holiest Sikh shrine. Widespread rioting followed the assassination; thousands of Sikhs were killed and some 50,000 left homeless. Rajiv, Indira Gandhi's son, replaced her as prime min. A gas leak at a Union Carbide chemical plant in Bhopal, Dec. 1984, eventually killed some 14,000 people.

Many died in religious, ethnic, and political conflicts during the late 1980s and early '90s. To suppress the Sikh insurgency in Punjab, Indian government troops attacked the Golden Temple again in 1988. Rajiv Gandhi was swept from office in 1989 amid charges of incompetence and corruption; he was assassinated May 21, 1991, while campaigning to regain power. Nationwide riots followed the destruction of a 16th-cent. mosque by Hindu militants in Dec. 1992. Ethnic clashes in Assam, in NW India, killed thousands in Feb. 1993. Bombs jolted Mumbai and Kolkata, Mar. 12-19, killing over 300.

India's first president from the lowest caste, K. R. Narayanan, took office July 1997. India conducted a series of nuclear tests in mid-May 1998, raising tensions with Pakistan. India blamed Pakistani-sponsored terrorist groups for an Oct. 1, 2001, suicide attack on the state legislature in Jammu and Kashmir (see below), in which at least 40 people died, and a Dec. 13 assault on the Indian parliament in New Delhi that left 13 people dead. Hindu-Muslim clashes in Gujarat Feb.-Mar. 2002 claimed more than 700 lives.

Led by Rajiv Gandhi's Italian-born widow, Sonia, the Congress Party won the most seats in 2004 parliamentary elections. When Hindu nationalists objected to her candidacy, Manmohan Singh, a Sikh economist, became prime minister instead.

The Indian Ocean tsunami of Dec. 26, 2004, left more than 16,000 people dead and over 647,000 displaced in India. Islamic extremists set off 7 bombs on commuter trains in Mumbai, July 11, 2006, killing some 200 people; 12 men were convicted, Sept. 11, 2015, of murder or other charges in connection with the bombings. The unmanned *Chandrayaan-1*, India's first lunar survey mission, was launched into space Oct. 22, 2008.

Ten Pakistanis linked to the Kashmir militant group Lashkar-e-Taiba stormed luxury hotels, a railway station, a Jewish center, and other sites in Mumbai, Nov. 26, 2008; by the time Indian army commandos took control three days later, the attackers had slaughtered 163 people. Nine of the terrorists were also killed. The lone surviving gunman, Ajmal Kasab, was executed by hanging Nov. 20, 2012.

In 2009 parliamentary elections, Prime Min. Manmohan Singh's United Progressive Alliance, headed by the Congress Party, gained a resounding victory. A triple bombing in Mumbai July 13, 2011, killed 26 people and injured about 140. Electricity blackouts July 30-31, 2012, left 670 mil people without power.

Several rapes in New Delhi in Nov.-Dec. 2012 prompted outrage and large protests for their mishandling by police and government inaction. Tougher laws against sexual violence were passed Feb. 4, 2013. The Hindu nationalist Bharatiya Janata party won a large majority in Apr.-May 2014 parliamentary elections; Narendra Modi became prime min.

Development of high-tech industries has propelled rapid economic growth since the 1990s; hundreds of millions have emerged from extreme poverty, although distribution of wealth remains highly uneven. Since 2011, India has had the world's third-largest GDP. To combat climate change, the government released a plan, Oct. 1, 2015, for reducing the rate of growth in India's carbon emissions. On Oct. 2, 2016, India ratified the UN climate change agreement negotiated in Paris, Dec. 2015. WHO data released in 2018 showed that 11 of the 12 world cities with the worst air pollution were in India.

To crack down on the large underground economy, Modi's government replaced almost all paper currency, Nov. 2016. Monsoon rains and flooding in Kerala, June-Aug. 2018, left more than 400 dead and displaced over 1 mil. The Supreme Court, Sept. 6, struck down a 19th-cent. law that made consensual gay sex a criminal offense.

Sikkim, bordered by Tibet, Bhutan, and Nepal, formerly British protected, became a protectorate of India in 1950. Area 2,740 sq mi; pop. (2011 census) 610,577; capital is Gangtok. In Sept. 1974, India's parliament voted to make Sikkim an associate Indian state, absorbing it into India.

Kashmir is a predominantly Muslim region in the NW that borders India, Pakistan, Afghanistan, and China. Muslim rule of the previously Hindu kingdom began in 1341; after almost 200 years under the Mughals, the area was incorporated into British India in 1846. Fighting broke out in the region between India and Pakistan in 1947 following independence from Britain. A cease-fire was negotiated by the UN Jan. 1, 1949; it gave Pakistan control of one-third of the area as Azad Kashmir, in the W and NW, and India the remaining two-thirds, as the Indian state of Jammu and Kashmir. Area 85,806 sq mi; pop. (2011 census) 12,541,302. Capitals: Srinagar (summer), pop. (2018 est.) 1,514,504; Jammu (winter), pop. (2018 est.) 692,531. Fighting in the area resumed during 1965 and 1971. China occupied about 14,000 sq mi in the Ladakh district after a war with India in 1962.

Since 1989, Indian security forces in Jammu and Kashmir have battled Islamic separatist fighters. India has charged Pakistan with aiding the separatists. Fighting was especially heavy in May-June 1999. A cease-fire between Indian and Pakistani troops along the line of control took effect Nov. 2003. Some breaches occurred, and fighting between Indian forces and Islamic militants continued. An earthquake Oct. 8, 2005, killed about 80,000 and left up to 3 mil homeless in Pakistani-held Kashmir and northern Pakistan. Weeks of violent protests, in which more than 90 died, followed the July 8, 2016, killing by Indian security forces of Kashmiri rebel leader Burhan Wani; 19 Indian soldiers were killed in a militant attack on an army base Sept. 18, 2016. Indian-separatist violence in 2017 left about 350 dead. After a period of intense cross-border shelling, India and Pakistan agreed on a new cease-fire, May 29, 2018. Indian security forces said, June 2018, that separatist fighters included a group affiliated with or inspired by ISIS. Estimates of conflict-related deaths since 1989 range from 40,000 to over 80,000.

France, 1952-54, peacefully yielded to India its five colonies, former French India: Pondicherry, Karikal, Mahe, and Yanaon were merged to become Pondicherry, now Puducherry, area 185 sq mi;

pop. (2011 census) 1,247,953. The colony of Chandernagor was incorporated into the state of West Bengal.

Indonesia
Republic of Indonesia

People: Population: 262,787,403 (4). **Age distrib.:** <15: 24.6%; 65+: 7.3%. **Growth:** 0.8%. **Migrants:** 0.1%. **Pop. density:** 375.7 per sq mi, 145.1 per sq km. **Urban:** 55.3%. **Ethnic groups:** Javanese 40.1%, Sundanese 15.5%, Malay 3.7%, Batak 3.6%, Madurese 3%, Betawi 2.9%, Minangkabau 2.7%, Buginese 2.7%, Bantenese 2%. **Languages:** Bahasa Indonesia (official; modified form of Malay), English, Dutch, local dialects (Javanese most widely spoken). **Religions:** Muslim 87.2%, Protestant 7%, Roman Catholic 2.9%.

Geography: Total area: 735,358 sq mi, 1,904,569 sq km (14); **Land area:** 699,451 sq mi, 1,811,569 sq km. **Location:** Archipelago SE of Asian mainland along the equator. Malaysia on N, Papua New Guinea on E, Timor-Leste on S. **Topography:** Comprises 17,508 islands (about 6,000 inhabited), including Java, Sumatra, Kalimantan (most of Borneo), Sulawesi (Celebes), and West Irian (Irian Jaya, the W half of New Guinea). Also Bangka, Billiton, Madura, Bali, Timor. Cooler climate in mountains and plateaus on the major isls.; tropical lowlands. **Arable land:** 13%. **Capital:** Jakarta, 10,516,927. **Cities:** Bekasi, 3,159,491; Surabaya, 2,902,504; Bandung, 2,537,934; Depok, 2,503,253.

Government: Type: Presidential republic. **Head of state and govt.:** Pres. Joko Widodo; b. 1961; in office: Oct. 20, 2014. **Local divisions:** 31 provinces, 1 autonomous province, 1 special region, 1 national capital district. **Defense budget:** $9 bil. **Active troops:** 395,500.

Economy: Industries: petroleum and nat. gas, textiles, automotive, elec. appliances, apparel, footwear, mining, cement, medical instruments and appliances. **Chief agric.:** rubber, palm oil, poultry, beef, shrimp, cocoa, coffee, medicinal herbs. **Natural resources:** petroleum, tin, nat. gas, nickel, timber, bauxite, copper, coal, gold, silver. **Water:** 7,839 cu m per capita. **Crude oil reserves:** 3.3 bil bbls. **Electricity prod.:** 221.3 bil kWh. **Labor force:** agric. 31.2%, industry 21.7%, services 47.1%. **Unemployment:** 4.2%.

Finance: Monetary unit: Rupiah (IDR) (14,955.24 = $1 U.S.). **GDP:** $3.2 tril; **per capita GDP:** $12,400; **GDP growth:** 5.1%. **Imports:** $149.9 bil; China 23.2%, Singapore 10.9%, Japan 10%, Thailand 6%, Malaysia 5.6%, South Korea 5.3%, U.S. 5.2%. **Exports:** $168.8 bil; China 13.6%, U.S. 10.6%, Japan 10.5%, India 8.4%, Singapore 7.6%, Malaysia 5.1%. **Tourism:** $12.5 bil. **Budget:** $213.3 bil. **Inflation:** 3.8%.

Transport: Railways: 5,070 mi (only partly operational). **Motor vehicles:** 90.6 per 1,000 pop. **Airports:** 186.

Communications: Telephone: 4.2 per 100 pop. **Mobile:** 173.8 per 100 pop. **Broadband:** 67.3 per 100 pop. **Internet** (2017): 32.3%.

Health: Expend.: 3.3%. **Life expect.:** 70.6 male; 76.0 female. **Births:** 15.9 per 1,000 pop. **Deaths:** 6.5 per 1,000 pop. **Infant mortality:** 21.9 per 1,000 live births. **Undernourished:** 7.7%. **HIV:** 0.4%.

Education: Compulsory: ages 7-15. **Literacy:** 95.4%.

Embassy: 2020 Massachusetts Ave. NW 20036; 775-5200.

Website: www.indonesia.go.id

Hindu and Buddhist civilization from India reached Indonesia nearly 2,000 years ago, taking root especially in Java. Islam spread along the maritime trade routes in the 15th cent., and became predominant by the 16th cent. The Dutch replaced the Portuguese as the area's most important European trade power in the 17th cent., securing territorial control over Java by 1750. The outer islands were subdued in the early 20th cent.

Following Japanese occupation, 1942-45, nationalists led by Sukarno and Hatta declared independence. The Netherlands ceded sovereignty in 1949. A republic was declared, Aug. 17, 1950, with Sukarno as president.

Irian Jaya, on New Guinea, remained under Dutch control but was transferred by the UN to Indonesia in 1963; it became the provinces of Papua and West Papua in the early 2000s. Pro-independence protests and an armed separatist movement have been met by a harsh government crackdown in recent years.

Sukarno suspended parliament in 1960 and was named president for life in 1963. He made close alliances with Communist governments. In Sept. 1965 an attempted coup was successfully put down, but Sukarno was forced to cede power to the army, led by Gen. Suharto. The regime blamed the coup on the Communist Party; more than 300,000 alleged Communists were killed in army-initiated massacres.

Parliament reelected Suharto to a seventh consecutive presidential term in 1998, as a severe economic downturn focused public anger on nepotism, cronyism, and corruption in the Suharto regime. Price increases in May sparked mass protests and then mob violence in Jakarta and other cities, claiming some 500 lives. Suharto resigned May 21, 1998. Abdurrahman Wahid, leader of Indonesia's largest Muslim organization, was elected president in 1999. In Aug. 2000, under pressure from the legislature, he agreed to share power with Vice Pres. Megawati Sukarnoputri, the daughter of the late Pres. Sukarno. Charging Wahid with incompetence and corruption, the legislature ousted him July 23, 2001, and Megawati became Indonesia's first woman president.

Clashes between Muslims and Christians in the Maluku (Molucca) Isls., 1999-2002, claimed about 5,000 lives. East Timor, a former Portuguese colony that Indonesia invaded in Dec. 1975 and controlled until Oct. 1999, became a fully independent country May 20, 2002, as Timor-Leste.

Separatists in Aceh, NW Sumatra, fought government troops, 1980s-2000s. A peace agreement granting Aceh greater autonomy was signed Aug. 15, 2005. Aceh adopted a strict penal code based on sharia law and sometimes enforced by vigilantes.

Investigators blamed Islamic terrorists for bombings that killed 202 people, mostly foreign tourists, at nightclubs in Bali, Oct. 12, 2002, and 12 people at a Marriott hotel in Jakarta, Aug. 5, 2003. A car bomb outside the Australian embassy, Sept. 9, 2004, killed 9. Susilo Bambang Yudhoyono, a retired general, defeated Megawati in a 2004 direct presidential runoff vote.

A massive earthquake off NW Sumatra, Dec. 26, 2004, triggered tsunamis that wreaked havoc in the Indian Ocean region. The death toll in Indonesia alone exceeded 165,000. On Java, an earthquake, May 27, 2006, killed 5,800.

Pres. Yudhoyono won a second 5-year term July 8, 2009. Suicide bombings at two Jakarta hotels July 17 left nine people dead. Police confirmed Sept. 17 that Noordin Muhammad Top, suspected of plotting the Jakarta attacks and other terrorist bombings, had been killed in a shootout.

The General Elections Commission, July 22, 2014, declared populist Jakarta governor Joko Widodo the presidential election winner. All 162 people aboard an AirAsia Indonesia flight were killed, Dec. 28, 2014, when the plane crashed into the Java Sea near Borneo.

Assaults by terrorist gunmen and bombers in Jakarta, Jan. 14, 2016, left 8 dead, including 4 attackers; ISIS claimed responsibility. Security forces, July 18, killed the suspected terrorist leader known as Santoso, whose group had declared allegiance to ISIS. A series of ISIS-inspired suicide bombings at churches and attacks on police, May 2018, left 13 victims dead.

Rainforest destruction and air pollution from fires to clear areas for agriculture have been major environmental problems in recent years. A Sept. 2016 study estimated that especially severe pollution from 2015 fires may have caused more than 100,000 premature deaths. A series of earthquakes on the island of Lombok, July-Aug. 2018, killed almost 500 and displaced hundreds of thousands. More than 2,000 died after an earthquake and tsunami struck central Sulawesi, Sept. 28.

Iran
Islamic Republic of Iran

People: Population: 83,024,745 (17). **Age distrib.:** <15: 24.2%; 65+: 5.5%. **Growth:** 1.2%. **Migrants:** 3.3%. **Pop. density:** 140.4 per sq mi, 54.2 per sq km. **Urban:** 74.9%. **Ethnic groups:** Persian, Azeri, Kurd, Lur, Baloch, Arab, Turkmen and Turkic tribes. **Languages:** Persian (official), Azeri Turkic and Turkic dialects, Kurdish, Gilaki and Mazandarani, Luri, Balochi, Arabic. **Religions:** Muslim (official) 99.4% (Shia 90%-95%, Sunni 5%-10%).

Geography: Total area: 636,372 sq mi, 1,648,195 sq km (17). **Land area:** 591,352 sq mi, 1,531,595 sq km. **Location:** Between the Middle East and S Asia. Iraq, Turkey on W; Armenia, Azerbaijan, Turkmenistan on N; Afghanistan, Pakistan on E. **Topography:** Interior highlands and plains surrounded by high mountains, up to 18,000 ft. Large salt deserts cover much of area, though there are oases and forests. Most of pop. inhabits N and NW. **Arable land:** 9%. **Capital:** Tehran, 8,895,947. **Cities:** Mashhad, 3,097,062; Esfahan, 2,040,574.

Government: Type: Theocratic republic. **Religious head:** Ayatollah Sayyed Ali Khamenei; b. 1939; in office: June 4, 1989. **Head of state and govt.:** Pres. Hassan Rouhani; b. 1948; in office: Aug. 4, 2013. **Local divisions:** 31 provinces. **Defense budget:** $16 bil. **Active troops:** 523,000.

Economy: Industries: petroleum, petrochemicals, gas, fertilizer, caustic soda, textiles, cement and other constr. materials. **Chief agric.:** wheat, rice, other grains, sugar beets, sugarcane, fruits, nuts, cotton; dairy prods., wool; caviar. **Natural resources:** petroleum, nat. gas, coal, chromium, copper, iron ore, lead, manganese, zinc, sulfur. **Water:** 1,732 cu m per capita. **Crude oil reserves:** 157.2 bil bbls. **Electricity prod.:** 265 bil kWh. **Labor force:** agric. 17.1%, industry 32.4%, services 50.5%. **Unemployment:** 12.5%.

Finance: Monetary unit: Rial (IRR) (41,785.60 = $1 U.S.). **GDP:** $1.6 tril; **per capita GDP:** $20,200; **GDP growth:** 4.3%. **Imports:** $70.5 bil; UAE 29.8%, China 12.7%. **Exports:** $92 bil; China 27.5%, India 15.1%, South Korea 11.4%, Turkey 11.1%, Italy 5.7%, Japan 5.3%. **Tourism:** $3.7 bil. **Budget:** $86.3 bil. **Inflation:** 10.5%.

Transport: Railways: 5,271 mi. **Motor vehicles:** 66.3 per 1,000 pop. **Airports:** 140.

Communications: Telephone: 38.4 per 100 pop. **Mobile:** 107.3 per 100 pop. **Broadband:** 33.8 per 100 pop. **Internet** (2017): 60.4%.

Health: Expend.: 7.6%. **Life expect.:** 72.8 male; 75.6 female. **Births:** 17.4 per 1,000 pop. **Deaths:** 5.3 per 1,000 pop. **Infant mortality:** 15.5 per 1,000 live births. **Undernourished:** 4.9%. **HIV:** 0.1%.

Education: Compulsory: ages 6-13. **Literacy:** 86.8%.

Permanent UN mission: 622 Third Ave., 34th Fl., New York, NY 10017; (212) 687-2020.

Website: www.president.ir

Ancestors of inhabitants of Iran, formerly known as Persia, came from the east during the second millennium BCE; they were an Indo-European group related to the Aryans of India. In 549 BCE, Cyrus the Great united the Medes and Persians in the Persian Empire; he conquered Babylonia in 538 BCE, and restored Jerusalem to the Jews. Alexander the Great conquered Persia in 333 BCE, but Persians regained independence in the next century under the Parthians, themselves succeeded by Sassanian Persians in 226 CE. Arabs brought Islam to Persia in the 7th cent., replacing the indigenous Zoroastrian faith. After Persian political and cultural autonomy was reasserted in the 9th cent., arts and sciences flourished.

Turks and Mongols ruled Persia in turn from the 11th cent. to 1502, when Ismael I established the Iranian Safavid dynasty and made Shiite Islam the official religion. The dynasty lasted until 1722. The British and Russian empires vied for influence in the 19th cent.; Britain severed Afghanistan from Iran in 1857.

Reza Khan, a military officer, became prime min., 1923, and shah in 1925. He began modernization, curbed foreign influence, and officially changed the country's name from Persia to Iran in 1935. Fearing the shah's Axis sympathies, British and Soviet troops forced him to abdicate, 1941; he was succeeded by his son, Mohammad Reza Pahlavi. The U.S. Central Intelligence Agency had a major role in the ouster, 1953, of Prime Min. Muhammad Mossadegh, who had nationalized the oil industry.

With U.S. backing, the shah brought economic and social change to Iran (White Revolution), but repression of opposition groups grew severe. Violent protests in 1978 eventually forced the shah to depart, Jan. 16, 1979. Shiite leader Ayatollah Ruhollah Khomeini, exiled by the shah in 1963, returned to Tehran, Feb. 1. Pro-Khomeini forces defeated government troops, Feb 11. Khomeini established an Islamic theocracy.

Iranian militants seized the U.S. embassy in Tehran Nov. 4, 1979, and took hostages, including 62 Americans. Despite international condemnations and U.S. efforts, including an abortive Apr. 1980 rescue attempt, the crisis continued. The U.S. broke diplomatic relations with Iran, Apr. 7. The shah died in Egypt, July 27. The hostage drama ended Jan. 20, 1981, when an accord, involving the release of frozen Iranian assets, was reached.

A dispute over the Shatt al-Arab waterway between Iran and Iraq led to a war between the two countries, 1980-88, killing hundreds of thousands. In Nov. 1986 it became known that the U.S., which had generally sided with Iraq during the war, had secretly shipped arms to Iran to gain that country's help in obtaining the release of U.S. hostages held in Lebanon. The revelation sparked a major scandal in the U.S. A U.S. Navy warship shot down an Iranian airliner, July 3, 1988, after mistaking it for an F-14 fighter jet; all 290 aboard died.

An earthquake struck northern Iran June 21, 1990, killing more than 45,000 and leaving 400,000 homeless. Some 1 mil Kurdish refugees fled from Iraq to Iran following the Persian Gulf War of 1991. To curb Iran's alleged support for international terrorism, the U.S. in 1996 authorized sanctions on foreign companies that invested there.

Mohammad Khatami, a moderate Shiite Muslim cleric, was elected president in 1997. During the next three years, hard-line Islamists clashed, sometimes violently, with reformers, who won a majority in 2000 parliamentary elections. Khatami was reelected in 2001 but continued to face resistance from religious conservatives.

An earthquake Dec. 26, 2003, in Bam, SE Iran, killed about 26,000 people. After the Guardian Council, dominated by religious conservatives, disqualified some 2,400 reformist candidates, hardliners won legislative elections Feb. 20, 2004.

The religiously conservative mayor of Tehran, Mahmoud Ahmadinejad, defeated former Pres. Hashemi Rafsanjani in a 2005 runoff election. U.S. Pres. George W. Bush's administration accused Iran of seeking to build nuclear weapons, aiding Shiite militias opposing government forces in the U.S.-led war in Iraq (2003-11), and supplying rockets to Hezbollah fighters in Lebanon for use against Israel.

Seeking to halt Iran's uranium-enrichment program, the UN Security Council imposed sanctions, 2006-07. After the Guardian Council disqualified about 1,700 reformist candidates, conservative allies of Ahmadinejad won parliamentary elections Mar.-Apr. 2008.

Ahmadinejad won the 2009 presidential election. His main opponent, former Prime Min. Mir Hussein Moussavi, claimed the vote count was fraudulent. Huge protests by Moussavi supporters in Tehran and other major cities were crushed. Tensions with the U.S. and European governments were heightened in late

Sept. 2009 by disclosures that Iran had been secretly enriching uranium at an underground site near Qom, and by Iranian tests of medium-range missiles. Iran agreed in Oct. to allow international inspection of the Qom site and to other nuclear safeguards.

The UN and U.S. toughened sanctions, June-July 2010. Iran accused Israel, the U.S., and other Western powers of carrying out cyberattacks against the country's nuclear facilities and of assassinating Iranian scientists. Iran announced, Jan. 2012, it was enriching uranium at its underground Fordo nuclear facility.

The moderate cleric Hassan Rouhani was elected president June 14, 2013. A 15-year agreement—signed July 14, 2015, by the U.S., UK, France, Germany, Russia, China, Iran, and the EU—required Iran to limit and partly dismantle its nuclear program and submit to international inspections in return for the lifting of most sanctions in stages. Sanctions were eased Jan. 16, 2016, after the Intl. Atomic Energy Agency reported Iran was complying with the agreement. Pro-Rouhani reformers won the largest bloc of seats in Feb. and Apr. 2016 parliamentary elections. Rouhani easily won reelection as president, May 19, 2017. Executive action by U.S. Pres. Donald Trump in July 2017 and legislation signed Aug. 2 imposed new sanctions not directly related to the nuclear agreement. Large-scale protests, mainly against poor economic conditions, occurred in dozens of cities around Iran, Dec. 2017-Jan. 2018, until suppressed by Revolutionary Guard forces. Pres. Trump announced, May 8, 2018, that the U.S. would withdraw from the 2015 Iran nuclear agreement and reimpose sanctions.

Playing a role in regional conflicts, Iran supported the Syrian government in its civil war, beginning 2012; Shiite militia forces in Iraq, beginning 2014; and Houthi rebels in Yemen's civil war, beginning 2014. ISIS claimed responsibility for two terrorist attacks in Tehran, June 7, 2017, that left at least 17 people dead. A Sept. 22, 2018, attack on a military parade in Ahvaz killed at least 25; ISIS and an Arab separatist group both claimed responsibility. Iran, Oct. 1, fired missiles at an ISIS target in Syria.

Iraq
Republic of Iraq

People: Population: 40,194,216 (36). **Age distrib.:** <15: 39%; 65+: 3.6%. **Growth:** 2.5%. **Migrants:** 1%. **Pop. density:** 238 per sq mi, 91.9 per sq km. **Urban:** 70.5%. **Ethnic groups:** Arab 75%-80%, Kurdish 15%-20%, other (incl. Turkmen, Yezidi, Shabak, Kaka'i) 5%. **Languages:** Arabic, Kurdish (both official); Turkmen, Syriac, Armenian (official in areas). **Religions:** Muslim (official) 95%-98% (Shia 64%-69%, Sunni 29%-34%).

Geography: Total area: 169,235 sq mi, 438,317 sq km (58). **Land area:** 168,868 sq mi, 437,367 sq km. **Location:** Middle East, occupying most of historic Mesopotamia. Jordan, Syria on W; Turkey on N; Iran on E; Kuwait, Saudi Arabia on S. **Topography:** Mostly an alluvial plain, including the Tigris and Euphrates Rivers, descending from mountains in N to desert in SW. Persian Gulf region is marshland. **Arable land:** 11.6%. **Capital:** Baghdad, 6,811,955. **Cities:** Mosul, 1,527,315; Basra, 1,298,903; Kirkuk, 980,857; Erbil, 821,302.

Government: Type: Federal parliamentary republic. **Head of state:** Pres. Barham Salih; b. 1960; in office Oct. 2, 2018. **Head of govt.:** Prime Min. Adel Abdul Mahdi; b. 1942; in office: Oct. 2, 2018. **Local divisions:** 18 governorates, 1 region (Kurdistan Regional Govt.). **Defense budget:** $19.3 bil. **Active troops:** 64,000.

Economy: Industries: petroleum, chemicals, textiles, leather, constr. materials, food proc., fertilizer, metal fabrication/proc. **Chief agric.:** wheat, barley, rice, vegetables, dates, cotton; cattle, sheep, poultry. **Natural resources:** petroleum, nat. gas, phosphates, sulfur. **Water:** 2,467 cu m per capita. **Crude oil reserves:** 148.8 bil bbls. **Electricity prod.:** 64.9 bil kWh. **Labor force:** agric. 18.7%, industry 19.7%, services 61.6%. **Unemployment:** 8.2%.

Finance: Monetary unit: Dinar (IQD) (1,193.31 = $1 U.S.). **GDP:** $658.8 bil; **per capita GDP:** $17,000; **GDP growth:** –0.8%. **Imports:** $36.5 bil; Turkey 27.8%, China 25.7%. **Exports:** $56.7 bil; India 21.2%, China 20.2%, U.S. 15.8%, South Korea 9.4%, Greece 5.3%. **Tourism:** $2.4 bil. **Budget:** $90.6 bil. **Inflation:** 0.2%.

Transport: Railways: 1,412 mi. **Motor vehicles:** 56.6 per 1,000 pop. **Airports:** 72.

Communications: Telephone: 7.6 per 100 pop. **Mobile:** 87.1 per 100 pop. **Broadband:** NA. **Internet** (2017): 49.4%.

Health: Expend.: 3.4%. **Life expect.:** 72.6 male; 77.2 female. **Births:** 30.0 per 1,000 pop. **Deaths:** 3.8 per 1,000 pop. **Infant mortality:** 37.5 per 1,000 live births. **Undernourished:** 27.7%. **HIV:** NA.

Education: Compulsory: ages 6-11. **Literacy:** 79.7%.

Embassy: 3421 Massachusetts Ave. NW 20007; 742-1600.

Website: www.pmo.iq

The Tigris-Euphrates valley, formerly called Mesopotamia, was the site of one of the earliest civilizations in the world. Mesopotamia ceased to be a separate entity after Persian, Greek, and Arab conquests. The Arabs founded Baghdad, from where the caliph ruled a vast Islamic empire in the 8th and 9th cents. Mongol and Turkish conquests led to a decline in the region's population, economy, cultural life, and irrigation system.

Britain secured a League of Nations mandate over Iraq after WWI. Independence under a king came in 1932. Rebellious army officers killed King Faisal II, July 1958, and established a leftist, pan-Arab republic. The Baath Arab Socialist Party increasingly dominated successive regimes. A Baath leader, Saddam Hussein, became president in 1979. He ruled as a dictator for more than two decades, repressing Iraq's Kurds and Shiites. Israeli planes destroyed a nuclear reactor near Baghdad in 1981, claiming it could be used to produce nuclear weapons.

After skirmishing intermittently for 10 months, Iraq and Iran entered into open warfare on Sept. 22, 1980. Iran repulsed early Iraqi advances, producing a long and costly stalemate; hundreds of thousands of Iraqis lost their lives during the 8-year conflict. Hussein used poison gas against Iraqi Kurds in 1988, killing more than 5,000 people in Halabja, the first mass use of poison gas against civilians since the Holocaust.

Iraq invaded Kuwait in 1990. Backed by the UN, a U.S.-led coalition launched air and missile attacks on Iraq, Jan. 16, 1991, and began a ground attack to retake Kuwait Feb. 23. Iraqi forces were defeated in four days. Some 175,000 Iraqis were taken prisoner, and Iraqi casualties were estimated at over 85,000. As part of the cease-fire agreement, Iraq agreed to scrap all poison gas and germ weapons and allow UN observers to inspect the sites. UN trade sanctions would remain in effect until Iraq complied with all terms.

Iraqi cooperation with UN weapons inspection teams was intermittent throughout the 1990s. Standoffs over inspections led to diplomatic crises 1997-98, culminating in intensive U.S. and British aerial bombardment of Iraqi military targets, Dec. 16-19, 1998. After two years of sporadic activity, U.S. and British warplanes struck sites near Baghdad mid-Feb. 2001.

Despite opposition from some countries, including France, Germany, and Russia, a U.S.-led coalition invaded Iraq Mar. 19, 2003. By Apr. 6 the British controlled Basra and other areas in the south, and the U.S. entered Baghdad Apr. 7. Hussein disappeared, the Iraqi government collapsed, and most of Iraq's armed forces dissolved into the civilian population. On May 1, U.S. Pres. George W. Bush declared the end of major combat. Searches failed to find chemical, biological, or nuclear weapons that the U.S. and other countries claimed Iraq had stockpiled.

The U.S.-led Coalition Provisional Authority was unable to maintain order following Hussein's fall. Reconstruction efforts were hampered by guerrilla attacks from Baath remnants, Islamic extremists, and others. U.S. troops killed two of Hussein's sons, Uday and Qusay, July 22, 2003, in Mosul. Saddam Hussein was captured in an underground hideout mid-Dec. 2003; tried and convicted for committing crimes against humanity in the 1980s, he was executed Dec. 30, 2006.

Photographs released in Apr. 2004 showed instances of physical abuse and sexual humiliation of Iraqi inmates by U.S. military personnel at Baghdad's Abu Ghraib prison in 2003.

On June 28, 2004, U.S. authorities transferred sovereignty to a transitional Iraqi government. Despite insurgent threats, an estimated 8 mil people in Iraq, mostly Shiites and Kurds, cast ballots Jan. 30, 2005, for a transitional national assembly. The assembly elected Jalal Talabani, a Kurd, as president; Ibrahim al-Jaafari, a Shiite, became prime min. Insurgents launched new waves of attacks. Rumors of a suicide bomber set off a stampede by Shiite pilgrims in northern Baghdad Aug. 31, killing close to 1,000 people. The U.S. blamed Jordanian militant Abu Musab al-Zarqawi, leader of al-Qaeda in Iraq, for directing a series of kidnappings, beheadings, and suicide bombings. He was killed by a U.S. airstrike, June 2006.

A new government elected in legislative elections Dec. 15, 2005, was installed May 20, 2006, headed by Shiite leader Nouri Kamel al-Maliki. The Iraqi civilian death toll averaged more than 2,800 per month in 2006.

A 2007 "surge" elevated U.S. troop strength from 132,000 in Jan. to 171,000 in Oct. Military and civilian casualties began dropping after mid-2007. A cease-fire by Shiite militias and a shift by Sunni clan leaders against al-Qaeda in Iraq contributed to the reduction in violence.

A Nov. 2008 agreement called for all U.S. forces to leave Iraq by Dec. 31, 2011. Inconclusive legislative elections were held Mar. 7, 2010. On Aug. 31, Pres. Barack Obama formally declared an end to the U.S. combat role, and Operation Iraqi Freedom was succeeded by Operation New Dawn. More than 9 months of political deadlock ended when Prime Min. Maliki was sworn in for a second term Dec. 21, heading a unity government that included Shiite, Sunni, and Kurdish factions.

U.S. troops completed their withdrawal from Iraq Dec. 15, 2011. From Mar. 2003 through Dec. 2011, more than 4,486 U.S. service members died in operations in Iraq; another 32,000 were wounded. British troop losses totaled 179; other allies, 139. More than 115,000 Iraqi civilians and over 10,000 police and security forces were killed. U.S. budgeted costs of the Iraq war exceeded $820 bil for the 2003-12 period.

Tensions manifested between Sunnis and Shiites after the U.S. departure. The Sunni insurgent group al-Qaeda in Iraq was blamed for ongoing violence; in periodic assaults throughout 2012, 4,573 civilians were killed. Violence accelerated; the UN reported Jan. 1, 2014, that violent attacks killed 8,868 people in Iraq during 2013, including at least 7,818 civilians. In 2014, 12,282 civilians were killed.

In parliamentary elections Apr. 30, 2014, Maliki's coalition won the largest bloc of seats. Shiite Haider al-Abadi, of Maliki's Dawa Party, became prime min. Sept. 8.

In Dec. 2013, the Sunni extremist Islamic State in Iraq and Syria (ISIS) began crossing from Syria into Iraq and seizing territory, including the city of Fallujah (Jan. 2014). The ISIS offensive intensified beginning in June 2014. The group took control of large areas of northern and central Iraq, including the cities of Mosul (Iraq's second-largest) and Tikrit, where ISIS killed 1,700 captured Shiite soldiers. ISIS imposed Islamic law, with harsh punishments, in areas it controlled while suppressing, killing, and sexually assaulting civilians who were non-Sunni Muslims or members of the Yazidi sect and other religious minorities. (Nadia Murad, a Yazidi sexual assault survivor, shared the 2018 Nobel Peace Prize for her activism against sexual violence in war.) The U.S., later joined by other nations, began, Aug. 8, airstrikes against ISIS targets; the U.S. provided military aid to Iraqi government forces and Kurdish fighters opposing ISIS, including ground troops to serve as advisers and trainers beginning in mid-2014.

Forces fighting ISIS in 2015-17 included government troops, Shiite militias (often backed by Iran), Sunni tribal militias, and Kurdish troops. Kurdish fighters made gains in northern Iraq, and government and Shiite forces completed recapturing Tikrit, Apr. 1, 2015. Ramadi, capital of Anbar province, captured by ISIS May 17, 2015, was retaken by government forces Dec. 28, 2015. Fallujah was retaken June 26, 2016. After a bloody 9-month campaign, Abadi proclaimed the recapture of Mosul, July 9, 2017. Abadi announced, Dec. 9, 2017, that all ISIS territory in Iraq had been retaken. However, in 2018, some ISIS fighters remained active or in hiding (perhaps 10,000-15,000 according to an Aug. UN report). The U.S. deactivated, Apr. 30, 2018, its land forces command in Baghdad; U.S. troop strength was about 5,200. UN estimates of all conflict-related civilian deaths totaled at least 7,515 in 2015, 6,878 in 2016, 3,298 in 2017, and 797 Jan.-Sept. 2018.

In May 12, 2018, parliamentary elections, a bloc headed by Shiite cleric Moqtada al-Sadr won the most seats, followed by a pro-Iranian coalition, with Abadi's coalition third. On Oct. 2, 2018, parliament elected Kurdish politician Barham Salih as president, and Shiite consensus candidate Adel Abdul Mahdi was designated prime min.

In a Sept. 25, 2017, referendum, called by the Kurdistan Regional Government—but deemed illegal by the Iraqi government—92.7% of participants voted for Kurdistan's independence from Iraq. Over the following month, Iraqi-government and Shiite-militia forces responded by driving Kurdish troops from territory outside the Kurdistan autonomous region that the Kurds had occupied during the fight against ISIS.

Ireland

People: Population: 5,068,050 (120). **Age distrib.:** <15: 21.4%; 65+: 13.3%. **Growth:** 1.1%. **Migrants:** 16.9%. **Pop. density:** 190.6 per sq mi, 73.6 per sq km. **Urban:** 63.2%. **Ethnic groups:** Irish 82.2%, other white 9.5%, Asian 2.1%. **Languages:** English (official; generally used), Irish (Gaelic or Gaeilge) (official; spoken mainly on western coast). **Religions:** Roman Catholic 78.3%, Church of Ireland 2.7%, none 9.8%.

Geography: Total area: 27,133 sq mi, 70,273 sq km (118); **Land area:** 26,596 sq mi, 68,883 sq km. **Location:** Atlantic O. just W of Great Britain. Northern Ireland (UK) on E. **Topography:** Central plateau surrounded by isolated groups of hills and mountains. Heavily indented Atlantic coastline. **Arable land:** 14.9%. **Capital:** Dublin, 1,201,426.

Government: Type: Parliamentary republic. **Head of state:** Pres. Michael D. Higgins; b. 1941; in office: Nov. 11, 2011. **Head of govt.:** Prime Min. Leo Varadkar; b. 1979; in office: June 14, 2017. **Local divisions:** 28 counties, 3 cities. **Defense budget:** $1 bil. **Active troops:** 9,100.

Economy: Industries: pharmaceuticals, chemicals, computer hardware and software, food prods., beverages and brewing, medical devices. **Chief agric.:** barley, potatoes, wheat; beef, dairy prods. **Natural resources:** nat. gas, peat, copper, lead, zinc, silver, barite, gypsum, limestone, dolomite. **Water:** 11,092 cu m per capita. **Electricity prod.:** 26.6 bil kWh. **Labor force:** agric. 5.4%, industry 19.2%, services 75.5%. **Unemployment:** 6.4%.

Finance: Monetary unit: Euro (EUR) (0.86 = $1 U.S.). **GDP:** $357.2 bil; **per capita GDP:** $75,500; **GDP growth:** 7.8%. **Imports:** $96 bil; UK 29%, U.S. 18.9%, France 12.1%, Germany 9.6%. **Exports:** $225.1 bil; U.S. 27.1%, UK 13.4%, Belgium 11%, Germany 8.1%, Switzerland 5.1%. **Tourism:** $5.6 bil. **Budget:** $87.2 bil. **Inflation:** 0.3%.

Transport: Railways: 2,011 mi. **Motor vehicles:** 484.6 per 1,000 pop. **Airports:** 16.

Communications: Telephone: 38.7 per 100 pop. **Mobile:** 102.9 per 100 pop. **Broadband:** 98.2 per 100 pop. **Internet** (2017): 84.5%.

Health: Expend.: 7.8%. **Life expect.:** 78.7 male; 83.5 female. **Births:** 13.8 per 1,000 pop. **Deaths:** 6.6 per 1,000 pop. **Infant mortality:** 3.6 per 1,000 live births. **Unemployment:** <2.5%. **HIV:** 0.2%.

Education: Compulsory: ages 6-15. **Literacy:** 99%.

Embassy: 2234 Massachusetts Ave. NW 20008; 462-3939.

Website: www.gov.ie

Celtic tribes invaded the islands about the 4th cent. BCE; their Gaelic culture and literature flourished in the 5th cent. CE, the same century in which St. Patrick converted the Irish to Christianity. Norse invasions began in the 8th cent., ending with defeat of the Danes by the Irish King Brian Boru in 1014. English invasions started in the 12th cent. For over 700 years the Anglo-Irish struggle continued with bitter rebellions and savage repressions. In the Irish Potato Famine, failure of the staple potato crop, 1845-49, caused 1 mil deaths from starvation and related diseases; up to 2 mil people emigrated, many to the U.S.

The Easter Monday Rebellion in 1916 failed but was followed by guerrilla warfare and harsh reprisals by British troops called the Black and Tans. The Dail Eireann (Irish parliament) reaffirmed independence in Jan. 1919. The British offered dominion status to Ulster (6 counties) and southern Ireland (26 counties) Dec. 1921. The constitution of the Irish Free State, a British dominion, was adopted Dec. 11, 1922. Northern Ireland remained part of the UK (see United Kingdom—Northern Ireland).

A new constitution adopted by plebiscite came into operation Dec. 29, 1937. It declared the name of the state Eire in the Irish language (Ireland in the English) and declared it a sovereign democratic state. On Dec. 21, 1948, the country was declared a republic rather than a dominion and withdrew from the Commonwealth. The British Parliament recognized both actions, 1949, but the six northeastern counties remained in the UK.

Irish governments have favored peaceful unification of all Ireland and cooperated with Britain against terrorist groups. After negotiators in Northern Ireland approved a peace settlement on Good Friday, Apr. 10, 1998, voters in the Irish Republic endorsed the accord, on May 22, and the Irish gave up their constitution's territorial claims on the north.

Expansion of educational opportunities and foreign investment in high-tech industries in the 1990s boosted Ireland's prosperity. In 1990, Mary Robinson became Ireland's first woman president. She was succeeded, 1997, by Mary McAleese, the first person from Northern Ireland to hold the office.

Responding to allegations of child sex abuse by Catholic clergy in Ireland, Pope Benedict XVI issued a public apology to victims and their families Mar. 2010. Pope Francis, visiting Ireland in Aug. 2018, criticized Church officials' "failure … adequately to address these repugnant crimes."

To aid Ireland's banks and prevent default after a 2008-10 financial crisis, EU finance ministers approved, Nov. 2010, an 85-bil euro emergency loan package that obligated Ireland to impose unpopular austerity measures. Fianna Fáil, the party that had dominated Irish politics since the 1930s, was defeated in Feb. 2011 elections, and Enda Kenny of the center-right Fine Gael became prime minister. Leo Varadkar of Fine Gael succeeded Kenny, June 14, 2017.

In a national referendum, May 22, 2015, voters approved changing the constitution to legalize same-sex marriage. In a May 25, 2018, referendum, voters repealed a 1983 constitutional amendment that had prohibited almost all abortions.

Israel
State of Israel

People: Population: 8,424,904 (98). **Age distrib.:** <15: 27.3%; 65+: 11.6%. **Growth:** 1.5%. **Migrants:** 23.6%. **Pop. density:** 1,073.3 per sq mi, 414.4 per sq km. **Urban:** 92.4%. **Ethnic groups:** Jewish 74.7% (Israel-born 76.3%, Europe/America/Oceania-born 16.2%, Africa-born 4.8%, Asia-born 2.7%), non-Jewish (mostly Arab) 25.2%. **Languages:** Hebrew (official), Arabic, English. **Religions:** Jewish 74.7%, Muslim 17.7%, Christian 2%.

Geography: Total area: 8,019 sq mi, 20,770 sq km (150); **Land area:** 7,849 sq mi, 20,330 sq km. **Location:** Middle East, on E end of Mediterranean Sea. Lebanon on N; Syria, West Bank, Jordan on E; Gaza Strip, Egypt on W. **Topography:** The Mediterranean coastal plain is fertile and well-watered. Judean Plateau in center. Semi-desert Negev region extends to apex at head of Gulf of Aqaba. The E border drops sharply into the Jordan Rift Valley, which incl. Lake Tiberias (Sea of Galilee) and the Dead Sea (1,339 ft below sea level), lowest point in Asia. **Arable land:** 13.7%. **Capital:** Jerusalem, 907,062. **Cities:** Tel Aviv-Jaffa, 4,010,977; Haifa, 1,134,843.

Government: Type: Parliamentary democracy. **Head of state:** Pres. Reuven Rivlin; b. 1939; in office: July 27, 2014. **Head of govt.:** Prime Min. Benjamin Netanyahu; b. 1949; in office: Mar. 31, 2009. **Local divisions:** 6 districts. **Defense budget:** $18.5 bil. **Active troops:** 176,500.

Economy: Industries: high-tech prods. (incl. aviation, communications, computer-aided design and manufactures, medical electronics, fiber optics), wood and paper prods. **Chief agric.:** citrus, vegetables, cotton; beef, poultry. **Natural resources:** timber, potash, copper ore, nat. gas, phosphate rock, magnesium bromide, clays, sand. **Water:** 221 cu m per capita. **Crude oil reserves:** 12.7 mil bbls. **Electricity prod.:** 60.4 bil kWh. **Labor force:** agric. 1.1%, industry 17.3%, services 81.6%. **Unemployment:** 4.2%.

Finance: Monetary unit: Shekel (ILS) (3.62 = $1 U.S.). **GDP:** $316.5 bil; **per capita GDP:** $36,300; **GDP growth:** 3.3%. **Imports:** $66.8 bil; U.S. 11.7%, China 9.5%, Switzerland 8%,

Germany 6.8%, UK 6.2%, Belgium 5.9%. **Exports:** $60.6 bil; U.S. 28.8%, UK 8.2%, Hong Kong 7%, China 5.4%. **Tourism:** $6.8 bil. **Budget:** $102.1 bil. **Inflation:** 0.2%.

Transport: Railways: 777 mi. **Motor vehicles:** 390.1 per 1,000 pop. **Airports:** 29.

Communications: Telephone: 38.9 per 100 pop. **Mobile:** 126.7 per 100 pop. **Broadband:** 93.4 per 100 pop. **Internet** (2017): 81.6%.

Health: Expend.: 7.4%. **Life expect.:** 80.8 male; 84.7 female. **Births:** 17.9 per 1,000 pop. **Deaths:** 5.2 per 1,000 pop. **Infant mortality:** 3.4 per 1,000 live births. **Undernourished:** <2.5%. **HIV:** NA.

Education: Compulsory: ages 5-17. **Literacy:** 97.8%. **Embassy:** 3514 International Dr. NW 20008; 364-5500. **Website:** www.gov.il

Occupying the southwest corner of the ancient Fertile Crescent, Israel contains some of the oldest known evidence of agriculture and of primitive town life. The Hebrews probably arrived early in the 2nd millennium BCE. Under King David and his successors (c. 1000 BCE-597 BCE), Judaism was developed and secured. After conquest by Babylonians, Persians, and Greeks, an independent Jewish kingdom was revived, 168 BCE, but Rome took over in the next century, suppressed Jewish revolts in 70 CE and 135 CE, and renamed Judea Palestine, after the earlier coastal inhabitants, the Philistines.

Arab invaders conquered Palestine in 636. The Arabic language and Islam prevailed within a few centuries, but a Jewish minority remained. The land was ruled from the 11th cent. as a part of non-Arab empires by Seljuks, Mamluks, and Ottomans (with a Crusader interval, 1098-1291).

After four centuries of Ottoman rule, the land was taken in 1917 by Britain, which pledged in the Balfour Declaration to support a Jewish homeland there. In 1920 a British Palestine Mandate was recognized; in 1922 the land east of the Jordan R. was detached.

Jewish immigration, begun in the late 19th cent., swelled in the 1930s and 1940s with refugees from Nazi Germany and survivors of the Holocaust; heavy Arab immigration from Syria and Lebanon also occurred. Arab opposition to Jewish immigration turned violent in 1920, 1921, 1929, and 1936. The UN General Assembly voted in 1947 to partition Palestine into an Arab and a Jewish state. Britain withdrew in May 1948.

Israel was declared independent May 14, 1948; Arabs rejected partition. Egypt, Jordan, Syria, Lebanon, Iraq, and Saudi Arabia invaded but failed to destroy the Jewish state, which gained territory. Separate armistices with the Arab nations were signed in 1949; Jordan occupied the West Bank, Egypt occupied Gaza. Neither granted Palestinian autonomy.

After persistent terrorist raids, Israel invaded Egypt's Sinai, Oct. 29, 1956, aided briefly by British and French forces. A UN cease-fire was arranged Nov. 6.

An uneasy truce between Israel and the Arab countries lasted until 1967, when Egypt reoccupied the Gaza Strip and closed the Gulf of Aqaba to Israeli shipping. In the Six-Day War, starting June 5, the Israelis took the Gaza Strip, occupied the Sinai Peninsula to the Suez Canal, and captured East Jerusalem, Syria's Golan Heights, and Jordan's West Bank. Together, the West Bank and Gaza comprise the Palestinian territories, now represented by the Palestinian Authority.

Egypt and Syria attacked Israel, Oct. 6, 1973 (Yom Kippur, the most solemn day in the Jewish calendar). Israel counterattacked, driving the Syrians back, and crossed the Suez Canal. A cease-fire took effect Oct. 24 and a UN peacekeeping force arrived. Under a 1974 disengagement agreement, Israel withdrew from the canal's west bank. Israeli forces raided Entebbe, Uganda, in 1976 and rescued 103 hostages who had been seized by Arab and German terrorists.

Israel's prime ministers, including David Ben-Gurion, Golda Meir, and Yitzhak Rabin, pursued a moderate socialist program, 1948-77. In 1977, the conservative opposition, led by Menachem Begin, was voted into office for the first time. Egypt's Pres. Anwar al-Sadat visited Jerusalem in 1977, and on Mar. 26, 1979, Egypt and Israel signed a formal peace treaty, ending 30 years of war. Israel returned the Sinai to Egypt in 1982.

Israeli forces invaded Lebanon, June 6, 1982, to destroy Palestine Liberation Organization (PLO) strongholds. After massive Israeli bombing of West Beirut, the PLO agreed to evacuate the city. Israeli troops entered West Beirut after newly elected Lebanese Pres. Bashir Gemayel was assassinated on Sept. 14. Israel drew widespread condemnation when Lebanese Christian forces, Sept. 16, entered two West Beirut refugee camps and slaughtered hundreds of Palestinians.

In 1989, violence escalated over the Israeli military occupation of the West Bank and Gaza Strip. In a series of uprisings known as the first intifada, Palestinian protesters defied Israeli troops, who forcibly retaliated. During the Persian Gulf War, 1991, Iraq fired Scud missiles at Israel.

Ongoing peace talks led to historic agreements between Israel and the PLO, Sept. 1993. The PLO recognized Israel's right to exist; Israel recognized the PLO as the Palestinians' representative. The two sides then signed, Sept. 13, an agreement (known as the Oslo Accord) for limited Palestinian self-rule in the West Bank and Gaza. A follow-up Sept. 1995 agreement (Oslo II) essentially divided the West Bank into areas under Israeli or Palestinian control. Israel and Jordan signed, July 25, 1994, in Washington, DC, a declaration ending their 46-year state of war.

Arab and Jewish extremists repeatedly challenged the peace process. On Nov. 4, 1995, an Orthodox Jewish Israeli assassinated Labor Party Prime Min. Yitzhak Rabin as he left a peace rally in Tel Aviv. Support for Rabin's successor, Shimon Peres, was shaken by a series of suicide bombings and rocket attacks against Israel by Islamic militants. Emphasizing security issues, the candidate of the conservative Likud bloc, Benjamin Netanyahu, was elected prime minister on May 29, 1996.

Under an interim accord signed by Netanyahu and PLO leader Yasir Arafat, Oct. 23, 1998, Israel agreed to yield more West Bank territory to the Palestinians, in exchange for new security guarantees. After May 1999 elections, the Labor Party's Ehud Barak replaced Netanyahu as prime minister.

Israel pulled virtually all its troops out of southern Lebanon in May 2000. Marathon summit talks in the U.S. between Barak and Arafat, July 11-25, failed. A second intifada began in late Sept. in Israel and the Palestinian territories. Barak called new elections for prime minister but lost Feb. 2001 to Ariel Sharon, a hardliner. The bloodshed intensified during the summer, as Palestinian suicide bombers attacked Israeli civilians, and Israel struck at Palestinian-controlled territory attempting to assassinate suspected terrorists.

Israel launched a major West Bank offensive Mar. 29, 2002, two days after a suicide bomber killed 26 Israeli Jews at a Passover celebration in Netanya.

Sharon's decision to pull all Israeli settlers and troops out of Gaza, approved by the cabinet Feb. 2005, led Israeli politics to be realigned. When right-wing Likud members opposed the plan, Sharon and Deputy Prime Min. Ehud Olmert broke with them and formed the centrist Kadima Party. Sharon suffered a massive stroke Jan. 4, 2006. Olmert became prime minister, led Kadima to victory in Mar. elections, and formed a broad coalition government.

Clashes in mid-2006 along the Gaza and Lebanon borders rapidly escalated into full-scale war. By Aug. 14, when a UN-sponsored cease-fire took hold, the estimated death toll from the war included nearly 1,150 Lebanese, almost 200 Gaza Palestinians, and 150 Israelis. Olmert, targeted in multiple corruption inquiries, announced his resignation July 30, 2008. (He was convicted on bribery charges, 2014 and 2015.) After a campaign overshadowed by a three-week war between Israel and Hamas in Gaza, both Kadima and Likud fell far short of a majority in Feb. 2009 elections. On Mar. 31, Netanyahu became prime min. for a second time.

Israel's relations with allies were strained when senior Hamas commander Mahmoud al-Mabhouh was killed Jan. 2010 in Dubai, allegedly by agents of the Israeli spy agency Mossad. There was further criticism of the Israeli government after its Mar. 2010 announcement that it would build 1,600 homes in Ramat Shlomo (a Jewish settlement in mostly Arab East Jerusalem), and later in the spring, when Israeli commandos killed 9 Turkish pro-Palestinian activists in clashes May 31 on board the *Mavi Marmara*, part of a flotilla seeking to break Israel's blockade of Gaza. Turkish-Israeli relations, downgraded by Turkey after the *Mavi Marmara* incident, were normalized under an agreement signed June 28, 2016.

Israel clashed with Palestinians in Gaza Oct.-Nov. 2012. In retaliation for the Gaza attacks, the hacker collective Anonymous launched cyberattacks on Israel before a cease-fire was declared Nov. 21, 2012.

Netanyahu's right-wing Likud-Yisrael Beiteinu political bloc narrowly won Jan. 22, 2013, parliamentary elections. Likud won the largest bloc of seats in Mar. 17, 2015, elections, and Netanyahu assembled a new coalition government.

Conflict between Israel and Hamas escalated in 2014. Rocket attacks from Gaza into Israel increased beginning in June. Israel blamed Hamas for the June 12 kidnapping and killing of 3 Israeli teenagers in the West Bank. Israel launched air and artillery attacks on targets in Gaza, including suspected missile launch sites, and Hamas intensified rocket attacks on Israel. Israeli ground forces entered Gaza July 17, in part to destroy tunnels used to infiltrate fighters into Israel. Israeli ground and air attacks caused high civilian casualties. Israel pulled out ground troops Aug. 5. By the time a cease-fire was agreed Aug. 26, more than 2,100 Palestinians were estimated to have died in the conflict; Israel reported 64 soldiers and 5 civilians killed.

Attacks by Palestinians and countermeasures by Israeli security forces resulted in the deaths of more than 30 Israelis and about 200 Palestinians in the 9 months ending June 30, 2016.

Tensions between Iran and Israel have grown over Iran's nuclear program, which Israel sees as an existential threat. An agreement to limit Iran's nuclear program, signed July 14, 2015, after U.S.-led negotiations, was criticized by Netanyahu as inadequate, and Netanyahu praised the U.S. decision in 2018 to withdraw from the accord. Israeli warplanes, May 10, staged extensive strikes against Iranian forces in Syria, after those forces fired rockets at the Israeli-controlled Golan Heights.

On May 14, 2018, the U.S. officially moved its embassy from Tel Aviv, where most embassies are located, to Jerusalem. The U.S., Aug.-Sept. 2018, announced the cutoff of hundreds of millions of dollars in direct and UN-administered Palestinian aid.

Controversial July 2018 legislation declared that "the Jewish people … have an exclusive right to national self-determination" in Israel; opponents included many non-Jewish Israeli groups.

Palestinian Territories

The Palestinian territories comprise the Gaza Strip, often called Gaza, and the West Bank, both occupied by Israel in 1967. Since 1996 the Palestinian Authority has been responsible for civil government in the territories. Elected president Jan. 20, 1996, PLO leader Yasir Arafat headed the Palestinian Authority until his death Nov. 11, 2004. Mahmoud Abbas, who had succeeded Arafat as PLO chairman and leader of the Fatah faction, was elected president Jan. 2005. (Abbas resigned as PLO chairman Aug. 22, 2015.) A victory by Hamas militants in Jan. 2006 legislative elections led to a power struggle with Abbas. In bitter fighting, Hamas ousted Fatah from Gaza, June 2007, but Abbas retained power in the West Bank. Fatah and Hamas reached a reconciliation agreement Apr. 27, 2011. However, Fatah-Hamas tensions increased in 2013. A new reconciliation agreement was completed Apr. 2014, but a unity government sworn in June 2, 2014, was unable to exert effective authority in Gaza. Another reconciliation accord was signed, Oct. 12, 2017, but implementation moved slowly.

In a 2011 UN speech, Abbas sought full UN membership for an independent Palestinian state; the General Assembly voted, Nov. 29, 2012, to make Palestine a non-member observer state. Speaking at the UN Sept. 30, 2015, Abbas said the Palestinian Authority would no longer be bound by the Oslo Accords and other power-sharing agreements with Israel, which he alleged had violated such agreements.

The **Gaza Strip** extends NE from the Sinai Peninsula for 25 mi, with the Mediterranean Sea to the W and Israel to the E. Nearly all the inhabitants are Palestinian Arabs. Area 139 sq mi; pop. (2018 est.) 1,836,713.

Israel captured Gaza from Egypt in the 1967 war. It remained under Israeli occupation until May 1994, when the Israeli Defense Forces largely withdrew. Agreements between Israel and the PLO in 1993 and 1994 provided for interim self-rule in Gaza, but Israel retained control over security. Israel forcibly evacuated all 9,000 Jewish settlers from Gaza by Aug. 22, 2005, and the last remaining Israeli soldiers pulled out Sept. 12. Israel established a fortified barrier on its Gaza border to block Palestinian infiltrators.

After the Hamas takeover, Israel declared Gaza a "hostile entity," Sept. 19, 2007, and intensified military and economic pressures. Hamas thwarted an Israeli blockade, Jan. 2008, blowing up part of the border wall between Gaza and Egypt. Retaliating for Hamas rocket and mortar attacks, Israel launched an aerial assault and ground offensive in Gaza, Dec. 2008-Jan. 2009. A UN report issued in 2009 found evidence of war crimes committed by both sides. After the *Mavi Marmara* incident, Israel June 2010 eased some restrictions on the flow of goods to Gaza. Egypt's new Islamist govt. lifted the blockade along its Gaza border May 28, 2011. However, Egypt's subsequent military government re-closed the border in 2013 and sought to destroy tunnels dug by Hamas to bring military and other equipment into Gaza. Egypt opened the Gaza border intermittently beginning in 2015.

Members of the Israeli Air Force, Oct. 31, 2012, assassinated Hamas's military chief, Ahmed al-Jabari, in the Gaza Strip. In 2017, Israel began building a below-ground barrier on the Gaza border in an effort to block Hamas tunneling. Large-scale, sometimes violent protests occurred, Mar.-May 2018, on the Gaza side of the Israeli border wall, accompanied by attempts to storm the wall and firing across the border into Israel; more than 100 protesters were killed by Israeli security forces. Cross-border violence, including Israeli airstrikes, flared again in July-Aug.

The **West Bank** is located W of the Jordan R. and Dead Sea, bounded by Jordan on the E and by Israel on the N, W, and S. The Palestinian Authority administers several major cities, but Israel retains control over much land, including Jewish settlements. Total area 2,263 sq mi, land area 2,178 sq mi; pop. (2018 est.) 2,798,494 (Palestinian only). The Palestinian Authority's National Security Force is a paramilitary organization of about 10,000 that maintains internal security in the West Bank.

In June 2002 the Israeli government began building a controversial security barrier in the West Bank to restrict Palestinian access to Israel and reduce infiltration by suicide bombers. In a nonbinding ruling, July 9, 2004, the World Court said the barrier violated international law. Israel has continued to allow the expansion of Jewish settlements; by 2018, over 435,000 Jewish settlers were living in the West Bank (not including more than 200,000 in East Jerusalem, which Israel annexed in 1967).

Italy
Italian Republic

People: Population: 62,246,674 (23). **Age distrib.:** <15: 13.6%; 65+: 21.7%. **Growth:** 0.2%. **Migrants:** 10%. **Pop. density:** 548.1 per sq mi, 211.6 per sq km. **Urban:** 70.4%. **Ethnic groups:** Italian (incl. small clusters of German-, French-, and Slovene-Italians in N; Albanian- and Greek-Italians in S). **Languages:** Italian (official), German, French, Slovene. **Religions:** Christian (overwhelmingly Roman Catholic) 80%, atheist and agnostic 20%.

Geography: Total area: 116,348 sq mi, 301,340 sq km (71); **Land area:** 113,568 sq mi, 294,140 sq km. **Location:** Southern Europe, jutting into Mediterranean Sea. France on W; Switzerland, Austria on N; Slovenia on E. **Topography:** Long boot-shaped peninsula, with Apennine Mts. running its length, extending SE from the Alps into Mediterranean, with islands of Sicily and Sardinia offshore. The alluvial Po Valley drains most of N. Rest of the country is rugged and mountainous, except for intermittent coastal plains like the Campania S of Rome. **Arable land:** 22.4%. **Capital:** Rome, 4,209,710. **Cities:** Milan, 3,132,060; Naples, 2,197,719; Turin, 1,786,059.

Government: Type: Parliamentary republic. **Head of state:** Pres. Sergio Mattarella; b. 1941; in office: Feb. 3, 2015. **Head of govt.:** Prime Min. Giuseppe Conte; b. 1964; in office: June 1, 2018. **Local divisions:** 20 regions (5 autonomous). **Defense budget:** $22.9 bil. **Active troops:** 174,500.

Economy: Industries: tourism, machinery, iron and steel, chemicals, food proc., textiles, motor vehicles, clothing, footwear. **Chief agric.:** fruits, vegetables, grapes, potatoes, sugar beets, soybeans, grain, olives; beef, dairy prods.; fish. **Natural resources:** coal, mercury, zinc, potash, marble, barite, asbestos, pumice, fluorspar, feldspar, pyrite (sulfur), nat. gas/crude oil reserves, fish. **Water:** 3,199 cu m per capita. **Crude oil reserves:** 487.8 mil bbls. **Electricity prod.:** 268.9 bil kWh. **Labor force:** agric. 3.9%, industry 26.3%, services 69.8%. **Unemployment:** 11.2%.

Finance: Monetary unit: Euro (EUR) (0.86 = $1 U.S.). **GDP:** $2.3 tril; **per capita GDP:** $38,100; **GDP growth:** 1.5%. **Imports:** $426.7 bil; Germany 16.3%, France 8.8%, China 7.1%, Netherlands 5.6%, Spain 5.3%. **Exports:** $499.1 bil; Germany 12.5%, France 10.3%, U.S. 9%, Spain 5.2%, UK 5.2%. **Tourism:** $44.2 bil. **Budget:** $927.7 bil. **Inflation:** 1.2%.

Transport: Railways: 12,540 mi. **Motor vehicles:** 701.6 per 1,000 pop. **Airports:** 98.

Communications: Telephone: 34.9 per 100 pop. **Mobile:** 141.3 per 100 pop. **Broadband:** 86.7 per 100 pop. **Internet** (2017): 61.3%.

Health: Expend.: 9%. **Life expect.:** 79.7 male; 85.2 female. **Births:** 8.5 per 1,000 pop. **Deaths:** 10.5 per 1,000 pop. **Infant mortality:** 3.2 per 1,000 live births. **Undernourished:** <2.5%. **HIV:** 0.2%.

Education: Compulsory: ages 6-17. **Literacy:** 99.2%.

Embassy: 3000 Whitehaven St. NW 20008; 612-4400.

Website: www.governo.it

Rome emerged as the major power in Italy after 500 BCE, dominating the Etruscans to the north and Greeks to the south. Under the Empire, which lasted until the 5th cent. CE, Rome ruled most of Western Europe, the Balkans, the Middle East, and North Africa. After Rome fell, Italy became a patchwork of kingdoms, principalities, and city-states until reunified, 1870.

The Fascist leader Benito Mussolini came to power, 1922, and aligned Italy with Nazi Germany in WWII. After Fascism was overthrown in 1943, Italy declared war on Germany and Japan and contributed to the Allied victory. It surrendered conquered lands and lost its colonies. Mussolini was killed by partisans Apr. 28, 1945. Victor Emmanuel III abdicated May 9, 1946; his son Humbert II was king until June 10, when Italy became a republic after a referendum, June 2-3. In the postwar decades, Italy had a succession of short-lived governments.

Christian Democratic leader and former Prime Min. Aldo Moro was abducted and murdered in 1978 by Red Brigade terrorists. The wave of left-wing political violence, including other kidnappings and assassinations, continued into the 1980s.

In Mar. 1994 voting, right-wing parties won a majority, dislodging Italy's long-powerful Christian Democratic Party. Italy led a 7,000-member peacekeeping force in Albania, Apr.-Aug. 1997, and contributed troops to the NATO-led security force (KFOR) that entered Kosovo in June 1999.

Supporters of Silvio Berlusconi, a multibillionaire media magnate, won the 2001 parliamentary elections. Berlusconi backed American-led military operations in Afghanistan (2001) and Iraq (2003). As of mid-2018, about 900 Italian troops were serving with the NATO mission in Afghanistan.

A coalition of center-left parties led by Romano Prodi scored a narrow win over Berlusconi in 2006 parliamentary voting; Berlusconi returned at the head of a center-right coalition after Apr. 2008 elections. Sluggish economic growth and rising public debt raised investors' concerns about Italy's financial stability. Berlusconi resigned Nov. 12, 2011, and Mario Monti, an economist, succeeded him Nov. 16. Italy's economic problems worsened. After Feb. 25, 2013, elections, a coalition government was announced Apr. 27, 2013, led by the center-left Democratic Party (PD). The PD's Matteo Renzi, prime minister as of Feb. 22, 2014, promised political reforms and initiatives to revive the economy. Berlusconi was sentenced, Apr. 15, 2014, to community service, following a 2012 conviction for tax fraud. He was convicted, July 8, 2015, of bribing a senator. Legalization of civil unions between same-sex couples won final parliamentary approval, May 11, 2016. In a Dec. 4, 2016, referendum, Renzi-backed government reforms were defeated. Renzi resigned; he was replaced, Dec. 12, by the PD's Paolo Gentiloni.

About 625,000 African, Middle Eastern, and SW Asian migrants fleeing violence and economic hardship crossed the Mediterranean from North Africa (mainly Libya) to Italy, 2014-17. More than 13,000 died trying to make the crossing. Beginning in the second half of 2017, efforts by Italy to work with the Libyan Coast Guard and various Libyan authorities to intercept smugglers' boats and stop trans-Mediterranean human trafficking sharply reduced migrant crossings. Migrant arrivals Jan.-Sept. 2018 totaled about 21,000. With resettlement proceeding slowly, about 165,000 migrants were living in refugee centers as of mid-2018; others lived in Rome and elsewhere. The government said, June 29, 2018, it would close Italian ports "all summer" to NGO Mediterranean migrant rescue ships.

In Mar. 4, 2018, elections, populist, anti-immigration parties critical of the EU made strong showings. A coalition government led by the Five Star Movement and the League took office June 1.

A highway bridge in Genoa collapsed, Aug. 14, 2018, killing at least 43.

Sicily, 9,927 sq mi, pop. (2014 est.) 5,094,937, is an island 180 by 120 mi, seat of an autonomous region that embraces the island of Pantelleria, 32 sq mi, and the Lipari group, 44 sq mi, including two active volcanoes: Vulcano (1,637 ft) and Stromboli (3,031 ft). From prehistoric times Sicily has been settled by various peoples; a Greek state had its capital at Syracuse. Rome took Sicily from Carthage 215 BCE. Mt. Etna, a 10,925-ft active volcano, is its tallest peak.

Sardinia, 9,301 sq mi, pop. (2014 est.) 1,663,859, lies in the Mediterranean, 115 mi W of Italy and 7½ mi S of Corsica. It is 160 mi long, 68 mi wide, and mountainous. Mining of various metals, historically important to the economy, has declined in recent decades, and tourism has increased. In 1720, Sardinia was added to the possessions of the Dukes of Savoy in Piedmont and Savoy to form the Kingdom of Sardinia. Elba, 86 sq mi, lies 6 mi W of Tuscany. Napoleon I lived in exile on Elba 1814-15.

Jamaica

People: Population: 2,812,090 (137). **Age distrib.:** <15: 26%; 65+: 8.7%. **Growth:** −0.05%. **Migrants:** 0.8%. **Pop. density:** 672.4 per sq mi, 259.6 per sq km. **Urban:** 55.7%. **Ethnic groups:** black 92.1%, mixed 6.1%. **Languages:** English, English patois. **Religions:** Protestant 64.8% (incl. Seventh-day Adventist 12%, Pentecostal 11%), none 21.3%.

Geography: Total area: 4,244 sq mi, 10,991 sq km (161); **Land area:** 4,182 sq mi, 10,831 sq km. **Location:** W Indies. Cuba to N, Haiti to E. **Topography:** Four-fifths of country is covered by mountains. **Arable land:** 11.1%. **Capital:** Kingston, 589,083.

Government: Type: Parliamentary democracy under constitutional monarchy. **Head of state:** Queen Elizabeth II, rep. by Gov.-Gen. Patrick Allen; b. 1951; in office: Feb. 26, 2009. **Head of govt.:** Prime Min. Andrew Holness; b. 1972; in office: Mar. 3, 2016. **Local divisions:** 14 parishes. **Defense budget:** $120 mil. **Active troops:** 3,950.

Economy: Industries: agriculture, mining, manufacture, constr., financial and insurance services, tourism, telecom. **Chief agric.:** sugarcane, bananas, coffee, citrus, yams, ackees, vegetables; poultry, goats, milk; shellfish. **Natural resources:** bauxite, gypsum, limestone. **Water:** 3,874 cu m per capita. **Electricity prod.:** 3.9 bil kWh. **Labor force:** agric. 18.6%, industry 15.4%, services 66%. **Unemployment:** 12.5%.

Finance: Monetary unit: Dollar (JMD) (137.19 = $1 U.S.). **GDP:** $26.1 bil; **per capita GDP:** $9,200; **GDP growth:** 1%. **Imports:** $5.8 bil; U.S. 40.6%, Colombia 6.8%, Japan 5.8%, China 5.8%. **Exports:** $1.3 bil; U.S. 39.1%, Netherlands 12.3%, Canada 8.4%. **Tourism:** $2.5 bil. **Budget:** $4 bil. **Inflation:** 4.4%.

Transport: Motor vehicles: 65.4 per 1,000 pop. **Airports:** 11. **Communications: Telephone:** 10.3 per 100 pop. **Mobile:** 107 per 100 pop. **Broadband:** 56.2 per 100 pop. **Internet:** 44.4%.

Health: Expend.: 5.9%. **Life expect.:** 72.7 male; 76.5 female. **Births:** 16.5 per 1,000 pop. **Deaths:** 7.6 per 1,000 pop. **Infant mortality:** 12.4 per 1,000 live births. **Undernourished:** 8.9%. **HIV:** 1.8%.

Education: Compulsory: ages 6-11. **Literacy:** 88.7%.
Embassy: 1520 New Hampshire Ave. NW 20036; 452-0660.
Website: jis.gov.jm

Jamaica was visited by Christopher Columbus, 1494, and ruled by Spain (under whom Arawak Indians died out) until seized by Britain, 1655. Jamaica won independence Aug. 6, 1962. The island's rich musical innovations include ska and reggae. Rastafarianism is an influential religious movement.

In 1974 Jamaica sought an increase in taxes paid by U.S. and Canadian bauxite mines. The socialist government acquired 50% ownership of the companies' Jamaican interests in 1976. Rudimentary welfare state measures were passed. Relations with the U.S. improved in the 1980s when Jamaican politics entered a more conservative phase.

Portia Simpson-Miller, leader of the People's National Party (PNP), became Jamaica's first female prime min., Mar. 30, 2006. The opposition Jamaica Labour Party (JLP) won the parliamentary elections of Sept. 3, 2007. While trying to arrest alleged gang leader Christopher (Dudus) Coke, police and soldiers clashed with residents in a section of Kingston in May 2010, leaving 76 people dead. Coke surrendered June 22, 2010. Extradited to the U.S., he pleaded guilty to racketeering charges in 2011. The PNP won Dec. 2011 elections; Simpson-Miller again became prime min.

After Simpson-Miller implemented unpopular austerity measures to obtain IMF financial assistance, the JLP won Feb. 25, 2016, elections; Andrew Holness became prime min.

Japan

People: Population: 126,168,156 (10). **Age distrib.:** <15: 12.7%; 65+: 28.4%. **Growth:** −0.2%. **Migrants:** 1.8%. **Pop. density:** 896.5 per sq mi, 346.2 per sq km. **Urban:** 91.6%. **Ethnic groups:** Japanese 98.5%, Korean 0.5%. **Languages:** Japanese. **Religions:** Shintoism 79.2%, Buddhism 66.8% (many practice both).

Geography: Total area: 145,914 sq mi, 377,915 sq km (61); **Land area:** 140,728 sq mi, 364,485 sq km. Consists of 4 main islands: Honshu ("mainland"), 87,805 sq mi; Hokkaido, 30,144 sq mi; Kyushu, 14,114 sq mi; Shikoku, 7,049 sq mi. **Location:** Archipelago off E coast of Asia. Russia to N, N. Korea and S. Korea to W. **Topography:** Deeply indented coast. The northern islands are continuation of the Sakhalin Mts. China's Kunlun range continues into southern islands. The ranges meet in Japanese Alps. Group of mostly extinct or inactive volcanoes, incl. Mt. Fuji (Fujiyama) (12,388 ft), cross Honshu E-W in a vast transverse fissure. **Arable land:** 11.5%. **Capital:** Tokyo, 37,468,302 (figure is for Major Metro area). **Cities:** Kinki Major Metro Area (MMA) (Osaka), 19,281,188; Chukyo MMA (Nagoya), 9,507,076; Kitakyushu-Fukuoka MMA, 5,550,683; Shizuoka-Hamamatsu MMA, 2,899,394; Sapporo, 2,664,966; Sendai, 2,306,451; Hiroshima, 2,095,220.

Government: Type: Parliamentary constitutional monarchy. **Head of state:** Emperor Akihito; b. 1933; in office: Jan. 7, 1989. **Head of govt.:** Prime Min. Shinzo Abe; b. 1954; in office: Dec. 26, 2012. **Local divisions:** 47 prefectures. **Defense budget:** $46 bil. **Active troops:** 247,150.

Economy: Industries: motor vehicles, electronic equip., machine tools, steel and nonferrous metals, ships, chemicals. **Chief agric.:** vegetables, rice, fish, poultry, fruit, dairy prods., pork, beef, flowers, potatoes/taros/yams, sugarcane, tea, legumes. **Natural resources:** negligible mineral resources, fish. **Water:** 3,397 cu m per capita. **Crude oil reserves:** 44.1 mil bbls. **Electricity prod.:** 976.4 bil kWh. **Labor force:** agric. 3.5%, industry 25.6%, services 70.9%. **Unemployment:** 2.8%.

Finance: Monetary unit: Yen (JPY) (111.60 = $1 U.S.). **GDP:** $5.4 tril; **per capita GDP:** $42,800; **GDP growth:** 1.7%. **Imports:** $625.7 bil; China 24.5%, U.S. 11%, Australia 5.8%. **Exports:** $683.3 bil; U.S. 19.4%, China 19%, South Korea 7.6%, Hong Kong 5.1%. **Tourism:** $34.1 bil. **Budget:** $1.9 tril. **Inflation:** 0.5%.

Transport: Railways: 16,970 mi. **Motor vehicles:** 603.9 per 1,000 pop. **Airports:** 142.

Communications: Telephone: 50.2 per 100 pop. **Mobile:** 133.5 per 100 pop. **Broadband:** 131.9 per 100 pop. **Internet** (2017): 90.9%.

Health: Expend.: 10.9%. **Life expect.:** 82.2 male; 89.0 female. **Births:** 7.5 per 1,000 pop. **Deaths:** 9.9 per 1,000 pop. **Infant mortality:** 2.0 per 1,000 live births. **Undernourished:** <2.5%. **HIV:** <0.1%.

Education: Compulsory: ages 6-14. **Literacy:** 99%.
Embassy: 2520 Massachusetts Ave. NW 20008; 238-6700.
Website: www.japan.go.jp

According to Japanese legend, the empire was founded by Emperor Jimmu, 660 BCE, but earliest records of a unified Japan date from 1,000 years later. Chinese influence was strong in the formation of Japanese civilization. Buddhism was introduced before the 6th cent. CE.

A feudal system, with locally powerful noble families and their samurai warrior retainers, dominated from 1192. Central power was held by successive families of shoguns (military dictators), 1192-1867, until recovered by Emperor Meiji, 1868. The Portuguese and Dutch had minor trade with Japan in the 16th and 17th cents.; U.S. Commodore Matthew C. Perry opened the country to U.S. trade in a treaty ratified 1854. Industrialization began in the late 19th cent. Military conflicts won Taiwan from China, 1894-95, and the southern half of Sakhalin from Russia, 1904-05. Japan annexed Korea, 1910.

In WWI Japan ousted Germany from Shandong in China and took over German Pacific islands. Japan took Manchuria in 1931 and launched full-scale war in China in 1937. Japan attacked Pearl Harbor Dec. 7, 1941, launching a war with the U.S. The U.S. dropped atomic bombs on Hiroshima, Aug. 6, and Nagasaki, Aug. 9, 1945. Japan surrendered Aug. 14.

In a new constitution adopted May 3, 1947, Japan renounced the right to wage war; the emperor renounced claims to divinity; and the Diet became the sole lawmaking authority. The U.S. and 48 other non-Communist nations signed a peace treaty with Japan on Sept. 8, 1951; on the same day, the U.S. signed a bilateral defense agreement with Japan. The peace treaty restored Japan's sovereignty effective Apr. 28, 1952.

Rebuilding after WWII, Japan emerged as one of the most powerful economies in the world. Japan's restrictive import policies allowed it to accumulate huge trade surpluses.

In 1968, the U.S. returned control of the Bonin Isls., Volcano Isls. (including Iwo Jima), and Marcus Isls to Japan. In 1972, the U.S.

returned Okinawa, the other Ryukyu Isls., and the Daito Isls., but the U.S. continued to maintain military bases on Okinawa.

The Liberal Democratic Party (LDP) governed Japan from the mid-1950s through early 1990s. In 1994, Tomiichi Murayama became Japan's first Socialist premier since 1947-48. With the country mired in a lengthy recession, the LDP regained power in 1996 and led Japan until 2009.

For the first time since WWII, Japan sent troops to an overseas war zone, when about 600 noncombat troops served in Iraq Feb. 2004-July 2006. Legislation formalizing a new constitutional interpretation allowing the military to take offensive action to aid an ally, such as the U.S., won final passage Sept. 19, 2015.

The 2008-09 global recession hit Japan hard, prompting a series of economic stimulus plans. The LDP suffered a crushing defeat in 2009 parliamentary elections, won by the opposition Democratic Party of Japan (DPJ).

A 9.0 magnitude earthquake and tsunami in the Pacific Ocean off Japan's east coast Mar. 11, 2011, left almost 21,000 people dead. Inundated by the tsunami, the Fukushima Daiichi nuclear power plant experienced meltdowns at three of its six nuclear reactors, spewing radiation over a large area. Japan shut down its nuclear reactors, and revised safety guidelines were announced in June 2013. The first power-plant reactor returned to service under the new guidelines Aug. 11, 2015.

Elections swept LDP candidates into office in Dec. 2012, and former Prime Min. Shinzo Abe became prime minister. Abe's LDP gained a two-thirds lower house "supermajority" in Dec. 14, 2014, elections. In a televised address Aug. 8, 2016, Emperor Akihito, 82, indicated a desire to abdicate, later scheduled for Apr. 30, 2019. Abe retained a two-thirds lower house majority in Oct. 22, 2017, parliamentary elections.

Japan had signed and ratified the 12-nation Trans-Pacific Partnership trade liberalization agreement that the U.S. withdrew from, Jan. 23, 2017. Japan then signed, Mar. 8, 2018, a revised 11-nation Comprehensive and Progressive Agreement for Trans-Pacific Partnership. Japan and the EU signed, July 17, 2018, a trade liberalization agreement. New U.S. tariffs on Japanese steel imports went into effect, Mar. 23, 2018.

Heavy rains caused severe flooding and landslides in SW Japan, July 2018, leaving at least 220 dead. Record heat in July killed more than 100.

Jordan
Hashemite Kingdom of Jordan

People: Population: 10,458,413 (86). **Age distrib.:** <15: 34.1%; 65+: 3.5%. **Growth:** 2%. **Migrants:** 33.3%. **Pop. density:** 305 per sq mi, 117.8 per sq km. **Urban:** 91%. **Ethnic groups:** Jordanian 69.3%, Syrian 13.3%, Palestinian 6.7%, Egyptian 6.7%. **Languages:** Arabic (official), English (widely understood among upper and middle classes). **Religions:** Muslim (official; predom. Sunni) 97.2%, Christian (majority Greek Orthodox) 2.2%.

Geography: Total area: 34,495 sq mi, 89,342 sq km (110); **Land area:** 34,287 sq mi, 88,802 sq km. **Location:** Middle East. Israel, West Bank on W; Saudi Arabia on S; Iraq on E; Syria on N. **Topography:** About 88% is arid. Fertile areas in W. Only port is on short Aqaba Gulf coast. Country shares Dead Sea (1,339 ft below sea level) with Israel. **Arable land:** 2.6%. **Capital:** Amman, 2,064,582.

Government: Type: Parliamentary constitutional monarchy. **Head of state:** King Abdullah II; b. 1962; in office: Feb. 7, 1999. **Head of govt.:** Prime Min. Omar al-Razzaz; b. 1960; in office: June 4, 2018. **Local divisions:** 12 governorates. **Defense budget:** $1.6 bil. **Active troops:** 100,500.

Economy: Industries: tourism, information tech., clothing, fertilizer, potash, phosphate mining, pharmaceuticals. **Chief agric.:** citrus, tomatoes, cucumbers, olives, strawberries, stone fruits; sheep, poultry, dairy. **Natural resources:** phosphates, potash, shale oil. **Water:** 123 cu m per capita. **Crude oil reserves:** 1 mil bbls. **Electricity prod.:** 17.9 bil kWh. **Labor force:** agric. 3.7%, industry 26.8%, services 69.5%. **Unemployment:** 14.9%.

Finance: Monetary unit: Dinar (JOD) (0.71 = $1 U.S.). **GDP:** $89.1 bil; **per capita GDP:** $12,500; **GDP growth:** 2.3%. **Imports:** $18.1 bil; China 13.6%, Saudi Arabia 13.6%, U.S. 9.9%. **Exports:** $7.7 bil; U.S. 24.9%, Saudi Arabia 12.8%, India 8.2%, Iraq 8.2%, Kuwait 5.4%. **Tourism:** $4.6 bil. **Budget:** $11.8 bil. **Inflation:** 3.3%.

Transport: Railways: 316 mi. **Motor vehicles:** 109.9 per 1,000 pop. **Airports:** 16.

Communications: Telephone (2016): 4.3 per 100 pop. **Mobile** (2016): 103.8 per 100 pop. **Broadband:** 118.8 per 100 pop. **Internet:** 62.3%.

Health: Expend.: 6.3%. **Life expect.:** 73.6 male; 76.6 female. **Births:** 23.6 per 1,000 pop. **Deaths:** 3.4 per 1,000 pop. **Infant mortality:** 13.7 per 1,000 live births. **Undernourished:** 13.5%. **HIV:** NA.

Education: Compulsory: ages 6-15. **Literacy:** 98%.

Embassy: 3504 International Dr. NW 20008; 966-2664.

Website: jordan.gov.jo

From ancient times to 1922 the lands to the east of the Jordan R. were culturally and politically united with the lands to the W. Arabs

conquered the area in the 7th cent.; the Ottomans took control in the 16th. Britain's 1920 Palestine Mandate covered both sides of the Jordan. In 1921, Abdullah, son of the ruler of Hejaz in Arabia, was installed by Britain as emir of an autonomous Transjordan, covering two-thirds of Palestine. An independent kingdom was proclaimed, 1946.

During the 1948 Arab-Israeli war, the West Bank and East Jerusalem were added to the kingdom, which changed its name to Jordan. These territories were lost to Israel in 1967, which swelled the number of Arab refugees on the East Bank.

Jordan and Israel signed a peace treaty, Oct. 26, 1994. King Hussein died Feb. 7, 1999, ending a nearly 47-year reign; his eldest son assumed the throne as Abdullah II. The king responded to Arab Spring protests, 2011-12, by somewhat liberalizing election laws in advance of Jan. 2013 and Sept. 2016 parliamentary elections. Abdullah appointed a new prime minister, June 4, 2018, after large-scale protests against proposed tax increases.

In 2014, Jordan joined the U.S.-led campaign of airstrikes and other military action against ISIS in Syria and Iraq. More than 670,000 Syrians fleeing civil war were living in Jordan as of Sept. 2018; about 67,000 Iraqi refugees were in Jordan, Aug. 2018.

Kazakhstan
Republic of Kazakhstan

People: Population: 18,744,548 (63). **Age distrib.:** <15: 26.1%; 65+: 7.9%. **Growth:** 1%. **Migrants:** 20%. **Pop. density:** 18 per sq mi, 6.9 per sq km. **Urban:** 57.4%. **Ethnic groups:** Kazakh (Qazaq) 63.1%, Russian 23.7%, Uzbek 2.9%, Ukrainian 2.1%. **Languages:** Kazakh or Qazaq, Russian (both official). **Religions:** Muslim 70.2%, Christian (mainly Russian Orthodox) 26.2%, atheist 2.8%.

Geography: Total area: 1,052,090 sq mi, 2,724,900 sq km (9); **Land area:** 1,042,360 sq mi, 2,699,700 sq km. **Location:** Central Asia. Russia on N; China on E; Kyrgyzstan, Uzbekistan, Turkmenistan on S. **Topography:** Extends from lower reaches of Volga in Europe to Altay Mts. on Chinese border. **Arable land:** 10.9%. **Capital:** Astana, 1,068,113. **Cities:** Almaty, 1,829,005.

Government: Type: Presidential republic. **Head of state:** Pres. Nursultan Nazarbayev; b. 1940; in office: Dec. 1, 1991. **Head of govt.:** Prime Min. Bakhytzhan Sagintayev; b. 1963; in office: Sept. 9, 2016. **Local divisions:** 14 provinces, 2 cities. **Defense budget:** $1.2 bil. **Active troops:** 39,000.

Economy: Industries: oil, coal, iron ore, manganese, chromite, lead, zinc, copper, titanium, bauxite, gold, silver, phosphates, sulfur, uranium. **Chief agric.:** grain (mostly spring wheat, barley), potatoes, vegetables, melons; livestock. **Natural resources:** petroleum, nat. gas, coal, iron ore, manganese, chrome ore, nickel, cobalt, copper, molybdenum, lead, zinc, bauxite, gold, uranium. **Water:** 6,150 cu m per capita. **Crude oil reserves:** 30 bil bbls. **Electricity prod.:** 100.6 bil kWh. **Labor force:** agric. 18.1%, industry 20.7%, services 61.2%. **Unemployment:** 4.9%.

Finance: Monetary unit: Tenge (KZT) (368.80 = $1 U.S.). **GDP:** $477.6 bil; **per capita GDP:** $26,300; **GDP growth:** 4%. **Imports:** $31.9 bil; Russia 38.9%, China 16.1%, Germany 5.1%. **Exports:** $49.3 bil; Italy 17.9%, China 11.9%, Netherlands 9.8%, Russia 9.3%, Switzerland 6.4%, France 5.9%. **Tourism:** $1.8 bil. **Budget:** $39 bil. **Inflation:** 7.4%.

Transport: Railways: 10,007 mi. **Airports:** 63.

Communications: Telephone: 20.3 per 100 pop. **Mobile:** 145.4 per 100 pop. **Broadband:** 71 per 100 pop. **Internet** (2017): 76.4%.

Health: Expend.: 3.9%. **Life expect.:** 66.2 male; 76.3 female. **Births:** 17.5 per 1,000 pop. **Deaths:** 8.2 per 1,000 pop. **Infant mortality:** 19.0 per 1,000 live births. **Undernourished:** <2.5%. **HIV:** 0.2%.

Education: Compulsory: ages 7-15. **Literacy:** 99.8%.

Embassy: 1401 16th St. NW 20036; 232-5488.

Website: www.government.kz

The region came under the Mongols' rule in the 13th cent. and gradually came under Russian rule, 1730-1853. It was admitted to the USSR as a constituent republic in 1936.

Kazakhstan's Dec. 16, 1991, declaration of independence became reality when the Soviet Union dissolved Dec. 26, 1991. The Communist Party chief, Nursultan Nazarbayev, was elected president unopposed. Dissent was suppressed. Nazarbayev encouraged Western investment in the oil industry, boosting the economy. Production began, Sept. 2013, at the Kashagan oil field, the largest outside the Middle East, in the Caspian Sea; it was suspended in Oct. 2013 due to gas leaks and resumed in Oct. 2016. Increased oil production boosted GDP growth in 2017.

Kazakhstan agreed, Feb. 1994, to dismantle nuclear missiles. Private land ownership was legalized Dec. 1995. Astana (formerly Akmola) became the nation's new capital, June 9, 1998. Reelected in 1999 and 2005, Pres. Nazarbayev was authorized to run for an unlimited number of terms under a constitutional amendment passed by parliament May 2007; he claimed more than 95% of the vote in the 2011 presidential election, and almost 98% in the 2015 election. Nazarbayev's Nur Otan party won 82% of the vote in Mar. 20, 2016, parliamentary elections.

An agreement to create a limited economic union of Kazakhstan, Russia, and Belarus was signed May 29, 2014 (Armenia and Kyrgyzstan joined in 2015).

Kenya
Republic of Kenya

People: Population: 48,397,527 (29). **Age distrib.:** <15: 39%; 65+: 3.1%. **Growth:** 1.6%. **Migrants:** 2.2%. **Pop. density:** 220.2 per sq mi, 85 per sq km. **Urban:** 27%. **Ethnic groups:** Kikuyu 22%, Luhya 14%, Luo 13%, Kalenjin 12%, Kamba 11%, Kisii 6%, Meru 6%. **Languages:** English, Kiswahili (both official); numerous indigenous langs. **Religions:** Christian 83% (incl. Protestant 47.7%, Catholic 23.4%), Muslim 11.2%.

Geography: Total area: 224,081 sq mi, 580,367 sq km (48); **Land area:** 219,746 sq mi, 569,140 sq km. **Location:** E Africa, on coast of Indian O. Uganda on W, Tanzania on S, Somalia on E, Ethiopia on N, South Sudan on NW. **Topography:** Northern three-fifths of country is arid. A low coastal area and a plateau 3,000-10,000-ft high is in S. The Great Rift Valley enters the country N-S, flanked by high mountains. **Arable land:** 10.2%. **Capital:** Nairobi, 4,385,853. **Cities:** Mombasa, 1,213,928.

Government: Type: Presidential republic. **Head of state and govt.:** Pres. Uhuru Kenyatta; b. 1961; in office: Apr. 9, 2013. **Local divisions:** 47 counties. **Defense budget:** $1.2 bil. **Active troops:** 24,100.

Economy: Industries: small-scale consumer goods (plastic, furniture, batteries, textiles, clothing, soap, cigarettes, flour), agric. prods., horticulture, oil refining, aluminum, steel, lead, cement. **Chief agric.:** tea, coffee, corn, wheat, sugarcane, fruit, vegetables; dairy prods., beef, fish, pork. **Natural resources:** limestone, soda ash, salt, gems, fluorspar, zinc, diatomite, gypsum, wildlife, hydropower. **Water:** 667 cu m per capita. **Electricity prod.:** 9.6 bil kWh. **Labor force:** agric. 38%, industry 14.3%, services 47.8%, India 15.5%, UAE 5.7%. **Unemployment:** 11.5%.

Finance: Monetary unit: Shilling (KES) (100.71 = $1 U.S.). **GDP:** $163.1 bil; **per capita GDP:** $3,500; **GDP growth:** 4.8%. **Imports:** $15.3 bil; China 22.5%, India 9.9%, UAE 8.7%, Saudi Arabia 5.1%. **Exports:** $5.8 bil; Uganda 10.8%, Pakistan 10.6%, U.S. 8.1%, Netherlands 7.3%, UK 6.4%. **Tourism:** $926 mil. **Budget:** $24.6 bil. **Inflation:** 8%.

Transport: Railways: 2,365 mi. **Motor vehicles:** 33.5 per 1,000 pop. **Airports:** 16.

Communications: Telephone: 0.1 per 100 pop. **Mobile:** 86.1 per 100 pop. **Broadband:** 26.2 per 100 pop. **Internet:** 16.6%.

Health: Expend.: 5.2%. **Life expect.:** 63.1 male; 66.1 female. **Births:** 22.6 per 1,000 pop. **Deaths:** 6.7 per 1,000 pop. **Infant mortality:** 36.1 per 1,000 live births. **Undernourished:** 19.1%. **HIV:** 4.8%.

Education: Compulsory: ages 6-17. **Literacy:** 78.7%.
Embassy: 2249 R St. NW 20008; 387-6101.
Website: www.president.go.ke

Arab colonies exported spices and slaves from the Kenya coast as early as the 8th cent. Britain obtained control in the 19th cent. Kenya won independence Dec. 12, 1963, four years after the end of the violent Mau Mau uprising. Jomo Kenyatta, the country's leader since independence, died Aug. 22, 1978. He was succeeded by his vice president, Daniel arap Moi.

During the first half of the 1990s, Kenya suffered widespread unemployment and high inflation. Tribal clashes in the western provinces claimed thousands of lives. Pres. Moi won a fourth term in Dec. 1997, in an election plagued by irregularities. A truck bomb explosion at the U.S. embassy in Nairobi, Aug. 7, 1998, killed more than 200 people and injured about 5,000. The U.S. blamed the attack on al-Qaeda.

Constitutionally barred from seeking another term, Pres. Moi was succeeded, Dec. 2002, by Mwai Kibaki of the opposition Democratic Party. After a disputed election Dec. 2007, Kenya's electoral commission declared Kibaki the winner over challenger Raila Odinga. Weeks of factional violence followed, leaving some 1,500 people dead and 600,000 displaced. Uhuru Kenyatta (Jomo Kenyatta's son) was declared, Mar. 10, 2013, the winner over Odinga in the Mar. 4 presidential election, amid accusations of vote-rigging. On Aug. 11, 2017, Kenyatta was again declared the victor over Odinga in Aug. 8 presidential voting; Odinga charged electoral fraud. After the Supreme Court, Sept. 1, nullified the result, Kenyatta won an Oct. 26 re-vote boycotted by Odinga.

Kenya sent troops to Somalia in 2011 (they joined with the African Union's AMISOM force in 2012) to combat the Somali Islamist extremist group al-Shabab. Al-Shabab carried out a series of deadly terrorist attacks in Kenya. An Apr. 2, 2015, attack on Garissa Univ. College killed 148 people. Scores of Kenyan troops have been killed by al-Shabab fighters in Somalia. The UNHCR estimated that more than 256,000 Somali refugees were living in Kenya as of July 31, 2018, a decline of about 80,000 from two years earlier. In May 2016, the Kenyan government announced plans to close the Dadaab refugee camp—then the world's largest—and tens of thousands of people were subsequently repatriated to Somalia, amid allegations of forced returns. A Feb. 2017 court ruling held it was unconstitutional to close the camp, which had almost 210,000 residents as of July 31, 2018.

Kiribati
Republic of Kiribati

People: Population: 109,367 (180). **Age distrib.:** <15: 29.3%; 65+: 4.3%. **Growth:** 1.1%. **Migrants:** 2.6%. **Pop. density:** 349.3 per sq mi, 134.9 per sq km. **Urban:** 54.1%. **Ethnic groups:** I-Kiribati 96.2%. **Languages:** I-Kiribati, English (both official). **Religions:** Roman Catholic 57.3%, Kiribati Uniting Church 31.3%, Mormon 5.3%.

Geography: Total area: 313 sq mi, 811 sq km (173); **Land area:** 313 sq mi, 811 sq km. **Location:** 33 atolls (Gilbert, Line, and Phoenix Isls.) in mid-Pacific scattered over an area of about 1.35 mil sq mi around the point where the International Date Line formerly crossed the Equator. The Date Line was moved in 1997 to follow Kiribati's E border. Nearest neighbors are Nauru to SW, Tuvalu and Tokelau Isls. (N.Z.) to S. **Topography:** Except Banaba (Ocean) Isl., all are low-lying, with soil of coral sand and rock fragments, subject to erratic rainfall. **Arable land:** 2.5%. **Capital:** Tarawa, 64,011 (figure is for Tarawa Isl.).

Government: Type: Presidential republic. **Head of state and govt.:** Pres. Taneti Maamau; b. 1960; in office: Mar. 11, 2016. **Local divisions:** 3 geographical units (no first-order admin. divisions). **Defense budget/active troops:** NA.

Economy: Industries: fishing, handicrafts. **Chief agric.:** copra, breadfruit, fish. **Natural resources:** phosphate (production discontinued in 1979), coconuts, fish. **Water:** NA. **Electricity prod.:** 24 mil kWh. **Labor force:** agric. 15%, industry 10%, services 75%. **Unemployment:** NA.

Finance: Monetary unit: Dollar (AUD) (1.39 = $1 U.S.). **GDP:** $226 mil; **per capita GDP:** $2,000; **GDP growth:** 3.1%. **Imports** (2013): $182.2 mil; Australia 29.3%, Fiji 17.3%, New Zealand 10.7%, China 5.8%, U.S. 5.8%, Singapore 5.1%. **Exports** (2013): $84.8 mil; Philippines 50.8%, Malaysia 17.2%, U.S. 11.4%, Bangladesh 5.8%, Fiji 5.4%. **Tourism:** $3 mil. **Budget:** $277.5 mil. **Inflation** (2014-15): 0.6%.

Transport: Airports: 4.

Communications: Telephone: 0.7 per 100 pop. **Mobile:** 39.6 per 100 pop. **Broadband:** 0.9 per 100 pop. **Internet:** 13.7%.

Health: Expend.: 7.6%. **Life expect.:** 64.3 male; 69.5 female. **Births:** 21 per 1,000 pop. **Deaths:** 7 per 1,000 pop. **Infant mortality:** 31.1 per 1,000 live births. **Undernourished:** 3.3%. **HIV:** NA.

Education: Compulsory: ages 6-14. **Literacy:** 97.7%.
Permanent UN mission: 800 Second Ave., Ste. 400A, New York, NY 10017; (212) 867-3310.
Website: www.president.gov.ki

A British protectorate since 1892, the Gilbert and Ellice Islands colony was completed with the inclusion of the Phoenix Islands, 1937. Tarawa Atoll was the scene of some of the bloodiest fighting in the Pacific during WWII.

Self-rule was granted 1971; the Ellice Islands separated from the colony in 1975 and became independent Tuvalu, 1978. Kiribati (pronounced *Kiribass*) independence was attained July 12, 1979. Under a treaty of friendship the U.S. relinquished its claims to several Line and Phoenix islands. Kiribati was admitted to the UN in 1999. Kiribati's land area is shrinking as a result of rising sea levels; in 2014, the government began buying land in Fiji to be used for agriculture and possible resettlement. Opposition candidate Taneti Maamau won the Mar. 9, 2016, presidential election.

Korea, North
Democratic People's Republic of Korea

People: Population: 25,381,085 (53). **Age distrib.:** <15: 20.6%; 65+: 9.5%. **Growth:** 0.5%. **Migrants:** 0.2%. **Pop. density:** 545.9 per sq mi, 210.8 per sq km. **Urban:** 61.9%. **Ethnic groups:** racially homogeneous; small Chinese community, a few ethnic Japanese. **Languages:** Korean. **Religions:** traditionally Buddhist and Confucianist. Autonomous religious activities almost nonexistent.

Geography: Total area: 46,540 sq mi, 120,538 sq km (97); **Land area:** 46,490 sq mi, 120,408 sq km. **Location:** Northern E Asia. China and Russia on N, S. Korea on S. **Topography:** Mountains and hills cover nearly entire country, with narrow valleys and small plains in between. N and E coasts are most rugged areas. **Arable land:** 19.5%. **Capital:** P'yongyang, 3,037,862.

Government: Type: Single-party state. **Head of state:** Kim Jong Un; b. 1983; officially assumed post Dec. 17, 2011. **Head of govt.:** Prem. Pak Pong Ju; b. 1939; in office: Apr. 1, 2013. **Local divisions:** 9 provinces, 3 cities. **Defense budget:** NA. **Active troops:** 1,280,000.

Economy: Industries: military prods.; machine building, elec. power, chemicals; mining, metallurgy; textiles, food proc.; tourism. **Chief agric.:** rice, corn, potatoes, wheat, soybeans, pulses, beef, pork. **Natural resources:** coal, iron ore, limestone, magnesite, graphite, copper, zinc, lead, prec. metals, hydropower. **Water:** 3,067 cu m per capita. **Electricity prod.:** 13.4 bil kWh. **Labor force:** agric. 67.1%, industry 17.5%, services 15.4%, Congo Republic 5.5%. **Unemployment:** 4.8%.

Finance: Monetary unit: Won (KPW) (900.03 = $1 U.S.). **GDP** (2015): $40 bil; **per capita GDP** (2015): $1,700; **GDP growth**

(2015): −1.1%. **Imports** (2016): $3.8 bil; China 91.9%. **Exports** (2016): $3 bil; China 86.3%. **Budget** (2007): $3.3 bil. **Inflation:** NA.

Transport: Railways: 4,620 mi. **Airports:** 39.

Communications: Telephone (2016): 4.7 per 100 pop. **Mobile** (2016): 14.2 per 100 pop. **Broadband:** NA. **Internet:** NA.

Health: Expend.: NA. **Life expect.:** 67.2 male; 75.0 female. **Births:** 14.6 per 1,000 pop. **Deaths:** 9.3 per 1,000 pop. **Infant mortality:** 21.4 per 1,000 live births. **Undernourished:** 40.8%. **HIV:** NA.

Education: Compulsory: ages 6-16. **Literacy:** 100%.

Permanent UN mission: 820 Second Ave., 13th Fl., New York, NY 10017; (212) 972-3105.

Website: www.korea-dpr.com

The Democratic People's Republic of Korea was founded May 1, 1948, in the zone occupied by Russia after WWII. Its armies tried to conquer the south, 1950. After three years of fighting, with Chinese and U.S. intervention, a cease-fire was proclaimed. A demilitarized zone (DMZ) was established, straddling the cease-fire line.

For the next four decades, a hard-line Communist regime headed by Kim Il Sung kept tight control over the nation's political, economic, and cultural life. The nation used its mineral and hydroelectric resources to develop its military strength. By the early 1990s, North Korea was widely believed to be developing nuclear weapons. The U.S. and North Korea signed an agreement, Oct. 21, 1994, providing for phased dismantling of North Korea's nuclear development program in return for U.S. energy aid and improved ties with the U.S.

Kim Il Sung died July 8, 1994. He was succeeded by his son, Kim Jong Il. Defections by high officials, a deteriorating economy, and severe food shortages plagued North Korea, beginning in the late 1990s. North Korea and Japan agreed to normalize relations in a Sept. 2002 summit.

In Oct. 2002, North Korea admitted to pursuing a secret nuclear weapons program in violation of past agreements. During 2003-09, as six-nation talks sponsored by China sought to resolve the nuclear issue, North Korea zigzagged, alternately stopping and resuming its nuclear program in order to win concessions. North Korea conducted its first nuclear explosion Oct. 9, 2006.

In Apr.-May 2009, North Korea suspended participation in the six-nation talks, expelled IAEA inspectors, tested multiple missiles, and exploded a nuclear device underground. The UN Security Council June 12 toughened sanctions on North Korea.

Kim Jong Il died Dec. 17, 2011. He was succeeded by his son Kim Jong Un. In an apparent move to consolidate his power, Kim Jong Un ordered the execution, Dec. 2013, of his uncle, Jang Song Thaek, who had been considered one of the most powerful political figures in North Korea.

North Korea conducted a nuclear test Feb. 10, 2013, and it negated, Mar. 11, 2013, the cease-fire agreement with the South that ended the Korean War. It conducted numerous short- and medium-range missile tests 2013-15. North Korea was apparently responsible for cyberattacks on Sony Pictures Entertainment, Nov. 2014, shortly before the studio's scheduled release of a comedy film about an attempt to assassinate Kim Jong Un; the U.S., June 8, 2018, filed criminal charges against a North Korean national. North Korea conducted its fourth nuclear weapons test on Jan. 6, 2016, and its fifth on Sept. 9. U.S. and UN sanctions were toughened in early 2016. North Korea continued missile tests, 2016-17, including its first ICBM launch, July 4, 2017. U.S. and UN sanctions were strengthened again Aug.-Sept. 2017. North Korea conducted its sixth nuclear test, Sept. 3, 2017.

On Apr. 27, 2018, Kim Jong Un became the first North Korean leader since the Korean War to set foot on South Korean soil, meeting in the DMZ with South Korean Pres. Moon Jae-in. The two leaders reached general agreements to work toward a peace treaty and denuclearization of the Korean Peninsula. North Korea said it destroyed, May 24, its nuclear test site. At a June 12 summit meeting in Singapore with U.S. Pres. Donald Trump, Kim again made a general denuclearization pledge. As post-summit U.S.-North Korea talks continued, North Korea began dismantling a missile test site in July. However, U.S. officials, and an Aug. UN report, concluded that North Korea was continuing its nuclear and missile programs.

Korea, South
Republic of Korea

People: Population: 51,418,097 (27). **Age distrib.:** <15: 13%; 65+: 14.6%. **Growth:** 0.4%. **Migrants:** 2.3%. **Pop. density:** 1,374 per sq mi, 530.5 per sq km. **Urban:** 81.5%. **Ethnic groups:** homogeneous. **Languages:** Korean, English (widely taught). **Religions:** Protestant 19.7%, Buddhist 15.5%, Catholic 7.9%, none 56.9%.

Geography: Total area: 38,502 sq mi, 99,720 sq km (107); **Land area:** 37,421 sq mi, 96,920 sq km. **Location:** Northern E Asia. N. Korea on N. **Topography:** Mountainous, with a rugged E coast. W and S coasts are deeply indented, with many islands and harbors. **Arable land:** 15%. **Capital:** Seoul, 9,963,497; Sejong City (admin. center). **Cities:** Busan, 3,466,898; Incheon, 2,763,344; Daegu, 2,221,234.

Government: Type: Presidential republic. **Head of state:** Pres. Moon Jae-in; b. 1953; in office: May 10, 2017. **Head of govt.:** Prime

Min. Lee Nak-yon; b. 1952; in office: June 1, 2017. **Local divisions:** 9 provinces, 6 metropolitan cities, 1 special city, 1 special self-governing city. **Defense budget:** $35.7 bil. **Active troops:** 625,000.

Economy: Industries: electronics, telecom, auto prod., chemicals, shipbuilding, steel. **Chief agric.:** rice, root crops, barley, vegetables, fruit, cattle, pigs, chickens, milk, eggs, fish. **Natural resources:** coal, tungsten, graphite, molybdenum, lead. **Water:** 1,386 cu m per capita. **Electricity prod.:** 516.5 bil kWh. **Labor force:** agric. 4.9%, industry 24.8%, services 70.3%. **Unemployment:** 3.7%.

Finance: Monetary unit: Won (KRW) (1,117.14 = $1 U.S.). **GDP:** $2 tril; **per capita GDP:** $39,400; **GDP growth:** 3.1%. **Imports:** $457.5 bil; China 20.5%, Japan 11.5%, U.S. 10.5%. **Exports:** $577.4 bil; China 25.1%, U.S. 12.2%, Vietnam 8.2%, Hong Kong 6.9%. **Tourism:** $13.4 bil. **Budget:** $303.3 bil. **Inflation:** 1.9%.

Transport: Railways: 2,472 mi. **Motor vehicles:** 440.2 per 1,000 pop. **Airports:** 71.

Communications: Telephone: 52.7 per 100 pop. **Mobile:** 124.9 per 100 pop. **Broadband:** 111.5 per 100 pop. **Internet** (2017): 95.1%.

Health: Expend.: 7.4%. **Life expect.:** 79.4 male; 85.8 female. **Births:** 8.3 per 1,000 pop. **Deaths:** 6.3 per 1,000 pop. **Infant mortality:** 3.0 per 1,000 live births. **Undernourished:** <2.5%. **HIV:** NA.

Education: Compulsory: ages 6-14. **Literacy:** NA.

Embassy: 2450 Massachusetts Ave. NW 20008; 939-5600.

Website: www.korea.net

The recorded history of Korea, once called the Hermit Kingdom, dates back to the 1st cent. BCE. It was united in a kingdom under the Silla Dynasty, 668 CE. It was at times associated with the Chinese empire; the treaty that concluded the Sino-Japanese war of 1894-95 recognized Korea's complete independence. In 1910 Japan forcibly annexed Korea as Chosun.

At the Potsdam conference, July 1945, near the end of WWII, the 38th parallel was designated as the line dividing Soviet (north) and U.S. (south) occupation zones. Russian troops entered Korea Aug. 10, 1945; U.S. troops entered Sept. 8.

The South Koreans formed the Republic of Korea in May 1948 with Seoul as the capital. Dr. Syngman Rhee was chosen president. A separate, Communist regime was formed in the North; its army attacked the south in June 1950, initiating the Korean War. UN troops, under U.S. command, supported South Korea in the war, which ended in an armistice (July 1953) leaving Korea divided by a demilitarized zone (DMZ) along the 38th parallel. The U.S. kept troops in South Korea (about 28,500 as of mid-2018).

Rhee's authoritarian rule became increasingly unpopular, forcing his resignation Apr. 26, 1960. In an army coup May 16, 1961, Gen. Park Chung-hee became chairman of a ruling junta. First elected president, 1963, Park was assassinated by the chief of the Korean intelligence agency, Oct. 26, 1979.

In May 1980, Gen. Chun Doo-hwan, head of military intelligence, ordered the brutal suppression of pro-democracy demonstrations in Kwangju. Chun became president, Aug. 27, 1980. On July 1, 1987, following anti-government protests, Chun agreed to democratic reforms. In Dec., Roh Tae-woo, a longtime ally of Chun's, was elected president.

Pres. Kim Young-sam took office in 1993. Convicted of mutiny, treason, and corruption, Chun was sentenced to death by a Seoul court, Aug. 26, 1996, for his role in the 1979 coup and 1980 Kwangju massacre; Roh received a 225-year prison sentence. Kim Dae-jung, a longtime dissident, won the presidential election Dec. 18, 1997. Chun and Roh were released and pardoned Dec. 22.

At a summit meeting in Pyongyang, June 13-15, 2000, Pres. Kim Dae-jung and North Korean leader Kim Jong Il agreed to work for reconciliation and eventual reunification of their two countries. On Oct. 13, 2000, Kim Dae-jung was named the winner of the Nobel Peace Prize. Roh Moo-hyun won the 2002 presidential election.

The IAEA, Sept. 2, 2004, said South Korea had acknowledged having secretly processed a small amount of uranium to near weapons-grade level in 2000, violating the Nuclear Non-Proliferation Treaty and a bilateral accord with North Korea (North Korea, 2006-17, conducted 6 nuclear weapons tests).

Conservative Park Geun-hye became South Korea's first female president in Dec. 19, 2012, elections. The sinking, Apr. 16, 2014, of the ferry *Sewol* off the South Korean coast caused the deaths of 304 people. Prime Min. Lee Wan-koo resigned, Apr. 27, 2015, after being implicated in a bribery scandal. Pres. Park was impeached for corruption by the National Assembly, Dec. 9, 2016, and removed from office, Mar. 10, 2017. A criminal trial on corruption charges ended, Apr. 6, 2018, in a conviction and 24-year prison sentence.

Following a series of North Korean missile tests, a U.S.-South Korean agreement to deploy an advanced U.S. missile defense system known as THAAD in South Korea was announced July 8, 2016.

Moon Jae-in of the Democratic Party, who campaigned on a policy of diplomatic engagement with North Korea, won the May 9, 2017, presidential election. Moon met with North Korean leader Kim Jong Un in the DMZ, Apr. 27, 2018; they agreed to work toward a peace treaty and denuclearization. Moon and Kim met again in the DMZ, May 26, to facilitate a U.S.-North Korea summit (held in June). Moon and Kim held a summit in North Korea, Sept. 18-20, 2018, for further talks on bilateral relations and de-nuclearization.

A U.S.-South Korea trade liberalization agreement went into effect Mar. 15, 2012. Revisions signed Sept. 24, 2018, were aimed in part at increasing U.S. auto exports.

Pyeongchang, South Korea, hosted the Winter Olympics, Feb. 9-25, 2018. South and North Korea marched in the opening ceremony under one flag, and a unified team competed in women's hockey.

Kosovo
Republic of Kosovo

People: Population: 1,907,592 (148). **Age distrib.:** <15: 24.7%; 65+: 7.4%. **Growth:** 0.7%. **Pop. density:** 453.8 per sq mi, 175.2 per sq km. **Ethnic groups:** Albanian 92.9%, Bosniak 1.6%, Serb 1.5%, Turk 1.1%. **Languages:** Albanian, Serbian (both official); Bosnian. **Religions:** Muslim 95.6%.

Geography: Total area: 4,203 sq mi, 10,887 sq km (162); **Land area:** 4,203 sq mi, 10,887 sq km. **Location:** SE Europe. Serbia on N, Montenegro on NW, Albania on SW, Macedonia on SE. **Topography:** Low flood basins surrounded by several high mountain ranges. **Arable land:** 27.4%. **Capital:** Pristina.

Government: Type: Parliamentary republic. **Head of state:** Pres. Hashim Thaci; b. 1968; in office: Apr. 7, 2016. **Head of govt.:** Prime Min. Ramush Haradinaj; b. 1968; in office: Sept. 9, 2017. **Local divisions:** 38 municipalities. **Defense budget:** NA. **Active troops:** Kosovo Security Force (non-military) only.

Economy: Industries: mineral mining, constr. materials, base metals, leather, machinery, appliances, foodstuffs and beverages. **Chief agric.:** wheat, corn, berries, potatoes, peppers, fruit; dairy; fish. **Natural resources:** nickel, lead, zinc, magnesium, lignite, kaolin, chrome, bauxite. **Water:** NA. **Electricity prod.:** 5.8 bil kWh. **Labor force:** agric. 4.4%, industry 17.4%, services 78.2%. **Unemployment:** NA.

Finance: Monetary unit: Euro (EUR) (0.86 = $1 U.S.). **GDP:** $19.6 bil; **per capita GDP:** $10,500; **GDP growth:** 4.1%. **Imports:** $3.2 bil; Germany 12.4%, Serbia 12.3%, Turkey 9.6%, China 9.1%, Italy 6.4%, Macedonia 5.1%, Albania 5%. **Exports:** $428 mil; Albania 16%, India 14%, Macedonia 12.1%, Serbia 10.6%, Switzerland 5.6%, Germany 5.4%. **Budget:** $2.2 bil. **Inflation:** 1.5%.

Transport: Railways: 207 mi. **Airports:** 3.

Communications: NA.

Health: Expend.: NA. **Life expect.:** 70.0 male; 74.5 female. **Births:** 16.0 per 1,000 pop. **Deaths:** 7.0 per 1,000 pop. **Infant mortality:** 32.6 per 1,000 live births. **Undernourished:** NA. **HIV:** NA.

Education: Compulsory: ages 6-15. **Literacy:** 91.9%.

Embassy: 2175 K St. NW, Ste. 300, 20037; 380-3581.

Website: www.rks-gov.net

Kosovo was part of the Roman and Byzantine empires before Serbs, a Slavic people, took control in the Middle Ages. After Ottoman Turks defeated Serb forces, 1389, Kosovo's population became predominantly Muslim and Kosovar (ethnic Albanian). Serbia regained control in the First Balkan War (1912-13). Kosovo entered the Kingdom of Serbs, Croats, and Slovenes as part of Serbia after World War I and became an autonomous province of Serbia, a constituent republic of Yugoslavia, after World War II.

Revoking provincial autonomy, Serbia began ruling Kosovo by force in 1989. Albanian secessionists proclaimed an independent Republic of Kosovo in July 1990. As Yugoslavia collapsed, the republics of Serbia (incl. Kosovo) and Montenegro proclaimed a new Federal Republic of Yugoslavia, 1992, under Pres. Slobodan Milosevic. Guerrilla attacks by the Kosovo Liberation Army (KLA) in 1997 brought a ferocious counteroffensive by Serbian authorities.

Fearful that the Serbs were employing "ethnic cleansing" tactics, NATO launched an air war against Yugoslavia, Mar.-June 1999; the Serbs retaliated by terrorizing the Kosovars. Hundreds of thousands fled, mostly to Albania and Macedonia. A 50,000-member multinational force (KFOR) entered Kosovo in June, and most refugees returned by Sept. 1, 1999. (Almost 3,900 KFOR troops remained in Kosovo as of mid-2018.)

From June 1999, Kosovo was administered by a UN mission (UNMIK). Kosovo declared independence, Feb. 17, 2008. More than 100 nations, including the U.S. and most EU members, have recognized Kosovo; Serbia and Russia have not. Kosovo and Serbia, Apr. 19, 2013, completed negotiating a power-sharing agreement between the northern Kosovo regions with a Serb majority and the Kosovo central government. A follow-up EU-brokered agreement was concluded Aug. 25, 2015. However, implementation of the 2013 accord was suspended by Kosovo's constitutional court, Nov. 10, 2015.

An EU special prosecutor reported, July 29, 2014, evidence of "unlawful killings" and other acts of ethnic cleansing against Serbs by the KLA in the late 1990s. Prime Min. Hashim Thaçi, who headed the KLA at that time, had denied any wrongdoing. After June 8, 2014, elections, Thaçi's party was unable to form a new government; conservative Isa Mustafa became prime min., Dec. 9, 2014. Parliament elected Thaçi president of Kosovo, Feb. 26, 2016. Mustafa lost a no-confidence vote, May 10, 2017, and elections were held June 11.

Former KLA commander Ramush Haradinaj became prime min., Sept. 9, heading a coalition govt.

Kuwait
State of Kuwait

People: Population: 2,916,467 (136). (Kuwait's Public Authority for Civil Information estimated its mid-2017 pop. to be 4.4 mil, with non-Kuwaitis making up about 69.5% of the pop.) **Age distrib.:** <15: 24.8%; 65+: 2.7%. **Growth:** 1.4%. **Migrants:** 75.5%. **Pop. density:** 423.9 per sq mi, 163.7 per sq km. **Urban:** 100%. **Ethnic groups:** Asian 37.8%, Kuwaiti 31.3%, other Arab 27.9%, African 1.9%. **Languages:** Arabic (official), English (widely spoken). **Religions:** Muslim (official) 76.7%, Christian 17.3%.

Geography: Total area: 6,880 sq mi, 17,818 sq km (153); **Land area:** 6,880 sq mi, 17,818 sq km. **Location:** Middle East, at N end of Persian Gulf. Iraq on N, Saudi Arabia on S. **Topography:** Flat, very dry, and extremely hot. **Arable land:** 0.4%. **Capital:** Kuwait City, 2,989,270.

Government: Type: Constitutional monarchy (emirate). **Head of state:** Emir Sheikh Sabah al-Ahmad al-Jabir al-Sabah; b. 1929; in office: Jan. 29, 2006. **Head of govt.:** Prime Min. Sheikh Jaber al-Mubarak al-Hamad al-Sabah; b. 1942; in office: Nov. 30, 2011. **Local divisions:** 6 governorates. **Defense budget:** $5.7 bil. **Active troops:** 15,500.

Economy: Industries: petroleum, petrochemicals, cement, shipbuilding and repair, water desalination, food proc., constr. materials. **Chief agric.:** fish. **Natural resources:** petroleum, fish, shrimp, nat. gas. **Water:** 5 cu m per capita. **Crude oil reserves:** 101.5 bil bbls (incl. half of Neutral Zone reserves). **Electricity prod.:** 63.8 bil kWh. **Labor force:** agric. 3.5%, industry 26.7%, services 69.8%. **Unemployment:** 2.1%.

Finance: Monetary unit: Dinar (KWD) (0.30 = $1 U.S.). **GDP:** $291.5 bil; **per capita GDP:** $66,200; **GDP growth:** −2.5%. **Imports:** $29.4 bil; China 13.5%, U.S. 13.3%, UAE 9.5%, Saudi Arabia 5.8%, Germany 5.4%, Japan 5%. **Exports:** $54.1 bil; South Korea 18.3%, China 17.4%, Japan 11.5%, India 11.2%, Singapore 6.3%, U.S. 5.7%. **Tourism:** $313 mil. **Budget:** $61.4 bil. **Inflation:** 2.2%.

Transport: Motor vehicles: 773.7 per 1,000 pop. **Airports:** 4.

Communications: Telephone: 13.1 per 100 pop. **Mobile:** 124.2 per 100 pop. **Broadband:** 66.8 per 100 pop. **Internet** (2017): 98%.

Health: Expend.: 4%. **Life expect.:** 76.9 male; 79.8 female. **Births:** 18.8 per 1,000 pop. **Deaths:** 2.3 per 1,000 pop. **Infant mortality:** 6.8 per 1,000 live births. **Undernourished:** <2.5%. **HIV:** <0.1%.

Education: Compulsory: ages 6-14. **Literacy:** 95.7%.

Embassy: 2940 Tilden St. NW 20008; 966-0702.

Website: www.pm.gov.kw

Kuwait is ruled by the Sabah dynasty, founded 1759. Britain ran foreign relations and defense from 1899 until independence in 1961. More than two-thirds of the population is non-Kuwaiti, including many Palestinians and non-Arab Asians, and cannot vote.

Oil exports provide most of Kuwait's income. Oil pays for free medical care and education for citizens. There is no income tax. Low global oil prices hurt the economy, 2014-17; government efforts to diversify the economy proceeded slowly.

Kuwait was attacked and overrun by Iraqi forces Aug. 1990. In Operation Desert Storm a U.S.-led coalition, with authorization from the UN Security Council, began bombing Iraq and Iraqi forces in Kuwait, Jan. 1991, then launched a ground assault Feb. 23. By Feb. 27, Iraqi forces were routed and Kuwait liberated.

Political rights were extended to women, May 16, 2005; the first female cabinet member was appointed June 12. Kuwait enacted a $5.2-bil program Mar. 2009 to bail out banks and investment companies battered by the global financial crisis. Prime Min. Jaber al-Mubarak al-Hamad al-Sabah, first appointed in 2011, remained in office after Nov. 26, 2016, elections, in which opposition candidates won 24 of 65 seats in the National Assembly; one woman was elected. A suicide bomber killed 27 people and wounded more than 200 at a Shiite mosque, June 26, 2015; an ISIS-affiliated Sunni extremist group claimed responsibility.

Kyrgyzstan
Kyrgyz Republic

People: Population: 5,849,296 (113). **Age distrib.:** <15: 30.4%; 65+: 5.4%. **Growth:** 1%. **Migrants:** 3.3%. **Pop. density:** 79 per sq mi, 30.5 per sq km. **Urban:** 36.4%. **Ethnic groups:** Kyrgyz 73.2%, Uzbek 14.6%, Russian 5.8%, other (incl. Uyghur, Tajik, Turk, Kazakh, Tatar, Ukrainian, Korean, German) 5.3%. **Languages:** Kyrgyz, Russian (both official); Uzbek. **Religions:** Muslim 75%, Russian Orthodox 20%.

Geography: Total area: 77,202 sq mi, 199,951 sq km (85); **Land area:** 74,055 sq mi, 191,801 sq km. **Location:** Central Asia. Kazakhstan on N, China on E, Uzbekistan on W, Tajikistan on S. **Topography:** Landlocked country nearly covered by Tien Shan and Pamir Mts.; avg. elevation 9,020 ft. Issyk-Kul, a large salt lake in NE, is 1 mi above sea level. **Arable land:** 6.7%. **Capital:** Bishkek, 996,319.

Government: Type: Parliamentary republic. **Head of state:** Pres. Sooronbay Jeenbekov; b. 1958; in office: Nov. 24, 2017. **Head of govt.:** Prime Min. Mukhammedkaliy Abylgaziyev; in office:

Apr. 20, 2018. **Local divisions:** 7 provinces, 2 cities. **Defense budget:** NA. **Active troops:** 10,900.

Economy: Industries: small machinery, textiles, food proc., cement, shoes, lumber, refrigerators, furniture, elec. motors. **Chief agric.:** cotton, potatoes, vegetables, grapes, fruits and berries; sheep, goats, cattle, wool. **Natural resources:** hydropower, gold, rare earth metals, coal, oil, nat. gas, nepheline, mercury, bismuth, lead, zinc. **Water:** 3,976 cu m per capita. **Crude oil reserves:** 40 mil bbls. **Electricity prod.:** 12.8 bil kWh. **Labor force:** agric. 26.7%, industry 22.2%, services 51.1%. **Unemployment:** 7.3%.

Finance: Monetary unit: Som (KGS) (69.02 = $1 U.S.). **GDP:** $23 bil; **per capita GDP:** $3,700; **GDP growth:** 4.5%. **Imports:** $4.3 bil; China 32.6%, Russia 24.8%, Kazakhstan 16.4%. **Exports:** $1.8 bil; Switzerland 59.1%, Uzbekistan 9.4%, Kazakhstan 5.1%. **Tourism:** $432 mil. **Budget:** $2.3 bil. **Inflation:** 3.2%.

Transport: Railways: 263 mi. **Airports:** 18.

Communications: Telephone: 6 per 100 pop. **Mobile:** 121.9 per 100 pop. **Broadband:** 46.1 per 100 pop. **Internet:** 34.5%.

Health: Expend.: 8.2%. **Life expect.:** 67.1 male; 75.6 female. **Births:** 21.6 per 1,000 pop. **Deaths:** 6.4 per 1,000 pop. **Infant mortality:** 25.0 per 1,000 live births. **Undernourished:** 6.5%. **HIV:** 0.2%.

Education: Compulsory: ages 6-15. **Literacy:** 99.5%.

Embassy: 2360 Massachusetts Ave. NW 20008; 449-9822.

Website: www.gov.kg

The region was inhabited around the 13th cent. by the Kyrgyz. It was annexed to Russia, 1864, and became a constituent republic of the USSR in 1936. Kyrgyzstan declared independence Aug. 31, 1991, ahead of the USSR disbanding Dec. 26, 1991.

In power since 1990, Pres. Askar Akayev won a third 5-year term in the 2000 election. Fraud by Akayev loyalists in parliamentary elections Feb.-Mar. 2005 sparked protests. Akayev fled the country, Mar. 24, and formally resigned, Apr. 4. His interim successor, former Prime Min. Kurmanbek Bakiyev, a leader of the "tulip revolution," won the 2005 presidential vote and was reelected 2009, when monitors reported numerous irregularities. He was ousted by opposition parties Apr. 7, 2010, after clashes between protesters and government security forces left at least 77 people dead; he left the country and was sentenced in absentia, July 25, 2014, to life in prison for his role in suppressing the protests.

Fighting in mid-June 2010 between majority Kyrgyz and minority Uzbeks in the southern cities of Osh and Jalalabad claimed up to 2,000 lives. A June 2010 referendum approved a new constitution. Almazbek Atambayev won the 2011 presidential election. Constitutional changes approved in a Dec. 2016 referendum strengthened the powers of the executive branch. Former Prime Min. Sooronbay Jeenbekov, backed by Atambayev, won the Oct. 15, 2017, presidential election. Jeenbekov ally Mukhammedkaly Abylgaziyev became prime min., Apr. 20, 2018.

Laos
Lao People's Democratic Republic

People: Population: 7,234,171 (101). **Age distrib.:** <15: 32.2%; 65+: 3.9%. **Growth:** 1.5%. **Migrants:** 0.7%. **Pop. density:** 81.2 per sq mi, 31.3 per sq km. **Urban:** 35%. **Ethnic groups:** Lao 53.2%, Khmou 11%, Hmong 9.2%, Phouthay 3.4%, Tai 3.1%, Makong 2.5%, Katong 2.2%, Lue 2%. **Languages:** Lao (official), French, English, ethnic langs. **Religions:** Buddhist 64.7%, none 31.4%.

Geography: Total area: 91,429 sq mi, 236,800 sq km (82); **Land area:** 89,112 sq mi, 230,800 sq km. **Location:** Indochina Peninsula in SE Asia. Myanmar, China on N; Vietnam on E; Cambodia on S; Thailand on W. **Topography:** Landlocked, dominated by jungle. Mountains along E border are source of E-W rivers. Mekong R. defines most of W border. **Arable land:** 6.6%. **Capital:** Vientiane, 664,754.

Government: Type: Communist state. **Head of state:** Pres. Bounnhang Vorachit; b. 1937; in office: Apr. 20, 2016. **Head of govt.:** Prime Min. Thongloun Sisoulith; b. 1945; in office: Apr. 20, 2016. **Local divisions:** 17 provinces, 1 capital city. **Defense budget:** NA. **Active troops:** 29,100.

Economy: Industries: mining, timber, elec. power, agric. proc., rubber, constr., garments. **Chief agric.:** sweet potatoes, vegetables, corn, coffee, sugarcane, tobacco, cotton, tea, peanuts, rice, cassava; water buffalo, pigs. **Natural resources:** timber, hydropower, gypsum, tin, gold, gems. **Water:** 49,030 cu m per capita. **Electricity prod.:** 11.5 bil kWh. **Labor force:** agric. 61.3%, industry 9.7%, services 29%. **Unemployment:** 0.7%.

Finance: Monetary unit: Kip (LAK) (8,510.96 = $1 U.S.). **GDP:** $49.2 bil; **per capita GDP:** $7,400; **GDP growth:** 6.8%. **Imports:** $5.9 bil; Thailand 59.1%, China 21.5%, Vietnam 9.8%. **Exports:** $2.9 bil; Thailand 42.6%, China 28.7%, Vietnam 10.4%. **Tourism:** $712 mil. **Budget:** $4.1 bil. **Inflation:** 0.8%.

Transport: Airports: 8.

Communications: Telephone: 16.4 per 100 pop. **Mobile:** 54.1 per 100 pop. **Broadband:** 34.7 per 100 pop. **Internet:** 21.9%.

Health: Expend.: 2.8%. **Life expect.:** 62.9 male; 67.1 female. **Births:** 23.2 per 1,000 pop. **Deaths:** 7.3 per 1,000 pop. **Infant mortality:** 48.4 per 1,000 live births. **Undernourished:** 16.6%. **HIV:** 0.3%.

Education: Compulsory: ages 6-10. **Literacy:** 79.9%.

Embassy: 2222 S St. NW 20008; 332-6416.

Website: www.na.gov.la

Laos became a French protectorate in 1893, but regained independence as a constitutional monarchy July 19, 1949. Conflicts among neutralist, Communist, and conservative factions created a chaotic political situation. Armed conflict increased after 1960.

The three factions formed a coalition government in June 1962 with neutralist Prince Souvanna Phouma as premier. A 14-nation conference in Geneva signed agreements, 1962, guaranteeing independence. By 1964 the leftist Pathet Lao had withdrawn from the coalition, and, with aid from North Vietnamese troops, renewed attacks. During the Vietnam War, U.S. planes (1964-73) dropped more than 2 mil tons of bombs on targets in Laos, principally the Ho Chi Minh trail, a supply line from North Vietnam to Communist forces in Laos, South Vietnam, and Cambodia. (Since the 1990s, the U.S., other nations, and the UN have provided aid to dismantle unexploded bombs.)

After Pathet Lao military gains in Laos, Souvanna Phouma, May 1975, ordered government troops to cease fighting; the Pathet Lao took control. The Lao People's Democratic Republic was proclaimed Dec. 3, 1975.

From the mid-1970s through the 1980s, Laos relied on Vietnam for military and financial aid. After easing its finance laws in 1988, Laos attracted investment from Thailand, China, South Korea, the U.S., and other nations. Laos was admitted to the Assn. of SE Asian Nations in 1997. The U.S. Congress approved normalization of trade with Laos in 2004. Laos opened its first stock exchange Jan. 11, 2011.

Despite environmental and safety concerns, since the 1990s, dozens of dams have been built or planned on Mekong R. tributaries, providing hydroelectricity for domestic use and export. A dam collapse in southern Laos, July 23, 2018, killed at least 35 and displaced thousands.

Latvia
Republic of Latvia

People: Population: 1,923,559 (147). **Age distrib.:** <15: 15.2%; 65+: 19.9%. **Growth:** −1.1%. **Migrants:** 13.2%. **Pop. density:** 80 per sq mi, 30.9 per sq km. **Urban:** 68.1%. **Ethnic groups:** Latvian 62%, Russian 25.4%, Belarusian 3.3%, Ukrainian 2.2%, Polish 2.1%. **Languages:** Latvian (official), Russian. **Religions:** Lutheran 19.6%, Orthodox 15.3%.

Geography: Total area: 24,938 sq mi, 64,589 sq km (122); **Land area:** 24,034 sq mi, 62,249 sq km. **Location:** E Europe, on Baltic Sea. Estonia on N; Russia on E; Belarus, Lithuania on S. **Topography:** Lowland with numerous lakes, marshes, and peat bogs. Principal river is W. Dvina (Daugava). Glacial hills in E. **Arable land:** 19.8%. **Capital:** Riga, 637,089.

Government: Type: Parliamentary republic. **Head of state:** Pres. Raimonds Vejonis; b. 1966; in office: July 8, 2015. **Head of govt.:** Prime Min. Maris Kucinskis; b. 1961; in office: Feb. 11, 2016. **Local divisions:** 110 municipalities, 9 cities. **Defense budget:** $507 mil. **Active troops:** 5,310.

Economy: Industries: processed foods, processed wood prods., textiles, processed metals, pharmaceuticals, railroad cars, synthetic fibers. **Chief agric.:** grain, rapeseed, potatoes, vegetables; pork, poultry; fish. **Natural resources:** peat, limestone, dolomite, amber, hydropower, timber. **Water:** 17,736 cu m per capita. **Electricity prod.:** 5.3 bil kWh. **Labor force:** agric. 7.5%, industry 24%, services 68.5%. **Unemployment:** 8.7%.

Finance: Monetary unit: Euro (EUR) (0.86 = $1 U.S.). **GDP:** $53.9 bil; **per capita GDP:** $27,600; **GDP growth:** 4.5%. **Imports:** $15.1 bil; Lithuania 17.6%, Germany 11.7%, Poland 8.7%, Estonia 7.6%, Russia 7.1%. **Exports:** $12.3 bil; Lithuania 15.8%, Russia 14%, Estonia 10.9%, Germany 6.9%, Sweden 5.7%. **Tourism:** $885 mil. **Budget:** $10.3 bil. **Inflation:** 2.9%.

Transport: Railways: 1,391 mi. **Motor vehicles:** 401.8 per 1,000 pop. **Airports:** 18.

Communications: Telephone: 17.5 per 100 pop. **Mobile:** 126.4 per 100 pop. **Broadband:** 77 per 100 pop. **Internet** (2017): 81.3%.

Health: Expend.: 5.8%. **Life expect.:** 70.4 male; 79.7 female. **Births:** 9.6 per 1,000 pop. **Deaths:** 14.5 per 1,000 pop. **Infant mortality:** 5.1 per 1,000 live births. **Undernourished:** <2.5%. **HIV:** NA.

Education: Compulsory: ages 5-15. **Literacy:** 99.9%.

Embassy: 2306 Massachusetts Ave. NW 20008; 328-2840.

Website: www.mk.gov.lv or latvia.lv

Prior to 1918, Latvia was occupied by the Russians and Germans. It was an independent republic, 1918-39. The Aug. 1939 Soviet-German agreement assigned Latvia to the Soviet sphere of influence. It was officially absorbed by the USSR in 1940. It was overrun by the German army in 1941, but retaken in 1945.

Latvia declared independence, Aug. 21, 1991. The last Russian troops in Latvia withdrew by Aug. 31, 1994. Responding to international pressure, Latvian voters, 1998, eased citizenship laws that had discriminated against some 500,000 ethnic Russians. Latvia joined the EU and NATO in 2004. It began using the euro as its currency Jan. 1, 2014.

Hit hard by recession, Latvia reached agreement Dec. 2008 on a $10.4-bil emergency loan from the EU, IMF, World Bank, and Nordic countries. Angered by the economic downturn and influence of wealthy oligarchs, voters approved a July 2011 referendum dissolving parliament. Prime Min. Valdis Dombrovskis's Unity Party came in third in Sept. 2011 elections, but he remained prime min. After more than 50 people died, Nov. 21, 2013, in a Riga supermarket roof collapse, Dombrovskis resigned. Laimdota Straujuma became Latvia's first woman prime min., Jan. 22, 2014. Her coalition won Oct. 4, 2014, elections, but she announced her resignation, Dec. 7, 2015, after agreeing to an unpopular EU refugee resettlement program. Maris Kucinskis became prime min., Feb. 11, 2016. NATO announced, Feb. 5, 2016, it would station troops in Latvia to deter Russian aggression; about 1,200 NATO troops were in Latvia in 2018.

Lebanon
Lebanese Republic

People: Population: 6,100,075 (109). **Age distrib.:** <15: 23.3%; 65+: 7%. **Growth:** −3.1%. **Migrants:** 31.9%. **Pop. density:** 1,544.4 per sq mi, 596.3 per sq km. **Urban:** 88.6%. **Ethnic groups:** Arab 95%, Armenian 4%. (Many Christian Lebanese identify not as Arab but as Phoenician, descendants of ancient Canaanites.) **Languages:** Arabic (official), French, English, Armenian. **Religions:** Muslim 54% (Sunni 27%, Shia 27%), Christian 40.5% (incl. Maronite Catholic 21%), Druze 5.6%.

Geography: Total area: 4,015 sq mi, 10,400 sq km (163); **Land area:** 3,950 sq mi, 10,230 sq km. **Location:** Middle East, on E end of Mediterranean Sea. Syria on E, Israel on S. **Topography:** Narrow coastal strip. Two N-S mountain ranges enclose the fertile Beqaa Valley. The Litani R. runs S through the valley. **Arable land:** 12.9%. **Capital:** Beirut, 2,385,271 (excl. Syrian refugees).

Government: Type: Parliamentary republic. **Head of state:** Pres. Michel Aoun; b. 1933; in office: Oct. 31, 2016. **Head of govt.:** Prime Min. Saad al-Hariri; b. 1970; in office: Dec. 18, 2016. **Local divisions:** 8 governorates. **Defense budget:** $1.9 bil. **Active troops:** 60,000.

Economy: Industries: banking, tourism, real estate and constr., food proc., wine, jewelry, cement, textiles, mineral and chem. prods., wood and furniture prods. **Chief agric.:** citrus, grapes, tomatoes, apples, vegetables, potatoes, olives, tobacco; sheep, goats. **Natural resources:** limestone, iron ore, salt, water (surplus in a water-deficit region). **Water:** 770 cu m per capita. **Electricity prod.:** 17.3 bil kWh. **Labor force:** agric. 3.2%, industry 20.3%, services 76.5%. **Unemployment:** 6.6%.

Finance: Monetary unit: Pound (LBP) (1,507.50 = $1 U.S.). **GDP:** $87.7 bil; **per capita GDP:** $19,400; **GDP growth:** 1.2%. **Imports:** $18.1 bil; China 10.2%, Italy 8.9%, Greece 7%, Germany 6.6%, U.S. 6.3%. **Exports:** $4.1 bil; China 13%, UAE 9.9%, South Africa 7.5%, Saudi Arabia 6.5%, Syria 6.5%, Iraq 5.8%. **Tourism:** $7 bil. **Budget:** $16 bil. **Inflation:** 4.3%.

Transport: Railways: 249 mi (unusable due to damage from fighting). **Motor vehicles:** 125 per 1,000 pop. **Airports:** 5.

Communications: Telephone (2016): 30.2 per 100 pop. **Mobile** (2016): 81.4 per 100 pop. **Broadband:** 67.2 per 100 pop. **Internet:** 76.1%.

Health: Expend.: 7.4%. **Life expect.:** 76.6 male; 79.3 female. **Births:** 14.1 per 1,000 pop. **Deaths:** 5.1 per 1,000 pop. **Infant mortality:** 7.2 per 1,000 live births. **Undernourished:** 10.9%. **HIV:** <0.1%. **Education:** Compulsory: ages 6-15. **Literacy:** 93.9%.

Embassy: 2560 28th St. NW 20008; 939-6300.

Website: www.pcm.gov.lb or www.presidency.gov.lb

Formed from five former Turkish Empire districts, Lebanon became independent Sept. 1, 1920, and was administered under French mandate 1920-41. French troops withdrew in 1946.

Under the 1943 National Covenant, all public positions were divided among the various religious communities, with Christians in the majority. By the 1970s, Muslims became the majority and demanded a larger political and economic role.

U.S. Marines intervened, May-Oct. 1958, during a Syrian-aided revolt. Continued raids against Israeli civilians, 1970-75, brought Israeli retaliation in southern Lebanon.

An estimated 60,000 were killed in a 1975-76 civil war. Palestinian units and leftist Muslims fought against Maronite militia (the Phalange) and other Christians. Several Arab countries provided support to various factions, while Israel aided Christian forces. Syria, which intervened in 1976 to fight Palestinian groups, largely policed a cease-fire.

Israeli forces invaded Lebanon June 6, 1982, attacking strongholds of the Palestine Liberation Organization (PLO). Israeli and Syrian forces engaged in the Bekaa Valley. On Aug. 21, the PLO evacuated W Beirut after massive Israeli bombings. Israeli troops entered W Beirut following the Sept. 14 assassination of newly elected Lebanese Pres. Bashir Gemayel. On Sept. 16, 1982, Lebanese Christian troops entered the Sabra and Shatila refugee camps and massacred hundreds of Palestinian civilians. An agreement May 17, 1983, between Lebanon, Israel, and the U.S. (but not Syria) provided for the withdrawal of Israeli troops; at least 30,000 Syrian troops remained in Lebanon, and Israel held onto a "security zone" in the south.

In 1983, some 50 people were killed in an explosion at the U.S. embassy, Apr. 18; 241 U.S. service members and 58 French soldiers died in separate Islamist suicide attacks, Oct. 23. The 1980s witnessed kidnappings of U.S., British, French, and Soviet citizens by Islamic militants.

A treaty signed May 22, 1991, between Lebanon and Syria recognized Lebanon as a separate state for the first time since 1943.

Israeli forces conducted air raids and artillery strikes against guerrilla bases and villages in southern Lebanon, causing over 200,000 to flee their homes July 25-29, 1993. Some 500,000 civilians fled in Apr. 1996 when Israel struck suspected guerrilla bases in the south. The economy revived in the 1990s, but Syria continued to dominate Lebanon's political affairs. Israel withdrew virtually all its troops from southern Lebanon by May 2000, leaving Hezbollah, an Iranian-backed Shiite Muslim guerrilla group, in control of much of the region.

Rafik al-Hariri, a former prime min. (1992-98, 2000-04), was killed by a truck bomb, Feb. 14, 2005. Many Lebanese blamed Syria. As anti-Syrian protests mounted, Syrian troops left Lebanon. An anti-Syrian bloc won May and June parliamentary elections. A new government was installed July 2005, headed by Fouad Siniora.

A Hezbollah rocket attack and border raid, July 2006, in which 3 Israeli soldiers were killed and 2 captured, triggered a massive escalation of hostilities. Hezbollah bombarded northern Israel with nearly 4,000 rockets, while Israeli air and ground forces assaulted suspected Hezbollah strongholds in southern Lebanon and southern Beirut. By Aug. 14, 2006, when a UN-sponsored cease-fire took hold, the war dead included nearly 1,150 Lebanese. To enforce the truce, thousands of Lebanese troops moved into southern Lebanon, and the small UN force already in Lebanon (UNIFIL) was expanded. As of Aug. 2018, UNIFIL had almost 10,500 uniformed personnel in Lebanon.

After more than 3 months of fighting in which over 400 people died, Lebanese forces Sept. 2, 2007, defeated Islamic militants at the Nahr al-Bared Palestinian refugee camp north of Tripoli. A 2008 power-sharing accord between the Siniora government and Hezbollah eased factional violence and paved the way for Gen. Michel Suleiman to become president, ending an 18-month stalemate. Factional disputes in parliament led to a lengthy delay in electing a successor when Suleiman's term expired in May 2014. Maronite Christian Michel Aoun, after gaining the support of Hezbollah, was elected president Oct. 31, 2016. Saad al-Hariri, a Sunni Muslim, became prime min., Dec. 18, 2016. Hezbollah and allied Shiite parties made gains in May 6, 2018, parliamentary elections. Hariri was designated, May 24, to form a new coalition government.

The Syrian civil war, in which Hezbollah fighters supported Syria's government (dominated by followers of the Alawite sect of Shiite Islam) and many opposition fighters were Sunni Muslims, spilled over into Lebanon beginning in 2012. In Tripoli, Sunnis and Alawites took part in firefights, Aug. 21-26, 2012, that left at least 17 dead. Syrian Sunni extremists fought the Lebanese army, June 2013 and Aug. 2014, fought Hezbollah in northern Lebanon in late 2014, and were apparently responsible for suicide bombings in Tripoli, Jan. 10, 2015, that killed 8. In an attack for which the Sunni extremist group ISIS claimed responsibility, suicide bombers killed at least 43 in a Shiite neighborhood of Beirut, Nov. 12, 2015. Hezbollah announced, May 14, 2016, that its top military commander had been killed by shellfire in Syria. Border fighting involving the Lebanese army, Hezbollah, and the Syrian army against ISIS occurred in Aug. 2017. The UNHCR estimated the number of Syrian refugees in Lebanon at about 976,000 as of Sept. 2018.

Lesotho
Kingdom of Lesotho

People: Population: 1,962,461 (146). **Age distrib.:** <15: 31.8%; 65+: 5.5%. **Growth:** 0.2%. **Migrants:** 0.3%. **Pop. density:** 167.4 per sq mi, 64.7 per sq km. **Urban:** 28.2%. **Ethnic groups:** Sotho 99.7%. **Languages:** Sesotho, English (both official); Zulu; Xhosa. **Religions:** Christian 80%, indigenous beliefs 20%.

Geography: Total area: 11,720 sq mi, 30,355 sq km (138); **Land area:** 11,720 sq mi, 30,355 sq km. **Location:** Southern Africa. Completely surrounded by South Africa. **Topography:** Landlocked and mountainous, 5,000 to 11,000 ft in elevation. **Arable land:** 9%. **Capital:** Maseru, 201,851.

Government: Type: Parliamentary constitutional monarchy. **Head of state:** King Letsie III; b. 1963; in office: Feb. 7, 1996. **Head of govt.:** Prime Min. Thomas Motsoahae (Tom) Thabane; b. 1939; in office: June 16, 2017. **Local divisions:** 10 districts. **Defense budget:** $53 mil. **Active troops:** 2,000.

Economy: Industries: food, beverages, textiles, apparel assembly, handicrafts, constr., tourism. **Chief agric.:** corn, wheat, pulses, sorghum, barley; livestock. **Natural resources:** water, diamonds, sand, clay, building stone. **Water:** 1,415 cu m per capita. **Electricity prod.:** 600 mil kWh. **Labor force:** agric. 10.4%, industry 40.5%, services 49.1%. **Unemployment:** 27.3%.

Finance: Monetary unit: Loti (LSL) (15.34 = $1 U.S.). **GDP:** $7 bil; **per capita GDP:** $3,600; **GDP growth:** 3.1%. **Imports:** $1.7 bil; South Africa 87.2%. **Exports:** $1 bil; South Africa 57%, U.S. 33.5%. **Tourism:** $48 mil. **Budget:** $1.2 bil. **Inflation:** 5.3%.

Transport: Airports: 3.

Communications: Telephone: 0.5 per 100 pop. **Mobile:** 106.6 per 100 pop. **Broadband:** 36.9 per 100 pop. **Internet:** 27.4%.

Health: Expend.: 8.4%. **Life expect.:** 53.0 male; 53.1 female. **Births:** 24.2 per 1,000 pop. **Deaths:** 15.1 per 1,000 pop. **Infant mortality:** 44.6 per 1,000 live births. **Undernourished:** 12.8%. **HIV:** 23.8%.

Education: Compulsory: ages 6-12. **Literacy:** 79.4%.

Embassy: 2511 Massachusetts Ave. NW 20008; 797-5533.

Website: www.gov.ls or www.lesothoemb-usa.gov.ls

Lesotho (once called Basutoland) became a British protectorate in 1868. Independence came Oct. 4, 1966. Livestock raising is a major industry; textiles, clothing, and diamonds are leading exports. Cultivation of marijuana for smuggling to South Africa is a significant source of income.

In Mar. 1990, King Moshoeshoe was exiled by the military government. Letsie III became king Nov. 12. In Mar. 1993, Ntsu Mokhehle, a civilian, was elected prime minister, ending 23 years of military rule. After a series of violent disturbances, the king dismissed the Mokhehle government Aug. 17, 1994; constitutional rule was restored Sept. 14.

Letsie abdicated and Moshoeshoe was reinstated Jan. 25, 1995. Moshoeshoe died in an automobile accident, Jan. 15, 1996. Letsie returned to power Feb. 7. South Africa and Botswana sent troops Sept. 1998 to help suppress violent anti-government protests. After parliamentary elections May 26, 2012, the left-leaning Thomas Motsoahae Thabane became prime min. He fled to South Africa, Aug.-Sept. 2014, when units of the military, which backed a political rival, attacked police forces loyal to Thabane. After Feb. 28, 2015, elections, former Prime Min. Pakalitha Mosisili (1998-2012) again became prime min. June 3, 2017, elections returned Thabane to office.

Liberia
Republic of Liberia

People: Population: 4,809,768 (124). **Age distrib.:** <15: 43.7%; 65+: 2.8%. **Growth:** 2.6%. **Migrants:** 2.1%. **Pop. density:** 129.3 per sq mi, 49.9 per sq km. **Urban:** 51.2%. **Ethnic groups:** Kpelle 20.3%, Bassa 13.4%, Grebo 10%, Gio 8%, Mano 7.9%, Kru 6%, Lorma 5.1%, Kissi 4.8%, Gola 4.4%. **Languages:** English (official), about 20 ethnic-group langs. **Religions:** Christian 85.6%, Muslim 12.2%.

Geography: Total area: 43,000 sq mi, 111,369 sq km (102); **Land area:** 37,189 sq mi, 96,320 sq km. **Location:** SW coast of W Africa. Sierra Leone on W, Guinea on N, Côte d'Ivoire on E. **Topography:** Marshy Atlantic coastline rises to low mountains and plateaus in forested interior. Six major rivers flow in parallel courses to the ocean. **Arable land:** 5.2%. **Capital:** Monrovia, 1,418,300.

Government: Type: Presidential republic. **Head of state and govt.:** Pres. George Weah; b. 1966; in office: Jan. 22, 2018. **Local divisions:** 15 counties. **Defense budget:** $14 mil. **Active troops:** 2,100.

Economy: Industries: mining, rubber and palm oil proc., diamonds. **Chief agric.:** rubber, coffee, cocoa, rice, cassava, palm oil, sugarcane, bananas; sheep, goats. **Natural resources:** iron ore, timber, diamonds, gold, hydropower. **Water:** 51,521 cu m per capita. **Electricity prod.:** 300 mil kWh. **Labor force:** agric. 43%, industry 12%, services 45.1%. **Unemployment:** 2.4%.

Finance: Monetary unit: Dollar (LRD) (154.26 = $1 U.S.). **GDP:** $6.1 bil; **per capita GDP:** $1,400; **GDP growth:** 2.5%. **Imports:** $1.2 bil; Singapore 29.8%, China 24.4%, South Korea 17.5%, Japan 9.4%. **Exports:** $202.1 mil; Germany 36.2%, Switzerland 14.2%, UAE 8.8%, U.S. 6.8%. **Tourism** (2015): $46 mil. **Budget:** $727.6 mil. **Inflation:** 12.4%.

Transport: Railways: 267 mi (mostly inoperable due to damage from fighting). **Motor vehicles:** 14.9 per 1,000 pop. **Airports:** 2.

Communications: Telephone (2016): 0.2 per 100 pop. **Mobile** (2016): 67.6 per 100 pop. **Broadband:** NA. **Internet:** 7.3%.

Health: Expend.: 15.2%. **Life expect.:** 61.6 male; 66.0 female. **Births:** 37.9 per 1,000 pop. **Deaths:** 7.4 per 1,000 pop. **Infant mortality:** 50.6 per 1,000 live births. **Undernourished:** 38.8%. **HIV:** 1.4%.

Education: Compulsory ages: 6-11. **Literacy:** 47.6%.

Embassy: 5201 16th St. NW 20011; 723-0437.

Website: www.emansion.gov.lr

Liberia was founded in 1822 by freed black slaves from the U.S. who settled at Monrovia with the aid of colonization societies. It became a republic July 26, 1847, with a constitution modeled on that of the U.S. Descendants of freed slaves dominated politics for much of the 19th and 20th centuries.

Under Pres. William V. S. Tubman, Liberia was a founding member of the UN in 1945. Tubman died in 1971 and was succeeded by his vice president, William R. Tolbert Jr. Charging rampant corruption, an Army Redemption Council of enlisted men staged a bloody predawn coup, Apr. 12, 1980, killing Pres. Tolbert and installing Sgt. Samuel Doe, an indigenous African, as head of state. In 1985, Doe was chosen president in a disputed election.

A civil war began Dec. 1989. In Sept. 1990, Pres. Doe was executed. Despite the introduction of a multinational peacekeeping force, the conflict intensified. Factional fighting devastated Monrovia in Apr. 1996. Ruth Perry became modern Africa's first female head of state Sept. 3, 1996, leading a transitional government. By then, the civil war had claimed more than 150,000 lives.

Former rebel leader Charles Taylor was elected president July 1997, in Liberia's first national election in 12 years. The UN imposed sanctions in 2001, to punish Liberia for aiding the Revolutionary United Front (RUF) insurgency in Sierra Leone.

A UN-sponsored war crimes tribunal indicted Taylor June 2003, for his role in the Sierra Leone conflict. With Liberian rebels threatening Monrovia, Taylor resigned Aug. 11 and went into exile. The UN authorized a 15,000-member peacekeeping force (UNMIL) Sept. 19 to help stabilize the nation. (The UNMIL mission officially ended Mar. 30, 2018.) A businessman, Charles Gyude Bryant, was sworn in Oct. 14, 2003, to head a power-sharing interim government. Ellen Johnson-Sirleaf won presidential elections in 2005 and 2011, and shared the 2011 Nobel Peace Prize. Charles Taylor went to trial at The Hague in 2007. He was convicted in 2012 of aiding and abetting war crimes and crimes against humanity, and sentenced to 50 years in prison. Former soccer star George Weah succeeded Johnson-Sirleaf after winning a Dec. 26, 2017, presidential runoff election. The U.S., Mar. 27, 2018, ended temporary residency status for thousands of Liberians who had come to the U.S. since the 1990s civil war, requiring them to leave the country by Mar. 31, 2019.

Liberia was seriously affected, 2014-16, by an Ebola virus epidemic. WHO reported a total of 10,675 Liberian cases, which caused 4,809 deaths.

Libya
State of Libya

People: Population: 6,754,507 (106). (Immigrants made up just over 12% of 2017 pop.) **Age distrib.:** <15: 25.5%; 65+: 4.4%. **Growth:** 1.5%. **Migrants:** 12.4%. **Pop. density:** 9.9 per sq mi, 3.8 per sq km. **Urban:** 80.1%. **Ethnic groups:** Berber and Arab 97%, other (incl. Greek, Maltese, Italian, Egyptian, Pakistani, Turk, Indian, Tunisian) 3%. **Languages:** Arabic (official), Italian, English, Berber. **Religions:** Muslim (official; virtually all Sunni) 96.6%, Christian 2.7%.

Geography: Total area: 679,362 sq mi, 1,759,540 sq km (16); **Land area:** 679,362 sq mi, 1,759,540 sq km. **Location:** Mediterranean coast of N Africa. Tunisia, Algeria on W; Niger, Chad on S; Sudan, Egypt on E. **Topography:** Desert and semidesert regions cover 92% of land with low mountains in N, higher mountains in S, and a narrow coastal zone. **Arable land:** 1%. **Capital:** Tripoli, 1,157,746.

Government: Type: In transition. **Head of state and govt.:** Prime Min. Faiez Mustafa Serraj is head of the internationally backed Government of National Accord; in office: Jan. 25, 2016. Competing leaders include Gen. Khalifa Haftar in eastern Libya. **Local divisions:** 22 districts. **Defense budget/active troops:** NA.

Economy: Industries: petroleum, petrochemicals, aluminum, iron and steel, food proc., textiles, handicrafts, cement. **Chief agric.:** wheat, barley, olives, dates, citrus, vegetables, peanuts, soybeans; cattle. **Natural resources:** petroleum, nat. gas, gypsum. **Water:** 112 cu m per capita. **Crude oil reserves:** 48.4 bil bbls. **Electricity prod.:** 35.5 bil kWh. **Labor force:** agric. 12.4%, industry 26.7%, services 60.9%. **Unemployment:** 17.7%.

Finance: Monetary unit: Dinar (LYD) (1.38 = $1 U.S.). **GDP:** $64.4 bil; **per capita GDP:** $10,000; **GDP growth:** 70.8%. **Imports:** $12.7 bil; China 13.5%, Turkey 11.3%, Italy 6.9%, South Korea 5.9%. **Exports:** $19.7 bil; Italy 19%, Spain 12.5%, France 11%, Egypt 8.6%, Germany 8.6%, China 8.3%. **Tourism** (2010): $60 mil. **Budget:** $22.3 bil. **Inflation** (2012-13): 2.6%.

Transport: Motor vehicles: 453.7 per 1,000 pop. **Airports:** 68. **Communications: Telephone** (2016): 21.8 per 100 pop. **Mobile** (2016): 121.7 per 100 pop. **Broadband:** 34.9 per 100 pop. **Internet:** 20.3%.

Health: Expend. (2011): 5%. **Life expect.:** 75.1 male; 78.7 female. **Births:** 17.2 per 1,000 pop. **Deaths:** 3.7 per 1,000 pop. **Infant mortality:** 10.5 per 1,000 live births. **Undernourished:** NA. **HIV:** NA.

Education: Compulsory: ages 6-14. **Literacy:** 91%.

Embassy: 2600 Virginia Ave. NW, Ste. 400, 20037; 944-9601.

Website: www.pm.gov.ly or www.embassyoflibyadc.org

First settled by Berbers, Libya was ruled in succession by Carthage, Rome, the Vandals, and the Ottomans. Italy ruled from 1912, and Britain and France after WWII. Libya became an independent constitutional monarchy Jan. 2, 1952. In 1969 a junta led by Col. Muammar al-Qaddafi seized power.

Under Qaddafi's dictatorship, dissent was suppressed and wars were waged with Egypt and Chad. During the 1980s, Libya was accused of promoting terrorism, such as the Apr. 5, 1986, bombing of a West Berlin nightclub, which killed 3, including a U.S. serviceman. The U.S. attacked what it called "terrorist-related targets" in Libya, Apr. 14, including Qaddafi's barracks.

Libyan agents were accused of planting bombs that blew up Pan Am Flight 103 over Lockerbie, Scotland, killing 270 people Dec. 21, 1988, and French UTA Flight 772 over Niger, killing 170 people Sept. 19, 1989. The UN imposed sanctions in 1992 for Libya's failure to cooperate in the Lockerbie and UTA cases.

Libya agreed in 2003 to renounce terrorism and settle compensation cases for the families of the Lockerbie and UTA bombing victims. The UN lifted sanctions in Sept., and in Dec., Libya renounced nuclear, chemical, and biological weapons and long-range missiles. Abdel Basset Ali al-Megrahi, a former Libyan agent sentenced to life in prison in 2001 for his role in the Lockerbie bombing, was freed by Scottish authorities on humanitarian grounds Aug. 20, 2009; he died in Tripoli, May 20, 2012.

Arab Spring rebels fought Qaddafi's forces throughout the spring of 2011. With diplomatic backing from the Arab League and the UN, NATO forces imposed an arms embargo and no-fly zone against Qaddafi. Aided by NATO, rebels took control of Tripoli Aug. 23, 2011, and began governing. Rebels killed Qaddafi Oct. 20, 2011. Ansar al-Shariah terrorists attacked the U.S. consulate and a CIA base in Benghazi Sept. 11, 2012, killing Ambassador J. Christopher Stevens and three other Americans. The U.S. captured, June 15, 2014, the alleged leader of the attack, Ahmed Abu Khattala; he was convicted, Nov. 28, 2017, on terrorism-related charges.

Violence between Islamists, rival militia groups, and pro-government forces intensified in 2013-14, and conflict continued in 2015-18. Parliamentary elections marred by violence were held June 25, 2014. The new parliament met in Tobruk because of Islamist militia control of Tripoli. A UN-backed Government of National Accord (GNA) was formed in Jan. 2016. The GNA had largely taken control in Tripoli by Apr. 2016 but was not recognized by the Islamist militias or the Tobruk government. ISIS seized territory in Libya and, by early 2016, controlled the city of Surt (Sirte). An offensive by pro-GNA and other militia forces, aided by U.S. airstrikes and special operations troops, had retaken most ISIS territory, including Surt, by Dec. 2016, although some ISIS fighters remained active. By mid-2017, forces led by former Libyan army Gen. Khalifa Haftar (loosely allied with the Tobruk government) gained control of large areas of eastern Libya, including oil installations and the city of Benghazi.

Beginning in 2014, Libya was a major transit route for African and other migrants trying to reach Europe. By mid-2017, efforts by Italy and other EU nations reduced migrant crossings of the Mediterranean. In mid-2018, about 680,000 migrants were in Libya, some living in harsh conditions in detention camps.

Liechtenstein
Principality of Liechtenstein

People: Population: 38,547 (190). (Immigrants made up about 65% of 2017 pop.) **Age distrib.:** <15: 15.2%; 65+: 17.9%. **Growth:** 0.8%. **Migrants:** 65.1%. **Pop. density:** 624 per sq mi, 240.9 per sq km. **Urban:** 14.3%. **Ethnic groups:** Liechtensteiner 66%. **Languages:** German (official). **Religions:** Roman Catholic (official) 75.9%, Protestant Reformed 6.5%, Muslim 5.4%, none 5.4%.

Geography: Total area: 62 sq mi, 160 sq km (191); **Land area:** 62 sq mi, 160 sq km. **Location:** Central Europe, in Alps. Switzerland on W, Austria on E. **Topography:** Rhine Valley occupies one-third of country, Alps in the rest. **Arable land:** 13.5%. **Capital:** Vaduz, 5,470.

Government: Type: Constitutional monarchy. **Head of state:** Prince Hans-Adam II; b. 1945; in office: Nov. 13, 1989. **Head of govt.:** Prime Min. Adrian Hasler; b. 1964; in office: Mar. 27, 2013. **Local divisions:** 11 communes. **Defense budget/active troops:** NA.

Economy: Industries: electronics, metal mfg., dental prods., ceramics, pharmaceuticals, food prods., precision instruments, tourism, optical instruments. **Chief agric.:** wheat, barley, corn, potatoes; livestock. **Natural resources:** hydroelectric potential. **Water:** NA. **Labor force:** agric. 0.8%, industry 36.9%, services 62.3%. **Unemployment:** NA.

Finance: Monetary unit: Franc (CHF) (0.97 = $1 U.S.). **GDP** (2014): $5 bil; **per capita GDP:** (2009) $139,100; **GDP growth** (2012): 1.8%. **Imports** (2016): $2 bil. **Exports** (2015): $3.2 bil. Data excl. trade with Switzerland. **Budget** (2012): $890.4 mil. **Inflation** (2015-16): −0.4%.

Transport: Railways: 6 mi (owned by Austrian Railway System). **Communications: Telephone:** 41.8 per 100 pop. **Mobile:** 122.9 per 100 pop. **Broadband:** NA. **Internet:** 98.1%.

Health: Expend.: NA. **Life expect.:** 79.8 male; 84.8 female. **Births:** 10.4 per 1,000 pop. **Deaths:** 7.6 per 1,000 pop. **Infant mortality:** 4.2 per 1,000 live births. **Undernourished:** NA. **HIV:** NA.

Education: Compulsory: ages 6-14. **Literacy:** 100%.
Embassy: 2900 K St. NW, Ste. 602B, 20007; 331-0590.
Website: www.liechtenstein.li

Liechtenstein became sovereign in 1806. It is united with Switzerland by a customs and monetary union. Many workers commute daily from Austria, Switzerland, and Germany.

On Aug. 15, 2004, Prince Hans-Adam II assigned day-to-day responsibilities for running the country to his son, Crown Prince Alois. Long regarded as a tax haven, Liechtenstein took steps, 2008-13, to ease banking secrecy laws.

Lithuania
Republic of Lithuania

People: Population: 2,793,284 (138). **Age distrib.:** <15: 15.1%; 65+: 19.9%. **Growth:** −1.1%. **Migrants:** 4.3%. **Pop. density:** 115.4 per sq mi, 44.6 per sq km. **Urban:** 67.7%. **Ethnic groups:** Lithuanian 84.1%, Polish 6.6%, Russian 5.8%. **Languages:** Lithuanian (official), Russian, Polish. **Religions:** Roman Catholic 77.2%, Russian Orthodox 4.1%, none 6.1%.

Geography: Total area: 25,212 sq mi, 65,300 sq km (121); **Land area:** 24,201 sq mi, 62,680 sq km. **Location:** Eastern Europe, on SE coast of Baltic. Latvia on N; Belarus on E, S; Poland, Russia on W. **Topography:** Lowland with hills in W and S. Many small lakes and rivers with marshes espec. in N and W. **Arable land:** 34.7%. **Capital:** Vilnius, 536,055.

Government: Type: Semi-presidential republic. **Head of state:** Pres. Dalia Grybauskaite; b. 1956; in office: July 12, 2009. **Head of govt.:** Prime Min. Saulius Skvernelis; b. 1970; in office: Dec. 13, 2016. **Local divisions:** 60 municipalities. **Defense budget:** $816 mil. **Active troops:** 18,350.

Economy: Industries: metal-cutting machine tools, elec. motors, TVs, refrigerators and freezers, petroleum refining, shipbuilding, furniture. **Chief agric.:** grain, potatoes, sugar beets, flax, vegetables; beef, milk, eggs; fish. **Natural resources:** peat, amber. **Water:** 8,513 cu m per capita. **Crude oil reserves:** 12 mil bbls. **Electricity prod.:** 3.6 bil kWh. **Labor force:** agric. 7.8%, industry 25%, services 67.2%. **Unemployment:** 7.1%.

Finance: Monetary unit: Euro (EUR) (0.86 = $1 U.S.). **GDP:** $91.2 bil; **per capita GDP:** $32,300; **GDP growth:** 3.8%. **Imports:** $30.4 bil; Russia 13%, Germany 12.3%, Poland 10.6%, Latvia 7.1%, Italy 5.2%, Netherlands 5.1%. **Exports:** $26.4 bil; Russia 15%, Latvia 9.9%, Poland 8.1%, Germany 7.3%, U.S. 5.2%, Estonia 5%. **Tourism:** $1.3 bil. **Budget:** $16.2 bil. **Inflation:** 3.7%.

Transport: Railways: 1,099 mi. **Motor vehicles:** 538.4 per 1,000 pop. **Airports:** 22.
Communications: Telephone: 16.8 per 100 pop. **Mobile:** 150.9 per 100 pop. **Broadband:** 76.8 per 100 pop. **Internet** (2017): 77.6%.
Health: Expend.: 6.5%. **Life expect.:** 69.9 male; 80.8 female. **Births:** 9.8 per 1,000 pop. **Deaths:** 14.8 per 1,000 pop. **Infant mortality:** 3.8 per 1,000 live births. **Undernourished:** <2.5%. **HIV:** 0.2%.
Education: Compulsory: ages 7-15. **Literacy:** 99.8%.
Embassy: 2622 16th St. NW 20009; 234-5860.
Website: lrvk.lrv.lt

Lithuania, briefly occupied by the German army, 1914-18, was annexed by the Soviet Union until 1919. In 1939 it rejoined the Soviet sphere of influence and was annexed by the USSR Aug. 3, 1940.

Lithuania declared its independence Mar. 11, 1990; independence was ratified by the Soviet Union Sept. 1991. The country became a full member of NATO and the EU in 2004; it began using the euro as its currency, Jan. 1, 2015. The center-left Social Democrats won Oct. 2012 parliamentary elections. Running as an independent and focusing on national security, Pres. Dalia Grybauskaite won reelection in a May 25, 2014, runoff. In an upset, the Peasants and Greens party won the most seats in Oct. 2016 parliamentary elections, and Saulius Skvernelis became prime min. Dec. 13.

Luxembourg
Grand Duchy of Luxembourg

People: Population: 605,764 (165). **Age distrib.:** <15: 16.7%; 65+: 15.1%. **Growth:** 1.9%. **Migrants:** 45.3%. **Pop. density:** 606.7 per sq mi, 234.2 per sq km. **Urban:** 91%. **Ethnic groups:** Luxembourger 52.1%, Portuguese 16%, French 7.6%, Italian 3.6%, Belgian 3.4%, German 2.2% (groups by nationality). **Languages:** Luxembourgish (national lang.), French, German (all official admin. and judicial langs.); Portuguese; Italian; English. **Religions:** Christian (predom. Roman Catholic) 70.4%, Muslim 2.3%, none 26.8%.

Geography: Total area: 998 sq mi, 2,586 sq km (169); **Land area:** 998 sq mi, 2,586 sq km. **Location:** Western Europe. Belgium on W, France on S, Germany on E. **Topography:** Heavy forests (Ardennes) cover N. Low, open plateau in S. **Arable land:** 24.2%. **Capital:** Luxembourg, 119,752.

Government: Type: Constitutional monarchy. **Head of state:** Grand Duke Henri; b. 1955; in office: Oct. 7, 2000. **Head of govt.:** Prime Min. Xavier Bettel; b. 1973; in office: Dec. 4, 2013. **Local divisions:** 12 cantons. **Defense budget:** $294 mil. **Active troops:** 900.

Economy: Industries: banking and financial services; constr.; real estate services; iron, metals, steel; information tech.; telecom; cargo transp. and logistics. **Chief agric.:** grapes, barley, oats, potatoes, wheat, fruits; dairy and livestock prods. **Natural resources:** iron ore (no longer exploited). **Water:** 6,172 cu m per capita. **Electricity prod.:** 757 mil kWh. **Labor force:** agric. 1%, industry 11.9%, services 87.1%. **Unemployment:** 5.5%.

Finance: Monetary unit: Euro (EUR) (0.86 = $1 U.S.). **GDP:** $62.7 bil; **per capita GDP:** $106,300; **GDP growth:** 3.5%. **Imports:** $22.4 bil; Belgium 32%, Germany 24.9%, France 11.1%, U.S. 5.7%. **Exports:** $18.4 bil; Germany 25.6%, Belgium 17%, France 14%, Netherlands 5.1%. **Tourism:** $4.5 bil. **Budget:** $27.3 bil. **Inflation:** 1.7%.

Transport: Railways: 171 mi. **Motor vehicles:** 760.3 per 1,000 pop. **Airports:** 1.
Communications: Telephone: 47.2 per 100 pop. **Mobile:** 136.1 per 100 pop. **Broadband:** 90.2 per 100 pop. **Internet** (2017): 97.8%.
Health: Expend.: 6%. **Life expect.:** 79.9 male; 85.0 female. **Births:** 11.6 per 1,000 pop. **Deaths:** 7.3 per 1,000 pop. **Infant mortality:** 3.4 per 1,000 live births. **Undernourished:** <2.5%. **HIV:** 0.3%.

Education: Compulsory: ages 4-15. **Literacy:** 100%.
Embassy: 2200 Massachusetts Ave. NW 20008; 265-4171.
Website: www.gouvernement.lu

Luxembourg, founded about 963, was ruled by Burgundy, Spain, Austria, and France from 1448 to 1815. It left the Germanic Confederation in 1866. Overrun by Germany in two world wars, Luxembourg ended its neutrality in 1948, when a customs union with Belgium and the Netherlands was adopted. Luxembourg was one of the six founding members (1951) of what became the European Union.

After Oct. 20, 2013, elections, Liberal Party leader Xavier Bettel became prime min. The Chamber of Deputies, June 18, 2014, legalized same-sex marriage. Bettel, May 15, 2015, became the first EU government head to marry a same-sex partner. Two former PricewaterhouseCoopers employees were convicted of theft, June 29, 2016, for leaking documents in 2014 indicating that hundreds of multinational corporations had reached tax-avoidance agreements with the Luxembourg government; both received suspended sentences and small fines.

Macedonia
Republic of Macedonia

People: Population: 2,118,945 (143). **Age distrib.:** <15: 16.2%; 65+: 13.4%. **Growth:** 0.2%. **Migrants:** 6.3%. **Pop. density:** 215.8 per sq mi, 83.3 per sq km. **Urban:** 58%. **Ethnic groups:** Macedonian 64.2%, Albanian 25.2%, Turkish 3.9%, Romani 2.7%. **Languages:** Macedonian, Albanian (both official); Turkish. **Religions:** Macedonian Orthodox 64.8%, Muslim 33.3%.

Geography: Total area: 9,928 sq mi, 25,713 sq km (146); **Land area:** 9,820 sq mi, 25,433 sq km. **Location:** SE Europe. Bulgaria on E, Greece on S, Albania on W, Serbia on N. **Topography:** Landlocked, mostly mountainous with deep river valleys, 3 large lakes. Country is bisected by Vardar R. **Arable land:** 16.5%. **Capital:** Skopje, 584,208.

Government: Type: Parliamentary republic. **Head of state:** Pres. Gjorge Ivanov; b. 1960; in office: May 12, 2009. **Head of govt.:** Prime Min. Zoran Zaev; b. 1974; in office: May 31, 2017. **Local divisions:** 70 municipalities, 1 city. **Defense budget:** $112 mil. **Active troops:** 8,000.

Economy: Industries: food proc., beverages, textiles, chemicals, iron, steel, cement, energy, pharmaceuticals. **Chief agric.:** grapes, tobacco, vegetables, fruits; milk, eggs. **Natural resources:** iron ore, copper, lead, zinc, chromite, manganese, nickel, tungsten, gold, silver, asbestos, gypsum, timber. **Water:** 3,080 cu m per capita. **Electricity prod.:** 6.1 bil kWh. **Labor force:** agric. 16.4%, industry 29.8%, services 53.8%. **Unemployment:** 22.4%.

Finance: Monetary unit: Denar (MKD) (53.09 = $1 U.S.). **GDP:** $31 bil (may not reflect country's large informal sector); **per capita GDP:** $14,900; **GDP growth:** 0%. **Imports:** $6.4 bil; Germany 11.9%, UK 10%, Greece 8%, Serbia 7.1%, China 5.9%, Italy 5.5%. **Exports:** $4.3 bil; Germany 46.7%, Bulgaria 6.1%. **Tourism:** $327 mil. **Budget:** $3.7 bil. **Inflation:** 1.3%.

Transport: Railways: 575 mi. **Airports:** 8.
Communications: Telephone: 17.3 per 100 pop. **Mobile:** 101.9 per 100 pop. **Broadband:** 59 per 100 pop. **Internet:** 72.2%.
Health: Expend.: 6.1%. **Life expect.:** 73.8 male; 78.2 female. **Births:** 10.8 per 1,000 pop. **Deaths:** 9.6 per 1,000 pop. **Infant mortality:** 7.8 per 1,000 live births. **Undernourished:** 4.1%. **HIV:** <0.1%.
Education: Compulsory: ages 6-18. **Literacy:** 97.8%.
Embassy: 2129 Wyoming Ave. NW 20008; 667-0501.
Website: www.vlada.mk

Muslim Turks ruled Macedonia from 1389 to 1912. In 1913, the area was incorporated into Serbia, which in 1918 became part of the Kingdom of Serbs, Croats, and Slovenes (later Yugoslavia). In 1946, Macedonia became a constituent republic of Yugoslavia.

Macedonia declared its independence Sept. 8, 1991, and was admitted to the UN in 1993. In the following decades, Greece, which objected to Macedonia's use of what it considered a Hellenic name, blocked Macedonia's bids to join NATO and the EU.

Ethnic Albanian guerrillas launched an offensive Mar. 2001 in NW Macedonia. An accord signed Aug. 13 paved the way for a NATO peacekeeping force. A law broadening the rights of ethnic Albanians was enacted Jan. 2002.

After a government wiretapping and corruption scandal, conservative Prime Min. Nikola Gruevski resigned Jan. 15, 2016. New elections, delayed by an abortive attempt to pardon wiretapping investigation targets, were held in Dec. 2016 but were inconclusive. Social Democratic party leader Zoran Zaev was injured when pro-Gruevski protesters stormed parliament, Apr. 27, 2017. Zaev formed a coalition and became prime min. May 31. On June 17, 2018, Macedonia and Greece signed an agreement for the former to change its name to North Macedonia. Macedonian voters approved the change in a Sept. 30 referendum but turnout was too low to validate the results; the agreement also required Macedonian constitutional amendments and Greek parliamentary approval.

In 2015 and early 2016, tens of thousands of migrants from the Middle East and SW Asia who landed in Greece tried to cross Macedonia on their way to N Europe. After building razor-wire border fencing and taking other steps to restrict the flow of migrants, Macedonia announced, Mar. 9, 2016, that its border with Greece was closed to migrants, and it used troops and tear gas to enforce the closure.

Madagascar
Republic of Madagascar

People: Population: 25,683,610 (52). **Age distrib.:** <15: 39.5%; 65+: 3.4%. **Growth:** 2.5%. **Migrants:** 0.1%. **Pop. density:** 114.4 per sq mi, 44.2 per sq km. **Urban:** 37.2%. **Ethnic groups:** Malayo-Indonesian (Merina and related Betsileo), Cotiers (mixed African/Malayo-Indonesian/Arab ancestry), French, Indian, Creole, Comoran. **Languages:** French, Malagasy (both official); English. **Religions:** Christian, indigenous religionist, Muslim.

Geography: Total area: 226,658 sq mi, 587,041 sq km (46); **Land area:** 224,534 sq mi, 581,540 sq km. **Location:** In Indian O., off SE coast of Africa. Comoro Isls. to NW, Mozambique to W. **Topography:** Humid coastal strip in E, fertile valleys in mountainous center plateau region, and a wider coastal strip on W. **Arable land:** 6%. **Capital:** Antananarivo, 3,058,387.

Government: Type: Semi-presidential republic. **Head of state:** Pres. Hery Rajaonarimampianina; b. 1958; in office: Jan. 25, 2014. **Head of govt.:** Prime Min. Christian Ntsay; b. 1961; in office: June 6, 2018. **Local divisions:** 6 provinces. **Defense budget:** $62 mil. **Active troops:** 13,500.

Economy: Industries: meat proc., seafood, soap, beer, leather, sugar, textiles, glassware, cement, auto assembly. **Chief agric.:** coffee, vanilla, sugarcane, cloves, cocoa, rice, cassava, beans, bananas, peanuts. **Natural resources:** graphite, chromite, coal, bauxite, rare earth elements, salt, quartz, tar sands, semiprec. stones, mica, fish, hydropower. **Water:** 13,906 cu m per capita. **Electricity prod.:** 1.5 bil kWh. **Labor force:** agric. 74.4%, industry 9.2%, services 16.4%. **Unemployment:** 1.8%.

Finance: Monetary unit: Ariary (MGA) (3,310.39 = $1 U.S.). **GDP:** $39.7 bil; **per capita GDP:** $1,600; **GDP growth:** 4.1%. **Imports:** $3.6 bil; China 18.7%, India 9.3%, France 6.4%, South Africa 5.6%, UAE 5.3%. **Exports:** $2.8 bil; France 24.8%, U.S. 16.5%, China 6.7%, Germany 6.5%, Japan 6%. **Tourism:** $750 mil.

Transport: Railways: 519 mi. **Motor vehicles:** 13.3 per 1,000 pop. **Airports:** 26.
Communications: Telephone: 0.3 per 100 pop. **Mobile:** 34.1 per 100 pop. **Broadband:** 10.5 per 100 pop. **Internet** (2017): 9.8%.
Health: Expend.: 5.2%. **Life expect.:** 65.1 male; 68.2 female. **Births:** 31.0 per 1,000 pop. **Deaths:** 6.4 per 1,000 pop. **Infant mortality:** 43.1 per 1,000 live births. **Undernourished:** 43.1%. **HIV:** 0.3%.
Education: Compulsory: ages 6-10. **Literacy:** 64.7%.
Embassy: 2374 Massachusetts Ave. NW 20008; 265-5525.
Website: www.primature.gov.mg

Madagascar was settled 2,000 years ago by Malayan-Indonesian people, whose descendants still predominate. A unified kingdom ruled in the 18th and 19th cent. The island became a French protectorate, 1885, and a colony, 1896. Independence came June 26, 1960.

Discontent with inflation and French domination led to a coup in 1972. The new regime nationalized French-owned financial interests, closed French bases and a U.S. space-tracking station, and obtained Chinese aid. The government conducted a program of arrests, expulsion of foreigners, and repression of strikes in 1979.

In 1990, Madagascar ended a ban on multiparty politics that had existed since 1975. Albert Zafy won the 1993 presidential election, ending the 17-year rule of Adm. Didier Ratsiraka, but was impeached and removed from office in 1996.

Marc Ravalomanana won a contentious presidential election over Ratsiraka Dec. 2001 and was reelected in 2006. A power struggle between Ravalomanana and the military-backed Andry Rajoelina led to Rajoelina's installation as head of a transitional regime, Mar. 17, 2009. Postponed presidential elections, held in late 2013, were won by Hery Rajaonarimampianina. Parliamentary elections were held Dec. 20, 2013. With economic conditions unimproved, Rajaonarimampianina changed prime ministers in Jan. 2015 and Apr. 2016. To comply with a High Constitutional Court ruling, the president named a new prime minister in June 2018.

Malawi
Republic of Malawi

People: Population: 19,842,560 (60). **Age distrib.:** <15: 46.2%; 65+: 2.7%. **Growth:** 3.3%. **Migrants:** 1.3%. **Pop. density:** 546.3 per sq mi, 210.9 per sq km. **Urban:** 16.9%. **Ethnic groups:** Chewa 35.1%, Lomwe 18.9%, Yao 13.1%, Ngoni 12%, Tumbuka 9.4%, Sena 3.5%. **Languages:** English (official), Chichewa (common), Chinyanja, Chiyao, Chitumbuka, Chilomwe, Chinkhonde. **Religions:** Protestant 27.2% (incl. Church of Central Africa Presbyterian 17.7%), Catholic 18.4%, Muslim 12.1%.

Geography: Total area: 45,747 sq mi, 118,484 sq km (98); **Land area:** 36,324 sq mi, 94,080 sq km. **Location:** SE Africa. Zambia on W, Mozambique on S and E, Tanzania on N. **Topography:** 560 mi N-S along Lake Nyasa (Lake Malawi), most of which belongs to Malawi. High plateaus and mountains line the Rift Valley along length of nation. **Arable land:** 40.3%. **Capital:** Lilongwe, 1,029,639.

Government: Type: Presidential republic. **Head of state and govt.:** Pres. Arthur Peter Mutharika; b. 1940; in office: May 31, 2014. **Local divisions:** 28 districts. **Defense budget:** $38 mil. **Active troops:** 10,700.

Economy: Industries: tobacco, tea, sugar, sawmill prods., cement, consumer goods. **Chief agric.:** tobacco, sugarcane, tea, corn, potatoes, cassava, sorghum, pulses, cotton, groundnuts, Macadamia nuts, coffee; cattle, goats. **Natural resources:** limestone; hydropower; unexploited deposits of uranium, coal, bauxite. **Water:** 1,004 cu m per capita. **Electricity prod.:** 2.1 bil kWh. **Labor force:** agric. 84.7%, industry 8.4%, services 6.9%. **Unemployment:** 5.9%.

Finance: Monetary unit: Kwacha (MWK) (726.47 = $1 U.S.). **GDP:** $22.4 bil; **per capita GDP:** $1,200; **GDP growth:** 4%. **Imports:** $2.4 bil; South Africa 20.7%, China 14.2%, India 11.6%, UAE 7%. **Exports:** $1.4 bil; Zimbabwe 13.1%, Mozambique 11.8%, Belgium 10.7%, South Africa 6.3%, Netherlands 5%. **Tourism:** $26 mil. **Budget:** $1.6 bil. **Inflation:** 12.2%.

Transport: Railways: 477 mi. **Motor vehicles:** 2 per 1,000 pop. **Airports:** 7.

Communications: Telephone: 0.09 per 100 pop. **Mobile:** 41.7 per 100 pop. **Broadband:** 18.5 per 100 pop. **Internet:** 11.5%.

Health: Expend.: 9.3%. **Life expect.:** 60.2 male; 64.3 female. **Births:** 40.7 per 1,000 pop. **Deaths:** 7.7 per 1,000 pop. **Infant mortality:** 42.1 per 1,000 live births. **Undernourished:** 26.3%. **HIV:** 9.6%.

Education: Compulsory: ages 6-13. **Literacy:** 62.1%.

Embassy: 2408 Massachusetts Ave. NW 20008; 721-0270.

Website: www.malawi.gov.mw

Bantus came to the land in the 16th cent., Arab slavers in the 19th. The area became the British protectorate Nyasaland in 1891. It became independent July 6, 1964, and a republic in 1966. After three decades as a one-party state under Pres. Hastings Kamuzu Banda, Malawi adopted a new constitution and, in multiparty elections held May 17, 1994, chose a new leader, Bakili Muluzi.

Bingu wa Mutharika, candidate of the ruling United Democratic Front, won a disputed 2004 presidential election. An effort by his former political allies to impeach him was halted by Malawi's Constitutional Court, Oct. 2005. Mutharika won reelection May 2009. Joyce Banda became Malawi's first female pres. after the death of Mutharika Apr. 5, 2012. Banda finished third in May 20-22, 2014, presidential elections. After her attempt to nullify the result was blocked in court, Peter Mutharika (the former president's brother) was declared the winner. El Niño-related drought left up to 8 mil in need of food aid in 2016.

Malaysia

People: Population: 31,809,660 (42). **Age distrib.:** <15: 27.5%; 65+: 6.3%. **Growth:** 1.3%. **Migrants:** 8.5%. **Pop. density:** 250.7 per sq mi, 96.8 per sq km. **Urban:** 76%. **Ethnic groups:** Bumiputera 61.7% (Malays and indigenous, incl. Orang Asli, Dayak, Anak Negeri), Chinese 20.8%, Indian 6.2%, non-citizen 10.4%. **Languages:** Bahasa Malaysia (official), English, Chinese, Tamil, Telugu, Malayalam, Panjabi, Thai. **Religions:** Muslim (official) 61.3%, Buddhist 19.8%, Christian 9.2%, Hindu 6.3%.

Geography: Total area: 127,355 sq mi, 329,847 sq km (66); **Land area:** 126,895 sq mi, 328,657 sq km. **Location:** SE tip of Asia, plus N coast of the island of Borneo. Thailand, Brunei on N; Indonesia on S. **Topography:** Most of W is covered by tropical jungle, including a central mountain range that runs N-S through the peninsula. Marshy W coast, sandy E coast. Wide swampy coastal plain with interior jungles and mountains in E. **Arable land:** 2.9%. **Capital:** Kuala Lumpur, 7,563,912. Putrajaya is referred to as federal govt. admin. center. **Cities:** Johor Bahru, 983,359.

Government: Type: Federal parliamentary constitutional monarchy. **Head of state:** King Muhammad V; b. 1969; in office: Dec. 13, 2016. **Head of govt.:** Prime Min. Mahathir Mohamad; b. 1925; in office: May 10, 2018. **Local divisions:** 13 states, 1 federal territory. **Defense budget:** $3.5 bil. **Active troops:** 109,000.

Economy: Industries: rubber and palm oil proc. and mfg., petroleum and nat. gas, light mfg., pharmaceuticals, medical tech., logging. **Chief agric.:** palm oil, rubber, cocoa, rice, pepper. **Natural resources:** tin, petroleum, timber, copper, iron ore, nat. gas, bauxite. **Water:** 19,122 cu m per capita. **Crude oil reserves:** 3.6 bil bbls. **Electricity prod.:** 141.9 bil kWh. **Labor force:** agric. 11%, industry 27.4%, services 61.6%. **Unemployment:** 3.4%.

Finance: Monetary unit: Ringgit (MYR) (4.14 = $1 U.S.). **GDP:** $930.8 bil; **per capita GDP:** $29,000; **GDP growth:** 5.9%. **Imports:** $163.4 bil; China 19.9%, Singapore 10.8%, U.S. 8.4%, Japan 7.6%, Thailand 5.8%. **Exports:** $188.2 bil; Singapore 15.1%, China 12.6%, U.S. 9.4%, Japan 8.2%, Thailand 5.7%. **Tourism:** $18.3 bil. **Budget:** $60.3 bil. **Inflation:** 3.9%.

Transport: Railways: 1,150 mi. **Motor vehicles:** 458.1 per 1,000 pop. **Airports:** 39.

Communications: Telephone: 20.8 per 100 pop. **Mobile:** 133.9 per 100 pop. **Broadband:** 91.7 per 100 pop. **Internet** (2017): 80.1%.

Health: Expend.: 4%. **Life expect.:** 72.6 male; 78.4 female. **Births:** 18.8 per 1,000 pop. **Deaths:** 5.2 per 1,000 pop. **Infant mortality:** 12.1 per 1,000 live births. **Undernourished:** 2.9%. **HIV:** 0.4%.

Education: Compulsory: ages 6-11. **Literacy:** 94.6%.

Embassy: 3516 International Ct. NW 20008; 572-9700.

Website: www.pmo.gov.my

European traders visited in the 16th cent.; Britain established control in 1867. Malaysia was created Sept. 16, 1963. It included Malaya (which gained independence in 1957 after the suppression of Communist rebels), plus the formerly British Singapore, Sabah (N Borneo), and Sarawak (NW Borneo). Singapore was separated in 1965.

Malaysia has abundant natural resources, though rainforest destruction has become a national environmental problem. Work on a federal administrative center at Putrajaya, south of Kuala Lumpur, was completed in 1999; it is linked by rail with Kuala Lumpur's city center and Cyberjaya, a hub for high-tech manufacturing and research.

National Front leader Najib Razak took over the premiership in 2009. In a close election (deemed fraudulent by the opposition), May 5, 2013, the governing coalition was returned to power.

A Malaysia Airlines flight to Beijing, carrying 239 passengers and crew, lost contact with air traffic control Mar. 8, 2014, shortly after takeoff from Kuala Lumpur and was presumed lost in the Indian Ocean. On July 17, 2014, a Malaysia Airlines flight from Amsterdam to Kuala Lumpur was shot down by a missile over eastern Ukraine, killing all 298 people onboard. An international team of investigators concluded, Sept. 2016, that the missile was Russian made and had been fired from an area controlled by pro-Russian separatists.

A security law enacted Dec. 3, 2015, gave the Malaysian government sweeping powers to conduct surveillance and searches and to suppress protests.

Beginning in 2015, Malaysian authorities (as well as officials in other countries) investigated possible ¬misappropriation of more than $4.5 bil from a government development fund (known as 1MDB), including more than $700 mil in transfers to bank accounts controlled by Prime Min. Najib. He denied wrongdoing, and the Malaysian government inquiry was closed, Jan. 2016. The U.S. Justice Dept., July 2016 and June 2017, initiated legal action to seize $1.7-bil worth of assets purchased with funds that passed through the U.S. The National Front lost May 9, 2018, elections. New Prime Min. Mahathir Mohamad reopened the 1MDB investigation. After police seized more than $270 mil worth of jewelry, cash, and other valuables from Najib and his wife, Najib was charged, in July, Aug., and Sept., with dozens of corruption-related offenses.

Maldives
Republic of Maldives

People: Population: 392,473 (170). **Age distrib.:** <15: 21.6%; 65+: 4.5%. **Growth:** −0.06%. **Migrants:** 15.4%. **Pop. density:** 3,411.1 per sq mi, 1,317 per sq km. **Urban:** 39.8%. **Ethnic groups:** South Indian, Sinhalese, Arab. **Languages:** Dhivehi (official), English (spoken by most govt. officials). **Religions:** Sunni Muslim (official).

Geography: Total area: 115 sq mi, 298 sq km (188); **Land area:** 115 sq mi, 298 sq km. **Location:** In Indian O. Nearest neighbor is India to NE. **Topography:** 19 atolls with 1,190 islands, 200 inhabited. None of the islands are over 5 sq mi in area; all are nearly flat. **Arable land:** 13%. **Capital:** Male, 176,851.

Government: Type: Presidential republic. **Head of state and govt.:** Pres. Abdulla Yameen Abdul Gayoom; b. 1959; in office: Nov. 17, 2013. (Pres.-elect Ibrahim Mohamed Solih was set to be inaugurated in Nov. 2018.) **Local divisions:** 21 admin. atolls. **Defense budget/active troops:** NA.

Economy: Industries: tourism, fish proc., shipping, boat building, coconut proc., woven mats, rope. **Chief agric.:** coconuts, corn, sweet potatoes; fish. **Natural resources:** fish. **Water:** 82 cu m per capita. **Electricity prod.:** 350 mil kWh. **Labor force:** agric. 7.5%, industry 24.8%, services 67.7%. **Unemployment:** 5%.

Finance: Monetary unit: Rufiyaa (MVR) (15.46 = $1 U.S.). **GDP:** $6.9 bil; **per capita GDP:** $19,100; **GDP growth:** 4.8%. **Imports** (2016): $2.1 bil; UAE 17.1%, India 13.5%, Singapore 13.3%, China 10.8%, Sri Lanka 6.7%, Malaysia 6%. **Exports** (2016): $256.2 mil; Thailand 42.8%, Sri Lanka 8.7%, Bangladesh 6.4%, France 6.2%, U.S. 6.1%, Germany 5%. **Tourism:** $2.7 bil. **Budget** (2016): $1.6 bil. **Inflation:** 2.7%.

Transport: Airports: 7.

Communications: Telephone: 4.7 per 100 pop. **Mobile:** 206.3 per 100 pop. **Broadband:** 72.7 per 100 pop. **Internet:** 59.1%.

Health: Expend.: 11.5%. **Life expect.:** 73.7 male; 78.5 female. **Births:** 16.1 per 1,000 pop. **Deaths:** 4.0 per 1,000 pop. **Infant mortality:** 21.3 per 1,000 live births. **Undernourished:** 11%. **HIV:** NA.

Education: Compulsory: NA. **Literacy:** 99.3%.

Embassy: 800 Second Ave., Ste. 400E, New York, NY 10017; (212) 599-6195.

Website: presidency.gov.mv

A British protectorate since 1887, the nation achieved independence July 26, 1965; long a sultanate, the Maldives became a republic in 1968. Rising sea levels threaten the island nation. The

Indian Ocean tsunami of Dec. 26, 2004, killed at least 82 people in the Maldives.

Pres. Maumoon Abdul Gayoom, in office 1978-2008, lost a 2008 runoff election to pro-democracy leader and former political prisoner Mohamed (Anni) Nasheed. Following protests over the arrest of a judge, Nasheed resigned Feb. 2012. He ran for president in 2013 but lost the Nov. 16 runoff to Abdulla Yameen Abdul Gayoom (the former president's half-brother). Nasheed, Mar. 2015, was convicted on terrorism charges and sentenced to 13 years in prison; while the case was appealed, Nasheed received political asylum in the UK in May 2016. The Maldives announced, Oct. 13, 2016, its withdrawal from the Commonwealth, which had criticized its human rights record. In 2017, the government detained political opponents. Troops intervened in July and Aug. 2017 to prevent opposition lawmakers from impeaching the parliament's speaker, an ally of Pres. Yameen. The Supreme Court voided Nasheed's 2015 conviction, Feb. 1, 2018, but the ruling was reversed Feb. 6, after two Supreme Court judges were arrested. Opposition candidate Ibrahim Mohamed Solih defeated Yameen in the Sept. 23 presidential election.

Mali
Republic of Mali

People: Population: 18,429,893 (64). **Age distrib.:** <15: 48%; 65+: 3%. **Growth:** 3%. **Migrants:** 2.1%. **Pop. density:** 39.1 per sq mi, 15.1 per sq km. **Urban:** 42.4%. **Ethnic groups:** Bambara 34.1%, Fulani (Peul) 14.7%, Sarakole 10.8%, Senufo 10.5%, Dogon 8.9%, Malinke 8.7%, Bobo 2.9%. **Languages:** French (official), Bambara, Peul/Foulfoulbe, Dogon, Maraka/Soninke, Malinke, Sonrhai/Djerma, Minianka, Tamacheq. **Religions:** Muslim 94.8%, Christian 2.4%.

Geography: Total area: 478,841 sq mi, 1,240,192 sq km (23); **Land area:** 471,118 sq mi, 1,220,190 sq km. **Location:** W Africa. Mauritania, Senegal on W; Guinea, Côte d'Ivoire, Burkina Faso on S; Niger on E; Algeria on N. **Topography:** Landlocked grassy plain in upper basins of the Senegal and Niger R., extending N into the Sahara. **Arable land:** 5.3%. **Capital:** Bamako, 2,446,749.

Government: Type: Semi-presidential republic. **Head of state:** Pres. Ibrahim Boubacar Keita; b. 1945; in office: Sept. 4, 2013. **Head of govt.:** Prime Min. Soumeylou Boubeye Maiga; b. 1954; in office: Dec. 31, 2017. **Local divisions:** 8 regions, 1 district. **Defense budget:** $644 mil. **Active troops:** 10,000.

Economy: Industries: food proc., constr., phosphate and gold mining. **Chief agric.:** cotton, millet, rice, corn, vegetables, peanuts; cattle, sheep, goats. **Natural resources:** gold, phosphates, kaolin, salt, limestone, uranium, gypsum, granite, hydropower. **Water:** 6,818 cu m per capita. **Electricity prod.:** 2.2 bil kWh. **Labor force:** agric. 57.6%, industry 8.5%, services 33.9%. **Unemployment:** 7.9%.

Finance: Monetary unit: CFA Franc (XOF) (566.17 = $1 U.S.). **GDP:** $41 bil; **per capita GDP:** $2,200; **GDP growth:** 5.3%. **Imports:** $3.9 bil; Senegal 24.4%, China 13.2%, Côte d'Ivoire 9%, France 7.3%. **Exports:** $3 bil; Switzerland 31.8%, UAE 15.4%, Burkina Faso 7.8%, Côte d'Ivoire 7.3%, South Africa 5%. **Tourism:** $200 mil. **Budget:** $3.6 bil. **Inflation:** 1.8%.

Transport: Railways: 368 mi. **Motor vehicles:** 1.7 per 1,000 pop. **Airports:** 8.

Communications: Telephone (2016): 1.1 per 100 pop. **Mobile** (2016): 112.4 per 100 pop. **Broadband:** 24.4 per 100 pop. **Internet:** 11.1%.

Health: Expend.: 5.8%. **Life expect.:** 58.6 male; 63.0 female. **Births:** 43.2 per 1,000 pop. **Deaths:** 9.6 per 1,000 pop. **Infant mortality:** 67.6 per 1,000 live births. **Undernourished:** 6%. **HIV:** 1.2%. **Education:** Compulsory: ages 7-15. **Literacy:** 33.1%. **Embassy:** 2130 R St. NW 20008; 332-2249. **Website:** primature.gov.ml

Until the 15th cent. the area was part of the great Mali Empire. Timbuktu (Tombouctou) was a center of Islamic study. French rule was secured, 1898. The Sudanese Rep. and Senegal became independent as the Mali Federation in 1960, but Senegal withdrew, and the Sudanese Rep. was renamed Mali.

A coup toppled a socialist regime led, 1960-68, by Pres. Modibo Keita. Famine struck in 1973-74, killing as many as 100,000 people.

The military, Mar. 1991, overthrew Pres. Moussa Traoré, who had ruled since 1968. Oumar Konare, a coup leader, was elected president, 1992. The government and a Tuareg rebel group signed a peace accord in 1994, but Taureg separatists remained active in the north. Twice condemned to death for crimes committed in office, Traoré had his sentences commuted to life imprisonment in 1997 and 1999; he was pardoned in 2002.

Amadou Toumani Touré, who led the 1991 coup, was elected president in 2002 and reelected 2007. After a Mar. 2012 coup, Islamist rebels, who had allied themselves with Taureg groups, seized control of the country's north. France entered the fight against the Islamists Jan. 10, 2013, and West African regional forces joined them Jan 17. The Islamists were pushed out of most of the territory they had seized. The UN Stabilization Mission in Mali (MINUSMA) was approved Apr. 25, 2013. Ibrahim Boubacar Keita was elected president Aug. 11, 2013. Attacks by Taureg rebels, as well as fighting against Islamists, continued in 2014 and early 2015. A new peace agreement with separatists and other Taureg fighters was signed May 15 and June 20, 2015 (although a Sept. 2018 UN report cited continued violence and criminal activity by some groups, as well as excessive force by Mali's military). Islamist extremist attacks continued. Gunmen killed 20 at a Bamako hotel, Nov. 20, 2015. A suicide bombing, Jan. 18, 2017, at a N Mali military camp left at least 75 dead. Apr. 2018 Islamist attacks on civilians in N Mali killed more than 40. Almost 14,000 MINUSMA uniformed personnel, as well as French and "G5" West African counterterrorism troops, were in Mali as of Aug. 31, 2018. Keita won a second a second term in an Aug. 12 runoff election.

Malta
Republic of Malta

People: Population: 449,043 (169). **Age distrib.:** <15: 14.3%; 65+: 20.5%. **Growth:** 0.2%. **Migrants:** 10.6%. **Pop. density:** 3,680.1 per sq mi, 1,421 per sq km. **Urban:** 94.6%. **Ethnic groups:** Maltese (descendants of ancient Carthaginians and Phoenicians with Italian, other Mediterranean stock). **Languages:** Maltese, English (both official). **Religions:** Roman Catholic (official) 90%+.

Geography: Total area: 122 sq mi, 316 sq km (187); **Land area:** 122 sq mi, 316 sq km. Island of Malta is 95 sq mi. Gozo, 26 sq mi, and Comino, 1 sq mi, are other islands in group. **Location:** Center of Mediterranean Sea. Nearest neighbor is Italy to N. **Topography:** Heavily indented coastline. Low hills cover interior. **Arable land:** 28%. **Capital:** Valletta, 212,768.

Government: Type: Parliamentary republic. **Head of state:** Pres. Marie-Louise Coleiro Preca; b. 1958; in office: Apr. 4, 2014. **Head of govt.:** Prime Min. Joseph Muscat; b. 1974; in office: Mar. 11, 2013. **Local divisions:** 68 localities. **Defense budget:** $64 mil. **Active troops:** 1,950.

Economy: Industries: tourism, electronics, shipbuilding and repair, constr., food and beverages, pharmaceuticals, footwear. **Chief agric.:** potatoes, cauliflower, grapes, wheat, barley, tomatoes, citrus, cut flowers, green peppers; pork, milk. **Natural resources:** limestone, salt. **Water:** 121 cu m per capita. **Electricity prod.:** 1.2 bil kWh. **Labor force:** agric. 1.3%, industry 19.4%, services 79.3%. **Unemployment:** 4%.

Finance: Monetary unit: Euro (EUR) (0.86 = $1 U.S.). **GDP:** $19.3 bil; **per capita GDP:** $42,000; **GDP growth:** 6.6%. **Imports:** $5.2 bil; Italy 23%, Germany 7.9%, UK 7.7%, Spain 5%. **Exports:** $2.6 bil; Germany 17.3%, France 10.2%, Italy 9.4%, Singapore 5.9%, Hong Kong 5.8%, U.S. 5.7%. **Tourism:** $1.7 bil. **Budget:** $4.4 bil. **Inflation:** 1.4%.

Transport: Motor vehicles: 826.8 per 1,000 pop. **Airports:** 1. **Communications: Telephone:** 55.8 per 100 pop. **Mobile:** 130 per 100 pop. **Broadband:** 71.4 per 100 pop. **Internet** (2017): 80.1%.

Health: Expend.: 9.6%. **Life expect.:** 80.6 male; 84.8 female. **Births:** 10.0 per 1,000 pop. **Deaths:** 7.9 per 1,000 pop. **Infant mortality:** 4.7 per 1,000 live births. **Undernourished:** <2.5%. **HIV:** NA. **Education:** Compulsory: ages 5-15. **Literacy:** 94.4%. **Embassy:** 2017 Connecticut Ave. NW 20008; 462-3611. **Website:** www.gov.mt

Malta was ruled by Phoenicians, Romans, Arabs, Normans, the Knights of Malta, France, and Britain (since 1814). It became independent Sept. 21, 1964, and a republic in 1974.

Malta became a full member of the EU May 1, 2004. Same-sex marriage was legalized in 2017.

The Labour Party won Mar. 9, 2013, and June 3, 2017, elections, the latter called early by Prime Min. Joseph Muscat in the face of corruption allegations. Daphne Caruana Galizia, a journalist reporting on corruption, was killed by a car bomb, Oct. 16, 2017. A judicial inquiry cleared Muscat and his wife, July 2018, of corruption charges.

Marshall Islands
Republic of the Marshall Islands

People: Population: 75,684 (187). **Age distrib.:** <15: 34.3%; 65+: 4.2%. **Growth:** 1.5%. **Migrants:** 6.2%. **Pop. density:** 1,083 per sq mi, 418.1 per sq km. **Urban:** 77%. **Ethnic groups:** Marshallese 92.1%, mixed Marshallese 5.9%. **Languages:** Marshallese, English (both official). **Religions:** Protestant 54.8%, Assembly of God 25.8%, Roman Catholic 8.4%, Bukot nan Jesus 2.8%.

Geography: Total area: 70 sq mi, 181 sq km (190); **Land area:** 70 sq mi, 181 sq km. **Location:** In N Pacific O.; made up of two 800-mi-long island chains, including atolls of Bikini, Enewetak, Kwajalein, Majuro, Rongelap, and Utirik. Nearest neighbors are Micronesia to W, Nauru and Kiribati to S. **Topography:** Low coral limestone and sand islands. **Arable land:** 11.1%. **Capital:** Majuro, 30,661.

Government: Type: Presidential republic in free association with U.S. **Head of state and govt.:** Pres. Hilda C. Heine; b. 1951; in office: Jan. 28, 2016. **Local divisions:** 24 municipalities. **Defense budget/active troops:** NA.

Economy: Industries: copra, tuna proc., tourism, craft items. **Chief agric.:** coconuts, tomatoes, melons, taro, breadfruit, fruits; pigs, chickens. **Natural resources:** coconut prods., marine prods., deep-seabed minerals. **Water:** NA. **Labor force:** agric. 11%, industry 16.3%, services 72.7%. **Unemployment:** NA.

Finance: Monetary unit: U.S. Dollar (USD) (1.00 = $1 U.S.). **GDP:** $189 mil; **per capita GDP:** $3,400; **GDP growth:** 1.9%. **Imports** (2013): $133.7 mil. **Exports** (2015): $47.2 mil. **Tourism:** $5 mil. **Budget** (2013): $113.9 mil. **Inflation:** 0.7%.

Transport: Airports: 4.

Communications: Telephone (2014): 4.5 per 100 pop. **Mobile** (2015): 29.2 per 100 pop. **Broadband:** NA. **Internet:** 29.8%.

Health: Expend.: 22.1%. **Life expect.:** 71.4 male; 76.0 female. **Births:** 23.8 per 1,000 pop. **Deaths:** 4.2 per 1,000 pop. **Infant mortality:** 18.7 per 1,000 live births. **Undernourished:** NA. **HIV:** NA.

Education: Compulsory: ages 5-17. **Literacy:** 98.3%.

Embassy: 2433 Massachusetts Ave. NW, 1st Fl., 20008; 234-5414.

Website: www.rmiparliament.org

The Marshall Islands were a German possession until WWI and were administered by Japan between the World Wars. After WWII, they were administered by the U.S. as part of the UN Trust Territory of the Pacific Islands. During 1946-58, Bikini and Enewetak Atolls were used as test sites for U.S. nuclear weapons.

The Compact of Free Association, ratified by the U.S. in 1986, gave the islands their independence. In the compact, the U.S. agreed to provide financial aid to the islands, maintain their defense, and compensate victims of nuclear testing; it was renewed Dec. 2003. Elected by parliament, Jan. 27, 2016, Hilda Heine became the country's first female president. Made up of low-lying atolls, the Marshall Islands is considered highly vulnerable to rising sea levels resulting from climate change.

Mauritania
Islamic Republic of Mauritania

People: Population: 3,840,429 (128). **Age distrib.:** <15: 38.2%; 65+: 3.8%. **Growth:** 2.1%. **Migrants:** 3.8%. **Pop. density:** 9.7 per sq mi, 3.7 per sq km. **Urban:** 53.7%. **Ethnic groups:** black Moor (Arab-speaking slaves, former slaves, and their descendants of African origin, enslaved by white Moors) 40%, white Moor or Beydane (Arab-Berber descent) 30%, Sub-Saharan Mauritanian (non-Arabic speaking) 30%. **Languages:** Arabic (official and national); Pulaar, Soninke, Wolof (all national langs.); French. **Religions:** Muslim (official) 100%.

Geography: Total area: 397,955 sq mi, 1,030,700 sq km (28); **Land area:** 397,955 sq mi, 1,030,700 sq km. **Location:** NW Africa. Western Sahara on N; Algeria, Mali on E; Senegal on S. **Topography:** Fertile Senegal R. valley in S gives way to wide central region of sandy plains and scrub trees. N is arid and extends into the Sahara. **Arable land:** 0.4%. **Capital:** Nouakchott, 1,205,414.

Government: Type: Presidential republic. **Head of state:** Pres. Mohamed Ould Abdel Aziz; b. 1956; in office: Aug. 5. 2009. **Head of govt.:** Prime Min. Yahya Ould Hademinein; b. 1953; in office: Aug. 21, 2014. **Local divisions:** 15 regions. **Defense budget:** $142 mil. **Active troops:** 15,850.

Economy: Industries: fish proc., oil prod., mining. **Chief agric.:** dates, millet, sorghum, rice, corn; cattle. **Natural resources:** iron ore, gypsum, copper, phosphate, diamonds, gold, oil, fish. **Water:** 2,802 cu m per capita. **Crude oil reserves:** 20 mil bbls. **Electricity prod.:** 1.3 bil kWh. **Labor force:** agric. 75.9%, industry 7.2%, services 16.9%. **Unemployment:** 9.9%.

Finance: Monetary unit: Ouguiya (MRO) (357.43 = $1 U.S.). **GDP:** $17.3 bil; **per capita GDP:** $4,400; **GDP growth:** 3.2%. **Imports:** $2.1 bil; Belgium 11.5%, UAE 11.3%, U.S. 9.2%, China 7.5%, France 7.4%, Netherlands 6.1%, Morocco 6%. **Exports:** $1.6 bil; China 31.2%, Switzerland 14.4%, Spain 10.1%, Germany 8.2%, Japan 8.1%. **Tourism:** $30 mil. **Budget:** $1.3 bil. **Inflation:** 2.3%.

Transport: Railways: 452 mi. **Motor vehicles:** 8 per 1,000 pop. **Airports:** 9.

Communications: Telephone: 1.3 per 100 pop. **Mobile:** 92.2 per 100 pop. **Broadband:** 30.2 per 100 pop. **Internet:** 18%.

Health: Expend.: 4.6%. **Life expect.:** 61.4 male; 66.2 female. **Births:** 29.9 per 1,000 pop. **Deaths:** 7.8 per 1,000 pop. **Infant mortality:** 50.5 per 1,000 live births. **Undernourished:** 11.3%. **HIV:** 0.3%.

Education: Compulsory: ages 6-14. **Literacy:** 52.1%.

Embassy: 2129 Leroy Pl. NW 20008; 232-5700.

Website: primature.gov.mr

A French protectorate from 1903, Mauritania became independent Nov. 28, 1960. It annexed the south of former Spanish Sahara (now Morocco-claimed Western Sahara) in 1976 but renounced its claim to the region after signing a peace treaty with the Saharan guerrillas of the Polisario Front, 1979.

During Jan.-June 2006, up to 10,000 people tried to emigrate in handmade boats from Mauritania to Spain's Canary Islands; more than 1,700 died. After decades of military rule, civilian rule was restored, 2006-07, but a 2008 military coup toppled the elected government. The coup leader, Gen. Mohamed Ould Abdel Aziz, won disputed presidential elections in 2009 and 2014. Security concerns, including a rising threat from al-Qaeda in the Islamic Maghreb, led the U.S. Peace Corps to remove its volunteers from Mauritania in Aug. 2009. In 2013, U.S. Special Operations troops began providing training and equipment to Mauritanian counterterrorism forces, to help

combat Islamic extremists. In 2017, Mauritania and 4 other nations created the anti-terrorism G5 Sahel Cross-Border Joint Force.

Major oil finds have recently been developed. Slavery, repeatedly abolished, continues to exist, despite legislation mandating prison terms for slaveholders enacted in 2007 and strengthened in 2015. The 2018 Global Slavery Index estimated that 90,000 people in Mauritania lived under conditions of servitude.

Mauritius
Republic of Mauritius

People: Population: 1,364,283 (151). **Age distrib.:** <15: 19.9%; 65+: 10.2%. **Growth:** 0.6%. **Migrants:** 2.3%. **Pop. density:** 1,740.6 per sq mi, 672.1 per sq km. **Urban:** 40.8%. **Ethnic groups:** Indo-Mauritian (approx. two-thirds of pop.), Creole, Sino-Mauritian, Franco-Mauritian. **Languages:** Creole, Bhojpuri, French, English (official). **Religions:** Hindu 48.5%, Roman Catholic 26.3%, Muslim 17.3%.

Geography: Total area: 788 sq mi, 2,040 sq km (171); **Land area:** 784 sq mi, 2,030 sq km. **Location:** In Indian O., 500 mi E of Madagascar, its nearest neighbor. **Topography:** A volcanic island nearly surrounded by coral reefs. A central plateau is encircled by peaks. **Arable land:** 36.5%. **Capital:** Port Louis, 149,365.

Government: Type: Parliamentary republic. **Head of state:** Acting Pres. Paramasivum Pillay "Barlen" Vyapoory; in office: Mar. 23, 2018. **Head of govt.:** Prime Min. Pravind Jugnauth; b. 1961; in office: Jan. 23, 2017. **Local divisions:** 9 districts, 3 dependencies. **Defense budget:** $218 mil. **Active troops:** No standing armed forces; 2,550 paramilitary. Special Mobile Force (part of police) and coast guard provide security.

Economy: Industries: food proc. (largely sugar milling), textiles, clothing, mining, chemicals, metal prods. **Chief agric.:** sugarcane, tea, corn, potatoes, bananas, pulses; cattle, goats; fish. **Natural resources:** fish. **Water:** 2,161 cu m per capita. **Electricity prod.:** 2.9 bil kWh. **Labor force:** agric. 7.3%, industry 26%, services 66.7%. **Unemployment:** 7.1%.

Finance: Monetary unit: Rupee (MUR) (34.49 = $1 U.S.). **GDP:** $27.5 bil; **per capita GDP:** $21,600; **GDP growth:** 3.9%. **Imports:** $4.5 bil; India 17.9%, China 15.7%, France 11.1%, South Africa 9.7%. **Exports:** $2.3 bil; France 16.7%, U.S. 12.5%, UK 12%, South Africa 9%, Madagascar 6.7%, Italy 6.6%, Spain 5.2%. **Tourism:** $1.7 bil. **Budget:** $3.3 bil. **Inflation:** 3.7%.

Transport: Motor vehicles: 194.8 per 1,000 pop. **Airports:** 2.

Communications: Telephone: 32.7 per 100 pop. **Mobile:** 145.4 per 100 pop. **Broadband:** 51.7 per 100 pop. **Internet:** 52.2%.

Health: Expend.: 5.5%. **Life expect.:** 72.6 male; 79.7 female. **Births:** 12.8 per 1,000 pop. **Deaths:** 7.1 per 1,000 pop. **Infant mortality:** 9.5 per 1,000 live births. **Undernourished:** 5.8%. **HIV:** NA.

Education: Compulsory: ages 5-15. **Literacy:** 92.7%.

Embassy: 1709 N St. NW 20036; 244-1491.

Website: www.govmu.org

Mauritius was uninhabited when settled in 1638 by the Dutch, who introduced sugarcane. France took over in 1721, bringing African slaves. Britain ruled from 1810, bringing Indian workers for the sugar plantations. Mauritius became independent, Mar. 12, 1968, and a republic, Mar. 12, 1992.

Mauritius topped the annual Ibrahim Index as the best-governed African country, 2006-17. Pres. Ameenah Gurib-Fakim resigned, Mar. 23, 2018, following allegations she used an NGO credit card to purchase $30,000 worth of luxury items for personal use.

Mexico
United Mexican States

People: Population: 125,959,205 (11). **Age distrib.:** <15: 26.6%; 65+: 7.3%. **Growth:** 1.1%. **Migrants:** 0.9%. **Pop. density:** 167.8 per sq mi, 64.8 per sq km. **Urban:** 80.2%. **Ethnic groups:** mestizo (Amerindian-Spanish) 62%, predom. Amerindian 21%, Amerindian 7%. **Languages:** Spanish, indigenous langs. (incl. Mayan, Nahuatl). **Religions:** Roman Catholic 82.7%, none 4.7%.

Geography: Total area: 758,449 sq mi, 1,964,375 sq km (13); **Land area:** 750,561 sq mi, 1,943,945 sq km. **Location:** Southern N America. U.S. on N, Guatemala and Belize on S. **Topography:** The Sierra Madre Occidental Mts. run NW-SE near the W coast; the Sierra Madre Oriental Mts. are near Gulf of Mexico. They join S of Mexico City. In between lies a dry central plateau (5,000-8,000 ft) with temperate vegetation. Coastal lowlands are tropical. About 45% of land is arid. **Arable land:** 11.8%. **Capital:** Mexico City, 21,580,827. **Cities:** Guadalajara, 5,022,674; Monterrey, 4,712,297; Puebla, 3,096,703; Toluca de Lerdo, 2,354,160; Tijuana, 2,058,213.

Government: Type: Federal presidential republic. **Head of state and govt.:** Pres. Enrique Peña Nieto; b. 1966; in office: Dec. 1, 2012. (Pres.-elect Andrés Manuel López Obrador, b. 1953, was set to be inaugurated Dec. 1, 2018.) **Local divisions:** 31 states, 1 city. **Defense budget:** $4.5 bil. **Active troops:** 277,150.

Economy: Industries: food/beverages, tobacco, chemicals, iron and steel, petroleum, mining, textiles, clothing, motor vehicles. **Chief agric.:** corn, wheat, soybeans, rice, beans, cotton, coffee, fruit, tomatoes; beef, poultry, dairy prods. **Natural resources:** petroleum, silver, copper, gold, lead, zinc, nat. gas, timber. **Water:**

3,637 cu m per capita. **Crude oil reserves:** 6.6 bil bbls. **Electricity prod.:** 294.8 bil kWh. **Labor force:** agric. 13.1%, industry 25.8%, services 61.1%. **Unemployment:** 3.4%.

Finance: Monetary unit: Peso (MXN) (19.39 = $1 U.S.). **GDP:** $2.5 tril; **per capita GDP:** $19,900; **GDP growth:** 2%. **Imports:** $417.3 bil; U.S. 46.4%, China 17.7%. **Exports:** $406.5 bil; U.S. 79.9%. **Tourism:** $21.3 bil. **Budget:** $314.9 bil. **Inflation:** 6%.

Transport: Railways: 9,562 mi. **Motor vehicles:** 331.6 per 1,000 pop. **Airports:** 243.

Communications: Telephone: 16 per 100 pop. **Mobile:** 88.5 per 100 pop. **Broadband:** 58.8 per 100 pop. **Internet** (2017): 63.9%.

Health: Expend.: 5.9%. **Life expect.:** 73.5 male; 79.2 female. **Births:** 18.1 per 1,000 pop. **Deaths:** 5.4 per 1,000 pop. **Infant mortality:** 11.3 per 1,000 live births. **Undernourished:** 3.8%. **HIV:** 0.3%.

Education: Compulsory: ages 4-17. **Literacy:** 94.5%.

Embassy: 1911 Pennsylvania Ave. NW 20006; 728-1600.

Website: www.gob.mx

Mexico was the site of advanced civilizations. The Mayans, an agricultural people, moved up from Yucatan, built huge stone pyramids and invented a calendar. The Toltecs were overcome by the Aztecs, who founded Tenochtitlan 1325 CE, now Mexico City. Hernán Cortés, Spanish conquistador, destroyed the Aztec empire, 1519-21. After three centuries of Spanish rule the people revolted, beginning in 1810. Spain recognized Mexican independence, 1821. Gen. Agustín Iturbide made himself emperor as Agustín I, 1822. A republic was declared in 1823.

Mexican territory extended into the present-day United States. Texas established a republic in 1836, and Mexico lost California and most of the SW in the U.S.-Mexican War, 1846-48.

The French supported an Austrian archduke on the Mexican throne as Maximilian I, 1864-67. He was deposed in an uprising led by Benito Juárez. Dictatorial rule by Porfirio Díaz, president 1877-80, 1884-1911, led to a period of rebellion and factional fighting. A new constitution in 1917 brought reform.

The Institutional Revolutionary Party (PRI) dominated politics from 1929 until the late 1990s. Radical opposition, including some guerrilla activity, was contained by strong measures. Gains in agriculture, industry, and social services were achieved, but poverty remained widespread. Vast oil reserves were discovered, 1970s-80s. About 10,000 people died when a magnitude 8.0 earthquake struck near Mexico City, Sept. 19, 1985.

After guerrillas of the Zapatista National Liberation Army (EZLN) rebelled Jan. 1994, a tentative peace accord was reached Mar. 2.

In 1997 elections, the PRI lost its congressional majority. The National Action Party won the 2000 and 2006 presidential elections. Despite a government crackdown on drug cartels, drug-related violence intensified. The death toll in the drug war exceeded 47,500, Dec. 2006-Sept. 2012. Enrique Peña Nieto (PRI) won the 2012 presidential election. He continued to combat drug gangs. Notorious drug cartel leader Joaquín Guzmán Loera, known as El Chapo, was captured, Feb. 22, 2014. He escaped, July 11, 2015, but was recaptured, Jan. 8, 2016, and extradited to the U.S. High levels of gang-related violence continued in 2016-18, as well as corruption-related violence and allegations of excessive force and extrajudicial actions by security officers. Vowing to reduce violence and corruption and to combat poverty, leftist Andrés Manuel López Obrador of the Moreno Party easily won the July 1, 2018, presidential election.

A Supreme Court decision, June 3, 2015, in effect legalized same-sex marriage nationwide.

The North American Free Trade Agreement (NAFTA) with the U.S. and Canada took effect Jan. 1, 1994. At U.S. insistence, negotiations on revising NAFTA began Aug. 16, 2017. While talks continued, new U.S. tariffs on Mexican steel and aluminum took effect June 1, 2018; Mexico announced retaliatory tariffs on U.S. steel and agricultural products June 5. A draft revised NAFTA pact, to be renamed the U.S.-Mexico-Canada Agreement, was completed Sept. 30, 2018—subject to signature of a final document and approval by the U.S. Congress, Mexican Senate, and Canadian cabinet.

Micronesia
Federated States of Micronesia

People: Population: 103,643 (182). **Age distrib.:** <15: 29.8%; 65+: 4.2%. **Growth:** –0.55%. **Migrants:** 2.6%. **Pop. density:** 382.4 per sq mi, 147.6 per sq km. **Urban:** 22.7%. **Ethnic groups:** Chuukese/Mortlockese 49.3%, Pohnpeian 29.8%, Kosraean 6.3%, Yapese 5.7%, Yap outer islander 5.1%. **Languages:** English (official), Chuukese, Kosrean, Pohnpeian, Yapese, Ulithian, Woleaian, Nukuoro, Kapingamarangi. **Religions:** Roman Catholic 54.7%, Protestant 41.1% (incl. Congregational 38.5%).

Geography: Total area: 271 sq mi, 702 sq km (177); **Land area:** 271 sq mi, 702 sq km. **Location:** Consists of 607 islands in four major island groups in W Pacific O. **Topography:** Mountainous islands and coral atolls; volcanic outcroppings on Pohnpei, Kosrae, and Truk. Tropical climate. **Arable land:** 2.9%. **Capital:** Palikir, 6,996.

Government: Type: Federal republic in free association with U.S. **Head of state and govt.:** Pres. Peter M. Christian; b. 1948; in office: May 11, 2015. **Local divisions:** 4 states. **Defense budget/active troops:** NA.

Economy: Industries: tourism, constr., specialized aquaculture, craft items. **Chief agric.:** taro, yams, coconuts, bananas, cassava, kava, Kosraen citrus, betel nuts, black pepper, fish, pigs, chickens. **Natural resources:** timber, marine prods., deep-seabed minerals, phosphate. **Water:** NA. **Labor force:** agric. 0.9%, industry 5.2%, services 93.9%. Two-thirds of labor force are govt. employees. **Unemployment:** NA.

Finance: Monetary unit: U.S. Dollar (USD) (1.00 = $1 U.S.). **GDP:** $347 mil (supplemented by grant aid from U.S.); **per capita GDP:** $3,400; **GDP growth:** 2%. **Imports** (2013): $258.5 mil. **Exports** (2013): $88.3 mil. **Tourism** (2015): $25 mil. **Budget** (FY2012/13): $192.1 mil. **Inflation** (2014-15): –0.5%.

Transport: Airports: 6.

Communications: Telephone: 6.6 per 100 pop. **Mobile:** 21.9 per 100 pop. **Broadband:** NA. **Internet:** 33.4%.

Health: Expend.: 13.1%. **Life expect.:** 71.3 male; 75.6 female. **Births:** 19.6 per 1,000 pop. **Deaths:** 4.2 per 1,000 pop. **Infant mortality:** 19.1 per 1,000 live births. **Undernourished:** NA. **HIV:** NA.

Education: Compulsory: ages 6-15. **Literacy:** 90.4%.

Embassy: 1725 N St. NW 20036; 223-4383.

Website: micronesia.fm

Micronesia, formerly known as the Caroline Islands, was ruled successively by Spain, Germany, Japan, and the U.S. The nation gained independence under a compact of free association with the U.S., Nov. 1986, and was admitted to the UN in 1991. Micronesian officials have repeatedly warned of the dangers to their country of rising sea levels linked to climate change.

Moldova
Republic of Moldova

People: Population: 3,437,720 (131). **Age distrib.:** <15: 18.3%; 65+: 13.1%. **Growth:** –1.1%. **Migrants:** 3.5%. **Pop. density:** 270.7 per sq mi, 104.5 per sq km. **Urban:** 42.6%. **Ethnic groups:** Moldovan 75.1%, Romanian 7%, Ukrainian 6.6%, Gagauz 4.6%, Russian 4.1%. **Languages:** Moldovan/Romanian (official), Russian, Gagauz, Ukrainian. **Religions:** Orthodox 90.1%.

Geography: Total area: 13,070 sq mi, 33,851 sq km (136); **Land area:** 12,699 sq mi, 32,891 sq km. **Location:** Eastern Europe. Romania on W; Ukraine on N, E, and S. **Topography:** Landlocked; mainly hilly plains with steppelands in S near Black Sea. **Arable land:** 55.5%. **Capital:** Chisinau, 509,707.

Government: Type: Parliamentary republic. **Head of state:** Pres. Igor Dodon; b. 1975; in office: Dec. 23, 2016. **Head of govt.:** Prime Min. Pavel Filip; b. 1966; in office: Jan. 20, 2016. **Local divisions:** 32 raions, 3 municipalities, 2 territorial units (1 autonomous). **Defense budget:** $29 mil. **Active troops:** 5,150.

Economy: Industries: sugar proc., vegetable oil, food proc., agric. machinery, foundry equip., refrigerators and freezers. **Chief agric.:** vegetables, fruits, grapes, grain, sugar beets, sunflower seeds, tobacco; beef, milk; wine. **Natural resources:** lignite, phosphorites, gypsum, limestone. **Water:** 3,015 cu m per capita. **Electricity prod.:** 5.7 bil kWh. **Labor force:** agric. 33.3%, industry 17.2%, services 49.6%. **Unemployment:** 4.5%.

Finance: Monetary unit: Leu (MDL) (16.71 = $1 U.S.). **GDP:** $20.1 bil; **per capita GDP:** $5,700; **GDP growth:** 4%. **Imports:** $4.8 bil; Romania 15.5%, Ukraine 11.4%, Russia 10.6%, China 10.4%, Germany 8.9%, Italy 6.9%, Turkey 6.1%. **Exports:** $2.4 bil; Romania 24.6%, Russia 13.7%, Italy 9.1%, Germany 6.2%, Ukraine 5.3%. **Tourism:** $312 mil. **Budget:** $2.9 bil (natl. public). **Inflation:** 6.6%.

Transport: Railways: 728 mi. **Airports:** 5.

Communications: Telephone: 28.2 per 100 pop. **Mobile:** 90.4 per 100 pop. **Broadband:** 55.5 per 100 pop. **Internet:** 71%.

Health: Expend.: 10.2%. **Life expect.:** 67.4 male; 75.4 female. **Births:** 11.2 per 1,000 pop. **Deaths:** 11.9 per 1,000 pop. **Infant mortality:** 11.7 per 1,000 live births. **Undernourished:** NA. **HIV:** 0.6%.

Education: Compulsory: ages 7-15. **Literacy:** 99.4%.

Embassy: 2101 S St. NW 20008; 667-1130.

Website: www.moldova.md

In 1918, Romania annexed all of Bessarabia, west of the Dniester R, that Russia had acquired from Turkey in 1812 by the Treaty of Bucharest. In 1924, the Soviet Union established the Moldavian Autonomous Soviet Socialist Republic on the eastern bank of the Dniester R (Trans-Dniester region, or Transnistria). It was merged with the Romanian-speaking districts of Bessarabia in 1940 to form the Moldavian SSR. During WWII, Romania, allied with Germany, occupied the area. It was recaptured by the USSR in 1944. Moldova declared independence Aug. 27, 1991, prior to the dissolution of the USSR Dec. 26, 1991.

Fighting erupted Mar. 1992 in Transnistria between Moldovan security forces and Slavic separatists—ethnic Russians and ethnic Ukrainians—who feared Moldova's merging with neighboring Romania. In a 1994 plebiscite, voters in Moldova supported independence. Defying the Moldovan government, voters in the breakaway Transnistria held legislative elections and approved a separatist constitution in 1995. A peace accord with Transnistria separatists was signed in Moscow in 1997. In a 2006 referendum, Transnistria voters overwhelmingly supported independence from Moldova and eventual union with Russia, which has troops in the region.

A fragile coalition of pro-Western parties won Moldova's parliamentary elections in 2009 and 2010. The pro-Western Nicolae Timofti, elected by parliament, became president in 2012. Moldova and the EU signed an Association Agreement, June 27, 2014. Pro-Western parties won a narrow majority in Nov. 30, 2014, parliamentary elections. A banking scandal involving the disappearance of about $1 bil in bad loans, 2010-14, caused political turmoil. Pavel Filip became prime min., Jan. 20, 2016, pledging to fight corruption and improve the economy. The Constitutional Court ruled, Mar. 4, that Moldova's president should be directly elected; pro-Russian Socialist Party candidate Igor Dodon won a Nov. 13, 2016, presidential runoff.

Monaco
Principality of Monaco

People: Population: 30,727 (192). (Immigrants made up almost 55% of pop. in 2017.) **Age distrib.:** <15: 10.3%; 65+: 33.2%. **Growth:** 0.3%. **Migrants:** 54.9%. **Pop. density:** 39,791.3 per sq mi, 15,363.5 per sq km. **Urban:** 100%. **Ethnic groups:** Monegasque 32.1%, French 19.9%, Italian 15.3%, British 5%, Belgian 2.3%, Swiss 2%. **Languages:** French (official), English, Italian, Monegasque. **Religions:** Roman Catholic (official) 90%.

Geography: Total area: 0.77 sq mi, 2 sq km (195); **Land area:** 0.77 sq mi, 2 sq km. **Location:** NW Mediterranean coast. France to W, N, and E. **Topography:** Principality rises from port up to Monaco-Ville on a high promontory. **Arable land:** 0%. **Capital:** Monaco.

Government: Type: Constitutional monarchy. **Head of state:** Prince Albert II; b. 1958; in office: Apr. 6, 2005. **Head of govt.:** Min. of State Serge Telle; b. 1955; in office: Feb. 1, 2016. **Local divisions:** no first-order admin. divisions. **Defense budget/active troops:** NA.

Economy: Industries: banking, insurance, tourism, constr. **Chief agric.:** none. **Natural resources:** none. **Water:** NA. **Labor force:** industry 16.1%, services 83.9%. **Unemployment:** NA.

Finance: Monetary unit: Euro (EUR) (0.86 = $1 U.S.). **GDP** (2015): $7.7 bil; **per capita GDP** (2015): $115,700; **GDP growth** (2015): 5.4%. **Imports:** $1.4 bil. **Exports:** $964.6 mil. Full customs integration with France. **Budget** (2011): $953.6 mil. **Inflation** (2009-10): 1.5%.

Transport: NA.

Communications: Telephone: 121.5 per 100 pop. **Mobile:** 85.2 per 100 pop. **Broadband:** 64.8 per 100 pop. **Internet:** 95.2%.

Health: Expend.: 2%. **Life expect.:** 85.5 male; 93.4 female. **Births:** 6.5 per 1,000 pop. **Deaths:** 10.1 per 1,000 pop. **Infant mortality:** 1.8 per 1,000 live births. **Undernourished:** NA. **HIV:** NA.

Education: Compulsory: ages 6-16. **Literacy:** 99%.

Embassy: 3400 International Dr. NW, Ste. 2K-100, 20008; 234-1530.

Website: www.gouv.mc

Monaco has belonged to the House of Grimaldi since 1297, except during the French Revolution when it was annexed by France (1793). It was placed under the protectorate of Sardinia in 1815. An 1861 treaty restored independence. The Prince of Monaco was an absolute ruler until the 1911 constitution. Monaco is noted for its climate, scenery, casinos, and Formula One Grand Prix auto race. It is one of Europe's top tourist spots and a tax haven for the wealthy. Prince Rainier III, who ruled Monaco from 1949, died in 2005 and was succeeded by his son, Albert II.

Mongolia

People: Population: 3,103,428 (133). **Age distrib.:** <15: 27%; 65+: 4.4%. **Growth:** 1.1%. **Migrants:** 0.6%. **Pop. density:** 5.2 per sq mi, 2 per sq km. **Urban:** 68.4%. **Ethnic groups:** Khalkh 81.9%, Kazak 3.8%, Dorvod 2.7%, Bayad 2.1%. **Languages:** Mongolian (official) (Khalkha dialect predom.), Turkic, Russian. **Religions:** Buddhist 53%, Muslim 3%, Shamanist 2.9%, none 38.6%.

Geography: Total area: 603,909 sq mi, 1,564,116 sq km (18); **Land area:** 599,831 sq mi, 1,553,556 sq km. **Location:** E Central Asia. Russia on N, China on E, W, and S. **Topography:** Mostly high plateau with mountains, salt lakes, and vast grasslands. Gobi Desert in S. **Arable land:** 0.4%. **Capital:** Ulaanbaatar, 1,520,381.

Government: Type: Semi-presidential republic. **Head of state:** Pres. Khaltmaa Battulga; b. 1963; in office: July 10, 2017. **Head of govt.:** Prime. Min. Ukhnaa Khurelsukh; b. 1968; in office: Oct. 4, 2017. **Local divisions:** 21 provinces, 1 municipality. **Defense budget:** $84 mil. **Active troops:** 9,700.

Economy: Industries: constr. and constr. materials, mining, oil, food and beverages, animal prods. proc., cashmere and natural fiber mfg. **Chief agric.:** wheat, barley, vegetables, forage crops; sheep, goats, cattle, camels, horses. **Natural resources:** oil, coal, copper, molybdenum, tungsten, phosphates, tin, nickel, zinc, fluorspar, gold, silver, iron. **Water:** 11,761 cu m per capita. **Electricity prod.:** 5.2 bil kWh. **Labor force:** agric. 30.4%, industry 19%, services 50.6%. **Unemployment:** 7%.

Finance: Monetary unit: Tugrik (MNT) (2,479.09 = $1 U.S.). **GDP:** $39.7 bil; **per capita GDP:** $13,000; **GDP growth:** 5.1%. **Imports:** $4.3 bil; China 32.6%, Russia 28.1%, Japan 8.4%. **Exports:** $6.2 bil; China 85%, UK 10.7%. **Tourism:** $396 mil. **Budget:** $3.2 bil. **Inflation:** 4.1%.

Transport: Railways: 1,128 mi. **Airports:** 15.

Communications: Telephone: 9.5 per 100 pop. **Mobile:** 126.4 per 100 pop. **Broadband:** 82 per 100 pop. **Internet:** 22.3%.

Health: Expend.: 3.9%. **Life expect.:** 66.0 male; 74.7 female. **Births:** 18.2 per 1,000 pop. **Deaths:** 6.3 per 1,000 pop. **Infant mortality:** 20.5 per 1,000 live births. **Undernourished:** 18.7%. **HIV:** <0.1%.

Education: Compulsory: ages 6-17. **Literacy:** 98.4%.

Embassy: 2833 M St. NW 20007; 333-7117.

Website: zasag.mn

Mongolia reached the zenith of its power in the 13th cent. when Genghis Khan and his successors conquered all of China and extended their influence as far west as Hungary and Poland. In later centuries, the empire dissolved and Mongolia became a province of China.

With the advent of the 1911 Chinese revolution, Mongolia, with Russian backing, declared its independence. A Communist regime was established, 1921. The Mongolian People's Revolutionary Party (MPRP) yielded its monopoly on power, 1990. A new constitution took effect, 1992.

Riots followed 2008 parliamentary elections, won by the ruling MPRP. In 2009 presidential voting, Tsakhiagiin Elbergdorj of the Democratic Party (DP) defeated incumbent Pres. Nambaryn Enkhbayar of the MPRP (renamed the Mongolian People's Party, or MPP, in 2010). The DP won 2012 legislative elections. Low commodity prices and reduced exports to China caused the economy to slump, and the MPP won June 29, 2016, parliamentary elections. The IMF approved a $5.5-bil bailout package, May 24, 2017. The DP's Khaltmaa Battulga won a July 7 presidential runoff vote. Parliament voted, Sept. 7, to oust Prime Min. Jargaltulga Erdenebat, whose government was accused of corruption. The MPP, Sept. 26, chose Khurelsukh Ukhnaa to replace Erdenebat.

Montenegro

People: Population: 614,249 (164). **Age distrib.:** <15: 18.2%; 65+: 15.1%. **Growth:** −0.34%. **Migrants:** 11.3%. **Pop. density:** 118.3 per sq mi, 45.7 per sq km. **Urban:** 66.8%. **Ethnic groups:** Montenegrin 45%, Serbian 28.7%, Bosniak 8.7%, Albanian 4.9%, Muslim 3.3%. **Languages:** Serbian, Montenegrin (official), Bosnian, Albanian, Serbo-Croat. **Religions:** Orthodox 72.1%, Muslim 19.1%, Catholic 3.4%.

Geography: Total area: 5,333 sq mi, 13,812 sq km (157); **Land area:** 5,194 sq mi, 13,452 sq km. **Location:** Balkan Peninsula in SE Europe. Bosnia and Herzegovina on N and W, Serbia on E, Albania on SE, Croatia on W. **Topography:** Mostly rugged and mountainous, with few arable regions, mostly along the Zeta R. Highly indented narrow coastline. **Arable land:** 0.6%. **Capital:** Podgorica, 177,177. Cetinje holds status of "Old Royal Capital."

Government: Type: Parliamentary republic. **Head of state:** Pres. Milo Djukanovic; b. 1958; in office: May 20, 2018. **Head of govt.:** Prime. Min. Dusko Markovic; b. 1958; in office: Nov. 28, 2016. **Local divisions:** 23 municipalities. **Defense budget:** $74 mil. **Active troops:** 1,950.

Economy: Industries: steelmaking, aluminum, agric. proc., consumer goods, tourism. **Chief agric.:** tobacco, potatoes, citrus fruits, olives, grapes; sheep; wine. **Natural resources:** bauxite, hydroelectricity. **Water:** NA. **Electricity prod.:** 2.9 bil kWh. **Labor force:** agric. 7.6%, industry 18%, services 74.3%. **Unemployment:** 16.1%.

Finance: Monetary unit: Euro (EUR) (0.86 = $1 U.S.). **GDP:** $11.1 bil; **per capita GDP:** $17,700; **GDP growth:** 4.2%. **Imports:** $2.6 bil. **Exports:** $422.2 mil. **Tourism:** $1 bil. **Budget:** $2.1 bil. **Inflation:** 2.4%.

Transport: Railways: 155 mi. **Airports:** 5.

Communications: Telephone: 24.2 per 100 pop. **Mobile:** 166.1 per 100 pop. **Broadband:** 60.7 per 100 pop. **Internet** (2017): 71.3%.

Health: Expend.: 6%. **Life expect.:** 74.5 male; 79.4 female. **Births:** 11.9 per 1,000 pop. **Deaths:** 10.4 per 1,000 pop. **Infant mortality:** 3.4 per 1,000 live births. **Undernourished:** <2.5%. **HIV:** <0.1%.

Education: Compulsory: ages 6-14. **Literacy:** 98.7%.

Embassy: 1610 New Hampshire Ave. NW 20009; 234-6108.

Website: www.gov.me

Part of the medieval Serbian Kingdom, Montenegro preserved its autonomy for centuries because of its mountainous terrain. After WWI, it was part of the Kingdom of Serbs, Croats, and Slovenes, later renamed Yugoslavia. Italian forces occupied parts of Montenegro during WWII. In 1945, with the establishment of a federal Yugoslavia under Communist rule, Montenegro became one of six constituent republics.

In Apr. 1992, after four other republics had declared independence, Montenegro and Serbia reconstituted themselves as the Federal Republic of Yugoslavia. Because of its ties with Serbia, Montenegro was a target of NATO airstrikes in the 1999 Kosovo war. On June 3, 2006, Montenegro declared independence, and it was admitted to the UN June 28. It applied, Dec. 15, 2008, to join the EU. Corruption allegations and violence, including attacks on journalists, linked to organized crime were concerns in EU negotiations. The governing, pro-Western Democratic Party of Socialists (DPS) won the most seats in Oct. 16, 2016, parliamentary elections; 20 Serbian nationals were arrested on election day, accused of plotting a coup, allegedly with Russian backing. Montenegro became a member of NATO, June 5, 2017. The DPS's Milo Djukanovic won the Apr. 15, 2018, presidential election.

Morocco
Kingdom of Morocco

People: Population: 34,314,130 (40). **Age distrib.:** <15: 25.5%; 65+: 7%. **Growth:** 1%. **Migrants:** 0.3%. **Pop. density:** 199.1 per sq mi, 76.9 per sq km. **Urban:** 62.5%. **Ethnic groups:** Arab-Berber 99%. **Languages:** Arabic (official), Berber langs. (incl. Tamazight [official]), French (lang. of business, govt., diplomacy). **Religions:** Muslim (official; virtually all Sunni) 99%.

Geography: Total area: 172,414 sq mi, 446,550 sq km (57); **Land area:** 172,317 sq mi, 446,300 sq km. **Location:** NW coast of Africa. Western Sahara on S, Algeria on E, Spain to N. **Topography:** Consists of 5 natural regions: mountain ranges (Riff in N, Middle Atlas, Upper Atlas, and Anti-Atlas); rich plains in W; alluvial plains in SW; well-cultivated plateaus in center; pre-Sahara arid zone extending from SE. **Arable land:** 18.2%. **Capital:** Rabat, 1,846,661. **Cities:** Dar-el-Beida (Casablanca), 3,683,566.

Government: Type: Parliamentary constitutional monarchy. **Head of state:** King Mohammed VI; b. 1963; in office: July 30, 1999. **Head of govt.:** Prime Min. Saad-Eddine al-Othmani; b. 1956; in office: Mar. 17, 2017. **Local divisions:** 11 regions (recognized; not incl. claimed region in territory of disputed Western Sahara). **Defense budget:** $3.5 bil. **Active troops:** 195,800.

Economy: Industries: automotive parts, phosphate mining and proc., aerospace, food proc., leather goods. **Chief agric.:** barley, wheat, citrus fruits, grapes, vegetables, olives. **Natural resources:** phosphates, iron ore, manganese, lead, zinc, fish, salt. **Water:** 844 cu m per capita. **Crude oil reserves:** 684 bbls. **Electricity prod.:** 28 bil kWh. **Labor force:** agric. 37.5%, industry 19.6%, services 43%. **Unemployment:** 9.3%.

Finance: Monetary unit: Dirham (MAD) (9.45 = $1 U.S.). **GDP:** $298.6 bil; **per capita GDP:** $8,600; **GDP growth:** 4.2%. **Imports:** $44.1 bil; Spain 16.7%, France 12.2%, China 9.2%, U.S. 6.9%, Germany 6%, Italy 5.9%. **Exports:** $24.6 bil; Spain 23.2%, France 22.6%. **Tourism:** $7.4 bil. **Budget:** $30.7 bil. **Inflation:** 0.8%.

Transport: Railways: 1,284 mi. **Motor vehicles:** 109.9 per 1,000 pop. **Airports:** 31.

Communications: Telephone: 5.7 per 100 pop. **Mobile:** 122.9 per 100 pop. **Broadband:** 46 per 100 pop. **Internet** (2017): 61.8%.

Health: Expend.: 5.5%. **Life expect.:** 74.2 male; 80.5 female. **Births:** 17.5 per 1,000 pop. **Deaths:** 4.9 per 1,000 pop. **Infant mortality:** 21.1 per 1,000 live births. **Undernourished:** 3.9%. **HIV:** <0.1%.

Education: Compulsory: ages 6-14. **Literacy:** 68.5%.

Embassy: 1601 21st St. NW 20009; 462-7980.

Website: www.maroc.ma

Berbers were the region's original inhabitants, followed by Carthaginians and Romans. Arabs conquered it in 683. In the 11th and 12th cents., a Berber empire ruled all NW Africa and most of Spain from Morocco.

Part of Morocco came under Spanish rule in the 19th cent.; France controlled the rest in the early 20th. Tribal uprisings lasted from 1911 to 1933. Independence was achieved Mar. 2, 1956. Tangier, an internationalized seaport, was incorporated into Morocco, 1956. Ifni, a Spanish enclave, was ceded in 1969.

King Hassan II assumed the throne in 1961, reigning until his death in 1999; he was succeeded by his eldest son. A bicameral legislature was established in 1997.

Five terrorist attacks, linked to al-Qaeda, in Casablanca May 16, 2003, left 45 people dead, including 12 suicide bombers. Following a series of suicide bombings in 2007, the government stepped up its campaign against militant Islamists. After Arab Spring street demonstrations Feb.-Mar. 2011, the monarchy implemented modest constitutional reforms. Throughout 2011, Moroccans staged protests over persistent unemployment, alleged unjust detentions, and lack of free speech. In Feb. 2016, Morocco opened the first phase of one of the world's largest concentrated solar power complexes, scheduled for completion by year-end 2018. The moderate Islamist Justice and Development Party (PJD) won a plurality in Oct. 7, 2016, parliamentary elections; the PJD's Saad-Eddine al-Othmani became prime min., Mar. 17, 2017. Large protests in the impoverished Rif region of northern Morocco, 2017-18, prompted a harsh response by security forces; 4 protesters received 20-year prison sentences, June 26, 2018.

Western Sahara

Western Sahara, formerly the protectorate of Spanish Sahara, is bounded on the N by Morocco, the NE by Algeria, the E and S by Mauritania, and the W by the Atlantic O. Phosphates are the major resource. Area 102,703 sq mi; pop. (2018 est.) 619,551. Capital is Laayoune; pop. (2018 est.) 232,388.

Spain withdrew in Feb. 1976. On Apr. 14, 1976, Morocco annexed over 70,000 sq mi, with the remainder annexed by Mauritania. The Polisario Front guerrilla movement, which proclaimed the region independent Feb. 27, launched attacks with Algerian support. After Mauritania signed a treaty with Polisario Aug. 5, 1979, Morocco occupied Mauritania's portion of Western Sahara.

After years of bitter fighting, Morocco controlled the main urban areas, and Polisario vast, sparsely populated desert areas. The two sides implemented a cease-fire in 1991, when a UN peacekeeping force (MINURSO) was established with a mandate to prepare for a referendum on self-determination as early as 1992. As of Aug. 31, 2018, MINURSO had about 200 personnel in Western Sahara. A referendum had still not been held. Morocco, which left the predecessor of the African Union (AU) in 1984 over recognition of Western Sahara, was readmitted to the AU, Jan. 31, 2017.

Mozambique
Republic of Mozambique

People: Population: 27,233,789 (50). **Age distrib.:** <15: 44.5%; 65+: 2.9%. **Growth:** 2.5%. **Migrants:** 0.8%. **Pop. density:** 89.7 per sq mi, 34.6 per sq km. **Urban:** 36%. **Ethnic groups:** African (incl. Makhuwa, Tsonga, Lomwe, Sena) 99.7%. **Languages:** Emakhuwa, Portuguese (official), Xichangana, Cisena, Elomwe, Echuwabo, other Mozambican langs. **Religions:** Roman Catholic 28.4%, Muslim 17.9%, Zionist Christian 15.5%, Protestant 12.2% (incl. Pentecostal 10.9%), none 18.7%.

Geography: Total area: 308,642 sq mi, 799,380 sq km (34); **Land area:** 303,623 sq mi, 786,380 sq km. **Location:** SE coast of Africa. Tanzania on N; Malawi, Zambia, Zimbabwe on W; South Africa, Swaziland on S. **Topography:** Coastal lowlands comprise nearly half the country with plateaus rising in steps to mountains along western border. **Arable land:** 7.2%. **Capital:** Maputo, 1,101,771. **Cities:** Matola, 1,635,392.

Government: Type: Presidential republic. **Head of state and govt.:** Pres. Filipe Jacinto Nyusi; b. 1959; in office: Jan. 15, 2015. **Local divisions:** 10 provinces, 1 city. **Defense budget:** $91 mil. **Active troops:** 11,200.

Economy: Industries: aluminum, petroleum prods., chemicals, textiles, cement, glass, asbestos, tobacco, food, beverages. **Chief agric.:** cotton, cashew nuts, sugarcane, tea, cassava, corn, coconuts, sisal, citrus and tropical fruits, potatoes, sunflowers; beef, poultry. **Natural resources:** coal, titanium, nat. gas, hydropower, tantalum, graphite. **Water:** 7,760 cu m per capita. **Electricity prod.:** 19.6 bil kWh. **Labor force:** agric. 73.3%, industry 4.3%, services 22.4%. **Unemployment:** 25%.

Finance: Monetary unit: Metical (MZN) (60.21 = $1 U.S.). **GDP:** $36.7 bil; **per capita GDP:** $1,200; **GDP growth:** 3%. **Imports:** $5 bil; South Africa 36.8%, China 7%, UAE 6.8%, India 6.2%. **Exports:** $4.8 bil; India 28.1%, Netherlands 24.4%, South Africa 16.7%. **Tourism:** $151 mil. **Budget:** $3.6 bil. **Inflation:** 15.1%.

Transport: Railways: 2,975 mi. **Motor vehicles:** 3.5 per 1,000 pop. **Airports:** 21.

Communications: Telephone: 0.3 per 100 pop. **Mobile:** 40 per 100 pop. **Broadband:** 49.5 per 100 pop. **Internet:** 17.5%.

Health: Expend.: 5.4%. **Life expect.:** 53.3 male; 54.9 female. **Births:** 37.8 per 1,000 pop. **Deaths:** 11.4 per 1,000 pop. **Infant mortality:** 64.0 per 1,000 live births. **Undernourished:** 30.5%. **HIV:** 12.5%.

Education: Compulsory: ages 6-12. **Literacy:** 58.8%.

Embassy: 1525 New Hampshire Ave. NW 20036; 293-7146.

Website: www.portaldogoverno.gov.mz

The first Portuguese post on the Mozambique coast was established in 1505 on the trade route to Asia. Mozambique became independent June 25, 1975, after a 10-year war against the Portuguese. The 1974 revolution in Portugal paved the way for an orderly transfer of power to Frelimo (Front for the Liberation of Mozambique).

The Frelimo government, headed by Pres. Samora Machel, a former guerrilla commander, gradually transitioned to a Communist system. Most of the country's whites emigrated. In the 1980s, severe drought and civil war caused famine and heavy loss of life. Pres. Machel was killed in a plane crash just inside the South African border, Oct. 19, 1986. Frelimo formally abandoned Marxist-Leninism in 1989, and a new constitution, effective Nov. 30, 1990, established multiparty elections and a free-market economy.

A 1992 peace agreement ended 15 years of hostilities (up to 1 mil killed) between the government and the Mozambique National Resistance (Renamo), which became the main opposition party. Repatriation of 1.7 mil Mozambican refugees ended June 1995.

In Feb.-Mar. 2000, floods killed more than 600 and devastated the economy. Another flood crisis, Jan.-Mar. 2008, left 700 dead and displaced 650,000.

Frelimo retained its hold on power under Pres. Joaquim Chissano (1986-2005) and his successor, Pres. Armando Guebuza (2005-15). Frelimo candidate Filipe Jacinto Nyusi won the Oct. 15,

2014, presidential election, and the party won legislative elections the same day. Clashes began in 2013 between government forces and Renamo, which challenged 2014 election results. A truce beginning Dec. 2016 paved the way for Frelimo-Renamo negotiations that led to May 2018 constitutional amendments decentralizing political power.

Natural gas reserves are estimated at 100 tril cu ft (third-largest in Africa). Beginning Oct. 2017, Islamist militants staged a series of attacks in the gas-rich Cabo Delgado region.

Myanmar
(Burma)
Union of Myanmar

People: Population: 55,622,506 (24). **Age distrib.:** <15: 26.6%; 65+: 5.7%. **Growth:** 0.9%. **Migrants:** 0.1%. **Pop. density:** 220.4 per sq mi, 85.1 per sq km. **Urban:** 30.6%. **Ethnic groups:** Burman (Bamar) 68%, Shan 9%, Karen 7%, Rakhine 4%, Chinese 3%, Indian 2%, Mon 2%. **Languages:** Burmese (official). **Religions:** Buddhist 87.9%, Christian 6.2%, Muslim 4.3%.

Geography: Total area: 261,228 sq mi, 676,578 sq km (39). **Land area:** 252,321 sq mi, 653,508 sq km. **Location:** Between S and SE Asia, on Bay of Bengal. Bangladesh, India on W; China, Laos, Thailand on E. **Topography:** Surrounding mountains on W, N, and E. Dense forests cover much of nation. N-S rivers provide habitable valleys, especially the Irrawaddy, navigable for 900 mi. Tropical monsoon climate. **Arable land:** 16.7%. **Capital:** Yangon (Rangoon), 5,157,461; Nay Pyi Taw (admin.), 500,218. **Cities:** Mandalay, 1,374,061.

Government: Type: Parliamentary republic. **Head of state and govt.:** Pres. Win Myint; b. 1951; in office: Mar. 30, 2018. **Local divisions:** 7 regions, 7 states, 1 union territory. **Defense budget:** $2.1 bil. **Active troops:** 406,000.

Economy: Industries: agric. proc.; wood/wood prods.; copper, tin, tungsten, iron; cement, constr. materials; pharmaceuticals, fertilizer. **Chief agric.:** rice, pulses, beans, sesame, groundnuts, sugarcane; fish. **Natural resources:** petroleum, timber, tin, antimony, zinc, copper, tungsten, lead, coal, marble, limestone, prec. stones, nat. gas, hydropower. **Water:** 21,671 cu m per capita. **Crude oil reserves:** 139 mil bbls. **Electricity prod.:** 15.5 bil kWh. **Labor force:** agric. 49.9%, industry 16.6%, services 33.5%. **Unemployment:** 0.8%.

Finance: Monetary unit: Kyat (MMK) (1,536.75 = $1 U.S.). **GDP:** $328.7 bil; **per capita GDP:** $6,200; **GDP growth:** 6.7%. **Imports:** $15.3 bil; China 31.4%, Singapore 15%, Thailand 11.1%, Saudi Arabia 7.5%, Malaysia 6.2%, Japan 6%, India 5.5%. **Exports:** $10.1 bil. China 36.5%, Thailand 21.8%, Japan 6.6%, Singapore 6.4%, India 5.9%. Trade figures are underestimates due to value of goods smuggled in from Thailand, China, Malaysia, India and smuggled out to Thailand, China, Bangladesh. **Tourism:** $2.2 bil. **Budget:** $11.5 bil. **Inflation:** 4.6%.

Transport: Railways: 3,126 mi. **Motor vehicles:** 0.7 per 1,000 pop. **Airports:** 36.

Communications: Telephone: 1 per 100 pop. **Mobile:** 89.8 per 100 pop. **Broadband:** 47.6 per 100 pop. **Internet:** 25.1%.

Health: Expend.: 4.9%. **Life expect.:** 67.0 male; 70.3 female. **Births:** 17.7 per 1,000 pop. **Deaths:** 7.3 per 1,000 pop. **Infant mortality:** 34.4 per 1,000 live births. **Undernourished:** 10.5%. **HIV:** 0.7%.

Education: Compulsory: ages 5-9. **Literacy:** 75.6%.

Embassy: 2300 S St. NW 20008; 332-3344.

Website: www.president-office.gov.mm

The Burmese arrived from Tibet before the 9th cent., displacing earlier cultures, and a Buddhist monarchy was established by the 11th cent. Burma was conquered by China's Mongol dynasty in 1272, then ruled by the Shan people as a Chinese tributary until the 16th cent. Britain subjugated Burma in three wars, 1824-84, and ruled the country as part of India until 1937, when Burma became self-governing. Full independence was achieved Jan. 4, 1948.

Gen. Ne Win dominated politics from 1962 to 1988, first as military ruler, then as constitutional president, advancing policies that increased economic socialization and international isolation. In 1987, the UN granted Burma, once the richest nation in SE Asia, less-developed status. Ne Win resigned July 1988, following anti-government riots. In Sept., the military seized power, under Gen. Saw Maung. In 1989 the country's name was changed to Myanmar.

Although the main opposition party won a decisive victory in 1990 multiparty elections, the military refused to surrender power. A key opposition leader, Aung San Suu Kyi, was held under house arrest, 1989-95, 2000-02, and 2003-10. The regime's poor human rights record and continued harassment of Suu Kyi and her supporters led to U.S.-imposed sanctions.

In late Sept. 2007, thousands of Buddhist monks led mass protests in Yangon; security forces cracked down by raiding monasteries, arresting monks, and firing on demonstrators. Cyclone Nargis, May 2-3, 2008, killed more than 138,000.

After the military dominated Nov. 2010 parliamentary elections, the ruling council was dissolved and an initially nominal civilian government returned, Mar. 30, 2011. Suu Kyi's National League for Democracy (NLD) won 43 of 45 parliamentary seats in an Apr. 1, 2012, election, and Suu Kyi traveled to Oslo, Norway, to accept the Nobel Peace Prize (awarded in absentia in 1991). The EU, Apr. 23,

and U.S., May 17, suspended most sanctions. The NLD won Nov. 8, 2015, parliamentary elections. Htin Kyaw of the NLD was elected president by the parliament, Mar. 15, 2016. Suu Kyi, constitutionally barred from the presidency, assumed the newly created post of state counsellor, Apr. 6, 2016, becoming the country's de facto leader. The U.S. announced, Sept. 14, 2016, that it would lift all remaining sanctions. Win Myint replaced Htin Kyaw as president in Mar. 2018. Fighting intensified in 2018 between government forces and rebels in northern Kachin state.

Violence against Rohingya Muslims in the NW intensified beginning in 2012. Almost all of Myanmar's more than 1 mil Rohingya are not recognized as citizens by the government, which by 2017 was confining about 120,000 in camps. Almost 100,000 Rohingya fled by boat, 2014-15, seeking asylum in other SE Asian countries. Attacks by the military beginning in Oct. 2016 (after Rohingya insurgents killed nine police officers) left hundreds of civilians dead and caused about 75,000 Rohingya to flee to Bangladesh by early 2017. Insurgent assaults, Aug. 25, 2017, on police and military outposts that killed 15 security officers led to new military and vigilante attacks on Rohingya. Hundreds of villages were burned, at least 10,000 were killed, and hundreds of thousands fled to Bangladesh (more than 727,000 Aug. 25, 2017-Sept. 15, 2018.) A UN panel recommended, Aug. 27, 2018, that Myanmar military leaders face trial for genocide.

Namibia
Republic of Namibia

People: Population: 2,533,224 (139). **Age distrib.:** <15: 36.5%; 65+: 3.9%. **Growth:** 1.9%. **Migrants:** 3.8%. **Pop. density:** 8 per sq mi, 3.1 per sq km. **Urban:** 50%. **Ethnic groups:** black 87.5%, white 6%, mixed 6.5%. Ovambo tribe about 50% of pop.; Kavangos tribe 9%. **Languages:** Oshiwambo langs., Nama/Damara, Afrikaans (common), Otjiherero langs., Kavango langs., Caprivi langs., English (official). **Religions:** Christian 80%-90% (Lutheran 50%+), indigenous beliefs 10%-20%.

Geography: Total area: 318,261 sq mi, 824,292 sq km (33). **Land area:** 317,874 sq mi, 823,290 sq km. **Location:** Southern Africa on Atlantic coast. Angola on N; Botswana, Zambia on E; South Africa on S. **Topography:** Three distinct regions incl. Namib Desert along the Atlantic, a mountainous central plateau with woodland savanna, and Kalahari Desert in E. True forests found in NE. Four rivers but little other surface water. **Arable land:** 1%. **Capital:** Windhoek, 404,280.

Government: Type: Presidential republic. **Head of state and govt.:** Pres. Hage Geingob; b. 1941; in office: Mar. 21, 2015. **Local divisions:** 14 regions. **Defense budget:** $415 mil. **Active troops:** 9,900.

Economy: Industries: meatpacking, fish proc., dairy prods., pasta, beverages, mining. **Chief agric.:** millet, sorghum, peanuts, grapes; livestock; fish. **Natural resources:** diamonds, copper, uranium, gold, silver, lead, tin, lithium, cadmium, tungsten, zinc, salt, hydropower, fish. **Water:** 16,230 cu m per capita. **Electricity prod.:** 1.5 bil kWh. **Labor force:** agric. 20.2%, industry 19.6%, services 60.2%. **Unemployment:** 23.3%.

Finance: Monetary unit: Dollar (NAD) (15.34 = $1 U.S.). **GDP:** $26.5 bil; **per capita GDP:** $11,300; **GDP growth:** –1.2%. **Imports:** $6.8 bil; South Africa 61.4%. **Exports:** $4.7 bil; South Africa 27.1%, Botswana 14.9%, Switzerland 12%, Zambia 5.7%. **Tourism:** $188 mil. **Budget:** $4.8 bil. **Inflation:** 6.1%.

Transport: Railways: 1,633 mi. **Motor vehicles:** 117.8 per 1,000 pop. **Airports:** 19.

Communications: Telephone: 7.6 per 100 pop. **Mobile:** 104.5 per 100 pop. **Broadband:** 66.1 per 100 pop. **Internet:** 31%.

Health: Expend.: 8.9%. **Life expect.:** 62.7 male; 66.2 female. **Births:** 26.8 per 1,000 pop. **Deaths:** 7.7 per 1,000 pop. **Infant mortality:** 33.8 per 1,000 live births. **Undernourished:** 25.4%. **HIV:** 12.1%.

Education: Compulsory: ages 7-13. **Literacy:** 81.9%.

Embassy: 1605 New Hampshire Ave. NW 20009; 986-0540.

Website: www.gov.na

Namibia was declared a German protectorate in 1890 and officially called South-West Africa. German troops putting down a rebellion killed tens of thousands of Herero and Nama people, 1904-08. South Africa seized the territory in 1915 during WWI. In 1966, the Marxist South-West Africa People's Organization (SWAPO) launched a guerrilla war for independence, aided by Angola and Cuba. The UN General Assembly named the area Namibia in 1968.

South Africa, Angola, and Cuba signed a U.S.-mediated agreement Dec. 22, 1988, to end South African administration of Namibia and provide for a cease-fire and transition to independence, in accordance with a 1978 UN plan. A constitution providing for multiparty government was adopted Feb. 9, 1990, and Namibia gained independence Mar. 21.

Walvis Bay, the principal deepwater port, under South African administration since 1922, was returned to Namibia in 1994. Separatist violence flared in the Caprivi Strip in the late 1990s. SWAPO, the leading political group since independence, dominated presidential and parliamentary elections, Nov. 28, 2014. Herero and Nama representatives initiated a lawsuit, Jan. 5, 2017, against Germany, seeking damages for the early 1900s genocide.

SPORTS

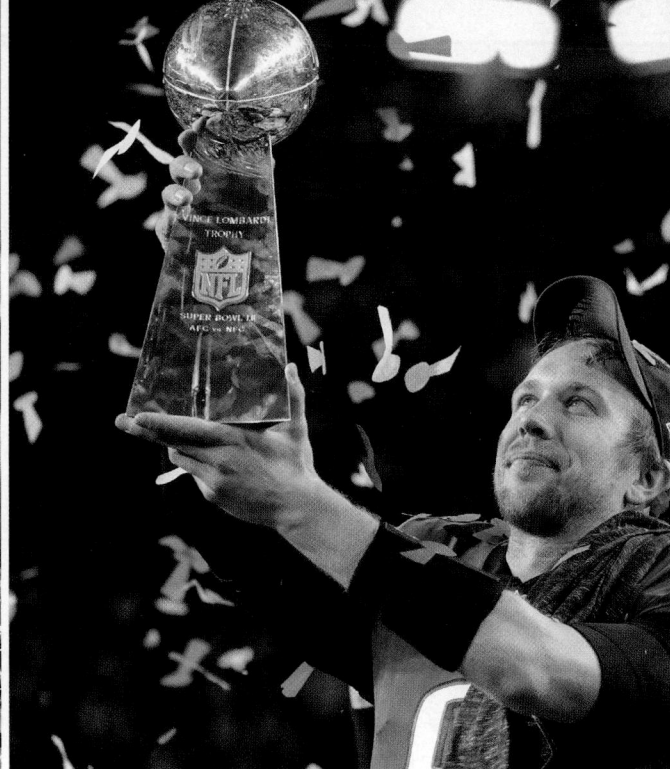

PLAN B Backup quarterback Tua Tagovailoa led Alabama to a second-half comeback and 26-23 victory over Georgia in the NCAA's College Football Playoff national championship game Jan. 8, 2018.

PHILADELPHIA'S FIRST Quarterback Nick Foles led the Philadelphia Eagles to the franchise's first-ever Super Bowl win, claiming the title, 41-33, over the New England Patriots Feb. 4, 2018.

FIGHTING TO WIN Arike Ogunbowale and her Notre Dame teammates defeated Mississippi St., 61-58, to claim the school's second NCAA Women's Basketball Championship Apr. 1, 2018

TITLE DEFENDED Japan's Yuzuru Hanyu won his second straight men's figure skating gold medal Feb. 17, 2018, at the Winter Olympic Games in Pyeongchang, South Korea.

SPORTS

TWO OUT OF THREE Villanova's Donte DiVincenzo claimed most outstanding player of the men's Final Four as the Wildcats defeated Michigan Apr. 2, 2018, to capture the team's second NCAA men's basketball title in three years.

THREE OUT OF FOUR For the third time since 2015, Golden State defeated Cleveland in the NBA Finals; Kevin Durant claimed the Finals MVP trophy June 8, 2018, for the second year in a row.

WORTH THE WAIT Alex Ovechkin and the Washington Capitals defeated the upstart Vegas Golden Knights in Game 5, June 7, 2018, to win the Caps' first Stanley Cup.

TRIPLE CROWN CAPTURED Justify, along with jockey Mike Smith, claimed the win in the Belmont Stakes June 9, 2018, and with it horse racing's Triple Crown.

WELL RESTED After taking nearly two years off following her gold medal-winning performance at the 2016 Olympic Games, gymnast Simone Biles won her record fifth U.S. national title Aug. 19, 2018.

LES BLEUS WIN France's Olivier Giroud and Kylian Mbappé celebrated their team's victory over Croatia, 4-2, July 15, 2018, in the final match of the 2018 FIFA Men's World Cup soccer tournament in Russia.

ROLE MODELS Athletes Sarah Klein, Tiffany Thomas Lopez, and Aly Raisman were among dozens of survivors of sexual abuse by convicted Michigan St. physician Larry Nassar honored for their courageous testimony at the ESPY Awards July 18, 2018.

OUT OF COURT Naomi Osaka won the U.S. Open women's singles title easily over Serena Williams Sept. 8, 2018, but more attention was paid to an altercation between Williams and an umpire than Osaka's first Grand Slam win.

ARTS

IN THE *BLACK* Chadwick Boseman and Michael B. Jordan starred in Marvel's *Black Panther*, which grossed $1.3 billion worldwide after opening Feb. 16, 2018.

"THAT'S WHAT I LIKE" Singer Bruno Mars (performing here with breakout star Cardi B) took home six Grammy Awards Jan. 28, 2018, including the year's best song, record, and album.

SHOW BUSINESS The revival of sitcom *Roseanne* was a ratings win for ABC, but it was canceled May 29, 2018, after its titular star tweeted a racist remark; a spinoff aimed to replicate that success without her.

BIG TIME Korean pop group BTS became the first K-pop act to have a No. 1 album on the Billboard 200 in May 2018.

EXCLUSIVE CLUB Tim Rice, John Legend, and Andrew Lloyd Webber claimed Emmys Sept. 9, 2018, and became 3 of just 15 career "EGOT" winners—entertainers who had won an Emmy, Grammy, Oscar, and Tony.

PEOPLE

TAKE YOUR DAUGHTER TO WORK Sen. Tammy Duckworth (D, IL) became the first U.S. senator to give birth while in office in Apr. 2018.

REAL AMERICAN HERO A Nashville police spokesperson called James Shaw Jr. a hero who "no doubt ... saved many lives" when he disarmed a gunman at a Tennessee Waffle House restaurant Apr. 22, 2018.

HOT AND COLD Tesla and SpaceX CEO Elon Musk drew attention for his companies' successes and for his sometimes-erratic behavior; he agreed Sept. 29, 2018, to pay a $20-million fine to settle charges that he misled investors in an Aug. tweet.

REAL-LIFE FAIRY TALE The UK's Prince Harry and American actress Meghan Markle were married at Windsor Castle near London, England, May 19, 2018.

FAREWELL

KOFI ANNAN
Apr. 8, 1938-Aug. 18, 2018

AVICII
Sept. 8, 1989-Apr. 20, 2018

ROGER BANNISTER
Mar. 23, 1929-Mar. 3, 2018

ANTHONY BOURDAIN
June 25, 1956-June 8, 2018

LINDA BROWN
Feb. 20, 1943-Mar. 25, 2018

BARBARA BUSH
June 8, 1925-Apr. 17, 2018

FATS DOMINO
Feb. 26, 1928-Oct. 24, 2017

ARETHA FRANKLIN
Mar. 25, 1942-Aug. 16, 2018

BILLY GRAHAM
Nov. 7, 1918-Feb. 21, 2018

STEPHEN HAWKING
Jan. 8, 1942-Mar. 14, 2018

TAB HUNTER
July 11, 1931-July 8, 2018

MARGOT KIDDER
Oct. 17, 1948-May 13, 2018

URSULA K. LE GUIN
Oct. 21, 1929-Jan. 22, 2018

JOHN MAHONEY
June 20, 1940-Feb. 4, 2018

WINNIE MANDELA
Sept. 26, 1936-Apr. 2, 2018

JOHN MCCAIN
Aug. 29, 1936-Aug. 25, 2018

STAN MIKITA
May 20, 1940-Aug. 7, 2018

V. S. NAIPAUL
Aug. 17, 1932-Aug. 11, 2018

CHARLOTTE RAE
Apr. 22, 1926-Aug. 5, 2018

BURT REYNOLDS
Feb. 11, 1936-Sept. 6, 2018

PHILIP ROTH
Mar. 19, 1933-May 22, 2018

NEIL SIMON
July 4, 1927-Aug. 26, 2018

KATE SPADE
Dec. 24, 1962-June 5, 2018

TOM WOLFE
Mar. 2, 1930-May 14, 2018

TWO OF A KIND Chinese researchers announced Jan. 24, 2018, that they had successfully cloned monkeys using the same cloning technique that created Dolly the sheep, proving the process could be used for primates.

LIFE CHANGING A major report released Oct. 8, 2018, by the UN's Intergovernmental Panel on Climate Change warned of dire consequences of global warming caused by greenhouse gases—such as food shortages, wildfires, flooded coastlines, and intense drought—by as early as 2040.

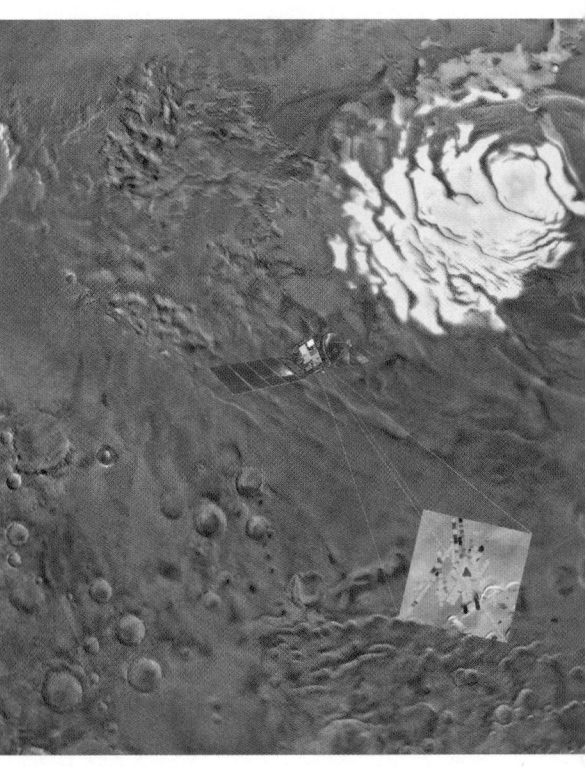

SPACE RACER SpaceX's long-anticipated Falcon Heavy rocket debuted Feb. 6, 2018, by launching its test payload, a Tesla Roadster, into space.

UNCHARTED WATERS An article published July 25, 2018, provided the best evidence yet of lake of liquid water on Mars.

Nauru
Republic of Nauru

People: Population: 9,692 (195). **Age distrib.:** <15: 31.2%; 65+: 2.9%. **Growth:** 0.5%. **Migrants:** 32.7%. **Pop. density:** 1,195.3 per sq mi, 461.5 per sq km. **Urban:** 100%. **Ethnic groups:** Nauruan 58%, other Pac. Islander 26%, Chinese 8%, European 8%. **Languages:** Nauruan (official), English (used in govt. and commerce). **Religions:** Protestant 60.4% (incl. Nauru Congregational 35.7%, Assembly of God 13%), Roman Catholic 33%.

Geography: Total area: 8.1 sq mi, 21 sq km (194); **Land area:** 8.1 sq mi, 21 sq km. **Location:** In W Pacific O. just S of equator. Nearest neighbor is Kiribati to E. **Topography:** Mostly a plateau bearing high-grade phosphate deposits, surrounded by a sandy shore and coral reef in concentric rings. **Arable land:** 0%. **Capital:** None official; govt. offices in Yaren district.

Government: Type: Parliamentary republic. **Head of state and govt.:** Pres. Baron Waqa; b. 1959; in office: June 11, 2013. **Local divisions:** 14 districts. **Defense budget/active troops:** NA.

Economy: Industries: phosphate mining, offshore banking, coconut prods. **Chief agric.:** coconuts. **Natural resources:** phosphates, fish. **Water:** NA. **Electricity prod.:** 25 mil kWh. **Labor force:** phosphate mining, public admin., education, transportation. **Unemployment:** NA.

Finance: Monetary unit: Australian Dollar (AUD) (1.39 = $1 U.S.). **GDP:** $159 mil; **per capita GDP:** $12,200; **GDP growth:** 4%. **Imports** (2013): $143.1 mil; Australia 67.5%, Fiji 9.2%, India 8.1%, Singapore 5.4%. **Exports** (2013): $125 mil; Nigeria 38.6%, Japan 16.6%, Australia 15.9%, South Korea 13.7%, New Zealand 5.7%. **Budget:** $113.4 mil. **Inflation:** 5.1%.

Transport: Airports: 1.

Communications: Telephone: NA. **Mobile** (2016): 87.2 per 100 pop. **Broadband:** NA. **Internet** (2011): 54%.

Health: Expend.: 4.8%. **Life expect.:** 63.6 male; 71.2 female. **Births:** 23.2 per 1,000 pop. **Deaths:** 5.9 per 1,000 pop. **Infant mortality:** 7.7 per 1,000 live births. **Undernourished:** NA. **HIV:** NA.

Education: Compulsory: ages 4-17. **Literacy:** NA.

Permanent UN mission: 801 2nd Ave., 3rd Fl., New York, NY 10017; (212) 937-0074.

Website: www.naurugov.nr

The British reached the island in 1798, but it was annexed to the German Empire in 1886. After WWI, Australia administered Nauru under a League of Nations mandate. Japan occupied the island during WWII. In 1947 Nauru was made a UN trust territory, administered by Australia. It became an independent republic Jan. 31, 1968.

Phosphate exports provided Nauru with high per capita revenues. Phosphate reserves, however, are nearly depleted, and environmental damage from strip mining has been severe. Rising sea levels linked to global climate change have eroded Nauru's coastline.

A Nov. 20, 2012, Amnesty Intl. report found inhumane living conditions at Australia's detention center on Nauru for refugees and undocumented immigrants intercepted trying to enter Australia by boat. An Australian government report, released Mar. 20, 2015, confirmed allegations of sexual and physical abuse of detainees by staff. Under a 2016 Australia-U.S. resettlement agreement, more than 260 refugees had left Nauru for the U.S. as of July 2018. As of Aug. 31, 2018, 173 refugees remained in the detention center. About 700 lived elsewhere in Nauru.

Nepal
Federal Democratic Republic of Nepal

People: Population: 29,717,587 (47). **Age distrib.:** <15: 29.5%; 65+: 5.3%. **Growth:** 1.1%. **Migrants:** 1.7%. **Pop. density:** 536.9 per sq mi, 207.3 per sq km. **Urban:** 19.7%. **Ethnic groups:** Chhettri 16.6%, Brahman-Hill 12.2%, Magar 7.1%, Tharu 6.6%, Tamang 5.8%, Newar 5%, Kami 4.8%, Muslim 4.4%, Yadav 4%, Rai 2.3%, Gurung 2%. **Languages:** Nepali (official), Maithali, Bhojpuri, Tharu, Tamang, Newar, Magar, Bajjika, Urdu. **Religions:** Hindu 81.3%, Buddhist 9%, Muslim 4.4%, Kirant 3.1%.

Geography: Total area: 56,827 sq mi, 147,181 sq km (93); **Land area:** 55,348 sq mi, 143,351 sq km. **Location:** Astride Himalaya Mts. China on N, India on S. **Topography:** The Himalayas across the N, hill country with fertile valleys across the center. S border region is part of flat, subtropical Ganges Plain. **Arable land:** 14.7%. **Capital:** Kathmandu, 1,329,732.

Government: Type: Federal parliamentary republic. **Head of state:** Pres. Bidhya Devi Bhandari; b. 1961; in office: Oct. 29, 2015. **Head of govt.:** Prime Min. KP Sharma Oli; b. 1952; in office: Feb. 15, 2018. **Local divisions:** 14 zones. **Defense budget:** $330 mil. **Active troops:** 96,600.

Economy: Industries: tourism, carpets, textiles; small rice, jute, sugar, oilseed mills; cigarettes, cement, brick prod. **Chief agric.:** pulses, rice, corn, wheat, sugarcane, jute, root crops; milk, water buffalo meat. **Natural resources:** quartz, water, timber, hydropower, lignite, copper, cobalt, iron ore. **Water:** 7,372 cu m per capita. **Electricity prod.:** 3.5 bil kWh. **Labor force:** agric. 71.7%, industry 8.1%, services 20.2%. **Unemployment:** 2.7%.

Finance: Monetary unit: Rupee (NPR) (115.03 = $1 U.S.). **GDP:** $78.6 bil; **per capita GDP:** $2,700; **GDP growth:** 7.5%. **Imports:** $11 bil; India 70.2%, China 7.5%. **Exports:** $818.7 mil; India 53.1%, U.S. 11.8%, Turkey 7.2%. **Tourism:** $630 mil. **Budget:** $8 bil. **Inflation:** 3.2%.

Transport: Railways: 33 mi. **Airports:** 11.

Communications: Telephone: 2.9 per 100 pop. **Mobile:** 123.2 per 100 pop. **Broadband:** 30.8 per 100 pop. **Internet:** 19.7%.

Health: Expend.: 6.1%. **Life expect.:** 70.6 male; 72.0 female. **Births:** 19.1 per 1,000 pop. **Deaths:** 5.6 per 1,000 pop. **Infant mortality:** 26.9 per 1,000 live births. **Undernourished:** 9.5%. **HIV:** 0.2%.

Education: Compulsory: NA. **Literacy:** 63.9%.

Embassy: 2131 Leroy Pl. NW 20008; 667-4550.

Website: nepal.gov.np

Nepal was originally a group of principalities, with the Gurkha principality becoming dominant about 1769. In 1951 King Tribhubana Bir Bikram, member of the Shah family, ended the system of rule by hereditary premiers of the Ranas family, who had kept the kings virtual prisoners, and established a cabinet system of government. Polygamy, child marriage, and the caste system were officially abolished in 1963. Political parties were legalized in 1990.

Nine members of Nepal's royal family, including King Birendra and Queen Aishwarya, died in a June 1, 2001, massacre. The killings were blamed on a 10th family member, Crown Prince Dipendra, who reportedly shot himself that night and died 3 days later, allowing Birendra's brother Gyanendra Bir Bikram Shah Dev to take the throne.

Citing the government's failure to stop a Maoist insurgency, King Gyanendra assumed absolute authority, Feb. 1, 2005, but after protests, he agreed, Apr. 24, 2006, to reinstate parliament. A new government, led by Prime Min. Girija Prasad Koirala, signed a peace accord with Maoist rebels Nov. 21 ending a decade-long civil war that claimed 13,000 lives. Maoists joined an interim parliament Jan. 2007 and entered the cabinet Apr. 1. A constituent assembly voted May 2008 to abolish the monarchy and make Nepal a republic. Maoist Baburam Bhattarai became prime min. Aug. 29, 2011. Bhattarai dissolved parliament May 27, 2012, when the deadline for a new constitution passed. Maoists suffered a defeat in Nov. 19, 2013, elections, in which moderate parties won the largest blocs.

The new constitution, establishing a federal system with seven states, was adopted Sept. 20, 2015. Protests beginning in Sept., largely by ethnic and religious groups fearing loss of autonomy, left more than 40 people dead. Khadga Prasad Sharma Oli, leader of a non-Maoist Communist party, was elected prime min. by parliament, Oct. 11, 2015. Bidhya Devi Bhandari (of Oli's party) was elected by parliament, Oct. 28, 2015, as Nepal's first female president. Oli, facing a no-confidence vote, announced his resignation, July 23, 2016. After a coalition of Communist parties won late 2017 legislative elections, Oli returned as prime min., Feb. 15, 2018.

A magnitude 7.8 earthquake near Kathmandu, Apr. 25, 2015, killed more than 8,000 people and displaced 2.8 mil. Historic temples and other sites were heavily damaged. A second quake, May 12, brought the combined death toll to over 8,600.

Netherlands
Kingdom of the Netherlands

People: Population: 17,151,228 (66). **Age distrib.:** <15: 16.3%; 65+: 19.1%. **Growth:** 0.4%. **Migrants:** 12.1%. **Pop. density:** 1,310.6 per sq mi, 506 per sq km. **Urban:** 91.5%. **Ethnic groups:** Dutch 77.4%, EU 6.2%, Turkish 2.3%, Moroccan 2.3%, Indonesian 2.1%, Surinamese 2%. **Languages:** Dutch (official). **Religions:** Roman Catholic 23.7%, Protestant 15.5% (incl. Dutch Reformed 6.5%), Islam 4.9%, none 50.1%.

Geography: Total area: 16,040 sq mi, 41,543 sq km (131); **Land area:** 13,086 sq mi, 33,893 sq km. **Location:** NW Europe on North Sea. Germany on E, Belgium on S. **Topography:** Land is flat with avg. elevation of 37 ft above sea level; much of land reclaimed and protected by some 1,500 mi of dikes. **Arable land:** 30.7%. **Capital:** Amsterdam, 1,131,690; s-Gravenhage (The Hague) (seat), 685,140. **Cities:** Rotterdam, 1,007,780.

Government: Type: Parliamentary constitutional monarchy. **Head of state:** King Willem-Alexander; b. 1967; in office: Apr. 30, 2013. **Head of govt.:** Prime Min. Mark Rutte; b. 1967; in office: Oct. 14, 2010. **Local divisions:** 12 provinces. **Defense budget:** $10.1 bil. **Active troops:** 35,410.

Economy: Industries: agroindustries, metal/engineering prods., elec. machinery/equip., chemicals. **Chief agric.:** vegetables, ornamentals, dairy, poultry and livestock prods. **Natural resources:** nat. gas, petroleum, peat, limestone, salt, sand and gravel. **Water:** 5,377 cu m per capita. **Crude oil reserves:** 81.1 mil bbls. **Electricity prod.:** 104.3 bil kWh. **Labor force:** agric. 2.2%, industry 16.5%, services 81.3%. **Unemployment:** 4.8%.

Finance: Monetary unit: Euro (EUR) (0.86 = $1 U.S.). **GDP:** $916.1 bil; **per capita GDP:** $53,600; **GDP growth:** 3.1%. **Imports:** $435.4 bil; China 16.4%, Germany 15.3%, Belgium 8.5%, U.S. 6.9%, UK 5.1%. **Exports:** $526.4 bil; Germany 24.2%, Belgium 10.7%, UK 8.8%, France 8.8%. **Tourism:** $15.9 bil. **Budget:** $342.3 bil. **Inflation:** 1.4%.

Transport: Railways: 1,900 mi. **Motor vehicles:** 568.7 per 1,000 pop. **Airports:** 23.

Communications: Telephone: 38.5 per 100 pop. **Mobile:** 120.5 per 100 pop. **Broadband:** 87.8 per 100 pop. **Internet** (2017): 93.2%.

Health: Expend.: 10.7%. **Life expect.:** 79.3 male; 83.8 female. **Births:** 10.9 per 1,000 pop. **Deaths:** 9.0 per 1,000 pop.

Infant mortality: 3.5 per 1,000 live births. **Undernourished:** <2.5%. **HIV:** 0.2%.

Education: Compulsory: ages 5-16. **Literacy:** 99%.

Embassy: 4200 Linnean Ave. NW 20008; 244-5300.

Website: www.government.nl

Julius Caesar conquered the region in 55 BCE, when it was inhabited by Celtic and Germanic tribes. After the empire of Charlemagne fell apart, the Netherlands (Holland, Belgium, Flanders) split among counts, dukes, and bishops, passed to Burgundy and thence to Spain. William the Silent, prince of Orange, led a confederation of the northern provinces, called Estates, in the Union of Utrecht, 1579; in 1581 they repudiated allegiance to Spain. The rise of the Dutch republic to naval, economic, and artistic eminence came in the 17th cent.

After a period of French hegemony, 1795-1813, the Congress of Vienna in 1815 formed a kingdom of the Netherlands, including Belgium, under William I. In 1830, Belgium seceded.

The Netherlands maintained its neutrality in WWI but was invaded during WWII and occupied by Germany, 1940-45. In 1949, after several years of fighting, the Netherlands granted independence to Indonesia.

The murder May 6, 2002, of right-wing populist leader Pim Fortuyn marked the first political assassination in modern Dutch history. Filmmaker Theo van Gogh was killed by an Islamic extremist Nov. 2, 2004. On Apr. 30, 2009, an attempted assassination of Queen Beatrix and other royal family members resulted in the deaths of 7 bystanders and the would-be assassin. Beatrix, 75, abdicated the throne to her son, Willem-Alexander, Apr. 30, 2013. A Malaysia Airlines flight from Amsterdam to Kuala Lumpur was shot down over eastern Ukraine, July 17, 2014; nearly 200 Dutch passport holders were among 298 killed. Prime Min. Mark Rutte's center-right People's Party won the most seats in Mar. 15, 2017, parliamentary elections, holding off a challenge from the anti-Islamic, right-wing Freedom Party, headed by Geert Wilders. Legislation to prohibit wearing face-covering garments, such as the burqa, in public facilities including schools and hospitals won final parliamentary approval in June 2018.

Dutch Dependencies

Constitutional changes effective Oct. 10, 2010, dissolved the political entity known as the Netherlands Antilles. **Curaçao** (area 171 sq mi), an island near the coast of Venezuela, and **Sint Maarten** (13 sq mi), occupying the southern one-third of the island of St. Martin, SE of Puerto Rico, were elevated to the status of autonomous countries. Bonaire, Saba, and Sint Eustatius became special municipalities. Sint Maarten suffered extensive damage from Hurricane Luis, Sept. 1995, and Hurricane Irma, Sept. 2017. Pop. of Curaçao, 150,241 (2018 est.); that of its capital, Willemstad, 144,037 (2018 est.). Sint Maarten, pop. 42,677 (2018 est.); capital is Philipsburg. Principal industries: Curaçao, tourism, petroleum refining and transshipment, light mfg.; Sint Maarten, tourism. International tourism receipts in 2017 were $551 mil for Curaçao, $630 mil for Sint Maarten. Per capita GDP of Sint Maarten was $66,800 (2014 est.). **Websites:** www.gobiernu.cw (Curaçao); www.sintmaartengov.org (Sint Maarten)

Aruba, about 26 mi west of Curaçao, was separated from the Netherlands Antilles on Jan. 1, 1986; it is an autonomous component of the Netherlands, with a status similar to Curaçao and Sint Maarten. Area: 69 sq mi; pop. (2018 est.) 116,576. Capital: Oranjestad; pop. (2018 est.) 29,877. Chief industries are tourism, petroleum transshipment facilities, banking. International tourism receipts in 2017 were $1.7 bil. **Website:** www.kabga.aw

New Zealand

People: Population: 4,545,627 (125). **Age distrib.:** <15: 19.6%; 65+: 15.6%. **Growth:** 0.8%. **Migrants:** 22.7%. **Pop. density:** 44.5 per sq mi, 17.2 per sq km. **Urban:** 86.5%. **Ethnic groups:** European 71.2%, Maori 14.1%, Asian 11.3%, Pacific peoples 7.6%. Respondents could identify more than one ethnic group. **Languages:** English (de facto official), Maori (de jure official), Samoan. **Religions:** Christian 44.3% (incl. Catholic 11.6%, Anglican 10.8%), no religion 38.5%.

Geography: Total area: 103,799 sq mi, 268,838 sq km (75); **Land area:** 102,138 sq mi, 264,537 sq km. **Location:** SW Pacific O. Nearest neighbors are Australia to W, Fiji and Tonga to N. **Topography:** Two main islands (North and South Isls.) are hilly and mountainous. The E coasts consist of fertile plains, incl. Canterbury Plains on South Isl. Volcanic plateau in center of North Isl. Glaciers and 15 peaks over 10,000 ft on South Isl. **Arable land:** 2.2%. **Capital:** Wellington, 411,346. **Cities:** Auckland, 1,556,875.

Government: Type: Parliamentary democracy under constitutional monarchy. **Head of state:** Queen Elizabeth II, rep. by Gov.-Gen. Patricia Lee Reddy; b. 1954; in office: Sept. 28, 2016. **Head of govt.:** Prime Min. Jacinda Ardern; b. 1980; in office: Oct. 26, 2017. **Local divisions:** 16 regions, 1 territory. **Defense budget:** $2.5 bil. **Active troops:** 9,000.

Economy: Industries: agric., forestry, fishing, logs and wood prods., mfg., mining, constr., financial services, real estate services, tourism. **Chief agric.:** dairy prods., sheep, beef, poultry, fruit, vegetables, wine, seafood, wheat, barley. **Natural resources:** nat. gas, iron ore, sand, coal, timber, hydropower, gold, limestone. **Water:** 72,201 cu m per capita. **Crude oil**

reserves: 51.8 mil bbls. **Electricity prod.:** 42.9 bil kWh. **Labor force:** agric. 6.6%, industry 20.2%, services 73.1%. **Unemployment:** 4.9%.

Finance: Monetary unit: Dollar (NZD) (1.53 = $1 U.S.). **GDP:** $188.6 bil; **per capita GDP:** $38,900; **GDP growth:** 3%. **Imports:** $38.7 bil; China 19%, Australia 12.1%, U.S. 10.5%, Japan 7.3%, Germany 5.3%. **Exports:** $37.4 bil; China 22.4%, Australia 16.4%, U.S. 9.9%, Japan 6.1%. **Tourism:** $10.3 bil. **Budget:** $71.9 bil. **Inflation:** 1.9%.

Transport: Railways: 2,565 mi. **Motor vehicles:** 902.3 per 1,000 pop. **Airports:** 39.

Communications: Telephone: 29.1 per 100 pop. **Mobile:** 136 per 100 pop. **Broadband:** 101.3 per 100 pop. **Internet:** 88.5%.

Health: Expend.: 9.3%. **Life expect.:** 79.2 male; 83.6 female. **Births:** 13.1 per 1,000 pop. **Deaths:** 7.6 per 1,000 pop. **Infant mortality:** 4.4 per 1,000 live births. **Undernourished:** <2.5%. **HIV:** 0.1%.

Education: Compulsory: ages 6-15. **Literacy:** 99%.

Embassy: 37 Observatory Cir. NW 20008; 328-4800.

Website: www.govt.nz

New Zealand comprises North Island, 43,911 sq mi; South Island, 58,084 sq mi; Stewart Island, 649 sq mi; Chatham Isls., 373 sq mi; and several groups of smaller islands. The Maori, a Polynesian group from the eastern Pacific, reached New Zealand before and during the 14th cent. The first European to sight New Zealand was Dutch navigator Abel Janszoon Tasman. The Maori refused to allow him to land. British Capt. James Cook explored the coasts, 1769-70.

British sovereignty was proclaimed and Maori land rights were recognized in the Treaty of Waitangi, 1840, with organized settlement beginning the same year. Representative institutions were granted in 1853. The Maori Wars, or New Zealand Wars, ended in 1870 with British victory. The colony became a dominion in 1907 and gained full independence in 1947.

A progressive tradition in politics began in the 19th cent., when New Zealand was known for social experimentation. Much of the nation's economy has been deregulated since the 1980s. Jenny Shipley of the National Party became the nation's first female prime min., Dec. 8, 1997, but the Labour Party, led by Helen Clark, won parliamentary elections, Nov. 27, 1999.

A measure establishing a supreme court and ending appeals to the UK Privy Council passed Oct. 14, 2003. A major settlement of Maori land claims dating from the 19th cent. was signed June 25, 2008.

A Christchurch earthquake, Feb. 22, 2011, killed 181 people and caused damage estimated at $11 bil to the central business district. Prime Min. John Key's handling of earthquake recovery and other disasters bolstered the popularity of his National Party (in office since 2008) in elections Nov. 26, 2011. New Zealand legalized same-sex marriage in a 77-44 parliamentary vote Apr. 17, 2013. Key's National Party won Sept. 20, 2014, parliamentary elections. On Dec. 5, 2016, Key announced he would step down, and Bill English became prime minister Dec. 12. After English's National Party fell short of a majority in Sept. 23, 2017, elections, Labour Party head Jacinda Ardern formed a coalition government, and she became prime minister, Oct. 26.

In 1965, the **Cook Islands** (area: 91 sq mi; 2018 est. pop.: 9,038), halfway between New Zealand and Hawaii, became self-governing. New Zealand retains responsibility for defense and foreign affairs. **Niue** (area: 100 sq mi; 2017 est. pop.: 1,618) attained the same status in 1974; it lies about 675 mi W of Cook Isls. Cyclone Heta devastated Niue Jan. 6, 2004. **Tokelau** (area: 4.6 sq mi; 2016 est. pop.: 1,499) comprises three atolls 300 mi N of Samoa. Two referendums on Tokelau self-government, held Feb. 13-15, 2006, and Oct. 20-24, 2007, failed to gain the required two-third majority. **Ross Dependency**, administered by New Zealand since 1923, comprises 160,000 sq mi of Antarctic territory. **Websites:** www.cookislands.gov.ck; www.gov.nu; www.tokelau.org.nz

Nicaragua
Republic of Nicaragua

People: Population: 6,085,213 (110). **Age distrib.:** <15: 26.6%; 65+: 5.5%. **Growth:** 1%. **Migrants:** 0.7%. **Pop. density:** 131.3 per sq mi, 50.7 per sq km. **Urban:** 58.5%. **Ethnic groups:** mestizo (mixed Amerindian/white) 69%, white 17%, black 9%, Amerindian 5%. **Languages:** Spanish (official), Miskito, Mestizo on Carib. coast. **Religions:** Roman Catholic 50%, Evangelical 33.2%.

Geography: Total area: 50,336 sq mi, 130,370 sq km (96); **Land area:** 46,328 sq mi, 119,990 sq km. **Location:** Central America. Honduras on N, Costa Rica on S. **Topography:** Both Caribbean and Pacific coasts are over 200 mi long. Cordillera Mts., with many volcanic peaks, run NW-SE through middle of country. **Arable land:** 12.5%. **Capital:** Managua, 1,047,923.

Government: Type: Presidential republic. **Head of state and govt.:** Pres. Daniel Ortega Saavedra; b. 1945; in office: Jan. 10, 2007. **Local divisions:** 15 departments, 2 autonomous regions. **Defense budget:** $84 mil. **Active troops:** 12,000.

Economy: Industries: food proc., chemicals, machinery and metal prods., knit and woven apparel, petroleum refining and distrib. **Chief agric.:** coffee, bananas, sugarcane, rice, corn, tobacco, cotton, sesame, soya, beans, beef, veal, pork, poultry, dairy prods., shrimp, lobsters, peanuts. **Natural resources:** gold, silver, copper, tungsten, lead, zinc, timber, fish. **Water:** 27,047 cu m per capita. **Electricity prod.:** 4.4 bil kWh. **Labor force:** agric. 29.4%, industry 17.7%, services 53%. **Unemployment:** 4.4%.

Finance: Monetary unit: Cordoba (NIO) (31.95 = $1 U.S.). **GDP:** $36.4 bil; **per capita GDP:** $5,800; **GDP growth:** 4.9%. **Imports:** $6.4 bil; U.S. 20.8%, China 14.3%, Mexico 11.1%, Costa Rica 7.9%, Guatemala 7%, El Salvador 5.6%. **Exports:** $3.6 bil; U.S. 44.2%, El Salvador 6.4%, Venezuela 5.5%, Costa Rica 5.5%. **Tourism:** $841 mil. **Budget:** $4.1 bil. **Inflation:** 3.9%.

Transport: Motor vehicles: 54.8 per 1,000 pop. **Airports:** 12. **Communications: Telephone:** 6 per 100 pop. **Mobile:** 131.6 per 100 pop. **Broadband:** 22.8 per 100 pop. **Internet:** 24.6%.

Health: Expend.: 7.8%. **Life expect.:** 71.5 male; 76.1 female. **Births:** 17.5 per 1,000 pop. **Deaths:** 5.2 per 1,000 pop. **Infant mortality:** 17.7 per 1,000 live births. **Undernourished:** 16.2%. **HIV:** 0.2%.

Education: Compulsory: ages 5-11. **Literacy:** 82.8%.
Embassy: 1627 New Hampshire Ave. NW 20009; 939-6570.
Website: www.asamblea.gob.ni

Nicaragua, inhabited by various Indian tribes, was conquered by Spain in 1552. After gaining independence from Spain, 1821, Nicaragua was united for a short period with Mexico, then with the United Provinces of Central America, before becoming an independent republic, 1838. U.S. Marines occupied the country at times in the early 20th cent., the last time from 1926 to 1933.

Gen. Anastasio Somoza Debayle held the presidency 1967-72, 1974-79. Martial law was imposed in Dec. 1974, after officials were kidnapped by Marxist Sandinista guerrillas. Nationwide strikes touched off a civil war, 1978, which ended when Somoza fled Nicaragua and the Sandinistas took control of Managua, July 1979. Somoza was assassinated in Paraguay, Sept. 17, 1980.

Relations with the U.S. were strained as a result of Nicaragua's aid to leftist guerrillas in El Salvador and U.S. backing of anti-Sandinista contra guerrilla groups, which fought the Sandinista government throughout the 1980s. In 1985 the U.S. House rejected Pres. Ronald Reagan's request for military aid to the contras. The subsequent diversion of funds to the contras from the proceeds of a secret arms sale to Iran caused a major scandal in the U.S.

In a stunning upset, Violeta Barrios de Chamorro defeated Sandinista leader Daniel Ortega Saavedra in national elections, Feb. 25, 1990. The conservative Arnoldo Alemán Lacayo defeated Ortega in the Oct. 1996 presidential election.

Drought and a drop in coffee prices precipitated an economic crisis in 2001. Enrique Bolaños Geyer, a conservative businessman, won the presidency that year. Ortega won the Nov. 2006 presidential election and was reelected Nov. 6, 2011. The Sandinista-controlled legislature gave final approval, Jan. 28, 2014, to constitutional changes removing presidential term limits. Amid allegations that opposition candidates were suppressed, Ortega easily won the Nov. 6, 2016, presidential election; Rosario Murillo Zambrana, Ortega's wife, was elected vice president. Months of protests, beginning Apr. 2018, against the Ortega government's policies and authoritarian rule resulted in hundreds of deaths, most at the hands of security forces or allied paramilitary groups.

Niger
Republic of Niger

People: Population: 19,866,231 (59). **Age distrib.:** <15: 48.7%; 65+: 2.6%. **Growth:** 3.2%. **Migrants:** 1.4%. **Pop. density:** 40.6 per sq mi, 15.7 per sq km. **Urban:** 16.4%. **Ethnic groups:** Hausa 53.1%, Zarma/Songhai 21.2%, Tuareg 11%, Fulani (Peul) 6.5%, Kanuri 5.9%. **Languages:** French (official), Hausa, Djerma. **Religions:** Muslim 80%, other (incl. indigenous beliefs and Christian) 20%.

Geography: Total area: 489,191 sq mi, 1,267,000 sq km (21). **Land area:** 489,076 sq mi, 1,266,700 sq km. **Location:** Interior of N Africa. Libya, Algeria on N; Mali, Burkina Faso on W; Benin, Nigeria on S; Chad on E. **Topography:** Mostly arid desert and mountains. Narrow savanna in S and Niger R. basin in the SW. **Arable land:** 13.3%. **Capital:** Niamey, 1,213,781.

Government: Type: Semi-presidential republic. **Head of state:** Pres. Mahamadou Issoufou; b. 1952; in office: Apr. 7, 2011. **Head of govt.:** Prime Min. Brigi Rafini; b. 1953; in office: Apr. 7, 2011. **Local divisions:** 7 regions, 1 capital district. **Defense budget:** $169 mil. **Active troops:** 5,300.

Economy: Industries: uranium mining, petroleum, cement, brick, soap, textiles, food proc., chemicals, slaughterhouses. **Chief agric.:** cowpeas, cotton, peanuts, millet, sorghum, cassava, rice; cattle, sheep, goats, camels, donkeys. **Natural resources:** uranium, coal, iron ore, tin, phosphates, gold, molybdenum, gypsum, salt, petroleum. **Water:** 1,711 cu m per capita. **Crude oil reserves:** 150 mil bbls. **Electricity prod.:** 499.4 mil kWh. **Labor force:** agric. 75.6%, industry 7.6%, services 16.8%. **Unemployment:** 0.4%.

Finance: Monetary unit: CFA Franc (XOF) (566.17 = $1 U.S.). **GDP:** $21.8 bil; **per capita GDP:** $1,200; **GDP growth:** 5.2%. **Imports:** $2.2 bil; France 28.8%, China 14.4%, Malaysia 5.7%, Nigeria 5.4%, Thailand 5.3%, U.S. 5.1%. **Exports:** $1.2 bil; France 30.2%, Thailand 18.3%, Malaysia 9.9%, Nigeria 8.3%, Mali 5%. **Tourism:** $77 mil. **Budget:** $1.7 bil. **Inflation:** 2.4%.

Transport: Motor vehicles: 13.2 per 1,000 pop. **Airports:** 10. **Communications: Telephone:** 0.5 per 100 pop. **Mobile:** 40.9 per 100 pop. **Broadband:** NA. **Internet** (2017): 10.2%.

Health: Expend.: 7.2%. **Life expect.:** 55.0 male; 57.7 female. **Births:** 43.6 per 1,000 pop. **Deaths:** 11.5 per 1,000 pop. **Infant mortality:** 79.4 per 1,000 live births. **Undernourished:** 14.4%. **HIV:** 0.3%.

Education: Compulsory: NA. **Literacy:** 19.1%.
Embassy: 2204 R St. NW 20008; 483-4224.
Website: www.gouv.ne

Niger was part of ancient and medieval African empires. European explorers reached the area in the late 18th cent. The French colony of Niger was established 1900-22 after the defeat of Tuareg fighters, who had invaded the area from the north a century before. The country became independent Aug. 3, 1960.

In 1993, Niger held its first free and open elections since independence; an opposition leader, Mahamane Ousmane, won the presidency. A peace accord Apr. 24, 1995, ended a Tuareg rebellion that began in 1990. After a coup, Jan. 27, 1996, the military retained control. On Apr. 9, 1999, Gen. Ibrahim Bare Mainassara, president since 1996, was assassinated. Elections held Oct. 17 and Nov. 24, 1999, under a new constitution, restored civilian rule.

Popularly elected in 1999 and 2004, Pres. Mamadou Tandja invoked emergency powers in 2009, seeking to remain in office for a third 5-year term. He was overthrown by a military junta Feb. 18, 2010. Civilian rule returned following Jan.-Mar. 2011 elections. Pres. Mahamadou Issoufou won reelection in a Mar. 20, 2016, runoff.

Terrorist attacks in Niger by an al-Qaeda-linked group, May 23, 2013, killed 21 soldiers. Beginning in Feb. 2015, the Nigeria-based Islamist extremist group Boko Haram staged attacks in southern Niger. Niger's parliament approved, Feb. 9, sending troops into Nigeria to fight Boko Haram. Niger joined 4 other regional nations in establishing, July 2, 2017, the G5 Sahel Cross-Border Joint Force to combat Islamist terrorism, organized crime, and human trafficking. An attack in W Niger by ISIS-affiliated militants, Oct. 4, 2017, killed 4 Niger soldiers, an interpreter, and 4 U.S. special operations troops. The UNHCR estimated, Aug. 2018, that Niger had more than 136,000 internally displaced persons and hosted almost 119,000 refugees from Nigeria, as well as more than 58,000 from Mali.

Nigeria
Federal Republic of Nigeria

People: Population: 203,452,505 (7). **Age distrib.:** <15: 42.5%; 65+: 3.3%. **Growth:** 2.5%. **Migrants:** 0.6%. **Pop. density:** 578.6 per sq mi, 223.4 per sq km. **Urban:** 50.3%. **Ethnic groups:** 250+ ethnic groups. Most populous, politically influential: Hausa and Fulani 29%, Yoruba 21%, Igbo (Ibo) 18%, Ijaw 10%, Kanuri 4%, Ibibio 3.5%, Tiv 2.5%. **Languages:** English (official), Hausa, Yoruba, Igbo (Ibo), Fulani, 500+ indigenous langs. **Religions:** Muslim 50%, Christian 40%, indigenous beliefs 10%.

Geography: Total area: 356,669 sq mi, 923,768 sq km (31); **Land area:** 351,649 sq mi, 910,768 sq km. **Location:** S coast of W Africa. Benin on W, Niger on N, Chad and Cameroon on E. **Topography:** 4 E-W regions: a coastal mangrove swamp, a tropical rain forest, a plateau of savanna and open woodland, and semi-desert in N. **Arable land:** 37.3%. **Capital:** Abuja, 2,918,518. **Cities:** Lagos, 13,463,421; Kano, 3,820,082; Ibadan, 3,382,598; Port Harcourt, 2,731,446.

Government: Type: Federal presidential republic. **Head of state and govt.:** Pres. Muhammadu Buhari; b. 1942; in office: May 29, 2015. **Local divisions:** 36 states, 1 territory. **Defense budget:** $1.5 bil. **Active troops:** 118,000.

Economy: Industries: crude oil, coal, tin, columbite; rubber prods., wood; hides/skins, textiles, cement and other constr. materials. **Chief agric.:** cocoa, peanuts, cotton, palm oil, corn, rice, sorghum, millet, cassava, yams, rubber; cattle, sheep; fish. **Natural resources:** nat. gas, petroleum, tin, iron ore, coal, limestone, niobium, lead, zinc. **Water:** 1,571 cu m per capita. **Crude oil reserves:** 37.5 bil bbls. **Electricity prod.:** 29.8 bil kWh. **Labor force:** agric. 36.6%, industry 11.6%, services 51.8%. **Unemployment:** 7%.

Finance: Monetary unit: Naira (NGN) (359.52 = $1 U.S.). **GDP:** $1.1 tril; **per capita GDP:** $5,900; **GDP growth:** 0.8%. **Imports:** $35.2 bil; China 21.1%, Belgium 8.7%, U.S. 8.4%, South Korea 7.5%. **Exports:** $40.8 bil; India 30.6%, U.S. 12.1%, Spain 6.6%, China 5.6%, France 5.5%. **Tourism:** $2.5 bil. **Budget:** $22.2 bil. **Inflation:** 16.5%.

Transport: Railways: 2,360 mi. **Motor vehicles:** 8.6 per 1,000 pop. **Airports:** 40.

Communications: Telephone: 0.07 per 100 pop. **Mobile:** 75.9 per 100 pop. **Broadband:** 21.8 per 100 pop. **Internet:** 25.7%.

Health: Expend.: 3.6%. **Life expect.:** 57.5 male; 61.1 female. **Births:** 35.2 per 1,000 pop. **Deaths:** 9.6 per 1,000 pop. **Infant mortality:** 63.3 per 1,000 live births. **Undernourished:** 11.5%. **HIV:** 2.8%.

Education: Compulsory: ages 6-14. **Literacy:** 59.6%.
Embassy: 3519 International Ct. NW 20008; 986-8400.
Website: www.nigeria.gov.ng

Early cultures in Nigeria date back to at least 700 BCE. From the 12th to the 14th cent., more advanced cultures developed in the Yoruba area, at Ife, and in the north, where Muslim influence prevailed. Portuguese and British slavers appeared in the 15th-16th cent. Britain seized Lagos, 1861, and gradually extended control inland until 1900. Nigeria became independent Oct. 1, 1960, and a republic Oct. 1, 1963.

On May 30, 1967, the Eastern Region seceded, proclaiming itself the Republic of Biafra, plunging the country into civil war. Casualties were estimated at over 1 mil, including many Biafrans (mostly Igbos) who died of starvation despite international relief efforts. The secessionists capitulated Jan. 12, 1970.

Nigeria emerged as one of the world's leading oil exporters in the 1970s, but much of the revenue has been squandered through corruption and mismanagement. Oil spills have polluted much of the Niger Delta region.

After 13 years of military rule, the nation made a peaceful return to civilian government Oct. 1979. Military rule resumed Dec. 31, 1983. An interim civilian government (in office Aug. 26, 1993) was ousted Nov. 17, 1993, in a coup led by Gen. Sani Abacha. His brutal rule ended June 8, 1998, when he died of an apparent heart attack. Abacha's successor, Gen. Abdulsalam Abubakar, promised elections and a return to civilian rule. Oluse-gun Obasanjo won the presidential vote Feb. 27, 1999, to lead Nigeria's first civilian government in 15 years.

The imposition of strict Islamic law in northern states led to clashes, Jan.-Mar. 2000, in which at least 800 people died. Fighting between Muslims and Christians Sept. 7-12 and Oct. 13-14, 2001, claimed an est. 600 lives. Christian militia members massacred about 630 Muslims at Yelwa, central Nigeria, May 2, 2004. Obasan-jo's chosen successor, Umaru Musa Yar'Adua, won a presidential election, Apr. 21, 2007, marred by violence and described as "not credible" by international monitors. Yar'Adua died May 5, 2010, and was succeeded by Vice Pres. Goodluck Jonathan, a southern Christian. Jonathan won reelection Apr. 16, 2011, over Muham-madu Buhari, a northern-based Muslim.

Boko Haram, a radical Islamist group based in NE Nigeria that seeks to establish an Islamist state, began terrorist attacks in 2009 against government forces and civilian targets. The group gained control of a large area in the NE and terrorist attacks escalated, 2013-15. In a message released Mar. 7, 2015, the group claimed allegiance to ISIS. Boko Haram also staged attacks in neighbor-ing Chad, Cameroon, and Niger; troops from those countries fought Boko Haram in Nigeria beginning in 2015. Vowing tougher action against Boko Haram, Buhari defeated Jonathan in the Mar. 28-29, 2015, presidential election. Subsequent government offensives retook a significant portion of the territory Boko Haram had seized, but in 2016-18, Boko Haram forces continued to control some areas of NE Nigeria and stage deadly attacks against civilians and secu-rity forces. Boko Haram split, in 2016, into ISIS-affiliated and non-affiliated factions. The Council on Foreign Relations estimated that, by mid-2018, more than 30,000 people had been killed as a result of Boko Haram attacks, clashes with security forces, and related actions. The UNHCR estimated that about 228,000 Nigerian refu-gees were in Niger, Cameroon, or Chad as of Aug. 31, 2018, and more than 1.9 mil Nigerians were internally displaced. Boko Haram kidnapped thousands of Nigerians and foreigners, including 276 girls abducted from their boarding school in Chibok in 2014; after a series of escapes, rescues, and releases, 113 girls remained in custody or unaccounted for in mid-2018.

In NW Nigeria, Dec. 2015, hundreds of members of a Shiite group, the Islamic Movement in Nigeria, were killed by security forces. A Judicial Commission of Inquiry concluded in 2016 that soldiers involved should be prosecuted; Amnesty International, Dec. 2017, criticized the government for failing to bring charges.

prod.: 142.4 bil kWh. **Labor force:** agric. 2.1%, industry 19.5%, services 78.5%. **Unemployment:** 4.2%.

Finance: Monetary unit: Krone (NOK) (8.39 = $1 U.S.). **GDP:** $380 bil; **per capita GDP:** $71,800; **GDP growth:** 1.8%. **Imports:** $79.9 bil; Sweden 11.4%, Germany 11%, China 9.8%, U.S. 6.8%, South Korea 6.7%, Denmark 5.4%. **Exports:** $102.8 bil; UK 21.1%, Germany 15.5%, Netherlands 9.9%, Sweden 6.6%, France 6.4%. **Tourism:** $5.4 bil. **Budget:** $198 bil. **Infla-tion:** 1.9%.

Transport: Railways: 2,641 mi. **Motor vehicles:** 621.6 per 1,000 pop. **Airports:** 67.

Communications: Telephone: 14 per 100 pop. **Mobile:** 107.8 per 100 pop. **Broadband:** 101.8 per 100 pop. **Internet** (2017): 96.5%.

Health: Expend.: 10%. **Life expect.:** 79.9 male; 84.1 female. **Births:** 12.2 per 1,000 pop. **Deaths:** 8.0 per 1,000 pop. **Infant mor-tality:** 2.5 per 1,000 live births. **Undernourished:** <2.5%. **HIV:** NA.

Education: Compulsory: ages 6-15. **Literacy:** 100%.

Embassy: 2720 34th St. NW 20008; 333-6000.

Website: www.regjeringen.no

The first ruler of Norway was Harald the Fairhaired, who came to power in 872 CE. Between 800 and 1000, Norway's Vikings raided and occupied widely dispersed parts of Europe. The country was united with Denmark, 1381-1814, and with Swe-den, 1814-1905. In 1905, the country became independent with Prince Charles of Denmark as king.

Norway remained neutral during WWI. In WWII, Germany attacked Norway Apr. 9, 1940, and held it until liberation May 8, 1945. The country abandoned its neutrality after the war and joined NATO. In a referendum Nov. 28, 1994, Norwegian voters rejected European Union membership.

Norway has one of the highest living standards in the world. Hydropower accounts for more than 90% of electricity produc-tion. The country is a leading producer and exporter of crude oil, with extensive reserves in the North Sea, and natural gas pro-duction has increased in recent years. Norway has used oil rev-enue to build up the world's largest sovereign wealth fund (more than $1 tril at the end of 2017).

A right-wing extremist, Anders Behring Breivik, confessed to killing 8 people with a car bomb in central Oslo and murdering another 69 at an island camp sponsored by the Labor Party's youth wing July 22, 2011. He was sentenced Aug. 24, 2012, to 21 years in prison, the maximum sentence. Parliament voted June 18, 2013, to make military service compulsory for women as well as men. Rightist parties, including the anti-immigration Progress Party, won the most seats in Sept. 9, 2013, elections; Conservative Party leader Erna Solberg became prime min. In 2015, about 31,000 migrants from the Middle East, SW Asia, and Africa applied for asylum in Norway. Solberg's coalition nar-rowly won Sept. 11, 2017, parliamentary elections. Norway won a record 39 medals at the 2018 Winter Olympics.

Svalbard is a group of mountainous islands in the Arctic O., area 23,956 sq mi, pop. (2017 est.) 2,583. The largest, Spitsber-gen (formerly called West Spitsbergen), 14,546 sq mi, seat of the governor, is about 370 mi N of Norway. By the 1920 Svalbard Treaty (in force 1925), major European powers recognized Nor-way's sovereignty over the archipelago.

Jan Mayen, area 146 sq mi, is a volcanic island located about 565 mi W-NW of Norway; it was annexed in 1929. The only peo-ple on Jan Mayen are military personnel and researchers. Norway operates a research station on volcanic Bouvet Isl., area 19 sq mi, in the South Atlantic O., about midway between South Africa and Antarctica. The UK waived its claim to the island in 1928.

Norway
Kingdom of Norway

People: Population: 5,372,191 (119). **Age distrib.:** <15: 18%; 65+: 16.9%. **Growth:** 0.9%. **Migrants:** 15.1%. **Pop. density:** 45.7 per sq mi, 17.7 per sq km. **Urban:** 82.2%. **Ethnic groups:** Nor-wegian (incl. Sami) 83.2%, other European 8.3%. **Languages:** Bokmal Norwegian, Nynorsk Norwegian (both official); Sami (offi-cial in 9 municipalities). **Religions:** Church of Norway (Evangeli-cal Lutheran) 71.5%, other Christian 3.9%, Muslim 2.8%.

Geography: Total area: 125,021 sq mi, 323,802 sq km (67); **Land area:** 117,484 sq mi, 304,282 sq km. **Location:** W part of Scandinavian peninsula in NW Europe (extends farther N than any European land). Sweden, Finland, Russia on E. **Topog-raphy:** Highly indented coast lined with tens of thousands of islands. Mountains and plateaus cover most of country, which is only 33% forested. **Arable land:** 2.2%. **Capital:** Oslo, 1,012,225.

Government: Type: Parliamentary constitutional monarchy. **Head of state:** King Harald V; b. 1937; in office: Jan. 17, 1991. **Head of govt.:** Prime Min. Erna Solberg; b. 1961; in office: Oct. 16, 2013. **Local divisions:** 18 counties. **Defense budget:** $6.1 bil. **Active troops:** 23,950.

Economy: Industries: petroleum and gas, shipping, fishing, aquaculture, food proc., shipbuilding, pulp/paper prods. **Chief agric.:** barley, wheat, potatoes; pork, beef, veal, milk; fish. **Natu-ral resources:** petroleum, nat. gas, iron ore, copper, lead, zinc, titanium, pyrites, nickel, fish, timber, hydropower. **Water:** 75,417 cu m per capita. **Crude oil reserves:** 6.4 bil bbls. **Electricity**

Oman
Sultanate of Oman

People: Population: 3,494,116 (130). (Immigrants made up about 45% of total pop. in 2017.) **Age distrib.:** <15: 30.1%; 65+: 3.6%. **Growth:** 2%. **Migrants:** 44.7%. **Pop. density:** 29.2 per sq mi, 11.3 per sq km. **Urban:** 84.5%. **Ethnic groups:** Arab, Balu-chi, South Asian (Indian, Pakistani, Sri Lankan, Bangladeshi), African. **Languages:** Arabic (official), English, Baluchi, Urdu, Indian dialects. **Religions:** Muslim (majority Ibadhi and Sunni) 85.9%, Christian 6.5%, Hindu 5.5%.

Geography: Total area: 119,499 sq mi, 309,500 sq km (70); **Land area:** 119,499 sq mi, 309,500 sq km. **Location:** SE coast of Arabian peninsula. United Arab Emirates, Saudi Arabia, Yemen on W. **Topography:** A narrow coastal plain, a range of barren mountains reaching 9,900 ft, and a wide, stony, mostly water-less plateau, avg. elevation 1,000 ft. An exclave at the tip of the Musandam peninsula controls access to the Persian Gulf. **Arable land:** 0.1%. **Capital:** Muscat, 1,446,563.

Government: Type: Absolute monarchy. **Head of state and govt.:** Sultan Qaboos bin Said al-Said; b. 1940; in office: July 23, 1970 (also prime min. since 1972). **Local divisions:** 11 gover-norates. **Defense budget:** $8.7 bil. **Active troops:** 42,600.

Economy: Industries: crude oil prod. and refining, nat. and liquefied nat. gas prod., constr., cement, copper, steel, chemi-cals, optic fiber. **Chief agric.:** dates, limes, bananas, alfalfa, vegetables; camels, cattle; fish. **Natural resources:** petroleum, copper, asbestos, marble, limestone, chromium, gypsum, nat.

gas. **Water:** 312 cu m per capita. **Crude oil reserves:** 5.4 bil bbls. **Electricity prod.:** 30.8 bil kWh. **Labor force:** agric. 6.5%, industry 38.2%, services 55.3%. **Unemployment:** 3.3%.

Finance: Monetary unit: Rial (OMR) (0.38 = $1 U.S.). **GDP:** $186.6 bil; **per capita GDP:** $45,200; **GDP growth:** –0.3%. **Imports:** $22.7 bil; UAE 35.5%, U.S. 27.8%. **Exports:** $31.9 bil; China 43.7%, UAE 11%, South Korea 7.9%. **Tourism:** $1.7 bil. **Budget:** $29.5 bil. **Inflation:** 1.6%.

Transport: Motor vehicles: 213.9 per 1,000 pop. **Airports:** 13. **Communications: Telephone:** 10.7 per 100 pop. **Mobile:** 149.8 per 100 pop. **Broadband:** 91.3 per 100 pop. **Internet:** 76.9%.

Health: Expend.: 3.8%. **Life expect.:** 73.9 male; 78.0 female. **Births:** 23.7 per 1,000 pop. **Deaths:** 3.3 per 1,000 pop. **Infant mortality:** 12.4 per 1,000 live births. **Undernourished:** 5.4%. **HIV:** NA.

Education: Compulsory: NA. **Literacy:** 93%.

Embassy: 2535 Belmont Rd. NW 20008; 387-1980.

Website: www.oman.om

Oman was originally called Muscat and Oman. A long history of rule by other lands, including Portugal in the 16th cent., ended with the ouster of the Persians in 1744. By the early 19th cent., Muscat and Oman controlled much of the Persian and Pakistan coasts.

British influence was confirmed in a 1951 treaty, and Britain helped suppress an uprising by traditionally rebellious interior tribes against control by Muscat in the 1950s.

On July 23, 1970, Sultan Said bin Taimur was overthrown by his son, Sultan Qaboos bin Said al-Said, who changed the nation's name to Sultanate of Oman. Petroleum and natural gas are major sources of income. Oman has strong military and economic ties to the U.S. but also has favorable relations with Iran. Sultan Qaboos shuffled his cabinet after Arab Spring protests Feb. 2011 and expanded the powers of the Majlis al-Shura, the lower house of parliament, Oct. 20, 2011.

Pakistan
Islamic Republic of Pakistan

People: Population: 207,862,518 (6). **Age distrib.:** <15: 30.8%; 65+: 4.6%. **Growth:** 1.4%. **Migrants:** 1.7%. **Pop. density:** 698.4 per sq mi, 269.6 per sq km. **Urban:** 36.7%. **Ethnic groups:** Punjabi 44.7%, Pashtun (Pathan) 15.4%, Sindhi 14.1%, Saraiki 8.4%, Muhajir 7.6%, Balochi 3.6%. **Languages:** Punjabi, Sindhi, Saraiki, Pashto or Pashtu, Urdu (official), Balochi, Hindko, English (official; lingua franca of elite and most govt. ministries). **Religions:** Muslim (official) 96.4% (Sunni 85%-90%, Shia 10%-15%).

Geography: Total area: 307,374 sq mi, 796,095 sq km (35); **Land area:** 297,637 sq mi, 770,875 sq km. **Location:** W part of S Asia. Iran on W, Afghanistan and China on N, India on E. **Topography:** The Indus R. rises in the Hindu Kush and Himalaya Mts. in the N, then flows 1,000 mi into Arabian Sea. Thar Desert, Eastern Plains flank Indus Valley. **Arable land:** 39.5%. **Capital:** Islamabad, 1,061,412. **Cities:** Karachi, 15,400,223; Lahore, 11,738,186; Faisalabad, 3,310,750; Rawalpindi, 2,156,119; Gujranwala, 2,109,839; Peshawar, 2,064,695.

Government: Type: Federal parliamentary republic. **Head of state:** Pres. Arif Alvi; b. 1949; in office: Sept. 9, 2018. **Head of govt.:** Prime Min. Imran Khan; b. 1952; in office: Aug. 18, 2018. **Local divisions:** 4 provinces, 1 territory, 1 capital territory; 2 admin. entities in Pakistan-administered part of disputed Jammu and Kashmir region. **Defense budget:** $9.7 bil. **Active troops:** 653,800.

Economy: Industries: textiles and apparel, food proc., pharmaceuticals, surgical instruments, constr. materials, paper prods., fertilizer, shrimp. **Chief agric.:** cotton, wheat, rice, sugarcane, fruits, vegetables; milk, beef, mutton, eggs. **Natural resources:** nat. gas, limited petroleum, poor quality coal, iron ore, copper, salt, limestone. **Water:** 1,306 cu m per capita. **Crude oil reserves:** 332.2 mil bbls. **Electricity prod.:** 104.6 bil kWh. **Labor force:** agric. 42%, industry 23.7%, services 34.3%. **Unemployment:** 4%.

Finance: Monetary unit: Rupee (PKR) (123.52 = $1 U.S.). **GDP:** $1.1 tril; **per capita GDP:** $5,400; **GDP growth:** 5.3%. **Imports:** $48.5 bil; China 27.4%, UAE 13.7%. **Exports:** $21.9 bil; U.S. 17.7%, UK 7.7%, China 6%, Germany 5.8%, Afghanistan 5.2%. **Tourism:** $352 mil. **Budget:** $59.3 bil. **Inflation:** 4.1%.

Transport: Railways: 7,383 mi. **Motor vehicles:** 18.2 per 1,000 pop. **Airports:** 108.

Communications: Telephone: 1.5 per 100 pop. **Mobile:** 73.4 per 100 pop. **Broadband:** 20.1 per 100 pop. **Internet:** 15.5%.

Health: Expend.: 2.7%. **Life expect.:** 66.4 male; 70.5 female. **Births:** 21.6 per 1,000 pop. **Deaths:** 6.3 per 1,000 pop. **Infant mortality:** 50.4 per 1,000 live births. **Undernourished:** 20.5%. **HIV:** 0.1%.

Education: Compulsory: ages 5-16. **Literacy:** 57.9%.

Embassy: 3517 International Ct. NW 20008; 243-6500.

Website: www.pakistan.gov.pk

Pakistan shares the 5,000-year history of the India-Pakistan subcontinent. At present-day Harappa and Mohenjo Daro, the Indus Valley civilization, with large cities and elaborate irrigation systems, flourished c. 4,000–2,500 BCE. Aryan invaders from the northwest conquered the region around 1,500 BCE, forging the Vedic civilization that dominated the region for over a thousand years. The first Arab invasion, 712 CE, introduced Islam. Present-

day Pakistan and India were part of the Mughal Empire from 1526 to 1857. Muslim power faded by the end of the 19th cent. as the British gained control.

Muhammad Ali Jinnah (1876-1948) was the principal architect of Pakistan. When the British withdrew, Aug. 14, 1947, two largely Islamic regions of British India acquired self-government as Pakistan, with dominion status in the Commonwealth. Pakistan was divided into West Pakistan and East Pakistan, nearly 1,000 mi apart on opposite sides of India. Kashmir, a predominantly Muslim region divided between Pakistan and India, has remained a source of conflict between the two countries.

Rioting and strikes broke out in the East after Pakistan's government, Mar. 1, 1971, postponed the constituent assembly, dominated by supporters of regional autonomy for East Pakistan. Armed conflict between East and West lasted from Mar. to Dec. 1971, with India siding with Easterners, who proclaimed the independent nation of Bangladesh. Thousands were killed, and some 10 mil Easterners fled to India. Full-scale war erupted between India and Pakistan, but Pakistan troops in the East surrendered Dec. 16; Pakistan agreed to a cease-fire in the West Dec. 17. On July 3, 1972, Pakistan and India signed a pact agreeing to troop withdrawals and peaceful conflict resolution.

Dec. 1970 elections brought Zulfikar Ali Bhutto to the presidency Dec. 20, 1971. Bhutto, who became prime min. in 1973, was overthrown in a military coup July 1977. Convicted of complicity in a 1974 political murder, he was executed Apr. 4, 1979. Millions of Afghan refugees entered Pakistan after the USSR invaded Afghanistan Dec. 1979 and after U.S.-led forces began fighting the Taliban in Afghanistan in 2001. Although millions of refugees have been repatriated, including those reportedly forced by Pakistan to return, almost 1.4 mil Afghan refugees were living in Pakistan as of Aug. 31, 2018.

Pres. Mohammad Zia ul-Haq was killed when his plane exploded in Aug. 1988. Following Nov. elections, Benazir Bhutto, daughter of Zulfikar Ali Bhutto, became prime min. and the first elected woman leader of a Muslim nation. She was accused of corruption and dismissed by the president, Aug. 1990. Bhutto returned to power Oct. 1993 but was dismissed Nov. 1996 amid further corruption charges. Responding to India's nuclear weapons tests, Pakistan conducted its own tests in 1998.

Prime Min. Nawaz Sharif fired, Oct. 1999, army chief Gen. Pervez Musharraf, whose supporters staged a bloodless coup. Musharraf assumed the presidency June 20, 2001. Following the Sept. 11, 2001, terrorist attacks on the U.S., Pres. Musharraf pledged cooperation with the U.S. in fighting Taliban and al-Qaeda militants within Pakistan and in neighboring Afghanistan. In return, the U.S. waived 1998 sanctions and offered Pakistan financial aid and debt relief. An earthquake that rocked Pakistan and the Pakistani-held region of Kashmir Oct. 8, 2005, killed about 80,000 people.

More than 140 people died Oct. 18, 2007, when suicide bombers struck Benazir Bhutto's convoy upon her return from more than eight years in exile. Musharraf, who had won the Oct. 6 presidential election, gave up his army post Nov. 25 and was sworn in as civilian president the next day. Bhutto was assassinated Dec. 27, 2007, after a rally in Rawalpindi.

Headed by Bhutto's widower, Asif Ali Zardari, the Pakistan Peoples Party led in parliamentary elections Feb. 18, 2008. Musharraf resigned Aug. 18 under threat of impeachment, and Zardari became president Sept. 9. Amid deteriorating security, U.S. and Pakistani forces clashed with the Taliban near the Afghan border, and Islamists carried out new suicide attacks. The government announced Feb. 16, 2009, a truce conceding de facto control of the strategic Swat Valley to the Taliban, but in May, government forces launched an offensive that reclaimed most of the region; the fighting displaced nearly 2 mil civilians. Catastrophic floods and monsoon rains, July-Aug. 2010, inundated one-fifth of Pakistan, leaving more than 1,750 people dead and displacing up to 20 mil.

A decade-long international effort came to an end May 2, 2011, when U.S. commandos killed al-Qaeda leader Osama bin Laden in Abbottabad. The raid, carried out by helicopter from Afghanistan, was launched without prior warning to Pakistani authorities. The U.S. has suspected some Pakistani military and other officials of covert links and assistance to Islamist extremist groups such as the Taliban and al-Qaeda.

On Oct. 9, 2012, 15-year-old Malala Yousafzai, who advocated for education rights for girls in Pakistan, was shot by the Taliban, sparking worldwide outrage. After treatment at a British hospital, she resumed her advocacy, for which she shared the 2014 Nobel Peace Prize. Two arrested Sept. 12, 2014, were convicted in Apr. 2015.

Musharraf returned to Pakistan Mar. 24, 2013, to attempt a political comeback. He was indicted in connection with Benazir Bhutto's assassination, Aug. 20, 2013, and charged with treason, Mar. 31, 2014. He was allowed to leave the country, Mar. 18, 2016, for medical treatment in Dubai. Former Prime Min. Nawaz Sharif was returned to office in May 11, 2013, elections. With Sharif accused of corruption, the Supreme Court ruled, July 28, 2017, that he could not serve in parliament, forcing him to step down as prime min. Sharif was convicted, July 6, 2018, but appealed the verdict. The party of former cricket star Imran Khan, the Pakistan Movement for Justice, with apparent backing from the military, won the most seats in July 25, 2018, parliamentary elections; Khan became prime min. Aug. 18. Arif Alvi, from Khan's party, was elected president Sept. 4, 2018.

A terrorist attack on a Peshawar school, Dec. 16, 2014, left about 150 dead. In 2007-14, an estimated 7,500 people died in terrorist attacks. Fighting between Pakistani forces and Islamic extremists resulted in more than 17,000 fatalities, 2007-14. Terrorist attacks and conflict between Islamic extremists and Pakistani forces, sometimes supported by U.S. drone strikes, continued in 2015-18. A suicide bomber killed about 70 people in a Lahore park, Mar. 27, 2016; a Taliban offshoot group claimed responsibility. An Aug. 8 suicide bombing at a hospital in Quetta killed more than 70; both a Taliban offshoot and ISIS claimed responsibility. At least 90 people were killed, Feb. 16, 2017, in a suicide bombing in Sehwan for which ISIS claimed responsibility. Pakistan reported that a U.S. drone strike in Afghanistan, June 13, 2018, killed the leader of the Pakistani Taliban. A July 13, 2018, Islamist extremist suicide bombing in Mastung left at least 149 dead.

Palau
Republic of Palau

People: Population: 21,516 (193). **Age distrib.:** <15: 19.4%; 65+: 8.5%. **Growth:** 0.4%. **Migrants:** 23%. **Pop. density:** 121.4 per sq mi, 46.9 per sq km. **Urban:** 79.9%. **Ethnic groups:** Palauan (Micronesian with Malayan/Melanesian admixtures) 73%, Asian 21.7%, Carolinian 2%. **Languages:** Palauan (official on most islands), English (official), Filipino. **Religions:** Roman Catholic 45.3%, Protestant 34.9% (incl. Evangelical 26.4%), Modekngei (indigenous to Palau) 5.7%, Muslim 3%.

Geography: Total area: 177 sq mi, 459 sq km (181); **Land area:** 177 sq mi, 459 sq km. **Location:** Archipelago (26 islands, more than 300 islets) in W Pacific O., about 530 mi SE of the Philippines. Micronesia to E, Indonesia to S. **Topography:** A mountainous main island and low coral atolls, usually fringed with large barrier reefs. **Arable land:** 2.2%. **Capital:** Ngerulmud.

Government: Type: Presidential republic in free association with U.S. **Head of state and govt.:** Pres. Tommy Remengesau; b. 1956; in office: Jan. 17, 2013. **Local divisions:** 16 states. **Defense budget/active troops:** NA.

Economy: Industries: tourism, fishing, subsistence agriculture. **Chief agric.:** coconuts, cassava, sweet potatoes; fish, pigs, chickens, eggs. **Natural resources:** forests, minerals (espec. gold), marine prods., deep-seabed minerals. **Water:** NA. **Labor force:** agric. 1.2%, industry 12.4%, services 86.4%. **Unemployment:** NA.

Finance: Monetary unit: U.S. Dollar (USD) (1.00 = $1 U.S.). **GDP:** $291 mil; **per capita GDP:** $16,200; **GDP growth:** –1%. **Imports** (2016): $179.3 mil; U.S. 33.4%, Guam 15.8%, Japan 15.7%, China 13.5%, South Korea 5.3%. **Exports** (2016): $117.5 mil; Japan 51.3%, U.S. 15.8%, India 13.8%, Guam 8%. **Tourism:** $141 mil. **Budget** (2012): $183.9 mil. **Inflation:** 1.3%.

Transport: Airports: 1.

Communications: Telephone (2015): 33.8 per 100 pop. **Mobile** (2015): 111.5 per 100 pop. **Broadband:** NA. **Internet:** NA.

Health: Expend.: 10.6%. **Life expect.:** 70.4 male; 77.0 female. **Births:** 11.3 per 1,000 pop. **Deaths:** 8.2 per 1,000 pop. **Infant mortality:** 10.3 per 1,000 live births. **Undernourished:** NA. **HIV:** NA.

Education: Compulsory: ages 6-17. **Literacy:** 96.6%.

Embassy: 1701 Pennsylvania Ave. NW, Ste. 300, 20036; 349-8598.

Website: palaugov.pw

Spain acquired the Palau Islands, 1886, and sold them to Germany, 1899. Japan seized them in 1914. U.S. forces occupied the islands in 1944; in 1947, they became part of the U.S.-administered UN Trust Territory of the Pacific Islands. In 1981, Palau became an autonomous republic. It ratified a compact of free association with the U.S. in 1993 and became an independent nation, Oct. 1, 1994. Oct. 2015 legislation provided for the creation of a 193,000 sq mi marine sanctuary, in which fishing and mineral development would be prohibited.

Panama
Republic of Panama

People: Population: 3,800,644 (129). **Age distrib.:** <15: 26.1%; 65+: 8.6%. **Growth:** 1.2%. **Migrants:** 4.7%. **Pop. density:** 132.4 per sq mi, 51.1 per sq km. **Urban:** 67.7%. **Ethnic groups:** mestizo (mixed Amerindian/white) 65%, Native American (incl. Ngabe 7.6%, Kuna 2.4%) 12.3%, black or African descent 9.2%, mulatto 6.8%, white 6.7%. **Languages:** Spanish (official), indigenous langs. **Religions:** Roman Catholic 85%, Protestant 15%.

Geography: Total area: 29,120 sq mi, 75,420 sq km (116); **Land area:** 28,703 sq mi, 74,340 sq km. **Location:** Central America. Costa Rica on W, Colombia on E. **Topography:** Two mountain ranges run length of isthmus. Tropical rain forests cover the Caribbean coast and E. **Arable land:** 7.6%. **Capital:** Panama City, 1,783,490.

Government: Type: Presidential republic. **Head of state and govt.:** Pres. Juan Carlos Varela; b. 1963; in office: July 1, 2014. **Local divisions:** 10 provinces, 3 indigenous regions. **Defense budget:** $746 mil. **Active troops:** No armed forces. 22,050 paramilitary only.

Economy: Industries: constr., brewing, cement/other constr. materials, sugar milling. **Chief agric.:** bananas, rice, corn, coffee, sugarcane, vegetables; livestock; shrimp. **Natural resources:** copper, mahogany forests, shrimp, hydropower. **Water:** 35,454 cu m per capita. **Electricity prod.:** 10 bil kWh. **Labor force:** agric. 15.1%, industry 18.2%, services 66.7%. **Unemployment:** 4.5%.

Finance: Monetary unit: Balboa (PAB) (1.00 = $1 U.S.). **GDP:** $103.9 bil; **per capita GDP:** $25,400; **GDP growth:** 5.4%. **Imports:** $21.2 bil; U.S. 24.4%, China 9.8%. **Exports:** $15.5 bil. Trade data incl. Colón Free Zone.; U.S. 18.9%, Netherlands 16.6%, China 6.5%, Costa Rica 5.4%, India 5.1%, Vietnam 5%. **Tourism:** $4.5 bil. **Budget:** $13.6 bil. **Inflation:** 0.9%.

Transport: Railways: 48 mi. **Motor vehicles:** 205.6 per 1,000 pop. **Airports:** 57.

Communications: Telephone: 14.7 per 100 pop. **Mobile:** 145.8 per 100 pop. **Broadband:** 29.7 per 100 pop. **Internet:** 54%.

Health: Expend.: 7%. **Life expect.:** 76.1 male; 81.9 female. **Births:** 17.6 per 1,000 pop. **Deaths:** 5.0 per 1,000 pop. **Infant mortality:** 9.6 per 1,000 live births. **Undernourished:** 9.2%. **HIV:** 1.0%.

Education: Compulsory: ages 4-14. **Literacy:** 95%.

Embassy: 2862 McGill Ter. NW 20008; 483-1407.

Website: www.presidencia.gob.pa

The coast of Panama was sighted by Rodrigo de Bastidas, sailing with Columbus for Spain in 1501, and was visited by Columbus in 1502. Vasco Núñez de Balboa crossed the isthmus and "discovered" the Pacific Ocean, Sept. 13, 1513. Spanish colonies were ravaged by Francis Drake, 1572-95, and Henry Morgan, 1668-71. Morgan destroyed the old city of Panama, which was founded in 1519. Freed from Spain, Panama joined Colombia in 1821.

Panama declared independence from Colombia Nov. 3, 1903, and granted use, occupation, and control of the Canal Zone to the U.S. Feb. 26, 1904. The U.S.-built Panama Canal opened Aug. 15, 1914. A 1978 treaty provided for a gradual takeover by Panama of the canal. The U.S. handed over control Dec. 31, 1999. A $5.3-bil project to expand the Panama Canal was approved by national referendum Oct. 22, 2006. Construction began Sept. 3, 2007; the first ship crossed the canal's new wider channel June 26, 2016.

Pres. Eric Arturo Delvalle was ousted by the National Assembly, Feb. 26, 1988, after he tried to fire Gen. Manuel Antonio Noriega, who was under a U.S. indictment on drug charges. U.S. troops invaded Panama Dec. 20, 1989, and Noriega surrendered Jan. 3, 1990. After two decades in a U.S. prison, Noriega was extradited to France Apr. 26, 2010; he was convicted of money laundering July 7 and received a 7-year sentence. France extradited him to Panama, Dec. 11, 2011, to serve a 20-year sentence for human rights violations. Noriega died May 29, 2017.

Juan Carlos Varela of the Panameñista Party won the May 4, 2014, presidential election. Information published beginning Apr. 3, 2016, from "Panama Papers" documents—leaked from a Panama City law firm—linked public officials and others in various countries to offshore bank accounts and companies created to conceal wealth or avoid taxes.

Papua New Guinea
Independent State of Papua New Guinea

People: Population: 7,027,332 (104). **Age distrib.:** <15: 32.9%; 65+: 4.4%. **Growth:** 1.7%. **Migrants:** 0.4%. **Pop. density:** 40.2 per sq mi, 15.5 per sq km. **Urban:** 13.2%. **Ethnic groups:** Melanesian, Papuan, Negrito, Micronesian, Polynesian. **Languages:** Tok Pisin, English, Hiri Motu (all official); some 839 indigenous langs. (many spoken by fewer than 1,000). **Religions:** Protestant 69.4% (incl. Evangelical Lutheran 19.5%, United Church 11.5%, Seventh-day Adventist 10%), Roman Catholic 27%.

Geography: Total area: 178,704 sq mi, 462,840 sq km (54); **Land area:** 174,850 sq mi, 452,860 sq km. **Location:** SE Asia; E half of island of New Guinea and about 600 nearby islands. Indonesia on W, Australia on S. **Topography:** Thickly forested mountains cover much of center, with lowlands along the coasts. Incl. some islands of Bismarck and Solomon groups, such as Admiralty Isls., New Ireland, New Britain, and Bougainville. **Arable land:** 0.7%. **Capital:** Port Moresby, 366,862.

Government: Type: Parliamentary democracy under constitutional monarchy. **Head of state:** Queen Elizabeth II, rep. by Gov.-Gen. Bob Dadae; in office: Feb. 28, 2017. **Head of govt.:** Prime Min. Peter O'Neill; b. 1965; in office: Aug. 2, 2011. **Local divisions:** 20 provinces, 1 autonomous region, 1 district. **Defense budget:** $71 mil. **Active troops:** 3,600.

Economy: Industries: copra crushing, palm oil proc., plywood prod., wood chip prod., mining, crude oil/petroleum prods. **Chief agric.:** coffee, cocoa, copra, palm kernels, tea, sugar, rubber, sweet potatoes; poultry, pork; shellfish. **Natural resources:** gold, copper, silver, nat. gas, timber, oil, fisheries. **Water:** 105,132 cu m per capita. **Crude oil reserves:** 183.8 mil bbls. **Electricity prod.:** 3.6 bil kWh. **Labor force:** agric. 20.6%, industry 7.6%, services 71.8%. **Unemployment:** 2.7%.

Finance: Monetary unit: Kina (PGK) (3.25 = $1 U.S.). **GDP:** $30.3 bil; **per capita GDP:** $3,700; **GDP growth:** 2.5%. **Imports:** $1.9 bil; Australia 30.1%, China 17.3%, Singapore 10.2%, Malaysia 8.2%. **Exports:** $9.5 bil; Australia 18.9%, Singapore 17.5%, Japan 13.8%, China 12.7%. **Tourism:** $1 mil. **Budget:** $4.8 bil. **Inflation** (2015-16): 6.7%.

Transport: Motor vehicles: 21.8 per 1,000 pop. **Airports:** 21.

Communications: Telephone (2016): 1.9 per 100 pop. **Mobile** (2016): 46.8 per 100 pop. **Broadband:** NA. **Internet:** 9.6%.

Health: Expend.: 3.8%. **Life expect.:** 65.3 male; 69.8 female.

Births: 23.3 per 1,000 pop. **Deaths:** 6.6 per 1,000 pop. **Infant mortality:** 35.3 per 1,000 live births. **Undernourished:** NA. **HIV:** 0.9%.

Education: Compulsory: NA. **Literacy:** 64.2%.

Embassy: 1779 Massachusetts Ave. NW, Ste. 805, 20036; 745-3680.

Website: www.pm.gov.pg

Human remains dating back at least 10,000 years have been found in the interior of New Guinea. European colonization began in the 19th cent., when the Dutch took control of the island's western half (now part of Indonesia). The southern half of eastern New Guinea was claimed by Britain in 1884 and transferred to Australia in 1905. Germany claimed the northern half in 1884, but Australia captured it in WWI. Self-government was achieved Dec. 1, 1973, and independence Sept. 16, 1975.

Secessionist rebels clashed with government forces on Bougainville 1988-97, claiming some 20,000 lives. A Bougainville autonomy agreement was signed Aug. 30, 2001. Sir Michael Somare, the nation's first prime min. (1975-80, 1982-85), regained the office in 2002 and was reelected by parliament Aug. 13, 2007. Somare took indefinite medical leave Apr. 2011; parliament, Aug. 2, elected Peter O'Neill as permanent replacement, but the Supreme Court, Dec. 12, ruled that action illegal. After June-July 2012 parliamentary elections, the new parliament elected O'Neill prime min., Aug. 3, 2012. After a weeks-long parliamentary election, beginning June 24, 2017—marred by violence and allegations of fraud—the newly seated parliament reelected O'Neill prime min., Aug. 2, 2017.

The Supreme Court, Apr. 26, 2016, ruled illegal Australia's detention center on Manus Island for migrants intercepted trying to reach Australia by boat. The center, where detainees endured harsh living conditions, was closed Oct. 31, 2017. Approximately 600 detainees, all male, were relocated to other Australian-run camps pending resettlement, some facing violence from an unwelcoming local population. Under a 2016 Australia-U.S. resettlement agreement, about 150 Manus Island detainees had left for the U.S. as of Sept. 2018.

The country has extensive energy resources. After the initial phase of a natural gas pipeline project was completed, shipments of liquefied natural gas through a new processing and shipping facility near Port Moresby began in May 2014.

Paraguay
Republic of Paraguay

People: Population: 7,025,763 (105). **Age distrib.:** <15: 24.1%; 65+: 7.3%. **Growth:** 1.2%. **Migrants:** 2.4%. **Pop. density:** 45.8 per sq mi, 17.7 per sq km. **Urban:** 61.6%. **Ethnic groups:** mestizo (mixed Spanish/Amerindian) 95%. **Languages:** Spanish, Guaraní (both official). **Religions:** Roman Catholic 89.6%, Protestant 6.2%.

Geography: Total area: 157,048 sq mi, 406,752 sq km (59); **Land area:** 153,399 sq mi, 397,302 sq km. **Location:** Landlocked country in central S America. Bolivia on N, Argentina on S, Brazil on E. **Topography:** Paraguay R. bisects country. Fertile plains, wooded slopes, grasslands to E. Gran Chaco plain, with marshes and scrub trees, to W. Extreme W is arid. **Arable land:** 12.1%. **Capital:** Asunción, 3,222,199.

Government: Type: Presidential republic. **Head of state and govt.:** Pres. Mario Abdo Benítez; b. 1971; in office: Aug. 15, 2018. **Local divisions:** 17 departments, 1 capital city. **Defense budget:** $264 mil. **Active troops:** 10,650.

Economy: Industries: sugar proc., cement, textiles, beverages, wood prods., steel. **Chief agric.:** cotton, sugarcane, soybeans, corn, wheat, tobacco, cassava, fruits, vegetables; beef, pork, eggs, milk. **Natural resources:** hydropower, timber, iron ore, manganese, limestone. **Water:** 58,412 cu m per capita. **Electricity prod.:** 55.2 bil kWh. **Labor force:** agric. 21.2%, industry 19.5%, services 59.3%. **Unemployment:** 4.6%.

Finance: Monetary unit: Guarani (PYG) (5,811.10 = $1 U.S.). **GDP:** $68.3 bil; **per capita GDP:** $9,800; **GDP growth:** 4.3%. **Imports:** $10.4 bil; China 31.3%, Brazil 23.4%, Argentina 12.9%, U.S. 7.4%. **Exports:** $11.5 bil; Brazil 31.9%, Argentina 15.9%, Chile 6.9%, Russia 5.9%. **Tourism:** $603 mil. **Budget:** $5.9 bil. **Inflation:** 3.6%.

Transport: Railways: 19 mi. **Motor vehicles:** 70 per 1,000 pop. **Airports:** 15.

Communications: Telephone: 4.3 per 100 pop. **Mobile:** 109.6 per 100 pop. **Broadband:** 41.7 per 100 pop. **Internet** (2017): 61.1%.

Health: Expend.: 7.8%. **Life expect.:** 74.9 male; 80.4 female.

Births: 16.6 per 1,000 pop. **Deaths:** 4.8 per 1,000 pop. **Infant mortality:** 18.1 per 1,000 live births. **Undernourished:** 11.2%. **HIV:** 0.5%.

Education: Compulsory: ages 5-17. **Literacy:** 95.1%.

Embassy: 2209 Massachusetts Ave. NW 20008; 483-6960.

Website: www.presidencia.gov.py

Guaraní Indians preceded Europeans in Paraguay, which was visited by Sebastian Cabot in 1527 and became a Spanish possession in 1535. Paraguay gained independence from Spain in 1811. It lost half its population and much of its territory to Brazil,

Uruguay, and Argentina in the War of the Triple Alliance, 1865-70. Large areas were won from Bolivia in the Chaco War, 1932-35. Gen. Alfredo Stroessner held the presidency 1954-89, until his ouster in a military coup.

Power struggles ensued between civilian and military leaders, 1993-97. The assassination of Vice Pres. Luis María Argaña, Mar. 23, 1999, was widely attributed to Pres. Raúl Cubas Grau and triggered protests and an impeachment vote; Cubas resigned Mar. 28. An attempted military coup was suppressed May 18, 2000.

Mass protests over the depressed economy led to the proclamation of a state of emergency July 15, 2002. Nicanor Duarte Frutos of the conservative Colorado Party won the presidency, Apr. 27, 2003.

Paraguayan authorities blamed a leftist group for the Sept. 2004 kidnapping and subsequent murder of Cecilia Cubas, daughter of former Pres. Cubas. Fernando Lugo, a former Catholic cleric known as the "bishop of the poor," won a presidential election Apr. 20, 2008, ending over six decades of Colorado rule. On June 22, 2012, Lugo was removed from office after his handling of a dispute between landless peasants and police left 17 dead June 15. Colorado candidate Horacio Cartes, a former tobacco magnate, was elected president Apr. 21, 2013. After an abortive 2017 attempt by Cartes to amend the constitution to allow him to seek another term, Mario Abdo Benítez of the Colorado Party narrowly won the Apr. 22, 2018, presidential election.

Peru
Republic of Peru

People: Population: 31,331,228 (44). **Age distrib.:** <15: 26%; 65+: 7.6%. **Growth:** 0.9%. **Migrants:** 0.3%. **Pop. density:** 63.4 per sq mi, 24.5 per sq km. **Urban:** 77.9%. **Ethnic groups:** Amerindian 45%; mestizo (mixed Amerindian/white) 37%; white 15%; black, Japanese, Chinese, other 3%. **Languages:** Spanish, Quechua, Aymara (all official). **Religions:** Roman Catholic 81.3%, Evangelical 12.5%.

Geography: Total area: 496,225 sq mi, 1,285,216 sq km (19); **Land area:** 494,209 sq mi, 1,279,996 sq km. **Location:** Pacific coast of S America. Ecuador, Colombia on N; Brazil, Bolivia on E; Chile on S. **Topography:** An arid coastal strip, 10-100 mi wide. The Andes cover one-quarter of land area. The uplands are well-watered, as are the eastern slopes reaching the Amazon Basin, which covers half of country. **Arable land:** 3.2%. **Capital:** Lima, 10,390,607. **Cities:** Arequipa, 899,796.

Government: Type: Presidential republic. **Head of state and govt.** Pres. Martín Vizcarra; b. 1963; in office: Mar. 23, 2018. **Local divisions:** 25 regions, 1 province. **Defense budget:** $2.1 bil. **Active troops:** 81,000.

Economy: Industries: mining, refining of minerals; steel, metal fabrication; petroleum extraction/refining, nat. gas and nat. gas liquefaction; fishing/fish proc., cement, glass, textiles. **Chief agric.:** artichokes, asparagus, avocados, blueberries, coffee, cocoa, cotton, sugarcane, rice, potatoes, corn, plantains, grapes and other fruits; poultry, beef, pork, dairy prods.; guinea pigs; fish. **Natural resources:** copper, silver, gold, petroleum, timber, fish, iron ore, coal, phosphate, potash, hydropower, nat. gas. **Water:** 59,916 cu m per capita. **Crude oil reserves:** 434.9 mil bbls. **Electricity prod.:** 46.6 bil kWh. **Labor force:** agric. 28.4%, industry 15.9%, services 55.7%. **Unemployment:** 3.6%.

Finance: Monetary unit: Sol (PEN) (3.32 = $1 U.S.). **GDP:** $424.4 bil; **per capita GDP:** $13,300; **GDP growth:** 2.5%. **Imports:** $38.8 bil; China 22.3%, U.S. 20.1%, Brazil 6%. **Exports:** $42.5 bil; China 26.5%, U.S. 15.2%, Switzerland 5.2%. **Tourism:** $3.7 bil. **Budget:** $65.5 bil. **Inflation:** 2.8%.

Transport: Railways: 1,152 mi. **Motor vehicles:** 82.5 per 1,000 pop. **Airports:** 59.

Communications: Telephone: 9.6 per 100 pop. **Mobile:** 121 per 100 pop. **Broadband:** 62 per 100 pop. **Internet** (2017): 48.7%.

Health: Expend.: 5.3%. **Life expect.:** 72.1 male; 76.4 female.

Births: 17.6 per 1,000 pop. **Deaths:** 6.1 per 1,000 pop. **Infant mortality:** 17.8 per 1,000 live births. **Undernourished:** 8.8%. **HIV:** 0.3%.

Education: Compulsory: ages 3-16. **Literacy:** 94.2%.

Embassy: 1700 Massachusetts Ave. NW 20036; 833-9860.

Website: www.peru.gob.pe

The powerful Inca Empire had its seat at Cuzco in the Andes and covered much of S America. A civil war had weakened the empire when Spaniard Francisco Pizarro began raiding Peru for its wealth, 1532. In 1533 he executed the Inca ruler, Atahualpa, and enslaved the people.

José de San Martín captured Lima from the Spanish in 1821; Simón Bolívar routed Spanish forces in 1824, and for much of the 19th cent., the country was governed by military leaders. Chile defeated Peru in the War of the Pacific, 1879-83. Right-wing groups allied with the military and the leftist APRA party vied for power in the first half of the 20th cent.

Peru returned to democratic leadership in 1980 but was plagued by economic problems and by leftist Shining Path (Sendero Luminoso) guerrillas. Conflict between guerrillas and government troops, 1980-2000, killed more than 69,000.

Elected president in June 1990, Alberto Fujimori, the son of Japanese immigrants, dissolved Congress, suspended parts of the constitution, and initiated press censorship, Apr. 1992. The leader of Shining Path was captured Sept. 12. Fujimori won reelection in 1995 and 2000, but his repressive antiterrorism tactics drew international criticism.

Scandals involving a top aide led Fujimori to resign Nov. 20, 2000; instead of accepting his resignation, Congress ousted him as "morally unfit." Fujimori was convicted in three separate proceedings, 2007-09, on charges that included complicity in a paramilitary death squad's killing of at least 25 people, 1991-92. He was convicted, Jan. 8, 2015, of misusing public funds during his 2000 campaign.

In a presidential runoff election June 5, 2011, Ollanta Humala Tasso, a leftist former military officer, defeated Keiko Fujimori, daughter of the former president. Pedro Pablo Kuczynski narrowly defeated Keiko Fujimori, Dec. 24, 2017, after allegedly receiving help from Fujimori's son to defeat an impeachment attempt (the Supreme Court overturned the pardon, Oct. 3, 2018). Again facing impeachment over a corruption scandal, Kuczynski announced his resignation, Mar. 21, 2018. He was replaced, Mar. 23, by Vice Pres. Martín Vizcarra. Early 2017 floods and mudslides killed over 100 and left more than 150,000 homeless.

An est. 400,000 or more Venezuelans, escaping economic hardship and repression, had entered Peru by Aug. 25, 2018, when the government instituted stricter border-crossing regulations.

Philippines
Republic of the Philippines

People: Population: 105,893,381 (13). **Age distrib.:** <15: 33.1%; 65+: 4.6%. **Growth:** 1.6%. **Migrants:** 0.2%. **Pop. density:** 919.8 per sq mi, 355.1 per sq km. **Urban:** 46.9%. **Ethnic groups:** Tagalog 28.1%, Cebuano 13.1%, Ilocano 9%, Bisaya/Binisaya 7.6%, Hiligaynon Ilonggo 7.5%, Bikol 6%, Waray 3.4%. **Languages:** Filipino (based on Tagalog), English (both official); 8 major dialects (incl. Tagalog). **Religions:** Catholic 82.9% (incl. Roman Catholic 80.9%), Muslim 5%, Evangelical 2.8%, Iglesia ni Kristo 2.3%.

Geography: Total area: 115,831 sq mi, 300,000 sq km (72); **Land area:** 115,124 sq mi, 298,170 sq km. **Location:** Archipelago in SE Asia. Malaysia, Indonesia on S; Taiwan on N. **Topography:** Comprises some 7,107 islands stretching 1,100 mi N-S. About 95% of area and pop. are on 11 largest islands, which are mountainous, except for the heavily indented coastlines and central plain on Luzon. **Arable land:** 18.7%. **Capital:** Manila, 13,482,468 (figure is for natl. capital region). **Cities:** Davao City, 1,744,980; Cebu City, 955,557.

Government: Type: Presidential republic. **Head of state and govt.:** Pres. Rodrigo Roa Duterte; b. 1945; in office: June 30, 2016. **Local divisions:** 80 provinces, 39 chartered cities. **Defense budget:** $2.8 bil. **Active troops:** 125,000.

Economy: Industries: semiconductors and electronics assembly, business process outsourcing, food/beverage mfg., constr. **Chief agric.:** rice, fish, livestock, poultry, bananas, coconuts/copra, corn, sugarcane. **Natural resources:** timber, petroleum, nickel, cobalt, silver, gold, salt, copper. **Water:** 4,757 cu m per capita. **Crude oil reserves:** 138.5 mil bbls. **Electricity prod.:** 78.6 bil kWh. **Labor force:** agric. 26%, industry 17.7%, services 56.3%. **Unemployment:** 2.4%.

Finance: Monetary unit: Peso (PHP) (53.57 = $1 U.S.). **GDP:** $875.6 bil; **per capita GDP:** $8,300; **GDP growth:** 6.7%. **Imports:** $92.8 bil; China 18.1%, Japan 11.4%, South Korea 8.8%, U.S. 7.4%, Thailand 7.1%, Indonesia 6.7%, Singapore 5.9%. **Exports:** $63.2 bil; Japan 16.4%, U.S. 14.6%, Hong Kong 13.7%, China 11%, Singapore 6.1%. **Tourism:** $7 bil. **Budget:** $56 bil. **Inflation:** 2.9%.

Transport: Railways: 48 mi. **Motor vehicles:** 39.3 per 1,000 pop. **Airports:** 89.

Communications: Telephone: 4 per 100 pop. **Mobile:** 110.4 per 100 pop. **Broadband:** 46.3 per 100 pop. **Internet:** 55.5%.

Health: Expend.: 4.4%. **Life expect.:** 66.1 male; 73.3 female. **Births:** 23.4 per 1,000 pop. **Deaths:** 6.1 per 1,000 pop. **Infant mortality:** 20.9 per 1,000 live births. **Undernourished:** 13.7%. **HIV:** 0.1%.

Education: Compulsory: ages 5-17. **Literacy:** 96.3%.
Embassy: 1600 Massachusetts Ave. NW 20036; 467-9300.
Website: www.gov.ph

Originally inhabited by Malay peoples, the archipelago was visited by Magellan, 1521. The Spanish founded Manila, 1571. Spain ceded the islands, named for King Philip II of Spain, to the U.S. for $20 mil, 1898, following the Spanish-American War. U.S. troops suppressed a guerrilla uprising in a brutal war, 1899-1905. Japan attacked the Philippines Dec. 8, 1941, and occupied the islands during WWII. Independence was proclaimed, July 4, 1946. A republic was established.

The repressive and corrupt regime of Pres. Ferdinand Marcos and his wife, Imelda, was in place 1965-86. The assassination of prominent opposition leader Benigno S. Aquino Jr., Aug. 21, 1983, sparked calls for Marcos's resignation. Marcos defeated Corazon Aquino, widow of the slain opposition leader, Feb. 16, 1986, in an allegedly fraudulent election. Mass protests and international pressure forced Marcos to flee the country Feb. 25, and Aquino became president.

Her government was plagued by a weak economy, widespread poverty, Communist and Muslim insurgencies, and lukewarm military support; an attempted coup Dec. 1, 1989, was defeated. Fidel Ramos won the May 1992 presidential election. The U.S. vacated the Subic Bay Naval Station in late 1992, ending its long military presence. However, a 2014 agreement gave U.S. forces increased access to Philippines bases. Some Muslim separatist guerrillas refused to abide by a cease-fire agreement signed Jan. 30, 1994, so a new treaty providing for expansion and development of an autonomous Muslim region on Mindanao was signed Sept. 2, 1996; the rebellion had claimed more than 120,000 lives since 1972.

Joseph (Erap) Estrada, a former movie actor, won the presidential election, May 11, 1998, but was impeached on bribery and corruption charges Nov. 13, 2000. Vice Pres. Gloria Macapagal Arroyo became president Jan. 20, 2001. Pres. Arroyo won reelection May 10, 2004. Former Pres. Estrada was convicted, Sept. 12, 2007, of taking more than $85 mil in bribes and kickbacks while in office; Pres. Arroyo pardoned him Oct. 25. Benigno "NoyNoy" Aquino III, the son of former Pres. Aquino (who died Aug. 1, 2009), defeated Estrada in the May 10, 2010, presidential election.

The government, Oct. 15, 2012, signed a new peace deal with Muslim rebels on Mindanao; violence had persisted after the 1996 accord. Yet another peace agreement, providing for a large measure of autonomy for Mindanao, was signed by the government and Moro Islamic Liberation Front, Mar. 27, 2014. The Abu Sayyaf Islamist guerrilla group rejected the accord. Abu Sayyaf and the rebel group Maute, both of which claimed allegiance to ISIS, continued to stage attacks.

Typhoon Haiyan, with winds up to 195 mph, struck the Philippines Nov. 8, 2013, killing more than 6,200 people and displacing over 4 mil. Vowing a tough crackdown on drug crime, Rodrigo Duterte was elected president, May 9, 2016. By the end of 2017, an estimated 12,000 or more drug suspects had been killed by police or vigilantes since Duterte took office, including about 4,000 acknowledged police killings; 1.3 mil drug suspects had surrendered as of mid-2017, according to government figures.

Duterte's government completed a new cease-fire agreement with Communist rebels, Aug. 26, 2016. Muslim rebels, May 2017, attacked and seized part of the city of Marawi; the military completed recapture of the ruined city Oct. 23. Legislation to implement the 2014 autonomy agreement was signed in July 2018.

Poland
Republic of Poland

People: Population: 38,420,687 (37). **Age distrib.:** <15: 14.8%; 65+: 17.5%. **Growth:** –0.2%. **Migrants:** 1.7%. **Pop. density:** 327.1 per sq mi, 126.3 per sq km. **Urban:** 60.1%. **Ethnic groups:** Polish 96.9%. **Languages:** Polish (official). **Religions:** Catholic 87.2%.

Geography: Total area: 120,728 sq mi, 312,685 sq km (69); **Land area:** 117,474 sq mi, 304,255 sq km. **Location:** On Baltic Sea in E central Europe. Germany on W; Czech Rep., Slovakia on S; Lithuania, Belarus, Ukraine on E; Russia on N. **Topography:** Mostly lowlands forming part of the Northern European Plain. The Carpathian Mts. along S border rise to 8,200 ft. **Arable land:** 35.6%. **Capital:** Warsaw, 1,767,798. **Cities:** Kraków, 767,178.

Government: Type: Parliamentary republic. **Head of state:** Pres. Andrzej Duda; b. 1972; in office: Aug. 6, 2015. **Head of govt.:** Prime Min. Mateusz Morawiecki; b. 1968; in office: Dec. 11, 2017. **Local divisions:** 16 provinces. **Defense budget:** $9.8 bil. **Active troops:** 105,000.

Economy: Industries: machine building, iron and steel, coal mining, chemicals, shipbuilding, food proc., glass, beverages, textiles. **Chief agric.:** potatoes, fruits, vegetables, wheat; poultry, eggs, pork, dairy. **Natural resources:** coal, sulfur, copper, nat. gas, silver, lead, salt, amber. **Water:** 1,567 cu m per capita. **Crude oil reserves:** 126 mil bbls. **Electricity prod.:** 155.3 bil kWh. **Labor force:** agric. 10.6%, industry 31.3%, services 58.1%. **Unemployment:** 4.9%.

Finance: Monetary unit: Zloty (PLN) (3.72 = $1 U.S.). **GDP:** $1.1 tril; **per capita GDP:** $29,500; **GDP growth:** 4.6%. **Imports:** $221.8 bil; Germany 27.9%, China 8%, Russia 6.4%, Netherlands 6%, Italy 5.3%. **Exports:** $221.4 bil; Germany 27.4%, Czechia 6.4%, UK 6.4%, France 5.6%. **Tourism:** $12.8 bil. **Budget:** $102.5 bil. **Inflation:** 2.1%.

Transport: Railways: 11,950 mi. **Motor vehicles:** 688.3 per 1,000 pop. **Airports:** 87.

Communications: Telephone (2016): 21.3 per 100 pop. **Mobile:** 130.5 per 100 pop. **Broadband:** 58.9 per 100 pop. **Internet** (2017): 76%.

Health: Expend.: 6.3%. **Life expect.:** 74.1 male; 82.0 female. **Births:** 9.3 per 1,000 pop. **Deaths:** 10.5 per 1,000 pop. **Infant mortality:** 4.4 per 1,000 live births. **Undernourished:** <2.5%. **HIV:** NA.

Education: Compulsory: ages 7-15. **Literacy:** 99.8%.
Embassy: 2640 16th St. NW 20009; 499-1700.
Website: www.poland.gov.pl

Slavic tribes in the area were converted to Latin Christianity in the 10th cent. Poland was a great power from the 14th to the 17th cent. In three partitions (1772, 1793, 1795) it was apportioned among Prussia, Russia, and Austria. Overrun by the Austro-German armies in WWI, it declared its independence on Nov. 11,

1918, and was recognized as independent by the Treaty of Versailles, June 28, 1919. Large territories to the east were taken in a war with Russia, 1921.

Germany and the USSR invaded Poland Sept. 1939 and divided the country. During the war, Nazis killed some 6 mil Polish citizens, half of them Jews. (Controversial Feb. 2018 legislation outlawed attributing to Poland any role in Nazi atrocities; a June amendment weakened penalties.) In compensation for territory ceded to the USSR when WWII ended, Poland received German territory comprising Silesia, Pomerania, West Prussia, and part of East Prussia. Communists, who aligned themselves with the USSR, dominated the 1947 election.

In 12 years of rule by Stalinists, large estates were abolished, industries nationalized, schools secularized, and Roman Catholic prelates jailed. Farm production fell off. Harsh working conditions caused a riot in Poznan, June 28-29, 1956. A new Politburo, committed to a more independent Polish Communism, was named Oct. 1956, with Wladyslaw Gomulka as first secretary of the party. Collectivization of farms was ended. Gomulka agreed to increase religious liberty.

In Dec. 1970 workers in port cities rioted because of price rises and new incentive wage rules. On Dec. 20 Gomulka resigned as party leader; he was succeeded by Edward Gierek. The rules were dropped and price rises revoked.

Independent trade union Solidarity gained strength in the 1980s, organizing strikes and making bold demands. Led by Lech Walesa, Solidarity helped to win political and economic reforms, including free elections, in an Apr. 5, 1989, accord. Candidates endorsed by Solidarity swept the parliamentary elections, June 4. Walesa became president Dec. 22, 1990.

A radical economic program designed to transform the economy into a free-market system led to inflation, unemployment, and a return to the political left in 1993 parliamentary elections. A former Communist, Aleksander Kwasniewski, defeated Walesa in the 1995 presidential election and was reelected 5 years later. Poland became a full member of NATO, Mar. 12, 1999, and entered the European Union May 1, 2004. At a July 2016 NATO summit in Warsaw, the alliance agreed to permanently station troops in Poland.

Lech Kaczynski of the conservative Law and Justice (PiS) party won a presidential runoff election Oct. 23, 2005. The center-right Civic Platform (PO) party won parliamentary elections Oct. 21, 2007. Pres. Kaczynski and many senior officials were killed in a plane crash Apr. 10, 2010. Parliament Speaker Bronislaw Komorowski of PO became president. Komorowski was defeated by Andrzej Duda of PiS in a May 24, 2015, presidential runoff. PiS won a majority of seats in Oct. 25, 2015, parliamentary elections. July 2017 legislation allowing the justice minister to appoint lower court judges drew criticism from EU leaders as a threat to the independence of the judiciary. Legislation effective July 2018 forcing the retirement of about two dozen Supreme Court judges was also condemned by the EU and prompted widespread protests.

Portugal
Portuguese Republic

People: Population: 10,355,493 (87). **Age distrib.:** <15: 14%; 65+: 20.3%. **Growth:** −0.3%. **Migrants:** 8.5%. **Pop. density:** 293.2 per sq mi, 113.2 per sq km. **Urban:** 65.2%. **Ethnic groups:** homogeneous Mediterranean pop. **Languages:** Portuguese, Mirandese (both official). **Religions:** Roman Catholic 81%, none 6.8%.

Geography: Total area: 35,556 sq mi, 92,090 sq km (109); **Land area:** 35,317 sq mi, 91,470 sq km. **Location:** SW extreme of Europe. Spain on N, E. **Topography:** Tajus R. bisects country NE-SW. N is cool and rainy, mountainous. S is drier, with warm climate and rolling plains. **Arable land:** 12.4%. **Capital:** Lisbon, 2,927,316. **Cities:** Porto, 1,306,934.

Government: Type: Semi-presidential republic. **Head of state:** Pres. Marcelo Rebelo de Sousa; b. 1948; in office: Mar. 9, 2016. **Head of govt.:** Prime Min. António Costa; b. 1961; in office Nov. 24, 2015. **Local divisions:** 18 districts, 2 autonomous regions. **Defense budget:** $2.4 bil. **Active troops:** 30,500.

Economy: Industries: textiles, clothing, footwear, wood and cork, paper and pulp, chemicals, fuels and lubricants, automobiles/auto parts, base metals. **Chief agric.:** grain, potatoes, tomatoes, olives, grapes; sheep, cattle, goats. **Natural resources:** fish, forests (cork), iron ore, copper, zinc, tin, tungsten, silver, gold, uranium, marble, clay, gypsum, salt, hydropower. **Water:** 7,478 cu m per capita. **Electricity prod.:** 49.2 bil kWh. **Labor force:** agric. 6.8%, industry 24.8%, services 68.3%. **Unemployment:** 8.9%.

Finance: Monetary unit: Euro (EUR) (0.86 = $1 U.S.). **GDP:** $313.4 bil; **per capita GDP:** $30,400; **GDP growth:** 2.7%. **Imports:** $74.3 bil; Spain 32%, Germany 13.7%, France 7.4%, Italy 5.5%, Netherlands 5.4%. **Exports:** $62.6 bil; Spain 25.2%, France 12.5%, Germany 11.3%, UK 6.6%, U.S. 5.2%. **Tourism:** $17.1 bil. **Budget:** $96.8 bil. **Inflation:** 1.4%.

Transport: Railways: 1,911 mi. **Motor vehicles:** 540.1 per 1,000 pop. **Airports:** 43.

Communications: Telephone: 46.8 per 100 pop. **Mobile:** 113.9 per 100 pop. **Broadband:** 61.1 per 100 pop. **Internet** (2017): 73.8%.

Health: Expend.: 9%. **Life expect.:** 77.7 male; 84.2 female. **Births:** 8.2 per 1,000 pop. **Deaths:** 10.6 per 1,000 pop. **Infant mortality:** 2.6 per 1,000 live births. **Undernourished:** <2.5%. **HIV:** 0.6%.

Education: Compulsory: ages 6-14. **Literacy:** 95.7%.
Embassy: 2012 Massachusetts Ave. NW 20036; 350-5400.
Website: www.portugal.gov.pt

Portugal, an independent state since the 12th cent., was a kingdom until a 1910 revolution drove out King Manoel II and a republic was proclaimed. Beginning in 1932, Prime Min. Antonio de Oliveira Salazar headed a repressive government. Illness forced his retirement in Sept. 1968.

On Apr. 25, 1974, a military junta led by Gen. Antonio de Spinola seized the government; Spinola became president. The new government granted independence to Guinea-Bissau, Mozambique, Cabo Verde, Angola, and São Tomé and Príncipe.

With the economy lagging, the Socialists won 2005 and 2009 parliamentary elections. After Portugal was given a 78-bil-euro bailout package from international lenders to avert default, the center-right Social Democratic Party won parliamentary elections June 2011. Austerity cuts caused widespread protests in Nov. 2012; the Constitutional Court ruled Apr. 5, 2013, that many of the cuts were illegal. Portugal completed loan repayments and exited the bailout program in May 2014. After parliamentary elections Oct. 4, 2015, Socialist António Costa became prime min., Nov. 24, leading an anti-austerity leftist coalition. Former Prime Min. António Guterres became UN secretary general, Jan. 1, 2017. June and Oct. 2017 wildfires in central and northern Portugal killed more than 100.

Azores Isls., in the Atlantic, 740 mi W of Portugal, have an area of 868 sq mi and a pop. (2014 est.) of 246,353. A 1951 agreement gave the U.S. rights to use defense facilities in the Azores. The **Madeira Isls.**, 350 mi off the NW coast of Africa, have an area of 306 sq mi and a pop. (2014 est.) of 258,686. Both groups were offered partial autonomy in 1976.

Qatar
State of Qatar

People: Population: 2,363,569 (140). **Age distrib.:** <15: 12.7%; 65+: 1.1%. **Growth:** 2%. **Migrants:** 65.2%. **Pop. density:** 528.4 per sq mi, 204 per sq km. **Urban:** 99.1%. **Ethnic groups:** non-Qatari 88.4%, Qatari 11.6%. **Languages:** Arabic (official), English. **Religions:** Muslim 67.7%, Christian 13.8%, Hindu 13.8%, Buddhist 3.1%.

Geography: Total area: 4,473 sq mi, 11,586 sq km (159); **Land area:** 4,473 sq mi, 11,586 sq km. **Location:** Middle East, occupying peninsula on W coast of Persian Gulf. Saudi Arabia on S. **Topography:** Mostly flat desert with some limestone ridges; scarce vegetation. **Arable land:** 1.1%. **Capital:** Doha (Ad-Dawhah), 633,401.

Government: Type: Absolute monarchy. **Head of state:** Emir Sheikh Tamim bin Hamad al-Thani; b. 1980; in office: June 25, 2013. **Head of govt.:** Prime Min. Sheikh Abdullah bin Nasser bin Khalifa al-Thani; b. 1959; in office: June 26, 2013. **Local divisions:** 8 municipalities. **Defense budget:** NA. **Active troops:** 11,800.

Economy: Industries: liquefied nat. gas, crude oil prod./refining, ammonia, fertilizer, petrochemicals, steel reinforcing bars. **Chief agric.:** fruits, vegetables; poultry, dairy prods., beef; fish. **Natural resources:** petroleum, nat. gas, fish. **Water:** 26 cu m per capita. **Crude oil reserves:** 25.2 bil bbls. **Electricity prod.:** 39 bil kWh. **Labor force:** agric. 1.3%, industry 55.1%, services 43.6%. **Unemployment:** 0.1%.

Finance: Monetary unit: Riyal (QAR) (3.64 = $1 U.S.). **GDP:** $340.6 bil; **per capita GDP:** $124,500; **GDP growth:** 2.1%. **Imports:** $26.7 bil; China 10.9%, U.S. 8.9%, UAE 8.5%, Germany 8.1%, UK 5.5%, India 5.4%, Japan 5.3%. **Exports:** $56.3 bil; Japan 17.3%, South Korea 16%, India 12.6%, China 11.2%, Singapore 8.2%, UAE 6.4%. **Tourism:** $6 bil. **Budget:** $51.8 bil. **Inflation:** 0.4%.

Transport: Motor vehicles: 183 per 1,000 pop. **Airports:** 4.
Communications: Telephone: 16.7 per 100 pop. **Mobile:** 148.3 per 100 pop. **Broadband:** 129.2 per 100 pop. **Internet:** 94.3%.
Health: Expend.: 3.1%. **Life expect.:** 76.9 male; 81.2 female. **Births:** 9.5 per 1,000 pop. **Deaths:** 1.6 per 1,000 pop. **Infant mortality:** 6.0 per 1,000 live births. **Undernourished:** NA. **HIV:** 0.1%.

Education: Compulsory: ages 6-14. **Literacy:** 97.3%.
Embassy: 2555 M St. NW 20037; 274-1600.
Website: portal.www.gov.qa

Qatar was under Bahrain's control until the Ottoman Turks took power, 1872 to 1915. In a treaty signed 1916, Qatar gave Great Britain responsibility for its defense and foreign relations. Qatar declared itself independent, Sept. 1, 1971. In municipal elections held Mar. 8, 1999, women participated for the first time as candidates and voters. Qatar's emir, Sheikh Hamad bin Khalifa al-Thani, abdicated in favor of his son, Sheikh Tamim bin Hamad al-Thani, June 25, 2013. A major producer and exporter of oil and natural gas, Qatar is one of the world's wealthiest nations per capita.

Since 2000, the U.S. Army has operated the Camp As-Sayliyah base near Doha. Beginning in 2003, the U.S. Air Force Central Command's operations center has been at Qatar's Al-Udeid air base, used since 2014 for airstrikes against ISIS. Qatar joined the U.S.-led anti-ISIS coalition. Qatar also joined Saudi-led airstrikes, beginning Mar. 2015, against Shiite Houthi rebels in Yemen but was expelled from that effort June 5, 2017. Beginning June 5, a Saudi-led group of Arab nations, alleging Qatari support for terrorist and sectarian groups, broke diplomatic relations with Qatar, expelled Qatari citizens, and imposed a travel and trade ban. On Aug. 24, Qatar restored full diplomatic relations with Iran (severed in 2016).

Romania

People: Population: 21,457,116 (58). **Age distrib.:** <15: 14.3%; 65+: 16.8%. **Growth:** –0.4%. **Migrants:** 1.9%. **Pop. density:** 241.7 per sq mi, 93.3 per sq km. **Urban:** 54%. **Ethnic groups:** Romanian 83.4%, Hungarian 6.1%, Romani 3.1%. **Languages:** Romanian (official), Hungarian. **Religions:** Eastern Orthodox 81.9%, Protestant 6.4%, Roman Catholic 4.3%.

Geography: Total area: 92,043 sq mi, 238,391 sq km (81); **Land area:** 88,761 sq mi, 229,891 sq km. **Location:** SE Europe, on the Black Sea. Moldova on E, Ukraine on N, Hungary and Serbia on W, Bulgaria on S. **Topography:** The Carpathian Mts. surround the N central Transylvanian plateau. The lower reaches of the Danube river system flow through plains S and E of the mountains. **Arable land:** 38.1%. **Capital:** Bucharest, 1,821,380.

Government: Type: Semi-presidential republic. **Head of state:** Pres. Klaus Iohannis; b. 1959; in office: Dec. 21, 2014. **Head of govt.:** Prime Min. Viorica Dancila; b. 1963; in office: Jan. 29, 2018. **Local divisions:** 41 counties, 1 municipality. **Defense budget:** $4 bil. **Active troops:** 69,300.

Economy: Industries: elec. machinery/equip., auto assembly, textiles/footwear, light machinery, metallurgy, chemicals, food proc. **Chief agric.:** wheat, corn, barley, sugar beets, sunflower seeds, potatoes, grapes; eggs, sheep. **Natural resources:** petroleum, timber, nat. gas, coal, iron ore, salt, hydropower. **Water:** 10,866 cu m per capita. **Crude oil reserves:** 600 mil bbls. **Electricity prod.:** 63 bil kWh. **Labor force:** agric. 22.9%, industry 29.1%, services 48%. **Unemployment:** 4.9%.

Finance: Monetary unit: Leu (RON) (4.00 = $1 U.S.). **GDP:** $481.5 bil; **per capita GDP:** $24,500; **GDP growth:** 7%. **Imports:** $78.1 bil; Germany 20%, Italy 10%, Hungary 7.5%, Poland 5.5%, France 5.3%, China 5%. **Exports:** $64.9 bil; Germany 23%, Italy 11.2%, France 6.8%. **Tourism:** $2.5 bil. **Budget:** $65.5 bil. **Inflation:** 1.3%.

Transport: Railways: 7,002 mi. **Motor vehicles:** 326.2 per 1,000 pop. **Airports:** 26.

Communications: Telephone: 19.8 per 100 pop. **Mobile:** 114.6 per 100 pop. **Broadband:** 73.7 per 100 pop. **Internet** (2017): 63.7%.

Health: Expend.: 5%. **Life expect.:** 72.1 male; 79.2 female. **Births:** 8.7 per 1,000 pop. **Deaths:** 12.0 per 1,000 pop. **Infant mortality:** 9.2 per 1,000 live births. **Undernourished:** <2.5%. **HIV:** 0.1%.

Education: Compulsory: ages 7-16. **Literacy:** 98.8%.
Embassy: 1607 23rd St. NW 20008; 332-4846.
Website: gov.ro

Romania's earliest known people merged with invading Proto-Thracians, preceding by centuries the Dacians. Rome occupied the Dacian kingdom, 106-271 CE; people and language were Romanized. The Turkey-dominated principalities of Wallachia and Moldavia were united in 1859, became Romania in 1861, and gained recognition as an independent kingdom, 1881.

After WWI, Romania acquired Bessarabia, Bukovina, Transylvania, and Banat. In 1940 it ceded Bessarabia and Northern Bukovina to the USSR, part of southern Dobrudja to Bulgaria, and northern Transylvania to Hungary. In 1941, Prem. Marshal Ion Antonescu led Romania in support of Germany against the USSR. He was overthrown in 1944, and Romania joined the Allies. After occupation by Soviet troops, a People's Republic was proclaimed, Dec. 30, 1947.

The domestic policies of Nicolae Ceausescu (in power 1965) were repressive. All industry was state-owned, and state farms and cooperatives owned almost all arable land. Ceausescu's security forces fired on anti-government demonstrators, Dec. 1989, killing hundreds, but when the army sided with the protesters, his regime fell. Charged with genocide and abuse of power, Ceausescu and his wife were executed Dec. 25, 1989.

A new constitution providing for a multiparty system took effect Dec. 8, 1991. Many state-owned companies were privatized in 1996. Romania became a full NATO member in 2004. It entered the European Union Jan. 1, 2007. Troops from Romania served with NATO-led forces in Afghanistan; almost 700 remained as of mid-2018. The Social Democratic Party's (PSD) Victor-Viorel Ponta became prime min. May 7, 2012. He ran for president in 2014 but lost the runoff to Klaus Iohannis. Large protests, blaming government incompetence for the deaths of more than 60 in a Bucharest nightclub fire, Oct. 30, 2015, led to the resignation, Nov. 4, 2015, of Ponta, already weakened by corruption allegations. The PSD won Dec. 11, 2016, parliamentary elections. A Jan. 2017 decree to thwart corruption investigations was repealed in Feb. after massive protests. The PSD's Viorica Dancila, a close ally of party leader Liviu Dragnea, became Romania's first female

prime min. Jan. 29, 2018. Dragnea was convicted, June 2018, on corruption-related charges. The country's top anti-corruption prosecutor was dismissed in July. Anti-corruption protests continued in 2018.

Russia
Russian Federation

People: Population: 142,122,776 (9). **Age distrib.:** <15: 17.2%; 65+: 14.7%. **Growth:** –0.1%. **Migrants:** 8.1%. **Pop. density:** 22.5 per sq mi, 8.7 per sq km. **Urban:** 74.4%. **Ethnic groups:** Russian 77.7%, Tatar 3.7%. **Languages:** Russian (official), Tatar. **Religions:** Russian Orthodox 15%-20%, Muslim 10%-15%.

Geography: Total area: 6,601,668 sq mi, 17,098,242 sq km (1); **Land area:** 6,323,482 sq mi, 16,377,742 sq km, more than 76% of total area of the former USSR and the largest country in the world. **Location:** Stretches from Eastern Europe across N Asia to the Pacific O. Finland, Norway, Estonia, Latvia, Belarus, Ukraine on W; Georgia, Azerbaijan, Kazakhstan, China, Mongolia, N. Korea on S; Kaliningrad exclave bordered by Poland on the S, Lithuania on the N and E. **Topography:** Every type of climate except distinctly tropical. European portion is low plain, grassy in S, wooded in N, with Ural Mts. on E, and Caucasus Mts. on S. Urals stretch N-S for 2,500 mi. Asiatic portion is vast plain, with mountains on S and in E; tundra covers extreme N with forest belt below; plains, marshes in W, desert in SW. **Arable land:** 7.5%. **Capital:** Moscow, 12,409,738. **Cities:** Saint Petersburg, 5,383,068; Novosibirsk, 1,635,618; Yekaterinburg, 1,482,148; Nizhniy Novgorod, 1,264,336; Kazan, 1,254,114; Chelyabinsk, 1,215,994.

Government: Type: Semi-presidential federation. **Head of state:** Pres. Vladimir Putin; b. 1952; in office: May 7, 2012. **Head of govt.:** Prime Min. Dmitri Medvedev; b. 1965; in office: May 8, 2012. **Local divisions:** 46 provinces (oblasts), 21 republics, 4 autonomous okrugs, 9 krays, 2 federal cities, 1 autonomous oblast. **Defense budget:** $45.6 bil. **Active troops:** 900,000.

Economy: Industries: coal, oil, gas, chemicals, metals; machine building; defense (incl. radar, missile prod.); shipbuilding; road, rail transp. equip.; communications equip.; agric. machinery, tractors, constr. equip. **Chief agric.:** grain, sugar beets, sunflower seeds, vegetables, fruits; beef, milk. **Natural resources:** oil, nat. gas, coal, minerals, rare earth elements, timber. Climate, terrain, and distance are obstacles to resource exploitation. **Water:** 31,543 cu m per capita. **Crude oil reserves:** 80 bil bbls. **Electricity prod.:** 1 tril kWh. **Labor force:** agric. 6.7%, industry 26.9%, services 66.4%. **Unemployment:** 5.2%.

Finance: Monetary unit: Ruble (RUB) (68.19 = $1 U.S.). **GDP:** $4 tril; **per capita GDP:** $27,800; **GDP growth:** 1.5%. **Imports:** $212.7 bil; China 21.2%, Germany 10.7%, U.S. 5.6%, Belarus 5%. **Exports:** $336.8 bil; China 10.9%, Netherlands 10%, Germany 7.1%, Belarus 5.1%. **Tourism:** $8.9 bil. **Budget:** $287.5 bil. **Inflation:** 3.7%.

Transport: Railways: 54,157 mi. **Motor vehicles:** 372.3 per 1,000 pop. **Airports:** 594.

Communications: Telephone: 21.7 per 100 pop. **Mobile:** 157.9 per 100 pop. **Broadband:** 75 per 100 pop. **Internet** (2017): 76%.

Health: Expend.: 5.6%. **Life expect.:** 65.6 male; 77.3 female. **Births:** 10.7 per 1,000 pop. **Deaths:** 13.4 per 1,000 pop. **Infant mortality:** 6.7 per 1,000 live births. **Undernourished:** <2.5%. **HIV:** 1.2%.

Education: Compulsory: ages 7-17. **Literacy:** 99.7%.
Embassy: 2650 Wisconsin Ave. NW 20007; 298-5700.
Website: government.ru

Slavic tribes began migrating into Russia from the W in the 5th cent. The first Russian state, centered in Novgorod and Kiev, was founded by Scandinavian chieftains in the 9th cent. In the 13th cent., Mongols overran the country. It recovered under the grand dukes and princes of Muscovy, or Moscow, and by 1480 freed itself from the Mongols. Ivan the Terrible was proclaimed Tsar, 1547. Peter the Great (1682-1725) extended the domain and, in 1721, founded the Russian empire. Western ideas and the beginnings of modernization spread through the empire in the 19th and early 20th cent.

Military reverses in the 1905 war with Japan and in WWI led to the breakdown of the Tsarist regime. The 1917 Revolution began in Mar. with a series of sporadic strikes for higher wages by factory workers. A provisional democratic government under Prince Georgi Lvov was established but a second provisional government, under Alexander Kerensky, followed in May. Vladimir Ilyich Lenin, Nov. 7, overthrew the Kerensky government and the freely elected Constituent Assembly in a Communist coup.

Soviet Union. Lenin's death Jan. 21, 1924, led to an internal power struggle won by Joseph Stalin. His brutal tactics, including purge trials, mass executions, and exile to work camps, resulted in millions of deaths.

Despite a Germany-USSR non-aggression pact signed in Aug. 1939, Germany invaded the Soviet Union, June 1941. Russian winter counterthrusts, 1941-42 and 1942-43; victory at Stalingrad (now Volgograd), Feb. 2, 1943 (2 mil total casualties); and resistance to the siege of Leningrad (now St. Petersburg) stopped the German advance. Russian armies drove the Germans from Eastern Europe and the Balkans in the next two years.

After WWII, Communists took over in countries throughout the region, extending the Soviet sphere of influence. The USSR and the U.S., the world's leading nuclear superpowers, became Cold War rivals. After Stalin died, Mar. 5, 1953, Nikita Khrushchev gained power and denounced Stalin, 1956, beginning "de-Stalinization."

Under Khrushchev the open antagonism of Poles and Hungarians toward Moscow's domination was suppressed in 1956. He aided the Cuban revolution under Fidel Castro but withdrew Soviet missiles from Cuba during a confrontation with U.S. Pres. John Kennedy, Sept.-Oct. 1962. Khrushchev was deposed, Oct. 1964, and replaced by Leonid I. Brezhnev. In Aug. 1968, Soviet forces invaded Czechoslovakia, crushing liberalization there.

Massive Soviet military aid to North Vietnam in the late 1960s and early 1970s helped ensure Communist victories throughout Indochina. In Dec. 1979, Soviet forces entered Afghanistan to support a pro-Soviet regime against U.S.-supported Muslim resistance fighters. In Apr. 1988, the Soviets agreed to withdraw their troops, ending a futile 8-year war.

Mikhail Gorbachev was chosen Communist Party gen. sec., Mar. 1985. In 1987 he initiated a program of political and economic reforms through openness (*glasnost*) and restructuring (*perestroika*). Gorbachev faced economic problems as well as ethnic and nationalist unrest in the republics. A coup by Communist hardliners Aug. 1991 was foiled with help from Russian Republic Pres. Boris Yeltsin. On Aug. 24, Gorbachev resigned as leader of the Communist Party. Several republics declared their independence. On Aug. 29, the Soviet Parliament voted to suspend all activities of the Communist Party. The Soviet Union officially broke up Dec. 26, 1991.

Russian Federation. Under Pres. Yeltsin, Russia took steps toward privatization, which caused inflation and a severe economic downturn. In June 1992, Yeltsin and U.S. Pres. George H. W. Bush agreed to massive arms reductions. In a referendum Dec. 12, 1993, a new constitution was approved. Russian troops fought rebels in the breakaway republic of Chechnya Dec. 1994-Aug. 1996, when a peace accord temporarily ended the conflict. On May 27, 1997, Yeltsin (reelected in 1996) signed a founding act, paving the way for NATO to admit Eastern European nations.

An Aug. 1999 operation to suppress Islamic rebels in the republic of Dagestan reignited the war in neighboring Chechnya, where Russia launched a full-scale assault. Yeltsin unexpectedly resigned Dec. 31, 1999, naming Prime Min. Vladimir Putin as his interim successor. Putin won presidential elections Mar. 2000. Putin's allies won legislative elections, Dec. 2003, and the president was reelected Mar. 2004.

A bomb in Grozny, May 9, 2004, killed Chechnya's pro-Moscow president, Akhmad Kadyrov. In another terrorist act linked to the Chechnya conflict, two passenger planes exploded in midair after taking off from Moscow Aug. 24, killing 90 people. Chechen rebels, Sept. 1, 2004, seized control of a school in Beslan, North Ossetia, taking more than 1,100 hostages. Russian troops stormed the school Sept. 3; more than 330 people, including 186 children, died. Putin cited the terrorist threat Sept. 13 in proposing a government overhaul that tightened his control over parliament and regional officeholders. Russian forces killed Chechen rebel leader Aslan Maskhadov, Mar. 8, 2005, and Chechen guerrilla leader Shamil Basayev, organizer of the terrorist attack at Beslan, July 10, 2006.

Constitutionally barred from seeking another term, Pres. Putin backed his protégé Prime Min. Dmitri Medvedev, who won the presidential election Mar. 2, 2008. Medvedev named Putin as prime min. A long-simmering conflict with Georgia erupted into open warfare Aug. 7-16. Russia dispatched troops to support secessionists in the enclaves of South Ossetia and Abkhazia; a cease-fire left thousands of Russian troops in the breakaway regions, which Russia recognized as independent, Aug. 26, 2008.

Russia declared, Apr. 16, 2009, that it had ended counterterrorism operations in Chechnya; from June through Aug., there was an upsurge of insurgent violence in Chechnya and neighboring Dagestan and Ingushetia. Suicide bombers from Dagestan struck two Moscow subway stations Mar. 29, 2010, killing 40 people. A bombing at a Moscow airport Jan. 24, 2011, killed 37.

Medvedev and U.S. Pres. Barack Obama, Apr. 8, 2010, signed a nuclear arms reduction treaty known as New START. Putin won 64% of the vote in the Mar. 4, 2012, presidential election, though there were claims of fraud. Three members of the anti-Putin punk-protest band Pussy Riot were convicted of hooliganism Aug. 17, 2012. Putin signed a law, June 30, 2013, effectively making it illegal to advocate publicly for gay rights. The Putin administration granted asylum to former U.S. National Security Agency contractor Edward Snowden Aug. 1, 2013.

Sochi, Russia, hosted the 2014 Winter Olympics Feb. 7-23, 2014. Although suicide bombings in Volgograd, for which Dagestan separatists claimed responsibility, killed 34, Dec. 29-30, 2013, there were no major security incidents at the Games.

After Ukraine's pro-Russian president was removed from office Feb. 22, 2014, Russia sent troops into Ukraine's Crimean Peninsula and annexed Crimea Mar. 18. A 12-mi. bridge linking Crimea to Russia was completed in May 2018. Russia also apparently provided military equipment and troops to pro-Russian separatists in eastern Ukraine fighting Ukrainian government forces beginning in Apr. 2014. The U.S. and EU imposed economic sanctions to protest Russia's Ukraine policies.

Russia supported Pres. Bashar al-Assad in Syria's civil war (2011-). In Sept. 2015, Russia sent combat aircraft, other military equipment, and troops to Syria. Russia began, Sept. 30, airstrikes against various rebel forces, including ISIS and an al-Qaeda affiliate, and against rebel-held areas, sometimes causing high civilian casualties. An ISIS-affiliated group claimed responsibility for planting a bomb on a Russian airliner that crashed in Egypt, Oct. 31, 2015, killing all 224 onboard. An al-Qaeda-linked group claimed it ordered a St. Petersburg suicide bombing, Apr. 3, 2017, that killed 15 victims.

More than 100 Russian athletes were barred from the 2016 Summer Olympics after the World Anti-Doping Agency presented evidence of a widespread state-sponsored program to provide athletes with banned drugs. Russia was officially barred from the 2018 Winter Olympics, although 169 individual Russian athletes were allowed to compete under the designation Olympic Athletes from Russia (OAR).

Putin's United Russia party won Sept. 18, 2016, parliamentary elections. With the media tightly controlled and amid allegations of fraud, Putin won a new 6-year term as president, Mar. 18, 2018, with about 77% of the vote.

U.S. government security agencies concluded in Dec. 2016 that Russia attempted to interfere in the 2016 U.S. presidential election, apparently to assist the candidacy of Donald Trump, using tactics such as cyberattacks and manipulation of social media. The U.S., Dec. 29, expelled 35 Russian diplomats. With Congress, July 2017, finalizing legislation strengthening sanctions, Russia ordered sharp staff reductions at U.S. diplomatic facilities. The U.S., Aug. 31, ordered the closure of three Russian diplomatic facilities. The U.S. indicted, Feb. 16, 2018, 16 Russian individuals or companies on charges related to 2016 election interference; 12 Russian intelligence officials were indicted, July 13, for hacking Democratic email accounts and other election-related activities. A U.S. grand jury, July 17, indicted Russian national Maria Butina for acting as a foreign agent in the U.S. At a July 16 meeting with Pres. Trump, Putin denied Russia had interfered in U.S. elections; speaking after the meeting, Trump appeared to accept the denial. At an Aug. 2 briefing, top Trump-administration intelligence officials stated that Russia was working to affect the 2018 elections as well. New U.S. sanctions went into effect, Aug. 22, following apparent Russian involvement in the poisoning, in the UK in Mar., of a former Russian intelligence officer.

Rwanda
Republic of Rwanda

People: Population: 12,187,400 (74). **Age distrib.:** <15: 41%; 65+: 2.5%. **Growth:** 2.3%. **Migrants:** 3.6%. **Pop. density:** 1,279.6 per sq mi, 494.1 per sq km. **Urban:** 17.2%. **Ethnic groups:** Hutu, Tutsi, Twa (Pygmy). **Languages:** Kinyarwanda (universal Bantu vernacular), French, English (all official). **Religions:** Protestant 49.5%, Roman Catholic 43.7%, Muslim 2%.

Geography: Total area: 10,169 sq mi, 26,338 sq km (145); **Land area:** 9,524 sq mi, 24,668 sq km. **Location:** E central Africa. Uganda on N, Dem. Rep. of the Congo on W, Burundi on S, Tanzania on E. **Topography:** Grassy uplands and hills cover most of country, with chain of volcanoes in NW. Nile R. source is in headwaters of the Kagera (Akagera) R. **Arable land:** 46.7%. **Capital:** Kigali, 1,057,836.

Government: Type: Presidential republic. **Head of state:** Pres. Paul Kagame; b. 1957; in office: Apr. 22, 2000 (de facto from Mar. 24). **Head of govt.:** Prime Min. Edouard Ngirente; b. 1973; in office: Aug. 30, 2017. **Local divisions:** 4 provinces, 1 city. **Defense budget:** $107 mil. **Active troops:** 33,000.

Economy: Industries: cement, agric. prods., small-scale beverages, soap, furniture, shoes, plastic goods, textiles, cigarettes. **Chief agric.:** coffee, tea, pyrethrum (insecticide made from chrysanthemums), bananas, beans, sorghum, potatoes; livestock. **Natural resources:** gold, tin ore, tungsten ore, methane, hydropower. **Water:** 1,146 cu m per capita. **Electricity prod.:** 600 mil kWh. **Labor force:** agric. 66.5%, industry 8.2%, services 25.4%. **Unemployment:** 1.3%.

Finance: Monetary unit: Franc (RWF) (878.16 = $1 U.S.). **GDP:** $24.6 bil; **per capita GDP:** $2,100; **GDP growth:** 6.1%. **Imports:** $2 bil; China 20.4%, Uganda 11%, India 7.2%, Kenya 7.1%, Tanzania 5.3%, UAE 5.1%. **Exports:** $908.9 mil; UAE 38.3%, Kenya 15.1%, Switzerland 9.9%, Dem. Rep. of the Congo 9.5%. **Tourism:** $438 mil. **Budget:** $2.3 bil. **Inflation:** 8.3%.

Transport: Airports: 4.

Communications: Telephone: 0.1 per 100 pop. **Mobile:** 72.2 per 100 pop. **Broadband:** 27 per 100 pop. **Internet:** 20%.

Health: Expend.: 7.9%. **Life expect.:** 62.6 male; 66.5 female. **Births:** 29.8 per 1,000 pop. **Deaths:** 6.3 per 1,000 pop. **Infant mortality:** 29.1 per 1,000 live births. **Undernourished:** 36.1%. **HIV:** 2.7%.

Education: Compulsory: ages 7-12. **Literacy:** 70.5%.

Embassy: 1875 Connecticut Ave. NW, Ste. 540, 20009; 232-2882.

Website: www.gov.rw

For centuries, the Tutsi dominated the Hutu majority. A civil war broke out in 1959 and Tutsi power was ended. Many Tutsi went into exile. Rwanda, which had been part of the Belgian UN trusteeship of Rwanda-Urundi, became independent July 1, 1962.

A large-scale massacre of Tutsi occurred in 1963. Hutu rivalries led to a bloodless coup July 1973 in which Hutu army officer Juvénal Habyarimana took power. After an invasion and coup attempt by Tutsi exiles in 1990, a multiparty democracy was established.

Renewed ethnic strife led to an Aug. 1993 peace accord between the government and rebels of the Tutsi-led Rwandan Patriotic Front (RPF). But after Habyarimana and Burundi Pres. Cyprien Ntaryamira were killed Apr. 6, 1994, in a suspicious plane crash, violence broke out. More than 1 mil may have died in massacres, mostly of Tutsi by Hutu militias, and in civil warfare as the RPF sought power. About 2 mil Tutsi and Hutu fled to camps in Zaire (now Dem. Rep. of the Congo, or DRC) and other countries; many died of disease. French troops under a UN mandate moved into SW Rwanda June 23 to establish a safe zone. The RPF claimed victory, installing a government led by a moderate Hutu president in July. French troops pulled out Aug. 22. A UN peacekeeping mission ended Mar. 8, 1996. More than 1 mil refugees, mostly Hutu, returned to Rwanda in Nov.-Dec. 1996.

Former Prime Min. Jean Kambanda pleaded guilty to genocide, May 1, 1998, before the UN-backed Intl. Criminal Tribunal for Rwanda (ICTR); he received a life sentence Sept. 4, 1998. RPF leader Maj. Gen. Paul Kagame became Rwanda's first Tutsi president Apr. 22, 2000.

Rwandans approved a new constitution, May 26, 2003, and reelected Pres. Kagame, Aug. 25. Steady economic growth began in 2003. Rwanda cut diplomatic ties with France Nov. 24, 2006, after a French judge linked Kagame to the 1994 deaths of Habyarimana and Ntaryamira. The country restored relations with France, Nov. 2009, the same month Rwanda joined the Commonwealth.

Accused of being one of the architects of the 1994 genocide, Col. Theoneste Bagosora was convicted and sentenced by the ICTR, Dec. 18, 2008, to life in prison (later reduced to 35 years). A Rwandan court Jan. 20, 2009, sentenced former Justice Min. Agnes Ntamabyariro to life in prison for her role in inciting the massacres. Up to 4,000 Rwandan troops fought that month alongside Congolese forces against Hutu militias in eastern DRC. After a campaign criticized as repressive by human rights groups, Pres. Kagame won reelection Aug. 9, 2010.

An Oct. 17, 2012, UN report found that the Rwanda military was backing a rebellion (2012-13) by the mostly-Tutsi M23 group in the DRC. More than 76,000 DRC refugees were living in Rwanda as of Aug. 31, 2018. Political unrest in Burundi beginning in early 2015 caused tens of thousands to flee to Rwanda, which hosted over 68,000 Burundian refugees as of Aug. 31, 2018. Shortly before the ICTR ceased operations, Dec. 31, 2015, one of its most-wanted fugitives, Ladislas Ntaganzwa, was arrested by Interpol in the DRC. His genocide trial in Rwanda began Apr. 4, 2016. Suppressing political opposition, Kagame won—with almost 99% of the vote—a new term as president in an Aug. 4, 2017, election.

Saint Kitts and Nevis
Federation of Saint Kitts and Nevis

People: Population: 53,094 (189). **Age distrib.:** <15: 20.1%; 65+: 9%. **Growth:** 0.7%. **Migrants:** 13.7%. **Pop. density:** 526.9 per sq mi, 203.4 per sq km. **Urban:** 30.8%. **Ethnic groups:** predominantly black; some British, Portuguese, Lebanese. **Languages:** English (official). **Religions:** Anglican, other Protestant, Roman Catholic.

Geography: Total area: 101 sq mi, 261 sq km (189); **Land area:** 101 sq mi, 261 sq km. **Location:** In N part of the Leeward group of Lesser Antilles in E Caribbean Sea. Antigua and Barbuda to E. **Topography:** Forested volcanic slopes on St. Kitts; beaches rising to central peak on Nevis. Tropical climate moderated by sea breezes. **Arable land:** 19.2%. **Capital:** Basseterre, 14,434.

Government: Type: Federal parliamentary democracy under constitutional monarchy. **Head of state:** Queen Elizabeth II, rep. by Gov.-Gen. Samuel W. T. Seaton; in office: Sept. 1, 2015. **Head of govt.:** Prime Min. Timothy Harris; b. 1964; in office: Feb. 16, 2015. **Local divisions:** 14 parishes. **Defense budget/active troops:** NA.

Economy: Industries: tourism, cotton, salt, copra, clothing, footwear, beverages. **Chief agric.:** sugarcane, rice, yams, vegetables, bananas; fish. **Water:** 432 cu m per capita. **Electricity prod.:** 208 mil kWh. **Labor force:** NA. **Unemployment:** NA.

Finance: Monetary unit: East Caribbean Dollar (XCD) (2.70 = $1 U.S.). **GDP:** $1.5 bil; **per capita GDP:** $26,800; **GDP growth:** 2.6%. **Imports:** $264.4 mil; U.S. 64.9%, Trinidad and Tobago 5%. 37.8%, Trinidad and Tobago 22.8%. **Exports:** $58.4 mil; Bangladesh 53%, U.S. 30.5%. **Tourism:** $141 mil. **Budget:** $370.4 mil. **Inflation:** 0.6%.

Transport: Railways: 31 mi. **Airports:** 2.

Communications: Telephone: 31.2 per 100 pop. **Mobile:** 138.9 per 100 pop. **Broadband:** 77.1 per 100 pop. **Internet:** 76.8%.

Health: Expend.: 5.6%. **Life expect.:** 73.7 male; 78.7 female. **Births:** 13.0 per 1,000 pop. **Deaths:** 7.2 per 1,000 pop. **Infant mortality:** 8.2 per 1,000 live births. **Undernourished:** NA. **HIV:** NA.

Education: Compulsory: ages 5-16. **Literacy:** 98%.
Embassy: 3216 New Mexico Ave. NW, 20016; 686-2636.
Website: www.gov.kn

St. Kitts (formerly St. Christopher; known by indigenous peoples as Liamuiga) and Nevis were reached by Columbus in 1493. They were settled by Britain in 1623 (ownership was disputed with France until 1713). The colony achieved self-government as an Associated State of the UK in 1967, becoming independent, Sept. 19, 1983. A secession referendum on Nevis, Aug. 10, 1998, fell short of the two-thirds majority required. Twenty years of Labour Party governments ended when an opposition coalition won a majority of seats in Feb. 16, 2015, legislative elections.

Saint Lucia

People: Population: 165,510 (178). **Age distrib.:** <15: 19.8%; 65+: 12.1%. **Growth:** 0.3%. **Migrants:** 7.2%. **Pop. density:** 707.4 per sq mi, 273.1 per sq km. **Urban:** 18.7%. **Ethnic groups:** black/African descent 85.3%, mixed 10.9%, East Indian 2.2%. **Languages:** English (official), French patois. **Religions:** Roman Catholic 61.5%, Protestant 25.5% (incl. Seventh-day Adventist 10.4%), none 5.9%.

Geography: Total area: 238 sq mi, 616 sq km (179); **Land area:** 234 sq mi, 606 sq km. **Location:** E Caribbean, second largest of Windward Isls. Martinique (Fr.) to N, St. Vincent to S. **Topography:** Mountainous, volcanic in origin; Soufrière Volcanic Centre in S. Wooded mountains run N-S. **Arable land:** 4.9%. **Capital:** Castries, 22,258.

Government: Type: Parliamentary democracy under constitutional monarchy. **Head of state:** Queen Elizabeth II, rep. by Gov.-Gen. Neville Cenac, b. 1939; in office: Jan. 12, 2018. **Head of govt.:** Prime Min. Allen Chastanet; in office: June 7, 2016. **Local divisions:** 10 districts. **Defense budget/active troops:** NA.

Economy: Industries: tourism, clothing, electronic components assembly, beverages, corrugated cardboard boxes, lime proc. **Chief agric.:** bananas, coconuts, vegetables, citrus, root crops, cocoa. **Natural resources:** forests, sandy beaches, pumice, mineral springs. **Water:** 1,622 cu m per capita. **Electricity prod.:** 358 mil kWh. **Labor force:** agric. 15.3%, industry 17.3%, services 67.4%. **Unemployment:** 21%.

Finance: Monetary unit: East Caribbean Dollar (XCD) (2.70 = $1 U.S.). **GDP:** $2.5 bil; **per capita GDP:** $14,400; **GDP growth:** 3%. **Imports:** $430.6 mil; U.S. 53.3%, Trinidad and Tobago 10.8%. **Exports:** $204.2 mil; U.S. 67.6%, UK 5.9%, Trinidad and Tobago 5.5%. **Tourism:** $404 mil. **Budget:** $430.7 mil. **Inflation:** 0.1%.

Transport: Airports: 2.

Communications: Telephone: 19.6 per 100 pop. **Mobile:** 98.8 per 100 pop. **Broadband:** 37 per 100 pop. **Internet:** 46.7%.

Health: Expend.: 6%. **Life expect.:** 75.4 male; 81.0 female. **Births:** 13.1 per 1,000 pop. **Deaths:** 7.8 per 1,000 pop. **Infant mortality:** 10.6 per 1,000 live births. **Undernourished:** NA. **HIV:** NA.

Education: Compulsory: ages 5-14. **Literacy:** NA.
Embassy: 1629 K St. NW, Ste. 1250, 20006; 364-6792.
Website: www.govt.lc

St. Lucia, ceded to Britain by France with the Treaty of Paris, 1814, gained independence Feb. 22, 1979. Investigation results announced Mar. 8, 2015, by Prime Min. Kenny Anthony found that 12 suspected criminals were put on a "death list" and killed by police in 2010-11. Pledging a tax cut and resolution of the police scandal, the conservative United Workers Party (UWP) defeated Anthony's Labor Party in June 6, 2016, elections; UWP leader Allen Chastanet became prime min.

Saint Vincent and the Grenadines

People: Population: 101,844 (183). **Age distrib.:** <15: 20.9%; 65+: 9.8%. **Growth:** -0.2%. **Migrants:** 4.2%. **Pop. density:** 678.1 per sq mi, 261.8 per sq km. **Urban:** 52.2%. **Ethnic groups:** black 66%, mixed 19%, East Indian 6%, European 4%, Carib Amerindian 2%. **Languages:** English, French patois. **Religions:** Protestant 75% (Anglican 47%, Methodist 28%), Roman Catholic 13%, other (incl. Hindu, Seventh-day Adventist, other Protestant) 12%.

Geography: Total area: 150 sq mi, 389 sq km (185); **Land area:** 150 sq mi, 389 sq km. **Location:** E Caribbean; St. Vincent (133 sq mi) and the northern islets of the Grenadines form a part of Windward chain. St. Lucia to N, Barbados to E, Grenada to S. **Topography:** St. Vincent is volcanic, with a ridge of thickly wooded mountains running its length. **Arable land:** 12.8%. **Capital:** Kingstown, 26,636.

Government: Type: Parliamentary democracy under constitutional monarchy. **Head of state:** Queen Elizabeth II, rep. by Gov.-Gen. Frederick Ballantyne; b. 1936; in office: Sept. 2, 2002. **Head of govt.:** Prime Min. Ralph Gonsalves; b. 1946; in office: Mar. 29, 2001. **Local divisions:** 6 parishes. **Defense budget/active troops:** NA.

Economy: Industries: tourism, food proc., cement, furniture, clothing, starch. **Chief agric.:** bananas, coconuts, sweet potatoes, spices. **Natural resources:** hydropower. **Water:** 913 cu m per capita. **Electricity prod.:** 155 mil kWh. **Labor force:** agric. 6.2%, industry 12.8%, services 81%. **Unemployment:** 18.3%.

Finance: Monetary unit: East Caribbean Dollar (XCD) (2.70 = $1 U.S.). **GDP:** $1.3 bil; **per capita GDP:** $11,500; **GDP growth:** 1%. **Imports:** $311.3 mil; U.S. 36.8%, Trinidad and Tobago 19.1%, UK 7%, China 5.8%. **Exports:** $51.3 mil; Jordan 40.7%, France 12.5%, Barbados 7%, St. Lucia 6.8%, Antigua and Barbuda 5.7%, U.S. 5.5%. **Tourism:** $101 mil. **Budget:** $259.3 mil. **Inflation:** 2.2%.

Transport: Airports: 5.

Communications: Telephone: 18.3 per 100 pop. **Mobile:** 105.7 per 100 pop. **Broadband:** 49.4 per 100 pop. **Internet** (2017): 65.6%.

Health: Expend.: 4.2%. **Life expect.:** 73.7 male; 77.9 female. **Births:** 13.0 per 1,000 pop. **Deaths:** 7.4 per 1,000 pop. **Infant mortality:** 11.7 per 1,000 live births. **Undernourished:** 5.7%. **HIV:** NA.

Education: Compulsory: ages 5-16. **Literacy:** 88%.

Embassy: 1627 K St. NW, Ste. 1202, 20006; 364-6730.

Website: www.gov.vc

St. Vincent received its name because of the belief (not supported by evidence) that Christopher Columbus landed there on Jan. 22, 1498 (St. Vincent's Day). Britain and France both laid claim to the island in the 17th and 18th cent.; the Treaty of Versailles, 1783, ceded it to Britain. Independence was attained Oct. 27, 1979.

Samoa
Independent State of Samoa

People: Population: 201,316 (177). **Age distrib.:** <15: 30.7%; 65+: 5.8%. **Growth:** 0.6%. **Migrants:** 2.5%. **Pop. density:** 184.8 per sq mi, 71.4 per sq km. **Urban:** 18.2%. **Ethnic groups:** Samoan 97.4%. **Languages:** Samoan (Polynesian), English (both official). **Religions:** Protestant 52.6% (incl. Congregationalist 29%, Methodist 12.4%), Roman Catholic 18.8%, Mormon 16.9%.

Geography: Total area: 1,093 sq mi, 2,831 sq km (168); **Land area:** 1,089 sq mi, 2,821 sq km. **Location:** S Pacific O. Nearest neighbors are Fiji to SW, Tonga to S. **Topography:** Main islands, Savaii (659 sq mi) and Upolu (432 sq mi), both ruggedly mountainous. Small islands of Manono and Apolima. **Arable land:** 2.8%. **Capital:** Apia, 36,066.

Government: Type: Parliamentary republic. **Head of state:** Tuimaleali'ifano Va'aletoa Sualauvi II; b. 1947; in office: July 21, 2017. **Head of govt.:** Prime Min. Tuilaepa Sailele Malielegaoi; b. 1945; in office: Nov. 23, 1998. **Local divisions:** 11 districts. **Defense budget/active troops:** NA.

Economy: Industries: food proc., building materials, auto parts. **Chief agric.:** coconuts, nonu, bananas, taro, yams, coffee, cocoa. **Natural resources:** hardwood forests, fish, hydropower. **Water:** NA. **Electricity prod.:** 127 mil kWh. **Labor force:** agric. 5.8%, industry 14.9%, services 79.3%. **Unemployment:** 8.2%.

Finance: Monetary unit: Tala (WST) (2.63 = $1 U.S.). **GDP:** $1.1 bil; **per capita GDP:** $5,700; **GDP growth:** 2.4%. **Imports** (2014): $341.3 mil; New Zealand 22%, Singapore 20.7%, U.S. 12.5%, China 10.1%, Australia 8.6%, Fiji 5.2%. **Exports** (2014): $27.5 mil; Australia 22.9%, New Zealand 22.8%, American Samoa 22.1%, Afghanistan 14.9%, U.S. 5.9%. **Tourism:** $165 mil. **Budget:** $272.8 mil. **Inflation:** 1.6%.

Transport: Airports: 1.

Communications: Telephone: 4.3 per 100 pop. **Mobile:** 63.2 per 100 pop. **Broadband:** 26.6 per 100 pop. **Internet:** 29.4%.

Health: Expend.: 5.6%. **Life expect.:** 71.3 male; 77.3 female. **Births:** 20.2 per 1,000 pop. **Deaths:** 5.4 per 1,000 pop. **Infant mortality:** 18.0 per 1,000 live births. **Undernourished:** 3.1%. **HIV:** NA.

Education: Compulsory: ages 5-12. **Literacy:** 99%.

Embassy: 800 Second Ave., 4th Fl., New York, NY 10017; (212) 599-6196.

Website: www.samoagovt.ws

Samoa (formerly Western Samoa) was a German colony, 1899 to 1914, when New Zealand landed troops and took over. It became a New Zealand mandate under the League of Nations and, in 1945, a New Zealand UN Trusteeship. An elected local government took office in Oct. 1959, and the country became fully independent Jan. 1, 1962. In 2011, Samoa moved west of the Intl. Date Line to reduce time differences with Australia and New Zealand. "Panama Papers" documents showed, in 2016, that the law firm from which the files leaked had set up thousands of shell companies in Samoa. The Legislative Assembly, July 4, 2017, elected Tuimaleali'ifano Va'aletoa Sualauvi II to a 5-year term as head of state.

San Marino
Republic of San Marino

People: Population: 33,779 (191). **Age distrib.:** <15: 15%; 65+: 19.8%. **Growth:** 0.7%. **Migrants:** 15.7%. **Pop. density:** 1,434.2 per sq mi, 553.8 per sq km. **Urban:** 97.2%. **Ethnic groups:** Sammarinese, Italian. **Languages:** Italian. **Religions:** Roman Catholic.

Geography: Total area: 24 sq mi, 61 sq km (192); **Land area:** 24 sq mi, 61 sq km. **Location:** Completely surrounded by Italy, in N center of that country, near Adriatic coast. **Topography:**

On slopes of Mt. Titano. **Arable land:** 16.7%. **Capital:** San Marino, 4,465.

Government: Type: Parliamentary republic. **Heads of state:** Two captains regent, elected by parliament from among its members, to 6-month term. **Head of govt.:** Sec. of State for Foreign and Political Affairs Nicola Renzi; b. 1979; in office: Dec. 27, 2016. **Local divisions:** 9 municipalities. **Defense budget/active troops:** NA.

Economy: Industries: tourism, banking, textiles, electronics, ceramics, cement, wine. **Chief agric.:** wheat, grapes, corn, olives; cattle, pigs, horses, beef, cheese, hides. **Natural resources:** building stone. **Water:** NA. **Labor force:** agric. 0.2%, industry 33.5%, services 66.3%. **Unemployment:** NA.

Finance: Monetary unit: Euro (EUR) (0.86 = $1 U.S.). **GDP:** $2.1 bil; **per capita GDP:** $58,600; **GDP growth:** 1.5%. **Imports** (2011): $2.6 bil. **Exports** (2011): $3.8 bil. **Budget** (2011): $715.1 mil. **Inflation:** 1%.

Transport: NA.

Communications: Telephone: 47.3 per 100 pop. **Mobile:** 113.8 per 100 pop. **Broadband:** NA. **Internet** (2011): 49.6%.

Health: Expend.: 6.8%. **Life expect.:** 80.8 male; 86.2 female. **Births:** 8.6 per 1,000 pop. **Deaths:** 8.8 per 1,000 pop. **Infant mortality:** 4.3 per 1,000 live births. **Undernourished:** NA. **HIV:** NA.

Education: Compulsory: ages 6-15. **Literacy:** 96%.

Embassy: 1711 N St. NW, 2nd Fl., 20036; 223-2418.

Website: www.sanmarino.sm

San Marino, founded in the 4th cent., claims to be the world's oldest republic. It has had a treaty of friendship with Italy since 1862. No coalition won a majority in Nov. 20, 2016, parliamentary elections. In second-round balloting, Dec. 4, the Adesso (Now) coalition of opposition parties took 58% of the vote and 35 of 60 seats.

São Tomé and Príncipe
Democratic Republic of São Tomé and Príncipe

People: Population: 204,454 (176). **Age distrib.:** <15: 41.2%; 65+: 2.8%. **Growth:** 1.7%. **Migrants:** 1.1%. **Pop. density:** 549.3 per sq mi, 212.1 per sq km. **Urban:** 72.8%. **Ethnic groups:** mestico, angolares (descendants of Angolan slaves), forros (descendants of freed slaves), servicais (contract laborers fr. Angola, Mozambique, Cabo Verde), tongas (children of servicais born on islands), Europeans (primarily Portuguese), Asians (mostly Chinese). **Languages:** Portuguese (official), Forro, Cabo Verdian, French, Angolar, English. **Religions:** Catholic 55.7%, Adventist 4.1%, Assembly of God 3.4%, New Apostolic 2.9%, none 21.2%.

Geography: Total area: 372 sq mi, 964 sq km (172); **Land area:** 372 sq mi, 964 sq km. **Location:** Gulf of Guinea about 125 mi off W central Africa. Gabon, Equatorial Guinea to E. **Topography:** Part of an extinct volcano chain; lush forests and croplands. **Arable land:** 9.1%. **Capital:** São Tomé, 80,099.

Government: Type: Semi-presidential republic. **Head of state:** Pres. Evaristo Carvalho; b. 1941; in office: Sept. 3, 2016. **Head of govt.:** Prime Min. Patrice Emery Trovoada; b. 1936; in office: Nov. 29, 2014. **Local divisions:** 6 districts, 1 autonomous region. **Defense budget/active troops:** NA.

Economy: Industries: light constr., textiles, soap, beer, fish proc., timber. **Chief agric.:** cocoa, coconuts, palm kernels, copra, cinnamon, pepper, coffee, bananas, papayas, beans; poultry; fish. **Natural resources:** fish, hydropower. **Water:** 11,456 cu m per capita. **Electricity prod.:** 66 mil kWh. **Labor force:** agric. 17.1%, industry 14.1%, services 68.8%. **Unemployment:** 13.5%.

Finance: Monetary unit: Dobra (STD) (21,144.14 = $1 U.S.). **GDP:** $676 mil; **per capita GDP:** $3,200; **GDP growth:** 4%. **Imports:** $127.7 mil; Portugal 54.7%, Angola 16.5%, China 5.6%. **Exports:** $10.9 mil; Guyana 43.7%, Germany 23.6%, Portugal 6%, Netherlands 5.5%. **Tourism:** $66 mil. **Budget:** $152.7 mil. **Inflation:** 5.7%.

Transport: Airports: 2.

Communications: Telephone: 2.7 per 100 pop. **Mobile:** 85 per 100 pop. **Broadband:** 24 per 100 pop. **Internet:** 28%.

Health: Expend.: 9.8%. **Life expect.:** 64.3 male; 67.1 female. **Births:** 31.5 per 1,000 pop. **Deaths:** 6.7 per 1,000 pop. **Infant mortality:** 44.1 per 1,000 live births. **Undernourished:** 10.2%. **HIV:** NA.

Education: Compulsory: ages 6-11. **Literacy:** 74.9%.

Permanent UN mission: 675 Third Ave., Ste. 1807, New York, NY 10017; (212) 651-8116.

Website: www.parlamento.st or www.state.gov/p/af/ci/tp/

The Portuguese reached the islands in 1471 and brought the first inhabitants—convicts and exiled Jews. Sugarcane planting was replaced by the slave trade as the chief economic activity until coffee and cocoa were introduced in the 19th cent.

Portugal agreed, 1974, to turn the colony over to the Gabon-based Movement for the Liberation of São Tomé and Príncipe; its East German-trained leader, Manuel Pinto da Costa, became the country's first president. Independence came July 12, 1975. Democratic reforms were instituted in 1987. In 1991, Miguel Trovoada won the first free presidential election.

After the Independent Democratic Action (ADI) party won legislative elections Aug. 1, 2010, Patrice Trovoada (son of the former president) became prime min. Pinto da Costa returned to power after a presidential runoff vote Aug. 7, 2011. The ADI won Oct. 12, 2014, legislative elections. Evaristo Carvalho of ADI unseated Pinto da Costa in an Aug. 7, 2016, presidential runoff. The country, long one of the world's poorest, has sought to develop oil deposits in the Gulf of Guinea and tourism. Seeking aid and investment, São Tomé broke diplomatic relations with Taiwan and established relations with China, Dec. 2016.

Saudi Arabia
Kingdom of Saudi Arabia

People: Population: 33,091,113 (41). (Immigrants made up about 37% of total pop. in 2017.) **Age distrib.:** <15: 25.7%; 65+: 3.3%. **Growth:** 1.6%. **Migrants:** 37%. **Pop. density:** 34.9 per sq mi, 13.5 per sq km. **Urban:** 83.8%. **Ethnic groups:** Arab 90%, Afro-Asian 10%. **Languages:** Arabic (official). **Religions:** Muslim (official). Citizens are 85%-90% Sunni and 10%-15% Shia; non-Muslims are not allowed Saudi citizenship.

Geography: Total area: 830,000 sq mi, 2,149,690 sq km (12); **Land area:** 830,000 sq mi, 2,149,690 sq km. **Location:** Occupies most of Arabian Peninsula in Middle East. Kuwait, Iraq, Jordan on N; Yemen, Oman on S; UAE, Qatar on E. **Topography:** Bordered by Red Sea on W. Highlands in W slope as barren desert to the Persian Gulf on E. **Arable land:** 1.6%. **Capital:** Riyadh, 6,906,595. **Cities:** Jiddah, 4,432,771; Mecca, 1,967,094; Medina, 1,429,634; Ad-Dammam, 1,197,400.

Government: Type: Absolute monarchy. **Head of state and govt.:** King Salman bin Abdul Aziz; b. 1924; in office: Jan. 23, 2015. **Local divisions:** 13 provinces. **Defense budget:** $76.7 bil. **Active troops:** 227,000.

Economy: Industries: crude oil prod., petroleum refining, basic petrochemicals, ammonia, industrial gases, caustic soda, cement, fertilizer. **Chief agric.:** wheat, barley, tomatoes, melons, dates, citrus; mutton, chickens, eggs, milk. **Natural resources:** petroleum, nat. gas, iron ore, gold, copper. **Water:** 76 cu m per capita. **Crude oil reserves:** 266.2 bil bbls (incl. half of Neutral Zone reserves). **Electricity prod.:** 318 bil kWh. **Labor force:** agric. 6.3%, industry 22.6%, services 71.2%. **Unemployment:** 5.5%.

Finance: Monetary unit: Riyal (SAR) (3.75 = $1 U.S.). **GDP:** $1.8 tril; **per capita GDP:** $54,800; **GDP growth:** –0.7%. **Imports:** $136.8 bil; China 15.4%, U.S. 13.6%, UAE 6.5%, Germany 5.8%. **Exports:** $231.3 bil; Japan 12.2%, China 11.7%, South Korea 9%, India 8.9%, U.S. 8.3%, UAE 6.7%. **Tourism:** $12.1 bil. **Budget:** $246.9 bil. **Inflation:** –0.2%.

Transport: Railways: 3,362 mi. **Motor vehicles:** 263 per 1,000 pop. **Airports:** 82.

Communications: Telephone: 11 per 100 pop. **Mobile:** 122.1 per 100 pop. **Broadband:** 78.5 per 100 pop. **Internet** (2017): 80.1%.

Health: Expend.: 5.8%. **Life expect.:** 74.2 male; 77.3 female. **Births:** 15.6 per 1,000 pop. **Deaths:** 3.3 per 1,000 pop. **Infant mortality:** 12.1 per 1,000 live births. **Undernourished:** 5.5%. **HIV:** NA.

Education: Compulsory: ages 6-14. **Literacy:** 94.7%.

Embassy: 601 New Hampshire Ave. NW 20037; 342-3800. **Website:** www.saudi.gov.sa

Arabia was divided among numerous warring groups and small kingdoms before Muhammad united it in the early 7th cent. His successors conquered the entire Middle East and North Africa, bringing Islam and the Arabic language. But Arabia soon returned to its former status.

Nejd, in central Arabia, long an independent state and center of the Wahhabi sect, fell under Turkish rule in the 18th cent. Ibn Saud, founder of the Saudi dynasty, overthrew the Turks, 1913. He captured Hasa, a Turkish province in eastern Arabia, also 1913; the Hejaz region in western Arabia, 1925; and most of Asir, in SW Arabia, by 1926. The discovery of oil in the 1930s transformed the nation. The Hejaz contains the holy cities of Islam—Medina and Mecca. About 2 mil Muslims make the pilgrimage (*hajj*) to Mecca annually.

Ibn Saud reigned until his death, Nov. 1953. Subsequent kings as of 2018 have been his sons. The king exercises authority with a Council of Ministers. The Islamic religious code is the law of the land. Alcohol and public entertainments are restricted. Women are subordinate to a male guardianship system. A royal decree, effective June 24, 2018, made it legal for women to drive. The government announced, Dec. 11, 2017, it would end a 35-year ban on movie theaters.

Saudi Arabia has often allied itself with and purchased arms from the U.S. and other Western nations. Saudi units, nevertheless, fought against Western ally Israel in the 1948 and 1973 Arab-Israeli wars. Beginning with the 1967 Arab-Israeli war, Saudi Arabia gave large financial gifts to Egypt, Syria, Jordan, and Palestinian groups. Saudi Arabia played a leading role in the 1973-74 Arab oil embargo against the U.S. and other nations.

After Iraq invaded Kuwait, Aug. 2, 1990, Saudi Arabia accepted the Kuwait royal family and more than 400,000 Kuwaiti refugees. Western and Arab troops also deployed on Saudi soil before and during the 1991 Persian Gulf War.

When 15 of the 19 al-Qaeda hijackers who carried out the Sept. 11, 2001, attacks on the U.S. were found to be Saudi, some in the U.S. blamed the Saudi government for allowing Muslim extremism to flourish in Saudi Arabia. Alarmed at guerrilla attacks that killed more than 100 people, mostly foreigners, in Saudi Arabia, 2003-04, the Saudis worked with the U.S. to increase antiterrorist activities. The U.S. completed a pullout of its combat forces from Saudi Arabia, Sept. 2003.

Municipal council elections, the first since 1963, were held in 2005; women were barred from voting. In 2011, King Abdullah announced that women would be allowed to vote and run for office in future municipal elections; women won 20 of 2,106 elective council seats in voting Dec. 12, 2015. In 2012, Saudi women competed in the Olympics for the first time. King Abdullah decreed, Jan. 11, 2013, that women would be permitted to hold 30 of the 150 seats on the government's advisory Shura council. Abdullah died, Jan. 23, 2015, and was succeeded by his half-brother Salman. King Salman, June 21, 2017, named as crown prince (heir to the throne) his son Mohammed bin Salman. Known as MBS, the crown prince took on increasing responsibilities.

Middle East Respiratory Syndrome (MERS), a viral disease, was first recognized in Saudi Arabia in 2012 and had spread to 26 other countries as of mid-2018. By Aug. 31, 2018, 2,248 total cases (1,871 in Saudi Arabia) had been confirmed; 798 people (724 in Saudi Arabia) had died.

Hoping to contain Arab Spring uprisings, a Saudi-led force suppressed protests in Bahrain Mar. 14, 2011. Saudi Arabia supplied weapons to anti-government rebels in Syria's civil war. Beginning Sept. 23, 2014, Saudi warplanes participated in U.S.-led airstrikes against ISIS in Syria. ISIS staged terrorist attacks inside Saudi Arabia, 2014-18, and the government arrested thousands of alleged ISIS supporters. Saudi Arabia led a coalition of Sunni nations that began airstrikes, Mar. 25, 2015, and took other military action against Iran-backed Shiite Houthi rebels in Yemen, causing high civilian casualties. In June 2017, Saudi Arabia, apparently concerned with Qatar's support for closer ties with Iran and alleged backing of militants, led a group of Arab nations that broke diplomatic relations with Qatar and imposed a travel and trade boycott.

Low oil prices reduced government revenue beginning in 2015. King Salman announced, Apr. 25, 2016, a plan for economic diversification and privatization by the year 2030. In what was said to be a government anti-corruption campaign, hundreds of business leaders and royal family members were detained, Nov. 2017-Jan. 2018, and more than $100 bil in assets taken. A number of rights activists and government critics were arrested in 2017-18.

Senegal
Republic of Senegal

People: Population: 15,020,945 (72). **Age distrib.:** <15: 41.2%; 65+: 3%. **Growth:** 2.4%. **Migrants:** 1.7%. **Pop. density:** 202.1 per sq mi, 78 per sq km. **Urban:** 47.2%. **Ethnic groups:** Wolof 41.6%, Pular 28.1%, Serer 15.3%, Mandinka 5.4%, Jola 3.4%. **Languages:** French (official), Wolof, Pular, Jola, Mandinka. **Religions:** Muslim (mostly four main Sufi brotherhoods) 96.1%, Christian (mostly Roman Catholic) 3.6%.

Geography: Total area: 75,955 sq mi, 196,722 sq km (86); **Land area:** 74,336 sq mi, 192,530 sq km. **Location:** W extreme of Africa. Mauritania on N, Mali on E, Guinea and Guinea-Bissau on S; surrounds The Gambia on three sides. **Topography:** Mostly low rolling plains, rising somewhat in SE. Swamp and jungles in SW. **Arable land:** 16.6%. **Capital:** Dakar, 2,978,419.

Government: Type: Presidential republic. **Head of state:** Pres. Macky Sall; b. 1961; in office: Apr. 2, 2012. **Head of govt.:** Prime Min. Mohammed Abdallah Boun Dionne; in office: July 6, 2014. **Local divisions:** 14 regions. **Defense budget:** $303 mil. **Active troops:** 13,600.

Economy: Industries: agric. and fish proc., phosphate mining, fertilizer prod., petroleum refining, zircon and gold mining, constr. materials, ship constr. and repair. **Chief agric.:** peanuts, millet, corn, sorghum, rice, cotton, tomatoes, green vegetables; cattle, poultry, pigs; fish. **Natural resources:** fish, phosphates, iron ore. **Water:** 2,576 cu m per capita. **Electricity prod.:** 3.7 bil kWh. **Labor force:** agric. 53.4%, industry 20.1%, services 26.5%. **Unemployment:** 4.9%.

Finance: Monetary unit: CFA Franc (XOF) (566.17 = $1 U.S.). **GDP:** $43.2 bil; **per capita GDP:** $2,700; **GDP growth:** 7.2%. **Imports:** $5.2 bil; France 16.3%, China 10.4%, Nigeria 8%, India 7.2%. **Exports:** $2.5 bil; Mali 14.8%, Switzerland 11.4%, India 6%, Côte d'Ivoire 5.3%, UAE 5.1%. **Tourism** (2015): $368 mil. **Budget:** $4.5 bil. **Inflation:** 1.3%.

Transport: Railways: 563 mi (only partly operational). **Airports:** 9.

Communications: Telephone: 1.8 per 100 pop. **Mobile:** 99.4 per 100 pop. **Broadband:** 26.1 per 100 pop. **Internet:** 25.7%.

Health: Expend.: 4%. **Life expect.:** 60.4 male; 64.7 female. **Births:** 32.9 per 1,000 pop. **Deaths:** 7.9 per 1,000 pop. **Infant mortality:** 48.0 per 1,000 live births. **Undernourished:** 11.3%. **HIV:** 0.4%.

Education: Compulsory: ages 6-16. **Literacy:** 57.7%.

Embassy: 2215 M St. NW 20037; 234-0540.

Website: www.sec.gouv.sn

Portuguese settlers arrived in the 15th cent., but French control grew from the 17th cent. The last independent Muslim state was subdued in 1893. Senegal became an independent republic Aug. 20, 1960, but French political and economic influence remained strong. Senegambia, a loose confederation of Senegal and The Gambia, was established in 1982 but dissolved seven years later.

Forty years of Socialist Party rule ended when Abdoulaye Wade, leader of the Senegalese Democratic Party (PDS), won a presidential runoff election, Mar. 19, 2000. A Senegalese ferry capsized Sept. 26, 2002, killing at least 1,863 people. A peace accord signed Dec. 30, 2004, with separatists in Cassamance Province sought to end a 22-year insurgency. Pres. Wade was reelected Feb. 25, 2007, but lost his bid for a third term Mar. 26, 2012, to Macky Sall, his former prime min. After a campaign marred by violence, Sall's coalition won a landslide victory in July 30, 2017, legislative elections.

Serbia
Republic of Serbia

People: Population: 7,078,110 (102). **Age distrib.:** <15: 14.4%; 65+: 19%. **Growth:** –0.5%. **Migrants:** 9.1%. **Pop. density:** 236.6 per sq mi, 91.4 per sq km. **Urban:** 56.1% (incl. Kosovo). **Ethnic groups:** Serb 83.3%, Hungarian 3.5%, Romani 2.1%, Bosniak 2%. **Languages:** Serbian (official), Hungarian. **Religions:** Orthodox 84.6%, Catholic 5%, Muslim 3.1%.

Geography: Total area: 29,913 sq mi, 77,474 sq km (115); **Land area:** 29,913 sq mi, 77,474 sq km. **Location:** Balkan Peninsula in SE Europe. Croatia, Bosnia and Herzegovina on W; Hungary on N; Romania, Bulgaria on E; Montenegro, Albania, Macedonia on S. **Topography:** Terrain varies widely—fertile plains drained by Danube, other rivers in N; limestone basins in E; mountains, hills in SE. **Arable land:** 29.6%. **Capital:** Belgrade, 1,389,351.

Government: Type: Parliamentary republic. **Head of state:** Pres. Aleksandar Vucic; b. 1970; in office: May 31, 2017. **Head of govt.:** Prime Min. Ana Brnabic; b. 1975; in office: June 29, 2017. **Local divisions:** 119 municipalities, 26 cities (of which 37 municipalities, 8 cities comprise the autonomous province of Vojvodina). **Defense budget:** $523 mil. **Active troops:** 28,150.

Economy: Industries: automobiles, base metals, furniture, food proc., machinery, chemicals, sugar, tires. **Chief agric.:** wheat, maize, sunflowers, sugar beets, grapes/wine, fruits (raspberries, apples, sour cherries), vegetables; beef, pork. **Natural resources:** oil, gas, coal, iron ore, copper, zinc, antimony, chromite, gold, silver, magnesium, pyrite, limestone, marble, salt. **Water:** 18,326 cu m per capita. **Crude oil reserves:** 77.5 mil bbls. **Electricity prod.:** 35.5 bil kWh. **Labor force:** agric. 19%, industry 24.4%, services 56.6%. **Unemployment:** 14.1%.

Finance: Monetary unit: Dinar (RSD) (101.92 = $1 U.S.). **GDP:** $105.5 bil; **per capita GDP:** $15,000; **GDP growth:** 1.8%. **Imports:** $19.2 bil; Germany 12.7%, Italy 10%, China 8.2%, Russia 7.3%. **Exports:** $14.7 bil; Italy 13.5%, Germany 12.8%, Bosnia and Herzegovina 8.2%, Russia 6%. **Tourism:** $1.3 bil. **Budget:** $16.9 bil (incl. central and local govt.). **Inflation:** 3.1%.

Transport: Railways: 2,367 mi. **Motor vehicles:** 291 per 1,000 pop. **Airports:** 10.

Communications: Telephone: 37.5 per 100 pop. **Mobile:** 124.1 per 100 pop. **Broadband:** 67.4 per 100 pop. **Internet** (2017): 70.3%.

Health: Expend.: 9.4%. **Life expect.:** 73.0 male; 79.0 female. **Births:** 8.9 per 1,000 pop. **Deaths:** 13.6 per 1,000 pop. **Infant mortality:** 5.7 per 1,000 live births. **Undernourished:** 5.6%. **HIV:** <0.1%.

Education: Compulsory: ages 7-14. **Literacy:** 98.8%.

Embassy: 2233 Wisconsin Ave. NW, Ste. 410, 20007; 332-0333.

Website: www.srbija.gov.rs

Serbia was a vassal principality of Turkey from 1389 to 1878, when the Treaty of Berlin established it as an independent kingdom. After the Balkan wars, Serbia annexed Old Serbia and Macedonia, 1913.

When the Austro-Hungarian empire collapsed after WWI, the Kingdom of Serbs, Croats, and Slovenes—Yugoslavia after 1929—was formed from the provinces of Croatia, Dalmatia, Bosnia, Herzegovina, Slovenia, Vojvodina, and the independent state of Montenegro.

After Nazi Germany's occupation 1941-45, Yugoslavia became a federal republic, headed by Josip Broz, a Communist, known as Marshal Tito. He rejected Stalin's dictatorship and accepted economic and military aid from the West. After Tito died in 1980, Yugoslavia held together for a decade before breaking apart. During 1991-95, Serbia, under Pres. Slobodan Milosevic, supported ethnic Serb fighters in Croatia and in Bosnia and Herzegovina, which had declared independence. The republics of Serbia and Montenegro proclaimed a new Federal Republic of Yugoslavia, Apr. 17, 1992. The UN imposed sanctions on the newly reconstituted Yugoslavia to end the bloodshed in Bosnia.

A peace agreement was reached in 1995. A UN-backed war crimes tribunal began in May 1996 to try suspects from the former Yugoslavia. Mass protests erupted when Milosevic refused to accept opposition victories in local elections, Nov. 17; non-Communist governments took office in Belgrade and other cities, Feb. 1997. Barred from running for a third term as Serbian president, Milosevic had himself inaugurated as president of Yugoslavia, July 23, 1997.

Serbian efforts to suppress a secessionist movement in Kosovo led in Mar.-June 1999 to a war with the U.S. and its NATO allies; they accused Milosevic of pursuing a policy of ethnic cleansing against the predominantly Muslim Kosovars (ethnic Albanians). NATO stationed a multinational force in Kosovo, which was placed under UN administration.

Milosevic initially refused to accept defeat by opposition leader Vojislav Kostunica in a 2000 presidential election but resigned Oct. 6 after mass demonstrations. Kostunica was sworn in the next day. Charged with corruption and abuse of power, Milosevic surrendered to Serbian authorities Apr. 1, 2001. He was extradited June 28 to The Hague, Netherlands, where a UN tribunal had indicted him for war crimes. His trial began Feb. 12, 2002. He was found dead in prison Mar. 11, 2006, before a verdict was reached.

A pact to reconstitute Yugoslavia as a new union of Serbia and Montenegro took effect Feb. 4, 2003. Zoran Djindjic, premier of the Republic of Serbia, was assassinated Mar. 12 in Belgrade, triggering a roundup of more than 4,500 people associated with organized crime and the Milosevic regime. Serbia's union with Montenegro disintegrated in 2006. Montenegrins voted for separation in a referendum May 21, and Montenegro became an independent republic June 3.

Kosovo declared independence from Serbia Feb. 17, 2008, but Serbia refused to recognize the new country. Following parliamentary elections in Serbia May 11, a pro-Western government under Mirko Cvetkovic took office July 7. To meet a requirement for EU membership, Serbia arrested, in 2008, former Bosnian Serb leader Radovan Karadzic, who was extradited to the Intl. Criminal Court in The Hague on charges of genocide and crimes against humanity; Karadzic was convicted and sentenced to 40 years in prison, Mar. 24, 2016. Serbia's parliament passed a resolution Mar. 31, 2010, apologizing for the 1995 massacre of 8,000 Bosnian Muslims (Bosniaks) by Bosnian Serbs at Srebrenica. Ratko Mladic, the former Bosnian Serb military commander accused of directing the Srebrenica massacre, was arrested in Serbia, May 2011, and sent to The Hague; he was convicted, Nov. 22, 2017, of genocide, war crimes, and crimes against humanity and sentenced to life in prison. After reaching an EU-brokered power-sharing deal with Kosovo Apr. 19, 2013, Serbia began accession negotiations for EU membership Jan. 21, 2014. Aleksandar Vucic, an advocate of EU membership and also close ties to Russia, became prime min. following Mar. 16, 2014, elections. He was elected president, Apr. 2, 2017. Ana Brnabić took office, June 29, as Serbia's first female prime min.

An estimated 815,000 refugees and other migrants, largely from the Middle East and SW Asia, passed through Serbia in 2015, most en route to N Europe. More than 90,000 entered Jan. 1-Mar. 9, 2016, when the government essentially closed Serbia's borders.

Vojvodina (8,304 sq mi) is a nominally autonomous province in northern Serbia with a pop. (2011 census) of 1,931,809, mostly Serbian. The capital is Novi Sad. **Website:** www.vojvodina.gov.rs

Seychelles
Republic of Seychelles

People: Population: 94,633 (185). **Age distrib.:** <15: 19.5%; 65+: 7.8%. **Growth:** 0.7%. **Migrants:** 13.6%. **Pop. density:** 538.7 per sq mi, 208 per sq km. **Urban:** 56.7%. **Ethnic groups:** mixed French, African, Indian, Chinese, and Arab. **Languages:** Seychellois Creole, English, French (all official). **Religions:** Roman Catholic 76.2%, Protestant 10.5%.

Geography: Total area: 176 sq mi, 455 sq km (182); **Land area:** 176 sq mi, 455 sq km. **Location:** In Indian O. 700 mi NE of Madagascar. Nearest neighbors are Madagascar and Somalia on NW. **Topography:** Archipelago of over 116 islands. One group is composed of coral; the Mahe group of isls., predominantly mountainous, is granite. **Arable land:** 0.3%. **Capital:** Victoria, 28,091.

Government: Type: Presidential republic. **Head of state and govt.:** Pres. Danny Faure; b. 1962; in office: Oct. 16, 2016. **Local divisions:** 25 admin. districts. **Defense budget:** NA. **Active troops:** 420.

Economy: Industries: fishing, tourism, beverages. **Chief agric.:** coconuts, cinnamon, vanilla, sweet potatoes, cassava, copra, bananas; tuna. **Natural resources:** fish, coconuts, cinnamon trees. **Water:** NA. **Electricity prod.:** 347 mil kWh. **Labor force:** agric. 3%, industry 23%, services 74%. **Unemployment:** NA.

Finance: Monetary unit: Rupee (SCR) (13.54 = $1 U.S.). **GDP:** $2.7 bil; **per capita GDP:** $28,900; **GDP growth:** 4.2%. **Imports:** $1 bil; UAE 13.4%, France 9.4%, Spain 5.7%, South Africa 5%. **Exports:** $495.4 mil; UAE 28.5%, France 24%, UK 13.8%, Italy 8.9%. **Tourism:** $483 mil. **Budget:** $557.2 mil. **Inflation:** 2.9%.

Transport: Airports: 7.

Communications: Telephone: 20.7 per 100 pop. **Mobile:** 176.6 per 100 pop. **Broadband:** 22.6 per 100 pop. **Internet:** 56.5%.

Health: Expend.: 3.4%. **Life expect.:** 70.7 male; 79.8 female. **Births:** 13.4 per 1,000 pop. **Deaths:** 7.0 per 1,000 pop. **Infant mortality:** 9.7 per 1,000 live births. **Undernourished:** NA. **HIV:** NA.

Education: Compulsory: ages 6-15. **Literacy:** 95.3%.

Permanent UN mission: 800 Second Ave., Ste. 400C, New York, NY 10017; (212) 972-1785.
Website: www.egov.sc
The islands were occupied by France in 1768 and seized by Britain in 1794. Ruled as part of Mauritius from 1814, Seychelles became a separate colony in 1903 and declared independence June 29, 1976. The tourism industry has been a major driver of economic growth since independence. The country's first president was ousted in a 1977 coup by socialist leader France Albert René. A new constitution, approved June 1993, provided for a multiparty state. René resigned Apr. 14, 2004. Vice Pres. James Michel succeeded him and won 2006, 2011, and 2015 elections (the last by 193 votes). After his party lost Sept. 2016 legislative elections, Michel resigned effective Oct. 16, and Vice Pres. Danny Faure became president.

Sierra Leone
Republic of Sierra Leone

People: Population: 6,312,212 (107). **Age distrib.:** <15: 41.7%; 65+: 3.8%. **Growth:** 2.4%. **Migrants:** 1.3%. **Pop. density:** 228.3 per sq mi, 88.1 per sq km. **Urban:** 42.1%. **Ethnic groups:** Temne 35.5%, Mende 33.2%, Limba 6.4%, Kono 4.4%, Fullah 3.4%, Loko 2.9%, Koranko 2.8%, Sherbro 2.6%, Mandingo 2.4%. **Languages:** English (official), Mende (principal vernacular in S), Temne (principal vernacular in N), Krio (English-based Creole, a lingua franca). **Religions:** Muslim 78.6%, Christian 20.8%.
Geography: Total area: 27,699 sq mi, 71,740 sq km (117); **Land area:** 27,653 sq mi, 71,620 sq km. **Location:** W coast of W Africa. Guinea on N and E, Liberia on S. **Topography:** Mangrove swamps in heavily indented, 210-mi coastline. Wooded hills rise to a plateau and mountains in E. **Arable land:** 21.9%. **Capital:** Freetown, 1,135,949.
Government: Type: Presidential republic. **Head of state and govt.:** Pres. Julius Maada Bio; b. 1964; in office: Apr. 4, 2018. **Local divisions:** 4 provinces, 1 area. **Defense budget:** $11 mil. **Active troops:** 8,500.
Economy: Industries: diamond mining, iron ore, rutile and bauxite mining, small-scale mfg. (beverages, textiles, footwear). **Chief agric.:** rice, coffee, cocoa, palm kernels, palm oil, peanuts, cashews; poultry, cattle, sheep, pigs; fish. **Natural resources:** diamonds, titanium ore, bauxite, iron ore, gold, chromite. **Water:** 24,795 cu m per capita. **Electricity prod.:** 175 mil kWh. **Labor force:** agric. 60.6%, industry 6.2%, services 33.3%. **Unemployment:** 4.5%.
Finance: Monetary unit: Leone (SLL) (8,394.11 = $1 U.S.). **GDP:** $11.5 bil; **per capita GDP:** $1,600; **GDP growth:** 3.5%. **Imports:** $1.6 bil; China 11.5%, U.S. 9.2%, Belgium 8.8%, UAE 7.7%, India 7.4%, Turkey 5.2%, Senegal 5.1%. **Exports:** $836.8 mil; Côte d'Ivoire 37.7%, Belgium 20.5%, U.S. 15.7%, China 10.2%, Netherlands 6.1%. **Tourism:** $41 mil. **Budget:** $962.6 mil. **Inflation:** 18.2%.
Transport: Motor vehicles: 4.8 per 1,000 pop. **Airports:** 1. **Communications: Telephone** (2016): 0.2 per 100 pop. **Mobile** (2016): 84.9 per 100 pop. **Broadband:** NA. **Internet:** 11.8%.
Health: Expend.: 18.3%. **Life expect.:** 56.4 male; 61.7 female. **Births:** 36.0 per 1,000 pop. **Deaths:** 10.2 per 1,000 pop. **Infant mortality:** 66.7 per 1,000 live births. **Undernourished:** 25.5%. **HIV:** 1.4%.
Education: Compulsory: ages 6-14. **Literacy:** 48.1%.
Embassy: 1701 19th St. NW 20009; 939-9261.
Website: statehouse.gov.sl
The British founded Freetown, 1787, as a haven for freed slaves. Full independence arrived Apr. 27, 1961. A one-party state was established by referendum in 1978.
Mutinous soldiers ousted Pres. Joseph Momoh, Apr. 30, 1992. A coup, Jan. 16, 1996, paved the way for multiparty elections and a return to civilian rule. A peace accord, signed Nov. 30 with the Revolutionary United Front (RUF), brought a temporary halt to a civil war that had claimed over 10,000 lives in five years.
After a May 25, 1997, coup, Nigeria's military restored Pres. Ahmad Tejan Kabbah to power on Mar. 10, 1998, but RUF rebels mounted a guerrilla counteroffensive, killing thousands of civilians and mutilating thousands more. A power-sharing agreement between the Kabbah government and the RUF, July 1999, was maintained by a UN mission (UNAMSIL). The accord collapsed in early May 2000, as RUF guerrillas took more than 500 UN peacekeepers hostage. Rebel leader Foday Sankoh was captured in Freetown, May 17. The hostages were freed by the end of May. A UN-sponsored disarmament program in 2001 reduced the level of violence. The Sierra Leone Special Court was created in 2002 to try war crimes. Government and rebel leaders declared an official end to the war Jan. 18; more than 50,000 people had died in the conflict. Kabbah won the May 14 presidential election.
Sankoh, an indicted war criminal, died in UN custody, July 29, 2003. Opposition leader Ernest Bai Koroma won a presidential runoff vote, Sept. 8, 2007. Three former RUF leaders were convicted of war crimes, Feb. 25, 2009. A 2012 cholera epidemic caused about 23,000 cases and 300 deaths. Koroma won reelection Nov. 17, 2012. An Ebola virus epidemic that began in Guinea in Dec. 2013 caused 14,124 cases and 3,956 deaths in Sierra Leone by the time WHO declared its public health emergency over, Mar. 29, 2016. After a campaign marred by violence, Julius

Maada Bio, a leader of the 1992 mutiny and 1996 coup, was declared the winner, Apr. 4, 2018, of a presidential runoff election.

Singapore
Republic of Singapore

People: Population: 5,995,991 (111). **Age distrib.:** <15: 12.8%; 65+: 10%. **Growth:** 1.8%. **Migrants:** 46%. **Pop. density:** 21,903.4 per sq mi, 8,457 per sq km. **Urban:** 100%. **Ethnic groups:** Chinese 74.3%, Malay 13.4%, Indian 9%, other (incl. Eurasian, Caucasian, Japanese, Filipino, Vietnamese) 3.2%. **Languages:** English, Mandarin, Malay, Tamil (all official); other Chinese dialects (incl. Hokkien, Cantonese, Teochew). **Religions:** Buddhist 33.2%, Christian 18.8%, Muslim 14%, Taoist 10%, Hindu 5%, none 18.5%.
Geography: Total area: 278 sq mi, 719 sq km (178); **Land area:** 274 sq mi, 709 sq km. **Location:** Off tip of Malayan Peninsula in SE Asia. Nearest neighbors are Malaysia on N, Indonesia on S. **Topography:** Flat, formerly swampy island with 40 nearby islets. **Arable land:** 0.8%. **Capital:** Singapore, 5,791,901.
Government: Type: Parliamentary republic. **Head of state:** Pres. Halimah Yacob; b. 1954; in office: Sept. 14, 2017. **Head of govt.:** Prime Min. Lee Hsien Loong; b. 1952; in office: Aug. 12, 2004. **Local divisions:** none. **Defense budget:** $10.2 bil. **Active troops:** 72,500.
Economy: Industries: electronics, chemicals, financial services, oil drilling equip., petroleum refining, biomedical prods., scientific instruments. **Chief agric.:** vegetables; poultry, eggs; fish, ornamental fish, orchids. **Natural resources:** fish, deep-water ports. **Water:** 107 cu m per capita. **Electricity prod.:** 47.5 bil kWh. **Labor force** (excl. non-residents): agric. 0.1%, industry 16.3%, services 83.6%. **Unemployment:** 2%.
Finance: Monetary unit: Dollar (SGD) (1.38 = $1 U.S.). **GDP:** $527 bil; **per capita GDP:** $93,900; **GDP growth:** 3.6%. **Imports:** $327.4 bil; China 13.9%, Malaysia 12%, U.S. 10.7%, Japan 6.3%, South Korea 5%. **Exports:** $372.9 bil; China 14.7%, Hong Kong 12.6%, Malaysia 10.8%, U.S. 6.6%, Indonesia 5.8%. **Tourism:** $19.7 bil. **Budget:** $63.1 bil (incl. operational and development expenditures). **Inflation:** 0.6%.
Transport: Motor vehicles: 139.3 per 1,000 pop. **Airports:** 9. **Communications: Telephone:** 34.7 per 100 pop. **Mobile:** 148.2 per 100 pop. **Broadband:** 144.6 per 100 pop. **Internet** (2017): 84.4%.
Health: Expend.: 4.3%. **Life expect.:** 82.8 male; 88.3 female. **Births:** 8.7 per 1,000 pop. **Deaths:** 3.5 per 1,000 pop. **Infant mortality:** 2.3 per 1,000 live births. **Undernourished:** NA. **HIV:** 0.2%.
Education: Compulsory: ages 6-11. **Literacy:** 97%.
Embassy: 3501 International Pl. NW 20008; 537-3100.
Website: www.gov.sg
Founded in 1819 by Sir Thomas Stamford Raffles, Singapore was a British colony until 1959, when it became autonomous within the Commonwealth. On Sept. 16, 1963, it joined with Malaya, Sarawak, and Sabah to form the Federation of Malaysia. Tensions between Malays, dominant in the federation, and ethnic Chinese, dominant in Singapore, led to an accord under which Singapore became a separate nation, Aug. 9, 1965.
Singapore is one of the world's largest ports and a major manufacturing, banking, and commerce center. Asian immigrant workers hold many low-paying jobs. The government, dominated by the People's Action Party (PAP), has taken strong actions to keep order and suppress dissent.
Singapore's first prime min., Lee Kuan Yew (in office 1959-90), credited with building the country's strong economy, died Mar. 23, 2015. His son, Lee Hsien Loong, took office as prime min., Aug. 12, 2004. The PAP won a landslide victory in Sept. 11, 2015, parliamentary elections.
Halimah Yacob became Singapore's first female president, Sept. 14, 2017.

Slovakia
Slovak Republic

People: Population: 5,445,040 (117). **Age distrib.:** <15: 15.2%; 65+: 16%. **Growth:** −0.02%. **Migrants:** 3.4%. **Pop. density:** 293.2 per sq mi, 113.2 per sq km. **Urban:** 53.7%. **Ethnic groups:** Slovak 80.7%, Hungarian 8.5%, Romani 2%. **Languages:** Slovak (official), Hungarian, Roma. **Religions:** Roman Catholic 62%, Protestant 8.2%, Greek Catholic 3.8%, none 13.4%.
Geography: Total area: 18,933 sq mi, 49,035 sq km (127); **Land area:** 18,573 sq mi, 48,105 sq km. **Location:** E central Europe. Poland on N, Hungary on S, Austria and Czech Rep. on W, Ukraine on E. **Topography:** Carpathian Mts. in N, fertile Danube plain in S. **Arable land:** 28.8%. **Capital:** Bratislava, 429,920.
Government: Type: Parliamentary republic. **Head of state:** Pres. Andrej Kiska; b. 1963; in office: June 15, 2014. **Head of govt.:** Prime Min. Peter Pellegrini; b. 1975; in office: Mar. 22, 2018. **Local divisions:** 8 regions. **Defense budget:** $1.1 bil. **Active troops:** 15,850.
Economy: Industries: automobiles; metal and metal prods.; electricity, gas, coke, oil, nuclear fuel; chemicals, synthetic fibers, wood and paper prods.; machinery. **Chief agric.:** grains, potatoes, sugar beets, hops, fruit; pigs, cattle, poultry. **Natural resources:** lignite, iron ore, copper and manganese ore, salt.

Water: 9,233 cu m per capita. **Crude oil reserves:** 9 mil bbls. **Electricity prod:** 24.8 bil kWh. **Labor force:** agric. 2.9%, industry 36.3%, services 60.8%. **Unemployment:** 8.1%.

Finance: Monetary unit: Euro (EUR) (0.86 = $1 U.S.). **GDP:** $179.4 bil; **per capita GDP:** $33,000; **GDP growth:** 3.4%. **Imports:** $78 bil; Germany 19.1%, Czechia 16.3%, Austria 10.3%, Poland 6.5%, Hungary 6.4%. **Exports:** $80.6 bil; Germany 20.7%, Czechia 11.6%, Poland 7.7%, France 6.3%, Italy 6.1%, UK 6%, Hungary 6%, Austria 6%. **Tourism:** $2.9 bil. **Budget:** $38.5 bil. **Inflation:** 1.3%.

Transport: Railways: 2,225 mi. **Motor vehicles:** 467.3 per 1,000 pop. **Airports:** 21.

Communications: Telephone: 13.9 per 100 pop. **Mobile:** 130.7 per 100 pop. **Broadband:** 78.7 per 100 pop. **Internet** (2017): 81.6%.

Health: Expend.: 6.9%. **Life expect.:** 73.9 male; 81.2 female. **Births:** 9.6 per 1,000 pop. **Deaths:** 9.9 per 1,000 pop. **Infant mortality:** 5.0 per 1,000 live births. **Undernourished:** 2.7%. **HIV:** <0.1%.

Education: Compulsory: ages 6-15. **Literacy:** NA.

Embassy: 3523 International Ct. NW 20008; 237-1054.

Website: www.government.gov.sk

Settled by Illyrian, Celtic, and Germanic peoples, Slovakia was incorporated into Great Moravia in the 9th cent. It became part of Hungary in the 11th cent. Overrun by Czech Hussites in the 15th cent., it was restored to Hungarian rule in 1526. The Slovaks disassociated themselves from Hungary after WWI and joined the Czechs of Bohemia to form the Republic of Czechoslovakia, Oct. 28, 1918.

Germany invaded Czechoslovakia, 1939, and declared Slovakia independent. Slovakia rejoined Czechoslovakia in 1945. Czechoslovakia split into two separate states—the Czech Republic and Slovakia—on Jan. 1, 1993.

Slovakia joined the EU and NATO in 2004. The country adopted the euro currency Jan. 1, 2009. In Mar. 10, 2012, legislative elections, Robert Fico's social-democratic party, Smer, won a majority. Fico ran for president in 2014 but lost a Mar. 29 runoff election to former businessman Andrej Kiska. Smer won the most seats but lost its majority in Mar. 5, 2016, elections in which far-right, anti-immigration parties made gains; Fico remained prime min. After a political scandal involving alleged links to organized crime and the murder of an investigative journalist, Peter Pellegrini of Smer replaced Fico, Mar. 22, 2018.

Slovenia
Republic of Slovenia

People: Population: 2,102,126 (144). **Age distrib.:** <15: 14.8%; 65+: 20.1%. **Growth:** 0.03%. **Migrants:** 11.8%. **Pop. density:** 270.2 per sq mi, 104.3 per sq km. **Urban:** 54.5%. **Ethnic groups:** Slovene 83.1%, Serb 2%, Croat 1.8%. **Languages:** Slovenian (official), Serbo-Croatian. **Religions:** Catholic 57.8%, Muslim 2.4%, Orthodox 2.3%, none 10.1%.

Geography: Total area: 7,827 sq mi, 20,273 sq km (151); **Land area:** 7,780 sq mi, 20,151 sq km. **Location:** SE Europe. Italy on W, Austria on N, Hungary on NE, Croatia on SE, S. **Topography:** Mostly hilly; more than half forested. **Arable land:** 9.1%. **Capital:** Ljubljana, 286,491.

Government: Type: Parliamentary republic. **Head of state:** Pres. Borut Pahor; b. 1963; in office: Dec. 22, 2012. **Head of govt.:** Prime Min. Marjan Sarec; b. 1977; in office: Aug. 17, 2018. **Local divisions:** 201 municipalities, 11 urban municipalities. **Defense budget:** $474 mil. **Active troops:** 7,250.

Economy: Industries: ferrous metallurgy and aluminum prods., lead and zinc smelting, electronics (incl. military), trucks, automobiles, elec. power equip., wood prods. **Chief agric.:** hops, wheat, coffee, corn, apples, pears; cattle, sheep, poultry. **Natural resources:** lignite, lead, zinc, building stone, hydropower, forests. **Water:** 15,411 cu m per capita. **Electricity prod:** 14.1 bil kWh. **Labor force:** agric. 4.9%, industry 32.6%, services 62.5%. **Unemployment:** 6.6%.

Finance: Monetary unit: Euro (EUR) (0.86 = $1 U.S.). **GDP:** $71.1 bil; **per capita GDP:** $34,400; **GDP growth:** 5%. **Imports:** $28.7 bil; Germany 16.5%, Italy 13.5%, Austria 9.3%, Turkey 5.8%. **Exports:** $30.2 bil; Germany 18.9%, Italy 10.7%, Austria 7.4%, Croatia 7.1%. **Tourism:** $2.7 bil. **Budget:** $19.3 bil. **Inflation:** 1.4%.

Transport: Railways: 764 mi. **Motor vehicles:** 629.4 per 1,000 pop. **Airports:** 7.

Communications: Telephone: 34.5 per 100 pop. **Mobile:** 117.5 per 100 pop. **Broadband:** 62.3 per 100 pop. **Internet** (2017): 78.9%.

Health: Expend.: 8.5%. **Life expect.:** 78.3 male; 84.2 female. **Births:** 9.2 per 1,000 pop. **Deaths:** 9.9 per 1,000 pop. **Infant mortality:** 1.6 per 1,000 live births. **Undernourished:** <2.5%. **HIV:** <0.1%.

Education: Compulsory: ages 6-14. **Literacy:** 99.7%.

Embassy: 2410 California St. NW 20008; 386-6601.

Website: www.vlada.si or e-uprava.gov.si

The Slovenes settled in their current territory during the 6th to 8th cent. They fell under German domination in the 9th cent. Modern Slovenian political history began after 1848 when the Slovenes, divided among several Austrian provinces, began their struggle for unification. In 1918 a majority of Slovenes became part of the Kingdom of Serbs, Croats, and Slovenes, later renamed Yugoslavia.

Slovenia declared independence June 25, 1991; attained full membership in the EU and NATO in 2004; and adopted the euro Jan. 1, 2007. In July 13, 2014, National Assembly elections, a new centrist party headed by Miro Cerar won the most seats, and Cerar became prime min. After Hungary, Oct. 2015, blocked migrants (many from the Middle East and SW Asia) trying to reach N Europe, large numbers entered Slovenia. Slovenia announced, Mar. 8, 2016, it was essentially closing its border to migrants. About 474,000 had entered Slovenia Oct. 1, 2015-Mar. 8, 2016. The anti-immigration Slovenian Democratic Party won the most seats in inconclusive June 3, 2018, National Assembly elections; 5 centrist parties agreed, Aug. 29, to form a coalition government.

Solomon Islands

People: Population: 660,121 (163). **Age distrib.:** <15: 34%; 65+: 4.3%. **Growth:** 1.9%. **Migrants:** 0.4%. **Pop. density:** 61.1 per sq mi, 23.6 per sq km. **Urban:** 23.7%. **Ethnic groups:** Melanesian 95.3%, Polynesian 3.1%. **Languages:** Melanesian pidgin (lingua franca in much of country), English (official), 120 indigenous langs. **Religions:** Protestant 73.4% (incl. Church of Melanesia 31.9%, South Sea Evangelical 17.1%, Seventh-day Adventist 11.7%, United Church 10.1%), Roman Catholic 19.6%.

Geography: Total area: 11,157 sq mi, 28,896 sq km (140); **Land area:** 10,805 sq mi, 27,986 sq km. **Location:** Melanesian Archipelago in W Pacific O. Nearest neighbor is Papua New Guinea to W. **Topography:** 10 large volcanic, rugged islands; 4 groups of smaller islands. **Arable land:** 0.7%. **Capital:** Honiara, 81,801.

Government: Type: Parliamentary democracy under constitutional monarchy. **Head of state:** Queen Elizabeth II, rep. by Gov.-Gen. Frank Ofagioro Kabui; in office: July 7, 2009. **Head of govt.:** Prime Min. Rick Hou(enipwela); b. 1958; in office: Nov. 16, 2017. **Local divisions:** 9 provinces, 1 city. **Defense budget/active troops:** NA.

Economy: Industries: fish (tuna), mining, timber. **Chief agric.:** cocoa, coconuts, palm kernels, rice, fruit; cattle, pigs; fish. **Natural resources:** fish, forests, gold, bauxite, phosphates, lead, zinc, nickel. **Water:** 76,594 cu m per capita. **Electricity prod.:** 90 mil kWh. **Labor force:** agric. 69.6%, industry 9.8%, services 20.6%. **Unemployment:** 2.1%.

Finance: Monetary unit: Dollar (SBD) (7.94 = $1 U.S.). **GDP:** $1.3 bil; **per capita GDP:** $2,200; **GDP growth:** 3.2%. **Imports:** $267 mil; China 21.9%, Australia 19.6%, Singapore 10.7%, Vietnam 7.5%, New Zealand 6.2%, Papua New Guinea 5%. **Exports:** $319 mil; China 64.5%, Italy 6.2%. **Tourism:** $67 mil. **Budget:** $406 mil. **Inflation:** 0.5%.

Transport: Airports: 1.

Communications: Telephone: 1.2 per 100 pop. **Mobile:** 76.1 per 100 pop. **Broadband:** 12.9 per 100 pop. **Internet:** 11%.

Health: Expend.: 8%. **Life expect.:** 73.1 male; 78.6 female. **Births:** 24.5 per 1,000 pop. **Deaths:** 3.8 per 1,000 pop. **Infant mortality:** 14.3 per 1,000 live births. **Undernourished:** 12.3%. **HIV:** NA.

Education: Compulsory: NA. **Literacy:** 84.1%.

Permanent UN Mission: 800 Second Ave., Ste. 400L, New York, NY 10017; (212) 599-6192.

Website: www.parliament.gov.sb

The Solomon Isls. were sighted 1568 by an expedition from Peru. Britain established a protectorate in the 1890s over most of the group, inhabited by Melanesians. The islands, including Guadalcanal, saw major WWII battles. They achieved self-government, Jan. 2, 1976, and formal independence, July 7, 1978.

To restore order after years of factional violence, including a coup attempt, June 5, 2000, an Australian-led regional security force arrived in July 2003—the Regional Assistance Mission to Solomon Islands (RAMSI).

Following Apr. 2006 elections, the first since RAMSI began, parliament's choice of Snyder Rini as prime min. led to two days of rioting in Honiara over alleged influence-buying by the ethnic Chinese business community. Rini resigned, Apr. 26, 2006. Former prime min. Manasseh Sogavare (2000-01, 2006-07) again became head of government following Nov. 19, 2014, parliamentary elections. RAMSI formally ended June 2017. After Sogavare, Nov. 6, 2017, lost a no-confidence vote, Rick Hou replaced him as prime minister.

Somalia
Federal Republic of Somalia

People: Population: 11,259,029 (81). **Age distrib.:** <15: 42.9%; 65+: 2.2%. **Growth:** 2.1%. **Migrants:** 0.3%. **Pop. density:** 46.5 per sq mi, 17.9 per sq km. **Urban:** 45%. **Ethnic groups:** Somali 85%, Bantu and other non-Somali 15%. **Languages:** Somali, Arabic (both official); Italian; English. **Religions:** Sunni Muslim (official).

Geography: Total area: 246,201 sq mi, 637,657 sq km (43); **Land area:** 242,216 sq mi, 627,337 sq km. **Location:** Eastern horn of Africa. Djibouti, Ethiopia, Kenya on W. **Topography:** Coastline extends for 1,700 mi. Hills cover the N; center and S are flat. **Arable land:** 1.8%. **Capital:** Mogadishu, 2,081,624.

Government: Type: Federal parliamentary republic. **Head of state:** Pres. Mohamed Abdullahi "Farmajo"; b. 1962; in office: Feb. 8, 2017. **Head of govt.:** Prime Min. Hassan Ali Khayre; b. 1968; in office: Mar. 1, 2017. **Local divisions:** 18 regions. **Defense budget:** NA. **Active troops:** 19,800.

Economy: Industries: light industries incl. sugar refining, textiles, wireless communication. **Chief agric.:** bananas, sorghum, corn, coconuts, rice, sugarcane, mangoes, sesame seeds, beans; cattle, sheep, goats; fish. **Natural resources:** uranium, largely unexploited reserves of iron ore, tin, gypsum, bauxite, copper, salt, nat. gas. **Water:** 1,363 cu m per capita. **Electricity prod.:** 345 mil kWh. **Labor force:** agric. 86.2%, industry 7.6%, services 6.2%, Djibouti 17%, India 15%, China 10.7%, Kenya 5.5%. **Unemployment:** 6%.

Finance: Monetary unit: Shilling (SOS) (576.94 = $1 U.S.). **GDP:** $18.7 bil; **GDP growth:** 1.8%. **Imports** (2014): $3.5 bil; China 17.6%, India 17.2%, Ethiopia 10.5%, Oman 10.3%, Kenya 6.9%, Turkey 5.3%. **Exports** (2014): $819 mil; Oman 31.7%, Saudi Arabia 18.7%, UAE 16.3%, Nigeria 5.1%. **Budget** (2014): $151.1 mil. **Inflation:** 1.5%.

Transport: Airports: 6.

Communications: Telephone (2016): 0.3 per 100 pop. **Mobile** (2016): 46.5 per 100 pop. **Broadband:** NA. **Internet:** 1.9%.

Health: Expend.: NA. **Life expect.:** 51.0 male; 55.4 female. **Births:** 39.3 per 1,000 pop. **Deaths:** 12.8 per 1,000 pop. **Infant mortality:** 93.0 per 1,000 live births. **Undernourished:** NA. **HIV:** 0.1%.

Education: Compulsory: NA. **Literacy:** NA.

Embassy: 1705 Desales St., Ste. 300, 20036; 296-0570.

Website: www.villasomalia.gov.so or www.state.gov/p/af/ci/so/

British Somaliland (present-day N Somalia) was formed in the 19th cent., as was Italian Somaliland (now central and S Somalia). Italy lost its African colonies in WWII. British Somaliland gained independence, June 26, 1960, and by prearrangement, merged, July 1, with the UN Trust Territory of Somalia to create the independent Somali Republic.

On Oct. 15, 1969, Somalia's first civilian president, Abdirashid Ali Sharmarke, was assassinated. Six days later, Maj. Gen. Muhammad Siad Barre led a military coup. In 1970, he declared the country a socialist state.

Somalia has laid claim to Ogaden, the huge eastern region of Ethiopia, peopled mostly by Somalis. Some 11,000 Cuban troops with Soviet arms defeated Somali army troops and ethnic Somali rebels in Ethiopia, 1978. As many as 1.5 mil refugees entered Somalia. Guerrilla fighting in Ogaden continued until 1988, when a peace agreement was reached with Ethiopia.

Fighting in Mogadishu led Siad Barre to flee the capital, Jan. 1991. Fighting between rival factions caused 40,000 casualties, 1991-92, and by mid-1992, the civil war, drought, and banditry combined to produce a famine that threatened some 1.5 mil people.

U.S. troops and the UN worked to safeguard food delivery, 1991-93, resulting in significant U.S. and other casualties; a failed mission Oct. 3-4, 1993, left 18 U.S. troops and more than 500 Somalis dead. The U.S. withdrew its peacekeeping forces Mar. 25, 1994.

When the last UN troops pulled out, Mar. 3, 1995, armed factions controlled different regions. A peace deal Jan. 29, 2004, led to the Aug. 22 inauguration of a transitional parliament, Somalia's first legislature in 13 years. Meeting in Nairobi, Kenya, the parliament chose Abdullahi Yusuf Ahmed as president; he was sworn in Oct. 14. Because Mogadishu was held by his rivals, Pres. Yusuf moved, July 26, 2005, to make his transitional capital at Jowhar. On June 5, an Islamist militia took over Mogadishu, defeating U.S.-backed secular warlords. Islamists held much of the central and southern regions.

With aid from Ethiopian troops, transitional govt. forces recaptured Mogadishu in Dec. 2006. The UN Security Council authorized, Feb. 20, 2007, an African Union peacekeeping mission to Somalia (AMISOM). An upsurge of fighting in Mogadishu, Feb.-Apr., killed hundreds of people and caused 350,000 to flee. Bombings and kidnappings escalated in 2007-08; many of the attacks on transitional authorities and their allies were blamed on al-Shabab, an al-Qaeda ally.

After Pres. Yusuf resigned Dec. 29, 2008, the transitional parliament, meeting in Djibouti Jan. 31, 2009, elected a moderate Islamist, Sheikh Sharif Sheikh Ahmed. Meanwhile, pirates carried out more than 200 attacks off the Horn of Africa in 2009. Pirates and Islamist insurgents continued to disrupt famine relief efforts in 2010-11. Pressured by AMISOM forces, al-Shabab pulled out of Mogadishu, Aug. 6, 2011, but continued to control much of southern Somalia. Somali leaders met in Feb. 2012 in Garowe, Somalia, and signed Feb. 18 the Garowe II Principles, which established the conditions to install the caretaker government sworn in Aug. 20. The new parliament elected activist-professor Hassan Sheik Mohamud president Sept. 10, 2012. Bombings and other attacks by al-Shabab, in Mogadishu and elsewhere, continued. Al-Shabab leader Ahmed Abdi Godane was killed by a U.S. airstrike Sept. 1, 2014, and U.S. drone strikes killed other high-ranking members of the group, 2014-15. AMISOM and Somali forces had pushed al-Shabab out of major towns by mid-2015. However, the group's terrorist attacks continued, and

it retook some towns by 2016. U.S. special operations troops (about 500 in mid-2018) assisted AMISOM forces (over 22,000 uniformed personnel in 2018) and Somali government forces. Delayed by violence, late 2016 indirect elections resulted in the seating of a new bicameral parliament Dec. 27. Parliament, Feb. 8, 2017, elected Prime Min. Mohamed Abdullahi Mohamed (2010-11) as Somalia's president. He pledged stronger action against Islamist militants, but further deadly al-Shabab attacks occurred. A truck bombing in Mogadishu, Oct. 14, killed more than 500. The U.S. intensified air strikes in Nov. Drought and warfare caused famine affecting more than 6 mil Somalis by 2017. Combat continued in 2018. Two U.S. service members were killed mid-2017 to mid-2018.

South Africa
Republic of South Africa

People: Population: 55,380,210 (26). **Age distrib.:** <15: 28.2%; 65+: 5.8%. **Growth:** 1%. **Migrants:** 7.1%. **Pop. density:** 118.1 per sq mi, 45.6 per sq km. **Urban:** 66.4%. **Ethnic groups:** black African 80.2%, colored (South African term for persons of mixed-race ancestry) 8.8%, white 8.4%, Indian/Asian 2.5%. **Languages:** isiZulu, isiXhosa, Afrikaans, English, Sepedi, Setswana, Sesotho, Xitsonga, siSwati, Tshivenda, isiNdebele (all official). **Religions:** Protestant 36.6% (incl. Zionist Christian 11.1%), Catholic 7.1%, none 15.1%.

Geography: Total area: 470,693 sq mi, 1,219,090 sq km (24); **Land area:** 468,909 sq mi, 1,214,470 sq km. **Location:** Southern extreme of Africa. Namibia, Botswana, Zimbabwe on N; Mozambique, Swaziland on E; surrounds Lesotho. **Topography:** Large interior plateau reaches close to the country's 1,739-mi coastline. Few major rivers or lakes. Rainfall is sparse in W, more plentiful in E. **Arable land:** 10.3%. **Capital:** Pretoria (admin.), 2,378,350; Cape Town (legis.), 4,430,367; Bloemfontein (judicial), 545,875. **Cities:** Johannesburg, 5,485,986; Ekurhuleni, 3,741,476; Durban, 3,133,729; Port Elizabeth, 1,230,819.

Government: Type: Parliamentary republic. **Head of state and govt.:** Pres. Cyril Ramaphosa; b. 1952; in office: Feb. 15, 2018. **Local divisions:** 9 provinces. **Defense budget:** $3.6 bil. **Active troops:** 66,350.

Economy: Industries: mining (platinum, gold, chromium), auto assembly, metalworking, machinery, textiles, iron and steel, chemicals, fertilizer, foodstuffs. **Chief agric.:** corn, wheat, sugarcane, fruits, vegetables; beef, poultry, mutton, wool, dairy prods. **Natural resources:** gold, chromium, antimony, coal, iron ore, manganese, nickel, phosphates, tin, rare earth elements, uranium, gem diamonds, platinum, copper, vanadium, salt, nat. gas. **Water:** 942 cu m per capita. **Crude oil reserves:** 15 mil bbls. **Electricity prod.:** 230.6 bil kWh. **Labor force:** agric. 5.6%, industry 23.4%, services 71.1%. **Unemployment:** 27.3%.

Finance: Monetary unit: Rand (ZAR) (15.34 = $1 U.S.). **GDP:** $765.6 bil; **per capita GDP:** $13,500; **GDP growth:** 1.3%. **Imports:** $80.2 bil; China 18.3%, Germany 11.9%, U.S. 6.6%. **Exports:** $78.3 bil; China 9.5%, U.S. 7.7%, Germany 7.1%. **Tourism:** $8.8 bil. **Budget:** $103.3 bil. **Inflation:** 5.2%.

Transport: Railways: 13,040 mi. **Motor vehicles:** 244.1 per 1,000 pop. **Airports:** 144.

Communications: Telephone: 6.4 per 100 pop. **Mobile:** 162 per 100 pop. **Broadband:** 58.6 per 100 pop. **Internet:** 54%.

Health: Expend.: 8.2%. **Life expect.:** 62.7 male; 65.6 female. **Births:** 19.9 per 1,000 pop. **Deaths:** 9.3 per 1,000 pop. **Infant mortality:** 29.9 per 1,000 live births. **Undernourished:** 6.1%. **HIV:** 18.8%.

Education: Compulsory: ages 7-15. **Literacy:** 94.4%.

Embassy: 3051 Massachusetts Ave. NW 20008; 232-4400.

Website: www.gov.za

San and KhoiKhoi people were the original inhabitants. Bantus, including Zulu, Xhosa, Swazi, and Sotho, occupied the area from northeastern to southern South Africa before the 17th cent.

The Dutch settled the Cape of Good Hope area, beginning in the 17th cent. Britain seized the Cape, 1806. Many Dutch trekked north and founded two republics, Transvaal and Orange Free State. Diamonds were discovered, 1867, and gold, 1886. The Dutch (Boers) resented encroachments by the British and others; the Anglo-Boer War followed, 1899-1902. Britain won and created, May 31, 1910, the Union of South Africa, incorporating two British colonies (Cape and Natal) with Transvaal and Orange Free State. After a referendum, the Union became the Republic of South Africa, May 31, 1961, and withdrew from the Commonwealth (it rejoined in 1994).

Daniel Malan's National Party, elected in 1948, made the policy of separate development of the races, or apartheid, official. Under apartheid, blacks were restricted to living and working in designated areas, attended separate schools, could hold only certain jobs, and were paid less than whites for similar work. Only whites could vote or run for public office. Persons of Asian Indian ancestry and those of mixed race ("coloureds") had limited political rights.

Protests against apartheid were suppressed. At Sharpeville on Mar. 21, 1960, government troops killed 69 black protesters. At least 600 persons, mostly Bantus, were killed in 1976 anti-apartheid riots. In 1986, Nobel Peace Prize winner Bishop Desmond Tutu called for Western nations to apply sanctions against South

Africa to force an end to apartheid. Pres. P. W. Botha offered blacks an advisory role in government starting in Apr. On May 19, South Africa attacked three neighboring countries—Zimbabwe, Botswana, Zambia—striking at guerrilla strongholds of the anti-apartheid African National Congress (ANC).

Some 2 mil South African black workers staged a strike, June 6-8, 1988. Pres. Botha, head of the government since 1978, resigned Aug. 14, 1989, and was replaced by F. W. de Klerk. In 1990 the government lifted its ban on the ANC. Anti-apartheid leader Nelson Mandela was freed Feb. 11 after more than 27 years in prison. In Feb. 1991, Pres. de Klerk pledged to end apartheid laws.

In 1993 negotiators agreed on basic principles for a new democratic constitution. South Africa's partially self-governing black territories, or "homelands," were incorporated into a national system of nine provinces. The ANC won elections Apr. 26-29, 1994, making Mandela president. The predominantly-Zulu Inkatha Freedom Party won control of the legislature in a mainly Zulu province. By then, fighting between the ANC and Inkatha (aided, during the apartheid era, by South African defense forces) had killed more than 14,000 people in the Zulu region.

A post-apartheid constitution became law Dec. 10, 1996. The ANC won elections, June 2, 1999, and ANC leader Thabo Mbeki became president. South Africa, Nov. 30, 2006, became the first African country to legalize same-sex marriage.

After Mbeki's former deputy president, Jacob Zuma, defeated him in a power struggle for the ANC leadership, Mbeki resigned his presidency, Sept. 21, 2008. Zuma became president after Apr. 22, 2009, elections. Thousands of miners struck for better wages at the Lonmin platinum mine near Marikana, Aug. 10, 2012. Protests at the mine left at least 10 dead, before police opened fire on protesters Aug. 16, killing 34 and wounding dozens. Mandela died Dec. 5, 2013.

Despite corruption charges, Zuma was reelected president by the National Assembly, May 21, 2014, following an ANC victory in May 7 parliamentary elections. With the economy weak and claims of corruption continuing, Zuma bowed to pressure from ANC leaders and resigned Feb. 14, 2018. Cyril Ramaphosa, head of the ANC since Dec. 2017, was elected president by the National Assembly, Feb. 15. Zuma went on trial, Apr. 6, 2018, on corruption-related charges.

South Sudan
Republic of South Sudan

People: Population: 10,204,581 (89). **Age distrib.:** <15: 42.3%; 65+: 2.5%. **Growth:** −1.2%. **Migrants:** 6.7%. **Pop. density:** 41 per sq mi, 15.8 per sq km. **Urban:** 19.6%. **Ethnic groups:** Dinka 35.8%; Nuer 15.6%; Shilluk, Azande, Bari, Kakwa, Kuku, Murle, Mandari, Didinga. **Languages:** English (official), Arabic (incl. Juba, Sudanese variants). **Religions:** animist, Christian.

Geography: Total area: 248,777 sq mi, 644,329 sq km (41). **Location:** NE Africa. Sudan on N, Uganda and Kenya on S, Ethiopia on E, Central African Rep. and Dem. Rep. of the Congo on W. **Topography:** The White Nile R. flows N through center of country and feeds the Sudd, a swampy area occupying more than 15% of the country's center; it is one of the world's largest wetlands. **Arable land:** NA. **Capital:** Juba, 368,914.

Government: Type: Presidential republic. **Head of state and govt.:** Pres. Salva Kiir Mayardit; b. 1951; in office: July 9, 2011. **Local divisions:** 10 states. **Defense budget:** $97 mil. **Active troops:** 185,000.

Economy: Chief agric.: sorghum, maize, rice, millet, wheat, gum arabic, sugarcane, mangoes, papayas, bananas, sweet potatoes, sunflower seeds, cotton, sesame seeds; cattle, sheep. **Natural resources:** hydropower, gold, diamonds, petroleum, hardwoods, limestone, iron ore, copper, chromium ore, zinc, tungsten, mica, silver. **Water:** 4,011 cu m per capita. **Crude oil reserves** (2017): 3.5 bil bbls. **Electricity prod.:** 310.3 mil kWh. **Labor force:** agric. 64.9%, industry 19%, services 16.1%. **Unemployment:** 11.5%.

Finance: Monetary unit: Pound (SSP) (147.27 = $1 U.S.). **GDP:** $18.7 bil; **per capita GDP:** $1,500; **GDP growth:** −11.1%. **Imports** (2016): $3.8 bil. **Exports** (2016): $1.1 bil. **Budget:** $298.6 mil. **Inflation:** 187.9%.

Transport: Railways: 154 mi. **Airports:** 3.

Communications: Telephone: NA. **Mobile:** 12 per 100 pop. **Broadband:** NA. **Internet:** 6.7%.

Health: Expend.: 2.5%. **Life expect.:** 43.2 male; 41.9 female. **Births:** 36.9 per 1,000 pop. **Deaths:** 19.3 per 1,000 pop. **Infant mortality:** 90.4 per 1,000 live births. **Undernourished:** NA. **HIV:** 2.4%.

Education: Compulsory: ages 6-13. **Literacy:** 27%. **Embassy:** 1015 31st St. NW, Ste. 300, 20007; 293-7940. **Website:** www.goss-online.org or www.state.gov/p/af/ci/su/

South Sudan was a region of the Republic of the Sudan when that country became independent in 1956. Northerners (mostly Arab Muslims) dominated, while southerners (mostly black Africans who practiced Christianity or traditional religions) were marginalized. Southern rebels waged war against the north, 1955-72, until an agreement was reached offering regional self-government for the south. Oil was discovered in the south in 1978.

Civil war broke out again in 1983. Fighting and related famine cost an estimated 2 mil lives and displaced millions of southerners. A peace accord was signed in 2005. A power-sharing agreement offered autonomy for southern Sudan and allowed for an independence referendum.

Almost 99% of southern Sudanese who voted in the referendum, Jan. 9-15, 2011, supported secession. The UN Security Council, July 8, authorized a peacekeeping force (UNMISS) for the area. South Sudan attained full independence July 9, 2011.

Pres. Salva Kiir fired Vice Pres. Riek Machar, July 23, 2013. Heavy fighting broke out in Juba in Dec. 2013 between government troops and rebels led by Machar. Forces of Kiir and Machar (who belong to different ethnic groups) battled throughout the country in 2014-15. Kiir and Machar signed a peace accord Aug. 2015, although a number of cease-fire violations occurred. Machar returned to Juba and resumed the vice presidency in Apr. 2016 but fled the country, Aug. 17; a new round of heavy fighting began July 7, and violence continued in 2017-18. UNMISS had about 16,000 uniformed personnel in South Sudan as of Aug. 31, 2018. As of Sept. 15, 2018, about 2.5 mil South Sudanese were refugees in neighboring countries. Almost 1.9 mil people were internally displaced in mid-2018, and millions faced severe food shortages. A new peace agreement was signed Sept. 12, 2018. A U.S.-funded study reported, Sept. 26, that South Sudan's civil war had caused, directly and indirectly (including disease and hunger), about 383,000 "excess deaths" since late 2013.

Spain
Kingdom of Spain

People: Population: 49,331,076 (28). **Age distrib.:** <15: 15.3%; 65+: 18.1%. **Growth:** 0.7%. **Migrants:** 12.8%. **Pop. density:** 256.1 per sq mi, 98.9 per sq km. **Urban:** 80.3%. **Ethnic groups:** mixed Mediterranean/Nordic. **Languages:** Castilian Spanish (official); Catalan, Galician, Basque (all official in areas). **Religions:** Roman Catholic 67.8%, atheist 9.1%, non-believer 18.4%.

Geography: Total area: 195,124 sq mi, 505,370 sq km (51). **Land area:** 192,657 sq mi, 498,980 sq km. **Location:** SW Europe. Portugal on W; France, Andorra on N; Morocco to S. **Topography:** High, arid plateau broken by mountain ranges and river valleys in interior. The NW is heavily watered, the S has lowlands and a Medit. climate. **Arable land:** 24.7%. **Capital:** Madrid, 6,497,124. **Cities:** Barcelona, 5,494,125.

Government: Type: Parliamentary constitutional monarchy. **Head of state:** King Felipe VI; b. 1968; in office: June 19, 2014. **Head of govt.:** Pres. Pedro Sánchez Pérez-Castejón; b. 1972; in office: June 2, 2018. **Local divisions:** 17 autonomous communities, 2 autonomous cities. **Defense budget:** $12.1 bil. **Active troops:** 121,200.

Economy: Industries: textiles/apparel (incl. footwear), food/beverages, metals/metal manufactures, chemicals, shipbuilding, automobiles, machine tools, tourism. **Chief agric.:** grain, vegetables, olives, wine grapes, sugar beets; citrus; beef, pork, poultry, dairy prods.; fish. **Natural resources:** coal, lignite, iron ore, copper, lead, zinc, uranium, tungsten, mercury, pyrites, magnesite, fluorspar, gypsum, sepiolite, kaolin, potash, hydropower. **Water:** 2,418 cu m per capita. **Crude oil reserves:** 150 mil bbls. **Electricity prod.:** 264.2 bil kWh. **Labor force:** agric. 4.1%, industry 19.5%, services 76.4%. **Unemployment:** 17.2%.

Finance: Monetary unit: Euro (EUR) (0.86 = $1 U.S.). **GDP:** $1.8 tril; **per capita GDP:** $38,300; **GDP growth:** 3.1%. **Imports:** $333.4 bil; Germany 14.2%, France 11.9%, China 6.9%, Italy 6.8%, Netherlands 5.1%. **Exports:** $301.5 bil; France 15.1%, Germany 11.3%, Italy 7.8%, Portugal 7.1%, UK 6.9%. **Tourism:** $68 bil. **Budget:** $535.9 bil. **Inflation:** 2%.

Transport: Railways: 10,005 mi. **Motor vehicles:** 585.1 per 1,000 pop. **Airports:** 99.

Communications: Telephone: 42.5 per 100 pop. **Mobile:** 113.2 per 100 pop. **Broadband:** 87.3 per 100 pop. **Internet** (2017): 84.6%.

Health: Expend.: 9.2%. **Life expect.:** 78.8 male; 85.0 female. **Births:** 9.0 per 1,000 pop. **Deaths:** 9.2 per 1,000 pop. **Infant mortality:** 3.3 per 1,000 live births. **Undernourished:** <2.5%. **HIV:** 0.4%.

Education: Compulsory: ages 6-15. **Literacy:** 98.3%. **Embassy:** 2375 Pennsylvania Ave. NW 20037; 452-0100. **Website:** www.lamoncloa.gob.es

Settled by Iberians, Basques, and Celts, Spain was successively ruled (wholly or in part) by Carthage, Rome, and the Visigoths. Muslims invaded Iberia from N Africa in 711. Reconquest of the peninsula by Christians from the N laid the foundations of modern Spain. In 1469 the kingdoms of Aragon and Castile were united by the marriage of Ferdinand II and Isabella I. Moorish rule ended with the fall of Granada, 1492, the year Spain's large Jewish community was expelled.

Spain established a colonial empire after Columbus's 1492 "discovery" of America. Cortés conquered Mexico, and Pizarro conquered Peru. Spain lost most of its American colonies in the early 19th cent. and Cuba, the Philippines, and Puerto Rico in the Spanish-American War, 1898.

Primo de Rivera became dictator, 1923. King Alfonso XIII revoked the dictatorship, 1930, but was forced into exile in 1931. A republic was proclaimed, which disestablished the church, curtailed its privileges, and secularized education. A Popular Front of socialists, Communists, republicans, and anarchists governed 1936-39.

Army officers under Francisco Franco revolted, 1936. Some 500,000 to 1 mil died in the Spanish Civil War before Franco's Nationalist forces won a complete victory Apr. 1, 1939. Franco ruled as a dictator. Spain was officially neutral in WWII but had cordial relations with Nazi Germany for most of the war.

After Franco's death, Nov. 20, 1975, Prince Juan Carlos became king. In free elections, June 1977, moderates and democratic socialists won the most votes. The king thwarted a 1981 coup attempt by right-wing military officers. The Socialist Workers' Party (PSOE), under Felipe González Márquez, won four consecutive general elections, 1982-93, but lost to a coalition of conservative and regional parties, 1996. Conservative Prime Min. José María Aznar won a parliamentary majority in the 2000 election.

Islamic extremists bombed four commuter trains in central Madrid, Mar. 11, 2004, killing 191 people. The PSOE won elections three days later, and Socialist leader José Luis Rodríguez Zapatero became prime min. Apr. 17. Spain legalized same-sex marriage in 2005.

Prime Min. Zapatero won a second term in 2008. Spain's economy suffered during the worldwide financial crisis; in May 2010, as the budget deficit mounted, the government introduced austerity measures to reassure international lenders. Mariano Rajoy's conservative Popular Party (PP) won Nov. 2011 elections. Spain received a 100-bil-euro EU bailout for its ailing banks in 2012. Spain's unemployment rate surpassed 26% in 2013. GDP began growing in 2014, after five years of decline; unemployment was about 17% in 2017.

Juan Carlos abdicated in favor of his son, who became King Felipe VI, June 19, 2014. Hurt by corruption scandals, the PP lost its majority in Dec. 20, 2015, legislative elections. When elections were repeated, June 26, 2016, the PP again fell short of a majority, but Rajoy was sworn in as head of a minority govt., Oct. 31, 2016. In the wake of a PP corruption conviction, Rajoy lost a no-confidence vote, June 1, 2018; the PSOE's Pedro Sánchez became prime min.

In one of a series of events linked by police to an Islamist extremist cell in Catalonia, 14 people were killed and more than 100 injured in Barcelona, Aug. 17, 2017, when a terrorist drove a van through a crowded pedestrian area; the suspect fled and apparently killed the driver of a car he stole. He was killed by police Aug. 21. The night of Aug. 17-18, one person was killed and several injured in Cambrils when five terrorists drove a car into pedestrians; the attackers were killed by police. Two suspected terrorists died in an explosion, Aug. 16, at a house in Alcanar apparently being used to make bombs.

Spain was the European entry point for about 42,000 African and Middle Eastern migrants (most arriving by boat), Jan.-Sept. 2018, the highest figure for any European country.

Catalonia and the **Basque Country** were granted autonomy, Jan. 1980, following overwhelming approval in home-rule referendums. But Basque extremists pushed for independence. The Basque separatist group ETA carried out bombings that killed about 830 since 1968. ETA declared a unilateral cease-fire Oct. 20, 2011. In a letter dated Apr. 16, 2018, and published May 2, the organization said it was disbanding. In Catalonia, voters approved expanded home-rule, June 18, 2006. Separatist parties won Catalonia's regional parliamentary elections Sept. 27, 2015. Measures passed in 2015 and 2016 to begin separation were blocked by Spain's Constitutional Court. Catalonia scheduled a separation referendum for Oct. 1, 2017, but Spanish authorities took steps to interfere with balloting, and national police clashed with independence advocates; 90% of voters favored separation. After the regional parliament, Oct. 27, voted to declare independence, the national government dissolved the parliament and removed pro-independence regional president Carles Puigdemont from office. In new regional parliamentary elections, Dec. 21, separatists again won a majority; the parliament elected separatist Quim Torra as regional president, May 14, 2018. **Website:** web.gencat.cat

The **Balearic** Isls. in the W Mediterranean, 1,927 sq mi, is an autonomous community of Spain; the islands include Majorca (Mallorca; capital Palma de Mallorca), Minorca, Cabrera, Ibiza, and Formentera. The Canary Isls., 2,807 sq mi, another autonomous community in the Atlantic W of Morocco, includes the islands of Tenerife, Palma, Gomera, Hierro, Grand Canary, Fuerteventura, and Lanzarote; Las Palmas and Santa Cruz are thriving ports. More than 1,700 people died trying to get from Mauritania to the Canary Isls. in rickety boats, Jan.-June 2006.

Ceuta and **Melilla**, small Spanish enclaves on Morocco's Mediterranean coast, gained limited autonomy in Sept. 1994. In 2014-18, thousands of African and Middle Eastern migrants crossed the borders between Morocco and the enclaves.

Spain has sought the return of Gibraltar, in British hands since 1704.

Sri Lanka
Democratic Socialist Republic of Sri Lanka

People: Population: 22,576,592 (57). **Age distrib.:** <15: 23.7%; 65+: 10%. **Growth:** 0.7%. **Migrants:** 0.2%. **Pop. density:** 904.7 per sq mi, 349.3 per sq km. **Urban:** 18.5%. **Ethnic groups:** Sinhalese 74.9%, Sri Lankan Tamil 11.2%, Sri Lankan Moor 9.2%, Indian Tamil 4.2%. **Languages:** Sinhala, Tamil (both official and national); English (commonly used in govt.). **Religions:** Buddhist (official) 70.2%, Hindu 12.6%, Muslim 9.7%, Roman Catholic 6.1%.

Geography: Total area: 25,332 sq mi, 65,610 sq km (120); **Land area:** 24,954 sq mi, 64,630 sq km. **Location:** Indian O. off SE coast of India. **Topography:** Coastal area and N half are flat; S central area is hilly and mountainous. **Arable land:** 20.7%. **Capital:** Colombo, 599,821; Sri Jayewardenepura Kotte (legis.), 103,248.

Government: Type: Presidential republic. **Head of state and govt.:** Pres. Maithripala Sirisena; b. 1951; in office: Jan. 9, 2015. **Local divisions:** 9 provinces. **Defense budget:** $1.7 bil. **Active troops:** 243,000.

Economy: Industries: rubber, tea, coconuts, tobacco and other agric. commodities; telecom, insurance, banking; tourism, shipping; clothing, textiles; cement, petroleum refining. **Chief agric.:** rice, sugarcane, grains, pulses, oilseed, spices, vegetables, fruit, tea, rubber, coconuts; milk, eggs, hides, beef; fish. **Natural resources:** limestone, graphite, mineral sands, gems, phosphates, clay, hydropower. **Water:** 2,549 cu m per capita. **Electricity prod.:** 12.7 bil kWh. **Labor force:** agric. 26.7%, industry 25.7%, services 47.7%. **Unemployment:** 4.1%.

Finance: Monetary unit: Rupee (LKR) (161.55 = $1 U.S.). **GDP:** $274.7 bil; **per capita GDP:** $12,800; **GDP growth:** 3.1%. **Imports:** $21.1 bil; India 22%, China 19.9%, Singapore 6.9%, UAE 5.7%. **Exports:** $10.9 bil; U.S. 24.6%, UK 9%, India 5.8%. **Tourism:** $3.9 bil. **Budget:** $16.7 bil. **Inflation:** 7.7%.

Transport: Railways: 971 mi. **Motor vehicles:** 48.9 per 1,000 pop. **Airports:** 15.

Communications: Telephone: 12.5 per 100 pop. **Mobile:** 135.1 per 100 pop. **Broadband:** 18.3 per 100 pop. **Internet:** 32.1%.

Health: Expend.: 3%. **Life expect.:** 73.7 male; 80.8 female. **Births:** 14.8 per 1,000 pop. **Deaths:** 6.3 per 1,000 pop. **Infant mortality:** 8.2 per 1,000 live births. **Undernourished:** 10.9%. **HIV:** <0.1%.

Education: Compulsory: ages 5-15. **Literacy:** 92.6%.
Embassy: 3025 Whitehaven St. NW 20008; 483-4025.
Website: www.gov.lk

The island was known to the ancient world as Taprobane (Greek for copper-colored) and later as Serendip (from Arabic). Colonists from N India subdued the indigenous Veddahs about 543 BCE; their descendants, the Buddhist Sinhalese, still form most of the population. Hindu descendants of Tamil immigrants from S India are the largest minority ethnic group.

Parts were occupied by the Portuguese in 1505 and the Dutch in 1658. The British seized the island in 1796. It became an independent member of the Commonwealth as Ceylon in 1948 before changing its name to Sri Lanka May 22, 1972.

Prime Min. Solomon W. R. D. Bandaranaike was assassinated Sept. 25, 1959. His widow, Sirimavo Bandaranaike, served as prime min. 1960-65, 1970-77, 1994-2000. In the 1970s, thousands of ultra-leftists were executed, while massive land reform and nationalization of foreign-owned plantations took place.

Tensions between Sinhalese and Tamil separatists erupted in the early 1980s and turned into a 20-year civil war that killed more than 60,000; another 20,000, mostly young Tamils, "disappeared" while in government custody. Pres. Ranasinghe Premadasa was assassinated May 1, 1993, by a Tamil rebel. A truce intended to bring an end to the civil war was signed Feb. 22, 2002.

More than 31,000 died in the Dec. 26, 2004, Indian Ocean tsunami. Prime Min. Mahinda Rajapaksa won the 2005 presidential election and was reelected in 2010. Thousands died during three years of fighting among government forces, paramilitary groups, and Tamil rebels beginning in Dec. 2005. About 7,000 noncombatants were killed Jan. 20-May 7, 2009. Tamil leader Vellupillai Prabhakaran was killed May 18-19, 2009, and Pres. Rajapaksa formally declared victory. Maithripala Sirisena defeated Rajapaksa in the Jan. 8, 2015, presidential election. Sirisena's coalition won Aug. 17 parliamentary elections. A Sept. 16, 2015, UN report documented numerous human rights violations by both sides in Sri Lanka's civil war, including widespread torture of detainees by government security forces. July 2017 and July 2018 UN reports concluded that torture of national-security detainees continued. WHO announced, Sept. 5, 2016, that Sri Lanka had eradicated malaria.

Loans and investments from China have financed a number of large infrastructure projects in recent years, including a new Port City under construction adjacent to Colombo and a new seaport; struggling to make loan payments, the Sri Lankan government turned over control of the seaport, Dec. 2017, to a state-owned Chinese company.

Sudan
Republic of the Sudan

(Pre-2012 data and communications statistics include South Sudan, which became independent July 9, 2011.)

People: Population: 43,120,843 (33). **Age distrib.:** <15: 43.1%; 65+: 3%. **Growth:** 2.9%. **Migrants:** 1.8%. **Pop. density:** 60 per sq mi, 23.2 per sq km. **Urban:** 34.6%. **Ethnic groups:** Sudanese Arab (approx. 70%), Fur, Beja, Nuba, Fallata.

Languages: Arabic, English (both official); Nubian; Ta Bedawie; Fur. **Religions:** Sunni Muslim, small Christian minority.

Geography: Total area: 718,723 sq mi, 1,861,484 sq km (15). **Location:** E end of Sahara desert zone. Egypt on N; Libya, Chad, Central African Republic on W; South Sudan on S; Ethiopia, Eritrea on E. **Topography:** The N consists of Libyan Desert in W and the mountainous Nubia Desert in E, with narrow Nile Valley between. Large rainy areas with fields, pastures, and forests in center. The S has rich soil, heavy rain. **Arable land:** 15.7%. **Capital:** Khartoum, 5,534,079.

Government: Type: Presidential republic. **Head of state and govt.:** Pres. Gen. Omar Hassan Ahmad al-Bashir; b. 1944; in office: Oct. 16, 1993 (de facto since June 30, 1989). **Local divisions:** 18 states. **Defense budget:** NA. **Active troops:** 104,300.

Economy: Industries: oil, cotton ginning, textiles, cement, edible oils, sugar, soap distilling, shoes, petroleum refining, pharmaceuticals, armaments. **Chief agric.:** cotton, groundnuts, sorghum, millet, wheat, gum arabic, sugarcane, cassava, mangoes, papayas, bananas, sweet potatoes, sesame seeds; animal feed, sheep. **Natural resources:** petroleum; small reserves of iron ore, copper, chromium ore, zinc, tungsten, mica, silver, gold; hydropower. **Water:** 940 cu m per capita. **Crude oil reserves** (2017): 1.5 bil bbls. **Electricity prod.:** 12.7 bil kWh. **Labor force:** agric. 53.3%, industry 19.2%, services 27.5%. **Unemployment:** 12.7%.

Finance: Monetary unit: Pound (SDG) (18.00 = $1 U.S.). **GDP:** $187 bil; **per capita GDP:** $4,600; **GDP growth:** 3.2%. **Imports:** $8.6 bil; UAE 12.7%, Egypt 10.6%, India 10.5%, Turkey 10.2%, Japan 7.6%, Saudi Arabia 6%. **Exports:** $3.8 bil; UAE 55.5%, Egypt 14.7%, Saudi Arabia 8.8%. **Tourism:** $1 bil. **Budget:** $13.4 bil. **Inflation** (2014-15): 16.9%.

Transport: Railways: 4,506 mi. **Motor vehicles:** 3.2 per 1,000 pop. **Airports:** 16.

Communications: Telephone: 0.4 per 100 pop. **Mobile:** 70.7 per 100 pop. **Broadband:** 25.2 per 100 pop. **Internet:** 28%.

Health: Expend.: 6.3%. **Life expect.:** 63.7 male; 68.1 female. **Births:** 34.2 per 1,000 pop. **Deaths:** 6.7 per 1,000 pop. **Infant mortality:** 44.2 per 1,000 live births. **Undernourished:** 25.2%. **HIV:** 0.2%.

Education: Compulsory: ages 6-13. **Literacy:** 75.9%.

Embassy: 2210 Massachusetts Ave. NW 20008; 338-8565.

Website: www.presidency.gov.sd

Northern Sudan, ancient Nubia, was settled by Egyptians in antiquity. The population was converted to Coptic Christianity in the 6th cent. Arab conquests brought Islam to the area in the 15th cent. In the 1820s, Egypt took over Sudan, defeating the last of the earlier empires, including the Fung. In the 1880s, Muhammad Ahmad, who called himself the Mahdi (leader of the faithful), and his followers, the dervishes, led a revolution. An Anglo-Egyptian force crushed the Mahdi's successors, 1898.

Sudan gained independence Jan. 1, 1956. In 1969, a Revolutionary Council took power, led by authoritarian Pres. Gaafar al-Nimeiry. He was overthrown, Apr. 6, 1985. Sudan held its first democratic parliamentary elections in 18 years in 1986. Brig. Omar Hassan Ahmad al-Bashir staged a bloodless military coup, June 30, 1989. He became president in 1993.

During 1955-72 and 1983-2005, rebels in the south (primarily Christians and followers of traditional religions) fought against government domination by mostly Arab-Muslim northern Sudan. War and related famine cost an estimated 2 mil lives. An accord ended the rebellion Jan. 9, 2005.

A rebellion in the Darfur region of western Sudan caused a new crisis, 2003-11. Marauding Arab militias, the *janjaweed*, reportedly acting in collusion with Sudanese government troops, looted and burned homes in Darfur and killed many African villagers. More than 7,000 African Union (AU) peacekeepers were ineffectual. By Sept. 2009, the Darfur war had killed about 300,000 people and displaced another 2.7 mil. A joint UN-AU force of up to 26,000 peacekeepers (UNMIS) was deployed Aug. 2007-July 2011.

The Intl. Criminal Court in The Hague, Netherlands, issued two arrest warrants for Pres. Bashir—in 2009 for war crimes and crimes against humanity in Darfur, and in 2010 for genocide. Bashir defied calls for his arrest. In Apr. 2010 and Apr. 2015, he won new 5-year terms in elections not deemed credible.

After southern Sudanese voted overwhelmingly for secession, Jan. 9-15, 2011, South Sudan attained full independence July 9. Border disputes between Sudan and South Sudan ensued. Conflict in Darfur flared up again in 2014-16, including attacks on civilians by pro-government militias; hundreds of thousands of people were displaced. Government bombings of rebel-held areas in the southern South Kordofan and Blue Nile states caused high civilian casualties. A UN-AU peacekeeping mission in Darfur (UNAMID) included almost 16,000 uniformed personnel as of Aug. 31, 2017. Finding evidence of reduced violence in Darfur, the UN Security Council voted, in 2017 and 2018, to reduce UNAMID forces, which totaled about 11,000 as of Aug. 31, 2018.

Suriname
Republic of Suriname

People: Population: 597,927 (166). **Age distrib.:** <15: 24.1%; 65+: 6.2%. **Growth:** 1%. **Migrants:** 8.5%. **Pop. density:** 9.9 per sq mi, 3.8 per sq km. **Urban:** 66.1%. **Ethnic groups:** Hindustani or East Indian (descended fr. 19th-cent. emigrants fr. northern India) 27.4%, Maroon (descendants of escaped African slaves) 21.7%, Creole (mixed white/black) 15.7%, Javanese 13.7%, mixed 13.4%. **Languages:** Dutch (official), English (widely spoken), Sranang Tongo (Surinamese), Caribbean Hindustani, Javanese. **Religions:** Protestant 23.6% (incl. Evangelical 11.2%, Moravian 11.2%), Hindu 22.3%, Roman Catholic 21.6%, Muslim 13.8%, none 7.5%.

Geography: Total area: 63,251 sq mi, 163,820 sq km (90); **Land area:** 60,232 sq mi, 156,000 sq km. **Location:** N shore of S America. Guyana on W, Brazil on S, French Guiana on E. **Topography:** Flat Atlantic coast, where dikes permit agriculture. Inland is forest belt. To S, hills cover three-fourths of country. **Arable land:** 0.4%. **Capital:** Paramaribo, 239,457.

Government: Type: Presidential republic. **Head of state and govt.:** Pres. Désiré Delano Bouterse; b. 1945; in office: Aug. 12, 2010. **Local divisions:** 10 districts. **Defense budget:** NA. **Active troops:** 1,840.

Economy: Industries: gold mining, oil, lumber, food proc., fishing. **Chief agric.:** rice, bananas, seabob shrimp, yellow-fin tuna, vegetables. **Natural resources:** timber, hydropower, fish, kaolin, shrimp, bauxite, gold; small amounts of nickel, copper, platinum, iron ore. **Water:** 182,320 cu m per capita. **Crude oil reserves:** 84.2 mil bbls. **Electricity prod.:** 2.2 bil kWh. **Labor force:** agric. 2.7%, industry 24.1%, services 73.2%. **Unemployment:** 8.1%.

Finance: Monetary unit: Dollar (SRD) (7.46 = $1 U.S.). **GDP:** $8.5 bil; **per capita GDP:** $14,600; **GDP growth:** 0%. **Imports:** $1.6 bil; U.S. 30.6%, Netherlands 14.8%, Trinidad and Tobago 11.4%, China 7.6%. **Exports:** $2 bil; Switzerland 38%, Hong Kong 21.9%, Belgium 10.1%, UAE 7.2%, Guyana 6.1%. **Tourism:** $46 mil. **Budget:** $805.5 mil. **Inflation:** 22%.

Transport: Motor vehicles: 266.8 per 1,000 pop. **Airports:** 6.

Communications: Telephone: 15.8 per 100 pop. **Mobile:** 141.3 per 100 pop. **Broadband:** 69.6 per 100 pop. **Internet:** 45.4%.

Health: Expend.: 6.5%. **Life expect.:** 70.3 male; 75.3 female. **Births:** 15.6 per 1,000 pop. **Deaths:** 6.1 per 1,000 pop. **Infant mortality:** 23.7 per 1,000 live births. **Undernourished:** 7.6%. **HIV:** 1.3%.

Education: Compulsory: ages 7-12. **Literacy:** 95.6%.

Embassy: 4201 Connecticut Ave. NW, Ste. 400, 20008; 629-4302.

Website: www.gov.sr or www.surinameembassy.org

The Netherlands acquired Suriname in 1667 from Britain. The 1954 Dutch constitution raised the colony to a level of equality with the Netherlands and the Netherlands Antilles. Independence was granted Nov. 25, 1975. Some 40% of the population (mostly E Indians, who opposed independence) immigrated to the Netherlands before independence.

Désiré "Dési" Bouterse, who masterminded coups in 1982 and 1990, was elected president by parliament, July 19, 2010. Bouterse had been convicted in absentia in the Netherlands, 1999, for drug trafficking. Named by the U.S. as a transshipment point for cocaine, Suriname signed the UN-supported Container Control Programme (CCP), Aug. 23, 2012, to improve inspection of shipping containers in its ports. Bouterse's son Dino, arrested in Panama in a sting operation and extradited to the U.S. in 2013, pleaded guilty, Aug. 29, 2014, to drug trafficking and terrorism charges; he was sentenced, Mar. 10, 2015, to 16 years in prison. Bouterse was elected by parliament to a new 5-year term, July 14, 2015. Suriname was affected, 2015-17, by a Zika virus outbreak (about 3,500 confirmed or suspected cases).

Sweden
Kingdom of Sweden

People: Population: 10,040,995 (91). **Age distrib.:** <15: 17.5%; 65+: 20.4%. **Growth:** 0.8%. **Migrants:** 17.6%. **Pop. density:** 63.4 per sq mi, 24.5 per sq km. **Urban:** 87.4%. **Ethnic groups:** Swedes with Finnish and Sami minorities. Most common countries of origin among immigrants: Syria, Finland, Iraq, Poland, Iran. **Languages:** Swedish (official). **Religions:** Church of Sweden (Lutheran) 63.5%, other (incl. Roman Catholic, Orthodox, Baptist, Muslim, Jewish, Buddhist) 8.1%.

Geography: Total area: 173,860 sq mi, 450,295 sq km (55); **Land area:** 158,431 sq mi, 410,335 sq km. **Location:** Scandinavian Peninsula in N Europe. Norway on W, Denmark on S (across Kattegat strait), Finland on E. **Topography:** Mountains along NW border cover 25% of Sweden. Flat or rolling terrain with several large lakes across central and southern areas. **Arable land:** 6.3%. **Capital:** Stockholm, 1,582,968.

Government: Type: Parliamentary constitutional monarchy. **Head of state:** King Carl XVI Gustaf; b. 1946; in office: Sept. 15, 1973. **Head of govt.:** Prime Min. Stefan Löfven; b. 1957; in office: Oct. 3, 2014. (Lost a Sept. 25, 2018, no-confidence vote.) **Local divisions:** 21 counties. **Defense budget:** $6 bil. **Active troops:** 29,750.

Economy: Industries: iron and steel, precision equip. (bearings, radio and phone parts, armaments), wood pulp and paper prods., processed foods, motor vehicles. **Chief agric.:** barley, wheat, sugar beets; meat, milk. **Natural resources:** iron ore, copper, lead, zinc, gold, silver, tungsten, uranium, arsenic, feldspar, timber, hydropower. **Water:** 17,793 cu m per capita. **Electricity prod.:** 159.3 bil kWh. **Labor force:** agric. 1.9%, industry 18.1%, services 80%. **Unemployment:** 6.7%.

Finance: Monetary unit: Krona (SEK) (9.08 = $1 U.S.). **GDP:** $520.9 bil; **per capita GDP:** $51,500; **GDP growth:** 2.4%. **Imports:** $154.8 bil; Germany 18.7%, Netherlands 8.9%, Norway 7.7%, Denmark 7.2%, China 5.5%, UK 5.1%. **Exports:** $169.7 bil; Germany 11%, Norway 10.2%, Finland 6.9%, U.S. 6.9%, Denmark 6.9%, UK 6.2%, Netherlands 5.5%. **Tourism:** $14.1 bil. **Budget:** $269.9 bil. **Inflation:** 1.8%.

Transport: Railways: 8,778 mi. **Motor vehicles:** 552.9 per 1,000 pop. **Airports:** 149.

Communications: Telephone: 28.2 per 100 pop. **Mobile:** 125.5 per 100 pop. **Broadband:** 125.2 per 100 pop. **Internet** (2017): 96.4%.

Health: Expend.: 11%. **Life expect.:** 80.3 male; 84.3 female. **Births:** 12.1 per 1,000 pop. **Deaths:** 9.4 per 1,000 pop. **Infant mortality:** 2.6 per 1,000 live births. **Undernourished:** <2.5%. **HIV:** NA.

Education: Compulsory: ages 7-15. **Literacy:** 99%.
Embassy: 2900 K St. NW 20007; 467-2600.
Website: sweden.se

The Swedes have lived in present-day Sweden for at least 5,000 years. Gothic tribes from Sweden played a major role in the disintegration of the Roman Empire. Other Swedes helped create the first Russian state in the 9th cent. The Swedes were Christianized from the 11th cent., and a strong centralized monarchy developed. The Riksdag, the first European parliament to represent all classes of society, was first called in 1435.

A revolt led by Gustavus I in 1521-23 freed Sweden from Danish rule (dating from 1397); he built up the government and military and established the Lutheran Church. In the 17th cent. Sweden was a major European power, gaining most of the Baltic seacoast. The Napoleonic wars, 1799-1815, in which Sweden acquired Norway (it became independent 1905), were the last in which Sweden participated.

The Social Democratic Party (SAP) has governed Sweden for most of the period since World War II. Prime Min. Olof Palme was shot to death in Stockholm, Feb. 28, 1986. Sweden entered the EU, Jan. 1, 1995. A center-right alliance defeated the SAP in Sept. 2006 and Sept. 2010 parliamentary elections. Parliament voted Apr. 1, 2009, to legalize same-sex marriage. The SAP won the largest bloc of seats in Sept. 14, 2014, elections, in which the anti-immigration Sweden Democrats (SD) won 49 seats. The SAP's Stefan Löfven became prime min., Oct. 3. Parliament approved, May 25, 2016, a defense cooperation agreement with NATO. A Sweden-U.S. defense cooperation agreement was signed June 8, 2016. In 2017, Sweden reintroduced (for men and women) a military draft, which had been abolished in 2010.

Almost 163,000 migrants, mostly from the Middle East, SW Asia, and Africa, applied for asylum in Sweden in 2015, about 29,000 in 2016, and more than 25,000 in 2017. Legislation tightening asylum rules was enacted June 21, 2016. Of applications decided, 2015-17, the government granted asylum to almost 127,000 people (54%) and did not grant asylum to about 110,000.

In Sept. 9, 2018, elections, an SAP-led center-left coalition and a Moderate Party-led center-right alliance both fell short of a majority, while the SD won 62 seats.

Switzerland
Swiss Confederation

People: Population: 8,292,809 (99). **Age distrib.:** <15: 15.2%; 65+: 18.3%. **Growth:** 0.7%. **Migrants:** 29.6%. **Pop. density:** 537 per sq mi, 207.3 per sq km. **Urban:** 73.8%. **Ethnic groups:** German 65%, French 18%, Italian 10%. **Languages:** German, French, Italian, Romansch (all official); English; Portuguese; Albanian; Serbo-Croatian; Spanish. **Religions:** Roman Catholic 37.3%, Protestant 24.9%, Muslim 5.1%, none 23.9%.

Geography: Total area: 15,937 sq mi, 41,277 sq km (132); **Land area:** 15,443 sq mi, 39,997 sq km. **Location:** In Alps Mts. in central Europe. France on W; Italy on S; Liechtenstein, Austria on E; Germany on N. **Topography:** The Alps cover 60% of land area; the Jura, near France, 10%. The midlands run NE-SW in-between. **Arable land:** 10.1%. **Capital:** Bern, 422,153. **Cities:** Zürich, 1,370,779.

Government: Type: Federal republic (formally a confederation). **Head of state and govt.:** President chosen on rotating basis from among 7-member Federal Council for 1-year term. **Local divisions:** 26 cantons. **Defense budget:** $4.8 bil. **Active troops:** 20,950.

Economy: Industries: machinery, chemicals, watches, textiles, precision instruments, tourism, banking, insurance. **Chief agric.:** grains, fruits, vegetables; meat, eggs, dairy prods. **Natural resources:** timber, salt. **Water:** 6,447 cu m per capita. **Electricity prod.:** 64.1 bil kWh. **Labor force:** agric. 3.5%, industry 20.7%, services 75.8%. **Unemployment:** 4.8%.

Finance: Monetary unit: Franc (CHF) (0.97 = $1 U.S.). **GDP:** $517.2 bil; **per capita GDP:** $61,400; **GDP growth:** 1.1%. **Imports:** $286.7 bil; Germany 20.9%, U.S. 7.9%, Italy 7.6%, UK 7.3%, France 6.8%, China 5%. **Exports:** $336.8 bil; Germany 15.2%, U.S. 12.3%, China 8.2%, India 6.7%, France 5.7%, UK 5.7%, Hong Kong 5.4%, Italy 5.3%. **Tourism:** $17 bil. **Budget:** $222.1 bil (federal, cantonal, and municipal). **Inflation:** 0.5%.

Transport: Railways: 3,512 mi. **Motor vehicles:** 624.9 per 1,000 pop. **Airports:** 40.

Communications: Telephone: 43.3 per 100 pop. **Mobile:** 133.2 per 100 pop. **Broadband:** 103.7 per 100 pop. **Internet** (2017): 93.7%.

Health: Expend.: 12.1%. **Life expect.:** 80.4 male; 85.2 female. **Births:** 10.5 per 1,000 pop. **Deaths:** 8.4 per 1,000 pop. **Infant mortality:** 3.6 per 1,000 live births. **Undernourished:** <2.5%. **HIV:** NA.

Education: Compulsory: ages 4-15. **Literacy:** 99%.
Embassy: 2900 Cathedral Ave. NW 20008; 745-7900.
Website: www.ch.ch

Switzerland, the former Roman province of Helvetia, traces its modern history to 1291, when three cantons created a defensive league. Other cantons were subsequently admitted to the Swiss Confederation, which obtained its independence from the Holy Roman Empire through the Peace of Westphalia (1648). The cantons were joined under a federal constitution in 1848.

Switzerland has maintained an armed neutrality since 1815 and has not been involved in a foreign war since 1515. It is the seat of many UN and other international agencies but only became a full UN member on Sept. 10, 2002.

Switzerland is a world banking center. The government announced, Mar. 1997, a $4.7-bil fund to compensate victims of the Nazi Holocaust and other catastrophes. Swiss banks agreed Aug. 12, 1998, to pay $1.25 bil in reparations. A June 2002 referendum decriminalized abortion. Two more referendums in 2005 harmonized travel, asylum, law enforcement, and labor policies with the EU; more rights for same-sex couples were also endorsed June 5, 2005.

The Swiss government bailed out the troubled banking giant UBS during the international financial crisis in Oct. 2008. In a Nov. 2009 referendum reflecting anti-Muslim sentiment, voters approved a constitutional ban on construction of new minarets on mosques. In a Feb. 9, 2014, referendum, voters narrowly approved a measure requiring the government to set immigration quotas within three years. However, Dec. 2016 immigration legislation rejected quotas, which could have jeopardized Switzerland's access to the EU single market. A Feb. 12, 2017, referendum made it easier for the grandchildren of immigrants to become citizens. Switzerland officially opened the 35-mi Gotthard Base Tunnel, the world's longest railway tunnel, June 1, 2016.

Syria
Syrian Arab Republic

People: Population: 19,454,263 (62). **Age distrib.:** <15: 31.4%; 65+: 4.3%. **Growth:** 7.4%. **Migrants:** 5.5%. **Pop. density:** 274.4 per sq mi, 105.9 per sq km. **Urban:** 54.2%. **Ethnic groups:** Arab 90.3%; Kurd, Armenian, other 9.7%. **Languages:** Arabic (official), Kurdish, Armenian, Aramaic, Circassian, French, English. **Religions:** Muslim 87% (official; incl. Sunni 74%; Alawi, Ismaili, Shia 13%), Christian 10%, Druze 3%.

Geography: Total area: 71,498 sq mi, 185,180 sq km (87); **Land area:** 70,900 sq mi, 183,630 sq km. (500 sq mi of area is occupied by Israel.) **Location:** Middle East, at E end of Medit. Sea. Lebanon, Israel on W; Jordan on S; Iraq on E; Turkey on N. **Topography:** A short Medit. coastline stretches E and S with fertile lowlands and plains, alternating with mountains and large desert areas. **Arable land:** 25.4%. **Capital:** Damascus, 2,319,545. **Cities:** Aleppo (Halab), 1,753,516; Homs (Hims), 1,295,317. (Pop. ests. are not based on solid evidence because of wartime instability.)

Government: Type: Presidential republic; highly authoritarian regime. **Head of state:** Pres. Bashar al-Assad; b. 1965; in office: July 17, 2000. **Head of govt.:** Prime Min. Imad Muhammad Dib Khamis; b. 1961; in office: June 22, 2016. **Local divisions:** 14 provinces. **Defense budget:** NA. **Active troops:** 142,500.

Economy: Industries: petroleum, textiles, food proc., beverages, tobacco, phosphate rock mining, cement. **Chief agric.:** wheat, barley, cotton, lentils, chickpeas, olives, sugar beets; beef, mutton. **Natural resources:** petroleum, phosphates, chrome and manganese ores, asphalt, iron ore, rock salt, marble, gypsum, hydropower. **Water:** 908 cu m per capita. **Crude oil reserves:** 2.5 bil bbls. **Electricity prod.:** 16.8 bil kWh. **Labor force:** agric. 22.9%, industry 32.8%, services 44.4%. **Unemployment:** 14.9%.

Finance: Monetary unit: Pound (SYP) (515.00 = $1 U.S.). **GDP** (2015): $50.3 bil; **per capita GDP** (2015): $2,900; **GDP growth** (2014): −36.5%. **Imports:** $5.6 bil; Russia 32.4%, Turkey 16.7%, China 9.5%. **Exports:** $1.8 bil; Lebanon 31.5%, Iraq 10.3%, Jordan 8.8%, China 7.8%, Turkey 7.5%, Spain 7.3%. **Tourism** (2010): $6.2 bil. **Budget:** $3.2 bil (govt. projections for FY2016). **Inflation** (2011-12): 36.7%.

Transport: Railways: 1,275 mi. **Motor vehicles:** 137.7 per 1,000 pop. **Airports:** 29.

Communications: Telephone: 14.9 per 100 pop. **Mobile:** 85.7 per 100 pop. **Broadband:** 10.4 per 100 pop. **Internet:** 31.9%.

Health: Expend. (2012): 3.6%. **Life expect.:** 72.8 male; 77.8 female. **Births:** 20.7 per 1,000 pop. **Deaths:** 4.0 per 1,000 pop. **Infant mortality:** 14.4 per 1,000 live births. **Undernourished:** NA. **HIV:** NA.

Education: Compulsory: ages 6-14. **Literacy:** 86.4%.
Embassy: 2215 Wyoming Ave. NW 20008; 232-6313.
Website: www.egov.sy

Syria was the center of the Seleucid Empire but later was absorbed into the Roman and Arab empires. Ottoman rule prevailed for four cents., until the end of WWI.

The state of Syria was formed from former Turkish districts, separated by the Treaty of Sevres, 1920, and divided into the states of Syria and Greater Lebanon. Both were administered under a French League of Nations mandate, 1920-41. The occupying French proclaimed Syria a republic Sept. 16, 1941; independence came Apr. 17, 1946. Syria joined the Arab invasion of Israel in 1948.

Syria belonged to the United Arab Republic from Feb. 1958 to Sept. 1961. The Socialist Baath party seized power Mar. 1963 and became the only legal party. The Alawite minority has dominated the government (Alawism is a sect of Shiite Islam).

In the June 1967 Arab-Israeli war, Israel seized and occupied the Golan Heights, from which Syria had shelled Israeli settlements. On Oct. 6, 1973, Syria and Egypt attacked Israel but failed to recapture the Golan Heights. Syrian troops entered Lebanon in 1976, during the Lebanese civil war, and remained a strong presence in the country. They fought Palestinian guerrillas and, later, Christian militiamen. Syria sided with Iran during the Iran-Iraq War, 1980-88.

Thousands died in the city of Hama Feb. 1982 when government forces crushed a Muslim Brotherhood uprising. Following Israel's invasion of Lebanon, June 6, 1982, Israeli planes destroyed 17 Syrian antiaircraft missile batteries in the Bekaa Valley, June 9, and some 25 Syrian planes. Israel and Syria agreed to a cease-fire June 11.

Hafez al-Assad, president of Syria since 1971, died June 10, 2000, and was succeeded by his son Bashar al-Assad. Israeli planes hit an alleged terrorist camp near Damascus Oct. 4, 2003. Syria aided fighters of the Lebanon-based Shiite group Hezbollah in their conflict with Israel and gave about 180,000 Lebanese temporary refuge when Israeli forces targeted Hezbollah, July-Aug. 2006. On Sept. 6, 2007, Israel bombed a secret site in N Syria where the Israelis believed Syria and North Korea were developing a nuclear facility; both countries denied the claim.

The Assad regime used troops and tanks during Arab Spring demonstrations in Mar. 2011, but the confrontations escalated into outright rebellion. A number of armed opposition groups fought Assad's forces and each other for control of territory. The Natl. Coalition for Syrian Revolutionary and Opposition Forces was formed Nov. 11, 2012; it gained international support, but its leadership was not recognized by many rebel groups. Hezbollah forces fought on the side of the Assad government, which was also backed by Iran. The U.S., Aug. 18, 2011, called on Assad to step down and imposed economic sanctions.

International intelligence communities announced, May 2013, increasing evidence that Assad's forces had used chemical and biological weapons. The EU and U.S, 2013, began to supply military support to rebel groups. (A CIA program to arm certain rebel groups, deemed to have had limited success, was ended in July 2017.) A chemical attack on an opposition-controlled Damascus suburb Aug. 21, 2013, killed more than 1,400. Assad and the rebels accused each other of the attack. Russian and U.S. negotiators reached an agreement with Syria requiring the Assad government to relinquish chemical weapons. International inspectors arrived in Syria Oct. 1, 2013, and the last known covered chemical weapons were believed to have been removed June 23, 2014. A UN report, Aug. 24, 2016, confirmed allegations that Assad's forces were using chlorine gas (not covered by the 2013 agreement). Syrian aircraft dropped chemical weapons prohibited by the 2013 agreement on a rebel-held town, Apr. 4, 2017; the U.S., Apr. 6, launched a cruise missile attack on the air base used by the planes. Israeli warplanes reportedly attacked, Sept. 7, 2017, Syrian military sites producing chemical weapons and missiles. An apparent chemical attack, Apr. 7, 2018, that killed dozens in a then-rebel-held area east of Damascus prompted U.S., UK, and French airstrikes, Apr. 13, on sites believed related to chemical weapons production. Israel was suspected in the Aug. 4 killing of a leading Syrian missile scientist.

By summer 2014, the Sunni extremist group ISIS (Islamic State in Iraq and Syria) controlled large areas in eastern and northern Syria. The night of Sept. 22-23, 2014, the U.S. began a campaign of airstrikes against ISIS and other Islamist extremist groups in Syria, supported by several Middle East countries and European and other allies. Russia, which backed Assad, sent warplanes and troops to Syria in Sept. 2015 and began its own air campaign, Sept. 30, against anti-government forces. Heavy Russian airstrikes, 2015-18, helped the Assad regime regain control of large areas, often with high civilian casualties. Syrian Kurdish and other rebel forces, with support from U.S. airstrikes and special operations troops, retook territory in northern and eastern Syria from ISIS, 2015-17. A U.S.-assisted campaign by Arab and Kurdish rebel groups against Raqqa (ISIS's self-proclaimed capital) captured the city by Oct. 2017. In 2018, ISIS controlled small pockets of Syrian territory and continued to stage attacks; coordinated suicide bombings and other attacks, July 25, killed more than 200 in southern Syria. U.S. and UN reports estimated the number of ISIS members in Syria at 10,000-15,000 in mid-2018.

In 2016-18, Turkish troops fought in Syria to attack Syrian Kurdish forces, support non-Kurdish rebels, and limit Kurdish-controlled areas.

Estimates of the total death toll in Syria's civil war since Mar. 2011 varied widely; the Syrian Observatory for Human Rights released an estimate of 511,000 in Mar. 2018. The UNHCR reported the number of Syrian refugees in Turkey, the Middle East, and North Africa at more than 5.6 mil as of Sept. 2018. By 2018, about 1 mil Syrians had applied for asylum in Europe. About 6.6 mil people were displaced within Syria as of mid-2018.

Taiwan

People: Population: 23,545,963 (55). **Age distrib.:** <15: 12.7%; 65+: 14.4%. **Growth:** 0.2%. **Pop. density:** 1,890.4 per sq mi, 729.9 per sq km. **Urban:** 78.2%. **Ethnic groups:** Han Chinese 95%+ (incl. Hoklo [approx. 70% of pop.], Hakka, other groups originating in mainland China), indigenous Malayo-Polynesian peoples 2.3%. **Languages:** Mandarin Chinese (official), Taiwanese (Min Nan), Hakka dialects. **Religions:** Buddhist 35.3%, Taoist 33.2%, Taoist/Confucian folk religionist 10%, Christian 3.9%.

Geography: Total area: 13,892 sq mi, 35,980 sq km (135); **Land area:** 12,456 sq mi, 32,260 sq km. **Location:** Off SE coast of China, between E and S China Seas. **Topography:** A mountain range forms backbone of island. The eastern half is very steep and craggy; western slope is flat, fertile, and well cultivated. **Arable land:** 16.7%. **Capital:** Taipei, 2,705,791. **Cities:** New Taipei City, 4,324,516; Taoyuan, 2,189,747.

Government: Type: Semi-presidential republic. **Head of state:** Pres. Tsai Ing-wen; b. 1956; in office: May 20, 2016. **Head of govt.:** Prem. Lai Ching-te (William); in office: Sept. 8, 2017. **Local divisions:** 13 counties, 3 cities, 6 special municipalities. **Defense budget:** $10.4 bil. **Active troops:** 215,000.

Economy: Industries: electronics, communications and information tech. prods., petroleum refining, chemicals, textiles, iron and steel, machinery, cement, food proc. **Chief agric.:** rice, vegetables, fruit, tea, flowers; pigs, poultry; fish. **Natural resources:** coal, nat. gas, limestone, marble, asbestos. **Water:** NA. **Crude oil reserves:** 2.4 mil bbls. **Electricity prod.:** 240.4 bil kWh. **Labor force:** agric. 4.8%, industry 35.6%, services 59.7%. **Unemployment:** 3.8%.

Finance: Monetary unit: New Dollar (TWD) (30.79 = $1 U.S.). **GDP:** $1.2 tril; **per capita GDP:** $50,300; **GDP growth:** 2.8%. **Imports:** $272.6 bil. **Exports:** $344.6 bil. **Tourism:** $12.3 bil. **Budget:** $91.7 bil. **Inflation:** 0.6%.

Transport: Railways: 1,002 mi. **Motor vehicles:** 335.4 per 1,000 pop. **Airports:** 35.

Communications: Telephone: 57.4 per 100 pop. **Mobile:** 121.8 per 100 pop. **Broadband:** NA. **Internet:** 79.7%.

Health: Expend.: NA. **Life expect.:** 77.2 male; 83.7 female. **Births:** 8.2 per 1,000 pop. **Deaths:** 7.6 per 1,000 pop. **Infant mortality:** 4.3 per 1,000 live births. **Undernourished:** 3.4%. **HIV:** NA.

Education: Compulsory: ages 6-14. **Literacy:** 98.5%.

Taipei Economic and Cultural Representative Office: 4201 Wisconsin Ave. NW 20016; 895-1800.
Website: www.taiwan.gov.tw

Large-scale immigration from China began in the 17th cent. The island came under mainland control after an interval of Dutch rule, 1620-62. Japan ruled Taiwan (also called Formosa), 1895-1945. The Kuomintang (Chinese Nationalist Party) government fled to Taiwan in 1949 and established the Republic of China under Chiang Kai-shek, who ruled until his death in 1975. The U.S. provided military aid to deter a Communist invasion.

In 1971, the UN expelled Taiwan and recognized the mainland government. The U.S. acknowledged the People's Republic of China, Dec. 15, 1978, and severed diplomatic relations with Taiwan. The U.S. and Taiwan have maintained strong economic, defense, and unofficial ties. Seeking Chinese aid and investment, the Dominican Rep. and Burkina Faso broke relations with Taiwan, May 2018, followed by El Salvador in Aug., reducing to 17 the number of countries maintaining diplomatic ties.

Land reform, government planning, U.S. aid and investment, and free universal education brought advances in industry, agriculture, and living standards. In 1987 martial law was lifted after 38 years, and in 1991 more than four decades of emergency rule ended. Taiwan held its first direct presidential election Mar. 23, 1996.

Five decades of Kuomintang rule ended when Chen Shui-bian, leader of the pro-independence Democratic Progressive Party (DPP), won the Mar. 2000 presidential election. Chen was wounded in an apparent assassination attempt Mar. 19, 2004, one day before he won a second term as president. Promising increased cooperation with China, Kuomintang candidate Ma Ying-jeou won the presidential election, Mar. 22, 2008, and was reelected Jan. 14, 2012.

The People's Republic considers Taiwan a rebel province of the mainland; in 1991, the Kuomintang dropped its claim to be the sole government of both. The first formal talks between representatives of Taiwan and China were held Feb. 11, 2014. The first summit meeting, between Ma and Chinese Pres. Xi Jin-ping, took place in Singapore, Nov. 7, 2015. Concern over recent Kuomintang pro-China policies helped the DPP win Jan. 16, 2016, presidential and legislative elections. The DPP's Tsai Ing-wen became Taiwan's first female president. The Constitutional Court, May 24, 2017, struck down Taiwan's law prohibiting same-sex marriage and gave lawmakers two years to pass new marriage legislation.

The Penghu Isls. (Pescadores), 49 sq mi, pop. (2011 est.) 96,597, lie between Taiwan and the mainland. Kinmen, fmr. Quemoy, pop. (2011 est.) 99,691, and Matsu, pop. (2011 est.) 10,106, lie just off the mainland.

Tajikistan
Republic of Tajikistan

People: Population: 8,604,882 (97). **Age distrib.:** <15: 32.1%; 65+: 3.4%. **Growth:** 1.6%. **Migrants:** 3.1%. **Pop. density:** 157.5 per sq mi, 60.8 per sq km. **Urban:** 27.1%. **Ethnic groups:** Tajik 84.3%, Uzbek (incl. Lakai, Kongrat, Katagan, Bar-los, Yuz) 13.8%, other (incl. Kyrgyz, Russian, Turkmen, Tatar, Arab) 2%. **Languages:** Tajik (official), Russian (used in govt. and business). **Religions:** Sunni Muslim 85%, Shia Muslim 5%.

Geography: Total area: 55,637 sq mi, 144,100 sq km (94); **Land area:** 54,637 sq mi, 141,510 sq km. **Location:** Central Asia. Uzbekistan on N and W, Kyrgyzstan on N, China on E, Afghanistan on S. **Topography:** Mountainous; contains the Pamirs, Trans-Alai mountain system. **Arable land:** 5.3%. **Capital:** Dushanbe, 872,653.

Government: Type: Presidential republic. **Head of state:** Pres. Emomali Rahmon; b. 1952; in office: Nov. 6, 1994. **Head of govt.:** Prime Min. Qohir Rasulzoda; b. 1961; in office: Nov. 23, 2013. **Local divisions:** 2 provinces, 1 autonomous province, 1 capital region, 1 district under republic admin. **Defense budget:** $192 mil. **Active troops:** 8,800.

Economy: Industries: aluminum, cement, coal, gold, silver. **Chief agric.:** cotton, grain, fruits, grapes, vegetables; cattle, sheep, goats. **Natural resources:** hydropower, petroleum, uranium, mercury, brown coal, lead, zinc, antimony, tungsten, silver, gold. **Water:** 2,583 cu m per capita. **Crude oil reserves:** 12 mil bbls. **Electricity prod.:** 17 bil kWh. **Labor force:** agric. 51.6%, industry 16.4%, services 32%. **Unemployment:** 10.3%.

Finance: Monetary unit: Somoni (TJS) (9.42 = $1 U.S.). **GDP:** $28.4 bil; **per capita GDP:** $3,200; **GDP growth:** 7.1%. **Imports:** $2.7 bil; Russia 38%, Kazakhstan 19%, China 8.7%. **Exports:** $794.7 mil; Turkey 27.5%, China 17.7%, Russia 13.4%, Switzerland 12.5%, Algeria 8.2%, Iran 7.1%. **Tourism:** $8 mil. **Budget:** $2.3 bil. **Inflation** (2015-16): 6%.

Transport: Railways: 423 mi. **Airports:** 17. **Communications: Telephone** (2016): 5.4 per 100 pop. **Mobile** (2016): 107.6 per 100 pop. **Broadband:** NA. **Internet:** 20.5%.

Health: Expend.: 6.9%. **Life expect.:** 65.2 male; 71.7 female. **Births:** 22.8 per 1,000 pop. **Deaths:** 5.9 per 1,000 pop. **Infant mortality:** 30.8 per 1,000 live births. **Undernourished:** NA. **HIV:** 0.3%.

Education: Compulsory: ages 7-15. **Literacy:** 99.8%. **Embassy:** 1005 New Hampshire Ave. NW 20037; 223-6090. **Website:** www.president.tj

Societies were settled in the region from about 3000 BCE. Invaders have included Iranians, Arabs (who converted the population to Islam), Mongols, Uzbeks, Afghans, and Russians. The USSR gained control 1918-25, making the region a part of the Uzbek SSR until the Tajik SSR was proclaimed, 1929.

Tajikistan declared independence Sept. 9, 1991. Factional fighting led to the installation of a pro-Communist regime, Jan. 1993. A new constitution establishing a presidential system was approved by referendum in 1994.

An estimated 55,000 died in clashes between Muslim rebels and loyalist troops (supported by Russia) by mid-1997, despite a series of peace accords. Constitutional changes including legalization of Islamic political parties were approved by referendum in 1999. Pres. Imomali Rakhmonov, first elected in 1994, won a Nov. 1999 election called a farce by human-rights observers. Leading opposition groups boycotted the Nov. 2006 election, again won by Rakhmonov (who changed his name to Rakhmon in 2007). He won the Nov. 2013 election with 84% of the vote. Constitutional changes in 2016 allowed Rakhmon to serve an unlimited number of terms.

Poverty and corruption are widespread. Much of the nation's income is supplied by international donors and by remittances from Tajiks working in Russia. After rebels murdered a Tajik general, July 21, 2012, the army killed about 30 militants, July 24. A former warlord surrendered, Aug. 13, in exchange for a troop withdrawal. In the 2010s, an estimated 1,300 Tajiks joined ISIS forces in Syria and Iraq. In an assault claimed by ISIS, four tourists (two U.S., two European) were fatally attacked while cycling in Tajikistan, July 29, 2018.

Tanzania
United Republic of Tanzania

People: Population: 55,451,343 (25). **Age distrib.:** <15: 43.4%; 65+: 3%. **Growth:** 2.7%. **Migrants:** 0.9%. **Pop. density:** 162.1 per sq mi, 62.6 per sq km. **Urban:** 33.8%. **Ethnic groups:** African 99% (of which 95% are Bantu consisting of 130+ tribes). **Languages:** Kiswahili or Swahili, English (primary lang. of commerce, admin., higher ed.) (both official); Arabic (widely spoken in Zanzibar). **Religions:** Christian 61.4%, Muslim 35.2%; almost entirely Muslim on Zanzibar.

Geography: Total area: 365,755 sq mi, 947,300 sq km (30); **Land area:** 342,009 sq mi, 885,800 sq km. **Location:** Coast of E Africa. Kenya, Uganda on N; Rwanda, Burundi, Dem. Rep. of the Congo on W; Zambia, Malawi, Mozambique on S. **Topography:** Hot, arid central plateau surrounded by lake region in W. Temperate highlands in N and S; coastal plains. Mt. Kilimanjaro (19,341 ft) is highest in Africa. **Arable land:** 15.2%. **Capital:** Dodoma (official; National Assembly meets here), 261,645; Dar es Salaam (de facto; exec. branch offices), 6,047,600. **Cities:** Mwanza, 1,003,267.

Government: Type: Presidential republic. **Head of state and govt.:** Pres. John Magufuli; b. 1959; in office: Nov. 5, 2015. **Local divisions:** 31 regions. **Defense budget:** $528 mil. **Active troops:** 27,000.

Economy: Industries: agric. proc.; mining; salt, soda ash; cement, oil refining, shoes, apparel, wood prods., fertilizer. **Chief agric.:** coffee, sisal, tea, cotton, pyrethrum (insecticide made from chrysanthemums), cashews, tobacco, cloves, corn, wheat, cassava; cattle, sheep, goats. **Natural resources:** hydropower, tin, phosphates, iron ore, coal, diamonds, gems, gold, nat. gas, nickel. **Water:** 1,800 cu m per capita. **Electricity prod.:** 6 bil kWh. **Labor force:** agric. 66.7%, industry 6%, services 27.3%. **Unemployment:** 2.2%.

Finance: Monetary unit: Shilling (TZS) (2,286.70 = $1 U.S.). **GDP:** $162.2 bil; **per capita GDP:** $3,200; **GDP growth:** 6%. **Imports:** $8.6 bil; India 16.5%, China 15.8%, UAE 9.2%, Saudi Arabia 7.9%, South Africa 5.1%. **Exports:** $5.2 bil; India 21.8%, South Africa 17.9%, Kenya 8.8%, Switzerland 6.7%, Belgium 5.9%, Dem. Rep. of the Congo 5.8%. **Tourism:** $2.3 bil. **Budget:** $9.3 bil. **Inflation:** 5.3%.

Transport: Railways: 2,838 mi. **Motor vehicles:** 1.9 per 1,000 pop. **Airports:** 10.

Communications: Telephone: 0.2 per 100 pop. **Mobile:** 69.7 per 100 pop. **Broadband:** 9.2 per 100 pop. **Internet:** 13%.

Health: Expend.: 6.1%. **Life expect.:** 61.6 male; 64.6 female. **Births:** 35.3 per 1,000 pop. **Deaths:** 7.5 per 1,000 pop. **Infant mortality:** 38.7 per 1,000 live births. **Undernourished:** 32%. **HIV:** 4.5%.

Education: Compulsory: ages 7-13. **Literacy:** 77.9%. **Embassy:** 1232 22nd St. NW 20037; 939-6125. **Website:** www.tanzania.go.tz

Arab colonization and slaving in Tanganyika began in the 8th cent.; Portuguese sailors explored the coast around 1500. Other Europeans followed.

In 1885 Germany established German East Africa, of which Tanganyika formed the bulk. Under Britain, it became a League of Nations mandate and after 1946, a UN trust territory. It became independent, Dec. 9, 1961, and a republic within the Commonwealth a year later.

Zanzibar, the Isle of Cloves, has an area of 640 sq mi and lies 23 mi off mainland Tanzania. The island of Pemba, area 380 sq mi, is 25 mi to the NE. Ethnic groups in Zanzibar include Arabs and Africans. Zanzibar and Pemba are major producers of cloves and clove oil.

Zanzibar was for centuries the center for Arab slave traders. Portugal ruled the region for two centuries until ousted by Arabs around 1700. Zanzibar became a British Protectorate in 1890; independence came Dec. 10, 1963. Revolutionary forces overthrew the Sultan, Jan. 12, 1964. The new government ousted Western diplomats and journalists, slaughtered thousands of Arabs, and nationalized farms.

The Republic of Tanganyika and the Republic of Zanzibar joined to form the United Republic of Tanzania, Apr. 26, 1964. Zanzibar retains internal self-government.

Until resigning as president in 1985, Julius K. Nyerere, a former Tanganyikan independence leader, dominated Tanzania's single-party government, which emphasized government planning and economic control. A multiparty system was established in 1992, and the economy was privatized in the 1990s.

A bomb at the U.S. embassy in Dar es Salaam, Aug. 7, 1998, killed 11 people and injured at least 70 others. The U.S. blamed the attack and a near-simultaneous embassy bombing in Kenya on Islamic terrorists associated with Osama bin Laden.

Jakaya Mrisho Kikwete of the ruling Chama Cha Mapinduzi (CCM) won the Dec. 2005 presidential election; he was reelected to a second 5-year term Oct. 2010. CCM candidate John Magufuli won the Oct. 25, 2015, presidential election. Zanzibar regional elections the same day were annulled because of voting irregularities and rerun Mar. 20, 2016; the CCM incumbent won Zanzibar's presidency in voting boycotted by the opposition.

Large natural gas deposits have been discovered in recent years; estimated recoverable gas reserves totaled at least 57 tril cubic ft in 2018.

Thailand
Kingdom of Thailand

People: Population: 68,615,858 (20). **Age distrib.:** <15: 16.7%; 65+: 11%. **Growth:** 0.3%. **Migrants:** 5.2%. **Pop. density:** 347.9 per sq mi, 134.3 per sq km. **Urban:** 49.9%. **Ethnic groups:** Thai 97.5%. **Languages:** Thai (official), English (secondary lang. of elite). **Religions:** Buddhist 94.6%, Muslim 4.3%.

Geography: Total area: 198,117 sq mi, 513,120 sq km (50); **Land area:** 197,256 sq mi, 510,890 sq km. **Location:** On Indochinese and Malayan peninsulas in SE Asia. Myanmar on W and N, Laos on N, Cambodia on E, Malaysia on S. **Topography:** A plateau dominates NE third of Thailand, dropping to fertile alluvial valley of Chao Phraya R. in center. Forested mountains with narrow fertile valleys are in N. Rain forests cover S peninsula region. **Arable land:** 32.9%. **Capital:** Bangkok (Krung Thep), 10,156,316. **Cities:** Chon Buri, 1,360,781.

Government: Type: Constitutional monarchy. **Head of state:** King Vajiralongkorn; b. 1952; in office: Dec. 1, 2016. **Head of govt.:** Prime Min. Prayuth Chan-ocha; b. 1954; in office: Aug. 25, 2014. **Local divisions:** 76 provinces, 1 municipality. **Defense budget:** $6.2 bil. **Active troops:** 360,850.

Economy: Industries: tourism, textiles and garments, agric. proc., beverages, tobacco, cement, light mfg. (jewelry, elec. appliances, computers and parts, integrated circuits, furniture). **Chief agric.:** rice, cassava, rubber, corn, sugarcane, coconuts, palm oil, pineapples, livestock, fish prods. **Natural resources:** tin, rubber, nat. gas, tungsten, tantalum, timber, lead, fish, gypsum, lignite, fluorite. **Water:** 6,454 cu m per capita. **Crude oil reserves:** 349.4 mil bbls. **Electricity prod.:** 168 bil kWh. **Labor force:** agric. 32.8%, industry 22.6%, services 44.7%. **Unemployment:** 1.1%.

Finance: Monetary unit: Baht (THB) (32.82 = $1 U.S.). **GDP:** $1.2 tril; **per capita GDP:** $17,900; **GDP growth:** 3.9%. **Imports:** $190 bil; China 20%, Japan 14.5%, U.S. 6.8%, Malaysia 5.4%. **Exports:** $228.2 bil; China 12.4%, U.S. 11.2%, Japan 9.5%, Hong Kong 5.2%. **Tourism:** $57.5 bil. **Budget:** $90.6 bil. **Inflation:** 0.7%.

Transport: Railways: 2,564 mi. **Motor vehicles:** 247.7 per 1,000 pop. **Airports:** 63.

Communications: Telephone: 4.2 per 100 pop. **Mobile:** 176 per 100 pop. **Broadband:** 94.7 per 100 pop. **Internet** (2017): 52.9%.

Health: Expend.: 3.8%. **Life expect.:** 71.9 male; 78.5 female. **Births:** 11.0 per 1,000 pop. **Deaths:** 8.1 per 1,000 pop. **Infant mortality:** 9.0 per 1,000 live births. **Undernourished:** 9%. **HIV:** 1.1%.

Education: Compulsory: ages 6-14. **Literacy:** 92.9%.

Embassy: 1024 Wisconsin Ave. NW 20007; 944-3600.

Website: www.thaigov.go.th

Thais began migrating from southern China during the 11th cent. and established a unified Thai kingdom, 1350. Known as Siam until 1939, Thailand is the only country in SE Asia never colonized by Europeans. King Mongkut and his son King Chulalongkorn, ruling successively from 1851 to 1910, modernized the country and signed trade treaties with Britain and France. A bloodless revolution in 1932 limited the monarchy. Thailand was an ally of Japan during WWII and of the U.S. during the postwar period. For decades, the military had a dominant role in governing the country.

By the end of the 1990s, according to UN estimates, more than 750,000 people in Thailand had HIV/AIDS, with 143,000 new infections in 1991 alone. A nationwide prevention campaign reduced the number of new HIV infections.

Beginning in 2004, security forces tried to suppress a Muslim insurgency in southern Thailand. By mid-2018, almost 7,000 people, mostly civilians, had been killed in insurgent attacks and actions by security forces.

Following elections in Jan. 2001, Thaksin Shinawatra became prime min. A military junta took power in a bloodless coup Sept. 19, 2006. Thaksin supporters won Dec. 2007 elections, and Samak Sundaravej became prime min. after civilian rule was restored Jan. 22, 2008. Thailand's Constitutional Court ousted Samak in Sept., and Thaksin's brother-in-law Somchai Wongsawat became prime min. Sept. 18. But a Constitutional Court ruling, Dec. 2, barred him from politics.

On Feb. 26, 2010, Thailand's Supreme Court ordered the seizure of about $1.4 bil of Thaksin's family assets. After Thaksin supporters, known as Red Shirts, staged mass rallies and began to build a fortified compound in Bangkok, a crackdown by Thai security forces May 14-19, 2010, left more than 90 people dead. Thaksin's sister, Yingluck Shinawatra, became Thailand's first female prime min. after parliamentary elections July 3, 2011. On May 7, 2014, she was removed from office by the Constitutional Court, and the military seized power in a May 22 coup. An interim legislature, with a majority of military members, was appointed July 31; it named coup leader Gen. Prayuth Chan-ocha as prime min. Aug. 21, 2014. Tried for criminal negligence, Yingluck fled the country before an Aug. 25, 2017, court

appearance. A guilty verdict and five-year prison sentence were announced Sept. 27.

A 2015 investigation resulted in charges against more than 100, including government and military officials, for involvement in human trafficking of migrants from Myanmar and Bangladesh. More than 60 traffickers were convicted, July 19, 2017. A bombing at the Erawan shrine in Bangkok, Aug. 17, 2015, killed 20. Thai police arrested two suspects, Aug. 29 and Sept. 1, said to be Uighur militants; in July, Thailand had deported more than 100 Uighur migrants to China. In an Aug. 7, 2016, referendum (opposition campaigning had been barred), voters approved a military-drafted new constitution and a companion measure that would effectively dilute the power of any one political party and increase the military's role in selecting prime ministers after a return to civilian rule. A series of 11 bombings, Aug. 11-12, 2016, mainly in tourist areas, killed four and injured dozens.

King Bhumibol, monarch since June 1946, died Oct. 13, 2016; crown prince Maha Vajiralongkorn succeeded him Dec. 1.

A large-scale effort to rescue 12 soccer-team members, aged 11-16, and a coach, trapped June 23, 2018, by flooding in the Tham Luang cave complex, was successfully completed July 10. One rescuer, a former Thai Navy SEAL, died July 6.

Timor-Leste
(East Timor)
Democratic Republic of Timor-Leste

People: Population: 1,321,929 (152). **Age distrib.:** <15: 40.4%; 65+: 3.9%. **Growth:** 2.3%. **Migrants:** 0.9%. **Pop. density:** 230.2 per sq mi, 88.9 per sq km. **Urban:** 30.6%. **Ethnic groups:** Austronesian (Malayo-Polynesian), Melanesian-Papuan, small Chinese minority. **Languages:** Tetun Prasa, Portuguese (both official); Indonesian, English, about 32 indigenous langs. **Religions:** Roman Catholic 97.6%.

Geography: Total area: 5,743 sq mi, 14,874 sq km (155); **Land area:** 5,743 sq mi, 14,874 sq km. **Location:** E half of Timor Isl. in SW Pacific O. Indonesia on W half of island. **Topography:** Rugged terrain, rising to 9,721 ft at Mt. Ramelau. **Arable land:** 10.4%. **Capital:** Dili, 281,135.

Government: Type: Semi-presidential republic. **Head of state:** Pres. Francisco Guterres; b. 1954; in office: May 20, 2017. **Head of govt.:** Prime Min. Taur Matan Ruak; b. 1956; in office: June 22, 2018. **Local divisions:** 13 admin. districts. **Defense budget:** $25 mil. **Active troops:** 1,330.

Economy: Industries: printing, soap mfg., handicrafts, woven cloth. **Chief agric.:** coffee, rice, corn, cassava, sweet potatoes, soybeans, cabbages, mangoes, bananas, vanilla. **Natural resources:** gold, petroleum, nat. gas, manganese, marble. **Water:** 6,932 cu m per capita. **Labor force:** agric. 25%, industry 15.2%, services 59.8%. **Unemployment:** 3.4%.

Finance: Monetary unit: U.S. Dollar (USD) (1.00 = $1 U.S.). **GDP:** $6.8 bil; **per capita GDP:** $5,400; **GDP growth:** –0.5%. **Imports** (2016): $558.6 mil. **Exports** (2016): $20 mil. **Tourism:** $73 mil. **Budget:** $2.2 bil. **Inflation:** 0.6%.

Transport: Airports: 2.

Communications: Telephone: 0.2 per 100 pop. **Mobile:** 119.3 per 100 pop. **Broadband:** 64.6 per 100 pop. **Internet:** 25.2%.

Health: Expend.: 3.1%. **Life expect.:** 67.1 male; 70.4 female. **Births:** 32.9 per 1,000 pop. **Deaths:** 5.8 per 1,000 pop. **Infant mortality:** 33.9 per 1,000 live births. **Undernourished:** 27.2%. **HIV:** NA.

Education: Compulsory: ages 6-14. **Literacy:** 67.5%.

Embassy: 4201 Connecticut Ave. NW, Ste. 504, 20008; 966-3202.

Website: timor-leste.gov.tl

The collapse of Portuguese rule in East Timor led to factional fighting, Aug. 1975, and an invasion by Indonesia in Dec. Indonesia annexed East Timor in 1976. In over two decades, some 200,000 Timorese died due to civil war, famine, and persecution by Indonesian authorities. In a referendum held Aug. 1999 under UN auspices, Timorese voted overwhelmingly for independence but were then terrorized by pro-Indonesian militias. An international peacekeeping force entered in Sept.; a UN interim administration formally took command Oct. 26, 1999. Pro-independence forces won elections for a constituent assembly Aug. 2001. Xanana Gusmão, a former guerrilla leader, won the presidential election Apr. 2002. As Timor-Leste, the territory became independent May 20.

José Ramos-Horta, a Nobel Peace Prize laureate, won a presidential runoff vote May 2007. After inconclusive parliamentary elections June 30, Ramos-Horta chose Gusmão as prime min. Gusmão-supported independent Taur Matan Ruak became president in a May 2012 runoff election. Gusmão's CNRT party won July parliamentary elections. The UN peacekeeping mission ended Dec. 31, 2012. Beginning in 2005, much of East Timor's budget consisted of revenue from offshore oil and natural gas deposits. Lower oil prices beginning in 2014, as well as depletion of oil fields and costly infrastructure projects, hurt the economy. Gusmão resigned Feb. 6, 2015, and was replaced as prime min. by Rui Maria de Araújo of the FRETILIN party. FRETILIN's Francisco Guterres won the Mar. 20, 2017, presidential election. After inconclusive July 22 parliamentary elections, FRETILIN's Mari Alkatiri became prime min. A coalition including the CNRT won new elections, May 12, 2018; Taur Matan Ruak became prime min. Ending a long dispute, Timor-Leste and Australia signed a treaty, Mar. 6, 2018, establishing the boundary between them in an oil- and gas-rich area of the Timor Sea.

Togo
Togolese Republic

People: Population: 8,176,449 (100). **Age distrib.:** <15: 40.1%; 65+: 3.5%. **Growth:** 2.6%. **Migrants:** 3.6%. **Pop. density:** 389.4 per sq mi, 150.3 per sq km. **Urban:** 41.7%. **Ethnic groups:** African (37 tribes; largest and most important are Ewe, Mina, Kabre) 99%. **Languages:** French (official, lang. of commerce), Ewe and Mina (in S), Kabye and Dagomba (in N). **Religions:** indigenous beliefs 51%, Christian 29%, Muslim 20%.

Geography: Total area: 21,925 sq mi, 56,785 sq km (123); **Land area:** 20,998 sq mi, 54,385 sq km. **Location:** S coast of W Africa. Ghana on W, Burkina Faso on N, Benin on E. **Topography:** Hills running SW-NE split Togo into two savanna plains regions. **Arable land:** 48.7%. **Capital:** Lomé, 1,745,744.

Government: Type: Presidential republic. **Head of state:** Pres. Faure Gnassingbé; b. 1966; in office: May 4, 2005. **Head of govt.:** Prime Min. Komi Klassou; b. 1960; in office: June 5, 2015. **Local divisions:** 5 regions. **Defense budget:** $89 mil. **Active troops:** 8,550.

Economy: Industries: phosphate mining, agric. proc., cement, handicrafts, textiles, beverages. **Chief agric.:** coffee, cocoa, cotton, yams, cassava, corn, beans, rice, millet, sorghum; livestock; fish. **Natural resources:** phosphates, limestone, marble. **Water:** 2,012 cu m per capita. **Electricity prod.:** 78.8 mil kWh. **Labor force:** agric. 37.8%, industry 17.3%, services 44.9%. **Unemployment:** 1.8%.

Finance: Monetary unit: CFA Franc (XOF) (566.17 = $1 U.S.). **GDP:** $12.9 bil; **per capita GDP:** $1,700; **GDP growth:** 4.4%. **Imports:** $2 bil; China 27.5%, France 9.1%. **Exports:** $1 bil; Benin 16.7%, Burkina Faso 15.2%, Niger 8.9%, India 7.3%, Mali 6.7%, Ghana 5.5%, Côte d'Ivoire 5.4%. **Tourism** (2015): $114 mil. **Budget:** $1.7 bil. **Inflation:** −0.8%.

Transport: Railways: 353 mi. **Motor vehicles:** 26.5 per 1,000 pop. **Airports:** 2.

Communications: Telephone: 0.5 per 100 pop. **Mobile:** 79.8 per 100 pop. **Broadband:** 19.6 per 100 pop. **Internet** (2017): 12.4%.

Health: Expend.: 6.6%. **Life expect.:** 63.1 male; 68.6 female. **Births:** 32.8 per 1,000 pop. **Deaths:** 6.8 per 1,000 pop. **Infant mortality:** 40.8 per 1,000 live births. **Undernourished:** 16.2%. **HIV:** 2.1%.

Education: Compulsory: ages 6-15. **Literacy:** 63.7%. **Embassy:** 2208 Massachusetts Ave. NW 20008; 234-4212. **Website:** www.primature.gouv.tg or www.state.gov/p/af/ci/to/

Togoland was administered by Germany and then by France and Britain. The French sector became the republic of Togo Apr. 27, 1960. In office since 1967, Pres. Gnassingbé Eyadéma was Africa's longest-serving head of state until his death Feb. 5, 2005. His son, Faure Gnassingbé, was installed as president, but African leaders pressured Togo to hold an election, which Gnassingbé won Apr. 24. Opposition parties disputed the result, and protests led to violent clashes in Lomé.

After a shootout at his home Apr. 12, 2009, former Defense Min. Kpatcha Gnassingbé, the president's brother, was arrested and accused of plotting a coup. Pres. Gnassingbé won reelection Mar. 4, 2010, to a second 5-year term. Weeks of anti-government protests led Prime Min. Gilbert Fossoun Houngbo to resign, July 13, 2012. Legislative elections were held July 25, 2013, with the ruling party maintaining its majority and the opposition claiming voting irregularities. Pres. Gnassingbé won a third term in Apr. 25, 2015, elections; the opposition disputed the result. More than a dozen people died and dozens were injured in large-scale protests, beginning Aug. 2017, demanding presidential term limits and the resignation of Pres. Gnassingbé.

Tonga
Kingdom of Tonga

People: Population: 106,398 (181). **Age distrib.:** <15: 33.3%; 65+: 6.6%. **Growth:** −0.1%. **Migrants:** 4.6%. **Pop. density:** 384.3 per sq mi, 148.4 per sq km. **Urban:** 23.1%. **Ethnic groups:** Tongan 97%. **Languages:** Tongan, English (both official). **Religions:** Protestant 64.1% (incl. Free Wesleyan Church 35%, Free Church of Tonga 11.9%), Mormon 18.6%, Roman Catholic 14.2%.

Geography: Total area: 288 sq mi, 747 sq km (176); **Land area:** 277 sq mi, 717 sq km. **Location:** Western S Pacific O. Nearest neighbors are Fiji to NW, Samoa to NE. **Topography:** Comprises 170 volcanic and coral islands, 36 inhabited. **Arable land:** 25%. **Capital:** Nuku'alofa, 22,904.

Government: Type: Constitutional monarchy. **Head of state:** King Tupou VI; b. 1959; in office: Mar. 18, 2012. **Head of govt.:**

Prime Min. 'Akilisi Pohiva; b. 1941; in office: Dec. 30, 2014. **Local divisions:** 5 island divisions. **Defense budget/active troops:** NA.

Economy: Industries: tourism, constr., fishing. **Chief agric.:** squash, coconuts, copra, bananas, vanilla beans, cocoa, coffee, sweet potatoes, cassava, taro, kava. **Natural resources:** fish. **Water:** NA. **Electricity prod.:** 50 mil kWh. **Labor force:** agric. 31.7%, industry 31.6%, services 36.8%. **Unemployment:** 1.1%.

Finance: Monetary unit: Pa'anga (TOP) (2.31 = $1 U.S.). **GDP:** $587 mil; **per capita GDP:** $5,600; **GDP growth:** 3.1%. **Imports:** $320.7 mil; New Zealand 33.3%, Fiji 11.7%, U.S. 9.8%, Singapore 9%, Australia 8.9%, China 7.9%, Japan 5.9%. **Exports:** $18.2 mil; Hong Kong 25.1%, New Zealand 22.6%, U.S. 14.3%, Japan 12.8%, Australia 10.5%. **Tourism** (2015): $40 mil. **Budget:** $134.6 mil. **Inflation** (2015-16): 2.6%.

Transport: Airports: 1.

Communications: Telephone (2016): 10.3 per 100 pop. **Mobile** (2016): 74.7 per 100 pop. **Broadband:** 56 per 100 pop. **Internet:** 40%.

Health: Expend.: 5.9%. **Life expect.:** 75.0 male; 78.3 female. **Births:** 21.8 per 1,000 pop. **Deaths:** 4.9 per 1,000 pop. **Infant mortality:** 10.9 per 1,000 live births. **Undernourished:** NA. **HIV:** NA.

Education: Compulsory: ages 4-18. **Literacy:** 99.4%. **Permanent UN mission:** 250 E. 51st St., New York, NY 10022; (917) 369-1025. **Website:** www.gov.to

First inhabited by ancestors of Polynesians c. 2000 BCE, Tonga was visited by the Dutch in the early 17th cent. and by British explorer James Cook in the 1770s. A series of civil wars ended, 1845, with establishment of the Tupou dynasty. In 1900, Tonga became a British protectorate. Tonga gained independence June 1970 and joined the Commonwealth. It joined the UN in 1999. George Tupou VI became king Mar. 18, 2012, following the death of his brother. Elections in Nov. 2010 gave the country its first democratically elected parliament. With the economy sluggish, almost two-thirds of directly elected members were voted out of office in Nov. 27, 2014, elections. In Nov. 16, 2017, elections, incumbent Prime Min. 'Akilisi Pohiva's Democratic Party won a majority.

Trinidad and Tobago
Republic of Trinidad and Tobago

People: Population: 1,215,527 (155). **Age distrib.:** <15: 19.2%; 65+: 11.1%. **Growth:** −0.2%. **Migrants:** 3.7%. **Pop. density:** 613.9 per sq mi, 237 per sq km. **Urban:** 53.2%. **Ethnic groups:** East Indian 35.4%, African 34.2%, mixed-other 15.3%, mixed African/East Indian 7.7%. **Languages:** English (official), Trinidadian Creole English, Tobagonian Creole English, Caribbean Hindustani, French, Spanish, Chinese. **Religions:** Protestant 32.1% (incl. Pentecostal/Evangelical/Full Gospel 12%), Roman Catholic 21.6%, Hindu 18.2%, Muslim 5%.

Geography: Total area: 1,980 sq mi, 5,128 sq km (166); **Land area:** 1,980 sq mi, 5,128 sq km. **Location:** In Caribbean, off E coast of Venezuela. **Topography:** Three low mountain ranges cross Trinidad E-W, with a well-watered plain between N and central ranges. Parts of E and W coasts are swamps. Tobago, 116 sq mi, lies 20 mi NE. **Arable land:** 4.9%. **Capital:** Port of Spain, 544,417.

Government: Type: Parliamentary republic. **Head of state:** Pres. Paula-Mae Weekes; b. 1958; in office: Mar. 19, 2018. **Head of govt.:** Prime Min. Keith Rowley; b. 1949; in office: Sept. 9, 2015. **Local divisions:** 9 regions, 3 boroughs, 2 cities, 1 ward. **Defense budget:** $596 mil. **Active troops:** 4,050.

Economy: Industries: petroleum and petroleum prods., liquefied nat. gas, methanol, ammonia, urea, steel prods., beverages. **Chief agric.:** cocoa, dasheen, pumpkin, cassava, tomatoes, cucumbers, eggplant, hot pepper, pommecythere, coconut water, poultry. **Natural resources:** petroleum, nat. gas, asphalt. **Water:** 2,824 cu m per capita. **Crude oil reserves:** 243 mil bbls. **Electricity prod.:** 9.7 bil kWh. **Labor force:** agric. 3.7%, industry 26.6%, services 69.7%. **Unemployment:** 4.8%.

Finance: Monetary unit: Dollar (TTD) (6.72 = $1 U.S.). **GDP:** $43 bil; **per capita GDP:** $31,400; **GDP growth:** −2.6%. **Imports:** $10.2 bil; U.S. 23.8%, Russia 15.3%, Colombia 11.1%, Gabon 10.5%, China 7.3%. **Exports:** $9.7 bil; U.S. 34.8%, Argentina 9%. **Tourism:** $464 mil. **Budget:** $7.8 bil. **Inflation:** 1.9%.

Transport: Motor vehicles: 336.1 per 1,000 pop. **Airports:** 2.

Communications: Telephone: 18.8 per 100 pop. **Mobile:** 148.3 per 100 pop. **Broadband:** 47.3 per 100 pop. **Internet:** 73.3%.

Health: Expend.: 6%. **Life expect.:** 70.5 male; 76.4 female. **Births:** 12.3 per 1,000 pop. **Deaths:** 8.9 per 1,000 pop. **Infant mortality:** 21.6 per 1,000 live births. **Undernourished:** 4.9%. **HIV:** 1.1%.

Education: Compulsory: ages 6-11. **Literacy:** 99%. **Embassy:** 1708 Massachusetts Ave. NW 20036; 467-6490. **Website:** www.ttconnect.gov.tt

Christopher Columbus sighted Trinidad in 1498. It became a British possession in 1802; in the 1800s tens of thousands of indentured servants and their families were brought from

India to work in agriculture. Trinidad and Tobago won independence Aug. 31, 1962. It became a republic in 1976. The nation, among the most prosperous in the Caribbean, produces oil and natural gas.

In July 1990, some 120 Muslim extremists captured the Parliament building and TV station and took about 50 hostages, including Prime Min. Arthur N. R. Robinson. After a six-day siege, the rebels surrendered.

Basdeo Panday, in office 1995-2001, was the nation's first prime min. of Indian ancestry. The country's first female prime min., Kamla Persad-Bissessar, leader of the People's Partnership coalition, took office May 26, 2010. After Sept. 7, 2015, elections, Keith Rowley of the People's National Movement became prime min. On Mar. 19, 2018, Paula-Mae Weekes became Trinidad's first female president.

Tunisia
Republic of Tunisia

People: Population: 11,516,189 (78). **Age distrib.:** <15: 25.3%; 65+: 8.2%. **Growth:** 1%. **Migrants:** 0.5%. **Pop. density:** 192 per sq mi, 74.1 per sq km. **Urban:** 68.9%. **Ethnic groups:** Arab 98%. **Languages:** Arabic (official), French (used in commerce), Berber (Tamazight). **Religions:** Muslim (official; Sunni) 99.1%.

Geography: Total area: 63,170 sq mi, 163,610 sq km (91); **Land area:** 59,985 sq mi, 155,360 sq km. **Location:** N coast of Africa. Algeria on W, Libya on E. **Topography:** The N is wooded and fertile. Grazing lands and orchards are in central coastal plains. The S is arid, approaching Sahara Desert. **Arable land:** 18.7%. **Capital:** Tunis, 2,290,777.

Government: Type: Parliamentary republic. **Head of state:** Pres. Béji Caïd Essebsi; b. 1926; in office: Dec. 31, 2014. **Head of govt.:** Prime Min. Youssef Chahed; b. 1975; in office: Aug. 27, 2016. **Local divisions:** 24 governorates. **Defense budget:** $826 mil. **Active troops:** 35,800.

Economy: Industries: petroleum, mining, tourism, textiles, footwear, agribusiness, beverages. **Chief agric.:** olives, olive oil, grain, tomatoes, citrus fruit, sugar beets, dates, almonds; beef, dairy prods. **Natural resources:** petroleum, phosphates, iron ore, lead, zinc, salt. **Water:** 410 cu m per capita. **Crude oil reserves:** 425 mil bbls. **Electricity prod.:** 18.3 bil kWh. **Labor force:** agric. 13.7%, industry 42.6%, services 43.7%. **Unemployment:** 15.4%.

Finance: Monetary unit: Dinar (TND) (2.77 = $1 U.S.). **GDP:** $135.4 bil; **per capita GDP:** $11,800; **GDP growth:** 1.9%. **Imports:** $23.3 bil; Italy 15.8%, France 15.1%, China 9.2%, Germany 8.1%. **Exports:** $14.2 bil; France 32.1%, Italy 17.3%, Germany 12.4%. **Tourism:** $1.3 bil. **Budget:** $11.9 bil. **Inflation:** 5.3%.

Transport: Railways: 1,350 mi (only partly operational). **Motor vehicles:** 144.4 per 1,000 pop. **Airports:** 15.

Communications: Telephone: 9.7 per 100 pop. **Mobile:** 124.3 per 100 pop. **Broadband:** 63 per 100 pop. **Internet** (2017): 55.5%.

Health: Expend.: 6.7%. **Life expect.:** 74.3 male; 77.6 female. **Births:** 17.4 per 1,000 pop. **Deaths:** 6.4 per 1,000 pop. **Infant mortality:** 11.7 per 1,000 live births. **Undernourished:** 4.9%. **HIV:** <0.1%.

Education: Compulsory: ages 6-14. **Literacy:** 81.8%.
Embassy: 1515 Massachusetts Ave. NW 20005; 862-1850.
Website: www.tunisie.gov.tn or www.pm.gov.tn

Site of ancient Carthage and a former Barbary state under the suzerainty of Turkey, Tunisia became a protectorate of France, May 12, 1881. The nation became independent Mar. 20, 1956, and ended the monarchy the following year. Habib Bourguiba, an independence leader, served as president until 1987, when he was deposed by his prime min., Zine al-Abidine Ben Ali, who then won five presidential elections, 1989-2009, all tightly controlled.

Arab Spring protests, which began Dec. 2010, ousted Ben Ali, Jan. 14, 2011. Prime Min. Hamadi Jebali, an Islamist leader of the moderate Ennahda party, took office after his party won Oct. 2011 elections. Jebali resigned Feb. 19, 2013, after failing to institute promised reforms. After a new constitution was approved, Jan. 26, 2014, the secular Nida Tunis party won the most seats in Oct. 26, 2014, legislative elections; Nida Tunis leader Beji Caid Essebsi was elected pres., Dec. 21, 2014. Youssef Chahed of Nida Tunis became prime min., Aug. 27, 2016.

Three Islamist extremist gunmen attacked a museum in Tunis, Mar. 18, 2015, killing 22. A gunman killed 38 foreign tourists at a resort hotel in Sousse, June 26. ISIS claimed responsibility for the Sousse attack and a suicide bombing in Tunis, Nov. 24, 2015, that left 12 victims dead. A sharp drop in tourism hurt the economy. More than 30 Islamist fighters, as well as about 20 security officers and civilians, were killed, Mar. 7, 2016, in attacks near the Libyan border.

July 2017 legislation gave women greater protection from abuse and sexual harassment. In Sept., the government lifted a ban on women marrying non-Muslims. Government austerity measures, introduced Jan. 2018, sparked large protests.

Turkey
Republic of Turkey

People: Population: 81,257,239 (18). **Age distrib.:** <15: 24.3%; 65+: 7.8%. **Growth:** 0.5%. **Migrants:** 6%. **Pop. density:** 273.4 per sq mi, 105.6 per sq km. **Urban:** 75.1%. **Ethnic groups:** Turkish 70%-75%, Kurdish 19%. **Languages:** Turkish (official), Kurdish. **Religions:** Muslim (mostly Sunni) 99.8%.

Geography: Total area: 302,535 sq mi, 783,562 sq km (36); **Land area:** 297,157 sq mi, 769,632 sq km. **Location:** Asia Minor, stretching into continental Europe; borders on Medit. and Black Seas. Bulgaria, Greece on W; Georgia, Armenia on N; Iran on E; Iraq, Syria on S. **Topography:** Center has wide plateaus with hot, dry summers and cold winters. High mountains ring the interior on all but W, with more than 20 peaks over 10,000 ft. Rolling plains in W; mild, fertile coastal plains in S and W. **Arable land:** 26.8%. **Capital:** Ankara, 4,919,074. **Cities:** Istanbul, 14,750,771; Izmir, 2,936,607; Bursa, 1,916,489; Adana, 1,729,859; Gaziantep, 1,631,568.

Government: Type: Parliamentary republic. **Head of state and govt.:** Pres. Recep Tayyip Erdogan; b. 1954; in office: Aug. 28, 2014. (The position of prime minister was eliminated in June 2018.) **Local divisions:** 81 provinces. **Defense budget:** $8 bil. **Active troops:** 355,200.

Economy: Industries: textiles, food proc., automobiles, electronics, mining, steel, petroleum, constr., lumber, paper. **Chief agric.:** tobacco, cotton, grain, olives, sugar beets, hazelnuts, pulses, citrus; livestock. **Natural resources:** coal, iron ore, copper, chromium, antimony, mercury, gold, barite, borate, strontium, emery, feldspar, limestone, magnesite, marble, perlite, pumice, pyrites (sulfur), clay, hydropower. **Water:** 2,690 cu m per capita. **Crude oil reserves:** 341.6 mil bbls. **Electricity prod.:** 248.9 bil kWh. **Labor force:** agric. 19.4%, industry 26.8%, services 53.8%. **Unemployment:** 11.3%.

Finance: Monetary unit: Lira (TRY) (6.67 = $1 U.S.). **GDP:** $2.2 tril; **per capita GDP:** $26,900; **GDP growth:** 7%. **Imports:** $196.8 bil; China 10%, Germany 9.1%, Russia 8.4%, U.S. 5.1%. **Exports** $157.3 bil; Germany 9.6%, UK 6.1%, UAE 5.9%, Iraq 5.8%, U.S. 5.5%, Italy 5.4%. **Tourism:** $22.5 bil. **Budget:** $190.4 bil. **Inflation:** 11.1%.

Transport: Railways: 7,461 mi. **Motor vehicles:** 213.7 per 1,000 pop. **Airports:** 91.

Communications: Telephone: 14 per 100 pop. **Mobile:** 96.4 per 100 pop. **Broadband:** 66.8 per 100 pop. **Internet** (2017): 64.7%.

Health: Expend.: 4.1%. **Life expect.:** 72.9 male; 77.7 female. **Births:** 15.4 per 1,000 pop. **Deaths:** 6.0 per 1,000 pop. **Infant mortality:** 16.9 per 1,000 live births. **Undernourished:** <2.5%. **HIV:** NA.

Education: Compulsory: ages 6-17. **Literacy:** 95.6%.
Embassy: 2525 Massachusetts Ave. NW 20008; 612-6700.
Website: www.tccb.gov.tr

Ancient inhabitants of Turkey were among the world's first agriculturalists. Such civilizations as the Hittite, Phrygian, and Lydian flourished in Asiatic Turkey (Asia Minor), as did much of Greek civilization. After the fall of Rome in the 5th cent., Constantinople (now Istanbul) was the capital of the Byzantine Empire for 1,000 years. It fell in 1453 to Ottoman Turks, who ruled a vast empire for over 400 years.

Just before WWI, Turkey, or the Ottoman Empire, ruled what is now Syria, Lebanon, Iraq, Jordan, Israel, Saudi Arabia, Yemen, and islands in the Aegean Sea. Turkey joined Germany and Austria in WWI, and its defeat resulted in the loss of territory and the fall of the sultanate. A secular republic was established Oct. 29, 1923. The first pres., Mustafa Kemal (later Kemal Ataturk), led Turkey until his death in 1938.

Turkey kept neutral during most of WWII. The country became a full member of NATO in 1952. Military coups overthrew civilian governments in 1960 and 1980. Turkey invaded nearby Cyprus July 20, 1974, to prevent that country from uniting with Greece, and Cyprus was divided into Greek and Turkish zones.

Turkey joined the U.S.-led force that ousted Iraq from Kuwait, 1991. Millions of Iraqi Kurdish refugees fled to Turkey's SE border region after the war. Turkish offensives in Kurdish areas of Turkey caused heavy casualties among separatist guerrillas and civilians. Kurdish militants raided Turkish diplomatic missions in some 25 Western European cities, June 24, 1993.

Tansu Ciller became Turkey's first woman prime min. July 5, 1993. The Islamic Welfare Party gained strength in the 1990s, and in June 1996, a coalition with Ciller's True Path Party was formed. The pro-Islamic government resigned June 18, 1997, under pressure from the military, which stepped up its campaign against Islamic fundamentalism in 1998.

Kurdish rebel leader Abdullah Öcalan was captured Feb. 15, 1999, and convicted of terrorism June 29. His organization, the Kurdistan Workers' Party (PKK), announced in 1999 that it would abandon its 14-year-old insurgency. Violence continued at a lower level, however, including attacks by both the PKK and Turkish forces.

Earthquakes in Apr. and Nov. 1999 killed over 17,000 people. The Islamic Justice and Development Party (AKP) led by Recep

Tayyip Erdogan won Nov. 3, 2002, parliamentary elections. Erdogan became prime min., May 14, 2003. After Erdogan's party scored a landslide win in 2007 elections, parliament chose an Islamic politician, Abdullah Gül, as president.

After anti-government protests in Taksim Square and elsewhere, 2013-14, Erdogan nevertheless won an Aug. 10, 2014, election to become Turkey's first popularly elected president. In an Apr. 16, 2017, referendum, accompanied by allegations of irregularities, voters narrowly approved constitutional amendments strengthening the president's powers and abolishing the post of prime minister after the next elections. Erdogan won the June 24, 2018, presidential election; the AKP won parliamentary elections the same day.

During Syria's civil war (2011-), Turkey became a haven for Syrian refugees (more than 3.5 mil as of Sept. 2018). Turkey was also a major transit route for hundreds of thousands of Syrian and other migrants trying to reach Europe. Under a Turkey-EU agreement, effective Mar. 20, 2016, Turkey pledged to crack down on smugglers ferrying migrants to Greece. The EU pledged to accelerate Turkey's application for membership (though accession talks stalled in 2017), provide aid to help Turkey care for refugees, and resettle some Syrians from Turkish refugee camps. Migrant crossings dropped sharply following the agreement.

Attacks beginning in Sept. 2014 by the Sunni extremist group ISIS against Kurdish areas in N Syria sent Syrian Kurds across the border into SE Turkey. Turkish government forces launched a new offensive against the PKK in SE Turkey, beginning in mid-2015, and Kurdish extremists staged terrorist attacks in Turkish cities, as well as attacks on government troops, 2015-18. Syrian Kurdish forces retook territory in Syria in 2015-17. Turkey began airstrikes, July 24, 2015, against PKK strongholds in N Iraq and later launched attacks on Syrian Kurdish fighters said to be affiliated with the PKK. Turkish ground troops fought in Syria, 2016-18, to help non-Kurdish rebels and limit areas controlled by Syrian Kurds.

Turkey began, July 2015, artillery and airstrikes against ISIS forces in N Syria and agreed to allow U.S. warplanes to use bases in Turkey to attack ISIS targets in Syria. About 20 terrorist attacks attributed to ISIS took place in Turkey by 2018. Suicide bombings at Istanbul's main airport, June 28, 2016, killed at least 45. On Aug. 20, a suicide bomber killed at least 54 at a wedding in SE Turkey. A gunman killed 39 at an Istanbul nightclub, Jan. 1, 2017.

A coup attempt against Erdogan by elements of the military, July 15-16, 2016, was put down by loyal military units. The abortive coup left at least 240 dead, and some 50,000 soldiers, government officials, and civilians (including journalists) were detained. Intensifying an ongoing crackdown on dissent, the government closed more than 100 media outlets and fired or suspended tens of thousands of judges, government officials, and teachers. About 1,200 schools were closed. More than 950 businesses were seized. The government blamed the coup on Muslim cleric Fethullah Gülen, living in the U.S.; Andrew Brunson, a U.S. Christian pastor, was arrested in Turkey in Oct. 2016 on espionage charges related in part to the failed coup. Tensions in U.S.-Turkish relations increased in Aug. 2018, contributing, along with economic problems, to a sharp drop in the lira's value. The U.S. imposed sanctions, Aug. 1, on high-level Turkish officials. Pres. Donald Trump said, Aug. 10, that tariffs on Turkish steel and aluminum (imposed Mar. 23) would be doubled. Turkey announced new tariffs on various U.S. goods, Aug. 15.

Turkmenistan

People: Population: 5,411,012 (118). **Age distrib.:** <15: 25.7%; 65+: 4.9%. **Growth:** 1.1%. **Migrants:** 3.4%. **Pop. density:** 29.8 per sq mi, 11.5 per sq km. **Urban:** 51.6%. **Ethnic groups:** Turkmen 85%, Uzbek 5%, Russian 4%. **Languages:** Turkmen (official), Russian, Uzbek. **Religions:** Muslim 89%, Eastern Orthodox 9%.

Geography: Total area: 188,456 sq mi, 488,100 sq km (52); **Land area:** 181,441 sq mi, 469,930 sq km. **Location:** Central Asia. Kazakhstan on N; Uzbekistan on N and E; Afghanistan, Iran on S. **Topography:** Kara Kum Desert occupies 80% of country. Bordered on W by Caspian Sea. **Arable land:** 4.1%. **Capital:** Ashgabat, 810,186.

Government: Type: Presidential republic; authoritarian. **Head of state and govt.:** Pres. Gurbanguly Berdymukhammedov; b. 1957; in office: Feb. 14, 2007 (acting from Dec. 21, 2006). **Local divisions:** 5 provinces, 1 independent city. **Defense budget:** NA. **Active troops:** 36,500.

Economy: Industries: nat. gas, oil, petroleum prods., textiles, food proc. **Chief agric.:** cotton, grain, melons; livestock. **Natural resources:** petroleum, nat. gas, sulfur, salt. **Water:** 4,609 cu m per capita. **Crude oil reserves:** 600 mil bbls. **Electricity prod.:** 21.2 bil kWh. **Labor force:** agric. 8.2%, industry 44.9%, services 46.8%. **Unemployment:** 3.4%.

Finance: Monetary unit: Manat (TMT) (3.50 = $1 U.S.). **GDP:** $103.5 bil; **per capita GDP:** $18,100; **GDP growth:** 6.5%. **Imports:** $4.8 bil; Turkey 24.2%, Algeria 14.4%, Germany 9.8%, China 8.9%, Russia 8%, U.S. 6.6%. **Exports:** $7.4 bil; China 83.7%, Turkey 5.1%. **Budget:** $4.7 bil. **Inflation:** 8%.

Transport: Railways: 3,177 mi. **Airports:** 21.

Communications: Telephone (2016): 11.7 per 100 pop. **Mobile** (2016). 151.4 per 100 pop. **Broadband:** NA. **Internet:** 18%.

Health: Expend.: 6.3%. **Life expect.:** 67.6 male; 73.9 female. **Births:** 18.9 per 1,000 pop. **Deaths:** 6.1 per 1,000 pop. **Infant mortality:** 33.1 per 1,000 live births. **Undernourished:** 5.5%. **HIV:** NA.

Education: Compulsory: ages 6-17. **Literacy:** 99.7%.

Embassy: 2207 Massachusetts Ave. NW 20008; 588-1500.

Website: www.turkmenistan.gov.tm

The region has been inhabited by Turkic peoples since the 10th cent. It became part of Russian Turkestan in 1881, and a constituent republic of the USSR in 1925. Turkmenistan declared independence Oct. 27, 1991, and became an independent state when the USSR disbanded Dec. 26, 1991.

Turkmenistan has extensive natural gas reserves and also oil reserves. Political power centers on the former Communist Party apparatus and authoritarian leadership. Gurbanguly Berdymukhammedov won the Feb. 2007 presidential election, considered fraudulent by international observers. He was reelected with 97% of the vote, Feb. 12, 2012, and with 98%, Feb. 12, 2017. The country's one-party system officially ended, Aug. 21, 2012. Constitutional changes in 2016 essentially allowed Berdymukhammedov to serve as president for life.

Tuvalu

People: Population: 11,147 (194). **Age distrib.:** <15: 29.3%; 65+: 6.3%. **Growth:** 0.9%. **Migrants:** 1.3%. **Pop. density:** 1,110.4 per sq mi, 428.7 per sq km. **Urban:** 62.4%. **Ethnic groups:** Tuvaluan 86.8%, Tuvaluan/I-Kiribati 5.6%, Tuvaluan/other 6.7%. **Languages:** Tuvaluan, English (both official); Samoan. **Religions:** Protestant 92.4% (incl. Congregational Christian Church of Tuvalu 85.7%).

Geography: Total area: 10 sq mi, 26 sq km (193); **Land area:** 10 sq mi, 26 sq km. **Location:** 9 islands forming NW-SE chain 360 mi long in SW Pacific O. Nearest neighbors are Kiribati to NE, Fiji to S. **Topography:** All low-lying atolls, no more than 15 ft above sea level, composed of coral reefs. **Arable land:** 0%. **Capital:** Funafuti, 7,042.

Government: Type: Parliamentary democracy under constitutional monarchy. **Head of state:** Queen Elizabeth II, rep. by Gov.-Gen. Iakoba Taeia Italeli; in office: Apr. 16, 2010. **Head of govt.:** Prime Min. Enele Sopoaga; b. 1956; in office: Aug. 5, 2013. **Local divisions:** 7 island councils, 1 town council. **Defense budget/active troops:** NA.

Economy: Industries: fishing. **Chief agric.:** coconuts; fish. **Natural resources:** fish, coconuts. **Water:** NA. **Labor force:** Pop. makes living mainly through exploitation of the sea, reefs, and atolls and from wages sent home by those abroad (mostly phosphate industry workers and sailors). **Unemployment:** NA.

Finance: Monetary unit: Australian Dollar (AUD) (1.39 = $1 U.S.). **GDP:** $42 mil; **per capita GDP:** $3,800; **GDP growth:** 3.2%. **Imports** (2013): $136.5 mil; Singapore 33.4%, South Korea 11.5%, Australia 10.8%, New Zealand 8%, Fiji 7.5%, Chile 6.1%, South Africa 5%, Japan 5%. **Exports** (2010): $600,000; U.S. 18.2%, Bosnia and Herzegovina 17%, Fiji 14.8%, Nigeria 14.2%, Germany 8.2%, South Africa 5.9%, Colombia 5.1%. **Budget:** $32.5 mil. **Inflation:** 2.4%.

Transport: NA.

Communications: Telephone (2016): 18 per 100 pop. **Mobile** (2016): 68.5 per 100 pop. **Broadband:** NA. **Internet:** 46%.

Health: Expend.: 15%. **Life expect.:** 65.0 male; 69.5 female. **Births:** 23.7 per 1,000 pop. **Deaths:** 8.4 per 1,000 pop. **Infant mortality:** 28.2 per 1,000 live births. **Undernourished:** NA. **HIV:** NA.

Education: Compulsory: ages 7-14. **Literacy:** NA.

Permanent UN Mission: 800 Second Ave., Ste. 400D, New York, NY 10017; (212) 490-0534.

Website: www.state.gov/p/eap/ci/tv/

The Ellice Islands separated from the British Gilbert and Ellice Islands Colony in 1975 and became Tuvalu; independence came Oct. 1, 1978. In 2000, Tuvalu joined the United Nations. A major drought that began in Nov. 2010 obliged the government to declare a state of emergency Sept. 28, 2011. Prime Min. Enele Sopoaga, in office since Aug. 5, 2013, formed a new government after Mar. 31, 2015, elections. Rising sea levels due to climate change are threatening to submerge the tiny island nation.

Uganda
Republic of Uganda

People: Population: 40,853,749 (35). **Age distrib.:** <15: 47.8%; 65+: 2%. **Growth:** 3.2%. **Migrants:** 3.9%. **Pop. density:** 536.8 per sq mi, 207.3 per sq km. **Urban:** 23.8%. **Ethnic groups:** Baganda 16.5%, Banyankole 9.6%, Basoga 8.8%, Bakiga 7.1%, Iteso 7%, Langi 6.3%, Bagisu 4.9%, Acholi 4.4%, Lugbara 3.3%. **Languages:** English (official), Ganda or Luganda (most widely used Niger-Congo lang.). **Religions:** Protestant 45.1% (incl. Anglican 32%, Pentecostal/Born Again/Evangelical 11.1%), Roman Catholic 39.3%, Muslim 13.7%.

Geography: Total area: 93,065 sq mi, 241,038 sq km (79); **Land area:** 76,101 sq mi, 197,100 sq km. **Location:** E Central Africa. South Sudan on N, Dem. Rep. of the Congo on W, Rwanda and Tanzania on S, Kenya on E. **Topography:** Mostly high plateau 3,000-6,000 ft high, with Ruwenzori Range in W (Mt. Margherita, 16,765 ft), volcanoes in SW. NE is arid, W and SW rainy. Lakes Victoria, Edward, Albert form much of borders. **Arable land:** 34.4%. **Capital:** Kampala, 2,986,352.

Government: Type: Presidential republic. **Head of state and govt.:** Pres. Yoweri Kaguta Museveni; b. 1944; in office: Jan. 29, 1986. **Local divisions:** 121 districts, 1 capital city. **Defense budget:** $436 mil. **Active troops:** 45,000.

Economy: Industries: sugar proc., brewing, tobacco, cotton textiles, cement, steel prod. **Chief agric.:** coffee, tea, cotton, tobacco, cassava, potatoes, corn, millet, pulses, cut flowers; beef, goat meat, milk, poultry, fish. **Natural resources:** copper, cobalt, hydropower, limestone, salt, gold. **Water:** 1,540 cu m per capita. **Crude oil reserves:** 2.5 bil bbls. **Electricity prod.:** 3.2 bil kWh. **Labor force:** agric. 69%, industry 6.9%, services 24.1%. **Unemployment:** 2.1%.

Finance: Monetary unit: Shilling (UGX) (3,768.29 = $1 U.S.). **GDP:** $88.7 bil; **per capita GDP:** $2,400; **GDP growth:** 4.5%. **Imports:** $4.6 bil; China 17.4%, India 13.4%, UAE 12.2%, Kenya 7.9%, Japan 6.4%, Saudi Arabia 6.3%. **Exports:** $2.9 bil; Kenya 17.7%, UAE 16.7%, Dem. Rep. of the Congo 6.6%, Rwanda 6.1%. **Tourism:** $918 mil. **Budget (2016):** $3.7 bil. **Inflation:** 5.2%.

Transport: Railways: 773 mi. **Motor vehicles:** 11.7 per 1,000 pop. **Airports:** 5.

Communications: Telephone: 0.6 per 100 pop. **Mobile:** 58.2 per 100 pop. **Broadband:** 33.7 per 100 pop. **Internet:** 21.9%.

Health: Expend.: 7.3%. **Life expect.:** 54.8 male; 57.8 female. **Births:** 42.4 per 1,000 pop. **Deaths:** 9.9 per 1,000 pop. **Infant mortality:** 54.6 per 1,000 live births. **Undernourished:** 41.4%. **HIV:** 5.9%.

Education: Compulsory: ages 6-12. **Literacy:** 78.4%.

Embassy: 5911 16th St. NW 20011; 726-0416.

Website: www.statehouse.go.ug

Britain obtained a protectorate over Uganda in 1894. The country became independent Oct. 9, 1962, and a republic within the Commonwealth a year later. In 1967, the traditional kingdoms, including the powerful Buganda state, were abolished.

Gen. Idi Amin seized power from Prime Min. Milton Obote in 1971. During his 8-year dictatorship, he was responsible for the deaths of up to 300,000 of his opponents. In 1972 he expelled nearly all of Uganda's 45,000 Asians. Tanzanian troops and Ugandan exiles and rebels ousted Amin, Apr. 11, 1979.

Obote, president from Dec. 1980, was ousted in a military coup July 1985. Guerrilla war and rampant human rights abuses had plagued Uganda under Obote's regime.

Conditions improved after Yoweri Museveni took power in Jan. 1986. In 1993 the Buganda and other traditional monarchies were restored for ceremonial purposes. Uganda helped Laurent Kabila seize power in the Dem. Rep. of the Congo (DRC; formerly Zaire) in 1997 but sent troops in 1998 to aid insurgents seeking his ouster. A withdrawal accord was signed Sept. 2002.

Pres. Museveni won reelection in 2001, 2006, 2011, and 2016; his political opponents, the U.S., and the EU considered the elections flawed. Several opposition politicians were arrested, Aug. 2018, and apparently abused in detention; anti-government protests were violently suppressed.

The rebel Lord's Resistance Army (LRA), led by Joseph Kony, began an insurgency against the Museveni government in 1986 and abducted tens of thousands of children to serve as soldiers and sex slaves. According to UN estimates, the LRA, 1987-2012, killed more than 100,000 people and displaced some 2.5 mil in Uganda and neighboring countries. Peace talks brokered by Sudan began July 2006, and LRA violence in Uganda diminished. A cease-fire accord was signed Feb. 23, 2008, by which time the LRA had largely moved its activities to the DRC and Central African Rep. (CAR). On Apr. 3, 2013, the U.S. offered a $5-mil reward for information leading to the capture of Kony, who had been charged with war crimes and crimes against humanity by the International Criminal Court in 2005. In Apr.-May 2017, although some LRA violence continued, the Ugandan military and U.S. special forces ended their operation in the CAR to capture Kony. As of Sept. 2018, he remained at large.

In 2007, Uganda began supplying troops to the African Union's peacekeeping force in Somalia. Suicide bombings July 11, 2010, killed 76 people watching a World Cup soccer match on outdoor video screens in Kampala; al-Shabab, a Somali al-Qaeda-linked Islamist group, claimed responsibility.

The UNHCR estimated that, as of July 31, 2018, more than 1 mil refugees from South Sudan were living in Uganda; as of Aug. 31, Uganda hosted about 317,000 refugees from the DRC.

Ukraine

People: Population: 43,952,299 (32). **Age distrib.:** <15: 15.9%; 65+: 16.5%. **Growth:** 0.04%. **Migrants:** 11.2%. **Pop. density:** 196.5 per sq mi, 75.9 per sq km. **Urban:** 69.4%. **Ethnic groups:** Ukrainian 77.8%, Russian 17.3%. **Languages:** Ukrainian (official), Russian. **Religions:** Orthodox (incl. Ukrainian Orthodox-Kyiv Patriarchate, Ukrainian Orthodox-Moscow Patriarchate).

Geography: Total area: 233,032 sq mi, 603,550 sq km (About 7.1% is occupied by Russia.) (45); **Land area:** 223,681 sq mi, 579,330 sq km. **Location:** Eastern Europe. Belarus on N; Russia on NE and E; Moldova, Romania on SW; Hungary, Slovakia, Poland on W. **Topography:** Part of E European plain with arable black soil. Carpathians in the SW, Crimean chain in the S. **Arable land:** 56.2%. **Capital:** Kiev, 2,956,706. **Cities:** Kharkiv, 1,435,895; Odesa, 1,011,187.

Government: Type: Semi-presidential republic. **Head of state:** Pres. Petro Poroshenko; b. 1965; in office: June 7, 2014. **Head of govt.:** Prime Min. Volodymyr Groysman; b. 1978; in office: Apr. 14, 2016. **Local divisions:** 24 provinces, 1 autonomous republic, 2 municipalities. **Defense budget:** $2.7 bil. **Active troops:** 204,000.

Economy: Industries: coal, elec. power, metals, machinery and transp. equip., chemicals, food proc. **Chief agric.:** grain, sugar beets, sunflower seeds, vegetables; beef, milk. **Natural resources:** iron ore, coal, manganese, nat. gas, oil, salt, sulfur, graphite, titanium, magnesium, kaolin, nickel, mercury, timber. **Water:** 3,911 cu m per capita. **Crude oil reserves:** 395 mil bbls. **Electricity prod.:** 152.1 bil kWh. **Labor force:** agric. 14.9%, industry 25.3%, services 59.8%. **Unemployment:** 9.5%.

Finance: Monetary unit: Hryvnia (UAH) (28.42 = $1 U.S.). **GDP:** $368.8 bil; **per capita GDP:** $8,700; **GDP growth:** 2.5%. **Imports:** $44.4 bil; Russia 14.5%, China 11.3%, Germany 11.2%, Poland 7%, Belarus 6.7%, U.S. 5.1%. **Exports:** $36.9 bil; Russia 9.2%, Poland 6.5%, Turkey 5.6%, India 5.5%, Italy 5.2%. **Tourism:** $1.3 bil. **Budget:** $38.9 bil (planned and consolidated). **Inflation:** 14.4%.

Transport: Railways: 13,504 mi. **Motor vehicles:** 226.6 per 1,000 pop. **Airports:** 108.

Communications: Telephone: 17.2 per 100 pop. **Mobile:** 133.5 per 100 pop. **Broadband:** 22.6 per 100 pop. **Internet:** 53%.

Health: Expend.: 6.1%. **Life expect.:** 67.7 male; 77.4 female. **Births:** 10.1 per 1,000 pop. **Deaths:** 14.3 per 1,000 pop. **Infant mortality:** 7.7 per 1,000 live births. **Undernourished:** 3.3%. **HIV:** 0.9%.

Education: Compulsory: ages 6-16. **Literacy:** 99.8%.

Embassy: 3350 M St. NW 20007; 349-2920.

Website: www.kmu.gov.ua

Ukrainians' Slavic ancestors inhabited the region well before the 1st cent. CE. In the 9th cent., the princes of Kiev established a strong state called Kievan Rus, which included much of present-day Ukraine. Internal conflicts led to the disintegration of the Ukrainian state by the 13th cent. Mongol rule was supplanted by Poland and Lithuania in the 14th and 15th cent. The N Black Sea coast and Crimea came under Turkish control in 1478. Ukrainian Cossacks, starting in the late 16th cent., rebelled against the occupiers of Ukraine: Russia, Poland, and Turkey.

An independent Ukrainian National Republic was proclaimed on Jan. 22, 1918. But in 1921, Ukraine's neighbors occupied and divided Ukrainian territory. In 1922, Ukraine became a constituent republic of the USSR. In 1932-33, the Soviet government engineered a famine in eastern Ukraine, and 6-7 mil Ukrainians died. During WWII the Ukrainian nationalist underground fought Nazi and Soviet forces. Over 5 mil Ukrainians died in the war. The reoccupation of Ukraine by Soviet troops in 1944 brought a renewed wave of repression.

The world's worst nuclear power plant disaster occurred in Chernobyl, Ukraine, in Apr. 1986; many thousands were killed or disabled as a result of the radiation leak.

Ukrainian independence was restored, Dec. 1991, with the Soviet Union's dissolution. Following a 1994 accord with Russia and the U.S., Ukraine's large nuclear arsenal was transferred to Russia for destruction.

President since 1994, Leonid Kuchma attempted to engineer the 2004 election of his handpicked successor, the Russian-backed Prime Min. Viktor Yanukovych. When Yanukovych was declared the winner in Nov., supporters of his main challenger, former Prime Min. Viktor Yushchenko, called the election fraudulent and staged massive protests (the Orange Revolution); the vote was annulled. An election rerun Dec. 26 gave Yushchenko the victory. Yushchenko's party fared poorly in Mar. 2006 parliamentary elections, and Yanukovych returned as prime min. in Aug.

Following Sept. 2007 elections, Yulia Tymoshenko, a former Orange Revolution ally of Yushchenko, became prime min., but she lost the presidential election to Yanukovych in Feb. 2010.

Large anti-Yanukovych protests began in Nov. 2013, following his decision not to sign a free trade pact with the EU. After dozens were killed in violent protests in Kiev, Feb. 18-20, 2014, parliament removed Yanukovych from office, Feb. 22. Pro-EU candidate Petro Poroshenko won a May 25, 2014, presidential election. Signing and ratification of the EU agreement were completed June 27 and Sept. 16. Pro-EU parties won a majority of seats in parliamentary elections, Oct. 26, 2014. Hurt by his perceived failure to reduce corruption, Prime Min. Arseniy Yatsenyuk resigned and was replaced by Volodymyr Groysman in Apr. 2016.

Aiding pro-Russian separatists, Russian forces entered Crimea in Mar. 2014, and Russia annexed the region Mar. 18. Fighting began in Apr. 2014 in eastern Ukraine between Ukrainian forces and pro-Russian separatists, widely reported to be aided by Russian military equipment and troops. A Russian missile fired by separatists or Russians apparently shot down a Malaysia Airlines commercial flight over eastern Ukraine, July 17, 2014, killing all 298 on board. A Feb. 12, 2015, cease-fire (known as the Minsk II Agreement) reduced violence, but fighting continued along the cease-fire line. By mid-2018, the death toll in Ukraine's civil war was more than 10,000, and 1.8 mil people were internally displaced; more than 470,000 Ukrainians had become refugees.

United Arab Emirates

People: Population: 9,701,315 (93). (UN estimated mid-2017 pop. to be 9.4 mil, with immigrants making up more than 88% of total pop.) **Age distrib.:** <15: 14.4%; 65+: 1.5%. **Growth:** 1.4%. **Migrants:** 88.4%. **Pop. density:** 300.6 per sq mi, 116 per sq km. **Urban:** 86.5%. **Ethnic groups:** South Asian 59.4% (incl. Indian 38.2%, Bangladeshi 9.5%, Pakistani 9.4%), Emirati 11.6%, Egyptian 10.2%, Philippine 6.1%. About 85% of pop. are noncitizens. **Languages:** Arabic (official), Persian, English, Hindi, Urdu. **Religions:** Muslim (official) 76%, Christian 9%.

Geography: Total area: 32,278 sq mi, 83,600 sq km (113); **Land area:** 32,278 sq mi, 83,600 sq km. **Location:** Middle East, on S shore of the Persian Gulf. Saudi Arabia on W and S, Oman on E. **Topography:** A barren, flat coastal plain gives way to uninhabited sand dunes on S. Hajar Mts. in E. **Arable land:** 0.4%. **Capital:** Abu Dhabi, 1,419,699. **Cities:** Dubai, 2,785,376; Sharjah, 1,570,849.

Government: Type: Federation of monarchies. **Head of state:** Pres. Sheikh Khalifa bin Zayed al Nahyan; b. 1948; in office: Nov. 3, 2004. **Head of govt.:** Prime Min. Sheikh Muhammad bin Rashid al-Maktum; b. 1949; in office: Jan. 5, 2006. **Local divisions:** 7 emirates: Abu Dhabi, Ajman, Dubai, Fujaira, Ras al-Khaimah, Sharjah, Umm al-Qaiwain. **Defense budget:** NA. **Active troops:** 63,000.

Economy: Industries: petroleum and petrochemicals, fishing, aluminum, cement, fertilizer, commercial ship repair, constr. materials. **Chief agric.:** dates, vegetables, watermelons; poultry, eggs; fish. **Natural resources:** petroleum, nat. gas. **Water:** 16 cu m per capita. **Crude oil reserves:** 97.8 bil bbls. **Electricity prod.:** 119.7 bil kWh. **Labor force:** agric. 0.4%, industry 38.9%, services 60.7%. **Unemployment:** 1.7%.

Finance: Monetary unit: Dirham (AED) (3.67 = $1 U.S.). **GDP:** $686.8 bil; **per capita GDP:** $67,700; **GDP growth:** 0.5%. **Imports:** $241.3 bil; China 8.5%, U.S. 6.8%, India 6.6%. **Exports:** $314.7 bil; India 10.1%, Iran 9.9%, Japan 9.3%, China 5.4%, Oman 5%. **Tourism:** $21 bil. **Budget:** $112.4 bil (not incl. emirate-level spending in Abu Dhabi and Dubai). **Inflation:** 2%.

Transport: Motor vehicles: 481.4 per 1,000 pop. **Airports:** 25. **Communications: Telephone:** 24.7 per 100 pop. **Mobile:** 210.9 per 100 pop. **Broadband:** 156.7 per 100 pop. **Internet** (2017): 94.8%.

Health: Expend.: 3.5%. **Life expect.:** 77.3 male; 80.1 female. **Births:** 9.8 per 1,000 pop. **Deaths:** 1.7 per 1,000 pop. **Infant mortality:** 5.5 per 1,000 live births. **Undernourished:** 2.5%. **HIV:** NA.

Education: Compulsory: ages 6-11. **Literacy:** 93.8%.

Embassy: 3522 International Ct. NW 20008; 243-2400.

Website: www.government.ae

The 7 "Trucial Sheikdoms" gave Britain control of defense and foreign relations in the 19th cent. They merged to become an independent state Dec. 2, 1971. Oil revenues have made the UAE one of the world's wealthiest countries. Foreigners make up most of the work force. International banking, investment, and construction boomed beginning in the late 1990s, and tourism became a major industry in the 21st cent., especially in Dubai.

Beginning in Sept. 2014, UAE warplanes took part in U.S.-led airstrikes against ISIS in Syria. In 2015, the UAE intervened in Yemen's civil war. It joined a Saudi-led coalition conducting airstrikes, beginning Mar. 25, 2015, against Shiite Houthi rebels in Yemen. UAE ground troops in Yemen trained anti-Houthi forces and assisted them in combat operations.

United Kingdom

United Kingdom of Great Britain and Northern Ireland

People: Population: 65,105,246 (22). **Age distrib.:** <15: 17.6%; 65+: 18.2%. **Growth:** 0.5%. **Migrants:** 13.4%. **Pop. density:** 697 per sq mi, 269.1 per sq km. **Urban:** 83.4%. **Ethnic groups:** white 87.2%, black/African/Caribbean/black British 3%, Asian/Asian British: Indian 2.3%. **Languages:** English; Scots, Scottish Gaelic, Welsh, Irish (all recognized regional langs.). **Religions:** Christian (incl. Anglican, Roman Catholic, Presbyterian, Methodist) 59.5%, Muslim 4.4%, none 25.7%.

Geography: Total area: 94,058 sq mi, 243,610 sq km (78); **Land area:** 93,410 sq mi, 241,930 sq km. **Location:** Off NW coast of Europe, across English Channel, Strait of Dover, North Sea. Ireland to W, France to SE. **Topography:** England is mostly rolling land, rising to Uplands of southern Scotland. Lowlands in center of Scotland, granite highlands in N. British Isles have milder climate than N Europe due to Gulf Stream and ample rainfall. Severn, 220 mi, and Thames, 215 mi, are longest rivers. **Arable land:** 24.8%. **Capital:** London, 9,046,485. **Cities:** Manchester, 2,690,445; Birmingham (West Midlands), 2,570,068; Leeds and Bradford (West Yorkshire), 1,864,036; Glasgow, 1,660,581; Belfast, 623,029; Edinburgh, 524,639; Cardiff, 470,816.

Government: Type: Parliamentary constitutional monarchy. **Head of state:** Queen Elizabeth II; b. 1926; in office: Feb. 6, 1952. **Head of govt.:** Prime Min. Theresa May; b. 1956; in office: July 13, 2016. **Local divisions:** 230 local authorities (England: 152;

Wales: 22; Scotland: 32; Northern Ireland: 11; 13 other dependent areas). **Defense budget:** $50.7 bil. **Active troops:** 150,250.

Economy: Industries: machine tools, elec. power equip., automation equip., railroad equip., shipbuilding, aircraft, motor vehicles and parts, electronics and communications equip. **Chief agric.:** cereals, oilseed, potatoes, vegetables; cattle, sheep, poultry; fish. **Natural resources:** coal, petroleum, nat. gas, iron ore, lead, zinc, gold, tin, limestone, salt, clay, chalk, gypsum, potash, silica sand, slate. **Water:** 2,271 cu m per capita. **Crude oil reserves:** 2.1 bil bbls. **Electricity prod:** 318.2 bil kWh. **Labor force:** agric. 1.1%, industry 18.4%, services 80.5%. **Unemployment:** 4.3%.

Finance: Monetary unit: Pound (GBP) (0.78 = $1 U.S.). **GDP:** $2.9 tril; **per capita GDP:** $44,100; **GDP growth:** 1.8%. **Imports:** $602.5 bil; Germany 13.7%, U.S. 9.5%, China 9.3%, Netherlands 8%, France 5.4%, Belgium 5%. **Exports:** $436.5 bil; U.S. 13.2%, Germany 10.5%, France 7.4%, Netherlands 6.2%, Ireland 5.6%. **Tourism:** $43.9 bil. **Budget:** $1.1 tril. **Inflation:** 2.6%.

Transport: Railways: 10,462 mi. **Motor vehicles:** 612.6 per 1,000 pop. **Airports:** 271.

Communications: Telephone: 50.1 per 100 pop. **Mobile:** 119.6 per 100 pop. **Broadband:** 91.4 per 100 pop. **Internet:** 94.8%.

Health: Expend.: 9.9%. **Life expect.:** 78.7 male; 83.2 female. **Births:** 12.0 per 1,000 pop. **Deaths:** 9.4 per 1,000 pop. **Infant mortality:** 4.2 per 1,000 live births. **Undernourished:** <2.5%. **HIV:** NA.

Education: Compulsory: ages 5-15. **Literacy:** 99%.

Embassy: 3100 Massachusetts Ave. NW 20008; 588-6500.

Website: www.gov.uk

The United Kingdom of Great Britain and Northern Ireland comprises England, Wales, Scotland, and Northern Ireland.

Queen and Royal Family. The ruling sovereign is Elizabeth II of the House of Windsor, elder daughter of King George VI. She succeeded to the throne Feb. 6, 1952, and was crowned June 2, 1953. She was married Nov. 20, 1947, to Lt. Philip Mountbatten (b. June 10, 1921), former Prince of Greece. He was created Duke of Edinburgh, and given the title H.R.H., Nov. 19, 1947; he was named Prince of the United Kingdom and Northern Ireland Feb. 22, 1957. Prince Charles Philip Arthur George (b. Nov. 14, 1948) is the Prince of Wales and heir apparent. His first son, William Philip Arthur Louis (b. June 21, 1982), is second in line to the throne. William's son George Alexander Louis (b. July 22, 2013) is third in line; William's daughter, Charlotte Elizabeth Diana (b. May 2, 2015), is fourth; his son Louis Arthur Charles (b. Apr. 23, 2018) is fifth. On May 19, 2018, Prince Charles's younger son, Henry Charles Albert David (Harry; sixth in line) married American actor Meghan Markle.

Parliament is the UK's legislative body, with certain powers over dependent units. It consists of two houses. The House of Commons has 650 members, elected by direct ballot and divided as follows: England, 533; Wales, 40; Scotland, 59; Northern Ireland, 18. The House of Lords (Oct. 2018) comprised 791 members: 90 hereditary peers, 676 life peers, and 25 archbishops and bishops of the Church of England.

Resources and Industries. Great Britain is a global trade and financial services center. As of 2017, service industries accounted for more than 80% of GDP; industry, 19%; agriculture, less than 1%. Manufacturing, historically important since the Industrial Revolution, has declined in economic significance, while finance, centered in London, has grown in importance. Coal production also historically important, has declined by more than 90% since 1970. Large oil and gas fields have been found in the North Sea; commercial oil production began in 1975. However, proved reserves are declining, and the country has been a net energy importer since 2005. The Walney Extension, which opened in the Irish Sea Sept. 2018, surpassed the London Array as the world's largest offshore wind farm.

Religion and Education. The Church of England is Protestant Episcopal. The queen is its temporal head, with rights of appointments to archbishoprics, bishoprics, and other offices. There are two provinces, Canterbury and York, each headed by an archbishop. Westminster Abbey (1050-1760) is the site of coronations and the tombs of Elizabeth I, Mary, Queen of Scots, kings, poets, and the Unknown Warrior. Celebrated British universities Oxford and Cambridge each date to the 13th cent.

History. Recent research indicates that Britain was separated from the European continent at least 200,000 years ago by a catastrophic flood that created the English Channel. Migrants across the Channel included the Celts, who arrived 2,500 to 3,000 years ago. Their language survives in Welsh and Gaelic enclaves.

England was part of the Roman Empire 43-410 CE, after which waves of Jutes, Angles, and Saxons arrived from German lands, followed by Danish raiders from the 8th through 11th cent. French-speaking Normans invaded in 1066, uniting the country with their dominions in France.

Opposition by nobles to royal authority forced King John to agree to the Magna Carta in 1215, a guarantee of rights and the rule of law. In the ensuing decades, the foundations of the parliamentary system were laid.

English dynastic claims to large parts of France led to the Hundred Years War, 1338-1453, an unsuccessful campaign. A long civil war, the War of the Roses, 1455-85, ended with the establishment of the Tudor monarchy. The economy prospered over long periods of domestic peace unmatched in continental Europe. The Church of England separated from the authority of the pope, 1534.

During the reign of Queen Elizabeth I, 1558-1603, England became a major naval power, leading to the founding of colonies in the New World and the expansion of trade with Europe and Asia. Scotland and England shared a single monarch after James VI of Scotland was crowned James I of England in 1603.

A struggle between Parliament and the Stuart kings led to a civil war, 1642-49, and the establishment of a republic under the Puritan Oliver Cromwell. The monarchy was restored in 1660, but the Glorious Revolution of 1688 confirmed the sovereignty of Parliament: a Bill of Rights was granted 1689. Scotland was united with England after the ratification of the Articles of Union of Scotland and England, May 1707.

Technological and entrepreneurial innovations led to the Industrial Revolution in the 18th cent. The 13 N American colonies were lost but replaced by growing empires in Canada, India, Australia, and elsewhere. Britain's role in the defeat of Napoleon, 1815, strengthened its position as the leading world power.

The limited extension of voting rights in 1832, 1867, and 1884; the formation of trade unions; and the development of universal public education were among the social changes that accompanied the spread of industrialization and urbanization in the 19th cent. (Men gained full voting rights in 1918 and women in 1928.) Large parts of Africa and Asia were added to the empire during the reign of Queen Victoria, 1837-1901.

Though victorious in WWI, Britain suffered huge casualties and economic dislocation. Ireland became independent in 1921, and independence movements became active in India and other colonies. The country suffered major bombing damage in WWII but rallied behind Prime Min. Winston Churchill and held off Germany until Allied victory was achieved, 1945.

In the postwar period, Britain lost its world leadership position to other powers. Labour governments passed socialist programs nationalizing some basic industries and expanding social security. In 1973, the UK joined the European Economic Community, which became the European Union (EU). Prime Min. Margaret Thatcher's Conservative governments, 1979-90, fostered private enterprise and began denationalization of key industries. Her Conservative successor, John Major, held power 1990-97. The Channel Tunnel linking Britain to the Continent was opened May 6, 1994.

The 1997 victory by the Labour Party made Tony Blair, 43, Britain's youngest prime min. since 1812. Diana, Princess of Wales, died in a car crash in Paris, Aug. 31. Britain played a leading role in the NATO air war against Yugoslavia, Mar.-June 1999, and contributed 12,000 troops to the multinational Kosovo security force.

After the Sept. 11 attacks on the U.S., the UK participated, beginning in 2001, in the Afghanistan war, maintaining as many as 9,500 troops in the country. About 650 remained in July 2018, when the government announced troop strength would increase to around 1,100 by Feb. 2019; British troops had suffered more than 450 fatalities since the war started. Blair, reelected in June 2001, committed British troops to the U.S.-led invasion of Iraq, Mar.-Apr. 2003. UK forces, which numbered 46,000 at the height of combat operations, almost entirely pulled out by mid-2009; 179 had died. Parliament approved British airstrikes against ISIS forces in Iraq (Sept. 26, 2014) and in Syria (Dec. 2, 2015).

In May 2005 elections, Blair became the first Labour prime min. to win 3 consecutive terms. Suicide bombings on 3 London underground trains and a bus, July 7, 2005, left 56 people dead and hundreds injured; police identified the bombers as 4 British Muslim men (3 of Pakistani origin).

Blair was succeeded by Gordon Brown, June 2007. Responding Oct. 13, 2008, to the worldwide financial crisis, Prime Min. Brown initiated a plan to provide three of Britain's largest banks with a capital infusion of up to $63 bil.

In the wake of Britain's deepest recession since WWII, voters rejected the Labour Party in May 2010 parliamentary elections. Conservatives and Liberal Democrats formed a coalition government; Conservative leader David Cameron became prime min. Cameron responded to the fiscal crisis with austerity measures meant to rein in debt. Parliament voted in favor of same-sex marriage July 16, 2013. The Conservatives won a House of Commons majority in May 7, 2015, elections. Tens of thousands of migrants to Europe from Africa, the Middle East, and SW Asia in 2015 tried to enter Britain. Anti-immigrant sentiment, including concerns about immigration from elsewhere in the EU, contributed to a 51.9%-48.1% referendum vote, June 23, 2016, favoring Britain's exit from the EU ("Brexit"). Cameron, who had campaigned for "remain," resigned as prime min. Conservative Theresa May replaced him, July 13. She formally notified the EU, Mar. 29, 2017, of Britain's intention to withdraw, triggering a two-year negotiation period on separation terms. In June 8 elections, the Conservatives lost their House of Commons majority, but May remained prime min.

A suicide bomber apparently with ISIS connections killed 22 victims and injured more than 100 at a concert in Manchester, May 22, 2017. On Mar. 22 in London, a terrorist (apparently inspired by Islamist extremism) had driven his car into pedestrians, killing 4, and fatally stabbed a police officer before he was killed by police. Also in London, June 3, three attackers fatally ran down with a van or stabbed eight victims before they were killed by police; ISIS claimed responsibility. At least 30 were injured, Sept. 15, when a bomb on a London Underground train partially

detonated; an Iraqi-born man was convicted, Mar. 16, 2018, of attempted murder.

Russia was the "highly likely" perpetrator, Prime Min. May said Mar. 12, 2018, of the Mar. 4 poisoning in Salisbury of a former Russian intelligence officer who became a British spy and his daughter; both survived. A British woman accidentally exposed to the nerve agent used died July 8. UK prosecutors, Sept. 5, charged (in absentia) two Russian agents with attempted murder.

When Cyprus gained independence, the UK retained the sovereign base areas of **Akrotiri** (47 sq mi) and **Dhekelia** (51 sq mi) on the island.

Wales

The Principality of Wales in western Britain has an area of 8,019 sq mi and a population (2017 est.) of 3,125,165. Cardiff is the capital, pop. (2017 est.) 362,756.

The creation of a 60-seat elected Welsh assembly with limited powers passed by a thin margin in a Sept. 18, 1997, referendum.

Early Anglo-Saxon invaders drove Celtic peoples into the mountains of Wales, where they developed a distinct nationality. Members of the ruling house of Gwynedd in the 13th cent. fought England but were crushed, 1283. Edward of Caernarvon, son of Edward I of England, was created Prince of Wales, 1301. **Website:** gov.wales

Scotland

Scotland occupies the northern 37% of the main British island, and the Hebrides, Orkney, Shetland, and smaller islands. Length 275 mi, breadth approx. 150 mi, area 30,414 sq mi, pop. (2017 est.) 5,424,800.

The Lowlands, a belt of land approx. 60 mi wide from the Firth of Clyde to the Firth of Forth, divide the farming region of the Southern Uplands from the granite Highlands of the N; they contain 75% of the population and most of the industry. The Highlands, famous for hunting and fishing, have been opened to industry by many hydroelectric power stations.

Edinburgh, pop. (2017 est.) 513,210, is the capital. Glasgow, pop. (2017 est.) 621,020, is Scotland's major port and shipbuilding center and has developed a services-based economy in the 21st cent., including financial services, healthcare, and engineering. Aberdeen, pop. (2017 est.) 228,800, is a major port and center of granite, fish-processing, and North Sea oil industries. Dundee, pop. (2017 est.) 148,710, NE of Edinburgh, is an industrial and fish-processing center.

History. Scotland was called Caledonia by the Romans who battled early Celtic tribes and occupied southern areas from the 1st to the 4th cent. Missionaries from Britain introduced Christianity in the 4th cent.; St. Columba, an Irish monk, converted most of Scotland in the 6th cent.

The Kingdom of Scotland was founded in 1018. William Wallace and Robert Bruce both defeated English armies 1297 and 1314, respectively. In 1603, James VI of Scotland, son of Mary, Queen of Scots, succeeded to the English throne as James I, and effected the Union of the Crowns. In 1707 Scotland received representation in the British Parliament, resulting from the union of formerly separate Parliaments. A 1997 proposal to create a regional legislature with limited taxing authority passed by a landslide. In 2011 elections for the 129-seat parliament, the pro-independence Scottish National Party (SNP) won a majority. In a referendum on independence Sept. 18, 2014, 55% of Scottish voters opposed separating from the UK. The SNP remained in power but lost its majority in May 5, 2016, parliamentary elections.

Memorials of Robert Burns, Sir Walter Scott, John Knox, and Mary, Queen of Scots, draw many tourists, as do the beauties of the Trossachs, Loch Katrine, Loch Lomond, and abbey ruins.

Industries. Engineering products are a key industry, with growing emphasis on office machinery, autos, electronics, and other consumer goods. Oil discoveries offshore in the North Sea stimulated onshore support industries.

Scotland produces fine woolens, worsteds, tweeds, silks, fine linens, and jute. It is known for its special breeds of cattle and sheep. Commercial fishing is an important industry. Whisky is a major export.

The Hebrides are a group of about 500 islands, 100 inhabited, off the W coast. The **Inner Hebrides** include Skye, Mull, and Iona, the last famous for the arrival of St. Columba, 563 CE. The **Outer Hebrides** include Lewis and Harris. Industries include sheep raising and weaving. The approx. 70 **Orkney Isls.** are to the NE. The capital is Kirkwall, on Pomona Isl. Fish curing, sheep raising, and weaving are occupations. NE of Orkney are the 200 **Shetland Isls.**, 24 inhabited, home of Shetland ponies. Orkney and Shetland are centers for the North Sea oil industry. **Website:** www.gov.scot

Northern Ireland

Northern Ireland was constituted in 1920 from 6 of the 9 counties of Ulster, the NE corner of Ireland. Area 5,452 sq mi, pop. (2017 est.) 1,870,834. Capital and chief industrial center, Belfast, pop. (2017 est.) 340,220.

Industries. Shipbuilding, including large tankers, has long been an important industry, centered in Belfast, the largest port. Linen is manufactured, along with apparel, rope, and twine. Growing diversification has added engineering products, synthetic fibers, and electronics. Major farm products include livestock, poultry, potatoes, and dairy foods.

Government and History. An act of the British Parliament, 1920, divided Northern from Southern Ireland, each with a parliament and government. When Ireland became a dominion, 1921, and later a republic, Northern Ireland chose to remain a part of the UK.

During 1968-69, Roman Catholics, then comprising about one-third of the population, claimed discrimination against them in voting rights, housing, and employment. Violence and terrorism intensified, involving branches of the Irish Republican Army (IRA; outlawed in the Irish Republic), Protestant groups, police, and British troops. Between 1969 and 2001, more than 3,500 were killed in sectarian violence in Northern Ireland, Ireland, England, and elsewhere. For most of this period, the Northern Ireland parliament was suspended, and Britain imposed direct rule.

A settlement reached on Good Friday, Apr. 10, 1998, and approved May 22 by voters in Northern Ireland and the Irish Republic, restored home rule and election of a 108-member assembly with safeguards for minority rights. Both Ireland and Great Britain agreed to relinquish constitutional claims on Northern Ireland. Elections to the assembly were held June 25. IRA dissidents seeking to derail the agreement detonated a bomb at Omagh Aug. 15 that killed 29 people and injured over 330.

London transferred authority to a Northern Ireland power-sharing government in 1999. Delays in IRA disarmament led to several suspensions of self-government. The IRA July 2005 renounced violence and ordered all units to disarm. The British responded by reducing their military presence in the region. On Sept. 26, an international monitoring group reported that the IRA had apparently scrapped its entire arsenal. The Northern Ireland legislature, suspended for 3½ years, reconvened May 15, 2006.

Religion and Education. According to the 2011 census, the population of Northern Ireland was 40.8% Catholic, 19.1% Presbyterian Church in Ireland, 13.7% Church of Ireland, and 10.1% no religion. Education is compulsory between the ages of 4 and 16 years. **Website:** www.northernireland.gov.uk

Channel Islands

The Channel Islands, area 75 sq mi, off the NW coast of France, the only parts of the former Dukedom of Normandy belonging to England, are Jersey, Guernsey, and the dependencies of Guernsey—Alderney, Brecqhou, Herm, Jethou, Lihou, and Sark. The Bailiwicks of **Jersey,** area 45 sq mi, pop. (2018 est.) 99,602, capital St. Helier, and **Guernsey,** area 30 sq mi, pop. (2018 est.) 66,697, capital St. Peter Port, have separate legal existences and lieutenant governors named by the Crown. The islands were the only British soil occupied by German troops in WWII. **Websites:** www.gov.je; www.gov.gg

Isle of Man

The Isle of Man, area 221 sq mi, pop. (2018 est.) 89,407, is in the Irish Sea, 20 mi from Scotland, 30 mi from Cumberland. It is rich in lead and iron. The island has its own laws and a lieutenant governor appointed by the Crown. The Tynwald (legislature) consists of the Legislative Council, partly elected, and House of Keys, elected. Capital: Douglas; pop. (2011 census, city proper) 27,938. Farming, tourism, and fishing (kippers, scallops) are chief occupations. Man is famous for the Manx tailless cat. **Website:** www.gov.im

Gibraltar

A dependency on the S coast of Spain, Gibraltar guards the entrance to the Mediterranean. Known as the Rock, Gibraltar has been in British possession since 1704. It is 3 mi long and 0.75 mi wide (total area, 2.25 sq mi) and reaches a max. elevation of 1,396 ft. A narrow isthmus connects it with the rest of the Iberian Peninsula. Pop. (2018 est.) 29,461.

Gibraltar has historically been—and remains—an object of contention between Britain and Spain. In 1967, residents voted almost unanimously to remain under British rule. A 1969 constitution increased Gibraltarian control of domestic affairs. Voters rejected a plan for the UK and Spain to share sovereignty, Nov. 7, 2002. Residents approved a new constitution Nov. 30, 2006. **Website:** www.gibraltar.gov.gi

British West Indies

A number of the Leeward Isls. are self-governing British possessions. Universal suffrage was instituted 1951-54; ministerial systems were set up 1956-60.

The Leeward Isls. associated with the UK are **Montserrat,** area 39 sq mi, pop. (2018 est.) 5,315. Brades Estate (2018 est. pop., 472) is de facto capital after Plymouth was abandoned in 1997 due to volcanic activity. The **British Virgin Isls.,** 58 sq mi, pop. (2018 est.) 35,802, capital Road Town (2018 est. pop., 15,137); and **Anguilla,** 35 sq mi, pop. (2018 est.) 17,422, capital The Valley (2018 est. pop., 1,402). Montserrat was devastated by the Soufrière Hills volcano, which began erupting July 18, 1995.

The three **Cayman Isls.,** a dependency, lie S of Cuba, NW of Jamaica. Pop. (2018 est.) 59,613, most of it on Grand Cayman. It is a free port; in the 1970s Grand Cayman became a tax-free refuge for foreign funds and branches of many Western banks were opened there. International tourism receipts in 2016 were $686 mil. Total area 102 sq mi. Capital: George Town; pop. (2018 est.) 34,875.

The **Turks and Caicos Isls.** are a dependency at the SE end of the Bahama Islands. Of about 40 islands, only 8 are inhabited; area 366 sq mi, pop. (2018 est.) 53,701; capital Cockburn Town (Grand Turk). Salt, shellfish, and conch shells are the main exports.

In Sept. 2017, Anguilla, the British Virgin Isls., and the Turks and Caicos Isls. suffered severe damage from Hurricane Irma. At least five people died and many were left homeless. Hurricane Maria further damaged the Turks and Caicos Isls.

Bermuda

Bermuda is a British dependency governed by a royal governor and an assembly, dating from 1620, the oldest legislative body among British dependencies. It is a group of about 150 small islands of coral formation, 20 inhabited, comprising 21 sq mi in the western Atlantic, 580 mi E of N. Carolina. Pop. (2018 est.) 71,176 (about 54% of African descent). Pop. density is high. Capital: Hamilton; pop. (2018 est.) 10,073.

Tourism is the major industry; tourism receipts in 2017 were $513 mil. Bermuda is also a haven for the offshore insurance industry. Exports include petroleum products, medicine. GDP per capita in 2016 was $99,400. In a referendum Aug. 15, 1995, voters rejected independence by nearly a 3-to-1 majority. **Website:** www.gov.bm

South Atlantic Territories

The **Falkland Isls.,** a dependency, lie 300 mi E of the Strait of Magellan at the southern end of S America.

The Falklands include 2 large islands and about 200 smaller ones, area 4,700 sq mi, pop. (2016 est.) 3,198. Capital Stanley, pop. (2018 est.) 2,269. The licensing of foreign fishing vessels is a major source of revenue. Fishing, tourism, and sheep farming are main industries; wool is the leading export. There are indications of large oil and gas deposits. Argentina claims the islands as Islas Malvinas; 97% of inhabitants are of British origin. Argentina invaded the islands Apr. 2, 1982. A British military task force sent to the area forced an Argentine surrender at Port Stanley, June 14, 1982. **Website:** www.falklands.gov.fk

British Antarctic Territory, S of 60° S lat., formerly a dependency of the Falkland Isls., was made a separate colony in 1962 and includes the South Shetland Isls., the South Orkney Isls., and the Antarctic Peninsula. A chain of meteorological stations is maintained.

South Georgia and the **South Sandwich Isls.,** formerly administered by the Falklands Isls., became a separate dependency in 1985. Total area of 1,507 sq mi. South Georgia, with no permanent population, is about 800 mi SE of the Falklands; the South Sandwich Isls. are uninhabited, about 470 mi SE of South Georgia. **Website:** www.sgov.gs

St. Helena, an island 1,200 mi off the W coast of Africa and 1,800 mi E of S America, 47 sq mi. Total area of St. Helena, Ascension, and Tristan da Cunha is 152 sq mi; total pop. (2018 est.) 7,841. Flax, lace, and rope-making are the chief industries. After Napoleon Bonaparte was defeated at Waterloo the Allies exiled him to St. Helena, where he lived from Oct. 16, 1815, to his death, May 5, 1821. Capital: Jamestown; pop. (2018 est.) 603. **Website:** www.sainthelena.gov.sh

Tristan da Cunha is the principal island, area 38 sq mi, in a group of islands of volcanic origin, total area 71 sq mi, halfway between the Cape of Good Hope and S America. The islands are part of the British overseas territory of St. Helena, Ascension, and Tristan da Cunha.

Ascension is an island of volcanic origin, 34 sq mi in area, 700 mi NW of St. Helena. It is part of the British overseas territory of St. Helena, Ascension, and Tristan da Cunha. It is a communications relay center for Britain, and has a U.S. satellite tracking center. The island is noted for sea turtles. **Website:** www.ascension-island.gov.ac

British Indian Ocean Territory (BIOT)

Formed Nov. 1965, with islands formerly dependencies of Mauritius or Seychelles: the Chagos Archipelago (including Diego Garcia), Aldabra, Farquhar, and Des Roches. The latter three were transferred to Seychelles, which became independent in 1976. Total area 21,004 sq mi, land area 23 sq mi. The Chagos civilian population was removed by the UK in the 1970s to make way for expansion of the U.S. military base on Diego Garcia. The UK has opposed islanders' efforts to return home; a Nov. 16, 2016, Foreign Office statement barred resettlement.

Pacific Ocean Territories

Pitcairn Isl. is in the Pacific, halfway between S America and Australia. The island was discovered in 1767 by Philip Carteret but was not inhabited until 23 years later when the mutineers of the *Bounty* landed there. Pop. (2016 est.) 54; descendants of mutineers and their Tahitian wives. It is administered by a British High Commissioner in New Zealand and a local Council. The uninhabited islands of Henderson, Ducie, and Oeno are in the Pitcairn group, area 18 sq mi. **Website:** www.government.pn

United States
United States of America

(Figures for U.S. may differ elsewhere in The World Almanac.*)*
People: Population: 329,256,465 (3). **Age distrib.:** <15: 18.6%; 65+: 16%. **Growth:** 0.6%. **Migrants:** 15.3%. **Pop. density:** 93.2 per sq mi, 36 per sq km. **Urban:** 82.3%. **Ethnic groups:** white 72.4%, black 12.6%, Asian 4.8%. About 16.3% of pop. is Hispanic (any race). **Languages:** English, Spanish, other Indo-European langs., Asian and Pacific island langs. No official natl. lang. **Religions:**

Protestant 46.5%, Roman Catholic 20.8%, Jewish 1.9%, Mormon 1.6%, other Christian 0.9%, Muslim 0.9%, Jehovah's Witness 0.8%, Buddhist 0.7%, Hindu 0.7%, unaffiliated 22.8%.

Geography: Total area: 3,796,742 sq mi, 9,833,517 sq km (3); **Land area:** 3,531,905 sq mi, 9,147,593 sq km. (Area is for 50 states and DC only.) **Location:** Primarily N America. Canada on N, Mexico on S; Pacific on W, Atlantic on E. **Topography:** Vast central plain, mountains in W, hills and low mountains in E. **Arable land:** 16.6%. **Capital:** Washington, DC, 5,206,593.

Government: Type: Constitutional federal republic. **Head of state and govt.:** Pres. Donald J. Trump; b. 1946; in office: Jan. 20, 2017. **Local divisions:** 50 states, 1 district. **Defense budget:** $602.8 bil. **Active troops:** 1,348,400.

Economy: Industries: petroleum, steel, motor vehicles, aerospace, telecom, chemicals, electronics, food proc., consumer goods, lumber, mining. **Chief agric.:** wheat, corn, other grains, fruits, vegetables, cotton; beef, pork, poultry, dairy prods.; fish. **Natural resources:** coal, copper, lead, molybdenum, phosphates, rare earth elements, uranium, bauxite, gold, iron, mercury, nickel, potash, silver, tungsten, zinc, petroleum, nat. gas, timber. **Water:** 9,538 cu m per capita. **Crude oil reserves** (2017): 35.2 bil bbls. **Electricity prod.** (2017): 4 tril kWh. **Labor force** (excl. unemployed): farming, forestry, fishing 0.7%; mfg., extraction, transp., crafts 20.3%; managerial, professional, technical 37.3%; sales and office 24.2%; other services 17.6%. **Unemployment:** 4.4%.

Finance: Monetary unit: Dollar (USD) (1.00 = $1 U.S.). **GDP:** $19.4 tril; **per capita GDP:** $59,500; **GDP growth:** 2.3%. **Imports:** $2.4 tril; China 21.6%, Mexico 13.4%, Canada 12.8%, Japan 5.8%, Germany 5%. **Exports:** $1.6 tril; Canada 18.3%, Mexico 15.7%, China 8.4%. **Tourism:** $210.7 bil. **Budget:** $4 tril (excl. approx. $2.3 tril of social benefits). **Inflation:** 2.1%.

Transport: Railways: 182,412 mi. **Motor vehicles:** 845.1 per 1,000 pop. **Airports:** 5,054.

Communications: Telephone: 37 per 100 pop. **Mobile:** 122 per 100 pop. **Broadband:** 120 per 100 pop. **Internet:** 76.2%.

Health: Expend.: 16.8%. **Life expect.:** 77.8 male; 82.3 female. **Births:** 12.4 per 1,000 pop. **Deaths:** 8.2 per 1,000 pop. **Infant mortality:** 5.7 per 1,000 live births. **Undernourished:** <2.5%. **HIV:** NA.

Education: Compulsory: ages 5-17. **Literacy:** 99%.
Website: www.usa.gov
See also U.S. History chapter; Chronology of the Year's Events.

Uruguay
Oriental Republic of Uruguay

People: Population: 3,369,299 (132). **Age distrib.:** <15: 19.9%; 65+: 14.4%. **Growth:** 0.3%. **Migrants:** 2.3%. **Pop. density:** 49.9 per sq mi, 19.3 per sq km. **Urban:** 95.3%. **Ethnic groups:** white 87.7%, black 4.6%, indigenous 2.4%. **Languages:** Spanish (official). **Religions:** Roman Catholic 47.1%, nondenominational 23.2%, non-Catholic Christians 11.1%, atheist or agnostic 17.2%.

Geography: Total area: 68,037 sq mi, 176,215 sq km (89); **Land area:** 67,574 sq mi, 175,015 sq km. **Location:** Southern S America, on Atlantic O. Argentina on W, Brazil on N. **Topography:** Rolling, grassy plains and hills, well-watered by rivers flowing W to Uruguay R. **Arable land:** 13.8%. **Capital:** Montevideo, 1,736,989.

Government: Type: Presidential republic. **Head of state and govt.:** Pres. Tabaré Vázquez; b. 1940; in office: Mar. 1, 2015. **Local divisions:** 19 departments. **Defense budget:** $513 mil. **Active troops:** 24,650.

Economy: Industries: food proc., elec. machinery, transp. equip., petroleum prods., textiles, chemicals, beverages. **Chief agric.:** cellulose, beef, soybeans, rice, wheat; dairy prods.; fish. **Natural resources:** hydropower, minor minerals, fish. **Water:** 50,175 cu m per capita. **Electricity prod.:** 13.6 bil kWh. **Labor force:** agric. 8.2%, industry 19.9%, services 71.9%. **Unemployment:** 7.9%.

Finance: Monetary unit: Peso (UYU) (32.14 = $1 U.S.). **GDP:** $78.2 bil; **per capita GDP:** $22,400; **GDP growth:** 3.1%. **Imports:** $8.7 bil; China 20%, Brazil 19.5%, Argentina 12.6%, U.S. 10.9%. **Exports:** $9 bil; China 19%, Brazil 16.1%, U.S. 5.7%, Argentina 5.4%. **Tourism:** $2.5 bil. **Budget:** $19.9 bil. **Inflation:** 6.2%.

Transport: Railways: 1,040 mi (operational). **Motor vehicles:** 322.8 per 1,000 pop. **Airports:** 11.

Communications: Telephone: 32.9 per 100 pop. **Mobile:** 147.5 per 100 pop. **Broadband:** 102 per 100 pop. **Internet:** 66.4%.

Health: Expend.: 9.2%. **Life expect.:** 74.4 male; 80.8 female. **Births:** 13.0 per 1,000 pop. **Deaths:** 9.4 per 1,000 pop. **Infant mortality:** 8.1 per 1,000 live births. **Undernourished:** <2.5%. **HIV:** 0.6%.

Education: Compulsory: ages 4-17. **Literacy:** 98.5%.
Embassy: 1913 I St. NW 20006; 331-1313.
Website: www.gub.uy

Spanish settlers began to supplant the indigenous Charrua Indians in 1624. Portuguese from Brazil arrived later, but Uruguay was attached to the Spanish Viceroyalty of Rio de la Plata in the 18th cent. Rebels fought against Spain beginning in 1810, with independence declared Aug. 25, 1825. To suppress Tupamaro guerrilla activities, a repressive military regime took power in 1973. Constitutional government was restored in 1985.

José (Pepe) Mujica, a former guerrilla who transformed his Marxist Tupamaro movement into a mainstream political party,

won a presidential runoff election Nov. 2009. Legislation legalizing same-sex marriage was signed into law May 3, 2013. A law passed in Dec. 2013 made Uruguay the first country to legalize marijuana nationwide. Former Pres. (2005-10) Tabaré Vázquez, the candidate of Mujica's Broad Front coalition, won a presidential runoff election, Nov. 30, 2014.

Uzbekistan
Republic of Uzbekistan

People: Population: 30,023,709 (46). **Age distrib.:** <15: 23.6%; 65+: 5.4%. **Growth:** 0.9%. **Migrants:** 3.6%. **Pop. density:** 182.8 per sq mi, 70.6 per sq km. **Urban:** 50.5%. **Ethnic groups:** Uzbek 80%, Russian 5.5%, Tajik 5%, Kazakh 3%, Karakalpak 2.5%. **Languages:** Uzbek (official), Russian, Tajik. **Religions:** Muslim (mostly Sunni) 88%, Eastern Orthodox 9%.

Geography: Total area: 172,742 sq mi, 447,400 sq km (56); **Land area:** 164,248 sq mi, 425,400 sq km. **Location:** Central Asia. Kazakhstan on N and W; Kyrgyzstan, Tajikistan on E; Afghanistan, Turkmenistan on S. **Topography:** Mostly plains and desert. **Arable land:** 10.3%. **Capital:** Tashkent, 2,463,969.

Government: Type: Presidential republic; highly authoritarian. **Head of state:** Pres. Shavkat Mirziyoyev; b. 1957; in office: Sept. 8, 2016. **Head of govt.:** Prime Min. Abdulla Aripov; b. 1961 in office: Dec. 14, 2016. **Local divisions:** 12 provinces, 1 autonomous republic, 1 city. **Defense budget:** NA. **Active troops:** 48,000.

Economy: Industries: textiles, food proc., machine building, metallurgy, mining, hydrocarbon extraction, chemicals. **Chief agric.:** cotton, vegetables, fruits, grain; livestock. **Natural resources:** nat. gas, petroleum, coal, gold, uranium, silver, copper, lead, zinc, tungsten, molybdenum. **Water:** 1,635 cu m per capita. **Crude oil reserves:** 594 mil bbls. **Electricity prod.:** 54.4 bil kWh. **Labor force:** agric. 21.9%, industry 37.7%, services 40.4%. **Unemployment:** 7.2%.

Finance: Monetary unit: Som (UZS) (7,827.23 = $1 U.S.). **GDP:** $222.6 bil; **per capita GDP:** $6,900; **GDP growth:** 5.3%. **Imports:** $11.4 bil; China 23.7%, Russia 22.5%, Kazakhstan 10.7%, South Korea 9.8%, Turkey 5.8%, Germany 5.6%. **Exports:** $11.4 bil; Switzerland 38.7%, China 15.5%, Russia 10.7%, Turkey 8.6%, Kazakhstan 7.7%. **Tourism** (2010): $121 mil. **Budget:** $19.9 bil. **Inflation:** 12.5%.

Transport: Railways: 2,884 mi. **Motor vehicles:** 80.2 per 1,000 pop. **Airports:** 33.

Communications: Telephone: 10.8 per 100 pop. **Mobile:** 76 per 100 pop. **Broadband:** 55.9 per 100 pop. **Internet:** 46.8%.

Health: Expend.: 6.2%. **Life expect.:** 71.2 male; 77.5 female. **Births:** 16.6 per 1,000 pop. **Deaths:** 5.4 per 1,000 pop. **Infant mortality:** 17.4 per 1,000 live births. **Undernourished:** 7.4%. **HIV:** 0.3%.

Education: Compulsory: ages 7-18. **Literacy:** 100%.
Embassy: 1746 Massachusetts Ave. NW 20036; 293-6803.
Website: www.gov.uz

The region was overrun by the Mongols under Genghis Khan in 1220. In the 14th cent., Uzbekistan became the center of a native Timurid empire. In later centuries Muslim feudal states emerged. Russian military conquest began in the 19th cent. The Uzbek SSR became a Soviet republic in 1925.

Uzbekistan gained independence when the Soviet Union disbanded Dec. 26, 1991, and was led by the authoritarian government of a former Communist, Islam A. Karimov.

Attacks by Islamic militants, Mar.-July 2004, killed more than 50 people. In June 2004, Russia's OAO Lukoil signed a $1-bil deal to develop Uzbekistan's natural gas fields.

After armed dissidents at Andizhan, east Uzbekistan, attacked government buildings and freed hundreds of prisoners, May 2005, Uzbek security forces killed many rebels and unarmed demonstrators. Karimov then launched a general crackdown on human rights activists. Karimov and Russian Pres. Vladimir Putin signed a military cooperation agreement, Nov. 2005.

Karimov remained in office following the expiration of his presidential term Jan. 22, 2007; despite a two-term constitutional limit, he ran for a third term Dec. 23 and won with an 88.1% majority. Karimov won a fourth term, with 90.4% of the vote, Mar. 29, 2015. The government announced, Sept. 2, 2016, that Karimov had died. Prime Min. Shavkat Mirziyoyev became interim president and won (with 88.6% of the vote) a flawed Dec. 4 presidential election. By 2018, Mirziyoyev had taken steps to reduce repression, including freeing some jailed dissidents, arresting some security officers accused of torture, and reducing forced labor in the annual cotton harvest.

Vanuatu
Republic of Vanuatu

People: Population: 288,037 (175). **Age distrib.:** <15: 34.9%; 65+: 4.1%. **Growth:** 1.8%. **Migrants:** 1.2%. **Pop. density:** 61.2 per sq mi, 23.6 per sq km. **Urban:** 25.3%. **Ethnic groups:** Melanesian 99.2%. **Languages:** 100+ local langs.; Bislama (creole), English, French (all official). **Religions:** Protestant 70% (incl. Presbyterian 27.9%, Anglican 15.1%, Seventh-day Adventist 12.5%), Roman Catholic 12.4%.

Geography: Total area: 4,706 sq mi, 12,189 sq km (158); **Land area:** 4,706 sq mi, 12,189 sq km. **Location:** More than

80 islands (about 65 inhabited) in SW Pacific, 1,200 mi NE of Brisbane, Australia. Fiji to E, Solomon Isls. to NW. **Topography:** Dense forest with narrow coastal strips of cultivated land. **Arable land:** 1.6%. **Capital:** Port Vila, 52,690.

Government: Type: Parliamentary republic. **Head of state:** Pres. Tallis Obed Moses; in office: July 6, 2017. **Head of govt.:** Prime Min. Charlot Salwai; b. 1963; in office: Feb. 11, 2016. **Local divisions:** 6 provinces. **Defense budget/active troops:** NA.

Economy: Industries: food and fish freezing, wood proc., meat canning. **Chief agric.:** copra, coconuts, cocoa, coffee, taro, yams, fruits, vegetables; beef; fish. **Natural resources:** manganese, hardwood forests, fish. **Water:** 37,793 cu m per capita. **Electricity prod.:** 55 mil kWh. **Labor force:** agric. 64.9%, industry 5.9%, services 29.2%. **Unemployment:** 5.2%.

Finance: Monetary unit: Vatu (VUV) (113.71 = $1 U.S.). **GDP:** $770 mil; **per capita GDP:** $2,700; **GDP growth:** 4.2%. **Imports:** $249.9 mil; Russia 35.2%, Australia 19.8%, New Zealand 9.8%, China 6.3%, Fiji 5.5%. **Exports:** $43.9 mil; Philippines 23.9%, Australia 16.5%, U.S. 10.4%, Japan 8.8%, Venezuela 8%. **Tourism** (2015): $228 mil. **Budget:** $206.9 mil. **Inflation** (2015-16): 0.8%.

Transport: Motor vehicles: 58 per 1,000 pop. **Airports:** 3.

Communications: Telephone: 1.3 per 100 pop. **Mobile:** 82.5 per 100 pop. **Broadband:** 22.3 per 100 pop. **Internet:** 24%.

Health: Expend.: 3.5%. **Life expect.:** 72.4 male; 75.7 female. **Births:** 23.5 per 1,000 pop. **Deaths:** 4.0 per 1,000 pop. **Infant mortality:** 13.9 per 1,000 live births. **Undernourished:** 7.1%. **HIV:** NA.

Education: Compulsory: NA. **Literacy:** 85.2%.

Permanent UN mission: 800 Second Ave., Ste. 400B, New York, NY 10017; (212) 661-4303.

Website: parliament.gov.vu

The Anglo-French condominium of the New Hebrides, administered jointly since 1906, became the independent Republic of Vanuatu on July 30, 1980. Cyclone Pam, Mar. 13-14, 2015, destroyed 96% of the country's crops and left 166,000 people in need of emergency assistance; the official death toll was 11. The speaker and 13 other members of parliament were convicted, Oct. 9, 2015, of accepting bribes in 2014 in exchange for voting no-confidence in the prime min. Pres. Baldwin Lonsdale died, June 17, 2017; Tallis Obed Moses was elected president by parliament, July 6.

Vatican City
The Holy See (Vatican City State)

People: Population: (2017) 1,000 (196). **Migrants:** 100%. **Pop. density:** (2017) 5,886.3 per sq mi, 2,272.7 per sq km. **Urban:** 100%. **Ethnic groups:** Italian, Swiss, Argentinian, other nationalities. **Languages:** Italian, Latin, French. **Religions:** Roman Catholic.

Geography: Total area: 0.17 sq mi, 0.44 sq km (196); **Land area:** 0.17 sq mi, 0.44 sq km. **Location:** Within the city of Rome, completely surrounded by Italy. **Arable land:** 0%.

Economy: Industries: printing; coins, medals, postage stamps prod.; mosaics, staff uniforms; worldwide banking, financial activities. **Water:** NA. **Labor force:** Essentially services with small amount of industry; nearly all dignitaries, priests, nuns, guards, and approx. 3,000 lay workers live outside the Vatican.

Finance: Monetary unit: Euro (EUR) (0.86 = $1 U.S.). **GDP:** NA; **per capita GDP:** NA. **Budget** (2013): $348 mil.

Apostolic Nunciature: 3339 Massachusetts Ave. NW 20008; 333-7171.

Website: www.vatican.va

The popes for many centuries, with brief interruptions, held temporal sovereignty over mid-Italy (the so-called Papal States), comprising an area of some 16,000 sq mi, with a population in the 19th cent. of more than 3 mil. This territory was incorporated in the new Kingdom of Italy (1861), the sovereignty of the pope being confined to the palaces of the Vatican and the Lateran in Rome and the villa of Castel Gandolfo, by an Italian law, May 13, 1871.

A Treaty of Conciliation, a concordat, and a financial convention with Italy were signed Feb. 11, 1929. They established the independent state of Vatican City and gave the Roman Catholic Church special status in Italy. The treaty (Lateran Agreement) was incorporated into Italy's Constitution (Article 7) in 1947. Italy and the Vatican signed an agreement in 1984 eliminating Roman Catholicism as the state religion and ending required religious education in Italian schools.

Vatican City includes the Basilica of Saint Peter, the Vatican Palace and Museum, the Vatican gardens, and neighboring buildings; 13 buildings in Rome, outside the boundaries, which house congregations or officers, enjoy extraterritorial rights. The legal system is based on the code of canon law, the apostolic constitutions, and laws especially promulgated for Vatican City by the pope.

Pope Benedict XVI, elected Apr. 19, 2005, announced he would resign Feb. 11, 2013, the first pontiff to do so since 1415. He became Pope Emeritus Feb. 28. Cardinal Jorge Mario Bergoglio, from Argentina, was elected Mar. 13, taking the name Francis. He became the first Latin American and first Jesuit pope. Cardinal George Pell, prefect of the Vatican's Secretariat for the Economy, was charged in Melbourne, June 29, 2017, with child sex abuse; he denied the charges. An Australian court ruled, May 1, 2018, that Pell stand trial on some charges. On Aug. 20, 2018, Pope Francis said the Church "did not act in a timely manner" regarding sex-abuse allegations in various countries, and he condemned "atrocities perpetrated by consecrated persons."

Venezuela
Bolivarian Republic of Venezuela

People: Population: 31,689,176 (43). **Age distrib.:** <15: 27%; 65+: 7.4%. **Growth:** 1.2%. **Migrants:** 4.5%. **Pop. density:** 93 per sq mi, 35.9 per sq km. **Urban:** 88.2%. **Ethnic groups:** Spanish, Italian, Portuguese, Arab, German, African, indigenous. **Languages:** Spanish (official), indigenous dialects. **Religions:** nominally Roman Catholic 96%, Protestant 2%.

Geography: Total area: 352,144 sq mi, 912,050 sq km (32); **Land area:** 340,561 sq mi, 882,050 sq km. **Location:** Carib. coast of S America. Colombia on W, Brazil on S, Guyana on E. **Topography:** Plains, called llanos, extend between Andes Mts. and Orinoco Delta. Orinoco stretches 1,600 mi and drains 80% of country. **Arable land:** 3.1%. **Capital:** Caracas, 2,934,560. **Cities:** Maracaibo, 2,178,861; Valencia, 1,860,329.

Government: Type: Federal presidential republic. **Head of state and govt.:** Pres. Nicolás Maduro Moros; b. 1962; in office: Apr. 19, 2013. **Local divisions:** 23 states, 1 capital district, 1 federal dependency consisting of 11 fed. controlled island groups. **Defense budget:** $1.1 bil. **Active troops:** 123,000.

Economy: Industries: agric. prods., livestock, raw materials, machinery and equip., transp. equip., constr. materials, medical equip., pharmaceuticals. **Chief agric.:** corn, sorghum, sugarcane, rice, bananas, vegetables, coffee; beef, pork, milk, eggs; fish. **Natural resources:** petroleum, nat. gas, iron ore, gold, bauxite, hydropower, diamonds. **Water:** 42,594 cu m per capita. **Crude oil reserves:** 302.3 bil bbls. **Electricity prod:** 114.4 bil kWh. **Labor force:** agric. 10.2%, industry 23.3%, services 66.5%. **Unemployment:** 7.7%.

Finance: Monetary unit: Bolivar (VEF) (9.99 = $1 U.S.). The govt., Aug. 20, 2018, introduced the sovereign bolivar (VES), which is equal to 100,000 of the former currency. **GDP:** $380.7 bil; **per capita GDP:** $12,100; **GDP growth:** −14%. **Imports:** $17.8 bil; U.S. 24.8%, China 14.2%, Mexico 9.5%. **Exports:** $29.2 bil; U.S. 34.8%, India 17.2%, China 16%, Netherlands Antilles 8.2%, Singapore 6.3%. **Tourism:** $473 mil. **Budget:** $160 bil. **Inflation** (2015-16): 254.9%.

Transport: Railways: 278 mi. **Motor vehicles:** 116.5 per 1,000 pop. **Airports:** 127.

Communications: Telephone: 18.5 per 100 pop. **Mobile:** 76.6 per 100 pop. **Broadband:** 44.6 per 100 pop. **Internet:** 60%.

Health: Expend.: 3.2%. **Life expect.:** 73.2 male; 79.3 female. **Births:** 18.5 per 1,000 pop. **Deaths:** 5.3 per 1,000 pop. **Infant mortality:** 11.9 per 1,000 live births. **Undernourished:** 11.7%. **HIV:** NA.

Education: Compulsory: ages 3-16. **Literacy:** 97.1%.

Embassy: 1099 30th St. NW 20007; 342-2214.

Website: www.presidencia.gob.ve or eeuu.embajada.gob.ve

Columbus first set foot on the South American continent on the peninsula of Paria, Aug. 1498. Alonso de Ojeda, 1499, called the land Venezuela, or Little Venice, because the native people had houses on stilts. Spanish colonialists dominated Venezuela until Simón Bolívar's victory near Carabobo in June 1821. The republic was formed after secession from the Colombian Federation in 1830. Military strongmen ruled Venezuela for much of its history. Beginning in 1959, the country had democratically elected governments.

Venezuela has the world's largest crude oil reserves, and oil accounts for more than 95% of export earnings and almost half of government revenues. The government, Jan. 1, 1976, nationalized the oil industry. The country also has large reserves of natural gas.

Two attempted coups were thwarted by loyalist troops in Feb. and Nov. 1992. Pres. Carlos Andrés Pérez was removed from office on corruption charges, May 1993, and convicted, May 1996, of mismanaging a $17-mil secret government fund.

A 1992 coup leader, Hugo Chávez, who ran as a populist, was elected president Dec. 1998. That month, voters approved a new constitution greatly increasing his powers.

Popular among the poor, Chávez alienated middle- and upper-class Venezuelans with economic and political reforms, and his foreign policy antagonized the U.S. Chávez countered U.S. attempts to isolate him by solidifying ties with Latin American leftist leaders and with Iran and Russia. With the economy surging, he won the Dec. 2006 presidential election. Venezuelan voters approved constitutional changes abolishing presidential term limits Feb. 15, 2009. Suffering from cancer, Chávez won reelection, Oct. 7, 2012. He died Mar. 5, 2013, before he could be sworn in. Vice Pres. Nicolás Maduro Moros won a narrow victory in Apr. 14, 2013, elections. With the economy hurt by low oil prices, declining oil production, and tight currency and price controls, GDP declined by about 4% in 2014, 6% in 2015, 16.5% in 2016, and 14% in 2017. The inflation rate was more than 120% in 2015, 300% in 2016, and 2,600% in 2017; estimates for 2018 were much higher. Shortages of food, medicine, and other goods were widespread. By Oct. 1, 2018, 1.9 mil. Venezuelans had emigrated since 2015, the UNHCR estimated—to Colombia, Brazil, Ecuador, Peru, Chile, and other nations.

Large anti-Maduro protests, Feb.-June 2014, were met with a harsh crackdown; more than 40 people died. The government arrested a number of opposition figures in 2014-15. Opposition leader Leopoldo López was convicted, Sept. 10, 2015, of inciting violence and received a 13+-year sentence. An opposition coalition won Dec. 6, 2015, legislative elections; the Supreme Court, made up mostly of Maduro loyalists, often overturned legislation. Looting and sometimes violent demonstrations, protesting shortages and calling for Maduro's removal, were widespread in

2016-17; about 125 died, Apr.-July 2017. Maduro, May 1, 2017, proposed a constituent assembly to write a new constitution. Assembly members, mainly Maduro supporters, were chosen July 30 in an election widely criticized as fraudulent. The assembly had broad interim governing powers; in a decree, Aug. 18, it largely took over the power to legislate. In a flawed election, May 20, 2018, Maduro won a new term as president. He survived a possible assassination attempt, Aug. 4, when drones exploded over a military parade where he was giving a speech.

Vietnam
Socialist Republic of Vietnam

People: Population: 97,040,334 (15). **Age distrib.:** <15: 23.3%; 65+: 6.4%. **Growth:** 0.9%. **Migrants:** 0.1%. **Pop. density:** 810.6 per sq mi, 313 per sq km. **Urban:** 35.9%. **Ethnic groups:** Kinh (Viet) 85.7%. **Languages:** Vietnamese (official), English, French, Chinese, Khmer. **Religions:** Buddhist 7.9%, Catholic 6.6%, none 81.8%.

Geography: Total area: 127,881 sq mi, 331,210 sq km (65); **Land area:** 119,719 sq mi, 310,070 sq km. **Location:** SE Asia, on E coast of Indochinese Peninsula. China on N; Laos, Cambodia on W. **Topography:** Long and narrow, with 1,400-mi coast. Densely settled Red R. Valley in N; narrow coastal plains in center; wide, often marshy Mekong R. Delta in S. Semi-arid plateaus and barren mountains, with some stretches of tropical rain forest, in rest of country. **Arable land:** 22.6%. **Capital:** Hanoi, 4,282,738. **Cities:** Ho Chi Minh City, 8,145,361; Can Tho, 1,444,343; Hai Phòng, 1,219,352.

Government: Type: Communist state. **Head of state:** Pres. Nguyen Phu Trong; b. 1944; in office: Oct. 23, 2018. **Head of govt.:** Prime Min. Nguyen Xuan Phuc; b. 1954; in office: Apr. 7, 2016. **Local divisions:** 58 provinces, 5 municipalities. **Defense budget:** $4.3 bil. **Active troops:** 482,000.

Economy: Industries: food proc., garments, shoes, machine-building, mining, coal, steel, cement, chemical fertilizer. **Chief agric.:** rice, coffee, rubber, tea, pepper, soybeans, cashews, sugarcane, peanuts, bananas; pork, poultry; seafood. **Natural resources:** phosphates, coal, manganese, rare earth elements, bauxite, chromate, offshore oil and gas deposits, timber, hydropower. **Water:** 9,461 cu m per capita. **Crude oil reserves:** 4.4 bil bbls. **Electricity prod.:** 146.9 bil kWh. **Labor force:** agric. 40.9%, industry 25.1%, services 34.1%. **Unemployment:** 2.1%.

Finance: Monetary unit: Dong (VND) (23,291.21 = $1 U.S.). **GDP:** $647.4 bil; **per capita GDP:** $6,900; **GDP growth:** 6.8%. **Imports:** $211.1 bil; China 25.8%, South Korea 20.5%, Japan 7.8%. **Exports:** $214 bil; U.S. 20.1%, China 14.5%, Japan 8%, South Korea 6.8%. **Tourism:** $8.9 bil. **Budget:** $54.4 bil. **Inflation:** 3.5%.

Transport: Railways: 1,616 mi. **Motor vehicles:** 6.2 per 1,000 pop. **Airports:** 38.

Communications: Telephone: 4.7 per 100 pop. **Mobile:** 125.6 per 100 pop. **Broadband:** 46.6 per 100 pop. **Internet:** 46.5%.

Health: Expend.: 5.7%. **Life expect.:** 71.4 male; 76.7 female. **Births:** 15.2 per 1,000 pop. **Deaths:** 5.9 per 1,000 pop. **Infant mortality:** 16.7 per 1,000 live births. **Undernourished:** 10.8%. **HIV:** 0.3%.

Education: Compulsory: ages 5-14. **Literacy:** 94.5%.
Embassy: 1233 20th St. NW, Ste. 400, 20036; 861-0737.
Website: vietnam.gov.vn

Settled by Viets from central China, Vietnam was held by China, 111 BCE-939 CE, and was a vassal state during subsequent periods. Conquest by France began in 1858 and ended in 1884 with the protectorates of Tonkin and Annam in the N and the colony of Cochin-China in the S.

Japan occupied Vietnam in 1940. Several groups formed the Vietminh (Independence) League, headed by Communist guerrilla leader Ho Chi Minh. In Aug. 1945, the Vietminh forced out Bao Dai, former emperor of Annam and head of a Japan-sponsored regime. France, seeking to reestablish colonial control, unsuccessfully battled Communist and nationalist forces, 1946-54.

Separate states formed in N. and S. Vietnam, with Communists under Ho Chi Minh (backed by Russia and China) controlling N. Vietnam and a non-Communist government (backed by the U.S.) controlling S. Vietnam. N. Vietnam aided Vietcong guerrillas who sought to take over S. Vietnam. U.S. troops and the S. Vietnamese army fought N. Vietnamese and Vietcong forces, including in border areas of Laos and Cambodia. Casualties of the war were as follows—combat deaths: U.S. 47,434 (Aug. 4, 1964-Jan. 27, 1973); S. Vietnam more than 200,000; other allied forces 5,225. Total U.S. fatalities numbered more than 58,000. Vietnamese civilian casualties were more than 1 mil. The war displaced more than 6.5 mil in S. Vietnam.

A never-implemented cease-fire agreement was signed in Paris Jan. 27, 1973, by the U.S., N. and S. Vietnam, and the Vietcong. The last U.S. troops left Vietnam Mar. 27, 1973. S. Vietnam surrendered Apr. 30, 1975. N. Vietnam assumed control. The country was officially reunited July 2, 1976.

Heavy fighting with Cambodia took place, 1977-80. China cut off economic aid, 1978, when 140,000 ethnic Chinese fled discrimination in Vietnam. Reacting to Vietnam's 1979 invasion of Cambodia, China attacked four Vietnamese border provinces, Feb. 1979.

Vietnam announced in 1987 reforms aimed at reducing central control of the economy. The U.S. ended, Feb. 1994, a 19-year embargo on trade with Vietnam. The U.S. extended full diplomatic recognition to Vietnam July 11, 1995. In Aug. 2012, the U.S. began cleaning up the herbicide Agent Orange, used to clear forests during the Vietnam War. Apparently to counter China's growing power in the South China Sea region, the U.S. lifted in 2016 its embargo on lethal arms sales to Vietnam. In Mar. 2018, the USS *Carl Vinson* became the first American aircraft carrier to visit Vietnam since the end of the Vietnam War.

Yemen
Republic of Yemen

People: Population: 28,667,230 (48). **Age distrib.:** <15: 39.2%; 65+: 2.8%. **Growth:** 2.2%. **Migrants:** 1.4%. **Pop. density:** 140.6 per sq mi, 54.3 per sq km. **Urban:** 36.6%. **Ethnic groups:** predom. Arab; also Afro-Arab, South Asian, European. **Languages:** Arabic (official). **Religions:** Muslim 99.1% (official; Sunni 65%, Shia 35%).

Geography: Total area: 203,850 sq mi, 527,968 sq km (49); **Land area:** 203,850 sq mi, 527,968 sq km. **Location:** Middle East, on S coast of the Arabian Peninsula. Saudi Arabia on N, Oman on E. **Topography:** Sandy coastal strip; well-watered fertile mountains in interior. **Arable land:** 2.4%. **Capital:** Sanaa, 2,779,317.

Government: Type: In transition. **Head of state:** Pres. Abd Rabbuh Mansur Hadi; b. 1950; in office: Feb. 25, 2012. **Head of govt.:** Prime Min. Maeen Abdulmalik Saeed; in office: Oct. 15, 2018. **Local divisions:** 22 governorates. **Defense budget:** NA. **Active troops:** 10,000-20,000. (20,000 insurgent forces in territory where govt. does not exercise effective control.)

Economy: Industries: crude oil prod. and petroleum refining, small-scale prod. of cotton textiles and leather goods, food proc., handicrafts, aluminum prods. **Chief agric.:** grains, fruits, vegetables, pulses, khat, coffee, cotton; dairy prods., livestock, poultry; fish. **Natural resources:** petroleum; fish; rock salt; marble; small deposits of coal, gold, lead, nickel, copper. **Water:** 78 cu m per capita. **Crude oil reserves:** 3 bil bbls. **Electricity prod.:** 5 bil kWh. **Labor force:** Most people employed in agric. and herding; services, constr., industry, and commerce account for less than one-fourth of labor force. **Unemployment:** 14%.

Finance: Monetary unit: Rial (YER) (250.29 = $1 U.S.). **GDP:** $38.6 bil; **per capita GDP:** $1,300; **GDP growth:** –13.8%. **Imports:** $4.6 bil; UAE 12.2%, China 12.1%, Turkey 8.7%, Brazil 7.3%, Saudi Arabia 6.5%, Argentina 5.5%. **Exports:** $501.2 mil; Egypt 29.4%, Thailand 16.7%, Belarus 13.5%, Oman 10.5%, UAE 6.5%, Saudi Arabia 5%. **Tourism** (2015): $100 mil. **Budget:** $5.2 bil. **Inflation** (2013-14): 8.1%.

Transport: Motor vehicles: 30.5 per 1,000 pop. **Airports:** 17.

Communications: Telephone (2016): 4.2 per 100 pop. **Mobile** (2016): 59.6 per 100 pop. **Broadband:** NA. **Internet:** 24.6%.

Health: Expend.: 6%. **Life expect.:** 64.0 male; 68.5 female. **Births:** 27.6 per 1,000 pop. **Deaths:** 5.9 per 1,000 pop. **Infant mortality:** 44.6 per 1,000 live births. **Undernourished:** 34.4%. **HIV:** NA.

Education: Compulsory: ages 6-14. **Literacy:** 70.1%.
Embassy: 2319 Wyoming Ave. NW 20008; 965-4760.
Website: www.yemen.gov.ye or www.yemenembassy.org

Yemen's territory once was part of the ancient biblical Kingdom of Sheba, or Saba. Yemen became independent in 1918, after centuries of Ottoman Turkish rule.

Imam Yahya ibn Muhammad ruled, 1904-48, and after his assassination was succeeded by his son, Imam Ahmed, 1948-62. Army officers headed by Brig. Gen. Abdullah al-Salal declared the country the Yemen Arab Republic, Sept. 1962. Ahmed's heir, the Imam Mohamad al-Badr, fled to the mountains where tribesmen joined royalist forces, aided by the Saudi monarchy. Fighting between royalists and republicans killed about 150,000 people until hostilities ended in 1970.

South Yemen, formed from the British colony of Aden and the British protectorate of South Arabia, became independent Nov. 1967. A Marxist state and a Soviet ally, it took the name People's Democratic Republic of Yemen in 1970. More than 300,000 Yemenis fled from the S to the N after independence, contributing to two decades of hostility between the two states.

The two countries were formally united May 21, 1990, but regional clan-based rivalries led to full-scale civil war in 1994. Secessionists declared a breakaway state in South Yemen, May 21, 1994, but northern troops captured the former southern capital of Aden in July.

While on a refueling stop in Aden, Oct. 12, 2000, the destroyer USS *Cole* was bombed, killing 17 Americans; the U.S. blamed the attack on al-Qaeda terrorists.

Clashes beginning in June 2004 between Yemeni government forces and Shiite rebels led by an anti-U.S. cleric, Hussein al-Houthi, left more than 200 people dead. The government announced Sept. 10 that Yemeni troops had killed al-Houthi.

During 2007-10, Shiite rebels in the northwest, secessionists in the south, Sunni militants in the east affiliated with al-Qaeda in the Arabian Peninsula (AQAP), and pirates in coastal waters challenged Yemeni government authority. In 2011, Arab Spring demonstrators demanded Pres. Ali Abdullah Saleh's resignation. Saleh was severely wounded June 3 in a rocket attack. Vice Pres. Abd Rabbuh Mansur Hadi became acting president. Anwar al-Awlaki, a U.S. citizen and radical Muslim cleric linked to several plots against the U.S., was killed Sept. 30, 2011, by a U.S. missile in northern Yemen. Hadi won an uncontested Feb. 2012 election but failed to stabilize the country.

Shiite rebels known as Houthis took over Sanaa in Sept. 2014 and gained control of much of western Yemen. A coalition of Sunni nations led by Saudi Arabia, which backed Hadi, began, Mar. 25, 2015, airstrikes against Houthi fighters and Houthi-controlled areas. The U.S. provided weaponry and logistical support. UAE ground troops aided pro-Hadi forces combating Houthi rebels. Airstrikes (including bombings of hospitals, markets, and schoolchildren) and other fighting caused high civilian casualties. A coalition offensive began in June 2018 against the strategic Houthi-controlled port of Hodeidah. Houthi rebels were aided by Iran and joined for a time by Yemeni military units loyal to Saleh; after a split in the Houthi-Saleh alliance, Houthi forces reportedly killed Saleh, Dec. 4, 2017. AQAP seized control of parts of southern Yemen. U.S. special operations troops aided the fight against AQAP; ongoing U.S. airstrikes against AQAP intensified beginning in 2017. The Sunni extremist group ISIS staged terrorist bombings and other attacks, 2015-18. Houthi forces fired missiles into Saudi Arabia. By 2018, perhaps tens of thousands had died in Yemen's civil war since Mar. 2015. As of Aug. 2018, more than 2 mil people were internally displaced. About 178,000 Yemenis were refugees in nearby countries. More than 22 mil people needed humanitarian assistance. A cholera epidemic that began in late 2016 had caused almost 1.2 mil cases and more than 2,500 deaths by Aug. 2018.

Zambia
Republic of Zambia

People: Population: 16,445,079 (70). **Age distrib.:** <15: 45.9%; 65+: 2.3%. **Growth:** 2.9%. **Migrants:** 0.9%. **Pop. density:** 57.3 per sq mi, 22.1 per sq km. **Urban:** 43.5%. **Ethnic groups:** Bemba 21%, Tonga 13.6%, Chewa 7.4%, Lozi 5.7%, Nsenga 5.3%, Tumbuka 4.4%, Ngoni 4%, Lala 3.1%, Kaonde 2.9%, Namwanga 2.8%, Lunda (northwestern) 2.6%, Mambwe 2.5%, Luvale 2.2%, Lamba 2.1%. **Languages:** Bantu langs. (incl. Bemba, Nyanja, Tonga, Lozi, Chewa, Nsenga, Tumbuka); English (official). **Religions:** Protestant 75.3%, Roman Catholic 20.2%.
Geography: Total area: 290,587 sq mi, 752,618 sq km (38); **Land area:** 287,028 sq mi, 743,398 sq km. **Location:** S central Africa. Dem. Rep. of the Congo on N; Tanzania, Malawi, Mozambique on E; Zimbabwe, Namibia on S; Angola on W. **Topography:** Mostly high plateau with thick forests, drained by several important rivers, including the Zambezi. **Arable land:** 5.1%. **Capital:** Lusaka, 2,523,844. Proposal to move the capital to Ngabwe was announced in 2017.
Government: Type: Presidential republic. **Head of state and govt.:** Pres. Edgar Lungu; b. 1956; in office: Jan. 25, 2015. **Local divisions:** 10 provinces. **Defense budget:** $337 mil. **Active troops:** 15,100.
Economy: Industries: copper mining and proc., emerald mining, constr., foodstuffs, beverages, chemicals, textiles, fertilizer, horticulture. **Chief agric.:** corn, sorghum, rice, peanuts, sunflower seeds, vegetables, flowers, tobacco, cotton, sugarcane, cassava, coffee; cattle, goats, pigs, poultry, milk, eggs, hides. **Natural resources:** copper, cobalt, zinc, lead, coal, emeralds, gold, silver, uranium, hydropower. **Water:** 6,464 cu m per capita. **Electricity prod.:** 13.3 bil kWh. **Labor force:** agric. 53.3%, industry 11.9%, services 34.8%. **Unemployment:** 7.8%.
Finance: Monetary unit: Kwacha (ZMW) (10.34 = $1 U.S.). **GDP:** $68.9 bil; **per capita GDP:** $4,000; **GDP growth:** 3.6%. **Imports:** $7.3 bil; South Africa 28.2%, Dem. Rep. of the Congo 20.8%, China 12.9%, Kuwait 5.4%. **Exports:** $8.1 bil; Switzerland 44.8%, China 16.1%, Dem. Rep. of the Congo 6.2%, Singapore 6%, South Africa 5.9%. **Tourism:** $683 mil. **Budget:** $7.1 bil. **Inflation:** 6.6%.
Transport: Railways: 1,942 mi (incl. 1,156 mi of Tanzania-Zambia Railway Authority). **Motor vehicles:** 22.8 per 1,000 pop. **Airports:** 8.
Communications: Telephone: 0.6 per 100 pop. **Mobile:** 78.6 per 100 pop. **Broadband:** 32.2 per 100 pop. **Internet:** 25.5%.
Health: Expend.: 5.4%. **Life expect.:** 51.4 male; 54.7 female. **Births:** 41.1 per 1,000 pop. **Deaths:** 12.0 per 1,000 pop. **Infant mortality:** 59.3 per 1,000 live births. **Undernourished:** 44.5%. **HIV:** 11.5%.
Education: Compulsory: ages 7-13. **Literacy:** 63.4%.
Embassy: 2200 R St. NW 20008; 234-4009.
Website: www.parliament.gov.zm
Ruled by the British as Northern Rhodesia, the country became the independent republic of Zambia within the Commonwealth Oct. 24, 1964. Independence leader Kenneth Kaunda governed as president, 1964-91. A Zambian government corporation in 1970 took over 51% of two foreign-owned copper-mining companies. Privately held land and other enterprises were nationalized in 1975. In the 1980s and 1990s, lowered copper prices hurt the economy and severe drought caused famine.

Oct. 1991 elections brought an end to Kaunda's one-party rule. The new government sought to sell state enterprises, including the copper industry. Pres. Frederick Chiluba won reelection Nov. 1996. In 2001, Chiluba endorsed Levy Patrick Mwanawasa, who won a disputed Dec. election. Food shortages threatened more than 2 mil Zambians in 2002. Mwanawasa won a second term in 2006. Accused of embezzling state funds as president, Chiluba was ordered by a British court—but refused—to pay $58 mil, June 2007.

Pres. Mwanawasa died Aug. 19, 2008. Vice Pres. Rupiah Banda became acting pres. He narrowly won the presidency in the Oct. 2008 election but lost to opposition leader Michael Sata Sept. 2011. Sata died in office, Oct. 28, 2014. Edgar Lungu of Sata's Patriotic Front party narrowly won a Jan. 2015 special election. Lungu narrowly won a new term in Aug. 11, 2016, elections that his main opponent claimed were marred by fraud. Lungu invoked emergency powers for 3 months, beginning in July 2017, after blaming opposition parties for a series of arson fires. Several European countries suspended aid payments, Sept. 2018, after allegations of government corruption and embezzlement of aid money.

The country has made progress in treating HIV/AIDS, but the disease afflicted 1.1 mil Zambians as of 2017.

Zimbabwe
Republic of Zimbabwe

People: Population: 14,030,368 (73). **Age distrib.:** <15: 38.6%; 65+: 4.5%. **Growth:** 1.7%. **Migrants:** 2.4%. **Pop. density:** 93.9 per sq mi, 36.3 per sq km. **Urban:** 32.2%. **Ethnic groups:** African (predom. Shona; Ndebele is second-largest ethnic group) 99.4%. **Languages:** Shona, Ndebele (both official and most widely spoken); English (official, used in business), 13 official minority langs. **Religions:** Protestant 74.8% (incl. Apostolic 37.5%, Pentecostal 21.8), Roman Catholic 7.3%, none 10.5%.
Geography: Total area: 150,872 sq mi, 390,757 sq km (60); **Land area:** 149,362 sq mi, 386,847 sq km. **Location:** Southern Africa. Zambia on N, Botswana on W, South Africa on S, Mozambique on E. **Topography:** High plateau rising to mountains on E border, sloping down on other borders. **Arable land:** 10.3%. **Capital:** Harare, 1,515,016.
Government: Type: Semi-presidential republic. **Head of state and govt.:** Pres. Emmerson Mnangagwa; b. 1942; in office: Nov. 24, 2017. **Local divisions:** 8 provinces, 2 cities with provincial status. **Defense budget:** $341 mil. **Active troops:** 29,000.
Economy: Industries: mining, steel, wood prods., cement, chemicals, fertilizer, clothing and footwear, foodstuffs, beverages. **Chief agric.:** tobacco, corn, cotton, wheat, coffee, sugarcane, peanuts; sheep, goats, pigs. **Natural resources:** coal, chromium ore, asbestos, gold, nickel, copper, iron ore, vanadium, lithium, tin, platinum group metals. **Water:** 1,282 cu m per capita. **Electricity prod.:** 9.4 bil kWh. **Labor force:** agric. 68.5%, industry 7.4%, services 24.1%. **Unemployment:** 5%.
Finance: Monetary unit: Dollar (ZWD) (361.90 = $1 U.S.). **GDP:** $34 bil; **per capita GDP:** $2,300; **GDP growth:** 3%. **Imports:** $5.6 bil; South Africa 47.8%, Zambia 20.5%. **Exports:** $3.8 bil; South Africa 50.3%, Mozambique 22.5%, UAE 9.8%. **Tourism:** $890 mil. **Budget:** $4.8 bil. **Inflation:** 0.9%.
Transport: Railways: 2,129 mi. **Motor vehicles:** 46.1 per 1,000 pop. **Airports:** 17.
Communications: Telephone: 1.6 per 100 pop. **Mobile:** 85.3 per 100 pop. **Broadband:** 38.1 per 100 pop. **Internet:** 23.1%.
Health: Expend.: 10.3%. **Life expect.:** 59.0 male; 63.2 female. **Births:** 34.0 per 1,000 pop. **Deaths:** 9.9 per 1,000 pop. **Infant mortality:** 31.9 per 1,000 live births. **Undernourished:** 46.6%. **HIV:** 13.3%.
Education: Compulsory: ages 6-12. **Literacy:** 86.5%.
Embassy: 1608 New Hampshire Ave. NW 20009; 332-7100.
Website: www.zim.gov.zw
Britain took over the area as Southern Rhodesia in 1923 from the British South Africa Co. (which, under Cecil Rhodes, had conquered it by 1897) and granted internal self-government. A 1961 constitution restricted voting to keep whites in power.

On Nov. 11, 1965, Prime Min. Ian D. Smith unilaterally declared independence. Britain termed the act illegal and demanded that the country (known as Rhodesia until 1980) enfranchise the black African majority. The UN imposed sanctions and, in May 1968, a trade embargo, as black nationalists launched guerrilla attacks.

After the country held its first universal-franchise election, Apr. 21, 1979, all parties accepted a cease-fire, Dec. 5. The country changed its name to Zimbabwe upon independence, Apr. 18, 1980. Robert Mugabe, the nation's first prime min., became executive president in 1987.

From the late 1990s, Mugabe's rule became increasingly repressive. A land redistribution campaign triggered violent attacks in Apr. 2000 against some white farmers. Whites made up less than 1% of the population but had held 70% of the land. Production of corn, the nation's food staple, subsequently declined sharply. Mugabe, relying on fraud and intimidation, won the Mar. 9-11, 2002, presidential election. During 2006-08, inflation soared to a yearly rate of more than 100,000%.

Mugabe clung to power after a widely discredited 2008 presidential election. Opposition groups, Jan. 18, 2013, condemned an increasing crackdown on Mugabe's critics. In the July 31, 2013, presidential election, Mugabe was once again declared the winner.

Drought caused food shortages in 2016. Police cracked down on strikes and demonstrations protesting deteriorating economic conditions. Mugabe lost the support of the military and his ZANU-PF party after dismissing Vice Pres. Emmerson Mnangagwa, Nov. 6, 2017, apparently to pave the way for Mugabe's wife to succeed him. Mugabe resigned under pressure, Nov. 21, and Mnangagwa became president, Nov. 24. Mnangagwa narrowly won the July 30, 2018, presidential election; the outcome was disputed by the opposition but upheld, Aug. 24, by the Constitutional Court.

SENIOR MOMENTS: MEMORABLE ACHIEVEMENTS BY AGING ATHLETES

In 2018, 42-year-old golfer Tiger Woods won his first tournament in five years, and 36-year-old Serena Williams made a stunning run to two Grand Slam singles finals within 13 months of a difficult childbirth. These two performances called to mind other athletic feats that prove age is just a number. Here are some of the greatest ever.

Auto Racing: Al Unser Sr.

Al Unser was initially left off the Penske team's slate for the 1987 Indianapolis 500. But when Danny Ongais crashed into the wall during the first week of practice, Unser took his place on the Penske team. He started in 20th position, and steadily worked his way through the pack before taking the lead in the 183rd lap when Roberto Guerrero stalled during a pit stop. Unser held off Guerrero to win his fourth Indy 500, tying A.J. Foyt for most Brickyard wins. Just five days shy of his 48th birthday, Unser became the oldest winner ever, surpassing the record set six years earlier by his older brother Bobby.

Baseball: Barry Bonds and Nolan Ryan

Barry Bonds never hit more than 46 season home runs before the age of 35, then—beginning at age 36—he turned in seasons of 49, 73 (all-time MLB record), 46, 45, and 45. At 43 years old and in his final season, he led MLB in walks (132) and on-base-percentage (.480). Widespread allegations of performance-enhancing drug use cast aspersions over Bonds's later achievements, but not so those of Nolan Ryan. The all-time MLB strikeouts leader started his career slowly but grew more dominant. Playing with the Texas Rangers in 1989, he struck out 301 batters and was an All-Star at age 42. Ryan threw his record sixth and seventh no-hitters at ages 43 and 44 in 1990 and 1991.

Honorable Mention: Negro Leagues pitching legend Satchel Paige made his MLB debut in 1948 at age 42 for Cleveland, which won the World Series that year. He retired five years later as a two-time All-Star with a 3.29 MLB-career ERA. Over 10 years later, in 1965, Paige made a one-night appearance with the Athletics, pitching three shutout innings. At 59, he was the oldest MLB player ever.

Basketball: Kareem Abdul-Jabbar

Kevin Willis was the oldest player to appear in more than one NBA game in a season, before retiring in 2007 at 44, and 43-year-old Robert Parish was the oldest to win an NBA title, in 1997. But they're all hangers-on compared to Kareem Abdul-Jabbar, who was an All-Star for the 18th time at age 40 (averaging 14.6 points per game) and for a 19th time a year later. Perhaps Abdul-Jabbar's most impressive season was 1984-85. The storied center averaged 22 points per game in the regular season and, at age 38, heated up even more in the NBA Finals as the Lakers faced their then-archrival Boston Celtics. Abdul-Jabbar was named the Finals MVP with 25.7 points and 9.0 rebounds per game.

Boxing: George Foreman

Twenty years after he lost the heavyweight championship to Muhammad Ali in the "Rumble in the Jungle" in then-Zaire in 1974, George Foreman made the unlikeliest of comebacks. Foreman challenged WBA and IBF heavyweight champion Michael Moorer in 1994. Foreman lost seven of the first nine rounds of what looked like a one-sided fight, then stunned the 26-year-old with a 10th-round knockout blow. The victory made Foreman, 45, the oldest heavyweight champion ever.

Honorable Mention: Bernard Hopkins captured the light heavyweight title at age 46 in 2011, becoming the oldest champ at any weight class. He broke that record two years later at 48 and continued fighting until he was 51.

Football: Tom Brady

Peyton Manning is the oldest quarterback to win a Super Bowl, taking home a ring from the Broncos victory in a defense-won Super Bowl 50 just six weeks before his 40th birthday in 2016. But Tom Brady claimed a comeback victory in Super Bowl LI at the age of 39 and was named the game's MVP. The following year, 40-year-old Brady threw for a Super Bowl-record 505 yards, though the Patriots lost.

Honorable Mention: George Blanda is the oldest man ever to play in an NFL game. The longtime quarterback for the Chicago Bears and Houston Oilers extended his career as a kicker for the Oakland Raiders and even kicked a 41-yard field goal in his last game ever, the 1975 AFC Championship, at the age of 48.

Golf: Jack Nicklaus

At an age when most golfers start thinking about whether to play the Senior Tour, Jack Nicklaus had a renaissance. Already regarded by many as the greatest golfer the game had ever seen, Nicklaus, at age 46, came out of nowhere on the final day to win the 1986 Masters, shooting a 9-under-par 65 to leapfrog eight other golfers on his way to a record sixth green jacket.

Honorable Mention: Julius Boros won the PGA Championship in 1968 at age 48. It was the third and last major championship for Boros after he turned pro in 1950.

Hockey: Gordie Howe

"Mr. Hockey" was a fixture of the sport for 33 seasons spanning five decades, 26 of them in the NHL. Though a wrist injury forced Gordie Howe into retirement in 1971 at the age of 43 after 25 seasons with the Detroit Red Wings, he returned to competition in 1973 with the upstart World Hockey Association. Playing alongside his sons Mark and Marty, Howe led the Houston Aeros to consecutive league championships and won the league's 1974 MVP award at the age of 46. Howe played one final NHL season in 1979-80 (after the NHL and WHA merged), during which he scored 15 goals in 80 games and celebrated his 52nd birthday.

Honorable Mention: Chris Chelios is the oldest player to win a Stanley Cup, at age 46, and remained in the NHL until the age of 48.

Olympic Games: Dara Torres

There's no shortage of ways to define oldest in the Olympic category, giving several nontraditional athletes a claim to fame. Sweden's Oscar Swahn is the oldest to win a gold medal (in shooting, in 1912, at age 64) and the oldest to win a medal of any kind (a silver in the running deer double-shot team event) eight years later at age 72. But American swimmer Dara Torres's accomplishments are even more age-limit defying. Torres won her first Olympic gold in Los Angeles as a 17-year-old in 1984 in the 4x100-meter freestyle relay, and her second eight years later in Barcelona. Eight years after that, in 2000, she won two gold and three bronze medals in Sydney and then retired. But Torres came out of retirement for the 2008 Games, and at age 41, as the oldest female swimmer in Olympic history, she won silver medals in the 50-meter freestyle and two relays.

Soccer: Dino Zoff

Dino Zoff became Italy's starting netminder in the 1974 World Cup but fared poorly as the team was eliminated in the first round. Eight years later, 40-year-old Zoff was captain of the 1982 Italian national team that defeated West Germany, 3-1, to win the World Cup. He was the oldest man to win the World Cup and to be awarded the Golden Glove (best goalkeeper of the tournament).

Honorable Mention: In 2018 Egypt's 45-year-old goalkeeper Essam El-Hadry set a new record for the oldest World Cup participant, but Egypt failed to win a single group stage game and was easily eliminated.

Tennis: Martina Navratilova

Martina Navratilova was a month shy of 50 when she and 28-year-old Bob Bryan won the 2006 Mixed Doubles Championship at the U.S. Open. It was the capper on a career that spanned decades since she won her first pro singles tournament at the age of 17 in 1974. In all, Navratilova won 18 Grand Slam singles titles, 31 doubles championships, and 10 mixed double crowns. She was especially invulnerable at Wimbledon, where she took home every singles championship in 1982-87.

Thoroughbred Racing: Mike Smith

At age 52, Mike Smith became the oldest jockey to win the Triple Crown of the Kentucky Derby, Preakness Stakes, and Belmont Stakes, riding Justify to first-place finishes in all three races in 2018. He was also the oldest ever Preakness and Belmont winner.

Honorable Mention: Bill Shoemaker is the oldest jockey to win any Triple Crown race, capturing his fourth Kentucky Derby (and 11th Triple Crown race overall) in 1986 at the age of 54, aboard 18-1 shot Ferdinand.

OLYMPIC GAMES

General Olympic Information

The modern Olympic Games, first held in Athens, Greece, in 1896, were the result of efforts by Baron Pierre de Coubertin, a French educator, to promote interest in education and culture and to foster better international understanding through love of athletics. His inspiration was the ancient Greek Olympic Games, most notable of the four Panhellenic celebrations. The games were combined patriotic, religious, and athletic festivals held every four years. The first such recorded festival was held in 776 BCE, when the Greeks began to keep their calendar by "Olympiads," or four-year spans between the games.

Coubertin enlisted 14 nations to send athletes to the first modern Olympics. Now athletes from more than 200 nations and territories compete in the Summer Olympics. The Winter Olympic Games, started in 1924, draw competitors from about 90 countries and territories.

Symbol: Five rings or circles, linked to represent the sporting friendship of all peoples. They also symbolize five geographic areas—Africa, America, Asia, Australia, and Europe. Each ring is a different color—blue, yellow, black, green, and red—which, with the color white, represent the colors of the world's flags.

Flag: The five-ring symbol on a plain white background.

Creed: "The most important thing in the Olympic Games is not to win but to take part, just as the most important thing in life is not the triumph but the struggle. The essential thing is not to have conquered but to have fought well."

Motto: Citius, Altius, Fortius. ("Faster, higher, stronger" in Latin)

Oath: "In the name of all the competitors I promise that we shall take part in these Olympic Games, respecting and abiding by the rules which govern them, committing ourselves to a sport without doping and without drugs, in the true spirit of sportsmanship, for the glory of sport and the honor of our teams."

Flame: The modern version of the flame was adopted in 1936. The torch used to kindle it is first lit by the sun's rays in Olympia, Greece, then carried to the site of the Games by relays of runners. Ships and planes are used when necessary.

Winter Olympic Games Sites, 1924-2022

1924	Chamonix, France	1956	Cortina d'Ampezzo, Italy	1980	Lake Placid, NY, U.S.	2006	Turin, Italy
1928	St. Moritz, Switzerland			1984	Sarajevo, Yugoslavia	2010	Vancouver, BC, Canada
1932	Lake Placid, NY, U.S.	1960	Squaw Valley, CA, U.S.	1988	Calgary, AB, Canada		
1936	Garmisch-Partenkirchen, Germany	1964	Innsbruck, Austria	1992	Albertville, France	2014	Sochi, Russia
		1968	Grenoble, France	1994	Lillehammer, Norway	2018	Pyeongchang, South Korea
1948	St. Moritz, Switzerland	1972	Sapporo, Japan	1998	Nagano, Japan		
1952	Oslo, Norway	1976	Innsbruck, Austria	2002	Salt Lake City, UT, U.S.	2022	Beijing, China

Summer Olympic Games Sites, 1896-2028

1896	Athens, Greece	1928	Amsterdam, Netherlands	1968	Mexico City, Mexico	2000	Sydney, Australia
1900	Paris, France	1932	Los Angeles, CA, U.S.	1972	Munich, W. Germany	2004	Athens, Greece
1904	St. Louis, MO, U.S.	1936	Berlin, Germany	1976	Montreal, QC, Canada	2008	Beijing, China
1906	Athens, Greece*	1948	London, England, UK	1980	Moscow, USSR	2012	London, England, UK
1908	London, England, UK	1952	Helsinki, Finland	1984	Los Angeles, CA, U.S.	2016	Rio de Janeiro, Brazil
1912	Stockholm, Sweden	1956	Melbourne, Australia	1988	Seoul, South Korea	2020	Tokyo, Japan
1920	Antwerp, Belgium	1960	Rome, Italy	1992	Barcelona, Spain	2024	Paris, France
1924	Paris, France	1964	Tokyo, Japan	1996	Atlanta, GA, U.S.	2028	Los Angeles, CA, U.S.

* = Games not recognized by International Olympic Committee. **Note:** Games VI (1916), XII (1940), and XIII (1944) were not celebrated.

2018 Winter Olympic Games

Pyeongchang, South Korea, Feb. 9-25, 2018

Nearly 3,000 (2,963) athletes representing 92 nations met in Pyeongchang, South Korea, to compete in a record 102 events in 15 sports during the XXIII Olympic Winter Games Feb. 9-25, 2018. South Korea was hosting the Games for the first time since 1988, when the Summer Olympics were held in Seoul. Norway won 39 medals, including 14 gold, to top the final medal count, followed by Germany (31), Canada (29), and the U.S. (23).

Host country South Korea and estranged neighbor North Korea agreed in Jan. 2018 to march together under a unified flag in the opening ceremony and to field a unified women's hockey team. The Intl. Olympic Committee barred Russia from competition due to a state-sponsored doping scandal; Russian athletes granted exemptions by the IOC were allowed to compete under the designation Olympic Athlete(s) from Russia (OAR).

Japanese superstar Yuzuru Hanyu became the first man to win back-to-back singles figure skating gold medals since 1952. OAR teammates Alina Zagitova and Evgenia Medvedeva claimed gold and silver, respectively, in the women's figure skating competition. Czech star Ester Ledecká became the first woman ever to win a gold medal in two different sports at a single Winter Games, claiming the top prize in both the Alpine super-G and snowboarding's parallel giant slalom.

Veteran U.S. snowboarder Shaun White won gold in the men's halfpipe for the third time in his four Olympic appearances, while 17-year-old American rookie Chloe Kim claimed gold in the women's halfpipe event. The U.S. women's hockey team beat Canada in dramatic fashion to claim their first gold medal in the sport since the event began in 1998. U.S. Alpine skiing legend Lindsey Vonn, seeking a comeback after missing the Sochi games due to injury, settled for a bronze medal in downhill; teammate Mikaela Shiffrin claimed gold and silver in the giant slalom and Alpine combined events, respectively. The U.S. men's curling team won gold for the first time since competition officially began in that sport in 1998.

The following six new medal events were introduced in 2018: Alpine skiing team, curling mixed doubles, snowboarding men's/women's big air, and speed skating men's/women's mass start. Two events from the 2014 Games in Sochi, snowboarding men's/women's parallel slalom, were eliminated.

2018 Winter Olympic Games: Final Medal Standings

Country	G	S	B	T	Country	G	S	B	T	Country	G	S	B	T
Norway	14	14	11	39	Austria	5	3	6	14	Poland	1	0	1	2
Germany	14	10	7	31	Japan	4	5	4	13	Slovenia	0	1	1	2
Canada	11	8	10	29	Italy	3	2	5	10	New Zealand	0	0	2	2
United States	9	8	6	23	China	1	6	2	9	Spain	0	0	2	2
Netherlands	8	6	6	20	Czech Republic	2	2	3	7	Hungary	1	0	0	1
South Korea	5	8	4	17	Finland	1	1	4	6	Ukraine	1	0	0	1
OAR	2	6	9	17	Great Britain	1	0	4	5	Belgium	0	1	0	1
Switzerland	5	6	4	15	Belarus	2	1	0	3	Kazakhstan	0	0	1	1
France	5	4	6	15	Slovakia	1	2	0	3	Latvia	0	0	1	1
Sweden	7	6	1	14	Australia	0	2	1	3	Liechtenstein	0	0	1	1

OAR = Olympic Athletes from Russia.

2018 Winter Olympics: Medal Winners

In 2018, Russian athletes competed under the designation Olympic Athlete(s) from Russia (OAR); Russia was banned from competition due to a state-sponsored doping scandal.
(G = Gold, S = Silver, B = Bronze)

Alpine Skiing

Team: G–Switzerland; S–Austria; B–Norway.

Men

Combined: G–Marcel Hirscher, Austria; S–Alexis Pinturault, France; B–Victor Muffat-Jeandet, France.

Downhill: G–Aksel Lund Svindal, Norway; S–Kjetil Jansrud, Norway; B–Beat Feuz, Switzerland.

Giant Slalom: G–Marcel Hirscher, Austria; S–Henrik Kristoffersen, Norway; B–Alexis Pinturault, France.

Slalom: G–Andre Myhrer, Sweden; S–Ramon Zenhäusern, Switzerland; B–Michael Matt, Austria.

Super-G: G–Matthias Mayer, Austria; S–Beat Feuz, Switzerland; B–Kjetil Jansrud, Norway.

Women

Combined: G–Michelle Gisin, Switzerland; S–Mikaela Shiffrin, U.S.; B–Wendy Holdener, Switzerland.

Downhill: G–Sofia Goggia, Italy; S–Ragnhild Mowinckel, Norway; B–Lindsey Vonn, U.S.

Giant Slalom: G–Mikaela Shiffrin, U.S.; S–Ragnhild Mowinckel, Norway; B–Federica Brignone, Italy.

Slalom: G–Frida Hansdotter, Sweden; S–Wendy Holdener, Switzerland; B–Katharina Gallhuber, Austria.

Super-G: G–Ester Ledecká, Czech Republic; S–Anna Veith, Austria; B–Tina Weirather, Liechtenstein.

Biathlon

Mixed Relay (2x6-km Women and 2x7.5-km Men): G–France (Dorin-Habert, Bescond, Desthieux, Fourcade); S–Norway (Olsbu, Eckhoff, Boe, Svendsen); B–Italy (Vittozzi, Wierer, Hofer, Windisch).

Men

10-km Sprint: G–Arnd Peiffer, Germany; S–Michal Krcmar, Czech Republic; B–Dominik Windisch, Italy.

12.5-km Pursuit: G–Martin Fourcade, France; S–Sebastian Samuelsson, Sweden; B–Benedikt Doll, Germany.

15-km Mass Start: G–Martin Fourcade, France; S–Simon Schempp, Germany; B–Emil Hegle Svendsen, Norway.

20-km Individual: G–Johannes Thingnes Boe, Norway; S–Jakov Fak, Slovenia; B–Dominik Landertinger, Austria.

4x7.5-km Relay: G–Sweden (Femling, Nelin, Samuelsson, Lindström); S–Norway (Birkeland, T. Boe, J. T. Boe, Svendsen); B–Germany (Lesser, Doll, Peiffer, Schempp).

Women

7.5-km Sprint: G–Laura Dahlmeier, Germany; S–Marte Olsbu, Norway; B–Veronika Vitkova, Czech Republic.

10-km Pursuit: G–Laura Dahlmeier, Germany; S–Anastasiya Kuzmina, Slovakia; B–Anaïs Bescond, France.

12.5-km Mass Start: G–Anastasiya Kuzmina, Slovakia; S–Darya Domracheva, Belarus; B–Tiril Eckhoff, Norway.

15-km Individual: G–Hanna Öberg, Sweden; S–Anastasiya Kuzmina, Slovakia; B–Laura Dahlmeier, Germany.

4x6-km Relay: G–Belarus (Skardino, Kryuko, Alimbekava, Domracheva); S–Sweden (Persson, Brorsson, Magnusson, Öberg); B–France (Chevalier, Dorin-Habert, Braisaz, Bescond).

Bobsled

Driver/pilot is listed first in parentheses.

Two-Man: G (tie)–Canada (Kripps, Kopacz) & Germany (Friedrich, Margis); B–Latvia (Melbardis, Strenga).

Four-Man: G–Germany (Friedrich, Bauer, Grothkopp, Margis); S–Germany (Walther, Kuske, Rödiger, Franke); B–S. Korea (Won, Jun, Seo, Kim).

Women: G–Germany (Jamanka, Buckwitz); S–U.S. (Meyers Taylor, Gibbs); B–Canada (Humphries, George).

Cross-Country Skiing

Men

Sprint Classic: G–Johannes Hoesflot Klaebo, Norway; S–Federico Pellegrino, Italy; B–Alexander Bolshunov, OAR.

15-km Free: G–Dario Cologna, Switzerland; S–Simen Hegstad Krüger, Norway; B–Denis Spitsov, OAR.

Skiathlon (15-km Classic + 15-km Free): G–Simen Hegstad Krüger, Norway; S–Martin Johnsrud Sundby, Norway; B–Hans Christer Holund, Norway.

50-km Mass Start Classic: G–Iivo Niskanen, Finland; S–Alexander Bolshunov, OAR; B–Andrey Larkov, OAR.

4x10-km Relay: G–Norway (Toenseth, Sundby, Krüger, Klaebo); S–OAR (Larkov, Bolshunov, Chervotkin, Spitsov); B–France (Gaillard, Manificat, Parisse, Backscheider).

Team Sprint Free: G–Martin Johnsrud Sundby & Johannes Hoesflot Klaebo, Norway; S–Denis Spitsov & Alexander Bolshunov, OAR; B–Maurice Manificat & Richard Jouve, France.

Women

Sprint Classic: G–Stina Nilsson, Sweden; S–Maiken Caspersen Falla, Norway; B–Yulia Belorukova, OAR.

10-km Free: G–Ragnhild Haga, Norway; S–Charlotte Kalla, Sweden; B (tie)–Marit Bjoergen, Norway & Krista Parmakoski, Finland.

Skiathlon (7.5-km Classic + 7.5-km Free): G–Charlotte Kalla, Sweden; S–Marit Bjoergen, Norway; B–Krista Parmakoski, Finland.

30-km Mass Start Classic: G–Marit Bjoergen, Norway; S–Krista Parmakoski, Finland; B–Stina Nilsson, Sweden.

4x5-km Relay: G–Norway (Östberg, Jacobsen, Haga, Bjoergen); S–Sweden (Haag, Kalla, Andersson, Nilsson); B–OAR (Nepryaeva, Belorukova, Sedova, Nechaevskaya).

Team Sprint Free: G–Kikkan Randall & Jessie Diggins, U.S.; S–Charlotte Kalla & Stina Nilsson, Sweden; B–Marit Bjoergen & Maiken Caspersen Falla, Norway.

Curling

Men: G–U.S.; S–Sweden; B–Switzerland.

Women: G–Sweden; S–S. Korea; B–Japan.

Mixed Doubles: G–Canada; S–Switzerland; B–Norway.

Figure Skating

Men: G–Yuzuru Hanyu, Japan; S–Shoma Uno, Japan; B–Javier Fernández, Spain.

Women: G–Alina Zagitova, OAR; S–Yevgenia Medvedeva, OAR; B–Kaetlyn Osmond, Canada.

Ice Dancing: G–Tessa Virtue & Scott Moir, Canada; S–Gabriella Papadakis & Guillaume Cizeron, France; B–Maia Shibutani & Alex Shibutani, U.S.

Pairs: G–Aljona Savchenko & Bruno Massot, Germany; S–Sui Wenjing & Han Cong, China; B–Meagan Duhamel & Eric Radford, Canada.

Team: G–Canada; S–OAR; B–U.S.

Freestyle Skiing

Men

Aerials: G–Oleksandr Abramenko, Ukraine; S–Jia Zongyang, China; B–Ilya Burov, OAR.

Moguls: G–Mikaël Kingsbury, Canada; S–Matt Graham, Australia; B–Daichi Hara, Japan.

Ski Cross: G–Brady Leman, Canada; S–Marc Bischofberger, Switzerland; B–Sergey Ridzik, OAR.

Ski Halfpipe: G–David Wise, U.S.; S–Alex Ferreira, U.S.; B–Nico Porteous, New Zealand.

Ski Slopestyle: G–Oystein Braaten, Norway; S–Nick Goepper, U.S.; B–Alex Beaulieu-Marchand, Canada.

Women

Aerials: G–Hanna Huskova, Belarus; S–Zhang Xin, China; B–Kong Fanyu, China.

Moguls: G–Perrine Laffont, France; S–Justine Dufour-Lapointe, Canada; B–Yulia Galysheva, Kazakhstan.

Ski Cross: G–Kelsey Serwa, Canada; S–Brittany Phelan, Canada; B–Fanny Smith, Switzerland.

Ski Halfpipe: G–Cassie Sharpe, Canada; S–Marie Martinod, France; B–Brita Sigourney, U.S.

Ski Slopestyle: G–Sarah Höfflin, Switzerland; S–Mathilde Gremaud, Switzerland; B–Isabel Atkin, Great Britain.

Ice Hockey

Men: G–OAR; S–Germany; B–Canada.

Women: G–U.S.; S–Canada; B–Finland.

Luge

Men's Singles: G–David Gleirscher, Austria; S–Chris Mazdzer, U.S.; B–Johannes Ludwig, Germany.

Men's Doubles: G–Germany (Wendl, Arlt); S–Austria (Penz, Fischler); B–Germany (Eggert, Benecken).

Women's Singles: G–Natalie Geisenberger, Germany; S–Dajana Eitberger, Germany; B–Alex Gough, Canada.

Mixed Team Relay: G–Germany (Arlt, Geisenberger, Ludwig, Wendl); S–Canada (Edney, Gough, Snith, Walker); B–Austria (Egle, Fischler, Gleirscher, Penz).

Nordic Combined

Large Hill/10 km: G–Johannes Rydzek, Germany; S–Fabian Riessle, Germany; B–Eric Frenzel, Germany.

Normal Hill/10 km: G–Eric Frenzel, Germany; S–Akito Watabe, Japan; B–Lukas Klapfer, Austria.

Team Large Hill/4x5-km Relay: G–Germany (Frenzel, Geiger, Riessle, Rydzek); S–Norway (Graabak, Riiber, Andersen, Schmid); B–Austria (Seidl, Gruber, Klapfer, Denifl).

Skeleton

Men: G–Yun Sung-bin, S. Korea; S–Nikita Tregubov, OAR; B–Dom Parsons, Great Britain.

Women: G–Lizzy Yarnold, Great Britain; S–Jacqueline Lölling, Germany; B–Laura Deas, Great Britain.

Ski Jumping

Men

Large Hill: G–Kamil Stoch, Poland; S–Andreas Wellinger, Germany; B–Robert Johansson, Norway.

Normal Hill: G–Andreas Wellinger, Germany; S–Johann Andre Forfang, Norway; B–Robert Johansson, Norway.

Team Large Hill: G–Norway (Tande, Stjernen, Forfang, Johansson); S–Germany (Geiger, Leyhe, Freitag, Wellinger); B–Poland (Kot, Hula, Kubacki, Stoch).

Women

Normal Hill: G–Maren Lundby, Norway; S–Katharina Althaus, Germany; B–Sara Takanashi, Japan.

Snowboarding

Men

Big Air: G–Sebastien Toutant, Canada; S–Kyle Mack, U.S.; B–Billy Morgan, Great Britain.

Halfpipe: G–Shaun White, U.S.; S–Ayumu Hirano, Japan; B–Scotty James, Australia.

Parallel Giant Slalom: G–Nevin Galmarini, Switzerland; S–Lee Sang-ho, S. Korea; B–Zan Kosir, Slovenia.

Slopestyle: G–Red Gerard, U.S.; S–Max Parrot, Canada; B–Mark McMorris, Canada.

Snowboard Cross: G–Pierre Vaultier, France; S–Jarryd Hughes, Australia; B–Regino Hernández, Spain.

Women

Big Air: G–Anna Gasser, Austria; S–Jamie Anderson, U.S.; B–Zoi Sadowski-Synnott, New Zealand.

Halfpipe: G–Chloe Kim, U.S.; S–Liu Jiayu, China; B–Arielle Gold, U.S.

Parallel Giant Slalom: G–Ester Ledecká, Czech Republic; S–Selina Jörg, Germany; B–Ramona Theresia Hofmeister, Germany.

Slopestyle: G–Jamie Anderson, U.S.; S–Laurie Blouin, Canada; B–Enni Rukajarvi, Finland.

Snowboard Cross: G–Michela Moioli, Italy; S–Julia Pereira de Sousa Mabileau, France; B–Eva Samková, Czech Republic.

Speed Skating

Men

500 m: G–Havard Lorentzen, Norway; S–Cha Min-kyu, S. Korea; B–Gao Tingyu, China.

1000 m: G–Kjeld Nuis, Netherlands; S–Havard Lorentzen, Norway; B–Kim Tae-yun, S. Korea.

1500 m: G–Kjeld Nuis, Netherlands; S–Patrick Roest, Netherlands; B–Kim Min-seok, S. Korea.

5000 m: G–Sven Kramer, Netherlands; S–Ted-Jan Bloemen, Canada; B–Sverre Lunde Pedersen, Norway.

10,000 m: G–Ted-Jan Bloemen, Canada; S–Jorrit Bergsma, Netherlands; B–Nicola Tumolero, Italy.

Mass Start: G–Lee Seung-hoon, S. Korea; S–Bart Swings, Belgium; B–Koen Verweij, Netherlands.

Team Pursuit: G–Norway (Bokko, Henriksen, Nilsen, Pedersen); S–S. Korea (Chung, Kim, Lee); B–Netherlands (Blokhuijsen, Kramer, Roest, Verweij).

Women

500 m: G–Nao Kodaira, Japan; S–Lee Sang-hwa, S. Korea; B–Karolina Erbanova, Czech Republic.

1000 m: G–Jorien ter Mors, Netherlands; S–Nao Kodaira, Japan; B–Miho Takagi, Japan.

1500 m: G–Ireen Wüst, Netherlands; S–Miho Takagi, Japan; B–Marrit Leenstra, Netherlands.

3000 m: G–Carlijn Achtereekte, Netherlands; S–Ireen Wüst, Netherlands; B–Antoinette de Jong, Netherlands.

5000 m: G–Esmee Visser, Netherlands; S–Martina Sáblíková, Czech Republic; B–Natalya Voronina, OAR.

Mass Start: G–Nana Takagi, Japan; S–Kim Bo-reum, S. Korea; B–Irene Schouten, Netherlands.

Team Pursuit: G–Japan (M. Takagi, Kikuchi, Sato, N. Takagi); S–Netherlands (Leenstra, van Beek, Wüst, de Jong); B–U.S. (Bergsma, Bowe, Manganello, Schoutens).

Speed Skating (Short Track)

Men

500 m: G–Wu Dajing, China; S–Hwang Dae-heon, S. Korea; B–Lim Hyo-jun, S. Korea.

1000 m: G–Samuel Girard, Canada; S–John-Henry Krueger, U.S.; B–Seo Yi-ra, S. Korea.

1500 m: G–Lim Hyo-jun, S. Korea; S–Sjinkie Knegt, Netherlands; B–Semion Elistratov, OAR.

5000-m Relay: G–Hungary (Burjan, Knoch, Liu S., Liu S.S.); S–China (Chen, Han, Ren, Wu, Xu); B–Canada (Cournoyer, Dion, Girard, Hamelin).

Women

500 m: G–Arianna Fontana, Italy; S–Yara van Kerkhof, Netherlands; B–Kim Boutin, Canada.

1000 m: G–Suzanne Schulting, Netherlands; S–Kim Boutin, Canada; B–Arianna Fontana, Italy.

1500 m: G–Choi Min-jeong, S. Korea; S–Li Jinyu, China; B–Kim Boutin, Canada.

3000-m Relay: G–S. Korea (Choi, Kim A., Kim Y., Lee, Shim); S–Italy (Fontana, Maffei, Peretti, Valcepina); B–Netherlands (Schulting, ter Mors, van Kerkhof, van Ruijven).

Winter Olympic Games Champions, 1924-2018

East and West Germany competed separately, 1968-88. In 1992, the Unified Team represented the former Soviet republics of Russia, Ukraine, Belarus, Kazakhstan, and Uzbekistan. In 2018, Russian athletes competed under the designation Olympic Athlete(s) from Russia (OAR); Russia was banned from competition due to a state-sponsored doping scandal. Not all sports are listed here, and many events are omitted. Point systems used for scoring have changed many times; those shown are of the point system in use at those Games. Times are shown in hour:minute:sec.

Alpine Skiing

Team

2018	Switzerland, Austria, Norway

Men's Downhill

		Time
1948	Henri Oreiller, France	2:55.0
1952	Zeno Colo, Italy	2:30.8
1956	Toni Sailer, Austria	2:52.2
1960	Jean Vuarnet, France	2:06.0
1964	Egon Zimmermann, Austria	2:18.16
1968	Jean-Claude Killy, France	1:59.85
1972	Bernhard Russi, Switzerland	1:51.43
1976	Franz Klammer, Austria	1:45.73
1980	Leonhard Stock, Austria	1:45.50
1984	Bill Johnson, United States	1:45.49
1988	Pirmin Zurbriggen, Switzerland	1:59.63
1992	Patrick Ortlieb, Austria	1:50.37
1994	Tommy Moe, United States	1:45.75
1998	Jean-Luc Cretier, France	1:50.11
2002	Fritz Strobl, Austria	1:39.13
2006	Antoine Deneriaz, France	1:48.80
2010	Didier Defago, Switzerland	1:54.31
2014	Matthias Mayer, Austria	2:06.23
2018	Aksel Lund Svindal, Norway	1:40.25

Men's Giant Slalom

		Time
1952	Stein Eriksen, Norway	2:25.0
1956	Toni Sailer, Austria	3:00.1
1960	Roger Staub, Switzerland	1:48.3
1964	François Bonlieu, France	1:46.71
1968	Jean-Claude Killy, France	3:29.28
1972	Gustavo Thoeni, Italy	3:09.62
1976	Heini Hemmi, Switzerland	3:26.97
1980	Ingemar Stenmark, Sweden	2:40.74
1984	Max Julen, Switzerland	2:41.18
1988	Alberto Tomba, Italy	2:06.37
1992	Alberto Tomba, Italy	2:06.98
1994	Markus Wasmeier, Germany	2:52.46
1998	Hermann Maier, Austria	2:38.51
2002	Stephan Eberharter, Austria	2:23.28
2006	Benjamin Raich, Austria	2:35.00
2010	Carlo Janka, Switzerland	2:37.83
2014	Ted Ligety, United States	2:45.29
2018	Marcel Hirscher, Austria	2:18.04

Men's Slalom

		Time
1948	Edi Reinalter, Switzerland	2:10.3
1952	Othmar Schneider, Austria	2:00.0
1956	Toni Sailer, Austria	3:14.7
1960	Ernst Hinterseer, Austria	2:08.9
1964	Josef Stiegler, Austria	2:11.13
1968	Jean-Claude Killy, France	1:39.73
1972	Francisco Fernandez-Ochoa, Spain	1:49.27
1976	Piero Gros, Italy	2:03.29
1980	Ingemar Stenmark, Sweden	1:44.26
1984	Phil Mahre, United States	1:39.41
1988	Alberto Tomba, Italy	1:39.47
1992	Finn Christian Jagge, Norway	1:44.39
1994	Thomas Stangassinger, Austria	2:02.02
1998	Hans-Petter Buraas, Norway	1:49.31
2002	Jean-Pierre Vidal, France	1:41.06
2006	Benjamin Raich, Austria	1:43.14
2010	Giuliano Razzoli, Italy	1:39.32
2014	Mario Matt, Austria	1:41.84
2018	Andre Myhrer, Sweden	1:38.99

Men's Combined

		Time
1936	Franz Pfnür, Germany	99.25 (pts.)
1948	Henri Oreiller, France	3.27 (pts.)
1988	Hubert Strolz, Austria	36.55 (pts.)
1992	Josef Polig, Italy	14.58 (pts.)
1994	Lasse Kjus, Norway	3:17.53
1998	Mario Reiter, Austria	3:08.06
2002	Kjetil André Aamodt, Norway	3:17.56
2006	Ted Ligety, United States	3:09.35
2010	Bode Miller, United States	2:44.92
2014	Sandro Viletta, Switzerland	2:45.20
2018	Marcel Hirscher, Austria	2:06.52

Men's Super Giant Slalom

		Time
1988	Franck Piccard, France	1:39.66
1992	Kjetil André Aamodt, Norway	1:13.04

Men's Super Giant Slalom

		Time
1994	Markus Wasmeier, Germany	1:32.53
1998	Hermann Maier, Austria	1:34.82
2002	Kjetil André Aamodt, Norway	1:21.58
2006	Kjetil André Aamodt, Norway	1:30.65
2010	Aksel Lund Svindal, Norway	1:30.34
2014	Kjetil Jansrud, Norway	1:18.14
2018	Matthias Mayer, Austria	1:24.44

Women's Downhill

		Time
1948	Hedi Schlunegger, Switzerland	2:28.3
1952	Trude Beiser-Jochum, Austria	1:47.1
1956	Madeleine Berthod, Switzerland	1:40.7
1960	Heidi Biebl, Germany	1:37.6
1964	Christl Haas, Austria	1:55.39
1968	Olga Pall, Austria	1:40.87
1972	Marie-Theres Nadig, Switzerland	1:36.68
1976	Rosi Mittermaier, W. Germany	1:46.16
1980	Annemarie Moser-Proell, Austria	1:37.52
1984	Michela Figini, Switzerland	1:13.36
1988	Marina Kiehl, W. Germany	1:25.86
1992	Kerrin Lee-Gartner, Canada	1:52.55
1994	Katja Seizinger, Germany	1:35.93
1998	Katja Seizinger, Germany	1:28.89
2002	Carole Montillet, France	1:39.56
2006	Michaela Dorfmeister, Austria	1:56.49
2010	Lindsey Vonn, United States	1:44.19
2014	Tina Maze, Slovenia	1:41.57
	Dominique Gisin, Switzerland (tie)	1:41.57
2018	Sofia Goggia, Italy	1:39.22

Women's Giant Slalom

		Time
1952	Andrea Mead Lawrence, United States	2:06.8
1956	Ossi Reichert, Germany	1:56.5
1960	Yvonne Ruegg, Switzerland	1:39.9
1964	Marielle Goitschel, France	1:52.24
1968	Nancy Greene, Canada	1:51.97
1972	Marie-Theres Nadig, Switzerland	1:29.90
1976	Kathy Kreiner, Canada	1:29.13
1980	Hanni Wenzel, Liechtenstein	2:41.66
1984	Debbie Armstrong, United States	2:20.98
1988	Vreni Schneider, Switzerland	2:06.49
1992	Pernilla Wiberg, Sweden	2:12.74
1994	Deborah Compagnoni, Italy	2:30.97
1998	Deborah Compagnoni, Italy	2:50.59
2002	Janica Kostelic, Croatia	2:30.01
2006	Julia Mancuso, United States	2:09.19
2010	Viktoria Rebensburg, Germany	2:27.11
2014	Tina Maze, Slovenia	2:36.87
2018	Mikaela Shiffrin, United States	2:20.02

Note: Beginning in 1980, the event time combined two runs.

Women's Slalom

		Time
1948	Gretchen Fraser, United States	1:57.2
1952	Andrea Mead Lawrence, United States	2:10.6
1956	Renee Colliard, Switzerland	1:52.3
1960	Anne Heggtveit, Canada	1:49.6
1964	Christine Goitschel, France	1:29.86
1968	Marielle Goitschel, France	1:25.86
1972	Barbara Ann Cochran, United States	1:31.24
1976	Rosi Mittermaier, W. Germany	1:30.54
1980	Hanni Wenzel, Liechtenstein	1:25.09
1984	Paoletta Magoni, Italy	1:36.47
1988	Vreni Schneider, Switzerland	1:36.69
1992	Petra Kronberger, Austria	1:32.68
1994	Vreni Schneider, Switzerland	1:56.01
1998	Hilde Gerg, Germany	1:32.40
2002	Janica Kostelic, Croatia	1:46.10
2006	Anja Paerson, Sweden	1:29.04
2010	Maria Riesch, Germany	1:42.89
2014	Mikaela Shiffrin, United States	1:44.54
2018	Frida Hansdotter, Sweden	1:38.63

Women's Combined

		Time
1936	Christl Cranz, Germany	97.06 (pts.)
1948	Trude Beiser-Jochum, Austria	6.58 (pts.)
1988	Anita Wachter, Austria	29.25 (pts.)
1992	Petra Kronberger, Austria	2.55 (pts.)
1994	Pernilla Wiberg, Sweden	3:05.16
1998	Katja Seizinger, Germany	2:40.74
2002	Janica Kostelic, Croatia	2:43.28

Women's Combined		Time
2006	Janica Kostelic, Croatia.	2:51.08
2010	Maria Riesch, Germany	2:09.14
2014	Maria Hoefl-Riesch, Germany	2:34.62
2018	Michelle Gisin, Switzerland.	2:20.90

Note: In 2010, a one-day super combined event replaced the traditional two-day combined event.

Women's Super Giant Slalom		Time
1988	Sigrid Wolf, Austria.	1:19.03
1992	Deborah Compagnoni, Italy	1:21.22
1994	Diann Roffe (Steinrotter), United States.	1:22.15
1998	Picabo Street, United States	1:18.02
2002	Daniela Ceccarelli, Italy	1:13.59
2006	Michaela Dorfmeister, Austria	1:32.47
2010	Andrea Fischbacher, Austria	1:20.14
2014	Anna Fenninger, Austria.	1:25.52
2018	Ester Ledecká, Czech Republic	1:21.11

Bobsled
(Driver/pilot in parentheses.)

Two-Man Bobsled		Time
1932	United States (Hubert Stevens)	8:14.74
1936	United States (Ivan Brown).	5:29.29
1948	Switzerland (Felix Endrich).	5:29.20
1952	Germany (Andreas Ostler)	5:24.54
1956	Italy (Dalla Costa).	5:30.14
1964	Great Britain (Anthony Nash)	4:21.90
1968	Italy (Eugenio Monti).	4:41.54
1972	W. Germany (Wolfgang Zimmerer)	4:57.07
1976	E. Germany (Meinhard Nehmer)	3:44.42
1980	Switzerland (Erich Schaerer)	4:09.36
1984	E. Germany (Wolfgang Hoppe)	3:25.56
1988	USSR (Janis Kipours).	3:54.19
1992	Switzerland (Gustav Weber).	4:03.26
1994	Switzerland (Gustav Weber).	3:30.81
1998	Canada (Pierre Lueders)	3:37.24
	Italy (Guenther Huber) (tie).	3:37.24
2002	Germany II (Christoph Langen)	3:10.11
2006	Germany (Andre Lange).	3:43.38
2010	Germany (Andre Lange).	3:26.65
2014	Russia (Alexander Zubkov)	3:45.39
2018	Canada (Justin Kripps).	3:16.86
	Germany (Francesco Friedrich) (tie).	3:16.86

Four-Man Bobsled		Time
1924	Switzerland (Eduard Scherrer).	5:45.54
1928	United States (William Fiske) (5-man)	3:20.50
1932	United States (William Fiske)	7:53.68
1936	Switzerland (Pierre Musy)	5:19.85
1948	United States (Francis Tyler)	5:20.10
1952	Germany (Andreas Ostler)	5:07.84
1956	Switzerland (Franz Kapus)	5:10.44
1964	Canada (Victor Emery).	4:14.46
1968	Italy (Eugenio Monti) (2 heats)	2:17.39
1972	Switzerland (Jean Wicki)	4:43.07
1976	E. Germany (Meinhard Nehmer)	3:40.43
1980	E. Germany (Meinhard Nehmer)	3:59.92
1984	E. Germany (Wolfgang Hoppe)	3:20.22
1988	Switzerland (Ekkehard Fasser)	3:47.51
1992	Austria (Ingo Appelt).	3:53.90
1994	Germany (Wolfgang Hoppe).	3:27.28
1998	Germany II (Christoph Langen)	2:39.41
2002	Germany II (Andre Lange)	3:07.51
2006	Germany (Andre Lange)	3:40.42
2010	United States (Steven Holcomb)	3:24.46
2014	Russia (Alexander Zubkov)	3:40.60
2018	Germany (Francesco Friedrich)	3:15.85

Two-Woman Bobsled		Time
2002	United States II (Jill Bakken)	1:37.76
2006	Germany (Sandra Kiriasis).	3:49.98
2010	Canada (Kaillie Humphries)	3:32.28
2014	Canada (Kaillie Humphries)	3:50.61
2018	Germany (Mariama Jamanka)	3:22.45

Cross-Country Skiing

Men's Individual Sprint		Time
2002	Tor Arne Hetland, Norway (1.5 km)	2:56.9
2006	Bjoern Lind, Sweden (1.3 km)	2:26.5
2010	Nikita Kriukov, Russia	3:36.3
2014	Ola Vigen Hattestad, Norway	3:38.39
2018	Johannes Hoesflot Klaebo, Norway	3:05.75

Men's 10 Kilometers		Time
1992	Vegard Ulvang, Norway	27:36.0
1994	Bjoern Daehlie, Norway	24:20.1
1998	Bjoern Daehlie, Norway	27:24.5
2002	Thomas Alsgaard, Norway	49:48.9
	Frode Estil, Norway (tie)[1]	49:48.9

(1) Both awarded gold after Johann Muehlegg of Spain was stripped of gold for a drug offense.

Men's 15 Kilometers		Time
1924	Thorleif Haug, Norway	1:14:31
1928	Johan Grottumsbraaten, Norway	1:37:01
1932	Sven Utterstrom, Sweden	1:23:07
1936	Erik-August Larsson, Sweden	1:14:38
1948	Martin Lundstrom, Sweden	1:13:50
1952	Hallgeir Brenden, Norway	1:01:34
1956	Hallgeir Brenden, Norway	0:49:39.0
1960	Haakon Brusveen, Norway.	0:51:55.5
1964	Eero Maentyranta, Finland.	0:50:54.1
1968	Harald Groenningen, Norway.	0:47:54.2
1972	Sven-Ake Lundback, Sweden	0:45:28.24
1976	Nikolai Balukov, USSR.	0:43:58.47
1980	Thomas Wassberg, Sweden	0:41:57.63
1984	Gunde Svan, Sweden	0:41:25.6
1988	Mikhail Deviatiarov, USSR	0:41:18.9
1992	Bjoern Daehlie, Norway	0:38:01.9
1994	Bjoern Daehlie, Norway	0:35:48.8
1998	Thomas Alsgaard, Norway.	1:07:01.7
2002	Andrus Veerpalu, Estonia.	0:37:07.4
2006	Andrus Veerpalu, Estonia.	0:38:01.3
2010	Dario Cologna, Switzerland	0:33:36.3
2014	Dario Cologna, Switzerland	0:38:29.7
2018	Dario Cologna, Switzerland	0:33:43.9

Note: Approx. 18-km course 1924-52.

Men's 30-Kilometer Pursuit		Time
1956	Veikko Hakulinen, Finland	1:44:06.0
1964	Eero Maentyranta, Finland.	1:30:50.7
1968	Franco Nones, Italy	1:35:39.2
1972	Vyacheslav Vedenine, USSR.	1:36:31.15
1976	Sergei Saveliev, USSR	1:30:29.38
1980	Nikolai Zimyatov, USSR.	1:27:02.80
1984	Nikolai Zimyatov, USSR.	1:28:56.3
1988	Aleksei Prokourorov, USSR.	1:24:26.3
1992	Vegard Ulvang, Norway.	1:22:27.8
1994	Thomas Alsgaard, Norway.	1:12:26.4
1998	Mika Myllylae, Finland	1:33:55.8
2002	Christian Hoffmann, Austria[1]	1:11:31.0
2006	Eugeni Dementiev, Russia.	1:17:00.8
2010	Marcus Hellner, Sweden	1:15:11.4

(1) Awarded gold after Johann Muehlegg of Spain was stripped of gold for a drug offense.

Men's Skiathlon		Time
2014	Dario Cologna, Switzerland	1:08:15.4
2018	Simen Hegstad Krüger, Norway.	1:16:20.0

Men's 50-Kilometer Mass Start		Time
1924	Thorleif Haug, Norway	3:44:32.0
1928	Per Erik Hedlund, Sweden.	4:52:03.0
1932	Veli Saarinen, Finland	4:28:00.0
1936	Elis Wiklund, Sweden.	3:30:11.0
1948	Nils Karlsson, Sweden	3:47:48.0
1952	Veikko Hakulinen, Finland	3:33:33.0
1956	Sixten Jernberg, Sweden.	2:50:27.0
1960	Kalevi Hamalainen, Finland	2:59:06.3
1964	Sixten Jernberg, Sweden.	2:43:52.6
1968	Ole Ellefsaeter, Norway	2:28:45.8
1972	Paal Tyldum, Norway	2:43:14.75
1976	Ivar Formo, Norway	2:37:30.05
1980	Nikolai Zimyatov, USSR.	2:27:24.60
1984	Thomas Wassberg, Sweden	2:15:55.8
1988	Gunde Svan, Sweden	2:04:30.9
1992	Bjoern Daehlie, Norway	2:03:41.5
1994	Vladimir Smirnov, Kazakhstan	2:07:20.3
1998	Bjoern Daehlie, Norway	2:05:08.2
2002	Mikhail Ivanov, Russia	2:06:20.8
2006	Giorgio di Centa, Italy.	2:06:11.8
2010	Petter Northug, Norway	2:05:35.5
2014	Alexander Legkov, Russia	1:46:55.2
2018	Iivo Niskanen, Finland	2:08:22.1

Men's 4x10-Kilometer Relay

		Time
1936	Finland, Norway, Sweden	2:41:33.0
1948	Sweden, Finland, Norway	2:32:08.0
1952	Finland, Norway, Sweden	2:20:16.0
1956	USSR, Finland, Sweden	2:15:30.0
1960	Finland, Norway, USSR	2:18:45.6
1964	Sweden, Finland, USSR	2:18:34.6
1968	Norway, Sweden, Finland	2:08:33.5
1972	USSR, Norway, Switzerland	2:04:47.94
1976	Finland, Norway, USSR	2:07:59.72
1980	USSR, Norway, Finland	1:57:03.46
1984	Sweden, USSR, Finland	1:55:06.30
1988	Sweden, USSR, Czechoslovakia	1:43:58.60
1992	Norway, Italy, Finland	1:39:26.00
1994	Italy, Norway, Finland	1:41:15.00
1998	Norway, Italy, Finland	1:40:55.70
2002	Norway, Italy, Germany	1:32:45.5
2006	Italy, Germany, Sweden	1:43:45.7
2010	Sweden, Norway, Czech Republic	1:45:05.4
2014	Sweden, Russia, France	1:28:42.0
2018	Norway, OAR, France	1:33:04.9

Men's Team Sprint

		Time
2006	Bjoern Lind & Thobias Fredriksson, Sweden	17:02.9
2010	Oeystein Pettersen & Petter Northug, Norway	19:01.0
2014	Sami Jauhojaervi & Iivo Niskanen, Finland	23:14.89
2018	Martin Johnsrud Sundby & Johannes Hoesflot Klaebo, Norway	15:56.26

Women's Individual Sprint

		Time
2002	Julia Tchepalova, Russia (1.5 km)	3:10.6
2006	Chandra Crawford, Canada (1.1 km)	2:12.3
2010	Marit Bjoergen, Norway	3:39.2
2014	Maiken Caspersen Falla, Norway	2:35.49
2018	Stina Nilsson, Sweden	3:03.84

Women's 5 Kilometers

		Time
1964	Claudia Boyarskikh, USSR	17:50.5
1968	Toini Gustafsson, Sweden	16:45.2
1972	Galina Koulacova, USSR	17:00.50
1976	Helena Takalo, Finland	15:48.69
1980	Raisa Smetanina, USSR	15:06.92
1984	Marja-Liisa Hamalainen, Finland	17:04.0
1988	Marjo Matikainen, Finland	15:04.0
1992	Marjut Lukkarinen, Finland	14:13.8
1994	Lyubov Yegorova, Russia	14:08.8
1998	Larissa Lazutina, Russia	17:37.9
2002	Beckie Scott, Canada[1]	25:09.9

(1) Awarded gold after Olga Danilova of Russia was stripped of gold and Larissa Lazutina of Russia was stripped of silver for drug offenses.

Women's 10 Kilometers

		Time
1952	Lydia Wideman, Finland	41:40.0
1956	Lyubov Kosyreva, USSR	38:11.0
1960	Maria Gusakova, USSR	39:46.6
1964	Claudia Boyarskikh, USSR	40:24.3
1968	Toini Gustafsson, Sweden	36:46.5
1972	Galina Koulacova, USSR	34:17.82
1976	Raisa Smetanina, USSR	30:13.41
1980	Barbara Petzold, E. Germany	30:31.54
1984	Marja-Liisa Hamalainen, Finland	31:44.2
1988	Vida Ventsene, USSR	30:08.3
1992	Lyubov Yegorova, Unified Team (Rus.)	25:53.7
1994	Lyubov Yegorova, Russia	27:30.1
1998	Larissa Lazutina, Russia	46.06.9
2002	Bente Skari, Norway	28:05.6
2006	Kristina Smigun, Estonia	27:51.4
2010	Charlotte Kalla, Sweden	24:58.4
2014	Justyna Kowalczyk, Poland	28:17.8
2018	Ragnhild Haga, Norway	25:00.5

Women's 15-Kilometer Pursuit

		Time
1992	Lyubov Yegorova, Unified Team (Rus.)	42:20.8
1994	Manuela Di Centa, Italy	39:44.5
1998	Olga Danilova, Russia	46:55.4
2002	Stefania Belmondo, Italy	39:54.4
2006	Kristina Smigun, Estonia	42:48.7
2010	Marit Bjoergen, Norway	39:58.1

Women's Skiathlon

		Time
2014	Marit Bjoergen, Norway	38:33.6
2018	Charlotte Kalla, Sweden	40:44.9

Women's 30-Kilometer Mass Start

		Time
1992	Stefania Belmondo, Italy	1:22:30.1
1994	Manuela Di Centa, Italy	1:25:41.6

Women's 30-Kilometer Mass Start

		Time
1998	Julija Tchepalova, Russia	1:22:01.5
2002	Gabriella Paruzzi, Italy	1:30:57.1
2006	Katerina Neumannova, Czech Republic	1:22:25.4
2010	Justyna Kowalczyk, Poland	1:30:33.7
2014	Marit Bjoergen, Norway	1:11:05.2
2018	Marit Bjoergen, Norway	1:22:17.6

Women's 4x5-Kilometer Relay

		Time
1956	Finland, USSR, Sweden (15 km)	1:09:01.0
1960	Sweden, USSR, Finland (15 km)	1:04:21.4
1964	USSR, Sweden, Finland (15 km)	0:59:20.2
1968	Norway, Sweden, USSR (15 km)	0:57:30.0
1972	USSR, Finland, Norway (15 km)	0:48:46.15
1976	USSR, Finland, E. Germany	1:07:49.75
1980	E. Germany, USSR, Norway	1:02:11.1
1984	Norway, Czechoslovakia, Finland	1:06:49.7
1988	USSR, Norway, Finland	0:59:51.1
1992	United Team, Norway, Italy	0:59:34.8
1994	Russia, Norway, Italy	0:57:12.5
1998	Russia, Norway, Italy	0:55:13.5
2002	Germany, Norway, Switzerland	0:49:30.6
2006	Russia, Germany, Italy	0:54:47.7
2010	Norway, Germany, Finland	0:55:19.5
2014	Sweden, Finland, Germany	0:53:02.7
2018	Norway, Sweden, OAR	0:51:24.3

Women's Team Sprint

		Time
2006	Lina Andersson & Anna Dahlberg, Sweden	16:36.9
2010	Evi Sachenbacher-Stehle & Claudia Nystad, Germany	18:03.7
2014	Marit Bjoergen & Ingvild Flugstad Oestberg, Norway	16:04.05
2018	Kikkan Randall & Jessie Diggins, United States	15:56.47

Curling

Men

1998	Switzerland, Canada, Norway
2002	Norway, Canada, Switzerland
2006	Canada, Finland, United States
2010	Canada, Norway, Switzerland
2014	Canada, Great Britain, Sweden
2018	United States, Sweden, Switzerland

Women

1998	Canada, Denmark, Sweden
2002	Britain, Switzerland, Canada
2006	Sweden, Switzerland, Canada
2010	Sweden, Canada, China
2014	Canada, Sweden, Great Britain
2018	Sweden, S. Korea, Japan

Mixed

2018	Canada, Switzerland, Norway

Figure Skating

Men's Singles

1908[1]	Ulrich Salchow, Sweden
1920[1]	Gillis Grafstrom, Sweden
1924	Gillis Grafstrom, Sweden
1928	Gillis Grafstrom, Sweden
1932	Karl Schaefer, Austria
1936	Karl Schaefer, Austria
1948	Richard Button, United States
1952	Richard Button, United States
1956	Hayes Alan Jenkins, United States
1960	David W. Jenkins, United States
1964	Manfred Schnelldorfer, Germany
1968	Wolfgang Schwartz, Austria
1972	Ondrej Nepela, Czechoslovakia
1976	John Curry, Great Britain
1980	Robin Cousins, Great Britain
1984	Scott Hamilton, United States
1988	Brian Boitano, United States
1992	Viktor Petrenko, Unified Team (Ukr.)
1994	Aleksei Urmanov, Russia
1998	Ilya Kulik, Russia
2002	Alexei Yagudin, Russia
2006	Yevgeny Plushenko, Russia
2010	Evan Lysacek, United States
2014	Yuzuru Hanyu, Japan
2018	Yuzuru Hanyu, Japan

(1) Event held during Summer Olympic Games.

Women's Singles

1908[1]	Madge Syers, Great Britain
1920[1]	Magda Julin-Mauroy, Sweden
1924	Herma von Szabo-Planck, Austria
1928	Sonja Henie, Norway

Women's Singles

1932	Sonja Henie, Norway
1936	Sonja Henie, Norway
1948	Barbara Ann Scott, Canada
1952	Jeanette Altwegg, Great Britain
1956	Tenley Albright, United States
1960	Carol Heiss, United States
1964	Sjoukje Dijkstra, Netherlands
1968	Peggy Fleming, United States
1972	Beatrix Schuba, Austria
1976	Dorothy Hamill, United States
1980	Anett Poetzsch, E. Germany
1984	Katarina Witt, E. Germany
1988	Katarina Witt, E. Germany
1992	Kristi Yamaguchi, United States
1994	Oksana Baiul, Ukraine
1998	Tara Lipinski, United States
2002	Sarah Hughes, United States
2006	Shizuka Arakawa, Japan
2010	Kim Yu-na, South Korea
2014	Adelina Sotnikova, Russia
2018	Alina Zagitova, OAR

(1) Event held during Summer Olympic Games.

Pairs

1908[1]	Anna Hubler & Heinrich Burger, Germany
1920[1]	Ludovika Jakobsson & Walter Jakobsson, Finland
1924	Helene Engelman & Alfred Berger, Austria
1928	Andree Joly & Pierre Brunet, France
1932	Andree Joly & Pierre Brunet, France
1936	Maxi Herber & Ernst Baier, Germany
1948	Micheline Lannoy & Pierre Baugniet, Belgium
1952	Ria Falk & Paul Falk, Germany
1956	Elisabeth Schwartz & Kurt Oppelt, Austria
1964	Ludmila Beloussova & Oleg Protopopov, USSR
1968	Ludmila Beloussova & Oleg Protopopov, USSR
1972	Irina Rodnina & Alexei Ulanov, USSR
1976	Irina Rodnina & Aleksandr Zaitzev, USSR
1980	Irina Rodnina & Aleksandr Zaitzev, USSR
1984	Elena Valova & Oleg Vassiliev, USSR
1988	Ekaterina Gordeeva & Sergei Grinkov, USSR
1992	Natalia Mishkutienok & Artur Dimitriev, Unified Team
1994	Ekaterina Gordeeva & Sergei Grinkov, Russia
1998	Oksana Kazakova & Artur Dmitriev, Russia
2002	Elena Berezhnaya & Anton Sikharulidze, Russia; Jamie Salé & David Pelletier, Canada (tie)
2006	Tatyana Totmianina & Maxim Marinin, Russia
2010	Shen Xue & Zhao Hongbo, China
2014	Tatiana Volosozhar & Maxim Trankov, Russia
2018	Aljona Savchenko & Bruno Massot, Germany

(1) Event held during Summer Olympic Games.

Ice Dancing

1976	Ludmila Pakhomova & Aleksandr Gorschkov, USSR
1980	Natalya Linichuk & Gennadi Karponosov, USSR
1984	Jayne Torvill & Christopher Dean, Great Britain
1988	Natalia Bestemianova & Andrei Bukin, USSR
1992	Marina Klimova & Sergei Ponomarenko, Unified Team
1994	Pasha Grishuk & Evgeny Platov, Russia
1998	Pasha Grishuk & Evgeny Platov, Russia
2002	Marina Anissina & Gwendal Peizerat, France
2006	Tatyana Navka & Roman Kostomarov, Russia
2010	Tessa Virtue & Scott Moir, Canada
2014	Meryl Davis & Charlie White, United States
2018	Tessa Virtue & Scott Moir, Canada

Mixed Team

2014	Russia, Canada, United States
2018	Canada, OAR, United States

Freestyle Skiing

Men's Aerials

		Points
1994	Andreas Schoenbaechler, Switzerland	234.67
1998	Eric Bergoust, United States	255.64
2002	Ales Valenta, Czech Republic	257.02
2006	Xiaopeng Han, China	250.77
2010	Alexei Grishin, Belarus	248.41
2014	Anton Kushnir, Belarus	134.50
2018	Oleksandr Abramenko, Ukraine	128.51

Men's Moguls

		Points
1992	Edgar Grospiron, France	25.81
1994	Jean-Luc Brassard, Canada	27.24
1998	Jonny Moseley, United States	26.93

Men's Moguls

		Points
2002	Janne Lahtela, Finland	27.97
2006	Dale Begg-Smith, Australia	26.77
2010	Alex Bilodeau, Canada	26.75
2014	Alex Bilodeau, Canada	26.31
2018	Mikaël Kingsbury, Canada	86.63

Men's Ski Cross

2010	Michael Schmid, Switzerland
2014	Jean Frederic Chapuis, France
2018	Brady Leman, Canada

Men's Ski Halfpipe

		Points
2014	David Wise, United States	92.00
2018	David Wise, United States	97.20

Men's Ski Slopestyle

		Points
2014	Joss Christensen, United States	95.80
2018	Oystein Braaten, Norway	95.00

Women's Aerials

		Points
1994	Lina Tcherjazova, Uzbekistan	166.84
1998	Nikki Stone, United States	193.00
2002	Alisa Camplin, Australia	193.47
2006	Evelyne Leu, Switzerland	202.55
2010	Lydia Lassila, Australia	214.74
2014	Alla Tsuper, Belarus	98.01
2018	Hanna Huskova, Belarus	96.14

Women's Moguls

		Points
1992	Donna Weinbrecht, United States	23.69
1994	Stine Lise Hattestad, Norway	25.97
1998	Tae Satoya, Japan	25.06
2002	Kari Traa, Norway	25.94
2006	Jennifer Heil, Canada	26.50
2010	Hannah Kearney, United States	26.63
2014	Justine Dufour-Lapointe, Canada	22.44
2018	Perrine Laffont, France	78.65

Women's Ski Cross

2010	Ashleigh McIvor, Canada
2014	Marielle Thompson, Canada
2018	Kelsey Serwa, Canada

Women's Ski Halfpipe

		Points
2014	Maddie Bowman, United States	89.00
2018	Cassie Sharpe, Canada	95.80

Women's Ski Slopestyle

		Points
2014	Dara Howell, Canada	94.20
2018	Sarah Höfflin, Switzerland	91.20

Ice Hockey

Men

1920[1]	Canada, United States, Czechoslovakia
1924	Canada, United States, Great Britain
1928	Canada, Sweden, Switzerland
1932	Canada, United States, Germany
1936	Great Britain, Canada, United States
1948	Canada, Czechoslovakia, Switzerland
1952	Canada, United States, Sweden
1956	USSR, United States, Canada
1960	United States, Canada, USSR
1964	USSR, Sweden, Czechoslovakia
1968	USSR, Czechoslovakia, Canada
1972	USSR, United States, Czechoslovakia
1976	USSR, Czechoslovakia, W. Germany
1980	United States, USSR, Sweden
1984	USSR, Czechoslovakia, Sweden
1988	USSR, Finland, Sweden
1992	Unified Team, Canada, Czechoslovakia
1994	Sweden, Canada, Finland
1998	Czech Republic, Russia, Finland
2002	Canada, United States, Russia
2006	Sweden, Finland, Czech Republic
2010	Canada, United States, Finland
2014	Canada, Sweden, Finland
2018	OAR, Germany, Canada

(1) Event held during Summer Olympic Games.

Women

1998	United States, Canada, Finland
2002	Canada, United States, Sweden
2006	Canada, Sweden, United States
2010	Canada, United States, Finland
2014	Canada, United States, Switzerland
2018	United States, Canada, Finland

Luge

Men's Singles

		Time
1964	Thomas Keohler, E. Germany	3:27.77
1968	Manfred Schmid, Austria	2:52.48
1972	Wolfgang Scheidel, E. Germany	3:27.58

Men's Singles	Time
1976 Detlef Guenther, E. Germany	3:27.688
1980 Bernhard Glass, E. Germany	2:54.796
1984 Paul Hildgartner, Italy	3:04.258
1988 Jens Mueller, E. Germany	3:05.548
1992 Georg Hackl, Germany	3:02.363
1994 Georg Hackl, Germany	3:21.571
1998 Georg Hackl, Germany	3:18.436
2002 Armin Zoeggeler, Italy	2:57.941
2006 Armin Zoeggeler, Italy	3:26.088
2010 Felix Loch, Germany	3:13.085
2014 Felix Loch, Germany	3:27.526
2018 David Gleirscher, Austria	3:10.702

Men's Doubles	Time
1964 Austria	1:41.62
1968 E. Germany	1:35.85
1972 Italy, E. Germany (tie)	1:28.35
1976 E. Germany	1:25.604
1980 E. Germany	1:19.331
1984 W. Germany	1:23.620
1988 E. Germany	1:31.940
1992 Germany	1:32.053
1994 Italy	1:36.720
1998 Germany	1:41.105
2002 Germany	1:26.082
2006 Austria	1:34.497
2010 Austria	1:22.705
2014 Germany	1:38.933
2018 Germany	1:31.697

Women's Singles	Time
1964 Ortun Enderlein, Germany	3:24.67
1968 Erica Lechner, Italy	2:28.66
1972 Anna M. Muller, E. Germany	2:59.18
1976 Margit Schumann, E. Germany	2:50.621
1980 Vera Zozulya, USSR	2:36.537
1984 Steffi Martin, E. Germany	2:46.570
1988 Steffi Walter, E. Germany	3:03.973
1992 Doris Neuner, Austria	3:06.696
1994 Gerda Weissensteiner, Italy	3:15.517
1998 Silke Kraushaar, Germany	3:23.779
2002 Sylke Otto, Germany	2:52.464
2006 Sylke Otto, Germany	3:07.979
2010 Tatjana Huefner, Germany	2:46.524
2014 Natalie Geisenberger, Germany	3:19.768
2018 Natalie Geisenberger, Germany	3:05.232

Mixed Team Relay	Time
2014 Germany, Russia, Latvia	2:45.649
2018 Germany, Canada, Austria	2:24.517

Nordic Combined

Men's Individual

1924	Thorleif Haug, Norway
1928	Johan Grottumsbraaten, Norway
1932	Johan Grottumsbraaten, Norway
1936	Oddbjorn Hagen, Norway
1948	Heikki Hasu, Finland
1952	Simon Slattvik, Norway
1956	Sverre Stenersen, Norway
1960	Georg Thoma, W. Germany
1964	Tormod Knutsen, Norway
1968	Franz Keller, W. Germany
1972	Ulrich Wehling, E. Germany
1976	Ulrich Wehling, E. Germany
1980	Ulrich Wehling, E. Germany
1984	Tom Sandberg, Norway
1988	Hippolyt Kempf, Switzerland
1992	Fabrice Guy, France
1994	Fred Barre Lundberg, Norway
1998	Bjarte Engen Vik, Norway
2002	Samppa Lajunen, Finland
2006	Georg Hettich, Germany

Men's 10-Kilometer Large Hill

2010	Bill Demong, United States
2014	Joergen Graabak, Norway
2018	Johannes Rydzek, Germany

Men's 10-Kilometer Normal Hill

2010	Jason Lamy Chappuis, France
2014	Eric Frenzel, Germany
2018	Eric Frenzel, Germany

Men's Team 4x5-Kilometer Relay

1988	W. Germany, Switzerland, Austria
1992	Japan, Norway, Austria
1994	Japan, Norway, Switzerland
1998	Norway, Finland, France
2002	Finland, Germany, Austria
2006	Austria, Germany, Finland
2010	Austria, United States, Germany
2014	Norway, Germany, Austria
2018	Germany, Norway, Austria

Ski Jumping

Men's Normal Hill	Points
1964 Veikko Kankkonen, Finland	229.9
1968 Jiri Raska, Czechoslovakia	216.5
1972 Yukio Kasaya, Japan	244.2
1976 Hans-Georg Aschenbach, E. Germany	252.0
1980 Toni Innauer, Austria	266.3
1984 Jens Weissflog, E. Germany	215.2
1988 Matti Nykaenen, Finland	230.5
1992 Ernst Vettori, Austria	222.8
1994 Espen Bredesen, Norway	282.0
1998 Jani Soininen, Finland	234.5
2002 Simon Ammann, Switzerland	269.0
2006 Lars Bystoel, Norway	266.5
2010 Simon Ammann, Switzerland	276.5
2014 Kamil Stoch, Poland	278.0
2018 Andreas Wellinger, Germany	259.3

Men's Large Hill	Points
1924 Jacob Tullin Thams, Norway	18.960
1928 Alfred Andersen, Norway	19.208
1932 Birger Ruud, Norway	228.1
1936 Birger Ruud, Norway	232.0
1948 Petter Hugsted, Norway	228.1
1952 Arnfinn Bergmann, Norway	226.0
1956 Antti Hyvarinen, Finland	227.0
1960 Helmut Recknagel, E. Germany	227.2
1964 Toralf Engan, Norway	230.7
1968 Vladimir Beloussov, USSR	231.3
1972 Wojciech Fortuna, Poland	219.9
1976 Karl Schnabl, Austria	234.8
1980 Jouko Tormanen, Finland	271.0
1984 Matti Nykaenen, Finland	231.2
1988 Matti Nykaenen, Finland	224.0
1992 Toni Nieminen, Finland	239.5
1994 Jens Weissflog, Germany	274.5
1998 Kazuyoshi Funaki, Japan	272.3
2002 Simon Ammann, Switzerland	281.4
2006 Thomas Morgenstern, Austria	276.9
2010 Simon Ammann, Switzerland	283.6
2014 Kamil Stoch, Poland	278.7
2018 Kamil Stoch, Poland	285.7

Men's Team	Points
1988 Finland, Yugoslavia, Norway	634.4
1992 Finland, Austria, Czechoslovakia	644.4
1994 Germany, Japan, Austria	970.1
1998 Japan, Germany, Austria	933.0
2002 Germany, Finland, Slovenia	974.1
2006 Austria, Finland, Norway	984.0
2010 Austria, Germany, Norway	1,107.9
2014 Germany, Austria, Japan	1,041.1
2018 Norway, Germany, Poland	1,098.5

Women's Normal Hill	Points
2014 Carina Vogt, Germany	247.4
2018 Maren Lundby, Norway	264.6

Snowboarding

Men's Big Air	Points
2018 Sebastien Toutant, Canada	174.25

Men's Halfpipe	Points
1998 Gian Simmen, Switzerland	85.2
2002 Ross Powers, United States	46.1
2006 Shaun White, United States	46.8
2010 Shaun White, United States	48.4
2014 Iouri Podladtchikov, Switzerland	94.75
2018 Shaun White, United States	97.75

Men's Parallel Giant Slalom

1998	Ross Rebagliati, Canada
2002	Philipp Schoch, Switzerland
2006	Philipp Schoch, Switzerland

Men's Parallel Giant Slalom

2010	Jasey Jay Anderson, Canada	
2014	Vic Wild, Russia	
2018	Nevin Galmarini, Switzerland	

Note: In 2002, the Giant Slalom became the Parallel Giant Slalom.

Men's Parallel Slalom

2014	Vic Wild, Russia

Men's Slopestyle

		Points
2014	Sage Kotsenburg, United States	93.50
2018	Red Gerard, United States	87.16

Men's Snowboard Cross

2006	Seth Wescott, United States
2010	Seth Wescott, United States
2014	Pierre Vaultier, France
2018	Pierre Vaultier, France

Women's Big Air

		Points
2018	Anna Gasser, Austria	185.00

Women's Halfpipe

		Points
1998	Nicola Thost, Germany	74.6
2002	Kelly Clark, United States	47.9
2006	Hannah Teter, United States	46.4
2010	Torah Bright, Australia	45.0
2014	Kaitlyn Farrington, United States	91.75
2018	Chloe Kim, United States	98.25

Women's Parallel Giant Slalom

1998	Karine Ruby, France
2002	Isabelle Blanc, France
2006	Daniela Meuli, Switzerland
2010	Nicolien Sauerbreij, Netherlands
2014	Patrizia Kummer, Switzerland
2018	Ester Ledecká, Czech Republic

Note: In 2002, the Giant Slalom became the Parallel Giant Slalom.

Women's Parallel Slalom

2014	Julia Dujmovits, Austria

Women's Slopestyle

		Points
2014	Jamie Anderson, United States	95.25
2018	Jamie Anderson, United States	83.00

Women's Snowboard Cross

2006	Tanja Frieden, Switzerland
2010	Maelle Ricker, Canada
2014	Eva Samková, Czech Republic
2018	Michela Moioli, Italy

Speed Skating

*= Olympic record

Men's 500 Meters

		Time
1924	Charles Jewtraw, United States	0:44.0
1928	C. Thunberg, Finland; B. Evensen, Norway (tie)	0:43.4
1932	John A. Shea, United States	0:43.4
1936	Ivar Ballangrud, Norway	0:43.4
1948	Finn Helgesen, Norway	0:43.1
1952	Kenneth Henry, United States	0:43.2
1956	Evgeniy Grishin, USSR	0:40.2
1960	Evgeniy Grishin, USSR	0:40.2
1964	Terry McDermott, United States	0:40.1
1968	Erhard Keller, W. Germany	0:40.3
1972	Erhard Keller, W. Germany	0:39.44
1976	Evgeny Kulikov, USSR	0:39.17
1980	Eric Heiden, United States	0:38.03
1984	Sergei Fokichev, USSR	0:38.19
1988	Uwe-Jens Mey, E. Germany	0:36.45
1992	Uwe-Jens Mey, Germany	0:37.14
1994	Aleksandr Golubev, Russia	0:36.33
1998	Hiroyasu Shimizu, Japan	0:35.59
2002	Casey FitzRandolph, United States	0:34.42
2006	Joey Cheek, United States	0:34.82
2010	Mo Tae-bum, S. Korea	0:69.82
2014	Michel Mulder, Netherlands	0:69.312
2018	Havard Lorentzen, Norway	0:34.41*

Note: In 2010 and 2014, results include the total of two 500-km race times.

Men's 1000 Meters

		Time
1976	Peter Mueller, United States	1:19.32
1980	Eric Heiden, United States	1:15.18
1984	Gaetan Boucher, Canada	1:15.80
1988	Nikolai Guiliaev, USSR	1:13.03
1992	Olaf Zinke, Germany	1:14.85
1994	Dan Jansen, United States	1:12.43
1998	Ids Postma, Netherlands	1:10.64
2002	Gerard van Velde, Netherlands	1:07.18*

Men's 1000 Meters

		Time
2006	Shani Davis, United States	1:08.89
2010	Shani Davis, United States	1:08.94
2014	Stefan Groothuis, Netherlands	1:08.39
2018	Kjeld Nuis, Netherlands	1:07.95

Men's 1500 Meters

		Time
1924	Clas Thunberg, Finland	2:20.8
1928	Clas Thunberg, Finland	2:21.1
1932	John A. Shea, United States	2:57.5
1936	Charles Mathiesen, Norway	2:19.2
1948	Sverre Farstad, Norway	2:17.6
1952	Hjalmar Andersen, Norway	2:20.4
1956	Y. Grishin, USSR; Y. Mikhailov, USSR (tie)	2:08.6
1960	R. Aas, Norway; Y. Grishin, USSR (tie)	2:10.4
1964	Ants Anston, USSR	2:10.3
1968	Cornelis Verkerk, Netherlands	2:03.4
1972	Ard Schenk, Netherlands	2:02.96
1976	Jan Egil Storholt, Norway	1:59.38
1980	Eric Heiden, United States	1:55.44
1984	Gaetan Boucher, Canada	1:58.36
1988	Andre Hoffmann, E. Germany	1:52.06
1992	Johann Koss, Norway	1:54.81
1994	Johann Koss, Norway	1:51.29
1998	Aadne Sondral, Norway	1:47.87
2002	Derek Parra, United States	1:43.95*
2006	Enrico Fabris, Italy	1:45.97
2010	Mark Tuitert, Netherlands	1:45.57
2014	Zbigniew Brodka, Poland	1:45.006
2018	Kjeld Nuis, Netherlands	1:44.01

Men's 5000 Meters

		Time
1924	Clas Thunberg, Finland	8:39.0
1928	Ivar Ballangrud, Norway	8:50.5
1932	Irving Jaffee, United States	9:40.8
1936	Ivar Ballangrud, Norway	8:19.6
1948	Reidar Liaklev, Norway	8:29.4
1952	Hjalmar Andersen, Norway	8:10.6
1956	Boris Shilkov, USSR	7:48.7
1960	Viktor Kosichkin, USSR	7:51.3
1964	Knut Johannesen, Norway	7:38.4
1968	F. Anton Maier, Norway	7:22.4
1972	Ard Schenk, Netherlands	7:23.61
1976	Sten Stensen, Norway	7:24.48
1980	Eric Heiden, United States	7:02.29
1984	Tomas Gustafson, Sweden	7:12.28
1988	Tomas Gustafson, Sweden	6:44.63
1992	Geir Karlstad, Norway	6:59.97
1994	Johann Koss, Norway	6:34.96
1998	Gianni Romme, Netherlands	6:22.20
2002	Jochem Uytdehaage, Netherlands	6:14.66
2006	Chad Hedrick, United States	6:14.68
2010	Sven Kramer, Netherlands	6:14.60
2014	Sven Kramer, Netherlands	6:10.76
2018	Sven Kramer, Netherlands	6:09.76*

Men's 10,000 Meters

		Time
1924	Julius Skutnabb, Finland	18:04.8
1928	Event not held because of thawing of ice	
1932	Irving Jaffee, United States	19:13.6
1936	Ivar Ballangrud, Norway	17:24.3
1948	Ake Seyffarth, Sweden	17:26.3
1952	Hjalmar Andersen, Norway	16:45.8
1956	Sigvard Ericsson, Sweden	16:35.9
1960	Knut Johannesen, Norway	15:46.6
1964	Jonny Nilsson, Sweden	15:50.1
1968	Jonny Hoeglin, Sweden	15:23.6
1972	Ard Schenk, Netherlands	15:01.35
1976	Piet Kleine, Netherlands	14:50.59
1980	Eric Heiden, United States	14:28.13
1984	Igor Malkov, USSR	14:39.90
1988	Tomas Gustafson, Sweden	13:48.20
1992	Bart Veldkamp, Netherlands	14:12.12
1994	Johann Koss, Norway	13:30.55
1998	Gianni Romme, Netherlands	13:15.33
2002	Jochem Uytdehaage, Netherlands	12:58.92
2006	Bob de Jong, Netherlands	13:01.57
2010	Lee Seung-hoon, S. Korea	12:58.55
2014	Jorrit Bergsma, Netherlands	12:44.45
2018	Ted-Jan Bloemen, Canada	12:39.77*

Men's Mass Start

2018	Lee Seung-hoon, S. Korea

Men's Team Pursuit

		Time
2006	Italy, Canada, Netherlands	3:44.46
2010	Canada, United States, Netherlands	3:41.37
2014	Netherlands, S. Korea, Poland	3:37.71
2018	Norway, S. Korea, Netherlands	3:37.32

Women's 500 Meters

		Time
1960	Helga Haase, Germany	0:45.9
1964	Lydia Skoblikova, USSR.	0:45.0
1968	Ludmila Titova, USSR	0:46.1
1972	Anne Henning, United States	0:43.33
1976	Sheila Young, United States	0:42.76
1980	Karin Enke, E. Germany	0:41.78
1984	Christa Rothenburger, E. Germany	0:41.02
1988	Bonnie Blair, United States	0:39.10
1992	Bonnie Blair, United States	0:40.33
1994	Bonnie Blair, United States	0:39.25
1998	Catriona Le May Doan, Canada	0:38.21
2002	Catriona Le May Doan, Canada	0:37.30
2006	Svetlana Zhurova, Russia.	0:38.23
2010	Lee Sang-hwa, S. Korea	0:76.09
2014	Lee Sang-hwa, S. Korea	0:74.70
2018	Nao Kodaira, Japan	0:36.94*

Note: In 2010 and 2014, results include the total of two 500-km race times.

Women's 1000 Meters

		Time
1960	Klara Guseva, USSR	1:34.1
1964	Lydia Skoblikova, USSR	1:33.2
1968	Carolina Geijssen, Netherlands	1:32.6
1972	Monika Pflug, W. Germany	1:31.40
1976	Tatiana Averina, USSR	1:28.43
1980	Natalya Petruseva, USSR	1:24.10
1984	Karin Enke, E. Germany	1:21.61
1988	Christa Rothenburger, E. Germany	1:17.65
1992	Bonnie Blair, United States	1:21.90
1994	Bonnie Blair, United States	1:18.74
1998	Marianne Timmer, Netherlands	1:16.51
2002	Chris Witty, United States	1:13.83
2006	Marianne Timmer, Netherlands	1:16.05
2010	Christine Nesbitt, Canada	1:16.56
2014	Zhang Hong, China	1:14.02
2018	Jorien ter Mors, Netherlands	1:13.56*

Women's 1500 Meters

		Time
1960	Lydia Skoblikova, USSR	2:52.2
1964	Lydia Skoblikova, USSR	2:22.6
1968	Kaija Mustonen, Finland	2:22.4
1972	Dianne Holum, United States	2:20.85
1976	Galina Stepanskaya, USSR	2:16.58
1980	Anne Borckink, Netherlands	2:10.95
1984	Karin Enke, E. Germany	2:03.42
1988	Yvonne van Gennip, Netherlands	2:00.68
1992	Jacqueline Boerner, Germany	2:05.87
1994	Emese Hunyady, Austria	2:02.19
1998	Marianne Timmer, Netherlands	1:57.58
2002	Anni Friesinger, Germany	1:54.02
2006	Cindy Klassen, Canada	1:55.27
2010	Ireen Wüst, Netherlands	1:56.89
2014	Jorien ter Mors, Netherlands	1:53.51*
2018	Ireen Wüst, Netherlands	1:54.35

Women's 3000 Meters

		Time
1960	Lydia Skoblikova, USSR	5:14.3
1964	Lydia Skoblikova, USSR	5:14.9
1968	Johanna Schut, Netherlands	4:56.2
1972	Christina Baas-Kaiser, Netherlands	4:52.14
1976	Tatiana Averina, USSR	4:45.19
1980	Bjoerg Eva Jensen, Norway	4:32.13
1984	Andrea Schoene, E. Germany	4:24.79
1988	Yvonne van Gennip, Netherlands	4:11.94
1992	Gunda Niemann, Germany	4:19.90
1994	Svetlana Bazhanova, Russia	4:17.43
1998	Gunda Niemann-Stirnemann, Germany	4:07.29
2002	Claudia Pechstein, Germany	3:57.70*
2006	Ireen Wüst, Netherlands	4:02.43
2010	Martina Sablikova, Czech Republic	4:02.53
2014	Ireen Wüst, Netherlands	4:00.34
2018	Carlijn Achtereekte, Netherlands	3:59.21

Women's 5000 Meters

		Time
1988	Yvonne van Gennip, Netherlands	7:14.13
1992	Gunda Niemann, Germany	7:31.57

Women's 5000 Meters

		Time
1994	Claudia Pechstein, Germany	7:14.37
1998	Claudia Pechstein, Germany	6:59.61
2002	Claudia Pechstein, Germany	6:46.91*
2006	Clara Hughes, Canada	6:59.07
2010	Martina Sablikova, Czech Republic	6:50.91
2014	Martina Sablikova, Czech Republic	6:51.54
2018	Esmee Visser, Netherlands	6:50.23

Women's Mass Start

2018	Nana Takagi, Japan

Women's Team Pursuit

		Time
2006	Germany, Canada, Russia	3:01.25
2010	Germany, Japan, Poland	3:02.82
2014	Netherlands, Poland, Russia	2:58.05
2018	Japan, Netherlands, United States	2:53.89*

Speed Skating (Short Track)

*= Olympic record

Men's 500 Meters

		Time
1998	Takafumi Nishitani, Japan	0:42.862
2002	Marc Gagnon, Canada	0:41.802
2006	Apolo Anton Ohno, United States	0:41.935
2010	Charles Hamelin, Canada	0:40.981
2014	Victor An, Russia	0:41.312
2018	Wu Dajing, China	0:39.584*

Men's 1000 Meters

		Time
1992	Kim Ki-hoon, S. Korea	1:30.76
1994	Kim Ki-hoon, S. Korea	1:34.57
1998	Kim Dong-sung, S. Korea	1:32.375
2002	Steven Bradbury, Australia	1:29.109
2006	Ahn Hyun-soo, S. Korea	1:26.739
2010	Lee Jung-su, S. Korea	1:23.747
2014	Victor An, Russia	1:25.325
2018	Samuel Girard, Canada	1:24.650

Men's 1500 Meters

		Time
2002	Apolo Anton Ohno, United States	2:18.541
2006	Ahn Hyun-soo, S. Korea	2:25.341
2010	Lee Jung-su, S. Korea	2:17.611
2014	Charles Hamelin, Canada	2:14.985
2018	Lim Hyo-jun, S. Korea	2:10.485*

Men's 5000-Meter Relay

		Time
1992	S. Korea, Canada, Japan	7:14.02
1994	Italy, United States, Australia	7:11.74
1998	Canada, S. Korea, China	7:06.075
2002	Canada, Italy, China	6:51.579
2006	S. Korea, Canada, United States	6:43.376
2010	Canada, S. Korea, United States	6:44.224
2014	Russia, United States, China	6:42.100
2018	Hungary, China, Canada	6:31.971*

Women's 500 Meters

		Time
1992	Cathy Turner, United States	0:47.04
1994	Cathy Turner, United States	0:45.98
1998	Annie Perreault, Canada	0:46.568
2002	Yang Yang (A), China	0:44.187
2006	Wang Meng, China	0:44.345
2010	Wang Meng, China	0:43.048
2014	Li Jianrou, China	0:45.263
2018	Arianna Fontana, Italy	0:42.569

Women's 1000 Meters

		Time
1998	Chun Lee-kyung, S. Korea	1:42.776
2002	Yang Yang (A), China	1:36.391
2006	Jin Sun-yu, S. Korea	1:32.859
2010	Wang Meng, China	1:29.213
2014	Park Seung-hi, S. Korea	1:30.761
2018	Suzanne Schulting, Netherlands	1:29.778

Women's 1500 Meters

		Time
2002	Ko Gi-hyun, S. Korea	2:31.581
2006	Jin Sun-yu, S. Korea	2:23.494
2010	Zhou Yang, China	2:16.993*
2014	Zhou Yang, China	2:19.140
2018	Choi Min-jeong, S. Korea	2:24.948

Women's 3000-Meter Relay

		Time
1992	Canada, United States, Unified Team	4:36.62
1994	S. Korea, Canada, United States	4:26.64
1998	S. Korea, China, Canada	4:16.26
2002	S. Korea, China, Canada	4:12.793
2006	S. Korea, Canada, Italy	4:17.040
2010	China, Canada, United States	4:06.610*
2014	S. Korea, Canada, Italy	4:09.498
2018	S. Korea; Italy; Netherlands	4:07.361

Paralympic Games

The XII Paralympic Winter Games were held Mar. 9-18, 2018, in the same Olympic venues that hosted the 2018 Winter Games in Pyeongchang, South Korea. A record 567 athletes from 49 delegations competed in 80 medal events across six sports. The United States led the medal tally with 36 total (13 gold), followed by the Neutral Paralympic Athletes (NPA) delegation with 24 (8 gold), Canada with 28 (8 gold), and France with 20 (7 gold).

More than 4,300 athletes from 159 countries met at the XV Paralympic Summer Games, held Sept. 7-18, 2016, in Rio de Janeiro, Brazil. A total of 529 gold medals were awarded in 23 sports. China claimed 239 total medals, outpacing Great Britain (147), Ukraine (117), and the United States (115). China also placed first in the number of gold medals, with 107.

The first Olympic Games for athletes with an impairment were held in Rome after the 1960 Summer Olympics; use of the name "paralympic" began with the 1964 games in Tokyo. The Paralympics are held by the Olympic host country in the same year and usually the same city and venue or venues. In 1976, the first Winter Paralympics were held in Ornskoldsvik, Sweden.

2016 Summer Olympic Games
Rio de Janeiro, Brazil, Aug. 5-21, 2016

Familiar names dominated the XXXI Summer Olympics in Rio de Janeiro, Brazil. The first-ever Games in South America set records for number of athletes (11,303) and nations participating (206, plus teams composed of refugees and of independent athletes). Thirty-two venues hosted 306 events in 28 different sports.

U.S. swimmer Michael Phelps won five gold medals and one silver, bringing the 31-year-old's career haul to 28 (including 23 gold medals) over four Olympiads. Fellow U.S. swimmer Katie Ledecky was the most decorated female athlete in Rio, with four golds and one silver, along with two new Olympic records. Hungary's Katinka Hosszú also set two new Olympic records on her way to three gold medals and one silver.

The U.S. excelled in women's gymnastics, cruising to the team gold medal behind the performances of 19-year-old Simone Biles and 22-year-old Aly Raisman. Biles and Raisman finished 1-2 in both the floor exercise and the individual all-around competitions; Biles also captured gold in the vault and bronze on the balance beam.

Jamaica's Usain Bolt defended his title as the world's fastest human, and completed an unprecedented feat, becoming the first man in history to win the 100-m run, the 200-m run, and the 4x100-m relay in three consecutive Olympics. South Africa's Wayde van Niekerk broke Michael Johnson's 17-year-old world record in the 400-m run.

Brazil's national team won its first-ever gold medal in soccer, avenging the 7-1 shellacking the team suffered against Germany in the 2014 World Cup semifinals, also played in Brazil. The medal win in the country's favorite sport was also a balm for months of speculation about whether Brazil could pull off staging the Games. Even in the last days before competition began, concerns lingered about public safety, incomplete facilities and arenas, water quality for the sailing and canoeing events, and the threat of Zika virus.

Less than a month before the Games began, the World Anti-Doping Agency released evidence of a comprehensive state-run doping program in Russia, and recommended banning all Russian athletes from the Games. The International Olympic Committee took a less punitive stance, and ultimately cleared more than two-thirds of Russia's contingent to compete at Rio.

2016 Summer Olympic Games: Final Medal Standings

Country	G	S	B	T
United States ..	46	37	38	121
China	26	18	26	70
Great Britain ...	27	23	17	67
Russia........	19	18	19	56
Germany......	17	10	15	42
France........	10	18	14	42
Japan	12	8	21	41
Australia	8	11	10	29
Italy..........	8	12	8	28
Canada.......	4	3	15	22
South Korea ...	9	3	9	21
Netherlands ...	8	7	4	19
Brazil.........	7	6	6	19
New Zealand ..	4	9	5	18
Azerbaijan.....	1	7	10	18
Spain	7	4	6	17
Kazakhstan....	3	5	9	17
Hungary	8	3	4	15
Denmark......	2	6	7	15
Kenya........	6	6	1	13
Uzbekistan	4	2	7	13
Jamaica	6	3	2	11
Cuba.........	5	2	4	11
Sweden.......	2	6	3	11
Ukraine.......	2	5	4	11
Poland	2	3	6	11
Croatia	5	3	2	10
South Africa ...	2	6	2	10
Czech Republic .	1	2	7	10
Belarus.......	1	4	4	9

Country	G	S	B	T
Colombia	3	2	3	8
Iran	3	1	4	8
Serbia........	2	4	2	8
Turkey........	1	3	4	8
Ethiopia.......	1	2	5	8
Switzerland....	3	2	2	7
North Korea ...	2	3	2	7
Georgia	2	1	4	7
Greece	3	1	2	6
Belgium.......	2	2	2	6
Thailand	2	2	2	6
Romania......	1	1	3	5
Malaysia	0	4	1	5
Mexico	0	3	2	5
Argentina	3	1	0	4
Slovakia	2	2	0	4
Armenia	1	3	0	4
Slovenia	1	2	1	4
Lithuania......	0	1	3	4
Norway.......	0	0	4	4
Indonesia	1	2	0	3
Taiwan	1	0	2	3
Bulgaria	0	1	2	3
Venezuela.....	0	1	2	3
Egypt	0	0	3	3
Tunisia	0	0	3	3
Bahrain.......	1	1	0	2
Vietnam	1	1	0	2
The Bahamas..	1	0	1	2
Côte d'Ivoire ...	1	0	1	2

Country	G	S	B	T
Independent Olympic Athletes.....	1	0	1	2
Algeria	0	2	0	2
Ireland........	0	2	0	2
India	0	1	1	2
Mongolia	0	1	1	2
Israel.........	0	0	2	2
Fiji...........	1	0	0	1
Jordan........	1	0	0	1
Kosovo	1	0	0	1
Puerto Rico....	1	0	0	1
Singapore.....	1	0	0	1
Tajikistan......	1	0	0	1
Burundi.......	0	1	0	1
Grenada......	0	1	0	1
Niger.........	0	1	0	1
Philippines	0	1	0	1
Qatar	0	1	0	1
Austria	0	0	1	1
Dominican Rep.	0	0	1	1
Estonia	0	0	1	1
Finland	0	0	1	1
Moldova	0	0	1	1
Morocco	0	0	1	1
Nigeria	0	0	1	1
Portugal	0	0	1	1
Trinidad and Tobago	0	0	1	1
UAE	0	0	1	1

Summer Olympic Games Champions, 1896-2016

* = Olympic record; (w) wind-aided; times are shown in hour:minute:sec.

The 1980 games were boycotted by 62 nations, including the U.S. The 1984 games were boycotted by the USSR and most Eastern bloc nations. East and West Germany competed separately, 1968-88. The 1992 Unified Team consisted of 12 former Soviet republics. The 1992 Independent Olympic Participants (IOP) were from Serbia, Montenegro, and Macedonia.

Not all sports are listed here, and many events are omitted, even within listed sports, particularly if the event has not been held in more recent Games. Point systems for scoring events have changed many times. Points shown are those under the point system in use at the time.

Basketball

Men

1936	United States, Canada, Mexico
1948	United States, France, Brazil
1952	United States, USSR, Uruguay
1956	United States, USSR, Uruguay
1960	United States, USSR, Brazil
1964	United States, USSR, Brazil
1968	United States, Yugoslavia, USSR
1972	USSR, United States, Cuba
1976	United States, Yugoslavia, USSR
1980	Yugoslavia, Italy, USSR
1984	United States, Spain, Yugoslavia

Men

1988	USSR, Yugoslavia, United States
1992	United States, Croatia, Lithuania
1996	United States, Yugoslavia, Lithuania
2000	United States, France, Lithuania
2004	Argentina, Italy, United States
2008	United States, Spain, Argentina
2012	United States, Spain, Russia
2016	United States, Serbia, Spain

Women

1976	USSR, United States, Bulgaria
1980	USSR, Bulgaria, Yugoslavia

Women

1984	United States, South Korea, China
1988	United States, Yugoslavia, USSR
1992	Unified Team, China, United States
1996	United States, Brazil, Australia
2000	United States, Australia, Brazil
2004	United States, Australia, Russia
2008	United States, Australia, Russia
2012	United States, France, Australia
2016	United States, Spain, Serbia

Boxing—Men

Weight class limits have changed many times since the first Olympic boxing events were held in 1904. The limits shown were used in the 2016 Olympic Games. The Super Heavyweight class was known as Heavyweight 1904-80.

Lt. Flyweight (49 kg/108 lbs)

1968	Francisco Rodriguez, Venezuela
1972	Gyorgy Gedo, Hungary
1976	Jorge Hernandez, Cuba
1980	Shamil Sabyrov, USSR
1984	Paul Gonzalez, United States
1988	Ivailo Hristov, Bulgaria
1992	Rogelio Marcelo, Cuba
1996	Daniel Petrov, Bulgaria
2000	Brahim Asloum, France
2004	Yan Bhartelemy Varela, Cuba
2008	Zou Shiming, China
2012	Zou Shiming, China
2016	Hasanboy Dusmatov, Uzbekistan

Flyweight (52 kg/115 lbs)

1904	George Finnegan, United States
1920	Frank Di Gennara, United States
1924	Fidel LaBarba, United States
1928	Antal Kocsis, Hungary
1932	Istvan Enekes, Hungary
1936	Willi Kaiser, Germany
1948	Pascual Perez, Argentina
1952	Nathan Brooks, United States
1956	Terence Spinks, Great Britain
1960	Gyula Török, Hungary
1964	Fernando Atzori, Italy
1968	Ricardo Delgado, Mexico
1972	Georgi Kostadinov, Bulgaria
1976	Leo Randolph, United States
1980	Peter Lesov, Bulgaria
1984	Steve McCrory, United States
1988	Kim Kwang-sun, S. Korea
1992	Choi Chol Su, N. Korea
1996	Maikro Romero, Cuba
2000	Wijan Ponlid, Thailand
2004	Yuriorkis Gamboa Toledano, Cuba
2008	Somjit Jongjohor, Thailand
2012	Robeisy Ramírez, Cuba
2016	Shakhobidin Zoirov, Uzbekistan

Bantamweight (56 kg/123 lbs)

1904	Oliver Kirk, United States
1908	A. Henry Thomas, Great Britain
1920	Clarence Walker, South Africa
1924	William Smith, South Africa
1928	Vittorio Tamagnini, Italy
1932	Horace Gwynne, Canada
1936	Ulderico Sergo, Italy
1948	Tibor Csik, Hungary
1952	Pentti Hamalainen, Finland
1956	Wolfgang Behrendt, E. Germany
1960	Oleg Grigoryev, USSR
1964	Takao Sakurai, Japan
1968	Valery Sokolov, USSR
1972	Orlando Martinez, Cuba
1976	Gu Yong Ju, N. Korea
1980	Juan Hernandez, Cuba
1984	Maurizio Stecca, Italy
1988	Kennedy McKinney, United States
1992	Joel Casamayor, Cuba
1996	Istvan Kovacs, Hungary

Bantamweight (56 kg/123 lbs)

2000	Guillermo Rigondeaux, Cuba
2004	Guillermo Rigondeaux, Cuba
2008	Badar-Uugan Enkhbat, Mongolia
2012	Luke Campbell, Great Britain
2016	Robeisy Ramírez, Cuba

Featherweight (57 kg/125 lbs)

1904	Oliver Kirk, United States
1908	Richard Gunn, Great Britain
1920	Paul Fritsch, France
1924	John Fields, United States
1928	Lambertus van Klaveren, Netherlands
1932	Carmelo Robledo, Argentina
1936	Oscar Casanovas, Argentina
1948	Ernesto Formenti, Italy
1952	Jan Zachara, Czechoslovakia
1956	Vladimir Safronov, USSR
1960	Francesco Musso, Italy
1964	Stanislav Stephashkin, USSR
1968	Antonio Roldan, Mexico
1972	Boris Kousnetsov, USSR
1976	Angel Herrera, Cuba
1980	Rudi Fink, E. Germany
1984	Meldrick Taylor, United States
1988	Giovanni Parisi, Italy
1992	Andreas Tews, Germany
1996	Somluck Kamsing, Thailand
2000	Bekzat Sattarkhanov, Kazakhstan
2004	Alexey Tishchenko, Russia
2008	Vasyl Lomachenko, Ukraine

Lightweight (60 kg/132 lbs)

1904	Harry Spanger, United States
1908	Frederick Grace, Great Britain
1920	Samuel Mosberg, United States
1924	Hans Nielsen, Denmark
1928	Carlo Orlandi, Italy
1932	Lawrence Stevens, South Africa
1936	Imre Harangi, Hungary
1948	Gerald Dreyer, South Africa
1952	Aureliano Bolognesi, Italy
1956	Richard McTaggart, Great Britain
1960	Kazimierz Pazdzior, Poland
1964	Jozef Grudzien, Poland
1968	Ronald Harris, United States
1972	Jan Szczepanski, Poland
1976	Howard Davis, United States
1980	Angel Herrera, Cuba
1984	Pernell Whitaker, United States
1988	Andreas Zülow, E. Germany
1992	Oscar De La Hoya, United States
1996	Hocine Soltani, Algeria
2000	Mario Kindelan, Cuba
2004	Mario Kindelan, Cuba
2008	Alexey Tishchenko, Russia
2012	Vasyl Lomachenko, Ukraine
2016	Robson Conceição, Brazil

Lt. Welterweight (64 kg/141 lbs)

1952	Charles Adkins, United States
1956	Vladimir Yengibaryan, USSR

Lt. Welterweight (64 kg/141 lbs)

1960	Bohumil Nemecek, Czechoslovakia
1964	Jerzy Kulej, Poland
1968	Jerzy Kulej, Poland
1972	Ray Seales, United States
1976	Ray Leonard, United States
1980	Patrizio Oliva, Italy
1984	Jerry Page, United States
1988	Viatcheslav Janovski, USSR
1992	Hector Vinent, Cuba
1996	Hector Vinent, Cuba
2000	Mahamadkadyz Abdullaev, Uzbekistan
2004	Manus Boonjumnong, Thailand
2008	Felix Diaz, Dominican Republic
2012	Roniel Iglesias, Cuba
2016	Fazliddin Gaibnazarov, Uzbekistan

Welterweight (69 kg/152 lbs)

1904	Albert Young, United States
1920	Albert Schneider, Canada
1924	Jean Delarge, Belgium
1928	Edward Morgan, New Zealand
1932	Edward Flynn, United States
1936	Sten Suvio, Finland
1948	Julius Torma, Czechoslovakia
1952	Zygmunt Chychia, Poland
1956	Nicolae Linca, Romania
1960	Giovanni Benvenuti, Italy
1964	Marian Kasprzyk, Poland
1968	Manfred Wolke, E. Germany
1972	Emilio Correa, Cuba
1976	Jochen Bachfeld, E. Germany
1980	Andres Aldama, Cuba
1984	Mark Breland, United States
1988	Robert Wangila, Kenya
1992	Michael Carruth, Ireland
1996	Oleg Saitov, Russia
2000	Oleg Saitov, Russia
2004	Bakhtiyar Artayev, Kazakhstan
2008	Bakhyt Sarsekbayev, Kazakhstan
2012	Serik Sapiyev, Kazakhstan
2016	Daniyar Yeleussinov, Kazakhstan

Lt. Middleweight (71 kg/156 lbs)

1952	Laszlo Papp, Hungary
1956	Laszlo Papp, Hungary
1960	Wilbert McClure, United States
1964	Boris Lagutin, USSR
1968	Boris Lagutin, USSR
1972	Dieter Kottysch, W. Germany
1976	Jerzy Rybicki, Poland
1980	Armando Martinez, Cuba
1984	Frank Tate, United States
1988	Park Si-hun, S. Korea
1992	Juan Lemus, Cuba
1996	David Reid, United States
2000	Yermakhan Ibraimov, Kazakhstan

Middleweight (75 kg/165 lbs)

1904	Charles Mayer, United States
1908	John Douglas, Great Britain
1920	Harry Mallin, Great Britain
1924	Harry Mallin, Great Britain

Middleweight (75 kg/165 lbs)

1928	Piero Toscani, Italy
1932	Carmen Barth, United States
1936	Jean Despeaux, France
1948	Laszlo Papp, Hungary
1952	Floyd Patterson, United States
1956	Gennady Schatkov, USSR
1960	Edward Crook, United States
1964	Valery Popenchenko, USSR
1968	Christopher Finnegan, Great Britain
1972	Vyacheslav Lemechev, USSR
1976	Michael Spinks, United States
1980	Jose Gomez, Cuba
1984	Shin Joon-sup, S. Korea
1988	Henry Maske, E. Germany
1992	Ariel Hernandez, Cuba
1996	Ariel Hernandez, Cuba
2000	Jorge Gutierrez, Cuba
2004	Gaydarbek Gaydarbekov, Russia
2008	James Degale, Great Britain
2012	Ryota Murata, Japan
2016	Arlen López, Cuba

Lt. Heavyweight (81 kg/179 lbs)

1920	Edward Eagan, United States
1924	Harry Mitchell, Great Britain
1928	Victor Avendaño, Argentina
1932	David Carstens, South Africa
1936	Roger Michelot, France
1948	George Hunter, South Africa

Lt. Heavyweight (81 kg/179 lbs)

1952	Norvel Lee, United States
1956	James Boyd, United States
1960	Cassius Clay, United States
1964	Cosimo Pinto, Italy
1968	Dan Poznyak, USSR
1972	Mate Parlov, Yugoslavia
1976	Leon Spinks, United States
1980	Slobodan Kacar, Yugoslavia
1984	Anton Josipovic, Yugoslavia
1988	Andrew Maynard, United States
1992	Torsten May, Germany
1996	Vassili Jirov, Kazakhstan
2000	Alexander Lebziak, Russia
2004	Andre Ward, United States
2008	Zhang Xiaoping, China
2012	Yegor Mekhontsev, Russia
2016	Julio César la Cruz, Cuba

Heavyweight (91 kg/201 lbs)

1984	Henry Tillman, United States
1988	Ray Mercer, United States
1992	Felix Savon, Cuba
1996	Felix Savon, Cuba
2000	Felix Savon, Cuba
2004	Odlanier Solis Fonte, Cuba
2008	Rakhim Chakhkiev, Russia
2012	Oleksandr Usik, Ukraine
2016	Evgeny Tishchenko, Russia

Super Heavyweight (91+ kg/201+ lbs)

1904	Samuel Berger, United States
1908	Albert Oldham, Great Britain
1920	Ronald Rawson, Great Britain
1924	Otto von Porat, Norway
1928	Arturo Rodriguez Jurado, Argentina
1932	Santiago Lovell, Argentina
1936	Herbert Runge, Germany
1948	Rafael Iglesias, Argentina
1952	H. Edward Sanders, United States
1956	T. Peter Rademacher, United States
1960	Franco De Piccoli, Italy
1964	Joe Frazier, United States
1968	George Foreman, United States
1972	Teofilo Stevenson, Cuba
1976	Teofilo Stevenson, Cuba
1980	Teofilo Stevenson, Cuba
1984	Tyrell Biggs, United States
1988	Lennox Lewis, Canada
1992	Roberto Balado, Cuba
1996	Vladimir Klitchko, Ukraine
2000	Audley Harrison, Great Britain
2004	Alexander Povetkin, Russia
2008	Roberto Cammarelle, Italy
2012	Anthony Joshua, Great Britain
2016	Tony Yoka, France

Boxing—Women

Flyweight (51 kg/112 lbs)

2012	Nicola Adams, Great Britain
2016	Nicola Adams, Great Britain

Lightweight (60 kg/132 lbs)

2012	Katie Taylor, Ireland
2016	Estelle Mossely, France

Middleweight (75 kg/165 lbs)

2012	Claressa Shields, United States
2016	Claressa Shields, United States

Gymnastics—Men

Floor Exercise

1932	István Pelle, Hungary
1936	Georges Miez, Switzerland
1948	Ferenc Pataki, Hungary
1952	William Thoresson, Sweden
1956	Valentin Muratov, USSR
1960	Nobuyuki Aihara, Japan
1964	Franco Menichelli, Italy
1968	Sawao Kato, Japan
1972	Nikolay Andrianov, USSR
1976	Nikolay Andrianov, USSR
1980	Roland Brückner, E. Germany
1984	Li Ning, China
1988	Sergei Kharkov, USSR
1992	Li Xiaoshuang, China
1996	Ioannis Melissanidis, Greece
2000	Igors Vihrovs, Latvia
2004	Kyle Shewfelt, Canada
2008	Zou Kai, China
2012	Zou Kai, China
2016	Max Whitlock, Great Britain

Horizontal Bar

1896	Hermann Weingärtner, Germany
1904	Anton Heida, United States; Edward Hennig, United States (tie)
1924	Leon Stukelj, Yugoslavia
1928	Georges Miez, Switzerland
1932	Dallas Denver Bixler, United States
1936	Aleksanteri Saarvala, Finland
1948	Josef Stalder, Switzerland
1952	Jakob "Jack" Günthard, Switzerland
1956	Takashi Ono, Japan
1960	Takashi Ono, Japan
1964	Boris Shakhlin, USSR
1968	Akinori Nakayama, Japan; Mikhail Voronin, USSR (tie)
1972	Mitsuo Tsukahara, Japan
1976	Mitsuo Tsukahara, Japan
1980	Stoyan Deltchev, Bulgaria
1984	Shinji Morisue, Japan
1988	Vladimir Artemov, USSR; Valeri Liukin, USSR (tie)
1992	Trent Dimas, United States
1996	Andreas Wecker, Germany
2000	Alexei Nemov, Russia
2004	Igor Cassina, Italy

Horizontal Bar

2008	Zou Kai, China
2012	Epke Zonderland, Netherlands
2016	Fabian Hambüchen, Germany

Individual All-Around

1900	Gustave Sandras, France
1904	Julius Lenhart, United States
1908	G. Alberto Braglia, Italy
1912	G. Alberto Braglia, Italy
1920	Giorgio Zampori, Italy
1924	Leon Stukelj, Yugoslavia
1928	Georges Miez, Switzerland
1932	Romeo Neri, Italy
1936	Karl-Alfred Schwarzmann, Germany
1948	Veikko Huhtanen, Finland
1952	Viktor Ivanovich Chukarin, USSR
1956	Viktor Ivanovich Chukarin, USSR
1960	Boris Shakhlin, USSR
1964	Yukio Endo, Japan
1968	Sawao Kato, Japan
1972	Sawao Kato, Japan
1976	Nikolay Andrianov, USSR
1980	Aleksandr Dityatin, USSR
1984	Koji Gushiken, Japan
1988	Vladimir Artemov, USSR
1992	Vitaly Scherbo, Unified Team (Belarus)
1996	Li Xiaoshuang, China
2000	Alexei Nemov, Russia
2004	Paul Hamm, United States
2008	Yang Wei, China
2012	Kohei Uchimura, Japan
2016	Kohei Uchimura, Japan

Parallel Bars

1896	Alfred Flatow, Germany
1904	George Eyser, United States
1924	August Güttinger, Switzerland
1928	Ladislav Vacha, Czechoslovakia
1932	Romeo Neri, Italy
1936	Konrad Frey, Germany
1948	Michael Reusch, Switzerland
1952	Hans Eugster, Switzerland
1956	Viktor Ivanovich Chukarin, USSR
1960	Boris Shakhlin, USSR
1964	Yukio Endo, Japan

Parallel Bars

1968	Akinori Nakayama, Japan
1972	Sawao Kato, Japan
1976	Sawao Kato, Japan
1980	Aleksandr Tkachev, USSR
1984	Bart Conner, United States
1988	Vladimir Artemov, USSR
1992	Vitaly Scherbo, Unified Team (Belarus)
1996	Roustam Sharipov, Ukraine
2000	Li Xiaopeng, China
2004	Valeri Goncharov, Ukraine
2008	Li Xiaopeng, China
2012	Feng Zhe, China
2016	Oleg Verniaiev, Ukraine

Pommel Horse

1896	Louis Zutter, Switzerland
1904	Anton Heida, United States
1924	Josef Wilhelm, Switzerland
1928	Hermann Hänggi, Switzerland
1932	István Pelle, Hungary
1936	Konrad Frey, Germany
1948	Paavo Johannes Aaltonen, Finland; Veikko Huhtanen, Finland; Heikki Savolainen, Finland (tie)
1952	Viktor Ivanovich Chukarin, USSR
1956	Boris Shakhlin, USSR
1960	Eugen Georg Oskar Ekman, Finland; Boris Shakhlin, USSR (tie)
1964	Miroslav Cerar, Yugoslavia
1968	Miroslav Cerar, Yugoslavia
1972	Viktor Klimenko, USSR
1976	Zoltan Magyar, Hungary
1980	Zoltan Magyar, Hungary
1984	Li Ning, China; Peter Glen Vidmar, United States (tie)
1988	Dmitri Bilozerchev, USSR; Zsolt Borkai, Hungary; Lubomir Geraskov, Bulgaria (tie)
1992	Pae Gil Su, N. Korea; Vitaly Scherbo, Unified Team (Belarus) (tie)
1996	Li Donghua, Switzerland
2000	Marius Daniel Urzica, Romania

Pommel Horse
2004 Teng Haibin, China
2008 Xiao Qin, China
2012 Krisztián Berki, Hungary
2016 Max Whitlock, Great Britain

Rings
1896 Ioannis Mitropoulos, Greece
1904 Hermann Glass, United States
1924 Francesco Martino, Italy
1928 Leon Stukelj, Yugoslavia
1932 George Gulack, United States
1936 Alois Hudec, Czechoslovakia
1948 Karl Frei, Switzerland
1952 Grant Shaginyan, USSR
1956 Albert Azaryan, USSR
1960 Albert Azaryan, USSR
1964 Takuji Hayata, Japan
1968 Akinori Nakayama, Japan
1972 Akinori Nakayama, Japan
1976 Nikolay Andrianov, USSR
1980 Aleksandr Dityatin, USSR
1984 Koji Gushiken, Japan;
     Li Ning, China (tie)
1988 Holger Behrendt, E. Germany;
     Dmitri Bilozerchev, USSR (tie)
1992 Vitaly Scherbo, Unified Team
     (Belarus)
1996 Juri Chechi, Italy
2000 Szilveszter Csollany, Hungary
2004 Dimosthenis Tampakos, Greece
2008 Chen Yibing, China

Rings
2012 Arthur Zanetti, Brazil
2016 Eleftherios Petrounias, Greece

Team Competition
1904 United States, United States,
     Unitedv States
1908 Sweden, Norway, Finland
1912 Italy, Hungary, Great Britain
1920 Italy, Belgium, France
1924 Italy, France, Switzerland
1928 Switzerland, Czechoslovakia,
     Yugoslavia
1932 Italy, United States, Finland
1936 Germany, Switzerland, Finland
1948 Finland, Switzerland, Hungary
1952 USSR, Switzerland, Finland
1956 USSR, Japan, Finland
1960 Japan, USSR, Italy
1964 Japan, USSR, Unified Team
     of Germany
1968 Japan, USSR, E. Germany
1972 Japan, USSR, E. Germany
1976 Japan, USSR, E. Germany
1980 USSR, E. Germany, Hungary
1984 United States, China, Japan
1988 USSR, E. Germany, Japan
1992 Unified Team, China, Japan
1996 Russia, China, Ukraine
2000 China, Ukraine, Russia
2004 Japan, United States, Romania
2008 China, Japan, United States
2012 China, Japan, Great Britain
2016 Japan, Russia, China

Vault
1896 Carl Schuhmann, Germany
1904 George Eyser, United States;
     Anton Heida, United States (tie)
1924 Frank Kriz, United States
1928 Eugen Mack, Switzerland
1932 Savino Guglielmetti, Italy
1936 Karl-Alfred Schwarzmann, Germany
1948 Paavo Johannes Aaltonen,
     Finland
1952 Viktor Ivanovich Chukarin, USSR
1956 Helmut Bantz, Unified Team of
     Germany; Valentin Muratov,
     USSR (tie)
1960 Takashi Ono, Japan;
     Boris Shakhlin, USSR (tie)
1964 Haruhiro Yamashita, Japan
1968 Mikhail Voronin, USSR
1972 Klaus Köste, E. Germany
1976 Nikolay Andrianov, USSR
1980 Nikolay Andrianov, USSR
1984 Lou Yun, China
1988 Lou Yun, China
1992 Vitaly Scherbo, Unified Team
     (Belarus)
1996 Alexei Nemov, Russia
2000 Gervasio Deferr, Spain
2004 Gervasio Deferr, Spain
2008 Leszek Blanik, Poland
2012 Yang Hak-seon, South Korea
2016 Ri Se Gwang, North Korea

Gymnastics—Women

Balance Beam
1952 Nina Bocharova, USSR
1956 Agnes Keleti, Hungary
1960 Eva Vechtova-Bosakova,
     Czechoslovakia
1964 Vera Caslavska, Czechoslovakia
1968 Natalya Kuchinskaya, USSR
1972 Olga Korbut, USSR
1976 Nadia Comaneci, Romania
1980 Nadia Comaneci, Romania
1984 Ecaterina Szabo, Romania;
     Simona Pauca, Romania (tie)
1988 Daniela Silivas, Romania
1992 Tatiana Lyssenko, Unified Team
     (Ukraine)
1996 Shannon Miller, United States
2000 Liu Xuan, China
2004 Catalina Ponor, Romania
2008 Shawn Johnson, United States
2012 Deng Linlin, China
2016 Sanne Wevers, Netherlands

Floor Exercise
1952 Agnes Keleti, Hungary
1956 Agnes Keleti, Hungary;
     Larisa Latynina, USSR (tie)
1960 Larisa Latynina, USSR
1964 Larisa Latynina, USSR
1968 Vera Caslavska, Czechoslovakia;
     Larisa Petrik, USSR (tie)
1972 Olga Korbut, USSR
1976 Nelli Kim, USSR
1980 Nelli Kim, USSR;
     Nadia Comaneci, Romania (tie)
1984 Ecaterina Szabo, Romania
1988 Daniela Silivas, Romania
1992 Lavinia Milosovici, Romania
1996 Lilia Podkopayeva, Ukraine
2000 Elena Zamolodchikova, Russia
2004 Catalina Ponor, Romania
2008 Sandra Izbasa, Romania
2012 Aly Raisman, United States
2016 Simone Biles, United States

Individual All-Around
1952 Mariya Gorokhovskaya, USSR
1956 Larisa Latynina, USSR
1960 Larisa Latynina, USSR
1964 Vera Caslavska, Czechoslovakia
1968 Vera Caslavska, Czechoslovakia
1972 Lyudmila Turischeva, USSR
1976 Nadia Comaneci, Romania
1980 Elena Davydova, USSR
1984 Mary-Lou Retton, United States
1988 Elena Shushunova, USSR
1992 Tatiana Gutsu, Unified Team
     (Ukraine)
1996 Lilia Podkopayeva, Ukraine
2000 Simona Amanar, Romania
2004 Carly Patterson, United States
2008 Nastia Liukin, United States
2012 Gabby Douglas, United States
2016 Simone Biles, United States

Team Competition
1928 Netherlands, Italy, Great Britain
1936 Germany, Czechoslovakia, Hungary
1948 Czechoslovakia, Hungary,
     United States
1952 USSR, Hungary, Czechoslovakia
1956 USSR, Hungary, Romania
1960 USSR, Czechoslovakia,
     Romania
1964 USSR, Czechoslovakia, Japan
1968 USSR, Czechoslovakia,
     E. Germany
1972 USSR, E. Germany, Hungary
1976 USSR, Romania, E. Germany
1980 USSR, Romania, E. Germany
1984 Romania, United States, China
1988 USSR, Romania, E. Germany
1992 Unified Team, Romania,
     United States
1996 United States, Russia, Romania
2000 Romania, Russia, United States
2004 Romania, United States, Russia
2008 China, United States, Romania

Team Competition
2012 United States, Russia, Romania
2016 United States, Russia, China

Uneven Bars
1952 Margit Korondi, Hungary
1956 Agnes Keleti, Hungary
1960 Polina Astakhova, USSR
1964 Polina Astakhova, USSR
1968 Vera Caslavska, Czechoslovakia
1972 Karin Janz, E. Germany
1976 Nadia Comaneci, Romania
1980 Maxi Gnauck, E. Germany
1984 Julianne McNamara, United States;
     Yan-Hong Ma, China (tie)
1988 Daniela Silivas, Romania
1992 Lu Li, China
1996 Svetlana Khorkina, Russia
2000 Svetlana Khorkina, Russia
2004 Emilie LePennec, France
2008 He Kexin, China
2012 Aliya Mustafina, Russia
2016 Aliya Mustafina, Russia

Vault
1952 Ekaterina Kalinchuk, USSR
1956 Larisa Latynina, USSR
1960 Margarita Nikolaeva, USSR
1964 Vera Caslavska, Czechoslovakia
1968 Vera Caslavska, Czechoslovakia
1972 Karin Janz, E. Germany
1976 Nelli Kim, USSR
1980 Natalia Shaposhnikova, USSR
1984 Ecaterina Szabo, Romania
1988 Svetlana Boginskaya, USSR
1992 Henrietta Onodi, Hungary;
     Lavinia Milosovici, Romania (tie)
1996 Simona Amanar, Romania
2000 Elena Zamolodchikova, Russia
2004 Monica Rosu, Romania
2008 Hong Un Jong, N. Korea
2012 Sandra Izbaşa, Romania
2016 Simone Biles, United States

Soccer

Men
1900 Great Britain, France, Belgium
1904 Canada, United States, United States
1908 Great Britain, Denmark, Netherlands
1912 Great Britain, Denmark, Netherlands
1920 Belgium, Spain, Netherlands
1924 Uruguay, Switzerland, Sweden

Men
1928 Uruguay, Argentina, Italy
1936 Italy, Austria, Norway
1948 Sweden, Yugoslavia, Denmark
1952 Hungary, Yugoslavia, Sweden
1956 USSR, Yugoslavia, Bulgaria
1960 Yugoslavia, Denmark, Hungary

Men
1964 Hungary, Czechoslovakia,
     Unified Team of Germany
1968 Hungary, Bulgaria, Japan
1972 Poland; Hungary; USSR,
     E. Germany (tie for bronze)
1976 E. Germany, Poland, USSR

Men		Men		Women	
1980	Czechoslovakia, E. Germany, USSR	2000	Cameroon, Spain, Chile	1996	United States, China, Norway
1984	France, Brazil, Yugoslavia	2004	Argentina, Paraguay, Italy	2000	Norway, United States, Germany
1988	USSR, Brazil, W. Germany	2008	Argentina, Nigeria, Brazil	2004	United States, Brazil, Germany
1992	Spain, Poland, Ghana	2012	Mexico, Brazil, South Korea	2008	United States, Brazil, Germany
1996	Nigeria, Argentina, Brazil	2016	Brazil, Germany, Nigeria	2012	United States, Japan, Canada
				2016	Germany, Sweden, Canada

Swimming and Diving—Men

50-Meter Freestyle		Time
1988	Matt Biondi, United States	0:22.14
1992	Aleksandr Popov, Unified Team (Rus.)	0:21.91
1996	Aleksandr Popov, Russia	0:22.13
2000	Anthony Ervin, United States	0:21.98
	Gary Hall Jr., United States (tie)	0:21.98
2004	Gary Hall Jr., United States	0:21.93
2008	Cesar Cielo Filho, Brazil	0:21.30*
2012	Florent Manaudou, France	0:21.34
2016	Anthony Ervin, United States	0:21.40

100-Meter Freestyle		Time
1896	Alfred Hajos, Hungary	1:22.2
1904	Zoltan de Halmay, Hungary (100 yds)	1:02.8
1908	Charles Daniels, United States	1:05.6
1912	Duke P. Kahanamoku, United States	1:03.4
1920	Duke P. Kahanamoku, United States	1:01.4
1924	Johnny Weissmuller, United States	0:59.0
1928	Johnny Weissmuller, United States	0:58.6
1932	Yasuji Miyazaki, Japan	0:58.2
1936	Ferenc Csik, Hungary	0:57.6
1948	Wally Ris, United States	0:57.3
1952	Clarke Scholes, United States	0:57.4
1956	Jon Henricks, Australia	0:55.4
1960	John Devitt, Australia	0:55.2
1964	Don Schollander, United States	0:53.4
1968	Mike Wenden, Australia	0:52.2
1972	Mark Spitz, United States	0:51.22
1976	Jim Montgomery, United States	0:49.99
1980	Jorg Woithe, E. Germany	0:50.40
1984	Ambrose "Rowdy" Gaines, United States	0:49.80
1988	Matt Biondi, United States	0:48.63
1992	Aleksandr Popov, Unified Team (Rus.)	0:49.02
1996	Aleksandr Popov, Russia	0:48.74
2000	Pieter van den Hoogenband, Netherlands	0:48.30
2004	Pieter van den Hoogenband, Netherlands	0:48.17
2008	Alain Bernard, France	0:47.21
2012	Nathan Adrian, United States	0:47.52
2016	Kyle Chalmers, Australia	0:47.58

200-Meter Freestyle		Time
1968	Mike Wenden, Australia	1:55.2
1972	Mark Spitz, United States	1:52.78
1976	Bruce Furniss, United States	1:50.29
1980	Sergei Kopliakov, USSR	1:49.81
1984	Michael Gross, W. Germany	1:47.44
1988	Duncan Armstrong, Australia	1:47.25
1992	Yevgeny Sadovyi, Unified Team (Rus.)	1:46.70
1996	Danyon Loader, New Zealand	1:47.63
2000	Pieter van den Hoogenband, Netherlands	1:45.35
2004	Ian Thorpe, Australia	1:44.71
2008	Michael Phelps, United States	1:42.96*
2012	Yannick Agnel, France	1:43.14
2016	Sun Yang, China	1:44.65

400-Meter Freestyle		Time
1904	C. M. Daniels, United States (440 yds)	6:16.2
1908	Henry Taylor, Great Britain	5:36.8
1912	George Hodgson, Canada	5:24.4
1920	Norman Ross, United States	5:26.8
1924	Johnny Weissmuller, United States	5:04.2
1928	Albert Zorilla, Argentina	5:01.6
1932	Clarence Crabbe, United States	4:48.4
1936	Jack Medica, United States	4:44.5
1948	William Smith, United States	4:41.0
1952	Jean Boiteux, France	4:30.7
1956	Murray Rose, Australia	4:27.3
1960	Murray Rose, Australia	4:18.3
1964	Don Schollander, United States	4:12.2
1968	Mike Burton, United States	4:09.0
1972	Brad Cooper, Australia	4:00.27
1976	Brian Goodell, United States	3:51.93
1980	Vladimir Salnikov, USSR	3:51.31
1984	George DiCarlo, United States	3:51.23
1988	Uwe Dassler, E. Germany	3:46.95
1992	Yevgeny Sadovyi, Unified Team (Rus.)	3:45.00
1996	Danyon Loader, New Zealand	3:47.97
2000	Ian Thorpe, Australia	3:40.59
2004	Ian Thorpe, Australia	3:43.10
2008	Park Tae-hwan, S. Korea	3:41.86
2012	Sun Yang, China	3:40.14*
2016	Mack Horton, Australia	3:41.55

1500-Meter Freestyle		Time
1908	Henry Taylor, Great Britain	22:48.4
1912	George Hodgson, Canada	22:00.0
1920	Norman Ross, United States	22:23.2
1924	Andrew Charlton, Australia	20:06.6
1928	Arne Borg, Sweden	19:51.8
1932	Kusuo Kitamura, Japan	19:12.4
1936	Noboru Terada, Japan	19:13.7
1948	James McLane, United States	19:18.5
1952	Ford Konno, United States	18:30.3
1956	Murray Rose, Australia	17:58.9
1960	John Konrads, Australia	17:19.6
1964	Robert Windle, Australia	17:01.7
1968	Mike Burton, United States	16:38.9
1972	Mike Burton, United States	15:52.58
1976	Brian Goodell, United States	15:02.40
1980	Vladimir Salnikov, USSR	14:58.27
1984	Michael O'Brien, United States	15:05.20
1988	Vladimir Salnikov, USSR	15:00.40
1992	Kieren Perkins, Australia	14:43.48
1996	Kieren Perkins, Australia	14:56.40
2000	Grant Hackett, Australia	14:48.33
2004	Grant Hackett, Australia	14:43.40
2008	Oussama Mellouli, Tunisia	14:40.84
2012	Sun Yang, China	14:31.02*
2016	Gregorio Paltrinieri, Italy	14:34.57

100-Meter Backstroke		Time
1904	Walter Brack, Germany (100 yds)	1:16.8
1908	Arno Bieberstein, Germany	1:24.6
1912	Harry Hebner, United States	1:21.2
1920	Warren Kealoha, United States	1:15.2
1924	Warren Kealoha, United States	1:13.2
1928	George Kojac, United States	1:08.2
1932	Masaji Kiyokawa, Japan	1:08.6
1936	Adolph Kiefer, United States	1:05.9
1948	Allen Stack, United States	1:06.4
1952	Yoshi Oyakawa, United States	1:05.4
1956	David Theile, Australia	1:02.2
1960	David Theile, Australia	1:01.9
1968	Roland Matthes, E. Germany	0:58.7
1972	Roland Matthes, E. Germany	0:56.58
1976	John Naber, United States	0:55.49
1980	Bengt Baron, Sweden	0:56.33
1984	Rick Carey, United States	0:55.79
1988	Daichi Suzuki, Japan	0:55.05
1992	Mark Tewksbury, Canada	0:53.98
1996	Jeff Rouse, United States	0:54.10
2000	Lenny Krayzelburg, United States	0:53.72
2004	Aaron Peirsol, United States	0:54.06
2008	Aaron Peirsol, United States	0:52.54
2012	Matt Grevers, United States	0:52.16
2016	Ryan Murphy, United States	0:51.97*

200-Meter Backstroke		Time
1964	Jed Graef, United States	2:10.3
1968	Roland Matthes, E. Germany	2:09.6
1972	Roland Matthes, E. Germany	2:02.82
1976	John Naber, United States	1:59.19
1980	Sandor Wladar, Hungary	2:01.93
1984	Rick Carey, United States	2:00.23
1988	Igor Polyanski, USSR	1:59.37
1992	Martin Lopez-Zubero, Spain	1:58.47
1996	Brad Bridgewater, United States	1:58.54
2000	Lenny Krayzelburg, United States	1:56.76
2004	Aaron Peirsol, United States	1:54.95
2008	Ryan Lochte, United States	1:53.94
2012	Tyler Clary, United States	1:53.41*
2016	Ryan Murphy, United States	1:53.62

100-Meter Breaststroke		Time
1968	Don McKenzie, United States	1:07.79
1972	Nobutaka Taguchi, Japan	1:04.94
1976	John Hencken, United States	1:03.11
1980	Duncan Goodhew, Great Britain	1:03.44
1984	Steve Lundquist, United States	1:01.65
1988	Adrian Moorhouse, Great Britain	1:02.04
1992	Nelson Diebel, United States	1:01.50

100-Meter Breaststroke

Year	Champion	Time
1996	Fred Deburghgraeve, Belgium	1:00.60
2000	Domenico Fioravanti, Italy	1:00.46
2004	Kosuke Kitajima, Japan	1:00.08
2008	Kosuke Kitajima, Japan	0:58.91
2012	Cameron van der Burgh, South Africa	0:58.46
2016	Adam Peaty, Great Britain	0:57.13*

200-Meter Breaststroke

Year	Champion	Time
1908	Frederick Holman, Great Britain	3:09.2
1912	Walter Bathe, Germany	3:01.8
1920	Hakan Malmrot, Sweden	3:04.4
1924	Robert Skelton, United States	2:56.6
1928	Yoshiyuki Tsuruta, Japan	2:48.8
1932	Yoshiyuki Tsuruta, Japan	2:45.4
1936	Tetsuo Hamuro, Japan	2:41.5
1948	Joseph Verdeur, United States	2:39.3
1952	John Davies, Australia	2:34.4
1956	Masura Furukawa, Japan	2:34.7
1960	William Mulliken, United States	2:37.4
1964	Ian O'Brien, Australia	2:27.8
1968	Felipe Muñoz, Mexico	2:28.7
1972	John Hencken, United States	2:21.55
1976	David Wilkie, Great Britain	2:15.11
1980	Robertas Zhulpa, USSR	2:15.85
1984	Victor Davis, Canada	2:13.34
1988	Jozsef Szabo, Hungary	2:13.52
1992	Mike Barrowman, United States	2:10.16
1996	Norbert Rozsa, Hungary	2:12.57
2000	Domenico Fioravanti, Italy	2:10.87
2004	Kosuke Kitajima, Japan	2:09.44
2008	Kosuke Kitajima, Japan	2:07.64
2012	Dániel Gyurta, Hungary	2:07.28
2016	Dmitriy Balandin, Kazakhstan	2:07.46

100-Meter Butterfly

Year	Champion	Time
1968	Doug Russell, United States	0:55.9
1972	Mark Spitz, United States	0:54.27
1976	Matt Vogel, United States	0:54.35
1980	Par Arvidsson, Sweden	0:54.92
1984	Michael Gross, W. Germany	0:53.08
1988	Anthony Nesty, Suriname	0:53.00
1992	Pablo Morales, United States	0:53.32
1996	Denis Pankratov, Russia	0:52.27
2000	Lars Froelander, Sweden	0:52.00
2004	Michael Phelps, United States	0:51.25
2008	Michael Phelps, United States	0:50.58
2012	Michael Phelps, United States	0:51.21
2016	Joseph Schooling, Singapore	0:50.39*

200-Meter Butterfly

Year	Champion	Time
1956	William Yorzyk, United States	2:19.3
1960	Michael Troy, United States	2:12.8
1964	Kevin J. Berry, Australia	2:06.6
1968	Carl Robie, United States	2:08.7
1972	Mark Spitz, United States	2:00.70
1976	Mike Bruner, United States	1:59.23
1980	Sergei Fesenko, USSR	1:59.76
1984	Jon Sieben, Australia	1:57.04
1988	Michael Gross, W. Germany	1:56.94
1992	Mel Stewart, United States	1:56.26
1996	Denis Pankratov, Russia	1:56.51
2000	Tom Malchow, United States	1:55.35
2004	Michael Phelps, United States	1:54.04
2008	Michael Phelps, United States	1:52.03*
2012	Chad le Clos, South Africa	1:52.96
2016	Michael Phelps, United States	1:53.36

200-Meter Individual Medley

Year	Champion	Time
1968	Charles Hickcox, United States	2:12.0
1972	Gunnar Larsson, Sweden	2:07.17
1984	Alex Baumann, Canada	2:01.42
1988	Tamas Darnyi, Hungary	2:00.17
1992	Tamas Darnyi, Hungary	2:00.76
1996	Attila Czene, Hungary	1:59.91
2000	Massimiliano Rosolino, Italy	1:58.98
2004	Michael Phelps, United States	1:57.14
2008	Michael Phelps, United States	1:54.23*
2012	Michael Phelps, United States	1:54.27
2016	Michael Phelps, United States	1:54.66

400-Meter Individual Medley

Year	Champion	Time
1964	Dick Roth, United States	4:45.4
1968	Charles Hickcox, United States	4:48.4
1972	Gunnar Larsson, Sweden	4:31.98
1976	Rod Strachan, United States	4:23.68
1980	Aleksandr Sidorenko, USSR	4:22.89
1984	Alex Baumann, Canada	4:17.41
1988	Tamas Darnyi, Hungary	4:14.75
1992	Tamas Darnyi, Hungary	4:14.23
1996	Tom Dolan, United States	4:14.90
2000	Tom Dolan, United States	4:11.76

400-Meter Individual Medley

Year	Champion	Time
2004	Michael Phelps, United States	4:08.26
2008	Michael Phelps, United States	4:03.84*
2012	Ryan Lochte, United States	4:05.18
2016	Kosuke Hagino, Japan	4:06.05

4x100-Meter Freestyle Relay

Year	Champion	Time
1964	United States	3:31.2
1968	United States	3:31.7
1972	United States	3:26.42
1984	United States	3:19.03
1988	United States	3:16.53
1992	United States	3:16.74
1996	United States	3:15.41
2000	Australia	3:13.67
2004	South Africa	3:13.17
2008	United States	3:08.24*
2012	France	3:09.93
2016	United States	3:09.92

4x200-Meter Freestyle Relay

Year	Champion	Time
1908	Great Britain	10:55.6
1912	Australasia (Australia and New Zealand)	10:11.6
1920	United States	10:04.4
1924	United States	9:53.4
1928	United States	9:36.2
1932	Japan	8:58.4
1936	Japan	8:51.5
1948	United States	8:46.0
1952	United States	8:31.1
1956	Australia	8:23.6
1960	United States	8:10.2
1964	United States	7:52.1
1968	United States	7:52.33
1972	United States	7:35.78
1976	United States	7:23.22
1980	USSR	7:23.50
1984	United States	7:15.69
1988	United States	7:12.51
1992	Unified Team	7:11.95
1996	United States	7:14.84
2000	Australia	7:07.05
2004	United States	7:07.33
2008	United States	6:58.56*
2012	United States	6:59.70
2016	United States	7:00.66

4x100-Meter Medley Relay

Year	Champion	Time
1960	United States	4:05.4
1964	United States	3:58.4
1968	United States	3:54.9
1972	United States	3:48.16
1976	United States	3:42.22
1980	Australia	3:45.70
1984	United States	3:39.30
1988	United States	3:36.93
1992	United States	3:36.93
1996	United States	3:34.84
2000	United States	3:33.73
2004	United States	3:30.68
2008	United States	3:29.34
2012	United States	3:29.35
2016	United States	3:27.95*

10-Kilometer Marathon

Year	Champion	Time
2008	Maarten van der Weijden, Netherlands	1:51:51.6
2012	Oussama Mellouli, Tunisia	1:49:55.1
2016	Ferry Weertman, Netherlands	1:52:59.8

Platform Diving

Year	Champion	Points
1904	Dr. G. E. Sheldon, United States	112.75
1908	Hjalmar Johansson, Sweden	183.75
1912	Erik Adlerz, Sweden	73.94
1920	Clarence Pinkston, United States	100.67
1924	Albert White, United States	97.46
1928	Pete Desjardins, United States	98.74
1932	Harold Smith, United States	124.80
1936	Marshall Wayne, United States	113.58
1948	Sammy Lee, United States	130.05
1952	Sammy Lee, United States	156.28
1956	Joaquin Capilla, Mexico	152.44
1960	Robert Webster, United States	165.56
1964	Robert Webster, United States	148.58
1968	Klaus Dibiasi, Italy	164.18
1972	Klaus Dibiasi, Italy	504.12
1976	Klaus Dibiasi, Italy	600.51
1980	Falk Hoffmann, E. Germany	835.65
1984	Greg Louganis, United States	710.91
1988	Greg Louganis, United States	638.61
1992	Sun Shuwei, China	677.31
1996	Dmitri Sautin, Russia	692.34
2000	Tian Liang, China	724.53
2004	Hu Jia, China	748.08
2008	Matthew Mitcham, Australia	537.95

Platform Diving	Points
2012 David Boudia, United States.	568.65
2016 Chen Aisen, China	545.35

Springboard Diving	Points
1908 Albert Zurner, Germany	85.50
1912 Paul Guenther, Germany	79.23
1920 Louis Kuehn, United States	675.40
1924 Albert White, United States	97.46
1928 Pete Desjardins, United States.	185.04
1932 Michael Galitzen, United States	161.38
1936 Richard Degener, United States.	163.57
1948 Bruce Harlan, United States	163.64
1952 David Browning, United States.	205.29
1956 Robert Clotworthy, United States	159.56
1960 Gary Tobian, United States	170.00
1964 Kenneth Sitzberger, United States	159.90
1968 Bernie Wrightson, United States	170.15
1972 Vladimir Vasin, USSR.	594.09
1976 Phil Boggs, United States	619.52
1980 Aleksandr Portnov, USSR	905.02
1984 Greg Louganis, United States	754.41
1988 Greg Louganis, United States	730.80

Springboard Diving	Points
1992 Mark Lenzi, United States	676.53
1996 Xiong Ni, China.	701.46
2000 Xiong Ni, China.	708.72
2004 Peng Bo, China	787.30
2008 He Chong, China	572.90
2012 Ilya Zakharov, Russia.	555.90
2016 Cao Yuan, China.	547.60

Synchronized Platform Diving	Points
2004 Tian Liang & Yang Jinghui, China	383.88
2008 Lin Yue & Huo Liang, China	468.18
2012 Cao Yuan & Zhang Yanquan, China	486.78
2016 Chen Aisen & Lin Yue, China	496.98

Synchronized Springboard Diving	Points
2004 Nikolaos Siranidis & Thomas Bimis, Greece	353.34
2008 Wang Feng & Qin Kai, China	469.08
2012 Luo Yutong & Qin Kai, China	477.00
2016 Jack Laugher & Chris Mears, Great Britain	454.32

Swimming and Diving—Women

50-Meter Freestyle	Time
1988 Kristin Otto, E. Germany.	0:25.49
1992 Yang Wenyi, China.	0:24.76
1996 Amy Van Dyken, United States	0:24.87
2000 Inge de Bruijn, Netherlands	0:24.32
2004 Inge de Bruijn, Netherlands	0:24.58
2008 Britta Steffen, Germany	0:24.06
2012 Ranomi Kromowidjojo, Netherlands	0:24.05*
2016 Pernille Blume, Denmark	0:24.07

100-Meter Freestyle	Time
1912 Fanny Durack, Australia	1:22.2
1920 Ethelda Bleibtrey, United States.	1:13.6
1924 Ethel Lackie, United States	1:12.4
1928 Albina Osipowich, United States	1:11.0
1932 Helene Madison, United States	1:06.8
1936 Hendrika Mastenbroek, Netherlands	1:05.9
1948 Greta Andersen, Denmark	1:06.3
1952 Katalin Szoke, Hungary	1:06.8
1956 Dawn Fraser, Australia.	1:02.0
1960 Dawn Fraser, Australia.	1:01.2
1964 Dawn Fraser, Australia.	0:59.5
1968 Jan Henne, United States.	1:00.0
1972 Sandra Neilson, United States	0:58.59
1976 Kornelia Ender, E. Germany.	0:55.65
1980 Barbara Krause, E. Germany	0:54.79
1984 Carrie Steinseifer, United States	0:55.92
Nancy Hogshead, United States (tie)	0:55.92
1988 Kristin Otto, E. Germany.	0:54.93
1992 Zhuang Yong, China.	0:54.64
1996 Li Jingyi, China.	0:54.50
2000 Inge de Bruijn, Netherlands	0:53.83
2004 Jodie Henry, Australia	0:53.84
2008 Britta Steffen, Germany	0:53.12
2012 Ranomi Kromowidjojo, Netherlands	0:53.00
2016 Simone Manuel, United States.	0:52.70*
Penny Oleksiak, Canada (tie).	0:52.70*

200-Meter Freestyle	Time
1968 Debbie Meyer, United States	2:10.5
1972 Shane Gould, Australia.	2:03.56
1976 Kornelia Ender, E. Germany.	1:59.26
1980 Barbara Krause, E. Germany	1:58.33
1984 Mary Wayte, United States.	1:59.23
1988 Heike Friedrich, E. Germany	1:57.65
1992 Nicole Haislett, United States	1:57.90
1996 Claudia Poll, Costa Rica.	1:58.16
2000 Susan O'Neill, Australia	1:58.24
2004 Camelia Potec, Romania	1:58.03
2008 Federica Pellegrini, Italy.	1:54.82
2012 Allison Schmitt, United States	1:53.61*
2016 Katie Ledecky, United States	1:53.73

400-Meter Freestyle	Time
1924 Martha Norelius, United States	6:02.2
1928 Martha Norelius, United States	5:42.8
1932 Helene Madison, United States	5:28.5
1936 Hendrika Mastenbroek, Netherlands	5:26.4
1948 Ann Curtis, United States	5:17.8
1952 Valerie Gyenge, Hungary	5:12.1
1956 Lorraine Crapp, Australia	4:54.6
1960 Chris von Saltza, United States	4:50.6
1964 Virginia Duenkel, United States	4:43.3
1968 Debbie Meyer, United States	4:31.8
1972 Shane Gould, Australia.	4:19.44

400-Meter Freestyle	Time
1976 Petra Thuemer, E. Germany	4:09.89
1980 Ines Diers, E. Germany	4:08.76
1984 Tiffany Cohen, United States	4:07.10
1988 Janet Evans, United States	4:03.85
1992 Dagmar Hase, Germany.	4:07.18
1996 Michelle Smith, Ireland.	4:07.25
2000 Brooke Bennett, United States	4:05.80
2004 Laure Manaudou, France	4:05.34
2008 Rebecca Adlington, Great Britain	4:03.22
2012 Camille Muffat, France	4:01.45
2016 Katie Ledecky, United States	3:56.46*

800-Meter Freestyle	Time
1968 Debbie Meyer, United States	9:24.0
1972 Keena Rothhammer, United States	8:53.68
1976 Petra Thuemer, E. Germany	8:37.14
1980 Michelle Ford, Australia	8:28.90
1984 Tiffany Cohen, United States	8:24.95
1988 Janet Evans, United States	8:20.20
1992 Janet Evans, United States	8:25.52
1996 Brooke Bennett, United States.	8:27.89
2000 Brooke Bennett, United States.	8:19.67
2004 Ai Shibata, Japan.	8:24.54
2008 Rebecca Adlington, Great Britain	8:14.10
2012 Katie Ledecky, United States	8:14.63
2016 Katie Ledecky, United States	8:04.79*

100-Meter Backstroke	Time
1924 Sybil Bauer, United States	1:23.2
1928 Marie Braun, Netherlands.	1:22.0
1932 Eleanor Holm, United States	1:19.4
1936 Dina Senff, Netherlands	1:18.9
1948 Karen Harup, Denmark.	1:14.4
1952 Joan Harrison, South Africa	1:14.3
1956 Judy Grinham, Great Britain	1:12.9
1960 Lynn Burke, United States	1:09.3
1964 Cathy Ferguson, United States	1:07.7
1968 Kaye Hall, United States.	1:06.2
1972 Melissa Belote, United States.	1:05.78
1976 Ulrike Richter, E. Germany.	1:01.83
1980 Rica Reinisch, E. Germany	1:00.86
1984 Theresa Andrews, United States	1:02.55
1988 Kristin Otto, E. Germany.	1:00.89
1992 Krisztina Egerszegi, Hungary	1:00.68
1996 Beth Botsford, United States	1:01.19
2000 Diana Mocanu, Romania	1:00.21
2004 Natalie Coughlin, United States	1:00.37
2008 Natalie Coughlin, United States	0:58.96
2012 Missy Franklin, United States.	0:58.33
2016 Katinka Hosszú, Hungary	0:58.45

200-Meter Backstroke	Time
1968 Lillian "Pokey" Watson, United States	2:24.8
1972 Melissa Belote, United States.	2:19.19
1976 Ulrike Richter, E. Germany.	2:13.43
1980 Rica Reinisch, E. Germany	2:11.77
1984 Jolanda de Rover, Netherlands	2:12.38
1988 Krisztina Egerszegi, Hungary	2:09.29
1992 Krisztina Egerszegi, Hungary	2:07.06
1996 Krisztina Egerszegi, Hungary	2:07.83
2000 Diana Mocanu, Romania	2:08.16
2004 Kirsty Coventry, Zimbabwe.	2:09.19
2008 Kirsty Coventry, Zimbabwe.	2:05.24
2012 Missy Franklin, United States.	2:04.06*
2016 Maya DiRado, United States.	2:05.99

100-Meter Breaststroke

		Time
1968	Djurdjica Bjedov, Yugoslavia	1:15.8
1972	Cathy Carr, United States	1:13.58
1976	Hannelore Anke, E. Germany	1:11.16
1980	Ute Geweniger, E. Germany	1:10.22
1984	Petra Van Staveren, Netherlands	1:09.88
1988	Tania Dangalakova, Bulgaria	1:07.95
1992	Yelena Rudkovskaya, Unified Team (Bel.)	1:08.00
1996	Penny Heyns, South Africa	1:07.73
2000	Megan Quann, United States	1:07.05
2004	Luo Xuejuan, China	1:06.64
2008	Leisel Jones, Australia	1:05.17
2012	Ruta Meilutyte, Lithuania	1:05.47
2016	Lilly King, United States	1:04.93*

200-Meter Breaststroke

		Time
1924	Lucy Morton, Great Britain	3:33.2
1928	Hilde Schrader, Germany	3:12.6
1932	Clare Dennis, Australia	3:06.3
1936	Hideko Maehata, Japan	3:03.6
1948	Nelly Van Vliet, Netherlands	2:57.2
1952	Eva Szekely, Hungary	2:51.7
1956	Ursula Happe, Germany	2:53.1
1960	Anita Lonsbrough, Great Britain	2:49.5
1964	Galina Prozumenshchikova, USSR	2:46.4
1968	Sharon Wichman, United States	2:44.4
1972	Beverly Whitfield, Australia	2:41.71
1976	Marina Koshevaia, USSR	2:33.35
1980	Lina Kachushite, USSR	2:29.54
1984	Anne Ottenbrite, Canada	2:30.38
1988	Silke Hoerner, E. Germany	2:26.71
1992	Kyoko Iwasaki, Japan	2:26.65
1996	Penny Heyns, South Africa	2:25.41
2000	Agnes Kovacs, Hungary	2:24.35
2004	Amanda Beard, United States	2:23.37
2008	Rebecca Soni, United States	2:20.22
2012	Rebecca Soni, United States	2:19.59*
2016	Rie Kaneto, Japan	2:20.30

100-Meter Butterfly

		Time
1956	Shelley Mann, United States	1:11.0
1960	Carolyn Schuler, United States	1:09.5
1964	Sharon Stouder, United States	1:04.7
1968	Lynn McClements, Australia	1:05.5
1972	Mayumi Aoki, Japan	1:03.34
1976	Kornelia Ender, E. Germany	1:00.13
1980	Caren Metschuck, E. Germany	1:00.42
1984	Mary T. Meagher, United States	0:59.26
1988	Kristin Otto, E. Germany	0:59.00
1992	Qian Hong, China	0:58.62
1996	Amy Van Dyken, United States	0:59.13
2000	Inge de Bruijn, Netherlands	0:56.61
2004	Petria Thomas, Australia	0:57.72
2008	Lisbeth Trickett, Australia	0:56.73
2012	Dana Vollmer, United States	0:55.98
2016	Sarah Sjöström, Sweden	0:55.48*

200-Meter Butterfly

		Time
1968	Ada Kok, Netherlands	2:24.7
1972	Karen Moe, United States	2:15.57
1976	Andrea Pollack, E. Germany	2:11.41
1980	Ines Geissler, E. Germany	2:10.44
1984	Mary T. Meagher, United States	2:06.90
1988	Kathleen Nord, E. Germany	2:09.51
1992	Summer Sanders, United States	2:08.67
1996	Susan O'Neill, Australia	2:07.76
2000	Misty Hyman, United States	2:05.88
2004	Otylia Jedrzejczak, Poland	2:06.05
2008	Liu Zige, China	2:04.18
2012	Jiao Liuyang, China	2:04.06*
2016	Mireia Belmonte, Spain	2:04.85

200-Meter Individual Medley

		Time
1968	Claudia Kolb, United States	2:24.7
1972	Shane Gould, Australia	2:23.07
1984	Tracy Caulkins, United States	2:12.64
1988	Daniela Hunger, E. Germany	2:12.59
1992	Lin Li, China	2:11.65
1996	Michelle Smith, Ireland	2:13.93
2000	Yana Klochkova, Ukraine	2:10.68
2004	Yana Klochkova, Ukraine	2:11.14
2008	Stephanie Rice, Australia	2:08.45
2012	Ye Shiwen, China	2:07.57
2016	Katinka Hosszú, Hungary	2:06.58*

400-Meter Individual Medley

		Time
1964	Donna de Varona, United States	5:18.7
1968	Claudia Kolb, United States	5:08.5
1972	Gail Neall, Australia	5:02.97
1976	Ulrike Tauber, E. Germany	4:42.77

400-Meter Individual Medley

		Time
1980	Petra Schneider, E. Germany	4:36.29
1984	Tracy Caulkins, United States	4:39.24
1988	Janet Evans, United States	4:37.76
1992	Krisztina Egerszegi, Hungary	4:36.54
1996	Michelle Smith, Ireland	4:39.18
2000	Yana Klochkova, Ukraine	4:33.59
2004	Yana Klochkova, Ukraine	4:34.83
2008	Stephanie Rice, Australia	4:29.45
2012	Ye Shiwen, China	4:28.43
2016	Katinka Hosszú, Hungary	4:26.36*

4x100-Meter Freestyle Relay

		Time
1912	Great Britain	5:52.8
1920	United States	5:11.6
1924	United States	4:58.8
1928	United States	4:47.6
1932	United States	4:38.0
1936	Netherlands	4:36.0
1948	United States	4:29.2
1952	Hungary	4:24.4
1956	Australia	4:17.1
1960	United States	4:08.9
1964	United States	4:03.8
1968	United States	4:02.5
1972	United States	3:55.19
1976	United States	3:44.82
1980	East Germany	3:42.71
1984	United States	3:43.43
1988	East Germany	3:40.63
1992	United States	3:39.46
1996	United States	3:39.29
2000	United States	3:36.61
2004	Australia	3:35.94
2008	Netherlands	3:33.76
2012	Australia	3:33.15
2016	Australia	3:30.65*

4x200-Meter Freestyle Relay

		Time
1996	United States	7:59.87
2000	United States	7:57.80
2004	United States	7:53.42
2008	Australia	7:44.31
2012	United States	7:42.92*
2016	United States	7:43.03

4x100-Meter Medley Relay

		Time
1960	United States	4:41.1
1964	United States	4:33.9
1968	United States	4:28.3
1972	United States	4:20.75
1976	East Germany	4:07.95
1980	East Germany	4:06.67
1984	United States	4:08.34
1988	East Germany	4:03.74
1992	United States	4:02.54
1996	United States	4:02.88
2000	United States	3:58.30
2004	Australia	3:57.32
2008	Australia	3:52.69
2012	United States	3:52.05*
2016	United States	3:53.13

10-Kilometer Marathon

		Time
2008	Larisa Ilchenko, Russia	1:59:27.7
2012	Éva Risztov, Hungary	1:57:38.2
2016	Sharon van Rouwendaal, Netherlands	1:56:32.1

Platform Diving

		Points
1912	Greta Johansson, Sweden	39.90
1920	Stefani Fryland-Clausen, Denmark	34.60
1924	Caroline Smith, United States	33.20
1928	Elizabeth B. Pinkston, United States	31.60
1932	Dorothy Poynton, United States	40.26
1936	Dorothy Poynton Hill, United States	33.93
1948	Victoria M. Draves, United States	68.87
1952	Patricia McCormick, United States	79.37
1956	Patricia McCormick, United States	84.85
1960	Ingrid Kramer, Germany	91.28
1964	Lesley Bush, United States	99.80
1968	Milena Duchkova, Czechoslovakia	109.59
1972	Ulrika Knape, Sweden	390.00
1976	Elena Vaytsekhouskaya, USSR	406.59
1980	Martina Jaschke, E. Germany	596.25
1984	Zhou Jihong, China	435.51
1988	Xu Yanmei, China	445.20
1992	Fu Mingxia, China	461.43
1996	Fu Mingxia, China	521.58
2000	Laura Wilkinson, United States	543.75
2004	Chantelle Newbery, Australia	590.31

Platform Diving	Points
2008 Chen Ruolin, China	447.70
2012 Chen Ruolin, China	422.30
2016 Ren Qian, China	439.25

Springboard Diving	Points
1920 Aileen Riggin, United States	539.90
1924 Elizabeth Becker, United States	474.50
1928 Helen Meany, United States	78.62
1932 Georgia Coleman, United States	87.52
1936 Marjorie Gestring, United States	89.27
1948 Victoria M. Draves, United States	108.74
1952 Patricia McCormick, United States	147.30
1956 Patricia McCormick, United States	142.36
1960 Ingrid Kramer, Germany	155.81
1964 Ingrid Engel-Kramer, Germany	145.00
1968 Sue Gossick, United States	150.77
1972 Micki King, United States	450.03
1976 Jenni Chandler, United States	506.19
1980 Irina Kalinina, USSR	725.91
1984 Sylvie Bernier, Canada	530.70

Springboard Diving	Points
1988 Gao Min, China	580.23
1992 Gao Min, China	572.40
1996 Fu Mingxia, China	547.68
2000 Fu Mingxia, China	609.42
2004 Guo Jingjing, China	633.15
2008 Guo Jingjing, China	415.35
2012 Wu Minxia, China	414.00
2016 Shi Tingmao, China	406.05

Synchronized Platform Diving	Points
2004 Lao Lishi & Li Ting, China	352.14
2008 Wang Xin & Chen Ruolin, China	363.54
2012 Chen Ruolin & Wang Hao, China	368.40
2016 Chen Ruolin & Liu Huixia, China	354.00

Synchronized Springboard Diving	Points
2004 Wu Minxia & Guo Jingjing, China	336.90
2008 Guo Jingjing & Wu Minxia, China	343.50
2012 He Zi & Wu Minxia, China	346.20
2016 Wu Minxia & Shi Tingmao, China	345.60

Tennis

Men's Singles
1896	John Boland, Great Britain
1900	Hugh Lawrence Doherty, Great Britain
1904	Beals Wright, United States
1908	Josiah George Ritchie, Great Britain
1912	Charles Lyndhurst Winslow, South Africa
1920	Louis Raymond, South Africa
1924	Vincent Richards, United States
1988	Miloslav Mecir, Czechoslovakia
1992	Marc Rosset, Switzerland
1996	Andre Agassi, United States
2000	Yevgeny Kafelnikov, Russia
2004	Nicolas Massu, Chile
2008	Rafael Nadal, Spain
2012	Andy Murray, Great Britain
2016	Andy Murray, Great Britain

Men's Doubles
1896	John Boland, Great Britain & Friedrick Traun, Germany
1900	Hugh Lawrence Doherty & Reginald Frank Doherty, Great Britain
1904	Edgar Leonard & Beals Wright, U.S.
1908	George Whiteside Hillyard & Reginald Frank Doherty, Great Britain
1912	Harry Austin Kitson & Charles Lyndhurst Winslow, South Africa
1920	Noel Turnbull & Maxwell Woosnam, Great Britain
1924	Vincent Richards & Francis Townsend Hunter, U.S.
1988	Kenneth Flach & Robert A. Seguso, United States
1992	Boris Becker & Michael Stich, Germany
1996	Mark Woodforde & Todd Woodbridge, Australia
2000	Sebastien Lareau & Daniel Nestor, Canada
2004	Fernando Gonzales & Nicolas Massu, Chile
2008	Roger Federer & Stanislas Wawrinka, Switzerland

Men's Doubles
2012	Mike Bryan & Bob Bryan, United States
2016	Marc López & Rafael Nadal, Spain

Women's Singles
1900	Charlotte Cooper, Great Britain
1908	Dorothy Katherine Chambers, Great Britain
1912	Marguerite Broquedis, France
1920	Suzanne Lenglen, France
1924	Helen Wills, United States
1988	Steffi Graf, W. Germany
1992	Jennifer Capriati, United States
1996	Lindsay Davenport, United States
2000	Venus Williams, United States
2004	Justine Henin-Hardenne, Belgium
2008	Elena Dementieva, Russia
2012	Serena Williams, United States
2016	Monica Puig, Puerto Rico

Women's Doubles
1920	Winifred Margaret McNair & Kathleen McKane, Great Britain
1924	Hazel Virginia Wightman & Helen Wills, United States
1988	Pam Shriver & Zina Garrison, United States
1992	Gigi Fernandez & Mary Joe Fernandez, United States
1996	Gigi Fernandez & Mary Joe Fernandez, United States
2000	Venus Williams & Serena Williams, United States
2004	Ting Li & Tian Tian Sun, China
2008	Serena Williams & Venus Williams, United States
2012	Serena Williams & Venus Williams, United States
2016	Ekaterina Makarova & Elena Vesnina, Russia

Mixed Doubles
2012	Victoria Azarenka & Max Mirnyi, Belarus
2016	Bethanie Mattek-Sands & Jack Sock, United States

Track and Field—Men

100-Meter Run	Time
1896 Thomas Burke, United States	0:12.0
1900 Francis Jarvis, United States	0:11.0
1904 Archie Hahn, United States	0:11.0
1908 Reginald Walker, South Africa	0:10.8
1912 Ralph Craig, United States	0:10.8
1920 Charles Paddock, United States	0:10.8
1924 Harold Abrahams, Great Britain	0:10.6
1928 Percy Williams, Canada	0:10.8
1932 Eddie Tolan, United States	0:10.3
1936 Jesse Owens, United States	0:10.3
1948 Harrison Dillard, United States	0:10.3
1952 Lindy Remigino, United States	0:10.4
1956 Bobby Morrow, United States	0:10.5
1960 Armin Hary, Germany	0:10.2
1964 Bob Hayes, United States	0:10.0
1968 Jim Hines, United States	0:09.95
1972 Valery Borzov, USSR	0:10.14
1976 Hasely Crawford, Trinidad and Tobago	0:10.06
1980 Allan Wells, Great Britain	0:10.25
1984 Carl Lewis, United States	0:09.99
1988 Carl Lewis, United States	0:09.92
1992 Linford Christie, Great Britain	0:09.96
1996 Donovan Bailey, Canada	0:09.84
2000 Maurice Greene, United States	0:09.87

100-Meter Run	Time
2004 Justin Gatlin, United States	0:09.85
2008 Usain Bolt, Jamaica	0:09.69
2012 Usain Bolt, Jamaica	0:09.63*
2016 Usain Bolt, Jamaica	0:09.81

200-Meter Run	Time
1900 Walter Tewksbury, United States	0:22.2
1904 Archie Hahn, United States	0:21.6
1908 Robert Kerr, Canada	0:22.6
1912 Ralph Craig, United States	0:21.7
1920 Allan Woodring, United States	0:22.0
1924 Jackson Scholz, United States	0:21.6
1928 Percy Williams, Canada	0:21.8
1932 Eddie Tolan, United States	0:21.2
1936 Jesse Owens, United States	0:20.7
1948 Mel Patton, United States	0:21.1
1952 Andrew Stanfield, United States	0:20.7
1956 Bobby Morrow, United States	0:20.6
1960 Livio Berruti, Italy	0:20.5
1964 Henry Carr, United States	0:20.3
1968 Tommie Smith, United States	0:19.83
1972 Valery Borzov, USSR	0:20.00
1976 Donald Quarrie, Jamaica	0:20.23
1980 Pietro Mennea, Italy	0:20.19
1984 Carl Lewis, United States	0:19.80

200-Meter Run		Time
1988	Joe DeLoach, United States	0:19.75
1992	Mike Marsh, United States	0:20.01
1996	Michael Johnson, United States	0:19.32
2000	Konstantinos Kenteris, Greece	0:20.09
2004	Shawn Crawford, United States	0:19.79
2008	Usain Bolt, Jamaica	0:19.30*
2012	Usain Bolt, Jamaica	0:19.32
2016	Usain Bolt, Jamaica	0:19.78

400-Meter Run		Time
1896	Thomas Burke, United States	0:54.2
1900	Maxwell Long, United States	0:49.4
1904	Harry Hillman, United States	0:49.2
1908	Wyndham Halswelle, Gr. Brit. (walkover)	0:50.0
1912	Charles Reidpath, United States	0:48.2
1920	Bevil Rudd, South Africa	0:49.6
1924	Eric Liddell, Great Britain	0:47.6
1928	Ray Barbuti, United States	0:47.8
1932	William Carr, United States	0:46.2
1936	Archie Williams, United States	0:46.5
1948	Arthur Wint, Jamaica	0:46.2
1952	George Rhoden, Jamaica	0:45.9
1956	Charles Jenkins, United States	0:46.7
1960	Otis Davis, United States	0:44.9
1964	Michael Larrabee, United States	0:45.1
1968	Lee Evans, United States	0:43.86
1972	Vincent Matthews, United States	0:44.66
1976	Alberto Juantorena, Cuba	0:44.26
1980	Viktor Markin, USSR	0:44.60
1984	Alonzo Babers, United States	0:44.27
1988	Steve Lewis, United States	0:43.87
1992	Quincy Watts, United States	0:43.50
1996	Michael Johnson, United States	0:43.49
2000	Michael Johnson, United States	0:43.84
2004	Jeremy Wariner, United States	0:44.00
2008	LaShawn Merritt, United States	0:43.75
2012	Kirani James, Grenada	0:43.94
2016	Wayde van Niekerk, South Africa	0:43.03*

800-Meter Run		Time
1896	Edwin Flack, Australia	2:11.0
1900	Alfred Tysoe, Great Britain	2:01.2
1904	James Lightbody, United States	1:56.0
1908	Mel Sheppard, United States	1:52.8
1912	James "Ted" Meredith, United States	1:51.9
1920	Albert Hill, Great Britain	1:53.4
1924	Douglas Lowe, Great Britain	1:52.4
1928	Douglas Lowe, Great Britain	1:51.8
1932	Thomas Hampson, Great Britain	1:49.8
1936	John Woodruff, United States	1:52.9
1948	Mal Whitfield, United States	1:49.2
1952	Mal Whitfield, United States	1:49.2
1956	Tom Courtney, United States	1:47.7
1960	Peter Snell, New Zealand	1:46.3
1964	Peter Snell, New Zealand	1:45.1
1968	Ralph Doubell, Australia	1:44.3
1972	Dave Wottle, United States	1:45.9
1976	Alberto Juantorena, Cuba	1:43.50
1980	Steve Ovett, Great Britain	1:45.40
1984	Joaquim Cruz, Brazil	1:43.00
1988	Paul Ereng, Kenya	1:43.45
1992	William Tanui, Kenya	1:43.66
1996	Vebjørn Rodal, Norway	1:42.58
2000	Nils Schumann, Germany	1:45.08
2004	Yuriy Borzakovskiy, Russia	1:44.45
2008	Wilfred Bungei, Kenya	1:44.65
2012	David Lekuta Rudisha, Kenya	1:40.91*
2016	David Lekuta Rudisha, Kenya	1:42.15

1500-Meter Run		Time
1896	Edwin Flack, Australia	4:33.2
1900	Charles Bennett, Great Britain	4:06.2
1904	James Lightbody, United States	4:05.4
1908	Mel Sheppard, United States	4:03.4
1912	Arnold Jackson, Great Britain	3:56.8
1920	Albert Hill, Great Britain	4:01.8
1924	Paavo Nurmi, Finland	3:53.6
1928	Harry Larva, Finland	3:53.2
1932	Luigi Beccali, Italy	3:51.2
1936	Jack Lovelock, New Zealand	3:47.8
1948	Henry Eriksson, Sweden	3:49.8
1952	Joseph Barthel, Luxembourg	3:45.2
1956	Ron Delany, Ireland	3:41.2
1960	Herb Elliott, Australia	3:35.6
1964	Peter Snell, New Zealand	3:38.1

1500-Meter Run		Time
1968	Kipchoge Keino, Kenya	3:34.91
1972	Pekka Vasala, Finland	3:36.33
1976	John Walker, New Zealand	3:39.17
1980	Sebastian Coe, Great Britain	3:38.4
1984	Sebastian Coe, Great Britain	3:32.53
1988	Peter Rono, Kenya	3:35.96
1992	Fermin Cacho Ruiz, Spain	3:40.12
1996	Noureddine Morceli, Algeria	3:35.78
2000	Noah Ngeny, Kenya	3:32.07*
2004	Hicham El Guerrouj, Morocco	3:34.18
2008	Asbel Kiprop, Kenya[1]	3:33.11
2012	Taoufik Makhloufi, Algeria	3:34.08
2016	Matthew Centrowitz, United States	3:50.00

(1) Originally won by Rashid Ramzi, Bahrain, who was stripped of the gold in 2009 due to doping.

3000-Meter Steeplechase		Time
1920	Percy Hodge, Great Britain	10:00.4
1924	Ville Ritola, Finland	9:33.6
1928	Toivo Loukola, Finland	9:21.8
1932	Volmari Iso-Hollo, Finland (about 3,450 m; extra lap by error)	10:33.4
1936	Volmari Iso-Hollo, Finland	9:03.8
1948	Tore Sjöstrand, Sweden	9:04.6
1952	Horace Ashenfelter, United States	8:45.4
1956	Chris Brasher, Great Britain	8:41.2
1960	Zdzislaw Krzyszkowiak, Poland	8:34.2
1964	Gaston Roelants, Belgium	8:30.8
1968	Amos Biwott, Kenya	8:51.0
1972	Kipchoge Keino, Kenya	8:23.64
1976	Anders Garderud, Sweden	8:08.02
1980	Bronislaw Malinowski, Poland	8:09.7
1984	Julius Korir, Kenya	8:11.80
1988	Julius Kariuki, Kenya	8:05.51
1992	Matthew Birir, Kenya	8:08.84
1996	Joseph Keter, Kenya	8:07.12
2000	Reuben Kosgei, Kenya	8:21.43
2004	Ezekiel Kemboi, Kenya	8:05.81
2008	Brimin Kiprop Kirpruto, Kenya	8:10.34
2012	Ezekiel Kemboi, Kenya	8:18.56
2016	Conseslus Kipruto, Kenya	8:03.28*

5000-Meter Run		Time
1912	Hannes Kolehmainen, Finland	14:36.6
1920	Joseph Guillemot, France	14:55.6
1924	Paavo Nurmi, Finland	14:31.2
1928	Ville Ritola, Finland	14:38.0
1932	Lauri Lehtinen, Finland	14:30.0
1936	Gunnar Höckert, Finland	14:22.2
1948	Gaston Reiff, Belgium	14:17.6
1952	Emil Zatopek, Czechoslovakia	14:06.6
1956	Vladimir Kuts, USSR	13:39.6
1960	Murray Halberg, New Zealand	13:43.4
1964	Bob Schul, United States	13:48.8
1968	Mohamed Gammoudi, Tunisia	14:05.0
1972	Lasse Viren, Finland	13:26.4
1976	Lasse Viren, Finland	13:24.76
1980	Miruts Yifter, Ethiopia	13:20.91
1984	Said Aouita, Morocco	13:05.59
1988	John Ngugi, Kenya	13:11.70
1992	Dieter Baumann, Germany	13:12.52
1996	Venuste Niyongabo, Burundi	13:07.96
2000	Million Wolde, Ethiopia	13:35.49
2004	Hicham El Guerrouj, Morocco	13:14.39
2008	Kenenisa Bekele, Ethiopia	12:57.82*
2012	Mo Farah, Great Britain	13:41.66
2016	Mo Farah, Great Britain	13:03.30

10,000-Meter Run		Time
1912	Hannes Kolehmainen, Finland	31:20.8
1920	Paavo Nurmi, Finland	31:45.8
1924	Ville Ritola, Finland	30:23.2
1928	Paavo Nurmi, Finland	30:18.8
1932	Janusz Kusocinski, Poland	30:11.4
1936	Ilmari Salminen, Finland	30:15.4
1948	Emil Zatopek, Czechoslovakia	29:59.6
1952	Emil Zatopek, Czechoslovakia	29:17.0
1956	Vladimir Kuts, USSR	28:45.6
1960	Pyotr Bolotnikov, USSR	28:32.2
1964	Billy Mills, United States	28:24.4
1968	Naftali Temu, Kenya	29:27.4
1972	Lasse Viren, Finland	27:38.4
1976	Lasse Viren, Finland	27:40.38
1980	Miruts Yifter, Ethiopia	27:42.7
1984	Alberto Cova, Italy	27:47.54

10,000-Meter Run		Time
1988	Brahim Boutayeb, Morocco	27:21.46
1992	Khalid Skah, Morocco	27:46.70
1996	Haile Gebrselassie, Ethiopia	27:07.34
2000	Haile Gebrselassie, Ethiopia	27:18.20
2004	Kenenisa Bekele, Ethiopia	27:05.10
2008	Kenenisa Bekele, Ethiopia	27:01.17*
2012	Mo Farah, Great Britain	27:30.42
2016	Mo Farah, Great Britain	27:05.17

Marathon		Time
1896	Spyridon Louis, Greece	2:58:50
1900	Michel Theato, France	2:59:45.0
1904	Thomas Hicks, United States	3:28:53.0
1908	John Hayes, United States	2:55:18.4
1912	Kenneth McArthur, South Africa	2:36:54.8
1920	Hannes Kolehmainen, Finland	2:32:35.8
1924	Albin Stenroos, Finland	2:41:22.6
1928	Boughera El Ouafi, France	2:32.57
1932	Juan Zabala, Argentina	2:31:36
1936	Kee-chung Sohn, Japan[1]	2:29:19.2
1948	Delfo Cabrera, Argentina	2:34:51.6
1952	Emil Zatopek, Czechoslovakia	2:23:03.2
1956	Alain Mimoun, France	2:25:00.0
1960	Abebe Bikila, Ethiopia	2:15:16.2
1964	Abebe Bikila, Ethiopia	2:12:11.2
1968	Mamo Wolde, Ethiopia	2:20:26.4
1972	Frank Shorter, United States	2:12:19.8
1976	Waldemar Cierpinski, E. Germany	2:09:55.0
1980	Waldemar Cierpinski, E. Germany	2:11:03.0
1984	Carlos Lopes, Portugal	2:09:21
1988	Gelindo Bordin, Italy	2:10:32
1992	Hwang Young-cho, S. Korea	2:13:23
1996	Josia Thugwane, South Africa	2:12:36
2000	Gezahegne Abera, Ethiopia	2:10:11
2004	Stefano Baldini, Italy	2:10:55
2008	Samuel Kamau Wanjiru, Kenya	2:06:32*
2012	Stephen Kiprotich, Uganda	2:08:01
2016	Eliud Kipchoge, Kenya	2:08:44

(1) Korean runner who competed under Japanese name Kitei Son.

4x100-Meter Relay		Time
1912	Great Britain	0:42.4
1920	United States	0:42.2
1924	United States	0:41.0
1928	United States	0:41.0
1932	United States	0:40.0
1936	United States	0:39.8
1948	United States	0:40.6
1952	United States	0:40.1
1956	United States	0:39.5
1960	Germany (U.S. disqualified)	0:39.5
1964	United States	0:39.0
1968	United States	0:38.24
1972	United States	0:38.19
1976	United States	0:38.33
1980	USSR	0:38.26
1984	United States	0:37.83
1988	USSR (U.S. disqualified)	0:38.19
1992	United States	0:37.40
1996	Canada	0:37.69
2000	United States	0:37.61
2004	Great Britain	0:38.07
2008	Trinidad and Tobago[1]	0:38.06
2012	Jamaica	0:36.84*
2016	Jamaica	0:37.27

(1) Due to team member Nesta Carter's doping, Jamaica was stripped of the victory in 2017.

4x400-Meter Relay		Time
1908	United States	3:29.4
1912	United States	3:16.6
1920	Great Britain	3:22.2
1924	United States	3:16.0
1928	United States	3:14.2
1932	United States	3:08.2
1936	Great Britain	3:09.0
1948	United States	3:10.4
1952	Jamaica	3:03.9
1956	United States	3:04.8
1960	United States	3:02.2
1964	United States	3:00.7
1968	United States	2:56.16
1972	Kenya	2:59.8
1976	United States	2:58.65
1980	USSR	3:01.1
1984	United States	2:57.91

4x400-Meter Relay		Time
1988	United States	2:56.16
1992	United States	2:55.74
1996	United States	2:55.99
2000	Nigeria[1]	2:58.68
2004	United States	2:55.91
2008	United States	2:55.39*
2012	The Bahamas	2:56.72
2016	United States	2:57.30

(1) The U.S. was stripped of the medal in 2012 after team member Antonio Pettigrew admitted to doping.

20-Kilometer Walk		Time
1956	Leonid Spirin, USSR	1:31:27.4
1960	Vladimir Golubnichy, USSR	1:34:07.2
1964	Kenneth Matthews, Great Britain	1:29:34.0
1968	Vladimir Golubnichy, USSR	1:33:58.4
1972	Peter Frenkel, E. Germany	1:26:42.4
1976	Daniel Bautista, Mexico	1:24:40.6
1980	Maurizio Damilano, Italy	1:23:35.5
1984	Ernesto Canto, Mexico	1:23:13
1988	Jozef Pribilinec, Czechoslovakia	1:19.57
1992	Daniel Plaza Montero, Spain	1:21:45
1996	Jefferson Perez, Ecuador	1:20:07
2000	Robert Korzeniowski, Poland	1:18:59
2004	Ivano Brugnetti, Italy	1:19:40
2008	Valeriy Borchin, Russia	1:19:01
2012	Chen Ding, China	1:18.46*
2016	Wang Zhen, China	1:19.44

50-Kilometer Walk		Time
1932	Thomas "Tommy" Green, Great Britain	4:50.10
1936	Harold Whitlock, Great Britain	4:30:41.4
1948	John Ljunggren, Sweden	4:41.52
1952	Giuseppe Dordoni, Italy	4:28:07.8
1956	Norman Read, New Zealand	4:30:42.8
1960	Donald Thompson, Great Britain	4:25:30
1964	Abdon Pamich, Italy	4:11:12.4
1968	Christoph Höhne, E. Germany	4:20:13.6
1972	Bernd Kannenberg, W. Germany	3:56:11.6
1980	Hartwig Gauder, E. Germany	3:49:24.0
1984	Raúl González, Mexico	3:47:26
1988	Vyacheslav Ivanenko, USSR	3:38.29
1992	Andrey Perlov, Unified Team (Rus.)	3:50:13
1996	Robert Korzeniowski, Poland	3:43:30
2000	Robert Korzeniowski, Poland	3:42:22
2004	Robert Korzeniowski, Poland	3:38:46
2008	Alex Schwazer, Italy	3:37:09
2012	Jared Tallent, Australia[1]	3:36:53*
2016	Matej Tóth, Slovakia	3:40:58

(1) Russia's Sergey Kirdyapkin was stripped of the gold medal in 2016 for doping.

110-Meter Hurdles		Time
1896	Thomas Curtis, United States	0:17.6
1900	Alvin Kraenzlein, United States	0:15.4
1904	Frederick Schule, United States	0:16.0
1908	Forrest Smithson, United States	0:15.0
1912	Frederick Kelly, United States	0:15.1
1920	Earl Thomson, Canada	0:14.8
1924	Daniel Kinsey, United States	0:15.0
1928	Sydney Atkinson, South Africa	0:14.8
1932	George Saling, United States	0:14.6
1936	Forrest Towns, United States	0:14.2
1948	William Porter, United States	0:13.9
1952	Harrison Dillard, United States	0:13.7
1956	Lee Calhoun, United States	0:13.5
1960	Lee Calhoun, United States	0:13.8
1964	Hayes Jones, United States	0:13.6
1968	Willie Davenport, United States	0:13.33
1972	Rod Milburn, United States	0:13.24
1976	Guy Drut, France	0:13.30
1980	Thomas Munkelt, E. Germany	0:13.39
1984	Roger Kingdom, United States	0:13.20
1988	Roger Kingdom, United States	0:12.98
1992	Mark McKoy, Canada	0:13.12
1996	Allen Johnson, United States	0:12.95
2000	Anier Garcia, Cuba	0:13.00
2004	Liu Xiang, China	0:12.91*
2008	Dayron Robles, Cuba	0:12.93
2012	Aries Merritt, United States	0:12.92
2016	Omar McLeod, Jamaica	0:13.05

400-Meter Hurdles		Time
1900	Walter Tewksbury, United States	0:57.6
1904	Harry Hillman, United States	0:53.0
1908	Charles Bacon, United States	0:55.0
1920	Frank Loomis, United States	0:54.0

400-Meter Hurdles

Year	Champion	Time
1924	F. Morgan Taylor, United States	0:52.6
1928	David, Lord Burghley, Great Britain	0:53.4
1932	Bob Tisdall, Ireland	0:51.7
1936	Glenn Hardin, United States	0:52.4
1948	Roy Cochran, United States	0:51.1
1952	Charles Moore, United States	0:50.8
1956	Glenn Davis, United States	0:50.1
1960	Glenn Davis, United States	0:49.3
1964	Rex Cawley, United States	0:49.6
1968	David Hemery, Great Britain	0:48.12
1972	John Akii-Bua, Uganda	0:47.82
1976	Edwin Moses, United States	0:47.64
1980	Volker Beck, E. Germany	0:48.70
1984	Edwin Moses, United States	0:47.75
1988	Andre Phillips, United States	0:47.19
1992	Kevin Young, United States	0:46.78
1996	Derrick Adkins, United States	0:47.54
2000	Angelo Taylor, United States	0:47.50
2004	Félix Sánchez, Dominican Republic	0:47.63
2008	Angelo Taylor, United States	0:47.25
2012	Félix Sánchez, Dominican Republic	0:47.63
2016	Kerron Clement, United States	0:47.73

Note: Event not held in 1912.

Discus Throw

Year	Champion	Dist.	
1896	Robert Garrett, United States	29.15m	(95' 7")
1900	Rudolf Bauer, Hungary	36.04m	(118' 3")
1904	Martin Sheridan, United States	39.28m	(128' 10")
1908	Martin Sheridan, United States	40.89m	(134' 1")
1912	Armas Taipale, Finland	45.21m	(148' 3")
1920	Elmer Niklander, Finland	44.68m	(146' 7")
1924	Clarence "Bud" Houser, U.S.	46.15m	(151' 4")
1928	Clarence "Bud" Houser, U.S.	47.32m	(155' 3")
1932	John Anderson, United States	49.49m	(162' 4")
1936	Ken Carpenter, United States	50.48m	(165' 7")
1948	Adolfo Consolini, Italy	52.78m	(173' 2")
1952	Sim Iness, United States	55.03m	(180' 6")
1956	Al Oerter, United States	56.36m	(184' 11")
1960	Al Oerter, United States	59.18m	(194' 2")
1964	Al Oerter, United States	61.00m	(200' 1")
1968	Al Oerter, United States	64.78m	(212' 6")
1972	Ludvik Danek, Czechoslovakia	64.40m	(211' 3")
1976	Mac Wilkins, United States	67.50m	(221' 5")
1980	Viktor Rashchupkin, USSR	66.64m	(218' 8")
1984	Rolf Danneberg, W. Germany	66.60m	(218' 6")
1988	Jürgen Schult, E. Germany	68.82m	(225' 9")
1992	Romas Ubartas, Lithuania	65.12m	(213' 8")
1996	Lars Riedel, Germany	69.40m	(227' 8")
2000	Virgilijus Alekna, Lithuania	69.30m	(227' 4")
2004	Virgilijus Alekna, Lithuania	69.89m	(228' 9¾")*
2008	Gerd Kanter, Estonia	68.82m	(225' 9½")
2012	Robert Harting, Germany	68.27m	(224')
2016	Christoph Harting, Germany	68.37m	(224' 3¾")

Hammer Throw

Year	Champion	Dist.	
1900	John Flanagan, United States	49.73m	(163' 1")
1904	John Flanagan, United States	51.23m	(168' 1")
1908	John Flanagan, United States	51.92m	(170' 4")
1912	Matt McGrath, United States	54.74m	(179' 7")
1920	Pat Ryan, United States	52.875m	(173' 5¾")
1924	Fred Tootell, United States	53.295m	(174' 10")
1928	Patrick O'Callaghan, Ireland	51.39m	(168' 7")
1932	Patrick O'Callaghan, Ireland	53.92m	(176' 11")
1936	Karl Hein, Germany	56.49m	(185' 4")
1948	Imre Németh, Hungary	56.07m	(183' 11½")
1952	József Csérmák, Hungary	60.34m	(197' 11")
1956	Harold Connolly, United States	63.19m	(207' 3")
1960	Vasily Rudenkov, USSR	67.10m	(202' 0")
1964	Romuald Klim, USSR	69.74m	(228' 10")
1968	Gyula Zsivótzky, Hungary	73.36m	(240' 8")
1972	Anatoly Bondarchuk, USSR	75.50m	(247' 8")
1976	Yuri Sedykh, USSR	77.52m	(254' 4")
1980	Yuri Sedykh, USSR	81.80m	(268' 4")
1984	Juha Tiainen, Finland	78.08m	(256' 2")
1988	Sergei Litvinov, USSR	84.80m	(278' 2")*
1992	Andrey Abduvaliyev, Unified Team	82.54m	(270' 9")
1996	Balázs Kiss, Hungary	81.24m	(266' 6")
2000	Szymon Ziolkowski, Poland	80.02m	(262' 6")
2004	Koji Murofushi, Japan	82.91m	(272')
2008	Primoz Kozmus, Slovenia	82.02m	(269' 1")
2012	Krisztián Pars, Hungary	80.59m	(264' 5")
2016	Dilshod Nazarov, Tajikistan	78.68m	(258' 1¾")

High Jump

Year	Champion	Height	
1896	Ellery Clark, United States	1.81m	(5' 11¼")
1900	Irving Baxter, United States	1.90m	(6' 2¾")

High Jump

Year	Champion	Height	
1904	Samuel Jones, United States	1.80m	(5' 11")
1908	Harry Porter, United States	1.90m	(6' 2¾")
1912	Alma Richards, United States	1.93m	(6' 4")
1920	Richmond Landon, United States	1.94m	(6' 4¼")
1924	Harold Osborn, United States	1.98m	(6' 6")
1928	Robert "Bob" King, United States	1.94m	(6' 4¼")
1932	Duncan McNaughton, Canada	1.97m	(6' 5½")
1936	Cornelius Johnson, United States	2.03m	(6' 8")
1948	John Winter, Australia	1.98m	(6' 6")
1952	Walter Davis, United States	2.04m	(6' 8¼")
1956	Charles Dumas, United States	2.12m	(6' 11½")
1960	Robert Shavlakadze, USSR	2.16m	(7' 1")
1964	Valery Brumel, USSR	2.18m	(7' 1¾")
1968	Dick Fosbury, United States	2.24m	(7' 4¼")
1972	Jüri Tarmak, USSR	2.23m	(7' 3¾")
1976	Jacek Wszola, Poland	2.25m	(7' 4½")
1980	Gerd Wessig, E. Germany	2.36m	(7' 8¾")
1984	Dietmar Mögenburg, W. Germany	2.35m	(7' 8½")
1988	Gennadi Avdeyenko, USSR	2.38m	(7' 9¾")
1992	Javier Sotomayor, Cuba	2.34m	(7' 8")
1996	Charles Austin, United States	2.39m	(7' 10")*
2000	Sergey Klyugin, Russia	2.35m	(7' 8½")
2004	Stefan Holm, Sweden	2.36m	(7' 8¾")
2008	Andrey Silnov, Russia	2.36m	(7' 8¾")
2012	Ivan Ukhov, Russia	2.38m	(7' 9¾")
2016	Derek Drouin, Canada	2.38m	(7' 9¾")

Javelin Throw

Year	Champion	Dist.	
1908	Eric Lemming, Sweden	54.82m	(179' 10")
1912	Eric Lemming, Sweden	60.64m	(198' 11")
1920	Jonni Myyrä, Finland	65.78m	(215' 9¾")
1924	Jonni Myyrä, Finland	62.96m	(206' 7")
1928	Erik Lundkvist, Sweden	66.60m	(218' 6")
1932	Matti Järvinen, Finland	72.71m	(238' 6½")
1936	Gerhard Stöck, Germany	71.84m	(235' 8")
1948	Kaj Tapio Rautavaara, Finland	69.77m	(228' 11")
1952	Cy Young, United States	73.78m	(242' 1")
1956	Egil Danielsen, Norway	85.71m	(281' 2½")
1960	Viktor Tsybulenko, USSR	84.64m	(277' 8")
1964	Pauli Nevala, Finland	82.66m	(271' 2")
1968	Janis Lusis, USSR	90.10m	(295' 7")
1972	Klaus Wolfermann, W. Germany	90.48m	(296' 10")
1976	Miklós Németh, Hungary	94.58m	(310' 4")
1980	Dainis Kula, USSR	91.20m	(299' 2")
1984	Arto Härkönen, Finland	86.76m	(284' 8")
1988	Tapio Korjus, Finland	84.28m	(276' 6")
1992	Jan Zelezny, Czechoslovakia	89.66m	(294' 2")
1996	Jan Zelezny, Czech Republic	88.16m	(289' 3")
2000	Jan Zelezny, Czech Republic	90.17m	(295' 9½")
2004	Andreas Thorkildsen, Norway	86.50m	(283' 10")
2008	Andreas Thorkildsen, Norway	90.57m	(297' 1¾")
2012	Keshorn Walcott, Trinidad & Tobago	84.58m	(277' 6")
2016	Thomas Röhler, Germany	90.30m	(296' 3")

Long Jump

Year	Champion	Dist.	
1896	Ellery Clark, United States	6.35m	(20' 10")
1900	Alvin Kraenzlein, United States	7.18m	(23' 6¾")
1904	Meyer Prinstein, United States	7.34m	(24' 1")
1908	Frank Irons, United States	7.48m	(24' 6½")
1912	Albert Gutterson, United States	7.60m	(24' 11¼")
1920	William Petersson, Sweden	7.15m	(23' 5½")
1924	William DeHart Hubbard, U.S.	7.45m	(24' 5¼")
1928	Ed Hamm, United States	7.73m	(25' 4½")
1932	Edward Gordon, United States	7.64m	(25' ¾")
1936	Jesse Owens, United States	8.06m	(26' 5½")
1948	Willie Steele, United States	7.82m	(25' 8")
1952	Jerome Biffle, United States	7.57m	(24' 10")
1956	Gregory Bell, United States	7.83m	(25' 8¼")
1960	Ralph Boston, United States	8.12m	(26' 7¾")
1964	Lynn Davies, Great Britain	8.07m	(26' 5¾")
1968	Bob Beamon, United States	8.90m	(29' 2½")*
1972	Randy Williams, United States	8.24m	(27' ½")
1976	Arnie Robinson, United States	8.35m	(27' 4¾")
1980	Lutz Dombrowski, E. Germany	8.54m	(28' ¼")
1984	Carl Lewis, United States	8.54m	(28' ¼")
1988	Carl Lewis, United States	8.72m	(28' 7½")
1992	Carl Lewis, United States	8.67m	(28' 5½")
1996	Carl Lewis, United States	8.50m	(27' 10¾")
2000	Ivan Pedroso, Cuba	8.55m	(28' ¾")
2004	Dwight Phillips, United States	8.59m	(28' 2¼")
2008	Irving Saladino, Panama	8.34m	(27' 4¼")
2012	Greg Rutherford, Great Britain	8.31m	(27' 3¼")
2016	Jeff Henderson, United States	8.38m	(27' 6")

	Pole Vault	Height	
1896	William Welles Hoyt, United States	3.30m	(10' 10")
1900	Irving Baxter, United States	3.30m	(10' 10")
1904	Charles Dvorak, United States	3.50m	(11' 6")
1908	Edward Cooke, United States	3.71m	(12' 2")
	Alfred Gilbert, United States (tie)	3.71m	(12' 2")
1912	Harry Stoddard Babcock, U.S.	3.95m	(12' 11½")
1920	Frank Foss, United States	4.09m	(13' 5")
1924	Lee Barnes, United States	3.95m	(12' 11½")
1928	Sabin Carr, United States	4.20m	(13' 9¼")
1932	Bill Miller, United States	4.31m	(14' 1¾")
1936	Earle Meadows, United States	4.35m	(14' 3¼")
1948	Guinn Smith, United States	4.30m	(14' 1¼")
1952	Robert Richards, United States	4.55m	(14' 11¼")
1956	Robert Richards, United States	4.56m	(14' 11½")
1960	Don Bragg, United States	4.70m	(15' 5")
1964	Fred Hansen, United States	5.10m	(16' 8¾")
1968	Bob Seagren, United States	5.40m	(17' 8½")
1972	Wolfgang Nordwig, E. Germany	5.50m	(18' ½")
1976	Tadeusz Slusarski, Poland	5.50m	(18' ½")
1980	Wladyslaw Kozakiewicz, Poland	5.78m	(18' 11½")
1984	Pierre Quinon, France	5.75m	(18' 10¼")
1988	Sergei Bubka, USSR	5.90m	(19' 4¼")
1992	Maksim Tarasov, Unified Team (Rus.)	5.80m	(19' ¼")
1996	Jean Galfione, France	5.92m	(19' 5")
2000	Nick Hysong, United States	5.90m	(19' 4¼")
2004	Timothy Mack, United States	5.95m	(19' 6¼")
2008	Steve Hooker, Australia	5.96m	(19' 6¾")
2012	Renaud Lavillenie, France	5.97m	(19' 7")
2016	Thiago Braz da Silva, Brazil	6.03m	(19' 9½")*

	Shot Put	Dist.	
1896	Robert Garrett, United States	11.22m	(36' 9¾")
1900	Richard Sheldon, United States	14.10m	(46' 3¼")
1904	Ralph Rose, United States	14.81m	(48' 7")
1908	Ralph Rose, United States	14.21m	(46' 7½")
1912	Pat McDonald, United States	15.34m	(50' 4")
1920	Ville Pörhölä, Finland	14.81m	(48' 7¼")
1924	Clarence "Bud" Houser, United States	14.99m	(49' 2¼")
1928	John Kuck, United States	15.87m	(52' ¾")
1932	Leo Sexton, United States	16.00m	(52' 6")
1936	Hans Woellke, Germany.	16.20m	(53' 1¾")
1948	Wilbur Thompson, United States	17.12m	(56' 2")
1952	W. Parry O'Brien, United States	17.41m	(57' 1½")
1956	W. Parry O'Brien, United States	18.57m	(60' 11¼")
1960	Bill Nieder, United States	19.68m	(64' 6¾")
1964	Dallas Long, United States	20.33m	(66' 8½")
1968	Randy Matson, United States	20.54m	(67' 4¾")
1972	Wladyslaw Komar, Poland	21.18m	(69' 6")
1976	Udo Beyer, E. Germany	21.05m	(69' ¾")
1980	Vladimir Kiselyov, USSR	21.35m	(70' ½")
1984	Alessandro Andrei, Italy	21.26m	(69' 9")
1988	Ulf Timmermann, E. Germany	22.47m	(73' 8¾")
1992	Michael Stulce, United States	21.70m	(71' 2½")
1996	Randy Barnes, United States	21.62m	(70' 11¼")
2000	Arsi Harju, Finland	21.29m	(69' 10¼")
2004	Adam Nelson, United States[1]	21.16m	(69' 5¼")
2008	Tomasz Majewski, Poland	21.51m	(70' 6¾")
2012	Tomasz Majewski, Poland	21.89m	(71' 9¾")
2016	Ryan Crouser, United States	22.52m	(73' 10½")*

(1) Yuriy Bilonog, Ukraine, was stripped of the gold medal in 2012 due to doping.

	Triple Jump	Dist.	
1896	James Connolly, United States	13.71m	(44' 11¾")
1900	Meyer Prinstein, United States	14.47m	(47' 5¾")
1904	Meyer Prinstein, United States	14.35m	(47' 1")
1908	Tim Ahearne, Gr. Brit.-Ireland	14.92m	(48' 11½")
1912	Gustaf Lindblom, Sweden	14.76m	(48' 5")
1920	Vilho Tuulos, Finland	14.505m	(47' 7")
1924	Anthony Winter, Australia	15.525m	(50' 11¼")
1928	Mikio Oda, Japan	15.21m	(49' 11")
1932	Chuhei Nambu, Japan	15.72m	(51' 7")
1936	Naoto Tajima, Japan	16.00m	(52' 6")
1948	Arne Ahman, Sweden	15.40m	(50' 6¼")
1952	Adhemar Ferreira da Silva, Brazil	16.22m	(53' 2¾")
1956	Adhemar Ferreira da Silva, Brazil	16.35m	(53' 7¾")
1960	Jozef Schmidt, Poland	16.81m	(55' 1½")
1964	Jozef Schmidt, Poland	16.85m	(55' 3½")
1968	Viktor Saneyev, USSR	17.39m	(57' ¾")
1972	Viktor Saneyev, USSR	17.35m	(56' 11¼")
1976	Viktor Saneyev, USSR	17.29m	(56' 8¾")
1980	Jaak Uudmäe, USSR	17.35m	(56' 11")
1984	Al Joyner, United States	17.26m	(56' 7½")
1988	Khristo Markov, Bulgaria	17.61m	(57' 9½")
1992	Mike Conley, United States	18.17m	(59' 7½")(w)
1996	Kenny Harrison, United States	18.09m	(59' 4¼")*
2000	Jonathan Edwards, Great Britain	17.71m	(58' 1¼")
2004	Christian Olsson, Sweden	17.79m	(58' 4½")
2008	Nelson Evora, Portugal.	17.67m	(57' 11¾")
2012	Christian Taylor, United States	17.81m	(58' 5¼")
2016	Christian Taylor, United States	17.86m	(58' 7¼")

	Decathlon	Points
1904	Thomas F. Kiely, Ireland.	6,036
1912	Jim Thorpe, United States[1]	8,412.995
1920	Helge Lovland, Norway	6,804.355
1924	Harold Osborn, United States.	7,710.775
1928	Paavo Yrjölä, Finland	8,053.29
1932	James Bausch, United States	8,462.23
1936	Glenn Morris, United States	7,900
1948	Robert Mathias, United States	7,139
1952	Robert Mathias, United States	7,887
1956	Milton Campbell, United States	7,937
1960	Rafer Johnson, United States.	8,392
1964	Willi Holdorf, Germany	7,887
1968	Bill Toomey, United States	8,193
1972	Nikolai Avilov, USSR	8,454
1976	Bruce Jenner, United States.	8,618
1980	Daley Thompson, Great Britain	8,495
1984	Daley Thompson, Great Britain	8,797
1988	Christian Schenk, E. Germany	8,488
1992	Robert Zmelik, Czechoslovakia	8,611
1996	Dan O'Brien, United States	8,824
2000	Erki Nool, Estonia.	8,641
2004	Roman Sebrle, Czech Republic	8,893*
2008	Bryan Clay, United States	8,791
2012	Ashton Eaton, United States	8,869
2016	Ashton Eaton, United States	8,893*

Note: Event not held in 1908. (1) Thorpe had been stripped of his medal for playing pro baseball prior to the Olympics. The Intl. Olympic Committee in 1982 posthumously restored his decathlon and pentathlon gold medals.

Track and Field—Women

	100-Meter Run	Time
1928	Elizabeth Robinson, United States	0:12.2
1932	Stella Walsh, Poland	0:11.9
1936	Helen Stephens, United States	0:11.5
1948	Fanny Blankers-Koen, Netherlands	0:11.9
1952	Marjorie Jackson, Australia	0:11.5
1956	Betty Cuthbert, Australia.	0:11.5
1960	Wilma Rudolph, United States	0:11.0
1964	Wyomia Tyus, United States	0:11.4
1968	Wyomia Tyus, United States	0:11.08
1972	Renate Stecher, E. Germany	0:11.07
1976	Annegret Richter, W. Germany	0:11.08
1980	Lyudmila Kondratyeva, USSR	0:11.06
1984	Evelyn Ashford, United States	0:10:97
1988	Florence Griffith-Joyner, United States	0:10.54*
1992	Gail Devers, United States	0:10.82
1996	Gail Devers, United States.	0:10.94
2000	No winner[1]	NA
2004	Yuliya Nestsiarenka, Belarus	0:10.93

	100-Meter Run	Time
2008	Shelly-Ann Fraser, Jamaica	0:10.78
2012	Shelly-Ann Fraser-Pryce, Jamaica	0:10.75
2016	Elaine Thompson, Jamaica	0:10.71

(1) Marion Jones, U.S., was stripped of her gold medal in 2007 due to doping; the Intl. Olympic Committee declined to award the medal to the runner-up, who was also suspected of doping.

	200-Meter Run	Time
1948	Fanny Blankers-Koen, Netherlands	0:24.4
1952	Marjorie Jackson, Australia	0:23.7
1956	Betty Cuthbert, Australia.	0:23.4
1960	Wilma Rudolph, United States	0:24.0
1964	Edith McGuire, United States	0:23.0
1968	Irena Szewinska, Poland	0:22.5
1972	Renate Stecher, E. Germany	0:22.40
1976	Bärbel Eckert, E. Germany.	0:22.37
1980	Bärbel Wöckel, E. Germany	0:22.03
1984	Valerie Brisco-Hooks, United States	0:21.81
1988	Florence Griffith-Joyner, United States	0:21.34*

200-Meter Run

Year	Champion	Time
1992	Gwen Torrence, United States	0:21.81
1996	Marie-Jose Perec, France	0:22.12
2000	Pauline Davis-Thompson, The Bahamas[1]	0:22.27
2004	Veronica Campbell, Jamaica	0:22.05
2008	Veronica Campbell-Brown, Jamaica	0:21.74
2012	Allyson Felix, United States	0:21.88
2016	Elaine Thompson, Jamaica	0:21.78

(1) Originally won by Marion Jones, U.S., who was stripped of the gold in 2007 due to doping.

400-Meter Run

Year	Champion	Time
1964	Betty Cuthbert, Australia	0:52.0
1968	Colette Besson, France	0:52.0
1972	Monika Zehrt, E. Germany	0:51.08
1976	Irena Szewinska, Poland	0:49.29
1980	Marita Koch, E. Germany	0:48.88
1984	Valerie Brisco-Hooks, United States	0:48.83
1988	Olga Bryzgina, USSR	0:48.65
1992	Marie-Jose Perec, France	0:48.83
1996	Marie-Jose Perec, France	0:48.25*
2000	Cathy Freeman, Australia	0:49.11
2004	Tonique Williams-Darling, The Bahamas	0:49.41
2008	Christine Ohuruogu, Great Britain	0:49.62
2012	Sanya Richards-Ross, United States	0:49.55
2016	Shaunae Miller, The Bahamas	0:49.44

800-Meter Run

Year	Champion	Time
1928	Lina Radke, Germany	2:16.8
1960	Lyudmila Shevtsova, USSR	2:04.3
1964	Ann Packer, Great Britain	2:01.1
1968	Madeline Manning, United States	2:00.9
1972	Hildegard Falck, W. Germany	1:58.55
1976	Tatyana Kazankina, USSR	1:54.94
1980	Nadezhda Olizarenko, USSR	1:53.43*
1984	Doina Melinte, Romania	1:57.60
1988	Sigrun Wodars, E. Germany	1:56.10
1992	Ellen Van Langen, Netherlands	1:55.54
1996	Svetlana Masterkova, Russia	1:57.73
2000	Maria Mutola, Mozambique	1:56.15
2004	Kelly Holmes, Great Britain	1:56.38
2008	Pamela Jelimo, Kenya	1:54.87
2012	Mariya Savinova, Russia	1:56.19
2016	Caster Semenya, South Africa	1:55.28

1500-Meter Run

Year	Champion	Time
1972	Lyudmila Bragina, USSR	4:01.04
1976	Tatyana Kazankina, USSR	4:05.48
1980	Tatyana Kazankina, USSR	3:56.06
1984	Gabriella Dorio, Italy	4:03.25
1988	Paula Ivan, Romania	3:53.96*
1992	Hassiba Boulmerka, Algeria	3:55.30
1996	Svetlana Masterkova, Russia	4:00.83
2000	Nouria Merah-Benida, Algeria	4:05.10
2004	Kelly Holmes, Great Britain	3:57.90
2008	Nancy Jebet Langat, Kenya	4:00.23
2012	Gamze Bulut, Turkey[1]	4:10.40
2016	Faith Chepngetich Kipyegon, Kenya	4:08.92

(1) Turkey's Asli Cakir Alpetkin was stripped of the gold medal in 2016 for doping.

3000-Meter Run

Year	Champion	Time
1984	Maricica Puica, Romania	8:35.96
1988	Tatyana Samolenko, USSR	8:26.53*
1992	Elena Romanova, Unified Team (Rus.)	8:46.04

3000-Meter Steeplechase

Year	Champion	Time
2008	Gulnara Galkina-Samitova, Russia	8:58.81*
2012	Habiba Ghribi, Tunisia[1]	9:08.37
2016	Ruth Jebet, Bahrain	8:59.75

(1) Russia's Yuliya Zaripova was stripped of the gold medal in 2016 for doping.

5000-Meter Run

Year	Champion	Time
1996	Wang Junxia, China	14:59.88
2000	Gabriela Szabo, Romania	14:40.79
2004	Meseret Defar, Ethiopia	14:45.65
2008	Tirunesh Dibaba, Ethiopia	15:41.40
2012	Meseret Defar, Ethiopia	15:04.25
2016	Vivian Cheruiyot, Kenya	14:26.17*

10,000-Meter Run

Year	Champion	Time
1988	Olga Bondarenko, USSR	31:05.21
1992	Derartu Tulu, Ethiopia	31:06.02
1996	Fernanda Ribeiro, Portugal	31:01.63

10,000-Meter Run

Year	Champion	Time
2000	Derartu Tulu, Ethiopia	30:17.49
2004	Xing Huina, China	30:24.36
2008	Tirunesh Dibaba, Ethiopia	29:54.66
2012	Tirunesh Dibaba, Ethiopia	30:20.75
2016	Almaz Ayana, Ethiopia	29:17.45*

Marathon

Year	Champion	Time
1984	Joan Benoit, United States	2:24:52
1988	Rosa Mota, Portugal	2:25:40
1992	Valentina Yegorova, Unified Team (Rus.)	2:32:41
1996	Fatuma Roba, Ethiopia	2:26:05
2000	Naoko Takahashi, Japan	2:23:14
2004	Mizuki Noguchi, Japan	2:26:20
2008	Constantina Tomescu, Romania	2:26:44
2012	Tiki Gelana, Ethiopia	2:23:07*
2016	Jemima Jelagat Sumgong, Kenya	2:24:04

4x100-Meter Relay

Year	Champion	Time
1928	Canada	0:48.4
1932	United States	0:46.9
1936	United States	0:46.9
1948	Netherlands	0:47.5
1952	United States	0:45.9
1956	Australia	0:44.5
1960	United States	0:44.5
1964	Poland	0:43.6
1968	United States	0:42.8
1972	West Germany	0:42.81
1976	East Germany	0:42.55
1980	East Germany	0:41.60
1984	United States	0:41.65
1988	United States	0:41.98
1992	United States	0:42.11
1996	United States	0:41.95
2000	The Bahamas	0:41.95
2004	Jamaica	0:41.73
2008	Russia	0:42.31
2012	United States	0:40.82*
2016	United States	0:41.01

4x400-Meter Relay

Year	Champion	Time
1972	East Germany	3:23.0
1976	East Germany	3:19.23
1980	USSR	3:20.2
1984	United States	3:18.29
1988	USSR	3:15.18*
1992	Unified Team	3:20.20
1996	United States	3:20.91
2000	United States[1]	3:22.62
2004	United States[2]	3:19.01
2008	United States	3:18.54
2012	United States	3:16.87
2016	United States	3:19.06

(1) Due to team member Marion Jones's doping, the U.S. was stripped of the victory in 2008. Jones's teammates won an appeal in 2010 to have their medals restored. (2) Team member Crystal Cox was stripped of her gold medal in 2012 due to doping.

20-Kilometer Walk

Year	Champion	Time
2000	Wang Liping, China	1:29:05
2004	Athanasia Tsoumeleka, Greece	1:29:12
2008	Olga Kaniskina, Russia	1:26:31
2012	Elena Lashmanova, Russia	1:25:02*
2016	Liu Hong, China	1:28:35

100-Meter Hurdles

Year	Champion	Time
1972	Annelie Ehrhardt, E. Germany	0:12.59
1976	Johanna Schaller, E. Germany	0:12.77
1980	Vera Komisova, USSR	0:12.56
1984	Benita Fitzgerald-Brown, United States	0:12.84
1988	Yordanka Donkova, Bulgaria	0:12.38
1992	Paraskevi Patoulidou, Greece	0:12.64
1996	Ludmila Engquist, Sweden	0:12.58
2000	Olga Shishigina, Kazakhstan	0:12.65
2004	Joanna Hayes, United States	0:12.37
2008	Dawn Harper, United States	0:12.54
2012	Sally Pearson, Australia	0:12.35*
2016	Brianna Rollins, United States	0:12.48

400-Meter Hurdles

Year	Champion	Time
1984	Nawal El Moutawakel, Morocco	0:54.61
1988	Debra Flintoff-King, Australia	0:53.17
1992	Sally Gunnell, Great Britain	0:53.23

400-Meter Hurdles

Year		Time
1996	Deon Hemmings, Jamaica	0:52.82
2000	Irina Privalova, Russia	0:53.02
2004	Faní Halkia, Greece	0:52.82
2008	Melaine Walker, Jamaica	0:52.64*
2012	Natalya Antyukh, Russia	0:52.70
2016	Dalilah Muhammad, United States	0:53.13

Discus Throw

Year		Dist.	
1928	Halina Konopacka, Poland	39.62m	(130' 0")
1932	Lillian Copeland, United States	40.58m	(133' 2")
1936	Gisela Mauermayer, Germany	47.63m	(156' 3")
1948	Micheline Ostermeyer, France	41.92m	(137' 6")
1952	Nina Ponomareva, USSR	51.42m	(168' 8")
1956	Olga Fikotová, Czechoslovakia	53.69m	(176' 1¾")
1960	Nina Ponomareva, USSR	55.10m	(180' 9")
1964	Tamara Press, USSR	57.27m	(187' 10¾")
1968	Lia Manoliu, Romania	58.28m	(191' 2")
1972	Faina Melnik, USSR	66.62m	(218' 7")
1976	Evelin Jahl, E. Germany	69.00m	(226' 4")
1980	Evelin Jahl, E. Germany	69.96m	(229' 6")
1984	Ria Stalman, Netherlands	65.36m	(214' 5")
1988	Martina Hellmann, E. Germany	72.30m	(237' 2")*
1992	Maritza Martén, Cuba	70.06m	(229' 10")
1996	Ilke Wyludda, Germany	69.66m	(228' 6")
2000	Ellina Zvereva, Belarus	68.40m	(224' 5")
2004	Natalya Sadova, Russia	67.02m	(219' 8¾")
2008	Stephanie Brown Trafton, U.S.	64.74m	(212' 4¾")
2012	Sandra Perkovic, Croatia	69.11m	(226' 9")
2016	Sandra Perkovic, Croatia	69.21m	(227' ¾")

Hammer Throw

Year		Dist.	
2000	Kamila Skolimowska, Poland	71.16m	(233' 5¾")
2004	Olga Kuzenkova, Russia	75.02m	(246' 1")
2008	Yipsi Moreno, Cuba[1]	75.20m	(246' 8¾")
2012	Anita Wlodarczyk, Poland[2]	77.60m	(254' 7")
2016	Anita Wlodarczyk, Poland	82.29m	(269' 11¾")*

(1) Belarus's Aksana Miankova was stripped of the gold medal for doping in 2016. (2) Russia's Tatyana Lysenko was stripped of the gold medal for doping in 2016.

High Jump

Year		Height	
1928	Ethel Catherwood, Canada	1.59m	(5' 2½")
1932	Jean Shiley, United States	1.67m	(5' 5½")
1936	Ibolya Csák, Hungary	1.60m	(5' 3")
1948	Alice Coachman, United States	1.68m	(5' 6")
1952	Esther Brand, South Africa	1.67m	(5' 5¾")
1956	Mildred McDaniel, United States	1.76m	(5' 9¼")
1960	Iolanda Balas, Romania	1.85m	(6' ¾")
1964	Iolanda Balas, Romania	1.90m	(6' 2¾")
1968	Miloslava Rezková, Czech.	1.82m	(5' 11½")
1972	Ulrike Meyfarth, W. Germany	1.92m	(6' 3½")
1976	Rosemarie Ackermann, E. Germany	1.93m	(6' 4")
1980	Sara Simeoni, Italy	1.97m	(6' 5½")
1984	Ulrike Meyfarth, W. Germany	2.02m	(6' 7½")
1988	Louise Ritter, United States	2.03m	(6' 8")
1992	Heike Henkel, Germany	2.02m	(6' 7½")
1996	Stefka Kostadinova, Bulgaria	2.05m	(6' 8¾")
2000	Yelena Yelesina, Russia	2.01m	(6' 7")
2004	Yelena Slesarenko, Russia	2.06m	(6' 9")*
2008	Tia Hellebaut, Belgium	2.05m	(6' 8¾")
2012	Anna Chicherova, Russia	2.05m	(6' 8¾")
2016	Ruth Beitia, Spain	1.97m	(6' 5½")

Javelin Throw

Year		Dist.	
1932	"Babe" Didrikson, United States	43.68m	(143' 4")
1936	Tilly Fleischer, Germany	45.18m	(148' 3")
1948	Herma Bauma, Austria	45.57m	(149' 6")
1952	Dana Zátopková, Czechoslovakia	50.47m	(165' 7")
1956	Inese Jaunzeme, USSR	53.86m	(176' 8")
1960	Elvira Ozolina, USSR	55.98m	(183' 8")
1964	Mihaela Penes, Romania	60.54m	(198' 7")
1968	Angéla Németh, Hungary	60.36m	(198' 0")
1972	Ruth Fuchs, E. Germany	63.88m	(209' 7")
1976	Ruth Fuchs, E. Germany	65.94m	(216' 4")
1980	Maria Colón, Cuba	68.40m	(224' 5")
1984	Tessa Sanderson, Great Britain	69.56m	(228' 2")
1988	Petra Felke, E. Germany	74.68m	(245' 0")
1992	Silke Renk, Germany	68.34m	(224' 2")
1996	Heli Rantanen, Finland	67.94m	(222' 11")

Javelin Throw

Year		Dist.	
2000	Trine Hattestad, Norway	68.91m	(226' 1")
2004	Osleidys Menendez, Cuba	71.53m	(234' 8")*
2008	Barbora Spotáková, Czech Republic	71.42m	(234' ¾")
2012	Barbora Spotáková, Czech Republic	69.55m	(228' 2¼")
2016	Sara Kolak, Croatia	66.18m	(217' 1½")

Note: New records were kept after javelin was modified in 1999.

Long Jump

Year		Dist.	
1948	Olga Gyarmati, Hungary	5.69m	(18' 8")
1952	Yvette Williams, New Zealand	6.24m	(20' 5¼")
1956	Elzbieta Krzesinska, Poland	6.35m	(20' 10")
1960	Vera Krepkina, USSR	6.37m	(20' 10¾")
1964	Mary Rand, Great Britain	6.76m	(22' 2¼")
1968	Viorica Viscopoleanu, Romania	6.82m	(22' 4½")
1972	Heidemarie Rosendahl, W. Germany	6.78m	(22' 3")
1976	Angela Voigt, E. Germany	6.72m	(22' ¾")
1980	Tatyana Kolpakova, USSR	7.06m	(23' 2")
1984	Anisoara Cusmir-Stanciu, Romania	6.96m	(22' 10")
1988	Jackie Joyner-Kersee, United States	7.40m	(24' 3½")*
1992	Heike Drechsler, Germany	7.14m	(23' 5¼")
1996	Chioma Ajunwa, Nigeria	7.12m	(23' 4¼")
2000	Heike Drechsler, Germany	6.99m	(22' 11¼")
2004	Tatyana Lebedeva, Russia	7.07m	(23' 2½")
2008	Maurren Higa Maggi, Brazil	7.04m	(23' 1¼")
2012	Brittney Reese, United States	7.12m	(23' 4¼")
2016	Tianna Bartoletta, United States	7.17m	(23' 6¼")

Pole Vault

Year		Height	
2000	Stacy Dragila, United States	4.60m	(15' 1")
2004	Elena Isinbaeva, Russia	4.91m	(16' 1¼')
2008	Elena Isinbaeva, Russia	5.05m	(16' 6¾")
2012	Jennifer Suhr, United States	4.75m	(15' 7")
2016	Ekateríni Stefanídi, Greece	4.85m	(15' 11")

Shot Put

Year		Dist.	
1948	Micheline Ostermeyer, France	13.75m	(45' 1½")
1952	Galina Zybina, USSR	15.28m	(50' 1½")
1956	Tamara Tyshkevich, USSR	16.59m	(54' 5¼")
1960	Tamara Press, USSR	17.32m	(56' 10")
1964	Tamara Press, USSR	18.14m	(59' 6¼")
1968	Margitta Gummel, E. Germany	19.61m	(64' 4")
1972	Nadezhda Chizhova, USSR	21.03m	(69' 0")
1976	Ivanka Khristova, Bulgaria	21.16m	(69' 5¼")
1980	Ilona Slupianek, E. Germany	22.41m	(73' 6¼")*
1984	Claudia Losch, W. Germany	20.48m	(67' 2")
1988	Natalya Lisovskaya, USSR	22.24m	(72' 11¾")
1992	Svetlana Krivelyova, Unified Team	21.06m	(69' 1¼")
1996	Astrid Kumbernuss, Germany	20.56m	(67' 5½")
2000	Yanina Karolchik, Belarus	20.56m	(67' 5½")
2004	Yumileidi Cumbá, Cuba	19.59m	(64' 3¼")
2008	Valerie Vili, New Zealand	20.56m	(67' 5½")
2012	Valerie Adams, New Zealand	20.70m	(67' 11")
2016	Michelle Carter, United States	20.63m	(67' 8¼")

Triple Jump

Year		Dist.	
1996	Inessa Kravets, Ukraine	15.33m	(50' 3½")
2000	Tereza Marinova, Bulgaria	15.20m	(49' 10½")
2004	Francoise Mbango Etone, Cameroon	15.30m	(50' 2¼")
2008	Francoise Mbango Etone, Cameroon	15.39m	(50' 6")*
2012	Olga Rypakova, Kazakhstan	14.98m	(49' 1¾")
2016	Caterine Ibargüen, Colombia	15.17m	(49' 9¼")

Heptathlon

Year		Points
1984	Glynis Nunn, Australia	6,390
1988	Jackie Joyner-Kersee, United States	7,291*
1992	Jackie Joyner-Kersee, United States	7,044
1996	Ghada Shouaa, Syria	6,780
2000	Denise Lewis, Great Britain	6,584
2004	Carolina Kluft, Sweden	6,952
2008	Natallia Dobrynska, Ukraine	6,733
2012	Jessica Ennis, Great Britain	6,955
2016	Nafissatou Thiam, Belgium	6,810

COLLEGE FOOTBALL

2017 CFP Championship: Alabama Comeback

The No. 4-ranked Alabama Crimson Tide came back from a 13-0 halftime deficit to defeat the No. 3 Georgia Bulldogs, 26-23 in overtime, Jan. 8, 2018, at Mercedes-Benz Stadium in Atlanta, GA, to claim the 2017 college football championship. With his team scoreless at the halftime mark, 'Bama head coach Nick Saban pulled starting quarterback Jalen Hurts, a sophomore, and sent in Tua Tagovailoa, a freshman who had never started a college game. Tagovailoa threw for 166 yards in the second half and overtime, with three touchdowns, including a 41-yard overtime pass to fellow freshman DeVonta Smith for the victory. The win was Alabama's 12th national title—their fifth in nine years—and Saban's sixth, matching him with Crimson Tide coaching legend Bear Bryant.

2017 College Football Final Rankings

College Football Playoff Rankings		Associated Press Poll		USA Today Coaches Poll	
Rank, team	**Rank, team**	**Rank, team**	**Rank, team**	**Rank, team**	**Rank, team**
1. Clemson	14. Notre Dame	1. Alabama	14. Oklahoma St.	1. Alabama	14. Oklahoma St.
2. Oklahoma	15. TCU	2. Georgia	15. Michigan St.	2. Georgia	15. Washington
3. Georgia	16. Michigan St.	3. Oklahoma	16. Washington	3. Oklahoma	16. Michigan St.
4. Alabama	17. LSU	4. Clemson	17. Northwestern	4. Clemson	17. Northwestern
5. Ohio St.	18. Washington St.	5. Ohio St.	18. LSU	5. Ohio St.	18. LSU
6. Wisconsin	19. Oklahoma St.	6. Central Florida	19. Mississippi St.	6. Wisconsin	19. Stanford
7. Auburn	20. Memphis	7. Wisconsin	20. Stanford	7. Central Florida	20. Mississippi St.
8. USC	21. Northwestern	8. Penn St.	21. South Florida	8. Penn St.	21. South Florida
9. Penn St.	22. Virginia Tech	9. TCU	22. Boise St.	9. TCU	22. Boise St.
10. Miami (FL)	23. Mississippi St.	10. Auburn	23. NC State	10. USC	23. NC State
11. Washington	24. NC State	11. Notre Dame	24. Virginia Tech	11. Notre Dame	24. Memphis
12. Central Florida	25. Boise St.	12. USC	25. Memphis	12. Auburn	25. Virginia Tech
13. Stanford		13. Miami (FL)		13. Miami (FL)	

Note: College Football Playoff ranking is as of Dec. 3, 2017, prior to bowl games and playoffs. Final AP and USA Today polls are as of Jan. 9, 2018 (after all bowls and championship game).

National College Football Championship Game Results, 1998-2017

The Bowl Championship Series (BCS) National Championship game (BCS ranked No. 1 vs. BCS No. 2) determined the NCAA's Football Bowl Subdivision (Div. I-A) champion in 1998-2013. The College Football Playoff (CFP) replaced the BCS at the end of the 2014 regular season. The four-team CFP consists of a semifinal round (rotating among the following six bowl games: Sugar, Rose, Orange, Cotton, Peach, and Fiesta) and a championship game played on a Monday night. A committee ranks 25 teams for the playoffs and selected other bowl games, using guidelines that include strength of schedule, head-to-head results, and won-loss records; preference is given to conference champions. Years shown here are for regular season, not year in which championship was played.

Year	Result	Year	Result	Year	Result
1998	Tennessee 23, Florida St. 16	2005	Texas 41, USC 38	2012	Alabama 42, Notre Dame 14
1999	Florida St. 46, Virginia Tech 29	2006	Florida 41, Ohio St. 14	2013	Florida St. 34, Auburn 31
2000	Oklahoma 13, Florida St. 2	2007	LSU 38, Ohio St. 24	2014	Ohio St. 42, Oregon 20
2001	Miami (FL) 37, Nebraska 14	2008	Florida 24, Oklahoma 14	2015	Alabama 45, Clemson 40
2002	Ohio St. 31, Miami (FL) 24	2009	Alabama 37, Texas 21	2016	Clemson 35, Alabama 31
2003[1]	LSU 21, Oklahoma 14	2010	Auburn 22, Oregon 19	2017	Alabama 26, Georgia 23 (OT)
2004[2]	USC 55, Oklahoma 19	2011	Alabama 21, LSU 0		

(1) AP named USC No. 1 in its final poll despite its not appearing in the BCS No. 1 vs. No. 2 matchup. (2) The BCS's Presidential Oversight Committee vacated USC's 2004 championship due to rules violations.

National College Football Champions, 1936-1997

Unofficial champion(s), as selected by the AP poll of writers and a separate poll of coaches. Where the polls disagreed, both teams are listed with the AP winner first. The AP poll started in 1936, the coaches poll in 1950.

Year	Champion(s)	Year	Champion(s)	Year	Champion(s)	Year	Champion(s)	Year	Champion(s)
1936	Minnesota	1949	Notre Dame	1962	USC	1974	Oklahoma/USC	1986	Penn St.
1937	Pittsburgh	1950	Oklahoma	1963	Texas	1975	Oklahoma	1987	Miami (FL)
1938	Texas Christian	1951	Tennessee	1964	Alabama	1976	Pittsburgh	1988	Notre Dame
1939	Texas A&M	1952	Michigan St.	1965	Alabama/Mich. St.	1977	Notre Dame	1989	Miami (FL)
1940	Minnesota	1953	Maryland	1966	Notre Dame	1978	Alabama/USC	1990	Colorado/GA Tech
1941	Minnesota	1954	Ohio St./UCLA	1967	USC	1979	Alabama	1991	Miami (FL)/Wash.
1942	Ohio St.	1955	Oklahoma	1968	Ohio St.	1980	Georgia	1992	Alabama
1943	Notre Dame	1956	Oklahoma	1969	Texas	1981	Clemson	1993	Florida St.
1944	Army	1957	Auburn/Ohio St.	1970	Nebraska/Texas	1982	Penn St.	1994	Nebraska
1945	Army	1958	LSU	1971	Nebraska	1983	Miami (FL)	1995	Nebraska
1946	Notre Dame	1959	Syracuse	1972	USC	1984	Brigham Young	1996	Florida
1947	Notre Dame	1960	Minnesota	1973	Notre Dame/	1985	Oklahoma	1997	Mich./Nebraska
1948	Michigan	1961	Alabama		Alabama				

Results of Major Bowl Games

Date indicates year the game was played; bowl games are generally played in late Dec. or early Jan. CFP = College Football Playoff semifinal game.

Rose Bowl Results, 1902-2018

1902	(Jan.) Michigan 49, Stanford 0	1928	Stanford 7, Pittsburgh 6	1941	Stanford 21, Nebraska 13
1916	Washington St. 14, Brown 0	1929	Georgia Tech 8, California 7	1942	Oregon St. 20, Duke 16
1917	Oregon 14, Pennsylvania 0	1930	USC 47, Pittsburgh 14	1943	Georgia 9, UCLA 0
1918-19	Service teams	1931	Alabama 24, Washington St. 0	1944	USC 29, Washington 0
1920	Harvard 7, Oregon 6	1932	USC 21, Tulane 12	1945	USC 25, Tennessee 0
1921	California 28, Ohio St. 0	1933	USC 35, Pittsburgh 0	1946	Alabama 34, USC 14
1922	Washington & Jefferson 0, California 0	1934	Columbia 7, Stanford 0	1947	Illinois 45, UCLA 14
		1935	Alabama 29, Stanford 13	1948	Michigan 49, USC 0
1923	USC 14, Penn St. 3	1936	Stanford 7, SMU 0	1949	Northwestern 20, California 14
1924	Navy 14, Washington 14	1937	Pittsburgh 21, Washington 0	1950	Ohio St. 17, California 14
1925	Notre Dame 27, Stanford 10	1938	California 13, Alabama 0	1951	Michigan 14, California 6
1926	Alabama 20, Washington 19	1939	USC 7, Duke 3	1952	Illinois 40, Stanford 7
1927	Alabama 7, Stanford 7	1940	USC 14, Tennessee 0	1953	USC 7, Wisconsin 0

1954 Michigan St. 28, UCLA 20	1976 UCLA 23, Ohio St. 10	1998 Michigan 21, Washington St. 16
1955 Ohio St. 20, USC 7	1977 USC 14, Michigan 6	1999 Wisconsin 38, UCLA 31
1956 Michigan St. 17, UCLA 14	1978 Washington 27, Michigan 20	2000 Wisconsin 17, Stanford 9
1957 Iowa 35, Oregon St. 19	1979 USC 17, Michigan 10	2001 Washington 34, Purdue 24
1958 Ohio St. 10, Oregon 7	1980 USC 17, Ohio St. 16	2002 Miami (FL) 37, Nebraska 14
1959 Iowa 38, California 12	1981 Michigan 23, Washington 6	2003 Oklahoma 34, Washington St. 14
1960 Washington 44, Wisconsin 8	1982 Washington 28, Iowa 0	2004 USC 28, Michigan 14
1961 Washington 17, Minnesota 7	1983 UCLA 24, Michigan 14	2005 Texas 38, Michigan 37
1962 Minnesota 21, UCLA 3	1984 UCLA 45, Illinois 9	2006 Texas 41, USC 38
1963 USC 42, Wisconsin 37	1985 USC 20, Ohio St. 17	2007 USC 32, Michigan 18
1964 Illinois 17, Washington 7	1986 UCLA 45, Iowa 28	2008 USC 49, Illinois 17
1965 Michigan 34, Oregon St. 7	1987 Arizona St. 22, Michigan 15	2009 USC 38, Penn St. 24
1966 UCLA 14, Michigan St. 12	1988 Michigan St. 20, USC 17	2010 Ohio St. 26, Oregon 17
1967 Purdue 14, USC 13	1989 Michigan 22, USC 14	2011 TCU 21, Wisconsin 19
1968 USC 14, Indiana 3	1990 USC 17, Michigan 10	2012 Oregon 45, Wisconsin 38
1969 Ohio St. 27, USC 16	1991 Washington 46, Iowa 34	2013 Stanford 20, Wisconsin 14
1970 USC 10, Michigan 3	1992 Washington 34, Michigan 14	2014 Michigan St. 24, Stanford 20
1971 Stanford 27, Ohio St. 17	1993 Michigan 38, Washington 31	2015 Oregon 59, Florida St. 20 (CFP)
1972 Stanford 13, Michigan 12	1994 Wisconsin 21, UCLA 16	2016 Stanford 45, Iowa 16
1973 USC 42, Ohio St. 17	1995 Penn St. 38, Oregon 20	2017 USC 52, Penn St. 49
1974 Ohio St. 42, USC 21	1996 USC 41, Northwestern 32	2018 Georgia 54, Oklahoma 48 [2OT]
1975 USC 18, Ohio St. 17	1997 Ohio St. 20, Arizona St. 17	(CFP)

Orange Bowl Results, 1935-2017

1935 (Jan.) Bucknell 26, Miami (FL) 0	1964 Nebraska 13, Auburn 7	1994 Florida St. 18, Nebraska 16
1936 Catholic U. 20, Mississippi 19	1965 Texas 21, Alabama 17	1995 Nebraska 24, Miami (FL) 17
1937 Duquesne 13, Mississippi St. 12	1966 Alabama 39, Nebraska 28	1996 Florida St. 31, Notre Dame 26
1938 Auburn 6, Michigan St. 0	1967 Florida 27, Georgia Tech 12	1996 (Dec.) Nebraska 41,
1939 Tennessee 17, Oklahoma 0	1968 Oklahoma 26, Tennessee 24	Virginia Tech 21,
1940 Georgia Tech 21, Missouri 7	1969 Penn St. 15, Kansas 14	1998 (Jan.) Nebraska 42,
1941 Mississippi St. 14,	1970 Penn St. 10, Missouri 3	Tennessee 17
Georgetown 7	1971 Nebraska 17, LSU 12	1999 Florida 31, Syracuse 10
1942 Georgia 40, TCU 26	1972 Nebraska 38, Alabama 6	2000 Michigan 35, Alabama 34 (OT)
1943 Alabama 37, Boston College 21	1973 Nebraska 40, Notre Dame 6	2001 Oklahoma 13, Florida St. 2
1944 LSU 19, Texas A&M 14	1974 Penn St. 16, LSU 9	2002 Florida 56, Maryland 23
1945 Tulsa 26, Georgia Tech 12	1975 Notre Dame 13, Alabama 11	2003 USC 38, Iowa 17
1946 Miami (FL) 13, Holy Cross 6	1976 Oklahoma 14, Michigan 6	2004 Miami (FL) 16, Florida St. 14
1947 Rice 8, Tennessee 0	1977 Ohio St. 27, Colorado 10	2005 USC 55, Oklahoma 19
1948 Georgia Tech 20, Kansas 14	1978 Arkansas 31, Oklahoma 6	2006 Penn St. 26, Florida St. 23
1949 Texas 41, Georgia 28	1979 Oklahoma 31, Nebraska 24	(3 OT)
1950 Santa Clara 21, Kentucky 13	1980 Oklahoma 24, Florida St. 7	2007 Louisville 24, Wake Forest 13
1951 Clemson 15, Miami (FL) 14	1981 Oklahoma 18, Florida St. 17	2008 Kansas 24, Virginia Tech 21
1952 Georgia Tech 17, Baylor 14	1982 Clemson 22, Nebraska 15	2009 Virginia Tech 20, Cincinnati 7
1953 Alabama 61, Syracuse 6	1983 Nebraska 21, LSU 20	2010 Iowa 24, Georgia Tech 14
1954 Oklahoma 7, Maryland 0	1984 Miami (FL) 31, Nebraska 30	2011 Stanford 40, Virginia Tech 12
1955 Duke 34, Nebraska 7	1985 Washington 28, Oklahoma 17	2012 West Virginia 70, Clemson 33
1956 Oklahoma 20, Maryland 6	1986 Oklahoma 25, Penn St. 10	2013 Florida St. 31, Northern Illinois 10
1957 Colorado 27, Clemson 21	1987 Oklahoma 42, Arkansas 8	2014 Clemson 40, Ohio St. 35
1958 Oklahoma 48, Duke 21	1988 Miami (FL) 20, Oklahoma 14	2014 (Dec.) Georgia Tech 49,
1959 Oklahoma 21, Syracuse 6	1989 Miami (FL) 23, Nebraska 3	Mississippi St. 34
1960 Georgia 14, Missouri 0	1990 Notre Dame 21, Colorado 6	2015 Clemson 37, Oklahoma 17 (CFP)
1961 Missouri 21, Navy 14	1991 Colorado 10, Notre Dame 9	2016 Florida St. 33, Michigan 32
1962 LSU 25, Colorado 7	1992 Miami (FL) 22, Nebraska 0	2017 Wisconsin 34, Miami (FL) 24
1963 Alabama 17, Oklahoma 0	1993 Florida St. 27, Nebraska 14	

Sugar Bowl Results, 1935-2018

1935 (Jan.) Tulane 20, Temple 14	1963 Mississippi 17, Arkansas 13	1992 Notre Dame 39, Florida 28
1936 TCU 3, LSU 2	1964 Alabama 12, Mississippi 7	1993 Alabama 34, Miami (FL) 13
1937 Santa Clara 21, LSU 14	1965 LSU 13, Syracuse 10	1994 Florida 41, West Virginia 7
1938 Santa Clara 6, LSU 0	1966 Missouri 20, Florida 18	1995 Florida St. 23, Florida 17
1939 TCU 15, Carnegie Tech 7	1967 Alabama 34, Nebraska 7	1995 (Dec.) Virginia Tech 28,
1940 Texas A&M 14, Tulane 13	1968 LSU 20, Wyoming 13	Texas 10
1941 Boston College 19, Tennessee 13	1969 Arkansas 16, Georgia 2	1997 (Jan.) Florida 52, Florida St. 20
1942 Fordham 2, Missouri 0	1970 Mississippi 27, Arkansas 22	1998 Florida St. 31, Ohio St. 14
1943 Tennessee 14, Tulsa 7	1971 Tennessee 34, Air Force 13	1999 Ohio St. 24, Texas A&M 14
1944 Georgia Tech 20, Tulsa 18	1972 Oklahoma 40, Auburn 22	2000 Florida St. 46, Virginia Tech 29
1945 Duke 29, Alabama 26	1972 (Dec.) Oklahoma 14, Penn St. 0	2001 Miami (FL) 37, Florida 20
1946 Oklahoma A&M 33,	1973 Notre Dame 24, Alabama 23	2002 LSU 47, Illinois 34
St. Mary's (CA) 13	1974 Nebraska 13, Florida 10	2003 Georgia 26, Florida St. 13
1947 Georgia 20, N. Carolina 10	1975 Alabama 13, Penn St. 6	2004 LSU 21, Oklahoma 14
1948 Texas 27, Alabama 7	1977 (Jan.) Pittsburgh 27, Georgia 3	2005 Auburn 16, Virginia Tech 13
1949 Oklahoma 14, N. Carolina 6	1978 Alabama 35, Ohio St. 6	2006 West Virginia 38, Georgia 35
1950 Oklahoma 35, LSU 0	1979 Alabama 14, Penn St. 7	2007 LSU 41, Notre Dame 14
1951 Kentucky 13, Oklahoma 7	1980 Alabama 24, Arkansas 9	2008 Georgia 41, Hawaii 10
1952 Maryland 28, Tennessee 13	1981 Georgia 17, Notre Dame 10	2009 Utah 31, Alabama 17
1953 Georgia Tech 24, Mississippi 7	1982 Pittsburgh 24, Georgia 20	2010 Florida 51, Cincinnati 24
1954 Georgia Tech 42, West Virginia 19	1983 Penn St. 27, Georgia 23	2011 Ohio St. 31, Arkansas 26
1955 Navy 21, Mississippi 0	1984 Auburn 9, Michigan 7	2012 Michigan 23, Virginia Tech 20
1956 Georgia Tech 7, Pittsburgh 0	1985 Nebraska 28, LSU 10	2013 Louisville 33, Florida 23
1957 Baylor 13, Tennessee 7	1986 Tennessee 35, Miami (FL) 7	2014 Oklahoma 45, Alabama 31
1958 Mississippi 39, Texas 7	1987 Nebraska 30, LSU 15	2015 Ohio St. 42, Alabama 35 (CFP)
1959 LSU 7, Clemson 0	1988 Syracuse 16, Auburn 16	2016 Mississippi 48, Oklahoma St. 20
1960 Mississippi 21, LSU 0	1989 Florida St. 13, Auburn 7	2017 Oklahoma 35, Auburn 19
1961 Mississippi 14, Rice 6	1990 Miami (FL) 33, Alabama 25	2018 Alabama 24, Clemson 6 (CFP)
1962 Alabama 10, Arkansas 3	1991 Tennessee 23, Virginia 22	

All-Time NCAA Bowl Subdivision (FBS) Statistical Leaders

Career Rushing Yards

Player, team	Yrs	Carries	Yds	Avg
Donnel Pumphrey, San Diego St.	2013-16	1,059	6,405	6.05
Ron Dayne, Wisconsin	1996-99	1,115	6,397	5.74
Ricky Williams, Texas	1995-98	1,011	6,279	6.21
Tony Dorsett, Pittsburgh	1973-76	1,074	6,082	5.66
DeAngelo Williams, Memphis	2002-05	969	6,026	6.22
Royce Freeman, Oregon	2014-17	947	5,621	5.94
Charles White, USC	1976-79	1,023	5,598	5.47
Travis Prentice, Miami (OH)	1996-99	1,138	5,596	4.92
Cedric Benson, Texas	2001-04	1,112	5,540	4.98
Justin Jackson, Northwestern	2014-17	1,142	5,440	4.76
Damion Fletcher, Southern Miss	2006-09	1,009	5,302	5.25

Career Rushing Yards/Game (min. 2,500 yds)

Player, team	Yrs	Carries	Yds	Avg/game
Ed Marinaro, Cornell	1969-71	918	4,715	174.6
O.J. Simpson, USC	1967-68	621	3,124	164.4
Herschel Walker, Georgia	1980-82	994	5,259	159.4
Garrett Wolfe, N. Illinois	2004-06	807	5,164	156.5
LeShon Johnson, N. Illinois	1992-93	592	3,314	150.6
Ron Dayne, Wisconsin	1996-99	1,115	6,397	148.8
Marshall Faulk, San Diego St.	1991-93	766	4,589	148.0
George Jones, San Diego St.	1995-96	486	2,810	147.9
Tony Dorsett, Pittsburgh	1973-76	1,074	6,082	141.4
Troy Davis, Iowa St.	1994-96	782	4,382	141.4

Career Passing Yards

Player, team	Yrs	Comp/att	Yds
Case Keenum, Houston	2007-11	1,546/2,229	19,217
Timmy Chang, Hawaii	2000-04	1,388/2,436	17,072
Landry Jones, Oklahoma	2009-12	1,388/2,183	16,646
Graham Harrell, Texas Tech	2005-08	1,403/2,010	15,793
Ty Detmer, BYU	1988-91	958/1,530	15,031
Kellen Moore, Boise St.	2008-11	1,157/1,658	14,667
Baker Mayfield, Texas Tech/Oklahoma	2013-17	1,026/1,497	14,607
Luke Falk, Washington St.	2014-17	1,404/2,055	14,486
Colt Brennan, Hawaii	2005-07	1,115/1,584	14,193
Rakeem Cato, Marshall	2011-14	1,153/1,838	14,079

Career Receiving Yards

Player, team	Yrs	Rec	Yds	Avg
Corey Davis, Western Michigan	2013-16	332	5,285	15.9
Trevor Insley, Nevada	1996-99	298	5,005	16.8
Ryan Broyles, Oklahoma	2008-11	349	4,586	13.1
Justin Hardy, E. Carolina	2011-14	387	4,541	11.7
Marcus Harris, Wyoming	1993-96	259	4,518	17.4
James Washington, Oklahoma St.	2014-17	225	4,467	19.8
Rashaun Woods, Oklahoma St.	2000-03	293	4,414	15.1
Ryan Yarborough, Wyoming	1990-93	229	4,357	19.03
Troy Edwards, Louisiana Tech	1996-98	280	4,352	15.54
Aaron Turner, Pacific	1989-92	266	4,345	16.33

Note: As of end of 2017 season. Prior to 2002, postseason games were not included in NCAA final football statistics or records. All postseason games were included for the 2002 season and thereafter. Career rushing yards per game rankings do not include active players.

All-Time NCAA Bowl Subdivision (FBS) Team Won-Lost Records

Team	Years	W	L	T	Total games	Pct.	Team	Years	W	L	T	Total games	Pct.
Michigan	138	943	339	36	1,318	0.729	Miami (FL)	92	623	354	19	996	0.635
Notre Dame	129	906	324	42	1,272	0.729	Georgia Southern[1] (2014)	54	377	216	10	603	0.633
Boise St. (1996)	50	438	165	2	605	0.726	Auburn	125	759	436	47	1,242	0.630
Ohio St.[1]	128	898	324	53	1,275	0.725	Florida	111	714	415	40	1,169	0.628
Alabama[1]	123	891	328	43	1,262	0.723	Washington	128	725	445	50	1,220	0.615
Oklahoma	123	884	323	53	1,260	0.723	Clemson	122	729	459	45	1,233	0.609
Texas	125	898	366	33	1,297	0.705	Virginia Tech	124	737	466	46	1,249	0.608
USC[1]	124	834	339	54	1,227	0.702	Arizona St.	105	607	388	24	1,019	0.607
Nebraska	128	893	380	40	1,313	0.695	Texas A&M	123	732	477	48	1,257	0.601
Penn St.	131	878	387	42	1,307	0.688	Michigan St.	121	694	453	44	1,191	0.601
Florida St.[1]	71	539	250	17	806	0.679	West Virginia	125	742	493	45	1,280	0.597
Tennessee	121	833	383	53	1,269	0.677	Central Mich.	117	617	411	36	1,064	0.597
Georgia	124	808	420	54	1,282	0.651	Miami (OH)	129	684	455	44	1,183	0.597
LSU	124	787	412	47	1,246	0.650	Georgia Tech	125	728	496	43	1,267	0.592
Appalachian St. (2014)	88	606	333	29	968	0.641	W. Kentucky (2009)	99	572	391	30	993	0.591

Note: As of end of 2017 season. Includes records as senior college only. Bowl and playoff games are included, and each tie game is computed as half won and half lost. Teams must have been in Div. I for at least 25 years to qualify. Year in parentheses indicates the first year of FBS membership, that is, reclassification to Bowl Subdivision (FBS) (formerly Div. I-A). Tiebreaker rule began with 1996 season. (1) Record adjusted by action of the NCAA Committee on Infractions.

Heisman Trophy Winners, 1935-2017

The Heisman Memorial Trophy is awarded annually to the nation's outstanding college football player by the Downtown Athletic Club.

Year	Winner, school, position	Year	Winner, school, position	Year	Winner, school, position
1935	Jay Berwanger, Chicago, HB	1963	Roger Staubach, Navy, QB	1991	Desmond Howard, Michigan, WR
1936	Larry Kelley, Yale, E	1964	John Huarte, Notre Dame, QB	1992	Gino Torretta, Miami (FL), QB
1937	Clinton Frank, Yale, HB	1965	Mike Garrett, USC, HB	1993	Charlie Ward, Florida St., QB
1938	David O'Brien, Texas Christian, QB	1966	Steve Spurrier, Florida, QB	1994	Rashaan Salaam, Colorado, RB
1939	Nile Kinnick, Iowa, HB	1967	Gary Beban, UCLA, QB	1995	Eddie George, Ohio St., RB
1940	Tom Harmon, Michigan, HB	1968	O.J. Simpson, USC, RB	1996	Danny Wuerffel, Florida, QB
1941	Bruce Smith, Minnesota, HB	1969	Steve Owens, Oklahoma, RB	1997	Charles Woodson, Michigan, CB
1942	Frank Sinkwich, Georgia, HB	1970	Jim Plunkett, Stanford, QB	1998	Ricky Williams, Texas, RB
1943	Angelo Bertelli, Notre Dame, QB	1971	Pat Sullivan, Auburn, QB	1999	Ron Dayne, Wisconsin, RB
1944	Leslie Horvath, Ohio St., QB	1972	Johnny Rodgers, Nebraska, RB-WR	2000	Chris Weinke, Florida St., QB
1945	Felix Blanchard, Army, FB	1973	John Cappelletti, Penn St., RB	2001	Eric Crouch, Nebraska, QB
1946	Glenn Davis, Army, HB	1974	Archie Griffin, Ohio St., RB	2002	Carson Palmer, USC, QB
1947	John Lujack, Notre Dame, QB	1975	Archie Griffin, Ohio St., RB	2003	Jason White, Oklahoma, QB
1948	Doak Walker, SMU, HB	1976	Tony Dorsett, Pittsburgh, RB	2004	Matt Leinart, USC, QB
1949	Leon Hart, Notre Dame, E	1977	Earl Campbell, Texas, RB	2005	Reggie Bush, USC, RB[1]
1950	Vic Janowicz, Ohio St., HB	1978	Billy Sims, Oklahoma, RB	2006	Troy Smith, Ohio St., QB
1951	Richard Kazmaier, Princeton, HB	1979	Charles White, USC, RB	2007	Tim Tebow, Florida, QB
1952	Billy Vessels, Oklahoma, HB	1980	George Rogers, S. Carolina, RB	2008	Sam Bradford, Oklahoma, QB
1953	John Lattner, Notre Dame, HB	1981	Marcus Allen, USC, RB	2009	Mark Ingram, Alabama, RB
1954	Alan Ameche, Wisconsin, FB	1982	Herschel Walker, Georgia, RB	2010	Cam Newton, Auburn, QB
1955	Howard Cassady, Ohio St., HB	1983	Mike Rozier, Nebraska, RB	2011	Robert Griffin III, Baylor, QB
1956	Paul Hornung, Notre Dame, QB	1984	Doug Flutie, Boston College, QB	2012	Johnny Manziel, Texas A&M, QB
1957	John Crow, Texas A&M, HB	1985	Bo Jackson, Auburn, RB	2013	Jameis Winston, Florida St., QB
1958	Pete Dawkins, Army, HB	1986	Vinny Testaverde, Miami (FL), QB	2014	Marcus Mariota, Oregon, QB
1959	Billy Cannon, LSU, HB	1987	Tim Brown, Notre Dame, WR	2015	Derrick Henry, Alabama, RB
1960	Joe Bellino, Navy, HB	1988	Barry Sanders, Oklahoma St., RB	2016	Lamar Jackson, Louisville, QB
1961	Ernest Davis, Syracuse, HB	1989	Andre Ware, Houston, QB	2017	Baker Mayfield, Oklahoma, QB
1962	Terry Baker, Oregon St., QB	1990	Ty Detmer, BYU, QB		

(1) Bush forfeited the trophy voluntarily Sept. 14, 2010, following revelations of NCAA rules violations while Bush was at USC.

College Football Coach of the Year, 1935-2017

The Coach of the Year has been selected by the American Football Coaches Assn. (AFCA) since 1935 as well as the Football Writers Assn. of America (FWAA) since 1957. When polls disagree, both winners are indicated.

1935 Lynn Waldorf, Northwestern
1936 Dick Harlow, Harvard
1937 Edward Mylin, Lafayette
1938 Bill Kern, Carnegie Tech
1939 Eddie Anderson, Iowa
1940 Clark Shaughnessy, Stanford
1941 Frank Leahy, Notre Dame
1942 Bill Alexander, Georgia Tech
1943 Amos Alonzo Stagg, Pacific (CA)
1944 Carroll Widdoes, Ohio St.
1945 Bo McMillin, Indiana
1946 Earl "Red" Blaik, Army
1947 Fritz Crisler, Michigan
1948 Bennie Oosterbaan, Michigan
1949 Bud Wilkinson, Oklahoma
1950 Charlie Caldwell, Princeton
1951 Chuck Taylor, Stanford
1952 Biggie Munn, Michigan St.
1953 Jim Tatum, Maryland
1954 Henry "Red" Sanders, UCLA
1955 Duffy Daugherty, Michigan St.
1956 Bowden Wyatt, Tennessee
1957 Woody Hayes, Ohio St.
1958 Paul Dietzel, LSU
1959 Ben Schwartzwalder, Syracuse
1960 Murray Warmath, Minnesota
1961 Paul "Bear" Bryant, Alabama (AFCA);
     Darrell Royal, Texas (FWAA)
1962 John McKay, USC
1963 Darrell Royal, Texas
1964 Ara Parseghian, Notre Dame &
     Frank Broyles, Arkansas (AFCA);
     Ara Parseghian, Notre Dame (FWAA)
1965 Tommy Prothro, UCLA (AFCA);
     Duffy Daugherty, Mich. St. (FWAA)
1966 Tom Cahill, Army
1967 John Pont, Indiana

1968 Joe Paterno, Penn St. (AFCA);
     Woody Hayes, Ohio St. (FWAA)
1969 Bo Schembechler, Michigan
1970 Charles McClendon, LSU &
     Darrell Royal, Texas (AFCA);
     Alex Agase, Northwestern (FWAA)
1971 Paul "Bear" Bryant, Alabama (AFCA);
     Bob Devaney, Nebraska (FWAA)
1972 John McKay, USC
1973 Paul "Bear" Bryant, Alabama (AFCA);
     Johnny Majors, Pittsburgh (FWAA)
1974 Grant Teaff, Baylor
1975 Frank Kush, Arizona St. (AFCA);
     Woody Hayes, Ohio St. (FWAA)
1976 Johnny Majors, Pittsburgh
1977 Don James, Washington (AFCA);
     Lou Holtz, Arkansas (FWAA)
1978 Joe Paterno, Penn St.
1979 Earle Bruce, Ohio St.
1980 Vince Dooley, Georgia
1981 Danny Ford, Clemson
1982 Joe Paterno, Penn St.
1983 Ken Hatfield, Air Force (AFCA);
     Howard Schnellenberger,
       Miami (FL) (FWAA)
1984 LaVell Edwards, Brigham Young
1985 Fisher De Berry, Air Force
1986 Joe Paterno, Penn St.
1987 Dick MacPherson, Syracuse
1988 Don Nehlen, W. Virginia (AFCA);
     Lou Holtz, Notre Dame (FWAA)
1989 Bill McCartney, Colorado
1990 Bobby Ross, Georgia Tech
1991 Don James, Washington
1992 Gene Stallings, Alabama
1993 Barry Alvarez, Wisconsin (AFCA);
     Terry Bowden, Auburn (FWAA)

1994 Tom Osborne, Nebraska (AFCA);
     Rich Brooks, Oregon (FWAA)
1995 Gary Barnett, Northwestern
1996 Bruce Snyder, Arizona St.
1997 Mike Price, Washington St.
1998 Phillip Fulmer, Tennessee
1999 Frank Beamer, Virginia Tech
2000 Bob Stoops, Oklahoma
2001 Larry Coker, Miami (FL) &
     Ralph Friedgen, Maryland (AFCA);
     Ralph Friedgen, Maryland (FWAA)
2002 Jim Tressel, Ohio St.
2003 Pete Carroll, USC (AFCA);
     Nick Saban, LSU (FWAA)
2004 Tommy Tuberville, Auburn (AFCA);
     Urban Meyer, Utah (FWAA)
2005 Joe Paterno, Penn St. (AFCA);
     Charlie Weis, Notre Dame (FWAA)
2006 Jim Grobe, Wake Forest (AFCA);
     Greg Schiano, Rutgers (FWAA)
2007 Mark Mangino, Kansas
2008 Kyle Whittingham, Utah (AFCA);
     Nick Saban, Alabama (FWAA)
2009 Gary Patterson, TCU
2010 Chip Kelly, Oregon
2011 Les Miles, LSU (AFCA);
     Mike Gundy, Oklahoma St. (FWAA)
2012 Brian Kelly, Notre Dame
2013 David Cutcliffe, Duke (AFCA);
     Gus Malzahn, Auburn (FWAA)
2014 Gary Patterson, TCU
2015 Dabo Swinney, Clemson (AFCA);
     Kirk Ferentz, Iowa (FWAA)
2016 Mike MacIntyre, Colorado
2017 Scott Frost, UCF

COLLEGE BASKETBALL

2018 Men's NCAA Tournament: Villanova Crushes Michigan

The Villanova Wildcats defeated the Michigan Wolverines, 79-62, at the Alamodome in San Antonio, TX, to claim their second national title in three years Apr. 2, 2018. Wildcats sophomore guard Donte DiVincenzo came in off the bench to score 31 points and was named the Final Four's most outstanding player. Villanova won each of their games in the 2018 tournament by double-digit margins, including a 95-79 semifinal win over Kansas in which 'Nova scored an NCAA tournament-record 18 three-pointers.

NCAA Men's Basketball Division I Champions, 1939-2018

Year	Champion	Final opponent	Score	Most outstanding player	Winning coach	Site
1939	Oregon	Ohio St.	46-33	Jimmy Hull, Ohio St.	Howard Hobson	Evanston, IL
1940	Indiana	Kansas	60-42	Marv Huffman, Indiana	Branch McCracken	Kansas City, MO
1941	Wisconsin	Washington St.	39-34	John Kotz, Wisconsin	Bud Foster	Kansas City, MO
1942	Stanford	Dartmouth	53-38	Howie Dallmar, Stanford	Everett Dean	Kansas City, MO
1943	Wyoming	Georgetown	46-34	Ken Sailors, Wyoming	Everett Shelton	New York, NY
1944	Utah	Dartmouth	42-40[1]	Arnold Ferrin, Utah	Vadal Peterson	New York, NY
1945	Oklahoma St.[2]	NYU	49-45	Bob Kurland, Oklahoma St.	Henry Iba	New York, NY
1946	Oklahoma St.[2]	North Carolina	43-40	Bob Kurland, Oklahoma St.	Henry Iba	New York, NY
1947	Holy Cross	Oklahoma	58-47	George Kaftan, Holy Cross	Alvin Julian	New York, NY
1948	Kentucky	Baylor	58-42	Alex Groza, Kentucky	Adolph Rupp	New York, NY
1949	Kentucky	Oklahoma St.	46-36	Alex Groza, Kentucky	Adolph Rupp	Seattle, WA
1950	CCNY	Bradley	71-68	Irwin Dambrot, CCNY	Nat Holman	New York, NY
1951	Kentucky	Kansas St.	68-58	Bill Spivey, Kentucky	Adolph Rupp	Minneapolis, MN
1952	Kansas	St. John's (NY)	80-63	Clyde Lovellette, Kansas	Forrest Allen	Seattle, WA
1953	Indiana	Kansas	69-68	B. H. Born, Kansas	Branch McCracken	Kansas City, MO
1954	La Salle	Bradley	92-76	Tom Gola, La Salle	Kenneth Loeffler	Kansas City, MO
1955	San Francisco	La Salle	77-63	Bill Russell, San Francisco	Phil Woolpert	Kansas City, MO
1956	San Francisco	Iowa	83-71	Hal Lear, Temple	Phil Woolpert	Evanston, IL
1957	North Carolina	Kansas	54-53[1]	Wilt Chamberlain, Kansas	Frank McGuire	Kansas City, MO
1958	Kentucky	Seattle	84-72	Elgin Baylor, Seattle	Adolph Rupp	Louisville, KY
1959	California	West Virginia	71-70	Jerry West, West Virginia	Pete Newell	Louisville, KY
1960	Ohio St.	California	75-55	Jerry Lucas, Ohio St.	Fred Taylor	San Francisco, CA
1961	Cincinnati	Ohio St.	70-65[1]	Jerry Lucas, Ohio St.	Edwin Jucker	Kansas City, MO
1962	Cincinnati	Ohio St.	71-59	Paul Hogue, Cincinnati	Edwin Jucker	Louisville, KY
1963	Loyola (IL)	Cincinnati	60-58[1]	Art Heyman, Duke	George Ireland	Louisville, KY
1964	UCLA	Duke	98-83	Walt Hazzard, UCLA	John Wooden	Kansas City, MO
1965	UCLA	Michigan	91-80	Bill Bradley, Princeton	John Wooden	Portland, OR
1966	UTEP[3]	Kentucky	72-65	Jerry Chambers, Utah	Don Haskins	College Park, MD
1967	UCLA	Dayton	79-64	Lew Alcindor[4], UCLA	John Wooden	Louisville, KY
1968	UCLA	North Carolina	78-55	Lew Alcindor[4], UCLA	John Wooden	Los Angeles, CA
1969	UCLA	Purdue	92-72	Lew Alcindor[4], UCLA	John Wooden	Louisville, KY
1970	UCLA	Jacksonville	80-69	Sidney Wicks, UCLA	John Wooden	College Park, MD
1971	UCLA	Villanova*	68-62	Howard Porter, Villanova*	John Wooden	Houston, TX
1972	UCLA	Florida St.	81-76	Bill Walton, UCLA	John Wooden	Los Angeles, CA
1973	UCLA	Memphis[5]	87-66	Bill Walton, UCLA	John Wooden	St. Louis, MO
1974	North Carolina St.	Marquette	76-64	David Thompson, NC State	Norm Sloan	Greensboro, NC

Year	Champion	Final opponent	Score	Most outstanding player	Winning coach	Site
1975	UCLA	Kentucky	92-85	Richard Washington, UCLA	John Wooden	San Diego, CA
1976	Indiana	Michigan	86-68	Kent Benson, Indiana	Bob Knight	Philadelphia, PA
1977	Marquette	North Carolina	67-59	Butch Lee, Marquette	Al McGuire	Atlanta, GA
1978	Kentucky	Duke	94-88	Jack Givens, Kentucky	Joe Hall	St. Louis, MO
1979	Michigan St.	Indiana St.	75-64	Magic Johnson, Michigan St.	Jud Heathcote	Salt Lake City, UT
1980	Louisville	UCLA*	59-54	Darrell Griffith, Louisville	Denny Crum	Indianapolis, IN
1981	Indiana	North Carolina	63-50	Isiah Thomas, Indiana	Bob Knight	Philadelphia, PA
1982	North Carolina	Georgetown	63-62	James Worthy, N. Carolina	Dean Smith	New Orleans, LA
1983	North Carolina St.	Houston	54-52	Hakeem Olajuwon, Houston	Jim Valvano	Albuquerque, NM
1984	Georgetown	Houston	84-75	Patrick Ewing, Georgetown	John Thompson	Seattle, WA
1985	Villanova	Georgetown	66-64	Ed Pinckney, Villanova	Rollie Massimino	Lexington, KY
1986	Louisville	Duke	72-69	Pervis Ellison, Louisville	Denny Crum	Dallas, TX
1987	Indiana	Syracuse	74-73	Keith Smart, Indiana	Bob Knight	New Orleans, LA
1988	Kansas	Oklahoma	83-79	Danny Manning, Kansas	Larry Brown	Kansas City, MO
1989	Michigan	Seton Hall	80-79[1]	Glen Rice, Michigan	Steve Fisher	Seattle, WA
1990	UNLV	Duke	103-73	Anderson Hunt, UNLV	Jerry Tarkanian	Denver, CO
1991	Duke	Kansas	72-65	Christian Laettner, Duke	Mike Krzyzewski	Indianapolis, IN
1992	Duke	Michigan	71-51	Bobby Hurley, Duke	Mike Krzyzewski	Minneapolis, MN
1993	North Carolina	Michigan	77-71	Donald Williams, N. Carolina	Dean Smith	New Orleans, LA
1994	Arkansas	Duke	76-72	Corliss Williamson, Arkansas	Nolan Richardson	Charlotte, NC
1995	UCLA	Arkansas	89-78	Ed O'Bannon, UCLA	Jim Harrick	Seattle, WA
1996	Kentucky	Syracuse	76-67	Tony Delk, Kentucky	Rick Pitino	E. Rutherford, NJ
1997	Arizona	Kentucky	84-79[1]	Miles Simon, Arizona	Lute Olson	Indianapolis, IN
1998	Kentucky	Utah	78-69	Jeff Sheppard, Kentucky	Tubby Smith	San Antonio, TX
1999	Connecticut	Duke	77-74	Richard Hamilton, Connecticut	Jim Calhoun	St. Petersburg, FL
2000	Michigan St.	Florida	89-76	Mateen Cleaves, Michigan St.	Tom Izzo	Indianapolis, IN
2001	Duke	Arizona	82-72	Shane Battier, Duke	Mike Krzyzewski	Minneapolis, MN
2002	Maryland	Indiana	64-52	Juan Dixon, Maryland	Gary Williams	Atlanta, GA
2003	Syracuse	Kansas	81-78	Carmelo Anthony, Syracuse	Jim Boeheim	New Orleans, LA
2004	Connecticut	Georgia Tech	82-73	Emeka Okafor, Connecticut	Jim Calhoun	San Antonio, TX
2005	North Carolina	Illinois	75-70	Sean May, N. Carolina	Roy Williams	St. Louis, MO
2006	Florida	UCLA	73-57	Joakim Noah, Florida	Billy Donovan	Indianapolis, IN
2007	Florida	Ohio St.	84-75	Corey Brewer, Florida	Billy Donovan	Atlanta, GA
2008	Kansas	Memphis	75-68[1]	Mario Chalmers, Kansas	Bill Self	San Antonio, TX
2009	North Carolina	Michigan St.	89-72	Wayne Ellington, N. Carolina	Roy Williams	Detroit, MI
2010	Duke	Butler	61-59	Kyle Singler, Duke	Mike Krzyzewski	Indianapolis, IN
2011	Connecticut	Butler	53-41	Kemba Walker, Connecticut	Jim Calhoun	Houston, TX
2012	Kentucky	Kansas	67-59	Anthony Davis, Kentucky	John Calipari	New Orleans, LA
2013[6]	Louisville	Michigan	82-76	Luke Hancock, Louisville	Rick Pitino	Atlanta, GA
2014	Connecticut	Kentucky	60-54	Shabazz Napier, Connecticut	Kevin Ollie	Arlington, TX
2015	Duke	Wisconsin	68-63	Tyus Jones, Duke	Mike Krzyzewski	Indianapolis, IN
2016	Villanova	North Carolina	77-74	Ryan Arcidiacono, Villanova	Jay Wright	Houston, TX
2017	North Carolina	Gonzaga	71-65	Joel Berry II, N. Carolina	Roy Williams	Glendale, AZ
2018	Villanova	Michigan	79-62	Donte DiVincenzo, Villanova	Jay Wright	San Antonio, TX

* = Declared ineligible after the tournament. (1) Overtime. (2) Then known as Oklahoma A&M. (3) Then known as Texas Western. (4) Changed name to Kareem Abdul-Jabbar in 1971. (5) Then known as Memphis State. (6) Title vacated by the NCAA Committee on Infractions in 2018.

All-Time Winningest Men's NCAA Division I Basketball Teams

Team	Yrs	Won	Lost	Pct.	Team	Yrs	Won	Lost	Pct.	Team	Yrs	Won	Lost	Pct.
Kentucky	115	2,263	699	0.764	Notre Dame	113	1,866	1,009	0.649	Indiana	118	1,817	1,034	0.637
N. Carolina	108	2,232	792	0.738	VCU	48	939	509	0.648	Weber State	56	1,044	597	0.636
Kansas	120	2,248	849	0.726	Utah	110	1,802	990	0.645	Purdue	120	1,777	1,026	0.634
Duke	113	2,144	881	0.709	Murray State	93	1,612	889	0.645	Memphis	97	1,542	903	0.631
UNLV	60	1,245	543	0.696	St. John's (NY)	111	1,833	1,016	0.643	NYU	100	1,332	783	0.630
UCLA	99	1,870	836	0.691	Illinois	113	1,778	991	0.642	Missouri State	106	1,654	975	0.629
Syracuse[1]	117	1,884	894	0.678	Temple	122	1,903	1,069	0.640	BYU	116	1,810	1,082	0.626
W. Kentucky	99	1,775	912	0.661	Arkansas	95	1,670	939	0.640	Texas	112	1,769	1,069	0.623
Arizona	113	1,796	931	0.659	Cincinnati	117	1,788	1,008	0.639	UAB	40	796	483	0.622
Villanova	98	1,749	924	0.654	Connecticut	115	1,696	957	0.639	NC State	106	1,713	1,054	0.619
Louisville[1]	104	1,702	915	0.650										

Note: Through 2017-18 season; winningest teams by percentage. Minimum 25 years as Div. I program. (1) Record adjusted by action of the NCAA Committee on Infractions.

National Invitation Tournament Champions, 1938-2018

The National Invitation Tournament (NIT), first played in 1938, is the oldest U.S. basketball tournament. The first National Collegiate Athletic Association (NCAA) national championship tournament was played one year later. In Aug. 2005, the NCAA agreed to purchase the NIT from the five New York City-area colleges that had run the NIT.

Year	Champion	Year	Champion	Year	Champion	Year	Champion	Year	Champion
1938	Temple	1955	Duquesne	1972	Maryland	1988	Connecticut	2004	Michigan
1939	Long Island Univ.	1956	Louisville	1973	Virginia Tech	1989	St. John's (NY)	2005	South Carolina
1940	Colorado	1957	Bradley	1974	Purdue	1990	Vanderbilt	2006	South Carolina
1941	Long Island Univ.	1958	Xavier (OH)	1975	Princeton	1991	Stanford	2007	West Virginia
1942	West Virginia	1959	St. John's (NY)	1976	Kentucky	1992	Virginia	2008	Ohio State
1943	St. John's (NY)	1960	Bradley	1977	St. Bonaventure	1993	Minnesota	2009	Penn State
1944	St. John's (NY)	1961	Providence	1978	Texas	1994	Villanova	2010	Dayton
1945	DePaul	1962	Dayton	1979	Indiana	1995	Virginia Tech	2011	Wichita State
1946	Kentucky	1963	Providence	1980	Virginia	1996	Nebraska	2012	Stanford
1947	Utah	1964	Bradley	1981	Tulsa	1997	Michigan	2013	Baylor
1948	St. Louis	1965	St. John's (NY)	1982	Bradley	1998	Minnesota	2014	Minnesota
1949	San Francisco	1966	Brigham Young	1983	Fresno State	1999	California	2015	Stanford
1950	CCNY	1967	Southern Illinois	1984	Michigan	2000	Wake Forest	2016	George Washington
1951	Brigham Young	1968	Dayton	1985	UCLA	2001	Tulsa	2017	TCU
1952	La Salle	1969	Temple	1986	Ohio State	2002	Memphis	2018	Penn State
1953	Seton Hall	1970	Marquette	1987	Southern Miss	2003	St. John's (NY)		
1954	Holy Cross	1971	North Carolina							

2018 Men's NCAA Basketball Tournament

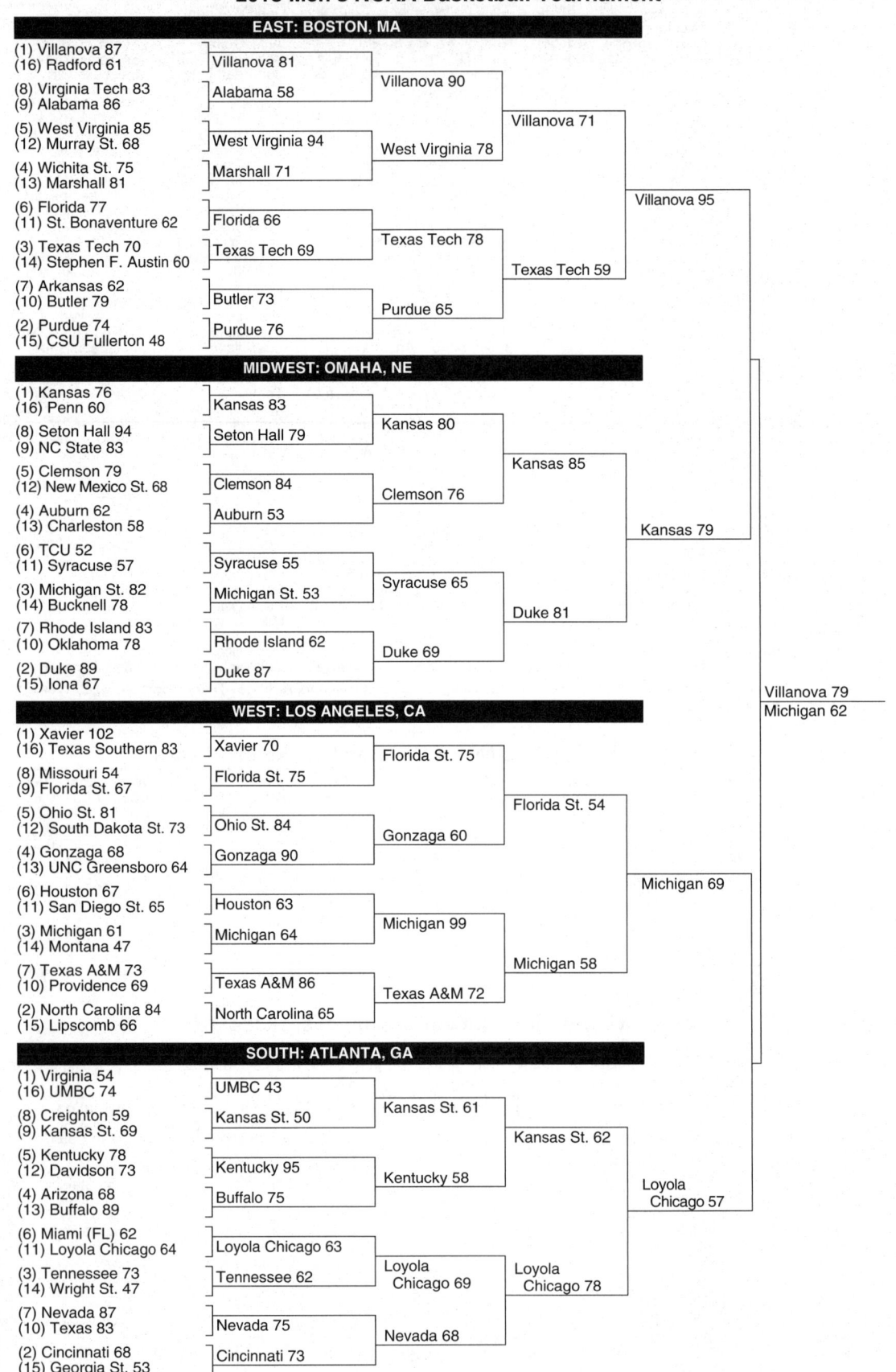

EAST: BOSTON, MA

(1) Villanova 87
(16) Radford 61 — Villanova 81
(8) Virginia Tech 83
(9) Alabama 86 — Alabama 58
Villanova 90

(5) West Virginia 85
(12) Murray St. 68 — West Virginia 94
(4) Wichita St. 75
(13) Marshall 81 — Marshall 71
West Virginia 78

Villanova 71

(6) Florida 77
(11) St. Bonaventure 62 — Florida 66
(3) Texas Tech 70
(14) Stephen F. Austin 60 — Texas Tech 69
Texas Tech 78

(7) Arkansas 62
(10) Butler 79 — Butler 73
(2) Purdue 74
(15) CSU Fullerton 48 — Purdue 76
Purdue 65

Texas Tech 59

Villanova 95

MIDWEST: OMAHA, NE

(1) Kansas 76
(16) Penn 60 — Kansas 83
(8) Seton Hall 94
(9) NC State 83 — Seton Hall 79
Kansas 80

(5) Clemson 79
(12) New Mexico St. 68 — Clemson 84
(4) Auburn 62
(13) Charleston 58 — Auburn 53
Clemson 76

Kansas 85

(6) TCU 52
(11) Syracuse 57 — Syracuse 55
(3) Michigan St. 82
(14) Bucknell 78 — Michigan St. 53
Syracuse 65

(7) Rhode Island 83
(10) Oklahoma 78 — Rhode Island 62
(2) Duke 89
(15) Iona 67 — Duke 87
Duke 69

Duke 81

Kansas 79

WEST: LOS ANGELES, CA

(1) Xavier 102
(16) Texas Southern 83 — Xavier 70
(8) Missouri 54
(9) Florida St. 67 — Florida St. 75
Florida St. 75

(5) Ohio St. 81
(12) South Dakota St. 73 — Ohio St. 84
(4) Gonzaga 68
(13) UNC Greensboro 64 — Gonzaga 90
Gonzaga 60

Florida St. 54

(6) Houston 67
(11) San Diego St. 65 — Houston 63
(3) Michigan 61
(14) Montana 47 — Michigan 64
Michigan 99

(7) Texas A&M 73
(10) Providence 69 — Texas A&M 86
(2) North Carolina 84
(15) Lipscomb 66 — North Carolina 65
Texas A&M 72

Michigan 58

Michigan 69

Villanova 79
Michigan 62

SOUTH: ATLANTA, GA

(1) Virginia 54
(16) UMBC 74 — UMBC 43
(8) Creighton 59
(9) Kansas St. 69 — Kansas St. 50
Kansas St. 61

(5) Kentucky 78
(12) Davidson 73 — Kentucky 95
(4) Arizona 68
(13) Buffalo 89 — Buffalo 75
Kentucky 58

Kansas St. 62

(6) Miami (FL) 62
(11) Loyola Chicago 64 — Loyola Chicago 63
(3) Tennessee 73
(14) Wright St. 47 — Tennessee 62
Loyola Chicago 69

(7) Nevada 87
(10) Texas 83 — Nevada 75
(2) Cincinnati 68
(15) Georgia St. 53 — Cincinnati 73
Nevada 68

Loyola Chicago 78

Loyola Chicago 57

Most Coaching Victories in Men's NCAA Division I Basketball Tournament

Coach, school(s), first/latest appearance	Wins	Tournaments	Championships
Mike Krzyzewski, Duke, 1984/2018	94	34	5
Roy Williams; Kansas, North Carolina; 1990/2018	77	28	3
Dean Smith, North Carolina, 1967/1997	65	27	2
Jim Boeheim, Syracuse, 1977/2018	55	33	1
Jim Calhoun; Northeastern, Connecticut; 1981/2012	49	22	3
Tom Izzo, Michigan St., 1998/2018	48	21	1
John Wooden, UCLA, 1950/1975	47	16	10
Lute Olson; Iowa, Arizona; 1979/2007	46	27	1
Bob Knight; Indiana, Texas Tech; 1973/2007	45	28	3
Denny Crum, Louisville, 1972/2000	42	23	2

Note: Through 2018 tournament. Coaches active in 2017-18 season in bold. Some records adjusted to reflect vacated victories.

NCAA Men's Basketball Division I All-Time Leaders

Season points

Player, school (season)	G	FG	3-FG	FT	PTS
Pete Maravich, LSU (1970)	31	522	NA	337	1,381
Elvin Hayes, Houston (1968)	33	519	NA	176	1,214
Frank Selvy, Furman (1954)	29	427	NA	355	1,209
Pete Maravich, LSU (1969)	26	433	NA	282	1,148
Pete Maravich, LSU (1968)	26	432	NA	274	1,138
Bo Kimble, Loyola Marymount (1990)	32	404	92	231	1,131
Hersey Hawkins, Bradley (1988)	31	377	87	284	1,125
Austin Carr, Notre Dame (1970)	29	444	NA	218	1,106
Austin Carr, Notre Dame (1971)	29	430	NA	241	1,101
Otis Birdsong, Houston (1977)	36	452	NA	186	1,090

Career points

Player, school (seasons)	G	FG	3-FG	FT	PTS
Pete Maravich, LSU (1968-70)	83	1,387	NA	893	3,667
Freeman Williams, Portland St. (1975-78)	106	1,369	NA	511	3,249
Lionel Simmons, La Salle (1987-90)	131	1,244	56	673	3,217
Alphonso Ford, Mississippi Valley St. (1990-93)	109	1,121	333	590	3,165
Doug McDermott, Creighton (2011-14)	145	1,141	274	594	3,150
Harry Kelly, Texas Southern (1980-83)	110	1,234	NA	598	3,066
Keydren Clark, St. Peter's (2003-06)	118	967	435	689	3,058
Hersey Hawkins, Bradley (1985-88)	125	1,100	118	690	3,008
Oscar Robertson, Cincinnati (1958-60)	88	1,052	NA	869	2,973
Danny Manning, Kansas (1985-88)	147	1,216	10	509	2,951

NA = Not available

Season points per game

Player, school (season)	G	FG	FT	PTS	PPG
Pete Maravich, LSU (1970)	31	522	337	1,381	44.5
Pete Maravich, LSU (1969)	26	433	282	1,148	44.2
Pete Maravich, LSU (1968)	26	432	274	1,138	43.8
Frank Selvy, Furman (1954)	29	427	355	1,209	41.7
Johnny Neumann, Mississippi (1971)	23	366	191	923	40.1
Freeman Williams, Portland St. (1977)	26	417	176	1,010	38.8
Billy McGill, Utah (1962)	26	394	221	1,009	38.8
Calvin Murphy, Niagara (1968)	24	337	242	916	38.2
Austin Carr, Notre Dame (1970)	29	444	218	1,106	38.1
Austin Carr, Notre Dame (1971)	29	430	241	1,101	38.0

Career points per game

Player, school (seasons)	G	FG	FT	PTS	PPG
Pete Maravich, LSU (1968-70)	83	1,387	893	3,667	44.2
Austin Carr, Notre Dame (1969-71)	74	1,017	526	2,560	34.6
Oscar Robertson, Cincinnati (1958-60)	88	1,052	869	2,973	33.8
Calvin Murphy, Niagara (1968-70)	77	947	654	2,548	33.1
Bo Lamar, La.-Lafayette (1972-73)	57	768	326	1,862	32.7
Frank Selvy, Furman (1952-54)	78	922	694	2,538	32.5
Rick Mount, Purdue (1968-70)	72	910	503	2,323	32.3
Darrell Floyd, Furman (1954-56)	71	868	545	2,281	32.1
Nick Werkman, Seton Hall (1962-64)	71	812	649	2,273	32.0
Willie Humes, Idaho St. (1970-71)	48	565	380	1,510	31.5

John R. Wooden Award Winners, 1977-2018

Awarded to the nation's outstanding men's college basketball player by the Los Angeles Athletic Club since 1977; awarded under the same name to women since 2004.

Year	Player, school
1977	Marques Johnson, UCLA
1978	Phil Ford, North Carolina
1979	Larry Bird, Indiana State
1980	Darrell Griffith, Louisville
1981	Danny Ainge, Brigham Young
1982	Ralph Sampson, Virginia
1983	Ralph Sampson, Virginia
1984	Michael Jordan, North Carolina
1985	Chris Mullin, St. John's (NY)
1986	Walter Berry, St. John's (NY)
1987	David Robinson, Navy
1988	Danny Manning, Kansas
1989	Sean Elliott, Arizona
1990	Lionel Simmons, La Salle
1991	Larry Johnson, UNLV
1992	Christian Laettner, Duke
1993	Calbert Cheaney, Indiana
1994	Glenn Robinson, Purdue
1995	Ed O'Bannon, UCLA
1996	Marcus Camby, Massachusetts

Year	Player, school
1997	Tim Duncan, Wake Forest
1998	Antawn Jamison, North Carolina
1999	Elton Brand, Duke
2000	Kenyon Martin, Cincinnati
2001	Shane Battier, Duke
2002	Jay Williams, Duke
2003	T. J. Ford, Texas
2004 (M)	Jameer Nelson, St. Joseph's
(W)	Alana Beard, Duke
2005 (M)	Andrew Bogut, Utah
(W)	Seimone Augustus, LSU
2006 (M)	J. J. Redick, Duke
(W)	Seimone Augustus, LSU
2007 (M)	Kevin Durant, Texas
(W)	Candace Parker, Tennessee
2008 (M)	Tyler Hansbrough, N. Carolina
(W)	Candace Parker, Tennessee
2009 (M)	Blake Griffin, Oklahoma
(W)	Maya Moore, Connecticut

Year	Player, school
2010 (M)	Evan Turner, Ohio State
(W)	Tina Charles, Connecticut
2011 (M)	Jimmer Fredette, Brigham Young
(W)	Maya Moore, Connecticut
2012 (M)	Anthony Davis, Kentucky
(W)	Brittney Griner, Baylor
2013 (M)	Trey Burke, Michigan
(W)	Brittney Griner, Baylor
2014 (M)	Doug McDermott, Creighton
(W)	Chiney Ogwumike, Stanford
2015 (M)	Frank Kaminsky, Wisconsin
(W)	Breanna Stewart, Connecticut
2016 (M)	Buddy Hield, Oklahoma
(W)	Breanna Stewart, Connecticut
2017 (M)	Frank Mason III, Kansas
(W)	Kelsey Plum, Washington
2018 (M)	Jalen Brunson, Villanova
(W)	A'ja Wilson, South Carolina

2018 Women's NCAA Basketball Tournament

ALBANY REGIONAL

(1) Connecticut 140
(16) St. Francis (PA) 52

Connecticut 71

(8) Miami (FL) 72
(9) Quinnipiac 86

Quinnipiac 46

Connecticut 72

(5) Duke 72
(12) Belmont 58

Duke 66

(4) Georgia 68
(13) Mercer 63

Georgia 40

Duke 59

Connecticut 94

(6) South Florida 79
(11) Buffalo 102

Buffalo 86

(3) Florida St. 91
(14) Little Rock 49

Florida St. 65

Buffalo 63

Connecticut 89

(7) California 62
(10) Virginia 68

Virginia 56

(2) South Carolina 63
(15) North Carolina A&T 52

South Carolina 66

South Carolina 79

South Carolina 65

SPOKANE REGIONAL

(1) Notre Dame 99
(16) CSU Northridge 81

Notre Dame 98

(8) South Dakota St. 74
(9) Villanova 81 (OT)

Villanova 72

Notre Dame 90

(5) DePaul 90
(12) Oklahoma 79

DePaul 79

(4) Texas A&M 89
(13) Drake 76

Texas A&M 80

Texas A&M 84

Notre Dame 84

(6) LSU 69
(11) Central Michigan 78

Central Michigan 95

(3) Ohio St. 87
(14) George Washington 45

Ohio St. 78

Central Michigan 69

Notre Dame 91 (OT)

(7) Green Bay 77
(10) Minnesota 89

Minnesota 73

(2) Oregon 88
(15) Seattle 45

Oregon 101

Oregon 83

Oregon 74

KANSAS CITY REGIONAL

(1) Mississippi St. 95
(16) Nicholls St. 50

Mississippi St. 71

(8) Syracuse 57
(9) Oklahoma St. 84

Oklahoma St. 56

Mississippi St. 71

(5) Maryland 77
(12) Princeton 57

Maryland 60

(4) NC State 62
(13) Elon 35

NC State 74

NC State 57

Mississippi St. 89

(6) Iowa 70
(11) Creighton 76

Creighton 64

(3) UCLA 71
(14) American 60

UCLA 86

UCLA 84

Mississippi St. 73 (OT)

(7) Arizona St. 73
(10) Nebraska 62

Arizona St. 65

(2) Texas 83
(15) Maine 54

Texas 85

Texas 75

UCLA 73

LEXINGTON REGIONAL

(1) Louisville 74
(16) Boise St. 42

Louisville 90

(8) Marquette 84
(9) Dayton 65

Marquette 72

Louisville 86

(5) Missouri 70
(12) Florida Gulf Coast 80

Florida Gulf Coast 70

(4) Stanford 82
(13) Gonzaga 68

Stanford 90

Stanford 59

Louisville 76

(6) Oregon St. 82
(11) Western Kentucky 58

Oregon St. 66

(3) Tennessee 100
(14) Liberty 60

Tennessee 59

Oregon St. 72

Louisville 63

(7) Michigan 75
(10) Northern Colorado 61

Michigan 58

(2) Baylor 96
(15) Grambling 46

Baylor 80

Baylor 67

Oregon St. 43

Notre Dame 61

Mississippi St. 58

Naismith Coach of the Year, 1987-2018

Year	Men's coach, school	Women's coach, school	Year	Men's coach, school	Women's coach, school
1987	Bob Knight, Indiana	Pat Summitt, Tennessee	2004	Phil Martelli, St. Joseph's	Pat Summitt, Tennessee
1988	Larry Brown, Kansas	Leon Barmore, Louisiana Tech	2005	Bruce Weber, Illinois	Pokey Chatman, LSU
1989	Mike Krzyzewski, Duke	Pat Summitt, Tennessee	2006	Jay Wright, Villanova	Sylvia Hatchell, North Carolina
1990	Bobby Cremins, Georgia Tech	Tara VanDerveer, Stanford	2007	Tony Bennett, Washington St.	Gail Goestenkors, Duke
1991	Randy Ayers, Ohio St.	Debbie Ryan, Virginia	2008	John Calipari, Memphis	Geno Auriemma, UConn
1992	Mike Krzyzewski, Duke	Chris Weller, Maryland	2009	Jamie Dixon, Pittsburgh	Geno Auriemma, UConn
1993	Dean Smith, North Carolina	Vivian Stringer, Iowa	2010	Jim Boeheim, Syracuse	Connie Yori, Nebraska
1994	Nolan Richardson, Arkansas	Pat Summitt, Tennessee	2011	Steve Fisher, San Diego St.	Tara VanDerveer, Stanford
1995	Jim Harrick, UCLA	Geno Auriemma, UConn	2012	Bill Self, Kansas	Kim Mulkey, Baylor
1996	John Calipari, UMass	Andy Landers, Georgia	2013	Jim Larrañaga, Miami (FL)	Muffet McGraw, Notre Dame
1997	Roy Williams, Kansas	Geno Auriemma, UConn	2014	Gregg Marshall, Wichita St.	Muffet McGraw, Notre Dame
1998	Bill Guthridge, North Carolina	Pat Summitt, Tennessee	2015	John Calipari, Kentucky	Courtney Banghart, Princeton
1999	Mike Krzyzewski, Duke	Carolyn Peck, Purdue			
2000	Mike Montgomery, Stanford	Geno Auriemma, UConn	2016	Jay Wright, Villanova	Geno Auriemma, UConn
2001	Rod Barnes, Mississippi	Muffet McGraw, Notre Dame	2017	Mark Few, Gonzaga	Geno Auriemma, UConn
2002	Ben Howland, Pittsburgh	Geno Auriemma, UConn	2018	Tony Bennett, Virginia	Vic Schaefer, Mississippi St.
2003	Tubby Smith, Kentucky	Gail Goestenkors, Duke			

2018 Women's NCAA Tournament: Notre Dame Beats the Buzzer

The Notre Dame Fighting Irish defeated the Mississippi State Bulldogs, 61-58, on Apr. 1, 2018, in the women's Division I basketball title game at Nationwide Arena in Columbus, OH. Two days after knocking perennially dominant UConn out of the Final Four with a last-minute jumper, Irish guard Arike Ogunbowale hit a three-point shot with under a second left to give Notre Dame its first title since 2001. Notre Dame head coach Muffet McGraw, the only woman head coach in the 2018 Final Four, claimed her second title and 800th win with the Irish.

NCAA Women's Basketball Division I Champions, 1982-2018

Year	Champion	Final opponent	Score	Most outstanding player	Winning coach	Site
1982	Louisiana Tech	Cheyney	76-62	Janice Lawrence, LA Tech	Sonja Hogg	Norfolk, VA
1983	USC	Louisiana Tech	69-67	Cheryl Miller, USC	Linda Sharp	Norfolk, VA
1984	USC	Tennessee	72-61	Cheryl Miller, USC	Linda Sharp	Los Angeles, CA
1985	Old Dominion	Georgia	70-65	Tracy Claxton, Old Dominion	Marianne Stanley	Austin, TX
1986	Texas	USC	97-81	Clarissa Davis, Texas	Jody Conradt	Lexington, KY
1987	Tennessee	Louisiana Tech	67-44	Tonya Edwards, Tennessee	Pat Summitt	Austin, TX
1988	Louisiana Tech	Auburn	56-54	Erica Westbrooks, LA Tech	Leon Barmore	Tacoma, WA
1989	Tennessee	Auburn	76-60	Bridgette Gordon, Tennessee	Pat Summitt	Tacoma, WA
1990	Stanford	Auburn	88-81	Jennifer Azzi, Stanford	Tara VanDerveer	Knoxville, TN
1991	Tennessee	Virginia	70-67 (OT)	Dawn Staley, Virginia	Pat Summitt	New Orleans, LA
1992	Stanford	W. Kentucky	78-62	Molly Goodenbour, Stanford	Tara VanDerveer	Los Angeles, CA
1993	Texas Tech	Ohio St.	84-82	Sheryl Swoopes, Texas Tech	Marsha Sharp	Atlanta, GA
1994	North Carolina	Louisiana Tech	60-59	Charlotte Smith, North Carolina	Sylvia Hatchell	Richmond, VA
1995	Connecticut	Tennessee	70-64	Rebecca Lobo, Connecticut	Geno Auriemma	Minneapolis, MN
1996	Tennessee	Georgia	83-65	Michelle Marciniak, Tennessee	Pat Summitt	Charlotte, NC
1997	Tennessee	Old Dominion	68-59	Chamique Holdsclaw, Tennessee	Pat Summitt	Cincinnati, OH
1998	Tennessee	Louisiana Tech	93-75	Chamique Holdsclaw, Tennessee	Pat Summitt	Kansas City, MO
1999	Purdue	Duke	62-45	Ukari Figgs, Purdue	Carolyn Peck	San Jose, CA
2000	Connecticut	Tennessee	71-52	Shea Ralph, Connecticut	Geno Auriemma	Philadelphia, PA
2001	Notre Dame	Purdue	68-66	Ruth Riley, Notre Dame	Muffet McGraw	St. Louis, MO
2002	Connecticut	Oklahoma	82-70	Swin Cash, Connecticut	Geno Auriemma	San Antonio, TX
2003	Connecticut	Tennessee	73-68	Diana Taurasi, Connecticut	Geno Auriemma	Atlanta, GA
2004	Connecticut	Tennessee	70-61	Diana Taurasi, Connecticut	Geno Auriemma	New Orleans, LA
2005	Baylor	Michigan St.	84-62	Sophia Young, Baylor	Kim Mulkey-Robertson	Indianapolis, IN
2006	Maryland	Duke	78-75 (OT)	Laura Harper, Maryland	Brenda Frese	Boston, MA
2007	Tennessee	Rutgers	59-46	Candace Parker, Tennessee	Pat Summitt	Cleveland, OH
2008	Tennessee	Stanford	64-48	Candace Parker, Tennessee	Pat Summitt	Tampa Bay, FL
2009	Connecticut	Louisville	76-54	Tina Charles, Connecticut	Geno Auriemma	St. Louis, MO
2010	Connecticut	Stanford	53-47	Maya Moore, Connecticut	Geno Auriemma	San Antonio, TX
2011	Texas A&M	Notre Dame	76-70	Danielle Adams, Texas A&M	Gary Blair	Indianapolis, IN
2012	Baylor	Notre Dame	80-61	Brittney Griner, Baylor	Kim Mulkey	Denver, CO
2013	Connecticut	Louisville	93-60	Breanna Stewart, Connecticut	Geno Auriemma	New Orleans, LA
2014	Connecticut	Notre Dame	79-58	Breanna Stewart, Connecticut	Geno Auriemma	Nashville, TN
2015	Connecticut	Notre Dame	63-53	Breanna Stewart, Connecticut	Geno Auriemma	Tampa, FL
2016	Connecticut	Syracuse	82-51	Breanna Stewart, Connecticut	Geno Auriemma	Indianapolis, IN
2017	South Carolina	Mississippi St.	67-55	A'ja Wilson, South Carolina	Dawn Staley	Dallas, TX
2018	Notre Dame	Mississippi St.	61-58	Arike Ogunbowale, Notre Dame	Muffet McGraw	Columbus, OH

NCAA Women's Basketball Division I All-Time Leaders

Season points					
Player, school (season)	G	FG	3-FG	FT	PTS
Kelsey Plum, Washington (2017)	35	379	115	236	1,109
Jackie Stiles, Missouri St. (2001)	35	365	65	267	1,062
Odyssey Sims, Baylor (2014) ..	37	362	98	232	1,054
Cindy Brown, Long Beach St. (1987).................	35	362	NA	250	974
Jerica Coley, FIU (2014)	33	345	51	231	972
Genia Miller, Cal St. Fullerton (1991).................	33	376	0	217	969
Chiney Ogwumike, Stanford (2014).................	37	402	4	159	967
Kelsey Plum, Washington (2016).................	37	308	78	266	960
Sheryl Swoopes, Texas Tech (1993).................	34	356	32	211	955
Alysha Clark, Middle Tennessee St. (2009)	34	343	12	237	935

Season points per game						
Player, school (season)	G	FG	3-FG	FT	PTS	PPG
Patricia Hoskins, Mississippi Valley St. (1989)..........	27	345	13	205	908	33.6
Andrea Congreaves, Mercer (1992).................	28	353	77	142	925	33.0
Kelsey Plum, Washington (2017)	35	379	115	236	1,109	31.7
Deborah Temple, Delta St. (1984)	28	373	NA	127	873	31.2
Andrea Congreaves, Mercer (1993).................	26	302	51	150	805	31.0
Wanda Ford, Drake (1986)	30	390	NA	139	919	30.6
Anucha Browne, Northwestern (1985).................	28	341	NA	173	855	30.5
LeChandra LeDay, Grambling (1988).................	28	334	36	146	850	30.4
Jackie Stiles, Missouri St. (2001)	35	365	65	267	1,062	30.3
Kim Perrot, La.-Lafayette (1990)	28	309	95	128	841	30.0

Career points

Player, school (seasons)	G	FG	3-FG	FT	PTS
Kelsey Plum, Washington (2014-17)	139	1,136	343	912	3,527
Kelsey Mitchell, Ohio St. (2015-18)	139	1,120	497	665	3,402
Jackie Stiles, Missouri St. (1998-2001)	129	1,160	221	852	3,393
Brittney Griner, Baylor (2010-13)	148	1,247	2	787	3,283
Patricia Hoskins, Mississippi Valley St. (1986-89)	110	1,196	24	706	3,122
Lorri Bauman, Drake (1981-84)	120	1,104	NA	907	3,115
Jerica Coley, FIU (2011-14)	131	1,099	160	749	3,107
Rachel Banham, Minnesota (2012-16)	144	1,081	354	577	3,093
Elena Delle Donne, Delaware (2010-13)	114	1,030	206	773	3,039
Maya Moore, Connecticut (2008-11)	154	1,171	311	383	3,036
Chamique Holdsclaw, Tennessee (1996-99)	148	1,233	36	523	3,025

Career points per game

Player, school (seasons)	G	FG	3-FG	FT	PTS	PPG
Patricia Hoskins, Mississippi Valley St. (1986-89)	110	1,196	24	706	3,122	28.4
Sandra Hodge, New Orleans (1981-84)	107	1,194	NA	472	2,860	26.7
Elena Delle Donne, Delaware (2010-13)	114	1,030	206	773	3,039	26.7
Jackie Stiles, Missouri St. (1998-2001)	129	1,160	221	852	3,393	26.3
Lorri Bauman, Drake (1981-84)	120	1,104	NA	907	3,115	26.0
Andrea Congreaves, Mercer (1990-93)	108	1,107	153	429	2,796	25.9
Cindy Blodgett, Maine (1995-98)	118	1,055	219	676	3,005	25.5
Valorie Whiteside, Appalachian St. (1985-88)	116	1,153	0	638	2,944	25.4
Kelsey Plum, Washington (2014-17)	139	1,136	343	912	3,527	25.4
Joyce Walker, LSU (1981-84)	117	1,259	NA	388	2,906	24.8
Kelsey Mitchell, Ohio St. (2015-18)	139	1,120	497	665	3,402	24.5

NA = Not available. **Note:** Career leaders played at least three seasons (in a four-year career) or two (in a three-season career) since official NCAA record-keeping began (1981-82).

Wade Trophy Winners, 1978-2018

Awarded by the National Assn. for Girls and Women in Sport and the Women's Basketball Coaches Assn. (WBCA) to the best college women's basketball player in terms of character, leadership, and player performance.

Year	Player, school	Year	Player, school	Year	Player, school
1978	Carol Blazejowski, Montclair St.	1992	Susan Robinson, Penn St.	2006	Seimone Augustus, LSU
1979	Nancy Lieberman, Old Dominion	1993	Karen Jennings, Nebraska	2007	Candace Parker, Tennessee
1980	Nancy Lieberman, Old Dominion	1994	Carol Ann Shudlick, Minnesota	2008	Candice Wiggins, Stanford
1981	Lynette Woodard, Kansas	1995	Rebecca Lobo, Connecticut	2009	Maya Moore, Connecticut
1982	Pam Kelly, Louisiana Tech	1996	Jennifer Rizzotti, Connecticut	2010	Maya Moore, Connecticut
1983	LaTaunya Pollard, Long Beach St.	1997	DeLisha Milton, Florida	2011	Maya Moore, Connecticut
1984	Janice Lawrence, Louisiana Tech	1998	Ticha Penicheiro, Old Dominion	2012	Brittney Griner, Baylor
1985	Cheryl Miller, USC	1999	Stephanie White-McCarty, Purdue	2013	Brittney Griner, Baylor
1986	Kamie Ethridge, Texas	2000	Edwina Brown, Texas	2014	Odyssey Sims, Baylor
1987	Shelly Pennefeather, Villanova	2001	Jackie Stiles, Missouri St.	2015	Breanna Stewart, Connecticut
1988	Teresa Weatherspoon, Louisiana Tech	2002	Sue Bird, Connecticut	2016	Breanna Stewart, Connecticut
1989	Clarissa Davis, Texas	2003	Diana Taurasi, Connecticut	2017	Kelsey Plum, Washington
1990	Jennifer Azzi, Stanford	2004	Alana Beard, Duke	2018	A'ja Wilson, South Carolina
1991	Daedra Charles, Tennessee	2005	Seimone Augustus, LSU		

NCAA Men's Baseball Division I Champions, 1947-2018

Year	Champion	Year	Champion	Year	Champion	Year	Champion	Year	Champion
1947	California	1962	Michigan	1977	Arizona St.	1991	LSU	2005	Texas
1948	USC	1963	USC	1978	USC	1992	Pepperdine	2006	Oregon St.
1949	Texas	1964	Minnesota	1979	Cal St. Fullerton	1993	LSU	2007	Oregon St.
1950	Texas	1965	Arizona St.	1980	Arizona	1994	Oklahoma	2008	Fresno St.
1951	Oklahoma	1966	Ohio St.	1981	Arizona St.	1995	Cal St. Fullerton	2009	LSU
1952	Holy Cross	1967	Arizona St.	1982	Miami (FL)	1996	LSU	2010	South Carolina
1953	Michigan	1968	USC	1983	Texas	1997	LSU	2011	South Carolina
1954	Missouri	1969	Arizona St.	1984	Cal St. Fullerton	1998	USC	2012	Arizona
1955	Wake Forest	1970	USC	1985	Miami (FL)	1999	Miami (FL)	2013	UCLA
1956	Minnesota	1971	USC	1986	Arizona	2000	LSU	2014	Vanderbilt
1957	California	1972	USC	1987	Stanford	2001	Miami (FL)	2015	Virginia
1958	USC	1973	USC	1988	Stanford	2002	Texas	2016	Coastal Carolina
1959	Oklahoma St.	1974	USC	1989	Wichita St.	2003	Rice	2017	Florida
1960	Minnesota	1975	Texas	1990	Georgia	2004	Cal St. Fullerton	2018	Oregon St.
1961	USC	1976	Arizona						

NCAA Women's Softball Division I Champions, 1982-2018

Year	Champion	Year	Champion	Year	Champion	Year	Champion	Year	Champion
1982	UCLA	1990	UCLA	1998	Fresno St.	2005	Michigan	2012	Alabama
1983	Texas A&M	1991	Arizona	1999	UCLA	2006	Arizona	2013	Oklahoma
1984	UCLA	1992	UCLA	2000	Oklahoma	2007	Arizona	2014	Florida
1985	UCLA	1993	Arizona	2001	Arizona	2008	Arizona St.	2015	Florida
1986	Cal St. Fullerton	1994	Arizona	2002	California	2009	Washington	2016	Oklahoma
1987	Texas A&M	1995	UCLA	2003	UCLA	2010	UCLA	2017	Oklahoma
1988	UCLA	1996	Arizona	2004	UCLA	2011	Arizona St.	2018	Florida St.
1989	UCLA	1997	Arizona						

NCAA Men's Hockey Division I Champions, 1948-2018

Year	Champion	Year	Champion	Year	Champion	Year	Champion	Year	Champion
1948	Michigan	1963	North Dakota	1977	Wisconsin	1991	North Michigan	2005	Denver
1949	Boston College	1964	Michigan	1978	Boston Univ.	1992	Lake Superior St.	2006	Wisconsin
1950	Colorado College	1965	Michigan Tech	1979	Minnesota	1993	Maine	2007	Michigan St.
1951	Michigan	1966	Michigan St.	1980	North Dakota	1994	Lake Superior St.	2008	Boston College
1952	Michigan	1967	Cornell	1981	Wisconsin	1995	Boston Univ.	2009	Boston Univ.
1953	Michigan	1968	Denver	1982	North Dakota	1996	Michigan	2010	Boston College
1954	Rensselaer	1969	Denver	1983	Wisconsin	1997	North Dakota	2011	Minnesota Duluth
1955	Michigan	1970	Cornell	1984	Bowling Green	1998	Michigan	2012	Boston College
1956	Michigan	1971	Boston Univ.	1985	Rensselaer	1999	Maine	2013	Yale
1957	Colorado College	1972	Boston Univ.	1986	Michigan St.	2000	North Dakota	2014	Union College
1958	Denver	1973	Wisconsin	1987	North Dakota	2001	Boston College	2015	Providence
1959	North Dakota	1974	Minnesota	1988	Lake Superior St.	2002	Minnesota	2016	North Dakota
1960	Denver	1975	Michigan Tech	1989	Harvard	2003	Minnesota	2017	Denver
1961	Denver	1976	Minnesota	1990	Wisconsin	2004	Denver	2018	Minnesota Duluth
1962	Michigan Tech								

NCAA Women's Hockey Champions, 2001-18

Year	Champion	Year	Champion	Year	Champion	Year	Champion	Year	Champion
2001	Minnesota Duluth	2005	Minnesota	2009	Wisconsin	2013	Minnesota	2016	Minnesota
2002	Minnesota Duluth	2006	Wisconsin	2010	Minnesota Duluth	2014	Clarkson	2017	Clarkson
2003	Minnesota Duluth	2007	Wisconsin	2011	Wisconsin	2015	Minnesota	2018	Clarkson
2004	Minnesota	2008	Minnesota Duluth	2012	Minnesota				

NCAA Division I Lacrosse Champions, 1982-2018

Year	Men	Women	Year	Men	Women	Year	Men	Women
1982	North Carolina	Massachusetts	1994	Princeton	Princeton	2006	Virginia	Northwestern
1983	Syracuse	Delaware	1995	Syracuse	Maryland	2007	Johns Hopkins	Northwestern
1984	Johns Hopkins	Temple	1996	Princeton	Maryland	2008	Syracuse	Northwestern
1985	Johns Hopkins	New Hampshire	1997	Princeton	Maryland	2009	Syracuse	Northwestern
1986	North Carolina	Maryland	1998	Princeton	Maryland	2010	Duke	Maryland
1987	Johns Hopkins	Penn St.	1999	Virginia	Maryland	2011	Virginia	Northwestern
1988	Syracuse	Temple	2000	Syracuse	Maryland	2012	Loyola (MD)	Northwestern
1989	Syracuse	Penn St.	2001	Princeton	Maryland	2013	Duke	North Carolina
1990	Syracuse[1]	Harvard	2002	Syracuse	Princeton	2014	Duke	Maryland
1991	North Carolina	Virginia	2003	Virginia	Princeton	2015	Denver	Maryland
1992	Princeton	Maryland	2004	Syracuse	Virginia	2016	North Carolina	North Carolina
1993	Syracuse	Virginia	2005	Johns Hopkins	Northwestern	2017	Maryland	Maryland
						2018	Yale	James Madison

Note: NCAA Championships began in 1971 for men, in 1982 for women. (1) Vacated due to an NCAA rules violation.

NCAA Division I Soccer Champions, 1982-2017

Year	Men	Women	Year	Men	Women	Year	Men	Women
1982	Indiana	North Carolina	1994	Virginia	North Carolina	2006	UC Santa Barbara	North Carolina
1983	Indiana	North Carolina	1995	Wisconsin	Notre Dame			
1984	Clemson	North Carolina	1996	St. John's (NY)	North Carolina	2007	Wake Forest	USC
1985	UCLA	George Mason	1997	UCLA	North Carolina	2008	Maryland	North Carolina
1986	Duke	North Carolina	1998	Indiana	Florida	2009	Virginia	North Carolina
1987	Clemson	North Carolina	1999	Indiana	North Carolina	2010	Akron	Notre Dame
1988	Indiana	North Carolina	2000	Connecticut	North Carolina	2011	North Carolina	Stanford
1989	Santa Clara; Virginia (tie)	North Carolina	2001	North Carolina	Santa Clara	2012	Indiana	North Carolina
			2002	UCLA	Portland	2013	Notre Dame	UCLA
1990	UCLA	North Carolina	2003	Indiana	North Carolina	2014	Virginia	Florida St.
1991	Virginia	North Carolina	2004	Indiana	Notre Dame	2015	Stanford	Penn St.
1992	Virginia	North Carolina	2005	Maryland	Portland	2016	Stanford	USC
1993	Virginia	North Carolina				2017	Stanford	Stanford

Note: NCAA Championships began in 1959 for men, in 1982 for women.

NCAA Division I Wrestling Champions, 1964-2018

Year	Champion	Year	Champion	Year	Champion	Year	Champion	Year	Champion
1964	Oklahoma St.	1975	Iowa	1986	Iowa	1997	Iowa	2008	Iowa
1965	Iowa St.	1976	Iowa	1987	Iowa St.	1998	Iowa	2009	Iowa
1966	Oklahoma St.	1977	Iowa St.	1988	Arizona St.	1999	Iowa	2010	Iowa
1967	Michigan St.	1978	Iowa	1989	Oklahoma St.	2000	Iowa	2011	Penn St.
1968	Oklahoma St.	1979	Iowa	1990	Oklahoma St.	2001	Minnesota	2012	Penn St.
1969	Iowa St.	1980	Iowa	1991	Iowa	2002	Minnesota	2013	Penn St.
1970	Iowa St.	1981	Iowa	1992	Iowa	2003	Oklahoma St.	2014	Penn St.
1971	Oklahoma St.	1982	Iowa	1993	Iowa	2004	Oklahoma St.	2015	Ohio St.
1972	Iowa St.	1983	Iowa	1994	Oklahoma St.	2005	Oklahoma St.	2016	Penn St.
1973	Iowa St.	1984	Iowa	1995	Iowa	2006	Oklahoma St.	2017	Penn St.
1974	Oklahoma	1985	Iowa	1996	Iowa	2007	Minnesota	2018	Penn St.

Selected NCAA Division I Teams

(Conferences and coaches listed are as of July 2018.)

Team	Nickname	Team colors	Conference	Basketball coach	Football coach
Air Force	Falcons	Blue & silver	Mountain West	Dave Pilipovich	Troy Calhoun
Akron	Zips	Blue & gold	Mid-American	John Groce	Terry Bowden
Alabama	Crimson Tide	Crimson & white	Southeastern	Avery Johnson	Nick Saban
Appalachian State	Mountaineers	Black & gold	Sun Belt	Jim Fox	Scott Satterfield
Arizona	Wildcats	Cardinal & navy	Pac-12	Sean Miller	Kevin Sumlin
Arizona State	Sun Devils	Maroon & gold	Pac-12	Bobby Hurley	Herm Edwards
Arkansas	Razorbacks	Cardinal & white	Southeastern	Mike Anderson	Chad Morris
Arkansas State	Red Wolves	Scarlet & black	Sun Belt	Mike Balado	Blake Anderson
Army	Black Knights	Black, gold, & gray	Independent#	Jimmy Allen	Jeff Monken
Auburn	Tigers	Burnt orange & navy blue	Southeastern	Bruce Pearl	Gus Malzahn
Ball State	Cardinals	Cardinal & white	Mid-American	James Whitford	Mike Neu
Baylor	Bears	Green & gold	Big 12	Scott Drew	Matt Rhule
Boise State	Broncos	Blue & orange	Mountain West	Leon Rice	Bryan Harsin
Boston College	Eagles	Maroon & gold	Atlantic Coast	Jim Christian	Steve Addazio
Bowling Green	Falcons	Orange & brown	Mid-American	Michael Huger	Mike Jinks
Brigham Young (BYU)	Cougars	Blue & white	Independent#	Dave Rose	Kalani Sitake
Brown*	Bears	Brown, red, & white	Ivy League	Mike Martin	Phil Estes
Butler	Bulldogs	Blue & white	Pioneer League#	LaVall Jordan	Jeff Voris
California	Golden Bears	Blue & gold	Pac-12	Wyking Jones	Justin Wilcox
Central Michigan	Chippewas	Maroon & gold	Mid-American	Keno Davis	John Bonamego
Cincinnati	Bearcats	Red & black	American Athletic	Mick Cronin	Luke Fickell
Citadel*	Bulldogs	Citadel blue & white	Southern	Duggar Baucom	Brent Thompson
Clemson	Tigers	Tiger orange & regalia	Atlantic Coast	Brad Brownell	Dabo Swinney
Colgate*	Raiders	Maroon, gray, & white	Patriot League	Matt Langel	Dan Hunt
Colorado	Buffaloes	Silver, black, & gold	Pac-12	Tad Boyle	Mike MacIntyre
Colorado State	Rams	Green & gold	Mountain West	Niko Medved	Mike Bobo
Columbia*	Lions	Columbia blue & white	Ivy League	Jim Engles	Al Bagnoli
Connecticut	Huskies	National flag blue & white	American Athletic	Dan Hurley	Randy Edsall
Cornell*	Big Red	Carnelian red & white	Ivy League	Brian Earl	David Archer
Dartmouth*	Big Green	Dartmouth green & white	Ivy League	David McLaughlin	Buddy Teevens
Delaware*	Blue Hens	Blue & gold	Colonial Athletic	Martin Ingelsby	Danny Rocco
Duke	Blue Devils	Duke blue & white	Atlantic Coast	Mike Krzyzewski	David Cutcliffe
East Carolina	Pirates	Purple & gold	American Athletic	Joe Dooley	Scottie Montgomery
Eastern Illinois*	Panthers	Blue & gray	Ohio Valley	Jay Spoonhour	Kim Dameron
Eastern Kentucky*	Colonels	Maroon & white	Ohio Valley	A. W. Hamilton	Mark Elder
Eastern Michigan	Eagles	Green & white	Mid-American	Rob Murphy	Chris Creighton
Eastern Washington*	Eagles	Red & white	Big Sky	Shantay Legans	Aaron Best
Florida	Gators	Orange & blue	Southeastern	Mike White	Dan Mullen
Florida A&M*	Rattlers	Orange & green	Mid-Eastern Athletic	Robert McCullum	Willie Simmons
Florida State	Seminoles	Garnet & gold	Atlantic Coast	Leonard Hamilton	Willie Taggart
Fresno State	Bulldogs	Red & blue	Mountain West	Justin Hutson	Jeff Tedford
Furman*	Paladins	Purple & white	Southern	Bob Richey	Clay Hendrix
Georgia	Bulldogs	Red & black	Southeastern	Tom Crean	Kirby Smart
Georgia Southern	Eagles	Blue & white	Sun Belt	Mark Byington	Chad Lunsford
Georgia Tech	Yellow Jackets	Old gold & white	Atlantic Coast	Josh Pastner	Paul Johnson
Gonzaga	Bulldogs, Zags	Navy blue, white, & red	West Coast	Mark Few	Does not compete
Harvard*	Crimson	Crimson, black, & white	Ivy League	Tommy Amaker	Tim Murphy
Hawaii	Rainbow Warriors	Green, black, white, silver	Mountain West#	Eran Ganot	Nick Rolovich
Holy Cross*	Crusaders	Royal purple	Patriot League	Bill Carmody	Bob Chesney
Houston	Cougars	Scarlet & white	American Athletic	Kelvin Sampson	Major Applewhite
Howard*	Bison	Blue & white	Mid-Eastern Athletic	Kevin Nickelberry	Mike London
Idaho	Vandals	Silver & vandal gold	Sun Belt	Don Verlin	Paul Petrino
Illinois	Fighting Illini	Orange & blue	Big Ten	Brad Underwood	Lovie Smith
Illinois State*	Redbirds	Red & white	Missouri Valley	Dan Muller	Brock Spack
Indiana	Hoosiers	Cream & crimson	Big Ten	Archie Miller	Tom Allen
Indiana State*	Sycamores	Royal blue & white	Missouri Valley	Greg Lansing	Curt Mallory
Iowa	Hawkeyes	Black & gold	Big Ten	Fran McCaffery	Kirk Ferentz
Iowa State	Cyclones	Cardinal & gold	Big 12	Steve Prohm	Matt Campbell
Jackson State*	Tigers	Blue & white	Southwestern Athletic	Wayne Brent	Tony Hughes
James Madison*	Dukes	Purple & gold	Colonial Athletic	Louis Rowe	Mike Houston
Kansas	Jayhawks	Crimson & blue	Big 12	Bill Self	David Beaty
Kansas State	Wildcats	Purple & white	Big 12	Bruce Weber	Bill Snyder
Kent State	Golden Flashes	Navy blue & gold	Mid-American	Rob Senderoff	Sean Lewis
Kentucky	Wildcats	Blue & white	Southeastern	John Calipari	Mark Stoops
Lafayette*	Leopards	Maroon & white	Patriot League	Fran O'Hanlon	John Garrett
Lehigh*	Mountain Hawks	Brown & white	Patriot League	Brett Reed	Andy Coen
Liberty*	Flames	Red, white, & blue	Big South	Ritchie McKay	Turner Gill
Louisiana State (LSU)	Fighting Tigers	Purple & gold	Southeastern	Will Wade	Ed Orgeron
Louisiana Tech	Bulldogs	Red & blue	Conference USA	Eric Konkol	Skip Holtz
Louisiana-Lafayette	Ragin' Cajuns	Vermilion & white	Sun Belt	Bob Marlin	Billy Napier
Louisiana-Monroe	Warhawks	Maroon & gold	Sun Belt	Keith Richard	Matt Viator
Louisville	Cardinals	Red & black	Atlantic Coast	Chris Mack	Bobby Petrino
Maine*	Black Bears	Blue & white	Colonial Athletic#	Richard Barron	Joe Harasymiak
Marshall	Thundering Herd	Kelly green & white	Conference USA	Dan D'Antoni	Doc Holliday
Maryland	Terrapins	Red, white, black, gold	Big Ten	Mark Turgeon	D. J. Durkin
Massachusetts	Minutemen	Maroon & white	Independent#	Matt McCall	Mark Whipple
Memphis	Tigers	Blue & gray	American Athletic	Anfernee "Penny" Hardaway	Mike Norvell
Miami (Florida)	Hurricanes	Orange & green	Atlantic Coast	Jim Larrañaga	Mark Richt
Miami (Ohio)	RedHawks	Red & white	Mid-American	Jack Owens	Chuck Martin
Michigan	Wolverines	Maize & blue	Big Ten	John Beilein	Jim Harbaugh
Michigan State	Spartans	Green & white	Big Ten	Tom Izzo	Mark Dantonio
Mid. Tennessee State	Blue Raiders	Royal blue & white	Conference USA	Nick McDevitt	Rick Stockstill
Minnesota	Golden Gophers	Maroon & gold	Big Ten	Richard Pitino	P. J. Fleck
Mississippi (Ole Miss)	Rebels	Cardinal red & navy blue	Southeastern	Kermit Davis	Matt Luke

Team	Nickname	Team colors	Conference	Basketball coach	Football coach
Mississippi State	Bulldogs	Maroon & white	Southeastern	Ben Howland	Joe Moorhead
Missouri	Tigers	Old gold & black	Southeastern	Cuonzo Martin	Barry Odom
Montana*	Grizzlies	Maroon & silver	Big Sky	Travis DeCuire	Bobby Hauck
Montana State*	Bobcats	Blue & gold	Big Sky	Brian Fish	Jeff Choate
Morgan State*	Bears	Blue & orange	Mid-Eastern Athletic	Todd Bozeman	Ernest T. Jones
Murray State*	Racers	Navy & gold	Ohio Valley	Matt McMahon	Mitch Stewart
Navy	Midshipmen	Navy blue & gold	American Athletic#	Ed DeChellis	Ken Niumatalolo
Nebraska	Cornhuskers	Scarlet & cream	Big Ten	Tim Miles	Scott Frost
Nevada	Wolf Pack	Silver & blue	Mountain West	Eric Musselman	Jay Norvell
Nevada-Las Vegas (UNLV)	Rebels	Scarlet & gray	Mountain West	Marvin Menzies	Tony Sanchez
New Hampshire*	Wildcats	Blue & white	Colonial Athletic#	Bill Herrion	Sean McDonnell
New Mexico	Lobos	Cherry & silver	Mountain West	Paul Weir	Bob Davie
New Mexico State	Aggies	Crimson & white	Western Athletic	Chris Jans	Doug Martin
Nicholls State*	Colonels	Red & gray	Southland	Austin Claunch	Tim Rebowe
North Carolina	Tar Heels	Carolina blue & white	Atlantic Coast	Roy Williams	Larry Fedora
North Carolina State	Wolfpack	Red & white	Atlantic Coast	Kevin Keatts	Dave Doeren
North Texas	Mean Green	Green & white	Conference USA	Grant McCasland	Seth Littrell
Northern Illinois	Huskies	Cardinal & black	Mid-American	Mark Montgomery	Rod Carey
Northern Iowa*	Panthers	Purple & old gold	Missouri Valley	Ben Jacobson	Mark Farley
Northwestern	Wildcats	Purple	Big Ten	Chris Collins	Pat Fitzgerald
Northwestern State*	Demons	Purple, white, & orange	Southland	Mike McConathy	Brad Laird
Notre Dame	Fighting Irish	Blue & gold	Independent#	Mike Brey	Brian Kelly
Ohio	Bobcats	Hunter green & white	Mid-American	Saul Phillips	Frank Solich
Ohio State	Buckeyes	Scarlet & gray	Big Ten	Chris Holtmann	Urban Meyer
Oklahoma	Sooners	Crimson & cream	Big 12	Lon Kruger	Lincoln Riley
Oklahoma State	Cowboys	Orange & black	Big 12	Mike Boynton Jr.	Mike Gundy
Oregon	Ducks	Green & yellow	Pac-12	Dana Altman	Mario Cristobal
Oregon State	Beavers	Orange & black	Pac-12	Wayne Tinkle	Jonathan Smith
Penn State	Nittany Lions	Blue & white	Big Ten	Patrick Chambers	James Franklin
Pennsylvania*	Quakers	Red & blue	Ivy League	Steve Donahue	Ray Priore
Pittsburgh	Panthers	Gold & blue	Atlantic Coast	Jeff Capel	Pat Narduzzi
Princeton*	Tigers	Orange & black	Ivy League	Mitch Henderson	Bob Surace
Purdue	Boilermakers	Old gold & black	Big Ten	Matt Painter	Jeff Brohm
Rice	Owls	Blue & gray	Conference USA	Scott Pera	Mike Bloomgren
Richmond*	Spiders	Red & blue	Colonial Athletic#	Chris Mooney	Russ Huesman
Rutgers	Scarlet Knights	Scarlet	Big Ten	Steve Pikiell	Chris Ash
Sam Houston State*	Bearkats	Orange & white	Southland	Jason Hooten	K. C. Keeler
San Diego State	Aztecs	Scarlet & black	Mountain West	Brian Dutcher	Rocky Long
San Jose State	Spartans	Gold, white, & blue	Mountain West	Jean Prioleau	Brent Brennan
South Carolina	Gamecocks	Garnet & black	Southeastern	Frank Martin	Will Muschamp
South Carolina State*	Bulldogs	Garnet & blue	Mid-Eastern Athletic	Murray Garvin	Oliver Pough
South Florida	Bulls	Green & gold	American Athletic	Brian Gregory	Charlie Strong
Southeast Missouri State*	Redhawks	Red, black, & white	Ohio Valley	Rick Ray	Tom Matukewicz
Southern California (USC)	Trojans	Cardinal & gold	Pac-12	Andy Enfield	Clay Helton
Southern Illinois*	Salukis	Maroon & white	Missouri Valley	Barry Hinson	Nick Hill
Southern Methodist (SMU)	Mustangs	Red & blue	American Athletic	Tim Jankovich	Sonny Dykes
Southern Mississippi	Golden Eagles	Black & gold	Conference USA	Doc Sadler	Jay Hopson
Stanford	Cardinal	Cardinal & white	Pac-12	Jerod Haase	David Shaw
Stephen F. Austin*	Lumberjacks	Purple & white	Southland	Kyle Keller	Jeff Byrd
Syracuse	Orange	Orange	Atlantic Coast	Jim Boeheim	Dino Babers
Temple	Owls	Cherry & white	American Athletic	Fran Dunphy	Geoff Collins
Tennessee	Volunteers	Orange & white	Southeastern	Rick Barnes	Jeremy Pruitt
Tennessee State*	Tigers	Reflex blue & white	Ohio Valley	Brian "Penny" Collins	Rod Reed
Tennessee Tech*	Golden Eagles	Purple & gold	Ohio Valley	Steve Payne	Dewayne Alexander
Texas	Longhorns	Burnt orange & white	Big 12	Shaka Smart	Tom Herman
Texas A&M	Aggies	Maroon & white	Southeastern	Billy Kennedy	Jimbo Fisher
Texas Christian (TCU)	Horned Frogs	Purple & white	Big 12	Jamie Dixon	Gary Patterson
Texas Southern*	Tigers	Maroon & gray	Southwestern Athletic	Johnny Jones	Michael Haywood
Texas State*	Bobcats	Maroon & gold	Sun Belt	Danny Kaspar	Everett Withers
Texas Tech	Red Raiders	Scarlet & black	Big 12	Chris Beard	Kliff Kingsbury
Toledo	Rockets	Midnight blue & gold	Mid-American	Tod Kowalczyk	Jason Candle
Troy	Trojans	Cardinal, silver, & black	Sun Belt	Phil Cunningham	Neal Brown
Tulane	Green Wave	Olive green & blue	American Athletic	Mike Dunleavy Sr.	Willie Fritz
Tulsa	Golden Hurricane	Old gold, royal blue, & crimson	American Athletic	Frank Haith	Philip Montgomery
UCLA	Bruins	Blue & gold	Pac-12	Steve Alford	Chip Kelly
Utah	Utes	Red & white	Pac-12	Larry Krystkowiak	Kyle Whittingham
Utah State	Aggies	Aggie blue, pewter, & white	Mountain West	Craig Smith	Matt Wells
UTEP (Texas-El Paso)	Miners	Dark blue, orange, & silver	Conference USA	Rodney Terry	Dana Dimel
Vanderbilt	Commodores	Black & gold	Southeastern	Bryce Drew	Derek Mason
Villanova*	Wildcats	Blue & white	Colonial Athletic#	Jay Wright	Mark Ferrante
Virginia	Cavaliers	Orange & blue	Atlantic Coast	Tony Bennett	Bronco Mendenhall
Virginia Tech	Hokies	Chicago maroon & burnt orange	Atlantic Coast	Buzz Williams	Justin Fuente
Wake Forest	Demon Deacons	Old gold & black	Atlantic Coast	Danny Manning	Dave Clawson
Washington	Huskies	Purple & gold	Pac-12	Mike Hopkins	Chris Petersen
Washington State	Cougars	Crimson & gray	Pac-12	Ernie Kent	Mike Leach
Weber State*	Wildcats	Purple & white	Big Sky	Randy Rahe	Jay Hill
West Virginia	Mountaineers	Old gold & blue	Big 12	Bob Huggins	Dana Holgorsen
Western Illinois*	Leathernecks	Purple & gold	Missouri Valley#	Billy Wright	Jared Elliott
Western Kentucky	Hilltoppers	Red & white	Conference USA	Rick Stansbury	Mike Sanford
Western Michigan	Broncos	Brown & gold	Mid-American	Steve Hawkins	Tim Lester
Wisconsin	Badgers	Cardinal & white	Big Ten	Greg Gard	Paul Chryst
Wyoming	Cowboys	Brown & gold	Mountain West	Allen Edwards	Craig Bohl
Yale*	Elis, Bulldogs	Yale blue & white	Ivy League	James Jones	Tony Reno
Youngstown State*	Penguins	Red & white	Missouri Valley#	Jerrod Calhoun	Bo Pelini

* = Football Championship Subdivision (FCS) team (formerly known as I-AA). # = Team competes in conference listed in football but not in basketball.

FOOTBALL

NFL 2017: Backup QB Foles Leads Eagles to Super Bowl Win

The Philadelphia Eagles lost starting quarterback Carson Wentz late in the season but still managed a Super Bowl title. Wentz, a second-year pro, set a franchise record with 33 touchdown passes before sustaining a season-ending knee injury in Week 14. Backup QB and former starter Nick Foles stepped in and the Eagles won a club record-tying 13 games and the NFC East title.

Foles passed for 352 yards and three touchdowns in the NFC Championship, a 38-7 win over the NFC North champion Minnesota Vikings, Jan. 21, 2018, at Lincoln Financial Field in Philadelphia. Minnesota's defense led the NFL during the regular season (allowing just 275.9 yards per game).

Old and new stars led the New Orleans Saints to their first NFC South title since 2011. Veteran Drew Brees achieved an NFL-record 12th consecutive season with at least 4,000 passing yards and his 72.0% season completion percentage was the league's best-ever. Saints running back Alvin Kamara and cornerback teammate Marshon Lattimore won the AP's two rookie of the year awards.

The L.A. Rams (11-5) captured their first NFC West title since 2003 under new head coach Sean McVay, who was just 30 years old when hired in Jan. 2017. Rams QB Jared Goff passed for 3,804 yards and 28 TDs, and running back Todd Gurley added an NFL-high 2,093 yards from scrimmage.

New England won its NFL-record ninth straight AFC East title. Forty-year-old QB Tom Brady won his third MVP award, leading the NFL with 4,577 passing yards. Brady earned his eighth AFC title with a pair of 4th quarter TD passes to Danny Amendola in 24-20 win over the Jacksonville Jaguars, Jan. 21, 2018, at Gillette Stadium in Foxborough, MA.

Jacksonville won its first AFC South title since 1999, with the second-best defense in the league (286.1 YPG allowed). A familiar trio led Pittsburgh (13-3) to the AFC North title. Quarterback Ben Roethlisberger passed for 4,251 yards, running back Le'Veon Bell had 1,291 rushing yards and 85 receptions, and wide receiver Antonio Brown topped the NFL in receiving yards (1,533).

Kansas City rookie Kareem Hunt led the league in rushing (1,327 yards) and QB Alex Smith passed for 4,042 yards as the Chiefs won their second straight AFC West title. The Chiefs were one game ahead of the L.A. Chargers, who played their first season in their new hometown after more than five decades in San Diego. Completion of the new stadium in Los Angeles, expected to be shared by both the Rams and Chargers, was pushed back to 2020 due to weather-related construction delays.

The league could not escape the political spotlight during the 2017 season. Pres. Donald Trump repeatedly criticized NFL players who made a statement of protest by not standing when the U.S. national anthem was played before games. Former 49ers QB Colin Kaepernick, who regularly kneeled during the anthem to protest racism and police brutality beginning with the 2016 preseason, went unsigned in 2017 after opting out of his contract in Mar.; he filed a collusion complaint against the NFL in Oct. 2017.

NFL Playoff Results, 2017

AFC Wild Card Games: Tennessee 22, Kansas City 21; Jacksonville 10, Buffalo 3
NFC Wild Card Games: Atlanta 26, L.A. Rams 13; New Orleans 31, Carolina 26
AFC Divisional Playoff Games: New England 35, Tennessee 14; Jacksonville 45, Pittsburgh 42
NFC Divisional Playoff Games: Philadelphia 15, Atlanta 10; Minnesota 29, New Orleans 24
AFC Championship Game: New England 24, Jacksonville 20
NFC Championship Game: Philadelphia 38, Minnesota 7
Super Bowl LII: Philadelphia 41, New England 33

Super Bowl LII: Philadelphia 41, New England 33

Philadelphia's late-season replacement quarterback Nick Foles passed for 373 yards and three touchdowns to lead the Philadelphia Eagles to a 41-33 triumph over the defending-champion New England Patriots in Super Bowl LII, Feb. 4, 2018, at U.S. Bank Stadium in Minneapolis, MN. The Eagles overcame a record-setting performance from New England QB Tom Brady to earn the franchise's first Super Bowl victory and their first NFL championship since 1960.

Foles, who won the Super Bowl MVP award, became the first player in Super Bowl history to throw and catch a TD pass in one game when he grabbed a one-yard toss on fourth down from tight end Trey Burton, which gave the Eagles a 22-12 lead at halftime.

New England was playing in its record 10th Super Bowl (5-3 under Belichick and 5-5 overall). The Eagles had lost in their two previous Super Bowl appearances, to the Patriots in Super Bowl XXXIX (2005) and to the Oakland Raiders in Super Bowl XV, after the 1980 season. The teams set an NFL record with 1,151 net yards gained, the most combined yards in a single NFL regular season or postseason game. Brady's 505 passing yards—an NFL postseason record—broke his Super Bowl-record 466 yards set just a year earlier.

Quarters

Team	1	2	3	4	Final
Philadelphia	9	13	7	12	41
New England	3	9	14	7	33

Total attendance: 67,612
Game length: 3:46

Scoring

Philadelphia: Jake Elliott, 25-yard field goal
New England: Stephen Gostkowski, 26-yard field goal
Philadelphia: Alshon Jeffery, 34-yard pass from Nick Foles (PAT failed)
Philadelphia: LeGarrette Blount, 21-yard run (2-point conversion failed)
New England: Gostkowski, 45-yard field goal
New England: James White, 26-yard run (PAT failed)
Philadelphia: Foles, 1-yard pass from Trey Burton (Elliott PAT)
New England: Rob Gronkowski, 5-yard pass from Tom Brady (Gostkowski PAT)
Philadelphia: Corey Clement, 22-yard pass from Foles (Elliott PAT)
New England: Chris Hogan, 26-yard pass from Brady (Gostkowski PAT)
Philadelphia: Elliott, 42-yard field goal
New England: Gronkowski, 4-yard pass from Brady (Gostkowski PAT)
Philadelphia: Zach Ertz, 11-yard pass from Foles (2-point conversion failed)
Philadelphia: Elliott, 46-yard field goal

Individual Statistics

Rushing

Philadelphia: Blount, 14-90; Ajayi, 9-57; Agholor, 1-9; Clement, 3-8.
New England: White, 7-45; Lewis, 9-39; Burkhead, 3-18; Brady, 1-6; Hogan, 1-4; Cooks, 1-1.

Passing

Philadelphia: Foles, 28-43, 373 yards, 3 TD, 1 int; Burton, 1-1, 1 yard, 1 TD, 0 int.
New England: Brady, 28-48, 505 yards, 3 TD, 0 int; Amendola, 0-1, 0 yards, 0 int.

Receiving

Philadelphia: Agholor, 9-84; Ertz, 7-67; Smith, 5-49; Clement, 4-100; Jeffery, 3-73; Foles, 1-1.
New England: Gronkowski, 9-116; Amendola, 8-152; Hogan, 6-128; White, 2-21; Burkhead, 1-46; Cooks, 1-23; Dorsett, 1-19.

Team Statistics

	Eagles	Patriots
First downs	25	29
Total net yards	538	613
Rushes-yards	27-164	22-113
Passing yards, net	374	500
Punt returns-yards	0-0	0-0
Kickoff returns-yards.	4-98	3-44
Interception returns-yards.	0-0	1-8
Field goals made-attempts	3-3	2-3
Pass attempts-completions-interceptions	44-29-1	49-28-0
Sacked-yards lost	0-0	1-5
Punts-average	1-41.0	0-0.0
Fumbles-lost	0-0	1-1
Penalties-yards.	6-35	1-5
Time of possession.	34:04	25:56

NFL Final Standings, 2017

(playoff seeding in parentheses)

AMERICAN FOOTBALL CONFERENCE

	W	L	T	Pct	PF	PA	Div
East Division							
New England (1)....	13	3	0	.813	458	296	5-1
*Buffalo (6)	9	7	0	.563	302	359	3-3
Miami	6	10	0	.375	281	393	2-4
NY Jets...........	5	11	0	.313	298	382	2-4
North Division							
Pittsburgh (2)	13	3	0	.813	406	308	6-0
Baltimore	9	7	0	.563	395	303	3-3
Cincinnati	7	9	0	.438	290	349	3-3
Cleveland	0	16	0	.000	234	410	0-6
South Division							
Jacksonville (3)	10	6	0	.625	417	268	4-2
*Tennessee (5)	9	7	0	.563	334	356	5-1
Indianapolis	4	12	0	.250	263	404	2-4
Houston	4	12	0	.250	338	436	1-5
West Division							
Kansas City (4).....	10	6	0	.625	415	339	5-1
L.A. Chargers	9	7	0	.563	355	272	3-3
Oakland	6	10	0	.375	301	373	2-4
Denver	5	11	0	.313	289	382	2-4

* = Wild card qualifier for playoffs. **Note:** New England won No. 1 AFC playoff seed over Pittsburgh based on head-to-head win percentage. Jacksonville and Tennessee won No. 3 and No. 5 seeds, respectively, based on win percentage in conference games. Buffalo won No. 6 seed over Baltimore based on strength of victory and over L.A. Chargers based on win percentage in conference games.

NATIONAL FOOTBALL CONFERENCE

	W	L	T	Pct	PF	PA	Div
East Division							
Philadelphia (1).....	13	3	0	.813	457	295	5-1
Dallas...........	9	7	0	.563	354	332	5-1
Washington........	7	9	0	.438	342	388	1-5
NY Giants.........	3	13	0	.188	246	388	1-5
North Division							
Minnesota (2)	13	3	0	.813	382	252	5-1
Detroit............	9	7	0	.563	410	376	5-1
Green Bay.........	7	9	0	.438	320	384	2-4
Chicago	5	11	0	.313	264	320	0-6
South Division							
New Orleans (4)....	11	5	0	.688	448	326	4-2
*Carolina (5)	11	5	0	.688	363	327	3-3
*Atlanta (6)	10	6	0	.625	353	315	4-2
Tampa Bay	5	11	0	.313	335	382	1-5
West Division							
L.A. Rams (3)	11	5	0	.688	478	329	4-2
Seattle	9	7	0	.563	366	332	4-2
Arizona...........	8	8	0	.500	295	361	3-3
San Francisco......	6	10	0	.375	331	383	1-5

* = Wild card qualifier for playoffs. **Note:** Philadelphia won NFC top playoff seed based on win percentage in common games. L.A. Rams won No. 3 NFC playoff seed based on head-to-head win percentage. New Orleans won NFC South title based on head-to-head win percentage.

NFL Individual Leaders: American Football Conference, 2017

(* = rookie)

PASSING

Player, team	Att	Comp	Pct comp	Yds	Yds/Att	Long	TD	Pct TD	Int	Rating
Alex Smith, Kansas City	505	341	67.5	4,042	8.0	79T	26	5.1	5	104.7
Tom Brady, New England	581	385	66.3	4,577	7.9	64T	32	5.5	8	102.8
Philip Rivers, L.A. Chargers	575	360	62.6	4,515	7.9	75T	28	4.9	10	96.0
Josh McCown, NY Jets...............	397	267	67.3	2,926	7.4	69T	18	4.5	9	94.5
Ben Roethlisberger, Pittsburgh...........	561	360	64.2	4,251	7.6	97T	28	5.0	14	93.4
Tyrod Taylor, Buffalo	420	263	62.6	2,799	6.7	47	14	3.3	4	89.2
Andy Dalton, Cincinnati	496	297	59.9	3,320	6.7	77T	25	5.0	12	86.6
Derek Carr, Oakland.................	515	323	62.7	3,496	6.8	87T	22	4.3	13	86.4
Blake Bortles, Jacksonville.............	523	315	60.2	3,687	7.0	75T	21	4.0	13	84.7
Jacoby Brissett, Indianapolis	469	276	58.8	3,098	6.6	80T	13	2.8	7	81.7
Jay Cutler, Miami	429	266	62.0	2,666	6.2	65T	19	4.4	14	80.8
Joe Flacco, Baltimore.................	549	352	64.1	3,141	5.7	66	18	3.3	13	80.4
Marcus Mariota, Tennessee	453	281	62.0	3,232	7.1	75T	13	2.9	15	79.3
Trevor Siemian, Denver	349	206	59.0	2,285	6.5	44	12	3.4	14	73.3
*DeShone Kizer, Cleveland	476	255	53.6	2,894	6.1	56T	11	2.3	22	60.5

RUSHING YARDS

Player, team	Yds	Att	Avg	Long	TD
*Kareem Hunt, Kansas City	1,327	272	4.9	69T	8
Le'Veon Bell, Pittsburgh........	1,291	321	4.0	27	9
LeSean McCoy, Buffalo	1,138	287	4.0	48T	6
Melvin Gordon, L.A. Chargers	1,105	284	3.9	87T	8
*Leonard Fournette, Jacksonville..	1,040	268	3.9	90T	9
C.J. Anderson, Denver	1,007	245	4.1	40	3
Alex Collins, Baltimore.........	973	212	4.6	50	6
Frank Gore, Indianapolis	961	261	3.7	21	3
Dion Lewis, New England	896	180	5.0	44	6
Marshawn Lynch, Oakland	891	207	4.3	51T	7

RECEPTIONS

Player, team	Rec	Yds	Avg	Long	TD
Jarvis Landry, Miami............	112	987	8.8	49	9
Keenan Allen, L.A. Chargers	102	1,393	13.7	51	6
Antonio Brown, Pittsburgh	101	1,533	15.2	57	9
DeAndre Hopkins, Houston	96	1,378	14.4	72T	13
Le'Veon Bell, Pittsburgh.........	85	655	7.7	42	2
Travis Kelce, Kansas City	83	1,038	12.5	44	8
Demaryius Thomas, Denver	83	949	11.4	40	5
Jack Doyle, Indianapolis	80	690	8.6	26	4
A.J. Green, Cincinnati	75	1,078	14.4	77T	8
Tyreek Hill, Kansas City.........	75	1,183	15.8	79T	7
Duke Johnson, Cleveland	74	693	9.4	41T	3
Delanie Walker, Tennessee	74	807	10.9	42	3

SCORING—KICKERS

Player, team	PAT	FG	Long	Pts
Stephen Gostkowski, New England ..	45/47	37/40	62	156
Chris Boswell, Pittsburgh..........	37/39	35/38	53	142
*Harrison Butker, Kansas City......	28/28	38/42	53	142
Justin Tucker, Baltimore	39/39	34/37	57	141
Ryan Succop, Tennessee	31/33	35/42	52	136
Stephen Hauschka, Buffalo	29/29	29/33	56	116

SCORING—NON-KICKERS

Player, team (position)	TD	Rush	Rec	2-Pt	Pts
DeAndre Hopkins, Houston (WR)....	13	0	13	0	78
Melvin Gordon, L.A. Chargers (RB) ..	12	8	4	0	72
Le'Veon Bell, Pittsburgh (RB)	11	9	2	0	66
*Kareem Hunt, Kansas City (RB)	11	8	3	0	66
*Leonard Fournette, Jacksonville (WR)	10	9	1	0	60
Dion Lewis, New England (RB)	10	7**	3	0	60
Antonio Brown, Pittsburgh (RB)	9	0	9	1	56
Jarvis Landry, Miami (RB)	9	0	9	0	54

** = Total includes one kickoff return.

INTERCEPTIONS

Player, team	No.	Yds	Avg	Long	TD
Kevin Byard, Tennessee	8	130	16.3	33	0
A.J. Bouye, Jacksonville	6	70	11.7	51	0
Eric Weddle, Baltimore	6	85	14.2	45T	1
Tre Boston, L.A. Chargers....	5	49	9.8	25	0
Micah Hyde, Buffalo	5	64	12.8	37	0
Marcus Peters, Kansas City ...	5	137	27.4	62	0
Jordan Poyer, Buffalo	5	33	6.6	19T	1

KICKOFF RETURNS

Player, team	No.	Yds	Avg	Long	TD
Dion Lewis, New England.....	23	570	24.8	103T	1
Akeem Hunt, Kansas City.....	25	611	24.4	42	0
*Adoree' Jackson, Tennessee..	25	578	23.1	57	0
Jakeem Grant, Miami	21	479	22.8	31	0
Alex Erickson, Cincinnati	32	663	20.7	41	0
Brandon Tate, Buffalo	28	548	19.6	29	0

PUNTING

Player, team	No.	Yds	Long	Avg
Brett Kern, Tennessee	75	3,728	74	49.7
Shane Lechler, Houston	92	4,507	68	49.0
Drew Kaser, L.A. Chargers	74	3,558	69	48.1
Britton Colquitt, Cleveland.....	80	3,811	67	47.6

Player, team	No.	Yds	Long	Avg
Marquette King, Oakland	69	3,270	65	47.4
Lachlan Edwards, NY Jets	94	4,378	70	46.6
Kevin Huber, Cincinnati	88	4,101	63	46.6

PUNT RETURNS

Player, team	No.	Yds	Avg	Long	TD
Michael Campanaro, Baltimore	27	291	10.8	77T	1
Jaydon Mickens, Jacksonville. .	27	287	10.6	72	1
Brandon Tate, Buffalo	20	193	9.7	40	0
Travis Benjamin, L.A. Chargers	27	257	9.5	65T	1
*Isaiah McKenzie, Denver.	21	183	8.7	44	0
Danny Amendola, New England	27	231	8.6	40	0

SACKS

Player, team	No.
Calais Campbell, Jacksonville	14.5
Joey Bosa, L.A. Chargers.	12.5
Cameron Heyward, Pittsburgh	12.0
Yannick Ngakoue, Jacksonville	12.0
Terrell Suggs, Baltimore	11.0
Melvin Ingram, L.A. Chargers	10.5
Khalil Mack, Oakland	10.5
Cameron Wake, Miami	10.5
Von Miller, Denver.	10.0
Jadeveon Clowney, Houston.	9.5
Justin Houston, Kansas City.	9.5

NFL Individual Leaders: National Football Conference, 2017

(* = rookie)

PASSING

Player, team	Att	Comp	Pct comp	Yds	Yds/Att	Long	TD	Pct TD	Int	Rating
Drew Brees, New Orleans	536	386	72.0	4,334	8.1	54T	23	4.3	8	103.9
Carson Wentz, Philadelphia	440	265	60.2	3,296	7.5	72T	33	7.5	7	101.9
Jared Goff, L.A. Rams.	477	296	62.1	3,804	8.0	94T	28	5.9	7	100.5
Matthew Stafford, Detroit	565	371	65.7	4,446	7.9	71T	29	5.1	10	99.3
Case Keenum, Minnesota	481	325	67.6	3,547	7.4	65T	22	4.6	7	98.3
Aaron Rodgers, Green Bay.	238	154	64.7	1,675	7.0	72	16	6.7	6	97.2
Russell Wilson, Seattle.	553	339	61.3	3,983	7.2	74T	34	6.1	11	95.4
Kirk Cousins, Washington.	540	347	64.3	4,093	7.6	74	27	5.0	13	93.9
Jameis Winston, Tampa Bay.	442	282	63.8	3,504	7.9	70	19	4.3	11	92.2
Matt Ryan, Atlanta	529	342	64.7	4,095	7.7	88T	20	3.8	12	91.4
Dak Prescott, Dallas	490	308	62.9	3,324	6.8	81T	22	4.5	13	86.6
Carson Palmer, Arizona	267	164	61.4	1,978	7.4	46	9	3.4	7	84.4
Cam Newton, Carolina	492	291	59.1	3,302	6.7	64	22	4.5	16	80.7
Eli Manning, NY Giants	571	352	61.6	3,468	6.1	77T	19	3.3	13	80.4
*Mitchell Trubisky, Chicago.	330	196	59.4	2,193	6.6	70	7	2.1	7	77.5
Brett Hundley, Green Bay	316	192	60.8	1,836	5.8	55T	9	2.8	12	70.6
C.J. Beathard, San Francisco	224	123	54.9	1,430	6.4	83T	4	1.8	6	69.2

RUSHING YARDS

Player, team	Yds	Att	Avg	Long	TD
Todd Gurley II, L.A. Rams. . . .	1,305	279	4.7	57T	13
Mark Ingram, New Orleans	1,124	230	4.9	72	12
Jordan Howard, Chicago	1,122	276	4.1	53	9
Ezekiel Elliott, Dallas	983	242	4.1	30	7
Carlos Hyde, San Francisco	938	240	3.9	61	8
Devonta Freeman, Atlanta	865	196	4.4	44	7
Latavius Murray, Minnesota	842	216	3.9	46	8
LeGarrette Blount, Philadelphia	766	173	4.4	68	2
Cam Newton, Carolina	754	139	5.4	69	6
Orleans Darkwa, NY Giants	751	171	4.4	75T	5

RECEPTIONS

Player, team	Rec	Yds	Avg	Long	TD
Larry Fitzgerald, Arizona.	109	1,156	10.6	37	6
Michael Thomas, New Orleans. .	104	1,245	12.0	43	5
Golden Tate, Detroit	92	1,003	10.9	71T	5
Adam Thielen, Minnesota	91	1,276	14.0	65T	4
Julio Jones, Atlanta.	88	1,444	16.4	53	3
*Alvin Kamara, New Orleans . . .	81	826	10.2	40	5
*Christian McCaffrey, Carolina . .	80	651	8.1	37	5
Doug Baldwin, Seattle.	75	991	13.2	54	8
Davante Adams, Green Bay	74	885	12.0	55T	10
Zach Ertz, Philadelphia	74	824	11.1	53	8

SCORING—KICKERS

Player, team	PAT	FG	Long	Pts
Greg Zuerlein, L.A. Rams.	44/46	38/40	56	158
Robbie Gould, San Francisco. . . .	28/30	39/41	52	145
Wil Lutz, New Orleans	47/50	31/36	53	140
Matt Bryant, Atlanta	35/35	34/39	57	137
Kai Forbath, Minnesota.	34/39	32/38	53	130
Matt Prater, Detroit	40/41	30/35	58	130

SCORING—NON-KICKERS

Player, team (position)	TD	Rush	Rec	2-Pt	Pts
Todd Gurley II, L.A. Rams (RB)	19	13	6	0	114
*Alvin Kamara, New Orleans (RB)	14	9**	5	1	86
Mark Ingram, New Orleans (RB) . .	12	12	0	0	72
Jimmy Graham, Seattle (TE)	10	0	10	1	62
Davante Adams, Green Bay (WR)	10	0	10	0	60
Alshon Jeffery, Philadelphia (WR)	9	0	9	3	60
Nelson Agholor, Philadelphia (WR)	9	1**	8	0	54
Ezekiel Elliott, Dallas (RB)	9	7	2	0	54
Jordan Howard, Chicago (RB)	9	9	0	0	54
Marvin Jones Jr., Detroit (WR)	9	0	9	0	54

** = Total includes one kickoff return (Kamara) and one fumble return (Agholor).

INTERCEPTIONS

Player, team	No.	Yds	Avg	Long	TD
Darius Slay, Detroit	8	73	9.1	37	0
Antoine Bethea, Arizona	5	51	10.2	21	0
*Marshon Lattimore, New Orleans	5	85	17.0	33	1
Harrison Smith, Minnesota	5	42	8.4	19	0
Kendall Fuller, Washington.	4	4	1.0	3	0
Damarious Randall, Green Bay . . .	4	35	8.8	21T	1
Patrick Robinson, Philadelphia . . .	4	36	9.0	19	0
D.J. Swearinger, Washington	4	32	8.0	31	0
*Marcus Williams, New Orleans . . .	4	12	3.0	12	0

KICKOFF RETURNS

Player, team	No.	Yds	Avg	Long	TD
Pharoh Cooper, L.A. Rams	34	932	27.4	103T	1
Tyler Lockett, Seattle.	37	949	25.6	99T	1
*Ryan Switzer, Dallas	24	600	25.0	61	0
Trevor Davis, Green Bay	31	707	22.8	34	0
Andre Roberts, Atlanta	38	860	22.6	61	0
*Tarik Cohen, Chicago	26	583	22.4	46	0

PUNTING

Player, team	No.	Yds	Long	Avg
Johnny Hekker, L.A. Rams	65	3,113	70	47.9
Andy Lee, Arizona	88	4,159	63	47.3
Thomas Morstead, New Orleans . .	60	2,822	68	47.0
Pat O'Donnell, Chicago	87	4,087	69	47.0
Michael Palardy, Carolina	71	3,269	63	46.0
Tress Way, Washington.	83	3,794	64	45.7
Donnie Jones, Philadelphia	67	3,033	62	45.3

PUNT RETURNS

Player, team	No.	Yds	Avg	Long	TD
*Jamal Agnew, Detroit.	29	447	15.4	88T	2
Pharoh Cooper, L.A. Rams	32	399	12.5	53	0
Trevor Davis, Green Bay	24	289	12.0	65	0
Marcus Sherels, Minnesota	39	372	9.5	46	0
*Tarik Cohen, Chicago	29	272	9.4	61T	1
*Trent Taylor, San Francisco	30	281	9.4	39	0

SACKS

Player, team	No.
Chandler Jones, Arizona	17.0
Demarcus Lawrence, Dallas	14.5
Everson Griffen, Minnesota	13.0
Cameron Jordan, New Orleans	13.0
Ryan Kerrigan, Washington	13.0
Ezekiel Ansah, Detroit	12.0
Mario Addison, Carolina	11.0
Aaron Donald, L.A. Rams	11.0
Julius Peppers, Carolina	11.0
Adrian Clayborn, Atlanta	9.5
Brandon Graham, Philadelphia	9.5

Super Bowl, 1967-2018

The Super Bowl was created as a condition of the merger between the American Football League (AFL, formed in 1959) and National Football League (NFL, formed in 1920). Announced June 8, 1966, the merger agreement stipulated that the leagues would play separate regular season schedules through the 1969 season but meet after each in an AFL-NFL Championship Game, unofficially dubbed the Super Bowl. The first Super Bowl, played at the Memorial Coliseum in Los Angeles on Jan. 15, 1967, did not sell out, unlike every Super Bowl game since. Each player on the victorious Green Bay Packers earned $15,000 for the win; the defeated Kansas City Chiefs each collected $7,500.

No.	Year	Winner	Opponent	Winning coach	Site
I	1967	*Green Bay Packers, 35	Kansas City Chiefs, 10	Vince Lombardi	Memorial Coliseum, Los Angeles, CA
II	1968	Green Bay Packers, 33	*Oakland Raiders, 14	Vince Lombardi	Orange Bowl, Miami, FL
III	1969	*NY Jets, 16	Baltimore Colts, 7	Weeb Ewbank	Orange Bowl, Miami, FL
IV	1970	Kansas City Chiefs, 23	*Minnesota Vikings, 7	Hank Stram	Tulane Stadium, New Orleans, LA
V	1971	Baltimore Colts, 16	*Dallas Cowboys, 13	Don McCafferty	Orange Bowl, Miami, FL
VI	1972	Dallas Cowboys, 24	*Miami Dolphins, 3	Tom Landry	Tulane Stadium, New Orleans, LA
VII	1973	*Miami Dolphins, 14	Washington Redskins, 7	Don Shula	Memorial Coliseum, Los Angeles, CA
VIII	1974	*Miami Dolphins, 24	Minnesota Vikings, 7	Don Shula	Rice Stadium, Houston, TX
IX	1975	*Pittsburgh Steelers, 16	Minnesota Vikings, 6	Chuck Noll	Tulane Stadium, New Orleans, LA
X	1976	Pittsburgh Steelers, 21	*Dallas Cowboys, 17	Chuck Noll	Orange Bowl, Miami, FL
XI	1977	*Oakland Raiders, 32	Minnesota Vikings, 14	John Madden	Rose Bowl, Pasadena, CA
XII	1978	*Dallas Cowboys, 27	Denver Broncos, 10	Tom Landry	Superdome, New Orleans, LA
XIII	1979	Pittsburgh Steelers, 35	*Dallas Cowboys, 31	Chuck Noll	Orange Bowl, Miami, FL
XIV	1980	Pittsburgh Steelers, 31	*L.A. Rams, 19	Chuck Noll	Rose Bowl, Pasadena, CA
XV	1981	Oakland Raiders, 27	*Philadelphia Eagles, 10	Tom Flores	Superdome, New Orleans, LA
XVI	1982	*San Francisco 49ers, 26	Cincinnati Bengals, 21	Bill Walsh	Silverdome, Pontiac, MI
XVII	1983	Washington Redskins, 27	*Miami Dolphins, 17	Joe Gibbs	Rose Bowl, Pasadena, CA
XVIII	1984	*L.A. Raiders, 38	Washington Redskins, 9	Tom Flores	Tampa Stadium, Tampa, FL
XIX	1985	*San Francisco 49ers, 38	Miami Dolphins, 16	Bill Walsh	Stanford Stadium, Stanford, CA
XX	1986	*Chicago Bears, 46	New England Patriots, 10	Mike Ditka	Superdome, New Orleans, LA
XXI	1987	NY Giants, 39	*Denver Broncos, 20	Bill Parcells	Rose Bowl, Pasadena, CA
XXII	1988	*Washington Redskins, 42	Denver Broncos, 10	Joe Gibbs	Jack Murphy Stadium, San Diego, CA
XXIII	1989	*San Francisco 49ers, 20	Cincinnati Bengals, 16	Bill Walsh	Joe Robbie Stadium, Miami, FL
XXIV	1990	San Francisco 49ers, 55	*Denver Broncos, 10	George Seifert	Superdome, New Orleans, LA
XXV	1991	NY Giants, 20	*Buffalo Bills, 19	Bill Parcells	Tampa Stadium, Tampa, FL
XXVI	1992	*Washington Redskins, 37	Buffalo Bills, 24	Joe Gibbs	Metrodome, Minneapolis, MN
XXVII	1993	Dallas Cowboys, 52	*Buffalo Bills, 17	Jimmy Johnson	Rose Bowl, Pasadena, CA
XXVIII	1994	*Dallas Cowboys, 30	Buffalo Bills, 13	Jimmy Johnson	Georgia Dome, Atlanta, GA
XXIX	1995	*San Francisco 49ers, 49	San Diego Chargers, 26	George Seifert	Joe Robbie Stadium, Miami, FL
XXX	1996	*Dallas Cowboys, 27	Pittsburgh Steelers, 17	Barry Switzer	Sun Devil Stadium, Tempe, AZ
XXXI	1997	Green Bay Packers, 35	*New England Patriots, 21	Mike Holmgren	Superdome, New Orleans, LA
XXXII	1998	Denver Broncos, 31	*Green Bay Packers, 24	Mike Shanahan	Qualcomm Stadium, San Diego, CA
XXXIII	1999	Denver Broncos, 34	*Atlanta Falcons, 19	Mike Shanahan	Pro Player Stadium, Miami, FL
XXXIV	2000	*St. Louis Rams, 23	Tennessee Titans, 16	Dick Vermeil	Georgia Dome, Atlanta, GA
XXXV	2001	Baltimore Ravens, 34	*NY Giants, 7	Brian Billick	Raymond James Stadium, Tampa, FL
XXXVI	2002	New England Patriots, 20	*St. Louis Rams, 17	Bill Belichick	Superdome, New Orleans, LA
XXXVII	2003	*Tampa Bay Buccaneers, 48	Oakland Raiders, 21	Jon Gruden	Qualcomm Stadium, San Diego, CA
XXXVIII	2004	New England Patriots, 32	*Carolina Panthers, 29	Bill Belichick	Reliant Stadium, Houston, TX
XXXIX	2005	New England Patriots, 24	*Philadelphia Eagles, 21	Bill Belichick	Alltel Stadium, Jacksonville, FL
XL	2006	Pittsburgh Steelers, 21	*Seattle Seahawks, 10	Bill Cowher	Ford Field, Detroit, MI
XLI	2007	Indianapolis Colts, 29	*Chicago Bears, 17	Tony Dungy	Dolphin Stadium, Miami Gardens, FL
XLII	2008	*NY Giants, 17	New England Patriots, 14	Tom Coughlin	Univ. of Phoenix Stadium, Glendale, AZ
XLIII	2009	Pittsburgh Steelers, 27	**Arizona Cardinals, 23	Mike Tomlin	Raymond James Stadium, Tampa, FL
XLIV	2010	*New Orleans Saints, 31	Indianapolis Colts, 17	Sean Payton	Sun Life Stadium, Miami Gardens, FL
XLV	2011	**Green Bay Packers, 31	Pittsburgh Steelers, 25	Mike McCarthy	Cowboys Stadium, Arlington, TX
XLVI	2012	NY Giants, 21	**New England Patriots, 17	Tom Coughlin	Lucas Oil Stadium, Indianapolis, IN
XLVII	2013	**Baltimore Ravens, 34	San Francisco 49ers, 31	John Harbaugh	Mercedes-Benz Superdome, New Orleans, LA
XLVIII	2014	**Seattle Seahawks, 43	Denver Broncos, 8	Pete Carroll	MetLife Stadium, East Rutherford, NJ
XLIX	2015	New England Patriots, 28	**Seattle Seahawks, 24	Bill Belichick	Univ. of Phoenix Stadium, Glendale, AZ
50 (L)	2016	Denver Broncos, 24	**Carolina Panthers, 10	Gary Kubiak	Levi's Stadium, Santa Clara, CA
LI	2017	New England Patriots, 34 (OT)	**Atlanta Falcons, 28	Bill Belichick	NRG Stadium, Houston, TX
LII	2018	Philadelphia Eagles, 41	**New England Patriots, 33	Doug Pederson	U.S. Bank Stadium, Minneapolis, MN

* = Team won the coin toss and elected to receive. ** = Team won the coin toss and elected to receive in the second half. OT = Overtime.

Super Bowl Sites, 2019-22

No.	Site	Date	No.	Site	Date
LIII	Mercedes-Benz Stadium, Atlanta, GA ...	Feb. 3, 2019	LVII	Univ. of Phoenix Stadium, Glendale, AZ	Feb. 2023
LIV	Hard Rock Stadium, Miami Gardens, FL	Feb. 2, 2020	LVIII	Mercedes-Benz Superdome, New Orleans, LA....................	Feb. 2024
LV	Raymond James Stadium, Tampa, FL ...	Feb. 7, 2021			
LVI	Inglewood, CA	Feb. 6, 2022			

Super Bowl MVPs, 1967-2018

Year	Most valuable player, team	Year	Most valuable player, team	Year	Most valuable player, team
1967	Bart Starr, Green Bay	1985	Joe Montana, San Francisco	2002	Tom Brady, New England
1968	Bart Starr, Green Bay	1986	Richard Dent, Chicago	2003	Dexter Jackson, Tampa Bay
1969	Joe Namath, NY Jets	1987	Phil Simms, NY Giants	2004	Tom Brady, New England
1970	Len Dawson, Kansas City	1988	Doug Williams, Washington	2005	Deion Branch, New England
1971	Chuck Howley, Dallas	1989	Jerry Rice, San Francisco	2006	Hines Ward, Pittsburgh
1972	Roger Staubach, Dallas	1990	Joe Montana, San Francisco	2007	Peyton Manning, Indianapolis
1973	Jake Scott, Miami	1991	Ottis Anderson, NY Giants	2008	Eli Manning, NY Giants
1974	Larry Csonka, Miami	1992	Mark Rypien, Washington	2009	Santonio Holmes, Pittsburgh
1975	Franco Harris, Pittsburgh	1993	Troy Aikman, Dallas	2010	Drew Brees, New Orleans
1976	Lynn Swann, Pittsburgh	1994	Emmitt Smith, Dallas	2011	Aaron Rodgers, Green Bay
1977	Fred Biletnikoff, Oakland	1995	Steve Young, San Francisco	2012	Eli Manning, NY Giants
1978	Randy White, Harvey Martin; Dallas	1996	Larry Brown, Dallas	2013	Joe Flacco, Baltimore
1979	Terry Bradshaw, Pittsburgh	1997	Desmond Howard, Green Bay	2014	Malcolm Smith, Seattle
1980	Terry Bradshaw, Pittsburgh	1998	Terrell Davis, Denver	2015	Tom Brady, New England
1981	Jim Plunkett, Oakland	1999	John Elway, Denver	2016	Von Miller, Denver
1982	Joe Montana, San Francisco	2000	Kurt Warner, St. Louis	2017	Tom Brady, New England
1983	John Riggins, Washington	2001	Ray Lewis, Baltimore	2018	Nick Foles, Philadelphia
1984	Marcus Allen, L.A. Raiders				

Super Bowl Single-Game Statistical Leaders

PASSING YARDS

Player, team	Year	Att/comp	Yds	TD
Tom Brady, New England	2018	48/28	505	3
Tom Brady, New England	2017	62/43	466	2
Kurt Warner, St. Louis	2000	45/24	414	2
Kurt Warner, Arizona	2009	43/31	377	3
Nick Foles, Philadelphia	2018	43/28	373	3
Kurt Warner, St. Louis	2002	44/28	365	1
Donovon McNabb, Philadelphia	2005	51/30	357	3
Joe Montana, San Francisco	1989	36/23	357	2

PASSING TOUCHDOWNS

Player, team	Year	Att/comp	Yds	TD
Steve Young, San Francisco	1995	36/24	325	6
Joe Montana, San Francisco	1990	29/22	297	5
Tom Brady, New England	2015	50/37	328	4
Troy Aikman, Dallas	1993	30/22	273	4
Doug Williams, Washington	1988	29/18	340	4
Terry Bradshaw, Pittsburgh	1979	30/17	318	4

SCORING

Player, team	Year	Pts	
James White, New England	2017	20	(3 TDs, 1 2-pt)
Terrell Davis, Denver	1998	18	(3 TDs)
Jerry Rice, San Francisco	1995	18	(3 TDs)
Ricky Watters, San Francisco	1995	18	(3 TDs)
Jerry Rice, San Francisco	1990	18	(3 TDs)
Roger Craig, San Francisco	1985	18	(3 TDs)
Don Chandler, Green Bay	1968	15	(4 FGs, 3 PATs)
Kevin Butler, Chicago Bears	1986	14	(3 FGs, 5 PATs)
Ray Wersching, San Francisco	1982	14	(4 FGs, 2 PATs)

RECEIVING YARDS

Player, team	Year	Rec	Yds	TD
Jerry Rice, San Francisco	1989	11	215	1
Ricky Sanders, Washington	1988	9	193	2
Isaac Bruce, St. Louis	2000	6	162	1

RUSHING YARDS

Player, team	Year	Att	Yds	TD
Timmy Smith, Washington	1988	22	204	2
Marcus Allen, L.A. Raiders	1984	20	191	2
John Riggins, Washington	1983	38	166	1

First-Round Selections in the 2018 NFL Draft

Held Apr. 26-28, 2018.

Team	Player	Pos.	College
1. Cleveland Browns	Baker Mayfield	QB	Oklahoma
2. NY Giants	Saquon Barkley	RB	Penn St.
3. NY Jets[1]	Sam Darnold	QB	USC
4. Cleveland Browns[2]	Denzel Ward	CB	Ohio St.
5. Denver Broncos	Bradley Chubb	DE	NC State
6. Indianapolis Colts[3]	Quenton Nelson	G	Notre Dame
7. Buffalo Bills[4]	Josh Allen	QB	Wyoming
8. Chicago Bears	Roquan Smith	LB	Georgia
9. San Francisco 49ers	Mike McGlinchey	OT	Notre Dame
10. Arizona Cardinals[5]	Josh Rosen	QB	UCLA
11. Miami Dolphins	Minkah Fitzpatrick	S	Alabama
12. Tampa Bay Buccaneers[6]	Vita Vea	DT	Washington
13. Washington Redskins	Da'ron Payne	DT	Alabama
14. New Orleans Saints[7]	Marcus Davenport	DE	Texas-San Antonio
15. Oakland Raiders[8]	Kolton Miller	OT	UCLA
16. Buffalo Bills[9]	Tremaine Edmunds	LB	Virginia Tech
17. Los Angeles Chargers	Derwin James	S	Florida St.
18. Green Bay Packers[10]	Jaire Alexander	CB	Louisville
19. Dallas Cowboys	Leighton Vander Esch	LB	Boise St.
20. Detroit Lions	Frank Ragnow	C	Arkansas
21. Cincinnati Bengals[11]	Billy Price	C	Ohio St.
22. Tennessee Titans[12]	Rashaan Evans	LB	Alabama
23. New England Patriots[13]	Isaiah Wynn	T	Georgia
24. Carolina Panthers	D.J. Moore	WR	Maryland
25. Baltimore Ravens[14]	Hayden Hurst	TE	South Carolina
26. Atlanta Falcons	Calvin Ridley	WR	Alabama
27. Seattle Seahawks[15]	Rashaad Penny	RB	San Diego St.
28. Pittsburgh Steelers	Terrell Edmunds	S	Virginia Tech
29. Jacksonville Jaguars	Taven Bryan	DT	Florida
30. Minnesota Vikings	Mike Hughes	CB	UCF
31. New England Patriots	Sony Michel	RB	Georgia
32. Baltimore Ravens[16]	Lamar Jackson	QB	Louisville

(1) From Colts. (2) From Texans. (3) From Jets. (4) From Buccaneers. (5) From Raiders. (6) From Bills through Bengals. (7) From Packers. (8) From Cardinals. (9) From Ravens. (10) From Seahawks. (11) From Bills. (12) From Ravens through Bills and Chiefs. (13) From Rams. (14) From Titans. (15) From Packers through Saints. (16) From Eagles.

Number One NFL Draft Choices, 1960-2018

Year	Team	Player, pos., college	Year	Team	Player, pos., college
1960	L.A. Rams	Billy Cannon, HB, LSU	1967	Baltimore Colts	Bubba Smith, DE, Michigan St.
1961	Minnesota	Tommy Mason, HB, Tulane	1968	Minnesota	Ron Yary, OT, USC
1962	Washington	Ernie Davis, HB, Syracuse	1969	Buffalo	O.J. Simpson, RB, USC
1963	L.A. Rams	Terry Baker, QB, Oregon St.	1970	Pittsburgh	Terry Bradshaw, QB, LA Tech
1964	San Francisco	Dave Parks, E, Texas Tech	1971	New England	Jim Plunkett, QB, Stanford
1965	NY Giants	Tucker Frederickson, RB, Auburn	1972	Buffalo	Walt Patulski, DE, Notre Dame
1966	Atlanta	Tommy Nobis, LB, Texas	1973	Houston	John Matuszak, DE, Tampa

Year	Team	Player, pos., college
1974	Dallas	Ed "Too Tall" Jones, DE, Tenn. St.
1975	Atlanta	Steve Bartkowski, QB, California
1976	Tampa Bay	Lee Roy Selmon, DE, Oklahoma
1977	Tampa Bay	Ricky Bell, RB, USC
1978	Houston	Earl Campbell, RB, Texas
1979	Buffalo	Tom Cousineau, LB, Ohio St.
1980	Detroit	Billy Sims, RB, Oklahoma
1981	New Orleans	George Rogers, RB, S. Carolina
1982	New England	Kenneth Sims, DT, Texas
1983	Baltimore Colts	John Elway, QB, Stanford
1984	New England	Irving Fryar, WR, Nebraska
1985	Buffalo	Bruce Smith, DE, Virginia Tech
1986	Tampa Bay	Bo Jackson, RB, Auburn
1987	Tampa Bay	Vinny Testaverde, QB, Miami (FL)
1988	Atlanta	Aundray Bruce, LB, Auburn
1989	Dallas	Troy Aikman, QB, UCLA
1990	Indianapolis	Jeff George, QB, Illinois
1991	Dallas	Russell Maryland, DL, Miami (FL)
1992	Indianapolis	Steve Emtman, DL, Washington
1993	New England	Drew Bledsoe, QB, Washington St.
1994	Cincinnati	Dan Wilkinson, DT, Ohio St.
1995	Cincinnati	Ki-Jana Carter, RB, Penn St.
1996	NY Jets	Keyshawn Johnson, WR, USC
1997	St. Louis	Orlando Pace, OT, Ohio St.
1998	Indianapolis	Peyton Manning, QB, Tennessee
1999	Cleveland	Tim Couch, QB, Kentucky
2000	Cleveland	Courtney Brown, DE, Penn St.
2001	Atlanta	Michael Vick, QB, Virginia Tech
2002	Houston	David Carr, QB, Fresno St.
2003	Cincinnati	Carson Palmer, QB, USC
2004	San Diego	Eli Manning, QB, Mississippi
2005	San Francisco	Alex D. Smith, QB, Utah
2006	Houston	Mario Williams, DE, NC State
2007	Oakland	JaMarcus Russell, QB, LSU
2008	Miami	Jake Long, OT, Michigan
2009	Detroit	Matthew Stafford, QB, Georgia
2010	St. Louis	Sam Bradford, QB, Oklahoma
2011	Carolina	Cam Newton, QB, Auburn
2012	Indianapolis	Andrew Luck, QB, Stanford
2013	Kansas City	Eric Fisher, OT, Central Michigan
2014	Houston	Jadeveon Clowney, DE, S. Carolina
2015	Tampa Bay	Jameis Winston, QB, Florida St.
2016	L.A. Rams	Jared Goff, QB, California
2017	Cleveland	Myles Garrett, DE, Texas A&M
2018	Cleveland	Baker Mayfield, QB, Oklahoma

American Football League Champions, 1960-69

Year	Eastern (W-L-T)	Western (W-L-T)	Championship
1960	Houston Oilers (10-4-0)	L.A. Chargers (10-4-0)	Houston 24, L.A. 16
1961	Houston Oilers (10-3-1)	San Diego Chargers (12-2-0)	Houston 10, San Diego 3
1962	Houston Oilers (11-3-0)	Dallas Texans (11-3-0)	Dallas 20, Houston 17 (2 OT)
1963	Boston Patriots (7-6-1)[1]	San Diego Chargers (11-3-0)	San Diego 51, Boston 10
1964	Buffalo Bills (12-2-0)	San Diego Chargers (8-5-1)	Buffalo 20, San Diego 7
1965	Buffalo Bills (10-3-1)	San Diego Chargers (9-2-3)	Buffalo 23, San Diego 0
1966	Buffalo Bills (9-4-1)	Kansas City Chiefs (11-2-1)	Kansas City 31, Buffalo 7
1967	Houston Oilers (9-4-1)	Oakland Raiders (13-1-0)	Oakland 40, Houston 7
1968	NY Jets (11-3-0)	Oakland Raiders (12-2-0)[2]	NY Jets 27, Oakland 23
1969	NY Jets (10-4-0)	Oakland Raiders (12-1-1)	Kansas City 17, Oakland 7[3]

(1) Defeated conference champion Buffalo Bills in divisional playoff. (2) Defeated conference champion Kansas City Chiefs in divisional playoff. (3) Kansas City Chiefs defeated NY Jets, and Oakland Raiders defeated Houston Oilers in divisional playoffs.

National Football League Champions, 1933-69

Year	Eastern (W-L-T)	Western (W-L-T)	Championship
1933	NY Giants (11-3-0)	Chicago Bears (10-2-1)	Chicago Bears 23, NY Giants 21
1934	NY Giants (8-5-0)	Chicago Bears (13-0-0)	NY Giants 30, Chicago Bears 13
1935	NY Giants (9-3-0)	Detroit Lions (7-3-2)	Detroit 26, NY Giants 7
1936	Boston Redskins (7-5-0)	Green Bay Packers (10-1-1)	Green Bay 21, Boston 6
1937	Washington Redskins (8-3-0)	Chicago Bears (9-1-0)	Washington 28, Chicago Bears 21
1938	NY Giants (8-2-1)	Green Bay Packers (8-3-0)	NY Giants 23, Green Bay 17
1939	NY Giants (9-1-1)	Green Bay Packers (9-2-0)	Green Bay 27, NY Giants 0
1940	Washington Redskins (9-2-0)	Chicago Bears (8-3-0)	Chicago Bears 73, Washington 0
1941	NY Giants (8-3-0)	Chicago Bears (10-1-0)[1]	Chicago Bears 37, NY Giants 9
1942	Washington Redskins (10-1-0)	Chicago Bears (11-0-0)	Washington 14, Chicago Bears 6
1943	Washington Redskins (6-3-1)[1]	Chicago Bears (8-1-1)	Chicago Bears, 41, Washington 21
1944	NY Giants (8-1-1)	Green Bay Packers (8-2-0)	Green Bay 14, NY Giants 7
1945	Washington Redskins (8-2-0)	Cleveland Rams (9-1-0)	Cleveland Rams 15, Washington 14
1946	NY Giants (7-3-1)	Chicago Bears (8-2-1)	Chicago Bears 24, NY Giants 14
1947	Philadelphia Eagles (8-4-0)[1]	Chicago Cardinals (9-3-0)	Chicago Cardinals 28, Philadelphia 21
1948	Philadelphia Eagles (9-2-1)	Chicago Cardinals (11-1-0)	Philadelphia 7, Chicago Cardinals 0
1949	Philadelphia Eagles (11-1-0)	L.A. Rams (8-2-2)	Philadelphia 14, L.A. Rams 0
1950	Cleveland Browns (10-2-0)[1]	L.A. Rams (9-3-0)[1]	Cleveland 30, L.A. Rams 28
1951	Cleveland Browns (11-1-0)	L.A. Rams (8-4-0)	L.A. Rams 24, Cleveland Browns 17
1952	Cleveland Browns (8-4-0)	Detroit Lions (9-3-0)[1]	Detroit 17, Cleveland Browns 7
1953	Cleveland Browns (11-1-0)	Detroit Lions (10-2-0)	Detroit 17, Cleveland Browns 16
1954	Cleveland Browns (9-3-0)	Detroit Lions (9-2-1)	Cleveland Browns 56, Detroit 10
1955	Cleveland Browns (9-2-1)	L.A. Rams (8-3-1)	Cleveland Browns 38, L.A. Rams 14
1956	NY Giants (8-3-1)	Chicago Bears (9-2-1)	NY Giants 47, Chicago Bears 7
1957	Cleveland Browns (9-2-1)	Detroit Lions (8-4-0)[1]	Detroit 59, Cleveland Browns 14
1958	NY Giants (9-3-0)[1]	Baltimore Colts (9-3-0)	Baltimore 23, NY Giants 17[2]
1959	NY Giants (10-2-0)	Baltimore Colts (9-3-0)	Baltimore 31, NY Giants 16
1960	Philadelphia Eagles (10-2-0)	Green Bay Packers (8-4-0)	Philadelphia 17, Green Bay 13
1961	NY Giants (10-3-1)	Green Bay Packers (11-3-0)	Green Bay 37, NY Giants 0
1962	NY Giants (12-2-0)	Green Bay Packers (13-1-0)	Green Bay 16, NY Giants 7
1963	NY Giants (11-3-0)	Chicago Bears (11-1-2)	Chicago 14, NY Giants 10
1964	Cleveland Browns (10-3-1)	Baltimore Colts (12-2-0)	Cleveland Browns 27, Baltimore 0
1965	Cleveland Browns (11-3-0)	Green Bay Packers (10-3-1)[1]	Green Bay 23, Cleveland Browns 12
1966	Dallas Cowboys (10-3-1)	Green Bay Packers (12-2-0)	Green Bay 34, Dallas 27
1967	Dallas Cowboys (9-5-0)	Green Bay Packers (9-4-1)	Green Bay 21, Dallas 17
1968	Cleveland Browns (10-4-0)	Baltimore Colts (13-1-0)	Baltimore 34, Cleveland Browns 0
1969	Cleveland Browns (10-3-1)	Minnesota Vikings (12-2-0)	Minnesota 27, Cleveland Browns 7

Note: Conference title games preceded NFL Championship from 1967-69. (1) Won divisional or conference playoff. (2) Won at 8:15 of sudden death overtime period.

NFL Divisional Champions and Wild Cards, 1970-95

The American Football League and National Football League officially merged in 1966. At the beginning of the 1970 season, the two leagues became the AFC and NFC conferences in the new NFL. Regular-season (W-L-T) records are in parentheses.

AMERICAN FOOTBALL CONFERENCE

Year	Eastern	Central	Western	Wild card
1970	Baltimore Colts (11-2-1)	Cincinnati Bengals (8-6-0)	Oakland Raiders (8-4-2)	Miami Dolphins (10-4-0)
1971	Miami Dolphins (10-3-1)	Cleveland Browns (9-5-0)	Kansas City Chiefs (10-3-1)	Baltimore Colts (10-4-0)
1972	Miami Dolphins (14-0-0)	Pittsburgh Steelers (11-3-0)	Oakland Raiders (10-3-1)	Cleveland Browns (10-4-0)
1973	Miami Dolphins (12-2-0)	Cincinnati Bengals (10-4-0)	Oakland Raiders (9-4-1)	Pittsburgh Steelers (10-4-0)
1974	Miami Dolphins (11-3-0)	Pittsburgh Steelers (10-3-1)	Oakland Raiders (12-2-0)	Buffalo Bills (9-5-0)
1975	Baltimore Colts (10-4-0)	Pittsburgh Steelers (12-2-0)	Oakland Raiders (11-3-0)	Cincinnati Bengals (11-3-0)
1976	Baltimore Colts (11-3-0)	Pittsburgh Steelers (10-4-0)	Oakland Raiders (13-1-0)	New England Patriots (11-3-0)
1977	Baltimore Colts (10-4-0)	Pittsburgh Steelers (9-5-0)	Denver Broncos (12-2-0)	Oakland Raiders (11-3-0)
1978	New England Patriots (11-5-0)	Pittsburgh Steelers (14-2-0)	Denver Broncos (10-6-0)	Houston Oilers (10-6-0) Miami Dolphins (11-5-0)
1979	Miami Dolphins (10-6-0)	Pittsburgh Steelers (12-4-0)	San Diego Chargers (12-4-0)	Houston Oilers (11-5-0) Denver Broncos (10-6-0)
1980	Buffalo Bills (11-5-0)	Cleveland Browns (11-5-0)	San Diego Chargers (11-5-0)	Houston Oilers (11-5-0) Oakland Raiders (11-5-0)
1981	Miami Dolphins (11-4-1)	Cincinnati Bengals (12-4-0)	San Diego Chargers (10-6-0)	Buffalo Bills (10-6-0) NY Jets (10-5-1)
1982	Strike abbreviated season. See note.			
1983	Miami Dolphins (12-4-0)	Pittsburgh Steelers (10-6-0)	L.A. Raiders (12-4-0)	Denver Broncos (9-7-0) Seattle Seahawks (9-7-0)
1984	Miami Dolphins (14-2-0)	Pittsburgh Steelers (9-7-0)	Denver Broncos (13-3-0)	L.A. Raiders (11-5-0) Seattle Seahawks (12-4-0)
1985	Miami Dolphins (12-4-0)	Cleveland Browns (8-8-0)	L.A. Raiders (12-4-0)	New England Patriots (11-5-0) NY Jets (11-5-0)
1986	New England Patriots (11-5-0)	Cleveland Browns (12-4-0)	Denver Broncos (11-5-0)	Kansas City Chiefs (10-6-0) NY Jets (10-6-0)
1987	Indianapolis Colts (9-6-0)	Cleveland Browns (10-5-0)	Denver Broncos (10-4-1)	Houston Oilers (9-6-0) Seattle Seahawks (9-6-0)
1988	Buffalo Bills (12-4-0)	Cincinnati Bengals (12-4-0)	Seattle Seahawks (9-7-0)	Cleveland Browns (10-6-0) Houston Oilers (10-6-0)
1989	Buffalo Bills (9-7-0)	Cleveland Browns (9-6-1)	Denver Broncos (11-5-0)	Houston Oilers (9-7-0) Pittsburgh Steelers (9-7-0)
1990	Buffalo Bills (13-3-0)	Cincinnati Bengals (9-7-0)	L.A. Raiders (12-4-0)	Houston Oilers (9-7-0) Kansas City Chiefs (10-6-0) Miami Dolphins (12-4-0)
1991	Buffalo Bills (13-3-0)	Houston Oilers (11-5-0)	Denver Broncos (12-4-0)	Kansas City Chiefs (10-6-0) L.A. Raiders (9-7-0) NY Jets (8-8-0)
1992	Miami Dolphins (11-5-0)	Pittsburgh Steelers (11-5-0)	San Diego Chargers (11-5-0)	Buffalo Bills (11-5-0) Houston Oilers (10-6-0) Kansas City Chiefs (10-6-0)
1993	Buffalo Bills (12-4-0)	Houston Oilers (12-4-0)	Kansas City Chiefs (11-5-0)	Denver Broncos (9-7-0) L.A. Raiders (10-6-0) Pittsburgh Steelers (9-7-0)
1994	Miami Dolphins (10-6-0)	Pittsburgh Steelers (12-4-0)	San Diego Chargers (11-5-0)	Cleveland Browns (11-5-0) Kansas City Chiefs (9-7-0) New England Patriots (10-6-0)
1995	Buffalo Bills (10-6-0)	Pittsburgh Steelers (11-5-0)	Kansas City Chiefs (13-3-0)	Miami Dolphins (9-7-0) Indianapolis Colts (9-7-0) San Diego Chargers (9-7-0)

NATIONAL FOOTBALL CONFERENCE

Year	Eastern	Central	Western	Wild card
1970	Dallas Cowboys (10-4-0)	Minnesota Vikings (12-2-0)	San Francisco 49ers (10-3-1)	Detroit Lions (10-4-0)
1971	Dallas Cowboys (11-3-0)	Minnesota Vikings (11-3-0)	San Francisco 49ers (9-5-0)	Washington Redskins (9-4-1)
1972	Washington Redskins (11-3-0)	Green Bay Packers (10-4-0)	San Francisco 49ers (8-5-1)	Dallas Cowboys (10-4-0)
1973	Dallas Cowboys (10-4-0)	Minnesota Vikings (12-2-0)	L.A. Rams (12-2-0)	Washington Redskins (10-4-0)
1974	St. Louis Cardinals (10-4-0)	Minnesota Vikings (10-4-0)	L.A. Rams (10-4-0)	Washington Redskins (10-4-0)
1975	St. Louis Cardinals (11-3-0)	Minnesota Vikings (12-2-0)	L.A. Rams (12-2-0)	Dallas Cowboys (10-4-0)
1976	Dallas Cowboys (11-3-0)	Minnesota Vikings (11-2-1)	L.A. Rams (10-3-1)	Washington Redskins (10-4-0)
1977	Dallas Cowboys (12-2-0)	Minnesota Vikings (9-5-0)	L.A. Rams (10-4-0)	Chicago Bears (9-5-0)
1978	Dallas Cowboys (12-4-0)	Minnesota Vikings (8-7-1)	L.A. Rams (12-4-0)	Atlanta Falcons (9-7-0) Philadelphia Eagles (9-7-0)
1979	Dallas Cowboys (11-5-0)	Tampa Bay Buccaneers (10-6-0)	L.A. Rams (9-7-0)	Chicago Bears (10-6-0) Philadelphia Eagles (11-5-0)
1980	Philadelphia Eagles (12-4-0)	Minnesota Vikings (9-7-0)	Atlanta Falcons (12-4-0)	Dallas Cowboys (12-4-0) L.A. Rams (11-5-0)
1981	Dallas Cowboys (12-4-0)	Tampa Bay Buccaneers (9-7-0)	San Francisco 49ers (13-3-0)	NY Giants (9-7-0) Philadelphia Eagles (10-6-0)
1982	Strike abbreviated season. See note.			
1983	Washington Redskins (14-2-0)	Detroit Lions (9-7-0)	San Francisco 49ers (10-6-0)	Dallas Cowboys (12-4-0) L.A. Rams (9-7-0)
1984	Washington Redskins (11-5-0)	Chicago Bears (10-6-0)	San Francisco 49ers (15-1-0)	L.A. Rams (10-6-0) NY Giants (9-7-0)
1985	Dallas Cowboys (10-6-0)	Chicago Bears (15-1-0)	L.A. Rams (11-5-0)	NY Giants (10-6-0) San Francisco 49ers (10-6-0)
1986	NY Giants (14-2-0)	Chicago Bears (14-2-0)	San Francisco 49ers (10-5-1)	L.A. Rams (10-6-0) Washington Redskins (12-4-0)

Year	Eastern	Central	Western	Wild card
1987	Washington Redskins (11-4-0)	Chicago Bears (11-4-0)	San Francisco 49ers (13-2-0)	Minnesota Vikings (8-7-0) New Orleans Saints (12-3-0)
1988	Philadelphia Eagles (10-6-0)	Chicago Bears (12-4-0)	San Francisco 49ers (10-6-0)	L.A. Rams (10-6-0) Minnesota Vikings (11-5-0)
1989	NY Giants (12-4-0)	Minnesota Vikings (10-6-0)	San Francisco 49ers (14-2-0)	L.A. Rams (11-5-0) Philadelphia Eagles (11-5-0)
1990	NY Giants (13-3-0)	Chicago Bears (11-5-0)	San Francisco 49ers (14-2-0)	New Orleans Saints (8-8-0) Philadelphia Eagles (10-6-0) Washington Redskins (10-6-0)
1991	Washington Redskins (14-2-0)	Detroit Lions (12-4-0)	New Orleans Saints (11-5-0)	Atlanta Falcons (10-6-0) Chicago Bears (11-5-0) Dallas Cowboys (11-5-0)
1992	Dallas Cowboys (13-3-0)	Minnesota Vikings (11-5-0)	San Francisco 49ers (14-2-0)	New Orleans Saints (12-4-0) Philadelphia Eagles (11-5-0) Washington Redskins (9-7-0)
1993	Dallas Cowboys (12-4-0)	Detroit Lions (10-6-0)	San Francisco 49ers (10-6-0)	Green Bay Packers (9-7-0) Minnesota Vikings (9-7-0) NY Giants (11-5-0)
1994	Dallas Cowboys (12-4-0)	Minnesota Vikings (10-6-0)	San Francisco 49ers (13-3-0)	Chicago Bears (9-7-0) Detroit Lions (9-7-0) Green Bay Packers (9-7-0)
1995	Dallas Cowboys (12-4-0)	Green Bay Packers (11-5-0)	San Francisco 49ers (11-5-0)	Philadelphia Eagles (10-6-0) Detroit Lions (10-6-0) Atlanta Falcons (9-7-0)

Note: A strike shortened the 1982 season from 16 to 9 games. The top eight teams in each conference played in a tournament to determine the conference champion.

NFL Playoff Results, 1996-2017

Year	Conference	Division	Winner (W-L-T)	Playoffs[1]	Year
1996	American	Eastern	New England Patriots (11-5-0)	Jacksonville* 30, Denver 27	1996
		Central	Pittsburgh Steelers (10-6-0)	New England 28, Pittsburgh 3	
		Western	Denver Broncos (13-3-0)	New England 20, Jacksonville* 6	
	National	Eastern	Dallas Cowboys (10-6-0)	Green Bay 35, San Francisco* 14	
		Central	Green Bay Packers (13-3-0)	Carolina 26, Dallas 17	
		Western	Carolina Panthers (12-4-0)	Green Bay 30, Carolina 13	
1997	American	Eastern	New England Patriots (10-6-0)	Pittsburgh 7, New England 6	1997
		Central	Pittsburgh Steelers (11-5-0)	Denver* 14, Kansas City 10	
		Western	Kansas City Chiefs (13-3-0)	Denver* 24, Pittsburgh 21	
	National	Eastern	NY Giants (10-5-1)	San Francisco 38, Minnesota* 22	
		Central	Green Bay Packers (13-3-0)	Green Bay 21, Tampa Bay* 7	
		Western	San Francisco 49ers (13-3-0)	Green Bay 23, San Francisco 10	
1998	American	Eastern	NY Jets (12-4-0)	Denver 38, Miami* 3	1998
		Central	Jacksonville Jaguars (11-5-0)	NY Jets 34, Jacksonville 24	
		Western	Denver Broncos (14-2-0)	Denver 23, NY Jets 10	
	National	Eastern	Dallas Cowboys (10-6-0)	Atlanta 20, San Francisco* 18	
		Central	Minnesota Vikings (15-1-0)	Minnesota 41, Arizona* 21	
		Western	Atlanta Falcons (14-2-0)	Atlanta 30, Minnesota 27 (OT)	
1999	American	Eastern	Indianapolis Colts (13-3-0)	Jacksonville 62, Miami* 7	1999
		Central	Jacksonville Jaguars (14-2-0)	Tennessee* 19, Indianapolis 16	
		Western	Seattle Seahawks (9-7-0)	Tennessee* 33, Jacksonville 14	
	National	Eastern	Washington Redskins (10-6-0)	Tampa Bay 14, Washington 13	
		Central	Tampa Bay Buccaneers (11-5-0)	St. Louis 49, Minnesota* 37	
		Western	St. Louis Rams (13-3-0)	St. Louis 11, Tampa Bay 6	
2000	American	Eastern	Miami Dolphins (11-5-0)	Oakland 27, Miami 0	2000
		Central	Tennessee Titans (13-3-0)	Baltimore* 24, Tennessee 10	
		Western	Oakland Raiders (12-4-0)	Baltimore* 16, Oakland 3	
	National	Eastern	NY Giants (12-4-0)	Minnesota 34, New Orleans 16	
		Central	Minnesota Vikings (11-5-0)	NY Giants 20, Philadelphia* 10	
		Western	New Orleans Saints (10-6-0)	NY Giants 41, Minnesota 0	
2001	American	Eastern	New England Patriots (11-5-0)	New England 16, Oakland 13 (OT)	2001
		Central	Pittsburgh Steelers (13-3-0)	Pittsburgh 27, Baltimore* 10	
		Western	Oakland Raiders (10-6-0)	New England 24, Pittsburgh 17	
	National	Eastern	Philadelphia Eagles (11-5-0)	Philadelphia 33, Chicago 19	
		Central	Chicago Bears (13-3-0)	St. Louis 45, Green Bay* 17	
		Western	St. Louis Rams (14-2-0)	St. Louis 29, Philadelphia 24	
2002	American	East	NY Jets (9-7-0)		2002
		North	Pittsburgh Steelers (10-5-1)	Oakland 30, NY Jets 10	
		South	Tennessee Titans (11-5-0)	Tennessee 34, Pittsburgh 31 (OT)	
		West	Oakland Raiders (11-5-0)	Oakland 41, Tennessee 24	
	National	East	Philadelphia Eagles (12-4-0)		
		North	Green Bay Packers (12-4-0)	Philadelphia 20, Atlanta* 6	
		South	Tampa Bay Buccaneers (12-4-0)	Tampa Bay 31, San Francisco 6	
		West	San Francisco 49ers (10-6-0)	Tampa Bay 27, Philadelphia 10	

Year	Conference	Division	Winner (W-L-T)	Playoffs[1]	Year
2003	American	East	New England Patriots (14-2-0)		2003
		North	Baltimore Ravens (10-6-0)	Indianapolis 38, Kansas City 31	
		South	Indianapolis Colts (12-4-0)	New England 17, Tennessee* 14	
		West	Kansas City Chiefs (13-3-0)	New England 24, Indianapolis 14	
	National	East	Philadelphia Eagles (12-4-0)		
		North	Green Bay Packers (10-6-0)	Carolina 29, St. Louis 23 (2 OT)	
		South	Carolina Panthers (11-5-0)	Philadelphia 20, Green Bay 17 (OT)	
		West	St. Louis Rams (12-4-0)	Carolina 14, Philadelphia 3	
2004	American	East	New England Patriots (14-2-0)		2004
		North	Pittsburgh Steelers (15-1-0)	Pittsburgh 20, NY Jets* 17 (OT)	
		South	Indianapolis Colts (12-4-0)	New England 20, Indianapolis 3	
		West	San Diego Chargers (12-4-0)	New England 41, Pittsburgh 27	
	National	East	Philadelphia Eagles (13-3-0)		
		North	Green Bay Packers (10-6-0)	Atlanta 47, St. Louis* 17	
		South	Atlanta Falcons (11-5-0)	Philadelphia 27, Minnesota* 14	
		West	Seattle Seahawks (9-7-0)	Philadelphia 27, Atlanta 10	
2005	American	East	New England Patriots (10-6-0)		2005
		North	Cincinnati Bengals (11-5-0)	Denver 27, New England 13	
		South	Indianapolis Colts (14-2-0)	Pittsburgh* 21, Indianapolis 18	
		West	Denver Broncos (13-3-0)	Pittsburgh* 34, Denver 17	
	National	East	NY Giants (11-5-0)		
		North	Chicago Bears (11-5-0)	Seattle 20, Washington* 10	
		South	Tampa Bay Buccaneers (11-5-0)	Carolina* 29, Chicago 21	
		West	Seattle Seahawks (13-3-0)	Seattle 34, Carolina* 14	
2006	American	East	New England Patriots (12-4-0)		2006
		North	Baltimore Ravens (13-3-0)	Indianapolis 15, Baltimore 6	
		South	Indianapolis Colts (12-4-0)	New England 24, San Diego 21	
		West	San Diego Chargers (14-2-0)	Indianapolis 38, New England 34	
	National	East	Philadelphia Eagles (10-6-0)		
		North	Chicago Bears (13-3-0)	New Orleans 27, Philadelphia 24	
		South	New Orleans Saints (10-6-0)	Chicago 27, Seattle 24 (OT)	
		West	Seattle Seahawks (9-7-0)	Chicago 39, New Orleans 14	
2007	American	East	New England Patriots (16-0-0)		2007
		North	Pittsburgh Steelers (10-6-0)	New England 31, Jacksonville* 20	
		South	Indianapolis Colts (13-3-0)	San Diego 28, Indianapolis 24	
		West	San Diego Chargers (11-5-0)	New England 21, San Diego 12	
	National	East	Dallas Cowboys (13-3-0)		
		North	Green Bay Packers (13-3-0)	Green Bay 42, Seattle 20	
		South	Tampa Bay Buccaneers (9-7-0)	NY Giants* 21, Dallas 17	
		West	Seattle Seahawks (10-6-0)	NY Giants* 23, Green Bay 20 (OT)	
2008	American	East	Miami Dolphins (11-5-0)		2008
		North	Pittsburgh Steelers (12-4-0)	Baltimore* 13, Tennessee 10	
		South	Tennessee Titans (13-3-0)	Pittsburgh 35, San Diego 24	
		West	San Diego Chargers (8-8-0)	Pittsburgh 23, Baltimore* 14	
	National	East	NY Giants (12-4-0)		
		North	Minnesota Vikings (10-6-0)	Arizona 33, Carolina 13	
		South	Carolina Panthers (12-4-0)	Philadelphia* 23, NY Giants 11	
		West	Arizona Cardinals (9-7-0)	Arizona 32, Philadelphia* 25	
2009	American	East	New England Patriots (10-6-0)		2009
		North	Cincinnati Bengals (10-6-0)	Indianapolis 20, Baltimore* 3	
		South	Indianapolis Colts (14-2-0)	NY Jets* 17, San Diego 14	
		West	San Diego Chargers (13-3-0)	Indianapolis 30, NY Jets* 17	
	National	East	Dallas Cowboys (11-5-0)		
		North	Minnesota Vikings (12-4-0)	New Orleans 45, Arizona 14	
		South	New Orleans Saints (13-3-0)	Minnesota 34, Dallas 3	
		West	Arizona Cardinals (10-6-0)	New Orleans 31, Minnesota 28 (OT)	
2010	American	East	New England Patriots (14-2-0)		2010
		North	Pittsburgh Steelers (12-4-0)	Pittsburgh 31, Baltimore* 24	
		South	Indianapolis Colts (10-6-0)	NY Jets* 28, New England 21	
		West	Kansas City Chiefs (10-6-0)	Pittsburgh 24, NY Jets* 19	
	National	East	Philadelphia Eagles (10-6-0)		
		North	Chicago Bears (11-5-0)	Green Bay* 48, Atlanta 21	
		South	Atlanta Falcons (13-3-0)	Chicago 35, Seattle 24	
		West	Seattle Seahawks (7-9-0)	Green Bay* 21, Chicago 14	
2011	American	East	New England Patriots (13-3-0)		2011
		North	Baltimore Ravens (12-4-0)	New England 45, Denver 10	
		South	Houston Texans (10-6-0)	Baltimore 20, Houston 13	
		West	Denver Broncos (8-8-0)	New England 23, Baltimore 20	
	National	East	NY Giants (9-7-0)		
		North	Green Bay Packers (15-1-0)	San Francisco 36, New Orleans 32	
		South	New Orleans (13-3-0)	NY Giants 37, Green Bay 20	
		West	San Francisco (13-3-0)	NY Giants 20, San Francisco 17 (OT)	

Year	Conference	Division	Winner (W-L-T)	Playoffs[1]	Year
2012	American	East	New England Patriots (12-4-0)		2012
		North	Baltimore Ravens (10-6-0)	Baltimore 38, Denver 35 (2 OT)	
		South	Houston Texans (12-4-0)	New England 41, Houston 28	
		West	Denver Broncos (13-3-0)	Baltimore 28, New England 13	
	National	East	Washington Redskins (10-6-0)		
		North	Green Bay Packers (11-5-0)	San Francisco 45, Green Bay 31	
		South	Atlanta Falcons (13-3-0)	Atlanta 30, Seattle* 28	
		West	San Francisco 49ers (11-4-1)	San Francisco 28, Atlanta 24	
2013	American	East	New England Patriots (12-4-0)		2013
		North	Cincinnati Bengals (11-5-0)	New England 43, Indianapolis 22	
		South	Indianapolis Colts (11-5-0)	Denver 24, San Diego* 17	
		West	Denver Broncos (13-3-0)	Denver 26, New England 16	
	National	East	Philadelphia Eagles (10-6-0)		
		North	Green Bay Packers (8-7-1)	Seattle 23, New Orleans* 15	
		South	Carolina Panthers (12-4-0)	San Francisco* 23, Carolina 10	
		West	Seattle Seahawks (13-3-0)	Seattle 23, San Francisco* 17	
2014	American	East	New England Patriots (12-4-0)		2014
		North	Pittsburgh Steelers (11-5-0)	New England 35, Baltimore* 31	
		South	Indianapolis Colts (11-5-0)	Indianapolis 24, Denver 13	
		West	Denver Broncos (12-4-0)	New England 45, Indianapolis 7	
	National	East	Dallas Cowboys (12-4-0)		
		North	Green Bay Packers (12-4-0)	Seattle 31, Carolina 17	
		South	Carolina Panthers (7-8-1)	Green Bay 26, Dallas 21	
		West	Seattle Seahawks (12-4-0)	Seattle 28, Green Bay 22 (OT)	
2015	American	East	New England Patriots (12-4-0)		2015
		North	Cincinnati Bengals (12-4-0)	New England 27, Kansas City* 20	
		South	Houston Texans (9-7-0)	Denver 23, Pittsburgh* 16	
		West	Denver Broncos (12-4-0)	Denver 20, New England 18	
	National	East	Washington Redskins (9-7-0)		
		North	Minnesota Vikings (11-5-0)	Arizona 26, Green Bay* 20 (OT)	
		South	Carolina Panthers (15-1-0)	Carolina 31, Seattle* 24	
		West	Arizona Cardinals (13-3-0)	Carolina 49, Arizona 15	
2016	American	East	New England Patriots (14-2-0)		2016
		North	Pittsburgh Steelers (11-5-0)	New England 34, Houston 16	
		South	Houston Texans (9-7-0)	Pittsburgh 18, Kansas City 16	
		West	Kansas City Chiefs (12-4-0)	New England 36, Pittsburgh 17	
	National	East	Dallas Cowboys (13-3-0)		
		North	Green Bay Packers (10-6-0)	Atlanta 36, Seattle 20	
		South	Atlanta Falcons (11-5-0)	Green Bay 34, Dallas 31	
		West	Seattle Seahawks (10-5-1)	Atlanta 44, Green Bay 21	
2017	American	East	New England Patriots (13-3-0)		2017
		North	Pittsburgh Steelers (13-3-0)	New England 35, Tennessee* 14	
		South	Jacksonville Jaguars (10-6-0)	Jacksonville 45, Pittsburgh 42	
		West	Kansas City Chiefs (10-6-0)	New England 24, Jacksonville 20	
	National	East	Philadelphia Eagles (13-3-0)		
		North	Minnesota Vikings (13-3-0)	Philadelphia 15, Atlanta* 10	
		South	New Orleans Saints (11-5-0)	Minnesota 29, New Orleans 24	
		West	Los Angeles Rams (11-5-0)	Philadelphia 38, Minnesota 7	

* = Wild card team. (1) Only the final two conference playoff rounds are shown.

American Football Conference Leaders, 1960-2017

(American Football League, 1960-69)

PASSING (BASED ON QB RATING POINTS)							RECEPTIONS			
Player, team	Rating	Att	Comp	Yds	TD	Year	Player, team	Rec	Yds	TD
Jack Kemp, L.A. Chargers	NA	406	211	3,018	20	1960	Lionel Taylor, Denver	92	1,235	12
George Blanda, Houston	NA	362	187	3,330	36	1961	Lionel Taylor, Denver	100	1,176	4
Len Dawson, Dallas Texans	NA	310	189	2,759	29	1962	Lionel Taylor, Denver	77	908	4
Tobin Rote, San Diego	NA	286	170	2,510	20	1963	Lionel Taylor, Denver	78	1,101	10
Len Dawson, Kansas City	NA	354	199	2,879	30	1964	Charley Hennigan, Houston	101	1,546	8
John Hadl, San Diego	NA	348	174	2,798	20	1965	Lionel Taylor, Denver	85	1,131	6
Len Dawson, Kansas City	NA	284	159	2,527	26	1966	Lance Alworth, San Diego	73	1,383	13
Daryle Lamonica, Oakland	NA	425	220	3,228	30	1967	George Sauer, NY Jets	75	1,189	6
Len Dawson, Kansas City	NA	224	131	2,109	17	1968	Lance Alworth, San Diego	68	1,312	10
Greg Cook, Cincinnati	NA	197	106	1,854	15	1969	Lance Alworth, San Diego	64	1,003	4
Daryle Lamonica, Oakland	NA	356	179	2,516	22	1970	Marlin Briscoe, Buffalo	57	1,036	8
Bob Griese, Miami	NA	263	145	2,089	19	1971	Fred Biletnikoff, Oakland	61	929	9
Earl Morrall, Miami	NA	150	83	1,360	11	1972	Fred Biletnikoff, Oakland	58	802	7
Ken Stabler, Oakland	88.3	260	163	1,997	14	1973	Fred Willis, Houston	57	371	1
Ken Anderson, Cincinnati	95.7	328	213	2,667	18	1974	Lydell Mitchell, Baltimore Colts	72	544	2
Ken Anderson, Cincinnati	93.9	377	228	3,169	21	1975	Reggie Rucker, Cleveland	60	770	3
							Lydell Mitchell, Baltimore Colts	60	554	4
Ken Stabler, Oakland	103.4	291	194	2,737	27	1976	MacArthur Lane, Kansas City	66	686	1
Bob Griese, Miami	87.8	307	180	2,252	22	1977	Lydell Mitchell, Baltimore Colts	71	620	4
Terry Bradshaw, Pittsburgh	84.7	368	207	2,915	28	1978	Steve Largent, Seattle	71	1,168	8
Dan Fouts, San Diego	82.6	530	332	4,082	24	1979	Joe Washington, Baltimore Colts	82	750	3
Brian Sipe, Cleveland	91.4	554	337	4,132	30	1980	Kellen Winslow, San Diego	89	1,290	9
Ken Anderson, Cincinnati	98.4	479	300	3,754	29	1981	Kellen Winslow, San Diego	88	1,075	10
Ken Anderson, Cincinnati	95.3	309	218	2,495	12	1982	Kellen Winslow, San Diego	54	721	6
Dan Marino, Miami	96.0	296	173	2,210	20	1983	Todd Christensen, L.A. Raiders	92	1,247	12
Dan Marino, Miami	108.9	564	362	5,084	48	1984	Ozzie Newsome, Cleveland	89	1,001	5
Ken O'Brien, NY Jets	96.2	488	297	3,888	25	1985	Lionel James, San Diego	86	1,027	6
Dan Marino, Miami	92.5	623	378	4,746	44	1986	Todd Christensen, L.A. Raiders	95	1,153	8
Bernie Kosar, Cleveland	95.4	389	241	3,033	22	1987	Al Toon, NY Jets	68	976	5
Boomer Esiason, Cincinnati	97.4	388	223	3,572	28	1988	Al Toon, NY Jets	93	1,067	5
Boomer Esiason, Cincinnati	92.1	455	258	3,525	28	1989	Andre Reed, Buffalo	88	1,312	9
Jim Kelly, Buffalo	101.2	346	219	2,829	24	1990	Haywood Jeffires, Houston	74	1,048	8
							Drew Hill, Houston	74	1,019	5
Jim Kelly, Buffalo	97.6	474	304	3,844	33	1991	Haywood Jeffires, Houston	100	1,181	7
Warren Moon, Houston	89.3	346	224	2,521	18	1992	Haywood Jeffires, Houston	90	913	9
John Elway, Denver	92.8	551	348	4,030	25	1993	Reggie Langhorne, Indianapolis	85	1,038	3

PASSING (BASED ON QB RATING POINTS)

Player, team	Rating	Att	Comp	Yds	TD
Dan Marino, Miami	89.2	615	385	4,453	30
Jim Harbaugh, Indianapolis	100.7	314	200	2,575	17
John Elway, Denver	89.2	466	287	3,328	26
Mark Brunell, Jacksonville	91.2	435	264	3,281	18
Vinny Testaverde, NY Jets	101.6	421	259	3,256	29
Peyton Manning, Indianapolis	90.7	533	331	4,135	26
Brian Griese, Denver	102.9	336	216	2,688	19
Rich Gannon, Oakland	95.5	549	361	3,828	27
Chad Pennington, NY Jets	104.2	399	275	3,120	22
Steve McNair, Tennessee	100.4	400	250	3,215	24
Peyton Manning, Indianapolis	121.1	497	336	4,557	49
Peyton Manning, Indianapolis	104.1	453	305	3,747	28
Peyton Manning, Indianapolis	101.0	557	362	4,397	31
Tom Brady, New England	117.2	578	398	4,806	50
Philip Rivers, San Diego	105.5	478	312	4,009	34
Philip Rivers, San Diego	104.4	486	317	4,254	28
Tom Brady, New England	111.0	492	324	3,900	36
Tom Brady, New England	105.6	611	401	5,235	39
Peyton Manning, Denver	105.8	583	400	4,659	37
Peyton Manning, Denver	115.1	659	450	5,477	55
Ben Roethlisberger, Pittsburgh	103.3	608	408	4,952	32
Andy Dalton, Cincinnati	106.2	386	255	3,250	25
Tom Brady, New England	112.2	432	291	3,554	28
Alex Smith, Kansas City	104.7	505	341	4,042	26

RECEPTIONS

Year	Player, team	Rec	Yds	TD
1994	Ben Coates, New England	96	1,174	7
1995	Carl Pickens, Cincinnati	99	1,234	17
1996	Carl Pickens, Cincinnati	100	1,180	12
1997	Tim Brown, Oakland	104	1,408	5
1998	O.J. McDuffie, Miami	90	1,050	7
1999	Jimmy Smith, Jacksonville	116	1,636	6
2000	Marvin Harrison, Indianapolis	102	1,413	14
2001	Rod Smith, Denver	113	1,343	11
2002	Marvin Harrison, Indianapolis	143	1,722	11
2003	LaDainian Tomlinson, San Diego	100	725	4
2004	Tony Gonzalez, Kansas City	102	1,258	7
2005	Chad Johnson, Cincinnati	97	1,432	9
2006	Andre Johnson, Houston	103	1,147	5
2007	Wes Welker, New England	112	1,175	8
	T.J. Houshmandzadeh, Cincinnati	112	1,143	12
2008	Andre Johnson, Houston	115	1,575	8
2009	Wes Welker, New England	123	1,348	4
2010	Reggie Wayne, Indianapolis	111	1,355	6
2011	Wes Welker, New England	122	1,569	9
2012	Wes Welker, New England	118	1,354	6
2013	Antonio Brown, Pittsburgh	110	1,499	8
2014	Antonio Brown, Pittsburgh	129	1,698	13
2015	Antonio Brown, Pittsburgh	136	1,834	10
2016	Antonio Brown, Pittsburgh	106	1,284	12
2017	Jarvis Landry, Miami	112	987	9

SCORING

Player, team	TD	XPM	FGM	Pts
Gene Mingo, Denver	6	33	18	123
Gino Cappelletti, Boston	8	48	17	147
Gene Mingo, Denver	4	32	27	137
Gino Cappelletti, Boston	2	35	22	113
Gino Cappelletti, Boston	7	36	25	155
Gino Cappelletti, Boston	9	27	17	132
Gino Cappelletti, Boston	6	35	16	119
George Blanda, Oakland	0	56	20	116
Jim Turner, NY Jets	0	43	34	145
Jim Turner, NY Jets	0	33	32	129
Jan Stenerud, Kansas City	0	26	30	116
Garo Yepremian, Miami	0	33	28	117
Bobby Howfield, NY Jets	0	40	27	121
Roy Gerela, Pittsburgh	0	36	29	123
Roy Gerela, Pittsburgh	0	33	20	93
O.J. Simpson, Buffalo	23	0	0	138
Toni Linhart, Baltimore Colts	0	49	20	109
Errol Mann, Oakland	0	39	20	99
Pat Leahy, NY Jets	0	41	22	107
John Smith, New England	0	46	23	115
John Smith, New England	0	51	26	129
Jim Breech, Cincinnati	0	49	22	115
Nick Lowery, Kansas City	0	37	26	115
Marcus Allen, L.A. Raiders	14	0	0	84
Gary Anderson, Pittsburgh	0	38	27	119
Gary Anderson, Pittsburgh	0	45	24	117
Gary Anderson, Pittsburgh	0	40	33	139
Tony Franklin, New England	0	44	32	140
Jim Breech, Cincinnati	0	25	24	97
Scott Norwood, Buffalo	0	33	32	129
David Treadwell, Denver	0	39	27	120
Nick Lowery, Kansas City	0	37	34	139
Pete Stoyanovich, Miami	0	28	31	121
Pete Stoyanovich, Miami	0	34	30	124
Jeff Jaeger, L.A. Raiders	0	27	35	132
John Carney, San Diego	0	33	34	135
Norm Johnson, Pittsburgh	0	39	34	141
Cary Blanchard, Indianapolis	0	27	36	135
Mike Hollis, Jacksonville	0	41	31	134
Steve Christie, Buffalo	0	41	33	140
Mike Vanderjagt, Indianapolis	0	43	34	145
Matt Stover, Baltimore	0	30	35	135
Mike Vanderjagt, Indianapolis	0	41	28	125
Priest Holmes, Kansas City	24	0	0	144
Priest Holmes, Kansas City	27	0	0	162
Adam Vinatieri, New England	0	48	31	141
Shayne Graham, Cincinnati	0	47	28	131
LaDainian Tomlinson, San Diego	31	0	0	186
Randy Moss, New England	23	0	0	138
Stephen Gostkowski, New England	0	40	36	148
Nate Kaeding, San Diego	0	50	32	146
Sebastian Janikowski, Oakland	0	43	33	142
Stephen Gostkowski, New England	0	59	28	143
Stephen Gostkowski, New England	0	66	29	153
Stephen Gostkowski, New England	0	44	38	158
Stephen Gostkowski, New England	0	51	35	156
Stephen Gostkowski, New England	0	52	33	151
Justin Tucker, Baltimore	0	27	38	141
Stephen Gostkowski	0	45	37	156

RUSHING YARDS

Year	Player, team	Yds	Att	TD
1960	Abner Haynes, Dallas Texans	875	156	9
1961	Billy Cannon, Houston	948	200	6
1962	Cookie Gilchrist, Buffalo	1,096	214	13
1963	Clem Daniels, Oakland	1,099	215	3
1964	Cookie Gilchrist, Buffalo	981	230	6
1965	Paul Lowe, San Diego	1,121	222	7
1966	Jim Nance, Boston	1,458	299	11
1967	Jim Nance, Boston	1,216	269	7
1968	Paul Robinson, Cincinnati	1,023	238	8
1969	Dickie Post, San Diego	873	182	6
1970	Floyd Little, Denver	901	209	3
1971	Floyd Little, Denver	1,133	284	6
1972	O.J. Simpson, Buffalo	1,251	292	6
1973	O.J. Simpson, Buffalo	2,003	332	12
1974	Otis Armstrong, Denver	1,407	263	9
1975	O.J. Simpson, Buffalo	1,817	329	16
1976	O.J. Simpson, Buffalo	1,503	290	8
1977	Mark van Eeghen, Oakland	1,273	324	7
1978	Earl Campbell, Houston	1,450	302	13
1979	Earl Campbell, Houston	1,697	368	19
1980	Earl Campbell, Houston	1,934	373	13
1981	Earl Campbell, Houston	1,376	361	10
1982	Freeman McNeil, NY Jets	786	151	6
1983	Curt Warner, Seattle	1,449	335	13
1984	Earnest Jackson, San Diego	1,179	296	8
1985	Marcus Allen, L.A. Raiders	1,759	380	11
1986	Curt Warner, Seattle	1,481	319	13
1987	Eric Dickerson, L.A. Rams-Ind.	1,288*	283	6
1988	Eric Dickerson, Indianapolis	1,659	388	14
1989	Christian Okoye, Kansas City	1,480	370	12
1990	Thurman Thomas, Buffalo	1,297	271	11
1991	Thurman Thomas, Buffalo	1,407	288	7
1992	Barry Foster, Pittsburgh	1,690	390	11
1993	Thurman Thomas, Buffalo	1,315	355	6
1994	Chris Warren, Seattle	1,545	333	9
1995	Curtis Martin, New England	1,487	368	14
1996	Terrell Davis, Denver	1,538	345	13
1997	Terrell Davis, Denver	1,750	369	15
1998	Terrell Davis, Denver	2,008	392	21
1999	Edgerrin James, Indianapolis	1,553	369	13
2000	Edgerrin James, Indianapolis	1,709	387	13
2001	Priest Holmes, Kansas City	1,555	327	8
2002	Ricky Williams, Miami	1,853	383	16
2003	Jamal Lewis, Baltimore	2,066	387	14
2004	Curtis Martin, NY Jets	1,697	371	12
2005	Larry Johnson, Kansas City	1,750	336	20
2006	LaDainian Tomlinson, San Diego	1,815	348	28
2007	LaDainian Tomlinson, San Diego	1,474	315	15
2008	Thomas Jones, NY Jets	1,312	290	13
2009	Chris Johnson, Tennessee	2,006	358	14
2010	Arian Foster, Houston	1,616	327	16
2011	Maurice Jones-Drew, Jacksonville	1,606	343	8
2012	Jamaal Charles, Kansas City	1,509	285	5
2013	Jamaal Charles, Kansas City	1,287	259	12
2014	Le'Veon Bell, Pittsburgh	1,361	290	8
2015	Chris Ivory, NY Jets	1,070	247	7
2016	DeMarco Murray, Tennessee	1,287	293	9
2017	Kareem Hunt, Kansas City	1,327	272	8

* = Includes 277 yards after being traded to NFC; 1,011 yards led AFC. NA = Not applicable/available. **Note:** Passer ratings for years prior to 1973 were determined by different measures and are not directly comparable to current passer ratings.

National Football Conference Leaders, 1960-2017
(National Football League, 1960-69)

PASSING (BASED ON QB RATING POINTS)

Player, team	Rating	Att	Comp	Yds	TD	Year
Milt Plum, Cleveland	NA	250	151	2,297	21	1960
Milt Plum, Cleveland	NA	302	177	2,416	18	1961
Bart Starr, Green Bay	NA	285	178	2,438	12	1962
Y. A. Tittle, NY Giants	NA	367	221	3,145	36	1963
Bart Starr, Green Bay	NA	272	163	2,144	15	1964
Rudy Bukich, Chicago	NA	312	176	2,641	20	1965
Bart Starr, Green Bay	NA	251	156	2,257	14	1966
Sonny Jurgensen, Washington	NA	508	288	3,747	31	1967
Earl Morrall, Baltimore Colts	NA	317	182	2,909	26	1968
Sonny Jurgensen, Washington	NA	442	274	3,102	22	1969
John Brodie, San Francisco	NA	378	223	2,941	24	1970
Roger Staubach, Dallas	NA	211	126	1,882	15	1971
Norm Snead, NY Giants	NA	325	196	2,307	17	1972
Roger Staubach, Dallas	94.6	286	179	2,428	23	1973
Sonny Jurgensen, Washington	94.5	167	107	1,185	11	1974
Fran Tarkenton, Minnesota	91.8	425	273	2,994	25	1975
James Harris, L.A. Rams	89.6	158	91	1,460	8	1976
Roger Staubach, Dallas	87.0	361	210	2,620	18	1977
Roger Staubach, Dallas	84.9	413	231	3,190	25	1978
Roger Staubach, Dallas	92.3	461	267	3,586	27	1979
Ron Jaworski, Philadelphia	91.0	451	257	3,529	27	1980
Joe Montana, San Francisco	88.4	488	311	3,565	19	1981
Joe Theismann, Washington	91.3	252	161	2,033	13	1982
Steve Bartkowski, Atlanta	97.6	432	274	3,167	22	1983
Joe Montana, San Francisco	102.9	432	279	3,630	28	1984
Joe Montana, San Francisco	91.3	494	303	3,653	27	1985
Tommy Kramer, Minnesota	92.6	372	208	3,000	24	1986
Joe Montana, San Francisco	102.1	398	266	3,054	31	1987
Wade Wilson, Minnesota	91.5	332	204	2,746	15	1988
Joe Montana, San Francisco	112.4	386	271	3,521	26	1989
Phil Simms, NY Giants	92.7	311	184	2,284	15	1990
Steve Young, San Francisco	101.8	279	180	2,517	17	1991
Steve Young, San Francisco	107.0	402	268	3,465	25	1992
Steve Young, San Francisco	101.5	462	314	4,023	29	1993
Steve Young, San Francisco	112.8	461	324	3,969	35	1994
Brett Favre, Green Bay	99.5	570	359	4,413	38	1995
Steve Young, San Francisco	97.2	316	214	2,410	14	1996
Steve Young, San Francisco	104.7	356	241	3,029	19	1997
Randall Cunningham, Minnesota	106.0	425	259	3,704	34	1998
Kurt Warner, St. Louis	109.2	499	325	4,353	41	1999
Trent Green, St. Louis	101.8	240	145	2,063	16	2000
Kurt Warner, St. Louis	101.4	546	375	4,830	36	2001
Brad Johnson, Tampa Bay	92.9	451	281	3,049	22	2002
Daunte Culpepper, Minnesota	96.4	454	295	3,479	25	2003
Daunte Culpepper, Minnesota	110.9	548	379	4,717	39	2004
Matt Hasselbeck, Seattle	98.2	449	294	3,459	24	2005
Drew Brees, New Orleans	96.2	554	356	4,418	26	2006
Tony Romo, Dallas	97.4	520	335	4,211	36	2007
Kurt Warner, Arizona	96.9	598	401	4,583	30	2008
Drew Brees, New Orleans	109.6	514	363	4,388	34	2009
Aaron Rodgers, Green Bay	101.2	475	312	3,922	28	2010
Aaron Rodgers, Green Bay	122.5	502	343	4,643	45	2011
Aaron Rodgers, Green Bay	108.0	552	371	4,295	39	2012
Nick Foles, Philadelphia	119.2	317	203	2,891	27	2013
Tony Romo, Dallas	113.2	435	304	3,705	34	2014
Russell Wilson, Seattle	110.1	483	329	4,024	34	2015
Matt Ryan, Atlanta	117.1	534	373	4,944	38	2016
Drew Brees, New Orleans	103.9	536	386	4,334	23	2017

RECEPTIONS

Year	Player, team	Rec	Yds	TD
1960	Raymond Berry, Baltimore Colts	74	1,298	10
1961	Jim Phillips, L.A. Rams	78	1,092	5
1962	Bobby Mitchell, Washington	72	1,384	11
1963	Bobby Joe Conrad, St. Louis Cardinals	73	967	10
1964	Johnny Morris, Chicago	93	1,200	10
1965	Dave Parks, San Francisco	80	1,344	12
1966	Charley Taylor, Washington	72	1,119	12
1967	Charley Taylor, Washington	70	990	9
1968	Clifton McNeil, San Francisco	71	994	7
1969	Dan Abramowicz, New Orleans	73	1,015	7
1970	Dick Gordon, Chicago	71	1,026	13
1971	Bob Tucker, NY Giants	59	791	4
1972	Harold Jackson, Philadelphia	62	1,048	4
1973	Harold Carmichael, Philadelphia	67	1,116	9
1974	Charles Young, Philadelphia	63	696	3
1975	Chuck Foreman, Minnesota	73	691	9
1976	Drew Pearson, Dallas	58	806	6
1977	Ahmad Rashad, Minnesota	51	681	2
1978	Rickey Young, Minnesota	88	704	5
1979	Ahmad Rashad, Minnesota	80	1,156	9
1980	Earl Cooper, San Francisco	83	567	4
1981	Dwight Clark, San Francisco	85	1,105	4
1982	Dwight Clark, San Francisco	60	913	5
1983	Roy Green, St. Louis Cardinals	78	1,227	14
	Charlie Brown, Washington	78	1,225	8
	Earnest Gray, NY Giants	78	1,139	5
1984	Art Monk, Washington	106	1,372	7
1985	Roger Craig, San Francisco	92	1,016	6
1986	Jerry Rice, San Francisco	86	1,570	15
1987	J. T. Smith, St. Louis Cardinals	91	1,117	8
1988	Henry Ellard, L.A. Rams	86	1,414	10
1989	Sterling Sharpe, Green Bay	90	1,423	12
1990	Jerry Rice, San Francisco	100	1,502	13
1991	Michael Irvin, Dallas	93	1,523	8
1992	Sterling Sharpe, Green Bay	108	1,461	13
1993	Sterling Sharpe, Green Bay	112	1,274	11
1994	Cris Carter, Minnesota	122	1,256	7
1995	Herman Moore, Detroit	123	1,686	14
1996	Jerry Rice, San Francisco	108	1,254	8
1997	Herman Moore, Detroit	104	1,293	8
1998	Frank Sanders, Arizona	89	1,145	3
1999	Muhsin Muhammad, Carolina	96	1,253	8
2000	Muhsin Muhammad, Carolina	102	1,183	6
2001	Keyshawn Johnson, Tampa Bay	106	1,266	1
2002	Randy Moss, Minnesota	106	1,347	7
2003	Torry Holt, St. Louis	117	1,696	12
2004	Joe Horn, New Orleans	94	1,399	11
	Torry Holt, St. Louis	94	1,372	10
2005	Steve Smith, Carolina	103	1,563	12
	Larry Fitzgerald, Arizona	103	1,409	10
2006	Mike Furrey, Detroit	98	1,086	6
2007	Larry Fitzgerald, Arizona	100	1,409	10
2008	Larry Fitzgerald, Arizona	96	1,431	12
2009	Steve Smith, NY Giants	107	1,220	7
2010	Roddy White, Atlanta	115	1,389	10
2011	Roddy White, Atlanta	100	1,296	8
2012	Calvin Johnson, Detroit	122	1,964	5
2013	Pierre Garcon, Washington	113	1,346	5
2014	Julio Jones, Atlanta	104	1,593	6
2015	Julio Jones, Atlanta	136	1,871	8
2016	Larry Fitzgerald, Arizona	107	1,023	6
2017	Larry Fitzgerald, Arizona	109	1,156	6

SCORING

Player, team	TD	XPM	FGM	Pts	Year
Paul Hornung, Green Bay	15	41	15	176	1960
Paul Hornung, Green Bay	10	41	15	146	1961
Jim Taylor, Green Bay	19	0	0	114	1962
Don Chandler, NY Giants	0	52	18	106	1963
Lenny Moore, Baltimore Colts	20	0	0	120	1964
Gale Sayers, Chicago	22	0	0	132	1965
Bruce Gossett, L.A. Rams	0	29	28	113	1966
Jim Bakken, St. Louis Cardinals	0	36	27	117	1967
Leroy Kelly, Cleveland	20	0	0	120	1968
Fred Cox, Minnesota	0	43	26	121	1969
Fred Cox, Minnesota	0	35	30	125	1970
Curt Knight, Washington	0	27	29	114	1971
Chester Marcol, Green Bay	0	29	33	128	1972

RUSHING YARDS

Player, team	Yds	Att	TD	Year
Jim Brown, Cleveland	1,257	215	9	1960
Jim Brown, Cleveland	1,408	305	8	1961
Jim Taylor, Green Bay	1,474	272	19	1962
Jim Brown, Cleveland	1,863	291	12	1963
Jim Brown, Cleveland	1,446	280	7	1964
Jim Brown, Cleveland	1,544	289	17	1965
Gale Sayers, Chicago	1,231	229	8	1966
Leroy Kelly, Cleveland	1,205	235	11	1967
Leroy Kelly, Cleveland	1,239	248	16	1968
Gale Sayers, Chicago	1,032	236	8	1969
Larry Brown, Washington	1,125	237	5	1970
John Brockington, Green Bay	1,105	216	4	1971
Larry Brown, Washington	1,216	285	8	1972

SCORING

Player, team	TD	XPM	FGM	Pts
David Ray, L.A. Rams	0	40	30	130
Chester Marcol, Green Bay	0	19	25	94
Chuck Foreman, Minnesota	22	0	0	132
Mark Moseley, Washington	0	31	22	97
Walter Payton, Chicago	16	0	0	96
Frank Corral, L.A. Rams	0	31	29	118
Mark Moseley, Washington	0	39	25	114
Ed Murray, Detroit	0	35	27	116
Ed Murray, Detroit	0	46	25	121
Rafael Septien, Dallas	0	40	27	121
Wendell Tyler, L.A. Rams	13	0	0	78
Mark Moseley, Washington	0	62	33	161
Ray Wersching, San Francisco	0	56	25	131
Kevin Butler, Chicago	0	51	31	144
Kevin Butler, Chicago	0	36	28	120
Jerry Rice, San Francisco	23	0	0	138
Mike Cofer, San Francisco	0	40	27	121
Mike Cofer, San Francisco	0	49	29	136
Chip Lohmiller, Washington	0	41	30	131
Chip Lohmiller, Washington	0	56	31	149
Morten Andersen, New Orleans	0	33	29	120
Chip Lohmiller, Washington	0	30	30	120
Jason Hanson, Detroit	0	28	34	130
Fuad Reveiz, Minnesota	0	30	34	132
Emmitt Smith, Dallas	22	0	0	132
Emmitt Smith, Dallas	25	0	0	150
John Kasay, Carolina	0	34	37	145
Richie Cunningham, Dallas	0	24	34	126
Gary Anderson, Minnesota	0	59	35	164
Jeff Wilkins, St. Louis	0	64	20	124
Marshall Faulk, St. Louis	26	0	0	160
Marshall Faulk, St. Louis	21	0	0	128
Jay Feely, Atlanta	0	42	32	138
Jeff Wilkins, St. Louis	0	46	39	163
David Akers, Philadelphia	0	41	27	122
Shaun Alexander, Seattle	28	0	0	168
Robbie Gould, Chicago	0	47	32	143
Mason Crosby, Green Bay	0	48	31	141
David Akers, Philadelphia	0	45	33	144
David Akers, Philadelphia	0	43	32	139
David Akers, Philadelphia	0	47	32	143
David Akers, San Francisco	0	34	44	166
Lawrence Tynes, NY Giants	0	46	33	145
Steven Hauschka, Seattle	0	44	33	143
Cody Parkey, Philadelphia	0	54	32	150
Graham Gano, Carolina	0	56	30	146
Matt Bryant, Atlanta	0	56	34	158
Greg Zuerlein, L.A. Rams	0	44	38	158

RUSHING YARDS

Year	Player, team	Yds	Att	TD
1973	John Brockington, Green Bay	1,144	265	3
1974	Lawrence McCutcheon, L.A. Rams	1,109	236	3
1975	Jim Otis, St. Louis Cardinals	1,076	269	5
1976	Walter Payton, Chicago	1,390	311	13
1977	Walter Payton, Chicago	1,852	339	14
1978	Walter Payton, Chicago	1,395	333	11
1979	Walter Payton, Chicago	1,610	369	14
1980	Walter Payton, Chicago	1,460	317	6
1981	George Rogers, New Orleans	1,674	378	13
1982	Tony Dorsett, Dallas	745	177	5
1983	Eric Dickerson, L.A. Rams	1,808	390	18
1984	Eric Dickerson, L.A. Rams	2,105	379	14
1985	Gerald Riggs, Atlanta	1,719	397	10
1986	Eric Dickerson, L.A. Rams	1,821	404	11
1987	Charles White, L.A. Rams	1,374	324	11
1988	Herschel Walker, Dallas	1,514	361	5
1989	Barry Sanders, Detroit	1,470	280	14
1990	Barry Sanders, Detroit	1,304	255	13
1991	Emmitt Smith, Dallas	1,563	365	12
1992	Emmitt Smith, Dallas	1,713	373	18
1993	Emmitt Smith, Dallas	1,486	283	9
1994	Barry Sanders, Detroit	1,883	331	7
1995	Emmitt Smith, Dallas	1,773	377	25
1996	Barry Sanders, Detroit	1,553	307	11
1997	Barry Sanders, Detroit	2,053	335	11
1998	Jamal Anderson, Atlanta	1,846	410	14
1999	Stephen Davis, Washington	1,405	290	17
2000	Robert Smith, Minnesota	1,521	295	7
2001	Stephen Davis, Washington	1,432	356	5
2002	Deuce McAllister, New Orleans	1,388	325	13
2003	Ahman Green, Green Bay	1,883	355	15
2004	Shaun Alexander, Seattle	1,696	353	16
2005	Shaun Alexander, Seattle	1,880	370	27
2006	Frank Gore, San Francisco	1,695	312	8
2007	Adrian Peterson, Minnesota	1,341	238	12
2008	Adrian Peterson, Minnesota	1,760	363	10
2009	Steven Jackson, St. Louis	1,416	324	4
2010	Michael Turner, Atlanta	1,371	334	12
2011	Michael Turner, Atlanta	1,340	301	11
2012	Adrian Peterson, Minnesota	2,097	348	12
2013	LeSean McCoy, Philadelphia	1,607	314	9
2014	DeMarco Murray, Dallas	1,845	392	13
2015	Adrian Peterson, Minnesota	1,485	327	11
2016	Ezekiel Elliott, Dallas	1,631	322	15
2017	Todd Gurley II, L.A. Rams	1,305	279	13

NA = Not applicable/available. **Note:** Passer ratings for years prior to 1973 were determined by different measures and are not directly comparable to current passer ratings.

NFL Most Valuable Player, 1957-2017

The Most Valuable Player is one of many awards given out annually by the Associated Press. Many other organizations give out annual awards honoring the NFL's best players, and those winners may differ from this list.

Year	Player, team	Year	Player, team	Year	Player, team
1957	Jim Brown, Cleveland	1978	Terry Bradshaw, Pittsburgh	1998	Terrell Davis, Denver
1958	Jim Brown, Cleveland	1979	Earl Campbell, Houston	1999	Kurt Warner, St. Louis
1959	Charlie Conerly, NY Giants	1980	Brian Sipe, Cleveland	2000	Marshall Faulk, St. Louis
1960	Norm Van Brocklin, Philadelphia	1981	Ken Anderson, Cincinnati	2001	Kurt Warner, St. Louis
1961	Paul Hornung, Green Bay	1982	Mark Moseley, Washington	2002	Rich Gannon, Oakland
1962	Jim Taylor, Green Bay	1983	Joe Theismann, Washington	2003	Peyton Manning, Indianapolis;
1963	Y. A. Tittle, NY Giants	1984	Dan Marino, Miami		Steve McNair, Tennessee
1964	Johnny Unitas, Baltimore	1985	Marcus Allen, Los Angeles	2004	Peyton Manning, Indianapolis
1965	Jim Brown, Cleveland	1986	Lawrence Taylor, NY Giants	2005	Shaun Alexander, Seattle
1966	Bart Starr, Green Bay	1987	John Elway, Denver	2006	LaDainian Tomlinson, San Diego
1967	Johnny Unitas, Baltimore	1988	Boomer Esiason, Cincinnati	2007	Tom Brady, New England
1968	Earl Morrall, Baltimore	1989	Joe Montana, San Francisco	2008	Peyton Manning, Indianapolis
1969	Roman Gabriel, Los Angeles	1990	Joe Montana, San Francisco	2009	Peyton Manning, Indianapolis
1970	John Brodie, San Francisco	1991	Thurman Thomas, Buffalo	2010	Tom Brady, New England
1971	Alan Page, Minnesota	1992	Steve Young, San Francisco	2011	Aaron Rodgers, Green Bay
1972	Larry Brown, Washington	1993	Emmitt Smith, Dallas	2012	Adrian Peterson, Minnesota
1973	O.J. Simpson, Buffalo	1994	Steve Young, San Francisco	2013	Peyton Manning, Denver
1974	Ken Stabler, Oakland	1995	Brett Favre, Green Bay	2014	Aaron Rodgers, Green Bay
1975	Fran Tarkenton, Minnesota	1996	Brett Favre, Green Bay	2015	Cam Newton, Carolina
1976	Bert Jones, Baltimore	1997	Brett Favre, Green Bay;	2016	Matt Ryan, Atlanta
1977	Walter Payton, Chicago		Barry Sanders, Detroit	2017	Tom Brady, New England

All-Time Professional (NFL and AFL) Football Records

(at end of 2017 season; * = active in 2017; (a) includes AFL statistics; ** = 2-pt conversions scored)

All-Time Defensive Leaders

Interceptions, career: 81, Paul Krause, Washington-Minnesota, 1964-79.

Interceptions, season: 14, Dick "Night Train" Lane, L.A. Rams, 1952.

Interception touchdowns, career: 12, Rod Woodson, Pittsburgh-San Francisco-Baltimore Ravens-Oakland, 1987-2003.

Interception touchdowns, season: 4; Ken Houston, Houston, 1971; Jim Kearney, Kansas City, 1972; Eric Allen, Philadelphia, 1993.

Sacks, career (since 1982): 200.0, Bruce Smith, Buffalo-Washington, 1985-2003.

Sacks, season (since 1982): 22.5, Michael Strahan, NY Giants, 2001.

All-Time Scoring Leaders by Points

Player	Yrs	TD	PAT	FG	Total
Morten Andersen	25	0	849	565	2,544
Adam Vinatieri*	22	0	808**	559	2,487
Gary Anderson	23	0	820	538	2,434
Jason Hanson.	21	0	665	495	2,150
John Carney	23	0	628	478	2,062
Matt Stover	19	0	591	471	2,004
George Blanda (a) . . .	26	9	943	335	2,002
Jason Elam	17	0	675	436	1,983
John Kasay.	20	0	587	461	1,970
Phil Dawson*	19	1	503	436	1,817
Sebastian Janikowski*	17	0	557	414	1,799
Norm Johnson	18	0	638	366	1,736
David Akers.	16	0	563	386	1,721
Nick Lowery	18	0	562	383	1,711

Points, season: 186, LaDainian Tomlinson, San Diego, 2006 (31 TDs).
Points, game: 40, Ernie Nevers, Chicago Cardinals vs. Chicago Bears, Nov. 28, 1929 (6 TDs, 4 PATs).
Touchdowns, season: 31, LaDainian Tomlinson, San Diego, 2006.
Touchdowns, game: 6; Ernie Nevers, Chicago Cardinals vs. Chicago Bears, Nov. 28, 1929 (6 rushing); Dub Jones, Cleveland Browns vs. Chicago Bears, Nov. 25, 1951 (4 rushing, 2 pass receptions); Gale Sayers, Chicago Bears vs. San Francisco, Dec. 12, 1965 (4 rushing, 1 pass reception, 1 punt return).

All-Time Scoring Leaders by Touchdowns

Player	Yrs	Rush	Rec	Ret	TD
Jerry Rice	20	10	197	1	208
Emmitt Smith	15	164	11	0	175
LaDainian Tomlinson . .	11	145	17	0	162
Randy Moss	14	0	156	1	157
Terrell Owens	15	3	153	0	156
Marcus Allen.	16	123	21	1	145
Marshall Faulk	12	100	36	0	136
Cris Carter	16	0	130	1	131
Marvin Harrison	13	0	128	0	128
Jim Brown.	9	106	20	0	126
Walter Payton	13	110	15	0	125
John Riggins.	14	104	12	0	116
Antonio Gates*	15	0	114	0	114
Lenny Moore	12	63	48	2	113
Shaun Alexander	9	100	12	0	112

Points after TD, season: 75, Matt Prater, Denver, 2013.
Consecutive points after TD: 523, Stephen Gostkowski, New England, 2006-16.
Field goals, career: 565, Morten Andersen, New Orleans-Atlanta-NY Giants-Kansas City-Minnesota-Atlanta, 1982-2007.
Field goals, season: 44, David Akers, San Francisco, 2011.
Field goals, game: 8, Rob Bironas, Tennessee vs. Houston, Oct. 21, 2007.
Longest field goal: 64 yards, Matt Prater, Denver vs. Tennesee, Dec. 8, 2013.

All-Time Rushing Leaders

(ranked by rushing yards; * = active in 2017)

Player	Yrs	Att	Yds	Avg	Long	TD
Emmitt Smith	15	4,409	18,355	4.2	75T	164
Walter Payton	13	3,838	16,726	4.4	76	110
Barry Sanders.	10	3,062	15,269	5.0	85	99
Curtis Martin.	11	3,518	14,101	4.0	70T	90
Frank Gore*	13	3,226	14,026	4.4	80T	77
LaDainian Tomlinson	11	3,174	13,684	4.3	85T	145
Jerome Bettis	13	3,479	13,662	3.9	71T	91
Eric Dickerson.	11	2,996	13,259	4.4	85T	90
Tony Dorsett	12	2,936	12,739	4.3	99T	77
Jim Brown.	9	2,359	12,312	5.2	80T	106

Player	Yrs	Att	Yds	Avg	Long	TD
Marshall Faulk	12	2,836	12,279	4.3	71T	100
Adrian Peterson*. . . .	11	2,574	12,276	4.8	82T	99
Edgerrin James	11	3,028	12,246	4.0	72	80
Marcus Allen.	16	3,022	12,243	4.1	61T	123
Franco Harris	13	2,949	12,120	4.1	75T	91
Thurman Thomas . . .	13	2,877	12,074	4.2	80T	65
Fred Taylor	13	2,534	11,695	4.6	80T	66
Steven Jackson.	12	2,764	11,438	4.1	59T	69
John Riggins.	14	2,916	11,352	3.9	66T	104
Corey Dillon	10	2,618	11,241	4.3	96T	82

Yards gained, season: 2,105, Eric Dickerson, L.A. Rams, 1984.
Yards gained, game: 296, Adrian Peterson, Minnesota vs. San Diego, Nov. 4, 2007.
Rushing TDs, career: 164, Emmitt Smith, Dallas-Arizona, 1990-2004.
Rushing TDs, season: 28, LaDainian Tomlinson, San Diego, 2006.

Rushing TDs, game: 6, Ernie Nevers, Chicago Cardinals vs. Chicago Bears, Nov. 28, 1929.
Rushing attempts, game: 45, Jamie Morris, Washington vs. Cincinnati, Dec. 17, 1988 (OT).
Longest run from scrimmage: 99 yards (TD), Tony Dorsett, Dallas vs. Minnesota, Jan. 3, 1983.

All-Time Receiving Leaders

(ranked by number of receptions; * = active in 2017)

Player	Yrs	No.	Yds	Avg	Long	TD
Jerry Rice	20	1,549	22,895	14.8	96T	197
Tony Gonzalez	17	1,325	15,127	11.4	73T	111
Larry Fitzgerald*	14	1,234	15,545	12.6	80T	110
Jason Witten*	15	1,152	12,448	10.8	69	68
Marvin Harrison	13	1,102	14,580	13.2	80T	128
Cris Carter	16	1,101	13,899	12.6	80T	130
Tim Brown.	17	1,094	14,934	13.7	80T	100
Terrell Owens	15	1,078	15,934	14.8	98T	153
Anquan Boldin	14	1,076	13,779	12.8	79T	82
Reggie Wayne	14	1,070	14,345	13.4	80	82

Player	Yrs	No.	Yds	Avg	Long	TD
Andre Johnson	14	1,062	14,185	13.4	77T	70
Steve Smith Sr.	16	1,031	14,731	14.3	80T	81
Isaac Bruce	16	1,024	15,208	14.9	80T	91
Hines Ward	14	1,000	12,083	12.1	85T	85
Randy Moss	14	982	15,292	15.6	82T	156
Brandon Marshall* . .	12	959	12,215	12.7	75T	82
Andre Reed	16	951	13,198	13.9	83T	87
Derrick Mason	15	943	12,061	12.8	79T	66
Art Monk.	16	940	12,721	13.5	79T	68
Antonio Gates*	15	927	11,508	12.4	72T	114

Yards gained, career: 22,895, Jerry Rice, San Francisco-Oakland-Seattle, 1985-2004.
Yards gained, season: 1,964, Calvin Johnson, Detroit, 2012.
Yards gained, game: 336, Willie "Flipper" Anderson, L.A. Rams vs. New Orleans, Nov. 26, 1989 (OT).
Pass receptions, season: 143, Marvin Harrison, Indianapolis, 2002.
Pass receptions, game: 21, Brandon Marshall, Denver vs. Indianapolis, Dec. 13, 2009.

Touchdown receptions, career: 197, Jerry Rice, San Francisco-Oakland-Seattle, 1985-2004.
Touchdown receptions, season: 23, Randy Moss, New England, 2007.
Touchdown receptions, game: 5; Bob Shaw, Chicago Cardinals vs. Baltimore Colts, Oct. 2, 1950; Kellen Winslow, San Diego vs. Oakland, Nov. 22, 1981; Jerry Rice, San Francisco vs. Atlanta, Oct. 14, 1990.

All-Time Passing Leaders

(minimum 1,500 attempts; ranked by quarterback rating points; * = active in 2017)

Player	Yrs	Att	Comp	Yds	TD	Int	Pts[1]
Aaron Rodgers* . . .	13	4,895	3,188	38,502	313	78	103.8
Russell Wilson*. . . .	6	2,834	1,815	22,176	161	56	98.8
Tom Brady*	18	8,805	5,629	66,159	488	160	97.6
Tony Romo	13	4,335	2,829	34,183	248	117	97.1
Steve Young	15	4,149	2,667	33,124	232	107	96.8
Drew Brees*	17	9,294	6,222	70,445	488	228	96.7
Peyton Manning . . .	17	9,380	6,125	71,940	539	251	96.5
Philip Rivers*	14	6,492	4,171	50,348	342	166	94.8
Ben Roethlisberger*	14	6,493	4,164	51,065	329	174	94.0
Kurt Warner	12	4,070	2,666	32,344	208	128	93.7
Kirk Cousins*	6	2,096	1,372	16,206	99	55	93.7

Player	Yrs	Att	Comp	Yds	TD	Int	Pts[1]
Matt Ryan*	10	5,593	3,630	41,796	260	126	93.4
Joe Montana.	15	5,391	3,409	40,551	273	139	92.3
Chad Pennington . .	11	2,471	1,632	17,823	102	64	90.1
Matt Schaub	13	3,274	2,093	24,867	133	90	89.1
Colin Kaepernick . .	6	1,692	1,011	12,271	72	30	88.9
Andy Dalton*	7	3,556	2,217	25,534	167	93	88.7
Matthew Stafford*. .	9	4,850	3,005	34,749	216	118	88.3
Carson Palmer* . . .	14	6,307	3,941	46,247	294	187	87.9
Derek Carr*	3	1,732	1,055	11,194	81	31	87.9
Daunte Culpepper. .	11	3,199	2,016	24,153	149	106	87.8

(1) Rating points based on performances in the following categories: percentage of completions, percentage of touchdown passes, percentage of interceptions, and average gain per pass attempt.

Yards gained, career: 71,940, Peyton Manning, Indianapolis-Denver, 1998-2015.

Yards gained, season: 5,477, Peyton Manning, Denver, 2013.

Yards gained, game: 554, Norm Van Brocklin, L.A. Rams vs. NY Yanks, Sept. 28, 1951 (27 completions in 41 attempts).

Touchdowns passing, career: 539, Peyton Manning, Indianapolis-Denver, 1998-2015.

Touchdowns passing, season: 55, Peyton Manning, Denver, 2013.

Touchdowns passing, game: 7; Sid Luckman, Chicago Bears vs. NY Giants, Nov. 14, 1943; Adrian Burk, Philadelphia vs. Washington, Oct. 17, 1954; George Blanda, Houston vs. NY Titans, Nov. 19, 1961; Y. A. Tittle, NY Giants vs. Washington, Oct. 28, 1962; Joe Kapp, Minnesota vs. Baltimore Colts, Sept. 28, 1969; Peyton Manning, Denver vs. Baltimore, Sept. 5, 2013; Nick Foles, Philadelphia vs. Oakland, Nov. 3, 2013; Drew Brees, New Orleans vs. NY Giants, Nov. 1, 2015.

Passes completed, career: 6,300, Brett Favre, Atlanta-Green Bay-NY Jets-Minnesota, 1991-2010.

Passes completed, season: 471, Drew Brees, New Orleans, 2016.

Passes completed, game: 45, Drew Bledsoe, New England vs. Minnesota, Nov. 13, 1994 (OT).

National Football League Franchise Origins

(Team: founding year, league. Home stadium location; subsequent history.)

Arizona Cardinals: 1920, American Professional Football Association (APFA)[1]. Chicago, 1920-59; St. Louis, 1960-87; Tempe, AZ, 1988-2005; Glendale, AZ, 2006-present.

Atlanta Falcons: 1966, NFL. Atlanta, GA, 1966-present.

Baltimore Ravens: 1996, NFL. Baltimore, 1996-present.

Buffalo Bills: 1960, American Football League (AFL)[2]. Buffalo, 1960-72; Orchard Park, NY, 1973-present.

Carolina Panthers: 1995, NFL. Clemson, SC, 1995; Charlotte, NC, 1996-present.

Chicago Bears: 1920, APFA. Decatur, IL, 1920; Chicago, 1921-present.

Cincinnati Bengals: 1968, AFL. Cincinnati, 1968-present.

Cleveland Browns: 1946, All-America Football Conference (AAFC)[3]. Cleveland, 1946-95; 1999-present.

Dallas Cowboys: 1960, NFL. Dallas, 1960-70; Irving, TX, 1971-2008; Arlington, TX, 2009-present.

Denver Broncos: 1960, AFL. Denver, 1960-present.

Detroit Lions: 1930, NFL. Portsmouth, OH, 1930-33; Detroit, 1934-74; Pontiac, MI, 1975-2001; Detroit, 2002-present.

Green Bay Packers: 1921, APFA. Green Bay, WI, 1921-present.

Houston Texans: 2002, NFL. Houston, 2002-present.

Indianapolis Colts: 1953, NFL[3]. Baltimore, 1953-83; Indianapolis, 1984-present.

Jacksonville Jaguars: 1995, NFL. Jacksonville, FL, 1995-present.

Kansas City Chiefs: 1960, AFL. Dallas, 1960-62; Kansas City, MO, 1963-present.

L.A. Chargers: 1960, AFL. Los Angeles, 1960; San Diego, 1961-2016. Los Angeles, 2017-present.

L.A. Rams: 1937, NFL. Cleveland, 1937-45; Los Angeles, 1946-79; Anaheim, CA, 1980-94; St. Louis, 1995-2015; L.A., 2016-present.

Miami Dolphins: 1966, AFL. Miami, 1966-2002; Miami Gardens, FL, 2003-present.

Minnesota Vikings: 1961, NFL. Bloomington, MN, 1961-81; Minneapolis, 1982-present.

New England Patriots: 1960, AFL. Boston, 1960-70; Foxborough, MA, 1971-present.

New Orleans Saints: 1967, NFL. New Orleans, 1967-2004; Baton Rouge and San Antonio, 2005; New Orleans, 2006-present.

NY Giants: 1925, NFL. New York, NY, 1925-73; 1975; New Haven, CT, 1973-74; E. Rutherford, NJ, 1976-present.

NY Jets: 1960, AFL. New York, NY, 1960-83; E. Rutherford, NJ, 1984-present.

Oakland Raiders: 1960, AFL. San Francisco, 1960-61; Oakland, CA, 1962-81; Los Angeles, 1982-94; Oakland, CA, 1995-present. The Raiders gained league approval, Mar. 2017, to move the franchise to Las Vegas, NV, for the start of the 2020 season.

Philadelphia Eagles: 1933, NFL. Philadelphia, 1933-present.

Pittsburgh Steelers: 1933, NFL. Pittsburgh, 1933-present.

San Francisco 49ers: 1946, AAFC. San Francisco, 1946-2013; Santa Clara, CA, 2014-present.

Seattle Seahawks: 1976, NFL. Seattle, 1976-present.

Tampa Bay Buccaneers: 1976, NFL. Tampa, FL, 1976-present.

Tennessee Titans: 1960, AFL. Houston, 1960-96; Memphis, 1997; Nashville, 1998-present.

Washington Redskins: 1932, NFL. Boston, 1932-36; Washington, DC, 1937-96; Landover, MD, 1997-present.

(1) The American Professional Football Association (APFA) was formed in 1920 to standardize the rules of professional football. In 1922, the name was changed to the National Football League (NFL). (2) The most successful of four leagues called the American Football League, or AFL (1926; 1936-37; 1940-41; 1960-69). Congress approved an NFL/AFL merger in 1966. The unified NFL began play in 1970 with 26 teams. (3) The All-America Football Conference (AAFC), 1946-49. In 1950, three of its teams joined the NFL (Baltimore, Cleveland, and San Francisco). The Baltimore franchise failed, but the NFL awarded the city a second one, also called the Colts, in 1953.

NFL Stadiums

(**A** = A-Turf Titan, **D** = DD Grassmaster (grass), **F** = FieldTurf, **G** = Grass, **M** = Matrix SoftTop Convertible Turf, **N** = Natural grass, **S** = Synthetic, **SM** = Sportexe Momentum, **U** = UBU Speed Series S5-M)

Team: stadium, location, surface (year built)	Capacity[1]	Team: stadium, location, surface (year built)	Capacity[1]
Bears: Soldier Field[2], Chicago, IL, N (1924)	61,500	**Giants:** MetLife Stadium[9], E. Rutherford, NJ, U (2010)	82,500
Bengals: Paul Brown Stadium, Cincinnati, OH, U (2000)	65,515	**Jaguars:** EverBank Field[10], Jacksonville, FL, G (1995)	64,428
Bills: New Era Field[3], Orchard Park, NY, A (1973)	71,870	**Jets:** MetLife Stadium[9], E. Rutherford, NJ, U (2010)	82,500
Broncos: Sports Authority Field at Mile High[4], Denver, CO, N (2001)	76,125	**Lions:** Ford Field, Detroit, MI, F (2002)	65,000
Browns: FirstEnergy Stadium[5], Cleveland, OH, G (1999)	67,431	**Packers:** Lambeau Field[11], Green Bay, WI, G (1957)	81,441
Buccaneers: Raymond James Stadium, Tampa, FL, G (1998)	65,890	**Panthers:** Bank of America Stadium[12], Charlotte, NC, G (1996)	75,525
Cardinals: University of Phoenix Stadium, Glendale, AZ, G (2006)	63,400	**Patriots:** Gillette Stadium, Foxborough, MA, F (2002)	66,829
Chargers: StubHub Center[6], Carson, CA, G (2003)	30,000	**Raiders:** Oakland-Alameda County Coliseum[13], Oakland, CA, G (1966)	56,057
Chiefs: Arrowhead Stadium, Kansas City, MO, G (1972; fully renovated 2010)	76,416	**Rams:** Los Angeles Memorial Coliseum[14], Los Angeles, CA, N (1923)	93,607
Colts: Lucas Oil Stadium, Indianapolis, IN, F (2008)	63,000	**Ravens:** M&T Bank Stadium[15], Baltimore, MD, SM (1998)	71,008
Cowboys: AT&T Stadium[7], Arlington, TX, M (2009)	80,000	**Redskins:** FedEx Field[16], Landover, MD, N (1997)	82,000
Dolphins: Hard Rock Stadium[8], Miami Gardens, FL, G (1987)	65,326	**Saints:** Mercedes-Benz Superdome[17], New Orleans, LA, U (1975)	73,208
Eagles: Lincoln Financial Field, Philadelphia, PA, N (2003)	69,596	**Seahawks:** CenturyLink Field[18], Seattle, WA, F (2002)	68,000
Falcons: Mercedes-Benz Stadium, Atlanta, GA, F (2017)	71,000	**Steelers:** Heinz Field, Pittsburgh, PA, N (2001)	68,400
49ers: Levi's Stadium, Santa Clara, CA, N (2014)	68,500	**Texans:** NRG Stadium[19], Houston, TX, S (2002)	71,795
		Titans: Nissan Stadium[20], Nashville, TN, N (1999)	69,143
		Vikings: U.S. Bank Stadium[21], Minneapolis, MN, U (2016)	66,655

(1) As of the start of the 2016 season. (2) Renovation in 2002 replaced interior of stadium. (3) Formerly Rich Stadium (1973-98); Ralph Wilson Stadium (1998-2015). (4) Formerly INVESCO Field at Mile High (2001-11). (5) Formerly Cleveland Browns Stadium (1999-2012). (6) Formerly San Diego Stadium (1967-80); San Diego Jack Murphy Stadium (1981-97). (7) Formerly Cowboys Stadium (2009-12). (8) Formerly Joe Robbie Stadium (1987-96); Pro Player Park/Stadium (1996-2005); Dolphin(s) Stadium (2005-09, 2010); Land Shark Stadium (2009); Sun Life Stadium (2010-16); New Miami Stadium (2016). (9) Formerly New Meadowlands Stadium (2010-11). (10) Formerly Alltel Stadium (1997-2007); Jacksonville Municipal Stadium (1946-97, 2007-09). (11) Formerly City Stadium (1957-65). Renovation completed in 2003 added 11,625 seats. (12) Formerly Ericsson Stadium (1996-2003). (13) Formerly Oakland-Alameda County Coliseum (1966-98); Network Associates Coliseum (1998-2004); McAfee Stadium (2004-08); Oakland Coliseum (2008-11); O.co Coliseum (2011-15). (14) The Rams relocated to Los Angeles prior to the 2016 season after 21 years in St. Louis from 1994-2015. (15) Formerly PSINet Stadium (1998-2002); Ravens Stadium (2002-03). (16) Formerly Jack Kent Cooke Stadium (1997-99). (17) Formerly Louisiana Superdome (1975-2011). (18) Formerly Seahawks Stadium (2002-04); Qwest Field (2004-11). (19) Formerly Reliant Stadium (2002-13). (20) Formerly Adelphia Coliseum (1999-2002); The Coliseum (2002-06); LP Field (2006-15). (21) The Vikings opened their new U.S. Bank Stadium in 2016 after playing at the Univ. of Minnesota's TCF Bank Stadium in 2014 and 2015.

Pro Football Hall of Fame

Located in Canton, OH. * = Member elected in Feb. 2018 and inducted Aug. 4, 2018. www.profootballhof.com

Herb Adderley
Troy Aikman
George Allen
Larry Allen
Marcus Allen
Lance Alworth
Morten Andersen
Doug Atkins
Morris "Red" Badgro
Lem Barney
Cliff Battles
Sammy Baugh
*Bobby Beathard
Chuck Bednarik
Bert Bell
Bobby Bell
Raymond Berry
Elvin Bethea
Jerome Bettis
Charles Bidwill
Fred Biletnikoff
George Blanda
Mel Blount
Terry Bradshaw
*Robert Brazile
Derrick Brooks
Bob Brown
Jim Brown
Paul Brown
Roosevelt Brown
Tim Brown
Willie Brown
Junious "Buck"
  Buchanan
Nick Buoniconti
Dick Butkus
Jack Butler
Earl Campbell
Tony Canadeo
Joe Carr
Harry Carson
Cris Carter
Dave Casper
Guy Chamberlin
Jack Christiansen
Earl "Dutch" Clark
George Connor
Jim Conzelman
Lou Creekmur
Larry Csonka
Curley Culp
Al Davis
Terrell Davis
Willie Davis
Dermontti Dawson
Len Dawson
Fred Dean
Edward DeBartolo Jr.
Joe DeLamielleure
Richard Dent
Eric Dickerson
Dan Dierdorf
Mike Ditka
Chris Doleman

Art Donovan
Tony Dorsett
John "Paddy" Driscoll
Bill Dudley
Tony Dungy
Kenny Easley
Glen "Turk" Edwards
Carl Eller
John Elway
Weeb Ewbank
Marshall Faulk
Brett Favre
Tom Fears
Jim Finks
Ray Flaherty
Len Ford
Dr. Daniel Fortmann
Dan Fouts
Benny Friedman
Frank Gatski
Bill George
Joe Gibbs
Frank Gifford
Sid Gillman
Otto Graham
Harold "Red" Grange
Bud Grant
Darrell Green
Joe Greene
Kevin Greene
Forrest Gregg
Bob Griese
Russ Grimm
Lou Groza
Ray Guy
Joe Guyon
George Halas
Charles Haley
Jack Ham
Dan Hampton
Chris Hanburger
John Hannah
Franco Harris
Marvin Harrison
Bob Hayes
Mike Haynes
Mel Hein
Ted Hendricks
Wilbur "Pete" Henry
Arnold Herber
Bill Hewitt
Gene Hickerson
Clarke Hinkle
Elroy "Crazylegs" Hirsch
Paul Hornung
Ken Houston
Robert "Cal" Hubbard
Sam Huff
Claude Humphrey
Lamar Hunt
Don Hutson
Michael Irvin
Rickey Jackson
Jimmy Johnson

John Henry Johnson
Charlie Joiner
David "Deacon" Jones
Jerry Jones
Stan Jones
Walter Jones
Henry Jordan
Sonny Jurgensen
Jim Kelly
Leroy Kelly
Cortez Kennedy
Walt Kiesling
Frank "Bruiser" Kinard
*Jerry Kramer
Paul Krause
Earl "Curly" Lambeau
Jack Lambert
Tom Landry
Dick "Night Train" Lane
Jim Langer
Willie Lanier
Steve Largent
Yale Lary
Dante Lavelli
Bobby Layne
Dick LeBeau
Alphonse "Tuffy"
  Leemans
Marv Levy
*Ray Lewis
Bob Lilly
Floyd Little
Larry Little
James Lofton
Vince Lombardi
Howie Long
Ronnie Lott
Sid Luckman
Roy "Link" Lyman
Tom Mack
John Mackey
John Madden
Tim Mara
Wellington Mara
Gino Marchetti
Dan Marino
George Preston Marshall
Curtis Martin
Bruce Mathews
Ollie Matson
Don Maynard
George McAfee
Mike McCormack
Randall McDaniel
Tommy McDonald
Hugh McElhenny
Johnny "Blood" McNally
Mike Michalske
Wayne Millner
Bobby Mitchell
Ron Mix
Art Monk
Joe Montana

Warren Moon
Lenny Moore
*Randy Moss
Marion Motley
Mike Munchak
Anthony Muñoz
George Musso
Bronko Nagurski
Joe Namath
Earle "Greasy" Neale
Ernie Nevers
Ozzie Newsome
Ray Nitschke
Chuck Noll
Leo Nomellini
Jonathan Ogden
Merlin Olsen
Jim Otto
Steve Owen
*Terrell Owens
Orlando Pace
Alan Page
Bill Parcells
Clarence "Ace" Parker
Jim Parker
Walter Payton
Joe Perry
Pete Pihos
Bill Polian
Fritz Pollard
John Randle
Hugh "Shorty" Ray
Andre Reed
Dan Reeves
Mel Renfro
Jerry Rice
Les Richter
John Riggins
Jim Ringo
Willie Roaf
Dave Robinson
Andy Robustelli
Art Rooney
Dan Rooney
Pete Rozelle
Ed Sabol
Bob St. Clair
Barry Sanders
Charlie Sanders
Deion Sanders
Warren Sapp
Gale Sayers
Joe Schmidt
Tex Schramm
Junior Seau
Lee Roy Selmon
Shannon Sharpe
Billy Shaw
Art Shell
Will Shields
Don Shula
O.J. Simpson
Mike Singletary

Jackie Slater
Bruce Smith
Emmitt Smith
Jackie Smith
Ken Stabler
John Stallworth
Dick Stanfel
Bart Starr
Roger Staubach
Ernie Stautner
Jan Stenerud
Dwight Stephenson
Michael Strahan
Hank Stram
Ken Strong
Joe Stydahar
Lynn Swann
Fran Tarkenton
Charley Taylor
Jason Taylor
Jim Taylor
Lawrence "LT" Taylor
Derrick Thomas
Emmitt Thomas
Thurman Thomas
Jim Thorpe
Mick Tingelhoff
Andre Tippett
Y. A. Tittle
LaDainian Tomlinson
George Trafton
Charley Trippi
Emlen Tunnell
Clyde "Bulldog" Turner
Johnny Unitas
Gene Upshaw
*Brian Urlacher
Norm Van Brocklin
Steve Van Buren
Doak Walker
Bill Walsh
Paul Warfield
Kurt Warner
Bob Waterfield
Mike Webster
Arnie Weinmeister
Randy White
Reggie White
Dave Wilcox
Aeneas Williams
Bill Willis
Larry Wilson
Ralph Wilson Jr.
Kellen Winslow
Alex Wojciechowicz
Ron Wolf
Willie Wood
Rod Woodson
Rayfield Wright
Ron Yary
Steve Young
Jack Youngblood
Gary Zimmerman

All-Time NFL Coaching Victories

(at end of 2017 season; ranked by overall career wins; * = active in 2017)

Coach	Team	Yrs	Regular Season				Overall			
			W	L	T	Pct	W	L	T	Pct
Don Shula	Baltimore Colts, Dolphins	33	328	156	6	.677	347	173	6	.666
George Halas	Bears	40	318	148	31	.682	324	151	31	.682
Bill Belichick*	Browns, Patriots	23	250	118	0	.679	278	129	0	.683
Tom Landry	Cowboys	29	250	162	6	.607	270	178	6	.603
Earl "Curly" Lambeau	Packers, Chicago Cardinals, Redskins	33	226	132	22	.631	229	134	22	.631
Chuck Noll	Steelers	23	193	148	1	.566	209	156	1	.572
Marty Schottenheimer	Browns, Chiefs, Redskins, Chargers	21	200	126	1	.613	205	139	1	.596
Dan Reeves	Broncos, Giants, Falcons	23	190	165	2	.535	201	174	2	.536
Andy Reid*	Eagles, Chiefs	19	183	120	1	.604	194	133	1	.593
Chuck Knox	L.A. Rams, Bills, Seahawks	22	186	147	1	.558	193	158	1	.550
Bill Parcells	Giants, Patriots, Jets, Cowboys	19	172	130	1	.569	183	138	1	.570
Tom Coughlin	Jaguars, Giants	20	170	150	0	.531	182	157	0	.537
Jeff Fisher	Houston/Tennessee Oilers, Titans; St. Louis/ L.A. Rams	22	173	165	1	.512	178	171	1	.510
Mike Shanahan	L.A. Raiders, Broncos, Redskins	20	170	138	0	.552	178	144	0	.553
Mike Holmgren	Packers, Seahawks	17	161	111	0	.592	174	122	0	.588
Joe Gibbs	Redskins	16	154	94	0	.621	171	101	0	.629
Paul Brown	Browns, Bengals	21	166	100	6	.624	170	108	6	.612
Bud Grant	Vikings	18	158	96	5	.621	168	108	5	.608
Bill Cowher	Steelers	15	149	90	1	.623	161	99	1	.619

Note: Official NFL records do not include All-America Football Conference statistics.

BASEBALL

Playoff Results, 2018

American League

American League Wild Card Game: NY Yankees 7, Oakland 2.
American League Division Series (ALDS): Boston defeated NY Yankees, 3 games to 1; Houston defeated Cleveland, 3 games to 0.
American League Championship Series (ALCS): Boston defeated Houston, 4 games to 1.

National League

National League Wild Card Game: Colorado 2, Chicago Cubs 1 (13 innings).
National League Division Series (NLDS): Milwaukee defeated Colorado, 3 games to 0; L.A. Dodgers defeated Atlanta, 3 games to 1.
National League Championship Series (NLCS): L.A. Dodgers defeated Milwaukee, 4 games to 3.

World Series, 2018: As Red Sox Win Again, Dodgers Lose Second Straight

The Boston Red Sox defeated the Los Angeles Dodgers in five games to win the 2018 World Series, their fourth MLB crown since 2004. Seeking their first title since 1988, the Dodgers went home empty-handed in their second straight trip to the Fall Classic, having lost to the Houston Astros in 2017.

The Red Sox slammed four home runs in their Series-clinching, 5-1 win in Game 5, Oct. 28, 2018, at Dodger Stadium in Los Angeles, CA. Left-hander David Price gave up only three hits in seven innings to earn his second win of the Series. Joe Kelly and Chris Sale each struck out the side in the eighth and ninth innings, respectively, to lift Boston to its first title since 2013. Journeyman first baseman Steve Pearce hit two of Boston's Game 5 home runs, a two-run shot in the first inning and a solo homer in the eighth. The veteran, acquired by the Red Sox in a June trade, hit three home runs in the Series and batted .333 with 8 RBI to earn World Series Most Valuable Player.

After the Red Sox won the first two games at Fenway Park in Boston, MA, the teams made history with the longest game in World Series history, a 7-hour, 20-minute marathon Game 3 at Dodger Stadium that began on Oct. 26. Dodgers infielder Max Muncy won the game in the 18th inning with a solo home run off Nathan Eovaldi, who entered in the 12th inning and threw 97 pitches. Both teams had scored a run in the 13th inning before Muncy's heroics brought the game to an end, 3-2, at 12:30 AM local time.

Eduardo Núñez slammed a pinch-hit, three-run homer in the seventh inning of Game 1 to power the Red Sox to an 8-4 victory over the Dodgers, Oct. 23, 2018, in Boston, as Matt Barnes earned the win in relief of Sale. After a shaky start in the ALDS and ALCS, Price started Game 2 and allowed only three hits in six innings. Kelly, Eovaldi, and Craig Kimbrel shut down the Dodgers in the last three innings of Boston's 4-2 victory Oct. 24 at Fenway. The Dodgers' hits all came in the fourth inning when they briefly went ahead, 2-1, but the Red Sox took the lead for good with three runs in the fifth inning, capped by J.D. Martinez's two-run single.

The Red Sox scored all of their Game 4 runs in the last three innings of a 9-6 victory Oct. 27 in Los Angeles. L.A. outfielder Yasiel Puig hit a three-run homer for a 4-0 Dodgers lead in the sixth, but Boston's Mitch Moreland started the comeback in the seventh with a pinch-hit, three-run homer off reliever Ryan Madson. Pearce drove in four runs in the game, with a game-tying solo homer in the eighth and a three-run double in Boston's five-run ninth inning.

Game 1

Oct. 23 at Fenway Park, Boston, MA. Attendance: 38,454. Game time: 3:52.

	1	2	3	4	5	6	7	8	9	R	H	E
L.A. Dodgers	0	1	1	0	1	0	1	0	0	4	8	0
Boston Red Sox	2	0	1	0	2	0	3	0	X	8	11	0

Winning pitcher: Matt Barnes
Losing pitcher: Clayton Kershaw

Game 2

Oct. 24 at Fenway Park, Boston, MA. Attendance: 38,644. Game time: 3:12.

	1	2	3	4	5	6	7	8	9	R	H	E
L.A. Dodgers	0	0	0	2	0	0	0	0	0	2	3	0
Boston Red Sox	0	1	0	0	3	0	0	0	X	4	8	0

Winning pitcher: David Price
Losing pitcher: Hyun-Jin Ryu
Save: Craig Kimbrel

Game 3

Oct. 26 at Dodger Stadium, Los Angeles, CA. Attendance: 53,114. Game time: 7:20.

	1	2	3	4	5	6	7	8	9	10	11	12	13	14	15	16	17	18	R	H	E
Boston Red Sox	0	0	0	0	0	0	1	0	0	0	0	0	1	0	0	0	0	0	2	7	1
L.A. Dodgers	0	0	1	0	0	0	0	0	0	0	0	0	1	0	0	0	0	1	3	11	1

Winning pitcher: Alex Wood
Losing pitcher: Nathan Eovaldi

Game 4

Oct. 27 at Dodger Stadium, Los Angeles, CA. Attendance: 54,400. Game time: 3:57.

	1	2	3	4	5	6	7	8	9	R	H	E
Boston Red Sox	0	0	0	0	0	0	3	1	5	9	8	1
L.A. Dodgers	0	0	0	0	0	4	0	0	2	6	9	0

Winning pitcher: Joe Kelly
Losing pitcher: Dylan Floro

Game 5

Oct. 28 at Dodger Stadium, Los Angeles, CA. Attendance: 54,367. Game time: 3:00.

	1	2	3	4	5	6	7	8	9	R	H	E
Boston Red Sox	2	0	0	0	0	1	1	1	0	5	8	0
L.A. Dodgers	1	0	0	0	0	0	0	0	0	1	3	0

Winning pitcher: David Price
Losing pitcher: Clayton Kershaw

Major League Baseball 2018: Red Sox Reign

The World Series-champion Boston Red Sox won a franchise-record 108 games under first-year manager Alex Cora and led the majors in team batting (.268) and runs (876). Outfielder Mookie Betts won the AL batting title with an MLB-best .346 average, ahead of teammate J.D. Martinez, who finished second in batting (.330) and home runs (43) and led the majors with 130 RBI. Betts (.640) and Martinez (.629) also finished 1-2 in the majors in slugging. Boston advanced to the Fall Classic by beating the defending champion Houston Astros in five games in the American League Championship Series. Boston's Jackie Bradley Jr. drove in nine runs in the ALCS and won series MVP.

The Astros also set a franchise record with 103 wins to win the AL West crown for the second year in a row. Astros veteran right-hander Justin Verlander (16-9, 2.52 ERA) led the AL with 290 strikeouts, ahead of teammate Gerrit Cole, with 276 strikeouts and 15 wins. Houston reached the ALCS when it swept its AL Division Series against Cleveland, which had won its third straight AL Central crown. The Red Sox defeated the NY Yankees in their AL Division Series in four games, including a Game 3, 16-1 win Oct. 8, 2018, at Yankee Stadium in the Bronx, NY. The Yankees beat Oakland, 7-2, in the AL Wild Card Game, Oct. 3, at Yankee Stadium. The Athletics (97-65) reached the postseason after three straight last-place finishes in the AL West.

The Dodgers made back-to-back trips to the World Series for the first time since 1977-78, and won the 2018 NL pennant in seven games over the Milwaukee Brewers. Cody Bellinger hit a go-ahead two-run homer and Yasiel Puig added a three-run shot in the Dodgers' 5-1 win over the Brewers in Game 7 of the NLCS Oct. 20 at Miller Park in Milwaukee, WI. After winning a tiebreaker game over the Colorado Rockies to claim the NL West crown, L.A. defeated the NL East champion Atlanta Braves, who were making their first postseason appearance since 2013, in four games in their NLDS.

Milwaukee beat the Chicago Cubs, 3-1, in tiebreaker game No. 163, Oct. 1, at Wrigley Field in Chicago to win the NL Central title. Brewers outfielder Christian Yelich, acquired from Miami in the offseason, became Milwaukee's first-ever batting champion with an NL-high .326 average, along with 36 home runs and 110 RBI. Milwaukee shut out Colorado twice in their NLDS to win a three-game sweep. Colorado had defeated the Chicago Cubs, 2-1 in 13 innings, in the NL Wild Card Game on Oct. 2 at Wrigley Field.

Japanese pitcher/designated hitter Shohei Ohtani made his MLB debut with the L.A. Angels in 2018, batting .285 with 22 homers while going 4-2 with a 3.31 ERA in 10 starts. Ohtani's pitching season was shortened by an elbow injury, but he joined Babe Ruth as the only two players in MLB history to record 20 or more home runs and make at least 10 pitching appearances in the same season. Angels veteran Albert Pujols joined the 3,000-hit club when he singled off Seattle's Mike Leake in L.A.'s 5-0 victory on May 4 at Safeco Field in Seattle.

Jacob deGrom was only 10-9 for the fourth-place NY Mets, but he led the majors with a stellar 1.70 ERA. The right-hander was second in the NL with 269 strikeouts behind Washington's Max Scherzer, who fanned an MLB-high 300 batters. Tampa Bay left-hander Blake Snell led the American League in both wins (21) and ERA (1.89).

National League Final Standings, 2018

(* = wild card)

Eastern Division

Team	W	L	PCT	GB	Home	Road	vs. East	vs. Central	vs. West	vs. AL
Atlanta	90	72	.556	—	43-38	47-34	49-27	18-14	15-19	8-12
Washington	82	80	.506	8	41-40	41-40	41-35	18-16	14-18	9-11
Philadelphia	80	82	.494	10	49-32	31-50	34-42	19-14	15-18	12-8
NY Mets	77	85	.475	13	37-44	40-41	40-36	13-20	16-17	8-12
Miami	63	98	.391	26.5	38-43	25-55	26-50	13-19	15-18	9-11

Central Division

Team	W	L	PCT	GB	Home	Road	vs. East	vs. Central	vs. West	vs. AL
Milwaukee	96	67	.589	—	51-30	45-37	20-13	40-37	23-10	13-7
Chicago Cubs*	95	68	.583	1	51-31	44-37	22-11	41-36	19-14	13-7
St. Louis	88	74	.543	7.5	43-38	45-36	16-16	41-35	20-14	11-9
Pittsburgh	82	79	.509	13	44-36	38-43	12-20	43-33	12-21	15-5
Cincinnati	67	95	.414	28.5	37-44	30-51	13-21	26-50	18-14	10-10

Western Division

Team	W	L	PCT	GB	Home	Road	vs. East	vs. Central	vs. West	vs. AL
L.A. Dodgers	92	71	.564	—	45-37	47-34	19-13	16-18	45-32	12-8
Colorado*	91	72	.558	1	47-34	44-38	23-11	14-18	41-36	13-7
Arizona	82	80	.506	9.5	40-41	42-39	17-17	16-16	39-37	10-10
San Francisco	73	89	.451	18.5	42-39	31-50	16-17	11-22	38-38	8-12
San Diego	66	96	.407	25.5	31-50	35-46	15-17	16-18	28-48	7-13

Note: The champions of the Central and Western Divisions were determined with a tie-breaking 163rd game at the end of the regular season.

American League Final Standings, 2018

(* = wild card)

Eastern Division

Team	W	L	PCT	GB	Home	Road	vs. East	vs. Central	vs. West	vs. NL
Boston	108	54	.667	—	57-24	51-30	52-24	19-14	21-12	16-4
NY Yankees*	100	62	.617	8	53-28	47-34	44-32	23-11	22-10	11-9
Tampa Bay	90	72	.556	18	51-30	39-42	41-35	21-11	21-13	7-13
Toronto	73	89	.451	35	40-41	33-48	30-46	18-15	12-21	13-7
Baltimore	47	115	.290	61	28-53	19-62	23-53	10-23	7-26	7-13

Central Division

Team	W	L	PCT	GB	Home	Road	vs. East	vs. Central	vs. West	vs. NL
Cleveland	91	71	.562	—	49-32	42-39	16-18	49-27	14-18	12-8
Minnesota	78	84	.481	13	49-32	29-52	18-16	42-34	10-22	8-12
Detroit	64	98	.395	27	38-43	26-55	15-17	33-43	10-24	6-14
Chicago White Sox	62	100	.383	29	30-51	32-49	16-16	30-46	10-24	6-14
Kansas City	58	104	.358	33	32-49	26-55	9-24	36-40	7-26	6-14

Western Division

Team	W	L	PCT	GB	Home	Road	vs. East	vs. Central	vs. West	vs. NL
Houston	103	59	.636	—	46-35	57-24	19-15	25-7	46-30	13-7
Oakland*	97	65	.599	6	50-31	47-34	21-11	26-8	38-38	12-8
Seattle	89	73	.549	14	45-36	44-37	19-15	23-9	41-35	6-14
L.A. Angels	80	82	.494	23	42-39	38-43	11-21	22-12	37-39	10-10
Texas	67	95	.414	36	34-47	33-48	12-21	18-15	28-48	9-11

National League Statistics, 2018

Individual statistics. Players recording fewer than 150 at-bats (batters) or fewer than 70 innings or 10 saves (pitchers) are not listed here. * = changed teams within NL during season; entry includes statistics for more than one team. # = changed teams to or from AL during season; entry includes only NL statistics. Team Batting and Team Pitching include players not shown separately.

Team Batting

Team	AVG	AB	R	H	HR	RBI
Chicago Cubs.........	.258	5,624	761	1,453	167	722
Atlanta Braves	.257	5,582	759	1,433	175	717
Colorado Rockies	.256	5,541	780	1,418	210	748
Washington Nationals...	.254	5,517	771	1,402	191	737
Cincinnati Reds	.254	5,532	696	1,404	172	665
Pittsburgh Pirates	.254	5,447	692	1,381	157	665
Milwaukee Brewers......	.252	5,542	754	1,398	218	711
Los Angeles Dodgers ...	.250	5,572	804	1,394	235	756
St. Louis Cardinals	.249	5,498	759	1,369	205	725
San Francisco Giants ...	.239	5,541	603	1,324	133	573
Miami Marlins	.237	5,488	589	1,303	128	554
Arizona Diamondbacks..	.235	5,460	693	1,283	176	658
San Diego Padres......	.235	5,486	617	1,289	162	583
New York Mets	.234	5,468	676	1,282	170	649
Philadelphia Phillies	.234	5,424	677	1,270	186	653

Team Pitching

Team	ERA	IP	H	BB	SO	SV
Los Angeles Dodgers ...	3.38	1,476.0	1,279	422	1,565	48
Chicago Cubs.........	3.65	1,476.1	1,319	622	1,333	46
Arizona Diamondbacks..	3.72	1,463.0	1,313	522	1,448	39
Milwaukee Brewers.....	3.73	1,461.0	1,259	553	1,428	49
Atlanta Braves	3.75	1,456.2	1,236	635	1,423	40
St. Louis Cardinals	3.85	1,455.1	1,354	593	1,337	43
San Francisco Giants ...	3.95	1,461.1	1,387	524	1,269	36
Pittsburgh Pirates	4.00	1,434.0	1,380	497	1,336	40
Washington Nationals....	4.04	1,446.0	1,320	487	1,417	40
New York Mets	4.07	1,460.2	1,364	484	1,446	41
Philadelphia Phillies	4.14	1,445.2	1,366	500	1,465	44
Colorado Rockies	4.33	1,452.1	1,377	525	1,409	51
San Diego Padres	4.40	1,457.0	1,430	519	1,399	36
Cincinnati Reds	4.63	1,441.0	1,491	532	1,258	38
Miami Marlins	4.76	1,442.0	1,388	605	1,249	30

Arizona Diamondbacks

Batters	AVG	AB	R	H	HR	RBI	OBP	SLG
David Peralta	.293	560	75	164	30	87	.352	.516
Paul Goldschmidt ..	.290	593	95	172	33	83	.389	.533
Eduardo Escobar#	.268	198	30	53	8	21	.327	.444
Ketel Marte	.260	520	68	135	14	59	.332	.437
A.J. Pollock	.257	413	61	106	21	65	.316	.484
Daniel Descalso ...	.238	349	54	83	13	57	.353	.436
Jon Jay#	.235	289	46	68	2	22	.304	.325
Nick Ahmed	.234	516	61	121	16	70	.290	.411
Jake Lamb	.222	207	34	46	6	31	.307	.348
Steven Souza Jr. ..	.220	241	21	53	5	29	.309	.369
Chris Owings	.206	281	34	58	4	22	.272	.302
John Ryan Murphy	.202	208	19	42	9	24	.244	.375
Jeff Mathis	.200	195	15	39	1	20	.272	.272
Jarrod Dyson	.189	206	29	39	2	12	.282	.257
Alex Avila	.165	194	13	32	7	20	.299	.304

Pitchers	ERA	W	L	IP	H	BB	SO	SV
T.J. McFarland	2.00	2	2	72.0	64	22	42	1
Clay Buchholz.....	2.01	7	2	98.1	80	22	81	0
Patrick Corbin.....	3.15	11	7	200.0	162	48	246	0
Zack Greinke	3.21	15	11	207.2	181	43	199	0
Archie Bradley	3.64	4	5	71.2	62	20	75	3
Brad Ziegler*......	3.91	2	6	73.2	71	25	50	10
Robbie Ray	3.93	6	2	123.2	97	70	165	0
Matt Koch	4.15	5	5	86.2	88	22	50	0
Brad Boxberger....	4.39	3	7	53.1	44	32	71	32
Zack Godley	4.74	15	11	178.1	177	81	185	0

Manager: Torey Lovullo

Atlanta Braves

Batters	AVG	AB	R	H	HR	RBI	OBP	SLG
Freddie Freeman ..	.309	618	94	191	23	98	.388	.505
Nick Markakis.....	.297	623	78	185	14	93	.366	.440
Ronald Acuña Jr. ..	.293	433	78	127	26	64	.366	.552
Johan Camargo ...	.272	464	63	126	19	76	.349	.457
Kurt Suzuki.......	.271	347	45	94	12	50	.332	.444
Charlie Culberson..	.270	296	47	80	12	45	.326	.466
Ender Inciarte	.265	597	83	158	10	61	.325	.380
Ozzie Albies	.261	639	105	167	24	72	.305	.452
Dansby Swanson ..	.238	478	51	114	14	59	.304	.395
Preston Tucker*....	.229	166	19	38	6	27	.299	.404
Tyler Flowers.....	.227	251	34	57	8	30	.341	.359
Ryan Flaherty.....	.217	161	17	35	2	13	.298	.292
José Bautista*.....	.203	325	52	66	13	48	.348	.378
Adam Duvall*	.195	384	48	75	15	61	.274	.365

Pitchers	ERA	W	L	IP	H	BB	SO	SV
Arodys Vizcaino ...	2.11	2	2	38.1	30	15	40	16
Aníbal Sánchez ...	2.83	7	6	136.2	106	42	135	0
Mike Foltynewicz ..	2.85	13	10	183.0	130	68	202	0
A.J. Minter.......	3.23	4	3	61.1	57	22	69	15
Sean Newcomb ...	3.90	12	9	164.0	137	81	160	0
Julio Teherán	3.94	9	9	175.2	122	84	162	0
Brandon McCarthy..	4.92	6	3	78.2	94	21	65	0

Manager: Brian Snitker

Chicago Cubs

Batters	AVG	AB	R	H	HR	RBI	OBP	SLG
Ben Zobrist	.305	455	67	139	9	58	.378	.440
Daniel Murphy*....	.299	328	40	98	12	42	.336	.454
Javier Báez.......	.290	606	101	176	34	111	.326	.554
Albert Almora Jr....	.286	444	62	127	5	41	.323	.378
Anthony Rizzo	.283	566	74	160	25	101	.376	.470
Kris Bryant	.272	389	59	106	13	52	.374	.460
Jason Heyward....	.270	440	67	119	8	57	.335	.395
Tommy La Stella ...	.266	169	23	45	1	19	.340	.331
Addison Russell ...	.250	420	52	105	5	38	.317	.340
Willson Contreras ..	.249	474	50	118	10	54	.339	.390
David Bote	.239	184	23	44	6	33	.319	.408
Kyle Schwarber....	.238	428	64	102	26	61	.356	.467
Ian Happ..........	.233	387	56	90	15	44	.353	.408
Victor Caratini.....	.232	181	21	42	2	21	.293	.304

Pitchers	ERA	W	L	IP	H	BB	SO	SV
Brandon Morrow ...	1.47	0	0	30.2	24	9	31	22
Steve Cishek	2.18	4	3	70.1	45	28	78	4
Pedro Strop.......	2.26	6	1	59.2	38	21	57	13
Cole Hamels#.....	2.36	4	3	76.1	61	23	74	0
Jon Lester........	3.32	18	6	181.2	174	64	149	0
Kyle Hendricks ...	3.44	14	11	199.0	184	44	161	0
Mike Montgomery..	3.99	5	6	124.0	131	39	86	0
José Quintana	4.03	13	11	174.1	162	68	158	0
Tyler Chatwood....	5.30	4	6	103.2	92	95	85	0

Manager: Joe Maddon

Cincinnati Reds

Batters	AVG	AB	R	H	HR	RBI	OBP	SLG
Scooter Gennett ...	.310	584	86	181	23	92	.357	.490
Jesse Winker	.299	281	38	84	7	43	.405	.431
José Peraza	.288	632	85	182	14	58	.326	.416
Joey Votto	.284	503	67	143	12	67	.417	.419
Eugenio Suárez ...	.283	527	79	149	34	104	.366	.526
Scott Schebler	.255	380	55	97	17	49	.337	.439
Phillip Ervin	.252	218	27	55	7	31	.324	.404
Tucker Barnhart ...	.248	460	50	114	10	46	.328	.372
Billy Hamilton	.236	504	74	119	4	29	.299	.327
Preston Tucker*....	.229	166	19	38	6	27	.299	.404
Devin Mesoraco* ..	.221	244	24	54	11	33	.303	.398
Adam Duvall*	.195	384	48	75	15	61	.274	.365

Pitchers	ERA	W	L	IP	H	BB	SO	SV
Jared Hughes	1.94	4	3	78.2	57	23	59	7
Raisel Iglesias	2.38	2	5	72.0	52	25	80	30
Michael Lorenzen ..	3.11	4	2	81.0	78	34	54	1
Luis Castillo	4.30	10	12	169.2	158	49	165	0
Anthony DeSclafani	4.93	7	8	115.0	118	30	108	0
Matt Harvey*......	4.94	7	9	155.0	165	37	131	0
Tyler Mahle	4.98	7	9	112.0	125	53	110	0
Sal Romano	5.31	8	11	145.2	155	53	105	0
Homer Bailey	6.09	1	14	106.1	141	33	75	0

Manager: Bryan Price, Jim Riggleman

Colorado Rockies

Batters	AVG	AB	R	H	HR	RBI	OBP	SLG
Nolan Arenado	.297	590	104	175	38	110	.374	.561
Trevor Story	.291	598	88	174	37	108	.348	.567
Charlie Blackmon ..	.291	626	119	182	29	70	.358	.502
Gerardo Parra.....	.284	401	52	114	6	53	.342	.372
Carlos González...	.276	463	71	128	16	64	.329	.467
DJ LeMahieu	.276	533	90	147	15	62	.321	.428
David Dahl	.273	249	31	68	16	48	.325	.534
Ian Desmond	.236	555	82	131	22	88	.307	.422
Ryan McMahon ..	.232	181	17	42	5	19	.307	.376
Chris Iannetta.....	.224	299	36	67	11	36	.345	.385
Tony Wolters......	.170	182	19	31	3	27	.292	.286

Pitchers	ERA	W	L	IP	H	BB	SO	SV
Adam Ottavino	2.43	6	4	77.2	41	36	112	6
Kyle Freeland	2.85	17	7	202.1	182	70	173	0
Germán Márquez ..	3.77	14	11	196.0	179	57	230	0
Wade Davis	4.13	3	6	65.1	43	26	78	43
Antonio Senzatela..	4.38	6	6	90.1	94	30	69	0
Tyler Anderson	4.55	7	9	176.0	165	59	164	0
Chad Bettis.......	5.01	5	2	120.1	121	47	80	0
Jon Gray.........	5.12	12	9	172.1	180	52	183	0

Manager: Bud Black

Los Angeles Dodgers

Batters	AVG	AB	R	H	HR	RBI	OBP	SLG
Justin Turner......	.312	365	62	114	14	52	.406	.518
David Freese*.....	.296	280	38	83	11	51	.359	.471
Matt Kemp	.290	462	62	134	21	85	.338	.481
Manny Machado#..	.273	267	36	73	13	42	.338	.487
Yasiel Puig	.267	405	60	108	23	63	.327	.494
Max Muncy.......	.263	395	75	104	35	79	.391	.582
Cody Bellinger	.260	557	84	145	25	76	.343	.470
Enrique Hernández	.256	402	67	103	21	52	.336	.470
Chris Taylor.......	.254	536	85	136	17	63	.331	.444
Joc Pederson	.248	395	65	98	25	56	.321	.522
Yasmani Grandal ..	.241	440	65	106	24	68	.349	.466
Chase Utley	.213	164	18	35	1	14	.305	.305
Logan Forsythe#...	.207	193	18	40	2	13	.270	.290
Austin Barnes.....	.205	200	32	41	4	14	.329	.290

Pitchers	ERA	W	L	IP	H	BB	SO	SV
Hyun-Jin Ryu	1.97	7	3	82.1	68	15	89	0
Walker Buehler....	2.62	8	5	137.1	95	37	151	0
Clayton Kershaw...	2.73	9	5	161.1	139	29	155	0
Kenley Jansen	3.01	1	5	71.2	54	17	82	38
Ross Stripling	3.02	8	6	122.0	123	22	136	0
Rich Hill	3.66	11	5	132.2	108	41	150	0
Alex Wood........	3.68	9	7	151.2	143	40	135	0
Kenta Maeda	3.81	8	10	125.1	115	43	153	2

Manager: Dave Roberts

Miami Marlins

Batters	AVG	AB	R	H	HR	RBI	OBP	SLG
Starlin Castro	.278	593	76	165	12	54	.329	.400
J.T. Realmuto	.277	477	74	132	21	74	.340	.484
Brian Anderson....	.273	590	87	161	11	65	.357	.400
Derek Dietrich....	.265	499	72	132	16	45	.330	.421
Miguel Rojas......	.252	488	44	123	11	53	.297	.346
Cameron Maybin#	.251	251	20	63	3	20	.338	.343
Martín Prado......	.244	197	16	48	1	18	.287	.305
JT Riddle	.231	308	28	71	9	36	.277	.377
Justin Bour*	.227	423	49	96	20	59	.341	.404
Bryan Holaday	.205	151	7	31	1	16	.261	.258
Lewis Brinson.....	.199	382	31	76	11	42	.240	.338

Pitchers	ERA	W	L	IP	H	BB	SO	SV
Brad Ziegler*......	3.91	2	6	73.2	71	25	50	10
José Ureña	3.98	9	12	174.0	155	51	130	0
Dan Straily	4.12	5	6	122.1	107	52	99	0
Caleb Smith	4.19	5	6	77.1	63	33	88	0
Kyle Barraclough ..	4.20	1	6	55.2	40	34	60	10
Trevor Richards....	4.42	4	9	126.1	121	54	130	0
Wei-Yin Chen	4.79	6	12	133.1	131	47	111	0

Manager: Don Mattingly

Milwaukee Brewers

Batters	AVG	AB	R	H	HR	RBI	OBP	SLG
Christian Yelich	.326	574	118	187	36	110	.402	.598
Lorenzo Cain	.308	539	90	166	10	38	.395	.417
Jesús Aguilar	.274	492	80	135	35	108	.352	.539
Domingo Santana..	.265	211	21	56	5	20	.328	.412
Jonathan Villar# ..	.261	257	26	67	6	22	.315	.377
Mike Moustakas#..	.256	195	20	50	8	33	.326	.441
Ryan Braun.......	.254	405	59	103	20	64	.313	.469
Hernán Pérez	.253	316	36	80	9	29	.290	.386
Manny Piña.......	.252	306	39	77	9	28	.307	.395
Travis Shaw	.241	498	73	120	32	86	.345	.480
Erik Kratz	.236	203	18	48	6	23	.280	.355
Orlando Arcia	.236	348	32	82	3	30	.268	.307
Eric Thames	.219	247	41	54	16	37	.306	.478

Pitchers	ERA	W	L	IP	H	BB	SO	SV
Jeremy Jeffress....	1.29	8	1	76.2	49	27	89	15
Josh Hader.......	2.43	6	1	81.1	36	30	143	12
Wade Miley.......	2.57	5	2	80.2	71	27	50	0
Jhoulys Chacín ...	3.50	15	8	192.2	153	71	156	0
Corey Knebel	3.58	4	3	55.1	38	22	88	16
Chase Anderson...	3.93	9	8	158.0	131	57	128	0
Junior Guerra	4.09	6	9	141.0	143	55	136	0
Jordan Lyles*	4.11	3	4	87.2	83	28	84	0
Gio Gonzalez*	4.21	10	11	171.0	167	80	148	0
Freddy Peralta	4.25	6	4	78.1	49	40	96	0
Brent Suter	4.44	8	7	101.1	102	19	84	0

Manager: Craig Counsell

New York Mets

Batters	AVG	AB	R	H	HR	RBI	OBP	SLG
Jeff McNeil	.329	225	35	74	3	19	.381	.471
Wilmer Flores	.267	386	43	103	11	51	.319	.417
Brandon Nimmo ...	.263	433	77	114	17	47	.404	.483
Asdrúbal Cabrera*	.262	546	68	143	23	75	.316	.458
Amed Rosario	.256	554	76	142	9	51	.295	.381
Austin Jackson* ...	.245	347	29	85	3	32	.299	.326
Michael Conforto ..	.243	543	78	132	28	82	.350	.448
Adrián González...	.237	169	15	40	6	26	.299	.373
Jay Bruce	.223	319	31	71	9	37	.310	.370
Devin Mesoraco*..	.221	244	24	54	11	33	.303	.398
Todd Frazier	.213	408	54	87	18	59	.303	.390
Kevin Plawecki	.210	238	33	50	7	30	.315	.370
José Bautista*.....	.203	325	52	66	13	48	.348	.378
José Reyes.......	.189	228	30	43	4	16	.260	.320

Pitchers	ERA	W	L	IP	H	BB	SO	SV
Jacob deGrom	1.70	10	9	217.0	152	46	269	0
Seth Lugo........	2.66	3	4	101.1	81	28	103	3
Jeurys Familia#....	2.88	4	4	40.2	36	14	43	17
Noah Syndergaard	3.03	13	4	154.1	148	39	155	0
Zack Wheeler	3.31	12	7	182.1	150	55	179	0
Steven Matz	3.97	5	11	154.0	134	58	152	0
Robert Gsellman ..	4.28	6	3	80.0	76	28	70	13
Matt Harvey*......	4.94	7	9	155.0	165	37	131	0
Jason Vargas	5.77	7	9	92.0	100	30	84	0

Manager: Mickey Callaway

Philadelphia Phillies

Batters	AVG	AB	R	H	HR	RBI	OBP	SLG
Maikel Franco	.270	433	48	117	22	68	.314	.467
Jorge Alfaro.......	.262	344	35	90	10	37	.324	.407
Asdrúbal Cabrera*..	.262	546	68	143	23	75	.316	.458
Nick Williams	.256	407	53	104	17	50	.324	.425
Odúbel Herrera....	.255	550	64	140	22	71	.310	.420
César Hernández ..	.253	605	91	153	15	60	.356	.362
Rhys Hoskins	.246	558	89	137	34	96	.354	.496
Carlos Santana....	.229	560	82	128	24	86	.352	.414
Justin Bour*	.227	423	49	96	20	59	.341	.404
Scott Kingery	.226	452	55	102	8	35	.267	.338
José Bautista*.....	.203	325	52	66	13	48	.348	.378
Andrew Knapp	.198	187	19	37	4	15	.294	.316
Aaron Altherr......	.181	243	28	44	8	38	.295	.333

Pitchers	ERA	W	L	IP	H	BB	SO	SV
Aaron Nola	2.37	17	6	212.1	149	58	224	0
Seranthony Domínguez	2.95	2	5	58.0	32	22	74	16
Jake Arrieta.	3.96	10	11	172.2	165	57	138	0
Zach Eflin	4.36	11	8	128.0	130	37	123	0
Nick Pivetta.	4.77	7	14	164.0	163	51	188	0
Vince Velasquez . . .	4.85	9	12	146.2	138	59	161	0
Héctor Neris	5.10	1	3	47.2	46	16	76	11

Manager: Gabe Kapler

Pittsburgh Pirates

Batters	AVG	AB	R	H	HR	RBI	OBP	SLG
Corey Dickerson . . .	.300	504	65	151	13	55	.330	.474
David Freese*	.296	280	38	83	11	51	.359	.471
Austin Meadows# . .	.292	154	16	45	5	13	.327	.468
Elías Díaz.	.286	252	33	72	10	34	.339	.452
Starling Marte	.277	559	81	155	20	72	.327	.460
Colin Moran	.277	415	49	115	11	58	.340	.407
Adam Frazier	.277	318	52	88	10	35	.342	.456
Josh Bell.	.261	501	74	131	12	62	.357	.411
Francisco Cervelli . .	.259	332	39	86	12	57	.378	.431
Gregory Polanco. . .	.254	461	75	117	23	81	.340	.499
Jordy Mercer	.251	394	43	99	6	39	.315	.381
Josh Harrison	.250	344	41	86	8	37	.293	.363
Sean Rodriguez . . .	.167	150	21	25	5	19	.277	.313

Pitchers	ERA	W	L	IP	H	BB	SO	SV
Felipe Vázquez	2.70	4	2	70.0	63	24	89	37
Trevor Williams	3.11	14	10	170.2	146	55	126	0
Jameson Taillon . . .	3.20	14	10	191.0	179	46	179	0
Joe Musgrove	4.06	6	9	115.1	113	23	100	0
Iván Nova	4.19	9	9	161.0	171	35	114	0
Chad Kuhl.	4.55	5	5	85.0	89	33	81	0
Steven Brault	4.61	6	3	91.2	84	57	82	0
Nick Kingham	5.21	5	7	76.0	79	26	69	0

Manager: Clint Hurdle

St. Louis Cardinals

Batters	AVG	AB	R	H	HR	RBI	OBP	SLG
José Martínez	.305	534	64	163	17	83	.364	.457
Marcell Ozuna	.280	582	69	163	23	88	.325	.433
Yairo Muñoz	.276	293	39	81	8	42	.350	.413
Harrison Bader	.264	379	61	100	12	37	.334	.422
Jedd Gyorko	.262	351	49	92	11	47	.346	.416
Yadier Molina	.261	459	55	120	20	74	.314	.436
Matt Carpenter	.257	564	111	145	36	81	.374	.523
Kolten Wong	.249	353	41	88	9	38	.332	.388
Tommy Pham#	.248	351	67	87	14	41	.331	.399
Paul DeJong	.241	436	68	105	19	68	.313	.433
Matt Adams*	.239	306	42	73	21	57	.309	.477
Greg Garcia	.221	181	15	40	3	15	.309	.304
Dexter Fowler	.180	289	40	52	8	31	.278	.298

Pitchers	ERA	W	L	IP	H	BB	SO	SV
Miles Mikolas	2.83	18	4	200.2	186	29	146	0
Carlos Martinez . . .	3.11	8	6	118.2	100	60	117	5
Michael Wacha	3.20	8	2	84.1	68	36	71	0
Jack Flaherty	3.34	8	9	151.0	108	59	182	0
John Gant	3.47	7	6	114.0	91	57	95	0
Bud Norris	3.59	3	6	57.2	51	21	67	28
Jordan Hicks.	3.59	3	4	77.2	59	45	70	6
Tyson Ross*	4.15	8	9	149.2	132	62	122	0
Austin Gomber	4.44	6	2	75.0	81	32	67	0
Luke Weaver	4.95	7	11	136.1	150	54	121	0

Manager: Mike Matheny, Mike Shildt

San Diego Padres

Batters	AVG	AB	R	H	HR	RBI	OBP	SLG
Franmil Reyes	.280	261	36	73	16	31	.340	.498
A.J. Ellis	.272	151	19	41	1	15	.378	.344
Travis Jankowski . . .	.259	347	45	90	4	17	.332	.346
Wil Myers	.253	312	39	79	11	39	.318	.446
Eric Hosmer	.253	613	72	155	18	69	.322	.398
José Pirela	.249	438	54	109	5	32	.300	.345

Batters	AVG	AB	R	H	HR	RBI	OBP	SLG
Hunter Renfroe	.248	403	53	100	26	68	.302	.504
Freddy Galvis	.248	602	62	149	13	67	.299	.380
Manuel Margot	.245	477	50	117	8	51	.292	.384
Christian Villanueva .	.236	351	42	83	20	46	.299	.450
Cory Spangenberg .	.235	298	35	70	7	25	.298	.362
Austin Hedges	.231	303	29	70	14	37	.282	.429
Carlos Asuaje	.196	189	15	37	2	19	.286	.280

Pitchers	ERA	W	L	IP	H	BB	SO	SV
Kirby Yates	2.14	5	3	63.0	41	17	90	12
Craig Stammen. . . .	2.73	8	3	79.0	65	17	88	0
Brad Hand#	3.05	2	4	44.1	33	15	65	24
Joey Lucchesi	4.08	8	9	130.0	125	43	145	0
Jordan Lyles*	4.11	3	4	87.2	83	28	84	0
Tyson Ross*	4.15	8	9	149.2	132	62	122	0
Robbie Erlin	4.21	4	7	109.0	112	12	88	0
Eric Lauer.	4.34	6	7	112.0	127	46	100	0
Clayton Richard . . .	5.33	7	11	158.2	159	60	108	0
Bryan Mitchell	5.42	2	4	73.0	85	43	38	0

Manager: Andy Green

San Francisco Giants

Batters	AVG	AB	R	H	HR	RBI	OBP	SLG
Buster Posey	.284	398	47	113	5	41	.359	.382
Andrew McCutchen#	.255	482	65	123	15	55	.357	.415
Brandon Crawford. .	.254	531	63	135	14	54	.325	.394
Joe Panik	.254	358	38	91	4	24	.307	.332
Brandon Belt.	.253	399	50	101	14	46	.342	.414
Alen Hanson	.252	294	36	74	8	39	.274	.425
Austin Slater	.251	199	21	50	1	23	.333	.307
Pablo Sandoval . . .	.248	230	22	57	9	40	.310	.417
Austin Jackson* . . .	.245	347	29	85	3	32	.299	.326
Evan Longoria	.244	480	51	117	16	54	.281	.413
Nick Hundley	.241	282	34	68	10	31	.298	.408
Gorkys Hernández .	.234	414	52	97	15	40	.285	.391
Hunter Pence	.226	235	19	53	4	24	.258	.332
Gregor Blanco	.217	189	19	41	2	12	.262	.317

Pitchers	ERA	W	L	IP	H	BB	SO	SV
Will Smith	2.55	2	3	53.0	37	15	71	14
Sam Dyson	2.69	4	3	70.1	56	20	56	3
Dereck Rodríguez. .	2.81	6	4	118.1	98	36	89	0
Madison Bumgarner	3.26	6	7	129.2	118	43	109	0
Derek Holland.	3.57	7	9	171.1	154	67	169	0
Hunter Strickland . .	3.97	3	5	45.1	43	21	37	14
Ty Blach	4.25	6	7	118.2	133	41	75	0
Andrew Suárez	4.49	7	13	160.1	163	45	130	0
Chris Stratton	5.09	10	10	145.0	153	54	112	0

Manager: Bruce Bochy

Washington Nationals

Batters	AVG	AB	R	H	HR	RBI	OBP	SLG
Anthony Rendon. . .	.308	529	88	163	24	92	.374	.535
Howie Kendrick. . . .	.303	152	17	46	4	12	.331	.474
Adam Eaton	.301	319	55	96	5	33	.394	.411
Daniel Murphy*	.299	328	40	98	12	42	.336	.454
Juan Soto	.292	414	77	121	22	70	.406	.517
Trea Turner	.271	664	103	180	19	73	.344	.416
Ryan Zimmerman. .	.264	288	33	76	13	51	.337	.486
Bryce Harper	.249	550	103	137	34	100	.393	.496
Mark Reynolds	.248	206	26	51	13	40	.328	.476
Matt Adams*	.239	306	42	73	21	57	.309	.477
Matt Wieters	.238	235	24	56	8	30	.330	.374
Wilmer Difo	.230	408	55	94	7	42	.298	.350
Michael A. Taylor. . .	.227	353	46	80	6	28	.287	.357
Pedro Severino. . . .	.168	190	14	32	2	15	.254	.247

Pitchers	ERA	W	L	IP	H	BB	SO	SV
Sean Doolittle	1.60	3	3	45.0	21	6	60	25
Max Scherzer	2.53	18	7	220.2	150	51	300	0
Jeremy Hellickson. .	3.45	5	3	91.1	78	20	65	0
Stephen Strasburg .	3.74	10	7	130.0	118	38	156	0
Gio Gonzalez*	4.21	10	11	171.0	167	80	148	0
Tanner Roark	4.34	9	15	180.1	181	50	146	0

Manager: Dave Martinez

American League Statistics, 2018

Individual statistics. Players recording fewer than 150 at-bats (batters) or fewer than 70 innings or 10 saves (pitchers) are not listed here. * = Changed teams within AL during season; entry includes statistics for more than one team. # = Changed teams to or from NL during season; entry includes only AL statistics. Team Batting and Team Pitching include players not shown separately.

Team Batting

Team	AVG	AB	R	H	HR	RBI
Boston Red Sox	.268	5,623	876	1,509	208	829
Cleveland Indians	.259	5,595	818	1,447	216	786
Tampa Bay Rays	.258	5,475	716	1,415	150	664
Houston Astros	.255	5,453	797	1,390	205	763
Seattle Mariners	.254	5,513	677	1,402	176	644
Oakland Athletics	.252	5,579	813	1,407	227	778
Minnesota Twins	.250	5,526	738	1,379	166	704
New York Yankees	.249	5,515	851	1,374	267	821
Kansas City Royals . . .	.245	5,505	638	1,350	155	606
Toronto Blue Jays	.244	5,477	709	1,336	217	680
Los Angeles Angels . .	.242	5,472	721	1,323	214	690
Detroit Tigers	.241	5,494	630	1,326	135	597
Chicago White Sox . . .	.241	5,523	656	1,332	182	639
Texas Rangers	.240	5,453	737	1,308	194	696
Baltimore Orioles	.239	5,507	622	1,317	188	593

Team Pitching

Team	ERA	IP	H	BB	SO	SV
Houston Astros	3.11	1,455.0	1,164	435	1,687	46
Tampa Bay Rays	3.74	1,448.1	1,236	501	1,421	52
Boston Red Sox	3.75	1,458.2	1,305	512	1,558	46
Cleveland Indians . . .	3.77	1,457.1	1,349	407	1,544	41
New York Yankees . . .	3.78	1,456.1	1,311	494	1,634	49
Oakland Athletics . . .	3.81	1,465.2	1,303	474	1,237	44
Seattle Mariners	4.13	1,448.2	1,396	400	1,328	60
Los Angeles Angels . .	4.15	1,437.1	1,353	546	1,386	35
Minnesota Twins	4.50	1,443.1	1,425	573	1,377	37
Detroit Tigers	4.58	1,425.1	1,423	491	1,215	37
Chicago White Sox . .	4.83	1,437.0	1,404	653	1,259	34
Toronto Blue Jays . . .	4.85	1,433.2	1,476	551	1,298	39
Texas Rangers	4.92	1,431.0	1,516	491	1,121	42
Kansas City Royals . .	4.94	1,432.0	1,542	549	1,157	33
Baltimore Orioles . . .	5.18	1,431.0	1,552	589	1,203	28

Baltimore Orioles

Batters	AVG	AB	R	H	HR	RBI	OBP	SLG
Manny Machado# . .	.315	365	48	115	24	65	.387	.575
Adam Jones	.281	580	54	163	15	63	.313	.419
Craig Gentry	.269	156	13	42	1	11	.321	.346
Danny Valencia	.263	255	28	67	9	28	.316	.408
Mark Trumbo	.261	330	41	86	17	44	.313	.452
Renato Núñez*	.258	236	28	61	8	22	.322	.419
Jonathan Villar# . . .	.258	209	28	54	8	24	.336	.392
Joey Rickard	.244	213	27	52	8	23	.300	.413
Jonathan Schoop# . .	.244	349	45	85	17	40	.273	.447
Trey Mancini	.242	582	69	141	24	58	.299	.416
Cedric Mullins	.235	170	23	40	4	11	.312	.359
Tim Beckham	.230	369	45	85	12	35	.287	.374
Caleb Joseph	.219	265	28	58	3	17	.254	.321
Jace Peterson*	.200	210	21	42	3	28	.310	.324
Chance Sisco	.181	160	13	29	2	16	.288	.269
Chris Davis	.168	470	40	79	16	49	.243	.296

Pitchers	ERA	W	L	IP	H	BB	SO	SV
Miguel Castro	3.96	2	7	86.1	75	50	57	0
Mychal Givens	3.99	0	7	76.2	61	30	79	9
Kevin Gausman# . . .	4.43	5	8	124.0	139	32	104	0
Brad Brach#	4.85	1	2	39.0	50	19	38	11
David Hess	4.88	3	10	103.1	106	37	74	0
Alex Cobb	4.90	5	15	152.1	172	43	102	0
Andrew Cashner . . .	5.29	4	15	153.0	177	65	99	0
Dylan Bundy	5.45	8	16	171.2	188	54	184	0
Mike Wright Jr.	5.55	4	2	84.1	101	36	74	0

Manager: Buck Showalter

Boston Red Sox

Batters	AVG	AB	R	H	HR	RBI	OBP	SLG
Mookie Betts	.346	520	129	180	32	80	.438	.640
J. D. Martinez	.330	569	111	188	43	130	.402	.629
Andrew Benintendi . .	.290	579	103	168	16	87	.366	.465
Xander Bogaerts . .	.288	513	72	148	23	103	.360	.522
Steve Pearce*	.284	215	35	61	11	42	.378	.512
Brock Holt	.277	321	41	89	7	46	.362	.411
Eduardo Núñez	.265	480	56	127	10	44	.289	.388
Hanley Ramirez . . .	.254	177	25	45	6	29	.313	.395
Mitch Moreland	.245	404	57	99	15	68	.325	.433
Ian Kinsler*	.240	487	66	117	14	48	.301	.380
Rafael Devers	.240	450	59	108	21	66	.298	.433
Jackie Bradley Jr. . .	.234	474	76	111	13	59	.314	.403
Blake Swihart	.229	192	28	44	3	18	.285	.328
Christian Vázquez . .	.207	251	24	52	3	16	.257	.283
Sandy León	.177	265	30	47	5	22	.232	.279

Pitchers	ERA	W	L	IP	H	BB	SO	SV
Chris Sale	2.11	12	4	158.0	102	34	237	0
Craig Kimbrel	2.74	5	1	62.1	31	31	96	42

Pitchers	ERA	W	L	IP	H	BB	SO	SV
Hector Velázquez . .	3.18	7	2	85.0	97	26	53	0
David Price	3.58	16	7	176.0	151	50	177	0
Nathan Eovaldi* . . .	3.81	6	7	111.0	105	20	101	0
Eduardo Rodríguez	3.82	13	5	129.2	119	45	146	0
Brian Johnson	4.17	4	5	99.1	104	38	87	0
Rick Porcello	4.28	17	7	191.1	177	48	190	0
Drew Pomeranz	6.08	2	6	74.0	87	44	66	0

Manager: Alex Cora

Chicago White Sox

Batters	AVG	AB	R	H	HR	RBI	OBP	SLG
Kevan Smith	.292	171	21	50	3	21	.348	.380
Ryan LaMarre*	.279	165	15	46	2	18	.322	.382
Omar Narváez	.275	280	30	77	9	30	.366	.429
Leury García	.271	258	23	70	4	32	.303	.376
José Abreu	.265	499	68	132	22	78	.325	.473
Welington Castillo . .	.259	170	17	44	6	15	.304	.406
Yolmer Sánchez . . .	.242	600	62	145	8	55	.306	.372
Tim Anderson	.240	567	77	136	20	64	.281	.406
Daniel Palka	.240	417	56	100	27	67	.294	.484
Avisail García	.236	356	47	84	19	49	.281	.438
Adam Engel	.235	429	49	101	6	29	.279	.336
Yoán Moncada	.235	578	73	136	17	61	.315	.400
Matt Davidson	.228	434	51	99	20	62	.319	.419
Nicky Delmonico . . .	.215	284	31	61	8	25	.296	.373

Pitchers	ERA	W	L	IP	H	BB	SO	SV
Joakim Soria#	2.56	0	3	38.2	35	10	49	16
Reynaldo López . . .	3.91	7	10	188.2	165	75	151	0
Carlos Rodón	4.18	6	8	120.2	97	55	90	0
Héctor Santiago . . .	4.41	6	3	102.0	101	60	103	2
James Shields	4.53	7	16	204.2	190	78	154	0
Dylan Covey	5.18	5	14	121.2	129	52	91	0
Lucas Giolito	6.13	10	13	173.1	166	90	125	0

Manager: Rick Renteria

Cleveland Indians

Batters	AVG	AB	R	H	HR	RBI	OBP	SLG
Michael Brantley . . .	.309	570	89	176	17	76	.364	.468
Melky Cabrera	.280	250	28	70	6	39	.335	.420
Francisco Lindor . . .	.277	661	129	183	38	92	.352	.519
José Ramírez	.270	578	110	156	39	105	.387	.552
Yan Gomes	.266	403	52	107	16	48	.313	.449
Tyler Naquin	.264	174	22	46	3	23	.295	.356
Greg Allen	.257	265	36	68	2	20	.310	.343
Leonys Martín*	.255	318	48	81	11	33	.323	.425
Yonder Alonso	.250	516	64	129	23	83	.317	.421
Josh Donaldson* . . .	.246	187	30	46	8	23	.352	.449
Edwin Encarnación	.246	500	74	123	32	107	.336	.474
Jason Kipnis	.230	530	65	122	18	75	.315	.389
Rajai Davis	.224	196	33	44	1	6	.278	.281
Brandon Guyer	.206	194	25	40	7	27	.300	.371
Roberto Pérez	.168	179	16	30	2	19	.256	.263

Pitchers	ERA	W	L	IP	H	BB	SO	SV
Trevor Bauer......	2.21	12	6	175.1	134	57	221	1
Corey Kluber......	2.89	20	7	215.0	179	34	222	0
Mike Clevinger...	3.02	13	8	200.0	164	67	207	0
Carlos Carrasco ...	3.38	17	10	192.0	173	43	231	0
Shane Bieber	4.55	11	5	114.2	130	23	118	0
Cody Allen	4.70	4	6	67.0	58	33	80	27
Adam Plutko	5.28	4	5	76.2	78	23	60	1
Josh Tomlin.......	6.14	2	5	70.1	92	12	46	0

Manager: Terry Francona

Detroit Tigers

Batters	AVG	AB	R	H	HR	RBI	OBP	SLG
Nicholas Castellanos	.298	620	88	185	23	89	.354	.500
José Iglesias......	.269	432	43	116	5	48	.310	.389
Jim Adduci	.267	176	19	47	3	21	.290	.386
John Hicks	.260	288	35	75	9	32	.312	.403
Leonys Martín*....	.255	318	48	81	11	33	.323	.425
Victor Martínez....	.251	467	32	117	9	54	.297	.353
Niko Goodrum	.245	444	55	109	16	53	.315	.432
Jeimer Candelario..	.224	539	78	121	19	54	.317	.393
Victor Reyes	.222	212	35	47	1	12	.239	.288
James McCann....	.220	427	31	94	8	39	.267	.314
Ronny Rodríguez ..	.220	191	22	42	5	20	.256	.335
JaCoby Jones	.207	429	54	89	11	34	.266	.364
Dixon Machado....	.206	214	20	44	1	21	.263	.290
Mikie Mahtook	.202	223	24	45	9	29	.276	.359

Pitchers	ERA	W	L	IP	H	BB	SO	SV
Mike Fiers*	3.56	12	8	172.0	166	37	139	0
Blaine Hardy......	3.56	4	5	86.0	79	22	66	1
Matthew Boyd....	4.39	9	13	170.1	146	51	159	0
Jordan Zimmermann	4.52	7	8	131.1	140	26	111	0
Francisco Liriano	4.58	5	12	133.2	127	73	110	0
Michael Fulmer....	4.69	3	12	132.1	128	46	110	0
Shane Greene	5.12	4	6	63.1	68	19	65	32

Manager: Ron Gardenhire

Houston Astros

Batters	AVG	AB	R	H	HR	RBI	OBP	SLG
José Altuve.......	.316	534	84	169	13	61	.386	.451
Yuli Gurriel	.291	537	70	156	13	85	.323	.428
Alex Bregman ...	.286	594	105	170	31	103	.394	.532
Tyler White	.276	210	27	58	12	42	.354	.533
George Springer...	.265	544	102	144	22	71	.346	.434
Tony Kemp	.263	255	37	67	6	30	.351	.392
Marwin González ..	.247	489	61	121	16	68	.324	.409
Josh Reddick	.242	433	63	105	17	47	.318	.400
Carlos Correa	.239	402	60	96	15	65	.323	.405
Max Stassi	.226	221	28	50	8	27	.316	.394
Evan Gattis.......	.226	407	49	92	25	78	.284	.452
Martín Maldonado*	.225	373	39	84	9	44	.276	.351
Brian McCann.....	.212	189	22	40	7	23	.301	.339
Jake Marisnick ...	.211	213	34	45	10	28	.275	.399

Pitchers	ERA	W	L	IP	H	BB	SO	SV
Collin McHugh	1.99	6	2	72.1	45	21	94	0
Roberto Osuna* ...	2.37	2	2	38.0	33	4	32	21
Justin Verlander ...	2.52	16	9	214.0	156	37	290	0
Ryan Pressly*.....	2.54	2	1	71.0	57	22	101	2
Gerrit Cole	2.88	15	5	200.1	143	64	276	0
Charlie Morton	3.13	15	3	167.0	130	64	201	0
Héctor Rondón	3.20	2	5	59.0	58	20	67	15
Dallas Keuchel ...	3.74	12	11	204.2	211	58	153	0
Lance McCullers Jr.	3.86	10	6	128.1	100	50	142	0
Ken Giles*........	4.65	0	3	50.1	54	7	53	26

Manager: A. J. Hinch

Kansas City Royals

Batters	AVG	AB	R	H	HR	RBI	OBP	SLG
Jon Jay#.........	.307	238	28	73	1	18	.363	.374
Whit Merrifield.....	.304	632	88	192	12	60	.367	.438
Adalberto Mondesí	.276	275	47	76	14	37	.306	.498
Jorge Soler	.265	223	27	59	9	28	.354	.466
Mike Moustakas#..	.249	378	46	94	20	62	.309	.468
Alex Gordon	.245	506	56	124	13	54	.324	.370
Lucas Duda#	.242	310	34	75	13	48	.310	.413
Rosell Herrera ...	.238	265	25	63	1	20	.292	.325
Salvador Pérez ...	.235	510	52	120	27	80	.274	.439
Alcides Escobar ...	.231	485	54	112	4	34	.279	.313
Hunter Dozier	.229	362	36	83	11	34	.278	.395
Jorge Bonifacio....	.225	236	31	53	4	23	.312	.360

Pitchers	ERA	W	L	IP	H	BB	SO	SV
Kelvin Herrera#....	1.05	1	1	25.2	19	2	22	14
Brad Keller	3.08	9	6	140.1	133	50	96	0
Kevin McCarthy ...	3.25	5	4	72.0	70	20	46	0
Wily Peralta.......	3.67	1	0	34.1	28	23	35	14
Brian Flynn	4.04	3	5	75.2	87	35	47	1
Heath Fillmyer....	4.26	4	2	82.1	78	32	57	0
Jakob Junis.......	4.37	9	12	177.0	182	43	164	0
Ian Kennedy	4.66	3	9	119.2	125	40	105	0
Danny Duffy	4.88	8	12	155.0	161	70	141	0
Eric Skoglund	5.14	1	6	70.0	66	19	49	0
Jason Hammel	6.02	4	14	127.0	168	39	92	0
Burch Smith	6.92	1	6	78.0	90	40	77	0

Manager: Ned Yost

Los Angeles Angels

Batters	AVG	AB	R	H	HR	RBI	OBP	SLG
Mike Trout	.312	471	101	147	39	79	.460	.628
Andrelton Simmons	.292	554	68	162	11	75	.337	.417
Shohei Ohtani.....	.285	326	59	93	22	61	.361	.564
David Fletcher....	.275	284	35	78	1	25	.316	.363
Justin Upton	.257	533	80	137	30	85	.344	.463
Albert Pujols	.245	465	50	114	19	64	.289	.411
Ian Kinsler*	.240	487	66	117	14	48	.301	.380
Martín Maldonado*	.225	373	39	84	9	44	.276	.351
Zack Cozart	.219	224	29	49	5	18	.296	.362
Jefry Marté	.216	194	28	42	7	22	.273	.371
Kole Calhoun	.208	491	71	102	19	57	.283	.369
Luis Valbuena.....	.199	266	23	53	9	33	.253	.335

Pitchers	ERA	W	L	IP	H	BB	SO	SV
Blake Parker......	3.26	2	1	66.1	63	19	70	14
Jaime Barria	3.41	10	9	129.1	117	47	98	0
Garrett Richards...	3.66	5	4	76.1	64	34	87	0
Tyler Skaggs	4.02	8	10	125.1	127	40	129	0
Andrew Heaney ...	4.15	9	10	180.0	171	45	180	0
Félix Peña........	4.18	3	5	92.2	87	28	85	0
Noé Ramirez.....	4.54	7	5	83.1	75	30	95	1
Nick Tropeano.....	4.74	5	6	76.0	68	31	64	0

Manager: Mike Scioscia

Minnesota Twins

Batters	AVG	AB	R	H	HR	RBI	OBP	SLG
Jorge Polanco.....	.288	302	38	87	6	42	.345	.427
Eddie Rosario.....	.288	559	87	161	24	77	.323	.479
Joe Mauer........	.282	486	64	137	6	48	.351	.379
Ryan LaMarre*....	.279	165	15	46	2	18	.322	.382
Eduardo Escobar#	.274	368	45	101	15	63	.338	.514
Robbie Grossman..	.273	396	50	108	5	48	.367	.384
Mitch Garver.....	.268	302	38	81	7	45	.335	.414
Jake Cave........	.265	283	54	75	13	45	.313	.473
Logan Forsythe#...	.258	178	19	46	0	14	.356	.292
Ehire Adrianza ...	.251	335	42	84	6	39	.301	.379
Tyler Austin*	.230	244	34	56	17	47	.287	.480
Brian Dozier#	.227	410	65	93	16	52	.307	.405
Max Kepler.......	.224	532	80	119	20	58	.319	.408
Johnny Field*	.222	221	28	49	9	21	.254	.403
Miguel Sanó	.199	266	32	53	13	41	.281	.398
Logan Morrison....	.186	318	41	59	15	39	.276	.368

Pitchers	ERA	W	L	IP	H	BB	SO	SV
Ryan Pressly*.....	2.54	2	1	71.0	57	22	101	2
Fernando Rodney*	3.36	4	3	64.1	62	32	70	25
Kyle Gibson	3.62	10	13	196.2	177	79	179	0
José Berríos	3.84	12	11	192.1	159	61	202	0
Jake Odorizzi	4.49	7	10	164.1	151	70	162	0
Lance Lynn	4.77	10	10	156.2	163	76	161	0
Trevor Hildenberger	5.42	4	6	73.0	75	26	70	7

Manager: Paul Molitor

New York Yankees

Batters	AVG	AB	R	H	HR	RBI	OBP	SLG
Miguel Andújar	.297	573	83	170	27	92	.328	.527
Aaron Judge	.278	413	77	115	27	67	.392	.528
Gleyber Torres	.271	431	54	117	24	77	.340	.480
Didi Gregorius ...	.268	504	89	135	27	86	.335	.494
Giancarlo Stanton.	.266	617	102	164	38	100	.343	.509
Adeiny Hechavarria#*	.249	253	32	63	5	28	.279	.336
Aaron Hicks	.248	480	90	119	27	79	.366	.467
Austin Romine	.244	242	30	59	10	42	.295	.417
Brett Gardner	.236	530	95	125	12	45	.322	.368
Tyler Austin*	.230	244	34	56	17	47	.287	.480
Neil Walker	.219	347	48	76	11	46	.309	.354
Jace Peterson* ...	.200	210	21	42	3	28	.310	.324
Greg Bird	.199	272	23	54	11	38	.286	.386
Gary Sánchez.....	.186	323	51	60	18	53	.291	.406

Pitchers	ERA	W	L	IP	H	BB	SO	SV
Aroldis Chapman	2.45	3	0	51.1	24	30	93	32
Chad Green	2.50	8	3	75.2	64	15	94	0
Luis Severino	3.39	19	8	191.1	173	46	220	0
J.A. Happ*	3.65	17	6	177.2	150	51	193	0
CC Sabathia	3.65	9	7	153.0	150	51	140	0
Masahiro Tanaka	3.75	12	6	156.0	141	35	159	0
Lance Lynn*	4.77	10	10	156.2	163	76	161	0
Sonny Gray	4.90	11	9	130.1	138	57	123	0
Domingo Germán	5.57	2	6	85.2	81	33	102	0

Manager: Aaron Boone

Oakland Athletics

Batters	AVG	AB	R	H	HR	RBI	OBP	SLG
Nick Martini	.296	152	26	45	1	19	.397	.414
Ramón Laureano	.288	156	27	45	5	19	.358	.474
Matt Chapman	.278	547	100	152	24	68	.356	.508
Stephen Piscotty	.267	546	78	146	27	88	.331	.491
Jed Lowrie	.267	596	78	159	23	99	.353	.448
Chad Pinder	.258	298	43	77	13	27	.332	.436
Marcus Semien	.255	632	89	161	15	70	.318	.388
Mark Canha	.249	365	60	91	17	52	.328	.449
Matt Olson	.247	580	85	143	29	84	.335	.453
Khris Davis	.247	576	98	142	48	123	.326	.549
Jonathan Lucroy	.241	415	41	100	4	51	.291	.325
Dustin Fowler	.224	192	19	43	6	23	.256	.354
Matt Joyce	.208	207	34	43	7	15	.322	.353

Pitchers	ERA	W	L	IP	H	BB	SO	SV
Blake Treinen	0.78	9	2	80.1	46	21	100	38
Lou Trivino	2.92	8	3	74.0	53	31	82	4
Yusmeiro Petit	3.00	7	3	93.0	76	18	76	0
Edwin Jackson	3.33	6	3	92.0	75	37	68	0
Fernando Rodney*	3.36	4	3	64.1	62	32	70	25
Mike Fiers*	3.56	12	8	172.0	166	37	139	0
Sean Manaea	3.59	12	9	160.2	141	32	108	0
Trevor Cahill	3.76	7	4	110.0	90	41	100	0
Daniel Mengden	4.05	7	6	115.2	103	26	72	0
Brett Anderson	4.48	4	5	80.1	90	13	47	0

Manager: Bob Melvin

Seattle Mariners

Batters	AVG	AB	R	H	HR	RBI	OBP	SLG
Jean Segura	.304	586	91	178	10	63	.341	.415
Robinson Canó	.303	310	44	94	10	50	.374	.471
Mitch Haniger	.285	596	90	170	26	93	.366	.493
Ben Gamel	.272	257	37	70	1	19	.358	.370
Dee Gordon	.268	556	62	149	4	36	.288	.349
Denard Span*	.261	437	63	114	11	58	.341	.419
Nelson Cruz	.256	519	70	133	37	97	.342	.509
Guillermo Heredia	.236	292	29	69	5	19	.318	.342
Ryon Healy	.235	493	51	116	24	73	.277	.412
Kyle Seager	.221	583	62	129	22	78	.273	.400
Mike Zunino	.201	373	37	75	20	44	.259	.410

Pitchers	ERA	W	L	IP	H	BB	SO	SV
Edwin Díaz	1.96	0	4	73.1	41	17	124	57
Alex Colomé*	3.04	7	5	68.0	59	21	72	12
Wade LeBlanc	3.72	9	5	162.0	151	40	130	0
James Paxton	3.76	11	6	160.1	134	42	208	0
Marco Gonzales	4.00	13	9	166.2	172	32	145	0
Mike Leake	4.36	10	10	185.2	207	34	119	0
Félix Hernández	5.55	8	14	155.2	159	59	125	0

Manager: Scott Servais

Tampa Bay Rays

Batters	AVG	AB	R	H	HR	RBI	OBP	SLG
Joey Wendle	.300	487	62	146	7	61	.354	.435
Wilson Ramos#	.297	293	30	87	14	53	.346	.488
Mallex Smith	.296	480	65	142	2	40	.367	.406
Matt Duffy	.294	503	59	148	4	44	.361	.366
Willy Adames	.278	288	43	80	10	34	.348	.406
Ji-Man Choi#	.269	160	21	43	8	27	.370	.506
Daniel Robertson	.262	282	46	74	9	34	.382	.415

Batters	AVG	AB	R	H	HR	RBI	OBP	SLG
Denard Span*	.261	437	63	114	11	58	.341	.419
Brad Miller#	.256	156	16	40	5	21	.322	.429
C.J. Cron	.253	501	68	127	30	74	.323	.493
Adeiny Hechavarria#*	.249	253	32	63	5	28	.279	.336
Johnny Field*	.222	221	28	49	9	21	.254	.403
Kevin Kiermaier	.217	332	44	72	7	29	.282	.370
Jesús Sucre	.209	182	9	38	1	17	.247	.253
Carlos Gómez	.208	360	42	75	9	32	.298	.336
Jake Bauers	.201	323	48	65	11	48	.316	.384

Pitchers	ERA	W	L	IP	H	BB	SO	SV
Blake Snell	1.89	21	5	180.2	112	64	221	0
Alex Colomé*	3.04	7	5	68.0	59	21	72	12
Yonny Chirinos	3.51	5	5	89.2	84	25	75	0
Nathan Eovaldi*	3.81	6	7	111.0	105	20	101	0
Ryan Yarbrough	3.91	16	6	147.1	140	50	128	0
Sergio Romo	4.14	3	4	67.1	65	20	75	25
Chris Archer#	4.31	3	5	96.0	102	31	102	0

Manager: Kevin Cash

Texas Rangers

Batters	AVG	AB	R	H	HR	RBI	OBP	SLG
Adrián Beltré	.273	433	49	118	15	65	.328	.434
Shin-Soo Choo	.264	560	83	148	21	62	.377	.434
Isiah Kiner-Falefa	.261	356	43	93	4	34	.325	.357
Nomar Mazara	.258	489	61	126	20	77	.317	.436
Renato Núñez*	.258	236	28	61	8	22	.322	.419
Elvis Andrus	.256	395	53	101	6	33	.308	.367
Jurickson Profar	.254	524	82	133	20	77	.335	.458
Rougned Odor	.253	474	76	120	18	63	.326	.424
Ronald Guzmán	.235	387	46	91	16	58	.306	.416
Robinson Chirinos	.222	360	48	80	18	65	.338	.419
Delino DeShields	.216	334	52	72	2	22	.310	.281
Joey Gallo	.206	500	82	103	40	92	.312	.498

Pitchers	ERA	W	L	IP	H	BB	SO	SV
José Leclerc	1.56	2	3	57.2	24	25	85	12
Keone Kela	3.44	3	3	36.2	28	14	44	24
Mike Minor	4.18	12	8	157.0	138	38	132	0
Cole Hamels#	4.72	5	9	114.1	115	42	114	0
Yovani Gallardo#	5.77	8	8	92.0	99	43	56	0
Bartolo Colon	5.78	7	12	146.1	172	25	81	0
Martin Pérez	6.22	2	7	85.1	116	36	52	0
Matt Moore	6.79	3	8	102.0	128	41	86	0

Manager: Jeff Banister, Don Wakamatsu

Toronto Blue Jays

Batters	AVG	AB	R	H	HR	RBI	OBP	SLG
Steve Pearce*	.284	215	35	61	11	42	.378	.512
Lourdes Gurriel Jr.	.281	249	30	70	11	35	.309	.446
Aledmys Díaz	.263	422	55	111	18	55	.303	.453
Kevin Pillar	.252	512	65	129	15	59	.282	.426
Kendrys Morales	.249	413	47	103	21	57	.331	.438
Luke Maile	.248	202	22	50	3	27	.333	.366
Josh Donaldson*	.246	187	30	46	8	23	.352	.449
Randal Grichuk	.245	424	60	104	25	61	.301	.502
Curtis Granderson#	.245	302	48	74	11	35	.342	.430
Justin Smoak	.242	505	67	122	25	77	.350	.457
Teoscar Hernández	.239	476	67	114	22	57	.302	.468
Devon Travis	.232	357	41	83	11	44	.275	.381
Yangervis Solarte	.226	468	50	106	17	54	.277	.378
Russell Martin	.194	289	37	56	10	25	.338	.325

Pitchers	ERA	W	L	IP	H	BB	SO	SV
Roberto Osuna*	2.37	2	2	38.0	33	4	32	21
J.A. Happ*	3.65	17	6	177.2	150	51	193	0
Ryan Borucki	3.87	4	6	97.2	96	33	67	0
Ken Giles*	4.65	0	3	50.1	54	7	53	26
Aaron Sanchez	4.89	4	6	105.0	106	58	86	0
Sam Gaviglio	5.31	3	10	123.2	140	38	105	0
Marcus Stroman	5.54	4	9	102.1	115	36	77	0
Marco Estrada	5.64	7	14	143.2	155	50	103	0
Jaime García#	5.93	3	6	74.1	76	38	69	0
Joe Biagini	6.00	4	7	72.0	96	24	53	0

Manager: John Gibbons

Major League Leaders, 2018
National League

Batting Average: Christian Yelich, Milwaukee, .326; Scooter Gennett, Cincinnati, .310; Freddie Freeman, Atlanta, .309; Anthony Rendon, Washington, .308; Lorenzo Cain, Milwaukee, .308.

On-Base Percentage: Joey Votto, Cincinnati, .417; Brandon Nimmo, NY Mets, .404; Christian Yelich, Milwaukee, .402; Lorenzo Cain, Milwaukee, .395; Bryce Harper, Washington, .393.

Slugging: Christian Yelich, Milwaukee, .598; Trevor Story, Colorado, .567; Nolan Arenado, Colorado, .561; Javier Báez, Chicago Cubs, .554; Jesús Aguilar, Milwaukee, .539.

Runs Scored: Charlie Blackmon, Colorado, 119; Christian Yelich, Milwaukee, 118; Matt Carpenter, St. Louis, 111; Ozzie Albies, Atlanta, 105; Nolan Arenado, Colorado, 104.

Runs Batted In: Javier Báez, Chicago Cubs, 111; Nolan Arenado, Colorado, 110; Christian Yelich, Milwaukee, 110; Jesús Aguilar, Milwaukee, 108; Trevor Story, Colorado, 108.

Hits: Freddie Freeman, Atlanta, 191; Christian Yelich, Milwaukee, 187; Nick Markakis, Atlanta, 185; Charlie Blackmon, Colorado, 182; José Peraza, Cincinnati, 182.

Doubles: Freddie Freeman, Atlanta, 44; Anthony Rendon, Washington, 44; Nick Markakis, Atlanta, 43; Matt Carpenter, St. Louis, 42; Trevor Story, Colorado, 42.

Triples: Ketel Marte, Arizona, 12; Javier Báez, Chicago Cubs, 9; Billy Hamilton, Cincinnati, 9; Ian Desmond, Colorado, 8; Manuel Margot, San Diego, 8; Brandon Nimmo, NY Mets, 8; Amed Rosario, NY Mets, 8; Chris Taylor, L.A. Dodgers, 8.

Home Runs: Nolan Arenado, Colorado, 38; Trevor Story, Colorado, 37; Matt Carpenter, St. Louis, 36; Christian Yelich, Milwaukee, 36; Jesús Aguilar, Milwaukee, 35; Max Muncy, L.A. Dodgers, 35.

Stolen Bases: Trea Turner, Washington, 43; Billy Hamilton, Cincinnati, 34; Starling Marte, Pittsburgh, 33; Lorenzo Cain, Milwaukee, 30; Ender Inciarte, Atlanta, 28.

Pitching Wins: Jon Lester, Chicago Cubs, 18; Miles Mikolas, St. Louis, 18; Max Scherzer, Washington, 18; Kyle Freeland, Colorado, 17; Aaron Nola, Philadelphia, 17.

Earned Run Average: Jacob deGrom, NY Mets, 1.70; Aaron Nola, Philadelphia, 2.37; Max Scherzer, Washington, 2.53; Miles Mikolas, St. Louis, 2.83; Kyle Freeland, Colorado, 2.85; Mike Foltynewicz, Atlanta, 2.85.

Strikeouts: Max Scherzer, Washington, 300; Jacob deGrom, NY Mets, 269; Patrick Corbin, Arizona, 246; German Márquez, Colorado, 230; Aaron Nola, Philadelphia, 224.

Saves: Wade Davis, Colorado, 43; Kenley Jansen, L.A. Dodgers, 38; Felipe Vázquez, Pittsburgh, 37; Brad Boxberger, Arizona, 32; Raisel Iglesias, Cincinnati, 30.

American League

Batting Average: Mookie Betts, Boston, .346; J.D. Martinez, Boston, .330; José Altuve, Houston, .316; Mike Trout, L.A. Angels, .312; Michael Brantley, Cleveland, .309.

On-Base Percentage: Mike Trout, L.A. Angels, .460; Mookie Betts, Boston, .438; J.D. Martinez, Boston, .402; Alex Bregman, Houston, .394; José Ramírez, Cleveland, .387.

Slugging: Mookie Betts, Boston, .640; J.D. Martinez, Boston, .629; Mike Trout, L.A. Angels, .628; José Ramírez, Cleveland, .552; Khris Davis, Oakland, .549.

Runs Scored: Mookie Betts, Boston, 129; Francisco Lindor, Cleveland, 129; J.D. Martinez, Boston, 111; José Ramírez, Cleveland, 110; Alex Bregman, Houston, 105.

Runs Batted In: J.D. Martinez, Boston, 130; Khris Davis, Oakland, 123; Edwin Encarnacion, Cleveland, 107; José Ramírez, Cleveland, 105; Xander Bogaerts, Boston, 103; Alex Bregman, Houston, 103.

Hits: Whit Merrifield, Kansas City, 192; J.D. Martinez, Boston, 188; Nicholas Castellanos, Detroit, 185; Francisco Lindor, Cleveland, 183; Mookie Betts, Boston, 180.

Doubles: Alex Bregman, Houston, 51; Miguel Andújar, NY Yankees, 47; Mookie Betts, Boston, 47; Nicholas Castellanos, Detroit, 46; Xander Bogaerts, Boston, 45.

Triples: Yolmer Sánchez, Chicago White Sox, 10; Mallex Smith, Tampa Bay, 10; Kevin Kiermaier, Tampa Bay, 9; Dee Gordon, Seattle, 8; Brett Gardner, NY Yankees, 7; Teoscar Hernández, Toronto, 7; Denard Span, Seattle/Tampa Bay, 7.

Home Runs: Khris Davis, Oakland, 48; J.D. Martinez, Boston, 43; Joey Gallo, Texas, 40; José Ramírez, Cleveland, 39; Mike Trout, L.A. Angels, 39.

Stolen Bases: Whit Merrifield, Kansas City, 45; Mallex Smith, Tampa Bay, 40; José Ramírez, Cleveland, 34; Adalberto Mondesí, Kansas City, 32; Mookie Betts, Boston, 30; Dee Gordon, Seattle, 30.

Pitching Wins: Blake Snell, Tampa Bay, 21; Corey Kluber, Cleveland, 20; Luis Severino, NY Yankees, 19; Carlos Carrasco, Cleveland, 17; J.A. Happ, NY Yankees/Toronto, 17; Rick Porcello, Boston, 17.

Earned Run Average: Blake Snell, Tampa Bay, 1.89; Trevor Bauer, Cleveland, 2.21; Justin Verlander, Houston, 2.52; Gerrit Cole, Houston, 2.88; Corey Kluber, Cleveland, 2.89.

Strikeouts: Justin Verlander, Houston, 290; Gerrit Cole, Houston, 276; Chris Sale, Boston, 237; Carlos Carrasco, Cleveland, 231; Corey Kluber, Cleveland, 222.

Saves: Edwin Díaz, Seattle, 57; Craig Kimbrel, Boston, 42; Blake Treinen, Oakland, 38; Aroldis Chapman, NY Yankees, 32; Shane Greene, Detroit, 32.

All-Time Major League Single-Season Leaders

Source: www.mlb.com; * = Active in 2018 season; records for "modern" era beginning in 1901.

Home Runs
Barry Bonds (2001)	73
Mark McGwire (1998)	70
Sammy Sosa (1998)	66
Mark McGwire (1999)	65
Sammy Sosa (2001)	64

Runs Scored
Babe Ruth (1921)	177
Lou Gehrig (1936)	167
Lou Gehrig (1931)	163
Babe Ruth (1928)	163
Chuck Klein (1930)	158
Babe Ruth (1920, 1927)	158

Hits
Ichiro Suzuki* (2004)	262
George Sisler (1920)	257
Lefty O'Doul (1929)	254
Bill Terry (1930)	254
Al Simmons (1925)	253
Rogers Hornsby (1922)	250
Chuck Klein (1930)	250

Runs Batted In
Hack Wilson (1930)	191
Lou Gehrig (1931)	184
Hank Greenberg (1937)	183
Jimmie Foxx (1938)	175
Lou Gehrig (1927)	175

Batting Average
Rogers Hornsby (1924)	.424
Nap Lajoie (1901)	.421
George Sisler (1922)	.420
Ty Cobb (1911)	.420
Ty Cobb (1912)	.410

Stolen Bases
Rickey Henderson (1982)	130
Lou Brock (1974)	118
Vince Coleman (1985)	110
Vince Coleman (1987)	109
Rickey Henderson (1983)	108

Walks (Batter)
Barry Bonds (2004)	232
Barry Bonds (2002)	198
Barry Bonds (2001)	177
Babe Ruth (1923)	170
Mark McGwire (1998)	162
Ted Williams (1947, 1949)	162

Strikeouts (Batter)
Mark Reynolds* (2009)	223
Adam Dunn (2012)	222
Chris Davis* (2016)	219
Yoán Moncada* (2018)	217
Chris Carter (2013)	212

Earned Run Average
Dutch Leonard (1914)	0.96
Mordecai "Three Finger" Brown (1906)	1.04
Bob Gibson (1968)	1.12
Christy Mathewson (1909)	1.14
Walter Johnson (1913)	1.14

Wins (Pitcher)
Jack Chesbro (1904)	41
Ed Walsh (1908)	40
Christy Mathewson (1908)	37
Walter Johnson (1913)	36
Joe McGinnity (1904)	35

Strikeouts (Pitcher)
Nolan Ryan (1973)	383
Sandy Koufax (1965)	382
Randy Johnson (2001)	372
Nolan Ryan (1974)	367
Randy Johnson (1999)	364

Saves
Francisco Rodríguez (2008)	62
Edwin Díaz* (2018)	57
Bobby Thigpen (1990)	57
Eric Gagne (2003)	55
John Smoltz (2002)	55
Trevor Hoffman (1998)	53
Randy Myers (1993)	53
Mariano Rivera (2004)	53

All-Time Major League Leaders

Source: www.mlb.com; * = Active in 2018 season; career records for players in "modern" era beginning in 1901 may include statistics from preceding years.

Games

Pete Rose	3,562
Carl Yastrzemski	3,308
Hank Aaron	3,298
Rickey Henderson	3,081
Ty Cobb	3,035
Eddie Murray	3,026
Stan Musial	3,026
Cal Ripken Jr.	3,001
Willie Mays	2,992
Barry Bonds	2,986

At Bats

Pete Rose	14,053
Hank Aaron	12,364
Carl Yastrzemski	11,988
Cal Ripken Jr.	11,551
Ty Cobb	11,429
Eddie Murray	11,336
Derek Jeter	11,195
Adrián Beltré*	11,068
Robin Yount	11,008
Dave Winfield	11,003

Runs Batted In

Hank Aaron	2,297
Babe Ruth	2,213
Alex Rodriguez	2,086
Barry Bonds	1,996
Lou Gehrig	1,995
Albert Pujols*	1,982
Stan Musial	1,951
Ty Cobb	1,938
Jimmie Foxx	1,922
Eddie Murray	1,917

Runs

Rickey Henderson	2,295
Ty Cobb	2,246
Barry Bonds	2,227
Hank Aaron	2,174
Babe Ruth	2,174
Pete Rose	2,165
Willie Mays	2,062
Alex Rodriguez	2,021
Stan Musial	1,949
Derek Jeter	1,923

Stolen Bases

Rickey Henderson	1,406
Lou Brock	938
Billy Hamilton	912
Ty Cobb	892
Tim Raines	808
Vince Coleman	752
Eddie Collins	745
Arlie Latham	739
Max Carey	738
Honus Wagner	722

Triples

Sam Crawford	309
Ty Cobb	297
Honus Wagner	252
Jake Beckley	243
Roger Connor	233
Tris Speaker	222
Fred Clarke	220
Dan Brouthers	205
Joe Kelley	194
Paul Waner	191

Batting Average

Ty Cobb	.367
Rogers Hornsby	.358
Joe Jackson	.356
Ed Delahanty	.346
Tris Speaker	.345
Ted Williams	.344
Billy Hamilton	.344
Dan Brouthers	.342
Babe Ruth	.342
Harry Heilmann	.342

Walks (Batter)

Barry Bonds	2,558
Rickey Henderson	2,190
Babe Ruth	2,062
Ted Williams	2,019
Joe Morgan	1,865
Carl Yastrzemski	1,845
Jim Thome	1,747
Mickey Mantle	1,733
Mel Ott	1,708
Frank Thomas	1,667

Strikeouts (Pitcher)

Nolan Ryan	5,714
Randy Johnson	4,875
Roger Clemens	4,672
Steve Carlton	4,136
Bert Blyleven	3,701
Tom Seaver	3,640
Don Sutton	3,574
Gaylord Perry	3,534
Walter Johnson	3,508
Greg Maddux	3,371

Saves

Mariano Rivera	652
Trevor Hoffman	601
Lee Smith	478
Francisco Rodríguez	437
John Franco	424
Billy Wagner	422
Dennis Eckersley	390
Joe Nathan	377
Jonathan Papelbon	368
Jeff Reardon	367

Shutouts

Walter Johnson	110
Grover Alexander	90
Christy Mathewson	79
Cy Young	76
Eddie Plank	69
Warren Spahn	63
Nolan Ryan	61
Tom Seaver	61
Bert Blyleven	60
Don Sutton	58

Losses

Cy Young	316
Nolan Ryan	292
Walter Johnson	279
Phil Niekro	274
Gaylord Perry	265
Don Sutton	256
Jack Powell	254
Eppa Rixey	251
Bert Blyleven	250
Robin Roberts	245
Warren Spahn	245

All-Time Home Run Leaders

Source: www.mlb.com; * = Active in 2018 season.

Player	HR	Player	HR	Player	HR	Player	HR
Barry Bonds	762	Manny Ramirez	555	Fred McGriff	493	Jason Giambi	440
Hank Aaron	755	Mike Schmidt	548	Adrián Beltré*	477	Paul Konerko	439
Babe Ruth	714	David Ortiz	541	Stan Musial	475	Andre Dawson	438
Alex Rodriguez	696	Mickey Mantle	536	Willie Stargell	475	Carlos Beltran	435
Willie Mays	660	Jimmie Foxx	534	Carlos Delgado	473	Juan Gonzalez	434
Albert Pujols*	633	Willie McCovey	521	Chipper Jones	468	Andruw Jones	434
Ken Griffey Jr.	630	Frank Thomas	521	Miguel Cabrera*	465	Cal Ripken Jr.	431
Jim Thome	612	Ted Williams	521	Dave Winfield	465	Mike Piazza	427
Sammy Sosa	609	Ernie Banks	512	Jose Canseco	462	Billy Williams	426
Frank Robinson	586	Eddie Mathews	512	Adam Dunn	462	Darrell Evans	414
Mark McGwire	583	Mel Ott	511	Carl Yastrzemski	452	Alfonso Soriano	412
Harmon Killebrew	573	Gary Sheffield	509	Jeff Bagwell	449	Mark Teixeira	409
Rafael Palmeiro	569	Eddie Murray	504	Vladimir Guerrero	449	Duke Snider	407
Reggie Jackson	563	Lou Gehrig	493	Dave Kingman	442		

Players With 3,000 Major League Hits

Source: www.mlb.com; * = Active in 2018 season.

Player	Hits	Player	Hits	Player	Hits	Player	Hits
Pete Rose	4,256	Paul Molitor	3,319	Paul Waner	3,152	Rickey Henderson	3,055
Ty Cobb	4,191	Eddie Collins	3,314	Robin Yount	3,142	Rod Carew	3,053
Hank Aaron	3,771	Willie Mays	3,283	Tony Gwynn	3,141	Lou Brock	3,023
Stan Musial	3,630	Eddie Murray	3,255	Alex Rodriguez	3,115	Rafael Palmeiro	3,020
Tris Speaker	3,515	Nap Lajoie	3,252	Dave Winfield	3,110	Cap Anson	3,011
Derek Jeter	3,465	Cal Ripken Jr.	3,184	Ichiro Suzuki*	3,089	Wade Boggs	3,010
Honus Wagner	3,430	Adrián Beltré*	3,166	Albert Pujols*	3,082	Al Kaline	3,007
Carl Yastrzemski	3,419	George Brett	3,154	Craig Biggio	3,060	Roberto Clemente	3,000

50 Home Run Club

Only Barry Bonds and Mark McGwire hit 70 or more home runs in a season. Five players—including Babe Ruth and Roger Maris—hit 60 or more, a feat Sammy Sosa accomplished for the third time in 2001.

HR	Player, team	Year	HR	Player, team	Year
73	Barry Bonds, San Francisco Giants	2001	54	Alex Rodriguez, NY Yankees	2007
70	Mark McGwire, St. Louis Cardinals	1998	54	Babe Ruth, NY Yankees	1920
66	Sammy Sosa, Chicago Cubs	1998	54	Babe Ruth, NY Yankees	1928
65	Mark McGwire, St. Louis Cardinals	1999	53	Chris Davis, Baltimore Orioles	2013
64	Sammy Sosa, Chicago Cubs	2001	52	George Foster, Cincinnati Reds	1977
63	Sammy Sosa, Chicago Cubs	1999	52	Aaron Judge, NY Yankees	2017
61	Roger Maris, NY Yankees	1961	52	Mickey Mantle, NY Yankees	1956
60	Babe Ruth, NY Yankees	1927	52	Willie Mays, San Francisco Giants	1965
59	Babe Ruth, NY Yankees	1921	52	Mark McGwire, Oakland A's	1996
59	Giancarlo Stanton, Miami Marlins	2017	52	Alex Rodriguez, Texas Rangers	2001
58	Jimmie Foxx, Philadelphia Athletics	1932	52	Jim Thome, Cleveland Indians	2002
58	Hank Greenberg, Detroit Tigers	1938	51	Cecil Fielder, Detroit Tigers	1990
58	Ryan Howard, Philadelphia Phillies	2006	51	Andruw Jones, Atlanta Braves	2005
58	Mark McGwire, Oakland A's/St. Louis Cardinals	1997	51	Ralph Kiner, Pittsburgh Pirates	1947
57	Luis Gonzalez, Arizona Diamondbacks	2001	51	Willie Mays, NY Giants	1955
57	Alex Rodriguez, Texas Rangers	2002	51	Johnny Mize, NY Giants	1947
56	Ken Griffey Jr., Seattle Mariners	1997	50	Brady Anderson, Baltimore Orioles	1996
56	Ken Griffey Jr., Seattle Mariners	1998	50	Albert Belle, Cleveland Indians	1995
56	Hack Wilson, Chicago Cubs	1930	50	Prince Fielder, Milwaukee Brewers	2007
54	José Bautista, Toronto Blue Jays	2010	50	Jimmie Foxx, Boston Red Sox	1938
54	Ralph Kiner, Pittsburgh Pirates	1949	50	Sammy Sosa, Chicago Cubs	2000
54	Mickey Mantle, NY Yankees	1961	50	Greg Vaughn, San Diego Padres	1998
54	David Ortiz, Boston Red Sox	2006			

Pitchers With 300 Major League Wins

Source: www.mlb.com

Pitcher	Wins	Pitcher	Wins	Pitcher	Wins	Pitcher	Wins
Cy Young	511	Charles "Kid" Nichols	361	Eddie Plank	326	Charley Radbourn	309
Walter Johnson	417	Greg Maddux	355	Nolan Ryan	324	Mickey Welch	307
Grover Alexander	373	Roger Clemens	354	Don Sutton	324	Tom Glavine	305
Christy Mathewson	373	Tim Keefe	342	Phil Niekro	318	Randy Johnson	303
Warren Spahn	363	Steve Carlton	329	Gaylord Perry	314	Robert "Lefty" Grove	300
James "Pud" Galvin	361	John Clarkson	328	Tom Seaver	311	Early "Gus" Wynn	300

Official Major League Perfect Games Since 1901

Date	Pitcher	Teams	Date	Pitcher	Teams
5/5/1904	Cy Young	Boston 3 vs. Phil. 0 (AL)	7/28/1994	Kenny Rogers	Texas 4 vs. California 0 (AL)
10/2/1908	Addie Joss	Clev. 1 vs. Chicago 0 (AL)	5/17/1998	David Wells	NY 4 vs. Minn. 0 (AL)
4/30/1922	Charlie Robertson	Chicago 2 vs. Detroit 0 (AL)	7/18/1999	David Cone	NY 6 vs. Montréal 0 (AL)
10/8/1956	Don Larsen	NY 2 (AL) vs. Brooklyn 0* (NL)	5/18/2004	Randy Johnson	Arizona 2 vs. Atlanta 0 (NL)
6/21/1964	Jim Bunning	Phil. 6 vs. NY 0 (NL)	7/23/2009	Mark Buehrle	Chicago 5 vs. Tampa Bay 0 (AL)
9/9/1965	Sandy Koufax	L.A. 1 vs. Chicago 0 (NL)	5/9/2010	Dallas Braden	Oakland 4 vs. Tampa Bay 0 (AL)
5/8/1968	Jim "Catfish" Hunter	Oakland 4 vs. Minn. 0 (AL)	5/29/2010	Roy Halladay	Phil. 1 vs. Florida 0 (NL)
5/15/1981	Len Barker	Clev. 3 vs. Toronto 0 (AL)	4/21/2012	Philip Humber	Chicago 4 vs. Seattle 0 (AL)
9/30/1984	Mike Witt	California 1 vs. Texas 0 (AL)	6/13/2012	Matt Cain	S.F. 10 vs. Houston 0 (NL)
9/16/1988	Tom Browning	Cincinnati 1 vs. L.A. 0 (NL)	8/15/2012	Felix Hernandez	Seattle 1 vs. Tampa Bay 0 (AL)
7/28/1991	Dennis Martinez	Montréal 2 vs. L.A. 0 (NL)			

* = World Series game. **Note:** Two pre-1901 National League pitchers are also credited with perfect games. Within one week in 1880, Lee Richmond (June 12, Worcester 1, Cleveland 0) and John "Monte" Ward (June 17, Providence 5, Buffalo 0) each threw a perfect game.

Most Career Major League No-Hitters

No.	Pitcher	No.	Pitcher
7	Nolan Ryan	2	Jake Arrieta, Homer Bailey, Mark Buehrle, Jim Bunning, Steve Busby, Carl Erskine, Bob Forsch, Pud Galvin, Roy Halladay, Ken Holtzman, Randy Johnson, Addie Joss, Dutch Leonard, Tim Lincecum, Jim Maloney, Christy Mathewson, Hideo Nomo, Allie Reynolds, Max Scherzer, Frank Smith, Warren Spahn, Bill Stoneman, Virgil Trucks, Johnny Vander Meer, Justin Verlander, Don Wilson
4	Sandy Koufax		
3	Larry Corcoran, Bob Feller, Cy Young		

Home Run Leaders by Season, 1901-2018

* = All-time single-season record for league since beginning of "modern" era in 1901.

	National League			American League	
Year	Player, team	HR	Year	Player, team	HR
1901	Sam Crawford, Cincinnati	16	1901	Nap Lajoie, Philadelphia	14
1902	Thomas Leach, Pittsburgh	6	1902	Socks Seybold, Philadelphia	16
1903	James Sheckard, Brooklyn	9	1903	Buck Freeman, Boston	13
1904	Harry Lumley, Brooklyn	9	1904	Harry Davis, Philadelphia	10
1905	Fred Odwell, Cincinnati	9	1905	Harry Davis, Philadelphia	8
1906	Timothy Jordan, Brooklyn	12	1906	Harry Davis, Philadelphia	12
1907	David Brain, Boston	10	1907	Harry Davis, Philadelphia	8
1908	Timothy Jordan, Brooklyn	12	1908	Sam Crawford, Detroit	7
1909	Red Murray, New York	7	1909	Ty Cobb, Detroit	9
1910	Fred Beck, Boston; Frank Schulte, Chicago	10	1910	Jake Stahl, Boston	10
1911	Frank Schulte, Chicago	21	1911	J. Franklin Baker, Philadelphia	11
1912	Henry Zimmerman, Chicago	14	1912	J. Franklin Baker, Phil.; Tris Speaker, Boston	10
1913	Gavvy Cravath, Philadelphia	19	1913	J. Franklin Baker, Philadelphia	12
1914	Gavvy Cravath, Philadelphia	19	1914	J. Franklin Baker, Philadelphia	9
1915	Gavvy Cravath, Philadelphia	24	1915	Robert Roth, Chicago-Cleveland	7
1916	Dave Robertson, NY; Fred "Cy" Williams, Chicago	12	1916	Wally Pipp, New York	12
1917	Gavvy Cravath, Phil.; Dave Robertson, NY	12	1917	Wally Pipp, New York	9

National League			American League		
Year	Player, team	HR	Year	Player, team	HR
1918	Gavvy Cravath, Philadelphia	8	1918	Babe Ruth, Boston; Tilly Walker, Philadelphia	11
1919	Gavvy Cravath, Philadelphia	12	1919	Babe Ruth, Boston	29
1920	Cy Williams, Philadelphia	15	1920	Babe Ruth, New York	54
1921	George Kelly, New York	23	1921	Babe Ruth, New York	59
1922	Rogers Hornsby, St. Louis	42	1922	Ken Williams, St. Louis	39
1923	Cy Williams, Philadelphia	41	1923	Babe Ruth, New York	41
1924	Jacques Fournier, Brooklyn	27	1924	Babe Ruth, New York	46
1925	Rogers Hornsby, St. Louis	39	1925	Bob Meusel, New York	33
1926	Hack Wilson, Chicago	21	1926	Babe Ruth, New York	47
1927	Hack Wilson, Chicago; Cy Williams, Philadelphia	30	1927	Babe Ruth, New York	60
1928	Hack Wilson, Chicago; Jim Bottomley, St. Louis	31	1928	Babe Ruth, New York	54
1929	Chuck Klein, Philadelphia	43	1929	Babe Ruth, New York	46
1930	Hack Wilson, Chicago	56	1930	Babe Ruth, New York	49
1931	Chuck Klein, Philadelphia	31	1931	Lou Gehrig, New York; Babe Ruth, New York	46
1932	Chuck Klein, Philadelphia; Mel Ott, New York	38	1932	Jimmie Foxx, Philadelphia	58
1933	Chuck Klein, Philadelphia	28	1933	Jimmie Foxx, Philadelphia	48
1934	Rip Collins, St. Louis; Mel Ott, New York	35	1934	Lou Gehrig, New York	49
1935	Walter Berger, Boston	34	1935	Jimmie Foxx, Phil.; Hank Greenberg, Detroit	36
1936	Mel Ott, New York	33	1936	Lou Gehrig, New York	49
1937	Joe Medwick, St. Louis; Mel Ott, New York	31	1937	Joe DiMaggio, New York	46
1938	Mel Ott, New York	36	1938	Hank Greenberg, Detroit	58
1939	John Mize, St. Louis	28	1939	Jimmie Foxx, Boston	35
1940	John Mize, St. Louis	43	1940	Hank Greenberg, Detroit	41
1941	Dolph Camilli, Brooklyn	34	1941	Ted Williams, Boston	37
1942	Mel Ott, New York	30	1942	Ted Williams, Boston	36
1943	Bill Nicholson, Chicago	29	1943	Rudy York, Detroit	34
1944	Bill Nicholson, Chicago	33	1944	Nick Etten, New York	22
1945	Tommy Holmes, Boston	28	1945	Vern Stephens, St. Louis	24
1946	Ralph Kiner, Pittsburgh	23	1946	Hank Greenberg, Detroit	44
1947	Ralph Kiner, Pittsburgh; John Mize, New York	51	1947	Ted Williams, Boston	32
1948	Ralph Kiner, Pittsburgh; John Mize, New York	40	1948	Joe DiMaggio, New York	39
1949	Ralph Kiner, Pittsburgh	54	1949	Ted Williams, Boston	43
1950	Ralph Kiner, Pittsburgh	47	1950	Al Rosen, Cleveland	37
1951	Ralph Kiner, Pittsburgh	42	1951	Gus Zernial, Chicago-Philadelphia	33
1952	Ralph Kiner, Pittsburgh; Hank Sauer, Chicago	37	1952	Larry Doby, Cleveland	32
1953	Ed Mathews, Milwaukee	47	1953	Al Rosen, Cleveland	43
1954	Ted Kluszewski, Cincinnati	49	1954	Larry Doby, Cleveland	32
1955	Willie Mays, New York	51	1955	Mickey Mantle, New York	37
1956	Duke Snider, Brooklyn	43	1956	Mickey Mantle, New York	52
1957	Hank Aaron, Milwaukee	44	1957	Roy Sievers, Washington	42
1958	Ernie Banks, Chicago	47	1958	Mickey Mantle, New York	42
1959	Ed Mathews, Milwaukee	46	1959	Rocky Colavito, Clev.; Harmon Killebrew, Wash.	42
1960	Ernie Banks, Chicago	41	1960	Mickey Mantle, New York	40
1961	Orlando Cepeda, San Francisco	46	1961	Roger Maris, New York	61*
1962	Willie Mays, San Francisco	49	1962	Harmon Killebrew, Minnesota	48
1963	Hank Aaron, Milwaukee; Willie McCovey, S.F.	44	1963	Harmon Killebrew, Minnesota	45
1964	Willie Mays, San Francisco	47	1964	Harmon Killebrew, Minnesota	49
1965	Willie Mays, San Francisco	52	1965	Tony Conigliaro, Boston	32
1966	Hank Aaron, Atlanta	44	1966	Frank Robinson, Baltimore	49
1967	Hank Aaron, Atlanta	39	1967	Harmon Killebrew, Minn.; Carl Yastrzemski, Boston	44
1968	Willie McCovey, San Francisco	36	1968	Frank Howard, Washington	44
1969	Willie McCovey, San Francisco	45	1969	Harmon Killebrew, Minnesota	49
1970	Johnny Bench, Cincinnati	45	1970	Frank Howard, Washington	44
1971	Willie Stargell, Pittsburgh	48	1971	Bill Melton, Chicago	33
1972	Johnny Bench, Cincinnati	40	1972	Dick Allen, Chicago	37
1973	Willie Stargell, Pittsburgh	44	1973	Reggie Jackson, Oakland	32
1974	Mike Schmidt, Philadelphia	36	1974	Dick Allen, Chicago	32
1975	Mike Schmidt, Philadelphia	38	1975	Reggie Jackson, Oak.; George Scott, Milw.	36
1976	Mike Schmidt, Philadelphia	38	1976	Graig Nettles, New York	32
1977	George Foster, Cincinnati	52	1977	Jim Rice, Boston	39
1978	George Foster, Cincinnati	40	1978	Jim Rice, Boston	46
1979	Dave Kingman, Chicago	48	1979	Gorman Thomas, Milwaukee	45
1980	Mike Schmidt, Philadelphia	48	1980	Reggie Jackson, New York; Ben Oglivie, Milw.	41
1981	Mike Schmidt, Philadelphia	31	1981	Tony Armas, Oakland; Dwight Evans, Boston; Bobby Grich, Cal.; Eddie Murray, Baltimore	22
1982	Dave Kingman, New York	37	1982	Gorman Thomas, Milw.; Reggie Jackson, Cal.	39
1983	Mike Schmidt, Philadelphia	40	1983	Jim Rice, Boston	39
1984	Dale Murphy, Atlanta; Mike Schmidt, Philadelphia	36	1984	Tony Armas, Boston	43
1985	Dale Murphy, Atlanta	37	1985	Darrell Evans, Detroit	40
1986	Mike Schmidt, Philadelphia	37	1986	Jesse Barfield, Toronto	40
1987	Andre Dawson, Chicago	49	1987	Mark McGwire, Oakland	49
1988	Darryl Strawberry, New York	39	1988	Jose Canseco, Oakland	42
1989	Kevin Mitchell, San Francisco	47	1989	Fred McGriff, Toronto	36
1990	Ryne Sandberg, Chicago	40	1990	Cecil Fielder, Detroit	51
1991	Howard Johnson, New York	38	1991	Jose Canseco, Oakland; Cecil Fielder, Detroit	44
1992	Fred McGriff, San Diego	35	1992	Juan Gonzalez, Texas	43
1993	Barry Bonds, San Francisco	46	1993	Juan Gonzalez, Texas	46
1994	Matt Williams, San Francisco	43	1994	Ken Griffey Jr., Seattle	40
1995	Dante Bichette, Colorado	40	1995	Albert Belle, Cleveland	50
1996	Andres Galarraga, Colorado	47	1996	Mark McGwire, Oakland	52
1997[1]	Larry Walker, Colorado	49	1997[1]	Ken Griffey Jr., Seattle	56
1998	Mark McGwire, St. Louis	70	1998	Ken Griffey Jr., Seattle	56
1999	Mark McGwire, St. Louis	65	1999	Ken Griffey Jr., Seattle	48
2000	Sammy Sosa, Chicago	50	2000	Troy Glaus, Anaheim	47
2001	Barry Bonds, San Francisco	73*	2001	Alex Rodriguez, Texas	52
2002	Sammy Sosa, Chicago	49	2002	Alex Rodriguez, Texas	57
2003	Jim Thome, Philadelphia	47	2003	Alex Rodriguez, Texas	47
2004	Adrián Beltré, Los Angeles	48	2004	Manny Ramirez, Boston	43
2005	Andruw Jones, Atlanta	51	2005	Alex Rodriguez, New York	48

National League			American League		
Year	Player, team	HR	Year	Player, team	HR
2006	Ryan Howard, Philadelphia	58	2006	David Ortiz, Boston	54
2007	Prince Fielder, Milwaukee	50	2007	Alex Rodriguez, New York	54
2008	Ryan Howard, Philadelphia	48	2008	Miguel Cabrera, Detroit	37
2009	Albert Pujols, St. Louis	47	2009	Carlos Peña, Tampa Bay; Mark Teixeira, New York	39
2010	Albert Pujols, St. Louis	42	2010	José Bautista, Toronto	54
2011	Matt Kemp, Los Angeles	39	2011	José Bautista, Toronto	43
2012	Ryan Braun, Milwaukee	41	2012	Miguel Cabrera, Detroit	44
2013	Pedro Alvarez, Pitt.; Paul Goldschmidt, Arizona	36	2013	Chris Davis, Baltimore	53
2014	Giancarlo Stanton, Miami	37	2014	Nelson Cruz, Baltimore	40
2015	Nolan Arenado, Colorado; Bryce Harper, Washington	42	2015	Chris Davis, Baltimore	47
2016	Nolan Arenado, Colorado; Chris Carter, Milwaukee	41	2016	Mark Trumbo, Baltimore	47
2017	Giancarlo Stanton, Miami	59	2017	Aaron Judge, New York	52
2018	Nolan Arenado, Colorado	38	2018	Khris Davis, Oakland	48

(1) In 1997, Mark McGwire hit 58 home runs, 34 with the Oakland Athletics (AL) and 24 with the St. Louis Cardinals (NL).

Batting Champions by Season, 1901-2018

* = All-time single-season record for league since beginning of "modern" era in 1901.

National League			American League		
Year	Player, team	AVG	Year	Player, team	AVG
1901	Jesse C. Burkett, St. Louis	.376	1901[1]	Nap Lajoie, Philadelphia	.426*
1902	Clarence Beaumont, Pittsburgh	.357	1902	Ed Delahanty, Washington	.376
1903	Honus Wagner, Pittsburgh	.355	1903	Nap Lajoie, Cleveland	.357
1904	Honus Wagner, Pittsburgh	.349	1904	Nap Lajoie, Cleveland	.382
1905	James Seymour, Cincinnati	.377	1905	Elmer Flick, Cleveland	.308
1906	Honus Wagner, Pittsburgh	.339	1906	George Stone, St. Louis	.358
1907	Honus Wagner, Pittsburgh	.350	1907	Ty Cobb, Detroit	.350
1908	Honus Wagner, Pittsburgh	.354	1908	Ty Cobb, Detroit	.324
1909	Honus Wagner, Pittsburgh	.339	1909	Ty Cobb, Detroit	.377
1910	Sherwood Magee, Philadelphia	.331	1910[2]	Ty Cobb, Detroit	.385
1911	Honus Wagner, Pittsburgh	.334	1911	Ty Cobb, Detroit	.420
1912	Henry Zimmerman, Chicago	.372	1912	Ty Cobb, Detroit	.410
1913	Jacob Daubert, Brooklyn	.350	1913	Ty Cobb, Detroit	.390
1914	Jacob Daubert, Brooklyn	.329	1914	Ty Cobb, Detroit	.368
1915	Larry Doyle, New York	.320	1915	Ty Cobb, Detroit	.369
1916	Hal Chase, Cincinnati	.339	1916	Tris Speaker, Cleveland	.386
1917	Edd Roush, Cincinnati	.341	1917	Ty Cobb, Detroit	.383
1918	Zach Wheat, Brooklyn	.335	1918	Ty Cobb, Detroit	.382
1919	Edd Roush, Cincinnati	.321	1919	Ty Cobb, Detroit	.384
1920	Rogers Hornsby, St. Louis	.370	1920	George Sisler, St. Louis	.407
1921	Rogers Hornsby, St. Louis	.397	1921	Harry Heilmann, Detroit	.394
1922	Rogers Hornsby, St. Louis	.401	1922	George Sisler, St. Louis	.420
1923	Rogers Hornsby, St. Louis	.384	1923	Harry Heilmann, Detroit	.403
1924	Rogers Hornsby, St. Louis	.424*	1924	Babe Ruth, New York	.378
1925	Rogers Hornsby, St. Louis	.403	1925	Harry Heilmann, Detroit	.393
1926	Eugene Hargrave, Cincinnati	.353	1926	Henry Manush, Detroit	.378
1927	Paul Waner, Pittsburgh	.380	1927	Harry Heilmann, Detroit	.398
1928	Rogers Hornsby, Boston	.387	1928	Goose Goslin, Washington	.379
1929	Lefty O'Doul, Philadelphia	.398	1929	Lew Fonseca, Cleveland	.369
1930	Bill Terry, New York	.401	1930	Al Simmons, Philadelphia	.381
1931	Chick Hafey, St. Louis	.349	1931	Al Simmons, Philadelphia	.390
1932	Lefty O'Doul, Brooklyn	.368	1932	Dale Alexander, Detroit-Boston	.367
1933	Chuck Klein, Philadelphia	.368	1933	Jimmie Foxx, Philadelphia	.356
1934	Paul Waner, Pittsburgh	.362	1934	Lou Gehrig, New York	.363
1935	Arky Vaughan, Pittsburgh	.385	1935	Buddy Myer, Washington	.349
1936	Paul Waner, Pittsburgh	.373	1936	Luke Appling, Chicago	.388
1937	Joe Medwick, St. Louis	.374	1937	Charlie Gehringer, Detroit	.371
1938	Ernie Lombardi, Cincinnati	.342	1938	Jimmie Foxx, Boston	.349
1939	John Mize, St. Louis	.349	1939	Joe DiMaggio, New York	.381
1940	Debs Garms, Pittsburgh	.355	1940	Joe DiMaggio, New York	.352
1941	Pete Reiser, Brooklyn	.343	1941	Ted Williams, Boston	.406
1942	Ernie Lombardi, Boston	.330	1942	Ted Williams, Boston	.356
1943	Stan Musial, St. Louis	.357	1943	Luke Appling, Chicago	.328
1944	Dixie Walker, Brooklyn	.357	1944	Lou Boudreau, Cleveland	.327
1945	Phil Cavarretta, Chicago	.355	1945	George Stirnweiss, New York	.309
1946	Stan Musial, St. Louis	.365	1946	Mickey Vernon, Washington	.353
1947	Harry Walker, St. Louis-Philadelphia	.363	1947	Ted Williams, Boston	.343
1948	Stan Musial, St. Louis	.376	1948	Ted Williams, Boston	.369
1949	Jackie Robinson, Brooklyn	.342	1949	George Kell, Detroit	.343
1950	Stan Musial, St. Louis	.346	1950	Billy Goodman, Boston	.354
1951	Stan Musial, St. Louis	.355	1951	Ferris Fain, Philadelphia	.344
1952	Stan Musial, St. Louis	.336	1952	Ferris Fain, Philadelphia	.327
1953	Carl Furillo, Brooklyn	.344	1953	Mickey Vernon, Washington	.337
1954	Willie Mays, New York	.345	1954	Roberto Avila, Cleveland	.341
1955	Richie Ashburn, Philadelphia	.338	1955	Al Kaline, Detroit	.340
1956	Hank Aaron, Milwaukee	.328	1956	Mickey Mantle, New York	.353
1957	Stan Musial, St. Louis	.351	1957	Ted Williams, Boston	.388
1958	Richie Ashburn, Philadelphia	.350	1958	Ted Williams, Boston	.328
1959	Hank Aaron, Milwaukee	.355	1959	Harvey Kuenn, Detroit	.353
1960	Dick Groat, Pittsburgh	.325	1960	Pete Runnels, Boston	.320
1961	Roberto Clemente, Pittsburgh	.351	1961	Norm Cash, Detroit	.361
1962	Tommy Davis, Los Angeles	.346	1962	Pete Runnels, Boston	.326
1963	Tommy Davis, Los Angeles	.326	1963	Carl Yastrzemski, Boston	.321
1964	Roberto Clemente, Pittsburgh	.339	1964	Tony Oliva, Minnesota	.323
1965	Roberto Clemente, Pittsburgh	.329	1965	Tony Oliva, Minnesota	.321
1966	Matty Alou, Pittsburgh	.342	1966	Frank Robinson, Baltimore	.316
1967	Roberto Clemente, Pittsburgh	.357	1967	Carl Yastrzemski, Boston	.326
1968	Pete Rose, Cincinnati	.335	1968	Carl Yastrzemski, Boston	.301
1969	Pete Rose, Cincinnati	.348	1969	Rod Carew, Minnesota	.332
1970	Rico Carty, Atlanta	.366	1970	Alex Johnson, California	.329
1971	Joe Torre, St. Louis	.363	1971	Tony Oliva, Minnesota	.337

	National League			American League	
Year	**Player, team**	**AVG**	**Year**	**Player, team**	**AVG**
1972	Billy Williams, Chicago	.333	1972	Rod Carew, Minnesota	.318
1973	Pete Rose, Cincinnati	.338	1973	Rod Carew, Minnesota	.350
1974	Ralph Garr, Atlanta	.353	1974	Rod Carew, Minnesota	.364
1975	Bill Madlock, Chicago	.354	1975	Rod Carew, Minnesota	.359
1976	Bill Madlock, Chicago	.339	1976	George Brett, Kansas City	.333
1977	Dave Parker, Pittsburgh	.338	1977	Rod Carew, Minnesota	.388
1978	Dave Parker, Pittsburgh	.334	1978	Rod Carew, Minnesota	.333
1979	Keith Hernandez, St. Louis	.344	1979	Fred Lynn, Boston	.333
1980	Bill Buckner, Chicago	.324	1980	George Brett, Kansas City	.390
1981	Bill Madlock, Pittsburgh	.341	1981	Carney Lansford, Boston	.336
1982	Al Oliver, Montréal	.331	1982	Willie Wilson, Kansas City	.332
1983	Bill Madlock, Pittsburgh	.323	1983	Wade Boggs, Boston	.361
1984	Tony Gwynn, San Diego	.351	1984	Don Mattingly, New York	.343
1985	Willie McGee, St. Louis	.353	1985	Wade Boggs, Boston	.368
1986	Tim Raines, Montréal	.334	1986	Wade Boggs, Boston	.357
1987	Tony Gwynn, San Diego	.370	1987	Wade Boggs, Boston	.363
1988	Tony Gwynn, San Diego	.313	1988	Wade Boggs, Boston	.366
1989	Tony Gwynn, San Diego	.336	1989	Kirby Puckett, Minnesota	.339
1990	Willie McGee, St. Louis	.335	1990	George Brett, Kansas City	.329
1991	Terry Pendleton, Atlanta	.319	1991	Julio Franco, Texas	.341
1992	Gary Sheffield, San Diego	.330	1992	Edgar Martinez, Seattle	.343
1993	Andres Galarraga, Colorado	.370	1993	John Olerud, Toronto	.363
1994	Tony Gwynn, San Diego	.394	1994	Paul O'Neill, New York	.359
1995	Tony Gwynn, San Diego	.368	1995	Edgar Martinez, Seattle	.356
1996	Tony Gwynn, San Diego	.353	1996	Alex Rodriguez, Seattle	.358
1997	Tony Gwynn, San Diego	.372	1997	Frank Thomas, Chicago	.347
1998	Larry Walker, Colorado	.363	1998	Bernie Williams, New York	.339
1999	Larry Walker, Colorado	.379	1999	Nomar Garciaparra, Boston	.357
2000	Todd Helton, Colorado	.372	2000	Nomar Garciaparra, Boston	.372
2001	Larry Walker, Colorado	.350	2001	Ichiro Suzuki, Seattle	.350
2002	Barry Bonds, San Francisco	.370	2002	Manny Ramirez, Boston	.349
2003	Albert Pujols, St. Louis	.359	2003	Bill Mueller, Boston	.326
2004	Barry Bonds, San Francisco	.362	2004	Ichiro Suzuki, Seattle	.372
2005	Derrek Lee, Chicago	.335	2005	Michael Young, Texas	.331
2006	Freddy Sanchez, Pittsburgh	.344	2006	Joe Mauer, Minnesota	.347
2007	Matt Holliday, Colorado	.340	2007	Magglio Ordoñez, Detroit	.363
2008	Chipper Jones, Atlanta	.364	2008	Joe Mauer, Minnesota	.328
2009	Hanley Ramirez, Florida	.342	2009	Joe Mauer, Minnesota	.365
2010	Carlos Gonzalez, Colorado	.336	2010	Josh Hamilton, Texas	.359
2011	José Reyes, New York	.337	2011	Miguel Cabrera, Detroit	.344
2012	Buster Posey, San Francisco	.336	2012	Miguel Cabrera, Detroit	.330
2013	Michael Cuddyer, Colorado	.331	2013	Miguel Cabrera, Detroit	.348
2014	Justin Morneau, Colorado	.319	2014	José Altuve, Houston	.341
2015	Dee Gordon, Miami	.333	2015	Miguel Cabrera, Detroit	.338
2016	DJ LeMahieu, Colorado	.348	2016	José Altuve, Houston	.338
2017	Charlie Blackmon, Colorado	.331	2017	José Altuve, Houston	.346
2018	Christian Yelich, Milwaukee	.326	2018	Mookie Betts, Boston	.346

(1) Nap Lajoie's 1901 batting average varies in historical records from .421 to .426. (2) Some baseball researchers have concluded that Ty Cobb actually hit .382 in 1910 while Nap Lajoie, Cleveland, hit .383.

Earned Run Average Leaders by Season, 1977-2018

	National League					American League			
Year	**Pitcher, team**	**G**	**IP**	**ERA**	**Year**	**Pitcher, team**	**G**	**IP**	**ERA**
1977	John Candelaria, Pittsburgh	33	230.2	2.34	1977	Frank Tanana, California	31	241.1	2.54
1978	Craig Swan, New York	29	207.1	2.43	1978	Ron Guidry, New York	35	273.2	1.74
1979	J. R. Richard, Houston	38	292.1	2.71	1979	Ron Guidry, New York	33	236.1	2.78
1980	Don Sutton, Los Angeles	32	212.1	2.20	1980	Rudy May, New York	41	175.1	2.46
1981	Nolan Ryan, Houston	21	149.0	1.69	1981	Sammy Stewart, Baltimore	29	112.1	2.32
1982	Steve Rogers, Montréal	35	277.0	2.40	1982	Rick Sutcliffe, Cleveland	34	216.0	2.96
1983	Atlee Hammaker, San Francisco	23	172.1	2.25	1983	Rick Honeycutt, Texas	25	174.2	2.42
1984	Alejandro Peña, Los Angeles	28	199.1	2.48	1984	Mike Boddicker, Baltimore	34	261.1	2.79
1985	Dwight Gooden, New York	35	276.2	1.53	1985	Dave Stieb, Toronto	36	265.0	2.48
1986	Mike Scott, Houston	37	275.1	2.22	1986	Roger Clemens, Boston	33	254.0	2.48
1987	Nolan Ryan, Houston	34	211.2	2.76	1987	Jimmy Key, Toronto	36	261.0	2.76
1988	Joe Magrane, St. Louis	24	165.1	2.18	1988	Allan Anderson, Minnesota	30	202.1	2.45
1989	Scott Garrelts, San Francisco	30	193.1	2.28	1989	Bret Saberhagen, Kansas City	36	262.1	2.16
1990	Danny Darwin, Houston	48	162.2	2.21	1990	Roger Clemens, Boston	31	228.1	1.93
1991	Dennis Martinez, Montréal	31	222.0	2.39	1991	Roger Clemens, Boston	35	271.1	2.62
1992	Bill Swift, San Francisco	30	164.2	2.08	1992	Roger Clemens, Boston	32	246.2	2.41
1993	Greg Maddux, Atlanta	36	267.0	2.36	1993	Kevin Appier, Kansas City	34	238.2	2.56
1994	Greg Maddux, Atlanta	25	202.0	1.56	1994	Steve Ontiveros, Oakland	27	115.1	2.65
1995	Greg Maddux, Atlanta	28	209.2	1.63	1995	Randy Johnson, Seattle	30	214.1	2.48
1996	Kevin Brown, Florida	32	233.0	1.89	1996	Juan Guzmán, Toronto	27	187.2	2.93
1997	Pedro Martinez, Montréal	31	241.1	1.90	1997	Roger Clemens, Toronto	34	264.0	2.05
1998	Greg Maddux, Atlanta	34	251.0	2.22	1998	Roger Clemens, Toronto	33	234.2	2.65
1999	Randy Johnson, Arizona	35	271.2	2.48	1999	Pedro Martinez, Boston	31	213.1	2.07
2000	Kevin Brown, Los Angeles	33	230.0	2.58	2000	Pedro Martinez, Boston	29	217.0	1.74
2001	Randy Johnson, Arizona	35	249.2	2.49	2001	Freddy Garcia, Seattle	34	238.2	3.05
2002	Randy Johnson, Arizona	35	260.0	2.32	2002	Pedro Martinez, Boston	30	199.1	2.26
2003	Jason Schmidt, San Francisco	29	207.2	2.34	2003	Pedro Martinez, Boston	29	186.2	2.22
2004	Jake Peavy, San Diego	27	166.1	2.27	2004	Johan Santana, Minnesota	34	228.0	2.61
2005	Roger Clemens, Houston	32	211.1	1.87	2005	Kevin Millwood, Cleveland	30	192.0	2.86
2006	Roy Oswalt, Houston	33	220.2	2.98	2006	Johan Santana, Minnesota	34	233.2	2.77
2007	Jake Peavy, San Diego	34	223.1	2.54	2007	John Lackey, Los Angeles	33	224.0	3.01
2008	Johan Santana, New York	34	234.1	2.53	2008	Cliff Lee, Cleveland	31	223.1	2.54
2009	Chris Carpenter, St. Louis	28	192.2	2.24	2009	Zack Greinke, Kansas City	33	229.1	2.16
2010	Josh Johnson, Florida	28	183.2	2.30	2010	Felix Hernandez, Seattle	34	249.2	2.27
2011	Clayton Kershaw, Los Angeles	33	233.1	2.28	2011	Justin Verlander, Detroit	34	251.0	2.40
2012	Clayton Kershaw, Los Angeles	33	227.2	2.53	2012	David Price, Tampa Bay	31	211.0	2.56
2013	Clayton Kershaw, Los Angeles	33	236.0	1.83	2013	Anibal Sanchez, Detroit	29	182.0	2.57
2014	Clayton Kershaw, Los Angeles	27	198.1	1.77	2014	Felix Hernandez, Seattle	34	236.0	2.14
2015	Zack Greinke, Los Angeles	32	222.2	1.66	2015	David Price, Detroit-Toronto	32	220.1	2.45
2016	Kyle Hendricks, Chicago	31	190.0	2.13	2016	Aaron Sanchez, Toronto	30	192.0	3.00
2017	Clayton Kershaw, Los Angeles	27	175.0	2.31	2017	Corey Kluber, Cleveland	29	203.2	2.25
2018	Jacob deGrom, NY Mets	32	217.0	1.70	2018	Blake Snell, Tampa Bay	31	180.2	1.89

Strikeout Leaders by Season, 1901-2018

* = All-time single-season record for league since beginning of "modern" era in 1901.

	National League			American League	
Year	Pitcher, team	SO	Year	Pitcher, team	SO
1901	Noodles Hahn, Cincinnati	239	1901	Cy Young, Boston	158
1902	Vic Willis, Boston	225	1902	Rube Waddell, Philadelphia	210
1903	Christy Mathewson, New York	267	1903	Rube Waddell, Philadelphia	302
1904	Christy Mathewson, New York	212	1904	Rube Waddell, Philadelphia	349
1905	Christy Mathewson, New York	206	1905	Rube Waddell, Philadelphia	287
1906	Fred Beebe, Chicago-St. Louis	171	1906	Rube Waddell, Philadelphia	196
1907	Christy Mathewson, New York	178	1907	Rube Waddell, Philadelphia	232
1908	Christy Mathewson, New York	259	1908	Ed Walsh, Chicago	269
1909	Orval Overall, Chicago	205	1909	Frank Smith, Chicago	177
1910	Earl Moore, Philadelphia	185	1910	Walter Johnson, Washington	313
1911	Rube Marquard, New York	237	1911	Ed Walsh, Chicago	255
1912	Grover Alexander, Philadelphia	195	1912	Walter Johnson, Washington	303
1913	Tom Seaton, Philadelphia	168	1913	Walter Johnson, Washington	243
1914	Grover Alexander, Philadelphia	214	1914	Walter Johnson, Washington	225
1915	Grover Alexander, Philadelphia	241	1915	Walter Johnson, Washington	203
1916	Grover Alexander, Philadelphia	167	1916	Walter Johnson, Washington	228
1917	Grover Alexander, Philadelphia	200	1917	Walter Johnson, Washington	188
1918	Hippo Vaughn, Chicago	148	1918	Walter Johnson, Washington	162
1919	Hippo Vaughn, Chicago	141	1919	Walter Johnson, Washington	147
1920	Grover Alexander, Chicago	173	1920	Stan Coveleski, Cleveland	133
1921	Burleigh Grimes, Brooklyn	136	1921	Walter Johnson, Washington	143
1922	Dazzy Vance, Brooklyn	134	1922	Urban Shocker, St. Louis	149
1923	Dazzy Vance, Brooklyn	197	1923	Walter Johnson, Washington	130
1924	Dazzy Vance, Brooklyn	262	1924	Walter Johnson, Washington	158
1925	Dazzy Vance, Brooklyn	221	1925	Lefty Grove, Philadelphia	116
1926	Dazzy Vance, Brooklyn	140	1926	Lefty Grove, Philadelphia	194
1927	Dazzy Vance, Brooklyn	184	1927	Lefty Grove, Philadelphia	174
1928	Dazzy Vance, Brooklyn	200	1928	Lefty Grove, Philadelphia	183
1929	Pat Malone, Chicago	166	1929	Lefty Grove, Philadelphia	170
1930	Bill Hallahan, St. Louis	177	1930	Lefty Grove, Philadelphia	209
1931	Bill Hallahan, St. Louis	159	1931	Lefty Grove, Philadelphia	175
1932	Dizzy Dean, St. Louis	191	1932	Red Ruffing, New York	190
1933	Dizzy Dean, St. Louis	199	1933	Lefty Gomez, New York	163
1934	Dizzy Dean, St. Louis	195	1934	Lefty Gomez, New York	158
1935	Dizzy Dean, St. Louis	190	1935	Tommy Bridges, Detroit	163
1936	Van Lingle Mungo, Brooklyn	238	1936	Tommy Bridges, Detroit	175
1937	Carl Hubbell, New York	159	1937	Lefty Gomez, New York	194
1938	Clay Bryant, Chicago	135	1938	Bob Feller, Cleveland	240
1939	Claude Passeau, Philadelphia-Chicago; Bucky Walters, Cincinnati	137	1939	Bob Feller, Cleveland	246
1940	Kirby Higbe, Philadelphia	137	1940	Bob Feller, Cleveland	261
1941	John Vander Meer, Cincinnati	202	1941	Bob Feller, Cleveland	260
1942	John Vander Meer, Cincinnati	186	1942	Tex Hughson, Boston; Bobo Newsom, Washington	113
1943	John Vander Meer, Cincinnati	174	1943	Allie Reynolds, Cleveland	151
1944	Bill Voiselle, New York	161	1944	Hal Newhouser, Detroit	187
1945	Preacher Roe, Pittsburgh	148	1945	Hal Newhouser, Detroit	212
1946	Johnny Schmitz, Chicago	135	1946	Bob Feller, Cleveland	348
1947	Ewell Blackwell, Cincinnati	193	1947	Bob Feller, Cleveland	196
1948	Harry Brecheen, St. Louis	149	1948	Bob Feller, Cleveland	164
1949	Warren Spahn, Boston	151	1949	Virgil Trucks, Detroit	153
1950	Warren Spahn, Boston	191	1950	Bob Lemon, Cleveland	170
1951	Warren Spahn, Boston; Don Newcombe, Brooklyn	164	1951	Vic Raschi, New York	164
1952	Warren Spahn, Boston	183	1952	Allie Reynolds, New York	160
1953	Robin Roberts, Philadelphia	198	1953	Billy Pierce, Chicago	186
1954	Robin Roberts, Philadelphia	185	1954	Bob Turley, Baltimore	185
1955	Sam Jones, Chicago	198	1955	Herb Score, Cleveland	245
1956	Sam Jones, Chicago	176	1956	Herb Score, Cleveland	263
1957	Jack Sanford, Philadelphia	188	1957	Early Wynn, Cleveland	184
1958	Sam Jones, St. Louis	225	1958	Early Wynn, Chicago	179
1959	Don Drysdale, Los Angeles	242	1959	Jim Bunning, Detroit	201
1960	Don Drysdale, Los Angeles	246	1960	Jim Bunning, Detroit	201
1961	Sandy Koufax, Los Angeles	269	1961	Camilo Pascual, Minnesota	221
1962	Don Drysdale, Los Angeles	232	1962	Camilo Pascual, Minnesota	206
1963	Sandy Koufax, Los Angeles	306	1963	Camilo Pascual, Minnesota	202
1964	Bob Veale, Pittsburgh	250	1964	Al Downing, New York	217
1965	Sandy Koufax, Los Angeles	382*	1965	Sam McDowell, Cleveland	325
1966	Sandy Koufax, Los Angeles	317	1966	Sam McDowell, Cleveland	225
1967	Jim Bunning, Philadelphia	253	1967	Jim Lonborg, Boston	246
1968	Bob Gibson, St. Louis	268	1968	Sam McDowell, Cleveland	283
1969	Ferguson Jenkins, Chicago	273	1969	Sam McDowell, Cleveland	279
1970	Tom Seaver, New York	283	1970	Sam McDowell, Cleveland	304
1971	Tom Seaver, New York	289	1971	Mickey Lolich, Detroit	308
1972	Steve Carlton, Philadelphia	310	1972	Nolan Ryan, California	329
1973	Tom Seaver, New York	251	1973	Nolan Ryan, California	383*
1974	Steve Carlton, Philadelphia	240	1974	Nolan Ryan, California	367
1975	Tom Seaver, New York	243	1975	Frank Tanana, California	269
1976	Tom Seaver, New York	235	1976	Nolan Ryan, California	327
1977	Phil Niekro, Atlanta	262	1977	Nolan Ryan, California	341
1978	J. R. Richard, Houston	303	1978	Nolan Ryan, California	260

National League			American League		
Year	Pitcher, team	SO	Year	Pitcher, team	SO
1979	J. R. Richard, Houston	313	1979	Nolan Ryan, California	223
1980	Steve Carlton, Philadelphia	286	1980	Len Barker, Cleveland	187
1981	Fernando Valenzuela, Los Angeles	180	1981	Len Barker, Cleveland	127
1982	Steve Carlton, Philadelphia	286	1982	Floyd Bannister, Seattle	209
1983	Steve Carlton, Philadelphia	275	1983	Jack Morris, Detroit	232
1984	Dwight Gooden, New York	276	1984	Mark Langston, Seattle	204
1985	Dwight Gooden, New York	268	1985	Bert Blyleven, Cleveland-Minnesota	206
1986	Mike Scott, Houston	306	1986	Mark Langston, Seattle	245
1987	Nolan Ryan, Houston	270	1987	Mark Langston, Seattle	262
1988	Nolan Ryan, Houston	228	1988	Roger Clemens, Boston	291
1989	Jose DeLeon, St. Louis	201	1989	Nolan Ryan, Texas	301
1990	David Cone, New York	233	1990	Nolan Ryan, Texas	232
1991	David Cone, New York	241	1991	Roger Clemens, Boston	241
1992	John Smoltz, Atlanta	215	1992	Randy Johnson, Seattle	241
1993	José Rijo, Cincinnati	227	1993	Randy Johnson, Seattle	308
1994	Andy Benes, San Diego	189	1994	Randy Johnson, Seattle	204
1995	Hideo Nomo, Los Angeles	236	1995	Randy Johnson, Seattle	294
1996	John Smoltz, Atlanta	276	1996	Roger Clemens, Boston	257
1997	Curt Schilling, Philadelphia	319	1997	Roger Clemens, Toronto	292
1998	Curt Schilling, Philadelphia	300	1998	Roger Clemens, Toronto	271
1999	Randy Johnson, Arizona	364	1999	Pedro Martinez, Boston	313
2000	Randy Johnson, Arizona	347	2000	Pedro Martinez, Boston	284
2001	Randy Johnson, Arizona	372	2001	Hideo Nomo, Boston	220
2002	Randy Johnson, Arizona	334	2002	Pedro Martinez, Boston	239
2003	Kerry Wood, Chicago	266	2003	Esteban Loaiza, Chicago	207
2004	Randy Johnson, Arizona	290	2004	Johan Santana, Minnesota	265
2005	Jake Peavy, San Diego	216	2005	Johan Santana, Minnesota	238
2006	Aaron Harang, Cincinnati	216	2006	Johan Santana, Minnesota	245
2007	Jake Peavy, San Diego	240	2007	Scott Kazmir, Tampa Bay	239
2008	Tim Lincecum, San Francisco	265	2008	A. J. Burnett, Toronto	231
2009	Tim Lincecum, San Francisco	261	2009	Justin Verlander, Detroit	269
2010	Tim Lincecum, San Francisco	231	2010	Jered Weaver, Los Angeles	233
2011	Clayton Kershaw, Los Angeles	248	2011	Justin Verlander, Detroit	250
2012	R.A. Dickey, New York	230	2012	Justin Verlander, Detroit	239
2013	Clayton Kershaw, Los Angeles	232	2013	Yu Darvish, Texas	277
2014	Johnny Cueto, Cincinnati;		2014	David Price, Tampa Bay-Detroit	271
	Stephen Strasburg, Washington	242			
2015	Clayton Kershaw, Los Angeles	301	2015	Chris Sale, Chicago	274
2016	Max Scherzer, Washington	284	2016	Justin Verlander, Detroit	254
2017	Max Scherzer, Washington	268	2017	Chris Sale, Boston	308
2018	Max Scherzer, Washington	300	2018	Justin Verlander, Houston	290

Cy Young Award Winners, 1956-2017

Year	Pitcher, team	Year	Pitcher, team	Year	Pitcher, team
1956	Don Newcombe, Brooklyn	1980	(NL) Steve Carlton, Philadelphia	1998	(NL) Tom Glavine, Atlanta
1957	Warren Spahn, Milwaukee		(AL) Steve Stone, Baltimore		(AL) Roger Clemens, Toronto
1958	Bob Turley, NY Yankees	1981	(NL) Fernando Valenzuela, L.A.	1999	(NL) Randy Johnson, Arizona
1959	Early Wynn, Chicago White Sox		(AL) Rollie Fingers, Milwaukee		(AL) Pedro Martinez, Boston
1960	Vernon Law, Pittsburgh	1982	(NL) Steve Carlton, Philadelphia	2000	(NL) Randy Johnson, Arizona
1961	Whitey Ford, NY Yankees		(AL) Pete Vuckovich, Milwaukee		(AL) Pedro Martinez, Boston
1962	Don Drysdale, L.A. Dodgers	1983	(NL) John Denny, Philadelphia	2001	(NL) Randy Johnson, Arizona
1963	Sandy Koufax, L.A. Dodgers		(AL) LaMarr Hoyt, Chicago		(AL) Roger Clemens, NY
1964	Dean Chance, L.A. Angels	1984	(NL) Rick Sutcliffe, Chicago	2002	(NL) Randy Johnson, Arizona
1965	Sandy Koufax, L.A. Dodgers		(AL) Willie Hernandez, Detroit		(AL) Barry Zito, Oakland
1966	Sandy Koufax, L.A. Dodgers	1985	(NL) Dwight Gooden, NY	2003	(NL) Eric Gagne, L.A.
1967	(NL) Mike McCormick, S.F.		(AL) Bret Saberhagen,		(AL) Roy Halladay, Toronto
	(AL) Jim Lonborg, Boston		Kansas City	2004	(NL) Roger Clemens, Houston
1968	(NL) Bob Gibson, St. Louis	1986	(NL) Mike Scott, Houston		(AL) Johan Santana, Minnesota
	(AL) Denny McLain, Detroit		(AL) Roger Clemens, Boston	2005	(NL) Chris Carpenter, St. Louis
1969	(NL) Tom Seaver, NY	1987	(NL) Steve Bedrosian, Phil.		(AL) Bartolo Colon, L.A.
	(AL) Denny McLain, Detroit;		(AL) Roger Clemens, Boston	2006	(NL) Brandon Webb, Arizona
	Mike Cuellar, Baltimore	1988	(NL) Orel Hershiser, L.A.		(AL) Johan Santana, Minnesota
1970	(NL) Bob Gibson, St. Louis		(AL) Frank Viola, Minnesota	2007	(NL) Jake Peavy, San Diego
	(AL) Jim Perry, Minnesota	1989	(NL) Mark Davis, San Diego		(AL) CC Sabathia, Cleveland
1971	(NL) Ferguson Jenkins, Chicago		(AL) Bret Saberhagen,	2008	(NL) Tim Lincecum, S.F.
	(AL) Vida Blue, Oakland		Kansas City		(AL) Cliff Lee, Cleveland
1972	(NL) Steve Carlton, Philadelphia	1990	(NL) Doug Drabek, Pittsburgh	2009	(NL) Tim Lincecum, S.F.
	(AL) Gaylord Perry, Cleveland		(AL) Bob Welch, Oakland		(AL) Zack Greinke, Kansas City
1973	(NL) Tom Seaver, NY	1991	(NL) Tom Glavine, Atlanta	2010	(NL) Roy Halladay, Philadelphia
	(AL) Jim Palmer, Baltimore		(AL) Roger Clemens, Boston		(AL) Felix Hernandez, Seattle
1974	(NL) Mike Marshall, L.A.	1992	(NL) Greg Maddux, Chicago	2011	(NL) Clayton Kershaw, L.A.
	(AL) Jim "Catfish" Hunter,		(AL) Dennis Eckersley, Oakland		(AL) Justin Verlander, Detroit
	Oakland	1993	(NL) Greg Maddux, Atlanta	2012	(NL) R.A. Dickey, NY
1975	(NL) Tom Seaver, NY		(AL) Jack McDowell, Chicago		(AL) David Price, Tampa Bay
	(AL) Jim Palmer, Baltimore	1994	(NL) Greg Maddux, Atlanta	2013	(NL) Clayton Kershaw, L.A.
1976	(NL) Randy Jones, San Diego		(AL) David Cone, Kansas City		(AL) Max Scherzer, Detroit
	(AL) Jim Palmer, Baltimore	1995	(NL) Greg Maddux, Atlanta	2014	(NL) Clayton Kershaw, L.A.
1977	(NL) Steve Carlton, Philadelphia		(AL) Randy Johnson, Seattle		(AL) Corey Kluber, Cleveland
	(AL) Sparky Lyle, NY	1996	(NL) John Smoltz, Atlanta	2015	(NL) Jake Arrieta, Chicago
1978	(NL) Gaylord Perry, San Diego		(AL) Pat Hentgen, Toronto		(AL) Dallas Keuchel, Houston
	(AL) Ron Guidry, NY	1997	(NL) Pedro Martinez, Montréal	2016	(NL) Max Scherzer, Washington
1979	(NL) Bruce Sutter, Chicago		(AL) Roger Clemens, Toronto		(AL) Rick Porcello, Boston
	(AL) Mike Flanagan, Baltimore			2017	(NL) Max Scherzer, Washington
					(AL) Corey Kluber, Cleveland

Most Valuable Players, 1931-2017

As selected by the Baseball Writers' Assn. of America. Prior to 1931, MVP honors were named by various sources.

National League

Year	Player, team	Year	Player, team	Year	Player, team
1931	Frank Frisch, St. Louis	1961	Frank Robinson, Cincinnati	1989	Kevin Mitchell, San Francisco
1932	Chuck Klein, Philadelphia	1962	Maury Wills, Los Angeles	1990	Barry Bonds, Pittsburgh
1933	Carl Hubbell, New York	1963	Sandy Koufax, Los Angeles	1991	Terry Pendleton, Atlanta
1934	Dizzy Dean, St. Louis	1964	Ken Boyer, St. Louis	1992	Barry Bonds, Pittsburgh
1935	Gabby Hartnett, Chicago	1965	Willie Mays, San Francisco	1993	Barry Bonds, San Francisco
1936	Carl Hubbell, New York	1966	Roberto Clemente, Pittsburgh	1994	Jeff Bagwell, Houston
1937	Joe Medwick, St. Louis	1967	Orlando Cepeda, St. Louis	1995	Barry Larkin, Cincinnati
1938	Ernie Lombardi, Cincinnati	1968	Bob Gibson, St. Louis	1996	Ken Caminiti, San Diego
1939	Bucky Walters, Cincinnati	1969	Willie McCovey, San Francisco	1997	Larry Walker, Colorado
1940	Frank McCormick, Cincinnati	1970	Johnny Bench, Cincinnati	1998	Sammy Sosa, Chicago
1941	Dolph Camilli, Brooklyn	1971	Joe Torre, St. Louis	1999	Chipper Jones, Atlanta
1942	Mort Cooper, St. Louis	1972	Johnny Bench, Cincinnati	2000	Jeff Kent, San Francisco
1943	Stan Musial, St. Louis	1973	Pete Rose, Cincinnati	2001	Barry Bonds, San Francisco
1944	Martin Marion, St. Louis	1974	Steve Garvey, Los Angeles	2002	Barry Bonds, San Francisco
1945	Phil Cavarretta, Chicago	1975	Joe Morgan, Cincinnati	2003	Barry Bonds, San Francisco
1946	Stan Musial, St. Louis	1976	Joe Morgan, Cincinnati	2004	Barry Bonds, San Francisco
1947	Bob Elliott, Boston	1977	George Foster, Cincinnati	2005	Albert Pujols, St. Louis
1948	Stan Musial, St. Louis	1978	Dave Parker, Pittsburgh	2006	Ryan Howard, Philadelphia
1949	Jackie Robinson, Brooklyn	1979	Keith Hernandez, St. Louis;	2007	Jimmy Rollins, Philadelphia
1950	Jim Konstanty, Philadelphia		Willie Stargell, Pittsburgh	2008	Albert Pujols, St. Louis
1951	Roy Campanella, Brooklyn	1980	Mike Schmidt, Philadelphia	2009	Albert Pujols, St. Louis
1952	Hank Sauer, Chicago	1981	Mike Schmidt, Philadelphia	2010	Joey Votto, Cincinnati
1953	Roy Campanella, Brooklyn	1982	Dale Murphy, Atlanta	2011	Ryan Braun, Milwaukee
1954	Willie Mays, New York	1983	Dale Murphy, Atlanta	2012	Buster Posey, San Francisco
1955	Roy Campanella, Brooklyn	1984	Ryne Sandberg, Chicago	2013	Andrew McCutchen,
1956	Don Newcombe, Brooklyn	1985	Willie McGee, St. Louis		Pittsburgh
1957	Hank Aaron, Milwaukee	1986	Mike Schmidt, Philadelphia	2014	Clayton Kershaw, Los Angeles
1958	Ernie Banks, Chicago	1987	Andre Dawson, Chicago	2015	Bryce Harper, Washington
1959	Ernie Banks, Chicago	1988	Kirk Gibson, Los Angeles	2016	Kris Bryant, Chicago
1960	Dick Groat, Pittsburgh			2017	Giancarlo Stanton, Miami

American League

Year	Player, team	Year	Player, team	Year	Player, team
1931	Lefty Grove, Philadelphia	1959	Nellie Fox, Chicago	1988	Jose Canseco, Oakland
1932	Jimmie Foxx, Philadelphia	1960	Roger Maris, New York	1989	Robin Yount, Milwaukee
1933	Jimmie Foxx, Philadelphia	1961	Roger Maris, New York	1990	Rickey Henderson, Oakland
1934	Mickey Cochrane, Detroit	1962	Mickey Mantle, New York	1991	Cal Ripken Jr., Baltimore
1935	Hank Greenberg, Detroit	1963	Elston Howard, New York	1992	Dennis Eckersley, Oakland
1936	Lou Gehrig, New York	1964	Brooks Robinson, Baltimore	1993	Frank Thomas, Chicago
1937	Charlie Gehringer, Detroit	1965	Zoilo Versalles, Minnesota	1994	Frank Thomas, Chicago
1938	Jimmie Foxx, Boston	1966	Frank Robinson, Baltimore	1995	Mo Vaughn, Boston
1939	Joe DiMaggio, New York	1967	Carl Yastrzemski, Boston	1996	Juan Gonzalez, Texas
1940	Hank Greenberg, Detroit	1968	Denny McLain, Detroit	1997	Ken Griffey Jr., Seattle
1941	Joe DiMaggio, New York	1969	Harmon Killebrew, Minnesota	1998	Juan Gonzalez, Texas
1942	Joe Gordon, New York	1970	John "Boog" Powell, Baltimore	1999	Ivan Rodriguez, Texas
1943	Spurgeon "Spud" Chandler,	1971	Vida Blue, Oakland	2000	Jason Giambi, Oakland
	New York	1972	Dick Allen, Chicago	2001	Ichiro Suzuki, Seattle
1944	Hal Newhouser, Detroit	1973	Reggie Jackson, Oakland	2002	Miguel Tejada, Oakland
1945	Hal Newhouser, Detroit	1974	Jeff Burroughs, Texas	2003	Alex Rodriguez, Texas
1946	Ted Williams, Boston	1975	Fred Lynn, Boston	2004	Vladimir Guerrero, Anaheim
1947	Joe DiMaggio, New York	1976	Thurman Munson, New York	2005	Alex Rodriguez, New York
1948	Lou Boudreau, Cleveland	1977	Rod Carew, Minnesota	2006	Justin Morneau, Minnesota
1949	Ted Williams, Boston	1978	Jim Rice, Boston	2007	Alex Rodriguez, New York
1950	Phil Rizzuto, New York	1979	Don Baylor, California	2008	Dustin Pedroia, Boston
1951	Yogi Berra, New York	1980	George Brett, Kansas City	2009	Joe Mauer, Minnesota
1952	Bobby Shantz, Philadelphia	1981	Rollie Fingers, Milwaukee	2010	Josh Hamilton, Texas
1953	Al Rosen, Cleveland	1982	Robin Yount, Milwaukee	2011	Justin Verlander, Detroit
1954	Yogi Berra, New York	1983	Cal Ripken Jr., Baltimore	2012	Miguel Cabrera, Detroit
1955	Yogi Berra, New York	1984	Willie Hernandez, Detroit	2013	Miguel Cabrera, Detroit
1956	Mickey Mantle, New York	1985	Don Mattingly, New York	2014	Mike Trout, Los Angeles
1957	Mickey Mantle, New York	1986	Roger Clemens, Boston	2015	Josh Donaldson, Toronto
1958	Jackie Jensen, Boston	1987	George Bell, Toronto	2016	Mike Trout, Los Angeles
				2017	José Altuve, Houston

Rookie of the Year, 1949-2017

(as selected by the Baseball Writers' Assn. of America)

1947: Jackie Robinson, Brooklyn, 1B (combined selection); 1948: Alvin Dark, Boston (NL), SS (combined selection).

National League

Year	Player, team, position	Year	Player, team, position	Year	Player, team, position
1949	Don Newcombe, Brooklyn, P	1956	Frank Robinson, Cincinnati, OF	1963	Pete Rose, Cincinnati, 2B
1950	Sam Jethroe, Boston, OF	1957	Jack Sanford, Philadelphia, P	1964	Richie Allen, Philadelphia, 3B
1951	Willie Mays, NY, OF	1958	Orlando Cepeda, San Francisco, 1B	1965	Jim Lefebvre, L.A., 2B
1952	Joe Black, Brooklyn, P	1959	Willie McCovey, San Francisco, 1B	1966	Tommy Helms, Cincinnati, 2B
1953	Jim Gilliam, Brooklyn, 2B	1960	Frank Howard, L.A., OF	1967	Tom Seaver, NY, P
1954	Wally Moon, St. Louis, OF	1961	Billy Williams, Chicago, OF	1968	Johnny Bench, Cincinnati, C
1955	Bill Virdon, St. Louis, OF	1962	Ken Hubbs, Chicago, 2B	1969	Ted Sizemore, L.A., 2B

Year	Player, team, position	Year	Player, team, position	Year	Player, team, position
1970	Carl Morton, Montréal, P	1986	Todd Worrell, St. Louis, P	2002	Jason Jennings, Colorado, P
1971	Earl Williams, Atlanta, C	1987	Benito Santiago, San Diego, C	2003	Dontrelle Willis, Florida, P
1972	Jon Matlack, NY, P	1988	Chris Sabo, Cincinnati, 3B	2004	Jason Bay, Pittsburgh, OF
1973	Gary Matthews, San Francisco, OF	1989	Jerome Walton, Chicago, OF	2005	Ryan Howard, Philadelphia, 1B
1974	Bake McBride, St. Louis, OF	1990	Dave Justice, Atlanta, 1B	2006	Hanley Ramirez, Florida, SS
1975	John Montefusco, San Francisco, P	1991	Jeff Bagwell, Houston, 1B	2007	Ryan Braun, Milwaukee, 3B
1976	Butch Metzger, San Diego, P; Pat Zachry, Cincinnati, P	1992	Eric Karros, L.A., 1B	2008	Geovany Soto, Chicago, C
		1993	Mike Piazza, L.A., C	2009	Chris Coghlan, Florida, OF
1977	Andre Dawson, Montréal, OF	1994	Raul Mondesi, L.A., OF	2010	Buster Posey, San Francisco, C
1978	Bob Horner, Atlanta, 3B	1995	Hideo Nomo, L.A., P	2011	Craig Kimbrel, Atlanta, P
1979	Rick Sutcliffe, L.A., P	1996	Todd Hollandsworth, L.A., OF	2012	Bryce Harper, Washington, OF
1980	Steve Howe, L.A., P	1997	Scott Rolen, Philadelphia, 3B	2013	José Fernández, Miami, P
1981	Fernando Valenzuela, L.A., P	1998	Kerry Wood, Chicago, P	2014	Jacob deGrom, NY, P
1982	Steve Sax, L.A., 2B	1999	Scott Williamson, Cincinnati, P	2015	Kris Bryant, Chicago, 3B
1983	Darryl Strawberry, NY, OF	2000	Rafael Furcal, Atlanta, SS	2016	Corey Seager, L.A., SS
1984	Dwight Gooden, NY, P	2001	Albert Pujols, St. Louis, OF	2017	Cody Bellinger, L.A., 1B
1985	Vince Coleman, St. Louis, OF				

American League

Year	Player, team, position	Year	Player, team, position	Year	Player, team, position
1949	Roy Sievers, St. Louis, OF	1972	Carlton Fisk, Boston, C	1994	Bob Hamelin, Kansas City, DH
1950	Walt Dropo, Boston, 1B	1973	Al Bumbry, Baltimore, OF	1995	Marty Cordova, Minnesota, OF
1951	Gil McDougald, NY, 3B	1974	Mike Hargrove, Texas, 1B	1996	Derek Jeter, NY, SS
1952	Harry Byrd, Philadelphia, P	1975	Fred Lynn, Boston, OF	1997	Nomar Garciaparra, Boston, SS
1953	Harvey Kuenn, Detroit, SS	1976	Mark Fidrych, Detroit, P	1998	Ben Grieve, Oakland, OF
1954	Bob Grim, NY, P	1977	Eddie Murray, Baltimore, DH	1999	Carlos Beltran, Kansas City, OF
1955	Herb Score, Cleveland, P	1978	Lou Whitaker, Detroit, 2B	2000	Kazuhiro Sasaki, Seattle, P
1956	Luis Aparicio, Chicago, SS	1979	John Castino, Minnesota, 3B;	2001	Ichiro Suzuki, Seattle, OF
1957	Tony Kubek, NY, IF-OF		Alfredo Griffin, Toronto, SS	2002	Eric Hinske, Toronto, 3B
1958	Albie Pearson, Washington, OF	1980	Joe Charboneau, Cleveland, OF	2003	Angel Berroa, Kansas City, SS
1959	Bob Allison, Washington, OF	1981	Dave Righetti, NY, P	2004	Bobby Crosby, Oakland, SS
1960	Ron Hansen, Baltimore, SS	1982	Cal Ripken Jr., Baltimore, SS	2005	Huston Street, Oakland, P
1961	Don Schwall, Boston, P	1983	Ron Kittle, Chicago, OF	2006	Justin Verlander, Detroit, P
1962	Tom Tresh, NY, IF-OF	1984	Alvin Davis, Seattle, 1B	2007	Dustin Pedroia, Boston, 2B
1963	Gary Peters, Chicago, P	1985	Ozzie Guillen, Chicago, SS	2008	Evan Longoria, Tampa Bay, 3B
1964	Tony Oliva, Minnesota, OF	1986	Jose Canseco, Oakland, OF	2009	Andrew Bailey, Oakland, P
1965	Curt Blefary, Baltimore, OF	1987	Mark McGwire, Oakland, 1B	2010	Neftali Feliz, Texas, P
1966	Tommie Agee, Chicago, OF	1988	Walt Weiss, Oakland, SS	2011	Jeremy Hellickson, Tampa Bay, P
1967	Rod Carew, Minnesota, 2B	1989	Gregg Olson, Baltimore, P	2012	Mike Trout, L.A., OF
1968	Stan Bahnsen, NY, P	1990	Sandy Alomar Jr., Cleveland, C	2013	Wil Myers, Tampa Bay, OF
1969	Lou Piniella, Kansas City, OF	1991	Chuck Knoblauch, Minnesota, 2B	2014	José Abreu, Chicago, 1B
1970	Thurman Munson, NY, C	1992	Pat Listach, Milwaukee, SS	2015	Carlos Correa, Houston, SS
1971	Chris Chambliss, Cleveland, 1B	1993	Tim Salmon, California, OF	2016	Michael Fulmer, Detroit, P
				2017	Aaron Judge, NY, OF

Major League Pennant Winners, 1901-75

	National League						American League				
Year	Winner	W	L	PCT	Manager	Year	Winner	W	L	PCT	Manager
1901	Pittsburgh	90	49	.647	Clarke	1901	Chicago	83	53	.610	Griffith
1902	Pittsburgh	103	36	.741	Clarke	1902	Philadelphia	83	53	.610	Mack
1903	Pittsburgh	91	49	.650	Clarke	1903	Boston	91	47	.659	Collins
1904	New York	106	47	.693	McGraw	1904	Boston	95	59	.617	Collins
1905	New York	105	48	.686	McGraw	1905	Philadelphia	92	56	.622	Mack
1906	Chicago	116	36	.763	Chance	1906	Chicago	93	58	.616	Jones
1907	Chicago	107	45	.704	Chance	1907	Detroit	92	58	.613	Jennings
1908	Chicago	99	55	.643	Chance	1908	Detroit	90	63	.588	Jennings
1909	Pittsburgh	110	42	.724	Clarke	1909	Detroit	98	54	.645	Jennings
1910	Chicago	104	50	.675	Chance	1910	Philadelphia	102	48	.680	Mack
1911	New York	99	54	.647	McGraw	1911	Philadelphia	101	50	.669	Mack
1912	New York	103	48	.682	McGraw	1912	Boston	105	47	.691	Stahl
1913	New York	101	51	.664	McGraw	1913	Philadelphia	96	57	.627	Mack
1914	Boston	94	59	.614	Stallings	1914	Philadelphia	99	53	.651	Mack
1915	Philadelphia	90	62	.592	Moran	1915	Boston	101	50	.669	Carrigan
1916	Brooklyn	94	60	.610	Robinson	1916	Boston	91	63	.591	Carrigan
1917	New York	98	56	.636	McGraw	1917	Chicago	100	54	.649	Rowland
1918	Chicago	84	45	.651	Mitchell	1918	Boston	75	51	.595	Barrow
1919	Cincinnati	96	44	.686	Moran	1919	Chicago	88	52	.629	Gleason
1920	Brooklyn	93	61	.604	Robinson	1920	Cleveland	98	56	.636	Speaker
1921	New York	94	59	.614	McGraw	1921	New York	98	55	.641	Huggins
1922	New York	93	61	.604	McGraw	1922	New York	94	60	.610	Huggins
1923	New York	95	58	.621	McGraw	1923	New York	98	54	.645	Huggins
1924	New York	93	60	.608	McGraw	1924	Washington	92	62	.597	Harris
1925	Pittsburgh	95	58	.621	McKechnie	1925	Washington	96	55	.636	Harris
1926	St. Louis	89	65	.578	Hornsby	1926	New York	91	63	.591	Huggins
1927	Pittsburgh	94	60	.610	Bush	1927	New York	110	44	.714	Huggins
1928	St. Louis	95	59	.617	McKechnie	1928	New York	101	53	.656	Huggins
1929	Chicago	98	54	.645	McCarthy	1929	Philadelphia	104	46	.693	Mack
1930	St. Louis	92	62	.597	Street	1930	Philadelphia	102	52	.662	Mack
1931	St. Louis	101	53	.656	Street	1931	Philadelphia	107	45	.704	Mack
1932	Chicago	90	64	.584	Hornsby, Grimm	1932	New York	107	47	.695	McCarthy

	National League						American League				
Year	Winner	W	L	PCT	Manager	Year	Winner	W	L	PCT	Manager
1933	New York	91	61	.599	Terry	1933	Washington	99	53	.651	Cronin
1934	St. Louis	95	58	.621	Frisch	1934	Detroit	101	53	.656	Cochrane
1935	Chicago	100	54	.649	Grimm	1935	Detroit	93	58	.616	Cochrane
1936	New York	92	62	.597	Terry	1936	New York	102	51	.667	McCarthy
1937	New York	95	57	.625	Terry	1937	New York	102	52	.662	McCarthy
1938	Chicago	89	63	.586	Grimm, Hartnett	1938	New York	99	53	.651	McCarthy
1939	Cincinnati	97	57	.630	McKechnie	1939	New York	106	45	.702	McCarthy
1940	Cincinnati	100	53	.654	McKechnie	1940	Detroit	90	64	.584	Baker
1941	Brooklyn	100	54	.649	Durocher	1941	New York	101	53	.656	McCarthy
1942	St. Louis	106	48	.688	Southworth	1942	New York	103	51	.669	McCarthy
1943	St. Louis	105	49	.682	Southworth	1943	New York	98	56	.636	McCarthy
1944	St. Louis	105	49	.682	Southworth	1944	St. Louis	89	65	.578	Sewell
1945	Chicago	98	56	.636	Grimm	1945	Detroit	88	65	.575	O'Neill
1946	St. Louis	98	58	.628	Dyer	1946	Boston	104	50	.675	Cronin
1947	Brooklyn	94	60	.610	Shotton	1947	New York	97	57	.630	Harris
1948	Boston	91	62	.595	Southworth	1948	Cleveland	97	58	.626	Boudreau
1949	Brooklyn	97	57	.630	Shotton	1949	New York	97	57	.630	Stengel
1950	Philadelphia	91	63	.591	Sawyer	1950	New York	98	56	.636	Stengel
1951	New York	98	59	.624	Durocher	1951	New York	98	56	.636	Stengel
1952	Brooklyn	96	57	.627	Dressen	1952	New York	95	59	.617	Stengel
1953	Brooklyn	105	49	.682	Dressen	1953	New York	99	52	.656	Stengel
1954	New York	97	57	.630	Durocher	1954	Cleveland	111	43	.721	Lopez
1955	Brooklyn	98	55	.641	Alston	1955	New York	96	58	.623	Stengel
1956	Brooklyn	93	61	.604	Alston	1956	New York	97	57	.630	Stengel
1957	Milwaukee	95	59	.617	Haney	1957	New York	98	56	.636	Stengel
1958	Milwaukee	92	62	.597	Haney	1958	New York	92	62	.597	Stengel
1959	Los Angeles	88	68	.564	Alston	1959	Chicago	94	60	.610	Lopez
1960	Pittsburgh	95	59	.617	Murtaugh	1960	New York	97	57	.630	Stengel
1961	Cincinnati	93	61	.604	Hutchinson	1961	New York	109	53	.673	Houk
1962	San Francisco	103	62	.624	Dark	1962	New York	96	66	.593	Houk
1963	Los Angeles	99	63	.611	Alston	1963	New York	104	57	.646	Houk
1964	St. Louis	93	69	.574	Keane	1964	New York	99	63	.611	Berra
1965	Los Angeles	97	65	.599	Alston	1965	Minnesota	102	60	.630	Mele
1966	Los Angeles	95	67	.586	Alston	1966	Baltimore	97	63	.606	Bauer
1967	St. Louis	101	60	.627	Schoendienst	1967	Boston	92	70	.568	Williams
1968	St. Louis	97	65	.599	Schoendienst	1968	Detroit	103	59	.636	Smith
1969	New York	100	62	.617	Hodges	1969	Baltimore	109	53	.673	Weaver
1970	Cincinnati	102	60	.630	Anderson	1970	Baltimore	108	54	.667	Weaver
1971	Pittsburgh	97	65	.599	Murtaugh	1971	Baltimore	101	57	.639	Weaver
1972	Cincinnati	95	59	.617	Anderson	1972	Oakland	93	62	.600	Williams
1973	New York	82	79	.509	Berra	1973	Oakland	94	68	.580	Williams
1974	Los Angeles	102	60	.630	Alston	1974	Oakland	90	72	.556	Dark
1975	Cincinnati	108	54	.667	Anderson	1975	Boston	95	65	.594	Johnson

Major League Pennant Winners, 1976-2018

National League

Year	East winner	W	L	PCT	Manager	West winner	W	L	PCT	Manager	Pennant winner
1976	Philadelphia	101	61	.623	Ozark	Cincinnati	102	60	.630	Anderson	Cincinnati
1977	Philadelphia	101	61	.623	Ozark	Los Angeles	98	64	.605	Lasorda	Los Angeles
1978	Philadelphia	90	72	.556	Ozark	Los Angeles	95	67	.586	Lasorda	Los Angeles
1979	Pittsburgh	98	64	.605	Tanner	Cincinnati	90	71	.559	McNamara	Pittsburgh
1980	Philadelphia	91	71	.562	Green	Houston	93	70	.571	Virdon	Philadelphia
1981(a)	Philadelphia	34	21	.618	Green	Los Angeles	36	21	.632	Lasorda	(c)
1981(b)	Montréal	30	23	.566	Williams, Fanning	Houston	33	20	.623	Virdon	Los Angeles
1982	St. Louis	92	70	.568	Herzog	Atlanta	89	73	.549	Torre	St. Louis
1983	Philadelphia	90	72	.556	Corrales, Owens	Los Angeles	91	71	.562	Lasorda	Philadelphia
1984	Chicago	96	65	.596	Frey	San Diego	92	70	.568	Williams	San Diego
1985	St. Louis	101	61	.623	Herzog	Los Angeles	95	67	.586	Lasorda	St. Louis
1986	New York	108	54	.667	Johnson	Houston	96	66	.593	Lanier	New York
1987	St. Louis	95	67	.586	Herzog	San Francisco	90	72	.556	Craig	St. Louis
1988	New York	100	60	.625	Johnson	Los Angeles	94	67	.584	Lasorda	Los Angeles
1989	Chicago	93	69	.574	Zimmer	San Francisco	92	70	.568	Craig	San Francisco
1990	Pittsburgh	95	67	.586	Leyland	Cincinnati	91	71	.562	Piniella	Cincinnati
1991	Pittsburgh	98	64	.605	Leyland	Atlanta	94	68	.580	Cox	Atlanta
1992	Pittsburgh	96	66	.593	Leyland	Atlanta	98	64	.605	Cox	Atlanta
1993	Philadelphia	97	65	.599	Fregosi	Atlanta	104	58	.642	Cox	Philadelphia

Year	Division	Winner	W	L	PCT	Manager	Playoffs	Pennant winner
1994(d)	East	Montréal	74	40	.649	Alou	—	—
	Central	Cincinnati	66	48	.579	Johnson		
	West	Los Angeles	58	56	.509	Lasorda		
1995	East	Atlanta	90	54	.625	Cox	Atlanta 3, Colorado* 1	Atlanta
	Central	Cincinnati	85	59	.590	Johnson	Cincinnati 3, Los Angeles 0	
	West	Los Angeles	78	66	.542	Lasorda	Atlanta 4, Cincinnati 0	
1996	East	Atlanta	96	66	.593	Cox	Atlanta 3, Los Angeles* 0	Atlanta
	Central	St. Louis	88	74	.543	La Russa	St. Louis 3, San Diego 0	
	West	San Diego	91	71	.562	Bochy	Atlanta 4, St. Louis 3	

Year	Division	Winner	W	L	PCT	Manager	Playoffs	Pennant winner
1997	East	Atlanta	101	61	.623	Cox	Atlanta 3, Houston 0	Florida*
	Central	Houston	84	78	.519	Dierker	Florida* 3, San Francisco 0	(Leyland)
	West	San Francisco	90	72	.556	Baker	Florida* 4, Atlanta 2	
1998	East	Atlanta	106	56	.654	Cox	Atlanta 3, Chicago* 0	San Diego
	Central	Houston	102	60	.630	Dierker	San Diego 3, Houston 1	
	West	San Diego	98	64	.605	Bochy	San Diego 4, Atlanta 2	
1999	East	Atlanta	103	59	.636	Cox	Atlanta 3, Houston 1	Atlanta
	Central	Houston	97	65	.599	Dierker, Galante	New York* 3, Arizona 1	
	West	Arizona	100	62	.617	Showalter	Atlanta 4, New York* 2	
2000	East	Atlanta	95	67	.586	Cox	St. Louis 3, Atlanta 0	New York*
	Central	St. Louis	95	67	.586	La Russa	New York* 3, San Francisco 1	(Valentine)
	West	San Francisco	97	65	.599	Baker	New York* 4, St. Louis 1	
2001	East	Atlanta	88	74	.543	Cox	Atlanta 3, Houston 0	Arizona
	Central	Houston	93	69	.574	Dierker	Arizona 3, St. Louis* 2	
	West	Arizona	92	70	.568	Brenly	Arizona 4, Atlanta 1	
2002	East	Atlanta	101	59	.631	Cox	St. Louis 3, Arizona 0	San Francisco*
	Central	St. Louis	97	65	.599	La Russa	San Francisco* 3, Atlanta 2	(Baker)
	West	Arizona	98	64	.605	Brenly	San Francisco* 4, St. Louis 1	
2003	East	Atlanta	101	61	.623	Cox	Chicago 3, Atlanta 2	Florida*
	Central	Chicago	88	74	.543	Baker	Florida* 3, San Francisco 1	(McKeon, Torborg)
	West	San Francisco	100	61	.621	Alou	Florida* 4, Chicago 3	
2004	East	Atlanta	96	66	.593	Cox	Houston* 3, Atlanta 2	St. Louis
	Central	St. Louis	105	57	.648	La Russa	St. Louis 3, Los Angeles 1	
	West	Los Angeles	93	69	.574	Tracy	St. Louis 4, Houston* 3	
2005	East	Atlanta	90	72	.556	Cox	St. Louis 3, San Diego 0	Houston*
	Central	St. Louis	100	62	.617	La Russa	Houston* 3, Atlanta 1	(Garner)
	West	San Diego	82	80	.506	Bochy	Houston* 4, St. Louis 2	
2006	East	New York	97	65	.599	Randolph	New York 3, Los Angeles* 0	St. Louis
	Central	St. Louis	83	78	.516	La Russa	St. Louis 3, San Diego 1	
	West	San Diego	88	74	.543	Bochy	St. Louis 4, New York 3	
2007	East	Philadelphia	89	73	.549	Manuel	Colorado* 3, Philadelphia 0	Colorado*
	Central	Chicago	85	77	.525	Piniella	Arizona 3, Chicago 0	(Hurdle)
	West	Arizona	90	72	.556	Melvin	Colorado* 4, Arizona 0	
2008	East	Philadelphia	92	70	.568	Manuel	Philadelphia 3, Milwaukee* 1	Philadelphia
	Central	Chicago	97	64	.602	Piniella	Los Angeles 3, Chicago 0	
	West	Los Angeles	84	78	.519	Torre	Philadelphia 4, Los Angeles 1	
2009	East	Philadelphia	93	69	.574	Manuel	Philadelphia 3, Colorado* 1	Philadelphia
	Central	St. Louis	91	71	.562	La Russa	Los Angeles 3, St. Louis 0	
	West	Los Angeles	95	67	.586	Torre	Philadelphia 4, Los Angeles 1	
2010	East	Philadelphia	97	65	.599	Manuel	San Francisco 3, Atlanta* 1	San Francisco
	Central	Cincinnati	91	71	.562	Baker	Philadelphia 3, Cincinnati 0	
	West	San Francisco	92	70	.568	Bochy	San Francisco 4, Philadelphia 2	
2011	East	Philadelphia	102	60	.630	Manuel	Milwaukee 3, Arizona 2	St. Louis*
	Central	Milwaukee	96	66	.593	Roenicke	St. Louis* 3, Philadelphia 2	(La Russa)
	West	Arizona	94	68	.580	Gibson	St. Louis* 4, Milwaukee 2	
2012	East	Washington	98	64	.605	Johnson	#St. Louis* 6, Atlanta* 3	San Francisco
	Central	Cincinnati	97	65	.599	Baker	St. Louis* 3, Washington 2	
	West	San Francisco	94	68	.580	Bochy	San Francisco 3, Cincinnati 2	
							San Francisco 4, St. Louis* 3	
2013	East	Atlanta	96	66	.593	González	#Pittsburgh* 6, Cincinnati* 2	St. Louis
	Central	St. Louis	97	65	.599	Matheny	St. Louis 3, Pittsburgh* 2	
	West	Los Angeles	92	70	.568	Mattingly	Los Angeles 3, Atlanta 1	
							St. Louis 4, Los Angeles 2	
2014	East	Washington	96	66	.593	Williams	#San Francisco* 8, Pittsburgh* 0	San Francisco*
	Central	St. Louis	90	72	.556	Matheny	San Francisco* 3, Washington 1	(Bochy)
	West	Los Angeles	94	68	.580	Mattingly	St. Louis 3, Los Angeles 1	
							San Francisco* 4, St. Louis 1	
2015	East	New York	90	72	.556	Collins	#Chicago* 4, Pittsburgh* 0	New York
	Central	St. Louis	100	62	.617	Matheny	Chicago* 3, St. Louis 1	
	West	Los Angeles	92	70	.568	Mattingly	New York 3, Los Angeles 2	
							New York 4, Chicago* 0	
2016	East	Washington	95	67	.586	Baker	#San Francisco* 3, New York* 0	Chicago
	Central	Chicago	103	58	.640	Maddon	Chicago 3, San Francisco* 1	
	West	Los Angeles	91	71	.562	Roberts	Los Angeles 3, Washington 2	
							Chicago 4, Los Angeles 2	
2017	East	Washington	97	65	.599	Baker	#Arizona* 11, Colorado* 8	Los Angeles
	Central	Chicago	92	70	.568	Maddon	Chicago 3, Washington 2	
	West	Los Angeles	104	58	.642	Roberts	Los Angeles 3, Arizona* 0	
							Los Angeles 4, Chicago 1	
2018	East	Atlanta	90	72	.556	Snitker	#Colorado* 2, Chicago* 1	Los Angeles
	Central	Milwaukee	96	67	.589	Counsell	Milwaukee 3, Colorado* 0	
	West	Los Angeles	92	71	.564	Roberts	Los Angeles 3, Atlanta 1	
							Los Angeles 4, Milwaukee 3	

American League

Year	East winner	W	L	PCT	Manager	West winner	W	L	PCT	Manager	Pennant winner
1976	New York	97	62	.610	Martin	Kansas City	90	72	.556	Herzog	New York
1977	New York	100	62	.617	Martin	Kansas City	102	60	.630	Herzog	New York
1978	New York	100	63	.613	Martin, Lemon	Kansas City	92	70	.568	Herzog	New York
1979	Baltimore	102	57	.642	Weaver	California	88	74	.543	Fregosi	Baltimore
1980	New York	103	59	.636	Howser	Kansas City	97	65	.599	Frey	Kansas City
1981(a)	New York	34	22	.607	Michael, Lemon	Oakland	37	23	.617	Martin	(c)
1981(b)	Milwaukee	31	22	.585	Rodgers	Kansas City	30	23	.566	Frey, Howser	New York
1982	Milwaukee	95	67	.586	Rodgers, Kuenn	California	93	69	.574	Mauch	Milwaukee
1983	Baltimore	98	64	.605	Altobelli	Chicago	99	63	.611	La Russa	Baltimore
1984	Detroit	104	58	.642	Anderson	Kansas City	84	78	.519	Howser	Detroit
1985	Toronto	99	62	.615	Cox	Kansas City	91	71	.562	Howser	Kansas City
1986	Boston	95	66	.590	McNamara	California	92	70	.568	Mauch	Boston
1987	Detroit	98	64	.605	Anderson	Minnesota	85	77	.525	Kelly	Minnesota
1988	Boston	89	73	.549	McNamara, Morgan	Oakland	104	58	.642	La Russa	Oakland
1989	Toronto	89	73	.549	Williams, Gaston	Oakland	99	63	.611	La Russa	Oakland
1990	Boston	88	74	.543	Morgan	Oakland	103	59	.636	La Russa	Oakland
1991	Toronto	91	71	.562	Gaston, Tenace	Minnesota	95	67	.586	Kelly	Minnesota
1992	Toronto	96	66	.593	Gaston	Oakland	96	66	.593	La Russa	Toronto
1993	Toronto	95	67	.586	Gaston	Chicago	94	68	.580	Lamont	Toronto

Year	Division	Winner	W	L	PCT	Manager	Playoffs	Pennant winner
1994(d)	East	New York	70	43	.619	Showalter	—	—
	Central	Chicago	67	46	.593	Lamont		
	West	Texas	52	62	.456	Kennedy		
1995	East	Boston	86	58	.597	Kennedy	Cleveland 3, Boston 0	Cleveland
	Central	Cleveland	100	44	.694	Hargrove	Seattle 3, New York* 2	
	West	Seattle	79	66	.545	Piniella	Cleveland 4, Seattle 2	
1996	East	New York	92	70	.568	Torre	Baltimore* 3, Cleveland 1	New York
	Central	Cleveland	99	62	.615	Hargrove	New York 3, Texas 1	
	West	Texas	90	72	.556	Oates	New York 4, Baltimore* 1	
1997	East	Baltimore	98	64	.605	Johnson	Baltimore 3, Seattle 1	Cleveland
	Central	Cleveland	86	75	.534	Hargrove	Cleveland 3, New York* 2	
	West	Seattle	90	72	.556	Piniella	Cleveland 4, Baltimore 2	
1998	East	New York	114	48	.704	Torre	New York 3, Texas 0	New York
	Central	Cleveland	89	73	.549	Hargrove	Cleveland 3, Boston* 1	
	West	Texas	88	74	.543	Oates	New York 4, Cleveland 2	
1999	East	New York	98	64	.605	Torre	New York 3, Texas 0	New York
	Central	Cleveland	97	65	.599	Hargrove	Boston* 3, Cleveland 2	
	West	Texas	95	67	.586	Oates	New York 4, Boston* 1	
2000	East	New York	87	74	.540	Torre	New York 3, Oakland 2	New York
	Central	Chicago	95	67	.586	Manuel	Seattle* 3, Chicago 0	
	West	Oakland	91	70	.565	Howe	New York 4, Seattle* 2	
2001	East	New York	95	65	.594	Torre	Seattle 3, Cleveland 2	New York
	Central	Cleveland	91	71	.562	Manuel	New York 3, Oakland* 2	
	West	Seattle	116	46	.716	Piniella	New York 4, Seattle 1	
2002	East	New York	103	58	.640	Torre	Anaheim* 3, New York 1	Anaheim*
	Central	Minnesota	94	67	.584	Gardenhire	Minnesota 3, Oakland 2	(Scioscia)
	West	Oakland	103	59	.636	Howe	Anaheim* 4, Minnesota 1	
2003	East	New York	101	61	.623	Torre	New York 3, Minnesota 1	New York
	Central	Minnesota	90	72	.556	Gardenhire	Boston* 3, Oakland 2	
	West	Oakland	96	66	.593	Macha	New York 4, Boston* 3	
2004	East	New York	101	61	.623	Torre	New York 3, Minnesota 1	Boston*
	Central	Minnesota	92	70	.568	Gardenhire	Boston* 3, Anaheim 0	(Francona)
	West	Anaheim	92	70	.568	Scioscia	Boston* 4, New York 3	
2005	East	New York	95	67	.586	Torre	Chicago 3, Boston* 0	Chicago
	Central	Chicago	99	63	.611	Guillen	Los Angeles 3, New York 2	
	West	Los Angeles	95	67	.586	Scioscia	Chicago 4, Los Angeles 1	
2006	East	New York	97	65	.599	Torre	Oakland 3, Minnesota 0	Detroit*
	Central	Minnesota	96	66	.593	Gardenhire	Detroit* 3, New York 1	(Leyland)
	West	Oakland	93	69	.574	Macha	Detroit* 4, Oakland 0	
2007	East	Boston	96	66	.593	Francona	Boston 3, Los Angeles 0	Boston
	Central	Cleveland	96	66	.593	Wedge	Cleveland 3, New York* 1	
	West	Los Angeles	94	68	.580	Scioscia	Boston 4, Cleveland 3	
2008	East	Tampa Bay	97	65	.599	Maddon	Tampa Bay 3, Chicago 1	Tampa Bay
	Central	Chicago	89	74	.546	Guillen	Boston* 3, Los Angeles 1	
	West	Los Angeles	100	62	.617	Scioscia	Tampa Bay 4, Boston* 3	
2009	East	New York	103	59	.636	Girardi	New York 3, Minnesota 0	New York
	Central	Minnesota	87	76	.534	Gardenhire	Los Angeles 3, Boston* 0	
	West	Los Angeles	97	65	.599	Scioscia	New York 4, Los Angeles 2	
2010	East	Tampa Bay	96	66	.593	Maddon	New York* 3, Minnesota 0	Texas
	Central	Minnesota	94	68	.580	Gardenhire	Texas 3, Tampa Bay 2	
	West	Texas	90	72	.556	Washington	Texas 4, New York* 2	
2011	East	New York	97	65	.599	Girardi	Detroit 3, New York 2	Texas
	Central	Detroit	95	67	.586	Leyland	Texas 3, Tampa Bay* 1	
	West	Texas	96	66	.593	Washington	Texas 4, Detroit 2	
2012	East	New York	95	67	.586	Girardi	#Baltimore* 5, Texas* 1	Detroit
	Central	Detroit	88	74	.543	Leyland	New York 3, Baltimore* 2	
	West	Oakland	94	68	.580	Melvin	Detroit 3, Oakland 2	
							Detroit 4, New York 0	
2013	East	Boston	97	65	.599	Farrell	#Tampa Bay* 4, Cleveland* 0	Boston
	Central	Detroit	93	69	.574	Leyland	Boston 3, Tampa Bay* 1	
	West	Oakland	96	66	.593	Melvin	Detroit 3, Oakland 2	
							Boston 4, Detroit 2	
2014	East	Baltimore	96	66	.593	Showalter	#Kansas City* 9, Oakland* 8	Kansas City*
	Central	Detroit	90	72	.556	Ausmus	Kansas City* 3, Los Angeles 0	(Yost)
	West	Los Angeles	98	64	.605	Scioscia	Baltimore 3, Detroit 0	
							Kansas City* 4, Baltimore 0	
2015	East	Toronto	93	69	.574	Gibbons	#Houston* 3, New York* 0	Kansas City
	Central	Kansas City	95	67	.586	Yost	Kansas City 3, Houston* 2	
	West	Texas	88	74	.543	Banister	Toronto 3, Texas 2	
							Kansas City 4, Toronto 2	
2016	East	Boston	93	69	.574	Farrell	#Toronto* 5, Baltimore* 2	Cleveland
	Central	Cleveland	94	67	.584	Francona	Toronto* 3, Texas 0	
	West	Texas	95	67	.586	Banister	Cleveland 3, Boston 0	
							Cleveland 4, Toronto* 1	
2017	East	Boston	93	69	.574	Farrell	#New York* 8, Minnesota* 4	Houston
	Central	Cleveland	102	60	.630	Francona	Houston 3, Boston 1	
	West	Houston	101	61	.623	Hinch	New York* 3, Cleveland 2	
							Houston 4, New York* 3	
2018	East	Boston	108	54	.667	Cora	#New York* 7, Oakland* 2	Boston
	Central	Cleveland	91	71	.562	Francona	Boston 3, New York* 1	
	West	Houston	103	59	.636	Hinch	Houston 3, Cleveland 0	
							Boston 4, Houston 1	

* = Wild-card team. If pennant winner is wild-card team, manager's name is given in parentheses. # = Single-game wild card playoff (debuted in 2012). (a) First half. (b) Second half. (c) Montréal, L.A., NY Yankees, and Oakland won the divisional playoffs. (d) In Aug. 1994, a players' strike began that caused the cancellation of the remainder of the season, the playoffs, and the World Series. Teams listed as division "winners" for 1994 were leading their divisions at the time of the strike.

World Series Results, 1903-2018

1903 Boston AL 5, Pittsburgh NL 3	1942 St. Louis NL 4, New York AL 1
1904 No series	1943 New York AL 4, St. Louis NL 1
1905 New York NL 4, Philadelphia AL 1	1944 St. Louis NL 4, St. Louis AL 2
1906 Chicago AL 4, Chicago NL 2	1945 Detroit AL 4, Chicago NL 3
1907 Chicago NL 4, Detroit AL 0, 1 tie	1946 St. Louis NL 4, Boston AL 3
1908 Chicago NL 4, Detroit AL 1	1947 New York AL 4, Brooklyn NL 3
1909 Pittsburgh NL 4, Detroit AL 3	1948 Cleveland AL 4, Boston NL 2
1910 Philadelphia AL 4, Chicago NL 1	1949 New York AL 4, Brooklyn NL 1
1911 Philadelphia AL 4, New York NL 2	1950 New York AL 4, Philadelphia NL 0
1912 Boston AL 4, New York NL 3, 1 tie	1951 New York AL 4, New York NL 2
1913 Philadelphia AL 4, New York NL 1	1952 New York AL 4, Brooklyn NL 3
1914 Boston NL 4, Philadelphia AL 0	1953 New York AL 4, Brooklyn NL 2
1915 Boston AL 4, Philadelphia NL 1	1954 New York NL 4, Cleveland AL 0
1916 Boston AL 4, Brooklyn NL 1	1955 Brooklyn NL 4, New York AL 3
1917 Chicago AL 4, New York NL 2	1956 New York AL 4, Brooklyn NL 3
1918 Boston AL 4, Chicago NL 2	1957 Milwaukee NL 4, New York AL 3
1919 Cincinnati NL 5, Chicago AL 3	1958 New York AL 4, Milwaukee NL 3
1920 Cleveland AL 5, Brooklyn NL 2	1959 Los Angeles NL 4, Chicago AL 2
1921 New York NL 5, New York AL 3	1960 Pittsburgh NL 4, New York AL 3
1922 New York NL 4, New York AL 0, 1 tie	1961 New York AL 4, Cincinnati NL 1
1923 New York AL 4, New York NL 2	1962 New York AL 4, San Francisco NL 3
1924 Washington AL 4, New York NL 3	1963 Los Angeles NL 4, New York AL 0
1925 Pittsburgh NL 4, Washington AL 3	1964 St. Louis NL 4, New York AL 3
1926 St. Louis NL 4, New York AL 3	1965 Los Angeles NL 4, Minnesota AL 3
1927 New York AL 4, Pittsburgh NL 0	1966 Baltimore AL 4, Los Angeles NL 0
1928 New York AL 4, St. Louis NL 0	1967 St. Louis NL 4, Boston AL 3
1929 Philadelphia AL 4, Chicago NL 1	1968 Detroit AL 4, St. Louis NL 3
1930 Philadelphia AL 4, St. Louis NL 2	1969 New York NL 4, Baltimore AL 1
1931 St. Louis NL 4, Philadelphia AL 3	1970 Baltimore AL 4, Cincinnati NL 1
1932 New York AL 4, Chicago NL 0	1971 Pittsburgh NL 4, Baltimore AL 3
1933 New York NL 4, Washington AL 1	1972 Oakland AL 4, Cincinnati NL 3
1934 St. Louis NL 4, Detroit AL 3	1973 Oakland AL 4, New York NL 3
1935 Detroit AL 4, Chicago NL 2	1974 Oakland AL 4, Los Angeles NL 1
1936 New York AL 4, New York NL 2	1975 Cincinnati NL 4, Boston AL 3
1937 New York AL 4, New York NL 1	1976 Cincinnati NL 4, New York AL 0
1938 New York AL 4, Chicago NL 0	1977 New York AL 4, Los Angeles NL 2
1939 New York AL 4, Cincinnati NL 0	1978 New York AL 4, Los Angeles NL 2
1940 Cincinnati NL 4, Detroit AL 3	1979 Pittsburgh NL 4, Baltimore AL 3
1941 New York AL 4, Brooklyn NL 1	1980 Philadelphia NL 4, Kansas City AL 2

1981 Los Angeles NL 4, New York AL 2
1982 St. Louis NL 4, Milwaukee AL 3
1983 Baltimore AL 4, Philadelphia NL 1
1984 Detroit AL 4, San Diego NL 1
1985 Kansas City AL 4, St. Louis NL 3
1986 New York NL 4, Boston AL 3
1987 Minnesota AL 4, St. Louis NL 3
1988 Los Angeles NL 4, Oakland AL 1
1989 Oakland AL 4, San Francisco NL 0
1990 Cincinnati NL 4, Oakland AL 0
1991 Minnesota AL 4, Atlanta NL 3
1992 Toronto AL 4, Atlanta NL 2
1993 Toronto AL 4, Philadelphia NL 2
1994 No series due to strike
1995 Atlanta NL 4, Cleveland AL 2
1996 New York AL 4, Atlanta NL 2
1997 Florida NL 4, Cleveland AL 3
1998 New York AL 4, San Diego NL 0
1999 New York AL 4, Atlanta NL 0
2000 New York AL 4, New York NL 1
2001 Arizona NL 4, New York AL 3
2002 Anaheim AL 4, San Francisco NL 3
2003 Florida NL 4, New York AL 2
2004 Boston AL 4, St. Louis NL 0
2005 Chicago AL 4, Houston NL 0
2006 St. Louis NL 4, Detroit AL 1
2007 Boston AL 4, Colorado NL 0
2008 Philadelphia NL 4, Tampa Bay AL 1
2009 New York AL 4, Philadelphia NL 2
2010 San Francisco NL 4, Texas AL 1
2011 St. Louis NL 4, Texas AL 3
2012 San Francisco NL 4, Detroit AL 0
2013 Boston AL 4, St. Louis NL 2
2014 San Fran. NL 4, Kansas City AL 3
2015 Kansas City AL 4, New York NL 1
2016 Chicago NL 4, Cleveland AL 3
2017 Houston AL 4, Los Angeles NL 3
2018 Boston AL 4, Los Angeles NL 1

World Series Most Valuable Player, 1955-2018

Year	Player, position, team
1955	Johnny Podres, P, Brooklyn
1956	Don Larsen, P, NY (AL)
1957	Lew Burdette, P, Milwaukee (NL)
1958	Bob Turley, P, NY (AL)
1959	Larry Sherry, P, Los Angeles (NL)
1960[1]	Bobby Richardson, 2B, NY (AL)
1961	Whitey Ford, P, NY (AL)
1962	Ralph Terry, P, NY (AL)
1963	Sandy Koufax, P, Los Angeles (NL)
1964	Bob Gibson, P, St. Louis
1965	Sandy Koufax, P, Los Angeles (NL)
1966	Frank Robinson, OF, Baltimore
1967	Bob Gibson, P, St. Louis
1968	Mickey Lolich, P, Detroit
1969	Donn Clendenon, 1B, NY (NL)
1970	Brooks Robinson, 3B, Baltimore
1971	Roberto Clemente, OF, Pittsburgh
1972	Gene Tenace, C, Oakland
1973	Reggie Jackson, OF, Oakland
1974	Rollie Fingers, P, Oakland
1975	Pete Rose, 3B, Cincinnati
1976	Johnny Bench, C, Cincinnati
1977	Reggie Jackson, OF, NY (AL)

Year	Player, position, team
1978	Bucky Dent, SS, NY (AL)
1979	Willie Stargell, 1B, Pittsburgh
1980	Mike Schmidt, 3B, Philadelphia
1981	Ron Cey, 3B, Los Angeles (NL);
	Pedro Guerrero, OF, Los Angeles;
	Steve Yeager, C, Los Angeles
1982	Darrell Porter, C, St. Louis
1983	Rick Dempsey, C, Baltimore
1984	Alan Trammell, SS, Detroit
1985	Bret Saberhagen, P, Kansas City
1986	Ray Knight, 3B, NY (NL)
1987	Frank Viola, P, Minnesota
1988	Orel Hershiser, P, Los Angeles (NL)
1989	Dave Stewart, P, Oakland
1990	José Rijo, P, Cincinnati
1991	Jack Morris, P, Minnesota
1992	Pat Borders, C, Toronto
1993	Paul Molitor, DH, Toronto
1994	No series due to strike
1995	Tom Glavine, P, Atlanta
1996	John Wetteland, P, NY (AL)
1997	Livan Hernandez, P, Florida
1998	Scott Brosius, 3B, NY (AL)

Year	Player, position, team
1999	Mariano Rivera, P, NY (AL)
2000	Derek Jeter, SS, NY (AL)
2001	Curt Schilling, P, Arizona;
	Randy Johnson, P, Arizona
2002	Troy Glaus, 3B, Anaheim
2003	Josh Beckett, P, Florida
2004	Manny Ramirez, OF, Boston
2005	Jermaine Dye, OF, Chicago (AL)
2006	David Eckstein, SS, St. Louis
2007	Mike Lowell, 3B, Boston
2008	Cole Hamels, P, Philadelphia
2009	Hideki Matsui, DH, NY (AL)
2010	Edgar Renteria, SS, San Francisco
2011	David Freese, 3B, St. Louis
2012	Pablo Sandoval, 3B, San Francisco
2013	David Ortiz, DH, Boston
2014	Madison Bumgarner, P, San Francisco
2015	Salvador Pérez, C, Kansas City
2016	Ben Zobrist, OF, Chicago (NL)
2017	George Springer, OF, Houston
2018	Steve Pearce, 1B, Boston

Note: World Series canceled in 1994 due to strike. (1) Richardson won the MVP although Pittsburgh beat New York.

World Series Won-Lost Records, by Franchise

Since beginning of "modern" era in 1901. Figures represent overall Series wins, not individual games.

Team	Wins	Losses
New York Yankees	27	13
St. Louis Cardinals	11	8
Boston Red Sox	9	4
Philadelphia/Kansas City/Oakland A's	9	5
New York/San Francisco Giants	8	12
Brooklyn/Los Angeles Dodgers	6	14
Pittsburgh Pirates	5	2
Cincinnati Reds	5	4
Detroit Tigers	4	7
Chicago White Sox	3	2
Washington Senators/Minnesota Twins	3	3
St. Louis Browns/Baltimore Orioles	3	4
Boston/Milwaukee/Atlanta Braves	3	6
Chicago Cubs	3	8

Team	Wins	Losses
Florida Marlins	2	0
Toronto Blue Jays	2	0
Kansas City Royals	2	2
New York Mets	2	3
Cleveland Indians	2	4
Philadelphia Phillies	2	5
Houston Astros	1	1
Arizona Diamondbacks	1	0
L.A./California/Anaheim/L.A. Angels	1	0
Colorado Rockies	0	1
Seattle Pilots/Milwaukee Brewers	0	1
Tampa Bay Rays	0	1
San Diego Padres	0	2
Texas Rangers	0	2

All-Time World Series Career Leaders
(through 2018)

Batting Leaders

Batter (min. 50 PA)	H	AB	AVG	Batter (min. 50 PA)	H	AB	AVG
1. David Ortiz	20	44	.455	6. Hal McRae	18	45	.400
2. Pablo Sandoval	20	47	.426	7. Lou Brock	34	87	.391
3. Johnny "Pepper" Martin	23	55	.418	8. Marquis Grissom	30	77	.390
4. Paul Molitor	23	55	.418	9. Thurman Munson	25	67	.373
5. Lance Berkman	16	39	.410	10. George Brett	19	51	.373

Games Played
Yogi Berra	75
Mickey Mantle	65
Elston Howard	54
Hank Bauer	53
Gil McDougald	53
Phil Rizzuto	52
Joe DiMaggio	51
Frankie Frisch	50
Pee Wee Reese	44
Roger Maris	41
Babe Ruth	41

Hits
Yogi Berra	71
Mickey Mantle	59
Frankie Frisch	58
Joe DiMaggio	54
Derek Jeter	50
Hank Bauer	46
Pee Wee Reese	46
Gil McDougald	45
Phil Rizzuto	45
Lou Gehrig	43

Runs
Mickey Mantle	42
Yogi Berra	41
Babe Ruth	37
Derek Jeter	32
Lou Gehrig	30
Joe DiMaggio	27
Roger Maris	26
Elston Howard	25
Gil McDougald	23
Jackie Robinson	22

Runs Batted In
Mickey Mantle	40
Yogi Berra	39
Lou Gehrig	35
Babe Ruth	33
Joe DiMaggio	30
Bill Skowron	29
Duke Snider	26

Home Runs
Mickey Mantle	18
Babe Ruth	15
Yogi Berra	12
Duke Snider	11
Lou Gehrig	10
Reggie Jackson	10
Joe DiMaggio	8
Frank Robinson	8
Bill Skowron	8

Stolen Bases
Lou Brock	14
Eddie Collins	14
Frank Chance	10
Dave Lopes	10
Phil Rizzuto	10
Frankie Frisch	9
Kenny Lofton	9
Honus Wagner	9
Johnny Evers	8

Pitching Leaders

Games Pitched
Mariano Rivera	24
Whitey Ford	22
Mike Stanton	20
Rollie Fingers	16
Ryan Madson	16
Jeff Nelson	16
Allie Reynolds	15
Bob Turley	15
Clay Carroll	14
Clem Labine	13
Andy Pettitte	13
Mark Wohlers	13
Jeremy Affeldt	12
Waite Hoyt	12
Catfish Hunter	12
Art Nehf	12

Wins
Whitey Ford	10
Bob Gibson	7
Allie Reynolds	7
Red Ruffing	7
Chief Bender	6
Lefty Gomez	6
Waite Hoyt	6
Three Finger Brown	5
Jack Coombs	5
Catfish Hunter	5
Christy Mathewson	5
Herb Pennock	5
Andy Pettitte	5
Vic Raschi	5

Strikeouts
Whitey Ford	94
Bob Gibson	92
Allie Reynolds	62
Sandy Koufax	61
Red Ruffing	61
Chief Bender	59
George Earnshaw	56
Andy Pettitte	56
John Smoltz	52
Roger Clemens	49
Waite Hoyt	49
Christy Mathewson	48
Bob Turley	46

Saves
Mariano Rivera	11
Rollie Fingers	6
Johnny Murphy	4
Robb Nen	4
Allie Reynolds	4
John Wetteland	4
Roy Face	3
Neftali Feliz	3
Firpo Marberry	3
Will McEnaney	3
Tug McGraw	3
Jonathan Papelbon	3
Herb Pennock	3
Troy Percival	3
Sergio Romo	3
Kent Tekulve	3
Todd Worrell	3

MLB Stadiums, 2018

Team	Stadium (year opened)	Surface	Distances (ft) LF	Center	RF	Seating capacity[1]
Arizona Diamondbacks	Chase Field (1998)	Grass	330	407	335	48,618
Atlanta Braves	SunTrust Park (2017)	Grass	335	400	325	41,084
Chicago Cubs	Wrigley Field (1914)	Grass	355	400	353	41,395
Cincinnati Reds	Great American Ball Park (2003)	Grass	328	404	325	42,319
Colorado Rockies	Coors Field (1995)	Grass	347	415	350	50,480
Los Angeles Dodgers	Dodger Stadium (1962)	Grass	330	395	330	56,000
Miami Marlins	Marlins Park (2012)	Grass	344	407	335	37,446
Milwaukee Brewers	Miller Park (2001)	Grass	344	400	345	41,900
New York Mets	Citi Field (2009)	Grass	335	408	330	41,922
Philadelphia Phillies	Citizens Bank Park (2004)	Grass	329	401	330	43,035
Pittsburgh Pirates	PNC Park (2001)	Grass	325	399	320	38,747
St. Louis Cardinals	Busch Stadium (2006)	Grass	336	400	335	44,494
San Diego Padres	Petco Park (2004)	Grass	336	396	322	40,209
San Francisco Giants	AT&T Park (2000)	Grass	339	399	309	41,915
Washington Nationals	Nationals Park (2008)	Grass	336	402	335	41,336
Baltimore Orioles	Oriole Park at Camden Yards (1992)	Grass	333	400	318	45,971
Boston Red Sox	Fenway Park (1912)	Grass	310	390	302	37,305[2]
Chicago White Sox	Guaranteed Rate Field (1991)	Grass	330	400	335	40,615
Cleveland Indians	Progressive Field (1994)	Grass	325	405	325	35,041
Detroit Tigers	Comerica Park (2000)	Grass	345	420	330	41,299
Houston Astros	Minute Maid Park (2000)	Grass	315	409	326	41,168
Kansas City Royals	Kauffman Stadium (1973)	Grass	330	410	330	37,903
Los Angeles Angels	Angel Stadium of Anaheim (1966)	Grass	347	396	348	45,477
Minnesota Twins	Target Field (2010)	Grass	339	404	328	38,885
New York Yankees	Yankee Stadium (2009)	Grass	318	408	314	47,309
Oakland Athletics	Oakland Coliseum (1968)	Grass	330	400	330	48,592
Seattle Mariners	Safeco Field (1999)	Grass	331	401	326	47,715
Tampa Bay Rays	Tropicana Field (1990)	Turf	315	404	322	31,042
Texas Rangers	Globe Life Park in Arlington (1994)	Grass	332	400	325	48,114
Toronto Blue Jays	Rogers Centre (1989)	Astroturf	328	400	328	49,286

(1) As of 2018 season. (2) For day games; night game capacity is 37,755.

Major League Franchise Shifts and Additions

1953: Boston Braves (NL) became Milwaukee Braves.
1954: St. Louis Browns (AL) became Baltimore Orioles.
1955: Philadelphia Athletics (AL) became Kansas City Athletics.
1958: New York Giants (NL) became San Francisco Giants.
1958: Brooklyn Dodgers (NL) became L.A. Dodgers.
1961: Washington Senators (AL) became Minnesota Twins.
1961: L.A. Angels enfranchised by the AL.
1961: Washington Senators enfranchised by the AL, replacing the former Washington club, whose franchise moved to Minneapolis-St. Paul.
1962: Houston Colt .45s enfranchised by the NL.
1962: New York Mets enfranchised by the NL.
1966: Milwaukee Braves (NL) became Atlanta Braves.
1968: Kansas City Athletics (AL) became Oakland Athletics.

1969: Kansas City Royals and Seattle Pilots enfranchised by the AL; Montréal Expos and San Diego Padres enfranchised by the NL.
1970: Seattle Pilots (AL) became Milwaukee Brewers.
1972: Washington Senators (AL) became Texas Rangers (Dallas-Fort Worth area).
1977: Toronto Blue Jays and Seattle Mariners enfranchised by the AL.
1993: Colorado Rockies (Denver) and Florida Marlins (Miami) enfranchised by the NL.
1998: Tampa Bay Devil Rays began play in the AL; Arizona Diamondbacks (Phoenix) began play in the NL (both teams enfranchised in 1995). Milwaukee Brewers moved from the AL to the NL.
2005: Montréal Expos (NL) became Washington Nationals.
2013: Houston Astros moved from the NL to the AL.

National Baseball Hall of Fame and Museum

Located in Cooperstown, NY. # = Player chosen in first year of eligibility (five seasons after retirement) or earlier. * = 2018 inductee.
www.baseballhall.org

#Aaron, Hank	Cronin, Joe	Herman, Billy	McCarthy, Joe	Sewell, Joe
Alexander, Grover	Cummings, W. A. "Candy"	Herzog, Whitey	McCarthy, Thomas	Simmons, Al
Alomar, Roberto	Cuyler, Hazen "Kiki"	Hill, Pete	#McCovey, Willie	Sisler, George
Alston, Walt	Dandridge, Ray	*Hoffman, Trevor	McGinnity, Joe	Slaughter, Enos
Anderson, George	Davis, George	Hooper, Harry	McGowan, Bill	Smith, Hilton
Anson, Cap	Dawson, Andre	Hornsby, Rogers	McGraw, John	#Smith, Ozzie
Aparicio, Luis	Day, Leon	Hoyt, Waite	McKechnie, Bill	#Smoltz, John
Appling, Luke	Dean, Jay Hanna "Dizzy"	Hubbard, Cal	McPhee, John "Bid"	Snider, Duke
Ashburn, Richie	Delahanty, Ed	Hubbell, Carl	Medwick, Joe	Southworth, Billy
Averill, Earl	Dickey, Bill	Huggins, Miller	Mendez, Jose	#Spahn, Warren
Bagwell, Jeff	Dihigo, Martín	Hulbert, William	Mize, Johnny	Spalding, Albert
Baker, Frank "Home Run"	#DiMaggio, Joe	Hunter, James "Catfish"	#Molitor, Paul	Speaker, Tris
Bancroft, Dave	#Doby, Larry	Irvin, Monte	#Morgan, Joe	#Stargell, Willie
#Banks, Ernie	Doerr, Bobby	#Jackson, Reggie	*Morris, Jack	Stearnes, Norman
Barlick, Al	Dreyfuss, Barney	Jackson, Travis	#Murray, Eddie	Stengel, Casey
Barrow, Edward G.	Drysdale, Don	Jenkins, Ferguson	#Musial, Stan	Sutter, Bruce
Beckley, Jake	Duffy, Hugh	Jennings, Hugh	Newhouser, Hal	Suttles, George "Mule"
Bell, James "Cool Papa"	Durocher, Leo	Johnson, Byron "Ban"	Nichols, Kid	Sutton, Don
#Bench, Johnny	#Eckersley, Dennis	#Johnson, Randy	Niekro, Phil	Taylor, Ben
Bender, Charles "Chief"	Evans, Billy	Johnson, Walter[1]	O'Day, Hank	Terry, Bill
Berra, Lawrence "Yogi"	Evers, John	Johnson, William "Judy"	O'Malley, Walter	#Thomas, Frank
Biggio, Craig	Ewing, Buck	*#Jones, Chipper	O'Rourke, Jim	*#Thome, Jim
Blyleven, Bert	Faber, Urban "Red"	Joss, Addie	Ott, Mel	Thompson, Sam
#Boggs, Wade	#Feller, Bob	#Kaline, Al	Paige, Satchel	Tinker, Joe
Bottomley, Jim	Ferrell, Rick	Keefe, Timothy	#Palmer, Jim	Torre, Joe
Boudreau, Lou	Fingers, Rollie	Keeler, William	Pennock, Herb	Torriente, Cristobal
Bresnahan, Roger	Fisk, Carlton	Kell, George	Perez, Tony	*Trammell, Alan
#Brett, George	Flick, Elmer H.	Kelley, Joe	Perry, Gaylord	Traynor, Harold J. "Pie"
#Brock, Lou	Ford, Whitey	Kelly, George	Piazza, Mike	Vance, Arthur "Dazzy"
Brouthers, Dan	Foster, Andrew "Rube"	Kelly, King	Plank, Ed	Vaughan, Joseph "Arky"
Brown, Mordecai	Foster, Bill	Killebrew, Harmon	Pompez, Alex	Veeck, Bill
Brown, Ray	Fox, Nellie	Kiner, Ralph	Posey, Cum(berland)	Waddell, Rube
Brown, Willard	Foxx, Jimmie	Klein, Chuck	#Puckett, Kirby	Wagner, Honus[1]
Bulkeley, Morgan C.	Frick, Ford	Klem, Bill	Radbourn, Charlie	Wallace, Roderick
Bunning, Jim	Frisch, Frank	#Koufax, Sandy	Raines, Tim	Walsh, Ed
Burkett, Jesse C.	Galvin, James "Pud"	Kuhn, Bowie	Reese, Pee Wee	Waner, Lloyd
Campanella, Roy	#Gehrig, Lou	La Russa, Tony	Rice, Jim	Waner, Paul
#Carew, Rod	Gehringer, Charles	Lajoie, Nap	Rice, Sam	Ward, John
Carey, Max	#Gibson, Bob	Landis, Kenesaw M.	Rickey, Branch	Weaver, Earl
#Carlton, Steve	Gibson, Josh	Larkin, Barry	#Ripken, Cal, Jr.	Weiss, George
Carter, Gary	Giles, Warren	Lasorda, Tommy	Rixey, Eppa	Welch, Mickey
Cartwright, Alexander	Gillick, Pat	Lazzeri, Tony	Rizzuto, Phil "Scooter"	Wells, Willie
Cepeda, Orlando	#Glavine, Tom	Lemon, Bob	Roberts, Robin	Wheat, Zach
Chadwick, Henry	Gomez, Lefty	Leonard, Buck	#Robinson, Brooks	White, Deacon
Chance, Frank	Gordon, Joe	Lindstrom, Fred	#Robinson, Frank	White, Sol
Chandler, Albert "Happy"	Goslin, Leon "Goose"	Lloyd, Pop	#Robinson, Jackie	Wilhelm, Hoyt
Charleston, Oscar	Gossage, Rich	Lombardi, Ernie	Robinson, Wilbert	Wilkinson, J. L.
Chesbro, John	Grant, Frank	Lopez, Al	#Rodríguez, Iván	Williams, Billy
Chylak, Nestor	Greenberg, Hank	Lyons, Ted	Rogan, Joe "Bullet"	Williams, Dick
Clarke, Fred	#Griffey, Ken, Jr.	Mack, Connie	Roush, Edd	Williams, Joe
Clarkson, John	Griffith, Clark	Mackey, James "Biz"	Ruffing, Red	#Williams, Ted
#Clemente, Roberto	Grimes, Burleigh	MacPhail, Larry	Ruppert, Jacob	Willis, Vic
Cobb, Ty[1]	Grove, Lefty	MacPhail, Lee	Rusie, Amos	Wilson, Hack
Cochrane, Mickey	*Guerrero, Vladimir	#Maddux, Greg	#Ruth, Babe[1]	Wilson, Jud
Collins, Eddie	#Gwynn, Tony	Manley, Effa	#Ryan, Nolan	#Winfield, Dave
Collins, James	Hafey, Charles "Chick"	Mantle, Mickey	Sandberg, Ryne	Wright, George
Combs, Earle	Haines, Jesse	Manush, Henry	Santo, Ron	Wright, Harry
Comiskey, Charles A.	Hamilton, Bill	Maranville, Walter	Santop, Louis	Wynn, Early
Conlan, John "Jocko"	Hanlon, Ned	Marichal, Juan	Schalk, Ray	#Yastrzemski, Carl
Connolly, Thomas H.	Harridge, Will	Marquard, Rube	Schmidt, Mike	Yawkey, Tom
Connor, Roger	Harris, Bucky	#Martinez, Pedro	Schoendienst, Red	Young, Cy
Cooper, Andy	Hartnett, Gabby	Mathews, Eddie	Schuerholz, John	Youngs, Ross
Coveleski, Stan	Harvey, Doug	Mathewson, Christy[1]	#Seaver, Tom	#Yount, Robin
Cox, Bobby	Heilmann, Harry	#Mays, Willie	Selee, Frank	
Crawford, Sam	#Henderson, Rickey	Mazeroski, Bill	Selig, Bud	

(1) Player inducted in 1936, the year of the first Hall of Fame election.

BASKETBALL

NBA 2018: Warriors Win Second Straight Title

The Golden State Warriors won their third NBA title in four years with a Game 4 victory, 108-85, over the Cleveland Cavaliers, June 8, 2018, at Quicken Loans Arena in Cleveland, OH. Warriors guard Stephen Curry scored 37 points and Kevin Durant added a triple-double with 20 points, 12 rebounds, and 10 assists. Durant averaged 28.8 points and 10.8 rebounds per game in the Warriors' sweep and was named NBA Finals Most Valuable Player for the second straight year. In Game 3, Durant scored 43 points with 13 rebounds and seven assists in a 110-102 road win on June 6, 2018.

The Warriors grabbed a 124-114 overtime win in Game 1 on May 31, 2018, at Oracle Arena in Oakland, CA. LeBron James scored a postseason career-high 51 points, but Golden State outscored Cleveland, 17-7, in overtime for the win. (The overtime was forced when Cleveland's J.R. Smith mistakenly ran down the clock on a tie score with 4.5 seconds left.) Playing in his eighth consecutive NBA Finals (and fourth straight against Golden State), James led all players in Finals scoring (34 PPG) and assists (10 APG) despite being swept. Curry, who missed part of the playoffs due to ankle and knee injuries, scored 33 points, including a Finals-record nine three-pointers as the Warriors bounced the Cavs, 122-103, in Game 2 on June 3, 2018, in Oakland.

Golden State advanced to its fourth straight NBA Finals by defeating the top-seeded Houston Rockets in the Western Conference Finals. Durant scored 34 points and Curry added 27 in a 101-92, Game 7 victory over the Rockets on May 28, 2018, at Toyota Center in Houston. The Rockets made only 7 of 44 three-point shot attempts in the Game 7 loss. Rockets guard James Harden won his first NBA scoring title (30.4 PPG) and first MVP award, leading Houston to an NBA-best 65 regular-season wins.

Houston followed a first-round playoff win over Minnesota by vanquishing Utah in a conference semifinal in five games. Jazz rookie Donovan Mitchell averaged 28.5 points in Utah's first-round playoff series win over 2017 MVP Russell Westbrook and the Oklahoma City Thunder. Westbrook became the first player in NBA history to average a triple-double for two straight seasons, with double digits in points (25.4), rebounds (10.1), and assists (10.3) in the 2017-18 regular season.

LeBron James scored 45 points in a 105-101 Cavs victory over the Indiana Pacers in Game 7 of an opening-round Eastern Conference playoff on Apr. 29, 2018. Cleveland then swept the Toronto Raptors in the semifinals, but needed all seven games to take down the second-seeded Boston Celtics in the Eastern Conference Finals. James tallied 35 points in Cleveland's 87-79 Game 7 victory May 27, 2018, at TD Garden in Boston. The Cavs traded All-Star guard Kyrie Irving to Boston before the season began, but Irving missed the playoffs entirely after suffering a late-season knee injury.

NBA Final Standings, 2017-18

(playoff seeding in parentheses)

Eastern Conference

Atlantic Division	W	L	PCT	GB
Toronto Raptors (1)	59	23	.720	—
Boston Celtics (2)	55	27	.671	4
Philadelphia 76ers (3)	52	30	.634	7
New York Knicks	29	53	.354	30
Brooklyn Nets	28	54	.341	31

Central Division	W	L	PCT	GB
Cleveland Cavaliers (4)	50	32	.610	—
Indiana Pacers (5)	48	34	.585	2
Milwaukee Bucks (7)	44	38	.537	6
Detroit Pistons	39	43	.476	11
Chicago Bulls	27	55	.329	23

Southeast Division	W	L	PCT	GB
Miami Heat (6)	44	38	.537	—
Washington Wizards (8)	43	39	.524	1
Charlotte Hornets	36	46	.439	8
Orlando Magic	25	57	.305	19
Atlanta Hawks	24	58	.293	20

Western Conference

Northwest Division	W	L	PCT	GB
Portland Trail Blazers (3)	49	33	.598	—
Oklahoma City Thunder (4)	48	34	.585	1
Utah Jazz (5)	48	34	.585	1
Minnesota Timberwolves (8)	47	35	.573	2
Denver Nuggets	46	36	.561	3

Pacific Division	W	L	PCT	GB
Golden State Warriors (2)	58	24	.707	—
L.A. Clippers	42	40	.512	16
L.A. Lakers	35	47	.427	23
Sacramento Kings	27	55	.329	31
Phoenix Suns	21	61	.256	37

Southwest Division	W	L	PCT	GB
Houston Rockets (1)	65	17	.793	—
New Orleans Pelicans (6)	48	34	.585	17
San Antonio Spurs (7)	47	35	.573	18
Dallas Mavericks	24	58	.293	41
Memphis Grizzlies	22	60	.268	43

Note: Miami earned the No. 6 seed due to a better head-to-head record (3-0) over Milwaukee. Oklahoma City earned the No. 4 seed due to a better head-to-head record (4-3) over Utah (4-4), which earned the No. 5 seed) and New Orleans (3-4, No. 6 seed). San Antonio earned the No. 7 seed due to a better head-to-head record (2-1) over Minnesota.

NBA Playoff Results, 2018

Eastern Conference
Toronto defeated Washington, 4 games to 2
Boston defeated Milwaukee, 4 games to 3
Philadelphia defeated Miami, 4 games to 1
Cleveland defeated Indiana, 4 games to 3
Cleveland defeated Toronto, 4 games to 0
Boston defeated Philadelphia, 4 games to 1
Cleveland defeated Boston, 4 games to 3

Western Conference
Houston defeated Minnesota, 4 games to 1
Golden State defeated San Antonio, 4 games to 1
New Orleans defeated Portland, 4 games to 0
Utah defeated Oklahoma City, 4 games to 2
Houston defeated Utah, 4 games to 1
Golden State defeated New Orleans, 4 games to 1
Golden State defeated Houston, 4 games to 3

Championship
Golden State defeated Cleveland, 4 games to 0 (124-114 (OT), 122-103, 110-102, 108-85)

NBA Regular Season Individual Highs, 2017-18

Minutes, game: 52, Russell Westbrook, Oklahoma City v. Philadelphia, Dec. 15 (3 OT); Ben Simmons, Philadelphia v. Oklahoma City, Dec. 15 (3 OT); DeMarcus Cousins, New Orleans v. Chicago, Jan. 22 (2 OT)
Points, game: 60, James Harden, Houston v. Orlando, Jan. 30
Field goals, game: 23, LeBron James, Cleveland v. Washington, Nov. 3
Field goal attempts, game: 37, Bradley Beal, Washington v. Portland, Dec. 5
3-pointers, game: 10, Stephen Curry, Golden State v. Memphis, Dec. 30; Kemba Walker, Charlotte v. Memphis, Mar. 22
3-point attempts, game: 18, Allen Crabbe, Brooklyn v. New Orleans, Feb. 10 (2 OT); Taurean Prince, Atlanta v. Philadelphia, Apr. 10

Free throws, game: 21, Anthony Davis, New Orleans v. Phoenix, Feb. 26
Free throw attempts, game: 29, Ben Simmons, Philadelphia v. Washington, Nov. 29
Rebounds, game: 30, Dwight Howard, Charlotte v. Brooklyn, Mar. 21
Assists, game: 25, Rajon Rondo, New Orleans v. Brooklyn, Dec. 27
Steals, game: 10, Lou Williams, L.A. Clippers v. Utah, Jan. 20
Blocks, game: 10, Anthony Davis, New Orleans v. Utah, Mar. 11
Minutes played, season: 3,026, LeBron James, Cleveland
Off. rebounds, season: 399, Andre Drummond, Detroit
Def. rebounds, season: 848, Andre Drummond, Detroit
Personal fouls, season: 285, Karl-Anthony Towns, Minnesota

NBA Finals MVP, 1969-2018

Year	Player, team	Year	Player, team	Year	Player, team
1969	Jerry West, L.A. Lakers	1985	Kareem Abdul-Jabbar, L.A. Lakers	2002	Shaquille O'Neal, L.A. Lakers
1970	Willis Reed, New York			2003	Tim Duncan, San Antonio
1971	Lew Alcindor (Kareem Abdul-Jabbar), Milwaukee	1986	Larry Bird, Boston	2004	Chauncey Billups, Detroit
		1987	Magic Johnson, L.A. Lakers	2005	Tim Duncan, San Antonio
1972	Wilt Chamberlain, L.A. Lakers	1988	James Worthy, L.A. Lakers	2006	Dwyane Wade, Miami
1973	Willis Reed, New York	1989	Joe Dumars, Detroit	2007	Tony Parker, San Antonio
1974	John Havlicek, Boston	1990	Isiah Thomas, Detroit	2008	Paul Pierce, Boston
1975	Rick Barry, Golden State	1991	Michael Jordan, Chicago	2009	Kobe Bryant, L.A. Lakers
1976	Jo Jo White, Boston	1992	Michael Jordan, Chicago	2010	Kobe Bryant, L.A. Lakers
1977	Bill Walton, Portland	1993	Michael Jordan, Chicago	2011	Dirk Nowitzki, Dallas
1978	Wes Unseld, Washington	1994	Hakeem Olajuwon, Houston	2012	LeBron James, Miami
1979	Dennis Johnson, Seattle	1995	Hakeem Olajuwon, Houston	2013	LeBron James, Miami
1980	Magic Johnson, L.A. Lakers	1996	Michael Jordan, Chicago	2014	Kawhi Leonard, San Antonio
1981	Cedric Maxwell, Boston	1997	Michael Jordan, Chicago	2015	Andre Iguodala, Golden State
1982	Magic Johnson, L.A. Lakers	1998	Michael Jordan, Chicago	2016	LeBron James, Cleveland
1983	Moses Malone, Philadelphia	1999	Tim Duncan, San Antonio	2017	Kevin Durant, Golden State
1984	Larry Bird, Boston	2000	Shaquille O'Neal, L.A. Lakers	2018	Kevin Durant, Golden State
		2001	Shaquille O'Neal, L.A. Lakers		

NBA Finals All-Time Statistical Leaders

(At the end of the 2018 NBA Finals. * = Active in 2017-18 season. Minimum 10 games played.)

Scoring average	GP	FG	FT	PTS	AVG	Scoring average	GP	FG	FT	PTS	AVG
Rick Barry	10	138	87	363	36.3	Bob Pettit	25	241	227	709	28.4
Michael Jordan	35	438	258	1,176	33.6	*LeBron James	49	520	257	1,383	28.2
*Kevin Durant	14	157	90	444	31.7	*Kyrie Irving	13	140	50	360	27.7
Jerry West	55	612	455	1,679	30.5	Hakeem Olajuwon	17	187	91	467	27.5
Shaquille O'Neal	30	340	185	865	28.8	Elgin Baylor	44	442	277	1,161	26.4

Games Played		Points		Rebounds		Assists	
Bill Russell	70	Jerry West	1,679	Bill Russell	1,718	Magic Johnson	584
Sam Jones	64	*LeBron James	1,383	Wilt Chamberlain	862	Bob Cousy	400
Kareem Abdul-Jabbar	56	Kareem Abdul-Jabbar	1,317	Elgin Baylor	603	*LeBron James	379
Jerry West	55	Michael Jordan	1,176	Kareem Abdul-Jabbar	502	Bill Russell	315
Tom Heinsohn	52	Elgin Baylor	1,161	*LeBron James	490	Jerry West	306

NBA Most Valuable Player, 1956-2018

Year	Player, team	Year	Player, team	Year	Player, team
1956	Bob Pettit, St. Louis	1977	Kareem Abdul-Jabbar, L.A. Lakers	1998	Michael Jordan, Chicago
1957	Bob Cousy, Boston	1978	Bill Walton, Portland	1999	Karl Malone, Utah
1958	Bill Russell, Boston	1979	Moses Malone, Houston	2000	Shaquille O'Neal, L.A. Lakers
1959	Bob Pettit, St. Louis	1980	Kareem Abdul-Jabbar, L.A. Lakers	2001	Allen Iverson, Philadelphia
1960	Wilt Chamberlain, Philadelphia	1981	Julius Erving, Philadelphia	2002	Tim Duncan, San Antonio
1961	Bill Russell, Boston	1982	Moses Malone, Houston	2003	Tim Duncan, San Antonio
1962	Bill Russell, Boston	1983	Moses Malone, Philadelphia	2004	Kevin Garnett, Minnesota
1963	Bill Russell, Boston	1984	Larry Bird, Boston	2005	Steve Nash, Phoenix
1964	Oscar Robertson, Cincinnati	1985	Larry Bird, Boston	2006	Steve Nash, Phoenix
1965	Bill Russell, Boston	1986	Larry Bird, Boston	2007	Dirk Nowitzki, Dallas
1966	Wilt Chamberlain, Philadelphia	1987	Magic Johnson, L.A. Lakers	2008	Kobe Bryant, L.A. Lakers
1967	Wilt Chamberlain, Philadelphia	1988	Michael Jordan, Chicago	2009	LeBron James, Cleveland
1968	Wilt Chamberlain, Philadelphia	1989	Magic Johnson, L.A. Lakers	2010	LeBron James, Cleveland
1969	Wes Unseld, Baltimore	1990	Magic Johnson, L.A. Lakers	2011	Derrick Rose, Chicago
1970	Willis Reed, New York	1991	Michael Jordan, Chicago	2012	LeBron James, Miami
1971	Lew Alcindor (Abdul-Jabbar), Milw.	1992	Michael Jordan, Chicago	2013	LeBron James, Miami
1972	Kareem Abdul-Jabbar, Milwaukee	1993	Charles Barkley, Phoenix	2014	Kevin Durant, Oklahoma City
1973	Dave Cowens, Boston	1994	Hakeem Olajuwon, Houston	2015	Stephen Curry, Golden State
1974	Kareem Abdul-Jabbar, Milwaukee	1995	David Robinson, San Antonio	2016	Stephen Curry, Golden State
1975	Bob McAdoo, Buffalo	1996	Michael Jordan, Chicago	2017	Russell Westbrook, Oklahoma City
1976	Kareem Abdul-Jabbar, L.A. Lakers	1997	Karl Malone, Utah	2018	James Harden, Houston

NBA Scoring Leaders, 1947-2018

(Average points per game; 58 games minimum in 2017-18; prior season minimums vary.)

Year	Player, team	PTS	AVG	Year	Player, team	PTS	AVG
1947	Joe Fulks, Philadelphia	1,389	23.2	1969	Elvin Hayes, San Diego	2,327	28.4
1948	Max Zaslofsky, Chicago	1,007	21.0	1970	Jerry West, L.A. Lakers	2,309	31.2
1949	George Mikan, Minneapolis	1,698	28.3	1971	Lew Alcindor (Kareem Abdul-Jabbar), Milw.	2,596	31.7
1950	George Mikan, Minneapolis	1,865	27.4	1972	Kareem Abdul-Jabbar, Milwaukee	2,822	34.8
1951	George Mikan, Minneapolis	1,932	28.4	1973	Nate Archibald, Kansas City-Omaha	2,719	34.0
1952	Paul Arizin, Philadelphia	1,674	25.4	1974	Bob McAdoo, Buffalo	2,261	30.6
1953	Neil Johnston, Philadelphia	1,564	22.3	1975	Bob McAdoo, Buffalo	2,831	34.5
1954	Neil Johnston, Philadelphia	1,759	24.4	1976	Bob McAdoo, Buffalo	2,427	31.1
1955	Neil Johnston, Philadelphia	1,631	22.7	1977	Pete Maravich, New Orleans	2,273	31.1
1956	Bob Pettit, St. Louis	1,849	25.7	1978	George Gervin, San Antonio	2,232	27.2
1957	Paul Arizin, Philadelphia	1,817	25.6	1979	George Gervin, San Antonio	2,365	29.6
1958	George Yardley, Detroit	2,001	27.8	1980	George Gervin, San Antonio	2,585	33.1
1959	Bob Pettit, St. Louis	2,105	29.2	1981	Adrian Dantley, Utah	2,452	30.7
1960	Wilt Chamberlain, Philadelphia	2,707	37.6	1982	George Gervin, San Antonio	2,551	32.3
1961	Wilt Chamberlain, Philadelphia	3,033	38.4	1983	Alex English, Denver	2,326	28.4
1962	Wilt Chamberlain, Philadelphia	4,029	50.4	1984	Adrian Dantley, Utah	2,418	30.6
1963	Wilt Chamberlain, San Francisco	3,586	44.8	1985	Bernard King, New York	1,809	32.9
1964	Wilt Chamberlain, San Francisco	2,948	36.9	1986	Dominique Wilkins, Atlanta	2,366	30.3
1965	Wilt Chamberlain, San Francisco-Phil.	2,534	34.7	1987	Michael Jordan, Chicago	3,041	37.1
1966	Wilt Chamberlain, Philadelphia	2,649	33.5	1988	Michael Jordan, Chicago	2,868	35.0
1967	Rick Barry, San Francisco	2,775	35.6	1989	Michael Jordan, Chicago	2,633	32.5
1968	Dave Bing, Detroit	2,142	27.1	1990	Michael Jordan, Chicago	2,753	33.6

Year	Player, team	PTS	AVG	Year	Player, team	PTS	AVG
1991	Michael Jordan, Chicago	2,580	31.5	2005	Allen Iverson, Philadelphia	2,302	30.7
1992	Michael Jordan, Chicago	2,404	30.1	2006	Kobe Bryant, L.A. Lakers	2,832	35.4
1993	Michael Jordan, Chicago	2,541	32.6	2007	Kobe Bryant, L.A. Lakers	2,430	31.6
1994	David Robinson, San Antonio	2,383	29.8	2008	LeBron James, Cleveland	2,250	30.0
1995	Shaquille O'Neal, Orlando	2,315	29.3	2009	Dwyane Wade, Miami	2,386	30.2
1996	Michael Jordan, Chicago	2,491	30.4	2010	Kevin Durant, Oklahoma City	2,472	30.1
1997	Michael Jordan, Chicago	2,431	29.6	2011	Kevin Durant, Oklahoma City	2,161	27.7
1998	Michael Jordan, Chicago	2,357	28.7	2012	Kevin Durant, Oklahoma City	1,850	28.0
1999	Allen Iverson, Philadelphia	1,284	26.8	2013	Carmelo Anthony, New York	1,920	28.7
2000	Shaquille O'Neal, L.A. Lakers	2,344	29.7	2014	Kevin Durant, Oklahoma City	2,593	32.0
2001	Allen Iverson, Philadelphia	2,207	31.1	2015	Russell Westbrook, Oklahoma City	1,886	28.1
2002	Allen Iverson, Philadelphia	1,883	31.4	2016	Stephen Curry, Golden State	2,375	30.1
2003	Tracy McGrady, Orlando	2,407	32.1	2017	Russell Westbrook, Oklahoma City	2,558	31.6
2004	Tracy McGrady, Orlando	1,878	28.0	2018	James Harden, Houston	2,191	30.4

NBA Champions, 1947-2018

Year	Eastern champion	Western champion	Champion	Winning coach	Opponent
		Regular season		Playoffs	
1947	Washington Capitols	Chicago Stags	Philadelphia	Ed Gottlieb	Chicago
1948	Philadelphia Warriors	St. Louis Bombers	Baltimore	Buddy Jeannette	Philadelphia
1949	Washington Capitols	Rochester	Minneapolis	John Kundla	Washington
1950[1]	Syracuse	Indianapolis	Minneapolis	John Kundla	Syracuse
1951	Philadelphia Warriors	Minneapolis	Rochester	Lester Harrison	New York
1952	Syracuse	Rochester	Minneapolis	John Kundla	New York
1953	New York	Minneapolis	Minneapolis	John Kundla	New York
1954	New York	Minneapolis	Minneapolis	John Kundla	Syracuse
1955	Syracuse	Ft. Wayne	Syracuse	Al Cervi	Ft. Wayne
1956	Philadelphia Warriors	Ft. Wayne	Philadelphia	George Senesky	Ft. Wayne
1957	Boston	St. Louis	Boston	Red Auerbach	St. Louis
1958	Boston	St. Louis	St. Louis	Alex Hannum	Boston
1959	Boston	St. Louis	Boston	Red Auerbach	Minneapolis
1960	Boston	St. Louis	Boston	Red Auerbach	St. Louis
1961	Boston	St. Louis	Boston	Red Auerbach	St. Louis
1962	Boston	L.A. Lakers	Boston	Red Auerbach	L.A. Lakers
1963	Boston	L.A. Lakers	Boston	Red Auerbach	L.A. Lakers
1964	Boston	San Francisco	Boston	Red Auerbach	San Francisco
1965	Boston	L.A. Lakers	Boston	Red Auerbach	L.A. Lakers
1966	Philadelphia	L.A. Lakers	Boston	Red Auerbach	L.A. Lakers
1967	Philadelphia	San Francisco	Philadelphia	Alex Hannum	San Francisco
1968	Philadelphia	St. Louis	Boston	Bill Russell	L.A. Lakers
1969	Baltimore	L.A. Lakers	Boston	Bill Russell	L.A. Lakers
1970	New York	Atlanta	New York	Red Holzman	L.A. Lakers

Year	Atlantic	Central	Midwest	Pacific	Champion	Winning coach	Opponent
1971	New York	Baltimore	Milwaukee	L.A. Lakers	Milwaukee	Larry Costello	Baltimore
1972	Boston	Baltimore	Milwaukee	L.A. Lakers	L.A. Lakers	Bill Sharman	New York
1973	Boston	Baltimore	Milwaukee	L.A. Lakers	New York	Red Holzman	L.A. Lakers
1974	Boston	Capital	Milwaukee	L.A. Lakers	Boston	Tom Heinsohn	Milwaukee
1975	Boston	Washington	Chicago	Golden State	Golden State	Al Attles	Washington
1976	Boston	Cleveland	Milwaukee	Golden State	Boston	Tom Heinsohn	Phoenix
1977	Philadelphia	Houston	Denver	L.A. Lakers	Portland	Jack Ramsay	Philadelphia
1978	Philadelphia	San Antonio	Denver	Portland	Washington	Dick Motta	Seattle
1979	Washington	San Antonio	Kansas City	Seattle	Seattle	Len Wilkens	Washington
1980	Boston	Atlanta	Milwaukee	L.A. Lakers	L.A. Lakers	Paul Westhead	Philadelphia
1981	Boston	Milwaukee	San Antonio	Phoenix	Boston	Bill Fitch	Houston
1982	Boston	Milwaukee	San Antonio	L.A. Lakers	L.A. Lakers	Pat Riley	Philadelphia
1983	Philadelphia	Milwaukee	San Antonio	L.A. Lakers	Philadelphia	Billy Cunningham	L.A. Lakers
1984	Boston	Milwaukee	Utah	L.A. Lakers	Boston	K. C. Jones	L.A. Lakers
1985	Boston	Milwaukee	Denver	L.A. Lakers	L.A. Lakers	Pat Riley	Boston
1986	Boston	Milwaukee	Houston	L.A. Lakers	Boston	K. C. Jones	Houston
1987	Boston	Atlanta	Dallas	L.A. Lakers	L.A. Lakers	Pat Riley	Boston
1988	Boston	Detroit	Denver	L.A. Lakers	L.A. Lakers	Pat Riley	Detroit
1989	New York	Detroit	Utah	L.A. Lakers	Detroit	Chuck Daly	L.A. Lakers
1990	Philadelphia	Detroit	San Antonio	L.A. Lakers	Detroit	Chuck Daly	Portland
1991	Boston	Chicago	San Antonio	Portland	Chicago	Phil Jackson	L.A. Lakers
1992	Boston	Chicago	Utah	Portland	Chicago	Phil Jackson	Portland
1993	New York	Chicago	Houston	Phoenix	Chicago	Phil Jackson	Phoenix
1994	New York	Atlanta	Houston	Seattle	Houston	Rudy Tomjanovich	New York
1995	Orlando	Indiana	San Antonio	Phoenix	Houston	Rudy Tomjanovich	Orlando
1996	Orlando	Chicago	San Antonio	Seattle	Chicago	Phil Jackson	Seattle
1997	Miami	Chicago	Utah	Seattle	Chicago	Phil Jackson	Utah
1998	Miami	Chicago	Utah	L.A. Lakers	Chicago	Phil Jackson	Utah
1999	Miami	Indiana	San Antonio	Portland	San Antonio	Gregg Popovich	New York
2000	Miami	Indiana	Utah	L.A. Lakers	L.A. Lakers	Phil Jackson	Indiana
2001	Philadelphia	Milwaukee	San Antonio	L.A. Lakers	L.A. Lakers	Phil Jackson	Philadelphia
2002	New Jersey	Detroit	San Antonio	Sacramento	L.A. Lakers	Phil Jackson	New Jersey
2003	New Jersey	Detroit	San Antonio	Sacramento	San Antonio	Gregg Popovich	New Jersey
2004	New Jersey	Indiana	Minnesota	L.A. Lakers	Detroit	Larry Brown	L.A. Lakers

Year	Atlantic	Central	Southeast	Northwest	Pacific	Southwest	Champion	Winning coach	Opponent
2005	Boston	Detroit	Miami	Seattle	Phoenix	San Antonio	San Antonio	Gregg Popovich	Detroit
2006	New Jersey	Detroit	Miami	Denver	Phoenix	San Antonio	Miami	Pat Riley	Dallas
2007	Toronto	Detroit	Miami	Utah	Phoenix	Dallas	San Antonio	Gregg Popovich	Cleveland
2008	Boston	Detroit	Orlando	Utah	L.A. Lakers	New Orleans	Boston	Glenn "Doc" Rivers	L.A. Lakers
2009	Boston	Cleveland	Orlando	Denver	L.A. Lakers	San Antonio	L.A. Lakers	Phil Jackson	Orlando
2010	Boston	Cleveland	Orlando	Denver	L.A. Lakers	Dallas	L.A. Lakers	Phil Jackson	Boston
2011	Boston	Chicago	Miami	OK City	L.A. Lakers	San Antonio	Dallas	Rick Carlisle	Miami
2012	Boston	Chicago	Miami	OK City	L.A. Lakers	San Antonio	Miami	Erik Spoelstra	OK City
2013	New York	Indiana	Miami	OK City	L.A. Clippers	San Antonio	Miami	Erik Spoelstra	San Antonio
2014	Toronto	Indiana	Miami	OK City	L.A. Clippers	San Antonio	San Antonio	Gregg Popovich	Miami
2015	Toronto	Cleveland	Atlanta	Portland	Golden State	Houston	Golden State	Steve Kerr	Cleveland
2016	Toronto	Cleveland	Miami	OK City	Golden State	San Antonio	Cleveland	Tyronn Lue	Golden State
2017	Boston	Cleveland	Washington	Utah	Golden State	San Antonio	Golden State	Steve Kerr	Cleveland
2018	Toronto	Cleveland	Miami	Portland	Golden State	Houston	Golden State	Steve Kerr	Cleveland

(1) The newly formed NBA combined the 11-team BAA (Basketball Assn. of Amer.) and six NBL (Natl. Basketball League) teams in the 1949-50 season and had three divisions for one year. The Minneapolis Lakers were co-champions of the soon-defunct Central Division.

All-NBA and All-Defensive Teams, 2017-18

	All-NBA Team			All-Defensive Team	
First Team	Second Team	Position	First Team		Second Team
LeBron James, Cleveland	Giannis Antetokounmpo, Milwaukee	**Forward**	Robert Covington, Philadelphia		Draymond Green, Golden State
Kevin Durant, Golden State	LaMarcus Aldridge (F/C), San Antonio	**Forward**	Anthony Davis (F/C), New Orleans		Al Horford (F/C), Boston
Anthony Davis (F/C), New Orleans	Joel Embiid, Philadelphia	**Center**	Rudy Gobert, Utah		Joel Embiid, Philadelphia
James Harden, Houston	Russell Westbrook, Oklahoma City	**Guard**	Victor Oladipo, Indiana		Dejounte Murray, San Antonio
Damian Lillard, Portland	DeMar DeRozan, Toronto	**Guard**	Jrue Holiday, New Orleans		Jimmy Butler (G/F), Minnesota

NBA Statistical Leaders, 2017-18

To qualify for averaged categories, player must be on pace to play 58 games in an 82-game season.

Scoring Average

Player, team	GP	FG	FT	PTS	AVG
James Harden, Houston	72	651	624	2,191	30.4
Anthony Davis, New Orleans	75	780	495	2,110	28.1
LeBron James, Cleveland	82	857	388	2,251	27.5
Damian Lillard, Portland	73	621	493	1,962	26.9
Giannis Antetokounmpo, Milwaukee	75	742	487	2,014	26.9
Kevin Durant, Golden State	68	630	359	1,792	26.4
Russell Westbrook, Oklahoma City	80	757	417	2,028	25.4
Kyrie Irving, Boston	60	534	232	1,466	24.4
LaMarcus Aldridge, San Antonio	75	687	334	1,735	23.1
Victor Oladipo, Indiana	75	640	294	1,735	23.1

Field Goal Percentage
(Minimum 300 field goals made)

Player, team	FGM	FGA	PCT
Clint Capela, Houston	441	676	.652
DeAndre Jordan, L.A. Clippers	373	578	.645
Montrezl Harrell, L.A. Clippers	348	548	.635
Steven Adams, Oklahoma City	448	712	.629
Enes Kanter, New York	422	713	.592
Taj Gibson, Minnesota	425	737	.577
John Collins, Atlanta	314	545	.576
Jonas Valanciunas, Toronto	390	687	.568
Derrick Favors, Utah	395	702	.563
Julius Randle, L.A. Lakers	504	904	.558

Free Throw Percentage
(Minimum 125 free throws made)

Player, team	FTM	FTA	PCT
Stephen Curry, Golden State	278	302	.921
Chris Paul, Houston	203	221	.919
Damian Lillard, Portland	493	538	.916
Marco Belinelli, Atlanta-Philadelphia	148	163	.908
Jamal Murray, Denver	229	253	.905
JJ Redick, Philadelphia	197	218	.904
Kyrie Irving, Boston	232	261	.889
Kevin Durant, Golden State	359	404	.889
Khris Middleton, Milwaukee	320	362	.884
Darren Collison, Indiana	127	144	.882

3-Point Field Goal Percentage
(Minimum 82 3-point field goals made)

Player, team	3-FGM	3-FGA	PCT
Darren Collison, Indiana	96	205	.468
Reggie Bullock, Detroit	125	281	.445
Otto Porter, Washington	138	313	.441
Joe Ingles, Utah	204	464	.440
Klay Thompson, Golden State	229	521	.440
Kyle Korver, Cleveland	164	376	.436
Anthony Tolliver, Detroit	159	365	.436
Jayson Tatum, Boston	105	242	.434
Buddy Hield, Sacramento	176	408	.431
Al Horford, Boston	97	226	.429

Rebounds per Game

Player, team	GP	OFF	DEF	TOT	AVG
Andre Drummond, Detroit	78	399	848	1,247	16.0
DeAndre Jordan, L.A. Clippers	77	329	842	1,171	15.2
Dwight Howard, Charlotte	81	255	757	1,012	12.5
Karl-Anthony Towns, Minnesota	82	238	774	1,012	12.3
Anthony Davis, New Orleans	75	187	645	832	11.1
Enes Kanter, New York	71	273	507	780	11.0
Joel Embiid, Philadelphia	63	143	547	690	11.0
Clint Capela, Houston	74	241	561	802	10.8
Nikola Jokic, Denver	75	195	608	803	10.7
Russell Westbrook, Oklahoma City	80	152	652	804	10.1

Assists per Game

Player, team	GP	AST	APG
Russell Westbrook, Oklahoma City	80	820	10.3
LeBron James, Cleveland	82	747	9.1
James Harden, Houston	72	630	8.8
Rajon Rondo, New Orleans	65	533	8.2
Ben Simmons, Philadelphia	81	661	8.2
Chris Paul, Houston	58	457	7.9
Draymond Green, Golden State	70	508	7.3
Jeff Teague, Minnesota	70	492	7.0
Kyle Lowry, Toronto	78	537	6.9
Damian Lillard, Portland	73	481	6.6
Spencer Dinwiddie, Brooklyn	80	524	6.6

Steals per Game

Player, team	GP	STL	AVG
Victor Oladipo, Indiana	75	177	2.36
Paul George, Oklahoma City	79	161	2.04
Eric Bledsoe, Phoenix-Milwaukee	74	149	2.01
Jimmy Butler, Minnesota	59	116	1.97
Russell Westbrook, Oklahoma City	80	147	1.84
Gary Harris, Denver	67	122	1.82
James Harden, Houston	72	126	1.75
Ben Simmons, Philadelphia	81	140	1.73
Robert Covington, Philadelphia	80	137	1.71
Thaddeus Young, Indiana	81	135	1.67

Blocked Shots per Game

Player, team	GP	BLK	AVG
Anthony Davis, New Orleans	75	193	2.57
Clint Capela, Houston	74	137	1.85
Myles Turner, Indiana	65	118	1.82
Joel Embiid, Philadelphia	63	111	1.76
Kevin Durant, Golden State	68	119	1.75
Andre Drummond, Detroit	78	127	1.63
Dwight Howard, Charlotte	81	131	1.62
John Henson, Milwaukee	76	109	1.43
Giannis Antetokounmpo, Milwaukee	75	106	1.41
Jusuf Nurkic, Portland	79	111	1.41

NBA Defensive Player of the Year, 1983-2018

Year	Player, team	Year	Player, team	Year	Player, team
1983	Sidney Moncrief, Milwaukee	1996	Gary Payton, Seattle	2007	Marcus Camby, Denver
1984	Sidney Moncrief, Milwaukee	1997	Dikembe Mutombo, Atlanta	2008	Kevin Garnett, Boston
1985	Mark Eaton, Utah	1998	Dikembe Mutombo, Atlanta	2009	Dwight Howard, Orlando
1986	Alvin Robertson, San Antonio	1999	Alonzo Mourning, Miami	2010	Dwight Howard, Orlando
1987	Michael Cooper, L.A. Lakers	2000	Alonzo Mourning, Miami	2011	Dwight Howard, Orlando
1988	Michael Jordan, Chicago	2001	Dikembe Mutombo, Philadelphia-	2012	Tyson Chandler, New York
1989	Mark Eaton, Utah		Atlanta	2013	Marc Gasol, Memphis
1990	Dennis Rodman, Detroit	2002	Ben Wallace, Detroit	2014	Joakim Noah, Chicago
1991	Dennis Rodman, Detroit	2003	Ben Wallace, Detroit	2015	Kawhi Leonard, San Antonio
1992	David Robinson, San Antonio	2004	Ron Artest, Indiana	2016	Kawhi Leonard, San Antonio
1993	Hakeem Olajuwon, Houston	2005	Ben Wallace, Detroit	2017	Draymond Green, Golden State
1994	Hakeem Olajuwon, Houston	2006	Ben Wallace, Detroit	2018	Rudy Gobert, Utah
1995	Dikembe Mutombo, Denver				

NBA Rookie of the Year, 1953-2018

Year	Player, team	Year	Player, team	Year	Player, team
1953	Don Meineke, Ft. Wayne	1975	Jamaal Wilkes, Golden State	1998	Tim Duncan, San Antonio
1954	Ray Felix, Baltimore	1976	Alvan Adams, Phoenix	1999	Vince Carter, Toronto
1955	Bob Pettit, Milwaukee	1977	Adrian Dantley, Buffalo	2000	Elton Brand, Chicago;
1956	Maurice Stokes, Rochester	1978	Walter Davis, Phoenix		Steve Francis, Houston
1957	Tom Heinsohn, Boston	1979	Phil Ford, Kansas City	2001	Mike Miller, Orlando
1958	Woody Sauldsberry, Philadelphia	1980	Larry Bird, Boston	2002	Pau Gasol, Memphis
1959	Elgin Baylor, Minneapolis	1981	Darrell Griffith, Utah	2003	Amar'e Stoudemire, Phoenix
1960	Wilt Chamberlain, Philadelphia	1982	Buck Williams, New Jersey	2004	LeBron James, Cleveland
1961	Oscar Robertson, Cincinnati	1983	Terry Cummings, San Diego	2005	Emeka Okafor, Charlotte
1962	Walt Bellamy, Chicago	1984	Ralph Sampson, Houston	2006	Chris Paul, New Orl./OK City
1963	Terry Dischinger, Chicago	1985	Michael Jordan, Chicago	2007	Brandon Roy, Portland
1964	Jerry Lucas, Cincinnati	1986	Patrick Ewing, New York	2008	Kevin Durant, Seattle
1965	Willis Reed, New York	1987	Chuck Person, Indiana	2009	Derrick Rose, Chicago
1966	Rick Barry, San Francisco	1988	Mark Jackson, New York	2010	Tyreke Evans, Sacramento
1967	Dave Bing, Detroit	1989	Mitch Richmond, Golden State	2011	Blake Griffin, L.A. Clippers
1968	Earl Monroe, Baltimore	1990	David Robinson, San Antonio	2012	Kyrie Irving, Cleveland
1969	Wes Unseld, Baltimore	1991	Derrick Coleman, New Jersey	2013	Damian Lillard, Portland
1970	Lew Alcindor (Kareem Abdul-Jabbar), Milwaukee	1992	Larry Johnson, Charlotte	2014	Michael Carter-Williams, Philadelphia
1971	Dave Cowens, Boston; Geoff Petrie, Portland	1993	Shaquille O'Neal, Orlando	2015	Andrew Wiggins, Minnesota
1972	Sidney Wicks, Portland	1994	Chris Webber, Golden State	2016	Karl-Anthony Towns, Minnesota
1973	Bob McAdoo, Buffalo	1995	Grant Hill, Detroit; Jason Kidd, Dallas	2017	Malcolm Brogdon, Milwaukee
1974	Ernie DiGregorio, Buffalo	1996	Damon Stoudamire, Toronto	2018	Ben Simmons, Philadelphia
		1997	Allen Iverson, Philadelphia		

NBA Sixth Man Award, 1983-2018

Year	Player, team	Year	Player, team	Year	Player, team
1983	Bobby Jones, Philadelphia	1995	Anthony Mason, New York	2007	Leandro Barbosa, Phoenix
1984	Kevin McHale, Boston	1996	Toni Kukoc, Chicago	2008	Manu Ginobili, San Antonio
1985	Kevin McHale, Boston	1997	John Starks, New York	2009	Jason Terry, Dallas
1986	Bill Walton, Boston	1998	Danny Manning, Phoenix	2010	Jamal Crawford, Atlanta
1987	Ricky Pierce, Milwaukee	1999	Darrell Armstrong, Orlando	2011	Lamar Odom, L.A. Lakers
1988	Roy Tarpley, Dallas	2000	Rodney Rogers, Phoenix	2012	James Harden, Oklahoma City
1989	Eddie Johnson, Phoenix	2001	Aaron McKie, Philadelphia	2013	J.R. Smith, New York
1990	Ricky Pierce, Milwaukee	2002	Corliss Williamson, Detroit	2014	Jamal Crawford, L.A. Clippers
1991	Detlef Schrempf, Indiana	2003	Bobby Jackson, Sacramento	2015	Lou Williams, Toronto
1992	Detlef Schrempf, Indiana	2004	Antawn Jamison, Dallas	2016	Jamal Crawford, L.A. Clippers
1993	Clifford Robinson, Portland	2005	Ben Gordon, Chicago	2017	Eric Gordon, Houston
1994	Dell Curry, Charlotte	2006	Mike Miller, Memphis	2018	Lou Williams, L.A. Clippers

NBA Player Draft First-Round Picks, 2018
(June 21, 2018)

Team	Player, position, school/team	Team	Player, position, school/team
1. Phoenix	Deandre Ayton, Center, Arizona	16. Phoenix[7]	Zhaire Smith, Guard, Texas Tech
2. Sacramento	Marvin Bagley III, Center, Duke	17. Milwaukee	Donte DiVincenzo, Guard, Villanova
3. Atlanta[1]	Luka Doncic, Guard, Real Madrid, Spain	18. San Antonio	Lonnie Walker IV, Guard, Miami
4. Memphis	Jaren Jackson Jr., Forward, Michigan State	19. Atlanta[8]	Kevin Huerter, Guard, Maryland
5. Dallas[2]	Trae Young, Guard, Oklahoma	20. Minnesota[9]	Josh Okogie, Guard, Georgia Tech
6. Orlando	Mohamed Bamba, Center, Texas	21. Utah	Grayson Allen, Guard, Duke
7. Chicago	Wendell Carter Jr., Center, Duke	22. Chicago[10]	Chandler Hutchison, Forward, Boise State
8. Cleveland[3]	Collin Sexton, Guard, Alabama	23. Indiana	Aaron Holiday, Guard, UCLA
9. New York	Kevin Knox, Forward, Kentucky	24. Portland	Anfernee Simons, Guard, IMG Academy
10. Philadelphia[4]	Mikal Bridges, Forward, Villanova	25. L.A. Lakers[11]	Moritz Wagner, Center, Michigan
11. Charlotte[5]	Shai Gilgeous-Alexander, Guard, Kentucky	26. Philadelphia	Landry Shamet, Guard, Wichita State
12. L.A. Clippers[6]	Miles Bridges, Forward, Michigan State	27. Boston	Robert Williams, Center, Texas A&M
13. L.A. Clippers	Jerome Robinson, Guard, Boston College	28. Golden State	Jacob Evans, Forward, Cincinnati
14. Denver	Michael Porter Jr., Forward, Missouri	29. Brooklyn[12]	Dzanan Musa, Forward, Cedevita, Croatia
15. Washington	Troy Brown, Guard, Oregon	30. Atlanta[13]	Omari Spellman, Forward, Villanova

(1) Rights traded to Dallas. (2) Rights traded to Atlanta. (3) From Brooklyn through Boston. (4) From L.A. Lakers; rights traded to Phoenix. (5) Rights traded to L.A. Clippers. (6) From Detroit; rights traded to Charlotte. (7) From Miami; rights traded to Philadelphia. (8) From Minnesota. (9) From Oklahoma City through Utah. (10) From New Orleans. (11) From Cleveland. (12) From Toronto. (13) From Houston through L.A. Clippers.

Number-One First-Round NBA Draft Picks, 1966-2018

Year	Team	Player, school/team	Year	Team	Player, school/team
1966	New York	Cazzie Russell, Michigan	1984	Houston	Hakeem Olajuwon, Houston
1967	Detroit	Jimmy Walker, Providence	1985	New York	Patrick Ewing, Georgetown
1968	San Diego	Elvin Hayes, Houston	1986	Cleveland	Brad Daugherty, North Carolina
1969	Milwaukee	Lew Alcindor (Kareem Abdul-Jabbar), UCLA	1987	San Antonio	David Robinson, Navy
			1988	L.A. Clippers	Danny Manning, Kansas
1970	Detroit	Bob Lanier, St. Bonaventure	1989	Sacramento	Pervis Ellison, Louisville
1971	Cleveland	Austin Carr, Notre Dame	1990	New Jersey	Derrick Coleman, Syracuse
1972	Portland	LaRue Martin, Loyola-Chicago	1991	Charlotte	Larry Johnson, UNLV
1973	Philadelphia	Doug Collins, Illinois State	1992	Orlando	Shaquille O'Neal, LSU
1974	Portland	Bill Walton, UCLA	1993	Orlando	Chris Webber[2], Michigan
1975	Atlanta	David Thompson[1], NC State	1994	Milwaukee	Glenn Robinson, Purdue
1976	Houston	John Lucas, Maryland	1995	Golden State	Joe Smith, Maryland
1977	Milwaukee	Kent Benson, Indiana	1996	Philadelphia	Allen Iverson, Georgetown
1978	Portland	Mychal Thompson, Minnesota	1997	San Antonio	Tim Duncan, Wake Forest
1979	L.A. Lakers	Earvin "Magic" Johnson, Michigan State	1998	L.A. Clippers	Michael Olowokandi, Pacific (CA)
1980	Golden State	Joe Barry Carroll, Purdue	1999	Chicago	Elton Brand, Duke
1981	Dallas	Mark Aguirre, DePaul	2000	New Jersey	Kenyon Martin, Cincinnati
1982	L.A. Lakers	James Worthy, North Carolina	2001	Washington	Kwame Brown, Glynn Academy (HS)
1983	Houston	Ralph Sampson, Virginia	2002	Houston	Yao Ming, Shanghai Sharks (China)

Year	Team	Player, school/team	Year	Team	Player, school/team
2003	Cleveland	LeBron James, St. Vincent-St. Mary (HS)	2010	Washington	John Wall, Kentucky
2004	Orlando	Dwight Howard, Southwest Atlanta Christian Academy (HS)	2011	Cleveland	Kyrie Irving, Duke
			2012	New Orleans	Anthony Davis, Kentucky
2005	Milwaukee	Andrew Bogut, Utah	2013	Cleveland	Anthony Bennett, UNLV
2006	Toronto	Andrea Bargnani, Benetton Treviso (Italy)	2014	Cleveland	Andrew Wiggins, Kansas
2007	Portland	Greg Oden, Ohio State	2015	Minnesota	Karl-Anthony Towns, Kentucky
2008	Chicago	Derrick Rose, Memphis	2016	Philadelphia	Ben Simmons, LSU
2009	L.A. Clippers	Blake Griffin, Oklahoma	2017	Philadelphia	Markelle Fultz, Washington
			2018	Phoenix	Deandre Ayton, Arizona

HS = High school. (1) Signed with Denver of the American Basketball Association (ABA). (2) Traded to Golden State for rights to Anfernee Hardaway and three future first-round draft choices.

All-Time NBA Statistical Leaders

(At the end of the 2017-18 season. * = Active in 2017-18 season.)

Scoring Average
(Minimum 400 games or 10,000 points)

	GP	PTS	AVG
Michael Jordan	1,072	32,292	30.1
Wilt Chamberlain	1,045	31,419	30.1
Elgin Baylor	846	23,149	27.4
*LeBron James	1,143	31,038	27.2
*Kevin Durant	771	20,913	27.1
Jerry West	932	25,192	27.0
Allen Iverson	914	24,368	26.7
Bob Pettit	792	20,880	26.4
George Gervin	791	20,708	26.2
Oscar Robertson	1,040	26,710	25.7

Field Goal Percentage
(Minimum 2,000 field goals made)

	FGM	FGA	PCT
*DeAndre Jordan	2,860	4,252	67.3
Artis Gilmore	5,732	9,570	59.9
*Tyson Chandler	3,483	5,847	59.6
*Dwight Howard	6,494	11,148	58.3
Shaquille O'Neal	11,330	19,457	58.2
Mark West	2,528	4,356	58.0
Steve Johnson	2,841	4,965	57.2
*Amir Johnson	2,479	4,333	57.2
Darryl Dawkins	3,477	6,079	57.2
James Donaldson	3,105	5,442	57.1

Free Throw Percentage
(Minimum 1,200 free throws made)

	FTM	FTA	PCT
Steve Nash	3,060	3,384	90.4
Mark Price	2,135	2,362	90.4
*Stephen Curry	2,271	2,514	90.3
Rick Barry	3,818	4,243	90.0
Peja Stojakovic	2,237	2,500	89.5
Chauncey Billups	4,496	5,029	89.4
Ray Allen	4,398	4,920	89.4
Calvin Murphy	3,445	3,864	89.2
*JJ Redick	1,618	1,818	89.0
Scott Skiles	1,548	1,741	88.9

3-Point Field Goal Percentage
(Minimum 250 3-point field goals made)

	3-FGM	3-FGA	PCT
Steve Kerr	726	1,599	45.4
Hubert Davis	728	1,651	44.1
Drazen Petrovic	255	583	43.7
*Stephen Curry	2,129	4,880	43.6
Jason Kapono	457	1,054	43.4
*Kyle Korver	2,213	5,130	43.1
Tim Legler	260	603	43.1
Steve Novak	575	1,337	43.0
Steve Nash	1,685	3,939	42.8
B.J. Armstrong	436	1,026	42.5

Minutes Played
Kareem Abdul-Jabbar	57,446
Karl Malone	54,852
*Dirk Nowitzki	50,572
Kevin Garnett	50,412
Jason Kidd	50,116
Elvin Hayes	50,000
Kobe Bryant	48,643
Wilt Chamberlain	47,859
John Stockton	47,766
Reggie Miller	47,620

Field Goals Attempted
Kareem Abdul-Jabbar	28,307
Karl Malone	26,210
Kobe Bryant	26,200
Michael Jordan	24,537
Elvin Hayes	24,272
John Havlicek	23,930
Wilt Chamberlain	23,497
*Dirk Nowitzki	23,358
*LeBron James	22,383
Dominique Wilkins	21,589

Points
Kareem Abdul-Jabbar	38,387
Karl Malone	36,928
Kobe Bryant	33,643
Michael Jordan	32,292
Wilt Chamberlain	31,419
*Dirk Nowitzki	31,187
*LeBron James	31,038
Shaquille O'Neal	28,596
Moses Malone	27,409
Elvin Hayes	27,313

Games Played
Robert Parish	1,611
Kareem Abdul-Jabbar	1,560
John Stockton	1,504
Karl Malone	1,476
*Dirk Nowitzki	1,471
Kevin Garnett	1,462
Kevin Willis	1,424
*Jason Terry	1,410
*Vince Carter	1,405
Tim Duncan	1,392

Field Goals Made
Kareem Abdul-Jabbar	15,837
Karl Malone	13,528
Wilt Chamberlain	12,681
Michael Jordan	12,192
Kobe Bryant	11,719
Shaquille O'Neal	11,330
*LeBron James	11,280
*Dirk Nowitzki	11,034
Elvin Hayes	10,976
Hakeem Olajuwon	10,749

Rebounds
Wilt Chamberlain	23,924
Bill Russell	21,620
Kareem Abdul-Jabbar	17,440
Elvin Hayes	16,279
Moses Malone	16,212
Tim Duncan	15,091
Karl Malone	14,968
Robert Parish	14,715
Kevin Garnett	14,662
Nate Thurmond	14,464

Personal Fouls
Kareem Abdul-Jabbar	4,657
Karl Malone	4,578
Robert Parish	4,443
Charles Oakley	4,421
Hakeem Olajuwon	4,383
Buck Williams	4,267
Elvin Hayes	4,193
Clifford Robinson	4,175
Kevin Willis	4,172
Shaquille O'Neal	4,146
Otis Thorpe	4,146

3-Point Field Goals Attempted
Ray Allen	7,429
Reggie Miller	6,486
*Jamal Crawford	6,175
*Jason Terry	6,010
Paul Pierce	5,816
Jason Kidd	5,701
*Vince Carter	5,650
Kobe Bryant	5,546
*Joe Johnson	5,331
*Kyle Korver	5,130

Assists
John Stockton	15,806
Jason Kidd	12,091
Steve Nash	10,335
Mark Jackson	10,334
Magic Johnson	10,141
Oscar Robertson	9,887
Isiah Thomas	9,061
Gary Payton	8,966
*Chris Paul	8,708
Andre Miller	8,524

Blocked Shots
Hakeem Olajuwon	3,830
Dikembe Mutombo	3,289
Kareem Abdul-Jabbar	3,189
Mark Eaton	3,064
Tim Duncan	3,020
David Robinson	2,954
Patrick Ewing	2,894
Shaquille O'Neal	2,732
Tree Rollins	2,542
Robert Parish	2,361

3-Point Field Goals Made
Ray Allen	2,973
Reggie Miller	2,560
*Jason Terry	2,282
*Kyle Korver	2,213
*Jamal Crawford	2,153
Paul Pierce	2,143
*Stephen Curry	2,129
*Vince Carter	2,106
Jason Kidd	1,988
*Joe Johnson	1,978

Steals
John Stockton	3,265
Jason Kidd	2,684
Michael Jordan	2,514
Gary Payton	2,445
Maurice Cheeks	2,310
Scottie Pippen	2,307
Clyde Drexler	2,207
Hakeem Olajuwon	2,162
Alvin Robertson	2,112
Karl Malone	2,085

NBA Coach of the Year, 1963-2018

Year	Coach, team	Year	Coach, team	Year	Coach, team
1963	Harry Gallatin, St. Louis	1982	Gene Shue, Washington	2001	Larry Brown, Philadelphia
1964	Alex Hannum, San Francisco	1983	Don Nelson, Milwaukee	2002	Rick Carlisle, Detroit
1965	Red Auerbach, Boston	1984	Frank Layden, Utah	2003	Gregg Popovich, San Antonio
1966	Dolph Schayes, Philadelphia	1985	Don Nelson, Milwaukee	2004	Hubie Brown, Memphis
1967	Johnny Kerr, Chicago	1986	Mike Fratello, Atlanta	2005	Mike D'Antoni, Phoenix
1968	Richie Guerin, St. Louis	1987	Mike Schuler, Portland	2006	Avery Johnson, Dallas
1969	Gene Shue, Baltimore	1988	Doug Moe, Denver	2007	Sam Mitchell, Toronto
1970	Red Holzman, New York	1989	Cotton Fitzsimmons, Phoenix	2008	Byron Scott, New Orleans
1971	Dick Motta, Chicago	1990	Pat Riley, L.A. Lakers	2009	Mike Brown, Cleveland
1972	Bill Sharman, L.A. Lakers	1991	Don Chaney, Houston	2010	Scott Brooks, Oklahoma City
1973	Tom Heinsohn, Boston	1992	Don Nelson, Golden State	2011	Tom Thibodeau, Chicago
1974	Ray Scott, Detroit	1993	Pat Riley, New York	2012	Gregg Popovich, San Antonio
1975	Phil Johnson, Kansas City-Omaha	1994	Lenny Wilkens, Atlanta	2013	George Karl, Denver
1976	Bill Fitch, Cleveland	1995	Del Harris, L.A. Lakers	2014	Gregg Popovich, San Antonio
1977	Tom Nissalke, Houston	1996	Phil Jackson, Chicago	2015	Mike Budenholzer, Atlanta
1978	Hubie Brown, Atlanta	1997	Pat Riley, Miami	2016	Steve Kerr, Golden State
1979	Cotton Fitzsimmons, Kansas City	1998	Larry Bird, Indiana	2017	Mike D'Antoni, Houston
1980	Bill Fitch, Boston	1999	Mike Dunleavy, Portland	2018	Dwane Casey, Toronto
1981	Jack McKinney, Indiana	2000	Glenn "Doc" Rivers, Orlando		

National Basketball Association Franchise Origins

Team, founding year (in NBA, Basketball Assn. of Amer. [BAA], or Amer. Basketball Assn. [ABA]), location, and subsequent history. Neutral sites and arena sites in the same metropolitan area not listed separately.

Atlanta Hawks: 1949, NBA, as Tri-Cities Blackhawks, 1949-51, Moline, IL. Milwaukee Hawks, 1951-55; St. Louis Hawks, 1955-68; Atlanta Hawks, 1968-present.
Boston Celtics: 1946, BAA, Boston, MA, 1946-present.
Brooklyn Nets: 1967, ABA, as New Jersey Americans, 1967-68, Teaneck, NJ. New York Nets, 1968-77; New Jersey Nets, 1977-2012; Brooklyn Nets, 2012-present.
Charlotte Hornets: 2004, NBA, as Charlotte Bobcats, 2004-14, Charlotte, NC. Charlotte Hornets, 2014-present.
Chicago Bulls: 1966, NBA, Chicago, IL, 1966-present.
Cleveland Cavaliers: 1970, NBA, Cleveland, OH, 1970-present.
Dallas Mavericks: 1980, NBA, Dallas, TX, 1980-present.
Denver Nuggets: 1967, ABA, as Denver Rockets, 1967-74, Denver, CO. Denver Nuggets, 1974-present.
Detroit Pistons: 1948, BAA, as Ft. Wayne Pistons, 1948-57, Ft. Wayne, IN. Detroit Pistons, 1957-present.
Golden State Warriors: 1946, BAA, as Philadelphia Warriors, 1946-62, Philadelphia, PA. San Francisco Warriors, 1962-71; Golden State Warriors, 1971-present, Oakland, CA.
Houston Rockets: 1967, NBA, as San Diego Rockets, 1967-71, San Diego, CA. Houston Rockets, 1971-present.
Indiana Pacers: 1967, ABA, Indianapolis, IN, 1974-present.
L.A. Clippers: 1970, NBA, as Buffalo Braves, 1970-78, Buffalo, NY. San Diego Clippers, 1978-84; L.A. Clippers, 1984-present.
L.A. Lakers: 1948, BAA, as Minneapolis Lakers, 1948-60, Minneapolis, MN. L.A. Lakers, 1960-present.
Memphis Grizzlies: 1995, NBA, as Vancouver Grizzlies, 1995-2001, Vancouver, BC, Canada. Memphis Grizzlies, 2001-present.
Miami Heat: 1988, NBA, Miami, FL, 1988-present.
Milwaukee Bucks: 1968, NBA, Milwaukee, WI, 1968-present.
Minnesota Timberwolves: 1989, NBA, Minneapolis, MN, 1989-present.
New Orleans Pelicans: 1988, NBA, as Charlotte Hornets, 1988-2002, Charlotte, NC. New Orleans Hornets, 2002-13 (Hornets played most home games in Oklahoma City, 2005-07, as city repaired Hurricane Katrina damage); New Orleans Pelicans, 2013-present.
New York Knicks: 1946, BAA, New York, NY, 1946-present.
Oklahoma City Thunder: 1967, NBA, as Seattle SuperSonics, 1967-2008, Seattle, WA. Oklahoma City Thunder, 2008-present.
Orlando Magic: 1989, NBA, Orlando, FL, 1989-present.
Philadelphia 76ers: 1949, NBA, as Syracuse Nationals, 1949-63, Syracuse, NY. Philadelphia 76ers, 1963-present.
Phoenix Suns: 1968, NBA, Phoenix, AZ, 1968-present.
Portland Trail Blazers: 1970, NBA, Portland, OR, 1970-present.
Sacramento Kings: 1948, BAA, as Rochester Royals, 1948-57, Rochester, NY. Cincinnati Royals, 1957-72; Kansas City-Omaha Kings, 1972-75; Kansas City Kings, 1975-85; Sacramento Kings, 1985-present.
San Antonio Spurs: ABA, as Dallas Chaparrals, 1967-73, Dallas, TX. San Antonio Spurs, 1973-present.
Toronto Raptors: 1995, NBA, Toronto, ON, Canada, 1995-present.
Utah Jazz: 1974, NBA, as New Orleans Jazz, 1974-79, New Orleans, LA. Utah Jazz, 1979-present, Salt Lake City.
Washington Wizards: 1961, NBA, as Chicago Packers, 1961-62, Chicago, IL. Chicago Zephyrs, 1962-63; Baltimore Bullets, 1963-73; Capital Bullets, 1973-74, Landover, MD; Washington Bullets, 1974-97; Washington Wizards, 1997-present.

NBA Home Courts

Team	Name (year built)	Capacity[1]	Team	Name (year built)	Capacity[1]
Atlanta	Philips Arena (1999)	15,711	Miami	AmericanAirlines Arena (1999)	19,600
Boston	TD Garden[2] (1995)	18,624	Milwaukee	Fiserv Forum (2018)	17,500[8]
Brooklyn	Barclays Center[3] (2012)	17,732	Minnesota	Target Center (1990)	19,356
Charlotte	Spectrum Center[4] (2005)	19,077	New Orleans	Smoothie King Center[9] (1999)	16,867
Chicago	United Center (1994)	20,917	New York	Madison Square Garden (IV) (1968)	19,812
Cleveland	Quicken Loans Arena[5] (1994)	20,562	Oklahoma City	Chesapeake Energy Arena[10] (2002)	18,203
Dallas	American Airlines Center (2001)	19,200	Orlando	Amway Center (2010)	18,846
Denver	Pepsi Center (1999)	19,520	Philadelphia	Wells Fargo Center[11] (1996)	20,328
Detroit	Little Caesars Arena (2017)	20,491	Phoenix	Talking Stick Resort Arena[12] (1992)	18,055
Golden State	Oracle Arena[6] (1966)	19,596	Portland	Moda Center[13] (1995)	19,441
Houston	Toyota Center (2003)	18,055	Sacramento	Golden 1 Center (2016)	17,500
Indiana	Bankers Life Fieldhouse[7] (1999)	17,923	San Antonio	AT&T Center[14] (2002)	18,460
L.A. Clippers	Staples Center (1999)	19,060	Toronto	Air Canada Centre (1999)	19,800
L.A. Lakers	Staples Center (1999)	18,997	Utah	Vivint Smart Home Arena[15] (1991)	19,911
Memphis	FedExForum (2004)	18,119	Washington	Capital One Arena[16] (1997)	20,356

(1) At the end of the 2017-18 season, unless noted. (2) FleetCenter, 1995-2005; TD Banknorth Garden, 2005-09. (3) The New Jersey Nets relocated to Brooklyn prior to the 2012-13 season. (4) Charlotte Bobcats Arena, 2005-08; Time Warner Cable Arena, 2008-16. (5) Gund Arena, 1994-2005. (6) Oakland Coliseum Arena, 1966-96; Arena in Oakland, 1997-2006. (7) Conseco Fieldhouse, 1999-2011. (8) Estimated capacity of Fiserv Forum prior to opening. (9) New Orleans Arena, 1999-2014; because of damage to New Orleans Arena due to Hurricane Katrina, the Hornets played 35 games in the Ford Center in Oklahoma City, OK, 3 games in New Orleans Arena, and 3 games at other locations during the 2005-06 season; in 2006-07, the Hornets played 35 games at the Ford Center and 6 games in New Orleans Arena. (10) Ford Center, 2008-11; the Seattle SuperSonics relocated to Oklahoma City prior to the 2008-09 season. (11) CoreStates Center, 1996-98; First Union Center, 1998-2003; Wachovia Center, 2003-10. (12) America West Arena, 1992-2006; US Airways Center, 2006-15. (13) The Rose Garden, 1995-2013. (14) SBC Center, 2002-06. (15) Delta Center, 1991-2006; EnergySolutions Arena, 2006-15. (16) MCI Center, 1997-2006; Verizon Center, 2006-17.

All-Time NBA Regular Season Coaching Victories

(At the end of the 2017-18 season, ranked by wins. * = Active in 2017-18 season.)

Coach	W	L	PCT	Coach	W	L	PCT	Coach	W	L	PCT
Don Nelson	1,335	1,063	.557	Larry Brown	1,098	904	.548	*Glenn "Doc" Rivers	846	624	.576
Lenny Wilkens	1,332	1,155	.536	Rick Adelman	1,042	749	.582	Cotton Fitzsimmons	832	775	.518
Jerry Sloan	1,221	803	.603	Bill Fitch	944	1,106	.460	Gene Shue	784	861	.477
Pat Riley	1,210	694	.636	Red Auerbach	938	479	.662	*Rick Carlisle	718	578	.554
*Gregg Popovich	1,197	541	.689	Dick Motta	935	1,017	.479	John MacLeod	707	657	.518
George Karl	1,175	824	.588	Jack Ramsay	864	783	.525	Red Holzman	696	603	.536
Phil Jackson	1,155	485	.704								

Naismith Memorial Basketball Hall of Fame

Located in Springfield, MA. * = 2018 inductee. + = Enshrined as both a player and coach. Referee inductees not shown.
www.hoophall.com

Players
Abdul-Jabbar, Kareem
*Allen, Ray
Archibald, Nate
Arizin, Paul
Barkley, Charles
Barlow, Thomas
Barry, Rick
Baylor, Elgin
Beaty, Zelmo
Beckman, John
Bellamy, Walt
Belov, Sergei
Bing, Dave
Bird, Larry
Blazejowski, Carol
Borgmann, Bennie
Bradley, Bill
Brennan, Joseph
Brown, Roger
Cervi, Al
Chamberlain, Wilt
*Cheeks, Maurice
Clayton, Zack
Cooper, Charles
Cooper, Cynthia
Cosic, Kresimir
Cousy, Bob
Cowens, Dave
Crawford, Joan
Cunningham, Billy
Curry, Denise
Dalipagic, Drazen
Dampier, Louis
Daniels, Mel
Dantley, Adrian
Davies, Bob
DeBernardi, Forrest
DeBusschere, Dave
Dehnert, Henry "Dutch"
Donovan, Anne
Drexler, Clyde
Dumars, Joe
Edwards, Teresa
Endacott, Paul
English, Alex
Erving, Julius
Ewing, Patrick
Foster, Bud
Frazier, Walt
Friedman, Max
Fulks, Joe
Gale, Lauren
Galis, Nick
Gallatin, Harry
Gates, William "Pop"
Gervin, George
Gilmore, Artis
Gola, Tom
Goodrich, Gail
Greer, Hal
Gruenig, Robert "Ace"
Guerin, Richard
Hagan, Cliff
Hanson, Victor
Harris-Stewart, Lusia
Havlicek, John

Hawkins, Cornelius "Connie"
Hayes, Elvin
Haynes, Marques
Haywood, Spencer
+Heinsohn, Tom
*Hill, Grant
Holman, Nat
Houbregs, Bob
Howell, Bailey
Hyatt, Chuck
Isaacs, John
Issel, Dan
Iverson, Allen
Jeannette, Harry "Buddy"
Johnson, Dennis
Johnson, Earvin "Magic"
Johnson, Gus
Johnson, William
Johnston, Neil
Jones, K. C.
Jones, Sam
Jordan, Michael
*Kidd, Jason
King, Bernard
Krause, Ed "Moose"
Kurland, Bob
Lanier, Bob
Lapchick, Joe
Leslie, Lisa
Lieberman, Nancy
Lovellette, Clyde
Lucas, Jerry
Luisetti, Angelo "Hank"
Macauley, Ed
Malone, Karl
Malone, Moses
Maravich, Pete
Marcari, Hortencia
Marciulionis, Sarunas
Martin, Slater
McAdoo, Bob
McClain, Katrina
McCracken, Emmett "Branch"
McCracken, Jack
McDermott, Bobby
McGinnis, George
McGrady, Tracy
McGuire, Dick
McHale, Kevin
Meneghin, Dino
Meyers, Ann
Mikan, George
Mikkelsen, Vern
Miller, Cheryl
Miller, Reggie
Ming, Yao
Monroe, Earl
Mourning, Alonzo
Mullin, Chris
Murphy, Calvin
Murphy, Charles "Stretch"
Mutombo, Dikembe
*Nash, Steve
Olajuwon, Hakeem

O'Neal, Shaquille
Page, Harlan "Pat"
Parish, Robert
Payton, Gary
Pereira, Maciel "Ubiratan"
Petrovic, Drazen
Pettit, Bob
Phillip, Andy
Pippen, Scottie
Pollard, Jim
Posey, Cumberland
*Radja, Dino
Ramsey, Frank
Reed, Willis
Richmond, Mitch
Risen, Arnie
Robertson, Oscar
Robinson, David
Rodgers, Guy
Rodman, Dennis
Roosma, John
Russell, Bill
Russell, John "Honey"
Sabonis, Arvydas
Sampson, Ralph
Sanders, Tom "Satch"
Schayes, Adolph
Schmidt, Ernest
Schmidt, Oscar
Schommer, John
*Scott, Charlie
Sedran, Barney
Semjonova, Uljana
+Sharman, Bill
*Smith, Katie
Staley, Dawn
Steinmetz, Chris
Stockton, John
Stokes, Maurice
Swoopes, Sheryl
Tatum, Reece "Goose"
Thomas, Isiah
Thompson, David
Thompson, John
*Thompson, Tina
Thurmond, Nate
Twyman, Jack
Unseld, Wes
Vandivier, Robert "Fuzzy"
Wachter, Ed
Walker, Chet
Walton, Bill
Wanzer, Bobby
*Washington, Ora Mae
West, Jerry
White, Jo Jo
White, Nera
+Wilkens, Lenny
Wilkes, Jamaal
Wilkins, Dominique
Woodard, Lynette
+Wooden, John
Worthy, James
Yardley, George

Coaches
Alexeeva, Lidia
Allen, Forrest C. "Phog"
Anderson, Harold
Auerbach, Arnold "Red"
Auriemma, Geno
Barmore, Leon
Barry, Justin "Sam"
Blood, Ernest
Boeheim, Jim
Brown, Larry
Calhoun, Jim
Calipari, John
Cann, Howard
Carlson, Clifford
Carnesecca, Lou
Carnevale, Ben
Carril, Pete
Case, Everett
Chancellor, Van
Chaney, John
Conradt, Jody
Crum, Denzil "Denny"
Daly, Chuck
Dean, Everett
Diaz-Miguel, Antonio
Diddle, Edgar
Drake, Bruce
*Driesell, Charles "Lefty"
Ferrándiz, Pedro
Gaines, Clarence
Gamba, Sandro
Gardner, James "Jack"
Gaze, Lindsay
Gill, Amory "Slats"
Gomelsky, Aleksandr
Gunter, Sue
Hannum, Alex
Harshman, Marv
Haskins, Don
Hatchell, Sylvia
+Heinsohn, Tom
Hickey, Edgar
Hobson, Howard
Holzman, William "Red"
Hughes, Robert
Hurley, Bob, Sr.
Iba, Hank
Izzo, Tom
Jackson, Phil
Julian, Alvin
Keaney, Frank
Keogan, George
Knight, Bob
Krzyzewski, Mike
Kundla, John
Lambert, Ward
Leonard, Bob
Lewis, Guy V.
Litwack, Harry
Loeffler, Kenneth
Lonborg, Arthur "Dutch"

Magee, Herb
McCutchan, Arad
McGraw, Muffet
McGuire, Al
McGuire, Frank
McLendon, John
Meanwell, Dr. Walter
Meyer, Ray
Miller, Ralph
Moore, Billie
Nelson, Don
Newell, Pete
Nikolic, Aleksandar
Novosel, Mirko
Olson, Robert "Lute"
Pitino, Rick
Ramsay, John "Jack"
Richardson, Nolan
Riley, Pat
Rubini, Cesare
Rupp, Adolph
Rush, Cathy
Sachs, Leonard
Self, Bill
+Sharman, Bill
Shelton, Everett
Sloan, Jerry
Smith, Dean
Stringer, C. Vivian
Summitt, Pat
Tarkanian, Jerry
Taylor, Fred
Thompson, John R.
VanDerveer, Tara
Wade, Margaret
Watts, Stan
+Wilkens, Lenny
Williams, Gary
Williams, Roy
Winter, Tex
+Wooden, John
Woolpert, Phil
Wootten, Morgan
Yow, Kay

Teams
1960 USA Men's Olympic Team
1966 Texas Western
1972-73-74 Immaculata Coll.
1992 USA Men's Olympic "Dream Team"
All American Red Heads
Buffalo Germans First Team
Harlem Globetrotters
New York Renaissance
Original Celtics

Contributors
Abbott, Senda Berenson
Barksdale, Don
Bee, Clair
Biasone, Danny
Brown, Hubert "Hubie"

Brown, Walter
Bunn, John
Buss, Jerry
Clifton, Nat
Colangelo, Jerry
Davidson, Bill
Douglas, Bob
Duer, Al
Embry, Wayne
Fagan, Cliff
Fisher, Harry
Fleisher, Larry
Gavitt, David
Gottlieb, Edward
Granik, Russ
Gulick, Dr. Luther
Harrison, Lester
Hearn, Francis "Chick"
Henderson, E. B.
Hepp, Dr. Ferenc
Hickox, Edward
Hinkle, Tony
Irish, Edward "Ned"
Jackson, Mannie
Jernstedt, Tom
Jones, R. William
Kennedy, Walter
Knight, Phil
Krause, Jerry
Lemon, Meadowlark
Liston, Emil
Lloyd, Earl
Lobo, Rebecca
McLendon, John
Mokray, Bill
Morgan, Ralph
Morgenweck, Frank
Naismith, Dr. James
Newton, C. M.
O'Brien, John
O'Brien, Larry
Olsen, Harold
Podoloff, Maurice
Porter, Henry V.
Raveling, George
Reid, William
Reinsdorf, Jerry
Ripley, Elmer
St. John, Lynn
Saperstein, Abe
Schabinger, Arthur
Stagg, Alonzo
Stankovic, Boris
Steitz, Edward
Stern, David
Taylor, Chuck
Teague, Bertha
*Thorn, Rod
Tower, Oswald
Trester, Arthur
Vitale, Dick
Wells, Clifford
Wilke, Lou
*Welts, Rick
Zollner, Fred

WNBA 2018: Stewart and Storm Claim Championship

The Seattle Storm won the WNBA Championship for the first time since 2010 with a three-game sweep over the Washington Mystics in the WNBA Finals. Breanna Stewart scored 30 points, and Natasha Howard added 29 points and 14 rebounds to lead the Storm past Washington, 98-82, in the Game 3 win, Sept. 12, 2018, at EagleBank Arena in Fairfax, VA. Stewart averaged 25.7 points in the three-game sweep and was voted WNBA Finals MVP.

Stewart also won the WNBA regular season MVP award, averaging a team-high 21.8 points and 8.4 rebounds and led the Storm to a five-game victory over Phoenix in the semifinals. Washington reached the WNBA Finals for the first time in franchise history with a five-game semifinals victory over Atlanta.

WNBA Final Standings, 2018

(playoff seeds in parentheses; top eight teams by PCT advance, regardless of conference; top two seeds receive a bye to the semifinals)

Eastern Conference	W	L	PCT	GB	Western Conference	W	L	PCT	GB
Atlanta Dream (2)	23	11	.676	—	Seattle Storm (1)	26	8	.765	—
Washington Mystics (3)	22	12	.647	1	Phoenix Mercury (5)	20	14	.588	6
Connecticut Sun (4)	21	13	.618	2	Los Angeles Sparks (6)	19	15	.559	7
Chicago Sky	13	21	.382	10	Minnesota Lynx (7)	18	16	.529	8
New York Liberty	7	27	.206	16	Dallas Wings (8)	15	19	.441	11
Indiana Fever	6	28	.176	17	Las Vegas Aces	14	20	.412	12

Note: Phoenix earned the No. 5 seed over Washington due to a better head-to-head record.

WNBA Playoff Results, 2018

First Round (single elimination)
(5) Phoenix 101, (8) Dallas 83
(6) Los Angeles 75, (7) Minnesota 68

Second Round (single elimination)
(3) Washington 96, (6) Los Angeles 64
(5) Phoenix 96, (4) Connecticut 86

Semifinals (best-of-five)
(1) Seattle defeated (5) Phoenix, 3 games to 2
(3) Washington defeated (2) Atlanta, 3 games to 2

WNBA Championship

Seattle defeated Washington, 3 games to 0 (Game 1: 89-76; 2: 75-73; 3: 98-82), in the best-of-five series

WNBA Statistical Leaders, 2018

Minutes played: 1,120, DeWanna Bonner, Phoenix
Total points: 742, Breanna Stewart, Seattle
Points per game: 23.0, Liz Cambage, Dallas
Field goal pct.: .619, Sylvia Fowles, Minnesota
3-point field goal pct.: .470, Briann January, Phoenix

Free throw pct.: .925, Diana Taurasi, Phoenix
Rebounds: 404, Sylvia Fowles, Minnesota
Assists: 258, Courtney Vandersloot, Chicago
Steals: 57, Maya Moore, Minnesota
Blocks: 87, Brittney Griner, Phoenix

WNBA Champions, 1997-2018

	Regular Season		Playoffs		
Year	Eastern champion	Western champion	Champion	Winning coach	Opponent
1997	Houston Comets	Phoenix Mercury	Houston	Van Chancellor	New York
1998	Cleveland Rockers	Houston Comets	Houston	Van Chancellor	Phoenix
1999	New York Liberty	Houston Comets	Houston	Van Chancellor	New York
2000	New York Liberty	Los Angeles Sparks	Houston	Van Chancellor	New York
2001	Cleveland Rockers	Los Angeles Sparks	Los Angeles	Michael Cooper	Charlotte
2002	New York Liberty	Los Angeles Sparks	Los Angeles	Michael Cooper	New York
2003	Detroit Shock	Los Angeles Sparks	Detroit	Bill Laimbeer	Los Angeles
2004	Connecticut Sun	Los Angeles Sparks	Seattle	Anne Donovan	Connecticut
2005	Connecticut Sun	Sacramento Monarchs	Sacramento	John Whisenant	Connecticut
2006	Connecticut Sun	Los Angeles Sparks	Detroit	Bill Laimbeer	Sacramento
2007	Detroit Shock	Phoenix Mercury	Phoenix	Paul Westhead	Detroit
2008	Detroit Shock	San Antonio Silver Stars	Detroit	Bill Laimbeer	San Antonio
2009	Indiana Fever	Phoenix Mercury	Phoenix	Corey Gaines	Indiana
2010	Washington Mystics	Seattle Storm	Seattle	Brian Agler	Atlanta
2011	Indiana Fever	Minnesota Lynx	Minnesota	Cheryl Reeve	Atlanta
2012	Connecticut Sun	Minnesota Lynx	Indiana	Lin Dunn	Minnesota
2013	Chicago Sky	Minnesota Lynx	Minnesota	Cheryl Reeve	Atlanta
2014	Atlanta Dream	Phoenix Mercury	Phoenix	Sandy Brondello	Chicago
2015	New York Liberty	Minnesota Lynx	Minnesota	Cheryl Reeve	Indiana
2016	New York Liberty	Minnesota Lynx	Los Angeles	Brian Agler	Minnesota
2017	New York Liberty	Minnesota Lynx	Minnesota	Cheryl Reeve	Los Angeles
2018	Atlanta Dream	Seattle Storm	Seattle	Dan Hughes	Washington

WNBA Finals MVP, 1997-2018

Year	Player, team	Year	Player, team	Year	Player, team
1997	Cynthia Cooper, Houston	2005	Yolanda Griffith, Sacramento	2012	Tamika Catchings, Indiana
1998	Cynthia Cooper, Houston	2006	Deanna Nolan, Detroit	2013	Maya Moore, Minnesota
1999	Cynthia Cooper, Houston	2007	Cappie Pondexter, Phoenix	2014	Diana Taurasi, Phoenix
2000	Cynthia Cooper, Houston	2008	Katie Smith, Detroit	2015	Sylvia Fowles, Minnesota
2001	Lisa Leslie, Los Angeles	2009	Diana Taurasi, Phoenix	2016	Candace Parker, Los Angeles
2002	Lisa Leslie, Los Angeles	2010	Lauren Jackson, Seattle	2017	Sylvia Fowles, Minnesota
2003	Ruth Riley, Detroit	2011	Seimone Augustus, Minnesota	2018	Breanna Stewart, Seattle
2004	Betty Lennox, Seattle				

WNBA Most Valuable Player, 1997-2018

Year	Player, team	Year	Player, team	Year	Player, team
1997	Cynthia Cooper, Houston	2005	Sheryl Swoopes, Houston	2012	Tina Charles, Connecticut
1998	Cynthia Cooper, Houston	2006	Lisa Leslie, Los Angeles	2013	Candace Parker, Los Angeles
1999	Yolanda Griffith, Sacramento	2007	Lauren Jackson, Seattle	2014	Maya Moore, Minnesota
2000	Sheryl Swoopes, Houston	2008	Candace Parker, Los Angeles	2015	Elena Delle Donne, Chicago
2001	Lisa Leslie, Los Angeles	2009	Diana Taurasi, Phoenix	2016	Nneka Ogwumike, Los Angeles
2002	Sheryl Swoopes, Houston	2010	Lauren Jackson, Seattle	2017	Sylvia Fowles, Minnesota
2003	Lauren Jackson, Seattle	2011	Tamika Catchings, Indiana	2018	Breanna Stewart, Seattle
2004	Lisa Leslie, Los Angeles				

WNBA Rookie of the Year, 1997-2018

Year	Player, team	Year	Player, team	Year	Player, team
1997	No award	2005	Temeka Johnson, Washington	2012	Nneka Ogwumike, Los Angeles
1998	Tracy Reid, Charlotte	2006	Seimone Augustus, Minnesota	2013	Elena Delle Donne, Chicago
1999	Chamique Holdsclaw, Washington	2007	Armintie Price, Chicago	2014	Chiney Ogwumike, Connecticut
2000	Betty Lennox, Minnesota	2008	Candace Parker, Los Angeles	2015	Jewell Loyd, Seattle
2001	Jackie Stiles, Portland	2009	Angel McCoughtry, Atlanta	2016	Breanna Stewart, Seattle
2002	Tamika Catchings, Indiana	2010	Tina Charles, Connecticut	2017	Allisha Gray, Dallas
2003	Cheryl Ford, Detroit	2011	Maya Moore, Minnesota	2018	A'ja Wilson, Las Vegas
2004	Diana Taurasi, Phoenix				

WNBA Scoring Leaders, 1997-2018

(Average points per game; 24 games or 480 point minimum, 2004-18; prior season minimums vary.)

Year	Player, team	PTS	AVG	Year	Player, team	PTS	AVG
1997	Cynthia Cooper, Houston	621	22.2	2008	Diana Taurasi, Phoenix	820	24.1
1998	Cynthia Cooper, Houston	680	22.7	2009	Diana Taurasi, Phoenix	631	20.4
1999	Cynthia Cooper, Houston	686	22.1	2010	Diana Taurasi, Phoenix	702	22.6
2000	Sheryl Swoopes, Houston	643	20.7	2011	Diana Taurasi, Phoenix	692	21.6
2001	Katie Smith, Minnesota	739	23.1	2012	Angel McCoughtry, Atlanta	514	21.4
2002	Chamique Holdsclaw, Washington	397	19.9	2013	Angel McCoughtry, Atlanta	711	21.5
2003	Lauren Jackson, Seattle	698	21.2	2014	Maya Moore, Minnesota	812	23.9
2004	Lauren Jackson, Seattle	634	20.5	2015	Elena Delle Donne, Chicago	725	23.4
2005	Sheryl Swoopes, Houston	614	18.6	2016	Tina Charles, New York	688	21.5
2006	Diana Taurasi, Phoenix	860	25.3	2017	Brittney Griner, Phoenix	569	21.9
2007	Lauren Jackson, Seattle	739	23.8	2018	Liz Cambage, Dallas	737	23.0

WNBA Rebounding Leaders, 1997-2018

(Average rebounds per game; 24 games or 240 rebounds minimum, 2004-18; prior season minimums vary.)

Year	Player, team	REB	RPG	Year	Player, team	REB	RPG
1997	Lisa Leslie, Los Angeles	266	9.5	2008	Candace Parker, Los Angeles	313	9.5
1998	Lisa Leslie, Los Angeles	285	10.2	2009	Candace Parker, Los Angeles	244	9.8
1999	Yolanda Griffith, Sacramento	329	11.3	2010	Tina Charles, Connecticut	398	11.7
2000	Natalie Williams, Utah	336	11.6	2011	Tina Charles, Connecticut	374	11.0
2001	Yolanda Griffith, Sacramento	357	11.2	2012	Tina Charles, Connecticut	345	10.5
2002	Chamique Holdsclaw, Washington	232	11.6	2013	Sylvia Fowles, Chicago	369	11.5
2003	Chamique Holdsclaw, Washington	294	10.9	2014	Courtney Paris, Tulsa	347	10.2
2004	Lisa Leslie, Los Angeles	336	9.9	2015	Courtney Paris, Tulsa	317	9.3
2005	Cheryl Ford, Detroit	322	9.8	2016	Tina Charles, New York	317	9.9
2006	Cheryl Ford, Detroit	363	11.3	2017	Jonquel Jones, Connecticut	403	11.9
2007	Lauren Jackson, Seattle	300	9.7	2018	Sylvia Fowles, Minnesota	404	11.9

WNBA Assist Leaders, 1997-2018

(Average assists per game; 24 games or 140 assists minimum, 2004-18; prior season minimums vary.)

Year	Player, team	AST	APG	Year	Player, team	AST	APG
1997	Teresa Weatherspoon, New York	172	6.1	2008	Lindsay Whalen, Connecticut	166	5.4
1998	Ticha Penicheiro, Sacramento	224	7.5	2009	Sue Bird, Seattle	179	5.8
1999	Ticha Penicheiro, Sacramento	226	7.1	2010	Ticha Penicheiro, Los Angeles	220	6.9
2000	Ticha Penicheiro, Sacramento	236	7.9	2011	Lindsay Whalen, Minnesota	199	5.9
2001	Ticha Penicheiro, Sacramento	172	7.5	2012	Lindsay Whalen, Minnesota	178	5.4
2002	Ticha Penicheiro, Sacramento	192	8.0	2013	Danielle Robinson, San Antonio	168	6.7
2003	Ticha Penicheiro, Sacramento	229	6.7	2014	Diana Taurasi, Phoenix	185	5.6
2004	Nikki Teasley, Los Angeles	207	6.1	2015	Courtney Vandersloot, Chicago	198	5.8
2005	Sue Bird, Seattle	176	5.9	2016	Sue Bird, Seattle	196	5.8
2006	Nikki Teasley, Washington	183	5.4	2017	Courtney Vandersloot, Chicago	218	8.1
2007	Becky Hammon, San Antonio	140	5.0	2018	Courtney Vandersloot, Chicago	258	8.6

All-Time WNBA Statistical Leaders

(At the end of the 2018 season. * = Active in 2018 season.)

Scoring Average
(Minimum 100 games)

Player	G	PTS	AVG	Player	G	PTS	AVG
Cynthia Cooper	124	2,601	21.0	Lauren Jackson	317	6,007	18.9
*Elena Delle Donne	159	3,247	20.4	*Maya Moore	271	4,984	18.4
*Breanna Stewart	101	2,019	20.0	*Tina Charles	297	5,423	18.3
*Diana Taurasi	431	8,549	19.8	*Candace Parker	293	5,113	17.5
*Angel McCoughtry	285	5,468	19.2	Lisa Leslie	363	6,263	17.3

Points

*Diana Taurasi	8,549
Tina Thompson	7,488
Tamika Catchings	7,380
*Cappie Pondexter	6,811
Katie Smith	6,452
Lisa Leslie	6,263
*Sue Bird	6,154
*Candice Dupree	6,057

Rebounds

*Rebekkah Brunson	3,356
Tamika Catchings	3,316
Lisa Leslie	3,307
Tina Thompson	3,070
*Sylvia Fowles	3,030
Taj McWilliams-Franklin	3,013
*Tina Charles	2,884
*Candice Dupree	2,775

Assists

*Sue Bird	2,831
Ticha Penicheiro	2,599
*Lindsay Whalen	2,348
*Diana Taurasi	1,835
Becky Hammon	1,708
*Cappie Pondexter	1,578
Tamika Catchings	1,488
Shannon Johnson	1,424

3-Point Field Goals Made

*Diana Taurasi	1,102
Katie Smith	906
*Sue Bird	855
Becky Hammon	829
Tina Thompson	748
Katie Douglas	727
Tamika Catchings	606
Kara Lawson	584

Steals

Tamika Catchings	1,074
Ticha Penicheiro	764
*Alana Beard	698
Sheryl Swoopes	657
*Sue Bird	652
Jia Perkins	634
Katie Douglas	623
*Sancho Lyttle; DeLisha Milton-Jones	619

Blocked Shots

Margo Dydek	877
Lisa Leslie	822
Lauren Jackson	586
*Sylvia Fowles	574
*Brittney Griner	574
Tangela Smith	557
Tammy Sutton-Brown	555
Ruth Riley	505

HOCKEY

Capitals, Ovechkin Win Their First Stanley Cup Finals in 2018

The Washington Capitals won their first Stanley Cup championship in 2018, beating the Vegas Golden Knights, the league's newest franchise. Lars Eller broke a 3-3 tie with a third-period goal that carried the Caps to a 4-3 win and the title in Game 5 of the Stanley Cup Final on June 7, 2018, at T-Mobile Arena in Las Vegas, NV. All-Star veteran left wing Alex Ovechkin, who topped the NHL with 49 goals during the regular season, led all scorers with 15 postseason goals and earned the Conn Smythe Trophy as the playoff's most valuable player.

The expansion Golden Knights won the team's emotional first-ever home game over Arizona Oct. 10, 2017, shortly after the Oct. 1 mass shooting that killed 58 people at a Las Vegas concert, and went on to amass 51 wins and 109 points, both of which set records for a first-year NHL franchise. Vegas advanced to the Stanley Cup Final by defeating the Winnipeg Jets in five games in the Western Conference finals.

Washington won 12 of its last 15 regular season games to capture the Metropolitan Division title, then defeated Columbus and the two-time defending Stanley Cup champion Pittsburgh Penguins in their first two playoff rounds. Washington needed seven games in the Eastern Conference finals to beat the Tampa Bay Lightning in the Caps' first Cup Final since 1998. Head coach Barry Trotz resigned shortly after leading the Caps to the Stanley Cup win and signed a deal with the NY Islanders.

The Ottawa Senators beat the Montréal Canadiens, 3-0, in the outdoor NHL 100 Classic, Dec. 16, 2017, at Lansdowne Park, Ottawa, ON, Canada, as part of the league's 100th anniversary celebration. Nearly 34,000 fans were in attendance, and temperature at game time hovered around 12 degrees Fahrenheit.

Final NHL Standings, 2017-18
(* = clinched playoff berth)

Standings are determined by total points. Teams earn two points for each win and one point for each game lost in overtime or in a shootout. ROW, which stands for Regulation plus Overtime Wins, is used to break ties between teams with the same number of points.

The top three finishers in each division qualify for the first 12 playoff seeds. Two additional wild-card playoff spots are awarded in each conference to the next two highest-placed finishers regardless of division.

Eastern Conference

Atlantic Division	W	L	OT	GF	GA	ROW	PTS
*Tampa Bay Lightning....	54	23	5	296	236	48	113
*Boston Bruins.........	50	20	12	270	214	47	112
*Toronto Maple Leafs....	49	26	7	277	232	42	105
Florida Panthers........	44	30	8	248	246	41	96
Detroit Red Wings.......	30	39	13	217	255	25	73
Montréal Canadiens.....	29	40	13	209	264	27	71
Ottawa Senators........	28	43	11	221	291	26	67
Buffalo Sabres.........	25	45	12	199	280	24	62

Metropolitan Division	W	L	OT	GF	GA	ROW	PTS
*Washington Capitals....	49	26	7	259	239	46	105
*Pittsburgh Penguins....	47	29	6	272	250	45	100
*Philadelphia Flyers.....	42	26	14	251	243	40	98
*Columbus Blue Jackets..	45	30	7	242	230	39	97
*New Jersey Devils......	44	29	9	248	244	39	97
Carolina Hurricanes.....	36	35	11	228	256	33	83
NY Islanders...........	35	37	10	264	296	32	80
NY Rangers	34	39	9	231	268	31	77

Western Conference

Central Division	W	L	OT	GF	GA	ROW	PTS
*Nashville Predators......	53	18	11	267	211	47	117
*Winnipeg Jets	52	20	10	277	218	48	114
*Minnesota Wild.........	45	26	11	253	232	42	101
*Colorado Avalanche	43	30	9	257	237	41	95
St. Louis Blues	44	32	6	226	222	41	94
Dallas Stars	42	32	8	235	225	38	92
Chicago Blackhawks......	33	39	10	229	256	32	76

Pacific Division	W	L	OT	GF	GA	ROW	PTS
*Vegas Golden Knights....	51	24	7	272	228	47	109
*Anaheim Ducks..........	44	25	13	235	216	40	101
*San Jose Sharks........	45	27	10	252	229	40	100
*L.A. Kings	45	29	8	239	203	43	98
Calgary Flames	37	35	10	218	248	35	84
Edmonton Oilers.........	36	40	6	234	263	31	78
Vancouver Canucks	31	40	11	218	264	31	73
Arizona Coyotes	29	41	12	208	256	27	70

Stanley Cup Playoff Results, 2018

Eastern Conference
Tampa Bay defeated New Jersey, 4 games to 1
Boston defeated Toronto, 4 games to 3
Washington defeated Columbus, 4 games to 2
Pittsburgh defeated Philadelphia, 4 games to 2
Tampa Bay defeated Boston, 4 games to 1
Washington defeated Pittsburgh, 4 games to 2
Washington defeated Tampa Bay, 4 games to 3

Western Conference
Nashville defeated Colorado, 4 games to 2
Winnipeg defeated Minnesota, 4 games to 1
Vegas defeated Los Angeles, 4 games to 0
San Jose defeated Anaheim, 4 games to 0
Winnipeg defeated Nashville, 4 games to 3
Vegas defeated San Jose, 4 games to 2
Vegas defeated Winnipeg, 4 games to 1

Stanley Cup Final
Washington defeated Vegas, 4 games to 1 (4-6, 3-2, 3-1, 6-2, 4-3)

Stanley Cup Champions, 1927-2018

Year	Champion	Coach	Final opponent	Year	Champion	Coach	Final opponent
1927	Ottawa	Dave Gill.........	Boston	1949	Toronto..........	Hap Day	Detroit
1928	NY Rangers	Lester Patrick.....	Montréal Maroons	1950	Detroit...........	Tommy Ivan	NY Rangers
				1951	Toronto..........	Joe Primeau......	Montréal
1929	Boston	Art Ross	NY Rangers	1952	Detroit...........	Tommy Ivan	Montréal
1930	Montréal Canadiens	Cecil Hart	Boston	1953	Montréal.........	Dick Irvin........	Boston
1931	Montréal Canadiens	Cecil Hart	Chicago	1954	Detroit...........	Tommy Ivan	Montréal
1932	Toronto..........	Dick Irvin........	NY Rangers	1955	Detroit...........	Jimmy Skinner	Montréal
1933	NY Rangers	Lester Patrick.....	Toronto	1956	Montréal.........	Toe Blake	Detroit
1934	Chicago	Tommy Gorman...	Detroit	1957	Montréal.........	Toe Blake	Boston
1935	Montréal Maroons	Tommy Gorman...	Toronto	1958	Montréal.........	Toe Blake	Boston
1936	Detroit...........	Jack Adams	Toronto	1959	Montréal.........	Toe Blake	Toronto
1937	Detroit...........	Jack Adams	NY Rangers	1960	Montréal.........	Toe Blake	Toronto
1938	Chicago	Bill Stewart.......	Toronto	1961	Chicago	Rudy Pilous	Detroit
1939	Boston	Art Ross	Toronto	1962	Toronto..........	Punch Imlach	Chicago
1940	NY Rangers	Frank Boucher	Toronto	1963	Toronto..........	Punch Imlach	Detroit
1941	Boston	Cooney Weiland...	Detroit	1964	Toronto..........	Punch Imlach	Detroit
1942	Toronto..........	Hap Day	Detroit	1965	Montréal.........	Toe Blake	Chicago
1943	Detroit...........	Jack Adams	Boston	1966	Montréal.........	Toe Blake	Detroit
1944	Montréal.........	Dick Irvin	Chicago	1967	Toronto..........	Punch Imlach	Montréal
1945	Toronto..........	Hap Day	Detroit	1968	Montréal.........	Toe Blake	St. Louis
1946	Montréal.........	Dick Irvin	Boston	1969	Montréal.........	Claude Ruel	St. Louis
1947	Toronto..........	Hap Day	Montréal	1970	Boston	Harry Sinden.....	St. Louis
1948	Toronto..........	Hap Day	Detroit	1971	Montréal.........	Al MacNeil.......	Chicago

Year	Champion	Coach	Final opponent	Year	Champion	Coach	Final opponent
1972	Boston	Tom Johnson	NY Rangers	1995	New Jersey	Jacques Lemaire	Detroit
1973	Montréal	Scotty Bowman	Chicago	1996	Colorado	Marc Crawford	Florida
1974	Philadelphia	Fred Shero	Boston	1997	Detroit	Scotty Bowman	Philadelphia
1975	Philadelphia	Fred Shero	Buffalo	1998	Detroit	Scotty Bowman	Washington
1976	Montréal	Scotty Bowman	Philadelphia	1999	Dallas	Ken Hitchcock	Buffalo
1977	Montréal	Scotty Bowman	Boston	2000	New Jersey	Larry Robinson	Dallas
1978	Montréal	Scotty Bowman	Boston	2001	Colorado	Bob Hartley	New Jersey
1979	Montréal	Scotty Bowman	NY Rangers	2002	Detroit	Scotty Bowman	Carolina
1980	NY Islanders	Al Arbour	Philadelphia	2003	New Jersey	Pat Burns	Anaheim
1981	NY Islanders	Al Arbour	Minnesota	2004	Tampa Bay	John Tortorella	Calgary
1982	NY Islanders	Al Arbour	Vancouver	2005	No competition (labor dispute; season canceled)		
1983	NY Islanders	Al Arbour	Edmonton	2006	Carolina	Peter Laviolette	Edmonton
1984	Edmonton	Glen Sather	NY Islanders	2007	Anaheim	Randy Carlyle	Ottawa
1985	Edmonton	Glen Sather	Philadelphia	2008	Detroit	Mike Babcock	Pittsburgh
1986	Montréal	Jean Perron	Calgary	2009	Pittsburgh	Dan Bylsma	Detroit
1987	Edmonton	Glen Sather	Philadelphia	2010	Chicago	Joel Quenneville	Philadelphia
1988	Edmonton	Glen Sather	Boston	2011	Boston	Claude Julien	Vancouver
1989	Calgary	Terry Crisp	Montréal	2012	Los Angeles	Darryl Sutter	New Jersey
1990	Edmonton	John Muckler	Boston	2013	Chicago	Joel Quenneville	Boston
1991	Pittsburgh	Bob Johnson	Minnesota	2014	Los Angeles	Darryl Sutter	NY Rangers
1992	Pittsburgh	Scotty Bowman	Chicago	2015	Chicago	Joel Quenneville	Tampa Bay
1993	Montréal	Jacques Demers	Los Angeles	2016	Pittsburgh	Mike Sullivan	San Jose
1994	NY Rangers	Mike Keenan	Vancouver	2017	Pittsburgh	Mike Sullivan	Nashville
				2018	Washington	Barry Trotz	Vegas

Presidents' Trophy, 1986-2018

Awarded annually to club with best regular season record. Records are Win-Loss-Tie, 1986-99; Win-Loss-Tie-Overtime Loss, 2000-04; Win-Loss-Overtime Loss, 2006-present. (Because of a labor dispute, the 2005 season was canceled.)

Year	Team	Record	Points	Year	Team	Record	Points	Year	Team	Record	Points
1986	Edmonton	56-17-7	119	1997	Colorado	49-24-9	107	2009	San Jose	53-18-11	117
1987	Edmonton	50-24-6	106	1998	Dallas	49-22-11	109	2010	Washington	54-15-13	121
1988	Calgary	48-23-9	105	1999	Dallas	51-19-12	114	2011	Vancouver	54-19-9	117
1989	Calgary	54-17-9	117	2000	St. Louis	51-19-11-1	114	2012	Vancouver	51-22-9	111
1990	Boston	46-25-9	101	2001	Colorado	52-16-10-4	118	2013	Chicago	36-7-5	77
1991	Chicago	49-23-8	106	2002	Detroit	51-17-10-4	116	2014	Boston	54-19-9	117
1992	NY Rangers	50-25-5	105	2003	Ottawa	52-21-8-1	113	2015	NY Rangers	53-22-7	113
1993	Pittsburgh	56-21-7	119	2004	Detroit	48-21-11-2	109	2016	Washington	56-18-8	120
1994	NY Rangers	52-24-8	112	2006	Detroit	58-16-8	124	2017	Washington	55-19-8	118
1995	Detroit	33-11-4	70	2007	Buffalo	53-22-7	113	2018	Nashville	53-18-11	117
1996	Detroit	62-13-7	131	2008	Detroit	54-21-7	115				

Most NHL Goals in a Season

Player	Team	Season	Goals	Player	Team	Season	Goals
Wayne Gretzky	Edmonton	1981-82	92	Jari Kurri	Edmonton	1984-85	71
Wayne Gretzky	Edmonton	1983-84	87	Mario Lemieux	Pittsburgh	1987-88	70
Brett Hull	St. Louis	1990-91	86	Bernie Nicholls	Los Angeles	1988-89	70
Mario Lemieux	Pittsburgh	1988-89	85	Brett Hull	St. Louis	1991-92	70
Phil Esposito	Boston	1970-71	76	Mike Bossy	NY Islanders	1978-79	69
Alexander Mogilny	Buffalo	1992-93	76	Mario Lemieux	Pittsburgh	1992-93	69
Teemu Selanne	Winnipeg	1992-93	76	Mario Lemieux	Pittsburgh	1995-96	69
Wayne Gretzky	Edmonton	1984-85	73	Phil Esposito	Boston	1973-74	68
Brett Hull	St. Louis	1989-90	72	Mike Bossy	NY Islanders	1980-81	68
Wayne Gretzky	Edmonton	1982-83	71	Jari Kurri	Edmonton	1985-86	68

NHL Regular Season Career Scoring Leaders

(Through end of 2017-18 season. * = Active in 2017-18 season.)

Player	Goals	Assists	Points	Player	Goals	Assists	Points	Player	Goals	Assists	Points
Wayne Gretzky	894	1,963	2,857	Bryan Trottier	524	901	1,425	Mike Gartner	708	627	1,335
*Jaromir Jagr	766	1,155	1,921	Adam Oates	341	1,079	1,420	Pierre Turgeon	515	812	1,327
Mark Messier	694	1,193	1,887	Doug Gilmour	450	964	1,414	Gilbert Perreault	512	814	1,326
Gordie Howe	801	1,049	1,850	Dale Hawerchuk	518	891	1,409	*Jarome Iginla	625	675	1,300
Ron Francis	549	1,249	1,798	Jari Kurri	601	797	1,398	Alex Delvecchio	456	825	1,281
Marcel Dionne	731	1,040	1,771	Luc Robitaille	668	726	1,394	Al MacInnis	340	934	1,274
Steve Yzerman	692	1,063	1,755	Brett Hull	741	650	1,391	Jean Ratelle	491	776	1,267
Mario Lemieux	690	1,033	1,723	Mike Modano	561	813	1,374	Peter Stastny	450	789	1,239
Joe Sakic	625	1,016	1,641	Johnny Bucyk	556	813	1,369	Phil Housley	338	894	1,232
Phil Esposito	717	873	1,590	Brendan Shanahan	656	698	1,354	Norm Ullman	490	739	1,229
Ray Bourque	410	1,169	1,579	Guy Lafleur	560	793	1,353	Jean Beliveau	507	712	1,219
Mark Recchi	577	956	1,533	Mats Sundin	564	785	1,349	Larry Murphy	288	929	1,217
Paul Coffey	396	1,135	1,531	Dave Andreychuk	640	698	1,338	Jeremy Roenick	513	703	1,216
Stan Mikita	541	926	1,467	Denis Savard	473	865	1,338	Bobby Clarke	358	852	1,210
Teemu Selanne	684	773	1,457					Bernie Nicholls	475	734	1,209
*Joe Thornton	397	1,030	1,427								

Leading NHL Career Goaltenders

(Through end of 2017-18 season. * = Active in 2017-18 season.)

Ranked by Shutouts				Ranked by Wins			
Martin Brodeur	125	*Roberto Luongo	76	Martin Brodeur	691	*Marc-Andre Fleury	404
Terry Sawchuk	103	Lorne Chabot	71	Patrick Roy	551	Grant Fuhr	403
George Hainsworth	94	Harry Lumley	71	Ed Belfour	484	Chris Osgood	401
Glenn Hall	84	Roy Worters	67	*Roberto Luongo	471	Dominik Hasek	389
Jacques Plante	82	Patrick Roy	66	Curtis Joseph	454	Mike Vernon	385
Dominik Hasek	81	*Henrik Lundqvist	63	Terry Sawchuk	447	John Vanbiesbrouck	374
Tiny Thompson	81	Turk Broda	61	Jacques Plante	437	Andy Moog	372
Alec Connell	81	Evgeni Nabokov	59	*Henrik Lundqvist	431	*Ryan Miller	370
Ed Belfour	76	John Ross Roach	58	Tony Esposito	423	Tom Barrasso	369
Tony Esposito	76	Clint Benedict	57	Glenn Hall	407	Rogie Vachon	353

Hart Memorial Trophy (MVP), 1927-2018

Year	Player, team	Year	Player, team	Year	Player, team
1927	Herb Gardiner, Montréal Canadiens	1957	Gordie Howe, Detroit	1987	Wayne Gretzky, Edmonton
1928	Howie Morenz, Montréal Canadiens	1958	Gordie Howe, Detroit	1988	Mario Lemieux, Pittsburgh
1929	Roy Worters, NY Americans	1959	Andy Bathgate, NY Rangers	1989	Wayne Gretzky, Los Angeles
1930	Nels Stewart, Montréal Maroons	1960	Gordie Howe, Detroit	1990	Mark Messier, Edmonton
1931	Howie Morenz, Montréal Canadiens	1961	Bernie Geoffrion, Montréal	1991	Brett Hull, St. Louis
1932	Howie Morenz, Montréal Canadiens	1962	Jacques Plante, Montréal	1992	Mark Messier, NY Rangers
1933	Eddie Shore, Boston	1963	Gordie Howe, Detroit	1993	Mario Lemieux, Pittsburgh
1934	Aurel Joliat, Montréal Canadiens	1964	Jean Beliveau, Montréal	1994	Sergei Fedorov, Detroit
1935	Eddie Shore, Boston	1965	Bobby Hull, Chicago	1995	Eric Lindros, Philadelphia
1936	Eddie Shore, Boston	1966	Bobby Hull, Chicago	1996	Mario Lemieux, Pittsburgh
1937	Babe Siebert, Montréal Canadiens	1967	Stan Mikita, Chicago	1997	Dominik Hasek, Buffalo
1938	Eddie Shore, Boston	1968	Stan Mikita, Chicago	1998	Dominik Hasek, Buffalo
1939	Toe Blake, Montréal	1969	Phil Esposito, Boston	1999	Jaromir Jagr, Pittsburgh
1940	Ebbie Goodfellow, Detroit	1970	Bobby Orr, Boston	2000	Chris Pronger, St. Louis
1941	Bill Cowley, Boston	1971	Bobby Orr, Boston	2001	Joe Sakic, Colorado
1942	Tom Anderson, Brooklyn Americans	1972	Bobby Orr, Boston	2002	Jose Theodore, Montréal
1943	Bill Cowley, Boston	1973	Bobby Clarke, Philadelphia	2003	Peter Forsberg, Colorado
1944	Babe Pratt, Toronto	1974	Phil Esposito, Boston	2004	Martin St. Louis, Tampa Bay
1945	Elmer Lach, Montréal	1975	Bobby Clarke, Philadelphia	2006	Joe Thornton, San Jose
1946	Max Bentley, Chicago	1976	Bobby Clarke, Philadelphia	2007	Sidney Crosby, Pittsburgh
1947	Maurice Richard, Montréal	1977	Guy Lafleur, Montréal	2008	Alexander Ovechkin, Washington
1948	Buddy O'Connor, NY Rangers	1978	Guy Lafleur, Montréal	2009	Alexander Ovechkin, Washington
1949	Sid Abel, Detroit	1979	Bryan Trottier, NY Islanders	2010	Henrik Sedin, Vancouver
1950	Chuck Rayner, NY Rangers	1980	Wayne Gretzky, Edmonton	2011	Corey Perry, Anaheim
1951	Milt Schmidt, Boston	1981	Wayne Gretzky, Edmonton	2012	Evgeni Malkin, Pittsburgh
1952	Gordie Howe, Detroit	1982	Wayne Gretzky, Edmonton	2013	Alexander Ovechkin, Washington
1953	Gordie Howe, Detroit	1983	Wayne Gretzky, Edmonton	2014	Sidney Crosby, Pittsburgh
1954	Al Rollins, Chicago	1984	Wayne Gretzky, Edmonton	2015	Carey Price, Montréal
1955	Ted Kennedy, Toronto	1985	Wayne Gretzky, Edmonton	2016	Patrick Kane, Chicago
1956	Jean Beliveau, Montréal	1986	Wayne Gretzky, Edmonton	2017	Connor McDavid, Edmonton
				2018	Taylor Hall, New Jersey

Conn Smythe Trophy (MVP in Playoffs), 1965-2018

Year	Player, team	Year	Player, team	Year	Player, team
1965	Jean Beliveau, Montréal	1983	Billy Smith, NY Islanders	2001	Patrick Roy, Colorado
1966	Roger Crozier, Detroit	1984	Mark Messier, Edmonton	2002	Nicklas Lidstrom, Detroit
1967	Dave Keon, Toronto	1985	Wayne Gretzky, Edmonton	2003	Jean-Sebastien Giguere, Anaheim
1968	Glenn Hall, St. Louis	1986	Patrick Roy, Montréal	2004	Brad Richards, Tampa Bay
1969	Serge Savard, Montréal	1987	Ron Hextall, Philadelphia	2006	Cam Ward, Carolina
1970	Bobby Orr, Boston	1988	Wayne Gretzky, Edmonton	2007	Scott Niedermayer, Anaheim
1971	Ken Dryden, Montréal	1989	Al MacInnis, Calgary	2008	Henrik Zetterberg, Detroit
1972	Bobby Orr, Boston	1990	Bill Ranford, Edmonton	2009	Evgeni Malkin, Pittsburgh
1973	Yvan Cournoyer, Montréal	1991	Mario Lemieux, Pittsburgh	2010	Jonathan Toews, Chicago
1974	Bernie Parent, Philadelphia	1992	Mario Lemieux, Pittsburgh	2011	Tim Thomas, Boston
1975	Bernie Parent, Philadelphia	1993	Patrick Roy, Montréal	2012	Jonathan Quick, Los Angeles
1976	Reggie Leach, Philadelphia	1994	Brian Leetch, NY Rangers	2013	Patrick Kane, Chicago
1977	Guy Lafleur, Montréal	1995	Claude Lemieux, New Jersey	2014	Justin Williams, Los Angeles
1978	Larry Robinson, Montréal	1996	Joe Sakic, Colorado	2015	Duncan Keith, Chicago
1979	Bob Gainey, Montréal	1997	Mike Vernon, Detroit	2016	Sidney Crosby, Pittsburgh
1980	Bryan Trottier, NY Islanders	1998	Steve Yzerman, Detroit	2017	Sidney Crosby, Pittsburgh
1981	Butch Goring, NY Islanders	1999	Joe Nieuwendyk, Dallas	2018	Alex Ovechkin, Washington
1982	Mike Bossy, NY Islanders	2000	Scott Stevens, New Jersey		

Calder Memorial Trophy (Best Rookie), 1933-2018

Year	Player, team	Year	Player, team	Year	Player, team
1933	Carl Voss, Detroit	1961	Dave Keon, Toronto	1989	Brian Leetch, NY Rangers
1934	Russ Blinco, Montréal Maroons	1962	Bobby Rousseau, Montréal	1990	Sergei Makarov, Calgary
1935	Dave Schriner, NY Americans	1963	Kent Douglas, Toronto	1991	Ed Belfour, Chicago
1936	Mike Karakas, Chicago	1964	Jacques Laperrière, Montréal	1992	Pavel Bure, Vancouver
1937	Syl Apps, Toronto	1965	Roger Crozier, Detroit	1993	Teemu Selanne, Winnipeg
1938	Cully Dahlstrom, Chicago	1966	Brit Selby, Toronto	1994	Martin Brodeur, New Jersey
1939	Frank Brimsek, Boston	1967	Bobby Orr, Boston	1995	Peter Forsberg, Quebec
1940	Kilby MacDonald, NY Rangers	1968	Derek Sanderson, Boston	1996	Daniel Alfredsson, Ottawa
1941	John Quilty, Montréal	1969	Danny Grant, Minnesota	1997	Bryan Berard, NY Islanders
1942	Grant Warwick, NY Rangers	1970	Tony Esposito, Chicago	1998	Sergei Samsonov, Boston
1943	Gaye Stewart, Toronto	1971	Gilbert Perreault, Buffalo	1999	Chris Drury, Colorado
1944	Gus Bodnar, Toronto	1972	Ken Dryden, Montréal	2000	Scott Gomez, New Jersey
1945	Frank McCool, Toronto	1973	Steve Vickers, NY Rangers	2001	Evgeni Nabokov, San Jose
1946	Edgar Laprade, NY Rangers	1974	Denis Potvin, NY Islanders	2002	Dany Heatley, Atlanta
1947	Howie Meeker, Toronto	1975	Eric Vail, Atlanta	2003	Barret Jackman, St. Louis
1948	Jim McFadden, Detroit	1976	Bryan Trottier, NY Islanders	2004	Andrew Raycroft, Boston
1949	Pentti Lund, NY Rangers	1977	Willi Plett, Atlanta	2006	Alexander Ovechkin, Washington
1950	Jack Gelineau, Boston	1978	Mike Bossy, NY Islanders	2007	Evgeni Malkin, Pittsburgh
1951	Terry Sawchuk, Detroit	1979	Bobby Smith, Minnesota	2008	Patrick Kane, Chicago
1952	Bernie Geoffrion, Montréal	1980	Ray Bourque, Boston	2009	Steve Mason, Columbus
1953	Gump Worsley, NY Rangers	1981	Peter Stastny, Quebec	2010	Tyler Myers, Buffalo
1954	Camille Henry, NY Rangers	1982	Dale Hawerchuk, Winnipeg	2011	Jeff Skinner, Carolina
1955	Ed Litzenberger, Chicago	1983	Steve Larmer, Chicago	2012	Gabriel Landeskog, Colorado
1956	Glenn Hall, Detroit	1984	Tom Barrasso, Buffalo	2013	Jonathan Huberdeau, Florida
1957	Larry Regan, Boston	1985	Mario Lemieux, Pittsburgh	2014	Nathan MacKinnon, Colorado
1958	Frank Mahovlich, Toronto	1986	Gary Suter, Calgary	2015	Aaron Ekblad, Florida
1959	Ralph Backstrom, Montréal	1987	Luc Robitaille, Los Angeles	2016	Artemi Panarin, Chicago
1960	Bill Hay, Chicago	1988	Joe Nieuwendyk, Calgary	2017	Auston Matthews, Toronto
				2018	Mathew Barzal, NY Islanders

Lady Byng Memorial Trophy (Most Gentlemanly Player), 1925-2018

Year	Player, team	Year	Player, team	Year	Player, team
1925	Frank Nighbor, Ottawa	1956	Dutch Reibel, Detroit	1987	Joe Mullen, Calgary
1926	Frank Nighbor, Ottawa	1957	Andy Hebenton, NY Rangers	1988	Mats Naslund, Montréal
1927	Billy Burch, NY Americans	1958	Camille Henry, NY Rangers	1989	Joe Mullen, Calgary
1928	Frank Boucher, NY Rangers	1959	Alex Delvecchio, Detroit	1990	Brett Hull, St. Louis
1929	Frank Boucher, NY Rangers	1960	Don McKenney, Boston	1991	Wayne Gretzky, Los Angeles
1930	Frank Boucher, NY Rangers	1961	Red Kelly, Toronto	1992	Wayne Gretzky, Los Angeles
1931	Frank Boucher, NY Rangers	1962	Dave Keon, Toronto	1993	Pierre Turgeon, NY Islanders
1932	Joe Primeau, Toronto	1963	Dave Keon, Toronto	1994	Wayne Gretzky, Los Angeles
1933	Frank Boucher, NY Rangers	1964	Ken Wharram, Chicago	1995	Ron Francis, Pittsburgh
1934	Frank Boucher, NY Rangers	1965	Bobby Hull, Chicago	1996	Paul Kariya, Anaheim
1935	Frank Boucher, NY Rangers	1966	Alex Delvecchio, Detroit	1997	Paul Kariya, Anaheim
1936	Doc Romnes, Chicago	1967	Stan Mikita, Chicago	1998	Ron Francis, Pittsburgh
1937	Marty Barry, Detroit	1968	Stan Mikita, Chicago	1999	Wayne Gretzky, NY Rangers
1938	Gordie Drillon, Toronto	1969	Alex Delvecchio, Detroit	2000	Pavol Demitra, St. Louis
1939	Clint Smith, NY Rangers	1970	Phil Goyette, St. Louis	2001	Joe Sakic, Colorado
1940	Bobby Bauer, Boston	1971	John Bucyk, Boston	2002	Ron Francis, Carolina
1941	Bobby Bauer, Boston	1972	Jean Ratelle, NY Rangers	2003	Alexander Mogilny, Toronto
1942	Syl Apps, Toronto	1973	Gil Perreault, Buffalo	2004	Brad Richards, Tampa Bay
1943	Max Bentley, Chicago	1974	John Bucyk, Boston	2006	Pavel Datsyuk, Detroit
1944	Clint Smith, Chicago	1975	Marcel Dionne, Detroit	2007	Pavel Datsyuk, Detroit
1945	Bill Mosienko, Chicago	1976	Jean Ratelle, NYR-Boston	2008	Pavel Datsyuk, Detroit
1946	Toe Blake, Montréal	1977	Marcel Dionne, Los Angeles	2009	Pavel Datsyuk, Detroit
1947	Bobby Bauer, Boston	1978	Butch Goring, Los Angeles	2010	Martin St. Louis, Tampa Bay
1948	Buddy O'Connor, NY Rangers	1979	Bob MacMillan, Atlanta	2011	Martin St. Louis, Tampa Bay
1949	Bill Quackenbush, Detroit	1980	Wayne Gretzky, Edmonton	2012	Brian Campbell, Florida
1950	Edgar Laprade, NY Rangers	1981	Rick Kehoe, Pittsburgh	2013	Martin St. Louis, Tampa Bay
1951	Red Kelly, Detroit	1982	Rick Middleton, Boston	2014	Ryan O'Reilly, Colorado
1952	Sid Smith, Toronto	1983	Mike Bossy, NY Islanders	2015	Jiri Hudler, Calgary
1953	Red Kelly, Detroit	1984	Mike Bossy, NY Islanders	2016	Anze Kopitar, Los Angeles
1954	Red Kelly, Detroit	1985	Jari Kurri, Edmonton	2017	Johnny Gaudreau, Calgary
1955	Sid Smith, Toronto	1986	Mike Bossy, NY Islanders	2018	William Karlsson, Vegas

James Norris Memorial Trophy (Best Defenseman), 1954-2018

Year	Player, team	Year	Player, team	Year	Player, team
1954	Red Kelly, Detroit	1975	Bobby Orr, Boston	1996	Chris Chelios, Chicago
1955	Doug Harvey, Montréal	1976	Denis Potvin, NY Islanders	1997	Brian Leetch, NY Rangers
1956	Doug Harvey, Montréal	1977	Larry Robinson, Montréal	1998	Rob Blake, Los Angeles
1957	Doug Harvey, Montréal	1978	Denis Potvin, NY Islanders	1999	Al MacInnis, St. Louis
1958	Doug Harvey, Montréal	1979	Denis Potvin, NY Islanders	2000	Chris Pronger, St. Louis
1959	Tom Johnson, Montréal	1980	Larry Robinson, Montréal	2001	Nicklas Lidstrom, Detroit
1960	Doug Harvey, Montréal	1981	Randy Carlyle, Pittsburgh	2002	Nicklas Lidstrom, Detroit
1961	Doug Harvey, Montréal	1982	Doug Wilson, Chicago	2003	Nicklas Lidstrom, Detroit
1962	Doug Harvey, NY Rangers	1983	Rod Langway, Washington	2004	Scott Niedermayer, New Jersey
1963	Pierre Pilote, Chicago	1984	Rod Langway, Washington	2006	Nicklas Lidstrom, Detroit
1964	Pierre Pilote, Chicago	1985	Paul Coffey, Edmonton	2007	Nicklas Lidstrom, Detroit
1965	Pierre Pilote, Chicago	1986	Paul Coffey, Edmonton	2008	Nicklas Lidstrom, Detroit
1966	Jacques Laperrière, Montréal	1987	Ray Bourque, Boston	2009	Zdeno Chara, Boston
1967	Harry Howell, NY Rangers	1988	Ray Bourque, Boston	2010	Duncan Keith, Chicago
1968	Bobby Orr, Boston	1989	Chris Chelios, Montréal	2011	Nicklas Lidstrom, Detroit
1969	Bobby Orr, Boston	1990	Ray Bourque, Boston	2012	Erik Karlsson, Ottawa
1970	Bobby Orr, Boston	1991	Ray Bourque, Boston	2013	P. K. Subban, Montréal
1971	Bobby Orr, Boston	1992	Brian Leetch, NY Rangers	2014	Duncan Keith, Chicago
1972	Bobby Orr, Boston	1993	Chris Chelios, Chicago	2015	Erik Karlsson, Ottawa
1973	Bobby Orr, Boston	1994	Ray Bourque, Boston	2016	Drew Doughty, Los Angeles
1974	Bobby Orr, Boston	1995	Paul Coffey, Detroit	2017	Brent Burns, San Jose
				2018	Victor Hedman, Tampa Bay

Art Ross Trophy (Highest Scorer), 1947-2018

Year	Player, team	Year	Player, team	Year	Player, team
1947	Max Bentley, Chicago	1971	Phil Esposito, Boston	1994	Wayne Gretzky, Los Angeles
1948	Elmer Lach, Montréal	1972	Phil Esposito, Boston	1995	Jaromir Jagr, Pittsburgh
1949	Roy Conacher, Chicago	1973	Phil Esposito, Boston	1996	Mario Lemieux, Pittsburgh
1950	Ted Lindsay, Detroit	1974	Phil Esposito, Boston	1997	Mario Lemieux, Pittsburgh
1951	Gordie Howe, Detroit	1975	Bobby Orr, Boston	1998	Jaromir Jagr, Pittsburgh
1952	Gordie Howe, Detroit	1976	Guy Lafleur, Montréal	1999	Jaromir Jagr, Pittsburgh
1953	Gordie Howe, Detroit	1977	Guy Lafleur, Montréal	2000	Jaromir Jagr, Pittsburgh
1954	Gordie Howe, Detroit	1978	Guy Lafleur, Montréal	2001	Jaromir Jagr, Pittsburgh
1955	Bernie Geoffrion, Montréal	1979	Bryan Trottier, NY Islanders	2002	Jarome Iginla, Calgary
1956	Jean Beliveau, Montréal	1980	Marcel Dionne, Los Angeles	2003	Peter Forsberg, Colorado
1957	Gordie Howe, Detroit	1981	Wayne Gretzky, Edmonton	2004	Martin St. Louis, Tampa Bay
1958	Dickie Moore, Montréal	1982	Wayne Gretzky, Edmonton	2006	Joe Thornton, Boston/San Jose
1959	Dickie Moore, Montréal	1983	Wayne Gretzky, Edmonton	2007	Sidney Crosby, Pittsburgh
1960	Bobby Hull, Chicago	1984	Wayne Gretzky, Edmonton	2008	Alexander Ovechkin, Washington
1961	Bernie Geoffrion, Montréal	1985	Wayne Gretzky, Edmonton	2009	Evgeni Malkin, Pittsburgh
1962	Bobby Hull, Chicago	1986	Wayne Gretzky, Edmonton	2010	Henrik Sedin, Vancouver
1963	Gordie Howe, Detroit	1987	Wayne Gretzky, Edmonton	2011	Daniel Sedin, Vancouver
1964	Stan Mikita, Chicago	1988	Mario Lemieux, Pittsburgh	2012	Evgeni Malkin, Pittsburgh
1965	Stan Mikita, Chicago	1989	Mario Lemieux, Pittsburgh	2013	Martin St. Louis, Tampa Bay
1966	Bobby Hull, Chicago	1990	Wayne Gretzky, Los Angeles	2014	Sidney Crosby, Pittsburgh
1967	Stan Mikita, Chicago	1991	Wayne Gretzky, Los Angeles	2015	Jamie Benn, Dallas
1968	Stan Mikita, Chicago	1992	Mario Lemieux, Pittsburgh	2016	Patrick Kane, Chicago
1969	Phil Esposito, Boston	1993	Mario Lemieux, Pittsburgh	2017	Connor McDavid, Edmonton
1970	Bobby Orr, Boston			2018	Connor McDavid, Edmonton

Vezina Trophy (Best Goaltender), 1927-2018

Before 1982, awarded to the goalie or goalies who played a minimum of 25 games for the team that allowed the fewest goals; since 1982, awarded to the most outstanding goalie, as determined by a vote of NHL general managers.

Year	Player, team	Year	Player, team	Year	Player, team
1927	George Hainsworth, Montréal Canadiens	1929	George Hainsworth, Montréal Canadiens	1932	Charlie Gardiner, Chicago
		1930	Tiny Thompson, Boston	1933	Tiny Thompson, Boston
1928	George Hainsworth, Montréal Canadiens	1931	Roy Worters, NY Americans	1934	Charlie Gardiner, Chicago
				1935	Lorne Chabot, Chicago

Year	Player, team	Year	Player, team	Year	Player, team
1936	Tiny Thompson, Boston	1964	Charlie Hodge, Montréal	1989	Patrick Roy, Montréal
1937	Normie Smith, Detroit	1965	Sawchuk, Bower; Toronto	1990	Patrick Roy, Montréal
1938	Tiny Thompson, Boston	1966	Lorne Worsley, Hodge; Montréal	1991	Ed Belfour, Chicago
1939	Frank Brimsek, Boston	1967	Hall, Denis DeJordy; Chicago	1992	Patrick Roy, Montréal
1940	Dave Kerr, NY Rangers	1968	Worsley, Rogatien Vachon; Montréal	1993	Ed Belfour, Chicago
1941	Turk Broda, Toronto	1969	Hall, Plante; St. Louis	1994	Dominik Hasek, Buffalo
1942	Frank Brimsek, Boston	1970	Tony Esposito, Chicago	1995	Dominik Hasek, Buffalo
1943	Johnny Mowers, Detroit	1971	Ed Giacomin, Gilles Villemure;	1996	Jim Carey, Washington
1944	Bill Durnan, Montréal		NY Rangers	1997	Dominik Hasek, Buffalo
1945	Bill Durnan, Montréal	1972	Esposito, Gary Smith; Chicago	1998	Dominik Hasek, Buffalo
1946	Bill Durnan, Montréal	1973	Ken Dryden, Montréal	1999	Dominik Hasek, Buffalo
1947	Bill Durnan, Montréal	1974	Bernie Parent, Philadelphia;	2000	Olaf Kolzig, Washington
1948	Turk Broda, Toronto		Tony Esposito, Chicago	2001	Dominik Hasek, Buffalo
1949	Bill Durnan, Montréal	1975	Bernie Parent, Philadelphia	2002	Jose Theodore, Montréal
1950	Bill Durnan, Montréal	1976	Ken Dryden, Montréal	2003	Martin Brodeur, New Jersey
1951	Al Rollins, Toronto	1977	Dryden, Michel Larocque; Montréal	2004	Martin Brodeur, New Jersey
1952	Terry Sawchuk, Detroit	1978	Dryden, Larocque; Montréal	2006	Miikka Kiprusoff, Calgary
1953	Terry Sawchuk, Detroit	1979	Dryden, Larocque; Montréal	2007	Martin Brodeur, New Jersey
1954	Harry Lumley, Toronto	1980	Bob Sauve, Don Edwards; Buffalo	2008	Martin Brodeur, New Jersey
1955	Terry Sawchuk, Detroit	1981	Richard Sevigny, Michel Larocque,	2009	Tim Thomas, Boston
1956	Jacques Plante, Montréal		Denis Herron; Montréal	2010	Ryan Miller, Buffalo
1957	Jacques Plante, Montréal	1982	Bill Smith, NY Islanders	2011	Tim Thomas, Boston
1958	Jacques Plante, Montréal	1983	Pete Peeters, Boston	2012	Henrik Lundqvist, NY Rangers
1959	Jacques Plante, Montréal	1984	Tom Barrasso, Buffalo	2013	Sergei Bobrovsky, Columbus
1960	Jacques Plante, Montréal	1985	Pelle Lindbergh, Philadelphia	2014	Tuukka Rask, Boston
1961	Johnny Bower, Toronto	1986	John Vanbiesbrouck, NY Rangers	2015	Carey Price, Montréal
1962	Jacques Plante, Montréal	1987	Ron Hextall, Philadelphia	2016	Braden Holtby, Washington
1963	Glenn Hall, Chicago	1988	Grant Fuhr, Edmonton	2017	Sergei Bobrovsky, Columbus
				2018	Pekka Rinne, Nashville

National Hockey League Franchise Origins

Team: founding year, league (NHL, World Hockey Association [WHA], or National Hockey Association of Canada [NHA]). Original location; subsequent history. Neutral sites and arena sites in the same metropolitan area not shown. * = Joined NHL in 1979 from defunct WHA.

Anaheim Ducks: 1993, NHL, as Mighty Ducks of Anaheim. Anaheim, CA, 1993-present. (Ducks, 2007-present.)

*Arizona Coyotes: 1972, WHA, as Winnipeg Jets. Winnipeg, MB, Canada, 1979-96; Phoenix Coyotes, 1996-2014; Arizona Coyotes, 2014-present.

Boston Bruins: 1924, NHL. Boston, 1924-present.

Buffalo Sabres: 1970, NHL. Buffalo, NY, 1970-present.

Calgary Flames: 1972, NHL, as Atlanta Flames. Atlanta, GA, 1972-80; Calgary, AB, Canada, 1980-present.

*Carolina Hurricanes: 1972, WHA, as Hartford Whalers. Hartford, CT, 1979-97; Carolina Hurricanes, Greensboro, NC, 1997-99; Raleigh, NC, 1999-present.

Chicago Blackhawks: 1926, NHL, as Chicago Black Hawks. Chicago, 1926-present. (Blackhawks, 1986-present.)

*Colorado Avalanche: 1972, WHA, as Quebec Nordiques. Quebec City, QC, Canada, 1979-95; Colorado Avalanche, Denver, 1995-present.

Columbus Blue Jackets: 2000, NHL. Columbus, OH, 2000-present.

Dallas Stars: 1967, NHL, as Minnesota North Stars. Bloomington, MN, 1967-93; Dallas Stars, Dallas, 1993-present.

Detroit Red Wings: 1926, NHL, as Detroit Cougars, 1926-30. Detroit Falcons, 1930-32; Detroit Red Wings, 1932-present.

*Edmonton Oilers: 1972, WHA. Edmonton, AB, Canada, 1979-present.

Florida Panthers: 1993, NHL. Miami, FL, 1993-98; Sunrise, FL, 1998-present.

Los Angeles Kings: 1967, NHL. Los Angeles, 1967-present.

Minnesota Wild: 2000, NHL. St. Paul, 2000-present.

Montréal Canadiens: 1909, NHA; joined NHL, 1917. Montréal, QC, Canada, 1909-present.

Nashville Predators: 1998, NHL. Nashville, TN, 1998-present.

New Jersey Devils: 1974, NHL, as Kansas City Scouts. Kansas City, MO, 1974-76; Colorado Rockies, Denver, CO, 1976-82; New Jersey Devils, East Rutherford, NJ, 1982-2007; Newark, NJ, 2007-present.

New York Islanders: 1972, NHL. Uniondale, NY, 1972-2015; Brooklyn, NY, 2015-present.

New York Rangers: 1926, NHL. New York City, 1926-present.

Ottawa Senators: 1992, NHL. Ottawa, ON, Canada, 1992-present.

Philadelphia Flyers: 1967, NHL. Philadelphia, 1967-present.

Pittsburgh Penguins: 1967, NHL. Pittsburgh, 1967-present.

St. Louis Blues: 1967, NHL. St. Louis, MO, 1967-present.

San Jose Sharks: 1991, NHL. Daly City, CA, 1991-93; San Jose, CA, 1993-present.

Tampa Bay Lightning: 1992, NHL. Tampa, FL, 1992-93; St. Petersburg, FL, 1993-96; Tampa, FL, 1996-present.

Toronto Maple Leafs: 1917, NHL, as Toronto (ON, Canada) Arenas, 1917-19. Toronto St. Patricks, 1919-26; Toronto Maple Leafs, 1926-present.

Vancouver Canucks: 1970, NHL. Vancouver, BC, Canada, 1970-present.

Vegas Golden Knights: 2017, NHL. Las Vegas, NV, 2017-present.

Washington Capitals: 1974, NHL. Landover, MD, 1974-97; Washington, DC, 1997-present.

Winnipeg Jets: 1999, NHL, as Atlanta Thrashers. Atlanta, GA, 1999-2011; Winnipeg, AB, Canada, 2011-present.

NHL Home Ice

Team	Name (year play began)	Capacity[1]	Team	Name (year play began)	Capacity[1]
Anaheim	Honda Center[2] (1993)	17,174	Nashville	Bridgestone Arena[10] (1997)	17,113
Arizona	Gila River Arena[3] (2003)	17,125	New Jersey	Prudential Center (2007)	16,514
Boston	TD Garden[4] (1995)	17,565	NY Islanders	Barclays Center (2015)	15,795
Buffalo	KeyBank Center[5] (1996)	19,070	NY Rangers	Madison Square Garden (IV) (1968)	18,006
Calgary	Scotiabank Saddledome[6] (1983)	19,289	Ottawa	Canadian Tire Centre[11] (1996)	17,373
Carolina	PNC Arena[7] (1999)	18,680	Philadelphia	Wells Fargo Center[12] (1996)	19,605
Chicago	United Center (1994)	19,717	Pittsburgh	PPG Paints Arena[13] (2010)	18,387
Colorado	Pepsi Center (1999)	17,809	St. Louis	Scottrade Center[14] (1994)	19,150
Columbus	Nationwide Arena (2000)	18,144	San Jose	SAP Center at San Jose[15] (1993)	17,562
Dallas	American Airlines Center (2001)	18,532	Tampa Bay	Amalie Arena[16] (1996)	19,092
Detroit	Little Caesars Arena (2017)	20,000*	Toronto	Air Canada Centre (1999)	18,819
Edmonton	Rogers Place (2016)	18,550	Vancouver	Rogers Arena[17] (1995)	18,865
Florida	BB&T Center[8] (1998)	19,250	Vegas	T-Mobile Arena (2017)	17,500*
Los Angeles	Staples Center (1999)	18,230	Washington	Capital One Arena[18] (1997)	18,506
Minnesota	Xcel Energy Center (2000)	17,954	Winnipeg	Bell MTS Place[19] (2004)	15,294
Montréal	Le Centre Bell[9] (1996)	21,288			

* = Estimate for 2017-18 season. (1) At the end of the 2017-18 season unless otherwise noted. (2) The Arrowhead Pond of Anaheim, 1993-2006. (3) Glendale Arena, 2003-06; Jobing.com Arena, 2006-14. (4) FleetCenter, 1995-2005; TD Banknorth Garden, 2005-09. (5) Marine Midland Arena, 1996-99; HSBC Arena, 1999-2011; First Niagara Center, 2011-16. (6) Olympic Saddledome, 1983-96; Canadian Airlines Saddledome, 1996-2000; Pengrowth Saddledome, 2000-10. (7) Raleigh Entertainment and Sports Arena, 1999-2002; RBC Center, 2002-11. (8) National Car Rental Center, 1998-2002; Office Depot Center, 2002-05; BankAtlantic Center, 2005-12. (9) Le Centre Molson, 1996-2002. (10) Nashville Arena, 1997-99; Gaylord Entertainment Center, 1999-2007; Sommet Center, 2007-10. (11) Corel Centre, 1996-2006; Scotiabank Place, 2006-13. (12) CoreStates Center, 1996-98; First Union Center, 1998-2003; Wachovia Center, 2003-10. (13) CONSOL Energy Center, 2010-16. (14) Kiel Center, 1994-2000; Savvis Center, 2000-06. (15) San Jose Arena, 1993-2001; Compaq Center, 2001-02; HP Pavilion at San Jose, 2002-13. (16) Ice Palace, 1996-2002; St. Pete Times Forum, 2002-12; Tampa Bay Times Forum, 2012-14. (17) General Motors Place, 1995-2010. (18) MCI Center, 1997-2006; Verizon Center, 2006-17. (19) MTS Centre, 2004-17.

SOCCER

France Wins 2018 FIFA Men's World Cup

France won its second FIFA World Cup men's soccer title with a 4-2 victory over Croatia, July 15, 2018, at Luzhniki Stadium in Moscow, Russia. Les Bleus scored first on a free kick by Antoine Griezmann, ruled an own goal by Croatia's Mario Mandzukic after he deflected the ball into Croatia's net. The new Video Assistant Referee (VAR) technology was used for the first time at the 2018 Men's World Cup tournament. When a video review confirmed a handball by Croatia's Ivan Perisic, France was awarded a penalty kick, which Griezmann converted to give Les Bleus a 2-1 lead. France added second-half goals by Paul Pogba and 19-year-old Kylian Mbappé—who became the first teenager to score a goal in a World Cup final match since 17-year-old Pelé in 1958—for a final score of 4-2, making it the highest scoring men's World Cup final since 1966.

Les Bleus goaltender and team captain Hugo Lloris recorded a pair of clean sheets en route to the finals, eliminating Uruguay in the quarterfinals, 2-0, July 6. Samuel Umtiti scored the only goal of the match in France's 1-0 semifinal win over Belgium, July 10. The Belgian squad won the third-place match, 2-0, against England, July 14 at St. Petersburg Stadium.

Croatia reached its first-ever World Cup final when Mandzukic scored in the 109th minute to defeat England, 2-1, in extra time in the semifinals, July 11. After playing to a 2-2 tie through extra time, Croatia won on penalty kicks, 4-3, defeating host Russia in the quarterfinals on July 7 at Fisht Stadium in Sochi.

England reached the semifinals for the first time since 1990. The Three Lions shut out Sweden, 2-0, in the quarterfinals July 7 at Samara Arena in Samara before their semifinal loss to Croatia. Defending champion Germany managed just one group match victory, 2-1, over Sweden June 23 at Fisht Stadium and failed to move on.

England's Harry Kane topped all scorers in the tournament with six goals and won the Golden Boot award. Veteran Croatia midfielder Luka Modric was voted the best player of the competition, taking home the Golden Ball award.

Men's World Cup Results, 2018

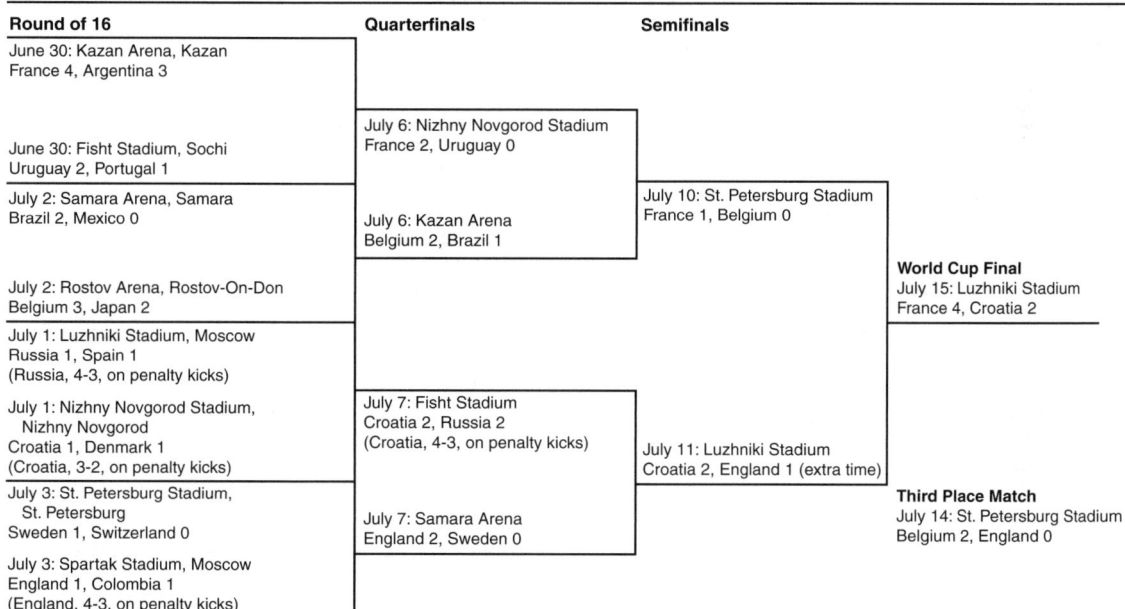

Round of 16

June 30: Kazan Arena, Kazan
France 4, Argentina 3

June 30: Fisht Stadium, Sochi
Uruguay 2, Portugal 1

July 2: Samara Arena, Samara
Brazil 2, Mexico 0

July 2: Rostov Arena, Rostov-On-Don
Belgium 3, Japan 2

July 1: Luzhniki Stadium, Moscow
Russia 1, Spain 1
(Russia, 4-3, on penalty kicks)

July 1: Nizhny Novgorod Stadium,
Nizhny Novgorod
Croatia 1, Denmark 1
(Croatia, 3-2, on penalty kicks)

July 3: St. Petersburg Stadium,
St. Petersburg
Sweden 1, Switzerland 0

July 3: Spartak Stadium, Moscow
England 1, Colombia 1
(England, 4-3, on penalty kicks)

Quarterfinals

July 6: Nizhny Novgorod Stadium
France 2, Uruguay 0

July 6: Kazan Arena
Belgium 2, Brazil 1

July 7: Fisht Stadium
Croatia 2, Russia 2
(Croatia, 4-3, on penalty kicks)

July 7: Samara Arena
England 2, Sweden 0

Semifinals

July 10: St. Petersburg Stadium
France 1, Belgium 0

July 11: Luzhniki Stadium
Croatia 2, England 1 (extra time)

World Cup Final
July 15: Luzhniki Stadium
France 4, Croatia 2

Third Place Match
July 14: St. Petersburg Stadium
Belgium 2, England 0

Men's World Cup Group Standings, 2018

(* = advanced to round of 16)

	MP	W	D	L	GF	GA	+/−	PTS
GROUP A								
Uruguay*	3	3	0	0	5	0	5	9
Russia*	3	2	0	1	8	4	4	6
Saudi Arabia	3	1	0	2	2	7	−5	3
Egypt	3	0	0	3	2	6	−4	0
GROUP B								
Spain*	3	1	2	0	6	5	1	5
Portugal*	3	1	2	0	5	4	1	5
Iran	3	1	1	1	2	2	0	4
Morocco	3	0	1	2	2	4	−2	1
GROUP C								
France*	3	2	1	0	3	1	2	7
Denmark*	3	1	2	0	2	1	1	5
Peru	3	1	0	2	2	2	0	3
Australia	3	0	1	2	2	5	−3	1
GROUP D								
Croatia*	3	3	0	0	7	1	6	9
Argentina*	3	1	1	1	3	5	−2	4
Nigeria	3	1	0	2	3	4	−1	3
Iceland	3	0	1	2	2	5	−3	1

	MP	W	D	L	GF	GA	+/−	PTS
GROUP E								
Brazil*	3	2	1	0	5	1	4	7
Switzerland*	3	1	2	0	5	4	1	5
Serbia	3	1	0	2	2	4	−2	3
Costa Rica	3	0	1	2	2	5	−3	1
GROUP F								
Sweden*	3	2	0	1	5	2	3	6
Mexico*	3	2	0	1	3	4	−1	6
South Korea	3	1	0	2	3	3	0	3
Germany	3	1	0	2	2	4	−2	3
GROUP G								
Belgium*	3	3	0	0	9	2	7	9
England*	3	2	0	1	8	3	5	6
Tunisia	3	1	0	2	5	8	−3	3
Panama	3	0	0	3	2	11	−9	0
GROUP H								
Colombia*	3	2	0	1	5	2	3	6
Japan	3	1	1	1	4	4	0	4
Senegal	3	1	1	1	4	4	0	4
Poland	3	1	0	2	2	5	−3	3

Men's World Cup Results, 1930-2018

Year	Winner	Final opponent	Score	Site	Year	Winner	Final opponent	Score	Site
1930	Uruguay	Argentina	4-2	Uruguay	1982	Italy	W. Germany	3-1	Spain
1934	Italy	Czechoslovakia	2-1#	Italy	1986	Argentina	W. Germany	3-2	Mexico
1938	Italy	Hungary	4-2	France	1990	W. Germany	Argentina	1-0	Italy
1950	Uruguay	Brazil	2-1	Brazil	1994	Brazil	Italy	0-0 (3-2)*	U.S.
1954	W. Germany	Hungary	3-2	Switzerland	1998	France	Brazil	3-0	France
1958	Brazil	Sweden	5-2	Sweden	2002	Brazil	Germany	2-0	Japan/S. Korea
1962	Brazil	Czechoslovakia	3-1	Chile	2006	Italy	France	1-1 (5-3)*	Germany
1966	England	W. Germany	4-2#	England	2010	Spain	Netherlands	1-0#	South Africa
1970	Brazil	Italy	4-1	Mexico	2014	Germany	Argentina	1-0#	Brazil
1974	W. Germany	Netherlands	2-1	W. Germany	2018	France	Croatia	4-2	Russia
1978	Argentina	Netherlands	3-1#	Argentina					

* = Match decided in penalty kicks (shootout score in parentheses). # = Match decided in extra time.

UEFA Champions League Results, 1956-2018

Year	Winner	Final opponent	Score	Year	Winner	Final opponent	Score
1956	Real Madrid	Reims	4-3	1987	Porto	Bayern Munich	2-1
1957	Real Madrid	Fiorentina	2-0	1988	PSV	Benfica	0-0 (6-5)*
1958	Real Madrid	AC Milan	3-2#	1989	AC Milan	Steaua	4-0
1959	Real Madrid	Reims	2-0	1990	AC Milan	Benfica	1-0
1960	Real Madrid	Eintracht Frankfurt	7-3	1991	Crvena Zvezda	Marseille	0-0 (5-3)*
1961	Benfica	FC Barcelona	3-2	1992	FC Barcelona	Sampdoria	1-0#
1962	Benfica	Real Madrid	5-3	1993	Marseille	AC Milan	1-0
1963	AC Milan	Benfica	2-1	1994	AC Milan	FC Barcelona	4-0
1964	Inter Milan	Real Madrid	3-1	1995	Ajax	AC Milan	1-0
1965	Inter Milan	Benfica	1-0	1996	Juventus	Ajax	1-1 (4-2)*
1966	Real Madrid	Partizan	2-1	1997	Borussia Dortmund	Juventus	3-1
1967	Celtic	Inter Milan	2-1	1998	Real Madrid	Juventus	1-0
1968	Manchester United	Benfica	4-1#	1999	Manchester United	Bayern Munich	2-1
1969	AC Milan	Ajax	4-1	2000	Real Madrid	Valencia	3-0
1970	Feyenoord	Celtic	2-1#	2001	Bayern Munich	Valencia	1-1 (5-4)*
1971	Ajax	Panathinaikos	2-0	2002	Real Madrid	Leverkusen	2-1
1972	Ajax	Inter Milan	2-0	2003	AC Milan	Juventus	0-0 (3-2)*
1973	Ajax	Juventus	1-0	2004	Porto	Monaco	3-0
1974	Bayern Munich	Atlético Madrid	5-1[1]	2005	Liverpool	AC Milan	3-3 (3-2)*
1975	Bayern Munich	Leeds United	2-0	2006	FC Barcelona	Arsenal	2-1
1976	Bayern Munich	St-Étienne	1-0	2007	AC Milan	Liverpool	2-1
1977	Liverpool	Borussia Mönchengladbach	3-1	2008	Manchester United	Chelsea	1-1 (6-5)*
1978	Liverpool	Club Brugge	1-0	2009	FC Barcelona	Manchester United	2-0
1979	Nottingham Forest	Malmö	1-0	2010	Inter Milan	Bayern Munich	2-0
1980	Nottingham Forest	Hamburg SV	1-0	2011	FC Barcelona	Manchester United	3-1
1981	Liverpool	Real Madrid	1-0	2012	Chelsea	Bayern Munich	1-1 (4-3)*
1982	Aston Villa	Bayern Munich	1-0	2013	Bayern Munich	Borussia Dortmund	2-1
1983	Hamburg SV	Juventus	1-0	2014	Real Madrid	Atlético Madrid	4-1#
1984	Liverpool	AS Roma	1-1 (4-2)*	2015	FC Barcelona	Juventus	3-1
1985	Juventus	Liverpool	1-0	2016	Real Madrid	Atlético Madrid	1-1 (5-3)*
1986	Steaua	FC Barcelona	0-0 (2-0)*	2017	Real Madrid	Juventus	4-1
				2018	Real Madrid	Liverpool	3-1

* = Match decided in penalty kicks (shootout score in parentheses). # = Match decided in extra time. (1) Aggregate score. First game, 1-1; second, 4-0.

UEFA European Football Championships, 1960-2016

The final rounds of the 2016 Union of European Football Associations (UEFA) European Championships were hosted by France and opened June 10, 2016, when the host country defeated Romania, 2-1, at Stade de France in Saint-Denis. France advanced to the Euro 2016 final match against Portugal, but Portugal prevailed, 1-0, in extra time on a goal by Éder in the 109th minute July 10 at Stade de France. Portugal had reached the final with a 2-0 victory over Wales on July 6 at Stade de Lyon in Lyon. France had defeated Germany, 2-0, in the other semifinal match July 7 at Stade Vélodrome in Marseilles. France's Antoine Griezmann was voted player of the tournament, with six goals and two assists.

Year	Winner	Final opponent	Score	Site	Year	Winner	Final opponent	Score	Site
1960	USSR	Yugoslavia	2-1#	France	1992	Denmark	Germany	2-0	Sweden
1964	Spain	USSR	2-1	Spain	1996	Germany	Czech Rep.	2-1#	England
1968	Italy	Yugoslavia	2-0	Italy	2000	France	Italy	2-1#	Belgium/Neth.
1972	W. Germany	USSR	3-0	Belgium	2004	Greece	Portugal	1-0	Portugal
1976	Czechoslovakia	W. Germany	2-2 (5-3)*	Yugoslavia	2008	Spain	Germany	1-0	Austria/Switz.
1980	W. Germany	Belgium	2-1	Italy	2012	Spain	Italy	4-0	Poland/Ukr.
1984	France	Spain	2-0	France	2016	Portugal	France	1-0#	France
1988	Netherlands	USSR	2-0	W. Germany					

* = Match decided in penalty kicks (shootout score in parentheses). # = Match decided in extra time.

Toronto FC Sets Points Record, Wins 2017 MLS Cup

In a rematch of the 2016 MLS Cup final, Toronto FC defeated the Seattle Sounders, 2-0, Dec. 9, 2017, at BMO Field in Toronto, ON, Canada. Veteran forward Jozy Altidore, who was voted MLS Cup MVP, broke a scoreless tie with a second-half goal, and Victor Vazquez added a stoppage time goal to give Toronto its first-ever MLS Cup championship. Toronto also won its first Supporters' Shield in 2017 with an MLS single-season record 69 points. The Reds reached the MLS Cup for the second year in a row after an aggregate win over the Columbus Crew in the Eastern Conference championship.

Seattle finished second in the West after the Portland Timbers during the regular season, but the Sounders were crowned Western Conference champions for the second straight year after they overpowered Houston in the conference finals, winning 5-0 on aggregate.

Major League Soccer expanded to 22 teams in 2017 with the addition of Atlanta United FC and Minnesota United FC. During its first season, Atlanta set an MLS single-season record in average attendance (48,200), reached the playoffs, and scored 70 goals (second-best in the regular season behind Toronto's 74).

A crowd of 61,428 attended the MLS All-Star Game on Aug. 2, 2017, at Soldier Field in Chicago. The MLS All-Stars and La Liga's Real Madrid played to a 1-1 tie, but Real won the match, 4-2, on penalty kicks.

Major League Soccer (MLS) Cup Results, 1996-2017

Year	Winner	Final opponent	Score	Site	MVP
1996	DC United	Los Angeles Galaxy	3-2 (OT)	Foxborough, MA	Marco Etcheverry
1997	DC United	Colorado Rapids	2-1	Washington, DC	Jaime Moreno
1998	Chicago Fire	DC United	2-0	Pasadena, CA	Peter Nowak
1999	DC United	Los Angeles Galaxy	2-0	Foxborough, MA	Ben Olsen
2000	Kansas City Wizards	Chicago Fire	1-0	Washington, DC	Tony Meola
2001	San Jose Earthquakes	Los Angeles Galaxy	2-1 (OT)	Columbus, OH	Dwayne De Rosario
2002	Los Angeles Galaxy	New England Revolution	1-0 (OT)	Foxborough, MA	Carlos Ruiz
2003	San Jose Earthquakes	Chicago Fire	4-2	Carson, CA	Landon Donovan
2004	DC United	Kansas City Wizards	3-2	Carson, CA	Alecko Eskandarian
2005	Los Angeles Galaxy	New England Revolution	1-0 (OT)	Frisco, TX	Guillermo Ramírez
2006	Houston Dynamo	New England Revolution	1-1 (4-3)*	Frisco, TX	Brian Ching
2007	Houston Dynamo	New England Revolution	2-1	Washington, DC	Dwayne De Rosario
2008	Columbus Crew	New York Red Bulls	3-1	Carson, CA	Guillermo Barros Schelotto
2009	Real Salt Lake	Los Angeles Galaxy	1-1 (5-4)*	Seattle, WA	Nick Rimando
2010	Colorado Rapids	FC Dallas	2-1 (OT)	Toronto, ON, Canada	Conor Casey
2011	Los Angeles Galaxy	Houston Dynamo	1-0	Carson, CA	Landon Donovan
2012	Los Angeles Galaxy	Houston Dynamo	3-1	Carson, CA	Omar Gonzalez
2013	Sporting Kansas City	Real Salt Lake	1-1 (7-6)*	Kansas City, KS	Aurelien Collin
2014	Los Angeles Galaxy	New England Revolution	2-1 (OT)	Carson, CA	Robbie Keane
2015	Portland Timbers	Columbus Crew	2-1	Columbus, OH	Diego Valeri
2016	Seattle Sounders FC	Toronto FC	0-0 (5-4)*	Toronto, ON, Canada	Stefan Frei
2017	Toronto FC	Seattle Sounders FC	2-0	Toronto, ON, Canada	Jozy Altidore

* = Match decided in penalty kicks (shootout score in parentheses). OT = Overtime.

Major League Soccer Final Standings, 2017

(Does not include playoff games)

Eastern Conference	W	L	T	GF	GA	GD	PTS	Western Conference	W	L	T	GF	GA	GD	PTS
Toronto FC	20	5	9	74	37	37	69	Portland Timbers	15	11	8	60	50	10	53
New York City FC	16	9	9	56	43	13	57	Seattle Sounders FC	14	9	11	52	39	13	53
Chicago Fire	16	11	7	61	47	14	55	Vancouver							
Atlanta United FC	15	9	10	70	40	30	55	Whitecaps FC	15	12	7	50	49	1	52
Columbus Crew SC . .	16	12	6	53	49	4	54	Houston Dynamo	13	10	11	57	45	12	50
New York Red Bulls . .	14	12	8	53	47	6	50	Sporting Kansas City	12	9	13	40	29	11	49
New England								San Jose Earthquakes	13	14	7	39	60	−21	46
Revolution	13	15	6	53	61	−8	45	FC Dallas	11	10	13	48	48	0	46
Philadelphia Union . . .	11	14	9	50	47	3	42	Real Salt Lake	13	15	6	49	55	−6	45
Montréal Impact	11	17	6	52	58	−6	39	Minnesota United FC	10	18	6	47	70	−23	36
Orlando City SC	10	15	9	39	58	−19	39	Colorado Rapids	9	19	6	31	51	−20	33
D.C. United	9	20	5	31	60	−29	32	L.A. Galaxy	8	18	8	45	67	−22	32

Major League Soccer Scoring Leaders, 2017

Player	Club	GP	Goals	Player	Club	GP	Goals
Nemanja Nikolic	Chicago Fire	34	24	Ignacio Piatti	Montréal Impact	28	17
David Villa	New York City FC	31	22	Bradley Wright-Phillips . .	New York Red Bulls	32	17
Diego Valeri	Portland Timbers	32	21	Sebastian Giovinco	Toronto FC	25	16
Josef Martinez	Atlanta United FC	20	19	CJ Sapong	Philadelphia Union	33	16
Ola Kamara	Columbus Crew FC	34	18	Jozy Altidore	Toronto FC	27	15

Landon Donovan MLS Most Valuable Player Award, 1996-2017

(Honda MLS Most Valuable Player Award, 1996-2007; Volkswagen MLS Most Valuable Player Award, 2007-14)

Year	Player, team	Year	Player, team	Year	Player, team
1996	Carlos Valderrama, Tampa Bay	2004	Amado Guevara, NY/NJ	2011	Dwayne De Rosario, D.C.
1997	Preki, Kansas City	2005	Taylor Twellman, New England	2012	Chris Wondolowski, San Jose
1998	Marco Etcheverry, D.C.	2006	Christian Gómez, D.C.	2013	Mike Magee, Chicago
1999	Jason Kreis, Dallas	2007	Luciano Emilio, D.C.	2014	Robbie Keane, L.A.
2000	Tony Meola, Kansas City	2008	Guillermo Barros Schelotto,	2015	Sebastian Giovinco, Toronto
2001	Alex Pineda Chacón, Miami		Columbus	2016	David Villa, New York City
2002	Carlos Ruiz, L.A.	2009	Landon Donovan, L.A.	2017	Diego Valeri, Portland
2003	Preki, Kansas City	2010	David Ferreira, Dallas		

North Carolina Courage Win 2018 NWSL Title

The North Carolina Courage ended a record-setting season with a 3-0 win over Portland Thorns FC to capture the 2018 NWSL title, Sept. 22, 2018, at Providence Park in Portland, OR. Jess McDonald scored twice in the match and was voted MVP of this year's championship game, which was a rematch of the 2017 final. The Courage set numerous regular season records en route to winning the NWSL Supporters' Shield, including most points (57), wins (17), goals (53), and fewest goals allowed (17).

Women's Professional Soccer Champions

Year	Winner	Final opponent	Score	Site	MVP
		Women's United Soccer Association champions			
2001	Bay Area CyberRays	Atlanta Beat	3-3 (4-2)*	Foxborough, MA	Julie Murray
2002	Carolina Courage	Washington Freedom	3-2	Atlanta, GA	Birgit Prinz
2003	Washington Freedom	Atlanta Beat	2-1	San Diego, CA	Abby Wambach
		Women's Professional Soccer champions			
2009	Sky Blue FC	Los Angeles Sol	1-0	Carson, CA	Heather O'Reilly
2010	FC Gold Pride	Philadelphia Independence	4-1	Hayward, CA	Marta
2011	Western New York Flash	Philadelphia Independence	1-1 (5-4)*	Rochester, NY	Christine Sinclair
		National Women's Soccer League champions			
2013	Portland Thorns FC	Western New York Flash	2-0	Rochester, NY	Tobin Heath
2014	FC Kansas City	Seattle Reign FC	2-1	Tukwila, WA	Lauren Holiday
2015	FC Kansas City	Seattle Reign FC	1-0	Portland, OR	Amy Rodriguez
2016	Western New York Flash	Washington Spirit	2-2 (3-2)*	Houston, TX	Sabrina D'Angelo
2017	Portland Thorns FC	North Carolina Courage	1-0	Orlando, FL	Lindsey Horan
2018	North Carolina Courage	Portland Thorns FC	3-0	Portland, OR	Jess McDonald

* = Match decided on penalty kicks (shootout score in parentheses). **Note:** The Women's United Soccer Association (WUSA) folded in 2003. Women's Professional Soccer (WPS) stopped operating in 2012, suspending its fourth season. In Apr. 2013, the National Women's Soccer League (NWSL) began play with eight teams competing: Boston Breakers, Chicago Red Stars, FC Kansas City, Portland Thorns FC, Seattle Reign FC, Sky Blue FC (New York/New Jersey), Washington Spirit, and Western New York Flash. The Houston Dash began play as an NWSL expansion team for the 2014 season; Orlando joined the league in 2016. In Jan. 2017, the Western New York Flash relocated to North Carolina and were renamed the North Carolina Courage. Kansas City and Boston ceased operation in 2017. Utah Royals joined the league in 2018, with former FC Kansas City assets.

U.S. Wins 2015 Women's World Cup Over Japan

The U.S. women's soccer team won the 2015 World Cup with a 5-2 victory over Japan July 5, 2015, at BC Place Stadium in Vancouver, BC, Canada. Veteran midfielder Carli Lloyd scored three goals in the first 16 minutes—the first-ever hat trick in a women's FIFA World Cup final match—as the U.S. captured its third World Cup title. Lloyd, who won the Golden Ball award as the tournament's top player, complemented a strong U.S. defense that allowed only three goals; U.S. goalkeeper Hope Solo won the Golden Glove as the tournament's top goalie. Lloyd tied Germany's Celia Sasic with six goals and one assist in the tournament, but Sasic won the Golden Boot award as top scorer based on fewer minutes played.

Canada served as host of the 2015 tournament, which was contested in six venues. Artificial turf was used for all Women's World Cup matches for the first time. Citing gender discrimination and concerns about turf causing more injuries and hotter playing conditions, a group of players filed a lawsuit against FIFA and the Canadian Soccer Assn. but eventually dropped it.

Women's World Cup Results, 2015

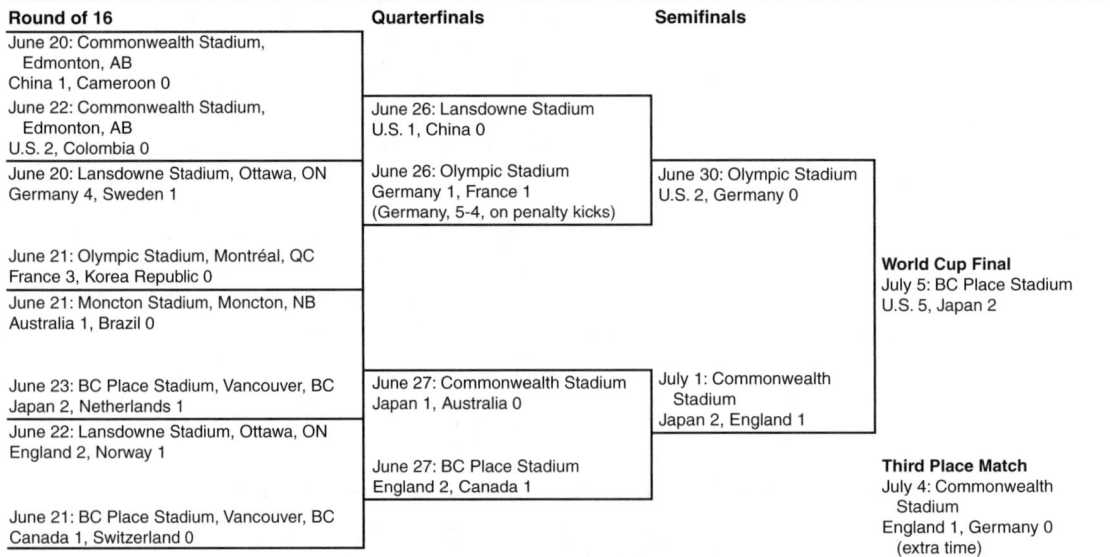

Women's World Cup Results, 1991-2015

Year	Winner	Final opponent	Score	Site	Year	Winner	Final opponent	Score	Site
1991	U.S.	Norway	2-1	China	2007	Germany	Brazil	2-0	China
1995	Norway	Germany	2-0	Sweden	2011	Japan	U.S.	2-2 (3-1)*	Germany
1999	U.S.	China	0-0 (5-4)*	Pasadena, CA, U.S.	2015	U.S.	Japan	5-2	Canada
2003	Germany	Sweden	2-1#	Carson, CA, U.S.					

* = Match decided in penalty kicks (shootout score in parentheses). # = Match decided in extra time.

Selected European Soccer League Champions, 1950-2018

Season	England: Premier League[1]	Spain: La Liga	Italy: Serie A	Germany: Bundesliga[2]
1949-50	Portsmouth FC	Atlético Madrid	Juventus	VfB Stuttgart
1950-51	Tottenham Hotspur	Atlético Madrid	AC Milan	Kaiserslautern
1951-52	Manchester United	FC Barcelona	Juventus	VfB Stuttgart
1952-53	Arsenal	FC Barcelona	Inter Milan	Kaiserslautern
1953-54	Wolverhampton Wanderers	Real Madrid	Inter Milan	Hannoverscher SV 96
1954-55	Chelsea	Real Madrid	AC Milan	Rot-Weiss Essen
1955-56	Manchester United	Athletic Bilbao	Fiorentina	Borussia Dortmund
1956-57	Manchester United	Real Madrid	AC Milan	Borussia Dortmund
1957-58	Wolverhampton Wanderers	Real Madrid	Juventus	Schalke 04
1958-59	Wolverhampton Wanderers	FC Barcelona	AC Milan	Eintracht Frankfurt
1959-60	Burnley FC	FC Barcelona	Juventus	Hamburg SV
1960-61	Tottenham Hotspur	Real Madrid	Juventus	FC Nuremberg
1961-62	Ipswich Town	Real Madrid	AC Milan	FC Cologne
1962-63	Everton	Real Madrid	Inter Milan	Borussia Dortmund
1963-64	Liverpool	Real Madrid	Bologna	FC Cologne
1964-65	Manchester United	Real Madrid	Inter Milan	Werder Bremen
1965-66	Liverpool	Atlético Madrid	Inter Milan	TSV 1860 Munich
1966-67	Manchester United	Real Madrid	Juventus	Eintracht Braunschweig
1967-68	Manchester City	Real Madrid	AC Milan	FC Nuremberg
1968-69	Leeds United	Real Madrid	Fiorentina	Bayern Munich
1969-70	Everton	Atlético Madrid	Cagliari	Borussia Mönchengladbach
1970-71	Arsenal	Valencia	Inter Milan	Borussia Mönchengladbach
1971-72	Derby County	Real Madrid	Juventus	Bayern Munich
1972-73	Liverpool	Atlético Madrid	Juventus	Bayern Munich
1973-74	Leeds United	FC Barcelona	Lazio	Bayern Munich
1974-75	Derby County	Real Madrid	Juventus	Borussia Mönchengladbach
1975-76	Liverpool	Real Madrid	Torino	Borussia Mönchengladbach
1976-77	Liverpool	Atlético Madrid	Juventus	Borussia Mönchengladbach
1977-78	Nottingham Forest	Real Madrid	Juventus	FC Cologne
1978-79	Liverpool	Real Madrid	AC Milan	Hamburg SV
1979-80	Liverpool	Real Madrid	Inter Milan	Bayern Munich
1980-81	Aston Villa	Real Sociedad	Juventus	Bayern Munich
1981-82	Liverpool	Real Sociedad	Juventus	Hamburg SV
1982-83	Liverpool	Athletic Bilbao	AS Roma	Hamburg SV
1983-84	Liverpool	Athletic Bilbao	Juventus	VfB Stuttgart
1984-85	Everton	FC Barcelona	Verona	Bayern Munich
1985-86	Liverpool	Real Madrid	Juventus	Bayern Munich
1986-87	Everton	Real Madrid	Napoli	Bayern Munich
1987-88	Liverpool	Real Madrid	AC Milan	Werder Bremen
1988-89	Arsenal	Real Madrid	Inter Milan	Bayern Munich
1989-90	Liverpool	Real Madrid	Napoli	Bayern Munich
1990-91	Arsenal	FC Barcelona	Sampdoria	FC Kaiserslautern
1991-92	Leeds United	FC Barcelona	AC Milan	VfB Stuttgart
1992-93	Manchester United	FC Barcelona	AC Milan	Werder Bremen
1993-94	Manchester United	FC Barcelona	AC Milan	Bayern Munich
1994-95	Blackburn Rovers	Real Madrid	Juventus	Borussia Dortmund
1995-96	Manchester United	Atlético Madrid	AC Milan	Borussia Dortmund
1996-97	Manchester United	Real Madrid	Juventus	Bayern Munich
1997-98	Arsenal	FC Barcelona	Juventus	FC Kaiserslautern
1998-99	Manchester United	FC Barcelona	AC Milan	Bayern Munich
1999-2000	Manchester United	Deportivo Coruña	Lazio	Bayern Munich
2000-01	Manchester United	Real Madrid	AS Roma	Bayern Munich
2001-02	Arsenal	Valencia	Juventus	Borussia Dortmund
2002-03	Manchester United	Real Madrid	Juventus	Bayern Munich
2003-04	Arsenal	Valencia	AC Milan	Werder Bremen
2004-05	Chelsea	FC Barcelona	None[3]	Bayern Munich
2005-06	Chelsea	FC Barcelona	Inter Milan[3]	Bayern Munich
2006-07	Manchester United	Real Madrid	Inter Milan	VfB Stuttgart
2007-08	Manchester United	Real Madrid	Inter Milan	Bayern Munich
2008-09	Manchester United	FC Barcelona	Inter Milan	VfL Wolfsburg
2009-10	Chelsea	FC Barcelona	Inter Milan	Bayern Munich
2010-11	Manchester United	FC Barcelona	AC Milan	Borussia Dortmund
2011-12	Manchester City	Real Madrid	Juventus	Borussia Dortmund
2012-13	Manchester United	FC Barcelona	Juventus	Bayern Munich
2013-14	Manchester City	Atlético Madrid	Juventus	Bayern Munich
2014-15	Chelsea	FC Barcelona	Juventus	Bayern Munich
2015-16	Leicester City	FC Barcelona	Juventus	Bayern Munich
2016-17	Chelsea	Real Madrid	Juventus	Bayern Munich
2017-18	Manchester City	FC Barcelona	Juventus	Bayern Munich

(1) Football League champions are listed prior to 1992-93 season, when the Premier League formed. (2) Regional champions are listed prior to 1963-64 season, when National Bundesliga formed. (3) Juventus was stripped of two titles in 2006 because of match-fixing.

FIFA Confederations Cup, 2017

A first-half goal by Lars Stindl was the only score of the match as Germany won its first-ever Confederations Cup by defeating Chile, 1-0, July 2, 2017, at St. Petersburg Stadium in St. Petersburg, Russia. Germany's Julian Draxler won the Golden Ball as the tournament's best player, and his teammate Timo Werner earned the Golden Boot with three goals and two assists.

FIFA Confederations Cup Results, 1997-2017

The FIFA Confederations Cup, now held every four years, is a tournament contested by six continental champions, the World Cup winner, and the host country.

Year	Winner	Final opponent	Score	Third place	Fourth place	Site
1997	Brazil	Australia	6-0	Czech Republic	Uruguay	Saudi Arabia
1999	Mexico	Brazil	4-3	U.S.	Saudi Arabia	Mexico
2001	France	Japan	1-0	Australia	Brazil	S. Korea/Japan
2003	France	Cameroon	1-0#	Turkey	Colombia	France
2005	Brazil	Argentina	4-1	Germany	Mexico	Germany
2009	Brazil	U.S.	3-2	Spain	South Africa	South Africa
2013	Brazil	Spain	3-0	Italy	Uruguay	Brazil
2017	Germany	Chile	1-0	Portugal	Mexico	Russia

= Match decided in extra time.

GOLF

Men's All-Time Leading Major Professional Championship Winners

Through Sept. 2018. * = Active PGA player in 2018; (a) = amateur.

Player	Masters	U.S. Open	British Open	PGA	Total
Jack Nicklaus	1963, '65-'66, '72, '75, '86	1962, '67, '72, '80	1966, '70, '78	1963, '71, '73, '75, '80	18
Tiger Woods*	1997, 2001-02, '05	2000, '02, '08	2000, '05-'06	1999-2000, '06-'07	14
Walter Hagen	—	1914, '19	1922, '24, '28-'29	1921, '24-'27	11
Ben Hogan	1951, '53	1948, '50-'51, '53	1953	1946, '48	9
Gary Player	1961, '74, '78	1965	1959, '68, '74	1962, '72	9
Tom Watson	1977, '81	1982	1975, '77, '80, '82-'83	—	8
Bobby Jones (a)	—	1923, '26, '29-'30	1926-27, '30	—	7
Arnold Palmer	1958, '60, '62, '64	1960	1961-62	—	7
Gene Sarazen	1935	1922, '32	1932	1922-23, '33	7
Sam Snead	1949, '52, '54	—	1946	1942, '49, '51	7
Harry Vardon	—	1900	1896, '98-'99, 1903, '11, '14	—	7
Nick Faldo	1989-90, '96	—	1987, '90, '92	—	6
Lee Trevino	—	1968, '71	1971-72	1974, '84	6

Men's All-Time Leading PGA Tournament Winners

Ranked by career wins in PGA Tour co-sponsored and/or approved tournaments through Sept. 2018. * = Active PGA player in 2017-18 season.

Player	Wins	Majors	Player	Wins	Majors	Player	Wins	Majors
Sam Snead	82	7	*Vijay Singh	34	3	Macdonald Smith	24	0
*Tiger Woods	80	14	Jimmy Demaret	31	3	Raymond Floyd	22	4
Jack Nicklaus	73	18	Horton Smith	30	2	Johnny Farrell	22	1
Ben Hogan	64	9	Lee Trevino	29	6	Jim Barnes	21	4
Arnold Palmer	62	7	Gene Littler	29	1	Craig Wood	21	2
Byron Nelson	52	5	Harry Cooper	29	0	*Davis Love III	21	1
Billy Casper	51	3	Leo Diegel	28	2	Willie Macfarlane	21	1
Walter Hagen	45	11	Paul Runyan	28	2	Lanny Wadkins	21	1
*Phil Mickelson	43	5	Henry Picard	26	2	Hale Irwin	20	3
Tom Watson	39	8	Tommy Armour	25	3	Greg Norman	20	2
Cary Middlecoff	39	3	Johnny Miller	25	2	Johnny Revolta	20	1
Gene Sarazen	38	7	Gary Player	24	9	Doug Sanders	20	0
Lloyd Mangrum	36	1						

Professional Golfers' Association Leading Money Winners, 1946-2018

Year	Player	Earnings	Year	Player	Earnings	Year	Player	Earnings
1946	Ben Hogan	$42,556	1971	Jack Nicklaus	$244,490	1995	Greg Norman	$1,654,959
1947	Jimmy Demaret	27,936	1972	Jack Nicklaus	320,542	1996	Tom Lehman	1,780,159
1948	Ben Hogan	32,112	1973	Jack Nicklaus	308,362	1997	Tiger Woods	2,066,833
1949	Sam Snead	31,593	1974	Johnny Miller	353,021	1998	David Duval	2,591,031
1950	Sam Snead	35,758	1975	Jack Nicklaus	298,149	1999	Tiger Woods	6,616,585
1951	Lloyd Mangrum	26,088	1976	Jack Nicklaus	266,438	2000	Tiger Woods	9,188,321
1952	Julius Boros	37,032	1977	Tom Watson	310,653	2001	Tiger Woods	5,687,777
1953	Lew Worsham	34,002	1978	Tom Watson	362,429	2002	Tiger Woods	6,912,625
1954	Bob Toski	65,819	1979	Tom Watson	462,636	2003	Vijay Singh	7,573,907
1955	Julius Boros	63,121	1980	Tom Watson	530,808	2004	Vijay Singh	10,905,166
1956	Ted Kroll	72,835	1981	Tom Kite	375,699	2005	Tiger Woods	10,628,024
1957	Dick Mayer	65,835	1982	Craig Stadler	446,462	2006	Tiger Woods	9,941,563
1958	Arnold Palmer	42,607	1983	Hal Sutton	426,668	2007	Tiger Woods	10,867,052
1959	Art Wall Jr.	53,167	1984	Tom Watson	476,260	2008	Vijay Singh	6,601,094
1960	Arnold Palmer	75,262	1985	Curtis Strange	542,321	2009	Tiger Woods	10,508,163
1961	Gary Player	64,540	1986	Greg Norman	653,296	2010	Matt Kuchar	4,910,477
1962	Arnold Palmer	81,448	1987	Curtis Strange	925,941	2011	Luke Donald	6,683,214
1963	Arnold Palmer	128,230	1988	Curtis Strange	1,147,644	2012	Rory McIlroy	8,047,952
1964	Jack Nicklaus	113,284	1989	Tom Kite	1,395,278	2013	Tiger Woods	8,553,439
1965	Jack Nicklaus	140,752	1990	Greg Norman	1,165,477	2014	Rory McIlroy	8,280,096
1966	Billy Casper	121,944	1991	Corey Pavin	979,430	2015	Jordan Spieth	12,030,465
1967	Jack Nicklaus	188,998	1992	Fred Couples	1,344,188	2016	Dustin Johnson	9,365,185
1968	Billy Casper	205,168	1993	Nick Price	1,478,557	2017	Justin Thomas	9,921,560
1969	Frank Beard	164,707	1994	Nick Price	1,499,927	2018	Justin Thomas	8,694,821
1970	Lee Trevino	157,037						

Note: The PGA tour introduced a new split season format in Oct. 2013, which concluded with the FedEx Cup in Sept. 2014. From 2014 on, year shown is the one in which season ended.

FedEx Cup Winners, 2007-18

The FedEx Cup, a season-long, $10-mil competition with points awarded by finishing rank in each tournament, divides the PGA Tour into a regular season consisting of 43 events, combined with a 4-event playoff that ends with the Tour Championship.

Year	Winner	Year	Winner	Year	Winner	Year	Winner	Year	Winner
2007	Tiger Woods	2010	Jim Furyk	2013	Henrik Stenson	2015	Jordan Spieth	2017	Justin Thomas
2008	Vijay Singh	2011	Bill Haas	2014	Billy Horschel	2016	Rory McIlroy	2018	Justin Rose
2009	Tiger Woods	2012	Brandt Snedeker						

Masters Golf Tournament Winners, 1940-2018

First contested in 1934 as Augusta National Invitation Tournament (name changed in 1939); not played, 1943-45.

Year	Winner	Year	Winner	Year	Winner	Year	Winner	Year	Winner
1940	Jimmy Demaret	1959	Art Wall Jr.	1975	Jack Nicklaus	1991	Ian Woosnam	2004	Phil Mickelson
1941	Craig Wood	1960	Arnold Palmer	1976	Ray Floyd	1992	Fred Couples	2005	Tiger Woods
1942	Byron Nelson	1961	Gary Player	1977	Tom Watson	1993	Bernhard Langer	2006	Phil Mickelson
1946	Herman Keiser	1962	Arnold Palmer	1978	Gary Player	1994	José María	2007	Zach Johnson
1947	Jimmy Demaret	1963	Jack Nicklaus	1979	Fuzzy Zoeller		Olazábal	2008	Trevor Immelman
1948	Claude Harmon	1964	Arnold Palmer	1980	Seve Ballesteros	1995	Ben Crenshaw	2009	Angel Cabrera
1949	Sam Snead	1965	Jack Nicklaus	1981	Tom Watson	1996	Nick Faldo	2010	Phil Mickelson
1950	Jimmy Demaret	1966	Jack Nicklaus	1982	Craig Stadler	1997	Tiger Woods	2011	Charl Schwartzel
1951	Ben Hogan	1967	Gay Brewer Jr.	1983	Seve Ballesteros	1998	Mark O'Meara	2012	Bubba Watson
1952	Sam Snead	1968	Bob Goalby	1984	Ben Crenshaw	1999	José María	2013	Adam Scott
1953	Ben Hogan	1969	George Archer	1985	Bernhard Langer		Olazábal	2014	Bubba Watson
1954	Sam Snead	1970	Billy Casper	1986	Jack Nicklaus	2000	Vijay Singh	2015	Jordan Spieth
1955	Cary Middlecoff	1971	Charles Coody	1987	Larry Mize	2001	Tiger Woods	2016	Danny Willett
1956	Jack Burke	1972	Jack Nicklaus	1988	Sandy Lyle	2002	Tiger Woods	2017	Sergio García
1957	Doug Ford	1973	Tommy Aaron	1989	Nick Faldo	2003	Mike Weir	2018	Patrick Reed
1958	Arnold Palmer	1974	Gary Player	1990	Nick Faldo				

U.S. Open Winners, 1940-2018

First contested in 1895; not played, 1942-45.

Year	Winner	Year	Winner	Year	Winner	Year	Winner	Year	Winner
1940	Lawson Little	1959	Billy Casper	1974	Hale Irwin	1989	Curtis Strange	2004	Retief Goosen
1941	Craig Wood	1960	Arnold Palmer	1975	Lou Graham	1990	Hale Irwin	2005	Michael Campbell
1946	Lloyd Mangrum	1961	Gene Littler	1976	Jerry Pate	1991	Payne Stewart	2006	Geoff Ogilvy
1947	Lew Worsham	1962	Jack Nicklaus	1977	Hubert Green	1992	Tom Kite	2007	Angel Cabrera
1948	Ben Hogan	1963	Julius Boros	1978	Andy North	1993	Lee Janzen	2008	Tiger Woods
1949	Cary Middlecoff	1964	Ken Venturi	1979	Hale Irwin	1994	Ernie Els	2009	Lucas Glover
1950	Ben Hogan	1965	Gary Player	1980	Jack Nicklaus	1995	Corey Pavin	2010	Graeme McDowell
1951	Ben Hogan	1966	Billy Casper	1981	David Graham	1996	Steve Jones	2011	Rory McIlroy
1952	Julius Boros	1967	Jack Nicklaus	1982	Tom Watson	1997	Ernie Els	2012	Webb Simpson
1953	Ben Hogan	1968	Lee Trevino	1983	Larry Nelson	1998	Lee Janzen	2013	Justin Rose
1954	Ed Furgol	1969	Orville Moody	1984	Fuzzy Zoeller	1999	Payne Stewart	2014	Martin Kaymer
1955	Jack Fleck	1970	Tony Jacklin	1985	Andy North	2000	Tiger Woods	2015	Jordan Spieth
1956	Cary Middlecoff	1971	Lee Trevino	1986	Ray Floyd	2001	Retief Goosen	2016	Dustin Johnson
1957	Dick Mayer	1972	Jack Nicklaus	1987	Scott Simpson	2002	Tiger Woods	2017	Brooks Koepka
1958	Tommy Bolt	1973	Johnny Miller	1988	Curtis Strange	2003	Jim Furyk	2018	Brooks Koepka

British Open Winners, 1946-2018

Officially called the Open Championship. First contested in 1860; not played, 1940-45.

Year	Winner	Year	Winner	Year	Winner	Year	Winner	Year	Winner
1946	Sam Snead	1961	Arnold Palmer	1976	Johnny Miller	1991	Ian Baker-Finch	2005	Tiger Woods
1947	Fred Daly	1962	Arnold Palmer	1977	Tom Watson	1992	Nick Faldo	2006	Tiger Woods
1948	Henry Cotton	1963	Bob Charles	1978	Jack Nicklaus	1993	Greg Norman	2007	Padraig Harrington
1949	Bobby Locke	1964	Tony Lema	1979	Seve Ballesteros	1994	Nick Price	2008	Padraig Harrington
1950	Bobby Locke	1965	Peter Thomson	1980	Tom Watson	1995	John Daly	2009	Stewart Cink
1951	Max Faulkner	1966	Jack Nicklaus	1981	Bill Rogers	1996	Tom Lehman	2010	Louis Oosthuizen
1952	Bobby Locke	1967	Roberto de Vicenzo	1982	Tom Watson	1997	Justin Leonard	2011	Darren Clarke
1953	Ben Hogan	1968	Gary Player	1983	Tom Watson	1998	Mark O'Meara	2012	Ernie Els
1954	Peter Thomson	1969	Tony Jacklin	1984	Seve Ballesteros	1999	Paul Lawrie	2013	Phil Mickelson
1955	Peter Thomson	1970	Jack Nicklaus	1985	Sandy Lyle	2000	Tiger Woods	2014	Rory McIlroy
1956	Peter Thomson	1971	Lee Trevino	1986	Greg Norman	2001	David Duval	2015	Zach Johnson
1957	Bobby Locke	1972	Lee Trevino	1987	Nick Faldo	2002	Ernie Els	2016	Henrik Stenson
1958	Peter Thomson	1973	Tom Weiskopf	1988	Seve Ballesteros	2003	Ben Curtis	2017	Jordan Spieth
1959	Gary Player	1974	Gary Player	1989	Mark Calcavecchia	2004	Todd Hamilton	2018	Francesco Molinari
1960	Kel Nagle	1975	Tom Watson	1990	Nick Faldo				

PGA Championship Winners, 1940-2018

First contested in 1916; not played, 1943.

Year	Winner	Year	Winner	Year	Winner	Year	Winner	Year	Winner
1940	Byron Nelson	1957	Lionel Hebert	1973	Jack Nicklaus	1989	Payne Stewart	2004	Vijay Singh
1941	Victor Ghezzi	1958	Dow Finsterwald	1974	Lee Trevino	1990	Wayne Grady	2005	Phil Mickelson
1942	Sam Snead	1959	Bob Rosburg	1975	Jack Nicklaus	1991	John Daly	2006	Tiger Woods
1944	Bob Hamilton	1960	Jay Hebert	1976	Dave Stockton	1992	Nick Price	2007	Tiger Woods
1945	Byron Nelson	1961	Jerry Barber	1977	Lanny Wadkins	1993	Paul Azinger	2008	Padraig Harrington
1946	Ben Hogan	1962	Gary Player	1978	John Mahaffey	1994	Nick Price	2009	Y.E.Yang
1947	Jim Ferrier	1963	Jack Nicklaus	1979	David Graham	1995	Steve Elkington	2010	Martin Kaymer
1948	Ben Hogan	1964	Bob Nichols	1980	Jack Nicklaus	1996	Mark Brooks	2011	Keegan Bradley
1949	Sam Snead	1965	Dave Marr	1981	Larry Nelson	1997	Davis Love III	2012	Rory McIlroy
1950	Chandler Harper	1966	Al Geiberger	1982	Ray Floyd	1998	Vijay Singh	2013	Jason Dufner
1951	Sam Snead	1967	Don January	1983	Hal Sutton	1999	Tiger Woods	2014	Rory McIlroy
1952	James Turnesa	1968	Julius Boros	1984	Lee Trevino	2000	Tiger Woods	2015	Jason Day
1953	Walter Burkemo	1969	Ray Floyd	1985	Hubert Green	2001	David Toms	2016	Jimmy Walker
1954	Melvin Harbert	1970	Dave Stockton	1986	Bob Tway	2002	Rich Beem	2017	Justin Thomas
1955	Doug Ford	1971	Jack Nicklaus	1987	Larry Nelson	2003	Shaun Micheel	2018	Brooks Koepka
1956	Jack Burke	1972	Gary Player	1988	Jeff Sluman				

PGA Tour Byron Nelson Award, 1980-2018

Awarded to the player with the best scoring average (1980-87) or adjusted scoring average (1988-present) who has competed in a minimum of 50 official rounds on the PGA Tour. The adjusted average is calculated using the average score of the field at each tournament.

Year	Winner	Average	Year	Winner	Average	Year	Winner	Average
1980	Lee Trevino	69.73	1993	Greg Norman	68.90	2006	Tiger Woods	68.11
1981	Tom Kite	69.80	1994	Greg Norman	68.81	2007	Tiger Woods	67.79
1982	Tom Kite	70.21	1995	Greg Norman	69.06	2008	Sergio García	69.12
1983	Raymond Floyd	70.61	1996	Tom Lehman	69.32	2009	Tiger Woods	68.05
1984	Calvin Peete	70.56	1997	Nick Price	68.98	2010	Matt Kuchar	69.61
1985	Don Pooley	70.36	1998	David Duval	69.13	2011	Luke Donald	68.86
1986	Scott Hoch	70.08	1999	Tiger Woods	68.43	2012	Rory McIlroy	68.87
1987	David Frost	70.09	2000	Tiger Woods	67.79	2013	Steve Stricker	68.95
1988	Greg Norman	69.38	2001	Tiger Woods	68.81	2014	Rory McIlroy	68.83
1989	Payne Stewart	69.485[1]	2002	Tiger Woods	68.56	2015	Jordan Spieth	68.91
1990	Greg Norman	69.10	2003	Tiger Woods	68.41	2016	Dustin Johnson	69.17
1991	Fred Couples	69.59	2004	Vijay Singh	68.84	2017	Jordan Spieth	68.85
1992	Fred Couples	69.38	2005	Tiger Woods	68.66	2018	Dustin Johnson	68.70

(1) Tie broken by more precise calculation.

Ryder Cup, 1927-2018

The Ryder Cup began in 1927 as a biennial team competition between U.S. and British pro male golfers. The British team expanded in 1973 to include players from Ireland and in 1979 to golfers from the rest of Europe. The 2018 Cup was held Sept. 28-30 at Le Golf National near Paris, France; the 2020 Cup will be held at Whistling Straits Golf Course in Mosel, WI.

Year	Winner, score	Year	Winner, score	Year	Winner, score	Year	Winner, score
1927	U.S., 9½-2½	1957	Great Britain, 7½-4½	1979	U.S., 17-11	1999	U.S., 14½-13½
1929	Great Britain, 7-5	1959	U.S., 8½-3½	1981	U.S., 18½-9½	2002	Europe, 15½-12½
1931	U.S., 9-3	1961	U.S., 14½-9½	1983	U.S., 14½-13½	2004	Europe, 18½-9½
1933	Great Britain, 6½-5½	1963	U.S., 23-9	1985	Europe, 16½-11½	2006	Europe, 18½-9½
1935	U.S., 9-3	1965	U.S., 19½-12½	1987	Europe, 15-13	2008	U.S., 16½-11½
1937	U.S., 8-4	1967	U.S., 23½-8½	1989	Draw, 14-14	2010	Europe, 14½-13½
1947	U.S., 11-1	1969	Draw, 16-16	1991	U.S., 14½-13½	2012	Europe, 14½-13½
1949	U.S., 7-5	1971	U.S., 18½-13½	1993	U.S., 15-13	2014	Europe, 16½-11½
1951	U.S., 9½-2½	1973	U.S., 19-13	1995	Europe, 14½-13½	2016	U.S., 17-11
1953	U.S., 6½-5½	1975	U.S., 21-11	1997	Europe, 14½-13½	2018	Europe, 17½-10½
1955	U.S., 8-4	1977	U.S., 12½-7½				

Women's All-Time Leading Major Professional Championship Winners

Through Sept. 2018. * = Active in 2018 LPGA season.

Player	ANA Inspiration[1]	KPMG Women's PGA[2]	U.S. Women's Open	Women's British Open[3]	Titleholders[4]	Western Open[5]	Total
Patty Berg	—	—	1946	—	1937-39, '48, '53, '55, '57	1941, '43, '48, '51, '55, '57-'58	15
Mickey Wright	—	1958, '60-'61, '63	1958-59, '61, '64	—	1961-62	1962-63, '66	13
Louise Suggs	—	1957	1949, '52	—	1946, '54, '56, '59	1946-47, '49, '53	11
Annika Sorenstam	2001-02, '05	2003-05	1995-96, 2006	2003	—	—	10
Babe Zaharias	—	—	1948, '50, '54	—	1947, '50, '52	1940, '44-'45, '50	10
Betsy Rawls	—	1959, '69	1951, '53, '57, '60	—	—	1952, '59	8
Juli Inkster*	1984, '89	1999-2000	1999, 2002	1984	—	—	7
Inbee Park*	2013	2013-15	2008, '13	2015	—	—	7
Karrie Webb*	2000, '06	2001	2000-01	1999, 2002	—	—	7

(1) Formerly the Nabisco Dinah Shore (1982-99), the Nabisco Championship (2000-01), and the Kraft Nabisco Championship (2002-14); designated major in 1983. (2) Formerly the LPGA Championship (1955-2014). (3) In 2001, the British Open replaced the du Maurier Classic as the LPGA's fourth major; wins in column prior to 2001 are for the Peter Jackson (1979-82) or du Maurier (1983-2000) Classic. (4) Titleholders Championship was a major, 1937-72. (5) Western Open was a major, 1930-67.

Ladies Professional Golf Association Leading Money Winners, 1954-2017

Year	Player	Earnings	Year	Player	Earnings	Year	Player	Earnings
1954	Patty Berg	$16,011	1976	Judy Rankin	$150,734	1997	Annika Sorenstam	$1,236,789
1955	Patty Berg	16,492	1977	Judy Rankin	122,890	1998	Annika Sorenstam	1,092,748
1956	Marlene Hagge	20,235	1978	Nancy Lopez	189,814	1999	Karrie Webb	1,591,959
1957	Patty Berg	16,272	1979	Nancy Lopez	197,489	2000	Karrie Webb	1,876,853
1958	Beverly Hanson	12,639	1980	Beth Daniel	231,000	2001	Annika Sorenstam	2,105,868
1959	Betsy Rawls	26,774	1981	Beth Daniel	206,998	2002	Annika Sorenstam	2,863,904
1960	Louise Suggs	16,892	1982	JoAnne Carner	310,400	2003	Annika Sorenstam	2,029,506
1961	Mickey Wright	22,236	1983	JoAnne Carner	291,404	2004	Annika Sorenstam	2,544,707
1962	Mickey Wright	21,641	1984	Betsy King	266,771	2005	Annika Sorenstam	2,588,240
1963	Mickey Wright	31,269	1985	Nancy Lopez	416,472	2006	Lorena Ochoa	2,592,872
1964	Mickey Wright	29,800	1986	Pat Bradley	492,021	2007	Lorena Ochoa	4,364,994
1965	Kathy Whitworth	28,658	1987	Ayako Okamoto	466,034	2008	Lorena Ochoa	2,763,193
1966	Kathy Whitworth	33,517	1988	Sherri Turner	350,851	2009	Jiyai Shin	1,807,334
1967	Kathy Whitworth	32,937	1989	Betsy King	654,132	2010	Na Yeon Choi	1,871,166
1968	Kathy Whitworth	48,379	1990	Beth Daniel	863,578	2011	Yani Tseng	2,921,713
1969	Carol Mann	49,152	1991	Pat Bradley	763,118	2012	Inbee Park	2,287,080
1970	Kathy Whitworth	30,235	1992	Dottie Mochrie	693,335	2013	Inbee Park	2,456,619
1971	Kathy Whitworth	41,181	1993	Betsy King	595,992	2014	Stacy Lewis	2,539,039
1972	Kathy Whitworth	65,063	1994	Laura Davies	687,201	2015	Lydia Ko	2,800,802
1973	Kathy Whitworth	82,864	1995	Annika Sorenstam	666,533	2016	Ariya Jutanugarn	2,550,947
1974	JoAnne Carner	87,094	1996	Karrie Webb	1,002,000	2017	Sung Hyun Park	2,335,883
1975	Sandra Palmer	76,374						

Women's All-Time Leading LPGA Tournament Winners

Ranked by career tournament wins through Sept. 2018. * = Active LPGA player in 2018.

Player	Wins	Majors	Player	Wins	Majors	Player	Wins	Majors
Kathy Whitworth	88	6	JoAnne Carner	43	2	Betsy King	34	6
Mickey Wright	82	13	Sandra Haynie	42	4	Beth Daniel	33	1
Annika Sorenstam	72	10	Babe Didrikson			*Juli Inkster	31	7
Patty Berg	60	15	Zaharias	41	10	Pat Bradley	31	6
Louise Suggs	60	11	*Karrie Webb	41	7	Amy Alcott	29	5
Betsy Rawls	55	8	Carol Mann	38	2	Lorena Ochoa	27	2
Nancy Lopez	48	3	Patty Sheehan	35	6	Jane Blalock	27	0

ANA Inspiration Winners, 1983-2018

Event began in 1972 and was designated a major championship in 1983. Formerly the Colgate Dinah Shore (1972-81), the Nabisco Dinah Shore (1982-99), the Nabisco Championship (2000-01), and the Kraft Nabisco Championship (2002-14).

Year	Winner	Year	Winner	Year	Winner	Year	Winner	Year	Winner
1983	Amy Alcott	1991	Amy Alcott	1998	Pat Hurst	2005	Annika Sorenstam	2012	Sun Young Yoo
1984	Juli Inkster	1992	Dottie Pepper	1999	Dottie Pepper	2006	Karrie Webb	2013	Inbee Park
1985	Alice Miller	1993	Helen Alfredsson	2000	Karrie Webb	2007	Morgan Pressel	2014	Lexi Thompson
1986	Pat Bradley	1994	Donna Andrews	2001	Annika Sorenstam	2008	Lorena Ochoa	2015	Brittany Lincicome
1987	Betsy King	1995	Nanci Bowen	2002	Annika Sorenstam	2009	Brittany Lincicome	2016	Lydia Ko
1988	Amy Alcott	1996	Patty Sheehan	2003	P. Meunier-Lebouc	2010	Yani Tseng	2017	So Yeon Ryu
1989	Juli Inkster	1997	Betsy King	2004	Grace Park	2011	Stacy Lewis	2018	Pernilla Lindberg
1990	Betsy King								

KPMG Women's PGA Championship Winners, 1955-2018

Formerly LPGA Championship (1955-2014).

Year	Winner	Year	Winner	Year	Winner	Year	Winner	Year	Winner
1955	Beverly Hanson	1968	Sandra Post	1981	Donna Caponi	1994	Laura Davies	2007	Suzann Pettersen
1956	Marlene Hagge	1969	Betsy Rawls	1982	Jan Stephenson	1995	Kelly Robbins	2008	Yani Tseng
1957	Louise Suggs	1970	Shirley Englehorn	1983	Patty Sheehan	1996	Laura Davies	2009	Anna Nordqvist
1958	Mickey Wright	1971	Kathy Whitworth	1984	Patty Sheehan	1997	Christa Johnson	2010	Cristie Kerr
1959	Betsy Rawls	1972	Kathy Ahern	1985	Nancy Lopez	1998	Se Ri Pak	2011	Yani Tseng
1960	Mickey Wright	1973	Mary Mills	1986	Pat Bradley	1999	Juli Inkster	2012	Shanshan Feng
1961	Mickey Wright	1974	Sandra Haynie	1987	Jane Geddes	2000	Juli Inkster	2013	Inbee Park
1962	Judy Kimball	1975	Kathy Whitworth	1988	Sherri Turner	2001	Karrie Webb	2014	Inbee Park
1963	Mickey Wright	1976	Betty Burfeindt	1989	Nancy Lopez	2002	Se Ri Pak	2015	Inbee Park
1964	Mary Mills	1977	Chako Higuchi	1990	Beth Daniel	2003	Annika Sorenstam	2016	Brooke Henderson
1965	Sandra Haynie	1978	Nancy Lopez	1991	Meg Mallon	2004	Annika Sorenstam	2017	Danielle Kang
1966	Gloria Ehret	1979	Donna Caponi	1992	Betsy King	2005	Annika Sorenstam	2018	Sung Hyun Park
1967	Kathy Whitworth	1980	Sally Little	1993	Patty Sheehan	2006	Se Ri Pak		

U.S. Women's Open Winners, 1946-2018

Year	Winner	Year	Winner	Year	Winner	Year	Winner	Year	Winner
1946	Patty Berg	1961	Mickey Wright	1976	JoAnne Carner	1991	Meg Mallon	2005	Birdie Kim
1947	Betty Jameson	1962	Murle Lindstrom	1977	Hollis Stacy	1992	Patty Sheehan	2006	Annika Sorenstam
1948	Babe Zaharias	1963	Mary Mills	1978	Hollis Stacy	1993	Lauri Merten	2007	Cristie Kerr
1949	Louise Suggs	1964	Mickey Wright	1979	Jerilyn Britz	1994	Patty Sheehan	2008	Inbee Park
1950	Babe Zaharias	1965	Carol Mann	1980	Amy Alcott	1995	Annika Sorenstam	2009	Eun-Hee Ji
1951	Betsy Rawls	1966	Sandra Spuzich	1981	Pat Bradley	1996	Annika Sorenstam	2010	Paula Creamer
1952	Louise Suggs	1967	Catherine Lacoste	1982	Janet Alex	1997	Alison Nicholas	2011	So Yeon Ryu
1953	Betsy Rawls	1968	Susie Berning	1983	Jan Stephenson	1998	Se Ri Pak	2012	Na Yeon Choi
1954	Babe Zaharias	1969	Donna Caponi	1984	Hollis Stacy	1999	Juli Inkster	2013	Inbee Park
1955	Fay Crocker	1970	Donna Caponi	1985	Kathy Baker	2000	Karrie Webb	2014	Michelle Wie
1956	Kathy Cornelius	1971	JoAnne Carner	1986	Jane Geddes	2001	Karrie Webb	2015	In Gee Chun
1957	Betsy Rawls	1972	Susie Berning	1987	Laura Davies	2002	Juli Inkster	2016	Brittany Lang
1958	Mickey Wright	1973	Susie Berning	1988	Liselotte Neumann	2003	Hilary Lunke	2017	Sung Hyun Park
1959	Mickey Wright	1974	Sandra Haynie	1989	Betsy King	2004	Meg Mallon	2018	Ariya Jutanugarn
1960	Betsy Rawls	1975	Sandra Palmer	1990	Betsy King				

Women's British Open Winners, 1979-2018

First contested as the Ladies' British Open in 1976; became the LPGA's fourth major championship in 2001, replacing the du Maurier Classic. Winners listed are for the Peter Jackson (1979-82) and du Maurier (1983-2000) Classic.

Year	Winner	Year	Winner	Year	Winner	Year	Winner	Year	Winner
1979	Amy Alcott	1987	Jody Rosenthal	1995	Jenny Lidback	2003	Annika Sorenstam	2011	Yani Tseng
1980	Pat Bradley	1988	Sally Little	1996	Laura Davies	2004	Karen Stupples	2012	Jiyai Shin
1981	Jan Stephenson	1989	Tammie Green	1997	Colleen Walker	2005	Jeong Jang	2013	Stacy Lewis
1982	Sandra Haynie	1990	Cathy Johnston	1998	Brandie Burton	2006	Sherri Steinhauer	2014	Mo Martin
1983	Hollis Stacy	1991	Nancy Scranton	1999	Karrie Webb	2007	Lorena Ochoa	2015	Inbee Park
1984	Juli Inkster	1992	Sherri Steinhauer	2000	Meg Mallon	2008	Jiyai Shin	2016	Ariya Jutanugarn
1985	Pat Bradley	1993	Brandie Burton	2001	Se Ri Pak	2009	Catriona Matthew	2017	In-Kyung Kim
1986	Pat Bradley	1994	Martha Nause	2002	Karrie Webb	2010	Yani Tseng	2018	Georgia Hall

Evian Championship, 2013-18

Began in 1994 as the Evian Masters; became the LPGA's fifth major tournament in 2013, when it was renamed the Evian Championship.

Year	Winner	Year	Winner	Year	Winner	Year	Winner
2013	Suzann Pettersen	2015	Lydia Ko	2017	Anna Nordqvist	2018	Angela Stanford
2014	Hyo Joo Kim	2016	In Gee Chun				

Solheim Cup, 1990-2017

The Solheim Cup began in 1990 as a biennial team competition between pro women golfers from the U.S. and Europe.

Year	Winner, score	Year	Winner, score	Year	Winner, score	Year	Winner, score
1990	U.S., 11½-4½	1998	U.S., 16-12	2005	U.S., 15½-12½	2013	Europe, 18-10
1992	Europe, 11½-6½	2000	Europe, 14½-11½	2007	U.S., 16-12	2015	U.S., 14½-13½
1994	U.S., 13-7	2002	U.S., 15½-12½	2009	U.S., 16-12	2017	U.S., 16½-11½
1996	U.S., 17-11	2003	Europe, 17½-10½	2011	Europe, 15-13		

TENNIS

Australian Open Champions, 1969-2018

First contested 1905 for men, 1922 for women. Became an open championship in 1969. Two tournaments held in 1977, in Jan. and Dec. No tournament held in 1986.

Men's Singles

Year	Champion	Final opponent
1969	Rod Laver	Andrés Gimeno
1970	Arthur Ashe	Dick Crealy
1971	Ken Rosewall	Arthur Ashe
1972	Ken Rosewall	Mal Anderson
1973	John Newcombe	Onny Parun
1974	Jimmy Connors	Phil Dent
1975	John Newcombe	Jimmy Connors
1976	Mark Edmondson	John Newcombe
1977	Roscoe Tanner	Guillermo Vilas
	Vitas Gerulaitis	John Lloyd
1978	Guillermo Vilas	John Marks
1979	Guillermo Vilas	John Sadri
1980	Brian Teacher	Kim Warwick
1981	Johan Kriek	Steve Denton
1982	Johan Kriek	Steve Denton
1983	Mats Wilander	Ivan Lendl
1984	Mats Wilander	Kevin Curren
1985	Stefan Edberg	Mats Wilander
1987	Stefan Edberg	Pat Cash
1988	Mats Wilander	Pat Cash
1989	Ivan Lendl	Miloslav Mecir
1990	Ivan Lendl	Stefan Edberg
1991	Boris Becker	Ivan Lendl
1992	Jim Courier	Stefan Edberg
1993	Jim Courier	Stefan Edberg
1994	Pete Sampras	Todd Martin
1995	Andre Agassi	Pete Sampras
1996	Boris Becker	Michael Chang
1997	Pete Sampras	Carlos Moya
1998	Petr Korda	Marcelo Rios
1999	Yevgeny Kafelnikov	Thomas Enqvist
2000	Andre Agassi	Yevgeny Kafelnikov
2001	Andre Agassi	Arnaud Clement
2002	Thomas Johansson	Marat Safin
2003	Andre Agassi	Rainer Schuettler
2004	Roger Federer	Marat Safin
2005	Marat Safin	Lleyton Hewitt
2006	Roger Federer	Marcos Baghdatis
2007	Roger Federer	Fernando Gonzalez
2008	Novak Djokovic	Jo-Wilfried Tsonga
2009	Rafael Nadal	Roger Federer
2010	Roger Federer	Andy Murray
2011	Novak Djokovic	Andy Murray
2012	Novak Djokovic	Rafael Nadal
2013	Novak Djokovic	Andy Murray
2014	Stanislas Wawrinka	Rafael Nadal
2015	Novak Djokovic	Andy Murray
2016	Novak Djokovic	Andy Murray
2017	Roger Federer	Rafael Nadal
2018	Roger Federer	Marin Cilic

Women's Singles

Year	Champion	Final opponent
1969	Margaret Smith Court	Billie Jean King
1970	Margaret Smith Court	Kerry Melville Reid
1971	Margaret Smith Court	Evonne Goolagong
1972	Virginia Wade	Evonne Goolagong
1973	Margaret Smith Court	Evonne Goolagong
1974	Evonne Goolagong	Chris Evert
1975	Evonne Goolagong	Martina Navratilova
1976	Evonne Goolagong Cawley	Renata Tomanova
1977	Kerry Reid	Dianne Balestrat
	Evonne Goolagong Cawley	Helen Gourlay
1978	Chris O'Neil	Betsy Nagelsen
1979	Barbara Jordan	Sharon Walsh
1980	Hana Mandlikova	Wendy Turnbull
1981	Martina Navratilova	Chris Evert Lloyd
1982	Chris Evert Lloyd	Martina Navratilova
1983	Martina Navratilova	Kathy Jordan
1984	Chris Evert Lloyd	Helena Sukova
1985	Martina Navratilova	Chris Evert Lloyd
1987	Hana Mandlikova	Martina Navratilova
1988	Steffi Graf	Chris Evert
1989	Steffi Graf	Helena Sukova
1990	Steffi Graf	Mary Joe Fernandez
1991	Monica Seles	Jana Novotna
1992	Monica Seles	Mary Joe Fernandez
1993	Monica Seles	Steffi Graf
1994	Steffi Graf	Arantxa Sánchez Vicario
1995	Mary Pierce	Arantxa Sánchez Vicario
1996	Monica Seles	Anke Huber
1997	Martina Hingis	Mary Pierce
1998	Martina Hingis	Conchita Martínez
1999	Martina Hingis	Amélie Mauresmo
2000	Lindsay Davenport	Martina Hingis
2001	Jennifer Capriati	Martina Hingis
2002	Jennifer Capriati	Martina Hingis
2003	Serena Williams	Venus Williams
2004	Justine Henin-Hardenne	Kim Clijsters
2005	Serena Williams	Lindsay Davenport
2006	Amélie Mauresmo	Justine Henin-Hardenne
2007	Serena Williams	Maria Sharapova
2008	Maria Sharapova	Ana Ivanovic
2009	Serena Williams	Dinara Safina
2010	Serena Williams	Justine Henin
2011	Kim Clijsters	Li Na
2012	Victoria Azarenka	Maria Sharapova
2013	Victoria Azarenka	Li Na
2014	Li Na	Dominika Cibulkova
2015	Serena Williams	Maria Sharapova
2016	Angelique Kerber	Serena Williams
2017	Serena Williams	Venus Williams
2018	Caroline Wozniacki	Simona Halep

French Open (Roland Garros) Champions, 1968-2018

First contested 1891 for men, 1897 for women. Became an open championship in 1968.

Men's Singles

Year	Champion	Final opponent
1968	Ken Rosewall	Rod Laver
1969	Rod Laver	Ken Rosewall
1970	Jan Kodes	Zeljko Franulovic
1971	Jan Kodes	Ilie Nastase
1972	Andrés Gimeno	Patrick Proisy
1973	Ilie Nastase	Nikki Pilic
1974	Björn Borg	Manuel Orantes
1975	Björn Borg	Guillermo Vilas
1976	Adriano Panatta	Harold Solomon
1977	Guillermo Vilas	Brian Gottfried
1978	Björn Borg	Guillermo Vilas
1979	Björn Borg	Victor Pecci
1980	Björn Borg	Vitas Gerulaitis
1981	Björn Borg	Ivan Lendl
1982	Mats Wilander	Guillermo Vilas
1983	Yannick Noah	Mats Wilander
1984	Ivan Lendl	John McEnroe
1985	Mats Wilander	Ivan Lendl
1986	Ivan Lendl	Mikael Pernfors
1987	Ivan Lendl	Mats Wilander
1988	Mats Wilander	Henri Leconte
1989	Michael Chang	Stefan Edberg
1990	Andres Gomez	Andre Agassi
1991	Jim Courier	Andre Agassi
1992	Jim Courier	Petr Korda
1993	Sergi Bruguera	Jim Courier
1994	Sergi Bruguera	Alberto Berasategui
1995	Thomas Muster	Michael Chang
1996	Yevgeny Kafelnikov	Michael Stich
1997	Gustavo Kuerten	Sergi Bruguera
1998	Carlos Moya	Alex Corretja
1999	Andre Agassi	Andrei Medvedev
2000	Gustavo Kuerten	Magnus Norman
2001	Gustavo Kuerten	Alex Corretja
2002	Albert Costa	Juan Carlos Ferrero
2003	Juan Carlos Ferrero	Martin Verkerk
2004	Gaston Gaudio	Guillermo Coria
2005	Rafael Nadal	Mariano Puerta
2006	Rafael Nadal	Roger Federer
2007	Rafael Nadal	Roger Federer
2008	Rafael Nadal	Roger Federer
2009	Roger Federer	Robin Soderling
2010	Rafael Nadal	Robin Soderling
2011	Rafael Nadal	Roger Federer
2012	Rafael Nadal	Novak Djokovic
2013	Rafael Nadal	David Ferrer
2014	Rafael Nadal	Novak Djokovic
2015	Stan Wawrinka	Novak Djokovic
2016	Novak Djokovic	Andy Murray
2017	Rafael Nadal	Stan Wawrinka
2018	Rafael Nadal	Dominic Thiem

Women's Singles

Year	Champion	Final opponent
1968	Nancy Richey	Ann Jones
1969	Margaret Smith Court	Ann Jones
1970	Margaret Smith Court	Helga Niessen
1971	Evonne Goolagong	Helen Gourlay
1972	Billie Jean King	Evonne Goolagong
1973	Margaret Smith Court	Chris Evert
1974	Chris Evert	Olga Morozova
1975	Chris Evert	Martina Navratilova
1976	Sue Barker	Renata Tomanova
1977	Mima Jausovec	Florenta Mihai
1978	Virginia Ruzici	Mima Jausovec
1979	Chris Evert Lloyd	Wendy Turnbull
1980	Chris Evert Lloyd	Virginia Ruzici
1981	Hana Mandlikova	Sylvia Hanika

Year	Champion	Final opponent	Year	Champion	Final opponent
1982	Martina Navratilova	Andrea Jaeger	2001	Jennifer Capriati	Kim Clijsters
1983	Chris Evert Lloyd	Mima Jausovec	2002	Serena Williams	Venus Williams
1984	Martina Navratilova	Chris Evert Lloyd	2003	Justine Henin-Hardenne	Kim Clijsters
1985	Chris Evert Lloyd	Martina Navratilova	2004	Anastasia Myskina	Elena Dementieva
1986	Chris Evert Lloyd	Martina Navratilova	2005	Justine Henin-Hardenne	Mary Pierce
1987	Steffi Graf	Martina Navratilova	2006	Justine Henin-Hardenne	Svetlana Kuznetsova
1988	Steffi Graf	Natalia Zvereva	2007	Justine Henin	Ana Ivanovic
1989	Arantxa Sánchez Vicario	Steffi Graf	2008	Ana Ivanovic	Dinara Safina
1990	Monica Seles	Steffi Graf	2009	Svetlana Kuznetsova	Dinara Safina
1991	Monica Seles	Arantxa Sánchez Vicario	2010	Francesca Schiavone	Samantha Stosur
1992	Monica Seles	Steffi Graf	2011	Li Na	Francesca Schiavone
1993	Steffi Graf	Mary Joe Fernandez	2012	Maria Sharapova	Sara Errani
1994	Arantxa Sánchez Vicario	Mary Pierce	2013	Serena Williams	Maria Sharapova
1995	Steffi Graf	Arantxa Sánchez Vicario	2014	Maria Sharapova	Simona Halep
1996	Steffi Graf	Arantxa Sánchez Vicario	2015	Serena Williams	Lucie Safarova
1997	Iva Majoli	Martina Hingis	2016	Garbiñe Muguruza	Serena Williams
1998	Arantxa Sánchez Vicario	Monica Seles	2017	Jelena Ostapenko	Simona Halep
1999	Steffi Graf	Martina Hingis	2018	Simona Halep	Sloane Stephens
2000	Mary Pierce	Conchita Martínez			

Wimbledon Champions, 1925-2018

First contested 1877 for men, 1884 for women. Became an open championship in 1968. Not held 1940-45.

Men's Singles

Year	Champion	Final opponent
1998	Pete Sampras	Goran Ivanisevic
1999	Pete Sampras	Andre Agassi
2000	Pete Sampras	Patrick Rafter
2001	Goran Ivanisevic	Patrick Rafter
2002	Lleyton Hewitt	David Nalbandian
2003	Roger Federer	Mark Philippoussis
2004	Roger Federer	Andy Roddick
2005	Roger Federer	Andy Roddick
2006	Roger Federer	Rafael Nadal
2007	Roger Federer	Rafael Nadal
2008	Rafael Nadal	Roger Federer
2009	Roger Federer	Andy Roddick
2010	Rafael Nadal	Tomas Berdych
2011	Novak Djokovic	Rafael Nadal
2012	Roger Federer	Andy Murray
2013	Andy Murray	Novak Djokovic
2014	Novak Djokovic	Roger Federer
2015	Novak Djokovic	Roger Federer
2016	Andy Murray	Milos Raonic
2017	Roger Federer	Marin Cilic
2018	Novak Djokovic	Kevin Anderson

Year	Champion	Final opponent
1925	René Lacoste	Jean Borotra
1926	Jean Borotra	Howard Kinsey
1927	Henri Cochet	Jean Borotra
1928	René Lacoste	Henri Cochet
1929	Henri Cochet	Jean Borotra
1930	Bill Tilden	Wilmer Allison
1931	Sidney B. Wood	Francis X. Shields
1932	Ellsworth Vines	Henry Austin
1933	Jack Crawford	Ellsworth Vines
1934	Fred Perry	Jack Crawford
1935	Fred Perry	Gottfried von Cramm
1936	Fred Perry	Gottfried von Cramm
1937	Donald Budge	Gottfried von Cramm
1938	Donald Budge	Henry Austin
1939	Bobby Riggs	Elwood Cooke
1946	Yvon Petra	Geoff E. Brown
1947	Jack Kramer	Tom P. Brown
1948	Bob Falkenburg	John Bromwich
1949	Ted Schroeder	Jaroslav Drobny
1950	Budge Patty	Frank Sedgman
1951	Dick Savitt	Ken McGregor
1952	Frank Sedgman	Jaroslav Drobny
1953	Vic Seixas	Kurt Nielsen
1954	Jaroslav Drobny	Ken Rosewall
1955	Tony Trabert	Kurt Nielsen
1956	Lew Hoad	Ken Rosewall
1957	Lew Hoad	Ashley Cooper
1958	Ashley Cooper	Neale Fraser
1959	Alex Olmedo	Rod Laver
1960	Neale Fraser	Rod Laver
1961	Rod Laver	Chuck McKinley
1962	Rod Laver	Martin Mulligan
1963	Chuck McKinley	Fred Stolle
1964	Roy Emerson	Fred Stolle
1965	Roy Emerson	Fred Stolle
1966	Manuel Santana	Dennis Ralston
1967	John Newcombe	Wilhelm Bungert
1968	Rod Laver	Tony Roche
1969	Rod Laver	John Newcombe
1970	John Newcombe	Ken Rosewall
1971	John Newcombe	Stan Smith
1972	Stan Smith	Ilie Nastase
1973	Jan Kodes	Alex Metreveli
1974	Jimmy Connors	Ken Rosewall
1975	Arthur Ashe	Jimmy Connors
1976	Björn Borg	Ilie Nastase
1977	Björn Borg	Jimmy Connors
1978	Björn Borg	Jimmy Connors
1979	Björn Borg	Roscoe Tanner
1980	Björn Borg	John McEnroe
1981	John McEnroe	Björn Borg
1982	Jimmy Connors	John McEnroe
1983	John McEnroe	Chris Lewis
1984	John McEnroe	Jimmy Connors
1985	Boris Becker	Kevin Curren
1986	Boris Becker	Ivan Lendl
1987	Pat Cash	Ivan Lendl
1988	Stefan Edberg	Boris Becker
1989	Boris Becker	Stefan Edberg
1990	Stefan Edberg	Boris Becker
1991	Michael Stich	Boris Becker
1992	Andre Agassi	Goran Ivanisevic
1993	Pete Sampras	Jim Courier
1994	Pete Sampras	Goran Ivanisevic
1995	Pete Sampras	Boris Becker
1996	Richard Krajicek	MaliVai "Mai" Washington
1997	Pete Sampras	Cedric Pioline

Women's Singles

Year	Champion	Final opponent
1925	Suzanne Lenglen	Joan Fry
1926	Kathleen McKane Godfree	Lili de Alvarez
1927	Helen Wills	Lili de Alvarez
1928	Helen Wills	Lili de Alvarez
1929	Helen Wills	Helen H. Jacobs
1930	Helen Wills Moody	Elizabeth Ryan
1931	Cilly Aussem	Hilde Krahwinkel
1932	Helen Wills Moody	Helen H. Jacobs
1933	Helen Wills Moody	Dorothy Round
1934	Dorothy Round	Helen H. Jacobs
1935	Helen Wills Moody	Helen H. Jacobs
1936	Helen H. Jacobs	Hilde Krahwinkel Sperling
1937	Dorothy Round	Jadwiga Jedrzejowska
1938	Helen Wills Moody	Helen H. Jacobs
1939	Alice Marble	Kay Stammers
1946	Pauline Betz	Louise Brough
1947	Margaret Osborne	Doris Hart
1948	Louise Brough	Doris Hart
1949	Louise Brough	Margaret Osborne duPont
1950	Louise Brough	Margaret Osborne duPont
1951	Doris Hart	Shirley Fry
1952	Maureen Connolly	Louise Brough
1953	Maureen Connolly	Doris Hart
1954	Maureen Connolly	Louise Brough
1955	Louise Brough	Beverly Fleitz
1956	Shirley Fry	Angela Buxton
1957	Althea Gibson	Darlene Hard
1958	Althea Gibson	Angela Mortimer
1959	Maria Bueno	Darlene Hard
1960	Maria Bueno	Sandra Reynolds
1961	Angela Mortimer	Christine Truman
1962	Karen Hantze-Susman	Vera Sukova
1963	Margaret Smith	Billie Jean Moffitt
1964	Maria Bueno	Margaret Smith
1965	Margaret Smith	Maria Bueno
1966	Billie Jean King	Maria Bueno
1967	Billie Jean King	Ann Haydon Jones
1968	Billie Jean King	Judy Tegart
1969	Ann Haydon Jones	Billie Jean King
1970	Margaret Smith Court	Billie Jean King
1971	Evonne Goolagong	Margaret Smith Court
1972	Billie Jean King	Evonne Goolagong
1973	Billie Jean King	Chris Evert
1974	Chris Evert	Olga Morozova
1975	Billie Jean King	Evonne Goolagong Cawley

Year	Champion	Final opponent	Year	Champion	Final opponent
1976	Chris Evert	Evonne Goolagong Cawley	1997	Martina Hingis	Jana Novotna
1977	Virginia Wade	Betty Stove	1998	Jana Novotna	Nathalie Tauziat
1978	Martina Navratilova	Chris Evert	1999	Lindsay Davenport	Steffi Graf
1979	Martina Navratilova	Chris Evert Lloyd	2000	Venus Williams	Lindsay Davenport
1980	Evonne Goolagong Cawley	Chris Evert Lloyd	2001	Venus Williams	Justine Henin
1981	Chris Evert Lloyd	Hana Mandlikova	2002	Serena Williams	Venus Williams
1982	Martina Navratilova	Chris Evert Lloyd	2003	Serena Williams	Venus Williams
1983	Martina Navratilova	Andrea Jaeger	2004	Maria Sharapova	Serena Williams
1984	Martina Navratilova	Chris Evert Lloyd	2005	Venus Williams	Lindsay Davenport
1985	Martina Navratilova	Chris Evert Lloyd	2006	Amélie Mauresmo	Justine Henin-Hardenne
1986	Martina Navratilova	Hana Mandlikova	2007	Venus Williams	Marion Bartoli
1987	Martina Navratilova	Steffi Graf	2008	Venus Williams	Serena Williams
1988	Steffi Graf	Martina Navratilova	2009	Serena Williams	Venus Williams
1989	Steffi Graf	Martina Navratilova	2010	Serena Williams	Vera Zvonareva
1990	Martina Navratilova	Zina Garrison	2011	Petra Kvitova	Maria Sharapova
1991	Steffi Graf	Gabriela Sabatini	2012	Serena Williams	Agnieszka Radwanska
1992	Steffi Graf	Monica Seles	2013	Marion Bartoli	Sabine Lisicki
1993	Steffi Graf	Jana Novotna	2014	Petra Kvitova	Eugenie Bouchard
1994	Conchita Martínez	Martina Navratilova	2015	Serena Williams	Garbiñe Muguruza
1995	Steffi Graf	Arantxa Sánchez Vicario	2016	Serena Williams	Angelique Kerber
1996	Steffi Graf	Arantxa Sánchez Vicario	2017	Garbiñe Muguruza	Venus Williams
			2018	Angelique Kerber	Serena Williams

U.S. Open Champions, 1925-2018

First contested 1881 for men, 1887 for women. The former U.S. National Championship became an open championship in 1968.

Men's Singles

Year	Champion	Final opponent	Year	Champion	Final opponent
1925	Bill Tilden	William Johnston	1987	Ivan Lendl	Mats Wilander
1926	René Lacoste	Jean Borotra	1988	Mats Wilander	Ivan Lendl
1927	René Lacoste	Bill Tilden	1989	Boris Becker	Ivan Lendl
1928	Henri Cochet	Francis Hunter	1990	Pete Sampras	Andre Agassi
1929	Bill Tilden	Francis Hunter	1991	Stefan Edberg	Jim Courier
1930	John Doeg	Francis X. Shields	1992	Stefan Edberg	Pete Sampras
1931	Ellsworth Vines	George Lott	1993	Pete Sampras	Cedric Pioline
1932	Ellsworth Vines	Henri Cochet	1994	Andre Agassi	Michael Stich
1933	Fred Perry	John Crawford	1995	Pete Sampras	Andre Agassi
1934	Fred Perry	Wilmer Allison	1996	Pete Sampras	Michael Chang
1935	Wilmer Allison	Sidney Wood	1997	Patrick Rafter	Greg Rusedski
1936	Fred Perry	Don Budge	1998	Patrick Rafter	Mark Philippoussis
1937	Don Budge	Gottfried von Cramm	1999	Andre Agassi	Todd Martin
1938	Don Budge	C. Gene Mako	2000	Marat Safin	Pete Sampras
1939	Bobby Riggs	S. Welby Van Horn	2001	Lleyton Hewitt	Pete Sampras
1940	Don McNeill	Bobby Riggs	2002	Pete Sampras	Andre Agassi
1941	Bobby Riggs	F. L. Kovacs	2003	Andy Roddick	Juan Carlos Ferrero
1942	F. R. Schroeder Jr.	Frank Parker	2004	Roger Federer	Lleyton Hewitt
1943	Joseph Hunt	Jack Kramer	2005	Roger Federer	Andre Agassi
1944	Frank Parker	Bill Talbert	2006	Roger Federer	Andy Roddick
1945	Frank Parker	Bill Talbert	2007	Roger Federer	Novak Djokovic
1946	Jack Kramer	Tom Brown Jr.	2008	Roger Federer	Andy Murray
1947	Jack Kramer	Frank Parker	2009	Juan Martín del Potro	Roger Federer
1948	Pancho Gonzales	Eric Sturgess	2010	Rafael Nadal	Novak Djokovic
1949	Pancho Gonzales	F. R. Schroeder Jr.	2011	Novak Djokovic	Rafael Nadal
1950	Arthur Larsen	Herbert Flam	2012	Andy Murray	Novak Djokovic
1951	Frank Sedgman	E. Victor Seixas Jr.	2013	Rafael Nadal	Novak Djokovic
1952	Frank Sedgman	Gardnar Mulloy	2014	Marin Cilic	Kei Nishikori
1953	Tony Trabert	E. Victor Seixas Jr.	2015	Novak Djokovic	Roger Federer
1954	E. Victor Seixas Jr.	Rex Hartwig	2016	Stan Wawrinka	Novak Djokovic
1955	Tony Trabert	Ken Rosewall	2017	Rafael Nadal	Kevin Anderson
1956	Ken Rosewall	Lewis Hoad	2018	Novak Djokovic	Juan Martín del Potro
1957	Malcolm Anderson	Ashley Cooper			
1958	Ashley Cooper	Malcolm Anderson		**Women's Singles**	
1959	Neale A. Fraser	Alejandro Olmedo	Year	Champion	Final opponent
1960	Neale A. Fraser	Rod Laver	1925	Helen Willis	Kathleen McKane
1961	Roy Emerson	Rod Laver	1926	Molla B. Mallory	Elizabeth Ryan
1962	Rod Laver	Roy Emerson	1927	Helen Wills	Betty Nuthall
1963	Rafael Osuna	F. A. Froehling III	1928	Helen Wills	Helen H. Jacobs
1964	Roy Emerson	Fred Stolle	1929	Helen Wills	Phoebe Holcroft-Watson
1965	Manuel Santana	Cliff Drysdale	1930	Betty Nuthall	Anna McCune Harper
1966	Fred Stolle	John Newcombe	1931	Helen Wills Moody	E. B. Whittingstall
1967	John Newcombe	Clark Graebner	1932	Helen H. Jacobs	Carolin A. Babcock
1968	Arthur Ashe	Tom Okker	1933	Helen H. Jacobs	Helen Wills Moody
1969	Rod Laver	Tony Roche	1934	Helen H. Jacobs	Sarah H. Palfrey
1970	Ken Rosewall	Tony Roche	1935	Helen H. Jacobs	Sarah Palfrey Fabyan
1971	Stan Smith	Jan Kodes	1936	Alice Marble	Helen H. Jacobs
1972	Ilie Nastase	Arthur Ashe	1937	Anita Lizana	Jadwiga Jedrzejowska
1973	John Newcombe	Jan Kodes	1938	Alice Marble	Nancye Wynne
1974	Jimmy Connors	Ken Rosewall	1939	Alice Marble	Helen H. Jacobs
1975	Manuel Orantes	Jimmy Connors	1940	Alice Marble	Helen H. Jacobs
1976	Jimmy Connors	Björn Borg	1941	Sarah Palfrey Cooke	Pauline Betz
1977	Guillermo Vilas	Jimmy Connors	1942	Pauline Betz	Louise Brough
1978	Jimmy Connors	Björn Borg	1943	Pauline Betz	Louise Brough
1979	John McEnroe	Vitas Gerulaitis	1944	Pauline Betz	Margaret Osborne
1980	John McEnroe	Björn Borg	1945	Sarah Palfrey Cooke	Pauline Betz
1981	John McEnroe	Björn Borg	1946	Pauline Betz	Patricia Canning
1982	Jimmy Connors	Ivan Lendl	1947	Louise Brough	Margaret Osborne
1983	Jimmy Connors	Ivan Lendl	1948	Margaret Osborne duPont	Louise Brough
1984	John McEnroe	Ivan Lendl	1949	Margaret Osborne duPont	Doris Hart
1985	Ivan Lendl	John McEnroe	1950	Margaret Osborne duPont	Doris Hart
1986	Ivan Lendl	Miloslav Mecir	1951	Maureen Connolly	Shirley Fry
			1952	Maureen Connolly	Doris Hart

Year	Champion	Final opponent	Year	Champion	Final opponent
1953	Maureen Connolly	Doris Hart	1986	Martina Navratilova	Helena Sukova
1954	Doris Hart	Louise Brough	1987	Martina Navratilova	Steffi Graf
1955	Doris Hart	Patricia Ward	1988	Steffi Graf	Gabriela Sabatini
1956	Shirley Fry	Althea Gibson	1989	Steffi Graf	Martina Navratilova
1957	Althea Gibson	Louise Brough	1990	Gabriela Sabatini	Steffi Graf
1958	Althea Gibson	Darlene Hard	1991	Monica Seles	Martina Navratilova
1959	Maria Bueno	Christine Truman	1992	Monica Seles	Arantxa Sánchez Vicario
1960	Darlene Hard	Maria Bueno	1993	Steffi Graf	Helena Sukova
1961	Darlene Hard	Ann Haydon	1994	Arantxa Sánchez Vicario	Steffi Graf
1962	Margaret Smith	Darlene Hard	1995	Steffi Graf	Monica Seles
1963	Maria Bueno	Margaret Smith	1996	Steffi Graf	Monica Seles
1964	Maria Bueno	Carole Caldwell Graebner	1997	Martina Hingis	Venus Williams
1965	Margaret Smith	Billie Jean Moffitt	1998	Lindsay Davenport	Martina Hingis
1966	Maria Bueno	Nancy Richey	1999	Serena Williams	Martina Hingis
1967	Billie Jean King	Ann Haydon Jones	2000	Venus Williams	Lindsay Davenport
1968	Virginia Wade	Billie Jean King	2001	Venus Williams	Serena Williams
1969	Margaret Smith Court	Nancy Richey	2002	Serena Williams	Venus Williams
1970	Margaret Smith Court	Rosemary Casals	2003	Justine Henin-Hardenne	Kim Clijsters
1971	Billie Jean King	Rosemary Casals	2004	Svetlana Kuznetsova	Elena Dementieva
1972	Billie Jean King	Kerry Melville	2005	Kim Clijsters	Mary Pierce
1973	Margaret Smith Court	Evonne Goolagong	2006	Maria Sharapova	Justine Henin-Hardenne
1974	Billie Jean King	Evonne Goolagong	2007	Justine Henin	Svetlana Kuznetsova
1975	Chris Evert	Evonne Goolagong Cawley	2008	Serena Williams	Jelena Jankovic
1976	Chris Evert	Evonne Goolagong Cawley	2009	Kim Clijsters	Caroline Wozniacki
1977	Chris Evert	Wendy Turnbull	2010	Kim Clijsters	Vera Zvonareva
1978	Chris Evert	Pam Shriver	2011	Samantha Stosur	Serena Williams
1979	Tracy Austin	Chris Evert Lloyd	2012	Serena Williams	Victoria Azarenka
1980	Chris Evert Lloyd	Hana Mandlikova	2013	Serena Williams	Victoria Azarenka
1981	Tracy Austin	Martina Navratilova	2014	Serena Williams	Caroline Wozniacki
1982	Chris Evert Lloyd	Hana Mandlikova	2015	Flavia Pennetta	Roberta Vinci
1983	Martina Navratilova	Chris Evert Lloyd	2016	Angelique Kerber	Karolina Pliskova
1984	Martina Navratilova	Chris Evert Lloyd	2017	Sloane Stephens	Madison Keys
1985	Hana Mandlikova	Martina Navratilova	2018	Naomi Osaka	Serena Williams

Davis Cup, 1950-2017

The Davis Cup began in 1900 as a competition between the U.S. and Great Britain and later expanded to include other countries.

Year	Result	Year	Result	Year	Result
1950	Australia 4, U.S. 1	1973	Australia 5, U.S. 0	1996	France 3, Sweden 2
1951	Australia 3, U.S. 2	1974	South Africa (default by India)	1997	Sweden 5, U.S. 0
1952	Australia 4, U.S. 1	1975	Sweden 3, Czechoslovakia 2	1998	Sweden 4, Italy 1
1953	Australia 3, U.S. 2	1976	Italy 4, Chile 1	1999	Australia 3, France 2
1954	U.S. 3, Australia 2	1977	Australia 3, Italy 1	2000	Spain 3, Australia 1
1955	Australia 5, U.S. 0	1978	U.S. 4, Great Britain 1	2001	France 3, Australia 2
1956	Australia 5, U.S. 0	1979	U.S. 5, Italy 0	2002	Russia 3, France 2
1957	Australia 3, U.S. 2	1980	Czechoslovakia 4, Italy 1	2003	Australia 3, Spain 1
1958	U.S. 3, Australia 2	1981	U.S. 3, Argentina 1	2004	Spain 3, U.S. 2
1959	Australia 3, U.S. 2	1982	U.S. 4, France, 1	2005	Croatia 3, Slovakia 2
1960	Australia 4, Italy 1	1983	Australia 3, Sweden 2	2006	Russia 3, Argentina 2
1961	Australia 5, Italy 0	1984	Sweden 4, U.S. 1	2007	U.S. 4, Russia 1
1962	Australia 5, Mexico 0	1985	Sweden 3, W. Germany 2	2008	Spain 3, Argentina 1
1963	U.S. 3, Australia 2	1986	Australia 3, Sweden 2	2009	Spain 5, Czech Republic 0
1964	Australia 3, U.S. 2	1987	Sweden 5, India 0	2010	Serbia 3, France 2
1965	Australia 4, Spain 1	1988	W. Germany 4, Sweden 1	2011	Spain 3, Argentina 1
1966	Australia 4, India 1	1989	W. Germany 3, Sweden 2	2012	Czech Republic 3, Spain 2
1967	Australia 4, Spain 1	1990	U.S. 3, Australia 2	2013	Czech Republic 3, Serbia 2
1968	U.S. 4, Australia 1	1991	France 3, U.S. 1	2014	Switzerland 3, France 1
1969	U.S. 5, Romania 0	1992	U.S. 3, Switzerland 1	2015	Great Britain 3, Belgium 1
1970	U.S. 5, W. Germany 0	1993	Germany 4, Australia 1	2016	Argentina 3, Croatia 2
1971	U.S. 3, Romania 2	1994	Sweden 4, Russia 1	2017	France 3, Belgium 2
1972	U.S. 3, Romania 2	1995	U.S. 3, Russia 2		

Note: The challenge round format, which guaranteed the previous year's winner a spot in the finals at home, was eliminated in 1972.

All-Time Grand Slam Singles Titles Leaders

Men	Australian Open	French Open[1]	Wimbledon	U.S. Open	Total
Roger Federer*	2004, '06-'07, '10, '17-'18	2009	2003-07, '09, '12, '17	2004-08	20
Rafael Nadal*	2009	2005-08, '10-'14, '17-'18	2008, '10	2010, '13, '17	17
Novak Djokovic*	2008, '11-'13, '15-'16	2016	2011, '14-'15, '18	2011, '15, '18	14
Pete Sampras	1994, '97	—	1993-95, 1997-2000	1990, '93, '95-'96, 2002	14
Roy Emerson	1961, '63-'67	1963, '67	1964-65	1961, '64	12
Björn Borg	—	1974-75, '78-'81	1976-80	—	11
Rod Laver	1960, '62, '69	1962, '69	1961-62, '68-'69	1962, '69	11
Bill Tilden	—	—	1920-21, '30	1920-25, '29	10
Andre Agassi	1995, 2000-01, '03	1999	1992	1994, '99	8
Jimmy Connors	1974	—	1974, '82	1974, '76, '78, '82-'83	8
Ivan Lendl	1989-90	1984, '86-'87	—	1985-87	8
Fred Perry	1934	1935	1934-36	1933-34, '36	8
Ken Rosewall	1953, '55, '71-'72	1953, '68	—	1956, '70	8

Women	Australian Open	French Open[1]	Wimbledon	U.S. Open	Total
Margaret Smith Court	1960-66, '69-'71, '73	1962, '64, '69-'70, '73	1963, '65, '70	1962, '65, '69-'70, '73	24
Serena Williams*	2003, '05, '07, '09-'10, '15, '17	2002, '13, '15	2002-03, '09-'10, '12, '15-'16	1999, 2002, '08, '12-'14	23
Steffi Graf	1988-90, '94	1987-88, '93, '95-'96, '99	1988-89, '91-'93, '95-'96	1988-89, '93, '95-'96	22
Helen Wills Moody	—	1928-30, '32	1927-30, '32-'33, '35, '38	1923-25, '27-'29, '31	19
Chris Evert	1982, '84	1974-75, '79-'80, '83, '85-'86	1974, '76, '81	1975-78, '80, '82	18
Martina Navratilova	1981, '83, '85	1982, '84	1978-79, '82-'87, '90	1983-84, '86-'87	18
Billie Jean King	1968	1972	1966-68, '72-'73, '75	1967, '71-'72, '74	12
Suzanne Lenglen	—	1920-23, '25-'26	1919-23, '25	—	12
Maureen Connolly	1953	1953-54	1952-54	1951-53	9
Monica Seles	1991-93, '96	1990-92	—	1991-92	9

* = Player active in 2018. (1) Prior to 1925, French Open entry was limited to members of French clubs.

AUTO RACING

Indianapolis 500 Winners, 1911-2018

At Indianapolis Motor Speedway in Indianapolis, IN. Not held 1917-18, 1942-45. * = Race record.

Year	Driver(s), car[1]	Avg. mph	Year	Driver(s), car[1]	Avg. mph
1911	Ray Harroun, Marmon	74.602	1968	Bobby Unser, Eagle-Offy	152.882
1912	Joe Dawson, National	78.719	1969	Mario Andretti, Hawk-Ford	156.867
1913	Jules Goux, Peugeot	75.933	1970	Al Unser, P.J. Colt-Ford	155.749
1914	René Thomas, Delage	82.474	1971	Al Unser, P.J. Colt-Ford	157.735
1915	Ralph DePalma, Mercedes	89.840	1972	Mark Donohue, McLaren-Offy	162.962
1916	Dario Resta, Peugeot	84.001	1973	Gordon Johncock, Eagle-Offy	159.036
1919	Howdy Wilcox, Peugeot	88.050	1974	Johnny Rutherford, McLaren-Offy	158.589
1920	Gaston Chevrolet, Frontenac	88.618	1975	Bobby Unser, Eagle-Offy	149.213
1921	Tommy Milton, Frontenac	89.621	1976	Johnny Rutherford, McLaren-Offy	148.725
1922	Jimmy Murphy, Duesenberg-Miller	94.484	1977	A. J. Foyt, Coyote-Foyt	161.331
1923	Tommy Milton, Miller	90.954	1978	Al Unser, Lola-Cosworth	161.363
1924	L. L. Corum/Joe Boyer, Duesenberg	98.234	1979	Rick Mears, Penske-Cosworth	158.899
1925	Peter DePaolo, Duesenberg	101.127	1980	Johnny Rutherford, Chaparral-Cosworth	142.862
1926	Frank Lockhart, Miller	95.904	1981	Bobby Unser, Penske-Cosworth	139.184
1927	George Souders, Duesenberg	97.545	1982	Gordon Johncock, Wildcat-Cosworth	162.029
1928	Louis Meyer, Miller	99.482	1983	Tom Sneva, March-Cosworth	162.117
1929	Ray Keech, Miller	97.585	1984	Rick Mears, March-Cosworth	163.612
1930	Billy Arnold, Summers-Miller	100.448	1985	Danny Sullivan, March-Cosworth	152.982
1931	Louis Schneider, Stevens-Miller	96.629	1986	Bobby Rahal, March-Cosworth	170.722
1932	Fred Frame, Wetteroth-Miller	104.144	1987	Al Unser, March-Cosworth	162.175
1933	Louis Meyer, Miller	104.162	1988	Rick Mears, Penske-Chevy Indy V8	144.809
1934	Bill Cummings, Miller	104.863	1989	Emerson Fittipaldi, Penske-Chevy Indy V8	167.581
1935	Kelly Petillo, Wetteroth-Offy	106.240	1990	Arie Luyendyk, Lola-Chevy Indy V8	185.981
1936	Louis Meyer, Stevens-Miller	109.069	1991	Rick Mears, Penske-Chevy Indy V8	176.457
1937	Wilbur Shaw, Shaw-Offy	113.580	1992	Al Unser Jr., Galmer-Chevy Indy V8A	134.477
1938	Floyd Roberts, Wetteroth-Miller	117.200	1993	Emerson Fittipaldi, Penske-Chevy Indy V8C	157.207
1939	Wilbur Shaw, Maserati	115.035	1994	Al Unser Jr., Penske-Mercedes Benz	160.872
1940	Wilbur Shaw, Maserati	114.277	1995	Jacques Villeneuve, Reynard-Ford Cosworth XB	153.616
1941	Floyd Davis/Mauri Rose, Wetteroth-Offy	115.117	1996	Buddy Lazier, Reynard-Ford Cosworth XB	147.956
1946	George Robson, Adams-Sparks	114.820	1997	Arie Luyendyk, G Force-Aurora	145.827
1947	Mauri Rose, Deidt-Offy	116.338	1998	Eddie Cheever Jr., Dallara-Aurora	145.155
1948	Mauri Rose, Deidt-Offy	119.814	1999	Kenny Brack, Dallara-Aurora	153.176
1949	Bill Holland, Deidt-Offy	121.327	2000	Juan Pablo Montoya, G Force-Oldsmobile	167.607
1950	Johnnie Parsons, Kurtis-Offy	124.002	2001	Helio Castroneves, Dallara-Oldsmobile	141.574
1951	Lee Wallard, Kurtis-Offy	126.244	2002	Helio Castroneves, Dallara-Chevrolet	166.499
1952	Troy Ruttman, Kuzma-Offy	128.922	2003	Gil de Ferran, G Force-Toyota	156.291
1953	Bill Vukovich, KK500A-Offy	127.740	2004	Buddy Rice, G Force-Honda	138.518
1954	Bill Vukovich, KK500A-Offy	130.840	2005	Dan Wheldon, Dallara-Honda	157.603
1955	Bob Sweikert, KK500D-Offy	128.209	2006	Sam Hornish Jr., Dallara-Honda	157.085
1956	Pat Flaherty, Watson-Offy	128.490	2007	Dario Franchitti, Dallara-Honda	151.774
1957	Sam Hanks, Salih-Offy	135.601	2008	Scott Dixon, Dallara-Honda	143.567
1958	Jimmy Bryan, Salih-Offy	133.791	2009	Helio Castroneves, Dallara-Honda	150.318
1959	Rodger Ward, Watson-Offy	135.857	2010	Dario Franchitti, Dallara-Honda	161.623
1960	Jim Rathmann, Watson-Offy	138.767	2011	Dan Wheldon, Dallara-Honda	170.265
1961	A. J. Foyt, Trevis-Offy	139.130	2012	Dario Franchitti, Dallara-Honda	167.734
1962	Rodger Ward, Watson-Offy	140.293	2013	Tony Kanaan, Dallara-Chevrolet	187.433*
1963	Parnelli Jones, Watson-Offy	143.137	2014	Ryan Hunter-Reay, Dallara-Honda	186.563
1964	A. J. Foyt, Watson-Offy	147.350	2015	Juan Pablo Montoya, Dallara-Chevrolet	161.341
1965	Jim Clark, Lotus-Ford	150.686	2016	Alexander Rossi, Dallara-Honda	166.634
1966	Graham Hill, Lola-Ford	144.317	2017	Takuma Sato, Dallara-Honda	155.395
1967	A. J. Foyt, Coyote-Ford	151.207	2018	Will Power, Dallara-Chevrolet	166.935

Note: The race was less than 500 mi in the following years: 1916 (300 mi), 1926 (400 mi), 1950 (345 mi), 1973 (332.5 mi), 1975 (435 mi), 1976 (255 mi), 2004 (450 mi), 2007 (415 mi). (1) Chassis-engine.

IndyCar Series Champions, 1996-2018

A breakaway group of Championship Auto Racing Teams (CART) drivers began the Indy Racing League (IRL) in 1994; it awarded its first championship in 1996. Known as the IndyCar Series in 2003-11 and as IndyCar from 2011 on. Merged with Champ Car World Series, 2008, under the IndyCar name.

Year	Driver	Year	Driver	Year	Driver	Year	Driver	Year	Driver
1996	Scott Sharp; Buzz Calkins (tie)	2000	Buddy Lazier	2005	Dan Wheldon	2010	Dario Franchitti	2015	Scott Dixon
1997	Tony Stewart	2001	Sam Hornish Jr.	2006	Sam Hornish Jr.	2011	Dario Franchitti	2016	Simon Pagenaud
1998	Kenny Brack	2002	Sam Hornish Jr.	2007	Dario Franchitti	2012	Ryan Hunter-Reay	2017	Josef Newgarden
1999	Greg Ray	2003	Scott Dixon	2008	Scott Dixon	2013	Scott Dixon	2018	Scott Dixon
		2004	Tony Kanaan	2009	Dario Franchitti	2014	Will Power		

Champ Car World Series Winners, 1959-2007

Known as U.S. Auto Club, 1959-78; Championship Auto Racing Teams (CART), 1979-2003; Champ Car World Series, 2004-07. The Vanderbilt Cup became the series championship trophy in 2000. Merged with Indy Racing League (now IndyCar) in 2008.

Year	Driver	Year	Driver	Year	Driver	Year	Driver	Year	Driver
1959	Rodger Ward	1969	Mario Andretti	1979	Rick Mears	1989	Emerson Fittipaldi	1999	Juan Montoya
1960	A. J. Foyt	1970	Al Unser	1980	Johnny Rutherford	1990	Al Unser Jr.	2000	Gil de Ferran
1961	A. J. Foyt	1971	Joe Leonard	1981	Rick Mears	1991	Michael Andretti	2001	Gil de Ferran
1962	Rodger Ward	1972	Joe Leonard	1982	Rick Mears	1992	Bobby Rahal	2002	Cristiano da Matta
1963	A. J. Foyt	1973	Roger McCluskey	1983	Al Unser	1993	Nigel Mansell	2003	Paul Tracy
1964	A. J. Foyt	1974	Bobby Unser	1984	Mario Andretti	1994	Al Unser Jr.	2004	Sébastien Bourdais
1965	Mario Andretti	1975	A. J. Foyt	1985	Al Unser	1995	Jacques Villeneuve	2005	Sébastien Bourdais
1966	Mario Andretti	1976	Gordon Johncock	1986	Bobby Rahal	1996	Jimmy Vasser	2006	Sébastien Bourdais
1967	A. J. Foyt	1977	Tom Sneva	1987	Bobby Rahal	1997	Alex Zanardi	2007	Sébastien Bourdais
1968	Bobby Unser	1978	Tom Sneva	1988	Danny Sullivan	1998	Alex Zanardi		

NASCAR Cup Series Champions, 1949-2017

Known as Strictly Stock, 1949; Grand National, 1950-70; Winston Cup, 1971-2003; Sprint Cup, 2004-16; Monster Energy NASCAR Cup, 2017.

Year	Driver	Year	Driver	Year	Driver	Year	Driver	Year	Driver
1949	Red Byron	1963	Joe Weatherly	1977	Cale Yarborough	1991	Dale Earnhardt	2005	Tony Stewart
1950	Bill Rexford	1964	Richard Petty	1978	Cale Yarborough	1992	Alan Kulwicki	2006	Jimmie Johnson
1951	Herb Thomas	1965	Ned Jarrett	1979	Richard Petty	1993	Dale Earnhardt	2007	Jimmie Johnson
1952	Tim Flock	1966	David Pearson	1980	Dale Earnhardt	1994	Dale Earnhardt	2008	Jimmie Johnson
1953	Herb Thomas	1967	Richard Petty	1981	Darrell Waltrip	1995	Jeff Gordon	2009	Jimmie Johnson
1954	Lee Petty	1968	David Pearson	1982	Darrell Waltrip	1996	Terry Labonte	2010	Jimmie Johnson
1955	Tim Flock	1969	David Pearson	1983	Bobby Allison	1997	Jeff Gordon	2011	Tony Stewart
1956	Buck Baker	1970	Bobby Isaac	1984	Terry Labonte	1998	Jeff Gordon	2012	Brad Keselowski
1957	Buck Baker	1971	Richard Petty	1985	Darrell Waltrip	1999	Dale Jarrett	2013	Jimmie Johnson
1958	Lee Petty	1972	Richard Petty	1986	Dale Earnhardt	2000	Bobby Labonte	2014	Kevin Harvick
1959	Lee Petty	1973	Benny Parsons	1987	Dale Earnhardt	2001	Jeff Gordon	2015	Kyle Busch
1960	Rex White	1974	Richard Petty	1988	Bill Elliott	2002	Tony Stewart	2016	Jimmie Johnson
1961	Ned Jarrett	1975	Richard Petty	1989	Rusty Wallace	2003	Matt Kenseth	2017	Martin Truex Jr.
1962	Joe Weatherly	1976	Cale Yarborough	1990	Dale Earnhardt	2004	Kurt Busch		

NASCAR Cup Series Rookie of the Year, 1958-2017

Year	Driver	Year	Driver	Year	Driver	Year	Driver	Year	Driver
1958	Shorty Rollins	1970	Bill Dennis	1982	Geoff Bodine	1994	Jeff Burton	2006	Denny Hamlin
1959	Richard Petty	1971	Walter Ballard	1983	Sterling Marlin	1995	Ricky Craven	2007	Juan Pablo Montoya
1960	David Pearson	1972	Larry Smith	1984	Rusty Wallace	1996	Johnny Benson	2008	Regan Smith
1961	Woodie Wilson	1973	Lennie Pond	1985	Ken Schrader	1997	Mike Skinner	2009	Joey Logano
1962	Tom Cox	1974	Earl Ross	1986	Alan Kulwicki	1998	Kenny Irwin	2010	Kevin Conway
1963	Billy Wade	1975	Bruce Hill	1987	Davey Allison	1999	Tony Stewart	2011	Andy Lally
1964	Doug Cooper	1976	Skip Manning	1988	Ken Bouchard	2000	Matt Kenseth	2012	Stephen Leicht
1965	Sam McQuagg	1977	Ricky Rudd	1989	Dick Trickle	2001	Kevin Harvick	2013	Ricky Stenhouse Jr.
1966	James Hylton	1978	Ronnie Thomas	1990	Rob Moroso	2002	Ryan Newman	2014	Kyle Larson
1967	Donnie Allison	1979	Dale Earnhardt	1991	Bobby Hamilton	2003	Jamie McMurray	2015	Brett Moffitt
1968	Pete Hamilton	1980	Jody Ridley	1992	Jimmy Hensley	2004	Kasey Kahne	2016	Chase Elliott
1969	Dick Brooks	1981	Ron Bouchard	1993	Jeff Gordon	2005	Kyle Busch	2017	Erik Jones

Daytona 500 Winners, 1959-2018

At Daytona International Speedway in Daytona Beach, FL.

Year	Driver, car	Avg. mph	Year	Driver, car	Avg. mph	Year	Driver, car	Avg. mph
1959	Lee Petty, Oldsmobile	135.521	1980	Buddy Baker, Oldsmobile	177.602	2001	Michael Waltrip, Chevrolet	161.783
1960	Junior Johnson, Chevrolet	124.740	1981	Richard Petty, Buick	169.651	2002	Ward Burton, Dodge	142.971
1961	Marvin Panch, Pontiac	149.601	1982	Bobby Allison, Buick	153.991	2003	Michael Waltrip, Chevrolet	133.870
1962	Fireball Roberts, Pontiac	152.529	1983	Cale Yarborough, Pontiac	155.979	2004	Dale Earnhardt Jr.,	
1963	Tiny Lund, Ford	151.566	1984	Cale Yarborough,			Chevrolet	156.345
1964	Richard Petty, Plymouth	154.334		Chevrolet	150.994	2005	Jeff Gordon, Chevrolet	135.173
1965	Fred Lorenzen, Ford	141.539	1985	Bill Elliott, Ford	172.265	2006	Jimmie Johnson, Chevrolet	142.667
1966	Richard Petty, Plymouth	160.627	1986	Geoff Bodine, Chevrolet	148.124	2007	Kevin Harvick, Chevrolet	149.335
1967	Mario Andretti, Ford	146.926	1987	Bill Elliott, Ford	176.263	2008	Ryan Newman, Dodge	152.672
1968	Cale Yarborough, Mercury	143.251	1988	Bobby Allison, Buick	137.531	2009	Matt Kenseth, Ford	132.816
1969	LeeRoy Yarbrough, Ford	157.950	1989	Darrell Waltrip, Chevrolet	148.466	2010	Jamie McMurray,	
1970	Pete Hamilton, Plymouth	149.601	1990	Derrike Cope, Chevrolet	165.761		Chevrolet	137.284
1971	Richard Petty, Plymouth	144.462	1991	Ernie Irvan, Chevrolet	148.148	2011	Trevor Bayne, Ford	130.326
1972	A. J. Foyt, Mercury	161.550	1992	Davey Allison, Ford	160.256	2012	Matt Kenseth, Ford	140.256
1973	Richard Petty, Dodge	157.205	1993	Dale Jarrett, Chevrolet	154.972	2013	Jimmie Johnson,	
1974	Richard Petty, Dodge	140.894	1994	Sterling Marlin, Chevrolet	156.931		Chevrolet	159.250
1975	Benny Parsons, Chevrolet	153.649	1995	Sterling Marlin, Chevrolet	141.710	2014	Dale Earnhardt Jr.,	
1976	David Pearson, Mercury	152.181	1996	Dale Jarrett, Ford	154.308		Chevrolet	145.290
1977	Cale Yarborough,		1997	Jeff Gordon, Chevrolet	148.295	2015	Joey Logano, Ford	161.939
	Chevrolet	153.218	1998	Dale Earnhardt, Chevrolet	172.712	2016	Denny Hamlin, Toyota	157.549
1978	Bobby Allison, Ford	159.730	1999	Jeff Gordon, Chevrolet	161.551	2017	Kurt Busch, Ford	143.187
1979	Richard Petty, Oldsmobile	143.977	2000	Dale Jarrett, Ford	155.669	2018	Austin Dillon, Chevrolet	150.545

Note: The race was less than 500 mi in the following years: 1965 (332.5 mi), 1966 (495 mi), 1974 (450 mi), 2003 (272.5 mi), 2009 (380 mi).

Coca-Cola 600 Winners, 1960-2018

At Charlotte Motor Speedway in Concord, NC. Known as the World 600, 1960-85. * = Rain-shortened.

Year	Driver, car	Avg. mph	Year	Driver, car	Avg. mph	Year	Driver, car	Avg. mph
1960	Joe Lee Johnson,		1979	Darrell Waltrip, Chevrolet	136.674	1999	Jeff Burton, Ford	151.367
	Chevrolet	107.735	1980	Benny Parsons, Chevrolet	119.265	2000	Matt Kenseth, Ford	142.640
1961	David Pearson, Pontiac	111.633	1981	Bobby Allison, Buick	129.326	2001	Jeff Burton, Ford	138.107
1962	Nelson Stacy, Ford	125.552	1982	Neil Bonnett, Ford	130.058	2002	Mark Martin, Ford	137.729
1963	Fred Lorenzen, Ford	132.418	1983	Neil Bonnett, Chevrolet	140.707	2003	Jimmie Johnson, Chevrolet	126.198*
1964	Jim Paschal, Plymouth	125.772	1984	Bobby Allison, Buick	129.233	2004	Jimmie Johnson, Chevrolet	142.763
1965	Fred Lorenzen, Ford	121.722	1985	Darrell Waltrip, Chevrolet	141.807	2005	Jimmie Johnson, Chevrolet	114.698
1966	Marvin Panch, Plymouth	135.042	1986	Dale Earnhardt, Chevrolet	140.406	2006	Kasey Kahne, Dodge	128.840
1967	Jim Paschal, Plymouth	135.832	1987	Kyle Petty, Ford	131.483	2007	Casey Mears, Chevrolet	130.222
1968	Buddy Baker, Dodge	104.207*	1988	Darrell Waltrip, Chevrolet	124.460	2008	Kasey Kahne, Dodge	135.772
1969	LeeRoy Yarbrough,		1989	Darrell Waltrip, Chevrolet	144.077	2009	David Reutimann, Toyota	120.899*
	Mercury	134.361	1990	Rusty Wallace, Pontiac	137.650	2010	Kurt Busch, Dodge	144.966
1970	Donnie Allison, Ford	129.680	1991	Davey Allison, Ford	138.951	2011	Kevin Harvick, Chevrolet	132.414
1971	Bobby Allison, Mercury	140.422	1992	Dale Earnhardt, Chevrolet	132.980	2012	Kasey Kahne, Chevrolet	155.687
1972	Buddy Baker, Dodge	142.255	1993	Dale Earnhardt, Chevrolet	145.504	2013	Kevin Harvick, Chevrolet	130.521
1973	Buddy Baker, Dodge	134.890	1994	Jeff Gordon, Chevrolet	139.445	2014	Jimmie Johnson, Chevrolet	145.484
1974	David Pearson, Mercury	135.720	1995	Bobby Labonte, Chevrolet	151.952	2015	Carl Edwards, Toyota	147.803
1975	Richard Petty, Dodge	145.327	1996	Dale Jarrett, Ford	147.581	2016	Martin Truex Jr., Toyota	160.655
1976	David Pearson, Mercury	137.352	1997	Jeff Gordon, Chevrolet	136.745*	2017	Austin Dillon, Chevrolet	138.800
1977	Richard Petty, Dodge	137.676	1998	Jeff Gordon, Chevrolet	136.424	2018	Kyle Busch, Toyota	136.692
1978	Darrell Waltrip, Chevrolet	138.355						

Brickyard 400 Winners, 1994-2018

At Indianapolis Motor Speedway in Indianapolis, IN.

Year	Driver, car	Avg. mph	Year	Driver, car	Avg. mph	Year	Driver, car	Avg. mph
1994	Jeff Gordon, Chevrolet	131.977	2003	Kevin Harvick, Chevrolet	134.554	2011	Paul Menard, Chevrolet	140.762
1995	Dale Earnhardt, Chevrolet	155.206	2004	Jeff Gordon, Chevrolet	115.037	2012	Jimmie Johnson, Chevrolet	137.680
1996	Dale Jarrett, Ford	139.508	2005	Tony Stewart, Chevrolet	118.782	2013	Ryan Newman, Chevrolet	153.485
1997	Ricky Rudd, Ford	130.814	2006	Jimmie Johnson, Chevrolet	137.182	2014	Jeff Gordon, Chevrolet	150.297
1998	Jeff Gordon, Chevrolet	126.772	2007	Tony Stewart, Chevrolet	117.379	2015	Kyle Busch, Toyota	131.656
1999	Dale Jarrett, Ford	148.194	2008	Jimmie Johnson, Chevrolet	115.117	2016	Kyle Busch, Toyota	128.940
2000	Bobby Labonte, Pontiac	155.912	2009	Jimmie Johnson, Chevrolet	145.882	2017	Kasey Kahne, Chevrolet	114.384
2001	Jeff Gordon, Chevrolet	130.790	2010	Jamie McMurray, Chevrolet	136.054	2018	Brad Keselowski, Ford	128.629
2002	Bill Elliott, Dodge	125.033						

Bass Pro Shops NRA Night Race Winners, 1961-2018

At Bristol Motor Speedway in Bristol, TN. Known as the Volunteer 500, 1961-75, '78-'79; Volunteer 400, 1976-77; Busch 500, 1980-90; Bud 500, 1991-93; Goody's 500, 1994-99; goracing.com 500, 2000; Sharpie 500, 2001-09; Irwin Tools, 2010-15. * = Rain-shortened.

Year	Driver, car	Avg. mph	Year	Driver, car	Avg. mph	Year	Driver, car	Avg. mph
1961	Jack Smith, Pontiac	68.373	1980	Cale Yarborough, Chevrolet	86.973	2000	Rusty Wallace, Ford	85.394
1962	Bobby Johns, Pontiac	73.320	1981	Darrell Waltrip, Buick	84.723	2001	Tony Stewart, Pontiac	85.106
1963	Fred Lorenzen, Ford	74.844	1982	Darrell Waltrip, Buick	94.318	2002	Jeff Gordon, Chevrolet	77.097
1964	Fred Lorenzen, Ford	78.044	1983	Darrell Waltrip, Chevrolet	89.430*	2003	Kurt Busch, Ford	77.421
1965	Ned Jarrett, Ford	61.826	1984	Terry Labonte, Chevrolet	85.365	2004	Dale Earnhardt Jr.,	
1966	Paul Goldsmith, Plymouth	77.963	1985	Dale Earnhardt, Chevrolet	81.388		Chevrolet	88.538
1967	Richard Petty, Plymouth	78.705	1986	Darrell Waltrip, Chevrolet	86.934	2005	Matt Kenseth, Ford	84.678
1968	David Pearson, Ford	76.310	1987	Dale Earnhardt, Chevrolet	90.373	2006	Matt Kenseth, Ford	90.025
1969	David Pearson, Ford	79.737	1988	Dale Earnhardt, Chevrolet	78.775	2007	Carl Edwards, Ford	89.006
1970	Bobby Allison, Dodge	84.880	1989	Darrell Waltrip, Chevrolet	85.554	2008	Carl Edwards, Ford	91.581
1971	Charlie Glotzbach,		1990	Ernie Irvan, Chevrolet	91.782	2009	Kyle Busch, Toyota	84.820
	Chevrolet	101.074	1991	Alan Kulwicki, Ford	82.028	2010	Kyle Busch, Toyota	99.071
1972	Bobby Allison, Chevrolet	92.735	1992	Darrell Waltrip, Chevrolet	91.198	2011	Brad Keselowski, Dodge	96.753
1973	Benny Parsons, Chevrolet	91.342	1993	Mark Martin, Ford	88.172	2012	Denny Hamlin, Toyota	84.402
1974	Cale Yarborough, Chevrolet	75.430	1994	Rusty Wallace, Ford	91.363	2013	Matt Kenseth, Toyota	90.279
1975	Richard Petty, Dodge	97.016	1995	Terry Labonte, Chevrolet	81.979	2014	Joey Logano, Ford	92.965
1976	Cale Yarborough, Chevrolet	99.175	1996	Rusty Wallace, Ford	91.267	2015	Joey Logano, Ford	96.890
1977	Cale Yarborough, Chevrolet	79.726	1997	Dale Jarrett, Ford	80.013	2016	Kevin Harvick, Chevrolet	77.968
1978	Cale Yarborough, Olds.	88.628	1998	Mark Martin, Ford	86.949	2017	Kyle Busch, Toyota	95.969
1979	Darrell Waltrip, Chevrolet	91.493	1999	Dale Earnhardt, Chevrolet	91.276	2018	Kurt Busch, Ford	89.538

NASCAR All-Star Race Winners, 1985-2018

At Charlotte Motor Speedway in Concord, NC. Known as The Winston, 1985-93, 1997-2003; The Winston Select, 1994-96; Nextel All-Star Challenge, 2004-07; NASCAR Sprint All-Star Challenge/Race, 2008-16; Monster Energy NASCAR All-Star Race, 2017-present.

Year	Driver, car	Year	Driver, car	Year	Driver, car
1985	Darrell Waltrip, Chevrolet	1997	Jeff Gordon, Chevrolet	2008	Kasey Kahne, Dodge
1986	Bill Elliott, Ford	1998	Mark Martin, Ford	2009	Tony Stewart, Chevrolet
1987	Dale Earnhardt, Chevrolet	1999	Terry Labonte, Chevrolet	2010	Kurt Busch, Dodge
1988	Terry Labonte, Chevrolet	2000	Dale Earnhardt Jr., Chevrolet	2011	Carl Edwards, Ford
1989	Rusty Wallace, Pontiac	2001	Jeff Gordon, Chevrolet	2012	Jimmie Johnson, Chevrolet
1990	Dale Earnhardt, Chevrolet	2002	Ryan Newman, Ford	2013	Jimmie Johnson, Chevrolet
1991	Davey Allison, Ford	2003	Jimmie Johnson, Chevrolet	2014	Jamie McMurray, Chevrolet
1992	Davey Allison, Ford	2004	Matt Kenseth, Ford	2015	Denny Hamlin, Toyota
1993	Dale Earnhardt, Chevrolet	2005	Mark Martin, Ford	2016	Joey Logano, Ford
1994	Geoff Bodine, Ford	2006	Jimmie Johnson, Chevrolet	2017	Kyle Busch, Toyota
1995	Jeff Gordon, Chevrolet	2007	Kevin Harvick, Chevrolet	2018	Kevin Harvick, Ford
1996	Michael Waltrip, Ford				

Formula One World Drivers' Champions, 1950-2017

Awarded by the Fédération Internationale de l'Automobile (FIA); champions determined through a series of Grand Prix races.

Year	Driver, country	Year	Driver, country	Year	Driver, country
1950	Giuseppe "Nino" Farina, Italy	1973	Jackie Stewart, Scotland, UK	1996	Damon Hill, England, UK
1951	Juan Manuel Fangio, Argentina	1974	Emerson Fittipaldi, Brazil	1997	Jacques Villeneuve, Canada
1952	Alberto Ascari, Italy	1975	Niki Lauda, Austria	1998	Mika Hakkinen, Finland
1953	Alberto Ascari, Italy	1976	James Hunt, England, UK	1999	Mika Hakkinen, Finland
1954	Juan Manuel Fangio, Argentina	1977	Niki Lauda, Austria	2000	Michael Schumacher, Germany
1955	Juan Manuel Fangio, Argentina	1978	Mario Andretti, United States	2001	Michael Schumacher, Germany
1956	Juan Manuel Fangio, Argentina	1979	Jody Scheckter, South Africa	2002	Michael Schumacher, Germany
1957	Juan Manuel Fangio, Argentina	1980	Alan Jones, Australia	2003	Michael Schumacher, Germany
1958	Mike Hawthorn, England, UK	1981	Nelson Piquet, Brazil	2004	Michael Schumacher, Germany
1959	Jack Brabham, Australia	1982	Keke Rosberg, Finland	2005	Fernando Alonso, Spain
1960	Jack Brabham, Australia	1983	Nelson Piquet, Brazil	2006	Fernando Alonso, Spain
1961	Phil Hill, United States	1984	Niki Lauda, Austria	2007	Kimi Raikkonen, Finland
1962	Graham Hill, England, UK	1985	Alain Prost, France	2008	Lewis Hamilton, England, UK
1963	Jim Clark, Scotland, UK	1986	Alain Prost, France	2009	Jenson Button, England, UK
1964	John Surtees, England, UK	1987	Nelson Piquet, Brazil	2010	Sebastian Vettel, Germany
1965	Jim Clark, Scotland, UK	1988	Ayrton Senna, Brazil	2011	Sebastian Vettel, Germany
1966	Jack Brabham, Australia	1989	Alain Prost, France	2012	Sebastian Vettel, Germany
1967	Denis Hulme, New Zealand	1990	Ayrton Senna, Brazil	2013	Sebastian Vettel, Germany
1968	Graham Hill, England, UK	1991	Ayrton Senna, Brazil	2014	Lewis Hamilton, England, UK
1969	Jackie Stewart, Scotland, UK	1992	Nigel Mansell, England, UK	2015	Lewis Hamilton, England, UK
1970	Jochen Rindt, Austria	1993	Alain Prost, France	2016	Nico Rosberg, Germany
1971	Jackie Stewart, Scotland, UK	1994	Michael Schumacher, Germany	2017	Lewis Hamilton, England, UK
1972	Emerson Fittipaldi, Brazil	1995	Michael Schumacher, Germany		

24 Hours of Le Mans Race, 2018

Toyota won the 86th running of the 24 Hours of Le Mans at Circuit de la Sarthe in Le Mans, France, June 16-17, 2018. It was Toyota's first victory in the endurance race in 19 attempts, and the first win for a Japanese manufacturer since Mazda won in 1991. Drivers Fernando Alonso of Spain, Kazuki Nakajima of Japan, and Sébastien Buemi of Switzerland completed 388 laps in the No. 8 TS050 Hybrid to bring Toyota the win. The Toyota No. 7 car, driven by Mike Conway, José María López, and Kamui Kobayashi, took second place, two laps behind.

BOXING

There are many boxing governing bodies, including the World Boxing Assn. (WBA; known as the National Boxing Assn. [NBA] until 1962), World Boxing Council (WBC), International Boxing Fed. (IBF), World Boxing Org., U.S. Boxing Assn., N. American Boxing Fed., and European Boxing Union. All have their own champions and divisions.

Boxing Champions by Class

Class (weight limit)	WBA Champion	WBC Champion	IBF Champion
Heavyweight (none)	Anthony Joshua, UK[1] Manuel Charr, Germany Trevor Bryan, U.S.[2]	Deontay Wilder, U.S.	Anthony Joshua, UK
Cruiserweight (200 lbs)	Oleksandr Usyk, Ukraine[1] Beibut Shumenov, Kazakhstan Arsen Goulamirian, Armenia[2]	Oleksandr Usyk, Ukraine	Oleksandr Usyk, Ukraine
Light Heavyweight (175 lbs)	Dmitry Bivol, Russia	Adonis Stevenson, Canada Oleksandr Gvozdyk, Ukraine[2]	Artur Beterbiev, Russia
Super Middleweight (168 lbs)	Callum Smith, UK[1] Rocky Fielding, UK	David Benavidez, U.S.	Jose Uzcategui, Venezuela
Middleweight (160 lbs)	Canelo Alvarez, Mexico[1] Ryota Murata, Japan	Canelo Alvarez, Mexico Jermall Charlo, U.S.[2]	Vacant
Super Welterweight/ Jr. Middleweight (154 lbs)	Jarrett Hurd, U.S.[1] Brian Carlos Castano, Argentina	Jermell Charlo, U.S.	Jarrett Hurd, U.S.
Welterweight (147 lbs)	Keith Thurman, U.S.[1] Manny Pacquiao, Philippines	Shawn Porter, U.S.	Errol Spence Jr., U.S.
Super Lightweight/ Jr. Welterweight (140 lbs)	Kiryl Relikh, Belarus	Jose Carlos Ramirez, U.S.	Vacant
Lightweight (135 lbs)	Vasiliy Lomachenko, Ukraine[1]	Mikey Garcia, U.S.	Mikey Garcia, U.S.
Super Featherweight/ Jr. Lightweight (130 lbs)	Gervonta Davis, U.S.[1] Alberto Machado, Puerto Rico	Miguel Berchelt, Mexico	Tevin Farmer, U.S.
Featherweight (126 lbs)	Leo Santa Cruz, Mexico[1] Jesus Rojas, Puerto Rico Jhack Tepora, Philippines[2]	Gary Russell Jr., U.S.	Josh Warrington, UK
Super Bantamweight/ Jr. Featherweight (122 lbs)	Daniel Roman, U.S.	Rey Vargas, Mexico	TJ Doheny, Ireland
Bantamweight (118 lbs)	Ryan Burnett, UK[1] Naoya Inoue, Japan Reymart Gaballo, Philippines[2]	Vacant	Emmanuel Rodriguez, Puerto Rico
Super Flyweight/ Jr. Bantamweight (115 lbs)	Khalid Yafai, UK	Srisaket Sor Rungvisai, Thailand	Jerwin Ancajas, Philippines
Flyweight (112 lbs)	Artem Dalakian, Ukraine	Cristofer Rosales, Nicaragua	Moruti Mthalane, South Africa
Jr. Flyweight (108 lbs)	Hekkie Budler, South Africa[1] Carlos Canizales, Venezuela	Ken Shiro, Japan	Vacant
Strawweight/ Mini Flyweight (105 lbs)	Knockout CP Freshmart, Thailand	Wanheng Menayothin, Thailand	Vacant

Note: As of Oct. 1, 2018. (1) Super champion. (2) Interim champion.

Ring Champions by Years

* = Abandoned/relinquished the title or was stripped of it. IBF champions listed only for heavyweight division. International Boxing Hall of Fame inductees in *italics*. For years with multiple champions, boxers are listed according to date of earliest title bout.

Heavyweights

1882-92	*John L. Sullivan*[1]	1978-79	*Muhammad Ali* (WBA*)[5]	1996	*Mike Tyson* (WBA/WBC*)
1892-97	*James J. Corbett*[2]	1978-83	*Larry Holmes* (WBC*)[6]	1996-97	Michael Moorer (IBF)
1897-99	*Bob Fitzsimmons*	1979-80	John Tate (WBA)	1996-99	*Evander Holyfield* (WBA/IBF)
1899-1905	*James J. Jeffries**[3]	1980-82	Mike Weaver (WBA)	1997-99	*Lennox Lewis* (WBC)
1905-06	Marvin Hart	1982-83	Michael Dokes (WBA)	1999-2001	*Lennox Lewis* (WBA*/WBC/IBF)
1906-08	*Tommy Burns*	1983-84	Gerrie Coetzee (WBA)	2000-01	*Evander Holyfield* (WBA)
1908-15	*Jack Johnson*	1983-85	*Larry Holmes* (IBF)[6]	2001-03	John Ruiz (WBA)
1915-19	*Jess Willard*	1984	Tim Witherspoon (WBC)	2001	Hasim Rahman (WBC/IBF)
1919-26	*Jack Dempsey*	1984-86	Pinklon Thomas (WBC)	2001-02	*Lennox Lewis* (IBF*)
1926-28	*Gene Tunney**	1984-85	Greg Page (WBA)	2001-04	*Lennox Lewis* (WBC)
1928-30	Vacant	1985-86	Tony Tubbs (WBA)	2002-06	Chris Byrd (IBF)
1930-32	*Max Schmeling*	1985-87	*Michael Spinks* (IBF*)	2003	Roy Jones Jr. (WBA*)
1932-33	*Jack Sharkey*	1986	Tim Witherspoon (WBA);	2004-05	John Ruiz (WBA)[7];
1933-34	Primo Carnera		Trevor Berbick (WBC)		*Vitali Klitschko* (WBC*)
1934-35	*Max Baer*	1986-87	*Mike Tyson* (WBC); James	2005-06	Hasim Rahman (WBC)
1935-37	*James J. Braddock*		"Bonecrusher" Smith (WBA)	2005-07	Nicolai Valuev (WBA)
1937-49	*Joe Louis**	1987	Tony Tucker (IBF)	2006-15	Wladimir Klitschko (IBF)
1949-51	*Ezzard Charles*	1987-90	*Mike Tyson* (WBA/WBC/IBF)	2006-08	Oleg Maskaev (WBC)
1951-52	*Joe Walcott*	1990	James "Buster" Douglas	2007-08	Ruslan Chagaev (WBA)
1952-56	*Rocky Marciano**		(WBA/WBC/IBF)	2008	Samuel Peter (WBC)
1956-59	*Floyd Patterson*	1990-92	*Evander Holyfield*	2008-09	Nikolai Valuev (WBA)
1959-60	*Ingemar Johansson*		(WBA/WBC/IBF)	2008-13	*Vitali Klitschko* (WBC*)
1960-62	*Floyd Patterson*	1992-93	Riddick Bowe (WBA/WBC*/IBF)	2009-11	David Haye (WBA)
1962-64	*Sonny Liston*	1992-94	*Lennox Lewis* (WBC)	2011-15	Wladimir Klitschko (WBA)
1964-67	*Cassius Clay (Muhammad Ali)**[4]	1993-94	*Evander Holyfield* (WBA/IBF)	2014-15	Bermane Stiverne (WBC)
1968-70	Jimmy Ellis[4]	1994	Michael Moorer (WBA/IBF)	2015-	Deontay Wilder (WBC)
1970-73	*Joe Frazier*	1994-95	Oliver McCall (WBC);	2015-	Tyson Fury (WBA*)
1973-74	*George Foreman*		*George Foreman* (WBA*/IBF*)	2015-16	Tyson Fury (IBF*)
1974-78	*Muhammad Ali*	1995-96	Bruce Seldon (WBA);	2016	Charles Martin (IBF)
1978	Leon Spinks (WBA/WBC*)[5];		Frank Bruno (WBC)	2016-	Anthony Joshua (IBF)
	Ken Norton (WBC)	1995	Frans Botha (IBF*)	2017-	Anthony Joshua (WBA)

(1) London Prize Ring (bare-knuckle champion). (2) First Marquis of Queensberry champion. (3) Jeffries vacated title (1905) and designated Marvin Hart and Jack Root as logical contenders. Hart def. Root in 12 rounds (1905); in turn was def. by Tommy Burns (1906), who claimed the title. Jack Johnson def. Burns (1908) and was recognized as champ. Johnson won the title by defeating Jeffries in the latter's attempted comeback (1910). (4) Title declared vacant by the WBA and others in 1967 after Ali refused military induction for religious reasons during the Vietnam War. Joe Frazier recognized as champ by six states, Mexico, and S. America. Jimmy Ellis won a tournament for the WBA title. (5) After Spinks def. Ali for the WBA title, the WBC recognized Ken Norton as champ. Ali def. Spinks in 1978 rematch for WBA title and retired in 1979. (6) Relinquished WBC title in Dec. 1983 to fight as champ of the new IBF. (7) James Toney def. Ruiz Apr. 30, 2005, to claim the title, but it was rescinded when Toney tested positive for steroids.

Light Heavyweights

Years	Champion
1903-05	Bob Fitzsimmons
1905-12	Philadelphia Jack O'Brien*
1912-16	Jack Dillon
1916-20	Battling Levinsky
1920-22	Georges Carpentier
1922-23	Battling Siki
1923-25	Mike McTigue
1925-26	Paul Berlenbach
1926-27	Jack Delaney*
1927-29	Tommy Loughran*
1930-34	Maxie Rosenbloom
1934-35	Bob Olin
1935-39	John Henry Lewis*
1939	Melio Bettina
1939-41	Billy Conn*
1941	Anton Christoforidis (NBA)
1941-48	Gus Lesnevich
1948-50	Freddie Mills
1950-52	Joey Maxim
1952-62	Archie Moore
1962-63	Harold Johnson
1963-65	Willie Pastrano
1965-66	Jose Torres
1966-68	Dick Tiger
1968-74	Bob Foster*
1974-77	John Conteh (WBC)
1974-78	Victor Galindez (WBA)
1977-78	Miguel Cuello (WBC)
1978	Mate Parlov (WBC)
1978-79	Mike Rossman (WBA); Marvin Johnson (WBC)
1979	Victor Galindez (WBA)
1979-81	Matthew Saad Muhammad (WBC)
1979-80	Marvin Johnson (WBA)
1980-81	Eddie Mustafa Muhammad (WBA)
1981-85	Michael Spinks (WBA)
1981-83	Dwight Muhammad-Qawi Braxton (WBC)
1983-85	Michael Spinks (WBC*)
1985-86	J. B. Williamson (WBC)
1986-87	Marvin Johnson (WBA); Dennis Andries (WBC)
1987	Thomas Hearns (WBC*)
1987	Leslie Stewart (WBA)
1987-91	Virgil Hill (WBA)
1987-88	Don Lalonde (WBC)
1988	Sugar Ray Leonard (WBC*)
1989	Dennis Andries (WBC)
1989-90	Jeff Harding (WBC)
1990-91	Dennis Andries (WBC)
1991-92	Thomas Hearns (WBA)
1991-94	Jeff Harding (WBC)
1992	Iran Barkley (WBA*)
1992-97	Virgil Hill (WBA)
1994-95	Mike McCallum (WBC)
1995-96	Fabrice Tiozzo (WBC*)
1996-97	Roy Jones Jr. (WBC)
1997	Montell Griffin (WBC); Dariusz Michalczewski (WBA*); Roy Jones Jr. (WBC)
1997-98	Lou Del Valle (WBA)
1998-2003	Roy Jones Jr. (WBA*/WBC*)
2003	Mehdi Sahnoune (WBA); Silvio Branco (WBA) Antonio Tarver (WBC)
2003-04	Roy Jones Jr. (WBA/WBC*)
2004	Antonio Tarver (WBA/WBC*)
2004-06	Fabrice Tiozzo (WBA)
2005-07	Tomasz Adamek (WBC)
2006-07	Silvio Branco (WBA)
2007-08	Chad Dawson (WBC*)
2007	Stipe Drews (WBA); Danny Green (WBA)
2008-09	Hugo Hernan Garay (WBA); Adrian Diaconu (WBC)
2009-11	Jean Pascal (WBC)
2009-10	Gabriel Campillo (WBA)
2010-14	Beibut Shumenov (WBA)
2011-12	Bernard Hopkins (WBC)
2012-13	Chad Dawson (WBC)
2013-	Adonis Stevenson (WBC)
2014	Bernard Hopkins (WBA)
2014-16	Sergey Kovalev (WBA)
2016-17	Andre Ward (WBA)
2017-	Dmitry Bivol (WBA)

Middleweights

Years	Champion
1884-91	Jack "Nonpareil" Dempsey
1891-97	Bob Fitzsimmons*
1897-1907	Tommy Ryan*
1907-08	Stanley Ketchel; Billy Papke
1908-10	Stanley Ketchel
1911-13	Vacant
1913	Frank Klaus; George Chip
1914-17	Al McCoy
1917-20	Mike O'Dowd
1920-23	Johnny Wilson
1923-26	Harry Greb
1926	Theodore "Tiger" Flowers
1926-31	Mickey Walker
1931-32	William "Gorilla" Jones (NBA)
1932-37	Marcel Thil
1938	Al Hostak (NBA); Solly Krieger (NBA)
1939-40	Al Hostak (NBA)
1940-47	Tony Zale
1947-48	Rocky Graziano
1948	Tony Zale; Marcel Cerdan
1949-51	Jake LaMotta
1951	"Sugar" Ray Robinson; Randy Turpin
1951-52	"Sugar" Ray Robinson*
1953-55	Carl "Bobo" Olson
1955-57	"Sugar" Ray Robinson
1957	Gene Fullmer; "Sugar" Ray Robinson
1957-58	Carmen Basilio
1958	"Sugar" Ray Robinson
1959	Gene Fullmer (NBA); "Sugar" Ray Robinson (NY)
1960	Gene Fullmer (NBA); Paul Pender (NY/MA)
1961	Gene Fullmer (NBA); Terry Downes (NY/MA/Europe)
1962	Gene Fullmer; Paul Pender (NY/MA*); Dick Tiger (NBA)
1963	Dick Tiger (universal)
1963-65	Joey Giardello
1965-66	Dick Tiger
1966-67	Emile Griffith
1967	Nino Benvenuti
1967-68	Emile Griffith
1968-70	Nino Benvenuti
1970-77	Carlos Monzon*
1977-78	Rodrigo Valdez
1978-79	Hugo Corro
1979-80	Vito Antuofermo
1980	Alan Minter
1980-87	"Marvelous" Marvin Hagler
1987	Sugar Ray Leonard (WBC*)
1987-89	Sumbu Kalambay (WBA)
1987-88	Thomas Hearns (WBC)
1988-89	Iran Barkley (WBC)
1989-90	Roberto Duran (WBC*)
1989-91	Mike McCallum (WBA*)
1990-93	Julian Jackson (WBC)
1992-93	Reggie Johnson (WBA)
1993-95	Gerald McClellan (WBC*)
1993-94	John David Jackson (WBA*)
1994-95	Jorge Castro (WBA)
1995	Julian Jackson (WBC)
1995-96	Quincy Taylor (WBC); Shinji Takehara (WBA)
1996-98	Keith Holmes (WBC)
1996-97	William Joppy (WBA)
1997	Julio Cesar Green (WBA)
1998-2001	William Joppy (WBA)
1998-99	Hacine Cherifi (WBC)
1999-2001	Keith Holmes (WBC)
2001	Felix Trinidad (WBA)
2001-05	Bernard Hopkins (WBC/WBA)
2005-06	Jermain Taylor (WBA)
2005-07	Jermain Taylor (WBC)
2006-07	Javier Castillejo (WBA)[1]
2007-12	Felix Sturm (WBA)
2007-10	Kelly Pavlik (WBC)
2009-11	Sebastian Zbik (WBC)
2010	Sergio Martinez (WBC)
2011-12	Julio Cesar Chavez Jr. (WBC)
2012	Daniel Geale (WBA*)
2012-14	Sergio Martinez (WBC)
2012-18	Gennady Golovkin (WBA)
2014-15	Miguel Cotto (WBC)
2015-16	Saul Alvarez (WBC*)
2016-18	Gennady Golovkin (WBC)
2018	Canelo Álvarez (WBA/WBC)

(1) Castillejo lost title to Mariano Carrera Dec. 2, 2006, but regained it Feb. 23, 2007, after Carrera tested positive for steroids.

Welterweights

Years	Champion
1892-94	"Mysterious" Billy Smith
1894-96	Tommy Ryan
1896	Kid McCoy*
1900	Rube Ferns; Matty Matthews
1901	Rube Ferns
1901-04	Joe Walcott
1904-06	Dixie Kid; Joe Walcott
1906	William "Honey" Mellody
1907-11	Mike Sullivan
1911-15	Vacant
1915-16	Ted Lewis
1916-17	Jack Britton
1917-19	Ted Lewis
1919-22	Jack Britton
1922-26	Mickey Walker
1926-27	Pete Latzo
1927-29	Joe Dundee
1929-30	Jackie Fields
1930	Jack Thompson; Tommy Freeman
1931	Tommy Freeman; Jack Thompson; Lou Brouillard
1932	Jackie Fields
1933	Young Corbett III; Jimmy McLarnin
1934	Barney Ross; Jimmy McLarnin
1935-38	Barney Ross
1938-40	Henry Armstrong
1940-41	Fritzie Zivic
1941-46	Fred Cochrane
1946	Marty Servo*
1946-51	"Sugar" Ray Robinson*[1]
1951	Johnny Bratton (NBA)
1951-54	Kid Gavilan
1954-55	Johnny Saxton
1955	Tony De Marco
1955-56	Carmen Basilio
1956	Johnny Saxton
1956-57	Carmen Basilio*
1958	Virgil Akins
1958-60	Don Jordan
1960-61	Benny Paret
1961	Emile Griffith
1961-62	Benny Paret
1962-63	Emile Griffith
1963	Luis Rodriguez
1963-66	Emile Griffith*
1966-69	Curtis Cokes
1969-70	Jose Napoles
1970-71	Billy Backus
1971-75	Jose Napoles
1975-76	Angel Espada (WBA); John Stracey (WBC)
1976-79	Carlos Palomino (WBC)
1976-80	Jose "Pipino" Cuevas (WBA)
1979	Wilfred Benitez (WBC)
1979-80	Sugar Ray Leonard (WBC)
1980	Roberto Duran (WBC)
1980-81	Thomas Hearns (WBA)
1980-82	Sugar Ray Leonard (WBC*/WBA*)
1983-85	Donald Curry (WBA); Milton McCrory (WBC)
1985-86	Donald Curry (WBC)
1986-87	Lloyd Honeyghan (WBC)
1987	Mark Breland (WBA)
1987-88	Marlon Starling (WBA); Jorge Vaca (WBC)
1988-89	Tomas Molinares (WBA*); Lloyd Honeyghan (WBC)
1989-90	Marlon Starling (WBA); Mark Breland (WBA)

1990-91	Maurice Blocker (WBC);	2000-02	Shane Mosley (WBC)	2009	Shane Mosley (WBA)
	Aaron Davis (WBA)	2001-02	Andrew Lewis (WBA)	2009-12	Vyacheslav Senchenko (WBA)
1991-92	Meldrick Taylor (WBA)	2002-03	Vernon Forrest (WBC)	2011	Victor Ortiz (WBC)
1991	Simon Brown (WBC)	2002	Ricardo Mayorga (WBA)	2011-15	Floyd Mayweather Jr. (WBC*)
1991-93	Buddy McGirt (WBC)	2003	Ricardo Mayorga	2012-13	Paulie Malignaggi (WBA)
1992-94	Crisanto Espana (WBA)		(WBA/WBC)	2013	Adrien Broner (WBA);
1993-97	Pernell Whitaker (WBC)	2003-05	Cory Spinks (WBA/WBC)		Marcos Maidana (WBA)
1994-98	Ike Quartey (WBA*)	2005-06	Zab Judah (WBA/WBC)	2014-15	Floyd Mayweather Jr. (WBA*)
1997-99	*Oscar De La Hoya* (WBC*)	2006	Carlos Baldomir (WBC);	2016-17	Danny Garcia (WBC)
1998-	James Page (WBA*)		Ricky Hatton (WBA*)	2016-	Keith Thurman (WBA)
2000		2006-08	Floyd Mayweather Jr. (WBC);	2017-18	Keith Thurman (WBC*)
1999-	*Felix Trinidad* (WBC*)		Miguel Cotto (WBA)	2018	Shawn Porter (WBC)
2000		2008	Antonio Margarito (WBA)		
2000	*Oscar De La Hoya* (WBC*)	2008-11	Andre Berto (WBC)		

(1) Robinson gained the title by defeating Tommy Bell in an elimination agreed to by the New York Commission and the National Boxing Association. Both claimed Robinson waived his title when he won the middleweight crown from Jake LaMotta in 1951.

Lightweights

1899-1902	Frank Erne	1970-72	*Ken Buchanan* (WBA)	1996-97	Jean-Baptiste Mendy (WBC)
1902-08	*Joe Gans*	1971-72	Pedro Carrasco (WBC)	1997-98	Steve Johnston (WBC)
1908-10	*Oscar "Battling" Nelson*	1972	Mando Ramos (WBC)	1998-99	Jean-Baptiste Mendy (WBA);
1910-12	*Ad Wolgast*	1972-79	*Roberto Duran* (WBA*)		Cesar Bazan (WBC)
1912-14	*Willie Ritchie*	1972	Chango Carmona (WBC)	1999-2000	Steve Johnston (WBC)
1914-17	*Freddie Welsh*	1972-74	Rodolfo Gonzalez (WBC)	1999	Julian Lorcy (WBA);
1917-25	*Benny Leonard**	1974-76	Ishimatsu Suzuki (WBC)		Stefano Zoff (WBA)
1925	Jimmy Goodrich;	1976-78	Esteban De Jesus (WBC)	1999-2000	Gilberto Serrano (WBA)
	Rocky Kansas	1978	*Roberto Duran* (WBC*)	2000-01	Takanori Hatakeyama (WBA)
1926-30	*Sammy Mandell*	1979-81	Jim Watt (WBC)	2000-02	Jose Luis Castillo (WBC)
1930	*Al Singer; Tony Canzoneri*	1979-80	Ernesto España (WBA)	2001	Julien Lorcy (WBA)
1930-33	*Tony Canzoneri*	1980-81	Hilmer Kenty (WBA)	2001-02	Raul Balbi (WBA)
1933-35	*Barney Ross**	1981	Sean O'Grady (WBA*);	2002-03	Leonard Dorin (WBA)
1935-36	*Tony Canzoneri*		Claude Noel (WBA)	2002-04	Floyd Mayweather Jr. (WBC*)
1936-38	*Lou Ambers*	1981-83	*Alexis Arguello* (WBC*)	2004	Lakva Sim (WBA)
1938	*Henry Armstrong*	1981-82	Arturo Frias (WBA)	2004-05	Jose Luis Castillo (WBC)
1939	*Lou Ambers*	1982-84	*Ray Mancini* (WBA)	2004-08	Juan Diaz (WBA)
1940	Lew Jenkins	1983-84	*Edwin Rosario* (WBC)	2005-06	Diego Corrales (WBC)
1941-43	*Sammy Angott*	1984-86	Livingstone Bramble (WBA)	2006	Joel Casamayor (WBC*)
1944	*Sammy Angott* (NBA);	1984-85	Jose Luis Ramirez (WBC)	2006-08	David Diaz (WBC)
	Juan Zurita (NBA)	1985-86	Hector "Macho" Camacho	2008	Nate Campbell (WBA*);
1945-51	*Ike Williams*		(WBC*)		Manny Pacquiao (WBC*)
	(NBA; later universal)	1986-87	*Edwin Rosario* (WBA)	2009-12	Juan Manuel Marquez (WBA*)
1951-52	*James Carter*	1987-88	*Julio Cesar Chavez* (WBA);	2009-10	Edwin Valero (WBC)
1952	Lauro Salas; *James Carter*		Jose Luis Ramirez (WBC)	2010-11	Humberto Soto (WBC*)
1953-54	*James Carter*	1988-89	*Julio Cesar Chavez*	2011-12	Antonio DeMarco (WBC)
1954	Paddy De Marco; *James Carter*		(WBA/WBC*)	2012-14	Adrien Broner (WBC)
1955	*James Carter*; Bud Smith	1989-90	*Edwin Rosario* (WBA);	2013-15	Richard Abril (WBA*)
1956	Bud Smith; *Joe Brown*		*Pernell Whitaker* (WBC)	2014	Omar Figueroa (WBC*)
1956-62	*Joe Brown*	1990	Juan Nazario (WBA)	2014-15	Jorge Linares (WBC)
1962-65	*Carlos Ortiz*	1990-92	*Pernell Whitaker* (WBC*/WBA*)	2015	Darleys Perez (WBA)
1965	*Ismael Laguna*	1992	Joey Gamache (WBA)	2015-16	Anthony Crolla (WBA)
1965-68	*Carlos Ortiz*	1992-96	Miguel Angel Gonzalez (WBC*)	2016-17	Dejan Zlaticanin (WBC)
1968-69	Carlos Teo Cruz	1992-93	Tony Lopez (WBA)	2016-18	Jorge Linares (WBA)
1969-70	Mando Ramos	1993	Dingaan Thobela (WBA)	2017-	Mikey Garcia (WBC)
1970	*Ismael Laguna*	1993-98	Orzubek Nazarov (WBA)	2018	Vasiliy Lomachenko (WBA)

Featherweights

1892-1900	*George Dixon* (disputed)	1970-72	Kuniaki Shibata (WBC)	1995-99	Luisito Espinosa (WBC)
1900-01	*Terry McGovern*;	1971-72	Antonio Gomez (WBC)	1996-98	*Wilfredo Vasquez* (WBA*)
	*Young Corbett II**	1972	Clemente Sanchez (WBC*)	1998	Freddie Norwood (WBA)
1901-12	*Abe Attell*	1972-74	Ernesto Marcel (WBA*)	1998-99	Antonio Cermeno (WBA)
1912-23	*Johnny Kilbane*	1972-73	Jose Legra (WBC)	1999	Cesar Soto (WBC)
1923	*Eugene Criqui*	1973-74	*Eder Jofre* (WBC*)	1999-2000	Freddie Norwood (WBA)
1923-25	*Johnny Dundee**	1974	*Ruben Olivares* (WBA)	1999	*Naseem Hamed* (WBC*)
1925-27	*Louis "Kid" Kaplan**	1974-75	Bobby Chacon (WBC)	2000-01	Guty Espadas Jr. (WBC)
1927-28	*Benny Bass; Tony Canzoneri*	1974-76	*Alexis Arguello* (WBA*)	2000-03	Derrick Gainer (WBA)
1928-29	Andre Routis	1975	*Ruben Olivares* (WBC)	2001-04	*Erik Morales* (WBC*)[1]
1929-32	*Battling Battalino**	1975-76	David Kotey (WBC)	2003-05	Juan Manuel Marquez (WBA*)
1932-34	Tommy Paul (NBA)	1976-80	*Danny "Little Red"*	2004-06	In-Jin Chi (WBC)
1933-36	*Freddie Miller*		*Lopez* (WBC)	2005-13	Chris John (WBA)
1936-37	*Petey Sarron*	1977	Rafael Ortega (WBC)	2006	Takashi Koshimoto (WBC);
1937-38	*Henry Armstrong**	1977-78	Cecilio Lastra (WBA)		Rodolfo Lopez (WBC)
1938-40	Joey Archibald	1978-85	Eusebio Pedroza (WBA)	2006-07	In-Jin Chi (WBC)
1940-41	Harry Jeffra	1980-82	*Salvador Sanchez* (WBC)	2007-08	Jorge Linares (WBC*)
1941	Joey Archibald	1982-84	Juan LaPorte (WBC)	2008	Oscar Larios (WBC)
1941-42	*Chalky Wright*	1984	*Wilfredo Gomez* (WBC)	2009	Takahiro Ao (WBC)
1942-48	*Willie Pep*	1984-88	*Azumah Nelson* (WBC)	2009-10	Elio Rojas (WBC)
1948-49	Sandy Saddler	1985-86	*Barry McGuigan* (WBA)	2010-11	Hozumi Hasegawa (WBC)
1949-50	*Willie Pep*	1986-87	Steve Cruz (WBA)	2011-12	Jhonny Gonzalez (WBC)
1950-57	*Sandy Saddler**	1987-91	Antonio Esparragoza (WBA)	2012-13	Daniel Ponce de León (WBC)
1957-59	*Hogan "Kid" Bassey*	1988-90	*Jeff Fenech* (WBC*)	2013	Abner Mares (WBC)
1959-63	Davey Moore	1990-91	Marcos Villasana (WBC)	2013-15	Jhonny Gonzalez (WBC)
1963-64	*Ultiminio "Sugar" Ramos*	1991-93	Park Yung Kyun (WBA);	2013-14	Simpiwe Vetyeka (WBA)
1964-67	*Vicente Saldivar**		Paul Hodkinson (WBC)	2014	Nonito Donaire (WBA)
1968	Raul Rojas (WBA)	1993	Goyo Vargas (WBC)	2014-15	Nicholas Walters (WBA*)
1968-69	Jose Legra (WBC)	1993-95	Kevin Kelley (WBC)	2015-	Gary Russell Jr. (WBC)
1968-71	Shozo Saijyo (WBA)	1993-96	Eloy Rojas (WBA)	2015-16	Leo Santa Cruz (WBC)
1969-70	Johnny Famechon (WBC)	1995	Alejandro Gonzalez (WBC);	2016-17	Carl Frampton (WBA)
1970	*Vicente Saldivar* (WBC)		Manuel Medina (WBC)	2017-	Leo Santa Cruz (WBA)

(1) Marco Antonio Barrera won unanimous decision over Morales, June 22, 2002, but refused WBC title. Morales regained WBC title with unanimous decision over Paulie Ayala, Nov. 16, 2002. Morales moved to Jr. Lightweight div. in 2004.

International Boxing Hall of Fame Inductees, 2018

Source: International Boxing Hall of Fame, 1 Hall of Fame Dr., Canastota, NY 13032. www.ibhof.com

Modern: Vitali Klitschko (45-2, 41 KO), Erik Morales (52-9, 36 KO), Ronald "Winky" Wright (51-6-1, 25 KO).
Old-Timer: Sid Terris (92-13-5, 12 KO).

Non-Participant: Klaus-Peter Kohl, promoter; Johnny Addie, ring announcer; Lorraine Chargin, promoter.
Observer: Steve Albert, broadcaster; Jim Gray, broadcaster.

Title-Changing Heavyweight Championship Bouts, 1889-2018

1889: July 8, John L. Sullivan def. Jake Kilrain, 75, Richburg, MS.
1892: Sept. 7, James J. Corbett def. John L. Sullivan, 21, New Orleans.
1897: Mar. 17, Bob Fitzsimmons def. James J. Corbett, 14, Carson City, NV.
1899: June 9, James J. Jeffries def. Bob Fitzsimmons, 11, Coney Island, NY. (Jeffries retired as champion in 1905.)
1905: July 3, Marvin Hart KOd Jack Root, 12, Reno, NV. (James J. Jeffries refereed, gave title to Hart. Jack O'Brien also claimed the title.)
1906: Feb. 23, Tommy Burns def. Marvin Hart, 20, Los Angeles.
1908: Dec. 26, Jack Johnson def. Tommy Burns, 14, Sydney, Australia. (Police halted contest.)
1915: Apr. 5, Jess Willard KOd Jack Johnson, 26, Havana, Cuba.
1919: July 4, Jack Dempsey KOd Jess Willard, Toledo, OH. (Willard failed to answer bell for 4th round.)
1926: Sept. 23, Gene Tunney def. Jack Dempsey, 10, Philadelphia. (Tunney retired as champion in 1928.)
1930: June 12, Max Schmeling def. Jack Sharkey on a foul, 4, New York City. (Resulted in the election of a successor to Gene Tunney.)
1932: June 21, Jack Sharkey def. Max Schmeling, 15, NYC.
1933: June 29, Primo Carnera KOd Jack Sharkey, 6, NYC.
1934: June 14, Max Baer KOd Primo Carnera, 11, NYC.
1935: June 13, James J. Braddock def. Max Baer, 15, NYC.
1937: June 22, Joe Louis KOd James J. Braddock, 8, Chicago. (Louis retired as champion in 1949.)
1949: June 22, Ezzard Charles def. Joe Walcott, 15, Chicago; NBA recognition only.
1951: July 18, Joe Walcott KOd Ezzard Charles, 7, Pittsburgh.
1952: Sept. 23, Rocky Marciano KOd Joe Walcott, 13, Philadelphia. (Marciano retired as champion in 1956.)
1956: Nov. 30, Floyd Patterson KOd Archie Moore, 5, Chicago.
1959: June 26, Ingemar Johansson KOd Floyd Patterson, 3, NYC.
1960: June 20, Floyd Patterson KOd Ingemar Johansson, 5, NYC.
1962: Sept. 25, Sonny Liston KOd Floyd Patterson, 1, Chicago.
1964: Feb. 25, Cassius Clay (Muhammad Ali) KOd Sonny Liston, 7, Miami Beach, FL. (Liston failed to answer bell for 7th round. In 1967, Ali was stripped of title for refusing military service.)
1970: Feb. 16, Joe Frazier KOd Jimmy Ellis, 5, NYC. (Frazier def. Ali, 15, NYC, on Mar. 8, 1971, in "Fight of the Century.")
1973: Jan. 22, George Foreman KOd Joe Frazier, 2, Kingston, Jamaica.
1974: Oct. 30, Muhammad Ali KOd George Foreman, 8, Kinshasa, Zaire (billed as the "Rumble in the Jungle").
1978: Feb. 15, Leon Spinks def. Muhammad Ali, 15, Las Vegas (WBC recognized Ken Norton as champion after Spinks refused to fight him before his rematch with Ali); June 9, (WBC) Larry Holmes def. Ken Norton, 15, Las Vegas; Sept. 15, (WBA) Muhammad Ali def. Leon Spinks, 15, New Orleans. (Ali retired as champion in 1979.)
1979: Oct. 20, (WBA) John Tate def. Gerrie Coetzee, 15, Pretoria, South Africa.
1980: Mar. 31, (WBA) Mike Weaver KOd John Tate, 15, Knoxville, TN.
1982: Dec. 10, (WBA) Michael Dokes KOd Mike Weaver, 1, Las Vegas.
1983: Sept. 23, (WBA) Gerrie Coetzee KOd Michael Dokes, 10, Richfield, OH; in Dec., Larry Holmes relinquished the WBC title and was named champion of the newly formed IBF.
1984: Mar. 9, (WBC) Tim Witherspoon def. Greg Page, 12, Las Vegas; Aug. 31, (WBC) Pinklon Thomas def. Tim Witherspoon, 12, Las Vegas; Dec. 1, (WBA) Greg Page KOd Gerrie Coetzee, 8, Sun City, Bophuthatswana, South Africa.
1985: Apr. 29, (WBA) Tony Tubbs def. Greg Page, 15, Buffalo, NY; Sept. 21, (IBF) Michael Spinks def. Larry Holmes, 15, Las Vegas. (Spinks relinquished title in Feb. 1987.)
1986: Jan. 17, (WBA) Tim Witherspoon def. Tony Tubbs, 15, Atlanta; Mar. 22, (WBC) Trevor Berbick def. Pinklon Thomas, 12, Miami; Nov. 22, (WBC) Mike Tyson KOd Trevor Berbick, 2, Las Vegas; Dec. 12, (WBA) James "Bonecrusher" Smith KOd Tim Witherspoon, 1, NYC.
1987: Mar. 7, (WBA) Mike Tyson def. James "Bonecrusher" Smith, 12, Las Vegas; May 30, (IBF) Tony Tucker KOd James "Buster" Douglas, 10, Las Vegas; Aug. 1, (IBF) Mike Tyson def. Tony Tucker, 12, Las Vegas. (Tyson became undisputed champion.)

1990: Feb. 11, (WBA/WBC/IBF) James "Buster" Douglas KOd Mike Tyson, 10, Tokyo, Japan; Oct. 25, (WBA/WBC/IBF) Evander Holyfield KOd James "Buster" Douglas, 3, Las Vegas.
1992: Nov. 13, (WBA/WBC/IBF) Riddick Bowe def. Evander Holyfield, 12, Las Vegas; in Dec., Lennox Lewis was named WBC champion after Bowe relinquished the WBC title rather than fight Lewis.
1993: Nov. 6, (WBA/IBF) Evander Holyfield def. Riddick Bowe, 12, Las Vegas.
1994: Apr. 22, (WBA/IBF) Michael Moorer def. Evander Holyfield, 12, Las Vegas; Sept. 24, (WBC) Oliver McCall KOd Lennox Lewis, 2, London, Eng.; Nov. 5, (WBA/IBF) George Foreman KOd Michael Moorer, 10, Las Vegas.
1995: In Mar., George Foreman was stripped of his WBA title for refusing to fight challenger Tony Tucker; in June, Foreman relinquished his IBF title rather than submit to a rematch with Axel Schulz; Apr. 8, (WBA) Bruce Seldon TKOd Tony Tucker, 7, Las Vegas; Sept. 2, (WBC) Frank Bruno def. Oliver McCall, 12, London, Eng.; Dec. 9, (IBF) Frans Botha def. Axel Schulz, 12, Stuttgart, Germany (Botha was subsequently stripped of title after testing positive for a steroid.)
1996: Mar. 16, (WBC) Mike Tyson KOd Frank Bruno, 3, Las Vegas; June 22, (IBF) Michael Moorer def. Axel Schulz, 12, Dortmund, Germany; Sept. 7, (WBA) Mike Tyson KOd Bruce Seldon, 1, Las Vegas (Tyson was subsequently stripped of WBC title after refusing to fight Lennox Lewis); Nov. 9, (WBA) Evander Holyfield KOd Mike Tyson, 11, Las Vegas.
1997: Feb. 7, (WBC) Lennox Lewis TKOd Oliver McCall, 5, Las Vegas; Nov. 8, (IBF) Evander Holyfield def. Michael Moorer, 8, Las Vegas.
1999: Nov. 13, (IBF) Lennox Lewis def. Evander Holyfield, 12, Las Vegas. (Lewis became undisputed champion.)
2000: In Apr., Lennox Lewis was stripped of his WBA title after refusing to fight challenger John Ruiz; Aug. 12, (WBA) Evander Holyfield def. John Ruiz, 12, Las Vegas.
2001: Mar. 3, (WBA) John Ruiz def. Evander Holyfield, 12, Las Vegas; Apr. 22, (WBC/IBF) Hasim Rahman KOd Lennox Lewis, 5, Brakpan, South Africa; Nov. 17, (WBC/IBF) Lennox Lewis KOd Hasim Rahman, 4, Las Vegas.
2002: In Sept., Lennox Lewis relinquished his IBF title; Dec. 14, (IBF) Chris Byrd def. Evander Holyfield, 12, Atlantic City, NJ.
2003: Mar. 1, (WBA) Roy Jones Jr. def. John Ruiz, 12, Las Vegas.
2004: Feb. 20, (WBA) John Ruiz gained title when Roy Jones Jr. relinquished it; Apr. 24, (WBC) Vitali Klitschko TKOd Corrie Sanders, 8, Los Angeles, to win title vacated by retirement of Lennox Lewis in Feb.
2005: Apr. 30, (WBA) James Toney def. John Ruiz, 12, NYC (title was returned to Ruiz after Toney tested positive for steroids); Nov. 9, (WBC) Hasim Rahman gained title when Vitali Klitschko retired due to an injury; Dec. 17, (WBA) Nikolai Valuev def. John Ruiz, 12, Berlin, Germany.
2006: Apr. 22, (IBF) Wladimir Klitschko TKOd Chris Byrd, 7, Mannheim, Germany; Aug. 12, (WBC) Oleg Maskaev TKOd Hasim Rahman, 12, Las Vegas.
2007: Apr. 14, (WBA) Ruslan Chagaev def. Nikolai Valuev, 12, Stuttgart, Germany. (An injured Chagaev was named champion in recess, July 2008.)
2008: Mar. 8, (WBC) Samuel Peter TKOd Oleg Maskaev, 6, Cancún, Mexico; Aug. 30, (WBA) Nikolai Valuev def. John Ruiz, 12, Berlin, Germany; Oct. 11, (WBC) Vitali Klitschko TKOd Samuel Peter, 8, Berlin, Germany.
2009: Nov. 7, (WBA) David Haye def. Nikolai Valuev, 12, Nuremberg, Germany.
2011: July 2, (WBA) Wladimir Klitschko def. David Haye, 12, Hamburg, Germany.
2014: May 10, (WBC) Bermane Stiverne TKOd Chris Arreola, 6, Los Angeles, to win title vacated in Dec. 2013.
2015: Jan. 17, (WBC) Deontay Wilder def. Bermane Stiverne, 12, Las Vegas; Nov. 28, (WBA/IBF) Tyson Fury def. Wladimir Klitschko, 12, Dusseldorf, Germany; in Dec., Fury was stripped of IBF title for refusing to fight mandatory challenger Vyacheslav Glazkov. (Fury relinquished WBA title Oct. 2016.)
2016: Jan. 16, (IBF) Charles Martin TKOd Vyacheslav Glazkov, 3, Brooklyn, NY; Apr. 9, (IBF) Anthony Joshua KOd Charles Martin, 2, London, Eng., UK.
2017: Apr. 29, (WBA) Anthony Joshua TKOd Wladimir Klitschko, 11, London, Eng., UK.

THOROUGHBRED RACING
Triple Crown Winners

The Kentucky Derby, Preakness Stakes, and Belmont Stakes make up the Triple Crown. Since 1920, colts have carried 126 lbs in Triple Crown events; fillies, 121 lbs.

Year	Horse	Jockey	Trainer	Year	Horse	Jockey	Trainer
1919	Sir Barton	J. Loftus	H. G. Bedwell	1946	Assault	W. Mehrtens	M. Hirsch
1930	Gallant Fox	E. Sande	J. Fitzsimmons	1948	Citation	E. Arcaro	H. A. Jones
1935	Omaha	W. Sanders	J. Fitzsimmons	1973	Secretariat	R. Turcotte	L. Laurin
1937	War Admiral	C. Kurtsinger	G. Conway	1977	Seattle Slew	J. Cruguet	W. H. Turner Jr.
1941	Whirlaway	E. Arcaro	B. A. Jones	1978	Affirmed	S. Cauthen	L. S. Barrera
1943	Count Fleet	J. Longden	G. D. Cameron	2015	American Pharoah	V. Espinoza	B. Baffert
				2018	Justify	M. Smith	B. Baffert

Kentucky Derby Winners, 1875-2018

Churchill Downs, Louisville, KY; inaug. 1875. Distance: 1-1/4 mi; 1-1/2 mi until 1896. 3-year-olds. Best time: 1:59-2/5, Secretariat (1973); 2018 time: 2:04.20. (Until 2001, times were measured in fifths of a second.)

Year	Horse	Jockey	Year	Horse	Jockey	Year	Horse	Jockey
1875	Aristides	O. Lewis	1923	Zev	E. Sande	1971	Canonero II	G. Avila
1876	Vagrant	R. Swim	1924	Black Gold	J. D. Mooney	1972	Riva Ridge	R. Turcotte
1877	Baden Baden	W. Walker	1925	Flying Ebony	E. Sande	1973	Secretariat	R. Turcotte
1878	Day Star	J. Carter	1926	Bubbling Over	A. Johnson	1974	Cannonade	A. Cordero
1879	Lord Murphy	C. Schauer	1927	Whiskery	L. McAtee	1975	Foolish Pleasure	J. Vasquez
1880	Fonso	G. Lewis	1928	Reigh Count	C. Lang	1976	Bold Forbes	A. Cordero
1881	Hindoo	J. McLaughlin	1929	Clyde Van Dusen	L. McAtee	1977	Seattle Slew	J. Cruguet
1882	Apollo	B. Hurd	1930	Gallant Fox	E. Sande	1978	Affirmed	S. Cauthen
1883	Leonatus	W. Donohue	1931	Twenty Grand	C. Kurtsinger	1979	Spectacular Bid	R. Franklin
1884	Buchanan	I. Murphy	1932	Burgoo King	E. James	1980	Genuine Risk[1]	J. Vasquez
1885	Joe Cotton	E. Henderson	1933	Brokers Tip	D. Meade	1981	Pleasant Colony	J. Velasquez
1886	Ben Ali	P. Duffy	1934	Cavalcade	M. Garner	1982	Gato Del Sol	E. Delahoussaye
1887	Montrose	I. Lewis	1935	Omaha	W. Saunders	1983	Sunny's Halo	E. Delahoussaye
1888	Macbeth II	G. Covington	1936	Bold Venture	I. Hanford	1984	Swale	L. Pincay
1889	Spokane	T. Kiley	1937	War Admiral	C. Kurtsinger	1985	Spend a Buck	A. Cordero
1890	Riley	I. Murphy	1938	Lawrin	E. Arcaro	1986	Ferdinand	W. Shoemaker
1891	Kingman	I. Murphy	1939	Johnstown	J. Stout	1987	Alysheba	C. McCarron
1892	Azra	A. Clayton	1940	Gallahadion	C. Bierman	1988	Winning Colors[1]	G. Stevens
1893	Lookout	E. Kunze	1941	Whirlaway	E. Arcaro	1989	Sunday Silence	P. Valenzuela
1894	Chant	F. Goodale	1942	Shut Out	W. Wright	1990	Unbridled	C. Perret
1895	Halma	J. Perkins	1943	Count Fleet	J. Longden	1991	Strike the Gold	C. Antley
1896	Ben Brush	W. Simms	1944	Pensive	C. McCreary	1992	Lil E. Tee	P. Day
1897	Typhoon II	F. Garner	1945	Hoop Jr.	E. Arcaro	1993	Sea Hero	J. Bailey
1898	Plaudit	W. Simms	1946	Assault	W. Mehrtens	1994	Go for Gin	C. McCarron
1899	Manuel	F. Taral	1947	Jet Pilot	E. Guerin	1995	Thunder Gulch	G. Stevens
1900	Lieut. Gibson	J. Boland	1948	Citation	E. Arcaro	1996	Grindstone	J. Bailey
1901	His Eminence	J. Winkfield	1949	Ponder	S. Brooks	1997	Silver Charm	G. Stevens
1902	Alan-a-Dale	J. Winkfield	1950	Middleground	W. Boland	1998	Real Quiet	K. Desormeaux
1903	Judge Himes	H. Booker	1951	Count Turf	C. McCreary	1999	Charismatic	C. Antley
1904	Elwood	F. Prior	1952	Hill Gail	E. Arcaro	2000	Fusaichi Pegasus	K. Desormeaux
1905	Agile	J. Martin	1953	Dark Star	H. Moreno	2001	Monarchos	J. Chavez
1906	Sir Huon	R. Troxler	1954	Determine	R. York	2002	War Emblem	V. Espinoza
1907	Pink Star	A. Minder	1955	Swaps	W. Shoemaker	2003	Funny Cide	J. Santos
1908	Stone Street	A. Pickens	1956	Needles	D. Erb	2004	Smarty Jones	S. Elliot
1909	Wintergreen	V. Powers	1957	Iron Liege	W. Hartack	2005	Giacomo	M. Smith
1910	Donau	F. Herbert	1958	Tim Tam	I. Valenzuela	2006	Barbaro	E. Prado
1911	Meridian	G. Archibald	1959	Tomy Lee	W. Shoemaker	2007	Street Sense	C. Borel
1912	Worth	C. Shilling	1960	Venetian Way	W. Hartack	2008	Big Brown	K. Desormeaux
1913	Donerail	R. Goose	1961	Carry Back	J. Sellers	2009	Mine That Bird	C. Borel
1914	Old Rosebud	J. McCabe	1962	Decidedly	W. Hartack	2010	Super Saver	C. Borel
1915	Regret[1]	J. Notter	1963	Chateaugay	B. Baeza	2011	Animal Kingdom	J. Velazquez
1916	George Smith	J. Loftus	1964	Northern Dancer	W. Hartack	2012	I'll Have Another	M. Gutierrez
1917	Omar Khayyam	C. Borel	1965	Lucky Debonair	W. Shoemaker	2013	Orb	J. Rosario
1918	Exterminator	W. Knapp	1966	Kauai King	D. Brumfield	2014	California Chrome	V. Espinoza
1919	Sir Barton	J. Loftus	1967	Proud Clarion	R. Ussery	2015	American Pharoah	V. Espinoza
1920	Paul Jones	T. Rice	1968	Forward Pass[2]	I. Valenzuela	2016	Nyquist	M. Gutierrez
1921	Behave Yourself	C. Thompson	1969	Majestic Prince	W. Hartack	2017	Always Dreaming	J. Velazquez
1922	Morvich	A. Johnson	1970	Dust Commander	M. Manganello	2018	Justify	M. Smith

Note: Two jockeys have won the Kentucky Derby five times: Eddie Arcaro and Bill Hartack. Willie Shoemaker won four times. Seven jockeys won three times: Isaac Murphy, Earle Sande, Angel Cordero, Gary Stevens, Kent Desormeaux, Calvin Borel, and Victor Espinoza. (1) Regret, Genuine Risk, and Winning Colors are the only fillies to have won the Derby. (2) Dancer's Image came in first but was disqualified after tests disclosed that the horse had run with a prohibited painkilling drug in his system. All wagers were paid on Dancer's Image, but Forward Pass was awarded the first-place money.

Fastest Winning Times for the Kentucky Derby

Until 2001, Kentucky Derby times were measured in fifths of a second.

Time	Horse	Jockey	Year	Time	Horse	Jockey	Year
1 min., 59-2/5 s.	Secretariat	Ron Turcotte	1973	2 min., 1.19 s.	Funny Cide	Jose Santos	2003
1 min., 59.97 s.	Monarchos	Jorge Chavez	2001	2 min., 1-1/5 s.	Thunder Gulch	Gary Stevens	1995
2 min.	Northern Dancer	Bill Hartack	1964		Affirmed	Steve Cauthen	1978
2 min., 1/5 s.	Spend a Buck	Angel Cordero Jr.	1985		Lucky Debonair	Bill Shoemaker	1965
2 min., 2/5 s.	Decidedly	Bill Hartack	1962	2 min., 1.31 s.	Nyquist	Mario Gutierrez	2016
2 min., 3/5 s.	Proud Clarion	Robert Ussery	1967	2 min., 1-2/5 s.	Barbaro	Edgar Prado	2006
2 min., 1 s.	Fusaichi Pegasus	Kent Desormeaux	2000		Whirlaway	Eddie Arcaro	1941
	Grindstone	Jerry Bailey	1996	2 min., 1-3/5 s.	Bold Forbes	Angel Cordero Jr.	1976
2 min., 1.13 s.	War Emblem	Victor Espinoza	2002		Hill Gail	Eddie Arcaro	1952
2 min., 1.19 s.	Funny Cide	Jose Santos	2003		Middleground	William Boland	1950

Preakness Stakes Winners, 1873-2018

Pimlico Race Course, Baltimore, MD; inaug. 1873. Distance: 1-3/16 mi. 3-year-olds. * = Horses ran in two divisions. Best time: 1:53, Secretariat (1973); 2018 time: 1:55.93.

Year	Horse	Jockey	Year	Horse	Jockey	Year	Horse	Jockey
1873	Survivor	G. Barbee	1924	Nellie Morse	J. Merimee	1972	Bee Bee Bee	E. Nelson
1874	Culpepper	M. Donohue	1925	Coventry	C. Kummer	1973	Secretariat	R. Turcotte
1875	Tom Ochiltree	L. Hughes	1926	Display	J. Malben	1974	Little Current	M. Rivera
1876	Shirley	G. Barbee	1927	Bostonian	A. Abel	1975	Master Derby	D. McHargue
1877	Cloverbrook	C. Holloway	1928	Victorian	R. Workman	1976	Elocutionist	J. Lively
1878	Duke of Magenta	C. Holloway	1929	Dr. Freeland	L. Schaefer	1977	Seattle Slew	J. Cruguet
1879	Harold	L. Hughes	1930	Gallant Fox	E. Sande	1978	Affirmed	S. Cauthen
1880	Grenada	L. Hughes	1931	Mate	G. Ellis	1979	Spectacular Bid	R. Franklin
1881	Saunterer	W. Costello	1932	Burgoo King	E. James	1980	Codex	A. Cordero
1882	Vanguard	W. Costello	1933	Head Play	C. Kurtsinger	1981	Pleasant Colony	J. Velasquez
1883	Jacobus	G. Barbee	1934	High Quest	R. Jones	1982	Aloma's Ruler	J. Kaenel
1884	Knight of Ellerslie	S. Fisher	1935	Omaha	W. Saunders	1983	Deputed	
1885	Tecumseh	J. McLaughlin	1936	Bold Venture	G. Woolf		Testamony	D. Miller
1886	The Bard	S. Fisher	1937	War Admiral	C. Kurtsinger	1984	Gate Dancer	A. Cordero
1887	Dunboyne	W. Donohue	1938	Dauber	M. Peters	1985	Tank's Prospect	P. Day
1888	Refund	F. Littlefield	1939	Challedon	G. Seabo	1986	Snow Chief	A. Solis
1889	Buddhist	G. Anderson	1940	Bimelech	F. A. Smith	1987	Alysheba	C. McCarron
1890	Montague	W. Martin	1941	Whirlaway	E. Arcaro	1988	Risen Star	E. Delahoussaye
1894	Assignee	F. Taral	1942	Alsab	B. James	1989	Sunday Silence	P. Valenzuela
1895	Belmar	F. Taral	1943	Count Fleet	J. Longden	1990	Summer Squall	P. Day
1896	Margrave	H. Griffin	1944	Pensive	C. McCreary	1991	Hansel	J. Bailey
1897	Paul Kauvar	C. Thorpe	1945	Polynesian	W. D. Wright	1992	Pine Bluff	C. McCarron
1898	Sly Fox	W. Simms	1946	Assault	W. Mehrtens	1993	Prairie Bayou	M. Smith
1899	Half Time	R. Clawson	1947	Faultless	D. Dodson	1994	Tabasco Cat	P. Day
1900	Hindus	H. Spencer	1948	Citation	E. Arcaro	1995	Timber Country	P. Day
1901	The Parader	F. Landry	1949	Capot	T. Atkinson	1996	Louis Quatorze	P. Day
1902	Old England	L. Jackson	1950	Hill Prince	E. Arcaro	1997	Silver Charm	G. Stevens
1903	Flocarline	W. Gannon	1951	Bold	E. Arcaro	1998	Real Quiet	K. Desormeaux
1904	Bryn Mawr	E. Hildebrand	1952	Blue Man	C. McCreary	1999	Charismatic	C. Antley
1905	Cairngorm	W. Davis	1953	Native Dancer	E. Guerin	2000	Red Bullet	J. Bailey
1906	Whimsical	W. Miller	1954	Hasty Road	J. Adams	2001	Point Given	G. Stevens
1907	Don Enrique	G. Mountain	1955	Nashua	E. Arcaro	2002	War Emblem	V. Espinoza
1908	Royal Tourist	E. Dugan	1956	Fabius	W. Hartack	2003	Funny Cide	J. Santos
1909	Effendi	W. Doyle	1957	Bold Ruler	E. Arcaro	2004	Smarty Jones	S. Elliot
1910	Layminster	R. Estep	1958	Tim Tam	I. Valenzuela	2005	Afleet Alex	J. Rose
1911	Watervale	E. Dugan	1959	Royal Orbit	W. Harmatz	2006	Bernardini	J. Castellano
1912	Colonel Holloway	C. Turner	1960	Bally Ache	R. Ussery	2007	Curlin	R. Albarado
1913	Buskin	J. Butwell	1961	Carry Back	J. Sellers	2008	Big Brown	K. Desormeaux
1914	Holiday	A. Schuttinger	1962	Greek Money	J. L. Rotz	2009	Rachel Alexandra	C. Borel
1915	Rhine Maiden	D. Hoffman	1963	Candy Spots	W. Shoemaker	2010	Lookin At Lucky	M. Garcia
1916	Damrosch	L. McAtee	1964	Northern Dancer	W. Hartack	2011	Shackleford	J. Castanon
1917	Kalitan	E. Haynes	1965	Tom Rolfe	R. Turcotte	2012	I'll Have Another	M. Gutierrez
1918*	War Cloud	J. Loftus	1966	Kauai King	D. Brumfield	2013	Oxbow	G. Stevens
	Jack Hare Jr.	C. Peak	1967	Damascus	W. Shoemaker	2014	California Chrome	V. Espinoza
1919	Sir Barton	J. Loftus	1968	Forward Pass	I. Valenzuela	2015	American Pharoah	V. Espinoza
1920	Man o' War	C. Kummer	1969	Majestic Prince	W. Hartack	2016	Exaggerator	K. Desormeaux
1921	Broomspun	F. Coltiletti	1970	Personality	E. Belmonte	2017	Cloud Computing	J. Castellano
1922	Pillory	L. Morris	1971	Canonero II	G. Avila	2018	Justify	M. Smith
1923	Vigil	B. Marinelli						

Belmont Stakes Winners, 1867-2018

Belmont Park, Elmont, NY; inaug. 1867. Distance: 1-1/2 mi. 3-year-olds. Best time: 2:24, Secretariat (1973); 2018 time: 2:28.18.

Year	Horse	Jockey	Year	Horse	Jockey	Year	Horse	Jockey
1867	Ruthless	J. Gilpatrick	1899	Jean Bereaud	R. R. Clawson	1933	Hurryoff	M. Garner
1868	General Duke	R. Swim	1900	Ildrim	N. Turner	1934	Peace Chance	W. D. Wright
1869	Fenian	C. Miller	1901	Commando	H. Spencer	1935	Omaha	W. Saunders
1870	Kingfisher	W. Dick	1902	Masterman	J. Bullman	1936	Granville	J. Stout
1871	Harry Bassett	W. Miller	1903	Africander	J. Bullman	1937	War Admiral	C. Kurtsinger
1872	Joe Daniels	J. Rowe	1904	Delhi	G. Odom	1938	Pasteurized	J. Stout
1873	Springbok	J. Rowe	1905	Tanya	E. Hildebrand	1939	Johnstown	J. Stout
1874	Saxon	G. Barbee	1906	Burgomaster	L. Lyne	1940	Bimelech	F. A. Smith
1875	Calvin	R. Swim	1907	Peter Pan	G. Mountain	1941	Whirlaway	E. Arcaro
1876	Algerine	W. Donohue	1908	Colin	J. Notter	1942	Shut Out	E. Arcaro
1877	Cloverbrook	C. Holloway	1909	Joe Madden	E. Dugan	1943	Count Fleet	J. Longden
1878	Duke of Magenta	L. Hughes	1910	Sweep	J. Butwell	1944	Bounding Home	G. L. Smith
1879	Spendthrift	S. Evans	1913	Prince Eugene	R. Troxler	1945	Pavot	E. Arcaro
1880	Grenada	L. Hughes	1914	Luke McLuke	M. Buxton	1946	Assault	W. Mehrtens
1881	Saunterer	T. Costello	1915	The Finn	G. Byrne	1947	Phalanx	R. Donoso
1882	Forester	J. McLaughlin	1916	Friar Rock	E. Haynes	1948	Citation	E. Arcaro
1883	George Kinney	J. McLaughlin	1917	Hourless	J. Butwell	1949	Capot	T. Atkinson
1884	Panique	J. McLaughlin	1918	Johren	F. Robinson	1950	Middleground	W. Boland
1885	Tyrant	P. Duffy	1919	Sir Barton	J. Loftus	1951	Counterpoint	D. Gorman
1886	Inspector B.	J. McLaughlin	1920	Man o' War	C. Kummer	1952	One Count	E. Arcaro
1887	Hanover	J. McLaughlin	1921	Grey Lag	E. Sande	1953	Native Dancer	E. Guerin
1888	Sir Dixon	J. McLaughlin	1922	Pillory	C. H. Miller	1954	High Gun	E. Guerin
1889	Eric	W. Hayward	1923	Zev	E. Sande	1955	Nashua	E. Arcaro
1890	Burlington	S. Barnes	1924	Mad Play	E. Sande	1956	Needles	D. Erb
1891	Foxford	E. Garrison	1925	American Flag	A. Johnson	1957	Gallant Man	W. Shoemaker
1892	Patron	W. Hayward	1926	Crusader	A. Johnson	1958	Cavan	P. Anderson
1893	Comanche	W. Simms	1927	Chance Shot	E. Sande	1959	Sword Dancer	W. Shoemaker
1894	Henry of Navarre	W. Simms	1928	Vito	C. Kummer	1960	Celtic Ash	W. Hartack
1895	Belmar	F. Taral	1929	Blue Larkspur	M. Garner	1961	Sherluck	B. Baeza
1896	Hastings	H. Griffin	1930	Gallant Fox	E. Sande	1962	Jaipur	W. Shoemaker
1897	Scottish Chieftain	J. Scherrer	1931	Twenty Grand	C. Kurtsinger	1963	Chateaugay	B. Baeza
1898	Bowling Brook	F. Littlefield	1932	Faireno	T. Malley	1964	Quadrangle	M. Ycaza

Year	Horse	Jockey	Year	Horse	Jockey	Year	Horse	Jockey
1965	Hail to All	J. Sellers	1983	Caveat	L. Pincay	2001	Point Given	G. Stevens
1966	Amberoid	W. Boland	1984	Swale	L. Pincay	2002	Sarava	E. Prado
1967	Damascus	W. Shoemaker	1985	Creme Fraiche	E. Maple	2003	Empire Maker	J. Bailey
1968	Stage Door Johnny	H. Gustines	1986	Danzig Connection	C. McCarron	2004	Birdstone	E. Prado
1969	Arts and Letters	B. Baeza	1987	Bet Twice	C. Perret	2005	Afleet Alex	J. Rose
1970	High Echelon	J. L. Rotz	1988	Risen Star	E. Delahoussaye	2006	Jazil	F. Jara
1971	Pass Catcher	W. Blum	1989	Easy Goer	P. Day	2007	Rags to Riches	J. Velazquez
1972	Riva Ridge	R. Turcotte	1990	Go and Go	M. Kinane	2008	Da' Tara	A. Garcia
1973	Secretariat	R. Turcotte	1991	Hansel	J. Bailey	2009	Summer Bird	K. Desormeaux
1974	Little Current	M. Rivera	1992	A.P. Indy	E. Delahoussaye	2010	Drosselmeyer	M. Smith
1975	Avatar	W. Shoemaker	1993	Colonial Affair	J. Krone	2011	Ruler On Ice	J. Valdivia Jr.
1976	Bold Forbes	A. Cordero	1994	Tabasco Cat	P. Day	2012	Union Rags	J. Velazquez
1977	Seattle Slew	J. Cruguet	1995	Thunder Gulch	G. Stevens	2013	Palace Malice	M. Smith
1978	Affirmed	S. Cauthen	1996	Editor's Note	R. Douglas	2014	Tonalist	J. Rosario
1979	Coastal	R. Hernandez	1997	Touch Gold	C. McCarron	2015	American Pharoah	V. Espinoza
1980	Temperence Hill	E. Maple	1998	Victory Gallop	G. Stevens	2016	Creator	I. Ortiz Jr.
1981	Summing	G. Martens	1999	Lemon Drop Kid	J. Santos	2017	Tapwrit	J. Ortiz
1982	Conquistador Cielo	L. Pincay	2000	Commendable	P. Day	2018	Justify	M. Smith

Annual Leading Jockey by Earnings, 1957-2017

Total purses earned by all horses that jockey raced in year listed; does not reflect what jockey earned.

Year	Jockey	Earnings	Year	Jockey	Earnings	Year	Jockey	Earnings
1957	Bill Hartack	$3,060,501	1977	Steve Cauthen	$6,151,750	1997	Jerry D. Bailey	$18,320,743
1958	Willie Shoemaker	2,961,693	1978	Darrel McHargue	6,029,885	1998	Gary Stevens	19,622,855
1959	Willie Shoemaker	2,843,133	1979	Laffit Pincay Jr.	8,193,535	1999	Pat Day	18,092,845
1960	Willie Shoemaker	2,123,961	1980	Chris McCarron	7,663,300	2000	Pat Day	17,479,838
1961	Willie Shoemaker	2,690,819	1981	Chris McCarron	8,397,604	2001	Jerry D. Bailey	22,597,720
1962	Willie Shoemaker	2,916,844	1982	Angel Cordero Jr.	9,483,590	2002	Jerry D. Bailey	19,271,814
1963	Willie Shoemaker	2,526,925	1983	Angel Cordero Jr.	10,116,697	2003	Jerry D. Bailey	23,354,960
1964	Willie Shoemaker	2,649,553	1984	Chris McCarron	12,045,813	2004	John R. Velazquez	22,220,261
1965	Braulio Baeza	2,582,702	1985	Laffit Pincay Jr.	13,353,299	2005	John R. Velazquez	20,799,923
1966	Braulio Baeza	2,951,022	1986	Jose Santos	11,329,297	2006	Garrett K. Gomez	20,122,592
1967	Braulio Baeza	3,088,888	1987	Jose Santos	12,375,433	2007	Garrett K. Gomez	22,800,074
1968	Braulio Baeza	2,835,108	1988	Jose Santos	14,877,298	2008	Garrett K. Gomez	23,344,351
1969	Jorge Velasquez	2,542,315	1989	Jose Santos	13,838,389	2009	Garrett K. Gomez	18,536,105
1970	Laffit Pincay Jr.	2,626,526	1990	Gary Stevens	13,881,198	2010	Ramon A. Dominguez	16,911,880
1971	Laffit Pincay Jr.	3,784,377	1991	Chris McCarron	14,441,083	2011	Ramon A. Dominguez	20,267,032
1972	Laffit Pincay Jr.	3,225,827	1992	Kent Desormeaux	14,193,006	2012	Ramon A. Dominguez	25,584,852
1973	Laffit Pincay Jr.	4,093,492	1993	Mike Smith	14,024,815	2013	Javier Castellano	26,214,007
1974	Laffit Pincay Jr.	4,251,060	1994	Mike Smith	15,979,820	2014	Javier Castellano	25,056,464
1975	Braulio Baeza	3,695,198	1995	Jerry D. Bailey	16,311,876	2015	Javier Castellano	28,120,809
1976	Angel Cordero Jr.	4,709,500	1996	Jerry D. Bailey	19,465,376	2016	Javier Castellano	26,826,241
						2017	José L. Ortiz	27,318,875

Breeders' Cup World Thoroughbred Championships, 1984-2018

The Breeders' Cup began in 1984 and through 2006, consisted of seven races at one track on one day. In 2007, it expanded to two days, and three new races debuted: Filly and Mare Sprint, Juvenile Turf, and Dirt. In 2008, a "Ladies' Day" for fillies and several more races debuted: Turf Sprint, Marathon (eliminated in 2014), and Juvenile Fillies Turf. In 2011, the Juvenile Sprint debuted; it was eliminated in 2013. In 2018, the 5½-furlong Juvenile Turf Sprint debuted and was won by Bulletin (jockey: J. Castellano).

Classic
Distance: 1-1/4 mi.

Year	Horse	Jockey	Year	Horse	Jockey	Year	Horse	Jockey
1984	Wild Again	P. Day	1996	Alphabet Soup	C. McCarron	2008	Raven's Pass	F. Dettori
1985	Proud Truth	J. Velasquez	1997	Skip Away	M. Smith	2009	Zenyatta	M. Smith
1986	Skywalker	L. Pincay Jr.	1998	Awesome Again	P. Day	2010	Blame	G. Gomez
1987	Ferdinand	W. Shoemaker	1999	Cat Thief	P. Day	2011	Drosselmeyer	M. Smith
1988	Alysheba	C. McCarron	2000	Tiznow	C. McCarron	2012	Fort Larned	B. Hernandez
1989	Sunday Silence	C. McCarron	2001	Tiznow	C. McCarron	2013	Mucho Macho Man	G. Stevens
1990	Unbridled	P. Day	2002	Volponi	J. Santos	2014	Bayern	M. Garcia
1991	Black Tie Affair	J. Bailey	2003	Pleasantly Perfect	A. Solis	2015	American Pharoah	V. Espinoza
1992	A.P. Indy	E. Delahoussaye	2004	Ghostzapper	J. Castellano	2016	Arrogate	M. Smith
1993	Arcangues	J. Bailey	2005	Saint Liam	J. Bailey	2017	Gun Runner	F. Geroux
1994	Concern	J. Bailey	2006	Invasor	F. Jara	2018	Accelerate	J. Rosario
1995	Cigar	J. Bailey	2007	Curlin	R. Albarado			

Juvenile
Distance: 1-1/16 mi, 1986 and since 1988; 1 mi, 1984-85, 1987.

Year	Horse	Jockey	Year	Horse	Jockey	Year	Horse	Jockey
1984	Chief's Crown	D. MacBeth	1996	Boston Harbor	J. Bailey	2007	War Pass	C. Velasquez
1985	Tasso	L. Pincay Jr.	1997	Favorite Trick	P. Day	2008	Midshipman	G. Gomez
1986	Capote	L. Pincay Jr.	1998	Answer Lively	J. Bailey	2009	Vale of York	A. Ajtebi
1987	Success Express	J. Santos	1999	Anees	G. Stevens	2010	Uncle Mo	J. Velazquez
1988	Is It True	L. Pincay Jr.	2000	Macho Uno	J. Bailey	2011	Hansen	R. Dominguez
1989	Rhythm	C. Perret	2001	Johannesburg	M. Kinane	2012	Shanghai Bobby	R. Napravnik
1990	Fly So Free	J. Santos	2002	Vindication	M. Smith	2013	New Year's Day	M. Garcia
1991	Arazi	P. Valenzuela	2003	Action This Day	D. Flores	2014	Texas Red	K. Desormeaux
1992	Gilded Time	C. McCarron	2004	Wilko	F. Dettori	2015	Nyquist	M. Gutierrez
1993	Brocco	G. Stevens	2005	Stevie Wonderboy	G. Gomez	2016	Classic Empire	J. Leparoux
1994	Timber Country	P. Day	2006	Street Sense	C. Borel	2017	Good Magic	J. Ortiz
1995	Unbridled's Song	M. Smith				2018	Game Winner	J. Rosario

Filly and Mare Sprint
Distance: 6 furlongs, 2007; 7 furlongs since 2008.

Year	Horse	Jockey	Year	Horse	Jockey	Year	Horse	Jockey
2007	Maryfield	E. Trujillo	2011	Musical Romance	J. Leyva	2015	Wavell Avenue	J. Rosario
2008	Ventura	G. Gomez	2012	Groupie Doll	R. Maragh	2016	Finest City	M. Smith
2009	Informed Decision	J. Leparoux	2013	Groupie Doll	R. Maragh	2017	Bar of Gold	I. Ortiz Jr.
2010	Dubai Majesty	J. Theriot	2014	Judy the Beauty	M. Smith	2018	Shamrock Rose	I. Ortiz Jr.

Juvenile Fillies

Distance: 1-1/16 mi, 1986 and since 1988; 1 mi, 1984-85, 1987. Outstandingly won the 1984 race by disqualification.

Year	Horse	Jockey
1984	Outstandingly	W. Guerra
1985	Twilight Ridge	J. Velasquez
1986	Brave Raj	P. Valenzuela
1987	Epitome	P. Day
1988	Open Mind	A. Cordero Jr.
1989	Go for Wand	R. Romero
1990	Meadow Star	J. Santos
1991	Pleasant Stage	E. Delahoussaye
1992	Eliza	P. Valenzuela
1993	Phone Chatter	L. Pincay Jr.
1994	Flanders	P. Day
1995	My Flag	J. Bailey
1996	Storm Song	C. Perret
1997	Countess Diana	S. Sellers
1998	Silverbulletday	G. Stevens
1999	Cash Run	J. Bailey
2000	Caressing	J. Velasquez
2001	Tempera	D. Flores
2002	Storm Flag Flying	J. Velasquez
2003	Halfbridled	J. Krone
2004	Sweet Catomine	C. Nakatani
2005	Folklore	E. Prado
2006	Dreaming of Anna	R. Douglas
2007	Indian Blessing	G. Gomez
2008	Stardom Bound	M. Smith
2009	She Be Wild	J. Leparoux
2010	Awesome Feather	J. Sanchez
2011	My Miss Aurelia	C. Nakatani
2012	Beholder	G. Gomez
2013	Ria Antonia	J. Castellano
2014	Take Charge Brandi	V. Espinoza
2015	Songbird	M. Smith
2016	Champagne Room	M. Gutierrez
2017	Caledonia Road	M. Smith
2018	Jaywalk	J. Rosario

Sprint

Distance: 6 furlongs.

Year	Horse	Jockey
1984	Eillo	C. Perret
1985	Precisionist	C. McCarron
1986	Smile	J. Vasquez
1987	Very Subtle	P. Valenzuela
1988	Gulch	A. Cordero Jr.
1989	Dancing Spree	A. Cordero Jr.
1990	Safely Kept	C. Perret
1991	Sheikh Albadou	P. Eddery
1992	Thirty Slews	E. Delahoussaye
1993	Cardmania	E. Delahoussaye
1994	Cherokee Run	M. Smith
1995	Desert Stormer	K. Desormeaux
1996	Lit de Justice	C. Nakatani
1997	Elmhurst	C. Nakatani
1998	Reraise	C. Nakatani
1999	Artax	J. Chaves
2000	Kona Gold	A. Solis
2001	Squirtle Squirt	J. Bailey
2002	Orientate	J. Bailey
2003	Cajun Beat	C. Velasquez
2004	Speightstown	J. Velazquez
2005	Silver Train	E. Prado
2006	Thor's Echo	C. Nakatani
2007	Midnight Lute	G. Gomez
2008	Midnight Lute	G. Gomez
2009	Dancing in Silks	J. Rosario
2010	Big Drama	E. Coa
2011	Amazombie	M. Smith
2012	Trinniberg	W. Martinez
2013	Secret Circle	M. Garcia
2014	Work All Week	F. Geroux
2015	Runhappy	E. Prado
2016	Drefong	M. Garcia
2017	Roy H	K. Desormeaux
2018	Roy H	P. Lopez

Mile

Year	Horse	Jockey
1984	Royal Heroine	F. Toro
1985	Cozzene	W. Guerra
1986	Last Tycoon	Y. St.-Martin
1987	Miesque	F. Head
1988	Miesque	F. Head
1989	Steinlen	J. Santos
1990	Royal Academy	L. Piggott
1991	Opening Verse	P. Valenzuela
1992	Lure	M. Smith
1993	Lure	M. Smith
1994	Barathea	F. Dettori
1995	Ridgewood Pearl	J. Murtagh
1996	Da Hoss	G. Stevens
1997	Spinning World	C. Asmussan
1998	Da Hoss	J. Velazquez
1999	Silic	C. Nakatani
2000	War Chant	G. Stevens
2001	Val Royal	J. Valdivia Jr.
2002	Domedriver	T. Thulliez
2003	Six Perfections	J. Bailey
2004	Singletary	D. Flores
2005	Artie Schiller	G. Gomez
2006	Miesque's Approval	E. Castro
2007	Kip Deville	C. Velasquez
2008	Goldikova	O. Peslier
2009	Goldikova	O. Peslier
2010	Goldikova	O. Peslier
2011	Court Vision	R. Albarado
2012	Wise Dan	J. Velazquez
2013	Wise Dan	J. Lezcano
2014	Karakatonie	S. Pasquier
2015	Tepin	J. Leparoux
2016	Tourist	J. Rosario
2017	World Approval	J. Velazquez
2018	Expert Eye	F. Dettori

Distaff

Distance: 1-1/8 mi since 1988; 1-1/4 mi, 1984-87; race known as Ladies' Classic, 2008-12.

Year	Horse	Jockey
1984	Princess Rooney	E. Delahoussaye
1985	Life's Magic	A. Cordero Jr.
1986	Lady's Secret	P. Day
1987	Sacahuista	R. Romero
1988	Personal Ensign	R. Romero
1989	Bayakoa	L. Pincay Jr.
1990	Bayakoa	L. Pincay Jr.
1991	Dance Smartly	P. Day
1992	Paseana	C. McCarron
1993	Hollywood Wildcat	E. Delahoussaye
1994	One Dreamer	G. Stevens
1995	Inside Information	M. Smith
1996	Jewel Princess	C. Nakatani
1997	Ajina	M. Smith
1998	Escena	G. Stevens
1999	Beautiful Pleasure	J. Chaves
2000	Spain	V. Espinoza
2001	Unbridled Elaine	P. Day
2002	Azeri	M. Smith
2003	Adoration	P. Valenzuela
2004	Ashado	J. Velazquez
2005	Pleasant Home	C. Velasquez
2006	Round Pond	E. Prado
2007	Ginger Punch	R. Bejarano
2008	Zenyatta	M. Smith
2009	Life Is Sweet	G. Gomez
2010	Unrivaled Belle	K. Desormeaux
2011	Royal Delta	J. Lezcano
2012	Royal Delta	M. Smith
2013	Beholder	G. Stevens
2014	Untapable	R. Napravnik
2015	Stopchargingmaria	J. Castellano
2016	Beholder	G. Stevens
2017	Forever Unbridled	J. Velazquez
2018	Monomoy Girl	F. Geroux

Turf

Distance: 1-1/2 mi.

Year	Horse	Jockey
1984	Lashkari	Y. St.-Martin
1985	Pebbles	P. Eddery
1986	Manila	J. Santos
1987	Theatrical	P. Day
1988	Great Communicator	R. Sibille
1989	Prized	E. Delahoussaye
1990	In the Wings	G. Stevens
1991	Miss Alleged	E. Legrix
1992	Fraise	P. Valenzuela
1993	Kotashaan	K. Desormeaux
1994	Tikkanen	M. Smith
1995	Northern Spur	C. McCarron
1996	Pilsudski	W. Swinburn
1997	Chief Bearhart	J. Santos
1998	Buck's Boy	S. Sellers
1999	Daylami	F. Dettori
2000	Kalanisi	J. Murtagh
2001	Fantastic Light	F. Dettori
2002	High Chaparral	M. Kinane
2003	(tie) High Chaparral	M. Kinane
	Johar	A. Solis
2004	Better Talk Now	R. Dominguez
2005	Shirocco	C. Soumillon
2006	Red Rocks	F. Dettori
2007	English Channel	J. Velasquez
2008	Conduit	R. Moore
2009	Conduit	R. Moore
2010	Dangerous Midge	F. Dettori
2011	St Nicholas Abbey	J. O'Brien
2012	Little Mike	R. Dominguez
2013	Magician	R. Moore
2014	Main Sequence	J. Velazquez
2015	Found	R. Moore
2016	Highland Reel	S. Heffernan
2017	Talismanic	M. Barzalona
2018	Enable	F. Dettori

Filly and Mare Turf

Distance: 1-3/8 mi, 1999-2000, 2004, 2006-07, 2010-11, 2018; 1-1/4 mi, 2001-03, 2005, 2008-09, 2012-14, 2016; 1-3/16 mi, 2015; 1-1/8 mi, 2017.

Year	Horse	Jockey	Year	Horse	Jockey	Year	Horse	Jockey
1999	Soaring Softly	J. Bailey	2006	Ouija Board	F. Dettori	2013	Dank	R. Moore
2000	Perfect Sting	J. Bailey	2007	Lahudood	A. Garcia	2014	Dayatthespa	J. Castellano
2001	Banks Hill	O. Peslier	2008	Forever Together	J. Leparoux	2015	Stephanie's Kitten	J. Velazquez
2002	Starine	J. Velazquez	2009	Midday	T. Queally	2016	Queen's Trust	F. Dettori
2003	Islington	K. Fallon	2010	Shared Account	E. Prado	2017	Wuheida	W. Buick
2004	Ouija Board	F. Dettori	2011	Perfect Shirl	J. Velazquez	2018	Sistercharlie	J. Velazquez
2005	Intercontinental	R. Bejarano	2012	Zagora	J. Castellano			

Juvenile Turf

Distance: 1 mi.

Year	Horse	Jockey	Year	Horse	Jockey	Year	Horse	Jockey
2007	Nownownow	J. Leparoux	2011	Wrote	R. Moore	2015	Hit It a Bomb	R. Moore
2008	Donativum	F. Dettori	2012	George Vancouver	R. Moore	2016	Oscar Performance	J. Ortiz
2009	Pounced	F. Dettori	2013	Outstrip	M. Smith	2017	Mendelssohn	R. Moore
2010	Pluck	G. Gomez	2014	Hootenanny	F. Dettori	2018	Line of Duty	W. Buick

Dirt Mile

Year	Horse	Jockey	Year	Horse	Jockey	Year	Horse	Jockey
2007	Corinthian	K. Desormeaux	2011	Caleb's Posse	R. Maragh	2015	Liam's Map	J. Castellano
2008	Albertus Maximus	G. Gomez	2012	Tapizar	C. Nakatani	2016	Tamarkuz	M. Smith
2009	Furthest Land	J. Leparoux	2013	Goldencents	R. Bejarano	2017	Battle of Midway	F. Prat
2010	Dakota Phone	J. Rosario	2014	Goldencents	R. Bejarano	2018	City of Light	J. Castellano

Turf Sprint

Distance: 6½ furlongs, 2008-09, 2012-14, 2016; 5 furlongs, 2010-11, 2017; 5½ furlongs, 2015, 2018.

Year	Horse	Jockey	Year	Horse	Jockey	Year	Horse	Jockey
2008	Desert Code	R. Migliore	2012	Mizdirection	M. Smith	2016	Obviously	F. Prat
2009	California Flag	J. Talamo	2013	Mizdirection	M. Smith	2017	Stormy Liberal	J. Rosario
2010	Chamberlain Bridge	J. Theriot	2014	Bobby's Kitten	J. Rosario	2018	Stormy Liberal	D. Van Dyke
2011	Regally Ready	C. Nakatani	2015	Mongolian Saturday	F. Geroux			

Juvenile Fillies Turf

Distance: 1 mi.

Year	Horse	Jockey	Year	Horse	Jockey	Year	Horse	Jockey
2008	Maram	J. Lezcano	2012	Flotilla	C. Lemaire	2016	New Money Honey	J. Castellano
2009	Tapitsfly	R. Albarado	2013	Chriselliam	R. Hughes	2017	Rushing Fall	J. Castellano
2010	More Than Real	G. Gomez	2014	Lady Eli	I. Ortiz Jr.	2018	Newspaperofrecord	I. Ortiz Jr.
2011	Stephanie's Kitten	J. Velazquez	2015	Catch a Glimpse	F. Geroux			

Eclipse Awards, 2017

The Eclipse Awards, honoring the Horse of the Year and other champions of thoroughbred racing, began in 1971 and are sponsored by the *Daily Racing Form*, the National Thoroughbred Racing Association, and the National Turf Writers Assn.

Horse of the Year: Gun Runner	**Older dirt female (4+ years old):** Forever Unbridled	**Trainer:** Chad Brown
2-year-old male: Good Magic		**Jockey:** José Ortiz
2-year-old female: Caledonia Road	**Male sprinter:** Roy H	**Apprentice jockey:** Evin Roman
3-year-old male: West Coast	**Female sprinter:** Unique Bella	**Breeder:** Clearsky Farms
3-year-old female: Abel Tasman	**Male turf horse:** World Approval	**Owner:** Juddmonte Farms, Inc.
Older dirt male (4+ years old): Gun Runner	**Female turf horse:** Lady Eli	
	Steeplechase horse: Scorpiancer	

HARNESS RACING
Harness Horse of the Year, 1947-2017

Chosen by the U.S. Trotting Assn. and the U.S. Harness Writers Assn.

Year	Horse	Year	Horse	Year	Horse	Year	Horse
1947	Victory Song	1965	Bret Hanover	1983	Cam Fella	2001	Bunny Lake
1948	Rodney	1966	Bret Hanover	1984	Fancy Crown	2002	Real Desire
1949	Good Time	1967	Nevele Pride	1985	Nihilator	2003	No Pan Intended
1950	Proximity	1968	Nevele Pride	1986	Forrest Skipper	2004	Rainbow Blue
1951	Pronto Don	1969	Nevele Pride	1987	Mack Lobell	2005	Rocknroll Hanover
1952	Good Time	1970	Fresh Yankee	1988	Mack Lobell	2006	Glidemaster
1953	Hi Lo's Forbes	1971	Albatross	1989	Matt's Scooter	2007	Donato Hanover
1954	Stenographer	1972	Albatross	1990	Beach Towel	2008	Somebeachsomewhere
1955	Scott Frost	1973	Sir Dalrae	1991	Precious Bunny	2009	Muscle Hill
1956	Scott Frost	1974	Delmonica Hanover	1992	Artsplace	2010	Rock N Roll Heaven
1957	Torpid	1975	Savoir	1993	Staying Together	2011	San Pail
1958	Emily's Pride	1976	Keystone Ore	1994	Cam's Card Shark	2012	Chapter Seven
1959	Bye Bye Byrd	1977	Green Speed	1995	CR Kay Suzie	2013	Bee a Magician
1960	Adios Butler	1978	Abercrombie	1996	Continental Victory	2014	JK She'salady
1961	Adios Butler	1979	Niatross	1997	Malabar Man	2015	Wiggle It Jiggleit
1962	Su Mac Lad	1980	Niatross	1998	Moni Maker	2016	Always B Miki
1963	Speedy Scot	1981	Fan Hanover	1999	Moni Maker	2017	Hannelore Hanover
1964	Bret Hanover	1982	Cam Fella	2000	Gallo Blue Chip		

Hambletonian Winners (3-year-old trotters), 1965-2018

Year	Horse	Driver	Year	Horse	Driver	Year	Horse	Driver
1965	Egyptian Candor	D. Cameron	1983	Duenna	S. Dancer	2001	Scarlet Knight	S. Melander
1966	Kerry Way	F. Ervin	1984	Historic Freight	B. Webster	2002	Chip Chip Hooray	E. Ledford
1967	Speedy Streak	D. Cameron	1985	Prakas	B. O'Donnell	2003	Amigo Hall	M. Lachance
1968	Nevele Pride	S. Dancer	1986	Nuclear Kosmos	U. Thoresen	2004	Windsong's Legacy	T. Smedshammer
1969	Lindy's Pride	H. Beissinger	1987	Mack Lobell	J. Campbell	2005	Vivid Photo	R. Hammer
1970	Timothy T	J. Simpson Sr.	1988	Armbro Goal	J. Campbell	2006	Glidemaster	J. Campbell
1971	Speedy Crown	H. Beissinger	1989	Park Avenue Joe	R. Waples	2007	Donato Hanover	R. Pierce
1972	Super Bowl	S. Dancer	1990	Harmonious	J. Campbell	2008	Deweycheatumnhowe	R. Schnittker
1973	Flirth	R. Baldwin	1991	Giant Victory	J. Moiseyev	2009	Muscle Hill	B. Sears
1974	Christopher T	B. Haughton	1992	Alf Palema	M. McNicholl	2010	Muscle Massive	R. Pierce
1975	Bonefish	S. Dancer	1993	American Winner	R. Pierce	2011	Broad Bahn	G. Brennan
1976	Steve Lobell	B. Haughton	1994	Victory Dream	M. Lachance	2012	Market Share	T. Tetrick
1977	Green Speed	B. Haughton	1995	Tagliabue	J. Campbell	2013	Royalty For Life	B. Sears
1978	Speedy Somolli	H. Beissinger	1996	Continental Victory	M. Lachance	2014	Trixton	J. Takter
1979	Legend Hanover	G. Sholty	1997	Malabar Man	M. Burroughs	2015	Pinkman	B. Sears
1980	Burgomeister	B. Haughton	1998	Muscles Yankee	J. Campbell	2016	Marion Marauder	S. Zeron
1981	Shiaway St. Pat	R. Remmen	1999	Self Possessed	M. Lachance	2017	Perfect Spirit	A. Svanstedt
1982	Speed Bowl	T. Haughton	2000	Yankee Paco	T. Ritchie	2018	Atlanta	S. Zeron

BOWLING
Professional Bowlers Association Tournament of Champions, 1965-2018

Year	Winner	Year	Winner	Year	Winner	Year	Winner
1965	Billy Hardwick	1978	Earl Anthony	1991	David Ozio	2007	Tommy Jones
1966	Wayne Zahn	1979	George Pappas	1992	Marc McDowell	2008	Michael Haugen Jr.
1967	Jim Stefanich	1980	Wayne Webb	1993	George Branham III	2009	Patrick Allen
1968	Dave Davis	1981	Steve Cook	1994	Norm Duke	2010	Kelly Kulick
1969	Jim Godman	1982	Mike Durbin	1996	Dave D'Entremont	2011	Mika Koivuniemi
1970	Don Johnson	1983	Joe Berardi	1997	John Gant	2012	Sean Rash
1971	Johnny Petraglia	1984	Mike Durbin	1998	Bryan Goebel	2013	Pete Weber
1972	Mike Durbin	1985	Mark Williams	1999	Jason Couch	2014	Jason Belmonte
1973	Jim Godman	1986	Marshall Holman	2000	Jason Couch	2015	Jason Belmonte
1974	Earl Anthony	1987	Pete Weber	2002	Jason Couch	2016	Jesper Svensson
1975	Dave Davis	1988	Mark Williams	2003	Patrick Healey Jr.	2017	E. J. Tackett
1976	Marshall Holman	1989	Del Ballard Jr.	2005	Steve Jaros	2018	Matt O'Grady
1977	Mike Berlin	1990	Dave Ferraro	2006	Chris Barnes		

Note: No tournament held in 2001 or 2004.

Professional Bowlers Association Leading Money Winners, 1962-2017
Total winnings from tournaments only. For 2000-13, year shown is year the PBA season ended.

Year	Bowler	Earnings	Year	Bowler	Earnings	Year	Bowler	Earnings
1962	Don Carter	$49,972	1980	Wayne Webb	$116,700	1998	Walter Ray Williams Jr.	$238,225
1963	Dick Weber	46,333	1981	Earl Anthony	164,735	1999	Parker Bohn III	240,912
1964	Bob Strampe	33,592	1982	Earl Anthony	134,760	2000	Norm Duke	143,325
1965	Dick Weber	47,674	1983	Earl Anthony	135,605	2002	Parker Bohn III	245,200
1966	Wayne Zahn	54,720	1984	Mark Roth	158,712	2003	Walter Ray Williams Jr.	419,700
1967	Dave Davis	54,165	1985	Mike Aulby	201,200	2004	Mika Koivuniemi	238,590
1968	Jim Stefanich	67,377	1986	Walter Ray Williams Jr.	145,550	2005	Patrick Allen	350,740
1969	Billy Hardwick	64,160	1987	Pete Weber	175,491	2006	Tommy Jones	301,700
1970	Mike McGrath	52,049	1988	Brian Voss	225,485	2007	Doug Kent	200,530
1971	Johnny Petraglia	85,065	1989	Mike Aulby	298,237	2008	Norm Duke	176,855
1972	Don Johnson	56,648	1990	Amleto Monacelli	204,775	2009	Norm Duke	199,130
1973	Don McCune	69,000	1991	David Ozio	225,585	2010	Walter Ray Williams Jr.	152,670
1974	Earl Anthony	99,585	1992	Marc McDowell	174,215	2011	Mika Koivuniemi	333,040
1975	Earl Anthony	107,585	1993	Walter Ray Williams Jr.	296,370	2012	Sean Rash	140,250
1976	Earl Anthony	110,833	1994	Norm Duke	273,753	2013	Sean Rash	248,317
1977	Mark Roth	105,583	1995	Mike Aulby	219,792	2014	Jason Belmonte	163,778
1978	Mark Roth	134,500	1996	Walter Ray Williams Jr.	241,330	2015	Jason Belmonte	178,542
1979	Mark Roth	124,517	1997	Walter Ray Williams Jr.	240,544	2016	E. J. Tackett	168,290
						2017	Jason Belmonte	238,912

World Chess Champions, 1886-2018
Source: U.S. Chess Federation, International Chess Federation (FIDE)
Official world champions since the title was first used. As of Oct. 2018.

Years	Champion, country	Years	Champion, country
1886-94	Wilhelm Steinitz, Austria	**1972-75**	Bobby Fischer, U.S.[2]
1894-1921	Emanuel Lasker, Germany	**1975-85**	Anatoly Karpov, USSR
1921-27	Jose R. Capablanca, Cuba	**1985-2000**	Garry Kasparov, USSR/Russia[3,4]
1927-35	Alexander Alekhine, France	**1993-99**	Anatoly Karpov, Russia (FIDE)[3]
1935-37	Max Euwe, Netherlands	**1999-2000**	Alexander Khalifman, Russia (FIDE)
1937-46	Alexander Alekhine, France[1]	**2000-02**	Viswanathan Anand, India (FIDE)
1948-57	Mikhail Botvinnik, USSR	**2000-06**	Vladimir Kramnik, Russia (classical)[4]
1957-58	Vassily Smyslov, USSR	**2002-04**	Ruslan Ponomariov, Ukraine (FIDE)
1958-59	Mikhail Botvinnik, USSR	**2004-05**	Rustam Kasimdzhanov, Uzbekistan (FIDE)
1960-61	Mikhail Tal, USSR	**2005-06**	Veselin Topalov, Bulgaria (FIDE)[5]
1961-63	Mikhail Botvinnik, USSR	**2006-07**	Vladimir Kramnik, Russia[5]
1963-69	Tigran Petrosian, USSR	**2007-13**	Viswanathan Anand, India
1969-72	Boris Spassky, USSR	**2013-**	Magnus Carlsen, Norway

(1) After Alekhine died in 1946, the title was vacant until 1948, when Botvinnik won the first world championship event sanctioned by FIDE. (2) Defaulted championship after refusing to accept FIDE rules for a championship match, Apr. 1975. (3) Kasparov broke with FIDE, Feb. 26, 1993. FIDE stripped Kasparov of his FIDE title Mar. 23. Kasparov defeated Nigel Short (UK) in a world championship match played Sept.-Oct. 1993 under the auspices of the Professional Chess Association (PCA), a new organization the two founded. FIDE held a championship match between Anatoly Karpov (Russia) and Jan Timman (Netherlands), which Karpov won in Nov. 1993. The PCA folded in 1995, but Kasparov was still considered the "classical" world champion. (That is, he defended his title against challengers; FIDE matches are arranged differently.) (4) In Nov. 2000, Kramnik defeated Kasparov for the classical world championship title. (5) Kramnik, the classical world champion since 2000, unified the chess titles by defeating Topalov on Oct. 13, 2006, at a world championship match.

U.S. and World Figure Skating Championships, 1952-2018

U.S. Champions			World Champions	
Men's winner	Women's winner	Year	Men's winner, country	Women's winner, country
Dick Button	Tenley Albright	1952	Dick Button, U.S.	Jacqueline du Bief, France
Hayes Jenkins	Tenley Albright	1953	Hayes Jenkins, U.S.	Tenley Albright, U.S.
Hayes Jenkins	Tenley Albright	1954	Hayes Jenkins, U.S.	Gundi Busch, W. Germany
Hayes Jenkins	Tenley Albright	1955	Hayes Jenkins, U.S.	Tenley Albright, U.S.
Hayes Jenkins	Tenley Albright	1956	Hayes Jenkins, U.S.	Carol Heiss, U.S.
David Jenkins	Carol Heiss	1957	David Jenkins, U.S.	Carol Heiss, U.S.
David Jenkins	Carol Heiss	1958	David Jenkins, U.S.	Carol Heiss, U.S.
David Jenkins	Carol Heiss	1959	David Jenkins, U.S.	Carol Heiss, U.S.
David Jenkins	Carol Heiss	1960	Alain Giletti, France	Carol Heiss, U.S.
Bradley Lord	Laurence Owen	1961	No competition[1]	No competition[1]
Monty Hoyt	Barbara Roles Pursley	1962	Don Jackson, Canada	Sjoukje Dijkstra, Netherlands
Tommy Litz	Lorraine Hanlon	1963	Don McPherson, Canada	Sjoukje Dijkstra, Netherlands
Scott Allen	Peggy Fleming	1964	Manfred Schnelldorfer, W. Germany	Sjoukje Dijkstra, Netherlands
Gary Visconti	Peggy Fleming	1965	Alain Calmat, France	Petra Burka, Canada
Scott Allen	Peggy Fleming	1966	Emmerich Danzer, Austria	Peggy Fleming, U.S.
Gary Visconti	Peggy Fleming	1967	Emmerich Danzer, Austria	Peggy Fleming, U.S.
Tim Wood	Peggy Fleming	1968	Emmerich Danzer, Austria	Peggy Fleming, U.S.
Tim Wood	Janet Lynn	1969	Tim Wood, U.S.	Gabriele Seyfert, E. Germany
Tim Wood	Janet Lynn	1970	Tim Wood, U.S.	Gabriele Seyfert, E. Germany
John Misha Petkevich	Janet Lynn	1971	Ondrej Nepela, Czechoslovakia	Beatrix Schuba, Austria
Ken Shelley	Janet Lynn	1972	Ondrej Nepela, Czechoslovakia	Beatrix Schuba, Austria
Gordon McKellen Jr.	Janet Lynn	1973	Ondrej Nepela, Czechoslovakia	Karen Magnussen, Canada
Gordon McKellen Jr.	Dorothy Hamill	1974	Jan Hoffmann, E. Germany	Christine Errath, E. Germany
Gordon McKellen Jr.	Dorothy Hamill	1975	Sergei Volkov, USSR	Dianne de Leeuw, Neth.
Terry Kubicka	Dorothy Hamill	1976	John Curry, UK	Dorothy Hamill, U.S.
Charles Tickner	Linda Fratianne	1977	Vladimir Kovalev, USSR	Linda Fratianne, U.S.
Charles Tickner	Linda Fratianne	1978	Charles Tickner, U.S.	Anett Poetzsch, E. Germany
Charles Tickner	Linda Fratianne	1979	Vladimir Kovalev, USSR	Linda Fratianne, U.S.
Charles Tickner	Linda Fratianne	1980	Jan Hoffmann, E. Germany	Anett Poetzsch, E. Germany
Scott Hamilton	Elaine Zayak	1981	Scott Hamilton, U.S.	Denise Biellmann, Switzerland
Scott Hamilton	Rosalynn Sumners	1982	Scott Hamilton, U.S.	Elaine Zayak, U.S.
Scott Hamilton	Rosalynn Sumners	1983	Scott Hamilton, U.S.	Rosalynn Sumners, U.S.
Scott Hamilton	Rosalynn Sumners	1984	Scott Hamilton, U.S.	Katarina Witt, E. Germany
Brian Boitano	Tiffany Chin	1985	Aleksandr Fadeev, USSR	Katarina Witt, E. Germany
Brian Boitano	Debi Thomas	1986	Brian Boitano, U.S.	Debi Thomas, U.S.
Brian Boitano	Jill Trenary	1987	Brian Orser, Canada	Katarina Witt, E. Germany
Brian Boitano	Debi Thomas	1988	Brian Boitano, U.S.	Katarina Witt, E. Germany
Christopher Bowman	Jill Trenary	1989	Kurt Browning, Canada	Midori Ito, Japan
Todd Eldredge	Jill Trenary	1990	Kurt Browning, Canada	Jill Trenary, U.S.
Todd Eldredge	Tonya Harding	1991	Kurt Browning, Canada	Kristi Yamaguchi, U.S.
Christopher Bowman	Kristi Yamaguchi	1992	Viktor Petrenko, Ukraine	Kristi Yamaguchi, U.S.
Scott Davis	Nancy Kerrigan	1993	Kurt Browning, Canada	Oksana Baiul, Ukraine
Scott Davis	Vacant[2]	1994	Elvis Stojko, Canada	Yuka Sato, Japan
Todd Eldredge	Nicole Bobek	1995	Elvis Stojko, Canada	Chen Lu, China
Rudy Galindo	Michelle Kwan	1996	Todd Eldredge, U.S.	Michelle Kwan, U.S.
Todd Eldredge	Tara Lipinski	1997	Elvis Stojko, Canada	Tara Lipinski, U.S.
Todd Eldredge	Michelle Kwan	1998	Alexei Yagudin, Russia	Michelle Kwan, U.S.
Michael Weiss	Michelle Kwan	1999	Alexei Yagudin, Russia	Maria Butyrskaya, Russia
Michael Weiss	Michelle Kwan	2000	Alexei Yagudin, Russia	Michelle Kwan, U.S.
Timothy Goebel	Michelle Kwan	2001	Yevgeny Plushenko, Russia	Michelle Kwan, U.S.
Todd Eldredge	Michelle Kwan	2002	Alexei Yagudin, Russia	Irina Slutskaya, Russia
Michael Weiss	Michelle Kwan	2003	Yevgeny Plushenko, Russia	Michelle Kwan, U.S.
Johnny Weir	Michelle Kwan	2004	Yevgeny Plushenko, Russia	Shizuka Arakawa, Japan
Johnny Weir	Michelle Kwan	2005	Stéphane Lambiel, Switzerland	Irina Slutskaya, Russia
Johnny Weir	Sasha Cohen	2006	Stéphane Lambiel, Switzerland	Kimmie Meissner, U.S.
Evan Lysacek	Kimmie Meissner	2007	Brian Joubert, France	Miki Ando, Japan
Evan Lysacek	Mirai Nagasu	2008	Jeffrey Buttle, Canada	Mao Asada, Japan
Jeremy Abbott	Alissa Czisny	2009	Evan Lysacek, U.S.	Yuna Kim, South Korea
Jeremy Abbott	Rachael Flatt	2010	Daisuke Takahashi, Japan	Mao Asada, Japan
Ryan Bradley	Alissa Czisny	2011	Patrick Chan, Canada	Miki Ando, Japan
Jeremy Abbott	Ashley Wagner	2012	Patrick Chan, Canada	Carolina Kostner, Italy
Max Aaron	Ashley Wagner	2013	Patrick Chan, Canada	Yuna Kim, South Korea
Jeremy Abbott	Gracie Gold	2014	Yuzuru Hanyu, Japan	Mao Asada, Japan
Jason Brown	Ashley Wagner	2015	Javier Fernández, Spain	Elizaveta Tuktamysheva, Russia
Adam Rippon	Gracie Gold	2016	Javier Fernández, Spain	Evgenia Medvedeva, Russia
Nathan Chen	Karen Chen	2017	Yuzuru Hanyu, Japan	Evgenia Medvedeva, Russia
Nathan Chen	Bradie Tennell	2018	Nathan Chen, U.S.	Kaetlyn Osmond, Canada

(1) Competition canceled after 18-member U.S. team died in plane crash en route. (2) Tonya Harding was stripped of the title for her involvement in an attack on rival Nancy Kerrigan.

Alpine Skiing Men's World Cup Champions, 1967-2018

Year	Champion, country	Year	Champion, country	Year	Champion, country
1967	Jean Claude Killy, France	1985	Marc Girardelli, Luxembourg	2002	Stephan Eberharter, Austria
1968	Jean Claude Killy, France	1986	Marc Girardelli, Luxembourg	2003	Stephan Eberharter, Austria
1969	Karl Schranz, Austria	1987	Pirmin Zurbriggen, Switzerland	2004	Hermann Maier, Austria
1970	Karl Schranz, Austria	1988	Pirmin Zurbriggen, Switzerland	2005	Bode Miller, U.S.
1971	Gustavo Thoeni, Italy	1989	Marc Girardelli, Luxembourg	2006	Benjamin Raich, Austria
1972	Gustavo Thoeni, Italy	1990	Pirmin Zurbriggen, Switzerland	2007	Aksel Lund Svindal, Norway
1973	Gustavo Thoeni, Italy	1991	Marc Girardelli, Luxembourg	2008	Bode Miller, U.S.
1974	Piero Gros, Italy	1992	Paul Accola, Switzerland	2009	Aksel Lund Svindal, Norway
1975	Gustavo Thoeni, Italy	1993	Marc Girardelli, Luxembourg	2010	Carlo Janka, Switzerland
1976	Ingemar Stenmark, Sweden	1994	Kjetil André Aamodt, Norway	2011	Ivica Kostelic, Croatia
1977	Ingemar Stenmark, Sweden	1995	Alberto Tomba, Italy	2012	Marcel Hirscher, Austria
1978	Ingemar Stenmark, Sweden	1996	Lasse Kjus, Norway	2013	Marcel Hirscher, Austria
1979	Peter Luescher, Switzerland	1997	Luc Alphand, France	2014	Marcel Hirscher, Austria
1980	Andreas Wenzel, Liechtenstein	1998	Hermann Maier, Austria	2015	Marcel Hirscher, Austria
1981	Phil Mahre, U.S.	1999	Lasse Kjus, Norway	2016	Marcel Hirscher, Austria
1982	Phil Mahre, U.S.	2000	Hermann Maier, Austria	2017	Marcel Hirscher, Austria
1983	Phil Mahre, U.S.	2001	Hermann Maier, Austria	2018	Marcel Hirscher, Austria
1984	Pirmin Zurbriggen, Switzerland				

Alpine Skiing Women's World Cup Champions, 1967-2018

Year	Champion, country	Year	Champion, country	Year	Champion, country
1967	Nancy Greene, Canada	1985	Michela Figini, Switzerland	2002	Michaela Dorfmeister, Austria
1968	Nancy Greene, Canada	1986	Maria Walliser, Switzerland	2003	Janica Kostelic, Croatia
1969	Gertrud Gabl, Austria	1987	Maria Walliser, Switzerland	2004	Anja Paerson, Sweden
1970	Michèle Jacot, France	1988	Michela Figini, Switzerland	2005	Anja Paerson, Sweden
1971	Annemarie Proell, Austria	1989	Vreni Schneider, Switzerland	2006	Janica Kostelic, Croatia
1972	Annemarie Proell, Austria	1990	Petra Kronberger, Austria	2007	Nicole Hosp, Austria
1973	Annemarie Proell, Austria	1991	Petra Kronberger, Austria	2008	Lindsey Vonn, U.S.
1974	Annemarie Proell, Austria	1992	Petra Kronberger, Austria	2009	Lindsey Vonn, U.S.
1975	Annemarie Proell, Austria	1993	Anita Wachter, Austria	2010	Lindsey Vonn, U.S.
1976	Rose Mittermaier, W. Germany	1994	Vreni Schneider, Switzerland	2011	Maria Höfl-Riesch, Germany
1977	Lise-Marie Morerod, Switzerland	1995	Vreni Schneider, Switzerland	2012	Lindsey Vonn, U.S.
1978	Hanni Wenzel, Liechtenstein	1996	Katja Seizinger, Germany	2013	Tina Maze, Slovenia
1979	Annemarie Moser-Proell, Austria	1997	Pernilla Wiberg, Sweden	2014	Anna Fenninger, Austria
1980	Hanni Wenzel, Liechtenstein	1998	Katja Seizinger, Germany	2015	Anna Fenninger, Austria
1981	Marie-Theres Nadig, Switzerland	1999	Alexandra Meissnitzer, Austria	2016	Lara Gut, Switzerland
1982	Erika Hess, Switzerland	2000	Renate Goetschl, Austria	2017	Mikaela Shiffrin, U.S.
1983	Tamara McKinney, U.S.	2001	Janica Kostelic, Croatia	2018	Mikaela Shiffrin, U.S.
1984	Erika Hess, Switzerland				

Tour de France, 2018

Welsh 32-year-old Geraint Thomas won the 105th edition of the Tour de France July 29, 2018, marking the sixth time in seven years cycling's premiere race was won by a British cyclist. The first stage of the 2,081-mi (3,349-km) Tour de France began July 7 in Noirmoutier-en-l'Île, France. The 21st and final stage ended in Paris, where Thomas claimed victory in 83 hr., 17 min., 13 sec., followed by Dutch rider Tom Dumoulin, 1 min., 51 sec. back, and Thomas's fellow Team Sky rider Chris Froome, 2 min., 24 sec. behind. France's Pierre Roger Latour won the white jersey as the best rider under age 25, and fellow countryman Julian Alaphilippe won the polka dot jersey as the best climber. Slovakia's Peter Sagan—who was disqualified after stage four of the 2017 Tour for causing a crash—reclaimed the green jersey as points leader, which he had previously won five consecutive years.

The 2019 Tour de France is scheduled to be held July 6-28. Its route will take cyclists from Brussels, Belgium, to Paris.

Tour de France Winners, 1903-2018

The Tour de France was first held in 1903. Sixty cyclists began the 1,509-mi (2,428-km) race at Montgeron, a suburb of Paris, and 21 cyclists finished the six-stage race 17 days later in Paris. The race route changes every year. Race not held, 1915-18, 1940-46.

Year	Winner, country	Year	Winner, country	Year	Winner, country
1903	Maurice Garin, France	1949	Fausto Coppi, Italy	1984	Laurent Fignon, France
1904	Henri Cornet, France	1950	Ferdi Kübler, Switzerland	1985	Bernard Hinault, France
1905	Louis Trousselier, France	1951	Hugo Koblet, Switzerland	1986	Greg LeMond, U.S.
1906	René Pottier, France	1952	Fausto Coppi, Italy	1987	Stephen Roche, Ireland
1907	Lucien Petit-Breton, France	1953	Louison Bobet, France	1988	Pedro Delgado, Spain
1908	Lucien Petit-Breton, France	1954	Louison Bobet, France	1989	Greg LeMond, U.S.
1909	François Faber, Luxembourg	1955	Louison Bobet, France	1990	Greg LeMond, U.S.
1910	Octave Lapize, France	1956	Roger Walkowiak, France	1991	Miguel Indurain, Spain
1911	Gustave Garrigou, France	1957	Jacques Anquetil, France	1992	Miguel Indurain, Spain
1912	Odile Defraye, Belgium	1958	Charly Gaul, Luxembourg	1993	Miguel Indurain, Spain
1913	Philippe Thys, Belgium	1959	Federico Bahamontes, Spain	1994	Miguel Indurain, Spain
1914	Philippe Thys, Belgium	1960	Gastone Nencini, Italy	1995	Miguel Indurain, Spain
1919	Firmin Lambot, Belgium	1961	Jacques Anquetil, France	1996	Bjarne Riis, Denmark
1920	Philippe Thys, Belgium	1962	Jacques Anquetil, France	1997	Jan Ullrich, Germany
1921	Léon Scieur, Belgium	1963	Jacques Anquetil, France	1998	Marco Pantani, Italy
1922	Firmin Lambot, Belgium	1964	Jacques Anquetil, France	1999	Vacant[1]
1923	Henri Pélissier, France	1965	Felice Gimondi, Italy	2000	Vacant[1]
1924	Ottavio Bottecchia, Italy	1966	Lucien Aimar, France	2001	Vacant[1]
1925	Ottavio Bottecchia, Italy	1967	Roger Pingeon, France	2002	Vacant[1]
1926	Lucien Buysse, Belgium	1968	Jan Janssen, Netherlands	2003	Vacant[1]
1927	Nicolas Frantz, Luxembourg	1969	Eddy Merckx, Belgium	2004	Vacant[1]
1928	Nicolas Frantz, Luxembourg	1970	Eddy Merckx, Belgium	2005	Vacant[1]
1929	Maurice Dewaele, Belgium	1971	Eddy Merckx, Belgium	2006	Óscar Pereiro, Spain[2]
1930	André Leducq, France	1972	Eddy Merckx, Belgium	2007	Alberto Contador, Spain
1931	Antonin Magne, France	1973	Luis Ocaña, Spain	2008	Carlos Sastre, Spain
1932	André Leducq, France	1974	Eddy Merckx, Belgium	2009	Alberto Contador, Spain
1933	Georges Speicher, France	1975	Bernard Thévenet, France	2010	Andy Schleck, Luxembourg[3]
1934	Antonin Magne, France	1976	Lucien Van Impe, Belgium	2011	Cadel Evans, Australia
1935	Romain Maes, Belgium	1977	Bernard Thévenet, France	2012	Bradley Wiggins, UK
1936	Sylvère Maes, Belgium	1978	Bernard Hinault, France	2013	Chris Froome, UK
1937	Roger Lapépie, France	1979	Bernard Hinault, France	2014	Vincenzo Nibali, Italy
1938	Gino Bartali, Italy	1980	Joop Zoetemelk, Netherlands	2015	Chris Froome, UK
1939	Sylvère Maes, Belgium	1981	Bernard Hinault, France	2016	Chris Froome, UK
1947	Jean Robic, France	1982	Bernard Hinault, France	2017	Chris Froome, UK
1948	Gino Bartali, Italy	1983	Laurent Fignon, France	2018	Geraint Thomas, UK

(1) Lance Armstrong, U.S., was stripped of his seven Tour titles Oct. 22, 2012; Armstrong dropped his fight against doping charges Aug. 23, 2012. (2) Floyd Landis, U.S., was stripped of the 2006 title, Sept. 20, 2007, for doping. Landis lost a final appeal of the ruling June 30, 2008. (3) Alberto Contador, Spain, was stripped of the 2010 title, Feb. 6, 2012, for doping.

Swimming World Records

Long course (50-m pools only) records, as of Oct. 2018. All times in minutes:seconds. * = Record pending ratification.

Men's Records

Freestyle

Distance	Record	Holder	Nationality	Location	Date
50 meters	0:20.91	César Cielo Filho	Brazil	São Paulo, Brazil	Dec. 18, 2009
100 meters	0:46.91	César Cielo Filho	Brazil	Rome, Italy	July 30, 2009
200 meters	1:42.00	Paul Biedermann	Germany	Rome, Italy	July 28, 2009
400 meters	3:40.07	Paul Biedermann	Germany	Rome, Italy	July 26, 2009
800 meters	7:32.12	Zhang Lin	China	Rome, Italy	July 29, 2009
1,500 meters	14:31.02	Yang Sun	China	London, England, UK	Aug. 4, 2012

Backstroke

50 meters	0:24.00*	Kliment Kolesnikov	Russia	Glasgow, Scotland, UK	Aug. 4, 2018
100 meters	0:51.85	Ryan Murphy	U.S.	Rio de Janeiro, Brazil	Aug. 13, 2016
200 meters	1:51.92	Aaron Peirsol	U.S.	Rome, Italy	July 31, 2009

Breaststroke

50 meters	0:25.95	Adam Peaty	UK	Budapest, Hungary	July 25, 2017
100 meters	0:57.10*	Adam Peaty	UK	Glasgow, Scotland, UK	Aug. 4, 2018
200 meters	2:06.67	Ippei Watanabe	Japan	Tokyo, Japan	Jan. 29, 2017

Butterfly

50 meters	0:22.27	Andriy Govorov	Ukraine	Rome, Italy	July 1, 2018
100 meters	0:49.82	Michael Phelps	U.S.	Rome, Italy	Aug. 1, 2009
200 meters	1:51.51	Michael Phelps	U.S.	Rome, Italy	July 29, 2009

Individual medley

200 meters	1:54.00	Ryan Lochte	U.S.	Shanghai, China	July 28, 2011
400 meters	4:03.84	Michael Phelps	U.S.	Beijing, China	Aug. 10, 2008

Freestyle relay

400 m (4×100)	3:08.24	Phelps, Weber-Gale, Jones, Lezak	U.S.	Beijing, China	Aug. 11, 2008
800 m (4×200)	6:58.55	Phelps, Berens, Walters, Lochte	U.S.	Rome, Italy	July 31, 2009

Medley relay

400 m (4×100)	3:27.28	Peirsol, Shanteau, Phelps, Walters	U.S.	Rome, Italy	Aug. 2, 2009

Women's Records

Freestyle

Distance	Record	Holder	Nationality	Location	Date
50 meters	0:23.67	Sarah Sjöström	Sweden	Budapest, Hungary	July 29, 2017
100 meters	0:51.71	Sarah Sjöström	Sweden	Budapest, Hungary	July 23, 2017
200 meters	1:52.98	Federica Pellegrini	Italy	Rome, Italy	July 29, 2009
400 meters	3:56.46	Katie Ledecky	U.S.	Rio de Janeiro, Brazil	Aug. 7, 2016
800 meters	8:04.79	Katie Ledecky	U.S.	Rio de Janeiro, Brazil	Aug. 12, 2016
1,500 meters	15:20.48	Katie Ledecky	U.S.	Indianapolis, IN	May 16, 2018

Backstroke

50 meters	0:27.06	Zhao Jing	China	Rome, Italy	July 30, 2009
100 meters	0:58.00	Kathleen Baker	U.S.	Irvine, CA	July 28, 2018
200 meters	2:04.06	Missy Franklin	U.S.	London, England, UK	Aug. 3, 2012

Breaststroke

50 meters	0:29.40	Lilly King	U.S.	Budapest, Hungary	July 30, 2017
100 meters	1:04.13	Lilly King	U.S.	Budapest, Hungary	July 25, 2017
200 meters	2:19.11	Rikke Moller Pedersen	Denmark	Barcelona, Spain	Aug. 1, 2013

Butterfly

50 meters	0:24.43	Sarah Sjöström	Sweden	Boras, Sweden	July 5, 2014
100 meters	0:55.48	Sarah Sjöström	Sweden	Rio de Janeiro, Brazil	Aug. 7, 2016
200 meters	2:01.81	Liu Zige	China	Jinan, China	Oct. 21, 2009

Individual medley

200 meters	2:06.12	Katinka Hosszú	Hungary	Kazan, Russia	Aug. 3, 2015
400 meters	4:26.36	Katinka Hosszú	Hungary	Rio de Janeiro, Brazil	Aug. 6, 2016

Freestyle relay

400 m (4×100)	3:30.05	Jack, Campbell, McKeon, Campbell	Australia	Gold Coast, Australia	Apr. 5, 2018
800 m (4×200)	7:42.08	Yang, Zhu, Liu, Pang	China	Rome, Italy	July 30, 2009

Medley relay

400 m (4×100)	3:51.55	Baker, King, Worrell, Manuel	U.S.	Budapest, Hungary	July 30, 2017

World Track and Field Outdoor Records

The International Association of Athletics Federations (IAAF), the world body of track and field, recognizes only records in metric distances, except for the mile. As of Oct. 2018. * = Record pending ratification.

Men's Records

Running

Event	Record	Holder	Nationality	Location	Date
100 meters	9.58 s.	Usain Bolt	Jamaica	Berlin, Germany	Aug. 16, 2009
200 meters	19.19 s.	Usain Bolt	Jamaica	Berlin, Germany	Aug. 20, 2009
400 meters	43.03 s.	Wayde Van Niekerk	South Africa	Rio de Janeiro, Brazil	Aug. 14, 2016
800 meters	1 min., 40.91 s.	David Lekuta Rudisha	Kenya	London, England, UK	Aug. 9, 2012
1,000 meters	2 min., 11.96 s.	Noah Ngeny	Kenya	Rieti, Italy	Sept. 5, 1999
1,500 meters	3 min., 26.00 s.	Hicham El Guerrouj	Morocco	Rome, Italy	July 14, 1998
1 mile	3 min., 43.13 s.	Hicham El Guerrouj	Morocco	Rome, Italy	July 7, 1999
2,000 meters	4 min., 44.79 s.	Hicham El Guerrouj	Morocco	Berlin, Germany	Sept. 7, 1999
3,000 meters	7 min., 20.67 s.	Daniel Komen	Kenya	Rieti, Italy	Sept. 1, 1996
3,000-meter stpl.	7 min., 53.63 s.	Saif Saaeed Shaheen	Qatar	Brussels, Belgium	Sept. 3, 2004
5,000 meters	12 min., 37.35 s.	Kenenisa Bekele	Ethiopia	Hengelo, Netherlands	May 31, 2004
10,000 meters	26 min., 17.53 s.	Kenenisa Bekele	Ethiopia	Brussels, Belgium	Aug. 26, 2005
20,000 meters	56 min., 26.00 s.	Haile Gebrselassie	Ethiopia	Ostrava, Czech Rep.	June 27, 2007
25,000 meters	1 hr., 12 min., 25.4 s.	Moses Cheruiyot Mosop	Kenya	Eugene, OR	June 3, 2011
Marathon	2 hr., 1 min., 39 s.*	Eliud Kipchoge	Kenya	Berlin, Germany	Sept. 16, 2018
110-meter hurdles	12.80 s.	Aries Merritt	U.S.	Brussels, Belgium	Sept. 7, 2012
400-meter hurdles	46.78 s.	Kevin Young	U.S.	Barcelona, Spain	Aug. 6, 1992
400 m (4×100)	36.84 s.	Carter, Frater, Blake, Bolt	Jamaica	London, England, UK	Aug. 11, 2012
800 m (4×200)	1 min., 18.63 s.	Ashmeade, Weir, Brown, Blake	Jamaica	Nassau, The Bahamas	May 24, 2014
1,600 m (4×400)	2 min., 54.29 s.	Valmon, Watts, Reynolds, Johnson	U.S.	Stuttgart, Germany	Aug. 22, 1993
3,200 m (4×800)	7 min., 2.43 s.	Mutua, Yiampoy, Kombich, Bungei	Kenya	Brussels, Belgium	Aug. 25, 2006

Field Events

Event	Record	Holder	Nationality	Location	Date
High jump	2.45 m (8' ½")	Javier Sotomayor	Cuba	Salamanca, Spain	July 27, 1993
Long jump	8.95 m (29' 4½")	Mike Powell	U.S.	Tokyo, Japan	Aug. 30, 1991
Triple jump	18.29 m (60' ¼")	Jonathan Edwards	UK	Gothenburg, Sweden	Aug. 7, 1995
Pole vault	6.14 m (20' 1¾")	Sergey Bubka	Ukraine	Sestriere, Italy	July 31, 1994
Discus	74.08 m (243' 0")	Jürgen Schult	E. Germany	Neubrandenburg, E. Germany	June 6, 1986
Hammer	86.74 m (284' 7")	Yuriy Sedykh	USSR	Stuttgart, W. Germany	Aug. 30, 1986
Javelin	98.48 m (323' 1")	Jan Zelezný	Czech Rep.	Jena, W. Germany	May 25, 1996
Shot put	23.12 m (75' 10¼")	Randy Barnes	U.S.	Westwood, CA	May 20, 1990
Decathlon	9,045 pts.	Ashton Eaton	U.S.	Beijing, China	Aug. 29, 2015

Women's Records

Running

Event	Record	Holder	Nationality	Location	Date
100 meters	10.49 s.	Florence Griffith-Joyner	U.S.	Indianapolis, IN	July 16, 1988
200 meters	21.34 s.	Florence Griffith-Joyner	U.S.	Seoul, S. Korea	Sept. 29, 1988
400 meters	47.60 s.	Marita Koch	E. Germany	Canberra, Australia	Oct. 6, 1985
800 meters	1 min., 53.28 s.	Jarmila Kratochvílová	Czechoslovakia	Munich, W. Germany	July 26, 1983
1,000 meters	2 min., 28.98 s.	Svetlana Masterkova	Russia	Brussels, Belgium	Aug. 23, 1996
1,500 meters	3 min., 50.07 s.	Genzebe Dibaba	Ethiopia	Monaco	July 17, 2015
1 mile	4 min., 12.56 s.	Svetlana Masterkova	Russia	Zürich, Switzerland	Aug. 14, 1996
2,000 meters	5 min., 25.36 s.	Sonia O'Sullivan	Ireland	Edinburgh, Scotland, UK	July 8, 1994
3,000 meters	8 min., 6.11 s.	Wang Junxia	China	Beijing, China	Sept. 13, 1993
3,000-meter stpl.	8 min., 44.32 s.	Beatrice Chepkoech	Kenya	Monaco	July 20, 2018
5,000 meters	14 min., 11.15 s.	Tirunesh Dibaba	Ethiopia	Oslo, Norway	June 6, 2008
10,000 meters	29 min., 17.45 s.	Almaz Ayana	Ethiopia	Rio de Janeiro, Brazil	Aug. 12, 2016
20,000 meters	1 hr., 5 min., 26.6 s.	Tegla Loroupe	Kenya	Borgholzhausen, Germany	Sept. 3, 2000
Marathon	2 hr., 15 min., 25.0 s.	Paula Radcliffe	UK	London, England, UK	Apr. 13, 2003
100-meter hurdles	12.20 s.	Kendra Harrison	U.S.	London, England, UK	July 22, 2016
400-meter hurdles	52.34 s.	Yuliya Pechenkina	Russia	Tula, Russia	Aug. 8, 2003
400 m (4×100)	40.82 s.	Madison, Felix, Knight, Jeter	U.S.	London, England, UK	Aug. 10, 2012
800 m (4×200)	1 min., 27.46 s.	Jenkins, Colander, Perry, Jones	U.S.	Philadelphia, PA	Apr. 29, 2000
1,600 m (4×400)	3 min., 15.17 s.	Ledovskaya, Nazarova, Pinigina, Bryzgina	USSR	Seoul, S. Korea	Oct. 1, 1988
3,200 m (4×800)	7 min., 50.17 s.	Olizarenko, Gurina, Borisova, Podyalovskaya	USSR	Moscow, USSR	Aug. 5, 1984

Field Events

Event	Record	Holder	Nationality	Location	Date
High jump	2.09 m (6' 10¼")	Stefka Kostadinova	Bulgaria	Rome, Italy	Aug. 30, 1987
Long jump	7.52 m (24' 8¼")	Galina Chistyakova	USSR	Leningrad, Russia	June 11, 1988
Triple jump	15.50 m (50' 10¼")	Inessa Kravets	Ukraine	Gothenburg, Sweden	Aug. 10, 1995
Pole vault	5.06 m (16' 7¾")	Yelena Isinbaeva	Russia	Zürich, Switzerland	Aug. 28, 2009
Discus	76.80 m (252' 0")	Gabriele Reinsch	E. Germany	Neubrandenburg, E. Germany	July 9, 1988
Hammer	82.98 m (272' 3")	Anita Wlodarczyk	Poland	Warsaw, Poland	Aug. 28, 2016
Javelin	72.28 m (237' 1¾")	Barbora Spotáková	Czech Rep.	Stuttgart, Germany	Sept. 13, 2008
Shot put	22.63 m (74' 3")	Natalya Lisovskaya	USSR	Moscow, Russia	June 7, 1987
Heptathlon	7,291 pts.	Jackie Joyner-Kersee	U.S.	Seoul, S. Korea	Sept. 24, 1988

Iditarod Trail Sled Dog Race, 2018

Joar Leifseth Ulsom won the 46th annual Iditarod Trail Sled Dog Race to Nome, AK, Mar. 14, 2018. The 31-year-old Norwegian finished the 998-mi course on the southern route to Nome in 9 days, 12 hr. Ulsom was the first person not named Seavey to win the race since 2011, and the second European ever to win it (after fellow Norwegian Robert Sorlie in 2003 and 2005).

The 2019 race was scheduled to begin Mar. 2 in Anchorage and again follow the 998-mi southern route.

Westminster Kennel Club Best-In-Show Dogs, 1985-2018

Year	Best-in-Show winner, breed	Year	Best-in-Show winner, breed
1985	Ch. Braeburn's Close Encounter, Scottish Terrier	2003	Ch. Torums Scarf Michael, Kerry Blue Terrier
1986	Ch. Marjetta's National Acclaim, Pointer	2004	Ch. Darbydale's All Rise Pouch Cove, Newfoundland
1987	Ch. Covy Tucker Hill's Manhattan, German Shepherd Dog	2005	Ch. Kan-Point's VJK Autumn Roses, Pointer (German Shorthaired)
1988	Ch. Great Elms Prince Charming II, Pomeranian		
1989	Ch. Royal Tudor's Wild As The Wind, Doberman Pinscher	2006	Ch. Rocky Top's Sundance Kid, Bull Terrier (Colored)
1990	Ch. Wendessa Crown Prince, Pekingese	2007	Ch. Felicity's Diamond Jim, Spaniel (English Springer)
1991	Ch. Whisperwind On A Carousel, Poodle (Standard)	2008	Ch. K-Run's Park Me In First, Beagle (15 Inch)
1992	Ch. Registry's Lonesome Dove, Fox Terrier (Wire)	2009	Ch. Clussexx Three D Grinchy Glee, Spaniel (Sussex)
1993	Ch. Salilyn's Condor, Spaniel (English Springer)	2010	Ch. Roundtown Mercedes Of Maryscot, Scottish Terrier
1994	Ch. Chidley Willum The Conqueror, Norwich Terrier	2011	GCh. Foxcliffe Hickory Wind, Scottish Deerhound
1995	Ch. Gaelforce Post Script, Scottish Terrier	2012	GCh. Palacegarden Malachy, Pekingese
1996	Ch. Clussexx Country Sunrise, Spaniel (Clumber)	2013	GCh. Banana Joe V Tani Kazari, Affenpinscher
1997	Ch. Parsifal Di Casa Netzer, Standard Schnauzer	2014	GCh. Afterall Painting The Sky, Fox Terrier (Wire)
1998	Ch. Fairewood Frolic, Norwich Terrier	2015	Ch. Tashtins Lookin For Trouble, Beagle (15 Inch)
1999	Ch. Loteki Supernatural Being, Papillon	2016	GCh. Vjk-Myst Garbonita's California Journey, Pointer (German Shorthaired)
2000	Ch. Salilyn 'N Erin's Shameless, Spaniel (English Springer)		
2001	Ch. Special Times Just Right, Bichon Frise	2017	GCh. Ch. Lockenhaus' Rumor Has It V Kenlyn, German Shepherd Dog
2002	Ch. Surrey Spice Girl, Poodle (Miniature)	2018	GCh. Belle Creek's All I Care About Is Love, Bichon Frise

World Marathon Majors Winners, 2006-18

Marathoners are awarded points relative to their finish in each race in the series; number of races and time period encompassed by each series varies.

Series	Men's winner, country	Women's winner, country	Series	Men's winner, country	Women's winner, country
I: 2006-07	Robert K. Cheruiyot, Kenya	Gete Wami, Ethiopia	VI: 2011-12	Geoffrey Mutai, Kenya	Mary Keitany, Kenya
II: 2007-08	Martin Lel, Kenya	Irina Mikitenko, Germany	VII: 2012-13	Tsegaye Kebede, Ethiopia	Priscah Jeptoo, Kenya
III: 2008-09	Samuel Wanjiru, Kenya	Irina Mikitenko, Germany	VIII: 2013-14	Wilson Kipsang, Kenya	Edna Kiplagat, Kenya*
IV: 2009-10	Samuel Wanjiru, Kenya	Irina Mikitenko, Germany*	IX: 2015-16	Eliud Kipchoge, Kenya	Mary Keitany, Kenya
V: 2010-11	Emmanuel Mutai, Kenya	Edna Kiplagat, Kenya*	X: 2016-17	Eliud Kipchoge, Kenya	Edna Kiplagat, Kenya*
			XI: 2017-18	Eliud Kipchoge, Kenya	Mary Keitany, Kenya

* = Winner adjusted following doping disqualifications.

Boston Marathon Winners, 1972-2018

All times in hour:minute:second format. * = Course record.

Men's winner, country	Time	Year	Women's winner, country	Time
Olavi Suomalainen, Finland	2:15:39	1972	Nina Kuscsik, U.S.	3:10:26
Jon Anderson, U.S.	2:16:03	1973	Jacqueline Hansen, U.S.	3:05:59
Neil Cusack, Ireland	2:13:39	1974	Michiko Gorman, U.S.	2:47:11
Bill Rodgers, U.S.	2:09:55	1975	Liane Winter, West Germany	2:42:24
Jack Fultz, U.S.	2:20:19	1976	Kim Merritt, U.S.	2:47:10
Jerome Drayton, Canada	2:14:46	1977	Michiko Gorman, U.S.	2:48:33
Bill Rodgers, U.S.	2:10:13	1978	Gayle S. Barron, U.S.	2:44:52
Bill Rodgers, U.S.	2:09:27	1979	Joan Benoit, U.S.	2:35:15
Bill Rodgers, U.S.	2:12:11	1980	Jacqueline Gareau, Canada	2:34:28
Toshihiko Seko, Japan	2:09:26	1981	Allison Roe, New Zealand	2:26:46
Alberto Salazar, U.S.	2:08:52	1982	Charlotte Teske, West Germany	2:29:33
Greg Meyer, U.S.	2:09:00	1983	Joan Benoit, U.S.	2:22:43
Geoff Smith, England, UK	2:10:34	1984	Lorraine Moller, New Zealand	2:29:28
Geoff Smith, England, UK	2:14:05	1985	Lisa Larsen Weidenbach, U.S.	2:34:06
Robert de Castella, Australia	2:07:51	1986	Ingrid Kristiansen, Norway	2:24:55
Toshihiko Seko, Japan	2:11:50	1987	Rosa Mota, Portugal	2:25:21
Ibrahim Hussein, Kenya	2:08:43	1988	Rosa Mota, Portugal	2:24:30
Abebe Mekonnen, Ethiopia	2:09:06	1989	Ingrid Kristiansen, Norway	2:24:33
Gelindo Bordin, Italy	2:08:19	1990	Rosa Mota, Portugal	2:25:24
Ibrahim Hussein, Kenya	2:11:06	1991	Wanda Panfil, Poland	2:24:18
Ibrahim Hussein, Kenya	2:08:14	1992	Olga Markova, Russia	2:23:43
Cosmas Ndeti, Kenya	2:09:33	1993	Olga Markova, Russia	2:25:27
Cosmas Ndeti, Kenya	2:07:15	1994	Uta Pippig, Germany	2:21:45
Cosmas Ndeti, Kenya	2:09:22	1995	Uta Pippig, Germany	2:25:11
Moses Tanui, Kenya	2:09:15	1996	Uta Pippig, Germany	2:27:12
Lameck Aguta, Kenya	2:10:34	1997	Fatuma Roba, Ethiopia	2:26:23
Moses Tanui, Kenya	2:07:34	1998	Fatuma Roba, Ethiopia	2:23:21
Joseh Chebet, Kenya	2:09:52	1999	Fatuma Roba, Ethiopia	2:23:25
Elijah Lagat, Kenya	2:09:47	2000	Catherine Ndereba, Kenya	2:26:11
Lee Bong-ju, South Korea	2:09:43	2001	Catherine Ndereba, Kenya	2:23:53
Rodgers Rop, Kenya	2:09:02	2002	Margaret Okayo, Kenya	2:20:43
Robert Kipkoech Cheruiyot, Kenya	2:10:11	2003	Svetlana Zakharova, Russia	2:25:20
Timothy Cherigat, Kenya	2:10:37	2004	Catherine Ndereba, Kenya	2:24:27
Hailu Negussie, Ethiopia	2:11:45	2005	Catherine Ndereba, Kenya	2:25:13
Robert Kipkoech Cheruiyot, Kenya	2:07:14	2006	Rita Jeptoo, Kenya	2:23:38
Robert Kipkoech Cheruiyot, Kenya	2:14:13	2007	Lidiya Grigoryeva, Russia	2:29:18
Robert Kipkoech Cheruiyot, Kenya	2:07:46	2008	Dire Tune, Ethiopia	2:25:25
Deriba Merga, Ethiopia	2:08:42	2009	Salina Kosgei, Kenya	2:32:16
Robert Kiprono Cheruiyot, Kenya	2:05:52	2010	Teyba Erkesso, Ethiopia	2:26:11
Geoffrey Mutai, Kenya	2:03:02*	2011	Caroline Kilel, Kenya	2:22:36
Wesley Korir, Kenya	2:12:40	2012	Sharon Cherop, Kenya	2:31:50
Lelisa Desisa, Ethiopia	2:10:22	2013	Rita Jeptoo, Kenya	2:26:25
Meb Keflezighi, U.S.	2:08:37	2014	Buzunesh Deba, Ethiopia[1]	2:19:59*
Lelisa Desisa, Ethiopia	2:09:17	2015	Caroline Rotich, Kenya	2:24:55
Lemi Berhanu Hayle, Ethiopia	2:12:45	2016	Atsede Baysa, Ethiopia	2:29:19
Geoffrey Kirui, Kenya	2:09:37	2017	Edna Kiplagat, Kenya	2:21:52
Yuki Kawauchi, Japan	2:15:58	2018	Desiree Linden, U.S.	2:39:54

(1) Kenya's Rita Jeptoo was stripped of the victory in Dec. 2016 due to doping.

New York City Marathon Winners, 1970-2018

All times in hour:minute:second format. * = Course record. Race not held, 2012.

Men's winner, country	Time	Year	Women's winner, country	Time
Gary Muhrcke, U.S.	2:31:38	1970	No finisher	
Norman Higgins, U.S.	2:22:54	1971	Beth Bonner, U.S.	2:55:22
Sheldon Karlin, U.S.	2:27:52	1972	Nina Kuscsik, U.S.	3:08:41
Tom Fleming, U.S.	2:19:25	1973	Nina Kuscsik, U.S.	2:57:07
Norbert Sander, U.S.	2:26:30	1974	Katherine Switzer, U.S.	3:07:29
Tom Fleming, U.S.	2:19:27	1975	Kim Merritt, U.S.	2:46:14
Bill Rodgers, U.S.	2:10:10	1976	Miki Gorman, U.S.	2:39:11
Bill Rodgers, U.S.	2:11:28	1977	Miki Gorman, U.S.	2:43:10
Bill Rodgers, U.S.	2:12:12	1978	Grete Waitz, Norway	2:32:30
Bill Rodgers, U.S.	2:11:42	1979	Grete Waitz, Norway	2:27:33
Alberto Salazar, U.S.	2:09:41	1980	Grete Waitz, Norway	2:25:42
Alberto Salazar, U.S.	2:08:13	1981	Allison Roe, New Zealand	2:25:29
Alberto Salazar, U.S.	2:09:29	1982	Grete Waitz, Norway	2:27:14
Rod Dixon, New Zealand	2:08:59	1983	Grete Waitz, Norway	2:27:00
Orlando Pizzolato, Italy	2:14:53	1984	Grete Waitz, Norway	2:29:30
Orlando Pizzolato, Italy	2:11:34	1985	Grete Waitz, Norway	2:28:34
Gianni Poli, Italy	2:11:06	1986	Grete Waitz, Norway	2:28:06
Ibrahim Hussein, Kenya	2:11:01	1987	Priscilla Welch, England, UK	2:30:17
Steve Jones, Wales, UK	2:08:20	1988	Grete Waitz, Norway	2:28:07
Juma Ikangaa, Tanzania	2:08:01	1989	Ingrid Kristiansen, Norway	2:25:30
Douglas Wakiihuri, Kenya	2:12:39	1990	Wanda Panfil, Poland	2:30:45
Salvador García, Mexico	2:09:28	1991	Liz McColgan, Scotland, UK	2:27:32
Willie Mtolo, South Africa	2:09:29	1992	Lisa Ondieki, Australia	2:24:40
Andres Espinosa, Mexico	2:10:04	1993	Uta Pippig, Germany	2:26:24
German Silva, Mexico	2:11:21	1994	Tegla Loroupe, Kenya	2:27:37
German Silva, Mexico	2:11:00	1995	Tegla Loroupe, Kenya	2:28:06
Giacomo Leone, Italy	2:09:54	1996	Anuta Catuna, Romania	2:28:43
John Kagwe, Kenya	2:08:12	1997	F. Rochat-Moser, Switzerland	2:28:43
John Kagwe, Kenya	2:08:45	1998	Franca Fiacconi, Italy	2:25:17
Joseph Chebet, Kenya	2:09:14	1999	Adriana Fernandez, Mexico	2:25:06
Abdelkader El Mouaziz, Morocco	2:10:09	2000	Ludmila Petrova, Russia	2:25:45
Tesfaye Jifar, Ethiopia	2:07:43	2001	Margaret Okayo, Kenya	2:24:21
Rodgers Rop, Kenya	2:08:07	2002	Joyce Chepchumba, Kenya	2:25:56
Martin Lel, Kenya	2:10:30	2003	Margaret Okayo, Kenya	2:22:31*
Hendrik Ramaala, South Africa	2:09:28	2004	Paula Radcliffe, England, UK	2:23:10
Paul Tergat, Kenya	2:09:30	2005	Jelena Prokopcuka, Latvia	2:24:41
Marilson Gomes dos Santos, Brazil	2:09:58	2006	Jelena Prokopcuka, Latvia	2:25:05
Martin Lel, Kenya	2:09:04	2007	Paula Radcliffe, England, UK	2:23:09
Marilson Gomes dos Santos, Brazil	2:08:43	2008	Paula Radcliffe, England, UK	2:23:56
Meb Keflezighi, U.S.	2:09:15	2009	Derartu Tulu, Ethiopia	2:28:52
Gebre Gebremariam, Ethiopia	2:08:14	2010	Edna Kiplagat, Kenya	2:28:20
Geoffrey Mutai, Kenya	2:05:06*	2011	Firehiwot Dado, Ethiopia	2:23:15
Geoffrey Mutai, Kenya	2:08:24	2013	Priscah Jeptoo, Kenya	2:25:07
Wilson Kipsang, Kenya	2:10:59	2014	Mary Keitany, Kenya	2:25:07
Stanley Biwott, Kenya	2:10:34	2015	Mary Keitany, Kenya	2:24:25
Ghirmay Ghebreslassie, Eritrea	2:07:51	2016	Mary Keitany, Kenya	2:24:26
Geoffrey Kamworor, Kenya	2:10:53	2017	Shalane Flanagan, U.S.	2:26:53
Lelisa Desisa, Ethiopia	2:05:59	2018	Mary Keitany, Kenya	2:22:48

Ironman Triathlon World Championships, 1978-2018

The Ironman Triathlon World Championship—a 2.4-mi ocean swim, 112-mi bike ride, and 26.2-mi run—is held annually in Kailua-Kona, HI. All times in hour:minute:second format. * = Course record.

Men's winner, country	Time	Year	Women's winner, country	Time
Gordon Haller, U.S.	11:46:58	1978	No finisher	—
Tom Warren, U.S.	11:15:56	1979	Lyn Lemaire, U.S.	12:55:00
Dave Scott, U.S.	9:24:33	1980	Robin Beck, U.S.	11:21:24
John Howard, U.S.	9:38:29	1981	Linda Sweeney, U.S.	12:00:32
Dave Scott, U.S.	9:08:23	1982	Julie Leach, U.S.	10:54:08
Dave Scott, U.S.	9:05:57	1983	Sylviane Puntous, Canada	10:43:36
Dave Scott, U.S	8:54:20	1984	Sylviane Puntous, Canada	10:25:13
Scott Tinley, U.S.	8:50:54	1985	Joanne Ernst, U.S.	10:25:22
Dave Scott, U.S.	8:28:37	1986	Paula Newby-Fraser, Zimbabwe	9:49:14
Dave Scott, U.S.	8:34:13	1987	Erin Baker, New Zealand	9:35:25
Scott Molina, U.S.	8:31:00	1988	Paula Newby-Fraser, Zimbabwe	9:01:01
Mark Allen, U.S.	8:09:15	1989	Paula Newby-Fraser, Zimbabwe	9:00:56
Mark Allen, U.S.	8:28:17	1990	Erin Baker, New Zealand	9:13:42
Mark Allen, U.S.	8:18:32	1991	Paula Newby-Fraser, Zimbabwe	9:07:52
Mark Allen, U.S.	8:09:08	1992	Paula Newby-Fraser, Zimbabwe	8:55:28
Mark Allen, U.S.	8:07:45	1993	Paula Newby-Fraser, Zimbabwe	8:58:23
Greg Welch, Australia	8:20:27	1994	Paula Newby-Fraser, Zimbabwe	9:20:14
Mark Allen, U.S.	8:20:34	1995	Karen Smyers, U.S.	9:16:46
Luc Van Lierde, Belgium	8:04:08	1996	Paula Newby-Fraser, Zimbabwe	9:06:49
Thomas Hellriegel, Germany	8:33:01	1997	Heather Fuhr, Canada	9:31:43
Peter Reid, Canada	8:24:20	1998	Natascha Badmann, Switzerland	9:24:16
Luc Van Lierde, Belgium	8:17:17	1999	Lori Bowden, U.S.	9:13:02
Peter Reid, Canada	8:21:01	2000	Natascha Badmann, Switzerland	9:26:16
Timothy Deboom, U.S.	8:31:18	2001	Natascha Badmann, Switzerland	9:28:37
Timothy Deboom, U.S.	8:29:56	2002	Natascha Badmann, Switzerland	9:07:54
Peter Reid, Canada	8:22:35	2003	Lori Bowden, Canada	9:11:55
Normann Stadler, Germany	8:33:29	2004	Natascha Badmann, Switzerland[1]	9:50:04
Faris al-Sultan, Germany	8:14:17	2005	Natascha Badmann, Switzerland	9:09:30
Normann Stadler, Germany	8:11:56	2006	Michellie Jones, Australia	9:18:31
Chris McCormack, Australia	8:15:34	2007	Chrissie Wellington, UK	9:08:45
Craig Alexander, Australia	8:17:45	2008	Chrissie Wellington, UK	9:06:23
Craig Alexander, Australia	8:20:21	2009	Chrissie Wellington, UK	8:54:02
Chris McCormack, Australia	8:10:37	2010	Mirinda Carfrae, Australia	8:58:36
Craig Alexander, Australia	8:03:56	2011	Chrissie Wellington, UK	8:55:08
Pete Jacobs, Australia	8:18:37	2012	Leanda Cave, U.S.	9:15:54
Frederik Van Lierde, Belgium	8:12:29	2013	Mirinda Carfrae, Australia	8:52:14
Sebastian Kienle, Germany	8:14:18	2014	Mirinda Carfrae, Australia	9:00:55
Jan Frodeno, Germany	8:14:40	2015	Daniela Ryf, Switzerland	8:57:57
Jan Frodeno, Germany	8:06:30	2016	Daniela Ryf, Switzerland	8:46:46
Patrick Lange, Germany	8:01:40	2017	Daniela Ryf, Switzerland	8:50:47
Patrick Lange, Germany	7:52:39*	2018	Daniela Ryf, Switzerland	8:26:18*

(1) First-place finisher Nina Kraft, Germany, admitted to using performance-enhancing drugs and was disqualified, Nov. 15, 2004.

James E. Sullivan Award Winners, 1930-2017

The James E. Sullivan Award, named after the former president of the Amateur Athletic Union (AAU), is given annually by the AAU to the amateur American athlete who "has done the most during the year to advance the cause of sportsmanship."

Year	Winner	Sport	Year	Winner	Sport	Year	Winner	Sport
1930	Bobby Jones	Golf	1963	John Pennel	Track	1993	Charlie Ward	Football, basketball
1931	Barney Berlinger	Track	1964	Don Schollander	Swimming			
1932	Jim Bausch	Track	1965	Bill Bradley	Basketball	1994	Dan Jansen	Speed skating
1933	Glenn Cunningham	Track	1966	Jim Ryun	Track			
1934	Bill Bonthron	Track	1967	Randy Matson	Track	1995	Bruce Baumgartner	Wrestling
1935	Lawson Little	Golf	1968	Debbie Meyer	Swimming	1996	Michael Johnson	Track
1936	Glenn Morris	Track	1969	Bill Toomey	Track	1997	Peyton Manning	Football
1937	Don Budge	Tennis	1970	John Kinsella	Swimming	1998	Chamique Holdsclaw	Basketball
1938	Don Lash	Track	1971	Mark Spitz	Swimming	1999	Coco Miller and	
1939	Joe Burk	Rowing	1972	Frank Shorter	Track		Kelly Miller	Basketball
1940	Greg Rice	Track	1973	Bill Walton	Basketball	2000	Rulon Gardner	Wrestling
1941	Leslie MacMitchell	Track	1974	Rick Wohlhuter	Track	2001	Michelle Kwan	Figure skating
1942	Cornelius Warmerdam	Track	1975	Tim Shaw	Swimming			
1943	Gilbert Dodds	Track	1976	Bruce Jenner	Track	2002	Sarah Hughes	Figure skating
1944	Ann Curtis	Swimming	1977	John Naber	Swimming			
1945	Doc Blanchard	Football	1978	Tracy Caulkins	Swimming	2003	Michael Phelps	Swimming
1946	Arnold Tucker	Football	1979	Kurt Thomas	Gymnastics	2004	Paul Hamm	Gymnastics
1947	John Kelly Jr.	Rowing	1980	Eric Heiden	Speed skating	2005	J. J. Redick	Basketball
1948	Robert Mathias	Track				2006	Jessica Long	Swimming
1949	Dick Button	Skating	1981	Carl Lewis	Track	2007	Tim Tebow	Football
1950	Fred Wilt	Track	1982	Mary Decker	Track	2008	Shawn Johnson	Gymnastics
1951	Rev. Robert Richards	Track	1983	Edwin Moses	Track	2009	Amy Palmiero-Winters	Ultra-marathon
1952	Horace Ashenfelter	Track	1984	Greg Louganis	Diving			
1953	Dr. Sammy Lee	Diving	1985	Joan Benoit Samuelson	Marathon	2010	Evan Lysacek	Figure skating
1954	Mal Whitfield	Track						
1955	Harrison Dillard	Track	1986	Jackie Joyner-Kersee	Track	2011	Andrew Rodriguez	Football
1956	Patricia McCormick	Diving	1987	Jim Abbott	Baseball	2012	Missy Franklin	Swimming
1957	Bobby Joe Morrow	Track	1988	Florence Griffith Joyner	Track	2013	John Urschel	Football
1958	Glenn Davis	Track	1989	Janet Evans	Swimming	2014	Ezekiel Elliott	Football
1959	Parry O'Brien	Track	1990	John Smith	Wrestling	2015	Keenan Reynolds	Football
1960	Rafer Johnson	Track	1991	Mike Powell	Track		Breanna Stewart	Basketball
1961	Wilma Rudolph Ward	Track	1992	Bonnie Blair	Speed skating	2016	Lauren Carlini	Volleyball
1962	James Beatty	Track				2017	Kyle Snyder	Wrestling

America's Cup Yacht Race, 1851-2017

An approximately 60-mi-long yacht race around the Isle of Wight during the London Exposition of 1851 became known as the first America's Cup after the New York Yacht Club won the race (and its prize cup) with the ship *America*. Prior to 1983, all yachts were American unless otherwise noted.

Year	Result (score)	Year	Result (score)
1851	America	1964	Constellation defeated Sovereign, England (4-0)
1870	Magic defeated Cambria, England (1-0)	1967	Intrepid defeated Dame Pattie, Australia (4-0)
1871	Columbia (first three races) and Sappho (last two races) defeated Livonia, England (4-1)	1970	Intrepid defeated Gretel II, Australia (4-1)
1876	Madeline defeated Countess of Dufferin, Canada (2-0)	1974	Courageous defeated Southern Cross, Australia (4-0)
1881	Mischief defeated Atalanta, Canada (2-0)	1977	Courageous defeated Australia, Australia (4-0)
1885	Puritan defeated Genesta, England (2-0)	1980	Freedom defeated Australia, Australia (4-1)
1886	Mayflower defeated Galatea, England (2-0)	1983	Australia II, Australia, defeated Liberty, U.S. (4-3)
1887	Volunteer defeated Thistle, Scotland (2-0)	1987	Stars & Stripes, U.S., defeated Kookaburra III, Aust. (4-0)
1893	Vigilant defeated Valkyrie II, England (3-0)	1988	Stars & Stripes, U.S., defeated New Zealand, NZ (2-0)
1895	Defender defeated Valkyrie III, England (3-0)	1992	America[3], U.S., defeated Il Moro di Venezia, Italy (4-1)
1899	Columbia defeated Shamrock, England (3-0)	1995	Team New Zealand, NZ, defeated Young America, U.S. (5-0)
1901	Columbia defeated Shamrock II, England (3-0)	2000	Team New Zealand, NZ, defeated Luna Rossa, Italy (5-0)
1903	Reliance defeated Shamrock III, England (3-0)	2003	Alinghi, Switzerland, defeated Team New Zealand, NZ (5-0)
1920	Resolute defeated Shamrock IV, England (3-2)	2007	Alinghi, Switzerland, defeated Emirates Team New Zealand, NZ (5-2)
1930	Enterprise defeated Shamrock V, England (4-0)		
1934	Rainbow defeated Endeavour, England (4-2)	2010	BMW Oracle Racing, U.S., defeated Alinghi 5, Switzerland (2-0)
1937	Ranger defeated Endeavour II, England (4-0)	2013	Oracle Team USA, U.S., defeated Emirates Team New Zealand, NZ (9-8)
1958	Columbia defeated Sceptre, England (4-0)		
1962	Weatherly defeated Gretel, Australia (4-1)	2017	Emirates Team New Zealand, NZ, defeated Oracle Team USA, U.S. (8-1)

Pro Rodeo Cowboys Association All-Around Champions, 1977-2017

Year	Winner, hometown	Earnings	Year	Winner, hometown	Earnings
1977	Tom Ferguson, Miami, OK	$76,730	1998	Ty Murray, Stephenville, TX	$264,673
1978	Tom Ferguson, Miami, OK	103,734	1999	Fred Whitfield, Hockley, TX	217,819
1979	Tom Ferguson, Miami, OK	96,272	2000	Joe Beaver, Huntsville, TX	225,396
1980	Paul Tierney, Rapid City, SD	105,568	2001	Cody Ohl, Stephenville, TX	296,419
1981	Jimmie Cooper, Monument, NM	105,862	2002	Trevor Brazile, Anson, TX	273,997
1982	Chris Lybbert, Coyote, CA	123,709	2003	Trevor Brazile, Anson, TX	294,839
1983	Roy Cooper, Durant, OK	153,391	2004	Trevor Brazile, Decatur, TX	253,170
1984	Dee Pickett, Caldwell, ID	122,618	2005	Ryan Jarrett, Summerville, GA	263,665
1985	Lewis Feild, Elk Ridge, UT	130,347	2006	Trevor Brazile, Decatur, TX	329,924
1986	Lewis Feild, Elk Ridge, UT	166,042	2007	Trevor Brazile, Decatur, TX	425,115
1987	Lewis Feild, Elk Ridge, UT	144,335	2008	Trevor Brazile, Decatur, TX	419,868
1988	Dave Appleton, Arlington, TX	121,546	2009	Trevor Brazile, Decatur, TX	346,779
1989	Ty Murray, Odessa, TX	134,806	2010	Trevor Brazile, Decatur, TX	507,921
1990	Ty Murray, Stephenville, TX	213,772	2011	Trevor Brazile, Decatur, TX	337,601
1991	Ty Murray, Stephenville, TX	244,230	2012	Trevor Brazile, Decatur, TX	298,626
1992	Ty Murray, Stephenville, TX	225,992	2013	Trevor Brazile, Decatur, TX	426,010
1993	Ty Murray, Stephenville, TX	297,896	2014	Trevor Brazile, Decatur, TX	494,369
1994	Ty Murray, Stephenville, TX	246,170	2015	Trevor Brazile, Decatur, TX	518,011
1995	Joe Beaver, Huntsville, TX	141,753	2016	Junior Nogueira, Presidente Prudente, Brazil	465,561
1996	Joe Beaver, Huntsville, TX	166,103	2017	Tuf Cooper, Decatur, TX	396,137
1997	Dan Mortensen, Manhattan, MT	184,559			

GENERAL INDEX

Note: Page numbers in boldface indicate key reference. Page numbers in italics indicate photo or illustration captions.

QUICK REFERENCE INDEX

For complete index, see pages 980-1007.